International Dictionary of Films and Filmmakers-4

WRITERS
and
PRODUCTION ARTISTS

International Dictionary of Films and Filmmakers

Volume 1
FILMS

Volume 2
DIRECTORS

Volume 3
ACTORS and ACTRESSES

Volume 4
WRITERS and PRODUCTION ARTISTS

International Dictionary of Films and Filmmakers- 4
WRITERS
and
PRODUCTION ARTISTS
FOURTH EDITION

EDITORS

TOM PENDERGAST

SARA PENDERGAST

ST. JAMES PRESS

AN IMPRINT OF THE GALE GROUP

DETROIT • NEW YORK • SAN FRANCISCO
LONDON • BOSTON • WOODBRIDGE, CT

Tom Pendergast, Sara Pendergast, *Editors*

Michael J. Tyrkus, *Project Coordinator*

Michelle Banks, Erin Bealmear, Laura Standley Berger, Joann Cerrito,
Jim Craddock, Steve Cusack, Nicolet V. Elert, Miranda H. Ferrara, Kristin Hart,
Melissa Hill, Laura S. Kryhoski, Margaret Mazurkiewicz, Carol Schwartz, and Christine Tomassini,
St. James Press Staff

Peter M. Gareffa, *Managing Editor*

Maria Franklin, *Permissions Manager*
Debra J. Freitas, *Permissions Assistant*
Mary Grimes, Leitha Etheridge-Sims, *Image Catalogers*

Mary Beth Trimper, *Composition Manager*
Dorothy Maki, *Manufacturing Manager*
Rhonda Williams, *Senior Buyer*

Cynthia Baldwin, *Product Design Manager*
Michael Logusz, *Graphic Artist*

Randy Bassett, *Image Database Supervisor*
Robert Duncan, *Imaging Specialists*
Pamela A. Reed, *Imaging Coordinator*
Dean Dauphinais, *Senior Editor, Imaging and Multimedia Content*

Library of Congress Cataloging-in-Publication Data
International dictionary of films and filmmakers / editors, Tom Pendergast, Sara Pendergast.—4th ed.
    p. cm.
        Contents: 1. Films — 2. Directors — 3. Actors and actresses — 4. Writers and production artists.
    ISBN 1-55862-449-X (set) — ISBN 1-55862-450-3 (v. 1) — ISBN 1-55862-451-1 (v. 2)
    — ISBN 1-55862-452-X (v. 3) — ISBN 1-55862-453-8 (v. 4)
        1. Motion pictures—Plots, themes, etc. 2. Motion picture producers and directors—Biography—
Dictionaries.   3. Motion picture actors and actresses—Biography—Dictionaries. 4. Screenwriters—
Biography—Dictionaries. I. Pendergast, Tom. II. Pendergast, Sara.

PN1997.8.I58 2000
791.43'03—dc2100-064024   CIP

Cover photograph—Karl Freund courtesy the Kobal Collection

Printed in the United States of America

St. James Press is an imprint of Gale Group
Gale Group and Design is a trademark used herein under license
10 9 8 7 6 5 4 3 2 1

CONTENTS

EDITORS' NOTE

This is a revised edition of the 4th volume of the *International Dictionary of Films and Filmmakers*, which also includes Volume 1, *Films*, Volume 2, *Directors*, and Volume 3, *Actors and Actresses*. The book contains 545 entries, consisting of a brief biography, a complete filmography, a selected bibliography of works by and about the entrant, and a critical essay written by a specialist in the field. There are 51 entrants new to this edition. Most of the entries from the previous edition have been retained here; all entries have updated filmographies and bibliographies; and many entries have updated critical essays. Since film is primarily a visual medium, the majority of entries are illustrated, either by a portrait or by a representative still from the entrant's body of work.

The entrants in this volume represent a wide range of writers and production artists, including art directors, cinematographers, costume designers, composers (and music directors, arrangers, and lyricists), editors, choreographers, stuntmen, special effects and sound technicians, makeup artists, and animators. The selection of entrants is once again based on the recommendations of the advisory board. It was not thought necessary to propose strict criteria for selection: the book is intended to represent the wide range of interests within North American, British, and West European film scholarship and criticism.

Thanks are due to the following: Nicolet V. Elert and Michael J. Tyrkus at St. James Press, for their efforts in preparing this collection for publication; Michael Najjar, for his tireless efforts in researching the entries; our advisers, for their wisdom and broad knowledge of international cinema; and our contributors, for their gracious participation. We have necessarily built upon the work of the editors who have preceded us, and we thank them for the strong foundation they created.

A Note on the Entries

Non-English language film titles are given in the original language or a transliteration of it, unless they are better known internationally by their English title. Alternate release titles in the original language(s) are found within parentheses, followed by release titles in English (American then British if there is a difference) and translations. The date of a film is understood to refer to its year of release unless stated otherwise.

In the list of films in each entry, information within parentheses following each film modifies, if necessary, then adds to the subject's principal function(s). The most common abbreviations used are:

an	animator
assoc	associate
asst	assistant
chor	choreographer
d	director
ed	editor
exec	executive
mus	music
ph	cinematographer or director of photography
pr	producer
prod des	production designer
ro	role
sc	scenarist or scriptwriter

The abbreviation ''co-'' preceding a function indicates collaboration with one or more persons. Other abbreviations that may be used to clarify the nature of an individual film are ''doc''—documentary; ''anim''—animation; and ''ep''—episode. A name in parentheses following a film title is that of the director. A film title in boldface type indicates that complete coverage of that film may be found in the *International Dictionary of Films and Filmmakers*, Volume 1: *Films*.

BOARD OF ADVISERS

CONTRIBUTORS

Richard Alwyn
Anthony Ambrogio
Roy Armes
Giselle Atterberry
Doreen Bartoni
Jeanine Basinger
John Baxter
Charles Ramírez Berg
Nina Bjornsson
Ronald Bowers
Jay Boyer
Anwar Brett
Stephen Brophy
Rick Broussard
Fred Camper
Ross Care
Richard Chatten
R. F. Cousins
Robert von Dassanowsky
Gertraud Steiner Daviau
Jerome Delamater
Denise Delorey
Charles Derry
Wheeler Winston Dixon
Robert Dixter
Susan Doll
Áine Doyle
Clyde Kelly Dunagan
Raymond Durgnat
Rob Edelman
Thomas L. Erskine
Mark W. Estrin
Greg S. Faller
Rodney Farnsworth
Susan Felleman
Patricia Ferrara
Peter Flynn
M. S. Fonseca
Alexa L. Foreman
John A. Gallagher
Sandra Garcia-Myers
Heidi Gensch
Shohini Ghosh
Tina Gianoulis
Jill Gillespie
Verina Glaessner
H. M. Glancy
Douglas Gomery
Martin A. Gostanian

Justin Gustainis
John Hagan
Kevin Jack Hagopian
John Halas
Robert A. Haller
Patricia King Hanson
Stephen L. Hanson
Leonard G. Heldreth
Mary Hess
Kyoko Hirano
Peter Hutchings
Dina Iordanova
Jill Gillespie
Mark Johnson
Nancy Jane Johnston
David Gonthier, Jr.
Philip Kemp
Tammy Kinsey
William Lafferty
Edith C. Lee
Peter Lev
David Levine
James Limbacher
Janet Lorenz
Jon Lupo
Richard Dyer MacCann
Geoffrey Macnab
Roger Manvell
Floyd W. Martin
Donald W. McCaffrey
John McCarty
Vacláv Merhaut
Lois Miklas
Joseph Milicia
Norman Miller
John E. Mitchell
James Morrison
John Mraz
Dominique Nasta
Richard R. Ness
Kim Newman
Martin F. Norden
Daniel O'Brien
Liam O'Leary
Carrie D. O'Neill
Linda Obalil
Vladimir Opěla
Dayna Oscherwitz

Maryann Oshana
Marc Oxoby
R. Barton Palmer
Sylvia Paskin
Soon-Mi Peten
Julian Petley
Philip Kemp
Rob Pinsel
Dominic Power
André Pozner
Victoria Price
Susan Perez Prichard
Ken Provencher
Lauren Rabinovitz
Bibekananda Ray
Allen Grant Richards
Arthur G. Robson
Chris Routledge
Marie Saeli
Richard Sater
Patrick J. Sauer
Eric Schaefer
H. Wayne Schuth
Leslie Felperin Sharman
Charles L. P. Silet
Anthony Slide
Edward S. Small
Cecile Starr
Christopher John Stephens
Dan Streible
Karel Tabery
Susan Tavernetti
J. P. Telotte
Suzanne Thomas
Tony Thomas
Frank Thompson
Doug Tomlinson
Lee Tsiantis
B. Urgošíková
Fiona Valentine
Ravi Vasudevan
Gregory Votolato
Milos Votruba
Mark Walker
Tomasz Warchol
Renee Ward
Graham Webb
Joanne L. Yeck

LIST OF ENTRANTS

K. A. Abbas
Ken Adam
Richard Addinsell
Adrian
Age and Scarpelli
Luis Alcoriza
John Alcott
G. R. Aldo
Henri Alekan
Alexander and Claire Alexeieff
Dede Allen
Jay Presson Allen
Nestor Almendros
John A. Alonzo
John Alton
William Alwyn
Preston Ames
Sergio Amidei
André Andrejew
Georges Annenkov
Malcolm Arnold
Joseph H. August
Jean Aurenche and Pierre Bost
Georges Auric
Tex Avery

Burt Bacharach
Angelo Badalamenti
Rick Baker
Barney Balaban
Michael Balcon
Lucien Ballard
Michael Ballhaus
Travis Banton
William George Barker
George S. Barnes
John Barry
Léon Barsacq
James Basevi
Ronald Bass
Saul Bass
Cecil Beaton
Sir Richard Rodney Bennett
Irving Berlin
Pandro S. Berman
James Bernard
Elmer Bernstein
Walter Bernstein
Adrian Biddle
Lajos Biro
Joseph Biroc
Anil Biswas
Billy Bitzer
Peter Biziou
Mel Blanc
Henry Blanke
Margaret Booth
Stephen Bosustow
Russell Boyd
Robert Boyle
Bruno Bozzetto

Charles Brackett
Leigh Brackett
Paulo Branco
Pierre Braunberger
J. R. Bray
Jiří Brdečka
Robert Breer
Albert R. Broccoli
Karl Brown
Nacio Herb Brown
Clyde Bruckman
John Bryan
Sidney Buchman
Wilfred Buckland
Henry Bumstead
Léonce-Henry Burel
Robert Burks
S. D. Burman
Ben Burtt
Carter Burwell

Sammy Cahn
Yakima Canutt
Jack Cardiff
Hoagy Carmichael
Ben Carré
James Carreras
Jean-Claude Carrière
Suso Cecchi D'Amico
Christopher Challis
Bansi Chandragupta
Borden Chase
Bob Clampett
Charles G. Clarke
T. E. B. Clarke
Ghislain Cloquet
William H. Clothier
Emile Cohl
Harry Cohn
Jack Cole
Henri Colpi
Betty Comden and Adolph
  Green
Bill Conti
Merian C. Cooper
Stanley Cortez
Curt Courant
Raoul Coutard
Noël Coward
Franco Cristaldi
Edward Cronjager
Floyd Crosby

Albert S. D'Agostino
William H. Daniels
Mason Daring
Beatrice Dawson
Richard Day
Acácio de Almeida
Basil Dean
Jean D'Eaubonne

Georges de Beauregard
Henri Decaë
Anatole de Grunwald
Dino De Laurentiis
Georges Delerue
Tonino Delli Colli
Louis de Rochemont
Adolph Deutsch
I. A. L. Diamond
Ernest Dickerson
Carmen Dillon
Todor Dinov
Walt Disney
Gianni Di Venanzo
Pino Donaggio
Danilo Donati
Max Douy
Hans Dreier
Paul Driessen
George Duning
Linwood Dunn
Philip Dunne
George Dunning
Marguerite Duras
Dulal Dutta
John Dykstra

Roger Edens
Arthur Edeson
Richard Edlund
Farciot Edouart
Hanns Eisler
Danny Elfman
Peter Ellenshaw
Yevgeni Enei
Julius and Philip Epstein
Joe Eszterhas
Bernard Evein

Verna Fields
Gabriel Figueroa
Gunnar Fischer
Oskar Fischinger
Gerry Fisher
Ennio Flaiano and Tullio Pinelli
Max and Dave Fleischer
Carl Foreman
William Fox
Marcel Fradetal
William A. Fraker
Freddie Francis
Arthur Freed
Karl Freund
Hugo Friedhofer
Jules Furthman

Henrik Galeen
Lee Garmes
Tony Gaudio
Léon Gaumont

Paul Gégauff
Piero Gherardi
Cedric Gibbons
Arnold Gillespie
Bert Glennon
Bob Godfrey
Menahem Golan and
    Yoram Globus
William Goldman
Jerry Goldsmith
Samuel Goldwyn
Anatoli Golovnya
Frances Goodrich and
    Albert Hackett
Stephen Goosson
Johnny Green
Paul Grimault
Anton Grot
Dave Grusin
Tonino Guerra
Burnett Guffey
Agnès Guillemot

Raymond and Robert Hakim
John Halas and Joy Batchelor
Conrad Hall
Ernest Haller
Gerry Hambling
Marvin Hamlisch
William Hanna and Joseph
    Barbera
Russell Harlan
Joan Harrison
Ray Harryhausen
Byron Haskin
Anthony Havelock-Allan
Fumio Hayasaka
John Michael Hayes
Edith Head
Ben Hecht
Hein Heckroth
Otto Heller
Buck Henry
Jim Henson
Robert Herlth
Jorge Herrera
Bernard Herrmann
Winton C. Hoch
Samuel Hoffenstein
Carl Hoffmann
Arthur Honegger
William Hornbeck
Harry Horner
John Houseman
Sidney Howard
James Wong Howe
John Hubley
Otto Hunte
Ross Hunter

Jacques Ibert
Thomas H. Ince
Irene
Ivan Ivanov-Vano
Ub Iwerks

Julius Jaenzon
Maurice Jarre
Paul Jarrico
Maurice Jaubert
Dorothy Jeakins
Henri Jeanson
George Jenkins
Talbot Jennings
Ruth Prawer Jhabvala
Nunnally Johnson
Chuck Jones
Quincy Jones
Alfred Junge
George Justin

Gus Kahn
Janusz Kaminski
Garson Kanin
Bronislau Kaper
Erich Kästner
Boris Kaufman
Michael Kidd
Howard W. Koch
Count "Sascha" Alexander
    Kolowrat-Krakowsky
Alexander Korda
Vincent Korda
Erich Wolfgang Korngold
Joseph Kosma
Laszlo Kovacs
Hanns Kräly
Robert Krasker
Norman Krasna
Milton Krasner
Hanif Kureishi
Yoji Kuri

Carl Laemmle, Sr. and Carl
    Laemmle, Jr.
Francis Lai
Giuseppe Lanci
Charles B. Lang
Sherry Lansing
Walter Lantz
Ring Lardner, Jr.
Joseph La Shelle
Jesse L. Lasky
Walter Lassally
Ernest Laszlo
Philip H. Lathrop
Charles Lederer
Michel Legrand
Ernest Lehman
Charles LeMaire
Jan Lenica
Boris Leven
Sonya Levien
Joseph E. Levine
Val Lewton
Pierre Lhomme
Carol Littleton
Marcus Loew
Anita Loos
Santo Loquasto
Jean Louis
Eugène Lourié

P. A. Lundgren
Len Lye

Charles MacArthur
Kenneth MacGowan
Jeanie Macpherson
Ben Maddow
Charles Magnusson
Daniel Mainwaring
David Mamet
Henry Mancini
Johnny Mandel
Daniel Mandell
Herman Mankiewicz
Frances Marion
Frank Marshall
Rudolph Maté
Muir Mathieson
June Mathis
Christian Matras
Carl Mayer
Louis B. Mayer
Donald McAlpine
Winsor McCay
Ted McCord
Robert McKimson
Norman McLaren
Lazare Meerson
Chris Menges
Alan Menken
William Cameron Menzies
Johnny Mercer
Ismail Merchant
Otto Messmer
Oskar Messter
Russell Metty
Ernö Metzner
Darius Milhaud
Arthur C. Miller
Seton I. Miller
Virgil Miller
Aleksandr Mindadze
Walter Mirisch
Subrata Mitra
Kazuo Miyagawa
Alexandre Mnouchkine
Hal Mohr
Ennio Morricone
Oswald Morris
Andrei Moskvin
Robby Müller
Yoshiro Muraki
Walter Murch
Dennis Muren
Nicholas Musuraca

Ronald Neame
Alfred Newman
Thomas Newman
Dudley Nichols
Govind Nihalani
Jack Nitzsche
Yuri Norstein
Alex North
Frank S. Nugent
Bruno Nuytten

Sven Nykvist

Willis H. O'Brien
Miroslav Ondříček
Orry-Kelly
Sam O'Steen

George Pal
Hermes Pan
Nick Park
Robert Parrish
Joe Pasternak
Charles Pathé
John Paxton
Clare Peploe
Hal Pereira
Georges Périnal
Jack P. Pierce
Harold Pinter
Franz Planer
Walter Plunkett
Van Nest Polglase
Sol Polito
Erich Pommer
Carlo Ponti
Ion Popescu-Gopo
Cole Porter
Zbigniew Preisner
Jacques Prévert
André Previn
Sergei Prokofiev
Alexander Ptushko
David Puttnam

Jean Rabier
David Raksin
Ken Ralston
J. Arthur Rank
Samson Raphaelson
Jean-Paul Rappeneau
Terence Rattigan
Lotte Reiniger
Walter Reisch
Ray Rennahan
Claude Renoir
Alma Reville
William H. Reynolds
Robert Riskin
Hal Roach
Alain Robbe-Grillet
Walter Röhrig
Helen Rose
Ralph Rosenblum
Leonard Rosenman
Charles Rosher
Hal Rosson
Nino Rota
Giuseppe Rotunno
Philippe Rousselot
Miklos Rozsa
Joseph Ruttenberg

Philippe Sarde
Alvin Sargent
Jacques Saulnier
John Monk Saunders

Tom Savini
James Schamus
Dore Schary
Joseph and Nicholas Schenck
Lalo Schifrin
Leon Schlesinger
Charles Schnee
Thelma Schoonmaker
Eugen Schüfftan
Stephen Schwartz
Aleksander Ścibor-Rylski
John Seale
John F. Seitz
William N. Selig
David O. Selznick
Jorge Semprun
Mario Serandrei
Leon Shamroy
Ravi Shankar
Irene Sharaff
Douglas Shearer
Sam Shepard
R. C. Sherriff
Robert E. Sherwood
Dmitri Shostakovich
Curt Siodmak
Douglas Slocombe
Dick Smith
Jack Martin Smith
Franco Solinas
Terry Southern
Charles Spaak
Dorothy Spencer
Sam Spiegel
Jan Stallich
Carl Stalling
Ladislaw Starewicz
Ray Stark
Jerzy Stefan Stawiński
Max Steiner
Donald Ogden Stewart
Vittorio Storaro
Herbert Stothart
Harry Stradling
Hunt Stromberg
Karl Struss
C. Gardner Sullivan
Robert L. Surtees
Jan Švankmajer
Jo Swerling
Richard Sylbert

Toru Takemitsu
Daniel Taradash
Dean Tavoularis
Paul Terry
Irving G. Thalberg
Mikis Theodorakis
Virgil Thomson
Dimitri Tiomkin
Edward Tisse
Jusho Toda
Gregg Toland
John Toll
Robert Towne
Alexandre Trauner

Jiří Trnka
Lamar Trotti
Dalton Trumbo
Douglas Trumbull
Eiji Tsuburaya

Geoffrey Unsworth
Sergei Urusevsky

Christine Vachon
Ernest Vajda
Helen Van Dongen
Vangelis
James Van Heusen
Theodora Van Runkle
Anthony Veiller
Alex Vetchinsky
Sacha Vierny
Will Vinton
Patrizia von Brandenstein
Elfi von Dassanowsky
Thea Von Harbou
Slavko Vorkapich
Dušan Vukotić

Fritz Arno Wagner
Georges Wakhévitch
Chris Walas
Jerry Wald
Joseph B. Walker
Hal B. Wallis
William Walton
Walter Wanger
Hermann Warm
Jack L. Warner
Lew Wasserman
David Watkin
Franz Waxman
The Westmore Family
Haskell Wexler
Lyle Wheeler
Albert Whitlock
Herbert Wilcox
John Williams
Richard Williams
Calder Willingham
Gordon Willis
Michael Wilson
Irwin Winkler
Stan Winston

Yoshikata Yoda
Freddie Young
Victor Young

Darryl F. Zanuck
Richard D. Zanuck
Cesare Zavattini
Karel Zeman
Hans Zimmer
Vilmos Zsigmond
Adolph Zukor

A

ABBAS, K. A.

Writer and Director. **Nationality:** Indian. **Born:** Khwaja Ahmad Abbas in Panipat, 7 June 1914. **Education:** Attended University of Aligarh. **Career:** Journalist, weekly columnist for *Blitz* magazine, and writer for various Hindi films; 1960s—suffered heart trouble and series of heart attacks. **Died:** 1 June 1987.

Films as Writer:

1943   *Naya Sansaar (New World)* (Acharya)
1946   *Dr. Kotnis Ki Amar Kahani (The Immortal Story of Dr. Kotnis)* (Shantaram)
1951   *Anhonee (The Impossible)* (+ d)
1952   ***Awara*** *(Awaara; The Vagabond)* (Kapoor)
1954   *Munna (Lost Child)* (+ d, pr)
1955   *Shree 420 (Mr. 420)* (Kapoor)
1965   *Aasman Mahal* (+ d)
1970   *Saat Hindustani (Seven Indians)* (+ d)
1973   *Achanak (Suddenly)* (Gulzar); *Bobby* (Kapoor)
1974   *Faasla (Distance)* (+ d)
1981   *The Naxalites*
1983   *Love in Goa*

Films as Director:

1947   *Dharti Ke Lal (Children of the Earth)*
1953   *Rahi*
1959   *Chaar Dil Chaar Rahen (Four Hearts, Four Roads; Four Faces of India)*; *One Thousand Nights on a Bed of Stones*
1972   *Do Boond Pani (2 Drops of Water)*

Publications

By ABBAS: book—

I Am not an Island: An Experiment in Autobiography, New Delhi, 1977.

By ABBAS: article—

"Social Realism in the Indian Cinema," in *Filmfare*, 2 June 1972.

On ABBAS: book—

Vasudev and Lenglet, editors, *Indian Cinema Superbazaar*, New Delhi, 1978.

On ABBAS: articles—

Indian Film Culture (New Delhi), no. 4, September 1964.
Film World, vol. 1, no. 10, October 1978.
Ghish, S., "K. A. Abbas: A Man in Tune with History," in *Screen* (Bombay), 19 June 1987.
Obituary in *Jump Cut* (Berkeley, California), no. 33, February 1988.

*   *   *

K. A. Abbas was representative of a generation of left-wing playwrights associated with the Indian People's Theatre Association (IPTA), who sought to draw upon indigenous and folk forms and idioms to communicate their radical ideas. This was evident in the first film Abbas directed, *Dharti Ke Lal (Children of the Earth)*, about the Bengal famine of 1943. But perhaps as important were questions of the topical: how films he had conceptualised would draw upon immediate events and articulate them as part of his *mise en scène*. In *Dharti Ke Lal* this led to IPTA using actual peasant unions to stage protest marches for the film. Otherwise, in ways which were less directly political in their articulation, Abbas drew upon his career as a journalist to fulfill these topical relations to contemporary life. Journalism was used to constitute the raw material of his scenarios, and also functioned as representative modern practice and metaphor.

Thus, his 1946 script, *Dr. Kotnis Ki Amar Kahani (The Immortal Story of Dr. Kotnis)*, drew on a real story, the commitment and premature death of a young doctor assigned to the Indian medical mission which helped the Chinese communists in Yenan, which had been recounted in Abbas's own book on the subject. And, in *Naya Sansaar (New World)*, journalism becomes the medium through which the struggle for a new rationality was represented. Perhaps as significantly, in *Naya Sansaar* Abbas employed an oedipal plot to frame his narrative of the emergence of a new notion of Indian personality, one founded on the conflict between a dynamic young reporter and his cautious editor.

If the drive for a new, Nehruvian truth, uncluttered by superstition and the impediments of traditional pieties motivated Abbas's heroes, it is significant that the individuated oedipal self through which these aspirations were voiced came to be narratively constrained. A key example is the later *Awara*, in which the polemic against social attitudes founded on hierarchical and genetic conceptions of the social order is somewhat denied its full power when the hero recovers the elevated social situation he had lost. Not only is the critique of social hierarchy cushioned by this; so too is the discourse of masculine aggression and conflict, for the oedipal antagonism against the father which structures the story is qualified, and held in check by an undercurrent that motivates the hero to recover his lost mother and the innocence of childhood. Underlying Abbas's stories, and their rationalist stances, there rests a certain nostalgia, an idea of loss that is more widely common in the Hindi popular cinema. Significantly, his 1954 film, *Munna*, while abandoning the musical and performative conventions of that cinema, nevertheless founds its story on a child's search for his mother. The archetypal mother came to cast a looming shadow, one which spoke of the loss and the drive to renegotiate a cultural mooring.

Finally, we should note a strongly didactic element in Abbas's writing, again quite common in traditional dramaturgy, and here yoked to progressive causes. His own efforts as director to use film to urge caste, religious, and regional amity, such as in *Chaar Dil Chaar Rahen* and *Saat Hindustani* were less successful than when these imperatives were combined with directors more attuned to the entertainment conventions of the popular Hindi cinema. This is especially apparent in Abbas's work with Raj Kapoor.

—Ravi Vasudevan

ADAM, Ken

Art Director. **Nationality:** British. **Born:** Klaus Adam in Berlin, Germany, February 1921; emigrated to the United Kingdom, 1934. **Education:** Attended Le Collège Français, Berlin; Craigend Park School, Edinburgh; St. Paul's School, London; Bartlett School of Architecture, University of London, 1937–39. **Military Service:** Served in Pioneer Corps and as a pilot in the Royal Air Force during World War II. **Career:** Articled with architectural firm C. W. Glover and Partners; 1947—draftsman on first film, *This Was a Woman*; then art director and production designer. **Awards:** British Academy Award, for *Dr. Strangelove*, 1964, and *The Ipcress File*, 1965; Academy Awards for Best Art Direction-Set Direction, for *Barry Lyndon*, 1975, and *The Madness of King George*, 1994; Honorary Doctorate, Royal College of Art, 1995. **Address:** c/o The Mirisch Agency, 10100 Santa Monica Boulevard, Los Angeles, CA 90067, U.S.A.

Films as Art Director/Production Designer:

1956   *Soho Incident* (*Spin a Dark Web*) (Sewell); *Child in the House* (de Lautour and Endfield)
1957   *Around the World in Eighty Days* (Anderson) (co); *The Devil's Pass* (Conyers); *Night of the Demon* (*Curse of the Demon*) (J. Tourneur)
1958   *Battle of the V1* (*Missile from Hell*; *Unseen Heroes*) (Sewell) (designs)
1959   *Gideon of Scotland Yard* (*Gideon's Day*) (Ford); *Beyond This Place* (*Web of Evidence*) (Cardiff); *The Angry Hills* (Aldrich); *10 Seconds to Hell* (Aldrich); *The Rough and the Smooth* (*Portrait of a Sinner*) (Siodmak); *In the Nick* (Hughes); *John Paul Jones* (Farrow) (co); *Ben-Hur* (Wyler) (research)
1960   *Let's Get Married* (Scott); *The Trials of Oscar Wilde* (*The Green Carnation*) (Hughes)
1961   *The Hellions* (Annakin) (designs)
1962   *Sodoma e Gomorra* (*Sodom and Gomorrah*) (Leone and Aldrich); *Dr. No* (Young); *In the Cool of the Night* (Stevens)
1964   **Dr. Strangelove: Or How I Learned to Stop Worrying and Love the Bomb** (Kubrick); *Woman of Straw* (Dearden); *Goldfinger* (Hamilton); *The Long Ships* (Cardiff) (designs)
1965   *The Ipcress File* (Furie); *Thunderball* (Young)

1966   *Funeral in Berlin* (Hamilton)
1967   *You Only Live Twice* (Gilbert)
1968   *Chitty Chitty Bang Bang* (Hughes)
1969   *Goodbye, Mr. Chips* (Ross)
1970   *The Owl and the Pussycat* (Ross)
1972   *Sleuth* (Mankiewicz)
1973   *The Last of Sheila* (Ross)
1975   *Barry Lyndon* (Kubrick)
1976   *The Seven-Per-Cent Solution* (Ross)
1977   *Salon Kitty* (*Madam Kitty*) (Brass); *The Spy Who Loved Me* (Gilbert)
1979   *Moonraker* (Gilbert)
1981   *Pennies from Heaven* (Ross) (+ assoc pr)
1985   *King David* (Beresford); *Agnes of God* (Jewison)
1986   *Crimes of the Heart* (Beresford)
1987   *The Deceivers* (Meyer)
1988   *Dead-Bang* (Frankenheimer)
1989   *The Freshman* (Bergman); *Dinosaurs* (Meyer)
1990   *The Doctor* (Haines)
1992   *Undercover Blues* (Ross)
1993   *Addams Family Values* (Sonnenfeld)
1994   *Boys on the Side* (Ross); *The Madness of King George* (Hytner)
1995   *Bogus* (Jewison)
1997   *In & Out* (Oz)
1999   *The Out-of-Towners* (Weisman)
2000   *The White Hotel*

Films as Draftsman and Assistant or Associate Art Director:

1947   *This Was a Woman* (Whelan)
1948   *Lucky Mascot* (*The Brass Monkey*) (Freeland); *Third Time Lucky* (Parry); *The Queen of Spades* (Dickinson); *Obsession* (*The Hidden Room*) (Dmytryk)
1949   *Dick Barton Strikes Back* (Parry); *Three Men and a Girl*
1950   *Your Witness* (*Eye Witness*) (Montgomery)
1952   *The Crimson Pirate* (Siodmak)
1953   *The Master of Ballantrae* (Keighley); *The Intruder* (Hamilton); *Star of India* (Lubin)
1955   *Helen of Troy* (Wise)

Publications

By ADAM: book—

"Moonraker," "Strangelove," and Other Celluloid Dreams, London, 1999.

By ADAM: articles—

"Designing Sets for Action," in *Films and Filming* (London), August 1956.
Screen International (London), 12 February 1977.
Positif (Paris), March 1977.
Cinéma (Paris), January 1978.
Film Comment (New York), January/February 1982.
American Film, February 1991.

Ken Adam

EPD Film (Frankfurt/Main), May 1994.
"Private View," in *Sight and Sound* (London), 1 September 1999.

On ADAM: articles—

Hudson, Roger, "Three Designers," in *Sight and Sound* (London), Winter 1964–65.
Monthly Film Bulletin (London), 1965.
Le Film Français (Paris), 1976.
National Film Theatre Booklet (London), October/November 1979.
American Film (Los Angeles), February 1991.
Köhler, Margret, "Wenn Film-Bilder Geschichte machen. Der Filmarchitekt Ken Adam," in *Film-dienst* (Cologne), 15 February 1994.

*   *   *

Born Klaus Adam in Berlin in 1921, Ken Adam emigrated to the United Kingdom in 1934. He studied architecture and became a freelance architect and interior designer. In 1947 he joined the film industry as a draftsman. An art director since 1948 and production designer since 1959, Adam has won awards for the low-key spy thriller *The Ipcress File* and the period adaptations *Barry Lyndon* and *The Madness of King George*, though it is his innovative and spectacular work on the James Bond adventure-fantasies for which he will be best remembered.

Adam's James Bond films characterized the modern look in the 1960s—slick, inventive, filled with modern gadgets and smooth, cold, clean surfaces. There was a love of the exotic with a dazzling display of conspicuous consumption. Colors were pure and bright. Everything gleamed and sparkled with movement. Plastic and steel were not only stylish, they were considered futuristic, and the future, people felt, "was now." The "back to nature" movement would have to wait till later in the decade. The only real things in the Bond movies were the mirrors on the floor. Meanwhile, Bond fans reveled in Adam's influential creations as the designer put the "mod" in modern.

To accommodate his mammoth designs for the Bond films, which ranged from a recreation of the interior of Fort Knox in *Goldfinger* to an underground space launch in *You Only Live Twice*, a special sound stage had to be built at Pinewood Studios where the films were made. It remains the largest single sound stage in the world.

Adam's ability to "come to the rescue" with ingenuity on a budget evidenced itself early in his career when the producer of *Night of the Demon* called him in at the last minute to render visible the titular beast that director Jacques Tourneur had insisted on keeping unseen in the belief that such things were best left to the audience's imagination. Adam responded economically with a design based on medieval woodcuts; shown only in a few brief closeups, his demon remains one of the most fearsome looking monsters in movie history. Years later, Adam applied similar ingenuity to bringing the macabre world of cartoonist Charles Addams to life on the screen in *Addams Family Values*.

Adam performed similar miracles on *Dr. Stangelove*, Stanley Kubrick's black comedy about a nuclear strike. Denied cooperation by the U.S. military due to the film's controversial theme, Kubrick relied on Adam to create everything from the interiors of the planes that drop the bombs to the "war room" where the U.S. president and Russian ambassador play cat and mouse with the fate of the world. Adam's "war room" set centered on a giant oval table with an ominous overhanging fixture that looked suspiciously like a nuclear mushroom cloud. This dramatically darkened room was lit only by this overhanging fixture and the electric arrows on the numerous maps that lined the walls, indicating the paths of nuclear destruction. The people surrounding the table seemed insignificant in scale, as individuals are to those who power the giant war machine.

Adam also designed *Sleuth*, an entertaining English thriller. One of its main characters, a successful mystery writer, lives to play games of physical and psychological sleight-of-hand. The story takes place at his home in the country, its rooms filled by games, puzzles, and mechanical toys; its garden is landscaped as an elaborate maze. It seemed the perfect place for a crime, a crime of the writer's own design. This wittily plotted tale shows Adam at his cleverest.

The Stanley Kubrick film *Barry Lyndon* was perhaps Adam's *magnum opus*. Every detail displayed a painstaking job of period reconstruction, each celluloid frame worthy of Gainsborough or Hogarth. His work on the later *The Madness of King George* showed equal devotion to detail. After the success of *The Madness of King George*, in the late 1990s Adam has been involved in disappointing mainstream comedies such as *In & Out* and *The Out-Of-Towners*. Set in contemporary America, neither film can have tested his considerable skills. Such projects are typical of the kind of films Adam has interspersed with more demanding work throughout his career. His next film release will be the rather more challenging *The White Hotel*, adapted from the D.M. Thomas novel of the same name and directed by Bosnian Emir Kusturica. How ironic it is that Adam, who leaped to prominence with his space-age designs for the hugely successful James Bond films, would receive his only two Oscars to date for films set in the far distant past.

—Edith C. Lee, updated by John McCarty,
further updated by Chris Routledge

ADDINSELL, Richard

Composer. **Nationality:** British. **Born:** London, England, 13 January 1904. **Family:** single. **Education:** Home schooled; attended Hertford School, Oxford, for 18 months; attended Royal College of Music for two semesters; studied in Berlin and Vienna, 1929–32. **Career:** Composed songs for London theater, 1925–28; scored first film, *Amateur Gentleman*, 1936. **Died:** London, England, 15 November 1977.

Films as Composer:

1936 *Amateur Gentleman* (Freeland)
1937 *Fire Over England* (Howard); *Dark Journey (The Anxious Years)* (Saville); *Farewell Again (Troopship)* (Whelan)
1938 *South Riding* (Saville); *Vessel of Wrath (The Beachcomber)* (Pommer)
1939 *Gaslight (Angel Street; Strange Case of Murder)* (Dickinson); *Goodbye, Mr. Chips* (Wood); *The Lion Has Wings* (Brunel/Hurst)
1940 *Contraband (Blackout)* (Powell)
1941 *Love on the Dole* (Baxter); *Dangerous Moonlight (Suicide Squadron)* (Hurst)
1942 *The Day Will Dawn (The Avengers)* (French); *The Big Blockade* (Frend)
1945 *Blithe Spirit* (Lean)
1949 *Under Capricorn* (Hitchcock); *The Passionate Friends (One Woman's Story)* (Lean)
1950 *Highly Dangerous* (Ward Baker); *The Black Rose* (Hathaway)
1951 *Tom Brown's Schooldays* (Parry); *Scrooge (A Christmas Carol)* (Hurst)
1952 *Encore* (French/Jackson)
1953 *Sea Devils* (Walsh)
1954 *Macbeth* (for TV) (Evans); *Beau Brummell* (Bernhardt)
1955 *Out of the Clouds* (Dearden/Relph)
1957 *The Prince and the Showgirl* (Olivier)
1957 *The Admirable Crichton (Paradise Lagoon)* (Gilbert)
1958 *A Tale of Two Cities* (Thomas)
1961 *The Greengage Summer (Loss of Innocence)* (Gilbert); *The Roman Spring of Mrs. Stone* (Quintero)
1962 *The War Lover* (Leacock)
1962 *Waltz of the Toreadors (The Amorous General)* (Guillermin)
1965 *Life at the Top* (Kotcheff)

Publications

On ADDINSELL: articles—

Lane, Philip, "British Light Music: Richard Addinsell," liner notes for *Marco Polo* compact disc 8.223732.
Long, Harry, "Hail, Britannia!, Richard Addinsell: Film Music," CD reviews, *Film Score Monthly Online Magazine*, 29 February 2000.

*   *   *

Composer Richard Stewart Addinsell was born in London on January 13, 1904. He was the son of a successful London businessman and a mother so protective of her youngest child that his major education came through home schooling. Addinsell briefly attended Hertford School, Oxford, where he began to read Law, but his interest in music soon led him—briefly—to the Royal College of Music. In 1926 Addinsell's natural musical gifts led to his writing songs for that year's Andre Charlot revue, and later travel in Europe visiting the continent's major musical and theatrical centers. Around this time Addinsell also began an enduring association with the theatrical writer, Clemence Dane, a collaboration which led to theater and film work with performers such as Gertrude Lawrence and Douglas Fairbanks, Jr.

These various contacts led to Addinsell's first work in British films, a feature entitled *The Amateur Gentleman*, which starred Fairbanks and was partially scripted by Dane. Ensuing British films such as *South Riding*, *Dark Journey*, *Fire Over England*, and the first of several British feature propaganda films, *The Lion Has Wings*, followed. In 1940 he scored his first international success with Metro-Goldwyn-Mayer's British production of *Goodbye, Mr. Chips*. He also scored MGM's early version of *Gaslight* which was later surpressed in the wake of the Ingrid Bergman American version.

1941 saw the debut of Addinsell's *chief d'oeuvre*, the "Warsaw Concerto" composed for the film *Dangerous Moonlight* (U.S. title: *Suicide Squadron*). The film itself is a melodrama involving a Polish air ace who had been a concert pianist before World War II. Themes from the "Warsaw" piece are heard throughout the film which then climaxes with a nearly complete performance of the concerto itself. This one-movement composition for piano and orchestra turned out to be the most striking element in the film for war-weary British audiences, and soon generated international interest as well. The celebrated Russian pianist and composer, Serge Rachmaninov, had been approached about doing the score, and when he refused it Addinsell cast his concerto in a Rachmaninovian mode of effusive, appealing lyricism. Indeed, the enduring popularity of the dramatic piece eventually eclipsed anything else the British composer was to create, and "Warsaw Concerto" eventually generated over a hundred separate recordings which sold in excess of three million copies.

"Warsaw Concerto" was also one of the first compositions to call attention to the specific art of composing for film, which was still an extremely specialized and esoteric calling in the early 1940s, and to the lucrative commercial potential of film music. (The popular success of Addinsell's work no doubt prompted the transcription of Miklos Rozsa's score for Alfred Hitchcock's *Spellbound* into a similar one-movement piano/orchestral synthesis which also achieved some popular success in 1945.) Addinsell's concerto remained popular for decades, and in the 1950s its lyrical main theme was adapted into an American popular song, "The World Outside." A pop version was recorded by Ray Coniff and his orchestra on the second volume of Coniff's *Concert in Rhythm* albums for Columbia.

Throughout the 1940s and 1950s Addinsell alternated film scoring with theatrical work, the latter including both composing and performing (as pianist/accompanist). He was especially known for his songwriting with the British actress/lyricist Joyce Grenfell, and for touring in her review of comic songs and sketches, *Joyce Grenfell Requests the Pleasure*. Addinsell also wrote extensively for the BBC. His most well-known films of this period include David Lean's production of Noel Coward's *Blithe Spirit*, which produced one of Addinsell's most lyrical waltz melodies, Alfred Hitchcock's *Under Capricorn*, and the British version of *Tom Brown's Schooldays*. Aside from his ubiquitous "Warsaw Concerto," one of Addinsell's best and most widely heard scores is for the 1951 British version of Dickens' *A Christmas Carol, Scrooge*. Starring Alistair Sim, this version of the oft-filmed tale has become a staple of holiday television viewing. Addinsell's imaginative and atmospheric score fuses his original themes and character motifs with traditional christmas carols, and explores a variety of styles and moods along the way, from the powerful opening cue which has been compared to music for a Universal horror classic, to a delicate music-box-style sequence for the wistful scene in which Tiny Tim gazes at clockwork toys in a shop window.

In the late 1950s and 1960s, the demise of the Hollywood studio system with its increasing emphasis on international co-productions led to some of Addinsell's more unusual and widely heard late work. In 1957 he scored the Marilyn Monroe production of Terance Ratigan's play, *The Sleeping Prince*, filmed as *The Prince and the Showgirl* with Monroe and Lawrence Olivier, and produced in London. For *The Roman Spring of Mrs. Stone*, Jose Quintero's 1961 film of the Tennessee Williams novel starring Vivien Leigh, Addinsell composed a moody main theme, and a lyrical cantilena for guitar and orchestra which underscores the main title credits and continues under the spoken prologue. 1961 also saw Addinsell composing what he refered to as one of his personal favorite scores, the pastoral *Greengage Summer*. Addinsell's last film was *Life at the Top*, the sequel to one of the classics of the New British Cinema of the 1960s, *Room at the Top*. After seeing his great friend, the couturier Victor Steibal, through a difficult demise due to muscular sclerosis, Addinsell himself died in his native London in November of 1977.

Addinsell was popular with film producers because he was also an accomplished pianist who could immediately capture (and play for them) the exact type of music they desired for their projects. He was a genius at scoring films, at capturing both mood and period, but (and here he is not unlike many other musicians who worked in films) he did not orchestrate, and so arrangers were needed to expand his music for full orchestra. Like the American composer/songwriter, Victor Young, Addinsell's reputation for attractive melodies and "light music" has somewhat overshadowed his prolific career in feature film scoring. But while the "Warsaw Concerto" remains the work for which Addinsell is best-remembered by the general public, the introduction of digital technology prompted a revival of interest in both Addinsell's film and light concert music, resulting in several CDs devoted to his film scores and miscellaneous pieces, including his "Smokey Mountains" concerto, and of course the ever-popular "Warsaw."

—Ross Care

ADRIAN, (Gilbert)

Costume Designer. **Nationality:** American. **Born:** Adrian Adolph Greenburg in Naugatuck, Connecticut, 3 March 1903; used the single name Adrian from 1921, then borrowed his father's given name, Gilbert, 1922. **Education:** Attended Parsons School of Fine and Applied Art (now Parsons School of Design), New York, 1921, and Paris branch, 1922. **Family:** Married the actress Janet Gaynor, 1939; son: Robin. **Career:** Costume designer for Broadway revues in early 1920s; 1925—in Hollywood: designer for Cecil B. De Mille, 1926–28; MGM, 1929–41; then freelance designer; also a painter (one-man shows, Knoedler Gallery, New York, 1949 and 1951); 1953–58—lived in Brazil. **Died:** In Hollywood, California, 13 September 1959.

Films as Costume Designer:

1924 *What Price Beauty* (Buckingham)
1925 *The Eagle* (Brown); *Cobra* (Henaberry); *Her Sister* (Franklin)
1926 *Fig Leaves* (Hawks); *Gigolo* (Howard); *Young April* (Crisp); *For Alimony Only* (W. De Mille); *The Volga Boatman* (C. De Mille)

Adrian

1927 *Almost Human* (Urson); *The Angel of Broadway* (Sjöström); *Chicago* (Urson); *Dress Parade* (Crisp); *His Dog* (K. Brown); *The Main Event* (Howard); *My Friend from India* (Hopper); *The Wise Wife* (Hopper); *The Country Doctor* (Julian); *The Fighting Eagle* (Crisp); *The Forbidden Woman* (Stein); *The Little Adventuress* (W. De Mille); *Vanity* (Crisp); *The Wreck of the Hesperus* (Clifton); *Love* (Goulding)

1928 *The Blue Danube* (Sloane); *A Ship Comes In* (Howard); *Skyscraper* (Higgin); *Walking Back* (Julian); *Dream of Love* (Niblo); *The Godless Girl* (C. De Mille); *Let 'er Go Gallagher* (Clifton); *Midnight Madness* (Weight); *Stand and Deliver* (Crisp); *A Woman of Affairs* (C. Brown); *A Lady of Chance* (Leonard); *The Masks of the Devil* (Sjöström)

1929 *Marianne* (Leonard); *The Bridge of San Luis Rey* (Brabin); *Dynamite* (C. De Mille); *A Single Man* (Beaumont) *Their Own Desire* (Hopper); *Wild Orchids* (Franklin); *The Last of Mrs. Cheyney* (Franklin); *Our Modern Maidens* (Conway); *Devil-May-Care* (Franklin); *The Single Standard* (Robertson); *The Thirteenth Chair* (Browning); *The Trial of Mary Dugan* (Veiller); *The Unholy Night* (L. Barrymore)

1930 *Not So Dumb* (K. Vidor); *Passion Flower* (W. De Mille); *The Rogue Song* (L. Barrymore); *This Mad World* (W. De Mille); *New Moon* (Conway); *The Divorcee* (Leonard); *Anna Christie* (C. Brown); *The Floradora Girl* (Beaumont); *In Gay Madrid* (Leonard); *The Lady of Scandal* (Franklin); *A Lady in Love* (Sjöström); *A Lady's Morals* (Franklin); *Let Us Be Gay* (Leonard); *Madam Satan* (C. De

Mille); *Montana Moon* (St. Clair); *Our Blushing Brides* (Beaumont); *Redemption* (Niblo); *Romance* (C. Brown)

1931 *Inspiration* (C. Brown); *Laughing Sinners* (Beaumont); *A Free Soul* (C. Brown); *The Squaw Man* (C. De Mille); *The Bachelor Father* (Leonard); *Five and Ten* (Leonard); *Strangers May Kiss* (Fitzmaurice); *The Guardsman* (Franklin); *Susan Lennox, Her Rise and Fall* (Leonard); *Arsene Lupin* (Conway)

1932 *Emma* (C. Brown); *Flying High* (Riesner); *Grand Hotel* (Goulding); *Strange Interlude* (Leonard); *Polly of the Circus* (Santell); *Rasputin and the Empress* (Boleslawsky); *Faithless* (Beaumont); *As You Desire Me* (Fitzmaurice); *Smilin' Through* (Franklin); *The Son-Daughter* (C. Brown); *The Wet Parade* (Fleming); *Huddle* (Wood); *But the Flesh Is Weak* (Conway); *Lovers Courageous* (Leonard); *Unashamed* (Beaumont); *Red Dust* (Fleming); *Red-Headed Woman* (Conway); *The Washington Masquerade* (Brabin); *The Mask of Fu Manchu* (Brabin)

1933 *The Barbarian* (Wood); *Peg o' My Heart* (Leonard); *Made on Broadway* (Beaumont); *Midnight Mary* (Wellman); *Queen Christina* (Mamoulian); *Dancing Lady* (Leonard); *Stage Mother* (Brabin); *When Ladies Meet* (Beaumont); *Hold Your Man* (Wood); *Another Language* (Griffith); *The Woman in His Life* (Seitz); *Bombshell* (Fleming); *Men Must Fight* (Selwyn); *Reunion in Vienna* (Franklin); *Looking Forward* (C. Brown); *Gabriel over the White House* (La Cava); *The White Sister* (Fleming); *The Secret of Madam Blanche* (Brabin); *Turn Back the Clock* (Selwyn); *Beauty for Sale* (Boleslawsky); *Dinner at Eight* (Cukor); *Storm at Daybreak* (Boleslawsky); *The Stranger's Return* (K. Vidor); *Going Hollywood* (Walsh); *The Solitaire Man* (Conway); *Penthouse* (Van Dyke); *Secrets* (Borzage) (co); *The Cat and the Fiddle* (Howard)

1934 *Operator 13* (Boleslawsky); *Forsaking All Others* (Van Dyke); *Riptide* (Goulding); *The Mystery of Mr. X* (Selwyn); *The Barretts of Wimpole Street* (Franklin); *Outcast Lady* (Leonard); *The Girl from Missouri* (Conway); *Men in White* (Boleslawsky); *The Painted Veil* (Boleslawsky); *What Every Woman Knows* (La Cava); *The Merry Widow* (Lubitsch); *Sadie McKee* (C. Brown)

1935 *No More Ladies* (Griffith); *After Office Hours* (Leonard); *Mark of the Vampire* (Browning); *I Live My Life* (Van Dyke); *China Seas* (Garnett); *Broadway Melody of 1936* (Leonard); *Reckless* (Fleming); *Anna Karenina* (C. Brown); *Naughty Marietta* (Van Dyke)

1936 *The Great Ziegfeld* (Leonard); *Romeo and Juliet* (Cukor) (co); *The Gorgeous Hussy* (C. Brown); *Love on the Run* (Van Dyke); *San Francisco* (Van Dyke); *Rose Marie* (Van Dyke); *Born to Dance* (Del Ruth); ***Camille*** (Cukor)

1937 *Parnell* (Stahl); *Maytime* (Leonard); *The Bride Wore Red* (Arzner); *The Double Wedding* (Thorpe); *Broadway Melody of 1938* (Del Ruth); *The Firefly* (Leonard); *Between Two Women* (Seitz); *The Last Gangster* (Ludwig); *Mannequin* (Borzage); *Conquest* (C. Brown)

1938 *The Girl of the Golden West* (Leonard); *Marie Antoinette* (Van Dyke) (co); *Love Is a Headache* (Thorpe); *The Toy Wife* (Thorpe) (co); *The Shopworn Angel* (Wallace); *Sweethearts* (Van Dyke); *The Shining Hour* (Borzage); *Three Loves Has Nancy* (Thorpe); *Vacation from Love* (Fitzmaurice); *Dramatic School* (Sinclair)

1939 *The Women* (Cukor); *Idiot's Delight* (C. Brown); **The Wizard of Oz** (Fleming); *Ice Follies of 1939* (Schunzel) (co); *It's a Wonderful World* (Van Dyke); *Broadway Serenade* (Leonard) (co); *Balalaika* (Schunzel); **Ninotchka** (Lubitsch)

1940 *Escape* (LeRoy); *Boom Town* (Conway) (co); *Bitter Sweet* (Van Dyke) (co); *The Mortal Storm* (Borzage) (co); *Pride and Prejudice* (Leonard) (co); *New Moon* (Leonard); *Broadway Melody of 1940* (Taurog) (co); *Waterloo Bridge* (LeRoy) (co); *Comrade X* (K. Vidor); *Strange Cargo* (Borzage); **The Philadelphia Story** (Cukor)

1941 *When Ladies Meet* (Leonard); *The Feminine Touch* (Van Dyke); *Smilin' Through* (Borzage) (co); *Two-Faced Woman* (Cukor); *Lady Be Good* (McLeod); *Dr. Jekyll and Mr. Hyde* (Fleming) (co); *They Met in Bombay* (C. Brown) (co); *Blossoms in the Dust* (LeRoy) (co); *Ziegfeld Girl* (Leonard); *A Woman's Face* (Cukor)

1942 *Woman of the Year* (Stevens); *Hers to Hold* (Ryan) (co); *Shadow of a Doubt* (Hitchcock) (co); *Hi Diddle Diddle* (Stone); *Keeper of the Flame* (Cukor)

1943 *His Butler's Sister* (Borzage); *The Powers Girl* (McLeod) (co)

1946 *Humoresque* (Negulesco) (co)

1947 *Rope* (Hitchcock)

1948 *Smart Woman* (Blatt)

1952 *Lovely to Look At* (LeRoy) (co)

Publications

By ADRIAN: articles—

"Dressing the Stars," in *The Picturegoer's Who's Who and Encyclopedia*, London, 1933.

"Setting Styles through the Stars," in *Ladies' Home Journal* (Philadelphia), February 1933.

"Do American Women Want American Clothes?," in *Harper's Bazaar* (New York), February 1934.

"Garbo Goes Different," in *Movie Classic* (New York), July 1935.

"Garbo as Camille," in *Vogue* (New York), 15 November 1936.

"Costumes," in *Romeo and Juliet: A Motion Picture Edition*, New York, 1936.

"Costumes for the Screen," in *Movie Merry-Go-Round*, edited by John Paddy Carstairs, London, 1937.

"Clothes," in *Behind the Screen*, edited by Stephen Watts, London, 1938.

On ADRIAN: book—

Tomerlin Lee, Sarah, editor, *American Fashion: The Life and Times of Adrian, Mainbocher, McCardell, Norell, Trigere*, New York, 1975.

On ADRIAN: articles—

Chierichetti, David, in *Hollywood Costume Design*, New York, 1976.
Leese, Elizabeth, in *Costume Design in the Movies*, New York, 1976.
LaVine, W. Robert, in *In a Glamorous Fashion*, New York, 1980.

Gibb, Bill, in *Films and Filming* (London), November 1983.
Wide Angle (Athens, Ohio), vol. 6, no. 4, 1985.
Architectural Digest, vol. 49, April 1992.
Los Angeles Times, 17 August 1995.

* * *

Known for his impeccable styling, Adrian influenced the history of fashion with his camera-tailored costumes that set cinematic precedents. Also to his credit is a potent iconography of American mythology that lingers even today.

Adrian envisioned Norma Shearer as "everywoman's" ideal. Loaded with class, Shearer wore the kinds of fashions on which the "best-dressed" lists thrive. For her "prestige" pictures, Adrian featured the ultimate in opulent elegance. In *Marie Antoinette*, for instance, her wardrobe rivaled the magnificence of the historical originals.

For Greta Garbo, MGM had originally planned to laden the Swedish actress with junk jewelry and paraphernalia. Adrian protested vehemently, "Never put anything fake on Garbo!" and proceeded to dress her in his finest creations. Though his lines were simple, he often added precious details, such as exquisite embroidery or special sleeve treatments. Instead of presenting her as a flashy *femme fatale*, he translated her beauty as ethereal fantasy. In *Camille* Adrian costumes told the tale. Garbo as martyr wore a golden chain around her neck, while her shoulders were bared and vulnerable. Stars across the gown associated her with the heavens. This image suggested a Christian saint more than a *demimonde* courtesan. In other films, Adrian designed heavily glittered garments to counteract Garbo's purity. The fabric symbolized adultery in *Wild Orchids* and moral decay in *Susan Lennox*. *Mata Hari* shed her sequins as she spiritually progressed, for no material could outshine Garbo's natural brilliance.

While Adrian's Garbo bore the timeless beauty of geometry, with her abstract, linear proportions paralleling contemporary European design, all-American Jean Harlow hit with Yankee hard sell. Exaggerated but clever, brassy yet bold, Harlow was dressed with panache. Her "white on white" look could be traced to a British decorating vogue. It stood for a contemporary decadence rather than traditional purity. Adrian revealed Harlow's round, provocative form in the guise of an earthly Venus.

Adrian's Joan Crawford evolved. Beginning as an unadulterated *moderne* flapper, she combined Garbo's geometry with Harlow's visual chutzpah. Later, as a sleek, sophisticated socialite, she spurred glorious dreams of wealth for Depression audiences. But it is for her masculine padded shoulder style that we remember her best. With a torso as assertive as a yield sign, Crawford typified the aggressive woman. When the working woman returned to fashion in the 1970s, so did Adrian's padded shoulders.

Throughout his career Adrian designed fantastic frivolities. From *Madam Satan* to *Ziegfeld Girl*, erotica akin to Erté's sumptuous extravaganzas paraded down MGM's runways. Adrian dressed the nymphs of the chorus as chimeric birds, sprites, and demons. But his ultimate contribution to American myth was in *The Wizard of Oz*, a colorful, childhood allegory that remains one of Hollywood's most frequently seen films.

—Edith C. Lee

AGE and SCARPELLI

AGE. Writer. Nationality: Italian. **Born:** Agenore Incrocci in Brescia, 4 July 1919. **Career:** Worked as journalist: 1945–49—radio writer; 1947—first film script, *I due orfanelli.*

SCARPELLI. Writer. Nationality: Italian. **Born:** Furio Scarpelli in Rome, 16 December 1919. **Family:** Son: the writer Giacomo Scarpelli. **Career:** Worked as journalist.

1949—first co-written script, *Totò cerca casa;* 1954–55—co-wrote the musical revues *Festival* and *Siamo tutti dottori.*

Films as Co-Writers (Selected Filmography):

1949 *Totò cerca casa* (Steno and Monicelli); *Il vedovo allegro* (Mattòli); *Totò le Moko* (Bragaglia)

1950 *Totò cerca moglie* (Bragaglia); *Totò Tarzan* (Mattòli); *47 morto che parla* (Bragaglia); *I cadetti di Guascogna* (Mattòli)

1951 *Arrivano i nostri* (Mattòli); *L'eroe sono io* (Bragaglia); *Signori in carrozza!* (Zampa); *Auguri e figli maschi* (Simonelli); *Una bruna indiavolata* (Bragaglia)

1952 *Totò a colori* (Steno); *Totò e le donne* (Steno and Monicelli); *Ragazze da marito* (De Filippo)

1953 *Ivan, il figlio del diavolo bianco* (Brignone); *Capitan Fantasma* (Zeglio); *Cinema d'altri tempi* (Steni); *L'incantevole nemica* (Gora); *Gli uomini, che mascalzoni!* (Pellegrini); *Napoletani a Milano* (De Filippo)

1954 *Le signorine delle 04* (Franciolini); *Casa Ricordi* (*House of Ricordi*) (Gallone); *Sinfonia d'amore* (*Schubert*) (Pellegrini)

1955 *Casta diva* (Gallone); *Bravissimo!* (d'Amico); *Il bigamo* (Emmer)

1956 *Racconti romani* (*Roman Tales*) (Franciolini); *La banda degli onesti* (Mastrocinque); *Peccato di castità* (Franciolini); *Tempo di villeggiatura* (Racioppi and Zampa); *Una pelliccia di visone* (Pellegrini); *Padri e figli* (*The Tailor's Maid; Fathers and Sons*) (Monicelli)

1957 *Il medico e lo stregone* (Monicelli); *Souvenir d'Italie* (Pietrangeli)

1958 *Totò, Peppino, e le fanatiche* (Mattòli); *I soliti ignoti* (*Big Deal on Madonna Street*) (Monicelli); *Nata di marzo* (Pietrangeli); *La Loi . . . c'est la loi* (*The Law Is the Law*) (Christian-Jaque); *Primo amore* (Camerini)

1959 *Audace colpo dei soliti ignoti* (*Fiasco in Milan*) (Loy); *Policarpo, ufficiale di scrittura* (Soldati); *La grande guerra* (*The Great War*) (Monicelli)

1960 *Il mattatore* (*Love and Larceny*) (Risi); *Risate di gioia* (*The Passionate Thief*) (Monicelli); *Tutti a casa* (*Everybody Go Home!*) (Comencini)

1961 *I due nemici* (*The Best of Enemies*) (Hamilton); *A cavallo della tigre* (Comencini)

1962 *Totò e Peppino divisi a Berlino* (Bianchi); *La marcia su Roma* (Risi); *Il commissario* (Comencini); *Il mafioso* (*Mafioso*) (Lattuada)

1963 *I compagni* (*The Organizer*) (Monicelli); *I mostri* (*Opiate '67; 15 from Rome*) (Risi); *Il maestro di Vigevano* (Petri)

1964 "Gente moderna" ("Modern People") ep. of *Alta infedeltà* (*High Infidelity*) (Monicelli); *Frenesia dell'estate* (Germi)

1965 *Casanova '70* (Monicelli); "Il complesso della schiava nubiana" ep. of *I complessi* (Rossi); *Io, io, io . . . e gli altri* (Blasetti)

1966 *Signore e signori* (*The Birds, the Bees, and the Italians*) (Germi); **Il buono, il brutto, il cattivo** (*The Good, the Bad, and the Ugly*) (Leone); *L'armata Brancaleone* (Monicelli); "Il marito di Olga" and "Il marito di Attilia" eps. of *I nostri mariti* (Monicelli and Risi)

1967 "Senso civico" ("Civic Sense") ep. of *Le streghe* (*The Witches*) (Bolognini); *Il tigre* (*The Tiger and the Pussycat*) (Risi); *Ti ho sposato per allegria* (*I Married You for Fun*) (Salce)

1968 *Riusciranno i nostri eroi a trovare l'amico misteriosamente scomparso in Africa?* (Scola); *Straziami ma di baci saziami* (*Tear Me but Satiate Me with Your Kisses*) (Risi); "La bambinaia" and "Perchè" eps. of *Capriccio all'italiana* (Monicelli and Bolognini)

1969 *Rosolino Paternò, soldato* (Loy)

1970 *Dramma della gelosia, tutti i particolari in cronaca* (*The Pizza Triangle; A Drama of Jealousy and Other Things*) (Scola); *Brancaleone alle crociate* (Monicelli)

1971 "Alberta" ep. of *Noi donne siamo fatte cosi* (*Women: So We Are Made*) (Risi); *In nome del popolo italiano* (*In the Name of the Italian People*) (Risi)

1972 *Senza famiglia nullatenenti, cercano affetto . . .* (Gassman)

1973 *Teresa la ladra* (Di Palma); *Vogliamo i colonnelli* (Monicelli)

1974 *Romanzo popolare* (Monicelli); *C'eravamo tanto amati* (*We All Loved Each Other So Much*) (Scola)

1975 *La donna della domenica* (*The Sunday Woman*) (Comencini)

1976 *L'Agnese va a morire* (Montaldo); *Signore e signori buonanotte* (Comencini and others); "Il superiore" and "Macchina d'amore" eps. of *Basta che non si sappia in giro* (Magni and Loy)

1977 *I nuovi mostri* (*The Monsters; Viva Italia!*) (Risi and Scola)

1979 *Temporale Rosy* (Monicelli)

1980 *La terrazza* (Scola)

1981 "Armando's Notebook" ep. of *Sunday Lovers* (Risi); *Nudo di donna* (*Portrait of a Woman, Nude*) (Manfredi); *Camera d'albergo* (Monicelli)

1982 *Spaghetti House* (Paradisi)

1983 *Il tassinaro* (Sordi)

1985 *Scemo di guerra* (Risi)

1988 *Una Botta di vita* (Oldoini)

1999 *Boom* (Zaccariello) (Age only)

Other Films:

1947 *I due orfanelli* (Mattòli) (Age only)

1949 *Vivere a sbafo* (Ferroni) (Age only)

1983 *Scherzo* (Wertmüller) (Age only); *Dagobert* (Risi) (Age only); *Un ragazzo, una ragazza* (Risi) (Scarpelli only); *Ballando ballando* (*Le Bal; The Ball*) (Scola) (Scarpelli only)

1984 *Cuori nella tormenta* (Oldoini) (Scarpelli only)

1985 *Maccheroni* (*Macaroni*) (Scola) (Scarpelli only); *I soliti ignoti vent'anni dopo* (Todini) (Age only)

1987 *La famiglia* (*The Family*) (Scola) (Scarpelli only)

1989 *Tempo di uccidere* (*The Short Cut; Le Raccourci; Time to Kill*) (Montaldo) (Scarpelli only)

1990   *Il viaggio di Capitan Fracassa* (*The Voyage of Captain Fracasse*; *Le Voyage du Capitaine Fracasse*) (Scola) (Scarpelli only)
1991   *La Pagaille* (Thomas) (Age only); *Il Conte Max* (De Sica) (Age only); *Zuppa di pesce* (Infascelli) (Age only)
1992   *Cattiva* (Lizzani) (Scarpelli only)
1994   *Il Postino* (*The Postman*) (Radford) (Scarpelli only with his son Giacomo)
1995   *Celluloide* (Lizzani) (Scarpelli only)

Publications

By AGE and SCARPELLI: books—

With Mario Monicelli, *Romanzo popolare*, Milan, 1974.
Age & Scarpelli in Commedia, edited by Claudio Trionfera, Rome, 1990.

By AGE: book—

Scriviamo un film, Parma, 1990.

By SCARPELLI: book—

With Ettore Scola, *Disegni per il cinema: Furio Scarpelli ed Ettore Scola*, Mantova, 1985.

By AGE and SCARPELLI: articles—

Jeune Cinéma (Paris), March 1975.
Positif (Paris), May 1977.
Cahiers du Cinéma (Paris), February 1979.
Avant-Scène (Paris), February 1981.
Bianco e Nero, July 1986.
CinémAction, March 1987.
Positif (Paris), May 1991.
CinémAction, October 1991.

By AGE: articles—

Image et Son (Paris), May 1977.
Cinéma (Paris), February 1978.
Cahiers du Cinéma (Paris), February 1979.

By SCARPELLI: articles—

Skoop, September-October 1986.
CinémAction (Courbevoie), January 1994.

*   *   *

Audiences familiar with popular Italian comedies from the sixties and early seventies cannot have missed the names of Age and Scarpelli from the credits. Apart from being the most representative writers of comedy "in the Italian style," they have marked the careers of many reputed filmmakers; a recent film historian has labeled them "the key binomial" in the evolution of Italian cinema. Both come from artistic milieus and get involved with theater, vaudeville, and satirical journals (they met as part of the staff of the famous magazine

Marc Aurelio) while still very young. They share with contemporaries such as Fellini, Monicelli, Risi, Scola, and Steno the taste for mordant verbal satire and its visualization, initially present in sketches and drawings, later to become subjects for feature-length films. Their first four-hand achievement is one of the numerous comedies starring the Keatonesque Totò, called *Totò cerca casa*, co-directed by one of their future habitués, director Mario Monicelli. Totò's innate sense for surrealist performance considerably influenced their screenwriting trajectory, allowing them to turn ordinary situations into models of irony and understatement. Another notable influence was Sergio Amidei, also known as the dean of postwar scriptwriting, with whom they wrote *Le signorine delle 04*; Amidei favors "the horizontal story," which allows several sub-stories to unfold simultaneously, as opposed to "the vertical story," in which plot-points lead to an expected finale.

After a couple of rather "operatic" productions such as *Casa Ricordi* and *Casta diva*, Age and Scarpelli eventually imposed their personal style, achieving an unprecedented blend between dramatic neorealism and satirical comedy. Their "youth-oriented" films, mainly directed by Monicelli, Comencini, and Risi (with whom they tried to set up a production company called "Film Cinque"), feature minor characters, small-time thieves, and homeless *vitelloni* whose humor, generosity, and wit facilitate audience identification: *I soliti ignoti*, *Tutti a casa*, *I compagni*, and *I mostri* (famous sketch-film with a sequel made 14 years later, *I nuovi mostri*) are just a few highlights of an outstandingly rich creative decade. The sixties also enabled the two screenwriters to desacralize various taboo subjects: war heroes are demystified (*La grande guerra* and *La marcia su Roma*) and middle-age icons ridiculed (*L'armata Brancaleone*); the sexual revolution, although incipient, is foregrounded (noteworthy in this respect is the collaboration with Pietro Germi, director of *Sedotta e abbandonata* and *Signore e signori*). Their versatile screenwriting style facilitated the revival of the Leone-Western (*Il buono, il brutto, il cattivo*) and turned a parodic melodrama by Ettore Scola (*Dramma della gelosia*) into a landmark Italian comedy from the early seventies. The subsequent production of Age and Scarpelli is more heterogeneous, although no less exciting: they were invited to write more scripts for sketch-films (i.e., *Noi donne siamo fatte cosi* by Dino Risi), while continuing to transgress political and historical taboos through ferocious farces (i.e., *Vogliamo i colonnelli* and its group of fascist nostalgics who set up a coup).

Nonetheless, 1974 proved a crucial year in the career of these modern-time Goldonis: they created one of their best comedies of manners, Monicelli's *Romanzo popolare*. The traditional love triangle staging the husband, his wife, and her lover is the pretext for analyzing the important gap separating urban and nonurban population, the North and the South, the "written" Italian language and the various dialects which Age and Scarpelli relish using in many of their scripts. In a totally different vein, *C'eravamo tanto amati* heralded a new beginning in their collaboration with Scola and coincided with a change in tone, an almost autumnal echoing of their common youth: the audience is confronted with individual destinies, their revolutionary ideals and their broken dreams. A few years later, in *La terrazza*, this autobiographical overture was further developed into an unconventional meditation of a group of aging intellectuals, one of them played by none other than Age.

The eighties witnessed a further diversification in the screenwriters' working style: they started collaborating with directors from the younger generation (Age with Fiorella Infascelli, Scarpelli with

Marco Risi), wrote scripts for actors' films (Manfredi, Sordi, etc.) and did not refrain from adapting famous novels (*Scemo di guerra*, after *Il deserto di Libia* by Mario Tobino) or from issuing "international products" (*Spaghetti House* and *Maccheroni*). Some of the above-mentioned films were scripted separately, others still in collaboration; Age and Scarpelli eventually decided to "part ways" in the mid-eighties, confessing above all a need for change and a natural impulse to help young filmmakers and start teaching on a more permanent basis. Such a decision did not prevent them from pursuing hectic careers, Age in France and Italy, Scarpelli mostly with Scola, but also more recently with his own son, Giacomo (for the Oscar-nominated *Il Postino*). Proving that they are still active and occasionally reunited into the nineties, Age and Scarpelli are credited for a 1996 musical revue, *Bobbi sa tutto*. Paraphrasing the musical, one could almost state that the "key binomial" definitely knows everything about successful screenwriting.

—Dominique Nasta

ALCORIZA, Luis

Writer and Director. **Nationality:** Mexican. **Born:** Badajóz, Spain, 5 September 1920; naturalized Mexican citizen. **Family:** Married the dancer and actress Raquel Rojas. **Career:** Actor from his teens; 1939—on stage in Mexico with Blanch Brothers' company; 1940—film debut as actor in *La torre de los suplicios*; 1946—first film as writer, *El ahijado de la muerte*; 1960—first film as director, *Los jovenes*. **Died:** December 1992.

Films as Writer (Often in Collaboration):

1946   *El ahijado de la muerte* (Foster)
1948   *Nocturno de amor* (Gómez Muriel); *Enredate y veras* (Orellana); *Flor de caña* (Orellana); *Negra consentida* (Soler); *Los amores de une viuda* (Soler)
1949   *La liga de las muchachas* (Cortés); *Un cuerpo de mujer* (Davison); *El gran calavera* (*The Great Madcap*) (Buñuel) (+ ro); *Tu, solo tu* (Delgado) (+ ro); *Yo quiero ser hombre* (Cardona)
1950   *Mala hembre* (Delgado); *Si me viera Don Porfirio* (Cortés); **Los olvidados** (*The Young and the Damned*) (Buñuel); *Huellas del pasado* (Crevenna); *El siete machos* (Delgado)
1951   *La hija del angaño* (*Daughter of Deceit*) (Buñuel); *Una gringuita en Mexico* (Soler); *Canasta uruguaya* (Cardona); *Los enredos de una gallega* (Soler); *Anillo de compromiso* (Gómez Muriel); *La Miel se fue de la luna* (Soler); *Carne de presidio* (Soler)
1952   *Se la paso la mano* (Soler); *Isla de mujeres* (Baledón)
1953   *El bruto* (*The Brute*) (Buñuel); *El* (*This Strange Passion*) (Buñuel); *Gitana tenias que ser* (Baledón); *La ilusión viaja en tranvia* (Buñuel)
1954   *El rio y la muerte* (*The River and Death*) (Buñuel); *La visita que no toco al timbre* (Soler); *Sombra verde* (Gavaldón); *. . . y mañana seran mujeres!* (Galindo); *La vida no vale nada* (González)

1955   *El rey de Mexico* (Baledón); *La tercera palabra* (Soler); *El inocente* (González)
1956   *La Mort en ce jardin* (*Gina*; *Evil Eden*; *Death in the Garden*) (Buñuel); *Escuela de rateros* (González)
1957   *A media luz los tres* (Soler)
1958   *El hombre de Alazan* (González); *El cariñoso* (Baledón); *Me gustan valentones* (Soler); *La tijera de oro* (Alazraki)
1959   *El hombre neustra de cada dia* (González); *El toro negro* (Alazraki); *La Fièvre monte à El Pao* (*Los ambiciosos*) (Buñuel); *El esqueleto de la señora Morales* (González); *Bala peridida* (Urueta); *Guantes de Oro* (Urueta)
1960   *Suicídate, mi amor* (Martínez Solares)
1962   *El ángel exterminador* (*The Exterminating Angel*) (Buñuel)
1979   *Fe, esperanza y caridad* (Bojorques)

Films as Writer and Director:

1960   *Los jovenes*
1961   *Tlayucan* (*The Pearl of Tlayucan*)
1962   *Tiburoneros*
1963   *Sapho 63*
1964   *El gangster*
1965   *Tarahumara*
1966   "*Divertimento*" ep. of *Juego peligroso*
1967   *La casa de cristal*
1968   *El oficio más antiguo*; *La puerta* (short)
1969   *Paraiso*
1971   *Mecánica nacional*
1972   *Esperanza*; *El muro de silencio*
1973   *Presagio*
1974   *Las fuerza vivas*
1980   *Tac, tac*
1986   *Terrór y encajes negros* (*Terror and Black Lace*)
1989   *Lo que importa es vivir* (*What's Important Is to Live*)

Publications

By ALCORIZA: book—

The Exterminating Angel and *Los olvidados* (scripts), in *Three Screen Plays by Luis Buñuel*, New York, 1969.

By ALCORIZA: articles:—

Tiempo de Cine, Spring 1965.
Cinemateca (Montevideo), January 1978.
Dirigido por . . . (Barcelona), February 1978.
Cineinforme, January 1982.
Dirigido por . . . (Barcelona), February 1982.

On ALCORIZA: articles—

Film Heritage (Dayton, Ohio), Fall 1965.
Filme Cultura (Rio de Janeiro), no. 7, 1967.
Hablemos de Cine (Lima), no. 61–62, 1971.

Huelva Festival Booklet, 1971.

Nevares, Beatriz Reyes, in *The Mexican Cinema*, Albuquerque, New Mexico, 1976.

Obituary in *Variety*, 14 December 1992.

*   *   *

Luis Alcoriza is best known for his script collaborations with fellow Spaniard Luis Buñuel, having worked on some of Buñuel's more intriguing Mexican films. But in his later life, Alcoriza emerged as one of the leading scenarists of modern Mexican cinema. After 1962 he scripted a number of important films (most of which he directed himself), which are his own peculiar blend of raucous entertainment and pointed social criticism. His unit of analysis is the group which, especially in his post-Buñuel period, he uses to symbolize Mexican society. This is a motif that is discernible in his Buñuel films as early as *Los olvidados* (the gang of street kids in Mexico City). Similarly, there are the bourgeois guests in *El ángel exterminador*, mysteriously trapped in their host's drawing room, the disparate band of refugees lost in the jungle in *La Mort en ce jardin*, and the political prisoners, bureaucrats, politicians, and hangers-on in the fictional South American dictatorship of *La Fièvre monte à El Pao*.

But whereas Buñuel's aims were existential, surrealist, and absurdist, Alcoriza's were satirical. Buñuel's films were bleak, detached commentaries on the human animal as he observed it, their undeniably dark side due to the fact that Buñuel's vision did not encompass redemption. Alcoriza's view was more hopeful. His scripts poke fun at human nature (particularly as it expresses itself in the Mexican national character), but like all true satirists, he criticizes in the hope of improving humanity. In Alcoriza's cinematic universe redemption is a goal worth striving for—is the *only* goal worth striving for. Asked why he chose to write and direct *Tarahumara*, his semidocumentary film about an isolated Mexican Indian tribe scratching out its meager existence in a remote region of Chihuahua, Alcoriza said: "I am not in agreement with the world in which I have to live, because I do not like our society. Today we try to reach other worlds, the moon, Mars . . . and the most elementary problems—hunger, justice, [human] dignity— have yet to be resolved." But Alcoriza believed this situation could be changed. Accordingly, his body of work reflects healthy indignation rather than Buñuel's typically distressing resignation.

Two of his more illustrious scripts (both for films he directed) are *Presagio*, coscripted by Gabriel García Márquez, about a village whose inhabitants come to believe that they are living under an evil spell, and *Mecánica nacional*, the story of a group of automobile racing fans, on their way to see the conclusion of an Acapulco-to-Mexico City auto race, who are thrown together for a day and a long night due to a traffic jam. In these and other Alcoriza films (*Tlayucan, Tiburoneros, El oficio más antiguo, Las fuerza vivas*) he fills an expansive canvas with a large cast of characters and succeeds in creating a Rabelaisian cross-section of Mexican society.

—Charles Ramírez Berg

ALCOTT, John

Cinematographer. **Nationality:** British. **Born:** London, 1931. **Career:** 1940s—clapper boy at Gainsborough Studios; 1983—moved to Hollywood. **Awards:** Berlin Film Festival Silver Bear Award for *Little Malcolm*, 1974; Academy Award and British Academy Award for *Barry Lyndon*, 1975. **Died:** Of heart attack, Cannes, 28 July 1986.

Films as Cinematographer:

1968   *2001: A Space Odyssey* (Kubrick) (additional photography)
1971   *Fangio* (Hudson); *A Clockwork Orange* (Kubrick)
1973   *David Niven* (Burder—doc)
1974   *Little Malcolm* (Cooper)
1975   *Barry Lyndon* (Kubrick)
1977   *The Fiesta Story* (Worth); *March or Die* (Richards); *The Disappearance* (Cooper)
1978   *Who Is Killing the Great Chefs of Europe? (Too Many Chefs)* (Kotcheff)
1980   *The Shining* (Kubrick); *Fort Apache, the Bronx* (Petrie); *Terror Train* (Spottiswoode)
1982   *The Beastmaster* (Coscarelli); *El triúnfo de un hombre llamado caballo* (Hough); *Vice Squad* (Sherman)
1984   *Greystoke: The Legend of Tarzan, Lord of the Apes* (Hudson); *Miracles* (Kouf)
1985   *Baby* (Norton)
1987   *No Way Out* (Donaldson); *White Water Summer* (Bleckner)

Films as Focus Puller:

1960   *The Singer Not the Song* (Baker)
1961   *Whistle Down the Wind* (Forbes)

Publications

By ALCOTT: article

American Cinematographer (Hollywood), vol. 6, no. 3, March 1985.

On ALCOTT: articles—

American Cinematographer (Hollywood), vol. 57, no. 3, March 1976.
Obituary, in *Variety* (New York), 6 August 1986.
American Cinematographer (Hollywood), vol. 68, no. 3, March 1987.

*   *   *

By the time of his tragically premature death in 1986, John Alcott had established himself as one of the world's leading directors of photography. In particular, his association with director Stanley Kubrick had put him at the forefront of technical and aesthetic developments in his field.

The son of Arthur Alcott, production controller at Gainsborough Studios throughout the 1940s, John Alcott began his movie career in the lowly position of clapper boy. After working as a focus puller on various films in the 1950s and 1960s (including Roy Baker's *The Singer Not the Song* and Bryan Forbes' *Whistle Down the Wind*), his big break came in the mid-sixties with his first film for Kubrick, *2001:*

A Space Odyssey. When that landmark film's original director of photography, Geoffrey Unsworth had to leave the project half-way through its two-year shooting schedule because of other commitments, Alcott, who had been his assistant, stepped ably into his shoes.

By all reports a modest and self-effacing man, Alcott preferred lighting that appeared natural and which did not draw attention to itself. As he himself put it, "It is possible then to emphasize colours more, on the streets and on the set." It was his work with Kubrick that gave Alcott the best opportunity to develop his ideas about "natural" lighting. One can indicate as examples of his skill the now famous scenes from *Barry Lyndon* which were shot entirely by candlelight. This was an idea that Kubrick and Alcott had discussed as far back as *2001* (it had originally been intended for Kubrick's abortive *Napoleon* project), but it was only in the 1970s that lens technology finally caught up with the imagination of these two great filmmakers. Similarly, in *The Shining* Alcott chose to light the elaborate hotel sets almost entirely with "practicals" (that is, sources of lighting which are visible on screen as an integral part of the set; e.g. chandeliers and other light fixtures).

Alcott also of course produced distinguished work with other directors. His numerous projects included a glossy comedy-romance (*Who Is Killing the Great Chefs of Europe?*), a Tarzan movie (*Greystoke*), thrillers (*No Way Out*, *Vice Squad*) and fantasies (*Baby*, *The Beastmaster*). Some of these films were better than others, but Alcott nearly always contributed something distinctive, even to the least interesting of films. A good example of this occurs in the generally undistinguished low-budget horror production *Terror Train*. At one point near the beginning of this film a group of masked partygoers board a train in the middle of the night. The scene is genuinely eerie (unlike the rest of the film), with its strange, dreamlike quality arising almost entirely from Alcott's lighting.

Alcott was one of a number of important behind-the-scenes figures in cinema whose input into various films often goes unheeded by critics and the public. The meticulousness of his work, as well as his complete lack of pretentiousness and his willingness to become involved in a wide range of projects (including some very unlikely ones) marked him out as one of cinema's great artist-technicians, someone who through his ability to push back the boundaries of what was technically possible and then think through some of the aesthetic consequences of this contributed to the development of film as an art form.

—Peter Hutchings

ALDO, G. R.

Cinematographer. **Nationality:** Italian. **Born:** Aldo Graziati in Scorze, 1 January 1902. **Career:** 1919—actor in France briefly, then still photographer in French film studios, and eventually cameraman; 1947—first film as cinematographer, *La terra trema*. **Died:** In a motor accident, 1953.

Films as Cinematographer:

1945   *Couleurs de Venise* (Faurez and Mercanton) (+ asst d)
1947   ***La terra trema*** (Visconti)

1948   *Les Derniers Jours de Pompéi* (*Gli ultimi giorni di Pompei*; *The Last Days of Pompeii*) (L'Herbier); *Cielo sulla palude* (Genina)
1950   *Taxi di notte* (*Singing Taxi Driver*) (Gallone); ***Miracolo a Milano*** (*Miracle in Milan*) (De Sica)
1951   *Domani e un altro giorno* (Moguy)
1952   *Othello* (Welles); *Tre storie proibite* (Genina); ***Umberto D*** (De Sica); *La provinciale* (*The Wayward Life*) (Soldati)
1953   *Stazione Termini* (*Indiscretion of an American Wife*) (De Sica)
1954   *Senso* (Visconti) (co)

Publications

On ALDO: articles—

Cinema Nuovo (Turin), 1 December 1953.
Bianco e Nero (Rome), December 1953.

*   *   *

G.R. Aldo, one of Italy's greatest cameramen, was a slow starter. Originally he had come to France in 1919 and appeared as an actor in a Jean Durand comedy. He abandoned this career to become a still photographer in the French film studios, continuing in the capacity for almost 20 years. He transferred his skills to working as an assistant cameraman and ultimately to lighting cameraman. In his humbler capacity he had worked with Marcel Carné and with Jean Cocteau on *La Belle et la bête*. In 1939 he was camera operator for Leonid Moguy's *L'Empreinte du Dieu* and also for Christian-Jaque on *La Symphonie fantastique*. With this experience behind him he visited Italy on location for Christian-Jaque's *Chartreuse de Parme* in 1947. He decided to remain in his native country and having been introduced to Visconti by his friend Antonioni, who knew him in Paris, he undertook the photography of *La terra trema*. His work on this made his reputation immediately. His sensitivity to location in this drama of poor Sicilian fishermen produced never-to-be-forgotten images in black-and-white. The physical beauty of the sea scenes and the contrasting landscapes never obscured the neorealistic approach of its director. It could be said that Aldo began and ended his career with Visconti for it was during the shooting of *Senso* in colour that he was killed in a motor accident on the Padua-Venice autostrada.

His output was not great but his artistry can be seen in three films of De Sica, *Miracolo a Milano*, *Umberto D*, and *Stazione Termini*. His exquisite work on Genina's *Cielo sulla palude*, a life of the child-saint Maria Goretti, brought out the beauty of the Pontine marshes in the changing seasons and the physical traits of peasant life and character. The film had, in the words of one critic, "the rhythm of an ancient sorrow." In 1952 Orson Welles made his version of *Othello* under conditions of great physical and financial difficulty. Forced to use the natural setting of Mogador in North Africa, Aldo illuminated the film with his striking images, and it became a feast for the eyes, turning the necessities of production into a virtue.

His style is never flamboyant and shows a subtle awareness of environment and subject but he could use every expressive device of the camera to penetrate the meaning of a scene. He played a key role in the neorealism of the Italian cinema.

—Liam O'Leary

ALEKAN, Henri

Cinematographer. **Nationality:** French. **Born:** Paris, 10 February 1909. **Education:** Attended the Conservatoire des Arts-et-Métiers and Institute of Optics. **Family:** Married to script supervisor/assistant director Nadia Starcevic. **Career:** Worked as assistant cameraman while a student; then bank clerk and puppeteer; 1931–36—assistant cameraman; 1932—helped form group, later union, of assistant cameramen; 1936–41—cameraman; 1940—briefly imprisoned by Germans during World War II: later worked in the Resistance (Legion of Honor); 1941—first film as cinematographer; 1944—founding member, IDHEC film school; 1946—co-founder, Académie du Cinema. TV work: *Le Taxi* (Marzelle), 1962, France; *The Henri Matisse Centennial at the Grand Palais* (Falkenberg/Namuth), 1970, U.S. acting debut in Wenders's *In Weiter Ferne, so Nah!* (*Far Away, So Close*), 1993. **Awards:** Prizes, for *L'Enfer de Rodin*, Prague Festival, 1957, and *Cerf-volant du bout du monde*, Karlory Vary Festival, 1958; César award for *The Trout*, 1982; Prix ESEC (École Supérieure Libre d'Études Cinématographiques), 1985. **Member:** Vice president, Film Production Technicians Union, 1958–65, president, 1965–68. **Address:** 46 rue de la Tourelle, 92100 Boulogne, France.

Films as Cinematographer:

1941   *Le Chariot de Thespis* (Canolle—short); *Robie est un ange* (Y. Allégret—destroyed)

1942   *Les Chevaux du Vercors* (Audry—short) (co); *Tu seras vedette* (Mineur—short); *Ceux du rail* (Clément—short); *Les Deux Timides* (Y. Allégret) (co)

1943   *Bell ouvrage* (Cloche—short); *Les Petites du Quai aux Fleurs* (M. Allégret—short); *Echec au roy* (Paulin); *La Symphonie du travail* (Cloche); *La Grande Pastorale* (Clément—short)

1944   *Chefs de demain* (Clément—short)

1945   **La Bataille du rail** (Clément); **La Belle et la bête** (Cocteau)

1947   *Les Maudits* (*The Damned*) (Clément); *Le Diable souffle* (Gréville)

1948   *Anna Karenina* (Duvivier); *Arch of Triumph* (Milestone) (2nd unit); *Un si jolie petite plage* (*Riptide*) (Y. Allégret)

1949   *La Marie du port* (Carné); *Les Amants de Vérone* (*The Lovers of Verona*) (Cayette)

1950   *Ma pomme* (Sauvajon)

1951   *Juliette ou la clé des songes* (Carné); *Parigi e sempre Parigi* (Emmer); "Mouche" ep. of *Trois femmes, trois âmes* (Michel); *La Voyage en Amérique* (Lavorel)

1952   *Stranger on the Prowl* (*Encounter*) (Losey) (+ ro); *La Sarre, pleins feux* (+ co-d—short); *Le Fruit défendu* (Verneuil)

1953   *Zoë* (Brabant); *Quand tu liras cette lettre* (Melville); *Roman Holiday* (Wyler) (co); *Les Amours finissent à l'aube* (Calef); *Julietta* (M. Allégret)

1954   *Le Port du désir* (Gréville); *Les Impures* (Chevalier); *La Reine Margot* (Dréville); *Frou-Frou* (Genina)

1955   *Les Héroes sont fatigués* (Ciampi); *La Meilleure Part* (Y. Allégret)

1956   *Typhon sur Nagasaki* (Ciampi); *La Salaire du péché* (de la Patellière); *Le Cas du Docteur Laurent* (le Chanois); "La Maison du bonheur" ep. of *Die Windrose* (Bellon)

1957   *L'Enfer de Rodin* (+ d—short)

1958   *Le Bourgeois Gentilhomme* (Meyer); *Cerf-volant du bout du monde* (Pigaut)

1959   *Le Mariage de Figaro* (Meyer); *Douze heures d'horloge* (Radvanyi)

1960   *Austerlitz* (Gance); *La Princesse de Clèves* (Delannoy); *Les Collants noirs* (*Un, deux, trois, quatre . . .*; *Black Tights*) (Young); *Le Secret du chevalier d'eon* (Audry) (co); *Un Oiseau s'en vole* (Canaille—short)

1961   "Ella" and "Antonia" eps. of *Les Parisiennes* (Poitrenaud and Boisrond)

1962   *Le Couteau dans la plaie* (*Five Miles to Midnight*) (Litvak)

1963   *El otro Cristobal* (Gatti); *Réunion des artistes* (Madanes)

1964   *Topkapi* (Dassin)

1965   *Lady L* (Ustinov)

1966   *Danger Grows Wild* (*The Poppy Is Also a Flower*) (Young); *Triple Cross* (Young)

1968   *Mayerling* (Young); *Ici et maintenant* (Bard—short)

1969   *Versailles* (Lamorisse—short); *L'Arbre de Noel* (*The Christmas Tree*) (Young)

1970   *Figures in a Landscape* (Losey) (co); *Giselle* (Farrel)

1971   *Soleil rouge* (*Red Sun*) (Young)

1975   *Jackpot* (Young)

1977   *Noire et Caline* (Leconte); *L'Ombre et la nuit* (Leconte)

1981   *The Territory* (Ruiz)

1982   *Techo de la ballena* (*The Roof of the Whale*) (Ruiz); *Der Stand der Dinge* (*The State of Things*) (Wenders); *Une Pierre dans la bouche* (Leconte); *The Trout* (Losey)

1983   *La Belle Captive* (Robbe-Grillet)

1984   *A Strange Love Affair* (de Kuyper); *Wunkanal Hinrichtung fur vier Stimmen* (*Exécution à quatre voix*) (Harlan); *Unser Nazi* (*Notre Nazi*) (Harlan)

1985   *The Perfect Kiss* (Demme)

1986   *Esther* (Gitai)

1987   ***Der Himmel über Berlin*** (*Wings of Desire*; *Sky over Berlin*; *Les Ailes du désir*) (Wenders)

1988   *Im Exil der ertrunkenen Tiger*

1989   *Berlin-Jérusalem* (Gitai); *J'écris dans l'espace* (Etaix); *Cézanne* (Jean-Marie Straub and Danièle Huillet); *La Danseuse de 14 ans* (short)

1992   *Golem—L'Esprit de l'exil* (*Golem—The Spirit of Exile*) (Gitai)

1993   *Golem—Le Jardin pétrifié* (*Golem—The Petrified Garden*) (Gitai)

Films as Camera Operator:

1936   *Mademoiselle Docteur* (Pabst)

1937   *La Danseuse rouge* (Paulin); *Drôle de drame* (*Bizarre Bizarre*) (Carné)

1938   *Le Drame de Shanghaï* (Pabst); *Quai des brumes* (*Port of Shadows*); (Carné); *Campement 13* (Constant); *L'Esclave blanche* (Sorkin); *Mollenard* (Siodmak)

1939   *Les Musiciens du ciel* (Lacombe); *L'Emigrante* (Y. Allégret and Joannon)

1940   *Sans lendemain* (Ophüls)

1941   *La Vénus aveugle* (Gance); *La Femme dans la nuit* (Gréville)

Publications

By ALEKAN: book—

Des lumières et des ombres, Paris, 1984.

By ALEKAN: articles—

Télécine (Paris), April 1961.
Cinéma (Paris), February 1973.
Le Technicien du Film (Paris), 15 January-15 February 1974.
Cinéma (Paris), June 1979.
Cinématographe (Paris), June 1981.
Film Français (Paris), 24 September 1982.
Positif (Paris), November 1982.
Cahiers du Cinéma (Paris), March 1983.
Cinéma (Paris), May 1983.
Le Technicien du Film (Paris), 15 May-15 June 1983.
Film Français (Paris), 31 August 1984.
Visions (Brussels), February 1985.
Skrien (Amsterdam), February/March 1985.
Première (Paris), June 1985
Postif (Paris), July/August 1985.
Films and Filming (London), no. 392, May 1987.
Revue du Cinéma (Paris), no. 431, October 1987.
Filmcritica (Montepulciano), September/October 1989.
Jeune Cinéma (Paris), no. 199, February-March 1990.
Framework, nos. 38/39, 1992.
Sight and Sound (London), vol. 3, no. 6, June 1993.
Film Français (Paris), no. 2519, August 1994.
Avant-Scène du Cinéma (Paris), no. 442, May 1995.
Filmvilag (Budapest), vol. 40, no. 2, 1997.

On ALEKAN: articles—

Unifrance (Paris), June/July 1951.
Lettres Françaises (Paris), 15 July 1970.
Focus on Film (London), no. 13, 1973.
Predal, R., in *Cinéma* (Paris), February 1973.
Film Français (Paris), 11 February 1977.
Vagnon, F., in *Cinéma Pratique* (Paris), April/May 1977.
Haustrate, G., and J. Petat, in *Cinéma* (Paris), June 1979.
Film Dope (London), no. 39, March 1988.
Première (Paris), no. 137, August 1988.
Film Français (Paris), nos. 2296/7, May 1990.
24 Images (Montreal), Summer 1992.
American Cinematographer (Hollywood), March 1996.

On ALEKAN: films:

1986 *Henri Alekan, des lumières et des hommes* (short) (Roth)
1988 *Alekan, la lumière* and *Alekan, la mémoire* (Dumoulin) (TV films as part of *Océaniques* series)

* * *

After studying optics and working as an assistant cameraman for several years, Henri Alekan abandoned film and worked as a bank clerk and puppeteer until 1931. Then he returned to film as an assistant cameraman, and worked with Eugen Schüfftan on several renowned films during the later 1930s: Pabst's *Mademoiselle Docteur* and *Le Drame de Shanghaï*, Carné's *Drôle de drame* and *Quai des brumes*, Siodmak's *Mollenard*, and Ophüls's *Sans lendemain*.

Alekan was imprisoned during the early years of World War II, but escaped and became a Resistance fighter. He found time to work on a series of short films (directed by Canolle, Audry, and Clément), and with both Yves and Marc Allégret. He persuaded Clément to revise his documentary *Ceux du rail*, and they collaborated with members of the ''Résistance Fer'' on the new version, centering on acts of sabotage and battles between the railway workers and the Germans. The film, *La Bataille du rail*, was greeted enthusiastically when it was shown in 1945, and considered the best French film about the Resistance.

Alekan's lyrical precision and sobriety, appropriate to the documentary subject, brought him an immediate reputation for sensitivity combined with realism. His next film was Cocteau's *La Belle et la bête*, a fairy tale with a cultivated poetic atmosphere. His earlier work with Schüfftan had opened his eyes to the potentialities of the camera; now his work with Cocteau would change his life. With Cocteau's help, he created a series of images often compared to such painters as de Hooch and Vermeer or de la Tour. The beauty of the film relies on the charm of Jean Marais and Josette Day, the leading players, on the splendor of the designs of sets and costumes of Christian Bérard, and above all on the harmony of the images and the ingenious utilization of values and the black-and-white contrasts caused by the play of light and shadows. Without becoming overly artful, Alekan was able to adapt his sense of the image to the needs of the scenario and the exigencies of the director, an ability he was able to maintain in all his future work.

After these two completely different films which showed his versatility of style, Alekan worked with a series of leading French directors, and made *Roman Holiday* with Wyler in 1953. Alekan's short film *L'Enfer de Rodin*, illustrating a double dream (of Dante and of Rodin), was widely praised, and in Gance's *Austerlitz* and Delannoy's *La Princesse de Clèves*, he was shown as masterful with color as he had been with black-and-white. Later outstanding films include *El otro Cristobal*, *Versailles*, *Figures in a Landscape*, *Der Stand der Dinge*, *The Trout*, and *Wings of Desire*, in which Alekan once more makes dazzling use of his talents in black-and-white cinematography.

In the mid-eighties Alekan teamed up with Amos Gitai, initially for *Esther*, then for the thematic trilogy dealing with exile and nationhood, *Berlin-Jérusalem*, *Golem—L'Esprit de l'exil*, and *Golem—Le Jardin pétrifié*. Each film tested Alekan's abiding aesthetic concerns with light, particularly in *Esther*, where the harsh sun of Haifa was ultimately turned to dramatic effect with painterly contrasts of light and shadow. In *Berlin-Jérusalem*, Alekan's formation through German expressionism is witnessed in dark and menacing atmospheric studio images of prewar Berlin, while for the sequences in Palestine, long traveling shots capture the ravaged, arid landscape to achieve a metaphorical resonance. If *Golem—L'Esprit de l'exil* is overly didactic in its representation of Paris as an inhospitable refuge for displaced foreigners, Alekan's images of despair, occasionally built from multiple exposures, retain a dark poetry. In *Golem: Le Jardin pétrifié*, the symbolic journey of an art collector's search for family heirlooms in Russia is registered in evocative landscape photography.

As an extremely active octogenarian, Alekan made his first American screen appearance in Wim Wenders's *In Weiter Ferne, so Nah!*, and in 1994 penned a vigorous protest against the relocation of

Langlois's beloved Cinémathèque. Reflecting on his career, he asserts his preference for black-and-white photography and generously acknowledges the importance of his chief electrician Louis Cochet to his achievements. Several exhibitions marked his eightieth birthday and, as a celebration of his contribution to cinematography, French television screened two film studies: *Alekan, la lumière* and *Alekan, la mémoire.*

—Karel Tabery, updated by R. F. Cousins

ALEXEIEFF, Alexander, and Claire PARKER

ALEXEIEFF. Director and animator. **Nationality:** Russian. **Born:** Alexander Alexeieff (also spelled Alexandre Alexieff) in Kazan, 5 August 1901. **Family:** Married 1) actress Alexandra Grinevsky, 1923 (divorced); 2) Claire Parker in 1941. **Died:** 1979.

PARKER. Director and animator. **Nationality:** American. **Born:** Boston, Massachusetts, 1907. **Died:** 1980.

1921—Alexeieff moved to Paris to study linguistics; scenic designer for Diaghilev's Ballets Russes; 1920s—active as artist, book illustrator, and stage designer; 1931—Claire Parker, then his student, collaborated with Alexeieff and his wife Alexandra Grinevsky on first pinboard (''l'écran d'épingles'') animation; 1933—*Night on Bald Mountain* a commercial failure, Alexeieff turned to advertising films for theatrical exhibitions; 1935–39—with collaborators Georges Violet and others, Alexeieff and Parker produced 25 films, mostly for sponsors or advertisers; some of these feature original scores by major composers such as Poulenc, Auric, and Milhaud; 1940—emigrated to U.S., married following year, continued work as illustrators; 1947—returned to Paris; 1952–64—produced 21 advertising films using ''totalization'' technique; 1957—designed logo used on films of distribution company Cocinor; 1962—produced animated prologue to Orson Welles's *The Trial*; through 1970—illustrated books (some using serial photos made on pinboard) total more than 40.

Films as Directors and Animators:

1933 *Une Nuit sur le Mont Chauve* (*Night on Bald Mountain*) (+ pr)
1935 *La Belle au bois dormant* (Puppet film)
1943 *En passant*
1962 Prologue to *Le Procès* (*The Trial*) (Welles)
1963 *Le Nez* (*The Nose*)
1966 *L'Eau*
1972 *Tableaux d'une exposition* (*Pictures at an Exhibition*)
1980 *Trois Themes* (*Three Themes*)

Advertising and Sponsored Films:

1936 *Lingner Werke*; *Opta empfangt*
1937 *Le Trône de France*; *Grands Feux*; *Parade des chapeaux*; *Franck Aroma*; *La Crème Simon*
1938 *Les Vêtements Sigrand*; *Huilor*; *L'Eau d'Evian*; *Les Fonderies Martin*; *Balatum*; *Les Oranges de Jaffa*; *Les Cigarettes Bastos*
1939 *Gulf Stream*; *Les Gaines Roussel*; *Cenpa*; *Le Gaz* (unfinished)
1951 *Fumées*
1952 *Masques*
1954 *Nocturne*; *Pure Beauté*; *Esso*; *Rimes*
1955 *La Sève de la terre*; *Le Buisson ardent*
1956 *Quatre Temps*; *Bain d'X* (Bendix)
1957 *Constance*; *Anonyme*; *Osram* (4 films); *Cent pour cent*
1959 *Automation*
1960 *La Dauphine Java*
1962 *Divertissement*; *A propos de Jivago*

Publications

By ALEXEIEFF and PARKER: books—

Alexandre Alexeieff, exhibition catalogue, National Library of Scotland, Edinburgh, 1967.
Alexandre Alexeieff, exhibition catalogue, by G. Rondolino, Cinema Incontri Abano Terme, Este, 1971.
Alexandre Alexeieff, exhibition catalogue, edited by G. Bendazzi, Ente provinciale per il turismo di Milano, Milan, 1973.
A. Alexeieff, C. Parker: Films et eaux-fortes, 1925–75, exhibition catalogue, Chateau d'Annecy, 1975.
Entretien avec A. Alexeieff et C. Parker, by N. Salomon, Annecy, 1980.
Pages d'Alexeieff, edited by G. Bendazzi, Milan, 1983.
A. Alexeieff ou la gravure animée, exhibition catalogue, Chateau d'Annecy, 1983.

By ALEXEIEFF and PARKER: articles—

''Circuit fermé!,'' in *Cinéma 57* (Paris), no. 14, 1957.
''L'Écran d'épingles,'' in *Technicien du Film* (Paris), no. 27, 1957.
''Reflections on Motion Picture Animation,'' in *Film Culture* (New York), no. 32, 1964.
Script, no. 10/12, 1964.
''Synthèse cinématographique des mouvements artificiels,'' in *IDHEC* (Paris), 1966.
Image et Son (Paris), no. 207, 1967.
''The Synthesis of Artificial Movements in Motion Picture Projection,'' in *Film Culture* (New York), no. 48–49, 1970.
''Chère Marthe,'' in *Bulletin d'Information ASIFA*, no. 1, 1972.
''Le Chant d'ombres et de lumières de 1 250 000 épingles,'' edited by H. Arnault, in *Cinéma Pratique* (Paris), no. 123, 1973.
''Alféoni par Alexeieff,'' edited by L. Olteanu, in *Nous Mêmes*, ASIFA, Bucharest, 1973.
''Cinema d'animazione: strategia e tattica,'' in *Filmcritica* (Rome), no. 31, 1980.

On ALEXEIEFF and PARKER: books—

Starr, Cecile, *Discovering the Movies*, New York, 1972.
Russett, R., and C. Starr., *Experimental Animation*, New York, 1976.

On ALEXEIEFF and PARKER: articles—

Cheronnet. L., "*Une Nuit sur le Mont Chauve*, film en gravure animée par A. Alexeieff et C. Parker," in *Art et Décoration* (Paris), no. 63, 1934.

Alberti, Walter, in *Il cinema di animazione*, Rome, 1957.

Martin, A., "Alexandre Alexeieff et les cinémas possibles," in *Cinéma 63* (Paris), no. 81, 1963.

Philippe, P., "Alexeieff nez à nez," in *Cinéma 63* (Paris), no. 81, 1963.

Starr, Cecile, "Notes on *The Nose*," in *Film Society Review* (New York), November 1965.

Rains, R. R., "The Road Less Travelled," in *The Lens & Speaker* (Univ. of Illinois Visual Aids Service), 15 January 1977.

Jouvanceau, J. P., and C. Gaudillière, "A. Alexeieff," in *Banc-Titre*, no. 25, 1982.

Robson, A. G., "Alexeieff's *The Nose*," in *Purdue University Film Studies* (Lafayette, Indiana), no. 6, 1982.

CinémAction (Conde-sur-Noireau), no. 51, April 1989.

Bendazzi, G., "Le courage de se nomer artiste," in *Plateau*, no. 5, 1984.

Vrielynck, R., "A. Alexeieff herdacht," in *Plateau*, no. 5, 1984.

On ALEXEIEFF and PARKER: films—

Alexeieff at the Pinboard, produced by Cinema Nouveau, Paris, 1960 (English version produced by Cecile Starr, 1972).

Pinscreen, produced by the National Film Board of Canada, 1972.

Annecy Impromptu, produced by S.F.P. Films, Paris, 1976 (English version distributed by Cecile Starr).

*   *   *

Even a brief scrutiny of Alexeieff's cinema must acknowledge his preliminary activities in other spheres, initially the severe challenge of designing and painting sets for the theatrical production companies of Paris. He also took up engraving, woodcuts, etching, and lithographs for book illustration, all of which profited from the assistance and critiques of his first wife, actress Alexandra Grinevsky, whose painting skills complemented his own.

Although Alexeieff and Claire Parker, who arrived in 1931, were participants in the avant-garde movements of Paris, as artists they remained largely separate from these spheres; their art is mainly a synthesis of their own experiences and conceptions. The key to their work lies in Alexeieff's engravings, especially a three-volume edition of Dostoevsky's *Brothers Karamozov* for which he created 100 lithographs. Until his edition of Pasternak's *Dr. Zhivago* in 1959 with 200 pinboard illustrations, the Dostoevsky work remained the most powerful example of "static film," i.e. a series of images joined together serially to create an implicit sense of movement, providing a visually powerful interpretation of the verbal narrative.

From this impetus Parker and Alexeieff conceived a desire to animate his engravings, to employ *chiaroscuro* with even more refinement than was possible with engravings. The blurred contours and indistinct forms of their poetic and anti-narrative films reflect the Freudian preoccupation with dreams of avant-garde cinema in the 1920s, to which they added a sense of theater and spectacle that invested the engravings with vivid drama.

At the same time as Alexeieff planned the pinboard with Parker, his student from Boston, Berthold Bartosch created *L'Idée*, described in its premiere announcement as "animated engravings." Less an influence than an inspiration, *L'Idée* became for Alexeieff and Parker an example of poetic animation, great art, arduous craftsmanship, and imaginative techniques.

All the pinboard films build their visual poetry upon the stimulus of a musical track devoid of dialogue. The only apparent anomaly in their use of the pinboard as a medium of visual poetry is *The Nose*, based on Gogol's short story. It is, however, more an homage to Gogol than a duplication of his narrative. Reducing his narrative to a slight strand, they build a finely detailed illustration of 19th-century Russia centered on a breathtaking realization of Kazan Cathedral. The story of an overreaching czarist clerk serves as the occasion for exploring spatial definitions in a new way.

Their final two pinboard films are derived from a single Mussorgsky composition. In the spirit of their first Mussorgsky-inspired film, four decades earlier, they continued to explore animated orchestrations of movement and time with their minds attuned to basic issues of mathematics and physics. In their first creative decade, Alexeieff and Parker focused more sharply on the ability of their medium to represent the free play of time and space, the intuitive interaction of visual and musical modes in a continual metamorphosis of contrapuntal relationships. *Pictures at an Exhibition* lacks the nightmarish quality of the initial film, but possesses quite different strengths. One pinboard in front of another establishes a visual dialogue, juxtaposing past and present in a sinuous and melancholy poetry that captures through interlaced allusions, the paradoxical relationship between youth and maturity.

In no pinboard film, least of all in their final one *Three Themes*, do Alexeieff and Parker try to simulate what they would call photographic prose. Their texture is suggestive rather than explicit, a three-part complementing and contrasting sonata; their goal is a heuristic creation of reality's depths where the mind and heart correspond freely. *Three Themes* is a fiftyfold slowdown of the normal *scherzo* pace of animation, a meditative elegy.

—Arthur G. Robson

ALLEN, Dede

Editor. **Nationality:** American. **Born:** Dorothea Carothers Allen in Cincinnati, Ohio, 1925. **Family:** Married the director Stephen Fleischman: one son and one daughter. **Career:** 1943—worked as messenger, then in sound laboratory and as assistant editor for Columbia; editor on commercial and industrial films before becoming feature-film editor. **Awards:** British Academy Award, for *Dog Day Afternoon*, 1975; Academy Award, for *Reds*, 1981. **Address:** c/o United Talent, 9560 Wilshire Boulevard, Suite 500, Beverly Hills, CA 90212, U.S.A.

Films as Editor:

1957   *Endowing Your Future* (Engel—short)
1958   *Terror from the Year 5000* (*Cage of Doom*) (Gurney)

Dede Allen

1959	*Odds against Tomorrow* (Wise)
1961	**The Hustler** (Rossen)
1964	*America, America* (*The Anatolian Smile*) (Kazan)
1965	*It's Always Now* (Wilmot—short)
1967	**Bonnie and Clyde** (Penn)
1968	*Rachel, Rachel* (Newman)
1970	*Alice's Restaurant* (Penn); *Little Big Man* (Penn)
1972	*Slaughterhouse-Five* (Hill)
1973	*Serpico* (Lumet) (co); *Vision of Eight* (Penn) (co)
1975	*Night Moves* (Penn); *Dog Day Afternoon* (Lumet)
1976	*The Missouri Breaks* (Penn) (co)
1977	*Slap Shot* (Hill)
1978	*The Wiz* (Lumet)
1981	*Reds* (Beatty) (co, + co-exec pr)
1984	*Harry & Son* (Newman); *Mike's Murder* (Bridges) (co)
1985	*The Breakfast Club* (Hughes)
1986	*Off Beat* (Dinner) (co)
1988	*The Milagro Beanfield War* (Redford) (co)
1989	*Let It Ride* (Pytka) (co)
1990	*Henry and June* (Kaufman) (co)
1991	*The Addams Family* (Sonnenfeld) (co)
2000	*Wonder Boys* (Hanson)

Film as Production Assistant:

1969	*Storia di una donna* (*Story of a Woman*) (Bercovici)

Publications

By ALLEN: articles—

Show (New York), May 1970.
Wide Angle (Athens, Ohio), vol. 2, no. 1, 1978.
American Film (Washington, D.C.), November 1985.
Film Quarterly (Berkeley), Fall 1992.

On ALLEN: articles—

Film Comment (New York), March/April 1977.
American Film (Washington, D.C.), December 1985.
Interview with Vincent LoBrutto in *Selected Takes*, 1991.

*   *   *

Between 1961 and 1981, Dede Allen reigned as American cinema's most celebrated editor. This period championed the auteur director and Allen emerged as an auteur editor, working with many of Hollywood's best auteurs (Arthur Penn, Sidney Lumet, Robert Wise, Robert Rossen, Elia Kazan, and George Roy Hill) and developing her own editorial signature.

Her first important feature film (after 16 years in the industry) was *Odds against Tomorrow*. Urged by Robert Wise to experiment, Allen developed one of her major techniques: the audio shift. Instead of stopping both a shot and its accompanying audio at the same time (the common practice), she would overlap sound from the beginning of the next shot into the end of the previous shot (or vice versa). The overall effect increased the pace of the film—something always happened, visually or aurally, in a staccato-like tempo.

When she started work on her next feature, *The Hustler*, the French Nouvelle Vague and the British "angry young men" films hit America. The realism of the British school and the radical editing of the French school made strong impressions on Allen. She credits Tony Gibbs's editing on *Look Back in Anger* (1959) as very influential. *The Hustler* employs a similar style: lengthy two-shots, unexpected shot/reverse-shot patterns, and strategically placed "jump cuts." "Jump cutting" helped launch the Nouvelle Vague, and before Allen began editing, Robert Rossen asked her to watch Jean-Luc Godard's *A bout de souffle*, one of the seminal films of the French movement. Although she felt the "jump cuts" were only partially successful, she incorporated the basic principle into *The Hustler* by using a straight cut instead of a dissolve or an invisible continuity edit. The combination of these two schools and the focus on character over a seamless narrative flow gives *The Hustler* its unique quality of realism and modernism.

With *Bonnie and Clyde* (the first of six films with Arthur Penn), Allen further developed the principle of the jump cut by marrying it to classical Hollywood editing and television commercial editing. Instead of using the jump cut as a modernist reflexive device or a stylistic flourish, Allen combined its spatial and temporal discontinuity with a clear narrative and strong character identification (from Hollywood) and nontraditional shot combinations and short duration shots (from television commercials). Allen's synthesis of the Nouvelle Vague, the "angry young men," Hollywood, and television defined her other major editing technique, what Andrew Sarris called "shock cutting . . . wild contrasts from one shot to the next, which give the film a jagged, menacing quality and create a sort of syncopated rhythm."

Bonnie's sexual frustration and ennui at the start of *Bonnie and Clyde* find perfect expression in a series of jump/shock cuts. The chaos of the gun fights and the immeasurably influential ending (which also shows Allen's debt to Eisenstein's montage) pushed screen violence to a new, visually stunning level.

In short, Allen must be credited with bringing modernist editing to Hollywood. Whether labeled American New Wave or Postclassical Hollywood, *The Hustler* and *Bonnie and Clyde* stand as benchmark films in the history of editing. And like *A bout de souffle*, *The Hustler* and *Bonnie and Clyde* deviated enough from the norm to be originally perceived as ''badly edited,'' a perception fully inverted today.

Allen's ''shock cutting'' in *Bonnie and Clyde* produced two long-lasting effects: 1) the American public began to recognize and openly discuss editing as an art form; and 2) the standard was set for rapid editing in every subsequent action film. From Sam Peckinpah to John Woo, editorial pacing continually moved toward shorter and flashier sequences. Her influence also manifests itself in other visual media; television commercials, music videos, animation, and children's television compress many images into very short sequences. Almost every music video owes its rapid, nontraditional editing constructs to Allen. In retrospect, Allen expresses concern about her contribution to increased editing tempo—''I wonder if we're raising enough people in a generation who are able to sit and look at a scene play out without getting bored if it doesn't change every two seconds. We talk an awful lot about cutting; we talk very little about not lousing something up by cutting just to make it move faster. I'm afraid that's the very thing I helped promulgate. . . . It may come to haunt us, because attention spans are short.''

Allen continued to refine her editorial signature (audio shifts, shock cutting, and montage) through her subsequent films, especially the temporal and spatial jumps of *Slaughterhouse-Five* and *Dog Day Afternoon* (her first Academy Award nomination). In *Dog Day Afternoon*, after a slow, tension-building opening, the protagonist's discovery of the SWAT team unleashes a brief moment of chaos which Allen augments into ten, breathless seconds of screen time by overlapping audio, intercutting multiple interior and exterior locations, and employing jarring shot combinations and temporal ellipses. Since Sidney Lumet used a double camera setup on Al Pacino and Chris Sarandon during their phone conversations, Allen used various takes of each, which produced jump cuts and violated screen direction, but intensified their performances. In *Reds*, Allen combined documentary editing and her signature narrative techniques to weave a historical and biographical tapestry of refined complexity. This documentary/narrative blend won her an Academy Award.

Since *Reds*, Allen's work remains consistently professional, especially in the usually overlooked dialogue scenes, but fails to convey the innovation of the sixties and seventies. This is not her fault. In the 1980s, not only did Hollywood become more an industry and less a developer of film artists, but Allen's techniques became fully integrated into everyday film and television editing. What once appeared radical became commonplace. When asked to edit *The Addams Family*, Allen needed to balance special effects, a greater emphasis on spectacle and set design, the demands of stars, shorter viewer attention span, a more cost-conscious Hollywood, and a script based on a 1960s television show. These constraints resulted in a polished film, but one with little of her signature, except for the loony glee of the vault slide and the intercutting of Gomez's train sequence. When working on independent projects, more of her creativity emerges. The curious jumble of edgy character interaction in *The Breakfast Club* and *Let It Ride* depends on the pacing her

editing provides. In *Henry and June*, she experimented with fades and partial fades to blur time and point of view.

Allen has co-edited most of her films since *Reds* with younger editors, providing invaluable training for them. Her mentoring of others has produced a new generation of top rank editors. After nearly 40 years in Hollywood, Allen's style, technical skill, ground-breaking films, and teaching secure her status as a legend of American editing.

—Greg S. Faller

ALLEN, Jay Presson

Writer. Nationality: American. **Born:** Jacqueline Presson in San Angelo, Texas, 3 March 1922. **Family:** Married the producer Lewis Maitland Allen (second marriage), 1955, one daughter: Brooke. **Career:** Writer: first novel published in 1948; 1963—film version of her play *Wives and Lovers* produced by Paramount; 1964—first film script, *Marnie*; 1969—play adaptation of the novel *The Prime of Miss Jean Brodie* published; also wrote screen version; 1976–80—creator and script consultant, TV series *Family*; 1980—produced first film, *Just Tell Me What You Want*, first of several films with Sidney Lumet. 1995—appeared on camera and provided commentary in the documentary *The Celluloid Closet*. **Agent:** ICM Agency, 40 West 57th Street, New York, New York 10019, U.S.A.

Films as Writer:

1964   *Marnie* (Hitchcock)
1969   *The Prime of Miss Jean Brodie* (Neame)
1972   *Cabaret* (Fosse); *Travels with My Aunt* (Cukor) (co)
1973   *The Borrowers* (Miller)
1975   *Funny Lady* (Ross) (co)
1980   *Just Tell Me What You Want* (Lumet) (+ co-pr)
1981   *Prince of the City* (Lumet) (co, + exec-pr)
1982   *Deathtrap* (Lumet) (+ pr)
1986   *The Morning After* (Lumet) (co)
1990   *Lord of the Flies* (Hook); *Year of the Gun* (Frankenheimer) (co)
1995   *Copycat* (Amiel) (co)

Films as Producer:

1980   *It's My Turn* (Weill)
1988   *Hothouse* (*The Center*) (Gyllenhaal)

Publications

By ALLEN: books—

Spring Riot (novel), New York, 1948.
Forty Carats (play), New York, 1969.
The Prime of Miss Jean Brodie (play), New York, 1969.
Just Tell Me What You Want (novel), New York, 1975.
A Little Family Business (play adapted from *Potiche* by Pierre Barillet), New York, 1983.

Jay Presson Allen

By ALLEN: article—

Los Angeles Times, 11 May 1975.
Filmkultura (Budapest), July-August 1983.

On ALLEN: articles—

Roddick, Nick, in *American Screenwriters*, edited by Robert E.
    Morsberger, Stephen O. Lesser, and Randall Clark, Detroit, 1984.
Francke, Lizzie, in *Script Girls: Women Screenwriters in Hollywood*,
    London, 1994.

*   *   *

Jay Presson Allen is a curiously overlooked screenwriter whose work has never received the attention it deserves. This may be in part because of a debut film which seemed inauspicious at the time, but which has grown in critical estimation: her screenplay for Alfred Hitchcock's *Marnie*. Although criticized at the time for what was regarded as facile psychoanalyzing, the screenplay is actually a finely constructed work, presenting with great subtlety, voyeurism, and yet sympathy, an emotionally disturbed woman who can hold her own with those female creations of Bergman and Antonioni of the same period, but who, perhaps typical of her American context, is able to overcome her problems. Providing Hitchcock with the screenplay for this, one of his two or three greatest films, is certainly a notable achievement, even more apparent if one is familiar with the original novel by Winston Graham and knows how well (and radically) Allen adapted the material. Her power to adapt brilliantly is present also in her screenplay for *The Prime of Miss Jean Brodie*, based on the novel by Muriel Spark, which once again presented sympathetically a three-dimensional, deeply disturbed woman.

Allen's greatest critical acclaim came for her adaptation for Bob Fosse of *Cabaret*, which not only threw out most of the sentimental trappings of the Broadway musical, but also had the courage to go back to the original Christopher Isherwood stories and to make explicit in the film itself the central homosexuality of the character generally patterned on Isherwood. By providing Fosse with a screenplay which allowed him to express his characteristic cynicism in great displays of technical razzle-dazzle, Allen made an inestimable contribution to the institution of the American musical; in its portrait of Nazism and German society, *Cabaret* claimed definitively for the musical a kind of laudable pretension and seriousness, as well as providing for Liza Minnelli one of the American cinema's great roles—yet another of Allen's portraits of neurotic women. Allen's most underrated screenplay is the surprising *Just Tell Me What You Want*, directed by Sidney Lumet, which offered an excellent Hollywood story and provided Ali McGraw the chance to turn in her most accomplished performance. Allen expanded the scope of her career somewhat by writing the screenplay for Sidney Lumet's *Prince of the City*, with its largely masculine milieu and adapting (again for Lumet) the thriller *Deathtrap*, perhaps her least interesting or successful project. Like many of her screenwriting colleagues, Allen became an occasional hyphenate, taking increased control of her work by functioning as her own producer as well. She also expanded into television and theater work. *Tru*, a one man show based on the life of Truman Capote which she wrote and directed, had great success on Broadway. Allen's theatrical follow-up was *The Big Love*, adapted from a novella by Florence Aadland. Cowritten with Allen's daughter, Brooke Allen, the play was produced by Allen's husband, Lewis Allen, and Home Box Office (HBO), and later appeared on the cable network. In 1994, Allen returned to film, discussing her work on *Cabaret* in *The Celluloid Closet*, a documentary on gay representations in Hollywood films. Allen also co-wrote the script for *Copycat*, a thriller featuring Sigourney Weaver as an agoraphobic psychologist. *Copycat*'s distraught detective (Holly Hunter) and paranoid psychologist are further examples of Allen's effective portraits of neurosis.

—Charles Derry, updated by Mark Johnson

Nestor Almendros (left) with Dustin Hoffman

ALMENDROS, Nestor

Cinematographer and Director. **Nationality:** Spanish. **Born:** Barcelona, 30 October 1930. **Education:** Attended University of Havana, Cuba, Ph.D.; Centro Sperimentale di Cinematografia, Rome, 1956–57; studied with Hans Richter, City College of New York. **Career:** 1948—emigrated with his family to Cuba; 1950—made amateur 8mm film with Tomas Gutiérrez Alea, *Una confusion contidiana*; 1957–59—taught Spanish, Vassar College, Poughkeepsie, New York; 1959–61—made documentaries for Cuban film institute (ICAIC); 1960s—worked in France as cinematographer: also director of TV documentaries (some 25 films in all), 1966—first feature film as cinematographer, Rohmer's *La Collectionneuse*; 1984—directed first full-length documentary, *Improper Conduct*. **Awards:** Academy Award for *Days of Heaven*, 1978; César award for *Le Dernier Métro*, 1980. **Died:** Of cancer, in New York, 4 March 1992.

Films as Cinematographer (Features):

1967   *La Collectionneuse* (Rohmer); *The Wild Racers* (Haller)
1969   *More* (Schroeder); *Ma nuit chez Maud* (*My Night at Maud's*) (Rohmer); *L'Enfant sauvage* (*The Wild Child*) (Truffaut)
1970   *Domicile conjugal* (*Bed and Board*) (Truffaut); *Le Genou de Claire* (*Claire's Knee*) (Rohmer)
1971   *Les Deux Anglaises et le continent* (*Two English Girls*) (Truffaut); *La Vallée* (*The Valley*) (Schroeder)
1972   *L'Amour l'après-midi* (*Chloe in the Afternoon*) (Rohmer)

1973   *Femmes au soleil* (Dreyfus); *The Gentleman Tramp* (Patterson)
1974   *La Gueule ouverte* (Pialat); *General Idi Amin Dada* (Schroeder); *Cockfighter* (*Born to Kill*) (Hellman); *Mes petites amoureuses* (Eustache)
1975   *L'Histoire d'Adèle H.* (*The Story of Adèle H.*) (Truffaut); *Maîtresse* (*The Mistress*) (Schroeder)
1976   *Die Marquise von O . . .* (*The Marquise of O . . .*) (Rohmer); *Des journées entières dans les arbres* (*Days in the Trees*) (Duras); *Cambio de sexo* (Aranda)
1977   *L'Homme qui aimait les femmes* (*The Man Who Loved Women*) (Truffaut); *La Vie devant soi* (*La Vie continue*) (Mizrahi); *Beaubourg* (Rossellini—doc); *Koko* (Schroeder—doc); *Goin' South* (Nicholson)
1978   *La Chambre verte* (*The Green Room*) (Truffaut); **Days of Heaven** (Malick); *Perceval le Gaullois* (Rohmer)
1979   *L'Amour en fuite* (*Love on the Run*) (Truffaut); *Kramer vs. Kramer* (Benton); *The Blue Lagoon* (Kleiser)
1980   *Le Dernier Métro* (*The Last Metro*) (Truffaut)
1982   *Still of the Night* (Benton); *Sophie's Choice* (Pakula); *Pauline à la plage* (*Pauline at the Beach*) (Rohmer); *Vivement dimanche!* (*Confidentially Yours*; *Finally, Sunday!*) (Truffaut)
1984   *Places in the Heart* (Benton)
1986   *Heartburn* (Nichols)
1987   *Nadine* (Benton)
1989   "Life Lessons" ep. of *New York Stories* (Allen, Coppola and Scorsese)
1990   *Billy Bathgate* (Benton)

Films as Cinematographer (Shorts):

1959   *58–59* (+ d, sc)
1960   *El acqua* (Gomez—doc); *El tomate* (Canel—doc); *Construcciones rurales* (Arenal—doc); *Coopertivas agropecurias* (Gutiérrez Alea—doc) (co)
1961   *Gente en la playa* (+ d, sc)
1964   "Place de l'Etoile" and "Saint-German-des-Pres" eps. of *Paris vu Par . . .* (*Paris Seen By . . .*) (Rohmer and Douchet); *Le Père Noel a les yeux bleus* (Eustache)
1969   *Les Bluets dans la tête* (Brach)

Other Films:

1960   *Escuela rural* (+ d—short):
1984   *Mauvaise conduite* (*Improper Conduct*) (+ co-d—feature doc)
1988   *Nadie escuchaba* (*Nobody Listened*) (+ co-pr, co-sc, co-d)

Publications

By ALMENDROS: book—

Un Homme à la caméra, Paris, 1980; as *A Man with a Camera*, New York, 1984.

By ALMENDROS: articles—

"Neorealist Cinematography," in *Film Culture* (New York), no. 20, 1959.
Film Dope (London), no. 1, December 1972.
Cinéma (Paris), January 1973.
Dirigido por . . . (Barcelona), April 1974.
Filmkritik (Munich), January 1976.
Cinématographe (Paris), Summer 1976.
Film Reader (Evanston, Illinois), no. 2, 1977.
"Buñuel, cinéaste hispanique," in *Cinématographe* (Paris), September 1977.
Revue du Cinéma (Paris), July-August 1978.
Film Comment (New York), September-October 1978.
On Rohmer in *Cinématographe* (Paris), February 1979.
On *Days of Heaven* in *American Cinematographer* (Hollywood), June 1979.
"Témoignage: mon expérience américaine," in *Cinématographe* (Paris), June 1979.
Ecran (Paris), 15 December 1979.
On *Kramer vs. Kramer* in *Millimeter* (New York), March 1980.
On *Kramer vs. Kramer* in *American Cinematographer* (Hollywood), May 1980.
Monthly Film Bulletin (London), May 1980.
Film Français (Paris), 3 October 1980.
American Cinematographer (Hollywood), September 1981.
Cinema e Cinema (Bologna), April-July 1982.
Mediafilm (Brussels), Winter 1982.
Millimeter (New York), February 1983.
Film Français (Paris), 18 March 1983.
Cahiers du Cinéma (Paris), April 1983.

On *Sophie's Choice* in *American Cinematographer* (Hollywood), April 1983.
"Bronte-Buñuel," in *Cinématographe* (Paris), September-October 1983.
In *Masters of Light: Conversations with Contemporary Cinematographers*, by Dennis Schaefer and Larry Salvato, Berkeley, California, 1984.
Sight and Sound (London), Spring 1984.
Cinématographe (Paris), March 1984.
"Sunrise," in *American Cinematographer* (Hollywood), April 1984.
On *Improper Conduct* in *American Film* (Washington, D.C.), September 1984.
Wide Angle (Athens, Ohio), vol. 7, no. 1–2, 1985.
Cinématographe (Paris), July 1985.
"Almendros and Documentary," in *Sight and Sound* (London), Winter 1985–86.
Films and Filming (London), June 1986 + filmo.
Film Comment (New York), vol. 23, no. 4, July-August 1987.
American Cinematographer (Hollywood), September 1987.
Kino (Warsaw), vol. 21, no. 11, November 1987.
Films and Filming (London), January 1988.
American Cinematographer (Hollywood), March 1989.
Cahiers du Cinéma (Paris), April and May 1989.

On ALMENDROS: articles—

Canby, Vincent, on *Claire's Knee* in *New York Times*, 28 February 1971.
Predal, R., in *Cinéma* (Paris), January 1973.
Film Français (Paris), 28 January 1977.
Avant-Scène (Paris), 1 November 1978.
Cinema 2002 (Madrid), December 1978.
Film Français (Paris), 2 February 1979.
Trusell, H., on *Goin' South* in *American Cinematographer* (Hollywood), March 1979.
Fieschi, J., in *Cinématographe* (Paris), no. 56, 1980.
Le Technicien du Film (Paris), 15 December 1979–15 January 1980.
Thevenet, Homero Alsina, in *Monthly Film Bulletin* (London), May 1980
Williams, A. L., in *American Cinematographer* (Hollywood), July 1980.
Cinéma Français (Paris), January 1981.
Sarris, Andrew, "The Cinematographer as Superstar," in *American Film* (Washington, D.C.), April 1981.
Carlesimo, C., "Painting with Light," in *American Film* (Washington, D.C.), April 1981.
Guttierez, Tomas, "Cuba Si, Almendros No!", in *Village Voice* (New York), 2 October 1984.
White, A., in *Films in Review* (New York), December 1984.
American Cinematographer (Hollywood), October 1988.
Filmcritica (Montepulciano), vol. 15, no. 391–392, January-February 1989.

*   *   *

Of the many splendid images Nestor Almendros recorded, two fleeting ones in *Kramer vs. Kramer* are remarkable for their pure visual power. The morning after Joanna has left Ted, he calls home from his office hoping she will answer, and the film cuts to two shots, one of their living room, one of the bedroom. Although we have seen the apartment earlier in the film, it is eerie how sad the rooms look without people: the colors are muted, the light is dim, the furnishings—the chairs, the lamp, the coffee table, the plant in the corner, the unanswered telephone on the bed—seem cold and oppressive in the semidarkness. The brief shots make the apartment's emptiness a metaphor for Ted Kramer's suddenly vacant life. Their poignant simplicity is not only a sterling example of Almendros's unaffected technical mastery, but an illustration of a common Almendros technique: producing telling images that capture a film's mood, crystalize its theme, and solidify its emotional content. One thinks of the rolling fields of wheat and the lone, erect farmhouse in *Days of Heaven*, Catherine Deneuve's luminously sculptured face in *Le Dernier Métro*, the dappled forest in *L'Enfant sauvage*, the spellbinding close-ups of Meryl Streep in *Sophie's Choice*, the crazed figure of Adèle H. wandering the sun-drenched streets of Barbados.

In his book of professional reminiscences, *A Man with a Camera*, Almendros demystifies much of the cinematographic process. For him, the images a director of photography records have less to do with technical trickery or special equipment than with sensibility. "The main qualities a director of photography needs," Almendros writes, "are plastic sensitivity and a solid cultural background. So-called cinematographic technique is only of secondary importance." Further, Almendros recognizes his responsibility of maintaining a cinematic tradition. The long-term function of the cinematographer, he believes, is to serve "as depository or transmitter of progress or discoveries in what has been called 'cinematographic language.'" Accordingly, the sum of Almendros's film work is more than a list of credits for films he has lighted, composed, and photographed; it is, as François Truffaut says in the preface of Almendros's book, a lustrous chronicle of an artistic vocation.

Cinematically, Almendros used standard photographic conventions expertly. Menacing or disturbed characters in his films often move through *chiaroscuro* spaces (thus the night is identified with the schizophrenic Nathan in *Sophie's Choice*, and the love-obsessed Adèle in *Histoire d'Adèle H.* cloaks herself in shadows and half-lights). *Film noir* lighting is employed to heighten suspense in thrillers such as the moody *Still of the Night*, the more light-hearted *Vivement dimanche!*, and the romantic *Le Dernier Métro*. And foreboding occurrences are sometimes underscored by darkness (the coming of the storm in *Places in the Heart*, Sophie's horrifying nighttime monologues recounting her tortured past in the Nazi concentration camps).

But beyond the inspired use of photographic language, an equally striking aspect of Almendros's work is his inversion of cinematographic clichés. More often than not Almendros contrasted a scene's mood with his visual rendering of it. Again and again in his films, the more emotionally complex a scene, the more brightly, naturally, and evenly it is lit. There is, for instance, the tangled bedroom farce that plays itself out amidst the sunny serenity in *Pauline à la plage*. Or the simple blacks and whites of Maud's apartment (the set was purposely painted in only those two colors) in *Ma nuit chez Maud*, which contrast sharply with the wide range of gray ambiguities—moral, sexual, and psychological—facing the protagonist during his snowbound night with Maud. A more emotionally charged instance is Joanna Kramer's disturbing departure from her husband in the full, flat glare of their well-lit apartment.

Almendros's use of this technique is subversive: undermining his pictorial perfection, he creates an unpredictable world. As a viewer

you appreciate the visual grace of the images, but become wary of lingering too long over a striking composition lest it explode in your face. In the cinematography of Almendros, tranquility is tenuous and likely to be violently shattered, like the sudden gunshot in broad daylight which kills the husband in *Places in the Heart*, the shooting of Richard Gere in *Days of Heaven* that breaks the river's mirror-like surface, or the last repose of Nathan and Sophie, locked in a deadly embrace as midday's golden light pours through the bedroom windows.

Almendros undercut his formal elegance because he realized that sorrow, pain, and sometimes evil lurk just beneath the surface of the finest, most evenly illuminated compositions. There is more to Almendros than pretty pictures. His camera eye sees down to the core of things, sees life's duplicitous nature, the coexistence of beauty and treachery, the terror that can underly the wondrous. In *Kramer vs. Kramer* the uniform lighting of the courtroom sequence creates a measured calmness counterpoised by the increasingly painful proceedings. What gives Almendros's visuals their charge is this kind of collision of surface with substance.

Most of Almendros's earliest credits as cinematographer were on the films of French New Wave directors, especially Truffaut and Rohmer. Beginning with *Days of Heaven* in 1978, he began working on American as well as European films, most often with Robert Benton; Almendros was the cinematographer of *Kramer vs. Kramer, Still of the Night, Places in the Heart, Nadine*, and *Billy Bathgate*. He also was the cinematographer of Truffaut's final features. Almendros himself directed or co-directed only a few films, the most notable of which were very personal expressions of his political/humanist beliefs and abhorrence of oppression in Castro's Cuba: *Mauvaise conduite* (*Improper Conduct*), which offers evidence of persecution against artistic and political dissenters and, especially, male homosexuals (which Vincent Canby called "something very rare in films—an intelligent attack on Fidel Castro's Cuban revolution" and "the first legitimately provocative anti-Castro film I've seen"); and the revealingly titled *Nadie escuchaba* (*Nobody Listened*), which further chronicles tyranny and human rights violations in Cuba.

But Almendros, who succumbed to cancer in 1992 at the all-too-young age of 61, will be best remembered as a cinematographer. In the preface to *A Man with a Camera*, Truffaut wrote that Almendros "loves the cinema religiously; he obliges us to share his faith, and proves that we can speak of light with words." Turning Truffaut's words around yields another truth: Almendros could speak with words of light.

—Charles Ramírez Berg, updated by Rob Edelman

ALONZO, John A.

Cinematographer, Director and Actor. **Nationality:** American. **Born:** Dallas, Texas, 1934. **Education:** Attended Dallas public schools. **Family:** Married Jan Murray. **Career:** Spent early childhood in Guadalajara, Mexico; worked with local theater while in high school; early 1950s—camera-pusher and cameraman, then director, WFAA-TV; 1956—puppet show created for Dallas TV; then in Hollywood working for KHJ-TV; also actor on TV and in films (credits include small role in *The Magnificent Seven*); 1964—cameraman for short film *The Legend of Jimmy Blue Eyes*; also did film documentaries for

Wolper Productions; 1970—first feature film as cinematographer, *Bloody Mama*; 1978—directed first film, *FM*. **Agent:** Scott Harris, Harris and Goldberg, 2121 Avenue of the Stars, No. 950, Los Angeles, CA 90067.

Films as Cinematographer:

1970   *Bloody Mama* (Corman)
1971   *Vanishing Point* (Sarafian); *Harold and Maude* (Ashby)
1972   *Sounder* (Ritt); *Get to Know Your Rabbit* (De Palma); *Pete 'n Tillie* (Ritt); *Lady Sings the Blues* (Furie)
1973   *The Naked Ape* (Driver)
1974   *Conrack* (Ritt); ***Chinatown*** (Polanski)
1975   *Once Is Not Enough* (Green); *The Fortune* (Nichols); *Farewell, My Lovely* (Richards)
1976   *The Bad News Bears* (Ritchie); *I Will, I Will . . . for Now* (Panama)
1977   ***Black Sunday*** (Frankenheimer); *Which Way Is Up?* (Schultz); ***Close Encounters of the Third Kind*** (Spielberg) (co)
1978   *Casey's Shadow* (Ritt); *The Cheap Detective* (Moore)
1979   *Norma Rae* (Ritt)
1980   *Tom Horn* (Wiard)
1981   *Back Roads* (Ritt)
1983   *Blue Thunder* (Badham); *Cross Creek* (Ritt); *Scarface* (De Palma)
1984   *Runaway* (Crichton)
1986   *Nothing in Common* (G. Marshall)
1987   *Overboard* (G. Marshall); *Real Men* (Ponzi)
1988   *Knightwatch* (F. Mann—for TV); *Physical Evidence* (Crichton)
1989   *Steel Magnolias* (Ross)
1990   *The Guardian* (Friedkin); *Internal Affairs* (Figgis); *Navy Seals* (Teague)
1992   *HouseSitter* (Oz); *Cool World* (Bakshi)
1993   *Meteor Man* (Townsend)
1994   *Clifford* (Flaherty); *World War II: When Lions Roared* (Sargent—for TV); *Star Trek: Generations* (Carson)
1995   *The Grass Harp* (Charles Matthau)
1998   *Letters from a Killer* (Carson)
1999   *Lansky* (McNaughton); *The Dancing Cow* (Goldstein)
2000   *Return to Me* (Hunt); *Fail Safe* (for TV)
2001   *Deuces Wild*

Other Films:

1960   *The Magnificent Seven* (Sturges) (uncredited bit part)
1961   *The Long Rope* (Witney) (role as Manuel); *Susan Slade* (Daves) (role as Manuel Alvarez)
1962   *Terror at Black Falls* (Sarafian) (role as Carlos Avila); *Hand of Death* (Nelson) (role as Carlos)
1964   *The Legend of Jimmy Blue Eyes* (cam—short); *Invitation to a Gunfighter* (Wilson) (role as Manuel)
1966   *Seconds* (Frankenheimer) (2nd cam)
1978   *FM* (d)
1979   *Champions: A Love Story* (d); *Portrait of a Stripper* (d)
1980   *Belle Starr* (d); *Blinded by the Light* (d)
1992   *Visions of Light: The Art of Cinematography* (as himself)

Publications

By ALONZO: articles—

On *Chinatown* in *American Cinematographer* (Hollywood), May 1975.
Millimeter (New York), March 1976.
On *Tom Horn* in *Filmmakers Monthly* (Ward Hill, Massachusetts), May 1980.
American Cinematographer (Hollywood), May 1983.
In *Masters of Light: Conversations with Contemporary Cinematographers*, by Dennis Schaefer and Larry Salvato, Berkeley, California, 1984.
Lighting Dimensions, November/December 1984.
American Cinematographer (Hollywood), October 1985.
American Cinematographer (Hollywood), March 1986.
American Cinematographer (Hollywood), May 1990.
American Cinematographer (Hollywood), April 1993.

On ALONZO: articles—

McGilligan, P., in *Take One* (Montreal), no. 2, 1978.
Cleaver, T., "*Scarface*," in *American Cinematographer* (Hollywood), December 1983.
McCarthy, T., in *Film Comment* (New York), March/April 1984.
Rose, P., on *Runaway* in *American Cinematographer* (Hollywood), January 1985.
Erbach, K., on *Nothing in Common* in *American Cinematographer* (Hollywood), March 1986.
Beeler, M., in *Cinefantastique* (Forest Park), vol. 26, no. 2, 1995.

*   *   *

John A. Alonzo represented—along with Vilmos Zsigmond, Gordon Willis, Conrad Hall, and others—a new breed of Hollywood cinematographer that entered the business during the 1970s whose work, like that of many new breed directors and editors at the time, challenged the classic style of Hollywood filmmaking by striving to be more experimental.

His career falls neatly into three segments. Initially, he journeyed to Los Angeles to make his fame and fortune as an actor; indeed for a short time he was the host of a locally produced children's show in Los Angeles. He got an uncredited bit part in *The Magnificent Seven*, John Sturges's western remake of Kurosawa's *Seven Samurai*, starring Yul Brynner. Bigger and better parts soon followed in such features as Delmer Daves's *Susan Slade* and the western *Invitation to a Gunfighter*, also starring Yul Brynner. On television, he had supporting roles in such hit series of the 1950s and 1960s as *Perry Mason, Cheyenne, Temple Houston, Destry, Bewitched* and *The Wild, Wild West*—where he appeared in two episodes, "The Night of the Golden Cobra" and "The Night of the Surreal McCoy." In the latter episode, he had the title role.

It was during this initial phase of his career that Alonzo decided he really wanted to work behind the camera. He spent many a day studying the work of great cinematographers, particularly Winton Hoch and James Wong Howe. It was Howe who helped him break into the industry. Howe was shooting *Seconds* in 1966 and needed a camera operator. Alonzo was picking up camera experience working on David Wolper television documentaries at the time, but had no union card. Howe and the director of *Seconds*, John Frankenheimer, sponsored Alonzo for union membership and his career was off and running. Between 1971 and 1974 Alonzo lensed such popular films as *Vanishing Point*, *Sounder*, *Lady Sings the Blues*, and director Roman Polanski's groundbreaking *Chinatown*.

For *Chinatown*, Alonzo was called upon to replace the film's original cinematographer, the legendary Stanley Cortez (*The Magnificent Ambersons*, *The Night of the Hunter*) whose old-guard methods of lighting and shooting Polanski found to be too slowly paced, causing the film to fall behind schedule. Alonzo's greater spontaneity both in the studio and on location—which stemmed from his experience shooting low budget films for Roger Corman, and greater familiarity with the day's newer, faster film speeds—made him an ideal replacement. His masterful evocation of a sun-baked Los Angeles of the 1930s darkened by shadows lurking everywhere with a hint of corruption virtually defined the cinematic style now known as *neo-noir*.

For *Chinatown* Alonzo earned his only (to date) Academy Award nomination. Though he didn't win, the Academy's acknowledgment of his brilliant work on *Chinatown* enabled him to pick and choose his next projects. There were a number of successful efforts such as *Norma Rae* in 1979 and *Scarface* in 1983 that defined this phase of his career. But there were no other major awards or breakthrough achievements. Thus, increasingly, Alonzo began to alternate work as a cinematographer with stabs at directing in an effort to gain more creative control.

He directed his first film, *FM* (an amusing, counter-cultural forerunner of the hit TV series *WKRP In Cincinnati*) in 1978. The TV movies *Champions: A Love Story*, and *Belle Starr*, as well as numerous videos for MTV followed. Alonzo's directorial career never really took off, however, and so he has had to settle for finding the top venues to exhibit his talent as a cinematographer. He is still much in demand. But most of the films Alonzo has lensed in the 1980s and 1990s-including *Meteor Man*, an entry in the big screen *Star Trek* franchise, *Internal Affairs*, *HouseSitter*, and others—only serve to remind us of a talent serving a system that has given him little opportunity to match the early promise of his masterful *Chinatown*.

—Douglas Gomery, updated by John McCarty

ALTON, John

Cinematographer. **Nationality:** Hungarian. **Born:** Sopron, Hungary, 5 October 1901. **Career:** Began film career at Cosmopolitan Studios, New York; Lab technician, MGM, 1924; cameraman, Paramount; worked on Spanish-language films in France and South America; returned to Hollywood, 1937 (some sources say 1939). **Awards:** Academy Award, with Alfred Gilks, for *An American in Paris*, 1952; Career Achievement Award, Los Angeles Film Critics Association, 1993. **Died:** Santa Monica, California, 2 June 1996.

Films as Cinematographer:

1933   *Los Tres Berretines* [uncredited] (+ d)
1934   *El Hijo de papá* (+ d, pr, sc)

1935   *Big Calibre* (Bradbury)
1937   *El Pobre Pérez* (Amadori)
1938   *Madreselva* (Amadori)
1939   *Caminito de Gloria* (Amadori); *Puerta cerrada* (Saslavsky)
1940   *Remedy for Riches* (Kenton); *Dr. Christian Meets the Women* (McGann); *Three Faces West* (*The Refugee*) (Vorhaus); *The Courageous Dr. Christian* (Vorhaus)
1941   *The Devil Pays Off* (Auer); *Forced Landing* (Wiles); *Melody for Three* (Kenton); *Power Dive* (Hogan)
1942   *The Affairs of Jimmy Valentine* (*Unforgotten Crime*) (Vorhaus); *Ice-Capades Revue* (*Ice-Capades*; *Rhythm Hits the Ice*) (Vorhaus); *Johnny Doughboy* (Auer); *Moonlight Masquerade* (Auer); *Mr. District Attorney in the Carter Case* (*The Carter Case*) (Vorhaus); *Pardon My Stripes* (Auer)
1944   *The Lady and the Monster* (*The Lady and the Doctor*; *Monster and Tiger Man*; *Tiger Man*) (Sherman); *Lake Placid Serenade* (Sekely); *Storm Over Lisbon* (*Inside the Underworld*) (Sherman); *The Sultan's Daughter* (Dreifuss); *Enemy of Women* (*Dr. Paul Joseph Goebbels*; *Mad Lover*; *The Private Life of Paul Joseph Goebbels*) (Zeisler); *Atlantic City* (McCarey)
1945   *Girls of the Big House* (Archainbaud); *Song of Mexico* (FitzPatrick); *Love, Honor and Goodbye* (Rogell); *I Was a Criminal* (*Captain of Koepenick*; *Passport to Heaven*) (Oswald)
1946   *Affairs of Geraldine* (Blair); *A Guy Could Change* (Howard); *The Madonna's Secret* (Thiele); *The Magnificent Rogue* (Rogell); *Murder in the Music Hall* (*Midnight Melody*) (English); *One Exciting Week* (Beaudine)
1947   *Driftwood* (Dwan); *The Ghost Goes Wild* (Blair); *Hit Parade of 1947* (McDonald); *T-Men* (Mann); *The Trespasser* (Blair); *Winter Wonderland* (Vorhaus); *Wyoming* (Kane); *Bury Me Dead* (*Back Home From the Dead*) (Vorhaus); *The Pretender* (Wilder)
1948   *Canon City* (Wilbur); *He Walked by Night* (Werker, Mann [uncredited]); *Hollow Triumph* (*The Scar*) (Sekely); *Raw Deal* (Mann); *The Spiritualist* (*The Amazing Mr. X*) (Vorhaus)
1949   *Captain China* (Foster); *The Crooked Way* (Florey); *Reign of Terror* (*Black Book*) (Mann); *Border Incident* (Mann); *Red Stallion in the Rockies* (Murphy)
1950   *Grounds for Marriage* (Leonard); *Mystery Street* (*Murder at Harvard*) (Sturges); *Devil's Doorway* (Mann); *Father of the Bride* (Minnelli)
1951   *It's a Big Country* (Brown, Hartman, Sturges, Thorpe, Vidor, Weis, Wellman); *An American in Paris* (ballet photography) (Minnelli); *The People Against O'Hara* (Sturges); *Father's Little Dividend* (Minnelli)
1952   *Talk About a Stranger* (Bradley); *Washington Story* (*Target for Scandal*) (Pirosh); *Apache War Smoke* (Kress)
1953   *I, the Jury* (Essex); *Take the High Ground!* (Brooks); *Count the Hours* (*Every Minute Counts*) (Siegel); *Battle Circus* (Brooks)
1954   *Cattle Queen of Montana* (Dwan); *Duffy of San Quentin* (*Men Behind Bars*) (Doniger); *Passion* (Dwan); *Witness to Murder* (Rowland); *Silver Lode* (Dwan)
1955   *The Big Combo* (Lewis); *Pearl of the South Pacific* (Dwan); *Escape to Burma* (Dwan); *Tennessee's Partner* (Dwan)
1956   *Slightly Scarlet* (Dwan); *Tea and Sympathy* (Minnelli); *The Teahouse of the August Moon* (Mann); *The Catered Affair* (*Wedding Breakfast*) (Brooks)

1957   *Designing Woman* (Minnelli)
1958   *The Brothers Karamazov* (*The Murderer Dmitri Karamazov*)
        (Brooks)
1959   *Lonelyhearts* (*Miss Lonelyheart*) (Donehue)
1960   *Elmer Gantry* (Brooks); *Twelve to the Moon* (*12 to the Moon*)
        (Bradley)
1966   *Mission: Impossible* (TV Series—pilot only)

Publications

By ALTON: book—

Painting with Light, Berkeley, 1995.

On ALTON: book—

Coursodon, Jean-Pierre, ed., *American Directors*, vol. 1, New
    York, 1983.

On ALTON: articles—

Comer, B., "John Alton, ASC to Be Saluted by Museum of the
    Moving Image," in *American Cinematographer* (Hollywood),
    vol. 75, no. 5, May 1994.
Obituary, in *Variety* (New York), vol. 363, no. 6, 10 June 1996.
Handzo, Stephen, *American Cinematographer* (Hollywood), September
    1996.
Obituary, in *EPD Film* (Frankfurt), vol. 13, no. 9, September 1996.
Obituary, in *Positif* (Paris), no. 427, September 1996.
Sarris, Andrew, in *Bright Lights* vol. 1, no. 4, Fall 1996.
Obituary, in *The Performing Arts, 1996. Film, Television, Radio,
    Theatre, Dance, Music, Cartoons, and Pop Culture*, by Harris M.
    Lentz III, Jefferson, N.C., 1997.

*   *   *

It is often claimed that film noir is more a matter of visual style
than of content. If so, cinematographers no less than directors and
screenwriters should perhaps be listed among the true auteurs of the
noir cycle, and John Alton would certainly rank as one of its prime
exponents. In the heyday of the cycle—especially in the early thrillers
of Anthony Mann and in Joseph H. Lewis's cult classic, *The Big
Combo*—Alton created archetypes of noir's main genre, the urban
thriller. But he also ingeniously extended the idiom into genres with
which it is less readily associated, such as the western and the
costume drama.

Alton's eclectic professional background provided ideal training
for the financial and stylistic economies of noir. Born in Hungary, he
started his film career at the Cosmopolitan Studios in New York
before heading for Hollywood to shoot low-budget silent westerns for
the notoriously fast-working "One Shot" Woody Van Dyke. From
there he moved to the Paramount studios at Joinville near Paris, then
spent six years heading up a new studio in Buenos Aires. on returning
to Hollywood in 1939 he found himself assigned to several years of
negligible B-movies. By the time he encountered Anthony Mann, he
knew just how to lend an aura of quality to the most shoestring
production.

For some years Alton had been trying to persuade the directors he
worked with that a cinematographer didn't simply "pump light into
a scene. The light has to tell something. There's a meaning, and it
establishes a mood." In Mann he at last found "a director I can really
sit down and talk with," someone sensitive to the subtleties of light
and shadow. In *T-Men*, their first film together, and its successors, his
"intense downbeat virtuosity," as Stephen Handzo put it, meshed
with Mann's acute spatial sense to produce "an unmistakable style:
deep perspective compositions with half-illuminated faces in the
foreground . . . distant backgrounds, ceilinged sets, pervasive darkness and gloom created through high-contrast lighting and filters,
angular composition, all creating a screen space at once expansive yet
oppressively fatalistic."

Mann readily paid tribute to Alton's skill in helping him achieve
the maximum effects with the minimum means. For *The Black Book*,
working to the usual modest budget, Alton contrived a richly atmospheric evocation of Revolutionary France, turbulent and treacherous,
largely from shadows and silhouettes. He created an equally alienated
visual mood for the location exteriors of *Border Incident*, as also for
Devil's Doorway, the first in Mann's great series of westerns.

Though his film noir work is in many ways his most interesting,
Alton was too professional a craftsman to limit himself to a single
style. His association with Allan Dwan, which began with *Driftwood*,
took in several of the veteran director's autumnal late westerns,
including *Silver Lode* and *Tennessee's Partner*. To these he brought
an austere lyricism, gently melancholy in its clarity, and long, elegant
but unobtrusive tracking shots. In Dwan's *Slightly Scarlet* he demonstrated another facet of his talent, matching James M. Cain's overheated melodrama with a Technicolor palate of startlingly garish hues
set off by areas of deep shadow. The result, according to Andrew
Sarris, was "one of the most eye-boggling American movies
ever made."

Other directors with whom Alton often worked included Vincente
Minnelli and Richard Brooks. His Minnelli films saw him turning the
glossy MGM house-style to advantage—as in *Father of the Bride*,
where Spencer Tracy's nightmare vision of the wedding ceremony
crumbling into disaster is all the more surreal for being shot with such
knife-edge crispness. Alton's sole Academy Award came for his
work on the climactic final ballet of *An American in Paris*, set to
Gershwin's tone poem. Whatever the pretensions of the ballet itself,
there is no gainsaying the virtuosity of Alton's lighting and camerawork.

For Brooks, Alton produced moodier, more downbeat effects,
sometimes—as in *The Brothers Karamazov*—deliberately jarring. In
an attempt to suggest the psychological turmoil of Dostoyevsky's
characters, he devised an expressionistic lighting scheme that threw
deep shadows of saturated primary colours, a technique widely
dismissed as crude and overemphatic. A similar approach, but more
subtly applied, worked far better in *Elmer Gantry*. John Fitzpatrick
noted how Alton's photography "catches the Dust Bowl reds and
browns by day and casts them against blue-black voids at night."
Many of the movie's nocturnal episodes, though filmed in colour,
convey a noirish feel of claustrophobic obsession.

Alton's last masterpiece of pure noir cinematography was *The Big
Combo*, routine gangland-vengeance stuff transmuted by its visual
treatment. Jean-Pierre Coursodon observed how "Lewis's carefully
studied spatial organization and positioning of actors, matched by
John Alton's masterful balance of sparse lighting and engulfing
darkness in predominantly deep-focus setups, create a dazzlingly rich
texture which at times . . . verges on the abstract." In its blend of trash

content and sheer overwrought style, *The Big Combo* strikingly exemplifies how, in the hands of a master like Alton, cinematography can on occasion take precedence over script, acting, and possibly even directing, in determining the key quality of the creative mix.

—Philip Kemp

ALWYN, William

Composer. **Nationality:** British. **Born:** Northampton, 7 November 1905. **Education:** Studied music at Royal Academy of Music, London 1920–23. **Career:** Played flute in an orchestra that accompanied silent films; 1927–55—Professor of Composition, Royal Academy of Music; 1936—score for first film, *The Future's in the Air*; also composed for radio, as well as orchestra and choral works; 1944–45—composer for newsreel *The Gen*. **Award:** Commander, Order of the British Empire, 1978. **Died:** 11 September 1985.

Films as Composer:

1936　*The Future's in the Air* (Shaw—short) (co); *New Worlds for Old* (Rotha—short)

1937　*Air Outpost* (Taylor—short); *Roads across Britain* (Cole—short); *Wings over Empire* (Legg—short)

1938　*Monkey into Man* (Hawes, Spice, and Alexander); *Zoo Babies* (Spice—short); *The Zoo and You* (Shaw—short); *The Birth of the Year* (Spice—short)

1939　*These Children Are Safe* (Shaw—short)

1940　*S.O.S.* (Eldridge—short); *The New Britain* (Keene—short)

1941　*Penn of Pennsylvania* (*The Courageous Mr. Penn*) (Comfort); *Architects of England* (Eldridge—short); *Night Watch* (Taylor—short); *Steel Goes to War* (Curthoys—short); *Queen Cotton* (Musk—short)

1942　*The Countrywomen* (Page—short); *Squadron Leader X* (Comfort); *They Flew Alone* (*Wings and the Woman*) (Wilcox); *The Harvest Shall Come* (Anderson—short); *Spring on the Farm* (Keene—short); *Life Begins Again* (Alexander—short); *Rat Destruction* (Cooper—short); *Western Isles* (Bishop—short); *Wales—Green Mountain, Black Mountain* (Eldridge—short); *Winter on the Farm* (Keene—short); *W.V.S.* (Birt—short); *Border Weave* (Curthoys—short); *Citizen of Tomorrow* (Smith—short)

1943　*Escape to Danger* (Comfort); *A.B.C.A.* (Riley—short); *The Crown of the Year* (Keene—short); *A Start in Life* (Smith—short); *Summer on the Farm* (Keene—short); *World of Plenty* (Rotha—short); **Fires Were Started** (*I Was a Fireman*) (Jennings); *Desert Victory* (R. Boulting); *Tunisian Victory* (R. Boulting and Capra) (co); *On Approval* (C. Brook); *Welcome to Britain* (Asquith and Meredith)

1944　*The Way Ahead* (*The Immortal Battalion*) (Reed); *French Town, September 1944* (Shaw—short); *Our Country* (Eldridge—short); *The Grassy Shires* (Keene—short); *Soldier—Sailor* (Shaw—short); *Medal for the General* (Elvey); *There's a Future in It* (Fenton—short); *Your Children's Eyes* (Strasser—short); *Country Town* (short)

1945　*The True Glory* (Reed and Kanin); *Great Day* (Comfort); *Your Children's Ears* (Pearl—short); *Land of Promise* (Rotha); *The Rake's Progress* (*Notorious Gentlemen*) (Gilliat); *Your Children's Teeth* (Massey—short); *Proud City* (Keene—short); *Worker and Warfront* series (Rotha); *Total War in Britain* (Rotha and Orrom—short); *Today and Tomorrow* (Carruthers—short)

1946　*I See a Dark Stranger* (*The Adventuress*) (Launder); *Home and School* (Bryant—short); *Green for Danger* (Gilliat); *Your Children and You* (Smith—short); *Each for All* (Tully—short)

1947　*Captain Boycott* (Launder); *Take My Life* (Neame); **Odd Man Out** (Reed); *The October Man* (Baker); *Approach to Science* (Mason—short); *A City Speaks* (Gysin—short); *A City Speaks* (Gysin—re-edited as *City Government*, 1948)

1948　*Escape* (Mankiewicz); *Three Dawns to Sydney* (Eldridge); *One Man's Story* (Munden and Shand—short); *The History of Mr. Polly* (Pellissier); *The Fallen Idol* (Reed); *The Winslow Boy* (Asquith); *So Evil My Love* (Allen) (co); *Your Children's Sleep* (Massy—short)

1949　*Morning Departure* (*Operation Disaster*) (Baker); *The Cure for Love* (Donat); *The Golden Salamander* (Neame); *The Rocking Horse Winner* (Pellissier); *Daybreak in Udi* (Bishop—short)

1950　*Madeleine* (Lean); *The Mudlark* (Negulesco); *State Secret* (*The Great Manhunt*) (Gilliat)

1951　*The Magic Box* (J. Boulting); *The Magnet* (Frend); *No Resting Place* (Rotha); *Night without Stars* (Pellissier); *Distant Thames* (*Royal River*) (Smith—short); *Lady Godiva Rides Again* (Launder); *The House in the Square* (*I'll Never Forget You*) (Baker); *Saturday Island* (*Island of Desire*) (Heisler); *Henry Moore* (Read—short)

1952　*Mandy* (*Crash of Silence*) (Mackendrick); *The Long Memory* (Hamer); *The Crimson Pirate* (Siodmak); *Royal Heritage* (Pine—short); *The Card* (*The Promoter*) (Neame)

1953　*Personal Affair* (Pellissier); *Malta Story* (Hurst); *The Master of Ballantrae* (Keighley); *The Million Pound Note* (*The Man with a Million*) (Neame)

1954　*The Seekers* (*Land of Fury*) (Annakin); *The Constant Husband* (Gilliat); *The Rainbow Jacket* (Dearden); *Svengali* (Langley); *Black on White* (Read—short)

1955　*The Ship That Died of Shame* (*P.T. Raiders*) (Dearden and Relph); *Bedevilled* (Leisen); *Geordie* (*Wee Geordie*) (Launder); *Zarak* (Young)

1956　*Safari* (Young); *Smiley* (Kimmins); *The Black Tent* (Hurst); *Odongo* (Gilling) (song only); *Fortune Is a Woman* (*She Played with Fire*) (Gilliat)

1957　*The Silent Enemy* (Fairchild); *Manuela* (*Stowaway Girl*) (Hamilton); *I Accuse!* (J. Ferrer); *The Smallest Show on Earth* (*Big Time Operators*) (Dearden); *Carve Her Name with Pride* (Gilbert)

1958　*A Night to Remember* (Baker)

1959　*Shake Hands with the Devil* (Anderson); *Killers of Kilimanjaro* (Thorpe); *Devil's Bait* (Scott); *Third Man on the Mountain* (Annakin)

1960　*Swiss Family Robinson* (Annakin); *The Professionals* (Sharp)

1961　*The Naked Edge* (Anderson); *In Search of the Castaways* (Stevenson); *Night of the Eagle* (*Burn, Witch, Burn*) (Hayers)

1962　*Life for Ruth* (*Walk in the Shadow*)

1963　*The Running Man* (Reed)

Publications

By ALWYN: books—

(Translator), *An Anthology of Twentieth Century French Poetry*, London, 1969.
Winter in Copenhagen, and Mirages, Southwold, Suffolk, 1971.
Daphne, Southwold, Suffolk, 1972.
(Translator), *The Prayers and Elegies of Francis Jammes*, Southwold, Suffolk, 1979.

By ALWYN: article—

"Composing for the Screen," in *Films and Filming* (London), March 1959.

On ALWYN: book—

Craggs, Stewart and Alan Poulton, *William Alwyn: A Catalogue of his Music*, Surrey, 1985

On ALWYN: articles—

Keller, K., "Film Music: Speech Rhythm," in *Musical Times* (London), 1955.
Hold, T., "The Music of William Alwyn," in *Composer* (Cleveland), nos. 43 and 44, 1972.
Pro Musica Sana (New York), Summer 1980 (additions in Fall 1980 issue).
Fistful of Soundtracks (London), October 1980.
Conway, Paul, "William Alwyn's Symphony no. 5: Exploring Hydriotaphia," in *Music Review*, August-November 1993.
Score (Lelystad), September 1996.

*   *   *

William Alwyn was the most successful British example of a composer dividing his creativity between absolute music and film composition. Between 1941 and 1963 he scored almost 80 films, while at the same time producing an extensive catalogue of concert, choral, and chamber works. It includes five symphonies, the opera *Miss Julie*, a piano concerto, a violin concerto, three concerti grossi, and several song cycles.

Alwyn studied the flute and the piano as a child. It was as a flautist that he first became aware of film scoring, when he was hired for an orchestra playing accompaniment to silent movies. Alwyn studied at the Royal Academy of Music in London and became a teacher of composition at the academy in 1925, a post he held until 1955. He was always among the most active forces in British music, serving as the chairman of the Composers' Guild, writing on musical topics for magazines, lecturing, serving on committees, all in addition to writing several volumes of poetry, translating French poetry, and painting. A number of his paintings were used to illustrate the covers of the recordings of his concert works.

Alwyn's first work for films was in 1936, when he was brought in to write a replacement score for the short documentary *The Future's in the Air*, which led to other assignments in this field. With *Penn of Pennsylvania* in 1941 he began his more than 20 years as Britain's most prolific composer of critically acclaimed films. Other composers—Walton, Bliss and Vaughan Williams—contributed occasional film scores of value but none matched the productivity or consistency of Alwyn. He was very much a part of the blossoming of the British film industry following the Second World War, and received praise for his contributions to such films as *The Rake's Progress*, *I See a Dark Stranger*, *The Fallen Idol*, *The Crimson Pirate*, *A Night to Remember*, and two films dealing with troubled Ireland—*Odd Man Out* and *Shake Hands with the Devil*, the latter being the only one of his film scores issued as a record album. He retired from the screen with *The Running Man* in 1963.

Despite his high academic standing and his success with serious music, Alwyn never considered film composition a lesser form. "I am passionately fond of films and I think all good film composers are. You must believe in pictures, have faith in your artistic medium, and you can produce good scores." He did, however, fully realize the different intent of concert and film music. "The whole art of the cinema is in its planning. It is coordination of a team, director, producer, designer, cameraman, musician, and actor, all working together and interlocking to obtain a dramatic whole in which no single aspect is predominant. I am always a little worried if somebody says to me, 'I liked your score for such-and-such a picture.' It makes me wonder whether I have stepped outside my brief, which is to provide music which is as indigenous to the film as the camera angles and the film sets."

—Tony Thomas

AMES, Preston

Art Director. **Nationality:** American. **Education:** Studied architecture in France. **Career:** Early 1930s—worked for the architect Arthur Brown, Jr., San Francisco, four years; 1936—hired as draftsman by MGM art department, after two years began working on films. **Awards:** Academy Award for *An American in Paris*, 1951; *Gigi*, 1958. **Died:** Of a heart attack in Los Angeles, California, 20 July 1983.

Films as Art Director:

1946   *Lady in the Lake* (Montgomery); *No Leave, No Love* (Martin); *The Show-Off* (Beaumont)
1948   *Three Daring Daughters* (Wilcox); *The Big City* (Taurog)
1949   *That Midnight Kiss* (Taurog); *Outriders* (Rowland); *The Doctor and the Girl* (Bernhardt)
1950   *Crisis* (Minnelli); *Two Weeks—with Love* (Rowland)
1951   ***An American in Paris*** (Minnelli); *Dear Brat* (Seiter); *Rhubarb* (Lubin); *Submarine Command* (Farrow); *Sailor Beware* (Walker)
1952   *The Wild North*
1953   ***The Band Wagon*** (Minnelli); *Torch Song* (Walters); *The Story of Three Loves* (Reinhardt and Minnelli)
1954   *Brigadoon* (Minnelli)
1955   *Kismet* (Minnelli)
1956   *Lust for Life* (Minnelli); *These Wilder Years* (Rowland)
1957   *Designing Woman* (Minnelli)
1958   *Gigi* (Minnelli)
1959   *Green Mansions* (M. Ferrer); *The Big Operator* (Haas)
1960   *Bells are Ringing* (Minnelli); *Home from the Hill* (Minnelli); *Where the Boys Are* (Levin)

1961   *The Honeymoon Machine* (Thorpe); *Wild in the Country* (Dunne)
1962   *All Fall Down* (Frankenheimer); *Jumbo* (*Billy Rose's Jumbo*) (Walters)
1963   *It Happened at the World's Fair* (Taurog)
1964   *A Global Affair* (Arnold); *The Unsinkable Molly Brown* (Walters)
1965   *Quick, Before It Melts* (Delbert Mann)
1966   *Made in Paris* (Sagal); *Penelope* (Hiller)
1968   *The Impossible Years* (Gordon); *Live a Little, Love a Little* (Taurog)
1970   *Airport* (Seaton); *Brewster McCloud* (Altman); *The Strawberry Statement* (Hagmann)
1972   *Lost Horizon* (Jarrott)
1973   *The Don Is Dead* (*Beautiful but Deadly*) (Fleischer)
1974   *Earthquake* (Robson)
1975   *Rooster Cogburn* (Millar); *Babe* (Kulik); *The Lives of Jenny Dolan* (Jameson); *The Prisoner of Second Avenue* (Frank)
1976   *Woman of the Year* (Taylor)
1977   *Damnation Alley* (Smight)
1978   *A Family Upside Down* (Rich); *The Cat from Outer Space* (Tokar)
1979   *Beyond the Poseidon Adventure* (Allen)
1981   *The Pursuit of D. B. Cooper* (Spottiswoode)
1982   *Bare Essence* (Grauman)

Publications

By AMES: articles—

"Art Direction: The Technical Approach to Design and Construction," in *IATSE Official Bulletin*, Winter 1963.
In *Hollywood Speaks! An Oral History*, by Mike Steen, New York, 1974.
Filmmakers Monthly (Ward Hill, Massachusetts), June 1979.
In *Dance in the Hollywood Musical*, by Jerome Delamater, Ann Arbor, Michigan, 1981.

On AMES: article—

Obituary, in *Variety* (New York), 27 July 1983.

*   *   *

Preston Ames's most notable successes in Hollywood art direction took place during MGM's golden musical era. His greatest work was produced while working with director Vincente Minnelli. His portfolio includes such titles as *An American in Paris*, *The Band Wagon*, *Brigadoon*, *Kismet*, *Lust for Life*, *Designing Woman*, *Bells Are Ringing*, and that adorable piece of Art Nouveau fluff, *Gigi*.

Minnelli was a highly visual director with a great concern for detail. In the 1930s the concern for decor had been the Hollywood norm, particularly at MGM. However, the self-depriving war years had tarnished the luster of the glamor capital's looking-glass. Then, in reaction to an era of sacrifice, opulence returned to America in the 1950s. Unfortunately, this was often at the expense of sophistication. Minnelli's iconoclastic artistic vision belied this trend. His demands for specific images often perplexed the studio and he often clashed with the iron wills of both the Art Department head Cedric Gibbons

and those new dictators of Hollywood—the special consultants from Technicolor. To work for such a creative maverick as Minnelli was an art director's dream, and such an opportunity came countless times to Ames.

Ames's most interesting assignments were for the Minnelli films *An American in Paris* and *Lust for Life*. The former was his first film with Minnelli, and somewhat appropriate since the American-born Ames had studied architecture in Paris and the film was about an American painter living in France. The movie, however, is far from a realistic depiction of life on the left bank. It is more a stateside fantasy of Paris life than *cinéma vérité*, colorful and quaint, with every set begging for a background of accordion music and spatially constructed for the Gene Kelly-Leslie Caron dance numbers. One of the less reproduced but fascinating designs was for a Follies Bergère-type number that did not feature the two principal dancers. "I'll Climb a Stairway to Paradise" had a long pink staircase with each stair electrically lit at the tap of the cabaret star's foot. At the base of its railing was a bevy of beautiful showgirls posing as ornaments and wearing enormous candelabras that would have made Carmen Miranda wince. It was an elaborate and difficult construction task, very uncomfortable for the showgirls, and it no doubt rekindled some fond memories for Cedric Gibbons about the good old days.

The most important number in the film, of course, was the "American in Paris" ballet. This production probably won the movie its many Academy Awards, including the one for Ames as art director. The credit cannot be given only to Ames, for costume designer Irene Sharaff also contributed a great deal to the sets. What made the film unique was its use of late 19th-century French art as the basis of design. It was not just the style and colors of painters such as Henri Rousseau, Toulouse-Lautrec and Raoul Dufy that were used. There was an attempt to emphasize the two-dimensional quality of these paintings on film, which, though a two-dimensional medium itself, almost exclusively aims at three-dimensional illusionism. (I should add that a similar attempt had been made as recently as 1944 in England when Olivier's *Henry V* used medieval illuminated manuscripts as a source for art direction.) Such an issue would be important to American artists of the 1950s, still battling with a general public unable to deal with non-objective art and mainly in love with impressionism for its "prettiness and charm."

Minnelli and Ames tried a similar approach when filming the Van Gogh biography *Lust for Life*. This time color played an even greater role. As Van Gogh's life progressed (or regressed) the colors of the film grew as intense as the colors in his paintings, indicating overwhelming madness.

Ames's films without Minnelli were not nearly as visually exciting. *Lost Horizon* as a musical remake was a pretentious flop, and *Airport*—well, there is only so much you can do with the inside of a plane. But due to his unusual achievements on the Minnelli films, we'll remember Ames well.

—Edith C. Lee

AMIDEI, Sergio

Writer. **Nationality:** Italian. **Born:** Trieste, 30 October 1904. **Career:** 1924—stage actor in Turin; 1926—entered films as assistant director for Brignone; 1935—first film as writer, *Don Bosco*. **Died:** Rome, 14 April 1981.

Films as Writer:

1935   *Don Bosco* (Allessandrini)

1938   *Il conte di Brechard* (Bonnard) (uncredited); *Pietro Micca* (Vergano)

1939   *Lotte nell'ombra* (Gambino); *Cose dell'altro mondo* (Malasomma); *Traversata nera* (Gambino)

1940   *La notte delle beffe* (Campogalliani); *Arditi civili* (Gambino); *Popo divorzieremo* (Malesomma); *La fanciulla di portici* (Bonnard) (uncredited)

1941   *Cuori nella tormenta* (Campogalliani); *Il prigioniero di Santa Cruz* (Bragaglia); *Il pozzo dei miracoli* (Righelli); *L'ultimo ballo* (Mastrocinque)

1942   *Giungla* (Malasomma); *La regina di Navarra* (Gallone); *Gioco pericoloso* (Malasomma); *Don Cesare di Bazan* (Freda); *Il figlio del corsaro rosso* (Elter); *La bisbetica domata* (Poggioli); *Harlem* (Gallone)

1943   *Gli ultimi filibustieri* (Elter); *Gelosia* (Poggioli); *Tristi amori* (Gallone); *T'amerò sempre* (Camerini)

1944   *Addio, amore!* (Franciolini); *Il cappello da prete* (Poggioli)

1945   **Roma città aperta** (*Open City*) (Rossellini)

1946   **Paisà** (*Paisan*) (Rossellini); **Sciuscià** (*Shoeshine*) (De Sica); *Cronoca nera* (Bianchi)

1947   *Fatalità* (Bianchi); *L'altra* (Bra gaglia); *Germania, anno zero* (*Germany, Year Zero*) (Rossellini)

1948   *Anni difficili* (*Difficult Years*) (Zampa); **Ladri di biciclette** (*The Bicycle Thief*) (De Sica); *La macchina ammazzacattivi* (Rossellini); *Sotto il sole di Roma* (*Under the Sun of Rome*) (Castellani)

1949   *Patto col diavolo* (Chiasrini); **Stromboli, terra di Dio** (*Stromboli*) (Rossellini)

1950   *Domenica d'agosto* (*Sunday in August*) (Emmer); *Vita da cani* (Steno and Monicclli)

1951   *Parigi è Sempre Parigi* (Emmer)

1952   *La ragasse di Piazza di Spagna* (*Three Girls from Rome*) (Emmer)

1953   *Anni facili* (*Easy Years*) (Zampa); *Destini di donne* (*Daughters of Destiny*) (Pagliero); *Villa Borghese* (*It Happened in the Park*) (Franciolini)

1954   *Cronache di poveri amanti* (Lizzani); *Le signorine dello 04* (Franciolini); *Terza liceo* (Emmer); *Secrets d'alcove* (*Il letto*; *The Bed*) (Decoin and others); *Die Angst* (*La paura*; *Fear*) (Rossellini)

1955   *Picasso* (Emmer—doc); *Il bigamo* (*The Bigamist*) (Emmer)

1956   *Una pelliccia di visone* (Pellegrini); *Racconti romani* (*Roman Tales*) (Franciolini); *Peccato di castità* (Franciolini)

1957   *Il momento più bello* (*The Most Wonderful Moment*) (Emmer)

1958   *Racconti d'estate* (*Love on the Riviera*; *Summer Tales*) (Franciolini)

1959   *Il Generale Della Rovere* (*General Della Rovere*) (Rossellini); *Viva l'Italia!* (Rossellini)

1961   *Fantasmi a Roma* (Pietrangeli)

1962   *Anni rugenti* (Zampa); *Copacabana Palace* (*Girl Game*; *The Saga of the Flying Hostesses*) (Steno); *Una domenica d'estate* (Petroni)

1963   *Il processo di Verona* (Lizzani)

1964   *La fuga* (Spinola); *Liolà* (*A Very Handy Man*) (Blasetti); *La vita agra* (Lizzani)

1966   *Fumo di Londra* (Sordi); *Scusi, lei e favorevole o contrario?* (Sordi)

1967   *Maigret a Pigalle* (Landi); *Cinq gars pour Singapour* (Toublanc-Michel) (Italian version only)

1968   *Colpo di sole* (Guerrini); *Il medico della Mutua* (Zampa)

1969   *Il Prof. Guido Tersilli, primario della clinica Villa Celeste convenzionato con le mutue* (Salce)

1970   *Il presidente del Borgorosso Football Club* (Filippo d'Amico)

1971   *Detenuto in attesa di giudizio* (*Why?*) (Loy)

1972   *La più bella serata della mia vita* (Scola)

1973   *Anastasia nio fratello* (Steno)

1977   *Un borghese piccolo piccolo* (Monicelli)

1979   *Le Temoin* (Mockey)

1981   *Storie di ordinaria follia* (*Tales of Ordinary Madness*) (Ferreri)

1982   *La Nuit de Varennes* (Scola)

Films as Assistant Writer or Assistant Director:

1926   *Maciste all'inferno* (Brignone); *Maciste nella gabbia dei Leoni* (Brignone); *Beatrice Cenci* (Negroni); *Transatlantisches* (Righelli)

1927   *Il carnevale di Venezia* (Almirante)

1928   *Gli ultimi zar* (Negroni); *La compagnia dei Matti* (Almirante)

1933   *Les Aventures du roi Pausole* (Granowsky)

1934   *Les Nuits moscovites* (Granowsky)

Publications

By AMIDEI: book—

Open City, Paisan, and *Germany, Year Zero* (scripts), in *Roberto Rossellini: The War Trilogy*, edited by Stefano Roncoroni, New York, 1973.

By AMIDEI: article—

Positif (Paris), April 1982.

On AMIDEI: articles—

Cinema Nuovo (Turin), 25 August 1955.
Revista del Cinematografo (Rome), June 1981.
Positif (Paris), April 1982.
Codelli, Lorenzo, "A invencao no Mercado Central," in *Filme Cultura*, January-April 1984.
Filmcritica (Siena), December 1990.

*   *   *

Roma città aperta (*Open City*) probably owes more to Sergio Amidei, one of its writers, than to its director, Roberto Rossellini. Amidei either directly experienced many of the events recreated in the film (the escape from German soldiers over the rooftops of Rome, sitting in a café with his romantic interest during an air raid), or witnessed them (the murder of a pregnant woman by soldiers while protesting an arrest). Further, he was probably responsible for the idea of combining two different stories he was working on with Rossellini and fellow writer Federico Fellini—one story based on the exploits of resistance priest Don Giuseppe Morosini and another about the partisan activities of Roman children against the Germans. And the landlady who warned him of the arrival of the German soldiers, as well as the young woman with whom he shared the air raid, both reprised their roles in the film.

Amidei and Rossellini were already close friends when they set to work on this project, and would work together on several other films over the next fifteen years before becoming estranged after the director commented negatively on *Il Generale Della Rovere* (*General Della Rovere*) in 1959. Their collaboration includes the other two films of Rossellini's "War Trilogy," *Paisà* (*Paisan*) and *Germania, anno zero* (*Germany, Year Zero*). This trilogy, together with De Sica's *Sciuscià* (*Shoeshine*) and *Ladri di biciclette* (*The Bicycle Thief*), to whose screenplays Amidei also contributed, are considered to be the central texts of the neorealist movement.

Amidei was much more politically committed than Rossellini or Fellini, but he joined them in their desires to move beyond the constraints of neorealist theory. Amidei collaborated with Rossellini on most of his films made with Ingrid Bergman, films generally greeted with howls of protest from Italian leftists at their apparent selling out of previously shared principles. Amidei's later work included comedies of manners, satires, and even fantasy (*La macchina ammazzacattivi*, begun but not completed by Rossellini) with younger directors such as Mario Monicelli and Marco Ferreri.

Amidei has, perhaps facetiously, described his work in these terms, "I'm a worker. Someone comes, asks me for something—a miniature, a fresco, a portrait, a country scene, a still life—and I do what I can. I'm like a Titian, a 16th-century artist (admitting the differences!)."

—Stephen Brophy

ANDREJEW, André

Art Director. **Nationality:** Russian. **Born:** Andrei Andrejev in St. Petersburg, 21 January 1887. **Education:** Studied architecture and painting at Academy of Fine Arts, Moscow. **Career:** Stage designer at Stanislavsky Theatre, Moscow, and for Max Reinhardt in Berlin and Vienna; 1923—first film designs; worked in France after the Nazis came to power; also worked in England. **Died:** In France, 1966.

Films as Art Director:

1923   *Die Macht der Finsternis* (C. Wiene); *Raskolnikoff* (*Crime and Punishment*) (R. Wiene)
1925   *Briefe, die ihn nicht erreichten* (Zelnik); *Das Geheimnis der alten Mamsell* (Marzbach); *Der Trödler von Amsterdam* (Janson)
1926   *An der schönen blauen Donau* (Zelnik); *Die Försterchristel* (Zelnik); *Die Lachende Grille* (Zelnik); *Die Mühle von Sanssouci* (Philippi); *Uberflüssige Menschen* (Rasumny); *Der Veilchenfresser* (Zelnik)
1927   *Alpentragödie* (Land); *Der goldene Abgrund* (Bonnard); *Im Luxuszug* (Schönfelder); *Die Spielerin* (Cutts); *Das tanzende Wien* (Zelnik); *Die Weber* (Zelnik); *Der Zigeunergaron* (Zelnik)
1928   *Thérèse Raquin* (*Shadows of Fear*) (Feyder); *Rapa-Nui* (Bonnard—short); *Die Büchse der Pandora* (*Pandora's Box*) (Pabst); *Die Heilige und ihr Narr* (Dieterle); *Der*

Herzensphotograph (Reichmann); *Heut tanzt Mariett* (Zelnik); *Der Ladenprinz* (Schönfelder); *Mary Lou* (Zelnik); *Wolga-Wolga* (Tourjansky); *Mein Herz ist eine jazzband* (Zelnik); *Zwei rote Rosen* (Land)
1929   *Diane* (Waschneck); *Die Liebe der Brüder Rott* (Waschneck); *Meineid* (Jacoby); *Der Narr seiner Liebe* (Tschechowa); *Revolte im Erzeihungshaus* (Asagaroff); *Sprengbagger 1010* (Achaz-Duisberg)
1930   *Die letzte Kompagnie* (Bernhardt)
1931   ***Die Dreigroschenoper*** (*The Threepenny Opera; The Beggar's Opera*) (Pabst); *Ihre Majestät die Liebe* (May); *Liebeskommando* (von Bolvary); *Die lustigen Weiber von Wien* (von Bolvary); *Der Raub der Mona Lisa* (von Bolvary)
1932   *Mirages de Paris* (Ozep) (co); *Don Quichotte* (*Don Quixote*) (Pabst)
1933   *Volga en flammes* (Tourjansky); *Dans les rues* (Trivas); *Cette vieille canaille* (Litvak)
1934   *Les Nuits moscovites* (Granowsky); *L'Or dans la rue* (Bernhardt); *The Dictator* (*The Loves of a Dictator*) (Saville)
1935   *Les Yeux noirs* (Tourjansky); *Whom the Gods Love* (Dean); *Tarass Boulba* (Granowsky); *Le Golem* (Duvivier)
1936   *Mayerling* (Litvak); *The Beloved Vagabond* (Bernhardt)
1937   *La Citadelle du silence* (L'Herbier); *Tarakanowa* (Ozep); *Dreaming Lips* (Czinner)
1938   *Le Drame de Shanghaï* (Pabst); *Lumières de Paris* (Pottier); *L'Esclave blanche* (Sorkin and Pabst); *Jeunes filles en détresse* (Pabst)
1939   *Les Musiciens du ciel* (Lacombe)
1940   *Paris-New York* (Mirande and Lacombe); *Elles étaient douze femmes* (Lacombe)
1941   *Caprices* (Joannon)
1942   *Le Dernier des six* (Lacombe); *La Symphonie pastorale* (Christian-Jaque); *L'Assassin habite au 21* (Clouzot); *Simplet* (Fernandel and Carlo-Rim); *La Fausse Maitresse* (Cayatte); *La Main du diable* (Tourneur); *Picpus* (Pottier)
1943   *Au Bonheur des dames* (Cayatte); *Le Corbeau* (*The Raven*) (Clouzot); *Mon Amour est près de toi* (Pottier); *La Ferme aux loups* (Pottier); *Pierre et Jean* (Cayatte)
1946   *Le Dernier sou* (Cayette—produced 1944)
1948   *Anna Karenina* (Duvivier); *The Winslow Boy* (Asquith)
1953   *The Man Between* (Reed); *Melba* (Milestone)
1954   *Mambo* (Rossen)
1955   *Alexander the Great* (Rossen)
1956   *Anastasia* (Litvak)

Publications

On ANDREJEW: article—

Cinématographe (Paris), March 1982.

*   *   *

Believing in creative freedom rather than academic reconstruction, André Andrejew fulfilled the 20th century's notion of the romantic, individualistic artist. The unusual titillated his imagination, and, much like the French Symbolists, Andrejew sought to reveal underlying truths through symbolic imagery.

Andrejew began his career as a film designer within the context of "German Expressionism," a movement obsessed with the outward depiction of man's internal traumas. *The Cabinet of Dr. Caligari*, designed by Hermann Warm, Walter Röhrig, and Walter Reimann, had emphasized this attitude through linear distortion and contrasts of lights and darks. However, *Caligari* remained highly two-dimensional—an appropriate surface treatment for its superficial story line (although the original author's intent had greater ambitions than the final scenario). Andrejew expanded *Caligari*'s conception into three dimensions in *Raskolnikoff* with twisted, jabbed spaces and jutting, discordant diagonals from plane to plane. This physical depth paralleled the psychological depth of Dostoevsky's source novel. In particular, Andrejew emphasized the staircase (a frequent motif in German cinema) as representative of the main character's twisted and tormented state.

Mingling fantasy with social reality, Andrejew furnished an ambiguously evil world for Pabst's *Pandora's Box*. Images of pain, cruelty, greed, innocence, and sacrifice balance precariously under a cloud of omnipresent sexuality, as Lulu, the *moderne*, lower-class outsider, threatens the teetering, respectable, older, upper-class Europeans, destroying them and later herself. Lulu's apartment imprisons anxious Expressionist lines in pillowcases and wallpaper, domesticating them into plausibility. Her mantle of knickknacks (as obtrusive as those in a 15th-century oil painting) includes an oriental grotesque, an incense burner, a tiny glass figurine of a lamb, and an empty, nine-branched candelabra (Jewish menorah?). On one wall hangs a picture of Lulu as Pierrot the musician. Yet, beyond this idyll lies an alcove hiding a secret past. Lulu's husband's bedchamber contains a relief of a praying figure as intense as Romanesque church carvings or prints by Edward Munch. Each time the sculpture appears, it elicits new meanings. Another scene visually compares a stuffed alligator to the brutal Rodrigo threatening a morally drowning Lulu.

As critics began to condemn any strongly stated art direction as distracting, Andrejew slightly toned down his style. Nonetheless, he maintained his belief in the importance of intrinsic meaning in design.

—Edith C. Lee

ANNENKOV, Georges

Costume Designer. **Nationality:** Russian. **Born:** Yuri Pavlovich Annenkov in Petropavlosk, 1 June 1889; occasionally billed as George Annet. **Career:** Stage designer in Russia in 1910s and early 1920s; 1924—emigrated to Germany, then to France, and worked as stage and film designer. **Died:** In Paris, July 1974.

Films as Costume Designer:

1926 *Faust* (Murnau)
1934 *Les Nuits moscovites* (*Moscow Nights*) (Granowsky)
1936 *Mayerling* (Litvak)
1937 *Mademoiselle Docteur* (Greville); *Nuits de feu* (L'Herbier); *Le Mensonge de Nina Petrowna* (Tourjansky); *Nostalgie* (*The Postmaster's Daughter*) (Tourjansky)
1938 *Le Drame de Shanghaï* (Pabst); *Tarakanowa* (Ozep)
1939 *Cavalcade d'amour* (Bernard)
1942 *Pontcarral, colonel d'empire* (Dellanoy); *La Duchesse de Langeais* (de Baroncelli)
1943 *L'Eternel Retour* (*The Eternal Return*) (Delannoy)
1944 *Le Bossu* (Delannoy)
1945 *Le Père Serge* (Gasnier-Raymond)
1946 *La Symphonie pastorale* (Delannoy); *Patrie* (Daquin); *L'Affaire du collier de la reine* (L'Herbier) (co)
1947 *La Colère des dieux* (Lamac); *La signora delle camelie* (Gallone)
1948 *La Chartreuse de Parme* (Christian-Jaque) (co); *La Leggenda di Faust* (Gallone)
1949 *Black Magic* (Ratoff); *La Valse brillante* (Boyer)
1950 *Lady Paname* (Jeanson) (co); **La Ronde** (Ophüls)
1952 *Le Plaisir* (Ophüls)
1953 ***Madame de . . .*** (*The Earrings of Madame De*) (Ophüls)
1955 **Lola Montès** (Ophüls)
1958 *Montparnasse 19* (*Modigliani of Montparnasse*) (Becker)
1964 *Pas question le samedi* (Joffé)

Publications

By ANNENKOV: books—

En habillant les vedettes, Paris, 1951.
Max Ophüls, Paris, 1962.
Russian Stage & Costume Designs for the Ballet, Opera & Theatre, Alexandria, 1967.

On ANNENKOV: article—

Avant-Scène (Paris), January 1969.
Obituary, in *Ecran* (Paris), October 1974.
Obituary, in *Cinema 74* (Paris), December 1974.

* * *

Georges Annenkov had worked as a stage and costume designer for 20 years before his work in French films, and he continued to do stage designs in France. His filmography is rather small for his years of activity, and his works from the 1940s have an overdone feel to them, especially the films immediately after the war when full-fleshed film design seemed de rigueur.

But his collaborations with Max Ophüls and his "team" (the art director Jean D'Eaubonne, the photographer Christian Matras, and, usually, the writer Jacques Natanson) on Ophüls's last four films display his sensitivity as well as his brilliance in costume design. The stylish variety of costumes in *La Ronde* and *Le Plaisir* testify to his long experience, and his ability not to let his command of the periods and styles overwhelm the thematic movements of the films themselves.

In *Madame de . . .*, the wardrobe, as well as the earrings, are used to promote insight into the underlying theme of the film: frivolity leading to understanding and finally tragedy. *Lola Montès* is a deliberate exercise in overabundance and opulence, and here, guided no doubt by Ophüls, Annenkov's use of the ''Baroque'' (a term used to both vilify and praise the film) is subtle and amusing. Cocteau, with whom Annenkov had worked on two films (*L'Eternel Retour* and *La Symphonie pastorale*), was interestingly enough one of those who signed an open letter defending the film after its disastrous opening, and only after the film's rehabilitation in the late 1960s has it come to be seen as a critique of excess rather than a film pandering to it.

ARNOLD, Malcolm

Composer. **Nationality:** British. **Born:** Northampton, England, 21 October 1921. **Education:** Attended the Royal College of Music, London, 1938–41. **Military Service:** British Army, 1944–45. **Family:** Married; two sons and one daughter. **Career:** 1941—joined London Philharmonic Orchestra as trumpeter (principal trumpet, 1942); 1945–46—played for the BBC Orchestra; 1946–48—rejoined the LPO; 1949—score for first fiction film, *Britannia Mews*; also composer of works for orchestra, incidental music for plays, the ballet *Homage to the Queen* (for 1953 coronation). **Awards:** Academy Award, for *The Bridge on the River Kwai*, 1957. Commander, Order of the British Empire, 1970. Knights Batchelor, 1993.

Malcolm Arnold

Films as Composer:

1947   *Avalanche Patrol* (Swain)

1948   *Charting the Seas* (Lowenstein); *Gates of Power* (Squire); *Badgers Green* (Irwin); *Women in Our Time* (Nolbandov—short)

1949   *Britannia Mews* (*The Forbidden Street*) (Negulesco); *The Frazers of Cabot Cove* (Swingler); *Drums for a Holiday* (Taylor); *Terra Incognito* (Verity)

1950   *Your Witness* (*Eye Witness*) (Montgomery)

1951   *Home at Seven* (Richardson)

1952   *The Ringer* (Hamilton); *The Sound Barrier* (*Breaking the Sound Barrier*) (Lean); *Stolen Face* (Fisher); *The Holly and the Ivy* (O'Ferrall); *Curtain Up* (Smart); *It Started in Paradise* (Compton Bennett); *Four Sided Triangle* (Fisher)

1953   *Albert, R.N.* (*Break to Freedom*) (Gilbert); *The Captain's Paradise* (Kimmins)

1954   *The Night My Number Came Up* (Norman); *Hobson's Choice* (Lean); *The Sea Shall Not Have Them* (Gilbert); *The Sleeping Tiger* (Losey); *The Beautiful Stranger* (*Twist of Fate*) (Miller); *The Belles of St. Trinian's* (Launder); *You Know What Sailors Are* (Annakin)

1955   *1984* (Anderson); *I Am a Camera* (Cornelius); *The Deep Blue Sea* (Litvak)

1956   *Tiger in the Smoke* (Baker); *Trapeze* (Reed); *Port Afrique* (Maté)

1957   *Island in the Sun* (Rossen); *The Bridge on the River Kwai* (Lean); *Wicked as They Come* (Hughes)

1958   *The Roots of Heaven* (Huston); *The Key* (Tully); *The Inn of the Sixth Happiness* (Robson); *Blue Murder at St. Trinian's* (Launder); *Dunkirk* (Norman)

1959   *Suddenly Last Summer* (Mankiewicz)

1960   *The Angry Silence* (Green); *Tunes of Glory* (Neame); *The Pure Hell of St. Trinian's* (Launder)

1961   *No Love for Johnnie* (Thomas); *Whistle Down the Wind* (Forbes); *On the Fiddle* (*Operation Snafu*) (Frankel)

1962   *The Lion* (Cardiff); *The Inspector* (*Lisa*) (Dunne)

1963   *Nine Hours to Rama* (*Nine Hours to Live*) (Robson); *Tamahine* (Leacock)

1964   *The Thin Red Line* (Marton); *The Chalk Garden* (Neame)

1965   *The Heroes of Telemark* (A. Mann)

1966   *Sky, West, and Crooked* (*Gypsy Girl*) (Mills); *The Great St. Trinian's Train Robbery* (Launder and Gilliat)

1967   *Africa—Texas Style!* (Marton)

1969   *Battle of Britain* (Hamilton) (co); *The Reckoning* (Gold)

1970   *David Copperfield* (Delbert Mann)

1975   *N.E.L. Offshore News* (doc) (co)

1980   *The Wildcats of St. Trinian's* (Launder)

Publications

By ARNOLD: articles—

''I Think of Music in Terms of Sound,'' in *Music and Musicians* (London), vol. 6, no. 11, 1956.

In *British Composers in Interview*, by M. Schafer, London, 1963.

On ARNOLD: book—

Poulton, Alan, *The Music of Malcolm Arnold: A Catalogue*, London, 1987.
Cole, Hugo, *Malcolm Arnold: An Introduction to His Music*, London, 1989.
Craggs, Stewart R., *Malcolm Arnold: A Bio-Bibliography*, Westport, 1998.

On ARNOLD: articles—

Fistful of Soundtracks (London), October 1980.
Soundtrack! (Hollywood), vol. 7, no. 26, 1988.
Soundtrack! (Hollywood), vol. 7, no. 27, September 1988.
Score (Lelystad), June 1993.

On ARNOLD: film—

1991 *Malcolm Arnold at 70* (Rusmanis)

*   *   *

One of the later recruits to the distinguished group of orchestral composers who worked for British films more especially during and after World War II, Malcolm Arnold began his main contribution to films in the 1950s. His first notable score was for David Lean's *The Sound Barrier*. Initially a trumpeter in the London Philharmonic Orchestra, Arnold had received his training at the Royal College of Music; as a composer he was outstanding for the range of his musical styles, which made him ideally adaptable as a composer for film, since he readily adjusted himself with an infectious enthusiasm to each individual film's dramatic needs, exploiting his evident skill in pastiche composition. This was demonstrated early in his notable screen career in his close collaboration with Lean on *The Sound Barrier*. In the opening sequence, in which a Spitfire fighter test pilot, while descending in a steep dive, inadvertently hits the sound barrier, the music blends brilliantly with the sound effects that represent the onset of the battering of the aircraft and the pilot's momentary loss of consciousness before he regains his self-control and manages to pull his aircraft out of trouble. Lean, as the former meticulous film editor-turned-director calculating every frame of every shot, required of his composer a split-second response to each nuance of the action, integrating momentary musical phrasing, or brief stretches of musical composition with the orchestration of the carefully selected sound effects. As the Spitfire lifts and soars so do the strings of Arnold's composition, and when the diving aircraft begins to batter, the music shifts into an ominous, chattering sound which ceases only when the half-swooning pilot pulls the craft out of its dangerous dive.

In another of Lean's films, *Hobson's Choice*—the film version of a celebrated stage comedy about an alcoholic Lancashire bootmaker and domestic tyrant, played by Charles Laughton—the opening scene again shows the inventive integration of Arnold's work. The film combines a vigorous and tuneful music hall-style pastiche with significant sound-effects—the squeaky pendant sign outside the old-fashioned bootshop, a striking city clock, slow pans accompanied by music over the variety of shoes on display, all culminating in a sudden zip-pan to the shopdoor as it crashes open and Hobson staggers back home with a monstrous, climactic belch.

For Arnold, film music only became a branch of musical creativity if it was fully integrated with the visual-aural action of the picture, an inventive component in a multiple art-form, as it is in ballet and opera. Bernard Herrmann (Hitchcock's key composer) used to claim that film is truly "melodrama"—music-drama. Otherwise, he claimed, film music becomes a mere hybrid, just background music, trying to exist *alongside*, not *with* the movie. His view was to be shared by most of the prominent British composers of the period who were also enthusiastic composers for film, including William Alwyn, Vaughan Williams, William Walton, Arnold Bax, and others. Though Alwyn preferred to begin composition at script stage, working closely with the director, Arnold, a very rapid worker, preferred to work only at the rough-cut stage of the picture. He also preferred to use small combinations of instruments rather than large orchestral effects—25 instruments only, for example, in the case of *Hobson's Choice*. He was to work with Lean again on *The Bridge on the River Kwai*, which earned him an Oscar; other prominent films for which he wrote the music were *The Inn of the Sixth Happiness* and *David Copperfield*.

—Roger Manvell

AUGUST, Joseph H.

Cinematographer. **Nationality:** American. **Born:** 1890. **Education:** Attended Colorado School of Mining. **Family:** Son: Joseph August, Jr. **Career:** 1911—entered films; 1913—first known film as cinematographer, *From the Shadows*; 1914—first of many films for William S. Hart; 1919—cofounder, American Society of Cinematographers. **Died:** In Hollywood, California, 25 September 1947.

Films as Cinematographer:

1913   *From the Shadows* (Barker—short); *The Heritage of Eve* (Barker—short); *The Iron Master* (Barker—short); *The Man Who Went Out* (Barker—short); *The Miser* (Barker—short);

1914   *The Fugitive* (*The Taking of Luke McVane*) (Hart and Smith—short); *The Imposter* (Barker—short); *On the Night Stage* (Barker—short; extended version: *The Bandit and the Preacher*, 1915); *The Passing of Two Gun Hicks* (*Two Gun Hicks*) (Hart and Smith—short); *Pinto Ben* (Barker—short);

1915   *Between Men* (Barker); *Cash Parrish's Pal* (*Double Crossed*) (Hart and Smith—short); *The City of Darkness* (Barker—short); *The Coward* (T. Ince and Barker); *The Conversion of Frosty Blake* (*The Gentleman from Blue Gulch*) (Hart and Smith—short; extended version: *The Convert/The Roughneck*, 1915); *The Darkening Trail* (Hart and Smith—short; extended version: *Hell Bound for Alaska*, 1915); *The Disciple* (Barker); *The Grit* (Hart and Smith—short); *His Hour of Manhood* (Barker); *The Iron Strain* (Barker); *Keno Bates, Liar* (Hart and Smith—short); *Rumpelstiltskin* (Barker); *The Silent Stranger* (Hart and Smith); *The Ruse* (Hart and Smith—short; extended version: *A Square Deal*, 1915)

1916   *Hell's Hinges*; *The Return of Drew Egan*; *Apostle of Vengeance* (Hart and Smith); *The Aryan* (Hart and Smith); *The Captive God* (Barker); *Civilization's Child* (Barker) (co);

The Deserter (Edwards) (co); The Devil's Double (Barker); The Last Act (Hart and Smith)

1917   The Cold Deck (Barker); The Desert Man (Hart); An Even Break (Hart); Golden Rule Kate (Barker); The Gunfighter (Hart); Truthful Tulliver (Hart); The Regenerates (Hart); The Silent Man (Hart); The Square Deal Man (Hart); Upholding the Law (Hart); Wolf Lowry (Hart)

1918   Blue Blazes Rawden (Hart); The Border Wireless (Hart); Branding Broadway (Hart); He Comes Up Smiling (Dwan); The Narrow Trail (Hart); Riddle Gawne (Hart); Selfish Yates (Hart); Shark Monroe (Hart); The Tiger Man (Hart); Wolves of the Rail (Hart)

1919   Poppy Girl's Husband (Hart); Breed of Men (Hillyer); John Petticoats (Hillyer); The Money Corral (Hillyer); Square Deal Sanderson (Hillyer); Wagon Tracks (Hillyer)

1920   Sand (Hillyer); The Testing Block (Hillyer); The Toll Gate (Hillyer); The Cradle of Courage (Hillyer)

1921   O'Malley of the Mounted (Hillyer); The Whistle (Hillyer); White Oak (Hillyer); Three Word Brand (Hillyer)

1922   Arabian Love (Storm); Travelin' On (Hillyer); Honor First (Storm); The Love Gambler (Franz); A California Romance (Storm)

1923   The Man Who Won (Wellman); Truxton King (Truxtonia) (Storm); Madness of Youth (Storm); The Temple of Venus (Otto); Big Dan (Wellman); Good-by Girls! (Storm); St. Elmo (Storm); Darkness and Daylight (Plummer); Cupid's Fireman (Wellman)

1924   Dante's Inferno (Otto); Not a Drum Was Heard (Wellman); The Folly of Vanity (Elvey and Otto) (co); The Vagabond Trail (Wellman)

1925   The Hunted Woman (Conway); Greater Than a Crown (Neill); The Fighting Heart (Ford); The Ancient Mariner (Otto and Bennett); Tumbleweeds (Baggot); Lightnin' (Ford)

1926   The Road to Glory (Hawks); Fig Leaves (Hawks); The Flying Horseman (Dull)

1927   The Beloved Rogue (Crosland); Two Arabian Knights (Milestone) (co); Come to My House (Green); Very Confidential (Tinling)

1928   Soft Living (Tinling); Don't Marry (Tinling); Honor Bound (Green); The Farmer's Daughter (Rosson or Taurog)

1929   Strong Boy (Ford); Salute (Ford); Seven Faces (Viertel) (co); The Black Watch (King of the Khyber Rifles) (Ford)

1930   Men without Women (Ford); Double Cross Roads (Werker) (co); On Your Back (McClintic); Up the River (Ford); Man Trouble (Viertel)

1931   Seas Beneath (Ford); Mr. Lemon of Orange (Blystone); Quick Millions (Brown); The Brat (Ford); Heartbreak (Werker); Charlie Chan's Chance (Blystone)

1932   Silent Witness (Varnel and Hough); As the Devil Commands (Neill); Mystery Ranch (Howard); Vanity Street (Grinde); No More Orchids (W. Lang); That's My Boy (Neill)

1933   Circus Queen Murder (Neill); Cocktail Hour (Schertzinger); Master of Men (Hillyer); Man's Castle (Borzage)

1934   No Greater Glory (Borzage); Twentieth Century (Hawks); Black Moon (Neill); Sisters under the Skin (The Romantic Age) (Burton); The Defense Rests (Hillyer); Among the Missing (Rogell); The Captian Hates the Sea (Milestone)

1935   The Whole Town's Talking (Passport to Fame) (Ford); I'll Love You Always (Bulgakov); The Informer (Ford); After the Dance (Bulgakov); Sylvia Scarlett (Cukor)

1936   Muss 'em Up (House of Fate) (C. Vidor) (co); Every Saturday Night (Tinling); Mary of Scotland (Ford); Grand Jury (Rogell); The Plough and the Stars (Ford)

1937   Sea Devils (Stoloff) (co); The Soldier and the Lady (Michael Strogoff) (Nicholls); Fifty Roads to Town (Taurog); There Goes My Girl (Holmes); Super-Sleuth (Stoloff); Music for Madam (Blystone); A Damsel in Distress (Stevens)

1938   The Saint in New York (Holmes) (co); Gun Law (Howard); Border G-Man (Howard); This Marriage Business (Cabanne)

1939   Man of Conquest (Nicholls); Gunga Din (Stevens); Nurse Edith Cavell (Wilcox) (co); The Hunchback of Notre Dame (Dieterle)

1940   Primrose Path (La Cava); Melody Ranch (Santley)

1941   All That Money Can Buy (The Devil and Daniel Webster) (Dieterle)

1945   They Were Expendable (Ford)

1948   Portrait of Jennie (Jennie) (Dieterle)

Publications

On AUGUST: articles—

Film Comment (New York), Summer 1972.
Focus on Film (London), no. 13, 1973.
Film Dope (Nottingham), March 1988.
Henderson, J. A., "Swan Song: Portrait of Jennie," in American Cinematographer (Hollywood), December 1996.

*   *   *

Screenwriter Dudley Nichols once wrote, ". . . Joe August was a great cameraman, perhaps the most experimental and audacious I have ever known." Much of his silent work has been lost or is available only in poor copies that do little justice to Joseph H. August's exemplary skill. But the films that survive—both silent and sound—eloquently support Nichols's appraisal.

August began in the business under the tutelage of Thomas Ince and soon was William S. Hart's photographer of choice. With only a couple of exceptions, August photographed every Hart feature from The Disciple to Tumbleweeds. Hart's westerns provided August with a wide range of stylistic challenges: the blazing religiosity of Hell's Hinges; the staid, almost geometric groupings of people and buildings in The Return of Drew Egan, the bright, expansive Truthful Tulliver, the desert panoramas of The Silent Man. August's eye for landscape distinguishes the Hart films; interiors, however, often look cramped and dull.

Though August was at home in the open western scenery, his work ranged farther afield during the 1920s. He provided startling images to moralistic fantasies like Dante's Inferno, The Temple of Venus, and The Ancient Mariner, and delighted in the unusual and experimental: he turns the camera upside-down for an effect in Big Dan, works with double exposure in Hart's Three Word Brand, utilizes Technicolor in Fig Leaves.

While the cliché would have it that the introduction of sound "nailed the camera to the floor," August found the new technology challenging and inspiring. His stunning camera work on John Ford films such as *Salute* and *Men without Women* is filled with elaborate tracking shots, underwater photography (at one point, he mounted a camera in a waterproof booth on top of a submarine and filmed the submersion), and other bravura techniques without sacrificing what Lindsay Anderson calls his ''voluptuous lighting'' which gives films like *The Black Watch* their ''remarkable visual distinction: strikingly *chiaroscuro*, boldly dramatic in composition, strongly dramatic in atmosphere.''

August worked often with Ford in the 1930s, oddly—considering that both men made their reputations in the genre—never in a western. Ford had August utilize double exposures to make twins of Edward G. Robinson in *The Whole Town's Talking* just as the cinematographer had done with William S. Hart in *Three Word Brand* (1921). Ford and August also worked together on the moody *Mary of Scotland*, *The Plough and the Stars* (an ''Irish'' film that seems to be composed equally of documentary and expressionist techniques), and *The Informer*, Ford's most overt excursion into the art film. *The Informer* seems more deliberate and obvious than much of Ford's best work but August's contribution is superb: stylized, shadowy, evocative.

However, Ford had no monopoly on August's services. Rowland Brown, Stevens, Dieterle, Cukor, and Borzage all brought out fresh facets of the cinematographer's talent. The cinematography in *Quick Millions* is fast-paced and hard-boiled; August suffuses *Man's Castle* with romantic mist; *A Damsel in Distress* is fluid and sun-lit; *Gunga Din* stylizes its roughhousing, mock-heroic images by placing the camera below eye level and undercranking.

Portrait of Jennie, August's last film, contains some of his most striking work: harsh, black-and-white contrasts in one scene, dreamy, misty romanticism in the next. Only in his late 50s when he died, August was a motion picture veteran of over 30 years. His career neatly spans the ''Golden Age.'' He weathered the technical innovations of the silent period, matter-of-factly took on sound, and gracefully exited the scene before television ever played havoc with the sensitive, glimmering, and audacious images to which he devoted his life.

—Frank Thompson

AURENCHE, Jean, and Pierre BOST

AURENCHE. Writer. **Nationality:** French. **Born:** Pierrelatte, 11 September 1904. **Career:** Worked for Etienne Damour advertising agency, then for the theatre director Charles Dullin; 1933—first film as actor and writer, *Monsieur Cordon*, and as writer and director, *Pirates du Rhône;* 1948—collaborated with Jean Anouilh on play *Humulus le muet;* collaborator on TV series *Molière pour rire et pour pleurer*, 1973, and *Lucien Leuwen*, 1973. **Awards:** César awards for *Let Joy Reign Supreme*, 1975; *Le Juge et l'assassin*, 1976; and *The Northern Star*, 1982. **Died:** September, 1992.

BOST. Writer. **Nationality:** French. **Born:** Lasalle, 5 September 1901. **Career:** 1924–27—journalist, *Gazette de France*, and editor of *Marianne* from 1938 and of *Marie Claire*; 1927–60—Secretary of the Senate; playwright and novelist from the 1920s, and writer for films from 1939, and for TV series *Molière pour rire et pour pleurer*, 1973, and *Lucien Leuwen*, 1973. **Died:** In 1976.

Films as Writer (Aurenche):

1933 *Pirates du Rhône* (+ co-d—short); *Bracos de Sologne* (+ co-d—short); *Monsieur Cordon* (P. Prévert—short) (+ ro)

1936 *Les Dégourdis de la onzième* (Christian-Jaque); *Vous n'avez rien à déclarer?* (Y. Allégret and Joannon)

1937 *L'Affaire Lafarge* (Chenal); *L'Affaire du courrier de Lyon (The Courier of Lyons)* (Lehmann)

1938 *Hôtel du Nord* (Carné); *Le Ruisseau* (Lehmann)

1939 *L'Héritier des Mondésir* (Valentin); *Cavalcade d'amour* (Bernard); *La Tradition de minuit* (Richebé); *L'Emigrante* (Y. Allégret and Joannon)

1941 *Madame Sans-Gêne* (Richebé)

1942 *Le Mariage de Chiffon* (Autant-Lara); *Domino* (Richebé); *Huit hommes dans un château* (Pottier); *Romance à trois* (Richebé); *Lettres d'amour* (Autant-Lara)

1943 *Le Moussaillon* (Gourguet); *Le Marchand de notes* (Grimault—short); *Les Petites du Quai aux Fleurs* (M. Allégret); *Adrien* (Fernandel); *L'Epouv antail* (Grimault—short)

1944 *Le Voleur de paratonnerres* (Grimault—short); *Sylvie et la fantôme (Sylvie and the Ghost; Sylvie and the Phantom)* (Autant-Lara)

1946 *Les J-3* (Richebé)

1947 *Les Amants du Pont Saint-Jean* (Decoin)

1951 *Gibier de potence* (Richebé)

1953 *Mam'zelle Nitouche* (Y. Allégret)

1956 *Notre-Dame de Paris (The Hunchback of Notre Dame)* (Delannoy)

1958 *La Femme et le pantin (The Female)* (Duvivier)

1960 *L'Affaire d'une nuit* (Verneuil)

1962 *Vive Henri IV, vive l'amour!* (Autant-Lara); *Vu du pont (A View from the Bridge)* (Lumet) (French version only)

1963 *Venere imperiale* (Delannoy)

1965 *Le Journal d'une femme en blanc* (Autant-Lara)

1966 *Le Nouveau Journal d'une femme en blanc (Une Femme en blanc se révolte* (Autant-Lara)

1967 ''Aujourd'hui'' ep. of *Le Plus Vieux Métier du monde (The Oldest Profession)* (Autant-Lara)

1969 *Les Patates* (Autant-Lara)

1975 *Que la fête commence (Let Joy Reign Supreme)* (Tavernier); *Le Juge et l'assassin (The Judge and the Assassin)* (Tavernier)

1981 *Coup de torchon (Clean Slate)* (Tavernier)

1982 *L'Etoile du nord (The Northern Star)* (Granier-Deferre)

1987 *Fucking Fernand* (Mordillat); *De guerre lasse* (Enrico) (co)

1988 *Le Palanquin des larmes* (Dorfmann)

Films as Writer (Bost):

1939 *L'Héritier des Mondésir* (Valentin)

1942 *L'Homme qui joue avec le feu* (De Limur); *Croisières sidérales* (Zwobada); *La Chèvre d'or* (Barberis); *Une Etoile au soleil* (Zwobada); *Madame et le mort* (Daquin); *Dernier atout* (Becker)

1944 *La Libération de Paris*

1945 *Patrie* (Daquin)

1947 *Les Jeux sont faits* (Delannoy)

1950 *Le Château de verre* (Clément)

1952 *La voce del silenzio* (Pabst); *La P . . . respectueuse (The Respectful Prostitute)* (Pagliero and Brabant)

1953	*Une Fille nommée Madeleine* (*Maddalena*) (Genina); *Le Guérisseur* (Ciampi)
1957	*Oeil pour oeil* (*An Eye for an Eye*) (Cayatte)
1958	*Le Vent se lève* (Ciampi)
1959	*Pantalaskas* (Paviot)
1961	*Che gioia vivere* (*Quelle joie de vivre*) (Clément)

Films as Cowriters:

1943	*Douce* (Autant-Lara)
1946	*La Symphonie pastorale* (Delannoy); *La Septième Porte* (Zwobada)
1947	***Le Diable au corps*** (*Devil in the Flesh*) (Autant-Lara)
1949	*Au-delà des grilles* (*The Walls of Malapaga*) (Clément); *Occupe-toi d'Amélie* (*Oh, Amelia*) (Autant-Lara)
1950	*Dieu a besoin des hommes* (*God Needs Men*) (Delannoy)
1951	*L'Auberge rouge* (Autant-Lara); ***Les Jeux interdits*** (*Forbidden Games*) (Clément); ''La Paresse'' and ''L'Orgeuil'' eps. of *Les Sept Péchés capitaux* (*The Seven Capital Sins*) (Dréville and Autant-Lara)
1952	''Jeanne d'Arc'' ep. of *Destinées* (*Daughters of Destiny*) (Delannoy)
1953	*Le Blé en herbe* (*The Game of Love*) (Autant-Lara); *Les Orgueilleux* (*The Proud and the Beautiful*) (Y. Allégret)
1954	*Le Rouge et le noir* (Autant-Lara)
1955	*Chiens perdus sans collier* (Delannoy); *Gervaise* (Clément)
1956	*La Traversée de Paris* (*Four Bags Full*) (Autant-Lara)
1958	*En cas de malheur* (*Love Is My Profession*) (Autant-Lara); *Le Joueur* (Autant-Lara)
1959	*La Jument verte* (*The Green Mare*) (Autant-Lara); *Le Chemin des écoliers* (Boisrond)
1960	*Les Régates de San Francisco* (Autant-Lara)
1961	*Tu ne tueras point* (Autant-Lara)
1962	*Le Crime ne paie pas* (*Crime Does Not Pay*) (Oury); *Le Rendez-vous* (Delannoy)
1963	*Le Meurtrier* (*Enough Rope*) (Autant-Lara)
1964	*Le Magot de Joséfa* (Autant-Lara); *Les Amitiés particulières* (*This Special Friendship*) (Delannoy); ''La Fourmi'' ep. of *Humour noir* (Autant-Lara)
1966	*Paris brûle-t-il?* (*Is Paris Burning?*) (Clément)
1967	*Le Franciscain de Bourges* (Autant-Lara)
1974	*L'Horloger de Saint-Paul* (*The Clockmaker*) (Tavernier)

Publications

By AURENCHE: books—

(Co-author), *Molière pour rire et pour pleurer*, Paris, 1973.
La suite à l'écran, Lyon, 1993.

By AURENCHE: articles—

Films and Filming (London), May 1959.
Cinéma (Paris), February 1962.
Positif (Paris), April 1975.
In *Les Scénaristes au travail*, edited by Christian Salé, Renens, Switzerland, 1981.

Image et Son/Ecran (Paris), November 1981.
Problèmes Audiovisuels (Aubervilliers, France), May-June 1983.

On AURENCHE: articles—

Cinémonde (Paris), 26 September 1952.
Avant-Scène (Paris), no. 15, 1962.
Avant-Scène (Paris), May 1974.
Cinéma de France (Paris), May 1981.
First Cut, no. 10, 1981.
Joris, L., and R. Pede, Obituary in *Film en Televisie et Video*, no. 426, November 1992.
Douin, Jean-Luc, ''De mémoire de cinéfils,'' in *Télérama* (Paris), 23 June 1993.
Masson, Alain, ''Eloquent et public,'' in *Positif* (Paris), January 1994.
Little, M.-N., ''Aurenche, Jean: La suite a l'ecran,'' in *French Review*, no. 4, 1996.

By BOST: books—

Hercule et mademoiselle, Paris, 1924.
Homicide par imprudence, Paris, 1925.
Les Vieillards, Paris, 1925.
Crise de croissance, Paris, 1926.
Faillite, Paris, 1928.
Anaïs, Paris, 1930.
Le Cirque et le music-hall, Paris, 1931.
Le Scandale, Paris, 1931, as *The Offence*, London, 1932.
Porte-Malheur, Paris, 1932.
Monsieur Ladmiral va bientôt mourir, Montrouge, 1945.
La Haute-Fourche, London, 1946.
With Pierre Darbon and Pierre Quet, *La Puissance et la gloire*, based on the novel by Graham Greene, Paris, 1953, as *The Power and the Glory*, London, 1959.
With C. A. Puget, *Un Nommé Judas*, Paris, 1954.
With others, *Molière pour rire et pour pleurer*, Paris, 1973.

By BOST: article—

Films and Filming (London), May 1959.

On BOST: articles—

Bianco e Nero (Rome), vol. 5, no. 7, 1943.
Avant-Scène (Paris), no. 15, 1962.
Avant-Scène (Paris), May 1974.
Obituary, in *Cinéma* (Paris), February 1976.
Little, Marie-Noelle, ''La Suite a l'ecran,'' in *French Review*, March 1996.

*   *   *

A prolific writer of over 80 scenarios, Jean Aurenche enjoyed a long and varied film career. His 30-year partnership with Pierre Bost brought several major literary classics to the screen, and in the late 1940s and early 1950s these soundly-crafted adaptations, mostly directed by Claude Autant-Lara, enjoyed both enormous popularity and, initially, critical approval. However, their influence on French film production in this period was condemned by André Bazin and his outspoken protégé, François Truffaut, for whom the notion of a so-called quality cinema beholden to a literary tradition was essentially a denial of cinema itself. The eventual triumph of New Wave concepts of film authorship and production methods may have marked the collapse of the Aurenche and Bost hegemony, but not the end of the partnership which lasted until Bost's death in 1976. After that, Aurenche enjoyed a productive association with Bernard Tavernier. Most recently, Aurenche's presence was discernible in the antiauthoritarian *Fucking Fernand* with its anarchic excesses and black humour, while the more traditional side of the scriptwriter's humanitarianism is witnessed in *De guerre lasse*, a study of love and friendship during the Occupation and characteristically structured through flashback and voice-over.

Aurenche's early ambition had been to write gags for Buster Keaton, but a more modest debut awaited him in the early 1930s when he began writing publicity films for the Maison Damour. Here collaboration with Marcel Carné, Jean Anouilh, Paul Grimault, Jacques Prévert, Max Ernst, and other former surrealists like Denis Tual eventually led to more serious undertakings. Tual introduced him to the German scriptwriter Hans Wilhem to gain experience, and early success followed with the scenario for Chenal's *L'Affaire Lafarge*, the reconstruction of a famous court case. From his friendship with Grimault came the coauthorship of celebrated cartoons: *Le Marchand de notes*, *L'Epouvantail*, and *Le Voleur de paratonnerres*, adapted from his own short story. With Anouilh he composed the surrealist sketch *Humulus le muet* and later coscripted his first feature films for Joannon, *Vous n'avez rien à déclarer?* and, for Christian-Jaque, *Les Dégourdis de la onzième*. Through Carné he worked with Henri Jeanson on a skillfully constructed adaptation of Eugène Dabit's melodramatic *Hôtel du Nord*, and this collaboration was renewed in the 1960s for Verneuil's *L'Affaire d'une nuit* and the disappointing costume drama *Vive Henri IV, vive l'amour!* directed by Autant-Lara. With Prévert responsible for the dialogue, Aurenche undertook his first adaptation for Autant-Lara, the melodramatic *L'Affaire du courrier de Lyon*, and the two writers again combined for Delannoy's colourful version of Hugo's *Notre-Dame de Paris*.

It was Autant-Lara who introduced Bost to Aurenche to help with the dialogue for his film *Douce*, taken from Michel Davet's simple story of a devoted governess in a bourgeois family. Their screen version cleverly subverts the original text by shifting the emphasis to expose middle-class complacency. Thereafter the two writers formed a unique partnership translating for the screen an impressive array of literary classics, including works by Aymé, Colette, Feydeau, Gide, Radiguet, Stendhal, and Zola. Their initial collaboration set the pattern for their approach to adaptation; Aurenche concerning himself mainly with the screenplay and Bost with the dialogue. Frequently their shared left-wing sympathies are reflected in the inflection given to their reworked film narratives. Although they worked for several directors their most memorable achievements are found in films by Delannoy, Clément, and Autant-Lara.

Their first international success came with Delannoy and their version of *La Symphonie pastorale*, after Gide's own script had been rejected. The original narrative exposes a pastor's self-deceiving relationship with Gertrude, a blind girl, and the tragic consequences his lack of self-awareness brings both for the girl and his family. Although the reworking is satisfactory in its own terms with a neatly balanced plot, clearly drawn characters, and thematic exposition of moral dilemmas, it is by the same token a betrayal and simplification of Gide's account of moral complexities and perceptions. The weakness in the film's narrative strategy lies in its inability to reproduce the

irony implicit in the restricted viewpoint of the self-deluding pastor, and, throughout, the audience is fully aware of the real situation. Similarly Gide's teasingly subtle symbolism becomes heavily explicit in the more concrete visual statement. Further films followed for Delannoy in the 1950s including *Chiens perdus sans collier*, a well-worked, socially conscious account of a judge's mission to save a group of delinquents, and *Dieu a besoin des hommes*, from a novel by Quefflec, which concerns a priest's fraught relationship with a superstitious fishing community. The film narrative is again tightly structured and allows for powerful visually composed scenes matched by forceful dialogue, but the ironical observation of the original is lost. Although collaboration with Delannoy continued in the 1960s none of the films redounded to the scriptwriters reputation.

Their association with René Clément began with *Au-delà des grilles* when they reshaped an existing Italian script into a tightly organized, but ultimately predictable, melodrama about a fugitive criminal played by Jean Gabin. The scenario for *Les Jeux interdits*, which depicts the life of two children growing up during the Occupation, was cowritten with the author François Boyer who had originally conceived his novel as a film-script. The result is a delicate, finely judged screen version which deftly projects the children's feelings. However, of their films for Clément, none has matched *Gervaise*, a generally faithful and sympathetic rendering of Zola's working-class masterpiece *L'Assommoir*, which deals with the social consequences of poverty and alcoholism. As the film title implies, the scenario shifts the emphasis from the study of general sociological issues to the depiction of the heroine's tragic fate. If the narrative framework retains the key elements the scope of the action is reduced, and some episodes, namely Goujet's involvement in a strike, his trial, and imprisonment have been invented. As with other adaptations, Aurenche and Bost have used a combination of flashback and voice-over to bind narrative elements together and to clarify characters' motivations.

It is through their sustained service to Autant-Lara both as a team and as individuals that the talents of Aurenche and Bost are most completely displayed. After *Douce* the two collaborated on an adaptation of Radiguet's *Le Diable au corps*, the first of three films with Gérard Philipe as the protagonist. Here he plays the selfish, immature lover of a woman whose husband is at the front during World War I. The film narrative is structured through a series of flashbacks which encourages a strong identification with the couple's situation, the tensions within the relationship, and the difficulties caused by social pressures. In the adaptation of Stendhal's *Le Rouge et le noir* Philipe was Julien Sorel, the gifted but unsure proletarian hero making his way in society as a charming seducer. The devices of flashback and first-person narrative are introduced to order the material of the novel, and although the key plot elements remain, there is inevitably considerable condensing and simplification of Stendhal's dense narrative. The tone and depth of the author's narration with its subtle articulations are sadly lacking. Sharp observations on the political intrigues and the social order, the insights afforded into the complex psychology of the assertive yet self-doubting hero have been sacrificed to episodes with an inherently dramatic, visual, appeal. Philipe was again the protagonist of *Le Joueur*, an adaptation of Dostoevsky's tale, but the script becomes a star vehicle and the subtleties and reflective nature of the original are lost in melodrama. Their version of Colette's delicately textured novel *Le Blé en herbe*, which tells of the burgeoning love between two adolescents and the seduction of the boy by a mature woman, is not without strengths, the script translating well many of the more tentatively intimate moments.

Farce and comedy were also part of the Aurenche and Bost repertoire. Their version of the Feydeau play *Occupe-toi d'Amélie* remains a cleverly wrought boulevard farce, adopting the form of a play within a film. In their adaptation of the Marcel Aymé comic story, *La Traversée de Paris*, telling of wartime blackmarketeering, episodes were invented and the proletarian taxi-driver is deliberately rendered more likeable than the aristocratic painter, played by Gabin. Less successful in its attempt to bring together a multiplicity of narrative threads was their version of Aymé's bucolic farce of seduction and intrigue, *La Jument verte*. Black comedy is at the heart of *L'Auberge rouge*, one of their few original scenarios. Here a murderous innkeeper and his wife systematically kill off their guests much to the consternation of an informed monk, played by Fernandel, who feels unable to break his vows of confidentiality. Antibourgeois, anti-Catholic, this disturbing farce is tightly worked but reveals a decidedly literary style. A much more serious, didactic tone is established for *Tu ne tueras point* which deals with conscientious objection. The plot, again dependent on flashback, is rather pedestrian and does not carry the weight of Autant-Lara's message.

The last important collaboration between Aurenche and Bost was for Bernard Tavernier with their free adaptation of Simenon's *L'Horloger d'Everton*. Retitled *L'Horloger de Saint-Paul*, the action moves from South America to Lyon. Characters and situations are modified to present a portrait of the French city and to depict an unusual friendship between the criminal's father, played by Philippe Noiret, and the investigating detective. The reshaping allows an exposition of current French political attitudes and the humanistic values dear to Tavernier. After Bost's death, Aurenche collaborated with the director on further scenarios with Noiret in the main role. The witty *Que la fête commence*, loosely adapted from *La Fille du Régent* by Dumas, is again used as a vehicle for contemporary comment, while *Le Juge et l'assassin* is a psychological study of power through the example of an overbearing magistrate. Black humour, though perhaps a little laboured, is the essence of *Coup de torchon* which deals with colonial rule in Africa through another figure of authority, that of a slovenly policeman, again brilliantly played by Noiret. In two of his films Tavernier acknowledges his debt to Aurenche. *Une Semaine de vacances* is dedicated to him, while within the narrative of *Coup de torchon* is found Aurenche's early advertising short *Au petit jour à Mexico on va fusiller un homme*. Homage is similarly paid to Bost with the delicately observed *Un Dimanche à la campagne*, a reworking of his early novel *Monsieur L'admiral va bientôt mourir*. With their strong literary flavour and social comment Tavernier's films appropriately renew the traditions established by Aurenche and Bost in the late 1940s.

Bost can claim a number of film credits independent of those in collaboration with Aurenche. He worked for a variety of directors, adapting both novels and plays as well as writing dialogue. An early 1940s script provided Becker with a taut police drama in *Dernier atout*, while for Daquin he wrote dialogue, notably for *Patrie*, adapted from a play by Sardou and dealing indirectly with the moral issues of Occupation and Resistance. His adaptation of the Soubiran novel *Les Hommes en blanc* for Habib inspired perhaps this director's most accomplished film, while also of considerable interest was Paviot's *Pantalaskas*, dealing with the difficulties of immigrant workers, for which he wrote the dialogue. His sober commentary enhances the documentary *La Libération de Paris*, which was pieced together from original footage.

Neither Aurenche nor Bost articulated any illuminating theory of adaptation. A rendering faithful to the original text while ensuring a visually engaging film readily understood by all seems to have been the basic aim. Their role was to stimulate the director, to work as closely as possible with him, and to allow for the needs of stars such as Philipe, Gabin, or Noiret. Dialogue was seen as an aspect of characterization rather than as a function of plot clarification. There is considerable truth in the basic charge levelled by Truffaut, namely that authors with quite different values and quite different narrative strategies are reduced to a sameness through the Aurenche and Bost treatment. Their well-tried formula closes open-ended plots, simplifies elusive, complex characters, and prefers strong visual development to reflective interiority. Their rejected script for *Le Journal d'un curé de campagne* understandably failed to satisfy Bernanos. Although their personal persuasions and values are occasionally discernible through their adaptations, they rarely treated a literary text as Balàzs would have wished, namely as raw material susceptible to a completely original restatement. Yet arguably they did impose their own identifiable style, based in an intelligent paring down of plots, a regular reliance on flashback and first-person narration in their reordering of material, together with frequently sharp, sensitive, and witty dialogue. Consummate craftsmen, fashioning to their own ends the disparate material of fellow authors, Aurenche and Bost represent a particular view of the cinema's relationship with literature. Their enterprise raises fundamental and unresolved questions about precisely what a film adaptation of a literary text should seek to achieve.

—R. F. Cousins

AURIC, Georges

Composer. **Nationality:** French. **Born:** Lodève, 15 February 1899. Studied at the Paris Conservatory, and under d'Indy at the Schola Cantorum, Paris, 1914–16. **Family:** Married Nora Smith, 1938. **Career:** Composer from age 15; member of the group Les Six; 1930—first film score, *Le Sang d'un poète*; composer of orchestra and choral works, and incidental music for plays; 1965—music for serialized TV work *Marc et Sylvie*, and for *L'Age heureux* 1966, *Le Trésor des Hollandais*, 1969, and *Zingari*, 1975. **Awards:** Venice Festival special award, 1952. **Died:** In Paris, 23 July 1983.

Films as Composer:

1930   *Le Sang d'un poète* (*The Blood of a Poet*) (Cocteau)
1931   *À nous la liberté* (Clair)
1934   *Lac-aux-dames* (M. Allégret)
1935   *Les Mystères de Paris* (Gandera)
1936   *Sous les yeux d'Occident* (*Razumov*) (M. Allégret)
1937   *L'Affaire Lafarge* (Chenal); *Un Déjeuner de soleil* (Cohen); *Gribouille* (*Heart of Paris*) (M. Allégret); *Tamara la complaisante* (Gandera); *Le Messager* (Rouleau) (co); *La Danseuse rouge* (Paulin) (co); *L'Alibi* (Chenal) (co)
1938   *Orage* (M. Allégret); *Les Oranges de Jaffa* (Alexeiff—short); *Trois minutes—les saisons* (short); *La Vie d'un homme* (short); *Huilor* (Alexeiff—short); *Entrée des artistes* (*The Curtain Rises*) (M. Allégret); *La Rue sans joie* (Hugon) (co); *Son oncle de Normandie* (Dréville)
1939   *La Mode rêvée* (L'Herbier—short); *Macao, l'enfer du jeu* (Delannoy); *The Alibi*

1940 *De la ferraille a l'acier victorieux* (Lallier—short)
1942 *Opéra-Musette* (Lefèvre and C. Renoir); *L'Assassin a peur la nuit* (Delannoy); *Monsieur et la souris* (Lacombe); *La Belle Aventure* (*Twilight*) (M. Allégret)
1943 *L'Eternel Retour* (*The Eternal Return*) (Delannoy); *Farandole* (Zwoboda)
1944 *Le Bossu* (Delannoy)
1945 *François Villon* (Zwoboda) (co); *Caesar and Cleopatra* (Pascal); **Dead of Night** (Cavalcanti and others); *La Part de l'ombre* (*Blind Desire*) (Delannoy)
1946 **La Belle et la bête** (*Beauty and the Beast*) (Cocteau); *La Symphonie pastorale* (Delannoy); *La Septième Porte* (Zwoboda)
1947 *Ruy Blas* (Billon); *Hue and Cry* (Crichton); *Les Jeux sont faits* (*The Chips Are Down*) (Delannoy); *L'Aigle à deux têtes* (*The Eagle with Two Heads*) (Cocteau); *Corridor of Mirrors* (Young); *It Always Rains on Sunday* (Hamer); *La Rose et le réséda* (Michel)
1948 *The Queen of Spades* (Dickinson); *Silent Dust* (Comfort); *Another Shore* (Crichton); *Noces du sable* (Zwoboda); *Les Parents terribles* (*The Storm Within*) (Cocteau); *Aux yeux du souvenir* (*Souvenir*) (Zwoboda);
1949 *Maya* (Bernard); **Passport to Pimlico** (Cornelius); *Ce siècle a cinquante ans* (Tual) (co); *The Spider and the Fly* (Hamer)
1950 *Orphée* (*Orpheus*) (Cocteau); *Cage of Gold* (Dearden); *Caroline chérie* (Pottier); *Fès* (Zwoboda—short); *Les Amants de Bras-Mort* (Pagliero)
1951 *Nex de cutr* (Y. Allégret); *Front de mer* (short); *Kermesse fantastique* (Mishek—short); *La P . . . respecteuse* (*The Respectful Prostitute*) (Pagliero and Brabant); *La Fête à Henriette* (Duvivier); *The Open Window* (Storck—short); *The Titfield Thunderbolt* (Crichton); *Moulin Rouge* (Huston); **The Lavender Hill Mob** (Crichton)
1953 *La Chair et le diable* (Josipovici); *L'Esclave* (Ciampi); **La Salaire de la peur** (*The Wages of Fear*) (Clouzot); *Roman Holiday* (Wyler)
1954 *Chéri Bibi* (Pagliero); *The Good Die Young* (Gilbert); **Du Rififi chez les hommes** (*Rififi*) (Dassin); *The Divided Heart* (Crichton); *Nagana* (Bromberger); *Abdullah the Great* (*Abdullah's Harem*) (Ratoff); *Father Brown* (*The Detective*) (Hamer)
1955 *La Femme et la fauve* (Sarrut and Asseo—short); *La Chaleur du foyer* (*Feeder de l'est*) (Gillet—short); *The Bespoke Overcoat* (Clayton—short); **Lola Montès** (Ophüls); *Les Hussards* (Joffé); *Gervaise* (Clément); *A Visit with Darius Milhaud* (Joseph) (+ appearance); *Walk into Paradise* (Robinson and Pagliero); *Licht und der Mensch* (Geesink);
1956 *Le Mystère Picasso* (*The Mystery of Picasso*) (Clouzot); *Notre-Dame de Paris* (Delannoy); *Heaven Knows, Mr. Allison* (Huston); *Les Aventures de Till l'Espiègle* (Philipe)
1957 *Celui qui doit mourir* (*He Who Must Die*) (Dassin); *Bonjour Tristesse* (Preminger); *Les Espions* (Clouzot); *The Story of Esther Costello* (Miller); *Walk into Hell*
1958 *Next to No Time* (Cornelius); *Dangerous Exile* (Hurst); *Les Bijoutiers du clair de lune* (*Heaven Fell That Night*) (Vadim); *Christine* (Gaspard-Huit)
1959 *The Journey* (Litvak); *La Princesse de Clèves* (Delannoy); *Sergent X . . .* (Borderie); *S.O.S. Pacific* (Green)
1960 *Le Testament d'Orphée* (*The Testament of Orpheus*) (Cocteau); *Schlüssakkord* (Liebeneiner)

1961 *Aimez-vous Brahms?* (*Goodbye Again*) (Litvak); *Bridge to the Sun* (Perier); *The Innocents* (Clayton); *Les Croulants se portent bien* (Boyer); *Le Rendez-vous de minuit* (Leenhardt)
1962 *La Chambre ardente* (*The Burning Court*) (Duvivier); *Smash en direct* (Dasque and Abadie—short) (co): *Carillons sans joie* (Brabant)
1963 *The Kremlin* (Vicas); *The Mind Benders* (Dearden)
1964 *Thomas l'imposteur* (Franju)
1965 *La Sentinelle endormie* (Dreville); *La Communale* (L'Hote)
1966 *La Grande Vadrouille* (Oury); *Danger Grows Wild* (*The Poppy Is Also a Flower*) (Young)
1968 *Thérèse and Isabelle* (Metzger); *Ce pays dont les frontières ne sont que fleurs* (Masson—short)
1969 *The Christmas Tree* (Young)

Other Films:

1924 *Entr'acte* (Clair—short) (ro)
1941 *Les Petits Riens* (Leboursier) (mus d)

Publications

By AURIC: autobiography—

Quand j'étais là, Paris, 1979.

By AURIC: articles—

Mein Film (Vienna), 22 August 1952.
Unifrance Film (Paris), no. 50, 1959.
Ecran Fantastique (Paris), no. 5, 1978.

On AURIC: books—

Schaeffner, A., *Georges Auric*, Paris, 1928.
Golea, A., *Georges Auric*, Paris, 1958.

On AURIC: articles—

Sight and Sound (London), April-June 1953.
Fistful of Soundtracks (London), October 1980.
Obituary, in *Revue du Cinéma* (Paris), no. 386, September 1983.
New Zealand Film Music Bulletin (Invercargill), November 1983.
The Annual Obituary 1983, Chicago and London, 1984.

*   *   *

Composer of some of the most delightfully whimsical motion picture scores in history, Georges Auric also had the added distinction of having written the first original score for a feature film: his music for Jean Cocteau's *The Blood of a Poet* (1930). Auric's quirky classicism is displayed in more than 75 scores from 1930 to 1969. He never lost sight of his own artistic vision, no matter the assignment he was given, and his screen music is shot through with echoes of Durey, Tailleferre, Poulenc, Honneger and Milhaud, the other members of ''The Group of Six'' (Auric was the sixth member). He worked with such major directors as Max Ophüls (*Lola Montès*), John Huston (*Moulin Rouge*), William Wyler, Otto Preminger, Jean Delannoy, and his scores range from the highly dramatic (*Bonjour Tristesse*) to the playful (*The Lavender Hill Mob, Passport to Pimlico*).

According to Cocteau's biographer, Francis Steegmuller, Auric early on acquired a taste for opium, but apparently never let the drug get the better of him, becoming what Steegmuller described as a "controlled, habitual smoker." He probably acquired his predilection for the drug from Cocteau, who was widely known to use opiates for relaxation and "brainstorming," and it is perhaps not too far-fetched to claim that a certain "twinkling etherealness" in Auric's music may be attributable to his use of the drug. Auric's best scores, including *The Blood of a Poet, A nous la liberté, Beauty and the Beast, The Eternal Return, Dead of Night, Rififi,* and *The Lavender Hill Mob,* all have a certain "celestial accent" (Cocteau's words) which makes them simultaneously fanciful and yet never too far removed from the mundane realities they must inevitably remain grounded in.

Almost alone among those composers who work specifically for films, Auric had a classical background which led him to create scores which stand quite well on their own as concert pieces, and interestingly, Auric's few detractors claim that at times his music forgets its supporting role and threatens to overpower the images it is supposed to accompany. Perhaps this explains why he worked so well, and so often, with Cocteau, whose visual style is boldly, even aggressively romantic. Cocteau's full blown imagery coupled with Auric's lush, yet light music meshed perfectly to create a fantastic world of full-blooded fantasy, a world at once more real and tangible than that of one's everyday existence.

Auric picked his assignments with great care, particularly after he became director of the Paris Opera in 1962. Although he won numerous prizes for his work at the Venice and Cannes Film Festivals, and elsewhere, Auric was always more interested in working on "difficult" or "experimental" projects than mainstream films. For example, one of his last films, *The Mind Benders,* directed by Basil Dearden, is a prescient tale of psychological research done by a group of university professors who subject themselves to long periods of sensory deprivation in "isolation tanks." That the film was ahead of its time is amply demonstrated by the fact that it was still considered a radical enough concept to be remade by Ken Russell in his uneven *Altered States.* Auric also worked on Cocteau's last project, *The Testament of Orpheus,* which, although arguably the least of Cocteau's efforts, is still an admirably evocative conclusion to the artist's illustrious multifaceted career. It is perhaps the highest possible tribute to Auric's work to say that his film scores are instantly recognizable, sincerely romantic, and, like the film scores of his fellow countryman George Delerue, glorious throwbacks to an earlier age of gentility, precision, and grace.

—Wheeler Winston Dixon

AVERY, Tex

Animator. **Nationality:** American. **Born:** Frederick Bean Avery in Taylor, Texas, 26 February 1907. **Education:** Attended North Dallas High School, graduated 1927. **Career:** 1930–35—animator with Universal-Walter Lantz Cartoons; 1936–41—worked at Warners (4 films in Bugs Bunny series: *A Wild Hare, Tortoise Beats Hare, The Heckling Hare,* and *All This and Rabbit Stew*); before 1941 credited as Fred Avery; 1942—brief period at Paramount, 3 films in *Speaking of Animals* series then moved to MGM beginning with *The Blitz Wolf;* 1954–55—directed for Walter Lantz; 1955—quit MGM; 1956–78—made commercials for Cascade Productions; 1979–80—with Hanna-Barbera Cartoons. **Awards:** First Prize, Venice Publicity Festival, for *Calo-Tiger,* 1958; Television Commercials Council Award, 1960; Annie Award, ASIFA 1974. **Died:** 26 August 1980.

Films as Director (often credited as supervisor):

1936   *Golddiggers of '49; The Blow-out; Plane Dippy; I'd Love to Take Orders from You; Miss Glory; I Love to Singa; Porky the Rain Maker; The Village Smithy; Milk and Money; Don't Look Now; Porky the Wrestler*

1937   *Picador Porky; I Only Have Eyes for You; Porky's Duck Hunt; Uncle Tom's Bungalow; Ain't We Got Fun; Daffy Duck and Egghead; Egghead Rides Again; A Sunbonnet Blue; Porky's Garden; I Wanna Be a Sailor; The Sneezing Weasel; Little Red Walking Hood*

1938   *The Penguin Parade; The Isle of Pingo Pongo; A Feud There Was; Johnny Smith and Poker-Huntas; Daffy Duck in Hollywood; Cinderella Meets Fella; Hamateur Night; The Mice Will Play; Daffy's Romance*

1939   *A Day at the Zoo; Thugs with Dirty Mugs; Believe It or Else; Dangerous Dan McFoo; Detouring America; Land of the Midnight Fun; Fresh Fish; Screwball Football; The Early Worm Gets the Bird*

1940   *Cross Country Detours; The Bear's Tale; A Gander at Mother Goose; Circus Today; A Wild Hare; Ceiling Hero; Wacky Wild Life; Of Fox and Hounds (+ voice of Willoughby the dog); Holiday Highlights*

1941   *The Crackpot Quail; Haunted Mouse; Tortoise Beats Hare; Hollywood Steps Out; Porky's Preview; The Heckling Hare (+ voice of Willoughby the dog); Aviation Vacation; All This and Rabbit Stew; The Bug Parade; Aloha Hooey; The Cagey Canary (completed by Bob Clampett); Crazy Cruise*

1942   *Speaking of Animals down on the Farm; Speaking of Animals in a Pet Shop; Speaking of Animals in the Zoo; The Blitz Wolf; The Early Bird Dood it; Dumb-Hounded*

1943   *Red Hot Riding Hood; Who Killed Who?; One Ham's Family; What's Buzzin', Buzzard?*

1944   *Screwy Squirrel; Batty Baseball; Happy-Go-Nutty; Big Heel-watha*

1945   *The Screwy Truant; The Shooting of Dan McGoo; Jerky Turkey; Swing Shift Cinderella; Wild and Woolfy*

1946   *Lonesome Lenny; The Hick Chick; Northwest Hounded Police; Henpecked Hoboes (+ voice of Junior)*

1947   *Hound Hunters (+ voice of Junior); Red Hot Rangers (+ voice of Junior); Uncle Tom's Cabana; Slap Happy Lion; King Size Canary; Little Tinker*

1948   *What Price Fleadom; Half-Pint Pygmy (+ voice of Junior); Lucky Ducky; The Cat That Hated People*

1949   *Bad Luck Blackie; Señor Droopy; The House of Tomorrow; Doggone Tired; Wags to Riches; Little Rural Riding Hood; Outfoxed; Counterfeit Cat*

1950   *Ventriloquist Cat; The Cuckoo Clock; Garden Gopher; The Chump Champ; The Peachy Cobbler*

1951   *Cock-a-Doodle Dog; Dare-Devil Droopy; Droopy's Good Deed; Symphony in Slang; The Car of Tomorrow; Droopy's Double Trouble; The Magical Maestro*

1952   *One Cab's Family; Rock-a-Bye Bear*

1953 *Little Johnny Jet; TV of Tomorrow; The Three Little Pups; Drag-a-long Droopy*

1954 *Billy Boy; Homesteader Droopy; Farm of Tomorrow; The Flea Circus; Dixieland Droopy; Crazy Mixed-Up Pup*

1955 *Field and Scream; The First Bad Man; Deputy Droopy* (co-d); *Cellbound* (co-d); *I'm Cold* (*Some Like It Not*); *Chilly Willy in the Legend of Rockabye Point* (*The Rockabye Legend*); *SH-H-H-H-H;* remakes of *Wags to Riches* and *Ventriloquist Cat*

1956 *Millionaire Droopy; Cat's Meow*

1958 *Polar Pests*

Publications

By AVERY: article—

Interview with Joseph Adamson, in *Take One* (Montreal), January-February 1970.

On AVERY: books—

Kyrou, Ado, *Le Surréalisme au cinéma*, Paris, 1952.
Benayoun, Robert, *Dessin animé après Walt Disney*, Paris, 1961.
Adamson, Joseph, *Tex Avery, King of Cartoons*, New York, 1975.
Brion, Patrick, *Tex Avery*, Paris, 1984.
Canemaker, John, *Tex Avery: Artist, Animator, & Director from the Golden Age of Animated Cartoons*, North Dighton, 1998.

On AVERY: articles—

Doniol Valcroze, Jacques, "Un Savoureaux Western animé," in *Revue du Cinéma* (Paris), February 1947.
"Le Dossier Tex Avery," in *Positif* (Paris), July-August 1963.
Canemakers, J., "The Hollywood Cartoon," in *Filmmakers Newsletter* (Ward Hill, Massachusetts), April 1974.
Kral, P., "Tex Avery ou le délire lucide," in *Positif* (Paris), June 1974.
Adamson, J., "Cartoonographies," in *Film Comment*, New York, January-February 1975.
Rosenbaum, J., "Dream Masters II: Tex Avery," in *Film Comment* (New York), January-February 1975.
Cohen, M. S. "Looney Tunes and Merrie Melodies," in *Velvet Light Trap* (Madison, Wisconsin), Autumn 1975.
Cornand, A., "Le Festival d'Annecy . . . ," in *Image et Son* (Paris), January 1977.
Jones, Chuck, "Confessions of a Cell Washer," in *Take One* (Montreal), September 1978.
Gaines, J., "The Showgirl and the Wolf," in *Cinema Journal* (Evanston, Illinois), Fall 1980.
Dagneau, G., "Tex Avery: L'accléré à 24 images seconde!," in *Cinéma* (Paris), October 1980.
Beltrán, A., "Dos bitos del ochenta," in *Contracampo* (Madrid), January 1981.
Colpart, G., "Look at Me, Folks, I'm Just Tex Avery," in *Image et Son* (Paris), January 1981.
Lenburg, Jeff, in *The Great Cartoon Directors*, Jefferson, North Carolina, 1983.
Cinéma (Paris), no. 335, 24 December 1985.
Schneider, Steve, in *That's All Folks!* New York, 1988.

Skrien, August-September 1992.
Smith, Lane, "The Artist At Work," in *Horn Book Magazine*, January-February 1993.
Film en Televisie, March 1993.
Sight and Sound, October 1993.
Time, 8 August 1994.
Klein, Tom, "Apprenticing the Master: Tex Avery at Universal (1929–1935)," in *Animation Journal* (Orange), Fall 1997.
Floquet, Pierre, "Tex Avery's Comic Language: A Transgressive Interpretation of Hunting," in *Animation Journal* (Orange), Fall 1997.
Corliss, Richard, "Cartoons are No Laughing Matter," in *Time*, 12 May 1997.

* * *

The cartoons of Tex Avery represent a style of animation that is the absolute antithesis to the Disney school of filmmaking. Whereas Disney strove for realism (with such technical devices as sound, Technicolor, and the multiplane camera), Avery strove for the absurd and the surreal. Avery's "logic" had no bounds and his cartoons exhibited an anything-goes policy. The characters in Avery's cartoons not only behaved in a crazy way, but actually seemed insane. Among the cartoon characters that he created were Daffy Duck, Screwball Squirrel, Droopy, and his most famous character, Bugs Bunny. Avery gave Bugs his familiar phrase "What's up Doc?," which was an expression in Avery's home town in Texas.

The most striking feature of Avery's animation style is the breakneck pace of gags. Avery believed in having as many gags as possible. While at Warner Brothers, Avery did a number of cartoons loosely structured as travelogues or newsreels. This simple framework gave Avery the opportunity to string together as many "black out" (short, self-contained) gags as could fit into seven minutes. Cartons like *Believe It or Else* and *Wacky Wild Life* were short on plot, but bursting with Avery's sight gags.

Another trademark of Avery's cartoons is the elasticity of his characters. It would be fair to say that Avery puts his characters through a wider range of physical distortions than any other cartoon director. For example, in *King Size Canary*, the dog, cat, bird and mouse grow to absurd proportions. In *Screwball Football* a character literally yells his head off. Naturally, none of these physical distortions ever proves to be fatal.

Another source of Avery's humor is the medium of animation itself. Many times the characters in Avery's cartoons refer to the cartoon world in which they live. For example, in *Porky's Preview*, Porky Pig draws his own cartoon starring himself. In *Screwball Squirrel*, Screwy accidentally runs clear off the side of the frame of the film. In *The Magical Maestro* a hair keeps bobbing up and down in the projection gate until one of the characters finally reaches over and pulls it out. Avery rarely lets the audience forget that they are watching cartoons.

Another feature often associated with Tex Avery's cartoons are his jokes based on sexual innuendos. For example, Avery's character of the Wolf (who appeared in *Red Hot Riding Hood* and *Wild and Woolfy* among others) represents the most elementary of sexual beings. In these cartoons the Wolf cannot control his desire for Red; his eyes pop out of his head, his jaw drops open, his tongue rolls out on the floor, and he literally falls to pieces. His lust is in no way subtle, and in fact, *Red Hot Riding Hood* had some trouble getting by the Hays Office because of the suggestion of bestiality. Nothing in

Avery's cartoons ever went beyond suggestion, but Avery subsequently adopted the habit of padding his scripts with extra and outlandish ''no-no's,'' which could then be dropped, in order that a few innuendoes could slip by the censors.

During the latter part of his career, Tex Avery achieved an unusual degree of recognition in television even though his work was uncredited. He created a number of award-winning animated commercials with such characters as the Raid bugs and the Frito Bandito. The short 30- or 60-second format of commercial advertising was an ideal outlet for Avery's fast-paced gags. His work has certainly influenced a number of younger animators, although no one has yet been able to completely match Avery's achievement: the totally crazy cartoon.

—Linda Obalil

B

BACHARACH, Burt

Composer. **Nationality:** American. **Born:** Kansas City, Missouri, 12 May 1928; son of the syndicated columnist Bert Bacharach; brought up in New York. **Education:** Studied musical theory at the Mannes School of Music in New York City; Berkshire Music Center; New School for Social Research, studying under Darius Milhaud, Bohuslav Martinu, and Henry Cowell; further study McGill University, Toronto; scholarship to study at the Music Academy of the West in Santa Barbara. **Military Service:** U.S. Army, 1950–52. **Family:** Married 1) Paula Stewart, 1953 (divorced 1958); 2) the actress Angie Dickinson, 1965 (divorced 1982); 3) the singer-songwriter Carole Bayer Sager, 1982 (divorced 1990); 4) Jane Hanson, 1991. **Career:** 1955— became member of ASCAP; 1957—teamed up with lyricist Hal David; 1958–61—toured America and Europe as musical director for Marlene Dietrich; 1962—Bacharach and David started to write for the singer Dionne Warwick; composed music for TV series *Any Day Now.* **Awards:** Academy Award for Best Song, for *Butch Cassidy*

and the Sundance Kid, 1969, and *Arthur*, 1981. **Address:** 10 Ocean Park Boulevard, Suite #4, Santa Monica, CA 90405–3556, U.S.A.

Films as Composer:

1965　*What's New, Pussycat?* (C. Donner)
1966　*After the Fox* (De Sica)
1967　***Casino Royale*** (Huston, Hughes, Parrish, McGrath, and Talmadge)
1969　*Butch Cassidy and the Sundance Kid* (Hill)
1972　*Lost Horizon* (Jarrott)
1981　*Arthur* (Gordon)
1982　*Night Shift* (R. Howard)
1988　*Arthur 2: On the Rocks* (Yorkin)
1992　*Love Hurts* (Yorkin)
1996　*Grace of My Heart* (Anders)
2000　*Isn't She Great*

Films as Songwriter:

1957　*Lizzie* (Haas); *The Sad Sack* (George Marshall)
1958　*The Blob* (Yeaworth Jr.); *Country Music Holiday* (Ganzer)
1961　*Love in a Goldfish Bowl* (Sher)
1962　*Forever My Love* (Marischka)
1963　*Who's Been Sleeping in My Bed?* (Daniel Mann); *Wives and Lovers* (Rich)
1964　*Send Me No Flowers* (Jewison); *A House Is Not a Home* (Rouse)
1965　*Bob and Carol and Ted and Alice* (Mazursky)
1966　*Alfie* (L. Gilbert)
1969　*April Fools* (Rosenberg)

Other Films:

1997　*Austin Powers: International Man of Mystery* (Roach) (ro as himself)
1999　*Austin Powers: The Spy Who Shagged Me* (Roach) (ro as himself)

Publications

On BACHARACH: book—

Karlin, Fred, and Rayburn Wright, *On the Track*, New York, 1990.

Burt Bacharach

On BACHARACH: articles—

Film Dope (London), March 1973.
Ecran (Paris), September 1975.
Fistful of Soundtracks, May 1981.
Film Dope (London), March 1990.
Interview (New York), February 1996.
Mojo, March 1996.
Q, July 1996.
New Yorker, 19 October 1998.

*   *   *

Burt Bacharach has achieved a singular place in the history of twentieth-century popular music. During the sixties, when pop music was becoming rock, Bacharach and lyricist Hal David wrote a string of hit records that were both melodically complex and seductive, romantic and suave. It is surprising that Bacharach has not composed scores for more films—so much of his work seems cinematic—the sound track, perhaps, of some romantic, sophisticated urban comedy in his head. Describing his compositional technique, he said ''I was thinking in terms of miniature movies. . . . Three and a half minute movies with peak moments and not just one intensity level the whole way through.''

Burt Bacharach's musical education began at an early age, studying cello, drums, and later piano. Being a music student in New York exposed himself to a variety of influences: ''I liked Berg and I liked Webern. . . . I hung out in New York watching Cage and Lou Harrison. I was aware of the angular side of music but I liked tunes too.'' His main influence, however, was Darius Milhaud, whom he studied under at the New School for Social Research, and who, Bacharach claims, taught him, ''Never to be ashamed to write something people can whistle.'' From 1958 to 1961 he was musical director for Marlene Dietrich, touring Europe and the United States with her. He teamed up with lyricist Hal David in 1957, and in 1962 they began to write for the singer Dionne Warwick, a three-way partnership that yielded 39 hit records.

Bacharach's involvement with film began in 1958, with the title song—written with veteran songwriter Mack David (Hal David's older brother)—for the low-budget horror film *The Blob*. This set a pattern for a significant amount of his writing for films, lending the Bacharach touch by furnishing individual songs rather than the creating an entire score. In some cases the songs have proved more memorable than the films in which they appeared. He has written title songs for *Whose Been Sleeping in My Bed?*, *Wives and Lovers*, *Send Me No Flowers*, and *A House Is Not a Home*. He has also contributed the song ''What the World Needs Now'' to *Bob and Carol and Ted and Alice*. Sometimes Bacharach's role can be confusing—''The Man Who Shot Liberty Valance,'' the hit he wrote for Gene Pitney is inspired by John Ford's film of the same name but is not featured in it. And for many the aching Bacharach ballad ''Alfie,'' used over the credit sequence in the American version of Lewis Gilbert's film, is more identified with *Alfie* than Sonny Rollins's coolly elegant modern jazz score.

Bacharach's first complete score for was Clive Donner's frantic sex comedy, scripted by Woody Allen, *What's New, Pussycat.''* Because of Bacharach's relative inexperience with film composition

most of the music used in the film was drawn from the buoyant title song: ''They took that one title theme, the title song, and one or two of the cues I'd written, and (producer) Charlie Feldman put them all through the movie because he fell in love with them.'' The result was a score that provided a perfect complement to the on-screen antics. Less successful was his score for the dire James Bond spoof *Casino Royale*, which does little more than underline the film's heavy-handed humor. It did, however, yield one classic Bacharach/David song, ''The Look of Love.''

Bacharach's greatest success as a film composer was with George Roy Hill's Western *Butch Cassidy and the Sundance Kid*, where Bacharach's score was crucial to the feel and the success of the film. The subject of the film was bleak: two middle-aged gunfighters, involved with one woman, unable to come to terms with the shrinking frontier, make a break for South America, where death instead of freedom awaits them. Thematically the film blends elements of Sam Peckinpah's *The Wild Bunch* with François Truffaut's *Jules et Jim*. Bacharach adds a defiantly upbeat and sunny score that, along with William Goldman's witty script, deflects much of the story's fatalism. The music nods towards period with occasional passages of pastiche ragtime, otherwise it is modern in tone, action choreographed with light scat choruses. In the film's most celebrated sequence Paul Newman and Katharine Ross careen across a meadow on a bicycle accompanied by ''Raindrops Keep Falling on My Head,'' one of Bacharach's most compulsively tuneful songs, perfectly matched by Hal David's nonsense lyrics. As if to emphasize the inspired incongruity, the sequence takes place in bright sunlight.

At the end of the sixties Bacharach and David and the playwright Neil Simon created the Tony award-winning Broadway show *Promise Her Anything*, based on Billy Wilder's film *The Apartment*. Bacharach provided music and songs for *Lost Horizon* Charles Jarrott's unsuccessful musical remake of the Frank Capra classic. After the partnership with Hal David foundered, Bacharach began a collaboration with his then wife, the singer/songwriter, Carole Bayer Sager. During the eighties Bacharach's most successful film score was for *Arthur*. The featured song, ''The Best that You Can Do,'' written by Bacharach, Sager, Christopher Cross, and Peter Allen, won an Academy Award for best song.

—Dominic Power

BADALAMENTI, Angelo

Composer. **Nationality:** American. **Born:** Brooklyn, New York, 22 March 1937; son of an Italian fish market owner. **Education:** Eastman School of Music. B.A.; Manhattan School of Music, M.A. 1960. **Family:** Married Lonny, 1968; two children: daughter Danielle and son Andre. **Career:** Accompanist to singers in the Catskills as a teen; taught at a Brooklyn junior high school before developing career as songwriter in the 1970s; hired for *Blue Velvet* as vocal coach for Isabella Rossellini but retained as composer, 1986; has scored all of David Lynch's films, TV productions, and other video material; composer for TV series *Inside the Actors Studio* (as Angelo

Angelo Badalamenti

Bagdelamenti), 1994, *The Profiler*, 1996–1998, *The Last Don*, 1997, and *Cracker*, 1997. **Awards:** Independent Spirit Award, for *Twin Peaks: Fire Walk with Me*, 1993.

Films as Composer:

1973   *Gordon's War* (Davis) (as Andy Badale)
1974   *Law and Disorder* (Passer) (as Andy Badale)
1986   *Blue Velvet* (Lynch)
1987   *Weeds* (Hancock); *Tough Guys Don't Dance* (Mailer); *Nightmare on Elm Street 3: Dream Warriors* (Russell)
1989   *Wait Until Spring, Bandini* (Deruddere); *Parents* (Balaban); *Cousins* (Schumacher); *National Lampoon's Christmas Vacation* (Chechik)
1990   *Industrial Symphony No. 1: The Dream of the Broken Hearted* (video) (Lynch); *The Comfort of Strangers* (Shrader); *Twin Peaks* (Lynch—for TV, pilot, and series); *Wild at Heart* (Lynch)
1992   *On the Air* (Lynch—for TV); *Twin Peaks: Fire Walk with Me* (Lynch)
1993   *Hotel Room* (Lynch—for TV)
1994   *Naked in New York* (Algrant); *Witch Hunt* (Shrader—for TV)
1995   *La Cité des enfants perdus* (*City of Lost Children*) (Caro and Jeunet)
1997   *Lost Highway* (Lynch); *The Blood Oranges* (Haas)

1999   *Story of a Bad Boy* (Donaghy); *Arlington Road* (Pellington); *Holy Smoke* (Campion); *Forever Mine* (Shrader); *The Straight Story* (Lynch)
2000   *Mulholland Drive* (Lynch—for TV); *The Beach* (Boyle)

Other Films:

1977   *Across the Great Divide* (Raffill) (lyricist)
1996   *Invasion of Privacy* (Hickox) (music theme)

Publications

By BADALAMENTI: books—

Floating into the Night (songs for voice and piano, words by David Lynch), Port Chester, New York, 1991.

By BADALAMENTI: articles—

''Angelo Badalamenti in Prague: 'I am the jazzman,''' interview in *Kinorevue* (Prague), October 1996.

On BADALAMENTI: articles—

Abrahams, Andrew, ''His Haunting Mood Music,'' in *People* (New York), 9 September 1990.
Woodard, Josef, ''Sonata for Cello and Cherry Pie,'' in *American Film*, 15 December 1990.

*   *   *

Only a few composers for films have the distinction of being deeply identified with a string of major works by a famed director, so that one can hardly think of the films without hearing the soundtrack: among the foremost pairings are Bernard Herrmann with Alfred Hitchcock and Nino Rota with Federico Fellini. Few, perhaps, would place David Lynch in the august company of Hitchcock and Fellini, but certainly many of the haunting moments of the American director's work have been accompanied by the music of Angelo Badalamenti, who since 1986's *Blue Velvet* has scored all of Lynch's films, TV work, and experimental videos. The composer has worked on other films, composed themes for TV shows, and collaborated on CDs with various singing artists, but his work with Lynch, notably *Blue Velvet, Twin Peaks* and *The Straight Story*, has been his most celebrated.

Blue Velvet's opening title music is relatively conventional, symphonic in style, appropriate enough for a moody, noirish film. Later, at suspenseful moments, as when Jeffrey is sneaking into Dorothy's apartment, the scoring is more sparse, and kept to the background, so that the low strings become indistinguishable from moaning sounds that might be wind blowing through a stairwell. In the first scene at the Slow Club, Badalamenti himself shows up as a pianist, with sax and bass, to accompany Dorothy (Isabella Rossellini) in a very slow version of ''Blue Velvet.'' But the composer truly comes into his own in the night scene between Jeffrey and Sandy in front of the church. The somber organ music appears to be coming from behind the stained glass windows glowing in the darkness, but as Sandy tells about her dream of robins and love, the music reaches a peak of hyper-sweet piety that seems a sly mockery of her speech. Later, when the young friends/crime-solvers kiss, the same music is played by strings, and later yet, at a dance and then as the couple converse by phone in a scene that could be captioned ''Teen Heartbreak,'' we hear a vocal version (''Mysteries of Love,'' sung by Julee Cruise, with lyrics by Lynch). In the film's ineffably weird epilogue, we hear the song again while the loving family watches the (mechanical) robin with its bug: at this point we have reached the classic moment of the Lynch/Badalamenti fusion.

If one may speak of a fully mature Badalamenti style, one can find it in his score for *Twin Peaks*, the TV series whose pilot film, directed by Lynch, was shown as a feature film in Europe and on video in the United States. The title track, like some spaced-out accompaniment to an unheard Country/Western song, seems on an endless loop with its repeated arpeggios and twangy steel-guitar-like notes. Later in the pilot film we do hear it backing a vocal line (though not remotely Country) sung by Julee Cruise, again with lyrics by Lynch—indeed, we see it performed, as the world's most improbable dance music for a biker roadhouse. A second important musical segment for *Twin Peaks* is the somber progression of notes, spare and tragic, first heard when the body of Laura Palmer is found; this segment often features a second part, when a piano enters and builds to a kind of soap-operatic pop climax, just short of parody—or well across the border—and thus perfect for various hyper-emotional scenes (the sheriff announcing Laura's death, or the love scene between the heartbroken teens James and Donna). A third category of *Twin Peaks* music is the sort that opens with finger-snapping in a '50s jazzy way, as if the Sharks and Jets of *West Side Story* are about to rumble. Various styles spin off from these openings: twangy guitar sounds for scenes with the hoodlum Bobby; a sax solo, suitable for a movie detective, used to introduce Agent Cooper; and other cool ''bad-girl'' music for the trampy Audrey. Like *Twin Peaks* itself, Badalamenti's music is vaguely ''period'' (1950s) yet contemporary, always either on the brink of parody or inhabiting some alternative universe beyond parody—in short, perfectly postmodern.

Badalamenti's music for the generally disliked feature-film prequel, *Twin Peaks: Fire Walk with Me*, is not just a reprise of his material for the series but new and more elaborately jazzy. His music for other Lynch films has varied in its importance: for example, though he contributed some New-Orleans-style accompaniments for *Wild at Heart*, the soundtrack for that film is memorable more for Chris' Isaak's eerie ''Wicked Game'' and the glorious orchestral outburst that opens the last of Richard Strauss' *Four Last Songs*. In some non-Lynch films too, notably *The Beach*, his original scoring is secondary to pop-group selections.

Badalamenti's contribution to films other than Lynch's has been quite varied in style. Joel Schumacher's *Cousins* uses very little soundtrack music in its first hour, except for some discreet flute-and-guitar and solo flute accompaniment to early scenes between the not-yet-lovers of the title. But there is also a little waltz on piano that gets orchestrated when the cousins run to each other on the train platform, and becomes a lovely if conventional ''big theme'' as the two become lovers and again when they marry at the end. For Paul Shrader's tale of murderous games in Venice, *The Comfort of Strangers*, Badalamenti comes up with a rather rich and dark Italianate tune, though with unusual 6-bar phrases, for the title music; but for various scenes of roaming about the haunted city he uses music of more Middle Eastern flavor, whether for solo flute, guitar, or strings with exotic percussion, as if the ghost of Othello were somewhere nearby. For *City of Lost Children* one might have expected music of a mocking grotesquerie to match the somewhat Terry-Gilliam-esque visuals, but although there

are certainly eerie moments, and a waltz for a hurdy-gurdy that recalls the more deranged sort of French grand organ music, Badalamenti's largely string score is more often alternately somber and tender.

Badalamenti's most memorable score of recent years is probably his contribution to Lynch's *The Straight Story*. Here the flavors are more distinctively American than usual, suitably enough for a genial and touching tale of an elderly man who travels from Iowa to Wisconsin by lawnmower to visit his ailing brother. But the score never attempts to be imitation Copland or folk music. The title music, mostly strings and piano, rises in intensity through long, irregular phrases, but holds back from the heart-on-sleeve sentimentality of the ''Laura Palmer'' theme. For the leisurely ''road music'' the composer features a solo fiddle, suggesting a very much slowed-down bluegrass or square dance style. Most strikingly of all, a melody for solo guitar is used to accompany scenes about parting, or love, or both. We first hear it as Alvin's daughter looks at a child playing near a sprinkler, while (we later learn) she thinks about her own children who were taken away from her. It will be used several times again, accumulating meaning, as when Alvin says goodbye to one of his most important helpers along the way, and most powerfully at the end, when Alvin reaches his long-estranged brother. Here, as is the case with many of the greatest film scores, the music tells us things the characters cannot possibly articulate.

—Joseph Milicia

BAKER, Rick

Special Effects Makeup Artist. **Nationality:** American. **Born:** Binghamton, New York, 1950. **Family:** Married Elaine Parkyn, 1974. **Career:** Worked for the TV production company Art Cloakey Productions, then for Dick Smith; also worked on music videos, including Michael Jackson's *Thriller*; established Cinovation Studios, 1993. **Awards:** Emmy Award, for *The Autobiography of Miss Jane Pittman*, 1974; Academy Award, for *An American Werewolf in London*, 1981, *Harry and the Hendersons*, 1987, *Ed Wood*, 1994, *The Nutty Professor*, 1996, and *Men in Black*, 1997; British Academy Award, for *Greystoke: The Legend of Tarzan, Lord of the Apes*, 1983, and *The Nutty Professor*, 1996.

Films as Special Effects Makeup Artist:

1971   *Schlock* (Landis)
1972   *The Thing with Two Heads* (Frost) (+ ro as policeman)
1973   *Live and Let Die* (Hamilton); *Black Caesar* (Cohen)
1974   *It's Alive* (Cohen); *The Autobiography of Miss Jane Pittman* (Korty—for TV)
1975   *Death Race 2000* (Bartel)
1976   *King Kong* (Guillermin) (+ title ro); *Zebra Force* (Tornatore); *Track of the Moon Beast* (Ashe); *Food of the Gods* (B. Gordon)
1977   *Incredible Melting Man* (Sachs)
1978   *The Fury* (De Palma); *It Lives Again* (Cohen)
1979   *An American Christmas Carol* (Till)

Rick Baker

1980   *The Howling* (Dante) (consultant only); *Tanya's Island* (Sole)
1981   *Funhouse* (Hooper); *Incredible Shrinking Woman* (Schumacher) (+ ro as Sidney); *An American Werewolf in London* (Landis)
1983   *Videodrome* (Cronenberg); *Greystoke: The Legend of Tarzan, Lord of the Apes* (Hudson); *Thriller* (Landis) (+ ro as zombie)
1984   *Starman* (Carpenter)
1985   *Cocoon* (R. Howard) (as consultant); *Into the Night* (Landis); *My Science Project* (Betuel); *Teen Wolf* (Daniel)
1986   *Max mon amour* (*Max, My Love*) (Oshima) (as chimp consultant); *Ratboy* (Locke); *Captain Eo* (Coppola)
1987   *Harry and the Hendersons* (Dear) (monster designer); *It's Alive III: Island of the Alive* (Cohen); *Beauty and the Beast* (Franklin—for TV)
1988   *Coming to America* (Landis); *Gorillas in the Mist* (Apted) (+ assoc producer)
1989   *Missing Link* (Hughes)
1990   *Gremlins 2: The New Batch* (Dante) (co-pr)
1991   *The Rocketeer* (Johnston)
1992   *Lorenzo's Oil* (Miller)
1993   *Body Bags* (Carpenter—for TV)
1994   *Wolf* (Nichols); *Baby's Day Out* (Johnson); *Ed Wood* (Burton)

1995   *Batman Forever* (Schumacher)
1996   *The Nutty Professor* (Shadyac)
1996   *Escape from L.A.* (Carpenter)
1997   *Men in Black* (Sonnenfeld)
1998   *Critical Care* (Lumet); *Mighty Joe Young* (Underwood)
1999   *Life* (Demme); *Wild Wild West* (Sonnenfeld)
2000   *How the Grinch Stole Christmas* (Howard); *Nutty II: The Klumps* (Segal)
2001   *The Visitor* (Burton)

Other Films:

1970   *Octaman* (Essex—for TV) (designer of Octaman costume)
1971   *The Incredible 2-Headed Transplant* (Lanza) (designer of gorilla suit)
1973   *The Exorcist* (Friedkin) (asst)
1976   *Squirm* (Lieberman) (design)
1977   **Star Wars** (Lucas) (sequence supervisor) (+ ro as Hem Dazon)
1994   *The Santa Clause* (Pasquin) (exec pr)

1996   *The Frighteners* (Jackson) (designer of The Judge)
1997   *Batman and Robin* (Schumaker) (designer of Nora Fries and
        copsicles); *The Devil's Advocate* (Hackford) (designer:
        demons)
1998   *Psycho* (Van Sant) (designer: Mrs. Bates)

Publications

By BAKER: articles—

Closeup (Little Neck, New York), no. 3, 1977.
Cinefantastique (New York), Spring 1978.
Starburst (London), October 1982.
American Cinematographer (Hollywood), June 1994.
Écran Fantastique (Neuilly), September 1996.

On BAKER: articles—

Écran Fantastique (Paris), no. 24, 1978.
Taylor, Al, and Sue Roy, in *Making a Monster*, New York, 1980.
Cinefantastique (New York), February 1982.
''Baker Issue'' of *Cinefex* (Riverside, California), April 1982.
Cinefantastique (New York), July/August 1982.
Écran Fantastique (Paris), October 1984.
Segnocinema (Vicenza), vol. 6, no. 21, January 1986.
Cinefex (Riverside), May 1991.
Cinefex (Riverside), December 1994.
Cinefex (Riverside), September 1996.
Écran Fantastique (Neuilly), September 1996.
Current Biography, vol. 58, no. 3, March 1997.
Cinefex (Riverside), June 1997.
American Cinematographer (Hollywood), June 1997.

*   *   *

If Dick Smith began the family of contemporary special makeup effects artists, Rick Baker is his eldest and most successful son. His early experiments with simple cosmetics apparently set the stage for the complex prosthetic appliances and creatures he would later design and create. Even though experienced enough at a young age to achieve professional results on shoestring budgets, his collaboration with Dick Smith on *The Exorcist* and his Emmy Award for *The Autobiography of Miss Jane Pittman* began Baker's rise to the top of his field.

Working in all genres, Baker excels at designing anthropomorphic creatures (the mutant killer babies of the *It's Alive* series, the cantina sequence aliens of *Star Wars*, Bigfoot in *Harry and the Hendersons*, the zombies of *Thriller*, the aliens in *Men in Black*, the Grinch), deformed humans *(The Thing with Two Heads, The Incredible Melting Man, Ratboy*, the geek in *Funhouse*, the beast of *Beauty and the Beast*, the judge in *The Frighteners*, the plastic surgery citizens of Beverly Hills in *Escape from L.A.*), and animals. In fact, one could argue that he ''specializes'' in creating animals. His apes *(The Incredible 2-Headed Transplant; King Kong; Greystoke: The Legend of Tarzan, Lord of the Apes; Gorillas in the Mist; Missing Link; Mighty Joe Young)* impress and wholly convince because the smallest ''human'' gestures and facial expressions carry through the layers of

makeup. His werewolves *(The Howling, An American Werewolf in London, Teen Wolf, Wolf)* frighten and disturb not simply because they are grotesque, but because they too convey a human agony.

An expert at combining mechanized appliances with masks, body suits, and cosmetics, Baker brought to life some of the most impressive special effects of the pre-digital effects era (before 1990). His full-body, on-screen transformations of *The Howling, An American Werewolf in London, Starman*, and *Videodrome* advanced the ability of film to graphically visualize metamorphoses without dissolves, mattes, stop-motion photography, or digital technology. Hydraulic devices implanted underneath an actor's makeup could alter any part of the human anatomy. The lengthy and detailed presentations of lycanthropic change in *The Howling* and *An American Werewolf in London* included extending fingers and legs, expanding torsos and faces, and growing fangs, claws, and hair. *Starman* employed the same techniques to show a new-born infant instantly growing into an adult male. These narratively grounded transformations yielded to pure hallucinations in *Videodrome*. The inorganic and the organic freely swap places: a television set becomes a lump of eroticized flesh and the protagonist's hand mutates into a living gun. These groundbreaking techniques set an industry standard—until digital effects supplanted them.

When digital effects became the dominant technology for rendering on-screen transformations, making Baker's mechanized appliances obsolete, Baker returned to more ''conservative'' cosmetic applications. Stating that how makeup *looks* proves more important than how it is done, he eschewed the very technology he propagated and moved towards a more ''human'' emphasis. In this way, Baker's recent award-winning work seems almost a homage to Jack Pierce and the Westmores. In *Coming to America, The Nutty Professor*, and *Nutty II: The Klumps*, Baker transformed Eddie Murphy into a number of eccentric characters; each one accomplished through ''traditional'' techniques employing full body and facial prosthetics. In *Gorillas in the Mist, Missing Link*, and *Mighty Joe Young*, Baker constructed ape suits and masks so flexible and responsive to the human form that, anecdotally, many viewers failed to realize they were watching actors playing apes. In *Wolf*, his makeup for Jack Nicholson and James Spader was actually subtle given its topic. Instead of on-screen, fully body werewolf metamorphoses, Baker showed isolated specifics: a hirsute palm, a pointed ear, a toothy smile, and most effectively, lupine eyes. The werewolf contact lenses he designed created a just noticeable distortion of pupil shape and color. In *Ed Wood*, Baker changed Martin Landau into Bela Lugosi and in *Wild Wild West* he created Kevin Kline's disguises by updating classical cosmetic techniques. Some of Baker's most accomplished recent work focuses on depicting the aged human body: Eddie Murphy becomes his own grandmother in *The Nutty Professor* and *Nutty II: The Klumps*; Albert Brooks plays an ld doctor in *Critical Care*; Martin Lawrence and Eddie Murphy turn into 90-year-olds during the course of *Life*. In all these examples, the makeup (whether prosthetic or cosmetic) does not draw attention to itself; it appears highly naturalistic.

Although Baker creates his effects without relying on digital technology, he does not retreat from it. Whatever the required effect, Baker and his Cinovation Studios crew will utilize any and all means to accomplish it. Combining models, puppets, and makeup with digital effects, Baker created an amazing menagerie of aliens for *Men in Black*. *Mighty Joe Young* employed the same combination of techniques and added to the mix actors in full gorilla costumes. *The Nutty Professor* and *Nutty II: The Klumps* used computer technology to depict rapid on-screen transformations between Buddy Love and Professor Klump. In *Wild Wild West*, Kenneth Branaugh's legs were digitally "amputated" to make his Dr. Loveless even more sinister. For *Life*, digital imaging aided the design of Murphy and Martin's prosthetic makeup.

Baker's five Oscars for special makeup effects (including the first one ever awarded by the Academy in 1981) place him as one of Hollywood's top production artists. His ability to utilize prosthetic technology, traditional cosmetics, puppets, mechanical appliances, and digital effects should keep Rick Baker in demand in a field which mutates as quickly as some of his own creations.

—Greg S. Faller

BALABAN, Barney

Theater Chain Owner, Producer. **Nationality:** American. **Born:** 8 June 1887 in Chicago, Illinois. **Education:** Attended local schools. **Family:** Married Tillie Urkov, 1929; son Leonard, daughter Judith. **Career:** After working in his immigrant father's grocery store, was hired by Western Union as a messenger; later was chief clerk in a cold-storage company. Opened a nickelodeon in Chicago in 1908 with his brother Abe and other members of his family; theatrical holdings grew into a prosperous, nationwide chain, though many of the principal houses were in the Chicago area; 1917—profited from his experience in the cold storage business to pioneer ice-cooled

Barney Balaban

refrigeration, a precursor to air conditioning, for his theaters. Control of theaters bought by Paramount in 1926, with much Paramount stock going to Balaban; with Katz, continued as manager of the chain; named first to the stockholders' board of Paramount in the early thirties, then to a directorship; 1936—named president; late 1940s—toured foreign theaters at invitation of State Department; 1964—relinquished presidency for chairmanship of the board; 1966—was eased out as Paramount came under control of Gulf and Western. **Died:** 8 March 1971.

Publications

On BALABAN: book—

Gomery, Douglas, *Shared Pleasures: A History of Movie Presentation in the United States*, Madison, Wisconsin, 1992.

*   *   *

Born in Chicago to parents who ran a small grocery store, Barney Balaban quit school at the age of twelve to work at a number of jobs in order to help support his parents and six younger brothers. It was in 1908, however, at the height of the nickelodeon craze, that Balaban embarked on the venture that would shape his career. Along with his parents and brothers, Balaban decided to rent a small movie theater; the idea, he was later to confess, was really his mother's, who, attending her first picture show, was impressed by the huge crowds that flocked to enjoy the new medium.

Balaban and his brother Abe expanded their holdings slowly; by 1914 they were managing three theaters. They also ran a restaurant, the Movie Inn, located in the downtown film business section; it was here that they met Sam Katz, who also worked in film exhibition and owned three downtown theaters. In 1916, the brothers went into partnership with Katz and embarked on an ambitious program of expansion. Seeing correctly that movie exhibition, which had initially drawn most of its paying customers from the working class, had more of a future with a middle-class clientele, Balaban & Katz determined to build and operate theaters that would appeal to this emerging audience. Because they were not affiliated with any of the major filmmakers, Balaban & Katz would not have access to the very best films then being made in the industry; so, they reasoned, economic success would come from designing and providing a total entertainment experience along the lines pioneered by Roxy Rothapfel's Rivoli and Rialto theaters in New York.

While Katz engineered a series of real estate deals to acquire prime property in upscale suburbs near mass transportation, even signing up as investors some of Chicago's richest tycoons, including William Wrigley, Jr. and John Hertz, Barney Balaban and his brother Abe set about making the resulting theaters attractive to middle-class customers. The Chicago firm of George and C.W. Rapp, soon to become one of the national leaders in "picture palace" design, was hired to create opulent and ornate designs that would accommodate huge crowds both within the auditorium and in the lobby, waiting for the next show. Exits and entrances were carefully planned so that the unending flow of patrons could easily come and go.

Much emphasis was placed on service, as Balaban attempted to run each establishment with the maximum of efficiency. Ushers, for example, were all to be young men, preferably college students, of a certain height and weight; careful training was given to all staff, who were to pamper patrons and cater efficiently to their needs. Though the ushers were to give the impression that they were present only to serve, actually they had another function—to make sure the auditorium was filled as quickly and completely as possible. Well-equipped restrooms provided middle-class patrons with familiar comforts, and most Balaban & Katz houses even featured free baby-sitting services, which certainly increased matinee attendance on weekdays. Because the films they exhibited were often second-rate, Barney Balaban directed his brother Abe to design the very best possible stage shows; film and show always ran 150 minutes, with films even shortened if they ran over the pre-set limit. The organists, stage attractions, and first-rate orchestras hired by Abe packed customers in seven days a week. Often the film on a given program was only an incidental attraction, certainly not responsible for box office success. Another marketing coup was Barney Balaban's inspiration alone. His experience in the meat-packing business had given him some knowledge of rudimentary cooling systems. He hired the best engineers in what was then an emerging field to create satisfactory air cooling for his theaters; this then required whole rooms full of expensive equipment in need of constant service, but the result was certainly profitable, especially in Chicago's often brutal summers, when crowds poured into Balaban & Katz theaters often simply to escape the oppressive heat. Along with Sam Katz and Abe, Barney Balaban was responsible for shaping the movie exhibition business in decisive ways, particularly by emphasizing the total experience provided by the house and thus encouraging what was soon to become a national obsession, "ging to the movies," a social activity indulged in often with little regard for what film was actually playing.

In 1925 Katz negotiated an alliance with Famous Players-Lasky, then the largest movie company in the world, and soon to be re-named Paramount Pictures. Katz himself was put in charge of the exhibition end of the business nationwide, centralizing operations for the resulting chain—Publix Theaters—in ways that would become a model for the industry. Barney Balaban stayed in Chicago to run what formerly had been Balaban & Katz, but soon was promoted to the Paramount board, eventually receiving a directorship. In 1936 Balaban was selected as president of the corporation. In an era of hard times that had seen several reorganizations of the company, and a descent into receivership, the choice of Balaban was a wise one. Moving to the New York offices, where he remained for thirty years, Balaban applied the same lessons of efficient management to the operation of the vertically integrated enterprise of a classic Hollywood studio. Costs were cut, operations made more efficient, and in the space of a year Paramount was again turning a profit, even as the other studios continued to struggle until the highly profitable war years. Balaban insisted that every expenditure meet with his prior approval. As a studio head, he was less interested in art than in the financial bottom line, staying with proven methods of making a collar, including the nearly exclusive use of stars who had already established reputations in vaudeville, radio, or the stage. But, just as he had done with air conditioning, Balaban was eager to invest in technological change; in 1939, at his direction, Paramount became an investor in the DuMont video company, which, in the early days of television, briefly became a fourth network. Balaban also thought that theater television might prove profitable, but, despite his efforts, this use of the new medium never gained enough popularity. After Paramount signed a consent decree in 1947 that forced the studio to divest itself of theatrical holdings, Balaban struggled to find a way to keep the company

profitable. Investment in a television station chain proved impossible because FCC regulations forbid ownership of stations by any corporation found guilty of monopoly practices. In the early 1950s, Paramount's fortunes declined despite Balaban's well-executed deal to sell the company's backlog of pre-1948 films to MCA for $50 million.

Unlike other studio heads, Balaban kept a low public profile, emerging into the limelight only to further his patriotic interest in promoting American films abroad. He proved such an able spokesman for the motion picture industry that he was invited to organize a tour abroad, backed by the State Department, to help rebuild Hollywood's overseas markets in the political and economic turmoil that resulted from the end of World War II. Paramount's corporate fortunes, however, did not improve during the general decline of the film business in the late 1950s and early 1960s. Balaban was forced gently from the presidency, and then from membership on the board by 1966, as what had been the most powerful of the majors became part of the international conglomerate Gulf and Western.

—R. Barton Palmer

BALCON, (Sir) Michael

Producer. **Nationality:** British. **Born:** Birmingham, 19 May 1896. **Education:** Attended George Dixon School, Birmingham. **Family:** Married Aileen Leatherman, 1924; one son; one daughter, the actress

Michael Balcon

Jill Balcon. **Career:** 1919—founder, with Victor Saville, Victory Motion Pictures, distributing company; 1921—first film produced, the documentary *The Story of Oil*; 1924—founder, with Graham Cutts, Gainsborough Pictures, Islington; 1926—organized Picadilly Pictures with Carlyle Blackwell; 1928—founder, with Maurice Ostrer and C. M. Wolf, Gainsborough Pictures Ltd.; 1931–36—in charge of production for Gaumont-British (who had taken over Gainsborough); 1936–38—head of production for MGM British; 1938–59—head of production for Ealing Studios (later Ealing Films); 1959–75—head of Bryanston Films; 1964–66—Chairman of British Lion. Knighted, 1948. **Died:** 16 October 1977.

Films as Producer (Features):

1925   *The Rat* (Cutts)

1926   *The Sea Urchin* (Cutts); *The Triumph of the Rat* (Cutts); *The Lodger: A Story of the London Fog* (*The Case of Jonathan Drew*) (Hitchcock); *The Mountain Eagle* (*Fear o' God*) (Hitchcock)

1927   *Blighty* (Brunel); *Downhill* (*When Boys Leave Home*) (Hitchcock); *The Rolling Road* (Cutts); *Easy Virtue* (Hitchcock); *One of the Best* (Hunter); *The Vortex* (Brunel)

1928   *A South Sea Bubble* (Hunter); *A Light Woman* (Brunel); *The First Born* (Mander); *The Wrecker* (von Bolvary)

1929   *The Return of the Rat* (Cutts); *Armistice* (Saville); *City of Play* (Clift); *Taxi for Two* (Esway); *Woman to Woman* (Saville)

1930   *Just for a Song* (Gundrey); *The Crooked Billet* (Brunel); *Journey's End* (Whale); *Balaclava* (*Jaws of Hell*) (Elvey); *Symphony in Two Flats* (Gundrey); *Ashes* (Birch); *A Warm Corner* (Saville)

1931   *P. C. Josser* (Rosmer); *Hot Heir* (Kellino); *Who Killed Doc Robin?* (Kellino); *Bull Rushes* (Kellino); *Third Time Lucky* (Forde); *The Sport of Kings* (Saville); *The Stronger Sex* (Gundrey); *Aroma of the South Seas* (Kellino); *The Ringer* (Forde); *The Lady of the Lake* (Fitzpatrick); *A Night in Montmartre* (Hiscott); *The Man They Could Not Arrest* (Hunter); *My Old China* (Kellino); *The Ghost Train* (Forde); *Hindle Wakes* (Saville); *The Calender* (*Bachelor's Folly*) (Hunter); *Michael and Mary* (Saville); *Sunshine Susie* (*The Office Girl*) (Saville)

1932   *Lord Babs* (Forde); *The Frightened Lady* (*Criminal at Large*) (Hunter); *The Faithful Heart* (*Faithful Hearts*) (Saville); *White Face* (Hunter); *Jack's the Boy* (*Night and Day*) (Forde); *Love on Wheels* (Saville); *Marry Me* (Thiele); *There Goes the Bride* (de Courville); *Rome Express* (Forde); *After the Ball* (Rosmer); *The Midshipman* (de Courville)

1933   *The Man from Toronto* (Hill); *The Good Companions* (Saville); *Soldiers of the King* (*The Woman in Command*) (Elvey); *King of the Ritz* (Gallone); *The Lucky Number* (Asquith); *Sleeping Car* (Litvak); *It's a Boy* (Whelan); *Falling for You* (Hulbert); *Britannia of Billingsgate* (Hill); *Orders Is Orders* (Forde); *The Ghoul* (Hunter); *I Was a Spy* (Saville); *The Fire Raisers* (Powell); *Just Smith* (Walls); *Friday the Thirteenth* (Saville); *Aunt Sally* (*Along Came Sally*) (Whelan); *The Constant Nymph* (Dean); *Turkey Time* (Walls)

1934   *Jack Ahoy!* (Forde); *Evergreen* (Saville); *A Cup of Kindness* (Walls); *Prince Charming* (Elvey); **Man of Aran** (Flaherty); *Wild Boy* (de Courville); *Chu Chin Chow* (Forde); *Wings over Everest* (Barkas and Montagu); *Little Friend* (Viertel); *My Old Dutch* (Hill); *Evensong* (Saville); *Jew Süss* (*Power*) (Mendes); *The Camels Are Coming* (Whelan); *Lady in Danger* (Walls); *Road House* (Elvey); *The Man Who Knew Too Much* (Hitchcock); *Dirty Work* (Walls); *Temptation* (Neufeld)

1935   *The Iron Duke* (Saville); *Things Are Looking Up* (de Courville); *Oh, Daddy!* (Cutts and Melford); *Fighting Stock* (Walls); *Bulldog Jack* (*Alias Bulldog Drummond*) (Forde); *Forever England* (*Born for Glory; Torpedo Raiders*) (Forde); **The 39 Steps** (Hitchcock); *The Clairvoyant* (*The Evil Mind*) (Elvey); *Me and Marlborough* (Saville); *Boys Will Be Boys* (Beaudine); *Stormy Weather* (Walls); *Car of Dreams* (Cutts and Melford); *The Passing of the Third Floor Back* (Viertel); *The Guv'nor* (*Mister Hobo*) (Rosmer); *First a Girl* (Saville); *The Tunnel* (*Transatlantic Tunnel*) (Elvey); *Foreign Affairs* (Walls)

1936   *King of the Damned* (Forde); *Jack of All Trades* (*The Two of Us*) (Stevenson and Hulbert); *First Offence* (Mason); *Rhodes of Africa* (*Rhodes, the Empire Builder*) (Viertel); *Pot Luck* (Walls); *Tudor Rose* (*Nine Days a Queen*) (Stevenson); *The Secret Agent* (Hitchcock); *It's Love Again* (Saville); *Where There's A Will* (Beaudine); *Seven Sinners* (*Doomed Cargo*) (de Courville); *Everything is Thunder* (Rosmer); *The Flying Doctor* (Mander); *East Meets West* (Mawson); *The Man Who Changed His Mind* (*The Man Who Lived Again; Doctor Maniac; Brain Snatcher*) (Stevenson); *Everybody Dance* (Reisner); *All In* (Varnel); *His Lordship* (*Man of Affairs*) (Mason); *Strangers on Honeymoon* (de Courville); *Sabotage* (*A Woman Alone*) (Hitchcock); *Windbag the Sailor* (Beaudine)

1937   *O.H.M.S.* (*You're in the Army Now*) (Walsh); *Head Over Heels* (Hale); *The Great Barrier* (*Silent Barriers*) (Rosmer); *King Solomon's Mines* (Stevenson)

1938   *A Yank at Oxford* (Conway); *The Gaunt Stranger* (*The Phantom Strikes*) (Forde); *The Ware Case* (Stevenson)

1939   *Let's Be Famous* (Forde); *There Ain't No Justice* (Tennyson); *The Four Just Men* (*The Secret Four*) (Forde); *Cheer Boys Cheer* (Forde); *Young Man's Fancy* (Stevenson); *Happy Families* (Forde)

1940   *Return to Yesterday* (Stevenson); *The Proud Valley* (Tennyson); *Let George Do It* (*Murder in Bergen*) (Varnel); *Saloon Bar* (Forde); *Convoy* (Tennyson); *Sailors Three* (*Three Cockeyed Sailors*) (Forde)

1941   *Spare a Copper* (Carstairs); *The Ghost of St. Michael's* (Varnel); *Turned Out Nice Again* (Varnel); *Ships with Wings* (Nolbandov); *Black Sheep of Whitehall* (Dearden and Hay)

1942   *The Big Blockade* (Frend); *The Foreman Went to France* (*Somewhere in France*) (Frend); *The Next of Kin* (Dickinson); *The Goose Steps Out* (Dearden and Hay); *Went the Day Well?* (*48 Hours*) (Cavalcanti)

1943   *Nine Men* (Watt); *The Bells Go Down* (Dearden); *Undercover* (*Underground Guerillas*) (Nolbandov); *My Learned Friend* (Dearden and Hay)

1944   *San Demetrio London* (Frend); *The Halfway House* (Dearden); *For Those in Peril* (Crichton); *The Return of the Vikings* (Frend); *They Came to a City* (Dearden); *Champagne Charlie* (Cavalcanti); *Fiddlers Three* (Watt)

1945   *Johnny Frenchman* (Frend); *Painted Boats* (*The Girl on the Canal*) (Crichton); **Dead of Night** (Dearden, Cavalcanti, and Hamer); *Pink String and Sealing Wax* (Hamer)
1946   *The Captive Heart* (Dearden); *The Overlanders* (Watt)
1947   *Hue and Cry* (Crichton); *Nicholas Nickleby* (*The Life and Adventures of Nicholas Nickleby*) (Cavalcanti); *The Loves of Joanna Godden* (Frend); *Frieda* (Dearden); *It Always Rains on Sunday* (Hamer)
1948   *Against the Wind* (Crichton); *Saraband for Dead Lovers* (*Saraband*) (Dearden); *Another Shore* (Crichton); *Scott of the Antarctic* (Frend)
1949   *Eureka Stockade* (Watt); **Passport to Pimlico** (Cornelius); *Whiskey Galore!* (*Tight Little Island*) (Mackendrick); **Kind Hearts and Coronets** (Hamer); *Train of Events* (Cole, Dearden and Crichton); *A Run for Your Money* (Frend)
1950   **The Blue Lamp** (Dearden); *Bitter Springs* (Smart); *Cage of Gold* (Dearden); *The Magnet* (Cole)
1951   *Pool of London* (Dearden); **The Lavender Hill Mob** (Crichton); *The Man in the White Suit* (Mackendrick); *Where No Vultures Fly* (*Ivory Hunter*) (Watt)
1954   *Lease of Life* (Frend)
1955   *The Night My Number Came Up* (Norman); *Armand and Michaela Denis* (series—3 films); *Touch and Go* (*The Light Touch*) (Truman); *The Ladykillers* (Mackendrick)
1956   *The Feminine Touch* (*The Gentle Touch*) (Jackson); *The Long Arm* (*The Third Key*) (Frend)
1959   *The Scapegoat* (Hamer)

Films as Producer (Shorts):

1925   Gainsborough *Burlesque* Films (Brunel)
1926   *The Steven Donoghue* Series (West)
1929   *In a Monastery Garden* (Brunel)
1930   *Sugar and Spice* Series (Oumansky); Gainsborough *Gems* Series
1931   *Harry Lauder Songs* Series (Pearson—8)
1940   *All Hands* (Carstairs); *Cable Laying* (Carstairs); *Dangerous Comment* (Carstairs—2); *Signals Office* (Carstairs); *Now You're Talking* (Carstairs)
1941   *Freedom Must Have Wings* (Bennett)
1942   *Go to Blazes* (Forde); *Mighty Penny* (Carstairs); *Raid on France* (Bennett); *Meet Mr. Joad* (Williams)
1943   *Did You Ever See a Dream Walking?* (Dearden); *Save Your Shillings and Smile* (Watt); *The Saving Grace* (Frend); *Fleet Air Arm* (Bennett)
1944   *Journal of Resistance*

Films as Co-Producer:

1921   *The Story of Oil* (Saville); *Liquid Sunshine* (Saville)
1923   *Woman to Woman* (Cutts)
1924   *The White Shadow* (*White Shadows*) (Cutts); *The Prude's Fall* (Cutts); *The Passionate Adventure* (Cutts)
1925   *The Blackguard* (Cutts)
1926   *The Pleasure Garden* (Hitchcock)

1928   *The Constant Nymph* (Brunel)
1963   *Sammy Going South* (*A Boy Ten Feet Tall*) (Mackendrick)

Publications

By BALCON: books—

Realism or Tinsel?, Brighton, 1943.
The Producer, London, 1945.
Twenty Years of British Film 1925–1945, London, 1947.
Film Production and Management, London, 1950.
Michael Balcon Presents . . . A Lifetime of Films, London, 1969.

By BALCON: articles—

''The Diary of a Talkie,'' in *Film Weekly* (London), 24 January 1931.
''The Function of the Producer,'' in *Cinema Quarterly* (London), Autumn 1933.
''Whither Film?,'' in *Film Art* (London), Winter 1934.
''How Films Are Made,'' in *The Listener* (London), 26 January 1938.
''Rationalise!,'' in *Sight and Sound* (London), Winter 1940–41.
''Propaganda and the Feature Producer,'' in *Cine-Technician* (London), February-March 1942.
''The British Film During the War,'' in *Penguin Film Review* (London), August 1946.
''The Eye Behind the Camera,'' in *Saraband for Dead Lovers*, London, 1948.
''The Technical Problems of *Scott of the Antarctic*,'' in *Sight and Sound* (London), Winter 1948–49.
''Film Comedy,'' in *The British Film Yearbook 1949–50*, edited by Peter Noble, London, 1950
''10 Years of British Films,'' in *Films in Britain 1951*, London, 1951.
''The Feature Carries on the Documentary Tradition,'' in *Quarterly of Film, Radio and Television* (Berkeley, California), Summer 1952.
''The Secret of Ealing Comedy,'' in *International Film Annual 1*, edited by George Campbell Dixon, London, 1957.
Interview with Penelope Houston, in *Sight and Sound* (London), Winter 1962–63.
Vision (London), March 1977.

On BALCON: books—

Danischewsky, Monja, editor, *Michael Balcon's 25 Years in Films*, London, 1947.
James, David, ''*Scott of the Antarctic*'': *The Film and Its Production*, London, 1948.
Anderson, Lindsay, *Making a Film: The Story of ''Secret People,''* London, 1952.
Slide, Anthony, editor, *Michael Balcon, Producer*, London, 1969.
Barr, Charles, *Ealing Studios*, London, 1977.
Perry, George, *Forever Ealing*, London 1981.
Brown, Geoff, editor, *Der Produzent: Michael Balcon und der englische Film*, Berlin, 1981.
Wilson, David, *Projecting Britain: Ealing Film Posters*, London, 1982.
Fleugel, Jane, editor, *Michael Balcon: The Pursuit of British Cinema*, New York, 1984.
Brown, Geoff, *Michael Balcon: Pursuit of Britain*, New York, 1990.

On BALCON: articles—

Clynton, Lionel, "Michael Balcon of Ealing," in *British Film Yearbook 1947–8*, edited by Peter Noble, London, 1947.

Dickinson, Thorold, "The Work of Sir Michael Balcon at Ealing Studios," in *The Year's Work in the Film 1950*, edited by Roger Manvell, London, 1951.

Koval, Francis, "The Studio: Sir Michael Balcon and Ealing," in *Films of Britain 1951*, London, 1951.

Baxter, Brian, in *National Film Theatre Booklet* (London), February-March and April-May 1973.

Barr, Charles, "'Projecting Britain and the British Character': Ealing Studios," in *Screen* (London), Spring and Summer 1974.

Pickard, Roy, "The Ealing Story," in *Films in Review* (New York), February 1975.

Baynham, Henri, "The Golden Age of Ealing Studios," in *British Journal of Photography* (London), 30 January, 12 March, 9 April, and 25 June 1976.

"Michael Balcon, 1896–1977," in *Sight and Sound* (London), Winter 1977–78.

Hall, Dennis John, "Balcon's Britain," in *Films* (London), February and March 1981.

"Ealing Studios," in *National Film Theatre Booklet* (London), November-December 1981, March 1982, and October-December 1982.

Salem, Charles, "The History of Ealing," in *Cinema* (London), November and December 1982, and January 1983.

Historical Journal of Film, Radio and Television, no. 3, 1992.

Segnocinema, January-February 1992.

Kythreotis, Anna, "Born Again: The Studio of Subversive British Comedies," in *New York Times*, 27 March 1994.

Richards, Jeffrey, "*Soldiers Three*: the 'Lost' Gaumont British Imperial Epic (Michael Balcon's Imperial Epic; Film Production Outfit)," in *Historical Journal of Film, Radio and Television*, March 1995.

Harding, Bruce, and E. Barnouw, "Sir Michael Balcon," in *Wide Angle* (Baltimore), vol. 17, no. 1–4, 1995.

Sedgwick, John, "Michael Balcon's Close Encounter with the American Market, 1934–36," in *Historical Journal of Film, Radio and Television*, August 1996.

Moat, Janet, "The Aileen and Michael Balcon Special Collection: an Introduction to British Cinema History," in *Historical Journal of Film, Radio and Television*, October 1996.

Kemp, Philip, "Paradise Postponed: Ealing, Rank and *They Came to a City*," in *Cineaste* (New York), Fall 1998.

*   *   *

Of the three producers whose influence, above all, shaped the British cinema—Alexander Korda, J. Arthur Rank and Michael Balcon—it was Balcon that in the end proved the strongest and the most lasting. Though he never enjoyed Korda's international prestige, nor Rank's financial might, he succeeded in creating a body of films recognizably stamped with his own image. To speak of a Denham film, or a Pinewood film, conveys no particular idea—but "an Ealing film" suggests, for better or worse, a very specific and very British style of movie, strongly marked by the personality of Balcon himself. Many of the outstanding qualities of British cinema, both during his lifetime and since, can be credited to Michael Balcon. And so, perhaps, can some of its faults.

Balcon's influence on British cinema long pre-dates his arrival at Ealing in 1938. He produced his first feature film in 1923 at Islington Studios, where he founded Gainsborough Pictures and gave Alfred Hitchcock his first chance to direct. As head of Gaumont-British in the 1930s he produced some of the most successful British films of the period: not only Hitchcock's thrillers, but Jessie Matthews musicals, Ben Travers farces, and the comedies of Jack Hulbert and Will Hay. There was also a string of slightly ungainly Anglo-German co-productions—and the occasional excursion into high seriousness such as Flaherty's *Man of Aran*, otherwise known as "Balcon's Folly."

After a brief, unhappy stint heading MGM's UK operation, Balcon took over from Basil Dean at Ealing, where he created the nearest the British film industry ever came to a studio after the classic Hollywood pattern. Like, say, Warners in the 1930s, Ealing had its roster of personnel—directors, writers, technicians, and so forth—on permanent salary, its pool of actors, its recurrent thematic preoccupations and, derived from all these, a recognizable house-style of filmmaking.

During this, "the happiest and most rewarding period of my working life," Balcon was able to realise his ambition of an indigenous, independent, national cinema, modest in its resources but international in scope. His aim, like that of every major British producer, was to get into the American market, but without aping the values, and the "hard technical perfection," of Hollywood movies. "We shall become international," he insisted, "by being national." To the "tinsel" of Hollywood he opposed the "realism" of Ealing—documentary-based productions, in authentic settings. Documentary, he contended, was less a question of factual, non-fiction subjects than of "an attitude of mind towards filmmaking."

Throughout his career Balcon was a great nurturer of young talent. At Ealing, presiding benevolently over "Mr Balcon's Academy for Young Gentlemen" (in Monja Danischewsky's famous phrase), he fostered a whole generation of filmmakers—not just directors like Alexander Mackendrick, Robert Hamer, Charles Crichton, Basil Dearden and Seth Holt, but producers, writers, cinematographers and actors—allowing them to develop their skills within an exceptionally tolerant and supportive atmosphere. He was, as Mackendrick remarked, "very mean with money, but extraordinarily generous with opportunities."

Inevitably, this benign environment had its drawbacks. Under Balcon's guidance, Ealing encouraged a consensus mentality that verged on complacency, a weakness for eccentricity dangerously akin to whimsy. Staunchly patriotic, he set out to make films "reflecting Britain and the British character," but it was a reflection contained within a carefully defined frame. Certain subjects—notably sex and religion—alarmed him, and featured rarely, if at all. Social institutions could be gently mocked, but never seriously attacked. Those directors—Hamer, Mackendrick, Cavalcanti—who expressed a darker vision did so only by defying, or subverting, the studio ethos.

Balcon has been accused of insularity, of turning his back on cinematic developments elsewhere—in Bertrand Tavernier's words, "a totally British talent but closed to the rest of the world." Certainly, Ealing never encouraged formal experimentation, and it's hard to imagine the swirling Baroque fantasies of Michael Powell fitting in there. In its latter years the studio retreated into a dated, toytown concept of England, and after its demise Balcon himself seemed a diminished figure, presiding uneasily at Bryanston over the brash outspokenness of the British New Wave.

Balcon's limitations, though, were the obverse of his strengths. And it is for his strengths that he was remarkable—for his vigorous, indefatigable championship of British filmmaking, for his skill in reconciling commercial appeal with creative integrity, for his knack of spotting, cultivating and teaming disparate talents. If his concept of cinema sometimes seemed unambitious, it was also—like the man himself—refreshingly free from pretension or rhetoric. It was typical of him that, looking back on his career, he assigned to others the credit for his achievement. "A film producer is only as good as the sum total of the quality of the colleagues with whom he works, and in this respect I have been uniquely fortunate."

—Philip Kemp

BALLARD, Lucien

Cinematographer. **Nationality:** American. **Born:** Miami, Oklahoma, 6 May 1908. **Education:** Attended the University of Oklahoma, Norman, and University of Pennsylvania, Philadelphia. **Family:** Married 2) the actress Merle Oberon, 1945 (divorced 1949), 3) Inez (died 1982). **Career:** 1929–35—general assistant, then assistant cameraman, Paramount; worked with von Sternberg; 1935—cinematographer for Columbia (first film as cinematographer, *Crime and Punishment*), then for RKO, 1939–41, and 20th Century-Fox, 1941–46 and 1951–55; 1945–49—made several films with his wife,

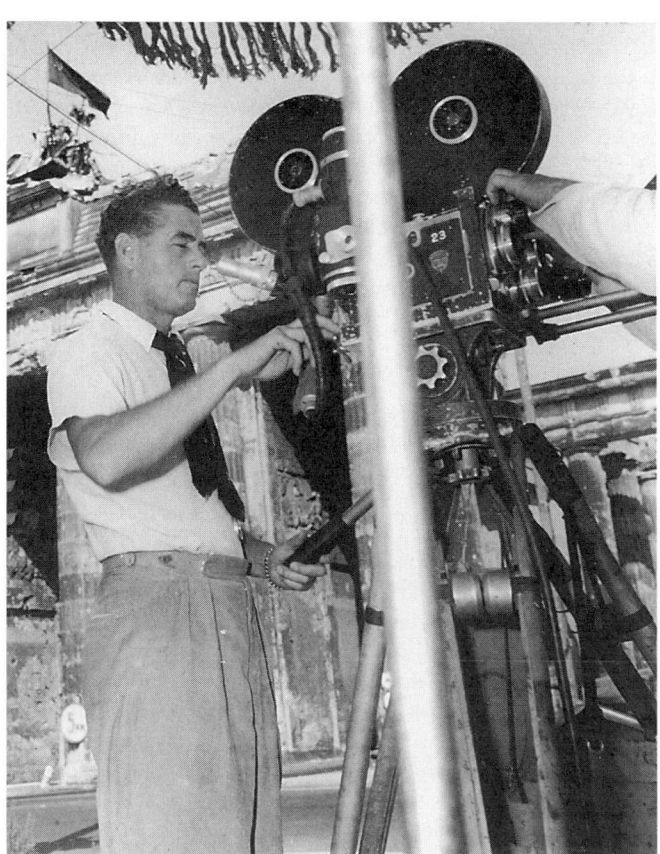

Lucien Ballard

Merle Oberon. **Died:** From injuries sustained in a cycling accident, in California, 1 October 1988.

Films as Cinematographer:

1935 *Crime and Punishment* (von Sternberg)
1936 *The King Steps Out* (von Sternberg); *Craig's Wife* (Arzner)
1937 *The Devil's Playground* (Kenton); *I Promise to Pay* (Lederman); *Racketeers in Exile* (Kenton); *Venus Makes Trouble* (Wiles); *Girls Can Play* (Hillyer); *The Shadow* (*The Circus Shadow*) (Coleman); *Life Begins with Love* (Ray McCarey); *Squadron of Honor* (Coleman); *From Bad to Worse* (Lord—short)
1938 *Penitentiary* (Brahm); *The Lone Wolf in Paris* (Rogell); *Highway Patrol* (Coleman); *Flight to Fame* (Coleman); *Rio Grande* (Nelson); *Home on the Range* (Lord—short); *Violent Is the Word for Curly* (Chase—short); *Three Little Sew and Sews* (Lord—short)
1939 *A Star Is Shorn* (Lord—short); *Let Us Live* (Brahm); *Blind Alley* (C. Vidor); *Coast Guard* (Ludwig); *The Thundering West* (Nelson); *Texas Stampede* (Nelson)
1940 *The Villain Still Pursued Her* (*She Done Him Wrong*) (Cline)
1941 *Wild Geese Calling* (Brahm)
1942 *Whispering Ghosts* (Werker); *Orchestra Wives* (Mayo); *The Undying Monster* (*The Hammond Mystery*) (Brahm)
1943 *Tonight We Raid Calais* (Brahm); *Bomber's Moon* (Fuhr); *Holy Matrimony* (Stahl)
1944 *The Lodger* (Brahm); *Sweet and Lowdown* (Mayo)
1945 *This Love of Ours* (Dieterle)
1946 *Temptation* (Pichel)
1947 *Night Song* (Cromwell)
1948 *Berlin Express* (Tourneur)
1951 *Let's Make It Legal* (Sale); *The House on Telegraph Hill* (Wise); *Fixed Bayonets!* (Fuller)
1952 *Return of the Texan* (Daves); *Diplomatic Courier* (Hathaway); *Don't Bother to Knock* (Baker); "The Clarion Call" ep. of *O. Henry's Full House* (*Full House*) (Hathaway); *Night without Sleep* (Baker)
1954 *New Faces* (Horner); *Prince Valiant* (Hathaway); *The Raid* (Fregonese)
1955 *White Feather* (Webb); *The Magnificent Matador* (*The Brave and the Beautiful*) (Boetticher); *Seven Cities of Gold* (Webb)
1956 *The Killer Is Loose* (Boetticher); *The Killing* (Kubrick); *The Proud Ones* (Webb); *A Kiss before Dying* (Oswald); *The King and Four Queens* (Walsh)
1957 *Band of Angels* (Walsh); *The Unholy Wife* (Farrow)
1958 *I Married a Woman* (Kanter); *Buchanan Rides Alone* (Boetticher); *Anna Lucasta* (Laven); *Murder by Contract* (Lerner); *City of Fear* (Lerner)
1959 *Al Capone* (Wilson); *The Rise and Fall of Legs Diamond* (Boetticher)
1960 *The Bramble Bush* (Petrie); *Pay or Die* (Wilson); *Desire in the Dust* (Claxton)
1961 *The Parent Trap* (Swift); *Marines, Let's Go* (Walsh); *Susan Slade* (Daves)
1962 *Ride the High Country* (*Guns in the Afternoon*) (Peckinpah); *Six-Gun Law* (Nyby)
1963 *Wives and Lovers* (Rich); *The Caretakers* (*Borderlines*) (Bartlett); *Wall of Noise* (Wilson); *Take Her, She's Mine* (Koster)

1964   *The New Interns* (Rich); *Roustabout* (Rich)
1965   *Dear Brigitte* (Koster); *The Sons of Katie Elder* (Hathaway); *Boeing Boeing* (Rich)
1966   *Nevada Smith* (Hathaway); *An Eye for an Eye* (Moore)
1967   *Hour of the Gun* (Sturges); *Will Penny* (Gries)
1968   *The Party* (Edwards); *How Sweet It Is!* (Paris); *Arruza* (Boetticher) (co)
1969   *A Time for Dying* (Boetticher); **The Wild Bunch** (Peckinpah); *True Grit* (Hathaway)
1970   *The Ballad of Cable Hogue* (Peckinpah); *The Hawaiians* (*Master of the Islands*) (Gries); *Elvis—That's the Way It Is* (Sanders)
1971   *What's the Matter with Helen?* (Harrington)
1972   *Junior Bonner* (Peckinpah); *The Getaway* (Peckinpah)
1974   *Thomasine and Bushrod* (Parks)
1975   *Breakout* (Gries)
1976   *Breakheart Pass* (Gries); *St. Ives* (Thompson); *From Noon till Three* (Gilroy); *Drum* (Carver); *Mikey and Nicky* (May) (co)
1978   *Rabbit Test* (Rivers)

Films as 2nd Cameraman:

1930   *Morocco* (von Sternberg)
1935   **The Devil Is a Woman** (von Sternberg)

Publications

By BALLARD: article—

In *The Art of the Cinematographer*, by Leonard Maltin, New York, 1978.

On BALLARD: articles—

Lightman, Herb A., on *The House on Telegraph Hill* in *American Cinematographer* (Hollywood), July 1951.
Harrington, Clifford, in *American Cinematographer* (Hollywood), August 1961.
Scott, Darrin, on *Ride the High Country* in *American Cinematographer* (Hollywood), July 1962.
Cinema (Beverly Hills), Fall 1969.
Film Comment (New York), Summer 1972.
Focus on Film (London). no. 13, 1973.
McGilligan, P., in *Take One* (Montreal), no. 2, 1978.
Focus on Film (London), January-February 1979.
Obituary in *Variety* (New York), 5 October 1988.

*   *   *

Lucien Ballard has to be ranked among the greatest of Hollywood cinematographers based on a distinguished career which stretched from the early days of talkies into the blockbuster era of the 1970s. During more than four decades he worked on an extraordinary number of visually interesting films, in particular *Buchanan Rides Alone*, *The Rise and Fall of Legs Diamond*, and *Ride the High Country*. His creative output seems to divide into five periods.

He began his career at Paramount as editor and assistant to the great cameraman Lee Garmes on Josef von Sternberg's *Morocco*, starring Marlene Dietrich. Taken under von Sternberg's wing as a protégé, Ballard worked on *The Devil Is a Woman* and *Crime and Punishment*. It is hard to think of a more inspirational training ground for exploring the possibilities of light and shadow in the cinema than to have worked with Josef von Sternberg in the 1930s.

Ballard then entered the next phase of his training when he struggled to make all forms of genre films a bit distinguished. The late 1930s saw his credits accumulate, even through work on many a two-reeler including the comedies of The Three Stooges, and Charlie Chase. His principal employer, the Columbia Pictures studio, may have been on "Poverty Row," but it afforded Ballard the perfect place to learn to shoot Hollywood films quickly and efficiently.

World War II, with many talented cameramen off working for the military, provided Lucien Ballard with his chance to move up to top Hollywood productions. He jumped from Columbia, the home of the "B" movie to Twentieth Century-Fox, a top studio. In the mid-1940s he became a bit of a celebrity as the husband of Merle Oberon and the cameraman who struggled with Howard Hughes to create the idiosyncratic Western, *The Outlaw*.

But then his career stuck and he returned to shooting lower-budget fare. He achieved a measure of excellence with *The Killer Is Loose* and *Buchanan Rides Alone* for Budd Boetticher, and *The Killing* for Stanley Kubrick. In 1962 his career took a turn for the better and he began to achieve fame as an exceptional cameraman with work for director Sam Peckinpah. Their *Ride the High Country* stands as one of the most beautiful of Westerns; *The Wild Bunch*, *The Ballad of Cable Hogue*, and *Junior Bonner* brought Ballard and Peckinpah much due recognition and acclaim. This final phase of Ballard's career was underlined with greatness for the clean, elegant visual style he brought to the Western just, ironically, as that form was passing from the movie screen.

—Douglas Gomery

BALLHAUS, Michael

Cinematographer. **Nationality:** German. **Born:** Berlin, 5 August 1935; family moved to Bavaria 1942; son of the actors Oskar Ballhaus and Lenna Huter. **Career:** Inspired to become a cinematographer after watching Ophüls's *Lola Montès*, 1950s; studied photography; employed as assistant cameraman for television; promoted to Director of Photography, 1960; began collaboration with Rainer Werner Fassbinder, 1971; settled in the United States, 1982. **Awards:** German Film Awards Film Strip of Gold-Outstanding Individual Achievement in Cinematography, for *Die Bitteren Tranen der Petra von Kant*, 1972; German Film Awards Film Strip of Gold-Outstanding Individual Achievement in Cinematography, for *Despair*, 1978; National Society of Film Critics Best Cinematography, Los Angeles Film Critics Association Award Best Cinematography, for *The Fabulous*

Michael Ballhaus

Baker Boys, 1989; Los Angeles Film Critics Association Best Cinematography, for *GoodFellas,* 1990; German Camera Awards Honorary Award, 1996. **Address:** c/o Lawrence A. Mirisch, Triad Artists, Inc., Los Angeles, CA, U.S.A.

Films as Cinematographer:

1971 *Whity* (Fassbinder); *Sand* (Politzsch); *Warnung vor einer Heiligen Nutte* (*Beware of a Holy Whore*) (Fassbinder)

1972 *Die Bitteren Tränen der Petra von Kant* (*The Bitter Tears of Petra von Kant*) (Fassbinder)

1973 *Tschetan, der Indianerjunge* (Bohm)

1974 *Martha* (Fassbinder)

1975 *Faustrecht der Freiheit* (*Fox and his Friends*) (Fassbinder)

1976 *Satansbraten* (*Satan's Brew*) (Fassbinder); *Sommergäste* (*Summer Guests*) (Stein); *Adolf & Marlene* (Lommel); *Also es war so . . .* (Thome); *Chinasisches Roulette* (*Chinese Roulette*) (Fassbinder); *Ich will doch nur, das Ihr mich liebt* (*I Only Want You to Love Me*) (Fassbinder)

1977 *Mütter Küsters fahrt zum Himmel* (*Mütter Küsters Goes to Heaven*) (Fassbinder); *Frauen in New York* (Fassbinder)

1978 *Despair* (Fassbinder); *Venedig—die Insel der Glückseligen am Rande am des Untergangs* (*The Team; Venice*) (Rischert);

Bolwieser (*The Stationmaster's Wife*) (Fassbinder); ***Deutschland im Herbst*** (*Germany in Autumn*) (Fassbinder); *Die Erste Polka* (Emmerich); *Der Kleine Godard* (Fassbinder)

1979 *Kaleidoskop: Valeska Gert* (*For Fun—for Play*) (Schlöndorff); ***Die Ehe der Maria Braun*** (*The Marriage of Maria Braun*) (Fassbinder) (+ro as Counsel); *Deutscher Frühling*

1980 *Der Aufstand* (*The Uprising*) (Lilienthal); *Gross und Klein* (Stein)

1981 *Looping* (Bockmayer)

1982 *Dear Mr. Wonderful* (*Citydreams*) (Lilienthal); *Friends and Husbands* (*Heller Wahn*) (von Trotta); *Der Zauberberg* (Geissendörfer)

1983 *Malou* (Merrapfel); *Baby It's You* (Sayles); *Edithes Tagebuch* (*Edith's Diary*) (Geissendörfer)

1984 *Reckless* (Foley); *Old Enough* (Silver); *Heartbreakers* (Roth); *Das Autogram* (Lilienthal)

1985 *After Hours* (Scorsese); *The Death of a Salesman* (Schlöndorff); *Private Conversations* (Blackwood)

1986 *The Color of Money* (Scorsese); *Under the Cherry Moon* (Prince)

1987 *Broadcast News* (James L. Brooks); *The Glass Menagerie* (Newman)

1988 *Baja Oklahoma* (Roth); *The Last Temptation of Christ* (Scorsese); *Dirty Rotten Scoundrels* (Oz); *Working Girl* (Nichols); *The House on Carroll Street* (Yates)

1989 *The Fabulous Baker Boys* (Kloves)

1990 ***GoodFellas*** (Scorsese); *Postcards from the Edge* (Nichols)

1991 *Guilty by Suspicion* (Winkler); *What about Bob?* (Oz); *The Mambo Kings* (Glimcher); *Fear No Evil* (Winkler)

1992 *Bram Stoker's Dracula* (Coppola)

1993 *The Age of Innocence* (Scorsese)

1994 *I'll Do Anything* (James L. Brooks)

1995 *Outbreak* (Petersen)

1996 *Der Tote vom anderen Ufer* (Krawinkel); *Sleepers* (Levinson)

1997 *Air Force One* (Petersen)

1998 *Primary Colors* (Nichols)

1999 *Wild Wild West* (Sonnenfeld)

2000 *What Planet Are You From?* (Nichols); *The Legend of Bagger Vance* (Redford); *The Gangs of New York* (Scorsese)

Other Films:

1970 *Fassbinder Produces Film No. 8* (d?for TV)

1992 *Visions of Light: The Art of Cinematography* (Glassman and McCarthy) (appearance)

1999 *The Thirteenth Floor* (Rusnak) (exec pr)

Publications

By BALLHAUS: articles—

Film, no. 4, April 1985.

Cinéma (Paris), no. 1, January 1986.

Cahiers du Cinéma (Paris), no. 397, June 1987.

Films in Review (Denville), November 1987.

EPD Film (Frankfurt/Main), March 1994.

On BALLHAUS: articles—

American Cinematographer (Hollywood), vol. 67, no. 11, November 1986, and vol. 68, no. 11, November 1987.
American Film (Washington, D.C.), vol. 13, no. 3, December 1987.
Film Comment (New York), vol. 25, no. 5, September/October 1989.
American Cinematographer (Hollywood), vol. 72, no. 3, March 1991.
American Cinematographer (Hollywood), November 1992.
American Cinematographer (Hollywood), October 1993.
Film & TV Kameramann (Munich), February 1995.
American Cinematographer (Hollywood), October 1996.
Variety (New York), 21 July 1997.

*   *   *

For decades, foreign cinematographers had little chance of getting anywhere in Hollywood. Nevertheless, a loosening of union restrictions in the late 1970s enabled a host of European "lensers" to colonize a corner of the American film industry. The new wave of emigré camera wizards—Nykvist, Storaro, and Robby Müller among them—had become so influential by 1989 that one critic, Todd McCarthy, was able to write in *Film Comment*: "The Yanks have been virtually wiped off the map . . . foreign lensers now utterly dominate."

At the helm of the invasion was an unassuming German cameraman, Michael Ballhaus—a relative of Max Ophüls—whose infatuation with the celluloid muse had started when he saw Ophüls at work on *Lola Montès*. Ballhaus cut his teeth as a cinematographer on pictures by several of the pioneers of the so-called "New German Cinema." Most notably, he shot 15 films for that tyrant of excess, Rainer Werner Fassbinder. Working with Fassbinder was never easy. Contemporaries recall him as a fiercely jealous, insanely competitive figure, a dynamic and mercurial director who liked to engender a mood of tension and fear on the set. Early collaborations between Fassbinder and Ballhaus hardly can be said to be distinguished by their cinematography. Fassbinder, in those days, operated at a breakneck pace, and was not overly concerned with allowing his cameraman the leisure to devise complex lighting patterns. Pictures such as *The Bitter Tears of Petra von Kant* were lit rapidly and crudely, and compulsive as these tales of role playing and sexual jealously may be to watch, they are certainly not shining advertisements for Ballhaus's skills.

Later collaborations, notably *Chinese Roulette* and *The Marriage of Maria Braun*, have more to recommend them. The former is set in a country house, and is full of exquisite pastoral compositions of twilights and dawns, shot in the "magic hour." The latter recreates postwar Germany in all its speedy splendor as the country rollicks into the Adenauer years. Moreover, in *The Marriage of Maria Braun*, Ballhaus does for Hanna Schygulla what von Sternberg did for Dietrich in *The Blue Angel*. (Ballhaus has a knack for photographing female stars: his work with Schygulla prefigures his later Hollywood movies such as *Working Girl* and *The Fabulous Baker Boys*, where he frames Melanie Griffith and Michelle Pfeiffer, respectively, with the same kind of teasing deference accorded Garbo in the 1930s.) Fassbinder's voracious appetite for cocaine in his latter years was a source of much stress to his colleagues: it is little wonder that around the time of his death Ballhaus fled west.

In 1984, he shot his first American film, *Baby It's You*, for John Sayles, and in his subsequent assignments, Ballhaus has shown extraordinary versatility. He has worked within the constraints of theatrical adaptation, shooting a dim and lugubrious *Death of a Salesman* for Volker Schlöndorff as well as Tennessee Williams's *The Glass Menagerie* for Paul Newman. Ballhaus has shot super-slick Mike Nichols movies such as *Working Girl*, *Postcards from the Edge*, *Primary Colors*, and *What Planet Are You From?*, which showed him as equally adept at photographing the urban sprawl of New York, the many shades of blue of California, and the vistas of the American South and Southwest. He was just as expert when working on soundstages, where he filmed practically all of *Bram Stoker's Dracula* for Francis Ford Coppola. Perhaps missing his former mentor, he even teamed up with another egotist, namely Prince, to shoot *Under the Cherry Moon*. Established as a veteran, he nurtured Steve Kloves in his remarkably assured directing debut, *The Fabulous Baker Boys*. While his well-earned reputation as a solid and reliable professional won him a range of other high-prestige Hollywood assignments, Ballhaus probably will be best remembered for his work with Scorsese; for the elaborate circular tracks he laid down so that the camera could prowl round the pool table as Newman and Cruise hustled their way through *The Color of Money*, and, by way of contrast, for his filming of dust and desert in *The Last Temptation of Christ*, and the elegant period detail of 1870s New York in *The Age of Innocence*. He certainly reached some kind of peak with his incredibly fluid camera work, perfectly complementing the quick-fire narrative, on the brilliant *GoodFellas*.

In Europe, Ballhaus asserts, filmmaking is by necessity an art: budgets are tight, and there is rarely the prospect of making much money. In the States, though, film is a business. One senses that Ballhaus is happier in Hollywood than he ever was in Germany. For a start, American directors are far less likely to interfere with the lighting than are their European counterparts. After his years with the erratic Fassbinder, the strict hierarchies of the Hollywood scene, where the director of photography rarely operates the camera and where everybody knows his or her role, must come as something of a relief. Having served his apprenticeship shooting films high on concept but low on finance and unlikely to reach a mass audience, Ballhaus—like fellow countryman Wolfgang Petersen, for whom he photographed *Outbreak* and *Air Force One*—now shows himself to be a consummate Hollywood professional, delighted with the opportunities that he is offered.

—Geoffrey Macnab, updated by Rob Edelman

BANTON, Travis

Costume Designer. **Nationality:** American. **Born:** Waco, Texas, 18 August 1894. **Education:** Attended Columbia University, New York, 1916; Arts Student League, New York; apprenticed to dressmaker Madame Frances, New York, 1916–19. **Military Service:** Served briefly in the United States Navy during World War I. **Career:** 1919–24—worked for Madame France and Couturiere Lucille, and established his own salon; 1924—first designs for film, *The Dressmaker from Paris*; 1925–27—assistant to Howard Greer; 1927–38—head designer at Paramount; 1938–39—private couturier with Greer; 1939–41—designer for 20th Century-Fox; 1941–45—private designer; 1945–48—freelance designer (mainly for Universal), then

Travis Banton

designer for manufacturers, and for his own salon. **Died:** In Hollywood, California, 2 February 1958.

Films as Costume Designer:

1917   *Poppy* (José) (asst)
1925   *The Dressmaker from Paris* (Bern); *Grounds for Divorce* (Bern); *The Little French Girl* (Brenon); *The Swan* (Buchowetski)
1926   *The Palm Beach Girl* (Kenton); *The Cat's Pajamas* (Wellman); *The Grand Duchess and the Waiter* (St. Clair); *Dancing Mothers* (Brenon); *The Blind Goddess* (Fleming); *The Popular Sin* (St. Clair); *Love 'em and Leave 'em* (Tuttle)
1927   *Children of Divorce* (Lloyd); *Beau Sabreur* (Waters); *Barbed Wire* (Lee); *It* (Badger); *Rolled Stockings* (Rosson)
1928   *Red Hair* (Badger); *Doomsday* (Lee); *The Fifty-Fifty Girl* (Badger); *His Tiger Lady* (Henley); *The Fleet's In* (St. Clair); *Docks of New York* (von Sternberg); *Sins of the Fathers* (Berger)
1929   *The Man I Love* (Wellman); *Abie's Irish Rose* (Fleming); *The Canary Murder Case* (St. Clair); *The Love Parade* (Lubitsch); *The Dance of Life* (Cromwell and Sutherland); *The Wild Party* (Arzner); *Four Feathers* (Schoedsack,

Cooper, and Mendes); *Charming Sinners* (Milton); *Interference* (Mendes); *The Case of Lena Smith* (von Sternberg)
1930   *Fast and Loose* (Newmeyer); *Slightly Scarlet* (Knopf and Gasnier); *Paramount on Parade* (Arzner and others); *Follow Thru'* (Schwab and Corrigan); *Morocco* (von Sternberg); *The Vagabond King* (Berger); *Safety in Numbers* (Schertzinger); *Monte Carlo* (Lubitsch); *Let's Go Native* (McCarey); *For the Defense* (Cromwell); *The Royal Family of Broadway* (Cukor and Gardner)
1931   *Dishonored* (von Sternberg); *Girls about Town* (Cukor); *The Mad Parade* (Beaudine); *Once a Lady* (McClintic); *An American Tragedy* (von Sternberg); *The Ladies' Man* (Mendes); *Tarnished Lady* (Cukor); *Up Pops the Devil* (Sutherland); *It Pays to Advertise* (Tuttle); **Dr. Jekyll and Mr. Hyde** (Mamoulian)
1932   *The Eagle and the Hawk* (Foster); *Blonde Venus* (von Sternberg); *Evening for Sale* (Walker); *He Learned about Women* (Corrigan); *The Man from Yesterday* (Viertel); *No Man of Her Own* (Ruggles); *Shanghai Express* (von Sternberg); *A Farewell to Arms* (Borzage); *The Phantom President* (Taurog); *Night after Night* (Mayo); **Trouble in Paradise** (Lubitsch); *Supernatural* (Halperin); *Stranger in Love* (*Intimate*) (Mendes)
1933   *Brief Moment* (Burton) (co); *The Crime of the Century* (Beaudine); *Design for Living* (Lubitsch); *Disgraced* (Kenton); *From Hell to Heaven* (Kenton); *Girl without a Room* (Murphy); *International House* (Sutherland); *A Lady's Profession* (McLeod); *Midnight Club* (Hall and Somnes); *Song of Songs* (Mamoulian); *Terror Abroad* (Sloane); *Three Cornered Moon* (Nugent); *Torch Singer* (Hall and Somnes)
1934   *All of Me* (Flood); *Belle of the Nineties* (McCarey); *Bolero* (Ruggles); *Death Takes a Holiday* (Leisen); *The Great Flirtation* (Murphy); *Here Is My Heart* (Tuttle); *Kiss and Make Up* (Thompson); *Menace* (Murphy); *The Scarlet Empress* (von Sternberg); *Search for Beauty* (Kenton); *You're Telling Me* (Kenton); *Cleopatra* (DeMille) (co); *Now and Forever* (Hathaway); *Nana* (Arzner)
1935   *Enter Madame!* (Nugent); *All the King's Horses* (Tuttle); *The Crusades* (DeMille); **The Devil Is a Woman** (von Sternberg); *The Gilded Lily* (Ruggles); *Goin' to Town* (Hall); *The Lives of a Bengal Lancer* (Hathaway); *Ruggles of Red Gap* (McCarey); *Rhumba* (Gering); *So Red the Rose* (K. Vidor)
1936   *The Bride Comes Home* (Ruggles); *Desire* (Borzage); *Yours for the Asking* (Hall); *Valiant Is the Word for Carrie* (Ruggles); *Rose of the Rancho* (Gering); *The Princess Comes Across* (Howard); *My Man Godfrey* (La Cava); *Love before Breakfast* (W. Lang); *Go West, Young Man* (Hathaway); *The Big Broadcast of 1937* (Leisen)
1937   *Maid of Salem* (Lloyd); *Angel* (Lubitsch); *Champagne Waltz* (Sutherland); *Artists and Models* (Walsh); *High, Wide, and Handsome* (Mamoulian); *I Met Him in Paris* (Ruggles); *Nothing Sacred* (Wellman) (co); *Swing High, Swing Low* (Leisen)
1938   *Bluebeard's Eighth Wife* (Lubitsch); *Fools for Scandal* (LeRoy) (co)
1939   *Made for Each Other* (Cromwell); *Eternally Yours* (Garnett) (co); *In Name Only* (Cromwell) (co); *The Great Commandment* (Pichel)

1940   *Chad Hanna* (H. King); *Down Argentine Way* (Cummings); *Lillian Russell* (Cummings); *The Mark of Zorro* (Mamoulian); *The Return of Frank James* (F. Lang); *Tin Pan Alley* (W. Lang); *Hudson's Bay* (Pichel); *Raffles* (Wood); *Slightly Honorable* (Garnett)

1941   *Blood and Sand* (Mamoulian); *Charley's Aunt* (Mayo); *Man Hunt* (F. Lang); *That Night in Rio* (Cummings); *A Yank in the R.A.F.* (H. King); *Moon over Miami* (W. Lang); *Western Union* (F. Lang); *How Green Was My Valley* (Ford); *Tobacco Road* (Ford); *The Great American Broadcast* (Mayo); *Sun Valley Serenade* (Humberstone); *Belle Starr* (Cummings); *Wild Geese Calling* (Brahm)

1942   *Confirm or Deny* (Mayo) (co)

1943   *What a Woman!* (Cummings)

1944   *Cover Girl* (C. Vidor) (co); *A Song to Remember* C. Vidor) (co)

1945   *Scarlet Street* (F. Lang); *Wonder Man* (Humberstone); *The Beautiful Cheat* (Barton); *Frontier Gal* (*The Bride Wasn't Willing*) (Lamont); *The Strange Affair of Uncle Harry* (Siodmak); *This Love of Ours* (Dieterle) (co); *She Wouldn't Say Yes* (Hall) (co)

1946   *Canyon Passage* (Tourneur); *Magnificent Doll* (Borzage) (co); *The Runaround* (Lamont); *Night in Paradise* (Lubin); *Tangier* (Waggner); *Sister Kenny* (Nichols)

1947   *I'll Be Yours* (Seitel) (co); *The Lost Moment* (Gabel); *Smash Up* (Heisler); *The Paradine Case* (Hitchcock)

1948   *A Double Life* (Cukor) (co); **Letter from an Unknown Woman** (Ophüls); *The Velvet Touch* (Gage); *The Secret beyond the Door* (F. Lang)

1950   *Never a Dull Moment* (Marshall)

1951   *Valentino* (Marshall) (co)

Publications

By BANTON: articles—

"Fashions for the Stars," in *Motion Picture Studio Insider*, May 1935.
"Amusing Fashions from *Auntie Mame*," in *Theatre Arts* (New York), February 1957.

On BANTON: articles—

Photoplay (New York), April, May, and June 1936.
Chierichetti, David, in *Hollywood Costume Design*, New York, 1976.
Leese, Elizabeth, in *Costume Design in the Movies*, New York, 1976.
LaVine, W. Robert, in *In a Glamorous Fashion*, New York, 1980.
Mann, William J., "Costume Design: Travis Banton," in *Architectural Digest* (Los Angeles), April 1996.
Shrewsbury, Judy, "Travis Banton et Adrian: Les créateurs de stars," in *Positif* (Paris), July-August 1996.

*   *   *

We characterize the European Baroque by its dramatic lighting, dynamic movement, frequent use of diagonals, repetition of motifs in infinite variation, forms built upon forms. Artists used lavish materials and embellished them with elaborate details. When individual works of art were brought together, sharing common styles and themes, they created even greater wholes. In the 1930s Travis Banton translated that spirit into pure Hollywood.

Banton's most "Baroque" examples of costume artistry were completed under director Joseph von Sternberg's visionary eye. Every detail in the von Sternberg films harmoniously meshed—scenery, costumes, makeup, even the postures of star Marlene Dietrich. Costume designer Banton, art director Hans Dreier, and photographer Lee Garmes, worked along with others toward an intricate and unified style.

Banton's careful choice of costume materials complemented the sophisticated lighting techniques found in von Sternberg productions. His fabric palette ranged from absorbent to highly reflective. The combined talents of Banton, von Sternberg and Dietrich constructed a *femme fatale* as ethereal as the sparkle of a diamond.

As moving pictures moved, so did costumes by Banton. Playing across his reflective surfaces, the light skimmed the screen like moonbeams on water. To increase this kinetic impact, Banton's couture sprouted feathers, fluttering veils, acres of chiffon, and anything else that moved with the slightest breeze or gesture. This assured Paramount that even in the midst of full-screen revolution, not an eye would stray from the star. *Shanghai Express* pitted guerilla leader Warner Oland against Marlene Dietrich, but she stole the scene, wearing hypnotic buttons that swung like swashbucklers on chandeliers.

Besides his technical and formal considerations, Banton concentrated on capturing the essential mystique. He created numerous guises to capture Dietrich's ambiguity—sexy masculine dress, elegant rags, etc. She even looked desirable in a gorilla suit. Dietrich glowed in glorious absurdity.

Love goddesses dressed by Banton spanned quite a range. Claudette Colbert alone crossed from temptress to dedicated wife. Banton "gilded" bawdy Mae West, investing her burlesque regalia with opulent class. Contrast West's grand-staircase curves with streamlined Carole Lombard, for whom Banton introduced a version of the bias cut to reveal her slender, natural form. Sculpting her body through drapery, he celebrated the anatomical ideal of the 1930s. Although West had the Rubensian body, Lombard's figure-caressing fabrics captured a sexuality just as potent.

—Edith C. Lee

BARBERA, Joseph

See **HANNA, William, and Joseph Barbera**

BARKER, (Sir) William George

Director, Producer, Entrepreneur. **Nationality:** British. **Born:** London, 1867. **Career:** Worked as a travelling salesman; became interested in amateur film production, turning professional in 1901 and founding the Autoscope Company, which specialized in "topical" or "reality" films; became director of the Warwick Trading Company in 1906, which specialized in news films; 1908—with the nickelodeon boom, he set up his own company, Barker Motion Photography Ltd., with offices in the London theatrical district (Soho) and studios at Ealing; continued making topicals for several years; 1911—began feature production; formed own stock company of players; 1918—left the production business because of unsolvable distribution problems. **Died**: 1951.

Feature Films as Director/Producer:

(undated) *The Anarchists Doom*; *The Great Bank Robbery*; *In the Hands of London Crooks*; *Jim the Fireman*; *The Last Round*; *Lights of London*; *The Fighting Parson*; *Greater Love Hath No Man*; *Younita*
1911 *Henry VIII*; *Princess Clementina*
1913 *The Great Bullion Robbery*; *London by Night*; *Sixty Years a Queen*; *East Lynne*
1914 *The Brother's Atonement*

Publications:

On BARKER: books—

Armes, Roy, *A Critical History of British Cinema*, New York, 1978.
Low, Rachael, *The History of the British Film Volume II*, Surrey, 1948.

*   *   *

Along with Cecil Hepworth and George Pearson, William Barker was responsible for the re-establishment of profitable British production in 1908, a boom that was prompted by the transference of exhibition from musical halls and fairgrounds to purpose-built theaters, known as nickelodeons, and the gradual shift to narrative films.

Interested first in filmmaking as an amateur, Barker saw the economic possibilities of the new medium and started making his own "topical" or "reality" films in the tradition of fellow British filmmakers Robert Paul and Birt Acres, themselves inspired by the success of the Lumière brothers in France. He abandoned the very primitive facilities of his Autoscope Company in 1906 to run the Warwick Trading Company, replacing founder Charles Urban, and soon turned the business into one of the country's most notable suppliers of topicals, for which there was then the greatest demand. He became one of the most important figures in the growing British film business.

The public's growing lack of interest in a steady diet of topicals, however, led to a radical change within the industry, with Barker very much in the forefront. The future, he saw clearly, lay in narrative films, and by 1911 he realized that longer, feature films would be most desirable, providing problems of exhibition and distribution could be solved so that larger production budgets could be justified. Like D. W. Griffith and Adolph Zukor in America, Baker saw that the most popular kind of film would likely be feature length productions starring famous actors, especially those from the legitimate stage. While he did not stop making the topicals that were still providing a steady income, Barker did pioneer the making of large-scale features, on the model of Italian costume epic spectaculars such as *Giulio Cesare* (1909), *Bruto* (1910), *San Francisco* (1911), and, particularly, *Fall of Troy* (1911). His initial choice of subject matter

was wise—a film on Henry VIII, perhaps the most famous of British monarchs; it was a subject that would prove popular and profitable again in the thirties with Alexander Korda's *The Private Life of Henry VIII* (1933). For his *Henry VIII*, Barker convinced the era's most famous Shakespearean actor, Sir Herbert Tree, to play the title role; only the promise of a huge salary convinced the reluctant Tree to take the part, but his superb performance made the film. British film historians are agreed that the film was the first truly important British feature, occupying roughly the place within the cinematic history of that country that Griffith's *The Birth of a Nation* does in the United States. Barker's film was an outstanding success at the box office and was instrumental in interesting a middle-class public in the cultural possibilities of the cinema.

Developing, again like Griffith, his own stock company of actors, Barker moved on to other historical subjects—most notably, *Sixty Years a Queen*, a slickly produced and patriotic homage to Queen Victoria. More important, however, for the growth and development of the industry was his elaborate mounting of *East Lynne*, which had started life as a novel by Mrs. Henry Wood and was soon adapted into one of the period's most successful and notable stage melodramas. As Griffith had, Barker discovered materials in the stage melodrama ideally suited to cinematic adaptation: stock characters, emotionally-heightened action, predictable but effective twists and turns of the plot, and young female main characters, potential victims of a male-dominated society, with whom the audience could easily identify. Barker's film version, directed by Bert Haldane, was the first six-reel British film and achieved an outstanding success with audiences. Though Barker and Haldane were not technically innovative in the manner of Griffith (the film's editing, without any intercutting, makes for a certain monotony that the basically static camera set-ups do not alleviate), *East Lynne* offers a well-told and coherent narrative, with an expert blending of interior scenes and appropriate exteriors.

During the same period, again following a popular trend undoubtedly inaugurated by Griffith (in *Musketeers of Pig Alley*), Barker produced a number of exciting crime melodramas that made much of London night life, particularly its seamier side. Despite his successes with audiences, however, Barker proved unable to solve persistent problems with distribution. He allowed *Henry VIII* to be hired for very limited runs at quite high prices, thus enabling him to keep distribution in the hands of one dealer, who would issue territorial rights for individual showmen. To keep prices and demand high, he allowed very few prints of any one film. Barker even went so far as to burn the twenty prints of *Henry VIII* after a release period of only six weeks in order to keep increasingly tattered prints from circulating and damaging the public image of the film business (and of course provding competition to newer films produced by him). No other producer went so far in an attempt to control the market, and Barker was by no means successful in solving the problem for British filmmakers with ensuring a distribution that would regularly reward the huge investment needed to make a top-quality feature.

Barker's films eventually became less noteworthy during the period from 1914 to 1917, and he was increasingly discouraged by the difficult business conditions the British industry suffered through as a result of wartime restrictions. The same general crisis that was soon to overtake all British production as a result of irresistible American competition forced him out of the industry by the end of the war in 1918.

—R. Barton Palmer

BARNES, George S.

Cinematographer. **Nationality:** American. **Born:** 1893. **Family:** Married seven times: fourth wife, the actress Joan Blondell, 1933 (divorced 1935). **Career:** 1918—photographer for Thomas Ince Productions: first film, *The Biggest Show on Earth*; photographed *Melody Masters* series in the 1930s. **Award:** Academy Award for *Rebecca*, 1940. **Died:** 30 May 1953.

Films as Cinematographer:

1918   *The Biggest Show on Earth* (Storm); *Desert Wooing* (Storm); *Fuss and Feathers* (Niblo); *The Marriage Ring* (Niblo); *Keys of the Righteous* (Storm); *Naughty! Naughty!* (Storm); *The Vamp* (Storm); *When Do We Eat?* (Storm)

1919   *Stepping Out* (Niblo); *Dangerous Hours* (Niblo); *Happy Though Married* (Niblo); *The Haunted Bedroom* (Niblo); *Law of Men* (Niblo); *Partners Three* (Niblo); *Virtuous Thief* (Niblo); *What Every Woman Learns* (Niblo); *The Woman in the Suitcase* (Niblo)

1920   *Her Husband's Friend* (Niblo); *Sex* (Niblo); *Hairpins* (Niblo); *The False Road* (Niblo)

1921   *Silk Hosiery* (Niblo); *The Heart Line* (Thompson); *The Beautiful Gambler* (Worthington); *The Bronze Bell* (Horne); *Opened Shutters* (Worthington)

1922   *The Real Adventure* (K. Vidor); *Woman, Wake Up!* (Harrison); *Peg o' My Heart* (K. Vidor); *Dusk to Dawn* (K. Vidor); *Conquering the Women* (K. Vidor)

1923   *Alice Adams* (Lee); *Desire* (Lee); *The Love Piker* (Hopper)

1924   *Janice Meredith* (*The Beautiful Rebel*) (Hopper) (co); *Yolanda* (Vignola) (co)

1925   *Zander the Great* (Hill) (co); *The Teaser* (Seiter); *The Dark Angel* (Fitzmaurice); *The Eagle* (Brown) (co)

1926   *Mademoiselle Modiste* (Leonard); *The Son of the Sheik* (Fitzmaurice); *The Winning of Barbara Worth* (H. King)

1927   *The Night of Love* (Fitzmaurice) (co); *Venus of Venice* (Neilan); *The Magic Flame* (H. King); *The Devil Dancer* (Niblo) (co)

1928   *Sadie Thompson* (Walsh) (co); *Two Lovers* (Niblo); *The Awakening* (Fleming); *Our Dancing Daughters* (Beaumont)

1929   *This Is Heaven* (Santell) (co); *The Rescue* (Brenon); *Bulldog Drummond* (Jones) (co); *The Trespasser* (Goulding) (co); *Condemned* (Ruggles) (co)

1930   *Raffles* (Fitzmaurice and D'Arrast) (co); *The Devil to Pay* (Fitzmaurice) (co); *A Lady's Morals* (*The Soul Kill*; *Jenny Lind*) (Franklin); *What a Widow!* (Dwan); *One Heavenly Night* (Fitzmaurice) (co)

1931   *Five and Ten* (*Daughter of Luxury*) (Leonard); *Unholy Garden* (Fitzmaurice) (co); *Street Scene* (K. Vidor)

1932   *The Greeks Had a Word for Them* (L. Sherman); *Polly of the Circus* (Santell); *The Wet Parade* (Fleming); *Society Girl* (Lanfield); *Blondie of the Follies* (Goulding); *Sherlock Holmes* (Howard)

1933   *Broadway Bad* (*Her Reputation*) (Lanfield); *Peg o' My Heart* (Leonard); *Goodbye Again* (Curtiz); *Footlight Parade* (Lloyd); *Havana Widows* (Enright)

1934   *Gambling Lady* (Mayo); *Massacre* (Crosland); *Smarty* (*Hit Me Again*) (Florey); *He Was Her Man* (Bacon); *Dames* (Enright) (co); *The Kansas City Princess* (Keighley); *Flirtation Walk* (Borzage) (co)

1935   *Gold Diggers of 1935* (Berkeley); *Traveling Saleslady* (Enright); *In Caliente* (Bacon) (co); *Broadway Gondolier* (Bacon); *The Irish in Us* (Bacon); *I Live for Love* (*I Live for You*) (Berkeley); *Stars over Broadway* (Keighley)

1936   *The Singing Kid* (Keighley); *Love Begins at Twenty* (*All One Night*) (McDonald); *Cain and Mabel* (Bacon); *Black Legion* (Mayo)

1937   *Marked Woman* (Bacon); *Ever Since Eve* (Bacon); *Variety Show* (Keighley) (co); *Hollywood Hotel* (Berkeley) (co); *The Barrier* (Selander)

1938   *Love, Honor, and Behave* (Logan); *The Beloved Brat* (*A Dangerous Age*) (Lubin); *Gold Diggers in Paris* (*The Gay Imposters*) (Enright) (co)

1939   *Jesse James* (H. King) (co); *Stanley and Livingstone* (H. King); *Our Neighbors, The Carters* (Murphy)

1940   *Parole Fixer* (Florey); *Rebecca* (Hitchcock); *Free, Blond, and 21* (Cortez); *Maryland* (H. King) (co); *The Return of Frank James* (F. Lang) (co); *Girl from Avenue A* (Brower) (co); *Hudson's Bay* (Pichel) (co)

1941   *Meet John Doe* (Capra); *That Uncertain Feeling* (Lubitsch); *Unholy Partners* (LeRoy); *Ladies in Retirement* (C. Vidor); *Remember the Day* (H. King); *Sex Hygiene* (Ford—short)

1942   *Rings on Her Fingers* (Mamoulian); *Nightmare* (Whelan); *Once upon a Honeymoon* (McCarey); *Broadway* (Seiter)

1943   *Mr. Lucky* (Potter)

1944   *Frenchman's Creek* (Leisen); *None but the Lonely Heart* (Odets); *Jane Eyre* (Stevenson)

1945   *The Spanish Main* (Borzage); *Spellbound* (Hitchcock); *The Bells of St. Mary's* (McCarey)

1946   *From This Day Forward* (Berry); *Sister Kenny* (Nichols); *Sinbad the Sailor* (Wallace)

1947   *Mourning Becomes Electra* (Nichols); *The Emperor Waltz* (Wilder)

1948   *Good Sam* (McCarey); *No Minor Vices* (Milestone); *The Boy with Green Hair* (Losey)

1949   *Force of Evil* (Polonsky); *The File on Thelma Jordan* (*Thelma Jordan*) (Siodmak); *Samson and Delilah* (DeMille)

1950   *Let's Dance* (McLeod); *Mr. Music* (Haydn); *Riding High* (Capra) (co)

1951   *Here Comes the Groom* (Capra)

1952   *The Greatest Show on Earth* (DeMille); *Somebody Loves Me* (Brecher); *Something to Live For* (Stevens); *Just for You* (Nugent); *Road to Bali* (Walker)

1953   *War of the Worlds* (Haskin); *Little Boy Lost* (Seaton)

Publications

On BARNES: articles—

Rowan, Arthur, "Filming the Circus," in *American Cinematographer* (Hollywood), December 1951.
Film Comment (New York), Summer 1972.
Focus on Film (London), no. 13, 1973.

*   *   *

George S. Barnes

An artist of great versatility, George S. Barnes was one of the masters of Hollywood cinematography, his handsome, stylish work best served in visually lush melodramas like *Rebecca*, *Jane Eyre*, and *Frenchman's Creek*. Barnes excelled in many genres—musicals (*Footlight Parade*, *Gold Diggers of 1935*), westerns (*Jesse James*), or science-fiction (*The War of the Worlds*)—but could also create a darker, more realistic visualization for social drama (*Black Legion*) and *film noir* (*Force of Evil*). Equally proficient in black-and-white (*Bulldog Drummond*, *Marked Woman*) or color (*Sinbad the Sailor*, *The Boy with Green Hair*), Barnes was in demand from top directors

like Hitchcock, Capra, DeMille, and McCarey, and such stars as Valentino, Swanson, Colman, Cooper, Bergman, and Crosby.

In the silent era, Barnes's finest achievements included *Janice Meredith*, a Revolutionary War drama in the Griffith style; the Valentino vehicle *The Son of the Sheik*, with its softly lit interiors and exhilarating desert photography of Arab horsemen; and *The Winning of Barbara Worth*, highlighted by a climactic and still impressive flood sequence. Barnes became Samuel Goldwyn's number one cameraman in 1925 with *The Dark Angel*, and his exquisite visuals became a Goldwyn hallmark in the late 1920s and early 1930s. He was responsible for the studio's important romantic team Ronald Colman and Vilma Banky, both in their solo vehicles (Colman's *Condemned* and *Raffles*, Banky's *The Awakening* and *This Is Heaven*) and their tandem efforts (*The Night of Love*, *The Magic Flame*, *Two Lovers*). Barnes's assistant and eventual co-photographer on the Goldwyn films was Gregg Toland, who learned cinematography under Barnes's tutelage. Toland's later work on *Dead End*, *Wuthering Heights*, and *Citizen Kane* shows Barnes's influence in the refinement of deep focus, expressive camera movement, and faultless lighting.

Bulldog Drummond exemplifies their artistry together. The film is an early precursor to the James Bond pictures, and allows for a bravura photographic style. Imaginative tracking shots, such as the opening at the men's club and later in the villains' hideout, are coupled with William Cameron Menzies's eccentric sets to create a visual feast. Tremendously mobile for one of the first talking pictures, *Bulldog Drummond* is set almost entirely at night, and Barnes and Toland eschew day-for-night for actual nocturnal exteriors.

Toland succeeded Barnes as Goldwyn's ace cameraman, and Barnes moved on to brief stints at MGM and Fox before settling at Warners. He was kept busy at the Warners factory, shooting 25 films between 1934 and 1937. He brought a gritty, realistic look to message movies like *Massacre*, *Black Legion*, and *Marked Woman*, but usually was assigned to musicals. He shot a trio of Busby Berkeley classics—*Footlight Parade* with the famous "Shanghai Lil" number; *Dames*; and *Gold Diggers of 1935* with its striking, lengthy "Lullaby of Broadway" sequence—and many lesser musicals, such as the ludicrous *Broadway Gondolier*. Barnes left Warners in 1938 for more rewarding films, and found himself very much in demand.

Henry King's *Jesse James* (co-photographed with W. Howard Greene) was a tremendous change from the sound-stage musicals, a lavish western adventure filmed on picturesque Missouri locations in dazzling three-strip Technicolor. Barnes imparts a staggering sense of movement to the proceedings, his exteriors bringing life to the vigorous action. Barnes also did the sequel in Technicolor, *The Return of Frank James*, this time with Fritz Lang directing. The color was just as vibrant, but Lang gave darker meaning to the film, reflected in Barnes's claustrophobic interiors.

Barnes's 1940s work is impeccable. He won an Oscar for Alfred Hitchcock's *Rebecca*, a black-and-white masterpiece. Manderley, the manor house of Daphne du Maurier's novel, was given a brooding, foreboding quality by Barnes's play of light and shadow. He also photographed *Spellbound* for Hitchcock, famed for the surrealistic Salvador Dali-designed dream sequence, a flashy, disproportionate, bizarre experiment. Robert Stevenson's *Jane Eyre* has much the same ominous feel of *Rebecca*, this time with a 19th-century period setting.

Barnes furnished a darker view than was normal for Frank Capra's films. In *Meet John Doe*, he painted the images in starkly defined high contrast, then softened the focus for the climactic rooftop scene in the snow. His later Capras, the Bing Crosby musicals *Riding High* and *Here Comes the Groom*, were by necessity much lighter in tone and text. Barnes's films for Leo McCarey during this period—*Once upon a Honeymoon*, *The Bells of St. Mary's*, and *Good Sam*—were slick studio jobs with a director noted for his straightforward, uncomplicated camera style. Barnes's main challenge in the McCarey films was to give the Hollywood glamour treatment to the stars—Cary Grant and Ginger Rogers in *Honeymoon*, Ingrid Bergman and Bing Crosby (as a nun and a priest, respectively) in *Bells*, and Gary Cooper and Ann

Sheridan in *Good Sam*. Crosby was so happy with Barnes's photography that he insisted on him for many of his subsequent features.

Barnes also distinguished himself with outstanding color work. *The Spanish Main* and *Sinbad the Sailor* have rich cartoon colors to suit their lusty adventures, while he etched subtler hues for the romantic *Frenchman's Creek*, again from a du Maurier novel. In his epics for Cecil B. DeMille, the Biblical *Samson and Delilah*, and the circus marathon *The Greatest Show on Earth*, Barnes employed garish colors for the director's showy vision.

A consummate cinematographer, George Barnes had a prolific career exemplified by a high degree of lighting sophistication, an intuitive mastery of deep-focus photography, and a creative sense of composition and camera movement. He helped set the Hollywood standard for studio cinematography, yet could also transcend the limitations of the system and paint artistically lasting works of cinema. Within the industry, Barnes was acclaimed as among the best in his field, and his Academy Award record is impressive. He was nominated for three films during the first Oscar season of 1927–28 with *Devil Dancer*, *The Magic Flame*, and *Sadie Thompson*, and, in addition to his win for *Rebecca*, he was nominated in both black-and-white (*Our Dancing Daughters*, *Spellbound*) and color (*The Spanish Main*, *Samson and Delilah*) categories.

—John A. Gallagher

BARRY, John

Composer. **Nationality:** British. **Born:** John Barry Prendergast in York, 3 November 1933. **Education:** Studied with Francis Jackson and Joseph William Russo. **Military Service:** Played in military band during military service. **Family:** Married 1) the actress Jane Birkin (divorced); 2) Laurie Barry. **Career:** Rock 'n' roll trumpeter, and composer-arranger-conductor for John Dankworth, Jack Parnell, and other bands; organized his own group, The John Barry Seven; 1960—score for first film, *Beat Girl*; has also written stage musicals and music for TV, including the mini-series *Eleanor and Franklin*, 1976. **Awards:** Academy Award, for *Born Free* (and the song "Born Free"), 1966, *The Lion in Winter*, 1968, *Out of Africa*, 1985, and *Dances with Wolves*, 1990; British Academy Award, for *The Lion in Winter*, 1968. **Agent:** ICM, 8899 Beverly Boulevard, Hollywood, CA 90048, U.S.A.

Films as Composer:

1960   *Beat Girl* (*Wild for Kicks*) (Grenville); *Never Let Go* (Guillermin)
1962   *The L-Shaped Room* (Forbes); *The Amorous Prawn* (*The Playgirl and the War Minister*) (Kimmins)
1963   *From Russia with Love* (Young); *Zulu* (Endfield)
1964   *A Jolly Bad Fellow* (*They All Died Laughing*) (Chaffey); *Seance on a Wet Afternoon* (Forbes); *Man in the Middle* (Hamilton); *Goldfinger* (Hamilton)

John Barry

1965 *The Party's Over* (Hamilton—produced 1962); *The Ipcress File* (Furie); *Four in the Morning* (Simmons); *King Rat* (Forbes); *Mister Moses* (Neame); *The Knack, and How to Get It* (Lester); *Thunderball* (Neame); *One Man and His Bank* (Cobham—short)

1966 *Born Free* (Hill); *The Quiller Memorandum* (Anderson); *Dutchman* (Harvey); *The Chase* (Penn); *The Wrong Box* (Forbes)

1967 *The Whisperers* (Forbes); *You Only Live Twice* (Gilbert)

1968 *Petulia* (Lester); *Deadfall* (Forbes); *Boom!* (Huston); *The Lion in Winter* (Harvey)

1969 **Midnight Cowboy** (Schlesinger); *On Her Majesty's Secret Service* (Hunt)

1970 *The Last Valley* (Clavell); *Monte Walsh* (Fraker); *The Appointment* (Lumet) (song)

1971 *A Clockwork Orange* (Kubrick); *Murphy's War* (Yates); *Follow Me* (*The Public Eye*) (Reed); *Walkabout* (Roeg); *They Might Be Giants* (Harvey); *Diamonds Are Forever* (Hamilton)

1972 *Alice's Adventures in Wonderland* (Sterling); *Mary, Queen of Scots* (Jarrott)

1973 *A Doll's House* (Garland); *The Glass Menagerie* (Harvey)

1974 *The Man with the Golden Gun* (Hamilton); *The Dove* (Jarrott); *The Little Prince* (Donen)

1975 *The Day of the Locust* (Schlesinger); *Love among the Ruins* (Cukor); *The Tamarind Seed* (Edwards)

1976 *Robin and Marian* (Lester); *King Kong* (Guillermin)

1977 *First Love* (Darling); *The Deep* (Yates); *The War between the Tates* (Philips); *White Buffalo* (Lee Thompson); *The Gathering* (Kleiser); *Eleanor and Franklin: The White House Years* (Petrie); *Young Joe, the Forgotten Kennedy* (Heffron)

1978 *Game of Death* (Clouse); *The Betsy* (Petrie)

1979 *Hanover Street* (Hyams); *Star Crash* (Coates); *Moonraker* (Gilbert); *The Black Hole* (Nelson); *Willa* (Darling and Guzman); *The Corn Is Green* (Cukor)

1980 *Inside Moves* (Donner); *Raise the Titanic!* (Jameson); *Somewhere in Time* (Szwarc)

1981 *The Legend of the Lone Ranger* (Fraker); *Body Heat* (Kasdan); *Murder by Phone* (*Bells*) (Anderson)

1982 *Hammett* (Wenders); *Frances* (Clifford)

1983 *Octopussy* (Glen); *High Road to China* (Hutton); *Svengali* (Harvey)

1984 *The Cotton Club* (Coppola); *Mike's Murder* (Bridges); *Until September* (Marquand)

1985 *Jagged Edge* (Marquand); *A View to a Kill* (Glen); *Out of Africa* (Pollack)

1986 *Howard the Duck* (Huyck); *A Killing Affair* (Saperstein); *My Sister's Keeper* (Saperstein); *Peggy Sue Got Married* (Coppola)

1987 *Hearts of Fire* (Marquand); *The Living Daylights* (Glen)

1988 *Masquerade* (Swaim)

1990 *Dances with Wolves* (Costner)

1992 *Chaplin* (Attenborough)

1993 *Deception* (Clifford); *Indecent Proposal* (Lyne); *My Life* (Rubin)

1994 *The Specialist* (Llosa)

1995 *Cry, the Beloved Country* (Roodt); *The Scarlett Letter* (Joffé)

1997 *Swept from the Sea* (Kidron)

1998 *Mercury Rising* (Becker); *Playing by Heart* (Carroll)

1999 *Goodbye Lover* (Score Withdrawn)

Film as Arranger:

1962 *Dr. No* (Young)

Publications

By BARRY: articles—

In *Knowing the Score*, by Irwin Bazelon, New York, 1975.
International Filmusic Journal, nos. 1, 2, and 3, 1979–80.
Segnocinema (Vicenza), vol. 6, no. 25, November 1986.
Soundtrack! (Hollywood), March 1988.

On BARRY: articles—

Films in Review (New York), October 1967.
Focus on Film (London), Winter 1970.
Films in Review (New York), April 1971.
Monthly Film Bulletin (London), October 1971.
Monthly Film Bulletin (London), August 1972.
Dirigido por . . . (Barcelona), July/August 1974.

Ecran (Paris), September 1975.

Focus on Film (London), Winter 1975–76.

Film Music Notebook (Calabasas, California), vol. 2, no. 4, 1976.

Soundtrack! (Hollywood), June 1978.

Fistful of Soundtracks (London), May 1981.

Filmusic (Leeds), 1982.

Soundtrack! (Hollywood), December 1983.

Soundtrack! (Hollywood), March 1984.

Soundtrack! (Hollywood), June 1984.

Soundtrack! (Hollywood), September 1986.

Soundtrack! (Hollywood), June 1994.

Soundtrack! (Hollywood), November 1994.

Film Score Monthly (Los Angeles), January/February/March 1996.

Film Score Monthly (Los Angeles), April 1996.

Soundtrack! (Hollywood), June 1996.

Film Score Monthly (Los Angeles), October 1996.

Film Score Monthly (Los Angeles), November 1996.

Billboard, v. 109, no. 41, 11 October 1997.

Billboard, v. 111, no. 27, 3 July 1999.

* * *

John Barry is one of cinema's most prolific and well-known composers. Europe has long provided the American movie industry with many of its leading musical artists, but no Englishman has ever equaled Barry's breadth of accomplishment and commercial success. Although movie music increasingly consists of collections of unrelated pop songs selected mainly for their ability to sell records, Barry's skills are still in demand among those who value dramatic and musical integration. Best known for his compositions for the James Bond films, Barry has in fact displayed an extraordinary versatility throughout his career. Jazz instrumentals, medieval music, blues motifs, rock variations, French ballads, and evocations of the Orient have all been featured in his work. He composes orchestral and solo textures with equal facility, and is as much at home with electronically generated sound as with that produced by acoustic instruments. Although he has been criticized for an excess of lushness, his professionalism, his competence in a diversity of idioms, and his keen understanding of the cinematic relevance of music have earned him wide respect.

By the time he entered the film industry, Barry was already acquainted with a wide range of musical genres. The son of a cinema-chain owner, he gravitated toward movies by way of a classical music training at an English cathedral, playing trumpet in an army band, arranging for several of Britain's top jazz orchestras, and leading the brass-laden rock 'n' roll group The John Barry Seven. After writing his first film score for the youth-oriented melodrama, *Beat Girl*, Barry was asked to arrange and direct Monty Norman's lively James Bond theme for *Dr. No*, the first of the 007 films. Norman has always received credit for the composition, with its plunking guitar and insistent brass, but Barry's input helped to make it one of the 1960's most recognizable signature tunes in any medium. Barry has since written most of the scores and about half the title songs for the Bond series. While all of these have achieved an effective synthesis of music and image, Barry's work for *Goldfinger* is perhaps the most exciting. Although the compositions have varied in musical quality, they have always been integral to the films' identity—as much a part of the total package as the arresting title sequences and 007 himself. Barry's distinctive use of brass has added urgency to the action

sequences, and his use of lush strings and woodwind melodies have enhanced the more romantic interludes. While he has been required to generate chart-busting title songs for the Bond films, he has always created thematic unity between the main number and the score as a whole.

Barry's work includes music which functions mainly to establish mood or signal changes of emotional pace. His unobtrusive score for *Jagged Edge* is a typical example. Yet he rejects the idea that film music must always be an appendage to the visual image, faithfully reflecting the events depicted on screen. His philosophy is that ''a film score should burn with its own fire, not merely glow in the dark like a pretty charcoal.'' While insisting that score and narrative should be in harmony, Barry believes that music can add dramatic dimension, either by augmenting expressed emotions and attitudes, or by communicating information not contained in the images or script. His sweeping pastorales for *Out of Africa*, for example, gave heightened expression to the protagonists' love for their adopted country, as well as for each other. In *The Lion in Winter*, choral fugues, sung in Latin, are used to establish the largely unarticulated influence of the Catholic Church on England's Henry II. As musical supervisor on *Midnight Cowboy*, he and director John Schlesinger used Fred Neil's up-tempo song ''Everybody's Talkin''' to supply much of the film's initial pace and meaning. Barry also employs musical understatement for dramatic effect. The emotional impact of the sober prison-camp drama *King Rat* owed much to Barry's delicate instrumentation.

Many of Barry's most lasting contributions to film music have been composed in a romantic vein. His love themes for *Robin and Marian*, his title song for *Moonraker*, and the gentle ballad sung by Louis Armstrong in *On Her Majesty's Secret Service* exemplify his skill at using music to call forth an affective response in the audience. Indeed, his score for *Somewhere in Time* was not only more memorable than the film, but was more effective than either script or acting in establishing the movie's romantic resonance. Although such compositions do not satisfy every taste—some critics describe them as ''soupy''—they are seldom inappropriate.

While Barry can scarcely be accused of a formulaic approach to film scoring, it is possible to identify certain trademarks in his music. Extensive use of flutes, horns, and strings, sustained low brass notes (''brass pedals''), and endless reworking of a single theme, serve to distinguish his work from that of his contemporaries. Although he may not always satisfy the aesthetic sensibilities of film-music critics, Barry has done more than most to keep alive the public's appreciation of movie scoring. In an era in which commercial pressure has eroded the relationship between music and film, this is a significant achievement.

—Fiona Valentine

BARSACQ, Léon

Art Director. **Nationality:** Russian. **Born:** the Crimea, 18 October 1906. **Education:** Attended the School of Decorative Arts, Paris. **Family:** Brother of the stage designer and director André Barsacq. **Career:** 1931–39—assistant designer for Perrier, Andrejew, and others; 1940—first film as art director, *Volpone*. **Died:** In Paris, 23 December 1969.

Films as Assistant Art Director:

1934   *Chansons de Paris* (de Baroncelli)
1935   *Touche-à-tour* (Dréville)
1936   *Le Coupable* (Bernard); *Courrier-Sud* (Billon); *Trois . . . six . . . neuf* (Rouleau)
1937   *Yoshiwara* (Ophüls)
1938   *L'Ange que j'ai vendu* (Bernheim); *J'étais une aventurière* (Bernard); *La Marseillaise* (Renoir)
1939   *Battement de coeur* (Decoin); *Le Monde tremblera* (Pottier)

Films as Art Director:

1940   *Volpone* (Tourneur)
1942   *Les Visiteurs du soir* (*The Devil's Envoys*) (Carné); *L'Honorable Catherine* (L'Herbier)
1943   *Les Mystères de Paris* (de Baroncelli); *Lumière d'été* (Gremillon) (co)
1945   **Les Enfants du paradis** (*Children of Paradise*) (Carné) (co); *Boule de suif* (Christian-Jaque)
1946   *L'Idiot* (*The Idiot*) (Lampin); *Le Chanteur inconnu* (Cayatte); *Le Silence est d'or* (Clair)
1947   *Les Dernières Vacances* (Leenhardt); *Eternel conflit* (Lampin) (co)
1949   *Pattes blanches* (Grémillon); *Maya* (Bernard); *Le Beauté du diable* (*Beauty and the Devil*) (Clair)
1950   *Le Château de verre* (Clément)
1951   *Deux sous de violettes* (Anouilh)
1952   *Rome ore 11* (*Rome 11 O'Clock*) (De Santis); *Les Belles de nuit* (*Beauties of the Night*) (Clair); *Les Amants de Tolède* (Decoin); *Violettes impériales* (Pottier); *La Dame aux camélias* (Bernard)
1953   *Leur dernière nuit* (Lacombe); *La Belle de Cadix* (Bernard)
1954   *Le Grand Jeu* (*Flesh and Women*) (Siodmak); *Bel-Ami* (Daquin); **Les Diaboliques** (*Diabolique*) (Clouzot); *Les Fruits de l'été* (Bernard)
1955   *Les Grandes Manoeuvres* (*The Grand Maneuver*) (Clair); *The Ambassador's Daughter* (Krasna)
1956   *Les Aventures de Till L'Espiègle* (Philipe); *Michel Strogoff* (Gallone)
1957   *Porte de Lilas* (*Gates of Paris*) (Clair); *Pot Bouille* (Duvivier)
1959   *Le Chemin des écoliers* (Boisrond); *Les Arrivistes* (Daquin); *Recours en grace* (Benedek)
1960   *La Croix des vivants* (*Cross of the Living*) (Govar)
1961   *Tout l'or du monde* (Clair)
1962   *The Longest Day* (Annakin, Marton, and Wicki) (co); "Les Deux Pigeons" ["The Two Pigeons"] ep. of *Les Quatres Vérités* (*Three Fables of Love*) (Clair)
1963   *Symphonie pour un massacre* (*Symphony for a Massacre*) (Deray); *Der Besuch* (*The Visit*) (Wicki)
1965   *Trois chambres à Manhattan* (Carné)
1966   *Le Soleil noir* (de la Patellière)
1967   *J'ai tué Raspoutine* (Hossein); *Diaboliquement vôtre* (Duvivier)
1968   *Phèdre* (Jourdan)

Film as Designer:

1948   *Tous les chemins mènent à Rome* (Boyer)

Publications

By BARSACQ: book—

Le Décor de film, Paris, 1970.

By BARSACQ: article—

"Le Décor de Lazare Meerson," in *Jacques Feyder*, Brussels, 1949.

On BARSACQ: article—

Cinématographe (Paris), March 1982.

*   *   *

Léon Barsacq was one of the leading art directors of his time. Yet his greater importance will almost certainly lie in his ideas about set design as an art and in his documentation of the history of film design. The Russian-born Barsacq trained in architecture and decorative arts in Paris before becoming an assistant designer on films by Andrei Andrejew and others. Among his early work as an art director, the most memorable settings appear in Marcel Carné's and Jacques Prévert's *Les Enfants du paradis*, for which Barsacq collaborated with Alexandre Trauner and Raymond Gabutti. In its density of detail, its visual richness and atmosphere, this was a masterpiece of style defying the austerity of occupied France.

In *Les Enfants du paradis* and other of his early films, such as *La Marseillaise*, directed by Jean Renoir, the elaboration of settings did not, perhaps, totally comply with Barsacq's premise that design should subordinate itself to narrative, simply lending atmospheric support. But as the complexities of style which dominate Occupation films gave way to a simpler imagery in the 1950s, Barsacq's work developed a more sketchlike style. His best sets achieve a delicate balance between realism and artifice. Barsacq was an elegant Beaux Arts draftsman whose drawings reflected his ability to find the essence of a setting without resorting to obvious trickery.

Barsacq's closest liaisons were with René Clair and Marcel Carné. Clair said of his designs, "reality paled alongside its imitation." Jean Renoir, too, was among his collaborators. Like the directors with whom he worked, Barsacq drew inspiration from such painters as Daumier, for the Boulevard du Crime in *Les Enfants du paradis*, and Breughel, for the sets in *Les Aventures de Till L'Espiègle*.

Barsacq worked among the French pioneers in the use of color during the early 1950s, the so-called "heroic" period of color film. Early color films with sets by Barsacq include Richard Pottier's *Violettes impériales* and Raymond Bernard's *La Dame aux camélias*. The expensive Technicolor process and the uncertain Belgian Gevacolor system were used until the introduction of the more controllable Eastmancolor, for which Barsacq designed sets in Calir's *Les Grandes Manoeuvres*. By limiting his palette of colors to neutral tones with only occasional use of strong color, Barsacq confirmed the aesthetic merit of color in producing atmospheric effects.

Barsacq's designs of the 1960s for films such as *The Longest Day* and *Trois Chambres à Manhattan*, have been treated with less interest by critics than his earlier work. This was due partly to the overwhelming fashion for *cinéma vérité* in the later 1950s and early 1960s, which attempted to abandon artificiality and contrivance in design and all other aspects of the film. But as a historian of film design, Barsacq was highly productive in his later years. Published in 1970, his book *Le Décor de film* not only contains a wealth of information, but also proposes a clear aesthetic postulate on film design and, consequently, has become the standard text on its subject.

—Gregory Votolato

BASEVI, James

Art Director. **Nationality:** British. **Born:** Plymouth, England, 1890. **Education:** Studied architecture. **Military Service:** British Army during World War I: colonel. **Career:** Emigrated to Canada, then to the United States, c. 1924; designer in late 1920s, and special effects director, mid-1930s, MGM; then art director, 1939–43, and supervising art director, 1943–44, 20th Century-Fox; 1945—head of art department, Vanguard Films; then freelance designer. **Awards:** Academy Award, for *The Song of Bernadette*, 1943. **Died:** 27 March 1962, in Bellflower, California.

Films as Art Director:

1925   *Soul Mates* (Conway); *The Circle* (Borzage); **The Big Parade** (K. Vidor); *Confessions of a Queen* (Sjöström); *The Tower of Lies* (Sjöström)
1926   *Bardelys the Magnificent* (Whatham) (co); *Dance Madness* (Leonard); *Love's Blindness* (Dillon); *The Temptress* (Niblo)
1938   *The Cowboy and the Lady* (Potter)
1939   *Raffles* (Wood); *Wuthering Heights* (Wyler); *The Real Glory* (Hathaway)
1940   *The Long Voyage Home* (Ford); *The Westerner* (Wyler)
1941   *Tobacco Road* (Ford); *A Yank in the R.A.F.* (H. King)
1942   *The Black Swan* (H. King); *Moontide* (Mayo); *Thunder Birds* (Wellman); *China Girl* (Hathaway); *Son of Fury* (Cromwell)
1943   *Bomber's Moon* (Fuhr); *Claudia* (Goulding); *The Dancing Masters* (St. Clair); *Guadalcanal Diary* (Seiler); *The Gang's All Here* (*The Girls He Left Behind*) (Berkeley); *Happy Land* (Pichel); *Heaven Can Wait* (Lubitsch); *Hello, Frisco, Hello* (Humberstone); *Holy Matrimony* (Stahl); *Jitterbugs* (St. Clair); *The Moon Is Down* (Pichel); *The Ox-Bow Incident* (*Strange Incident*) (Wellman); *Paris after Dark* (*The Night Is Ending*) (Moguy); *The Song of Bernadette* (H. King); *Stormy Weather* (Stone); *Sweet Rosie O'Grady* (Cummings); *They Came to Blow Up America* (Ludwig); *Wintertime* (Brahm)
1944   *Lifeboat* (Hitchcock); *Bermuda Mystery* (Stroloff); *Buffalo Bill* (Wellman); *The Eve of St. Mark* (Stahl); *Four Jills in a Jeep* (Weiter); *Greenwich Village* (W. Lang); *Home in Indiana* (Hathaway); *Jane Eyre* (Stevenson); *In the Meantime, Darling* (Preminger); *Ladies of Washington* (L. King); *The Keys of the Kingdom* (Stahl); *The Lodger* (Brahm); *Pin-Up Girl* (Humberstone); *The Purple Heart* (Milestone); *Roger Touhy, Gangster* (*The Last Gangster*) (Florey); *The Sullivans* (Bacon); *Tampico* (Mendes); *Wilson* (H. King)
1945   *Spellbound* (Hitchcock)

1946   *Claudia and David* (W. Lang); *The Dark Corner* (Hathaway); *Duel in the Sun* (K. Vidor); *Home, Sweet Homicide* (Bacon); *It Shouldn't Happen to a Dog* (Leeds); *Johnny Comes Flying Home* (Stoloff); *Somewhere in the Night* (Mankiewicz); *Strange Triangle* (*Strange Alibi*) (McCarey); *Margie* (H. King); *13 Rue Madeline* (Hathaway); *If I'm Lucky* (Seiler); **My Darling Clementine** (Ford) (co)
1947   *The Brasher Doubloon* (*The High Window*) (Brahm); *Captain from Castile* (H. King); *The Homestretch* (Humberstone); *Carnival on Costa Rica* (Ratoff); *The Late George Apley* (Mankiewicz); *The Shocking Miss Pilgrim* (Seaton); *Boomerang!* (Kazan); *Thunder in the Valley* (*Bob, Son of Battle*) (L. King)
1948   *Fort Apache* (Ford); *Three Godfathers* (Ford)
1949   *Mighty Joe Young* (Schoedsack); *She Wore a Yellow Ribbon* (Ford)
1950   *To Please a Lady* (Brown); *Wagonmaster* (Ford); *Across the Wide Missouri* (Wellman)
1951   *Night into Morning* (Markle); *The People against O'Hara* (J. Sturges); *Just This Once* (Weis)
1952   *My Man and I* (Wellman)
1953   *Battle Circus* (R. Brooks); *Island in the Sky* (Wellman)
1954   **East of Eden** (Kazan)
1956   **The Searchers** (Ford)

Films as Special Effects Artist:

1929   *The Mysterious Island* (Hubbard)
1937   *History Is Made at Night* (Borzage); *Dead End* (Wyler); *The Hurricane* (Ford)
1938   *The Adventures of Marco Polo* (Mayo); *Blockade* (Dieterle)

*   *   *

During Hollywood's Golden Age, James Basevi was one of the most successful and innovative set designers and special effects men working for the major studios. He made films with many of the greatest directors of his time including William Wyler, William Wellman, John Ford, and Elia Kazan. Both in collaboration with other leading designers and on his own, Basevi created some of the most memorable visual images in American film history.

Within a short time after his arrival in Hollywood around 1924, Basevi was an assistant to the highly influential Cedric Gibbons, working on silent classics such as *The Big Parade*. Among numerous consultancies and collaborations, Basevi's work with Richard Day is particularly notable. Their films together include *Bardelys the Magnificent*, *The Hurricane*, and *Captain from Castile*.

During the 1930s Basevi proved to be one of the greatest masters of special effects. In 1935, as head of MGM's special effects department, he collaborated with Arnold Gillespie on the lengthy and memorable earthquake sequence in *San Francisco*. This was, at that time, the most ambitious and technically exacting recreation of a natural catastrophe ever attempted; and even with the passage of many years, it remains extremely convincing. For John Ford's *The Hurricane*, a 1937 vehicle for Dorothy Lamour, Basevi devised a 600-foot miniature set representing a tropical island village which was to be deluged by a gigantic tidal wave. The wave effect was produced by releasing many thousands of gallons of water onto the model in a controlled manner through tall, specially designed and constructed channels. The result is one of the most believable storms ever filmed using studio miniatures.

As art director at Twentieth Century-Fox Studios from 1939 to 1944, later as head of the art department at Vanguard Films, and in subsequent freelance work, Basevi demonstrated a special skill in creating highly atmospheric images of the Old West. His sets for John Ford's *My Darling Clementine* and *She Wore a Yellow Ribbon* display the visual conventions of the Western genre at their most refined and persuasive.

—Gregory Votolato

BASS, Ronald

Nationality: American. **Born:** Ronald Jay Bass in Los Angeles, 1943. **Education:** Became a voracious reader while bedridden as a child; attended Stanford University, where he studied political science; awarded a Woodrow Wilson fellowship to Yale University, where he continued his studies; graduated from Harvard Law School. **Family:** Married Gail Weinstein (divorced); married Christine Steinmann; two daughters, Jennifer and Sasha. **Career:** Began working in the motion picture industry as an entertainment lawyer, 1967; re-worked *Voleur*, a novel he had written while a teen-ager, which was published as *The Perfect Thief*, 1978; wrote two additional novels, *Lime's Crisis*, 1982, and *The Emerald Illusion*, 1984; abandoned his law practice to write full-time, 1984; authored his first produced screenplay, *Code Name: Emerald*, based on *The Emerald Illusion*, 1985; worked as executive producer on two network TV series, *Maloney* and *Dangerous Minds*, 1996; signed an exclusive three-year writing and producing deal with Sony Pictures Entertainment, 1998; was one of 30 screenwriters to sign a pact with Sony Pictures Entertainment that will enable them to earn at least two per cent of a film's gross receipts, plus upfront fees, 1999. **Awards:** Best Original Screenplay Academy Award (shared with Barry Morrow), for *Rain Man*, 1988; ShoWest Convention Screenwriter of the Year, 1998. **Address:** c/o Beth Swafford, Creative Artists Agency, 9830 Wilshire Blvd., Beverly Hills, CA 90212, USA.

Films as Writer: (sometimes credited as Ron Bass)

1985   *Code Name Emerald* (*Emerald*) (Sanger) (based on his novel)
1986   *Black Widow* (Rafelson)
1987   *Gardens of Stone* (Coppola)
1988   *Rain Man* (Levinson) (co-sc)
1991   *Sleeping With the Enemy* (Ruben)
1993   *The Joy Luck Club* (Wang) (co-sc, + co-pr)
1994   *When a Man Loves a Woman* (Mandoki) (co-sc, + co-exec pr, ro as AA Man #1); *The Enemy Within* (Darby—for TV) (co-sc); *Reunion* (Grant—for TV) (co-sc)
1995   *Waiting to Exhale* (Whitaker) (+ co-exec pr); *Dangerous Minds* (Smith)
1997   *My Best Friend's Wedding* (Hogan) (+ co-pr)
1998   *How Stella Got Her Groove Back* (Sullivan) (co-sc, + co-exec pr); *What Dreams May Come* (Ward) (+ co-exec pr); *Stepmom* (Columbus) (co-sc, + co-exec pr)

1999   *New Kid on the Block* (Hogan); *Border Line* (Kwapis—for TV) (co-sc, + story); *Invisible Child* (Silver—for TV) (co-sc); *Swing Vote* (Anspaugh—for TV) (co-sc); *Entrapment* (Amiel) (co-sc, + co-story, co-exec pr); *Snow Falling on Cedars* (Hicks) (co-sc, + co-pr)
2000   *Passion of Mind* (Berliner) (co-sc) (+ co-pr)
2001   *The Shipping News*

Publications

By BASS: books—

The Perfect Thief, New York, 1978.
Lime's Crisis, New York, 1982.
The Emerald Illusion, New York, 1984.
With Scott Hicks, *Snow Falling on Cedars: The Shooting Script*, New York, 1999.

By BASS: articles—

"Joy & Luck in Hollywood," interview with Jeff Schwager, in *MovieMaker* (Los Angeles), January 1994.
"*My Best Friend's Wedding*," interview in *Romantic Times* (Brooklyn, New York), July 1997.

On BASS: books—

Schanzer, Karl and Thomas Lee Wright, *American Screenwriters: The Insiders' Look at the Art, the Craft, and the Business of Writing Movies*, New York, 1993.

On BASS: articles—

Weinraub, Bernard, "When a Man (a Lawyer!) Writes About Women," in *New York Times*, 24 April 1994.
Bart, Peter, "Bass-o-Matic," in *Gentlemen's Quarterly* (New York), October 1998.
Strauss, Bob, "It's Quality and Quantity for Passionate Screenwriter," in *Los Angeles Daily News*, 19 October 1998.
Friend, Tad, "Letter from Hollywood: The Two-Billion-Dollar Man," in *New Yorker*, 24 January 2000.
"Film: The Most Powerful Writer in the World," in *The Independent* (London), 21 May 2000.

*   *   *

In 1988, Ron Bass had only a trio of produced screenplays to his credit. That year, he won an Academy Award for co-writing *Rain Man*, which remains among the most fondly recalled films of its era. Since then, he has been one of Hollywood's most prolific and in-demand screenwriters, establishing himself as a reliable scripter whose films generally are inspirational in content as they spotlight human needs, desires, and relations. Furthermore, in an industry in which the screenwriter often is undervalued, if not the object of outright scorn, Bass's savvy business sense, combined with his professional roots as an entertainment lawyer, have allowed him to cannily market himself as a high-profile—and highly-paid—scenarist.

Bass occasionally will be associated with a popcorn action movie. One such title is *Code Name: Emerald*, his first screen credit, a by-the-numbers espionage yarn based on one of his novels. Another is *Entrapment*, a tired older man-younger woman romantic thriller featuring Sean Connery and Catherine Zeta-Jones. However, the majority of his scripts tell humanistic stories and feature characters who are struggling to find happiness and inner peace within themselves and in their relationships with others.

Many of his scripts feature strong female characters; even *Entrapment* pits an insurance investigator who is as tough as she is attractive against a sly veteran thief. Bass's screenplays have examined the plights of, and delineated issues related to, minority women: *The Joy Luck Club* (based on the novel by Amy Tan); and *Waiting to Exhale* and *How Stella Got Her Groove Back* (both adaptations of books by Terry McMillan). They have explored the complexities of relations between the races: *Dangerous Minds*, about a "white bread" teacher/ex-marine who struggles to inspire her African-American and Hispanic charges; and *Snow Falling on Cedars*, in which a Japanese-American fisherman is accused of murder and a white reporter covering the case finds that the man's Japanese-American wife was his own boyhood love. Some are inter-generational sagas: *Gardens of Stone*, spotlighting a veteran soldier who believes the war in Vietnam is a folly and a young, raw, anxious-for-combat recruit. They have examined the intricacies of friendship: *My Best Friend's Wedding*, in which a woman is jarred when the man who has been her best pal becomes engaged to another. Or, they have charted the complexities of inter-familial relationships and crises, focusing on characters who patronize, disregard, or despise each other but come to understandings: *When a Man Loves a Woman* (about an alcoholic wife-mother and her mildly condescending husband); *Stepmom* (in which a cancer-stricken ex-wife-mother first opposes but then unites with her former husband's girlfriend); and, of course, *Rain Man* (in which a self-absorbed young man establishes a bond with his autistic older brother).

Bass's most fanciful screenplays explore other-worldly existences, alternative realities that are the outgrowths of an individual's dreams, or an individual's death. *What Dreams May Come* depicts a concrete, fully-visualized afterlife for its main character, who dies, ends up in heaven, and then must venture from paradise to save his wife/soulmate, who has committed suicide and gone to hell. In *Passion of Mind*, a woman concocts a make-believe reality in her dreams, and then must ascertain which of her lives is authentic and which is illusion. Both of these films explore their main characters' deep-seated longings, fears, and fantasies—and, by extension, those of the viewer.

Quite a few of Bass's scripts are adaptations of novels. He has transformed books by such diverse writers as Tan, McMillan, Nicholas Proffitt (*Gardens of Stone*), Nancy Price (*Sleeping With the Enemy*), Charles W. Bailey II and Fletcher Knebel (*Seven Days in May*, the source material for the TV movie *The Enemy Within*), LouAnne Johnson (*My Posse Don't Do Homework*, the source material for *Dangerous Minds*), Richard Matheson (*What Dreams May Come*), and David Guterson (*Snow Falling on Cedars*). With regard to how he goes about adapting a novel into a screenplay, Bass once observed, "My basic view of film is that, literature is about what happens within people, while film is more about what happens between people. So the basic tool for me is the two-shot, a scene

between two people interacting in a way that illuminates for them and for us who they are, what they want, and where they're going."

At a point in time in which a majority of Hollywood movies seem to be about special effects or teens intent on losing their virginity, Bass's films spotlight character development and explore human emotions. His strength is in writing dramatic scenes, in which characters reveal their innermost feelings or connect with others—and he has come to be depended upon for his ability to fashion such sequences. The original draft of *Stepmom*, an autobiographical effort penned by Gigi Levangie, was a blend of comedy and drama. It was deemed unacceptable by the potential stars, Susan Sarandon and Julia Roberts. Bass eventually was hired to rework the script, to excise the comic aspects and highlight the dramatic ones—resulting in Sarandon's and Roberts's agreeing to sign onto the project.

Conversely, to some, Bass's screenplays are unabashedly sentimental, not to mention formulaic. They wallow in touchy-feely emotion and, in the grand Hollywood tradition, they have manufactured happy endings. The production notes of his films may refer to him as "one of the film industry's preeminent screenwriter(s)" and add that his films "have earned well over $1 billion in box-office revenues worldwide." However, one critic has even gone so far as to label him a "powerful industry hack."

Bass started out in the business as an entertainment lawyer—an industry type whom his creative counterpart might disdainfully label a "suit"—and so it is no surprise that most of his films, for better or worse, are strictly and safely mainstream. For example, during the 1990s, dozens of independent features offered in-depth explorations of the romantic lives and lifestyles of gays and lesbians. In Hollywood movies, homosexuals finally have a non-disapproving presence, but only as poignantly tragic figures (in *Philadelphia*), comic figures (*The Birdcage*), and, most notoriously, as sexually neutered buddies (*As Good as It Gets* and Bass's *My Best Friend's Wedding*, in which the heroine and her gay sidekick set out to torpedo her pal's nuptials). So Bass's screenplays usually are tame, and rarely are cutting-edge. And he fully understands and accepts his role within the filmmaking process. He has noted that "you judge a writer's work by what the final film looks like, but there are a lot of other people whose decisions (come into how a) film is going to be presented, and ultimately of course the author of every film is the director. He's the guy that makes the final decisions."

With this in mind, Bass has endured the everyday indignities of the screenwriter. Many of his scripts have been rejected and gone unproduced, or have been altered by others; Elaine May, for one, was hired to make revisions on *Dangerous Minds*. Yet he is no underpaid, underappreciated ink-stained wretch. Given his background as an entertainment lawyer, Bass fully understands the sources of power in the motion picture industry. And so he has astutely established himself as a mini-writing factory, penning several screenplays at once and charging $2-million per script. Assisting him are six writer-researchers, who are known as his Team—and who a number of his friends have dubbed The Ronettes.

Since *The Joy Luck Club* in 1993, he also has received a producer credit on many of the films he has scripted. In the late 1990s, he agreed to an exclusive three-year writing and producing deal with Sony Pictures Entertainment. Then he was among a group of 30 screenwriters who signed a landmark, controversial pact with Sony that will result in their earning at least two per cent of a movie's gross receipts, in addition to upfront fees. The deal was negotiated without input from either the Writers Guild of America or the scenarists' managers and agents.

—Rob Edelman

BASS, Saul

Title Designer and Director. **Nationality:** American. **Born:** New York City, 8 May 1920. **Education:** Studied under Howard Trafton, Art Students League, New York, 1936–39; under Gyorgy Kepes, Brooklyn College, 1944–45. **Family:** Married Elaine Makatura, 1961, one daughter and one son. **Career:** 1936–46—freelance designer, New York; 1946—founded Saul Bass and Associates, Los Angeles (became Saul Bass/Herb Yager and Associates, 1978); 1954—first film as title designer, *Carmen Jones*; 1962—first film as director, *Apples and Oranges*; also designed trailers, film posters, commercials, title credits for television, package design, and corporation logos. **Awards:** Academy Award, for short film *Why Man Creates*, 1968. **Died:** 25 April 1996.

Films as Title Designer:

1954 *Carmen Jones* (Preminger)
1955 *The Big Knife* (Aldrich); *The Man with the Golden Arm* (Preminger); *The Racers* (*Such Men Are Dangerous*) (Hathaway); *The Seven Year Itch* (Wilder); *The Shrike* (J. Ferrer)
1956 *Attack!* (Aldrich); *Storm Center* (Taradash)
1957 *Saint Joan* (Preminger); *Edge of the City* (*A Man Is Ten Feet Tall*) (Ritt); *Around the World in Eighty Days* (Anderson); *Bonjour Tristesse* (Preminger); *The Pride and the Passion* (Kramer); *The Young Stranger* (Frankenheimer)
1958 *The Big Country* (Wyler); *Cowboy* (Daves); **Vertigo** (Hitchcock)
1959 *Anatomy of a Murder* (Preminger); **North by Northwest** (Hitchcock)
1960 *Ocean's Eleven* (Milestone); **Psycho** (Hitchcock); *The Facts of Life* (Frank); *Spartacus* (Kubrick)
1961 *Exodus* (Preminger); **West Side Story** (Wise and Robbins); *Something Wild* (Garfein)
1962 *Walk on the Wild Side* (Dmytryk); *Advise and Consent* (Preminger)
1963 *The Cardinal* (Preminger); *Nine Hours to Rama* (Robson)
1964 *The Victors* (Foreman)
1965 *In Harm's Way* (Preminger); *Bunny Lake Is Missing* (Preminger)
1966 *Grand Prix* (Frankenheimer); *Not with My Wife, You Don't* (Panama); *Seconds* (Frankenheimer)
1971 *Such Good Friends* (Preminger)
1976 *That's Entertainment, Part II* (Kelly—compilation)
1987 *Broadcast News* (J. Brooks)
1988 *Big* (P. Marshall)
1989 *The War of the Roses* (DeVito)
1990 **GoodFellas** (Scorsese)
1991 *Cape Fear* (Scorsese)
1992 *Mr. Saturday Night* (Crystal)
1993 *The Age of Innocence* (Scorsese)
1995 *Casino* (Scorsese)

Other Films:

1962 *Apples and Oranges* (pr, + d—short)
1964 *From Here to There* (pr, + d, co-sc—short); *History of Adventure* (d—short); *Packaging Story* (d—short); *The Searching Eye* (d, + co-sc—short)
1968 *Why Man Creates* (d, + co-sc—short)
1973 *Phase IV* (d)
1977 *One Hundred Years of the Telephone* (d—short)
1978 *Notes on the Popular Arts* (d—short)
1980 *The Solar Film* (d—short)
1983 *The Quest* (co-d)

Publications

By BASS: articles—

''Film Titles,'' in *Graphis*, vol. 16, no. 89, 1960.
Cinema (Beverly Hills, California), Fall 1968.
American Cinematographer (Hollywood), March 1977.
Interview by P. Murat and B. Génin, in *Banc-Titre* (Paris), April 1984.
Interview with Bass and Billy Wilder by P. Kirkham, in *Sight and Sound* (London), June 1995.
Interview by Pamela Haskin, in *Film Quarterly* (Berkeley), Fall 1996.

On BASS: book—

Nelson, G., *Saul Bass*, New York, 1967.
Morgenstern, Joe, *Saul Bass: A Life in Film Design*, Santa Monica, 1997.

On BASS: articles—

Print (New York), May/June 1958.
Foster, Frederick, in *American Cinematographer* (Hollywood), June 1962.
Gid, R., in *Graphis*, vol. 19, no. 106, 1963.
Rondolino, G., in *Filmzelezione* (Bologna), no. 15–16, 1963.
Allen, Bob, in *American Cinematographer* (Hollywood), December 1963.
Skoop (Amsterdam), March 1968.
Bianco e Nero (Rome), September/October 1968.
Jacobs, Lewis, in *The Emergence of Film Art*, 1969.
Communication Arts (Palo Alto, California), August/September 1969.
Sohn, David A., in *Film: The Creative Eye*, London, 1970.
Cinéma (Paris), January and March 1970.
Industrial Design (New York), March 1971.
Film Reader (Evanston, Illinois), no. 1, 1975.

Saul Bass

Cinema Papers (Melbourne), January 1977.

Image et Son (Paris), April 1981.

Film Comment (New York), May/June 1982.

Broadcast (London), 18 April 1986.

Rodman, Howard, "The Name behind the Title," in *Village Voice* (New York), 12 July 1988.

Skrien (Amsterdam), no. 165, April/May 1989.

Woudhuysen, James, "Bass Profundo" in *Design Week* (London), 22 September 1989.

Kirkham, Pat, "Looking for the Simple Idea," in *Sight and Sound* (London), February 1994.

Naughton, John, "Credit Where Credit's Due," in *Empire* (London), March 1994.

Glucksman, Mary, "Due Credit," in *Screen International* (London), 13 May 1994.

Kirkham, Pat, "Bright Lights Big City," in *Sight and Sound* (London), January 1996.

Lally, K., "Arresting Images," in *Film Journal* (New York), March 1996.

Obituary, in *Variety* (New York), 29 April 1996.

Obituary, in *Classic Images* (Muscatine), June 1996.

Obituary, in *International Documentary*, June 1996.

Wollen, Peter, and Pat Kirkham, "Compulsion/The Jeweller's Eye," in *Sight & Sound* (London), April 1997.

Supanick, Jim, "Saul Bass: 'to hit the ground running'," in *Film Comment* (New York), March-April 1997.

"Saul Bass (Commercial Artist)," in *Communications Arts*, March-April 1999.

*   *   *

If any one person can be credited with having introduced the idea of "high concept"—the single striking image or pithy phrase that immediately sums up a creative work—to the movie industry, it would have to be Saul Bass. Not that the term existed when Bass, then known as one of America's brightest graphic designers, was called in to create the poster and title design for Otto Preminger's *Carmen Jones*. Bass preferred to talk in terms of Single Appropriate Image, in contrast to the then prevalent style of selling films, which he drily summed up as "the See! See! See! approach. See the missionaries boiled in oil, see the volcano destroy the island, see the virgins of the temple! The theory was that if you talked about a film in pieces, there would be something for everyone." Instead of crassly duplicating the function of the trailer, Bass saw his task as "finding a metaphor for the film, rather than an actuality from it."

The single image he created for *Carmen Jones* was a rose, in flames; taken with the title, that said it all. His design for Preminger's next film, *The Man with the Golden Arm*, was yet more audacious: the jagged diagram of an arm groping downward, contorted with agony. Like so many of Bass's concepts, it relied on the simplest and most effective style of design, a silhouette. Initially Preminger wanted a static image for the title sequence, but after "some towering discussions" Bass won his battle to animate the arm, making it jerk in torment to the rhythm of Elmer Bernstein's doomy, small-hours jazz score. Not for the last time, Bass's title sequence packed a more formidable punch than the movie that followed it. The prowling black alley cat that prefaced *Walk on the Wild Side* was so patently the best thing in the film that, once word got around, people would come to see the credit sequence, then get up and leave once the film started.

Knowing that nothing is more universally recognizable than stylized images of the human face or body, Bass drew on this primal source for some of his most memorable designs. The paper cut-out doll, suggesting at once childish innocence and the lethal sharpness of a blade, introduced the kidnap drama of *Bunny Lake Is Missing*. For *Exodus*, clenched fists grasping at a rifle: anger, desperation, revolt, revenge, all in one charged outline. A voluptuous pair of bare female thighs (in a style borrowed from Matisse) heralded the sophisticated sex comedy *Such Good Friends*. *Bonjour Tristesse* was evoked by a made-up face (a nod here to Picasso) decorated with a single fat tear. Most famous of all was the sectioned human body that suggested both a chalked forensic outline on the ground, and the title of the film: *Anatomy of a Murder*. So potent was the concept that it has been widely plagiarized ever since.

All these organic images were for Preminger films. For Hitchcock and Wilder, two film-makers with a cooler, more analytical eye, Bass often played with abstract designs. For *The Seven Year Itch*, a sex farce rather than sex comedy, Bass created the abstract equivalent of the multiple doors of a Feydeau intrigue: a patchwork of colored rectangles that one by one slid aside to reveal the film's title and credits lurking coyly behind them. *Vertigo*'s credit sequence started with the close-up of an eye wide with horror, out of which spun dizzying, spidery vortices. Thin lines, criss-crossing each other straight up and diagonally, gave *North by Northwest* its sense of direction before resolving themselves into the huge impersonal skyscraper from which Cary Grant is about to emerge. Lines again for *Psycho*, but this time thick and destructive, bludgeoning in from the sides of the screen to split apart the names of the cast, as Norman Bates is mentally split, as Marion Crane will be split by his knife.

Working in close collaboration with his wife Elaine (whose name deserves to stand with his on many of his films), Bass restlessly began to explore ways in which the title sequence could become part of the narrative itself, acting as a launch pad. "My view . . . was that something could happen during the credits that could help the film, so that the establishing shots aren't carrying the total burden." From encapsulating the film, through setting the mood, it was a small step to using the credits to tell part of the story. In *The Big Country*, Gregory Peck's journey from the urbane east coast to the frontier is conveyed, vividly and succinctly, in the title sequence. For Carl Foreman's *The Victors* Bass paid homage to the great montage-maker Slavko Vorkapich with a montage that whisked through the major events of history between World Wars I and II. Sometimes his credit sequences served as epilogue rather than prologue, as in *Around the World in Eighty Days*, allowing the audience to put names to all the multiple cameos they had seen, or *West Side Story*, where Bass intended the

credits—scrawled as graffiti on tenement blocks—to act as "a sort of decompression chamber, to give the audience a chance to pull themselves together after the terrible denouement."

Having supplied the beginnings and ends of films, Bass made the logical move into directing sequences within the body of the film. Though Hitchcock always denied it, it is widely believed that Bass not only storyboarded but directed the notorious shower murder in *Psycho*; certainly no one disputes that he directed many of the car-racing sequences in Frankenheimer's *Grand Prix* and the climactic battle scene in *Spartacus*. His own foray into feature directing, though, the science-fiction film *Phase IV*, proved competent but strangely anonymous, as if Bass's creative urge needed the compression and concentration of the brief span to function at full throttle.

Bass's title designs defined a whole era of American filmmaking, and were hugely influential. Among his followers was Maurice Binder, who designed the "walking gun" titles for the Bond films. For a time, perhaps inevitably for the creator of such a specific look, Bass fell out of fashion and concentrated on his industrial design work. Between 1971 and 1987 he designed credits for only a single feature, the compilation film *That's Entertainment, Part II*. But in the last decade of his life he was back in demand, eagerly embracing new technologies to create intricate title designs for four of Scorsese's films. Beautiful, complex, and hypnotic, this late work lacks something of the stark immediacy of his classic period. But Bass's status as the first and so far the only auteur of title design seems, for the moment, safe from challenge.

—Philip Kemp

BEATON, (Sir) Cecil

Costume Designer. **Nationality:** British. **Born:** Cecil Walter Hardy Beaton in London, 14 January 1904. **Education:** Attended Heath Mount School, London; Harrow School; St. Cyprian's School, Eastbourne; St. John's College, Cambridge, 1922–25. **Career:** 1925–26—clerk, Schmiegelow cement company, London; then freelance portrait and fashion photographer (contract with Condé Nast Publications, particularly for *Vogue* magazine, 1930-mid-1950s); also stage designer from 1925, and costume and set designer for films from 1941. **Awards:** Academy Awards for *Gigi*, 1958; *My Fair Lady*, 1964. Chevalier, Legion of Honor, 1960; Commander, Order of the British Empire, 1957; Knighted, 1972. **Died:** In Broadchalke, Wiltshire, 18 January 1980.

Films as Costume Designer:

1941   *Kipps* (*The Remarkable Mr. Kipps*) (Recd); *Major Barbara* (Pascal); *Dangerous Moonlight* (*Suicide Squadron*) (Hurst)
1946   *Beware of Pity* (Elvey)
1947   *Anna Karenina* (Duvivier)
1948   *An Ideal Husband* (Korda)
1957   *The Truth about Women* (Box)
1959   *The Doctor's Dilemma* (Asquith)
1970   *On a Clear Day You Can See Forever* (Minnelli) (co)

Cecil Beaton

Other Films:

1942   *The Young Mr. Pitt* (Reed) (costume design + art d)
1958   *Gigi* (Minnelli) (costume + pr design)
1965   *My Fair Lady* (Cukor) (costume + pr design)

Publications

By BEATON: books—

The Book of Beauty, London, 1930.
Scrapbook, London, 1937.
New York, London, 1938, as *Portrait of New York*, New York, 1938.
My Royal Past (as Baroness von Bulop), London, 1939, revised edition, 1960.
Time Exposure, text by Peter Quennell, London, 1941.
History under Fire, text by James Pope-Hennessy, London, 1941
Winged Squadrons, London, 1942.
Near East, London, 1943.

(Editor) *British Photographers*, London, 1944.
Face to Face with China, text by H. B. Rattenburg, London, 1945.
Far East, London, 1945.
Air of Glory, London, 1946.
Indian Album, London, 1946.
Chinese Album, London, 1946.
(Editor) Whistler, Rex, *Designs for the Theatre*, London, 1947.
Ashcombe: The Story of a 15 Year Lease, London, 1947.
The School for Scandal, text by Sheridan, London, 1949.
Ballet, London, 1951.
Photobiography, London, 1951.
With Kenneth Tynan, *Persona Grata*, London, 1953.
The Glass of Fashion, London, 1954.
It Gives Me Great Pleasure, London, 1955, as *I Take Great Pleasure*, New York, 1955.
The Face of the World, London, 1957.
Images, London, 1959.
The Importance of Being Earnest, text by Wilde, London, 1960.
The Wandering Years: Diaries 1922–39, London, 1961.
Quail in Aspic: The Life Story of Count Charles Korsetz, London, 1962.

Royal Portraits, London, 1963.

My Fair Lady, London, 1964, as *Cecil Beaton's Fair Lady*, New York, 1964.

The Years Between: Diaries 1939–44, London, 1965.

The Best of Beaton, London, 1968.

(Editor) *Fashion*, London, 1971.

My Bolivian Aunt: A Memoir, London, 1971.

The Happy Years: Diaries 1944–48, London, 1972, as *Memories of the 40's*, New York, 1972.

Salisbury, A New Approach to the City and Its Neighbourhood, text by Hugh de Shortt, London, 1972.

The Strenuous Years: Diaries 1948–55, London, 1973.

With Gail Buckland, *The Magic Image: The Genius of Photography from 1839 to the Present Day*, London, 1975.

The Restless Years: Diaries 1955–63, London, 1976.

The Parting Years: Diaries 1963–74, London, 1978.

Self-Portrait with Friends: The Selected Diaries, edited by Richard Buckle, London, 1979.

War Photographs 1939–45, London, 1981.

Beaton in Vogue, edited by Josephine Ross, London, 1986.

By BEATON: article—

Interview with Penelope Tree, in *Inter/View* (New York), April 1973.

On BEATON: books—

Danziger, James, editor, *Beaton*, London, 1980.

Vickers, Hugo, *Cecil Beaton: The Authorized Biography*, London, 1985.

Mellor, David, editor, *Cecil Beaton*, London, 1994.

Souhami, Diana, *Greta & Cecil*, London, 1994.

Spencer, Charles, *Cecil Beaton Stage and Film Designs*, Academy Editions, 1995.

Vickers, Hugo, *Loving Garbo: The Story of Greta Garbo, Cecil Beaton, and Mercedes de Acosta*, London, 1995.

On BEATON: articles—

Chierichetti, David, in *Hollywood Costume Design*, New York, 1976.

LaVine, W. Robert, in *In a Glamorous Fashion*, New York, 1980.

The Annual Obituary 1980, New York, 1981.

Richardson, John, "The Eternally Fashionable Cecil Beaton," in *Vanity Fair* (New York), August 1986.

Perl, Jed, "Grand Delusions: The Luxurious Worlds of Fragonard and Beaton," in *Vogue*, vol. 178, February 1988.

Wade, Marcia J., in *Horizon*, vol. 31, March 1988.

Roth, Evelyn, "On Being and Beaton," in *American Photographer*, vol. 23, December 1989.

Hastings, S., "Strange Interlude," in *New Yorker*, 11 July 1994.

"Cecil Beaton, Philippe Garner and David Alan Mellor," in *Metro*, no. 102, 1995.

Diederichsen, Diedrich, "Stage Frights: Art Trends in Berlin, Germany," in *Artforum*, April 1998.

Schonauer, David, "Fame's Birth," in *American Photo*, January 2000.

*   *   *

Cecil Beaton is best known as a photographer, whose major work included fashion images for *Vogue* and *Harper's Bazaar*, images of the Second World War for the British government, and portraits of prominent figures from society, the performing arts, and the movies. In terms of motion pictures, Beaton will be remembered for his designs for *Gigi* and *My Fair Lady*.

His designs for these films can be described as elegant and swanky. In both there is a high degree of realistic detail and attention to historical accuracy in furnishings and costumes. Nevertheless there are striking and unusual aspects within a mostly realistic design framework. *My Fair Lady*'s Ascot sequence, for example, is costumed entirely in black and white, but with such variety that there is no sense of dullness caused by the lack of color. Many of the costumes have organic or geometric shapes and surreal designs that recall those found in the paintings of Miro, Dali, or Picasso (all of whom had been subjects for Beaton's camera).

Beaton's experiences with fashion photography and his fascination with Hollywood's make-believe world during the early 1930s made him well-suited for designing films that emphasized dramatic and lavish costuming. His first trip to the United States in 1929 brought him to the attention of Condé Nast, for whom he worked in the following decade, making periodic trips to this country from England. In 1931 and the years following he photographed such stars as Gary Cooper, Orson Welles, Buster Keaton, Carole Lombard, Tallulah Bankhead, Marlene Dietrich, and John Wayne, often using frames of sets or other structural elements as dramatic contrasts to the figures. He continued to photograph stars throughout his life, and had a complex, but intense professional relationship with Greta Garbo from 1944 to 1955.

Beaton had experience as a theatre designer in London and New York in the 1940s and 1950s; his *My Fair Lady* film sets are expansions of the theatre designs. His experience with stage design and with the world of fashion gave him a sensibility to fabrics and to the human figure, and this, combined with his understanding of photography, a medium requiring the ability to perceive the world two-dimensionally, made him successful as a screen designer. His output on that medium was small, but well represents a particular approach to film design—lavish appearances made memorable by the use of unusual and effective details.

—Floyd W. Martin

BENNETT, Sir Richard Rodney

Composer. **Nationality:** British. **Born:** Broadstairs, Kent, England, 29 March 1936, one of three children of Rodney Bennett, a lyricist and author of children's book, and the former Joan Spink, a violinist/pianist/composer/critic who studied with Gustav Holst. **Family:** Single. **Education:** Leighton Park School, a private school in Reading, U.K.; Royal Academy of Music, composition study with Lennox Berkeley, Howard Ferguson, 1953–56; Private study with Pierre Boulez, Paris, France, 1957–58. **Career:** 1952—composed first work in serial idiom, "Put Away the Flutes" for soprano, chorus, and orchestra; 1956–1966—scored miscellaneous British shorts including *The Song of the Clouds* and *The World Assured*, the latter

Richard Rodney Bennett

a documentary about insurance; 1957—scored first feature film, *Interpol* (American title: *Pickup Alley*); 1961—one act opera, "The Ledge," staged at Sadler's Wells; 1963—scored *Billy Liar*; 1965—full length opera, "The Mines of Sulphur" received various international productions; 1966—Symphony #1 premiered at Royal Festival Hall, London; 1967—attained international cinematic prominence with *Far From the Madding Crowd*, score nominated for an Academy Award and became Bennett's first original soundtrack released on LP; 1968—Piano Concerto #1 premiered by Stephen Bishop and City of Birmingham Symphony Orchestra; 1970–71—visiting professor of composition, Peabody Conservatory of Music, Baltimore, Maryland, USA; 1971—score for *Nicholas and Alexandra* is nominated for an Academy Award,; 1974—score for *Murder on the Orient Express* nominated for Academy Award; 1977—scored film of the internationally successful British play, *Equus*, made Commander of the Order of the British Empire; 1981—"Isadora," a controversial dance-theater piece based on the life of Isadora Duncan, premiered by the Royal Ballet, London; 1984–1999—scored miscellaneous television productions; 1987—Symphony #3, commissioned by the Elgar Foundation, marked Bennett's return to tonal concert writing; 1992—scored *Enchanted April*, a film made for British television which becomes a popular theatrical release in the US; 1996—scored the Canadian film, *Swann*; 1998—Knighted; scored *The Tale of Sweeney Todd* for British television; 1999—scored *Gorbenhurst* for British television. **Awards:** Arnold Bax Society Prize, 1964; Ralph Vaughan Williams Award for Composer of the Year, 1965; Anthony Asquith Award for Film Music for *Murder On The Orient Express*, 1975; knighted, 1998. **Agent:** (film) Ian Amos, 107 Otho Court, August

Close, Brentford Dock, Middlesex TW8 8PZ, England; (performing) Caroline Oakes, Clarion/Seven Muses, 47 Whitehall Park, London N19 3TW, England.

Films as Composer:

1957   *Pickup Alley* (*Interpol*) (Gilling)
1958   *Face in the Night* (*Menace in the Night*) (Comfort); *The Man Inside* (Gilling); *The Safecracker* (Milland); *Indiscreet* (Donen)
1959   *Blind Date* (*Change Meeting*) (Losey); *The Angry Hills* (as Richard Bennett) (Aldrich); *The Devil's Disciple* (Hamilton); *The Man Who Could Cheat Death* (Fisher)
1961   *The Mark* (Green)
1962   *The Wrong Arm Of The Law* (Owen); *Satan Never Sleeps* (*The Devil Never Sleeps; Flight from Terror*) (McCarey); *Only Two Can Play* (Gilliat)
1963   *Billy Liar* (Schlesinger); *Doctor Who* (TV series) (C. Carry/ M. Barry); *Heavens Above*
1965   *One Way Pendulum* (Yates); *The Nanny* (Holt)
1966   *The Witches* (*The Devil's Own*) (Frankel)
1967   *Far from the Madding Crowd* (Schlesinger) *Billion Dollar Brain* (Russell)
1968   *Secret Ceremony* (Losey)
1969   *Figures in a Landscape* (Losey); *The Buttercup Chain* (Ellis Miller)
1971   *Nicholas and Alexandria* (Schaffner)
1972   *Lady Caroline Lamb* (Bolt)
1973   *Voices* (*Nightmare*) (Billington)
1974   *Murder on the Orient Express* (Lumet)
1975   *Permission to Kill* (Frankel)
1976   *Sherlock Holmes in New York* (TV) (Sagal)
1977   *Equus* (Lumet)
1978   *The Brink's Job* (*Big Stickup at Brink's*) (Friedkin)
1979   *Yanks* (Schlesinger)
1982   *The Return of the Soldier* (Bridges)
1984   *The Ebony Tower* (TV) (Knights)
1985   *Tender Is the Night* (TV mini-series) (Knights)
1987   *Strange Interlude* (TV) (Wise)
1988   *The Attic: The Hiding of Anne Frank* (TV) (Erman)
1992   *Enchanted April* (Newell)
1994   *Four Weddings and a Funeral* (Newell)
1996   *Swann* (Gyles)
1998   *The Tale of Sweeney Todd* (TV) (Schlesinger)
2000   *Gorbenhurst* (TV)

Publications

By BENNETT: articles—

"A Conversation with Richard Rodney Bennett," interview with Elmer Bernstein, in *Elmer Bernstein's Filmmusic Notebook*, vol. II, no. 1, 1976

"In Conversation with Richard Rodney Bennett," interview with John Caps, in *Soundtrack Collectors Newsletter*, vol. II, no. 7, July 1976

"Interview with Tom Sutcliffe," in *Manchester Guardian Weekly*, May 10, 1981.

On BENNETT: books—

Seabrook, Mike, *Richard Rodney Bennett*, Scholar Press, 1997.

*   *   *

Composing for film and television has been only one aspect of the prolific musical career of the British composer/pianist Richard Rodney Bennett. Aside from his film scores Bennett has worked equally prodigiously in concert music and opera, and has maintained a successful ''secondary'' career performing vintage popular music. In addition, Bennett was once a devotee of the new Vienna serialist school of Schoenberg and his disciples, and in the 1960s was a key member of an emerging school of new British concert composers which included Peter Maxwell-Davies, Elizabeth Luytens, and Thea Musgrave.

Bennett, however, began his professional musical career as a jazz pianist. At age 19, Bennett broke into film music when Howard Ferguson, one of Bennett's professors at the Royal Academy, introduced him to conductor John Hollingsworth in 1955 and he began scoring British short films. Feature scores soon followed (including his first, *Interpol* in 1957, and Hammer's *The Man Who Could Cheat Death* in 1959), these leading to a 1963 score for John Schlesinger's *Billy Liar*, a key film in the British cinema renaissance which evolved from the emerging international popularity of foreign (or ''art'') films in the post-studio era 1950s.

It was Bennett's association with Schlesinger which led to his first international cinematic success, a lush symphonic score for *Far from the Madding Crowd*, released by MGM in 1967. Here Bennett's atmospheric lyricism aptly captured the pantheism of Thomas Hardy's mythic Wessex countryside through the use of traditional British folk themes fused with his own folk-like motifs. The score was also a landmark of symphonic orchestral scoring for an era in which film music had become increasingly dominated by rock/pop effects. Bennett's extended cue for the scene in which Sergeant Troy seduces Bathsheba with a virtuoso display of swordsplay is one of the most striking fusions of music, image, and drama in late 20th-century film music. While the Hardy film itself was a commercial disappointment, Bennett's score became a contemporary classic, and Schlesinger would go on to direct one of the most popular American films of the 1970s, *Midnight Cowboy* in 1969.

That same year Bennett scored *Billion Dollar Brain* for another British director soon to create a major splash on the international film scene: Ken Russell. *Brain* was a manifestation of the James Bond/secret agent craze launched in the early 1960s, and was the third in a series based on Len Deighton's ''Harry Palmer'' novels. It chronicles the fantastic efforts of a mad American general to invade communist Russia, and Russell's stylish production makes several visual references to Eisenstein. Likewise, Bennett's sleekly contemporary music pays homage to Prokovief, Shostakovich and other 20th-century Russian composers. Orchestrated solely for multiple pianos, brass, percussion, and an early electronic instrument, the Ondes Martinot, Bennett's cohesive, yet sonically adventurous score includes of a kind of aural Op Art-style Main Title (and a languorous love theme cleverly derived from it), and an extended cue for the film's climactic sequence, a homage to Eisenstein's ''Battle On The Ice'' sequence from *Ivan the Terrible*. These two contrasting but distinctive scores led to Bennett's scoring more prestigious productions on the international film scene of the 1970s. He created another

big symphonic score evoking both the lyricism and brooding melancholy of Tchaikowsky for Franklin Schaffner's epic of the last days of the Romanov dynasty, *Nicholas and Alexandra* in 1971. This was followed by darkly rhapsodic music for *Lady Caroline Lamb*, Robert Bolt's 1972 film about the scandalous affair between Lord Byron and the wife of a prominent British aristocrat. (The *Lady Caroline* score was also developed and recorded as a concert piece for viola and orchestra). Sidney Lumet's 1974 *Murder On The Orient Express*, based on one of Agatha Christie's Hercule Poirot mysteries, provided a change of pace with a pastiche score which indulged Bennett's interest in period popular music, while still providing the opportunity for a number of orchestral cues in the mode of Ravel and the French impressionists.

While scoring these major international productions Bennett remained active in the more intimate realm of native British cinema. He scored several small films for American expatriate director, Joseph Losey, including *Secret Ceremony* in 1968, and *Figures In A Landscape* in 1970. For the former (a notoriously ambiguous and rather Pinteresque exercise with Elizabeth Taylor and Mia Farrow) Bennett created a delicately minimalist, partially serialized score for a chamber ensemble which aptly captured the enigmatic quality of Losey's strange film.

In 1977 Bennett produced another major score for Lumet's depressingly literal adaptation of Peter Schaffer's international stage success, *Equus*. Orchestrated solely for lower strings, Bennett's music effectively played against Schaffer's poetic, if overwrought script with a somberly melancholy yet compassionate lyricism. Bennett's last major score for the 1970s was for another Schlesinger film, 1979's *Yanks*, a modern romance about American soldiers stationed in Britain during World War II.

By the 1980s Bennett had veered away from big film scores to pursue his interest in popular music, particularly the classic songs of great American songwriters such as Porter, Warren, Gershwin, and Berlin, and to further pursue his career as a pianist, accompanist, and sometimes singer on the New York cabaret scene. The composer also scored a number of television productions during this period, among them a *Tender Is The Night* mini-series, *Strange Interlude*, and *The Attic: The Hiding of Anne Frank*. In 1992 a film which he had scored for British television, *Enchanted April*, was successfully released as a theatrical film in the United States. Along with his popular cabaret performances and solo recordings Bennett's other recent work has been for the popular *Four Weddings and A Funeral* (1994). This followed by another all-string chamber style score for the poetic murder mystery *Swann* (Canadian film, 1996). In 1998 Bennett scored another John Schlesinger film, *The Tale of Sweeney Todd*, produced for British television, a score which Bennett himself considers one of his finest. His most recent score was for another British mini-series, *Gorbenhurst*.

Concerning his film work (about which the composer has become very selective) Sir Richard Rodney Bennett has commented: ''I realized very early that I was never going to make by living by writing string quartets. But I wanted to write music and I didn't want to have to do anything else.'' Bennett has called his film work ''a means to an end,'' a way for him ''to live as a composer,'' but in the process has nonetheless created some of the most brilliant, varied, and original scores in the history of late-20th-century film. In a conversation on film music with American film composer Elmer Bernstein, Bennett also offered these comments: ''on the other hand, you've got to be born to it. It is *not* hack work as far as I'm concerned. I've never had any consistent theory about film music. I try to simply respond freshly to everything I see. Every picture I do to stimulate myself, and in order not to let myself do anything I've done before.''

—Ross Care

BERLIN, Irving

Composer and Songwriter. **Nationality:** American. **Born:** Israel Isidore Baline in Temun, Siberia, 11 May 1888; family emigrated to the U.S., 1892. **Career:** As a boy sang on street corners in New York's Lower East Side; 1902—ran away from home and sang in cafés in the Bowery; 1907—hired as singing waiter at Nigger Mike's Saloon; hired by publishing firm as songwriter; 1911—wrote ''Alexander's Ragtime Band,'' followed by numerous scores for the stage including the Ziegfeld Follies; 1927—moved to Hollywood and began scoring films. **Awards:** Academy Award for ''White Christmas,'' 1942. **Died:** In New York, 22 September 1989.

Films as Songwriter/Composer:

1927   *The Jazz Singer* (Crosland)
1928   *The Awakening* (Fleming)
1929   *Cocoanuts* (Santley) (+ original play); *Coquette* (Sam Taylor); *Glorifying the American Girl* (Webb); *Lady of the Pavements* (D. W. Griffith); *Hallelujah* (Vidor)

Irving Berlin

1930   *Puttin' on the Ritz* (Schenk); *Mammy* (Curtiz) (+ original play); *The Bad One* (Fitzmaurice)
1931   *Reaching for the Moon* (Goulding) (+ story)
1934   *Kid Millions* (Goldwyn); *Top Hat* (Sandrich)
1936   *Follow the Fleet* (Sandrich)
1937   *On the Avenue* (Del Ruth): *Way out West*
1938   *Carefree* (Sandrich); *Alexander's Ragtime Band* (King)
1939   *Second Fiddle* (Lanfield)
1942   *Holiday Inn* (Sandrich) (+ story); *Louisiana Purchase* (Cummings) (co)
1943   *This is the Army* (Curtiz) (+ story + ro)
1944   *Christmas Holiday* (Siodmak)
1946   *Blue Skies* (Heisler); *The Jolson Story* (Green)
1948   *Easter Parade* (Walters)
1950   *Annie Get Your Gun* (Sidney) (+ original play)
1953   *Call Me Madam* (Walter Lang): *Run for the Hills*
1954   *White Christmas* (Curtiz); *There's No Business Like Showbusiness* (Walter Lang) (songs)
1957   *Sayonara* (Logan) (song)

Film as Writer of Original Story:

1926   *Stop, Look and Listen*

Publication:

On BERLIN: books—

Freedland, Michael, *Irving Berlin*, London, 1974.
Woollcott, Alexander, *The Story of Irving Berlin*, New York, 1982.
Bergreen, Lawrence, *As Thousands Cheer*, London, 1990.
Barrett, Mary Ellin, *Irving Berlin: A Daughter's Memoir*, New York and London, 1995.
Furia, Philip, *Irving Berlin: A Life in Song*, New York, 1998.

On BERLIN: articles—

Films in Review (New York), vol. 9, no. 5, May 1958.
Hemmings, Roy, in *The Melody Lingers On*, New York, 1986.
The Listener (London), vol. 119, no. 3061, 5 May 1988.
Obituary, in *Classic Images* (Muscatine, Iowa), no. 173, November 1989.
Hayes, H., ''Of Life and Love, Of Happiness and Friendship,'' in *New York Times*, Section 2, 28 March 1993.
Hamm, Charles, ''Genre, Performance and Ideology in the Early Songs of Irving Berlin,'' in *Popular Music*, May 1994.
Schiff, David, ''For Everyman, By Everyman: In Creating Himself According to the Nation's Enthusiams for His Songs, Irving Berlin helped create a National Identity,'' in *Atlantic Monthly*, March 1996.
''A Song for America, The Lost Generation Wobbles,'' in *Newsweek*, June 28, 1999.

* * *

Irving Berlin's career as a songwriter was so long that he out-lived some of the copyrights of his early works. Although he was hit-making as early as ''Alexander's Ragtime Band'' in 1911, he was obviously barred from the cinema until 1927, when he got in at the earliest possible moment by providing "Blue Skies," a tune featured in *The Jazz Singer*, the first musical movie. The burst of song and dance activity that naturally followed Al Jolson's warbling found Berlin's work featured in a clutch of late 1920s and early 1930s musicals, most notably the Marx Brothers' *Cocoanuts* ("When My Dreams Come True," the first song Berlin wrote expressly for a film, "Monkey Doodle-Doo," "The Tale of a Shirt") and the all-black *Hallelujah* ("Waiting at the End of the Road," "Swanee Shuffle") in 1929, but also *Glorifying the American Girl* ("Blue Skies" again), *Puttin' on the Ritz* (the first film titled after a Berlin tune), and *The Jazz Singer* follow-up *Mammy* (with a Technicolor sequence, and "Let Me Sing and I'm Happy"). However, once the first burst of screen musicals died down, Berlin had to wait until 1935 to be offered something worthwhile in the way of a credit.

Top Hat, the first of the great Astaire-Rogers musicals, features only one forgettable song—"The Piccolino," which is unfortunately the climax of the picture—but otherwise boasts four soon-to-be-standard numbers, all mounted with the maximum of RKO elegance, "No Strings," "Cheek to Cheek," "Top Hat, White Tie and Tails" and "Isn't This a Lovely Day to Be Caught in the Rain?" Here, Berlin's deft but unfussy tunes and simple but perfect lyrics are at their best, expressing neither the lyrical nor musical sophistication of George Gershwin or Cole Porter—beside whom Berlin still looks like the Compleat Tin Pan Alley Professional—and yet never seeming cheap, obvious or cynical. *Top Hat* was followed by the underrated *Follow the Fleet*, which is a better all-round movie than *Top Hat*—with a more congenial navy-and-showbiz New York setting as opposed to the stuffily trivial London and continental high society of the earlier film—with an almost equally good score, led off by "Let's Face the Music and Dance" but featuring also "I'm Puttin' All My Eggs in One Basket," "Let Yourself Go," "We Saw the Sea" and "But Where Are You?"

Berlin would create hit-packed scores for Astaire movies again—for *Carefree* ("I Used to Be Color Blind") and *Holiday Inn* ("White Christmas," for which he won an Oscar)—as well as a few lesser talents (*Second Fiddle*, for Sonja Henie) but *Top Hat* and *Follow the Fleet* were the peak of his contribution purely to cinema, most of the other Berlin movies being adapted from stage successes (*Louisiana Purchase*, *This Is the Army*, *Call Me Madam*, *Annie Get Your Gun*) or built around clutches of pre-existing songs (*On the Avenue*, *Alexander's Ragtime Band*, *Blue Skies*, *Easter Parade*, *White Christmas*, *There's No Business Like Show Business*).

Meanwhile, individual Berlin songs persistently turned up, the most lavishly overproduced number perhaps being the "A Pretty Girl Is Like a Melody" riot of bad taste in *The Great Ziegfeld*. Berlin songs also appear in *Kid Millions* ("Mandy"), *The Story of Vernon and Irene Castle* ("Syncopated Walk"), *Hello, Frisco, Hello* ("Doin' the Grizzly Bear"), *The Powers Girl* ("A Pretty Girl Is Like a Melody"), *The Jolson Story* ("Let Me Sing and I'm Happy"), *The Fabulous Dorseys* ("Everybody's Doin' It"), *Big City* ("God Bless America," "What'll I Do?"), *Jolson Sings Again* ("Let Me Sing and I'm Happy," again), *Meet Danny Wilson* ("How Deep is the Ocean?"), *Love Me or Leave Me* ("Shaking the Blues Away"), *The Great Gatsby* ("What'll I Do?"), *Pennies from Heaven* ("Let's Face the Music and Dance," soundtrack poached from *Follow the Fleet*) and *The Purple Rose of Cairo* ("Cheek to Cheek," poached from *Top Hat*). Strangely, Steven Spielberg's *Always*, whose mood obviously derives from the Berlin song, opts to use Jerome Kern's inapt "Smoke Gets in Your Eyes" instead.

While Porter, Gershwin, Richard Rogers and Stephen Sondheim aspire to lift the musical comedy to a High Art level, Berlin was simply content to do the best possible work within the framework of a three-minute popular song, and demonstrated an astonishing versatility within those limits, turning to comedy ("Oh, How I Hate to Get Up in the Morning," "Doin' What Comes Nat'rally"), romance ("Cheek to Cheek," "Always"), social comment ("Let's Have Another Cup of Coffee, Let's Have Another Piece of Pie"), patriotism ("God Bless America," a song so ingrained in the national psyche it's hard to remember someone sat down and wrote it, "Three Cheers for the Red, White and Blue") holiday sentiment ("Easter Parade," "White Christmas"), and show stopping razzamatazz ("When the Midnight Choo-Choo Leaves for Alabam," "There's No Business Like Show Business"). Almost always sunny and optimistic, the only variety of standard Berlin appeared never to master was the lovelorn torch song, which he either turned around into a renewal of hope ("Blue Skies") or played for laughs ("You Can't Get a Man with a Gun"). After the 1950s, his output declined, but his oeuvre probably includes more lasting songs than any other composer this century.

—Kim Newman

BERMAN, Pandro S.

Producer. **Nationality:** American. **Born:** Pandro Samuel Berman in Pittsburgh, Pennsylvania, 28 March 1905; son of the film executive Harry M. Berman; sometimes billed as Pan Berman. **Education:** Attended schools in Philadelphia, New Castle, Pennsylvania, and New York City. **Family:** Married 1) Viola Newman, 1927 (divorced), son: Michael, daughters: Susan and Cynthia; 2) Kathryn Hereford, 1960 (died 1993). **Career:** 1925—assistant director, then film editor at RKO; assistant to William LeBaron and David O. Selznick; 1931–40—producer, RKO, then at MGM until 1967; retired 1970. **Awards:** Irving M. Thalberg Award, 1976; David O. Selznick Lifetime Achievement Award, Motion Picture Producers Guild of America, 1992. **Died:** In Beverly Hills, California, 13 July 1996.

Films as Producer:

1931   *Way Back Home* (Seiter); *The Gay Diplomat* (Boleslawsky)
1932   *Symphony of Six Million* (*Melody of Life*) (La Cava); *Age of Consent* (La Cava); *The Half-Naked Truth* (La Cava); *What Price Hollywood?* (Cukor); *Men of Chance* (Archainbaud)
1933   *Ann Vickers* (Cromwell); *Morning Glory* (L. Sherman); *One Man's Journey* (Robertson); *The Silver Cord* (Cromwell)
1934   *The Gay Divorcee* (*The Gay Divorce*) (Sandrich); *The Life of Vergie Winters* (Santell); *Age of Innocence* (Moeller); *Of Human Bondage* (Cromwell); *The Little Minister* (Wallace); *The Gridiron Flash* (Tyron); *Wednesday's Child* (Robertson); *The Fountain* (Cromwell); *Spitfire* (Cromwell); *Richest Child in the World* (Seiter); *Stingaree* (Wellman); *By Your Leave* (Corrigan)
1935   *Roberta* (Seiter); *Romance in Manhattan* (Roberts); *Alice Adams* (Stevens); *Laddie* (Stevens); **Top Hat** (Sandrich);

Pandro S. Berman

Freckles (Killy and Hamilton); *Sylvia Scarlett* (Cukor); *Break of Hearts* (Moeller); *I Dream Too Much* (Cromwell); *In Person* (Seiter); *Star of Midnight* (Roberts)

1936   *Follow the Fleet* (Sandrich); *Mary of Scotland* (Ford); *Winterset* (Santell); *Swing Time* (Stevens); *A Woman Rebels* (Sandrich); *That Girl from Paris* (Jason); *Muss 'em Up* (C. Vidor); *The Big Game* (Nicholls)

1937   *Stage Door* (La Cava); *A Damsel in Distress* (Stevens); *Shall We Dance?* (Sandrich); *Quality Street* (Stevens); *Christopher Strong* (Arzner); *The Soldier and the Lady* (*Michael Strogoff*) (Nicholls)

1938   *Room Service* (Seiter); *Vivacious Lady* (Stevens); *Carefree* (Sandrich); *Having Wonderful Time* (Santell); *The Mad Miss Manton* (Jason); *Mother Carey's Chickens* (Lee)

1939   *Gunga Din* (Stevens); *In Name Only* (Cromwell); *The Hunchback of Notre Dame* (Dieterle); *Love Affair* (McCarey); *The Story of Vernon and Irene Castle* (Potter) (co); *The Flying Irishman* (Jason); *Boy Slaves* (Wolfson)

1941   *Ziegfeld Girl* (Leonard); *Love Crazy* (Conway); *Honky Tonk* (Conway)

1942   *Rio Rita* (Simon); *Somewhere I'll Find You* (Ruggles)

1943   *Slightly Dangerous* (Ruggles); *Marriage Is a Private Affair* (Leonard)

1944   *Dragon Seed* (Conway and Bucquet); *The Seventh Cross* (Zinnemann); *National Velvet* (Brown)

1945   ***The Picture of Dorian Gray*** (Lewin)

1946   *Undercurrent* (Minnelli)

1947   *Sea of Grass* (Kazan); *If Winter Comes* (Saville); *Living in a Big Way* (La Cava)

1948   *The Three Musketeers* (Sidney)

1949   *Madame Bovary* (Minnelli); *The Bribe* (Leonard); *The Doctor and the Girl* (Bernhardt)

1950   *Father of the Bride* (Minnelli)

1951   *Father's Little Dividend* (Minnelli); *Soldiers Three* (Garnett); *The Light Touch* (R. Brooks)

1952   *The Prisoner of Zenda* (Thorpe); *Ivanhoe* (Thorpe); *Lovely to Look At* (LeRoy); *Battle Circus* (R. Brooks)

1953   *The Knights of the Round Table* (Thorpe); *All the Brothers Were Valiant* (Thorpe)

1954   *The Long, Long Trailer* (Minnelli)

1955   *The Blackboard Jungle* (R. Brooks); *Quentin Durward* (*The Adventures of Quentin Durward*) (Thorpe)

1956 *Bhowani Junction* (Cukor); *Tea and Symphony* (Minnelli); *The Great American Pastime* (Hoffman)
1957 *Something of Value* (R. Brooks); *Jailhouse Rock* (Thorpe)
1958 *The Brothers Karamazov* (R. Brooks); *The Reluctant Debutante* (Minnelli)
1960 *All the Fine Young Cannibals* (Anderson); *Butterfield 8* (Daniel Mann); *Key Witness* (Karlson)
1962 *Sweet Bird of Youth* (R. Brooks)
1963 *The Prize* (Robson)
1964 *Honeymoon Hotel* (Levin)
1965 *A Patch of Blue* (Green)
1969 *Justine* (Cukor)
1970 *Move* (Rosenberg)

Films as Assistant Director:

1925 *Midnight Molly* (Ingraham); *Smooth as Satin* (R. Ince); *Lady Robinhood* (R. Ince); *Alias Mary Flynn* (R. Ince)

Films as Editor:

1928 *Beyond London* (Terriss); *Phantom of the Range* (Dugan); *Fangs of the Wild* (Storm); *Stocks and Blondes* (Murphy); *Taxi 13* (Neilan); *The Texas Tornado* (Clark)
1929 *Trial Marriage* (Kenton) (co)

Publications

On BERMAN: articles—

Film Daily (New York), 8 July 1953.
Cinématographe (Paris), May 1984.
Obituary in *New York Times*, 15 July 1996.
Obituary in *Variety* (New York), 26 August 1996.
Obituary in *Classic Images* (Muscatine), September 1996.

*   *   *

Pandro S. Berman was one of the great line producers in Hollywood history. Working for RKO in the 1930s he supervised the creation of such classic Fred Astaire-Ginger Rogers musicals as *The Gay Divorcee*, *Top Hat*, *Follow the Fleet*, and *Swing Time*. At MGM in the 1940s Berman produced such hits as *National Velvet* starring Elizabeth Taylor and *Father of the Bride*, again starring Taylor, this time with Spencer Tracy.

Berman's career spanned three important eras in the history of the movies. The first was his apprenticeship in the 1920s. In those days one learned all aspects of the film industry at the feet of the masters at work; no one went to film school. It was on-the-job-training at its best. Indeed Berman never went to college; he went into the film business directly from high school. His father, a minor executive at powerful Universal Pictures, secured Pandro's first job at a minor studio, Film Booking Office. Little did they know that before the end of the 1920s Film Booking Office would merge into one of the major studios and become part of RKO. Such luck is the foundation of many a great career.

Berman worked hard at his new job. He worked his way up to chief film editor, and then became an assistant to William LeBaron and

David O. Selznick, two of the myriad of early production chiefs at RKO in the late 1920s and early 1930s. From this position of power he teamed Astaire with Rogers and helped remake the history of the Hollywood musical. He also assisted the careers of Katharine Hepburn and Cary Grant, plus director George Stevens.

But RKO was always on shaky grounds financially and thus any producer had to work twice as hard as one at the studio then at the top, Metro-Goldwyn-Mayer. Thus it was not surprising that Berman was drawn to MGM in 1940 to work for Louis B. Mayer. Berman's early MGM films will not be remembered as great classics, but nearly all made money. He built the career of a young Elizabeth Taylor from *National Velvet* to *Father of the Bride* to *Ivanhoe* to *Cat on a Hot Tin Roof* and *Butterfield 8*.

Berman's output as a producer slowed considerably in the late 1950s and early 1960s. With the change of power at MGM in 1956 he became in effect an independent producer distributing through the studio. And Berman did well by MGM. When the studio was entering its darkest days in the 1960s, Berman produced many of its rare hits: consider that in 1964 *The Prize* starring Paul Newman and Edward G. Robinson finished 19th in *Variety*'s listing of top money-making films of the year. Two years later *A Patch of Blue* starring Sidney Poitier, Elizabeth Hartman, and Shelley Winters finished tenth. But MGM slid further and further downhill. Berman gracefully retired from the studio in 1967 after working there for more than 35 years. He switched to Fox for his two final productions (neither of which did well at the box office), *Justine* and *Move*.

Pandro S. Berman survived almost everyone from his generation of producers from the Golden Age of Hollywood, and thus gracefully retired in 1970. The Academy of Motion Picture Arts and Sciences honored this ultimate insider with the Irving Thalberg Award in 1976 for his consistent creation of profitable films.

—Douglas Gomery

BERNARD, James

Composer. **Nationality:** British. **Born:** 20 September 1925. **Education:** Attended Wellington College; Royal College of Music, London. **Military Service:** Royal Air Force during World War II. **Career:** Assistant to Benjamin Britten; then freelance musician: composer for radio and television, and for films from mid-1950s; 1963—composer of stage musical *Virtue in Danger*; 1980—semi-retired to Jamaica; 1994—returned to London and to composing. **Awards:** Academy Award, for writing, for *Seven Days to Noon*, 1950. **Address:** c/o London Management, 235 Regent Street, London W.1, England.

Films as Composer:

1955 *The Quatermass Experiment* (*The Creeping Unknown*) (Guest)
1956 *Pacific Destiny* (Rilla); *X—the Unknown* (Norman); *The Door in the Wall* (Alvey)
1957 *The Curse of Frankenstein* (Fisher); *Quatermass II* (*Enemy from Space*) (Guest); *Windom's Way* (Neame); *Across the Pacific* (Annakin)
1958 *Dracula* (*Horror of Dracula*) (Fisher); *Nor the Moon by Night* (*Elephant Gun*) (Annakin); *The Immortal Land* (Wright—doc)

1959   *The Hound of the Baskervilles* (Fisher); *The Stranglers of Bombay* (Fisher)
1960   *The Terror of the Tongs* (Bushell); *A Place for Gold* (Wright—doc)
1961   *The Damned* (*These Are the Damned*) (Losey)
1963   *Kiss of the Vampire* (*Kiss of Evil*) (Sharp)
1964   *The Gorgon* (Fisher)
1965   *Dracula—Prince of Darkness* (Fisher); *She* (Day); *The Secret of Blood Island* (Lawrence)
1966   *The Plague of the Zombies* (Gilling)
1967   *Frankenstein Created Woman* (Fisher); *Torture Garden* (Francis) (co)
1968   *Dracula Has Risen from the Grave* (Francis); *The Devil Rides Out* (*The Devil's Bride*) (Fisher)
1969   *Frankenstein Must Be Destroyed* (Fisher)
1970   *The Horror of Frankenstein* (Sangster); *Taste the Blood of Dracula* (Sasdy); *The Scars of Dracula* (Baker)
1973   *Frankenstein and the Monster from Hell* (Fisher)
1974   *The Legend of the Seven Golden Vampires* (*The Seven Brothers Meet Dracula*) (Baker)
1985   *Murder Elite* (Whatham)
1997   *Flesh and Blood* (Newsom)
1998   *Universal Horror* (for TV)

Film as Co-writer, with Paul Dehn:

1950   *Seven Days to Noon* (J. & R. Boulting)

Publications

By BERNARD: articles—

Soundtrack (Belgium), September 1992.
Soundtrack (Belgium), June 1996.

On BERNARD: articles—

Films in Review (New York), January 1971.
Little Shoppe of Horrors (Waterloo, Iowa), February 1974.
Little Shoppe of Horrors (Waterloo, Iowa), April 1978.
Fistful of Soundtracks (London), May 1981.
Filmusic (Leeds), 1982.
Larson, R. D., ''Music from the Hammer Films,'' in *Soundtrack!* (Hollywood), vol. 9, no. 35, September 1990.
Dark Terrors (Cornwall, England), 1993
Scarlet Street (Glen Rock), Spring 1995.
Bender, J., '''The Devil Rides Out': the Film Music of James Bernard'' in *Film Score Monthly* (Los Angeles), September 1996.
Soundtrack (Belgium), September 1996.
Madison, B. and Sullivan, D., ''He Who Must Be Replayed!'' in *Scarlet Street* (Glen Rock), no. 22, 1996.

*   *   *

James Bernard created the musical identity of Hammer Films, the great British ''gothic'' studio, which flourished at Hammer's studios in Bray between 1958 and 1964. Bernard's most conspicuous accomplishment in the area of film scoring is undoubtedly his musical

''signature'' for *Dracula*, directed by Terence Fisher, Hammer's major house director. Bernard also wrote the scores for such ''Hammer horrors'' as *The Quatermass Experiment*, *X—the Unknown*, *Quatermass II*, and *The Curse of Frankenstein*. His major work for the company includes his haunting work on the 1959 *The Hound of the Baskervilles*, his score for Joseph Losey's prescient *The Damned*, his gorgeous piano music for *Kiss of the Vampire*, and his sensuous main theme for *She*. But in addition to his work for Hammer, Bernard has a long career in classical music composition which helped him immeasurably as a composer of film scores.

Educated at Wellington College, Bernard met the eminent composer Benjamin Britten at age 17, when Britten was asked to judge a school music competition. Britten was impressed with young Bernard's work, and urged him to continue composing. In 1947, after service in the Royal Air Force, Bernard entered the Royal College of Music, again on the advice of Benjamin Britten. He studied composition under Herbert Howells, and then labored as Britten's assistant on his opera *Billy Budd*. Bernard said later that his work with Britten during this period refined his skill as an arranger and orchestrator.

In 1951, Bernard left Britten's employ, seeking freelance work as a composer to create his own reputation. He found work at the BBC, and John Hollingsworth conducted a number of Bernard's scores for the network. In 1954, Hammer hired Hollingsworth to work up a score for their forthcoming science-fiction film *The Quatermass Experiment*. Hollingsworth immediately asked Bernard to score the film, and it thus emerged as the first science-fiction/horror film from the studio that truly bore the stamp of all the major collaborators during Hammer's peak period. The enormous commercial and critical success of this film assured Bernard's reputation with the public, but it also effectively typed Bernard as primarily a composer of horror scores. This is unfortunate, since it led to his being only spottily employed since the time of Hammer's demise as a production organization. No one can deny, however, that Bernard has a musical sensibility which seems most at home in the gothic genre, and the best Bernard scores are brooding melancholic visions of a temporal world shot through with peril and temptation.

Bernard admits to a real affinity for the character of *Dracula*, although he, along with everyone else connected with that series of films, feels that the later Dracula films trailed off in quality. Bernard orchestrates all his own music, but leaves the conducting to others. His own favorite scores include *The Devil Rides Out*, the *Dracula* scores, and *She*. He writes all of his scores first on a piano, composing at his home in Chelsea, in a quiet room near the back of his house which is reserved for his work. He sees the film twice through altogether; then he likes to break the film down reel-by-reel, stopping during the projection to discuss cues with the film's musical director. According to Bernard, he writes his scores (40 to 50 minutes in length) in roughly four weeks, which is all that most producers will allow him. He builds each score ''round two or three main themes, and perhaps one or two subsidiary themes. I do not give a theme to every character in the film—it would become much too complicated. In horror films, I am always pleased when there is an opportunity for a love-theme (as in *Taste the Blood of Dracula*), or at any rate something romantic, as a contrast to the main horror theme.''

Some have accused Bernard of being too simplistic, repetitive, and insistent in his music, and one can see where this criticism is founded. Bernard's theme for *Dracula*, for example, is a *very* simple three-note signature (Drac-u-la) which repeats itself in the score at least 50 times during the course of the film. Bernard piles on the brass sections for the ''shock'' moments in some of his films, and he often borrows from himself, or uses some of his trademark ''developmental'' devices, such as repeating a main theme over and over while moving up or down in registers.

Yet, along with Bernard Robinson's settings, Jimmy Sangster's scripts, Terence Fisher's and Freddie Francis's direction, and the iconic presences of actors Christopher Lee and Peter Cushing, James Bernard's music is an integral part of the Hammer vision, both commercially and artistically. His scores may lack the subtlety of Elizabeth Lutyen's work on such films as Freddie Francis's *Paranoiac* or Terence Fisher's *The Earth Dies Screaming*, but Bernard's brooding romanticism is an energetic and engaging component of many of Hammer's finest efforts.

—Wheeler Winston Dixon

BERNSTEIN, Elmer

Composer. **Nationality:** American. **Born:** New York City, 4 April 1922. **Education:** Attended Walden School; New York University; trained as pianist; also studied composition with Roger Sessions and Stefan Wolpe. **Military Service:** Composer for U.S. Army Air Force radio shows during World War II. **Family:** Married 1) Pearl Glusman,

Elmer Bernstein

1946, two sons: composer Peter Bernstein; writer Gregory Bernstein; 2) Eve Adamson, 1965, two daughters. **Career:** After military service, worked as a concert pianist; also worked in the United Nations radio department; scored first film, *Saturday's Hero*, 1951; composed for the TV series *Johnny Staccato*, 1959–60; composed for the TV series *Riverboat*, 1959–61; composed for the TV series *Owen Marshall, Counselor at Law*, 1971–74; composed for the TV series *Ellery Queen*, 1975–76; composed for the TV mini-series *Captains and the Kings*, 1976. **Awards:** Best Motion Picture Score Golden Globe, for *To Kill a Mockingbird,* 1962; Best Original Music Score Golden Globe, for *Hawaii,* 1966; Best Original Music Score Academy Award, for *Thoroughly Modern Millie*, 1967; Los Angeles Film Critics Association Career Achievement Award, 1991; Cinequest San Jose Film Festival Maverick Tribute Award, 1998. **Address:** c/o Academy of Motion Pictures Arts and Sciences, 8949 Wilshire Boulevard, Beverly Hills, CA 90211, U.S.A.

Films as Composer:

1951 *Saturday's Hero* (*Idols in the Dust*) (Miller); *Boots Malone* (Dieterle)
1952 *Sudden Fear* (Miller); *Battles of Chief Pontiac* (Feist)
1953 *Never Wave at a WAC* (*The Private Wore Skirts*) (McLeod); *Robot Monster* (Tucker); *Miss Robin Crusoe* (Frenke); *Cat Women of the Moon* (Hilton)
1954 *Make Haste to Live* (Seiter); *Silent Raiders* (Bartlett); *Career: Medical Technologists* (Churchill—short)
1955 *The Eternal Sea* (Auer); *Storm View from Pompey's Head* (*Secret Interlude*) (Dunne); *The Man with the Golden Arm* (Preminger); *House, after Five Years of Living* (C. & R. Eames—short)
1956 *The Ten Commandments* (DeMille); *Men in War* (A. Mann); *Fear Strikes Out* (Mulligan); *Eames Lounge Chair* (C. & R. Eames—short)
1957 *Drango* (Bartlett and Bricken); *The Naked Eye* (Stoumen); **Sweet Smell of Success** (Mackendrick); *The Tin Star* (A. Mann); *Toccata for Toy Trains* (C. & R. Eames—short); *The Information Machine* (C. & R. Eames—short)
1958 *Desire under the Elms* (Delbert Mann); *God's Little Acre* (A. Mann); *Kings Go Forth* (Daves); *The Buccaneer* (Quinn); *Anna Lucasta* (Laven); *Saddle the Wind* (Parrish); *Some Came Running* (Minnelli)
1959 *The Miracle* (Rapper); *The Story on Page One* (Odets); *Two Baroque Churches in Germany* (C. & R. Eames—short); *Glimpses of the U.S.A.* (C. & R. Eames—short); *Israel* (Zebba—short)
1960 *From the Terrace* (Robson); *The Magnificent Seven* (J. Sturges); *Introduction to Feedback* (C. & R. Eames—short)
1961 *By Love Possessed* (J. Sturges); *The Young Doctors* (Karlson); *The Comancheros* (Curtiz); *Summer and Smoke* (Glenville); *IBM Mathematics Peep Show* (C. & R. Eames—short)
1962 *The House of Silence* (C. & R. Eames—short); *Ilud* (Ritt); *Walk on the Wild Side* (Dmytryk); *A Girl Named Tamiko* (J. Sturges); *Birdman of Alcatraz* (Frankenheimer); *The Great Escape* (J. Sturges); *To Kill a Mockingbird* (Mulligan); *Rampage* (Karlson)
1963 *The Caretakers* (*Borderlines*) (Bartlett); *Kings of the Sun* (Lee Thompson); *The Carpetbaggers* (Dmytryk); *Love with the Proper Stranger* (Mulligan)

1964   *The World of Henry Orient* (Hill); *Think* (C. & R. Eames—short); *Four Days in November* (Stuart); *Baby the Rain Must Fall* (Mulligan); *Some Sort of Cage* (Allyn and Baldwin—short)

1965   *The Hallelujah Trail* (J. Sturges); *The Reward* (Bourguignon); *7 Women* (Ford); *The Sons of Katie Elder* (Hathaway); *Cast a Giant Shadow* (Shavelson); *IBM at the Fair* (C. & R. Eames—short); *Westinghouse A.B.C.* (C. & R. Eames—short); *The Smithsonian Institution* (C. & R. Eames—short); *IBM Puppet Show* (C. & R. Eames—short)

1966   *The Silencers* (Karlson); *Hawaii* (Hill); *Return of the Seven* (Kennedy)

1967   *Thoroughly Modern Millie* (Hill); *The Scalphunters* (Pollack); *A Computer Glossary* (C. & R. Eames—short)

1968   *I Love You, Alice B. Toklas!* (Averback); *Where's Jack* (Clavell); *The Bridge at Remagen* (Guillermin); *Guns of the Magnificent Seven* (Wendkos); *Powers of Ten* (C. & R. Eames—short)

1969   *True Grit* (Hathaway); *The Gypsy Moths* (Frankenheimer); *The Midas Run* (*A Run on Gold*) (Kjellin); *A Walk in the Spring Rain* (Green); *Tops* (C. & R. Eames—short); *The Liberation of L. B. Jones* (Wyler)

1970   *Cannon for Cordoba* (Wendkos); *Doctors' Wives* (Schaefer)

1971   *Big Jake* (G. Sherman); *The Tell-Tale Heart* (Carver—short); *Blind Terror* (*See No Evil*) (Fleischer); *Light, Strong and Beautiful* (Tardio—short); *Owen Marshall, Counselor at Law* (Kulik)

1972   *The Magnificent Seven Ride!* (McCowan); *The Amazing Mr. Blunden* (Jeffries); *The Rookies* (Taylor); *Deadly Honeymoon* (Silverstein)

1973   *Cahill, United States Marshal* (*Cahill*) (McLaglen); *Incident on a Dark Street* (Kulik)

1974   *The Man from Independence* (Smight); *Men of the Dragon* (Falk); *McQ* (J. Sturges); *The Trial of Billy Jack* (Laughlin); *Gold* (Hunt); *Report to the Commissioner* (*Operation Undercover*) (Katselas)

1975   *Ellery Queen* (*Too Many Suspects*) (Greene)

1976   *The Shootist* (Siegel); *The Incredible Sarah* (Fleischer); *Serpico: The Deadly Game* (Collins)

1977   *Billy Jack Goes to Washington* (Laughlin); *The 3,000 Mile Chase* (Mayberry)

1978   *National Lampoon's Animal House* (Landis); *Bloodbrothers* (Mulligan)

1979   *Charleston* (Arthur); *The Great Santini* (*The Ace*) (Carlino); *Meatballs* (Reitman); *Zulu Dawn* (Hickox)

1980   *Airplane!* (Abrahams and D. & J. Zucker); *Moviola: This Year's Blonde* (Erman); *Saturn 3* (Donen)

1981   *Honky Tonk Freeway* (Schlesinger) (co); *Going Ape!* (Kronsberg); *Stripes* (Reitman); *An American Werewolf in London* (Landis); *Heavy Metal* (Potterton—animation)

1982   *The Chosen* (Kagan); *Five Days One Summer* (Zinnemann); *Airplane II: The Sequel* (Finkleman)

1983   *Trading Places* (Landis); *The Entity* (Furie); *Class* (Carlino); *Thriller* (Landis) (co); *Spacehunter: Adventures in the Forbidden Zone* (Johnson)

1984   *Bolero* (Derek) (co); *Ghostbusters* (Reitman); *Prince Jack* (Lovitt)

1985   *Spies Like Us* (Landis); *Marie Ward* (Donaldson); *The Black Cauldron* (Berman and Rich—animation)

1986   *Legal Eagles* (Reitman); *Three Amigos!* (Landis)

1987   *Amazing Grace and Chuck* (Newell); *Leonard, Part 6* (Welland)

1988   *Da* (Clark); *Funny Farm* (Hill); *The Good Mother* (Nimoy)

1989   *Slipstream* (Lisberger); *My Left Foot* (Sheridan)

1990   *The Field* (Sheridan); *The Grifters* (Frears)

1991   *A Rage in Harlem* (Duke); *Cape Fear* (Scorsese); *Rambling Rose* (Coolidge); *Oscar* (Landis)

1992   *A River Runs through It* (Redford); *The Babe* (Hiller)

1993   *The Age of Innocence* (Scorsese); *Lost in Yonkers* (Coolidge); *Mad Dog and Glory* (McNaughton); *The Good Son* (Ruben); *The Cemetery Club* (Duke)

1994   *Canadian Bacon* (Moore)

1995   *Devil in a Blue Dress* (Demme); *Roommates* (Yates); *Frankie Starlight* (Lindsay-Hogg)

1996   *Bulletproof* (Dickerson)

1997   *Puppies for Sale* (Krauss); *Buddy* (Thompson); *Rough Riders* (Milius—for TV) (theme only); *Hoodlum* (Duke); *The Rainmaker* (Coppola)

1998   *Twilight* (Benton)

1999   *Chinese Coffee* (Pacino); *The Deep End of the Ocean* (Grosbard); *Introducing Dorothy Dandridge* (Coolidge—for TV); *Happy Face Murders* (Trenchard-Smith—for TV); *Bringing Out the Dead* (Scorsese); *Wild Wild West* (Sonnenfeld)

2000   *Keeping the Faith* (Norton)

2001   *Chinese Coffee*

Other Films:

1960   *The Rat Race* (Mulligan) (mus, + bit ro)

1974   *Mister Quilp* (Tuchner) (mus d)

1975   *From Noon till Three* (Gilroy) (mus, + bit ro)

1977   *Slap Shot* (Hill) (mus supervision)

1992   *Music for the Movies: Bernard Herrmann* (Waletzky) (doc) (ro)

1998   *Digging to China* (Hutton) (score pr, orch)

Publications

By BERNSTEIN: articles—

Filme Cultura (Rio de Janeiro), May/June 1969.

"What Ever Happened to Great Movie Music?," in *High Fidelity* (New York), July 1972.

Film Music Notebook (Calabasas, California), Fall 1974.

"The Annotated Friedkin," in *Film Music Notebook* (Calabasas, California), Winter 1974.

Film Music Notebook (Calabasas, California), Winter 1974–75.

Interview with Irwin Bazelton, in *Knowing the Score*, New York, 1975.

Film Music Notebook (Calabasas, California), Spring 1975.

Film Music Notebook (Calabasas, California), Summer 1975.

"Film Composers vs. the Studios," in *Film Music Notebook* (Calabasas, California), vol. 2, no. 1, 1976.

Film Music Notebook (Calabasas, California), nos. 2 and 3, 1976.

"On Film Music," *Journal of the University Film Association* (Carbondale, Illinois), Fall 1976.

Film Music Notebook (Calabasas, California), vol. 2, no. 4 and vol. 3, no. 1, 1977.

Interview with Jerry Goldsmith, in *Film Music Notebook* (Calabasas, California), vol. 3, no. 2, 1977.

Interview with John Addison, in *Film Music Notebook* (Calabasas, California), vol. 3, no. 3, 1977.

"The Aesthetics of Film Scoring," in *Film Music Notebook* (Calabasas, California), no. 1, 1978.

Interview with Henry Mancini, in *Film Music Notebook* (Calabasas, California), vol. 4, no. 1, 1978.

Interview with Bronislau Kaper, in *Film Music Notebook* (Calabasas, California), vol. 4, no. 2, 1978.

Films and Filming (London), March 1978.

In *Film Score*, edited by Tony Thomas, South Brunswick, New Jersey, 1979.

Millimeter (New York), April 1979.

Soundtrack! (Hollywood), June and September 1983.

Soundtrack! (Hollywood), March 1986.

Soundtrack (Belgium), March 1992.

On BERNSTEIN: articles—

Godfrey, Lionel, "The Music Makers: Elmer Bernstein and Jerry Goldsmith," in *Films and Filming* (London), September 1966.

Focus on Film (London), January/February 1970.

Films in Review (New York), December 1971.

Thomas, Tony, in *Music for the Movies*, South Brunswick, New Jersey, 1973.

Dirigido por . . . (Barcelona), January 1974.

Scheff, Michael, in *Film Music Notebook* (Calabasas, California), Winter 1974–75.

Ecran (Paris), September 1975.

Séquences (Montreal), October 1980.

Soundtrack! (Hollywood), Summer 1981.

Fistful of Soundtracks (London), July 1981.

Soundtrack! (Hollywood), December 1981.

Score (Leystad, Netherlands), March 1982.

Cinefantastique (New York), January 1985.

Palmer, Christopher, in *The Composer in Hollywood*, New York, 1990.

Positif (Paris), July-August 1993.

Walsh, J.S., "The Ten Most Influential Film Composers," in *Film Score Monthly* (Los Angeles), January/February/March 1996.

Sight & Sound (London), May 1996.

Wolthius, J.J.C., and R. Valkenburg, "Elmer Bernstein," in *Score* (Ak Lelystad, Netherlands), June 1996.

*   *   *

In 1967, Elmer Bernstein won an Oscar for scoring *Thoroughly Modern Millie*, which is ironic because it is not typical of his work and is far less interesting than his other Oscar-nominated scores, among them *The Man with the Golden Arm*, *The Magnificent Seven*, *Summer and Smoke*, *To Kill a Mockingbird*, *Hawaii*, and *The Age of Innocence*. The first of these was marked by an arresting use of jazz colors and rhythms; the theme from *The Magnificent Seven* remains possibly the most recognizable of all Western movie themes; and the score for *To Kill a Mockingbird* is generally thought to be the most evocative for any film set in the Deep South.

Bernstein showed artistic aptitude as a child. He won a number of prizes for paintings but by the age of 12 it was apparent that his major talent was music. He studied piano with Henrietta Michelson of the Juilliard School of Music but she was so impressed with his ability to improvise that she took him to see Aaron Copland. He arranged

lessons in composition with Israel Sitowitz, resulting in a scholarship that enabled Bernstein to study with Roger Sessions.

Completing his music education at New York University, Bernstein was still intent on a career as a concert pianist and began giving recitals in his late teens. At 21 he was inducted into the Army Air Corps and assigned duty as an arranger with the Armed Forces Radio Service. One of his first jobs was making arrangements for Glenn Miller's newly formed Army Air Corps band. In time he was given assignments scoring radio documentaries and in the course of the next three years arranged and composed for about 80 of them. He returned to being a concert pianist after his military service but in 1949 he accepted an offer to score a radio program for the United Nations, which led to similar film offers, and finally one from Columbia Pictures.

Bernstein was brought to Hollywood in 1951 and given two films, *Saturday's Hero* and *Boots Malone*. After a dozen modest films Bernstein drew comment with *The Man with the Golden Arm*, plus a goodly sale on the record album, and his success thereafter was assured. His music for DeMille's *The Ten Commandments* proved his ability to handle the mightiest of screen fare, but it was with his scores for films of Americana, such as *Desire under the Elms*, *God's Little Acre*, and *Summer and Smoke*, and such Westerns as *The Magnificent Seven*, *The Scalphunters*, *True Grit*, and *The Shootist* that Bernstein seemed truly at home. As the years passed, he has remained an active and vital force in the film industry, easily adapting himself to changing tastes. After working on *National Lampoon's Animal House* in 1978, Bernstein went on to score a number of comedies starring *Saturday Night Live* alumni (including *Meatballs*, *Stripes*, *Trading Places*, *Ghostbusters*, and *Spies Like Us*). Meanwhile, he continued working on more serious films, winning acclaim for his evocative scores of *My Left Foot*, *The Grifters*, *A River Runs through It*, and *Age of Innocence*, and his adaptation of Bernard Herrmann's original score of *Cape Fear*, commissioned for Martin Scorsese's 1991 remake. In the late 1990s, approaching his eightieth birthday, Bernstein remained ever-active, composing the scores for films as varied as Francis Coppola's *The Rainmaker*, Robert Benton's *Twilight*, Barry Sonnenfeld's *Wild Wild West*, and Scorsese's *Bringing Out the Dead*. Active as a guest conductor with symphony orchestras and for a ten-year period the president of the Los Angeles Young Musicians Foundation, Bernstein has also been involved in film music preservation, starting his own record label, Film Music Collection, in 1974 and recording scores by the likes of Rozsa, Newman, Tiomkin, Steiner, and others. Few men have done more to maintain high standards in film scoring than Bernstein. "Music really is an art whose life begins where pictures and words leave off," he has declared. "You receive it through an emotional medium. Music is basically an emotional fantasy. It is for this reason that I think it functions so ideally in film."

—Tony Thomas, updated by Rob Edelman

BERNSTEIN, Walter

Writer. **Nationality:** American. **Born:** Brooklyn, 20 August 1919. **Family:** Married to the literary agent Gloria Loomis; several children from a previous marriage. **Education:** Graduated from Dartmouth College, 1940. **Military Service:** Drafted into the U.S. Army, 1941; served as a correspondent for the Army weekly *Yank* during World

Walter Bernstein

War II. **Career:** Secured first writing job reviewing films for the *Daily Dartmouth*, a student newspaper, circa 1938; wrote a musical comedy while stationed at Fort Benning, GA, 1941; wrote for *New Yorker*, *Argosy*, *Life*, *Sports Illustrated*, and *Collier's* during the 1940s and 1950s; co-edited a newsletter, *Facts About the Blacklist*, during the 1950s. **Awards:** Writers Guild of America-East, Ian McLellan Hunter Memorial Award for Lifetime Achievement in Writing, 1994; Gotham Awards, Writer Award, 1996; Human Family Educational and Cultural Institute, Humanitas Prize, PBS/Cable Category, for *Miss Evers' Boys*, 1997. **Agent:** Arlene Donovan, International Creative Management, 40 W. 57th St., New York, NY 10019, U.S.A.

Films as Writer:

1948 *Kiss the Blood Off My Hands* (Foster)
1959 *That Kind of Woman* (Lumet); *The Wonderful Country* (Parrish)
        (uncredited)
1960 *Heller in Pink Tights* (Cukor); *A Breath of Scandal* (Curtiz)
        (uncredited); *The Magnificent Seven* (Sturges) (uncredited)
1961 *Paris Blues* (Ritt)
1962 *Something's Got to Give* (Cukor)
1964 *Fail-Safe* (Lumet)
1965 *The Train* (Frankenheimer) (uncredited)
1966 *The Money Trap* (Kennedy)
1970 *The Molly Maguires* (Ritt) (+ pr)
1976 *The Front* (Ritt)

1977 *Semi-Tough* (Ritchie)
1978 *The Betsy* (Petrie)
1979 *An Almost Perfect Affair* (Ritchie); *Yanks* (Schlesinger)
1980 *Little Miss Marker* (+ d)
1985 *The Legend of Billie Jean* (Robbins)
1988 *The House on Carroll Street* (Yates)
1991 *Women & Men 2: In Love There Are No Rules* (for TV) (+ d)
1994 *Doomsday Gun* (Young—for TV)
1995 *The Affair* (Seed—for TV) (story only)
1997 *Miss Evers' Boys* (Sargent—for TV)
1999 *Durango* (Shields—for TV)
2000 *Fail Safe* (Frears—for TV)

Other Films:

1950 *Panic in the Streets* (Kazan) (ro)
1976 *Hollywood on Trial* (Helpern) (doc) (ro)
1977 *Annie Hall* (Allen) (ro)
1985 *The Last Days of Marilyn Monroe* (Olgiati) (doc) (ro)

Publications

By BERNSTEIN: books—

Keep Your Head Down, New York, 1945.
Inside Out: A Memoir of the Blacklist, New York, 1996.

By BERNSTEIN: articles—

"What Blacklist," interview with Patricia Aufderheide, in *Film Comment* (New York), January-February 1988.
"Conversation with Blacklisted Writer Walter Bernstein," interview with David Walsh, World Socialist Web Site wsws.org, February 1999.

*   *   *

If for no other reason, Walter Bernstein will be remembered for his sheer longevity as a film and television screenwriter. Incredibly, his screenplays have spanned a period from the 1940s to the 2000s and may well qualify him as the longest-working writer of produced films and television programs in history.

Bernstein began his screenwriting career in 1947, shortly after he had published a collection of World War II essays originally written for the *New Yorker* and the Army weekly *Yank*. The anthology, *Keep Your Head Down*, was so strong that it landed him a ten-week contract as a writer with Columbia Pictures. He moved to Hollywood and soon began working with Columbia's Robert Rossen. Though he learned much about the craft of screenwriting from Rossen during that period, he did not actually write his first script until the ten-week stint was over. His agent, Harold Hecht, and actor Burt Lancaster had just formed an independent film company, Norma Productions, and Hecht hired Bernstein at $500 a week, doubling the writer's Columbia salary. Paired with the more experienced writer Ben Maddow, Bernstein created the screenplay for his first film: *Kiss the Blood Off*

My Hands, an adaptation of a British thriller novel and regarded by Bernstein as ''an offbeat melodrama that borrowed (stole) heavily from Hitchcock.''

The tyro screenwriter had little time to savor his breakthrough accomplishment, however. He left Hollywood in December 1947—a mere six months after he had arrived and before *Kiss the Blood Off My Hands* had even opened—in the wake of the anti-Communist investigation of the movie industry launched by the House Committee on Un-American Activities (HUAC). Bernstein, who had joined the Communist Party a year after his Army discharge, could see the destructive effects of HUAC's inquisition and returned to his native New York in the hope of writing film screenplays on the East Coast. Instead, he found steady work as a writer for the fledgling medium of television.

Bernstein's early success as a TV writer could not shield him from the icy effects of the Cold War and the anti-Communist fervor of the time. He was blacklisted in 1950 and was unable to write television scripts under his own name until 1961, though several film directors did hire him openly as early as 1959. Routinely harassed by the FBI during the 1950s, Bernstein wrote many TV scripts under various pseudonyms (principally ''Paul Bauman'') for some of early television's most prestigious anthology programs, including *You Are There*, *Playhouse 90*, and *Studio One*. Working behind a ''front'' for producer David Susskind, Bernstein also adapted Thornton Wilder's *The Bridge of San Luis Rey* and Mark Twain's *The Prince and the Pauper* for television. His script for the latter production won a Christopher Award, which he was unable to collect because of the blacklist.

Following his return to Hollywood under his own name in 1959, Bernstein crafted screenplays for movies that ranged widely in their content; westerns, thrillers, comedies, and melodramas became his stock in trade, with the screenplays for *Fail-Safe*, *The Train*, *The Molly Maguires*, and *Semi-Tough* among his best. Unquestionably the most heartfelt of Bernstein's screenplays were for those films that dealt with the blacklisting era: *The Front*, for which he received Oscar and Writers Guild of America (WGA) screenplay nominations; and *The House on Carroll Street*, a film that Bernstein unapologetically turned into a melodrama to deliver his views. ''With melodrama you're never going to go very deep,'' he said. ''What you can do is to state a social issue, draw the lines, and you can't do a hell of a lot more than that. But that's a lot. It's not disgraceful. It's a very American form—stories in the way people expect to hear them.''

Since the 1990s, Bernstein has written exclusively for television. His work there has included his much-admired screenplay for *Miss Evers' Boys* and a rewrite of his *Fail Safe* script for a production performed live on network TV in April 2000. In a sense, his writing career had returned full circle with the new *Fail Safe* screenplay, since much of his early work had been for live television as well.

Despite the heavy demands of his writing career, Bernstein has found time to share his knowledge with up-and-coming filmmakers. He has been an Adjunct Professor of Film at Columbia University's School of the Arts for years, taught at New York University, and also served as an advisor at the Sundance Institute's Screenwriters Lab for several summers. He has also worked as a teacher of a different sort, reminding people of Hollywood's dark days during the 1940s and 1950s. He was vociferous in his complaints, for example, when Elia Kazan, a Hollywood director who informed on his leftist colleagues during the blacklisting era, was soon to receive a Lifetime Achievement Oscar. As he told interviewer David Walsh in early 1999, ''I don't think they should give Kazan an award. It's true, it's been a long

time [since Kazan testified before HUAC], but this was a man who damaged the industry that is now giving him the award. . . . He hurt a lot of people.''

Bernstein's dedication to screenwriting may be found in a simple remark in his memoir, *Inside Out*: ''I write movies; focus is all.'' Judging from the breadth and depth of his work, the span of his career, and the passion of his beliefs, Bernstein must surely be among the most focused of writers ever to have their work appear on the large and small screens.

—Martin F. Norden

BIDDLE, Adrian

Cinematographer. Nationality: English. **Career:** Worked as assistant cameraman for Ridley Scott, 1970s. **Address:** British Film Institute, 127 Charing Cross Rd, London, WC2, England; Home Farm, Ripley Rd., East Clandon, Surrey, England GU4 75G.

Films as Cinematographer:

1986   *Aliens* (Cameron)
1987   *The Princess Bride* (Reiner)
1988   *The Dawning* (Knights); *Willow* (Howard)
1990   *The Tall Guy* (Smith)
1991   *Thelma and Louise* (Scott)
1992   *1492: The Conquest of Paradise* (Scott)
1994   *City Slickers II: The Legend of Curly's Gold* (Weiland)
1995   *Judge Dredd* (Cannon)
1996   *101 Dalmatians* (Herek)
1997   *Fierce Creatures* (Young and Schepisi) (co-ph); *The Butcher Boy* (Jordan); *Event Horizon* (Anderson)
1998   *Holy Man* (Herek)
1999   *The Mummy* (Sommers); *The World is Not Enough* (Apted)
2000   *102 Dalmations*
2001   *The Mummy Returns*; *The Weight of Water*

Other Films:

1977   *The Duellists* (Scott) (camera focus)
1979   *Alien* (Scott) (co-camera focus)

Publications:

By BIDDLE: articles—

Fisher, Bob, ''*1492: Conquest of Paradise*. Epic Film Recounts Legendary Epoch,'' interview in *American Cinematographer* (Hollywood), vol. 73, no. 10, October 1992.

Magid, Ron, ''Unearthly Terrors/Scare Tactics,'' in *American Cinematographer* (Hollywood), vol. 78, no. 8, August 1997.

On BIDDLE: articles—

Gainsborough, John, "Black-and-white All Over," in *American Cinematographer* (Hollywood), vol. 77, no. 11, November 1996.

* * *

Whatever the advances in computer-generated imagery, there will always be a place in films for a top grade director of photography. Working alongside such big name directors as Ridley Scott, James Cameron, Rob Reiner and Neil Jordan, cameraman Adrian Biddle specialises in high profile mainstream projects that tend to aim for the elusive "thinking person's blockbuster" category. Much of Biddle's work to date has been in big budget fantasy-adventure cinema, whether high-tech science fiction, mythical sword and sorcery, or borderline *fantastique* such as the James Bond franchise. To his credit, Biddle's undeniable lighting skill has never been swamped by the regular deluges of special effects in his movies, the two elements usually complementing rather than competing with each other.

Having served as a focus puller on Ridley Scott's *Alien*, Biddle's somewhat belated debut as lighting cameraman for the first sequel plunged him straight into the deep end of effects-heavy movie making. James Cameron's visual style is as dynamic as his storytelling, and he had Biddle working with quantities of smoke, mist, steam, strobes, flashes, flames, and gunfire. What could have been tired sci-fi cliches—blue and red washes, metallic greys, clinical whites, "spooky" backlighting—are handled with great assurance. Demonstrating an aptitude for sharply defined images, Biddle also gives liquid substances a curiously visceral quality: the condensation on Ripley's cryogenic pod, water splashing into a see-through cup, rain falling on the planet surface, sweat on Sigourney Weaver's finely chiselled face, even the gross-out drool from the aliens' mouths. Lurking in the shadows, the aliens are barely visible much of the time, light occasionally glinting off their exo-skeletonal bodies. When the shooting starts, Biddle's camera picks out every drop of acid blood spurting from the blasted creatures. He is equally assured during the quieter, more intimate moments, bathing a close-up scene between Ripley and orphan Newt in orange light, a moment of warmth in the overall darkness.

Ron Howard's violent fairytale *Willow* demonstrates Biddle's abilities outside the studio, the spectacular, if sombre British and New Zealand locations providing a realistic counterpoint to the fantastical plot and CGI bonanza. While the Industrial Light and Magic company provide a wealth of trolls, pixies, shapeshifters, and two-headed behemoths, Biddle's "natural" style of lighting emanates from more plausible points of origin: flickering torchlight, moonlight from a dungeon window, sunlight through trees. Forsaking the all-out sensory assault of *Aliens*, the film has more than its share of visual highlights: the forbidding grey stone of wicked Queen Bavmorda's realm, the island prison with a mountain range backdrop, a silhouetted procession of soldiers through a snowy wasteland, the final rainswept battle in the castle grounds.

Reunited with Ridley Scott a decade on from *Alien*, Biddle made his mark away from the fantasy genre. Dispensing with the tech-noir visuals of *Alien* and *Blade Runner*, *Thelma and Louise* offers increasingly ironic tourist brochure views of the American southwest as the protagonists travel down Route 66, taking in John Ford favourite Monument Valley along the way (Biddle's work netted him an Academy Award nomination). Few paying customers turned up to appreciate his photography for Scott's flop commemorative epic *1492*, which evokes both the dazzling spectacle and squalid brutality of the period.

The Mummy, an *Indiana Jones*-style reworking of the old horror favourite, is virtually a two-hour showcase for Industrial Light and Magic's CGI division. Those transfixed by the procession of scuttling scarab beetles, walking cadavers, firestorms, locust swarms, and transmigrating souls might miss out on the film's more subtle visual pleasures, such as burning torches flickering in the cavernous darkness of an Egyptian tomb. Working with largely orange-gold hues, Biddle provides some striking backdrops, notably the Sahara Desert and a ruined "lost city" built inside the crater of an inactive volcano. Sand and sky are rendered in sharp, bright tones, giving no hint of the dark, malevolent powers dormant beneath the ground. As with all of Biddle's best work, these images convey a sense of tangibility, texture, and atmosphere that even ILM's digital bag of tricks cannot equal.

—Daniel O'Brien

BIRO, Lajos

Writer. **Nationality:** Hungarian. **Born:** Nagyvárad, 22 August 1880. **Family:** Married Yolan Veszi; two daughters. **Career:** Editor of several newspapers in Budapest before 1919; playwright and fiction writer in Vienna; 1924–32—worked in Hollywood; 1932—scriptwriter and executive director, London Films. **Died:** In London, 1948.

Films as Writer:

1927   *The Way of All Flesh* (Fleming)
1928   *The Last Command* (Von Sternberg); *The Yellow Lily* (A. Korda); *The Night Watch* (A. Korda); *The Haunted House* (Christensen); *Adoration* (Lloyd)
1930   *Women Everywhere* (A. Korda)
1931   *The Ghost Train* (Forde); *Michael and Mary* (Saville)
1932   *Wedding Rehearsal* (A. Korda); *Service for Ladies* (A. Korda); *The Faithful Heart* (*Faithful Hearts*) (Saville)
1933   **The Private Life of Henry VIII** (A. Korda); *Strange Evidence* (Milton)
1934   *Catherine the Great* (Czinner); *The Private Life of Don Juan* (A. Korda)
1935   *The Scarlet Pimpernel* (Young); *Sanders of the River* (Z. Korda): *Rembrandt*
1937   *Under the Red Robe* (Sjöström); *Knight without Armor* (Feyder); *The Return of the Scarlet Pimpernel* (Schwarz); *Over the Moon* (Freeland and Howard); *Dark Journey* (*The Anxious Years*) (Saville); **Things to Come** (Menzies) (co): *The Man Who Could Work Miracles*
1938   *The Drum* (*Drums*) (Z. Korda); *The Divorce of Lady X* (Whelan)
1939   *The Four Feathers* (Z. Korda): *Hotel Imperial*
1940   *The Thief of Bagdad* (Powell, Berger, and Whelan); *The Way of All Flesh*
1943   *Five Graves to Cairo* (Wilder)
1945   *A Royal Scandal* (Preminger)

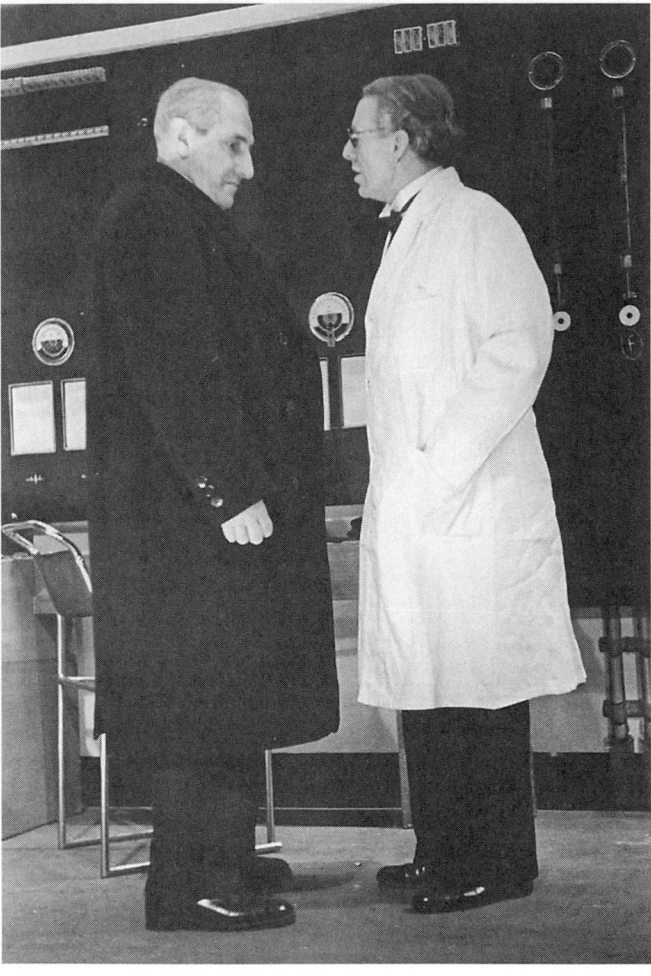

Lajos Biro

1948   *An Ideal Husband* (A. Korda)
1955   *Storm over the Nile*

Publications

By BIRO: books—

Bálványrombolók, Nagyvárad, 1901.
A fekete ostor és más novellák, Budapest, 1911.
A vízözön, és egyéb elbeszélések, Budapest, 1911.
Kunszállási emberek, Budapest, 1912, as *The Last Command*, London, 1929.
Tavaszi ünnep, Budapest, 1913.
1913, Budapest, 1914.
A diadalmas asszony, Budapest, 1921.
Harminc novella, Budapest, 1922.
Nyári zivatar, Budapest, 1922.
Házasság, Budapest, 1926.
With others, *The Last Command* (script), in *Motion Picture Continuities*, edited by Frances Taylor, New York, 1929.
A Molitor-ház, Budapest, 1931.
With Arthur Wimperis, *The Private Life of Henry VIII* (script), edited by Ernest Betts, London, 1934.

Gods and Kings: Six Plays, London, 1945.
Szolgák országa, Budapest, 1957.

On BIRO: article—

Film Kultura (Budapest), December 1985.

*   *   *

A prolific and celebrated Hungarian writer of the old school, Lajos Biro was originally a journalist and drama critic who, based in Vienna, published some 30 volumes of romantic plays, novels, and short stories, much of this work translated into German and other languages. He left Hungary after the First World War and worked variously in Rome, Paris, and Berlin as well as Hollywood, where in 1924 he became primarily a successful screenwriter for silent film. His earlier credits included an acknowledgement for his play *The Czarina* as the basis for Ernst Lubitsch's film *Forbidden Paradise*, while another of his plays, *Hotel Imperial*, was adapted three times for the screen, the last as Billy Wilder's *Five Graves to Cairo*.

In the 1930s Biro became one of the highly creative team of Hungarian film writers, artists, and executives assembled in England by Alexander Korda for his newly established production company, London Films. He was to remain in close association with Korda until his death in 1948. He co-scripted Korda's first British film, *Service for Ladies*; he acted as staff "dramaturge," or script supervisor, not only on those films Korda himself directed, such as *The Private Life of Henry VIII*, *Rembrandt*, and *An Ideal Husband*, but those he produced, including Czinner's *Catherine the Great* (another adaptation of *The Czarina*), Harold Young's *The Scarlet Pimpernel*, Jacques Feyder's *Knight without Armour*, Tim Whelan's *The Divorce of Lady X*, and Zoltan Korda's *Sanders of the River*, *The Drum*, *The Four Feathers*, and *The Thief of Bagdad*. No doubt Korda's implicit trust in Biro began with their early association and collaboration in Hungary and subsequently in Hollywood. He also worked on H. G. Wells's film *The Man Who Could Work Miracles* and (uncredited) Korda's abortive production of *I, Claudius*, and at one stage acted as script adviser to Winston Churchill when Korda invited the future Prime Minister to prepare a script about his ancestor, the Duke of Marlborough.

—Roger Manvell

BIROC, Joseph

Cinematographer. **Nationality:** American. **Born:** New York City, 12 February 1903. **Education:** Attended Emerson High School, Union City, New Jersey. **Military Service:** U.S. Signal Corps during World War II: filmed the liberation of Paris. **Career:** Camera operator during the 1930s; 1947—first feature film as cinematographer, *It's a Wonderful Life*; 1952—shot the first 3-D feature film, *Bwana Devil*; much work for TV, including episodes for *Superman*, *Richard Diamond*, and *Four Star Theatre*, and the mini-series *The Money-changers*, 1976, *Washington: Behind Closed Doors*, 1977, *Little Women*, 1978, and *Scruples*, 1980. **Awards:** Academy Award, for *The Towering Inferno*, 1974; Life Achievement Award, American Society of Cinematographers, 1989. **Died:** 7 September 1996, in Woodland Hills, California.

Films as Cinematographer:

1947 *It's a Wonderful Life* (Capra) (co); *Magic Town* (Wellman); *A Miracle Can Happen* (*On Our Merry Way*) (K. Vidor and Fenton) (co)

1948 *My Dear Secretary* (Martin)

1949 *Roughshod* (Robson); *Mrs. Mike* (L. King); *Johnny Allegro* (*Hounded*) (Tetzlaff)

1950 *The Killer that Stalked New York* (*The Frightened City*) (McEnvoy)

1951 *Cry Danger* (Parrish); *All that I Have* (Claxton)

1952 *Without Warning* (Laven); *The Bushwackers* (*The Rebel*) (Amateau); *Red Planet Mars* (Horner); *Bwana Devil* (Oboler); *Loan Shark* (Friedman)

1953 *The Twonky* (Oboler); *Vice Squad* (*The Girl in Room 17*) (Laven); *Donovan's Brain* (Feist); *The Glass Wall* (Shane); *The Tall Texan* (Williams); *Appointment in Honduras* (J. Tourneur); *Charade* (Kellino) (co)

1955 *Bengazi* (Brahm); *Ghost Town* (Miner)

1956 *Quincannon, Frontier Scout* (*Frontier Scout*) (Selander); *Nightmare* (Shane); *Attack!* (Aldrich); *The Black Whip* (Warren); *Tension at Table Rock* (Warren)

1957 *The Ride Back* (Miner); *The Garment Jungle* (V. Sherman); *China Gate* (Fuller); *Run of the Arrow* (Fuller); *The Unknown Terror* (Warren); *Forty Guns* (Fuller); *The Amazing Colossal Man* (Gordon)

1958 *Underwater Warrior* (Marton); *Home before Dark* (LeRoy)

1959 *Born Reckless* (Koch); *The FBI Story* (LeRoy); *Verboten!* (Fuller); *The Bat* (Wilbur)

1960 *Ice Palace* (V. Sherman); *Thirteen Ghosts* (Castle)

1961 *Gold of the Seven Saints* (Douglas); *Operation Eichmann* (Springsteen); *The Devil at Four O'Clock* (Brecher); *Sail a Crooked Ship* (Brecher)

1962 *Convicts Four* (*Reprieve*) (Kaufman); *Hitler* (Heisler); *Confessions of an Opium Eater* (*Evils of Chinatown*) (Zugsmith)

1963 *Bye Bye Birdie* (Sidney); *Toys in the Attic* (Hill); *Under the Yum Yum Tree* (Swift); *Gunfight at Comanche Creek* (MacDonald)

1964 *Viva Las Vegas* (*Love in Las Vegas*) (Sidney); *Bullet for a Badman* (Springsteen); *Ride the Wild Surf* (Taylor); *Promises, Promises* (Donovan); *Kitten with a Whip* (Heyes); *Hush . . . Hush, Sweet Charlotte* (Aldrich); *The Young Lovers* (Goldwyn) (co)

1965 *I Saw What You Did* (Castle); *The Flight of the Phoenix* (Aldrich)

1966 *The Russians Are Coming, the Russians Are Coming* (Jewison); *The Swinger* (Sidney); *Warning Shot* (Kulik); *Who's Minding the Mint?* (Morris)

1967 *Enter Laughing* (C. Reiner); *Tony Rome* (Douglas); *Fitzwilly* (*Fitzwilly Strikes Back*) (Delbert Mann)

1968 *The Detective* (Douglas); *The Legend of Lylah Clare* (Aldrich); *Lady in Cement* (Douglas); *The Killing of Sister George* (Aldrich)

1969 *Whatever Happened to Aunt Alice?* (Katzin); *Too Late the Hero* (Aldrich)

1970 *Mrs. Pollifax—Spy* (Martinson)

1971 *Escape from the Planet of the Apes* (Taylor); *The Grissom Gang* (Aldrich); *The Organization* (Medford); *Brian's Song* (Kulik)

1972 *Ulzana's Raid* (Aldrich); *Gidget Gets Married* (Swackhamer); *Playmates* (Flicker); *The Crooked Hearts* (Sandrich)

1973 *Cahill, United States Marshal* (*Cahill*) (McLaglen); *Emperor of the North* (Aldrich)

1974 *Blazing Saddles* (M. Brooks); *The Longest Yard* (*The Mean Machine*) (Aldrich); *Shanks* (Castle); *The Towering Inferno* (Guillermin) (co); *Wonder Woman* (McEveety); *Honky Tonk* (Taylor); *Thursday's Game* (Moore) (produced 1971)

1975 *Hustle* (Aldrich)

1976 *The Duchess and the Dirtwater Fox* (Frank)

1977 *The Choirboys* (Aldrich); *SST—Death Flight* (*SST: Disaster in the Sky*) (Rich)

1978 *A Family Upside Down* (Rich); *The Clone Master* (Medford)

1980 *Kenny Rogers as the Gambler* (Lowry)

1981 *. . . All the Marbles* (*The California Dolls*) (Aldrich)

1982 *Hammett* (Wenders) (co); *Airplane II: The Sequel* (Finkleman); *Desperate Lives* (Lewis)

1984 *The Jerk, Too* (Schultz—for TV)

1985 *Father of Hell Town* (Medford—for TV); *A Death in California* (Mann—for TV)

1986 *A Winner Never Quits* (Damski—for TV); *Outrage!* (Grauman—for TV)

Other Films:

1934 *Where Sinners Meet* (*The Dover Road*) (Ruben) (asst cameraman); *The Gay Divorcee* (*The Gay Divorce*) (Sandrich) (asst cameraman)

1935 *Laddie* (Stevens) (cameraman); *Break of Hearts* (Moeller) (cameraman)

1940 *Tom Brown's Schooldays* (Stevenson) (cameraman)

1963 *Four for Texas* (Aldrich) (2nd unit ph)

Publications

By BIROC: articles—

"Hollywood Launches 3-D Production," in *American Cinematographer* (Hollywood), August 1952.

"Photographing *Washington: Behind Closed Doors*," in *American Cinematographer* (Hollywood), November 1977.

Photoplay (London), August 1979.

American Cinematographer (Hollywood), July 1981.

On BIROC: articles—

Focus on Film (London), no. 13, 1973.

Patterson, R., on *Hammett* in *American Cinematographer* (Hollywood), November 1982.

Basinger, Jeanine, in *The* It's a Wonderful Life *Book*, 1987.

American Cinematographer (Hollywood), March 1989.

Obituary, in *American Cinematographer* (Hollywood), November 1996.

Obituary, in *Cinefantastique* (Forest Park), vol. 28, no. 6, 1996.

*   *   *

Joseph Biroc's cinematography has a no-nonsense competence that does not draw attention to itself. His images are always at the service of the story, never showy in or of themselves. It is easy to dismiss Biroc as a modest talent or (worse yet) to ignore him altogether; but a look at his filmography reveals a body of work of impressive skill, variety, vitality, and innovation.

Biroc learned the ropes as a cinematographer in the Army Signal Corps during World War II and did not begin working in Hollywood until his mid-forties. He received his first screen credit as co-photographer with Joseph Walker on Frank Capra's *It's a Wonderful Life*, and he applied Walker's teachings to the Capra-esque (though directed by William Wellman) *Magic Town*. Biroc wasted no time in proving his uncommon versatility; he provided some admirably hard-boiled images for films noir *Johnny Allegro* and *Cry Danger* and proved equal to the challenges of 3-D in *Bwana Devil* (the first film made in the process), special effects on a dimestore budget in *The Amazing Colossal Man*, and CinemaScope in *The Devil at Four O'Clock* and *Bye Bye Birdie*.

Biroc's long association with Robert Aldrich—beginning with *Attack!* and continuing until the director's untimely death in 1982—gave the cinematographer some of his most challenging assignments. Aldrich's work is strongly individualistic (eccentric, even) and Biroc was a trusted ally for translating that maverick vision into powerful and telling images. If the Aldrich films were all that survived of Biroc's work his career would still strike one as unusually provocative. From the punchy, gritty images of *Attack!* to the lush color stylings in *The Legend of Lylah Clare*, the austere landscapes of the survival in the desert drama *The Flight of the Phoenix*, the berserk pyrotechnics of *The Grissom Gang* to the sad dignity of *Ulzana's Raid* and the neon raunch of the world of female wrestling in . . . *All the Marbles*, Biroc and Aldrich worked together with a sympathy of purpose as productive as Griffith and Bitzer, Capra and Walker, and Bergman and Nykvist.

Other directors have not been as demanding of Biroc, and *The Swinger*; *The Russians Are Coming, the Russians Are Coming*; *Who's Minding the Mint?*; and *The Duchess and the Dirtwater Fox* can count his professional sheen as one of their few attributes. Biroc's name continues to appear on such box-office hits as *Airplane!* Though he has become one of cinematography's Grand Old Men, his work retains the muscle and clarity that has always distinguished it from that of his more prosaic peers. For that work, the American Society of Cinematographers bestowed on him its prestigious life achievement award in 1989.

—Frank Thompson, updated by John McCarty

BISWAS, Anil

Composer. **Nationality:** Indian. **Born:** Barisal, East Bengal (now Bangladesh), 1914. **Career:** 1930—moved to Calcutta: actor, singer, and assistant music director, Rangmahal Theatre, 1932–34; 1934—moved to Bombay; 1935—composed background music for *Dharam Ki Devi*; 1936–42—composer for Sagar Movietones; 1942—joined Bombay Talkies; 1957—worked on two films in the USSR; 1963–65—director of National Orchestra for All India Radio (AIR), and chief producer of light Hindustani music from 1965; television work

includes title music for popular serial *Humlog*. **Address:** K-11/12, South Extension Part-II, New Delhi 110049, India.

Films as Composer/Music Director:

1935   *Dharam Ki Devi*
1936   *Pratima (Prem Murti)*; *Prem Bandhan*; *Sher Ka Panja*
1937   *Bull Dog*; *Dukhiyari*; *Gentleman Daku*; *Insaf*; *Jagirdar*; *Kokila*; *Maha Geet*
1938   *Dynamite*; *Gramaphone Singer*; *Hum Tum aur Woh*; *Nirala Hindustan*; *Abhilasha*; *300 Din Ke Baad*; *Vatan*
1939   *Jeevan Sathi*; *Ek Hi Raasta*
1940   *Alibaba*; *Aurat*; *Pooja*
1941   *Aasraa*; *Bahen*; *Nai Roshani*
1942   *Apna Paraya*; *Gareeb*; *Jawani*; *Roti*; *Vijaya*
1943   *Hamari Baat*; *Basant*; *Kismat*
1944   *Char Ankhen*; *Jwar Bhata*
1945   *Pahli Nazar*
1946   *Milan*
1947   *Bhookh*; *Manjudhar*; *Nayya*
1948   *Anokha Pyar*; *Gajre*; *Veena*
1949   *Girls' School*; *Jeet*; *Ladali*
1950   *Arzoo*; *Beqasoor*; *Lajawab*
1951   *Aaraam*; *Badi Bahu*; *Do Sitare*; *Taran*
1952   *Do Raha*
1953   *Aakash*; *Farib*; *Ham Dard*; *Julianwale*; *Baag ki Jyoti*; *Mehmaan*; *Rahi*
1954   *Maan*; *Mahatma Kabir Munna*; *Naaz*; *Waris*
1955   *Farar*
1956   *Heer*; *Paisa hi paisa*
1957   *Abhiman*; *Jalti Nishani*; *Afanasi Nikitin*; *Pardeshi*
1958   *Sanskar*
1959   *Char dil Char rahen*
1960   *Angulimaal*; *Mira ka Chitra*; *Superman ki Wapasi*
1961   *Lucky Number*; *Savitri*
1962   *Hame Khelne Do*; *Sautela Bhai*
1964   *Raju aur Gangaram*
1965   *Chhoti Chhoti Baten*

Publications

On BISWAS: book—

Anil Biswas: Tribute—A Collection of Essays on the Occasion of His Fiftieth Year of Music Composition for Films, Bangalore, 1986.

*   *   *

The music Anil Biswas has composed for films is a reflection of his active and eventful life. Born at a time when a wave of patriotism was sweeping the country, young Biswas became an active underground worker and a revolutionary. This patriotic militancy and stirring optimism came to be manifested in the music that he composed for Hindi films.

Biswas began composing film music in 1931, but the first film in which he was credited with composing the entire score is the 1935

Dharam Ki Devi. The memorable scores that followed bore ample testimony not only to a wide variety of songs but to an element of orchestration that accompanied each composition. By then, he had formed an orchestra of 12 musicians, a number considered "extraordinary" by the industry. Orchestration had always fascinated him, particularly the adaptation of Indian *ragas* within a Western discipline. When Biswas began work with the Bombay film industry, music-recording was in its infancy. Once when Biswas, an accomplished singer, played the role of a blind performer, the camera, mike, and orchestra had to be moved down the road with him as he sang.

Biswas's immense popularity is due not only to the songs that he composed but also to his background scores. He paid careful attention to instrumental scores for creating mood and ambiance. He also pioneered the adaptation of folk and classical forms within modern film music. He felt that only the "temple" and the "field," symbolizing the Indian classical and folk traditions respectively, could salvage contemporary Indian music from colonial fetters. His fame also rests on his ability to create music with which ordinary Indians can identify.

—Shohini Ghosh

BITZER, Billy

Cinematographer. **Nationality:** American. **Born:** Johan Gottlieb Wilhelm Bitzer in Roxbury, Massachusetts, 21 April 1872; brother of the photographer John C. Bitzer. **Education:** Trained as silversmith: studied electrical engineering, Cooper Union, New York. **Family:** Married Ethel (Bitzer), son: Eden Griffith Bitzer. **Career:** 1894—joined Magic Introduction Company, later called American Mutoscope, then Biograph Company, and photographed (with Laurie Dickson); projected first Mutoscope films, shown in 1896; in the next dozen years photographed many newsreel and popular interest subjects; 1908—first film shot for D. W. Griffith, *A Calamitous Elopement*: shot most of Griffith's films until 1924 (in Hollywood after 1913); 1926—founder, International Photographers of the Motion Picture Industries (twice president); worked in a New York photographic shop in late 1930s; 1939—began assembling old cameras and restoring film prints and documents for Museum of Modern Art. **Died:** Of heart disease, Woodland Hills, California, 29 April 1944.

Films as Cinematographer:

1896 *William McKinley at Canton, Ohio*; *Hard Wash*
1897 *President McKinley's Inauguration*; *Mutoscope Shorts*
1898 *U.S.S. Maine, Havana Harbor*; *Spanish-American War Scenes*
1899 *Jim Jeffries-Jim Sharkey Fight*; *Ambulance Corps Drill*; *Children Feeding Ducklings*; *How Ducks Are Fattened*; *Train on Jacob's Ladder, Mt. Washington*; *Frankenstein Trestle, White Mts.*; *Canadian Pacific Railroad Shots*; *Union Pacific Railroad Shots*; *The Picturesque West*
1900 *Galveston Hurricane Shots*; *Polo Games, Brooklyn*; *The Interrupted Message* (+ d, sc); *Tough Kid's Waterloo*; *Grand Trunk Railroad Scenes*; *Water Duel*; *Love in the Suburbs*; *Last Alarm*; *U.S. Naval Militia*; *Council Bluffs to Omaha—Train Scenic*; *Childhood's Vow*; *At Breakneck Speed* (Fall River, Mass.)
1901 *Middies Shortening Sail*; *Boats under Oars*; *Pan-American Exposition Electric Tower*; *Union Pacific Railroad Scenes*; *In the Grazing Country*; *Fattened for the Market*
1902 *St. Louis Exposition*
1903 *I Want My Dinner*; *N.Y. City Fire Dept.*; *American Soldier in Love and War*; *Boy in the Barrel*; *Dude and the Burglar*; *Don't Get Gay with Your Manicure*; *Model Courtship*; *Jeffries-Corbett Fight* (restaged); *Happy Hooligan Earns His Dinner*; *How Mike Got the Soap in His Eyes*; *In the N.Y. Subway*; *Kidnapper*; *Physical Culture Girls*; *Poor Old Fido*; *President T. R. Roosevelt, July 4th*; *Professor of the Drama*; *Pajama Girl*; *Sweets for the Sweet*; *Shocking Incident*; *She Fell Fainting in His Arms*; *Too Ardent Lover*; *Unprotected Female*; *Unfaithful Wife*; *Wages of Sin*; *Widow*; *Willie's Camera*; *Why Foxy Grandpa Escaped Ducking*; *Weighing the Baby*; *You Will Send Me to Bed, Eh?*
1904 *Auto Boat on the Hudson*; *Vanderbilt Cup Auto Race*; *Holland Submarine Torpedo Boat*; *Children in the Surf*; *Coney Island Police Patrol Chicken Thief*; *First Baby*; *Hero of Liao Yang*; *Judge Alton B. Parker*; *Lost Child*; *Moonshiners*; *Person*; *Racing the Chutes at Dreamland*; *Seashore Baby*; *Slocum Disaster*; *Speed Test of Tarantula*; *Swimming Class*; *Two Bottle Babies*; *Widow and the Only Man*
1905 *Al Treloar Muscle Exercises*; *Athletic Girl and Burglar*; *Auto Races, Ormonde, Fla.*; *Ballroom Tragedy*; *Barnstormers*; *Between the Dances*; *Chauncy Explains*; *Country Courtship*; *Dream of the Racetrack Fiend*; *Deer Stalking with Camera*; *Departure of Train from Station*; *Deadwood Sleeper*; *Everybody Works but Father*; *Firebug*; *Flight of Ludlows Aerodrome*; *Fun on the Joy Line*; *Gee, If Me Mudder Could See Me*; *Gossipers*; *Great Jewel Mystery*; *Henpecked Husband*; *His Move*; *Horse Thief*; *Impossible Convicts*; *Kentucky Feud*; *Leap Frog Railway*; *Ludlow's Aeroplane*; *Lifting the Lid*; *Mobilizing Mass. State Troops*; *Moose Hunt in Canada*; *Mystery of the Jewel Casket*; *Nan Paterson's Trial*; *Oslerizing Papa*; *Pipe Dream*; *Quail Shooting*; *Pinehurst*; *Reuben in the Subway*; *River Pirates*; *Reception of British Fleet*; *Salmon Fishing, Quebec*; *Sparring at N.Y. Athletic Club*; *Simple Life*; *Spirit of '76*; *Trout Fishing, Rangeley Lakes*; *Turkey Hunt, Pinehurst*; *Two Topers*; *Under the Bamboo Tree*; *Wine Opener*; *Wedding*; *Wrestling, N.Y. Athletic Club*
1906 *At the Monkey House*; *Black Hand*; *Country Schoolmaster*; *Critic*; *Dr. Dippy's Sanitarium*; *Fox Hunt*; *Friend in Need Is Friend Indeed*; *Gateway to the Catskills*; *Grand Hotel to Big Indian*; *Hallroom Boys*; *Holdup of Rocky Mt. Express*; *In the Haunts of Rip Van Winkle*; *In the Heart of the Catskills*; *Lighthouse*; *Married for Millions*; *Masqueraders*; *Mr. Butt-In*; *Mr. Hurry-Up*; *Night of the Party*; *Paymaster*; *Poughkeepsie Regatta*; *San Francisco*; *Society Ballooning*; *Subpoena Server*; *Trial Marriages*; *Through Austin Glen*; *Valley of Esopus*; *Village Cut-Up*
1907 *Crayono*; *Deaf-Mutes Ball*; *Dr. Skinum*; *Elopement*; *Falsely Accused*; *Fencing Master*; *Fights of Nations*; *Hypnotist's Revenge*; *If You Had a Wife Like This*; *Jamestown Exposition*; *Love Microbe*; *Model's Ma*; *Mrs. Smithers' Boarding School*; *Neighbors*; *Professional Jealousy*; *Rube Brown in*

Town; Tenderloin Tragedy; Terrible Ted; Truants; Under the Old Apple Tree; Wife Wanted; Yale Laundry

1908   Bobby's Kodak; Classmates; Lonesome Junction; Snowman; Boy Detective; Princess in the Vase; Yellow Peril; Caught by Wireless; Famous Escape; Her First Adventure; Old Isaacs, the Pawnbroker; His Day of Rest; Hulda's Lovers; King of the Cannibal Islands; King's Messenger; Mixed Babies; Music Master; Romance of an Egg; Sculptor's Nightmare; When Knights Were Bold; At the French Ball; Invisible Fluid; Man in the Box; Night of Terror; 'Ostler Joe; Outlaw; Over the Hills to the Poorhouse; Thompson's Night Out; Black Viper; Fight for Freedom; Kentuckian; A Calamitous Elopement; Deceived Slumming Party; The Man and the Woman; Betrayed by a Handprint; Monday Morning in a Coney Island Police Court; Smoked Husband; The Stolen Jewels; Where the Breakers Roar; The Zulu's Heart; The Barbarian, Ingomar; Concealing a Burglar; The Devil; Father Gets in the Game; Mr. Jones at the Ball; The Planter's Wife; Romance of a Jewess; Vaquero's Vow; After Many Years; The Guerilla; The Ingrate; Money Man; Pirate's Gold; Song of the Shirt; Taming of the Shrew; The Christmas Burglars; The Clubman and the Tramp; The Feud and the Turkey; The Reckoning; The Test of Friendship; Valet's Wife; The Curtain Pole; Mrs. Jones Entertains; The Maniac Cook; A Wreath in Time; The Honor of Thieves; The Criminal Hypnotist; The Sacrifice; The Welcome Burglar; A Rural Elopement; Mrs. Jones Has a Card Party; The Hindoo Dagger; The Salvation Army Lass; Love Finds a Way; Tragic Love; The Girls and a Daddy

1909   Those Boys; The Cord of Life; Trying to Get Married; The Fascinating Mrs. Frances; Those Awful Hats; Jones and the Lady Book Agent; The Drive for Life; The Brahma Diamond; The Politician's Love Story; The Jones Have Amateur Theatricals; Edgar Allan Poe; The Roue's Heart; His Ward's Love; At the Altar; The Prussian Spy; The Medicine Bottle; The Deception; The Lure of the Gown; Lady Helen's Escapade; A Fool's Revenge; The Wooden Leg; I Did It, Mama; A Burglar's Mistake; The Voice of the Violin; A Little Child Shall Lead Them; The French Duel; Jones and His New Neighbors; A Drunkard's Reformation; The Winning Coat; A Rude Hostess; The Eavesdropper; Confidence; Lucky Jim; A Sound Sleeper; A Troublesome Satchel; 'Tis an Ill Wind; The Suicide Club; Resurrection; One Busy Hour; A Baby's Shoe; Eloping with Auntie; The Cricket on the Hearth; The Jilt; Eradicating Auntie; What Drink Did; Her First Biscuit; The Violin Maker of Cremona; Two Memories; The Lonely Villa; The Peach-Basket Hat; The Son's Return; His Duty; A New Trick; The Necklace; The Way of Man; The Faded Lillies; The Message; The Friend of the Family; Was Justice Served?; Mrs. Jones' Lover; The Mexican Sweetheart; The Country Doctor; Jealousy and the Man; The Renunciation; The Cardinal's Conspiracy; The Seventh Day; Tender Hearts; A Convict's Sacrifice; Sweet and Twenty; The Slave; They Would Elope; Mrs. Jones' Burglar; The Mended Lute; Indian Runner's Romance; With Her Card; The Better Way; His Wife's Visitor; The Mills of the Gods; Oh, Uncle!; The Sealed Room; 1776, or Hessian Renegades; The Little Darling; In Old Kentucky; The Children's Friend; Comata, The Sioux;

Getting Even; The Broken Locket; A Fair Exchange; The Awakening; Pippa Passes; Leather Stocking; Fools of Fate; Wanted, a Child; The Little Teacher; A Change of Heart; His Lost Love; Lines of White on the Sullen Sea; The Gibson Goddess; In the Watches of the Night; The Expiation; What's Your Hurry?; The Restoration; Nursing a Viper; Two Women and a Man; The Light That Came; A Midnight Adventure; The Open Gate; Sweet Revenge; The Mountaineer's Honor; In the Window Recess; The Trick that Failed; The Death Disk; Through the Breakers; In a Hempen Bag; A Corner in Wheat; The Redman's View; The Test; A Trap for Santa Claus; In Little Italy; To Save Her Soul; Choosing a Husband; The Rocky Road; The Dancing Girl of Butte; Her Terrible Ordeal; The Call; The Honor of the Family; On the Reef; The Last Deal; One Night and Then—; The Cloister's Touch; The Woman from Mellon's; The Duke's Plan; The Englishman and the Girl

1910   The Final Settlement; His Last Burglary; Taming a Husband; The Newlyweds; The Thread of Destiny; In Old California; The Man; The Converts; Faithful; The Twisted Trail; Gold Is Not All; As It Is in Life; A Rich Revenge; Romance of the Western Hills; Thou Shalt Not; The Way of the World; The Unchanging Sea; The Gold Seekers; The Two Brothers; Unexpected Help; Ramona; Over Silent Paths; The Impalement; In the Season of Buds; A Child of the Ghetto; In the Border States; A Victim of Jealousy; The Face at the Window; The Marked Timetable; A Child's Impulse; Muggsy's First Sweetheart; The Purgation; A Midnight Cupid; What the Daisy Said; A Child's Faith; The Call to Arms; Serious Sixteen; A Flash of Light; As the Bells Rang Out; The Arcadian Maid; House with the Closed Shutters; Her Father's Pride; A Salutary Lesson; The Usurer; Sorrows of the Unfaithful; In Life's Cycle; Wilful Peggy; A Summer Idyll; The Modern Prodigal; Rose o' Salem Town; Little Angels of Luck; A Mohawk's Way; The Oath and the Man; The Iconoclast; Examination Day at School; That Chink in Golden Gulch; The Broken Doll; The Banker's Daughters; The Message of the Violin; Two Little Waifs; Waiter No. 5; The Fugitive; Simple Charity; Song of the Wildwood Flute; A Child's Strategem; Sunshine Sue; A Plain Song; His Sister-in-Law; The Golden Supper; The Lesson; When a Ma Loves; Winning Back His Love; His Trust; His Trust Fulfilled; A Wreath of Orange Blossoms; The Italian Barber; The Two Paths; Conscience; Three Sisters; A Decree of Destiny; Fate's Turning; What Shall We Do with Our Old?; The Diamond Star; The Lily of the Tenements; Heart Beats of Long Ago

1911   Fisher Folks; His Daughter; The Lonedale Operator; Was He a Coward?; Teaching Dad to Like Her; The Spanish Gypsy; The Broken Cross; The Chief's Daughter; A Knight of the Road; Madame Rex; His Mother's Scarf; How She Triumphed; In the Days of '49; The Two Sides; The New Dress; Enoch Arden (2 parts); The White Rose of the Wilds; The Crooked Road; A Romany Tragedy; A Smile of the Child; The Primal Call; The Jealous Husband; The Indian Brothers; The Thief and the Girl; Her Sacrifice; Blind Princess and the Poet; The Last Drop of Water; Bobby the Coward; A Country Cupid; The Ruling Passion; The Rose of Kentucky; The Sorrowful Example; Sword and Hearts; The

Stuff Heroes Are Made Of; Old Confecioner's Mistake; The Unveiling; The Eternal Mother; Dan the Dandy; Revenue Man and the Girl; The Squaw's Love; Italian Blood; The Making of a Man; Her Awakening; The Adventures of Billy; The Long Road; The Battle; Love in the Hills; The Trail of the Books; Through Darkened Vales; Saved from Himself; A Woman Scorned; The Miser's Heart; The Failure; Sunshine through the Dark; As in a Looking-Glass; A Terrible Discovery; The Voice of the Child; A Tale of the Wilderness; The Baby and the Stork; The Old Bookkeeper; A Sister's Love; For His Son; The Transformation of Mike; A Blot on the Scutcheon; Billy's Strategem; The Sunbeam; A String of Pearls; The Root of Evil

1912 *The Mender of the Nets; Under Burning Skies; A Siren of Impulse; Iola's Promise; The Goddess of Sagebrush Gulch; The Girl and Her Trust; The Punishment; Fate's Interception; The Female of the Species; Just Like a Woman; One Is Business, the Other Crime; The Lesser Evil; The Old Actor; A Lodging for the Night; His Lesson; When Kings Were the Law; A Beast at Bay; An Outcast among Outcasts; Home Folks; A Temporary Truce; The Spirit Awakened; Lena and the Geese; An Indian Summer; The Schoolteacher and the Waif; Man's Lust for Gold; Man's Genesis; Heaven Avenges; A Pueblo Legend; The Sands of Dee; Black Sheep; The Narrow Road; A Child's Remorse; The Inner Circle; An Unseen Enemy; Two Daghters of Eve; Friends; So Near Yet So Far; A Feud in the Kentucky Hills; In the Aisles of the Wild; The One She Loved; The Painted Lady; The Musketeers of Pig Alley; Heredity; Gold and Glitter; My Baby; The Informer; Brutality; The New York Hat; My Hero; The Burglar's Dilemma; A Cry for Help; The God Within; The Unwelcome Guest; Pirate Gold; The Massacre; Oil and Water; Three Friends; The Telephone Girl and the Lady; Fate; Adventure in the Autumn Woods; A Chance Deception; The Tenderhearted Boy; A Misappropriated Turkey; Brothers; Drink's Lure, Love in an Apartment Hotel*

1913 *Broken Ways; A Girl's Strategem; Near to Earth; A Welcome Intruder; The Sheriff's Baby; The Hero of Little Italy; The Perfidy of Mary; A Misunderstood Boy; The Little Tease; The Lady and the Mouse; The Wanderer; The House of Darkness; Olaf, an Atom; His Mother's Son; Just Gold; The Gold; The Yaqui Cur; The Ranchero's Revenge; A Timely Interception; Death's Marathon; The Sorrowful Shore; The Mistake; The Mothering Heart; Her Mother's Oath; During the Roundup; The Coming of Angelo; An Indian's Loyalty; Two Men of the Desert*

1914 *In Prehistoric Days; Judith of Bethulia; The Battle at Elderbush Gulch; The Battle of the Sexes; The Escape; Home, Sweet Home; The Avenging Conscience*

1915 **The Birth of a Nation**

1916 **Intolerance**

1918 *Hearts of the World; The Great Love; The Greatest Thing in Life*

1919 *A Romance in Happy Valley; The Girl Who Stayed Home; True-Heart Susie; Scarlet Days;* **Broken Blossoms**; *The Greatest Question*

1920 *The Idol Dancer; The Love Flower; Way Down East*

1923 *The White Rose*

1924 *America*

1928 *Drums of Love; The Battle of the Sexes*
1929 *Lady of the Pavements*

Publications

By BITZER: book—

Billy Bitzer: His Story, New York, 1973.

By BITZER: article—

"I Remember," in *Cine-Technician* (London), September/October 1944.

On BITZER: articles—

Owen, Kenneth, "The Man Behind," in *Photoplay* (New York), August 1915.

Sterling, Philip, in *New Theatre* (New York), April 1937.

Arnheim, Rudolph, in *Intercine* (Rome), January 1938.

Stern, S., in *Films in Review* (New York), October 1952.

Image (Rochester, New York), March 1958.

Mitchell, George J., "Billy Bitzer, Pioneer and Innovator," in *American Cinematographer* (Hollywood), December 1964.

Lightman, Herb A., "The Film Artistry of D. W. Griffith and Billy Bitzer," in *American Cinematographer* (Hollywood), January 1969.

Focus on Film (London), no. 13, 1973.

Silent Picture (London), no. 18, 1973.

Spehr, Paul, in *Backstage*, 12 November 1976.

Williams, Martin, in *Griffith: First Artist of the Movies*, New York, 1980.

Gish, Lillian, "Griffith et Billy Bitzer," in *Cinématographe* (Paris), June 1981.

Brown, Karl, in *American Cinematographer* (Hollywood), January 1983.

Schickel, Richard, in *D. W. Griffith*, London, 1984.

McDonough, T., "Tender Is the Light," in *American Film* (Washington, D.C.), April 1984.

Turconi, Davide, "'Hic sunt leones': The First Decade of American Film Comedy," in *Griffithiana*, September 1996.

*   *   *

Billy Bitzer's career as a cinematographer spanned the silent film era, and his development as a cameraman provides a history of early filmmaking. Because he worked primarily with D. W. Griffith, the foremost director in silent film, he is permanently linked with Griffith in film history. The two worked so closely together that their collaboration amounted to a kind of partnership, one that produced the most outstanding films of the 1910s, among them *Broken Blossoms*, *Intolerance*, *The Birth of a Nation*, and *Judith of Bethulia*. In the 1920s, however, with the exception of *Way Down East* (1920), Griffith's career declined, as did Bitzer's. In addition to cultural changes brought on by World War I there were changes in cinematic style: German expressionism proved incompatible in content and technique with Griffith and Bitzer, who did not adapt well to a changed movie industry.

A former electrician with the Magic Introduction Company, Bitzer became a photographer when the company acquired the Mutoscope camera and changed its name to American Mutoscope and then Biograph. Among his earliest newsreels were William McKinley's receiving the presidential nomination in Canton, Ohio, and the Jim Jeffries-Jack Sharkey championship prizefight—he used 40 lights over the ring. He began making short fiction films in 1900 (he wrote, photographed, and directed *The Interrupted Message*, his first film). When Griffith came to Biograph, Bitzer had quite a bit of experience. When the two began working together in 1908, however, both men had to become cinematographic students in order to shoot the complex narratives Griffith had designed. Although Bitzer has been credited with the creation of the close-up, soft-focus photography, the iris shot, the fade-out, and backlighting, many of these techniques had been used before (Griffith credited Georges Méliès with some of these innovations); but Bitzer and Griffith were the first team to use these techniques to advance and enhance the narrative. Some of the cinematic "effects" were the results of accidents or mistakes; in his autobiography Bitzer recounts the accidental-discovery story of double exposure, as well as of the "reverse light" effect. He learned to shoot into the sun using a shaded lens, used the close-up to advance the narrative in *The Mender of Nets*, and, after Hendrik Sartov, a special effects photographer, joined the Griffith team, achieved the soft-focus effect which made *Broken Blossoms* an artistic triumph— the diffused, softened lighting on the Chinese rescuer is contrasted with the documentary photography accorded Battling Burrows. His first use of backlighting was in *The Politician's Love Story*, and he used Rembrandt lighting and profile portrait-effect in *Edgar Allan Poe*, fireside-light in *A Drunkard's Reformation*, parallel-action montage in *The Lonely Villa*, and morning-light effect in *Pippa Passes*. Sartov's arrival, however, heralded the beginning of Bitzer's decline. As he noted in his autobiography, "With the entrance of Sartov, I became the pupil." Sartov received cinematography credit for Griffith's *Dream Street*, and after *Way Down East* Bitzer was only one of several cameramen on the last five Griffith films.

—Thomas L. Erskine

BIZIOU, Peter

Cinematographer. **Nationality:** British. **Awards:** Best Artistic Contribution, Cannes Film Festival, for *Another Country*, 1984; Academy Award for Best Cinematography, British Academy Award for Best Cinematography, British Society of Cinematographers Best Cinematography Award, for *Mississippi Burning*, 1989.

Films as Cinematographer:

1969   *L'Échelle blanche* (Secret World) (Freeman)
1976   *Bugsy Malone* (Parker)
1979   *Life of Brian* (*Monty Python's Life of Brian*) (Jones)
1981   *Time Bandits* (Gilliam)
1982   *Pink Floyd The Wall* (*The Wall*) (Parker and Scarfe)
1984   *Another Country* (Kanievska)
1986   *Nine 1/2 Weeks* (Lyne)
1988   *A World Apart* (Menges); *Mississippi Burning* (Parker)

1990   *Rosencrantz and Guildenstern Are Dead* (Stoppard)
1992   *City of Joy* (*La Cité de la joie*) (Joffé); *Fatale* (*Damage*) (Malle)
1993   *In the Name of the Father* (Sheridan)
1994   *The Road to Wellville* (Parker)
1995   *Richard III* (Loncraine)
1998   *The Truman Show* (Weir)

Publications

On BIZIOU: articles—

Levin, L., "Nine and One-Half Weeks, a Love Story," in *American Cinematographer* (Hollywood), vol. 66, no. 8, August 1985.
Kauffmann, Stanley, *The New Republic* (New York), vol. 191, 9 July 1984.
Rudolph, E., "This Is Your Life," in *American Cinematographer* (Hollywood), vol. 79, June 1998.

*   *   *

Peter Biziou has quietly built a solid reputation as one of the finest cinematographers of his generation that Britain has produced. Of Welsh extraction, he began his career building models, graduated to lighting commercials, and began his career behind the camera with his friend and long time collaborator, director Alan Parker. His journeyman years spent making commercials have heavily influenced his style without inhibiting his creativity: in making Peter Weir's *The Truman Show* (1998) he relied on that "unreal" look to create an insular world lit by too-brilliant sunlight: as Weir put it, "I was taken with the way Peter uses light, his choice of lenses and his overall look. I loved his work with directors Alan Parker and Jim Sheridan. He takes chances, yet one always sees what one needs to see. I also knew that Peter is selective and only takes on films to which he feels he can offer something unique." *The Truman Show* itself is a showcase for the cinematographer's art: when the director Christof (Ed Harris) says abruptly, "Cue the sun" and a fireball shoots up in response (a stunning effect requiring Biziou's strategy and elaborate digital enhancement) or the vignettes that alert the viewer to the presence of the many spying cameras recording Truman Burbank's life. To give "a more obvious, menacing feel," Biziou used gobos placed in front of the lens and explored the use of wide angle lenses often used in commercials, as well as all the ingenious "Truman-cams." His ability to translate Weir's wish for a hyper-real, light-soaked Norman Rockwell world is in keeping with his reputation as an inventive, intuitive artisan who compliments and completes a director's vision.

His work on literary adaptations is much admired: the audacious *Richard III* (1995), fashioned by Ian McKellen and director Richard Loncraine, owes much to Biziou's smoke-filled, hazy ambiance which signifies the creeping evil of Richard's homicidal ambition. A deco palette of soft browns and tan interiors is punctuated by bold flashes of color (usually a vivid red, of lipstick, fire, or blood) or by the sleek menace of gleaming black leather crypto-Nazi outfits: *Richard III* invents a fascist state a la Leni Riefenstahl, and Biziou's precise lighting and camera work creates the proper shock of recognition, from a Marat-style death scene to a stunning, flag-waving political rally. Similarly, Tom Stoppard's *Rosencrantz and Guildenstern Are Dead* (1990) was saved from excessive staginess in large part by Biziou's work, and 1994's *The Road To Wellville*, a film otherwise disliked, was praised for its handsome photography.

Director Adrian Lyne praised Biziou's ability to deliver the exact look he wanted—an expensive, lush 1980s style eroticism that again hearkened back to the desired style of commercials—for his controversial *Nine 1/2 Weeks* (1985). The visual style of that film is what audiences responded to more than Lyne's typically juiced-up script, and which complimented leading lady Kim Basinger (whose career took off after this film). Biziou is also beloved of Monty Python fans: his work on *Life of Brian* (1979) and especially Terry Gilliam's cult favorite *Time Bandits* (1981) added much to the artistic success of those films. *Time Bandits'* conceit of time travel allowed Biziou to create a variety of visual styles to suggest historical passages and Gilliam's trademark, an otherworldly atmosphere and fantastic set design. The first employed a naturalistic style that added to its hilarious quality, while Gilliam's fantasy is otherworldly and surreal. Similarly, Biziou's work enhanced the cult artiness of Alan Parker's hypnotic midnight movie favorite *Pink Floyd—The Wall* (1982) and *Bugsy Malone* (1976) which established both Parker and Biziou, who met while still making commercials in the United Kingdom in the 1970s.

Peter Biziou finally received critical acclaim for his work in *Another Country*, the high-toned public school saga of spy Guy Burgess. He went for a look of "slightly sour sunlight" to suggest the oppressive nature of the place, and for this film he was awarded "Best Artistic Achievement" at the 1984 Cannes Film Festival. Admitted to the ranks of the British Cinematographer's Society, Biziou began to receive assignments more worthy of his talents. The versatile Biziou has proved most capable of handling assignments that require evoking difficult history: his work on Parker's *Mississippi Burning*, a fictionalized but gripping story of three murdered civil rights workers in 1964, catapulted him into the exclusive company of the best British cinematographers, capped by his Academy Award in 1989. The opening sequence (as the doomed men are chased by the Klan) is Biziou at his most powerful, and his artistic restraint helps to curtail Parker's characteristic excesses. Film historian Duncan Petrie noted that he used long lenses (between 70mm and 80mm) to give "an observational look" to the opening sequence, and further noted that Biziou has not been absorbed into the Hollywood scene, preferring to pick his projects and showing a preference for British films.

His work on Jim Sheridan's *In the Name of the Father* (1994) and Chris Menges' *A World Apart* (1988) shows Biziou's affinity for thoughtful, potentially controversial films. Biziou is as well known for his collegiality as his professional acumen: in an interview with *American Cinematographer* he was careful to credit everyone who helped achieve the astonishing look of *The Truman Show* and was generous with his praise. As a cinematographer, Peter Biziou has made good films exceptional and memorable, and his art has rescued many others: his body of work shows an artist of remarkable talent and sensitivity.

—Mary Hess

BLANC, Mel

Voice Artist. **Nationality:** American. **Born:** Melvin Jérome Blank in San Francisco, California, 30 May 1908; raised in Portland, Oregon. **Family:** Married Estelle Rosenberg, 1933; son: Noel. **Career:** 1927—sang on radio show *The Hoot Owls* with his wife; wrote and produced

Mel Blanc

and performed all characters in the daily show *Cobwebs and Nuts*; 1928—played bass and violin in San Francisco's NBC Radio Orchestra; 1937—began voice characterization for Warners' *Merrie Melodies* and *Looney Tunes* cartoons, including Bugs Bunny and Daffy Duck; regular performer on *The Jack Benny Show*; 1961—serious car accident. Television work included the voice of Barney Rubble in the *Flintstones*, Mr. Spacely in *The Jetsons* and Twiki in *Buck Rogers in the 25th Century*. **Died:** Of heart disease, Los Angeles, California, 10 July 1989.

Films as Voice Artist for Warner Bros.:

1937   *Porky the Wrestler*; *Porky's Road Race*; *Picador Porky*; *Porky's Romance*; *Porky's Duck Hunt*; *Porky and Gabby*; *Porky's Building*; *Porky's Super Service*; *Porky's Badtime Story*; *Porky's Railroad*; *Get Rich Quick Porky*; *Porky's Garden*; *Rover's Rival*; *The Case of the Stuttering Pig*; *Porky's Double Trouble*; *Porky's Hero Agency*

1938   *Daffy Duck and Egghead*; *Porky's Poppa*; *Porky at the Crocadero*; *What Price Porky*; *Porky's Phoney Express*; *Porky's Five and Ten*; *Porky's Hare Hunt*; *Injun Trouble*; *Porky the Fireman*; *Porky's Party*; *Porky's Spring Planting*; *Porky and Daffy*; *Wholly Smoke*; *Porky in Wackyland*; *Porky's Naughty Nephew*; *Porky in Egypt*; *The Daffy Doc*; *Daffy Duck in Hollywood*; *Porky the Gob*

1939   *The Lone Stranger and Porky*; *It's an Ill Wind*; *Porky's Tire Trouble*; *Porky's Movie Mystery*; *Prest-O Change-O*;

Chicken Jitters; Daffy Duck and the Dinosaur; Porky and Teabiscuit; Kristopher Kolumbus, Jr.; Polar Pals; Scalp Trouble; Old Glory; Porky's Picnic; Wise Quacks; Hare-Um Scare-Um; Porky's Hotel; Jeepers Creepers; Naughty Neighbors; Pied Piper Porky; Porky the Giant Killer; The Film Fan

1940 *Porky's Last Stand; The Early Worm Gets the Bird; Africa Squeaks; Mighty Hunters; Ali Baba Bound; Busy Bakers; Elmer's Candid Camera; Pilgrim Porky; Cross Country Doctors; Confederate Honey; Slap Happy Pappy; The Bear's Tale; The Hardship of Miles Standish; Porky's Poor Fish; Sniffles Takes a Trip; You Ought to Be in Pictures; A Gander at Mother Goose; The Chewin' Bruin; Tom Thumb in Trouble; Circus Today; Porky's Baseball Broadcast; Little Blabbermouse; The Egg Collector; A Wild Hare; Ghost Wanted; Patient Porky; Ceiling Hero; Malibu Beach Party; Calling Dr. Porky; Stage Fright; Prehistoric Porky; Holiday Highlights; Good Night Elmer; The Sour Puss; Wacky Wildlife; Bedtime for Sniffles; Porky's Hired Hand; Of Fox and Hounds; The Timid Toreador; Shop, Look and Listen*

1941 *Elmer's Pet Rabbit; Porky's Snooze Reel; The Fighting 69½th; Sniffles Bells the Cat; The Haunted Mouse; The Crackpot Quail; The Cat's Tale; Joe Glow the Firefly; Tortoise Beats Hare; Porky's Bear Facts; Goofy Groceries; Toy Trouble; Porky's Preview; The Trial of Mr. Wolf; Porky's Ant; Farm Frolics; Hollywood Steps Out; A Coy Decoy; Hiawatha's Rabbit Hunt; Porky's Prize Pony; The Wacky Worm; Meet John Doughboy; The Heckling Hare; Inki and the Lion; Aviation Vacation; We, the Animals, Squeak; Sport Champions; The Henpecked Duck; Snow Time for Comedy; All This and Rabbit Stew; Notes to You; The Brave Little Bat; The Bug Parade; Robinson Crusoe, Jr.; Rookie Revue; Saddle Silly; The Cagey Canary; Porky's Midnight Matinee; Rhapsody in Rivets; Wabbit Twouble; Porky's Pooch*

1942 *Hop, Skip and a Chump; Porky's Pastry Pirates; The Bird Came C.O.D.; Aloha Hooey; Who's Who in the Zoo; Porky's Cafe; Conrad the Sailor; Crazy Cruise; The Wabbit Who Came to Supper; Saps in Chaps; Horton Hatches the Egg; Dog Tired; Daffy's Southern Exposure; The Wacky Wabbit; The Draft Horse; Nutty News; Lights Fantastic; Hobby Horse Laffs; Hold the Lion, Please; Gopher Goofy; Double Chaser; Wacky Blackouts; Bugs Bunny Gets the Boid; Foney Fables; The Ducktators; The Squawkin' Hawk; Eatin' on the Cuff; Fresh Hare; The Impatient Patient; Fox Pop; The Dover Boys; The Hep Cat; The Sheepish Wolf; The Daffy Duckaroo; The Hare-Brained Hypnotist; A Tale of Two Kitties; My Favorite Duck; Ding Dog Daddy; Case of the Missing Hare*

1943 *Coal Black and de Sebben Dwarfs; Confessions of a Nutzy Spy; Pigs in a Polka; Tortoise Wins by a Hare; Fifth Column Mouse; To Duck or Not to Duck; Flop Goes the Weasel; Hop and Go; Super Rabbit; The Unbearable Bear; The Wise Quacking Duck; Greetings Bait; Tokio Jokio; Jack-Wabbit and the Beanstalk; The Aristo-Cat; Yankee Doodle Daffy; Wackiki Wabbit; Tin Pan Alley Cats; Porky Pig's Feat; Scrap Happy Daffy; Hiss and Make Up; A Corny Concerto; Fin 'n' Catty; Falling Hare; Inki and the Minah Bird; Daffy the Commando; An Itch in Time; Puss 'n' Booty*

1944 *Little Red Riding Rabbit; What's Cookin', Doc?; Meatless Flyday; Tom Turk and Daffy; Bugs Bunny and the Three Bears; I Got Plenty of Mutton; The Weakly Reporter; Tick Tock Tuckered; Bugs Bunny Nips the Nips; The Swooner Crooner; Russian Rhapsody; Duck Soup to Nuts; Angel Puss; Slightly Daffy; Hare Ribbin'; Brother Brat; Hare Force; From Hand to Mouse; Birdy and the Beast; Buckaroo Bugs; Goldilocks and the Jivin' Bears; Plane Daffy; Lost and Foundling; Booby Hatched; The Old Grey Hare; The Stupid Cupid; Stage Door Cartoon*

1945 *Odor-able Kitty; Herr Meets Hare; Draftee Daffy; The Unruly Hare; Trap Happy Porky; Life with Feathers; Behind the Meat Ball; Hare Trigger; Ain't That Ducky; A Gruesome Twosome; A Tale of Two Mice; Wagon Heels; Hare Conditioned; Fresh Airedale; The Bashful Buzzard; Peck Up Your Troubles; Hare Tonic; Nasty Quacks*

1946 *Book Revue; Baseball Bugs; Holiday for Shoestrings; Quentin Quail; Baby Bottleneck; Hare Remover; Daffy Doodles; Hollywood Canine Canteen; Hush My Mouse; Hair-Raising Hare; Kitty Kornered; Hollywood Daffy; Acrobatty Bunny; The Eager Beaver; The Great Piggy Bank Robbery; Bacall to Arms; Of Thee I Sting; Walky Talky Hawky; Racketeer Rabbit; Fair and Worm-er; The Big Snooze; The Mouse-merized Cat; Mouse Menace; Rhapsody Rabbit; Roughly Squeaking*

1947 *One Meat Brawl; The Goofy Gophers; The Gay Anties; Scentimental Over You; A Hare Grows in Manhattan; The Birth of a Notion; Tweetie Pie; Rabbit Transit; Hobo Bobo; Along Came Daffy; Inki At the Circus; Easter Yeggs; Crowing Pains; A Pest in the House; The Foxy Duckling; House Hunting Mice; Little Orphan Airedale; Doggone Cats; Slick Hare; Mexican Joyride; Catch As Cats Can; A Horsefly Fleas*

1948 *Gorilla My Dreams; Two Gophers from Texas; A Feather in His Hare; What Makes Daffy Duck; What's Brewin', Bruin?; Daffy Duck Slept Here; A Hick, a Slick and a Chick; Back Alley Oproar; I Taw a Putty Tat; Rabbit Punch; Hop, Look and Listen; Nothing But the Tooth; Buccaneer Bunny; Bone, Sweet Bone; Bugs Bunny Rides Again; The Rattled Rooster; The Upstanding Sitter; The Shell Shocked Egg; Haredevil Hare; You Were Never Duckier; Dough Ray Me-ow; Hot Cross Bunny; The Pest That Came to Dinner; Hare Splitter; Odor of the Day; The Foghorn Leghorn; A Lad in His Lamp; Daffy Dilly; Kit for Kat; The Stupor Salesman; Riff Raffy Daffy; My Bunny Lies over the Sea; Scaredy Cat*

1949 *Wise Quackers; Hare Do; Holiday for Drumsticks; The Awful Orphan; Porky Chops; Mississippi Hare; Paying the Piper; Daffy Duck Hunt; Rebel Rabbit; Mouse Wreckers; High Diving Hare; The Bee-devilled Bruin; Curtain Razor; Bowery Bugs; Mouse Mazurka; Long-haired Hare; Henhouse Henry; Knights Must Fall; Bad Ol' Putty Tat; The Greyhound Hare; Often an Orphan; The Windblown Hare; Dough for the Do-do; Fast and Furry-ous; Each Dawn I Crow; Frigid Hare; Swallow the Leader; Bye Bye Bluebeard; For Scentimental Reasons; Hippety Hopper; Which Is Witch?; Bear Feat; Rabbit Hood; A Ham in a Role*

1950 *Home Tweet Home; Hurdy Gurdy Hare; Boobs in the Woods; Mutiny on the Bunny; The Lion's Busy; The Scarlet Pumpernickel; Homeless Hare; Strife with Father; The Hypochondri-Cat; Big House Bunny; The Leghorn Blows* at Midnight; His Bitter Half; An Egg Scramble; What's Up, Doc?; All Abir-r-rd; 8 Ball Bunny; It's Hummer Time; Golden Yeggs; Hillbilly Hare; Dog Gone South; The Ducksters; A Fractured Leghorn; Bunker Hill Bunny; Canary Row; Stooge for a Mouse; Pop 'im Pop; Bushy Hare; Caveman Inki; Dog Collared; Rabbit of Seville; Two's a Crowd

1951   Hare We Go; A Fox in a Fix; Canned Feud; Rabbit Every Monday; Putty Tat Trouble; Corn Plastered; Bunny Hugged; Scent-imental Romeo; A Bone for a Bone; Fair-haired Hare; A Hound for Trouble; Early to Bet; Rabbit Fire; Room and Bird; Chow Hound; French Rabbit; The Wearing of the Grin; Leghorn Swoggled; His Hare Raising Tale; Cheese Chasers; Lovelorn Leghorn; Tweety's S.O.S.; Ballot Box Bunny; A Bear for Punishment; Sleepy Time Possum; Drip-Along Daffy; Tweet, Tweet, Tweety; The Prize Pest

1952   Who's Kitten Who?; Operation: Rabbit; Feed the Kitty; Gift Wrapped; Foxy by Proxy; Thumb Fun; 4 Carrot Rabbit; Little Beau Pepe; Kiddin' the Kitten; Water, Water Every Hare; Little Red Rodent Hood; Sock a Doodle Doo; Beep, Beep; Hasty Hare; Ain't She Tweet; The Turn-Tale Wolf; Cracked Quack; Oily Hare; Hoppy Go Lucky; Going! Going! Gosh!; Bird in a Guilty Cage; Mouse Warming; Rabbit Seasoning; The Egg-cited Rooster; Tree for Two; The Super Snooper; Rabbit's Kin; Terrier Stricken; Fool Coverage; Hare Lift

1953   Don't Give Up the Sheep; Snow Business; A Mouse Divided; Forward March Hare; Kiss Me Cat; Duck Amuck; Upswept Hare; A Peck 'o' Trouble; Fowl Weather; Muscle Tussle; Southern Fried Rabbit; Ant Pasted; Much Ado about Nutting; There Auto Be a Law; Hare Trimmed; Tom-Tom Tomcat; Wild over You; Duck Dodgers in the 24 1/2th Century; Bully for Bugs; Plop Goes the Weasel; Cat-Tails for Two; A Street Cat Named Sylvester; Zipping Along; Duck! Rabbit! Duck; Easy Peckin's; Catty Cornered; Of Rice and Hen; Cats A-weigh; Robot Rabbit; Punch Trunk

1954   Dog Pounded; Captain Hareblower; I Gopher You; Feline Frame-Up; Wild Wife; No Barking; Bugs and Thugs; The Cat's Bah; Design for Leaving; Bell Hoppy; No Parking Hare; Doctor Jerkyll's Hide; Claws for Alarm; Little Boy Boo; Devil May Hare; Muzzle Tough; The Oily American; Bewitched Bunny; Satan's Waitin'; Stop, Look and Hasten; Yankee Doodle Bugs; Gone Batty; Goo Goo Goliath; By Word of Mouse; From A to Z-Z-Z; Quack Shot; Lumber Jack Rabbit; My Little Duckaroo; Sheep Ahoy; Baby Buggy Bunny

1955   Pizzicato Pussycat; Feather Duster; Pests for Guests; Beanstalk Bunny; All Fowled Up; Stork Naked; Lighthouse Mouse; Sahara Hare; Sandy Claws; The Hole Idea; Ready, Set, Zoom!; Hare Brush; Past Perfumance; Tweety's Circus; Rabbit Rampage; Lumber Jerks; This Is a Life?; Double or Mutton; Jumpin' Jupiter; A Kiddie's Kitty; Hyde and Hare; Dime to Retire; Speedy Gonzales; Knight-mare Hare; Two Scents Worth; Red Riding Hoodwinked; Roman Legion Hare; Heir Conditioned; Guided Muscle; Pappy's Puppy; One Froggy Evening

1956   Bugs Bonnets; Too Hop to Handle; Weasel Stop; The High and the Flighty; Broomstick Bunny; Rocket Squad; Tweet and Sour; Heaven Scent; Mixed Master; Rabbitson Crusoe; Gee Whiz-z-z; Tree Cornered Tweety; The Unexpected Pest; Napoleon Bunny-Part; Tugboat Granny; Stupor Duck; Barbary Coast Bunny; Rocket Bye Baby; Half-fare Hare; Raw! Raw! Rooster; Slap-Happy Mouse; A Star Is Bored; Deduce, You Say; Yankee Dood It; Wideo Wabbit; There They Go-Go-Go; Two Crows from Tacos; The Honeymousers; To Hare Is Human

1957   The Three Little Bops; Tweet Zoo; Scrambled Aches; Ali Baba Bunny; Go Fly a Kit; Tweety and the Beanstalk; Bedevilled Rabbit; Boyhood Daze; Cheese It, the Cat; Fox Terror; Piker's Peak; Steal Wool; Boston Quackie; What's Opera, Doc?; Tobasco Road; Birds Anonymous; Ducking the Devil; Bugsy and Mugsy; Zoom and Bored; Greedy for Tweety; Touché and Go; Show Biz Bugs; Mouse-taken Identity; Gonzales' Tamales; Rabbit Romeo

1958   Don't Axe Me; Tortilla Flaps; Hare-less Wolf; A Pizza Tweety Pie; Robin Hood Daffy; Hare-way to the Stars; Whoa, Be Gone; A Waggily Tale; Feather Bluster; Now Hare This; To Itch His Own; Dog Tales; Knighty Night Bugs; Weasel While You Work; A Bird in a Bonnet; Hook, Line and Stinker; Pre-hysterical Hare; Gopher Broke; Hip, Hip—Hurry!; Cat Feud

1959   Baton Bunny; Mouse Placed Kitten; China Jones; Hare-abian Nights; Trick or Tweet; The Mouse That Jack Built; Apes of Wrath; Hot Rod and Reel; A Mutt in a Rut; Backwoods Bunny; Really Scent; Mexicali Shmoes; Tweet and Lovely; Wild and Wooly Hare; The Cat's Paw; Here Today, Gone Tamale; Bonanza Bunny; A Broken Leghorn; Wild About Hurry; A Witch's Tangled Hare; Unnatural Hare; Tweet Dreams; People Are Bunny

1960   Fastest with the Mostest; West of the Pesos; Horse Hare; Wild Wild World; Goldimouse and the Three Cats; Person to Bunny; Who Scent You?; Hyde and Go Tweet; Rabbit's Feat; Crockett-Doodle-Do; Mouse and Garden; Ready, Woolen and Able; Mice Follies; From Hare to Heir; The Dixie Fryer; Hopalong Casualty; Trip for Tat; Doggone People; High Note; Lighter Than Hare

1961   Cannery Woe; Zip 'n' Snort; Hoppy Daze; The Mouse on 57th Street; Strangled Eggs; Birds of a Father; 'D' Fightin' Ones; The Abominable Snow Rabbit; Lickety Splat; A Scent of the Matterhorn; The Rebel without Claws; Compressed Hare; The Pied Piper of Guadalupe; Prince Violent; Daffy's Inn Trouble; What's My Lion; Beep Prepared; The Last Hungry Cat; Nelly's Folly

1962   Wet Hare; A Sheep in the Deep; Fish and Slips; Quackodile Tears; Crow's Feat; Mexican Boarders; Bill of Hare; Zoom at the Top; The Slick Chick; Louvre Come Back to Me; Honey's Money; The Jet Cage; Mother Was a Rooster; Good Noose; Shishkabugs; Martian Through Georgia

1963   Devil's Feud Cake; Fast Buck Duck; The Million-Hare; Mexican Cat Dance; Now Hear This; Woolen Under Where; Hare-breadth Hurry; Banty Raids; Chili Weather; The Unmentionables; Aqua Duck; Mad As a Mars Hare; Claws in the Lease; Transylvania 6–5000; To Beep or Not to Beep

1964   Dumb Patrol; A Message to Gracias; Bartholomew versus the Wheel; Freudy Cat; Dr. Devil and Mr. Hare; Nuts and Volts; The Iceman Ducketh; War and Pieces; Hawaiian Aye Aye; False Hare; Senorella and the Glass Huarache; Pancho's Hideaway; Road to Andalay

1965   *It's Nice to Have a Mouse around the House; Cats and Bruises; The Wild Chase; Moby Duck; Assault and Peppered; Well Worn Daffy; Suppressed Duck; Corn on the Cop; Rushing Roulette; Run, Run Sweet Road Runner; Tease for Two; Tired and Feathered; Boulder Wham; Chili Con Corny; Just Plane Beep; Harried and Hurried; Go Go Amigo; Highway Runnery; Chaser on the Rocks*

1966   *Astroduck; Shot and Bothered; Mucho Locos; Mexican Mousepiece; The Solid Tin Coyote; Out and Out Rout; Daffy Rents; Clippety Clobbered; A Haunting We Will Go; Snow Excuse; A Squeak in the Deep; Feather Finger; Swing Ding Amigo; Sugar and Spies; A Taste of Catnip*

1967   *Daffy's Diner; The Quacker Tracker; The Music Mice-Tro; The Spy Swatter; Speedy Ghost to Town; Rodent to Stardom; Go Away Stowaway; Cool Cat; Merlin the Magic Mouse; Fiesta Fiasco*

1968   *Hocus Pocus Powwow; Norman Normal; Big Game Haunt; Skyscraper Caper; Hippydrome Tiger; A Feud with a Dude; The Door; See Ya Later Gladiator; 3-Ring Wing-Ding; Flying Circus; Bunny and Claude; Chimp and Zee*

1969   *The Great Carrot Train Robbery; Fistic Mystic; Rabbit Stews and Rabbits Too; Shamrock and Roll; Bugged by a Bee; Injun Trouble*

1988   *The Duxorcist*

Other Films as Voice Artist/Actor:

1940   *Pinocchio* (Disney)
1949   *Neptune's Daughter* (Buzzell)
1964   *Kiss Me Stupid* (Wilder)
1986   *Heathcliff: The Movie* (Bianchi); *Howard the Duck* (Huyck); *Porky Pig in Hollywood* (Avery)
1988   *Daffy Duck's Quackbusters* (Ford); *Who Framed Roger Rabbit?* (Zemeckis); *The Night of the Living Duck*
1989   *Entertaining the Troops* (Mugge)
1990   *Jetsons: The Movie* (Hanna)

Publications

By BLANC: book—

That's Not All Folks: My Life in the Golden Age of Cartoons and Radio, New York, 1988.

On BLANC: books—

Christman, Trent, *Brass Button Broadcasters: A Lighthearted Look at Fifty Years of Military Broadcasting*, Paducah, 1992.

On BLANC: articles—

Films in Review (New York), vol. 13, no. 1, January 1962.
Obituary in *Hollywood Reporter*, vol. 308, no. 18, 11 July 1989.
Obituary in, *Variety* (New York), 12 July 1989.
Classic Images (Muscatine, Iowa), no. 170, August 1989, and see also no. 173, November 1989.

TV Guide (London), vol. 38, no. 27, 7 July 1990.
Catsos, G. J.M., "A Master of Animated Art: Chuck Jones," in *Filmfax* (Evanston), August/September 1992.

*   *   *

Mel Blanc's vocal talents are so universally known that he seems a little strange, adrift almost, in that handful of feature films—*Neptune's Daughter, Kiss Me Stupid*—or archive TV shows—*The Jack Benny Show*—in which he appears live. A pudgy comic actor very unlike the wiry cartoon creatures he voiced, he could well lay claim to being one of the most versatile performers in the cinema for his contributions to the marvellous characterizations—engineered, of course, by animator-directors like Bob Clampett, Tex Avery, Chuck Jones, Frank Tashlin, Robert McKimson and Friz Freleng—of a fifty-year run of cartoons, from *Picador Porky* in 1937 to *Who Framed Roger Rabbit?* and *The Duxorcist* in 1988. Often playing against himself—as in the incredible confrontations between Bugs Bunny and Daffy Duck or Bugs and Yosemite Sam—Blanc created, adapted and incarnated the voices of an unparalleled run of Warner Brothers characters—Porky Pig and Elmer Fudd are just about the only major characters he *didn't* originate, and he swiftly took over Porky from Joe Dougherty—keeping them consistent even when, as in *Duck Amuck*, almost everything about their physical form was in a constant state of flux.

The jewels of Blanc's career are the sustained film-to-film performances as Bugs Bunny, Daffy Duck and Sylvester P. Pussycat. Bugs is the archetypal Warner Bros. character, a snarling, wise-talking urban rabbit who stands next to Disney's cute animal tykes as Humphrey Bogart does to Shirley Temple. Permanently chomping on a carrot and sneering "nyahh, what's up doc?" at hapless opponents, Bugs is, even more than Mickey Mouse, the great versatile creation of the cartoon short, at home in any historical period or geographical locale—emerging from a tunnel in a Mexican bullring or the Abominable Snowman-haunted Himalayas, he can fish out a map and muse "I knew I should have taken that left turn at Albuquerque"—and the equal of any bullying hunter, predator, rabbit chef, monster or do-badder in sight, without ever seeming, as Mighty Mouse does, like a moralizing twit. Daffy and Sylvester are subtler achievements, especially considering that they started out with exactly the same lisp: Daffy the money-grubbing coward, doomed to horrible failure in every enterprise, hopelessly outclassed by the smarts of Bugs ("you're dethpicable!") or the natural innocence of Porky or Elmer, occasionally prone to fits of absolute raving insanity, ridiculously miscast in the hero roles (*Duck Dodgers in the 241/2th Century, Robin Hood Daffy*) he insists Jack Warner give him; Sylvester the hopeless carnivore without the heart to consume his prey ("suffering succotash"), eternally the victim of the sinisterly benign Tweety Pie or the deceptively sweet-looking Grandma, sometimes (as in the sublime *Birds Anonymous*) desperately at odds with his own hunger-fuelled nature, or even stuck with the role reversal (*Snow Business*) of being at odds in a snowbound cabin with a mouse so hungry he wants to eat a cat.

Besides this trio of masterful characterizations, Blanc also managed to pull off a succession of one-joke creatures, helping them last beyond their debut appearances into modest series of their own: Pepe le Pew, a Charles Boyer-cum-Maurice Chevalier voiced romantic skunk whose bizarre French expressions prefigure Inspector Clouseau ("ahh, la belle femme skunque fatale"); Foghorn Leghorn, a Southern rooster always eager to give unwanted advice to others as he struts around the yard; Wile E. Coyote, in his rare speaking roles as he abandons his pursuit of the Road Runner to try, unwisely, for a substitute diet of Bugs Bunny; Marvin the Martian, the strangle-voiced Thing From Another World who wants to disintegrate Earth to make room for a freeway; Barney Rubble, Fred Flintstone's bumbling neighbor, doubling also as the voice of Dino the Dinosaur; Woody Woodpecker, devising the voice and laugh and then passing them on to a succession of others when an exclusive contract with Warners prevented him from continuing with Walter Lantz; the Tasmanian Devil, inarticulate but a furiously munching fiend, appetite incarnate; Speedy Gonzalez, the one-gag mouse with the perky Mexican accent; and Yosemite Sam, ''the blood-thirstiest, shoot-'em firstiest, gosh-darn worstiest bandit North, South, East and *West* of the Pecos!,'' originally a pint-sized cowboy with a huge moustache but later a pirate or a black knight.

Cartoons are essentially driven by sight gags, sometimes to the extent of throwing in captions to the pictures, but Warners also believed in a riot of sound. This was exemplified not only by Blanc's many voices—gaining him sole credit even on cartoons where the likes of Stan Freberg did some of the work—but also by Carl W. Stalling's ferocious and furious orchestral accompaniment. Some of Blanc's greatest moments find him bursting into song, in the mock-Wagnerian shenanigans of *What's Opera, Doc?* or *The Rabbit of Seville*, not to mention Bugs' occasional bursts of ''What Do They Do in a Rainy Night in Rio?'' or ''Singing in the Bathtub,'' and he also scored novelty hits with ''I'm Glad to Be Bugs Bunny,'' ''The Woody Woodpecker Song'' and, immortally, ''I Tort I Taw a Putty Tat.''

—Kim Newman

BLANKE, Henry

Producer. **Nationality:** German. **Born:** Berlin, 30 December 1901; son of the painter Wilhelm Blanke. **Career:** 1920—joined UFA, Berlin: personal assistant to Ernst Lubitsch, and accompanied him to Hollywood, 1922; 1927–28—worked for Warner Brothers in Hollywood, then headed their production in Germany, 1928–30, their foreign productions in Hollywood, 1930–31, supervised their American output, 1931–32, and then producer, 1932–61 (sometimes termed ''production supervisor'' under Hal B. Wallis). **Died:** 28 May 1981.

Films as Producer:

1933   *Female* (Curtiz); *Bureau of Missing Persons* (Del Ruth); *The Mystery of the Wax Museum* (Curtiz); *Lady Killer* (Del Ruth); *I Loved a Woman* (Green); *Convention City* (Mayo)

1934   *Fashions of 1934* (*Fashion Follies of 1934*) (Dieterle); *Madame Du Barry* (Dieterle); *Fog Over Frisco* (Dieterle); *Journal of a Crime* (Keighley); *Gambling Lady* (Mayo); *Dragon Murder Case* (Humberstone); *The Firebird* (Dieterle); *British Agent* (Curtiz); *Dr. Monica* (Keighley)

1935   *The Story of Louis Pasteur* (Dieterle); *Secret Bride* (Dieterle); *The White Cockatoo* (Crosland); *The Girl from 10th Avenue* (Green); *A Midsummer Night's Dream* (Reinhardt and Dieterle); *I Am a Thief* (Florey)

1936   *The Petrified Forest* (Mayo); *Anthony Adverse* (LeRoy); *The Green Pastures* (Connelly and Keighley); *The White Angel* (Dieterle); *Satan Met a Lady* (Dieterle); *Green Light* (Borzage); *The Case of the Velvet Claw* (Clemens)

1937   *The Life of Emile Zola* (Dieterle); *Call It a Day* (May); *Confession* (May)

1938   *Jezebel* (Wyler) (co); ***The Adventures of Robin Hood*** (Curtiz and Keighley); *Four Daughters* (Curtiz); *White Banners* (Goulding); *Juarez* (Dieterle) (co)

1939   *The Old Maid* (Goulding) (co); *Four Wives* (Curtiz); *Daughters Courageous* (Curtiz); *We Are Not Alone* (Goulding)

1940   *The Sea Hawk* (Curtiz) (co); *A Dispatch from Reuters* (*This Man Reuter*) (Dieterle); *Saturday's Children* (V. Sherman); *Four Mothers* (Keighley)

1941   ***The Maltese Falcon*** (Huston) (co); *The Great Lie* (Goulding) (co); *Blues in the Night* (Litvak); *Out of the Fog* (Litvak); *The Sea Wolf* (Curtiz)

1942   *The Gay Sisters* (Rapper)

1943   *The Constant Nymph* (Goulding); *Old Acquaintance* (V. Sherman); *Edge of Darkness* (Milestone)

1944   *The Mask of Dimitrios* (Negulesco)

1945   *Roughly Speaking* (Curtiz)

1946   *Deception* (Rapper); *My Reputation* (Bernhandt); *Of Human Bondage* (Goulding); *One More Tomorrow* (Godfrey)

1947   *Cry Wolf* (Godfrey); *Deep Valley* (Negulesco); *Escape Me Never* (Godfrey); *The Woman in White* (Godfrey)

1948   ***The Treasure of the Sierra Madre*** (Huston); *Winter Meeting* (Windust); *June Bride* (Windust)

1949   *The Fountainhead* (K. Vidor); *Beyond the Forest* (K. Vidor)

1950   *Bright Leaf* (Curtiz)

1951   *Lightning Strikes Twice* (K. Vidor); *Come Fill the Cup* (Douglas); *Goodbye, My Fancy* (V. Sherman); *Tomorrow Is Another Day* (Feist); *Room for One More* (Taurog)

1952   *The Iron Mistress* (Douglas); *Operation Secret* (Seiler)

1953   *So Big* (Wise); *She's Back on Broadway* (Douglas); *So This Is Love* (*The Grace Moore Story*) (Douglas)

1954   *Phantom of the Rue Morgue* (Del Ruth); *Lucky Me* (Donohue); *King Richard and the Crusaders* (Butler); *Young at Heart* (Douglas)

1955   *The McConnell Story* (*Tiger in the Sky*) (Douglas); *Sincerely Yours* (Douglas)

1956   *Serenade* (A. Mann)

1958   *Too Much, Too Soon* (Napoleon);

1959   *The Nun's Story* (Zinnemann); *The Miracle* (Rapper); *Westbound* (Boetticher)

1960   *Ice Palace* (V. Sherman); *Cash McCall* (Pevney)

1961   *The Sins of Rachel Cade*Douglas)

1962   *Hell Is for Heroes* (Siegel)

Films as Assistant Director:

1924   *The Marriage Circle* (Lubitsch); *Three Women* (Lubitsch)

1926   *My Official Wife* (Stein); *The Third Degree* (Curtiz)

1927   *Brass Knuckles* (Bacon); *The College Widow* (Mayo); *Dearie* (Mayo); *The Desired Woman* (Curtiz); *Don't Tell the Wife* (Stein); *Ginsberg the Great* (Haskin); *Matinee Ladies* (Haskin); *A Million Bid* (Curtiz)

1928   *Across the Atlantic* (Bretherton); *Rinty of the Desert* (Lederman)

Publications

On BLANKE: articles—

Obituary, in *Variety* (New York), 3 June 1981.
Obituary, in *Cinematographe* (Paris), July 1981.
Filme (Berlin), July-August 1981.

*   *   *

Henry Blanke represents one of those individuals of little public fame, but who had immense power as a producer during Hollywood's Golden Age of the 1930s and 1940s. His immediate boss, Jack L. Warner, was, of course, well known, as were the stars over whose careers he had so much influence, including Humphrey Bogart, Bette Davis and Olivia de Havilland. But in his more than 30 years at Warners, Henry Blanke supervised the creation of hundreds of films, including such motion picture classics as *The Adventures of Robin Hood*, *Juarez*, *The Maltese Falcon*, and *The Treasure of the Sierra Madre*.

Blanke came to Hollywood as part of the then-famous European connection so active during the 1920s. In the two decades before the World War II dozens of directors, producers, and even stars (most notably Marlene Dietrich) emigrated from impoverished European film communities to Hollywood to seek fame and fortune. No European film industry, even that in Germany, could come close to challenging Hollywood. As a native-born German, Blanke made his connection with Hollywood by helping Warners create versions of their films for foreign audiences. Once in the United States he brought the noted director William Dieterle from Germany into Warners's fold.

With the coming of sound Warners became a major Hollywood studio. Quickly Blanke moved into third position of power at the studio, behind only the founding brother Jack and Warners's ace assistant Hal Wallis. When Wallis left for Paramount in the mid-1940s, Blanke had no rival other than the brothers Warner themselves. He would leave the company only when it was sold to outsiders in the 1950s.

Blanke seemed to have his greatest success with vehicles designed for stars Paul Muni, Errol Flynn, and Bette Davis. Muni starred in the Academy Award-winning *The Life of Emile Zola* in 1937, as well as *Juarez* the following year, both Blanke productions. Flynn essayed *The Adventures of Robin Hood* and *The Sea Hawk* for Blanke's production unit. *The Petrified Forest* helped Davis become a major star, and *Jezebel* earned her an Academy Award for Best Actress in 1938. These and 11 other Davis films were produced directly by Henry Blanke.

Blanke's films for Warners after World War II did not seem to match his pre-war efforts. But make no mistake about it—they made the company millions of dollars. But the studio system in which Blanke had labored for more than 30 years came to an end in the 1950s and his skills were no longer needed at Warners. Blanke left for an independent deal at Paramount but that union produced only one film, *Hell Is for Heroes*, his final effort as a producer, issued in 1962. Henry Blanke was the product of an earlier era when the studio system produced, year-in and year-out, the classic narrative films which continue to define the Golden Age of American movie making.

—Douglas Gomery

BOOTH, Margaret

Editor. **Nationality:** American. **Born:** 1898; sister of the actor Elmer Booth. **Career:** Entered films as "joiner" for Griffith; then worked in Paramount Laboratories; 1921—assistant editor for Mayer (later MGM); 1939–68—supervising film editor, MGM. **Awards:** Special Academy Award, 1977.

Films as Editor:

1924   *Why Men Leave Home* (Stahl) (co); *Husbands and Lovers* (Stahl) (co)
1925   *Fine Clothes* (Stahl) (co)
1926   *Memory Lane* (Stahl); *The Gay Deceiver* (Stahl)
1927   *The Enemy* (Niblo); *Bringing Up Father* (Conway); *Lovers?* (Stahl); *In Old Kentucky* (Stahl) (co)
1928   *Telling the World* (Wood) (co); *The Mysterious Lady* (Niblo); *A Lady of Chance* (Leonard)
1929   *The Bridge of San Luis Rey* (Brabin); *Wise Girls* (Kempy) (Hopper)
1930   *The Rogue Song* (L. Barrymore); *Redemption* (Niblo); *Strictly Unconventional* (Burton); *The Lady of Scandal* (*The High Road*) (Franklin); *A Lady's Morals* (*The Soul Kiss*; *Jenny Lind*) (Franklin)
1931   *New Moon* (Conway); *The Southerner* (*The Prodigal*) (Pollard); *It's a Wise Child* (Leonard); *The Cuban Love Song* (Van Dyke); *Five and Ten* (*Daughter of Luxury*) (Leonard);

Margaret Booth

Susan Lenox, Her Fall and Rise (The Rise of Helga) (Leonard)
1932 Lovers Courageous (Leonard); Smilin' Thru (Franklin); Strange Interlude (Strange Interval) (Leonard); The Son-Daughter (Franklin)
1933 White Sister (Fleming); Peg o' My Heart (Leonard); Storm at Daybreak (Boleslavsky); Bombshell (Fleming); Dancing Lady (Leonard)
1934 Riptide (E. Goulding); The Barretts of Wimpole Street (Franklin)
1935 Reckless (Fleming); Mutiny on the Bounty (Lloyd)
1936 Romeo and Juliet (Cukor)
1937 **Camille** (Cukor)

Films as Editorial Supervisor:

1937 A Yank at Oxford (Conway)
1970 The Owl and the Pussycat (Ross); To Find a Man (Huston)
1972 Fat City (Huston)
1973 The Way We Were (Pollack)
1975 The Sunshine Boys (Ross); The Black Bird (Giler) (uncredited)
1976 Murder by Death (Moore)
1977 The Goodbye Girl (Ross)
1978 California Suite (Ross)
1979 Chapter Two (Moore) (+ assoc pr)
1980 Seems Like Old Times (Sandrich) (+ assoc pr)
1982 Annie (Huston)

Other Films:

1963 The V.I.P.s (Asquith) (prod adviser)
1978 The Cheap Detective (Moore) (assoc pr)
1982 The Toy (Donner) (assoc pr)
1985 The Slugger's Wife (Ashby) (exec pr)

Publications

By BOOTH: articles—

Film Weekly (London), 9 October 1937.
"The Cutter," in Behind the Screen, edited by Stephen Watts, London, 1938.
Focus on Film (London), Summer/Autumn 1976.

On BOOTH: articles—

Film Comment (New York), March/April 1977.
American Cinemeditor (Los Angeles, California), Spring/Summer 1977.
American Film (Washington, D.C.), October 1979.
Film Dope (Nottingham), March 1982.

*   *   *

Margaret Booth was one of the great film editors in Hollywood history. She started out as a patcher (film joiner) for D. W. Griffith and ended her career some 60 years later as one of the true insiders at MGM. The classic Hollywood film is surely defined by its characteristics of editing. Booth was one of the innovators who shepherded the classic Hollywood editing style through the coming of sound, color, and wide-screen.

Like many of her contemporaries, Booth joined the American film industry without any formal training. She took her first job with D. W. Griffith's company right out of high school. She then moved to Famous Players and the Mayer studios. By the early 1930s she ranked as one of the top editors at MGM. In 1939 she was appointed MGM's supervising film editor, a position she held until the studio collapsed in 1968.

Booth was, if anything, a survivor. Once she left MGM, she began to work as a freelance editor on such 1970s blockbusters as The Way We Were, The Sunshine Boys, and Murder by Death. She was one of those rare individuals whose career encompassed the history of Hollywood from its beginnings through the studio years into the age of television.

There have been few opportunities for women behind the camera in Hollywood. "Film editing," noted the New York Times in 1936, "is one of the few important functions in a studio in which women play a substantial part." And at MGM Booth was able to advance in the ranks so that she held a position of substantial creative power in the 1930s and 1940s. Her patron was Louis B. Mayer himself, for Booth had worked as a secretary with the old Mayer studio before it ever merged into MGM.

Booth's career neatly divides into two parts. During the first, up through her appointment as head of editing at MGM, she cut many a noted film. These include a number of MGM classics: The Barretts of Wimpole Street, Romeo and Juliet, and Camille. Somewhat surprisingly for one with so much industry power and influence, Booth received only one Academy Award nomination for film editing. This was for the 1935 version of Mutiny on the Bounty. She did not win the award. However it should be noted that Booth did get an Honorary Oscar in 1977 to denote "sixty-two years of exceptionally distinguished service to the motion picture industry as film editor."

In the second half of her career Margaret Booth worked strictly as an editing supervisor. In her own words she did no actual editing for 30 years. But she assigned those who did, and approved their work and performance. As such she held immense power and continued the tradition of a style of classic editing for which Hollywood films of the studio years have now become famous. All filmmakers from the late 1930s through the late 1960s who worked at MGM had, in the end, to go through Booth to have the final editing of sound and image approved. Thus for three decades she represented one of the truly important but relatively unknown powers in the history of Hollywood filmmaking.

—Douglas Gomery

BOST, Pierre
See **AURENCHE, Jean, and Pierre BOST**

BOSUSTOW, Stephen

Animator, Writer, Designer, Director and Producer. **Nationality:** Canadian. **Born:** Victoria, British Columbia, 6 November 1911; family moved to California when Bosustow was a boy. **Career:** 1922—won first art prize at school; worked with Ub Iwerks; worked for the Walter Lantz Organisation at Universal Studios; 1934–41—writer and sketcher at Walt Disney's studio; laid off after participating in workers' strike; 1944—produced *Hell Bent for Election* for Roosevelt's election campaign; 1945—founded UPA (United Producers of America) Animation Studio; 1960—sold UPA. **Award:** Academy Award, *Magoo's Puddle Jumper*, 1956. **Died:** Of pneumonia, 4 July 1981.

Films as Producer at UPA:

1945   *Flathatting* (Hubley)
1946   *The Brotherhood of Man* (Hubley and Cannon)
1948   *Robin Hoodlum* (Hubley)
1949   *The Magic Fluke* (Hubley); *Ragtime Bear* (Hubley); *Punchy Deleon* (Hubley); *The Miner's Daughter* (Cannon); *Giddy Yap* (Babbitt); *Trouble Indemnity* (Burness); *The Popcorn Story* (Babbitt); *Bungled Bungalow* (Burness)
1950   *Spellbound Hound* (Hubley)
1951   *Gerald McBoing Boing* (Cannon); *The Family Circus* (Babbitt); *Bare Faced Flatfoot* (Burness); *Georgie and the Dragon* (Cannon); *Fuddy Duddy Buddy* (Hubley); *Wonder Gloves* (Cannon); *Grizzly Golfer* (Burness)
1952   *Rooty Toot Toot* (Hubley); *The Four Poster* (Hubley); *The Oompahs* (Cannon); *Sloppy Jalopy* (Burness); *Dog Snatcher* (Burness); *Willie the Kid* (Cannon); *Pink and Blue Blues* (Burness); *Pete Hothead* (Burness); *Hotsy Footsy* (Hurtz); *Madeline* (Cannon); *Captains Outrageous* (Burness)
1953   *Christopher Crumpet* (Cannon); *A Unicorn in the Garden* (Hurtz); *The Tell-Tale Heart* (Parmelee); *Little Boy with a Big Heart* (Cannon); *The Emperor's New Clothes* (Parmelee); *Safety Spin* (Burness); *Gerald McBoing Boing's Symphony* (Cannon); *Magoo's Masterpiece* (Burness); *Magoo Slept Here* (Burness)
1954   *Destination Magoo* (Burness); *Bringing Up Mother* (Hurtz); *Ballet-Oop* (Cannon); *Magoo Goes Skiing* (Burness); *The Man on the Flying Trapeze* (Parmelee); *Fudget's Budget* (Cannon); *Kangaroo Courting* (Burness); *How Now Boing Boing* (Cannon)
1955   *When Magoo Flew* (Burness); *Magoo Makes News* (Burness); *Spare the Child* (Liss); *Four Wheels and No Brake* (Parmelee); *Magoo's Check-Up* (Burness); *Baby Boogie* (Julian); *Magoo's Express* (Burness); *Madcap Magoo* (Burness); *Christopher Crumpet's Playmate* (Cannon); *Stage Door Magoo* (Burness); *Rise of Duton Lang* (Evans)
1956   *Gerald McBoing Boing on the Planet Moo* (Cannon); *Magoo's Puddle Jumper* (Burness); *Magoo's Caine Mutiny* (Burness); *Magoo Goes West* (Burness); *Calling Dr. Magoo* (Burness); *The Jaywalker* (Cannon); *Magoo Beats the Heat* (Burness); *Trailblazer Magoo* (Burness); *Magoo's Problem Child* (Burness); *Meet Mother Magoo* (Burness)
1957   *Magoo Goes Overboard* (Burness); *Matador Magoo* (Burness); *Magoo Breaks Par* (Burness); *Magoo's Glorious Fourth* (Burness); *Magoo's Masquerade* (Larriva); *Magoo Saves the Bank* (Burness); *Rock Hound Magoo* (Burness); *Magoo's Moose Hunt* (Cannon); *Magoo's Private War* (Larriva)
1958   *Trees and Jamaica Daddy* (Keller); *Sailing and Village Band* (Keller); *Magoo's Young Manhood* (Burness); *Scoutmaster Magoo* (Cannon); *The Explosive Mr Magoo* (Burness); *Magoo's Three Point Landing* (Burness); *Magoo's Cruise* (Larriva); *Love Comes to Magoo* (McDonald); *Spring and Saganaki* (Keller); *Gumshoe Magoo* (Turner)
1959   *1001 Arabian Nights* (Kinney); *Bwana Magoo* (McDonald); *Picnics Are Fun and Dino's Serenade* (Keller); *Magoo's Homecoming* (Turner); *Merry Minstrel Magoo*; *Magoo's Lodge Brother* (Larriva); *Terror Faces Magoo* (Ishii)

Publications

By BOSUSTOW: book—

Chief By Birthright, 1981.

On BOSUSTOW: articles—

Montgomery, John, in *The Summing Up in Comedy Films*, 1954.
American Cinematographer (Hollywood), vol. 46, no. 11, November 1965.
Obituary in *Variety* (New York), 15 July 1981.

*   *   *

The name of Stephen Bosustow is inseparably linked with the United Productions of America. This important artist was not only its founder but also its spiritual father. At the end of the forties and the beginning of the fifties, this corporation became the greatest rival of Walt Disney as a result of Bosustow's artistic way of looking at animated—especially cartoon—film, but also it served as a creative base for young artists. Now Bosustow could realize his dreams and ideas both in his own films (the first such film—*Brotherhood of Man*—raised a sharp reaction and brought about notable success) and in serial stories and series with characteristic figures such as Mr. Magoo, the little boy Gerald McBoing Boing, and others.

The importance of this cartoon filmmaker, scriptwriter, art designer and director consists, above all, in the fact that he was the initiator of new trends and currents. He created conditions for artistic development of modern animation in the United States and to a pleiad of talented artists such as the painter Saul Stenberg, the designer Thurber, Robert Cannon, Peter Burness, Ted Parmelee and others. The basis of the work of this group headed by Bosustow was inspired by modern artistic tendencies, abstraction and children's drawing, and the graphic development of modern posters and caricature. Bosustow gave way to personalities: he did not restrain them by his own style and challenged the established ''rules'' of American cartoon film from the point of view of both content and graphic form. Thus he broke conventions and established new values. He abandoned gags and the settled ''O-style'' which was characteristic of the cartoon slapstick of that time. He did not portray animals and did not tell fables but dealt with problems of human beings in cartoon films for adults.

In comparison with Disney and his technical perfection of animation and naturalistic detailed drawings, Bosustow returned to a simpler form of drawing and animation. He often used linear drawing. The scene expressed only the essential, and partial animation stressed absurdity or even the grotesque. This shows in his feature films where he aimed at effectiveness of scenes regardless of the principles of perspective in his desire to make the scenes visually more attractive.

Stephen Bosustow's tendencies influenced others such as Hy Hirsch, Ernest Pintoff, Gene Deitch and, to some extent, even Walt

Disney himself. They influenced the commercial trick film and the works of Tex Avery, Walter Lantz, Paul J. Smith, and others. Thus Bosustow could be called the founder of the modern American school of animation.

—Vacláv Merhaut

BOYD, Russell

Cinematographer. **Nationality:** Australian. **Born:** 1944 in Australia. **Career:** Worked at Cinesound, Melbourne; shot commercials for Supreme Films, Paddington, late 1960s; first feature credit as director of photography for *Between Wars*, 1974; cinematographer for dozens of Australian and American films; television credits include *A Town Like Alice*, 1981. **Awards:** Australian Cinematographers Society (ACS) Cinematographer of the Year, for *Between Wars*, 1976; British Academy Award (BAFTA) for Best Cinematography, 1977, and Academy of Science Fiction, Horror and Fantasy Films Saturn Award for Best Cinematography, 1979, for *Picnic at Hanging Rock*; Australian Film Institute (AFI) Award for Best Achievement in Cinematography, for *Break of Day*, 1977; AFI Award for Best Achievement in Cinematography, for *The Last Wave*, 1978; AFI Award for Best Achievement in Cinematography, 1981, and ACS Cinematographer of the Year, 1982, for *Gallipoli*; AFI Raymond Longford Award for significant contribution to Australian filmmaking, 1988. **Address:** 52 Sutherland Street, Cremorne NSW 2090, Australia. **Agent:** Smith/Gosnell/Nicholson & Assoc., PO Box 1166, 1515 Palisades Dr., Pacific Palisades, CA 90272–2113, U.S.A.

Films as Cinematographer:

1974   *Between Wars* (Thornhill)
1975   *Picnic at Hanging Rock* (Weir); *The Man From Hong Kong* (Wang and Trenchard-Smith); *The Golden Cage* (Kuyululu)
1976   *Summer of Secrets* (Sharman); *Break of Day* (Hannam)
1977   *Gone to Ground* (Dobson); *The Singer and the Dancer* (Armstrong); *The Last Wave* (Weir)
1979   *Just Out of Reach* (Blagg); *Dawn!* (Hannam); *The Chain Reaction* (Barry and Miller)
1980   *. . . Maybe This Time* (McGill)
1981   *Gallipoli* (Weir); *A Town Like Alice* (Stevens—for TV)
1982   *The Year of Living Dangerously* (Weir); *Starstruck* (Armstrong)
1983   *Tender Mercies* (Beresford); *Phar Lap* (Wincer); *Stanley: Every Home Should Have One* (Storm)
1984   *A Soldier's Story* (Jewison); *Mrs. Soffel* (Armstrong)
1986   *Burke & Wills* (Clifford); *"Crocodile" Dundee* (Faiman); *The Perfectionist* (Thomson)
1987   *High Tide* (Armstrong)
1988   *The Rescue* (Fairfax); *"Crocodile" Dundee II* (Cornell)
1989   *In Country* (Jewison); *Blood Oath* (Wallace); *Sweet Talker* (Jenkins)
1990   *Almost an Angel* (Cornell); *Prisoners of the Sun* (Wallace)
1991   *Turtle Beach* (Wallace)
1992   *Forever Young* (Miner); *White Men Can't Jump* (Shelton)
1994   *Cobb* (Shelton)
1995   *Operation Dumbo Drop* (Wincer)
1996   *Tin Cup* (Shelton)
1997   *Liar Liar* (Shadyac)
1998   *Dr. Dolittle* (Thomas)
1999   *Company Man* (Askin)

Other Films:

1997   *Oscar and Lucinda* (Armstrong) (additional camera)

Publications

By BOYD: articles—

"The 'New Vintage' Cinematographers of Australia Speak Out," interview in *American Cinematographer* (Hollywood), September 1976.

On BOYD: articles—

Bachmann, Gideon, "Films in Australia," in *Sight and Sound* (London), Winter 1976–77.
Dawson, Jan, "Picnic Under Capricorn," in *Sight and Sound* (London), Spring 1976.
Murray, Scott, editor, *The New Australian Cinema*, London, 1980.
Chase, Donald, "Russell Boyd," in *American Cinematographer* (Hollywood), December 1984.
McCarthy, Todd, "Speed of Light," in *Film Comment* (New York), September-October 1989.
O'Regan, Tom, "Australian Film in the 1970s: The Ocker and the Quality Film," in *Oz Film: Australian Film in the Reading Room*, http://kali.murdoch.edu.au/continuum/film/1970s.html, February 7, 1997.
Australian Film Commission and Australian Film Finance Corporation Limited, "Report on the Film and Television Production Industry," http://www.ffc.gov.au, November 5, 1999.

*   *   *

Australian cinematographer Russell Boyd came to prominence in 1975 for lensing Peter Weir's *Picnic at Hanging Rock*. He was part of the New Wave that revitalized the Australian motion picture industry by introducing the "quality" film, a hybrid of art cinema and classic Hollywood conventions. Technically skilled and imaginative, Boyd and his peers—producers, directors, screenwriters, and cinematographers—had their first features in the can before their 30th birthdays. These productions dominated Australian screens and received international acclaim.

Boyd was an overnight sensation whose career had started unassumingly years earlier. He first became interested in the production of television commercials, news, and documentaries while working at Cinesound in Melbourne. After moving to Sydney in the mid-1960s he started his apprenticeship as a cameraman at Supreme Films in Paddington: there he shot commercials every day for five years. Boyd's feature film break came when director Michael Thornhill hired him as director of photography for *Between Wars* (1974), and the effort earned him the Cinematographer of the Year award from the Australian Cinematographers Society (ACS). Boyd made his worldwide mark with *Picnic at Hanging Rock*, while he was still making a name for himself. Along with many young and talented filmmakers, he continued to work throughout the 1970s on domestic productions, promoting the growth of "an authentic Australian cinema." Part of the Australian film drain of the early 1980s, Boyd journeyed to Los Angeles to work on features helmed by Aussie directors Bruce Beresford (*Tender Mercies*, 1983) and Gillian Armstrong (*Mrs. Soffel*, 1984). Unlike many of his compatriots, he also continued to shoot films Down Under. With smash hit "*Crocodile*" *Dundee* in 1986, Boyd proved that an Australian production could have the same slick look as its American competition. His craftsmanship put him in demand behind the camera on both continents, but his choice of projects grew more commercial. In the 1990s, for example, he shot the Australian film *Turtle Beach* and then a number of mainstream American movies including *White Men Can't Jump, Tin Cup, Liar Liar*, and *Dr. Dolittle*.

Pinpointing Boyd's personal style is difficult. He is the first to admit "the contrast between one picture and the next can be extraordinary" for a cinematographer like himself, who tailors different looks for different films. In addition, depending upon the demands of a scene, he shifts back and forth between the British and the American system. If the lighting design is complex, Boyd adopts the British "lighting cameraman" model: he concentrates on the lighting, while the camera operator works more closely with the director to set the shot. When working in the American style, Boyd collaborates more significantly with the director to determine the camera angle, composition, and choreography. Although many of Boyd's credits have come from collaborating with the same directors (Peter Weir, Gillian Armstrong, Norman Jewison, Ron Shelton), he has achieved considerably different looks on each of their projects.

Boyd distinguishes between a "cameraman's picture" and a performance piece. He earned lavish praise for his conspicuously artistic photography in *Picnic at Hanging Rock*, a "cameraman's picture" with a lyrical style intrinsic to the drama. He based its look on the Impressionist period of Australian art, covering his camera lens with a yellow-dyed net to simulate the golden light in the turn-of-the-century paintings. He created the hallucinatory, hypnotic feel of the picnic sequences by shooting at different camera speeds. To enhance the romantic image of the Victorian schoolgirls, Boyd backlit their hair and used longer focal-length lenses to capture them in the middleground, surrounded by wildflowers and grass rendered out of focus in the foreground and background planes. His tight framing and extreme angles convey a sense of claustrophobia and impending doom when the girls start winding their way up Hanging Rock, the site of their puzzling disappearance. Boyd's pictorialism greatly contributed to the drama's mystery and atmosphere.

When shooting a performance piece like Norman Jewison's *A Soldier's Story* (1984), based on Charles Fuller's Pulitzer Prize-winning play, Boyd uses conventional compositions to support the acting and direction. In a 1984 article, Boyd explains, "To me, *A Soldier's Story* is pretty much performance and the director's choreography of the scenes. It doesn't have—and can't support—a very strong visual style." He subordinates style to the needs of the theatrical piece, often making the camerawork disappear so that nothing detracts from the acting.

Regardless of the project, Boyd's working methodology remains the same. Valuing creative collaboration, he has studied paintings and period photographs with directors and production designers to help determine the appropriate look for a film. His favorite tools include adjustable Fresnel spotlights and color-compensating filters placed at the camera lens rather than at the lamps. Boyd is known for his exceptional night work, which includes the evening murder sequence

that sets the plot of *A Soldier's Story* into motion, and his flair for photographing scenery in movies as diverse as *Tender Mercies* and *Tin Cup*, both shot in Texas.

Except for winning a British Academy Award for *Picnic at Hanging Rock*, Boyd has never collected a major cinematography award outside the Australian film industry. Several factors contribute to the lack of recognition. Boyd adapts his style to a film's shifting modes and moods, an approach that affords him less visibility than those cinematographers who constantly capture beautiful pictures or select projects on the basis of showcasing their talent. During the last decade, while feature film production and budgets have remained static in Australia, Boyd has accepted more and more work on mainstream American projects. Often he adjusted to new crews containing personnel with little experience working together. As a result, his 40 films as director of photography are a mixture of notable outings and average, impersonal jobs. Instead of developing into the visual artist promised by his earlier work, Boyd has become a hardworking, accomplished craftsman.

—Susan Tavernetti

BOYLE, Robert

Art Director. **Nationality:** American. **Born:** Los Angeles, California, 1910. **Education:** Attended the University of Southern California, Los Angeles, B. Arch. 1933. **Family:** Married. **Career:** Worked for several architectural firms, and acting extra; 1933—sketch artist and draftsman, Paramount, then worked for Universal, RKO, and Universal again. **Agent:** The Gersh Agency Inc., 232 North Canon Drive, Beverly Hills, CA 90210, U.S.A.

Films as Art Director or Production Designer:

1942   *Saboteur* (Hitchcock)
1943   *Flesh and Fantasy* (Duvivier); *Shadow of a Doubt* (Hitchcock); *Good Morning, Judge* (Yarbrough); *South of Tahiti* (*White Savage*) (Lubin)
1946   *Nocturne* (Marin)
1947   *They Won't Believe Me* (Pichel); *Ride the Pink Horse* (Montgomery)
1948   *Another Part of the Forest* (Gordon); *An Act of Murder* (*Live Today for Tomorrow*) (Gordon); *For the Love of Mary* (de Cordova)
1949   *The Gal Who Took the West* (*The Western Story*) (de Cordova); *Abandoned* (Newman)
1950   *Buccaneer's Girl* (de Cordova); *Louisa* (Hall); *The Milkman* (Barton); *Sierra* (Grenen); *Mystery Submarine* (Sirk)
1951   *Iron Man* (Pevney); *Mark of the Renegade* (Fregonese); *The Lady Pays Off* (Sirk); *Weekend with Father* (Sirk)
1952   *Bronco Buster* (Boetticher); *Lost in Alaska* (Yarbrough); *Yankee Buccaneer* (de Cordova); *Back at the Front* (G. Sherman)
1953   *Girls in the Night* (Arnold); *The Beast from 20,000 Fathoms* (Lourié); *Gunsmoke* (Juran); *Abbott and Costello Go to Mars* (Lamont); *Ma and Pa Kettle on Vacation* (Lamont); *It Came from Outer Space* (Arnold); *East of Sumatra* (Boetticher)

1954   *Ma and Pa Kettle at Home* (Lamont); *Johnny Dark* (G. Sherman); *Ride Clear of Diablo* (Hibbs)

1955   *Chief Crazy Horse* (G. Sherman); *Kiss of Fire* (Newman); *The Private War of Major Benson* (Hopper); *Lady Godiva* (Lubin); *Running Wild* (La Cava)

1956   *Never Say Goodbye* (Hopper); *A Day of Fury* (Jones); *Congo Crossing* (Pevney)

1957   *The Night Runner* (Biberman); *The Brothers Rico* (Karlson); *Operation Mad Ball* (Quine)

1958   *Buchanan Rides Alone* (Boetticher); *Wild Heritage* (Haas)

1959   *The Crimson Kimono* (Fuller); **North by Northwest** (Hitchcock)

1962   *Cape Fear* (Lee Thompson) (co)

1963   **The Birds** (Hitchcock); *The Thrill of It All* (Jewison) (co)

1964   *Marnie* (Hitchcock)

1965   *Do Not Disturb* (Levy) (co); *The Reward* (Bourguignon) (co)

1966   *The Russians Are Coming, the Russians Are Coming* (Jewison)

1967   *Fitzwilly* (Delbert Mann); *In Cold Blood* (R. Brooks); *How to Succeed in Business without Really Trying* (Swift)

1968   *The Thomas Crown Affair* (Jewison)

1969   *Gaily, Gaily* (*Chicago, Chicago*) (Jewison)

1970   *The Landlord* (Ashby)

1971   *Fiddler on the Roof* (Jewison)

1972   *Portnoy's Complaint* (Lehman)

1974   *Mame* (Saks)

1975   *Bite the Bullet* (R. Brooks)

1976   *Leadbelly* (Parks)

1978   *Winter Kills* (Richert)

1980   *Private Benjamin* (Zieff)

1983   *Staying Alive* (Stallone)

1986   *Jumpin' Jack Flash* (P. Marshall)

1987   *Dragnet* (T. Mankiewicz)

1988   *Troop Beverly Hills* (Kanew)

1991   *To Meteoro vima tou pelargou* (*The Suspended Step of the Stork*) (Angelopoulos)

Publications

By BOYLE: articles—

Film Comment (New York), May/June 1978.
Cahiers du Cinéma (Paris), June 1982.

On BOYLE: article—

Films and Filming (London), March/April 1970.

*   *   *

During his 46 years as an independent Hollywood art director, Robert Boyle worked on a variety of films, applying his technique and the tricks of the art director's trade to make realistic looking sets and locations. He created images that would not only enhance the story but also cement it to time and place. From Hitchcock's *Saboteur* to *Troop Beverly Hills*, Boyle worked on such films as *The Russians Are Coming, the Russians Are Coming*; *The Thomas Crown Affair*; and the original *Cape Fear*. But along with these impressive films, Boyle also served as art director on such films as *Abbott and Costello Go to Mars* and *It Came from Outer Space*, as well as a few Ma and Pa Kettle films. Westerns such as *Bronco Buster* and such costume films as *Buccaneer's Girl* were also part of Boyle's oeuvre.

Boyle began his career in the thirties when film sets started to move away from the style that was more suitable to the theater, from which they had been borrowed. Film studios began to maintain large art departments and art department heads were appointed to be responsible for the ultimate style of the studio. At Paramount, where Boyle was associated with Wiard Ihnen, the art department head was Hans Drier, a German architect. Drier brought a flair for the modern to Paramount, having been influenced by Bauhaus artists and the Swiss architect, Le Corbusier. It was said that Drier's Paramount was able to make sets look more like the real thing.

Although trained as an architect, Boyle started out as a sketch artist and assistant designer. He was, however, able to use his architectural skills to design the realistic sets that were in demand by the studios during the thirties. Developing his skills at this time made Boyle a believer in film sets and the total control the art director could exercise over them. He also found that it was easier to design a location than to find one. After reading a script, Boyle would put into reality the images he conceived from the story. On the film set, Boyle would be able to use all the tricks of his trade to design and build a believable set.

As films changed and location filming became more popular, Boyle adapted as well. He used his tricks to make the location shots more controllable. Using mattes to improve the mood and floodlights to correct existing conditions—or adding bits and pieces to the location—Boyle used anything to try to create the preconceived image he got from the script. Although he worked on memorable films by other great directors, it is his work with Hitchcock for which Boyle is best known. He first worked as an art director on Hitchcock's *Saboteur* in 1942, then worked on four more Hitchcock films—*Shadow of a Doubt*, *North by Northwest*, *Marnie*, and *The Birds*, receiving an Oscar nomination for his work on *North by Northwest*.

Hitchcock wanted to use actual locations for *North by Northwest*, including Grand Central Station and Mount Rushmore. Since filming at Mount Rushmore was limited, the sequence was filmed on a stage using rear projections to create the illusion that it was filmed on location. For Grand Central Station, Boyle used a maximum of light to create a proper set. Boyle said he flooded the station with so much light he wondered if Paramount could pay the bill. He also showed his adaptability with location shooting by using an ideal site for the crop-duster assault on Cary Grant. The image is one of a lone figure in the dusty field with no cover in sight desperately trying to flee the airplane. The contrast between the impeccably dressed Grant, the dust from the fields, and the emptiness of the landscape combine to create a memorable scene.

The most startling and perhaps the most technically complex film Boyle has worked on is *The Birds*. Boyle drew his inspiration from Edvard Munch's painting ''The Cry'' for his overall look. For the technical challenge, he turned to the Disney studios for their special effects technology. Using mattes, and a borrowed special effect prism from Disney, he was able to exercise total control of the imagery and to make convincing illusions. One of the more famous scenes is the bird's-eye view of the fire in the town of Bodega Bay. Boyle had to create the entire scene using mattes; even the apparently moving smoke was part of the mattes. The only actual ''real'' objects were the gas, the phone booth, the car and, of course, the fire. The filming of the fire was done in the studio parking lot, and the town was added in matte by matte to create the final image. Boyle said they could not film the fire on location because the town in the movie was actually a composite of several towns. Boyle created Bodega Bay by using bits and pieces from one town or another, another example of his ability to take control and create his vision of the story while on location.

Marnie was to be his last film with Hitchcock, and Boyle went on to work with Norman Jewison for several films. He was nominated for an Academy Award for his work on *Gaily, Gaily*—a lavish production set in Chicago in 1910 in which he successfully incorporated historic landmarks and period scenes in and around Chicago. *Fiddler on the Roof*, Jewison's film version of the theater production, was shot on location in Yugoslavia. The film called for real houses, real animals and real landscapes. Boyle again was nominated for an Academy Award for his work on this film, the look of which was described as gritty and realistic.

Boyle continued to show his adaptability and versatility well into the 1980s working on such films as *Private Benjamin*, *Staying Alive* (Stallone's sequel to *Saturday Night Fever*), *Jumpin' Jack Flash*, and finishing his career with the film version of *Dragnet* in 1987 and *Troop Beverly Hills* in 1988.

—Renee Ward

BOZZETTO, Bruno

Animator. **Nationality:** Italian. **Born:** Milan, 3 March 1938. **Education:** Studied the classics, law, and geology in school and university. **Career:** 1958–59—freelance animated film designer: first film as animator, *Tapum*, 1958; 1959–60—studied animation under John Halas, London; since 1959—director, Bruno Bozzetto Film, Milan, making advertising and entertainment films. **Address:** Bruno Bozzetto Film, Via Melchoirre Gioia 55, 20124 Milan, Italy.

Films as Animator:

1958   *Tapum!, la storia delle armi*
1959   *La storie delle invenzioni*
1960   *Un Oscar per il Signor Rossi*
1961   *Alpha Omega*
1963   *I Due Castelli*; *Il Signor Rossi va a Sciare*
1964   *Il Signor Rossi al mare*
1965   *West and Soda*
1966   *Il Signor Rossi compra l'automobile*
1967   *Una vita in scatola*; *L'uomo e il suo mondo*
1968   *Vip mio fratello superuomo*
1969   *Ego*
1970   *Il Signor Rossi al camping*
1971   *Sottaceti*
1972   *Oppio per oppio*; *Il Signor Rossi al Safari Fotografico*
1973   *Opera*; *La cabina*
1974   *Self Service*; *Il Signor rossi a Venezia*
1975   *Gli Sport del Signor Rossi*
1976   *Il Signor Rossi cerca la Felicita*; *La Piscinia*; *Allegro non troppo*
1977   *I sogni del Signor Rossi*; *Le Vacanze del Signor Rossi*; *Striptease*
1978   *Baby Story*
1979   *Happy Birthday*
1980   *Giallo automatico*; *Sandwich*; *Ma come fanno a farli cosi' belli?* (4 films); *Lilliput-put* (13 films)
1981–83   *Quark* (35 films)
1981   *Homo Technologicus* (7 films)
1982   *Tennis Club*; *Sporting*; *Homo Technologicus* (8 films)
1983   *La Pillola*; *Milano Zero*; *Sigmund*; *Nel Centro del Mirino*; *Homo Technologicus* (6 films)
1984   *Moa Moa*; *Sandwich*; *Homo Technologicus* (8 films)
1985   *El Dorado*; *Homo Technologicus* (5 films)
1986   *Spiaggia privata*; *Spider*; *Quark Economia* (13 films)
1987   *Sotto il ristorante Cinese* (*Below the Chinese Restaurant*); *Baeus*; *Quark* (5 films)
1988   *Sigmund* (for TV); *Mini Quark* (29 films); *Quark* (6 films); *Mister Tao*
1990   *Cavalette*; *Big Bang*
1991   *Dancing*; *Ski Love*
1992   *Tulilem*
1993   *Maleducazione in Montagna*; *Educazione al Cinema*; *Drop*
1995   *Help?*

Publications

By BOZZETTO: articles—

Cinema International, no. 16, 1967.
Filmblatter, 2 February 1968.
Banc-Titre (Paris), October 1982.
Segnocinema (Vicenza), vol. 7, no. 28, May 1987.

On BOZZETTO: book—

Bendazzi, G., *Bruno Bozzetto: Animazione primo amore*, Milan, 1972.

On BOZZETTO: articles—

Rivista del Cinematografo (Rome), July 1964.
Film a Doba (Prague) no. 2, 1965.
Halas, John, and Robert Delpire, in *Film and TV Graphics*, edited by Walter Herdeg, Zurich, 1967.
Cinema International, no. 15, 1967.
Rivista del Cinematografo (Rome), January 1967.
Image et Son (Paris), November 1967.
Cineforum (Bergamo), November 1968.
Rivista del Cinematografo (Rome), June 1975.
Film Guia, June/July 1975.
Edera, Bruno, in *Full Length Animated Feature Films*, London, 1977.
Canemaker, John, in *Film News*, Summer 1979.
Film Library Quarterly (New York), vol. 13, no. 4, 1980.
Banc-Titre (Paris), December 1980.
Bastiancich, A., "Italie: visages de Bruno Bozzetto," in *CinémAction* (Conde-sur-Noireau), no. 51, April 1989.

*   *   *

Bruno Bozzetto's early education consisted of classical studies and some years at university devoted to law and geology, but since entering animation and design at the age of 17, he has succeeded in a field that was primarily dominated by the Hollywood-based studios, such as those of Walt Disney, Hanna-Barbera, and more recently, Filmation and Ralph Bakshi.

Bozzetto's main attributes are his consistency of output and his inimitable style of grotesque, highly individual caricature. He can define with simple outlines the true essence of a personality which is instantly recognizable and commands interest. As a film cartoonist, he is able to expand a character with the right behavior patterns and to create a complementary personality in depth. One of his stock characters, Il Signor Rossi, who appears in numerous short cartoons from 1960 onwards and in three of his feature-length films, became the symbol of the Italian "little man"; resourceful, determined, greedy, and vain, he charmingly puts his family interests above all others.

Bozzetto's rare asset is his ability to coordinate and control story continuity, characterization of personalities, development of story, complementary sound effects and music (which underline the behavior of his figures), humor (which never steps out of context of the subject), and ideas (which are within the bounds of the technical flexibility of animation) to achieve the final effect. His sharp, European wit differs from the American (which is more physical), inasmuch as he comments satirically on human shortcomings, such as greed and stupidity. Nevertheless, his humor is light, it never swings over into preaching, and is fixed firmly within the limits of traditional Italian comedy.

His large output, which includes several series for television and six full-length animated feature films, reached a peak with *Allegro non troppo* in 1976. A parody on a grand symphony concert, it plays on the unexpected happenings which could occur during such an event. The film combines pleasing graphic design, close relationships between choreography of movement and music, and a degree of visual progression which few animated films have achieved. Several of Bozzetto's shorter films, such as *Alpha Omega*, *Opera*, *Ego*, and *Self Service*, all classic cautionary tales for our time, exemplify his integration of graphic design, storytelling, and European humor.

—John Halas

BRACKETT, Charles

Writer and Producer. **Nationality:** American. **Born:** Saratoga Springs, New York, 26 November 1892. **Education:** Attended Williamstown College, Williamstown, Massachusetts, B.A. 1915; Harvard Law School, Cambridge, Massachusetts, LL.B., 1920. **Family:** Married 1) Elizabeth Barrows Fletcher, 1920 (died 1948); two daughters; 2) Lillian Fletcher, 1953. **Career:** Served in the United States Army in World War I: 2nd lieutenant, and vice-consul in St. Nazaire, France (Medal of Honor, France); 1920–25—practicing lawyer, and also writer: first novel, *The Counsel of the Ungodly*, 1920; 1926–29—drama critic, *The New Yorker*; 1930—joined father's law firm (also board member, Adirondacks Trust Company): retained these positions throughout his career; 1934—first film as writer, *Enter Madam!*; 1937–50—collaborator with Billy Wilder; 1943—first film as producer, *Five Graves to Cairo*; 1949–55—president, Motion Picture Academy; 1954—worked mainly as producer; 1962—retired. **Awards:** Academy Award (producer and writer) for *The Lost Weekend*, 1945; *Sunset Boulevard*, 1950; *Titanic*, 1953; Writers Guild Award for *Sunset Boulevard*, 1950; Writers Guild Laurel Award, 1956, and

Charles Brackett

Founders Award, 1966; Special Academy Award, 1957. **Died:** In Beverly Hills, California, 9 March 1969.

Films as Writer:

1934   *Enter Madam!* (Nugent)
1935   *College Scandal* (*The Clock Strikes Eight*) (Nugent); *The Crusades* (De Mille); *The Lost Outpost* (*The Last Outpost*) (Gasnier and Barton); *Without Regret* (Young)
1936   *Woman Trap* (Young); *Rose of The Rancho* (Gering)
1937   *Live, Love, and Learn* (Fitzmaurice)
1938   *Bluebeard's Eighth Wife* (Lubitsch)
1939   *Midnight* (Leisen); **Ninotchka** (Lubitsch)
1940   *Arise, My Love* (Leisen)
1941   *Hold Back the Dawn* (Leisen); *Ball of Fire* (Hawks)
1942   *The Major and the Minor* (Wilder)
1944   *Skirmish on the Home Front* (Short)

Films as Writer and Producer:

1943   *Five Graves to Cairo* (Wilder)
1945   ***The Lost Weekend*** (Wilder)
1946   *To Each His Own* (Leisen)
1948   *The Emperor Waltz* (Wilder); *A Foreign Affair* (Wilder); *Miss Tatlock's Millions* (Haydn)
1950   ***Sunset Boulevard*** (Wilder)

1951   *The Mating Season* (Leisen); *The Model and the Marriage
        Broker* (Cukor)
1953   *Niagara* (Hathaway); *Titanic* (Negulesco)

Films as Producer:

1944   *The Uninvited* (Allen)
1954   *Garden of Evil* (Hathaway); *Woman's World* (Negulesco)
1955   *The Girl in the Red Velvet Swing* (Fleischer) (+ co-sc); *The
        Virgin Queen* (Koster)
1956   *Teenage Rebel* (Goulding) (+ co-sc); *The King and I* (Walter
        Lang); *D-Day, the Sixth of June* (Koster)
1957   *The Wayward Bus* (Vicas)
1958   *The Gift of Love* (Negulesco); *Ten North Frederick* (Dunne);
        The Remarkable Mr. Pennypacker (Levin)
1959   *Journey to the Center of the Earth* (Levin) (+ co-sc); *Blue
        Denim* (*Blue Jeans*) (Dunne)
1960   *High Time* (Edwards)
1962   *State Fair* (J. Ferrer)

Publications

By BRACKETT: fiction—

The Counsel of the Ungodly, New York, 1920.
Week-End, New York, 1925.
That Last Infirmity, New York, 1926.
American Colony, New York, 1929.
Entirely Surrounded, New York, 1934.

By BRACKETT: other books—

With Billy Wilder, *The Lost Weekend* in *The Best Film Plays of 1945*
    (screenplay), edited by John Gassner and Dudley Nichols, 1946.
With Billy Wilder and Walter Reisch, *Ninotchka* (screenplay), 1966.

By BRACKETT: articles—

"Putting the Picture on Paper," in *American Cinematographer*
    (Hollywood), December 1951.
In *Writing on Life*, by Lincoln Barnett, New York, 1951.
On Lubitsch, in *Cahiers du Cinéma* (Paris), no 198.

On BRACKETT: articles—

Films in Review (New York), March 1960.
Film Comment (New York), Winter 1970–71.
Corliss, Richard, in *Talking Pictures*, New York, 1974.
Film Comment (New York), May-June 1982.
Frank, Sam, in *American Screenwriters*, edited by Robert E.
    Morsberger, Stephen O. Lesser, and Randall Clark, Detroit, Michi-
    gan, 1984.

*   *   *

Who was Charles Brackett? Just a secretary to Billy Wilder? That
premise has been proferred numerous times and when one looks at
Brackett's work outside the 14 pictures he did with Wilder, there

appears to be some truth in it. Yet in all fairness, Brackett was, like
many of his screenwriting colleagues, a chameleon who adapted to
the influence exerted by his collaborators at the time.

Brackett was a graduate of Harvard Law School and a practicing
lawyer for some six years before his second novel, *Week-End*, landed
him a job as drama critic on *The New Yorker*. In 1932, he signed
a writing contract with Paramount and the ten or so pictures he
worked on before joining forces with Billy Wilder are mostly
forgettable. His first collaboration with Wilder was the screenplay for
Bluebeard's Eighth Wife, directed by Ernst Lubitsch. This sophisticated, witty story of greed on the French Riviera owed much to
Wilder's dark humor, but Brackett's contribution should not be
diminished. Wilder's films all have a streak of cruelty running
through them, and Brackett's chief talent was his ability to be
a mellowing buffer to this characteristic, to "Americanize" Wilder's
Viennese idiom and to provide the "bridging dialogue" between
Wilder's perceptive but sarcastic ideas.

They continued this extremely successful collaboration through
1950—frequently being joined by two other writers—Walter Reisch
and Richard Breen—and their combined filmographies include some
of Hollywood's most memorable and sophisticated films: *Midnight*,
Ninotchka, *Ball of Fire*, *A Foreign Affair*, *The Lost Weekend*, and
Sunset Boulevard, the last two winning Academy Awards. Brackett's
reaction to Wilder's dark side is revealed in a comment he made about
Sunset Boulevard in 1952: "[Norma Desmond] was also tragic.
Perhaps we should have told about her with a more audible lump in
our throats. We thought it effective to suppress the pitying sounds and
let the audience find the pity for themselves." It is obvious that
Wilder is not of the "lump in our throats" school of filmmaking, and
his treatment of *Sunset Boulevard* as a real horror story is what makes
it the greatest film about Hollywood.

Brackett, on the other hand, was very definitely of a more
sentimental nature and the work he wrote and produced without
Wilder proves this. His best work without Wilder was the extremely
romantic women's picture *To Each His Own*, the sensuous marital
suspenser *Niagara*, and the melodramatic *Titanic*, which earned him,
and Reisch, Academy Awards. And as a producer he proved extremely successful with middle-of-the-road sentimental entertainments such as *The Virgin Queen*, *The King and I*, *The Remarkable Mr.
Pennypacker*, and *State Fair*.

While Wilder is the dominant force behind Brackett's best films,
the contribution to the collaborative art of the motion picture by such
writers as Brackett must not be underestimated. Without the leveling
force of a Brackett, Wilder's films would probably never have found
the wide audience they did.

—Ronald Bowers

BRACKETT, Leigh

Writer. **Nationality:** American. **Born:** Leigh Douglass Brackett in
Los Angeles, California, 7 December 1915. **Family:** Married the
writer Edmond Hamilton, 1946 (died 1977). **Career:** Freelance
writer; first novel published, *No Good from a Corpse*, 1944; 1945—
first film as writer, *The Vampire's Ghost*; 1946—first of several films
for Howard Hawks, *The Big Sleep*; also worked for TV series
Checkmate, *Suspense*, and *Alfred Hitchcock Presents*. **Died:** In
Lancaster, California, 18 March 1978.

Leigh Brackett

Films as Writer:

1945 *The Vampire's Ghost* (Selander)
1946 ***The Big Sleep*** (Hawks); *Crime Doctor's Manhunt* (Castle)
1959 ***Rio Bravo*** (Hawks)
1961 *Gold of the Seven Saints* (Douglas)
1962 *Hatari!* (Hawks)
1967 *El Dorado* (Hawks)
1970 *Rio Lobo* (Hawks)
1973 *The Long Goodbye* (Altman)
1980 ***The Empire Strikes Back*** (Kershner)

Publications

By BRACKETT: fiction—

No Good from a Corpse, New York, 1944.
Stranger at Home (ghost-written for George Sanders), New York, 1946.
Shadow over Mars, New York, 1951, as *The Nemesis from Terra*, New York, 1961.
The Starman, New York, 1952, as *The Galactic Breed*, New York, 1955, as *The Starman of Llyrdis*, New York, 1976.
The Sword of Rhiannon, New York, 1953.
The Big Jump, New York, 1955.
The Long Tomorrow, New York, 1955.
The Tiger among Us, New York, 1957, as *Fear No Evil*, London, 1960, as *13 West Street*, New York, 1962.

An Eye for an Eye, New York, 1957.
Rio Bravo (novelization of screenplay), New York, 1959.
Alpha Centauri—or Die!, New York, 1963.
Follow the Free Wind, New York, 1963.
People of the Talisman, the Secret of Sinharat, New York, 1964.
The Coming of the Terrans (stories), New York, 1967.
Silent Partner, New York, 1969.
The Halflings and Other Stories, New York, 1973.
The Ginger Star, New York, 1974.
The Best of Leigh Brackett (stories), New York, 1977.
Eric John Stark, Outlaw of Mars, New York, 1982.

By BRACKETT: other books—

With William Faulkner and Jules Furthman, *The Big Sleep* (screenplay), in *Film Scripts One*, edited by George P. Garrett, O. B. Harrison, Jr., and Jane Gelfmann, 1971.
(Editor) *The Best of Planet Stories 1*, New York, 1975.
The Book of Skaith (includes *The Hound of Skaith* and *The Reavers of Skaith*), New York, 1976.
(Editor) *The Best of Edmond Hamilton*, New York, 1977.
(Editor) *Strange Adventures in Other Worlds*, New York, 1975.
With Lawrence Kasdan, *The Empire Strikes Back* (screenplay), in *The Empire Strikes Back Notebook*, edited by Diane Attias and Lindsay Smith, New York, 1980.

By BRACKETT: articles—

Take One (Montreal), September-October 1972.
Films in Review (New York), August-September 1976.

On BRACKETT: book—

Arbur, Rosemarie, *Leigh Brackett, Marion Zimmer Bradley, Anne McCaffrey: A Primary and Secondary Bibliography*, Boston, Massachusetts, 1982.
Carr, John L., *Leigh Brackett: American Writer*, Polk City, 1986.
Benson, Gordon; Jr., *Leigh Brackett & Edmond Hamilton: The Enchantress & the World Wrecker: A Working Bibliography*, San Bernardino, 1988.

On BRACKETT: articles—

Biografären, October 1966.
Film Comment (New York), Winter 1970–71.
Cinéma (Paris), July 1977.
Take One (Montreal), November 1978.
Monthly Film Bulletin (London), July 1980.
Silver, Alain, and Elizabeth Ward, in *American Screenwriters*, edited by Robert M. Morsberger, Stephen O. Lesser, and Randall Clark, Detroit, Michigan 1984.

*   *   *

Upon being asked about Leigh Brackett's work on *El Dorado* in the book *Hawks on Hawks*, director Howard Hawks replied: "She wrote that like a man. She writes good." Therein lies not only

Hawks's opinion of Brackett but also his screen heroes' reaction to a person who comes through in a tight spot. ''You were good back there'' (*Big Sleep*), ''You were good in there tonight'' (*Rio Bravo*), were the best compliments that a Hawks character could pay. And Brackett did come through for Hawks, writing screenplays for five of his films, beginning with *The Big Sleep*.

By the time that Brackett began working with Hawks, the director already had a definite style. The ''Hawksian woman'' as she is now known—a strong-willed character who gambles, drinks, can use a gun, and still remains feminine—had made appearances in previous films. Hawks normally shaped his action around two or more men and their reaction to pressure and to the Hawksian woman. Brackett's contribution as one of Hawks's screenwriters was to hone the male-female relationships, and to connect scenes and action that Hawks gave her. Hawks preferred his writers to be present on the set, and there was constant rewriting as dialogue was changed and then changed again. During their period together, Brackett and Hawks produced ensemble films in which the hero is helped by a group of oddball characters who surround him and aid him in a life or death situation. In four of the five films that they did together (*Rio Bravo*, *Hatari!*, *El Dorado*, *Rio Lobo*), John Wayne was that hero.

Brackett believed, as Hawks did, that the usual Hollywood leading ladies were not very strong or interesting, and the Hawksian woman was a necessary character in their films. The screenwriter and the director also agreed that you had to depend on yourself because others can fail you in any situation—especially love. And while the characters of their films reject help in a tight situation, they receive it from unexpected places. On the subject of love, the characters usually have an unlucky past record with someone who left them, and they are wary of new relationships. Both the hero and the heroine tentatively approach a possible relationship by sarcastic bantering back and forth, testing the waters, aware that it might not last. Even the first kiss is a test: ''I'm glad we tried it a second time. It's better when two people do it,'' Feathers tells Chance in *Rio Bravo*. But once started, the relationship is strong.

Without Hawks, Brackett wrote the script for *The Long Goodbye*, directed by Robert Altman and, like *The Big Sleep*, based on a Raymond Chandler story. This script, however, was more brutal than anything that Brackett wrote for Hawks, and it portrayed a modern-day Marlowe who, like the 1940s detective, has definite values of honor and trust and downplays danger with a flippant attitude. This Marlowe reacts to events with ''O.K. with me,'' but, unlike his '40s counterpart, he is truly alone. He is betrayed by everyone, including his cat, and in the end he shoots a friend, Terry, who has deceived him. Brackett admitted that she changed the ending of the Chandler story because she felt Marlowe could not walk away from such a betrayal. Later, in *Take One*, she explained, in typically graphic terms, ''It seemed that the only satisfactory ending was for the cruelly-diddled Marlowe to blow Terry's guts out . . . something the old Marlowe would never have done.''

Shortly before she died Brackett wrote a draft for *The Empire Strikes Back*. Concerned for the most part with Luke Skywalker's battle against evil (in others and in himself), the film has Brackett touches—most obviously the strong sarcastic Leia, the daring Han Solo, and their relationship. When Solo attempts to kiss her, Leia says, ''Being held by you isn't quite enough to get me excited.'' But the attraction was there, and like Vivian and Marlowe, and Feathers and Chance, it is only a matter of time.

—Alexa L. Foreman

BRANCO, Paulo

Producer. **Nationality:** Portuguese. **Born:** José Condeixa de Araújo Branco in Lisbon, 3 June 1950. **Education:** Attended the Instituto Superior Tecnico, Lisbon, 1967–71. **Family:** Two children. **Career:** 1971–73—gambler in London; 1972—assistant director on Antonio-Pedro Vasconcelos's film *Perdido per cem*; also organized the Cine-Club of Paris-Pullman cinema, London; 1973–77—helped organize the Cinéma Olympic, the Artistic Voltaire, and the Action-République, and the Cahiers du Cinéma Festival, all in Paris; 1977—founded Hors-Champ distribution company; 1979—founded V.O. Filmes production company: first film as producer, *Oxalá* by Vasconcelos.

Films as Producer:

1979   *Oxalá* (Vasconcelos); *Aurelia Steiner—Vancouver* (Duras)
1980   *Loin de Manhattan* (Biette); *Conversa Acabada* (Botelho); *Silvestre* (Montiro)
1981   *Le Territoire* (*The Territory*) (Ruiz); *Francisca* (de Oliveira); *Amor de perdicao* (de Oliveira); *Ana* (Reis and Cordeiro); *A estrangeira* (Grilo); *Fim de estação* (Silva); *Aspern* (de Gregorio)
1982   *Les Trois couronnes du matelot* (*The Sailor's Three Crowns*) (Ruiz); *Der Stand der Dinge* (*The State of Things*) (Wenders) (co); *O Lugar do morto* (Vasconcelos)
1983   *Dans la ville blanche* (Tanner) (+ ro); *Pointe de fuite* (Ruiz) (+ ro); *Jusqu'à la nuit* (Martiny)
1984   *Les Amants terribles* (Dubroux); *Maine-Océan* (Rozier); *Notre mariage* (Sarmiento); *Angola* (Ruiz); *Der Rosenkönig* (Schroeter); *Ninguém Daus Vezes* (Mello) (co); *Le Meilleur de la ville* (Victor) (co); *Les Destins de Manoel* (Ruiz)
1985   *L'Île au trésor* (Ruiz); *L'Eveillé du Pont de l'Alma* (*The Insomniac at the Bridge*) (Ruiz); *Le Soulier de satin* (de Oliveira); *Vertiges* (Laurent); *Gardien de la nuit* (Limosin); *Faubourg St. Martin* (Guiguet); *O Outono* (Canijo)
1986   *Across the Heart* (R. Kramer); *Les Mendiants* (Jacquot); *Eden-misère* (Laurent); *Mon cas* (de Oliveira); *Agosta* (Mello)
1988   *Tres menos eu* (*Three Minus Me*) (Canijo) (co)
1990   *Nao ou a vã gloria de mandar* (*No, or the Vain Glory of Command*; *Non, ou la vaine gloire de commande*) (de Oliveira); *Le Trésor des Îles Chiennes* (*Land of the Dead*) (Ossang) (co); *Border Film* (Dubroux); *Une Flame dans mon coeur* (*A Flame in My Heart*) (Tanner)
1991   *L'Homme qui a perdu son ombre* (*The Man Who Lost His Shadow*) (Tanner) (co); *A divina comedia* (*The Divine Comedy*) (de Oliveira); *Bis ans Ende der Welt* (*Until the End of the World*) (Wenders) (exec)
1992   *O Último Mergulho* (*The Last Dive*) (Monteiro); *No Dia dos Meus Anos* (*On My Birthday*) (Botelho); *O Fim do Mundo* (Grilo); *O Dia do Desespero* (*The Day of Despair*) (de Oliveira); *Das Tripas Coração* (*Twin Flames*) (Pinto); *Un Paraguas para tres* (*An Umbrella for Three*) (Vega) (assoc)
1993   *Madregilda* (Regueiro) (assoc); *Les Gens normaux n'ont rien d'exceptionnel* (*Normal People Are Nothing Exceptional*) (Laurence Ferreira Barbosa) (co); *L'Absence* (*The Absence*) (Handke); *Vale Abraão* (*Abraham Valley*) (de Oliveira)

1994 *Mil e Uma* (*A Thousand and One*) (Moraes); *Le Livre de cristal* (*Crystal Book*) (Plattner); *Fado majeur et mineur* (*Fado, Major and Minor*) (Ruiz); *Casa de Lava* (*Down to Earth*) (Costa); *A Caixa* (*Blind Man's Bluff*) (de Oliveira); *Longe Daqui* (Guerra); *Três Palmeiras* (*Three Palm Trees*) (Botelho); *Lisbon Story* (Wenders)
1995 *O Convento* (*The Convent*) (de Oliveira)
1996 *No Sex Last Night* (*Double Blind*) (Calle and Shephard); *Le Journal de séducteur* (*Diary of a Seducer*) (Dubroux); *Le Coeur fantôme* (Garrel); *Cinco Dias, Cinco Noites* (Fonseca e Costa); *Trois vies et une seule mort* (*Three Lives and Only One Death*) (Ruiz); *Os Olhos da Ásia* (*The Eyes of Asia*); *Party* (de Oliveira); *For Ever Mozart* (Godard); *Few of Us* (Bartas); *Caméléone* (Cohen)
1997 *Transatlantique* (Laurent); *O Homem do Comboio* (Bruxelas and Rezende); *Pour rire!* (Belvaux); *Généalogies d'un crime* (*Genealogies of a Crime*) (Ruiz); *Viagem ao Princípio do Mundo* (*Voyage to the Beginning of the World*) (de Oliveira); *A Casa* (*The House*) (Bartas); *J'ai horreur de l'amour* (*I Hate Love*) (Laurence Ferreira Barbosa); *Porto Santo* (Vicente Jorge Silva); *Ossos* (*Bones*) (Costa); *Alors voilà* (Piccoli)
1998 *Trois ponts sur la rivière* (Biette); *On a très peu d'amis* (Monod); *Sapatos Pretos* (Canijo); *Requiem* (Tanner); *Inquietude* (*Anxiety*) (de Oliveira); *Comic Act* (Hazan); *L'Inconnu de Strasbourg* (Sarmiento); *Traffic* (Botelho); *Longe da Vista* (Grilo); *L'Examen de minuit* (*Midnight Exam*) (Dubroux); *L'Ennui* (Kahn)
1999 *Lila Lili* (Vermillard); *La Nouvelle Ève* (The New Eve) (Corsini); *Le Temps retrouvé* (Time Regained) (Ruiz) (exec); *As Bodas de Deus* (Monteiro); *A Carta* (*The Letter*) (de Oliveira)
2000 *El Mar;* (*The Sea*); *Tarde Demais*; *La Fidélité;* (*Fidelity*); *La Captive;* (*The Captive*); *Palavra e Utopia*

Other Films:

1972 *Perdido per cem* (Vasconcelos) (asst d)
1983 *Les Tricheurs* (Schroeder) (exec pr); *Vidas* (Telles) (ro); *La Ville des pirates* (*City of Pirates*) (Ruiz) (exec pr)
1984 *De grens* (*Frontiers*) (de Winter) (exec pr)
1989 *Piano panier* (ro as António)
1999 *Les Infortunes de la beauté* (ro as Le gardien)

Publications

By BRANCO: articles—

Cinema e Cinema (Bologna), October/December 1982.
"Les Rôles des producteurs—la porte étroite," in *Cahiers du Cinéma* (Paris), May 1985.
Screen International (London), 4–18 May 1985.
Cahiers du Cinéma (Paris), January 1986.

On BRANCO: articles—

Celuloide (Rio Maior, Portugal), July 1981.
Cahiers, no. 458, July/August 1992.

Cahiers, no. 464, February 1993.
Les Cine-Fiches de Grand Angle (Mariembourg), April 1997.
Variety (New York), 22 December 1997.

*   *   *

In the first three years of the 1980s, Paulo Branco changed the axis of film production in Portugal. Since 1983, Branco has been the Portuguese pole of European production, putting his mark as producer on some of the most important European vanguard cineastes, Raoul Ruiz, Wim Wenders, Marguerite Duras, Werner Schroeter, and Alain Tanner, without mentioning his particular relationship with Manoel de Oliveira.

In Portugal, where production depended exclusively on financial assistance from the state, Branco, in association with Antonio-Pedro Vasconcelos, formed V.O. Filmes and started a small revolution, creating a system of complicated personal relations that has permitted him to produce a number of films unknown since the best years of the "cinema novo," a movement equivalent to the New Wave in France. The prestige he acquired in France as a distributor (showing films by Straub, de Oliveira, Ruiz, and Welles in France, and a variety of films in the Portuguese market) was such that he was able to attract to Portugal important European filmmakers, integrating them into his production system which relies, in equal proportion, on a love of film, rapid production, and a multiplication of financing which Branco, with his gambler's instinct, calls "controlled risks." Another factor in his success is the "clan" spirit he elicits, evident on the continued presence on his productions of the cinematographer Acácio de Almeida, the sound recorder Joaquim Pinto, and the set designer María José Branco.

The filmmaker most amenable to Paulo Branco's production system is Raoul Ruiz, a Chilean radical living in France. Since *Le Territoire*, most of Ruiz's films have been produced by Branco with financial backing through television, film festivals, cultural institutions, and "advance over receipts," a type of state support for film production in France. The secret of multiple production can be explained in part by the films' low budgets much below standard costs, and in part by the aesthetic and stylistic similarity between Ruiz and Branco. Ruiz's cinema thrives on an illusionist representation in which improvisation is a strong part. As Branco has said, "$600,000 or $700,000 on a film of Ruiz represents four times more money than on a normal film. Nothing is ever wasted. The amount of the budget is the amount actually spent."

Because of the difficulty in financing films by new filmmakers or films that go beyond the routinely commercial, Branco has used a system whereby he produces two films simultaneously, one, financially certain, financing a second film of uncertain standing. For instance, Wenders's *Der Stand der Dinge* supported Ruiz's *Le Territoire*, and Ruiz's *La Ville des pirates* was produced using a diversion of part of the budget of *Les Tricheurs* by Barbet Schroeder.

The production of the films of Manoel de Oliveira is, however, different from the usual system. Unlike Ruiz, de Oliveira is a perfectionist unable to surrender the most minor elements of his conception of a film. His films require a long and rigorous preparation, similar to that of large-scale European films. For *Le Soulier de satin*, however, Branco was able to provide a production of 50 sets, a cast of 7 months with a crew of 75 people. His Portuguese budget of $1,800,000, however, would have been $9,000,000 had the film been produced in France, yet this film, as well as *Francisca* and *Mon cas*, attains an unexpected splendor.

Though one cannot say that Branco has sparked a new aesthetic movement, his production system has been able to make films by new "auteurs," and new films by established makers (think of *Dans la ville blanche* by Tanner and *Der Stand der Dinge* by Wenders), and to make at the same time a type of European series B film which does not lack a characteristic mark of elegance.

—M. S. Fonseca

BRAUNBERGER, Pierre

Producer. **Nationality:** French. **Born:** Paris, 29 July 1905. **Education:** Attended the Lycée Voltaire, Paris. **Family:** Married the actress Gisèle Hauchecorne, 1964; two sons. **Career:** General film experience in Germany, England, and the United States in early 1920s; 1926–30—formed several production companies, notably Pierre Braunberger Productions; 1929—founded Société du Cinéma du Panthéon, and opened Cinéma du Panthéon; operated Billancourt studios from early 1930s; 1945—founded Panthéon productions, and built Lhomond studios: later companies include Films de la Pléiade, France Opéra Films, and Films du Jeudi. Officer, Legion of Honor. **Died:** In Paris, 1990.

Films as Producer/Executive Producer (Shorts):

1924   *Entr'acte* (Clair)
1925   *Rien que les heures* (Cavalcanti)
1926   *Voyage au Congo* (M. Allégret and Gide)
1927   *La P'tite Lili* (Cavalcanti)
1929   *Un Chien andalou* (Buñuel)
1937   *Records 37* (Brunius)
1945   *Gitans d'Espagne* (Castanier); *Six si petits* (Bertrand); *Chambre 34* (Barma)
1946   *Une Partie de campagne* (*A Day in the Country*) (Renoir—produced 1936); *Paris 1900* (Vèdres) (+ sc); *Le Bâton* (Gibaud); *L'Homme* (Margaritis); *Monsieur Badin* (Régnier)
1947   *Les Petites Annonces* (Barma); *Illusion* (Rougeul); *La Cathédrale* (Béranger)
1948   *Transports urbains* (Gibaud); *Journal masculin* (Barma); *Versailles et ses fantômes* (Béranger); *Van Gogh* (Resnais); *Actualités burlesques* (Margaritis); *Rondo est sur la piste* (Henry)
1949   *Guernica* (Resnais and Hessens); *Les Actualités: ça c'est des nouvelles!* (Margaritis)
1950   *Histoire de pin-up girls* (Gibaud); *Gauguin* (Resnais); *Toulouse-Lautrec* (Hessens)
1951   *La Course de tauraux* (*Bullfight*) (+ d, sc); *Pompon rouge* (Lalande); *Le Fils de l'eau* (Rouche—compilation); *L'Art Haut-Rhénan* (Gibaud); *Station mondaine* (Gibaud); *Palais-Royale* (Béranger); *Le Dictionnaire des pin-up girls* (Gibaud)
1952   *Avec André Gide* (M. Allégret—compilation); *En quête de Marie* (Gibaud)
1953   *La Seine et ses marchands* (Gibaud); *Chagall* (Hessens)
1954   *Ballade parisienne* (Gibaud); *Croissance de Paris* (Gibaud)
1955   *Impressions de New York* (Reichenbach); *New York ballade* (Reichenbach); *Visages de Paris* (Reichenbach); *Paris qui ne dort pas* (Reichenbach); *Une Lettre pour vous* (Vétusto);

Mammy Water (*Ma mère l'eau*) (Rouch); *Les Maîtres fous* (Rouch)
1956   *Paris d'hier et d'aujourd'hui* (*Hier et aujourd'hui*) (Gibaud); *Symphonie New York* (Reichenbach); *Le Grand Sud* (Reichenbach); *Houston Texas* (Reichenbach); *Novembre à Paris* (Reichenbach); *Toute la mémoire du monde* (Resnais); *Le Coup de berger* (Rivette); *Les Abeilles* (Dhuit); *Surprise-boogie* (Pierru); *Soir de fête* (Pierru)
1957   *O Saisons, o châteaux* (Varda); *Les Marines* (Reichenbach); *Au pays de Porgy and Bess* (Reichenbach); *L'Américain se détend* (Reichenbach); *L'Eté indien* (Reichenbach); *Carnaval à la Nouvelle Orléans* (Reichenbach); *Alberobello, "Au pays des trulli"* (Reichenbach); *Ballade sur les fils* (Vétusto); *L'Oeil du maître* (Vétusto); *Eygalières, commune de France* (Vétusto); *La Santé à l'étable* (Vétusto); *La Vie dans l'herbe* (Dhuit); *Fantaisie sur quatre cordes* (Pierru); *Tous les garçons s'appellent Patrick* (Godard); *Les surmenés* (Doniol-Valcroze); *Terre d'insectes* (Calderon); *Terre d'oiseaux* (Calderon and Dragesco)
1958   *Le Printemps de la mer* (Gibaud); *Le Chant du Styrène* (Resnais); *Bonjour, Monsieur La Bruyère* (Doniol-Valcroze); *Les Eglises romanes en Saintange* (Bazin and Doniol-Valcroze); *Elèves-maîtres* (Vétusto); *Ces gens de Paris* (Fabiani); *Au bon coin* (Kerchbron); *Recherches* (Agam); *Charlotte et son Jules* (Godard); *Terre sous-marine* (Calderon); *Une Histoire d'eau* (Godard and Truffaut); *Le Vivarium* (Calderon); *La Montagne aux météores* (Bissirieus); *La Vie des termites* (Grasse and Dragesco); *L'Amérique insolite* (Reichenbach); *Moi, un noir* (Rouch)
1959   *Drôles d'actualités* (Pierru)
1960   *L'Abeille et les hommes* (Dhuit); *Photo-souvenir* (Fabiani); *La Jeune Fille et l'étoile* (Pierru); *Aventures en Laponie* (Bissirieux); *Ile Maurice* (Rossif); *Prélude à l'Asie* (Rossif); *La Soif des bêtes* (Dragesco and Calderon); *Tant qu'il est temps: le cancer* (Vétusto and Doniol-Valcroze)
1961   *Le Soleil éteint* (Gilles); *Les Guêpes* (Dhuit); *Les Oiseaux d'Afrique* (Dragesco and Calderon); *L'Amour existe* (Pialat); *La Frontière* (Cayrol and Durand); *Calligraphie japonaise* (Alechinsky); *Cinq cents balles* (Rippert); *Dans la réserve africaine* (Calderon and Dragesco); *La Machine à parler d'amour* (Rossi, i.e. Japrisot); *Quatorze juillet* (Hurtado); *Le match de catch* (Bekretaoui); *La Pyramide humaine* (Rouche)
1962   *Jeu 1* (Reichenbach); *Exemple Etretat* (Lepeuve); *Venir du Havre* (Lepeuve); *Le Menuisier* (Blue); *L'Idée fixe* (Triangle) (Rossi, i.e. Japrisot); *Sirène* (Hurtado); *Dante n'avait rien vu* (Hurtado); *Delphica* (Korber); *Retour à New York* (Reichenbach); *A la mémoire du rock* (Reichenbach); *L'Amérique Lunaire* (Reichenbach); *Le Paris des mannequins* (Reichenbach); *Le Paris des photographes* (Reichenbach); *Le Petit Café* (Reichenbach)
1963   *Illuminations* (Reichenbach); *Gestes de France* (Reichenbach); *Histoire d'un petit garçon devenu grand* (Gilles and Reichenbach); *La Douceur du village* (Reichenbach); *Captain Cap* (Hurtado); *Havre sac* (Lepeuve); *L'Endormi* (Blue); *Le Voleur* (Blue); *1880* (Clerfeuille); *Dé partement 66* (Laporte); *Suivez l'oeuf* (Robin); *Plus qu'on ne peut donner* (Chevassu); *L'Epouse infernale* (Korber); *La Dame à la longue vue* (Korber); *Eve sans trêve* (Korber); *Auto-portrait* (Patris); *Le Monde des marais* (Dhuit); *Les*

Hommes de la Wahgi (Villeminot); *Gaspard fait du cheval* (Matalon); *Artifices* (Reichenbach); *Gaspard a un rendez-vous* (Matalon); *La Vie des oiseaux en Mauritanie* (Dragesco)

1964   *Gaspard se marie* (Matalon); *La Princesse muette* (Blue); *Les Albigeois* (Laporte); *Altitude 8625* (Korber); *La Rentrée* (Korber); *La Rose de mon jardin* (Grimblat); *Paolo, le petit pecheur* (Labrit); *La Parachutistes* (Jean-Pierre and Jean-Paul Janssen); *L'Avatar botanique de Mlle. Flora* (Barbillon); ''Véronique et Marie-France'' ep. of *Le Fleur de l'age, ou les adolescents* (*The Adolescents*) (Rouche)

1965   *Lomelin* (Reichenbach); *Paris au jour d'hiver* (Gilles); *Dunoyer de Segonzac* (Reichenbach and Lepeuve); *La Vengeance d'une orpheline russe* (F. and M. Lepeuve); *La Goumbé des jeunes noceurs* (Rouch); *L'Affaire des poissons* (Barbillon); *Les Hommes du Sepik* (Villeminot); *Week-end total* (Calderon); *Le Drame du taureau* (Clergue); *Pierre Boulez* (Fano); *Corrida d'hier et d'aujourd'hui* (Popelin); *Au Guadalquiviz* (Puzenat); *Le Dernier Refuge* (Puzenat); *Lourdes* (Gion); *La Longue Nuit* (Seban)

1966   *Aurora* (Reichenbach); *Equivoque 1900* (Lepeuve); *L'Incertaine Vocation de Médéric de Plougastel* (Barbillon); *Chanson de gestes* (Gilles); *Linarès, le jeune toréro* (Clergue); *Dans Arles où sont les Alyscamps* (Clergue); *Soleil* (Thorn); *Une Misanthrope* (Pirès); *La Direction d'acteurs par Jean Renoir* (G. Braunberger); *Stéphane et la garde chasse* (Duval)

1967   *Lumière* (M. Allégret); *Exposition 1900* (M. Allégret); *Concerto Brandenbourgeois* (Reichenbach); *L'Etoile de mer* (Puzenat); *Le Phare* (Clergue); *La Sixième Face du Pentagone* (Marker); *Vive eau* (Roger); *Soleil de pierre* (Baux); *L'Emploi du temps* (Demoine); *Les Toros* (Flaujac); *Delta de sel* (Clergue)

1968   *Au peril de la mer* (Roger); *Du cuir en juin* (G. Braunberger); *Début du siècle* (M. Allégret); *Jeunesse de France* (M. Allégret); *La Grande-Bretagne et les Etats-Unis de 1896 à 1900* (M. Allégret); *Je vous salue, Paris* (Reichenbach); *Mario Prassinos* (Clergue); *Les Seigneurs des mers du sud* (Villeminot); *L'Entrainement du toréro* (Clergue); *Vivre à San Francisco* (de Gaspari)

1969   *Monique à Vichy* (Reichenbach); *La Fête des morts* (Reichenbach); *Le Mariage des dieux* (Reichenbach); *Suite en si mineur* (Reichenbach); *Méditerréenne* (Clergue); *Sables* (Clergue); *L'Art de la turlutte* (Pirès); *Les Flamands Roses de Camargue* (Clergue); *La Fête des mères* (Pirès); *Le Deuxième Ciel* (Roger); *Europe continentale avant 1900* (M. Allégret); *Europe méridionale au temps des rois* (M. Allégret); *Au champ de vapeur* (Roger); *Cinéma cinéma* (Lajournade); *Libre de ne pas l'être* (Lajournade); *Comme je te veux* (Comolli); *Kill Patrice, un shérif pas comme les autres* (Reichenbach); *L'Avant-veille du grand soir* (Fansten); *L'Oniromane* (Ginet); *L'Armoire* (Moulin); *Et quand vient le soir* (Desclercs); *Trois hommes dur un cheval* (Moussy); *Les Moissons de l'espoir* (Reichenbach)

1970   *Gromaire* (Reichenbach); *A fleur d'eau* (Reichenbach); *L'Opéra de quatres pesos* (Reichenbach); *Visage mysterieux d'Océanie* (Villeminot); *Dressage de chevaux sauvages* (Clergue); *La Tortue et le renard* (J. and C. Clerfeuille);

Le Droit d'asile (Lajournade); *En attendant l'auto* (G. Braunberger); *Un Coup pur pour rien* (Comolli); *Chambre de bonne* (Moulin); *Les Voisins n'aiment pas la musique* (Fansten); *Le Chasseur* (Reichenbach); *Un Lion nommé l'Américain* (Rouch); *On ira lui porter des oranges* (Wachsberger); *L'Autre* (Grandjouan)

1971   *Prison à l'américaine* (Reichenbach); *Voyage en Camardie* (Clergue); *La Mort ne tue jamais personne* (Reichenbach); *Eliette, ou instants de la vie d'une femme* (Reichenbach); *La Forêt calcinée* (*Le Feu*) (Clergue); *Le Renard et le corbeau* (J. and C. Clerfeuille); *Hans Hartung* (Ferlet); *Le Révolte* (Berny); *Le Laboratoire de l'angoisse* (Leconte); *Narcissus/Echo* (Foldes); *Le Leçon de musique* (Scorpion); *La Vie sentimentale de Georges le Tueur* (Berger)

Films as Producer/Executive Producer (Features):

1924   *Monsieur Beaucaire* (Olcott) (asst)

1925   *La Fille de l'eau* (Renoir)

1926   *Nana* (Renoir) (+ ro)

1927   *Sur un air de Charleston* (*Charleston*) (Renoir); *En rade* (*Sea Fever*) (Cavalcanti); *Yvette* (Cavalcanti)

1928   *Tire au flanc* (Renoir)

1929   *La Route est belle* (Florey)

1930   ***L'Age d'or*** (Buñuel); *L'Armour chante* (Florey)

1931   *Les Amants de minuit* (M. Allégret and Genina); *Mam'zelle Nitouche* (M. Allégret); *On purge Bébé* (Renoir); *La Chienne* (Renoir); *Fantômas* (Féjos); *l'Amour à l'américaine* (Féjos and Haymann); *Baleydier* (Mamy)

1932   *Le Blanc et le noir* (M. Allégret and Florey); *La Petite Chocolatière* (M. Allégret)

1934   *Sans famille* (M. Allégret)

1936   *Vous n'avez rien à déclarer?* (Joannon)

1937   *Forfaiture* (L'Herbier)

1939   *Menaces* (Gréville)

1946   *Paris 1900* (Vedrès) (+ sc)

1948   *Les Aventures des Pieds-Nickelés* (Aboulker)

1949   *Le Trésor des Pieds-Nickelés* (Aboulker)

1950   *Le Tampon du capiston* (Labro); *Bertrand, coeur de lion* (Dhery)

1951   *La Crime du bouif* (Cerf); *Jocelyn* (de Casembroot); *La Vie de Jésus* (*En souvenir de moi*) (Gibaud)

1953   *Julietta* (M. Allégret)

1959   *L'Eau à la bouche* (*Game for Six Lovers*) (Doniol-Valcroze); *Ein Engel auf Erden* (*Angel on Earth*) (von Radvanyi)

1960   ***Tirez sur le pianiste*** (*Shoot the Piano Player*) (Truffaut)

1961   *Cuba si!* (Marker); *La Dénonciation* (*The Immoral Moment*) (Doniol-Valcroze); *La Temps du ghetto* (*The Witness*) (Rossif); *Un Coeur gros comme ça* (*The Winner*) (Reichenbach)

1962   ***Vivre sa vie*** (*My Life to Live*) (Godard); *Virginie* (Boyer)

1963   *Muriel* (Resnais); *L'Amour avec des si . . .* (Lelouch); *La Difficulté d'être infidèle* (*Bonne à tout faire*) (Toublanc-Michel); *La Bestaire d'amour* (Calderon)

1964   *La Punition* (Rouch); *De l'amour* (Aurel); *La Femme spectacle* (*Night Women*) (Lelouch); *Une Fille et des fusils* (*To Be a Crook*) (Lelouch)

113

1965 *La Chasse au lion à l'arc* (*The Lion Hunters*) (Rouch); *Les Grands Moments* (Lelouch)
1966 *Mamaia* (Varéla); *Martin Soldat* (Deville)
1967 *Jaquar* (Rouch)
1968 *Erotissimo* (Pirès); *Plaisir d'amour* (Reichenbach); *L'Astragale* (Casaril) (+ art d)
1969 **Ma nuit chez Maud** (*My Night at Maud's*) (Rohmer)
1970 *Medicine Ball Caravan* (*We Have Come for Your Daughters*) (Reichenbach); *Petit à petit* (Rouch); *Etes-vous fiancée à un marin grec ou à un pilote de ligne?* (Aurel)
1971 *Fantasia chez les ploucs* (Pirès); *On n'arrête pas le printemps* (Gilson); *Catch Me a Spy* (Clément); *La Cavale* (Mitrani); *Je, tu, elles . . .* (Foldes); *La Fin des Pyrénées* (Lajournade); *J'ai tout donnée* (Reichenbach)
1973 *Elle court, elle court, la banlieu* (Pirès)
1974 *Comment réussir . . . quand on est con et pleurnichard* (Audiard); *Comme un pot de fraises* (Aurel); *L'Agression* (Pirès)
1975 *Attention les yeux* (Pirès)
1976 *Sex O'Clock U.S.A.* (Reichenbach)
1978 *Les Héroines du mal* (Borowczyk)
1979 *Collections privées* (Jaeckin); *Le Risque de vivre* (Calderon)
1984 *Dionysos* (Rouch); *Kusameikyu*
1990 *Les Chevaliers de la table ronde* (Llorca)

Publications

By BRAUNBERGER: book—

Pierre Braunberger: producteur: cinemamemoire, Paris, 1987.

By BRAUNBERGER: articles—

Cinéma (Paris), March 1961.
Film (London), Spring 1963.
Cinéma (Paris), no. 94, 1965.
Kosmorama (Copenhagen), December 1970.
Cinéma (Paris), February 1972.
Cinéma Française (Paris), no. 12, 1977.
Ecran (Paris), September 1978.
Film Français (Paris), 23 December 1983.
Cinéma Française (Paris), 31 August 1984.
Film Français (Paris), 31 August 1984.
Cinéma (Paris), 27 November-3 December 1985.

On BRAUNBERGER: articles—

Avant-Scène (Paris), 15 October 1962.
Cinéma Française (Paris), December 1980.
Alion, Y., "Pierre Braunberger, le limier du cinéma," in *Revue du Cinéma* (Paris), no. 432, November 1987.
Obituary in *Variety* (New York), 26 November 1990.
Thüna, Ulrich von, "Pierre Braunberger: 29.7.1905 -17.11.1990," in *EPD Film* (Frankfurt), January 1991.
Obituary, in *Revue du Cinéma* (Paris), January 1991.
Obituary, in *Positif* (Paris), February 1991.

Maillis, Annie, "La course de taureaux de P. Braunberger," in *Archives: Institut Jean Vigo* (Perpignan), March 1996.
Serceau, D., "Pierre Braunberger: Rouch a du genie mais il ne maitrise pas toujours son imagination debordante," in *Cinémaction* (Courbevoie), no. 4, 1996.

*   *   *

The French film industry, never as centralised as the British or American, left more leeway for "small" producers of whom Pierre Braunberger became the doyen: in love with film, eclectic in his tastes, interested in the arts, and joyously practical in commerce. In another respect he was quite unique: as producer, distributor, and exhibitor, he extended the 1920s avant-garde and cradled the 1950s New Wave, alongside diverse commercial features and shorts. Born into a medical family, he fell in love with cinema after seeing Feuillade's *Fantômas* and DeMille's *The Cheat*. He learned the trade as film-buyer for Brockliss of London, then, in the United States, he was French adviser for Fox and secretary to Thalberg, then publicity executive for Paramount in Paris. As a crucial learning experience, he cites his heroic struggle, in Miami in 1923, to finish a fiction film despite a hurricane—only to be sacked for not filming the hurricane instead. The lesson stayed with him, and his survival in a shaky industry depended on combining strict economy with an openness to improvisation and location work; whence his congeniality for Renoir, Rouch, Reichenbach and the nascent New Wave, whose commercial "godfather" he can claim to be.

His decisive encounter, through their mutual friend Pierre Lestringuez, was with Renoir, for whom he functioned as administrative producer, organising the completion of Renoir's first two films, both unfinished. Another enduring association was with brothers Yves and Marc Allégret. At studio Films he distributed avant-garde films so energetically that his, quite inadvertent, "monopoly" covered even the USA. From 1930–39 and 1945–65, his Panthéon Cinema was the major showcase for art and experimental shorts, and for Anglophone product shown only undubbed and unsubtitled, through respect for the integrity of the image. His commercial productions, first in tandem with another exhibitor, Roger Richebé, then solo as Panthéon Films, introduced to films Sacha Guitry, Fernandel, the Préverts, and Simone Simon. After the Second World War, first as Panthéon, then as Les Films de la Pléiade, and latterly in collaboration with his wife, Gisèle Braunberger, as Les Films du Jeudi, he promoted Resnais, Melville, Rouch, Reichenbach (an art dealer who became a pioneer of "globe-trotting" direct cinema, making 36 films for Braunberger). By 1986 his producer filmography ran to 88 features and 300 shorts, from spoofs and interest films to underappreciated efforts by Peter Foldes and Jacques Doniol-Valcroze, editor of *Cahiers du Cinéma*.

Preoccupation with directorial credits has overshadowed producer creativity, much as a critical preference for single consistent themes has obscured diversity of interest. Braunberger typifies a type of art-sensitive opportunist, juggling, usually on a shoestring, Festival kudos, commercial viability, and his own spread of enthusiasms; and providing creative collaboration without cramping a director's style. He was also an innovator. In 1924 he showed Renoir mercury vapour lamps, then unknown in French film production, but used by Braunberger, Sr. for the medical treatment of his patients. *La Route est belle* (1929) was the first French talkie. *Paris 1900*, the first elaborate compilation film, was Braunberger's concept. His too, the realisation that *Partie de campagne*, shelved as unfinished, needed only two intertitles to become, not merely showable, but truly complete, a lyrical gem. Around 1930, when an avant-garde film proved dismally unshowable, Braunberger projected the negative, eliciting Panthéon applause, and launching its successful career. He believed that a similar dodge later, showing reels out of order, inspired the extensive resort to "arbitrary" devices by Godard, the director whom, with Renoir, Braunberger most admired.

—Raymond Durgnat

BRAY, J. R.

Animator. **Nationality:** American. **Born:** Addison, Michigan, 25 August 1879. **Career:** 1906–10—newspaper cartoonist; 1914—set up the Bray Studio Inc. and drew the first *Colonel Heezaliar* cartoon; 1917—formed the Bray Hurd Process Company, which controlled licencing for cel animation; 1920—produced the first commercial colour animated film *The Debut of Thomas Cat*. **Died:** 1978.

Films as Animator (Selected List):

1910   *The Artist's Dream (The Dachshund and the Sausage)*
1914   *Colonel Heezaliar, Naturalist; Colonel Heezaliar's African Hunt; Colonel Heezaliar, Shipwrecked; Colonel Heezaliar, Explorer; Colonel Heezaliar, Farmer; Colonel Heezaliar in Mexico; Colonel Heezaliar in the Wilderness; Colonel Heezaliar in Africa*
1915   *Colonel Heezaliar and the Zeppelin; Colonel Heezaliar At the Bat; Colonel Heezaliar At the Front; Colonel Heezaliar— Ghost Breaker; The Adventures of Colonel Heezaliar— He's a Daredevil; Colonel Heezaliar and the Torpedo; Colonel Heezaliar, Dog Fancier; Colonel Heezaliar Foils the Enemy; Colonel Heezaliar in the Haunted Castle; Colonel Heezaliar in the Trenches; Colonel Heezaliar, War Aviator; Colonel Heezaliar, War Dog; Colonel Heezaliar Invents a New Kind of Shell; Colonel Heezaliar Runs the Blockade; Colonel Heezaliar Signs the Pledge; Ramiet and Julio; Rastus' Rabid Rabbit Hunt*
1916   *Colonel Heezaliar and the Bandits; Colonel Heezaliar at the Vaudeville Show; Colonel Heezaliar Captures Villa; Colonel Heezaliar's Bachelor Quarters; Colonel Heezaliar on Strike; Colonel Heezaliar Plays Hamlet; Colonel Heezaliar Gets Married*
1917   *Colonel Heezaliar, Detective; Colonel Heezaliar on the Jump; Colonel Heezaliar, Spy Dodger; Colonel Heezaliar, Temperance Advocate*
1920   *The Best Mouse Loses; The Chinese Honeymoon; Family Affair; The Great Cheese Robbery; Happy Hooldini and Lampoons; His Last Legs; Jerry and the 5.15 Train; Kats Is Kats; Knock on the Window, the Door Is in a Jamb; The Debut of Thomas Cat*
1921   *How I Became Krazy; Izzy Able the Detective; The Awful Spook; The Chicken Thief*
1923   *Colonel Heezaliar's Mysterious Case; Colonel Heezaliar*
1924   *Colonel Heezaliar, Nature Faker; Colonel Heezaliar's Ancestors; Colonel Heezaliar's Horseplay; Colonel Heezaliar's Knighthood; Colonel Heezaliar, Skypilot*
1925   *The Adventures of Togo and Dinky; A Fitting Gift*
1926   *Captain Kidd*

Publications

On BRAY: articles—

Canemaker, Jon, "Profile of a Living Animation Legend: J.R. Bray," in *Filmmaker's Newsletter* (Ward Hill, Massachusetts), vol. 8, no. 3, January 1975.

"Bray-Hurd: the key animation patents," in *Film & History*, no. 2, 1988.

Callahan, D., "Cel animation: mass production and marginalization in the animated film industry," in *Film & History*, no. 2, 1988.

Langer, Mark, "La parola a John Randolph Bray, pioniere dell'animazione," in *Griffithiana* (Baltimore), May 1995.

Langer, Mark, "The Reflections of John Randolph Bray," in *Griffithiana* (Baltimore), May 1995.

*   *   *

Many media and artistic techniques can be used to create the illusion of movement in an animated film, like charcoal, paint on glass, computer graphics, or the manipulation of objects like clay, sand, or models with the use of frame-by-frame exposure by a camera. The most common method, however, is "cel" animation, a technique so popular it almost seems alone to define "animation" in the popular imagination. The control of its patent was wielded primarily by John Randolph Bray from 1917 onwards, although the use of "cels" or panes of celluloid on which images are painted was actually patented by Earl Hurd in 1915. Bray himself took over several crucial patents on the registration and use of translucent sheets for backgrounds in 1914, and in 1917, in order to avoid a costly legal battle with Hurd, they together formed the Bray Hurd Process Company, to which all animators had to apply for a license to use the cel technique. These technical accomplishments alone would be enough to ensure Bray's place in the history of film, but in addition, he was also responsible for drawing and producing the first commercially distributed animated cartoon (*The Artist's Dream* or *The Dachshund and the Sausage*) (1910), founding the first commercial animation studio organized along Taylorist principles of production, and producing the first colour cartoon (*The Debut of Thomas Cat*; 1920); he was, as Donald Crafton has appropriately called him, "the Henry Ford of Animation."

Like most of the animators of the silent period, Bray came to the medium from a background in newspaper cartoons, starting in 1906 with single panel cartoons for *Judge*, moving on to a full-page comic strip called "The Teddy Bears," a well-drawn if somewhat prosaic series based on the exploits of a group of magical stuffed toys. Inspired by Porter's film *The "Teddy" Bears* (1907) which used stop motion photography to animate real toys, Bray experimented with animating his own drawings of frolicsome furry animals, but abandoned the project eventually. His second attempt, *The Artist's Dream*, about a greedy Dachshund who explodes after overindulging in sausages, was more successful once Bray realized that time could be saved enormously by minimizing detail. This second film was made around 1910 or 1911, but not released until 1913. Unlike Winsor McCay's first two films, *Little Nemo* (1911) and *The Story of a Mosquito* (1912) (or all his films for that matter) which Bray had seen on the vaudeville stage and which were made by laboriously tracing over every single line frame-by-frame, Bray, inspired by his experience in journalism, printed his backgrounds and then experimented with using translucent pages that could be laid over the changing character drawings. He realized he could further save time by having a staff of artists each responsible for the different stages of the process, and in 1914 he formed Bray Studios, Incorporated and went into production of the *Colonel Heezaliar* series, based on a character part Teddy Roosevelt, part Baron Munchausen, featuring his fantastic exploits abroad. Only seven films in 1914, according to Crafton, were actually animated by Bray himself. After that he delegated the work to his staff, many of whom went on to be famous in the field, like Walter Lantz, Max and Dave Fleischer, Paul erry, Cy Young, and Shamus Culhane.

Culhane described Bray as "a sallow, lean man with a very military bearing. It was hard to believe he was ever a humorist." Indeed, once the theatrical cartoon department was established and running smoothly, Bray began to devote his energies to the production of animated military training and educational films, a specialized but lucrative market that he exploited in the best tradition of sound business management, with the help of his strong-willed wife Margaret, who was endowed with considerable business acumen in her own right. This part of the corporation has survived up to the present, run by Bray's descendants, while the theatrical cartoon department, depleted of talented staff and ideas, ran aground with the advent of sound cartoons.

Although it was the largest independent animation studio of the silent period, its output, though popular at the time, has not been canonized with the same reverence accorded now to the *Felix the Cat* series by Otto Messmer, or Fleischer's *Out of the Inkwell* series, lacking as it did in commensurate wit and invention. Nonetheless, the products of the Bray Studio helped to establish the place of the animated cartoon in the theatrical program, and the technique that he and Hurd patented remains an exceptional contribution to the art of animation. In his 90s, concerning cel animation, Bray remarked, "I'm very much pleased that they haven't been able to improve on the process. It's still the same old process that I invented." Although it does now seem that cel animation is gradually being assisted and replaced by more widely available computer technology, Bray's hierarchical model of production remains an industry standard, and his position as a key figure in animation and film history remains irrefutable.

—Leslie Felperin Sharman

BRDEČKA, Jiří

Animator and Writer. **Nationality:** Czech. **Born:** Jiří Brnečka in Hranice, Moravia, 24 December 1917. **Education:** Studied at an art college, Prague; studied art history, Charles University, Prague,

1936–39. **Career:** Writer, journalist, and illustrator; 1940—first appearance of story *Limonádový Joe* (later versions as play, novel, and animated film); 1943–44—animator for Richard Dillenz Studio (later Prag-Film); 1946—wrote scripts for Trnka's animated films, and joined Bratri Triku Studio after the war; 1947—first film as director of animation; 1951—first fiction film as scriptwriter. **Died:** 2 June 1982.

Animated Films as Writer:

1946 *Pérák a SS* (*The Springer and the SS-Men*) (Trnka); *Dárek* (*The Gift*) (Trnka)
1947 *Sváb* (*The Cockroach*) (Mann); *Vzucholod a láska* (*Love and the Zeppelin*) (+ d)
1948 *Císařuv slavík* (*The Emperor's Nightingale*) (Trnka); *Andelský kabát* (*The Angel's Coat*) (Hofman)
1949 *Papírové nokturno* (*Paper Nocturne*) (Hofman); *Arie prérie* (*The Song of the Prairie*) (Trnka)
1950 *Káslání a kýchani* (*Cough and Sneeze*) (Mozís); *Mouchy* (*Flies*) (Mozís); *Neviditelní neprátelé* (*Invisible Enemy*) (Mozís); *Vitamin C*
1953 **Staré povesti ceské** (*Old Czech Legends*) (Trnka); *O svetle* (*On Light*) (Srámek); *O skleničku vic* (*A Drop Too Much*) (Pojar)
1956 *Ztracená varta* (*The Lost Sentry*) (Makovec)
1958 *Historie blechatého psa* (*Story of a Dog Who Had Fleas*) (Mudrnáč); *Vynález zkásy* (*An Invention for Destruction*; *The Fabulous World of Jules Verne*) (K. Zeman)

Animated Films as Director and Writer:

1958 *Jak se človek naucil létat* (*A Comic History of Aviation*; *How Man Learned to Fly*)
1959 *Drahoušek Klementýna* (*My Darling Clementine*); *Pozor!* (*Look Out!*; *Attention*)
1960 *Naše Karkulka* (*Our Little Red Riding Hood*)
1961 *Clovek pod vodou* (*Man Under Water*); *Zavada není na vašem přijímaci* (*The Television Fan*)
1962 *Rozum a cit* (*Reason and Emotion*); *Zmrzly dřevař* (*The Frozen Logger*)
1963 *Spatne namalovaná slepice* (*Gallina Vogelbirdie*; *The Grotesque Chicken*); *Jak na to* (*How to Keep Slim*)
1964 *Slóvce M* (*The Letter M*; *The Minstrel's Song*)
1965 *Dezertér* (*The Deserter*); *Blaho lásky* (*The Joy of Love*; *She and He*)
1966 *Do lesíčka na čekanou* (*Forester's Song*; *Let's Go Hunting in the Woods*); *Proč se usmíváš, Mona Lisa?* (*Why Do You Smile, Mona Lisa?*)
1968 *Moc osudu* (*The Power of Destiny*); *Pomsta* (*Vengeance*)
1969 *Metamorfeus*
1970 *Jak se moudrý Aristoteles stal jeste moudřejšim* (*Wise Aristotle Gets Still Wiser*; *Aristotle*)
1971 *Jsouc na rece mlynár jeden* (*There Was a Miller on the River*)
1973 *Tvár* (*The Face*)

1974 *Accordion Song*
1975 *What I Didn't Say to the Prince*
1978 *Aaamour*

Animated Films as Cowriter:

1959 *Proč UNESCO?* (*Why UNESCO?*) (Trnka); *Sen noci svatojánske* (*A Midsummer Night's Dream*) (Trnka); *Bombománie* (*Bomb Mania*) (Pojar); *Stastny lev* (*The Happy Lion*) (Bedrich)
1960 *Sláva* (*Fame*) (Pojar); *Prak a drank* (*The Catapult and the Kite*) (Topaldjikov); *Jak zařídit byt* (*How to Furnish a Flat*) (Pojar); *Mikromakrokosmos* (*Little-Big-Cosmos*)
1961 **Baron Prášil** (*Baron Munchausen*) (Zeman)
1962 *Sroublkova dobrodružství* (*Screw's Adventures*) (Vystrcil)
1970 *Tři čarovná péra* (*Three Magic Feathers*) (Rozkopal)

Other Animated Films:

1959 *Tucet mých tatínku* (*My Twelve Fathers*) (Hofman) (codesign)

Films as Writer:

1951 *Císařuv pekař a pekaruv cisař* (*The Emperor's Baker and the Baker's Emperor*) (Fric)
1952 *Velké dobrodružství* (*Great Adventure*) (Makovek)
1954 *Kavárna na hlavní třide* (*Cafe in the Main Street*) (Hubácek); *Severní přístav* (*Northern Harbour*) (Makovek)
1955 *Bly jednou jeden Král* (*There Was Once a King*) (B. Zeman)
1956 *Obusku, z pytle ven!* (*Stick, Start Beating!*) (Pleskot)
1957 *Snadný život* (*Easy Life*) (Makovek); *Vlčí jáma* (*Wolf Trap*) (Weiss); *Ztracenci* (*Three Men Missing*) (Makovek)
1959 *Tukuvá láska* (*Appassionata*) (Weiss)
1960 *Cerná sobota* (*Saturday Night*) (Hubácek)
1961 *Lidé za kamerou* (*People behind the Camera*) (Hofman—doc)
1963 *Až přijde kocour* (*That Cat*) (Jasny)
1964 *Limonádnový Joe* (*Lemonade Joe*) (Lipsky)
1968 "Last Golem" ep. of *Pražské noci* (*Prague Nights*) (+ d + co-sc of other episodes)
1972 *Román o ruži* (*Story of a Rose*) (+ d—short)
1982 *Tajemstvi hradu v Karpatech* (*The Mysterious Castle in the Carpathians*) (Lipsky)

Other Films:

1963 *Spanilá jízda* (*The Glorious Campaign*) (Danek) (ro)

Publications

By BRDEČKA: books—

Limonádový Joe, Prague, 1940.
Kelty bez pozlatka (*Guns without Glamour*), Prague, 1956.
Faunovo znacne pokrocile adpoledne (*The Faun's Rather Late Afternoon*), Prague, 1966.

By BRDEČKA: articles—

"De la difficulté d'être cinéaste d'animation tchecoslovague," in *Annecy Festival Catalogue*, 1963.
Continental Film Review (London), January 1977.
Film a Doba (Prague), September 1982.
Film a Doba (Prague), November 1983.

On BRDEČKA: articles—

Jeune Cinema (Paris), no. 3–4, 1964–65.
Film a Doba (Prague), vol. 11, no. 3. 1965.
Image et Son (Paris), November 1967.
Film a Doba (Prague), vol. 33, no. 12, December 1967.
Film a Doba (Prague), February 1983.
Film a Doba (Prague), December 1987.

* * *

It is not altogether accurate to call Jiří Brdečka an animator. That is, of course, what he was—but the breadth of his other interests is impressive: he was also a draughtsman, film critic, novelist, scriptwriter, and film director.

In 1940 he worked as a film critic for *Lidové Noviny* (later known as *Svobodné*). For two years he worked on publicity for Lucernafilm, and in 1943 he studied animation at the AFIT Special Effects Studio. Soon after that, he did the animation of an octopus in the animated film *Wedding in the Coral Sea*, the first film of the future Bratri Triku Studio, which he joined after the war. He returned to animated film and collaborated with Trnka on the scripts for such films as *The Gift*, *The Springer and the SS-Men*, *The Emperor's Nightingale*, *The Song of the Prairie*, *Old Czech Legends*, *Why UNESCO?*, and *A Midsummer Night's Dream*. With Pojar he collaborated on *A Drop Too Much*, *Fame*, and *Bombománie*. During a career that lasted almost 40 years, he also collaborated on the scripts for a number of feature, live-action films, including *The Emperor's Baker and the Baker's Emperor* (with Fric); *Wolf Trap* (with Jiri Weiss); *That Cat* (with Vojtěch Jasny); and *Lost People* (Miloš Makovec). He also adapted his own novel for Oldrich Lipsky's film *Lemonade Joe*.

In 1947 Brdečka made his debut as a director of animated films, with *Love and the Zeppelin*, visually inspired by Art Nouveau. In this film he lovingly and humorously portrays the world of discoverers, inventors and pioneers of science. He returned to this theme on two more occasions, with the films *How Man Learned to Fly* and *Man Under Water*, which involve some of the most demanding material ever attempted by an animated film—particularly the sketch "Wisdom and Teaching." As J. Bocek has commented: "This animated ballet captures a philosophical debate between the author and the audience. The conflict between reason and feeling reflects nothing less than the basic issues of life and worldliness."

The Grotesque Chicken is Brdečka's most famous film: it is his artistic declaration of faith in the imagination and in creativity. Many of his other films have their origin in a visual inspiration transformed into the grotesque—for example, *Why Do You Smile, Mona Lisa?* In others, particularly those inspired by music, Brdecka was attempting to impose on the serious, the tragic, and the lyrical his own touch of humour.

Brdečka was the kind of intellectual filmmaker, rich in inventiveness, who fully mastered all the elements of cinematography. He portrayed with both cunning and a gentle irony the history of inventions, philosophical essays, folk songs, myths, and fairy tales. Above all, he was the consummate story-teller who was able to transform his visual, literary, and musical inspirations into individualistic works of art. He brought new ideas and new expressive means to both the animated and the feature film.

—Vladimir Opěla

BREER, Robert

Animator. **Nationality:** American. **Born:** Detroit, Michigan, 30 September 1926. **Education:** Attended Stanford University, B.A. 1949. **Career:** 1944—began painting; 1949—moved to Paris, painting in mode of neo-plasticism; exhibitions at Denise René Gallery and elsewhere; 1952—made first film; 1955—following one-person painting show, interest shifted to filmmaking; 1958—ceased painting; began making mutoscopes; 1959—returned to United States, settled in New York; 1971—film style shifted from abstract to more eclectic mode including use of rotoscoping and photographed images; 1973—film teacher at Cooper Union; 1981—painted large mural outside Film Forum, New York City; 1996—*Now You See It!*, a thaumatrope-like spinning disk installed at the American Museum of the Moving Image, New York City. **Agent:** Film-Makers' Cooperative, 175 Lexington Avenue, New York, NY 10016, U.S.A. **Address:** 80 Sparkill Avenue, Tappan, NY 10983, U.S.A.

Films as Animator:

1952 *Form Phases I*
1953 *Form Phases II*; *Form Phases III*
1954 *Form Phases IV*; *Image by Images I (endless loop): Un Miracle*
1955 *Image by Image II*; *Image by Image III*
1956 *Image by Images IV*; *Motion Pictures*; *Cats*; *Recreation I*
1956–57 *Recreation II*
1957 *Jamestown Baloos*; *A Man and His Dog Out for Air*
1958 *Par Avion*
1958–59 *Cassis Colank*; *Chutes de pierres, danger du mort* (Fano) (sequence only)
1959 *Eyewash*; *Trailer*
1960 *Homage to Jean Tinguely's Homage to New York* (live-action); *Inner and Outer Space*
1961 *Blazes*; *Kinetic Art Show—Stockholm*
1962 *Pat's Birthday* (live-action); *Horse over Tea Kettle*
1963 *Breathing*
1964 *Fist Fight*
1966 *66*
1968 *69*; *PBL 2* (for PBL TV); *PBL 3* (for PBL TV)
1970 *70*
1971 *Elevator* (for CTW TV); *What?* (for CTW TV)
1972 *Gulls and Buoys*
1974 *Fuji*

1975 *Etc.*; *Rubber Cement*
1977 *77*
1978 *LMNO*
1979 *TZ*
1981 *Swiss Army Knife with Rats and Pigeons*
1982 *Trial Balloons*
1986 *Bang!*
1988 *A Frog on the Swing*; *Blue Monday* (video)
1993 *Sparkill Ave!*

Publications

By BREER: articles—

"On Two Films," in *Film Culture* (New York), Summer 1961.
Interview with Guy Cote, in *Film Culture* (New York), Winter 1962–63.
"Robert Breer on His Work," in *Film Culture* (New York), Fall 1966.
Interview with Jonas Mekas and P. Adams Sitney, in *Film Culture* (New York), Spring 1973.
"Tape Recorded Interview with Robert Breer," with Paul Cummings, in *Archives of American Art* (New York), 10 July 1973.
The American Film Institute Report (Washington, D.C.), Summer 1974.
"Independent Film: Talking with Robert Breer," with L. Fischer, in *University Film Study Newsletter* (Cambridge, Massachusetts), no. 1, 1976.
Paris-New York, exhibition catalog, Centre Pompidou, Paris, 1977.
Velvet Light Trap (Madison, Wisconsin), no. 24, Fall 1989.

On BREER: books—

Hulten, K. G., *The Machine as Seen at the End of the Mechanical Age*, exhibition catalog, New York, 1969.
Hanhardt, John, and others, *A History of the American Avant-Garde Cinema*, exhibition catalog, The American Federation of Arts, New York, 1976.
Russett, Robert, and Cecile Starr, *Experimental Animation*, New York, 1976.
Hein, Birgit, *Film as Film*, Arts Council of Great Britain, 1979.
Moore, Sandy, *Robert Breer*, St. Paul, Minnesota, 1980.
Mendelson, Lois, *Robert Breer: A Study of His Work in the Context of the Modernist Tradition*, Metuchen, New Jersey, 1982.

On BREER: articles—

Burch, Noël, "Images by Images, *Cats*, *Jamestown Baloos*, *A Man and His Dog Out for Air* (films by Robert Breer)," in *Film Quarterly* (Berkeley, California), Spring 1959.
Mancia, A., and W. Van Dyke, "Four Artists as Filmakers," in *Art in America* (New York), January 1967.
Rosenstein, H., "Motionless Motion," in *Art News* (New York), November 1967.
Mekas, Jonas, "Movie Journal," in *Village Voice* (New York), 24 April 1969.
Tomkins, Calvin, "Onward and Upward with the Arts," in *New Yorker*, 3 October 1970.

Michelson, Annette, ''Intellectual Cinema: A Reconsideration,'' in *Yale University Art Gallery Catalogue* (New Haven, Connecticut), April/May 1973.

Hammen, Scott, ''*Gulls and Buoys*, an Introduction to the Remarkable Range of Pleasures Available from the Films of Robert Breer,'' in *Afterimage* (Rochester, New York), December 1974.

Fischer, Lucy, ''Avant Garde Film (Homage to Robert Breer),'' in *Soho Weekly News* (New York), 3 April 1975.

Camper, Fred, ''Animated Dissection,'' in *Soho Weekly News* (New York), 20 May 1976.

Taubin, Amy, ''At Long Last Breer,'' in *Soho Weekly News* (New York), 14 April 1977.

Hoberman, J., ''A Mixed Bag of Tricks,'' in *Village Voice* (New York), 22 January 1979.

Carroll, Noel, ''The Other Cinema,'' in *Soho Weekly News* (New York), 25 January 1979.

Tournes, A., ''Robert Breer: l'avant-garde revient aux sources,'' in *Jeune Cinéma* (Paris), March 1979.

Hoberman, J., ''Robert Breer's Animated World,'' in *American Film* (Washington, D.C.), September 1980.

Camper, Fred, ''Robert Breer: *Fuji*, *77*, *LMNO* and *TZ*,'' in *Ten Years of Living Cinema*, New York, 1982.

Taylor, G. ''The Cinema of Ontology: Sound-Image Abstraction in Robert Breer's *TZ*,'' in *Wide Angle*, vol. 15, no. 1, 1993.

* * *

Robert Breer's work as a filmmaker has been primarily in animation. He has made two live-action films (*Pat's Birthday* and *Homage to Jean Tinguely's Homage to New York*), and many of his other films contain photographed images, but his films generally are made one or a few frames at a time, which is what distinguishes them from live-action cinema. He is arguably the most extraordinary maker of animated films the cinema has given us since Méliès.

Just as many avant-garde live-action filmmakers have defined their work—in terms radically opposed to the ''illusionistic'' mainstream of commercial film—so Breer defines his work in direct opposition to mainstream commercial animation. The Hollywood cartoon, and many of its offshoots, are based on continuous movements of characters through connected spaces. Breer's films are full of disjunctive breaks, multiple and discontinuous spaces and rhythms, and acknowledgments, often humorous, of the animation process itself and the animator's presence.

The tremendous richness of Breer's cinema comes not from a simple exclusion of continuities, but rather from the attempt to *include* as much as possible. Thus he situates his films at a number of ''thresholds.'' A burst of continuous movement will suddenly arrest itself in a freeze frame. Extremely jerky and irregular rhythms will unexpectedly become continuous ones. A drawn object will appear to rotate in three dimensions, creating the illusion of depth; a moment later we find ourselves watching a flat surface once again. The sound track will oscillate between apparently synchronous effects that match the action, a more abstract accompaniment, and sounds that are intentionally, often humorously, ill at odds with the images. The audience thus finds itself presented with a virtual panoply of styles and techniques. The effect is that the audience is held literally at the edge of its perception by a continual unfolding of surprises. Each time

a brief section (''brief'' being generally only a few seconds) establishes some form of continuity, the film leaps outside the pattern just established into some new realm. While it should be apparent from this that Breer's attitude toward his medium and its materials locates him clearly within the modernist tradition, the effect of his work is unique. Time and space are profoundly fragmented, and the film and its viewer are placed firmly in the infinitely uncertain realm of the instant.

In the first two decades of Breer's filmmaking, he utilized a variety of approaches and styles. His earliest films, such as the *Form Phases* series, are abstract, and grew out of his work as an abstract painter. Mondrian was an early inspiration, and some of the abstract films seem to be questing after idealized, perfect forms. There are hand-drawn and animated films, such as *A Man and His Dog Out for Air* and *PBL 2*, in which tension is created between line as representation of figure and line as an abstraction. There are some highly eclectic works, such as *Eyewash* and *Fist Fight*, in which cut-outs, various kinds of animation, and live-action photography are intermixed. There are ''abstract'' animations such as *66*, *69*, and *70*, which are amazing for their fusion of purity and complexity. It should also be mentioned that Breer has made kinetic sculptures, works that move along the floor so slowly their movement can barely be seen, and a number of constructions inspired by early ''pre-cinema'' devices such as thaumatropes; these works again play at the threshold between movement and stillness.

In 1972, Breer's filmmaking entered a new period, in which he mirrors the eclecticism of his earlier filmography within individual films. Abstract animation, animation that mimics photographed scenes, and actual photographs are combined with dense, collage-like sound tracks to produce a visionary mixture of humor and surprise, whimsy and ecstatic delight. The use of rotoscoping in *Gulls and Buoys* and *Fuji*, and of photographs combined with drawings based on them in many other films, also creates a relationship between these films and daily seeing: every object, every landscape, seems to harbor underlying abstract shapes and movements. In the ''kitchen sink'' multiplicity of these films, different kinds of image material interact in multiple ways, resulting in a new, and profoundly energized form of seeing: traces of recognizable objects perpetually oscillate between their existence as identifiable places and things and the multitudinous abstract shapes and colors that they contain, or suggest.

—Fred Camper

BROCCOLI, Albert R.

Producer. **Nationality:** American. **Born:** New York City, 5 April 1909. **Military Service:** US Navy, 1942–47. **Family:** Married Dana Natol Wilson; sons, Michael Wilson and Anthony; daughters, Christina and Barbara. **Education:** City College of New York. **Career:** Worked as an agronomist before landing a job in 1938 with 20th Century Fox, first as a messenger, then as a publicist, and finally as an assistant director in 1941–42; 1947–48—assistant director for RKO; 1948—became a successful theatrical agent with Charles Feldman, then moved to London where he founded Warwick Pictures with Irving

Albert R. Broccoli

Allen; produced with Allen a series of mostly B pictures released through Columbia; 1959—ended partnership with Allen; produced a few further films with Harold Huth and John R. Sloan; 1961—teamed with Harry Saltzman to found Eon Productions Ltd.; 1962—produced *Dr. No*, first of a number of James Bond adaptations; 1974—broke with Saltzman after *The Man with the Golden Gun;* retained rights to Bond series, which continues under auspices of Broccoli's Warfield Productions. **Award**: Irving Thalberg Lifetime Achievement Award, 1982. **Died**: 27 June 1996.

Films as Producer:

1954   *The Black Knight* (with Irving Allen and Phil C. Samuel); *Hell Below Zero* (with Allen and George W. Willoughby); *Paratrooper* (with Allen)

1955   *The Cockleshell Heroes* (with Allen); *A Prize of Gold* (with Allen and Samuel)

1956   *Zarak* (with Adrian D. Worker); *Odongo* (with Islin Auster)

1957   *How to Murder a Rich Uncle* (with John Paxton); *Fire Down Below* (with Allen); *Pickup Alley* (with Allen)

1958   *The Man Inside* (with Allen and Harold Huth); *Tank Force* (with Allen)

1959   *The Bandit of Zhobe* (with Allen); *Idol on Parade* (with Huth)

1960   *Killers of Killimanjaro* (with John R. Sloan); *In the Nick* (with Huth); *Jazz Boat* (with Huth); *Let's Get Married* (with Sloan); *The Trials of Oscar Wilde* (with Huth)

1961   *Johnny Nobody* (with Sloan, released in 1965)

1962   *Dr. No* (with Harry Saltzman)

1963   *Call Me Bwana* (with Saltzman); *From Russia with Love* (with Saltzman)

1964   *Goldfinger* (with Saltzman)

1967   *You Only Live Twice* (with Saltzman)

1968   *Chitty Chitty Bang Bang* (with Saltzman)

1969   *On Her Majesty's Secret Service* (with Saltzman)

1971   *Diamonds are Forever* (with Saltzman)

1973   *Live and Let Die* (with Saltzman)

1974   *The Man with the Golden Arm* (with Saltzman)

1977   *The Spy Who Loved Me*

1979   *Moonraker*

1981   *For Your Eyes Only*

1983   *Octopussy*

1985   *A View to a Kill*
1987   *The Living Daylights* (with Michael Wilson)
1989   *Licence to Kill* (with Wilson)

Publications

On BROCCOLI: articles—

"25th Anniversary of James Bond," in *Variety* (New York), 13
    May 1987.
Brown, C., "Golden Boy," in *Premiere* (Boulder), April 1996.
Obituary, in *Variety* (New York), 1–14 July 1996.
Calley, J., "Letters: Bitter Suite," in *Premiere* (Boulder), July 1996.
Obituary, in *Film-Dienst* (Cologne), July 1996.
Obituary, in *Classic Images* (Muscatine), August 1996.

*   *   *

Albert "Cubby" Broccoli is the subject of what is perhaps the film industry's greatest rags to riches story; a down at the heels producer of low budget action films in the early 1960s, he became in a few short years the genius behind the James Bond films, the most financially successful and popular series ever produced by the commercial film industry. As a result, from a marginal figure, Broccoli became one of the most important figures in international filmmaking. Always eager to enter film production, Broccoli had worked his way rapidly up the industry ladder with an impressive display of energy, enthusiasm, and intelligence. Starting as a messenger boy at Fox, he talked his way into assistant directing within three years, only to be interrupted by the outbreak of World War II. Broccoli served for the duration of hostilities and beyond, attempting in the late 1940s to resume his work behind the camera. However his career took another direction as he became associated with Charles Feldman, a noted theatrical agent and producer (who was responsible for, among other notable successes, bringing largely intact to the screen Elia Kazan's stage production of Tennessee Williams' *A Streetcar Named Desire*). Working with the highflying Feldman gave Broccoli a yen for deal making and production, but the economic woes of the industry at the time in America made breaking into this area, even as an enterprising independent, no easy task. Broccoli saw better possibilities in England, which was also experiencing a downturn in exhibition, but where, because of currency regulations, a good many American-financed, mostly low budget films were being shot, with a view toward exhibition in the US as well as in the UK.

In partnership with another emigré deal maker, Irving Allen, Broccoli set up Warwick Films, which planned to make largely low-budget action and/or costume films. Some of these are eminently forgettable: *Zarak*, *Odongo*, and *The Bandit of Zhobe* stand out in this category. Others are rather interesting "small" films, especially two World War II productions, *Paratrooper* and *The Cockleshell Heroes*. *The Trial of Oscar Wilde*, though in some sense an exploitation film, also offers a sensitive and often profound treatment of a difficult subject. In any case, the years with Warwick gave Broccoli a good deal of insight into what aspects of British cultural mythology could be sold to American audiences. He also developed a feel for British popular culture. Making war and adventure films taught Broccoli how to tell an exciting story on a limited budget, and he was not slow to realize the importance of cheesecake and "love interests" to energize and eroticize the narrative.

Warwick Films was not doing well by the end of the 1950s. One of Broccoli's last productions for the company, the appropriately titled *Johnny Nobody*, could not even secure an American release until 1965, when Broccoli had become the darling of exhibitors and distributors. Because he was used to mining pulp and popular literature for source materials, it is hardly surprising that Broccoli discovered and subsequently reworked one of Ian Fleming's James Bond narratives. This is a project he began after entering into partnership with Harry Saltzman, an experienced deal maker in his own right who had clear ideas about popular taste. Beginning with *Dr. No*, whose huge financial success fueled the series of Fleming adaptations, Broccoli and Saltzman invented a formula that had mass and sustained appeal at a time when other producers were wondering what kind of films to make for an Anglo-American culture in the throes of profound and far-reaching changes. Broccoli and Saltzman remade James Bond into the very epitome of a cultural icon born in 1950s America—the playboy. Like the implied reader of Hugh Hefner's magazine of the same name (a cultural product that achieved the same kind of phenomenal success as the Bond films themselves), Bond was single and single-mindedly devoted to pleasure in the forms of expensive clothes, food, liquor, fast cars, and faster women. If he was still to some degree an action hero of the old school—good with his fists, quick-witted, physically daring, and cool under fire—James Bond, under the careful shaping of Broccoli and Saltzman, became a very different kind of male figure, one whose selfishness and emotional shallowness suited a generation brought up on the idea of unending consumption. It is a tribute to the genius of Broccoli and Saltzman that they recognized early the necessary connection of their James Bond to Hefner's new masculine ideal, striking a deal with the magazine that effectively "tied inrdquo; each new Bond film to a *Playboy* special issue in which some or all of the female stars were featured in various states of tasteful undress.

The Bond films, in many ways, are very similar to the adventure/action productions Broccoli oversaw for Warwick early in his career—the difference is an artful and highly effective expansion of production values. The Bond films of the 1960s featured what were, for the time, unusual and elaborate special effects and scenes of spectacle; they emphasized visual beauty in terms of exotic locations, sumptuous interiors (particularly for the villains, who are always rich), and of course a gallery of attractive women, the most important of whom is the "Bond girl," for whom James develops a special affection since she always belongs to the villain. Under Broccoli and Saltzman's careful generalship (these were never directors' pictures in any true sense), the Bond films developed a well-deserved reputation for excess—mostly in terms of visual spectacle—that always far outweighed any emphasis on theme or even ideas. Even more so than Fleming's novels, which relate complexly to the fact of the Cold War, the Bond films ignore the real world of politics for the more enjoyable one of pure escapism. Thus they retained their popularity even in the face of immense cultural change, proving eminently adaptable even to twists and turns in gender politics (the later "Bond girls" are provided with a more feminist inflection).

Though all of Fleming's novels have been filmed and new scripts must be devised for each production, the series pioneered by Broccoli and Saltzman has entered its fourth decade of popularity, becoming a phenomenon unparalleled in screen history.

—R. Barton Palmer

BROWN, Karl

Cinematographer, Director, and Writer. **Nationality:** American. **Born:** Pennsylvania, 1897. **Family:** Married the actress Edna Mae Cooper, c. 1918. **Career:** 1912–13—laboratory assistant, then in charge of negative processing, Kinemacolor Company, New York (moved to Hollywood, 1913); 1914—first film work, as still photographer on *The Spoilers*; 1914–20—assistant and special effects photographer for D. W. Griffith; served in the United States Army during World War I; 1920–26—cinematographer for Paramount; 1920s—associate editor, *American Cinematographer*; 1927—directed first film, *His Dog*; then director and writer. **Died:** Of kidney failure in California, 25 March 1990.

Films as Cinematographer:

1920   *The City of Masks* (Heffron); *The Fourteenth Man* (Henabery); *The Life of the Party* (Henabery)

1921   *Brewster's Millions* (Henabery); *The Dollar-a-Year Man* (Cruze); *Gasoline Gus* (Cruze); *The Traveling Salesman* (Henabery); *Crazy to Marry* (Cruze)

1922   *One Glorious Day* (Cruze); *Is Matrimony a Failure?* (Cruze); *The Dictator* (Cruze); *The Old Homestead* (Cruze); *Thirty Days* (Cruze)

1923   *The Covered Wagon* (Cruze); *Ruggles of Red Gap* (Cruze)

1924   *The Fighting Coward* (Cruze); *The Enemy Sex* (Cruze); *Merton of the Movies* (Cruze); *The City That Never Sleeps* (Cruze); *The Garden of Weeds* (Cruze)

1925   *The Goose Hangs High* (Cruze); *Welcome Home* (Cruze); *Marry Me* (Cruze); *Beggar on Horseback* (Cruze); *The Pony Express* (Cruze)

1926   *Mannequin* (Cruze)

Films as Assistant and Special Effects Photographer:

1914   *The Spoilers* (Campbell); *The Avenging Conscience* (Griffith); *Golden Days*

1915   **The Birth of a Nation** (Griffith)

1916   *The Mystery of the Leaping Fish* (Emerson—short); *Daphne and the Pirate* (Cabanne); **Intolerance** (Griffith); *The Flying Torpedo* (Emerson)

1918   *The Great Love* (Griffith)

1919   **Broken Blossoms** (Griffith)

Films as Director:

1927   *His Dog*; *Stark Love* (+ pr + co-sc)

1930   *Prince of Diamonds*

1932   *Flames* (*Fire Alarm*)

1937   *Michael O'Halloran* (*Any Man's Wife*)

1938   *Barefoot Boy*; *Numbered Woman* (*Private Nurse*); *Under the Big Top* (*The Circus Comes to Town*)

Films as Writer:

1929   *The Mississippi Gambler* (Barker) (co)

1933   *Fast Workers* (Browning)

1934   *Stolen Sweets* (Thorpe); *City Park* (Thorpe); *One in a Million* (Strayer); *The Curtain Falls* (Lamont)

1935   *The Calling of Dan Matthews* (Rosen); *Tarzan Escapes* (McKay)

1936   *In His Steps* (*Sins of the Children*) (+ d); *White Legion* (+ d); *Hearts in Bondage* (Ayres)

1937   *Join the Marines* (Staub); *Girl Loves Boy* (Mansfield); *Federal Bullets* (+ d)

1938   *Gangster's Boy* (Nigh); *Port of Missing Girls* (+ d)

1939   *A Woman Is the Judge* (Nigh); *The Man They Could Not Hang* (Grinde); *My Son Is Guilty* (*Crime's End*) (Barton)

1940   *The Man with Nine Lives* (*Behind the Door*) (Grinde); *Gangs of Chicago* (Lubin); *Military Academy* (Lederman); *Before I Hang* (MacDonald); *Girl from Havana* (Landers)

1941   *Mr. District Attorney* (Morgan); *Prairie Pioneers* (Orlebeck); *Rookies on Parade* (Santley); *I Was a Prisoner on Devil's Island* (Landers); *Under Fiesta Stars* (McDonald); *Harvard, Here I Come* (*Here I Come*) (Landers)

1942   *Phantom Killer* (Beaudine); *Hitler—Dead or Alive* (Grinde)

1943   *The Ape Man* (*Lock Your Doors*) (Beaudine)

1945   *The Chicago Kid* (McDonald)

Publications

By BROWN: books—

With Leonard Fields, *The Mississippi Gambler* (novelization), New York, 1929.
Incorrigible (novel), New York, 1947.
The Cup of Trembling (novel), New York, 1953.
Adventures with D. W. Griffith, New York, 1973.

By BROWN: articles—

On D. W. Griffith in *Sight and Sound* (London), Summer 1973.
''Flashback: A Director's Best Friend,'' in *American Film* (Washington, D.C.), October 1982.
''Billy Bitzer: A Reminiscence,'' in *American Cinematographer* (Hollywood), November 1983.
''The Blind Leading the Blind,'' in *American Film* (Washington, D.C.), December 1984.
''Spfx 101: An Introductory Course,'' in *American Film* (Washington, D.C.), September 1985.

On BROWN: articles—

Filme Cultura (Rio de Janeiro), November-December 1969.
Quarterly Journal of the Library of Congress (Washington, D.C.), Summer-Fall 1980.
Turner, George E., ''A Hollywood Saga: Karl Brown,'' in *American Cinematographer* (Hollywood), October 1982.

Films in Review (New York), vol. 37, no. 4, April 1986.
Obituary, in *Variety* (New York), 4 April 1990.
Obituary, in *American Cinematographer* (Hollywood), June 1990.

*   *   *

Karl Brown became associated with the movies in Hollywood when both were young. Brown's credits include photographing *The Covered Wagon* in the early 1920s and directing *Stark Love* (1927), a semi-documentary shot in North Carolina; and writing scripts for Columbia and Republic Studios between 1926 and 1945. Brown's career is most memorable in his association with D. W. Griffith between 1913 and 1919.

Brown's 1973 *Adventures with D. W. Griffith* is one of the best sources describing Griffith's working methods. Brown began as an assistant to the cameraman Billy Bitzer, and thus learned how to operate cameras, light scenes, and keep written records of various shots. His book makes clear that he was more than simply an assistant cameraman; he was a jack-of-all-trades for the Griffith organization. Brown describes in extensive detail the planning, shooting, and post-production aspects of Griffith's three masterpieces, *Birth of a Nation*, *Intolerance*, and *Broken Blossoms*.

For the last film Brown was in charge of the opening sequence showing ships on the Thames seen from the Limehouse district of London. He was shown a picture and then organized a series of miniature flats, groundrows, moving boats, and a trough of water. He lit the scene so that when photographed it provided a Whistler-like illusion of a London dockside. This one example is typical of the pictorial values Griffith emphasized and which he expected from his collaborators. It also shows how good a student of both Griffith and Bitzer Brown had become.

Brown's career as author and screenwriter included work for Columbia, Republic, and a few independent producers. Most of these films are gangster pictures, courtroom dramas, military situations, or horror stories. Had not Brown had good notes and recollections and been encouraged to publish them, he would probably be almost forgotten today. It is fitting, however, that a person who spent so much time on the routine tasks of filmmaking in its early Hollywood years will now be remembered because of his thoughtful book. Now, as then, moviemaking is a collaborative effort, and while a few key individuals receive major credit, no work would succeed without the many workers who, like Brown, also make fundamental contributions.

—Floyd W. Martin

BROWN, Nacio Herb

Composer. **Nationality:** American. **Born:** Deming, New Mexico, 22 February 1896. **Education:** Attended Manual Arts High School, Los Angeles. **Family:** Married the actress Anita Page. **Career:** Vaudeville accompanist, then worked in clothing store and real estate; song writer from 1920; 1929—songs for first film, *The Broadway Melody*; worked for MGM for 10 years, then for both MGM and 20th Century-Fox. **Died:** San Francisco, California, 28 September 1964.

Films as Composer:

1929   *The Broadway Melody* (Beaumont); *Untamed* (Conway); *The Hollywood Revue of 1929* (Reisner); *Marianne* (Leonard)
1930   *Whoopee!* (Freeland); *Good News* (Grinde); *Montana Moon* (St. Clair); *Lord Byron of Broadway* (Nigh and Beaumont); *One Heavenly Night* (Fitzmaurice)
1932   *A Woman Commands* (Stein)
1933   *The Barbarian* (Wood); *Stage Mother* (Brabin); *Going Hollywood* (Walsh); *Hold Your Man* (Wood); *Peg o' My Heart* (Leonard)
1934   *Hollywood Party* (Dwan); *Hide-Out* (Van Dyke); *Student Tour* (Riesner); *Riptide* (Goulding); *Sadie McKee* (Brown)
1935   *Broadway Melody of 1936* (Del Ruth); *China Seas* (Garnett); *A Night at the Opera* (Wood)
1936   *The Devil Is a Sissy* (Van Dyke); *San Francisco* (Van Dyke); *After the Thin Man* (Van Dyke)
1937   *Broadway Melody of 1938* (Del Ruth); *Thoroughbreds Don't Cry* (Green)
1939   *Babes in Arms* (Berkeley); *The Ice Follies of 1939* (Schünzel)
1940   *Two Girls on Broadway* (Simon)
1941   *Ziegfeld Girl* (Leonard)
1943   *Wintertime* (Brahm); *Swing Fever* (Whelan)
1944   *Greenwich Village* (W. Lang)
1946   *Holiday in Mexico* (Sidney)
1948   *The Kissing Bandit* (Benedek); *On an Island with You* (Thorpe)
1949   *The Bribe* (Leonard)
1950   *Pagan Love Song* (Alton)
1952   ***Singin' in the Rain*** (Kelly and Donen)

Publications

On BROWN: articles—

Craig, Warren, in *The Great Songwriters of Hollywood*, San Diego, California, 1980.
Hemming, Roy, in *The Melody Lingers On: The Great Songwriters and Their Movie Musicals*, New York, 1986.

*   *   *

After bidding goodnight to Kathy Selden, the woman with whom he has fallen in love, Don Lockwood waves his limousine on and begins strolling down a rain-drenched street. Even the most casual movie musical fan knows what happens next. Gene Kelly, cast as Lockwood, begins ''doodle-doo-dooing.'' He closes his umbrella, unconcerned with the rain storming down over him, and starts singing the lyrics to and dancing to the melody of the song for which the movie is named, *Singin' in the Rain*.

The man who wrote the melody, Nacio Herb Brown, was one of the most successful of all Hollywood studio composers working during the first quarter-century of the film musical. And ''Singin' in the Rain,'' with lyrics by Arthur Freed, is perhaps the one song which remains most closely identified with not only the MGM musical but the era itself. In the first sequence of *That's Entertainment!*, a compilation featuring the very best MGM musical numbers, ''Singin' in the Rain'' is performed initially by Cliff (''Ukelele Ike'') Edwards (in a rainstorm and accompanied by a dancing chorus) in *The Hollywood Revue of 1929*. Then in the 1930s, Jimmy Durante sits at his piano and

Nacio Herb Brown (left) with Arthur Freed

scat-sings to its rhythm. Next, during the 1940s, Judy Garland sings it in her own inimitable style. Finally, in the 1950s, Kelly, Donald O'Connor, and Debbie Reynolds harmonize before the opening credits of *Singin' in the Rain*. (The song is performed in the latter two more times, in Kelly's solo and by Reynolds at the finale.)

Brown began composing for the screen in the late 1920s, just as the movies were learning to sing and dance as well as talk. He retired in 1950, the year before his career was paid homage to in *Singin' in the Rain* (which is credited as being "suggested by the song," and is set in the era when Brown's career was beginning).

For the next two decades, Brown composed scores and songs for MGM musicals (often, but not always, in collaboration with Freed). His melodies feature no Gershwinesque phrasing. Unlike the sophisticated world described in Cole Porter's lyrics, or the playful quadruple rhymes of Betty Comden and Adolph Green, Brown's music is more at home with lyrics that are simple, lilting, and irrepressibly romantic. It elicits a naive, happy-go-lucky lightheartedness. This carefree, cheerful aura is the hallmark of the MGM musical.

In addition to the little song, all but two of the tunes performed in *Singin' in the Rain* originally were included in other studio releases: *The Broadway Melody* ("You Were Meant for Me," "The Wedding

of the Painted Doll," and "The Broadway Melody"); *San Francisco* ("Would You?"); *Sadie McKee* ("All I Do Is Dream of You"); *The Broadway Melody of 1936* ("You Are My Lucky Star," "I've Got a Feeling You're Fooling," and "Broadway Rhythm"); *Lord Byron of Broadway* ("Should I?"); and *Babes in Arms* ("Good Morning"). In each, Brown's music nicely complements the eternal optimism of Freed's lyrics: "All I do is dream of you the whole night through"; "life was a song, you came along . . . you were meant for me, and I was meant for you"; "good mornin', good mornin' . . . rainbows are shinin' through"; "no skies of gray on that Great White Way, that's the Broadway melody"; and, finally, "I'm singin' in the rain. . . . What a glorious feeling. I'm happy again."

The word *again* in the latter places the song within a time frame. Most of Brown and Freed's compositions were for films made during the American Depression and the Second World War, and their optimism reflects a need to focus on life's bright side. The songs are colorful; they do not dwell on the problems of the present, but offer the message that the viewer also will one day "be happy again." (Interestingly, Brown's MGM connection allowed him to continue enjoying this same pleasure during the Depression. He first began composing as a hobby; he successfully ran a menswear shop in Los

Angeles, and was one of the first to invest in land in Beverly Hills. Brown had spurned Irving Thalberg's invitation to write for the talkies, until the Wall Street crash supposedly severely altered his economic status.)

A Depression-era Warners musical might feature characters visibly stifled by the economic constraints of the era, or social commentary (in such song lyrics imploring the listener to "remember my forgotten man"). Not so an MGM musical, and certainly not so an MGM musical with a Nacio Herb Brown score. Whatever problems the characters endure will not be all that permanent or serious because you know that, at any moment, someone is bound to burst into tune, to be singin' in a rainstorm to a Nacio Herb Brown melody.

—Rob Edelman

BRUCKMAN, Clyde

Writer and Director. **Nationality:** American. **Born:** Clyde Adolph Bruckman in San Bernardino, California, 1894. **Family:** Married Gladys (Bruckman). **Career:** 1916–19—newspaper reporter; 1920—title writer for Monty Banks-Bull Montana comedies at Warner Bros.; 1921–25—writer and director with Buster Keaton unit; mainly a director from 1926 to 1936; 1939—joined Columbia under Jules White and worked there into the 1950s, writing also for Keaton's and Abbott and Costello's TV shows. **Died:** (Suicide) in Santa Monica, California, 4 January 1955.

Films as Writer (Shorts):

1920   *Three in a Closet* (Lyons and Moran)
1923   *A Punctured Prince* (Fay) (gags only); *Rob 'em Good* (Stromberg); *Glad Rags* (Fay) (gags only)
1925   *Remember When?* (Edwards—short)
1936   *Three Little Beers* (Lord); *Half Shot Shooters* (Black)
1937   *Grips, Grunts, and Groans* (Black); *Whoops! I'm an Indian* (Lord); *3 Dumb Clucks* (Lord); *Cash and Carry* (Lord)
1939   *Moochin' through Georgia* (White); *Pest from the West* (White); *Andy Clyde Gets Spring Chicken* (White); *Three Sappy People* (White); *Nothing but Pleasure* (White)
1940   *You Nazty Spy!* (White); *Rockin' thru the Rockies* (White); *Pardon My Berth Marks* (White); *The Taming of the Snood* (White); *Nutty but Nice* (White); *Pleased to Mitt You* (White); *From Nurse to Worse* (White); *The Spook Speaks* (White)
1941   *Fresh as a Freshman* (White); *So Long, Mr. Chumps* (White); *Black Eyes and Blues* (White); *I'll Never Heil Again* (White); *General Nuisance* (White); *In the Sweet Pie and Pie* (White); *Yankee Doodle Andy* (White); *Mitt Me Tonight* (White); *Loco Boy Makes Good* (White)
1942   *Glove Birds* (White); *Olaf Laughs Last* (White); *Tireman Spare My Tires* (White); *Three Smart Saps* (White); *Sock-a-bye Baby* (White); *Spook Louder* (Lord); *Shot in the Escape* (White); *Farmer for a Day* (White); *I Can Hardly Wait* (White); *Pitchin' in the Kitchen* (White); *Dizzy Pilots* (White)
1944   *The Yoke's on Me* (White)
1945   *A Miner Affair* (White)

1946   *Uncivil War Brides* (White); *Honeymood Blues* (Bernds); *Three Little Pirates* (Bernds); *Andy Plays Hookey* (Bernds)
1947   *The Scooper Dooper* (Bernds); *Fright Night* (Bernds); *Out West* (Bernds); *Nervous Shakedown* (Lord); *Rolling Down to Rio* (White); *Brideless Groom* (Bernds); *Should Husbands Marry?* (Lord); *Wedlock Deadlock* (Bernds)
1948   *Pardon My Clutch* (Bernds); *Tall, Dark and Gruesome* (Lord)
1952   *The Gink at the Sink* (White); *Up in Daisy's Penthouse* (White)
1953   *Love's A-Poppin'* (White); *Goof on the Roof* (White); *Pals and Gals* (White)
1954   *Two April Fools* (White)
1955   *Wham-Bam-Slam!* (White); *Husbands Beware* (White)

Films as Writer (Features):

1923   *The Three Ages* (Keaton and Cline); *The Rouged Lips* (Shaw) (titles only); *Our Hospitality* (Keaton and Blystone)
1924   ***Sherlock, Jr.*** (Keaton); *The Navigator* (Keaton and Crisp)
1925   *Seven Chances* (Keaton); *Keep Smiling* (Pratt)
1926   *For Heaven's Sake* (Taylor)
1928   *The Cameraman* (Sedgwick) (co)
1938   *Professor Beware* (Nugent)
1942   *Blondie Goes to College* (*The Boss Said No*) (Strayer)
1943   *Honeymoon Lodge* (Lilley); *So's Your Uncle* (Yarborough); *Swingtime Johnny* (Cline)
1944   *Week-end Pass* (Yarborough); *Moon over Las Vegas* (Yarborough); *South of Dixie* (Yarborough); *Twilight on the Prairie* (Yarborough)
1945   *Under Western Skies* (Yarborough); *Her Lucky Night* (Lilley); *She Gets Her Man* (Kenton)

Films as Director:

1926   ***The General*** (co + co-sc)
1927   *Horse Shoes* ; *A Perfect Gentleman* ; *Love 'em and Feed 'em* (short); *Call of the Cuckoo* (short); *Putting Pants on Philip* (short)
1928   *The Battle of the Century* (short); *Leave 'em Laughing* (short); *The Finishing Touch* (short)
1929   *Welcome Danger* (+ co-sc)
1930   *Feet First* (+ co-sc)
1931   *Everything's Rosie*
1932   *Movie Crazy*
1933   *The Human Fish* (short); *Too Many Highballs* (short); *The Fatal Glass of Beer* (short)
1935   *Horse Collars* (short); *Spring Tonic* (co); *Man on the Flying Trapeze* (*The Memory Expert*)

Publications

On BRUCKMAN: articles—

Blesh, Rudi, in *Keaton*, New York, 1966.
Adamson, Joseph, III, in *American Screenwriters*, edited by Robert E. Morsberger, Stephen O. Lesser, and Randall Clark, Detroit, Michigan, 1984.

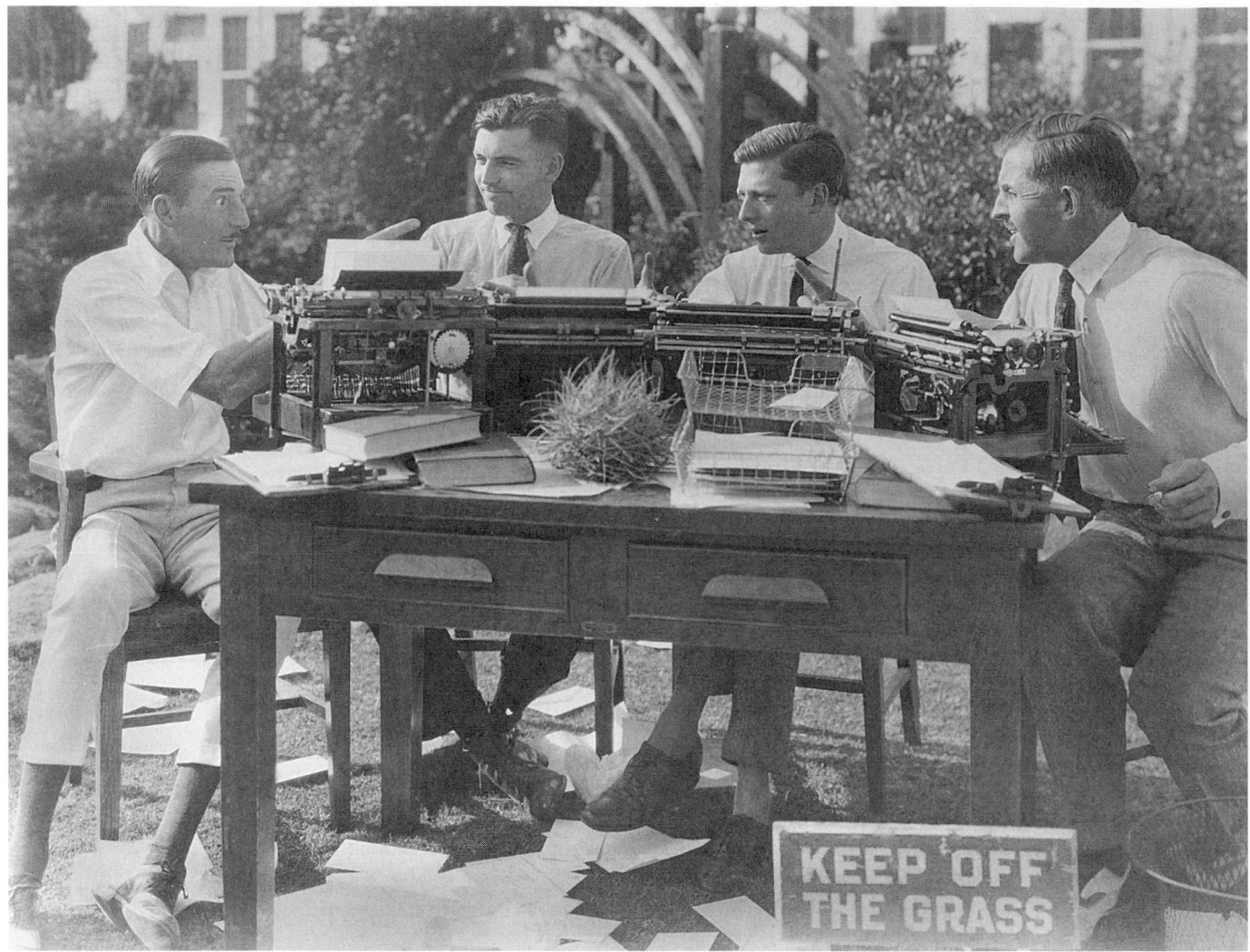

Clyde Bruckman (second from left) with Hugh Fay, Hunt Stromberg, and David Kirkland

Pratfall, vol. 2, no. 6–9, 1985.
Positif (Paris), June 1994.
Sanders, J., and D. Lieberfeld, ''Dreaming in Pictures,'' in *Film Quarterly* (Berkeley), no. 4, 1994.

*   *   *

The intention of a comedy craftsman is not only to create a comic situation, but to build on it, complicate it, top it, and give the comedian room to work in his own unique personality. The gagman/director Clyde Bruckman was one of the most sought after talents of comedy's Golden Age.

Harry Brand lured Bruckman away from Warner Bros. to work for Buster Keaton in 1921. Along with Joe Mitchell, Jean Havez, and Eddie Cline, Bruckman fashioned the blissfully odd mechanical world of which the poker-faced Keaton was the center, controlling nothing. The story lines for these shorts were strong and remarkably serious for their time, but with logical twists that snowballed into the chase. The daring acrobatic stunts and incredible sight gags rank as some of the best on film today. Although he didn't receive screen credit until his feature films with Keaton, Bruckman had a hand in many early pictures, most noticeably *Cops*.

As the medium grew from one- and two-reelers to feature-length productions, Keaton and his stable of gag writers pushed themselves into creating more deliberately paced sequences. Buster insisted that impossible or ''cartoon gags'' be discontinued, though he used them rarely anyway. When complications arose (or worse, if they didn't), they'd break for baseball in the backlot or continue playing cards until a better idea came along. This freewheeling approach to screen collaboration worked at the Keaton Studio, especially for Bruckman. ''In such a situation, gags are never a problem. You feel good. Your mind's at ease, and working.''

It was Bruckman who showed Keaton a Civil War novel about a Confederate raid into Northern lines, and knew the comic possibilities in it. This became *The General*, which he cowrote and codirected with Keaton. Their story was scripted by Al Boasberg and Charles Smith, and used fewer than 50 title cards. Six of the seven reels involved a pursuit of locomotives at full steam, one manned by an army of Northern spies and the other by Keaton alone. *The General* is a marvel of sustained ingenuity and, though unsuccessful in its first release, remains what many consider the last great silent comedy.

Harold Lloyd needed a person of Bruckman's talent to get his timid "glasses character" into mighty and hilarious situations. A businesslike comic, Lloyd sometimes found sitting in on gagwriting sessions unsettling. "Our lack of method is deplorable, but sometimes it works."

Lloyd often used Bruckman in tight situations, such as turning the silent *Welcome Danger* into a sound picture (a painful early lesson in postdubbing) and directing *Feet First*, Lloyd's first venture as a "sound comedian." The latter's climax had Harold roll onto a painter's scaffold in a mail sack that becomes hooked on the side of a skyscraper. His attempts to escape provided the thrills that audiences screamed for, yet it was the Harold Lloyd Corporation that later sent Bruckman's own career out the window.

Producer Hal Roach sought Bruckman to direct comedian Max Davidson in *Call of the Cuckoo* in 1927. Stan Laurel and Oliver Hardy were featured in secondary roles, and Bruckman's credit in the development of this comedy team is notable in the next four pictures he directed. Bruckman's ability to milk a single embarrassing situation, that of *Putting Pants on Philip* (with Stan as a woman-crazy Scottish nephew of Ollie), was praised by film historian William K. Everson for design and editing. This might have been part Leo McCarey's handiwork, part Stan Laurel's, part Bruckman's, and surely the uncredited editor's.

What is important was something special in the foolishness of Laurel and Hardy, and they seized upon it. Here was a case of two characters groping for a screen persona, and Bruckman's direction established them as a team—a couple of children innocently creating a mounting choreography of chaos. *The Battle of the Century* had the banana peel and pie fight spectacular to end them all, *Leave 'em Laughing* a hysterical traffic jam with the boys convulsed by laughing gas, and *The Finishing Touch* carpentry sight gags galore.

W. C. Fields was known to eat directors alive. Bruckman directed Fields *twice*. *The Fatal Glass of Beer*, produced by Mack Sennett, was a patchwork burlesque of long-winded dramas of the demon drink set in the Yukon. There is hardly any structure to it, but the nightmarish lunacy of this film made it a cult classic. Fields himself called upon Bruckman to fill in as the director of *Man on the Flying Trapeze* during a flu epidemic.

Bruckman worked best with comics who established their own screen personalities and knew what they wanted. From the simpleminded Stan Laurel to the malevolent W.C. Fields, the all-around guy Harold Lloyd to the analytical Buster Keaton, Clyde Bruckman adapted to the rhythms of each of these contrasting comic characters, subordinating "specialty" gags for the excellence of the picture as a whole. Using this same surefire material for other comedians got him into big trouble.

By the mid-1930s, one of the last bastions of the comedy short was Jules White's unit at Columbia Pictures. Bruckman worked as director for The Three Stooges in *Horse Collars* in 1935. Later, for the most part, he wrote stories and screenplays directed by White. Among the best of these were his collaborations with Felix Adler in the Hitler lampoons *You Nazty Spy!*, a favorite of Moe's and Jules White's and Larry's, and its sequel *I'll Never Heil Again*.

1939 brought a happy reunion for Buster Keaton and Clyde Bruckman at Columbia Pictures, making two-reelers again. Keaton had done one feature with Bruckman at MGM in 1928, was fired in 1933, and since then had batted around in shabby Educational Comedies and miscellaneous jobs. Even though Bruckman wasn't providing fresh material, Keaton was giving it all he had. The film historian Leonard Maltin calls *Pest from the West* "one of Keaton's

funniest pictures." Keaton made ten shorts at Columbia from 1939 to 1941, seven of these with Bruckman.

Time and budget restrictions at the Columbia short-subject department (averaging three days and using leftover sets) required the elastic ability to land on your feet, and Bruckman was already on a downward slide. Alcoholism and bouts with depression had dissipated a lot of his talents. He was drawing from past routines, sometimes word for word, and not crafting them to the artist. In 1945 and early 1946, the Harold Lloyd Corporation filed three suits against Universal Studios and two against Columbia Pictures for alleged plagiarism of Lloyd's films, naming writers who had previously worked with him. Bruckman was named in all five. In 1947, the Lloyd Corporation collected. The court's judgment held that the Universal films *So's Your Uncle*, *She Gets Her Man*, and *Her Lucky Night* contained material lifted from the Lloyd comedies *Movie Crazy*, *Welcome Danger*, and *The Freshman*, respectively. The Stooges' two-reelers *Three Smart Saps* and *Loco Boy Makes Good* contained material borrowed from *The Freshman* and *Movie Crazy*.

Being sued closed almost every avenue for employment. With his reputation shattered and his drinking getting worse, Bruckman was becoming more and more unreliable. And, like Buster Keaton, he found the assembly-line method of story conferences in the industry made him lose confidence in his own ideas. In the 1950s television was growing and it had a huge appetite. Bruckman worked on *The Buster Keaton Comedy Show*, one of the pioneering live television shows, and from 1951 to 1953 on *The Abbott and Costello Show*, one of the first syndicated comedy series. (Joseph Adamson III writes that Bruckman did uncredited work for Abbott and Costello's 1944 feature *In Society*.) Much of his material for these shows was derived from his old pencraft, as well as vaudeville and burlesque routines. The Golden Age was over, and Bruckman became a tragic casualty: he killed himself in Santa Monica in 1955.

—Rob Pinsel

BRYAN, John

Producer/Production Designer. **Nationality:** British. **Born:** London, 1911. **Career:** Nominated for Oscar for Set Design for *Caesar and Cleopatra*, 1947. **Awards:** Oscar for *Great Expectations*, 1947; British Academy Award (BAFTA) for *Becket*, 1965. **Died:** 10 June 1969.

Films as Producer:

1952   *The Card* (*The Promoter*) (Neame)
1953   *The Million Pound Note* (*Man with a Million*) (Neame)
1954   *The Purple Plain* (Parrish)
1956   *The Spanish Gardener* (Leacock)
1957   *The Secret Place* (Donner)
1958   *Windom's Way* (Neame); *The Horse's Mouth* (Neame)
1960   *There Was a Crooked Man* (Mankiewicz)
1962   *The Girl on the Boat* (Kaplan)
1964   *Tamahine* (Leacock)
1966   *Caccia alla volpe* (*After the Fox*) (de Sica)
1968   *The Touchables* (Freeman)

Films as Production Designer:

1937   *The Song of the Road* (Baxter)
1946   *Great Expectations* (Lean)
1947   *Blanche Fury* (Allégret); *Take My Life* (Neame)
1948   *Oliver Twist* (Lean) (also set designer)
1949   *The Passionate Friends* (One Woman's Story (USA)) (Lean)
       (also set decorator)
1950   *The Golden Salamander* (Neame)
1951   *Pandora and the Flying Dutchman* (Lewin); *The Magic Box*
       (Boulting)
1964   *Becket* (Glenville)
1968   *Great Catherine* (Flemyng)

Films as Art Director:

1938   *Pygmalion* (Asquith and Howard)
1939   *A Stolen Life* (Czinner)
1941   *Dangerous Moonlight* (Suicide Squadron) (Hurst)
1942   *King Arthur Was a Gentleman* (Varnel)
1943   *Dear Octopus* (The Randolph Family) (French); *Millions Like
       Us* (Launder and Gilliat); *Sabotage Agent* (Adventures of
       Tartu; Tartu) (Bucquet)
1944   *2,000 Women* (House of 1,000 Women; Two Thousand Women)
       (Launder); *Fanny by Gaslight* (Man of Evil) (Asquith);
       Love Story (A Lady Surrenders) (Arliss); *Time Flies* (Forde)
1945   *Caravan* (Charell); *The Wicked Lady* (Arliss)
1946   *Caesar and Cleopatra* (Pascal)

Other Films:

1936   *Things to Come* (Menzies) (asst art d, uncredited)
1950   *Madeleine* (The Strange Case of Madeleine) (Lean) (set
       decorator)

Publications:

On BRYAN: books—

Low, Rachel, *Filmmaking in 1930s Britain*, London, 1985.
Cook, David, *A History of Narrative Film*, London, 1996.
McFarlane, Bryan, editor, *An Autobiography of British Cinema*,
    London, 1996.

*   *   *

A little-known but key figure in British cinema from the 1940s until the 1960s, John Bryan involved himself in most areas of film production. Bryan's work with directors David Lean and Ronald Neame on films like *Great Expectations*, *Oliver Twist*, *The Card* and *The Million Pound Note*, has proved to be the most enduring, and the films also rank among the directors' best work. Unlike many of his contemporaries who went on to make names for themselves in Hollywood, Bryan continued to work in the British film industry even as it began to struggle in the 1960s.

Bryan's career began in the 1930s as a production designer and art director on films such as *The Song of the Road* and *Pygmalion*. In many ways, these films were to shape Bryan's career, idealizing as they do an England of the past; in many of his later films Bryan was required to create sets and locations reminiscent of an earlier age. *The Song of the Road* tells the story of a man and his horse made redundant by the introduction of motorized trucks. The England it portrays is a comfortable, conservative one, and the main character, adhering to the values of honesty and hard-work and having a firm grip on his social position, is a peculiarly English hero of the time. *Pygmalion*, which was later to be adapted as the musical *My Fair Lady*, won an Oscar for its writers, and for George Bernard Shaw, the writer of the original play—although it was originally trailed in the United States as being based on a play by Shakespeare. The film is notable for the detail of its settings and the overall quality of the production, which marked Bryan out as an impressive talent in only his second film.

Bryan spent most of the 1930s and early 1940s working as art director at Pinewood Studios, where he contributed to notable films such as *The Wicked Lady* and the Bernard Shaw adaptation, *Caesar and Cleopatra*. *The Wicked Lady* is notable mainly for its period detail and had to be re-shot for American release in order that the women's costumes should meet the requirements of the Hays Code. Apart from its production values, *Caesar and Cleopatra*, benefits from a talented cast, including Vivien Leigh as Cleopatra, and Claude Rains as an unlikely Caesar.

It was after Word War II, when he teamed up with Lean, Neame, and Anthony Havelock-Allen, that Bryan entered the most successful period in his career. As production designer on Lean's *Great Expectations*, Bryan combined his talent for historically stylised versions of England with Lean's gothic imagination to create a Dickens adaptation that is decidedly British in its look. A comparative viewing of William Wyler's 1939 adaptation of *Wuthering Heights*, for which the Yorkshire moors were recreated, complete with transplanted heather, in the California hills, will confirm the Britishness of the look of Lean's film. Bryan also worked with Lean on another Dickens adaptation, as production designer for the exemplary *Oliver Twist*, a film which is superior in every respect to Carol Reed's commendable 1968 musical version, *Oliver!* Although Bryan and Lean collaborated on only two films, the dark settings and confident visual style mark *Great Expectations* and *Oliver Twist* out as two of the finest British films ever made.

As a producer, working with Ronald Neame, Bryan found almost immediate success, with *The Card* and *The Million Pound Note* becoming two of the best British films of the 1950s. Although he produced the films of other directors it was his collaborations with Neame that have proved the most long-lasting. Later in his career as a producer, as the British film industry entered a period of rapid decline, Bryan was less fortunate in his choice of film projects, and *The Touchables*, his last film as producer, was an unmitigated failure. As a production designer, Bryan was more consistent, and his penultimate film, *Becket*, is among the highlights of his career. Based on a play by Jean Anouilh, *Becket* is rather slow-paced, but the relative lack of action only serves to highlight the magnificence of the English locations.

John Bryan's career spanned the most successful period in British film making, and he was an important figure among the group of producers, directors, and cinematographers who gathered around

David Lean and Cineguild in the 1940s and early 1950s. He became adept at recreating archetypal English landscapes and interiors, but he was also capable of dramatic exaggeration, as in the gothic bleakness of the country churchyard in *Great Expectations*. Oddly, his career began and ended with adaptations of George Bernard Shaw plays; first *Pygmalion*, and then, in 1968, the over-adorned *Great Catherine*.

—Chris Routledge

BUCHMAN, Sidney

Writer and Producer. **Nationality:** American. **Born:** Duluth, Minnesota, 27 March 1902. **Education:** Attended the University of Minnesota, St. Paul; Oxford University. **Career:** 1929—assistant stage manager, Old Vic Theatre, London; 1930—play *This One Man* produced in New York (later play is *Storm Song*); 1931–34—staff writer at Paramount; 1934–42—writer at Columbia, then Vice-President and Assistant Production Chief, 1942–51; 1951—questioned by the House Un-American Committee, admitted being a Communist Party member, 1938–45, and blacklisted from 1953; moved to Europe; 1961—hired by 20th Century-Fox as writer-producer, and worked in Europe for the rest of his career; lived in Cannes after 1965. **Awards:** Academy Award for *Here Comes Mr. Jordan*, 1941; Writers Guild Laurel Award, 1965. **Died:** Of cancer in Cannes, 23 August 1975.

Films as Writer:

1927   *Matinee Ladies* (Haskin) (co)
1931   *Daughter of the Dragon* (Corrigan) (dialogue)
1932   *No One Man* (Corrigan); *Thunder Below* (Wallace); *If I Had a Million* (Lubitsch and others); *The Sign of the Cross* (DeMille)
1933   *From Hell to Heaven* (Kenton); *Right to Romance* (Santell)
1934   *All of Me* (Flood); *Whom the Gods Destroy* (W. Lang); *His Greatest Gamble* (Robertson); *Broadway Bill* (*Strictly Confidential*) (Capra)
1935   *I'll Love You Always* (Bulgakov); *Love Me Forever* (Schertzinger); *She Married Her Boss* (La Cava)
1936   *The Music Goes 'Round* (Schertzinger); *The King Steps Out* (von Sternberg); *Adventure in Manhattan* (*Manhattan Madness*) (Ludwig); *Theodora Goes Wild* (Boleslawsky)
1938   *Holiday* (Cukor)
1939   **Mr. Smith Goes to Washington** (Capra)
1940   *The Howards of Virginia* (*The Tree of Liberty*) (Lloyd)
1941   *Here Comes Mr. Jordan* (Hall)
1942   *The Talk of the Town* (Stevens)
1944   *A Song to Remember* (C. Vidor) (+ pr)
1945   *Over 21* (C. Vidor) (+ pr)
1949   *Jolson Sings Again* (Levin) (+ pr)
1951   *Saturday's Heroes* (*Idols in the Dust*) (Miller)
1961   *The Mark* (Green) (+ co-pr)
1963   *Cleopatra* (Mankiewicz)

1966   *The Group* (Lumet) (+ pr)
1971   *La Maison sous les arbres* (*The Deadly Trap*) (Clément) (+ co-pr)

Films as Producer:

1937   *She Married an Artist* (Gering)
1948   *To the Ends of the Earth* (Stevenson)

Publications

By BUCHMAN: scripts—

Mr. Smith Goes to Washington and *Here Comes Mr. Jordan* in *Twenty Best Film Plays*, edited by John Gassner and Dudley Nichols, New York, 1943.
Over 21 in *The Best Film Plays of 1945*, edited by John Gassner and Dudley Nichols, New York, 1946.

On BUCHMAN: articles—

Kael, Pauline, "The Making of *The Group*," in *Kiss Kiss Bang Bang*, New York, 1968.
Positif (Paris), June 1969
Film Comment (New York), Winter 1970–71.
Film Comment (New York), September-October 1972.
Corliss, Richard, in *Talking Pictures*, New York, 1974.
Film Guia, October-November 1975.

*   *   *

Sidney Buchman wrote, alone or in collaboration, some of the best socially oriented screenplays in the American cinema, such as *Mr. Smith Goes to Washington* and *The Talk of the Town*, managing to make his messages palatable to audiences in the guise of entertainment. In this, he was aided by such arbiters of public taste as the directors Frank Capra and George Stevens and the enticing screen stars Jean Arthur, James Stewart, and Cary Grant. Ironically, Buchman was ultimately a victim of the Hollywood blacklist in the 1950s, and although he was involved in other film projects he never regained the momentum he had built up in 15 years of inspired screenwriting.

After serving as an assistant stage manager in London at the Old Vic Theatre, Buchman tried his hand at playwrighting, with no success. He joined Paramount in the early 1930s as a junior writer; his most notable credits there—DeMille's *The Sign of the Cross*, and the omnibus *If I Had a Million*—were cowritten with a multitude of scenarists, and Buchman did not flourish until he joined Harry Cohn's Columbia Pictures in 1934. The year is significant; it saw Columbia legitimized as a major studio with the Oscar-winning success of Capra's *It Happened One Night*. Buchman became Cohn's favorite writer, and he had a hand in most of the studio's important productions. He would frequently be asked to polish scripts, and he toiled without screen credit on Capra's *Broadway Bill* and *Lost Horizon*,

Sidney Buchman (left) with Irene Dunne and Charles Vidor

McCarey's *The Awful Truth*, Zoltan Korda's *Sahara*, and Alfred Green's *The Jolson Story*. In 1942 Cohn appointed Buchman to the position of production supervisor, and he eventually became a vice-president of production. His Sidney Buchman Productions produced the comedy *Over 21*, from the Ruth Gordon play, and the Jolson sequel, *Jolson Sings Again*, before the blacklist took effect. He admitted to the House Un-American Activities Committee that he had been a member of the Communist party in his youth, but refused to name names, and was subsequently fined, given a suspended sentence, and unofficially blacklisted. The producer who had benefited most from his skills, Harry Cohn, did not come to his aid, and Buchman became a European exile. The story is all the more ironic when one considers that Buchman's scripts for *She Married Her Boss*, *Theodora Goes Wild*, *Holiday*, *Mr. Smith Goes to Washington*, *The Howards of Virginia*, *Here Comes Mr. Jordan*, and *The Talk of the Town* were among Columbia's biggest moneymakers.

Gregory LaCava's *She Married Her Boss* was a domestic comedy, a warm farce with telling situations. Buchman's script for Richard Boleslawsky's *Theodora Goes Wild* was based on a Mary McCarthy story, with Irene Dunne in the title role as a small-town novelist whose juicy book causes a scandal. The premise of the rural idealist in

the big city was later adapted for Capra's *Mr. Smith Goes to Washington*. While *Mr. Smith* was officially based on the story "The Gentleman from Montana" by Lewis R. Foster, it clearly has a partial inspiration in *Theodora*. James Stewart excels as the naive Senator who tackles the corrupt political machine in Washington. A courageous paean to democracy, *Mr. Smith Goes to Washington* boasted carefully drawn characters, thoughtful and at times humorous dialogue, and a narrative that builds to a monumental filibuster by Stewart in the U.S. Senate.

George Stevens's *The Talk of the Town* also couched its ideology in mass entertainment, using a comedic situation to say some important things about justice. Jean Arthur harbors fugitive Cary Grant in her house, while Ronald Colman, a dedicated professor of law, rents a room from her. The Colman character is forced to rethink his rigid application of law in a humanistic comedy of social manners. Buchman could also write straight farcical material, as witness *Here Comes Mr. Jordan*, as well as epic drama, such as *The Howards of Virginia*, a Revolutionary War film about America's founding fathers.

Buchman lived in Europe after the blacklist, and returned to motion pictures with a contract from 20th Century-Fox in the early 1960s. *The Mark*, directed by Guy Green, is a thinly disguised allegory about a convict released from prison and forced to adapt to a new society, a metaphor for Buchman's situation at the time. The multimillion dollar turkey *Cleopatra* followed, but he had more success with his adaptation of Mary McCarthy's novel *The Group*, which he also produced.

In *Talking Pictures*, Richard Corliss pointed out the similarity between Buchman and Robert Riskin, another writer who was favored at Columbia. Both Buchman and Riskin wrote lengthy scripts, both wrote uncommonly fast, both used the dramatic device of opposing characters from rural and urban backgrounds, and both were ''easy-going populists'' who had Frank Capra as their ideal director. Corliss maintains that Buchman's writing was much richer than Riskin's; the record tends to bear him out. Unfortunately, Buchman's populism was eventually undermined by the real life tyranny of Senator McCarthy.

—John A. Gallagher

BUCKLAND, Wilfred

Art Director. **Nationality:** American. **Born:** 1866. **Family:** Married; one son. **Career:** Stage director; 1914—joined Famous Players-Lasky as first credited art director; worked on many early films of Cecil B. DeMille. **Died:** (Suicide) 18 July 1946.

Films as Art Director for DeMille and/or Apfel:

1914   *The Squaw Man*; *The Ghost Breaker*; *Brewster's Millions*; *The Man on the Box*; *The Virginian*; *The Call of the North*; *What's His Name*; *The Man from Home*; *Rose of the Ranch*; *The Girl of the Golden West*
1915   *The Unafraid*, *The Captive*; *The Warrens of Virginia*; *Carmen*; *The Cheat*; *The Wild Goose Chase*; *The Arab*; *Chimmie Fadden*; *Kindling*; *Maria Rosa*; *Chimmie Fadden Out West*; *Temptation*
1916   *The Golden Chance*; *The Trail of the Lonesome Pine*; *The Heart of Nora Flynn*; *The Dream Girl*; *Joan the Woman*
1917   *A Romance of the Redwoods*; *The Little American*; *The Woman God Forgot*; *The Devil-Stone*
1918   *The Whispering Chorus*; *Old Wives for New*; *We Can't Have Everything*; *Till I Come Back to You*; *The Squaw Man*; *Don't Change Your Husband*
1919   *For Better, for Worse*; *Male and Female*
1923   *Adam's Rib*

Other Films as Art Director:

1918   *Less than Kin* (Crisp); *Stella Maris* (Neilan)
1919   *The Grim Game* (Willat)
1920   *Conrad in Search of His Youth* (W. De Mille)
1921   *A Perfect Crime* (Dwan)
1922   *The Deuce of Spades* (Ray); *The Masquerader* (Young); *Omar the Tentmaker* (Young); *Robin Hood* (Dwan) (co)

1924   *Icebound* (W. De Mille)
1927   *The Forbidden Woman* (Stein) (co); *Almost Human* (Urson)

Publications

By BUCKLAND: articles—

''Getting Belasco Atmosphere,'' in *Moving Picture World* (New York), 30 May 1914.
''When the Leaves Begin to Fall,'' in *Theatre*, October 1918.

On BUCKLAND: article—

In *The Art of Hollywood*, edited by John Hambley, London, 1979.

*   *   *

In his autobiography, *I Blow My Own Horn*, Jesse L. Lasky wrote, ''As the first *bona fide* art director in the industry, and the first to build architectural settings for films, Buckland widened the scope of pictures tremendously by throwing off the scenic limitations of the stage.''

Lasky's comments are at the same time correct and inaccurate. Wilfred Buckland did, quite obviously, understand the difference between stage and screen settings. Through the use of klieg lights, he introduced artificial lighting, which helped develop the early film industry. In the countless films on which he was art director, usually without screen credit, produced by Lasky and later Famous Players-Lasky in the 1910s, Buckland demonstrates an ability to create any type of set, ancient or modern. Unquestionably, he helped to expand the relationship between the director and the art director; he proved that the art director as much as the director is responsible for the look of the film—something which has come to be taken for granted. The best proof of this is Cecil B. DeMille's *Male and Female*, which is best remembered for its bathroom sequence with Gloria Swanson. That bathroom owes as much to the imagination of Buckland as to DeMille's obsession with vulgarity.

At the same time, Buckland had been a stage director (notably for David Belasco) prior to entering films, and many of his interior sets for the 1910s dramas, starring Blanche Sweet, Geraldine Farrar, or Wallace Reid, have a Victorian stuffiness to them which is inexorably linked to the theatre. Even the outrageous DeMille sets are so far divorced from reality as to have their origins in Victorian and Edwardian theatre rather than screen reality.

Buckland's last major contribution to art direction was the creation of the castle setting for Douglas Fairbanks's *Robin Hood*. His was an extraordinary architectural achievement, and a fitting climax to a career which paved the way for Cedric Gibbons, William Cameron Menzies, and others. Buckland had established the importance of the art director, but, quite obviously, he lacked the youth—he was almost 60 when he worked on *Robin Hood*—and vitality to continue in a major position within the industry.

Sadly, the tragedy of Wilfred Buckland's death overshadows the importance of his career. He shot and killed his mentally ill son, fearing what might happen to the boy after his death, and then killed himself.

—Anthony Slide

BUMSTEAD, Henry

Art Director. **Nationality:** American. **Born:** 17 March 1915 in Ontario, California. **Career:** Art director from 1948; received Academy Award nominations for *Vertigo*, 1958; and *Unforgiven*, 1992. **Awards:** Academy Awards for *To Kill a Mockingbird*, 1962; *The Sting*, 1973. **Address:** Smith, Gosnell, Nicholson and Associates, Pacific Palisades, CA, U.S.A.

Films as Art Director:

1948   *Saigon* (Fenton); *The Sainted Sisters* (Russell); *My Own True Love* (Bennett)

1949   *Song of Surrender* (Leisen); *Top 'o the Morning* (Miller); *My Friend Irma* (Marshall)

1950   *The Furies* (A. Mann); *No Man of Her Own* (*The Lie*) (Leisen); *My Friend Irma Goes West* (Walker); *The Goldbergs* (Hart); *The Redhead and the Cowboy* (Fenton)

1952   *Aaron Slick from Punkin Crick* (Binyon); *Jumping Jacks* (Taurog); *Come Back, Little Sheba* (Daniel Mann)

1953   *The Stars Are Singing* (Taurog)

1954   *Knock on Wood* (Panama and Frank); *The Bridges at Toko-Ri* (Robson)

1955   *The Man Who Knew Too Much* (Hitchcock); *Run for Cover* (Ray); *Lucy Gallant* (Parrish)

1956   *That Certain Feeling* (Panama and Frank); *The Leather Saint* (Ganzer); *The Vagabond King* (Curtiz); *Hollywood or Bust* (Tashlin)

1958   *I Married a Monster from Outer Space* (Fowler); *As Young As We Are* (Girard); **Vertigo** (Hitchcock)

1959   *The Hangman* (Curtiz)

1960   *The Bellboy* (Lewis); *Cinderfella* (Tashlin)

1961   *Come September* (Mulligan); *The Great Imposter* (Mulligan)

1962   *The Spiral Road* (Mulligan); *To Kill a Mockingbird* (Mulligan)

1963   *A Gathering of Eagles* (Delbert Mann)

1964   *The Brass Bottle* (Keller); *Bullet for a Badman* (Springsteen); *Father Goose* (Nelson)

1965   *The War Lord* (Schaffner)

1966   *Beau Geste* (Heyes); *Blindfold* (Dunne); *Gunpoint* (Bellamy)

1967   *Banning* (Winston); *Tobruk* (Hillier)

1968   *The Secret War of Harry Frigg* (Smight); *What's So Bad about Feeling Good?* (Seaton)

1969   *Topaz* (Hitchcock); *Tell Them Willie Boy Is Here* (Polonsky); *A Man Called Gannon* (Goldstone)

1970   *The Movie Murderer* (Sagal); *McCloud: Who Killed Miss U.S.A.?* (*Portrait of a Dead Girl*) (Colla)

1972   *Joe Kidd* (J. Sturges); *Slaughterhouse-Five* (Hill) (+ ro); *High Plains Drifter* (Eastwood); *The Victim* (Daugherty); *The Adventures of Nick Carter* (Krasny)

1973   *The Sting* (Hill)

1974   *The Front Page* (Wilder); *Honky Tonk* (Taylor)

1975   *The Great Waldo Pepper* (Hill)

1976   *Family Plot* (Hitchcock)

1977   *Don't Push, I'll Charge When I'm Ready* (Lande—produced 1969)

1978   *Same Time Next Year* (Mulligan); *House Calls* (Zieff)

1979   *The Concorde—Airport '79* (*Airport 80—The Concorde*) (Rich); *A Little Romance* (Hill)

1982   *The World According to Garp* (Hill)

1984   *Harry & Son* (Newman); *The Little Drummer Girl* (Hill)

1986   *Psycho III* (Perkins)

1988   *Funny Farm* (Hill); *A Time of Destiny* (Nava) (+ ro)

1989   *Her Alibi* (Beresford)

1990   *Almost an Angel* (Cornell); *Ghost Dad* (Poitier)

1991   *Cape Fear* (Scorsese)

1992   **Unforgiven** (Eastwood)

1993   *A Perfect World* (Eastwood)

1994   *The Stars Fell on Henrietta* (Keich)

1997   *Absolute Power* (Eastwood); *Midnight in the Garden of Good and Evil* (Eastwood); *Home Alone 3* (Gosnell)

1999   *True Crime* (Eastwood)

2000   *Space Cowboys* (Eastwood)

Publications

By BUMSTEAD: article—

American Cinematographer (Hollywood), May 1974.

On BUMSTEAD: articles—

Button, Simon, Review of *Home Alone 3* in *Total Film* (London), January 1998.

McCarthy, Todd, "Eastwood Shows His True Grit," in *Variety* (New York), 15 March 1999.

*   *   *

Embarking on his 1955 remake of *The Man Who Knew Too Much*, Alfred Hitchcock asked cameraman Robert Burks to recommend the best designer among those currently at work for Paramount under Hal Pereira. Roland Anderson and John Meehan had won Oscars, but Burks suggested Henry Bumstead, then designing Michael Curtiz's *The Vagabond King*, a period musical starring the Mario Lanza-surrogate Oreste Kirkop.

Bumstead did the art direction on four Hitchcock films, including *Vertigo*, one of his finest, and went on to an Oscar-winning career. Until then he had mainly worked for Paramount's second-string directors like Mitchell Leisen, who as an ex-designer himself had had his own ideas of how *Song of Surrender* and *No Man of Her Own* should look. Hitchcock was no less specific about his wants, but Bumstead, sensing the director's tastes, not only reflected but amplified them. The London suburban chapel haunted by Bernard Miles and Brenda de Banzie in *The Man Who Knew Too Much* improved on Alfred Junge's 1934 original, while the new addition of a taxidermist's shop lined with stuffed animal heads prefigures Norman Bates's office in *Psycho*. Less flamboyantly, a Moroccan restaurant in the same film shows the eye for authentic detail that was to enliven Bumstead's later design.

In 1957, Hitchcock called on Bumstead again for *Vertigo*. He told him he conceived the film as almost motionless, a series of *tableaux vivants* which would demand particularly evocative set design. As a further hint he suggested Bumstead "try to use a lot of mirrors," emphasizing the dual role played by Kim Novak and the moral ambivalence of the James Stewart character. Bumstead turned these suggestions into one of the most visually distinctive of all Hollywood films. The empty picture gallery where Kim Novak contemplates what appears to be her own portrait, Barbara Bel Geddes's San Francisco apartment with its vertiginous view from the kitchen window, the Spanish mission church tower around which much of the film hinges, all fulfill the requirement of great design, telling us part of the story even before we see a moment of action.

Bumstead would later design *Topaz* and *Family Plot* for Hitchcock but in neither case did the story demand much besides simple backgrounds, both being shot on mainly existing locations, though Bumstead did put much effort into turning Hitchcock's chosen graveyard for the latter into an effective setting. He also worked on *No Bail for the Judge*, the 1959 Audrey Hepburn thriller that Hitchcock cancelled when the star rejected the script. Bumstead had meanwhile become a member of the Hitchcock entourage, a dubious honour. It was the designer who drove Hitchcock to his naturalisation ceremony in April 1955, a favour for which the director rewarded him with one of his practical jokes, calling him in and asking his secretary casually, ''Dolores, how would you like to screw Henry Bumstead?'' Hitchcock's appreciation of the *Vertigo* sets was as typically egocentric and cutting. Impressed by Bumstead's design for Tom Helmore's book-lined red leather 19th-century office, Hitchcock asked him to redo his own study in the same style. When he got no acknowledgement for his work Bumstead asked the director's wife if he'd been satisfied. Prompted, Hitch rang with his thanks—and a request that Bumstead similarly renovate the house's gates and furniture.

On the foundation of his Hitchcock films Bumstead built a distinguished career. He won an Oscar nomination (shared by tradition with Universal design supervisor Alexander Golitzen) for the Sharecropper Gothic sets of *To Kill a Mockingbird* and gained considerable acclaim for his work on Franklin Shaffner's 1965 *The War Lord*, which recreated with atmospheric accuracy a world of magic and superstition in 11th-century Brittany. Guy Stockwell's muttered comment, ''This place has the dimensions of heresy'' as he rides through a forest festooned with charms and fetishes is an implied endorsement of Bumstead's authenticity.

In 1973, Bumstead won an Oscar for *The Sting*, not so much for the film's meticulous recreation of 1920s cafes, bookie joints, and train interiors, as for decades of imaginative design. He continued to work with such cosy materials on films like *Her Alibi*, but it was in the area of exterior and, in particular, western designs that his reputation increased during the 1980s and 1990s.

He had already designed his share of such productions during the 1960s, notably George Roy Hill's film of the post-First World War barnstormers, *The Great Waldo Pepper*, and Abraham Polonsky's socially-conscious Native American drama *Tell Them Willie Boy Is Here*, employing a style on which he enlarged in *Cape Fear* for Martin Scorsese and *A Perfect World* for Clint Eastwood. In particular, however, *High Plains Drifter* inaugurated a long and fruitful collaboration with Eastwood, establishing a distinctive vision of frontier architecture that was to prove highly influential. Raw as a wreck and dumped down in the most bare and hostile of plateaus, the town in *High Plains Drifter* is human habitation reduced to the barest of bones, an effect heightened when Eastwood's vengeful gunman forces it to be literally painted red in retribution for its betrayal. Bumstead exploited this vision further in *Unforgiven*, that bleakest of 1990s revisionist westerns.

The collaboration with Eastwood has become a regular arrangement in the second half of the 1990s, with Bumstead bringing his talent for American landscapes to bear on Eastwood's penchant for thrillers in unremarkable films such as *Absolute Power*, *Midnight in the Garden of Good and Evil*, and *True Crime*. His work with director James Keach on *The Stars Fell on Henrietta*, a film set during the oil boom, reworks much of the cinematic imagery of the West that he helped establish. In contrast, the ill-conceived sequel *Home Alone 3* could not be saved even by Bumstead's instinct for imaginative detail.

—John Baxter, updated by Chris Routledge

BUREL, Léonce-Henry

Cinematographer and Director. **Nationality:** French. **Born:** Indret, 23 November 1892. **Education:** Studied art at the University of Nantes and the Institute of Fine Arts, Paris. **Career:** Photo-engraver and photo-typographer; 1913—directed films for Cosmographe, and photographed films for Henri Wulschleger, for Eclair, and for Le Somptier; 1916—first of many films for Abel Gance; 1918—official photographer of armistice celebrations in Paris and London. **Award:** Venice Festival prize for *Diary of a Country Priest*, 1950. **Died:** 21 March 1977.

Films as Cinematographer:

1915 *Alsace* (Pouctal); *La Folie du Docteur Tube* (Gance)
1916 *La Fleur des ruines* (Gance); *L'Enigme de dix heures* (Gance); *L'Heroïsme de Paddy* (Gance); *Le Fou de la falaise* (Gance); *Ce que les flots racontent* (Gance); *Les Mouettes* (Mariaud); *Fioritures* (*L a Source de beauté*) (Gance); *Barberousse* (Gance); *Les Gaz mortels* (*La Brouillard sur la ville*) (Gance)
1917 *Le Droit à la vie* (Gance); *La Zone de la mort* (Gance); *Mater Dolorosa* (Gance)
1918 *La Dixième Symphonie* (Gance)
1919 *J'accuse* (Gance)
1921 *L'Hirondelle et la mésange* (Antoine); *Mademoiselle de la seiglière* (Antoine)
1922 *L'Arlésienne* (Antoine)
1923 *Visages d'enfants* (Feyder); *La Roue* (Gance); *La Femme inconnue* (de Baroncelli)
1924 *Salammbo* (*Der Kampf um Karthago*) (Maradon)
1925 *Michel Strogoff* (Tourjansky); *L'Image* (Feyder); **Feu Mathias Pascal** (*The Late Mathias Pascal*; *The Living Dead Man*) (L'Herbier)
1927 **Napoléon** (Gance) (co); *Casanova* (Wolkoff); *Morgane la Sirène* (Perret); *La Danseuse orchidé* (Perret); *L'Equipage* (Tourneur)
1928 *Nuits de princes* (D'Herbier); *Vénus* (Mercanton)
1929 *The Three Passions* (Ingram); *Frivolités* (Mazeline and Le Héneff); *Le Requin* (Chomettre); *Le Secret de Delhia* (Menessier)
1930 *Le Mystère de la chambre jaune* (L'Herbier); *Die Fremde* (Sauer)—also French version, *L'Etrangère* (Ravel); *Die Königin einer Nacht* (Wendhausen) (co)—also French version, *La Femme d'une nuit* (L'Herbier)
1931 *Un Soir de rafle* (Gallone); *L'Aiglon* (Tourjansky); *Baroud* (*Love and Morocco*) (Ingram)

1932   *Danton* (Roubaud); *La Femme nue* (Paulin); *Il a été perdu une mariée* (Joannon)

1933   *On n'a pas besoin d'argent* (Paulin); *L'Abbé Constantin* (Paulin); *Les Deux "Monsieurs" de Madame* (Jacquin); *Le Fakir du Grand Hotel* (Billon); *Mariage à responsabilité limité* (de Limur); *Coralie et Cie.* (Cavalcanti)

1934   *L'Auberge du petit dragon* (de Limur); *Un Homme en or* (Dréville); *Le Petit Jacques* (Roudes); *Toboggan* (Decoin)

1935   *Son autre amour* (Marchard and Remy); *L'Homme à l'oreille cassée* (Boudrioz); *Touche-à-tout* (Dréville)

1936   *Hélène* (Benoît-Levy and Epstein); *Les Petites Alliées* (Dréville); *La Dernière Valse* (Mitler); *La Gondole delle chimera* (Genina)

1937   *Mirages* (Ryder); *Mademoiselle ma mère* (Decoin); *Abus de confiance* (Decoin); *La Mort du cygne* (Benoît-Levy and Epstein)

1938   *Les Filles du Rhone* (Paulin); *Retour à l'aube* (Decoin); *Carrefour* (Bernhardt); *Education de prince* (Esway)

1939   *L'Homme du Niger* (de Baroncelli); *Le Club des soupirants* (Gleize); *Pour le maillot jaune* (Stelli) (co)

1941   *La Vénus aveugle* (Gance); *Ne le criez pas sur les toits* (Daniel-Norman)

1942   *La Belle Aventure* (*Twilight*) (M. Allégret); *Feu sacré* (Cloche and Choux)

1943   *Les Mystères de Paris* (de Baroncelli)

1945   *Etrange destin* (Cuny); *La Route du bagne* (Mathot)

1946   *Rocambole* (de Baroncelli); *La Revanche de Baccarat* (de Baroncelli); *La Colère des dieux* (Lamac); *Dernier refuge* (Maurette); *La Fugitif* (Bibel)

1947   *Carrefour du crime* (Sachs)

1948   *Métier de fous* (Hunebelle); *Suzanne et ses brigands* (Ciampi); *Le Mystère Barton* (Spaak); *Tous les deux* (Cuny); *Les Casse-Pieds* (Dréville)

1949   *La Ronde des heures* (Ryder); *La Valse brillante* (Boyer)

1950   *Banco de prince* (Dulud); *Bille de clown* (Wall); *La Vie chantée* (Noël-Noël); ***Le Journal d'un curé de campagne*** (*Diary of a Country Priest*) (Bresson)

1951   *La Vérité sur Bébé Donge* (Decoin); *La Demoiselle et son revenant* (M. Allégret)

1952   *Mon gosse de Père* (Mathot)

1953   "Riviera-Express" ep. of *Secrets d'alcove* (Habib); *L'Envers du paradis* (Gréville); *La Route Napoléon* (Delannoy); *L'Etrange Désir de Monsieur Bard* (Radvanyi)

1955   *Marianne de ma jeunesse* (Duvivier); *La Madone des sleepings* (Diamant-Berger); *Tant qu'il y aura des femmes* (Gréville); *Vous pigez?* (Chevalier); *Toute la ville accuse* (*Les Mille et un millions*) (Boissol); *Bonjour sourire* (*Sourire aux lèvres*) (Sautet)

1956   *Mon curé chez les pauvres* (Diamant-Berger); ***Un Condamné à mort s'est échappé*** (*Le Vent souffle où il veut*; *A Condemned Man Escapes*) (Bresson)

1957   *Les Fanatiques* (Joffe); *Quand sonnera midi* (Gréville)

1958   *Cette nuit-là* (Cazeneuve)

1959   ***Pickpocket*** (Bresson)

1961   *Un Soir sur la plage* (Boisrond)

1962   *Le Procès de Jeanne d'Arc* (*The Trial of Joan of Arc*) (Bresson)

1963   *Un Drole de paroissien* (Mocky); *Chair de poule* (Duvivier)

1964   *Dernier tiercé* (Pottier)

1966   *Les Compagnons de la marguerite* (Mocky)

Films as Director:

1913   *Les Rapaces diurnes et nocturnes* (short); *L'Industrie du verre* (short); *La Pousse des plantes* (short); *La Floraison* (short)

1922   *La Conquête des Gaules* (co)

1929   *L'Evadée* (co)

1932   *Le Fada*

Publications

By BUREL: articles—

Cinéma (Paris), July-August 1972.
Cinéma (Paris), July-August 1974.
Sight and Sound (London), Winter 1976–77.

On BUREL: articles—

Focus on Film (London), no. 13, 1977.
Cinéma (Paris), May 1977.

*   *   *

A cinematographer is like a chameleon, in that his job is to capture whatever diverse moods and images are required by his director. Abel Gance and Robert Bresson are a pair of directors with profoundly different aesthetics. So, if these two are among the most revered French filmmakers of the pre-*Nouvelle Vague*, then Léonce-Henry Burel (who photographed several of Gance and Bresson's most representative images) must not only be a master of versatility, but one of the greatest of all French cinematographers.

This could be the case if only for longevity: Burel's career spans seven decades, with credits that include a healthy share of French cinema classics from Gance's *Mater Dolorosa* in 1917 and his first version of *J'accuse* in 1919 through Bresson's *Les Procès de Jeanne d'Arc* (*The Trial of Joan of Arc*) in 1962. Indeed, in *The Parade's Gone By . . .* , Kevin Brownlow calls the cinematographer "brilliant;" in his book on the reconstruction of Gance's 1927 epic, *Napoléon* (on which Burel served as a chief cameraman), Brownlow refers to him as "one of the finest cinematographers Europe has ever known."

Burel established his reputation as the photographer of Gance's most important early films, culminating with his work on *Napoléon* as part of a team of cinematographers. Much of Burel's initial collaboration with Gance predates the German Expressionism of the 1920s: in *La Folie du Docteur Tube*, he uses mirrors to create images that are fragmented, abstracted; in close-ups in *Barberousse*, the camera is set below the actor's face, resulting in stark, expressive imagery; in *Mater Dolorosa*, light and shade are utilized to vividly emphasize facial expressions.

J'accuse features images which depict the devastation of war in grand, panoramic terms. It is highlighted by the famous, allegorical "Return of the Dead" sequence, in which thousands of deceased First World War soldiers collectively rise from the battlefields and march off to see if their sacrifices were in vain. Burel's camera captures Gance's vision in vividly eerie detail. And later, in *La Roue*, he stunningly photographs the various objects relating to the film's grimy railroad and snowy mountain settings. They become key elements within each sequence, not simply backgrounds.

Whatever Burel's specific contribution to *Napoléon*, the film remains a landmark of cinematographic innovation. It is crammed with majestic images, including detailed battle sequences, and is a startling example of the creative use of the camera. There is camera movement to imitate a ship in a storm at sea; spectacular lighting; handheld cameras attached to horses, pendulums, even a toboggan; and, finally, color sequences (the latter, according to Georges Sadoul, was Burel's major contribution to *Napoléon*).

As the Gance films feature images that portray reality in expressive, panoramic terms, and that are intended to stir the senses, Burel's films with Robert Bresson (including *Le Journal d'un curé de campagne*, *Un Condamné à mort s'est échappé*, *Pickpocket* and *Le Procès de Jeanne d'Arc*) offer visuals that explore their characters' inner workings. His dusky blacks and glaring greys are perfect accompaniments to Bresson's highly personal vision: pastoral and intimate depictions of reality as a still-life, with the resulting emotion deriving from images that are austere, that evolve from the filmmaker's particular world view.

Burel's work with Bresson is interior and philosophical; here, dialogue and other interaction between the characters, along with the shots of faces and objects that are necessary to Bresson's art, take precedence over compositions that are overtly dramatic. Contrasted with *J'accuse* or *Napoléon*, there is a visual monotony, but that is precisely Bresson's scheme. His concern is the characters and their sensitivities, how they look when they ask questions and give answers.

Burel's own career as a director—he made a trio of features between 1922 and 1932—remains minor. But his work with Gance and Bresson—he also collaborated with a gallery of other filmmakers, including Feyder, Renoir, L'Herbier, Benoit-Levy and Maurice Tourneur—is indicative of his outstanding ability to capture images that fit each filmmakers' diversely varying cinematic vision.

—Rob Edelman

BURKS, Robert

Cinematographer. **Natonality:** American. **Born:** California, 1910. **Career:** 1937–44—special effects photographer at Warners; 1950s-60s—close collaboration with the director Alfred Hitchcock. **Award:** Academy Award for *To Catch a Thief*, 1955. **Died:** In Newport Beach, California, 1968.

Films as Cinematographer:

1944 *Jammin' the Blues* (Mili); *Make Your Own Bed* (Godfrey)
1945 *Escape in the Desert* (Blatt); *Hitler Lives!* (Siegel); *Star in the Night* (Siegel)
1948 *To the Victor* (Daves); *A Kiss in the Dark* (Daves)
1949 *Task Force* (Daves) (co); *The Fountainhead* (King Vidor); *Beyond the Forest* (King Vidor)
1950 *The Glass Menagerie* (Rapper)
1951 *Room for One More* (Taurog); *Close to My Heart* (Keighley); *The Enforcer* (*Murder Inc.*) (Windust); ***Strangers on a Train*** (Hitchcock); *Tomorrow Is Another Day* (Feist); *Come Fill the Cup* (Douglas)
1952 *Mara Maru* (Douglas); *I Confess* (Hitchcock)

1953 *The Desert Song* (Humberstone); *Hondo* (Farrow) (co); *The Boy from Oklahoma* (Farrow); *So This Is Love* (*The Grace Moore Story*) (Douglas)
1954 *Dial M for Murder* (Hitchcock); ***Rear Window*** (Hitchcock)
1955 *To Catch a Thief* (Hitchcock); *The Man Who Knew Too Much* (Hitchcock); *The Trouble with Harry* (Hitchcock)
1956 *The Vagabond King* (Curtiz); *The Wrong Man* (Hitchcock)
1957 *The Spirit of St. Louis* (Wilder) (co)
1958 ***Vertigo*** (Hitchcock); *The Black Orchid* (Ritt)
1959 ***North By Northwest*** (Hitchcock); *But Not for Me* (Walter Lang)
1960 *The Rat Race* (Mulligan); *The Great Impostor* (Mulligan)
1961 *The Pleasure of His Company* (Seaton)
1962 *The Music Man* (da Costa)
1963 ***The Birds*** (Hitchcock)
1964 *Marnie* (Hitchcock)
1965 *Once a Thief* (Nelson); *A Patch of Blue* (Green)
1966 *A Covenant with Death* (Johnson)
1967 *Waterhole #3* (Graham)

Films as Special Effects Photographer:

1937 *Marked Woman* (Bacon) (co)
1940 *Brother Orchid* (Bacon) (co); *A Dispatch from Reuters* (*This Man Reuter*) (Dieterle); *They Drive by Night* (*The Road to Frisco*) (Walsh); *The Story of Dr. Ehrlich's Magic Bullet* (*Dr. Ehrlich's Magic Bullet*) (Dieterle)
1941 *King's Row* (Wood); *Highway West* (McGann)
1942 *In This Our Life* (Huston) (co)
1944 *Arsenic and Old Lace* (Capra) (co)
1945 *Pride of the Marines* (*Forever in Love*) (Daves); *God Is My Co-Pilot* (Florey)
1946 *Night and Day* (Curtiz); *The Verdict* (Siegel)
1947 *The Two Mrs. Carrolls* (Godfrey); *My Wild Irish Rose* (Butler); *Possessed* (Bernhardt); *The Unfaithful* (Sherman); *Cry Wolf* (Godfrey); *The Unsuspected* (Curtiz)
1948 *The Woman in White* (Godfrey); *Key Largo* (Huston) (co); *Romance on the High Seas* (*It's Magic*) (Curtiz); *Smart Girls Don't Talk* (Bare)
1949 *John Loves Mary* (Butler); *The Younger Brothers* (Marin)
1952 *The Miracle of Our Lady of Fatima* (*The Miracle of Fatima*) (Brahm)

Publications

On BURKS: articles—

Film Comment (New York), vol. 8, no. 2, Summer 1972.
Focus on Film (London), no. 13, 1973.

*   *   *

Robert Burks was perhaps Alfred Hitchcock's most important collaborator on the director's films of the fifties and early sixties. To be sure, of the crucial collaborators from this period, such as the film editor George Tomasini and the composer Bernard Herrmann, Burks worked with Hitchcock most consistently. He photographed Hitchcock's films from *Strangers on a Train* (1951) to *Marnie* (1964), with the crucial exception of *Psycho* (1960), for which Hitchcock attempted to achieve a different visual texture by using his television crew. (*Psycho* was photographed by John Russell.) These are the films on which Burks's reputation as a cinematographer largely rests, and what is immediately striking about them is their visual range. Indeed, throughout the fifties, Hitchcock made two distinct types of films. For Paramount, he made big-budget films in color with established stars and crowd-pleasing suspense tactics (*Rear Window*, *The Man Who Knew Too Much*). For the more adventurous Warner Bros. studio, he made films with lower budgets, usually in black-and-white featuring lesser-known actors, and exploring forms of irony and pessimism that became the dominant tones of Hitchcock's late work. Amazingly, Burks was capable of shooting both the bleakly neorealist *The Wrong Man* (1956) and the jubilantly colorful *To Catch a Thief* (1955); both the delicately shaded *Strangers on a Train* and the deliriously deep-toned *Vertigo* (1958).

If this set of films illustrates Burks's range, it is perhaps in the later films that Burks's experiments with color are most audacious. It may well be, of course, that Hitchcock was a decisive influence on these experiments. Certainly nothing in the bland colors Burks provided for Morton da Costa's overblown *The Music Man* (1962) prepares one for the extraordinary palette of *Marnie* with its feverish color contrasts, its nauseous yellows and bile-greens set against burnished or full-hued auburns and blues. The film was much criticized at the time of its release for its presumed visual clumsiness. Now, however, it seems very much a precursor of sixties art-cinema, especially of such a film as Antonioni's *Red Desert* (1966). Moreover, the film's visual distinction lies not only in its play with color but in Burks's manipulation of telephoto and wide-angle lenses, particularly in the climactic flashback scene. Thus *Marnie*, Burks's last film with Hitchcock, emerges as in many ways his most extraordinary achievement.

—James Morrison

BURMAN, S. D.

Composer and Musical Director. **Nationality:** Indian. **Born:** Kumar (Prince) Sachin Dev Burman in Comilla (now in Bangladesh), 1 October 1906. **Education:** Graduated from Calcutta University; studied Indian classical music with Bhishmadev Chatterjee, Badal Khan, Alauddin Khan, and others. **Career:** Served in the court of Maharaja of Tripura; 1932—radio singer on Calcutta station; also made popular recordings of East Bengal folk songs; 1934—small singing role in Urdu film *Selima*; 1937—first film as musical director, *Rajgi*; 1944—settled in Bombay; 1945—composed first songs for film, *Shikari*; compiled collection of Indian folk songs. **Awards:** Sangeet Natak Akademi (Academy of Music and Plays) award, 1957; President of India Padmashree award, 1969; India National Film award for *Aradhana*, 1969; *Zindagi, Zindagi*, 1972. **Died:** In Bombay, 31 October 1977.

Films as Composer and Musical Director:

1937   *Rajgi* (mus d only)
1945   *Shikari*
1946   *Aath Din*
1947   *Chittor Vijay*; *Dil Ki Rani*; *Do Bhai*

1948   *Vidya*
1949   *Kamal*; *Shabnam*
1950   *Asfar*; *Mashal*; *Pyar*
1951   *Baaji*; *Bahar*; *Ek Naujawan*; *Sazaa*
1952   *Jaal*; *Lal Kunwar*
1953   *Arman*; *Babla*; *Jeewan Jyoti*; *Shahen Shah*
1954   *Angarey*; *Chalis Baba Ek Chor*; *Radha Krishna*; *Taxi Driver*
1955   *Davdas*; *House No. 44*; *Madh Bhare Nain*; *Munimji*; *Society*
1956   *Funtoosh*
1957   *Miss India*; *Nao Do Egarah*; *Paying Guest*; *Pyasaa*
1958   *Chalti Ka Naam Gaddi*; *Kala Pani*; *Lajwanti*; *Sitaron Se Aagey*; *Solva Saal*
1959   *Insaan Jag Utha*; **Kaagaz Ke Phool**
1960   *Apna Haath Jaganath*; *Bombai Ka Babu*; *Bewaqoof*; *Ek Ke Baad Ek*; *Kala Bazar*; *Manzil*; *Miya Bibi Raji*
1962   *Baat Ek Raat Ki*; *Dr. Vidya*; *Naughty Boy*
1963   *Bandini*; *Meri Soorat*; *Teri Ankhen*; *Tere Ghar Ke Saamne*
1964   *Benazir*; *Kaise Kahoon*; *Ziddi*
1965   *The Guide*; *Teen Deviyan*
1967   *Jewel Thief*
1969   *Aradhana*; *Jyoti*; *Talash*
1970   *Ishq par Zor Nahin*; *Prem Pujari*
1971   *Gambler*; *Naya Zamana*; *Sharmeelee*; *Tere Mere Sapne*
1972   *Anuraag*; *Yeh Gulistan Hamara*; *Zindagi Zindagi*
1973   *Abhiman*; *Chhupa Rustam*; *Jugnu*; *Phagun*
1974   *Prem Nagar*; *Sagina*; *Us Paar*
1975   *Chupke Chupke*; *Mili*
1976   *Arjun Pandit*; *Baroon*; *Deewanjee*
1977   *Tyaag*

Films as Actor:

1934   *Selima*
1935   *Bidrohi*

Publications

On BURMAN: articles—

Rangoonwalla, Feroze, in *Screen* (Bombay), 4 August 1978.
Rangoonwalla, Feroze, in *Screen* (Bombay), 11 August 1978.
Ragendran, Girija, in *Screen* (Bombay), 27 October 1978.

*   *   *

S. D. Burman migrated to Bombay early in his singing career (1944) and soon climbed to the top, despite the city's cut-throat competition. Burman stayed in Bombay for more than three decades, but he continued to hold Bengal dear and it is from there that he drew his creative sustenance. His childhood exposure to the vast paddy fields and swollen, serpentine rivers of East Bengal and to the folk music of Chittagong and Comilla influenced his slightly nasal, long-drawn style of singing, evoking mood and landscape. His name on a cinema poster or advertisement was enough to guarantee box-office success in the 1950s and beyond.

Burman sang or wrote the music for over 500 songs in Hindi films from Bombay alone, in addition to his numerous recordings in Calcutta and Bombay, and though he amassed a fortune, he remained a humble, unassuming man all his life. His fame in Bombay did not rest on orchestration like Anil Biswas's or on using Indian classical music like Naushad, but on giving haunting and inimitable tunes, rather like Hemanta Mukherjee, to the work of such lyricists as Gopal Singh Nepali, Harikrishna ''Premi,'' Y. N. Joshi, Raja Mehdi Ali Khan, ''Madhukar,'' Anjum Pilibhiti, Prem Dhavan, Qamar Jalalabadi, Narendra Sharma, Rajendra Krishna, Shahir Ludhianvi, Shailendra, Kaifi Azmi, P. L. Santoshi, S. Athaiya, Majrooh Sultanpuri, Gulzar, Hasrat, Shakeel Badayuni, Anand Bakshi, Neeraj, Vijay Anand, Fani Badayuni, and Yogesh.

S. D. Burman's memory will be preserved among millions of his admirers through his lilting tunes, whether it was a melancholy *Bhatiali* of East Bengal or a love song in an indifferent Hindi film. His tunes transcend space and time and transport a listener to a milieu of romance or nostalgia. He took five to six days to decide a tune, test and retest it, before going ahead with the composition. No wonder they abide.

—Bibekananda Ray

BURTT, Ben

Sound Technician. **Nationality:** American. **Born:** Benjamin Burtt Jr., in Syracuse, New York, 1948. **Education:** Attended Allegheny College, Meadville, Pennsylvania, B.S. in physics; University of Southern California film school, Los Angeles, three years. **Career:** Assistant on several Roger Corman films; then sound designer for Lucasfilm: first sound engineering film work on *Star Wars*, 1977; also designed the *Star Wars* radio series sound. **Awards:** Academy Award, for *Star Wars*, 1977, *Raiders of the Lost Ark*, 1981, *E.T.—The Extra-Terrestrial*, 1982, and *Indiana Jones and the Last Crusade*, 1989.

Films as Sound Technician:

1974 *Killdozer* (London)
1977 **Star Wars** (Lucas)
1978 *Invasion of the Body Snatchers* (Kaufman)
1979 *Alien* (Scott)
1980 **The Empire Strikes Back** (Kershner)
1981 **Raiders of the Lost Ark** (Spielberg)
1982 **E.T.—The Extra-Terrestrial** (Spielberg); *The Dark Crystal* (Henson)
1983 **Return of the Jedi** (Marquand); *WarGames* (Badham)
1984 *Indiana Jones and the Temple of Doom* (Spielberg)
1989 *Indiana Jones and the Last Crusade* (Spielberg)
1989 *Always* (Spielberg)
1999 **Star Wars: Episode I—The Phantom Menace** (Lucas) (+ ed)

Other Films:

1986 *The Great Heep* (Smith) (sc)
1990 *Blue Planet* (d)
1992 *The Young Indiana Jones Chronicles* (series for TV) (d)
1994 *Destiny in Space* (d)
1995 *Young Indiana Jones and the Attack of the Hawkmen* (d)
1996 *Special Effects: Anything Can Happen* (d,ed, co-sc)

Publications

By BURTT: article—

Cinefantastique (New York), Spring 1978.
American Cinematographer (Los Angeles), August 1996.

On BURTT: article—

Mancini, Marc, in *Film Comment* (New York), November/December 1983.
Weaver, J.M., in *Skrien* (Amsterdam), February/March 1995.
Garcia, F., in *Cinefantastique* (Forest Park), vol. 28, no. 8, 1997.
Chiarella, Chris, in *Films in Review* (Denville), vol. 48, no. 1–2, January-February 1997.

*   *   *

As head supervisor of Skywalker Sound (formerly Sprocket Systems), Ben Burtt is chiefly known as George Lucas's personal sound designer, creating the now telltale sound effects for Lucas's *Star Wars* trilogy. Equally impressive is Burtt's insistence on using original sounds, or distorting classical sounds through electronic processing. Rather than rely on stock sounds, computers, or synthesizers, Burtt finds his own sounds and reinvents them in the laboratory. This dedication to sounds discovered in the physical world leads Burtt to unusual sources. A *Star Wars* laser blast, for example, is Burtt tapping a radio wire in the Mojave Desert. The rolling boulder in *Raiders of the Lost Ark* is a station wagon coasting down a gravel road. Animals are primary sources for a slew of creatures and machines: Chewbacca's growl, E.T.'s voice, and even a *Star Wars* TIE-Fighter derive from sounds of bears, seals, elephants, dogs, cats, badgers, racoons, lions, and walruses.

Burtt has few peers in his orchestration of jarring, realistic sound effects in large-scale action sequences: the truck chase in *Raiders* has more than 200 camera cuts, and Burtt's attention to nearly every detail—the loud crank of the truck's hood ornament as Indiana Jones pulls it off, the smash of a windshield as a Nazi falls through it— shows he is a precise, gifted editor. But his expertise is in science-fiction/fantasy pictures whose settings and characters are without ''natural'' sounds. The spacecraft and creatures out of *E.T.*, *Alien*, *The Dark Crystal*, and the *Star Wars* films have no voice beyond Burtt's invention.

Rarely is a Burtt sound effect limited to one noise for one event; he prefers mixes—overlapping or sequential effects arranged in a sound montage. These montages vary in length from a split second (the Millenium Falcon's door opening in *Star Wars*) to several minutes (the birth of a pod person in *Invasion of the Body Snatchers*). Many of Burtt's assigned pictures have long passages without dialogue; the only sounds in these sequences come from Burtt and the musician (John Williams is a frequent collaborator), and to a large extent, Burtt's effects have to tell the story. *Body Snatchers* is a prime example: the exhausted heroes have to keep quiet to elude the pod people, who alert each other with a horrifying scream devised by Burtt—the only confirmation of their alien identity.

Burtt is especially adept at creating offscreen action with offscreen sounds. A scene crowded with chattering aliens and futuristic machinery (the cantina in *Star Wars*, Jabba's palace in *Return of the Jedi*, the holding docks in *The Empire Strikes Back*) depends on background noise for ambience and authenticity. In the *Star Wars* pictures,

Burtt creates an intergalactic hubbub so busy and familiar it is irresistibly funny, if a little sophomoric: gluttonous monsters slobber and belch (see also—or hear—The Dark Crystal's infamous banquet scene); Jabba's palace minions hoot and holler at Luke's fight against the Rancor with catcalls, whistles, and yee-hahs; robots beep and argue in languages that need no translation. The background effects in Star Wars almost always suggest an Earthly setting, bridging Lucas's galaxy with our own through an aural similarity.

At times the offscreen sound effects provide more than mere background: they depict actions we cannot see, or supply information withheld from the camera. This dependence on the sound expert to ''fill in'' crucial elements absent from the screen is, of course, fiscally prudent: Yoda's resurrection of Luke's X-Wing Fighter from a bog in Empire is largely conveyed through close-ups of Yoda and a burbling, sloshing sound inserted by Burtt (as well as some stirring music by Williams)—a more cost-effective method than simply air-lifting the whole fighter. But the closeups and the sloshing are also dramatically effective: they leave more to the imagination. In several pictures, Burtt's offscreen montages heighten suspense or inject humor into a scene. They range from a quick fistfight in Indiana Jones and the Temple of Doom—we hear an offscreen Indy punch out a Thuggee guard, who slides on-screen through a group of slave children who had been watching the fight with their mouths open—to Ripley's mad, prolonged scurrying through the corridors of the Nostromo in Alien, accompanied by endlessly overlapping hisses and shudders that both suggest and cloak the sounds of the monster chasing her. The Star Wars radio series, released after Jedi, owes its success entirely to Burtt's mastery of audio drama.

Given Burtt's painstaking technique, it's not surprising that he's a perfectionist who expects theaters to do justice to his effects. Dissatisfied with the poor quality of sound equipment in most theaters showing Jedi, Burtt designed a surround speaker system that more advanced theaters have adopted: all dialogue issues from two speakers in the bottom center of the screen, while a network of speakers all around the theater broadcast the more spectacular sound effects in digital stereo. Although the system is expensive, and not every film can benefit from surround sound—few films are on the massive scale of Lucas's and Spielberg's—a monotrack system quashes many of Burtt's compositions.

Perhaps disenchanted with most theatrical sound systems, Burtt has avoided the feature film industry in recent years, concentrating on such projects as 1990's Blue Planet, an IMAX film released only in those theaters equipped with IMAX screens two stories high. IMAX theaters are a sound expert's dream, featuring a multitrack, floor-rumbling speaker system more complex than Cinerama and twice as loud. A towering IMAX image from Blue Planet, coupled with pristine, undistorted sounds mixed in Burtt's laboratory, inspire awe in the audience, a response as rare as the talents worthy of evoking it. In terms of audio-visual extravagance, Burtt has broken the sound barrier.

—Ken Provencher

BURWELL, Carter

Composer. **Nationality:** American. **Born:** New York, 18 November 1955. **Education:** Harvard, B.A. in Fine Arts; studied computer animation, Massachusetts Institute of Technology; studied computers and music, New York Institute of Technology. **Career:** Played keyboards in band The Same, and toured with David Hykes and The Harmonic Choir, late 1970s-early 1980s; chosen by Joel and Ethan Coen to score their first film, Blood Simple, 1984. **Awards:** Chicago Film Critics Association Award for Best Music, for Fargo, 1996; Los Angeles Film Critics Association Award for Best Music, for Gods and Monsters, 1998. **Agent:** Creative Artists Agency, 9830 Wilshire Blvd., Beverly Hills, CA 90212–1825, U.S.A.

Films as Composer:

1984 Blood Simple (Coen and Coen)
1985 A Hero of Our Time (Almereyda)
1986 Psycho III (Perkins)
1987 Raising Arizona (Coen and Coen)
1988 Pass the Ammo (Beaird); It Takes Two (Beaird); The Beat (Mones)
1989 Checking Out (Leland)
1990 Miller's Crossing (Coen and Coen)
1991 Doc Hollywood (Caton-Jones); Barton Fink (Coen and Coen); Scorchers (Beaird)
1992 Buffy the Vampire Slayer (Kuzui); Waterland (Gyllenhaal); Storyville (Frost)
1993 This Boy's Life (Caton-Jones); Kalifornia (Sena); A Dangerous Woman (Gyllenhaal); And the Band Played On (Spottiswoode—for TV); Wayne's World 2 (Surjik)
1994 It Could Happen to You (Bergman); The Hudsucker Proxy (Coen and Coen); Airheads (Lehmann)
1995 Children Remember the Holocaust (doc) (Gordon); Bad Company (Harris); Rob Roy (Caton-Jones); A Goofy Movie (Lima); The Celluloid Closet (doc) (Epstein and Friedman); Two Bits (Foley)
1996 The Chamber (Foley); Fargo (Coen and Coen); Fear (Foley); Joe's Apartment (Payson)
1997 Girls Night Out (Paci); Picture Perfect (Coron); Assassin(s) (Kassovitz); Conspiracy Theory (Donner); The Locusts (Kelley); The Spanish Prisoner (Mamet); The Jackal (Caton-Jones)
1998 Gods and Monsters (Condon); The Big Lebowski (Coen and Coen); Velvet Goldmine (Haynes); The Hi-Lo Country (Frears)
1999 The Corruptor (Foley); The General's Daughter (West); Being John Malkovich (Jonze); Three Kings (Russell); Mystery, Alaska (Roach)
2000 Hamlet (Almereyda); What Planet Are You From? (Nichols); High Fidelity (Frears)

Publications

On BURWELL: articles—

Herson, Bob, ''Off the Beaten Track,'' in Cineaste (New York), vol. 23, no. 4, 1998.
San, Helen, ''Carter Burwell: Passion Under Pressure,'' at Cinemusic Online, http://www.cinemusic.net/spotlight/1999/cb-spotlight.html, February 1999.

*   *   *

Carter Burwell is among the most chameleonic of modern film composers. Though his music certainly has recognizable traits, his work for the first seven films by Joel and Ethan Coen is greatly varied in style—far from instantly identifiable, at least when compared to the scores of Angelo Badalamenti for David Lynch, or Bernard Herrmann for Alfred Hitchcock (or for anyone else). In the mid-to-late 1990s Burwell has also been among the most prolific of American film composers, averaging five scores per year while working on everything from risk-taking independent films to big summer spectacles—e.g., from *Being John Malkovich* to *Conspiracy Theory*, with *A Goofy Movie* for good measure. One can single out particular musical characteristics of a Burwell score—favorite chord progressions, a fondness for wistful little themes for solo piano or occasionally celesta or the like against soft strings—but perhaps what his scores most have in common is a general "thoughtfulness" and subtlety, compared to the "blast-'em-with-the-big-theme-again" philosophy of many current Hollywood composers. While "self-effacing" would be the wrong term for Burwell, he does appear to subscribe to the classic position that movie music should seldom call attention to itself, but always serve the drama.

A look at the Coen brothers' first three films reveals some of Burwell's range. His first film score, for *Blood Simple* (a noirish thriller with black comedy very close to the Coens' later *Fargo*), is nothing if not understated, but effective in its quiet way. Lightly scored (mainly with a synthesizer), the music is neither conventionally suspenseful nor grotesquely humorous, though there are occasional menacing groaning sounds; more often we hear a pensive sort of solo piano music ("eerie" would be overstating the case). *Raising Arizona* is inventive in completely different ways. The cartoonish and mostly illegal activities of the redneck characters are fittingly accompanied by banjo music of the *Bonnie and Clyde* variety, though with the addition of yodeling vocals and odd bits like a Country version of Beethoven's "Ode to Joy." Yet there are also musical moments that are almost indefinable in mood, though somehow "right," like the abrupt, possibly teasing, synthesizer notes when Nicholas Cage's character is attempting to steal one of the quints. (One might have thought the scene called for the kind of comical suspense music one hears in a Warner Brothers cartoon, but Burwell rarely goes for the conventional.) The historical gangster drama *Miller's Crossing* does not use music for most of its dialogue, and some violent scenes are backed by old-fashioned songs for Irish tenor ("Danny Boy" and "Good Night, Sweetheart") to ironic effect; but Burwell comes up with a stately, very Irish-sounding theme—this is his first orchestral score—for the opening and final credits and some scenes between Tom and Verna, with solo oboe playing a traditional melody and cymbals punctuating the bigger restatements.

As for the Coens' more recent *Fargo*, with its murder spree in Minnesota, the title music, strangely enough, has a medieval or folk flavor, modal with harp and what sound like viols; later drums introduce a bigger, more solemn version of the music in a more definite minor key. Hearing the music alone, one might expect something more along the lines of *Ivanhoe*, but in fact the "medieval" theme will be used again to introduce the crime-solving police officer Marge, and played even as she dines at Hardee's. The film does contain what seems mock-ominous music, as during shots of the Paul Bunyan statue, yet the score as a whole is very far from either suspenseful or satirical in any obvious way, though it does keep a sort of ironic distance from the action. Curiously, it even makes certain scenes (e.g., ones involving Marge) touching that might otherwise seem deliberately ludicrous. Much the same might be said about

Burwell's score for Spike Jonze's *Being John Malkovich*, where the plot itself is sufficiently weird without any need for a joking soundtrack; if anything, the score could be called wistful, as in the puppet music.

Burwell's music for directors besides the Coens is equally varied. For example, Richard Donner's *Conspiracy Theory* is the sort of film that calls for a great deal of soundtrack music, filled as it is with suspense sequences, extensive driving on the streets of New York, and a much more prominent love drama than most thrillers contain. Burwell does offer some fairly typical "thriller music," including one theme with a *Peter Gunn* rhythm for some street scenes, and some jazzy passages that may recall the scores of John Barry, but much of his contribution is extremely subtle. As is often the case for this composer, some of the action scenes are accompanied so deftly (but not softly, and not routinely) that one hardly notices how well the music is doing its job. For the romance between Mel Gibson and Julia Roberts, music is particularly needed to convey the true feelings of the hero, who is extremely inarticulate and motivated by repressed memories; again Burwell's music is stirring without being either sentimental or grandiose.

For Richard Condon's *Gods and Monsters*, about the twilight years of the "forgotten" film director James Whale and his troubled involvement with a young gardener on his estate—a story with echoes of *Death in Venice* and *Sunset Boulevard*—Burwell again avoids heavy sentimentality, especially of the sort which Franz Waxman used for Whale's *The Bride of Frankenstein*, scenes from which are shown in Condon's film. We do get a sad waltz during a dream near the very end, and a solo violin passage that gently connects to the Hermit's playing for the Monster in Whale's movie; but as usual, it is very hard to attach a simple emotional label to most of Burwell's score, whose main theme is more a delicately orchestrated series of chords than an identifiable tune. For certain dramatic scenes late in the film the music editors do seem to have laid on the music rather mindlessly and almost inaudibly, but for the flashbacks and fantasies that Whale (Ian McKellen) slips into, the music is hauntingly appropriate.

In line with what could be called a non-egotistical approach to scoring, Burwell has also proven a successful collaborator and adapter. In a film like *Velvet Goldmine*, about glam-rock musicians of the 1970s, his synthesizer and guitar accompaniments discreetly contribute to the mostly pop score. For *Rob Roy*, he combines his own themes with traditional Celtic music performed by folk specialists. For the Coens' *The Hudsucker Proxy* he features music by Aram Khatchaturian, chiefly the love theme from the ballet *Spartacus* (truly a "big theme" of practically Max Steiner dimensions, with its "Stormy Weather" first notes), for mocking effect. Like film composers of an older generation Burwell is good at evoking exotic settings—but rather than compose in the "Hollywood-Oriental" styles once standard for pictures set in China or the Middle East, he uses authentic instruments and creates unusual pastiches of Western and other music. An example is his score for *The Corruptor*, a Hong-Kong-action-comes-to-NY-Chinatown thriller, featuring actual Chinese stringed instruments and woodwinds but with an American pop-rhythm accompaniment. *Three Kings*, with its Gulf War setting, has an especially eclectic score: it uses Middle Eastern sounds, but also does not hesitate to borrow a chorus from Handel for a drive across the desert. Some stretches of military action have only a drum set accompaniment, while music connected to "treasure" is quiet, with chime-like sounds, later overlaid with Middle Eastern music when the soldiers find the gold.

''Never obvious'' could practically be this composer's motto. For better or worse, there is nothing in Burwell's music like Trevor Jones' stirring main theme for Michael Mann's *Last of the Mohicans*. A recurring theme for *Rob Roy* is about as close as he comes to such a style: a tender melody, first played by folk instruments, but suitable for statement by full orchestra during the film's grander moments. Still, the moody, thoughtful scores he has created for an astonishing variety of films have made him one of the distinguished film composers of his generation.

—Joseph Milicia

CAHN, Sammy

Lyricist. **Nationality:** American. **Born:** Samuel Cohen in New York City, 18 June 1913. **Family:** Married 1) Gloria Delson, 1945 (divorced 1964); one son and one daughter; 2) Tita Curtis, 1970. **Career:** Violinist in vaudeville band, then formed band with Saul Chaplin; lyricist from 1935, often working with composers Jules Styne, Jimmy Van Heusen; 1974—appeared on Broadway in *Words and Music*. **Awards:** Academy Awards for songs ''Three Coins in the Fountain,'' 1954; ''All the Way,'' 1957; ''High Hopes,'' 1959; ''Call Me Irresponsible,'' 1963. **Died:** 15 January 1993.

Films as Lyricist:

1940   *Argentine Nights* (Rogell); *Ladies Must Live* (Smith)
1941   *Time Out for Rhythm* (Salkow); *Go West, Young Lady* (Strayer); *Sing for Your Supper* (Barton); *Rookies on Parade* (Santley); *Two Latins from Manhattan* (Barton); *Honolulu Lu* (Barton)

Sammy Cahn

1942   *Two Yanks in Trinidad* (Ratoff); *Johnny Doughboy* (Auer); *Blondie Goes to College* (Strayer); *Blondie's Blessed Event* (Strayer); *Youth on Parade* (Rogell)
1943   *Crazy House* (Cline); *Lady of Burlesque* (Wellman); *Let's Face It* (Lanfield); *Thumbs Up* (Santley); *The Heat's On* (Ratoff)
1944   *Follow the Boys* (Sutherland); *Knickerbocker Holiday* (Brown); *Jam Session* (Barton); *Carolina Blues* (Jason); *Step Lively* (Whelan); *Jamie* (Curtiz); *A Song to Remember* (C. Vidor); *Tonight and Every Night* (Saville)
1945   *Anchors Aweigh* (Sidney); *The Stork Club* (Walker); *Thrill of a Romance* (Thorpe)
1946   *The Kid from Brooklyn* (McLeod); *Cinderella Jones* (Berkeley); *Earl Carroll Sketchbook* (Rogell); *Tars and Spars* (Green); *The Sweetheart of Sigma Chi* (Bernhard); *It Happened in Brooklyn* (Whorf)
1947   *Ladies Man* (Russell)
1948   *Romance on the High Seas* (Curtiz); *Sons of Adventure* (Canutt); *Two Guys from Texas* (Butler); *Miracle of the Bells* (Pichel)
1949   *It's a Great Feeling* (Butler); *Borderline* (Seiter); *Always Leave Them Laughing* (Del Ruth); *Anna Lucasta* (Rapper)
1950   *Young Man with a Horn* (Curtiz); *The Toast of New Orleans* (Taurog); *The West Point Story* (Del Ruth)
1951   *Rich, Young and Pretty* (Taurog); *Sugarfoot* (Marin); *Two Tickets to Broadway* (Kern); *Double Dynamite* (Cummings)
1952   *April in Paris* (Butler); *She's Working Her Way Through College* (Humberstone); *Stazione Termini* (*Indiscretion of an American Wife*) (De Sica)
1953   *Because You're Mine* (Hall); *Peter Pan* (Luske, Geronimi, and Jackson); *Three Sailors and a Girl* (Del Ruth) (+ pr)
1954   *Three Coins in the Fountain* (Negulesco); *Vera Cruz* (Aldrich)
1955   *The Tender Trap* (Walters); *Love Me or Leave Me* (C. Vidor); *The Court Jester* (Panama and Frank); *Anything Goes* (Lewis); *Pete Kelly's Blues* (Webb); *You're Never Too Young* (Taurog); *How to Be Very, Very Popular* (Johnson); *Ain't Misbehavin'* (Buzzell); *The Seven Year Itch* (Wilder)
1956   *Meet Me in Las Vegas* (Rowland); *Written on the Wind* (Sirk); *Quincannon, Frontier Scout* (Selander); *Serenade* (A. Mann); *Somebody Up There Likes Me* (Wise); *Forever Darling* (Hall); *The Opposite Sex* (Miller) *Pardners* (Taurog); *Beau James* (Shavelson)
1957   *Pal Joey* (Sidney); *The Joker Is Wild* (C. Vidor); *Until They Sail* (Wise); *Ten Thousand Bedrooms* (Thorpe); *Don't Go Near the Water* (Walters); *This Could Be the Night* (Wise)
1958   *The Long Hot Summer* (Ritt); *Indiscreet* (Donen); *Paris Holiday* (Oswald); *Some Came Running* (Minnelli); *Home Before Dark* (LeRoy); *Rock-a-Bye Baby* (Tashlin); *The Sound and the Fury* (Ritt); *Party Girl* (Ray); *Kings Go Forth* (Daves)

1959 *A Hole in the Head* (Capra); *Who Was That Lady?* (Sidney); *The Best of Everything* (Negulesco); *Career* (Anthony); *They Came to Cordura* (Rossen); *This Earth Is Mine* (H. King); *Say One for Me* (Tashlin); *Holiday for Lovers* (Levin); *Journey to the Center of the Earth* (Levin); *Night of the Quarter Moon* (Haas)

1960 *High Time* (Edwards); *Wake Me When It's Over* (LeRoy); *Let's Make Love* (Cukor); *Oceans Eleven* (Milestone); *The World of Suzie Wong* (Quine)

1961 *The Pleasure of His Company* (Seaton); *Pocketful of Miracles* (Capra); *By Love Possessed* (J. Sturges)

1962 *Boys' Night Out* (Gordon); *The Road to Hong Kong* (Panama); *How the West Was Won* (Ford, Marshall, and Hathaway); *Gigot* (Kelly)

1963 *My Six Loves* (Champion); *Papa's Delicate Condition* (Marshall); *Come Fly with Me* (Levin); *Come Blow Your Horn* (Yorkin); *Johnny Cool* (Asher); *Under the Yum Yum Tree* (Swift); *4 for Texas* (Aldrich)

1964 *Robin and the 7 Hoods* (Douglas); *Honeymoon Hotel* (Levin); *Looking for Love* (Weis); *The Pleasure Seekers* (Negulesco); *Where Love Has Gone* (Dmytryk)

1965 *Licensed to Kill* (*The Second Best Secret Agent in the Whole Wide World*) (Shonteff) (song in US version)

1966 *The Oscar* (Rouse); *Texas Across the River* (Gordon)

1967 *The Bobo* (Parrish); *Thoroughly Modern Millie* (Hill); *The Cool Ones* (Nelson); *The Odd Couple* (Saks); *Jack and the Beanstalk* (Kelly)

1968 *Star!* (Wise); *A Flea in Her Ear* (Charon); *Bandolero!* (McLaglen)

1969 *The Great Bank Robbery* (Averback)

1971 *Journey Back to Oz* (Sutherland)

1973 *The Heartbreak Kid* (May); *A Touch of Class* (Frank)

1974 *Paper Tiger* (Annakin)

1975 *Whiffs* (Post); *I Will, I Will . . . for Now* (Panama)

1976 *The Duchess and the Dirtwater Fox* (Frank) (co)

1977 *Fingers* (Toback)

1978 *The Stud* (Masters)

1982 *Heidi's Song* (Taylor—animation)

Publications

By CAHN: book—

I Should Care (autobiography), New York, 1974.

On CAHN: articles—

Craig, Warren, in *The Great Songwriters of Hollywood*, San Diego, California, 1980.

Schwartz, Jonathan, "Call him irreplaceable," in *Gentleman's Quarterly*, July 1991.

Frank, Michael, "Sammy Cahn," in *Architectural Digest*, April 1992.

Obituary in *Variety*, 25 January 1993.

Obituary in *Classic Images* (Muscatine), April 1993.

*   *   *

Sammy Cahn was one of the mainstays of Hollywood's popular music industry during its Golden Age from the 1930s to the 1960s. In a remarkable career from 1942 to 1975 he worked as a lyricist with four different composers to garner some 25 Academy Award nominations for best original song. He won four times and will always be remembered for the words to such popular classics as "Three Coins in the Fountain," "All the Way," and "High Hopes." Cahn proved to be a survivor by adapting to the changing musical tastes of a nation. From the Broadway-inspired musical tunes of the 1940s he moved smoothly to ballads for the 1950s and 1960s.

Songwriter Jules Styne and lyricist Cahn churned out hit after hit during the 1940s. They were one of a select team of composer/lyricists who wrote the year's top ten hits, year in and year out. In the 1940s the movies, by and large, introduced the major popular musical hits, and Styne and Cahn contrived their share for such stars as Frank Sinatra in *Anchors Aweigh* and Danny Kaye in *The Kid from Brooklyn*.

But movie music moved into different forms, and Cahn, ever the professional, adapted. In the 1950s he teamed with Nicholas Brodszky to write several forgettable songs from movies such as *The Toast of New Orleans* and *Love Me or Leave Me*. But with "Three Coins in the Fountain," a major hit in 1953, Cahn's career was off again. The reason was a new partner, Jimmy Van Heusen, and the renewed career of hit-maker Frank Sinatra.

The late 1950s and the early 1960s were a "Golden Age" for Cahn and Van Heusen. Together with Sinatra they provided hit after hit in the face of a revolution in popular music—rock and roll. "All the Way" and "High Hopes" came to be Sinatra standards. Unfortunately the Sinatra rage ended with the coming of the Beatles. Yet Cahn and Van Heusen kept on with the formula music which had worked so well before, and provided the forgettable theme song from the gigantic bust *Star!* Musical idioms had changed and the contributions of Sammy Cahn would fade into the world of nostalgia.

Sammy Cahn, thus, stands as yet another example of the multitude of top professionals who labored to create the great Hollywood movies of the past. Though working in a niche of the business that is not often taken very seriously, Cahn does deserve a note as one of the film industry's (as well as the popular music industry's) great talents.

—Douglas Gomery

CANUTT, Yakima

Stuntman and Second Unit Director. **Nationality:** American. **Born:** Enos Edward Canutt in Colfax, Washington, 29 November 1895. **Family:** Sons: actors/stuntmen Tap and Joe Canutt. **Career:** Ranch hand, then joined wild west show at age 17: became rodeo "world champion"; 1919—first film appearance as actor/stuntman; 1927–35—second unit director for Mascot; 1935–48—head of Republic stunt unit. **Award:** Special Academy Award, 1966. **Died:** In Hollywood, California, 24 May 1986.

Films as Actor/Stuntman:

1919 *Lighting Bryce* (Hurst—serial)

1922 *The Heart of a Texan* (Hurst)

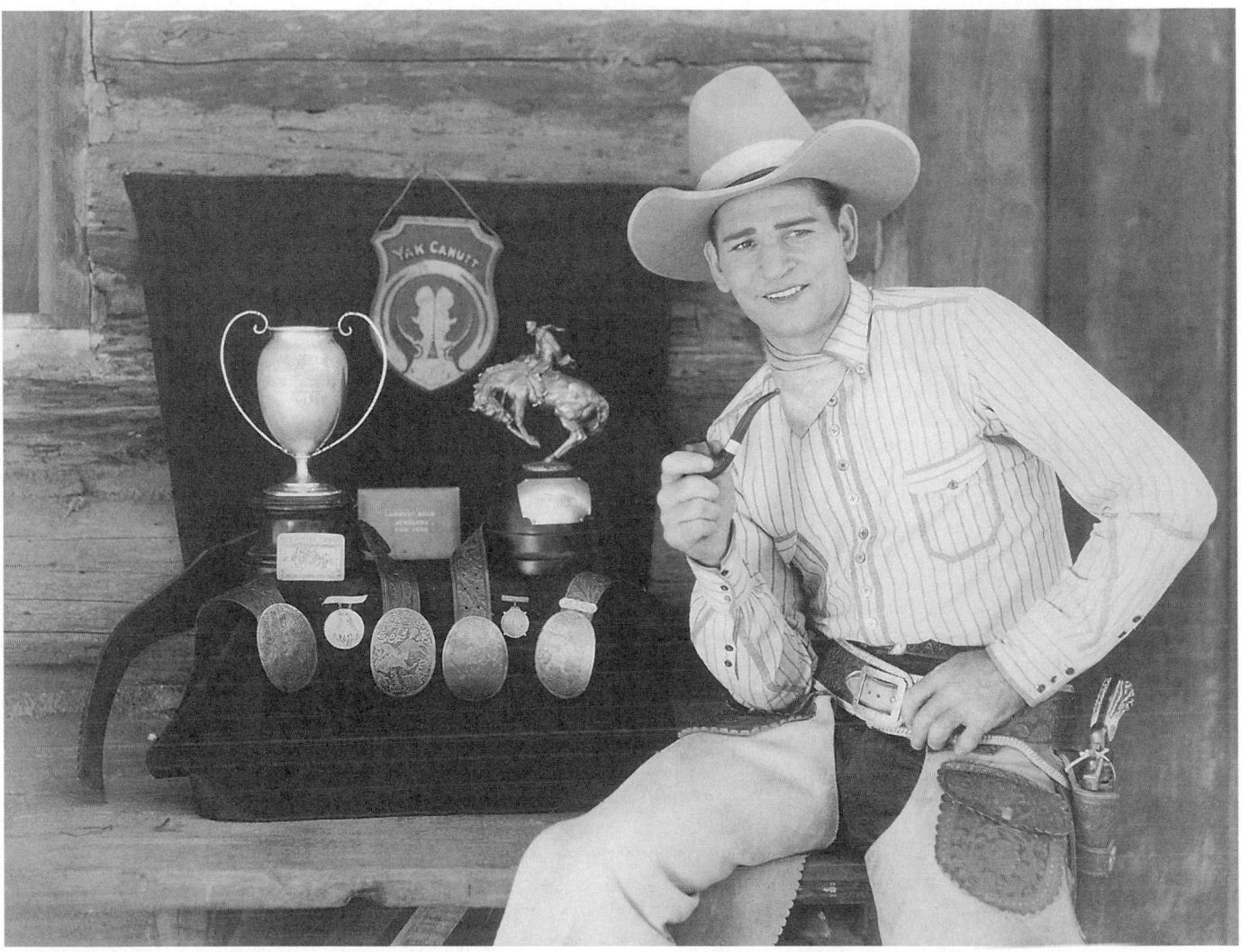

Yakima Canutt

1923 *The Forbidden Range* (Hart)
1924 *The Days of '49* (Jaccard and Marchand—serial; released as feature *California in '49*, 1924); *The Desert Hawk* (De La Mothe); *Ridin' Mad* (Jaccard); *Sell 'em Cowboy* (*Alias Texas Pete Owens*) (Hayes); *Branded a Bandit* (Hurst); *The Riddle Rider* (Craft—serial)
1925 *The Cactus Cure* (Hayes); *Romance and Rustlers* (Wilson); *Scar Hanan* (*The Man with the Scar*) (Wilson, Linden, and Cunliff) (+ co-sc); *Risin' Comet* (Wilson); *A Two-Fisted Sheriff* (Wilson and Hayes); *White Thunder* (*The White Rider*) (Wilson); *Wolves of the Road* (Hayes); *The Strange Rider* (Hayes); *The Human Tornado* (Wilson)
1926 *The Devil Horse* (Jackman); *The Fighting Stallion* (Wilson); *Desert Greed* (*Greed of Gold*) (Jaccard); *Hellhound of the Plains* (Wilson)
1927 *The Outline Breaker* (Jaccard); *Open Range* (Smith)
1928 *The Vanishing West* (Thorpe—serial)
1929 *The Three Outcasts* (Smith) (+ co-sc as Enos Edwards); *Bad Men's Money* (*Mad Man's Money*) (McGowan); *Captain Cowboy* (McGowan); *Riders of the Storm* (McGowan); *A Texan's Honor*

1930 *Firebrand Jordan* (Neitz); *Ridin' Law* (Webb); *Bar L Ranch* (Webb); *The Lonesome Trail* (Mitchell); *Canyon Hawks* (Neitz); *Westward Bound* (Webb); *The Texan* (*The Big Race*) (Smith)
1931 *Hurricane Horseman* (*The Mexican*) (Schaefer); *Pueblo Terror* (*Paradise Valley*) (Neitz); *Battling with Buffalo Bill* (Taylor—serial); *The Fighting Test* (Horner); *The Vanishing Legion* (Eason—serial); *The Lightning Warrior* (Kline and Schaefer—serial)
1932 *Cheyenne Cyclone* (*Smashing Through*) (Schaefer); *Two-Fisted Justice* (Durlan); *Wyoming Whirlwind* (Schaefer); *The Last Frontier* (Bennet—serial; released as feature *The Black Ghost*, 1932); *The Devil Horse* (Brower—serial); *The Shadow of the Eagle* (Beebe—serial); *Hurricane Express* (Schaefer and McGowan—serial); *The Last of the Mohicans* (Eason and Beebe—serial); *Raider of the Golden Gulch* (Smith) (+ co-sc)
1933 *The Telegraph Trail* (Wright); *Law and Lawless* (Schaefer); *The Three Musketeers* (Schaefer and Clark—serial; released as feature *Desert Command*, 1948); *Via Pony Express* (Collins); *Wolf Dog* (Clark and Fraser—serial); *Fighting*

143

Texans (*Randy Strikes Oil*) (Schaefer); *Sagebrush Trail* (Schaefer); *Scarlet River* (Brower); *Battling Buckaroos* (*His Last Adventure*) (Drake); *Fighting with Kit Carson* (Schaefer and Clark—serial); *The Mystery Squadron* (Clark and Howard—serial)

1934   *The Lucky Texan* (Bradbury); *West of the Divide* (Bradbury); *Texas Tornado* (Drake); *Blue Steel* (Bradbury); *The Man from Utah* (Bradbury); *Randy Rides Alone* (Fraser); *The Star Packer* (Bradbury); *Man from Hell* (Collins); *Fighting Through* (Fraser); *'Neath the Arizona Skies* (Fraser); *Carrying the Mail* (Franum and Emmett—short); *The Lost Jungle* (Schaefer and Clark—serial); *Monte Carlo Nights* (Nigh); *The Trail Beyond* (Bradbury); *Burn-'em-Up Barnes* (Clark and Schaefer—serial); *Law of the Wild* (Schaefer and Eason—serial); *Mystery Mountain* (Brower and Eason—serial); *Outlaw Rule* (Luby); *Blazing Guns* (Heinz); *The Desert Man* (Emmett—short); *Pals of the West* (Emmett—short)

1935   *The Lawless Frontier* (Bradbury); *Circle of Death* (London); *Paradise Canyon* (Pierson); *The Dawn Rider* (Bradbury); *Westward Ho* (Bradbury); *Lawless Range* (Bradbury); *Cyclone of the Saddle* (Clifton); *The Farmer Takes a Wife* (Fleming); *The Phantom Empire* (Brower and Eason—serial); *Rough Ridin' Rangers* (*The Secret Stranger*) (Clifton); *Dante's Inferno* (Lachman); *The Fighting Marine* (Eason—serial)

1936   *The Oregon Trail* (Pembroke); *King of the Pecos* (Kane); *The Lonely Trail* (Kane); *Winds of the Wasteland* (Wright); *The Vigilantes Are Coming* (*The Mounties Are Coming*) (Wright and Taylor—serial); *Wildcat Trooper* (*Wild Cat*) (Clifton); *Ghost Town Gold* (Kane); *The Clutching Hand* (Herman—serial); *The Black Coin* (Herman—serial); *Roarin' Lead* (Wright and Newfield); *Rose Marie* (Van Dyke); *Ten Laps to Go* (Clifton); *The Lawless Nineties* (Kane); *The Trail of the Lonesome Pine* (Hathaway); *San Francisco* (Van Dyke); *The Charge of the Light Brigade* (Curtiz); *The Big Show* (Wright)

1937   *The Bold Caballero* (*The Bold Cavalier*) (Root); *The Riders of the Whistling Skull* (*The Golden Trail*) (Wright); *Hit the Saddle* (Wright); *Trouble in Texas* (Bradbury); *Gunsmoke Ranch* (Kane); *Come on Cowboys* (Kane); *The Painted Stallion* (Witney, James, and Taylor—serial); *Range Defenders* (Wright); *Prairie Thunder* (Eason); *Riders of the Rockies* (Bradbury); *Riders of the Dawn* (Bradbury); *Zorro Rides Again* (Witney and English—serial); *The Mysterious Pilot* (Bennet—serial); *In Old Chicago* (H. King); *Rootin' Tootin' Rhythm* (*Rhythm on the Range*) (Wright); *S.O.S. Coastguard* (Witney and James—serial); *Ali Baba Goes to Town* (Butler)

1938   *The Secret of Treasure Island* (Clifton—serial); *The Lone Ranger* (Witney and English—serial); *Heart of the Rockies* (Kane); *Santa Fe Stampede* (G. Sherman); *The Girl of the Golden West* (Leonard); *Heroes of the Hills* (G. Sherman); *Pals of the Saddle* (G. Sherman); *Dick Tracy Returns* (Witney and English—serial); *Overland Stage Raiders* (G. Sherman); *Storm over Bengal* (Salkow)

1939   *Man of Conquest* (Nicholls); *Wyoming Outlaw* (G. Sherman); *The Kansas Terrors* (G. Sherman); *Cowboys from Texas* (G. Sherman); *Zorro's Fighting Legion* (Witney and English—serial); **Gone with the Wind** (Fleming); *Jesse*

James (H. King); *The Lone Ranger Rides Again* (Witney and English—serial); *Dodge City* (Curtiz); *The Night Riders* (G. Sherman); *The Oregon Trail* (Beebe—serial); *Captain Fury* (Roach); *Daredevils of the Red Circle* (Witney and English—serial); *The Light That Failed* (Wellman)

1940   *Pioneers of the West* (Orelbeck); *Ghost Valley Raiders* (G. Sherman); *The Ranger and the Lady* (Kane); *Under Texas Skies* (G. Sherman); *Frontier Vengeance* (Watt); *Young Bill Hickok* (Kane); *Virginia City* (Curtiz); *One Million B.C.* (*Man and His Mate*) (Roach and Roach Jr.); *Shooting High* (Green); *Deadwood Dick* (Horne—serial); *Boom Town* (Conway); *Oklahoma Renegades* (Watt); *Prairie Schooners* (*Through the Storm*) (Nelson)

1941   *Prairie Pioneers* (Orelbeck); *The Great Train Robbery* (Kane); *Gauchos of Eldorado* (Orelbeck); *White Eagle* (Horne—serial); *Western Union* (F. Lang); *Jungle Girl* (Witney and English—serial); *Kansas Cyclone* (G. Sherman); *Bad Man of Deadwood* (Kane); *King of the Texas Rangers* (Witney and English—serial)

1942   *Shadows on the Sage* (Orlebeck); *Spy Smasher* (Witney—serial)

1943   *Pride of the Plains* (Fox); *King of the Cowboys* (Kane); *Santa Fe Scouts* (Bretherton); *Song of Texas* (Kane); *Calling Wild Bill Hickok* (Bennet); *For Whom the Bell Tolls* (Wood)

1944   *Hidden Valley Outlaws* (Bretherton); *Zorro's Black Whip* (Grissell and Bennet—serial); *The Tiger Woman* (*Perils of the Darkest Jungle*) (Bennet and Grissell—serial)

1945   *Sunset in El Dorado* (McDonald)

1950   *The Showdown* (D. & S. McGowan); *Rocky Mountain* (Keighley)

Films as Stuntman and 2nd Unit Director:

1931   *The Galloping Ghost* (Schaefer and Eason—serial)

1939   *Stagecoach* (Ford)

1940   *Dark Command* (Walsh)

1941   *They Died with Their Boots On* (Walsh)

1943   *In Old Oklahoma* (Rogell)

1945   *Flame of Barbary Coast* (Kane); *The Topeka Terror* (Bretherton); *Dakota* (Kane); *Manhunt of Mystery Island* (+ co-d—serial); *Sheriff of Cimarron* (+ d); *Federal Operator 99* (+ co-d—serial)

1946   *Cyclone* (Springsteen); *Under Nevada Skies* (McDonald); *Angel and the Badman* (Grant)

1947   *Twilight on the Rio Grande* (McDonald); *That's My Man* (*Will Tomorrow Ever Come?*) (Borzage); *Northwest Outpost* (*End of the Rainbow*) (Dwan); *Wyoming* (Kane)

1949   *Red Stallion in the Rockies* (Murphy); *Hellfire* (Springsteen); *The Doolins of Oklahoma* (*The Great Manhunt*) (Douglas)

1950   *Devil's Doorway* (A. Mann)

1952   *Last of the Comanches* (*The Sabre and the Arrow*) (De Toth); *Ivanhoe* (Thorpe); *Hangman's Knot* (Huggins)

1955   *The Far Horizons* (Mate)

1957   *Old Yeller* (Stevenson)

1958   *In Love and War* (Dunne)

1959   *Ben-Hur* (Wyler)

1960   *Spartacus* (Kubrick)

1961   *El Cid* (A. Mann)

1962   *How the West Was Won* (Hathaway, Ford, and Marshall)

1966   *Khartoum* (Dearden)
1969   *Where Eagles Dare* (Hutton)
1970   *Rio Lobo* (Hawks)
1975   *Breakheart Pass* (Gries)
1985   *High on the Range*

Other Films:

1947   *G-Men Never Forget* (co-d—serial)
1948   *Dangers of the Canadian Mounted* (co-d); *Oklahoma Bad-
       lands* (d); *Carson City Raiders* (d); *Adventures of Frank
       and Jesse James* (co-d—serial); *Sons of Adventure* (d)
1954   *The Lawless Rider* (d)
1977   *Equus* (Lumet) (technical consultant)

Publications

By CANUTT: book—

Stunt Man: The Autobiography of Yakima Canutt, New York, 1979.

On CANUTT: articles—

Classic Film Collector (Indiana, Pennsylvania), Summer 1967.
Filme Cultura (Rio de Janeiro), November-December 1969.
Ecran (Paris), May 1978.
Classic Images (Indiana, Pennsylvania), May 1984.
Classic Images (Indiana, Pennsylvania), October 1984.
Obituary in *Variety* (New York), 28 May 1986.
Cineforum, vol. 31, no. 304, May 1991.
Rhodes, S., ''Hangin' On,'' in *Filmfax* (Evanston), February/
       March 1994.
Wyatt, E., ''The Lost Films of Yakima Canutt,'' in *Films of the
       Golden Age* (Muscatine), Spring 1997.

*   *   *

In 1966, Yakima Canutt was given a special Academy Award ''for
creating the profession of stuntman as it exists today and for the
development of many safety devices used by stuntmen everywhere.''
Canutt helped legitimize the stuntman, and though he had peers such
as Harvey Parry, Gil Perkins, and Dave Sharpe, it was Canutt whose
work was best known and most widely publicized, largely through his
40-year association with John Wayne. Canutt graduated from stuntman
for the stars to second unit director, staging action scenes for the likes
of John Ford (*Stagecoach*), William Wellman (*The Light That Failed*),
Raoul Walsh (*Dark Command*), and Howard Hawks (*Rio Lobo*), as
well as big-budget spectacles like *Ben-Hur*, *Spartacus*, and *El Cid*.

Canutt came from a rodeo background, and was a star on the Wild
West Show circuits as a teenager. A newspaper labeled him ''The
Cowboy from Yakima (Washington),'' and the nickname stuck.
Canutt's rodeo speciality was bareback bronco riding, helping him
win five world championship cowboy titles. He entered silents doing
unbilled stunts, but quickly became a cowboy star in a series of silent
westerns, performing his own daring stunts. His voice prevented him

from succeeding in talking pictures, and he opted for full-time stunt
work, with occasional bit parts, mostly as Indians or heavies.

Canutt doubled for many stars, including Clarke Gable, Errol
Flynn, Tyrone Power, and Henry Fonda. He first worked with John
Wayne in a 1932 Mascot serial, *The Shadow of the Eagle*, and through
a series of B-westerns for Monogram, helped develop Wayne's
physical persona, teaching him how to fake punches for the screen. He
went to Republic in 1935 with Wayne, and through a score of
westerns doubled Wayne while playing small roles in which he
inevitably tangled in knockdown, drag out fisticuffs with the star.

When Wayne was boosted to the big time with *Stagecoach*, he
recommended Canutt to director John Ford. Canutt was hired to direct
second unit action on the film, as well as perform some of his most
celebrated stunts. In addition to saddle-and-horse falls, Canutt did the
famous transfer stunt (his personal favorite), shot on the flats at
Victorville, California. Playing an Indian, Canutt jumps from his
galloping horse onto the stagecoach team's lead horses then works his
way over six charging team horses towards the carriage. Wayne
shoots him, he falls between the horses, is dragged along the ground at
full speed, then finally drops to the ground as stage and horses pass
over him. As second unit director, Canutt staged the sequence of the
stagecoach in the river crossing. Miraculously, Canutt emerged
unhurt, although he did suffer injuries doubling for Gable on *San
Francisco* (six broken ribs while saving a panicked stuntwoman) and
Boom Town (a punctured lung when he was tossed from a wagon into
a bass drum). Canutt also doubled for Gable as Rhett Butler in the
burning of Atlanta sequence for *Gone with the Wind*, and played a bit
as a renegade who terrorizes Vivien Leigh.

Canutt had staged action for directors as early as his starring role in
The Devil Horse with Rex, King of the Wild Horses, and after
Stagecoach, he concentrated in this area. He handled second unit for
Raoul Walsh on the westerns *Dark Command* (featuring a spectacular
cliff jump by Canutt and three other stuntmen) and *They Died with
Their Boots On* (in which Canutt doubled Flynn for Custer's Last
Stand and helped supervise the battle sequence). Republic hired him
as a director in 1944 and assigned him B-westerns with Sunset
Carson, Rocky Lane, and Clayton Moore. After four years of low
budgets, Canutt signed as second unit director with MGM.

Canutt found his forte as a second unit action man, and in this
capacity was responsible for some of the best action sequences of the
1950s and 1960s. He specialized in medieval epics (Richard Thorpe's
Ivanhoe, Anthony Mann's *El Cid*) and biblical spectacles (William
Wyler's *Ben-Hur*, Stanley Kubrick's *Spartacus*). His most memora-
ble set pieces include the jousts in *Ivanhoe* and *El Cid*; the sieges in *El
Cid* and Basil Dearden's *Khartoum*; the revolt of the slaves in
Spartacus; the attack on the Nazi fortress in Brian Hutton's *Where
Eagles Dare*; and especially the celebrated chariot race between
Charlton Heston and Stephen Boyd in *Ben-Hur*.

—John A. Gallagher

CARDIFF, Jack

Cinematographer and Director. **Nationality:** British. **Born:** Yarmouth,
Norfolk, England, 18 September 1914. **Family:** Married; three sons.
Career: Child actor from age four to fourteen. 1928—joined British

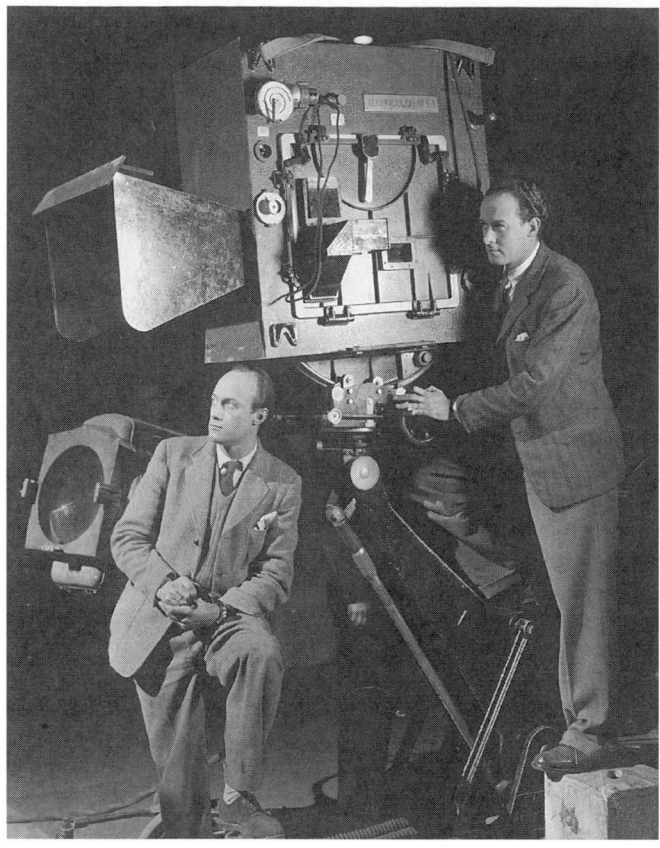

Jack Cardiff (left) with Geoffrey Unsworth

International as runner and general assistant; expert on color photography by 1935; 1940s—made first films as cinematographer; worked for Crown Film Unit during World War II; 1958—first film as director, *Intent to Kill*; television work includes the mini-series *The Far Pavilions* and *The Last Days of Pompeii*, both in 1984. **Awards:** Academy Award, for *Black Narcissus*, 1947; Golden Globe, Directors' Guild of America and New York Critics' awards, for *Sons and Lovers*, 1960; International award, American Society of Cinematographers, for Outstanding Achievement, 1994. **Address:** c/o L'Epine Smith and Carney Associates, 10 Wyndham Place, London W1H 1AS, England.

Films as Cinematographer:

1937–40 *World Window* (*Rome Symphony*; *The Eternal Fire*; *Fox Hunting the Roman Compagna*; *Jerusalem*; *Petra*; *Wanderers of the Desert*; *Arabian Bazaar*; *Ruins of Palmyra and Baalbek*; *A Road in India*; *River Thames—Yesterday*; *Indian Temples*; *Jungle*; *Delhi*; *The Sacred Ganges*; *A Village in India*; *Indian Durbar*) (Gentilomo, Francisci, Nieter, Blasetti, and Hanau—docs)
1938 *Paris on Parade* (Fitzpatrick—short)
1939 *Main Street of Paris* (Bernard—short)
1940 *Peasant Island* (Taylor—short)
1941 *Green Girdle* (Keene—short); *Queen Cotton* (Musk—short); *Western Isles* (Bishop—short); *Plastic Surgery in Wartime* (Sainsbury—short)

1942 *Colour in Clay* (Catling—short); *Border Weave* (Curthoys—short); *Out of the Box* (Bishop—short); *The Great Mr. Handel* (Walker) (co); *This Is Colour* (Ellitt—short); ***The Life and Death of Colonel Blimp*** (*Colonel Blimp*) (Powell and Pressburger)
1943 *Scottish Mazurka* (Nieter—short)
1944 *Western Approaches* (*The Raider*) (Jackson); *Steel* (Riley—short) (co)
1945 *Caesar and Cleopatra* (Pascal) (co)
1946 ***A Matter of Life and Death*** (*Stairway to Heaven*) (Powell and Pressburger)
1947 ***Black Narcissus*** (Powell and Pressburger)
1948 ***The Red Shoes*** (Powell and Pressburger); *Scott of the Antarctic* (Frend) (co)
1949 *Under Capricorn* (Hitchcock)
1950 *The Black Rose* (Hathaway); *Montmartre* (Bernard—short)
1951 *Montmartre Nocturne* (Bernard—short); *Paris* (Bernard—short); *Pandora and the Flying Dutchman* (Lewin); *The Magic Box* (J. Boulting); ***The African Queen*** (Huston)
1952 *It Started in Paradise* (Bennett)
1953 *The Master of Ballantrae* (Keighley)
1954 *Il maestro di Don Giovanni* (*Crossed Swords*) (Krims); *The Barefoot Contessa* (Mankiewicz)
1956 *War and Peace* (K. Vidor); *The Brave One* (Rapper)
1957 *Legend of the Lost* (Hathaway); *The Prince and the Showgirl* (Olivier)
1958 *The Vikings* (Fleischer); *The Diary of Anne Frank* (Stevens) (co)
1959 *The Journey* (Litvak)
1960 *Fanny* (Logan)
1968 *The Girl on a Motorcycle* (*Naked under Leather*; *La Motocyclette*) (+ d, co-sc)
1973 *Scalawag* (Douglas)
1976 *Ride a Wild Pony* (Chaffey)
1978 *Death on the Nile* (Guillermin); *The Prince and the Pauper* (*Crossed Swords*) (Fleischer)
1981 *Ghost Story* (Irvin); *The Dogs of War* (Irvin)
1983 *Scandalous* (Cohen); *Wicked Lady* (Winner)
1984 *Conan the Destroyer* (Fleischer)
1985 *Cat's Eye* (Teague); *Rambo: First Blood, Part II* (Cosmatos)
1986 *Tai-Pan* (Duke)
1987 *Million Dollar Mystery* (Fleischer)
1988 *Call from Space* (Fleischer)
1989 *Magic Balloon* (Neame)
1991 *Vivaldi's Four Seasons*
1998 *The Dance of Shiva* (Payne)

Films as Director:

1958 *Intent to Kill*
1959 *Beyond This Place* (*Web of Evidence*)
1960 *Scent of Mystery* (*Holiday in Spain*); *Sons and Lovers*
1961 *My Geisha*
1962 *The Lion*; *Satan Never Sleeps* (additional segments only)
1963 *The Long Ships*
1964 *Young Cassidy*
1965 *The Liquidator*
1967 *The Mercenaries* (*Dark of the Sun*)

1973   *Penny Gold*
1974   *The Mutations*

Other Films:

1929   *The Informer* (Robison) (asst)
1930   *Loose Ends* (Walker) (asst)
1935   *The Ghost Goes West* (Clair) (cam)
1936   *As You Like It* (Czinner) (cam); *Wings of the Morning* (Schuster) (cam)
1937   *Knight without Armor* (Feyder) (cam)

Publications

By CARDIFF: articles—

On *Under Capricorn* in *American Cinematographer* (Hollywood), October 1949.
On *The Black Rose* in *American Cinematographer* (Hollywood), November 1950.
Screen International (London), 7 February 1976.
Time Out (London), 1–7 August 1985.
Cinématographe (Paris), no. 117, March 1986.
American Cinematographer (Hollywood), March 1990.
American Cinematographer (Hollywood), March 1994.

On CARDIFF: articles—

Lightman, Herb A., on *The Red Shoes* in *American Cinematographer* (Hollywood), March 1949.
Edwards, M., in *Sight and Sound* (London), Summer 1951.
Cinéma (Paris), 1 November 1952.
Hill, Derek, in *American Cinematographer* (Hollywood), December 1956.
Cinéma (Paris), February 1968.
Filme Cultura (Rio de Janeiro), April/May 1970.
Focus on Film (London), no. 13, 1973.
Luft, Herbert G., in *Films in Review* (New York), April 1974.
Films Illustrated (London), August 1974.
Reiss, D.S., in *Filmmakers Monthly* (Ward Hill, Massachusetts), March 1981.
In Camera (Hemel Hempstead, Hertfordshire), Spring 1990.
Filmfax (Evanston), April-May 1993.
Eyepiece (Greenford), vol. 15, no. 6, 1994/1995.

*   *   *

Like Freddie Francis, Jack Cardiff made the transition from director of photography to director in the 1960s and gradually drifted back to his old job in the 1970s and 1980s, leaving behind him an interesting but not especially successful body of directorial work, from the prestige of *Sons and Lovers* (for which, ironically, Francis won an Oscar for best cinematography) through the trendy idiocy of *The Girl on a Motorcycle* (also known, in honor of Marianne Faithfull's fetishist introductory scene, as *Naked under Leather*) to the grotesque mad-scientist melodrama of *The Mutations* (a horror movie a good deal freakier, funnier, stupider, and trashier than Francis's run of professional and faintly stodgy contributions to the

genre). Otherwise, Cardiff the director seemed mainly there to collect scraps from the table: allowed to finish *Young Cassidy* when John Ford fell ill, and doing what he could with the mismatch of Rod Taylor and Julie Christie in a project that meant a lot to Ford and nothing apparently to Cardiff; permitted to make in *The Long Ships* a sequel to *The Vikings*—a film he had photographed—and failing to match Richard Fleischer's bold swashbuckling approach to the original; stepping in to do additional sequences for *Satan Never Sleeps*, the ailing Leo McCarey's last film; stuck with the standing joke of *Scent of Mystery*, a gimmick attempt to introduce Odorama to the cinema 20 years before *Polyester*, with various smells and perfumes pumped into the auditorium to coincide with the on-screen action; and yet again unable to make Rod Taylor seem charismatic in the cut-price Bond imitation *The Liquidator*, although Cardiff and Taylor both seem to have been uncharacteristically enthused by *Dark of the Sun*.

Once the directorial doodles have been set aside, Cardiff has one of the most impressive records of pictorial achievement in the cinema, starting as a camera operator and second unit cameraman with Korda and the Archers in the 1930s—working on *Knight without Armor*, *The Ghost Goes West*, the early Technicolor *Wings of the Morning* (Britain's first full-color film), and *The Life and Death of Colonel Blimp* before being promoted to director of photography with the documentary *Western Approaches* and the lavish, prestigious, slightly boring *Caesar and Cleopatra*. He first made himself noticed, however, with three color masterpieces for Michael Powell and Emeric Pressburger, *A Matter of Life and Death*, *Black Narcissus*, and *The Red Shoes*. Here, in an atmosphere of fantasy, violence, and eroticism, Cardiff was allowed a very un-English lack of restraint, and came through with a procession of images that go beyond the chocolate-box prettiness of Technicolor into very dangerous areas indeed, especially in the striking use of strong reds—the scarlet of Kathleen Byron's dress and lipstick in *Narcissus*, the shoes themselves in *The Red Shoes*—and a knack for making unconventional beauties into screen goddesses. Kim Hunter, a most unlikely candidate, looks extraordinary in uniform in *A Matter of Life and Death*, and the later films find turbulent depths in the cool exteriors of Deborah Kerr and Kathleen Byron, all the more disturbing since they are supposed to be playing nuns, and Moira Shearer. Unsurprisingly, Cardiff would later be called in to highlight the faces and figures of Ava Gardner (*Pandora and the Flying Dutchman*, *The Barefoot Contessa*), Audrey Hepburn (*War and Peace*), Marilyn Monroe (*The Prince and the Showgirl*), Sophia Loren (*Legend of the Lost*), Janet Leigh (*The Vikings*) and Leslie Caron (*Fanny*).

After his period with the Archers, Cardiff became a prestige international director of photography, especially adept at American productions with a European or period flavor. *Under Capricorn*, for Alfred Hitchcock, is labyrinthine and elegant, the Hollywood Englishman calling upon some of the innovations of the Archers to reinvigorate his Selznicked-to-the-ground studio style. *Pandora*, directed by the delirious Albert Lewin with unrestrained Ava and uptight Flying Dutchman James Mason, is three degrees steamier even than *Black Narcissus*, to the point when its magic, eroticism, and monomania is almost, but not quite, ludicrous. *The African Queen*, made in color under grueling conditions, is unfussy about its exotic backgrounds, spirited in its action, and modestly competent when it comes to keeping its unglamorized stars center screen and registering the nuances of their performances. If some of the 1950s "big pictures"—*The Magic Box*, *The Prince and the Showgirl*, *War and Peace*, *The Journey*, *The Brave One*—look stuffy today, that has more to do with the then-prevalent ideas of "quality" than with any inherent limitations in Cardiff's approach. And before temporarily abandoning the camera for the megaphone, Cardiff did do his best for *The Vikings*, a still-underrated classic of the demented melodrama following up Cardiff's work on *The Black Rose* and *The Master of Ballantrae*. Here, Cardiff captured Kirk Douglas walking on the oars, Ernest Borgnine jumping into a pit of starving wolves, Tony Curtis ripping Janet Leigh's dress so she can row better, and plenty of *Boys' Own* boat and swordplay.

Returning in the 1970s and 1980s as a photographer, Cardiff found himself on familiar ground—swashbuckling and faraway places—with *Scalawag*, *The Prince and the Pauper*, *Death on the Nile*, and *Conan the Destroyer*, then perhaps recaptured some of the discomfort of *The African Queen* and sadomasochistic action man feel of *The Vikings* in *Rambo: First Blood, Part II*, in which he followed Stallone's glistening torso through mud, blood, leeches, machine gun bandoliers, electric torture, and nonstop jungle engagements. It was as if he had never been away.

—Kim Newman

CARMICHAEL, Hoagy

Composer. **Nationality:** American. **Born:** Hoagland Howard Carmichael in Bloomington, Indiana, 22 November 1899. **Education:** Studied Law at Indiana University, Bloomington. **Family:** Married Ruth Mary Meinardi, 1936; two sons. **Career:** Law practice; then band leader, songwriter, and arranger; 1924—first recorded song; 1936—songs for first film, *Anything Goes*; also composer for Broadway, and performer on radio from 1944, and in films and TV. **Award:** Academy Award for song ''In the Cool Cool Cool of the Evening,'' 1951. **Died:** 27 December 1981.

Films as Composer:

1936   *Anything Goes* (Milestone)
1938   *Every Day's a Holiday* (Sutherland); *College Swing* (Walsh); *Sing, You Sinners* (Ruggles)
1941   *Road Show* (Roach Jr., and Douglas)
1942   *Mr. Bug Goes to Town* (Fleischer)
1943   *True to Life* (Marshall)
1944   *To Have and Have Not* (Hawks) (+ ro)
1945   *Johnny Angel* (Martin) (+ ro); *The Stork Club* (Walker) (+ ro)
1946   *Canyon Passage* (Tourneur) (+ ro); ***The Best Years of Our Lives*** (Wyler) (+ ro)
1947   *Night Song* (Cromwell) (+ ro)
1950   *Johnny Holiday* (Holdbeck) (+ ro)
1951   *Here Comes the Groom* (Capra)
1952   *Belles on Their Toes* (Levin) (+ ro); *The Las Vegas Story* (Stevenson) (+ ro)
1953   *Gentlemen Prefer Blondes* (Hawks)
1955   *Timberjack* (Kane) (+ ro); *Three for the Show* (Potter)

Film as Actor:

1950   *Young Man with a Horn* (Curtiz)

Publications

By CARMICHAEL: books—

The Stardust Road, New York, 1948.
With Stephen Longstreet, *Sometimes I Wonder*, New York, 1965.

On CARMICHAEL: books—

Hoagy Carmichael: Stardust Memories, Miami, 1985.
Hasse, John E., *The Classic Hoagy Carmichael*, Indianapolis, 1988.
Bradley, Arthur, *Silver Threads*, El Paso, 1994.

On CARMICHAEL: articles—

Picturegoer (London), 18 January 1947.
The Listener (London), 11 December 1975.
Obituary in *Films & Filming*, March 1982.
Furness, Adrian, in *TV Times* (London), 14–20 August 1982.
Hemming, Roy, in *The Melody Lingers On: The Great Songwriters and Their Movie Musicals*, New York, 1986.
Zinsser, William, ''From Natchez to Mobile, from Memphis to St. Joe,'' in *American Scholar*, Spring 1994.

*   *   *

Hoagy Carmichael

Born in Bloomington, Indiana, into a rich and privileged background, Hoagy Carmichael first studied law and even undertook a law practice for a brief period until a chance meeting with the legendary jazz pianist and cornet player, Bix Beiderbecke, completely bowled him over. He took up his musical career then and there, playing piano with Jean Goldkette's band. He never had a formal music lesson in his life—he simply played by ear. Carmichael went on to compose great classics like "Stardust," "Rockin' Chair," "Georgia on My Mind," "Old Buttermilk Sky," "Skylark" and "Lazy Bones." Carmichael's drawling style of singing derived from a black jazz tradition. His phrasing was so very effortless, so lazy, that when he sang, it was Beale Street or Bourbon Street come to bluesy life.

In the 1940s Hoagy Carmichael went to Hollywood where he wrote film tunes as well as making screen appearances (often as a piano-playing character complete with hat over his eyes, a match stuck between his lips and sitting slouched at the keyboard—an image as memorable as that of Dooley Wilson, ("Sam" in *Casablanca*) in such films as *To Have and Have Not*, *Johnny Angel*, *The Best Years of Our Lives* and *Young Man with a Horn* (inspired by Beiderbecke), *Night Song*, *The Las Vegas Story*, *Belles on Their Toes* and *Timberjack*. His role in the movie *Canyon Passage* made his lean face familiar to millions. In the film he wore a top hat while singing his own composition "Old Buttermilk Sky." He wrote the memorable "In the Cool Cool Cool of the Evening" performed by Bing Crosby for *Here Comes the Groom* which won an Academy Award in 1951.

Carmichael, like Irving Berlin, Richard Rodgers and Cole Porter, has become a household name in the English-speaking world. He had a knack for writing songs which were both memorable and freshsounding and on the occasions when he did collaborate with lyricists, his choice was always impeccable—Johnny Mercer and Sammy Lerner were among his partners. His most famous song was the heavenly "Stardust" which he wrote while still a struggling lawyer. He scribbled the song on the front pages of a lawbook while waiting for business in Florida but he did not get it recorded till several years later. "I figured there ought to be work for a good lawyer because there was all that selling and reselling going on. There probably was too—only I wasn't a good lawyer. A note, to me, was something that belonged on a musical staff. . . ." His death in 1981 was a great loss to American popular music and film.

—Sylvia Paskin

CARRÉ, Ben

Art Director. **Nationality:** French. **Born:** Paris, 1883; emigrated to the United States, 1912. **Education:** Studied scenic painting at Atelier Amable studios, Paris. **Family:** Married Ann (Carré). **Career:** 1901–06—scene painter at Paris Opéra, Comédie Française, and other theatres; 1906–12—designer and scene painter for Pathé Gaumont Studios, Paris; 1912–18—designer for Eclair Studios, Fort Lee, New Jersey; associated with Maurice Tourneur; 1918–37—art director for various Hollywood studios; 1937–69—background designer and painter for MGM; 1964—designed murals for General Motors Pavilion, New York World's Fair; 1969—retired to become easel painter. **Died:** In Hollywood, California 28 May 1978.

Films as Art Director:

1907 *La Course aux potirons* (*The Pumpkin Race*) (Cohl)
1909 *Le Huguenot* (Feuillade); *La Mort de Mozart* (Feuillade)
1910 *Le Festin de Balthazar* (Feuillade)
1911 *Aux lions les chrétiens* (Feuillade)
1914 *The Dollar Mark* (Lund); *Mother* (Tourneur); *The Man of the Hour* (Tourneur); *The Wishing Ring* (Tourneur); *The Pit* (Tourneur)
1915 *Alias Jimmy Valentine* (Tourneur); *Hearts in Exile* (Young); *The Boss* (Chautard); *The Ivory Snuff Box* (Tourneur); *A Butterfly on the Wheel* (Tourneur); *The Pawn of Fate* (Tourneur); *Camille* (Capellani)
1916 *A Girl's Folly* (Tourneur); *The Hand of Peril* (Tourneur); *The Closed Road* (Tourneur); *La Vie de Bohème* (Capellani); *The Rail Rider* (Tourneur); *The Velvet Paw* (Tourneur); *The Dark Silence* (Capellani); *The Deep Purple* (Young); *The Rack* (Chautard)
1917 *Trilby* (Tourneur); *The Cub* (Tourneur); *The Undying Flame* (Tourneur); *The Whip* (Tourneur); *The Law of the Land* (Tourneur); *Exile* (Tourneur); *Barbary Sheep* (Tourneur); *The Rise of Jenny Cushing* (Tourneur); *The Pride of the Clan* (Tourneur); *Poor Little Rich Girl* (Tourneur)
1918 *The Blue Bird* (Tourneur) (co); *Rose of the World* (Tourneur); *Prunella* (Tourneur) (co); *A Doll's House* (Tourneur); *Woman* (Tourneur); *Sporting Life* (Tourneur)
1919 *The White Heather* (Tourneur); *The Life Line* (Tourneur); *Victory* (Tourneur); *The Broken Butterfly* (Tourneur)
1920 *Stronger than Death* (Bryand and Blanché); *The River's End* (Neilan); *In Old Kentucky* (Neilan and Green); *Go and Get It* (Neilan and Symonds); *For the Soul of Rafael* (Garson); *My Lady's Garter* (Tourneur); *Treasure Island* (Tourneur) (co)
1921 *Don't Ever Marry* (Neilan and Heerman); *Dinty* (Neilan and McDermott); *Man, Woman, and Marriage* (Holubar); *Bob Hampton of Placer* (*Custer's Last Stand*) (Neilan); *The Wonderful Thing* (Brenon)
1922 *The Light in the Dark* (Brown); *When the Desert Calls* (Smallwood) *Queen of the Moulin Rouge* (Smallwood); *What Fools Men Are* (Terwilliger)
1923 *Wife in Name Only* (Terwilliger)
1924 *Thy Name Is Woman* (Niblo); *The Goldfish* (Storm); *Cytherea* (*The Forbidden Way*) (Fitzmaurice); *Tarnish* (Fitzmaurice); *The Red Lily* (Fitzmaurice); *In Hollywood with Potash and Perlmutter* (*So This Is Hollywood*) (Green)
1925 *Lights of Old Broadway* (*Merry Wives of Gotham*) (Bell); **The Phantom of the Opera** (Julian) (co); *The Masked Bride* (Cabanne and von Sternberg) (co)
1926 *Mare Nostrum* (Ingram); *La Bohème* (K. Vidor) (co); *The Book* (*The Yokel*) (Wellman) (co); *Don Juan* (Crosland); *The Better 'ole* (Reisner); *My Official Wife* (Stein); *When a Man Loves* (Crosland)
1927 *The King of Kings* (DeMille) (co); *Old San Francisco* (Crosland); *Soft Cushions* (Cline); **The Jazz Singer** (Crosland)
1928 *The Red Dance* (*The Red Dancer of Moscow*) (Walsh); *The River Pirate* (Howard); *The Air Circus* (Hawks and Seiler)
1929 *The Iron Mask* (Dwan) (co); *The Woman from Hell* (Erickson); *The Valiant* (Howard); *The Cockeyed World* (Walsh); *Frozen Justice* (Dwan); *Hot for Paris* (Walsh) (co)

1930   *City Girl* (Murnau) (co); *River's End* (Curtiz)
1931   *Women of All Nations* (Walsh) (co); *The Black Camel*
         (MacFadden); *Riders of the Purple Sage* (MacFadden)
1933   *Sailor's Luck* (Walsh)
1935   *Dante's Inferno* (Lachman) (co); *A Night at the Opera*
         (Wood) (co)
1936   *Let's Sing Again* (Neumann); *The Mine with the Iron Door*
         (Howard) (co); *Great Guy* (Blystone)
1937   *231/2 Hours Leave* (Blystone)

Publications

By CARRÉ: articles—

Film Comment (New York), May-June 1978.
Griffithiana, no. 44/45, May/September 1992.

On CARRÉ: articles—

Everson, William K., in *Films in Review* (New York), November 1977
Hambley, John, (ed.), in *The Art of Hollywood*, London, 1979.
Brownlow, Kevin, in *Sight and Sound* (London), Winter 1979–80.
Brownlow, Kevin, ''Ben Carré,'' in *Griffithiana* (Gemona, Italy),
     September 1988.
Positif (Paris), no. 344, October 1989.
Brownlow, Kevin, ''Ben Carré,'' in *Griffithiana,* May-September 1992.

*   *   *

Ben Carré had one of the longest careers in the history of cinema. He began his movie career as a contemporary of Méliès, Lumière, and Emile Cohl, and retired in 1969 at the age of 82. For 63 years he applied his classical training in painting and practical experience in theatre design to the production of French and American films. His expertise in *trompe l'oeil* painting techniques provided the early French cinema with a depth and locale the studio productions otherwise lacked. Reportedly to enliven the actors' performances, he provided sets in full color, an uncommon practice since everything was photographed in black-and-white. During the mid-1930s, Carré withdrew from his prominent role as art director because of ill health and contented himself with background painting. He also experimented with miniatures and glass paintings, and created many vivid and memorable images, especially the Emerald City in *The Wizard of Oz*, the Smith house in *Meet Me in St. Louis*, and the numerous Impressionist settings for the climactic ballet of *An American in Paris.*

Carré was also one of the first (if not *the* first) Hollywood art directors. He created opulent and picturesque sets which alternated between extreme realism and bold abstraction. His 34-film collaboration with Maurice Tourneur during the 1910s represented the major peak of his career. As William K. Everson said: ''Their early work together, combining stylized pictorial inventiveness with tasteful, charming storytelling, represents one of the most felicitous teamings of visual talents in all film history.'' Overseeing every aspect of set production for Tourneur, Carré displayed the first cohesive sense of film design seen in Hollywood and possibly the world. Films ranging from *The Pawn of Fate* and *The Hand of Peril*, through *Trilby, Poor*

Little Rich Girl, and *The Blue Bird*, to *Treasure Island* demonstrate the two styles associated with Carré. He was best at visualizing the fantastic, employing highly stylized sets, shadowy backgrounds, glass paintings, and miniatures in an expressionistic manner. The sets for *Poor Little Rich Girl* and *The Blue Bird* seem to anticipate German Expressionism by suggesting a character's interior perspective through light and decor. Yet his designs for *Pawn of Fate* (an entire farm in Normandy), *Trilby* (the backstreets of Paris), and *The Hand of Peril* (a nine-room apartment set) successfully achieved a realism which influenced Rex Ingram and Erich von Stroheim.

The film most closely associated with Carré's name is *The Phantom of the Opera*. Combining imagination with a fond memory of the Paris Opéra, he created the haunting subterranean chambers inhabited by the Phantom. The film summarizes his encompassing talents by merging opposing sensibilities: concrete physical reality with a stylized netherworld of horror. Carré's retirement to easel painting provided a fitting closure to a career of great significance, one that is just recently being reevaluated.

—Greg S. Faller

CARRERAS, (Sir) James

Producer. **Nationality:** British. **Born:** 30 January 1909. **Education:** Attended Manchester Grammar School. **Family:** Married Vera St. John, 1926; son: Michael. **Career:** 1925—managed cinema in Manchester; joined his father in managing the Blue Hall circuit of theatres;

James Carreras

1939–45—Colonel in Army; 1948–72—Chairman of Hammer Film Productions; 1968—Hammer awarded the Queen's Award to Industry; 1972—sold shares in Hammer to his son. **Awards:** MBE, 1944; knighted (''for services to youth''), 1970. **Died:** In Henley on Thames, 9 June 1990.

Films as Executive Producer:

1947   *River Patrol* (Hart)
1948   *Dick Barton—Special Agent* (Goulding)
1949   *Dick Barton Strikes Back* (Grayson); *Dr. Morelle—the Case of the Missing Heiress* (Grayson); *Celia* (Searle); *The Adventures of PC 49* (Grayson)
1950   *Dick Barton at Bay* (Grayson); *The Man in Black* (Searle); *Meet Simon Cherry* (Grayson); *Room to Let* (Grayson); *Someone at the Door* (Searle); *What the Butler Saw* (Grayson); *The Lady Craved Excitement* (Searle)
1951   *The Rossiter Case* (Searle); *To Have and to Hold* (Grayson); *The Dark Light* (Sewell); *Cloudburst* (Searle); *The Black Widow* (Sewell); *A Case for PC 49* (Searle)
1952   *Death of an Angel* (Saunders); *Whispering Smith Hits London (Whispering Smith vs. Scotland Yard)* (Searle); *The Last Page (Man Bait)* (Fisher); *Never Look Back* (Searle); *Wings of Danger* (Fisher); *Stolen Face* (Fisher); *Lady in the Fog (Scotland Yard Inspector)* (Newfield); *Mantrap (Man in Hiding)* (Fisher); *The Gambler and the Lady* (Jenkins and Fisher)
1953   *Four Sided Triangle* (Fisher); *Spaceways* (Fisher); *The Flanagan Boy (Bad Blonde)* (Le Borg); *The Saint's Return (The Saint's Girl Friday)* (Friedman)
1954   *Face the Music (The Black Glove)* (Fisher); *The Stranger Came Home (The Unholy Four)* (Fisher); *Blood Orange (Three Stops to Murder)* (Fisher); *Life with the Lyons* (Guest); *The House across the Lake (Heat Wave)* (Hughes); *Five Days (Paid to Kill)* (Tully); *36 Hours (Terror Street)* (Tully); *Men of Sherwood Forest* (Guest); *Mask of Dust (A Race for Life)* (Fisher)
1955   *The Quatermass Xperiment (The Creeping Unknown)* (Guest); *The Lyons in Paris* (Guest); *Break in the Circle* (Guest); *Third Party Risk (Deadly Game)* (Birt); *Murder By Proxy (Blackout)* (Fisher); *Cyril Stapleton and the Show Band* (Michael Carreras); *The Glass Cage (The Glass Tomb)* (Tully); *The Eric Winstone Band Show* (Michael Carreras); *The Right Person* (Cotes)
1956   *X the Unknown* (Norman); *Just for You* (Michael Carreras); *A Man on the Beach* (Losey); *Parade of the Bands* (Michael Carreras); *Eric Winstone's Stagecoach* (Michael Carreras); *Women without Men* (Williams); *Copenhagen* (Michael Carreras); *Dick Turpin—Highwayman* (Paltenghi)
1957   *The Steel Bayonet* (Michael Carreras); *The Curse of Frankenstein* (Fisher); *Quatermass II (Enemy from Space)* (Guest); *The Edmundo Ross Half Hour* (Michael Carreras); *Day of Grace* (Searle); *The Abominable Snowman* (Guest); *Danger List* (Arliss); *Clean Sweep* (Rogers)
1958   *The Camp on Blood Island* (Guest); *The Snorkel* (Green); *The Revenge of Frankenstein* (Fisher); *Dracula (Horror of Dracula)* (Fisher); *Further up the Creek* (Guest); *Man with a Dog* (Arliss)

1959   *I Only Arsked* (Tully); *The Hound of the Baskervilles* (Fisher); *Ten Seconds to Hell* (Aldrich); *The Ugly Duckling* (Comfort); *Operation Universe* (Bryan); *Yesterday's Enemy* (Guest); *The Mummy* (Fisher); *The Man Who Could Cheat Death* (Fisher); *Don't Panic Chaps!* (Pollock)
1960   *The Stranglers of Bombay* (Fisher); *Hell Is a City* (Guest); *The Curse of the Werewolf* (Fisher); *The Brides of Dracula* (Fisher); *Never Take Sweets from a Stranger* (Frankel); *The Two Faces of Dr. Jekyll (House of Fright)* (Fisher); *Sword of Sherwood Forest* (Fisher)
1961   *Pirates of Blood River* (Gilling); *The Damned (These Are the Damned)* (Losey); *Visa to Canton (Passport to China)* (Michael Carreras); *The Full Treatment (Stop Me before I Kill)* (Guest); *A Weekend with Lulu* (Carstairs); *Taste of Fear (Scream of Fear)* (Holt); *Watch it Sailor!* (Rilla); *The Terror of the Tongs* (Bushell)
1962   *The Phantom of the Opera* (Fisher); *Captain Clegg (Night Creatures)* (Scott); *The Pirates of Blood River* (Gilling)
1963   *The Devil-Ship Pirates* (Sharp); *Maniac* (Michael Carreras); *Paranoiac* (Francis); *The Damned (These Are the Damned)* (Losey); *The Scarlet Blade (The Crimson Blade)* (Gilling); *Cash on Demand* (Lawrence)
1964   *The Evil of Frankenstein* (Thompson); *Kiss of the Vampire* (Sharp); *Nightmare* (Francis); *The Gorgon* (Fisher); *The Curse of the Mummy's Tomb* (Michael Carreras); *Fanatic (Die! Die! My Darling!)* (Narizzano)
1965   *She* (Day); *The Secret of Blood Island* (Lawrence); *Hysteria* (Francis); *The Brigand of Kandahar* (Gilling); *The Nanny* (Holt)
1966   *One Million Years B.C.* (Chaffey); *Dracula—Prince of Darkness* (Fisher); *The Plague of the Zombies* (Gilling); *Rasputin—The Mad Monk* (Sharp); *The Reptile* (Gilling); *The Old Dark House* (Castle); *The Witches (The Devil's Own)* (Frankel)
1967   *The Viking Queen* (Chaffey); *Frankenstein Created Woman* (Fisher); *The Mummy's Shroud* (Gilling); *Quartermass and the Pit (Five Million Years to Earth)* (Baker); *A Challenge for Robin Hood* (Pennington-Richards)
1968   *The Anniversary* (Baker); *The Vengeance of She* (Owen); *The Devil Rides Out (The Devil's Bride)* (Fisher); *Slave Girls (Prehistoric Women)* (Michael Carreras); *Dracula Has Risen from the Grave* (Franics); *The Lost Continent* (Carreras)
1969   *Frankenstein Must Be Destroyed* (Fisher); *Moon Zero Two* (Baker)
1970   *Taste the Blood of Dracula* (Sasdy); *Crescendo* (Gibson); *Horror of Frankenstein* (Sangster); *Scars of Dracula* (Baker); *The Vampire Lovers* (Baker); *When Dinosaurs Ruled the Earth* (Guest)
1971   *Creatures the World Forgot* (Chaffey); *Lust for a Vampire* (Sangster); *Countess Dracula* (Sasdy); *On the Buses* (Booth); *Hands of the Ripper* (Sasdy); *Twins of Evil* (Hough); *Dr. Jekyll and Sister Hyde* (Baker); *Blood from the Mummy's Tomb* (Holt and Michael Carreras)
1972   *Shock (The Creeping Unknown)* (Francis); *Dracula A.D. 1972* (Gibson); *Vampire Circus* (Stark); *Fear in the Night* (Sangster); *Straight On till Morning* (Collingson); *Mutiny on the Buses* (Booth); *Demons of the Mind* (Sykes)

Publications

On CARRERAS: articles—

Films and Filming (London), vol. 6, no. 1, October 1959.
Little Shoppe of Horrors (Waterloo, Iowa), no. 4, April 1978.
Obituary in *Variety* (New York), 13 June 1990.
Obituary in *New York Times*, 13 June 1990.

*   *   *

The reputation of James Carreras rests on the output of a single, low-budget production company, Hammer Films—and specifically on the movies it produced between 1954 and 1970. During that period Hammer established, for the first time, an indigenously British style of horror movie; and if Carreras himself had relatively little to do with the creation of that style, he deserves every credit for fostering and encouraging it, in the teeth of virulent critical outrage.

Carreras has sometimes been compared to Michael Balcon. Like Balcon, he ran a small, self-contained studio on paternalist lines—in his case at Bray in Berkshire, in a rambling 19th-century country house whose Gothic architecture provided ready-made sets for numerous Hammer movies. Bray, like Ealing, offered supportive opportunities to beginners and continuous employment to a regular team of actors and technicians. But where Balcon was closely concerned with the style and ethical stance of the films he produced, Carreras—as he readily admitted—cared only about saleability. "If tomorrow the public decided it wanted Strauss waltzes," he once observed, "we'd be in the Strauss waltz business."

Hammer was founded in 1948 as the production arm of Exclusive Films, a distribution company set up by Carreras's father Enrique and his partner William Hinds, a one-time music hall performer whose stage name was Will Hammer. James Carreras, having served a pre-war apprenticeship as usher, cashier and projectionist in his father's chain of cinemas, returned after his war service to take over the running of the newly formed Hammer. His corporate policy was brutally simple: to make films guaranteed to show a profit.

Since the minuscule budgets scarcely ran to star actors, Hammer often went for presold subjects—films based on characters well known from British radio or TV. So when in 1953 the BBC broadcast a hugely popular science fiction TV serial, *The Quatermass Experiment*, Hammer promptly snapped up the rights. The film version (respelt *Xperiment* to exploit the British censor's new adults-only "X" certificate) went down well both in Britain and the USA, as did two follow-ups—*X the Unknown* and *Quatermass II*.

Shrewdly deducing that it was the horrific, rather than the sci-fi, element of these films that was hooking audiences, Carreras looked round for similar properties and realised that not since the great Universal cycle of the 1930s had the classic Gothic myths of Dracula and Frankenstein appeared on screen—and never in colour. *The Curse of Frankenstein* launched Hammer's horror cycle, along with the careers of Peter Cushing and Christopher Lee, and—according to David Pirie—"reintroduced into Britain the cinema of action and spectacle, of imagination and myth." It also set the style for its successors: full-blooded, sensual stories, straightforwardly told, in plush period settings that owed nothing to Universal's shadowy Germanic expressionism.

Such elements, though, should probably be credited less to Carreras than to his collaborators—in particular to his partner, the producer/screenwriter Anthony (son of William) Hinds, the director Terence

Fisher, the screenwriter Jimmy Sangster, art director Bernard Robinson, and cinematographer Jack Asher. What James Carreras contributed was consummate salesmanship—or perhaps showmanship might be a better term. Hammer's films were promoted with fairground razzmatazz and vigorously presold to foreign distributors, especially in the United States. By the late 1960s, over 80 per cent of Hammer's revenue came from overseas earnings, an achievement that won the company the Queen's Award for Industry.

Having no particular commitment to horror, Carreras was always ready to explore other avenues. In the wake of *Psycho*, Hammer produced a run of psychological thrillers—*Maniac, Paranoiac, Hysteria* and so on—and the success of *One Million Years B.C.* inspired several more fur-bikini sagas. Where this serviceable, down-to-earth approach showed its limitations was when a filmmaker tried to subvert the studio formula for imaginative ends, as Losey did with *The Damned*. Neither Carreras nor anyone else at Bray could grasp what Losey was after, and the film wound up badly mutilated.

This may also explain why the most intriguing and distinctive horror films of the period were left to Hammer's rivals—Gordon Hessler's *Scream and Scream Again* for Amicus, or Michael Reeves's *Witchfinder General* for Tigon. Though even here Hammer could claim some indirect input, since both Tigon and Amicus were operating within a market that Carreras had opened up for them.

By the end of the 1960s, Hammer horror, initially so reviled by squeamish critics, had become respectable enough to feature in retrospectives at the National Film Theatre in London. But with the cutback in American financing, Hammer's market was shrinking, and in 1969 Bray studios were sold. Soon afterwards James Carreras withdrew from control of the company, handing it over to his son Michael, and within three years Hammer had ceased production.

—Philip Kemp

CARRIÈRE, Jean-Claude

Writer. **Nationality:** French. **Born:** Colombières, 19 (or 17) September 1931. **Career:** Often worked with the director Luis Buñuel, as well as Jacques Deray, Pierre Etaix, Jean-Luc Godard, Louis Malle, and Volker Schlöndorff; 1968—directed short *La Pince à ongles*; 1985—directed feature *L'Unique*. **Awards:** Best Short Subject—Live Action Academy Award, for *Heureux anniversaire,* 1961; Best Screenplay British Academy Award, for *Le Charme discret de la bourgeoisie,* 1972; Best Writing—Original Cesar Award, for *Le Retour de Martin Guerre*, 1982; Best Adapted Screenplay British Academy Award, for *The Unbearable Lightness of Being,* 1988; Catalonian International Film Festival Best Screenplay, for *At Play in the Fields of the Lord,* 1990; Writers Guild of America Laurel Award for Screen Writing Achievement, 2000.

Films as Writer/Co-writer:

1961 *Rupture* (+ co-d—short); *Heureux anniversaire* (+ co-d, pr—short)
1962 *Le Soupirant* (*The Suitor*) (Etaix)

Jean-Claude Carrière (right) with Gregory Peck

1963 *Nous n'irons plus au bois* (Etaix; expanded into *Tant qu'on a la santé*, 1965); *Insomnie* (Etaix) (+ ro); *Le Bestaire d'amour* (Calderon); *Le Journal d'une femme de chambre* (*The Diary of a Chambermaid*) (Buñuel) (+ ro as The Priest)

1964 *Yoyo* (Etaix); *La Reine verte* (*The Green Queen*) (Mazoyer)

1965 *Viva Maria!* (Malle); *Cartes sur table* (Franco)

1966 ***Belle de jour*** (Buñuel); *Miss Muerte* (*The Diabolical Dr. Z*) (Franco); *Hotel Paradiso* (Glenville)

1967 *Le Voleur* (*The Thief of Paris*) (Malle)

1968 *La Pince à ongles* (+ d—short); *La Piscine* (*The Swimming Pool*) (Deray); *Le Grand Amour* (Etaix)

1969 *La Voie Lactée* (*The Milky Way*) (Buñuel) (+ ro as Priscillian)

1970 *L'Alliance* (de Chalonge) (+ ro as Hugues); *Taking Off* (Forman); *Borsalino* (Deray)

1971 *Un Peu de soleil dans l'eau froide* (Deray) (+ ro)

1972 *La cagna* (*Liza*) (Ferreri); *Le Moine* (*The Monk*) (Kyrou); *Le Droit d'aimer* (Le Hung); *Un Homme est mort* (*The Outside Man*) (Deray); ***Le Charme discret de la bourgeoisie*** (*The Discreet Charm of the Bourgeoisie*) (Buñuel)

1973 *France S.A.* (*France Société anonyme*) (Corneau)

1974 *Dorotheas Rache* (Fleischmann); *Grandeur nature* (*Life Size*) (Berlanga); *La Fantôme de la liberté* (*The Phantom of Liberty*) (Buñuel); *La Chair de l'orchidée* (Chereau); *La Femme aux bottes rouges* (J. Buñuel); *Sérieux comme le plaisir* (Benayoun) (+ ro)

1975 *Leonor* (J. Buñuel); *Les Oeufs brouillés* (Santoni); *La Faille* (Fleischmann)

1976 *Le Gang* (Deray)

1977 *Julie Pot de Colle* (de Broca); *Le Diable dans la boîte* (Lary); *Cet obscur objet de désir* (*That Obscure Object of Desire*) (Buñuel)

1978 *Photo souvenir* (Sechan) (+ ro); *Un Papillon sur l'épaule* (Deray); *Chausette surprise* (*Surprise Sock*) (Davy) (+ ro as Fournier) (Davy)

1979 *Ils sont grands ces petits* (*These Kids Are Grown-Ups*) (Santoni); *L'Associé* (*The Associate*) (Gainville); *Le Tambour* (*The Tin Drum*) (Schlöndorff)

1981 *Die Falschung* (*Circle of Deceit*) (Schlöndorff)

1982 *Danton* (Wajda); *Le Retour de Martin Guerre* (*The Return of Martin Guerre*) (Vigne)

1983 *Un Amour de Swann* (*Swann in Love*) (Schlöndorff); *La Tragédie de Carmen* (*The Tragedy of Carmen*) (Brook)

1986 *Max mon amour* (*Max, My Love*) (Oshima); *Wolf at the Door* (Carlsen)

1987 *Les Exploits d'un jeune Don-Juan* (Mingozzi); *Les Possédés* (*The Possessed*) (Wajda)

1988 *The Unbearable Lightness of Being* (Kaufman); *La Nuit bengali* (Klotz)

1989 *Valmont* (Forman); *Hard to Be a God* (Fleischmann); *J'écris dans l'éspace* (Etaix); *The Mahabharata*

1990 ***Cyrano de Bergerac*** (Rappeneau); *At Play in the Fields of the Lord* (Babenco); *Milou en mai* (*May Fools*) (Malle)

1991 *Bouvard et Pecuchet* (Verhaeghe—for TV) (+ ro as Narrator)

1992 *La Controverse de Valladolid* (Verhaeghe—for TV); *Le Retour de Casanova* (*Casanova's Return*) (Niermans)

1993 *Sommersby* (Amiel) (based on *Le Retour de Martin Guerre*; sc)

1994 *Le hussard sur le toit* (*The Horseman on the Roof*) (Rappeneau); *The Night and the Moment* (Tato) (+ ro as The Governor); *La Duchesse de Langeais* (Verhaeghe—for TV); *Associations de bienfaiteurs* (Verhaeghe—mini for TV)

1995 *Le roi des aulnes* (*The Ogre*) (Schlöndorff); *Capitaine Cyrano* (Failevic)

1996 *Une femme explosive* (Deray—for TV)

1997 *Chinese Box* (Wang) (+ co-story)

1998 *La Guerre dans le Haut Pays* (*War in the Highlands*) (Reusser); *Attaville, le veritable histoire des fourmis* (Calderon) (commentary only); *Clarissa* (Deray—for TV)

2000 *Salsa* (Joyce Buñuel)

Other Films:

1976 *Le jardin des supplices* (Gion) (ro)

1984 *Vive les femmes!* (Confortes) (ro as Le sourd-muet)

1993 *Eugenie Grandet* (Verhaeghe—for TV) (ro as Narrator)

Publications

By CARRIÈRE: books—

Lézard, Paris, 1957.
Monsieur Hulot's Holiday (novelization), London, 1959.
L'Alliance, Paris, 1963.

L'Aide-mémoire, Paris, 1968.

With Luis Buñuel, *La Moine*, Paris, 1971.

Mon Oncle (novelization), London, 1972.

(Translator) *Le Clou brûlant*, by José Bergamin, Paris, 1972.

With Luis Buñuel, *Le Charme discret de la bourgeoisie* (script), in *Avant-Scène* (Paris), April 1973.

La Pari, Paris, 1973.

(Translator) *Harold et Maude*, by Colin Higgins, Paris, 1974.

With Daniel Vigne, *Le Retour de Martin Guerre*, Paris, 1982.

Credo, Paris, 1983.

With Jean Audouze and Michel Cassé, *Conversations sur l'invisible*, Paris, 1988.

Les mots et la chose, Paris, 1990.

La paix des braves, Paris, 1991.

Le Mahabharata, Paris, 1992.

La Controverse de Valladolid, Paris, 1993.

The Secret Language of Film, New York, 1994.

Simon Le Mage, Paris, 1994.

With H. H., le Dalaï-Lama, *La force du buddhisme*, Paris, 1995.

With Jean Audouze, *Régards sur le visible*, Paris, 1996.

By CARRIÈRE: articles—

Cinéma (Paris), February 1965.

Positif (Paris), July 1966.

Jeune Cinéma (Paris), September 1968.

Positif (Paris), March 1969.

Cinéma (Paris), July/August 1970.

Kosmorama (Copenhagen), December 1970.

Cinémonde (Paris), March 1971.

In *Les scénaristes au travail*, by Christian Salé, Paris, 1981.

Cinéaste (Paris), vol. 13, no. 1, 1983.

"Luis Buñuel," in *Cinéma* (Paris), September 1983.

Avant-Scène (Paris), February 1984.

Cinématographe (Paris), February 1984.

Technicien du Film (Paris), October/November 1984.

Cahiers du Cinéma (Paris), May 1985.

American Film (Washington, D.C.), December 1985.

24 Images (Montreal), Autumn 1986.

Cinéma (Paris), 1 October 1986.

Revue Belge du Cinéma (Brussels), Winter 1986.

CinémAction (Conde-sur-Noireau), no. 44, June 1987.

Skrien (Amsterdam), no. 164, February/March 1989.

Cinéma (Paris), May 1990.

Interview by Vincent Amiel, in *Positif* (Paris), October 1993.

Interview by Omid Rohani, in *Film International* (Tehran), Winter 1993.

Interview by Pierre Beylot and Raphaëlle Moine, in *Cinemaction* (Paris), March 1996.

Interview with I. Wiese, in *Z Filmtidsskrift* (Oslo), no. 3, 1996.

On CARRIÈRE: articles—

Focus on Film (London), Spring 1975.

Focus on Film (London), Summer 1975.

Focus on Film (London), Winter 1975–76.

Positif (Paris), December 1977/January 1978.

Film Français (Paris), 3 February 1978.

Télérama (Paris), 13–19 July 1985.

Millard, Kathryn, "Henri and Georgette Go Writing," in *Film News* (Sydney), April 1995.

*   *   *

As a screenwriter, Jean-Claude Carrière is still best known for his association with Luis Buñuel, with whom he collaborated regularly from *Le Journal d'une femme de chambre* onwards. Yet of all his screenplays, only six (or seven if one counts *Le Moine*, eventually directed by Ado Kyrou) were written for Buñuel. To date, Carrière has produced well over 80 screenplays and teleplays for a long and prestigious list of directors that includes Malle, Schlöndorff, Wajda, Forman, Godard, Oshima, Philip Kaufman, Carlos Saura, Hector Babenco, Wayne Wang, and Pierre Etaix. He also writes for the stage (most notably for Peter Brook's international theater company); he has written novels, and has occasionally acted and directed.

Unlike many prolific scenarists, though, Carrière rarely lapses into lazy or slipshod writing, and the overall standard of his work has remained consistently high. Nor, despite his literary background, does his dialogue feel overwritten or stilted. He himself, while wary of laying down rules and guidelines, maintains that a screenwriter should above all aim for clarity and avoid self-indulgence. "Good dialogue doesn't draw attention to itself," he has observed. "You penetrate it without effort. It's like the sound of a mill to the miller; he only hears it when it stops."

Carrière took up screenwriting at a time when the New Wave filmmakers, reacting against the confined, studio-bound style of the "*cinéma de qualité*," were also rejecting the rigid tyranny of the traditional script. Carrière entirely concurred, since he considered the scenario "at once useful and superfluous, simply a stage in the existence and development of a film." A script, he believes, "doesn't stop when it's written, it continues during the shooting and often during the editing." It should be flexible enough to "allow a degree of freedom, not just to the director, but to the actors." At the same time, he expresses reservations about wholly improvisational approaches, which can lead to shapelessness and banality. "I think we have to strike a balance between the script being all-powerful, and it being nonexistent."

The role of improvisation, for Carrière, comes much earlier in the creative process. "The scenario is created when you and the director act it out together, improvising." To achieve this, he tries to establish with his director "a near telepathic communication," which "requires on both sides a receptiveness and a trust which can never be taken for granted. Like all good relationships, it has to be constantly worked at, and shielded against the effects of personal vanity." The scriptwriter must on occasion be prepared to submerge his ego, since ultimately "it's the director's film, and you're there to help him, to facilitate him."

Not that there is anything in the least anonymous about Carrière's work. From his films there emerges a dryly humorous personality, alert to the absurdities of life, profoundly mistrustful of all absolutes and authorities. Having a sharp eye for middle-class ritual, he particularly enjoys prodding at the pretensions of "the French bourgeoisie in all its self-satisfied myopia." Pessimistic but too ironic for tragedy, left-leaning but too skeptical for dogma, Carrière presents a world in which the surreal, the unpremeditated, or simply the spectacle of sheer bloody-minded human resilience, can serve to keep alive an intrigued sense of unexplored potential. ''The best quality for a screenwriter,'' he has remarked, ''is an unsatisfied curiosity.''

Carrière's unselfishly craftsmanlike approach to screenwriting is exemplified by his work on *Cyrano de Bergerac*, one of his biggest international hits. Both Carrière and his director, Jean-Paul Rappeneau, were determined, in the teeth of widespread skepticism, to preserve the play's convention of having all the dialogue in rhymed alexandrine couplets. By judiciously pruning Rostand's sometimes clotted verse, adding in a few extra scenes and some fragments of skillful Rostand-pastiche, Carrière produced a script that moved at a smart cinematic pace while staying faithful to the spirit of the original. So faithful, indeed, that even devotees of the play scarcely registered that changes had been made. Carriere also served Rappeneau well in *Le hussard sur le toit*, which like *Cyrano* is an energetic, deliciously romantic historical epic. *Le hussard* is crammed with sweeping, eye-popping imagery; on visual terms, Rappeneau does an especially fine job of contrasting the lushly beautiful French countryside and the deadly dangers confronting his idealistic and honorable Italian aristocrat-soldier-revolutionary hero. Simultaneously, Carriere's smart, literate dialogue propels the story along while keeping the characters lively and engaging.

The subtlety, and the understated ironies, of Carrière's style can on occasion prove self-defeating. In his work with Buñuel, he once explained, ''we chose the path of what is probable, but just at the limit, at the borderline of the probable.'' It is a balance, as he acknowledges, that is ''very difficult to maintain,'' and in some films his writing, perhaps aiming to avoid extravagance, can verge towards over-neatness. What his skilled adaptation of Kundera's *The Unbearable Lightness of Being* gains in clarity and narrative coherence, it loses in moral complexity and the joy of inconsequentiality. And the straight-faced surrealism of *Max mon amour*, ill-served by Oshima's literal-minded direction, falls sadly flat.

Some critics have suggested that even Bunuel was rendered ''respectable'' by his association with Carrière, trading the earthiness and carnality of his earlier Spanish-language movies for French urbanity and sophistication—no longer outraging his bourgeois audiences, but titillating them with pleasurable shocks. But it can equally be argued that in Carrière, whom he called ''the writer closest to me,'' Buñuel found the ideal collaborator in the expression of his cruel, insidious vision, his elegantly austere sensuality. And certainly Carrière achieved in his work with Buñuel a mastery of style and structure that he may subsequently have equaled but has yet to surpass. Had he written nothing else, he would rank high among contemporary screenwriters for these six films alone.

—Philip Kemp, updated by Rob Edelman

CECCHI D'AMICO, Suso

Writer. **Nationality:** Italian. **Born:** Giovanna Cecchi in Rome, 21 July 1914; daughter of the writer Emilio Cecchi. **Education:** Studied in Rome and Cambridge. **Career:** Journalist; translator of English-language plays; 1946—first film as writer, *Mio figlio professore*; 1977—co-writer for TV mini-series *Gesù di Nazareth* (*Jesus of Nazareth*); writer for TV, *Una moglie*, 1987, *Quattro storie di donne*, 1990. **Awards:** Best script award, Sindicato Nazionale Giornalisti Cinematografici Italiani, for *Speriamo che sia femmina*, 1986. **Address:** via Paisiello 27, 00198 Rome, Italy.

Films as Writer:

1946 *Mio figlio professore* (*Professor My Son*) (Castellani); *Vivere in pace* (*To Live in Peace*) (Zampa); *Roma città libera* (Pagliero)

1947 *Il delitto di Giovanni Episcopo* (*Flesh Will Surrender*) (Lattuada); *L'onorevole Angelina* (*Angelina*) (Zampa)

1948 *Fabiola* (Blasetti); **Ladri di biciclette** (*The Bicycle Thief*) (De Sica); *Patto col diavolo* (Chiarini); *Cielo sulla palude* (*Heaven over the Marshes*) (Genina)

1949 *Le mura di Malapaga* (*The Walls of Malapaga*) (Clément) (co-sc Italian version); *Prohibito rubare* (*Guaglio*) (Comencini)

1950 *Miracolo a Milano* (*Miracle in Milan*) (De Sica); *E primavera* (*It's Forever Springtime*) (Castellani); *E più facile che un cammello* (Zampa); *Romazo d'amore* (*Toselli*) (Coletti)

1951 *Due mogli sono troppe* (*Honeymoon Deferred*) (Camerini); *Bellissima* (Visconti)

1952 ''Primo amore'' ep. of *Altri tempi* (*Times Gone By*) (Blasetti); *Processo alla città* (*A Town on Trial*) (Zampa); *Buongiorno, elefante!* (*Hello Elephant!*) (Franciolini); *I vinti* (*I nostri figli*) (Antonioni); *Il mondo le condanna* (*His Last Twelve Hours*) (Franciolini)

1953 *Siamo donne* (*We the Women*) (Visconti); ''Il pupo'' ep. of *Tempi nostri* (*Anatomy of Love*) (Blassetti); *Febbre di vivere* (Gora); *La signora senza camelie* (*Camille without Camelias*) (Antonioni); *Cento anni d'amore* (de Felice)

1954 *Graziella* (Bianchi); *Senso* (Visconti); *L'allegro squadrone* (Moffa); *Peccato che sia una canaglia* (*Too Bad She's Bad*) (Blasetti); *Proibito* (Monicelli)

1955 *Le amiche* (*The Girlfriends*) (Antonioni)

1956 *La fortuna di essere donna* (Blasetti); *La finestra sul Luna Park* (Comencini); *Kean* (Gassman); *Difendo il mio amore* (Sherman) (co)

1957 *Le notti bianche* (*White Nights*) (Visconti); *Mariti in città* (Comencini)

1958 *Nella città l'inferno* (*And the Wild, Wild Women*) (Castellani); *La sfida* (*The Challenge*) (Rosi); *I soliti ignoti* (*Big Deal on Madonna Street*) (Monicelli)

1959 *Estate violenta* (*Violent Summer*) (Zurlini); *I magliari* (Rosi)

1960 *La contessa azzurra* (Gora); *Rocco e i suoi fratelli* (*Rocco and His Brothers*) (Visconti); *Risate di gioia* (*The Passionate Thief*) (Monicelli); *It Started in Naples* (Shavelson)

1961 *Salvatore Giuiliano* (Rosi); *Il relitto* (*The Wastrel*) (Cacoyannis); *I due nemici* (*The Best of Enemies*) (Hamilton)

1962 ''Il lavoro'' (''The Job'') and ''Renzo e Luciana'' (''Renzo and Luciana'') eps. of *Boccaccio '70* (Visconti and Monicelli); ''Le Lièvre et la tortue'' (''The Tortoise and the Hare'') ep. of *Les Quatre Vérités* (*Three Fables of Love*) (Blasetti)

1963 *Il gattopardo* (*The Leopard*) (Visconti); *Gli indifferenti* (*Time of Indifference*) (Maselli)

1965 *Casanova '70* (Monicelli); *Vaghe stelle dell'orsa* (*Sandra*) (Visconti)

1966   *Io, io, io . . . e gli altri* (Blasetti); ''Queen Armenia'' ep. of *Le fate* (*The Queens*) (Monicelli); *Spara forte, più forte . . . non capisco* (*Shout Loud, Louder . . . I Don't Understand*) (De Filippo); *The Taming of the Shrew* (Zeffirelli)

1967   *Lo straniero* (*The Stranger*) (Visconti); *L'uomo, l'orgoglio, la vendetta* (*Man, Pride and Vengeance*) (Bazzoni)

1969   *Metello* (Bolognini); *Infanzia, vocazione, e prime esperienze di Giacomo Casanova, Veneziano* (Comencini); *Senza sapere nulla di lei* (Comencini)

1971   *La mortadella* (*Lady Liberty*) (Monicelli)

1972   *Pinocchio* (Comencini—for TV); *Fratello sole, sorella luna* (*Brother Sun, Sister Moon*) (Zeffirelli); *Il diavolo nel cervello* (Sollima); *I figli chiedono perche* (Zanchin)

1973   *Ludwig* (Visconti); *Amore e ginnastica* (L. F. d'Amico)

1974   *Gruppo di famiglia in un interno* (*Conversation Piece*) (Visconti); *Prete, fai un miracolo* (Chiari); *Amore amaro* (Vancini) (co)

1976   *L'innocente* (*The Innocent*) (Visconti); *Caro Michele* (Monicelli); *Dimmi che fai tutto per mei* (Festa Campanile)

1980   *La velia* (Ferrero)

1983   *Lighea* (Tuzii) (co); *Les Mots pour le dire* (Pinheiro) (co)

1984   *Cuore* (Comencini—for TV); *Uno scandale per bene* (Festa Campanile); *Bertoldo, Bertoldino e Cacasenno* (Monicelli) (co)

1985   *Le due vite di Mattia Pascal* (Monicelli) (co)

1986   *I soliti ignoti vent'anni dopo* (*Big Deal on Madonna Street. . . 20 Years Later*) (Todini) (co); *Speriamo che sia femmina* (*Let's Hope It's a Girl*) (Monicelli) (co); *La storia* (Comencini) (co)

1987   *L'inchiesta* (Damiani) (co); *Oci ciornie* (*Dark Eyes*) (Mikhalkov) (co); *I picari* (Monicelli)

1988   *Ti presento un'amica* (Massaro)

1989   *Stradivari* (Battiato) (co)

1990   *Il male oscuro* (Monicelli); *Rossini, Rossini* (Monicelli)

1992   *Parenti serpenti* (Monicelli) (co)

1993   *La fine e nota* (Cristina Comencini); *Cari fottutissimi amici* (Monicelli) (co)

1995   *Facciamo paradiso* (Monicelli)

1996   *Bruno aspetta in macchina* (*Bruno is Waiting on the Car*) (Camerini)

1998   *La Stanza dello scirocco* (*The Room of the Scirocco*) (Sciarra); *Der Letzte Sommer-Wenn Du nicht willst* (Pucitta)

1999   *Panni sporchi* (Monicelli); *Un Amico magico: il maestro Nino Rota* (Monicelli); *Il Dolce cinema* (Scorsese—for TV)

2000   *Il Cielo Cade* (*The Sky Will Fall*)

Publications

By CECCHI D'AMICO: books—

(Translator with Emilio Cecchi) *Otello* in *Teatro*, by Shakespeare, vol. 3, Florence, 1961.

With others, *Bicycle Thieves* (script), London, 1968, as *The Bicycle Thief*, New York, 1968.

With others, *Miracle in Milan* (script), New York, 1968.

With Luchino Visconti, *Senso* and *La terra trema* (scripts), in *Two Screenplays*, New York, 1970.

With others, *The Job, Rocco and His Brothers*, and *White Nights* (scripts), in *Three Screenplays*, New York, 1970.

By CECCHI D'AMICO: articles—

Positif (Paris), September 1985.
Revista del Cinematografo, vol. 62, September 1992.
Revista del Cinematografo, vol. 63, 1993.
EPD Film (Frankfurt/Main), April 1993.
CinémAction (Conde-sur-Noireau), January 1994.

On CECCHI D'AMICO: book—

Hochkofler, Matilde, and Orio Caldiron, *Suso Cecchi d'Amico, scriveri du cinema*, Bari, 1988.

On CECCHI D'AMICO: articles—

Sight and Sound (London), Winter 1986–87.
Filmihullu (Helsinki), no. 2, 1989.
Iskussstvo Kino (Moscow), no. 5, 1997.

*   *   *

Suso Cecchi d'Amico is undoubtedly best known as Visconti's regular scriptwriter, however her work, either alone or in collaboration, with a large number of other directors is at the core of a long list of films which embodies the development of postwar Italian cinema from Blasetti to De Sica, from Rosi to Zeffirelli and Antonioni. It is undoubtedly a tribute to her work that her scripts achieve a certain ''transparency,'' becoming all-but-inextricable from the finished film itself.

She has all too modestly described her work as akin to that of the artisan. This emphasizes her professionalism, the literate well-craftedness of her scripts, and her endless adaptability to the contrasting needs of filmmakers working within competing stylistic conventions. It glosses over the acuteness of her appraisal of particular projects and particular directors. Luigi Comencini may be no great stylist, as she has remarked, his films stand or fall by their overall effect. *Cuore* is a tender and ironic melodrama but anchored cogently to moments in Italian history. Zampa may be a minor talent but with *Vivere in pace* Cecchi d'Amico wrote to the project's integrity and antiheroic pacifism. Her script gives Genina's strange melodrama about a peasant girl's rape and subsequent sanctification, *Heaven over the Marshes*, a much-needed steely quality.

Writing for De Sica made other demands. Cecchi d'Amico has spoken of his need ''to borrow from and reproduce'' reality, a need that predated any theorization of neorealism. The moral catch-22 behind *The Bicycle Thief* lends De Sica's slice-of-life a bitter edge. Her collaboration with Francesco Rosi has been equally rewarding. A trial transcript provided the source for *Salvatore Giuliano's* script, the framework for a film of epic dimension honed from events both sordid and sadly routine. But where she worked with a director whose own drive was towards honing away excesses and revealing a structure, the results were less happy. Where Antonioni saw his films as the bare rendition of reality, Cecchi d'Amico saw contemporary fables.

It was the opportunity posed by working for Visconti with his concern for the firm location of characters within a specific time, place, and history that drew from her her best work. She has said that his clarity of vision and sureness made him an easy person to work for, and there is an obvious complementarity between her spareness and Visconti's rhetorical visual style. Initial efforts for him required copious pruning to adapt them to his particular "cinematic rhythm." So completely did Visconti make his projects his own that they escape the category of "literary adaptation," and are rewritten and reformed to his own vision. Where a subject interested him but a suitable text could not be found, Cecchi d'Amico has spoken of the preparation of a script only after a considerable amount of research had been done. Even a contemporary subject might have a literary analogue. Thus Dostoyevsky was a touchstone for *Rocco and His Brothers*.

Rocco, an original story, knits its moral conundrum into a precisely located mise-en-scène, as it follows the attempts of a Southern peasant family to adjust to a new life in the North, and in doing so charts the stresses attendant upon Italy's own path to industrialization. The script's major coup is the withholding of an explicit statement of the immigrant's code of morality until the final section, where it acquires an especially revelatory force, marking a passage from the certainties of an agrarian society, to notions of compromise embodied in a trade-off between rights and duties. The concern for morality and betrayal, personal and national history present here also underlie many of her other projects for Visconti, *The Innocent*, *Senso*, *Ludwig*, and *Conversation Piece*.

The same concerns give her extraordinary gallery of female characters a memorable distinctiveness. Often transgressive they are always true to their time and place and never airbrushed into stereotype. Another consistent thread has been her collaborations with Monicelli, a director known for his humorously ironic tales of bourgeois life. The recent *Il male oscuro* was scripted with Tonino Guerra from a prizewinning sixties novel (translated as *Incubus* in the United States) by Giuseppe Berto. It studies the relationships between a mediocre writer undergoing analysis, his younger wife, and his obsessive, ambivalent relationship with his father. The family theme is continued with *Parenti serpenti*, also made in the nineties, an examination of the tensions that arise as three generations of an extended family attempt Christmas together. Humor and irony also underlie her contributions to the script for Mikhalkov's *Oci ciornie*.

Her experience of writing a supposedly "Ben Hecht" script for Wyler's *Roman Holiday* (she took the job out of admiration for the director), which involved stringing together a series of banal generic elements, merely confirmed her observations of the wholly pernicious effect of Hollywood's postwar incursion into Italian filmmaking. (The Italian industry was, in her opinion, to be destroyed and the country opened up as a market for U.S. product.) There were other international co-productions occasionally; the Taylor-Burton *The Taming of the Shrew* for which her early experience as a translator into Italian of English literature might have, in part, prepared her, and on which she worked with Paul Dehn. But her preoccupations lay elsewhere. Cecchi d'Amico has always believed in the necessity of developing a national cinema that would "tell its own stories." It has been an unstinting dedication to this principle which underlies her work.

—Verina Glaessner

CHALLIS, Christopher

Cinematographer. **Nationality:** British. **Born:** London, 18 March 1919. **Education:** Wimbledon College. **Career:** Camera assistant on newsreels from late teens; apprentice technician at Technicolor laboratory; second unit cameraman (credits include *The Thief of Bagdad* 1940); cameraman with the Royal Air Force Film Unit during World War II (credits include *Theirs Is the Glory* 1945); post-war return to film industry as camera operator (including uncredited work on *A Matter of Life and Death* 1946), graduating to lighting cameraman in 1947; retired 1985. **Address:** c/o British Society of Cinematographers, 11 Crost Road, Gerard's Cross, Buckinghamshire SL9 9AE, England.

Films as Cinematographer:

1947 *End of the River* (+ uncredited assoc d) (Twist)
1949 *The Small Back Room* (*Hour of Glory*) (Powell/Pressburger)
1950 *Gone to Earth* (*The Wild Heart*) (Powell/ Pressburger) (new scenes for U.S. version uncredited director, Rouben Mamoulian); *The Elusive Pimpernel* (*The Fighting Pimpernel*) (Powell/Pressburger)
1951 *The Tales of Hoffmann* (Powell/Pressburger)
1952 *Angels One Five* (co-ph) (O'Ferrall); *Twenty-Four Hours of a Woman's Life* (Saville)
1953 *Genevieve* (Cornelius); *Saadia* (Lewin); *The Story of Gilbert and Sullivan* (Gilliat)
1954 *Twice Upon a Time* (Pressburger); *Malaga* (*Fire Over Africa*) (Sale); *The Flame and the Flesh* (Brooks)
1955 *The Sorcerer's Apprentice* (short) (Powell); *Oh Rosalinda!* (Powell/Pressburger); *Quentin Durward* (*The Adventures of Quentin Durward*) (Thorpe); *Raising a Riot* (Toye), *Footsteps in the Fog* (Lubin)
1956 *The Battle of the River Plate* (*The Pursuit of the Graf Spee*) (Powell/Pressburger); *Ill Met By Moonlight* (*Night Ambush*) (Powell/Pressburger); *The Spanish Gardener* (Leacock)
1957 *Miracle in Soho* (Amyes); *Windom's Way* (Neame)
1958 *Floods of Fear* (Crichton); *Rooney* (Pollack); *The Captain's Table* (Lee)
1959 *Blind Date* (*Chance Meeting*) (Losey)
1960 *Sink the Bismark* (Gilbert); *The Grass is Greener* (Donen); *Surprise Package* (Donen); *Never Let Go* (Guillermin)
1961 *Flame in the Streets* (Baker); *Five Golden Hours* (Zampi); *An Evening With the Royal Ballet* (co-ph)
1962 *HMS Defiant* (*Damn the Defiant*) (Gilbert)
1963 *The Long Ships* (Cardiff); *The Victors* (Foreman)
1964 *A Shot in the Dark* (Edwards); *The Americanization of Emily* (co-ph) (Hiller)
1965 *Those Magnificent Men in Their Flying Machines* (Annakin); *Return from the Ashes* (Thompson)
1966 *Arabesque* (Donen); *Kaleidoscope* (Smight)
1967 *Two for the Road* (Donen)
1968 *A Dandy in Aspic* (Mann & uncredited Laurence Harvey); *Chitty Chitty Bang Bang* (Hughes)
1969 *Staircase* (Donen)
1970 *The Private Life of Sherlock Holmes* (Wilder)
1971 *Villain* (Tuchner); *Catch Me a Spy* (Clement); *Mary Queen of Scots* (Jarrott)
1972 *Follow Me* (*The Public Eye*) (Reed); *The Boy Who Turned Yellow* (Powell/Pressburger)
1974 *The Little Prince* (Donen)
1975 *Mister Quilp* (*The Old Curiosity Shop*) (Tuchner)
1976 *The Incredible Sarah* (Fleischer)
1977 *The Deep* (Yates)

Christopher Challis

1978	*Force Ten from Navarone* (Hamilton)
1979	*The Riddle of the Sands* (Maylam)
1980	*The Mirror Crack'd* (Hamilton)
1981	*Evil Under the Sun* (Hamilton)
1984	*Top Secret!* (Abrahams, Zucker, Zucker)
1985	*Steaming* (Losey)

Other Films:

1948   *The Red Shoes* (cam op only) (Powell/Pressburger)

Publications

On CHALLIS: books—

Powell, Michael, *A Life in Movies*, London, 1986.
Walker, Alexander, *Hollywood, England*, London, 1986.
Powell, Michael, *Million Dollar Movie*, London, 1992.

Macdonald, Kevin, *Emeric Pressburger. The Life and Death of a Screenwriter*, London, 1994.
Howard, James, *Michael Powell*, London, 1996.

On CHALLIS: articles—

Watson, John H., "The Private Life of Sherlock Holmes and The Curious Case of the Missing Footage," *Movie Collector*, vol. 1, no. 7, July-August 1994, and vol. 1, no. 8, November/December 1994.

*   *   *

Christopher Challis belongs to a select group of cameramen who honed their skills in the relatively thriving post-war British film industry, attracting Hollywood interest with a series of impressive credits. Probably best known for his work with the celebrated Powell-Pressburger partnership, The Archers, Challis' career spanned five decades and virtually every film genre, ranging from historical romance (*Mary Queen of Scots*) to *Airplane*-style comedy (*Top Secret!*). Challis' technical skill was allied to a strong visual sense, both in the studio and on location, most notably in his rich Technicolor photography for the Archers productions *Gone to Earth* and *Tales of Hoffmann*. Equally adept with black and white, Challis also adapted successfully to the various widescreen formats, whether Cinemascope, Vistavision, Technirama or Panavision. In demand at home and abroad throughout the 1960s and 1970s, Challis found few projects—or directors—to test his abilities, finally calling it a day after nearly forty years.

Along with the likes of Ronald Neame, Geoffrey Unsworth, Freddie Francis, and Jack Cardiff, Challis served an invaluable apprenticeship under Powell and Pressburger, making his debut as lighting cameraman on the Archers-produced *End of the River*, his stylish black and white photography enhancing an otherwise unremarkable effort. Challis hit his stride with *The Small Back Room*, also in high contrast black and white. A little uncertain in its dramatic effects, this wartime tale of a physically and emotionally crippled bomb disposal expert (David Farrar) has undeniable visual authority. The location work is vivid, taking in the Thames Embankment, Stonehenge, the Welsh countryside, and a windswept seafront, the backdrop for the climactic bomb dismantling. Back in the studio, Powell requested "Caligari lighting" (the use of a shadowy, distorted, nightmarish backdrop to reflect an equally disturbed state of mind typical of 1920s German cinema) for the famous hallucinatory sequence where Farrar imagines himself crushed by a giant whisky bottle, an expressionist touch as striking as it is unsubtle. Other visual highlights include a "sculpted" effect for close-ups of leading lady Kathleen Byron; film noir-style lighting as Farrar and Byron kiss, their faces wreathed in shadow; and shots from underneath a metal walkway, feet passing overhead as blurred shadows. There is even a ripple effect shot from Farrar's point of view as sweat pours down his face during the bomb disposal scene. *The Tales of Hoffmann* marked the peak of Challis' Technicolor work with The Archers, making ingenious use of gauzes to produce in-camera optical effects. Shooting without sound to a prerecorded score, Challis and his crew dispensed with the cumbersome camera blimp, normally required to muffle motor noise, enabling the newly mobile equipment to be as elaborately "choreographed" as the performers. According to Powell, the Technicolor Company rated the photography in The Archers' films as the best in the world.

Challis became The Archers' regular cameraman at a time when the duo's creative powers were showing signs of decline. *Gone to Earth* renders the nineteenth century Shropshire landscape in dazzling shades of green and red, yet the story lacks conviction. *Ill Met By Moonlight*, the last Archers production, was actually criticised for its supposedly murky black and white photography, one reviewer retitling the film 'Ill lit by moonlight'.

Away from The Archers, Challis became a mainstay of the Rank Organisation during the 1950s, lending his talents to the smash hit *Genevieve*, and worked with leading British directors such as Sidney Gilliat, Lewis Gilbert, Charles Crichton and Roy Ward Baker. Challis' Hollywood credits from this period include the lively medieval swashbuckler *Quentin Durward*, notable for its vibrant widescreen imagery. Hollywood-backed productions seldom called for the kind of visual imagination evident in the Archers films. *A Shot in the Dark*, for example, found Challis largely constricted by Blake Edwards' penchant for subdued colour and long, static takes. An elaborate crane shot in the opening sequence, charting multiple amorous liaisons in a French villa, shows what could have been.

Challis' only long-term collaborator after The Archers was choreographer turned director Stanley Donen. In truth, their six films together are largely undistinguished, with the exception of the literate romantic comedy *Two for the Road*. Stranded with a "problematic" script for the chic thriller *Arabesque*, Donen went all out for visual dazzle, the disorienting shifts in focus and off-kilter camera angles accentuating rather than disguising the flimsy content.

Unlike fellow Archers graduates Cardiff, Neame, and Francis, Challis never turned to directing. Joining forces with Cardiff for *The Long Ships*, he probably felt he'd made the right decision. Leaving aside the clumsy dialogue, plodding pace, and questionable casting, this Vikings versus Moors adventure has only moments of visual flair, notably a stylised prologue involving silhouetted figures superimposed against still backdrops of mosaics and engravings.

Ironically, Challis' most impressive film from the latter period of his career, Billy Wilder's *The Private Life of Sherlock Holmes*, was one of his least satisfying assignments. While Challis rated both Powell and Donen as great visual directors, he felt Wilder was unable to picture what he wanted in advance, preoccupied with the script and performances. Challis also clashed with production designer Alexander Trauner, claiming that the latter built his intricate sets without regard to the practicalities of filmmaking and showed total ignorance of process shots, flaws evident in the finished film. Nevertheless, *Private Life* contains some striking imagery: Holmes lurking in shadow operating a remote control pipe with a foot pump; the palatial corridor of the Diogenes Club; a cycle ride by the shores of Loch Ness; Queen Victoria's torch-lit nighttime visit to a secret government base beneath a ruined castle.

For much of the 1970s, Challis lent a glossy veneer to otherwise bland big budget productions, whether biopics, musicals, thrillers or Agatha Christie adaptations. A belated reunion with Powell and Pressburger resulted in *The Boy Who Turned Yellow*, a modest juvenile fantasy produced for the Rank-backed Children's Film Foundation. Having secured Panavision equipment for this 55 minute epic, Challis captured the locations—the Tower of London, Chalk Farm Underground Station—as effectively as he did for *The Small Back Room*. Times had changed but Challis remained a true professional.

—Daniel O'Brien

CHANDRAGUPTA, Bansi

Art Director. **Nationality:** Indian. **Born:** Sialkot (now in Pakistan), 1924. **Education:** Attended schools in Kashmir; studied painting in Calcutta. **Career:** 1950—assistant art director on Jean Renoir's *The River*; 1955—first film as art director, *Pather Panchali*, first of many films by Satyajit Ray; directed several documentaries; President, Art Directors Association, Bombay. **Died:** In New York, 27 June 1981.

Films as Art Director:

1955   *Pather Panchali* (*Father Panchali*) (Ray)
1956   *Aparajito* (*The Unvanquished*) (Ray)
1957   *Parash Pathar* (Ray); *Seema*
1958   *Jalsaghar* (*The Music Room*) (Ray)
1959   *Apur Sansar* (*The World of Apu*) (Ray)
1960   *Devi* (*The Goddess*) (Ray)

1961   *Rabindranath Tagore* (Ray—doc); *Teen Kanya* (*Two Daughters*) (Ray)
1962   *Abhijan* (*Expedition*) (Ray)
1963   *Mahanagar* (*The Big City*) (Ray)
1964   **Charulata** (*The Lonely Wife*) (Ray)
1965   *Kapurush-o-Mahapurush* (*The Coward and the Saint*) (Ray)
1966   *Nayak* (*The Hero*) (Ray)
1970   **Aranyer Din Ratri** (*Days and Nights in the Forest*) (Ray)
1972   *Maya Darpan* (Shahani)
1973   *27 Down* (Kaul)
1977   *Shatranj Ke Khilari* (*The Chess Player*) (Ray)
1981   *36 Chowringhee Lane* (A. Sen)
1982   *Aarohan* (*Ascending Scale*) (Benegal)

Films as Director:

1978   *Glimpses of West Bengal* (doc)
1979   *Ganga Sagar* (doc)
1980   *Happening in Calcutta* (doc)

Publications

By CHANDRAGUPTA: articles—

Montage, July 1966.
Madhuri, 16 November 1978.
In *The New Generation, 1960–1980*, edited by Uma de Cunha, New Delhi, 1981.
Obituary in *Variety*, 1 July 1981.

*   *   *

Bansi Chandragupta, by far India's best production designer, aspired to be a painter and went to Calcutta to study painting at the insistence of Subho Tagore, but friendship with Satyajit Ray in the late 1940s attracted him to the career of art director, then an unheard-of concept in Bengali or Indian cinema. Ardent and long viewing of Western films with Ray, mostly at the Calcutta Film Society (founded by Ray and his friend Chidananda Dasgupta, later a noted film critic), nurtured his imagination for realistic production sets, then lacking in most studio-oriented Indian films.

Opportunity came with Renoir's *The River* on the recommendation of Ray and Harisadhan Dasgupta. But the most satisfying beginning was made with designing outdoor sets for Ray's *Pather Panchali*, e.g., the hut in which Apu spends his childhood and other locales of the Bengali village. His most accomplished work that marked him out in later life were studio sets for Ray's *Charulata*, *Nayak*, and *Shatranj Ke Khilari*. He designed the bogey of the high-speed train for the shooting of *Nayak* so flawlessly that it was mistaken by most viewers as a real railway compartment. He recreated the mid-nineteenth century milieu of the British general Outram and the pre-Mutiny Muslim habitats of Lucknow in *Shatranj*. His ambition to switch over to directing was cut short by his untimely death, though he made three documentaries for the West Bengal Government.

Chandragupta's ideas on art direction and production design were very unconventional. Although a pioneer and ardent advocate of location shooting, he told an interviewer later in life that "outdoor shooting cannot compare with the excellence of indoor setting where factual details can be more easily established." It is surprising to hear from him that "85 per cent of Ray's films are shot indoors." For his most acclaimed work, in *Shatranj*, he was helped by Ray who studied pre-Mutiny Lucknow thoroughly, and by the paintings of Gaziuddin Hyder, a Nawab of Audh, preserved in the Victoria Memorial, Calcutta. The throne of Wazed Ali, for example, was copied from one such painting. Bansi was critical of set design in the commercial Hindi films of Bombay which were crudely expensive, gaudy, unrealistic, and generally outside the purview of directors. "Spending on sets is not infractuous but it is also challenging to design sets within a limited budget." For good set designing, there should be close collaboration between the director, the scriptwriter, and the designer. A set should not be a replica of what already exists, but built with a view to its photogenic appeal. "Anything that is not effective through the lens, is a waste of good money and effort," he told an interviewer in 1966.

—Bibekananda Ray

CHASE, Borden

Writer. **Nationality:** American. **Born:** Frank Fowler in Brooklyn, New York, 11 January 1900. **Family:** Married the pianist Lee Keith (first of three wives); daughter: Barrie Chase. **Career:** Left school at 14; worked as boxer, taxi driver, high diver in a carnival, shipyard worker, bootlegger, deep sea diver, sandhog (tunnel digger) on Holland and Eighth Avenue subway tunnels, and as a writer; 1935— first film as writer, *Under Pressure*; first novel, *East River*, published; then freelance fiction and film writer; TV work includes pilots for *Daniel Boone* and *Laredo* series, 1960s. **Died:** 8 March 1971.

Films as Writer:

1935   *Under Pressure* (Walsh)
1941   *Blue, White, and Perfect* (Leeds) (story)
1943   *Harrigan's Kid* (Reisner) (story)
1944   *Destroyer* (Seiter); *The Fighting Seabees* (Ludwig)
1945   *This Man's Navy* (Wellman); *Flame of the Barbary Coast* (Kane)
1946   *I've Always Loved You* (*Concerto*) (Borzage)
1947   *Tycoon* (Wallace)
1948   **Red River** (Hawks); *The Man from Colorado* (Levin)
1950   *The Great Jewel Robbery* (Godfrey); *Montana* (Enright); *Winchester '73* (A. Mann)
1951   *Iron Man* (Pevney); *Lone Star* (Sherman)
1952   *Bend of the River* (*Where the River Bends*) (A. Mann); *The World in His Arms* (Walsh)
1953   *Sea Devils* (Walsh)
1954   *His Majesty O'Keefe* (Haskin); *Vera Cruz* (Aldrich) (story)
1955   *The Far Country* (A. Mann); *Man without a Star* (K. Vidor)
1956   *Backlash* (J. Sturges)
1957   *Night Passage* (Neilson)
1958   *Ride a Crooked Trail* (Hibbs)

1965   *Los Pistoleros de Casa Grande* (*Gunfighters of Casa Grande*)
        (Rowland)
1969   *A Man Called Gannon* (Goldstone); *Backtrack*
        (Bellany—for TV)

Publications

By CHASE: fiction—

East River, New York, 1935.
Sandhog, New York, 1938.
Lone Star, New York, 1942.
Diamonds of Death, New York, 1947.
Blazing Guns on the Chisholm Trail, New York, 1948, as *Red River*,
    New York, 1948.
Viva Gringo!, New York, 1961.

By CHASE: nonfiction—

Sandhog: The Way of the Life of the Tunnel Builders, Evanston,
    Illinois, 1941.

By CHASE: article—

Interview with Jim Kitses in *The Hollywood Screenwriter*, edited by
    Richard Corliss, New York, 1972.

On CHASE: articles—

Script (Belgium), no. 3, 1962.
Présence du Cinéma (Paris), June 1962.
Film Comment (New York), Winter 1970–71.

*   *   *

Borden Chase pursued a successful screenwriting career from the
mid-1930s into the 1970s by creating tough heroes who faced danger
and death in the uncivilized days of the American West. His most
famous films, such as *Red River* (with Charles Schnee) and *Bend of
the River*, were all Westerns, although he also wrote war films
(*Fighting Seabees, Destroyer*), detective films (*Blue, White, and
Perfect*), and even romantic melodramas (Frank Borzage's *I've
Always Loved You*, which is also based on Chase's own short story
"Concerto"). However, his success at depicting complex conflicts
between two strong men kept him working in the Western format after
a certain point in his career, and today his name is associated almost
exclusively with that genre.

Chase left school at fourteen, and roamed the country, trying his
hand at boxing, taxi driving, bootlegging, sandhogging, and even
serving a hitch in the navy. Realizing this colorful existence could be
put to use in storytelling, he started a professional writing career. His
background led him easily to writing for the pulps (*Argosy* and
Detective Fiction) and for slick successful magazines (*The Saturday
Evening Post* and *Liberty*). This success led him inevitably to Hollywood, where his brand of well-plotted, clear stories about strong men
found a welcome market.

Among Chase's most successful works are three Western films
starring James Stewart and directed by Anthony Mann: *Winchester
'73* (with Robert L. Richards), *Bend of the River*, and *The Far
Country*. These films typify the characters and conflicts associated
with Chase's work. First of all, two strong men are involved in an
arduous journey across the western terrain, with units of society either
contained within the journey itself (as a wagon train) or as various
stops along the way (western towns, mining towns, etc.). The primary
involvement of the movie is the conflict between two men, who tend
to be deeply linked by some common bond. It may be an actual blood
relationship (*Winchester '73*), a mutual past experience (*Bend of the
River*), a competition over an economic goal (*The Far Country*), or an
adoptive father-son link as in his Howard Hawks film, *Red River*. In
some cases the conflict is internal, the hero against the evil inside
himself. Although Chase created strong females in films like *Lone
Star*, *Vera Cruz*, and *Flame of the Barbary Coast*, most Chase stories
are male conflicts. Chase once said "That I believe is the greatest love
story in all of the world. I don't mean sexual. I have always believed
that a man can actually love and respect another man more so than he
can a woman. . . . That's the theory I've worked on. There is a closer
relationship between two men than between a man and a woman."

Straightforward dialogue, and absence of pretentious philosophiz-
ing, and clearly delineated action mark the story progressions, which
culminate in unambiguous resolutions. Any ambiguities lie in the
maturity of the characterizations, in which the two men are neither
totally good nor totally bad. In this regard, Chase made a major
contribution to what is thought of as the "adult" or "psychological"
Westerns of the 1950s. Even when Chase's original script endings
were altered, as in the case of *Red River*, the story and the characters
he created were not destroyed. (Charles Schnee wrote a new ending
for *Red River*, in which the two heroes, John Wayne and Montgomery
Clift, end up in a showdown resolved by the intervention of the
leading lady.)

The Chase Western story is presented in a physical progression
across a larger-than-life landscape, an epic journey west which allows
forces of good and evil to interact. In *Red River*, there is a cattle drive.
In *Bend of the River*, a wagon train moves west. In *Vera Cruz*,
a stagecoach progresses into Mexico. And in perhaps Chase's most
commercially successful Western, *Winchester '73*, a search for a stolen
rifle moves the story across the American West, and also through
a microcosm of typical Western genre events: a final shootout, an
Indian uprising, a last stand, a bank robbery, a saloon fight, an Indian
attack on the cavalry, and more. The issue of the Chase Western script
is not whether man will settle the West and live in it. It is assumed he
will, or that he already has. The question is more universal and
appropriate to modern life: Will the uncivilized forces within man
create a Wild West in perpetuity by winning out over his better
instincts?

—Jeanine Basinger

CLAMPETT, Bob

Animator. **Nationality:** American. **Born:** San Diego, California,
1915 (?). **Education:** Attended Otis Art Institute, Los Angeles.
Career: Cartoonist for Los Angeles *Times* while still in school, then
strip cartoon contract with King Features; 1931—joined Warner
Brothers as animator, working mainly on *Bosko and Buddy* series;
director of animation 1937; 1948—briefly a consultant to Columbia,
then worked mainly in television: puppet series *Time for Beany* from
1949; other series include *Thunderbolt the Wonder Colt, Buffalo*

Billy, Top o' the Morning, Wm. Shakespeare Wolf, and *Beany and Cecil;* also made commercials. **Died:** In 1985.

Films as Animator:

1936   *When's Your Birthday* (Beaumont) (sequence)
1937   *Get Rich Quick Porky; Injun Trouble; Porky in Wackyland; Porky's Bedtime Story; Porky's Hero Agency; Porky's Poppa; Rover's Rival*
1938   *The Daffy Doc; The Lone Stranger and Porky; Porky and Daffy; Porky in Egypt; Porky's Five and Ten; Porky's Naughty Nephew; Porky's Party; What Price Porky*
1939   *Ali Baba Bound; Chicken Jitters; The Film Fan; Jeepers Creepers; Kristopher Kolumbus, Jr.; Naughty Neighbors; Patient Porky; Pied Piper Porky; Polar Pals; Porky's Hotel; Porky's Last Stand; Porky's Movie Mystery; Porky's Picnic; Porky's Tire Trouble; Scalp Trouble; Wise Quacks*
1940   *Africa Squeaks; The Chewin' Bruin; Farm Frolics; Pilgrim Porky; Porky's Poor Fish; Porky's Snooze Reel* (co); *Prehistoric Porky; Slap Happy Pappy; The Sour Puss; The Timid Toreador* (co); *We, the Animals Squeak*
1941   *A Coy Decoy; Goofy Groceries; The Henpecked Duck; Meet John Doughboy; Porky's Pooch; Robinson Crusoe, Jr.; Wabbit Twouble*
1942   *Bugs Bunny Gets the Boid; Cagey Canary* (co); *Crazy Cruise; Eatin' on the Cuff; The Hep Cat; Horton Hatches the Egg; The Impatient Patient* (co); *A Tale of Two Kitties; Wacky Blackout; The Wacky Wabbit; Any Bonds Today* (co)
1943   *Coal Black and de Sebben Dwarfs; A Corny Concerto; Falling Hare; An Itch in Time; Tin Pan Alley Cats; Tortoise Wins By a Hare; The Wise Quacking Duck; Booby Traps*
1944   *Birdy and the Beast; Buckaroo Bugs; Draftee Daffy; Hare Ribbin'; The Old Grey Hare; Russian Rhapsody; Slightly Daffy; Tick Tock Tuckered; What's Cookin' Doc?*
1945   *Baby Bottleneck; The Bashful Buzzard; Book Revue; A Gruesome Twosome; Wagon Heels*
1946   *Bacall to Arms; The Big Snooze; The Great Piggy Bank Robbery; Kitty Kornered; The Goofy Gophers* (co)
1947   *It's a Grand Old Nag* (+ pr)
1952   *Bwana Devil* (Oboler) (prologue, + ro)
1975   *Bugs Bunny—Superstar* (compilation) (+ ro)

Publications

By CLAMPETT: articles—

Funnyworld, Summer 1970.
Classic Film Collector (Indiana, Pennsylvania), Summer 1971.
The Velvet Light Trap (Madison, Wisconsin), Fall 1975.
Classic Images (Muscatine, Iowa), June 1984.
''Creating the Warner Bros. Animation Style: an interview with Bob Clampett,'' with T. Andrae, in *Animatrix* (Los Angeles), no. 9, 1995–1996.

On CLAMPETT: articles—

Technicien du Film (Paris), 15 December 1982–15 January 1983.
Lenburg, Jeff, in *The Great Cartoon Directors,* London, 1983.

Obituary in *Variety* (New York), 9 May 1984.
Obituary in *Film Comment* (New York), November-December 1984.
Classic Images (Muscatine, Iowa), December 1984.
Corliss, Richard, in *Films in Review* (New York), November 1985.
Schneider, Steve, in *That's All Folks,* New York, 1988.

*   *   *

Arguably one of the most creative and instrumental cartoon directors at Warner Brothers during the 1930s and 1940s, Bob Clampett started his cartooning career while still at school when King Features offered him a job drawing a newspaper Sunday strip. His earliest contact with animated cartoons was when he joined the Harman-Ising unit at Warner Brothers as an inbetweener; he was soon working as an animator on the very first *Merrie Melody* cartoon. At this early stage it is difficult to pick out one person's contribution, but Clampett was soon animating and suggesting stories and gags for most of the cartoons in production.

After his apprenticeship was served, Clampett was elevated to a full director to fill the space left by Frank Tashlin. Clampett made a hopeful start on an animated version of Edgar Rice Burrough's science-fiction stories *John Carter on Mars,* but it unfortunately never came to fruition. His first directorial role was an animated segment for a Joe E. Brown feature called *When's Your Birthday,* in which the zodiac signs become animated. Chiefly directing *Porky Pig* cartoons, he injected a wild, flighty surrealism close to that of his colleague Tex Avery, yet in a style all his own. The ludicrousness of a ''rubberized'' dog (*Porky's Tire Trouble*), a camel doing a highland fling (*Porky in Egypt*) or Daffy Duck inflating and deflating like a balloon, having just escaped being in an iron lung (*The Daffy Doc*) are all excellent examples of the Clampett philosophy of throwing logic to the wind.

Not until the war years and his being allowed color did Clampett pull out all the stops and inflict on audiences his own particular no-holds-barred kinds of zaniness. Armed with some excellent animators (Bob McKimson and Rod Scribner, among others) and his layout man Mike Sasanoff, who helped with just about every aspect connected with the production, Clampett made some of the wildest, most bizarre shorts ever put out by Warners. Parodies were also a good stock-in-trade for Clampett. His *Corny Concerto* flattens Disney's *Fantasia* by using Elmer Fudd as Deems Taylor to introduce the mayhem, including Bugs Bunny as a ballerina. *Coal Black and de Sebben Dwarfs* ribs Disney's *Snow White* by putting the whole cast in blackface, while *Bacall to Arms* deflates the Humphrey Bogart feature *To Have and Have Not* and *Kitty Kornered* parodies the effect Orson Welles's radio broadcast of *The War of the Worlds* had on the general public.

Only one really perennial character was to emerge from Clampett's pen, that of (''I T'ot I Taw a Putty Tat!'') Tweety-Pie, and Tweety only survived when refined, remodelled, and placed in a Award-winning cartoon directed by Friz Freleng after Bob had left Warners. It would seem as though Clampett's characters were too bizarre to survive the test of time and become standard Warner featured stars.

After leaving Warners, Clampett helped other Warner drop-outs to remodel Columbia cartoons and made a pilot cartoon to launch Republic Pictures' Trucolor color system. But his true glory was yet to come—in television—*and* with puppets. *Time for Beanie* was the most successful and popular children's puppet show on TV in the 1950s, watched by young and old alike. It reached out to all ages with its action, adventure, in-jokes, and dreadful puns featuring Cecil the

Sea-Sick Sea Serpent, Dishonest John, Cap'n Huffenpuff, and, of course, Beanie, whose propeller cap became a necessity for every American child in that era. The popularity of this puppet show inspired Clampett to revert to form and make an animated series of Beanie, syndicated throughout the world.

—Graham Webb

CLARKE, Charles G.

Cinematographer. **Nationality:** American. **Born:** Charles Gallorsy Clarke in Potter Valley, California, 10 March 1899. **Career:** 1916—assistant cameraman to Allen Siegler at Universal; 1917–18—served in United States Army; 1918—worked in film laboratories at National (also editor) and Oliver Morosco Company; 1922—first cameraman, Jesse Lasky Company; 1927–33—cinematographer for Fox and for 20th Century-Fox, 1937–62; 1966—co-director, Milestone of the Movies; past president, American Society of Cinematographers. **Died:** In Beverly Hills, California, 1 July 1983.

Films as Cinematographer:

1922   *The Half Breed* (Taylor) (co, + ed)
1923   *Salomy Jane* (*The Law of the Sierras*) (Melford); *The Light That Failed* (Melford)
1924   *Flaming Barriers* (Melford); *The Dawn of a Tomorrow* (Melford); *Tiger Love* (Melford); *The Top of the World* (Melford)
1925   *Friendly Enemies* (Melford); *Without Mercy* (Melford)
1926   *Rocking Moon* (Melford); *Whispering Smith* (*The Open Switch*) (Melford); *One Minute to Play* (Wood); *Going Crooked* (Melford); *Upstream* (*Footlight Glamor*) (Ford); *Singed* (Wray); *A Racing Romeo* (Wood); *Ham and Eggs at the Front* (Del Ruth)
1928   *Sharp Shooters* (*Three Naval Rascals*) (Blystone); *Four Sons* (Ford) (co); *The Red Dance* (*The Red Dancer of Moscow*) (Walsh) (co); *Plastered in Paris* (Stoloff); *Riley the Cop* (Ford)
1929   *The Sin Sister* (Klein) (co); *Not Quite Decent* (Cummings); *The Veiled Woman* (Flynn); *The Exalted Flapper* (Tinling); *Masquerade* (Birdwell) (co); *Words and Music* (Tinling) (co); *Nix on Dames* (Gallaher); *A Song of Kentucky* (Seiler)
1930   *Temple Tower* (Gallaher); *So This Is London* (Blystone); *Oh, for a Man!* (MacFadden); *Men on Call* (Blystone)
1931   *Girls Demand Excitement* (Felix); *Annabelle's Affairs* (Werker); *Good Sport* (MacKenna)
1932   *Too Busy to Work* (Blystone); *Second Hand Wife* (*The Illegal Divorce*) (MacFadden)
1933   *Hot Pepper* (Blystone)
1934   *The Cat and the Fiddle* (Howard) (co); *Tarzan and His Mate* (Gibbons) (co); *Viva Villa!* (Conway) (co); *Evelyn Prentice* (Howard)
1935   *The Winning Ticket* (Reisner); *Shadow of Doubt* (Seitz); *The Casino Murder Case* (Martin); *Woman Wanted* (Seitz); *Pursuit* (Martin) (co); *The Perfect Gentleman* (Whelan)

1936   *The Garden Murder Case* (Marin); *Moonlight Murder* (Marin); *Trouble for Two* (*The Suicide Club*) (Rubin); *All American Chump* (*Country Bumpkin*) (Marin)
1937   *Under Cover of Night* (Seitz); *Man of the People* (Marin); *The Thirteenth Chair* (Seitz); *Stand-in* (Garnett)
1938   *Safety in Numbers* (St. Clair); *Charlie Chan in Honolulu* (Humberstone)
1939   *Pardon Our Nerve* (Humberstone); *The Return of the Cisco Kid* (Leeds); *Mr. Moto Takes a Vacation* (Foster); *Frontier Marshal* (Dwan)
1940   *Young As You Feel* (St. Clair); *Viva Cisco Kid* (Foster); *Yesterday's Heroes* (Leeds); *For Beauty's Sake* (Traube); *Street of Memories* (Traube)
1941   *Romance of the Rio Grande* (Leeds); *Murder among Friends* (McCarey); *Dead Men Tell* (Lachman); *The Cowboy and the Blonde* (McCarey); *The Bride Wore Crutches* (Traube); *Accent on Love* (McCarey); *The Last of the Duanes* (Tinling); *Cadet Girl* (McCarey); *Marry the Boss's Daughter* (Freeland); *The Perfect Snob* (McCarey)
1942   *A Gentleman at Heart* (McCarey); *It Happened in Flatbush* (McCarey); *Moontide* (Mayo); *Thru Different Eyes* (Loring); *Careful, Soft Shoulders* (Garrett); *Time to Kill* (Leeds)
1943   *Hello, Frisco, Hello* (Humberstone) (co); *Wintertime* (Brahm) (co); *Guadalcanal Diary* (Weiler)
1944   *Tampico* (Mendes); *Ladies of Washington* (L. King)
1945   *Thunderhead, Son of Flicka* (L. King); *Molly and Me* (Seiler); *Junior Miss* (Seaton)
1946   *Smokey* (L. King); *Margie* (H. King)
1947   *Miracle on 34th Street* (*The Big Heart*) (Seaton); *Captain from Castile* (H. King) (co); *Thunder in the Valley* (*Bob, Son of Battle*) (L. King)
1948   *The Iron Curtain* (Wellman); *Green Grass of Wyoming* (L. King); *That Wonderful Urge* (Sinclair)
1949   *Sand* (L. King); *Slattery's Hurricane* (De Toth)
1950   *The Big Lift* (Seaton); *I'll Get By* (Sale)
1951   *Golden Girl* (Bacon); *The Academy Awards Film* (Carleton-Hunt) (co)
1952   *Red Skies of Montana* (Newman); *Kangaroo* (Milestone); *Stars and Stripes Forever* (*Marching Along*) (Koster)
1953   *Destination Gobi* (Wise); *City of Bad Men* (Jones); *Vesuvius Express* (O. Lang—short); *The Coronation Parade* (Hathaway—short)
1954   *Night People* (Johnson); *Suddenly* (Allen); *Black Widow* (Johnson); *Prince of Players* (Dunne); *The Bridges at Toko-Ri* (Robson) (co)
1955   *Violent Saturday* (Fleischer); *The Virgin Queen* (Koster)
1956   *Carousel* (H. King); *The Man in the Gray Flannel Suit* (Johnson); *The Dark Wave* (Negulesco—short); *Three Brave Men* (Dunne)
1957   *Oh, Men! Oh, Women!* (Johnson); *The Wayward Bus* (Vicas); *Stopover Tokyo* (Breen)
1958   *The Barbarian and the Geisha* (Huston); *The Hunters* (Powell); *These Thousand Hills* (Fleischer)
1959   *The Sound and the Fury* (Ritt); *Holiday for Lovers* (Levin); *A Private's Affair* (Walsh); *Hound Dog Man* (Siegel)
1960   *Flaming Star* (Wiegel)
1961   *Return to Peyton Place* (J. Ferrer); *Madison Avenue* (Humberstone)

Other Films:

1916 *Shoes* (Weber) (asst)
1921 *The Son of Tarzan* (*Jungle Trail of the Son of the Tarzan*)
         (Revier and Flaven—serial) (2nd unit ph)
1922 *Burning Sands* (*The Dweller in the Desert*) (Melford) (asst);
         Ebb Tide (Melford) (asst)
1923 *Slippery McGee* (Ruggles) (2nd unit ph + ed)
1935 *Mutiny on the Bounty* (Lloyd) (2nd unit ph)
1937 *Pigskin Champions* (d—short)
1938 *Suez* (Dwan) (2nd unit ph)
1950 *Three Came Home* (Negulesco) (2nd unit ph)
1966 *Milestones of the Movies* (co-d)

Publications

By CLARKE: books—

Early Film Making in Los Angeles, Los Angeles, California, 1976.
Professional Cinematography, Hollywood, 1964, 5th edition, 1980.

By CLARKE: articles—

On *The Big Lift* in *American Cinematographer* (Hollywood), May 1950.
On *Kangaroo* in *American Cinematographer* (Hollywood), July 1952.
"Practical Filming Techniques for Three-Dimension and Wide-
      Screen Motion Pictures," in *American Cinematographer* (Holly-
      wood), March 1953.
"CinemaScope Photographic Techniques," in *American Cinema-
      tographer* (Hollywood), June 1955.
"And Now 55mm," in *American Cinematographer* (Hollywood),
      December 1955.
"Shooting Night Scenes in Daylight," in *American Cinematographer*
      (Hollywood), December 1956.
"The Case of the Inventor of Motion Pictures," in *American Cinema-
      tographer* (Hollywood), November 1961.
"How to Film Night Scenes in Daylight," in *American Cinema-
      tographer* (Hollywood), May 1966.
"What Is a 'Director of Photography,'" in *American Cinema-
      tographer* (Hollywood), May 1967.
American Cinematographer (Hollywood), June 1974.
Film Dope (London), no. 7, April 1975.

On CLARKE: articles—

Focus on Film (London), no. 13, 1973.
Cinéma (Paris), July-August 1973.
Obituary in *Variety* (New York), 13 July 1983.
Obituary in *American Cinematographer* (Hollywood), November 1983.
Film Dope (Nottingham), March 1985.

*   *   *

A commentator once noted that Charles G. Clarke "doesn't work
at photography . . . he is in love with it." It is an apt comment on
a cinematographer whose contribution to the screen as a cameraman
is equalled by his devotion to acquiring and preserving (through
donations to the Academy of Motion Picture Arts and Sciences) many
early and rare books, papers, and artifacts.

Clarke was a pioneer in technical innovations in cinematography,
including the introduction of a battery-operated camera motor, the
development of matte photography, and a device for composing
artificial clouds. He was heavily involved with the American Society
of Cinematographers, and edited several editions of its *Cinematographers Manual*. He was a consummate filmmaker, and yet, at the
same time, it is difficult to identify him as a great cameraman.

Although the films on which Clarke worked are widely known and
admired, the cinematography in them is not particularly outstanding.
Or, at least, he makes his camerawork seem so matter-of-fact that it is
never noted as a major critical issue in the film. Indeed, his films very
clearly emphasize his own comment that "There are two kinds of
cinematographers—those who know and those who put on a show."
He dismissed his work simply: "You work out a pleasing composition, take a light reading and shoot. It's that simple."

A prolific cinematographer, Clarke has no discernible style, as do
the better-known cameramen. His photography is so innocuous that
despite the critical furor over the "colorization" of black-and-white
features, there were no arguments with the plans to "colorize"
Clarke's work on *Miracle on 34th Street*. If Clarke is best-known for
anything, it is for his outdoor work on difficult locations for features
such as *Mutiny on the Bounty*, *Viva Villa!*, and *The Good Earth*. As
one of the leading cameramen at 20th Century-Fox, to which he was
under long-term contract, Clarke was considered reliable enough to
photograph the first Technicolor Monopack feature, *Thunderhead*.
His style could easily be changed to suit an Alice Faye musical such as
Hello Frisco, Hello or a John Ford production, such as *Four Sons*,
which Clarke always considered his best work.

—Anthony Slide

CLARKE, T. E. B.

Writer. **Nationality:** British. **Born:** Thomas Ernest Bennett Clarke in
Watford, Hertfordshire, England, 7 June 1907. **Education:** Attended
Cambridge University. Lived in Australia (where he edited the
magazine *The Red Heart*) and Argentina in the late 1920s and early
1930s. **Family:** Married Joyce Steel, 1932 (died 1983); two children.
Career: 1932—first of several books published; reporter for the
Daily Sketch, London; 1940–43—served with the War Reserve
Police, London; 1944—first film as writer, *For Those in Peril*.
Award: Academy Award and Venice Festival Award for *The Laven-
der Hill Mob*, 1952. Officer, Order of the British Empire, 1952. **Died:**
In Surrey, 11 February 1989.

Films as Writer:

1944 *For Those in Peril* (Crichton) (co); *The Halfway House*
         (Dearden) (co); *Champagne Charlie* (Cavalcanti) (co-lyrics)
1945 *Johnny Frenchman* (Frend); "The Golfing Story" ep. of
         Dead of Night (Crichton) (additional dialogue)
1946 *Hue and Cry* (Crichton)
1948 *Against the Wind* (Crichton); **Passport to Pimlico** (Cornel-
         ius); "The Engine Driver" ep. of *Train of Events* (Cole);
         The Blue Lamp (Dearden)
1950 *The Magnet* (Frend)

T. E. B. Clarke

1951   *The Lavender Hill Mob* (Crichton); "The Ant and the Grass-
        hopper" ep. of *Encore* (Jackson)
1952   *The Titfield Thunderbolt* (Crichton)
1954   *The Rainbow Jacket* (Dearden)
1955   *Who Done It?* (Relph and Dearden)
1957   *Barnacle Bill* (*All at Sea*) (Frend)
1958   *A Tale of Two Cities* (Thomas); *Gideon's Day* (*Gideon of
        Scotland Yard*) (Ford); *Law and Disorder* (Crichton) (co)
1960   *Sons and Lovers* (Cardiff) (co)
1963   *The Horse without a Head* (Chaffey)
1966   *A Man Could Get Killed* (Neame and Owen) (co)
1978   *A Hitch in Time* (Darnley-Smith)
1979   *High Rise Donkey* (Forlong)

Publications

By CLARKE: books—

Go South—Go West, London, 1932.
Jeremy's England, London, 1934.
Cartwright Was a Cad, London, 1937.
Two and Two Make Five, London, 1938.
What's Yours? The Student's Guide to Publand, London, 1938.
Mr. Spirket Reforms, London, 1940.
Encore (script), London, 1951.
The World Was Mine, London, 1964.

The Wide Open Door, London, 1966.
The Wrong Turning, London, 1971.
Intimate Relations, London, 1971.
This Is Where I Came In (autobiography), London, 1974.
Highlights and Shadows, New York, 1989.

By CLARKE: article—

Picturegoer (London), 16 July 1949.

On CLARKE: articles—

Obituary in *Variety* (New York), 15 February 1989.
Obituary in *Skoop*, April 1989.

*   *   *

If any one person can be credited with inventing Ealing Comedy, it would have to be T. E. B. Clarke. Not that Michael Balcon's studio had produced no comedies prior to Clarke's arrival; but they had largely been vehicles for such superannuated British comics as George Formby or Will Hay—crude, slapdash productions in the broad music-hall tradition, lacking any distinctively Ealing look or tone. With *Hue and Cry*, Clarke's first comedy, something fresh had unmistakably arrived.

Hue and Cry—like its more accomplished successor, *Passport to Pimlico*—draws on the Ealing documentary heritage, making effective use of the blitzed buildings and bomb-craters of postwar London. Its humour is soundly based in character and observation, without recourse to tired comic routines. And, like all Clarke's comedies, it celebrates a degree of anarchy—the liberating power of fantasy to break through the drab, commonsense fabric of everyday life. A group normally subject to the prosaic weight of authority (schoolboys, in this case) suddenly find themselves able to wriggle free, to realise—at least for a time—their daydreams. (The plot stems from an isolated image conceived by the film's producer, Henry Cornelius: "the impression that for one glorious hour boys have taken over the city.")

Yet—as so often in Clarke's work, and indeed in Ealing generally—the anarchy is limited, controlled, ultimately unambitious, feeding safely back into the society which surrounds and, in the end, contains it. The boys "take over the city" for no more subversive purpose than to round up a gang of crooks. Similarly, in *Passport to Pimlico* the Londoners who have joyfully thrown off the burdens of austerity and bureaucracy soon feel themselves constrained to reimpose their own versions of these things, and finally return, thankfully, to the cosily regulated world of ration-books. ("Never thought I'd welcome the sight of these again.") The status quo is teased, rumpled a little, but never seriously endangered.

Of all the Clarke comedies, *The Lavender Hill Mob* comes closest to shattering these self-prescribed limits. Alec Guinness's downtrodden, patronized bank clerk does get away with his stolen bullion, does enjoy the high life in South America—but even here convention imposes, in the last reel, a well-spoken Interpol detective, complete with handcuffs. The script, which won an Oscar and a prize at Venice, includes some of Clarke's most inventive and enjoyable writing. The "seduction scene" has become deservedly famous: Guinness circling restlessly around the more slow-witted Stanley Holloway, slily insinuating, until realization dawns in Holloway's eyes—"By Jove, Holland, it's a good job we're both honest men." The distance, though, between this, archetype of the good-natured Ealing mainstream, and the darker vision of Hamer or Mackendrick, can readily be estimated by comparison with *The Ladykillers*. Both movies feature Guinness as gang boss; but the brutal deaths of the later film would be unthinkable in *Lavender Hill Mob*, wrecking its gentle make-believe.

"Its good humour," Charles Barr wrote of *Lavender Hill Mob* (and the judgment holds good for all Clarke's comedies), "has the effect of continuously endorsing the 'social' values even while the plot is ostensibly defying them." This endorsement figures even more clearly in his non-comedies such as *The Blue Lamp*, seminal ancestor of every British TV police series ever since. In the closing scenes, police and criminal underworld unite to trap a young cop-killer. The episode recalls *M*, but with none of Lang's Brechtian irony ("Child-murderers are bad for business"); the delinquent in *The Blue Lamp* has broken a set of rules acknowledged equally by cops and villains, and thus placed himself beyond the communal pale.

The best comedy, it can be argued, needs an element of cruelty in the mix. But cruelty seems to have been something absent from the character of Clarke, an exceptionally genial and tolerant man, and in the post-*Lavender Hill* comedies the kindliness threatens to become stifling. *The Titfield Thunderbolt*, *Barnacle Bill*: fantasy shades off into whimsy, individuality into eccentricity. There are still enjoyable moments, but it's hard not to lose patience with the pervasive air of parochial self-indulgence as Ealing's vision turns increasingly in on itself. "This little, close-knit community," Clarke commented in a TV interview, "had really failed to see how life was changing round about us."

After Ealing closed down, many of its alumni seemed to lose their way, missing the supportive team atmosphere that Balcon had created. Clarke was no exception; the handful of films he scripted for other producers show little sign of his distinctive quirkiness, and he largely withdrew from screenwriting midway through the 1960s. To judge from his autobiography, it was as much with relief as with regret.

—Philip Kemp

CLOQUET, Ghislain

Cinematographer. **Nationality:** Belgian. **Born:** Ghislain Pierre Cloquet in Antwerp, 18 April 1924. **Education:** Attended schools in Brussels and Paris; studied film at École National de Photographie et Cinématographie, 1943–44, and IDHEC, 1946–47. **Military Service:** World War II service, 1945–46. **Family:** Married Sophie Becker. **Career:** Cameraman from 1947; 1954–62—in charge of courses, IDHEC, and director of studies, 1974–81; co-founder, Institut National des Arts du Spectacle; 1963–64—under contract to Television Française: later TV work includes—*Double-vue* series (in Belgium), 1963, and *Charles Aznavour—Music Hall de France*, 1969. **Awards:** Academy Award, César award, and British Academy Award, for *Tess*, 1979. **Died:** 2 November 1981.

Films as Cinematographer:

1950 *Curare et curarisants de synthèse* (Lemoigne); *Une ligne sans incident* (Magnin—short); *Soldats d'eau douce* (Leduc—short)

1952 *Saint-Tropez, devoir de vacances* (Paviot—short)

1953 *Les Statues meurent aussi* (Resnais and Marker—short); *Lumière et l'invention du cinématographe* (*Louis Lumière*) (Paviot—short); *Statues d'épouvante* (*Le Cubisme*; *L'École de Paris*) (Hessens—short)

1954 *Neiges* (Languepin—short) (co); *Pantomimes* (Paviot—short); *Contes à dormir debout* (Brabant—short); *La Belle Journée* (Gibaud—short); *Aux frontières de l'homme* (Védrès and Rostand—short)

1955 *Deux bobines et un fil* (Villier—short); **Nuit et brouillard** (Resnais—short)

1956 *Toute la mémoire du monde* (Resnais—short); *Le Ciel est par-dessus le toit* (*Ma famille et mon toit*) (Decourt—short); *Brahim* (Fléchet)

1957 *Le Mystère de l'Atelier Quinze* (Resnais and Heinrich—short) (co); *Me and the Colonel* (Glenville) (2nd unit); *Un Amour de poche* (Kast)

1958 *Chopin* (Mitry and Olembert—short) (co); *Le Bel Age* (Kast) (co)

1959 *Classe tous risques* (Sautet); *Le Trou* (Jacques Becker)

1960 *Les Honneurs de la guerre* (Dewever) (co); *Description d'un combat* (Marker); *L'Exécution* (Cazeneuve—for TV)

1961 *Un nommé la Rocca* (Jean Becker); *La Belle Américaine* (Dhery)

1962 *Carillons sans joie* (Brabant)

1963 *Le Poulet* (Berri—short); *Un Panier de chats* (Villa—for TV); *La Belle Marinière* (Marchand—for TV); *Touiste encore* (Malle and Ertaud; another version: *Vive le Tour!*, 1965); *Le Feu follet* (*The Fire Within. A Time to Live, a Time to Die*) (Malle)

1964 *Le Pain et le vin* (Witta—short); *La Chambre* (Mitrani—for TV)

1965 *Mickey One* (A. Penn); *Pas de caviar pour Tante Olga* (Jean Becker)

1966 *Au hasard Balthazar* (*Balthasar*) (Bresson); *L'Homme au crâne rasé* (*Die man die zijn Haar kort liet knippen*; *The Man Who Had His Hair Cut Short*) (Delvaux)

1967 *Mouchette* (Bresson); *Loin du Viêt-nam* (Varda) (co); *Les Demoiselles de Rochefort* (*The Young Girls of Rochefort*) (Demy)

1968 *Benjamin ou les mémoires d'un puceau* (Deville); *Un Soir, un train* (Delvaux); *Mazel tov ou le mariage* (Berri)

1969 *La Maison des Bories* (Doniol-Valcroze); *Une Femme douce* (Bresson)

1970 *La Décharge* (Baratier); *C'était un jour comme les autres* (Chartier—short)

1971 *Peau d'âne* (*Donkey Skin*) (Demy); *Faustine et le bel été* (Companeez); *Rendez-vous à Bray* (Delvaux); *Pouce!* (Badal)

1972 *Nathalie Granger* (Duras); *Au rendez-vous de la mort joyeuse* (J. Buñuel)

1973 *L'Histoire très bonne et très joyeuse de Colinot Trousse-Chemise* (Companeez); *Belle* (Delvaux)

1974 *Dites-le avec des fleurs* (Grimblat); *Le Boucher, la star, et l'orpheline* (Savary) (co)

1975	*Love and Death* (Allen); *Monsieur Albert* (Renard); *La Ville Bidon* (Baratier)
1978	*The Secret Lives of Plants* (Green) (co)
1979	*Tess* (Polanski) (co)
1980	*Chère inconnue* (*I Sent a Letter to My Love*) (Mizrahi)
1981	*Four Friends* (*Georgia's Friends*) (A. Penn)

Films as Camera Operator:

1947	*Blanc comme neige* (Berthomieu)
1948	*Cent ans de mission* (Méhu—short); *Mademoiselle de la Ferté* (Dallier)
1949	*La Perspective* (*Le Dessin de perspective*) (Régnier—short); "Le Retour de Jean" ep. of *Retour à la vie* (Clouzot); *Un Certain Monsieur* (Ciampi); *La Profession de géomètre expert* (Gibaud—short); *Moissons d'aujourd'hui* (*Chevaux d'acier*) (Dupont—short); *Pétrole de la Gironde* (Lemoigne—short)
1950	*Braque* (Bureau—short); *L'Espoir au village* (de Boissac—short); *Hommes des oasis* (Régnier—short); *Les Musiciens de la mine* (Méhu—short); *Avalanche* (Segard)
1951	*La Petite Diligence* (Croses—short); *Labor Goes to School* (Croses—short); *The Green Glove* (Maté)
1952	*Il est minuit, Docteur Schweitzer* (Haguet)
1953	*La Classe de mathématiques* (Lecomte—short); *La Classe de lettres* (Lecomte—short); *La Classe d'histoire* (Lecomte—short); *L'Homme à l'oeillet blanc* (Severac—short); *Le Grand Pavois* (Pinoteau)
1954	*Napoléon* (Guitry) (2nd unit)
1955	*Les Possédés* (Brabant)
1957	*Les aventures d'Arsène Lupin* (*The Adventures of Arsène Lupin*) (Jacques Becker)
1958	*Le Piège* (Brabant); *Les Naufrageurs* (Brabant)

Publications

By CLOQUET: articles—

Cinéma (Paris), January 1965.
Revue du Cinéma (Morges, Switzerland), October/December 1969.
Le Technicien du Film (Paris), April/May 1974.
Le Technicien du Film (Paris), May/June 1974.
Film Reader (Evanston, Illinois), January 1977.
Ecran (Paris), 15 September 1979.
American Cinematographer (Hollywood), May 1981.

On CLOQUET: articles—

Focus on Film (London), no. 13, 1973.
Film Dope, April 1975.
Cinéma Français (Paris), May 1980.
Pour le Cinéma Belge (Brussels), May/June 1980.
Russell, Sharon A., in *Semiotics and Lighting*, Ann Arbor, Michigan, 1981.

Filme (Berlin), November/December 1981.
Sainderich, G.-P., in *Cahiers du Cinéma* (Paris), December 1981.
Obituary in *Films and Filming*, January 1982.
Film Dope (Nottingham), December 1983.

*   *   *

Ghislain Cloquet's outstanding contribution to the development of postwar European camerawork was twofold. First, his rich experience as camera operator and cinematographer on short fictions and documentaries for cinema or television allowed him to foreground the lightweight technique at a time when cinema was still very "heavy." Cloquet subsequently established, thanks to his masterly use of the camera, a perfect compatibility between the liberation of technique and the exactness of framed shots. Second, his generous nature and his desire to train capable technicians while widening their artistic scope, led him to form not only reputed present-day cinematographers (Bruno Nuytten and Charlie Van Damme, among many others), but also whole generations of European film-makers who attended the French IDHEC and the no less famous Belgian INSAS, a film school Cloquet and André Delvaux founded in the early sixties.

Though Belgian-born, Cloquet moved to France very early, as during the fifties there was no ongoing production in his native country. In spite of having started his apprenticeship on the sets of great cinematographers such as Louis Page, Christian Matras, and Edmond Séchan, Cloquet considered himself a self-made artisan and strove to attain perfect harmony between the director's general concept of a film and his visual translation of it. The results of his fulfilled ambition are visible throughout his collaboration with Alain Resnais on his most challenging documentaries (*Les Statues meurent aussi*, *Nuit et brouillard*, and *Toute la mémoire du monde*).

The same went for Resnais's friend Chris Marker, whom Cloquet overtly admired for his capacity to extensively use the cinematographer's potential, especially during the shooting of the famous *Description d'un combat*. International recognition came, however, with a feature-length film—unfortunately Jacques Becker's last—*Le Trou*, in which Cloquet's lighting managed to effectively dramatize an action unfolding in a circumscribed, unspectacular setting. Throughout Louis Malle's psychological study of a young bourgeois's suicidal ego, *Le Feu follet*, Cloquet related perfectly to the director's style and rendered the symbolism of ordinary places, such as hotel rooms, taxis, or Parisian cafés. His partnership with Nouvelle Vague directors included films by Pierre Kast and Agnès Varda.

The latter's husband, Jacques Demy, an atypical creator for his generation, requested from Cloquet a color photography very close to magic: *Les Demoiselles de Rochefort* and *Peau d'âne*, made a few years later, still enchant audiences over the world. During the same decade, Cloquet's work also helped materialize some of the most relevant metaphysical films of this century. While shooting *Au hasard Balthazar* and *Mouchette*, he tried his utmost to satisfy Robert Bresson's demanding mise en scène: the director wanted him to frame each shot as a sensual, dense entity inside which shades of daylight, raindrops falling over a countryscape or mysterious gazes from Balthazar, the sacred donkey, were supposed to be part of a spiritual visual event. Such an experience seems to have had an impact on his fruitful collaboration with André Delvaux, master of what is commonly called "magic realism" on the screen. Cloquet served both as camera operator and as cinematographer for most of Delvaux's films: *L'Homme au crâne rasé*; *Un soir, un train*; *Rendez-vous à Bray*; and *Belle* all received worldwide praise for their camerawork. The black-and-white photography used for *L'Homme au crâne rasé* works up a striking ambiguity between dream and reality, while images shot in color for the three other films are a deliberate reminder of Flemish and French masters.

Cloquet's name has nonetheless been associated with less sophisticated directors such as Claude Berri, Jean Becker, and Nina Companeez. It is precisely after having seen *Faustine et le bel été* by Companeez that Woody Allen decided to hire the Belgian cinematographer for *Love and Death*, asking him to find evocative Russian locations around Paris and to keep a consistent balance between the poetic and the parodic elements of a multilayered visual fiction. Cloquet had previously worked with another U.S. director, Arthur Penn, for *Mickey One*, and one of his last films was another successful Penn vehicle, *Four Friends*. Cloquet's last—but not least—challenge consisted in brilliantly succeeding the reputed Geoffrey Unsworth, who died unexpectedly before having time to complete the shooting of Polanski's *Tess*. Apart from receiving an Academy Award—for his work on *Tess*—Cloquet was offered the opportunity, one year before his untimely death, to bring his opinions back to the forefront and to reaffirm what he has always cherished, namely the importance of rigorous training for a discipline where art and technical ability were meant to be one.

—Dominique Nasta

CLOTHIER, William H.

Cinematographer. **Nationality:** American. **Born:** Decatur, Illinois, 1903. **Military Service:** U.S. Army Air Corps during World War II: captain. **Career:** 1923—newsreel photographer for Paramount; 1927—did aerial photography for *Wings*; 1929—contract with RKO; mid-1930s—worked as photographer in Mexico and Spain; 1953–54—photographed the television series *Gang-Busters*. **Awards:** Presidential Award, American Society of Cinematographers, 1994. **Died:** 7 January 1996.

Films as Cinematographer:

1932   *The Lost Squadron* (Archimbaud and Sloane); *The Conquerors* (Wellman) (aerial ph)
1935   *Maria Elena* (Sevilla); *El 113* (Sevilla)
1936   *Rinconcito madrileno* (Artola); *Lola Triana* (del Campo)
1944   *Memphis Belle* (Wyler—short)
1947   *For You I Die* (Reinhardt)
1948   *Sofia* (Reinhardt)
1950   *Once a Thief* (W. Wilder)
1952   *Confidence Girl* (Stone)
1953   *Phantom from Space* (W. Wilder); *Island in the Sky* (Wellman) (aerial ph); *Killers from Space* (W. Wilder)
1954   *The High and the Mighty* (Wellman) (aerial ph); *Track of the Cat* (Wellman)

1955   *Gang-Busters* (Karn) (+ co-pr); *Top of the World* (Foster) (aerial ph); *The Sea Chase* (Farrow); *Blood Alley* (Wellman); *Sincerely Yours* (Douglas); *Good-bye, My Lady* (Wellman)
1956   *Seven Men from Now* (Boetticher); *Gun the Man Down* (McLaglen); *The Man in the Vault* (McLaglen)
1957   *Dragoon Wells Massacre* (Schuster); *Fort Dobbs* (Douglas); *Bombers B-52* (*No Sleep till Dawn*) (Douglas); *Darby's Rangers* (*The Young Invaders*) (Wellman); *Lafayette Escadrille* (*Hell Bent for Glory*) (Wellman); *Jet Pilot* (aerial photography) (von Sternberg)
1958   *China Doll* (Borzage); *Escort West* (Lyon)
1959   *The Horse Soldiers* (Ford)
1960   *The Alamo* (Wayne); *Tomboy and the Champ* (Lyon)
1961   *Ring of Fire* (Stone); *The Deadly Companions* (Peckinpah); *The Comancheros* (Curtiz); **The Man Who Shot Liberty Valance** (Ford)
1962   *Merrill's Marauders* (Fuller)
1963   *Donovan's Reef* (Ford); *McLintock!* (McLaglen)
1964   *A Distant Trumpet* (Walsh); *Cheyenne Autumn* (Ford)
1965   *Shenandoah* (McLaglen); *The Rare Breed* (McLaglen)
1966   *Stagecoach* (Douglas); *Way . . . Way Out* (Douglas)
1967   *The Way West* (McLaglen); *The War Wagon* (Kennedy); *Firecreek* (McEveety)
1968   *The Devil's Brigade* (McLaglen); *Bandolero!* (McLaglen); *Hellfighters* (McLaglen)
1969   *The Undefeated* (McLaglen)
1970   *The Cheyenne Social Club* (Kelly); *Chisum* (McLaglen); *Rio Lobo* (Hawks)
1971   *Big Jake* (G. Sherman)
1973   *The Train Robbers* (Kennedy)

Films as Cameraman:

1927   *Wings* (Wyler) (aerial ph); *Underworld* (*Paying the Penalty*) (von Sternberg)
1928   *The Last Command* (von Sternberg); *The Patriot* (Lubitsch); *Sins of the Fathers* (Berger)
1929   *Rio Rita* (Reed)
1930   *Hit the Deck* (Reed); *The Silver Horde* (Archainbaud); *Cimarron* (Ruggles)
1933   **King Kong** (Cooper and Schoedsack)
1939   *Gunga Din* (Stevens)
1942   *Name, Age, Occupation* (Lorentz—short)
1948   *Fort Apache* (Ford) (asst)

Publications

By CLOTHIER: articles—

On Film, 1970.
Filmmakers Newsletter (Ward Hill, Massachusetts), April 1973.
Take One (Montreal), no. 8, 1975.
American Cinematographer (Hollywood), November 1977.
Interview in *Five American Cinematographers*, by Scott Eyman, London, 1987.

On CLOTHIER: articles—

Clark, Donald, and Christopher Andersen, in *John Wayne's* The Alamo*: The Making of the Epic Film: in TODD-AO*, Secaucus, New Jersey, 1994.
Obituary, in *Classic Images* (Muscatine), February 1996.
Obituary, in *American Cinematographer* (Hollywood), March 1996.
Obituary, in *Classic Images* (Muscatine), March 1996.

* * *

"I never saw a mountain I wouldn't climb," said the cinematographer William H. Clothier, "if I thought I could make my shot better, or get up on a rooftop, or in an airplane, anything to improve a shot." In the course of 45 years, Clothier climbed many a mountain, and risked his life in all types of aircraft to achieve the most effective photography. A favorite Clothier setup involved digging a pit for his camera and crew, then charging John Ford's cavalry over it for a spectacular low-angle shot. Whether filming Westerns in Monument Valley, or documentary footage of aerial combat during World War II, Clothier was the preeminent location cameraman. His sense of composition and penchant for dangerous settings appealed to such action-oriented directors as Ford, William Wellman, Raoul Walsh, and Howard Hawks, and Clothier photographed their last films.

It took Clothier 20 years to rise to the status of Hollywood director of photography, but he brought with him a wealth of rich and varied cinematic experience. He broke into pictures at the age of 20, painting sets at Warner Brothers. He worked his way up to assistant cameraman on low-budget Westerns before joining Harry Perry's camera crew on William Wellman's aviation spectacular *Wings*. A contract with Paramount followed, and Clothier assisted such veteran cinematographers as Bert Glennon (his strongest influence) and Victor Milner. With the advent of sound, he moved to RKO, where he did the beautiful aerial cinematography in Wellman's *The Conquerors*, and assisted on *Cimarron*, *The Silver Horde*, and *King Kong*. Clothier spent the rest of the 1930s as a first cameraman in the fledgling Mexican and Spanish film industries, and shot newsreels of the Spanish Civil War for Paramount. He returned to America to work as Joseph August's assistant cameraman on *Gunga Din*, and during World War II served as a photographic officer in the U.S. Eighth Air Force. In this capacity he shot William Wyler's historic documentary *Memphis Belle*, a color film shot in combat situations in the European skies.

After the war, Clothier began a relationship with John Ford, working first as a camera operator for Archie Stout on *Fort Apache*. He also made his first Hollywood film as a director of photography, the low-budget *For You I Die*. He renewed his association with William Wellman in 1953 shooting the aerials for *Island in the Sky* and *The High and the Mighty*, the former in black and white, the latter in color and CinemaScope, both offering Clothier's visual sense of space and composition. With Archie Stout's retirement, Clothier became Wellman's regular cameraman, and he shot the remainder of Wellman's films. *Track of the Cat* was a fascinating experiment, a black-and-white film in color. In the exteriors, the snow and forest were shot in low-light situations to create a black-and-white look. In the interiors the actors were clothed in black and white except for

Robert Mitchum's red jacket and Diana Lynn's yellow sleeves. The cumulative effect was visually remarkable, and a statement against the typical garish color of Hollywood product. The other Wellman films have good pictorial values as well—*Blood Alley* was comic-book color, recreating China in San Rafael, California; *Good-bye, My Lady* profited from Georgia swamp locations; *Darby's Rangers* featured a memorable combat terrain filmed entirely on a misty soundstage; and *Lafayette Escadrille* contains some breathtaking aerial scenes shot at dawn, although the dogfights were reused from Wellman's earlier *Men with Wings*.

Clothier's work for John Ford is also distinguished. The main title sequence of *The Horse Soldiers* showcases a classic Clothier shot, a long view of 30 Union troopers galloping along a railroad track, silhouetted against the sky. *The Man Who Shot Liberty Valance* is black-and-white symbolism, a story about right and wrong, and the building of a myth, given eloquence by the simplicity of Clothier's cinematography. By contrast, Ford's *Donovan's Reef* with its bright colors and Hawaiian locations, and *Cheyenne Autumn*, filmed in color and Super Panavision 70mm to emphasize the epic qualities of the piece, reveal another side of Clothier's talent.

Clothier's films for Wellman and Ford, most of which starred John Wayne, made him the actor's favorite cameraman, and he was enlisted to shoot Wayne's Todd-AO epic *The Alamo*. It is one of his best-looking pictures, visualized in the style of Frederic Remington's Western paintings. Clothier went on to shoot the majority of Wayne's pictures, all on Western and Mexican locations. Many of them, including *McLintock!*, *The Undefeated*, and *Chisum*, were directed by the former Wellman/Ford assistant director Andrew McLaglen.

Clothier's style embraced landscape and location in the classic manner of Remington and Russell, and his films share a common trait of beautiful compositions. Win Sharples, Jr., once commented on the shot across the dunes towards a line of horsemen in Burt Kennedy's *The Train Robbers*, and it sums up the essence of Clothier's work: "There was that clean, strong recording of the image—the composition coming out of that instinctive placing of the camera, a matter of an inch or two adjustment in the set-up, and the lighting just perfect—a real Clothier shot."

—John A. Gallagher

COHL, Emile

Animator. **Nationality:** French. **Born:** Emile Eugène Jean Louis Courtet in Paris, 4 January 1857. **Education:** The Ecole Professionnelle, Pantin, 1864; Ecole Turgot, Paris, 1870. **Family:** Married 1) Marie Servat, 1879 (separated 1889); child: Andrée; 2) Suzanne Delpy, 1896; child: André. **Career:** 1872—apprenticed to jeweller; 1875–76—military service; 1878—studied under Andre Gill; 1879—caricaturist and illustrator of journals; 1881—designer for theatre, wrote comedies; 1884—founded portraiture company; 1907—worked at Gaumont animating his drawings; 1910—left Gaumont for Pathé; 1911—made films combining live-action and animation; 1912—joined Société Française des Films-Eclair, left for U.S.; began *Newlywed* series of cartoons; 1914—returned to France; 1919–23—made animated commercials. **Died:** In Paris, 20 January 1938.

Films as Animator, Director, and Writer:

1908   *Le Violoniste (L'Agent et le violoniste; Violon et agent); Fantasmagorie (Metamorphosis; Black and White); Le Prince azur; La Monnaie de 1.000F; Blanche comme neige; La Vengeance de Riri; La Séquestrée; La Force de l'enfant; Le Veau; Le Coffre-fort; Et si nous buvions un coup; Le Journal animé (Mon Journal); L'Hôtel du silence; Le Cauche-mar du Fantoche (The Puppet's Nightmare; Living Blackboard); L'Automate; Un Drame chez les fantoches (A Love Affair in Toyland; Mystical Love-Making); Les Allumettes animées (Animated Matches); Le Cerceau magique (Magic Hoop); Le Petit Soldat qui devient Dieu; Les Freres Boutdebois (Acrobatic Toys; Brothers Wod); N.I. ni-c'est fini*

1909   *Les Transfigurations; Soyons doncs sportifs (A Sportive Puppet); La Valise diplomatique (La Bourse; The Ambassador's Despatch); L'Omelette fantastique (Magic Eggs); Les Beaux-Arts de Jocko (The Automatic Monkey; Jacko the Artist); La Lampe qui file (The Smoking Lamp); Japon de fantaisie (Japanese Magic; A Japanese Fantasy); L'Agent de poche (Pocket Policeman); Les Joyeaux Microbes (The Merry Microbes); Moderne Ecole; Les Gricheux; Le Docteur Carnaval; L'Eventail animé (Historical Fan; Magic Fan); Clair de lune espagnol (The Man in the Moon; The Moon-Struck Matador); Les Locataires d'à côté (Next Door Neighbors); Les Couronnes (Laurels); Le Linge turbulent; La Bataille d'Austerlitz (The Battle of Austerlitz); Monsieur Clown chez les Lilliputiens; Porcelaines tendres (Sevres Porcelain); Les Chapeaux des belles dames; L'Armée d'Agenor (L'Ecole du soldat); Génération spontanée (Les Générations comiques; Magic Cartoons); Les Chaussures matrimoniales; La Lune dans son tablier (Moon for Your Love); Don Quichotte (Don Quixote); Un Coup de Jarnác (Jarnac's Treacherous Blow); Un Chirurgien distrait; Les Lunettes féeriques (X-Ray Glasses); Affairs de coeur (Affairs of Hearts)*

1910   *Cadres fleuris (Floral Studies); Le Binettoscope (The Comedy-Graph); Rêves enfantins; En route; Les Chaines; Singeries humaines (The Jolly Whirl); Le Songe d'un garçon de café (Le Rêve du garçon de café; The Hasher's Delirium; Café Waiter's Dream); Le Champion du jeu à la mode (Solving the Puzzle); Le Mobilier fidèle; Le Petit Chantecler; Les Douze Travaux d'Hercule (Hercules and the Big Stick); Le Tout Petit Faust (The Beautiful Margaret); Le Peintre neo-impressioniste; Les Qautre Petits Tailleurs (The Four Little Tailors); L'Enfance de l'art; Les Beaux Arts mysterieux; Monsieur Stop; Le Placier est tenance; Toto devient anarchiste; Histoire de chapeaux (Headdresses of Different Periods); La Telecoutre sans fil; Rien n'est impossible à l'homme; Dix Siècles d'elegance; Monsieur de Crac (Le Baron de Crac; The Wonderful Adventures of Herr Munchausen); Le Grand Machin et le petit chose; Bonsoirs russes; Bonsoirs (in 8 languages); Les Chefs d'oeuvres de Bébé; La Musicomanie (last film for Gaumont)*

1911   *Le Retapeur de Cervelles (Brains Repaired); Les Aventures d'un bout de papier; Le Musée des grotesques; Les Bestioles Artistes; Les Fantaisies d'Agenor maltrace; Jobard est demande en mariage; Jobard ne peut pas rire; Jobard a tué sa belle-mere; Jobard change de bonne; Jobard garçon de recettes; Jobard amoureux timide; Jobard portefaix par amour; Jobard ne peut pas voir les femmes travailler; Jobard fiance par interim (Jobard chauffeur); La Vengeance des esprits; La Boite diabolique*

1912   *Les Exploits de feu-follet; Les Jouets animés (Les Joujoux savants); Les Allumettes fantaisies (Les Allumettes magiques); Les Extraordinaires Exercices de la famille Coeur-de-Bois; Campbell Soups; Les Metamorphoses comiques; Dans la Vallée d'Ossau; Quelle drôle de blanchisserie; Une Poule mouillée qui se sèche; Poulot n'est pas sage; Ramoneur malgré lui; Le Mari a mal aux dents; Le Premier Jour de Vacances de Poulot; Jeunes Gens a marier; Le Prince de galles et fallières; La Marseillaise; Fruits et légumes vivants; Moulai Hafid et Alphonse XIII*

1913–14   *Bewitched Matches; Clara and Her Mysterious Toys; A Vegetarian's Dream; Unforeseen Metamorphosis (Exposition de Caricatures); Le Ousititi de Toto*

1915   *Le Voisin trop gourmand; La Trompette anti-neurasthenique; Ses Ancêtres; Fantaisies truquées; La Blanchisserie américaine; Fruits et legumes animés; Les Braves Petits Soldats de plomb; Le Terrible Bout de papier; Un Drame sur la planche à chaussures*

1916   *Les Exploits de Farfadet; Les Tableaux futuristes et incohérents; Pulcherie et ses meubles; Les Evasions de Bob Walter; Mariage par suggestion; Les Victuailles de Gretchen se revoltent; Figures de cire et tetes de bois; Croquemitaine et Rosalie; Jeux de cartes; La Journée de Flambeau (Flambeau, chien perdu); Flambeau au pays des surprises (Flambeau aux lignes); La Main mystérieuse; Les Fiancailles de Flambeau; Les Aventures de Clementine; La Maison du Fantoche (Fantoche cherche un logement); La Campagne de France 1814-(?); Pages d'histoire numbers 1 and 2; numerous publicity and educational films*

1917   *L'Enlevement de Dejanire Goldebois; L'Avenir devoile par les lignes des pieds*

1922–23   Numerous publicity films for Publi-Cine

Newlywed Series—

1912–14   *When He Wants a Dog He Wants a Dog; Business Must Not Interfere; He Wants What He Wants When He Wants It; Poor Little Chap He Was Only Dreaming; He Loves to Watch the Flight of Time; He Ruins His Family Reputation; He Slept Well; He Was Not Ill, Only Unhappy; It Is Hard to Please Him, But It Is Worth It; He Poses for His Portrait; He Loves to Be Amused; He Likes Things Upside-Down; He Doesn't Care to Be Photographed*

Other Titles, Possibly Belonging to *Newlywed* Series—

1912–14   *Pick-me-up est un sportsman; La Baignoire; Il aime le bruit; Carte américaine; Il joue avec Dodo*

The Moving World Series—

1912–1922   Films, 15 to 25 meters long, based on news events
            of the day

*Eclair Journal*Series—

1915   4 films, 10 to 12 meters long
1916   32 films, most between 10 and 30 meters long, and on subjects
       relating to the War

*Les Aventures des Pieds-Nickles*Series—

1916   Numbers 1 through 5

Other Films:

1908   *Le Mouton enragé*; *Le Miracle des roses*

Publications

On COHL: books—

Duca, Lo, *Les Dessins animés—histoire, esthétique*, Paris, 1948.
Crafton, Donald, *Emile Cohl: Caricature and Film*, Princeton, New
   Jersey, 1990.

On COHL: articles—

Auriol, Jean, "Les Premiers dessins animés cinématographiques:
   Emile Cohl," in *La Revue du Cinéma* (Paris), January 1930.
Dauven, L.R., "En visite chez M. Emile Cohl," in *Pour Vous* (Paris),
   August 1933.
d'Allemagne, Henry, "Emile Cohl (Emile Courtet), créateur du
   dessin animé sur pellicule cinématographique," in *Bulletin de la
   Société d'Encouragement pour l'Industrie Nationale* (Paris), March-
   April 1937.
Łapierre, Marcel, "Trois Hommes ont inventé le dessin animé—
   Reynaud, Cohl et Disney," in *Paris-Soir*, 28 April 1937.
Martin, André, "Le Dessin animé revient à ses origines," in *Arts*
   (Paris), 20 August 1958.
Courtet-Cohl, Pierre, "Les Beaux-arts mystérieuses—portrait d'Emile
   Cohl," in *Catalogue des Huitieme Journées Internationales du
   Cinéma d'Animation*, Annecy, 1971.
Maillet, Raymond, "Les Pionniers français de l'animation," in
   Ecran (Paris), January 1973.
Maillet, R., "Emile Cohl 1857–1938," in *Avant-Scène* (Paris), 15
   June 1978.
Maillet, Raymond, "Emile Cohl 1857–1938," in *Anthologie du
   Cinéma vol. 10*, Paris, 1979.
CinémAction (Conde-sur-Noireau), no. 51, April 1989.
Cosandey, R., "Émile Cohl: animation, dessins animés, ou film à
   trucs?," in *Positif*, no. 371, January 1992.

Cosandey, R., "Le peintre neo-impressionniste d'Émile Cohl ou la
   cause commune," in *Positif*, no. 371, January 1992.
Crafton, D., "Emile Cohl and American Eclair's animated cartoons,"
   in *Griffithiana*, no. 47, March 1983.
Cherchi Usai, Paolo, "Émile Cohl l'artista," in *Segnocinema* (Vicenza),
   November-December 1990.
Abel, Richard, "An Incomparably Incoherent Cinema," in *Persist-
   ence of Vision* (Maspeth), no. 9, 1991.
Animation Journal (Orange), Fall 1992.
Jeune Cinéma (Paris), January 1993.
Crafton, Donald, "Emile Cohl and American Éclair's Animated
   Cartoons," in *Griffithiana* (Baltimore), May 1993.
McLaren, N., "Hyllest til Emile Cohl," in *Z Filmtidsskrift* (Oslo),
   no. 2, 1997.

*   *   *

The invention of animated cartoons goes back to the invention of
film itself making it difficult to trace its exact origins. However, one
of the first (if not the first) to discover this art form was Emile Cohl.
Before he began his career as a film animator (aged 50), Cohl had
achieved some fame in France as a newspaper caricaturist and
political satirist. With his background as a cartoonist it seemed only
natural that he should add movement to his drawings.

Before Cohl's work, both drawn and object animation was used
only as a novelty in "trick" films, such as those done by George
Méliès and J. Stuart Blackton. Cohl expanded the form so that an
entire story could be told using animation. One of Cohl's first films,
Fantasmagorie, ran only two minutes, but was composed of 700
drawings narrating the adventures of a little clown.

Cohl's animation style is rather surreal and also makes good use of
the medium. The cartoons are not formally structured, but the images
flow easily from one to another as objects melt into other shapes. For
example, an elephant turns into a house or a window changes into
a man. These films have had an obvious influence on later animated
films, such as George Dunning's *Yellow Submarine*, or the pink
elephant sequence in Walt Disney's *Dumbo*.

Emile Cohl's films also contain many technical innovations used
in later cartoons. For example, *Clair de lune espagnol* uses matte
photography to combine animation with live-action. Although it is
a "simple" split-screen technique, it is amazing that Cohl registered
any synchronization at all between the live and animated halves since
these scenes must have been composed in-the-camera.

Emile Cohl was the first animator to have to deal with the
pressures of studio production schedules. While at the Gaumont
Studios in France he was required to complete a film every two
weeks. This time pressure forced him to take several shortcuts. In
some cases his animated films were lengthened with live-action
footage; at other times he was forced to use cut-out animation. (Cut-
out animation uses a single figure with movable limbs in order to save
time by not having to redraw the figure every frame.) Cohl naturally
disliked the look of the cut-out animation because of its obviously
limited motion. His situation at Gaumont Studios can be compared to
television animation today where time and money limits the potential
of the animators in favor of more product.

In 1912 Cohl moved to New Jersey to work for the Eclair Studios.
In America Cohl worked on a number of cartoons known as *The

Newlyweds, marking the first time that a continuing set of characters appeared in a cartoon series. Of course, many competitors, such as Krazy Kat and Mickey Mouse, soon followed.

Though Cohl's films were extremely well received in America (where his French films were distributed by Gaumont), he was, unfortunately, given no credit. The production companies received all the praise and the true artist went unknown. However, the influence which Emile Cohl has had on the shape of the animated cartoon is invaluable, the basis for the art form as it exists today.

—Linda Obalil

COHN, Harry

Producer. **Nationality:** American. **Born:** New York City, 27 July 1891. **Family:** Married 1) Rose Barker (divorced); 2) the actress Joan Perry, 1941: two sons, one daughter. **Career:** 1906—song plugger in vaudeville; 1913—personal secretary to Carl Laemmle at IMP (to become Universal) Studios; 1920—with Jack Warner, partnered Joseph Brandt in forming CBC Film Sales Company, soon to become Columbia; 1924—the studio produced its first full-length features, and took up premises in Hollywood; 1929—became president of the company; 1937—Columbia began the first of over sixty sound serials. **Awards:** 45 Academy Awards for films produced by Columbia, including five for *It Happened One Night*, 1934; and eight for

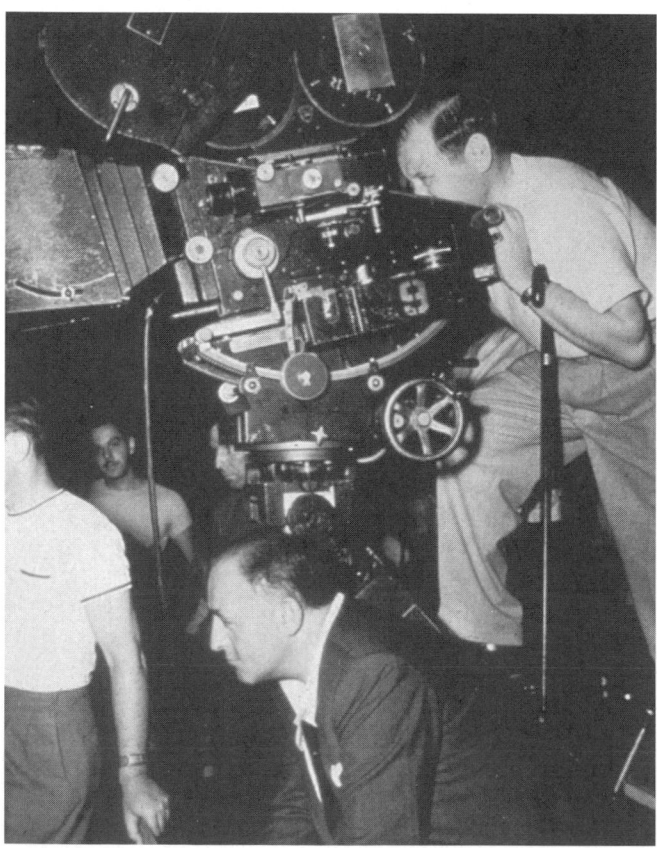

Harry Cohn

From Here to Eternity, 1953. **Died:** In Phoenix, Arizona, 27 February 1958.

Films as Executive Producer:

1918   *My Four Years in Germany*
1922   *Only a Shop Girl* (Le Saint)
1923   *Her Accidental Husband* (Fitzgerald); *Mary of the Movies* (McDermott); *Temptation* (Le Saint)
1924   *More to Be Pitied Than Scorned*; *The Barefoot Boy* (Kirkland); *Yesterday's Wife* (Le Saint)
1926   *The Way of the Strong* (Capra)
1927   *The Blood Ship* (Seitz)
1928   *Submarine* (Capra); *The Matinee Idol* (Capra); *Say It with Sables* (Capra); *The Power of the Press* (Capra); *That Certain Thing* (Capra); *So This Is Love* (Capra)
1929   *Flight* (Capra); *The Donovan Affair* (Capra); *Younger Generation* (Capra)
1930   *Vengeance* (Mayo); *Ladies of Leisure* (Capra); *Rain or Shine* (Capra)
1931   *Miracle Woman* (Capra); *The Criminal Code* (Hawks); *Dirigible* (Capra); *Platinum Blonde* (Capra)
1932   *American Madness* (Capra); *Love Affair* (McCarey); *Forbidden* (Capra)
1933   *Bitter Tea of General Yen* (Capra); *Man's Castle* (Borzage)
1934   ***It Happened One Night*** (Capra); *Twentieth Century* (Hawks); *One Night of Love* (Schertzinger); *Lady for a Day* (Capra); *Broadway Bill* (Capra); *Lady by Choice* (Burton)
1935   *The Whole Town's Talking* (Ford); *Crime and Punishment* (von Sternberg); *In Spite of Danger* (Hillyer); *She Couldn't Take It* (Garnett); *She Married Her Boss* (La Cava)
1936   *Mr. Deeds Goes to Town* (Capra); *The King Steps Out* (von Sternberg); *Love Me Forever* (Schertzinger); *Theodora Goes Wild* (Boleslawsky); *It's All Yours* (Nugent)
1937   *Lost Horizon* (Capra); *The Awful Truth* (McCarey); *What Price Vengeance* (Lord); *When You're in Love* (Riskin); *I'll Take Romance* (E. Griffith)
1938   *Holiday* (Cukor); *You Can't Take It with You* (Capra); *There's Always a Woman* (Hall); *There's That Woman Again* (Hall); *Juvenile Court* (Lederman)
1939   ***Mr. Smith Goes to Washington*** (Capra); *Golden Boy* (Mamoulian); *Only Angels Have Wings* (Hawks); *Good Girls Go to Paris* (Hall); ***His Girl Friday*** (Hawks)
1940   *Angels Over Broadway* (Hecht and Garmes); *Arizona* (Ruggles); *Too Many Husbands* (Ruggles); *He Stayed for Breakfast* (Hall); *The Lady in Question* (Charles Vidor)
1941   *Adam Had Four Sons* (Ratoff); *Here Comes Mr. Jordan* (Hall); *The Face behind the Mask* (Florey); *This Thing Called Love* (Hall); *Our Wife* (Hall); *You'll Never Get Rich* (Lanfield)
1942   *The Talk of the Town* (Stevens); *You Were Never Lovelier* (Seiter); *Flight Lieutenant* (Salkow); *My Sister Eileen* (Hall); *They All Kissed the Bride* (Hall)
1943   *The More the Merrier* (Stevens)
1944   *Cover Girl* (C. Vidor); *Together Again* (C. Vidor); *A Song to Remember* (Seiter)

1945   *Tonight and Every Night* (Saville); *Over 21* (C. Vidor)

1946   *Dead Reckoning* (Cromwell); *The Jolson Story* (Buchman); ***Gilda*** (C. Vidor)

1947   *Johnny O' Clock* (Rossen); *Down to Earth* (Hall)

1948   ***The Lady from Shanghai*** (Welles)

1949   ***All the King's Men*** (Rossen); *The Reckless Moment* (Ophüls); *Knock on Any Door* (Ray); *Jolson Sings Again* (Buchman)

1950   *Born Yesterday* (Cukor); *In a Lonely Place* (Ray)

1951   *M* (Losey); *Death of a Salesman* (Benedek)

1952   *The Marrying Kind* (Cukor); *Affair in Trinidad* (Sherman)

1953   *It Should Happen to You* (Cukor); ***The Big Heat*** (Lang); *The Wild One* (Benedek); ***From Here to Eternity*** (Zinnemann); *The Member of the Wedding* (Zinnemann); *Miss Sadie Thompson* (Bernhardt)

1954   *The Caine Mutiny* (Dmytryk); ***On the Waterfront*** (Kazan); *Phfft!* (Robson)

1955   *The Man from Laramie* (Mann); *The Long Gray Line* (Ford); *Five Against the House* (Karlson)

1956   *Jubal* (Daves); *Picnic* (Logan); *The Solid Gold Cadillac* (Quine); *The Harder They Fall* (Robson); *Storm Center* (Taradash); *The Eddie Duchin Story* (Sidney)

1957   *3:10 to Yuma* (Daves); *Pal Joey* (Sidney); *Night of the Demon* (Tourneur); *The Bridge on the River Kwai* (Lean); *Full of Life* (Quine); *Fire Down Below* (Parrish)

Publications

On COHN: books—

Thomas, Bob, *King Cohn*, New York, 1967, 1990.
Larkin, Rochelle, *Hail Columbia*, 1975 + filmo.
Dick, Bernard F., *The Merchant Prince of Poverty Row: Harry Cohn of Columbia Pictures*, Louisville, 1993.

On COHN: articles—

Films in Review (New York), vol. 9, no. 4, April 1958.
Views & Reviews, vol. 1, no. 4, Spring 1970, and vol. 2, no. 1, Summer 1970.
Film en Televisie (Brussels), no. 308, January 1983.
Classic Images (Muscatine, Iowa), no. 145, July 1987.
Sight and Sound (London), vol. 57, no. 1, Winter 1987–88.
Gabler, Neal, in *An Empire of Their Own: How the Jews Invented Hollywood*, New York, 1988.
Leifert, Don, "The Horrors of Columbia: Karloff & Cohn," in *Filmfax* (Evanston), April-May 1991.
Rubin, Mann, "The Day Harry Cohn Died," in *Creative Screenwriting* (Washington, D.C.), Summer 1994.
Cohn, H., "From the Mailbag: Offended by Honor to Riefenstahl," in *Classic Images* (Muscatine), November 1997.
Tobin, Yann, "Prés des yeux, près du coeur: Les gros plans de "La Dame de Shanghai," in *Positif* (Paris), July-August 1998.

*   *   *

President and head of production for Columbia Pictures, Harry Cohn was a late-comer in the main second wave of motion picture business tycoons. Starting with $250 in 1920 and facing the competition of Paramount, Universal, Fox, First National, Warner Brothers—and after 1925, MGM—he steered his company from Poverty Row to the status of a major studio. Thanks in large part to hiring Frank Capra as director in 1928 and Robert Riskin as writer in 1931, he could claim at the time of his death 45 Academy Awards for his films.

His father (a tailor) was born in Germany, his mother in Russia. Their family of five children shared four rooms with the two grandmothers on 88th Street in New York City. Harry quit school at 14 to take his first paying job in the "choir" of a popular play, *The Fatal Wedding* (which at one time included in its touring company Mary Pickford and family).

Brother Jack had moved from advertising to Universal Pictures, where he learned lab work and editing and collaborated with George Loane Tucker in the surreptitious production of *Traffic in Souls* (1913), a five-reel film about the white slave traffic. Harry, who had been working as a "song-plugger," both live and on film, was hired by Carl Laemmle as his secretary. By 1920, they were certain they knew enough about movies to start their own shop. Taking Joe Brandt with them, they set up a company named by their initials CBC—soon to be known, because of its rockbottom budgets, as Corned Beef and Cabbage Productions.

Beginning with a nonfiction series about movie stars called *Screen Snapshots*, and *The Hall Room Boys*, based on a comic strip, the new company became Columbia while making its first feature film, *More to Be Pitied Than Scorned* (1924). In 1929 the brothers bought out their partner. Jack, as head of sales and distribution, stayed in New York. Harry produced the pictures in Hollywood. They quarreled constantly.

Skilled at betting on talent, Harry nevertheless refused to offer long-term contracts, but watched for cheaper opportunities: actors "on the way up and on the way down." He was quick to accept the chance L.B. Mayer gave him to "punish" a young newcomer at MGM, Clark Gable, by loaning him out. Riskin's handling of the inexpensive short story, *Night Bus*, under Capra's direction, brought Columbia the five top Oscars for *It Happened One Night* (1934).

Jack Cohn was equally mean in denying Columbia expansion into theaters. This minimized real estate burdens and risks but put pressure on the company to make outstanding popular films and win time on the screens of the theater chains. Capra did it with comedy in *Mr. Deeds Goes to Town*, *Mr. Smith Goes to Washington*, and *You Can't Take It with You*. After Capra left to try independence, the studio continued to be a source of top-notch films, and there were still some major successes in terms of Academy Awards. Cohn himself was in effect executive producer for *From Here to Eternity* which won eight Oscars in 1953. *On the Waterfront* also got eight awards in 1954, and *The Bridge on the River Kwai* seven in 1957, but both of these were produced on the new "independent" basis by Sam Spiegel—an augury of the Hollywood transition away from studio boss rule.

Generally viewed as the most vulgar, loud-mouthed, and autocratic of all the studio bosses, Cohn customarily shouted insults at writers until they stoutly defended their work—after which he claimed to have more confidence in them. Hated and feared by some, sneered at by others for his limited education and experience, he could not seem to operate without four-letter words. Yet when he died there were many, like Jack Lemmon and Glenn Ford, who said he "would be missed."

In an early statement about his views on film making (1928) Harry Cohn stressed economy—original scripts, fewer scenes and set-ups, fewer close-ups. He tried to create stars—Rita Hayworth, Kim

Novak. But his unique loyalty was to the talent of the writer, even though it was very often a love-hate relationship. It is suitable that the index of films in Larkin's studio profile called *Hail, Columbia* lists only titles, dates, and screenwriters.

He was also conscious of what might be called an American style. Knowing that theater bookers might not watch new releases beyond the first reel or two, he said: "Like newspaper writers, we put a punch in the first reel of our picture that demands immediate respect and attention." Then, "if your picture has novelty, human appeal, humor, and pathos without being too morbid, your chances are very good."

He knew what was in the scripts. According to the Bob Thomas biography, Capra confronted him in 1933 with last-minute qualms on *Lady for a Day*—a picture which later won four Academy Award nominations. "Do you realize you're spending $300,000 on a picture in which the heroine is seventy years old?" Cohn thought about it, but told him to go ahead: "All I know is—the story packs a wallop."

—Richard Dyer MacCann

COLE, Jack

Choreographer. **Nationality:** American. **Born:** New Brunswick, New Jersey, 27 April 1914. **Education:** Studied with Ted Shawn, Ruth St. Denis, Charles Weidman, Doris Humphrey, and others. **Career:** Dancer with Denishawn Concert Dancers, 1930–32, and the Humphrey-Weidman Dance Group, 1932–33; 1933—dancer on Broadway in *The School for Husbands*; 1937—danced with his own group;

Jack Cole with Marilyn Monroe

1943—choreographed the Broadway musical *Something for the Boys*; later shows include *Kismet*, 1953, *Jamaica*, 1957, *Candide*, 1959, *A Funny Thing Happened on the Way to the Forum*, 1962, and *Foxy*, 1964. **Died:** 17 February 1974.

Films as Choreographer:

1944   *Kismet* (Dieterle); *Cover Girl* (C. Vidor); *Jammin' the Blues* (Burks—short); *Tonight and Every Night* (Saville)
1946   *Gilda* (C. Vidor); *The Jolson Story* (Green); *The Thrill of Brazil* (Simon) (co)
1947   *Down to Earth* (Hall)
1951   *On the Riviera* (W. Lang); *Meet Me after the Show* (Sale)
1952   *The Merry Widow* (Bernhardt); *David and Bathsheba* (H. King)
1953   *The I Don't Care Girl* (Bacon); *Gentlemen Prefer Blondes* (Hawks); *The Farmer Takes a Wife* (Levin)
1954   *River of No Return* (Preminger); *There's No Business Like Show Business* (W. Lang)
1955   *Three for the Show* (Potter); *Kismet* (Minnelli); *Gentlemen Marry Brunettes* (Sale)
1957   *Les Girls* (Cukor)
1959   *Some Like It Hot* (Wilder)
1960   *Let's Make Love* (Cukor)

Films as Actor:

1941   *Moon over Miami* (W. Lang); *Designing Woman* (Minnelli)

Publications

By COLE: article—

In *Dance in the Hollywood Musical*, by Jerome Delamater, Ann Arbor, Michigan, 1981.

On COLE: article—

Kisselgoff, Anna, "Recalling an Innovator of Film Choreography," in the *New York Times*, section C, 7 February 1994.

*   *   *

Credited as one of the primary influences in show business choreography, Jack Cole combined modern dance, jazz, and ethnic—particularly oriental—movement into a unique style that he exploited in a variety of commercial settings. Although he began as a modern dancer with Ruth St. Denis and Ted Shawn, he soon became involved with stage and night club performances and maintained those affiliations long after becoming a significant force in Hollywood. Working primarily at Columbia, Twentieth Century-Fox, and, occasionally, MGM, Cole provided individual dances in many musical and nonmusical films as well as choreographing all the numbers in a variety of musicals. Cole's importance outweighs the films—and, indeed, the stage shows—he worked on. As mentor to a number of major dancers, as an innovator of dance movement, and as a filmmaker concerned with the relationship of camera and dance, Jack Cole provided a model for filming dance but often in films that have reputations inferior to his own.

During his stint at Columbia, Cole founded a permanent troupe of twelve dancers who formed the core of his work on such films as *Tonight and Every Night*, *Down to Earth*, and *The Jolson Story*. The troupe provided the studio with the equivalent of one of its departments: trained professionals, under contract, ready at any moment to rehearse for a film. Gwen Verdon, Carol Haney, and Matt Mattox were members of Cole's unit at Columbia, and each helped perpetuate Cole's influence. Although jazz and modern dance were the basis of their education with him, they also studied ballet and ethnic dance. Cole recognized the need for variety in their training and the possibilities inherent in using that variety in his choreography. Gwen Verdon has discussed the way in which Cole integrated all aspects of dance into a theatrical whole: "When we danced with him . . . , we had to do absolutely authentic dances, but in jazzy costumes to jazz music." The understanding of how to use different forms of dance, combine them with unexpected kinds of music, and adapt them to the needs of the show or film led to remarkable innovations. It also led to frustration, for, as Glenn Loney has suggested in a series of articles in *Dance Magazine*, "he seldom had major artistic control; instead, he tailored his contribution to the demands of others."

In spite of a difficult and iconoclastic personality, Cole was admired in Hollywood. He was often called on in difficult situations, to help temperamental stars, as with Marilyn Monroe in *Some Like It Hot*, or to provide material that would seem authentic, as with the biblical epic *David and Bathsheba*. His work is most evocative, though, in musicals, and he demonstrated his diverse interests in many films: a modern-dance parody of Marlon Brando in *Les Girls*; Latin American influences in "Heat Wave" from *There's No Business Like Show Business*; oriental dance in *Kismet*. Always concerned with photographing dance, Cole insisted on tight control of the shooting and editing of the material he prepared and tried to work with directors to integrate the dances into the totality of a film. He seldom had the opportunity, however, to influence the films beyond the musical numbers. Fortunately, the record of his work on film survives and gives credence to the claim that he provided the legacy inherited by Bob Fosse and others.

The dancer Barrie Chase has articulated Cole's contribution to contemporary dance style: "his combining of modern, oriental and jazz movement, his way of digging into the ground, of breaking down dance steps and body movement, of exact counting of every part of every step." Never happy working in Hollywood, Cole was, however, important as a teacher and innovator. He made occasional screen appearances (in *Designing Woman*, for example), but always returned to the stage and the classroom for sustenance. Perhaps Cole's independent spirit worked against him in Hollywood, for those who succeeded in developing the musical genre were, by nature, collaborators. Cole, on the other hand, was unique, and, although willing to tailor his material to the needs of a film, rarely agreed to a subordinate role. His ideas have become part of the vocabulary of contemporary dance and are present in films far removed from his direct contact, but his real genius may have been his ability to link innovation with show business savvy. Marilyn Monroe doing "Diamonds Are a Girl's Best Friend" in *Gentlemen Prefer Blondes* demonstrates that Jack Cole had a remarkable theatrical flair. Jack Cole's style will endure because it makes artistic endeavor part of popular expression.

—Jerome Delamater

COLPI, Henri

Editor and Director. **Nationality:** Swiss. **Born:** Brigue, 15 July 1921. **Education:** Studied editing at IDHEC, Paris, 1945–47. **Career:** 1949—Editor, Ciné-Digest; 1948—editor of first film, *Fourvière;* also edited advertising shorts, worked for TV, and directed. **Address:** 33 rue Bonaparte, 75006 Paris, France.

Films as Editor (Shorts):

1948   *Fourvière* (Maudru); *Super-Pacific* (Maudru)
1950   *Les Déchaînés* (*Surboum*) (Keigel) (+ asst d); *L'Amour d'un métier* (Gérard)
1951   *Des rails sous les palmiers* (Colson-Malleville) (+ asst d); *La Chanson du pavé* (Gérard); *Ce soir . . . le cirque* (Gérard); *La Fabrication industrielle des solutés injectables* (Gérard); *Disques d'hier et d'aujourd'hui* (Gérard); *Finlande* (Bonnière); *Norvège* (Bonnière); *Sarre, pleins feux* (Bonnière and Alekan)
1952   *Baba-Ali* (Colson-Malleville); *Le Petit Monde des étangs* (Colson-Malleville); *Rencontres sur le Rhin* (Bonnière); *La Fabrication industrielle des comrimés et dragées* (Gérard) (+ asst d)
1953   *Le Barrage du Châtelot* (Colson-Malleville) (+ asst d); *A tout casser* (*Stock-Cars*) (Dupont); *Architecture de lumière* (+ co-d)
1954   *Du point de vue d'Anton* (Colson-Malleville); *L'Enquête aboutit* (Delbez and others) (+ asst d)
1955   **Nuit et brouillard** (*Night and Fog*) (Resnais)
1956   *Monsieur La Bruyère* (Doniol-Valcroze); *Routes barrées* (Collet); *Matériaux nouveaux, demeures nouvelles* (+ d)
1957   *La Déroute* (Kyrou); *Morts en vitrine* (Vogel) (co); *La Jaconde* (Gruel); *Chères vieilles choses* (Vogel)
1958   *Le Siècle a soif* (Vogel) (co); *La Mer et les jours* (Vogel) (co); *Les Hommes de la baleine* (Ruspoli); *Du côté de la côte* (Varda); *La Première Nuit* (Franju)
1959   *Paris la belle* (P. Prévert); *Monsieur Tête* (Gruel and Lenica)
1966   *Symphonie Nr. 7 von Ludwig von Beethoven* (+ d); *Symphonie Nr. 9 von Franz Schubert* (+ d)
1967   *Le Coeur des pierres* (Bettetini); *Symphonie Nr. 3 in Es-dur, Opus 55 "Eroica" von Ludwig von Beethoven* (+ d)
1972   *Une Belle Journée* (Tacchella)

Films as Editor (Features):

1947   *Les Jeux sont faits* (Delannoy) (asst)
1952   *Si ça vous chante* (Loew)
1956   *Le Mystère Picasso* (*The Mystery of Picasso*) (Clouzot)
1957   *A King in New York* (Chaplin)
1959   **Hiroshima mon amour** (Resnais) (co)
1961   **L'Année dernière à Marienbad** (*Last Year at Marienbad*) (Resnais) (co); *Une Aussi Longue Absence* (*A Long Absence*) (+ d, lyrics)
1963   *Codine* (+ d, co-sc)
1964   *Fascinante Amazônie* (Lambert)
1966   *Mona, l'étoile sans nom* (+ d, co-sc)

1969   *Femme noire, femme nue* (Ecaré); *Détruire, dit-elle* (*Destroy, She Said*) (Duras)

1970   *Heureux qui comme Ulysse* (+ d, co-sc)

1973   *L'Ile mystérieuse* (*The Mysterious Island*) (+ co-d, co-sc)

1976   *Chantons sous l'occupation* (Halimi); *Bilitis* (Hamilton) (+ co-d)

1981   *Les Fruits de la passion* (*The Fruits of Passion*) (Tereyama)

1983   *L'Hirondelle et la mésange* (Antoine—produced 1920); *Le Grand frère* (Girod); *La Fuite en Avant* (Zerbib)

1989   *Australia* (Andrien)

Other Films:

1948   *Les Enfants dorment la nuit* (Bonnière—short) (asst d); *Les Chants retrouvés* (Breteuil—short) (asst d)

1953   *Les Statues meurent aussi* (Resnais and Marker—short) (uncredited sound ed)

1961   *Regard sur la folie* (Ruspoli) (technical adviser)

1986   *Offret* (*The Sacrifice*) (Tarkovsky) (editorial consultant)

1987   *Rue des Arcrives* (co-d, with Lubtchansky, Ikhlef, Boutang, Patris)

Publications

By COLPI: books—

(Editor) *Le Cinéma et ses hommes*, 1947.
Défense et illustration de la musique dans le film, Paris, 1963.

By COLPI: articles—

With Louis Mercorelles and Richard Roud, ''Alain Resnais and *Hiroshima Mon Amour*,'' in *Sight and Sound* (London), Winter 1959–60.
''Musique d' Hiroshima,'' in *Cahiers du Cinéma* (Paris), January 1960.
Image et Son (Paris), no. 144, 1961.
Film Français (Paris), 15 May 1961.
''Debasement of the Art of Montage,'' in *Film Culture* (New York), Summer 1961.
Télécine (Paris), no. 103, 1962.
Cinéma (Paris), November 1962.
Avant-Scène (Paris), September 1963.
Image et Son (Paris), May 1970.
Cinéma (Paris), July-August 1980.
Cinématographe (Paris), November 1980.
Cinématographe (Paris), June 1982.
Cinématographe (Paris), July-August 1983.
Cinématographe (Paris), April 1984.
Cinématographe (Paris), March 1985.

On COLPI: articles—

Positif (Paris), June 1962.
Cahiers du Cinéma (Paris), December 1962.
Cinéma (Paris), no. 104, 1966.

Film Ideal (Madrid), no. 216, 1969.
Chaplin (Stockholm), no. 2, 1970.
Film Comment (New York), March-April 1977.
Bref (Paris), no. 20, Spring 1994.

*   *   *

Henri Colpi's education at IDHEC, his experience as a film writer and as editor of *Ciné-Digest*, together with his early work as assistant director and editor of short films, give his editorial work a notable authority and maturity. Work for Resnais (*Nuit et brouillard, Hiroshima mon amour*, and *L'Année dernière à Marienbad*), Clouzot (*Le Mystère Picasso*), and Chaplin (*A King in New York*) on long films; and for Gruel, Kyrou, Franju, Varda, and Pierre Prévert on short films—his activity in this second group corresponding to the apogee of the French short film—reveals his astonishing sensibility and assurance in a variety of styles, seen in the actual editing by his choice and arrangements of plain and visual sequences.

As a director as well, Colpi becomes a complete man of the cinema. After a few short films, Colpi made his long-film debut with *Une Aussi Longue Absence*, based on a scenario conceived by Marguerite Duras. The film, which surprises by its maturity (and also by its deliberate rhythm), tells the story of a woman who thinks her missing husband has reappeared as a tramp. This intimate drama rests on a profound and poetic humanism, despite its realism. In spite of critical attention, the film was not popular, and in the next ten years Colpi succeeded in directing only three more long films. *Codine*, a faithful adaptation of a work by Panait Istrati, contains color images of great beauty. *Mona, l'étoile sans nom*, while containing plastic qualities and a poetic atmosphere, seems compromised by a commercial system working against the director. But his next film, *Heureux qui comme Ulysse* (Fernandel's last film), is a notable success: Colpi manages to translate into visual images all the poetry of Provence, and to render through the story of a man and his horse a homage to liberty.

Later work includes a TV series, *L'Ile mystérieuse* (with a shorter cinema version), and an edited version of André Antoine's silent film *L'Hirondelle et la mésange*, evidently never before prepared for viewing, a resurrection unique in cinema.

—Karel Tabery

COMDEN, Betty, and Adolph GREEN

COMDEN. Writer and Lyricist. **Nationality:** American. **Born:** Betty Cohen in Brooklyn, New York, 3 May 1919.

GREEN. Writer and Lyricist. **Nationality:** American. **Born:** The Bronx, New York, 2 December 1918. **Family:** Married 1) the actress Allyn McLerie (divorced); 2) Phyllis Newman, 1960.

Career: 1940–44—Comden and Green performed with Judy Holliday, John Frank, and Alvin Hammer in cabaret group The Revuers; 1944—wrote first Broadway musical, *On the Town* (later musicals include *Billion Dollar Baby*, 1945, *Bonanza Beyond*, 1947, *Two on the Aisle*, 1951, *Wonderful Town*, 1953, *Bells Are Ringing*, 1956, *Say Darling*, 1958, *Do Re Mi*, 1960, *Subways Are for Sleeping*, 1961,

Betty Comden and Adolph Green

Fade Out—Fade In, 1964, *Hallelljah Baby*, 1967, *Applause*, 1970, *Lorelei, or Gentlemen Still Prefer Blondes*, 1974, *By Bernstein*, 1975, and *On the Twentieth Century*, 1978); 1947—first film as writers, *Good News*. **Awards:** Writers Guild Award, for *On the Town*, 1949, *Singin' in the Rain*, 1952, and *Bells Are Ringing*, 1960.

Films as Writers and Lyricists:

1947 *Good News* (Walters)
1948 *Take Me Out to the Ball Game* (*Everybody's Cheering*) (Berkeley) (lyricists only); *The Barkleys of Broadway* (Walters) (sc only)
1949 **On the Town** (Donen and Kelly)
1952 **Singin' in the Rain** (Donen and Kelly)
1953 **The Band Wagon** (Minnelli) (sc only)
1955 *It's Always Fair Weather* (Donen and Kelly)
1958 *Auntie Mame* (da Costa) (sc only)
1960 *Bells Are Ringing* (Minnelli)
1964 *What a Way to Go!* (Lee Thompson)

Films as Actress: Comden:

1944 *Greenwich Village* (W. Lang)
1984 *Garbo Talks* (Lumet)
1989 *Slaves of New York* (Ivory) (as Mrs. Wheeler)

Films as Actor: Green:

1944 *Greenwich Village* (W. Lang)
1979 *Simon* (Brickman) (as commune leader)
1982 *My Favorite Year* (Benjamin) (as Leo Silver)
1985 *Lily in Love* (Makk) (as Jerry Silber)
1989 *I Want to Go Home* (Resnais)
1996 *The Substance of Fire* (Sullivan) (as Mr. Musselblatt)

Publications

By COMDEN and GREEN: books—

Singin' in the Rain (script), New York, 1972.
Comden and Green on Broadway, New York, 1981.
On the Twentieth Century (play), New York, 1981.

By COMDEN and GREEN: articles—

Cahiers du Cinéma (Paris), January 1966, translated in *Cahiers du Cinéma in English*, no. 2, 1966.
Positif (Paris), no. 343, September 1989.
Films in Review (Denville), vol. 43, no. 3–4, March-April 1992.
Films in Review (Denville), vol. 43, no. 5–6, May-June 1992.

On COMDEN and GREEN: article—

Film Comment (New York), Winter 1970–71.
Laffel, Jeff, "Betty Comden and Adolph Green (part 1)," in *Films in Review* (Denville), March-April, 1992.
Laffel, Jeff, "Betty Comden and Adolph Green (part 2)," in *Films in Review* (Denville), May-June, 1992.
Isherwood, Charles, "Carnegie Hall Celebrates Betty Comden and Adolf Green," in *Variety* (New York), 27 September 1999.

*   *   *

Betty Comden and Adolph Green came to Hollywood from New York, where as two-fifths of a group called The Revuers they wrote and performed songs and sketches in a series of cabaret, radio, and theater shows in the early 1940s. When the group disbanded, Comden and Green wrote the book and lyrics for the Broadway production of *On the Town*, in which they also acted and which, five years later, they adapted for the screen, their roles now played by Ann Miller and Jules Munshin.

The experience gained and associations formed in this early period of their partnership—despite the decision to play a mostly backstage, offscreen role in their later ventures—significantly influenced their writing. They prepared their own material because The Revuers were originally too poor to hire writers, while the group's gradual word-of-mouth success at a Greenwich Village cellar nightclub assumed certain musical-comedy proportions of its own and influenced plot developments in a number of Comden-Green screenplays. ("Within the measure of possibility," they once told an interviewer, "we always make use of elements in our personal lives." The writing couple played by Oscar Levant and Nanette Fabray in *The Band Wagon* provides perhaps the wittiest testimony to that practice.) Moreover, the episodic nature of the sketch form and Comden and Green's ability to integrate it with satiric songs proved particularly adaptable to the more extended requirements of musical comedy, whose heyday at MGM they magically helped to shape. Their original screenplays for *Singin' in the Rain* and *The Band Wagon*, for example, emerged from sets of songs they were told to incorporate into each film's story line, not an uncommon process in the making of a musical.

The genre of musical comedy is thus particularly dependent upon the world of show business itself, as screenwriters seek contexts for their characters to perform production numbers from a "realistic" base in an essentially unrealistic art form. As in *Singin' in the Rain* and *Band Wagon*, lead characters in a musical tend to be performers in rehearsal for a musical play or film within the film. (Note Comden and Green's delicious parody of the writer's desperate search for musical excuses within the story line as Cosmo Brown—Donald O'Connor—transforms *Singin' in the Rain*'s dueling cavalier into a dancing one.) In this regard, even when (as in *On the Town*) their main characters are not literally performers, Comden and Green's work is infused with the exhilarating appearance of that "Hey kids, let's put on a show" spontaneity so endemic to the spirit of the classic Hollywood musical. (Consider, for example, the madcap element of carnival embedded in the *Singin' in the Rain* and *Band Wagon* dialogue, or the joyous sense of liberation captured in their lyrics to "New York, New York" as the three sailors disembark for shore leave in *On the Town*.)

But the deep affection for the world of entertainment that shines through their work is wittily balanced by Comden and Green's satiric pleasure in the industry's absurdities. Their screenplays abound with pretentious directors (Jeffrey Cordova in *The Band Wagon*), dollar-hungry movie moguls (R. F. Simpson in *Singin' in the Rain*), and egomaniacal stars (Astaire/Rogers in *The Barkleys of Broadway*, Lina Lamont in *Singin' in the Rain*) all courting potential comic disaster. Television provides the target for their nastiest satire in *It's Always Fair Weather*, a film considerably ahead of its time and predating such brilliantly bitter musicals as *Cabaret*, *All That Jazz*, and *Pennies from Heaven*.

—Mark W. Estrin

CONTI, Bill

Composer. **Nationality:** American. **Born:** Providence, Rhode Island, 13 April 1942. **Family:** Married Shelby Cox; children: Rachela, Nicola. **Education:** Louisiana State University, B.A. in piano and composition, 1964; Juilliard School of Music, M.A., 1967. **Career:** Was a piano prodigy as a child; organized his own band, 1957; scored his first films in Italy while traveling with a jazz combo, late 1960s; composed original music for many TV series and mini-series, most notably *Dynasty, Falcon Crest, Cagney & Lacey, Lifestyles of the Rich and Famous, The Colbys, American Gladiators, North and South, North and South II,* and *Napoleon and Josephine: A Love*

Story, 1976–89; his recording of "Gonna Fly Now" (the theme from *Rocky*) became a number one pop music hit, 1977; began stint as Music Director of yearly Academy Awards ceremony, 1970s. **Awards:** Best Original Score Academy Award, for *The Right Stuff*, 1984; ASCAP Film and Television Music Award for *Primetime Live*, 1989; Emmy Award for Outstanding Achievement in Music Direction, for *The 64th Academy Awards*, 1992; ASCAP Golden Soundtrack Award for Lifetime Achievement, 1995. **Agent:** Kraft-Benjamin Agency, 8491 West Sunset Blvd., Suite 492, West Hollywood, CA 90069–1911, U.S.A.

Films as Composer:

1969 *Juliette de Sade (Heterosexual)* (Kiefer); *Un Sudario a la medida (A Candidate for a Killing)* (Elorrieta)

1970 *Il Giardino dei Finzi-Contini (The Garden of the Finzi-Continis)* (De Sica)

1972 *Liquid Subway*

1973 *Blume in Love* (Mazursky)

1974 *Harry and Tonto* (Mazursky)

1975 *Pacific Challenge* (Amram)

1976 *Next Stop, Greenwich Village* (Mazursky); *The Displaced Person* (Jordan—for TV); *Rocky* (Avildsen) (+ "Gonna Fly Now" theme); *Smash-Up on Interstate 5* (Moxey—for TV)

1977 *Handle with Care (Citizens Band)* (Demme) (+ song "You Heard the Song"); *A Sensitive, Passionate Man* (Newland—for TV) (+ co-wrote title song); *Kill Me If You Can (The Caryl Chessman Story)* (Kulik—for TV); *In the Matter of Karen Ann Quinlan* (Jordan—for TV)

1978 *Uncle Joe Shannon* (Hanwright); *Slow Dancing in the Big City* (Avildsen); *Paradise Alley* (Stallone) (+ song "Too Close to Paradise"); *Five Days from Home* (Peppard); *The Big Fix* (Kagan); *Ring of Passion (Countdown to the Big One)* (Lewis— for TV); *An Unmarried Woman* (Mazursky); *F.I.S.T.* (Jewison); *The Pirate (Harold Robbins' The Pirate)* (Annakin—for TV)

1979 *The Seduction of Joe Tynan* (Schatzberg); *The Fantastic Seven (Steel Glory, Stunt Seven)* (Peyser—for TV); *Dreamer* (Nosseck) (+ song "Reach for the Top"); *Goldengirl* (Sargent) (+ song "Slow Down, I'll Find You"); *A Man, a Woman, and a Bank (A Very Big Withdrawal)* (Black) (+ song "When You Smile at Me"); *Rocky II* (Stallone)

1980 *Private Benjamin* (Zieff); *The Formula* (Avildsen); *Gloria* (Cassavetes)

1981 *For Your Eyes Only* (Glen) (+ co-wrote title theme); *Carbon Copy* (Schultz) (+ song "I'm Gonna Get Closer to You"); *Victory (Escape to Victory)* (Huston); *Neighbors* (Avildsen)

1982 *That Championship Season* (Miller); *Split Image* (Kotcheff) (+ songs); *Rocky III* (Stallone) (+ song "Pushin'"); *I, the Jury* (Heffron); *Farrell for the People* (Wendkos—for TV)

1983 *Without a Trace* (Jaffe); *Two of a Kind* (Herzfeld); *The Right Stuff* (Kaufman); *The Terry Fox Story* (Thomas—for TV); *Bad Boys* (Rosenthal)

1984 *Mass Appeal* (Jordan); *Grand Canyon: The Hidden Secrets* (Merrill) (doc); *The Bear* (Sarafian) (+ co-wrote song "I'll

Bill Conti

Be Home Again''); *Unfaithfully Yours* (Zieff); *The Karate Kid* (Avildsen) (+ songs); *The Coolangatta Gold* (*The Gold and the Glory*) (Auzins)

1985   *Stark* (Holcomb—for TV); *Rocky IV* (Stallone); *Beer* (*The Selling of America*) (Kelly); *Gotcha!* (Kanew)

1986   *Stark: Mirror-Image* (*Stark II*) (Nosseck—for TV); *Nomads* (McTiernan) (+ co-wrote songs); *Niagara: Miracles, Myths and Magic* (Merrill) (doc); *F/X* (Mandel); *The Boss' Wife* (Steinberg); *Big Trouble* (Cassavetes); *The Karate Kid, Part II* (Avildsen) (+ song ''Two Looking for One'')

1987   *Io e papa* (*Papa and Me*) (Capitani—for TV); *Happy New Year* (Avildsen); *Broadcast News* (Brooks); *Baby Boom* (Shyer) (+ song ''Everchanging Times''); *A Prayer for the Dying* (Hodges); *Masters of the Universe* (Goddard)

1988   *A Night in the Life of Jimmy Reardon* (Richert); *I Love N.Y.* (Bozzacchi, Smithee); *For Keeps* (Avildsen); *Betrayed* (Costa-Gavras); *Le Grand Bleu* (*The Big Blue*) (*Le grand bleu*) (Besson)

1989   *The Karate Kid III* (Avildsen); *Lean on Me* (Avildsen); *Murderers Among Us: The Simon Wiesenthal Story* (Gibson—for TV); *Bionic Showdown: The Six Million Dollar Man and the Bionic Woman* (Levi—for TV); *Cohen and Tate* (Red); *Lock Up* (Flynn)

1990   *The Fourth War* (Frankenheimer); *A Captive in the Land* (Berry); *Backstreet Dreams* (*Backstreet Strays*) (Hitzig); *The Operation* (*Bodily Harm*) (Wright—for TV); *Rocky V* (Avildsen)

1991   *Necessary Roughness* (Dragoti); *Grand Canyon* (Kasdan); *By the Sword* (Kagan); *Year of the Gun* (Frankenheimer); *Dynasty: The Reunion* (Moore—for TV)

1992   *Nails* (Flynn—for TV)

1993   *Rookie of the Year* (Stern); *The Adventures of Huck Finn* (Sommers); *Bound By Honor* (*Blood In. . . Blood Out*) (Hackford)

1994   *Yellowstone* (doc); *8 Seconds* (*The Lane Frost Story*) (Avildsen); *The Next Karate Kid* (Cain); *The Scout* (Ritchie)

1995   *Napoleon* (Andreacchio); *Bushwhacked* (*The Tenderfoot*) (Beeman)

1996   *Spy Hard* (Friedberg); *Entertaining Angels: The Dorothy Day Story* (Rhodes)

1998   *Wrongfully Accused* (Proft); *The Real Macaw* (Andreacchio); *Winchell* (Mazursky—for TV)

1999   *The Thomas Crown Affair* (McTiernan)
2000   *Sugihara: Conspiracy of Goodness*

Publications

By CONTI: articles—

"A Few Easy Pieces: Interviews with Composers Bill Conti and Jerry Goldsmith," interview in *Millimeter* (New York), April 1979.

"Working Abroad: Two Composers," interview with D. Koeser, in *Cinema Papers* (North Melbourne, Australia), February/March 1985.

"Bill Conti," interview with S. Simak, in *CinemaScore* (Sunnyvale, California), Summer 1987.

"A Conversation with Bill Conti," interview with D. Cavanagh and P.A. Maclean, in *Soundtrack! The Collector's Quarterly* (Belgium), September 1992.

On CONTI: articles—

Barbano, N., "Musik," in *Kosmorama* (Copenhagen), September 1980.

Santiago, T., "A Film Music Seminar," in *Soundtrack! The Collector's Quarterly* (Belgium), March 1984.

Feldman, G., "Filmusic: Bill Conti," in *American Premiere* (Beverly Hills, California), no. 2, 1985.

Scott, V., "Scrapbook: Conti Scores Catchy Themes," in *Soundtrack! The Collector's Quarterly* (Belgium), June 1985.

Lehti, S., "*The Right Stuff*/*North and South*/Bill Conti," in *Soundtrack! The Collector's Quarterly* (Belgium), December 1986.

Pecqueriaux, J. and others, "Bill Conti-Filmography/Discography," in *Soundtrack! The Collector's Quarterly* (Belgium), December 1986.

Darnton, Nina, "At the Movies," in *New York Times*, 22 May 1987.

Tucker, G.M., "Bill Conti's '*Neighbors*'/The Undiscovered Score," in *CinemaScore* (Sunnyvale, California), Summer 1987.

Silverman, M.S., "Organizers of Oscar Telecast Plan a Few Changes This Year," in *Variety* (New York), 10 February 1988.

Blocker, S., "Conti Doesn't Write Music for Prosperity," in *Wisconsin Journal*, 22 January 1995.

*   *   *

Bill Conti is a prolific, all-purpose composer-arranger who in his thirty-plus year career has written musical themes for every conceivable medium and genre: blockbuster and B-list Hollywood action-adventures and comedies; television series and mini-series; independent and foreign-language productions; and even television commercials, specials, and news and variety programs. In 1987, for example, he composed the music for such diverse films as *Broadcast News* and *Masters of the Universe*, *Baby Boom* and *A Prayer for the Dying*—not to mention the Italian-made *Io e Papa*, the television series *Ohara* and *Mariah*, and the mini-series *Napoleon and Josephine: A Love Story*. Early in his career Conti found himself in Italy, where he scored one prestigious film, Vittorio De Sica's *Il Giardino dei Finzi-Continis*. He began composing scores and themes for long-forgotten television series and made-for-TV movies and worked with Paul Mazursky, writing music for *Blume in Love, Harry and Tonto*, and *Next Stop, Greenwich Village*. Yet in the mid-1970s, Conti still was relatively unheralded. Then he won the assignment that would establish him as one of the most celebrated composers of his era. He was hired to write the music for an obscure, low-budget feature about a club fighter who gets the opportunity to tangle in the ring with the World Heavyweight Champion. The star and screenwriter was an unsung actor named Sylvester Stallone. The film was *Rocky*, and Conti's rousing, inspirational theme song, "Gonna Fly Now," was an immediate audience-grabber. Along with Vangellis's *Chariots of Fire* theme and Randy Newman's music for *The Natural*, "Gonna Fly Now" remains among the most familiar and beloved sports-oriented movie themes. Musically-speaking, Conti's overall score is neither complex nor creative, but it is undeniably effective in imparting a mood of self-confidence and triumph.

Conti's music for *Rocky* transcends the motion picture medium—and not just because, back in 1977, "Gonna Fly Now" reached number one on the pop music charts. In subsequent years, the song has come to symbolize the courage and spirit of the underdog. Decades after *Rocky* first came to movie theaters, one might attend an athletic event and find some scrappy, Rocky-like challengers entering the boxing ring or playing field to the soaring trumpet that opens "Gonna Fly Now."

Given the phenomenal success of Rocky, it is no surprise that Conti went on to compose the theme music for the television series *American Gladiators*. In fact, quite a few of his future projects involved creating musical sounds to parallel the emotion inherent in athletic activity: *Goldengirl*; *Dreamer*; *The Terry Fox Story*; *The Karate Kid* and its sequels; *Rookie of the Year*; *The Scout*; *Necessary Roughness*. One of Conti's very best scores, for *The Right Stuff*, amplifies the heroics of pioneer American astronauts. The names of the themes on the soundtrack—including "Breaking the Sound Barrier," "Yeager's Triumph," "A Close Call," "Returning Home," "Last Embrace," and "Final Meeting"—mirror the composer's approach to conveying the tension and emotion of the story.

Across the decades, Conti has maintained professional relationships with his *Rocky* co-workers. Immediately following the film's success, he composed for projects that were outgrowths of *Rocky*: *Slow Dancing in the Big City* (a *Rocky* clone helmed by its director, John G. Avildsen); *Paradise Alley* (directed and scripted by and starring Sylvester Stallone); *Uncle Joe Shannon* (scripted by and starring *Rocky* supporting actor Burt Young); *F.I.S.T.* and *Victory* (both starring Stallone)—and, of course, the inevitable *Rocky* sequels. In particular, Conti has remained Avildsen's house composer, scoring a majority of the filmmaker's projects well into the 1990s.

As a composer working in a commercial medium, Conti is as pragmatic as he is prolific. He accepts the reality that his role as composer is to serve his director. If the filmmaker is not musically oriented, Conti will relish the resulting artistic freedom. However, if the filmmaker knows exactly what he wants for the soundtrack, Conti will provide those sounds. He understands that movie music primarily must be emotional; it is one of the components that keeps the viewer involved in the on-screen activity.

For Conti, composing ultimately is a job. Upon completing work on one project, which may be a much-hyped potential blockbuster or Oscar contender, he will dutifully move on to the next, which might be an obscure television show or made-for-TV movie.

—Rob Edelman

COOPER, Merian C.

Producer. **Nationality:** American. **Born:** Jacksonville, Florida, 24 October 1893 (some sources give 1894). **Education:** Attended Lawrenceville School; United States Naval Academy, Annapolis, Maryland, 1911–15; Georgia Institute of Technology, Atlanta, graduated 1917. **Military Service:** Served in the United States infantry, 1916, then in Aviation Corps: captain; 1918–20—served with the Kosciusko Flying Squadron: Lt. Colonel; then news correspondent; served as colonel with Army Air Corps during World War II: chief of staff to General Claire Chennault in China: retired as brigadier general. **Career:** Merchant seaman and newspaperman; 1920s—collaborated with Ernest B. Schoedsack on documentaries and other films; joined RKO, and succeeded David O. Selznick as Vice President in Charge of Production, 1933; 1936—Vice President, Selznick International Pictures; 1947—formed Argosy Pictures with John Ford; 1952—coproducer of first Cinerama film. **Award:** Special Academy Award, 1952. **Died:** 21 April 1973.

Films as Producer:

1925   *Grass: A Nation's Battle for Life (Grass: The Epic of a Lost Tribe)* (+ co-d + co-ph + ro)
1927   *Chang* (+ co-d)
1928   *Gow, the Head Hunter* (doc)
1929   *The Lost Empire* (doc—produced 1924); *The Four Feathers* (+ co-d + co-ph)

Merian C. Cooper

1932   *The Most Dangerous Game (The Hounds of Zaroff)* (Schoedsack and Pichel); *The Phantom of Crestwood* (Ruben)
1933   **King Kong** (+ co-d + co-sc); *Lucky Devils* (R. Ince); *Professional Sweetheart* (Seiter); *Bed of Roses* (La Cava); *The Right to Romance* (Santell)
1934   *La Cucaracha* (Corrigan—short)
1935   *Becky Sharp* (Mamoulian); *She* (Pichel and Holden); *The Last Days of Pompeii* (Schoedsack)
1936   *Dancing Pirate* (Corrigan)
1938   *The Toy Wife (Frou Frou)* (Thorpe)
1939   *Stagecoach* (Ford) (uncredited)
1940   *The Long Voyage Home* (Ford)
1942   *Jungle Book (Rudyard Kipling's Jungle Book)* (Z. Korda) (uncredited); *Eagle Squadron* (Lubin) (uncredited)
1947   *The Fugitive* (Ford)
1948   *Fort Apache* (Ford); *Three Godfathers* (Ford)
1949   *Mighty Joe Young* (Schoedsack); *She Wore a Yellow Ribbon* (Ford)
1950   *Rio Grande* (Ford); *Wagonmaster* (Ford)
1952   *The Quiet Man* (Ford); *This Is Cinerama* (Rose) (+ uncredited co-d)
1953   *The Sun Shines Bright* (Ford)
1956   **The Searchers** (Ford); *The Best of Cinerama* (compilation)

Films as Executive Producer:

1933   *The Silver Cord* (Cromwell); *Melody Cruise* (Sandrich); *Double Harness* (Cromwell); *Morning Glory* (L. Sherman); *Ann Vickers* (Cromwell); *Ace of Aces* (Ruben); *Chance at Heaven* (Seiter); *Little Women* (Cukor); *After Tonight (Sealed Lips)* (Archainbaud); *Flying Down to Rio* (Freeland)
1934   *The Lost Patrol* (Ford); *Spitfire* (Cromwell); *Sing and Like It* (Seiter); *Success at Any Price* (Ruben); *Finishing School* (Tuchcok and Nicholls); *Stingaree* (Wellman)

Publications

By COOPER: books—

With Edward A. Salisbury, *The Sea Gypsy*, New York, 1924.
Grass, New York, 1925.

By COOPER: article—

Midi-Minuit Fantastique (Paris), June 1963.

On COOPER articles—

"King Kong Was a Dirty Old Man," in *Esquire* (New York), April 1951.
Films in Review (New York), January 1966.
American Film (Washington, D.C.), December-January 1977.
Avant-Scène (Paris), 15 November 1982.
Cinématographe (Paris), May 1984.
"The big picture," in *Boxoffice* (Chicago), no. 128, October 1992.
Clayton, J., "*King Kong*: the ultimate fantasy," in *Classic Images* (Muscatine, Iowa), no. 205, July 1992.

Boxoffice (Chicago), October 1992.

Mcgurl, M., "Making it Big: Picturing the Radio Age in *King Kong*," in *Critical Inquiry*, no. 3, 1996.

*   *   *

Merian C. Cooper, first a journalist, then an explorer, then a scriptwriter/producer, then an executive producer, was given a special Academy Award in 1952 "for his many innovations and contributions to the art of the motion pictures." He and Ernest B. Schoedsack were executive producers for the original *King Kong*, which made so many innovations in the horror-fantasy genre. In 1932 and 1933, RKO/Radio was suffering from the Depression, which was only then seriously affecting the film industry. In a desperate attempt to avoid the bankruptcy of RKO, Cooper and Schoedsack made a $500,000 gamble—a gigantic budget then—and won the bet with a tremendous financial success with *King Kong*. He was also the main writer of the script. Two decades later he opened a new frontier in film when he became a pioneer in the wide-screen process by producing *This Is Cinerama* in 1952.

Cooper's real contribution to cinema, however, was that he joined forces with John Ford to create Argosy Film Pictures in 1941. In the early days, the two men had a distribution deal with Darryl F. Zanuck of 20th Century-Fox where the latter approved the story and cost of each production. Cooper, however, managed also to arrange the international distribution for *The Fugitive* with Alexander Korda. Cooper continued to make other deals that had the effect of freeing Ford from the importunity of producers, whom he generally despised. It is no accident that, with Cooper as his producer or coproducer, Ford made the film that critics now claim to be the finest he or any other American made.

Ford has a great amount of power in Argosy; for example, in a letter dated 19 May 1959 (now a part of the Lilly Library collection) a colleague of Cooper and Ford writes that Ford "makes all vital decisions" in financial matters. In an earlier letter (2 April 1947) Cooper writes about a proposed script to Ford: "In my opinion, in its present form and with its dialogue, it is not a money picture." At Cooper's advice, the script was set aside. Letters in the same collection suggest how important Cooper was in negotiating a good deal for *The Searchers*—a deal that allowed Ford the creative freedom his particular talent needed. Cooper's contributions to Ford's career are demonstrated by the names of a mere few of the films he had a hand in: the entire Calvary Trilogy, *Three Godfathers*, *The Quiet Man*; it is also demonstrated by the general mediocrity of the films Ford made at the same time without Cooper.

—Rodney Farnsworth

CORTEZ, Stanley

Cinematographer. **Nationality:** American. **Born:** Stanislaus Krantz in New York City, 4 November 1908; brother of the actor Ricardo Cortez. **Education:** Attended New York University. **Military Service:** Photographer for Signal Corps during World War II. **Career:** 1920s—worked with portrait photographers Edward Steichen, Pirie MacDonald, and Bachrach; then worked for various studios in New York and Hollywood as assistant and cameraman; 1932—directed the short film *Scherzo*; 1936—first film as cinematographer, *Four Days'*

Wonder; after the war, under personal contract to David O. Selznick, Orson Welles, Walter Wanger, etc.; also worked for television. **Died:** 23 December 1997, in Hollywood, California, of a heart attack.

Films as Cinematographer:

1932	*Scherzo* (+ d, sc—short)
1936	*Four Days' Wonder* (Salkow)
1937	*The Wildcatter* (Collins); *Armored Car* (Foster)
1938	*The Black Doll* (Garrett) (co); *The Last Express* (Garrett); *Lady in the Morgue* (*The Case of the Missing Blonde*) (Garrett); *Danger on the Air* (Garrett); *Personal Secretary* (Garrett); *Exposed* (Schuster)
1939	*Risky Business* (Lubin); *They Asked for It* (McDonald); *For Love or Money* (*Tomorrow at Midnight*) (Rogell); *Hawaiian Nights* (Rogell); *The Forgotten Woman* (Young); *Laugh It Off* (*Lady Be Gay*) (Rogell)
1940	*Alias the Deacon* (Cabanne); *Love, Honor, and Oh, Baby!* (Lamont); *The Leatherpushers* (Rawlins); *Margie* (Garrett and Smith); *Meet the Wildcat* (Lubin); *A Dangerous Game* (Rawlins)
1941	*The Black Cat* (Rogell); *San Antonio Rose* (Lamont); *Moonlight in Hawaii* (Lamont); *Badlands of Dakota* (Green); *Sealed Lips* (Waggner); *Bombay Clipper* (Rawlins)
1942	*Eagle Squadron* (Lubin); ***The Magnificent Ambersons*** (Welles)
1943	*The Powers Girl* (*Hello Beautiful*) (McLeod); *Flesh and Fantasy* (Duvivier)
1944	*Since You Went Away* (Cromwell) (co)
1947	*Smash-Up* (*A Woman Destroyed*) (Heisler); *Secret behind the Door* (F. Lang)
1948	*Smart Woman* (Blatt)
1949	*The Man on the Eiffel Tower* (Meredith)
1950	*The Underworld Story* (*The Whipped*) (Endfield); *The Admiral Was a Lady* (Rogell)
1951	*The Basketball Fix* (*The Big Decision*) (Feist); *Fort Defiance* (Rawlins); *De l'autre côté de l'eau* (*From the Other Side of the Water*) (Darene—short) (co)
1952	*Stronghold* (Sekely); *Models, Inc.* (*Call Girl*; *That Kind of Girl*) (LeBorg); *Abbott and Costello Meet Captain Kidd* (Lamont)
1953	*The Neanderthal Man* (Dupont); *The Diamond Queen* (Brahm); *Dragon's Gold* (Wisberg and Pollexfen); *Shark River* (Rawlins); *Riders to the Stars* (Carlson)
1954	*Black Tuesday* (Fregonese)
1955	***The Night of the Hunter*** (Laughton)
1956	*Man from Del Rio* (Horner)
1957	*Top Secret Affair* (*Their Secret Affair*) (Potter); *The Three Faces of Eve* (Johnson)
1959	*Thunder in the Sun* (Rouse); *Vice Raid* (Cahn)
1960	*The Angry Red Planet* (Melchior); *Dinosaurus!* (Yeaworth); *Back Street*
1962	*Madmen of Mandoras* (*Return of Mr. H*) (Bradley)
1963	*Shock Corridor* (Fuller); *A Comedy Tale of Fanny Hill* (Goodwins—short); *Nightmare in the Sun* (Lawrence)
1964	*The Naked Kiss* (Fuller)
1965	*Young Dillinger* (Morse); *The Navy versus the Night Monsters* (*Monsters in the Night*) (Hoey)
1966	*Blue* (Narizzano): *The Bridge at Remagen* (Guillermin)
1969	*Tell Me that You Love Me, Junie Moon* (Preminger) (co)

1971   *The Date* (Hansley); *Do Not Fold, Spindle, or Mutilate* (Post)
1977   *Un autre homme, une autre chance* (*Another Man, Another Woman*) (Lelouch)

Film as Cameraman:

1935   *Gold Diggers of 1935* (Berkeley)

Publications

By CORTEZ: articles—

On *Blue* in *American Cinematographer* (Hollywood), July 1968.
In *Sources of Light*, edited by Charles Higham, London, 1970.
American Cinematographer (Hollywood), November 1976.
Cinématographe (Paris), June 1981.
On *The Night of the Hunter* in *American Cinematographer* (Hollywood), December 1982.

On CORTEZ: articles—

Lightman, Herb A., on *Back Street* in *American Cinematographer* (Hollywood), November 1961.
Lightman, Herb A., on *The Bridge at Remagen* in *American Cinematographer* (Hollywood), November 1969.
Film Comment (New York), Summer 1972.
Focus on Film (London), no. 13, 1973.
McGilligan, P., in *Take One* (Madison, Wisconsin), no. 2, 1978.
American Cinematographer (Hollywood), January 1990.
Obituary, in *Variety* (New York), 5 January 1998.

*   *   *

Stanley Cortez, while a solid contributor to Hollywood hack works, played an important part in the creation of a handful of transcendent masterpieces: *The Magnificent Ambersons*, *The Night of the Hunter*, *The Three Faces of Eve*, and *Shock Corridor*. Cortez was also able to give otherwise mediocre works a certain interest by means of experimental techniques.

Before Cortez started making films, he worked as a designer of elegant sets for several portrait photographers' studios. This work may well have instilled in him his great talent: a strong feeling for space and an ability to move his camera through that space in such a way as to embody it in film's two-dimensional format. Cortez lent an additional depth to his spatial capability by making the set into an objective correlative of the characters' psyche. He had his first job in cinema with Pathé News, which later allowed him to give his films the newsreel-like touch when necessary. During the 1920s and the early 1930s, he worked his way up the ladder that has become usual for Hollywood cameramen—camera assistant, camera operator, and cinematographer (or first cameraman). He managed to work for some of the great Hollywood cameramen, among them Karl Struss, Charles Rosher, and Arthur C. Miller. On the side, Cortez managed to do an experimental film, *Scherzo*, that drew on the techniques of Slavko Vorkapich; critics who have seen it have referred to this short as a "symphony of light."

Cortez's early films as cinematographer are not of the first rank, but they often had offbeat subjects that allowed him to experiment. In *The Forgotten Woman* he did an extreme close-up of the actress's eyes to create a sense of seeing into her mind. Then in 1942 Cortez had his big chance of working with Orson Welles on *The Magnificent Ambersons*. Cortez saw the set for the film before being appointed first cameraman. His spatial sense told him that film among these sets would be a tremendous challenge. Welles's cinematic genius told him that Cortez's mastery of studio space was exactly what this film—having a house as its main setting, indeed, its main character—demanded. Much of Cortez's great work was cut out later by the studio. There is the famous long take where the camera seems to explore the now empty Amberson mansion. The camera (a hand-held Mitchell) in this and another similar shot had to enter various rooms which were literally created and dismantled on cue and within seconds by the crew. The film contained documentary-like moments—for example, the opening shots which look like period photographs or engravings. These vignettes of turn-of-the-century life are carefully framed and often done in triangularly posed three-shots that give an atmosphere of bygone formality and order. *The Magnificent Ambersons* uses Tolandesque techniques such as depth of field with the new Plus-X film and the Waterhouse stops; *Eagle Squadron* carries these techniques even further.

In his later years, Cortez showed skill in filming psychological dramas. In a relatively minor work, *Smash-Up*, Cortez created the sense of drunkenness by doing subjective shots with flashing lights placed inside the camera, instead of using the banal distorted-lens shot. Charles Laughton gave Cortez another challenge—*The Night of the Hunter*. The extraordinary film demanded trial underwater shots and expressionistically lighted sets. The camera movements have a musical quality about them, and with the possible exception of the work of Charles Rosher and Karl Struss on *Sunrise*, *Night of the Hunter* contains the most beautiful camera ballet and shots of light on water ever done. As Cortez says, the camera work is musically conceived. In *The Three Faces of Eve*, Cortez found his actress Joanne Woodward would be to him what Garbo was to Daniels and Dietrich to Garmes. Cortez's subtle modulations of lighting match Woodward's equally subtle changes of expression, and both together create the sense of Eve, a psychologically split personality, becoming someone else. The labyrinthine hallways and rooms of the studio set representing a mental hospital for Samuel Fuller's *Shock Corridor* is transformed by Cortez's camera into a symbol of incarceration and insanity.

—Rodney Farnsworth

COURANT, Curt

Cinematographer. **Nationality:** German. **Born:** 1895 (?); also known as Kurt or Curtis. **Family:** Son, the cinematographer Willy Kurant. **Career:** Early work as cameraman for German and Italian films;

1917—first film work on *Hilde Warren und der Tod*; 1933—left Germany after rise of Nazis, worked in France and England.

Films as Cinematographer:

1917   *Hilde Warren und der Tod* (May) (co)

1920   *Das Mädchen aus der Ackerstrasse* (Schünzel); *Hamlet* (Glade) (co); *Präsident Barrada* (Lund)

1921   *Das Mädel vom Piccadilly* (Zelnik); *Der Abenteurer*

1922   *Peter de Grosse (Peter the Great)* (Buchowetzki); *Der Pantoffelheld* (Schünzel)

1923   *Das Paradies im Schnee* (Jacoby) (co)

1924   *Quo Vadis?* (D'Annunzio and Jacoby); *Komödianten des Lebens* (Jacoby); *Zwei Kinder* (Hilber)

1925   *Liebesfeuer* (Stein)

1926   *Die Insel der Träume* (Stein); *Ich liebe dich* (Stein); *Die Fahrt ins Abenteuer* (Mack); *Gräfin Plättmamsell* (David); *Die Flucht in die Nacht (The Flight in the Night)* (Palermi); *Die kleine vom Variété* (Schwarz); *Wehe, wenn die lossgelassen* (Froehlich); *Die Welt will belogen sein* (Felner) (co); *Heinrich der Vierte* (Palermi)

1927   *Der fesche Erzherzog* (Land); *Die Czardasfürsten* (Schwarz); *Familientag im Hause Prellstein* (Steinhoff); *Der Kampf des Donald Westhof* (Wendhausen)

1928   *Schuldig* (Meyer) (co); *Geheimnisse des Orients* (Wolkoff) (co); *Hurrah! Ich lebe!* (Thiele) (co)

1929   *Die Frau, nach der Mann sich sehnt* (Lang); *Das brennende Herz (The Burning Heart)* (Berger); *Die Frau im Mond (The Woman in the Moon)* (Lang) (co)

1930   *Der Hampelmann* (Emo); *L'Homme qui assassina* (Bernhardt and Tarride); *Der König von Paris* (Mittler) (co); *Die singende Stadt* (Gallone) (co); *Der weisse Teufal* (Wolkoff) (co)

1931   *Le Chanteur inconnu* (Tourjansky); *Der Mann, der den mord Being* (Bernhardt); *Meine Cousine aus Warschau (Ma cousine de Varsovie)* (Boese and Gallone); *Son altesse l'amour* (Schmidt and Peguy); *Wer nimmt die Liebe ernst?* (Engel)

1932   *Coeur de Lilas* (Litvak); *Un Fils d'Amérique* (Gallone); *Gitta entdeckt ihr Herz* (Froelich); *Die—oder Keine* (Froelich); *L'Homme qui ne sais pas dire non* (Hilpert); *Rasputin (Der Dämon der Frauen)* (Trotz)

1933   *Ces messieurs de la santé* (Colombier); *Cette vieille canaille* (Litvak); *Ciboulette* (Autant-Lara); *Ich will dich liebe lehren* (Hilpert) (co); *Scampolo, ein Kind der Strasse* (Steinhoff); *The Perfect Understanding* (Gardner)

1934   *Le Voleur* (Tourneur); *Amok* (Ozep); *The Man Who Knew Too Much* (Hitchcock); *The Iron Duke* (Saville)

1935   *The Passing of the Third Floor Back* (Viertel)

1936   *Broken Blossoms* (Septan); *Spy of Napoleon* (Knowles); *The Man in the Mirror* (Elvey)

1937   *Le Mensonge de Nina Petrowna* (Tourjansky); *Le Puritain* (Musso); *Tarakanova* (Ozep); *Dusty Ermine* (Vorhaus)

1938   **La Bête humaine** *(The Human Beast)* (Renoir); *Le Drame de Shanghaï* (Pabst); *Lumières de Paris* (Pottier); *La Maison du Maltais* (Chenal)

1939   **Le Jour se lève** *(Daybreak)* (Carné); *Louise* (Gance); *Monsieur Bretonneau* (Esway)

1940   *De Mayerling à Sarajevo (Mayerling to Sarajevo)* (Ophüls)

1947   *Monsieur Verdoux* (Chaplin) (co)

1961   *It Happened in Athens* (Marton)

Publications

By COURANT: article—

"Cameramen in the Golden Age of Cinema," in *Film Culture* (New York), no. 9, 1965.

On COURANT: article—

Focus on Film (London), no. 13, 1973.

*   *   *

Most of Curt Courant's work as a cinematographer was done in Germany before 1933, and he is recognized as one of the best of his profession, especially on melodramas and spectaculars. He worked for Gallone, Froelich, Thiele, May, and Buchowetzki, as well as making two films for Fritz Lang (including *Die Frau im Mond*). In the early 1930s, he made several French-language versions of German Films, but when he left Germany with the rise of the Nazis, he worked first in England, where he was partly responsible for the wonderful incongruities of Hitchcock's *The Man Who Knew Too Much* (1934). Though he made films with Max Ophüls and Charlie Chaplin in the 1940s, his most famous films are two he made in 1938 and 1939, *La Bête humaine* and *Le Jour se lève*. These two films, directed by Renoir and Carné, respectively, represent the final flourishing of what is often called "poetic realism," a concept which to current thinking looks very much like romanticism. The mood of poetic intensity, the melancholy and bittersweet fatalism, and the dreaminess that pervade both films—though much stronger in *Le Jour se lève*—centers on proletarian heroes (almost anti-heroes) caught up in psychological intensities they cannot quite understand or control. The despair they represented in the late 1930s has been muted into nostalgia, but they are still powerful and moving films.

COUTARD, Raoul

Cinematographer and Director. **Nationality:** French. **Born:** Paris, 16 September 1924. **Military Service:** Served with French forces in Indochina, 1945–50. **Career:** Worked in photographic laboratories; 1951–56—still photographer and combat reporter for *Life*, *Paris-Match*, and other magazines in the Far East; also photographer for French Ministry of Information; 1956—first film as cinematographer; 1967—first film as director; also made television advertisements. **Awards:** Jean Vigo prize, for *Hoa-Binh*, 1969; César award, for *Le Crabe-Tambour*, 1977; Venice Festival prize, for *Prénom Carmen*, 1983. **Died:** At Troyes, 5 September 1993.

Films as Cinematographer:

1956   *Paradiso terrestre* (Emmer) (co)

1957   *Thau le pêcheur* (Schöndörffer—short); *La Passe du diable* (Dupont and Schöndörffer)

1958 *Ramuntcho* (Schöndörffer)
1959 *Pêcheur d'Islande* (Schöndörffer); *Nicky et Kitty* (Mercier—short)
1960 ***A bout de souffle*** (*Breathless*) (Godard); *Les Grandes Personnes* (Valère); *Chronique d'un été* (Rouch and Morin) (co); *Tirez sur le pianiste* (*Shoot the Piano Player*) (Truffaut)
1961 *Lola* (Demy); ***Jules et Jim*** (*Jules and Jim*) (Truffaut); *Une Femme est une femme* (Godard); *Tire-au-flanc 62* (de Givray) (+ ro)
1962 *La Poupée* (Baratier); ***Vivre sa vie*** (Godard); "Antoine et Colette" ep. of *L'Amour à vingt ans* (*Love at Twenty*) (Truffaut); *Et Satan conduit le bal* (Dabat); *Vacances portugaises* (Kast); *Bourdelle, sculpteur monumental* (Navarra—short) (co)
1963 *Le Petit Soldat* (Godard—produced 1960); *Les Carabiniers* (Godard); *Als tween druppels water* (*Spitting Image*) (Rademakers); *Les Baisers* (Tavernier and others); ***Le Mépris*** (***Contempt***) (Godard) (+ ro); "Le Grand Escroc" ep. of *Les Plus Belles Escroqueries du monde* (Godard); *La Difficulté d'être infidèle* (Troublanc-Michel)
1964 *Bande à part* (Godard); *Les 317e Section* (Schöndörffer); *Je vous salue, Maria* (Lévy); *Un Monsieur de compagnie* (*Male Companion*) (de Broca); *La Peau douce* (*The Soft Skin*) (Truffaut); *La Femme mariée* (Godard); *L'Avatar botanique de Mlle. Flora* (Barbillon—short); *Petit jour* (Pierre—short) (co)
1965 ***Alphaville*** (Godard); *Pierrot le fou* (Godard); *Les Voix d'Orly* (Lachenay—short); *Scruggs* (*A Game Called Scruggs*) (Hart)
1966 *L'Horizon* (Rouffio); *Made in U.S.A.* (Godard); *Riom le beau* (Guilbert—short)
1967 *The Sailor from Gibraltar* (Richardson); *L'Espion* (*The Defector*) (Levy); *Deux ou trois choses que je sais d'elle* (Godard); ***Weekend*** (Godard); *La Chinoise* (Godard); *Concerto Brandebourgeois* (Reichenbach—short) (co); *La Mariée était en noir* (*The Bride Wore Black*) (Truffaut); *Vive eau* (Roger—short)
1968 *L'Éoile du sud* (*The Southern Star*) (Hayers); *Rocky Road to Dublin* (Lennon); *Au péril de la mer* (Roger—short)
1969 *Z* (Costa-Gavras) (+ ro)
1970 *L'Aveu* (*The Confession*) (Costa-Gavras) (+ ro); *Jolly Green* (+ d, sc—short); *Etes-vous fiancée à un marin grec ou à un pilote de ligne?* (Aurel); *La Liberté en croupe* (Molinaro)
1971 *L'Explosion* (Simenon) (+ ro); *Le Trèfle à cinq feuilles* (Freess); *Les Aveux les plus doux* (Molinaro); *The Jerusalem File* (Flynn)
1972 *Embassy* (Hessler); *Le Gang des otages* (Molinaro)
1973 *L'Emmerdeur* (Molinaro)
1974 *Comme un pot de fraises!* (Aurel)
1977 *Le Crabe-Tambour* (Schöndörffer)
1979 *La Légion sauté sur Kolwezi* (+ d)
1982 *Passion* (Godard)
1983 *Le Diagonale du fou* (*Dangerous Moves*) (Dembo); *Prénom Carmen* (*First Name Carmen*) (Godard)
1984 *La Garce* (Pascal); *Du Sel sur la peau* (Deges)
1986 *Max mon amour* (*Max, My Love*) (Oshima)
1987 *Fuegos* (Arias)
1988 *Blanc de chine* (Granier-Deferre); *Brennende Betten* (*Burning Beds*) (Frankenberg) *Ne réveillez pas un flic qui dort* (Pinheiro); *Peaux de vaches* (Mazuy)

1990 *La femme fardeé* (Pinheiro); *Bethune: The Making of a Hero* (*Dr. Bethune*) (Borsos); *Il gèle en enfer* (Mocky)
1991 *Les Enfants volants* (*The Flying Children*) (Nicloux) (co)
1992 *La Vie crevée* (*The Punctured Life*) (Nicloux)
1993 *La Naissance de l'amour* (Garrel)
1994 *Faut-pas rire au bonheur* (*Happiness Is No Joke*) (Nicloux)

Films as Director:

1967 *Singal l'antilope sacrée* (short); *Tu es danse et vertige* (short)
1969 *Hoa-Binh* (*Peace*) (+ co-sc)
1980 *La Légion saute sur Kolweizi*
1982 *SAS à San Salvador* (*SAS—Terminate with Extreme Prejudice*)

Publications

By COUTARD: articles—

Cinéma (Paris), January 1965.
"Light of Day," in *Sight and Sound* (London), Winter 1965–66.
Braucout, Guy, "Raoul Coutard pour des raisons simplement humaines," in *Les Lettres Françaises* (Paris), 11 March 1970.
Films and Filming (London), June 1970.
Show (New York), 17 September 1970.
Revue du Cinéma (Paris), February 1971.
Cinéma Français (Paris), no. 33, 1980.
Cinématographe (Paris), July 1981.
Le Technicien du Film (Paris), July/September 1982.
Filmkritik (Munich), July 1983.
Film Français (Paris), 19 October 1984.

On COUTARD: articles—

Monthly Film Bulletin (London), 1963.
Film (Hanover), no. 9, 1965.
Lennon, Peter, "La Vie Coutard," in *The Guardian* (London) 15 December 1966.
Chaplin (Stockholm), no. 2, 1970.
Lennon, Peter, "The Film World's Cool Hand Luke," in *The Daily Telegraph* (London), 17 July 1970.
Kent, Leticia, "Coutard: War Can Be Beautiful," in *New York Times*, 12 September 1971.
Focus on Film (London), no. 13, 1973.
Film Français (Paris), 3 February 1978.
Canby, Vincent, in *New York Times*, 19 February 1984.
Bergery, B., "Raoul Coutard: Revolutionary of the Nouvelle Vague," in *American Cinematographer* (Hollywood), March 1997.
Solman, G., "Remembering Raoul," in *Variety's On Production* (Los Angeles), no. 2, 1997.

*   *   *

Most readily identified with Godard and, to a lesser extent, Truffaut, Raoul Coutard's unorthodox, technically unsophisticated but highly imaginative photography became an expression of French

New Wave values. In the era of lightweight cameras and fast film-stock which prized inventiveness and naturalness above the studied, polished images of the fifties, he was at home working quickly with hand-held cameras in locations invariably underlit by textbook standards. His direct, simplified approach to filming also broke with traditional aesthetics by drawing attention to the camera in films such as *A bout de souffle* or *Le Petit Soldat*. His challenging innovations were so rapidly assimilated as to become, in many respects, the new orthodoxy of the sixties both in France and further afield. His influence in America, for example, shows in the work of Konrad Hall, Laszlo Kovaks, Gordon Willis, and Vilmos Zsigmond.

The qualities of freshness and resourcefulness inherent in Coutard's approach are attributable to an absence of formal training and to his fieldwork experience, initially as an army photographer in Indochina and later as a daring photojournalist for *Radar*, *Paris-Match*, and *Life*.

Feature work ensued with *Ramuntcho*, a film about smugglers in the Basque country and *Pêcheur d'Islande*, with the life of deep-sea fishermen as its subject. Remarkable for its images of stormy seas, the film anticipates by two decades Coutard's award-winning photography of ships and dramatic seascapes in *Le Crabe-Tambour*.

The sixties brought collaboration with a variety of directors including Demy, Kast, Valère, Richardson, and Costa-Gavras, though most notably with Godard and Truffaut. His work for Valère in *Les Grandes Personnes*, with its Parisian setting captured in flat, naturalistic lighting, reveals the influence of Decaë. For Demy's *Lola*, with its striking slow motion sequences at the fairground, he obtained the distinctively rich blacks and whites by using Gevaert 36 film; for Costa-Gavras in *Z* the political message of the investigative documentary is effectively pointed by subjective shots and informative close-ups.

Coutard's association with Truffaut resulted in films which were remarkable for their atmospheric qualities and their sympathetic treatment of character. In *Tirez sur le pianiste*, the pastiched mood of the American B movie is established as the camera tracks through dark streets and, in terms of characterization, a slow pan round Charlie's room becomes a delicate revelation of his painful past; in *La Mariée était en noir*, homage to Hitchcock is found in the play of tracking shots and close-ups to create tension and engender audience identification; in *Jules et Jim*, the richly varied camerawork reflects the pattern of moods dictated by the mercurial Catherine. In his work with Truffaut, Coutard excelled in conveying the full weight of the psychological moment. In *Tirez sur le pianiste* a lengthy close-up of a finger hesitating above a doorbell renders the violinist's apprehension before the audition while rapid camera movements brilliantly convey Charlie's panic and desperation as he rushes, too late, to his suicidal wife. In *Jules et Jim*, Coutard captures the sheer exuberance of the sun-drenched bicycle rides, or the innocent joy of childish games, or the initial awkwardness, then exhilaration, of the reunion as the camera hesitantly, then excitedly, links the protagonists, or conveys the depth of Jim's feelings with the camera soaring above the trees to deny the distance between the chalet and the hotel.

Nevertheless, it is above all in his contribution to Godard's subversive cinema of ideas during the sixties and in the early eighties that Coutard revolutionized approaches to cinematography. There were frequent experiments with film stock. For *A bout de souffle* a raw newsreel quality was achieved by using Ilford HPS photographic film; for *Les Carabiniers*, a special processing was employed to produce the documentary realism of harsh blacks and whites rather than muted grays; in *Vivre sa vie* starkly contrasting monochrome images underpin the bleak depiction of prostitution; in *La Femme mariée* or *Le Petit Soldat* dehumanization is conveyed in clinically

detached photography of characters against empty white backgrounds while the chilling mood of alienation in *Alphaville* derives from the camera's emphasis of inhumane architecture and the harsh neon lights of Paris by night. Coutard's color photography for Godard was equally experimental. In *Le Mépris* the symbolic play of reds, blues, and yellows is emphasized by the use of film stock which enhances sensitivity; in *Une Femme est une femme* color is used for dramatic purposes to serve the mood; in *La Chinoise* primary colors translate the brutality of the Vietnam war, and in *Deux ou trois choses que je sais d'elle*, the display of brightly-colored commercial products exposes the temptations of Western materialism. With the luxuriant color of *Pierrot le fou*, there are elements of unusual beauty in the reflection of traffic lights on the car windshield or in the images of the protagonists walking through long grass as the car blazes. In *Passion*, concerned as it is with light and pictorial representation, Coutard's experience as a lighting cameraman was invaluable.

Coutard's use of long tracking shots—from the hand-held camera in a bath chair for the sequence at Orly airport in *Une Femme mariée* to the shocking ten-minute account of the murderous traffic jam in *Weekend*—has been daring. Equally challenging has been the use of the distancing longshot in *Pierrot le fou*, *Week-end* or *Les Carabiniers*, and, in *Deux ou trois choses que je sais d'elle*, for example, the use of the extreme close-up of a coffee cup to achieve a degree of abstraction or, in *Vivre sa vie*, a telling concentration on Nana's pen as she struggles over an illiterate letter.

In the nineties Coutard enabled a new generation of filmmakers to bring their vision to the screen. For Garrel he provided aptly prosaic black-and-white images of workaday Paris as a framework for the mid-life crises explored in *La Naissance de l'amour*, while in three films for Nicloux, he again conveyed bleak, soulless moods through restrained camerawork. In *Les Enfants volants*, he worked with Jean Badal to provide a controlled, dispassionate portrait of the deranged and murderous protagonist; in *La Vie crevée*, his camera perceptively observes the maneuvers of a manipulative older male (Michel Piccoli) destroying the previously happy relationships of two young couples, while in *Faut-pas rire au bonheur*, long takes characterize the unfolding of the director's gloomy tale of chance encounters set in Coutard's familiar nighttime Paris.

Although Coutard enjoyed a measure of polite recognition as a director with films such as *Hoa-Binh*, it is essentially his work as a cinematographer that has determined his reputation. He is justly acknowledged to be not only the unrivaled interpreter of the Godardian vision, but also the most consistently adventurous and influential of the New Wave cameramen.

—R. F. Cousins

COWARD, (Sir) Noël

Producer, Writer, and Actor. **Nationality:** British. **Born:** Noël Pierce Coward in Teddington, Middlesex, England, 16 December 1899. **Education:** Attended Chapel Road School. **Career:** Child actor, writer for revues in late 1910s; 1924—first successful play, *The Vortex*, followed by a series of comedies, musicals (often writing the music and lyrics), and dramas; also a stage director of his own and

Noël Coward

other plays; 1942—first film as writer (also producer and co-director), *In Which We Serve*; cabaret entertainer from the 1950s. **Awards:** Special Academy Award for *In Which We Serve*, 1942. Knighted, 1970. **Died:** 26 March 1973.

Films as Producer:

1942   *In Which We Serve* (+ co-d + sc + mus + ro)
1944   *This Happy Breed* (Lean)
1945   *Blithe Spirit* (Lean); **Brief Encounter** (Lean) (+ co-sc)

Films as Writer:

1945   *Journal de la résistance* (Grémillon) (commentary, + narrator)
1949   *The Astonished Heart* (Fisher and Darnborough) (+ mus + ro)
1952   *Meet Me Tonight* (Pelissier) (+ mus)
1955   *Cavalcade* (Allen)

Films as Actor:

1918   *Hearts of the World* (Griffith)
1935   *The Scoundrel* (Hecht and MacArthur)
1956   *Around the World in Eighty Days* (Anderson)

1959   *Our Man in Havana* (Reed)
1960   *Surprise Package* (Donen)
1963   *Paris When It Sizzles* (Quine)
1965   *Bunny Lake Is Missing* (Preminger)
1968   *Boom!* (Losey)
1969   *The Italian Job* (Collinson)

Publications

By COWARD: plays—

I'll Leave It to You, London, 1920.
The Young Idea, London, 1922
The Rat Trap, London, 1924.
The Vortex, London, 1925.
Hay Fever, London, 1925.
Fallen Angels, London, 1925.
Easy Virtue, London, 1926.
The Queen Was in the Parlour, London, 1926.
This Was a Man, London, 1926.
The Marquise, London, 1927.
Home Chat, London, 1927.
Sirocco, London, 1927.
Bitter-Sweet, London, 1929.
Private Lives, London, 1930.
Post-Mortem, London, 1931.
Cavalcade, London, 1932.
Design for Living, London, 1933.
Play Parade, 6 vols., London, 1933–62.
Conversation Piece, London, 1934.
Pointe Valaine, London, 1935.
Tonight at 8:30, 3 vols., London, 1936.
Operette, London, 1938.
Curtain Calls, New York, 1940.
Blithe Spirit, London, 1941.
Australian Broadcast, London, 1941.
Present Laughter, London, 1943.
This Happy Breed, London, 1943.
Peace in Our Time, London, 1947.
Quadrille, London, 1952.
South Sea Bubble, London, 1954.
Relative Values, London, 1954.
After the Ball, London, 1954.
Nude with Violin, London, 1957.
Look after Lulu, London, 1959.
Waiting in the Wings, London, 1960.
Suite in Three Keys, London, 1966.
Plays, 4 vols., London, 1979.
The Collected Stories of Noel Coward, New York, 1986.
Three Plays by Noel Coward, Garden City, 1997.

By COWARD: other books—

A Withered Nosegay (non-fiction), London, 1922.
Chelsea Buns (verse), London, 1925.

The Collected Sketches and Lyrics, London, 1931.
Spangled Unicorn (verse), London, 1932.
Present Indicative (autobiography), London, 1937.
To Step Aside (stories), London, 1939.
Middle East Diary (non-fiction), London, 1944.
Brief Encounter (script), in *Three British Screen Plays*, edited by Roger Manvell, London, 1950.
Star Quality (stories), London, 1951.
The Noel Coward Song-Book, London, 1953.
Future Indefinite (autobiography), London, 1954.
(Editor) *The Last Bassoon*, London, 1960.
Pomp and Circumstance (novel), London, 1960.
Collected Short Stories, London, 1962, augmented edition, 1969.
Pretty Polly Barlow (stories), London, 1964, as *Polly Barlow*, New York, 1965.
The Lyrics of Noël Coward, London, 1965.
Not Yet the Dodo, (verse), London, 1967.
Bon Voyage (stories), London, 1967.
Diaries, edited by Graham Payn and Sheridan Morley, London, 1982.
Collected Verse, edited by Graham Payn and Martin Tickner, London, 1984.
The Complete Stories, London, 1985.
Autobiography, London, 1986.

By COWARD: articles—

Picturegoer (London), August 1927.
Picturegoer (London), 29 April 1933.
Photoplay (New York), February 1935.
The Listener (London), 7 April 1966.
Revue du Cinéma International, April 1971.

On COWARD: books—

Braybrooke, Patrick, *The Amazing Mr. Noël Coward*, London, 1933.
Graecen, Robert, *The Art of Noël Coward*, London, 1957.
Levin, Milton, *Noël Coward*, New York, 1968.
Morley, Sheridan, *A Talent to Amuse: A Biography of Noël Coward*, London, 1969.
Castle, Charles, *Noël*, London, 1972.
Merchant, William, *Privilege of His Company: Noël Coward Remembered*, London, 1975.
Lesley, Cole, *The Life of Noël Coward*, London, 1976, as *Remembered Laughing*, New York, 1976.
Yaraventilimath, C. R., *Jesting Jeremiah: A Study of Noël Coward's Comic Vision*, Dharwad, 1978.
Lesley, Cole, *Noël Coward and His Friends*, London, 1979.
Lahr, John, *Coward the Playwright*, London, 1982.
Fisher, Clive, *Noël Coward*, London, 1992.
Cole, Stephen, *Noël Coward: A Bio-bibliography*, Westport, Connecticut, London, 1993.
Payn, Graham, *My Life with Noël Coward*, New York, 1994.
Hoare, Philip, *Noël Coward*, Sinclair-Stevenson, 1995.
Morella, Joseph, and George Mazzei, *Genius and Lust: The Creative and Sexual Lives of Noel Coward and Cole Porter*, New York, 1995.
Browne, Phyllis, *Thanks for the Tea, Mrs. Browne: My Life with Noel*, Dublin, 1998.
Hoare, Philip, *Noel Coward*, Chicago, 1998.
Mander, Raymond, *Theatrical Companion to Coward*, New York, 1999.

On COWARD: articles—

Picturegoer (London), 27 April 1935.
Photoplay (New York), June 1935.
Picturegoer (London), 15 February 1947.
Obituary in *Cinéma* (Paris), May 1973.
Films in Review (New York), March 1975.
Lahr, John, in *Automatic Vaudeville*, New York, 1984.
Baker, Bob, ''In Which He Served,'' in *Sight & Sound* (London), Summer 1990.
Stillwater, Marianne, ''Noël Coward et David Lean,'' in *Cinéma* (Paris), July-August 1991.
Gottlieb, S., ''Kissing and Telling in Hitchcock's *Easy Virtue*,'' in *Hitchcock Annual* (Gambier), no. 1, 1992.

*   *   *

Noël Coward, bright young man of the 1920s and 1930s and darling of cafe society for over five decades, wore many creative caps in addition to his chief vocation as playwright. Likewise his ventures into films were under a number of guises—actor, screenwriter, producer, and director.

As a playwright he saw most of his plays adapted for the screen but with little actual involvement on his part—*Bitter Sweet*, *Private Lives*, *Design for Living*, and *Blithe Spirit*. In 1933, the American production of his play, *Cavalcade*—the saga of a British family between the Boer War and the First World War—won the Academy Award as Best Picture of the Year. As an actor, he did two bit parts in 1918 in D. W. Griffith's *Heart of the World*. Later acting roles included *Around the World in Eighty Days*, *Bunny Lake Is Missing*, and *Boom!* As a screenwriter he was less prolific, but his output includes two hallmark films—*In Which We Serve*, based upon his original screenplay, and *Brief Encounter*, which he adapted from his one-act play *Still Life*. Curiously, neither of these films rely on the flippant, sometimes sarcastic, and often effete subject matter of many of his famous plays. Instead they were inspiring, realistic depictions of the English during the Second World War.

In Which We Serve was Coward's admirable effort to boost British wartime morale, a propaganda film with lasting value. The germination for the film began with Louis Mountbatten's description of life aboard the *HMS Kelly* prior to its sinking during the Battle of Crete. Coward developed the screenplay, and also produced the film, wrote the music, co-directed with David Lean, and acted the role of the ship's captain. Told in sober, documentary style with the use of flashbacks, it is flagwaver of considerable merit which earned Coward a special Academy Award.

Brief Encounter remains one of the screen's most durable romantic films. For all its simplicity—the story of an extramarital affair between two happily married, middle-class people—the film is a moving and convincing account of basic human emotions. Coward wrote the screenplay with David Lean and Anthony Havelock-Allan; Coward produced and Lean directed. The complete opposite of Hollywood's glossy women's pictures, *Brief Encounter* is sparingly directed by Lean, and beautifully acted by Celia Johnson and Trevor Howard.

—Ronald Bowers

CRISTALDI, Franco

Producer. **Nationality:** Italian. **Born:** Turin, 3 October 1924. Studied law: degree. **Career:** Documentary film producer after World War II, and feature film producer from early 1950s; founded Vides Cinematografica, and in 1982 Vides Internationale; also TV producer: executive producer of mini-series *Marco Polo*, 1982; 1977— President, International Federation of Film Producers Association. **Died:** In July 1992.

Films as Producer:

1954   *La pattaglia sperduta* (Nelli)
1955   *Il seduttore* (Rossi); *Camilla* (Emmer); *Un eroe dei nostri tempi* (Monicelli)
1956   *Mio figlio Nerone* (*Nero's Mistress*) (Steno); *Kean* (Gassman)
1957   *Rascel Fifi* (Leoni); *L'uomo di paglia* (Germi); *I notti bianchi* (*White Nights*) (Visconti)
1958   *La sfida* (*The Challenge*) (Rosi); *I soliti ignoti* (*Big Deal on Madonna Street*) (Monicelli); *La loi . . . c'est la loi* (*The Law Is the Law*) (Christian-Jaque)
1959   *Audace colpo dei soliti ignoti* (*Fiasco in Milan*) (Loy); *Un ettaro di cielo* (Casadio); *Rascel Marine* (Leoni); *I magliari* (Rosi)
1960   *I delfini* (Maselli); *Vento del sud* (Provenzale); *Kapò* (Pontecorvo)
1961   *L'assassino* (*The Lady Killer of Rome*) (Petri); *Fantasmi a Roma* (Pietrangeli); *Un giorno da leone* (Loy); *Giorno per giorno disperatamente* (Giannetti); **Salvatore Giuliano** (Rosi)
1962   *Divorzio all'italiana* (*Divorce, Italian Style*) (Germi); *Arrivano i Titani*; (*My Son, the Hero*) (Tessari)
1963   *La ragazzi di Bube* (*Bebo's Girl*) (Comencini); *I compagni* (*The Organizer*) (Monicelli); *Omicron* (Gregoretti); *Mare matto* (Castellani)
1964   *Sedotta e abbandonata* (*Seduced and Abandoned*) (Germi); *Les Plus Belles Escroqueries du monde* (*The Beautiful Swindlers*) (Godard and others); *Gli indifferenti* (*Time of Indifference*) (Maselli)
1965   *Vaghe stelle dell'orsa* (*Sandra*) (Visconti); *L'antimiracolo* (Piccon)
1967   *Una rosa per tutti* (*A Rose for Everyone*) (Rossi); *La Cine è vicina* (*China Is Near*) (Bellocchio)
1968   *Ruba al prossimo tuo* (*A Fine Pair*) (Maselli) (exec pr)
1971   *Krasnaya palatka* (*The Red Tent*) (Klalatazov); *Nel nome del padre* (*In the Name of the Father*) (Bellocchio); *L'udienza* (Ferreri); **Le Souffle au coeur** (*Murmur of the Heart*) (Malle)
1972   *Il caso Mattei* (*The Mattei Affair*) (Rosi); *Lady Caroline Lamb* (Bolt) (exec pr)

1973   *A proposito Lucky Luciano* (*Re: Lucky Luciano*) (Rosi); *Lacombe Lucien* (Malle)
1974   *Amarcord* (Fellini)
1975   *Beata Loro*
1976   *Qui comincia l'avventura* (Di Palma)
1979   *Ogro* (*Operation Ogre*) (Pontecorvo) (co); **Cristo si è fermato a Eboli** (*Christ Stopped at Eboli*) (Rosi); *Ratataplan* (Nichetti) (co)
1980   *Café Express* (Loy); *Ho fatto splash* (Nichetti); *Il Cappotto di Astrakan* (Vicario)
1982   *Domani si balla* (Nichetti)
1983   *Marco Polo* (for TV); *Arrivano i miei* (Salerno); *E la nave va* (*And the Ship Sails On*) (Fellini)
1986   *Garibaldi—the General* (Magni); *The Name of the Rose* (Annaud)
1989   *Vanille fraise* (Oury)
1990   *Cinema Paradiso* (Tornatore); *C'era un castello con 40 cani* (*Au bonheur des chiens*) (Tessari)

Publications

By CRISTALDI: articles—

Rivista del Cinematografo (Rome), January-February 1980.
Positif (Paris), no. 316, June 1987.

On CRISTALDI: articles—

Film Français (Paris), 4 May 1984.
Delli Colli, Laura, in *Les métiers du cinéma*, Paris, 1986.
Obituary, in *New York Times*, vol. 141, 3 July 1992.
Obituary, in *Variety* (New York), 13 July 1992.
RIvista del Cinematografo (Rome), September 1992.
Skoop, 5 September 1992.
Cinema Sud (Avellino, Italy), December-January-February 1992–1993.

*   *   *

As an occasional, if reluctant, producer for Luchino Visconti and a longtime associate of Francesco Rosi, Franco Cristaldi was responsible in the 1960s and 1970s for some of Italy's most uncompromising cinema, while shrewd marketing of his Pietro Germi and Mario Monicelli productions made them among the best-known European films to circulate in the United States.

Born in 1924, Cristaldi began producing documentaries. In 1952 he founded Vides Cinematografica and moved into features as Italy's youngest producer. Half a dozen minor projects attracted the attention of the prestigious but profligate Luchino Visconti, the budget overruns of whose *Senso* had scared off more experienced financiers. Cristaldi, Visconti and writer Suso Cecchi d'Amico collaborated to make *I notti bianchi*, intended as a cheap vehicle to launch their friend Marcello Mastroianni as a serious actor. Shortly before filming was to begin in Livorno, Visconti, impressed by Maria Schell's Venice Golden Lion for *Gervaise*, hired her, at a fee Cristaldi considered exorbitant. But Visconti refused to recast, and further announced his preference for a studio shoot over locations. Sets of city streets, canals and railway lines were built at Cinecittà, made even more expensive

Franco Cristaldi (with cigarette) with Suso Cecchi D'Amice and Marcello Mastrioanni (left)

when Visconti demanded huge tulle curtains to create the effect of fog. Hoping to spread costs, Cristaldi commissioned a comedy script from d'Amico to employ the *Notti bianchi* sets, but delays forced them out of Cinecittà before the film, *I soliti ignoti*, could start shooting under Mario Monicelli. *I notti bianchi* won a Silver Lion at Venice but failed commercially. On the other hand, Monicelli's farce about feckless crooks trying to pull a robbery became Cristaldi's first success, even (as *Big Deal on Madonna Street*) in the U.S.A. Cristaldi also married one of its stars, Claudia Cardinale.

Over the next five years Cristaldi financed a range of films distinguished by tough socialist subject matter. Monicelli's assistant Gillo Pontecorvo brought him the concentration camp drama *Kapò*, whose starkness prefigures Monicelli's *I compagni*, the story of a turn of the century union agitator working in Cristaldi's native Turin, and Francesco Rosi's *Salvatore Giuliano*. The films established Vides as Italy's preeminent producer of socially conscious cinema but were too bleak to enjoy wide English-language release. In particular *Salvatore Giuliano*, recut and retitled *The Bandit's Revenge*, fared badly.

In 1959, Visconti approached Cristaldi to produce *Rocco and his Brothers*. Committed to a mixed French and Italian cast, the director had already chosen Annie Girardot for a major role. When Cristaldi

suggested Brigitte Bardot or Pascale Petit, Visconti, replying acidly that he could see hiring them as manicurists but not as actresses, moved the project to Goffredo Lombardo's Titanus and broke with Cristaldi ''after a series of telegrams,'' recalled the producer, ''that could never be published in a respectable book. I am even surprised the postal service agreed to send them.'' Cristaldi returned to social satire, backing Pietro Germi's highly successful *Divorzio all'italiana* and *Sedotta e abbandonata*, films that overturned the rocks of Italian regional life, showing the clichéd warm-hearted Italian as greedy, treacherous and priapic. Stefania Sandrelli was established as a star, Germi won an Oscar for *Divorce*'s story and screenplay, and Cristaldi was launched decisively as an international producer.

In 1964, Visconti proposed another collaboration. Aware that Cardinale, who had worked with him on *The Leopard*, was anxious to do so again, Visconti induced Cristaldi to back *Vaghe stelle dell'orsa*, his version of *Elektra* with Cardinale and Jean Sorel as incestuous aristocratic siblings. The film made little money, but probably paid off in scandal and critical esteem. Cristaldi also funded two further vehicles for Cardinale, *A Rose for Everyone* on Brazilian locations and *Ruba al prossimo tuo*, a crime comedy with Rock Hudson, leeringly retitled *A Fine Pair* for the U.S.A.

Consistently interested in socialist/humanist projects through the 1970s, Cristaldi continued the collaboration with Francesco Rosi that had begun with 1958's *La sfida*. Though he funded *China Is Near* and *In the Name of the Father* by belligerent left-wing director Marco Bellochio, Cristaldi was not drawn to the new crop of young Italian filmmakers. His main involvement with the newer generation was with French directors, notably Louis Malle, whose *Viva Maria*, *Le Souffle au Coeur*, *Lacombe Lucien*, and *Black Moon* Vides backed. He also financed Fellini's autobiographical *Amarcord*.

In 1977, Cristaldi became head of the International Federation of Film Producers Associations, a post which briefly reduced his activities in feature film, though he did produce the 1982 TV mini-series *Marco Polo* and Rosi's *Cristo si è fermato a Eboli*. Based on Carlo Levi's account of his exile by the Fascists to a remote village, the latter was distributed as both feature film and TV mini-series, a rare art cinema use of this Hollywood technique. In 1990, Cristaldi demonstrated he had not lost his skill at merchandising Italian cinema to the world when the Sicilian comedy *Cinema Paradiso*, which he produced, became an international success.

—John Baxter

CRONJAGER, Edward

Cinematographer. **Nationality:** American. **Born:** 1904. **Family:** Married the actress Kay Sutton (divorced). **Career:** Assistant cameraman from the early 1920s; 1925—first film as cinematographer, *Womanhandled*; then worked for Paramount, Fox, and other studios; 1950s—television work for Ziv company. **Died:** In 1960.

Films as Cinematographer:

1925 *Womanhandled* (La Cava)
1926 *Let's Get Married* (La Cava); *Say It Again* (La Cava); *The Quarterback* (Newmeyer)
1927 *Paradise for Two* (La Cava); *Knockout Reilly* (St. Clair); *Man Power* (Badger); *Shanghai Bound* (Reed); *The Gay Defender* (La Cava)
1928 *Sporting Goods* (St. Clair); *Easy Come, Easy Go* (Tuttle); *Warming Up* (Newmeyer); *Moran of the Marines* (Strayer); *What a Night!* (Sutherland)
1929 *Redskin* (Schertzinger); *Nothing but the Truth* (Schertzinger); *The Wheel of Life* (Schertzinger); *Fashions in Love* (Schertzinger); *Fast Company* (Sutherland); *The Love Doctor* (M. Brown); *Seven Keys to Baldpate* (Barker)
1930 *Lovin' the Ladies* (M. Brown); *He Knew Women* (Herbert and Shores); *Shooting Straight* (Archainbaud); *Cimarron* (Ruggles)
1931 *Young Donovan's Kid* (*Donovan's Kid*) (Niblo); *The Public Defender* (Ruben); *Secret Service* (Ruben)
1932 *The Lost Squadron* (Archainbaud) (co); *Road of the Dragon* (Ruggles); *Hell's Highway* (R. Brown); *The Conquerors* (Wellman); *No Other Woman* (Ruben); *Sweepings* (Cromwell); *Diplomaniacs* (Seiter); *Professional Sweetheart* (Seiter); *No Marriage Ties* (Ruben); *If I Were Free* (*Behold We Live*) (Nugent)

1934 *Spitfire* (Cromwell); *Strictly Dynamite* (Nugent); *Down to Their Last Yacht* (*Hawaiian Nights*) (Sloane); *Kentucky Kernels* (*Triple Trouble*) (Stevens); *Lightning Strikes Twice* (Holmes)
1935 *Enchanted April* (Beaumont); *Roberta* (Seiter); *The Nitwits* (Stevens); *Jalna* (Cromwell); *In Person* (Seiter)
1936 *Yellow Dust* (Fox); *Special Investigator* (L. King); *Swing It* (Goodwins—short); *The Texas Rangers* (K. Vidor); *Three Married Men* (Buzzell); *One in a Million* (Lanfield)
1937 *Nancy Steele Is Missing* (Marshall); *Wake Up and Live* (Lanfield); *Thin Ice* (*Lovely to Look At*) (Lanfield) (co); *Wife, Doctor, and Nurse* (W. Lang)
1938 *Island in the Sky* (Leeds); *Rascals* (Humberstone); *Gateway* (Werker); *Keep Smiling* (*Miss Fix-It*) (Leeds)
1939 *Winner Take All* (Brower); *The Gorilla* (Dwan); *Chicken-Wagon Family* (Leeds); *The Escape* (Cortez); *Heaven with a Barbed Wire Fence* (Cortez); *Too Busy to Work* (Brower); *Everything Happens at Night* (Cummings)
1940 *I Was an Adventuress* (Ratoff) (co); *The Girl in 313* (Cortez); *Young People* (Dwan); *The Gay Caballero* (Brower); *Youth Will Be Served* (Brower)
1941 *Western Union* (F. Lang) (co); *A Very Young Lady* (Schuster); *Sun Valley Serenade* (Humberstone); *Hot Spot* (*I Wake Up Screaming*) (Humberstone); *Rise and Shine* (Dwan)
1942 *To the Shores of Tripoli* (Humberstone) (co); *Friendly Enemies* (Dwan); *The Pied Piper* (Pichel); *Girl Trouble* (Schuster); *Life Begins at 8:30* (*The Light of Heart*) (Pichel)
1943 *Margin for Error* (Preminger); *Heaven Can Wait* (Lubitsch); *The Gang's All Here* (*The Girls He Left Behind*) (Berkeley)
1944 *Home in Indiana* (Hathaway)
1945 *Nob Hill* (Hathaway); *Colonel Effingham's Raid* (*Man of the Hour*) (Pichel)
1946 *Do You Love Me?* (Ratoff); *Canyon Passage* (J. Tourneur)
1947 *Honeymoon* (*Two Men and a Girl*) (Keighley); *Desert Fury* (Allen) (co); *A Miracle Can Happen* (*On Our Merry Way*) (K. Vidor and Fenton) (co)
1948 *Relentless* (G. Sherman); *Don't Trust Your Husband* (*An Innocent Affair*) (Bacon); *The Countess of Monte Cristo* (de Cordova)
1950 *The Capture* (J. Sturges); *House by the River* (F. Lang)
1951 *I'd Climb the Highest Mountain* (H. King); *Best of the Badmen* (Russell); *Two Tickets to Broadway* (Kern) (co)
1952 *Lure of the Wilderness* (Negulesco); *Bloodhounds of Broadway* (Jones)
1953 *Treasure of the Golden Condor* (Davies); *Powder River* (L. King); *Beneath the 12 Mile Reef* (Webb)
1954 *The Siege at Red River* (Maté)
1958 *Devil's Partner* (Rondeau)
1959 *The Girl in Lover's Lane* (Rondeau)
1960 *The Threat* (Rondeau)

*   *   *

The Cronjager family is perhaps the most prolific dynasty of cameramen who have ever worked in motion pictures. Their collective work, which extends back to the one-reelers of the earliest part of the twentieth century continues through to the present day with feature films and television.

The earliest members of the Cronjager family to work in pictures were Henry and Jules, who shot scores of films between the turn of the century and the mid-1920s. Henry, the more famous of the brothers, was the head cameraman for Klaw & Ehrlanger in the early teens after working at Edison and then Biograph, where he worked on some of the D. W. Griffith films. The best remembered film on which he worked was undoubtedly Henry King's *Tol'able David*, made in 1921. In the late 1920s two other Cronjager brothers, Henry and Edward, began to make films while they were still in their early twenties. Because they shared the same first name, the younger Henry's filmography is often intertwined with the elder Henry's, especially during the 1920s when both were active.

Edward Cronjager has attained perhaps the greatest fame because of his extensive work during the 1930s and 1940s on a wide variety of major studio productions, mostly at Twentieth Century-Fox. *Cimarron*, the Edna Ferber Oscar-winning saga directed by Wesley Ruggles, was a triumph for Edward, who was nominated for an Oscar for his fine work (the first of five such nominations over the course of the next 20 years), and received ecstatic notices. The Oklahoma land rush sequence, one of the most famous from any western, compares favorably with the same sequence in the 1961 version which benefited from color and advanced technology, but did not surpass the original in design or scope.

Perhaps Cronjager's most famous work was that which he did on several of Sonja Henie's pictures at Fox, including her best-known film, *Sun Valley Serenade*. He was noted for his spectacular work with the black ice sequences which were characteristic of her films, and Henie insisted on several occasions that Cronjager be taken off other projects to work on her pictures.

In 1943 Cronjager made *Heaven Can Wait*, directed by Ernst Lubitsch at Fox and the vivid color brought him his third Oscar nomination. D. W. Griffith reportedly was so impressed with the photography on the film that he called it the best color footage ever made. Vivid color continued to be important in Cronjager's later work. In *Canyon Passage*, directed by Jacques Tourneur, the "Ole Buttermilk Sky" described in Hoagy Carmichael's title song came to life spectacularly under Cronjager's photographic direction. The last film of significance which Cronjager shot was *Beneath the 12 Mile Reef*, with innovative underwater photography that far surpassed the mundane plot.

Although he continued to work sporadically for several years, including some uncredited work on *Desiree* in 1954, ill health greatly curtailed his career until his death.

—Patricia King Hanson

CROSBY, Floyd

Cinematographer. **Nationality:** American. **Born:** Floyd Delafield Crosby in New York City, 12 December 1899. **Family:** Son: the rock musician David Crosby. **Career:** Worked in cotton industry and on Wall Street in stock exchange; 1927—photographer for William Beebe in Haiti, and worked on documentary films in 1930s; after World War II—freelance cinematographer on entertainment films; TV work includes episodes for *Reader's Digest*, *Court of Last Appeal*, *Author's Playhouse*, and other series. **Award:** Academy Award for *Tabu*, 1931. **Died:** In Ojai, California, 30 September 1985.

Films as Cinematographer:

1931   *Tabu* (Murnau and Flaherty)
1932   *Matto Grosso* (+ co-d) (co)
1937   **The River** (Lorentz) (co)
1940   *The Fight for Life* (Lorentz); *The Power and the Land* (Ivens—short) (co)
1941   **The Land** (Flaherty—short) (co)
1942   *Power for Defense* (Gerke and Bolte—short) (co); *Name, Age, Occupation* (Lorentz—short; produced 1939)
1947   *Rural Co-op* (Lorentz—short); *My Father's House* (Kilne)
1950   *Of Men and Music* (Reis) (co)
1951   *The Brave Bulls* (Rossen) (co)
1952   **High Noon** (Zinnemann)
1953   *Man in the Dark* (Landers); *Mystery Lake* (Lansburgh); *Stormy, the Thoroughbred with an Inferiority Complex* (Landsburgh—short) (co); *The Steel Lady* (*The Treasure of Kalifa*) (Dupont); *Man Crazy* (Lerner)
1954   *Monster from the Ocean Floor* (Ordung); *Five Guns West* (Corman); *The Fast and the Furious* (Ireland and Sampson); *The Snow Creature* (W. Wilder)
1955   *The Naked Street* (Shane); *Apache Woman* (Corman); *Shack Out on 101* (Dein); *Hell's Horizon* (Gries)
1957   *She-Gods of Shark Reef* (*Shark Reef*) (Corman); *Naked Paradise* (Corman); *Rock All Night* (Corman); *Attack of the Crab Monsters* (Corman); *Carnival Rock* (Corman); *Ride Out for Revenge* (Girard); *Hell Canyon Outlaws* (*The Tall Trouble*) (Landers); *Reform School Girl* (Bernds)
1958   *Suicide Battalion* (Cahn); *War of the Satellites* (Corman); *The Cry Baby Killer* (Addiss); *Hot Rod Gang* (*Fury Unleashed*) (Landers); *Machine Gun Kelly* (Corman); *Teenage Caveman* (*Out of the Darkness*) (Corman); *Wolf Larsen* (Jones); *The Old Man and the Sea* (Sturges) (co); *The Screaming Skull* (Nicol); *I, Mobster* (*The Mobster*) (Corman)
1959   *Crime and Punishment, U.S.A.* (Sanders); *The Wonderful Country* (Parrish) (co); *Blood and Steel* (Kowalski); *The Rookie* (O'Hanlon); *Terror at Black Falls* (*Ordeal at Dry Red*) (Sarafian)
1960   *Twelve Hours to Kill* (Cahn); *The Fall of the House of Usher* (*House of Usher*) (Corman); *High-Powered Rifle* (Dexter); *Freckles* (McLaglen); *Walk Tall* (Dexter); *Operation Bottleneck* (Cahn); *The Little Shepherd of Kingdom Come* (McLaglen); *The Gambler Wore a Gun* (Cahn)
1961   *A Cold Wind in August* (Singer); *The Pit and the Pendulum* (Corman); *The Purple Hills* (Dexter); *The Explosive Generation* (Kulik); *Seven Women from Hell* (Webb); *The Two Little Bears* (Hood); *The Broken Land* (Bushelman); *Hand of Death* (Nelson); *Woman Hunt* (Dexter)
1962   *The Premature Burial* (Corman); *Tales of Terror* (Corman); *The Firebrand* (Dexter)
1963   *The Raven* (Corman); *The Yellow Canary* (Kulik); *Black Zoo* (Gordon); *The Young Racers* (Corman); *The Haunted Palace* (Corman); *X* (*The Man with the X-Ray Eyes*) (Corman); *The Comedy of Terrors* (Tourneur)
1964   *Bikini Beach* (Asher); *Pajama Party* (Weis); *Indian Paint* (Foster)
1965   *Beach Blanket Bingo* (Asher); *Sergeant Deadhead* (Taurog); *Sallah* (Kishon); *How to Stuff a Wild Bikini* (*How to Fill a Wild Bikini*) (Asher)
1966   *Fireball 500* (Asher)

1967 *The Cool Ones* (Nelson)
1972 *Sweet Kill* (*The Arousers*) (Hanson) (co)

Other Films:

1938 *Doctor Rhythm* (Tuttle) (cam)
1955 *Oklahoma* (Zinnemann) (2nd unit ph)

Publications

On CROSBY: articles—

Lightman, Herb A., "A Study in Horror Film Photography," *American Cinematographer* (Hollywood), October 1961.
Film Comment (New York), Summer 1972.
Focus on Film (London), no. 13, 1973.
Obituary in *Variety* (New York), 9 October 1985.
Obituary in *American Cinematographer* (Hollywood), December 1985.

*   *   *

Although Floyd Crosby's work as a cinematographer stretches back to *Tabu* (1931) and *The River* (1937), he achieved his greatest measure of commercial and artistic success in the late 1950s and early 1960s as director of photography for the American director Roger Corman, working on a series of low-budget horror and science fiction films. Crosby was born in 1899 in New York City, and after a brief period on Wall Street, he began working as a still photographer, before turning to cinematography around 1930. Crosby rapidly made a name for himself as a cameraman, working with such pioneer documentarists as Robert Flaherty, Joris Ivens, and Pare Lorentz. In 1931, Crosby won the Academy Award for his work on *Tabu*, directed by Flaherty and F.W. Murnau. But following this early period of celebrity and success, Crosby shied away from the Hollywood mainstream. Except for a few assignments, such as *Fight for Life* in 1940 and *My Father's House* in 1947, he remained a fringe figure in the film community, known for his uncompromising standards and his lack of interest in studio politics.

In 1951, however, he went back to work on Robert Rossen's *The Brave Bulls* and shot Fred Zinnemann's classic antiwestern *High Noon* the following year. These films showed that Crosby had lost none of his skill as a cinematographer. He was much in demand as a result of his speed and craftsmanship on both projects, but still refused to become tied to any particular producer or director. That is, until he met Corman. The two first worked together on *Five Guns West* in 1954 and immediately hit it off. "He needed a lot less coaching than a lot of other young directors," Crosby remembered later. "He knew what he wanted, he worked fast, and it was fun. Suddenly we were a team." In an interview I conducted with Corman on 21 April 1986, he remembered working with Crosby with equal fondness. "He was a rarity," Corman reminisced. "He worked fast, which is important to me, and yet his stuff was always good. No matter how fast I moved, Floyd kept right up, and he could light a setup in 10–15 minutes flat, or even faster if need be, and we'd go. That's unusual—lots of people are fast, but you don't want to see the results. With Floyd, you didn't have that problem. Plus, he knew how to set up these really complicated dolly shots *quickly*. He was the best, and working with him was always a pleasure, professionally and personally."

For Corman, Crosby shot *War of the Satellites*, *Machine Gun Kelly*, *I, Mobster*, *The Fall of the House of Usher*, *The Pit and the Pendulum*, *The Premature Burial*, *Tales of Terror*, and many other films. Most of these films were for American International Pictures, or AIP, Corman's "home company." Eventually Crosby worked on other AIP projects not directed by Corman, including *Bikini Beach*, *Pajama Party*, *How to Stuff a Wild Bikini*, and *Fireball 500*. After his work as a cophotographer of the undistinguished programmer *The Arousers*, Crosby retired from the industry.

But it is his atmospheric, imaginative work for Corman which is Floyd Crosby's most enduring achievement. The unlikely alliance between Crosby, the seasoned veteran (he was 56 when he shot his first film for Corman), and Corman, the brash young neophyte of 1950s cinema, remains one of the most prolific and resonant partnerships in film.

—Wheeler Winston Dixon

D'AGOSTINO, Albert S.

Art Director. **Nationality:** American. **Born:** New York City, 27 December 1893; billed as Al D'Agostino in early years in Hollywood. **Career:** Stage designer for four years; then worked in art departments of several Hollywood companies: for MGM, for four years, Selznick, and Universal; 1939–58—supervising art director, RKO: collaborated on entire output of the company; 1943—directed the film *Zombies on Broadway*. **Died:** 14 March 1970.

Films as Art Director/Production Designer:

1921   *Salvation Nell* (Webb) (co)
1928   *Ramona* (Carewe)
1929   *She Goes to War* (H. King) (co)
1930   *Today* (Nigh)
1933   *Headline Shooter* (Brower) (co); *Midshipman Jack* (Cabanne) (co); *One Man's Journey* (Robertson) (co); *Blood Money* (R. Brown) (co); *I Cover the Waterfront* (Cruze)
1934   *Palooka* (Stoloff); *The Man Who Reclaimed His Head* (Ludwig); *Finishing School* (Tuchock and Nicholls)
1935   *Werewolf of London* (Walker); *The Raven* (Landers); *She Gets Her Man* (Kenton); *The Mystery of Edwin Drood* (Walker); *King Solomon of Broadway* (Crosland); *Manhattan Moon* (Walker); *Three Kids and a Queen* (Ludwig)
1936   *The Invisible Ray* (Hillyer); *Love before Breakfast* (W. Lang); *Dracula's Daughter* (Hillyer)
1937   *A Doctor's Diary* (C. Vidor); *John Meade's Woman* (Wallace); *Her Husband Lies* (Ludwig); *The Great Gambini* (C. Vidor)
1938   *The Gladiator* (Sedgwick)
1940   *The Stranger on the Third Floor* (Ingster)
1941   *Mr. and Mrs. Smith* (Hitchcock)
1942   *Cat People* (Tourneur); ***The Magnificent Ambersons*** (Welles)
1943   *I Walked with a Zombie* (Tourneur); *This Land Is Mine* (Renoir); *The Leopard Man* (Tourneur); *The Ghost Ship* (Robson); *The Seventh Victim* (Robson); *Zombies on Broadway* (+ d)
1944   *Tender Comrade* (Dmytryk); *Murder My Sweet* (Dmytryk); *The Curse of the Cat People* (Fritsch and Wise); *Mademoiselle Fifi* (Wise); *None but the Lonely Heart* (Odets)
1945   *The Body Snatcher* (Wise); *The Spiral Staircase* (Siodmak); *The Enchanted Forest* (Landers); *The Bells of St. Mary's* (McCarey); *Cornered* (Dmytryk); *Isle of the Dead* (Robson); *The Brighton Strangler* (Nosseck)
1946   *Till the End of Time* (Dmytryk); *Bedlam* (Robson); *From This Day Forward* (Berry); ***Notorious*** (Hitchcock); *The Locket* (Brahm); *The Falcon's Adventure* (Berke) (co); *The Stranger* (Welles); *Back to Bataan* (Dmytryk); *Lady Luck* (Marin); *Badman's Territory* (Whelan)
1947   *Dick Tracy Meets Gruesome* (Rawlins); ***Crossfire*** (Dmytryk); *The Woman on the Beach* (Renoir); *The Long Night* (Litvak); *Mourning Becomes Electra* (Nichols); *Night Song* (Cromwell); *Tycoon* (Wallace); *Rachel and the Stranger* (Foster); ***Out of the Past*** (***Build My Gallows High***) (Tourneur)
1948   *Berlin Express* (Tourneur); *Blood on the Moon* (Wise); *The Boy with Green Hair* (Losey); *I Remember Mama* (Stevens); ***They Live by Night*** (***The Twisted Road***) (Ray)
1949   *The Set-Up* (Wise); *Adventure in Baltimore* (Wallace); *The Window* (Tetzlaff)
1951   *The Thing* (Nyby)
1952   *Beware My Lovely* (Horner); *The Lusty Men* (Ray); *Clash by Night* (F. Lang); *Macão* (von Sternberg); *The Big Sky* (Hawks); *Angel Face* (Preminger)
1953   *Androcles and the Lion* (Erskine); *The Hitch-Hiker* (Lupino); *Devil's Canyon* (Werker); *Second Chance* (Maté)
1954   *The French Line* (Bacon); *Susan Slept Here* (Tashlin)
1955   *Underwater* (J. Sturges)
1956   *Back from Eternity* (Farrow); *The Conqueror* (Powell); *Great Day in the Morning* (Tourneur); *I Married a Woman* (Kanter)
1957   *Jet Pilot* (von Sternberg—produced 1950); *The Unholy Wife* (Farrow); *Run of the Arrow* (Farrow)

Publications

On D'AGOSTINO: article—

Dorst, Gary, in *Cinefantastique* (New York), Summer 1971.

*   *   *

Albert S. D'Agostino's career as supervising art director at RKO in the 1940s has always been overshadowed by the more conspicuous career of Van Nest Polglase whose regime in the same position at the studio extended over the flamboyant 1930s. Polglase's designs were large and opulent, D'Agostino's smaller and more conservative, though no less impressive in their ability to stretch a budget while using the sets to underpin character psychology.

Though he created sets for dramas of some of the industry's top directors, D'Agostino's work is most closely associated with the horror and mystery genres, particularly with the low-budget efforts of producer Val Lewton. Much of his early work for Universal on films such as *The Raven*, *Dracula's Daughter*, and *Werewolf of London* continued that studio's gothic tradition of dank dungeons and fantastic laboratories. The move from Universal to RKO was a move from the shuffling monster school of horror to a brand of narrative grounded in psychological causality. Consciously creepy sets gave way to spaces that were often more normal at first glance but were in fact braced by considerable psychic influence. A dream sequence in *The Stranger on the Third Floor*, a D'Agostino collaboration with Polglase, found direct projection of a character's psychological state in a series of minimal, expressionistic sets. The protagonist's sense of guilt is conveyed in sets that grow increasingly abstract to the point where a jail cell is suggested by merely a bed and the shadows of bars. Not all of D'Agostino's work is as overt in its linkage of characters' subconscious states with physical surroundings due to simple narrative strictures, hence often a single, realistic setting would serve as a psychological metaphor for an entire film.

D'Agostino was able deftly to balance a sense of reality with metaphoric undercurrents reflecting the interior state of characters. Most of the films designed by D'Agostino and Walter Keller for the Lewton thrillers feature at least one set that serves the metaphoric function. *I Walked with a Zombie* and *The Leopard Man* both contain fountains which act as central staging points for action and as the psychic centers of the films. In the former film, a fountain in the form of St. Sebastian materializes the characters' personal sense of martyrdom and pain. Like the seemingly random narrative of *The Leopard Man*, and the fate which afflicts its characters, the ball suspended by the waters of a fountain at the center of that film appears to be controlled by larger, intangible forces. *Isle of the Dead* recreates the Arnold Bocklin painting that inspired the movie and centers much of the film's polemic about faith and death on a parapet on which a votive fire burns. The key set for *The Seventh Victim* is a room, decorated with only a chair and a noose, which becomes a manifestation of the heroine's philosophy of life and death. Also crucial to the film, as with many designed by D'Agostino, is the staircase, often functioning as a path to sexual invitation or initiation. The double staircase in *The Seventh Victim* is a conspicuous symbol of the choices in life available to the characters in the film.

While D'Agostino's sets were often motivated by psychology, designs were also prompted by budgetary concerns. The massive, ornate staircase from *The Magnificent Ambersons* was reused numerous times in slightly altered forms, and the 18th-century English insane asylum in *Bedlam* was a frugal refitting of sets left from *The Bells of St. Mary's*. James Agee and others lauded the Lewton unit for its ability to create convincing period sets on almost nonexistent budgets, with 19th-century Edinburgh (*The Body Snatcher*) and the small French village caught up in the Franco-Prussian War (*Mademoiselle Fifi*) often singled out as examples of D'Agostino and Keller's most evocative work.

Much of the Polglase influence continued in D'Agostino's work, notably in the expressionist motives favored by Polglase for thrillers. These characteristics became exploited fully in the studio's extensive production of the *film noir* in the post-war years. D'Agostino continued and refined some of the Polglase tenets while leaving his own unique mark on the studio. By linking characters to their surroundings on a psychological level rather than simply placing them in handsomely designed spaces, Albert D'Agostino added a degree of depth to art direction that had been largely lacking since the Expressionist period in Germany.

—Eric Schaefer

DANIELS, William H.

Cinematographer. **Nationality:** American. **Born:** Cleveland, Ohio, 1 December 1895 (or 1900); brother of the director Jack Daniels. Attended the University of Southern California, Los Angeles. **Family:** Married Betty Lee Gaston, 1943; two daughters and one son. **Career:** 1917—assistant cameraman for Triangle/KB; 1918–24—worked for Universal, then for MGM, 1924–43, Universal, 1945–58, and MGM, 1958–70; 1961–63—president, American Society of Cinematographers. **Awards:** Academy Award for *The Naked City*, 1948. **Died:** 14 June 1970.

Films as Assistant/2nd Cameraman:

1917   *Robinson Crusoe* (short)
1919   *Blind Husbands* (von Stroheim)
1920   *The Devil's Passkey* (von Stroheim)
1922   *The Long Chance* (Conway)

Films as Cinematographer:

1922   *Foolish Wives* (von Stroheim) (co)
1923   *Merry-Go-Round* (von Stroheim and Julian) (co)
1924   *Helen's Babies* (Seiter) (co)
1925   *Women and Gold* (Hogan); *Greed* (von Stroheim) (co); *The Merry Widow* (von Stroheim) (co); *MGM Studio Tour* (short)

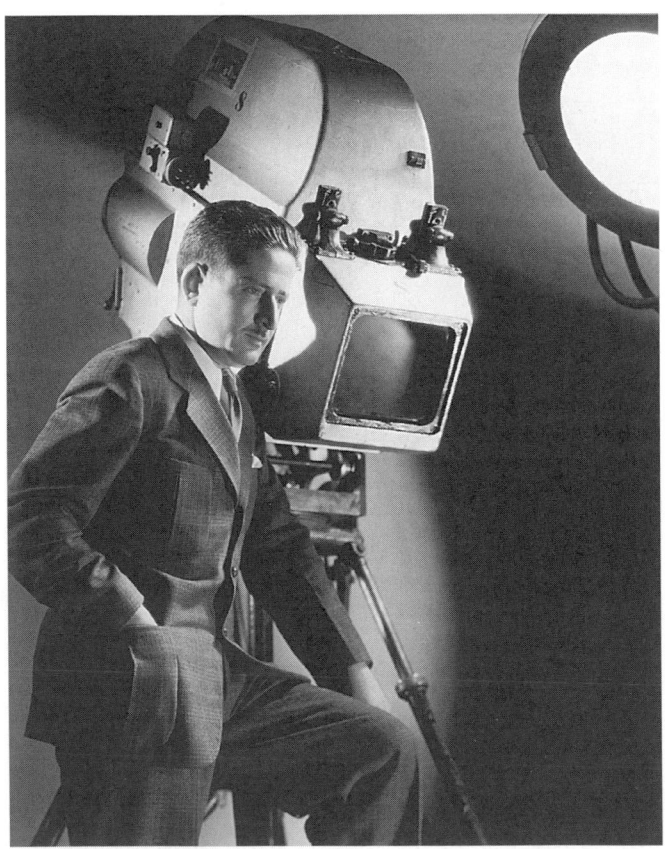

William H. Daniels

1926   *Dance Madness* (Leonard) (co); *The Torrent* (Bell); *The Boob (The Yokel)* (Wellman); *Monte Carlo (Dreams of Monte Carlo)* (Cabanne); *Money Talks* (Mayo); *Bardelys the Magnificent* (K. Vidor); *The Temptress* (Niblo) (co); *Altars of Desire* (Cabanne); *Flesh and the Devil* (Brown)

1927   *Captain Salvation* (Robertson); *Tillie, the Toiler* (Henley); *Love (Anna Karenina)* (Goulding); *On ze Boulevard* (Millarde) (co)

1928   *The Latest from Paris* (Wood); *Bringing Up Father* (Conway); *Telling the World* (Wood); *The Actress (Trelawny of the Wells)* (Franklin); *The Mysterious Lady* (Niblo); *A Woman of Affairs* (Brown); *Dream of Love* (Niblo) (co); *A Lady of Chance* (Leonard) (co)

1929   *Wild Orchids* (Franklin); *The Trial of Mary Dugan* (Veiller); *The Last of Mrs. Cheyney* (Franklin); *Wise Girls (Kempy)* (Hopper); *The Kiss* (Feyder); *Their Own Desire* (Hopper)

1930   *Anna Christie* (Brown); *Montana* (St. Clair); *Strictly Unconventional* (Burton) (co); *Le Spectre vert* (Feyder—French version of L. Barrymore's *The Unholy Night*); *Romance* (Brown); *Si l'empereur savait ça!* (Feyder—French version of L. Barrymore's *His Glorious Night*); *Olympia* (Feyder—German version of *His Glorious Night*); *A Free Soul* (Brown); *Strangers May Kiss* (Fitzmaurice); *Susan Lenox: Her Fall and Rise (The Rise of Helga)* (Leonard)

1932   *Mata Hari* (Fitzmaurice); *Lovers Courageous* (Leonard); *Grand Hotel* (Goulding); *As You Desire Me* (Fitzmaurice); *Skyscraper Souls* (Selwyn)

1933   *Rasputin and the Empress (Rasputin, the Mad Monk)* (Boleslawsky); *The White Sister* (Fleming); *The Stranger's Return* (K. Vidor); *Broadway to Hollywood (Ring Up the Curtain)* (Mack) (co); *Dinner at Eight* (Cukor); *Christopher Bean* (Wood)

1934   *Queen Christina* (Mamoulian); *The Barretts of Wimpole Street* (Franklin); *The Painted Veil* (Boleslawsky)

1935   *Naughty Marietta* (Van Dyke); *Anna Karenina* (Brown); *Rendezvous* (Howard)

1936   *Rose-Marie* (Van Dyke); *Romeo and Juliet* (Cukor); **Camille** (Cukor) (co)

1937   *Personal Property* (Van Dyke); *Broadway Melody of 1938* (Del Ruth); *Double Wedding* (Thorpe); *The Last Gangster* (Ludwig); *Beg, Borrow, or Steal* (Thiele)

1938   *Marie Antoinette* (Van Dyke); *Three Loves Has Nancy* (Thorpe); *Dramatic School* (Sinclair)

1939   *Idiot's Delight* (Brown); *Stronger than Desire* (Fenton); **Ninotchka** (Lubitsch); *Another Thin Man* (Van Dyke)

1940   *The Shop around the Corner* (Lubitsch); *The Mortal Storm* (Borzage); *New Moon* (Leonard)

1941   *So Ends Our Night* (Cromwell); *Back Street* (Stevenson); *They Met in Bombay* (Brown); *Shadow of the Thin Man* (Van Dyke); *Design for Scandal* (Taurog) (co); *Dr. Kildare's Victory (The Doctor and the Debutante)* (Van Dyke)

1942   *For Me and My Gal* (Berkeley) (co); *Keeper of the Flame* (Cukor)

1943   *Girl Crazy* (Taurog) (co)

1947   *Brute Force* (Dassin); *Lured (Personal Column)* (Sirk)

1948   **The Naked City** (Dassin); *For the Love of Mary* (de Cordova); *Family Honeymoon* (Binyon)

1949   *The Life of Riley* (Brecher); *Illegal Entry* (de Cordova); *Abandoned* (Newman); *The Gal Who Took the West* (de Cordova)

1950   *Woman in Hiding* (Gordon); *Winchester '73* (A. Mann); *Harvey* (Koster); *Deported* (Siodmak)

1951   *Thunder on the Hill* (Bonaventure) (Sirk); *The Lady Pays Off* (Sirk); *Bright Victory (Lights Out)* (Robson)

1952   *When in Rome* (Brown); *Pat and Mike* (Cukor); *Glory Alley* (Walsh); *Plymouth Adventure* (Brown); *Never Wave at a WAC (The Private Wore Skirts)* (McLeod)

1953   *Forbidden* (Maté); *Thunder Bay* (A. Mann); *The Glenn Miller Story* (A. Mann); *War Arrow* (G. Sherman)

1954   *The Far Country* (A. Mann); *Strategic Command* (A. Mann)

1955   *Six Bridges to Cross* (Pevney); *Foxfire* (Pevney); *The Shrike* (J. Ferrer); *The Girl Rush* (Pirosh); *The Benny Goodman Story* (Davies)

1956   *Away All Boats* (Pevney); *The Unguarded Moment* (Keller); *Istanbul* (Pevney)

1957   *Night Passage* (A. Mann and Neilson); *Interlude* (Sirk); *My Man Godfrey* (Koster)

1958   *Voice in the Mirror* (Keller); *Cat on a Hot Tin Roof* (Brooks); *Some Came Running* (Minnelli); *A Stranger in My Arms* (Kautner)

1959   *A Hole in the Head* (Capra); *Never So Few* (J. Sturges)

1960   *Can-Can* (W. Lang); *All the Fine Young Cannibals* (Anderson); *Ocean's Eleven* (Milestone)

1961   *Come September* (Mulligan)

1962   *Jumbo (Billy Rose's Jumbo)* (Walters); *How the West Was Won* (Hathaway)

1963   *Come Blow Your Horn* (Yorkin); *The Prize* (Robson)

1964   *Robin and the Seven Hoods* (Douglas) (+ assoc pr)

1965   *Von Ryan's Express* (Robson); *Marriage on the Rocks* (Donohue) (+ pr)

1966   *Assault on a Queen* (Donohue) (+ assoc pr)

1967   *In Like Flint* (Douglas); *Valley of the Dolls* (Robson)

1968   *The Impossible Years* (Gordon)

1969   *Marlowe* (Bogart); *The Maltese Bippy* (Panama)

1970   *Move* (Rosenberg)

Film as Associate Producer:

1965   *None But the Brave* (Sinatra)

Publications

By DANIELS: articles—

"Photography at 40,000 Feet," in *American Cinematographer* (Hollywood), September 1955.

"Cinerama Goes Dramatic," in *American Cinematographer* (Hollywood), January 1962.

Sight and Sound (London), Autumn 1967.

In *Sources of Light*, edited by Charles Higham, London, 1970.

Image (Rochester, New York), no. 1, 1979.

On DANIELS: articles—

Foster, Frederick, on *Six Bridges to Cross* in *American Cinematographer* (Hollywood), February 1955.

Rowan, Arthur, on *Night Passage* in *American Cinematographer* (Hollywood), March 1957.

Film Comment (New York), Summer 1972.
Focus on Film (London), no. 13, 1973.
Apecinema (Brussels), no. 4, 1974–75.
Bedford, Pat, in *American Cinematographer* (Hollywood), March 1983.

*   *   *

William H. Daniels gained considerable stature as a creative artist, even though he began his career by working well within the tradition of the Hollywood silents. In 1918, Daniels began working as cinematographer at Universal Studio, making serials and one-reel comedies. During the early 1920s he worked with Erich von Stroheim, whose obsession with detail is a Hollywood legend and who may very well have instilled in Daniels (although on a healthier scale) the eye for detail that was to become his own hallmark. The demands that von Stroheim made upon Daniels's lighting and photographic skills were tremendous, given the time: outdoor shots in Death Valley, shots taken deep in a gold mine (according to Daniels, in 132-degree heat) or a junk-man's cabin. Many of the shots over which Daniels took such great pains were cut out of the final version of *Greed*, but the discipline of shooting them left its mark on Daniels, who was about to face his greatest challenge—filming Greta Garbo.

Daniels achieved a major triumph in photographing Garbo in *Flesh and the Devil*. This cinematographer elegantly tailored his style, which called for the heavy use of gauzes and filters, to capture the sophisticated beauty of Garbo. He often lit Garbo with sidelights in half-tone, creating a *chiaroscuro* effect in which one half of the actress's face is lit, the other in shadows. However, unlike the way Lee Garmes consistently lit Dietrich, Daniels varied his lighting—often showing great imagination by improvising effects that can only be called romantic, in the broadest sense. These effects often lend the subtlest detail, and Daniels felt that the invention of details was his contribution to the director's vision.

It is no surprise that of the sound films made by Garbo, the most significant were photographed by William Daniels. In *Anna Christie* Daniels and Garbo achieved moments of real poetry—in spite of some stiffness caused by the relative newness of sound. In the adventurous film adaptation of Luigi Pirandello's *As You Desire Me*, Daniels was again working with von Stroheim—as well as Garbo. Considering the difficulty of the original play, the finished result is fascinating. *Queen Christina* is a masterpiece. This film includes one rare moment of pure cinema: the famous scene showing Garbo moving around the room in the inn where she first knew love. Daniels freely admitted that the realistic elements were added under the influence of von Stroheim—the sources of light placed so as to seem as if the fire were the only source of light. The cinematographer, however, failed to acknowledge that the lighting and filming have an expressive side, which transcends the actual. In this scene, Daniels achieves the goal of conveying the drama through light as the director does through speech and action. In *Anna Karenina* we feel the lighting's aptness both for the reality and the psyche of the film—whether it is a tryst of lovers in a sun-dappled, leafy arbor or a flashing light of a passing train on Garbo's face. Even the virtuoso tracking shot over the officers' banquet table has the dramatic purpose of creating the elegant brutality of Tzarist Russia—a world of contradictions that eventually crush the protagonist. *Ninotchka*, for all its shallowness, is a flawlessly photographed and lit apotheosis of cinematic Art Nouveau. It is these films' magical mixture of Daniels and Garbo, of the actual and the glamorous, that represent the best of what is quintessentially Hollywood. It would be wrong to perceive

Daniels merely as the best glamor director of the most glamorous of studios—MGM. He never lost touch with the deeper dramatic, psychological significance of a shot.

It is difficult after these films with Garbo to see Daniels's career as anything other than a decline. However, he did achieve some successes. He won the Academy Award for *The Naked City*, an acknowledgment of the realistic side of his talent. Nevertheless, a romantic mixture of life and daydreams remained his forte. *Pat and Mike* is a sun-filled world of tennis courts and golf courses. Katharine Hepburn was never photographed in any other film better than she is in this 1952 romantic comedy. In *Valley of the Dolls*, mediocre as it is otherwise, the face of Barbara Parkins, especially in the scenes set in New England, calls forth something vaguely reminiscent of the old Daniels-Garbo magic. Daniels combined romanticism with realism; and, like all great portraitists, his ultimate achievement was only as good as the face and personality he rendered.

—Rodney Farnsworth

DARING, Mason

Composer. **Nationality:** American. **Born:** Philadelphia, Pennsylvania, 21 September 1949. **Career:** Played folk music in New England coffeehouses; worked as video director and editor; began composing for movies on John Sayles' first feature film, *Return of the Secaucus Seven*; composer of music for TV series, including *Something Wilder* (1994).

Films as Composer:

1980   *Return of the Secaucus 7* (Sayles)
1983   *Lianna* (Sayles)
1984   *The Brother from Another Planet* (Sayles)
1985   *Osa* (Egorov); *Key Exchange* (Kellman)
1987   *Matewan* (Sayles) (+ ro as Picker)
1988   *Jenny's Song* (Barzyk—for TV); *Eight Men Out* (Sayles)
1989   *Day One* (Sargent—for TV)
1990   *Murder in Mississippi* (Young—for TV); *Little Vegas* (Lang)
1991   *Dogfight* (Savoca); *City of Hope* (Sayles) (+ ro as Peter); *Wild Hearts Can't Be Broken* (Miner)
1992   *Passion Fish* (Sayles) (+ musician)
1993   *Stolen Babies* (Laneuville—for TV); *Ed and His Dead Mother* (*Bon Appetit, Mama*) (Wacks) (+ musician); *The Ernest Green Story* (Laneuville—for TV)
1994   *Getting Out* (Korty—for TV); *The Last Outlaw* (Murphy—for TV); *On Promised Land* (Tewkesbury—for TV); *The Secret of Roan Inish* (Sayles); *She Lives to Ride* (Stone); *The Old Curiosity Shop* (Connor—mini, for TV)
1995   *Letter to My Killer* (Meyers—for TV)
1996   *Hidden in America* (Bell—for TV); *Odyssey of Life* (Agaton—for TV) (NOVA theme); *The Great War* (miniseries—for TV); **Lone Star** (Sayles); *Einstein Revealed* (Jones—for TV) (NOVA theme)
1997   *Cold Around the Heart* (Ridley); *Men with Guns* (*Hombres armados*) (Sayles) (+ musician); *The Ripper* (Meyer—for TV); *Hitchhiking Vietnam: Letters From the Trail* (Muller); *Prefontaine* (James)

1998   *The Opposite of Sex* (Roos); *Evidence of Blood* (Mondshein—
            for TV); *From the Earth to the Moon* (mini—for TV)
1999   *Limbo* (Sayles); *Music of the Heart* (Craven); *A Walk on the
            Moon* (Goldwyn)
2000   *Private Lies* (Horman—for TV); *Where the Heart Is* (Wil-
            liams); *George Wallace: Settin' the Woods on Fire* (McCabe
            and Stekler)

Publications

By DARING: articles—

Daring, Mason, telephone conversations with Philip Kemp,
    Spring 2000.

On DARING: books—

Sayles, John, *Thinking in Pictures*, Boston, 1987.

On DARING: articles—

Ellis, Andy, and James Rotondi, ''You Oughta Be in Pictures:
    Soundtrack Savvy from Marc Bonilla and Mason Daring,'' in
    Guitar Player, vol. 31, no. 4, April 1997.

                              *   *   *

Anyone who knows the films of John Sayles will have heard a lot
of Mason Daring's music, though perhaps without realising it. Not
because Daring's scores are colourless or undistinguished—quite the
reverse, indeed. But as a composer, he displays the chameleon ability
to feel his way into a remarkably wide range of musical idioms,
adopting their stylistic garb with uncanny fluency. The creator of the
lilting Irish folk score of *The Secret of Roan Inish* also composed the
zydeco dances for *Passion Fish*, the mountain music and Italian
popular song of *Matewan*, the country and western, rhythm and blues,
and Mexican folk music of *Lone Star*. There's never any sense of
pastiche in Daring's scores; rather it is a matter of assimilation
from within.

Daring may be unique among film composers in having entered
the industry as a lawyer, though he studied music at college. ''I was in
a band signed to Columbia,'' he explains, ''and the deal fell through
halfway through making the record. So in a panic I thought, I'll go to
law school. Then no sooner had I enrolled than I really started to play
music and led a dual life for a few years, playing music live and
producing records for people, and studying law and finally being
a lawyer.'' It was through his work as an entertainment lawyer that
Daring met John Sayles. ''I heard this fellow wanted to make his own
movie and was looking for a lawyer. I said, 'Forget it—those people
never really make the movie and I never get paid,' They said, 'His
name is John Sayles.' Now I'd just read his novel *Union Dues*—one
of the best books I'd ever read. I said, 'Forget what I just said—I'll
hold his coat.'''

The film was Sayles' first as director, *Return of the Secaucus 7*.
Soon discovering his attorney's other talents, Sayles invited Daring to
contribute the film's score. ''I'd done music for a number of short
films and commercials, so I said sure. And that was pretty much my
last job in the law. I wasn't really cut out for it, anyway.''

Setting up as a full-time composer, Daring went on to score all
Sayles' subsequent features except *Baby It's You*. His reputation for
versatility soon gained him other commissions, including five from
Disney: two TV films, a Dickens mini-series, *The Old Curiosity Shop*,
with Tom Courtenay and Peter Ustinov, and two features, *Wild
Hearts Can't Be Broken* and *Prefontaine* from Jared Leto and Amy
Locane, makers of the groundbreaking documentary *Hoop Dreams*.
He also scored a western, *The Last Outlaw* with Mickey Rourke, for
Home Box Office (HBO), ''because I wanted to do a film with
a bunch of guys on horseback shooting each other. It was great fun,
but one's enough.''

Much of Daring's work has been for PBS, including themes for the
long-running shows *Nova* and *Frontline*, and a documentary, *George
Wallace: Setting the Woods on Fire*, about the racist 1968 presidential
candidate George Wallace. His longest project to date is the eight-
hour KCET/BBC series *The Great War* (1996). ''It was five months
out of my life. But it was a challenge, and I thought it was great.''

Daring's association with Sayles has now lasted through eleven
movies. ''John starts with the music much earlier. He and I talk about
it even before he shoots. He knows exactly what he wants it to do.''
Daring wholeheartedly endorses Sayles' comment that ''when it
works movie music is like a natural voice, like the only sound the
picture up there could possibly make.'' ''That's exactly it,'' he
agrees, ''the music should arise from the scene. I usually write source
music for him, whereas almost everybody else buys the music in. It's
not just a budgetary thing, he wants it to have a certain effect.''

Daring dismisses the view that film music represents a compromise for the composer. ''It's not compromise,'' he insists, ''it's
opportunity.'' He relishes the challenge of finding exactly the right
instrument for a given film. For *Matewan* he unearthed a dobro,
a modified guitar from the 1920s with an inset metal plate that makes
the notes (as Sayles put it) ''bend into a question at the end.'' Much of
the otherworldly flavour of *Roan Inish* (Daring's own personal
favourite among his scores) comes from the yearning wail of the
Uillean pipes, which he learned to play for the occasion. In *Limbo* the
''voice of the film'' was provided by an e-bow, an electromagnetic
device held over an electric guitar to give ''an eerie sound, like whale
sounds or gulls' cries.''

Limbo, set in Alaska, was less folk-based than Daring's previous
scores for Sayles. By contrast, *Hombres armados* (*Men with Guns*),
Sayles's first foreign-language movie, made intense use of folk
idioms. The film is set in a fictional Latin American country ''like
Guatemala but it's not. So my score's intended to be pan-Hispanic
music, from all around Central and South America. And almost every
instrument is wooden, except for a little trumpet and French horn:
Spanish guitar, marimba, wooden percussion. I didn't set out to do
that; it just happened that way.''

Recently Daring has moved into scoring big-budget mainstream
films, starting with Wes Craven's *Music of the Heart* and Matt
Williams' directorial debut *Where the Heart Is*. He describes both
projects as ''a pleasure from start to finish,'' but plans to continue
working on smaller independent films as well. At his studio in
Marblehead, Massachusetts, near Boston, he produces his own music
and acts as producer for a number of other artists, which involves
being ''a cross between the Wizard of Oz and a den mother.'' He sees
himself as being exceptionally lucky to have become someone ''who
actually gets paid to write music. It's a wonderful job, but somebody
has to do it.''

—Philip Kemp

DAWSON, Beatrice

Costume Designer. **Nationality:** British. **Born:** 1908. **Career:** Begin as costume designer in the theatre, 1945. **Died:** 16 April 1976.

Films as Costume Designer:

1948   *Night Beat*; *London Belongs to Me* (*Dulcimer Street*)
1949   *Dear Mr. Prohack*; *Trottie True* (*The Gay Lady*)
1950   *State Secret* (*The Great Manhunt*)
1951   *The Reluctant Widow*; *Pandora and the Flying Dutchman*
1952   *Penny Princess*; *The Importance of Being Earnest*; *The Pickwick Papers*
1954   *Macbeth* (for TV); *Grand National Night* (*Wicked Wife*)
1955   *Footsteps in the Fog*; *Svengali*; *Dance Little Lady*
1957   *The Prince and the Showgirl*
1958   *A Tale of Two Cities*
1960   *Faces in the Dark*; *Expresso Bongo*; *Macbeth* (for TV)
1961   *The Full Treatment* (*Stop Me Before I Kill!*) (*Treatment*); *The Day the Earth Caught Fire* (*The Day the Sky Caught Fire*)
1962   *The Adventures of Sir Francis Drake* (for TV); *Waltz of the Toreadors* (*The Amorous General*)
1963   *The Servant*; *The L-Shaped Room*
1964   *The Beauty Jungle* (*Contest Girl*); *Woman of Straw*
1965   *The Intelligence Men* (*Spylarks*); *Life at the Top*; *Masquerade* (*Operation Masquerade*) (*A Shabby Tiger*); *Where the Spies Are*
1966   *Promise Her Anything*; *Modesty Blaise*
1967   *Accident*
1968   *Mrs. Brown, You've Got a Lovely Daughter*; *Guns in the Heather* (*The Secret of Boyne Castle*) (*Spy Busters*); *Only When I Larf*
1969   *The Assassination Bureau*
1970   *The Man Who Haunted Himself*; *The Last Grenade*
1972   *Zee and Co.* (*X, Y and Zee*) (+ wardrobe designer)
1973   *The Merchant of Venice* (for TV); *A Doll's House*
1974   *Brief Encounter* (for TV)
1976   *The Bawdy Adventures of Tom Jones*

Other Films:

1957   *The Abominable Snowman of the Himalayas* (*The Snow Creature*) (dress designer)

*   *   *

Beatrice "Bumble" Dawson, the prolific and versatile British costume designer, began her career in the theatre with a production of *The Duchess of Malfi* at the Haymarket Theatre in 1945. She started her film work with the 1948 postwar drama *Night Beat* for British Lion Film Corporation. Dawson continued working for both film and the stage throughout her career. With *Trottie True* (1949), the lavish costume musical about a Gaiety Girl who graduates from the stage to marriage with a peer, Dawson herself found the success that elevated her to the top rank of Britain's designers. Actress Jean Kent, a lovely redhead, was the first of the screen beauties to be showcased by

Dawson's elegant costumes—the film itself is chiefly noted for its brilliant use of Technicolor.

Dawson's next major assignment was *Pandora and the Flying Dutchman*, remarkable for its exquisite star, Ava Gardner, and it marked Dawson's first collaboration with cinematographer Jack Cardiff. While a critical failure, *Pandora* gave Dawson true international exposure. Selected for Anthony Asquith's definitive version of Wilde's *The Importance of Being Earnest*, Dawson's designs artfully used applied floral motifs made popular by British designer Norman Hartnell. Other prestige projects followed, with Dawson gaining a reputation for period costume at a time when Britain (particularly through the agency of J. Arthur Rank) used handsome, expensive prestige productions to penetrate the American market and boost Britain's sagging film industry. Her work in the film adaptation of Dickens' *The Pickwick Papers* garnered an Academy Award nomination for black and white costume design, and she would similarly produce memorable designs for the classic *Tale of Two Cities* in 1958. Reunited with cinematographer Jack Cardiff for *The Prince and the Showgirl*, her resourcefulness helped on an admittedly difficult shoot. One costume, a slinky beaded white gown, had to be replaced several times because Marilyn Monroe spilled food on the front repeatedly. Dawson remade the dress in two parts, with a front that could be quickly replaced if it was soiled.

Another significant and successful working relationship was with writer/director Val Guest, who directed *Dance Little Lady* (a ballet drama cashing in on the *Red Shoes* craze) and *Expresso Bongo*, meant to sell the career of rocker Cliff Richard (in the latter, some costumes were provided by Balmain). Dawson showed a flair for modern dress which served her well in the British film industry of the 1950s and 1960s, which began to turn from literary adaptations to working class dramas (*Life at the Top*, *The L-Shaped Room*) and later to sleek, pop-influenced confections like *Masquerade* and *Modesty Blaise*. Dawson worked nonstop throughout these years, in one high profile film after another, for eminent directors such as Joseph Losey (*The Servant*, *Accident*), as she and the British film industry were the beneficiaries of American investment in British films in the 1960s. *Waltz of the Toreadors* (starring Peter Sellers), an international success, showed her to be as skillful designing for color as she had been for black-and-white, and made her work better known to a wider audience. British fashion had finally come into its own, and 1968 found her back at work creating turn-of-the-century attire for the stylish hit *The Assassination Bureau*, where she dressed the willowy Diana Rigg, who looked as comfortable in Dawson's creations as she did in a leather catsuit on television's *The Avengers*. Despite their excellent work, British designers were occasionally snubbed by foreign stars: sometimes a star would require her own designer for a production, as was the case in *I Could Go On Singing*, where Judy Garland's wardrobe was by Hollywood design diva Edith Head. For 1964's otherwise unprepossessing *Woman of Straw*, Dawson received professional acclaim for her work with a BAFTA nomination for color costume and also one for black-and-white for *Of Human Bondage*. Star Gina Lollobrigida consented to make the film if she could be dressed by Dior, a common practice by European actresses used to acquiring a designer wardrobe in exchange for making a mediocre film.

Continuing her highly successful interpretation of 19th century period costume, Dawson created the wardrobe for 1973's *A Doll's House* (the version starring Claire Bloom—Jane Fonda and Joseph Losey's version of the Ibsen play was made the same year) and received another BAFTA nomination. Her last film, the unfortunate

The Bawdy Adventures of Tom Jones (1976)—described as ''a nudie musical'' and ''dull'' by critics—at least allowed her to costume British actress Joan Collins in the role of highwaywoman Black Bess. Beatrice Dawson continued her theatre work (dressing stage great Dame Judith Anderson among many others), did films for television (the remake of *Brief Encounter* [1974]), and remained professionally active until her death at 68.

—Mary Hess

DAY, Richard

Art Director. **Nationality:** American. **Born:** Victoria, British Columbia, Canada, 9 May 1896; emigrated to the United States, 1918. **Family:** Married; six children. **Career:** Set decorator for Erich von Stroheim at MGM, Paramount, and United Artists during the 1920s; 1928–38—worked independently with Goldwyn and United Artists, then with 20th Century-Fox, 1939–43, and freelance. **Awards:** Academy Award for *The Dark Angel*, 1935; *Dodsworth*, 1936; *How Green Was My Valley*, 1941; *This above All*, 1942; *My Gal Sal*, 1942; *A Streetcar Named Desire*, 1951; *On the Waterfront*, 1954. **Died:** In Hollywood, 23 May 1972.

Films as Art Director:

1918 *Blind Husbands* (von Stroheim)
1919 *The Devil's Passkey* (von Stroheim)
1922 **Foolish Wives** (von Stroheim)
1923 *Merry-Go-Round* (Julian and von Stroheim)
1925 **Greed** (von Stroheim); *The Merry Widow* (von Stroheim); *Bright Lights* (Leonard); *The Only Thing* (Conway); *His Secretary* (Henley)
1926 *Beverley of Graustark* (Franklin); *Bardelys the Magnificent* (K. Vidor)
1927 *The Show* (Browning); *Mr. Wu* (Nigh); *Tillie the Toiler* (Henley); *The Unknown* (Browning); *Adam and Evil* (Leonard); *After Midnight* (Bell); *The Road to Romance (Romance)* (Robertson); *Tea for Three* (Leonard); *The Student Prince in Old Heidelberg* (Franklin); *The Enemy* (Niblo)
1928 *The Divine Woman* (Sjöström); *Wickedness Preferred* (Henley); *Rose-Marie* (Hubbard); *The Big City* (Browning); *Circus Rookies* (Sedgwick); *Laugh, Clown, Laugh* (Brenon); *The Actress (Trelawny of the Wells)* (Franklin); *Forbidden Hours* (Beaumont); *Our Dancing Daughters* (Beaumont); *Excess Baggage* (Cruze); *While the City Sleeps* (Conway); *The Wedding March* (von Stroheim); *West of Zanzibar* (Browning)
1929 *The Bridge of San Luis Rey* (Brabin); *The Idle Rich* (W. De Mille); *A Man's Man* (Cruze); *Wonder of Women* (Brown); *The Girl in the Show* (Selwyn); *The Unholy Night* (L. Barrymore); *The Hollywood Revue of 1929* (Reisner); *Wise Girls (Kempy)* (Hopper); *The Thirteenth Chair* (Browning); *The Kiss* (Feyder); *Their Own Desire* (Hopper); *Devil*

May Care (Franklin); *Untamed* (Conway); *Gus Edwards' Song Revue* (Edwards—short); *Song Shop* (Lee—short)
1930 *Anna Christie* (Brown) (also German and French versions directed by Feyder); *In Gay Madrid* (Leonard); *Whoopee!* (Freeland); *Sins of the Children (The Richest Man in the World)* (Wood); *Madame Satan* (C. DeMille); *Le Spectre vert* (Feyder—French version of *The Unholy Night*); *The Devil to Pay* (Fitzmaurice)
1931 *The Front Page* (Milestone); *Indiscreet* (McCarey); *Street Scene* (K. Vidor); *The Unholy Garden* (Fitzmaurice); *Palmy Days* (Sutherland); *Arrowsmith* (Ford)
1932 *The Greeks Had a Word for Them* (L. Sherman); *Rain* (Milestone); *Cynara* (K. Vidor); *The Kid from Spain* (McCarey)
1933 *Hallalujah I'm a Bum! (Hallelujah I'm a Tramp)* (Milestone); *Secrets* (Borzage); *The Bowery* (Walsh); *The Masquerader* (Wallace); *Roman Scandals* (Tuttle); *Gallant Lady* (La Cava)
1934 *Moulin Rouge* (Lanfield); *Nana* (Arzner); *The Affairs of Cellini* (La Cava); *Born to Be Bad* (L. Sherman); *The House of Rothschild* (Werker); *The Last Gentleman* (Lanfield); *Bulldog Drummond Strikes Back* (Del Ruth); *Kid Millions* (Del Ruth); *Looking for Trouble* (Wellman); *We Live Again* (Mamoulian); *The Mighty Barnum* (W. Lang)
1935 *Folies Bergere (The Man from the Folies Bergere)* (Del Ruth); *Clive of India* (Boleslawsky); *Cardinal Richelieu* (Lee); *The Call of the Wild* (Wellman); *The Dark Angel* (Franklin); *Barbary Coast* (Hawks); *Metropolitan* (Boleslawsky); *Splendor* (Nugent)
1936 *Strike Me Pink* (Taurog); *These Three* (Wyler); *One Rainy Afternoon* (Lee); *Dodsworth* (Wyler); *The Gay Desperado* (Mamoulian); *Come and Get It* (Hawks and Wyler); *Beloved Enemy* (Potter)
1937 *Woman Chases Man* (Blystone); *Stella Dallas* (K. Vidor); *Dead End* (Wyler); *The Hurricane* (Ford)
1938 *The Goldwyn Follies* (Marshall); *The Cowboy and the Lady* (Potter); *The Adventures of Marco Polo* (Mayo); *Charlie Chan in Honolulu* (Humberstone)
1939 *The Little Princess* (W. Lang); *The Gorilla* (Dwan); *The Hound of the Baskervilles* (Lanfield); *The Return of the Cisco Kid* (Leeds); *Rose of Washington Square* (Ratoff); **Young Mr. Lincoln** (Ford); *Frontier Marshal* (Dwan); *Quick Millions* (St. Clair); *The Adventures of Sherlock Holmes* (Werker); *Charlie Chan at Treasure Island* (Foster); *The Escape* (Cortez); *Hollywood Cavalcade* (Cummings); *Pack Up Your Troubles (We're in the Army Now)* (Humberstone); *Drums along the Mohawk* (Ford); *Day-Time Wife* (Ratoff); *City of Darkness* (Leeds); *Swanee River* (Lanfield); *The Honeymoon's Over* (Forde); *Everything Happens at Night* (Cummings); *City of Chance* (Cortez)
1940 *Little Old New York* (H. King); *The Blue Bird* (W. Lang); *He Married His Wife* (Del Ruth); **The Grapes of Wrath** (Ford); *The Man Who Wouldn't Talk* (Burton); *Charlie Chan in Panama* (Foster); *Star Dust* (W. Lang); *Johnny Apollo* (Hathaway); *Shooting High* (Green); *I Was an Adventuress* (Ratoff); *Lilian Russell* (Cummings); *Girl in 313* (Cortez); *Earthbound* (Pichel); *Four Sons* (Mayo); *Manhattan Heartbeat* (Burton); *Maryland* (H. King); *The Man I Married*

Richard Day with Ingrid Bergman

(Pichel); *Girl from Avenue A* (Brower); *The Return of Frank James* (F. Lang); *Pier 13* (Forde); *Young People* (Dwan); *Charlie Chan at the Wax Museum* (Shores); *Yesterday's Heroes* (Leeds); *The Gay Caballero* (Brower); *Down Argentine Way* (Cummings); *The Great Profile* (W. Lang); *The Mark of Zorro* (Mamoulian); *Street of Memories* (Traube); *Tin Pan Alley* (W. Lang); *Youth Will Be Served* (Brower); *Murder over New York* (Lachman); *Jennie* (Burton); *Chad Hanna* (H. King); *Hudson's Bay* (Pichel); *Michael Shayne, Private Detective* (Forde)

1941   *For Beauty's Sake* (Traube); *Remember the Day* (H. King); *Romance of the Rio Grande* (Leeds); *Western Union* (F. Lang); *Tobacco Road* (Ford); *That Night in Rio* (Cummings); *The Great American Broadcast* (Mayo); *Blood and Sand* (Mamoulian); *The Cowboy and the Blonde* (McCarey); *Man Hunt* (F. Lang); *A Very Young Lady* (Schuster); *Moon over Miami* (W. Lang); *The Bride Wore Crutches* (Traube); *Accent on Love* (McCarey); *Dance Hall* (Pichel); *Dressed to Kill* (Forde); *Charley's Aunt* (*Charley's American Aunt*) (Mayo); *Wild Geese Calling* (Brahm); *Private Nurse* (Burton); *Sun Valley Serenade* (Humberstone); *Belle Starr*

(Cummings); *Charlie Chan in Rio* (Lachman); *We Go Fast* (McGann); *The Last of the Duanes* (Tinling); *Man at Large* (Forde); *A Yank in the R.A.F.* (H. King); *Great Guns* (Banks); *Riders of the Purple Sage* (Tinling); *Weekend in Havana* (W. Lang); *Rise and Shine* (Dwan); *How Green Was My Valley* (Ford); *Swamp Water* (*The Man Who Came Back*) (Renoir)

1942   *The Lone Star Ranger* (Tinling); *Son of Fury* (Cromwell); *Roxie Hart* (Wellman); *Song of the Islands* (W. Lang); *Rings on Her Fingers* (Mamoulian); *My Gal Sal* (Cummings); *The Man Who Wouldn't Die* (Leeds); *It Happened in Flatbush* (McCarey); *Whispering Ghosts* (Werker); *Moontide* (Mayo); *The Magnificent Dope* (W. Lang); *Through Different Eyes* (Loring); *The Postman Didn't Ring* (Schuster); *Ten Gentlemen from West Point* (Hathaway); *This above All* (Litvak); *Footlight Serenade* (Ratoff); *A-Haunting We Will Go* (Werker); *Little Tokyo, U.S.A.* (Brower); *Orchestra Wives* (Mayo); *The Loves of Edgar Allan Poe* (Lachman); *Berlin Correspondent* (Forde); *Careful, Soft Shoulders* (Garrett); *Just Off Broadway* (Leeds); *Iceland* (*Katina*) (Humberstone); *Girl Trouble* (Schuster);

Manila Calling (Leeds); *The Man in the Trunk* (St. Clair); *Tales of Manhattan* (Duvivier); *Springtime in the Rockies* (Cummings); *That Other Woman* (McCarey); *The Ox-Bow Incident (Strange Incident)* (Wellman); *Thunder Birds* (Wellman); *China Girl* (Hathaway); *The Undying Monster (The Hammond Mystery)* (Brahm); *Time to Kill* (Leeds); *The Black Swan* (H. King); *Dr. Renault's Secret* (Lachman); *Quiet, Please, Murder* (Larkin); *Life Begins at 8:30 (The Light at Heart)* (Pichel)

1943   *The Meanest Man in the World* (Lanfield); *Dixie Dugan* (Brower); *Immortal Sergeant* (Stahl); *He Hired the Boss* (Loring); *Chetniks! (Chetniks—the Fighting Guerillas)* (L. King); *Margin for Error* (Preminger); *My Friend Flicka* (Schuster); *Tonight We Raid Calais* (Brahm); *Crash Dive* (Mayo); *Coney Island* (W. Lang)

1946   *The Razor's Edge* (Goulding); *Anna and the King of Siam* (Cromwell)

1947   *Boomerang* (Kazan); *Moss Rose* (Ratoff); *Miracle on 34th Street (The Big Heart)* (Seaton); *The Ghost and Mrs. Muir* (Mankiewicz); *Mother Wore Tights* (W. Lang); *I Wonder Who's Kissing Her Now* (Bacon); *Captain from Castile* (H. King)

1948   *Joan of Arc* (Fleming); *Force of Evil* (Polonsky)

1949   *My Foolish Heart* (Robson)

1950   *Our Very Own* (Miller); *Edge of Doom (Stronger than Fear)* (Robson)

1951   *Cry Danger* (Parrish); *I Want You* (Robson); **A Streetcar Named Desire** (Kazan)

1952   *Hans Christian Andersen* (C. Vidor)

1954   **On the Waterfront** (Kazan)

1959   *Solomon and Sheba* (K. Vidor)

1960   *Exodus* (Preminger)

1961   *Something Wild* (Garfein)

1964   *Goodbye Charlie* (Minnelli); *Cheyenne Autumn* (Ford)

1965   *The Greatest Story Ever Told* (Stevens); *The Chase* (Penn)

1966   *The Happening* (Silverstein)

1967   *The Valley of the Dolls* (Robson)

1968   *The Boston Strangler* (Fleischer); *The Sweet Ride* (Hart)

1970   *Tora! Tora! Tora!* (Fleischer); *Tribes (The Soldier Who Declared Peace)* (Sargeant)

Film as Technical Advisor:

1944   *Up in Arms* (Nugent)

Publications

On DAY: articles—

Fowler, Gene, foreword to *The Mighty Barnum: A Screen Play*, New York, 1934.

In *The Art of Hollywood*, edited by John Hambley, London, 1979.

*   *   *

Richard Day put on the screen some of the seediest sets in Hollywood history. The constructions for *Dead End* so appalled the producer Samuel Goldwyn that the mogul wondered why his money couldn't have been used to build a better slum! Despite his proclivity for suggesting human blight, Day was equally at ease designing for drawing-room dramas and musical extravaganzas. What unities can be found in such versatility?

Day's film career began with his apprenticeship to director Erich von Stroheim, who was possessed by a violent forcefulness akin to the German Expressionists. Attracted to fantasy and symbolism in spirit, he belonged with the German social realists such as George Grosz. Yet von Stroheim's meticulous attention to detail recalled the American realists (such as Thomas Eakins), with their fascination for everyday minutiae. Although Day absorbed these traditions, he equally shared the sensibilities of the American regionalist school. His classically balanced urban scenes recalled Edward Hopper's works, serene even in their turmoil. His humble, rural environments interpreted the countryside with the same poignancy found in paintings by Thomas Hart Benton.

Day's films were lush with details. His expressions of poverty included every crack in the wall, thick coats of dust, peeling paint, and the fading floral wallpaper of an out-of-date print. Stairways creaked, and laundry blocked the sky like a Piranesi prison. On the other hand, for the old-world wealthy, Day gilt grand staircases with elaborate ornamentation. His swags of velvet drapery regally dressed the richly veined marble colonnades. The "moderne chic" danced on floors of patent leather-black gleam. White multiplatform steps, kaleidoscopic mirrors, and Deco glass sculpture well served the slick set's "swells." Despite their apparent disparities, each style shared Day's love of the particular.

In the 1950s the "new breed" of actors and directors found Day's work well suited to their needs. Day could capture the brutal snap and underlying sensitivity dominating the works of such directors as Elia Kazan. As always, Day invested the commonplace with potent symbolism. His intensely ambient spaces suggested inner psychologies—a critical factor in artistic works of the time. However, despite Day's topicality, his modus operandi had barely changed since his collaborations with von Stroheim.

Day achieved richness through magnification of the specific. Amassing details, he combined visual intricacy with depth of content. As a result, his tragic visions spoke with the boldest tones. Day filled even his saddest images with a poetry that von Stroheim denied, thus giving his viewer a bittersweet sense of hope.

—Edith C. Lee

de ALMEIDA, Acácio

Cinematographer. **Nationality:** Portuguese. **Born:** Acácio Augusto de Almeida in Souto, 29 June 1938. **Education:** Studied cinematography at the Centro Universitário de Lisboa, 1963–65. **Career:** Assistant to cinematographers Jean Rabier and others; 1967—first film as cinematographer, *Sete Balas para Selma*; 1969—co-founder, the cooperative Centro Português de Cinema; 1980s—associated as cameraman on several films by Raúl Ruiz; also associated with the producer Paulo Branco.

Films as Cinematographer:

1965   *Ilhas Encantadas* (Vilardebó) (asst); *Domingo à Tarde* (Macedo) (asst)

1967   *Sete Balas para Selma* (Macedo)

1968   *A Cruz de Ferro* (do Canto) (asst)

1970   *O Cerco* (Telles)

1971   *Queridísimos Verdugos* (Patiño)

1972   *O Passado e o Presente (Past and Present)* (de Oliveira); *A Sagrada Família* (Monteiro); *India* (Faria)

1974   *Meus Amigos* (Telles); *Brandos Costumes* (Santos)

1975   *As armas e o Povo* (doc) (co); *Deus, Pátria, Autoridade* (Simões); *Que Farei Eu Com Esta Espada* (Monteiro); *Gente da Praia da Vieira* (Campos)

1976   *Trás-os-Montes* (Reis and Cordeiro); *Máscaras* (Delgado); *Continuar a Viver* (Telles); *A Lei da Terra—Alentejo 76* (Grupo Zero)

1977   *Veredas* (Monteiro); *Que fait-on ce dimanche* (Essid)

1978   *Histórias Selvagems* (Campos)

1980   *Bom Povo Português* (Simões); *Passagem ou a Meio Caminho* (Mello)

1981   *Dina e Django* (Nordland); *Conversa Acabada* (Botelho); *Silvestre* (Monteiro)

1982   *A Ilha dos Amores* (Rocha) (co); *Gestos e Fragmentos* (Santos); *Aspern* (de Gregorio); *Ana* (Reis and Cordeiro); *A Estrangeira* (Grilo); *Le Cercle des passions* (D'Anna)

1983   *Dans la ville blanche (In the White City)* (Tanner); *Vidas* (Telles); *Point de fuite* (Ruiz); *La Ville des pirates (City of Pirates)* (Ruiz)

1984   *Ninguém Duas Vezes* (Mello); *Maine-Océan* (Rozier); *Notre mariage* (Sarmiento); *Les Destins de Manoel* (Ruiz); *Jusqu'à la nuit* (Martiny); *Vertiges* (Laurent)

1985   *Um Adeus Português* (Botelho); *L'Ile au trésor (Treasure Island)* (Ruiz); *Dans un miroir* (Ruiz); *Régime sans pain* (Ruiz)

1986   *A Flor do Mar* (Monteiro); *Mammame* (Ruiz); *Balada da Praia dos Cães* (Fonseca and Costa); *Agosta* (Mello); *Les Mendiants* (Jacquot)

1988   *El placer de matar (The Pleasure of Killing)* (Rotaeta); *Étoile (Ballet)* (Del Monte); *La Maschera (The Mask)* (Infascelli)

1989   *A rosa de areia (Desert Rose)* (Cordeiro) (co-pr); *O Sangue* (Costa); *Il Maestro (The Maestro)* (Hänsel)

1990   *Une Flame dans mon coeur (A Flame in My Heart)* (Tanner); *Terra Fria (Cold Land)* (Campos) (+ pr)

1992   *Zuppa di pesce* (Infascelli)

1995   *Pandora* (da Cunha Telles); *La Leyenda de Balthasar el Castrado* (Miñon); *Fugueuses* (Trintignant)

1996   *Un Asunto privado* (Arias)

1998   *A Tempestade da Terra* (Fernando D'Almeida e Silva); *Os Mutantes (The Mutants)* (Villaverde); *A Sombra dos Abutres (In the Shadow of the Vultures)* (Vieira) (+ exec pr); *L'Inconnu de Strasbourg* (Sarmiento)

1999   *Yerma* (Távora); *Mal*

Film as Cameraman:

1981   *Le Territoire (The Territory)* (Ruiz)

1987   *O Bobo (The Jester)*

Publications:

On de ALMEIDA: articles—

Holland, Jonathan, "La Novia De Medianoche," in *Variety* (New York), 1 December 1997.

*   *   *

The most notable aspects of the photography of Acácio de Almeida are his intuitions and his craftsmanship. Because of the noncommercial nature of the directors he has worked with (Manoel de Oliveira, Raúl Ruiz, Alain Tanner, António Reis, and César Monteiro, among others), de Almeida's work is determined by aesthetic imperatives. In almost all his films, for example, de Almeida functions as both director of photography and camera operator, paying equal attention to lighting and framing each shot. The phrase "cinematographic technique" applies perfectly to his sensibility and to his intimate style associated with the appearance of objects in the frame and with fast film sensitive to a minimum of light.

Since *Trás-os-Montes* (1976), a film by António Reis and Margarida Cordeiro vigorously defended by *Cahiers du Cinéma*, de Almeida's photography testifies to his taste for low-key lighting and the utilization of a single light source. In the case of *Trás-os-Montes*, his use of a candle's flame has suggested the influence of the painter Georges de la Tour. Not without some irony, de Almeida rejects the idea of any cultural influence on his work, noting that he grew up in a rural area without electric light.

There is, however, an influence that de Almeida has not rejected—that of Nestor Almendros who photographed François Truffaut's *L'Amour en fuite* in 1978. De Almeida shares with Almendros the same preoccupation—to discover in nature and daily life inspiration for his light. The lighting in de Almeida's films, as in the European films of Almendros, always seek to reconstruct and represent the principles of natural light.

Notwithstanding having begun his career at the peak of the "*cinema novo*," an aesthetic movement that developed in Portugal under the influence of the Nouvelle Vague and the South American *cinema novo*, de Almeida can only vaguely be linked to the movement. For de Oliveira's *O Passado e o Presente*, for instance, situated on the aesthetic edge of the movement, de Almeida used high-key lighting and complex sequence shots, neither of which corresponds to the principal characteristics of *cinema novo*.

It is with *Trás-os-Montes*, a film situated between fiction and documentary, that de Almeida finds his style. Alain Tanner's *Dans la ville blanche*, a film which contrasts the brilliant light of Lisbon with the "soft lights" of the interiors, begins de Almeida's European series, which attains its highest point in his collaboration with Raúl Ruiz, a Chilean filmmaker exiled in France.

The "Raúl Ruiz-Paulo Branco system" of filmmaking, in which de Almeida is a continuing figure, lends itself to a permanent inventive delirium that attempts to explore to the fullest the magical outpouring of cinema. In this context, de Almeida's photography gains an extraordinary liberty, evident in the theater of shadows in *La Ville des pirates* and in the games of light, contrasting dull and vivid tones, in *L'Ile au trésor*. In these films, without abandoning realism, de Almeida's photography shows its magic as never before.

—M. S. Fonseca

DEAN, Basil

Producer and Director. **Nationality:** British. **Born:** Croydon, Surrey, 27 September 1888. **Military Service:** 1914—joined Cheshire Regiment: head of War Office theatres, 1917–18. **Family:** Married 1) Esther Van Gruisen (divorced); 2) Lady Mercy Greville (divorced); 3) the actress Victoria Hopper (divorced). **Career:** 1907–11—member of the Horniman Repertory Company, Manchester; 1919–26—cofounding director, with Alec L. Rea, theatrical production company Reandean; 1926—cowrote the play *The Constant Nymph* with Margaret Kennedy, based on Kennedy's novel (and later filmed); 1926–64—head of Basil Dean Productions, (and L.B. Dean Productions, 1939–46); 1932—founder, Associated Talking Pictures (later Ealing Studios); 1939—founding director, Entertainments National Service Association (ENSA); 1942—director, National Service Entertainment; 1948—organized first British Repertory Theatre Festival, London. **Award:** Commander, Order of the British Empire, 1947. **Died:** 22 April 1978.

Films as Producer and Director:

1928   *The Return of Sherlock Holmes*
1930   *Escape* (+ sc); *Birds of Prey* (*The Perfect Alibi*) (+ sc)
1932   *Nine till Six*; *The Impassive Footman* (*Woman in Bondage*); *Looking at the Bright Side* (co-d + co-sc)
1933   *Loyalties*
1934   *Autumn Crocus* (+ sc); *Sing As We Go*

Basil Dean

1935   *Lorna Doone*; *Look Up and Laugh*
1936   *Whom the Gods Love* (*Mozart*)
1937   *The Show Goes On* (+ co-sc)

Films as Producer:

1931   *A Honeymoon Adventure* (*Footsteps in the Night*) (Elvey) (+ co-sc); *Sally in Our Alley* (Elvey)
1932   *The Water Gipsies* (Elvey) (+ co-sc); *The Sign of Four* (Lee and Cutts); *Love on the Spot* (Cutts)
1933   *Three Men in a Boat* (Cutts); *Skipper of the Osprey* (Walker)
1934   *Love, Life, and Laughter* (Elvey); *Java Head* (Ruben)
1935   *No Limit* (Banks); *Midshipman Easy* (*Men of the Sea*) (Reed) (co)
1936   *Queen of Hearts* (Banks); *The Lonely Road* (*Scotland Yard Commands*) (Flood)
1937   *Feather Your Nest* (Beaudine)
1938   *I See Ice* (Kimmins); *It's in the Air* (*George Takes the Air*) (Kimmins)

Other Films:

1928   *The Constant Nymph* (Brunel) (co-sc)
1933   *The Constant Nymph* (d + co-sc)
1937   *The First and the Last* (*21 Days*; *21 Days Together*) (d)
1938   *Penny Paradise* (co-pr + co-sc)

Publications

By DEAN: books—

The Repertory Theatre (lecture), Liverpool, 1911.
With Barry V. Jackson, *Fifinella* (play), London, 1912.
With Margaret Kennedy, *The Constant Nymph* (play), London, 1926.
With Margaret Kennedy, *Come with Me* (play), London, 1928.
The Theatre in Reconstruction, Tonbridge, Kent, 1945.
Hassan (play), London, 1951.
The Theatre at War, London, 1956.
Seven Ages and *Mind's Eye: An Autobiography 1888–1972*, London, 2 vols., 1970–72.

By DEAN: articles—

"Talking Pictures," in *Nineteenth Century and After* (London), December 1929.
Picturegoer (London), July 1930.

On DEAN: article—

Historical Journal of Film, Radio and Television (Abingdon, Oxford), Vol. 10, no. 1, March 1990.

*   *   *

A major figure in British theatrical history, Basil Dean is all too often overlooked in the study of British film history. His fame as the creator of Ealing Studios is overshadowed by the importance placed on his successor, Michael Balcon. Because of the general opinion that British cinema failed to exist on an international level prior to Alexander Korda's production of *The Private Life of Henry VIII* in 1933, Dean's work in the development of a major studio, Associated Talking Pictures (arguably the first British company to be incorporated after the coming of sound), and its collaborative activities with the American RKO Radio Pictures, has been neglected. (Coincidentally, in 1937, Korda and Dean worked together, far from amicably, on *21 Days*, which Dean had originally produced on the stage, and which was intended as a starring vehicle for Laurence Olivier and Vivien Leigh.)

More importantly, Basil Dean has not received recognition for understanding the screen potential of British music hall stars and for his work in developing two of those stars, Gracie Fields and George Formby, into the most popular British screen personalities of the 1930s. Dean's screen career led directly from his work in the theatre, as he wrote the screenplay for Margaret Kennedy's *The Constant Nymph* and directed John Galsworthy's *Escape*, both of which had been highspots in his stage career. Basil Dean further learned the rudiments of motion picture production from a trip to New York, where he directed one feature for Paramount, *The Return of Sherlock Holmes*, a surprisingly competent production for one unfamiliar with American production techniques.

In 1930 Somerset Maugham had advised Dean that ''it would be grand if the pictures ceased to be an outrage to the intelligence of an educated person.'' Dean sought to heed Maugham's suggestion, initially by adapting works by A.A. Milne and John Galsworthy, among others, for the screen. Later, he realized that British films had the potential for depicting the working-class view of British society. The theatre belonged to the middle and upper classes. The screen belonged to the masses. He developed two North Country comedy performers, Gracie Fields and George Formby, and used their personae to show the grit and determination, the humor and pathos of working-class society. Fields and Formby were already familiar to theatregoers in Britain. Dean was able to create films which brought these performers away from the confines and limitations of the stage and helped show the world the unsentimental reality of British working-class life. His finest achievement is, unquestionably, *Sing As We Go*, which boasts a screenplay by J. B. Priestley, and captures the drama of life in the Lancashire cotton mills. It is one of the finest social realistic portraits of North Country British working-class society.

During the years that Dean was a producer, he helped further the careers of many individuals at Ealing studios, notably David Lean (then an editor), Carol Reed, Thorold Dickinson, and Basil Dearden. In many respects, his films from 1931–38 are the forerunners of the popular Ealing comedies of the late 1940s and early 1950s. Indeed, Dean claimed up to his death that his Ealing comedies, which relied more on personalities than situations, had stood the test of time better than those of his highly promoted Ealing heir, Michael Balcon.

—Anthony Slide

D'EAUBONNE, Jean

Art Director. **Nationality:** French. **Born:** Jean Adrien D'Eaubonne in Talence, 8 March 1903. **Education:** Trained as sculptor and painter with Antoine Bourdelle, Paris. **Career:** Painter and poster designer;

assistant to Lazare Meerson and Jean Perrier on films in the late 1920s, then art director; 1940–45—lived in Switzerland; 1957–68—lived in Hollywood. **Awards:** Venice Festival prize, for *La Ronde*, 1950. **Died:** In July 1970.

Films as Art Director/Production Designer:

1928   *Le Perroquet vert* (Milva) (asst)
1930   *Tarakanova* (Bernard); **Le Sang d'un poète** (*The Blood of a Poet*) (Cocteau); *Le Défenseur* (Ryder); *La Ronde des heures* (Ryder); *Azais* (Hervil)
1931   *Coup de roulis* (de la Cour); *Le Juif polonais* (Kemm); *Coquecigrole* (Berthomieu); *Pour un sou d'amour* (Grémillon) (co); *Amour et discipline* (Kemm)
1932   *Le Truc au Brésilien* (Cavalcanti); *Les Vignes du seigneur* (Hervil); *L'Amour et la veine* (Banks)
1933   *Mademoiselle Josette ma femme* (Berthomieu); *Mannequins* (Hervil); *Ame de clown* (Noé and Didier); *L'Ami Fritz* (de Baroncelli); *Coralie et Cie* (Cavalcanti); *La Femme idéale* (Berthomieu)
1934   *Maître Bolbec et son mari* (Natanson); *Le Petit Jacques* (Roudes); *La Reine de Biarritz* (Toulout); *L'Aristo* (Berthomieu)
1935   *Le Clown Bux* (Natanson); *Les Beaux Jours* (M. Allégret); *Le Chant de l'amour* (Roudes); *Marie des angoisses* (Bernheim)
1936   *Le Roman d'un spahi* (Bernheim); *La Flamme* (Berthomieu); *Jenny* (Carné); *L'Amant de Madame Vidal* (Berthomieu); *Anne-Marie* (Bernard)
1937   *La Chaste Suzanne* (*The Girl in the Taxi*) (Berthomieu); *Police mondaine* (Bernheim and Chamborant); *L'Habit vert* (Richebé); *Un Déjeuner de soleil* (Cravenne); *Légions d'honneur* (Gleize); *L'Homme sans nom* (Vallée)
1938   *Les Gens du voyage* (Feyder); *Le Train pour Venise* (Berthomieu); *Carrefour* (Bernhardt); *Trois valses* (Berger); *Un de la Canebière* (Pujol); *Les Gangsters du Chateau d'If* (Pujol)
1939   *Nuit de décembre* (Bernhardt); *L'Enfer des anges* (Christian-Jaque) (designs); *De Mayerling à Sarajevo* (*Mayerling to Sarajevo*) (Ophüls)
1942   *La Loi du nord* (Feyder—produced 1939); *Une Femme disparait* (Feyder)
1945   *Étoile sans lumière* (Blistène)
1946   *Macadam* (*Backstreets of Paris*) (Blistène and Feyder); *La Foire aux chimères* (Chenal)
1947   *Black Magic* (*Cagliostro*) (Ratoff)
1948   *La Chartreuse de parme* (Christian-Jaque); *L'Impasse des Deux Anges* (M. Tourneur); *Hans le marin* (Villiers)
1949   *Le Paradis des pilotes perdus* (Lapmin); *Je n'aime que toi* (Montazel); *Pas de week-end pour notre amour* (Montazel); *Lady Paname* (Jeanson)
1950   **Orphée** (Cocteau); **La Ronde** (Ophüls); *La Dame de Chez Maxim's* (Aboulker) (designs); *Ma pomme* (Sauvajon); *Olivia* (Audry)
1951   *Nuits de Paris* (Baum)
1952   *Le Plaisir* (*House of Pleasure*) (Ophüls); **Casque d'or** (Jacques Becker); *Plaisirs de Paris* (Baum); *La Fête à Henriette* (Duvivier); ''Lysistrata'' ep. of *Destinées* (*Daughters of Destiny*) (Christian-Jaque)

1953   *Rue de l'Estrapade* (Jacques Becker); *Jeunes mariés* (Grangier); *Le Mystère du Palace Hôtel* (Steckel and Berna); **Madame de . . .** (*The Earrings of Madame De . . .*) (Ophüls); *Cet homme est dangereux* (Sacha); *Julietta* (M. Allégret)

1954   *Touchez pas au Grisbi* (*Grisbi*) (Jacques Becker); *Mam'zelle Nitouche* (Y. Allégret); *Scènes de ménage* (Berthomieu); *Bonnes à tuer* (Decoin); *Les Amants du Tage* (Verneuil)

1955   *Marianne de ma jeunesse* (Duvivier); **Lola Montès** (*The Sins of Lola Montes*) (Ophüls); *L'Affaire des poisons* (Decoin); *Le Secret de Soeur Angèle* (Joannon)

1956   *Le Long des trottoirs* (Moguy); *Paris-Palace-Hôtel* (Verneuil); *L'Homme aux clés d'or* (Joannon); *La Mariée est trop belle* (Gaspard-Huit); *Bonsoir Paris, bonjour l'amour* (Baum); *OSS 117 n'est pas mort* (Sacha); *Jusqu'au dernier* (Billon)

1957   *Amère victoire* (*Bitter Victory*) (N. Ray); *Une Manche et la belle* (Verneuil); *Quand la femme s'en mêle* (Y. Allégret); *Montparnasse 19* (*Modigliani of Montparnasse*) (Jacques Becker)

1958   *The Reluctant Debutante* (Minnelli); *Christine* (Gaspard-Huit); *Nina* (Boyer)

1959   *Ein Engel auf Erden* (*Angel on Earth*) (Radvanyi); *Suspense au 2e Bureau* (de St. Maurice)

1960   *Katja* (*The Magnificent Sinner*) (Siodmak); *Les Magiciennes* (*Double Deception*) (Friedman); *Crack in the Mirror* (Fleischer); *The Big Gamble* (Fleischer)

1961   *Madame Sans-Gêne* (*Madame*) (Christian-Jaque)

1962   *L'Affaire Nina B* (*The Nina B Affair*) (Siodmak); *Love Is a Ball* (Swift)

1963   *Charade* (Donen)

1964   *Paris When It Sizzles* (Quine); *Le Repas des fauves* (Christian-Jaque)

1965   *Lady L* (Ustinov) (co); *Cartes sur table* (Franco)

1966   *Galia* (*I and My Lovers*) (Lautner); *Avec les peaux des autres* (Deray)

1967   *Fleur d'oseille* (Lautner); *La Pacha* (Lautner)

1968   *Custer of the West* (Siodmak) (co); *Girl on a Motorcycle* (Cardiff) (co); *Johnny Banco* (Y. Allégret); *Faut pas prendre les enfants du Bon Dieu pour des canards sauvages* (Audiard)

1969   *Une Veuve en or* (Audiard); *Sur la route de Salina* (Lautner)

1970   *Elle boit pas, elle fume pas, elle drague pas, mais . . . elle cause!* (Audiard); *Sapho* (Farrel); *Laisse aller, c'est une valse* (Lautner); *Le Cri du cormoran le soir, au-dessus des jonques* (Audiard)

1971   *Le Drapeau noir flotte sur la marmite* (Audiard)

Publications

On D'EAUBONNE: articles—

Technique/L'Exploitation Cinématographe (Paris), no. 331, September 1971.
Cinématographe (Paris), no. 76, March 1982.
Positif (Paris), no. 331, September 1988.

*   *   *

After studying under the sculptor Antoine Bourdelle in Paris, Jean d'Eaubonne initially found work at the Epinay studios as a publicity artist and scenery painter before graduating to set design. He later moved to the Jacques Haïk studios as a now fully experienced production designer and art director. This thorough grounding in the fundamentals of his craft was invaluable to a career that involved, over four decades, an association with some 70 directors and work on more than 130 films, mainly in European studios but also in Hollywood. His apprenticeship to filmmaking was completed as assistant to Jean Perrier and then to Lazare Meerson for Feyder's *Les Nouveaux Messieurs*.

If many of d'Eaubonne's multifarious films are unremarkable, several rightfully merit critical recognition and, in 1950, his magnificent design for Max Ophüls's *La Ronde* was duly rewarded at the Venice Film Festival. Essentially practical, resourceful and unassuming, Jean d'Eaubonne calmly coped with last-minute script changes necessitating alterations to already constructed sets. Such was the case with *Madame de . . .*, where Ophüls's revisions required a balcony for the general's quarters, previously deemed below street level. In *Lola Montès* tact and lateral thinking were required when the innkeeper, refusing to see his inn repainted brick red, eventually allowed a temporary cladding of red tiles. Sadly, d'Eaubonne discarded most of his models and production designs.

D'Eaubonne's work first came to notice with Cocteau's *Le Sang d'un poète*, where his understanding of the plastic arts informed a conception in which statues were but part of the real world. The spare, but highly suggestive design, derived from an intimate knowledge of Cocteau's work, served to perfection the poet-filmmaker's vision. This fertile relationship was renewed 20 years later when Cocteau returned to the theme of creativity with *Orphée*. Once again d'Eaubonne responded brilliantly, providing everyday locations which merged magically with trompe l'oeil sets suggesting the otherworldliness of the princess: the disquieting, ruinous house with its unreal rooms equipped with potent mirrors and passageways to the underworld.

The thirties and war-torn forties brought work with leading poetic realist directors, notably Grémillon, Carné, and Feyder, though sometimes for indifferent films. After Grémillon's uninspired, early sound comedy *Pour un sou d' amour*, came the powerful poetic realism of Carné's *Jenny*, with its memorable location work at the Canal Saint-Martin, followed by four films for the ubiquitous Feyder in Germany, France, and Switzerland. In Munich, d'Eaubonne surmounted communication problems to provide convincing French-looking streets for Feyder's traveling circus film, *Les Gens du voyage*, but the Paris production of *La Loi du Nord* disappointed with flimsy evocations of America and Norway. During the Nazi occupation, the thriller *Une Femme disparaît* was filmed in Switzerland, and the authentic feel to d'Eaubonne's work did not return until the Parisian street settings of the postwar *Macadam*.

After the liberation the resuscitation of the French film industry led to big-budget productions in heavily subsidized studios. Typical was Christian-Jaque's version of *La Chartreuse de Parme* for which d'Eaubonne designed impressively complex and costly sets. The golden decade of the fifties, with an emphasis on high production values, saw d'Eaubonne's creative talents flourish, particularly in his all-important association with Ophüls. D'Eaubonne's stylized Vienna for *La Ronde*, with its glittering theaters, extravagant restaurants, and misty riverside settings, was followed by an even more lavish design for *Madame de . . .*, where palatial apartments, magnificent ballrooms, and sweeping staircases set the tone of opulence and frivolity. In *Le Plaisir*, striking contrasts were achieved between the ornate artificiality of Maupassant's Maison Tellier brothel and the idyllic, redemptive countryside locations for Madame's day out with her girls.

Similarly, in *Lola Montès*, the heroine's giddy, tinsel world of the circus is set against the more ordered and substantial setting of the Bavarian palace. In each undertaking, d'Eaubonne deftly satisfied through location and set design, Ophüls's expressionist style.

In the fifties d'Eaubonne was frequently required to create a studio Paris and this he largely achieved without slipping into lazy, well-worn clichés. For Jeanson's *Lady Paname*, he provided the capital of the belle époque, while for Jacques Becker he created a turn-of-the-century Paris to frame the tragic love story, *Casque d'Or*. Thereafter came fashionable domestic settings for the latter director's light-hearted comedy, *Rue de l'Estrapade*, the bohemian milieu of cafés and studios for Modgliani's final days in *Montparnasse 19*, while in the seminal gangster film *Touchez pas au Grisbi*, d'Eaubonne served the narrative with luxurious apartments and expensive nightclubs. With Baum came lightweight films exploiting the city's romantic image: *Nuits de Paris*; *Plaisirs de Paris*, and *Bonjour Paris, bonjour l'amour*.

The sixties saw American and British interest in Parisian locations. For Donen's thriller *Charade*, the scenic *quais*, the colonnade of the Palais Royal, and the Comédie Française were deployed, while for Quine's *Paris When It Sizzles*, more conventional tourist locations were used. Among d'Eaubonne's more imaginative creations was the lavish Parisian brothel for Ustinov's *Lady L*.

More exotic locations were also d'Eaubonne's remit. For Verneuil's *Les Amants du Tage*, colorful Portuguese beaches provided the essential romantic atmosphere; for Siodmark's Civil War spectacular, *Custer of the West*, arid Spanish locations stood in for Montana, with man-made rapids completing plot requirements. D'Eaubonne's portfolio of American productions also included Nicholas Ray's Benghazi desert war film *Bitter Victory*; Minnelli's sparkling *The Reluctant Debutante*, with its aristocratic London settings; Swift's American comedy vehicle, *Love Is a Ball*; and Fleischer's murder story, *Crack in the Mirror*, produced entirely in Paris. Towards the end of his career, d'Eaubonne served Lautner with conventional settings for mainstream detective thrillers while at the same time working with Audiard on films which played anarchically against the thriller formula.

The range and diversity of d'Eaubonne's portfolio confirm not only his eclecticism but also his acknowledged professionalism. Directors and producers recognized in d'Eaubonne a gifted, self-effacing craftsman who would skillfully meet their needs, whether through spare, suggestive sets for the experimental Cocteau, solid, detailed constructions and atmospheric locations for the poetic realists such as Carné or Feyder, or though lavish theatrical designs for the expressionist Ophüls.

—R. F. Cousins

de BEAUREGARD, Georges

Producer. **Nationality:** French. **Born:** Edgar Denys Nau de Beauregard in Marseilles, 23 December 1920. **Education:** Studied law. **Military Service:** During World War II. **Career:** Journalist; 1947—founded Agence Universel Presse; entered film business as distributor; then film producer in Spain; 1960—founded Rome-Paris-Films; 1973—founded Bela Productions. **Award:** Special César award, 1983. **Died:** 10 September 1984.

Films as Producer or Coproducer:

1955   *Muerte de un ciclista* (*Death of a Cyclist*; *Age of Infidelity*) (Bardem)
1956   *Calle Mayor* (*The Lovemaker*) (Bardem)
1957   *La Passe du diable* (Dupont and Schöndörffer)
1958   *Ramuntscho* (Schöndörffer)
1959   *Pecheur d'Islande* (Schöndörffer)
1960   *Adieu Philippine* (Rozier); ***A bout de souffle*** (*Breathless*) (Godard)
1961   ***Lola*** (Demy); ***Cléo de 5 à 7*** (*Cleo from 5 to 7*) (Varda); *Une Femme est une femme* (*A Woman Is a Woman*) (Godard)
1962   *L'Oeil du malin* (*The Third Lover*) (Chabrol)
1963   *Léon Morin—prêtre* (Melville); *Landru* (*Bluebeard*) (Chabrol); *Le Petit Soldat* (Godard—produced 1960); *Le Doulos* (*Doulos—the Finger Man*) (Melville); ***Le Mépris*** (*Contempt*) (Godard); *Les Carabiniers* (Godard); *Les Baisers* (Berri and others)
1964   *La Chance et l'amour* (Tavernier and others); *Le Vampire de Düsseldorf* (Hossein); *La 317e Section* (Schöndörffer)
1965   *Pierrot le fou* (Godard); *Marie-Chantal contre le Dr. Kha* (Chabrol)
1966   *Objectif 500 millions* (Schöndörffer); *Un Choix d'assassins* (Fourastie); *Le Ligne de démarcation* (*Line of Demarcation*) (Chabrol); *Made in U.S.A.* (Godard); *Suzanne Simonin, la religieuse de Denis Diderot* (*La Religieuse*; *The Nun*) (Rivette)
1967   *La Collectioneuse* (Rohmer); *Lamiel* (Fourastie)
1968   *L'Amour fou* (Rivette); *48 heures d'amour* (St. Laurent)
1969   *Le Petit Bournat* (Toublanc-Michel)
1970   *Le Mur de l'Atlantique* (Camus)
1972   *Le Bar de la fourche* (Levent)
1973   *Prêtres interdits* (de la Patellière); *Gross Paris* (Grangier)
1975   *Numéro deux* (Godard); *Les Fougères bleues* (Schöndörffer)
1977   *Le Crabe-Tambour* (Schöndörffer)
1979   *Tout dépend des filles* (Fabre); *La Légion saute sur Kolwezi* (Coutard)
1980   *Le Cheval d'orgueil* (Chabrol)
1982   *L'Honneur d'un capitaine* (Schöndörffer)

Publications

By de BEAUREGARD: articles—

Cinématographe (Paris), 10 September 1960.
Cinéma (Paris), no. 94, 1965.
Film Quarterly (Berkeley, California), Spring 1967.

On de BEAUREGARD: articles—

Avant-Scène (Paris), 15 February 1964.
Ciné Française (Paris), no. 8, 1965.
Film Français (Paris), 2 March 1982.
Film Français (Paris), 1 October 1982.
Cinématographe (Paris), May 1984.
Cinéma (Paris), October 1984.

Cahiers du Cinéma (Paris), November 1984.
Obituary in *Revue du Cinéma* (Paris), no. 399, November 1984.

* * *

Georges de Beauregard is best known as one of the producers of the French New Wave filmmakers of the late 1950s and early 1960s. His adventurous spirit and enthusiasm for negotiation and financial risk corresponded to the audacious confidence of the generation of directors, headed by Jean-Luc Godard, Claude Chabrol, and François Truffaut, that swept aside the classicism of the ''tradition of quality'' and established a new, more vital form of filmmaking. In a sense, the New Wave was at least as great a revolution in production as in direction; the small-budget films of Georges de Beauregard (like those produced by Pierre Braunberger), shot on location and without stars, put an end to the dominance of French cinema by the solid yet somewhat stale work of studio-bound directors such as Claude Autant-Lara, Christian-Jaque, and Jean Delannoy. A fresher, more personal style of filmmaking developed, in which the camera was assimilated to the pen of a writer and the director, assuming virtual total control of his or her work, could become an ''auteur.''

Even though de Beauregard was not the *first* producer of the films of the young generation of directors to emerge from the ranks of the critics of the *Cahiers du Cinéma* (Chabrol's *Le Beau Serge* and *Les Cousins*, and Truffaut's *Les Quatre Cents Coups* had already proved the financial credibility of small-budget filmmaking), his courage was nevertheless great in producing the first full-length feature films of Jean-Luc Godard (*A bout de souffle*), Jacques Demy (*Lola*), Jacques Rozier (*Adieu Philippine*), and Agnès Varda (*Cléo de 5 à 7*), and later such contentious works as Godard's second film, *Le Petit Soldat* (banned until 1963) and Jacques Rivette's *Suzanne Simonin, la religieuse de Denis Diderot*. This courage was backed by a strong faith in his directors and in the need for innovation in the French cinema. For de Beauregard, confidence in the originality of ideas, rather than youth for the sake of youth, often determined his decisions to produce; he was equally ready, for example, to produce *Le Doulos*, a highly personal thriller by Jean-Pierre Melville who had been directing feature films since 1947, as the first works of the impressive *Cahiers du Cinéma* critics, or, in *Les Baisers*, a film composed of sketches, to reveal the talents of five new directors at once: Bertrand Toublanc, Claude Berri, Bertrand Tavernier, Charles Bitsch, and J-F Hauduroy.

The great achievement of de Beauregard was that this flair for newness and vitality did not operate in terms of an esoteric underground marginality, but most often corresponded to what the general public wanted. Maintaining an awareness of the importance of the demands of the public (both domestic and international) assured the financial success of films as innovative as *A bout de souffle* and proved that formal inventiveness and originality, as demonstrated by the New Wave, need not be the exclusive privilege of an avant-garde minority.

The path by which de Beauregard came to film production reveals the origins of the taste for risk that characterizes the bold nature of many of his productions. After several years in the army and work in journalism (he founded the Agence Universel Presse in 1947), de Beauregard became involved in the selling of American films to French distributors (including films by Lubitsch and Milestone) and the export of French films to Brazil. He moved to Spain in 1950, where he continued to import American films, and eventually applied his entrepreneurial flair to film production. After one film by Miguel

Iglésia, he produced two films by the militant anti-Francist Juan Antonio Bardem, *Muerte de un ciclista* and *Calle Mayor*, which courageously portrayed life under Franco and greatly contributed to a renaissance in Spanish cinema. The courage in producing such politically bold films as those of Bardem prefigures de Beauregard's career in France, marked by the formal audacities of the New Wave and the confrontations with French censors for both *Le Petit Soldat* and *Suzanne Simonin*. De Beauregard's military career, on the other hand, accounts for another facet of his productions: a number of larger budget films which reveal a nostalgia for the camaraderie of the military and, true to his own personality, a strong dose of adventure. The clearest examples of this aspect of his work are Pierre Schöndörffer's *La Passe du diable*, *La 317e Section*, *Objectif 500 millions*, *Le Crabe-Tambour*, and *L'Honneur d'un capitaine*, and Raoul Coutard's *La Légion saute sur Kolwezi*.

But whatever sort of film de Beauregard was producing, he remained true to the notion of the director as ''auteur,'' seeing it as his role both to provide the necessary material means for a production and to encourage an atmosphere that suited and stimulated the creative temperament of the director and his collaborators. It is this which made him and his production company, Rome-Paris-Films (established in 1960 with Carlo Ponti), so respected by directors. For such excellent relationships with his directors, for his encouragement of new talent, and for demonstrating, especially in his early New Wave productions, that successful cinema does not necessarily require exhorbitant budgets and studio facilities, Georges de Beauregard will be remembered as an exemplary producer.

—Richard Alwyn

DECAË, Henri

Cinematographer and Director. **Nationality:** French. **Born:** Saint-Denis, 31 July 1915. **Education:** Attended the Ecole Technique de Photographie et de Cinématographie. **Career:** Made amateur films as a boy; worked for Poste Parisien as sound engineer and editor; Air Force cameraman during World War II; 1941—shot first film (also co-director); 1945—photo-journalist, *Petit Parisien*; late 1940s— shot first long films. **Died:** 7 March 1987.

Films as Cinematographer (Shorts):

1941   *Eau vive* (+ co-d)
1942   *Glaciers* (+ d); *Premier prix du conservatoire* (Guy-Grand) (co)
1943   *Au-delà du visible* (+ d)
1945   *A tous les vents* (+ d); *Chanson de rue* (Sevestre); *Marseille, premier port de France* (Mineur)
1946   *Hommes et bêtes* (Mineur); *L'Accordéon et ses vedettes* (Sevestre); *Sport de la voile* (Sevestre and Motard)
1947   *Les Drames du Bois de Boulogne* (Loew)
1948   *Un Homme à la mer* (Loew); *Sous les palmes de Marrakech* (Mineur); *Marrakech, capitale du Sud* (Mineur); *Le Mellah de Marrakech* (Mineur)
1949   *Pensez à ceux qui sont en-dessous!* (+ d); *Surveillez votre tenue* (+ d); *Evitez le désordre* (+ d); *Ne compromettez pas vos loisirs* (+ d); *Apprenez à soulever une charge* (+ d);

Faites soigner vos égratignures (+ d); *Bons baisers de Dinard* (Loew)

1950 *A cheval* (+ d); *Cher vieux Paris!* (de Gastyne); *Le Premier Pas* (Chartier); *Paré pour accoster* (Loew)

1951 *Visite au Haras* (+ d); *Le Garde-chasse* (+ d); *Caroline au pays natal* (de Gastyne); *Vacances blanches* (de Gastyne); *La Course de taureaux* (Braunberger); *La Lutte contre le gaspillage* (Sevestre); *Escale à Paris* (Lukine) (co)

1952 *Caroline du Sud* (de Gastyne)

1953 *Cow-boys français* (Vaudremont); *La Beauté de l'effort* (de Gastyne); *Avec les gens de voyage* (de Gastyne) (co); *L'Homme et la bête* (de Gastyne) (co); *Le Grand Cirque s'en va* (de Gastyne) (co); *A tout casser* (*Stock-cars*) (Dupont) (co); *L'Egypte éternelle* (de Gastyne); *Un Monde troublant* (de Gastyne) (Vaudremont); *Navigation marchande* (*Marine marchande*) (Franju)

1955 *Mer Caribe* (de Hubsch) (co); *La Grande Terre* (Vaudremont)

1956 *L'Enfant au fennec* (Dupont); *Coureurs de brousse* (Dupont); *Israel . . . terre retrouvée* (de Gastyne) (co); *Propre à rien* (de Gastyne) (co)

1957 *La Voix des anches* (Leduc); *De bouche à oreille* (Leduc); *Neuf à trois, ou la journée d'une vedette* (Leduc); *Piano, mon ami* (Leduc); *Confidences d'un piano* (Leduc); *Robinson* (de Gastyne) (co); *Les Plus Beaux Jours* (de Gastyne)

1958 *Bois et cuivres* (Leduc) (co); *Les Cuivres à la voix d'or* (Leduc); *Le Château du passé* (de Gastyne) (co)

1960 *Images d'hier et d'aujourd'hui* (Leduc) (co); *Ce monde banal* (Wagner)

1961 *Le Village du milieu des brumes* (Chartier)

1962 *Football* (Languepin)

1963 *Le Marionnettiste* (Languepin)

1967 *Toutankhamon et son royaume* (de Gastyne—produced 1952)

Films as Cinematographer (Features):

1948 *Le Silence de la mer* (Melville)

1950 *Les Enfants terribles* (Melville); *Bertrand, coeur de lion* (Dhéry)

1951 *Au coeur de la Casbah* (*Maria-Pilar*) (Cardinal)

1954 *Crève-Coeur* (Dupont)

1956 *Bob le flambeur* (Melville) (+ voice); *S.O.S. Noronha* (Rouquier)

1957 *Le Désir mène les hommes* (Roussell) (*Bitter Reunion*) (Chabrol); *Un Témoin dans la ville* (Molinaro); *Les Amants* (*The Lovers*) (Malle)

1959 **Les Quatre Cents Coups** (*The 400 Blows*) (Truffaut); *Les Cousins* (*The Cousins*) (Chabrol); *Plein soleil* (*Web of Passion; Leda*) (Chabrol); *La Sentence* (Valère)

1960 *Les Bonnes Femmes* (Chabrol)

1961 *Che gioia vivere* (*Quelle joie de vivre*) (Clément); *Cybèle, ou les dimanches de Ville d'Avray* (*Sundays and Cybèle*) (Bourguignon)

1962 ''La Luxure,'' ''La Paresse,'' and ''L'Orgueil'' eps. of *Les Sept Péchés capitaux* (*The Seven Deadly Sins*) (Demy, Godard, and Vadim); *Vie privée* (*A Very Private Affair*) (Malle); *Le Jour et l'heure* (*The Day and the Hour*) (Clément)

1963 *Léon Morin, prêtre* (Melville); *La Tulipe noire* (*The Black Tulip*) (Christian-Jaque); *Dragées au poivre* (Baratier); *La Porteuse de pain* (Cloche); *L'Aîné des Ferchaux* (Melville)

1964 *Week-end à Zuydcoote* (Verneuil); **La Ronde** (*Circle of Love*) (Vadim); *Les Félins* (*Joy House; The Love Cage*) (Clément); *Le Corniaud* (Oury)

1965 *Viva Maria!* (Malle)

1966 *Le Voleur* (*The Thief of Paris*) (Malle); *Hotel Paradiso* (Glenville)

1967 *The Night of the Generals* (Litvak); **Le Samourai** (Melville) (co); *Diaboliquement vôtre* (Duvivier); *The Comedians* (Glenville)

1969 *Le Clan des siciliens* (*The Sicilian Clan*) (Verneuil); *Castle Keep* (Pollack)

1970 *The Only Game in Town* (Stevens); *Hello-Goodbye* (Negulesco)

1971 *Two People* (Wise); *La Folie des grandeurs* (Oury); *Jo* (Girault); *La Luz del fin del mundo* (*The Light at the Edge of the World*) (Billington)

1972 *Le Cercle rouge* (Melville); *Le Droit d'aimer* (Le Hung)

1973 *Don Juan 1973, ou si Don Juan était une femme* (*Ms. Don Juan*) (Vadim) (co); *Les Aventures de Rabbi Jacob* (Oury)

1974 *Isabelle devant le désir* (Berckmans); *La Moutarde me monte au nez* (Zidi)

1975 *La Course à l'échalotte* (Zidi); *Operation Daybreak* (Gilbert)

1976 *Seven Nights in Japan* (Gilbert)

1977 *Bobby Deerfield* (Pollack); *Le Point de mire* (Tramont); *Mort d'un pourri* (Lautner)

1978 *Ils sont foux, ces sorciers!* (Lautner); *The Boys from Brazil* (Schaffner); *Flic ou voyou* (Lautner)

1979 *An Almost Perfect Affair* (Ritchie); *The Hard Way* (Dryhurst); *Le Guignolo* (Lautner)

1980 *The Island* (Ritchie); *Le Coup du parapluie* (Oury); *Inspecteur la bavure* (Zidi); *Est-ce bien raisonnable* (Lautner)

1983 *Exposed* (Toblack)

1984 *Les Parents ne sont pas simples cette année*; *Le Vengeance du serpent à plumes*

Other Films:

1946 *Le Charcutier de Machonville* Yvernel—short) (cam)

1948 *Le Silence de la mer* (Melville—short) (co-ed)

1950 *Trois hommes en Corse* (d—short)

1951 *Faits d'hiver* (d—short)

Publications

By DECAË: articles—

Cinéma Français (Paris), March 1954.
Films and Filming (London), February 1967.
Revue du Cinéma (Morges, Switzerland), January 1971.
Cinématographe (Paris), July 1981.

On DECAË: articles—

Cinéma (Paris), November-December 1961.
Monthly Film Bulletin (London), 1963.
Cinéma (Paris), no. 91, 1964.
Chaplin (Stockholm), no. 2, 1970.
Focus on Film (London), September-October 1970.
Focus on Film (London), no. 13, 1973.

Maillet, J. C., in *Cinéma Pratique* (Paris), November-December 1973.

Film Français (Paris), 4 February 1977.

Avant-Scène (Paris), 1 February 1981.

Obituary in *Revue du Cinéma* (Paris), no. 427, May 1987.

Revue du Cinéma (Paris), no. 432, November 1987.

*   *   *

Scornful of cinematography which drew attention to itself at the expense of a film's aesthetic coherence, Henri Decaë modestly regarded the cinematographer as an invisible technician serving the director's vision. He rejected the notion of a "Decaë style," arguing that every film required a fresh approach and that different directors made individual demands on his skills. The characteristic feature of his practice was a flexible attitude to constantly changing technical challenges. To ensure aesthetic unity, he advocated close collaboration between director and camera crew: production strategies in respect of narrative intentions or options regarding the creation of tone or atmosphere were best arrived at collectively. More inclined to leave framing to others, Decaë was above all concerned with lighting to promote the required mood or the appropriate exposure of actors. With colour, no less than with monochrome, he sought to suggest meaning rather than simply to record action. In a career embracing both the austere and the spectacular, the modest documentary and the large-budget movie, working creatively in both black-and-white and in colour, Henri Decaë successfully served directors on both sides of the Atlantic for over forty years.

After graduating from the Vaugirard cinema school, he joined Poste Parisien as a sound recordist and editor, but it was as an Air Force photographer that he developed his ability to work quickly and inventively under pressure. His first film, *Eau vive*, was a nature documentary processed by the Jean Mineur laboratories. This contact with the publicity filmmaker led to over forty shorts in genres as disparate as the travelogue, the educational documentary, the publicity short or the nature film. In turn Decaë worked with, amongst others, Dupont, Leduc and Loew, but his principal collaboration was with Marc de Gastyne for whom he shot fourteen films. His association with Jean Mineur also led to a remarkable debut in features as Melville's cameraman for *Le Silence de la mer*.

If the film is a tribute to Melville's commitment to a project for which he had little money, it is also a magnificent testimony to Decaë's adaptability and resourcefulness. Making do with discarded lengths of studio negative (often with different emulsions), meagre lighting equipment, and unreliable hand-held cameras (occasionally used surreptitiously in unauthorised locations), Decaë achieved a film of striking visual quality. This spare approach to filming, born out of pure necessity, was to be hailed a decade later as the way forward by young directors seeking to break away from the tyranny of prohibitively expensive studio productions. The New Wave generation was fortunate to have available lightweight cameras and fast film stock requiring little artificial lighting, and was able to benefit from Decaë's no-nonsense, direct method and his inventive resourcefulness. The cinematographer readily drew on his documentary experience to produce striking images imbued with a sense of raw authenticity and immediacy for, among others, Truffaut and Chabrol. Decaë's knowledge of film stock was invaluable, preferring the softer and faster Gevaert monochrome to Kodak, and later, Eastmancolor for its superior colour range. In Melville's *Bob le flambeur*, for example, the brilliant evocation of Paris by night was achieved using specially produced ultra-fast film stock.

Characteristics of Decaë's style include his atmospheric work in monochrome. For Truffaut he captured the doleful greyness of the Parisian suburbs in *Les Quatre Cents Coups*; for Melville, in *Léon Morin, prêtre*, he evoked the grinding mood of austerity and repression in occupied France through dull, flat tones; for Chabrol, in *Le Beau Serge*, he conjured up the bleakness of autumnal landscapes drained of colour, and, in *Les Bonnes Femmes* the harsh realities of life for urban working girls, while for Clément's thriller *Les Félins* he brilliantly developed tension through high contrast images.

Decaë's handling of colour registers was no less masterful. Muted hues were produced for shadowy gangster films such as Melville's *Le Samourai* or for Malle's *Le Voleur*. Warmer colours shaped the mood of Melville's *L'Aîné des Ferchaux* as did more sensual colour tones for Malle's *Les Amants* or the rich range of glowing reds for Clément's powerful *Plein soleil*, while for Chabrol's *A double tour* images of bourgeois decadence were expressed by an overripe palette. However, it was in Malle's *Viva Maria!* with its bright costumes, gaudy caravans, and fireworks lighting up the night sky, that Decaë exploited to the full the colour spectrum.

Invariably his resourcefulness resolved technical difficulties. To convey Antoine Doinel's point of view from inside the rotor in *Les Quatre Cents Coups*, he strapped himself to the central pole, while in *Plein soleil* to film the storm-tossed boat he secured himself to the mast. Technical challenges of a different order were posed in *Le Samourai*—particularly impressive are the shadows of passing cars seen on Jeff Costello's ceiling and the tracking of the gangster in the underlit Metro.

The long tracking shot is almost a stylistic marker in Decaë's films. Apart from the Melville gangster canon and Toback's affectionate homage to the French master in *Exposed*, the tracking shot features prominently in, amongst other films, *Les Quatre Cents Coups*, here to detail Antoine's escape from the reformatory, and in *Ascenseur pour l'échafaud* to chart Jeanne Moreau's distracted walk through Paris in the early hours.

Decaë's urban landscapes, from the early monochromes of *Les Quatre Cents Coups* and *Les Bonnes Femmes* through to the colour compositions in his gangster movies such as *Le Clan des siciliens* or *Exposed*, are richly atmospheric. His country landscapes are equally memorable, from the documentary notations of village life in *Le Beau Serge* and the delicately conjured parkland in *Les Amants* to the rolling Mexican landscapes of *Viva Maria!* and the beautiful rural compositions of Gilbert's *Seven Nights in Japan*.

In the mid-sixties, after the initial impact of the New Wave began to fade, Decaë turned his attention to the less adventurous, studio-based cinema of Lautner, Oury, Vernuiel and Zidi, and to collaboration with American directors such as Pollack, Stevens, and Wise. His corpus of transatlantic films testifies to his international recognition as an artist and serves to consolidate his already considerable reputation. However, Decaë's place in cinema history ultimately rests on his formative influence within the New Wave movement, as the liberating cinematographer whose initiatives made possible a whole new approach to cinematic practice.

—R. F. Cousins

de GRUNWALD, Anatole

Producer and Writer. **Nationality:** Russian. **Born:** St. Petersburg, 25 December 1910. **Education:** Attended the Sorbonne, Paris; Caius College, Cambridge, England. **Family:** Brother, the film producer Dimitri de Grunwald. **Career:** 1943–45—producer and writer at Two Cities Films; 1946—formed independent production company International Screenplays with Terence Rattigan; 1959—producer at MGM. **Award:** National Film Award for "the best British picture made during WWII," *The Way to the Stars*, 1945. **Died:** In London, 13 January 1967.

Films as Producer and Writer:

1949   *Now Barabbas was a Robber . . .* (Parry)
1951   *Flesh and Blood* (Kimmins)
1952   *Treasure Hunt* (Carstairs); *The Holly and the Ivy* (O'Ferrall);   *Three Men and a Girl* (*Golden Arrow*) (Parry)
1958   *The Doctor's Dilemma* (Asquith)
1959   *Libel* (Asquith)

Films as Writer:

1938   *French without Tears* (Asquith) (co)
1940   *Spy for a Day* (*Live and Let Live*) (Zampi) (co)
1941   *Cottage to Let* (*Bombsight Stolen*) (Asquith) (co); *Pimpernel*   *Smith* (Howard); *Tomorrow We Live* (King)
1943   *The First of the Few* (Howard)
1948   *Bond Street* (Parry) (co); *Home at Seven* (*Murder on Monday*)   (Richardson)
1952   *Women of Twilight* (*Twilight Women*) (Parry)
1953   *Innocents in Paris* (Parry)

Films as Producer:

1943   *The Demi-Paradise* (Asquith)
1945   *The Way to the Stars* (*Johnny in the Clouds*) (Asquith)
1948   *The Winslow Boy* (Asquith); *The Queen of Spades* (Dickinson)
1962   *Come Fly with Me* (Levin); *I Thank a Fool* (Stevens)
1963   *The V.I.Ps* (*International Hotel*) (Asquith)
1964   *The Yellow Rolls-Royce* (Asquith)

Publications

By de GRUNWALD: articles—

"The Champagne Set—from Two Cities to *The Yellow Rolls-Royce*,"   in *Films and Filming* (London), vol. 11, no. 5, February 1965.
Kine Weekly, no. 2313, 10 May 1969.

On de GRUNWALD: article—

Obituary in *Daily Cinema*, no. 9320, 18 January 1967.

*   *   *

"Tolly," as Anatole de Grunwald was nicknamed, came from a Russian diplomatic and academic family; an air of affable distinction imbued most of his productions. On leaving Cambridge he submitted scenarios to Gaumont-British, who, in crisis, could only offer a year's apprenticeship, unpaid, in their scenario department. Eventually Mario Zampi brought him into the company, and *French without Tears* was the first of many collaborations with its playwright, Terence Rattigan, and its director, Anthony Asquith. A romantic comedy of Englishmen in France, it combined several de Grunwald specialities: "typical Englishness," windows into Europe, adaptations of stage plays, "drawing-room" discussions of issues, and sophisticated dialogue. In a word: personal diplomacy, where politeness may conceal intelligence, and sharp purpose survive due form.

Until he rejoined Two Cities in 1943, his writing jobs were mainly melodramas of Occupied Europe, as the free nations imagined it. In retrospect, *Tomorrow We Live* looks astonishingly like *'Allo, 'Allo*, BBC TV's 1984 Resistance burlesque, thanks to its melodramatist director, George King, and his invincibly English cast. But de Grunwald came into his own while working on *Pimpernel Smith* and *The First of the Few* with Leslie Howard, whose refined Englishness went with a sensitive cosmopolitanism. Howard initiated de Grunwald in the finer points of American tastes, which other English producers too quickly assumed they understood. In *The Demi-Paradise* Laurence Olivier played a Bolshevik engineer who comes to appreciate an apparently overgentrified English industrialist; its two-way sentimentality suited the times. *The Way to the Stars*, about gentle frictions between a "Yank" aircrew and the English, was inspired by the poem which it featured—John Pudney's gently Housemanesque "Johnny-Head-in-the-Air," and promptly became one of the best-loved war films.

Labour Government Minister Ernest Bevin asked de Grunwald to make a film about British justice, and another about British goods. Rattigan's play, *The Winslow Boy*, inspired by the Archer-Shee case, was the first, and *The Yellow Rolls-Royce*, much later, the second. Gradually de Grunwald's interests shifted to his own company, International Screenplays. Its most celebrated film was Thorold Dickinson's *The Queen of Spades*, which also sparked a well-known courtroom battle over credits with playwright Rodney Ackland.

De Grunwald then combined independent productions with executive production of Korda's lower-budget films. His own films included several "cross-section" or "omnibus" films (a then-prevalent genre, with loosely connected tales proceeding episodically or in parallel), like *Now Barrabas Was a Robber . . .* (convicts), *Innocents in Paris* (Englishmen abroad), and *Bond Street* (women associated with a wedding trousseau). The Korda films inclined to "filmed theatre," notably *Home at Seven*, directed by Ralph Richardson. R. C. Sherriff's play, about an amnesiac bank clerk suspected of murder, forefronts a theme hovering over many de Grunwald films. A protagonist who might be mesmerised by circumstances into accepting his plight, gropes for control of his own life—not brashly, American-style, but almost blindly, and by quietly persistent negotiation which elicits modest support from others—by, in short, the diplomacies of everyday life. In *The Winslow Boy* and *Libel* the syndrome centres on courtroom battles. *The Doctor's Dilemma*, from Shaw's play, centre-stages the converse theme, a "superior" individual achieving a just, not exaggerated, estimate of his social rights. *The Queen of Spades* endows with expressionist force the theme of "the trap and the spell." This theme imbues with a little poetry de Grunwald's other-wise routine "little people" subjects.

Soon after Korda's death de Grunwald moved to MGM, where his last three films were mounted with a slap-up lavishness suiting American ostentation. *The V.I.Ps* and *The Yellow Rolls-Royce* re-united him with Rattigan and Asquith, but stressed the self-made super-rich and famous, notably Burton and Taylor as a divorcing couple. De Grunwald reputedly intended the films as rejoinders to kitchen-sink misery, and encouragements to self-help; with Asquith, a very compassionate socialist, directing, their individualism could only be nonabrasive. They are upmarket "omnibus" films, the form suiting an interest in moments of interpersonal decision.

De Grunwald's *cinéma de qualité*, rooted in middle-class middle-brow stage pieces, may have struck younger critics as talkative and unfilmic, and geared to old-fashioned issues and attitudes, but wider audiences shared the director's fascination with personal diplomacy, which is indeed a profound and complex matter.

—Raymond Durgnat

DE LAURENTIIS, Dino

Producer. **Nationality:** Italian. **Born:** Torre Annunciata, 8 August 1919. **Education:** Attended Centro Sperimentale di Cinematografia, Rome. **Military Service:** During World War II. **Family:** Married 1) the actress Silvana Mangano, 1949 (deceased), one son (deceased), three daughters; 2) the producer Martha Schumacher. **Career:** Worked as extra, actor, propman, unit manager, and assistant director while still in school; 1939—produced his first film, *Troppo tardi t'ho conosciuta;* early 1950s—co-founded Ponti-De Laurentiis produc-tion company with Carlo Ponti: dissolved, 1957; built Dinocittà studio in early 1960s: sold to Italian government, early 1970s; resettled in the United States with Embassy Pictures, and, in 1985, De Laurentiis Entertainment Group (resigned as chairman of the board, 1988). **Awards:** Academy Award, for *La strada*, 1954, and *Nights of Cabiria*, 1956. **Address:** De Laurentiis Communications, 8670 Wilshire Boulevard, Beverly Hills, California 90211, U.S.A.

Films as Producer:

1939   *Troppo tardi t'ho conosciuta* (Caraccioli)
1941   *L'amore canta* (Poggioli)
1942   *Margherita fra i tre* (Perilli); *Malombra* (Soldati)
1943   *La donna della montagne* (Castellani)
1946   *Il miserie del Signor Travet* (Soldati); *Il bandito* (Lattuada)

1947   *La figlia del capitano* (Camerini); *Il passatore* (Coletta)
1948   *Riso amaro* (*Bitter Rice*) (de Santis); *Molti sogni per le strade* (*Women Trouble*) (Camerini)
1949   *Il lupo della Sila* (*Lure of the Sila*) (Coletti)
1950   *Il brigante Mussolini* (Camerini); *Napoli milionaria* (de Filippo); *Adamo e Eva* (Mattòli)
1951   *Guardie e ladri* (*Cops and Robbers*) (Steno and Monicelli); *Botta e risposta* (Soldati); *Romanticismo* (Fracassi); *Sensualità* (Fracassi); *Totò a colori* (*Totò in Color*) (Steno)
1952   *Anna* (Lattuada) (co); *Europa '51* (Rossellini); *I tre corsari* (Soldati); *La tratta delle bianche* (*Girls Marked Danger*) (Comencini); *Jolanda, la figlia del Corsaro Nero* (Soldati)
1953   *Anni facili* (*Easy Years*) (Zampa); *Dov'è la libertà?* (Rossellini); *La Lupa* (*The She-Wolf*) (Lattuada)
1954   *Ulisse* (*Ulysses*) (Camerini); **La strada** (Fellini); *La romana* (*Woman of Rome*) (Zampa)
1955   *Il coraggio* (Paolella); *Mambo* (Rossen); *L'oro di Napoli* (*Gold of Naples*) (De Sica); *La donna del fiume* (Soldati); *La bella mugnaia* (*The Miller's Beautiful Wife*) (Camerini)
1956   *Guendalina* (Lattuada); *La banda degli honesti* (Mastrocinque); *Totò, Peppino, e . . . la malafemmina* (Mastrocinque); *War and Peace* (K. Vidor); *La notti di Cabiria* (*Nights of Cabiria; Cabiria*) (Fellini)
1958   *Barrage contre le Pacifique* (*La diga sul Pacifico; The Sea Wall; This Angry Age*) (Clément); *La tempesta* (*Tempest*) (Lattuada); *Fortunella* (de Filippo)
1959   *La grande guerra* (*The Great War*) (Monicelli)
1960   *Giovanna e le altre* (*Five Branded Women*) (Ritt); *Crimen* (*. . . and Suddenly It's Murder*) (Camerini); *Tutti a casa* (*Every-body Go Home!*) (Comencini); *Il gobbo* (*The Hunchback of Rome*) (Lizzani)
1961   *I due nemici* (*The Best of Enemies*) (Hamilton); *Il giudizia universale* (*The Last Judgment*) (De Sica); *Barabba* (*Barabbas*) (Fleischer); *Io amo, tu ami* (*I Love, You Love*) (Blasetti)
1962   *Mafioso* (Lattuada)
1963   *Il boom* (De Sica); *Il diavolo* (*To Bed or Not to Bed*) (Polidoro)
1965   *La Bibbia* (*The Bible . . . in the Beginning*) (Huston)
1966   *Se tutte le donne del mondo* (*Kiss the Girls and Make Them Die*) (Levin and Maiuri)
1967   *Lo straniero* (*The Stranger*) (Visconti); *Le streghe* (*The Witches*) (Visconti and others)
1968   *La sbarco di Anzio* (*Anzio; The Battle for Anzio*) (Coletti and Dmytryk); *Barbarella* (Vadim); *Diabolik* (*Danger: Diabolik*) (Bava); *Fraulein Doktor* (Lattuada); *Banditi a Milano* (*The Violent Four*) (Lizzani); *Romeo and Juliet* (Zeffirelli)
1969   *Una breve stagione* (*A Brief Season*) (Castellani)
1970   *Waterloo* (Bondarchuk); *La spina dorsale del diavolo* (Kennedy)
1971   *The Deserter* (Kennedy)
1972   *Joe Valachi—i segreti di Cosa Nostra* (*The Valachi Papers*) (Kennedy)
1973   *The Stone Killer* (Winner); *Serpico* (Lumet)
1975   *Mandingo* (Fleischer)
1976   *Casanova* (Fellini); *Drum* (Carter); *King Kong* (Guillermin); *Ansikte mot ansikte* (*Face to Face*) (Bergman); *Buffalo Bill and the Indians* (Altman); *The Shootist* (Siegel)
1977   *Das Schlangenei* (*The Serpent's Egg*) (Bergman)

Dino De Laurentiis

1979   *Hurricane* (Troell); *Flash Gordon* (Hodges)

1981   *Ragtime* (Forman); *Conan the Barbarian* (Milius)

1984   *Conan the Destroyer* (Fleischer); *Firestarter* (Lester)

1985   *Year of the Dragon* (Cimino); *Red Sonja* (Fleischer); *Marie* (Donaldson); *Cat's Eye* (Teague); *Silver Bullet* (Attias)

1990   *Desperate Hours* (Cimino)

1991   *Sometimes They Come Back* (McLoughlin—for TV)

1992   *Once upon a Crime* (*Criminals*; *Over My Dead Body*; *Troublemakers*; *Returning Napoleon*) (Levy)

1993   *Body of Evidence* (Edel)

1995   *Solomon & Sheba* (Young—for TV); *Assassins* (Donner) (exec); *Slave of Dreams* (Young—for TV)

1996   *Unforgettable* (Dahl)

1997   *Breakdown* (Mostow)

Films as Executive Producer:

1954   *Un giorno in pretura* (*A Day in Court*) (Steno) (co)

1961   *Maciste contre il vampiro* (*Goliath and the Vampire*) (Gentilomo and Corbucci)

1974   *Death Wish* (Winner)

1975   *Three Days of the Condor* (Pollack)

1977   *La orca* (*Orca*) (E. Visconti); *The White Buffalo* (Lee Thompson)

1978   *The Brink's Job* (Friedkin); *King of the Gypsies* (Pierson)

1983   *The Dead Zone* (Cronenberg)

1984   *The Bounty* (Donaldson)

1985   *Dune* (Lynch)

1986   *Tai Pan* (Duke); *Crimes of the Heart* (Beresford); *Blue Velvet* (Lynch); *Maximum Overdrive* (Stephen King)

Publications

By DE LAURENTIIS: articles—

Bianco e Nero (Rome), no. 7–8, 1961.

Interview (New York), January 1973.

Film Français (Paris), 11 June 1976.

American Film (Washington, D.C.), December/January 1977.

American Cinematographer (Hollywood), January 1977.

Ciné Revue (Paris), 6 January 1977.
Film Comment (New York), January/February 1977.
Ciné Revue (Paris), 15 May 1980.
Stills (London), June/July 1984.

On DE LAURENTIIS: articles—

Films and Filming (London), January 1957.
Film Français (Paris), 15 June 1984.
National Film Theatre Booklet (London), July 1984.
American Film (Washington, D.C.), November 1984.
Film Français (Paris), 28 December 1984.
Cinema Papers (Melbourne), March 1987.
Time, 11 January 1988.
Variety (New York), 24 February 1988.
Variety (New York), 3 February 1992.
Astronomy, November 1994.
Variety (New York), 10 May 1999.

* * *

One of the most colorful, prolific, and successful producers in the contemporary motion picture business, Dino De Laurentiis has proven his entrepreneurial skills time and again, growing from an independent Italian producer into an international conglomerate. His product, from low-budget neorealist works to multimillion dollar spectacles, has always stressed entertainment value, and no matter what the era, he has managed to overcome the exigencies of the fickle motion picture industry to produce consistently crowd-pleasing fare. In the 1950s and 1960s it was the epic; in the 1970s and 1980s a flow of Charles Bronson and Arnold Schwarzenegger action movies, and a series of Stephen King horror shows. De Laurentiis has been a popular media figure with his flamboyant personality and high profile; very much a mogul in the tradition of Samuel Goldwyn, he maintains a strong degree of production value with talented directors, actors, writers, and technicians. What other producer, for example, has produced films by Fellini, Bergman, Rossellini, De Sica, Visconti, Vidor, Huston, Lumet, Forman, Altman, Friedkin, Pollack, Cimino, and Cronenberg, to name but a few? Their films bear the De Laurentiis imprimatur; at the same time, he has shown his fondness for such impersonal, reliable directorial technicians as Richard Fleischer, John Guillermin, and Michael Winner on many of his bread-and-butter pictures.

De Laurentiis attended the Centro Sperimentale di Cinematografia in Rome at the age of 16, then gained practical filmmaking experience in the Italian film industry as an actor, prop man, assistant director, and unit manager. By the age of 20, he had produced his first major film, *L'amore canta*, then organized Realcine in Turin in order to arrange financing for his productions. World War II disrupted his progress, and Realcine was destroyed during the war. De Laurentiis was at the heart of the postwar neorealism movement in Italy, helping to revitalize the Italian cinema. He scored his first international success with Giuseppe de Santis's *Bitter Rice*, a stark drama of the women who work the rice fields of the Po Valley, starring Silvana Mangano (whom De Laurentiis married shortly thereafter). The producer solidified his status when he formed the Ponti-De Laurentiis Production Company with Carlo Ponti in the early 1950s.

Together, De Laurentiis and Ponti produced films by Roberto Rossellini (*Europa '51*), Vittorio De Sica (*Gold of Naples*), and Federico Fellini (*La strada*). *Europa '51*, starring Rossellini's wife Ingrid Bergman, was a bleak disappointment, typical of the Rossellini-Bergman films, but it did give the producers the prestige of a former Hollywood star. They had much better fortune with De Sica and Fellini—*Gold of Naples* is an exceptional anthology of four vignettes dealing with Neapolitan life, while *La strada* has become a classic of world cinema, a beautiful and affecting drama of a loutish circus performer and the young woman he abuses, brilliantly directed by Fellini and acted by Anthony Quinn and Giulietta Massina. *La strada* won De Laurentiis and Ponti an Academy Award for Best Foreign Film, and worldwide recognition as the preeminent producers in Italy.

De Laurentiis realized the box-office appeal of epics during the 1950s, when small-screen television began stealing motion picture audiences. Another advantage was attracting big-name stars to increase the size of their potential audience, and with this in mind Ponti and De Laurentiis produced two gargantuan spectacles, Mario Camerini's *Ulysses*, starring Kirk Douglas and Silvana Mangano, and King Vidor's *War and Peace* with Henry Fonda and Audrey Hepburn. *Ulysses*, indirectly based on Homer's saga of ancient Greece, sold on the strength of Douglas's marquee value; it is a tedious, talky picture. *War and Peace* was more successful, with the Tolstoy novel condensed into two hours and 30 minutes, marked by vivid imagery of the Napoleonic Wars, and King Vidor's eye for character and landscape.

De Laurentiis and Ponti went their separate ways after these films, and De Laurentiis created a new independent production company. *Nights of Cabiria*, a Fellini film about a wistful prostitute (played by Massina), won De Laurentiis another Best Foreign Film Oscar, and later served as the basis for the Broadway musical and film *Sweet Charity*. Although he still produced Italian movies such as *Cabiria* and Mario Monicelli's *The Great War*, a comedy-drama set during World War I, De Laurentiis continued with a policy of U.S.-Italo co-productions, frequently releasing in America through Paramount, filming in Italy with English-speaking stars and directors. In the early 1960s, he constructed a vast studio complex outside Rome and used it as a base of operations for production, as well as leasing it to other independents. In addition to such steamy dramas as Martin Ritt's *Five Branded Women* and René Clément's *This Angry Age*, De Laurentiis made money from epics such as Richard Fleischer's *Barabbas* and particularly from *The Bible . . . in the Beginning*, directed by John Huston with an all-star cast reverently recreating the great tales of the Old Testament. De Laurentiis had another prestigious blockbuster with Franco Zeffirelli's adaptation of *Romeo and Juliet*. For once the Shakespeare tragedy was correctly cast with teenagers in the leads, and the picture struck a chord with the rebellious young generation of the late 1960s.

De Laurentiis moved to America in the early 1970s, after Italy imposed tight tax restrictions on the film industry. Since then his career has expanded rapidly. He continued to support individualistic filmmakers such as Fellini (*Casanova*) and Ingmar Bergman (*Face to Face*, *The Serpent's Egg*), and experienced noble failures with Robert Altman's *Buffalo Bill and the Indians* and William Friedkin's *The Brink's Job*, but began to rely more and more on sure-fire mass appeal material. A series of Charles Bronson action films—*The Valachi Papers*, *The Stone Killer*, and *Death Wish*—were huge moneymakers, and employed a graphic, streetwise realism. Although De Laurentiis still made important films such as Sidney Lumet's *Serpico* (the true story of New York police corruption), Sydney Pollack's CIA thriller *Three Days of the Condor*, Don Siegel's *The Shootist*, (a nostalgic Western and John Wayne's last movie), and Milos Forman's impressive turn-of-the-century epic *Ragtime*, he found it profitable to exploit more popular genres.

For a time in the 1970s, it seemed as though the producer was dedicated to such overwrought kitsch as *Mandingo*, *Orca*, and *Hurricane*. Of these only *Mandingo* was a resounding box-office hit, spawning a sequel, *Drum*. While he had enjoyed a science-fiction success with Roger Vadim's sexy *Barbarella*, De Laurentiis's other sci-fi films, *Flash Gordon* and David Lynch's $50 million *Dune* did not perform well. Much stronger were the *Conan* films; Robert E. Howard's classic sword and sorcery adventures were faithfully transmitted to the screen with Arnold Schwarzenegger in the title role. John Milius directed *Conan the Barbarian;* Richard Fleischer handled the inferior sequel *Conan the Destroyer*, as well as a related adventure, *Red Sonja*. After a well-mounted remake of *The Bounty* with Mel Gibson as Fletcher Christian and Anthony Hopkins as Captain Bligh under Roger Donaldson's direction, De Laurentiis opened new studios in Wilmington, North Carolina. In 1985 he acquired Embassy Pictures and formed De Laurentiis Entertainment Group, a new distribution and production company, making many of its films at the North Carolina studios. Again, there was a familiar pattern to the De Laurentiis product, with prestigious films (*Crimes of the Heart*), epics (*Tai-Pan*), action movies (*Desperate Hours*), and occasionally the offbeat (*Blue Velvet*). Horror pictures have been the mainstay of De Laurentiis's output in recent years, especially the successful Stephen King movies—*The Dead Zone*, *Firestarter*, *Cat's Eye*, *Silver Bullet*, and *Maximum Overdrive*. De Laurentiis has seemingly beat the system by surviving as an independent producer for 50 years, capping his career with a thriving distribution company. It is no surprise. For 50 years, De Laurentiis has been making movies, not just deals, and his prodigious body of work is rare indeed in today's film industry. Few producers possess his sense of daring—he was the only producer to hire Michael Cimino, for example, after the *Heaven's Gate* debacle, and their film, *Year of the Dragon*, helped Cimino back on his feet—or his sense of showmanship, whether promoting the sublime or the banal.

—John A. Gallagher

DELERUE, Georges

Composer. **Nationality:** French. **Born:** Roubaix, 12 March 1925. Studied under Milhaud and Henry Busser at the Paris Conservatory. **Family:** Married Micheline Gautron, 1959; one daughter and one step-daughter. **Career:** Conductor, composer, of orchestra and stage works; 1950—first work for films; also much work for TV; 1984—worked in Hollywood. **Awards:** Academy Award for *A Little Romance*, 1979; Commandeur de l'ordre des Arts et des Lettres. **Died:** In Los Angeles, California, 20 March 1992.

Films as Composer (Shorts):

1950   *Le Mystère du Quai Conti* (Lacoste)
1952   *Les Ingénieurs de la mer* (Renaud)
1953   *''L'Aventure'' et ses Terre-Nuevas* (Renaud); *Au rythme du siècle* (Champetier); *Berre, cité du pétrole* (Champetier); *Avec les pilotes de porte-avions* (Galey)
1954   *La Grande Cité* (Angkor) (Rouy); *Madagascar* (Rouy); *Au pays de Guillaume le Conquérant* (Wronecki); *Regards sur l'Indochine* (Rouy)

1955   *Ame d'argile* (Toublanc-Michel); *La Cité d'argent* (Galey); *Première croisière* (Renaud)
1956   *Tu enfanteras sans douleur* (Fabiani and Dalmas); *La Rue chinoise* (Loriquet); *Marche française* (Fabiani and Vogel); *Le Corbusier, l'architecte du bonheur* (Kast) (co)
1957   *Portrait de la France* (Fabiani); *Morts en vitrine* (Vogel); *Les Surmenés* (Doniol-Valcroze); *Courses d'obstacles* (Berr); *Chères vieilles choses* (Vogel)
1958   *Les Centrales de la mine* (Gillet); *I'Ile de sein* (Vogel); *L'Opéra-Mouffe* (Varda); *Mam' zelle Souris* series (Paviot) (co); *OCIL 1958* (Berr); *Europe* (Biro, Pagliero, and Weber); *La Première Nuit* (Franju); *Du côté de la côte* (Varda); *Le Sourire* (Bourguignon); *Images pour Baudelaire* (Kast); *Zinc laminé et architecture* (Berr); *Le Siècle a soif* (Vogel); *Le Dragon de Komodo* (Bourdelon); *Des ruines et des hommes* (Kast and Lioret)
1959   *La Mer et les jours* (Vogel); *Le Montreur d'ombres* (Bourguignon); *Images des mondes perdus* (Lifschitz); *L'Age des artères* (Berr); *Prélude pour orchestre, voix, et caméra* (Arcady); *L'Etoile de mer* (Bourguignon); *Le Mal des autres* (Logereau); *Entre la terre et le ciel* (Volardebo); *Escale* (Bourguignon); *Une Question d'assurance* (Kast); *Images de Sologne* (de Roubaix); *Le Pont de Tancarville* (Champetier)
1960   *Allumorphoses* (Rhein); *Plaisir de plaire* (Lecomte); *Dorothea Tanning, ou le regard ébloui* (Desvilles); *Des hommes . . . une doctrine* (Catenys); *La Fleuve invisible* (Vilardebo); *Naissance du plutonium* (Hulin); *Diagnostic C.I.V.* (Fabiani); *Le Vaisseau sur la colline* (Marcilly); *Picasso, romancero du picador* (Desvilles); *Architecture et chauffage d'aujourd'hui* (Berr); *Les Etudiants* (Grospierre); *Sahara an IV* (Gerard); *Prenez des gants* (Billon) (co); *Brevet de pilote No. 1: Bleriot* (Galey); *El Gassi* (Heinrich); *Fruits communs* (Forestier); *Des gouts et des couleurs* (Gerard); *Neuf étages tout acier* (Wronecki) (co)
1961   *Les Hommes du pétrole* (Heinrich and Chapot); *Son et Lumière* (Béranger); *Les Guêpes* (Dhuit); *L'Amour existe* (Pialat); *Enez Eussa* (*L'Ile d'Ouessant*) (Page and Gestin); *La Parole est du fleuve* (Vetusto and Oswald); *Horizons nouveaux* (Gillet); *La Balayeur* (Desvilles); *Les Chevaux de Vaugirard* (Grospierre)
1962   *Les Autogrimpeurs* (Languepin); *Les Héros de l'air* (Laurent and Mitry); *Chateaux stop . . . sur la Loire* (Vernick and Desvilles); *Le Champ du possible* (Toublanc-Michel); *On a volé la mer* (Salvy); *La Naturalisée* (Cuniot); *Le Bureau des mariages* (Bellon); *Exemple Etretat* (Lepeuve); *Six petites bougies* (Cotton); *Le Chemin de la terre* (Menezgoz); *Le Rendez-vous d'Asnières* (Gruel); *Un Prince belge de l'Europe: Charles-Joseph de Ligne* (*Prince de Ligne*) (Kupissonoff); *Palissades* (Potignat); *La Contrebasse* (Fasquel); *Le Cousin de Callao* (Pierre); *Exposition Française à Moscou* (Pagliero) (co)
1963   *Route sans sillage* (Menegoz); *Le Monde des marais* (Dhuit); *Le Bosphore* (Pialat); *Le Soir de notre vie* (Valentin); *Corne d'or* (Pialat); *Eves futures* (Baratier)
1964   *Apparences* (Kupissonoff); *A* (Lenica); *La Rose et le sel* (Champion); *L'Impasse d'un matin* (Desvilles); *La Montagne vivante* (Dhuit)
1965   *Le Voix d'orly* (Lachenay); *Vive le Tour!* (Malle and Ertaud); *Le Dernier Refuge* (Puzenat)

1966   *Une Alchimie* (Kupossonoff); *La Revue blanche* (Ferreux); *Le Cours d'une vie* (Desvilles and Darribehaude) (co); *Louis Lecoin* (Desvilles and Darribehaude) (co)

1967   *Paris au temps des cerises: La Commune* (Desvilles and Darribehaude) (co); *Le Temps redonné* (Fabiani and Levi-Alvares) (co)

1968   *Le Violon de Crémone* (Kupissonoff)

1969   *Le Jeu de la puce* (Desvilles)

Films as Composer (Features):

1959   *Le Bel Age* (Kast) (co); **Hiroshima mon amour** (Resnais) (waltz); *Une Fille pour l'été* (Molinaro); *Marche ou crève* (Lautner)

1960   *Classe tous risques* (*The Big Risk*) (Sautet); *Les Jeux de l'amour* (de Broca); "La Femme seule" ep. of *La Française et l'amour* (*Love and the Frenchwoman*) (Le Chanois); **Tirez sur le pianiste** (*Shoot the Piano Player*) (Truffaut); *Arretez les tambours* (Lautner); *La Recreation* (Moreuil); *La Mort de Belle* (Molinaro); *La Morte-Saison de amours* (Kast)

1961   *Le Farceur* (*The Joker*) (de Broca); *L'Amant de cinq jours* (*The Five Day Lover*) (de Broca); *Une Aussi Longue Absence* (*The Long Absence*) (Colpi); *En plein cirage* (Lautner); *La Denonciation* (Don iol-Valcroze); *Le Petit Garçon de l'ascenseur* (Granier-Deferre)

1962   *L'Amour à vingts ans* (*Love at 20*) (Truffaut and Ophüls); *Le Monte-charge* (Bluwal); *Le Crime ne paie pas* (*Crime Does Not Pay*) (Oury); *Le Bonheur est pour demain* (Fabiani) (co); **Jules et Jim** (*Jules and Jim*) (Truffaut); *Jusqu'au bout du monde* (Villiers); *L'Immortelle* (Robbe-Grillet); *Rififi à Tokyo* (Deray); *Vacances portugaises* (Kast); *Cartouche* (de Broca); *L'Affaire Nina B.* (*The Nina B. Affair*) (Siodmak)

1963   *L'Abominable Homme des douanes* (M. Allégret); *Hitler . . . connais pas* (Blier); *Nunca pasa nada* (Bardem); *L'Honorable Stanislas, agent secret* (Dudrumet); *L'Aîné des Ferchaux* (Melville); *Le Journal d'un fou* (Coggio); *Chair de poule* (Duvivier); **Le Mépris** (*Contempt*) (Godard); *L'Homme de Rio* (*That Man from Rio*) (de Broca); *Du grabuge chez les veuves* (Poitrenaud); *French Dressing* (Russell); *Cent Mille Dollars au soleil* (Verneuil); *Muriel* (Resnais) (song)

1964   *Des pissenlits par la racine* (Lautner); *La Peau douce* (*The Soft Skin*) (Truffaut); *The Pumpkin Eater* (Clayton); *Le Gros Coup* (Valere); *L'Amour à la chaîne* (de Givray); *L'Autre Femme* (Villiers); *Laissez tirer les tireurs* (Lefranc); *L'Insoumis* (Cavalier); *Un Monsieur de compagnie* (*Male Companion*) (de Broca); *Lucky Jo* (Deville); *L'Age ingrat* (Grangier); *Mata-Hari, Agent H-21* (Richard); *Le Corniaud* (Oury)

1965   *Los pianos mécanicos* (*The Uninhibited*) (Barden); *Rapture* (Guillermin); *Viva Maria!* (Malle); *Pleins feux sur Stanislas* (Dudrumet); *Les Tribulations d'un chinois en Chine* (*Up to His Ears*) (de Broca); *Le Bestiaire d'amour* (Calderon)

1966   *Le Roi de coeur* (*King of Hearts*) (de Broca); *A Man for All Seasons* (Zinnemann); *La Vingt-cinquième heure* (*The 25th Hour*) (Verneuil); *Le Vieil Homme et l'enfant* (*The Two of Us*) (Berri); *Mona, l'étoile sans nom* (Colpi); *Jeudi on chantera comme dimanche* (de Heusch); *Derrière la fenêtre* (Schmidt) (co)

1967   *Our Mother's House* (Clayton); *Oscar* (Molinaro); *La Petite Vertu* (Korber)

1968   *Les Cracks* (Joffé); *Les Gommes* (Deroisy); *Interlude* (Billington); *Nobody Runs Forever* (*The High Commissioner*) (Thomas); *Le Diable par la queue* (*The Devil by the Tail*) (de Broca)

1969   *Le Cerveau* (Oury); *A Walk with Love and Death* (Huston); *Hibernatus* (Molinaro); *Women in Love* (Russell); *Anne of the Thousand Days* (Jarrott); *Les Caprices de Maria* (*Give Her the Moon*) (de Broca)

1970   **Il conformista** (*The Conformist*) (Bertolucci); *Heureux qui comme Ulysse* (Colpi); *Comptes à rebours* (Pigaut); *The Horsemen* (Frankenheimer)

1971   *La Promesse de l'aube* (*Promise at Dawn*) (Dassin); *Les Aveux les plus doux* (Molinaro); *L'Ingénu* (Carbonnaux); *Deux anglaises et le continent* (*Two English Girls*) (Truffaut); *Mira* (Rademakers)

1972   *Malpertuis* (Kumel); *Chère Louise* (de Broca); *Une Belle Fille comme moi* (*Such a Gorgeous Kid Like Me*) (Truffaut); *Quelque part, quelqu'un* (Bellno)

1973   *The Day of the Jackal* (Zinnemann); *La Nuit américaine* (*Day for Night*) (Truffaut); *Angela* (Van Der Heyde); *The Day of the Dolphins* (Nichols); *La Femme de Jean* (Bellon)

1974   *La Gifle* (*The Slap*) (Pinoteau); *L'Important c'est d'aimer* (*The Most Important Thing: Love*) (Zulawski)

1975   *L'Incorrigible* (de Broca); *Calmos* (Blier); *Jamais plus toujours* (Bellon); *Oublie-moi Mandoline* (Wyn); *Police Python 357* (Corneau)

1977   *Julia* (Zinnemann); *Julie Pot de Colle* (de Broca); *Le Point de mire* (*Focal Point*) (Tramont); *Tendre poulet* (*Dear Inspector*) (de Broca); *Va voir Maman . . . Papa travaille* (*Go See Mother . . . Father Is Working*; *Your Turn, My Turn*) (Leterrier); *Preparez vos mouchoirs* (*Get Out Your Handkerchiefs*) (Blier)

1978   *La Petite Fille en velour bleu* (*The Little Girl in Blue Velvet*) (Bridges); *Le Cavaleur* (*Practice Makes Perfect*) (de Broca)

1979   *L'Amour en fuite* (*Love on the Run*) (Truffaut); *A Little Romance* (Hill); *An Almost Perfect Affair* (Ritchie)

1980   *Le Dernier Métro* (*The Last Metro*) (Truffaut); *Garde a vue* (*Under Suspicion*) (Miller)

1981   *Rich and Famous* (Cukor); *True Confessions* (Grosbard); *Richard's Things* (Harvey); *La Femme d'à côté* (*The Woman Next Door*) (Truffaut); *La Passante du Sans-Souci* (*La Passante*) (Rouffio)

1982   *A Little Sex* (Paltrow); *La Vie continue* (Mizrahi); *The Escape Artist* (Deschanel); *Partners* (Borrows)

1983   *Vivement dimanche!* (*Finally, Sunday!*) (Truffaut); *L'Eté meurtrier* (*One Deadly Summer*) (Becker); *The Black Stallion Returns* (Dalva); *Man, Woman, and Child* (Richards); *Silkwood* (Nichols); *Exposed* (Toback)

1984   *Femmes de personne* (*Nobody's Women*) (Frank); *Love Thy Neighbor* (Bill)

1985   *Agnes of God* (Jewison); *Maxie* (Aaron)

1986   *Conseil de famille* (Costa Gavras); *Crimes of the Heart* (Beresford); *Déscente aux enfers* (Girod); *Mesmerized* (Laughlin); *Platoon* (Stone); *Salvador* (Stone)

1987   *Un Homme amoureux* (*A Man in Love*) (Kurys); *The Lonely Passion of Judith Hearne* (Clayton); *Maid to Order* (Jones); *The Pick-Up Artist* (Toback); *Summer Heat* (Gleason)

1988   *Paris by Night* (Hare); *Beaches* (G. Marshall); *Biloxi Blues* (Nichols); *Chouans!* (de Broca); *Heartbreak Hotel* (Columbus); *The House on Carroll Street* (Yates); *Memories of Me* (Winkler); *Popielusko*; *A Summer Story* (Haggard); *Twins* (Reitman)

1989   *Der Aten*; *Hard to Be a God* (Fleischmann); *Her Alibi* (Beresford); *La Révolution française* (Guillermin); *Seven Minutes* (Meyer); *Steel Magnolias* (Ross); *Strapless* (Hare)

1990   *Mister Johnson* (*Mr. Johnson*) (Beresford); *Cadence* (Sheen); *Joe versus the Volano* (Shanley); *A Show of Force* (Barretto)

1991   *La Reine blanche* (Hubert); *Curly Sue* (Hughes)

1992   *Céline* (Brisseau); *The Josephine Baker Story* (Gibson—for TV)

Films as Music Director:

1954   *La Pointe-Courte* (Varda—short)
1955   **Nuit et brouillard** (Resnais—short)
1956   *Dimanche à Pekin* (Marker—short); *Novembre à Paris* (Reichenbach—short); *Toute la mémoire du monde* (Resnais—short); *Les Sorcières de Salem* (Rouleau—short)
1957   *Le Mystère de l'atelier 15* (Resnais and Heinrich—short); *La Joconde* (Gruel—short); *Lettre de Sibérie* (Marker—short); *Le Chant du styrène* (Resnais—short); *Notre-Dame, cathédrale de Paris* (Franju—short)
1958   *André Masson et les quatre éléments* (Grémillon—short)
1959   *Haim Soutine* (Brabo—short); *Vacances au paradis* (L'Hôte—short)
1961   *L'Ondomane* (Arcady)
1962   *Marquet* (Megret); *Mais où sont les nègres d'antan?* (Martin and Boschet)
1963   *. . . à Valparaiso* (Ivens)

Film as Arranger:

1957   *Si le roi savait ça* (Canaille—short)

Publications

By DELERUE: articles—

Cinéma (Paris), no. 89, 1964.
Ecran (Paris), September 1975.
Cinéma (Paris), July-August 1980.
Soundtrack! (Hollywood), August and Fall 1980.
Soundtrack! (Hollywood), June 1982.
Télérama (Paris), 9–15 March 1985.
Cahiers du Cinéma (Paris), no. 393, March 1987.
Soundtrack! (Hollywood), vol. 7, no. 27, September 1988.
Soundtrack! (Hollywood), vol. 9, no. 33, March 1990.

On DELERUE: articles—

Chaplin (Stockholm), no. 2, 1970.
Films in Review (New York), March 1970.

Film Français (Paris), 2 February 1979.
Soundtrack! (Hollywood), April 1980.
Film Français (Paris), 16 January 1981.
Film Français (Paris), 2 March 1984.
Soundtrack! (Hollywood), vol. 8, nos. 29, 30 and 31, March, June and September 1989.

*   *   *

A former student of the French composer Darius Milhaud, Georges Delerue created some of the most aggressively romantic film music in cinema history. Delerue's many scores include his work for Jean-Luc Godard's *Contempt*, François Truffaut's *Shoot the Piano Player* and *Jules and Jim*, as well as the music for the classic films *Hiroshima mon amour*, *The Pumpkin Eater*, *That Man from Rio*, *King of Hearts*, and *A Man for All Seasons*. Indeed, one of the hallmarks of Delerue's career was his ability to compose excellent scores with remarkable facility and speed, borrowing from himself from time to time, but on the whole creating work of vigor, beauty, and instantly identifiable originality.

As Truffaut's principal scorer, Delerue's music for both the director's early and late films (*Day for Night* and *Love on the Run* being two of the later efforts) became as much a part of the director's vision as Truffaut's lyrical visual compositions and gently elegiac evocations of youthful excess and innocence. Delerue's music is typically lushly orchestrated, with delicately melancholic undertones, and a remarkable sense of both ''place,'' and the irrecoverable past. Delerue's music for *Day for Night* is in many ways the culmination of his long collaboration with the gifted director. In this gently tragic film of the passion that must necessarily go into the making of any movie, Delerue becomes a character in Truffaut's ''movie within the movie,'' as he plays his ''proposed'' score over a long distance telephone hookup for Truffaut's approval. Truffaut listens as he peruses a number of books on film history which have just arrived for him; within 30 seconds, he has approved the score and hung up. Clearly, Truffaut has worked with Delerue for so long on so many projects that there is an unspoken language between them; Truffaut does not need to hear the entire score to know what Delerue is up to. In this scene, both men are professionals, each working under a tight deadline to create a work of art. They have no time for pleasantries, but they need none. The finished film will be a coherent whole, with the music perfectly underscoring Truffaut's visuals, which Delerue has, at that point, not even seen. Delerue's score for *Contempt*, one of Jean-Luc Godard's most deeply felt and somber works, and also a film about the making of a film (albeit more tangentially than *Day for Night*), comprises little more than 15 minutes of music in all. But Delerue's two main themes, with variations, are repeated continually throughout the film by Godard, lending a tragic intensity to the doomed romance of the scriptwriter (Michel Piccoli) and his wife (Brigitte Bardot). Delerue's music also meshes expertly with the film within *Contempt*, Fritz Lang's fragmented attempt to make a film of the *Odyssey* for producer Jack Palance. By the end of the film, Delerue's score has become, through insistent repetition, a metaphor for the inexorable sweep of events which governs the characters' actions. Certainly, both scores are remarkable achievements, and they stand as some of the finest work Delerue ever produced.

One is constantly struck by the fact that Delerue's scores for individual films seem to be part of one large whole. Many of his soundtracks seem, on first hearing, to be quite similar, and certainly his scores repeat a number of themes which are obviously dear to the composer's heart. However, the variations which Delerue created from these themes are unique, and one can no more criticize him for this practice than one could call Bach to task for writing *The Goldberg Variations*. Delerue never tried to be what he was not: he was a romantic, a man with one foot in the early 20th century (Milhaud, Honegger, Auric, Poulenc), and the other foot firmly striding forward.

Although it has not generally been commented upon, my own feeling is that Delerue was most deeply influenced as a composer by the work of Jean-Jacques Grünenwald, the brilliant French composer who wrote the music for Robert Bresson's masterpieces *Les Dames du Bois de Boulogne* (1945) and *Diary of a Country Priest* (1950). Grünenwald's scores are invariably more austere and tragic than Delerue's, but they share a common interest in full orchestral arrangements, and a sense of depth which refuses to be wholly frivolous. There is at times a frank commerciality in some of Delerue's music, as in his perfunctory score for *A Man for All Seasons*, which seems dashed off with little care or concern. In addition to his work in films, Delerue wrote regularly for French TV, the stage, and the ballet. With this considerable output, it is inevitable that some of his work was second-rate, and perhaps this willingness to work on almost any project sometimes mitigated against his wider acceptance as one of the truly great film composers. But although the number of his scores is prodigious, Delerue displayed an unwavering sensibility which was entirely his own, and in his best work he succeeded brilliantly.

—Wheeler Winston Dixon

DELLI COLLI, Tonino

Cinematographer. **Nationality:** Italian. **Born:** Antonio Delli Colli in Rome, 20 November 1923. **Career:** Worked as camera assistant; 1943—first film as cinematographer, *Finalmente sì;* 1951—shot first Italian color film, *Totò a colori.* **Awards:** Silver Ribbon, Italian National Syndicate of Film Journalists, 1965, for *Il vangelo secondo Matteo*, 1968, for *La Cina è vicina*, 1982, for *Tales of Ordinary Madness*, 1985, for *Once Upon a Time in America*, 1987, for *Der Name der Rose*, 1998, for *Marianna Ucrìa*; British Academy Award, Best Cinematography, for *Once Upon a Time in America*, 1985; David di Donatello Award, Best Cinematography, for *Marianna Ucrìa*, 1997, and for *La Vita è bella*, 1998.

Films as Cinematographer:

1943   *Finalmente sì* (Kish); *Il paese senza pace* (*Le Baruffe Chiozzotte*) (Menardi)
1945   *O Sole mio* (Gentilomo) (co)
1946   *Trepidazione* (Frenguelli); *Felicità perduta* (Ratti) (co)
1947   *La lunga manica* (Mantici—short); *Il quirinale* (Mantici—short)
1948   *L'isola di Montecristo* (Sequi); *La città dolente* (Bonnard)
1949   *L'esperienza del cubismo* (Pelligrini—short); *Liszt* (Micucci—short); *La strada* (*Fugitive Lady*) (Salkow); *Nerone e Messalina* (Zeglio)
1950   *Arte e realtà* (Giovannini and Mayer—short); *Alina* (Pastina); *Il voto* (Bonnard); *Io sono il Capataz!* (Simonelli)
1951   *Milano Miliardaria* (Metz, Marchesi, and Girolami); *Totò a colori* (*Totò in Color*) (Steno); *Gli undici moschettieri*

(Saraceni and De Concini); *Jolanda la figlia del corsaro nero* (Soldati); *I tre corsari* (Soldati); *Fratelli d'italia* (Saraceni); *Gioventù alla sbarra* (Cerio)
1953   *Dov'è la libertà?* (Rossellini) (co); *Totò e le donne* (Steno and Monicelli); *Il sacco di Roma* (Cerio); *Ti ho sempre amato* (Costa); *Amori di mezzo secolo* (Pellegrini and others)
1954   *Rosso e nero* (Paolella); *Tradita* (*La notte delle nozze*) (Bonnard); *L'ombra* (Bianchi); *Le signorine della 04* (Franciolini)
1955   *Angelo bianco* (Matarazzo); *L'intrusa* (Matarazzo); *Piccola posta* (Steno); *Accadde al penitenziario* (Bianchi)
1956   *Donatella* (Monicelli); *Una voce, una chitarra, un po' di luna* (Gentilomo); *Poveri ma belli* (*Poor but Beautiful*) (D. Risi); *Buon appetito* (Saraceni—short); *Vecchie amicizie* (Saraceni—short); *Il Nilo di pietra* (Rondi—short)
1957   *Femmine tre volte* (Steno); *La nonna Sabella* (*Grandmother Sabella*) (D. Risi); *Susanna tutta panna* (Steno); *Seven Hills of Rome* (Rowland); *Belle ma povere* (*Beautiful But Poor*) (D. Risi); *Adorabili e bugiarde* (Malasomma)
1958   *Venezia, la luna, e tu* (*Venice, the Moon, and You*) (D. Risi); *Marinai, donne e guai* (Simonelli) (co); *Primo amore* (Camerini); *Poveri milionari* (*Poor Millionaires*) (D. Risi); *L'amico del giaguaro* (Bennati)
1959   *Le cameriere* (Bragaglia); *Il Mondo di notte* (Vanzi)
1960   *Il ladro di Bagdad* (*The Thief of Bagdad*) (Lubin and Vailati)
1961   *Morgan il pirata* (*Morgan the Pirate*) (Zeglio and De Toth); *Le meraviglie di Aladino* (*The Wonders of Aladdin*) (Levin); *Accattone* (Pasolini); *Il nuovi angeli* (Gregoretti) (co); *Le spadaccino di Siena* (*La congiura dei dieci*; *The Swordsman of Siena*) (Perier)
1962   *Mamma Roma* (Pasolini); *La monaca di Monza* (Gallone); *La bella di Lodi* (Missiroli)
1963   "La ricotta" ep. of *Rogopag* (Pasolini); *El verdugo* (Berlanga); "Naples" ep. of *Les Plus Belles Escroqueries du monde* (Gregoretti); "Amore e alfabeto" and "Amore e morte" eps. of *Amore in quattro dimensioni* (Mida and Guerrini)
1964   *Liolà* (Blasetti) (co); "Il generale" ep. of *Amore pericolosi* (Giannetti); ***Il vangelo secondo Matteo*** (*The Gospel According to St. Matthew*) (Pasolini); "La doccia" ep. of *Extraconiugale* (Franciosa); *Comizi d'amore* (Pasolini) (co)
1965   *Le soldatesse* (*The Camp Followers*) (Zurlini); *Les Sultans* (Delannoy); *La mandragola* (*The Love Root*) (Lattuada); "Le Monstre" and "Mourir pour vivre" eps. of *Le Lit à deux places* (Puccini)
1966   *Andremo in città* (N. Risi); *Uccellacci e uccellini* (*The Hawks and the Sparrows*) (Pasolini) (co); ***Il buono, il brutto, il cattivo*** (*The Good, the Bad, and the Ugly*) (Leone)
1967   *La Cina è vicina* (Bellocchio); *Questi fantasmi* (Castellani); "Che cosa sono le nuvole?" ep. of *Capriccio all'italiana* (Pasolini)
1968   "William Wilson" ep. of *Histoires extraordinaires* (*Spirits of the Dead*) (Malle); *Il giorno della civetta* (Damiani); *Niente rose per OSS 177* (Cerrato and Desagnat); *C'era una volta il west* (*Once upon a Time in the West*) (Leone); *Metti, una sera a cena* (Patroni Griffi)
1969   *Porcile* (*Pigsty*) (Pasolini) (co); *Rosolino Paterno, soldato...* (Loy)
1970   *Pussycat, Pussycat, I Love You* (Amateau)
1971   *Il Decamerone* (*The Decameron*) (Pasolini); *Cometogether* (Swimmer); *Homo eroticus* (Vicario)

1972   *I racconti di Canterbury* (*The Canterbury Tales*) (Pasolini); *Los amigos* (*Deaf Smith and Johnny Ears*) (Cavara); *Pilgrimage* (Montresor); *Un uomo da rispettare* (*A Man to Respect*; *The Master Touch*; *Hearts and Minds*) (Lupo)

1973   *Storie scellarate* (Citti); *Paolo il caldo* (Vicario); *Peccato veniale* (Samperi); *Lacombe Lucien* (Malle)

1974   *Mio Dio, come sono caduta in basso!* (Comencini)

1975   *Salo o le 120 giornate di Sodoma* (*Salo—The 120 Days of Sodom*) (Pasolini); *Pasqualino Settebellezza* (*Seven Beauties*) (Wertmüller)

1976   *Caro Michele* (Monicelli); *Anima persa* (*Lost Soul*) (D. Risi)

1977   *I nuovi mostri* (*Viva Italia*) (Monicelli); *Un Taxi mauve* (*The Purple Taxi*) (Boisset)

1978   *Primo amore* (*First Love*) (D. Risi); *Viaggio con Anita* (*Travels with Anita*) (Monicelli)

1979   *Caro Papà* (*Dear Father*) (D. Risi); *Revenge* (Wertmüller)

1980   *Macabro* (*Macabre*) (Bava)

1981   ''Armando's Notebook'' ep. of *Sunday Lovers* (D. Risi); *Storie di ordinaria follia* (*Stories of Ordinary Madness*) (Ferreri)

1983   *Zeder: Voices from Darkness* (Avati); *Trenchcoat* (Tuchner)

1984   ***Once upon a Time in America*** (Leone); *Il futore e donna* (*The Future Is a Woman*) (Ferreri)

1986   *Ginger e Fred* (Fellini); *The Name of the Rose* (Annaud)

1987   *Intervista* (*The Interview*) (Fellini)

1989   *Stradivari* (Battiato)

1990   *Die Ruckkehr* (*L'Africana*) (von Trotta); *Le voce della luna* (*The Voice of the Moon*) (Fellini)

1991   *Una storia semplice* (*A Simple Story*) (Greco); *Specialmente la domenica* (*Especially on Sunday*) (Tornatore and others)

1992   *Bitter Moon* (Polanski)

1993   *La Soif de l'or* (*The Thirst for Gold*) (Oury)

1994   *Death and the Maiden* (Polanski)

1995   *Facciamo paradiso* (Monicelli)

1996   *Marianna Ucrìa* (Faenza)

1997   *La Vita è bella* (*Life is Beautiful*) (Benigni)

Film as Camera Assistant:

1940   *La fanciulla di portici* (Bonnard)

Publications

By DELLI COLLI: articles—

Rivista del Cinematografo (Rome), July 1965.
Bianco e Nero (Rome), April/June 1986.

On DELLI COLLI: articles—

Focus on Film (London), no. 13, 1973.
Delli Colli, Laura, in *Les métiers du cinéma*, Paris, 1986.
Kauffmann, Stanley, in *New Republic*, 7 December 1992.

*　　*　　*

''Metta, metta, Tonino
il cinqanta, non abbia paura

che le luce sfondi—faciamo
questo carrello contro natura!''

Tonino Delli Colli is probably the only cinematographer who has had a poem addressed to him. A self-avowedly ''instinctive'' practitioner of his craft, Delli Colli holds a crucial position between genre cinema at its most dazzlingly ambitious (in the hands of Sergio Leone) and art cinema as embodied in the intensely innovative and challenging films of Pier Paolo Pasolini, author of the above verse.

It is an impossible task to find a visual signature common to Delli Colli's work with Rossellini, Louis Malle, Dino Risi, Bellocchio, or Federico Fellini, and that is without taking into account his strictly generic output—a string of films made with the Italian comic star Totò. And he is indeed the last person to wish such a common denominator to be apparent.

His approach is less to impose a common visual style upon a number of disparate projects than to apply an identical strategy. Thus the needs and wishes of the director are identified as precisely as possible and reconciled as closely as possible with the constraints and opportunities offered by a particular location (Delli Colli prefers location shooting) or set. Also to be taken into account are the needs of the performers—whether established stars (such as Magnani, who preferred to be lit a certain way, or Totò, whose vision, towards the end of his life, was failing) or nonprofessionals unused to the camera. Never a cinephile, Delli Colli's fascination has always been, and remains with the basic medium of photography—light, and its varying qualities depending on time, weather, geography and the subtle balances required between natural and artificial light.

Working on *Accattone* with Pasolini signaled a move away from genre cinema which Delli Colli has sustained up to the present, but it was not something which changed his working methods. He has remained pragmatic, approaching each project as it comes, with a precise and increasingly practiced eye for nuances in the quality of light and the possibilities film offers for going ''contro natura.''

Delli Colli's response to Pasolini's poetic demands is characteristically phlegmatic. Pasolini, he has said, could write of a ''cinquanta'' (a kind of lens), but he would not know what to do with one. On *Accattone* Delli Colli confronted a director innocent of any technical knowledge of film, but with a crystal clear idea of how he wanted the finished film to look. Delli Colli was shown Chaplin's *City Lights* and Dreyer's *Joan of Arc* (later reference points were to be early Italian religious painters and, for *Mamma Roma*, the paintings of Mantegna). To achieve the film's grainy look, Delli Colli took as inspiration such ''yellow press'' scandal sheets as *Lo Specchio* and shot on the then rarely-used Ferrania film.

In Sergio Leone he confronted someone whose starting point was also genre cinema and who had also had experience working as an assistant director but whose demands were, like Pasolini's, in a sense transgressive. Like Pasolini, Leone is concerned about rewriting myths and constructing a kind of prehistoric world. Behind it all is a very different dynamic, rhetorical and romantic and predicated on Leone's obsessive need to extend the dramatic moment far beyond its ''natural'' duration. Thus Delli Colli was able to bring into play an avidly mobile camera, ritualistically circling and tracking shots, zooms, and large close-ups, all of which tied the viewer into a dramatic space quite other than that of everyday experience.

Ideally, he has said, a cinematographer and a director must work as one, each automatically knowing what the other wants and can do, otherwise one works on a solely technical register. And for the best directors, he has said, it is impossible to make a bad shot; their knowledge of camera angle and framing will be so precise.

If there are times when one might wish for a different cinematic style, harsher, say for Malle's *Lacombe Lucien*, they are outweighed by wonder at the extraordinary breadth of range encompassed by Delli Colli's work—the sharply evocative images of *The Gospel According to St. Matthew*, the extraordinary sense of another time and place in *The Decameron* or *Oedipus*, the potent meld of romance and history in Leone's Westerns, the acerbic poetry of *Accattone* matching exquisitely the rawness of the nonprofessional players, the sterility of *Salo* and, more recently, the parade of Fellinian leitmotifs in *The Voice of the Moon*.

—Verina Glaessner

de ROCHEMONT, Louis

Producer. **Nationality:** American. **Born:** Louis Clark de Rochemont in Chelsea, Massachusetts, 13 January 1899. **Education:** Attended Massachusetts Institute of Technology, Cambridge; Naval Aviation School; Harvard Naval Cadet School. **Military Service:** British Military Intelligence, 1916–17; officer in U.S. Navy, 1917–23. **Family:** Married Virginia Shaler, 1929, son: the filmmaker Louis de Rochemont III, daughter: Virginia. **Career:** 1923–29—cameraman for International and for Pathé News; director of short-film program, 20th Century-Fox (*Adventures of a Newsreel Cameraman* and *Magic Carpets of Movietone* series); 1933—created (with Roy E. Larsen) *The March of Time* series of newsreels; 1940—first feature; 1943–46—producer, 20th Century-Fox; then founder, Louis de Rochemont Associates: producer of *The Earth and Its Peoples* educational series, and made films in Cinerama and other wide-screen processes. **Awards:** Special Academy Award, for *The March of Time*, 1936. **Died:** 23 December 1978.

Films as Producer:

1933–43   *The March of Time* (series)
1933   *The Cry of the World* (doc)
1934   *The First World War* (doc)
1940   *The Ramparts We Watch* (+ d—doc)
1942   *We Are the Marines* (+ d—doc)
1944   *The Fighting Lady* (Steichen) (+ ed)
1945   *The House on 92nd Street* (Hathaway)
1947   *13 Rue Madeleine* (Hathaway); *Boomerang!* (Kazan)
1949   *Lost Boundaries* (Werker)
1951   *The Whistle at Eaton Falls* (Siodmak)
1952   *Walk East on Beacon* (Werker)
1953   *Martin Luther* (Pichel)
1954   *Animal Farm* (Halas and Batchelor—animation)
1955   *Cinerama Holiday*
1958   *Windjammer* (L. de Rochemont III)
1960   *Man on a String* (de Toth)
1961   *The Roman Spring of Mrs. Stone* (Quintero)

Publications

By de ROCHEMONT: article—

Sight and Sound (London), Spring 1941.

On de ROCHEMONT: book—

Fielding, Raymond, *The March of Time 1935–1951*, New York, 1978.

On de ROCHEMONT: articles—

Screen and Audience, London, 1947.
Lightman, Herb A., "*13 Rue Madeleine*: Documentary Style in the Photoplay," in *American Cinematographer* (Hollywood), March 1947.
Current Biography, New York, 1949.
Lyons, Eugene, "Louis de Rochemont, Maverick of the Movies," in *Reader's Digest* (Pleasantville, New York), July 1949.
Gehman, Richard B., in *Theatre Arts* (New York), October 1951.
Films in Review (New York), May 1958.
"A Black Filmmaker Remembers Louis de Rochemont," in *Film Library Quarterly* (New York), vol. 12, no. 4, 1979.
Culbert, David, "A Documentary Note on Wilson: Hollywood Propaganda for World Peace," in *Historical Journal of Film, Radio, and Television* (Abingdon), vol. 3, no. 2, 1983.
Lafferty, William, "A Reappraisal of the Semi-Documentary in Hollywood 1945–1948," in *Velvet Light Trap* (Madison, Wisconsin), Summer 1983.
Dunlap, Donald, "*The March of Time* and *The Ramparts We Watch* (1940)," in *Historical Journal of Film, Radio, and Television* (Abingdon), vol. 5, no. 2, 1985.
Sakmyster, Thomas, "Nazi Documentaries of Intimidation: *Feldzug in Polen* (1940), *Feuertaufe* (1940) and *Sieg im Westen* (1941)," in *Historical Journal of Film, Radio and Television* (Abingdon), October 1996.

*   *   *

Louis de Rochemont is best remembered today for his involvement with Roy Larsen in producing *Time* magazine's innovative and popular newsreel *The March of Time* and for pioneering in a postwar Hollywood subgenre, the so-called "semidocumentary." Generally overlooked, however, is de Rochemont's far-ranging work in the early days of American newsreels, his early embracing of the compilation documentary, his later activity in adapting new wide-screen processes to the documentary mode, and his extensive educational film production outside the Hollywood industry.

According to Raymond Fielding, de Rochemont's passion for journalism had its origin in his enthusiasm for Richard Harding Davis's novel *Gallegher*, in which the title character is a teenaged reporter dedicated to "scoops." During his youth de Rochemont emulated Gallegher, prowling his hometown in Massachusetts for news, and, when news was not forthcoming, manufacturing it. As a freelance motion picture cameraman during his high school days, de Rochemont regularly supplied regional movie theaters with short films of local happenings, and in 1916 achieved some renown when he successfully coaxed a Maine sheriff to "reenact" his jailing of a suspected German saboteur. According to Fielding, it is from this initial "re-creation" that evolved de Rochemont's sustained belief

Louis de Rochemont

that, just as a reporter and editor can re-create events with words, so can the newsreel cameraman re-create those events in images. While serving with Pathé News as an assistant newsreel editor, he reportedly expressed to a colleague his dissatisfaction with the current form of newsreels—claiming that they just depicted an event, never explaining its causes or what it may portend—and vowed to "someday revolutionize the newsreel." By 1935 de Rochemont received the opportunity to do just that.

After his stint in the navy (during which he still pursued freelance newsreel photography) and with various newsreel concerns, particularly Fox Movietone, de Rochemont in 1933 launched his *March of the Years* series of historical reenactments, which he admitted had been inspired by *Time*'s radio program *The March of Time*. The radio program anticipated the newsreel. The program employed a prodigious coterie of actors who mimicked the voices of current newsmakers, re-creating their statements to the press, and, if no statements had been recorded, voicing a writer's interpretations of what those statements might have been. Roy Larsen at *Time* determined that de Rochemont would be the ideal person to take *The March of Time* to the screen, based upon his extensive newsreel experience at Fox Movietone and his demonstrated penchant for filmic re-creation.

Today, such re-creation seems an atavistic and even dishonest approach to the news. Nevertheless, it must be realized that this is solely from a contemporary viewpoint within a society permeated by instantaneous telecommunications technology; 60 years ago, lacking the technology, audiences and producers alike generally accepted John Grierson's dictum that the essence of cinematic truth was "the creative interpretation of actuality." For the next eight years, de Rochemont oversaw the production of the newsreel, dubbed "a new kind of pictorial journalism" by *Time*. Almost from the beginning, the newsreel found itself involved in controversy: although the impersonations by actors of famous persons (such as President Roosevelt) frequently annoyed those so depicted, it was the series' increasing political trenchancy that caused the most furor. Like the opinions voiced about Charles Foster Kane in the *March of Time* imitation at the beginning of *Citizen Kane*, Time-Life's newsreel similarly suffered schizoid assessments of its political bent. Despite its progressively more pointed depictions of Hitler, the American left claimed the series was an agent of fascism, while the conservative minions of Henry Luce at *Time* regarded it as distinctly left-wing, a sentiment shared within areas of American political life. Throughout its run, the series was plagued by the capriciousness of local and state censor boards, and at times caused such controversy that the Hays Office considered censoring it before release.

Despite whatever political imbroglios *The March of Time* precipitated, the political leanings of de Rochemont, an intensely private man, were never fully manifest; nevertheless, virtually all of his film work was marked by a general liberalism in social matters. While at Fox in 1933, he helped edit Laurence Stalling's compilation documentary *The First World War*, a film using wartime footage. Perhaps based upon this experience, the same year de Rochemont independently produced his compilation documentary *The Cry of the World*, described by Fielding as ''a powerful indictment of war and oppression,'' a film that anticipated many of the formal compilation techniques which such filmmakers as Emil de Antonia would use years later. By 1938, de Rochemont, with Larsen's backing, produced a feature-length film, *The Ramparts We Watch*, which sought to explicate for audiences the international tensions of the day by presenting a dramatic narrative depicting the causes of the Great War 25 years earlier. In its conception, the use of nonactors and location shooting to point up social concerns, the film mirrored contemporary production in England (such as Jennings's *Fires Were Started*) and prefigured many aspects of postwar Italian neorealism. In terms of de Rochemont's career, it also prefigured his success seven years later as a producer of semidocumentaries.

In 1943 de Rochemont left *The March of Time*, apparently because his often idiosyncratic and expensive filmmaking techniques, as well as his undistinguished managerial abilities, increasingly riled his corporate superiors, an aspect of his professional nature that would continue to plague his later dealings with the studios. In August 1943 Darryl F. Zanuck hired de Rochemont as a producer, apparently intending him to work on Twentieth Century-Fox's bio-film of Woodrow Wilson, a statesman whose concern with international peace reflected that of de Rochemont's *Cry of the World* and *The Ramparts We Watch*. Instead de Rochemont found himself producing Edward Steichen and William Wyler's naval documentary *The Fighting Lady*, an assignment for which de Rochemont's documentary work and naval background were perfectly suited. By 1945, though, de Rochemont had begun production of *The House on 92nd Street*, the first of three features produced by de Rochemont for Zanuck which would ultimately become known as semidocumentaries. The origin of the term ''semidocumentary'' is unclear, although it quickly found common usage in the Hollywood trade press; de Rochemont himself thought the term ''documentary'' to be ''the kiss of death'' at the box office, it signifying to audiences the type of film produced by the government during the 1930s, what he called ''arty avant-garde'' films such as *The Plow that Broke the Plains*, of which de Rochemont, apparently, was not too fond.

De Rochemont preferred the term ''pictorial journalism'' to describe his features, the same term that *Time* had used to describe *The March of Time*. All of de Rochemont's features during this period followed a set production philosophy: all were based upon actual incidents involving some aspects of law enforcement or detection, filmed on location, and, to an extent unheard of in Hollywood, all made extensive use of nonprofessional actors.

Some critics, such as Paul Schrader, have attributed Hollywood's postwar appropriation of de Rochemont's filmmaking technique to audiences' desire for a more realistic depiction of the world, conditioned particularly by society's wartime experience. This may be, but other more tangible reasons explain the appearance of the semidocumentary. De Rochemont's brand of filmmaking not only reflected that of the Italian neorealist films then finding quick popular

and critical acceptance in the United States, but the particular economies of production of such filmmaking were highly attractive to a Hollywood film industry beleaguered by studio labor strife, escalating production costs, and a diminishing box office. Based upon relatively inexpensive properties (generally magazine articles), using relatively unknown low-priced talent, and shot on locations far away from Hollywood's labor demands, de Rochemont's films for Zanuck found a receptive audience while well suited to Hollywood's stringent postwar cost-cutting. After two years, however, de Rochemont's general dislike of the Hollywood system and resistance to Zanuck's supervision led to his departure from Twentieth Century-Fox. According to de Rochemont, Zanuck insisted that he use ''star'' names (such as James Cagney in *13 Rue Madeleine*) over de Rochemont's objections (the producer believing that such star presences deflected audiences' attention from the story and the films' realistic aura). De Rochemont and Zanuck feuded over publicity and screen credits, and de Rochemont left when Zanuck began charging de Rochemont's productions with studio overheads, despite none of his films ever using the Fox lot. He went to MGM in 1948, but soon left when it balked at producing *Lost Boundaries*, dealing with what was at the time a highly controversial racial theme.

To produce *Lost Boundaries*, de Rochemont again entered independent production, bankrolling much of the film himself. The film proved a somewhat notorious critical and financial success, being censored in some parts of the country, but it gained de Rochemont a contract with Columbia which assured him a high degree of creative autonomy while guaranteeing production financing, leading to two more films in the semidocumentary vein: *The Whistle at Eaton Falls*, dealing with both sides of a contemporary labor problem, and *Walk East on Beacon*, a reprise of de Rochemont's earlier interest in factual espionage films.

After his Columbia productions, both de Rochemont's Hollywood career and the semidocumentary vogue went into decline, as television news and French and Canadian experiments with *cinéma vérité* began to alter audiences' perceptions of what constituted cinematic reality. De Rochemont produced an historical re-creation of Martin Luther's life, an American-German co-production shot in Europe—a project apparently initiated by his former *March of Time* colleague Lothar Wolff. After handling the release of John Halas and Joy Batchelor's animated feature *Animal Farm*, de Rochemont entered Cinerama production, a multiple-camera widescreen system. De Rochemont had always maintained a keen interest in technological innovation in film since his days at *Time*, perhaps explaining his exploration of the potential of Cinerama. He produced the second Cinerama film, *Cinerama Holiday*; ostensibly the story of two couples, one American and one European, who explore the other's homeland; the film was actually a thinly veiled pretense for reproducing glorious American and European landscapes through Cinerama. Using Cinemiracle, a rival process acquired by Cinerama, de Rochemont produced *Windjammer* with his son Louis III directing; as the slightly fictionalized depiction of a Norwegian training ship's visit to the United States, the film was slightly reminiscent of de Rochemont's early semidocumentaries.

The early 1960s saw de Rochemont's last two feature films. In 1960 he produced a film strongly evocative of his first Twentieth Century-Fox productions, a generally well-received espionage drama filmed on location, *Man on a String*; the next year de Rochemont undertook a radically different project for him, producing José Quintero's screen version of Tennessee Williams's novella *The Roman Spring of Mrs. Stone*, which, despite its impressive cast, received but lukewarm critical acclaim. After that film, de Rochemont would never produce a feature film again. As a newsreel innovator in the 1930s and producer of distinctive Hollywood features in the 1940s, features that broke away from established Hollywood practice in both production technique and, especially with *Lost Boundaries*, content, de Rochemont achieved high visibility both within and without the motion picture industry. By the 1950s, however, de Rochemont's particular brand of "pictorial journalism," in light of new trends in documentary production and television news, had lost its luster. Although de Rochemont did not remain active in feature film production, he did remain active in industrial and educational film production: until his death Louis de Rochemont Associates was a prolific producer of nontheatrical films, ranging from foreign language educational films (the 143-part *Nous Parlons Français*) to basketball instructional films to a series of informational and promotional films for the American Medical Association.

—William Lafferty

DEUTSCH, Adolph

Composer and Arranger. **Nationality:** American. **Born:** London, England, 20 October 1897; emigrated to the United States with his parents, 1910. **Education:** Studied composition and piano with Clara Wieck Schumann, Royal Academy of Music, London, 1906–10. **Family:** Married 1) Hermina Selz, one son; 2) Dianne Axzelle. **Career:** Worked in accessories department, Ford Motor Company, Buffalo; music arranger with Ager Yeller and Bornstein and with Henry Busse and Arnold Johnson, both in New York, in the 1920s; with Paul Ash, Chicago Oriental Theatre, New York, and with Paramount Studios, Long Island; 1931—first film as music director, *The Smiling Lieutenant*; 1935–37—radio work with Paul Whiteman's Music Hall; 1937–46—musical director and composer, Warner Brothers, and then worked with MGM, 1948–62. **Awards:** Academy Award for *Annie Get Your Gun*, 1950; *Seven Brides for Seven Brothers*, 1954; *Oklahoma!*, 1955. **Died:** In Palm Desert, California, 1 January 1980.

Films as Composer or Arranger:

1936   *Mr. Deeds Goes to Town* (Capra)
1937   *Tovarich* (Litvak); *Submarine D-1* (Bacon); *They Won't Forget* (LeRoy); *The Great Garrick* (Whale); *Mr. Dodd Takes the Air* (Green); *Swing Your Lady* (Enright)
1938   *Fools for Scandal* (LeRoy); *Racket Busters* (Bacon); *Valley of the Giants* (Keighley) (co); *Broadway Musketeers* (Farrow); *Heart of the North* (Seiler); *Four's a Crowd* (Curtiz); *Cowboy from Brooklyn* (Bacon)
1939   *Angels Wash Their Faces* (Enright); *Off the Record* (Flood); *The Kid from Kokomo* (Seiler); *Indianapolis Speedway* (Bacon); *Espionage Agent* (Bacon); *The Oklahoma Kid* (Bacon) (co); *Gone with the Wind* (Fleming) (co)
1940   *They Drive by Night* (*The Road to Frisco*) (Walsh); *Torrid Zone* (Keighley); *Castle on the Hudson* (*Years Without Days*) (Litvak); *Saturday's Children* (V. Sherman); *East of the River* (Green); *Flowing Gold* (Green); *The Fighting 69th* (Keighley); *Three Cheers for the Irish* (Bacon); *Tugboat Annie Sails Again* (Seiler)
1941   ***The Maltese Falcon*** (Huston); ***High Sierra*** (Walsh); *The Great Mr. Nobody* (Stoloff); *Kisses for Breakfast* (Seiler); *Underground* (V. Sherman); *Manpower* (Walsh); *Singapore Woman* (Negulesco)
1942   *Across the Pacific* (Huston); *All Through the Night* (V. Sherman); *Juke Girl* (Bernhardt); *The Big Shot* (Seiler); *Lucky Jordan* (Tuttle); *Larceny* (Bacon); *You Can't Escape* (Graham); *George Washington Slept Here* (Keighley)
1943   *Action in the North Atlantic* (Bacon); *Nothern Pursuit* (Walsh)
1944   *Uncertain Glory* (Walsh); *The Doughgirls* (Kern)
1945   *The Mask of Dimitrios* (Negulesco); *Danger Signal* (Florey); *Escape in the Desert* (Blatt)
1946   *Nobody Lives Forever* (Negulesco); *Three Strangers* (Negulesco); *Shadow of a Woman* (Santley)
1947   *Blaze of Noon* (Farrow); *Ramrod* (de Toth)
1948   *Whispering Smith* (Fenton); *Julia Misbehaves* (Conway)
1949   *Intruder in the Dust* (Brown); *Little Women* (LeRoy); *The Stratton Story* (Wood)
1950   *Mrs. O'Malley and Mr. Malone* (Taurog); *The Big Hangover* (Krasna); *Father of the Bride* (Minnelli); *Stars in My Crown* (Tourneur); *Pagan Love Song* (Alton); *The Yellow Cab Man* (Donohue)
1951   *Soldiers Three* (Garnett)
1952   *The Belle of New York* (Walters)
1953   *Torch Song* (Walters); ***The Band Wagon*** (Minnelli)
1954   *Seven Brides for Seven Brothers* (Donen) (co); *The Long, Long Trailer* (Minnelli); *Deep in My Heart* (Donen)
1955   *Oklahoma!* (Zinnemann); *Interrupted Melody* (Bernhardt); *Battle of Gettysburg* (Hoggman—doc)
1956   *Tea and Sympathy* (Minnelli); *The Rack* (Laven)
1957   *Funny Face* (Donen); *Les Girls* (Cukor)
1958   *The Matchmaker* (Anthony)
1959   ***Some Like It Hot*** (Wilder)
1960   ***The Apartment*** (Wilder)
1961   *Go Naked in the World* (MacDougall)

Films as Music Director:

1931   *The Smiling Lieutenant* (Lubitsch)
1948   *Take Me Out to the Ball Game* (Berkeley)
1950   *Annie Get Your Gun* (Sidney) (co)
1951   *Show Boat* (Sidney) (co)
1952   *Million Dollar Mermaid* (LeRoy)

Publications

By DEUTSCH: articles—

"Collaboration Between the Screen Writer and the Composer," in *Proceedings of the Writers' Congress* (Berkeley, California), 1944.
"Three Strangers" in *Hollywood Quarterly*, January 1946.

On DEUTSCH: articles—

Rivista del Cinematografo (Rome), May 1980.
The Annual Obituary 1980, New York, 1981.

*   *   *

Adolph Deutsch was one of those great unrecognized talents who collectively worked behind the scenes to help create the great MGM musicals of the 1950s. Deutsch worked on nearly all of them. He was nominated for Academy Awards for scoring *The Band Wagon* from Arthur Freed's unit, and he won Oscars for his work on two minor musical efforts, *Annie Get Your Gun* and *Oklahoma!*, as well as for *Seven Brides for Seven Brothers*.

Deutsch's career in music divides neatly into three parts. This classically trained musician earned his spurs as an arranger in New York, serving an apprenticeship on many Broadway shows, helping such composers as Irving Berlin, Richard Rogers, and George Gershwin. Like others in the 1930s, he also dabbled, because the money was so good, in the fledgling radio industry. Indeed he toiled full-time on *Paul Whiteman's Music Hall,* a network radio program, for three years before moving to even bigger money in Hollywood.

Deutsch moved to California in the late 1930s to work for Warner Brothers, and scored such films as *High Sierra*, *The Maltese Falcon*, and *Action in the North Atlantic*. But probably his greatest fame within the Hollywood community came with a "loan out" in 1939 when he helped Max Steiner, a fellow Warner contract musician, with the three-hour score for *Gone with the Wind*.

After World War II Deutsch moved to MGM and became part of the team under producer Arthur Freed which created the greatest set of musicals in movie history. He also scored non-musical films such as *Father of the Bride* and *The Stratton Story*. Like many of the great "unknown" musicians of his era, Deutsch understood that his function was to help, not star in the movie, "A film musician is like a mortician—he can't bring the body back to life but he's expected to make it look better." Deutsch was part of an MGM music department which many critics argue may never have been equalled.

—Douglas Gomery

DIAMOND, I. A. L.

Writer and Producer. **Nationality:** American. **Born:** Itek Dommnici, Romania, 7 June 1920; emigrated to the United States, 1929. **Education:** Attended Boys High School, Brooklyn, New York; Columbia University, New York, 1938–41. **Family:** Married Barbara Bentley, 1945. **Career:** 1941–43—junior writer at Paramount; 1944—first film as writer, *Murder in the Blue Room*; 1951–55—writer for 20th Century-Fox; 1955—began collaboration with Billy Wilder; 1959—began producing his own films. **Awards:** Writers Guild Award for *Love in the Afternoon*, 1957; *Some Like It Hot*, 1959; *The Apartment*, 1960 (also Academy Award and New York Film Critics Award); Writers Guild Laurel Award, 1979. **Died:** In Beverly Hills, California, 21 April 1988.

I. A. L. Diamond

Films as Writer:

1944   *Murder in the Blue Room* (Goodwins)
1946   *Never Say Goodbye* (Kern); *Two Guys from Milwaukee* (*Royal Flush*) (Butler); *Love and Learn* (de Cordova)
1947   *Always Together* (de Cordova)
1948   *Romance on the High Seas* (*It's Magic*) (Curtiz) (additional dialogue); *Two Guys from Texas* (*Two Texas Knights*) (Butler)
1949   *The Girl from Jones Beach* (Godfrey); *It's a Great Feeling* (Butler) (story)
1951   *Love Nest* (Newman); *Let's Make It Legal* (Sale)
1952   *Monkey Business* (Hawks); *Something for the Birds* (Wise)
1956   *That Certain Feeling* (Panama and Frank)
1957   *Love in the Afternoon* (Wilder)
1958   *Merry Andrew* (Kidd)

Films as Writer and Co-associate Producer:

1959   ***Some Like It Hot*** (Wilder)
1960   ***The Apartment*** (Wilder)
1961   *One, Two, Three* (Wilder)
1963   *Irma La Douce* (Wilder)
1964   *Kiss Me, Stupid* (Wilder)
1966   *The Fortune Cookie* (*Meet Whiplash Willie*) (Wilder)
1969   *Cactus Flower* (Saks) (sc only)
1970   *The Private Life of Sherlock Holmes* (Wilder)

1972   *Avanti!* (Wilder) (co-sc)
1974   *The Front Page* (Wilder) (co-sc)
1978   *Fedora* (Wilder)
1981   *Buddy Buddy* (Wilder)

Publications

By DIAMOND: scripts (with Billy Wilder)—

Some Like It Hot, New York, 1959.
Irma La Douce, New York, 1963.
The Apartment, and *The Fortune Cookie*, New York, 1970.

By DIAMOND: articles—

Cinema (London), October 1969.
American Film (Washington, DC), May 1982.
Films and Filming (London), May 1982.

On DIAMOND: articles—

Sight and Sound (London), Winter 1969–70.
Show (New York), June 1970.
Focus on Film (London), Summer 1973.
Frank, Sam, in *American Screenwriters*, edited by Robert E. Morsberger, Stephen O. Lesser, and Randall Clark, Detroit, Michigan, 1984.
Obituary in *Variety* (New York), 27 April 1988.

*   *   *

I. A. L. Diamond's talent as a writer emerged at Columbia University, where, in 1941, his newsworthy contribution to the school's annual Varsity Show resulted in a story in the *New York Times*. Paramount Studios read of his success and offered him a ten-week contract as a junior writer. Diamond gave up his plans to attend Columbia School of Journalism and headed for Hollywood. The studio picked up his option, but his screenwriting efforts went unproduced. So in 1943 Diamond left Paramount, wrote one screenplay for Universal, and eventually negotiated a contract with Warner Bros. There he worked on several box-office successes, particularly the Dennis Morgan-Jack Carson vehicles (*Two Guys from Milwaukee*, *Two Guys from Texas*, and *It's a Great Feeling*), but these and Diamond's other comedy assignments were frothy diversions at best. His work at 20th Century-Fox in the early 1950s was in the same vein; the most memorable of these films is *Monkey Business*, a screwball-style comedy directed by Howard Hawks. During these years Diamond's work lacked distinction, his opportunities for stylistic development hindered by the collaborative nature of the studio system. He left Fox after only three films and began freelancing.

Coincident with his first notoriety, it was once again his talent at writing sketches rather than screenplays that brought Diamond his next opportunity. The writer-director Billy Wilder, impressed by the skits Diamond wrote for a Writers Guild dinner, asked him to cowrite a screenplay. Wilder had worked with several writers since his breakup with the writer-producer Charles Brackett, but had failed to

find the ideal collaborator. Though their personalities were dramatically different, Diamond's withdrawn, introverted qualities proved to be the perfect balance for Wilder's extrovert nature. They not only shared a common European immigrant background, but the same dry sense of humor.

Beginning with *Love in the Afternoon*, their partnership spanned 25 years and a dozen films. While popular and critical reception of the pictures varied, their combined talents created some of the best and most enduring comedy/dramas of the late 1950s and early 1960s. Witty dialogue and sophisticated sexual situations marked their stories. They openly challenged the long-standing assumption that *all* Hollywood productions should be family oriented, and provided moviegoers with tasteful, adult entertainment. Their most satisfying pictures combined cynicism with sentiment, playing the two extremes against each other until the softer side of human nature won out. Frequently focused on illicit sex, their scenarios were also about love and the emotional vicissitudes of intimate relationships.

Innocence was sometimes ascribed to the female characters (Audrey Hepburn in *Love in the Afternoon* or Marilyn Monroe in *Some Like It Hot*) and sometimes to the males (Jack Lemmon in *The Apartment* or Joe E. Brown in *Some Like It Hot*). Their most popular and complicated exposé of male/female relationships, *Some Like It Hot*, showed masculinity taking on a new kind of innocence when two sexually savvy musicians (Tony Curtis and Jack Lemmon), disguise themselves as women to escape Chicago gangsters.

For Diamond and Wilder cynicism knew neither sexual nor age boundaries; it belonged to the middle-aged male (Gary Cooper in *Love in the Afternoon* and Fred MacMurray in *The Apartment*), to the youthful bachelor (Curtis and Lemmon in *Some Like It Hot*), and to the simple working girl (Shirley MacLaine in *The Apartment* and *Irma La Douce*). They poked fun at modern mores (*Avanti!*), at the American Dream (*One, Two, Three*), at ambition (*Kiss Me, Stupid*), and at greed (*The Fortune Cookie*). Their repeated casting of stars such as Lemmon, MacLaine, and Walter Matthau gave an additional continuity to their work. Particularly effective was the teaming of Lemmon and Matthau in a series of films (*The Fortune Cookie*, *The Front Page*, and *Buddy Buddy*) focusing on male relationships.

During the 1970s their work lost the bite and zest of the earlier pieces, perhaps because the genuine sentiment of the team's contemporary satires was replaced by a less appealing nostalgia. Attempting to recapture the lost innocence of another time, their productions of *The Private Life of Sherlock Holmes*, *The Front Page*, and *Fedora* lacked meaning for modern audiences.

Diamond took one significant respite from Wilder to adapt the Broadway success *Cactus Flower*. The material proved a perfect outlet for his urbane repartee.

—Joanne L. Yeck

DICKERSON, Ernest

Cinematographer and Director. **Nationality:** American. **Born:** Newark, New Jersey, 1952. **Education:** Degrees from Howard University School of Architecture and New York University Graduate School of Film. **Family:** Married twice; second wife, Traci; one daughter and one son. **Career:** Filmed surgical procedures for Howard University

Ernest Dickerson

Medical School and commercials for Nike; cinematographer for all of Spike Lee's films, 1981–92; began career as a director with PBS documentary *Spike & Co.: Do It A Capella*, 1990; photographed television series *Tales from the Darkside* and *Law and Order*, 1990; filmed music videos for Anita Baker, Bruce Springsteen, Miles Davis, the Neville Brothers, and others; founded Original Film, a bi-coastal company formed to produce television commercials and public service announcements, 1992. **Awards:** New York Film Critics Circle Award, Best Cinematography, for *Do the Right Thing*, 1989; L.A. Outfest Grand Jury Award for Outstanding American Narrative Feature, for *Blind Faith*, 1999. **Agent:** Dolores Robinson Agency, 10683 Santa Monica Blvd., Los Angeles, CA, 90025, U.S.A.

Films as Cinematographer:

1982   *Joe's Bed-Stuy Barbershop: We Cut Heads* (Lee)
1984   *The Brother From Another Planet* (Sayles)
1985   *Krush Groove* (Schultz)
1986   *She's Gotta Have It* (Lee) (+ ro)
1987   *Enemy Territory* (Manoogian); *Eddie Murphy Raw* (doc) (Townsend)
1988   *School Daze* (Lee)
1989   ***Do the Right Thing*** (Lee)
1990   *The Laserman* (Wong); *Def by Temptation* (Bond); *Ava & Gabriel* (de Rooy); *Mo' Better Blues* (Lee)
1991   *Jungle Fever* (Lee)
1992   *Cousin Bobby* (doc) (Demme); *Malcolm X* (Lee)

Films as Director:

1992   *Juice* (+ co-sc)
1994   *Surviving the Game*
1995   *Tales From the Crypt: Demon Knight*
1996   *Bulletproof*
1998   *Ambushed; Blind Faith* (for TV); *Futuresport* (for TV)
1999   *Strange Justice* (for TV)
2000   *Bones*

Publications

By DICKERSON: articles—

Interview with Jacquie Jones, "Peer Pressure," in *Black Film Review* (New York), 1993.

On DICKERSON: books—

Lee, Spike, *Spike Lee's Gotta Have It: Inside Guerrilla Filmmaking*, New York, 1987.
Lee, Spike, *Do the Right Thing* (journal, production notes, and script), New York, 1989.

On DICKERSON: articles—

Dyson, Michael Eric, "Out of the Ghetto," in *Sight & Sound* (London), October 1992.
Harrell, Al, "Malcolm X: One Man's Legacy, to the Letter," in *American Cinematographer* (Hollywood), November 1992.
Ravo, Nick, "Ernest Dickerson Would Rather Be Called Director," in *New York Times*, 18 April 1993.
Chan, Kenneth, "The Construction of Black Male Identity in Black Action Films of the Nineties," in *Cinema Journal* (Austin, Texas), Winter 1998.
Jefferson, Margo, "Television as Storyteller, Shaping History into Legend," in *New York Times*, 6 September 1999.

*   *   *

Ernest Dickerson's career has so far divided rather decisively into two parts: until 1991, he was exclusively a cinematographer, and since 1992, he has been exclusively a director. He was Spike Lee's director of photography on all his films from student projects (culminating in the hour-long *Joe's Bed-Stuy Barbershop: We Cut Heads*) through *Malcolm X*, creating a distinctive look that sets these films apart from Lee's post-Dickerson work. As a director he began auspiciously with *Juice*, one of the best of the youth-crime dramas of the early 1990s, but went on to make a series of genre films that received little critical notice or box office success. Recent forays into social melodrama rather than action-thriller suggest that he may be finding a voice for himself in a different genre while continuing to engage himself in stories of the ongoing struggles of blacks in America.

Spike Lee's book on the making of his first feature, *She's Gotta Have It*, describes how Dickerson was an important collaborator. It was the latter's idea to shoot the film in black and white (and the dance scene in color), and he directed the scenes in which Lee appears onscreen as Mars Blackmon. Shot in super 16mm, the film is handsomely realized, most strikingly in its inventive lighting and framing for each of the sex scenes between Nola and one of her three lovers.

Do the Right Thing, Lee's third feature, is visually remarkable in many ways, beginning with the fact that it appears to take place on a single hot day and night on a Brooklyn street. Actually, the film was shot on location over the course of several weeks in varying weather, even occasionally in rain (as in Radio Raheem's first encounter with some youths sitting on an apparently sunny stoop). Dickerson very precisely drew up a scheme noting the time of day each scene must take place, in order to create the sense of inexorable movement from sweltering dawn to glowing dusk. He has commented on his choice of hot colors for the night sequences too (rather than the typical blues that suggest a cooling down), and on the need—for this and all films with a cast of people of color—to choose the right lighting and film stocks to bring out the full rich range of light and dark skin tones. *Do the Right Thing* is filled with so many memorable shots that every viewer might have different favorites: e.g., the first shot after the opening credits, a remarkable pullback from the lips of Senor Love Daddy (Samuel L. Jackson) at his radio mike to a wide view of the street where the whole film will take place; or the radiant late-afternoon look of Jade (Joie Lee) in her pink dress and hat. Of Dickerson's other films for Lee, one might single out '*Mo Better Blues* for its "jazzy" camera movements to suggest the improvisatory nature of the music, and *Malcolm X* for its shifting color schemes for the different phases of Malcolm's life.

Dickerson's first feature as director, completed before *Malcolm X*, remains in many ways his most accomplished. Based on his own preliminary script, *Juice* traces the lives of four Harlem youths spiraling out of control. (Dickerson gave all four actors their first major screen roles, with Omar Epps and music star Tupac Shakur going on to important film careers, tragically short in the case of the latter.) The plot may be a bit schematic, with Q (Epps) aspiring to win fame in the hip hop world of DJ contests, while Bishop (Shakur) watches *White Heat* rather too intensely, identifying himself with James Cagney's lunatic gangster, whom he sees "taking destiny in his own hands" and "going out in a blaze." Bishop lures his pals into a grocery-store robbery that he turns into murder, then psychotically seeks to slay each of his now former buddies. But Dickerson gives the drama a rich texture and density, partly by including memorable minor characters (notably those played by Queen Letifah and Samuel L. Jackson), but especially through the photography and pacing. He places his characters solidly within Harlem settings which are full of detail without any shots seeming self-consciously picturesque or cluttered. He finds striking locations, like a deserted courtyard which seems like the bottom of a well, into which the friends flee after the robbery and where Bishop slays one of them—or the 125th St. Viaduct, under which Bishop chases Q. Also effective is the overall arc of the drama from bright daylight in the first half to predominantly night in the second half, as the story turns from kids playing hooky and stealing records to murder and pursuit. The DJ contest is excitingly portrayed with restless camera and fast editing, while a funeral scene, right after an intense police grilling, slows down the pace at a point where the drama needs it. Shakur's sudden creepy appearances onscreen in the second haf are rather horror-movie in style, but his performance is disturbing in its intensity. *Juice* may be a little weak in its final resolution, and it has been criticized for placing blame for ruined lives on individual psychosis rather than larger social forces of racism, but Dickerson has defended his film in terms of its being explicitly about peer pressure.

Dickerson's subsequent films continue to tell troubled stories of African Americans, most often using action-melodrama as a vehicle. *Surviving the Game*, one of many remakes of 1932's *The Most Dangerous Game*, updates the tale of a madman hunting humans for sport by having a group of affluent "weekend warrior" types spouting jargon about "embracing the animal within" themselves and getting in touch with their "prime masculine essence," while their victims are ghetto loners lured to a remote wilderness with promises of a job. The film plays down naked racism by having references only to "the poor" or to "someone like you" (i.e., the hero, played by Ice-T), and casting Charles S. Dutton (rather implausibly) as one of the vicious hunters. All the same, the satisfaction of the drama comes from seeing an unarmed but resourceful black man outwit his mostly white pursuers. To Dickerson's credit, the film has original touches like having the hunt played out in woods ironically bathed in splendid golden light, rather than going for a noirish look; and although the villains do a lot of scene-chewing, the director allows one of them, Gary Busey, the opportunity to deliver at leisure a chilling, brilliantly acted monologue. Unfortunately, the final scene of the film, back in a ghetto alleyway, is so improbable and ineptly staged that everyone involved seems to have given up on the project.

One can imagine Dickerson having a lark with the horror-movie conventions of *Demon Knight*, his third project; but *Bulletproof*—an "action-comedy" featuring a black cop and white crook, friends turned enemies, fleeing both police and mobsters—accomplishes little other than providing Adam Sandler some good opportunities to display his distinctive humor (most notably a Whitney Houston imitation). Hampered by the script, Dickerson finds no way to make the co-star, Damon Wayans, anything but thick-headed and unamusing, while the quite graphic violence seems at odds with the light comedy, and the combination of mysogyny and constant jokes about homosexual acts and the quarreling friends being "sweet on" each other give the film a most peculiar tone. Production values are undistinguished except for some handsome lighting (as in nearly all of Dickerson's projects). One other genre piece, *Futuresport*, was originally a pilot for a TV series, shot both for a network showing and for an R-rated videotape release. This is Dickerson's first directorial foray into science fiction, though less *Blade Runner* than *Max Headroom*—indeed, both the look of this near-future world and the plot seem directly derived from that 1980s series. It does boast some snazzy footage of the titular game—a kind of co-ed hockey played on floating skateboards—and Wesley Snipes has fun with a Rasta accent as a mysterious possible villain, but the film is otherwise far from a major achievement.

Ambushed, on the other hand, deserves more recognition than it has received to date. Its virtues are those of a "B" movie of the 1940s, with haunting, powerful scenes embedded in hokey melodrama and some unconvincing action (including more than one ambush). The plot involves another unlikely pair on the run: here, a black cop and a vicious-mouthed 12-year-old son of a neo-Nazi, fleeing both a corrupt police force and gangs of murderous racists. The setting is some Southern state of today where black children are regularly kidnapped, black men are routinely threatened with lynching, and less-than-fully-racist white children are murdered by their fathers, without any police interference. Yet the film features some genuinely moving scenes between fathers and sons or surrogate sons, and an atmospheric climax in a deserted industrial complex, with lots of canted angles. At its best moments, *Ambushed* seems to have a "B"-movie conviction abut its own preposterous situations and dialogue.

More recently Dickerson has tried his hand at domestic melo-drama, with mixed results. In *Blind Faith* his usual eye for striking lighting effects is in evidence, but he does little to make plausible (or compellingly lurid) a plot, set in the 1950s, in which the first black cop in his Bronx precinct (Charles Dutton in one of his rare unconvincing performances) helps cover up the white gang murder of a young black homosexual, even though he knows that doing so will cause his own gay son to be sentenced to death for a murder that was really self-defense. Far more successful is *Strange Justice*, a retelling of the Anita Hill/Clarence Thomas controversy. While the producer and head writer claim to have scrupulously (or perhaps calculatedly) taken a neutral position on who was telling the truth, with the drama focusing upon media exploitation, one might suspect Dickerson and his leading actors (Regina Taylor and Delroy Lindo) of giving more credence to Hill's side. Whether or not it was Dickerson's own idea to stage the climactic speeches at the hearing as "heightened" drama (veering into fantasy, most theatrically when Thomas strips off his shirt and pulls his tie in a noose, before we snap back to the "real" hearing), the scenes work, and the whole film features nuanced performances. Though Dickerson has not yet achieved the status of well-known "auteur" among critics or public, works as varied as *Juice* and *Strange Justice* reveal an important artist whose best work may be yet to come.

—Joseph Milicia

DILLON, Carmen

Art Director. **Nationality:** British. **Born:** Cricklewood, London, 1908. **Education:** Attended New Hall Convent, Chelmsford, Essex; qualified as architect. **Career:** Actress and designer for amateur dramatics; 1934—assistant to Ralph Brinton, Wembley Studios; then long association with Two Cities and Rank. **Awards:** Academy Award, for *Hamlet*, 1948; Venice Festival prize, for *The Importance of Being Earnest*, 1952. **Died:** 1995.

Films as Art Director:

1937   *The Five Pound Man* (Parker)
1938   *Who Goes Next?* (Elvey)
1939   *French without Tears* (Asquith) (asst); *The Mikado* (Schertzinger) (asst)
1940   *Freedom Radio* (*The Voice in the Night*) (Asquith)
1941   *Quiet Wedding* (Asquith)
1942   *Unpublished Story* (French); *The First of the Few* (*Spitfire*) (L. Howard)
1943   *The Gentle Sex* (L. Howard); *The Demi-Paradise* (*Adventure for Two*) (Asquith)
1945   **Henry V** (Olivier); *The Way to the Stars* (*Johnny in the Clouds*) (Asquith)
1946   *Carnival* (Haynes); *School for Secrets* (Ustinov)
1947   *White Cradle Inn* (*High Fury*) (French)
1948   *Vice Versa* (Ustinov); *Woman Hater* (Young); *Hamlet* (Olivier)
1949   *Cardboard Cavalier* (Forde)
1950   *The Reluctant Widow* (Knowles); *The Woman in Question* (Asquith); *The Rocking-Horse Winner* (Pelissier)
1951   *The Browning Version* (Asquith)

Carmen Dillon

1952   *The Story of Robin Hood and His Merrie Men* (*The Story of Robin Hood*) (Annakin); *The Importance of Being Earnest* (Asquith); *Meet Me Tonight* (Pelissier)
1953   *The Sword and the Rose* (Annakin); *Rob Roy, the Highland Rogue* (French)
1954   *Doctor in the House* (Thomas); *One Good Turn* (Carstairs)
1955   *Richard III* (Olivier); *Doctor at Sea* (Thomas); *Simon and Laura* (Box)
1956   *The Iron Petticoat* (Thomas) *Checkpoint* (Thomas)
1957   *The Prince and the Showgirl* (Olivier); *Miracle in Soho* (Amyes)
1958   *A Tale of Two Cities* (Thomas)
1959   *Sapphire* (Dearden)
1960   *No Kidding* (*Beware of Children*) (Thomas); *Watch Your Stern* (Thomas); *Carry on Constable* (Thomas); *Please Turn Over* (Thomas); *Kidnapped* (Stevenson); *Make Mine Mink* (Asher)
1961   *The Naked Edge* (Anderson); *Raising the Wind* (*Roommates*) (Thomas)
1962   *Carry on Cruising* (Thomas); *Twice 'round the Daffodils* (Thomas)
1963   *The Iron Maiden* (*The Swingin' Maiden*) (Thomas)
1964   *The Chalk Garden* (Neame)
1965   *The Battle of the Villa Fiorita* (Daves); *The Intelligence Men* (*Spylarks*) (Asher)
1966   *Sky, West, and Crooked* (*Gypsy Girl*) (Mills)
1967   **Accident** (Losey)
1968   *A Dandy in Aspic* (A. Mann and Harvey); *Otley* (Clement)
1969   *Sinful Davey* (Huston)

1970   *The Rise and Rise of Michael Rimmer* (Billington)
1971   *Catch Me a Spy* (Clement); *The Go-Between* (Losey)
1973   *Lady Caroline Lamb* (Bolt); *The Nelson Affair* (*A Bequest to
         the Nation*) (Jones)
1974   *Butley* (Pinter)
1975   *In This House of Brede* (Schaefer—for TV); *Love among the
         Ruins* (Cukor—for TV)
1977   *Julia* (Zinnemann)
1979   *The Corn Is Green* (Cukor—for TV)

Publications

By DILLON: article—

"The Function of the Art Director," in *Films and Filming* (London),
    May 1957.

On DILLON: articles—

Picturegoer (London), 16 July 1949.
Cinema Studio (London), November 1951.
Focus on Film (London), Spring 1973.

*   *   *

Carmen Dillon was born in 1908 in London. As did so many art
directors, she originally studied architecture. Dillon worked as a set
dresser and art director on many pictures for Two Cities and Rank,
and for nearly a quarter of century she was the only woman art
director working in English films.

Early in her career Dillon collaborated with the great British art
directors Paul Sheriff and Roger Furse. She assisted Sheriff on
Olivier's *Henry V*, and the sets of Olivier's *Hamlet* were by Dillon
with design by Furse. These two pictures were very significant in the
history of film design. *Henry V* changed style from a "realistic" look
at a historic (Elizabethan) time, to a historic theatrical setting, and
finally to a re-creation of the style, color, and spatial sense of
medieval illuminated manuscripts. It was a daring and successful
undertaking. As a contrast to the highly colored spectacle of *Henry V*,
Olivier filmed the tragedy of *Hamlet* in black and white. The
impression was that of an etching. The design emphasized spaces,
with ominous repeating arches and geometric platforms, giving
a sense of modern minimal theater as well as that of a dark and
drafty castle.

Dillon did several historical reconstruction films. *The Importance
of Being Earnest* and *The Go-Between* amply illustrate her skills as
a researcher. In 1977 Dillon worked with Gene Callahan and Willy
Holt on *Julia*. This film had great potential as a costumer. Art Deco
was enjoying a revival and there were enough scenes of the wealthy,
the bohemians, and the decadents for some standard streamlining and
a bit of neon here and there. But the picture had none of that. Except
for a calendar on the wall and the political events taking place it could
have represented any time. This is critical. It gives the film a timeless
meaning that speaks beyond a particular era and style. This story does
not only tell specifically about Julia fighting Nazi atrocities but also
how a brave human can stand up against injustice and evil. It is not
just about the author Lillian Hellman and her deep relationship with
a childhood companion, but of the strength of loving friendships.
Furthermore, this film concerns nonmaterialistic characters who care

more about feelings and ideas than decor. Dillon must convey
that tone.

Julia uses clean simple lines. Dillon emphasizes few objects, and
then with the precision of a still life. Objects, when shown, have
specific relationships to the story. They are never there just for local
color. Again, the sets are painted with the sparcity of a modern
minimalist stage set. Often, particularly in the scenes of Hellman and
Dashiell Hammett, darkness forms a cover. At times it serves as
a protective blanket, at others as a threat of the unknown. Sometimes
it serves for dramatic composition. Light also plays many roles—
exposing, attacking, enlightening. Scene after scene features silhouettes and outlines, lamps and lighting fixtures. Ceilings are shown,
giving a feeling of claustrophobia.

Dillon characterizes Julia's childhood in strongly lit reflective
surfaces broadcasting to the viewer the opulent wealth of her family.
There are few objects—the highly polished silver, the crystal chandeliers, the red velvet chairs. The rest of the house is almost bare, even
the few hanging paintings blend into the blankness of the walls. The
tall arches throughout oppress and intimidate. The staircase at the end
of the film serves a similar function. Julia's room, in contrast, feels
cozy, an all-white interior which symbolizes purity rather than
coldness.

In *Julia* Dillon's free use of space and lighting as key elements in
design goes back to her earlier work on *Hamlet*. These elements
project inner feelings and serve a purpose other than that of decorative
surface trappings. Dillon's versatility allows her to use detail or to
eliminate it, in her pursuit of achieving an appropriate narrative effect.

—Edith C. Lee

DINOV, Todor

Animator. **Nationality:** Bulgarian. **Born:** Greece, 1919; grew up in
Sofia, Bulgaria. **Education:** Studied art in Sofia; studied under
Ivanov-Vano at the Institute of Motion Picture Arts, Moscow, two
years. **Career:** Caricaturist and journalist; 1953—first animated film,
Marko the Hero; 1969—directed first live-action film; taught visual
communications, University of Sofia.

Films as Animator:

1953   *Junak Markos* (*Marko the Hero*)
1956   *The Little Guardian Angel*
1959   *Prometheus*
1960   *Story of a Twig*
1962   *The Lightning Conductor*
1963   *Jealously*; *The Apple*
1965   *The Daisy*
1969   *Ikonostast* (co-d live-action)
1970   *Prometheus XX*
1971   *Chain Reaction*
1974   *Lamjata* (live-action)
1975   *Perpetual Motion*
1977   *Baruten Bukvar* (live-action)
1980   *The Rain of Paris*
1986   *Grehut na Malitsa*

Publications

By DINOV: articles—

Kinoiskustvo, vol. 19, no. 2, 1964.
Image et son (Paris), June/July 1971.
Cinema TV Digest, Spring 1973.
Bulgarian Film (Sofia), no.4, 1984.

On DINOV: articles—

Kinoiskustvo, vol. 19, no. 7, 1964.
Iskusstvo Kino (Moscow), no. 4, 1966.
Bulgarian Film (Sofia), no. 6, 1968.
Bulgarian Film (Sofia), no. 8, 1979.
Bulgarian Film (Sofia), no. 4, 1985.
Kino (Sofia), June 1994.

* * *

Todor Dinov is reputed to be the veteran of Bulgarian animation from its birth in the mid-1950s. He studied figurative art in Sofia in his formative years and was among the students selected to continue their studies in Moscow. There he found a place in the Institute of Motion Picture Arts where he learned his technique and approach to animation from the great Russian master, Ivanov-Vano for two years. Ivanov-Vano's influence has prevailed all through Dinov's life, though Dinov was able to expand his interests over a much broader field. He had a period in journalism, acted as a caricaturist for a local newspaper, and published satirical magazines. One of the later ones, *A Propos*, a collection of drawings and articles by well-known humorists, enjoyed an international success in 1983. Nevertheless, Dinov achieved his reputation through his animated films.

Dinov's first production, *Marko the Hero*, was made in the Sofia Animated Film Studio in 1953. While he understands how to appeal to the public, he never compromises his serious outlook and his belief that good will eventually overcome bad. He has also been consistent with his visual style. His work is graphically pleasing without being revolutionary and experimental beyond the reach of his audience. As the Bulgarian animation studio expanded and the second generation of animators emerged, including Donyo Donev and Stoyan Dukov (eventually they were known as the Three Big Ds), Dinov took time off to try his skills as scriptwriter and as director of live-action films, as so many animators have done when the opportunity arises. Possibly more than others of the former Eastern Bloc, Dinov has succeeded with some of his live films and has become established as one of the popular Bulgarian directors, as well as a supremely talented animator.

—John Halas

DISNEY, Walt

Animator. **Nationality:** American. **Born:** Walter Elias Disney in Chicago, 5 December 1901. **Education:** Attended McKinley High School, Chicago; Kansas City Art Institute, 1915. **Family:** Married Lillian Bounds, 1925; children: Diane, Sharon. **Career:** 1918—in France with Red Cross Ambulance Corps, arriving just after Armistice; 1919—returned to Kansas, became commercial art studio

Walt Disney

apprentice, met Ub Iwerks; with Iwerks briefly in business, doing illustrations and ads; 1920—joined Kansas City Film Ad Co., making cartoon commercials for local businesses; 1922—incorporated Laugh-o-Gram Films, first studio, went bankrupt; 1923—to Hollywood, contract with M. J. Winkler, began *Alice in Cartoonland* series; soon joined by Iwerks; 1927—ended *Alice* series, began *Oswald the Lucky Rabbit* series; salary dispute with Winkler; formed Walt Disney Productions; 1928—*Steamboat Willie* released, first synchronized sound cartoon, featuring Mickey Mouse; made deal with Pat Powers for independent distribution; 1930—began distributing through Columbia; 1932—*Flowers and Trees*, first cartoon in Technicolor and first to win an Academy Award; released through United Artists; 1937—*Snow White*, first feature-length cartoon, marked innovative use of multi-plane camera, developed by Disney Studios; began releasing through RKO; 1941—strike by Disney staff belonging to Cartoonists Guild; Art Babbitt fired, later rehired; changes introduced included credit titles on cartoon shorts; 1944—"Mickey Mouse" is password on D-Day invasion of Europe; 1945—"True Life Adventure" series began, Disney's first live-action films; 1951–60—Disney developed several television programs; 1954—formed Buena Vista Distributing Co. for release of Disney and occasionally other films; hosting *Disneyland* TV series (later *Walt Disney Presents, Walt Disney's Wonderful World of Color, The Wonderful World of Disney*); 1955—Disneyland opened, Anaheim, California; *The Mickey Mouse Club* premiered on TV; 1960—*Walt Disney's Wonderful World of Color* premiered on television; 1971—Walt Disney World opened in Orlando, Florida. **Awards:** Special Academy Award, 1932; Special Academy Award for contributions to sound, with William Garity and John N.A.

Hawkins, 1941; Irving G. Thalberg Award, 1941; Best Director for his work as a whole, Cannes Film Festival, 1953. **Died:** California, 15 December 1966.

Films as Director, Animator and Producer:

1920   *Newman Laugh-O-Grams* series
1922   *Cinderella; The Four Musicians of Bremen; Goldie Locks and the Three Bears; Jack and the Beanstalk; Little Red Riding Hood; Puss in Boots*
1923   *Alice's Wonderland; Tommy Tucker's Tooth; Martha*

(Alice Series)

1924   *Alice and the Dog Catcher; Alice and the Three Bears; Alice Cans the Cannibals; Alice Gets in Dutch; Alice Hunting in Africa; Alice's Day at Sea; Alice's Fishy Story; Alice's Spooky Adventure; Alice's Wild West Show; Alice the Peacemaker; Alice the Piper; Alice the Toreador*
1925   *Alice Chops the Suey; Alice Gets Stung; Alice in the Jungle; Alice Loses Out; Alice on the Farm; Alice Picks the Champ; Alice Plays Cupid; Alice Rattled by Rats; Alice's Balloon Race; Alice's Egg Plant; Alice's Little Parade; Alice's Mysterious Mystery; Alice Solves the Puzzle; Alice's Ornery Orphan; Alice Stage Struck; Alice's Tin Pony; Alice the Jail Bird; Alice Wins the Derby*
1926   *Alice Charms the Fish; Alice's Monkey Business; Alice in the Wooly West; Alice the Fire Fighter; Alice Cuts the Ice; Alice Helps the Romance; Alice's Spanish Guitar; Alice's Brown Derby; Clara Cleans Her Teeth*
1927   *Alice the Golf Bag; Alice Foils the Pirates; Alice at the Carnival; Alice's Rodeo (Alice at the Rodeo); Alice the Collegiate; Alice in the Alps; Alice's Auto Race; Alice's Circus Daze; Alice's Knaughty Knight; Alice's Three Bad Eggs; Alice's Picnic; Alice's Channel Swim; Alice in the Klondike; Alice's Medicine Show; Alice the Whaler; Alice the Beach Nut; Alice in the Big League*

(Oswald the Lucky Rabbit Series)

1927   *Trolley Troubles; Oh, Teacher; The Ocean Hop; All Wet; The Mechanical Cow; The Banker's Daughter; Great Guns; Rickety Gin; Empty Socks; Harem Scarem; Neck 'n Neck*
1928   *The Ol' Swimmin' 'ole; Africa Before Dark; Rival Romeos; Bright Lights; Sagebrush Sadie; Ozzie of the Mounted; Ride 'em Plow Boy!; Hungry Hoboes; Oh, What a Knight; Sky Scrappers; Poor Papa; The Fox Chase; Tall Timber; Sleigh Bells; Hot Dog*

Films as Head of Walt Disney Productions, co-d with Ub Iwerks:

(Mickey Mouse Series)

1928   ***Steamboat Willie***
1929   *Plane Crazy* (made as silent, 1928, but released with synch sound); *The Gallopin' Gaucho* (made as silent, 1928, but released with synch sound); *The Barn Dance; The Opry House; When the Cat's Away; The Barnyard Battle; The*

Plow Boy; The Karnival Kid; Mickey's Choo Choo; The Jazz Fool; Jungle Rhythm; The Haunted House
1930   *The Barnyard Concert* (sole director); *Just Mickey (Fiddling Around)* (sole director); *The Cactus Kid* (sole director)

(Silly Symphonies Series)

1929   *The Skeleton Dance; El Terrible Toreador; The Merry Dwarfs* (sole director)
1930   *Night* (sole director)
1935   *The Golden Touch* (sole director)

Other Films as Head of Walt Disney Productions:

1937   ***Snow White and the Seven Dwarfs*** (Hand)
1940   *Pinocchio* (Sharpsteen); ***Fantasia*** (Sharps teen)
1941   *The Reluctant Dragon* (Luske, Handley, Beebe, Verity, Blystone and Werker) (+ ro); *Dumbo* (Sharpsteen)
1942   *Bambi* (Hand); *Saludos Amigos* (Ferguson) (+ ro)
1943   *Victory through Air Power* (Hand and Potter)
1944   *The Three Caballeros* (Ferguson)
1946   *Make Mine Music* (Grant); *Song of the South* (Jackson and Foster)
1947   *Fun and Fancy Free* (Sharpsteen)
1948   *Melody Time* (Sharpsteen); *So Dear to My Heart* (Luske and Schuster)
1949   *Ichabod and Mr. Toad (The Adventures of Ichabod and Mr. Toad)* (Sharpsteen)
1950   *Cinderella* (Sharpsteen); *Treasure Island* (Haskin)
1951   *Alice in Wonderland* (Sharpsteen)
1952   *The Story of Robin Hood and His Merrie Men* (Annakin)
1953   *Peter Pan* (Luske, Geronimi, and Jackson); *The Sword and the Rose* (Annakin); *Rob Roy, the Highland Rogue* (French)
1954   *20,000 Leagues under the Sea* (Fleischer); *The Littlest Outlaw (El pequino proscrito)* (Gavaldon)
1955   *Lady and the Tramp* (Luske, Geronimi and Jackson); *Davy Crockett and the River Pirates*
1956   *The Great Locomotive Chase* (Lyon); *Westward Ho the Wagons!* (Beaudine)
1957   *Johnny Tremain* (Stevenson); *Old Yeller* (Stevenson)
1958   *The Light in the Forest* (Daugherty); *Sleeping Beauty* (Geronimi); *Tonka* (L. Foster)
1959   *The Shaggy Dog* (Barton); *Darby O'Gill and the Little People* (Stevenson); *Third Man on the Mountain* (Annakin); *Toby Tyler, or Ten Weeks with a Circus* (Barton)
1960   *Kidnapped* (Stevenson); *Pollyanna* (Swift); *Ten Who Dared* (Beaudine); *Swiss Family Robinson* (Annakin); *One Hundred and One Dalmatians* (Reitherman, Luske and Geronimi); *The Absent-Minded Professor* (Stevenson)
1961   *Moon Pilot* (Neilson); *In Search of the Castaways* (Stevenson); *Nikki, Wild Dog of the North* (Couffer and Haldane); *The Parent Trap* (Swift); *Greyfriars Bobby* (Chaffey); *Babes in Toyland* (Donohue)
1962   *Son of Flubber* (Stevenson); *The Miracle of the White Stallions (Flight of the White Stallions)* (Hiller); *Big Red* (Tokar); *Bon Voyage* (Neilson); *Almost Angels (Born to Sing)* (Previn); *The Legend of Lobo* (Algar and Couffer)
1963   *Savage Sam* (Tokar); *Summer Magic* (Neilson); *The Incredible Journey* (Markle); *The Sword in the Stone* (Reitherman);

The Misadventures of Merlin Jones (Stevenson); *The Three Lives of Thomasina* (Chaffey)

1964   *A Tiger Walks* (Tokar); *The Moon-Spinners* (Neilson); *Mary Poppins* (Stevenson); *Emil and the Detectives* (Tewksbury); *Those Calloways* (Tokar); *The Monkey's Uncle* (Stevenson)

1965   *That Darn Cat* (Stevenson)

1966   *The Ugly Dachshund* (Tokar); *Lt. Robin Crusoe, U.S.N.* (Paul) (story under pseudonym Retlaw Yensid); *The Fighting Prince of Donegal* (O'Herlihy); *Follow Me, Boys!* (Tokar); *Monkeys, Go Home!* (McLaglen); *The Adventures of Bullwhip Griffin* (Neilson); *The Gnome-Mobile* (Stevenson)

1967   *The Jungle Book* (commentary) (Reitherman)

Publications

By DISNEY, book—

Sketch Book, Old Saybrook, CT, 1993.

By DISNEY: articles—

''What I've Learned from Animals,'' in *American Magazine*, February 1953.

''The Lurking Camera,'' in *Atlantic Monthly* (New York), August 1954.

''Too Long at the Sugar Bowls: Frances C. Sayers Raps with Disney,'' in *Library Journal* (New York), 15 October 1965.

On DISNEY: books—

Rotha, Paul, *Celluloid, the Film Today*, New York, 1931.

Bardeche, Maurice, and Robert Brasillach, *Histoire du Cinéma*, Paris, 1935.

Field, Robert D., *The Art of Walt Disney*, New York, 1942.

Eisenstein, Sergei, *Film Sense*, translated and edited by Jay Leyda, New York, 1947.

Clair, René, *Reflections on the Cinema*, translated by Vera Traill, London, 1953.

Manvell, Roger, and J. Huntley, *The Technique of Film Music*, New York, 1957.

Martin, Pete, (ed.), *The Story of Walt Disney*, New York, 1957. McGowan, Kenneth, *Behind the Screen: The History and Techniques of Motion Pictures*, New York, 1965.

Stephenson, Ralph, *Animation in the Cinema*, New York, 1967.

Bessy, Maurice, *Walt Disney*, Paris, 1970.

Kurland, Gerald, *Walt Disney: The Master of Animation*, New York, 1971.

Maltin, Leonard, *The Disney Films*, New York, 1973, revised edition, 1984.

Thomas, Frank, and Ollie Johnston, *Disney Animation: The Illusion of Life*, New York, 1982.

Bruno, Eduardo, and Enrico Ghezzi, *Walt Disney*, Venice, 1985.

Mosley, Leonard, *The Real Walt Disney*, London, 1986.

Schickel, Richard, *The Disney Version: The Life, Times, Art and Commerce of Walt Disney*, London, 1986.

Culhane, Shamus, *Talking Animals and Other People*, New York, 1986 + filmo.

Taylor, John, *Storming the Magic Kingdom*, New York, 1987.

Grant, John, *Encyclopaedia of Walt Disney's Animated Characters*, New York, 1987.

Thomas, Frank, and Ollie Johnston, *Too Funny for Words*, New York, 1987.

Holliss, Richard, and Brian Sibley, *The Disney Studio Story*, London, 1988.

Duchene, Alain, *Walt Disney n'est pas mort!*, Paris, 1989.

Ford, Barbara, *Walt Disney*, New York, 1989.

Grover, Ron, *The Disney Touch*, Homewood, Illinois, 1991.

Jackson, Kathy Merlock, *Walt Disney: A Bio-bibliography*, Westport, CT, 1993.

Merritt, Russell, *Walt in Wonderland: The Silent Films of Walt Disney*, Gemona, 1993.

Fanning, Jim, *Walt Disney*, New York, 1994.

Smoodkin, Eric, (ed.), *Disney Discourse: Producing the Magic Kingdom*, New York, 1994.

Thomas, Bob, *Walt Disney: An American Original*, New York, 1994.

West, John G., Jr., *The Disney Live-action Productions*, Milton, WA, 1994.

Eliot, Marc, *Walt Disney: Hollywood's Dark Prince, A Biography*, Deutsch, 1995.

Finch, Christopher, *The Art of Walt Disney: From Mickey Mouse to the Magic Kingdom*, New York, 1995.

Bell, Elizabeth, Lynda Haas, and Laura Sells, editors, *From Mouse to Mermaid: The Politics of Film, Gender, and Culture*, Bloomington, Indiana, 1995.

Cole, Michael D. *Walt Disney: Creator of Mickey Mouse*, Springfield, NJ, 1996.

Watts, Steven, *The Magic Kingdom: Walt Disney and the American Way of Life*, Boston, 1997.

Sherman, Robert B., and Richard M. Sherman, *Walt's Time: From Before to Beyond*, Santa Clarita, California, 1998.

On DISNEY: articles—

''The Mechanized Mouse,'' in *The Saturday Review of Literature* (New York), 11 November 1933.

Mann, Arthur, in *Harper* (New York), May 1934.

Bragdon, Claude, ''Straws in the Wind,'' in *Scribner's Magazine* (New York), July 1934.

Boone, Andrew R., ''A Famous Fairytale is Brought to the Screen as the Pioneer Feature Length Cartoon in Color,'' in *Popular Science Monthly* (New York), 1938.

Jeanne, René, ''Comment naquirent les dessins animés,'' in *Revue des Deux Mondes* (Paris), 15 March 1938.

Moellenhoff, F., ''Remarks on the Popularity of Mickey Mouse,'' in *American Imago*, (Detroit, Michigan) no. 3, 1940.

Boone, R., ''Mickey Mouse Goes Classical,'' in *Popular Science Monthly* (New York), January 1941.

Ahl, Frances Norene, ''Disney Techniques in Educational Film,'' in *The Social Studies*, December 1941.

''Walt Disney: Great Teacher,'' in *Fortune* (New York), August 1942.

''Mickey Mouse and Donald Duck Work for Victory,'' in *Popular Science Monthly* (New York), September 1942.

Mosdell, D., ''Film Review,'' in *Canadian Forum*, November 1946.

Wallace, Irving, ''Mickey Mouse and How He Grew,'' in *Colliers* (New York), 9 April 1949.

''A Silver Anniversary for Walt and Mickey: Disney's Magic Wand Has Enriched the World with Birds, Beasts and Fairy Princesses,'' in *Life* (New York), 2 November 1953.

"Disney Comes to Television," in *Newsweek* (New York), 12 April 1954.

Fishwick, Marshall, "Aesop in Hollywood: The Man and the Mouse," in *Saturday Review* (New York), 10 July 1954.

"Cinema: Father Goose—Walt Disney: To Enchanted Worlds on Electronic Wings," in *Time* (New York), 27 December 1954.

McEvoy, J.P., "McEvoy in Disneyland: A Visit with the Wonderful Wizard of Filmdom," in *Reader's Digest* (Pleasantville, New York), February 1955.

"A Wonderful World: Growing Impact of the Disney Art," in *Newsweek* (New York), 18 April 1955.

Powell, Dilys, "Hayley Mills on the Pickford Path," in *New York Times*, 13 August 1961.

Sadoul, Georges, "Sur le 'huitième art'," in *Cahiers du Cinéma* (Paris), June 1962.

Special Disney issue of *National Geographic* (Washington, D.C.), August 1963.

"The Wide World of Walt Disney," in *Newsweek* (New York), 31 December 1963.

Whitaker, Frederic, "A Day with Disney," in *American Artist* (New York), September 1965.

Aubriant, Michel, "Le vrai Walt Disney est mort il y a des années mais ne soyons pas injustes . . . ," in *Paris Presse*, 21 December 1966.

Comolii, Jean-Louis, and Michel Delahaye, "Le Cinéma à l'expo de Montréal," in *Cahiers du Cinéma* (Paris), April 1967.

"Disney without Walt . . . Is Like a Fine Car without an Engine. Will the Great Entertainment Company Find a New Creative Boss? Or Will It Slowly Lose Momentum?," in *Forbes* (New York), 1 July 1967.

Tucker, N., "Who's Afraid of Walt Disney," in *New Society*, no.11, 1968.

Gessner, Robert, "Letters to the Editor: Class in *Fantasia*," in *The Nation* (New York), 30 November 1970.

"The Ten Greatest Men of American Business—As You Picked Them," in *Nation's Business*, March 1971.

Pérez, F., "Walt Disney, una pedagogía reaccionaria," in *Cine Cubano* (Havana), no. 81–83, 1973.

Murray, J.C., "Lest We Forget," in *Lumiere* (Melbourne), November 1973.

Stuart, A., "Decay of an American Dream," in *Films and Filming* (London), November 1973.

Special Disney issue of *Kosmorama* (Copenhagen), November 1973.

Canemaker, J., "A Visit to the Walt Disney Studio," in *Filmmakers Newsletter* (Ward Hill, Massachusetts), January 1974.

Sklar, Robert, in *Movie Made America: A Social History of American Movies*, New York, 1975.

Rosenbaum, Jonathan, "Dream Masters," in *Film Comment* (New York), January-February 1975.

Smith, D.R., "Ben Sharpsteen . . . 33 Years with Disney," in *Millimeter* (New York), April 1975.

Beckerman, H., "Animation Kit: Movies, Myth and Us," in *Filmmakers Newsletter* (Ward Hill, Massachusetts), September 1975.

Brody, M., "The Wonderful World of Disney: Its Psychological Appeal," in *American Imago* (Detroit, Michigan), no. 4, 1976.

"Disney Night at the A.S.C.," in *American Cinematographer* (Los Angeles), February 1977.

Paul, W., "Art, Music, Nature and Walt Disney," in *Movie* (London), Spring 1977.

Schupp, P., "Mickey a cinquante ans," in *Sequences* (Montreal), January 1979.

Canemaker, J., "Disney Animation: History and Technique," in *Film News* (New York), January-February 1979.

Hulett, S., "A Star Is Drawn," in *Film Comment* (New York), January-February 1979.

Canemaker, J., "Disney Design: 1928–1979," in *Millimeter* (New York), February 1979.

Barrier, M., "'Building a Better Mouse': Fifty Years of Disney Animation," in *Funnyworld* (New York), Summer 1979.

Smith, D.R., "Disney Before Burbank: The Kingswell and Hyperion Studios," in *Funnyworld* (New York), Summer 1979.

Cawley, J., Jr., "Disney Out-Foxed: The Tale of Reynard at the Disney Studio," in *American Classic Screen* (Shawnee Mission, Kansas), July-August 1979.

"Journals: Tom Allen from New York," in *Film Comment* (New York), September-October 1981.

Griffithiana (Gemona, Italy), no. 34, December 1988.

CinémAction (Conde-sur-Noireau), no. 51, April 1989.

Kosmorama (Copenhagen), vol. 35, no. 188, Summer 1989.

Animatrix, no. 6, 1990/1992.

Cineforum, no. 319, 1992.

Skoop, October 1992.

Plateau, no. 2, 1993.

The South Atlantic Quarterly, no. 1, 1993.

New York Times, 6 May 1993.

New York Times, 8 May 1993.

Positif, no. 388, June 1993.

New York Times, 13 July 1993.

New York Times, 18 July 1993.

Newsweek, 26 July 1993.

*   *   *

Before Walt Disney, there was Emile Cohl (the "first animator," who made over 250 films in the early years of the twentieth century); Winsor McCay (whose Gertie the Dinosaur, created in 1914, was the original animated personality); John Randolph Bray (the Henry Ford of animation, whose technological and organizational contributions revolutionized the art form); and Otto Messmer, inventor of Felix the Cat, the Charlie Chaplin of animated characters and the most popular cartoon creation of the 1920s, entertaining audiences before Mickey Mouse ever uttered a squeak.

So why is Walt Disney synonymous with animation? How could *Fantasia*, *Snow White and the Seven Dwarfs*, and *Bambi* have been re-released to theaters every few years and then marketed to home video, to delight generations of children? Simply because no other animator ever duplicated the Disney studio's appealingly lifelike cartoon characters and wonderful flair for storytelling.

First, Disney was an innovator, a perfectionist who was forever attempting to improve his product and explore the medium to its fullest potential. He was the first to utilize sound in animation, in *Steamboat Willie*, which was the third Mickey Mouse cartoon. The soundtrack here is more than just a gimmick: for example, in an animal concert, a cow's udder is played like a bagpipe and its teeth are transformed into a xylophone. The musical accompaniment thus emerges from the background, becoming an integral element in the film's structure.

In *Flowers and Trees*, Disney was the first to utilize three-strip Technicolor in animation, a process devised by Joseph Arthur Ball:

three different negatives, each recording a primary color, replaced the single camera film previously used. *Snow White and the Seven Dwarfs* was the first full-length cartoon feature: during the production, Disney staffers developed the multiplane method of realistically creating the illusion of perspective and depth. The camera, operated by several technicians, filled an entire room. A sequence was drawn and painted on several panes of glass, with each one carefully placed and rigidly held down. Cels of the animated characters were placed on the various planes, which would then be moved past the camera at varying speeds. Those close to the camera would go by rapidly; those in the rear would be moved more slowly.

Just as significantly, however, Disney was a master organizer and administrator. As a result, from the 1930s on, the Disney Studio practically monopolized the animation industry. He established an industrialized assembly line, employing hundreds of animators and technicians who regularly churned out high-quality, Academy Award-caliber product. In the early 1930s, he opened distribution offices in London and Paris. He instigated large merchandising campaigns to reap additional profits via T-shirts, toys, and watches. Today, Disneyland and Disneyworld are living monuments to his memory. And it is not surprising that Disney eventually stretched his talents beyond pure animation, first combining cartoons with actors and, finally, producing live-action features, wildlife documentaries, and television series. In 1950, he produced *Treasure Island*, his first non-animated feature. In 1953, he made his first nature documentary, *The Living Desert*. The following year, he premiered his weekly television anthology series, which aired for decades. And he established the Buena Vista company as a distribution outlet for his films.

Yet Walt Disney's ultimate legacy remains his animated stories, and the narrative elements which lifted them above his competition. His characters are not just caricatures who insult each other, bash each other with baseball bats, or push each other off cliffs. They are lifelike, three-dimensional creatures with personalities all their own: they are simple, but never simplistic, and rarely, if ever, fail to thoroughly involve the viewer.

It is virtually impossible to rank the best of Disney's animated features in order of quality or popularity. *Snow White*, with its enchanting storyline and sweet humor, remains a joy for audiences many decades after its release. It is the perfect romantic fairy tale, with Snow White and her Prince Charming in a happy-ever-after ending, the comic relief of the lovable dwarfs, and the villainy of the evil Queen. The film's financial history is typical of most Disney features: originally budgeted at $250,000, it eventually cost $1,700,000 to produce. It earned $4.2 million in the United States and Canada alone when first released; by the mid-1990s, it had grossed over $175-million.

Jiminy Cricket singing "When You Wish Upon a Star" is the highlight of *Pinocchio*. *Bambi* is easily the most delicate of all Disney features. And there is *Fantasia*, a series of animated sequences set to musical classics conducted by Leopold Stokowski and performed by the Philadelphia Orchestra: Tchaikovsky's *The Nutcracker Suite*, Dukas's *The Sorcerer's Apprentice*, Stravinsky's *The Rite of Spring*, and Beethoven's *Symphony No.6 in F Major*, among others. *Fantasia* is ambitious, innovative, controversial— how dare anyone attempt to visually interpret music?— and, ultimately, timeless.

Since Disney's death in 1966, his studio has had its failures and triumphs. After a dry spell in the late 1960s and 1970s, it established a subsidiary, Touchstone Pictures, which successfully debuted in 1984 with the PG-rated *Splash*. In the intervening years, the studio struck deals with the likes of Bob and Harvey Weinstein of Miramax

Films and Merchant-Ivory Productions, and marketed such traditionally un-Disney-like fare as *Pulp Fiction, Kids, Pretty Woman*, and *The Hand That Rocks the Cradle*. But the studio remains mostly synonymous with animation. In the 1990s, it produced a string of animated features which ranks with its classics of decades past: *The Lion King, Pocahontas, Beauty and the Beast,* and *Aladdin*. As of 1996, *The Lion King* rated number five on *Variety's* list of all-time money-earning champs, taking in over $312 million. Also ranked in the top 50 were other animated and non-animated Disney fare, which certifies the studio's status as a major Hollywood player: *Aladdin* (number 16, $217-million); *Toy Story* (number 24, $182 million); *Pretty Woman* (number 26, $178 million); the previously mentioned *Snow White* (number 29); *Three Men and a Baby* (number 34, $167 million); *Who Framed Roger Rabbit?* (number 42, $154 million); *Beauty and the Beast* (number 49, $145 million); and *The Santa Clause* (number 50, $144 million).

In 1991, *Beauty and the Beast* became the first animated film ever nominated for a Best Picture Academy Award. And in 1995 came *Toy Story*, a groundbreaking feature produced completely on computer.

An essay on Walt Disney would be incomplete without a note on Mickey Mouse, the most famous of all Disney creations and one of the world's most identifiable and best-loved characters. Appropriately, Disney himself was the voice of Mickey, who was originally named Mortimer. The filmmaker himself best explained the popularity of his mouse: ". . . Mickey is so simple and uncomplicated, so easy to understand, that you can't help liking him."

With pen, pencil, ink, and paint, Walt Disney created a unique, special world. Max and Dave Fleischer, Walter Lantz, Chuck Jones, and many others may all be great animators, but Disney is unarguably the most identifiable name in the art form.

—Rob Edelman

DI VENANZO, Gianni

Cinematographer. **Nationality:** Italian. **Born:** Teramo, 18 December 1920. **Career:** Camera assistant from early 1940s; 1949—first film as cinematographer, *Cantoria d'Angeli*. **Died:** 3 March 1966.

Films as Cameraman:

1947   *La terra trema* (Visconti)
1949   *La Beauté du diable* (Clair)
1950   ***Miracolo a Milano*** (*Miracle in Milan*) (De Sica)

Films as Cinematographer:

1949   *Cantoria d'Angeli* (Hamza—short); *La scuola di Severino* (Guerrini—short); *Pesca a Mazzara del Vallo* (Fallette— short); *Ponti e porte de Roma* (Hamza—short); *La primavera del papa* (Hamza—short)
1950   *Procida* (Fasano—short); *S. Carlino* (Fasano—short); *Carrara* (Lomazi—short)
1951   *Achtung banditi!* (Lizzani)
1953   *Cronache di poveri amanti* (Lizzani); *Terra straniera* (Corbucci); *Amore in città* (*Love in the City*) (Risi and others)

1954   *Donne e soldati* (Malerba and Marchi); *Le ragazze de San Frediano* (Zulini)

1955   *Le amiche* (Antonioni); *Gli sbandati* (Maselli); *Quando tramonta il sole* (Brignone); *Le scapolo* (*El soltero*) (Pietrangeli

1956   *Difendo il mio amore* (*Defend My Love*; *I'll Defend You My Love*) (V. Sherman); *Terrore sulla città* (Majano); *Kean* (Gassman); *Su or Letizia* (Camerini)

1957   *Il grido* (*The Outcry*) (Antonioni); *Rascel fifi* (Leoni); *Un ettaro di cielo* (Casadio)

1958   *La sfida* (*The Challenge*) (Rosi); *La Loi . . . c'est la loi* (*The Law Is the Law*) (Christian-Jaque); *I soliti ignoti* (*Big Deal on Madonna Street*) (Monicelli); *La prima notte* (*Les Noces vénetiennes*) (Cavalcanti); *Rascel marine* (Leoni)

1959   *Nel blu dipinto di blu* (*Volare*) (Tellini); *I magliari* (Rosi); *Il nemico di mia moglie* (Puccini); *Vento del sud* (Provenzale)

1960   *I delfini* (Maselli); **La notte** (*The Night*) (Antonioni); *Crimen* (Camerini); *Un mandarino per Teo* (Mattoli)

1961   *Il carabiniere a cavallo* (Lizzani); *Salvatore Giuliano* (Rosi)

1962   **L'eclisse** (*The Eclipse*) (Antonioni); *Eve* (Losey)

1963   **Otto e mezzo** (*8 1/2*) (Fellini); *Le mani sulla città* (*Hands over the City*) (Rosi); *I basilischi* (*The Lizards*) (Wertmüller); *Gli indifferenti* (*Time of Indifference*) (Maselli); *La ragazzi di Bube* (*Bebo's Girl*) (Comencini)

1964   "Gente moderna" ep. of *Alta infedeltá* (*High Infidelity*) (Monicelli); "La moglia bionda" ep. of *Oggi, dommani, e dopodomani* (Salce); "La balena bianca" ep. of *La Donna e una cosa meravigliosa* (Bolognini)

1965   *Il momento della verità* (*The Moment of Truth*) (Rosi) (co); *Giulietta degli spirit* (*Juliet of the Spirits*) (Fellini); *Il morbidone* (Franciosa) (co); *La decima vittima* (*The 10th Victim*) (Petri)

1967   *The Honey Pot* (Mankiewicz)

Publications

On DI VENANZO: articles—

Film (Hanover), no. 5, 1966.
Rosi, Francesco, in *Filmcritica* (Rome), February 1966.
Cahiers du Cinéma (Paris), April 1966.
Gillett, John, in *Sight and Sound* (London), Summer 1966.
Focus on Film (London), no. 13, 1973.
Gerely, A., in *Film und Ton* (Munich), November 1977.
White, Armand, in *Film Comment* (New York), March/April 1986.

*   *   *

Di Venanzo began his career during World War II as camera assistant to Aldo Tonti, Otello Martelli and others, working on the films of key neorealist directors such as Visconti, Rossellini, De Santis and De Sica. Given his training in the flat documentary style favored by these filmmakers, as well as the more somber approach of Tonti, it is all the more surprising that he developed in his work with Antonioni the bleached-out, shimmering whiteness that now so strongly evokes classic Italian black and white cinematography.

Working with Antonioni, particularly on *Le amiche*, he also developed a capacity for filming complex and changing groupings of actors, experience that proved useful when he worked with Fellini on *Otto e mezzo*. Fellini's masterpiece can also be seen as Di Venanzo's, with its subtle gradations of light and shadow essential in helping the viewer to navigate this complex assemblage of dream, memory, imagination and reality.

Di Venanzo put his early experience as a cameraman to good use also in his work with Francesco Rosi, particularly in *Salvatore Giuliano* and *Le mani sulla città*. In these films he recreated the documentary feeling of neorealism, adding another level of chronological signification to each. For Lina Wertmüller's first film, *I basilischi* (*The Lizards*), he helped to develop a pared-down visual language that focuses on the essentail details of her comedy.

Di Venanzo worked as cinematographer with important directors on films which proved to be central to their careers. He was universally lauded by them for his perfectionism and the variety of his photographic talents. John Gillett says these opinions were based on Di Venanzo's ". . . extraordinary ability to establish a rapport with each director; a facility for sensing the particular textures they sought after; and sheer tenacity in getting those precise effects on to celluloid." His untimely death at 45 from hepatitis has cast him into an undeserved obscurity in film history. Had he survived he would surely equal, and perhaps surpass, the reputation now held only by Vittorio Storaro among Italian cinematographers.

—Stephen Brophy

DONAGGIO, Pino

Composer. **Nationality:** Italian. **Born:** Burano, 24 November 1941. **Education:** Studied the violin at Venice Conservatory and Verdi Conservatory, Milan; also studied under Ugo Amendola. **Career:** Singer and songwriter; 1973—first film score, for *Don't Look Now*.

Films as Composer:

1973   *Don't Look Now* (Roeg)

1975   *Corruzione al palazzo di giustizia* (*Corruption in the Halls of Justice*) (Aliprandi)

1976   *Un sussurro nel buio* (Aliprandi)

1977   *Carrie* (De Palma)

1978   *Piranha* (Dante); *Nero Veneziamo* (*Damned in Venice*) (Liberatore); *Amore, piombo, e furore* (*China 9, Liberty 37*) (Hellman)

1979   *Tourist Trap* (Schmoeller); *Senza buccia* (Aliprandi); *Home Movies* (De Palma)

1980   *The Howling* (Dante); *Dressed to Kill* (De Palma); *Augh! Augh!* (Toniato); *Desideria, la vita interiore* (*Desire, the Interior Life*) (Barcelloni); *Al di là del bene a del male* (*Beyond Evil*) (Cavani)

1981   *Tattoo* (B. Brooks); *The Fan* (Bianchi); *Blow Out* (De Palma); *Il gatto nero* (*The Black Cat*) (Fulci); *Venezia, carnevale, un amore* (Lanfanchi)

1982   *Morte in Vaticano* (*Death in the Vatican*) (Aliprandi); *Oltre la porta* (*Behind the Door*) (Cavani); *Jugando con la muerte* (*Playing with Death*; *Target Eagle*) (de la Loma); *Tex* (Hunter)

1983   *Hercules* (Coates)

1984 *Over the Brooklyn Bridge (Alby's Delight)* (Golan); *Body Double* (De Palma); *Déjà vu* (Richmond); *Agatha Christie's Ordeal by Innocence* (Davis)
1985 *Sotto il vestito niente* (Vanzini); *The Berlin Affair* (Cavani)
1986 *Sette chili in sette giorni* (Verdone); *Il caso moro* (Ferrara); *Hotel Colonial* (Torrini); *Crawlspace* (Schmoeller)
1987 *The Barbarians* (Deodato); *Dancers* (Ross); *Going Bananas* (Davidson); *Jenatsch* (Schmid); *La monaca di Monza* (Odorisio); *Scirocco* (Lado)
1988 *La Partita (The Match; The Gamble)* (Vanzina); *Appointment with Death* (Winner); *Catacombs* (Schmoeller); *High Frequency* (Rosati); *Kansas* (D. Stevens); *Phantom of Death* (Deodato); *Sacrilege* (Odorisio); *Zelly and Me* (Rathbone)
1989 *Indio* (De Anda); *Night Games* (Vadim)
1990 *Meridian—Kiss of the Beast* (Band); *Rito d'amore* (Lado); *Two Evil Eyes* (Romero)
1992 *Raising Cain* (De Palma); *Indio 2—The Revolt* (Dawson); *A Fine Romance (Tchin-Tchin; Cin Cin)* (Saks); *La Setta (The Devil's Daughter)* (Soavi); *Trauma* (Argento); *Così fan tutte (All Women Do It)* (Brass); *Missione d'amore* (Risi—mini for TV)
1993 *Curse IV: The Ultimate Sacrifice* (Schmoeller); *Pakt mit dem Tod* (Sánchez Silva); *Giovanni Falcone* (Ferrara); *Dove siete' Io sono qui (Where Are You? I'm Here)* (Cavani—for TV)
1994 *Oblivion* (Irvin); *La Chance (Power and Lovers)* (Lado); *Botte di Natale (The Night Before Christmas)* (Hill)
1995 *Soldato ignoto* (Aliprandi); *Segreto di stato (State Secret)* (Ferrara); *Palermo Milano solo andata* (Fragasso); *Mollo tutto* (Sánchez Silva); *Marciando nel buio* (Spano); *Un Eroe borghese (Ordinary Hero)* (Placido); *Inka Connection* (Gremm—mini for TV); *Never Talk to Strangers* (Hall)
1996 *Oblivion 2: Backlash* (Irvin); *Festival* (Avati); *L'Arcano incantatore (Mysterious Encounter)* (Avati); *Squillo* (Vanzina); *Nach uns die Sintflut* (Rothemund—for TV)
1997 *La Terza luna* (Bellinelli); *Il Carniere (The Game Bag)* (Zaccaro); *Le Ragazze di Piazza di Spagna* (Lazotti and Sánchez Silva—series for TV); *Die Stunden vor dem Morgengrauen* (Gremm)
1999 *Die Sünde der Engel* (Gremm—for TV); *Coppia omicida* (Fragasso); *Il Tesoro di Damasco* (Sánchez Silva) (mini-series for TV); *Monella* (Brass); *Il Mio West (My West)* (Veronesi); *Prima del tramonto* (Incerti); *Morte di una ragazza perbene* (Perelli—for TV)
2000 *Up at the Villa*; *Mr. Hughes*

Publications

By DONAGGIO: article—

Soundtrack! (Hollywood), June 1984.
Soundtrack! (Hollywood), September 1994.

On DONAGGIO: articles—

Fistful of Soundtracks (London), July 1981.
Film Comment (New York), September/October 1981.
Elley, Derek, in *Films and Filming* (London), January 1982.
Score (Bologna), June 1983.
Soundtrack! (Hollywood), vol. 18, June 1986.
Segnocinema (Vicenza), vol. 6, no. 25, November 1986.
CinémAction (Conde-sur-Noireau), no. 62, January 1992.
Variety (New York), 14 June 1993.
Soundtrack! (Hollywood), vol. 13, March 1994.
Variety (New York), 22 December 1997.

*   *   *

Pino Donaggio's association with Brian De Palma on a number of the director's deliberately Hitchcockian thrillers has led to the composer's being compared to Bernard Herrmann, and inevitably coming up the loser.

Herrmann provided De Palma with the intense scores for two of the director's earliest Hitchcock pastiches, *Sisters* and *Obsession*. *Carrie*, Donaggio's first score for De Palma, was to have been a Herrmann assignment too, but the composer died suddenly. Donaggio has been replacing Herrmann for De Palma ever since.

Early on, Donaggio had established a distinct and recognizable musical voice all his own, characterized by lyrical melodies—usually for woodwinds backed by guitar or piano—juxtaposed against suspense cues provided by jarring chords and sharply sustained string lines.

In general Donaggio's scores, often conducted by Natale Massara, show an ability to adapt to a variety of classical and contemporary stylings. Donaggio likes to experiment with a broad range of musical styles, such as the Giorgio Moroder-style effects in *Body Double* or the pop presentation of a Rossini-style overture for the comedy *Home Movies*.

His stylistic signature of using the same instrumentation for both love themes and suspenseful passages evidenced itself in his first major score, for Nicolas Roeg's *Don't Look Now*. The score's lyrical themes give way to trills in the upper registers of the woodwinds, high-pitched strings, and jarring chords on piano, guitar, and harp. *Don't Look Now* shows evidence of Donaggio's classical training as well as his background in jazz and pop, and also shows his ability to deliberately compose against the tone of the film by providing richly melodic themes identified with the characters rather than the terrifying events that are occurring.

By employing Herrmannesque orchestrations and compositional elements in his subsequent work for De Palma, Donaggio has significantly muted this early voice, becoming a sort of ersatz-Herrmann instead—and, therefore, complicit in the negative comparison that haunts him.

His recent, often very different work, in genres other than the De Palma thriller may, in time, bring an end to the invited Herrmann comparisons and lead to his being recognized for his own individual, often lyrical, style. Donaggio has been associated with Joe Dante (*Piranha*, *The Howling*) and more recently with Liliana Cavani (*Behind the Door*, *The Berlin Affair*). Donaggio has provided scores for Westerns (*Amore, piombo, e furore*), political thrillers (*Corruzione al palazzo di giustizia*), contemporary dramas (*Tex*), and light romantic films (*Over the Brooklyn Bridge*).

Despite the diversity of subject matter and use of various musical styles, these scores are more characteristic of the real—i.e., non-Herrmann—Donaggio, than his work for De Palma.

—Richard R. Ness, updated by John McCarty

DONATI, Danilo

Costume Designer. **Nationality:** Italian. **Born:** Luzzara, 1926. **Education:** Studied art in Florence. **Career:** Supervising art director for the TV network RAO; 1955—first stage designs for operas produced by Visconti, Rome: later designs for Visconti's stage productions of *The Crucible*, 1955, *Contessa Giulia*, 1957, and *Impresario delle Smirne*, 1957; 1962—first costume designs for film, *The Steppe*. **Awards:** Academy Award and British Academy Award, for *Romeo and Juliet*, 1968, and *Casanova*, 1976.

Films as Costume Designer:

1962 *La steppa* (*The Steppe*) (Lattuada); *Rogopag* (Pasolini and others)
1964 ***Il vangelo secondo Matteo*** (*The Gospel According to St. Matthew*) (Pasolini)
1965 *La mandragola* (*Mandragola*; *The Love Root*) (Lattuada)
1966 *El Greco* (Salce); *Uccellacci e uccellini* (*The Hawks and the Sparrows*) (Pasolini); *The Taming of the Shrew* (Zeffirelli) (co)
1967 *Edipo re* (*Oedipus Rex*) (Pasolini)
1968 *Romeo and Juliet* (Zeffirelli): *La cintura di castità* (*On My Way to the Crusades, I Met a Girl Who . . .*) (Festa Campinile)
1969 *Porcile* (*Pigsty*) (Pasolini); *Medea* (Pasolini); *Satyricon* (Fellini); *La monaca di Monza* (*The Lady of Monza*) (E. Visconti)
1970 *I clowns* (*The Clowns*) (Fellini)
1971 *Il decameron* (*The Decameron*) (Pasolini)
1972 *Roma* (Fellini); *I racconti di Canterbury* (*The Canterbury Tales*) (Pasolini); *Fratello sole, sorella luna* (*Brother Sun, Sister Moon*) (Zeffirelli)
1974 *Il fiore delle mille e una notte* (*A Thousand and One Nights*) (Pasolini); *Amarcord* (Fellini)
1975 *Salo, o le 120 giornate di Sodoma* (*Salo—The 120 Days of Sodom*) (Pasolini)
1976 *Caligula* (Brass); *Casanova* (Fellini)
1979 *Hurricane* (Troell)
1980 *Flash Gordon* (Hodges)
1985 *Red Sonja* (Fleischer)
1986 *Ginger e Fred* (Fellini)
1987 *Intervista* (*The Interview*) (Fellini) (art designer)
1989 *Francesco* (*St. Francis of Assisi*) (Cavani)
1994 *Il Mostro* (*The Monster*) (Benigni and Filippi)
1996 *I Magi randagi* (*We Free Kings*) (Citti) (+ production designer); *Nostromo* (Reid) (miniseries for TV)
1997 *La Vita è bella* (Benigni) (+ production designer)

Publications

On DONATI: articles—

Variety (New York), 22 December 1997.
Interiors, April 1999.

*   *   *

When one recalls the films of Federico Fellini, Franco Zeffirelli, and Pier Paolo Pasolini, one inevitably visualizes the creations of Danilo Donati. Those outrageous hats of the Pharisees in *The Gospel According to St. Matthew*, the richly colored gowns in *Romeo and Juliet* and *The Taming of the Shrew*, bizarre interpretations of history in *Satyricon* and *Casanova*, eye-popping fashion shows for clowns in *The Clowns* and for the well-dressed pope in *Roma*, all these examples illustrate the strength of the Donati vision keeping pace with the powerful images of modern movie masters.

Donati was born in Italy and had originally trained in Florence as a muralist and fresco painter. He had also spent several years as supervising art director at RAO, Italy's national television network. In addition to his cinema work, Donati designed theatrical productions (including the early stage and opera presentations of Luchino Visconti) and public spectacles.

It is hard to characterize Donati's work only because he is interested in so many different elements of creation. In his costumes, for example, he uses inventive shapes, sometimes modified from tradition, sometimes entirely fanciful. Color is important. Usually his hues are unbelievably rich, but at other times they are purposefully subdued or faded. Fabrics are important. Specially created textiles were made for *Satyricon* so that they would in no way resemble anything contemporary.

Donati often uses light reflective surfaces such as sequins or materials such as feathers or furs that create eye-catching movement on the screen. His approach to costume decoration rivals the great Hollywood costume designers of the 1930s. Donati not only uses these techniques, he understands their function. Furthermore, Donati costumes interact with each other; as lovely as they may be individually, they work together to form visual unities (or even contrasts when necessary—as seen in the dinner party of the Spanish and French in *Casanova*) and themes.

Donati's oeuvre conjures up monuments to opulence in the minds of many; even lesser films, such as *Caligula* and the entertaining Dino De Laurentiis production of *Flash Gordon* were memorable due to their outlandish Donati designs. Nevertheless, Donati equally excels in depicting realism. Consider an earthier work of Fellini, such as *Amarcord*, or the scruffy peasants peopling Pasolini's *The Decameron*: Donati pays as great an attention to details in the rags of the poor and the mundane attire of the middle class, as he would for robes of a Renaissance princess. Often Donati will contrast the ultraglamorous or unusual with the more humble in the same movie.

It is important to note that Donati worked with highly individualistic directors with well-developed visual senses and strong opinions on what they wanted. Zeffirelli's productions were to be like exquisite oil paintings. Donati's works for Pasolini were to be revolutionary new interpretations of well-known tales. And as for the films of Fellini . . . well, they are simply Fellini!

Cooperation is essential when a director tries to create a statement of great complexity. Donati's directors have had very specific visual conceptions they wished to convey. Observe their cast selections: Donati costumes would have to compete with those ravishing faces featured in Zeffirelli films. Pasolini and Fellini extras could have stepped out of the sketch books of Leonardo da Vinci. Of course, Donati did not compete with great men's visions; he complemented them. Donati's designs integrate well within the dreams of his directors and at the same time they are distinctively Donati.

—Edith C. Lee

DOUY, Max

Art Director. **Nationality:** French. **Born:** Issy-Les-Moulineaux, 20 June 1914; brother of the designer Jacques Douy. **Education:** Studied architecture. **Career:** 1930–41—assistant art director for Jacques Colombier, Lucien Aguettand, Lazare Meerson, Alexandre Trauner, Serge Pimenoff, and Eugène Lourié; then art director for films, stage plays, and television (including the mini-series Lucien Leuwen, 1973). **Awards:** Cannes Film Festival award, for Occupe-toi d'Amélie, 1949; César award, for Le Malevil, 1980.

Films as Assistant Art Director:

1930 *Le Poignard malais* (Goupillières); *Le Rêve* (de Baroncelli); *Levy et Cie* (Hugon); *Kopfüber ins Gluck* (Steinhoff); *Das gelbe Haus des King-Fu* (Grune); *La Petite Lise* (Grémillon); *Accusée, levez-vous!* (M. Tourneur)

1931 *La Bête errante* (de Gastyne); *Les Croix de bois* (Bernard); *Grains de beauté* (Caron); *Paris-Mediterranée* (May); *Partir* (M. Tourneur); *Le Roi du cirage* (Colombier)

1932 *Au nom de la loi* (M. Tourneur); *L'Ane de Bruidan* (Ryder); *Enlevez-moi* (Perret); *Mirages de Paris* (Ozep); *Les Gaietés de l'escadron* (M. Tourneur)

1933 *Les Deux Orphelines* (M. Tourneur); *Chotard et Cie* (Renoir); *Tout pour rien* (Pujol); *Charlemagne* (Colombier); *Ces messieurs de la Santé* (Colombier); *Totò* (J. Tourneur); *Les Deux Canards* (Schmidt); *Il était une fois* (Perret); *Léopold le bienaimé* (Brun); *Le Paquebot Tenacity* (Duvivier); *Théodore et Cie* (Colombier)

1934 *L'Atalante* (Vigo); *Les Misérables* (Bernard—3 parts); *Dactylo se marie* (May and Pujol); *Sapho* (Perret); *Mam'zelle Spahi* (de Vaucorbeil); *Zouzou* (M. Allégret); *Tartarin de tarascon* (Bernard)

1935 *La Rosière des Halles* (de Limur); *Le Bonheur* (L'Herbier); *L'École des cocottes* (Colombier); *Le Clown Bux* (Natanson); *Princess Tam-Tam* (Gréville); *Le Bébé de l'escadron* (Sti)

1937 *Ces dames aux chapeaux verts* (Cloche); *Ramuntcho* (Barberis)

1938 *Le Paradis de Satan* (Gandera); *Werther* (Le Roman de Werther) (Ophüls); *La Bête humaine* (The Human Beast) (Renoir)

1939 *L'Enfer du jeu* (Macao, l'enfer du jeu) (Delannoy); *La Règle du jeu* (The Rules of the Game) (Renoir); *Air pur* (Clair—unfinished)

1940 *Sans lendemain* (Ophüls)

1941 *Nous les gosses* (Daquin); *Le Pavillon brûle* (de Baroncelli); *Ce n'est pas moi* (de Baroncelli); *La Maison des sept jeunes filles* (Valentin); *La Duchesse de Langeais* (de Baroncelli)

Films as Art Director:

1942 *Le Dernier atout* (Jacques Becker)

1943 *Lumière d'été* (Grémillon); *Adieu . . . Léonard!* (P. Prévert); *Feu Nicolas* (Houssin)

1944 *Le Ciel est à vous* (Grémillon)

1945 *Falbalas* (Paris Frills) (Jacques Becker); *La Ferme du pendu* (Dréville); *Les Dames du Bois de Boulogne* (Bresson); *François Villon* (Zwobada)

1946 *L'Affaire du collir de la reine* (The Queen's Necklace) (L'Herbier); *Pétrus* (M. Allégret)

1947 *Le Diable au corps* (Devil in the Flesh) (Autant-Lara); *Quai des Orfèvres* (Clouzot)

1948 *Le Mystère de la chambre jaune* (Aisner); *Manon* (Clouzot)

1949 *Occupe-toi d'Amélie* (Oh Amelia!) (Autant-Lara); *Le Parfum de la dame en noir* (Daquin); "Le Retour de Jean" ep. of *Retour à la vie* (Clouzot); *La Belle que voilà* (Le Chanois)

1950 *Terreur en Oklahoma* (Heinrich and Paviot—short); *Sans laisser d'adresse* (Le Chanois); *Adventures of Captain Fabian* (Marshall)

1951 *Agence matrimoniale* (Le Chanois); *L'Auberge rouge* (The Red Inn) (Autant-Lara)

1952 Linking sketch and "L'Orgueil" ("Pride") ep. of *Les Septs Péchés capitaux* (The Seven Capital Sins) (Lacombe and Autant-Lara)

1953 *Le Bon Dieu sans confession* (Autant-Lara); *Le Blé en herbe* (The Game of Love) (Autant-Lara)

1954 *L'Affaire Maurizius* (Duvivier); *Le Rouge et le noir* (Autant-Lara)

1955 *French Can-Can* (Only the French Can) (Renoir); *Les Mauvaises Rencontres* (Astruc); *Cela s'appelle l'aurore* (Buñuel); *Mutter Courage und ihre Kinder* (Staudte—unfinished)

1956 *Marguerite de la nuit* (Autant-Lara); *La Traversée de Paris* (Four Bags Full) (Autant-Lara)

1957 *Tamango* (Berry)

1958 *Celui qui doit mourir* (He Who Must Die) (Dassin); *En cas de malheur* (Love Is My Profession) (Autant-Lara); *Le Joueur* (Autant-Lara)

1959 *Les Dragueurs* (Mocky); *La Jument verte* (The Green Mare) (Autant-Lara)

1960 *Les Régates de San Francisco* (Autant-Lara); *Le Bois des amants* (Autant-Lara); *Le panier à crabes* (Lisbona)

1961 *Tu ne tueras point* (Non uccidere; Thou Shalt Not Kill) (Autant-Lara); *Le Comte de Monte Cristo* (The Story of the Count of Monte Cristo) (Autant-Lara—2 parts); "La Colère" ("Anger") ep. of *Les Sept Péchés capitaux* (The Seven Capital Sins) (Dhomme) (adviser)

1962 *Phaedra* (Dassin); *Vive Henri IV, vive l'amour* (Autant-Lara); *Mandarin, bandit gentilhomme* (Le Chanois)

1963 *Le Meurtrier* (Enough Rope) (Autant-Lara)

1964 *Le Magot de Joséfa* (Autant-Lara); "La Fourmi" ep. of *Humour noir* (Autant-Lara); *Topkapi* (Dassin); *Patate* (Friend of the Family) (Thomas)

1965 *Le Journal d'une femme en blanc* (A Woman in White) (Autant-Lara); *Thunderball* (Young) (uncredited); *Un Monde nouveau* (A Young World) (De Sica); *Fantômas se déchaîne* (Hunebelle)

1966 *La Seconde Vérité* (Christian-Jaque); *Le Nouveau Journal d'une femme en blanc* (Une Femme en blanc se revolte) (Autant-Lara); *Atout coeur à Tokyo pour OSS 177* (Boisrond)

1967 *Fantômas contre Scotland Yard* (Hunebelle); "Aujourd'hui" ep. of *Le Plus Vieux Métier du monde* (The Oldest Profession) (Autant-Lara); *Le Franciscain de Bourges* (Autant-Lara)

1969 *Catherine, il suffit d'un amour* (Borderie); *Les Patates* (Autant-Lara); *Castle Keep* (Pollack)

1970 *Tang* (Michel)

1971   *Joseph Balsamo* (Hunebelle); *Bouevard du Rhum* (Enrico); *La Cavale* (Mitrani)

1972   *Les Caids* (Enrico); *Le Moine* (Kyrou); *L'Insolent* (Roy)

1973   *A nous quatre, Cardinal* (Hunebelle); *Les Quatre Charlots mousequetaires* (Hunebelle)

1975   *Section speciale* (Special Section) (Costa-Gavras); *Le Sauvage* (Rappeneau)

1976   *La Victoire en chantant* (Annaud); *Vous n'aurez pas l'Alsace et la Lorraine* (Coluche)

1979   *Moonraker* (Gilbert)

1980   *Le Malevil* (de Chalonge)

1981   *Les quarantième rugissante* (de Chalonge)

1984   *Monsieur de Pourceaugnas* (Mitrani)

Publications

By DOUY: books—

With Jacques Douy, *Décors de Cinéma*, 1993.

By DOUY: articles—

Film Français (Paris), 28 November 1975.
Positif (Paris), July-August 1981.
Positif (Paris), September 1981.

On DOUY: articles—

Unifrance (Paris), May 1950.
Cinéma Français (Paris), 24 February 1951.
Film Français (Paris), 17 June 1977.
Cinématographe (Paris), March 1982.

*   *   *

Max Douy was one of the most prolific art directors of French cinema. Having regularly collaborated on the films of Claude Autant-Lara since *Le Diable au corps*, he contributed greatly to the French ''tradition of quality'' which the New Wave critics and filmmakers so virulently attacked. This work with Autant-Lara was often in the service of narratives in which stylized poetry (in the manner of the collaborations between Lazare Meerson and René Clair, or Alexandre Trauner and Marcel Carné) was less important than sober issues of character psychology and morality. Consequently, his sets often were conceived in order to complement a visual style which foregrounded dialogue rather than décor and their relationship to narrative requirements frequently made them persuasively, although discreetly, realistic. Indeed, Douy's skill was such that sets for exteriors often could be mistaken for real locations. For example, the garden of the Jaubert family and the streets in which Gérard Philipe meets the husband of Micheline Presle and asks him for a light for his cigarette in *Le Diable au corps*, or the small provincial square of *Le Ciel est à vous*.

Douy vigorously defended such a use of studio sets for exteriors against the location shooting that emerged with the New Wave. The greater control of work conditions and of lighting, especially important for color films, complied with his insistence on quality professionalism. For *L'Auberge rouge*, Douy said that only 17 shots were actual exterior locations; everything else, including the little bridge and the credits, were studio sets. His designs for interiors, such as the reconstruction of the Véfour Restaurant and Harry's Bar in *Le Diable au corps*, Bernard Blier's and Suzy Delair's apartment in *Quai des Orfèvres* (based on Douy's own apartment), could also be convincingly realistic.

Nevertheless, the vast experience of Douy led him to work in many styles. Although the most successful films on which he worked usually required an efficiently unobtrusive impression of the real that suited the needs of a somewhat solemn psychological realism, he was also responsible for more flamboyant designs: the widely acclaimed theatrical sets of *Occupe-toi d'Amélie*, so wittily used by Autant-Lara; the stylization of *Le Rouge et le noir*, an important part of the simplification of Stendhal's novel in order to avoid a crushing décor and to facilitate concentration on characters and dialogue; the expressionistic quality of the sets for *Marguerite de la nuit*, translucent and colored and lit from behind; the silhouettes of the theatrical flats that reconstruct a familiar yet strangely unreal Paris for *La Traversée de Paris*; or the gothic designs for *Castle Keep* in which the sets have the force of a character.

Yet whatever the degree of reality inherent in Douy's designs, they were always conceived and constructed to serve the subject of the film; stylization was never the result of gratuitous ostentation. Indeed, Douy's insistence on filmmaking as a team activity, thoroughly opposed to the New Wave's individualistic notions of ''auteur,'' excluded all possibility of any such gratuitous brilliance that could run contrary to the needs of a narrative. His preferred way of working involved very close preproduction collaboration with the director and other members of the team. He preferred to prepare drawings of the sets as they were to appear on the screen, taking into account the focal length of the lens used, and consequently he designed and built his sets according to the dramatic necessity of camera angles and camera and actor movement. Such a method, developed in France during the 1930s by art directors such as Jacques Colombier and Jean Perrier (to whom Douy was assistant), involves meticulous shot by shot preparation and not only ensures that the sets serve the requirements of the narrative, but is also economical and allows directors to concentrate on the direction of actors during the shooting. Such an intense collaboration is especially characteristic of Douy's work with Autant-Lara, Henri-Georges Clouzot, and Jean-Paul Le Chanois.

Douy's thorough professionalism was the result of a long career, begun at the age of 16. He worked for 12 years as an assistant art director, serving apprenticeship to most of the great designers of the 1930s: at Pathé-Natan he worked not only with Jean Perrier and Jacques Colombier, but also with Lucien Aguettand and Guy de Castyne. He later worked with Francis Jourdain on the cluttered and realistic sets of Jean Vigo's *L'Atalante*, and with Lazare Meerson on Marc Allégret's *Zouzou* and Edmond Gréville's *Princesse Tam-Tam*. Collaborating with Eugene Lourié on Jean Renoir's *La Bête humaine* and *La Règle du jeu*, Douy worked on sets which have the same force of realism as his later designs for *Le Diable au corps*.

—Richard Alwyn

DREIER, Hans

Art Director. **Nationality:** German. **Born:** Bremen, 21 August 1885. **Education:** Studied engineering and architecture, Munich University. **Military Service:** Served in the German army during World War

I. **Career:** Supervising architect for German government in the Cameroons; 1919–23—designer for UFA/EFA, Berlin; 1923–28—art director, and then head designer and supervising art director, 1928–51, Paramount, Hollywood. **Awards:** Academy Award for *Frenchman's Creek*, 1945, *Sunset Boulevard*, 1950, *Samson and Delilah*, 1950. **Died:** In Bernardsville, New Jersey, 24 October 1966.

Films as Art Director:

1919   *Der letzte Zeuge* (Gartner); *Lillis Ehe* (Speyer); *Der Teufel und die Madonna* (Boese and Speyer); *Maria Magdalena* (Schünzel); *Seelenverkäufer* (Boese); *Seine Beichte* (Moest); *Die Duplizität der Ereignisse* (Gärtner)

1920   *Das Frauenhaus von Brescia* (Moest); *Der Marquis d'Or* (Schünzel); *Der Reigen* (Oswald); *Die Fürstin Woronzoff* (Gärtner); *Florentinische Nachte* (Wienskowitz and Wassung); *Kurfurstendamm (Ein Höllenspuk in 6 Akten)* (Oswald); *Lady Godiva* (Moest); *Maria Tudor* (Gärtner); *Max, der Vielgeprüfte* (Grunwald); *Nachtgestvalten* (Oswald); *Napoleon und die kleine Wäscherin* (Gärtner); *Sizilianische Blutrache* (Gärtner); *Ut Mine Stromtid* (Moest); *Die Stimme* (Gärtner); *Manolescus Memoiren* (Oswald)

1921   *Danton (All for a Woman)* (Buchowertzki); *Das Rätsel der Sphinx* (Gärtner); *Lady Hamilton* (Oswald); *Die grosse und die kleine Welt* (Mack); *Fahrendes Volk* (Gärtner); *Die Liebschaftenden des Hektor Dalmore* (Oswald)

1922   *Fridericus Rex: Ein Königsschicksal* (von Csrépy); *Peter der Grosse* (Buchowetzki)

1923   *Boheme* (Righelli); *Die Frau mit den Millionen* (Wolff)

1924   *Forbidden Paradise* (Lubitsch)

1925   *East of Suez* (Walsh)

1927   *Underworld* (von Sternberg); *The Student Prince* (Lubitsch)

1928   *The Last Command* (von Sternberg); *The Dragnet* (von Sternberg); *The Patriot* (Lubitsch); *The Street of Sin* (Stiller); *The Docks of New York* (von Sternberg)

1929   *A Dangerous Woman* (Lee); *Betrayal* (Milestone); *The Case of Lena Smith* (von Sternberg); *Thunderbolt* (von Sternberg); *The Love Parade* (Lubitsch)

1930   *Monte Carlo* (Lubitsch); *The Vagabond King* (Berger); *Morocco* (von Sternberg)

1931   *An American Tragedy* (von Sternberg); *Dishonored* (von Sternberg); *The Smiling Lieutenant* (Lubitsch); **Dr. Jekyll and Mr. Hyde** (Mamoulian)

1932   *Love Me Tonight* (Mamoulian); *The Man I Killed (Broken Lullaby)* (Lubitsch); *One Hour with You* (Lubitsch and Cukor); *A Farewell to Arms* (Borzage); *Trouble in Paradise* (Lubitsch); *Shanghai Express* (von Sternberg)

1933   *This Day and Age* (DeMille); *Design for Living* (Lubitsch); *Song of Songs* (Mamoulian); *Duck Soup* (McCarey); *White Woman* (Walker); *I'm No Angel* (Ruggles); *One Sunday Afternoon* (Roberts)

1934   *Kiss and Make Up* (Thompson); *Ladies Should Listen* (Taurog); *We're Not Dressing* (Taurog); *Cleopatra* (DeMille); *Six of a Kind* (McCarey); *Now and Forever* (Hathaway); *It's a Gift* (McLeod); **The Scarlet Empress** (von Sternberg); *Belle of the Nineties* (McCarey)

1935   *The Crusades* (DeMille); *So Red the Rose* (K. Vidor); *Paris in the Spring* (Milestone); *The Lives of a Bengal Lancer* (Hathaway); **The Devil Is a Woman** (von Sternberg); *Ruggles of Red Gap* (McCarey); *Rumba* (Gering); *Peter Ibbetson* (Hathaway); *Enter Madam* (Nugent); *Wings in the Dark* (Flood); *The Last Outpost* (Barton and Gasnier); *Goin' to Town* (Hall)

1936   *Hollywood Boulevard* (Florey); *Wedding Present* (Wallace); *Go West, Young Man* (Hathaway); *Desire* (Borzage); *Klondike Annie* (Walsh); *Anything Goes (Tops Is the Limit)* (Milestone); *The General Died at Dawn* (Milestone); *Mississippi* (Sutherland); *The Trail of the Lonesome Pine* (Hathaway); *The Plainsman* (DeMille); *Poppy* (Sutherland); *The Big Broadcast of 1937* (Leisen); *Border Flight* (Lovering); *Desert Gold* (Hogan); *F-Man* (Cline); *Girl of the Ozarks* (Shea); *Give Us This Night* (Hall); *Lady Be Careful* (Reed); *The Preview Murder Mystery* (Florey); *The Princess Comes Across* (Howard); *The Texas Rangers* (K. Vidor); *Yours for the Asking* (Hall)

1937   *Angel* (Lubitsch); *Artists and Models* (Walsh); *The Buccaneer* (DeMille); *Easy Living* (Leisen); *Bulldog Drummond Comes Back* (L. King); *High, Wide, and Handsome* (Mamoulian); *Hold 'em, Navy* (Neumann); *I Met Him in Paris* (Ruggles); *King of Gamblers* (Florey); *Interns Can't Take Money* (Santell); *Night Club Scandal* (Murray); *Make Way for Tomorrow* (McCarey); *Mountain Music* (Florey); *Partners in Crime* (Murphy); *Souls at Sea* (Hathaway); *Swing High, Swing Low* (Leisen); *This Way Please* (Florey); *Thrill of a Lifetime* (Archainbaud); *True Confessions* (Ruggles); *Turn Off the Moon* (Seiler); *Wells Fargo* (Lloyd)

1938   *The Arkansas Traveler* (Santell); *You and Me* (F. Lang); *Artists and Models Abroad* (Leisen); *Zaza* (Cukor); *The Big Broadcast of 1938* (Leisen); *College Swing* (Walsh); *Bluebeard's Eighth Wife* (Lubitsch); *Hunted Men* (L. King); *Bulldog Drummond in Africa* (L. King); *Campus Confessions* (Archainbaud); *Bulldog Drummond's Peril* (Hogan); *Give Me a Sailor* (Nugent); *If I Were King* (Lloyd); *Illegal Traffic* (L. King); *Prison Farm* (L. King); *Sing You Sinners* (Ruggles); *Sons of the Legion* (Hogan); *Stolen Heaven* (Stone); *Thanks for the Memory* (Archainbaud)

1939   *Arrest Bulldog Drummond* (Hogan); *Beau Geste* (Wellman); *Bulldog Drummond's Bride* (Hogan); *Café Society* (Griffith); *The Cat and the Canary* (Nugent); *Disbarred* (Florey); *Disputed Passage* (Borzage); *Geronimo* (Sloane); *The Gracie Allen Murder Case* (Green); *Grand Jury Secrets* (Hogan); *The Great Victor Herbert* (Stone); *Invitation to Happiness* (Ruggles); *The Light That Failed* (Wellman); *Man about Town* (Sandrich); *Never Say Die* (Nugent); *Our Neighbors, the Carters* (Murphy); *One Thousand Dollars a Touchdown* (Hogan); *Persons in Hiding* (L. King); *Rulers of the Sea* (Lloyd); *Some Like It Hot* (Archainbaud); *Union Pacific* (DeMille); *Night of Nights* (Milestone); *St. Louis Blues* (Walsh)

1940   *Arise My Love* (Leisen); *Victory* (Cromwell); *North West Mounted Police* (DeMille); *The Biscuit Eater* (Heisler); *Buck Benny Rides Again* (Sandrich); *Christmas in July* (P. Sturges); *Comin' round the Mountain* (Archainbaud); *Dr. Cyclops* (Schoedsack); *Emergency Squad* (Dmytryk); *The Farmer's Daughter* (Hogan); *Golden Gloves* (Dmytryk); *The Great McGinty* (P. Sturges); *I Want a Divorce* (Murphy); *Love Thy Neighbor* (Sandrich); *Mystery Sea Raider* (Phy);

(Dmytryk); *Opened by Mistake* (Archainbaud); *A Night at Earl Carroll's* (Neumann); *The Ghost Breakers* (Marshall); *Queen of the Mob* (Hogan); *Rangers of Fortune* (Wood); *Remember the Night* (Leisen); *Road to Singapore* (Schertzinger); *Safari* (Griffith); *Seventeen* (L. King); *Those Were the Days* (Reed); *Typhoon* (L. King); *Untamed* (Archainbaud); *Women without Names* (Florey)

1941   *Aloma of the South Seas* (Santell); *Bahama Passage* (Griffith); *Birth of the Blues* (Schertzinger); *Buy Me That Town* (Forde); *Caught in the Draught* (Butler); *Glamour Boy* (Murphy); *Henry Aldrich for President* (Bennett); *Hold Back the Dawn* (Leisen); *I Wanted Wings* (Leisen); *Louisiana Purchase* (Cummings); *New York Town* (C. Vidor); *Night of January 16th* (Clemens); *Nothing but the Truth* (Nugent); *One Night in Lisbon* (Griffith); *The Shepherd of the Hills* (Hathaway); *Skylark* (Sandrich); *There's Magic in Music* (Stone); *Virginia* (Griffith); *West Point Widow* (Siodmak); **Sullivan's Travels** (Sturges)

1942   *Beyond the Blue Horizon* (Santell); *Dr. Broadway* (A. Mann); *The Forest Rangers* (Marshall); *The Glass Key* (Heisler); *The Great Man's Lady* (Wellman); *Henry Aldrich, Editor* (Bennett); *Holiday Inn* (Sandrich); *I Married a Witch* (Clair); *Lucky Jordan* (Tuttle); *The Major and the Minor* (Wilder); *Mrs. Wiggs of the Cabbage Patch* (Murphy); *My Favorite Blonde* (Lanfield); *A Night in New Orleans* (Clemens); *My Heart Belongs to Daddy* (Siodmak); *Pacific Blackout* (Murphy); *Palm Beach Story* (P. Sturges); *Priorities on Parade* (Rogell); *Reap the Wild Wind* (DeMille); *Road to Morocco* (Butler); *Star Spangled Rhythm* (Marshall); *Street of Chance* (Hively); *Sweater Girl* (Clemens); *Take a Letter, Darling* (Leisen); *This Gun for Hire* (Tuttle); *Wake Island* (Farrow)

1943   *China* (Farrow); *The Crystal Ball* (Nugent); *Five Graves to Cairo* (Wilder); *For Whom the Bell Tolls* (Wood); *The Good Fellows* (Graham); *Happy Go Lucky* (Bernhardt); *Henry Aldrich Gets Glamour* (Bennett); *Henry Aldrich Haunts a House* (Bennett); *Henry Aldrich Swings It* (Bennett); *Hostages* (Tuttle); *Lady Bodyguard* (Clemens); *No Time for Love* (Leisen); *Riding High* (Marshall); *Salute for Three* (Murphy); *So Proudly We Hail* (Sandrich); *True to Life* (Marshall); *Young and Willing* (Griffith)

1944   *And Now Tomorrow* (Pichel); *And the Angels Sing* (Binyon); **Double Indemnity** (Wilder); *Frenchman's Creek* (Leisen); *Going My Way* (McCarey); *The Great Moment* (P. Sturges); *Hail the Conquering Hero* (P. Sturges); *Henry Aldrich, Boy Scout* (Bennett); *Here Comes the Waves* (Sandrich); *Henry Aldrich Plays Cupid* (Bennett); *Henry Aldrich's Little Secret* (Bennett); *The Hitler Gang* (Farrow); *The Hours before the Dawn* (Tuttle); *Lady in the Dark* (Leisen); *The Man in Half Moon Street* (Murphy); *Ministry of Fear* (F. Lang); *The Miracle of Morgan's Creek* (P. Sturges); *The National Barn Dance* (Bennett); *Practically Yours* (Leisen); *Our Hearts Were Young and Gay* (Allen); *Rainbow Island* (Murphy); *Standing Room Only* (Lanfield); *Till We Meet Again* (Borzage); *The Story of Dr. Wassell* (DeMille); *The Uninvited* (Allen); *You Can't Ration Love* (Fuller)

1945   *The Affairs of Susan* (Seiter); *Duffy's Tavern* (Walker); *Hold That Blonde* (Marshall); *Incendiary Blonde* (Marshall); *Kitty* (Leisen); **The Lost Weekend** (Wilder); *Love Letters*

(Dieterle); *Masquerade in Mexico* (Leisen); *A Medal for Benny* (Pichel); *Miss Susie Slagle's* (Berry); *Murder, He Says* (Marshall); *Out of This World* (Walker); *Road to Utopia* (Walker); *Salty O'Rourke* (Walsh); *The Story Club* (Walker); *The Unseen* (Allen); *You Came Along* (Farrow)

1946   *The Blue Dahlia* (Marshall); *The Bride Wore Boots* (Pichel); *California* (Farrow); *Monsieur Beaucaire* (Marshall); *O.S.S.* (Pichel); *Our Hearts Were Growing Up* (Russell); *The Searching Wind* (Dieterle); *To Each His Own* (Leisen); *The Strange Love of Martha Ivers* (Milestone); *Two Years before the Mast* (Farrow); *The Virginian* (Gilmore); *The Well-Groomed Bride* (Lanfield)

1947   *Suddenly It's Spring* (Leisen); *Blaze of Noon* (Farrow); *Calcutta* (Farrow); *Dear Ruth* (Russell); *Easy Come, Easy Go* (Farrow); *Golden Earrings* (Leisen); *I Walk Alone* (Haskin); *The Imperfect Lady* (Allen); *Ladies' Man* (Russell); *My Favorite Brunette* (Nugent); *The Perils of Pauline* (Marshall); *The Road to Rio* (McLeod); *The Trouble with Women* (Lanfield); *Unconquered* (DeMille); *Variety Girl* (Marshall); *Welcome Stranger* (Nugent); *Where There's Life* (Lanfield); *Wild Harvest* (Garnett)

1948   *The Accused* (Dieterle); *Beyond Glory* (Farrow); *The Big Clock* (Farrow); *Dream Girl* (Leisen); *The Emperor Waltz* (Wilder); *A Foreign Affair* (Wilder); *Hazard* (Marshall); *Isn't It Romantic?* (McLeod); *Miss Tatlock's Millions* (Haydn); *My Own True Love* (Bennett); *The Night Has a Thousand Eyes* (Farrow); *The Paleface* (McLeod); *Saigon* (Fenton); *The Sainted Sisters* (Russell); *Sealed Verdict* (Allen); *Sorry, Wrong Number* (Litvak); *Whispering Smith* (Fenton)

1949   *Alias Nick Beal* (Farrow); *Bride of Vengeance* (Leisen); *A Connecticut Yankee in King Arthur's Court* (Garnett); *The File on Thelma Jordan* (Siodmak); *The Great Gatsby* (Nugent); *The Great Lover* (Hall); *Dear Wife* (Haydn); *My Friend Irma* (Marshall); *Red, Hot, and Blue* (Farrow); *Rope of Sand* (Dieterle); *Samson and Delilah* (DeMille); *Song of Surrender* (Leisen); *Sorrowful Jones* (Lanfield); *Streets of Laredo* (Fenton); *Top o' the Morning* (Miller)

1950   *Dark City* (Dieterle); **Sunset Boulevard** (Wilder); *No Man of Her Own* (Leisen); *Riding High* (Capra); *Paid in Full* (Dieterle); *Captain Carey, U.S.A.* (Leisen); *My Friend Irma Goes West* (Wallis); *The Furies* (A. Mann); *Union Station* (Maté); *Copper Canyon* (Farrow); *Let's Dance* (McLeod); *Fancy Pants* (Marshall); *Mr. Music* (Haydn); *September Affair* (Dieterle); *Branded* (Maté)

1951   *Appointment with Danger* (Allen); *A Place in the Sun* (Stevens)

1957   *A Farewell to Arms* (C. Vidor)

Publications

By DREIER: articles—

"Motion Picture Sets," in *Journal of the Society of Motion Picture Engineers* (Easton, Pennsylvania), November 1931.

"Designing the Sets," in *We Make the Movies*, edited by Nancy Naumburg, New York, 1937.

"Les Decors," in *Silence, on tourne*, Paris, 1948.

On DREIER: articles—

Thompson, David, in *American Film* (Washington, D.C.), February 1977.
In *The Art of Hollywood*, edited by John Hambley, London, 1979.
Dickstein, M., "Out of the Past: *Sunset Boulevard* Revisited," in *Chaplin* (Stockholm), vol. 31, no. 1, 1989.
Girard, Martin, "Hollywood gothique: *Sunset Blvd.*," in *Séquences* (Haute-Ville), April 1994.
Lambert, Gavin, "Origins of the *Sunset Boulevard* Mansion: An Academy Award-winning Design That Blurred Fact and Fiction," in *Architectural Digest* (Los Angeles), April 1998.

* * *

The influx of talented Germans who invaded Hollywood in the 1920s to change the course of American filmmaking included art director Hans Dreier. Like other German moviemakers, inspired by Expressionist art movements and the theater of Max Reinhardt, Dreier conveyed moments of horror and intensity by using such stylistic devices as violent lines, exaggerated spaces, and dramatic *chiaroscuro*.

Dreier's films with Josef von Sternberg rank among the art director's most expressionistic. His torturous, Russo-Byzantine *The Scarlet Empress* and moody *Shanghai Express* produced in viewers an empathetic anxiety towards the characters' situations. In many ways, these films served as precursors to the *film noir*. Dreier's early training as an architect enabled him to manipulate space expertly. He finished these environments with such evocative details as posters peeling from aging walls and discarded clothing draped on idle chairs. This type of ambience continued to appear in his work as late as 1950 with his designs (done in collaboration with John Meehan) for Billy Wilder's *Sunset Boulevard*.

Dreier's alternative style can be compared to early, German-period epics of Fritz Lang and Ernst Lubitsch; in these, the artist sacrifices accuracy for effect. For Cecil B. DeMille's *Cleopatra* and *The Crusades*, Dreier produced a curious hybrid—an international *moderne* translation of a 19th-century academic interpretation of a historic time. Retaining those elements conforming to contemporary taste, revelling in emblem and drapery, this style suggested the past but in popular proportions.

Dreier developed a different style for Lubitsch's later films, in which he illustrated the decadent aristocracy's fantastic world—as delectable as a Viennese pastry. Slightly restrained, yet still ornate, his curves whipped gaily with the rhythms of light operetta, rather than those of an intricate, rococo string quartet.

Director Rouben Mamoulian depended on Dreier to adapt previous visual treatments for his particular directorial ends. Mamoulian often based his works on other directors' special genres, but injected his own insights along the way. *Love Me Tonight* paid homage to Lubitsch, for instance, while *Song of Songs* paid respects to von Sternberg's image of Marlene Dietrich. Mamoulian's *Dr. Jekyll and Mr. Hyde* contrasted Dreier's updated Beaux Arts neoclassicism with Expressionism, as Jekyll's respectably ordered universe clashed with Hyde's chaotic disrepute to illustrate the theme of man's dual nature. With his own disparate styles, it might be said that Dreier illustrated just such a coexistence in his work.

—Edith C. Lee

DRIESSEN, Paul

Animator. **Nationality:** Dutch. **Born:** Nijmegen, 1940. **Education:** Attended the Academy of Arts, Utrecht. **Career:** Early 1960s—worked in animation studio making films for television, Hilversum; 1968—made his first animated film, *The Story of Little John Bailey*; since 1970—worked from his studio in the Netherlands with Nico Crama, and also from the National Film Board of Canada and the Canadian Broadcasting Corporation; 1996, story consultant for *Quest*. **Address:** c/o National Film Board of Canada, Studio A, P.O. Box 6100, Montreal PQ H3C 3H5, Canada.

Films as Animator:

1968 *The Story of Little John Bailey*
1972 *Le Bleu perdu*; *Air*
1974 *Cat's Cradle* (*Au bout du fil*)
1975 *An Old Box*
1977 *David*; *The Killing of an Egg*
1980 *On Land, at Sea, and in the Air*; *Elbowing* (*Jeu de coudes*)
1982 *Home on the Rails*; *The Same Old Story*; *Oh What a Knight*
1983 *Spotting a Cow*
1986 *Elephantrio*
1995 *The End of the World in Four Seasons* (+ d)

Publications

By DRIESSEN: articles—

Séquences (Montreal), January 1978.
Skoop (Amsterdam), July 1978.
Skrien (Amsterdam), April 1981.
Positif (Paris), June 1987.
CinémAction (Conde-sur-Noireau), no. 51, April 1989.

On DRIESSEN: articles—

Cinema Canada, March 1979.
24 Images (Montreal), no. 43, Summer 1989.
Film a Doba (Prague), Summer 1994.
24 Images (Montreal), no. 80, December-January 1995–96.

* * *

Paul Driessen is a highly original artist whose work can be recognized instantly. His films have three basic elements which make them different from others: the drawings look like scribbles which could just as well come from the pen of a child; his stories are not for children but primarily have adult appeal; and his humor is purely visual. He makes a character out of a dot and plays with contrasting dimensions and fantasy to such an extent that they become ridiculous. Apart from these values, his graphic treatment of contrasting black-and-white tonal forms provides a vibrance seldom experienced on the screen.

Driessen feels he is lucky not to have known anything about animation up to the time he met Jim Hiltz in 1964, since he was not influenced by any particular style. Thereafter he truly earned the label

"The Flying Dutchman." In 1970 he went to Canada and since then divides his time in commuting between the National Film Board of Canada, the Canadian Broadcasting Corporation in Montreal, and his studio in Holland where he works with producer Nico Crama.

He recognizes the differences of the two continents. In Holland he enjoys its quiet isolation working alone; in Canada he likes the contact with other animators and the excellent equipment available. The unifying theme in his films is visual imagery, abstract cartoon ideas, and the mystic content of the stories. He categorizes his films as crazy tendencies in such productions as *Cat's Cradle* and *On Land, at Sea and in the Air*; short gags such as *The Killing of an Egg, Elbowing*, and *Oh What a Knight*; dramatic structures such as *An Old Box, David*, and *Spotting a Cow*. Visual gags play a significant role in all of them. Driessen states: "I like spending time on my back in the sun, dreaming up new ideas, a small but important part of my schedule. So little time, so much to do."

—John Halas

DUNING, George

Composer and Arranger. **Nationality:** American. **Born:** Richmond, Indiana, 25 February 1908. **Education:** Attended the Cincinnati Conservatory of Music and the University of Cincinnati; also studied with Mario Castelnuovo-Tedesco. **Military Service:** U.S. Navy, arranger and conductor for the Armed Forces Radio Service during World War II. **Career:** Band arranger; then musical director for Kay Kyser's radio program, eight years; 1939—first film as arranger, the Kay Kyser film *That's Right, You're Wrong*; 1944–62—contract arranger, and after 1947, composer, Columbia; then freelance composer; TV work includes the mini-series *The Dream Merchants*, 1980, and *Goliath Awaits*, 1981; 1983—retired.

Films as Arranger:

1939 *That's Right, You're Wrong* (Butler)
1944 *Show Business* (Marin); *Carolina Blues* (Jason)
1946 *Singing in the Corn* (*Give and Take*) (Lord)

Films as Composer:

1947 *Down to Earth* (Hall); *Lust for Gold* (Simon); *The Guilt of Janet Ames* (Levin); *I Love Trouble* (Simon); *The Corpse Came C.O.D.* (Levin); *Her Husband's Affairs* (Simon); *Johnny O'Clock* (Rossen)
1948 *To the Ends of the Earth* (Stevenson); *The Dark Past* (Maté); *Gallant Blade* (Levin); *The Man from Colorado* (Levin); *The Untamed Breed* (Lamont); *The Return of October* (Lewis)
1949 *Jolson Sings Again* (Levin); *Slightly French* (Sirk); *The Undercover Man* (Lewis); *The Doolins of Oklahoma* (Douglas); *And Baby Makes Three* (Levin); *Lust for Gold* (Simon); *Johnny Allegro* (*Hounded*) (Tetzlaff); *Shockproof* (Sirk)
1950 *No Sad Songs for Me* (Maté); *Convicted* (Levin); *Between Midnight and Dawn* (Douglas); *The Pretty Girl* (Levin);

Harriet Craig (V. Sherman); *Cargo to Capetown* (McEvoy); *The Flying Missile* (Levin)
1951 *The Barefoot Mailman* (McEvoy); *The Mob* (Parrish); *Lorna Doone* (Karlson); *Two of a Kind* (Levin); *Sunny Side of the Street* (Quine); *The Family Secret* (Levin); *The Lady and the Bandit* (Murphy); *Man in the Saddle* (de Toth); *Scandal Sheet* (*The Dark Page*) (Karlson)
1952 *Sound Off* (Quine); *All Ashore* (Quine); *Paula* (Maté); *Last of the Comanches* (de Toth); *Assignment in Paris* (Parrish); *Captain Pirate* (*Captain Blood, Fugitive*) (Murphy); *Affair in Trinidad* (V. Sherman); **From Here to Eternity** (Zinnemann)
1953 *Salome* (Dieterle); *Miss Sadie Thompson* (Bernhardt)
1954 *Three for the Show* (Potter); *Picnic* (Logan); *The Long Gray Line* (Ford)
1955 *The Man from Laramie* (A. Mann); *Soldier of Fortune* (Dmytryk); *Tight Spot* (Karlson); *Five against the House* (Karlson); *Count Three and Pray* (G. Sherman); *The Queen Bee* (MacDougall); *Three Stripes in the Sun* (*The Gentle Sergeant*) (Murphy); *My Sister Eileen* (Quine)
1956 *Nightfall* (J. Tourneur); *Storm Center* (Taradash); *You Can't Run Away from It* (Powell); *Full of Life* (Quine); *The Eddy Duchin Story* (Sidney)
1957 *The Shadow on the Window* (Asher); *Pal Joey* (Sidney); *Jeanne Eagels* (Sidney); *3:10 to Yuma* (Daves); *Operation Mad Ball* (Quine); *The Brothers Rico* (Karlson)
1958 *Gunman's Walk* (Karlson); *Houseboat* (Shavelson); *Cowboy* (Daves); *Bell, Book and Candle* (Quine)
1959 *Me and the Colonel* (Glenville); *It Happened to Jane* (Quine); *The Last Angry Man* (Daniel Mann); *Gidget* (Wendkos); *The Wreck of the Mary Deare* (Anderson)
1960 *Let No Man Write My Epitaph* (Leacock); *Man on a String* (de Toth); *The Wackiest Ship in the Navy* (Murphy); *All the Young Men* (Bartlett); *Strangers When We Meet* (Quine); *The World of Suzie Wong* (Quine)
1961 *Cry for Happy* (Marshall); *Gidget Goes Hawaiian* (Wendkos); *The Devil at 4 O'Clock* (LeRoy)
1962 *Thirteen West Street* (Leacock); *Who's Got the Action?* (Daniel Mann); *The Notorious Landlady* (Quine); *Two Rode Together* (Ford); *That Touch of Mink* (Delbert Mann); *Sail a Crooked Ship* (Brecher)
1963 *Toys in the Attic* (Hill); *Critic's Choice* (Weis); *Island of Love* (DaCosta); *Who's Been Sleeping in My Bed?* (A. Mann)
1964 *Ensign Pulver* (Logan)
1965 *Brainstorm* (Conrad); *Dear Brigitte* (Koster); *My Blood Runs Cold* (Conrad)
1966 *Any Wednesday* (Miller)
1967 *Quarantined* (L. Penn); *But I Don't Want to Get Married!* (Paris)
1971 *Yuma* (Post); *Black Noon* (Kowalski)
1972 *The Woman Hunter* (Kowalski); *The Great American Tragedy* (Lee Thompson); *Climb an Angry Mountain* (Horn)
1973 *Arnold* (Fenady); *Honor Thy Father* (Wendkos); *Terror in the Wax Museum* (Fenady)
1975 *The Abduction of Saint Anne* (*They've Kidnapped Anne Benedict*) (Falk)
1980 *The Man with Bogart's Face* (Day); *The Top of the Hill* (Grauman); *The Dream Merchants* (Sherman—for TV)
1981 *Goliath Awaits* (Connor—for TV)
1983 *Zorro and Son* (Beaumont and Myerson—series for TV)

Publications

By DUNING: articles—

''*Salome*,'' in *Film and TV Music* (New York), March/April 1953.
''*From Here to Eternity*,'' in *Film and TV Music* (New York), March/April 1954.
''A Hoosier in Hollywood,'' in *Soundtrack* (Hollywood), September 1994.
''An Interview with George Duning,'' in *Cue Sheet* (Hollywood), vol. 12, no. 1, 1996.

On DUNING: articles—

Morton, Lawrence, in *Quarterly of Film, Radio, and Television* (Berkeley, California), Winter 1951.
Lacombe, Alain, in *Hollywood*, Paris, 1983.
Steiner, Fred, in *Quarterly of the Library of Congress*, 1983.
Thomas, Tony, ''1987 Career Achievement Award To Be Presented to George Duning,'' in *Cue Sheet* (Hollywood), November 1987.
Larson, Randal, in *Soundtrack*, September 1990.
Karlin, Fred, in *Listening to Movies*, 1994.

* * *

Virtually an epitome of the solid, reliable craftsman in the days of high studio productivity, George Duning was for a 17-year period the mainstay composer of Columbia Pictures. During that period, when he proved himself adept at almost every kind of film scoring, Duning was nominated for an Oscar five times for *Jolson Sings Again*, *No Sad Songs for Me*, *From Here to Eternity*, *Picnic*, and *The Eddy Duchin Story*.

Born to musician parents, Duning never considered any path for himself other than music. He majored in theory at the Cincinnati Conservatory of Music. He also excelled in playing the trumpet and earned his first money performing with jazz groups and dance bands. Years later he would study composition with the esteemed Italian Mario Castelnuovo-Tedesco, but Duning's first work of writing music came in the popular field, making band arrangements. The next step was radio, where he gained a reputation as a fast and inventive arranger. Duning became the musical director for the Lucky Strike radio program *Kay Kyser's Kollege of Musical Knowledge* and held that post for eight years. His first film experience came in 1939 when Kyser was contracted by RKO to make a series of movies, starting with *That's Right, You're Wrong*. The last of the Kyser films, *Carolina Blues*, was made at Columbia and resulted in that studio putting Duning under contract as an arranger. Soon afterwards he joined the U.S. Navy and spent almost three years arranging and conducting programs for the Armed Forces Radio Service.

After his discharge Duning rejoined Columbia as an arranger and orchestrator but pestered the studio to give him a chance to write original dramatic compositions. His ability in this regard was well proven with *Johnny O'Clock*, and from then until he left Columbia in 1962 Duning scored at least half a dozen films each year. Thereafter, until his retirement in 1983, he freelanced. He claims never to have made a listing of his scores but estimates that the total number of feature and television films in which he has worked in various capacities probably totals 300. Of these he is especially proud of *Picnic*, the love theme of which is among the most acclaimed pieces

of film scoring; *3:10 to Yuma*; *Cowboy*; *Bell, Book and Candle*; *The World of Suzie Wong*; and *Toys in the Attic*.

A quiet, modest man, never a seeker of publicity, Duning is particularly well regarded in the Hollywood music community. Arthur Morton, who orchestrated most of Duning's scores during the Columbia years, says, ''George never took any easy means. He always had a shrewd sense of what would and wouldn't work in scoring films, of what you could and couldn't do. George is a first-class musician and working with him was a pleasure.''

—Tony Thomas

DUNN, Linwood

Special Effects Technician. **Nationality:** American. **Born:** Linwood Gale Dunn in Brooklyn, New York, 27 December 1904. **Education:** Attended Manual Training High School, Brooklyn. **Career:** Trainee projectionist; also played in band; 1925—assistant cameraman on Pathé serials, New York, then in Hollywood with Pathé, 1926–29; 1929–56—director of special effects, RKO: co-designer, Acme-Dunn Optical Printer; 1946—founder, Film Effects of Hollywood; President, American Society of Cinematographers. **Awards:** Academy Technical Award, 1946, 1980; Gordon E. Sawyer Award, 1984. **Died:** 15 May 1998, in Los Angeles, California, of cancer.

Films as Special Effects Technician (selected list):

1930	*Danger Lights* (Seitz); *Cimarron* (Ruggles)
1932	*The Most Dangerous Game* (Schoedsack and Pichel); *Bird of Paradise* (K. Vidor)
1933	*Flying Down to Rio* (Freeland); **King Kong** (Cooper and Schoedsack)
1934	*Down to Their Last Yacht* (Sloane)
1935	*She* (Pichel and Holden); *The Last Days of Pompeii* (Cooper and Schoedsack)
1938	**Bringing Up Baby** (Hawks)
1939	*Gunga Din* (Stevens); *The Hunchback of Notre Dame* (Dieterle)
1940	*The Swiss Family Robinson* (Ludwig)
1941	**Citizen Kane** (Welles)
1942	*The Navy Comes Through* (Sutherland); **Cat People** (J. Tourneur)
1943	*Bombardier* (Wallace)
1944	*Days of Glory* (J. Tourneur); *Experiment Perilous* (J. Tourneur)
1945	*A Game of Death* (Wise)
1949	*Mighty Joe Young* (Schoedsack)
1951	*The Thing* (Nyby)
1952	*Androcles and the Lion* (Erskine)
1953	*The French Line* (Bacon)
1961	**West Side Story** (Wise and Robbins)
1963	*It's a Mad, Mad, Mad, Mad World* (Kramer) (co)
1965	*The Great Race* (Edwards) (co); *La Bibbia* (*The Bible . . . in the Beginning*) (Huston)
1966	*Hawaii* (Hill) (co); *What Did You Do in the War, Daddy?* (Edwards) (co)
1969	*Airport* (Seaton)
1970	*Darling Lili* (Edwards) (co)
1976	*King Kong* (Guillermin)

Publications

By DUNN: book—

With George E. Turner, *The ASC Treasury of Visual Effects*, Hollywood, 1983.

By DUNN: articles—

"Effects and Titles for *West Side Story*," in *American Cinematographer* (Hollywood), December 1961.
"The 'Mad, Mad' World of Special Effects," in *American Cinematographer* (Hollywood), March 1965.
Journal of University Film Association (Carbondale, Illinois), vol. 26, no. 4, 1974.
Wide Angle (Athens, Ohio), vol. 1, no. 1 (revised), 1979.
Classic Images (Muscatine, Iowa), December 1982.
American Cinematographer (Hollywood), December 1985.

On DUNN: articles—

Brosnan, John, in *Movie Magic*, New York, 1974.
American Cinematographer (Hollywood), April 1985.
Eyman, Scott, in *Five American Cinematographers*, Metuchen, New Jersey, 1987.
Turner, George, in *American Cinematographer* (Hollywood), February 1990.
Obituary, in *Variety* (New York), 1 June 1998.

*   *   *

The name of Linwood Dunn is almost synonymous with the art of special effects: he created effects for several hundred motion pictures. Dunn was a production assistant cameraman with a Pathé serial unit in Astoria, Long Island, went to Hollywood in 1926, and in 1929 joined RKO Radio Pictures where he created all types of visual effects while working in their photographic effects department. Dunn developed highly creative uses for the optical printer, which he first used in 1928. The printer consisted of a modified motion picture camera set up on a solid base with a special precision motion picture projector—both driven in synchronization while the camera photographed the film carried in the projector. Through this film-copying process, the image in the projector could be modified in unlimited ways: superimposition of one or more images; various types of transitional effects from scene-to-scene; changes in size, screen quality, action speed; conversion from one screen format to another; and the introduction of many other modifications limited only by the imagination and skill of the operating cameraperson. The optical effects printer is truly the heart of the motion picture visual effects techniques. Its facilities have been utilized by practically every movie subsequently made. Dunn also carried on the development of complex traveling mattes, rear projection, and many other types of special photographic effects.

While he was at RKO, Dunn's work included effects for many major productions. He assisted the noted special effects expert Willis H. O'Brien on the classic *King Kong* after he convinced O'Brien that the optical printer could do certain complicated animation composites effectively (and speedily) and thus relieve O'Brien from occasional retakes of the animation. Dunn was then assigned to the optical effects for the entire production. In *Citizen Kane*, he used matte paintings, optical printing, rear projection, and miniatures to compensate for the minimal use of sets, and for the need to modify scenes during editing.

With the United States at war in 1942, Eastman Kodak commissioned Dunn to develop an effects optical printer for the armed forces motion picture units in various locations throughout the world, for which he received an Academy citation in 1946. When World War II ended, Dunn founded his own special effects studio and laboratory, Film Effects of Hollywood, while still continuing his work with RKO until the studio ceased operations in 1956. Film Effects pioneered the expansion of 16mm film into the production field, being the first to create sophisticated optical effects for the wider use of this medium. Also it became one of the first visual effects companies to offer a variety of effects to the growing number of independent production companies, effects that had previously been available primarily to those major studios that could afford their own elaborate special effects departments. The company handled the special effects for the NBC-TV series *Star Trek*, and was a consultant to Twentieth Century-Fox on *Star Wars* in 1977.

Towards the end of his life, Dunn was in great demand as a speaker and gave his comprehensive special effects film lecture at more than 100 institutions. In this presentation, he demonstrated how he used three separate filmed images of Katharine Hepburn, Cary Grant, and a leopard—optically combining them by split screen for *Bringing Up Baby*—and also described the methods of a variety of other sophisticated special effects from major films.

—James Limbacher

DUNNE, Philip

Writer and Director. **Nationality:** American. **Born:** New York City, 11 February 1908; son of the writer Finley Peter Dunne. **Education:** Attended St. Bernard's School, New York; Middlesex School, Massachusetts; Harvard University, Cambridge, Massachusetts, 1925–29, no degree. **Family:** Married Amanda Duff, 1939; three daughters. **Career:** 1929—worked for Guaranty Trust Company, New York; 1930–31—story reader, Fox Company; 1933—first film as writer, *Student Tour*; 1937–62—writer, 20th Century-Fox: also a director: first film as director, *The View from Pompey's Head*, 1955; 1942—staff member, Nelson Rockefeller's Office of the Coordinator of Inter-American Affairs; 1942–46—Chief of Production, Office of War Information, Overseas Branch; 1952 and 1956—speechwriter for Adlai Stevenson's presidential campaigns, and for John F. Kennedy's 1960 campaign. **Awards:** Writers Guild Laurel Award, 1961, and Valentine Davies Award, 1973. **Died:** June 1992.

Films as Writer:

1933   *Student Tour* (Bell)
1934   *The Count of Monte Cristo* (Lee)
1935   *The Melody Lingers On* (Burton)
1936   *The Last of the Mohicans* (Seitz)
1937   *Lancer Spy* (Ratoff); *Breezing Home* (Carruth) (co-story)
1938   *Suez* (Dwan)

Philip Dunne (foreground) with Richard Egan and Dana Wynter

1939 *The Rains Came* (Brown); *Swanee River* (Lanfield); *Stanley and Livingston* (H. King)
1940 *Johnny Apollo* (Hathaway)
1941 *How Green Was My Valley* (Ford)
1942 *Son of Fury* (Cromwell)
1947 *The Late George Apley* (Mankiewicz); *Forever Amber* (Preminger); *The Ghost and Mrs. Muir* (Mankiewicz)
1948 *The Luck of the Irish* (Koster); *Escape* (Mankiewicz)
1949 *Pinky* (Kazan)
1951 *Anne of the Indies* (Tourneur); *David and Bathsheba* (King)
1952 *Lydia Bailey* (Negulesco); *Way of a Gaucho* (Tourneur) (+ pr)
1953 *The Robe* (Koster)
1954 *Demetrius and the Gladiators* (Daves); *The Egyptian* (Curtiz)
1965 *The Agony and the Ecstasy* (Reed)

Films as Writer and Director:

1955 *The View from Pompey's Head* (+ pr)
1956 *Hilda Crane*
1957 *Three Brave Men*

1958 *Ten North Frederick*; *Blue Denim* (*Blue Jeans*)
1966 *Blindfold* (co-sc)

Films as Director:

1955 *Prince of Players*
1958 *In Love and War*
1961 *Wild in the Country*
1962 *Lisa* (*The Inspector*)

Publications

By DUNNE: books—

How Green Was My Valley (screenplay), in *Twenty Best Film Plays*, edited by John Gassner and Dudley Nichols, New York, 1943.
(Editor), *Mr. Dooley Remembers*, by Finley Peter Dunne, Boston, Massachusetts, 1963.
Take Two: A Life in Movies and Politics, New York, 1980.

247

By DUNNE: articles—

"The Documentary and Hollywood," in *Hollywood Quarterly*, January 1946.
"The Animal Called a Writer," in *Films and Filming* (London), September 1961.
Film Comment (New York), Winter 1970–71.
In *Blueprint on Babylon*, by J.D. Marshall, Los Angeles, California, 1978.
In *Backstory: Interviews with Screenwriters of Hollywood's Golden Age*, edited by Pat McGilligan, Berkeley, California, 1986.

On DUNNE: articles—

Stempel, Tom, in *American Screenwriters*, edited by Robert E. Morsberger, Stephen O. Lesser, and Randall Clark, Detroit, Michigan, 1984.
Dunne, John Gregory, "*How Green Was My Valley*: The Screenplay for Darryl F. Zanuck Film Production Directed by John Ford," in *New York Review of Books*, 16 May 1991.
Callenbach, Ernest, "*How Green Was My Valley*: The Screenplay for the John Ford Directed Film," in *Film Quarterly* (Berkeley), Fall 1991.
Obituary in *The New York Times*, 4 June 1992.
Obituary in *Variety* (New York), 8 June 1992.
Obituary in *Facts on File*, 11 June 1992.
Obituary in *Classic Images* (Muscatine), July 1992.

*   *   *

One of Hollywood's most respected screenwriters, Philip Dunne is best known for his successful adaptations of literary works. Throughout a 25-year association with 20th Century-Fox—which later included stints as both a producer and a director—Dunne wrote films noted for their intelligence, strongly developed characters, and frequent social commentary. He was also one of the film industry's leading liberal political activists—a role which found him labeled a Communist sympathizer in many quarters during the McCarthy era—as a principal organizer of the Writers Guild, and a sometime political speech writer for candidates ranging from Franklin Roosevelt to John F. Kennedy.

Although Dunne initially tried his hand at banking after leaving Harvard, literature had played an important role in his childhood (his father was the noted humorist Finley Peter Dunne) and his inclination toward writing was perhaps a natural one. Arriving in Hollywood in 1930, he was hired by Fox as a reader, then fired and rehired a year later as a junior writer, a position which found him assisting on various screenplays in a minor capacity. In 1934, he received his first chance as a full-fledged writer when he and Rowland Lee were assigned to co-author an adaptation of *The Count of Monte Cristo*. The film proved a success and Dunne began a long and fruitful collaboration with the studio, writing screenplays for such films as *Stanley and Livingstone*, *The Ghost and Mrs. Muir*, and *The Robe*. His work was characterized by its attention to details of character and human interaction and his literate handling of dialogue and the mechanics of storytelling.

During most of Dunne's tenure at Fox the studio was run by Darryl F. Zanuck, whose thoroughness in overseeing film productions extended to participating in script and story conferences. Zanuck was known for his willingness to tackle controversial social issues in the films he produced, and Dunne was assigned to write two of the most notable: *How Green Was My Valley*, the story of a Welsh mining family, and *Pinky*, which deals with the subject of racism. Both of these films represent Dunne's work at its best, displaying his talent for literary adaptation, his sensitivity to social and political problems, and his reliance on characters as the source of true dramatic conflict.

How Green Was My Valley, based on the novel by Richard Llewellyn and directed by John Ford, focuses on the hardships endured by one family, the Morgans, Welsh coal miners whose strong family bonds are torn apart by disagreements over labor strikes and the formation of a miners' union. Although the film's setting is Wales, the issue of unionization was an extremely controversial one in the United States at the time of its release, and *How Green Was My Valley* helped put a human face on the many nameless workers plagued by unsafe or unjust conditions both in America and abroad.

Pinky dealt with an issue much closer to home. The film stars Jeanne Crain as a light-skinned young black girl who is able to "pass for white" until she is forced to confront her own sense of identity and pride when she falls in love with a white doctor. The film was one of the first to confront the subject of racism, and it takes the issue a step further than does the book, *Quality*, on which it is based. *Quality* ends with the doctor rejecting the girl after learning she is black. Dunne and his cowriter, Dudley Nichols, altered this slightly, with the doctor now offering to marry Simons if she will continue to "pass"; Crain refusing, realizing at last that self-hatred is perhaps the most damaging form of prejudice. It is a perceptive alteration on the writers' part and one which allows the young heroine to grow throughout the course of the story.

Despite his tinkering with *Pinky's* conclusion, Dunne has been among the most successful adapters of literature because of his respect for the original author's intentions. He has stated in interviews that the three keys to adapting a novel are remaining true to the essence of the book and its author's style, allowing the characters to tell the story, and selecting the right scenes to retain for the screen. Michael Mann so highly regarded Dunne's adaptation skills, that he credited Dunne's 1936 screenplay as the source for his own 1992 film version of *The Last of the Mohicans*, rather than the original novel by James Fenimore Cooper.

Dunne's own autobiography, *Take Two: A Life in Movies and Politics*, is among the best-written and most informative books on Hollywood and the craft of screenwriting, and he has remained a vocal critic over the years of the auteur theory, likening the screenwriter to an architect and the director to a building contractor who imposes his own style on the architect's blueprints. Dunne's outings as a director have included such films as *Prince of Players* with Richard Burton and *Ten North Frederick* with Gary Cooper, but it is as a screenwriter that Dunne will be remembered, with the intelligence, insight, and concern for the human condition that mark his work, remaining rare and valued qualities on the screen.

—Janet Lorenz

DUNNING, George

Animator. **Nationality:** Canadian. **Born:** Toronto, Ontario, 1920. **Education:** Attended Ontario College of Art. **Career:** Freelance illustrator; 1943–48—worked for the animation unit of the National Film Board of Canada: first film as director, *Chants populaires*, 1943;

1948–50—worked for Unesco in Paris; 1950–55— worked in Canada; 1955–56—worked in New York on *The Gerald McBoing Boing Show*; 1957—formed T.V. Cartoons Ltd. (later TVC London): made commercials, worked for the National Coal Board, Ford Motors, and other companies; television work included producing *The Beatles* series in the UK, 1964, the *Cool McCool* series in the U.S.A., 1966. **Died:** In 1979.

Films as Animator:

1943	"Auprès de ma blonde" ep. of *Chants populaires*
1944	*Grim Pastures, or the Fight for Fodder*
1945	*The Three Blind Mice*
1946	"J'ai tant dansé" ep. of *Chants populaires*; *Cadet Rousselle*
1947	*Upright and Wrong* (co)
1948	*Family Tree* (co)
1958	*The Wardrobe*
1961	*Visible Manifestations*
1962	*The Ever-Changing Motor Car*; *Mr. Know-How in Hot Water*; *The Apple*; *The Flying Man*
1964	*The Ladder*
1965	*Safety Boots*
1967	*The Chair*
1968	*Yellow Submarine*; *Lazy River*
1969	*Hands, Knees, and Bumps-a-Daisy*
1970	*Moon Rock*
1972	*Damon the Mower*; *Horses of Death*
1973	*How Not to Lose Your Head While Shotfiring* (co); *The Maggot*
1977	*Teamwork* (co)

Other Films:

1944	*Keep Your Mouth Shut* (asst d)
1967	*Canada Is My Piano* (Sewell) (pr)

Publications

By DUNNING: article—

Animafilm (Warsaw), January-March 1980.

On DUNNING: articles—

Films and Filming (London), June 1964.
Roudévitch, Michel, in *Cinéma* (Paris), no. 98, 1965.
Filmmakers Newsletter (Ward Hill, Massachusetts), July-August 1973.
Cornand, André, "Le Festival d'Annecy et les Recontres internationales du cinéma d'animation," in *Image et Son*, January 1977.
Obituary in *Cinéma* (Paris), July-August 1979.

*   *   *

George Dunning, like his contemporaries John Hubley and Norman McLaren, can best be described as an "experimentalist," having used every medium to make animated films, including cut-outs, painting on glass, and direct painting onto film as well as more orthodox methods such as cel and paper. Most of his early energies were directed toward commercials, and once he had formed his UK company, sponsors were eager for his particular brand of animated television advertising. While working on commercial projects, Dunning's enthusiasm still found outlets in projects done for his own personal satisfaction in his spare time and usually at his own expense.

Damon the Mower, a visual interpretation of Andrew Marvell's poem, is photographed as a pencil-test which enhances the quality rather than loses it. He always attempts to bring the right technique to each of his films. In *The Apple*, the humorous story of a man trying to reach an apple high in a tree, Dunning draws his characters in simple outline with the apple being the only colored object on the screen. *The Flying Man* is painted directly onto glass in a different fashion of artwork entirely.

Each new film Dunning produced reflected the fact that he was still experimenting. This proved true in his highly acclaimed film *Yellow Submarine*, which includes every style and technique from water color on cel ("Lucy in the Sky with Diamonds") and Rotoscope to early forms of computer animation. Unfortunately, due to ill health Dunning was never able to finish his pet project of several years, Shakespeare's *The Tempest*. His company carries on in his memory, chalking up awards for such masterpieces as Raymond Briggs's *The Snowman* (1982). No doubt Dunning would approve.

—Graham Webb

DURAS, Marguerite

Writer. **Nationality:** French. **Born:** Marguerite Donnadieu in Giadinh, French Indo-China, 1914. **Education:** Educated in mathematics, law and political science at the Sorbonne, Paris. **Career:** Published first novel, *Les Impudents*, 1943; subsequently novelist, journalist and playwright; directed first film, *La Musica*, 1966. **Awards:** Prix Goncourt for novel *L'Amant*, 1984; CICAE Award, CIDALC Award, and Silver Berlin Bear Honorable Mention, Berlin International Film Festival, all for *Les Enfants*, 1985; **Died:** 3 March 1996, in Paris, France.

Films as Writer:

1959	***Hiroshima mon amour*** (Resnais)
1960	*Moderato Cantabile* (Brook) (co-adapt from her novel)
1961	*Une Aussi longue absence* (*The Long Absence*) (Colpi) (co-sc from her novel)
1964	*Nuit noire, Calcutta* (Karmitz) (short)
1965	"Les rideaux blancs" (Franju) episode of *Der Augenblick des Friedens* (*Un Instant de la paix*) (for W. German TV)
1966	*10:30 P.M. Summer* (Dassin) (co-sc uncredited, from her novel) (*Dix heures et demie du soir en été*); *La Voleuse* (Chapot) (+ dialogue); *La Musica* (+ co-d)
1969	*Détruire, dit-elle* (*Destroy She Said*) (+ d)
1971	*Jaune le soleil* (+ d, pr, co-ed, from her novel *Abahn, Sabana, David*)
1972	*Nathalie Granger* (+ d, music)
1974	*La Femme du Ganges* (+ d)
1975	***India Song*** (+ d, voice)
1976	*Des journées entières dans les arbres* (*Days in the Trees*) (+ d); *Son Nom de Venises dans Calcutta desert* (+ d)

Marguerite Duras

1977   *Baxter, Vera Baxter* (+ d); *Le Camion* (+ d, role)
1978   *Le Navire Night* (+ d)
1978/79   *Aurelia Steiner* (4-film series): *Cesarée* (1978) (+ d); *Les Mains négatives* (1978) (+ d); *Aurelia Steiner— Melbourne* (1979) (+ d); *Aurelia Steiner—Vancouver* (1979) (+ d)
1981   *Agatha et les lectures illimitées* (*Agatha*) (+ d)
1991   *L'Amant* (*The Lover*) (co-sc)

Other Films:

1985   *Les Enfants* (*The Children*) (d)

Publications

By DURAS: screenplays—

Hiroshima mon amour, Paris, 1959.
Moderato Cantabile, with Gérard Jarlot and Peter Brook, 1960.
Une Aussi longue absence, with Gérard Jarlot, Paris, 1961.

10:30 P.M. Summer, with Jules Dassin, Paris, 1966.
La Musica, Paris, 1966.
Detruire, dit-elle, Paris, 1969; as *Destroy, She Said*, New York, 1970.
Les rideaux blancs, Paris, 1966.
Jaune le soleil, Paris, 1971
Nathalie Granger, suivi de La Femme du Gange, Paris, 1973.
India Song—texte—theatre—film, Paris, 1975; as *India Song*, New York, 1976.
Des journées entières dans les arbres, Paris, 1976.
Son Nom de Venises dans Calcutta desert, Paris, 1976.
Le Camion, Paris, 1977.
Le Navire Night, Césarée, Les Mains négatives, Aurelia Steiner, Paris, 1979.
Vera Baxter; ou, Les Plages de l'Atlantique, Paris, 1980.
Agatha, Paris, 1981.
Les Enfants, Paris, 1985.

By DURAS: fiction—

Les Impudents, Paris, 1943.
La Vie tranquille, Paris, 1944.

Un Barrage contre le Pacifique, Paris, 1950; as *The Sea Wall*, New York, 1952; as *A Sea of Troubles*, London, 1953.

Le Marin de Gibraltar, Paris, 1952; as *The Sailor From Gibraltar*, London and New York, 1966.

Les Petits Chevaux de Tarquinia, Paris, 1953; as *The Little Horses of Tarquinia*, London, 1960.

Des journées entières dans les arbres, Paris, 1954; as *Whole Days in the Trees*, New York, 1981.

Le Square, Paris, 1955.

Moderato Cantabile, Paris, 1958, and New York, 1987.

Dix heures et demi du soir en été, Paris, 1960; as *Ten-Thirty on a Summer Night*, London, 1962.

L'Après-midi de Monsieur Andesmas, Paris, 1962; as *The Afternoon of Monsieur Andesmas*, London, 1964.

Le Ravissement de Lol V. Stein, Paris, 1964; as *The Ravishing of Lol V. Stein*, New York, 1967; as *The Rapture of Lol V. Stein*, London, 1967.

Le Vice-consul, Paris, 1966; as *The Vice-Consul*, London, 1968, New York, 1987.

L'Amante anglaise, Paris, 1967, New York, 1968.

Abahn, Sabana, David, Paris, 1970.

L'Amour, Paris, 1971.

Ah! Ernesto, with Bernard Bonhomme, Paris, 1971.

La Maladie de la mort, Paris, 1983; as *The Malady of Death*, New York, 1986.

L'Amant, Paris, 1984; as *The Lover*, New York, 1985.

Hiroshima mon amour, translated by Richard Seaver, New York, 1987.

Les Yeux bleus cheveux noirs, Paris, 1987; as *Blue Eyes, Black Hair*, London and New York, 1988.

Emily L., Paris, 1987, New York, 1989.

The Lover, introduction by Maxine Hong Kingston, translated by Barbara Bray, New York, 1998.

By DURAS: plays—

Théâtre 1 (includes *Les Eaux et forets, Le Square, La Musica*), Paris, 1965.

Théâtre 2 (includes *Susanna Andler; Yes, peut-étre; Le Shaga; Des journées entières dans les arbres; Un Homme est venu me voir*), Paris, 1968.

L'Homme assis dans le couloir, Paris, 1980.

L'Homme Atlantique, Paris, 1982.

Savannah Bay, Paris, 1982.

The Square, Edinburgh, 1986.

Yes, peut-etre, Edinburgh, 1986.

By DURAS: other books—

Les Parleuses, with Xaviere Gauthier, Paris, 1974.

Étude sur l'oeuvre littéraire, théâtrale, et cinématographique, with Jacques Lacan and Maurice Blanchot, Paris, 1976.

Territoires du féminin, with Marcelle Marini, Paris, 1977.

Les Lieux de Duras, with Michelle Porte, Paris, 1978.

L'Été 80, Paris, 1980.

Outside: Papiers d'un jour, Paris, 1981, Boston 1986.

The War: A Memoir, New York, 1986.

The Physical Side, London, 1990.

By DURAS: articles—

"Conversation with Marguerite Duras," with Richard Roud, in *Sight and Sound* (London), Winter 1959/60.

"Marguerite Duras en toute liberté," interview with F. Dufour, in *Cinéma* (Paris), April 1972.

"Du livre au film," in *Image et Son* (Paris), April 1974.

"India Song, a Chant of Love and Death," interview with F. Dawson, in *Film Comment* (New York), November/December 1975.

"India Song and Marguerite Duras," interview with Carlos Clarens, in *Sight and Sound* (London), Winter 1975/76.

Interview with J.-C. Bonnet and J. Fieschi, in *Cinématographe* (Paris), November 1977.

"Les Yeux verts," special issue written and edited by Duras, of *Cahiers du Cinéma* (Paris), June 1980.

Interview with D. Fasoli, in *Filmcritica* (Florence), June 1981.

Interview with A. Grunert, in *Filmfaust* (Frankfurt), February-March 1982.

"The places of Marguerite Duras," an interview with M. Porte, in *Enclitic* (Minneapolis), Spring 1983.

Interview with P. Bonitzer, C. Tesson, and Serge Toubiana, in *Cahiers du Cinéma* (Paris), July-August 1985.

Interview with Jean-Luc Godard, in *Cinéma* (Paris), 30 December 1987.

Interview with Colette Mazabrard, in *Cahiers du Cinéma* (Paris), December 1989.

"Jacquot filme Duras," in *Cahiers du Cinéma* (Paris), May 1993.

On DURAS: books—

Bernheim, N.-L., *Marguerite Duras tourne un film*, Paris, 1976.

Ropars-Wuilleumier, Marie-Claire, *La Texte divisé*, Paris, 1981.

Trastulli, Daniela, *Dalla parola all imagine: Viaggio nel cinema di Marguerite Duras*, Geneva, 1982.

Borgomano, Madeleine, *L'Écriture filmique de Marguerite Duras*, Paris, 1985.

Brossard, Jean-Pierre, editor, *Marguerite Duras: Cinéaste, écrivain*, La Chaux-de-Fonde, 1985.

Guers-Villate, Yvonne, *Continuité/discontinuité de l'oeuvre Durassienne*, Brussels, 1985.

Fernandes, Marie-Pierre, *Travailler avec Duras: La musica deuxième*, Paris, 1986.

Selous, Trista, *The Other Woman: Feminism and Femininity in the Work of Marguerite Duras*, New Haven, Connecticut, 1988.

Vircondelet, Alain, *Duras: A Biography*, translated by Thomas Buckley, Normal, Illinois, 1994.

Adler, Laure, *Marguerite Duras: A Life*, translated by Anne-Marie Glasheen, Chicago, 2000.

On DURAS: articles—

Gollub, Judith, "French Writers Turned Film Makers," in *Film Heritage* (New York), Winter 1968/69.

"Reflections in a Broken Glass," in *Film Comment* (New York), November/December 1975.

Lakeland, M.J., "Marguerite Duras in 1977," in *Camera Obscura* (Berkeley), Fall 1977.

Van Wert, W.F., "The Cinema of Marguerite Duras: Sound and Voice in a Closed Room," in *Film Quarterly* (Berkeley), Fall 1979.

Seni, N., ''Wahrnehungsformen von Zeit und Raum am Beispiel der Filme von Marguerite Duras und Chantal Akerman,'' in *Frauen und Film* (Berlin), September 1979.

''Marguerite Duras à l'action,'' in *Positif* (Paris), July/August 1980.

Andermatt, V., ''Big mach (on the truck),'' in *Enclitic* (Minneapolis), Spring 1980.

Lyon, E., ''Marguerite Duras: Bibliography/Filmography,'' in *Camera Obscura* (Berkeley), Fall 1980.

Murphy, C.J., ''The role of desire in the films of Marguerite Duras,'' in *Quarterly Review of Film Studies* (New York), Winter 1982.

Fedwik, P., ''Marguerite Duras: Feminine Field of Nostalgia,'' in *Enclitic* (Minneapolis), Fall 1982.

Sarrut, B., ''Marguerite Duras: Barrages against the Pacific,'' in *On Film* (Los Angeles), Summer 1983.

Murphy, C.J., ''New narrative regions: The role of desire in the films and novels of Marguerite Duras,'' in *Literature/Film Quarterly* (Salisbury, Maryland), April 1984.

Le Masson, H., ''La voix tatouee,'' in *Cahiers du Cinéma* (Paris), January 1985.

McWilliams, D., ''Aesthetic tripling: Marguerite Duras's *Le navire Night*,'' in *Literature/Film Quarterly* (Salisbury, Maryland), January 1986.

Cottent-Hage, M., ''Le camion de Marguerite Duras, ou comment assurer la libre circulation,'' in *Post Script* (Commerce), vol. 7, no. 1, Fall 1987.

Williams, Bruce, ''Splintered Perspectives: Counterpoint and Subjectivity in the Modernist Film Narrative,'' in *Film Criticism* (Meadville), vol. 15, no. 2, Winter 1991.

Grange, M.F., ''Corps filmique entre lisible et visible chez Marguerite Duras,'' in *Cinémas* (Montreal), vol. 3, no. 1, Autumn 1992.

Vajdovich, G., ''Antiregény és anitfilm,'' in *Filmkultura* (Budapest), April 1995.

Johnston, Trevor, ''French Lessons,'' in *Time Out* (London), 18 October 1995.

DuPont, J., ''The Enduring Duras,'' in *Village Voice* (New York), 9 April 1996.

Obituary, in *EPD Film* (Frankfurt), April 1996.

Obituary, in *Kino* (Sofia), no. 2, 1996.

Obituary, in *Classic Images* (Muscatine), May 1996.

Obituary, in *Skrien* (Amsterdam), June-July 1996.

Roy, André, ''Marguerite Duras, moderne,'' in *24 Images* (Montreal), no. 82, Summer 1996.

Everett, Wendy, ''Director as Composer: Marguerite Duras and the Musical Analogy,'' in *Literature/Film Quarterly* (Salisbury), April 1998.

*   *   *

Marguerite Duras brought the same qualities that made her a lyrical yet powerful novelist and playwright to her screenplays. Duras' work, originally influenced by such American writers as Hemingway and Steinbeck, drew on her unique life which began in what was then Indochina and is now Vietnam. She left Asia in the early 1930s for Paris and began publishing novels that were celebrated for their untraditional narrative structure. For Duras, certainty and a linear plot gave way to work that explored, instead, ambiguity and silences. She was, she said, exploring the ''interplay of love and destruction.''

She turned to screenwriting in 1959 when French director Alain Resnais asked her to write the screenplay for his film, *Hiroshima,* *Mon Amour,* which closely resembled the novel, *Moderato Cantiblis* (1958), that established her literary reputation. The film explores the brief extra-marital relationship between a French woman (played by Emmanuelle Riva) and a Japanese architect (played by Eiji Okada.) The film won critical acclaim (the International Critics Prize at the Cannes Film Festival and the New York Film Critics Best Foreign Language Film Award) in part for the innovative use of flashbacks to the war when the woman was involved with a German soldier. The haunting story, which was able to juxtapose such seemingly disparate themes as Hiroshima and love, reflected Duras' preoccupation with desire, death, love and memory. Although Duras was nominated for an Academy Award for her work as a screenwriter, she was unhappy enough with the result that she claimed she would never again let anyone else direct her words on the screen.

Duras continued to write for the screen and began to direct as well. In 1975 her screenplay for *India Song* demonstrated Duras' continuing connection to the Asia of her youth, a place that is, for her, emblematic of an unattainable desire and unknowable longing which, sought through memory, can only, finally, be resolved in death. The 1977 adaptation of her novel, *Le Camion,* which she directed, features a scene in which Duras herself reads star Gerard Depardieu the scenario of the film, which focuses on a truck driver and a mysterious woman hitch-hiker. Duras directed in order to be able to ''preserve textual obscurity.''

Her 1985 novel, *L'aimant* (*The Lover*), perhaps her finest work, returned to the Indochina of her youth. *The New York Times Book Review* praised it for the same qualities that infused the film (released in 1991): its ''masterly balance between formalism and powerful emotional effect.'' Duras was uniquely capable of creating what has been called cinematic prose, or ''literary films.'' Her innovative work as a screenwriter and director paved the way for such minimalist women filmmakers as Chantal Ackerman who followed in the wake of Duras' artistic legacy.

—Nina Bjornsson

DUTTA, Dulal

Editor. **Nationality:** Indian. **Born:** Chandannagar, West Bengal, 1925. **Career:** Assistant editor in Bombay; 1955—first film as editor, *Pather Panchali,* by Satyajit Ray; in addition to Ray's films, edited films by Satyen Bose, Asit Sen, Ajoy Kar, Tarun Mazumdar, and others.

Films as Editor for Satyajit Ray:

1955   ***Pather Panchali*** (*Father Panchali*)
1956   ***Aparajito*** (*The Unvanquished*)
1957   *Parash Pathar* (*The Philosopher's Stone*)
1958   *Jalsaghar* (*The Music Room*)
1959   ***Apur Sansar*** (*The World of Apu*)
1960   *Devi* (*The Goddess*)
1961   *Rabindranath Tagore* (doc); *Teen Kanya* (*Two Daughters*)
1962   *Kanchanjanga*; *Abhijan* (*Expedition*)
1963   *Mahanagar* (*The Big City*)
1964   ***Charulata*** (*The Lonely Wife*)

1965   *Kapurush-o-Mahapurush* (*The Coward and the Saint*)
1966   *Nayak* (*The Hero*)
1967   *Chiriakhana* (*The Zoo*)
1969   *Goopy Gyne Bagha Byne* (*The Adventures of Goopy and Bagha*)
1970   **Aranyer Din Ratri** (*Days and Nights in the Forest*); **Pratidwandi** (*The Adversary*)
1971   *Seemabaddha*; *Sikkim* (doc)
1972   *The Inner Eye* (doc)
1973   *Asani Sanket* (*Distant Thunder*)
1974   *Sonar Kella* (*The Golden Fortress*)
1975   *Jana Aranya* (*The Middleman*)
1976   *Bala* (doc)
1977   *Shatranj Ke Khilari* (*The Chess Players*)
1978   *Joi Baba Felunath* (*The Elephant God*)
1979   *Heerak Rajar Deshe* (*The Kingdom of Diamonds*)
1982   *Ghare Bahire* (*The Home and the World*)
1989   *Ganashatru* (*An Enemy of the People*)
1990   *Shakha Proshakha* (*The Branches of the Tree*)
1991   *Agantuk* (*The Stranger*)

Films as Editor for Sandip Ray:

1994   *Uttoran* (*The Broken Journey*)
1995   *Target*

*   *   *

When Satyajit Ray gathered a crew of friends together to make a film of Bibhuti Banerjee's novel, *Pather Panchali*, editor Dulal Dutta seemed to be an old veteran in comparison with the inexperience of the others. He had previously worked on two movies. He went on to collaborate many times with Ray, gaining worldwide fame for this association. Ray later commented on the amateur appearance of his first work: "Judged on the level of craftsmanship, there was much that was wrong with my film. . . . The early part clearly shows we were groping with the medium. Shots are held for too long, cuts come at the wrong points, the pace falters." Other critics have more generously judged that the director and his editor allowed the material, the natural rhythms of the village life and landscape, to dictate the rambling style of the film.

Dutta, under Ray's close supervision, developed a cutting style of great economy, but one which could reveal the poetry of the content. Akira Kurosawa commented that "his work can be described as flowing composedly, like a big river." Dutta's editing skills are most apparent in scenes of dialogue, such as the picnic and memory game in *Aranyer Din Ratri*. Ray described in a 1966 article, "Some Aspects of My Craft," the alternative assemblages Dutta would put together for him: "These offer endless variations of emphasis, unlimited scope for pointing up shades of feeling. It is not unusual for an important dialogue scene to be cut in half a dozen different ways before a final satisfactory form is achieved."

Dutta has worked with other directors, including James Ivory on his first film, *The Householder*. But he has otherwise lived an almost reclusive life in the film community of Calcutta, rarely being seen in public.

—Stephen Brophy

DYKSTRA, John

Special Effects Supervisor. **Nationality:** American. **Born:** Long Beach, California, 3 June 1947. **Education:** Attended Long Beach State University. **Career:** 1971—first film, *Silent Running*; 1973—left film to work for Berkeley's Institute of Urban Development; 1975—returned to movies as first head of George Lucas's special-effects lab, Industrial Light and Magic; 1977—special-effects supervisor on *Star Wars*; 1978—left ILM to form his own effects company, Apogee, which produced visual effects for television's *Battlestar: Galactica*, served as visual-effects supervisor and producer of first five episodes; 1979—received Academy Award nomination for work on *Star Trek: The Motion Picture*; 1982—dismantled Apogee Productions commercial division; 1995—pioneered use of computer-generated images as special-effects supervisor on *Batman Forever*. **Awards:** Academy Awards for best visual effects, and scientific/technical special Academy Award for invention of the Dykstraflex motion-control computerized camera system, both for *Star Wars*, 1977.

Films as Special Effects Crew:

1971   *Silent Running* (Trumbull); *The Andromeda Strain* (Wise)
1977   **Star Wars** (Lucas) (special photographic effects supervisor)
1978   *Battlestar: Galactica* (Colla) (effects-unit supervisor, co-pr)
1979   *Star Trek: The Motion Picture* (Wise) (special photographic effects supervisor); *Avalanche Express* (Robson)
1982   *Firefox* (Eastwood) (supervisor)
1985   *Lifeforce* (Hooper) (supervisor)
1986   *Invaders from Mars* (Hooper) (supervisor)
1988   *My Stepmother Is an Alien* (Benjamin) (supervisor); *The Unholy* (Vila)
1995   *Batman Forever* (Schumacher) (visual effects supervisor)
1997   *Batman & Robin* (Schumacher) (visual effects)
1999   *Stuart Little* (Minkoff) (senior visual effects supervisor)
2001   *Spider-Man*

Publications

By DYKSTRA: article—

"Directing Effects," in *Back Stage* (Hollywood), 19 April 1985.
"*My Stepmother is an Alien* Sci-fi comedy. Full Array of Tricks for Stepmother," in *American Cinematographer* (Hollywood), December 1988.
American Cinematographer (Hollywood), July 1995.
"Digitizing the Dynamic Duo," in *American Cinematographer* (Hollywood), December 1997.

On DYKSTRA: articles—

Back Stage-Shoot (Hollywood), 16 October 1992.
Clark, Michael, on *Batman Forever*, in *Shoot* (Hollywood), 14 July 1995.

Reid, C., ''John Dykstra Effects Supervisor,'' in *Cinefantastique* (Forest Park), vol. 29, no. 1, 1997.

Vaz, M.C., ''Freeze Frames,'' in *Cinefex* (Riverside), September 1997.

*   *   *

John Dykstra is arguably the most respected and sought after special effects supervisor working in Hollywood. He has built a deservedly stellar reputation for ingenuity, organizational skill, and thorough preproduction planning. In the 1970s, he set the visual-effects standard for both the *Star Wars* trilogy and the *Star Trek* films, two of Hollywood's most popular science-fiction film series. Dykstra is also a pioneer in the use of computer technology for visual effects, from the computer-controlled Dykstraflex camera system developed for *Star Wars*, to the extensive use of computer-generated image animation in *Batman Forever*.

Dykstra started his career studying at Long Beach State as an industrial designer. According to *Star Wars* promotional material, he was kicked out of school before earning a degree. He began working with Douglas Trumbull, a veteran effects director (whose work included effects for Victor Fleming's *Wizard of Oz* and Stanley Kubrick's *2001: A Space Odyssey*), as part of the effects crew on Trumbull's science-fiction thriller *Silent Running*. From Trumbull, he learned techniques on matte filming and miniature work, skills he would put to great use throughout his career. Following his apprenticeship with Trumbull, Dykstra joined Berkeley's Institute of Urban Development, where he was involved in a sophisticated project coupling cinematography and visual effects with the construction of miniature cityscape models. Here, he further honed his skills with miniatures and camera effects. In June 1975, George Lucas and Gary Kurtz asked him to handle visual effects for a film they were working on called *Star Wars*. As a result, Dykstra became the first head of Lucas's new special effects studio, Industrial Light and Magic.

Industrial Light and Magic would evolve into the premier Hollywood special-effects studio, doing the effects for all three *Star Wars* films as well as *Terminator II* and *Jurassic Park*, among other films. Dykstra won two Academy Awards in 1977 for his work on *Star Wars*. The first award was for best visual effects, while the second was a scientific/technical special award for his invention and development of the Dykstraflex motion-control camera system. The innovation of combining computer programing with camera work would be an essential link to the computer-generated imaging currently being utilized by Hollywood's special-effects producers.

In 1978, Dykstra left ILM to form Apogee, his own special-effects company. Through Apogee, he produced the first five episodes of the television series *Battlestar: Galactica*. He also supervised the special effects for the motion-picture version of *Battlestar: Galactica*. Later, he worked with director Robert Wise on the first motion picture version of an older television science-fiction phenomenon, *Star Trek*. In 1979, Dykstra earned another Academy Award nomination for his work on *Star Trek: The Motion Picture*.

Dykstra dismantled Apogee in the fall of 1982, due to the lack of commercial work, the company's primary source of clientele. This turned out to be only a minor setback. Over the next decade, he would work with esteemed directors Clint Eastwood (on *Firefox*), Tobe Hooper (*Lifeforce* and *Invaders from Mars*), and Richard Benjamin (*My Stepmother Is an Alien*). Though none of these movies was a blockbuster, he continued to innovate, maintaining his reputation for creativity and organization.

This reputation resulted in a job as visual-effects supervisor on *Batman Forever*. Dykstra's work here proved worthy of his reputation: *Batman Forever* was the top box-office draw for 1995, largely due to the special effects as well as Jim Carrey's over-the-top performance as the Riddler. The effects called for by director Joel Schumacher and the script were more than a single effects studio could deliver on its own, thus Dykstra decided to subcontract with many different effects labs.

Much of the organization of this picture was deciding what to do with real actors and sets, what to do in miniature, and what to do in computer-generated images, or CGI. Dykstra determined that the stunts called for were too dangerous for a human stuntman to perform. As a result, many of the film's stunts were ''performed'' by high-end computer-generated animation. These animated segments were compiled by Dykstra at his Warner Bros. office in Burbank, where he was linked with the firms via real-time digital fiber, letting him judge the quality of each shot as it was being crafted. Dykstra and his crew combined computer imaging from the many subcontracted firms, each firm responsible for a different element (such as lighting, blurring motion, background matte paintings, etc.) of the final composite.

John Dykstra's contribution to cinema is substantial: from the Dykstraflex motion-control camera system utilized in *Star Wars*, to the computer-generated image animation of *Batman Forever*, Dykstra has proved himself to be an organized supervisor and an innovative special effects visionary.

—Mark Johnson

EDENS, Roger

Music Director and Composer. **Nationality:** American. **Born:** Hillsboro, Texas, 9 November 1905. **Career:** Piano accompanist for ballroom dancers; 1935—joined MGM as musical supervisor, composer, and later as associate producer. **Awards:** Academy Awards for *Easter Parade*, 1948, *On the Town*, 1949, and *Annie Get Your Gun*, 1950. **Died:** In Hollywood, 13 July 1970.

Films as Music Director/Supervisor:

1934   *Kid Millions* (Del Ruth)
1935   *Broadway Melody of 1936* (Del Ruth)
1936   *San Francisco* (Van Dyke); *Born to Dance* (Del Ruth); *The Great Ziegfeld* (Leonard)
1937   *Broadway Melody of 1938* (Del Ruth) (song); *A Day at the Races* (Wood); *Rosalie* (Van Dyke)
1938   *Love Finds Andy Hardy* (Seitz); *Everybody Sing* (Marin)
1939   ***The Wizard of Oz*** (Fleming); *Babes in Arms* (Berkeley) (songs)
1940   *Strike Up the Band* (Berkeley); *Go West* (Buzzell); *Little Nelly Kelly* (Taurog) (songs)
1941   *Kathleen* (Bucquet); *Ziegfeld Girl* (Leonard) (songs); *Lady Be Good* (McLeod); *Babes on Broadway* (Berkeley)
1942   *Panama Hattie* (McLeod)
1943   *Presenting Lily Mars* (Taurog); *Cabin in the Sky* (Minnelli)
1944   *Thousands Cheer* (Sidney); *Ziegfeld Follies* (Minnelli) (songs); **Meet Me in St. Louis** (Minnelli) (+ assoc pr)
1945   *Yolanda and the Thief* (Minnelli) (+ assoc pr); *The Harvey Girls* (Sidney) (+ assoc pr)
1947   *Good News* (Walters) (songs, + assoc pr)
1948   *Words and Music* (Taurog); *Easter Parade* (Walters) (songs); *The Pirate* (Minnelli)
1949   ***On the Town*** (Donen)
1950   *Annie Get Your Gun* (Sidney)
1952   ***Singin' in the Rain*** (Kelly and Donen) (song)
1954   *Deep in My Heart* (Donen) (song, + pr); ***A Star Is Born*** (Cukor) (song)
1957   *Funny Face* (Donen) (songs, + pr)
1962   *Jumbo* (Walters) (songs, + assoc pr)

Other Films:

1948   *Take Me Out to the Ball Game* (Berkeley) (composer)
1951   *Show Boat* (Sidney) (assoc pr); ***An American in Paris*** (Minnelli) (assoc pr)
1953   ***The Band Wagon*** (Minnelli) (assoc pr)
1964   *The Unsinkable Molly Brown* (Walters) (assoc pr)
1969   *Hello Dolly!* (Kelly) (assoc pr)

Publications

By EDENS: article—

Sight and Sound (London), Spring 1958.

*   *   *

If the musical genre reached its artistic and commercial peak with the MGM/Arthur Freed vehicles of the 40s and 50s, then some of the credit must go to Roger Edens. Composer, lyricist, arranger, producer, and associate of Freed's, Edens built a career in Hollywood that was synonymous with the genre that typified the glamour and extravagance of the Golden Age of Hollywood. He worked behind the limelight that fell on Ethel Merman, Eleanor Powell, Mickey Rooney, Fred Astaire, Gene Kelly, and, most especially, Judy Garland. His lyrics and compositions included "I've got a Feeling You're Fooling," "Think Pink," "Bonjour Paris," and "Dear Mr. Gable," Garland's breakthrough number from *Broadway Melody of 1938* (1937).

A former ballroom pianist, Edens began his film career at Paramount, where he was hired in 1933 to write material for the studio's Ethel Merman pictures. From there he moved to MGM in 1935, where he would remain until the decline of the musical in the mid- to late-'50s. He began as musical supervisor working on such early chorus-line pictures as *The Broadway Melody of 1938*, *Born to Dance* (1936), and *Everybody Sing* (1938). It was at Warners, however, where Busby Berkeley was staging the glamorous, kaleidoscopic numbers for such films as *42nd Street* (1933) and *Footlight Parade* (1933), that the genre was achieving its fullest expression. Edens found himself working on imitations of Berkeley's mechanical, impersonal style. In *Born to Dance* for example, Eleanor Powell dances to the Cole Porter tune "Swingin' the Jinx Away" while encircled by hundreds of singers and dancing sailors on the prow of a huge glittering battleship. In *Gotta Sing, Gotta Dance: A Pictorial History of the Film Musical* (London: Hamlyn, 1971) by John Kobol, Edens is reported to have referred to the scene as "that really monstrous epitome of nonsense" (p. 133).

Edens's discomfort with the baroque, non-narrative spectacle of the Berkeley style was shared by fellow lyricist and future producer Arthur Freed. Freed had set about refining the musical, moving the genre toward a more integrated form, with music and narration as integral parts of the overall plot. *Babes in Arms* (1939), Freed's debut as producer, employing Edens as lyricist and a more subdued Berkeley as director, begins an inexorable movement toward such plot-integrated, character-driven musicals as *Ziegfeld Girl* (1941), *Ziegfeld Follies* (1944), and *Take Me Out to the Ballgame* (1948), all of which were worked on by Edens as supervisor and sometimes composer.

The Freed unit as MGM, of which Edens was becoming an increasingly integral part, sought a new intimacy in the genre. Freed's "integrated musicals" became more character bound, employing such stars as Fred Astaire, Judy Garland, and Gene Kelly to add a warmth and personality previously left wanting in the en masse chorus-line picture.

Through his various approaches to the genre, Edens was seeking a way to achieve this through lyrics and composition. His work as music supervisor/arranger on *The Wizard of Oz* (1939) contributed to the film's groundbreaking integration of music and plot. While "Over the Rainbow" establishes the theme of the picture, and songs like "Off to See the Wizard" propel the narrative, numbers such as "If I Only Had a Brain" establish characterization. In short, the music routines fulfill plot functions—creating character, theme, and movement.

Elevated in the early '40s to the position of associate producer, Edens found himself with even greater control and influence over the genre. Freed was beginning to view him as indispensable; by mere suggestion Edens could veto even the most major ideas from his collaborator/boss. He was Freed's right-hand man on *Meet Me in St. Louis* (1944), *Easter Parade* (1948), *On the Town* (1949), *Annie Get Your Gun* (1950), and *An American in Paris* (1951). During this period, the musical reached its most perfect form. Extraneous numbers such as Garland and Astaire's "A Couple of Swells" from *Easter Parade* were skillfully and believably worked into the storyline. Others, such as those in *On the Town* attained an almost minimalist quality, foregrounding not the excess and artificiality of the genre, but a realism (in terms of both character and landscape) heretofore left untapped. By the end of the '40s, Edens had earned three Academy Awards, and the musical, with MGM at the crest of the wave, was the most popular genre of the industry.

In 1954, at the prompting of Freed, Edens began to produce. His first project, *Deep in My Heart* (1954) was a minor success. However, *Funny Face* (1957), his next assignment as producer, was far more accomplished. Though the "Freed Unit" had begun to disband (due to a sudden and inexorable decline in popularity), Edens moved many of the MGM craftsmen to Paramount and there, with his frequent collaborator, director Stanley Donen, produced one of the last great musicals of the Hollywood era. Starring Audrey Hepburn and Fred Astaire, *Funny Face* used a tantalizing, sophisticated mixture of color and music to enter the world of fashion photography and fairy-tale romance.

Following *Funny Face* Edens's career began to fade. The genre was now outmoded and his final two productions, *The Unsinkable Molly Brown* (1964) and *Hello Dolly* (1969) were further evidence to the fact. Overblown and splashy, they conformed to the emerging philosophy of what is bigger is better, and performed poorly at the box office.

Edens died in 1970 at the cusp of a new era in American cinema. He was sixty-five years of age and his career in the industry had spanned over half his lifetime. Though his contributions to the genre's development were substantial, Edens worked continuously in the collaborative environment of the studio system. His career runs alongside that of great musical talents of the time, and his impact on the genre must be viewed in the light of his peers. Indeed, the story of Edens's career is not only the story of the great American genre of song and dance, but also that of the factory system itself.

—Peter Flynn

EDESON, Arthur

Cinematographer. **Nationality:** American. **Born:** New York City, 24 October 1891. **Education:** Attended College of the City of New York. **Military Service:** United States Army, 1918. **Career:** Negative retoucher and platinum printer for New York portrait photographers; 1911—extra at Eclair Studios, Fort Lee, New Jersey; also studio still photographer; 1914—first film as cinematographer, *A Gentleman from Mississippi*; 1919—co-founder, American Society of Cinematographers (president, 1949–50); 1950—retired. **Died:** In 1970.

Films as Cinematographer:

1914   *A Gentleman from Mississippi* (Sergeant); *The Dollar Mark* (Lund)
1915   *The Deep Purple* (Young); *Wildfire* (Middleton); *Hearts in Exile* (*Hearts Afire*) (Young)
1916   *The Devil's Toy* (Knoles); *Miss Petticoats* (Knoles); *The Gilded Cage* (Knoles); *Bought and Paid For* (Knoles)
1917   *A Woman Alone* (Davenport); *A Square Deal* (Knoles); *The Master Hand* (Knoles) (+ asst d); *The Social Leper* (Knoles); *The Page Mystery* (Knoles); *In Again—Out Again* (Emerson); *The Stolen Paradise* (Knoles); *The Price of Pride* (Knoles); *Wild and Woolly* (Emerson); *Souls Adrift* (Knoles); *Baby Mine* (Robertson and Ballin); *Reaching for the Moon* (Emerson); *Nearly Married* (Withey)
1918   *Jack Spurlock, Prodigal* (Harbaugh); *Mr. Fixit* (Dwan); *The Savage Woman* (Mortimer); *The Road through the Dark* (Mortimer)
1919   *Cheating Cheaters* (Dwan); *The Better Wife* (Earle); *Hushed Hour* (Mortimer); *Eyes of Youth* (Parker)
1920   *The Forbidden Woman* (Garson); *For the Soul of Rafael* (Garson); *Mid Channel* (Garson); *Hush* (Garson)
1921   *Good Women* (Gasnier); *The Three Musketeers* (Niblo)
1922   *The Worldly Madonna* (Garson); *Robin Hood* (Dwan)
1924   *The End of the World* (Keays); *The Thief of Bagdad* (Walsh); *Inez from Hollywood* (*The Good Bad Girl*) (Green)
1925   *The Lost World* (Hoyt) (co); *Waking Up the Town* (Cruze) (co); *One Way Street* (Dillon); *The Talker* (Green); *Her Sister from Paris* (Franklin); *Stella Dallas* (H. King)
1926   *Partners Again* (H. King); *The Bat* (West); *Sweet Daddies* (Santell); *Subway Sadie* (Santell); *Just Another Blonde* (Santell)
1927   *McFadden's Flats* (Wallace); *The Patent Leather Kid* (Santell) (co); *The Drop Kick* (*Glitter*) (Webb) (co); *The Gorilla* (Santell)
1928   *A Thief in the Dark* (Ray); *Me, Gangster* (Walsh)
1929   *In Old Arizona* (Walsh and Cummings); *Girls Gone Wild* (Seiler) (co); *The Cock-Eyed World* (Walsh); *Romance of the Rio Grande* (Santell)
1930   **All Quiet on the Western Front** (Milestone); *The Big Trail* (Walsh) (co); *The Man Who Came Back* (Walsh)
1931   *Doctors' Wives* (Borzage); *Always Goodbye* (McKenna and Menzies); *Waterloo Bridge* (Whale); **Frankenstein** (Whale)
1932   *The Impatient Maiden* (Whale); *Strangers of the Evening* (Humberstone); *Fast Companions* (*Information Kid*)

(Neuman); *The Last Mile* (Bischoff); *Those We Love* (Florey); *The Old Dark House* (Whale); *Flesh* (Ford)

1933   *The Constant Woman* (Schertzinger); *A Study in Scarlet* (Marin); *The Life of Jimmy Dolan* (*The Kid's Last Fight*) (Mayo); *The Big Brain* (*Enemies of Society*) (Archainbaud); *The Invisible Man* (Whale); *His Double Life* (Hopkins and W. De Mille)

1934   *Palooka* (*The Great Schnozzle*) (Stoloff); *The Merry Frinks* (*The Happy Family*) (Green); *Here Comes the Navy* (Bacon); *Maybe It's Love* (McGann)

1935   *Devil Dogs of the Air* (Bacon); *While the Patient Slept* (Enright); *Dinky* (Lederman and Bretherton); *Going Highbrow* (Florey) (co-ph); *Mutiny on the Bounty* (Lloyd); *Ceiling Zero* (Hawks)

1936   *The Golden Arrow* (Green); *Satan Met a Lady* (Dieterle); *Hot Money* (McGann); *China Clipper* (Enright); *Gold Diggers of 1937* (Bacon)

1937   *The Go Getter* (Berkeley); *Mr. Dodd Takes the Air* (Green); *The Footloose Heiress* (Clements); *They Won't Forget* (LeRoy); *Submarine D-1* (Bacon); *Swing Your Lady* (Enright); *The Kid Comes Back* (*Don't Pull Your Punches*) (Eason)

1938   *Boy Meets Girl* (Bacon); *Cowboy from Brooklyn* (*Romance and Rhythm*) (Bacon); *Racket Busters* (Bacon); *Mr. Chump* (Clements)

1939   *Wings of the Navy* (Bacon); *Nancy Drew—Reporter* (Clements); *Sweepstakes Winner* (McGann); *No Place to Go* (Morse); *Each Dawn I Die* (Keighley); *Kid Nightingale* (Amy)

1940   *Castle on the Hudson* (*Years without Days*) (Litvak); *They Drive by Night* (*The Road to Frisco*) (Walsh); *Tugboat Annie Sails Again* (Seiler); *Lady with Red Hair* (Bernhardt)

1941   *Kisses for Breakfast* (Seiler); *Sergeant York* (Hawks) (co); **The Maltese Falcon** (Huston)

1942   *The Male Animal* (Nugent); *Across the Pacific* (Huston); **Casablanca** (Curtiz)

1943   *Thank Your Lucky Stars* (Butler)

1944   *Shine On, Harvest Moon* (Butler); *The Mask of Dimitrios* (Negulesco); *The Conspirators* (Negulesco)

1946   *Three Strangers* (Negulesco); *Two Guys from Milwaukee* (*Royal Flush*) (Butler); *Never Say Goodbye* (Kern); *Nobody Lives Forever* (Negulesco); *The Time, the Place and the Girl* (Butler) (co-ph)

1947   *Stallion Road* (Kern); *My Wild Irish Rose* (Butler) (co)

1948   *Two Guys from Texas* (*Two Texas Knights*) (Butler) (co); *The Fighting O'Flynn* (Pierson)

Publications

On EDESON: articles—

Film Comment (New York), Summer 1972.
Focus on Film (London), no. 13, 1973.
Films in Review (New York), January 1975, March 1975.
Mitchell, G.J., ''Making *All Quiet on the Western Front*,'' in *American Cinematographer* (Hollywood), September 1985.
Kauffmann, Stanley, ''*Casablanca*,'' in *New Republic*, 4 May 1992.
Krebs, Josef, ''*The Old Dark House*,'' in *Stereo Review's Sound & Vision*, October 1991.

*   *   *

Arthur Edeson's style is a perfect example of the approach and merger of two schools and aesthetics of world cinema. Like Hal Mohr, Arthur Miller, or Charles Rosher, Edeson was one of the master craftsmen of the old American school, whose principal work was on the side of realism, considered by most historians to represent the zenith of Hollywood photography. Edeson built on the influence of German Expressionism, brought to America by German cinematographers during the 1920s.

Notable among Edeson's 1920s work are his films for Douglas Fairbanks, especially three which gained Gold Medal Awards (the immediate predecessor of the Oscar): Fred Niblo's *The Three Musketeers*, Allan Dwan's *Robin Hood*, and Raoul Walsh's *The Thief of Bagdad*. One of Edeson's great strengths was his ability to capture the spirit of large-scale scenarios: for *Robin Hood*, for instance, with a scenario by Wilfred Buckland, through the use of double exposures and glass shots, and, notably for the scenes in the castle's interior, through the use of natural light. In *The Thief of Bagdad* his photography creates an atmosphere almost unreal, matching the William Cameron Menzies scenario, and bringing a fascination to Walsh's film.

In fact, in the late 1920s and early 1930s Walsh was the director to whose work Edeson was most linked. The realism of the photography of *Me, Gangster* and *In Old Arizona* (the first sound film to be shot outside a studio) prepares for that of *The Big Trail*, the culminating collaboration of the two men. Filmed in the first wide-screen process (70 mm), known as Grandeur, this epic reveals Edeson's mastery of composition, using frame enlargement dramatically. *The Big Trail* is both pictorial and documentary, with a spectacular use of space, sensitive to the archetypical sequences of the western, including a buffalo charge, an Indian attack, and a fantastic river crossing.

The visual drama of *The Big Trail*, based in part on epic realism, is counterpointed admirably in his work as cinematographer for James Whale. (His work for Whale is anticipated by his collaboration with Karl Freund, one of the great German photographers, on *All Quiet on the Western Front*, filmed with a mute camera and with sound added later, and one of the most widely praised American war films.) In *Frankenstein*, his first film with Whale, Edeson was seen to have assimilated and controlled the ''expressionist heritage,'' synthesizing it into an appropriate style—attaining a fantastic and mysterious realism without losing the mobility of the camera. *Frankenstein* is a classic ''horror movie,'' above all owing to its visual conception which suggests the silent German film, especially *The Cabinet of Dr. Caligari*, due to its paradigmatic opening scene in which Frankenstein and his assistant watch a funeral, and to Edeson's camera angles and camera movement. *The Old Dark House* and *The Invisible Man* are also classics of their genres. In the first of these, the potentialities of illumination to create zones of shadows give the film an irony approaching black comedy; in the second, there is a masterful combination of Edeson's photography and John Fulton's special effects.

In the late 1930s and early 1940s Edeson worked for Warner Brothers within the parameters of the studio style, but utilizing his own below-eye-level shots and strong angular compositions Edeson was able to produce the sinister and threatening *Maltese Falcon* and the devastatingly romantic *Casablanca*. This alone is enough for Edeson to merit a place of honor in American film. Without obsessively darkening the set, without a geometrical lighting leading to remote shadows, obscuring rather than suggesting, *The Maltese Falcon* can be said to have invented a genre—the *film noir*—and to have highlighted a visage that Louise Brooks called "the face of St. Bogart."

—M. S. Fonseca

EDLUND, Richard

Special Effects Technician. **Nationality:** American. **Born:** Fargo, North Dakota, 6 December 1940. **Education:** Attended high school in California; University of Southern California film school, Los Angeles. **Military Service:** Made training films while serving in the U.S. Navy. **Career:** Assistant to special effects technician Joe Westheimer; then worked as cable car driver and photographer; designed Candy Apple Neon lettering while working for Bob Abel; 1975–83—worked for George Lucas's company; founded the Industrial Light and Magic Company; 1983—joined Douglas Trumbull's Entertainment Effects group, the Boss Film Corporation. **Awards:** Academy Award, for *Star Wars*, 1977, *The Empire Strikes Back*, 1980, *Raiders of the Lost Ark*, 1981, and *Return of the Jedi*, 1983; Academy Technical Award, 1981 (2 awards); British Academy Award, for *Poltergeist*, 1982, and *Return of the Jedi*, 1983.

Films as Special Effects Technician:

1977   *Star Wars* (Lucas)
1979   *The China Syndrome* (Lumet)
1980   *The Empire Strikes Back* (Kershner)
1981   *Raiders of the Lost Ark* (Spielberg)
1982   *Poltergeist* (Spielberg)
1983   *Return of the Jedi* (Marquand)
1984   *2010* (Hyams); *Ghostbusters* (Reitman)
1985   *Fright Night* (Holland)
1986   *Big Trouble in Little China* (Carpenter); *The Boy Who Could Fly* (Castle); *Legal Eagles* (Reitman); *Solarbabies* (Johnson); *Poltergeist II* (Gibson)
1987   *Date with an Angel* (McLoughlin); *Leonard, Part 6* (Weiland); *Masters of the Universe* (Goddard); *The Monster Squad* (Dekker)
1988   *Big Top Pee-Wee* (Kleiser); *Die Hard* (McTiernan); *Elvira, Mistress of the Dark* (Signorelli); *Vibes* (Kwapis)
1989   *Farewell to the King* (Milius) (ph—special water unit)
1990   *Ghost* (Zucker); *Solar Crisis* (Sarafian) (+ co-pr)
1992   *Alien 3* (Fincher)
1995   *Species* (Donaldson)
1996   *Multiplicity* (Ramis)
1997   *Air Force One* (Petersen)
1998   *Desperate Measures* (Schroeder)
2000   *Bedazzled* (Ramis)

Publications

By EDLUND: articles—

Cinefantastique (New York), Spring 1978.
American Cinematographer (Hollywood), June 1980.
Filmmakers Monthly (Ward Hill, Massachusetts), June 1980.
Cahiers du Cinéma (Paris), June 1982.
Ecran Fantastique (Paris), October 1983.
Film Comment (New York), July/August 1984.
Screen International (London), 15–22 December 1984.
Photoplay (London), March 1985.
On Location (Hollywood), April 1985.
American Cinematographer (Hollywood), December 1988.
American Cinematographer (Hollywood), August 1993.
American Cinematographer (Hollywood), July 1996.

On EDLUND: articles—

Aisenberg, Adam, in *American Film* (Washington, D.C.), June 1983.
American Cinematographer (Hollywood), April and June 1984.
American Cinematographer (Hollywood), January 1985.
Cinefex (Riverside, California), no. 25, February 1986.
American Cinematographer (Hollywood), June 1986.
Cinefantastique (Forest Park), vol. 27, no. 7, 1996.
Cinefex (Riverside, California), March 1996.
Cinefex (Riverside, California), September 1996.
Variety (New York), 21 July 1997.

*   *   *

Richard Edlund's career as a special effects expert began when he was hired as part of the visual effects team for *Star Wars*. The film, a phenomenal critical and popular success, breathed life into the science-fiction genre, and established the director/producer George Lucas as a powerful member of Hollywood's new generation of filmmakers. It was a significant film in the history of Hollywood for other, less apparent reasons as well. With its innovative visual effects, it changed the course of that aspect of the industry. Edlund's career has developed as rapidly as the special effects business itself.

The backbone of the science-fiction film is the matte shot, which can combine a prepositioned live-action sequence with separate footage of painted backgrounds to create the illusion that the characters are existing in another time and place; or matte shots can also bring together several individual components, such as animated sequences, model shots, and shots with miniatures, to create scenes impossible to produce in another manner. Some of the first matte shots were done in the camera, while later ones were produced using an optical printing process. Because of the complex space battles that Lucas planned for *Star Wars*, neither of these methods were adequate.

The system developed for *Star Wars* was a combination of producing the mattes inside the camera and optical printing. It was Edlund who helped develop the motion-control camera which was used for creating the in-camera mattes. This camera, linked to a computer, was capable of repeating the same movements with an exact precision. Few viewers realize the complexities of producing one shot of a flying spaceship. The ship, the lights on the ship, and the flame coming from the tail are all shot separately. With the motion-control camera, these components, which must all move on the same perspective, are recorded one at a time on a single piece of film with each pass of the camera. Once this image of the spaceship is complete, it then becomes a component in a larger matte, perhaps of a battle with many ships, assembled on the optical printer. Before *Star Wars* and the development of the motion-control camera, and other technical innovations, this type of complex process shot was not possible.

Given the complicated nature of the special effects and the time and technology it took to produce them (there were more than 300 special effects shots in *Star Wars*), it is no wonder that a different approach to assembling an effects crew was necessary. A large group of experts (including Edlund) was gathered for *Star Wars*, resulting in the formation of Industrial Light and Magic (ILM), a visual effects company, where the equipment and crew needed to produce the effects for a given film were housed together.

The success of *Star Wars* and its sequels, and of *Close Encounters of the Third Kind* to some extent, caused a renaissance in the special effects industry. Edlund believes that that renaissance is still peaking and that "the new grammar of special film effects is still being developed." Since *Star Wars*, leaps and bounds have been made in the technology, and Edlund's motion-control camera has been modified and improved many times.

Edlund himself has developed a number of pieces of effects equipment, including a snorkel lens, which is used inside a cloud tank. On big-budget science-fiction or adventure films, visual effects houses have replaced the lone special effects expert as the creators of large-scale effects. After *Star Wars*, ILM, (including Edlund), went on to do the visual effects for *The Empire Strikes Back*, *The Return of the Jedi*, and *Raiders of the Lost Ark*. On each of these films, Edlund and other members of the ILM crew won Academy Awards for their innovative work. While at ILM, Edlund also headed the special effects unit on *Poltergeist*. His work for that film was also nominated for an Oscar.

In the early 1980s Edlund boosted his career when he became the head of the large special effects crew for *2010*, the sequel to *2001: A Space Odyssey*. Though he worked with a crew of 100 for 16 months and was associated with the effects house Entertainment Effect Group, he was virtually in charge of most of the effects. For *2010* Edlund made decisions concerning the special type of cameras and camera equipment necessary for the effects shots, the cloud tanks, the motion-control system, how to shoot the mattes, at what camera speed to shoot the miniatures, what size film stock to use, and the effects of the different types of film emulsion for various shots.

At the request of special effects pioneer Douglas Trumbull, Edlund became the supervising head of Trumbull's effects house, Boss Film, in the mid-1980s. Boss is a completely self-contained effects company, with a number of departments—including a creature department, an animation and rotoscope division, a matte department, and much more—headed by experts in the field. When a studio hires Boss Film, it is in charge of producing all the special and mechanical effects for that film, with each department handling the appropriate effect. Edlund heads the whole creative force.

Because of the complex nature of today's special effects, the large number of people needed to produce them for each film, and their technical nature, it would seem that any attempt to discuss an overall approach to a film's effects would be impossible. Edlund, however, likes to group his films into two categories—those that are complete fantasies, that have little basis in the world as the audience knows it (the *Star Wars* trilogy, *Masters of the Universe*); and those that depend on the audience's familiarity with certain characters, situations, and locales (*2010*, *Poltergeist*, and the smash hit, *Ghost*). Edlund seems to have a certain fondness for the latter, as they present more of a challenge in terms of making the effects more believable. For example, Edlund went to great pains in *2010* to make the images of Jupiter familiar to the audience by playing off their expectations based on NASA footage from *Voyager 2*, which had been shown on television.

In the 1990s, Edlund continues to dominate much of the special effects industry, and has taken advantage of recent developments in digital technology. Films such as ILM's *Terminator 2* and *Jurassic Park* show how fantastical images can emerge on-screen via computer enhancement, and look completely realistic. Edlund and Boss Films have not fallen behind. In 1992, IBM delivered to Boss a $1.2 million Power Visualization System (PVS), whose output data of 100 megabytes per second (roughly 100 times the average Ethernet networked work station), make models and matte shots nearly obsolete. With a PVS to create digital images, anything within the effects expert's imagination can be reproduced on film. Edlund marvels at the new technology: "Suddenly we have a godlike capability." And yet he has not abandoned more traditional methods. For *Species*, Edlund supervised construction of an animatronic monster equipped with motion sensors. This fierce, agile creature leaps and growls with the speed of a jungle cat. As with many of Edlund's creations, it remains the sole spark of originality in an otherwise mediocre film.

Edlund is a pivotal figure in the visual effects renaissance brought about by the success of techniques and innovations pioneered in *Star Wars*. Since then, Edlund has moved up the ladder from being one member of a visual effects team to becoming board chairman of one of Hollywood's largest special effects houses.

—Susan Doll, updated by Ken Provencher

EDOUART, Farciot

Special Effects Technician. **Nationality:** American. **Born:** California, 1895. **Family:** Married. **Military Service:** U.S. Army Engineers, Camouflage Division of Corps of Engineers during World War I, then with the Signal Corps. **Career:** 1915—joined Realart Studio as assistant cameraman; then worked for the Red Cross in Europe until 1921; 1922—joined Lasky Company, and worked as special effects photographer after it became Paramount, until 1974. **Awards:** Academy Award for *I Wanted Wings*, 1941, *Reap the Wild Wind*, 1942; Technical Academy Award, 1937, 1939, 1943 (2 awards), 1947, 1955 (2 awards); Special Academy Award, 1938. **Died:** In Kenwood, California, 17 March 1980.

Films as Special Effects Photographer (selected list):

1933   *Alice in Wonderland* (McLeod)
1935   *Lives of a Bengal Lancer* (Hathaway)
1936   *Peter Ibbetson* (Hathaway)
1938   *The Texans* (Hogan); *Spawn of the North* (Hathaway)
1939   *Union Pacific* (DeMille)
1940   *Dr. Cyclops* (Schoedsack)
1941   *I Wanted Wings* (Leisen); *Virginia* (Griffith); ***Sullivan's Travels*** (P. Sturges); *Aloma of the South Seas* (Santell)

1942   *Reap the Wild Wind* (DeMille)
1943   *So Proudly We Hail* (Sandrich)
1944   *The Story of Dr. Wassell* (DeMille)
1945   ***The Lost Weekend*** (Wilder)
1946   *The Virginian* (Gilmore)
1947   *Unconquered* (DeMille)
1948   *The Emperor Waltz* (Wilder)
1950   ***Sunset Boulevard*** (Wilder)
1951   *Ace in the Hole* (Wilder); *When Worlds Collide* (Maté)
1955   *Artist and Models* (Tashlin)
1956   *The Mountain* (Dmytryk)
1958   *The Colossus of New York* (Lourié); *The Space Children* (Arnold); ***Vertigo*** (Hitchcock); *Houseboat* (Shavelson)
1961   *Blue Hawaii* (Taurog); ***Breakfast at Tiffany's*** (Edwards); *One-Eyed Jacks* (Brando); *The Pleasure of His Company* (Seaton)
1963   *Donovan's Reef* (Ford); *Hud* (Ritt); *It's a Mad, Mad, Mad, Mad World* (Kramer)
1964   *The Carpetbaggers* (Dmytryk); *The Disorderly Orderly* (Lewis)
1965   *In Harm's Way* (Preminger); *Red Line 7000* (Hawks); *Ship of Fools* (Kramer); *Village of the Giants* (Gordon)
1966   *This Property Is Condemned* (Pollack)
1967   *Barefoot in the Park* (Saks); *El Dorado* (Hawks); *Warning Shot* (Kulik)
1968   ***Rosemary's Baby*** (Polanski)

Publications

On EDOUART: articles—

American Cinematographer (Hollywood), June 1942, July 1974.
Fry, Ron, and Pamela Fourzon, in *The Saga of Special Effects*, Englewood Cliffs, New Jersey, 1977.
Obituary in *Variety* (New York), 26 March 1980.
Obituary in *Journal of the Society of Motion Picture and Television Engineers* (Scarsdale), July 1980.

*   *   *

The name most closely associated with classic rear-screen projection effects is Farciot Edouart. Rear-screen projection is a technique which composites studio sequences with location or effects shots by projecting images on a screen behind the live action and then simultaneously photographing them. Developed during the late 1920s, it was first used in *Just Imagine* in 1930. According to *American Cinematographer*, Edouart was the second technician to employ rear-screen projection in feature films.

Edouart's concentration and expertise in this field is made clear by the ten Academy Awards he received between 1937 and 1955. Seven of the awards were technical and directly involved improvements on the rear-screen projection process, most notably his improvement of the triple-headed background projector and a process which transferred color transparencies to glass plates, then projected and rephotographed them.

Edouart's filmography avoids much overt science-fiction or fantasy. This fact is not all that surprising, since rear-screen projection as practiced by Edouart was used to render a heightened reality and project authenticity of locale, as in *Spawn of the North*, *Union Pacific*, *Aloma of the South Seas*, *Ace in the Hole*, *The Mountain*, and *Blue*

Hawaii. However, some of his best-remembered work foregrounds technology as it plays with the unreal. *Dr. Cyclops* and *When Worlds Collide* (both created by Edouart and Gordon Jennings, a frequent collaborator) used rear-screen projection to depict the very small in an oversized environment: the 12-inch-tall explorers struggling to survive in a world usually taken for granted (*Dr. Cyclops*) or the scientists coping with Earth's destruction by a renegade planet (*When Worlds Collide*). *Vertigo* and *It's a Mad, Mad, Mad, Mad World* employed similar techniques to visualize the private fantasies of the film's protagonists: the morbid obsession to recreate the lost ideal woman (*Vertigo*) or the comic lunacy of the promise of untold wealth (*It's a Mad, Mad, Mad, Mad World*).

Edouart stands as an expert technician whose efforts were made in the service of a film's overall design. Professionalism prevented him from creating special effects for their own end and consequently much of his work passes undetected. Although this may deny recognition by the general public, it actually attests to Edouart's consummate skills.

—Greg. S. Faller

EISLER, Hanns

Composer. **Nationality:** German. **Born:** Leipzig, 6 July 1898. **Education:** Studied with Schoenberg at Vienna Conservatory. **Military Service:** Served in German army, 1916–18. **Career:** Taught at Klindworth-Scharwenka Conservatory, Berlin, 1925–33; also wrote incidental music for stage works of Brecht and others; 1930—first score for film, *Das Lied vom Leben*; 1933—left Germany with rise of Nazis; 1936–48—lived in the United States, professor of music at New School of Social Research, New York (in charge of their Film Music Project, 1940–42), and Los Angeles University; 1948—deported from U.S.; lived in Vienna, then in East Berlin; professor at Music Institute (later named after him). **Died:** In Berlin, 6 September 1962.

Films as Composer:

1930   *Das Lied vom Leben* (*Song of Life*) (Granowsky) (co)
1931   *Niemansland* (*No Man's Land*) (Trivas) (co)
1932   *Kuhle Wampe, oder Wem gehört die Welt?* (Dudow); *Pesn o geroyazh* (*Komsomol*; *Song of Heroes*; *Youth Speaks*) (Ivens)
1933   *Dans les rues* (Trivas); ***Nieuwe gronden*** (*New Earth*) (Ivens—short)
1934   *Le Grand Jeu* (Feyder)
1935   *Abdul the Damned* (Grune)
1936   *La Vie est à nous* (Renoir) (song)
1938   *The 400 Million* (*China's 400 Million*) (Ivens)
1940   *White Flood* (Maddow, Field, and Meyers—short); *Rain* (Ivens) (new score for 1929 film *Regen*)
1941   *Pete Roleum and His Cousins* (Losey—short); *A Child Went Forth* (Losey and Ferno—short); *Our Russian Front* (Ivens and Milestone—short); *The Forgotten Village* (Kline)

Hanns Eisler (center)

1942 *China Fights* (Yuan)
1943 *Hangmen Also Die!* (F. Lang)
1944 *None But the Lonely Heart* (Odets)
1945 *Jealousy* (Machaty); *The Spanish Main* (Borzage)
1946 *Deadline at Dawn* (Clurman); *Scandal in Paris* (Sirk) (co)
1947 *The Woman on the Beach* (Renoir); *So Well Remembered* (Dmytryk)
1948 *Krizova trojka* (*Three Crosses*) (Gajer)
1949 *Unser täglich Brot* (*Our Daily Bread*) (Dudow)
1950 *Der Rat der Götter* (Maetzig)
1951 *Das Leben unserer Präsidenten* (*Leben Wilhelm Piecks*) (Thorndike)
1952 *Frauenschicksale* (Dudow)
1953 *Schicksal am Lenkrad* (Vergano)
1954 *Bel Ami* (Daquin)
1955 *Herr Puntila und sein Knecht Matti* (Cavalcanti); **Nuit et brouillard** (*Night and Fog*) (Resnais)
1956 *Les Sorcières de Salem* (*The Witches of Salem*) (Rouleau)
1958 *Geschwader Fledermaus* (Engel)
1959 *Trübe Wasser* (*Les Arrivistes*) (Daquin)
1962 *Unbändiges Spanien* (J. and K. Stein); *Esther* (Trosch)

Other Films:

1936 *Pagliacci* (*A Clown Must Laugh*) (Grune) (arranger)
1955 *Gasparone* (Paryla) (adaptation, + co-sc)
1956 *Fidelio* (Felsenstein) (adaptation, + co-sc)

Publications

By EISLER: books—

With Theodore Adorno, *Composing for the Films*, New York, 1947, 1994.
Reden und Aufsätze, Berlin, 1959.
With H. Bunge, *Fragen Sie mehr über Brecht: Hanns Eisler in Gesprach*, Munich, 1970.
Materialen zu einer Dialektik der Musik, Berlin, 1973.
Musik und Politik, edited by G. Mayer, Berlin, 1973.
A Rebel in Music: Selected Writings, edited by Manfred Grabs, New York, 1978.

By EISLER: articles—

Film und Fernsehen (letters) (Berlin), no. 7, 1983.
Film und Fernsehen (letters) (Berlin), no. 4, 1985.

On EISLER: books—

Brockhaus, H. A., *Hanns Eisler*, Leipzig, 1961.
Notowicz, N., and J. Elsner, *Hanns Eisler*, Leipzig, 1966.
Klemm, E., *Hanns Eisler*, Berlin, 1973.
Betz, Albrecht, *Hanns Eisler*, Munich, 1976, as *Hanns Eisler, Political Musician*, Cambridge, 1982.
Hennenberg, Fritz, *Hanns Eisler*, Rowohlt, 1987.
Blake, David, editor, *Hanns Eisler*, Newark, 1995.
Fischbach, Fred, *Hanns Eisler: Le Musicien et la Politique*, Bern, 1999.

On EISLER: articles—

Films in Review (New York), May 1962.
Film und Fernsehen (Berlin), nos. 6 and 7, 1981.
Kinemathek (Berlin), June 1983.
Stilwell, R., "Theodor Adorno and Hanns Eisler: Composing for the Films," in *Screen* (Oxford), no. 4, 1995.
"Hanns Eisler and Film Music," in *Historical Journal of Film, Radio and Televsion* (Abingdon), October 1998.

*   *   *

Hanns Eisler was a well-known composer of orchestral and stage works (collaborating especially with Bertolt Brecht) before his first film compositions, and he was always a musical theoretician, stressing the revolutionary function of music: his "Solidaritätslied" appeared in the film *Kuhle Wampe*, and other "revolutionary" songs include the "Einbeitsfrontlied" and the East German national anthem. About his work for the film *Komsomol*, he said: "In composing music to a revolutionary film the composer is faced with new and difficult problems, especially when the film deals with such an important theme as youth constructing socialism." In that film, he used music based on recordings of the noise of blast furnaces as well as folk songs. His other early films also have music based on his firm ideas about the relation of music to film content. He disliked the use of *leitmotifs*, since he felt it led to a poverty of composition, and stressed "musical commentary" as opposed to "illustration, mood-painting." For *Das Lied vom Leben* he used a ballad of the life awaiting a newborn child; for *Niemansland* he showed the "stultifying and narcotic effect" of military music. Often, in fact, he set music *against* the action of the film in order to encourage a thoughtful, rather than a sentimental, reaction to it—a lesson he might have learned from Brecht's alienation effect. *Kuhle Wampe* is divided into episodes by the musical forms used, so any sentimental reaction to this film about unemployment is neutralized. In *New Earth* his compositions operate under the principle that machinery should be accompanied by natural sound and men by music: he used the usual instrumentation as well as banjo, accordion, and jazz-type percusson, with a blues tune used in the central section of men carrying heavy equipment. For *White Flood*, a documentary about glaciers, he used an invention, a *scherzo*, an etude (for a snow storm), and a sonata finale, while in *Rain* he utilized the 12-tone technique ("14 Ways of Describing Rain"). His stay in Hollywood (which he detested) was not as productive as his early documentary period, though he received an Oscar nomination for *Hangmen Also Die!*

ELFMAN, Danny

Composer. **Nationality:** American. **Born:** Los Angeles (one source lists Amarillo, Texas), 29 May 1953; brother of Richard Elfman, founder of Oingo Boingo and film director. **Education:** Educated in Los Angeles public schools; toured with an avant-garde theater troupe playing conga; spent a year in West Africa. **Family:** Married (separated); two children: Lola, Mali. **Career:** Rock musician with group Mystic Nights of Oingo Boingo, 1971–79; singer, songwriter, and guitarist for rock group Oingo Boingo 1979–1986; recorded solo albums, including *So-Lo* (1984) and *Music for a Darkened Theater* (1990); film composer, from 1980; composer of music for television series, including *Amazing Stories* (1985), *Pee Wee's Playhouse* (1986), *The Simpsons* (1989), *Batman: Animated Series* (1992), and *Dilbert* (1999). **Awards:** Grammy Award, Best Instrumental Composition, for "The Batman Theme" from *Batman*, 1989; Academy of Science Fiction, Horror, and Fantasy Films Saturn Award for Best Musical Score, for *Mars Attacks!*, 1997; Academy of Science Fiction, Horror, and Fantasy Films Saturn Award for Best Music, for *Men in Black*, 1998; Academy of Science Fiction, Horror, and Fantasy Films Saturn Award for Best Music, and Golden Satellite Award for Best Original Score, for *Sleepy Hollow*, 2000; Fantosporto Special Career Award, 2000. **Agent:** Blue Focus Management, 15233 Ventura Blvd., Suite 2A, Sherman Oaks, CA 91403, U.S.A.

Danny Elfman

Films as Composer:

1980	*Forbidden Zone* (+ arranger, ro as Satan)
1985	*Pee Wee's Big Adventure*
1986	*Back To School* (+ ro as Oingo Boingo band member); *Wisdom*; *The Texas Chainsaw Massacre 2* (song)
1987	*Summer School*
1988	*Midnight Run*; *Scrooged*; *Hot to Trot*; *Big Top Pee Wee*; *Delores Claiborne*
1989	*Batman*; *Ghostbusters II*
1990	*Dick Tracy*; *Edward Scissorhands*; *Nightbreed*; *Darkman*; *Leatherface: Texas Chainsaw Massacre III* (song); *The Flash* (main theme—for TV)
1991	*Pure Luck* (main theme)
1992	*Batman Returns* (+ music producer); *Buffy the Vampire Slayer* (song "We Close Our Eyes"); *Article 99*
1993	*Sommersby*; *Army of Darkness* (*Evil Dead 3*); *Nightmare Before Christmas* (+ assoc pr, ro as Jack Skellington [singing])
1994	*Black Beauty*; *Shrunken Heads* (main theme); *Darkman II: The Return of Durant* (musical themes)
1995	*Delores Claiborne* (+ music producer); *Dead Presidents* (+ music producer); *To Die For*; *Great People of the Bible and How They Lived* (video)
1996	*Extreme Measures* (+ music producer); *The Frighteners*; *Mars Attacks!*; *Mission Impossible*; *Bordello of Blood* (theme); *Freeway*; *Farewell: Live from the Universal Amphitheatre Halloween* (video) (+ sc, exec pr, performer); *Darkman III: Die Darkman Die* (musical themes)
1997	*Good Will Hunting* (+ score producer); *Flubber*; *Men in Black*; *Scream 2* ("Cassandra" aria)
1998	*A Simple Plan*; *Modern Vampires*; *A Civil Action* (+ score producer)
1999	*Anywhere But Here* (+ songs); *My Favorite Martian*; *Instinct*; *Sleepy Hollow*

Films as Actor:

1977	*Hot Tomorrows* (as singer)
1981	*Urgh! A Music War* (as Oingo Boingo member)
1992	*The Magical World of Chuck Jones* (as himself)

Other Films:

1998	*Pyscho* (music adaptor, producer, and supervisor)

Publications

On ELFMAN: books—

Karlin, Fred, *Listening to Movies: The Film Lover's Guide to Film Music*, New York, 1994.
Marill, Alvin H., *Keeping Score: Film and Television Music, 1988–1997*, Landham, Maryland, 1998.
Craggs, Stewart A., *Soundtracks: An International Dictionary of Composers for Film*, Aldershot, England, and Brookfield, Vermont, 1998.

On ELFMAN: articles—

Gorbman, Claudia, "Narrative Film Music," in *Yale French Studies*, vol. 60, 1988.
"A Sweet and Scary Treat," in *Time*, 11 October 1993.
Hoberman, Jonathan, "Puppet Regimes," in *Village Voice*, vol. 38, 19 October 1993.
Katz, Alyssa, "Elf Esteem," in *Village Voice*, vol. 38, 9 November 1993.
"The Evolution of Elfman," in *Film Score Monthly*, vol. 4, no. 1, January 1999.
"Danny Elfman: Music for a Darkened People," at http://elfman.filmmusic.com, June 2000.

* * *

Danny Elfman's shadowy scores of exaggerated comic-book quality are most closely associated with the films of director Tim Burton: *Batman, Batman Returns, Beetlejuice, Pee Wee's Big Adventure, Edward Scissorhands, Nightmare Before Christmas*, and *Mars Attacks!* Yet, his most catchy tune is perhaps the Jetson's-like theme of the animated television series *The Simpsons*. Elfman is a self-taught musician who can (and does) play virtually every instrument. In an interview for *Time*, Elfman resisted the label "genius," instead describing himself as "a good observer [who's] very tenacious." During his youth, Elfman was exposed to symphonies and classical film scores. His favorite composers are highly imagistic Eastern European composers such as Bartok, Prokofiev, Shostokovich, and Stravinsky. Yet, he is the first to admit that his exposure to classical music has been filtered through film. Alfred Hitchcock's composer Bernard Hermann (*Psycho, Vertigo, The Man Who Knew Too Much*) is Elfman's all-time favorite, with Nino Rota (Fellini's *8 1/2* and Coppola's *The Godfather*) a close runner-up. His ongoing fascination with Hermann was one of the reasons Elfman joined up for the 1999 remake of *Psycho*, in which one can hear distinct homages that are reminiscent of the original score without being derivative. Elfman also credits Cab Calloway, Gilbert and Sullivan, Ravel, Camille Saint-Saens, Dr. Seuss, Max Steiner, and Franz Waxman as inspirations. The "dark cheeriness" of songs, lyrics, score, and vocals for main character that Elfman composed for *Nightmare Before Christmas* are reminiscent of Kurt Weill, the German cabaret composer.

Elfman started playing the violin in high school. In his first gig, he played conga drums while touring France and Belgium with an avant-garde troupe, Grand Magic Circus. When eighteen, he spent a year in West Africa, after which he joined up with his brother's group, The Mystic Knights, otherwise known as the prequel to Oingo Boingo. Elfman taught himself composition by transcribing the jazz music of Duke Ellington. Elfman received his first taste of international stardom when Oingo Boingo's theme song for the film *Weird Science* (1985) made Billboard's Top 40. He remained active in the rock group until the band's retirement in 1996.

Although Elfman's first composition for film was the low-budget cult film made by his brother, Richard, *Forbidden Zone* (1980), Elfman entered the Hollywood scene in 1985 when Tim Burton approached Elfman to score *Pee Wee's Big Adventure* based solely on Elfman's work with Oingo Boingo. Elfman subsequently composed the music for all three Pee Wee sequels and the television series that resulted from the film's popularity. Burton and Elfman have enjoyed a lucrative and creatively inspirational partnership ever since.

After winning a Grammy for the neo-gothic soundtrack for Burton's *Batman* (1989), Elfman has had his pick of film projects. However, Elfman usually chooses to share his distinctive sound in films featuring alienated characters and macabre story-lines similar to Burton's portraits of melancholy and misunderstood outsiders. His music intensifies the atmosphere of bizarre, mysterious, and haunting alienation that complement Burton's highly stylized, moody films. In these films, music becomes part of a mosaic of poetic effects that turn the film into a composite of suspense. His quirky, gloomy musical style reflects the essential quality of the comic books that inspired some of films such as *Batman*, *Darkman*, and *Dick Tracy*, the latter leading to his second Grammy nomination. In *Nightmare*, for example, Elfman ''wraps minor scales, dissonance, and witchy vocals into a child-accessible soundtrack,'' explains Alyssa Katz. Against Elfman's elaborate musical backdrop, the spectator enters a different world in which Elfman's music becomes part of the ethereal mood. Film critic Jonathan Hoberman sums up Elfman's music for *Nightmare before Christmas*, Elfman's personal favorite, as ''a near perfect balance between nasty and cute.'' *Nightmare*, a ''funhouse of funereal glamour'' according to a film review in *Time*, balances a succession of funny, tragic, ironic characters in exaggeratedly dramatic situations.

In an interview, Elfman has said that ''writing the melody is the easy part. Art comes from what you do with the melody.'' His music is indeed artful: his haunting melodies match the rhythm of animated sequences, just as his changes in instrumental color highlight dramatic effect. His scores provide emotional support, accentuate the pacing of the films, and enhance the mood of the setting. Elfman creates a textured fabric that drapes over the narrative to magical effect. The music in *Scissorhands*, for example, emphasizes the character's alienation and increasing uncertainty as he becomes a cultural cast-off.

As counterpart to his exaggerated portraits of lonely outsiders, Elfman's interest in the gothic and creepy led to his participation in several horror films, including *Delores Claiborne*, *Psycho*, *Tales from the Crypt*, and *Sleepy Hollow*. Elfman has composed eerie music for many ghostly, otherwordly characters including those from *Beetlejuice*, *Scrooged*, *My Favorite Martian*, and *Modern Vampires*. Of the 300 films Elfman has been involved in, he readily admits to regretting at least a third of them. Moreover, his candid acknowledgement of the commercial enterprise of film composition, in which creative vision is frequently sacrificed for heightened sales, is part of Elfman's appeal. He has proven his independence in thought, action, and music.

—Jill Gillespie

ELLENSHAW, Peter

Special Effects Technician. **Nationality:** British. **Born:** London, England, 24 May 1913. **Military Service:** Royal Air Force during World War II. **Family:** Married c. 1942, son: the special effects man Harrison Ellenshaw. **Career:** Worked as special effects man for Alexander Korda from mid-1930s; worked for Walt Disney from early 1950s, until 1953 in England, then in the United States: also worked on Disney television films and Disneyland rides; also a painter: regular exhibits at Hammer Gallery, New York. **Awards:** Academy Award, for *Mary Poppins*, 1964, and *Bedknobs and Broomsticks*, 1971.

Peter Ellenshaw

Films as Special Effects Technician:

1940   *The Thief of Bagdad* (Powell, Berger, and Whelan)
1946   ***A Matter of Life and Death*** (*Stairway to Heaven*) (Powell and Pressburger)
1947   ***Black Narcissus*** (Powell and Pressburger)
1950   *Treasure Island* (Haskin)
1951   *Quo Vadis* (LeRoy)
1952   *The Story of Robin Hood and His Merrie Men* (*The Story of Robin Hood*) (Annakin); *The Sword and the Rose* (Annakin)
1953   *Rob Roy, the Highland Rogue* (French)
1954   *20,000 Leagues under the Sea* (Fleischer); *Davy Crockett, King of the Wild Frontier* (Foster)
1956   *The Great Locomotive Chase* (Lyon)
1957   *Johnny Tremain* (Stevenson)
1958   *The Light in the Forest* (Daugherty)
1960   *Pollyanna* (Swift); *Swiss Family Robinson* (Annakin); *Spartacus* (Kubrick)
1961   *The Absent-Minded Professor* (Vitarelli) (co)
1962   *In Search of the Castaways* (Bolton)
1963   *Son of Flubber* (Stevenson) (co); *Summer Magic* (Neilson)
1964   *Mary Poppins* (Stevenson) (co)
1966   *The Fighting Prince of Donegal* (O'Herlihy); *Lt. Robin Crusoe U.S.N.* (Paul) (co-hairstylist)
1967   *The Adventures of Bullwhip Griffin* (Neilson); *The Gnome-Mobile* (Stevenson); *The Happiest Millionaire* (Tokar); *Monkeys, Go Home!* (McLaglen) (co)

1968   *Blackbeard's Ghost* (Stevenson); *Never a Dull Moment*
          (Paris) (co)
1969   *The Love Bug* (Stevenson)
1971   *Bedknobs and Broomsticks* (Stevenson)
1973   *The Island at the Top of the World* (Stevenson)
1979   *The Black Hole* (Nelson)

Publications

By ELLENSHAW: books—

*Peter Ellenshaw: Selected Works, Nineteen Twenty-Nine to Nineteen
     Eighty-Three*, Shreveport, 1983.

By ELLENSHAW: articles—

Ecran Fantastique (Paris), no. 14, 1980.
American Cinematographer (Hollywood), January 1980.
Screen International (London), 19–26 January 1980.
Films Illustrated (London), March 1980.
Film Review (London), April 1980.
Filme (Berlin), January-February 1981.

On ELLENSHAW: articles—

Culhane, John, "The Remarkable Visions of Peter Ellenshaw," in
     American Film (Washington, D.C.), September 1979.
Movie Maker (Hemel Hempstead, Hertfordshire), March 1980.

*   *   *

Peter Ellenshaw made a career out of mixing fantasy with reality to make make-believe worlds come to life and also, conversely, mixing reality with fantasy to allow the real world to enter into animated or make-believe environments. He began his career in 1934 as a matte artist and was an assistant to W. Percy Day, an early advocate (and possibly the inventor) of matte painting in Europe. Ellenshaw worked for several British directors—including Michael Powell—painting fanciful backgrounds that would have been too expensive to build as sets. He provided the matte painting and the hanging miniature that represented the blue and pink city of *The Thief of Bagdad* and the matte painting of the heavens in *A Matter of Life and Death*. He also worked on all of Alexander Korda's films.

Because Disney Studios had a large sum of revenues in England which they were not able to transfer stateside, they decided to open a production company in England. In 1948, when they established their British branch, Disney began to make period feature movies with English actors. Their first films were *Treasure Island*, *The Story of Robin Hood and His Merrie Men*, *The Sword and the Rose*, and *Rob Roy, the Highland Rogue*. Ellenshaw, joining Disney at this time, worked on all four. He began as a matte artist and special effects artist, and later in his career became a production designer. It was the start of a long association. Over the next four decades, Ellenshaw worked on the largest and most-challenging projects the Disney studios made— and won two Academy Awards for his work.

When Disney decided to make *20,000 Leagues under the Sea*, Ellenshaw moved to Hollywood to work on the film. This was Disney's most ambitious film thus far. The story called for spectacular special effects, underwater filming, and location shooting far from the studios—not to forget the most important special effect, the designing and building of the giant squid.

While Ellenshaw continued to work on other well-known films such as *Pollyanna*, *Swiss Family Robinson*, and even the blockbuster, *Spartacus*, it is his work on *Mary Poppins* that is the best known. Filming *Mary Poppins* was a feat only the Disney studio could accomplish. First, the Disney creators were coming from the world of animation and they had a different slant on storytelling. Second, they had a history of successful special effects. For *Mary Poppins*, they incorporated wonderful adventures in flying or racing that defied logic and merged the worlds of dream and reality. Ellenshaw's special effects became one of the great delights of the film.

Ellenshaw's special effects are an intrinsic part of the Mary Poppins story. For the gravity-defying special effects, the flying effects used for *The Absent-Minded Professor*, a black-and-white movie, were adapted to color film. The flying effects enabled fantasy to enter the real world as Mary Poppins arrives from somewhere above with an umbrella keeping her aloft, as the wind blows hard and carries away all the other nannies; Ed Wynn floats to the ceiling every time he laughs; and pieces of paper float up the chimney. All seems effortless and real, indeed a mix between fantasy and reality. The real mixes with fantasy as Dick Van Dyke dances with cartoon penguins, and carousel horses come to life to run a race which, of course, Mary Poppins wins. The mattes used to create the rooftop scenes to the "Step in Time" sequence are breathtaking. For his work on this film, Ellenshaw won his first Academy Award.

Ellenshaw later won his second Academy Award as art director for *Bedknobs and Broomsticks* and was also nominated for another Academy Award as production designer on *The Island at the Top of the World*. *Bedknobs and Broomsticks* was filled with special effects and many critics felt that they were the redeeming factor of the movie. Many of the special effects were similar to those in *Mary Poppins*: a bedstead flies like a magic carpet, animation is nicely mixed with live action, and the characters ride into seven fantastic worlds.

The Island at the Top of the World is a story set in 1907. An Englishman commissions a spaceship to take him to a mythical, arctic Shangri-La. Ellenshaw produced splendid visual effects for the authentic looking Viking settlement and mysterious valley on the edge of the volcano. Many critics again felt that the special effects redeemed the movie.

For Disney's super-production *The Black Hole*, Ellenshaw was asked to come out of retirement to be the production designer and special effects director. This was the largest project attempted up till that time by Disney. It was also important work for Ellenshaw who would later see his work on *The Black Hole* as part of an exhibit at the Museum of Modern Art. The sets are eye-catching, almost distracting. For the interior of the Spaceship Cygnus, Ellenshaw achieved a dated modern look by borrowing from Chagall and Mondrian. Inside, it is comfy, not austere. There are big picture windows replacing the usual small portholes. Bunks beds have space art hanging on the walls. The ambience is friendly and inviting.

Ellenshaw exclusively used mattes in *The Black Hole*—simple mattes as well as complex running mattes—and his son executed all 150 mattes, a world record. The special effects work on *The Black Hole* is considered to be technically superior to *Star Wars*, *Star Trek*, and *Close Encounters of the Third Kind*, although *The Black Hole* did not attract the same box-office attention. The design of the movie is considered to be a point of departure from *Star Wars*. *The Black Hole* was Peter Ellenshaw's last movie and a fitting close for someone who was described as one of the screen's masters of visual effects, and the film garnered him another Academy Award nomination, for best visual effects.

—Renee Ward

ENEI, Yevgeni

Art Director. **Nationality:** Hungarian. **Born:** Austria-Hungary, 1890. **Education:** Attended Fine Arts Academy, Budapest. **Career:** Entered films in mid-1920s, working with both the formalist group FEKS (mainly for Kozintsev and Trauberg), and for the realist group KEM (especially for Ermler). **Died:** In 1971.

Films as Art Director:

1925   *Mishki protiv Youdenitsa* (*Mishka against Yudenich*) (Kozintsev and Trauberg); *V tylu u belych* (*Tchaikovsky and Rachimanova*); *Napoleon-Gaz* (Timoshenko)

1926   *Severnoe siianie* (*Mirage in the North*) (Foregger); *Katka bumazhnyi ranet* (*Katka's Reinette Apple*) (Johanson and Ermler); *Chyortovo koleso* (*The Devil's Wheel*) Kozintsev and Trauberg); *Shinel* (*The Cloak*) (Kozintsev and Trauberg)

1927   *S.V.D.* (*Soyuz Velikogo Dela*; *The Club of the Big Deed*) (Kozintsev and Trauberg); *Bratichka* (*Little Brother*) (Kozintsev and Trauberg); *Chiuzoi pidzak* (Schpiss)

1928   *Devushka s dalekoi reki* (*The Girl from the Distant River*) (Chervyakov) (co); *Dom v sugribakh* (*The House in the Snow-Drifts*) (Ermler)

1929   *Oblomok imperii* (*Fragment of an Empire*) (Kozintsev and Trauberg); ***Novyi Vavilon*** (*The New Babylon*) (Kozintsev and Trauberg); *Flag nazii* (*Flags of Nations*) (Schmidgof) (co); *Chornyi parus* (*The Black Sail*) (Yutkevich)

1930   *Dvadzatdva neshchastia* (*22 Misfortunes*) (Gerasimov and Bartenev)

1931   *Odna* (*Alone*) (Kozintsev and Trauberg)

1932   *Ich puti razoshchlis* (Federov); *Snaiper* (Timoshenko)

1935   ***Yunost Maksima*** (*The Youth of Maxim*) (Kozintsev and Trauberg)

1937   ***Vozvrashcheniye Maksima*** (*The Return of Maxim*) (Kozintsev and Trauberg)

1939   ***Vyborgskaya Storona*** (*The Vyborg Side*) (Kozintsev and Trauberg)

1947   *Pirogov* (Kozintsev (co); *Zhizn v tsitadel* (*Life in the Citadel*) (Rappaport) (co)

1949   *Academician Ivan Pavlov* (Roshal) (co)

1952   *Jambul* (Dzigan) (co)

1955   *Ovod* (*The Gadfly*) (Fainzimmer)

1956   *Prostiye lyudi* (*Simple People*) (Kozintsev and Trauberg—produced 1945) (co)

1957   *Don Cesar de Bazan* (Shapiro); *Don Quixote* (Kozintsev)

1958   *Den pervyi* (*The First Day*) (Ermler)

1963   *Hamlet* (Kozintsev) (co)

1967   *Katerina Izmailova* (Shapiro)

1971   *Karol Lear* (*King Lear*) (Kozintsev)

Publications

On ENEI: articles—

Soviet Film (Moscow), no. 10, 1970.

Silaneva, T. A., in *Designers of the Soviet Cinema*, Moscow, 1972 (text partly in English).

*   *   *

Yevgeni Enei's career extended from the mid-1920s to 1971, and he combined in his work the delightful eccentricity and wonderment of the early filmmakers Kozinstev and Trauberg with the later dedication to Soviet psychological realism of Ermler and the Kozinstev-Trauberg team in the 1930s. His brilliance was revealed in the striking sets for *The New Babylon*: the fantastic department store of the Paris Commune of 1870 perfectly matches Kozinstev and Trauberg's extravagant political views. Working again with the cinematographer Andrei Moskvin on Kozinstev and Trauberg's *Alone*, he used a variety of white tones in close collaboration with the cinematography. Later in his career, he proved adept at providing rather solid biographical films, such as *Pirogov*. *The New Yorker* called *Don Quixote* one of the most beautiful color compositions ever assembled in a film. Enei maximized the potential and richness of color film while successfully avoiding a garishly unrestrained palette of hues. Shot in the Crimea under a scathing sun, the film enjoys a landscape of chalky white that serves as a perfect backdrop against which to silhouette the characters of the knight errant, his devoted companion, and those whom the two encounter. In the film, art direction provides Enei with a means of communicating character; for example, the stark black cloaks and stiff white ruffles perfectly frame the cold, arrogant faces of the aristocrats at the duke's court, while costuming for the ragged don heightens both his tragedy and his absurdity. *Don Quixote is* considered by most to be the best of the Soviet offerings in the State Department's U.S.-U.S.S.R. Cultural Exchange Agreement of that year.

Enei shared excellent company in developing *Hamlet*. Grigori Kozinstev, not only a talented director but also a respected Shakespeare scholar, both directed and wrote the script, based on poet Boris Pasternak's admired Russian translation. In addition, the film is supported by composer Dmitri Shostakovich's turbulent, foreboding musical score. Visual spectacle supports the film's epic tone and features impressive black-and-white tableaux that are nothing short of visual poetry. Exterior shots are of a funereal grayness with chiaroscuro reminiscent of Russian film patriarch Sergei Eisenstein. Interior scenes, by contrast, contain warm lighting amid labyrinthine stone corridors where courtiers adorned with courtly robes, furs, and elegant raiment course a doomed path. Beyond the excellent costuming, settings contribute to the quality of the picture. Above a violent, storm-lashed sea is poised upon a cliff of forbidding rocks an ancient, turreted castle (a real castle located in Estonia). Visual imagery is carefully composed and powerfully displayed. For example, riders on horseback seem winged with the fluttering of capes and soldiers hurtling over the castle's drawbridge provide potent spectacle. Fortinbras's troops replete with artillery—hundreds of cavalry and pikemen covering miles of bleak landscape—make their way toward the Baltic coastline. Period accuracy was ensured with the use of actual sixteenth- and seventeenth-century weapons and authentic armor lent to the film by Leningrad's Hermitage. Enei's attention to detail is evident throughout *Hamlet*, as is characteristic of his work in general. The portrait of the royal court is one teeming not only with royalty, courtiers, soldiers, and ladies but also with stable boys, cooks, fishmongers, and peasants—giving the film a social context generally absent from previous interpretations of the play. A final example of Enei's meticulous art direction is evidenced in Polonius's death scene. When Prince Hamlet kills the Lord Chamberlain in his mother's bed chamber, the old man falls, tearing down a curtain to expose rows of mannequins draped in the queen's finery. The film's social consciousness continues to the final climactic scene. The choice to set Hamlet's death beyond the walls of the brooding castle provides the film with an opportunity to reveal how the microcosm impacts the macrocosm, how the world of the king affects the lives of the people. Hundreds of peasants stood witness to the death of their prince.

Enei worked again with Kozinstev in producing another Shakespeare classic, *King Lear*. It is useful to contrast Kozinstev's *Lear* with Britain's Peter Brook's version of the same play, filmed the same year. Indeed, the two directors corresponded and shared production notes. Brook's version has been criticized as being visually dead, a nightmare vision of emptiness serving as a symbol for the meaninglessness and hopelessness of the universe. The play itself is certainly grim enough; however, Kozinstev and Enei manage not to lose themselves in morbidity and despair. As is his custom, Enei gives careful attention to the films accouterments, which are tactilely rich despite a stark, at times even sterile backdrop. Costumes and sets are appropriate both to the subject and to the emotional content of each scene.

Enei's most famous works, however, are the two Maxim films he made for Kozinstev and Trauberg in the mid-1930s. This outstanding fictional sequence, so rooted in reality that millions of viewers in the Soviet Union believed it represented the life of a real man, had a precedent in Ermler's silent *Fragment of an Empire*, described by Paul Rotha as "the epitome of the Soviet sociological propaganda film." The Maxim films do more than put words and sounds to a silent sociological biography: the disparate images that Maxim encounters in his early life, the amazing views of the city, always from Maxim's perspective, suggest the way a mind actually thinks and grows.

—Carrie D. O'Neill

EPSTEIN, Julius and Philip

Writers. **Nationality:** American. **Born:** New York City, 22 August 1909 (twins). **Education:** Attended public schools in New York; Pennsylvania State University, University Park, Julius graduated 1931, Philip graduated 1932. **Family:** Julius married 1) Frances Sage, 1936 (divorced 1945); 2) Ann Lazlo, 1949. **Career:** Philip worked as an actor, Julius as a press agent and boxer; 1933—moved to Hollywood: Julius's first film as writer, *Living on Velvet*, 1935, and Philip's first film as writer, *Love on a Bet*, 1936; 1939—began collaborating on films; Julius continued writing alone after Philip's death in 1952; TV work includes the mini-series *The Pirate*, 1978. **Awards:** Academy Award for *Casablanca*, 1943; Writers Guild Laurel Award,

Julius and Philip Epstein

1955. **Address:** (Julius) c/o ICM, 8899 Beverly Blvd., Los Angeles, California 90048, U.S.A. **Died:** Philip died 9 February 1952.

Films as Writer (Julius):

1935 *Living on Velvet* (Borzage); *In Caliente* (Bacon); *Little Big Shot* (Curtiz); *I Live for Love* (Berkeley); *Stars Over Broadway* (Keighley); *Broadway Gondolier* (Bacon)
1936 *Sons o' Guns* (Bacon)
1937 *Confession* (May)
1938 *Secrets of an Actress* (Keighley); *Four Daughters* (Curtiz)
1954 *Young at Heart* (Douglas) (co)
1955 *The Tender Trap* (Walters)
1957 *Kiss Them for Me* (Donen)
1958 *The Brothers Karamazov* (Brooks) (co-adaptation only)
1959 *Take a Giant Step* (Leacock) (co, + pr)
1960 *Tall Story* (Logan)
1961 *Fanny* (Logan)
1962 *The Light in the Piazza* (Green)
1964 *Send Me No Flowers* (Jewison)
1965 *Return from the Ashes* (Thompson)
1966 *Any Wednesday* (Miller) (+ pr)
1972 *Pete 'n' Tillie* (Ritt) (+ co-pr)
1975 *Once Is Not Enough* (Green)
1978 *House Calls* (Ziett) (co-sc); *Cross of Iron* (Peckinpah) (co)
1983 *Reuben, Reuben* (Miller)

Films as Writer (Philip):

1936 *Love on a Bet* (Jason); *The Bride Walks Out* (Jason); *Grand Jury* (Rogell)
1937 *New Faces of 1937* (Jason)
1938 *The Mad Miss Manton* (Jason); *There's That Woman Again* (Hall)

Films as Co-Writers:

1939 *Daughters Courageous* (Curtiz); *Four Wives* (Curtiz)
1940 *Saturday's Children* (V. Sherman); *No Time for Comedy* (Keighley)
1941 *Strawberry Blonde* (Walsh); *The Bride Came C.O.D.* (Keighley); *The Man Who Came to Dinner* (Keighley); *Honeymoon for Three* (Bacon)
1942 *The Male Animal* (Nugent)
1943 *Casablanca* (Curtiz)
1944 *Mr. Skeffington* (V. Sherman) (+ pr); *Arsenic and Old Lace* (Capra); *One More Tomorrow* (Godfrey) (additional dialogue only)
1948 *Romance on the High Seas* (Curtiz)
1949 *Chicken Every Sunday* (Seaton); *My Foolish Heart* (Robson)
1951 *Take Care of My Little Girl* (Negulesco)
1953 *Forever Female* (Rapper)
1954 *The Last Time I Saw Paris* (Brooks); *The Brothers Karamazov*

Publications

By Julius and Philip EPSTEIN: book—

With Howard Koch, *Casablanca* (script), in *The Best Film Plays of 1943–44*, edited by John Gassner and Dudley Nichols, New York, 1945.

By Julius EPSTEIN: articles—

Films in Review (New York), November 1984.
Film en Televisie (Brussels), no. 392, January 1990.

On Julius and Philip EPSTEIN: articles—

Film Comment (New York), Winter 1970–71.
Focus on Film (London), Spring 1973.
Kilbourne, Don, in *American Screenwriters*, edited by Robert E. Morsberger, Stephen O. Lesser, and Randall Clark, Detroit, Michigan, 1984.
Zolotow, Maurice, "Don't Call Me Mr. Casablanca," in *Los Angeles Magazine*, vol. 33, September 1988.
Case, Brian, "As Time Goes By," in *Time Out* (London), 1 July 1992.
Written By. . . Journal: The Writers Guild of America, West (Los Angeles), March and August 1997.

*   *   *

If *Casablanca* represents the ultimate in the Hollywood studio film, then it is no surprise that the Epstein brothers rank among the best screenwriters to emerge from the Hollywood studio system.

Their combined talents span almost 50 years of filmmaking, resulting in an impressive list of well-wrought screenplays.

The identical twins, Julius and Philip, both graduated from Pennsylvania State University, after which Philip took up acting and Julius became a professional boxer. Julius's athletic career was shortlived, however, when he found work as a radio publicist, wrote a few one-act plays, and moved to California where he began his career in Hollywood as a ghostwriter. He quickly broke into more credible screenwriting when he sold an original story, *Living on Velvet*, to Warner Brothers in 1935. Sharing this first screen credit with another Warners writer, Jerry Wald (soon to become well known as a producer), Epstein signed a seven-year contract with the studio.

Julius collaborated with Wald on a series of pictures, and worked on a routine Kay Francis vehicle, *Confession*, before he got his big break writing with the veteran screenwriter Lenore Coffee on *Four Daughters*. The team was honored with the first of Epstein's four Academy Award nominations.

While Julius was making inroads at Warners, Philip made his way to California. After collaborating with Julius on a play (*And the Stars Remain*), Philip worked with various writers on routine pictures, mostly comedies, for RKO, Paramount, and Columbia. In 1938, following the popularity of *Four Daughters*, he joined Julius at Warners and they became an indivisible writing team until Philip's death from cancer in 1952.

Their first joint assignment to duplicate the success of *Four Daughters* represents typical studio logic. The same cast, plus the same basic storyline, equals another hit. So the Epsteins repeated the film's blend of domestic conflict and romance in *Daughters Courageous* and in a sequel, *Four Wives*. These were followed by a decade-long, series of successes, many of which were adaptations of Broadway plays. The studio capitalized on the writers' talents at sophisticated, often rapier-like, dialogue, depending on the pair to adapt the material faithfully when it was good and to improve on it when it wasn't.

Beginning with a remake of Maxwell Anderson's *Saturday's Children*, the brothers became increasingly skilled at pace and comic timing. Whether delivered by Jimmy Stewart and Rosalind Russell (*No Time for Comedy*), Monty Wooley (*The Man Who Came to Dinner*), Henry Fonda (*The Male Animal*), or Cary Grant (*Arsenic and Old Lace*), the Epsteins' dialogue was bright, pointed, and modern. Even a nostalgic period piece like *Strawberry Blonde* was enlivened by James Cagney's smart remarks and the quick tongue of Olivia de Havilland's forward-thinking suffragette.

With their names appearing on only one conspicuous failure, *One More Tomorrow* (based on Philip Barry's *Animal Kingdom*), the Epsteins proved themselves virtually guaranteed box-office. Their resultant power enabled them to work at home (a rarity at Warner Bros.), not obligated to "punch in" on the studio time clock.

Ironically, their biggest success, *Casablanca*, was the adaptation of a theatrical failure, *Everybody Comes to Rick's*. Working with Howard Koch, the Epsteins turned it into an Academy Award-winning screenplay. In spite of the film's classic stature, however, Julius Epstein still insists that it is the worst kind of Hollywood "junk."

In 1944, the Epstein's attempted their first film in the capacity of both writers and producers with *Mr. Skeffington*. Although the picture was a box-office success and won both Bette Davis and Claude Rains Oscar nominations, production problems made the film an unpleasant experience. They also tried writing for the stage (*Chicken Every Sunday* and *That's the Ticket*) and briefly joined Frank Capra on *Why*

We Fight, a government-made documentary series. None of these ventures proved satisfying, so, they returned to screenwriting. After leaving Warners in 1948, the Epsteins wrote five more screenplays together, two of which, *The Last Time I Saw Paris* and *The Brothers Karamazov*, were released after Philip's death.

Julius continued to freelance throughout the 1950s, 1960s, and less frequently during the 1970s; his most successful scripts were still comedies. He preferred working alone to collaboration, and on several occasions, *Take a Giant Step*, *Any Wednesday*, and *Pete 'n' Tillie*, acted as producer/writer. In 1969, he attempted playwriting again with *But Seriously*—and in 1978 adapted Harold Robbins's *The Pirate* for television.

Today, Julius Epstein describes himself as a cynic, despite the number of romantic films he and his brother wrote over the years. The tone of those pictures, he insists, was shaped by the times, the tastes of the audiences, the demands of the studio, and Hollywood's prevailing censorship. He prefers honesty to sentiment and values adult entertainment over youth-oriented exploitation films. He names *Reuben, Reuben* as the type of film he would have rather written all along.

—Joanne L. Yeck

ESZTERHAS, Joe

Screenwriter. **Nationality:** American. **Born:** Joseph A. Eszterhas, 23 November 1944, in Csakanydoroszlo, Hungary; immigrated to United States, naturalized citizen. **Family:** Married 1) Geri (a police reporter; divorced); 2) Naomi Baka; children (first marriage): Steven, Susie. **Career:** Reporter for *Cleveland Plain Dealer*, Cleveland, Ohio, in early 1970s; began as staff writer, became senior editor, *Rolling Stone*, San Francisco, California, 1971–74; screenwriter, novelist, and freelance journalist, 1974—. **Agent:** Rosalie Swedlin, Creative Artists Agency, 1888 Century Park E., Suite 1400, Los Angeles, CA 90067, U.S.A.

Films as Screenwriter:

1978	*F.I.S.T.* (Jewison)
1983	*Flashdance* (Lyne)
1985	*Jagged Edge* (Marquand)
1987	*Hearts of Fire* (Marquand); *Big Shots* (Mandel)
1988	*Betrayed* (Costa-Gavras) (+ exec pr)
1989	*Checking Out* (Leland)
1990	*Music Box* (Costa-Gavras) (+ exec pr)
1992	*Basic Instinct* (Verhoeven)
1993	*Nowhere to Run* (Harmon); *Sliver* (Noyce) (+ exec pr)
1995	*Showgirls* (Verhoeven); *Jade* (Friedkin) (+ exec pr)
1997	*An Alan Smithee Film: Burn Hollywood Burn* (Smithee, Hiller) (ro as Himself); *One Night Stand* (Figgis) [uncredited]; *Original Sin*; *Telling Lies in America* (Ferland)
1998	*Male Pattern Baldness* (Thomas)
2000	*Blaze of Glory*

Publications

By ESZTERHAS: books—

With Michael D. Roberts, *Thirteen Seconds: Confrontation at Kent State*, New York, 1970.
Charlie Simpson's Apocalypse, New York, 1974.
Nark!: A Tale of Terror, San Francisco, 1974.
F.I.S.T. (novel; based on screenplay of the same title), New York, 1978.

By ESZTERHAS: articles—

Grant, S., and A. McGregor, ''Sex Crimes. Divide and Conquer,'' in *Time Out* (London), no. 1131, 22 April 1992.
''Telling Lies in America,'' in *Scenario* (Rockville, Maryland), vol. 3, no. 4, 1997.

On ESZTERHAS: books—

Wolfe, Tom, and E. W. Johnson, editors, *The New Journalism*, New York, 1973.
Love, Robert, *The Best of Rolling Stone: 25 Years of Journalism on the Edge*, New York, 1993.

On ESZTERHAS: articles—

American Film, 3 December 1989.
Chicago Tribune, 18 April 1983; 28 August 1988; 19 January 1990.
Esquire, 9 May 1978.
Film Comment, January-February 1990.
Los Angeles Times, 15 April 1983; 4 October 1985; 2 October 1987; 26 August 1988; 30 October 1989.

Joe Eszterhas

Newsweek, 28 November 1970; 14 January 1974.

New York Times, 15 April 1983; 4 October 1985; 2 October 1987; 30 May 1993.

New York Times Book Review, 27 January 1974; 7 July 1974.

San Francisco Chronicle, 5 June 1994.

Sight and Sound, October 1996.

Time, 31 May 1993.

Washington Post, 26 January 1974; 10 October 1985; 26 August 1988; 19 January 1990.

* * *

The phenomenal success in 1992 of his notorious *Basic Instinct* (the film earned a reported $365 million in initial release, not to mention lucrative video earnings) made Joe Eszterhas a celebrity and Hollywood's best-paid screenwriter. Eszterhas has been in the public eye ever since, which is quite unusual in his profession. With its fearful, resigned misogyny, its unflattering portrayal of lesbianism as delightfully lewd and criminal-minded, and its equation of heterosexual pleasure with deadly violence, *Basic Instinct* pushed the limits of what could be accommodated in an ''R'' rated film. The film's self-consciously sleazy transgressiveness, hyped by a skillful advertising campaign, found a deep resonance in an America finally coming to grips with the psychosexual consequences of the AIDS crisis. Distracted by its soft-core pornography (which hinted at more than it showed), audiences were untroubled by a script that lacked dramatic intensity and development, but was riddled with implausibilities. Director Paul Verhoeven's frantic pacing helped plaster over the structural problems that Eszterhas's one-dimensional characters and shaky plot presented.

Nothing in Eszterhas's earlier career would have predicted that he would either be involved in such a project or be able to carry it off successfully. Brought from his native Hungary to America as a child, he persevered in mastering a new language and culture, eventually graduating from Ohio State University. As a journalist, first for Cleveland's *Plain Dealer* and then for *Rolling Stone* magazine, Eszterhas showed himself a talented, courageous, and energetic writer. He wrote a competent investigative history of the Kent State killings and then penned a novel that won a National Book Award. He established himself as a kind of proletarian intellectual. This background proved useful when he turned to screenwriting. His first project was *F.I.S.T.*, an unusual Hollywood film in that it was devoted to the union movement in the trucking industry during the 1930s; it is thus a kind of pseudo-autobiography of Jimmy Hoffa. Unfortunately, the project became more of a Sylvester Stallone vehicle, and on these terms it was a failure. Both this film and the subsequent *Flashdance*, which proved an outstanding success, are in part autobiographical. They are Horatio Alger stories in which those at the margins of respectable society discover how through their own efforts they can make lives for themselves in an America that is more or less a land of opportunity.

Quite soon afterward, however, Eszterhas turned to the thriller genre, a time-honored Hollywood type which he would soon prove instrumental in transforming, furthering, if not setting, the fashion for the erotic thriller that would prove a Hollywood staple in the 1990s. *Jagged Edge* centers around an *homme fatal*, a handsome businessman who protests his innocence of the brutal, bondage killing of his rich wife. His beautiful attorney, charmed by her client, at first believes him innocent, but later discovers he is guilty after nearly becoming his next victim. Established in the 1940s by noir classics

such as *Dead Reckoning* and *Lady from Shanghai*, these conventions make for effective filmmaking when fleshed out with interesting characters and plot twists. *Jagged Edge* is somewhat predictable, but manages to be intriguing throughout. The same cannot be said for *Betrayed*, which gives the thriller narrative a political twist. Here the woman in danger is an FBI agent assigned to study a white supremacist group who manages to fall in love with a charismatic man before learning that he is one of the worst perpetrators of neo-fascist violence. Eszterhas's plotting is spotty at best, and the film as a whole relies too much on melodramatic clichés to make its obvious points; the direction by the talented Costa-Gavras, who invented the political thriller in the 1960s with such films as Z, cannot save this poor script. Despite this failure, screenwriter and director teamed up a second time to make a quite similar film, which, with fewer holes in its plot and more interestingly drawn characters, proved more successful. *Music Box* focuses on a beautiful young attorney whose Hungarian immigrant father is suddenly accused of complicity in the murder and deportation of Budapest's Jews during the final yar of the war. She defends him successfully against the charges, but then, not entirely satisfied with his protestations of innocence, follows up a lead that reveals undeniable photographic evidence of his guilt. Though emotionally torn, she turns over her evidence to the press and legal authorities. *Music Box* offers a compelling story, principally because of the screenwriter's intelligent attention to historical and psychological detail. Here too Eszterhas was on home ground, drawing on his own knowledge of the postwar Hungarian immigrant community.

Basic Instinct's success, however, encouraged Eszterhas to abandon, at least temporarily, respectable filmmaking for exploitation. Three subsequent scripts—*Jade*, *Sliver*, and *Showgirls* (another collaboration with Verhoeven)—obviously try to repeat the box office magic of *Basic Instinct* by focusing on rough sex, homosexuality, autoeroticism, and deadly violence. In each case, a righteous misogyny prevails, even when Eszterhas, apparently, thinks he is offering a positive model of women's liberation. All three films proved offensive, which seemed to be their obvious intention, but none achieved the notoriety of its model and so could not find an audience, in spite of massive expenditures on television advertising.

Lately, Eszterhas appears to have reinvented himself and returned to the kind of writing that made him a success as a journalist and novelist. *Telling Lies in America* is an autobiographical tale, tracing the struggles of a 17 year-old Hungarian immigrant named Karchy to find his way in America. Hooking up with a sharpster named Magic, who turns him on to what he thinks is success—money, women, and power. Karchy, however, soon learns that Magic is only using him as a convenient way to mask illegal activities that are the true source of his only apparent and position. Karchy rejects the glamorous but illicit life modeled for him by Magic and determines to make his own way, now that he is through ''telling lies.'' The story, perhaps, is a parable for the direction in which the undeniably talented Eszterhas now intends taking his career.

—R. Barton Palmer

EVEIN, Bernard

Art Director. **Nationality:** French. **Born:** Saint-Mazaire, 5 January 1929. **Education:** Attended School of Fine Arts, Nantes; IDHEC, Paris. **Career:** Art director in films from early 1950s (often in collaboration with Jacques Saulnier); also stage designer, including works directed by Barrault, Rivette, and Hossein; 1961—first of many films for the director Jacques Demy.

Films as Art Director:

1952   *La Danseuse nue* (Louis) (asst); *Douze heures de bonheur* (*Jupiter*) (Grangier) (asst); *On ne badine pas avec l'amour* (Desailly) (+ costumes)

1957   *Le Bel Indifférent* (Demy—short)

1958   *Les Amants* (*The Lovers*) (Malle) (co)

1959   **Les Quatre Cents Coups** (*The 400 Blows*) (Truffaut); *Les Cousins* (*The Cousins*) (Chabrol) (co); *A double tour* (*Web of Passion*; *Leda*) (Chabrol) (co); *La Sentence* (Valère) (co); *Les Jeux de l'amour* (de Broca) (co)

1960   *Les Scélérants* (Hossein) (co); *Zazie dans le métro* (*Zazie*) (Malle); *Les Grandes Personnes* (*Time Out for Love*) (Valère)

1961   *L'Amant de cinq jours* (*The Five Day Lover*) (de Broca); *Lola* (Demy) (+ costumes); *Une Femme est une femme* (*A Woman Is a Woman*) (Godard); *Le Rendez-vous de minuit* (Leenhardt); **Cléo de cinq à sept** (*Cleo from 5 to 7*) (Varda) (+ costumes); **L'Année dernière à Marienbad** (*Last Year at Marienbad*) (Resnais) (costumes only)

1962   *Vie privée* (*A Very Private Affair*) (Malle); *Cybèle, ou les dimanches de Ville d'Avray* (*Sundays and Cybèle*) (Bourguignon); "La Luxure" ("Lust") ep. of *Les Sept Péchés capitaux* (*The Seven Capital Sins*) (Demy); *Le Combat dans l'île* (Cavalier); *Le Jour et l'heure* (*The Day and the Hour*) (Clément)

1963   *La Baie des anges* (*Bay of the Angels*) (Demy); *Le Feu follet* (*The Fire Within*) (Malle)

1964   *Les Parapluies de Cherbourg* (*The Umbrellas of Cherbourg*) (Demy); *Aimez-vous des femmes* (*A Taste for Women*) (Léon) (designs); *L'Insoumis* (Cavalier); *Comment épouser un premier ministre* (Boisrond)

1965   *Viva Maria!* (Malle); *Paris au mois d'août* (*Paris in the Month of August*) (Granier-Deferre)

1966   *Qui êtes-vous, Polly Maggoo?* (Klein)

1967   *Les Demoiselles de Rochefort* (*The Young Girls of Rochefort*) (Demy); *Woman Times Seven* (*Sept Fois Femme*) (De Sica); "Mademoiselle Fifi" ep. of *Le Plus Vieux Métier du monde* (*The Oldest Profession*) (de Broca)

1968   *Adolphe, ou l'age tendre* (Roublanc-Michel)

1969   *Sweet Hunters* (Guerra)

1970   *L'Aveu* (*The Confession*) (Costa-Gavras)

1971   *Le Bateau sur l'herbe* (Brach)

1973   *L'Evènement le plus important depuis que l'homme a marché sur la lune* (*A Slightly Pregnant Man*) (Demy); *Le Grand Bazar* (Zidi); *Le Hasard et la violence* (Labro)

1974   *La Merveilleuse Visite* (Carné) (designs)

1976   *L'Alpagueur* (Labro); *Néa* (Kaplan); *Le Jouet* (Veber)

1977   *La Vie devant soi* (*Madame Rosa*) (Mizrahi)

1978   *Lady Oscar* (Demy)

1979   *Tous vedettes* (Lang)

1981   *Chère inconnue* (*I Sent a Letter to My Love*) (Mizrahi); *Une Merveilleuse Journée* (Vital)

1982   *Une Chambre en ville* (*A Room in Town*) (Demy)

1984   *Notre histoire* (*Our Story*) (Blier)

1986   *La Rumba* (Hanin); *Thérèse* (Cavalier)

1988   *Trois places pour le 26* (Demy)

Publications

By EVEIN: articles—

Télécine (Paris), no. 104, 1962.
Cinéma (Paris), no. 90, 1966.
Image et Son (Paris), April 1968.
Cinéma (Paris), July/August 1981.
Cahiers du Cinéma (Paris), December 1982.
Cahiers du Cinéma (Paris), December 1990.

On EVEIN: articles—

Film Français (Paris), 18 February 1977.
Film Français (Paris), 3 February 1978.
Film Français (Paris), 1 March 1982.
Cahiers du Cinéma (Paris), no. 342, December 1982.
Positif (Paris), February 1990.

*   *   *

Until 1960, French production design specialized in elegant but often over-theatrical re-creations of urban life. Into this calm pond, the Nouvelle Vague, with its hit-and-run shooting style, minuscule budgets, and studied naturalism, threw a rock. When the ripples cleared, two designers dominated the remade French cinema. Between them, Jacques Saulnier and his collaborator Bernard Evein—both young, both graduates of the highly theoretical Institut des Hautes Études Cinematographiques—designed for most of the New Wave directors who had any need of (or money for) décor.

Except for *Les Quatre Cents Coups*, they never worked for the naturalistic Truffaut, nor for Godard, except on his sole attempt at a musical, *Une femme est une femme*. But Philippe de Broca, Claude Chabrol, Jacques Demy, and Louis Malle used them often, and when the partnership broke up in 1961 after *Last Year at Marienbad* (Saulnier sets/Evein costumes), Evein became an almost permanent member of Demy's *équipe*.

Demy's ebullience and Malle's taste for erotic melodrama suited Evein equally well, since both invited forceful visual statements. He wove a colorful high-life cocoon around Brigitte Bardot in *Vie privée*, but no less skillfully established a mood of wintry despair for a suicidal Maurice Ronet in *Le Feu follet* and Corinne Marchand in Agnès Varda's *Cléo de cinq à sept*. Evein's designs of an old pavilion in a choked grove and an orphanage by a frozen lake for Serge Bourguignon's *Sundays and Cybèle*, the fable of a war veteran's obsession with a young girl, turned the Paris suburb of Ville d'Avray into a chill extension of the Freudian landscape.

Evein's triumphs, however, remain Demy's *Lola*, *Les Parapluies de Cherbourg*, and *Les Demoiselles de Rochefort*. Born near Nantes (where Demy lived as a student), Evein was sympathetic to the movement carrying the Nouvelle Vague away from Paris. The trilogy captures the atmosphere of France's Atlantic coast port towns: cold, wet and empty in winter, but in summer blazing with sun, and filled with sailors and tourists.

Parapluies, and *Demoiselles* in particular, re-instilled in the New Wave some of its lost thirties theatricality. Both are so perfectly integrated by Demy that it is hard to separate design from lighting, costumes from character, music from story. For the former, Evein repainted the port city's old plaster walls in vivid primaries. The green, rose, red, and purple complement Michel Legrand's parlando operatic score, the photography of Jean Rabier (mainly known for Chabrol's gaudier thrillers) and Demy's sensual direction of the doomed love affair between Catherine Deneuve and Nino Castelnuovo.

Rochefort, in the warmer south, is equally well exploited in the sprightly *Demoiselles*. Evein stresses the honey-colored stone of the old town and its pastel shutters, the tones of which he picks up in interiors and costumes of white, pink, and blue—candy colors, just right for this sunny musical. Nothing Evein has done since matches the vividness and visual unity of these delightful films. Sadly, ill-health brought a premature end to Evein's career in 1990.

—John Baxter

FIELDS, Verna

Editor. **Nationality:** American. **Family:** Married the film editor Sam Fields (died 1954); two sons. **Career:** Assistant editor on Hollywood films in the 1940s, and on TV series *The Whistler*, 1954–55, *The Lone Ranger*, 1954–57, *Death Valley Days*, 1955–58, *Sky King*, 1955–58, *Wanted: Dead or Alive*, 1959–60, and *The Tom Ewell Show*, 1960–61; taught film editing, University of Southern California, Los Angeles; film editor from 1960; 1976–82—vice-president of Feature Productions, Universal. **Awards:** Academy Award for *Jaws*, 1975. **Died:** 30 November 1982.

Films as Editor:

1944   *Belle of the Yukon* (Seiter) (asst); *Casanova Brown* (Wood) (asst); *The Woman in the Window* (F. Lang) (asst)
1945   *Along Came Jones* (Heisler) (asst)
1960   *The Savage Eye* (Maddow, Meyers, and Strick); *Studs Lonigan* (Lerner); *The Sword and the Dragon* (English-language version of *Ilya Mourometz*) (Ptushko)
1963   *An Affair of the Skin* (Maddow); *Cry of Battle* (Lerner) (supervisor)
1964   *The Bus* (Wexler) (co)
1966   *Country Boy* (Kane); *Deathwatch* (Morrow)
1967   *The Legend of the Boy and the Eagle* (Couffer) (co); *Search for the Evil One* (Kane); *Track of Thunder* (Kane)
1968   *The Wild Racers* (Haller) (co)
1969   *Medium Cool* (Wexler)
1971   *Point of Terror* (Nicol) (supervisor)
1972   *What's Up, Doc?* (Bogdanovich)
1973   *American Graffiti* (Lucas) (co); *Paper Moon* (Bogdanovich)
1974   *Daisy Miller* (Bogdanovich); *The Sugarland Express* (Spielberg) (co)
1975   *Jaws* (Spielberg)

Other Films:

1956   *While the City Sleeps* (F. Lang) (sound ed)
1958   *Snowfire* (D. & S. McGowan) (sound ed)
1961   *El Cid* (A. Mann) (sound ed)
1963   *The Balcony* (Strick) (sound ed); *A Face in the Rain* (Kershner) (sound ed)
1967   *Targets* (Bogdanovich) (sound ed)
1968   *Journey to the Pacific* (d)
1969   *It's a Good Day* (d)

Publications

By FIELDS: articles—

American Film (Washington, D.C.), June 1976.
Films and Filming (London), February 1977.
Mise-en-Scène (Cleveland, Ohio), Spring 1980.
"Working with Time: Verna Fields Prevails," an interview with J. Padroff, in *Millimeter*, December 1980.
American Premiere (Los Angeles, California), vol. 3, no. 5, 1982.

On FIELDS: articles—

Cinema (Beverly Hills, California), no. 35, 1976.
Film Comment (New York), March-April 1977.
Action (Los Angeles, California), January-February 1978.
Slate, L., "Women & Film: One Year Later," in *American Premiere*, July 1982.
Obituary in *Variety* (New York), 8 December 1982.

*   *   *

Verna Fields became one of the American film industry's most famous editors during the 1970s, and in the process was able to accumulate considerable power. Since she had helped with so many blockbusters of the decade, including *Jaws* and *American Graffiti*, Fields was promoted by a grateful Universal Pictures into the executive suite. She held that vice-presidency until her death in 1982.

Unfortunately all this fame and power at the end of her long career only served to remind close observers of the American film industry that like in other multi-billion dollar institutions, few women ever accumulated a measure of true power. However, since the beginnings of the film industry, film editing had been one of the few arenas open to women. Fields, like Margaret Booth before her (at MGM), used this opening to become a force at a major Hollywood studio.

Indeed during the heyday of the "Movie Brats" of the 1970s, many looked to Fields as a symbolic breakthrough. Here was a person who had worked on many a low-budget independent film being elevated into a real position of power. She was so "in" that in 1974 *Newsweek* featured an article on her—one of the few in a popular magazine about a film editor.

Verna Fields' father helped her move into the film industry. Through him she met her husband Sam Fields, who was a film editor, in the 1940s. Sam died in 1954, leaving two sons to support. Verna returned to work that year and learned her craft on television fare such as *The Lone Ranger*, *Wanted: Dead or Alive*, *Death Valley Days*, and *Sky King*. She made her big splash in Hollywood as the sound editor for *El Cid*.

But her greatest impact came when she began to teach film editing to a generation of students at the University of Southern California.

She then operated on the fringes of the film business, for a time making documentaries for the Office of Economic Opportunity. The end of that Federal Agency pushed her back into mainstream Hollywood then being overrun by her former USC students.

Cutting *What's Up, Doc?* for Peter Bogdanovich represented her return, but her real influence began when she helped a former USC student, George Lucas, persuade Universal to distribute *American Graffiti.* A grateful Lucas, the story goes, presented her with a brand new BMW automobile in return. *Jaws* for Steven Spielberg "made" Fields' career.

She was quoted in the 1970s, at the height of her influence, saying that she believed editing should be invisible. She sought to downplay her own influence, preferring to let the director dictate the terms. Thus she worked in a variety of projects equally well—from melodrama to comedy to classic genre films. Certainly that is precisely what the new young Hollywood generation liked about her. She was a great technician who was sympathetic to their projects and visions. She wanted to help them—unlike the rest of the Hollywood establishment of the day which fought their very entry into the system. It is for this support that Fields will long be remembered.

—Douglas Gomery

FIGUEROA, Gabriel

Cinematographer. **Nationality:** Mexican. **Born:** Mexico City, 24 April 1907. **Education:** Studied design and the violin at Academia de San Carlos and National Conservatory. **Family:** Married; one son and one daughter. **Career:** Worked in portrait photography studio; 1932— entered films as still photographer; 1935–36—studied cinematography as assistant to Gregg Toland in Hollywood, then worked in Mexican cinema; 1936—first film as cinematographer, *Allá en el rancho grande.* **Awards:** Venice Festival award, for *La perla,* 1947; *La malquerida,* 1949. **Died:** 27 April 1997, in Mexico City, Mexico, of a stroke following heart surgery.

Films as Cinematographer:

1934   *El escándalo* (Urueta)
1936   *Allá en el rancho grande* (de Fuentes); *¡Vámonos con Pancho Villa!* (de Fuentes) (co); *Cielito lindo* (O'Quigley) (co)
1937   *Jalisco nunca pierde* (Urueta); *Las mujeres mandan* (de Fuentes); *Bajo el cielo de México* (de Fuentes)
1938   *Canción del alma* (Urueta); *La Adelita* (Gómez); *Mi candidato* (Urueta); *Refugiados en Madrid* (Galindo); *Padre de más de cuatro* (O'Quigley); *Los millones de Chaflan* (Aguilar); *Mientras México duerme* (Galindo); *La casa del ogro* (de Fuentes)
1939   *La bestia negra* (*Mi negra o su negra*) (Soria); *La noche de los mayas* (Urueta); *Papacito lindo* (de Fuentes)
1940   *Los de abajo* (*Con la División del Norte*) (Urueta); *¡Que viene mi marido!* (Urueta); *Allá en el trópico* (de Fuentes); *La canción del milagro* (Aguilar); *El jefe Máximo* (de Fuentes); *Con su amable permiso* (Soler); *El monje loco* (Galindo)
1941   *Creo en Dios* (de Fuentes); *Ni sangre ni arena* (Galindo); *Mi viuda alegre* (Delgado); *El rápido de las 9.15* (Galindo);

¡Ay, qué tiempos, señor don Simón! (Bracho); *El gendarme desconocido* (Delgado); *La casa del rencor* (Solares); *La gallina clueca* (de Fuentes)
1942   *Cuando viajan las estrellas* (Gout); *Virgen de medianoche* (Galindo); *Los tres mosqueteros* (Delgado); *Historia de un gran amor* (Bracho); *El verdugo de Sevilla* (Soler); *La virgen que forjó una patria* (Bracho)
1943   *El circo* (Delgado); *Flor Silvestre* (Fernández); *El espectro de la novia* (Cardona); *Distinto amanecer* (Bracho); *María Candelária* (*Xochimilco*) (Fernández)
1944   *La mujer sin cabeza* (Cardona); *El as negro* (Cardona); *El corsario negro* (Urueta); *Adiós, Mariquita linda* (Gómez) (co); *Las abandonadas* (Fernández); *Bugambilia* (Fernández)
1945   *Un día con el diablo* (Delgado); *Cantaclaro* (Bracho); *Más allá del amor* (Bustamante); *La perla* (*The Pearl*) (Fernández)
1946   *Su última aventura* (Solares); *Enamorada* (Fernández)
1947   *La casa colorado* (Morayta); *Río escondido* (*Hidden River*) (Fernández); *The Fugitive* (Ford); *Tarzan and the Mermaids* (Florey) (co)
1948   *María de la O* (Bustamante); *Maclovia* (Fernández); *Dueña y señora* (Davison); *Pueblerina* (Fernández)
1949   *Salón México* (Fernández); *Medianoche* (Davison); *Opio* (*Laddroga Maldita*) (Peón); *El embajador* (Davison); *La malquerida* (Fernández); *Un cuerpo de mujer* (Davison); *Duelo en las montañas* (Fernández); *Del odio nació el amor* (*The Torch; Beloved; The Bandit General*) (Fernández)
1950   *Prisión de suenos* (Urruchua); *Nuestras vidas* (Peón); *Una dia de vida* (Fernández); *Los olvidados* (*The Young and the Damned*) (Buñuel); *El gavilan pollero* (González); *Victimas del pecado* (Fernández); *Islas Marías* (Fernández); *Siempre tuya* (Fernández)
1951   *Pecado* (Amadori); *Los pobres van al cielo* (Salvador); *La bien amada* (Fernández); *El mar y tú* (Fernández)
1952   *Hay un niño en su futuro* (Cortés); *Ahí viene Martín Corona* (Zacarías); *Un gallo en corral ajeno* (Soler); *El bombero atómico* (Delgado—produced 1950); *El enamorado* (*El regreso de Martín Corona*) (Zacarías); *Ni pobres ni ricos* (Cortés); *El rebozo de Soledad* (*Soledad*) (Gavaldón); *Cuando levanta la niebla* (Fernández); *La histérico* (Delgado); *El señor fotografo* (Delgado); *Dos tipos de cuidado* (Rodríguez); *Ansiedad* (Zacarías); *El* (Buñuel)
1953   *Camelia* (Galvaldón); *El niño y la niebla* (Gavaldón); *La rosa blanca* (*Momentos de la vida de Martí*) (Fernández); *Llevame en tus brazos* (Bracho)
1954   *La Mujer X* (Soler); *La rebelión de los colgados* (Crevenna); *Estafa de amor* (Delgado); *El monstruo de la sombra* (Urquiza); *Pueblo, canto y esperanza* (Gonzáles)
1955   *Cautiva del recuerdo* (Gavaldón); *La escondida* (Galvadón); *La Tierra del Fuego se apaga* (Fernández); *La doncella de piedra* (Delgado); *Historia de un amor* (Galvadón)
1956   *Una cita de amor* (Fernández); *El bolero de Raquel* (Delgado); *Canasta de cuentos mexicanos* (Bracho); *Suenos de oro* (Zacarías); *Mujer en condominio* (González)
1957   *Flor de mayo* (*Beyond All Limits; A Mexican Affair*) (Gavaldón); *Maricruz* (Zacarías); *La sonrisa de la Virgen* (Rodríguez); *Aquí está Heraclio Bernal* (Gavaldón); *La venganza de Heraclio Bernal* (Gavaldón); *La rebelión de la sierra* (Gavaldón); *Una golfa* (Demicheli)

1958   *La cucaracha* (Rodríguez); *Nazarin* (Buñuel); *El puño del amo* (Fernández); *Carabina 30–30* (Delgado); *Impaciencia del corazon* (Davison); *Café Colón* (Alaraki); *Isla para dos* (Davison)

1959   *Macaro* (Gavaldón); *Sonotas* (Bardem) (co); *La fièvre monte à El Pao* (*Los Ambiciosos*) (Buñuel)

1960   *The Young Ones* (*La joven*) (Buñuel); *La muchacha* (Zacarías); *Juana Gallo* (Zacarías)

1961   *Los hermanos del hierro* (Rodríguez); *El tejedor de milagros* (del Villar); *Animas Trujano, el hombre importante* (Rodríguez)

1962   *El angel exterminador* (*The Exterminating Angel*) (Buñuel); *La bandida* (Rodríguez); *Días de otoño* (Gavaldón)

1963   *El hombre de papel* (Rodríguez); *Entrega immediata* (Delgado); *En la mitad del mundo* (Pereda)

1964   *El gallo de oro* (Gavaldón); *The Night of the Iguana* (Huston); *Escuela para solteras* (Zacarías); *Los tres calaveras* (Cortés); *Los cuatro Juanes* (Zacarías)

1965   ''Las dos Elenas'' and ''Lola de mi vida'' eps. of *Amor, amor, amor* (José Ibáñez and Ponce); ''Un alma pura'' ep. of *Los bienamados* (Juan Ibáñez); *Simón del desierto* (Buñuel); *Cargamento prohibibo* (Delgado); *¡Viva Benito Canales!* (Delgado)

1966   *Pedro Páramo* (Velo); *El asesino se embarca* (Delgado); *El escapulario* (González); *Domingo salvaje* (del Villar); *The Chinese Room* (Zugsmith); *Las angeles de Puebla* (del Villar)

1967   *Mariana* (Guerrero); *El jinete fantasma* (Zugsmith)

1968   *Corazón salvaje* (Davison) (co); *La puerta* (Alcoriza); *Pax?* (Rilla—short)

1969   *The Big Cube* (Davison)

1970   *Two Mules for Sister Sara* (Siegel); *Kelly's Heroes* (Hutton)

1971   *Los hijos de Satanas* (Baledón); *Hijazo de mi vidaza* (Baledón); *María* (Davison)

1972   *La rosa blanca* (Gavaldón—produced 1961); *El señor de Osanto* (Hermosillo); *El monasterio de los buitres* (del Villar)

1973   *Interval* (Daniel Mann); *Once upon a Scoundrel* (Schaefer); *El amor tiene cara de mujer* (Davison); *Los perros de Dios* (del Villar); *Presagio* (Alcoriz)

1974   *El llanto de la tortuga* (del Villar)

1975   *Coronación* (Olhovich); *Maten al león* (Estrada)

1976   *La vida cambia* (Torres); *Balún Canán* (Alasraki); *Cananea* (Violante); *Los aztecas* (Boudou)

1977   *Divinas palabras* (Juan Ibáñez); *La casa del pelicano* (Véjar)

1978   *The Children of Sanchez* (Bartlett); *D.F.* (González); *Te quiero* (Davison)

1980   *El jugador de ajedrez* (J. Buñuel); *México mágico* (Tavera, Zermeño, and Mandoki)

1981   *México 2000* (González); *El héroe desconocido* (Pastor)

1983   *El corazón de la noche* (Hermosilla)

1984   *Under the Volcano* (Huston)

Other Films:

1932   *Revolución* (Torres) (still ph)

1933   *Almas encontradas* (Sevilla) (still ph)

1935   *El primo Basilio* (Nájera) (cam); *María Elena* (Sevilla) (cam)

Publications

By FIGUEROA: articles—

American Cinematographer (Hollywood), February 1975.
Signore, December 1982.
Dicine, nos. 8 and 9, 1984.
Skrien (Amsterdam), no. 172, June/July 1990.

On FIGUEROA: books—

Chalaman, Nuria, *Gabriel Figueroa: La Mirada en el Centro*, Mexico, M.A. Porrua, 1993.
Isaac, Alberto, *Conversaciones con Gabriel Figueroa*, Mexico, Universidad de Guadalajara, 1993.

On FIGUEROA: articles—

Goméz Sicre, J., in *Américas*, May 1950.
Sadoul, Georges, in *Ecran* (Paris), 21 August 1950.
Cinema (Rome), 1 October 1950.
Otro Cine (Barcelona), January/February 1959.
Focus on Film (London), no. 13, 1973.
de la Colina, José, in *Artes Visuales*, Autumn 1977.
Heraldo del Cine (Buenos Aires), 20 July 1984.
Jump Cut, no. 50, March 1993.
Dey, Tom, ''ASC Hails Career of Gabriel Figueroa,'' in *American Cinematographer* (Hollywood), March 1995.
Obituary, in *Variety* (New York), 5 May 1997.
Obituary, in *Time*, 12 May 1997.
Obituary, in *EPD Film* (Frankfurt/Main), June 1997.
Obituary, in *Sight & Sound* (London), June 1997.
''Figueroa Passes Away,'' in *American Cinematographer* (Hollywood), July 1997.
Obituary, in *Psychotronic Video* (New York), no. 25, 1997.

*   *   *

The outstanding cinematographer of Mexico, Gabriel Figueroa received some 19 international and more than 40 national awards. Figueroa conceived of photography as interpretive, likening it to an actor's rendering of a script. He argued that though the camera ought to be essentially unobtrusive, it must establish a dialogue with the spectators through the vigor, force, and beauty it creates. This cameraman worked with almost all the important directors of Mexican cinema, and some international greats—John Ford, Luis Buñuel, John Huston, and Don Siegel. He is best known, however, for his role in forging the classical Mexican film style, which he brought into being along with director Emilio Fernández in their films of the 1940s: *María Candelária*, *Flor Silvestre*, *Bugambilia*, *La perla*, *Enamorada*, and *Río escondido*.

The classical Mexican film aesthetic is based on that country's rural environment, particularly its sun and clouds. Figueroa believed that the single most important aspect of cinematography is illumination, and the light given off by the Mexican sun is dramatic and piercing. Thus he drew a distinction between filmmaking in, for example, London, where there is little natural light and Mexico, where the sun is one of the elements that creates the ambience, and therefore must be interpreted. The same can be said for the monumental masses of rolling clouds which mark the Mexican landscape. In Europe, cineastes have jokingly referred to "Figueroa's clouds"; and there is a famous anecdote in which Buñuel (who detested expressive photography) held up shooting during *Los olvidados* until a cloud had disappeared. Nevertheless, these billowing cloud formations are a vital part of the Mexican panorama—though they were highlighted through Figueroa's use of infrared filters. If the more picturesque human elements of this aesthetic—stony Indian faces set off by dark rebozos and white shirts, *charros* and their stallions galloping through majestic cactus, fishermen and their nets reflected in swirling ocean tides—have been rightly criticized for their historic immobility, Figueroa's use of Mexico's sun and clouds still provided a striking context for these films' narratives.

The influences that were important in the creation of Figueroa's style were manifold, as befits an international artist. Figueroa stated that Edward Tisse's use of sunlight and composition of frames in Eisenstein's never-finished *Que Viva Mexico* were an important example for him. A more direct influence was Gregg Toland, under whom Figueroa studied in Hollywood and whom he accompanied during the filming of *The Best Years of Our Lives*. Toland's use of artificial light impressed Figueroa greatly, as did his own studies of classical artists such as Vermeer and Rembrandt. Nonetheless, Figueroa contended that the single most important inspiration for his art came from the Mexican muralists, particularly David Alfaro Siquieros, whose perspective and analytical force were determinant for the cinematographer. If Figueroa achieved international recognition, it was finally due to the degree to which he immersed himself in his country's natural beauty, its artists, and its culture.

—John Mraz

FISCHER, Gunnar

Cinematographer. **Nationality:** Swedish. **Born:** Ljungby, 18 November 1910. **Education:** Studied in Stockholm and Copenhagen. **Family:** Son: the cinematographer Peter Fischer. **Career:** Entered films as second cameraman in the 1930s; 1942—first film as cinematographer, *It Is My Music*; 1948—first of several films for Ingmar Bergman, *Port of Call*; TV work includes series *Raskens*, 1974; also illustrator of children's books; 1975—retired.

Films as 2nd Cameraman:

1935   *Smålänningar (People of Småland)* (Rodin)
1936   *Samvetsömma Adolf (Conscientious Adolf)* (Wallen); *Johan Ulfstjerna* (Edgren); *Hans, hon, och pengarna (He, She, and the Money)* (Henrikson); *Aventyret (Adventure)* (Branner); *65, 66, och jag (Privates 65, 66, and I)* (Henrikson)
1937   *Klart till drabbning (Clear the Decks for Action)* (Adolphson); *Sara lär sig folkvett (Sara Learns Manners)* (Molander); *Pappas pojke (Rich Man's Son)* (Martin)
1938   *Blixt och dunder (Thunder and Lightning)* (Henrikson); *Goda vänner, trogna grannar (Good Friends and Faithful Neighbors)* (Hildebrand)
1939   *Valfångare (Whalers)* (Henrikson); *Emilie Högqvist* (Molander)

1941   *Lärarinna på vift (Schoolmistress on the Spree)* (Larsson); *Dunungen (Downy Girl)* (Hildebrand)
1942   *Flickan i fönstret mittemot (Girl in the Window Opposite)* (Jerring); *Jacobs stege (Jacob's Ladder)* (Molander)

Films as Cinematographer:

1942   *Det är min musik (It Is My Music)* (Larsson)
1943   *Natt i hamn (Night in the Harbor)* (Faustman) (+ co-sc)
1945   *Två människor (Two People)* (Dreyer); *Blåjackor (Bluejackets)* (Husberg); *Tant Grun, Tant Brun, och Tant Gredelin (Aunt Green, Aunt Brown, and Aunt Lilac)* (Lindstrom)
1947   *Krigsmans erinran (Soldier's Duties)* (Faustman); *Tappa inte sugen (Don't Give Up)* (Kjellgren)
1948   *Hamnstad (Port of Call)* (Bergman); *Soldat Bom (Private Bom)* (Kjellgren)
1949   *Törst (Thirst)* (Bergman); *Ports of Industrial Scandinavia: Sweden's East Coast* (Colleran—short)
1950   *Till glädje (To Joy)* (Bergman); *Sånt händer inte här (High Tension)* (Bergman)
1951   *Sommarlek (Summer Interlude)* (Bergman)
1952   *Kvinnors väntan (Waiting Women)* (Bergman); *I dimma dold (Hidden in the Fog)* (Kjellgren)
1953   *Sommaren med Monika (Summer with Monika)* (Bergman); *Gycklarnas afton (The Naked Night; Sawdust and Tinsel)* (Bergman) (co); *Vi tre debutera (We Three Debutantes)* (Ekman)
1954   *Seger i mörker (Victory in the Dark)* (Folke); *Gabrielle* (Ekman); *Ballettens born (Ballet Girl)* (A. Henning-Jensen—short)
1955   *Stampen (Pawn Shop)* (Lagerkvist); *Egen ingång (Private Entrance)* (Ekman); **Sommarnattens leende** *(Smiles of a Summer Night)* (Bergman); *Den hårda leken (The Tough Game)* (Kjellgren)
1957   *Det sjunde inseglet (The Seventh Seal)* (Bergman); *Möten i skymningen (Twilight Meeting)* (Kjellin); **Smultronstället** *(Wild Strawberries)* (Bergman); *Lek på regnbågen (Playing on the Rainbow)* (Kjellgren); *Batavernas trohetsed (The Batavians' Oath of Fidelity)* (Derkert—short) (co)
1958   *Du är mitt äventyr (You Are My Adventure)* (Olin); *Ansiktet (The Magician; The Face)* (Bergman)
1959   *Det svänger på slottet (Swinging at the Castle)* (Kjellin); *Hans Brinker, or the Silver Skates* (Foster)
1960   *Djävulens öga (The Devil's Eye)* (Bergman); *Ett glass vin (A Glass of Wine)* (Werner—short)
1961   *Pojken i trädet (The Boy in the Tree)* (Sucksdorff); *Two Living, One Dead* (Asquith); *Een blandt mange (One among Many)* (A. Henning-Jensen); *Lustgården (Pleasure Garden)* (Kjellin)
1962   *Siska* (Kjellin); *Kort är sommaren (Pan; Short Is the Summer)* (B. Henning-Jensen); *Vittnesbörd om henne (Testimonies)* (Donner—short)
1963   *Min kära är en ros (My Love Is Like a Rose)* (Ekman); *Mamsell Josabeth (Miss Josabeth)* (+ d—short); *För vänskaps skull (For Friendship)* (Abramson)
1964   *491* (Sjöman)
1965   *Juninatt (June Night)* (Liedholm); *Ojojoj eller sången om den eldröda hummern (Well Well Well)* (Axelman); *Väntande*

vatten (*Waiting Water*) (Werner—short); *Drottningholms slottsteater* (*The Drottningholm Palace Theatre*) (+ d—short)

1966   *Adamson i Sverige* (*I Need a Woman*) (Ericsson) (co); *Slut* (*The End*) (Forsberg—short); *Pianolektionen* (*The Piano Lesson*) (Nordin—short)

1967   "Han-Hon" ("He-She"), "Birgit Nilsson," and "Smycket" ("The Necklace"), eps. of *Stimulantia* (Donner, Arnbom, and Molander); *Djävulens instrument* (*The Devil's Instrument*) (+ d—short); *Ola och Julia* (*Ola and Julia*) (Halldoff) (co); *Ack, du är some en ros* (*Oh, You Are Like a Rose*) (+ d, sc—short)

1968   *Svarta palmkronor* (*Black Palm Trees*) (Lindgren); *Made in Sweden* (Bergenstrahle)

1969   *Miss and Mrs. Sweden* (Gentele); *Krakguldet* (*Fool's Gold*) (Krantz)

1970   *Is* (*Ice*) (Lindman)

1972   *Din stund pa jorden* (*Your Time on Earth*) (Sjöstrand)

1973   *Parade* (Tati) (co)

1976   *Raskens* (Sjöstrand—mini-series for TV)

Other Films:

1943   *Stora Skrällen* (*Big Crash*) (Jerring) (cam)

1951   *Biffen och bananen* (*Biffen and the Banana*) (Husberg) (cam)

1971   *Beröringen* (*The Touch*) (Bergman) (titles ph)

*   *   *

Gunnar Fischer was the director of photography on the films that first brought Ingmar Bergman worldwide renown. Like most Swedish cinematographers, he is a master of practical lighting and operates his own camera. His style is heavily influenced both by the facial landscapes of Carl Dreyer, for whom he worked, and by the psychological landscapes of Victor Sjöström, whom he knew. Fischer is thus in the mainstream of the Scandinavian tradition. His work features some of the closest and most intensely psychological close-ups and two-shots in film history. He favors a cold, bleak lighting that lends many of Bergman's early films a sense of despair the director may not have intended. In Fischer's films, one is constantly in a world governed by a changeable moral atmosphere which is signified by variations in light, from harshly overexposed noontimes to backlit twilights.

His early films for Bergman have a misleading flavor of Italian neorealism, not surprising given their period, but as the emphasis of Bergman's films is on moral conflict so the cinematography's harshness indicates a psychological or emotional rather than social barrenness. For example, the emotionally devastated clown at the end of *Sawdust and Tinsel* is photographed in growing isolation from the onlookers, and the film is overexposed to convey a spiritual nakedness which is outside of social criticism.

The pseudo-neorealist harshness of the 1940s gives way to the symbolic dreamscape of the 1950s in *Wild Strawberries*. Here the shift from past to present, from memory to actuality to dream, is signified largely by changes in light: a soft-focus, bright light for the past, a darker light for the present, an overexposed world or an intensely dark one filled with fearfully sharp contrasts and huge faces for dreams. In *The Seventh Seal*, the shift from one moral world to another is conveyed through lighting. A bright and soft natural light indicates characters at peace, while heavy filters and backlighting

indicate moral doubt, and harsh contrasts in overexposed film indicate hollow spirituality. Although Fischer's lighting effects on Bergman's black-and-white films vary extraordinarily in technique, often within the same film, they nonetheless convey an aesthetic unity.

Fischer's lighting is too extreme to be easily interpreted by others, but he is one of several European cinematographers responsible for the popular equation between harsh, black-and-white cinematography and art films in American culture in the 1950s and 1960s. Indirectly, he has influenced such Hollywood art films as *Who's Afraid of Virginia Woolf?* Fischer and Bergman parted company after *The Devil's Eye*. Bergman's style was mellowing, and he was gaining more technical expertise and authority. When he could not persuade Fischer to soften his lighting techniques, Bergman switched to Sven Nykvist as his director of photography. Since Fischer's retirement in 1975, he has lectured on film lighting at various Scandinavian universities.

—Patricia Ferrara

FISCHINGER, Oskar

Animator. **Nationality:** German. **Born:** Gelnhausen, near Frankfurt-am-Main, Germany, 22 June 1900. **Education:** Attended local technical school. **Family:** Married Elfriede, 1931, five children. **Career:** 1915—became draftsman in architect's office; 1916—employed at turbine factory in Frankfurt, rose to post of senior engineer; c.1920—became interested in animated design, worked on experimental series of films from 1921 to 1926; 1928–29—worked with Fritz Lang on *Die Frau im Mond*; 1930—started making sound films; 1933—first experimented with color; 1936—fled Germany for America, settled in Hollywood; 1938—worked on opening sequence of *Fantasia*, but quit after disagreement with Disney; 1941–42—worked for Orson Welles on a projected section about Louis Armstrong of *It's All True*; 1950—invented Lumigraph, a device for playing light images. **Awards:** Special Prize at Venice, for *Komposition in Blau*, 1935; Grand Prix, Brussels Exhibition, for *Motion Painting No 1*, 1947. **Died:** Of a stroke, in Hollywood, 1 February (some sources give 31 January) 1967.

Films as Animator/Director:

(some filmographies of Fischinger's work discount the four early experimental *Studien* and number *Studie Nr 5* [1929] as *Nr 1*)

1921–26   *Wachsexperimente*

1922–25   *Studien 1–4*

1922–27   *Orgelstäbe*

1924–26   *Münchener Bilderbogen* (*Pierrette I*)

1926   *Spiralen*

1927   *R-I, ein Formspiel von Oskar Fischinger*; *Seelische Konstruktionen* (*Spiritual Constructions*); *Sintflut*; *München-Berlin Wanderung*

1929   *Studie Nr 5*

1930   *Studie Nr 6*; *Studie Nr 7*; *Studie Nr 8*; *Studie Nr 9*; *Studie Nr 10*

1931   *Studie Nr 11*; *Studie Nr 12* (unfinished); *Studie Nr 13*; *Liebesspiel*

1932   *Studie Nr 14*; *Studie Nr 15*; *Studie Nr 16*; *Koloraturen*

1933 *Studie Nr 17*; *Studie Nr 18*; *Kreise*
1934 *Ein Spiel in Farben* (colorized version of *Studie Nr 15*); *Quadrate*; *Muratti greift ein* (*Muratti Marches On*); *Reise im Schweiz*
1935 *Komposition in Blau* (*Lichtkonzert Nr 1*); *Lichtkonzert Nr 2* (unfinished)
1936 *Allegretto*
1937 *An Optical Poem*
1941 *American March*
1942 *Radio Dynamics*
1947 *Motion Painting No 1*
1952 *Stereo Film* (pilot fragment)
1960 *Motion Painting No 2* (unfinished)

Other Films:

1928 *Dein Schicksal* (Metzner) (animation seqences)
1929 *Die Frau in Mond* (F. Lang) (special effects)
1930 *Das Hohelied der Kraft* (Schongen) (special effects)
1936 *Big Broadcast of 1937* (Leisen) (special effects, unused)
1939 *Fantasia* (Disney) (orig des)

Publications

By FISCHINGER: article—

"My Statements Are in My Work," in *Art in Cinema: a Symposium on the Avant-Garde Film,* edited by Frank Stauffacher, New York, 1968.

On FISCHINGER: book—

Westbrock, Ingrid, *Das Werbefilm*, Hildesheim, 1983.

On FISCHINGER: articles—

Brett, Guy, "Abstract Films of Oskar Fischinger," in *Times* (London), 4 November 1968.
Moritz, William, "The Films of Oskar Fischinger," in *Film Culture* (New York), 1974.
Moritz, William, "Fischinger at Disney or, Oskar in the Mousetrap," in *Millimeter* (New York), February 1977.
Canemaker, John, "On the Road with Mrs. Oskar Fischinger," in *Funnyworld* (New York), Summer 1978.
Gough-Yates, Kevin, "German Avant-Garde Film," in *Art Monthly* (London), June 1989.
Film a Doba (Prague), October 1990.
Film-Dienst (Cologne), 4 February 1992.
Moritz, W., "Gasparcolor: Perfect Hues for Animation," in *Animation Journal* (Orange), no. 1, 1996.
Summer, Edward, "*Toy Story*: 15,587,175,628 Pixels of Joy!" in *Films in Review*, March-April 1996.

* * *

Towards the end of his life, Oskar Fischinger prepared a short artistic credo under the title of "My Statements Are in My Work." It is an uncompromising, even dogmatic document, dismissing as mere "mountain ranges of soap bubbles" virtually all the feature films ever made, and equally scathing about the work of most of his fellow animators ("on a very low artistic level . . . a mass product of factory proportions"). Only the solitary, dedicated creative artist, working in lonely purity, may hope to create true cinematic art. "The Creative Spirit shall be unobstructed through realities or anything that spoils his absolute *pure* creation. . . . The real artist should *not care* if he is understood or misunderstood by the masses. He should listen only to his Creative Spirit and satisfy his highest ideals."

It is only fair to note that these words were written after Fischinger had suffered long years of frustration and disappointment in Hollywood. But anyone who came across this article before seeing any of Fischinger's films might well be led to expect a solemn, self-consciously elevated experience. Certainly it gives no hint of the wit, energy, and joie de vivre—in short, the sheer accessibility—of his work.

Fischinger's earliest experiments in abstract animation (or, as he preferred to call it, "absolute film") sprang from the same post-World War I European artistic ferment that gave rise to surrealism, dadaism, expressionism, and the Bauhaus movement. The influence of such artists as Klee, Kandinsky, and Mondrian is evident on his work, along with his own professional background as an engineer. As early as 1921 he invented what might be seen as the most primitive ancestor of computer animation: a machine synchronizing a camera with a mechanism that sliced thin slivers off a prepared block of wax, so that the designs embedded in the wax would be gradually revealed and filmed as moving shapes. Walther Ruttmann, whose pioneering animation work greatly impressed Fischinger, made ingenious use of this machine in the "evil magic" sequence he contributed to Lotte Reiniger's *Die Abenteuer des Prinzen Achmed* (1926).

Although other artists and filmmakers—Ruttmann, Hans Richter, Fernand Léger, Len Lye—explored abstract animation, Fischinger was exceptional in devoting almost his entire career to the genre. The long series of *Studien* forms the core of his black-and-white work. Like emanations of pure energy, they populate the screen with flashing, darting shapes: blips, dashes, curves, circles, explosions of light that zip and swoop and scurry as if propelled by unseen winds. Sometimes they suggest birds or fishes chasing each other in play, at other times sheets of paper, the notes on a plainsong stave or even signals in some unknown language. From 1930 onwards Fischinger's films were accompanied by music, but he always emphasized that this was all that the music was—an accompaniment, aimed at helping the audience accept the abstract shapes. None of his films, he insisted, was intended to illustrate the music, and they could be viewed in silent form with no loss of effect.

While Fischinger's black-and-white work is mainly two-dimensional in effect, he seized on the possibilities of color to lend depth and body to his designs. *Komposition in Blau*—which won a prize in Venice and brought him international fame—choreographs cubes, cylinders, and columns into an exuberant ballet that recalls the (almost equally abstract) patterns created by Busby Berkeley. The same irrepressible high spirits bubble through *Muratti greift ein* (*Muratti Marches On*), Fischinger's most famous advertising work—whole troupes of cigarettes strutting, marching, dancing and ice-skating in formation—and his first American film, *Allegretto*. Set to a jazzy, Gershwinesque score, this exploits the potential of cel animation to deploy complex, overlapping patterns of shimmering shapes in what William Moritz called "California colors—the pinks and turquoises and browns of desert sky and sand, the orange of poppies and the green of avocadoes.'' The influence on the early films of Norman McLaren, such as *Boogie Doodle*, is unmissable.

All too predictably, Fischinger's hopes of pursuing his exploration of abstract animation within the context of the Hollywood studios were soon dashed. His most frustrating experience was working for Disney on *Fantasia*—all the more so because it was he who had first suggested the idea of the film, or at any rate of the Bach Toccata and Fugue section of it, to Leopold Stokowski. Although the released version was partly based on his original designs, he disowned it as a tasteless vulgarization. Disheartened by the lack of interest in his ideas, Fischinger's output slowed, and during the last 25 years of his life he completed only one film, *Motion Painting No 1*, painted in oil on plexiglass. Intricate and imaginative, it bemused his patrons at the Guggenheim Foundation, who withheld further support.

Given the integrity of Fischinger's resolve in sticking to his chosen field of animation, it may seem perverse to wish he had allowed himself more versatility. But a rare mature excursion into figurative animation, the *Seelische Konstruktionen* (*Spiritual Constructions*) of 1927, suggests uncommon—and largely undeveloped— aptitude for that field as well. Prefaced by the words "Mir ist so merkwürdig, als sei die Welt betrunken" (I have the strange feeling that the whole world is drunk), it depicts two boozy silhouettes who swell, distort, clash and devour each other. As well as strikingly anticipating the world of Jan Svankmajer (*Dimensions of Dialogue*), the *Constructions* reveal a flair for Rabelaisian mayhem that Fischinger could well have exploited alongside his "absolute" work—perhaps even to the benefit of both styles.

—Philip Kemp

FISHER, Gerry

Cinematographer. **Nationality:** British. **Born:** London, 1926. **Military Service:** Royal Navy during World War II. **Family:** Married. **Career:** Worked for Kodak and De Havilland Aircraft; 1946—joined Alliance Riverside as clapper boy; then worked for Wessex Films, Shepperton, and British Lion as camera assistant and focus puller, and from 1957 as cameraman; 1967—first film as cinematographer, *Accident*. **Address:** Smith, Gosnell, Nicholson and Associates, Pacific Palisades, California, U.S.A.

Films as Cameraman:

1957   *The Bridge on the River Kwai* (Lean)
1958   *The Journey* (Litvak)
1959   *Tarzan's Greatest Adventure* (Guillermin); *The Devil's Disciple* (Hamilton); *Suddenly, Last Summer* (Mankiewicz)
1960   *The Millionairess* (Asquith); *The Sundowners* (Zinnemann)
1961   *The Road to Hong Kong* (Panama)
1962   *Guns of Darkness* (Asquith); *Live Now, Pay Later* (Lewis); *55 Days at Peking* (Ray)
1963   *The V.I.P.s* (Asquith); *Night Must Fall* (Reisz)
1964   *Circus World* (*The Magnificent Showman*) (Hathaway); *Guns at Batasi* (Guillermin); *The Yellow Rolls-Royce* (Asquith)
1965   *Bunny Lake Is Missing* (Preminger)

1966   *Modesty Blaise* (Losey)
1967   ***Casino Royale*** (Huston and others)

Films as Cinematographer:

1967   ***Accident*** (Losey); *The Mikado* (Burge); *Sebastian* (Greene)
1968   *The Seagull* (Lumet); *Amsterdam Affair* (O'Hara); *Interlude* (Billington); *Secret Ceremony* (Losey)
1969   *Hamlet* (Richardson); *All the Right Noises* (O'Hara)
1970   *Ned Kelly* (Richardson); *Macho Callahan* (Kowalski); *The Go-Between* (Losey)
1971   *Blind Terror* (*See No Evil*) (Fleischer); *Man in the Wilderness* (Sarafian)
1972   *Malpertuis* (Kumel); *The Man and the Snake* (Rydman— short); *The Amazing Mr. Blunden* (Jeffries); *The Offence* (Lumet)
1973   *A Bequest to the Nation* (*The Nelson Affair*) (Jones); *A Doll's House* (Losey); *Butley* (Pinter); *Catholics* (Gold)
1974   *Spys* (Kershner); *Juggernaut* (Lester); *Dogpound Shuffle* (*Spot*) (Bloom)
1975   *Brannigan* (Hickox); *The Romantic Englishwoman* (Losey); *The Adventure of Sherlock Holmes' Smarter Brother* (G. Wilder)
1976   *Aces High* (Gold); *Comme un boomerang . . .* (Giovanni)
1977   *Mr. Klein* (Losey); *The Island of Dr. Moreau* (Taylor); *The Last Remake of Beau Geste* (Feldman); *Once upon a Time . . . Is Now* (Billington) (co); *Exorcist II* (Boorman)
1978   *Fedora* (B. Wilder); *Les Routes du sud* (Losey)
1979   *Don Giovanni* (Losey)
1980   *Wise Blood* (Huston); *Wolfen* (Wadleigh); *The Ninth Configuration* (*Twinkle, Twinkle, Killer Kane*) (Blatty)
1981   *Victory* (*Escape to Victory*) (Huston)
1982   *Lovesick* (Brickman); *Yellowbeard* (Damski)
1983   *Les mots pour le dire* (Pinheiro); *Better Late than Never* (Forbes)
1984   *The Holcroft Covenant* (Frankenheimer)
1985   *Highlander* (Mulcahy); *Man on Fire* (Chouraqui)
1986   *Running on Empty* (Lumet); *Dead Bang* (Frankenheimer)
1987   *Black Rainbow* (Hodges); *The Fourth War* (Frankenheimer)
1988   *Exorcist III* (Blatty)
1991   *Company Business* (*Patriots*) (Meyer)
1992   *The Positively True Adventures of the Alleged Texas Cheerleader-Murdering Mom* (Ritchie—for TV); *Diggstown* (*Midnight Sting*) (Ritchie)
1993   *Cops and Robbersons* (Ritchie)
1994   *Dandelion Dead* (Hodges—for TV)
1995   *When Saturday Comes* (Geiss)
1997   *K* (Arcady)
1999   *Furia* (Aja)

Publications

By FISHER: articles—

On *The Adventures of Sherlock Holmes' Smarter Brother* in *American Cinematographer* (Hollywood), October 1975.
On *The Island of Dr. Moreau* in *American Cinematographer* (Hollywood), August 1977.

On FISHER: article—

Eyles, A., in *Focus on Film* (London), Summer 1975.

* * *

Gerry Fisher's filmography encompasses such quintessentially Hollywood enterprises as *Suddenly, Last Summer* and *The V.I.P.s* as well as such routine jobs of work as *Exorcist II*. He has worked with major stars such as the Burtons and John Wayne and with such thoughtfully mainstream and contrasting directors as Billy Wilder (*Fedora*) and Sidney Lumet (*The Seagull*). A more telling thread begins perhaps with the studio work he performed for Jack Hildyard and takes in such definitively British films of their period as *The Bridge on the River Kwai* (on which David Lean promoted him to cameraman) and *The Yellow Rolls-Royce*. A self-avowedly "location sort of cameraman really," however, his career is definitively linked to that of Joseph Losey's with whom he collaborated on some of that director's most assured, enigmatic and "English" work. The collaboration began with *Accident*, Fisher's first film as a lighting cameraman. It was the first time he was free to read a script and consider how he would visualize the action. Despite the visibility of tracks in the final sequence, the result of the demands of the ratio and the constraints of a small budget which precluded reshooting the scene, the film boasts cinematography that perfectly meets the director's needs in the creation of a very particularly English, and rather desultory, wasteland of the spirit and the emotions. On *Secret Ceremony*, a Borgesian fable set in an architecturally and decoratively distinctive mansion in London, Fisher allowed the colors and contours of the house itself to determine both the dominant colors of the film and also the wandering camera movements. The effect made the house something of a character in itself rather than merely, as happened in *The Romantic Englishwoman*, an expressive setting for the performers. With *The Go-Between*, again a decidedly English story, this time of cross-class and intergenerational conflict and passions played out through notions of manners and etiquette, Fisher drew on his own childhood memories—of the particular play of sunlight on wood for example. This brought to the film a tactile precision which productively undercut its inherent nostalgia.

On *Don Giovanni*, Losey's film of Mozart's opera, Fisher was able to make great play with the magical and grandiose aspects of the film's Palladian setting. He was also faced with the difficulty of filming the singers in such a way that the effort of singing remained visible—and therefore convincing—but did not become so obvious as to distract from the narrative. While quite aware of the constraints placed on the cameraman by a performer's limitations (the fact that Bogarde could not play tennis had necessitated inventive hand-held camera work on *Accident*), Fisher is also careful to acknowledge the catalyst that a certain performance can be for framing and the selection of camera angles. A project such as *The Adventures of Sherlock Holmes' Smarter Brother*, Gene Wilder's first attempt at directing, placed other demands on the cinematographer's resourcefulness. While taking Fisher back into the studio, it also necessitated involvement in the project almost from inception. In photographing it Fisher tried to give weight to the serious and romantic elements of the story, while at the same time giving the project enough visual clarity for the sight gags.

On the whole, Fisher remains a cinematographer rather at the mercy of his material and directors. His work is never less than professional, but not always distinctive. Given, however, a director whose very personal vision he can share, and with whom he can fully collaborate he can produce work of matchless quality.

—Verina Glaessner

FLAIANO, Ennio, and Tullio PINELLI

FLAIANO. Writer. **Nationality:** Italian. **Born:** Pescara, 5 March 1910. **Education:** Studied architecture in Rome. **Career:** Architect; then journalist; drama critic, *Offi*; contributor to *Mondo*; 1942—film writing debut for *La danza del fuoco*. **Died:** 20 November 1972.

PINELLI. Writer. **Nationality:** Italian. **Born:** Turin, 24 June 1908. **Education:** Degree in law. **Career:** Attorney until 1942; also playwright in Turin dialect (plays produced include '*L Sôfà d'la marchesa 'd Mômbarôn*, 1932; *I porta*, 1936; *Crotta, lupo, Pegaso*, and *Lo Stilita*, 1938; *L'arcidiavolo di Radicofani* and *I padri etruschi*, 1941; *Il padre nudo* and *Lotta con l'angelo*, 1942; *La leggenda dell'assassino*, 1949; *Gorgonio*, 1952; *Mattutino* and *L'inferno*, 1954; *Ciarlatano*, 1967; *Santa Marina*, 1970; *Giardino delle Sfingi*, 1975); film writer from 1945. **Awards:** Ufficiale di Cavalleria. **Address:** Via Lucio Cassio 13, Rome 00189, Italy.

Films as Writers:

1950 *Luci del varietà* (*Variety Lights*) (Fellini and Lattuada)
1952 *Lo sceicco bianco* (*The White Sheik*) (Fellini)
1953 *I vitelloni* (Fellini); *Riscatto* (Girolami)
1954 *La strada* (Fellini)
1955 *Il bidone* (*The Swindle*) (Fellini)
1956 *Le notti di Cabiria* (*The Nights of Cabiria*; *Cabiria*) (Fellini)
1957 *Fortunella* (De Filippo)
1960 *La dolce vita* (Fellini)
1962 "La tentazioni di Dottor Antonio" ("The Temptations of Dr. Antonio") ep. of *Boccaccio '70* (Fellini)
1963 *8½* (*Otto e mezzo*) (Fellini)
1965 *Giulietta degli spiriti* (*Juliet of the Spirits*) (Fellini)

Films as Writer—Flaiano:

1942 *La danza del fuoco* (Simonelli); *Pastor Angelicus* (Marcellini)
1943 *Inviati speciali* (Marcellini); *L'abito nero da sposa* (Zampa)
1945 *La freccia nel fianco* (Lattuada)
1946 *Roma città libera* (*La notte porta consiglio*) (Pagliero); *L'ultimo paradiso* (Quilici)
1948 *Fuga in Francia* (*Flight into France*) (Soldati)
1949 *Cintura di castità* (Mastrocinque)
1951 *Parigi è sempre Parigi* (Emmer); *Guardie e ladri* (*Cops and Robbers*) (Steno)
1952 *Fanciulle di lusso* (*Luxury Girls*) (Vorhaus and Mussetta); "Elizabeth" ("Due donne") ep. of *Destini di donne* (*Daughters of Destiny*) (Pagliero); *Il mondo le condanna* (Franciolini)
1953 *Dov'è la libertà?* (Rossellini); "Scene all'aperto" ep. of *Tempi nostri* (Blasseti); *Canzoni, canzoni, canzoni* (Paolella); *Vesire gli ignudi* (Pagliero); *Villa Borghese* (*It Happened in the Park*) (Franciolini)

1954   *La donna del fiurne* (Soldati); *Camilla* (Emmer); *Peccato che sia una canaglia* (*Too Bad She's Bad*) (Blasetti); *La romana* (*Woman of Rome*) (Zampa); *La vergine moderna* (Pagliero)

1955   *Totò e Carolina* (Monicelli—produced 1953); *Il segno di Venere* (*The Sign of Venus*) (Risi); *La fortuna di essere donna* (*Lucky to Be a Woman*) (Blasetti)

1956   *Calabuch* (Berlanga); *Terrore sulla città* (Majano)

1958   *Un ettaro di cielo* (Casadio); *Racconti d'estate* (*Love on the Riviera*; *Summer Tales*) (Franciolini)

1960   *La ragazza in vetrina* (Emmer); *Un amore a Roma* (*Love in Rome*) (Risi); *Fantasmi a Roma* (Pietrangeli); **La notte** (*The Night*) (Antonioni)

1962   *Hong Kong un addio* (Polidoro)

1963   **El verdugo** (*Not on Your Life*) (Berlanga)

1964   *Tonio Kroger* (Thiele)

1965   *Una moglie americana* (*Run for Your Wife*) (Polidoro); *La decima vittima* (*The 10th Victim*) (Petri); *Rapture* (Guillermin)

1966   *Io, io, io . . . e gli altri* (Blasetti)

1967   "Ere préhistorique" ("Prehistoric Era") and "Nuits romaines" ("Roman Nights") eps. of *Le Plus Vieux Métier du monde* (*The Oldest Profession*) (Indovina and Bolognini); *I protagonisti* (Fondato)

1969   *Vivi, o preferibilmente morti* (Tessari); *Colpe rovente* (Zuffi); *Red* (Carle)

1972   *La Cagna* (*Liza*) (Ferreri)

1987   *L'inchiesta* (*The Inquiry*) (co)

Films as Writer—Pinelli:

1945   *L'adultera* (Coletti)

1946   *Le miserie del signor Travet* (Soldati)

1947   *La figlia del capitano* (Camerini); *Il passatore* (Coletti)

1948   *Senza pietà* (*Without Pity*) (Lattuada); "Il miracolo" ("The Miracle") ep. of *Amore* (*The Ways of Love*) (Rossellini); *Come persi la guerra* (Borghesio)

1949   *Il mulino del Po* (*The Mill on the Po*) (Lattuada); *In nome della legge* (*In the Name of the Law*) (Germi)

1950   *Il cammino della speranza* (*The Path of Hope*) (Germi)

1951   *La città si difende* (Germi); *Cameriera bella presenza offresi* (Pastina)

1952   *Wanda, la peccatrice* (Coletti)

1953   "Un' agenzia matrimoniale" ep. of *Amore in città* (*Love in the City*) (Fellini); *Pieta per chi cade* (Costa); *Traviata '53* (Cottafavi)

1954   *Sinfonia d'amore—Schubert* (Pellegrini); *Gli amori di Manon Lescaut* (Costa)

1960   *Adua e le compagne* (*Love à la carte*) (Petrangeli)

1961   *Senilita* (Bolognini)

1963   *Le steppa* (*The Steppe*) (Lattuada)

1965   "Il trattato di eugenetica" ("Treatise in Eugenics") ep. of *Le bambole* (Comencini)

1966   *San Francesco* (Cavani)

1967   *L'immorale* (*The Climax*) (Germi)

1968   *Galileo* (Cavani); *Serafino* (Germi)

1970   *Il giardino dei Finzi-Contini* (*The Garden of the Finzi-Contini*) (De Sica)

1973   *Alfredo, Alfredo* (Germi)

1975   *Amici miei* (*My Friends*) (Germi and Monicelli)

1976   *Per le antiche scale* (*Down the Ancient Stairs*) (Bolognini)

1978   *Viaggio con Anita* (*Travels with Anita*) (Monicelli)

1980   *Cristoforo Colombo* (Lattuada)

1983   *Amici miei atto II* (Monicelli)

1984   *Amici miei III* (Loy)

1985   *Speriamo che sia femmina* (Monicelli)

1986   *Ginger e Fred* (Fellini)

1990   *La voce della luna* (*The Voice of the Moon*) (Fellini)

Publications

By FLAIANO and PINELLI: books—

With others, *La dolce vita* (script), edited by T. Kesich, Rocca San Casciano, 1959, translated as *La Dolce Vita*, New York, 1961.

With others, *Juliet of the Spirits* (script), New York, 1965.

Three Screenplays by Federico Fellini (includes *Il bidone* [*The Swindle*], *The Temptations of Doctor Antonio*, and *I vitelloni*), New York, 1970.

With Federico Fellini, *Moraldo in the City* (script), edited by John C. Stubbs, Urbana, Illinois, 1983.

By FLAIANO: books—

La guerra spiegata ai poveri (play), Turin, 1946.

Tempo di uccidere (novel), Milan, 1947, as *Miriam*, London, 1949.

Diario notturno (novel), Milan, 1956.

La donna nell armadio (play), Turin, 1957.

Una e una notte (novel), Milan, 1959.

Un marziano a Roma (play), Turin, 1960.

With Antonioni and Tonino Guerra, *La notte* (script) in *Screenplays by Michelangelo Antonioni*, New York, 1963.

Il gioco e il massacro (novel), Milan, 1970.

Opere, Milan, 1970.

La conversazione continuamente interrotta (play), Turin, 1972.

Le ombre bianche, Milan, 1972.

La solitudine del satiro (novel), Milan, 1973.

Autobiografia del Blu di Prussia, Milan, 1974.

Diario degli errori, edited by Emma Giammattei, Milan, 1976.

Lettere d'amore al cinema, edited by Christina Bragaglia, Milan, 1978.

Melampo, Turin, 1978.

Storie inedite per film mai fatti, Milan, 1984.

By PINELLI: books—

Re Hassan (libretto), Milan, 1938.

La pulce d'oro (libretto), Milan, 1940.

La croce deserta (libretto), Milan, 1950.

With Fellini, *La strada* (script), in *Cinema Nuovo* (Turin), September/October 1954.

With others, *Otto e mezzo* (script), edited by Camilla Cederna, Bologna, 1965.

Il giardino della sfingi e altri commedie, Turin, 1975.

With L. Benvenutti and P. De Bernardi, *Amici miei* (script), Milan, 1976.

By PINELLI: article—

Positif (Paris), no. 351, May 1990.

CinémAction (Courbevoie), January 1994.

Positif (Paris), July-August 1995.
Filmvilag (Budapest), vo. 38, no. 2, 1995.

On FLAIANO: book—

Berterelli, Gian Carlo, and Pier Marco de Santi, *Omaggio a Flaiano*, Pisa, 1986.

On FLAIANO: articles—

Cineforum (Bergamo, Italy), vol. 23, no. 221, January/February 1983.
Revue de la Cinémathèque (Montreal), December 1990/January 1991.

On PINELLI: articles—

Barbetti, E., in *Teatro*, vol. 2, 1950.
Tassone, in *Positif* (Paris), July 1985.
Chion, Michel, "Fellini roman," in *Cahiers du Cinéma* (Paris), December 1993.

*   *   *

Ennio Flaiano and Tullio Pinelli, important Italian playwrights and screenwriters each in his own right, are known internationally as collaborators with Federico Fellini on *all* of his first nine features and two shorts (though only Pinelli worked on the first of the latter), from *Luci del varietà* (1950) through *Giulietta degli spiriti* (1965). Fellini met Pinelli in 1947 as a fellow scenarist; they worked together on at least seven films for other directors, notably Roberto Rossellini and Alberto Lattuada, between 1947 and 1951. Flaiano joined the team for Fellini's first feature (co-directed by Lattuada). Both writers always received credit, listed after Fellini himself, for screenplay, and often one or the other for original story (again with Fellini) as well. Yet they never worked together on a film for any other director, with the exception of Eduardo De Filippo's *Fortunella* (1957)—on which Fellini worked as well.

Critics have been fond of neatly contrasting Pinelli and Flaiano as reflecting opposing sides of the master: e.g., as "respectively the devout mystical side and the skeptical, ironic side" of Fellini (*Times Literary Supplement*, 1961); or as his "mystical" (again) and "comical or irreverent" sides (Edward Murray, *Fellini the Artist*, 1976); or Pinelli as "methodical, rational, well-balanced . . . serious, dramatic and full of enthusiasm" and Flaiano as "casual and skeptical, hating vagueness and over-emphasis, in fact he is anti-poetic. It is he who has always played the part of the devil's advocate between Fellini and Pinelli, by avoiding excess lyricism and anchoring himself to reality. He suggests theories for social satire to Fellini" (Angelo Solmi, *Fellini*, 1962). Fellini himself, in a 1962 interview, while less neatly characterizing Pinelli as a "most serious" and "most fruitful" playwright and Flaiano "the subtle writer, the delicate humorist, the ardent chronicler of Italian life," agreed that the two were "temperamentally quite different but . . . basically complementary; that is, when they are working together, I feel that each is giving the best of himself."

It appears impossible to separate out the exact contributions of each to the final films because of the trio's informal working methods

and Fellini's changes at the shooting stage, though it is sometimes on record as to who contributed dialogue to which scenes. (These working methods, it should be added, are fairly typical for the Italian film industry.) According to the director, he would typically get an idea, then tell his scenarists about it "without dramatizing it at all, just as if I were telling a story." At some point in this early stage one or more of the three would do "field research," whether interviewing swindlers for *Il bidone*, strolling on the Via Veneto for *La dolce vita*, or visiting spas for *8½*. At later meetings "we behave in such a way as to avoid the heavy, formal atmosphere of a working session . . . we chat around the subject, and develop it. . . . Then, when the story begins to have a fairly precise thread in it, we often divide up the work. Pinelli takes some scenes, Flaiano others, and I take others myself, but we do all we can to give this creation . . . the greatest possible freedom . . . because I shouldn't be able to work with a very carefully constructed screenplay. . . . I need to be given freedom within an extremely elastic screenplay, not in order to improvise, exactly, but so that I can enrich a character or a situation while the film is actually being made."

Angelo Solmi's biography of Fellini provides glimpses of how the trio worked on two particular films. For *La strada*, Pinelli wandered on foot in the Turin region to observe gypsies at village fairs. The subsequent scenario he and Fellini devised was a "compromise between the carefree tone Fellini had in mind and Pinelli's more dramatic one," but still more "somber and legendary . . . magical" than the completed film was to be. Flaiano was then called in to "say derogatory things about *La strada* for three months. . . . I condemned a vagueness of atmosphere, certain affectations in the characters," and insisted the story should "come down to earth" and the "symbolism should be integrated with the narrative." Flaiano still gave Fellini the credit for balancing the neorealist and poetic elements of the film.

For *Le notti di Cabiria* each wrote dialogue for different scenes. Flaiano successfully fought to keep the episode with the film star, which Fellini had been inclined to remove. The final scene of the film originated when Flaiano recalled an actual murder of a prostitute and Pinelli suggested it be the model for the end of the film and of Cabiria; Fellini and Flaiano insisted that Cabiria should live, but it was Pinelli, bowing to their demand, who all the same was the one to develop the scene in detail.

During the making of *Giulietta degli spiriti*, Pinelli and Flaiano became increasingly alienated from the director's vision. By the time the film was completed Flaiano felt shabbily treated by Fellini and ceased to have any professional or social contact with him. Pinelli too, after nearly 20 years of working with Fellini, no longer collaborated with the director, who established a whole new team of artists and technicians for his later films, with the notable carryover of the composer Nino Rota. Yet 20 years after *Giulietta*, Fellini returned to Pinelli for assistance on the screenplay for *Ginger e Fred* and again for work on *La voce della luna*.

Recent biographies of Fellini (e.g., Hollis Alpert's 1986 *Fellini: A Life*) and studies of his films (Peter Bondanella's 1992 *The Cinema of Federico Fellini*) give more prominent attention to Pinelli than to Flaiano, if only because of the former's longer working relationship with the director and his continuing availability for interviews. Yet it may be fairly said of both men that however much in the service of Fellini's vision they worked, the two screenwriters made incalculably important contributions to an unbroken series of astonishingly fine, original, and varied films.

—Joseph Milicia

FLEISCHER, Max and Dave

Animators. **Nationality:** American. **Born:** Max in Vienna, 17 July 1883 (or 1885); Dave in New York City, 14 July 1894. **Education:** Max studied at New York Art Students League, Cooper Union, and Mechanics and Tradesmen's School. **Military Service:** U.S. Army, 1917; edited live action training films, 1917–18. **Career:** 1887— Fleischer family moved to New York City; before 1912—Dave worked as theater usher and in engraving company; 1912—Dave a cutter for Pathé Films; before 1914—Max an errand boy for Brooklyn *Daily Eagle* and for Boston photoengraver; 1914—Max a commercial artist for Crouse-Hinds, and *Popular Science Monthly* art editor; 1915—Max invented Rotoscope, device for tracing live-action film for conversion to animation; 1916—employed by John Randolph Bray at Paramount, producing animation sequences for *Bray Pictograph* series; joined by Dave as assistant and Rotoscope model; 1917–18—Max made Army instructional films; 1919—brothers formed Out of the Inkwell, Inc. production company; 1925—distribution company Red Seal Pictures acquired; 1929—Fleischer Studios, Inc. formed, distributing through Paramount; 1936—produced medium-length *Popeye the Sailor Meets Sinbad the Sailor*; 1939—studio moved from New York to Miami; 1939—first full-length feature *Gulliver's Travels*; 1941—second feature *Mr. Bug Goes to Town*, a financial failure; Paramount withdrew loans, shutting down studio; 1942—Dave became head of Columbia cartoon dept. Max produced instructional films for Jam-Handy company; 1944—Dave moved to Universal, held various positions until1967 retirement; 1962—Max formed a new Out of the Inkwell, Inc.; 1963—Max retired. **Died:** Max Fleischer died in 1972; Dave Fleicher died in 1979.

Films as Director:

(Max Fleischer as Director):

1915   *Out of the Inkwell* (+ pr + sc + an, Dave asst d, Rotoscope model)
1918   *How to Read an Army Map*; *How to Fire a Lewis Gun*; *How to Fire a Stokes Mortar*

(Dave Fleischer as director, Max as producer of cartoon shorts, both collaborating on scripts):

1927   advertising cartoon: *That Little Big Fellow*
1930   *Marriage Wows*; *Radio Riot*; *Hot Dog*; *Fire Bugs*; *Wise Flies*; *The Grand Uproar*; *Sky Scraping*; *Up to Mars*
1931   advertising cartoons: *Graduation Day in Bugland* (for Listerine Co.); *Suited to a T.* (for India Tea Co.); *Hurry Doctor* (for Texaco); *In My Merry Oldsmobile* (for Oldsmobile Co.); *Texas in 1999* (for Texaco); *A Jolt for General Germ* (for Listerine Co.?); other cartoons: *Ace of Spades*; *Teacher's Pest*; *Tree Saps*; *The Cow's Husband*; *The Male Man*; *Twenty Legs under the Sea*; *Step on It*; *The Herring Murder Case*
1934   *Poor Cinderella*; *Little Dutch Mill*
1935   *An Elephant Never Forgets*; *The Song of the Birds*; *The Kids in the Shoe*; *Dancing on the Moon*; *Time for Love*; *Musical Memories*

1936   *Somewhere in Dream Land*; *The Little Stranger*; *The Cobweb Hotel*; *Greedy Humpty Dumpty*; *Hawaiian Birds*; *Play Safe*; *Christmas Comes But Once a Year*
1937   *Bunny-mooning*; *Chicken à la King*; *A Car-Tune Portrait*; *Peeping Penguins*; *Educated Fish*; *Little Lamby*
1938   *Hold It*; *Hunky and Spunky*; *All's Fair at the Fair*; *The Playful Polar Bears*; *The Tears of an Onion*
1939   *Always Kickin'*; *Aladdin and His Wonderful Lamp* (2-reeler); *Small Fry*; *Barnyard Brat*; *The Fresh Vegetable Mystery* (in 3-D)
1940   *Little Lambkin*; *Ants in the Plants*; *Kick in Time*; *Snubbed by a Snob*; *You Can't Shoe a Horsefly*; *The Dandy Lion*; *King for a Day*; *Sneak, Snoop and Snitch*; *The Constable*; *Mommy Loves Puppy*; *Bring Himself Back Alive*
1941   *All's Well*; *Pop and Mom in Wild Oysters*; *Two for the Zoo*; *Zero, the Hound*; *Twinkletoes Gets the Bird*; *Raggedy Ann and Andy* (2-reeler); *Swing Cleaning*; *Sneak, Snoop and Snitch in Triple Trouble*; *Fire Cheese*; *Twinkletoes—Where He Goes Nobody Knows*; *Copy Cat*; *Gabby Goes Fishing*; *The Wizard of Arts*; *It's a Hap-hap-happy Day*; *Vitamin Hay*; *Twinkletoes in Hat Stuff*

Superman Series—

1941   *Superman*; *Superman in The Mechanical Monsters*
1942   *Superman in Billion Dollar Limited*; *Superman in The Arctic Giant*; *Superman in The Bulleteers*; *The Raven* (2-reeler); *Superman in The Magnetic Telescope*; *Superman in Electric Earthquake*; *Superman in Volcano*; *Superman in Terror on the Midway*

Out of the Inkwell Series—

1919   *The Clown's Pup*; *The Tantalizing Fly*; *Slides*
1920   *The Boxing Kangaroo*; *The Chinaman*; *The Circus*; *The Clown's Little Brother*; *The Ouija Board*; *Perpetual Motion*; *Poker (The Card Game)*; *The Restaurant*
1921   *The Automobile Ride*; *Cartoonland*; *The First Man to the Moon*; *Fishing*; *Invisible Ink*; *November*; *The Sparring Partner*
1922   *Birthday*; *Bubbles*; *The Challenge*; *The Dresden Doll*; *The Fish* (possibly alternative title for *Fishing*, 1921); *The Hypnotist*; *Jumping Beans*; *Mosquito*; *Pay Day*; *Reunion*; *The Show*
1923   *Balloons*; *The Battle*; *Bedtime*; *The Contest*; *False Alarm*; *Flies*; *The Fortune Teller*; *Fun from the Press* (series of 3 inserts); *Laundry*; *Modeling*; *The Puzzle*; *Shadows*; *Surprise*; *Trapped*; *The Einstein Theory of Relativity* (d Max only; live action, in 2-reel version, and 4-reel with some cartoon sequences)
1924   *The Cure*; *Ko-Ko in 1999*; *Ko-Ko the Hot Shot*; *League of Nations*; *The Masquerade*; *The Runaway*; *Vacation*; *Vaudeville*
1925   *Big Chief Ko-Ko*; *The Cartoon Factory*; *Ko-Ko Celebrates the Fourth*; *Ko-Ko Eats*; *Ko-Ko in Toyland*; *Ko-Ko Nuts*; *Ko-Ko on the Run*; *Ko-Ko Packs 'em*; *Ko-Ko Sees Spooks*; *Ko-Ko's Thanksgiving*; *Ko-Ko the Barber*; *Ko-Ko Trains Animals*; *Mother Goose Land*; *The Storm*

1926 *Ko-Ko at the Circus*; *Ko-Ko Baffles the Bulls*; *Ko-Ko Gets Egg-cited*; *Ko-Ko Hot After It*; *Ko-Ko Kidnapped*; *Ko-Ko's Paradise*; *Ko-Ko Steps Out*; *Ko-Ko the Convict*; *Toot! Toot!*; *The Fadeaway*; *It's the Cat's*

1927 *Inklings* (series of 18); *East Side, West Side* (Song Car-Tune?); *Ko-Ko Back Tracks*; *Ko-Ko Makes 'em Laugh*; *Ko-Ko Plays Pool*; *Ko-Ko's Kane*; *Ko-Ko the Knight*; *Ko-Ko Hops Off*; *Ko-Ko the Kop*; *Ko-Ko Explores*; *Ko-Ko Chops Suey*; *Ko-Ko's Klock*; *Ko-Ko Kicks*; *Ko-Ko's Quest*; *Ko-Ko the Kid*; *Ko-Ko Needles the Boss*

1928 *Ko-Ko's Kink*; *Ko-Ko's Kozy Korner*; *Koko's Germ Jam*; *Ko-Ko's Bawth*; *Ko-Ko Smokes*; *Ko-Ko's Tattoo*; *Ko-Ko's Earth Control*; *Ko-Ko's Hot Dog*; *Ko-Ko's Haunted House*; *Ko-Ko Lamps Aladdin*; *Ko-Ko Squeals*; *Ko-Ko's Field Daze*; *Ko-Ko Goes Over*; *Ko-Ko's Catch*; *Ko-Ko's War Dogs*; *Ko-Ko's Chase*; *Ko-Ko Heaves-Ho*; *Ko-Ko's Big Pull*; *Ko-Ko Cleans Up*; *Ko-Ko's Parade*; *Ko-Ko's Dog-Gone*; *Telefilm*; *Ko-Ko in the Rough*; *Ko-Ko's Magic*; *Ko-Ko on the Track*; *Ko-Ko's Act*; *Ko-Ko's Courtship*

1929 *No Eyes Today*; *Noise Annoys Ko-Ko*; *Ko-Ko Beats Time*; *Ko-Ko's Reward*; *Ko-Ko's Hot Ink*; *Ko-Ko's Crib*; *Ko-Ko's Saxaphonies*; *Ko-Ko's Knock-down*; *Ko-Ko's Signals*; *Ko-Ko's Focus*; *Ko-Ko's Conquest*; *Ko-Ko's Harem-Scarem*; *Ko-Ko's Big Sale*; *Ko-Ko's Hypnotism*; *Chemical Ko-Ko*; *Noah's Lark* (sound)

Song Car-Tune Series—

1924 *Come Take a Trip in My Airship*; *Mother, Mother, Mother, Pin a Rose on Me*; *Oh, Mabel!*; *Old Folks at Home*; *Echo and Narcissus*; *The Proxy Lover: A Fable of the Future*

1925 *Daisy Bell*; *Dixie*; *Good-bye My Lady Love*; *I Love a Lassie*; *My Bonnie*; *Suwanee River*; *Evolution* (d Max only; part-live action feature)

1926 *By the Light of the Silvery Moon*; *Comin' through the Rye*; *Darling Dolly Gray*; *Has Anybody Here Seen Kelly?*; *In the Good Old Summertime*; *My Old Kentucky Home*; *Oh You Beautiful Doll*; *Old Black Joe*; *Pack Up Your Troubles*; *Sailing, Sailing over the Bounding Main*; *Sweet Adeline*; *Take a Trip*; *Ta-Ra-Ra-Boom-Der-A*; *Trail of the Lonesome Pine*; *Tramp, the Boys are Marching*

Carrie of the Chorus Live-Action Series—

1926 *Berth Mark*; *Another Bottle, Doctor* (not released); *Morning Judge*

Screen Songs Series—

1929 *The Sidewalks of New York*; *Yankee Doodle Boy*; *Old Black Joe*; *Ye Olde Melodies*; *Daisy Bell*; *Mother Pin a Rose on Me* (remake of 1924 title); *Chinatown My Chinatown*; *Dixie* (remake of 1925 title); *Good-bye My Lady Love* (remake of 1925 title); *My Pony Boy*; *Smiles*; *Oh You Beautiful Doll* (remake of 1926 title); *After the Ball*; *Put on Your Old Gray Bonnet*; *I've Got Rings on My Fingers*

1930 *Bedelia*; *In the Shade of the Old Apple Tree*; *I'm Afraid to Come Home in the Dark*; *La Paloma*; *Prisoner's Song*; *I'm*

Forever Blowing Bubbles; *Yes! We Have No Bananas*; *Come Take a Trip in My Airship* (remake of 1924 title); *In the Good Old Summer Time* (remake of 1926 title); *A Hot Time in the Old Town Tonight*; *The Glow Worm*; *The Stein Song*; *Strike Up the Band*; *My Gal Sal*; *Mariutch*; *On a Sunday Afternoon*; *Row, Row, Row*

1931 *By the Beautiful Sea*; *I Wonder Who's Kissing Her Now*; *I'd Climb the Highest Mountain*; *Somebody Stole My Gal*; *Any Little Girl That's a Nice Little Girl*; *Alexander's Ragtime Band*; *And the Green Grass Grew All Around*; *My Wife's Gone to the Country*; *That Old Gang of Mine*; *Mr. Gallagher and Mr. Shean*; *You're Driving Me Crazy*; *Little Annie Rooney*; *Kitty from Kansas City* (also *Betty Boop* series); *By the Light of the Silvery Moon* (remake of 1926 title); *My Baby Just Cares for Me*; *Russian Lullaby*; *Please Go 'way and Let Me Sleep*

1932 *Sweet Jenny Lee*; *Show Me the Way to Go Home*; *When the Red Red Robin Comes Bob Bob Bobbin' Along*; *Wait Till the Sun Shines, Nellie*; *Just One More Chance*; *Oh! How I Hate to Get Up in the Morning*; *Shine On Harvest Moon*; *I Ain't Got Nobody*; *You Try Somebody Else*; *Rudy Vallee Melodies*; *Down among the Sugar Cane*; *Just a Gigolo*; *School Days*; *Sleepy Time Down South*; *Sing a Song*; *Time on My Hands*

1933 *Dinah*; *Ain't She Sweet*; *Reaching for the Moon*; *Aloha Oe*; *Popular Melodies*; *The Peanut Vendor*; *Song Shopping*; *Boilesk*; *Sing, Sisters, Sing!*; *Down by the Old Mill Stream*; *Stoopnocracy*; *When Yuba Plays the Rumba on the Tuba*; *Boo, Boo, Theme Song*; *I Like Mountain Music*; *Sing, Babies, Sing*

1934 *Keeps Rainin' All the Time*; *Let's All Sing Like the Birdies Sing*; *Tune Up and Sing*; *Lazybones*; *This Little Piggie Went to Market*; *She Reminds Me of You*; *Love Thy Neighbor*

1935 *I Wished on the Moon*; *It's Easy to Remember*

1936 *No Other One*; *I Feel Like a Feather in the Breeze*; *I Don't Want to Make History*; *The Hills of Old Wyomin'*; *I Can't Escape from You*; *Talking through My Heart*

1937 *Never Should Have Told You*; *Twilight on the Trail*; *Please Keep Me in Your Dreams*; *You Came to My Rescue*; *Whispers in the Dark*; *Magic on Broadway*

1938 *You Took the Words Right Out of My Heart*; *Thanks for the Memory*; *You Leave Me Breathless*; *Beside a Moonlit Stream*

Betty Boop Series—

1930 *Swing, You Sinner*; *Accordion Joe*; *Mysterious Mose*; *Dizzy Dishes*; *Barnacle Bill*

1931 *Silly Scandals*; *Bimbo's Initiation*; *Bimbo's Express*; *Minding the Baby*; *In the Shade of the Old Apple Sauce*; *Mask-a-Raid*; *Jack and the Beanstalk*; *Dizzy Red Riding Hood*; *Betty Co-ed*; *The Bum Bandit*

1932 *Minnie the Moocher*; *Swim or Sink*; *Crazy Town*; *The Dancing Fool*; *A-Hunting We Will Go*; *Chess-nuts*; *Let Me Call You Sweetheart* (also *Screen Song*); *Hide and Seek*; *Admission Free*; *The Betty Boop Limited*; *Stopping the Show*; *Betty Boop's Bizzy Bee*; *Betty Boop M.D.*; *Betty Boop's Bamboo Isle*; *Betty Boop's Ups and Downs*; *Romantic Melodies* (also *Screen Song*); *Betty Boop for President*; *I'll Be Glad*

When You're Dead, You Rascal (also *Screen Song*); *Betty Boop's Museum*; *Any Rags*; *Boop-Oop-a-Doop*; *The Robot*

1933 *Betty Boop's Ker-choo*; *Betty Boop's Crazy Inventions*; *Is My Palm Read*; *Betty Boop's Penthouse*; *Snow White*; *Betty Boop's Birthday Party*; *Betty Boop's May Party*; *Betty Boop's Big Boss*; *Mother Goose Land*; *The Old Man of the Mountain*; *I Heard*; *Morning, Noon, and Night*; *Betty Boop's Hallowe'en Party*; *Parade of the Wooden Soldiers*

1934 *Ha! Ha! Ha!*; *Betty in Blunderland*; *Betty Boop's Rise to Fame* (compilation of sequences from *Stopping the Show*, *Betty Boop's Bamboo Isle*, and *The Old Man of the Mountain*, + new material); *Betty Boop's Life Guard*; *There's Something about a Soldier*; *Betty Boop's Little Pal*; *Betty Boop's Prize Show*; *Keep in Style*; *When My Ship Comes In*; *She Wronged Him Right*; *Red Hot Mama*

1935 *Baby Be Good*; *Taking the Blame*; *Stop That Noise*; *Swat the Fly*; *No! No! A Thousand Times No!*; *A Little Soap and Water*; *A Language All My Own*; *Betty Boop and Grampy*; *Judge for a Day*; *Making Stars*; *Betty Boop with Henry the Funniest Living American*; *Little Nobody*

1936 *Betty Boop and the Little King*; *Not Now*; *Betty Boop and Little Jimmy*; *We Did It*; *A Song a Day*; *More Pep*; *You're Not Built That Way*; *Happy You and Merry Me*; *Training Pigeons*; *Grampy's Indoor Outing*; *Be Human*; *Making Friends*

1937 *House Cleaning Blues*; *Whoops! I'm a Cowboy*; *The Hot Air Salesman*; *Pudgy Takes a Bow-wow*; *Pudgy Picks a Fight*; *The Impractical Joker*; *Ding Dong Doggie*; *The Candid Candidate*; *Service with a Smile*; *The New Deal Show*; *The Foxy Hunter*; *Zula Hula*

1938 *Riding the Rails*; *Be Up to Date*; *Honest Love and True*; *Out of the Inkwell*; *Swing School*; *Pudgy and the Lost Kitten*; *Buzzy Boop*; *Pudgy and the Watchman*; *Buzzy Boop at the Concert*; *Sally Swing*; *On with the New*; *Thrills and Chills*

1939 *My Friend the Monkey*; *So Does an Automobile*; *Musical Mountaineers*; *The Scared Crows*; *Rhythm on the Reservation*; *Yip, Yip, Yippy*

Popeye Series—

1933 *I Yam What I Yam*; *Blow Me Down*; *I Eats My Spinach*; *Season's Greetinks*; *Wild Elephinks* (all cartoons also *Betty Boop* series)

1934 *Sock a Bye Baby*; *Let's You and Him Fight*; *Can You Take It?*; *The Man on the Flying Trapeze*; *Shoein' Hosses*; *Strong to the Finich*; *Shiver Me Timbers!*; *Axe Me Another*; *A Dream Walking*; *The Two-Alarm Fire*; *The Dance Contest*; *We Aim to Please*

1935 *Be Kind to Aminals*; *Pleased to Meet Cha*; *The Hyp-nut-tist*; *Choose Your Weppins*; *Beware of Barnacle Bill*; *For Better or Worser*; *Dizzy Divers*; *You Gotta Be a Football Hero*; *King of the Mardi Gras* (also *Betty Boop* Series); *Adventures of Popeye* (compilation with sequences from *I Eats My Spinach*, *Popeye the Sailor*, and *Axe Me Another*); *The Spinach Overture*

1936 *Vim, Vigor and Vitaliky*; *A Clean Shaven Man*; *Brotherly Love*; *I-ski Love-ski You-ski*; *Bridge Ahoy!*; *What No Spinach?*; *I Wanna Be a Life Guard*; *Let's Get Movin'*; *Never Kick a Woman*; *Little Swee' Pea*; *Hold the Wire*; *Popeye the*

Sailor Meets Sinbad the Sailor (2-reeler); *The Spinach Roadster*; *I'm in the Army Now* (compilation)

1937 *The Paneless Window Washer*; *Organ Grinder's Swing*; *My Artistical Temperature*; *Hospitaliky*; *The Twisker Pitcher*; *Morning, Noon, and Night Club*; *Lost and Foundry*; *I Never Changes My Altitude*; *I Like Babies and Infinks*; *The Football Toucher Downer*; *Protek the Weakerist*; *Popeye the Sailor Meets Ali Baba's Forty Thieves* (2-reeler); *Fowl Play*

1938 *Let's Celebrake*; *Learn Polikeness*; *The House Builder-Upper*; *Big Chief Ugh-Amugh-Ugh*; *I Yam Love Sick*; *Plumbing Is a Pipe*; *The Jeep*; *Bulldozing the Bull*; *Mutiny Ain't Nice*; *Goonland*; *A Date to Skate*; *Cops Is Always Right*

1939 *Leave Well Enough Alone*; *Customers Wanted*; *Wotta Nitemare*; *Ghosks in the Bunk*; *Hello, How Am I?*; *It's the Natural Thing to Do*; *Never Sock a Baby*

1940 *Shakespearian Spinach*; *Females Is Fickle*; *Stealin' Ain't Honest*; *My Feelin's Is Hurt*; *Onion Pacific*; *Wimmin Is a Myskery*; *Nurse Mates*; *Fightin' Pals*; *Doing Imposikible Stunts*; *Wimmin Hadn't Oughta Drive*; *Puttin' on the Act*; *Popeye Meets William Tell*; *My Pop, My Pop*; *Poopdeck Pappy*; *Eugene, the Jeep*

1941 *Problem Pappy*; *Quiet! Pleeze*; *Olive's Sweepstake Ticket*; *Flies Ain't Human*; *Popeye Meets Rip Van Winkle*; *Olive's Boithday Presink*; *Child Psykolojiky*; *Pest Pilot*; *I'll Never Crow Again*; *The Mighty Navy*; *Nix on Hypnotricks*

1942 *Kickin' the Conga 'round*; *Blunder Below*; *Fleets of Stren'th*; *Pip-eye, Pup-eye, Poop-eye and Peep-eye*; *Many Tanks*; *Olive Oyl and Water Don't Mix*; *Baby Wants a Bottle-ship*

Stone Age Cartoons Series—

1940 *Way Back When a Triangle Had Its Points*; *Way Back When a Nag Was Only a Horse*; *Way Back When a Night Club Was a Stick*; *Granite Hotel*; *The Foul Ball Player*; *The Ugly Dino*; *Wedding Belts*; *Way Back When a Razzberry Was a Fruit*; *The Fulla Bluff Man*; *Springtime in the Rockage*; *Pedagogical Institution (College to You)*; *Way Back When Women Had Their Weigh*

Other Films:

1923 *Adventures in the Far North* (*Captain Kleinschmidt's Adventures in the Far North*) (Kleinschmidt) (co-pr and ed Max only; live action)

1929 *Finding His Voice* (co-d Max only; for Western Electric Co.)

Screen Gems Series—

1942 *Song of Victory* (Wickersham) (Dave pr); *The Gullible Canary* (Geiss) (Dave pr); *The Dumbconscious Mind* (Sommer and Hubley) (Dave pr); *Tito's Guitar* (Wickersham) (Dave pr); *Malice in Slumberland* (Geiss) (Dave pr); *Toll Bridge Troubles* (Wicker) (Dave pr); *King Midas, Junior* (Sommer and Hubley) (Dave pr); *Cholly Polly* (Geiss) (Dave pr)

1943 *Slay It with Flowers* (Wickersham) (Dave pr); *The Vitamin G-Man* (Sommer and Hubley) (Dave pr); *There's Something about a Soldier* (Geiss) (Dave pr); *Kindly Scram* (Geiss) (Dave pr); *Prof. Small and Mr. Tall* (Sommer and Hubley) (Dave pr); *Willoughby's Magic Hat* (Wickersham) (Dave pr); *Plenty Below Zero* (Wickersham) (Dave pr); *Duty and the Beast* (Geiss) (Dave pr); *Mass Mouse Meeting* (Geiss) (Dave pr); *Tree for Two* (Wickersham) (Dave pr); *He Can't Make It Stick* (Sommer and Hubley) (Dave pr); *The Fly in the Ointment* (Sommer) (Dave pr); *Dizzy Newsreel* (Geiss) (Dave pr); *A-Hunting We Won't Go* (Wickersham) (Dave pr); *The Rocky Road to Ruin* (Sommer) (Dave pr); *Room and Bored* (Wickersham) (Dave pr); *Imagination* (Wickersham) (Dave pr); *Nursery Crimes* (Geiss) (Dave pr); *The Cocky Bantam* (Sommer) (Dave pr); *Way Down Yonder in the Corn* (Wickersham) (Dave pr); *The Playful Pest* (Sommer) (Dave pr); *Polly Wants a Doctor* (Swift) (Dave pr)

1944 *Sadie Hawkins Day* (Wickersham) (Dave pr); *The Herring Murder Mystery* (Roman) (Dave pr); *Magic Strength* (Wickersham) (Dave pr); *Lionel Lion* (Sommer) (Dave pr); *Amoozin' But Confoozin'* (Marcus) (Dave pr); *Giddy-yapping* (Swift) (Dave pr); *The Dream Kids* (Wickersham) (Dave pr); *The Disillusioned Bluebird* (Swift) (Dave pr); *Tangled Travels* (Geiss) (Dave pr); *Trocadero* (Nigh) (Dave pr, live action + d animated sequences + ro)

Sing and Be Happy Series, live action with cartoon inserts—

1946 *Merrily We Sing* (Moore) (Dave anim spvr); *A Bit of Blarney* (Moore) (Dave anim spvr); *The Singing Barbers* (Moore) (Dave anim spvr)

1947 *Let's Sing a College Song* (Moore) (Dave anim spvr); *Let's Sing a Western Song* (Moore) (Dave anim spvr); *Kernels of Corn* (Moore) (Dave anim spvr); *Let's Go Latin* (Moore) (Dave anim spvr); *Manhattan Memories* (Moore) (Dave anim spvr)

1948 *Lamp Post Favorites* (Moore) (Dave anim spvr); *Singin' the Blues* (Parker) (Dave anim spvr); *Spotlight Serenade* (Parker) (Dave anim spvr); *Choo Choo Swing* (Cowan) (Dave anim spvr); *River Melodies* (Parker) (Dave anim spvr); *Clap Your Hands* (Cowan) (Dave anim spvr); *Hits of the Nineties* (Parker) (Dave anim spvr); *Let's Sing a Love Song* (Parker) (Dave anim spvr); *Sing While You Work* (Parker) (Dave anim spvr); *Songs of the Seasons* (Parker) (Dave anim spvr); *The Year Around* (Cowan) (Dave anim spvr)

1949 *Minstrel Mania* (Cowan) (Dave anim spvr); *Songs of Romance* (Cowan) (Dave anim spvr); *Sailing with a Song* (Cowan) (Dave anim spvr); *Singing Along* (Cowan) (Dave anim spvr); *Francis* (Lubin) (Dave live action, storyboard only)

Cartoon Melody Series, live action with cartoon inserts—

1950 *Brother John* (Cowan) (Dave anim spvr); *Lower the Boom* (Cowan) (Dave anim spvr); *Peggy, Peg and Polly* (Cowan) (Dave anim spvr)

1951 *Bedtime for Bonzo* (de Cordova) (Dave, live action + d anim sequences for trailer); *Bubbles of Song* (Cowan) (Dave anim spvr); *Readin' 'ritin' and 'rithmetic* (Cowan) (Dave anim spvr); *Down the River* (Cowan) (Dave anim spvr);

Hilly Billy (Cowan) (David anim spvr); *MacDonald's Farm* (Cowan) (Dave anim spvr); *Reuben, Reuben* (Cowan) (Dave anim spvr); *Uncle Sam's Songs* (Cowan) (Dave anim spvr)

1952 *Memory Song Book* (Cowan) (Dave anim spvr); *Songs That Live* (Cowan) (Dave anim spvr); *Toast of Song* (Cowan) (Dave anim spvr)

Publications

By the FLEISCHERS: books—

Fleischer, Max, *Betty Boop*, New York, 1975.
Fleischer, Max, *Betty Boop's Sunday Best*, Northampton, Massachusetts, 1995.

On the FLEISCHERS: books—

Garvie, Charles, *The Betty Boop Book*, London, 1984.
Cabarga, Leslie, *The Fleischer Story*, New York, 1988.

On the FLEISCHERS: articles—

de Bree, K., ''Max Fleischer, de koning van de voorfilm,'' in *Skoop* (Amsterdam), vol. 8, no. 5, 1972.
Beylie, Claude, ''Les Epinards par la racine,'' (obituary for Max), in *Ecran* (Paris), November 1972.
Langer, M., ''Max and Dave Fleischer,'' in *Film Comment* (New York), January-February 1975.
Fernett, G., ''Even Popeye Couldn't Hold Fleischer's Studio Together,'' in *Classic Film Collector* (Muscatine, Iowa), Winter 1978.
Baker, B., ''Max & Dave Fleischer,'' in *Film Dope* (London), February 1979.
De Bree, K., ''In Memoriam Dave Fleischer,'' in *Skoop* (Amsterdam), August 1979.
Obituary for Dave, in *Variety* (New York), 4 July 1979.
Moret, H., obituary for Dave, in *Ecran* (Paris), 20 October 1979.
Cahiers de la Cinémathèque (Perpignan), Summer-Autumn 1980.
Maltin, Leonard, in *Of Mice and Magic*, New York, 1980.
Culhane, Shamus, in *Talking Animals and Other People*, New York, 1986.
''The Perfect Film,'' in *Animation Journal* (Orange), Fall 1992.
Langer, Mark, ''The Fleischer Rotoscope Patent,'' in *Animation Journal* (Orange), Spring 1993.
Butters, Patrick, ''Respectable Collectibles: Animated Cartoon Cels as Collectibles from Disney, Warner Bros and Max Fleischer Studios,'' in *Insight on the News*, 1 February 1999.
Deneroff, Harvey, ''The Innovators 1930–1940: The Thin Black Line,'' in *Sight & Sound* (London), June 1999.

* * *

Max and Dave Fleischer were important innovators in American animation in the 1920s and 1930s. Their cartoon series, which included *Out of the Inkwell*, *Betty Boop*, *Popeye*, and *Superman*, relied on a flair for ingenuity and comic imagination that made their work stylistically distinctive. The best of the Fleischer brothers' work features an unselfconscious surrealism and fluid imagery unparalleled in pre-Second World War animation.

Max Fleischer emigrated with his family in 1887 from Vienna to New York City, where his brother Dave was born seven years later. Max studied art at the Art Students League and Cooper Union in New York City. After his schooling, he became a staff artist on the *Brooklyn Daily Eagle*. There he met cartoonist John R. Bray, whose subsequent move into animation later furthered Fleischer's own career. By 1915, Max was an art editor at *Popular Science Monthly*. His job heightened his interest in mechanics and inspired him to invent a machine that would enable an animator to trace over live-action film frame-by-frame. Fleischer was assisted by his brothers Joe and Dave in his new invention, the Rotoscope.

The Fleischers put the Rotoscope to use in a series of cartoons produced by Bray and called *Out of the Inkwell*. The series featured the ''out-of-the-inkwell'' appearances and adventures of a cartoon clown (later named Ko-Ko) in live-action settings. Max and Dave collaborated on the *Out of the Inkwell* series for Bray until 1921, when they established their own company. Max took over responsibility for managing the business and distributing the films. Dave, meanwhile, assumed creative directorship over all the company's cartoons. The Fleischers released their cartoons from 1921 to 1927 through their own distribution company, Red Seal Pictures. After Red Seal collapsed in 1927, they distributed through Paramount pictures until they were forced out of business in 1942.

The brothers' success increased in the late 1920s with *Talkartoons*, a series of sound cartoons. One of the *Talkartoons'* characters became so popular that she got her own series. Betty Boop, modelled after the flapper actress Helen Kane and individualized by Mae Questel's vocals, was the first sexualized cartoon character. Frequently likened to actress Mae West for her suggestive body language and natural insouciance, Betty Boop appealed to adults as well as to children. The best of the series capitalized on good-natured sexual innuendo, constantly metamorphosing images, and thinly veiled Freudian symbolism. But in 1934, Hollywood's new Production Code called for so much revision that a sanitized and desexed Betty Boop destroyed the series' imaginative flair, though it continued until 1939.

When Betty's popularity waned, another Fleischer cartoon character became the studio's main attraction. The *Popeye* series, based on the Elzie Segar comic strip character, featured new songs, comic twists, and a more ambitious graphic style that used perspective and a range of values. The peak of the series came in the late 1930s in three two-reel Popeyes (*Popeye the Sailor Meets Sinbad the Sailor*, *Popeye the Sailor Meets Ali Baba's Forty Thieves*, and *Aladdin and His Wonderful Lamp*). The three films featured Technicolor, and the first two used Max Fleischer's Turntable Camera, a device for photographing animation cels in front of revolving miniature sets that created three-dimensional effects.

Soon after, the Fleischers attempted to compete with Walt Disney's successful animated feature, *Snow White and the Seven Dwarfs*. They made two feature-length cartoons. *Gulliver's Travels* and *Mr. Bug Goes to Town*. The financial failure of the latter prompted Paramount pictures to foreclose on the Fleischers' company. Paramount took over the management, renamed the studio (Famous Studio), and fired the Fleischers. The two brothers, who had not been speaking to each other for some time, went their separate ways.

Dave worked at Columbia Pictures cartoon studio and Universal studios. He retired in 1969. Max worked on a series of industrial and educational projects, mechanical inventions, and television animation, but he never achieved his former success. He died in 1972 at the Motion Picture Country Home, where he had been a resident for almost ten years.

—Lauren Rabinovitz

FOREMAN, Carl

Writer and Producer. **Nationality:** American. **Born:** Chicago, Illinois, 13 July 1914. **Education:** Attended Crane College; University of Illinois, Urbana, 1932–33; Northwestern University, Evanston, Illinois, 1935–36; John Marshall Law School, 1936–37. **Military Service:** 1942–45—worked in Frank Capra's Army Documentary Unit. **Family:** Married 1) Estelle Barr; one daughter; 2) Evelyn Smith; one son and one daughter. **Career:** 1937–38—worked as newspaper reporter, and public relations manager for stage personalities; 1938–42—worked in Hollywood as reader and story analyst, gag writer for Bob Hope and Cantor radio programs: jobs with MGM and Columbia; studied screenwriting at the League of American Writers School under Robert Rossen and Dore Schary; 1941—first film as writer, *Spooks Run Wild*; 1946—formed Screen Plays Inc. with Stanley Kramer and George Glass; 1952—investigated by the House Un-American Activities Committee, and blacklisted; moved to Great Britain; used pseudonym for next writing job; 1958—first film as producer, *The Key*; 1963–64—conducted screenwriting class in Israel; 1975—returned to the United States; 1977—formed High Noon

Carl Foreman (right) on the set of *The Victors*

production company: contract with Universal as producer-writer; 1980—contract with Warner Bros.. **Awards:** Writers Guild Robert Meltzer Award for *The Men*, 1950; *High Noon*, 1952; Academy Award for *The Bridge on the River Kwai* (awarded to Pierre Boulle because of the blacklisting), 1957; Writers Guild Laurel Award, 1968, and Valentine Davies Award, 1976; Honorary Companion, Order of the British Empire, 1970. **Member:** 1965–71—Board of Governors, British Film Institute; 1975–83—Advisory Board, American Film Institute. **Died:** Of cancer in Beverly Hills, California, 26 June 1984.

Films as Writer:

1941   *Spooks Run Wild* (Rosen)
1942   *Rhythm Parade* (Bretherton and Gould)
1945   *Dakota* (Kane) (story)
1948   *So This Is New York* (Fleischer); *Let's Go to the Movies* (Gladden) (co-story)
1949   *Champion* (Robson); *Home of the Brave* (Robson); *The Clay Pigeon* (Fleischer)
1950   *The Men* (Zinnemann); *Young Man with a Horn* (*Young Man of Music*) (Curtiz); *Cyrano de Bergerac* (Gordon)
1952   **High Noon** (Zinnemann)
1955   *The Sleeping Tiger* (Losey) (co-sc as Derek Frey)
1957   *The Bridge on the River Kwai* (Lean) (co-sc, uncredited)

Films as Writer and Producer:

1958   *The Key* (Reed)
1961   *The Guns of Navarone* (Thompson)
1963   *The Victors* (+ d)
1969   *Mackenna's Gold* (Thompson) (co-pr)
1972   *Young Winston* (Attenborough)
1978   *Force 10 from Navarone* (Hamilton) (story)
1981   *When Time Ran Out* (*Earth's Final Fury*) (Goldstone)

Films as Producer/Executive Producer:

1959   *The Mouse That Roared* (Arnold)
1966   *Born Free* (Hill)
1969   *Otley* (Clement)
1970   *The Virgin Soldiers* (Dexter)
1971   *Living Free* (Couffer)
1979   *The Golden Gate Murders* (Grauman)

Publications

By FOREMAN: books—

A Cast of Lions, London, 1966.
High Noon (screenplay), in *Film Scripts One*, edited by George P. Garrett, O. B. Harrison, Jr., and Jane Gelfmann, New York, 1971.
Young Winston (script), New York, 1972.

By FOREMAN: articles—

Interview with Penelope Houston and Kenneth Cavander, in *Sight and Sound* (London), Summer 1958.
Sight and Sound (London), Summer 1961.
Journal of the Producers of America, December 1968.
Interview with Bernard Tavernier, in *Positif* (Paris), February 1969.
Films and Filming (London), November 1969.
Film Comment (New York), Winter 1970–71.
Chaplin (Stockholm), no. 7, 1972.
Film Making, March 1972.
Films and Filming (London), August 1972.
Take One (Montreal), May 1973.
American Film (Washington, D.C.), April 1979.

On FOREMAN: articles—

Films and Filming (London), June 1957.
Films and Filming (London), September 1963.
Show (New York), December 1972.
In *American Screenwriters*, edited by Robert E. Morsberger, Stephen O. Lesser, and Randall Clark, Detroit, Michigan, 1984.
Obituary in *Variety* (New York), 4 July 1984.
Obituary in *Revue du Cinéma* (Paris), no. 398, October 1984.
The Annual Obituary 1984, Chicago, 1985.
Hodson, Joel, ''Who Wrote *Lawrence of Arabia*?: Sam Spiegel and David Lean's Denial of Credit to a Blacklisted Screenwriter,'' in *Cineaste* (New York), October 1994.
Foreman, Jonathan, ''Witch-Hunt: Carl Foreman's Experience of McCarthyism and the Hollywood Blacklist,'' in *Index on Censorship*, November-December 1995.
Robb, David, ''Naming the Right Names: Amending the Hollywood Blacklist,'' in *Cineaste* (New York), Spring 1996.
Foreman, Amanda, and Jonathan Foreman, ''Our Dad Was No Commie,'' in *New Statesman*, 26 March 1999.

*   *   *

In 1982, talking about his planned writing and direction of Philip Hallie's *Lest Innocent Blood Be Shed*, Carl Foreman said that the book excited him because it is ''about conquering fear and doing what you have to do.'' Twenty years earlier, Foreman had been drawn into the challenge of making a film about the early life of Winston Churchill because ''the central theme of alienation was . . . one that men and women everywhere would recognize and respond to.''

These themes—the struggle with fear within, maintaining self-respect in the context of the external world, and acknowledging the continuing alienation of the individual—recur in all of the films Foreman wrote and produced after 1949. During the making of *High Noon*, his personal experience and that of the screen character played by Gary Cooper intersected: Foreman, by refusing to ''name names'' before the House Un-American Activities Committee, and Cooper's lawman, by refusing to flee when pursued by a trio of killers—both against the background of apathetic society—similarly found exile. Foreman's exile began in 1952 when he was blacklisted and denied the producer's credit on *High Noon*. By 1958, working with Columbia Pictures in Great Britain, his name could again appear in the credits of the films he wrote. But the shadow of the blacklist remained, and Foreman made most of his subsequent films in Europe. It was not until the day before he died that the Academy of Motion Picture Arts and Sciences officially acknowledged that Foreman (and Michael Wilson) were the Oscar-winning screenwriters for *The Bridge on the River Kwai*.

Born in Illinois to Russian immigrants, Foreman attended Northwestern University and the John Marshall Law School, but left to become a newspaper reporter, public relations man for theater actors, radio writer for Bob Hope and Eddie Cantor, and eventually a writer for marginal films in Hollywood. During the Second World War he was part of Frank Capra's film unit and worked on *Know Your Enemy: Japan* with Joris Ivens. This experience, he said, transformed him. After the war ended Foreman, Stanley Kramer, and George Glass created an independent production company, Screen Plays, Inc., which released impressive low-budget films between 1948 and 1952 (when the company was purchased by Columbia). Foreman wrote *Home of the Brave*, *The Men*, *Champion*, and *High Noon*, for example. With the last film he became a producer so he could protect his creative contributions as a writer. As a writer-producer, he became the principal author of his films while working with experienced filmmakers like Carol Reed, J. Lee Thompson, and Richard Attenborough. Only with *The Victors* in 1963 did he actually direct, as well as write and produce. Acting as a producer only, he had at least two major successes, *The Mouse That Roared* in 1959 and *Born Free* in 1966.

As a writer Foreman took risks, from the flashbacks of *Home of the Brave*, to the "real time" of *High Noon*, to the "interview-camera" of *Young Winston*. Despair surfaced in *The Key*, one of his most affecting films (with major performances by Sophia Loren, William Holden, and Trevor Howard), but the impression most often left by his movies is that courage and conviction do make a difference, and that the nobility of the human spirit can endure.

—Robert A. Haller

FOX, William

Producer. **Nationality:** American. **Born:** Wilhelm Fried in Tulchva, Hungary, 1 January 1879; family moved to New York when Fox was nine months old. **Career:** Peddler in the garment industry; 1904—went into the penny arcade business; bought cinemas in New York; moved into distribution with the Greater New York Film Rental Co.; launched the Fox production studio in New York with the one-reeler *Life's Show Window*; 1912—succeeded in bringing legal action against the Motion Picture Trust for restraint of trade; 1915—merged his production, distribution and exhibition interests; 1917—Fox Studio moved to Los Angeles; 1925—pioneered Movietone Sound for newsreels, bought out Loew's Inc. and its production wing, MGM; bought the Gaumont Theatre Chain in Britain; 1929—taken to court on the grounds that his purchase of Loew's constituted restraint of trade; 1930—seriously injured in car crash; sold his interests in Fox, and retired from film production; 1942–43—imprisoned for bribing a judge in bankruptcy proceedings. **Died:** Of heart disease in New York, 8 May 1952.

Films as Producer:

1915   *A Fool There Was* (Powell)
1917   *The Silent Lie* (Walsh)

1919   *Should a Husband Forgive?* (Walsh)
1920   *The Strongest* (Walsh)
1921   *Beyond Price* (Dawley); *The Big Punch* (Ford); *The Blushing Bride* (Furthman); *Bucking the Line* (Harbaugh); *The Cheater Reformed* (Dunlap); *Children of the Night* (Dillon); *Cinderella of the Hills* (Mitchell); *A Connecticut Yankee at King Arthur's Court* (Flynn); *Desert Blossoms* (Rosson); *Dynamite Allen* (Henderson); *Ever Since Eve* (Mitchell); *Footfalls* (Brabin)
1922   *Arabia* (Reynolds); *Arabian Love* (Storm); *The Boss of Camp Four* (Van Dyke); *The Broadway Peacock* (Brabin); *A California Romance* (Storm); *Calvert's Valley* (Dillon); *Catch My Smoke* (Beaudine); *Chasing the Moon* (Sedgwick); *The Crusader* (Mitchell); *Do and Dare* (Sedgwick); *Elope If You Must* (Wallace); *The Fighting Streak* (Rosson); *A Fool There Was* (Flynn); *For Big Stakes* (Reynolds); *A Friendly Husband* (Blystone); *The Fast Mail* (Durning)
1923   *The Face on the Barroom Floor* (Ford); *The Footlight Ranger* (Dunlap); *Big Dan* (Wellman); *Boston Blackie* (Dunlap); *Brass Commandments* (Reynolds); *Bucking the Barrier* (Campbell); *The Buster* (Campbell); *Cameo Kirby* (Ford); *Cupid's Fireman* (Wellman); *The Custard Cup* (Brenon); *Does It Pay?* (Horan); *The Eleventh Hour* (Durning); *Eyes of the Forest* (Hillyer)
1924   *The Arizona Express* (Buckingham); *The Brass Bowl* (Storm); *Circus Cowboy* (Wellman); *Curlytop* (Elvey); *Dante's Inferno* (Otto); *Darwin Was Right* (Seiler); *Daughters of the Night* (Clifton); *The Deadwood Coach* (Reynolds); *The Desert Outlaw* (Mortimer); *Flames of Desire* (Clift); *The Folly of Vanity* (Elvey)
1925   *The Road to Glory* (Hawks); *East Lynne* (Flynn); *The Arizona Romeo* (Mortimer); *The Duncers* (Flynn); *The Desert's Price* (Van Dyke); *Dick Turpin* (Blystone); *Durand of the Badlands* (Reynolds); *The Everlasting Whisper* (Blystone); *Every Man's Wife* (Elvey); *The Fighting Heart* (Ford); *The Fool* (Millarde)
1926   *Bertha, the Sewing Machine Girl* (Cummings); *Black Paradise* (Neill); *The Blue Eagle* (Ford); *The Canyon of Light* (Stoloff); *The City* (Neill); *The Country Beyond* (Cummings); *The Cowboy and the Countess* (Neill); *Desert Valley* (Dunlap); *The Dixie Merchant* (Borzage); *The Silver Treasure* (Lee); *Early to Wed* (Borzage); *The Family Upstairs* (Blystone); *Fig Leaves* (Hawks); *The Fighting Buckaroo* (Neill); *The First Year* (Borzage); *The Flying Horseman* (Dull)
1927   *The Arizona Wildcat* (Neill); *The Auctioneer* (Green); *Black Jack* (Dull); *Blood Will Tell* (Flynn); *The Broncho Twister* (Dull); *Chain Lightning* (Hillyer); *The Circus Ace* (Stoloff); *Colleen* (O'Connor); *Come to My House* (Green); *The Cradle Snatchers* (Hawks); *East Side, West Side* (Dwan); *The Gay Retreat* (Stoloff)
1928   *Fazil* (Hawks); *Blindfold* (Klein); *The Branded Sombrero* (Hillyer); *Chicken à la King* (Lehrman); *The Cowboy Kid* (Carruth); *Daredevil's Reward* (Forde); *Don't Marry* (Tinling); *Dressed to Kill* (Cummings); *Dry Martini* (D'Arrast); *The Farmer's Daughter* (Taurog); *Fleetwing* (Hillyer); *Four Sons* (Ford); *The Gateway of the Moon* (Wray)
1929   *The River* (Borzage); *Four Devils* (Murnau); *Behind That Curtain* (Cummings); *Big Time* (K. Hawks); *Black Magic*

William Fox (left)

(Seitz); *The Black Watch* (Ford); *Blue Skies* (Werker); *Cameo Kirby* (Cummings); *Captain Lash* (Blystone); *Chasing Through Europe* (Butler); *Christina* (Howard); *The Cock-Eyed World* (Walsh); *The Exalted Flapper* (Tinling); *The Far Call* (Dwan); *Frozen Justice* (Dwan); *Fugitives* (Beaudine); *Fox Movietone Follies of 1929* (Butler)

1930   *The Arizona Kid* (Santell); *The Big Party* (Blystone); *Born Reckless* (Ford); *Cheer Up and Smile* (Lanfield); *City Girl* (Murnau); *Common Clay* (Fleming); *Crazy That Way* (MacFadden); *A Devil with Women* (Cummings); *Double Cross Roads* (Werker); *Fox Movietone Follies of 1930* (Stoloff)

Publications

On FOX: books—

Sinclair, Upton, *Upton Sinclair Presents William Fox*, 1933.
Allvine, Glendon, *The Greatest Fox of Them All*, 1969.

On FOX: articles—

Obituary in *Motion Picture Herald* (Hollywood), vol. 187, no.7, 17 May 1952.
Cinématographe (Paris), no. 100, May 1984.
Classic Images (Muscatine, Iowa), no. 111, September 1984.
Zierold, Norman, "The Film's Forgotten Man: William Fox," in *The First Tycoons*, edited by Richard Dyer MacCann, London, 1987.
Woods, R., "*Over the Hill* Put William Fox over the Top," in *Classic Images* (Muscatine, Iowa), no. 222, December 1993.

*   *   *

William Fox was one of the true pioneers of the American motion picture industry. From his base in New York City, he established a chain of early movie and vaudeville theaters. He stubbornly defied the takeover attempts of the Motion Picture Patents Company. Thereafter he prospered. During the 1910s Fox set up a film production unit to feed his growing number of theaters, eventually incorporating as the Fox Film Corporation.

In 1914 the Fox Company made its first film in Los Angeles; three years later it set up a permanent operation in California, eventually building a studio lot complex located at Sunset and Western. By 1920 the Fox company had offices for distribution throughout the world, and an ever expanding chain of movie palaces. Indeed, in the mid-1920s, Fox personally sought to create a set of the greatest movie palaces in the world, each bearing his name. Soon thousands each day sought movie fun at several thousand-seat Fox theaters in Brooklyn, Detroit, St. Louis, Philadelphia, San Francisco, and Atlanta. By the late 1920s, the Fox theater chain had movie houses in almost every major town west of the Rocky mountains.

But it was the coming of sound that established Fox as a major player in the American motion picture business. During the early days of talkies, from 1925 through 1928, William Fox and his assistants adapted a version of AT&T's pioneering technology for recording and playing back sound-on-film. Others continued to use sound-on-disc, but by the early 1930s, the sound-on-film technology had become the world film industry standard.

In 1926, Fox signed to help pioneer sound because he felt such a technical change might improve his company's newsreel business. Like the Warner Bros., at first Fox did not believe in a future for feature-length talkies, but reasoned that the public certainly might prefer newsreels with sound. Fox never made a better business decision. Skillfully Fox Film engineers labored to integrate sound-on-film with accepted silent newsreel techniques. On the final day of April 1927, five months before the opening of *The Jazz Singer*, Fox Film presented its first sound newsreel at the ornate, 5000 seat Roxy Theater located at the crossroads of the entertainment world in Times Square. The process of innovation was off and running.

Less than a month later Fox stumbled across the publicity coup of the decade when he was able to tender the only footage *with sound* of the takeoff and triumphant return of aviator Charles Lindbergh. Fox newsreel cameramen soon travelled all over the globe in search of stories "with a voice." Theater owners queued up to wire their houses simply to be able to show Fox Movietone newsreels. To movie fans of the day Fox Movietone News offered as much an attraction as any feature-length talkie.

But the coming of the Great Depression did not prove kind to the fortunes of Fox. In 1925 Fox had gone so far as to borrow millions to temporarily take over Loew's, Inc., and its noted filmmaking unit, Metro-Goldwyn-Mayer. But this investment, coupled with the existing mortgages on the Fox movie palaces and the financing he took on to innovate sound-on-film meant William Fox and his corporation owed millions. With the Depression came a decline in movie attendance, and Fox was not able to pay his loans back. Soon he lost his company; it was merged with 20th Century Pictures in 1935. Fox thereafter attempted to make a grand return to the film business, but a conviction on court tampering charges, time in jail, and advancing age prevented him from ever doing so.

—Douglas Gomery

FRADETAL, Marcel

Cinematographer. **Nationality:** French. **Born:** Villefranche-sur-Saone, 1908. **Military Service:** 1928–30. **Career:** 1928—grip, Billancourt Studios; 1931–39—assistant cameraman, then cinematographer after

World War II; 1948—first of many films for Georges Franju, *Le Sang des bêtes*; 1952—directed the film *Hommes d'aujourd'hui*; also worked for TV, including the series *Villages de Paris*, 1962, *Féminin singulier*, 1964–65, and others.

Films as Assistant Cameraman:

1931　*La Vagabonde* (Bussi); *Le Train des suicides* (Gréville); *Chassé-croisé* (H. Diamant-Berger); *Tout s'arrange* (H. Diamant-Berger); *Ma tante d'Honfleur* (M. Diamant-Berger); *Prisonnier de mon coeur* (Tarride); *Le Coeur de Paris* (Benoît-Lévy and Epstein)

1932　*Vampyr* (*The Dream of Allan Gray*) (Dreyer); *L'Enfant du miracle* (M. Diamant-Berger); *La Bonne Aventure* (H. Diamant-Berger); *Clair de lune* (H. Diamant-Berger); *Les Trois Mousquetaires* (H. Diamant-Berger—2 parts); *L'Homme à la barbiche* (Valray—short)

1933　*La Maternelle* (Benoît-Lévy and Epstein); *Plein aux as* (Houssein); *Miquette et sa mère* (H. and M. Diamant-Berger)

1934　*Cartouche* (Blondeau); *Jeanne* (Marret); *Comédie Française* (Perret—short); *Les Deux Couverts* (Perret—short); *Trois cents à l'heure* (Rozier)

1935　*Fanfare d'amour* (Pottier); *Paris, mes amours* (Blondeau); *Le Gagnant* (Y. Allégret—short)

1936　*Arsène Lupin, détective* (H. Diamant-Berger); *Vous n'avez rien à déclarer?* (Joannon); *Les Hommes nouveaux* (L'Herbier)

1937　*Double crime sur la ligne Maginot* (Gandera); *L'Affaire Lafarge* (Chenal); *L'Alibi* (Chenal); *La Fessée* (Caron)

1938　*Tempête sur l'Asie* (Oswald); *Ultimatum* (Wiene and Siodmak); *Gibraltar* (Ozep); *Conflit* (Moguy)

1939　*Entente cordiale* (L'Herbier); *Pièges* (*Personal Column*) (Siodmak)

1947　*Farrebique* (Rouquier) (+ uncredited ph)

Films as Cinematographer:

(shorts)

1946　*L'Oeuvre scientifique de Pasteur* (*Pasteur*) (Rouquier and Painlevé); *Le Charcutier de Machonville* (Yvernel); *Jeux d'enfants* (Painlevé)

1947　*La Caravane de la lumière* (Colson-Malleville); *Les Doigts de lumière* (Colson-Malleville); *Le Oued, la ville aux mille coupoles* (Colson-Malleville) (co)

1948　**Le Sang des bêtes** (Franju); *Le Chaudronnier* (Rouquier)

1950　*Champions juniors* (Blondy) (co); *Le Sel de la terre* (Rouquier); *En passant par la Lorraine* (Franju); *A Votre santé!* (Thévenard) (co); *Le Barrage du Chatelot* (Colson-Malleville) (co)

1951　*Une Année se meurt* (Loew); *Le Fleuve: Le Tarn* (*Les Eaux vives*) (Mitry); *Au pays des grandes causses* (Mitry); *Hôtel des Invalides* (Franju); *Renaissance du Havre* (Camus)

1952　*L'Homme en marche* (Lallier and Rivoalen); *Aux confins d'une ville* (Loew); *Sécurité et hygiène du travail dans la fabrication du sucre et de l'alcool* (Dumas); *Le Lycée sur la colline* (Rouquier)

1953 *Recontres sur le Rhin* (Bonnière); *Monsieur et Madame Curie*
      (Franju)
1954 *La Moisson sera belle* (Villet)
1956 *Le Théâtre National Populaire* (Franju); *Sur le pont d'Avignon*
      (Franju)
1957 *Notre Dame, cathédrale de Paris* (Franju); *Le Bel Indifférent*
      (Demy); *Celle qui n'était plus* (Gérard)
1958 *Le Musée Grévin* (Masson and Demy)
1959 *Cités du ciel* (See)
1960 *Sahara, au IV* (Gérard); *Le Huitième Jour* (Hanoun); *Pleins*
      feux sur l'assassin (Franju)
1961 *La Chèvre* (Grospierre); *Le Petit Chasseur* (Grospierre);
      Jardins de Paris (de Vaucorbeil)
1963 *Voici des fleurs* (de Vaucorbeil) (co); *Houat* (Magrou); *La*
      Machine à parler d'amour (Japrisot)
1967 *Les Yeux d'elstir* (Magrou)
1971 *Jusques au feu exclusivement* (Ginsey)

(features)

1949 *Faits divers à Paris* (Kirsanoff)
1961 *Vacances en enfer* (Kerchbron); *Le Temps du ghetto* (Rossif)
1963 *Judex* (Franju)
1964 *Thomas l'imposteur* (*Thomas the Imposter*) (Franju)
1970 *La Faute de l'Abbé Mouret* (Franju)
1971 *La Ligne d'ombre* (Franju)
1974 *Penelope, folle de son corps* (Magrou)

Film as Director:

1952 *Hommes d'aujourd'hui*

*   *   *

Although Marcel Fradetal is most readily identified with the director Georges Franju, his career has evolved through association with several filmmakers. In the 1930s he worked under various leading cameramen, notably Rudolph Maté on Dreyer's atmospheric *Vampyr*, Maurice Desfassieux on Henri Diamant-Berger's *Les Trois Mousquetaires*, and Ted Pahle on L'Herbier's *Entente cordiale*. Their influence is discernible in his work.

With the postwar interest in documentary film, often promoted by government agencies, Fradetal was engaged by diverse directors. Initially hired by Georges Rouquier and Jean Painlevé for *L'Oeuvre scientifique de Pasteur*, he then contributed to Rouquier's celebrated filming of the farming year in *Farrebique*, his account of the coppersmith's trade in *Le Chaudronnier*, and his documentary about irrigation schemes in the Camargue, *Le Sel de la terre*. Blending lyricism with factual detail Fradetal's camera delicately captures the still unviolated peace and natural beauty of the marshes at daybreak. He worked not only for established directors such as Painlevé, Perret, and Kirsanoff but also for relative newcomers. For the film critic Jacques Loew he made the reflective *Une Année se meurt*; for the film theorist Jean Mitry the nature studies *Le Fleuve: Le Tarn* and *Au pays des grandes causses*; for Jacques Demy *Le Bel Indifférent*, adapted from a Cocteau sketch; and for Marcel Camus, his first film, *Renaissance du Havre*, depicting the reconstruction of the war-damaged channel port. Travelogues also formed part of Fradetal's repertoire

with films for Marie-Anne Colson-Malleville, such as *Le Oued, la ville aux mille coupoles*. Both the range of subjects treated—science, sport, nature, history, travel—together with his widespread collaboration, confirms Fradetal's reputation in the documentary field. The 1960s brought features and television documentaries. For Marcel Hanoun he filmed *Le Huitième Jour*, for Frédéric Rossif the moving account of a doomed Warsaw ghetto, *Le Temps du ghetto*, and after several successful television documentaries for Jean Kerchbron, his feature *Vacances en enfer*.

It is essentially his 30-year collaboration with Georges Franju, however, that has cemented Fradetal's reputation. The association began in the 1940s with *Le Sang des bêtes*, and a series of documentaries, features, and eventually television films followed. Franju initially hired Fradetal because of his work with Maté whose insistence on lighting and composition corresponded to Franju's own preoccupations.

Le Sang des bêtes opens gently with images of the Parisian outskirts and a surreal wasteland in which incongruous objects are isolated by the camera: an elegant table, an ornate lamp swinging from a tree, a Renoir painting, all trappings of civilization, but, divorced from their usual contexts, they invite reappraisal. Inside the abattoir the camera calmly records every aspect of the butcher's trade unsensationally moving between medium shot and close-up to note the details. This apparently innocent eye is, however, deceptive. Startling images imprint themselves. Gray walls, an indifferent executioner, a white horse slaughtered, decapitated sheep with stumpy legs still kicking, an atmosphere thick and steamy with hot blood. Death and mutilation are again tellingly revealed in *Hôtel des Invalides*. The dark, cold metal of weaponry, the stunted trees and limbless victims of war expose the painful realities of the heroic ideal. Close-ups emphasize the ugly consequences of violence, oppressive lighting reinforces the far from triumphant mood, and the slow tracking shot reviewing the representation of heroically charging cavalrymen completes the subversive irony of the visual composition. Traditional tourist images are undermined in *Sur le pont d'Avignon* and *Notre Dame, cathédrale de Paris*, for which both color and CinemaScope were used. Postcard views of Avignon emphasize the tourist's limited perspective of the town while in *Notre Dame* aesthetic responses and religious indifference are juxtaposed through the beauty of the stained glass and rows of empty cathedral chairs. Similarly arresting images punctuate *En passant par la Lorraine* where the dark sky is lit by white hot metal pouring from enormous furnaces, set against nature in rich cornfields.

Fradetal's camerawork is equally vital to Franju's features. In *Pleins feux sur l'assassin* an eerie son-et-lumière sequence at a castle is created, and in contrast an accelerated funeral, à la Clair, irreverently conveys the joy of the dead man's beneficiaries. In *Judex*, a homage to Feuillade and the early serial, Fradetal brilliantly reproduces the orthochromatic tonal qualities of the silent cinema to create a visual symphony of light and dark effects as good and evil join battle. The screen version of Cocteau's *Thomas l'imposteur* exposing the heroic myth renders concrete the writer's imagery, such as the horse with its mane ablaze, while beautifully composed luminous shots of Belgian beaches with sea mists rolling across the trenches combine to produce a hauntingly atmospheric film about the realities and the unreality of war. For Zola's *La Faute de l'Abbé Mouret*, Fradetal achieved powerful, almost surrealist images such as the statue of the Virgin appearing to rise spontaneously from a packing case, but the essentially poetic quality of Zola's work is often disappointingly labored in the visual transcription.

The quality of Fradetal's camerawork ultimately resides in his experienced, sensitive, and appropriate response to his material. Where his camera is required to observe unobtrusively it does so, and where images of pristine clarity are expected then Fradetal provides them. Nevertheless, where a synthesizing image, or a telling close-up, or an atmospheric composition, or a specifically paced tracking shot is needed, he imaginatively satisfies his director's wishes. A self-effacing professional, Fradetal has left his mark both on fictional as well as documentary cinema.

—R. F. Cousins

FRAKER, William A.

Cinematographer and Director. **Nationality:** American. **Born:** Los Angeles, California, 29 September 1923. **Education:** Attended the University of Southern California Cinema School, Los Angeles, B.A. **Military Service:** Coast Guard during World War II. **Family:** Married Denise (Fraker), children, including the photographer Bill Fraker Jr. **Career:** TV work from mid-1950s—commercials, inserts, loader on *Lone Ranger* series, then assistant and cameraman for *The Adventures of Ozzie and Harriet* series, seven years; 1961—first film as cinematographer, *Forbid Them Not*; 1970—first film as director, *Monte Walsh*; director of TV series *Wiseguy*, 1987–1990, and *B.L. Stryker: The Dancer's Touch*, 1989; past president, American Society

William A. Fraker

of Cinematographers. **Address:** The Gersh Agency, Inc., 232 North Canon Drive, Beverly Hills, CA 90210, U.S.A.

Films as Cameraman:

1964   *Father Goose* (Nelson); *The Wild Seed* (*Fargo*) (Hutton)
1965   *Morituri* (*The Saboteur Code Name "Morituri"*) (Wicki)
1966   *The Professionals* (R. Brooks)

Films as Cinematographer:

1959   *The Young Guns* (Band) (asst)
1961   *Forbid Them Not* (Kimble) (+ co-pr)
1967   *Games* (Harrington); *The Fox* (Rydell); *Fade-In* (Taylor); *The President's Analyst* (Flicker)
1968   *Rosemary's Baby* (Polanski); *Bullitt* (Yates)
1969   *Paint Your Wagon* (Logan)
1970   *Dusty and Sweets McGee* (Mutrux) (+ ro)
1973   *The Day of the Dolphin* (Nichols)
1974   *Rancho Deluxe* (Perry)
1975   *Aloha Bobby and Rose* (Mutrux); *Coonskin* (Bakshi) (co); **One Flew over the Cuckoo's Nest** (Forman) (co); *The Killer inside Me* (Kennedy)
1976   *Lipstick* (L. Johnson) (co); *Gator* (B. Reynolds)
1977   *Exorcist II: The Heretic* (Boorman); *Looking for Mr. Goodbar* (R. Brooks); **Close Encounters of the Third Kind** (Spielberg) (co); *American Hot Wax* (Mutrux)
1978   *Heaven Can Wait* (Beatty and Henry)
1979   *Old Boyfriends* (Tewkesbury); *1941* (Spielberg)
1980   *Divine Madness* (Ritchie); *Hollywood Knights* (Mutrux)
1982   *Sharkey's Machine* (B. Reynolds); *The Best Little Whorehouse in Texas* (Higgins)
1983   *WarGames* (Badham)
1984   *Protocol* (Ross); *Irreconcilable Differences* (Shyer)
1985   *Murphy's Romance* (Ritt); *Fever Pitch* (R. Brooks)
1986   *SpaceCamp* (Winer)
1987   *Baby Boom* (Shyer); *Burglar* (Ogorodnikov)
1989   *Chances Are* (Ardolino); *An Innocent Man* (Yates)
1990   *The Freshman* (Andrew Bergman)
1992   *Memoirs of an Invisible Man* (Carpenter); *Honeymoon in Vegas* (Andrew Bergman)
1993   *Tombstone* (Cosmatos); *There Goes My Baby* (Mutrux)
1994   *Street Fighter* (De Souza)
1995   *Death in Small Doses* (Locke—for TV); *Father of the Bride Part II* (Shyer)
1996   *The Island of Dr. Moreau* (Frankenheimer)
1997   *Vegas Vacation* (Kessler)
2000   *Town and Country* (Chelsom); *Rules of Engagement* (Friedkin)

Films as Director:

1970   *Monte Walsh*
1971   *A Reflection of Fear*
1981   *The Legend of the Lone Ranger*
1990   *The Flash* (series for TV)

Publications

By FRAKER: articles—

American Cinematographer (Hollywood), June 1977.
On *Exorcist II: The Heretic* in *American Cinematographer* (Hollywood), August 1977.
On *1941* in *American Cinematographer* (Hollywood), December 1979.
Filmmakers Monthly (Ward Hill, Massachusetts), December 1979.
Filmmakers Monthly (Ward Hill, Massachusetts), October 1980.
On *The Legend of the Lone Ranger* in *American Cinematographer* (Hollywood), July 1981.
American Cinematographer (Hollywood), September 1982.
In *Masters of Light: Conversations with Contemporary Cinematographers*, by Dennis Schaefer and Larry Salvato, Berkeley, California, 1984.
American Cinematographer (Hollywood), April 1984.
American Cinematographer (Hollywood), November 1985.
American Cinematographer (Hollywood), November 1987.
American Cinematographer (Hollywood), April 1989.

On FRAKER: articles—

Focus on Film (London), Winter 1970.
American Cinematographer (Hollywood), May 1978.
McGilligan, Patrick, in *American Film* (Washington, D.C.), April 1979.
American Cinematographer (Hollywood), May 1979.
Williams, A. L., in *American Cinematographer* (Hollywood), July 1980.
McCarthy, T., in *Film Comment* (New York), March/April 1984.
Turner, George, on *WarGames* in *American Cinematographer* (Hollywood), April 1984.
Block, Bruce A., in *American Cinematographer* (Hollywood), October 1984.
American Cinematographer (Hollywood), April 1986.
American Cinematographer (Hollywood), November 1986.
American Cinematographer (Hollywood), November 1991.
Skrien (Amsterdam), June/July 1993.
American Cinematographer (Hollywood), September 1996.

*   *   *

By 1970 most of the older Hollywood cinematographers, those who established their careers during the height of the studio system, had retired, and a new, younger group seemed to fill the ranks almost immediately. Some of these new craftsmen had gone to film school, while many had gained experience and honed their craft as camera operators and directors of photography for television series. Among this new cadre were cinematographers now considered to be the best in Hollywood—Vilmos Zsigmond, Laszlo Kovacs, Nestor Almendros, and William A. Fraker. According to Todd McCarthy, Fraker was in many ways "the Dean" of these so-called New Breed cinematographers.

Fraker came from a family of photographers. His grandfather worked in photography and his father had been a noted Hollywood studio photographer during the 1920s. After World War II, Fraker's grandmother encouraged him to pursue a profession in the photographic arts, so Fraker entered the University of Southern California's School of Cinema on the G.I. Bill. After paying his dues as a camera operator, camera assistant, and director of photography on various

television series, Fraker worked as a cinematographer on his first feature film in 1967. *Games*, an offbeat drama filmed in less than a month, received some attention at the time for Fraker's interesting photography.

Since then he has worked on many major American films for a number of prominent directors, including Roman Polanski's *Rosemary's Baby*, Peter Yates's *Bullitt*, Milos Forman's *One Flew over the Cuckoo's Nest*, Richard Brooks's *Looking for Mr. Goodbar*, and Steven Spielberg's *Close Encounters of the Third Kind* and *1941*. Though he has never won an Academy Award, Fraker has been nominated several times, including twice for *1941*—for both cinematography and special effects, the only time in the history of the Academy that this has occurred.

Though Fraker's film career has consisted mostly of big-budget, mainstream Hollywood features (no experimental films, documentaries, or exploitation films, and very few low-budget, "small" features), he has worked in a number of genres. His filmography is fairly diverse in that respect, including everything from the musical Western *Paint Your Wagon* to the horror film *Exorcist II: The Heretic* to the romantic feminist comedy *Baby Boom*. Discerning a personal style or specialty is difficult in Fraker's work because he believes that the cinematographer should make every film look different. The look of the film should be dictated by various aspects of the film itself, according to Fraker, who stated, "I don't agree with a cinematographer putting his stamp on a picture." There are many variables to creating that "look," including the location, the sets, the actors, and, most importantly, the director's interpretation of the material. Fraker's approach to cinematography is to understand exactly what a director wants in terms of the visual interpretation of a scene and to use all of his experience and knowledge of lighting, cameras, lenses, cranes, and dollies to make real that vision.

Interestingly, Fraker has directed three films himself. The opportunity to direct arose from his relationship with Lee Marvin on the set of *Paint Your Wagon*. Marvin requested that Fraker direct his next film, *Monte Walsh*, a melancholy and gritty Western that emphasized the drudgery and hardships of Western life. Fraker also directed *A Reflection of Fear*, a moody but stylized murder mystery, and the financial and critical disaster *The Legend of the Lone Ranger*. According to Fraker, he finds directing an interesting challenge but only "an occasional exhilarating experience," preferring to remain one of Hollywood's prominent cinematographers.

In 1993 Fraker appeared before the camera for a 90-minute American Film Institute documentary, *Visions of Light: The Art of Cinematography*. Along with some of the other great cinematographers of today, Fraker outlines his overall approach to his craft, and illuminates some of his specific technical choices, most notably on *Rosemary's Baby*.

—Susan Doll, updated by Denise Delorey

FRANCIS, Freddie

Cinematographer and Director. **Nationality:** British. **Born:** Islington, London, 22 December 1917. **Education:** Studied engineering. **Military Service:** British Army, with duties for Army Kinetograph Services, 1939–46. **Family:** Married Pamela Mann, son: the production manager Kevin Francis. **Career:** 1936—joined Gaumont-British

Freddie Francis (left)

as clapper loader; then camera assistant at British and Dominions and at Pinewood; after military service, cameraman for London Films; 1956—first film as cinematographer, *A Hill in Korea*; 1962—first film as director, *Two and Two Make Six*; also TV director. **Awards:** Academy Award, for *Sons and Lovers*, 1960, and *Glory*, 1989. **Agent:** CCA Personal Management Ltd., 4 Court Lodge, 48 Sloane Square, London SW1W 8AT, England.

Films as Cameraman:

1947 *The Macomber Affair* (Z. Korda) (2nd unit); *Mine Own Executioner* (Kimmins); *Night Beat* (Huth)
1948 *The Small Back Room* (Powell and Pressburger)
1949 *Golden Salamander* (Neame)
1950 *Gone to Earth* (*The Wild Heart*) (Powell and Pressburger); *The Elusive Pimpernel* (Powell and Pressburger)
1951 *The Tales of Hoffman* (Powell and Pressburger); *Outcast of the Islands* (Reed); *Angels One Five* (O'Ferrall)
1952 *24 Hours of a Woman's Life* (*Affair in Monte Carlo*) (Saville); *Moulin Rouge* (Huston)

1953 *Rough Shoot* (*Shoot First*) (Parrish); *Twice upon a Time* (Pressburger); *Beat the Devil* (Huston)
1954 *Monsieur Ripois* (*Knave of Hearts*; *Lovers*; *Happy Lovers*) (Clément); *Beau Brummell* (Bernhardt)
1955 *The Sorcerer's Apprentice* (Powell—short)
1956 *Moby Dick* (Huston)

Films as Cinematographer:

1956 *A Hill in Korea* (*Hell in Korea*) (Aymes); *Moby Dick* (2nd unit); *Dry Rot* (Elbey) (2nd unit)
1957 *Time without Pity* (*No Time for Pity*) (Losey); *The Scamp* (Rilla)
1958 *Next to No Time!* (Cornelius); *Virgin Island* (Jackson); ***Room at the Top*** (Clayton)
1959 *Battle of the Sexes* (Crichton)
1960 *Never Take Sweets from a Stranger* (*Never Take Candy from a Stranger*) (Frankel); *Sons and Lovers* (Cardiff); ***Saturday Night and Sunday Morning*** (Reisz)
1961 *The Innocents* (Clayton); *The Horsemasters* (Fairchild)

1964   *Night Must Fall* (Reisz)
1980   *The Elephant Man* (Lynch)
1981   *The French Lieutenant's Woman* (Reisz)
1984   *Memed My Hawk* (Ustinov); *The Jigsaw Man* (Young);
          Dune (Lynch)
1985   *Code Name: Emerald* (Sanger)
1988   *Clara's Heart* (Mulligan)
1989   *Brenda Starr* (Miller) (co); *Dark Tower* (Barnett); *Glory*
          (Zwick); *Her Alibi* (Beresford)
1991   *Cape Fear* (Scorsese); *The Man in the Moon* (Mulligan)
1992   *School Ties* (Mandel)
1993   *A Life in the Theater* (Mosher—for TV)
1994   *Princess Caraboo* (Austin)
1995   *Rainbow* (Hoskins)
1999   *The Straight Story* (Lynch)

Films as Director:

1962   *Two and Two Make Six* (*A Change of Heart*; *The Girl
          Swappers*); *Vengeance* (*The Brain*); *Paranoiac*
1963   *Nightmare*
1964   *The Evil of Frankenstein*; *Hysteria*; *Traitor's Gate*
1965   *The Skull*; *The Psychopath*; *Dr. Terror's House of Horrors*
1966   *The Deadly Bees*
1967   *They Came from beyond Space*; *Torture Garden*
1968   *Dracula Has Risen from the Grave*; *The Intrepid Mr.
          Twigg* (short)
1969   *Mumsy, Nanny, Sonny, and Girly*
1970   *Trog*
1971   *Gebissen wird nur Nachts—Happening der Vampire* (*Vam-
          pire Happening*)
1972   *Tales from the Crypt*; *The Creeping Flesh*
1973   *Tales that Witness Madness*; *Craze*
1974   *Son of Dracula* (*Count Downe*)
1975   *The Ghoul*; *Legend of the Werewolf*
1977   *Golden Rendezvous* (co)
1985   *The Doctor and the Devils*
1987   *Dark Tower*
1989   *Tales from the Crypt* (series for TV)

Publications

By FRANCIS: articles—

Film (Hanover, New Hampshire), August 1968.
Photon (New York), no. 22, 1972.
Little Shoppe of Horrors (Waterloo, Iowa), March 1973.
Bizarre (Asheville, North Carolina), August 1974.
Filmmaking, August and September 1978.
On *The Elephant Man* in *Millimeter* (New York), March 1981.
Eyepiece (London), July/August 1982.
Classic Images (Muscatine), October 1992.

Sight & Sound (London), November 1992.
Sight & Sound (London), September 1994.

On FRANCIS: books—

Dixon, Wheeler Winston, *The Films of Freddie Francis*, Metuchen,
    New Jersey, 1991.
McCarty, John, *The Fearmakers: The Screen's Directorial Masters
    of Suspense and Terror*, New York, 1994.
Jensen, Paul. M., *The Men Who Made the Monsters*, New York, 1996.

On FRANCIS: articles—

Filmmaking, September 1971.
Monthly Film Bulletin (London), June 1973.
Nolan J. E., in *Films in Review* (New York), August/September 1974.
Film Review (London), August 1975.
Mandell, P., on *Dune* in *American Cinematographer* (Hollywood),
    December 1984.
Gentry, R., in *Millimeter* (New York), February 1985.
On *Glory* in *American Cinematographer* (Hollywood), Novem-
    ber 1990.
Revue du Cinema, no. 484, July/August 1992.
Kelleher, E., "Double Oscar Winner Francis Reflects on His Two-
    Hatted Career," in *Film Journal* (New York), September 1992.
Iles, T., "Amorphic Cinematography Seminar," in *Image Technol-
    ogy* (London), July 1997.
Bradley, Matthew R., "The Good and Evil of Freddie Francis," in
    Filmfax (Evanston, Illinois), February-March 2000.

                              *   *   *

One of the world's most accomplished cameramen, as well as an excellent director of gothic films, Freddie Francis brings a camera-man's eye and his own uniquely despairing sensibility to his numer-ous cinematographic assignments, and to the many horror films he has directed in his long career.

Francis started at 17 as a clapper boy, rapidly advancing to the position of camera assistant. After service during World War II in The Royal Army Kinematographic Unit, he returned to the industry as a full-fledged camera operator, working on a number of films for maverick British director Michael Powell (*The Small Back Room*, *The Tales of Hoffman*) and maverick American director John Huston, including *Moulin Rouge*, *Moby Dick*, and *Beat the Devil*. Francis says his experiences on *Moby Dick* were what finally convinced him that he had served a long enough apprenticeship as a camera operator. "We [Huston and I] got on very well — so well he wouldn't let me advance." Francis was also somewhat miffed that he did not receive the full credit due him on the film, for in addition to doing all the "live" second-unit work for *Moby Dick* (which included shooting Portuguese fisherman in vulnerable longboats hunting whales with hand-hurled harpoons), he also supervised the special effects se-quences in the studio; these involved constructing twenty mini-Mobys built to crunch whaling boat floors as well as bleed and roll dead out in the studio tank doubling for the ocean. "When I finished that film I said, 'Right, that's enough; now I want to do my own film as Director of Photography.'" That film was *A Hill in Korea*, a war picture with a cast that included Robert Shaw, Stephen Boyd, and a young Michael Caine. "The cast was fantastic," he says. "They were all yet unknown. It would be hard to collect such an excellent group of players today."

However, when *A Hill in Korea* came out, the Suez crisis was very much in the news and war seemed imminent; because of this the film did relatively little business at the box office. But, as Francis noted, his work as director of photography got noticed and landed him work on a number of important British films of the late 1950s and early 1960s. "I became a sort of darling of the British New Wave," he says. During this period, he shot *Room at the Top*, *Saturday Night and Sunday Morning*, and *The Innocents*, establishing himself as one of the most active and innovative British cinematographers. In 1960 he won an Academy Award for his brilliant black-and-white work on *Sons and Lovers*. It was during this period that the critic Pauline Kael wrote, "I don't know where this photographer Freddie Francis sprang from. You may recall that in the last year, just about every time a British movie is something to look at, it turns out to be his—in each case with a different director." Although he received many offers to direct because of his enormous success, he turned them all down because "I was quite happy at that point photographing other people's films—except that now and then there were some unexciting ones. I thought 'If I direct, then I can't stand around criticizing other people's work. If it's not exciting, it'll be *my* fault.'"

Finally, in 1962, he took the plunge. He credits Michael Powell and John Huston as influencing his approach to directing. "They were both great adventurers, and once they started a film, they went off into the great unknown and enjoyed everything about it," he says. "They had a cavalier attitude toward the whole thing. [Working with them] you never knew what was going to happen next. It was always a great adventure." He directed some sequences added to the science-fiction thriller *The Day of the Triffids* for which he received no screen credit, then made his official bow as a director with the indifferent *Two and Two Make Six*. "I decided to do a film with a script I didn't much like. Stupidly, I thought I could make a good movie anyway. But, of course, you can't. The result was slightly disastrous. So it seemed to me I had to follow that film with a lot of other films very quickly, simply to establish myself as a *director*, rather than a Director of Photography." *The Brain*, a British-German co-production, followed shortly thereafter (the film is yet another version of *Donovan's Brain*, which nevertheless strongly benefits from an excellent performance by Bernard Lee and Francis's atmospheric set-ups), and then Francis received an invitation which would forever change the course of his career. "Tony Hinds, who ran a studio called Hammer Films at that time, is a very close friend of mine, and he was going to do a psychological horror film called *Paranoiac*, starring a young Oliver Reed. So I did the film, and I loved making it. It was a very happy experience. And then that finished, and Tony said 'Do another, and do another,' and the next thing I knew, I was typecast. I had achieved my goal—I had directed a lot of films in a short period of time—but I was embroiled in *that* genre—the *horror* genre." By his own admission, Francis has no particular affinity for gothic cinema, unlike Hammer's house director, the gifted Terence Fisher, and he soon found he disliked being forced to work on horror films and nothing else.

Not that his films were aesthetically unsuccessful. *Paranoiac*, *Nightmare*, *Dr. Terror's House of Horrors*, *The Skull*, and perhaps *Torture Garden* are all accomplished pieces of work, which Francis feels "visually transcended" their source material. In many ways, he is absolutely right. Francis's horror films have been discussed at length in numerous books and magazines, the most incisive of which is undoubtedly David Pirie's excellent book, *Heritage of Horror*. But Francis himself is reluctant to make claims for his work, or even discuss it at length. By the time of *Trog*, probably Francis's worst film as director, he had clearly given up. What marked his early work was a fluid, continually dollying camera, deep compositions, and effective, low-keyed lighting. By *Trog*, everything is flatly lit, and routinely shot, and the film is obviously the work of a man who no longer cares about what he is doing. *Tales from the Crypt* (Francis's most successful film commercially) is slightly better, but still relies on zooms where before Francis had once used the more participatory tracking camera style.

After making two films with his son, Kevin Francis, Francis simply quit directing films, and went back, after a rest, to being a director of photography on David Lynch's *The Elephant Man*. Francis liked the script, and the lead, John Hurt (who Francis had worked with in *The Ghoul* in 1975), but the finished product has many shortcomings stylistically, due mostly to David Lynch's rather static use of the camera. But it put Francis back in the industry's eye as a director of photography. He won his second Oscar for his brilliant photography of the Civil War film *Glory*, which boasts some of the most breathtakingly colorful nighttime battle scenes ever brought to the screen. For director Martin Scorsese, he photographed the thriller *Cape Fear* (a remake of the 1962 film of the same title), and handled the second unit work in the film's finale where (shades of *Moby Dick*) a model boat is convincingly tossed about in a storm created in a studio tank. Working again with David Lynch, he shot *Dune* and later *The Straight Story* in 1999.

As a result of the success of *The Elephant Man*, Francis returned to directing when Mel Brooks, the executive producer of that film, agreed to back *The Doctor and the Devils* by Dylan Thomas, a project Francis had long wanted to make. Filming began on 17 January 1985. Despite the film's horrific content, Francis was quite determined to play the horror angle down. While acknowledging grudgingly that there was a similarity in the plot lines of the Thomas screenplay and the famous series of murders of Burke and Hare, he refused to take the matter any further.

Francis does little preplanning of shots before he gets on the set. He walks around the set with the head grip, the director of photography, and the camera operator, and "blocks" the camera setups out in a very informal manner. I was able to watch him doing this on the day before filming began, and it was impressive to watch him set up a complex dolly shot, one which introduces the set and several of the main characters, with more than 150 extras in the background, by coolly strolling about the set and saying, "Right! We start from here, to here, then turn, then end up here. Got it?" And everyone would nod yes, and that was it.

The Doctor and the Devils, unhappily, never received a very wide release, and Francis's work as a "horror specialist" continues to mitigate against most serious appreciation of his work as a director. This is unfortunate, because at his best, even though Francis seemingly disdains much of his own directorial work, his cinematic sensibility is restrained, melancholic, and altogether believable. The brooding cynicism which pervades the world of his films *The Skull*, *Paranoiac*, *Hysteria*, *Nightmare*, and others, is uniquely Francis's own, and by itself his work as a director would be a considerable achievement. But when one figures in his remarkable accomplishments as a director of photography, Francis emerges as a major figure in the history of cinema.

—Wheeler Winston Dixon, updated by John McCarty

FREED, Arthur

Producer and Lyricist. **Nationality:** American. **Born:** Arthur Grossman in Charleston, South Carolina, 9 September 1894. **Military Service:** 1917–19—served during World War I as sergeant. **Career:** Piano player for music publisher, Chicago; later appeared with the Marx Brothers and Gus Edwards in vaudeville; toured in vaudeville, and began writing songs and special material (first hit song, ''I Cried for You,'' 1923); 1924—opened The Orange Grove Theatre, Los Angeles, and presented straight and musical plays; 1929–39—lyricist for MGM; 1939—producer for MGM: in charge of special musical unit; 1963–66—President, Motion Picture Academy. **Awards:** Irving G. Thalberg Award, 1951; Academy Award for *An American in Paris*, 1951; Special Academy Award, 1967; Chevalier, Legion of Honor. **Died:** 12 April 1973.

Arthur Freed (right) with Nacio Herb Brown

Films as Lyricist:

1929 *The Broadway Melody* (Beaumont); *The Pagan* (Van Dyke); *Marianne* (Leonard); *The Hollywood Revue of 1929* (Reisner); *Untamed* (Conway)

1930 *Lord Byron of Broadway* (*What Price Melody?*) (Nigh and Beaumont); *Montana Moon* (St. Clair); *Good News* (Grinde); *Those Three French Girls* (Beaumont); *A Lady's Morals* (*The Soul Kiss*; *Jenny Lind*) (Franklin)

1933 *The Barbarian* (*A Night in Cairo*) (Wood); *Peg o' My Heart* (Leonard); *Hold Your Man* (Wood); *Stage Mother* (Brabin); *College Coach* (*Football Coach*) (Wellman); *Going Hollywood* (Walsh); *Blondie of the Follies* (Goulding); *Riptide* (Goulding); *Sadie McKee* (Brown); *Hollywood Party*; *Hide-Out* (Van Dyke); *Student Tour* (Reisner)

1935 *China Seas* (Garnett); *A Night at the Opera* (Wood); *Broadway Melody of 1936* (Del Ruth)

1936 *San Francisco* (Van Dyke); *The Devil Is a Sissy* (*The Devil Takes the Count*) (Van Dyke); *After the Thin Man* (Van Dyke)

1937 *Broadway Melody of 1938* (Del Ruth)

1939 *The Ice Follies of 1939* (Schünzel)

1940 *Two Girls on Broadway* (*Choose Your Partner*) (Simon)

Films as Producer:

1939 *The Wizard of Oz* (Fleming) (assoc); *Babes in Arms* (Berkeley) (+ lyrics)

1940 *Strike Up the Band* (Berkeley) (+ lyrics); *Little Nellie Kelly* (Taurog) (+ lyrics)

1941 *Lady Be Good* (McLeod) (+ lyrics); *Babes on Broadway* (Berkeley)

1942 *Panama Hattie* (McLeod); *For Me and My Gal* (Berkeley)

1943 *Du Barry Was a Lady* (Del Ruth); *Best Foot Forward* (Buzzell); *Girl Crazy* (Taurog); *Cabin in the Sky* (Minnelli)

1944 *Meet Me in St. Louis* (Minnelli) (+ lyrics, dubbed Leon Ames)

1945 *The Clock* (*Under the Clock*) (Minnelli) (+ lyrics, bit ro); *Yolanda and the Thief* (Minnelli) (+ lyrics); *The Harvey Girls* (Sidney)

1946 *Ziegfeld Follies* (Minnelli—produced 1944) (+ lyrics); *Till the Clouds Roll By* (Whorf)

1947 *Summer Holiday* (Mamoulian); *Good News* (Walters) (+ lyrics)

1948 *The Pirate* (Minnelli); *Easter Parade* (Walters); *Words and Music* (Taurog); *The Barkleys of Broadway* (Walters); *Take Me Out to the Ballgame* (*Everybody's Cheering*) (Berkeley)

1949 *Any Number Can Play* (LeRoy) (+ lyrics); *On the Town* (Donen and Kelly)

1950 *Annie Get Your Gun* (Sidney); *Crisis* (Brooks); *Pagan Love Song* (Alton) (+ lyrics); *Royal Wedding* (*Wedding Bells*) (Donen)

1951 *Show Boat* (Sidney); *An American in Paris* (Minnelli); *The Belle of New York* (Walters); *Singin' in the Rain* (Donen and Kelly)

1953 *The Band Wagon* (Minnelli)

1954 *Brigadoon* (Minnelli)

1955 *It's Always Fair Weather* (Donen and Kelly); *Kismet* (Minnelli)

1956 *Invitation to the Dance* (Kelly)

1957 *Silk Stockings* (Mamoulian)

1958 *Gigi* (Minnelli)

1960   *Bells Are Ringing* (Minnelli); *The Subterraneans* (MacDougall)
        (+ lyrics)
1961   *Light in the Piazza* (Green)

Publications

On FREED: articles—

Galling, Dennis, in *Films in Review* (New York), November 1964,
    (corrections in December 1964).
Fordin, Hugh, in *The World of Entertainment: Hollywood's Greatest
    Musicals*, New York, 1975.
Craig, Warren, in *The Great Songwriters of Hollywood*, San Diego,
    California, 1980.
Braudy, Leo, "Film Genre: A Dialogue: The Thirties and Fourties,"
    in *Post Script* (Commerce), Spring-Summer 1982.
National Film Theatre booklet (London), May 1980.
Cinématographe (Paris), May 1984.
Wald, Malvin, "At War with M-G-M," in *Creative Screenwriting*
    (Washington, D.C.), Spring 1994.
Rimoldi, O.A., "Produced by Aruthur Freed," in *Films in Review*
    (New York), July-August 1994; September-October 1994.
Restif, Henri, "Fred, Busby, Gene et Arthur," in *Avant-Scène du
    Cinéma* (Paris), February 1996.
Tinkcom, Matthew, "Working Like a Homosexual: Camp Visual
    Codes and the Labor of Gay Subjects in the MGM Freed Unit," in
    Cinema Journal (Austin), Winter 1996.
Elley, Derek, "Musicals Great Musicals: The Arthur Freed Unit at
    MGM," in *Variety* (New York), 16 December 1996.

*   *   *

Few producers have been as closely associated with or as instrumental in the development of a specific film genre as Arthur Freed. Freed's contributions to the Hollywood musical helped shape the look and style that dominated the genre in the 1940s, reaching a peak in the 1950s with such films as *Singin' in the Rain*, *The Band Wagon*, and *An American in Paris*. Working at MGM with a group that included many of the best directors, performers, songwriters, and technicians of the day, he oversaw the production of films which have become classics of the form and his influence is felt in the image which persists of the American musical.

Freed's own development as a producer grew naturally out of his early career as a lyricist. Together with his most frequent collaborator, the composer Nacio Herb Brown, Freed wrote dozens of popular songs, including such standards as "Broadway Rhythm," "Singin' in the Rain" and "You Are My Lucky Star," and he continued his work as a songwriter intermittently throughout his years as a producer. It was as a lyricist that Freed had originally come to MGM, but by the late 1930s he had begun urging Louis B. Mayer to allow him to produce, and in 1938 he received his chance when the studio began developing L. Frank Baum's children's fantasy, *The Wizard of Oz*, for the screen. With Mervyn LeRoy as its producer and Freed as associate producer, the film became one of MGM's most successful features and secured for Freed a far more autonomous position within the studio hierarchy.

Freed's particular skill was his ability to recognize exceptional talent in those around him, and he began gathering together a group of individuals whose aptitude in the musical field was second to none. This group became known as the "Freed Unit," and its members included artists and technicians representing all aspects of the process involved in producing musical films. Some worked exclusively for Freed while others made films for outside producers as well, but all did work under the Freed Unit banner that ranks with their best. The composer Roger Edens became Freed's trusted colleague and associate producer, while Vincente Minnelli, Stanley Donen, Busby Berkeley, and Charles Walters were among the Unit's leading directors. Freed had been instrumental in signing 13-year-old Judy Garland to a contract with MGM in the mid-1930s, and she became—along with Fred Astaire and Gene Kelly—one of the performers most closely associated with the producer. (Lena Horne and June Allyson were also among those recruited by Freed for the studio.) Cole Porter, Irving Berlin, and Oscar Hammerstein all wrote songs for Freed, and his production staff drew on the finest art directors, costume designers, musicians, and choreographers the industry had to offer.

The result of Freed's efforts was the formation of the Hollywood equivalent of a theatrical stock company, with many of the collaborators forming close working relationships which lasted throughout the better part of three decades. The films produced under the aegis of the Freed Unit brought the members of the company together in varying combinations and raised the art of the musical film to new heights. Bright, colorful, and energetic, these films were increasingly characterized by elegantly mounted productions and elaborate musical numbers, the most acclaimed of which was the 20-minute "American in Paris" ballet from the movie of the same name.

That film represented the Unit in full flower, however, and Freed's initial efforts were on a somewhat more modest scale. His early films are exemplified by the series of black-and-white, so-called "backyard" musicals he produced starring Judy Garland and Mickey Rooney. The films all follow the same general format: a problem, usually financial, arises in the context of the story's small-town setting and Mickey and Judy solve the crisis by putting on a show in a barn or the high school gym.

Garland was also the star of the film which began a transition in the Freed Unit's style—*Meet Me in St. Louis*. Directed by Vincente Minnelli, the film is a warm, simple family story and a painstakingly recreated period piece, shot in richly evocative color and marked by production values which reflected an increasing confidence on the studio's part in the potential success of Freed's projects. The majority of the Unit's subsequent films were also in color, a development which lent itself splendidly to the patterns of a choreographed dance routine. Minnelli, in particular, translated the changeover from black-and-white into a cinematic style noted for its vivid imagery. Working later with both Gene Kelly (*The Pirate*, *An American in Paris*) and Fred Astaire (*The Band Wagon*) and backed by Freed and the resources of his production staff, Minnelli created musical numbers that are elaborate yet witty and refined—carefully escalating orchestrations of color, music, and movement that use the screen much as a painter uses a canvas.

Freed produced musicals which stretched the genre in other directions as well. In 1949 *On the Town* became the first musical ever shot on location, as the codirectors Gene Kelly and Stanley Donen staged the film's production numbers on the streets of New York City, an unheard-of idea at that time. The process gave the film a vibrant energy and realism impossible to capture on a studio set, and it remains one of Freed's most innovative and successful projects.

The two films which best reflect the Freed Unit's influence on the musical both appeared in the early 1950s—*Singin' in the Rain* and *An American in Paris*. Although both star Gene Kelly, they are quite different in style and execution, each in its own way displaying the artistry and breadth of talent characteristic of the films Freed produced. Like *On the Town*, *Singin' in the Rain* was co-directed by Kelly and Stanley Donen, and the film tells its behind-the-scenes Hollywood love story with a lively energy that can encompass the extravagant ''Broadway Ballet'' number, Donald O'Connor's comical ''Make 'em Laugh,'' and Kelly's famous rendition of the film's title song. Boisterous and colorful, *Singin' in the Rain* is pure entertainment made in the best traditions of Hollywood movie-making.

An American in Paris, directed by Vincente Minnelli, cast the ballet-trained Leslie Caron opposite Kelly, and the film is a fusion of varying dance styles and elements of French and American culture. The ''American in Paris'' ballet takes place on a vast set which recalls the styles of several French Impressionist painters as Kelly and Caron mix classical dance with jazz and a touch of Broadway hoofing in one of the most ambitious musical numbers ever filmed. As its producer, Freed received the film's Academy Award for Best Picture (he would receive his second Oscar for *Gigi* seven years later). *An American in Paris* remains an outstanding example of the scope of imagination and talent that marked the work of the Freed Unit.

The musicals produced by Arthur Freed reflect the collaboration of an extraordinary group of gifted individuals, all working under the guiding hand of a man whose instincts and taste set the standard for their achievements, and the films themselves are among the best the genre has to offer. Freed's influence in shaping the style of the Hollywood musical during its Golden Age remains unsurpassed and the form continues to bear the stamp of his talents.

—Janet Lorenz

FREUND, Karl

Cinematographer and Director. **Nationality:** German. **Born:** Königinhof, Bohemia, 16 January 1890; grew up in Berlin. **Military Service:** 1914—served briefly in Austrian Army. **Career:** Apprenticed to rubber stamp manufacturer; then projectionist; 1907—first film as photographer, *Der Hauptmann von Köpenick*; 1908—worked as newsreel cameraman for Pathé; 1910—worked for Sascha-Film, Vienna, and then for Union Templehof Studio, 1912–14, and for Oskar Messtner in Berlin, 1914–19; 1919–26—operated film processing laboratory; 1926–28—production head of Fox-Europa; 1928—formed Movie Colour Ltd. in London; 1929—emigrated to the United States, and worked as cinematographer for Universal, 1930–35, MGM, 1935–47, and Warner Bros., 1947–50; 1932—first film as director, *The Mummy*; then worked as supervising photographer for Desilu Productions on their TV series *I Love Lucy*, *Our Miss Brooks*, *December Bride*, and other series, 1951–59; also head of Photo Research Corporation, Burbank, California (developed Norwich light meter and TV cameras). **Awards:** Academy Award for *The Good Earth*, 1937, Technical Academy Award, 1954. **Died:** In 1969.

Karl Freund

Films as Cinematographer:

1907   *Der Hauptmann von Köpenick*; *Das Lied von der Glocke*
1911   *Der Liebling der Frauen*; *Nachtfalter* (Gad); *Heisses Blut* (Gad) (co); *Der fremde Vogel* (Gad) (co)
1912   *Die Firma heiratet* (Wilhelm)
1913   *Die Filmprimadonna* (Gad); *Engelein* (Gad)
1914   *Zapatas Bande* (Gad) (co); *Das Kind ruft* (Gad) (co); *Das Feuer* (Gad) (co); *Der Hund von Baskerville, part 1* (Meinert); *Die ewige Nacht* (Gad) (co); *Engeleins Hochzeit* (Gad) (co); *Eine venezianische Nacht* (Reinhardt)
1915   *Vordertreppe und Hintertreppe* (Gad) (co); *Frau Eva* (*Arme Eva*) (Wiene)
1916   *Abseits vom Blück* (Biebrach); *Gelöste Ketten* (Beibrach); *Der Mann im Spiegel* (Wiene)
1917   *Die Ehe der Luise Rohrbach* (Biebrach); *Die Prinzessin von Neutralien* (Biebrach); *Gefangene Seele* (Biebrach); *Bummelstudenten* (Biebrach); *Christa Hartungen* (Biebrach)
1918   *Das Geschlecht derer von Ringwall* (Biebrach)
1919   *Rausch* (Lubitsch); *Die Arche* (Oswald); *Die letzten Menschen* (Oswald)
1920   *Satanas* (Murnau); *Katharina die Grosse* (Schünzel); *Der Januskopf* (*Janus-Faced*) (Murnau) (co); *Der Golem, wie er in die Welt kam* (Wegener) (co); *Der Bucklige und die Tänzerin* (Murnau); *Der verlorene Schatten* (Gliese); *Die Spinnen* (Lang)
1921   *Louise de Lavallière* (Burghardt); *Der Schwur des Peter Hertaz* (Halm); *Verlogene Moral* (*Brandherd*; *Totenklaus*;

Torgus) (Kobe); *Die Ratten* (Kobe); *Der Roman der Christine von Herre* (Berger)

1922 *Marizza, genannt die Schmuggler-Madonna* (Murnau); *Kinder der Finsternis* (Dupont—2 parts); *Herzog Ferrantes Ende* (Wegener); *Die brennende Acker* (*Burning Soil*) (Murnau); *Lucrezia Borgia* (Oswald) (co)

1923 *Die Austreibung* (*Driven from Home*) (Murnau)

1924 *Die Finanzen des Grossherzogs* (*The Grand Duke's Finances*) (Murnau) (co); **Der letzte Mann** (*The Last Laugh*) (Murnau); *Michael* (Dreyer) (co, + ro)

1925 **Variété** (*Variety*) (Dupont)

1926 *Tartüff* (*Tartuffe*) (Murnau)

1927 **Metropolis** (Lang) (co); *Doña Juana* (Czinner) (co)

1928 *A Knight in London* (Pick) (co)

1929 *Fräulein Else* (Czinner) (co)

1930 **All Quiet on the Western Front** (Milestone); *The Boudoir Diplomat* (St. Clair)

1931 **Dracula** (Browning); *The Bad Sister* (Henley); *Personal Maid* (Bell); *Up for Murder* (*Fires of Youth*) (Bell); *Strictly Dishonorable* (Stahl) (co)

1932 *Murders in the Rue Morgue* (Florey); *Scandal for Sale* (Mack); *Back Street* (Stahl); *Airmail* (Ford); *Afraid to Talk* (Cahn)

1933 *The Kiss Before the Mirror* (Whale)

1936 *The Great Ziegfeld* (Leonard) (co); **Camille** (Cukor) (co)

1937 *The Good Earth* (Franklin); *Parnell* (Stahl); *Man-Proof* (Thorpe); *Conquest* (*Marie Walewska*) (Brown)

1939 *Tail Spin* (Del Ruth); *Rose of Washington Square* (Ratoff); *Golden Boy* (Mamoulian) (co); *Burricade* (Ratoff); *Balalaika* (Schünzel); *Green Hell* (Whale)

1940 *Florian* (Marin); *Pride and Prejudice* (Leonard); *We Who Are Young* (Bucquet); *Keeping Company* (Simon)

1941 *Blossoms in the Dust* (LeRoy) (co); *The Chocolate Soldier* (Del Ruth)

1942 *Tortilla Flat* (Fleming); *A Yank at Eton* (Taurog) (co); *The War Against Mrs. Hadley* (Bucquet)

1943 *DuBarry Was a Lady* (Del Ruth); *The Cross of Lorraine* (Garnett) (co); *Cry Havoc* (Thorpe); *A Guy Named Joe* (Fleming) (co)

1944 *The Seventh Cross* (Zinnemann); *The Thin Man Goes Home* (Thorpe)

1945 *Without Love* (Bucquet); *Dangerous Partners* (Cahn)

1946 *A Letter for Evie* (Dassin); *Two Smart People* (Dassin); *Undercurrent* (Minnelli)

1947 *This Time for Keeps* (Thorpe); *That Hagen Girl* (Godfrey)

1948 *Wallflower* (de Cordova); *Key Largo* (Huston); *The Decision of Christopher Blake* (Godfrey)

1949 *South of St. Louis* (Enright); *Montana* (Enright)

1950 *Bright Leaf* (Curtiz)

1960 *Open Windows* (Leisen)

Other Films:

1926 *Madam wünscht keine Kinder* (*Madame Wants No Children*) (Z. Korda) (pr spvr)

1927 **Berlin—Die Symphonie einer Grossstadt** (*Berlin—Symphony of a Great City*) (Ruttmann) (co-pr, co-sc); *Die Abenteuer eines Zehnmarkscheinen* (Viertel) (pr spvr); *Der Sohn der Hagar* (Wendhausen) (pr spvr)

1932 *The Mummy* (d)

1933 *Moonlight and Pretzels* (*Moonlight and Melody*) (d)

1934 *Madame Spy* (d); *The Countess of Monte Cristo* (d); *Uncertain Lady* (d); *I Give My Love* (d); *Gift of Gab* (d)

1935 *Mad Love* (*The Hands of Orlac*) (d)

Publications

By FREUND: articles—

Close-Up (London), January 1929.
Film (Hanover), no. 9, 1965.
Chaplin (Stockholm), no. 1, 1974.
Chaplin (Stockholm), no. 2, 1974.

On FREUND: articles—

Close-Up (London), March 1930.
Luft, Herbert G., in *Films in Review* (New York), February 1963.
Deschner, Donald, in *Cinema* (Beverly Hills, California), Fall 1969.
Luft, Herbert G., in *Film Journal*, Spring 1971.
Mundy, Robert, in *Cinema* (London), Summer 1971.
Film Comment (New York), Summer 1972.
Focus on Film (London), no. 13, 1973.
Brosnan, John, in *Movie Magic*, New York, 1974.
Gerely, A., in *Film und Ton* (Munich), July 1977.
Filme (Berlin), May-June 1981.
Avant-Scène (Paris), March 1985.
American Cinematographer (Hollywood), April 1987.
Pitman, Randy, "The Mummy," in *Library Journal*, 1 September 1991.
Holt, W.G., "The Mummy," in *Filmfax*, no. 36, December/January 1992/93.
Senn, B., "The Golden Age of Horror," in *Midnight Marquee*, no. 45, Summer 1993.
Mank, G.W., "Gift of Gab: The Mystery of the Lost Karloff and Lugosi Movie," in *Scarlet Street*, no. 10, Spring 1993.

*   *   *

During a career that lasted nearly 50 years, cinematographer Karl Freund contributed his artfully innovative camerawork to more than 100 German and American films, including the classic *Metropolis* and the solid *Key Largo*. Unfortunately, superlative examples of filmmaking are not the sole entries in Freund's filmography. Numerous forgettable or already forgotten comedies, romances, and musicals are also present, a perhaps inevitable consequence of Freund's long career. Symptomatic of his commitment to perfection was his refusal to discriminate a "programmer" from a masterpiece, which provided many of the films he lit and shot with their only noteworthy feature: excellent cinematography.

In 1905, when he was 15 years old, Freund quit his apprenticeship with a manufacturer of rubber stamps to work as an assistant projectionist for a Berlin film company. Displaying a prodigious technical inventiveness toward and understanding of lighting and the motion picture camera, Freund graduated within two years from projectionist to cameraman. As one of Germany's motion picture pioneers, Freund spent his earliest years in film shooting an assortment of material, from shorts and newsreel footage to several of the actress Asta Nielsen's films (*Nachtfalter, Engelein*) and the early efforts of, among others, directors F.W. Murnau (*Satanas*) and Fritz Lang (*Die Spinnen*).

In the 1920s Freund worked at Ufa, Germany's great government-supported film studio, where he collaborated with Murnau, Lang, and others on a number of the films that collectively created the golden age of the German cinema, films such as Murnau's *Der letzte Mann* and E.A. Dupont's *Variety*. For the revolutionary *Der letzte Mann*, the camera became both narrator and character, relating and interpreting the story of the demoted doorman so lucidly that title cards were superfluous. Freund and scriptwriter Carl Mayer enriched the simple plot of Murnau's film with artistically purposeful camera movement and lighting that set the expressionistic sobriety of the film proper against the high-key clarity of its controversial epilogue.

Between 1926 and 1928 Freund served as production head of Fox-Europa and participated in creating the sole experimental film of his career, Walter Ruttmann's *Berlin—Symphony of a Great City*, for which Freund developed a high-speed film stock that made shooting outside at night without artificial lighting as feasible as shooting during the daytime. In 1929, Freund's experiments with a color process for 35mm film took him first to New York and then to Hollywood where, following the failure of the process, he joined Universal as a cinematographer.

One of Freund's earliest assignments at Universal was to shoot Lewis Milestone's *All Quiet on the Western Front* (whether Freund devised and executed the butterfly scene that ends the film remains an unsettled issue). Freund also shot two horror films for Universal, Tod Browning's *Dracula* and Robert Florey's *Murders in the Rue Morgue*, the perfect showcase for Freund's abilities with *chiaroscuro* lighting. In 1933, Universal assigned Freund to direct his first motion picture, *The Mummy*. He would direct six more films at Universal before his contract ended in 1935.

Shortly after moving to MGM that same year, Freund directed his final picture, the macabre *Mad Love*, a remake of Robert Wiene's *Orlacs Hände*. In 1937, Freund received an Academy Award for the exceptional camerawork and special effects of *The Good Earth*. Other projects that occupied him during his dozen years with MGM were Rouben Mamoulian's *Golden Boy*, on which Freund collaborated with cinematographer Nicholas Musaraca; his first color film, *Blossoms in the Dust*; and a string of Spencer Tracy's films (*Tortilla Flat, A Guy Named Joe, The Seventh Cross*). While under contract to MGM, Freund also established the Photo Research Corporation in Burbank, where he developed a highly successful incident exposure meter.

Filming John Huston's *Key Largo* was the highlight of Freund's three years with Warner Bros. (1947–50). Although Freund is never named in James Agee's essay on Huston, "Undirectable Director," Agee does comment on the rightness of the camerawork in *Key Largo*: "The lighting is stickily fungoid. The camera is sneakily 'personal'; working close and in almost continuous motion, it enlarges the ambiguous suspensefulness of almost every human move."

In the summer of 1951, Freund was directing his Photo Research Corporation when Lucille Ball, with whom he had worked at MGM, contacted him about the new television series that she and Desi Arnaz wanted to film live with three simultaneously operating 35mm motion picture cameras, a then relatively unprecedented and difficult approach. Freund joined the staff of the *I Love Lucy* show as director of photography, inventing an overhead lighting system that was responsible for the exceptional quality of the program's images. Freund supervised the photography of more than 400 episodes of *I Love Lucy*

before resigning from the series in 1956; he retired from television altogether three years later. In the final decade of his life, Freund presided over Photo Research, continuing his efforts to improve the machinery of his art.

—Nancy Jane Johnston

FRIEDHOFER, Hugo

Composer and Arranger. **Nationality:** American. **Born:** Hugo Wilhelm (or William) Friedhofer in San Francisco, California, 3 May 1902. **Education:** Studied with Domenica Brescia, Respighi, Nadia Boulanger, Schoenberg, and others into the 1940s. **Career:** Cellist with the People's Symphony Orchestra and San Francisco Symphony Orchestra, in 1920s; arranger for stage bands; 1929—orchestrator for first film, *Sunny Side Up*, and worked as arranger for Fox until 1935; 1935–38—orchestrator for Warner Bros., working mainly with Korngold and Steiner; 1938—first original score, for *The Adventures of Marco Polo*. **Awards:** Academy Award for *The Best Years of Our Lives*, 1946; Venice Festival award for *Ace in the Hole*, 1951. **Died:** In Hollywood, California, 17 May 1981.

Films as Orchestrator or Musical Director:

1929   *Sunny Side Up* (Butler); *Happy Days* (Stoloff); *Seven Faces* (Viertel)

1930   *The Golden Calf* (Webb); *Scotland Yard* (Howard); *The Big Trail* (Walsh); *A Devil with Women* (Cummings); *The Dancers* (Sprague); *Just Imagine* (Butler); *The Princess and the Plumber* (Korda); *Men on Call* (Blystone); *The Man Who Came Back* (Walsh)

1931   *Always Goodbye* (Menzies and MacKenna); *Skyline* (Taylor); *Daddy Long Legs* (Santell); *Transatlantic* (Howard); *The Spider* (Menzies and MacKenna); *Heartbreak* (Werker); *The Yellow Ticket* (Walsh)

1932   *Devil's Lottery* (Taylor); *Careless Lady* (MacKenna); *Amateur Daddy* (Blystone); *The Woman in Room 13* (H. King); *The Trial of Vivienne Ware* (Howard); *Almost Married* (Menzies); *Mystery Ranch* (Howard); *Rebecca of Sunnybrook Farm* (Santell); *A Passport to Hell* (Lloyd); *The First Year* (Howard); *The Painted Woman* (Blystone); *Sherlock Holmes* (Howard); *Second Hand Wife* (MacFadden)

1933   *The Face in the Sky* (Lachman); *Dangerously Yours* (Tuttle); *Broadway Bad* (Lanfiedl); *Bondage* (Santell); *Zoo in Budapest* (Lee); *It's Great to Be Alive* (Werker); *My Lips Betray* (Blystone); *The Good Companions* (Saville); *As Husbands Go* (MacFadden)

1934   *Orient Express* (Martin); *Coming Out Party* (Blystone); *George White's Scandals* (Freeland); *Now I'll Tell* (Burke); *Change of Heart* (Blystone); *The World Moves On* (Ford); *Servant's Entrance* (Lloyd)

1935   *The Little Colonel* (Butler); *Orchids to You* (Seiter); *George White's 1935 Scandals* (White); *Curly Top* (Cummings); *Dante's Inferno* (Lachman); *Here's to Romance* (Green); *Way Down East* (H. King); *Last of the Pagans* (Thorpe); *Captain Blood* (Curtiz)

1936   *Rose of the Rancho* (Gering); *The Green Pastures* (Connelly and Keighley); *The Prisoner of Shark Island* (Ford); *The Trail of the Lonesome Pine* (Hathaway); *Sins of Man* (Brower and Ratoff); *White Fang* (Butler) (co); *The Great O'Malley* (Dieterle); *The Charge of the Light Brigade* (Curtiz); *God's Country and the Woman* (Keighley)

1937   *Green Light* (Borzage); *Kid Galahad* (Curtiz); *The Prince and the Pauper* (Keighley) (co); *The Life of Emile Zola* (Dieterle); *Another Dawn* (Dieterle) (co); *Swing Your Lady* (Enright)

1938   **The Adventures of Robin Hood** (Curtiz and Keighley) (co); *Gold Is Where You Find It* (Curtiz); *Jezebel* (Wyler); *Crime School* (Seiler) (co); *Four Daughters* (Curtiz); *Racket Busters* (Bacon); *Valley of the Giants* (Keighley); *The Sisters* (Litvak); *Angels with Dirty Faces* (Curtiz); *The Dawn Patrol* (Goulding)

1939   *Made for Each Other* (Cromwell); *The Oklahoma Kid* (Bacon) (co); *Dodge City* (Curtiz); *Dark Victory* (Goulding); *The Old Maid* (Goulding); *Juarez* (Dieterle); *You Can't Get Away with Murder* (Seiler) (co); *The Private Lives of Elizabeth and Essex* (Curtiz) (co); **Gone with the Wind** (Fleming) (co)

1940   *Dr. Ehrlich's Magic Bullet* (Dieterle); *All This, and Heaven Too* (Litvak); *Virginia City* (Curtiz); *The Fighting 69th* (Keighley); *City for Conquest* (Litvak); *The Sea Hawk* (Curtiz) (co); *The Mark of Zorro* (Mamoulian); *The Letter* (Wyler); *Santa Fe Trail* (Curtiz)

1941   *The Sea Wolf* (Curtiz); *The Bride Came C.O.D.* (Keighley); *Dive Bomber* (Curtiz); *Sergeant York* (Curtiz); *One Foot in Heaven* (Rapper); *The Gay Parisian* (short)

1942   *In This Our Life* (Huston); *Prelude to War* (Capra—doc); *Desperate Journey* (Walsh); **Now, Voyager** (Rapper); *Kings Row* (Wood)

1943   **Casablanca** (Curtiz); *The Constant Nymph* (Goulding); *Wintertime* (Brahm); *Watch on the Rhine* (Shumlin); *The Gang's All Here* (Berkeley)

1944   *The Woman in the Window* (F. Lang); *Four Jills in a Jeep* (Seiter) (co); *Arsenic and Old Lace* (Capra); *Between Two Worlds* (Blett)

1945   *Along Came Jones* (Heisler); **Mildred Pierce** (Curtiz); *Devotion* (Bernhardt—produced 1943)

1946   *Cloak and Dagger* (F. Lang); *A Stolen Life* (Bernhardt); *Of Human Bondage* (Goulding)

1947   *A Song Is Born* (Hawks); *The Man I Love* (Walsh); *The Beast with Five Fingers* (Florey); *Cheyenne* (Walsh); *Escape Me Never* (Godfrey)

1954   *Deep in My Heart* (Donen)

1965   *The Greatest Story Ever Told* (Stevens)

1945   *The Corn Is Green* (Rapper); *Brewster's Millions* (Dwan); *Getting Gertie's Garter* (Dwan)

1946   *The Bandit of Sherwood Forest* (G. Sherman and Levin); **Gilda** (Vidor) (co); *So Dark the Night* (Lewis); **The Best Years of Our Lives** (Wyler)

1947   *Body and Soul* (Rossen); *Wild Harvest* (Garnett); *The Bishop's Wife* (Koster); *The Swordsman* (Lewis)

1948   *Adventures of Casanova* (Gavaldon); *Black Bart* (G. Sherman) (co); *Sealed Verdict* (Allen); *Joan of Arc* (Fleming); *Enchantment* (Reis)

1949   *Bride of Vengeance* (Leisen); *Roseanna McCoy* (Reis) (co)

1950   *Guilty of Treason* (Feist); *Three Came Home* (Negulesco); *Captain Carey, U.S.A.* (*After Midnight*) (Leisen); *No Man of Her Own* (Leisen); *Broken Arrow* (Daves); *Edge of Doom* (Robson); *Two Flags West* (Wise); *The Sound of Fury* (*Try and Get Me*) (Endfield)

1951   *Queen for a Day* (Lubin); *Ace in the Hole* (*The Big Carnival*) (Wilder)

1952   *The San Francisco Story* (Parrish) (co); *Rancho Notorious* (F. Lang); *The Marrying Kind* (Cukor); *The Outcasts of Poker Flat* (Newman); *Lydia Bailey* (Negulesco); *Just for You* (Nugent); *Above and Beyond* (Frank and Panama); "The Secret Sharer" and "The Bride Comes to Yellow Sky" eps. of *Face to Face* (Brahm and Windust)

1953   *Plunder of the Sun* (Farrow) (co); *Thunder in the East* (C. Vidor); *Island in the Sky* (Wellman); *Hondo* (Farrow) (co)

1954   *Vera Cruz* (Aldrich)

1955   *White Feather* (Webb); *Violent Saturday* (Fleischer); *Soldier of Fortune* (Dmytryk); *Seven Cities of Gold* (Webb); *The Rains of Ranchipur* (Negulesco)

1956   *The Harder They Fall* (Robson); *Between Heaven and Hell* (Fleischer); *The Revolt of Mamie Stover* (Walsh)

1957   *Oh, Men! Oh, Women!* (Mockridge); *Boy on a Dolphin* (Negulesco); *An Affair to Remember* (McCarey); *The Sun Also Rises* (H. King)

1958   *The Young Lions* (Dmytryk); *The Bravados* (H. King) (co); *The Barbarian and the Geisha* (Huston); *In Love and War* (Dunne)

1959   *Woman Obsessed* (Hathaway); *This Earth Is Mine* (H. King); *The Blue Angel* (Dmytryk); *Never So Few* (J. Sturges)

1960   *One Eyed Jacks* (Brando)

1961   *Homicidal* (Castle)

1962   *Geronimo* (Laven); *Beauty and the Beast* (Cahn)

1964   *The Secret Invasion* (Corman)

1969   *The Over-the-Hill Gang* (Harbrough)

1971   *Von Richtofen and Brown* (*The Red Baron*) (Corman)

1973   *Private Parts* (Bartel)

1975   *A Walk in the Forest* (Hood—short)

1977   *The Companion* (Hood)

Films as Composer:

1938   *The Adventures of Marco Polo* (Mayo); *Topper Takes a Trip* (McLeod)

1943   *China Girl* (Hathaway); *Chetniks!* (L. King); *They Came to Blow Up America* (*School for Sabotage*) (Ludwig); *Paris after Dark* (Moguy)

1944   *The Lodger* (Brahm); *Lifeboat* (Hitchcock); *Roger Tuohy, Gangster* (Florey); *Home in Indiana* (Hathaway); *Wing and a Prayer* (Hathaway)

Publications

By FRIEDHOFER: articles—

Interview with Elmer Bernstein, in *Film Music Notebook* (Calabasas, California), Fall 1974.
American Film (Washington, D.C.), June 1977.
In *Film Score*, edited by Tony Thomas, South Brunswick, New Jersey, 1979.

On FRIEDHOFER: books—

Danly, Linda, editor, *Hugo Friedhofer: The Best Years of His Life: A Hollywood Master of Music for the Movies*, Lanham, 1999.

On FRIEDHOFER: articles—

Sternfield, Frederick W., in *Musical Quarterly* (London), October 1947.
Morton, Lawrence, in *Quarterly of Film, Radio, and Television* (Berkeley, California), Winter 1951.
Thomas, Anthony, in *Films in Review* (New York), October 1965.
Films in Review (New York), March 1966.
Thomas, Tony, in *Music for the Movies*, South Brunswick, New Jersey, 1973.
Films in Review (New York), December 1975.
Films in Review (New York), May 1979.
Films in Review (New York), August-September 1981.
Bertolina, Gian Carlo, in *Rivista del Cinematografo* (Rome), June-August 1982.
Lacombe, Alain, in *Hollywood*, Paris, 1983.
Sherk, W.M., "The Art of Film Music: Special Emphasis on Hugo Friedhofer, Alex North, David Raskin, Leonard Rosenman," in *Cue Sheet* (Hollywood), no. 1, 1995.
Danly, L., "Hugo Friedhofer's Westerns," in *Cue Sheet* (Hollywood), no. 2, 1995.
Scheer, R., "Soundtrack," in *Filmbulletin* (Winterthur), no. 6, 1995.
Kalinak, Kathryn, "The Art of Film Music: Special Emphasis on Hugo Friedhofer, Alex North, David Raskin and Leonard Rosenman," in *Historical Journal of Film, Radio and Television*, March 1996.

* * *

There was always a disparity between Hugo Friedhofer's high regard among other film composers and his lack of public identity. With no interest in publicity or promotion, he was considered by his colleagues as the master of film composition and a man to whom they turned for advice. Friedhofer arrived in Hollywood in 1929 and became a witness, and participator, in the entire development of film scoring. He wrote more than 70 scores, but he was also a collaborator, adapter, arranger, orchestrator and utility composer on many others. Segments of scores, even main titles, of films attributed to other composers were actually written by Friedhofer. As an orchestrator he had few peers; in fact, he was so highly regarded in that capacity that it became necessary for him to end that aspect of his career in order to proceed as a composer. Fifteen of Erich Korngold's scores were orchestrated by Friedhofer, as were more than 50 by Max Steiner.

Friedhofer was the son of a cellist, who encouraged Hugo to take up the instrument. He was employed as a cellist with small groups and hired for a two-year period with the People's Orchestra of San Francisco. In 1925 he joined the orchestra of the Granada, a leading movie theatre, and gradually became more interested in making arrangements for film accompaniment than performing. The coming of sound caused him to lose this livelihood, but a violinist friend, George Lipschultz, had been contracted as a music director at the Fox Studios in Los Angeles and he offered Friedhofer a job as an arranger.

His first assignment was *Sunny Side Up*, followed by a continual stream of such movies. He also worked for Alfred Newman, who gave Friedhofer his first chance to write an original score, *The Adventures of Marco Polo*. It was not, however, until 1943 that he was able to break away from his constant chores as an orchestrator, when Newman hired him as a composer at 20th Century-Fox. Two years later he began freelancing, and in 1946 he won an Oscar for what is considered a landmark in American film music, *The Best Years of Our Lives*. His other nominated scores included *The Woman in the Window*, *The Bishop's Wife*, *Joan of Arc*, *Above and Beyond*, *Boy on a Dolphin*, and *The Young Lions*. Others of his scores held in high regard are *Broken Arrow*, *Vera Cruz*, *The Sun Also Rises*, and *One Eyed Jacks*.

Of his craft, Friedhofer said, "It is not important for the audience to be aware of the technique by which music affects them, but affect them it must. Film music is absorbed, you might say, through the pores. But the listener should be aware, even subliminally, of continuity, of a certain binder that winds through the film experience. A score must relate, it must integrate."

—Tony Thomas

FURTHMAN, Jules

Writer. **Pseudonym:** Stephen Fox. **Nationality:** American. **Born:** Julius Grinnell Furthmann in Chicago, Illinois, 5 March 1888. **Education:** Attended Northwestern University Preparatory School, Evanston, Illinois, 1904–05. **Family:** Married Sybil Travilla, 1921. **Career:** Magazine and newspaper writer in early 1910s; 1915—began

Jules Furthman

writing film stories for American, Fox, and Paramount studios (used the pseudonym Stephen Fox, 1918–20); 1920–23—under contract to Fox, and later to Paramount, 1926–32, and MGM, 1932–39; then freelance writer; 1960—retired. **Died:** Of a stroke in Oxford, England, 22 September 1966.

Films as Writer (used pseudonym Stephen Fox, 1918–20):

1915 *Steady Company* (De Grasse—short) (story); *Bound on the Wheel* (De Grasse—short); *Mountain Justice* (De Grasse—short) (story); *Chasing the Limited* (McRae—short) (story); *A Fiery Introduction* (Giblyn—short) (story); *Little Blonde in Black* (Leonard—short) (story); *Quits* (De Grasse—short) (story)

1917 *The Frame-Up* (Sloman); *Souls in Pawn* (H. King)

1918 *The Camouflage Kiss* (Millarde); *More Trouble* (Warde); *A Japanese Nightingale* (Fitzmaurice); *All the World to Nothing* (H. King); *The Mantle of Charity* (Sloman); *Hobbs in a Hurry* (H. King); *Wives and Other Wives* (Ingraham); *When A Man Rides Alone* (H. King)

1919 *Where the West Begins* (H. King); *Brass Buttons* (H. King); *Some Liar* (H. King); *A Sporting Chance* (H. King) (story); *This Hero Stuff* (H. King) (story); *Six Feet Four* (H. King); *Victory* (Tourneur); *The Lincoln Highwayman* (Flynn) (adaptation)

1920 *The Valley of Tomorrow* (Flynn) (story); *Treasure Island* (Tourneur); *Would You Forgive?* (Dunlap); *Leave It to Me* (Flynn); *The Twins of Suffering Creek* (Dunlap); *A Sister to Salome* (LeSaint); *The White Circle* (Tourneur) (co-adaptation); *The Man Who Dared* (Flynn); *The Skywayman* (Hogan); *The Great Redeemer* (Brown) (co-adaptation); *The Texan* (Reynolds); *The Iron Rider* (Dunlap); *The Land of Jazz* (co-story, + d)

1921 *The Cheater Reformed* (Dunlap); *The Big Punch* (Ford); *High Gear Jeffrey* (Sloman); *Singing River* (Giblyn); *The Last Trail* (Flynn); *The Roof Tree* (Dillon); *The Blushing Bride* (+ d); *Colorado Pluck* (*Colorado Jim*) (+ d)

1922 *Gleam O'Dawn* (Dillon); *The Ragged Heiress* (Beaumont); *Arabian Love* (Storm); *The Yellow Stain* (Dillon); *Strange Idols* (Durning); *Calvert's Valley* (*Calvert's Folly*) (Dillon); *The Love Gambler* (Franz); *A California Romance* (Storm) (story); *Pawn Ticket 210* (Dunlap)

1923 *Lovebound* (Otto); *St. Elmo* (*St. Elmo Murray*) (Storm); *North of Hudson Bay* (*North of the Yukon*) (Ford); *The Acquittal* (Brown); *Condemned* (Rosson)

1924 *Try and Get It* (Tate); *Call of the Mate* (Neitz)

1925 *Sackcloth and Scarlet* (H. King); *Any Woman* (H. King); *Before Midnight* (Adolfi); *Big Pal* (Adolfi)

1926 *The Wise Guy* (*Into the Light*) (Lloyd) (story); *You'd Be Surprised* (Rosson); *Hotel Imperial* (Stiller)

1927 *Casey at the Bat* (Brice); *Fashions for Women* (Arzner) (co-adaptation); *The Way of All Flesh* (Fleming); *Barbed Wire* (Lee); *City Gone Wild* (Cruze); *Underworld* (von Sternberg)

1928 *The Dragnet* (von Sternberg); *The Docks of New York* (von Sternberg)

1929 *Abie's Irish Rose* (Fleming); *The Case of Lena Smith* (von Sternberg); *Thunderbolt* (von Sternberg); *New York Nights* (Milestone)

1930 *Common Clay* (Fleming); *Del mismo barro* (Howard); *Ladron de amor* (*Cuando el amor rie*) (Howard and Scully); *Renegades* (Fleming); *Morocco* (von Sternberg)

1931 *Body and Soul* (Santell); *Merely Mary Ann* (H. King); *The Yellow Ticket* (*The Yellow Passport*) (Walsh); *Over the Hill* (H. King)

1932 *Shanghai Express* (von Sternberg); *Blonde Venus* (von Sternberg)

1933 *The Girl in 419* (Somnes and Hall) (story); *Bombshell* (*Blonde Bombshell*) (Fleming)

1935 *China Seas* (Garnett); *Mutiny on the Bounty* (Lloyd)

1936 *Come and Get It!* (Hawks and Wyler)

1938 *Spawn of the North* (Hathaway)

1939 *Only Angels Have Wings* (Hawks)

1940 *The Way of All Flesh* (L. King) (co-story)

1941 *The Shanghai Gesture* (von Sternberg)

1943 *The Outlaw* (Hughes)

1944 *To Have and Have Not* (Hawks)

1946 **The Big Sleep** (Hawks)

1947 *Moss Rose* (Ratoff); *Nightmare Alley* (Goulding)

1950 *Pretty Baby* (Windust) (co-story)

1951 *Peking Express* (Dieterle) (adaptation)

1957 *Jet Pilot* (von Sternberg) (+ pr)

1958 **Rio Bravo** (Hawks); *Girl on the Subway* (Rich) (co-story)

Publications

By FURTHMAN: books—

With William Faulkner and Leigh Brackett, *The Big Sleep* (screenplay) in *Film Scripts One*, edited by George P. Garrett, O. B. Harrison, Jr., and Jane Gelfmann, New York, 1971.
Morocco and *Shanghai Express* (screenplays), New York, 1973.
With William Faulkner, *To Have and Have Not* (screenplay), edited by Bruce F. Kawin, Madison, Wisconsin, 1980.

On FURTHMAN: articles—

Présence du Cinéma (Paris), June 1962.
Koszarski, Richard, in *The Hollywood Screenwriter*, edited by Richard Corliss, New York, 1972.
Pennington, Renée D., in *American Screenwriters*, edited by Robert E. Morsberger, Stephen O. Lesser, and Randall Clark, Detroit, Michigan, 1984.
National Film Theatre booklet (London), April 1984.

*   *   *

Jules Furthman's output of film stories and scripts numbers something over one hundred projects, most of which were silent films that unfortunately no longer exist. Because so few of his early films are extant, Furthman's reputation as a screenwriter is somewhat unfairly determined by his later work in sound movies. His reputation is further restricted by the fact that he wrote for two of Hollywood's most famous directors, Howard Hawks and Josef von Sternberg, and their preeminence as moviemakers has greatly overshadowed Furthman's contribution to their collective projects.

Furthman began writing for films in 1915, and for the next dozen years he supplied stories and screenplays and occasionally dialogue titles for scores of silent movies, most of them westerns and run-of-the-mill romances and adventure films. His first major break came when he and his brother were involved (without credit) in writing the script for Josef von Sternberg's *Underworld*, a collaboration which continued on von Sternberg's next movie, *The Dragnet*, and on *Thunderbolt* which was filmed in 1929. Jules also wrote solo two additional von Sternberg projects, *The Docks of New York* and *The Case of Lena Smith*. All of these early von Sternberg films deal with the lower classes, often criminals, who eke out an existence in the "underworld" of American society. They most often focus on men and women who have endured hard lives but remain capable of warmth and love.

The second half of Furthman's collaboration with von Sternberg began after the filming of *The Blue Angel* in Germany when the director brought the star, Marlene Dietrich, back to America with him. Furthman was to script three of the six films von Sternberg and Dietrich made together in Hollywood: *Morocco*, *Shanghai Express*, and *Blonde Venus*. The first two were adventure films in which the character played by Dietrich, although used and abandoned by the central male character, followed him nevertheless into the dangers of the future. The third film also dealt with a self-sacrificing woman who falls from respectability to prostitution in order to finance an operation for her scientist husband, and after several plot twists is reintegrated back into the rather smug world of her family and husband. Although Dietrich became the focus of these films, as she was of von Sternberg's obsession, the scripts Furthman wrote remain remarkably unified. All of the scripts involve the discrepancy between classes and how traditional notions of morality determine such differences. In all cases the good/bad woman proves to be worthy of admiration because of her self-sacrificing nature and because of the basic purity of heart which she has retained although her life has been subjected to extremes of poverty and vice.

By the early 1930s Furthman was working at MGM, where he remained throughout the decade except when he was loaned out for projects at other studios. He won his only Academy Award nomination during this period for his work on the adaptation of *Mutiny on the Bounty* in 1935. In 1936 Furthman coauthored a script of Edna Ferber's *Come and Get It!* for Howard Hawks and William Wyler, which began the screenwriter's most memorable collaboration with a director. In 1939 Furthman again worked for Hawks and wrote *Only Angels Have Wings*, the first of their three major collaborations. *Only Angels Have Wings* was based loosely on Hawks's experience flying in South America and starred Jean Arthur and Cary Grant. It is one of the earliest of Hawks's adventure films in which a newcomer is initiated into a smaller group of individuals who are facing some sort of danger. Furthman repeated the situation in *To Have and Have Not*, a film he cowrote with William Faulkner based on Ernest Hemingway's novel. This plot format was repeated one more time by Furthman in his final script for Hawks, and as it turned out, of his career, when he wrote *Rio Bravo*, a western starring John Wayne, which also has an acknowledged relationship to the earlier von Sternberg film, *Underworld*.

In between working for Hawks, Furthman wrote one more film for von Sternberg, *The Shanghai Gesture*, a melodrama set in a brothel; and he also scripted Howard Hughes's notorious film, *The Outlaw*. Furthman also adapted Raymond Chandler's *The Big Sleep* for Hawks, a successful vehicle for Humphrey Bogart and Lauren Bacall who worked so well together in *To Have and Have Not*. In all of these projects Furthman proved himself an adaptable and professional craftsman.

Unlike some of his colleagues, Jules Furthman has proved a difficult artist to categorize. Some critics have characterized him as the perfect Hollywood writer, self-effacing and undistinctive, one who could grind out dialogue and scripts to order; adventures, melodrama, love stories, westerns, it did not make any difference, Furthman could do them with efficiency and speed. Other film scholars have isolated what they describe as Furthman's distinctive talents which bridge various acting styles and directors to produce individual characterization and dialogue. It is too early for any sort of final judgment on Furthman's place in the Hollywood pantheon, but the controversy over his worth as an artist has stirred a healthy debate about the place of the screenwriter in the collaborative effort of film.

—Charles L. P. Silet

GALEEN, Henrik

Writer. **Nationality:** Danish (or Belgian, Czech, or Dutch). **Born:** Denmark (Belgium, Czechoslovakia, and the Netherlands are also given in various sources), 1882; given name also spelled Henryk and Heinrich. **Career:** Journalist (?), then actor; 1906—assistant to Max Reinhardt at Deutsches Theater, Berlin; later acted in Switzerland, England, and France; film actor as early as 1910; 1914—first film as writer and codirector, *Der Golem*; 1933—emigrated to the United States, then disappeared from view. **Died:** In 1949.

Films as Writer:

1914   *Der Golem* (*The Golem*) (+ co d, ro—short)
1919   *Die beiden Gatten der Frau Ruth* (Biebrach—short); *Die rollende Kugel* (Biebrach); *Peter Schlemihl* (Rye) (+ ro)
1920   *Der Golem, wie er in die Welt kam* (*The Golem*) (Wegener); *Der verbotene Weg* (+ d); *Judith Trachtenberg* (+ d)
1921   *Die geliebte Roswolskys* (Basch); **Nosferatu: Eine Symphonie des Grauens** (*Nosferatu the Vampire*) (Murnau)
1923   *Stadt in Sicht* (+ d)
1924   *Die Liebesbriefe der Baronin von S.* (+ d); *Auf gefährlichen Spuren* (*Verwehte Spuren*) (Piel) (+ ro); *Das Wachsfigurenkabinett* (*Waxworks*) (Leni)
1925   *Das Fräulein vom Amt* (*Liebe und Telephon*) (Schwarz); *Zigano, der Brigant vom Monte Diavolo* (*Zigano*) (Piel) (+ ro)
1926   *Der Student von Prag* (*The Student of Prague*); *The Man Who Cheated Life* (+ d); *Achtung Harry! Augen auf!* (*Sechs Wochen unter den Apachen*) (Piel)
1927   *Alraune* (*Mandrake*; *Unholy Love*; *A Daughter of Destiny*) (+ d); *Sein grösster Bluff* (*Er oder ich*) (Piel)
1928   *Die Dame mit der Maske* (Thiele)
1931   *Schatten der Unterwelt* (Piel)

Other Films:

1913   *Der Student von Prag* (Rye) (asst d)
1923   *Das Haus ohne Lachen* (ro)
1929   *After the Verdict* (d)
1933   *Salon Dora Green* (*Die Falle*) (d)

Publications

By GALEEN: books—

The Golem and *Nosferatu* (screenplays) in *Films of Tyranny*, edited by Richard B. Byrne, Madison, Wisconsin, 1966.
Nosferatu (screenplay) in *Masterworks of the German Cinema*, edited by Roger Manvell, London, 1973.
Nosferatu (screenplay) in *Murnau*, by Lotte Eisner, Berkeley, California, 1973.
Das Wachsfigurenkabinett: Drehbuch von Henrik Galeen zu Paul Lenis Film von 1923, Munchen, 1994.

On GALEEN: article—

Filmkultura, no. 12, January 1993.

*   *   *

Henrik Galeen, who was possibly of Danish, Dutch or Czech origin, became an actor in the early German theatre and (from 1910) in the German cinema. He was very soon to widen his career in film and establish himself both as a screenwriter and director of some importance, especially in the development of the Expressionist movement during the 1920s. As Lotte Eisner, in her invaluable book on the German Expressionist film, *The Haunted Screen*, has pointed out, Expressionist stylization in the art direction for fantasy and horror subjects actually preceded by some years its notable popularization in *The Cabinet of Dr. Caligari* of 1919; it appeared for example in the earliest version of *The Student of Prague*, directed by Stellan Rye in 1913, in which the actor-director Paul Wegener starred. The following year Wegener made his early version of the mythological film, *The Golem*, also employing a pioneer form of the Expressionist style in order to establish the medieval form of magic of this strange Jewish legend. He was assisted by Galeen as both scriptwriter and director, and Galeen also acted in the film.

After this Galeen either directed, codirected, or wrote a number of silent films (*Peter Schlemihl*, *Judith Trachtenberg*), including coscripting another (1920) version of *The Golem*, directed by Wegener, who also played the title role. Among Galeen's greatest contributions to German cinema was the script for *Nosferatu the Vampire*, directed by one of Germany's most distinguished filmmakers, F.W. Murnau. Murnau's working script survives, and is the subject of detailed comment and generous quotation by Lotte Eisner in her book *Murnau*. Galeen's script was written in the Expressionist style much resembling blank verse established by Carl Mayer, who was in process of becoming Germany's outstanding scriptwriter for silent film; and the talents of Galeen and Murnau fused in this, still one of the most

Henrik Galeen (seated in center)

effective of the period's German ''haunted'' films. Galeen went on to write and direct more routine films (*Stadt in Sicht, Die Liebesbriefe der Baronin von S.*) before scripting another influential film in the Expressionist style, *Waxworks*, which Paul Leni directed, and which Siegfried Kracauer points out in his book *From Caligari to Hitler* as developing further the theme of tyranny in all its varied forms which Galeen had originated in *Nosferatu*. The film is a three-part feature fantasizing the power-crazed ''tyrants'' Harun-al-Raschid, Ivan the Terrible, and Jack the Ripper. In 1926 he directed and coscripted a later version of *The Student of Prague* starring Conrad Veidt and Werner Krauss, again one of the most effective of Germany's silent ''haunted'' films, with emphasis on the psychology of Baldwin (Veidt) in his struggle with his *doppelgäner*, or alter ego, revealed as a hidden aspect of his own, individual psyche, and displaying Galeen's special skill in handling both fantasy and horror. *Alraune* (which Galeen coscripted and directed) followed, a study of a destructive *femme fatale* (Brigitte Helm), a woman created by artificial insemination as the child of a prostitute and a criminal who had been hanged.

Galeen bridged the silent and early sound film periods with less interesting work, coming to Britain for a short while, where he directed *After the Verdict* in 1929, a film scripted by Alma Reville, made during the difficult changeover from silent to sound film technique. He left Germany for the U.S. in 1933, when Hitler came to power, but made no films there. There are several references to his collaboration with Siegfried Kracauer on *From Caligari to Hitler*, but following this there appears to be no record of his activities.

—Roger Manvell

GARMES, Lee

Cinematographer and Director. **Nationality:** American. **Born:** Peoria, Illinois, 27 May 1898. **Education:** Attended North Denver High School, Colorado. **Career:** 1916—painter's assistant for Thomas Ince, then property boy and camera assistant; 1923—cinematographer on first films, *Fighting Blood* series; late 1920s—helped develop crab dolly; producer and director in the 1930s; later worked in TV. **Award:** Academy Award for *Shanghai Express*, 1932. **Died:** 31 August 1978.

Films as Cameraman:

1918   *The Hope Chest* (Clifton)
1919   *Chicken à la King* (short); *I'll Get Him Yet* (Clifton); *Nugget Nell* (Clifton); *Nobody Home* (Clifton)
1921   *Sweet Cookie* (Schlank—short)

Films as Cinematographer:

1923   *Fighting Blood* series (St. Clair and Lehrman—shorts)
1924   *The Telephone Girl* series (St. Clair—shorts); *Find Your Man* (St. Clair); *The Lighthouse by the Sea* (St. Clair) (co)
1925   *The Pacemaker* series (Ruggles—shorts); *Crack o' Dawn* (Rogell); *Goat Getter* (Rogell); *Keep Smilin'* (Pratt and Austin) (co)
1926   *The Grand Duchess and the Waiter* (St. Clair); *The Carnival Girl* (Tate); *A Social Celebrity* (St. Clair); *The Palm Beach Girl* (Kenton); *The Show Off* (St. Clair); *The Popular Sin* (St. Clair)
1927   *The Garden of Allah* (Ingram) (co); *Rose of the Golden West* (Fitzmaurice); *The Private Life of Helen of Troy* (Z. Korda) (co); *The Love Mart* (Fitzmaurice)
1928   *The Little Shepherd of Kingdom Come* (Santell); *The Yellow Lily* (Z. Korda); *The Barker* (Fitzmaurice); *Waterfront* (Seiter)
1929   *His Captive Woman* (Fitzmaurice); *Love and the Devil* (Z. Korda); *Prisoners* (Seiter); *Say It with Songs* (Bacon); *The Great Divide* (Barker) (co); *Disraeli* (Green)
1930   *Lillies of the Field* (Z. Korda); *The Other Tomorrow* (Bacon); *Spring Is Here* (Dillon); *Song of the Flame* (Crosland); *Whoopee!* (Freeland) (co); *Bright Lights* (Curtiz); *Morocco* (von Sternberg)
1931   *Fighting Caravans* (Brower and Burton); *Dishonored* (von Sternberg); *Kiss Me Again* (*The Toast of the Legion*) (Seiter) (co); *City Streets* (Mamoulian); *An American Tragedy* (von Sternberg); *Confessions of a Co-ed* (*Her Dilemma*) (Burton and Murphy)
1932   *Shanghai Express* (von Sternberg); **Scarface** (Hawks) (co); *Smilin' Through* (Franklin); *Strange Interlude* (*Strange Interval*) (Leonard); *Call Her Savage* (Dillon)
1933   *The Face in the Sky* (Lachman); *Zoo in Budapest* (Lee); *My Lips Betray* (Blystone); *Shanghai Madness* (Blystone); *I Am Suzanne* (Lee)
1934   *George White's Scandals* (White, Freeland, and Lachman); *Crime without Passion* (Hecht and MacArthur) (+ assoc d)
1935   *Once in a Blue Moon* (Hecht and MacArthur) (+ assoc d); *The Scoundrel* (Hecht and MacArthur) (+ assoc d)
1939   **Gone with the Wind** (Fleming) (co—uncredited)
1940   *The Conquest of the Air* (Z. Korda and others) (co); *Angels over Broadway* (+ co-d)
1941   *Lydia* (Duvivier) (+ assoc pr)
1942   *Jungle Book* (Z. Korda) (co, + assoc pr); *Footlight Serenade* (Ratoff); *China Girl* (Hathaway)
1943   *Forever and a Day* (Clair and others) (co); *Flight for Freedom* (Mendes); *Stormy Weather* (Stone) (co); *Jack London* (Santell) (co)

1944   *None Shall Escape* (De Toth); *Since You Went Away* (Cromwell) (co); *Guest in the House* (Brahm)
1945   *Paris Underground* (*Madame Pimpernel*) (Ratoff); *Love Letters* (Dieterle)
1946   *Spectre of the Rose* (+ co-pr + co-d); *Duel in the Sun* (K. Vidor) (co); *Young Widow* (Marin); *The Searching Wind* (Dieterle)
1947   *The Secret Life of Walter Mitty* (McLeod); *Nightmare Alley* (Goulding); *The Paradine Case* (Hitchcock)
1948   *Caught* (Ophüls)
1949   *Roseanna McCoy* (Reis); *The Fighting Kentuckian* (Waggner); *My Foolish Heart* (Robson); *Our Very Own* (Miller)
1950   *My Friend Irma Goes West* (Walker)
1951   *Actors and Sin* (+ co-d); *That's My Boy* (Walker); *Detective Story* (Wyler); *Saturday's Hero* (*Idols in the Dust*) (Miller); *Thunder in the East* (C. Vidor)
1952   *The Captive City* (Wise); *The Lusty Men* (Ray)
1953   *Outlaw Territory* (Hannah Lee) (+ co-pr + co-d)
1954   *Abdulla the Great* (*Abdullah's Harem*) (Ratoff)
1955   *Land of the Pharoahs* (Hawks) (co); *The Desperate Hours* (Wyler); *Man with the Gun* (*The Trouble Shooter*) (Wilson)
1956   *The Bottom of the Bottle* (*Beyond the River*) (Hathaway); *D Day, the Sixth of June* (Koster); *The Sharkfighters* (Hopper); *The Big Boodle* (*Night in Havana*) (Wilson)
1957   *Never Love a Stranger* (Stevens)
1959   *The Big Fisherman* (Borzage); *Happy Anniversary* (Miller)
1961   *Misty* (Clark)
1962   *Ernest Hemingway's Adventures of a Young Man* (Ritt); *Ten Girls Ago* (Daniels)
1963   *Lady in a Cage* (Grauman)
1966   *A Big Hand for the Little Lady* (*Big Deal at Dodge City*) (Cook)
1967   *How to Save a Marriage and Ruin Your Life* (Cook)
1972   *Why?* (Stoloff)

Other Films:

1934   *The Nephew of Paris* (d—short)
1937   *The Sky's the Limit* (co-d); *Dreaming Lips* (co-d); *The Lilac Domino* (Zelnik) (assoc pr)
1940   *Beyond Tomorrow* (Sutherland) (pr)

Publications

By GARMES: articles—

"Photography," in *Behind the Screen: How Films Are Made*, edited by Stephen Watts, London, 1938.
"Lighting Translucent Backings," in *American Cinematographer* (Hollywood), November 1949.
Sight and Sound (London), Autumn 1967.
In *Sources of Light*, by Charles Higham, London, 1970.
On *Why?* in *American Cinematographer* (Hollywood), October 1972.

Journal of the University Film Association (Carbondale, Illinois), vol. 26, no. 4, 1974.

Wide Angle (Athens, Ohio), vol. 1, no. 3, 1976.

Journal of the University Film Association (Carbondale, Illinois), Fall 1976.

Boxoffice (Kansas City), 24 April 1978.

On GARMES: articles—

Wayne, Palma, in *Saturday Evening Post* (Philadelphia, Pennsylvania), 22 July 1933.

Cue (New York), 9 February 1935.

Foster, Frederick, in *American Cinematographer* (Hollywood), March 1949.

Foster, Frederick, in *American Cinematographer* (Hollywood), August 1959.

Monthly Film Bulletin (London), September 1967.

Monthly Film Bulletin (London), October 1971.

Film Comment (New York), Summer 1972.

Lightman, Herb A., in *American Cinematographer* (Hollywood), October 1972.

Focus on Film (London), no. 13, 1973.

Collura, J., in *Classic Images* (Muscatine, Iowa), September 1983.

American Cinematographer (Hollywood), October 1985.

Anez, N., ''Westerns,'' in *Films in Review* (New York), November-December 1994.

*   *   *

Lee Garmes admitted to having been strongly influenced by Rembrandt. Like the Dutch painter, the director used north light by lighting the set from an opening facing north. He desired to achieve a low-key light, with lots of deep shadows and a lack of strong headlights. Critics have referred to his light as ''painterly.'' Most details are omitted; only significant elements of the scene and actors are highlighted. In *The Garden of Allah* Garmes draws upon the north-light effect, which had first been developed by John F. Seitz. In the courtroom scene in *An American Tragedy* most of the light comes from a window facing north.

These stylistic traits date from influences gained in Garmes's silent-film work. From working with John Leezer, he learned to filter out unwanted detail by means of gauze over the lens. Near the end of the First World War, Garmes got a hack job filming slapstick comedies for Gale Henry. The films' budgets were so low that the cameramen had no lights and used an open stage with reflectors that caught and directed the sunlight. In *The Grand Duchess and the Waiter* Garmes and the director Mal St. Clair sought to achieve a subtly varying grisaille effect by lighting and by creating sets painted in different shades of grey. In *The Little Shepherd of Kingdom Come* Garmes completely replaced the arc with Mazda lights and lead-sheet reflectors. *Morocco*, Garmes's first masterpiece, evoked North Africa with a torrid mix of sun and shadows, created by covering the ''streets'' with lattice-work and filming at high noon. Garmes filmed Marlene Dietrich with the north-light effect—his trademark, and hers from then on. He further added to the Dietrich image by lighting her in a low key and filming her in the misty atmosphere of *Shanghai Express*. In *Zoo in Budapest* Garmes created a verdant, parklike effect by placing lacy plants in front of the camera—they appear as a hazy blur.

Even when working with color, he always strove for a soft effect and a certain vagueness. He worked on the opening portions of *Gone with the Wind*, and sought a soft-toned color; however, David O. Selznick took Garmes off the film because the producer preferred harsh, picture-postcard colors. Garmes claims credit for planning the Atlanta railway-yard shot; but so do Val Lewton and others.

Of his later works, Garmes felt that his best work was *The Big Fisherman*, but perhaps a more interesting piece, cinematographically speaking, is his work on *How to Save a Marriage*, where he achieves a subtle form of expressionistic lighting varied to convey the moods of the protagonist.

—Rodney Farnsworth

GAUDIO, Tony

Cinematographer. **Nationality:** Italian. **Born:** Gaetano Antonio Gaudio in Cosenza, 1885. **Education:** Attended an art school, Rome. **Family:** Brother of the cinematographer Eugene Gaudio. **Career:** Assistant to his father and elder brother, portrait photographers; 1903–06—photographed hundreds of short subjects for Italian film companies

Tony Gaudio with Ann Blyth

(first title: *Napoleon Crossing the Alps*); 1906–08—made "song slides" for Al Simpson, New York; 1908—worked in Vitagraph laboratories, New York, then supervised construction of Laemmle laboratories, New York; 1910–12—chief of cinematographers at Laemmle's Imp Company; then worked for Biograph and other companies; 1922—invented the Mitchell camera finder; also invented the camera focusing microscope; 1923–24—President, American Society of Cinematographers; 1930–43—at Warner Bros.. **Award:** Academy Award for *Anthony Adverse*, 1936. **Died:** In 1951.

Films as Cinematographer:

1903   *Napoleon Crossing the Alps*

1908   *Madame Nicotine*

1910   *Submarine*

1911   *Pictureland; Their First Misunderstanding* (T. Ince and Tucker); *The Dream* (T. Ince and Tucker); *Maid or Man* (T. Ince); *At the Duke's Command; The Mirror; While the Cat's Away; Her Darkest Hours* (T. Ince); *Artful Kate* (T. Ince); *A Manly Man* (T. Ince); *The Message in the Bottle* (T. Ince); *The Fisher-Maid* (T. Ince); *In Old Madrid* (T. Ince); *Sweet Memories of Yesterday* (T. Ince); *The Stampede; Second Sight; The Fair Dentist; For Her Brother's Sake* (T. Ince and Tucker); *Back to the Soil; In the Sultan's Garden* (T. Ince); *The Master and the Man; The Lighthouse Keeper; For the Queen's Honor* (+ ro); *A Gasoline Engagement; At a Quarter of Two; Science; The Skating Bug; The Call of the Song; The Toss of a Coin; The Sentinel Asleep; The Better Way; His Dress Shirt; The Nose's Story; From the Bottom of the Sea*

1914   *Classmates* (Kirkwood); *Strongheart* (Powell or Kirkwood); *The Woman in Black* (Marsten); *The Cricket on the Hearth* (Marsten)

1916   *The Unpardonable Sin* (O'Neill); *The Masked Rider ; Mister 44* (Otto); *The River of Romance* (Balshofer); *Big Tremaine* (Balshofer)

1917   *Pidgin Island* (Balshofer); *The Promise* (Balshofer); *The Hidden Children* (Apfel); *The Haunted Pajamas* (Balshofer); *The Hidden Spring* (Hopper); *Under Handicap* (Balshofer); *Paradise Garden* (Balshofer); *The Square Deceiver* (Balshofer); *The Avenging Trail* (F. Ford)

1918   *Broadway Bill* (Balshofer); *The Landloper* (Irving); *Lend Me Your Name* (Balshofer); *Pals First* (Carewe)

1919   *Man of Honor* (Balshofer and Lockwood); *In Wrong* (Kirkwood); *The Inferior Sex* (Henabery)

1920   *Fighting Shepherdess* (José); *Her Kingdom of Dreams* (Neilan); *The Mark of Zorro* (Niblo); *The Forbidden Thing* (Dwan); *Kismet* (Gasnier); *Whispering Devils* (Garson); *In Old Kentucky* (Neilan)

1921   *The Other Woman* (Sloman); *The Ten Dollar Raise* (Sloman); *The Sin of Martha Queed* (*Sins of the Parents*) (Dwan); *Shattered Idols* (Sloman); *Pilgrims of the Nights* (Sloman)

1922   *The Woman He Loved* (*How a Man Loves*) (Sloman); *The Eternal Flame* (Floyd); *East Is West* (Franklin)

1923   *The Voice from the Minaret* (Lloyd) (co); *Adam and Eva* (Vignola) (co); *Within the Law* (Lloyd); *Ashes of Vengeance* (Lloyd); *The Song of Love* (Franklin and Marion)

1924   *Secrets* (Borzage); *Husbands and Lovers* (Stahl); *The Only Woman* (Olcott)

1925   *The Lady* (Borzage); *Déclassée* (*The Social Exile*) (Vignola); *Graustark* (Buchowetzki)

1926   *The Gay Deceiver* (*The Mask of Comedy*) (Stahl) (co); *The Temptress* (Niblo) (co); *Upstage* (Bell); *The Blonde Saint* (Gade)

1927   *An Affair of the Follies* (Webb); *The Notorious Lady* (Baggot); *Two Arabian Knights* (Milestone) (co)

1928   *The Gaucho* (Jones); *The Racket* (Milestone)

1929   *She Goes to War* (H. King) (co); *On with the Show* (Crosland); *Tiger Rose* (Archainbaud); *General Crack* (Crosland)

1930   *Hell's Angels* (Hughes); **Little Caesar** (LeRoy); **All Quiet on the Western Front** (Milestone) (2nd cam)

1931   *The Lady Who Dared* (*The Devil's Playground*) (Beaudine)

1932   *Sky Devils* (Sutherland); *Tiger Shark* (Hawks); *The Mask of Fu Manchu* (Brabin)

1933   *Blondie Johnson* (Enright); *Ex-Lady* (Florey); *The Silk Express* (Enright); *The Narrow Corner* (Green); *Private Detective 62* (Curtiz); *Voltaire* (Adolfi); *Ladies Must Love* (Dupont); *The World Changes* (LeRoy); *Lady Killer* (Del Ruth)

1934   *Upperworld* (Del Ruth); *Mandalay* (Curtiz); *Fog over Frisco* (Dieterle); *The Man with Two Faces* (Mayo); *The Dragon Murder Case* (Humberstone); *Happiness Ahead* (LeRoy); *Bordertown* (Mayo)

1935   *The White Cockatoo* (Crosland); *Sweet Music* (Green) (co); *Oil for the Lamps of China* (LeRoy); *Go into Your Dance* (*Casino de Paree*) (Maro); *Front Page Woman* (Curtiz); *Little Big Shot* (Curtiz); *The Case of the Lucky Legs* (Mayo); *Dr. Socrates* (Dieterle)

1936   *The Story of Louis Pasteur* (Dieterle); *The White Angel* (Dieterle); *Anthony Adverse* (LeRoy); *God's Country and the Woman* (Keighley) (co)

1937   *The King and the Chorus Girl* (*Romance Is Sacred*) (LeRoy); *Kid Galahad* (Dieterle); *Another Dawn* (Dieterle); *The Life of Emile Zola* (Dieterle)

1938   *Torchy Blane in Panama* (*Trouble in Panama*) (Clemens); **The Adventures of Robin Hood** (Curtiz and Keighley) (co); *The Amazing Dr. Clitterhouse* (Litvak); *Gardens of the Moon* (Berkeley); *Secrets of an Actress* (Keighley) (co); *The Sisters* (Litvak); *The Dawn Patrol* (Goulding)

1939   *Juarez* (Dieterle); *The Old Maid* (Goulding); *We Are Not Alone* (Goulding)

1940   *The Fighting 69th* (Keighley); *'Till We Meet Again* (Goulding); *Brother Orchid* (Bacon); *The Letter* (Wyler); *Knute Rockne—All-American* (*A Modern Hero*) (Bacon)

1941   **High Sierra** (Walsh); *The Great Lie* (Goulding); *Affectionately Yours* (Bacon); *Navy Blues* (Bacon) (co); *The Man Who Came to Dinner* (Keighley)

1942   *Larceny Inc.* (Bacon); *Wings for the Eagle* (Bacon); *You Can't Escape Forever* (Graham)

1943   *Action in the North Atlantic* (Bacon) (co); *The Constant Nymph* (Goulding); *Background to Danger* (Walsh); *Corvette K-225* (*The Nelson Touch*) (Rosson)

1944   *Days of Glory* (Tourneur); *Experiment Perilous* (Tourneur); *I'll Be Seeing You* (Dieterle); *A Song to Remember* (C. Vidor) (co)

1946 *The Bandit of Sherwood Forest* (G. Sherman and Levin) (co); *I've Always Loved You* (*Concerto*) (Borzage); *Swell Guy* (Tuttle)

1947 *That's My Man* (*Will Tomorrow Ever Come?*) (Borzage); *Love from a Stranger* (*A Stranger Walked In*) (Whorf)

1949 *The Red Pony* (Milestone)

Publications

On GAUDIO: articles—

Film Comment (New York), Summer 1972.
Focus on Film (London), no. 13, 1973.
Tibbetts, John C., ''*The Gaucho*,'' in *Films in Review*, July-August 1996.

*   *   *

Gaetano (Tony) Gaudio, along with Sol Polito, Barney McGill, and Sid Hickox, helped create the Warner Bros. photographic style of the 1930s, crisp and economic, with a strong influence of German Expressionism. Warners, unlike MGM and Paramount, did not demand pretty pictures, and these cameramen were able to light for mood and atmosphere. Gaudio was extremely versatile and able to handle all types of pictures, from big-budget extravaganzas to B-movies like the *Torchy Blane* series.

Gaudio was a pioneer cinematographer; as early as 1911 he was the chief cameraman for Carl Laemmle's Universal Pictures. In the 1920s he photographed two Douglas Fairbanks adventures, *The Mark of Zorro* and *The Gaucho*, and worked with top directors like Marshal Neilan, Allan Dwan, and Frank Borzage. He contributed to some of the earliest Technicolor sequences (*The Gaucho*, *On with the Show*, *General Crack*), as well as the seminal war films *All Quiet on the Western Front* (second camera to Arthur Edeson) and *Hell's Angels*, handling the dialogue scenes with Harry Perry on the aerial cinematography.

Gaudio hit his stride when he signed with Warner Bros. in 1930. He shot Mervyn LeRoy's gangster classic *Little Caesar* in a harsh style befitting the gritty subject. Throughout the 1930s Gaudio handled Warners' most prestigious films, such as LeRoy's *Oil for the Lamps of China* and *Anthony Adverse*, and William Dieterle's *Story of Louis Pasteur* and *Life of Emile Zola*. The LeRoy films were among the studio's most ambitious projects and, with the Dieterle biographies, gave Warners unaccustomed Oscar status. Gaudio's work met with critical acclaim, and he won an Academy Award for his impressive work on *Anthony Adverse*.

After shooting Warners' first three-strip Technicolor film, *God's Country and the Woman*, Gaudio was reteamed with that picture's director William Keighley for *The Adventures of Robin Hood*, a color spectacle with Errol Flynn in the title role. Keighley and Gaudio started the picture on a difficult location and work went too slowly, prompting producer Hal Wallis to replace them with director Michael Curtiz and cameraman Sol Polito, although they all shared screen credit. Gaudio's footage included the first meeting in the forest between Robin and Little John, portions of the archery tournament, the banquet in the woods, and the fight between Robin and Friar Tuck. Gaudio was director of photography on another Flynn picture, Edmund Goulding's *The Dawn Patrol*, a remake of Howard Hawks' 1930

World War I aviation story. Aerial scenes from the original were used in the Goulding version, and Gaudio was responsible for the claustrophobic interiors.

Gaudio was a regular cameraman for Bette Davis. For *Ex-Lady*, an early attempt to turn her into a sex symbol, Gaudio gave Davis the glamour treatment. By the time he shot *Bordertown*, the studio realized her histrionic talents, and Gaudio brought a stark realism to the seedy Mexican setting. *Kid Galahad* gave him the opportunity to contrast high-key Art Deco scenes with the smoky interiors of the boxing ring. Gaudio deglamorized Davis in two period films, *Juarez* and *The Old Maid*, gave the contemporaneous *The Great Lie* a shining look, and reached the zenith of his Warner days with William Wyler's *The Letter*. One of Davis' best remembered vehicles, *The Letter* is distinguished by Gaudio's moody cinematography, especially the memorable opening shot, a slow track through a Malaysian rubber plantation that sets the tone for the whole picture.

Gaudio lit Raoul Walsh's crime masterwork *High Sierra* in an ultrarealistic, documentary-like fashion. Gaudio left Warners in 1943, and his subsequent work lacks the same consistency he had previously demonstrated, although he achieved some fine color cinematography on *A Song to Remember* and *The Red Pony*. Like many of the technicians during the Golden Age of Hollywood, Gaudio was at his best in the highly departmentalized confines of the studio system.

—John A. Gallagher

GAUMONT, Léon

Producer. **Nationality:** French. **Born:** Paris, 10 May 1864. **Education:** Attended College of Sainte-Barbe. **Career:** After military service, managed an incandescent lamp factory; 1895—formed the Gaumont Company to market cinema apparatus; marketed the Demeny Bioscope; 1896—produced the first actualité films; 1898—opened London office; 1899—first films made in England; 1903—introduced the Gaumont Chronophone and Chronomegaphone as a prelude to talking pictures; 1905—built the first great French movie studio and produced colour pictures with Chronochrome; 1912—showed popular ''rural scenes'' in colour; 1929—retired from movies. **Award:** Exhibition Prize of France for ''having contributed in greatest measure to the progress of photography.'' **Died:** In Sainte-Maxime, 10 August 1946.

Films as Producer (selected list):

1895–97 *Une Caravane au Jardin d'Acclimatation*; *Les Grandes Eaux de Versailles*; *Le Déjeuner des oiseaux au Kursaal de Vienne*; *La Sortie des usines Panhard et Levessor*; *Défilé d'artillerie à la revue du 14 juillet 1896*; *L'Arrivée du Président de la République au pesage* (*Grand Prix de Paris 1896*); *Le Fardier*; *La Charmeuse de serpents*

1898 *La Vie du Christ*

1899 *Les Méfaits d'un tête de veau* (Guy); *Monnaie de lapin* (Guy); *Les Dangers de l'alcoolisme* (Guy); *Mauvaise soupe* (Guy);

Léon Gaumont (center)

Mésaventure d'un charbonnier (Guy); Le Tonnelier (Guy); Chanteurs des cours (Guy); Angélus (Guy); La Bonne Absinthe (Guy)

1900   L'Ascension du Mont-Blanc; Cyrano de Bergerac; Précieuses ridicules

1901   Au bal de flore (Guy); Fredaines de Pierrette (Guy); Défilé de vaches laitières; Baignades dans le torrent; Pédiluve; Laboureur; Marché a la volaille; Récolte des betteraves; Sortie d'un vapeur du port du Havre; Bataille de boules de neige

1902   Sage-femme de première classe (La Fée aux choux) (Gallet)

1903   Illusioniste renversant; Modelage express

1904   L'Assassinat du courrier de Lyon (Gallet); Nos bons étudiants (Gallet); Paris la nuit (Guy); Volé par les bohemiens (Gallet); L'Assassinat de la rue du Temple (Gallet); Les Petits Coupeurs de bois verts (Gallet); Le Cake-Walk de la pendule (Guy); La Passion (Guy); Histoire d'un crime (Gallet)

1905   La Esmérelda (Jasset); Réhabilitation; Robert Macaire; Une Noceau Lac Saint-Fargeau

1906   Rêves d'un fumeur d'Opium (Jasset); La Vie du Christ (Jasset)

1907   The Mikado; Vive le sabotage!; Father Buys a Ladder; La Course des belles mères; Towser and the Tramp; L'Homme aimanté; Un Facteur trop ferré; Le Lecteur distrait; L'Aveugle; L'Ordonnance; La Bataille d'oreillers; Toto aéronaute; L'Apprenti; L'Arroseur arrosé; Le Planton du colonel; Le Cocher de fiacre endormi; La Lecon de boxe comique; Zigomar serial

1908   Un Drame chez les fantoches

1909   Nick Carter serial (Jasset); Morgan le Pirate (Jasset); Le Vantour de la Sierra (Jasset); Meskal le contrabandier (Jasset)

1910   Morgan le pirate serial (Jasset); Hérodiade (Jasset)

1911   Dans la vie (Perret); Zigomar (Jasset); Nick Carter (Jasset); La Fin de Don Juan (Jasset)

1913   Bouquets de fleurs; Voyage à la Côte d'Azur; Carnaval à Nice; Majorca; Balao (Jasset); Zigomar peau d'anguille (Jasset); Protea I (Jasset); L'enfant de Paris (Perret); La Force de l'argent (Perret); Erreur tragique (Perret); Les Léonce (Perret)

1915   Un Drame au château d'Acre (Gance); L'Héröisme de Paddy (Gance); Strass et cie (Gance); La Fleur des ruines (Gance);

Le Périscope (Gance); *La Folie du Dr. Tube* (Gance); *La Fiancée du diable* (Perret); *Les Mystères de l'ombre*

1916 *Le Droit à la vie* (Gance); *Les Gaz mortels* (Gance); *Le Bluff* (Feyder); *L'Homme de compagnie* (Feyder); *L'Instinct est maître* (Feyder)

1917 *Les Vieilles Femmes de l'hospice* (Feyder); *Le Ravin sans fond* (Feyder); *Mater dolorosa* (Gance); *Zone de mort* (Gance); *Barberousse* (Gance)

1918 ***La Haine***; *La Dixième Symphonie* (Gance)

1919 *J'accuse* (Gance); *Rose France* (L'Herbier); *Phantasmes* (L'Herbier); *La Faute d'orthographie* (Feyder); *Ames d'orient* (Poirier)

1920 *L'Homme du large* (L'Herbier)

1921 *El Dorado* (L'Herbier)

Films as Producer (directed by Feuillade):

1909 *Judith et Holopherne*; *La Possession de l'enfant*; *La Légende des phares*; *Le Huguenot*; *La Mort*; *La Fille du cantonnier*

1910 *Les Sept Pechés capitaux*; *Le Pater*; *1814*; *La Fille de Jephté*; *La Roi de Thulé*; *Bienvenuto Cellini*; *Esther*; *Chef-Lieu de Canton*

1911 *Aux lions les chrétiens*; *Les Vipères*; *Le Roi Lear au village*; *Le Poison*; *Le Trust*; *Les Souris blanches*; *En grève*; *La Tare*

1912 *Les Braves Gens*; *Le Nain*; *La Hantise*; *L'Oubliette*; *Le Proscrit*

1913 *L'Agonie de Byzance*; *S'affranchir*; *Série des bouts de Zari*; *Les Yeux ouverts*; *La Rose blanche*; *L'Angoisse*; *Fantômas*; *Juve contre Fantômas*; *Le Mort qui tue*

1914 *Fantômas contre Fantômas*; *La Vie drôle*; *Le Faux Magistrat*

1915–16 ***Les Vampires*** serial (10 episodes)

1916 ***Judex*** serial (12 episodes)

1918 *La Nouvelle Mission de Judex*; *Vendemiaire*

1919 *Tin-minh*; *L'Homme sans visage*; *L'Engrenage*; *Nocturne*; *Enigme*

Publications

On GAUMONT: books—

Établissements Gaumont 1895–1929, Paris, 1935.
Sadoul, Georges, *Les Pionniers du Cinéma*, Paris, 1947.
Fescourt, Henri, *La Foi et les montagnes*, Paris, 1959.

On GAUMONT: articles—

La Technique cinématographique (Paris), no. 128, January 1953.
Montgomery, John, "The First Comedies," in *Comedy Films*, 1954.
Film Français (Paris), no. 1755, 2 February 1979.
Avant-Scène (Paris), no. 334, November 1984.
Cine Cubano, no. 132, 1991.
Variety, vol. 346, 20 January 1992.
Variety, vol. 347, 20 July 1992.
Variety, vol. 351, 12 July 1993.
Film Journal, vol. 96, December 1993.

Variety (New York), 24–30 January 1994.
Turman, Suzanna, "Gaumont (Gaumont Film Company)," in *Films in Review* (Denville), January-February 1994.
"100 Years of Cinema (Studio History) (Gaumont 100th Anniversary," in *Variety* (New York), 12 December 1994.
Les Cahiers de la Cinematheque (Perpignan), December 1995.
Positif (Paris), April 1996.

*　　*　　*

After 1895, and the success of the Lumière films, France was a hive of invention and film projects. Unlike his compatriot and rival, Charles Pathé, Léon Gaumont came from a comfortable background, running a well-established photographic and optical apparatus business. He was financially well-connected, and in 1895 was able to found the Léon Gaumont company with a capital of 200,000 francs. He acquired the rights to inventions by a man called Demeny, and with the help of his partner was able to give the illusion of living portraits by marketing the chronophotograph. It was only a short step to involvement with the newly fledged cinema, and he opened his film studio, soon to be known as "Cité Elge" after his initials, at Buttes-Chaumont. This became one of the largest studios in Europe, managed by Gaumont's secretary, Alice Guy, who was to become an important figure in American cinema and is often cited as the first woman director.

Gaumont's first films were simple vaudeville sketches, comedies, moral tales, and, of course, imitations of other people's film successes. As his enterprise expanded and developed, documentaries, newsreels, scientific and educational programmes were embarked upon.

His organisation now spread to other countries, and in England, for example, Colonel Bromhead opened the first Gaumont Cinema in 1901. The first British Gaumont production was *The Life of Richard Wagner*, and the *Gaumont Graphic* soon took its place among British newsreels. Documentaries included *The Ascent of Mont Blanc* and the *National Pilgrimage to Lourdes of 1902*. In 1913, Gaumont established his Vitorine Studios in Nice, which was to form the basis of Rex Ingram's studio.

The sound-film was of special interest to Gaumont, and in 1903 he introduced the chronophone which he circulated worldwide. His technical section was constantly experimenting with improvements, and he introduced early wide-screen and elaborate amplification systems. Although talkies did not really come into their own until the end of the twenties, nevertheless Gaumont maintained his interest in the area and was associated with the first modern French sound film, *Eau de nil*.

Gaumont took a particular interest in the American cinema, and was a close friend of George Eastman, the raw-film manufacturer. He championed the independent filmmakers of Europe against the Edison Trust controls, but the First World War was a big blow to European cinema, particularly that of France. American films were encroaching, with technical innovation and big star names that were extremely popular with French audiences. Gaumont ruefully remarked, "We made munitions for war in our factories. They made movies, and they have conquered us."

Gaumont attracted many talented people to his studios. After Guy left, he replaced her with Victorin Jasset, the maker of the famous *Zigomar* serial, and following him came perhaps the most famous name in the Gaumont team—Louis Feuillade. It was he who gave the films a particular colouring, with his famous serials *Fantômas*, *Les*

Vampires, and *Judex*. The worldwide popularity of these films and their special visual richness make them today classics of a great period of French filmmaking.

As the French film developed visually and artistically, the Gaumont company found a home for such diverse and innovative talents as Léon Poirier (*Jocelyn*, *La Brière*), Marcel L'Herbier (*Rose France*, *El Dorado*), Jacques Feyder (*La Faute d'orthographie*), Léonce Perret (comedian, and director of *L'enfant de Paris*), and Abel Gance (actor, and director of *La Folie du Dr. Tube*).

By 1925, Gaumont had increased his capital by an arrangement with MGM, but by 1938 his financial structures began to crumble. Today, his name is still familiar, but the extent of his achievement is past history. There was little in the field of cinema that he did not tackle. He handled production and worldwide distribution, ran supercinemas, developed colour and sound, and made huge technical innovations. He was a harsh taskmaster, never less than frank if the work of one of his employees displeased him, and in the early days, so they say, this giant of the French cinema stood at the doors of his studio with watch in hand, checking the arrival of every one of his staff.

—Liam O'Leary

GÉGAUFF, Paul

Writer. **Pseudonym:** Martial Matthieu. **Nationality:** French. **Born:** Blötzheim, 10 August 1922. **Education:** Attended schools in Mulhouse and Basle, and educated at home. **Family:** Married the actress Danielle (Gégauff) (divorced). **Career:** Writer of fiction in the 1950s; cofounder, Cine-Club du Quartier Latin; 1959—first feature film as writer, *Les Cousins*; occasional actor. **Died:** (Murdered) in Gjoevic, Norway, 25 December 1983.

Films as Writer:

1950   *Journal d'un scélérat* (Rohmer) (+ ro)
1959   *Les Cousins* (*The Cousins*) (Chabrol); *Plein Soleil* (*Purple Noon*) (Clément); *A double tour* (*Leda; Web of Passion*) (Chabrol); *Le Signe du lion* (*The Sign of Leo*) (Rohmer)
1960   *Les Bonnes Femmes* (Chabrol)
1961   *Les Godelureaux* (Chabrol)
1962   *Les Reflux—L'Enfer au paradis* (+ d); *Un Chien dans un jeu de quilles* (Collin)
1963   *Ophélia* (Chabrol) (as Martial Matthieu); *Les Grands Chemins* (*Of Flesh and Blood*) (Marquand)
1964   "*L'Homme qui vendit la Tour Eiffel*" ep. of *Les Plus Belles Escroqueries du monde* (*The Beautiful Swindlers*) (Chabrol); *Le Gros Coup* (Valère)
1967   *Le Scandale* (*The Champagne Murders*) (Chabrol); *Diaboliquement vôtre* (*Diabolically Yours*) (Duvivier)
1968   *Les Biches* (*The Does*) (Chabrol); *Delphine* (Le Hung); *La Femme écarlate* (*The Scarlet Woman*) (Valère)
1969   *Que la bête meure* (*This Man Must Die*; *Killer!*) (Chabrol); *More* (Schroeder)
1970   *Les Novices* (Casaril); *Qui?* (Keigel)

1972   *La Decade prodigieuse* (*Ten Days' Wonder*) (Chabrol); *Docteur Popaul* (*Scoundrel in White*) (Chabrol); *La Vallée* (*The Valley*) (Schroeder)
1974   *Une Invitation à la chasse* (Chabrol)
1975   *Une Partie de plaisir* (*A Piece of Pleasure*; *Love Match*) (Chabrol) (+ ro); *Les Magiciens* (Chabrol)
1979   *Brigade mondaine* (*La Secte de Marrakech*) (Matalon); *Historien om en moder* (*The Story of a Mother*) (Weeks)
1981   *Les Folies d'elodie* (*Naughty Blue Knickers*) (Génovès)

Films as Actor:

1963   *Le Vice et la vertu* (*Vice and Virtue*) (Vadim)
1966   *La Ligne de démarcation* (*Line of Demarcation*) (Chabrol)
1967   **Week-end** (*Weekend*) (Godard)
1972   *Hellé* (Vadim)

Publications

By GÉGAUFF: books—

Les Mauvais Plaisants, Paris, 1951.
Le Toit des autres, Paris, 1952.
Rebus, Paris, 1957.
Une Partie de plaisir, Paris, 1958.
Tous mes amis, Paris, 1969.

By GÉGAUFF: articles—

Image et Son (Paris), January 1971.
Télérama (Paris), 18 January 1975.
Monthly Film Bulletin (London), August 1977.

On GÉGAUFF: articles—

Cahiers du Cinéma (Paris), December 1962.
Chaplin (Stockholm), no. 2, 1970.
Dirigido por . . . (Barcelona), August 1977.
Obituary in *Revue du Cinéma* (Paris), February 1984.
Obituary in *Cinématographe*, March 1984.
Pawelczak, Andy, "*Purple Noon*," in *Films in Review*, September-October 1996.
Buss, Robin, "*Plein Soleil*," in *Times Literary Supplement*, 29 August 1997.
Reader, Keith, "*Plein Soleil/Delitto in pieno sole/Blazing Sun/Purple Noon*," in *Sight and Sound* (London), September 1997.

*   *   *

Paul Gégauff and Claude Chabrol first met in the early 1950s at the Ciné-Club du Quartier Latin. Gégauff at this time was already a published novelist; Chabrol was a university student. A few years later Chabrol was one of the leading directors of the French New Wave, and Gégauff was his screenwriter.

The nature of the Chabrol-Gégauff collaboration is difficult to pin down. Chabrol is a fine writer himself, and he often takes cowriting credit in his films with Gégauff. Also, Chabrol has certain "signature" traits—a murder mystery plot, a bourgeois milieu, a pervasive atmosphere of guilt and complicity—no matter who writes the script. However, the Chabrol-Gégauff films do seem to be both crueler and more complexly plotted than the films Chabrol has written on his own.

The first Chabrol-Gégauff film was *Les Cousins*, one of the key films of the early New Wave. *Les Cousins* tells the story of a naive country cousin and a cynical city cousin, both students in contemporary Paris, and of the young woman to whom both are attracted. As in many Chabrol-Gégauff films, the characters are either repressed or decadent, with other, healthier possibilities almost entirely excluded.

With the commercial and critical success of *Les Cousins*, Chabrol and Gégauff were able to make more experimental narratives such as *A double tour* and *Les Bonnes Femmes*. The title of *A double tour* refers to a technique of scrambling chronology to show the same time period from more than one point of view. The murder mystery plot has Leda, a beautiful artist, killed by the son of her married lover. One interesting aspect of this film is its mixture of spontaneous, free characters and repressed, violent characters—both within the same family setting. Chabrol and Gégauff seem more adept at presenting the repressed characters, but they also try their hand at New Wave spontaneity à la Truffaut. *Les Bonnes Femmes* describes the lives and dreams of four Parisian shopgirls. Notably distanced and unsentimental, the film shows the young women as limited in imagination and self-knowledge.

Between 1967 and 1975 Chabrol and Gégauff collaborated on six feature films. *Les Biches*, the best known of them, returns to the triangular relationship of *Les Cousins*, but with greater rigor and intensity. The triangle here features two women (one inexperienced, one decadent) and one man; all possible relationships, including a lesbian affair, are worked out. The tangled motives and desires of the characters lead inevitably to a concluding murder. *Les Biches* is a subtle exploration of love and cruelty that marks the peak of the Chabrol-Gégauff collaboration.

Une Partie de plaisir, the last Chabrol-Gégauff film, is about the breakup of a marriage after the husband decides that he and his wife should take other lovers. The intimacies and cruelties of a relationship are here presented without the melodramatic touches (murders, hidden motives, surprises) of other Chabrol-Gégauff films. Curiously, Gégauff himself plays one lead in the film, his wife Danielle (they were separated at the time) the other. Nevertheless, Gégauff maintained that his script was only marginally autobiographical.

Gégauff's films with Chabrol are generally austere, beautifully made explorations of characters with limited self-knowledge who exist in highly defined and often repressive social environments. In his work with Barbet Schroeder, Gégauff turns to looser, freer, more exotic subjects. Both *More* and *The Valley* are clearly films of the late 1960s-early 1970s "youth culture," concerned with the sexual revolution, the use of drugs, the search for a new consciousness. But the cynical Gégauff does not suddenly turn sentimental in these films—the freedom of *More* is destroyed by heroin addiction; the freedom of *The Valley* may be an illusion.

Paul Gégauff also wrote four novels and one short-story collection. His literary work anticipates some themes of his scripts—cruelty, decadence, characters of limited self-understanding—and

showcases a dark sense of humor. One story, set in Parisian film circles, satirizes the pretensions of film acting.

—Peter Lev

GHERARDI, Piero

Art Director. **Nationality:** Italian. **Born:** Poppi, Arezzo, 20 November 1909. **Education:** Mainly self-taught in art and architecture. **Career:** Practicing architect in the 1930s; then set decorator and art director after 1945 (also designed costumes); stage designer in Italy and Britain. **Awards:** Academy Award for *La dolce vita*, 1961, *8½*, 1963. **Died:** In Rome, 8 June 1971.

Films as Art Director:

1946 *Daniele Cortis* (Soldati)
1947 *Amanti senza amore* (Franciolini)
1948 *Senza pietà* (*Without Pity*) (Lattuada); *Proibito rubare* (*Guaglio*) (Comencini); *Fuga in Francia* (Soldati)
1949 *Campane a martello* (*Children of Change*) (Zampa); *Napoli milionaria* (de Filippo) (co)
1950 *Cinema d'altri tempi* (Steno) (+ costumes); *Her Favourite Husband* (*The Taming of Dorothy*) (Soldati); *Romanzo d'amore* (*Toselli*) (Coletti); *Camicie rosse* (Alessandrini)
1951 *Sensualità* (Fracassi)
1953 *Anni facili* (*Easy Years*) (Zampa)
1954 *Proibito* (Monicelli) (+ costumes)
1956 *Le notti di Cabiria* (*Nights of Cabiria*) (Fellini)
1957 *Padri e figli . . .* (*Fathers and Sons*) (Monicelli); *La grande strada azzurra* (Pontecorvo) (co); *Il medico e lo stregone* (Monicelli) (+ costumes)
1958 *I soliti ignoti* (*Big Deal on Madonna Street*) (Monicelli) (+ costumes)
1960 **La dolce vita** (Fellini); *Kapò* (Pontecorvo); *Risate di gioia* (*The Passionate Thief*) (Monicelli) (co); *Sotto dieci bandiere* (*Under Ten Flats*) (Coletti); *Crimen* (Camerini)
1961 *Il carabiniere a cavallo* (Lizzani); *Il re di Poggioreala* (Coletti)
1962 "Renzo e Luciana" ep. of *Boccaccio '70* (Monicelli)
1963 **Otto e mezzo** (*8½*) (Fellini) (+ costumes); *La ragazza di Bube* (*Bebo's Girl*) (Comencini)
1964 "Peccato nel Pomeriggio" ep. of *Alta infedeltà* (*High Infidelity*) (Petri); "Fatabene fratelli" ep. of *Tre notti d'amore* (*Three Nights of Love*) (Comencini) (+ costumes)
1965 *Giulietta degli spiriti* (*Juliet of the Spirits*) (Fellini) (+ costumes); *Madamigella di Maupin* (Bolognini); *L'armata Brancaleone* (Monicelli) (+ costumes)
1966 "Fata Armenia" ep. of *Le fate* (*The Queens*) (Monicelli)
1969 *The Appointment* (Lumet) (+ costumes); *Queimada!* (*Burn!*) (Pontecorvo) (+ costumes); *Infanzia, vocatione, e prime esperienza di Giacomo Casanova, veneziano* (Comencini) (+ costumes)

Other Films:

1945   *Notte di tempesta* (Franciolini) (set decorator)
1946   *Eugenia Grandet* (Soldati) (set decorator)
1951   *Iolanda la figlia del corsaro nero* (Soldati) (set decorator)
1956   *War and Peace* (K. Vidor) (set decorator)
1960   *Il gobbo* (*The Hunchback of Rome*) (Lizzani) (costumes)
1962   *Violenza segreta* (Moser) (costumes)
1964   "La telefonata" and "Il trattato di eugenetica" eps. of *Le bambole* (*The Dolls*) (Risi and Comencini) (costumes)
1966   *Se tutte le donne del mondo . . .* (*Operazione Paradiso; Kiss the Girls and Make Them Die*) (Levin and Maiuri) (co-costumes)
1967   *Diabolik* (*Danger: Diabolik*) (Bava) (co-costumes)
1971   *Le avventure di Pinocchio* (Comencini) (costumes)

Publications

By GHERARDI: article—

Sight and Sound (London), Winter 1969–70.

On GHERARDI: film—

Piero Gherardi, 1967.

*   *   *

Piero Gherardi collaborated with Federico Fellini on his major films of the late 1950s and early 1960s. The styles of these films show an infusion of new artistic qualities into the established practices of neorealist films of the late 1940s. In *La dolce vita*, *8½*, and *Juliet of the Spirits*, there still was the use of some actual locations and some nonprofessional actors, characteristics of the neorealist movement. But Gherardi and Fellini brought certain surrealistic images into their films, such as the opening of *La dolce vita*, in which a statue of Christ with outstretched arms is suspended from a helicopter. Though such a situation is plausible the image is striking and memorable because it juxtaposes familiar objects with an unusual context.

The sets and costumes of *8½* and *Juliet of the Spirits* established the dreamlike quality of the films. The spa in *8½* is not a real location but a set, modeled not on an existing place but on the memories of one Gherardi had visited as a child. Similarly, the train station is a memory—all the viewer sees are a locomotive, a platform, and some steam. In *Juliet of the Spirits* the conservative heroine's surroundings are mostly white, while the interiors of the house of her liberated friend Suzy are red, yellow, and violet. Juliet's house, an environment of purity, is contrasted to Suzy's, which has the atmosphere of circus and brothel. Gherardi considered a costume as more than a mere covering for a character; it reveals that character and defines the personality. Likewise, his sets did more than give documentary information about a place. Gherardi often mixed the ordinary with the simplified or the surrealistic. In so doing, he emphasized the artificial quality of films and helped to focus attention on characters and situations whose components were as complex as the visual elements.

—Floyd W. Martin

GIBBONS, Cedric

Art Director. **Nationality:** American. **Born:** New York, 23 March 1893. **Family:** Married the actress Dolores Del Rio, 1930 (divorced 1941). **Military Service:** U.S. Navy, 1916–17. **Career:** 1917–18—art director for Edison, then for Goldwyn, 1918–23, and for MGM from 1924–56: supervising art director for many years. **Awards:** Academy Award for *The Bridge of San Luis Rey*, 1928–29; *The Merry Widow*, 1934; *Pride and Prejudice*, 1940; *Blossoms in the Dust*, 1941; *Gaslight*, 1944; *The Yearling*, 1946; *Little Women*, 1949; *An American in Paris*, 1951; *The Bad and the Beautiful*, 1952; *Julius Caesar*, 1953; *Somebody Up There Likes Me*, 1956; Special Award, 1950. **Died:** In Westwood, California, 26 July 1960.

Films as Art Director (selected list):

1919   *The World and Its Women* (Lloyd)
1921   *Beating the Game* (Schertzinger); *The Invisible Power* (Lloyd); *Made in Heaven* (Schertzinger); *An Unwilling Hero* (Badger)
1922   *Come on Over* (Green); *Remembrance* (Hughes); *Yellow Men and Gold* (Willat)
1923   *Broadway Gold* (Dillon and Cooper); *Gimme* (Hughes); *Jazzmania* (Leonard); *Look Your Best* (Hughes)
1924   *Circe the Enchantress* (Leonard); *He Who Gets Slapped* (Sjöström); *His Hour* (K. Vidor); *The Snob* (Bell); *So This Is Marriage* (Henley); *Three Weeks* (Crosland)
1925   *Wife of the Centaur* (K. Vidor); *Ben-Hur* (Niblo); **The Big Parade** (K. Vidor); *Bright Lights* (Leonard); *Cheaper to Marry* (Leonard); *The Circle* (Borzage); *Confessions of a Queen* (Sjöström); *Daddy's Gone a-Hunting* (Borzage); *The Denial* (Henley); *The Dixie Handicap* (Barker); *Exchange of Wives* (Henley); *Excuse Me* (Goulding); *Fine Clothes* (Stahl); *The Great Divide* (Barkee); *Greed* (von Stroheim); *His Secretary* (Henley); *Lady of the Night* (Bell); *Man and Maid* (Schertzinger); *The Mystic* (Browning); *The Masked Bride* (von Sternberg and Cabanne); *The Merry Widow* (von Stroheim); *The Only Thing* (Conway); *Sally, Irene, and Mary* (Goulding); *A Slave of Fashion* (Henley); *Soul Mates* (Conway); *The Sporting Venus* (Neilan); *The Tower of Lies* (Sjöström); *The Unholy Three* (Conway); *The Way of a Girl* (Vignola)
1926   *Bardelys the Magnificent* (K. Vidor); *Beverly of Graustark* (Franklin); *The Black Bird* (Browning); *Blarney* (De Sano); *La Boheme* (K. Vidor); *The Boob* (Wellman); *The Boy Friend* (Bell); *Brown of Harvard* (Conway); *Dance Madness* (Leonard); *Exit Smiling* (Taylor); *The Exquisite Sinner* (von Sternberg and Rosen); *The Fire Brigade* (Nigh); *The Flaming Forest* (Barker); *Flesh and the Devil* (Brown); *The Gay Deceiver* (Stahl); *Love's Blindness* (Dillon); *Lovey Mary* (Baggot); *Memory Lane* (Stahl); *Money Talks* (Mayo); *Monte Carlo* (Cabanne); *Paris* (Goulding); *The Road to Mandalay* (Browning); *The Scarlet Letter* (Sjöström); *Tell It to the Marines* (Hill); *The Temptress* (Stiller and Niblo); *There You Are!* (Sedgwick); *Tin Hats* (Sedgwick); *The Torrent* (Bell); *Upstage* (Bell); *Valencia* (Buchowetzki); *The Waning Sex* (Leonard)

Cedric Gibbons (left)

1927   *Adam and Evil* (Leonard); *After Midnight* (Bell); *Altars of Desire* (Cabanne); *Annie Laurie* (Robertson); *Becky* (McCarthy); *Body and Soul* (Barker); *The Bugle Call* (Sedgwick); *Buttons* (Hill); *The Callahans and the Murphys* (Hill); *Captain Salvation* (Robertson); *The Demi-Bride* (Leonard); *The Enemy* (Niblo); *The Fair Co-ed* (Wood); *Foreign Devils* (Van Dyke); *Frisco Sally Levy* (Beaudine); *Heaven on Earth* (Rosen); *In Old Kentucky* (Stahl); *A Little Journey* (Leonard); *London after Midnight* (Browning); *Love* (Goulding); *The Lovelorn* (McCarthy); *Lovers?* (Stahl); *Man, Woman, and Sin* (Bell); *Mr. Wu* (Nigh); *Mockery* (Christensen); *On ze Boulevard* (Millarde); *Quality Street* (Franklin); *The Red Mill* (Goodrich, i.e. Arbuckle); *The Road to Romance* (Robertson); *Rookies* (Wood); *The Show* (Browning); *Slide, Kelly, Slide* (Sedgwic); *Spring Fever* (Sedgwick); *The Student Prince in Old Heidelberg* (Lubitsch); *The Taxi Driver* (Millarde); *Tea for Three* (Leonard); *Tillie the Toiler* (Henley); *Twelve Miles Out* (Conway); *The Understanding Heart* (Conway); *The Unknown* (Browning); *Women Love Diamonds* (Goulding); *Anna Karenina* (Buckowetzki—unfinished)

1928   *Across to Singapore* (Nigh); *The Actress* (Franklin); *The Baby Cyclone* (Sutherland); *Baby Mine* (Leonard); *Beau Broadway* (St. Clair); *The Big City* (Browning); *Bringing Up Father* (Conway); *Brotherly Love* (Reisner); *The Cardboard Lover* (Leonard); *A Certain Young Man* (Henley); *Circus Rookies* (Sedgwick); *The Cossacks* (Hill); ***The Crowd*** (K. Vidor); *The Divine Woman* (Sjöström); *Dream of Love* (Niblo); *Excess Baggage* (Cruze); *Forbidden Hours* (Beaumont); *Four Walls* (Nigh); *Honeymoon* (Golden); *A Lady of Chance* (Leonard); *The Latest from Paris* (Wood); *Laugh, Clown, Laugh* (Brenon); *The Masks of the Devil* (Sjöström); *The Mysterious Lady* (Niblo); *Our Dancing Daughters* (Beaumont); *The Patsy* (K. Vidor); *Rose-Marie* (Hubbard); *Show People* (K. Vidor); *The Smart Set* (Conway); *Telling the World* (Wood); *West of Zanzibar* (Bowning); *While the City Sleeps* (Conway); *Wickedness Preferred* (Henley); ***The Wind*** (Sjöström); *A Woman of Affairs* (Brown)

1929   *Alias Jimmy Valentine* (Conway); *All at Sea* (Goulding); *Bellamy Trial* (Bell); *The Bridge of San Luis Rey* (Brabin); *The Broadway Melody* (Beaumont); *China Bound* (Reisner);

Desert Nights (Nigh); *Devil-May-Care* (Franklin); *The Duke Steps Out* (Cruze); *Dynamite* (De Mille); *The Flying Fleet* (Hill); *The Girl in the Show* (Selwyn); **Hallelujah** (K. Vidor); *His Glorious Night* (L. Barrymore); *The Hollywood Revue of 1929* (Reisner); *The Idle Rich* (W. De Mille); *It's a Great Life* (Wood); *The Kiss* (Conway); *The Last of Mrs. Cheyney* (Franklin); *Madame X* (L. Barrymore); *A Man's Man* (Cruze); *Marianne* (Leonard); *The Mysterious Island* (Hubbard); *Navy Blues* (Brown); *Our Modern Maidens* (Conway); *The Pagan* (Van Dyke); *A Single Man* (Beaumont); *The Single Standard* (Robertson); *So This Is College* (Wood); *Speedway* (Beaumont); *Spite Marriage* (Sedgwick); *Their Own Desire* (Hopper); *The Thirteenth Chair* (Browning); *Tide of Empire* (Dwan); *The Trial of '98* (Brown); *The Trial of Mary Dugan* (Veiller); *The Unholy Night* (L. Barrymore); *Untamed* (Conway); *Voice of the City* (Mack); *Where East Is East* (Browning); *Wild Orchids* (Franklin); *Wise Girls* (Hopper); *Wonder of Women* (Brown)

1930   *Anna Christie* (Brown); *The Big House* (Hill); *Billy the Kid* (K. Vidor); *The Bishop Murder Case* (Grinde); *Call of the Flesh* (Brabin); *Caught Short* (Reisner); *Chasing Rainbows* (Reisner); *Children of Pleasure* (Lloyd); *The Divorcee* (Leonard); *Doughboys* (Sedgwick); *The Floradora Girl* (Beaumont); *Free and Easy* (Sedgwick); *The Girl Said No* (Wood); *Good News* (Grinde); *In Gay Madrid* (Leonard); *The Lady of Scandal* (Franklin); *A Lady to Love* (Sjöström); *A Lady's Morals* (Franklin); *Let Us Be Gay* (Leonard); *Lord Byron of Broadway* (Nigh and Beaumont); *Love in the Rough* (Reisner); *Madam Satan* (De Mille); *Men of the North* (Roach); *Min and Bill* (Hill); *Montana Moon* (St. Clair); *Not So Dumb* (K. Vidor); *Olympia* (Feyder—German version of *A Lady to Love*; he also directed *Si l'empereur savaitça!*, the French version); *Our Blushing Brides* (Beaumont); *Paid* (Wood); *Passion Flower* (W. De Mille); *Redemption* (Niblo); *Remote Control* (St. Clair and Grinde); *The Rogue Song* (L. Barrymore); *Romance* (Brown); *The Sea Bat* (Ruggles); *The Ship from Shanghai* (Brabin); *Sins of the Children* (Wood); *Strictly Unconventional* (Burton); *They Learned about Women* (Conway); *This Mad World* (W. De Mille); *Those Three French Girls* (Beaumont); *The Unholy Three* (Conway); *Le Spectre vert* (Feyder—French version of previous film); *War Nurse* (Selwyn); *Way for a Sailor* (Wood); *Way Out West* (Niblo); *The Woman Racket* (Ober and Kelly); *Wu Li Chang* (Grinde—Spanish version of *Mr. Wu*)

1931   *Private Lives* (Franklin); *Susan Lenox, Her Fall and Rise* (Leonard)

1932   *Grand Hotel* (Goulding); **Freaks** (Browning)

1933   *Dinner at Eight* (Cukor); *Queen Christina* (Mamoulian)

1934   *Men in White* (Boleslawsky); *The Painted Veil* (Boleslawsky); **The Thin Man** (Van Dyke); *The Barretts of Wimpole Street* (Franklin); *David Copperfield* (Cukor); *Anna Karenina* (Brown); *The Merry Widow* (Lubitsch)

1935   *Mark of the Vampire* (Browning); *China Seas* (Garnett); *A Tale of Two Cities* (Conway); *Naughty Marietta* (Van Dyke); *Mutiny on the Bounty* (Lloyd); *Mad Love* (Freund); *Reckless* (Fleming); *A Night at the Opera* (Wood)

1936   *The Devil-Doll* (Browning); *The Great Ziegfeld* (Leonard); *The Gorgeous Hussy* (Brown); *Small Town Girl* (Wellman); *Wife vs. Secretary* (Brown); *Romeo and Juliet* (Cukor); *San Francisco* (Van Dyke); **Fury** (F. Lang)

1937   *The Good Earth* (Franklin); *Conquest* (Brown); *Big City* (Borzage); *A Day at the Races* (Wood); *Broadway Melody of 1938* (Del Ruth); *The Emperor's Candlesticks* (Fitzmaurice); *The Firefly* (Leonard); *The Last of Mrs. Cheyney* (Boleslawsky); *Saratoga* (Conway); *Navy Blue and Gold* (Wood); *Captains Courageous* (Fleming); **Camille** (Cukor); *Madame X* (Wood)

1938   *The Girl of the Golden West* (Leonard); *The Great Waltz* (Duvivier); *Lord Jeff* (Wood); *Three Comrades* (Borzage); *Arsene Lupin Returns* (Fitzmaurice); *Marie Antoinette* (Van Dyke)

1939   *Balalaika* (Schünzel); **The Wizard of Oz** (Fleming); *Another Thin Man* (Van Dyke); **Ninotchka** (Lubitsch); *Remember?* (McLeod); *Maisie* (Marin)

1940   *Boom Town* (Conway); **The Philadelphia Story** (Cukor); *Pride and Prejudice* (Leonard)

1941   *The Chocolate Soldier* (Del Ruth); *H. M. Pulham, Esq.* (K. Vidor); *Love Crazy* (Conway); *Honky Tonk* (Conway); *Unholy Partners* (LeRoy); *Barnacle Bill* (Thorpe); *Blossoms in the Dust* (LeRoy)

1942   **Mrs. Miniver** (Wyler)

1943   *Bataan* (Garnett); *A Guy Named Joe* (Fleming); *Cabin in the Sky* (Minnelli); *The Cross of Lorraine* (Garnett); *The Human Comedy* (Brown); *Lassie Come Home* (Wilcox); *Thousands Cheer* (Sidney)

1944   *Gaslight* (Cukor); *Kismet (Oriental Dream)* (Dieterle); *Madame Curie* (LeRoy); *The Seventh Cross* (Zinnemann); *Thirty Seconds over Tokyo* (LeRoy); **Meet Me in St. Louis** (Minnelli)

1945   *The Picture of Dorian Grey* (Lewin); *Yolanda and the Thief* (Minnelli)

1946   *The Postman Always Rings Twice* (Garnett); *Ziegfeld Follies* (Minnelli—produced 1944); *The Green Years* (Saville); *The Yearling* (Brown)

1947   *Lady in the Lake* (Montgomery); *Song of Love* (Brown)

1948   *The Pirate* (Minnelli); *Command Decision* (Wood); *The Three Musketeers* (Sidney)

1949   **On the Town** (Kelly and Donen); *Madame Bovary* (Minnelli); *Battle Ground* (Wellman); *The Great Singer* (Siodmak); *Little Women* (LeRoy); **Adam's Rib** (Cukor)

1950   *Annie Get Your Gun* (Sidney); **The Asphalt Jungle** (Huston)

1951   **An American in Paris** (Minnelli); *Showboat* (Sidney); *Quo Vadis* (LeRoy); *The Tall Target* (A. Mann)

1952   *The Bad and the Beautiful* (Minnelli); **Singin' in the Rain** (Kelly and Donen); *Lovely to Look At* (LeRoy)

1953   *Scaramouche* (Sidney); *Julius Caesar* (Mankiewicz); **The Band Wagon** (Minnelli); *The Actress* (Cukor)

1954   *Executive Suite* (Wise); *Jupiter's Darling* (Sidney); *Bad Day at Black Rock* (Sturges)

1955   *Blackboard Jungle* (Brooks); *Kismet* (Minnelli); *Love Me or Leave Me* (C. Vidor)

1956   *Somebody Up There Likes Me* (Wise); *I'll Cry Tomorrow* (D. Mann); *The Swan* (A. Mann); *Lust for Life* (Minnelli); *High Society* (Walters); *Forbidden Planet* (Wilcox)

Film as Director:

1934   *Tarzan and His Mate*

Publications

By GIBBONS: articles—

"Motion Picture Sets," in *The Theatre and Motion Pictures*, edited by Warren E. Cox, Chicago, 1933.
"Every Home's a Stage," in *Ladies' Home Journal* (Philadelphia, Pennsylvania), July 1933.
"Designs of Settings for Romeo and Juliet," in *Romeo and Juliet: A Moving Picture Edition*, New York, 1936.
"The Art Director," in *Behind the Screen: How Films Are Made*, edited by Stephen Watts, London, 1938.

On GIBBONS: articles—

Lachenbruch, Jerome, "Interior Decoration for the 'Movies': Studies from the Work of Cedric Gibbons and Gilbert White," in *Arts and Decoration* (New York), January 1921.
Flint, Ralph, in *Creative Art*, October 1932.
Stuart, Betty Thornley, "Movie Set Up," in *Collier's* (New York), 30 September 1933.
Erengis, George P., in *Films in Review* (New York), April 1965.
Hambley, John, in *The Art of Hollywood*, London, 1979.
Cinématographe (Paris), February 1982.
Webb, Michael, "Pioneering Art Director Who Brought Modernism to the Movies: Cedric Gibbons and the MGM Style," in *Architectural Digest*, vol. 47, April 1990.
Gill, Brendan, "Cedric Gibbons and Dolores Del Rio: The Art Director and the Star of *Flying Down to Rio* in Santa Monica," in *Architectural Digest*, vol. 49, April 1992.

*   *   *

The production designer Cedric Gibbons, though little-known to many filmgoers, strongly influenced many of Hollywood's greatest films. Born in New York in the last decade of the 19th century, Gibbons, already educated in art and architecture, began his movie career just as the film industry started rolling. He obtained an assistant's job at the Edison Studios and worked there from 1915 to 1917. Gibbons made a major mark on film design at this time when he insisted on the use of three-dimensional scenery rather than painted backdrops.

In 1918 Gibbons left Edison for a position as art director at Goldwyn's in New York. Later he moved with Goldwyn and company to California. In 1924 came a significant turning point. MGM studios was formed, and Gibbons became its supervising art director.

It is not easy to determine which of the films in his very vast filmography can really be completely credited to Gibbons. Any film coming out of MGM would list Gibbons as art director. Gibbon's greatest contributions would go to the "prestige" pictures, such as *Marie Antoinette*, *Ben-Hur*, or *Camille*. He collaborated on many of the other MGM movies and merely approved the rest. Those pictures produced after his heart attack in 1946 would have even less of his touch. But it is misleading to assume Gibbons blindly accepted the ideas of others, taking credit for their creations. Gibbons felt strongly about what was right and wrong for MGM and getting his approval was no easy task. Vincente Minnelli described the Gibbons reign as a "medieval fiefdom, its overlord accustomed to doing things in a certain way." As stifling as this might be to the creativities of other artists and directors at MGM, this attitude served its purpose. MGM films shared a distinctive "look." This was achieved because all employees responsible in any way for the visual appearance of the film—from props to costumes to special effects—had to confer with Gibbons. He maintained MGM's visual continuity and maintained this control through the decades.

Several qualities characterize the MGM picture during the Gibbons rule, particularly elegance and glamor in his films from the 1930s. It did not matter if the scene or the moment called for it; the floors would still be highly polished and the chandelier crystal. Luxury and the elaborate were encouraged. A Gibbons-approved set could be as active as one of the dancers during a production number, littered with booms and turntables.

Like the popular British and French interior designers between the wars, Gibbons preferred all-white rooms. The harsh contrast of shapes and shadows that one would find in the German expressionist-influenced studios such as Warner Brothers or Universal would never be found at MGM. Gibbons sets were the height of escapist fantasy, as light and witty as a Cole Porter tune.

Gibbons also preferred to have MGM sets sculptural, perhaps harking back to his days as an artist and architect. This penchant for the three-dimensional might have been part of the reason for Vincente Minelli's animosity towards Gibbons, for Minelli films such as *An American in Paris* require a two-dimension emphasis for artistic effect. Fortunately, in spite of the difficulties, *An American in Paris* managed to gain Gibbons's dictatorial approval (and ironically enough won him an Oscar).

Gibbons retired in 1956 and died in 1960. He had been nominated for 37 Academy Awards in his career and had won 11. In addition, he is credited with designing the original Oscar statuette. This streamlined, planar sculpture is an appropriate homage to Gibbons's *oeuvre* and serves as a reminder of the film industry's more glorious and powerful past.

—Edith C. Lee

GILLESPIE, Arnold

Special Effects Technician and Art Director. **Nationality:** American. **Born:** A. Arnold Gillespie in El Paso, Texas, 14 October 1899. **Education:** Attended Columbia University, New York; Art Students League, New York. **Career:** 1922–24—assistant art director at Paramount; 1924–36—art director, MGM; 1936–65—head of MGM's special effects department, working on some 600 films. **Awards:** Academy Award for *Thirty Seconds over Tokyo*, 1944; *Green Dolphin Street*, 1947; *Plymouth Adventure*, 1952; *Ben-Hur* 1959; Technical Award, 1963. **Died:** 3 May 1978.

Films as Art Director (selected list):

1922   *Manslaughter* (De Mille) (asst)

1923   *Adam's Rib* (De Mille) (asst)

1926   *Ben-Hur* (Niblo); *The Black Bird* (Browning); *Brown of Harvard* (Conway); *Lovey Mary* (Baggot); *The Road to Mandalay* (Browning); *Upstage* (Bell); *There You Are!* (Sedgwick); *Valencia* (Buchowetzki); *Tell It to the Marines* (Hill); *La Bohème* (K. Vidor)

1927   *Altars of Desire* (Cabanne); *Women Love Diamonds* (Goulding); *The Demi-Bride* (Leonard); *Heaven on Earth* (Rosen); *Body and Soul* (Barker); *The Fair Co-Ed* (Wood); *London after Midnight* (Browning); *Buttons* (Hill)

1928   *The Latest from Paris* (Wood); *The Divine Woman* (Sjöström); **The Crowd** (Hill); *Tarzan the Ape Man* (Van Dyke)

1933   *Turn Back the Clock* (Selwyn); *Tarzan and His Mate* (Gibbons); *Operator 13* (Boleslawsky); *Laughing Boy* (Van Dyke); *The Girl from Missouri* (Conway); *Eskimo* (Van Dyke)

1934   *Fugitive Lovers* (Boleslawsky)

1935   *Mutiny on the Bounty* (Lloyd); *The Last of the Pagans* (Thorpe); *Exclusive Story* (Seitz); *Small Town Girl* (Wellman); *Speed* (Marin)

Films as Special Effects Technician (selected list):

1936   *San Francisco* (Van Dyke)

1937   *The Good Earth* (Franklin); *Captains Courageous* (Fleming)

1938   *Test Pilot* (Fleming)

1939   **The Wizard of Oz** (Fleming)

1940   *Waterloo Bridge* (LeRoy); *Boom Town* (Conway); *Comrade X* (K. Vidor)

1941   *Flight Command* (Borzage)

1942   **Mrs. Miniver** (Wyler)

1943   *Bataan* (Garnett); *The Heavenly Body* (Hall)

1944   *Thirty Seconds over Tokyo* (LeRoy); *The White Cliffs of Dover* (Brown)

1945   *The Clock* (Minnelli); *Yolanda and the Thief* (Minnelli); *Valley of Decision* (Garnett)

1946   *The Green Years* (Saville)

1947   *Green Dolphin Street* (Saville); *The Beginning of the End* (Taurog)

1948   *Command Decision* (Wood)

1949   *The Secret Garden* (Wilcox)

1951   *Quo Vadis?* (LeRoy)

1952   *Plymouth Adventure* (Brown)

1954   *Green Fire* (Marton); *Seven Brides for Seven Brothers* (Donen)

1956   *Forbidden Planet* (Wilcox)

1958   *Torpedo Run* (Pevney)

1959   *Ben-Hur* (Wyler); **North by Northwest** (Hitchcock)

1960   *Cimarron* (A. Mann)

1961   *Atlantis, the Lost Continent* (Pal)

1962   *The Four Horsemen of the Apocalypse* (Minnelli); *The Horizontal Lieutenant* (Thorpe); *Jumbo* (*Billy Rose's Jumbo*) (Walters); *Mutiny on the Bounty* (Reed and Milestone)

1963   *How the West Was Won* (Ford, Hathaway, and Marshall); *The Prize* (Robson); *A Ticklish Affair* (Sidney)

1964   *The Unsinkable Molly Brown* (Walters)

1965   *The Greatest Story Ever Told* (Stevens)

Publications

By GILLESPIE: articles—

In *Hollywood Speaks! An Oral History*, by Mike Steen, New York, 1974.
The Velvet Light Trap (Madison, Wisconsin), Spring 1978.
Film Comment (New York), May-June 1978.

*   *   *

The complete filmography of Arnold Gillespie is one of the largest in Hollywood, reaching nearly 600 films and almost evenly divided between art direction and special visual effects. He worked on both versions of *Ben-Hur* and *Mutiny on the Bounty*, created the visceral quality of the 1906 San Francisco earthquake in *San Francisco*, the alien beauty of *Forbidden Planet*, and the maleficent nightmare of *The Wizard of Oz*. Gillespie's work in *The Wizard of Oz* demonstrated the imagination, ingenuity, and patience that became his trademark. To produce the witch's skywriting of "surrender Dorothy," he used a mixture of sheep dip and nigrosine dye released through a stylus into milk in a glass tank. The attack of the flying monkeys required the hanging of 2,200 piano wires from the sound stage's ceiling.

When Gillespie began special effects work for MGM, the studio was an efficient organization, all facets of production departmentalized. He was head of the Special Effects Department under the titular guidance of Cedric Gibbons' Art Department and in charge of the crews who worked with miniatures, rear screen projection, and full-scale mechanical effects. The other aspects of visual effects fell under two other main departments; the Optical Department (matte paintings and optical printing) and the Animation Department. Gillespie seemed particularly intrigued with miniatures (Circus Maximus in the original *Ben-Hur*, the sea battle in the 1959 remake, the tank chase in *Comrade X*, the ships in *Torpedo Run*, and the raft sequence in *How the West Was Won*) and full-scale mechanicals (Robbie the Robot in *Forbidden Planet* and the four *Bountys* used for the 1962 version of *Mutiny on the Bounty*). But his forte lay in designing solutions for odd effects never before photographed. As in the skywriting effect described above, he usually employed liquids in a glass tank. To create the plague of locusts in *The Good Earth*, Gillespie dumped coffee grounds into a water tank, filmed their dispersal upside-down, and then superimposed the image with shots of the crops. For the atomic explosion in *The Beginning of the End*, he visualized a mushroom cloud before photographs and information were declassified by the government. By releasing blood bags under water and superimposing the image with a background shot, Gillespie manufactured an effect so believable and accurate that government officials thought he had access to secret materials. The footage was later used by the United States Air Corps in their instructional films.

Gillespie had the talent and a studio system to make the remarkable, the unexperienced, the fantastic, and the cataclysmic very believable and authentic. As he described his profession in a *Film*

Comment interview, ''The whole physical end of movies, in my opinion, was so interesting because whether the picture was modern, whether it was in the future, whether it was a dream world like *The Wizard of Oz* or in Outer Space like *Forbidden Planet*, it was illusion made real.''

—Greg S. Faller

GLENNON, Bert

Cinematographer and Director. **Nationality:** American. **Born:** Bert Lawrence Glennon in Anaconda, Montana, 19 November 1893 (or 1895). **Education:** Attended Stanford University, California, graduated 1912. **Military Service:** Pursuit pilot instructor during World War I. **Career:** 1912—stage manager for theater entrepreneur Oliver Morosco; c. 1913—worked for Keystone and Famous Players, then laboratory superintendent for Clune Film Corporation, four years; 1915—first film as cinematographer, *The Stingaree* (serial); 1928—directed first film, *The Perfect Crime*. **Died:** In 1967.

Films as Cinematographer:

1915   *The Stingaree* (Horne—serial)
1919   *Lighting Bryce* (Hurst—serial)
1920   *The Man from Kangaroo* (Lucas and Meredyth) (+ asst d); *Shadow of Lightning Ridge* (Lucas) (+ asst d); *The Jackaroo of Coolabong* (*The Fighting Breed*) (Lucas) (+ asst d); *Parted Curtains* (Bracken); *Kentucky Colonel* (Seiter) (co); *The Torrent* (Paton) (co)
1921   *The Dangerous Moment* (De Sano); *Cheated Love* (Baggot); *The Kiss* (Conway); *A Daughter of the Law* (Conway); *Moonlight Follies* (Baggot); *Nobody's Fool* (Baggot)
1922   *Domestic Relations* (Withey); *The Woman Who Walked Alone* (Melford); *Ebb Tide* (Melford); *Burning Sands* (*The Dweller in the Desert*) (Melford)
1923   *Java Head* (Melford); *You Can't Fool Your Wife* (Melford); *The Ten Commandments* (DeMille) (co)
1924   *Triumph* (DeMille); *Changing Husbands* (Urson and Iribe); *Open All Night* (*One Parisian ''Knight''*) (Bern); *Worldly Goods* (Bern)
1925   *Tomorrow's Love* (Bern); *The Dressmaker from Paris* (Bern); *Are Parents People?* (St. Clair); *Wild Horse Mesa* (Seitz); *Flower of Night* (Bern); *A Woman of the World* (St. Clair)
1926   *The Crown of Lies* (Buchowetzki); *Good and Naughty* (St. Clair); *Hotel Imperial* (Stiller)
1927   *Barbed Wire* (Lee); *Underworld* (*Paying the Penalty*) (von Sternberg); *We're All Gamblers* (Cruze); *The Woman on Trial* (Stiller); *The City Gone Wild* (Cruze)
1928   *The Last Command* (von Sternberg); *The Street of Sin* (*King of Soho*) (Stiller); *The Patriot* (Lubitsch)
1932   *Blonde Venus* (von Sternberg); *The Half Naked Truth* (La Cava)
1933   *So This Is Harris!* (Sandrich—short); *Christopher Strong* (Arzner); *Gabriel over the White House* (La Cava); *Melody Cruise* (Sandrich); *Morning Glory* (L. Sherman); *Alice in Wonderland* (McLeod) (co)

1934   *She Was a Lady* (MacFadden); *Grand Canary* (Cummings); ***The Scarlet Empress*** (von Sternberg); *Hell in the Heavens* (Blystone)
1935   *Lottery Lover* (Thiele); *Ginger* (Seiler); *Thunder in the Night* (Archainbaud); *Bad Boy* (Blystone); *Show Them No Mercy* (*Tainted Money*) (Marshall)
1936   *The Prisoner of Shark Island* (Ford); *Half Angel* (Lanfield); *Little Miss Nobody* (Blystone); *Dimples* (Seiter); *Can This Be Dixie?* (Marshall) (co); *Lloyd's of London* (H. King)
1937   *The Hurricane* (Ford); *Adventures of Marco Polo* (2nd unit)
1939   *Stagecoach* (Ford); ***Young Mr. Lincoln*** (Ford); *Second Fiddle* (Lanfield) (co); *The Rains Came* (Brown) (co); *Drums along the Mohawk* (Ford); *Swanee River* (Lanfield)
1940   *Our Town* (Wood); *The Howards of Virginia* (*The Tree of Liberty*) (Lloyd)
1941   *Virginia* (Griffith) (co); *The Reluctant Dragon* (Werker) (co); *One Night in Lisbon* (Griffith); *Dive Bomber* (Curtiz) (co); *They Died with Their Boots On* (Walsh)
1942   *Juke Girl* (Bernhardt); *Desperate Journey* (Walsh)
1943   *Mission to Moscow* (Curtiz); *This Is the Army* (Curtiz) (co); *The Desert Song* (Florey)
1944   *Destination Tokyo* (Daves); *The Very Thought of You* (Daves); *Hollywood Canteen* (Daves)
1945   *San Antonio* (Butler)
1946   *One More Tomorrow* (Godfrey); *Shadow of a Woman* (Santley)
1947   *The Red House* (Daves); *Mr. District Attorney* (Sinclair); *Copacabana* (Green)
1948   *Ruthless* (Ulmer)
1949   *Ichabod and Mr. Toad* (*The Adventures of Ichabod and Mr. Toad*) (Kinney, Algar, and Geronimi) (co); *Red Light* (Del Ruth)
1950   *Wagonmaster* (Ford); *Rio Grande* (Ford)
1951   *Operation Pacific* (Waggner); *The Sea Hornet* (Kane); *About Face* (Del Ruth); *The Big Trees* (Feist)
1952   *The Man behind the Gun* (Feist); *Riding Shotgun* (De Toth); *Thunder over the Plains* (de Toth)
1953   *House of Wax* (De Toth); *The Moonlighter* (Rowland)
1954   *The Mad Magician* (Brahm); *Crime Wave* (*The City Is Dark*) (De Toth)
1955   *Davy Crockett and the River Pirates* (Foster) (co)
1960   *Sergeant Rutledge* (Ford)
1961   *Lad—A Dog* (Avakian and Martinson)
1963   *The Man from Galveston* (Conrad)

Films as Director:

1928   *The Perfect Crime*; *The Gang War* (*All Square*)
1929   *The Air Legion*
1930   *Girl of the Port*; *Around the Corner*; *Paradise Island*
1931   *In Line of Duty*
1932   *South of Santa Fe*

Other Films:

1922   *Moran of the Lady Letty* (Melford) (cam)
1930   *Second Wife* (Mack) (co-sc)

Publications

On GLENNON: articles—

Film Comment (New York), Summer 1972.
Focus on Film (London), no. 13, 1973.

*   *   *

Bert Glennon was a visual stylist whose cinematography enhanced the best work of such disparate directors as John Ford and Josef von Sternberg. Glennon exemplifies the professional Hollywood craftsperson overshadowed by volatile, individualistic directors, his name rarely mentioned in film histories despite such credits as DeMille's *The Ten Commandments*, von Sternberg's *Underworld* and *The Scarlet Empress*, and Ford's epochal 1939 trio—*Stagecoach*, *Young Mr. Lincoln*, and *Drums Along the Mohawk*.

There were two Glennon styles—the glossy soft-focus of his 1920s Paramounts, and the dramatic, often minimalist, realism he employed at 20th Century-Fox in the late 1930s and at Warners ten years later. Along with Victor Milner, Glennon helped define the corporate Paramount look, with assignments for such directors of sophisticated fare as DeMille (*Triumph*), Lubitsch (*The Patriot*), Malcolm St. Clair (*Are Parents People?*, *A Woman of the World*, *Good and Naughty*), Rowland V. Lee (*Barbed Wire*), and Mauritz Stiller (*Hotel Imperial*, *The Street of Sin*—co-photographed by Milner and Harry Fischbeck).

Glennon's two great silent triumphs were *The Ten Commandments* and *Underworld*. The DeMille epic was the most spectacular production up to that time, with Glennon in charge of a crew steeped with photographic talent, including Edward S. Curtis, Archie Stout, J. Peverell Marley, and Donald Keyes. The contemporary story is well handled, but the film is most satisfying in the Biblical sequences, many shot in reverential tableaux, with sweeping camera movements on the action scenes. The most powerful moments include the Golden Calf sequence, Moses (Theodore Roberts) receiving the Commandments, and the famous parting of the Red Sea, all handled by Glennon in a documentary-like fashion. A prologue of the Israelites fleeing Egypt was cophotographed in two-strip Technicolor with Ray Rennahan.

Underworld foreshadowed many later crime films, uniting elements of that genre which would become commonplace, including Glennon's *chiaroscuro* photography. There are many fine photographic touches—the underworld ball, the police car chase—rendered in a crisp, economic manner. *Underworld* was a much more starkly lit work than was common at Paramount, but in his next film for von Sternberg, *The Last Command*, Glennon reverted to the softer studio style. His mobile camera makes both *Underworld* and *The Last Command* among the most visually pleasing films of the late silent era.

Glennon directed eight programmers between 1928 and 1930, making the transition to sound on such inaccessible titles as *Gang War* and *Syncopation*. If the films do exist, they would be interesting rediscoveries, since Glennon had by then shot nearly 40 features. He returned to cinematography in 1932 with von Sternberg's *Blonde Venus*, shooting interiors (Paul Ivano handled the exteriors). Among the scenes Glennon worked on is the "Hot Voodoo" number, with icon Marlene Dietrich emerging from a gorilla suit. Glennon shot two striking films for Gregory La Cava (*The Half Naked Truth* and *Gabriel over the White House*), and two important films for the young

Katharine Hepburn, Dorothy Arzner's *Christopher Strong* and Lowell Sherman's *Morning Glory*. These were all contemporary films, slickly shot by Glennon, and helped reestablish him as a quality cinematographer.

Glennon reunited with von Sternberg on *The Scarlet Empress*, which cast Dietrich as Russia's Catherine the Great. Glennon achieved an extraordinary Baroque look, with dazzling camera movement complemented by von Sternberg's eccentric *mise en scène* and lavish art direction by Hans Dreier, Peter Ballbusch, and Richard Kollorsz. Truly one of the most photographically stunning works in American cinema, *The Scarlet Empress* was a Glennon masterwork, culminating his contributions to the von Sternberg canon. Typically, the director made no mention of Bert Glennon in his autobiography.

Glennon moved to Fox in 1934, and inexplicably toiled on B-movies, routine products except for George Marshall's gritty antikidnapping film *Show Them No Mercy*. His fortunes improved when Darryl Zanuck merged his 20th Century Pictures with the failing Fox and assigned him to shoot *The Prisoner of Shark Island*, the first of eight John Ford films shot by Glennon. The story of Dr. Samuel Mudd, the man who treated John Wilkes Booth's wound after the Lincoln assassination and found himself incarcerated as an unwitting accomplice, the film reveals Ford's passion for the era, nicely realized by Glennon. The Shark Island prison sequences are dark and gloomy, contrasted with the juleps-and-magnolia South symbolized by Mudd's family. Like much of Ford's best work, there is a silent film-feel to the cinematography. When Goldwyn borrowed Ford to make *The Hurricane*, a high-budget romantic adventure highlighted by the titular spectacle, the director brought along Glennon, who this time counterpointed South Seas exotica with prison sequences reminiscent of *Prisoner of Shark Island*.

Glennon's position as a master cinematographer was confirmed with the 1939 Ford films. *Stagecoach* deserves its reputation as one of the great westerns. Picturesque Monument Valley vistas and expert action sequences were expertly captured by Glennon, making *Stagecoach* one of the best looking black-and-white movies ever made. In a direct stylistic contrast to the von Sternberg films, there is little camera movement, and rare use of close-ups, the notable exception being the Indians on the bluff in a preattack sequence.

Smaller in scope, *Young Mr. Lincoln* impeccably recreated Indiana and Illinois of the 1830s and 1840s, a simple, Griffithian style which appealed to both Glennon and Ford. While an uncredited Arthur Miller shot the riverside locations, Glennon was responsible for the bulk of the film's classical look, with the fight in the clearing particularly well rendered. *Drums along the Mohawk* was a much more difficult film. Forced by Zanuck's release schedule to rush from *Lincoln* to *Drums*, the filmmakers were plagued by minimal preparation, an unpolished script, and a rugged location in Utah's Wasatch Mountains. Summer storms played havoc with matching shots, and to compound problems, the film was shot in three-strip Technicolor, Ford's first in color. Despite these rigors, *Drums Along the Mohawk* is exquisitely photographed, as perfect an exercise in color as *Stagecoach* was for black-and-white. There are many notable exteriors in this Revolutionary War drama, such as Henry Fonda and Claudette Colbert travelling west by oxcart; John Carradine's raid with the Mohawks upon the settlers; the siege of Fort Stanwix; and Henry Fonda's run through the forest, chased by Mohawk warriors.

It was ten years before Glennon worked with Ford again, but the occasion and the project was a special one—*Wagonmaster*. Ford told Peter Bogdanovich that *Wagonmaster* was one of the films that "came closest to being what I had wanted to achieve." A western masterwork written largely by Ford, the film is graced by Glennon's newsreel quality cinematography. Glennon also shot Ford's *Rio Grande* in stark black-and-white, the third and last of the John Wayne cavalry trilogy, and in *Sergeant Rutledge* he balanced dramatic exteriors of the black ''Buffalo Soldiers'' of the western Indian Wars with the sparse sound stage dramatics of the trial sequence.

Glennon did superlative work for another strong director, Raoul Walsh, on *They Died with Their Boots On*, in which he photographed a spectacular recreation of Custer's Last Stand; and *Desperate Journey*, a slam-bang Second World War adventure highlighted by an exhilarating car chase. Glennon had a chance to create a stylized, romantic look for *Our Town*, and a well-done *film noir*, Edgar Ulmer's *Ruthless*, then closed his career at Warners with some of the best 3-D photography (*House of Wax*, *The Moonlighter*, *The Mad Magician*).

—John A. Gallagher

GODFREY, Bob

Animator. **Nationality:** British. **Born:** West Maitland, New South Wales, Australia, 1921; emigrated with his parents to the United Kingdom, 1927. **Career:** 1949—background artist, Larkins animation studio; then member of Grasshopper Group; 1954—cofounder, Biographic Cartoon Films for producing short animated films and advertisements; 1964—formed Bob Godfrey Films; television work includes series *The Do-It-Yourself Film Animation Show* (as writer and narrator), 1974, *Roobarb*, 1974, *Noah and Nelly in . . . SkylArk*, 1976, and *Henry's Cat*, 1983–86. **Awards:** Academy Award for *Great*, 1975; MBE, 1986; Senior Fellw, Royal College of Art, 1989.

Films as Director (Animation):

1952   *The Big Parade* (co); *Formation* (co)
1954   *Watch the Birdie* (co)
1958   *Polygamous Polonius*
1959   *The Do-It-Yourself Cartoon Kit* (co)
1963   *A Productivity Primer*
1964   *The Rise and Fall of Emily Sprod* (+ ro); *Alf, Bill, and Fred*
1967   *Rope Trick*; *What Ever Happened to Uncle Fred?*; *The Fearless Vampire Killers, or Pardon Me, But Your Teeth Are in My Neck* (*Dance of the Vampires*) (Polanski) (animation sequence)
1968   *Two Off the Cuff* (co, + voice)
1969   *Colloids* (Jessop) (animation sequences)
1970   *Henry 9 'til 5* (+ voice); *The Electron's Tale* (co); *Love and Marriage* (*Sex, Love and Marriage*) (Gould) (animation sequences)
1971   *Kama Sutra Rides Again* (+ voice); *The Magnificent Seven Deadly Sins* (Stark) (animation sequences)
1972   *It's a 2' 6'' above the Ground World* (*The Love Ban*) (Thomas) (animation sequences)
1973   *Is This a Record?* (Turpin) (animation sequences)
1975   *Great*
1976   *The Key*
1977   *Dear Margery Boobs* (+ voice)
1978   *Marx for Beginners* (co)

1979   *Dream Doll* (co); *Instant Sex*
1980   *Bio Woman*
1985   *Polygamous Polonius Revisited*; *Beaks to the Grindstone*; *A Journalist's Tale*
1989   *Revolution—La Belle France*
1990   *Wicked Willie*
1991   *Happy Birthday Switzerland*
1992   *What a Hog!*
1993   *Small Talk*
1994   *1066 and All That*; *Know Your Europeans*
1995   *Kevin Saves the World* (+ production designer); *Know Your Europeans: The United Kingdom*

Films as Director (Live-Action):

1960   *The Battle of New Orleans* (+ ro)
1961   *That Noise*; *What Kind of Fool Am I?*
1962   *Plain Man's Guide to Advertising* (+ voice)
1963   *Morse Code Melody*
1965   *One Man Band*; *L'Art pour l'art* (+ ro)
1967   *Bang*

Films as Actor:

1955   *Bride and Groom* (Daborn and Potterton)
1966   *Just Like a Woman* (Fuest)
1968   *The Bliss of Mrs. Blossom* (McGrath)
1970   *Today Mexico, Tomorrow . . . the World* (Shillingford)
1975   *I'm Not Feeling Myself Tonight* (McGrath)
1977   *Sensations* (Shillingford and Grant)
1980   *The Falls* (Greenaway)
1982   *Henry's Cat* (Godfrey)

Other Films:

1965   *You Must Be Joking* (Winner) (titles designs)
1967   *Ouch!* (Bryant) (titles designs)
1968   *Twenty-Nine* (Cummins) (graphics)
1971   *And Now for Something Completely Different* (Macnaughton) (animation ph)
1979   *Dream Doll* (Godfrey) (pr)
1993   *Small Talk* (pr)

Publications

By GODFREY: articles—

Cinema Papers (Melbourne), August-September 1980.
Screen International (London), 25 September-2 October 1982.
Video Business, 12 September 1984.

On GODFREY: articles—

Roudévitch, Michel, in *Cinéma* (Paris), no. 98, 1965.
Movie Maker (Hemel Hempstead, Hertfordshire), April 1967.

Image et Son (Paris), November 1967.

Lockey, Nicola, in *Broadcast*, 2 April 1979.

Banc-Titre (Paris), September 1982.

National Film Theatre booklet (London), March 1985.

Holton, Gillian, ''Simply Great,'' in *Stage Screen and Radio* (London), April 1995.

*   *   *

One way and another, Bob Godfrey's films have attracted a good deal of attention, not all of it invariably favourable. *Great* won him an Oscar; but feminists have condemned much of his work for misogyny—a charge to which he himself is now inclined to plead guilty—and several Godfrey cartoons have had ''X'' certificates slapped on them by alarmed censorship boards. *Kama Sutra Rides Again* was the first cartoon to receive an ''R'' (adults only) rating in Australia, which did it no harm at all at the box office. It also gained a special award from Yugoslav film-buffs as ''The Film Most Likely to be Understood All Over the World,'' much to Godfrey's delight. ''I am completely communication-oriented. . . . If the art gets in the way—stamp it out, I say. I'm a plagiarist, I will desecrate, I will mutilate, I'll do anything in order to get the message across.''

He first achieved wide recognition with *The Do-It-Yourself Cartoon Kit*, a spirited and irreverent send-up of animated-film conventions which Ralph Stephenson described as ''one of the funniest cartoons ever made.'' The film signalled what Michel Roudévitch called, in tangy French, Godfrey's ''penchants pour l'hétéroclite, le saugrenu, le coq-à-l'âne'' (taste for the offbeat, preposterous and parodic), as well as locating him squarely in a British comic-surrealist tradition descending from Lewis Carroll via the Goons, and leading on to Monty Python. (Godfrey's influence is clearly evident in the work of Terry Gilliam, the Pythons' animator.)

Another fecund source of imagery was Donald McGill, maestro of the ribald seaside postcard. McGill's vast, predatory women and nervously randy little men peopled the long series of bawdy comedies, from *Polygamous Polonius* through *Henry 9 'til 5* and *Kama Sutra Rides Again* to *Instant Sex* and *Dream Doll*, for which Godfrey is now best known. In these ''sexual punch-ups'' (his own term) he mocked his audiences, prodded impudently at the boundaries of censorship, and exposed the fears and anxieties haunting the male libido. Repeatedly, his anti-heroes take refuge in reassuringly manageable surrogates (masturbation fantasies, inflatable life-size dolls, cans of ''Instant Sex''), rather than confront the terrifying prospect of a real, live woman. If some feminists have berated Godfrey for misogyny, others have felt more inclined to thank him for providing them with so much first-rate ammunition.

As the series progressed, the mood underlying the broad knockabout of Godfrey's sex comedies appeared to darken, the depiction of emotional inadequacy to grow more bleak. The frenetically varied couplings of *Kama Sutra Rides Again* suggest, as Tom Ryan observed, ''nightmare rather than satisfaction.'' Most sombre of all is *Dream Doll*, codirected with Zlatko Grgic of the Zagreb studios. Despite problems during the making—Godfrey summed up coproduction as ''like directing a jellyfish''—he was proud of the final result, ''which took on a kind of Croatian doom—a sort of comedy *noir*. . . . Some of my films are very patchy, but this one really flows.'' The ending, in which the Chaplinesque little man is transported heavenwards by a whole flotilla of inflatable women, deliberately parodies Lamorisse's *Le Ballon rouge*; when *Dream Doll* was premiered at Annecy, the French were not amused.

Godfrey's most ambitious work to date is the Oscar-winning *Great*, a 30-minute musical treatment of the life of the Victorian inventor-engineer, Isambard Kingdom Brunel. Visually and verbally exuberant, it packs in all the notable events of Brunel's stupendous career, along with a wealth of songs, jokes, and miscellaneous objects—including Union Jacks, exploding hats, and multiple appearances by Queen Victoria, who makes her entrance rising majestically out of a lavatory bowl. This gives fair notice of the overall level of humour, but it would take a jaundiced viewer to object, given the film's abundant energy, high spirits, and evident affection for its subject. Even so, according to Godfrey, the Brunel Society did object: ''They said it was full of historical inaccuracies and lewd innuendoes. And why not, I say.'' In recent years Godfrey has made determined efforts to escape narrow typecasting as the maker of ''male anxiety films.'' (''I think Maggie [Thatcher] used up all my misogyny,'' he commented in a 1993 television programme. ''I haven't got any left, I used up so much on her.'') But not even the award of an OBE—which arrived, much to Godfrey's glee, while a hanged effigy of Mrs Thatcher was on public display outside his studio—has conferred respectability. There have been collaborations with the left-anarchist cartoonist Steve Bell, whose scabrous political wit meshed well with the vigour of Godfrey's style of animation, and a loose ongoing series of portraits of European nations, unrepentantly rich in irreverence and crude stereotypes. Godfrey's main current activity is in the field of children's television, exercising his anarchic (and only slightly less lewd) humour in such series as *Roobarb, Henry's Cat* and *The Bunbury Tails*. He remains fascinated and excited by the unlimited potential of his medium—''You can do the impossible. We leave the possible to the TV news''—and as iconoclastic as ever. ''One of the things I want to do is *Hamlet*. With robots. Get rid of the poetry and keep all the violence and the paranoia.''

—Philip Kemp

GOLAN, Menahem, and Yoram GLOBUS

GOLAN. Producer and Director. **Nationality:** Israeli. **Born:** Tiberias, Palestine (now Israel), 31 May 1929. **Education:** Studied directing at the Old Vic School and the London Academy of Music and Drama, filmmaking at New York University. **Military Service:** Served as pilot in the Israeli Air Force during the war of independence. **Family:** Married; three children. **Career:** Apprentice at Habimah Theatre, Tel Aviv; after stage studies, directed plays in Israel; after film studies, worked as assistant to Roger Corman; later became head of 21st Century Film Corporation. **Address:** 21st Century Film Corporation, 7000 West Third Street, Los Angeles, CA 90048, U.S.A.

GLOBUS. Producer. **Nationality:** Israeli. **Born:** Palestine (now Israel), c. 1943. **Career:** Became CEO of Pathé International (previously Cannon), later MGM-Pathé; founded production company, Melrose Entertainment. **Address:** c/o 5757 Wilshire Boulevard, Suite 721, Los Angeles, CA 90036, U.S.A.

Menahem Golan and Yoram Globus

1963—Golan and Globus formed the production and distribution company Noah Films; 1979—bought Cannon International and moved operations to Los Angeles; 1986—bought the United Kingdom ABC cinema chain and Elstree Studios; 1989—dissolved partnership.

Films as Producers/Executive Producers:

1963   *The Young Racers* (Corman) (Golan = prop master only); *El Dorado* (+ Golan = d)

1964   *Sallah Shabati* (*Sallah*) (Kishon)

1966   *Mivtza Kahir* (*Trunk to Cairo*) (+ Golan = d); *La Fille de la mer morte* (+ Golan = d)

1969   *What's Good for the Goose* (Golan = d, + co-sc only)

1970   *Margo* (+ Golan = d); *Lupo* (+ Golan = d)

1971   *Ani Ohev Otach Rosa* (*I Love You, Rosa*) (Mizrahi); *Queen of the Road* (+ Golan = d, + sc)

1972   *Escape to the Sun* (+ Golan = d, + co-sc)

1973   *The House on Chelouche Street* (Mizrahi); *Kazablan* (+ Golan = d)

1974   *Lepke* (+ Golan = d)

1975   *Diamonds* (*Tevye and His Seven Daughters*) (+ Golan = d, + co-sc)

1976   *The Passover Plot* (Campus)

1977   *Operation Thunderbolt* (*Entebbe*) (+ Golan = d); *The Uranium Conspiracy* (+ Golan = d); *Eskimo Limon* (*Lemon Popsicle*) (Davidson)

1978   *It's a Funny, Funny World* (Shessel)

1979   *Der Magier* (*The Magician of Lublin*) (+ Golan = d); *Imi Hageneralit* (*My Mother the General*) (Zilberg); *Yotz 'im Kavua* (*Going Steady*) (Davidson)

1980   *The Apple* (*Star Rock*) (+ Golan = d)

1981   *New Year's Evil* (Alston); *Body and Soul* (Browers); *Enter the Ninja* (Globus = pr, Golan = d, + co-sc)

1982   *That Championship Season* (Miller); *Hospital Massacre* (Davidson); *Sapiches* (*Private Popsicle*; *Lemon Popsicle IV*) (Davidson); *Ahava Ilemeth* (*The Secret of Yolanda*) (Silberg); *The Last American Virgin* (Davidson); *Nana* (Wolman); *House of the Long Shadows* (Walker)

1983   *Ten to Midnight* (Lee Thompson); *One More Chance* (Firstenberg); *Hercules* (Coates); *Revenge of the Ninja* (Firstenberg); *The Ultimate Solution of Grace Quigley*

(Harvey); *Roman Zair* (*Baby Love*; *Lemon Popsicle V*) (Wolman); *The Wicked Lady* (Winner)

1984 *I'm Almost Not Crazy: John Cassavetes—the Man and His Work* (Ventura—doc); *Over the Brooklyn Bridge* (*Alby's Delight*) (+ Golan = d); *The Seven Magnificent Gladiators* (Mattel); *Bolero* (Derek); *Missing in Action* (Zito); *Breakdance 2: Electric Boogaloo* (Firstenberg); *Exterminator 1* (Buntzman); *Ninja III: The Domination* (Firstenberg); *Sword of the Valiant* (Wecks); *Love Streams* (Cassavetes); *Sahara* (McLaglen); *The Naked Face* (Forbes); *Agatha Christie's Ordeal by Innocence* (David); *Mata Hari* (Harrington); *Déjà vu* (Richmond); *Hot Resort* (Robins); *Thunder Alley* (Cardone); *The Ambassador* (Lee Thompson)

1985 *King Solomon's Mines* (Lee Thompson); *Runaway Train* (Konchalovsky); *Lifeforce* (Hooper); *Invasion U.S.A.* (Zito); *Rappin'* (Silberg); *Eskimo Ohgen* (*Eskimo Limon 6*; *Up Your Anchor*; *Lemon Popsicle 6*) (Wolman); *The Berlin Affair* (Cavani)

1986 *The Delta Force* (+ Golan = d, + co-sc); *Cobra* (Cosmatos); *Invaders from Mars* (Hooper); *The Texas Chainsaw Massacre II* (Hooper); *Over the Top* (+ Golan = d); *Assassination* (Hunt); *52 Pick-Up* (Frankenheimer); *America 3000* (Engelbach); *Avenging Force* (Firstenberg); *Dangerously Close* (Pyun); *Duet for One* (Konchalovsky); *Dumb Dicks* (Ottoni); *Field of Honor* (Scheersmaker); *Firewalker* (Lee Thompson); *Hashigaon Hagadol* (Alter); *Journey to the Center of the Earth* (Lemorande); *K'Fafoth*; *Lightning—The White Stallion* (Levey); *Malkat Hakita*; *Murphy's Law* (Lee Thompson); *The Naked Cage* (Nicholas); *Number One with a Bullet* (Smight); *Otello* (Zeffirelli); *POW—the Escape* (Amir); *Salome* (d'Anna)

1987 *Business as Usual* (Barrett); *Rumpelstiltskin* (Irving); *Allan Quatermain and the Lost City of Gold* (Nelson); *American Ninja II* (Firstenberg); *Assassination* (Hunt); *The Barbarians* (Deodato); *Barfly* (Schroeder); *Beauty and the Beast* (Marner); *Dancers* (Ross); *Death Wish 4: The Crackdown* (Lee Thompson); *Down Twisted* (Pyun); *Dutch Treat* (Davidson); *The Emperor's New Clothes* (Irving); *Going Bananas* (Davidson); *Gor* (Kiersch); *Hansel and Gretel* (Talan); *King Lear* (Godard); *The Kitchen Toto* (Hook); *Mascara* (Conrad); *Masters of the Universe* (Goddard); *Red Riding Hood* (Adam Brooks); *Shy People* (Konchalovsky); *Sleeping Beauty* (Irving); *Snow White* (Berz); *Street Smart* (Schatzberg); *Superman IV: The Quest for Peace* (Furie); *Surrender* (Belson); *Too Much* (Rochat); *Tough Guys Don't Dance* (Mailer); *Undercover* (Stockwell)

1988 *D.C. Follies*; *Hanna's War* (*Innocent Heroes*) (+ Golan = d); *The Threepenny Opera* (+ Golan = d); *Alien from L.A.* (Pyun); *Appointment with Death* (Winner); *Bloodsport* (Arnold); *Braddock: Missing in Action III* (Norris); *A Cry in the Dark* (Schepisi); *Doin' Time on Planet Earth* (Matthau); *Wall of Tyrany* (*Freedom Fighter*) (Davis); *Haunted Summer* (Passer); *Hero and the Terror* (Tannen); *Manifesto* (Makavejev); *Messenger of Death* (Lee Thompson); *Powaqqatsi* (Reggio); *Puss in Boots* (Marner); *Salsa* (Davidson); *Cyborg* (Pyun) *Mack the Knife* (+ Golan = d, + sc); *Kinjite* (Lee Thompson); *Rockula* (Bercovici); *Sinbad of the Seven Seas*; *Young Love: Lemon Popsicle VII*

Films as Producer—Golan:

1987 *Die Papierene Brucke* (Beckermann); *The Hanoi Hilton* (Chetwynd)

1989 *Captain America* (Pyun); *The Phantom of the Opera* (Little); *The Rose Garden* (Rademakers); *Bad Jim* (Ware)

1990 *Bullseye!* (Winner) (co); *The Fifth Monkey* (Rochat); *Captain America* (Pyun); *The Forbidden Dance* (Clark); *Night of the Living Dead* (Savini); *Street Hunter* (Gallagher)

1991 *Terror of Manhattan* (Clark); *Invader* (Cook); *Badlanders* (Gazarian); *Three Days to a Kill* (Williamson) (co); *Rage* (Maharaj) (co); *Mad Dog Coll* (*Killer Instinct*) (Stein) (co)

1992 *Dance Macabre* (Clark); *The Finest Hour* (*Desert Shield*; *S.E.A.L.S.* (Dotan)

1993 *Teenage Bonnie and Klepto Clyde* (Shepphird) (exec); *Silent Victim* (Golan—for TV)

1994 *Dead Center* (Carver)

1999 *Delta Force One: The Lost Patrol* (Zito); *Cattle Call* (Guigui) (exec)

Films as Producer—Globus:

1989 *A Man Called Sarge* (Gillard); *Secret of the Ice Cave* (Gabrea)

1990 *Delta Force 2* (*Stranglehold: Delta Force 2*; *Delta Force 2: The Columbian Connection*) (Norris) (co)

1992 *Tipat Mazal* (*A Bit of Luck*); *Lelakek Tatut* (*Licking the Raspberry*) (Barbash)

1993 *Tobe Hooper's Night Terrors* (Hooper) (exec); *The Mummy Lives* (O'Hara) (exec); *Hellbound* (Norris) (exec); *Street Knight* (Magnoli) (exec)

1995 *Chain of Command* (Worth) (exec)

1999 *Delta Force One: The Lost Patrol* (Zito)

Publications

By GOLAN and GLOBUS: articles—

Screen International (London), 21–28 March 1981.
Screen International (London), 16–23 January 1982.
American Premiere (Los Angeles, California), April 1982.
Screen International (London), May 1982.
Screen International (London), 10–17 March 1984.
Ecran Fantastique (Paris), December 1984.
Screen International (London), 4–18 May 1985.
Ciné Revue (Paris), 30 January 1986.
Cinématographe (Paris), no. 119, May 1986.
EPD Film (Frankfurt), vol. 4, no. 9, September 1987.

On GOLAN and GLOBUS: book—

Yule, Andrew, *Hollywood a Go-Go: An Account of the Cannon Phenomenon*, London, 1987.

On GOLAN and GLOBUS: articles—

Cinema TV Today (London), 8 June 1974.
Screen International (London), 7 October 1978.
Screen International (London), 22–29 January 1983.

Sight and Sound (London), Summer 1983.
Film Comment (New York), November/December 1983.
Stills (London), June/July 1984.
Friedman, Robert, in *American Film* (Washington, D.C.), July/
August, 1986.
Sight and Sound (London), Autumn 1986.

On GLOBUS: articles—

Hovde, B., "Moguler pa kreditt," in *Z Filmtidsskrift* (Oslo), no. 2, 1995.

On GOLAN: articles—

Abittan, G., "Le cinema Israelien: de la propagande a la critique," in
Avant-Scene Cinema (Paris), July 1994.
Weiner, R., "Catching Up With Golan's Fresh Act," in *Variety* (New
York), October 17/23, 1994.
Kino (Munich), no. 2, 1996.

*   *   *

The Israeli film producers Menahem Golan—a patriot who changed his name after the taking of the Golan Heights and directed *Operation Thunderbolt* about the Entebbe rescue—and Yoram Globus are cousins who bought the Cannon Group, a floundering film company, in 1979 for a mere $350,000, soon turning it into Hollywood's most prosperous independent film company, with revenues reaching $150 million in 1986. Cannon achieved this meteoric ascent by making exploitation films cheaply and quickly, and by adhering to a number of innovative though sometimes questionable business tactics.

The average Cannon film cost about $5 million to make, whereas a film from a major studio such as Paramount, Columbia, or Universal often costs two to three times that amount. Because studios allocate enormous budgets for talent, production crews, publicity, and the use of studio equipment, many productions must gross $20 million just to break even. As a result, a film thought to possess box-office potential is booked in as many theaters as possible in hopes of drawing huge audiences and profits. If the film is a flop, however, the loss to the studio can be astronomical. By working outside the Hollywood system and avoiding many of its expensive accouterments, an independent company such as Cannon could keep production costs down, although the savings frequently came at the expense of quality. Many independent companies are too small and financially insecure to distribute their own films and, ironically, rely on the stronger distribution arm of a major studio. Again, risk and costs are minimized, yet so is the chances of reaping huge profits.

As independent producers, Golan and Globus found additional ways to reduce costs, maximize profits, and at the same time attract name stars and directors. Cannon persuaded a number of stars to forfeit their million dollar-plus salaries in exchange for smaller salaries and profit sharing. To safeguard further against loss, Cannon sold its films' cable, home video, and overseas exhibition rights in advance of production, thereby guaranteeing a marketplace for even the poorest films. Impatient with Hollywood excess, Golan, the company's chairman and chief artistic decision maker, rigorously kept films from going over schedule or budget. Golan also refused to read scripts, much to the consternation of agents and lawyers. Instead, he made fast decisions on what he felt to be promising story ideas. This brashness, combined with the production of exploitation films

such as *Bolero*, *Schizoid*, *Death Wish IV*, and *Invasion, U.S.A.*, earned Golan and Globus a sort of "bad boys" reputation in Hollywood.

Indeed, Golan and Globus surprised the film community in 1982 with their production of Jason Miller's Pulitzer Prize-winning drama *That Championship Season*. The film was a commercial failure but it did suggest that Cannon was interested in serious filmmaking. Commercial success also eluded its esoteric productions of Robert Altman's *Fool for Love* and John Cassavetes's *Love Streams*, which cost little to make. Interestingly enough, neither of these films would have been made by a major studio today, the audience for them being too limited. Responding to the artistic restrictions of a profit-motivated studio system, directors such as Roman Polanski, Bill Forsyth, Hector Babenco, John Huston, and Jean-Luc Godard turned to Cannon for help. And in their determination to upgrade their image, Golan and Globus afforded a generous amount of artistic freedom to those who could work within their budgetary constraints. Nevertheless, most of Cannon's "prestige" projects—Anthony Harvey's *The Ultimate Solution of Grace Quigley*, Andrei Konchalovsky's *Runaway Train*— are as ill-judged, clodhopping, and embarrassing as their coattail-riding Charles Bronson vehicles (*Assassination*) or Israeli sex comedies (the *Lemon Popsicle* series).

As Cannon's artistic ambitions expanded, so did its assets and financial burdens. In 1985 Cannon produced 23 films, more than any other film company in the United States. Its acquisition of Thorn EMI Screen Entertainment, a production and distribution company, and the Commonwealth Theaters, the sixth-largest theater chain in the country, proved Cannon a force to be reckoned with. This risky move, however, also resulted in high production costs and crippling debts. Though Golan and Globus managed to get in on the beginnings of certain exploitation fads (teenage sex, breakdance musicals, vigilante action, Chuck Norris), they showed a lack of Corman-style savvy by staying with them long after the market had passed on, and floundered badly by producing a slate of live-action fairy-tale adaptations that crucially missed the Disney market.

Among the films Golan himself chose to direct was the obvious commercial loser *Over the Top*, a Sylvester Stallone vehicle about arm-wrestling, for which Cannon unwisely laid out a star-level salary. Golan always had a knack of pulling middlebrow properties from the Cannon list for his own directorial exercises and making stodgy embarrassments such as *The Magician of Lublin*, *Over the Brooklyn Bridge*, *Hanna's War*, and *The Threepenny Opera*. In Cannon's heyday, the trade press were thick with portfolios of ads for upcoming projects, many of which (*Citizen Joe*, *Spider-Man*) never came to pass.

After acquiring the ABC chain, Cannon had to be helped out by European financiers, and Golan and Globus took an unaccustomed back seat. In 1989, Golan declared a desire to produce "artier" works, dissolved the Golan-Globus partnership, and established an independent production company, 21st Century which eventually specialized in direct-to-video offerings (*Night Terrors*, *The Mummy Lives*) from the likes of longtime hacks Tobe Hooper and Harry Alan Towers. Globus, meanwhile, although still involved with MGM-Pathé (previously Cannon), has his own production company, Melrose Entertainment, which makes action-adventure movies in the best Cannon tradition. After the collapse of his film career, Golan resuscitated himself by putting on a blockbusting stage production of *The Sound of Music* in Tel Aviv, controversial mostly because the Nazis in the play were speaking Hebrew.

—Heidi Gensch, updated by Kim Newman

GOLDMAN, William

Writer. **Nationality:** American. **Born:** Chicago, Illinois, 12 August 1931; brother of the writer James Goldman. **Education:** Attended Highland Park High School; Oberlin College, Ohio, B.A. 1952; Columbia University, New York, M.A. 1956. **Military Service:** U.S. Army, 1952–54: corporal. **Family:** Married Ilene Jones, 1961 (divorced), two daughters. **Career:** Writer: first novel published 1957; author of two plays with James Goldman, *Blood, Sweat, and Stanley Poole*, 1961, and *A Family Affair*, 1962; 1964—first film as writer, *Masquerade*. **Awards:** Academy Award, Writers Guild Award, and British Academy Award, for *Butch Cassidy and the Sundance Kid*, 1969; Academy Award and Writers Guild Award, for *All the President's Men*, 1976. **Address:** 50 East 77th Street, New York, NY 10021, U.S.A.

Films as Writer:

1964 *Masquerade* (Dearden) (co)
1966 *Harper* (*The Moving Target*) (Smight)
1969 *Butch Cassidy and the Sundance Kid* (Hill)
1972 *The Hot Rock* (*How to Steal a Diamond in Four Uneasy Lessons*) (Yates)

William Goldman

1974 *The Stepford Wives* (Forbes)
1975 *The Great Waldo Pepper* (Hill)
1976 *All the President's Men* (Pakula); *Marathon Man* (Schlesinger)
1977 *A Bridge Too Far* (Attenborough)
1978 *Magic* (Attenborough)
1979 *Mr. Horn* (Starrett); *Butch and Sundance: The Early Days* (Lester) (idea)
1987 *Heat* (Richards); *The Princess Bride* (R. Reiner)
1990 *Misery* (R. Reiner); *The Lions of Salvo* (de Palma)
1992 *Year of the Comet* (Yates); *Memoirs of an Invisible Man* (Carpenter) (co); *Chaplin* (Attenborough) (co)
1993 *Last Action Hero* (McTiernan) (co)
1994 *Maverick* (Donner)
1996 *The Chamber* (Foley) (co); *The Ghost and the Darkness* (Hopkins)
1997 *Absolute Power* (Eastwood); *Fierce Creatures* (Schepisi and Young) (uncredited)
1999 *The General's Daughter* (West) (co)

Films Based on Goldman's Writings:

1963 *Soldier in the Rain* (Nelson)
1968 *No Way to Treat a Lady* (Smight)

Publications

By GOLDMAN: fiction—

The Temple of Gold, New York, 1957.
Your Turn to Curtsy, My Turn to Bow, New York, 1958.
Soldier in the Rain, New York, 1960.
Boys and Girls Together, New York, 1964.
No Way to Treat a Lady, New York, 1964.
The Thing of It Is . . ., New York, 1967.
Father's Day, New York, 1971.
The Princess Bride, New York, 1973.
Marathon Man, New York, 1974.
Wigger (for children), New York, 1974.
Magic, New York, 1976.
Tinsel, New York, 1979.
Control, New York, 1982.
The Color of Light, New York, 1984.
The Silent Gondoliers, New York, 1984.
Heat, New York, 1985, as *Edged Weapons*, London, 1985.
Brothers, New York, 1986.
William Goldman: Four Screenplays, New York, 1997.
William Goldman: Five Screenplays, All the President's Men, Harper, The Great Waldo Papper, Magic & Maverick, New York, 1998.

By GOLDMAN: other writings—

With James Goldman, *Blood, Sweat and Stanley Poole* (play), New York, 1962.
With James Goldman, *A Family Affair* (play), New York, 1962.
Butch Cassidy and the Sundance Kid (screenplay), New York, 1969.
The Season: A Candid Look at Broadway (nonfiction), New York, 1969.
The Great Waldo Pepper (screenplay), New York, 1975.
The Story of A Bridge Too Far, New York, 1977.

Adventures in the Screentrade: A Personal View of Hollywood and Screenwriting, New York, 1983.
With Mike Lupica, *Wait till Next Year: The Story of a Season When What Should've Happened Didn't and What Could've Gone Wrong Did*, New York, 1988.
Hype and Glory (nonfiction), New York, 1990.
The Big Picture: Who Killed Hollywood? And Other Essays, New York, 2000.
Which Lie Did I Tell? More Adventures in the Screen Trade, New York, 2000.

By GOLDMAN: articles—

Films Illustrated (London), July 1976.
Filmmakers Newsletter (Ward Hill, Massachusetts), October 1977.
In *The Craft of the Screenwriter*, by John Brady, New York, 1981.
Films (London), May 1984.
Cahiers du Cinéma (Paris), February 1991.
Positif (Paris), no. 361, March 1991.
Disaster Movies, no. 38, New York, 1992.
Cinema 66, no. 20, New York, 1993.
Sins of Omission, no. 6, New York, 1993.
''Butch Cassidy and the Nazi Dentist,'' no. 5, *Esquire*, 1994.
The Pig and the Hunk, no. 8, New York, 1996.
''Tracking *The Ghost and the Darkness*,'' in *Premiere* (Boulder), November 1996.
''From Brando to Paltrow,'' in *Premiere* (Boulder), December 1996.
Film en Televisie + Video (Brussels), July 1997.
''William Goldman on Norman Jewison,'' in *The Toronto Star*, 18 April 1999.
''The Gray '90s: Nobody Knows Anything,'' in *Premiere* (Boulder), November 1999.

On GOLDMAN: book—

Andersen, Richard, *William Goldman*, Boston, 1979.

On GOLDMAN: articles—

American Film (Washington, D.C.), January/February 1976.
Cinéma (Paris), August/September 1977.
Cinéma (Paris), August/September 1978.
National Film Theatre Booklet (London), April 1984.
Stone, Botham, in *American Screenwriters, 2nd series*, edited by Randall Clark, Detroit, 1986.
Radio Times (London), 19 February 1994.
Feeney, Mark, ''The Goldman Standard: Oscar-Winning Screenwriter Says It's Easy: Work Hard, Stay Scared, and Above All Be Lucky,'' in *The Boston Globe*, 8 March 2000.
Welkos, Robert W. ''Profile: He Knows They Don't Know,'' in *The Los Angeles Times*, 2 April 2000.
Sragow, Michael, ''Famous Screenwriters School,'' in *The New York Times Book Review*, 9 April 2000.

*   *   *

William Goldman is a master craftsman of streamlined scripts with well-delineated characters and crisp dialogue. For Goldman, screenwriting is carpentry. ''The single most important thing contributed by the screenwriter,'' he once said, ''is the structure.'' Accordingly, Goldman's scripts are fast-paced models of plot design.

Butch Cassidy and the Sundance Kid was an important screenplay even before it was produced. In 1967 it sold for the then unheard-of price of $400,000, setting an industrial precedent that helped American screenwriters gain recognition and clout. The film was extremely popular, but suffered critically in comparison with Peckinpah's *The Wild Bunch*, released a few months earlier. Where *The Wild Bunch* was a gritty, intensely graphic revisionist Western, *Butch Cassidy* appeared lightweight, flip, and coy. And *Butch Cassidy*'s freeze-frame ending (which came directly from Goldman's script) seemed tame and retrograde compared to *The Wild Bunch*'s apocalyptic bloodbath. But for all its cuteness, *Butch Cassidy* was revisionist too. Goldman's heroes were imperfect (Sundance cannot swim, and Butch, notorious leader of the Hole in the Wall Gang, confesses he has never killed anyone) and drawn on a human rather than heroic scale (Butch and Sundance spend most of the film running away from the railroad agents, strenuously avoiding the obligatory Western confrontation). Goldman parodied train robberies, bank holdups, and tight-lipped face-offs. He made a joke of the gathering-of-the-posse scene (de rigueur since *The Great Train Robbery*) by writing one in which the local marshal fails to persuade the townsfolk to rush out after Butch and Sundance. (''It's up to us to do something!'' exhorts the marshal. ''What's the point?'' answers one uninterested citizen.) Perhaps most revisionist of all was Goldman's arch, smart-alecky dialogue. Having his characters speak like witty urbanites was an experiment that might have failed, but it worked, and its originality was no small part of the film's charm. If *The Wild Bunch* madeus think about violence in Westerns, *Butch Cassidy and the Sundance Kid* made us question Western conventions.

Although Goldman has adapted other authors' works as well as his own, he is not, by his own admission, ruthless enough when the source is his. This may account for the absence of Goldman's usually hard-driving plotting in *Marathon Man* and *Magic*, both adapted from his best-selling novels. Szell's torturing of Babe with a dental drill is unforgettable, but the main action in *Marathon Man* is muddled. *Magic* develops some keen moments of tension, but it fizzles where it should pop, and pales badly in comparison with its generic ancestor, Michael Redgrave's ventriloquist sequence in *Dead of Night*. But in adapting others' works for the screen Goldman is expert. Indeed, it seems the longer and more intricate the original, the better his final script. His adaptations for *A Bridge Too Far* and *All the President's Men*, both based on nonfiction books about complex historical events, are clean and economical translations, especially considering the problems he faced.

In *A Bridge Too Far* Goldman was required to make commercially palatable what was essentially a noncommercial property. Cornelius Ryan's book documented a crucial but (in the United States) little-known Allied operation that defies simple summarization (unless it would be ''We lost''). Goldman cut through the book's tangled historical web and provided an easily understood, straight-line narrative by making the film, as he says, ''the ultimate cavalry-to-the-rescue story'': the Allies need to take a series of bridges and relieve 35,000 soldiers who have parachuted in behind enemy lines. But the loss suffered by the Allies when they came up one bridge short of their objective dictated a deflated ending, which no doubt had something to do with the film's disappointing reception.

In *All the President's Men* Goldman had to find a way to interest audiences in a talky political story, lacking in action and climactic confrontations, with an ending viewers already knew. Goldman's solution was to model the film on late 1940s-early 1950s investigative reporter films noir (Goldman's script preface specified that the film should have "a black-and-white feel") and give it racehorse pacing (another prefatory script note: "This film is written to go like a streak"). He structured the film as a dramatic progression of clues uncovered by the giant-killing investigators, Woodward and Bernstein, and built a solid foundation for a gripping thriller.

Goldman is a pragmatic professional about his work and about the baroque process of going from script to screen. In *Adventures in the Screen Trade* Goldman looks at the movie business sans rose-colored glasses and comes up with screenwriting rules of thumb such as what he considers to be the key movie industry fact: "NOBODY KNOWS ANYTHING." And there is this clear-eyed observation, which may explain why Goldman continues to describe himself as a novelist who writes screenplays rather than the other way around. This thoroughly professional screenwriter feels that in the final analysis screenwriting—because of built-in industrial limitations—will ruin a serious writer. "I truly believe," Goldman writes, "that if all you do with your life is write screenplays, it ultimately has to denigrate the soul. . . . Because you will spend your always-decreasing days . . . writing Perfect Parts for Perfect People."

During the first half of the 1980s, Goldman went through a fallow period when none of his scripts were produced. However, these doldrums ended in 1986, when Goldman sold his screenplay of *The Princess Bride* (based on his 1973 novel of the same name). He remained busy throughout the decade of the 1990s (a period whose films Goldman has characterized as the most lackluster in the history of American cinema) and beyond. In the spring of 2000, he published two nonfiction books. *Which Lie Did I Tell? More Adventures in the Screen Trade* was a sequel to Goldman's popular 1983 memoir, *Adventures in the Screen Trade*. The second book, *The Big Picture: Who Killed Hollywood? And Other Essays* collects short pieces that Goldman originally wrote for *Premiere* and other popular magazines.

—Charles Ramirez Berg, updated by John McCarty,
further updated by Justin Gustainis

GOLDSMITH, Jerry

Composer. **Nationality:** American. **Born:** Jerrald Goldsmith in Los Angeles, California, 1929. **Education:** Attended Dorsey High School; studied piano with Jakob Gimpel at Los Angeles City College, and film music under Miklos Rozsa at University of California, Los Angeles. **Family:** Son: the composer Joel Goldsmith. **Career:** 1952—joined CBS as clerk, then radio composer; 1955—composer for TV; composer of theme music and background music for many TV series, and music for TV films and mini-series (*QB VII*, 1974, *Masada*, 1981); 1957—first score for film, *Black Patch*; also composer of orchestra and choral works, and conductor. **Awards:** Academy Award, for *The Omen*, 1976. **Agent:** ICM, 8899 Beverly Boulevard, Los Angeles, CA 90048, U.S.A.

Films as Composer:

1957   *Black Patch* (Miner)
1958   *City of Fear* (Lerner)

Jerry Goldsmith

1959   *Face of a Fugitive* (Wendkos)
1960   *Studs Lonigan* (Lerner)
1962   *Lonely Are the Brave* (Miller); *The Spiral Road* (Mulligan); *Freud* (*Freud: The Secret Passion*) (Huston); *A Gathering of Eagles* (Delbert Mann)
1963   *The List of Adrian Messenger* (Huston); *The Stripper* (*Woman of Summer*) (Schaffner); *The Prize* (Robson); *Lilies of the Field* (Nelson); *Take Her, She's Mine* (Koster); *Seven Days in May* (Frankenheimer); *Fate Is the Hunter* (Nelson); *Rio Conchos* (Douglas)
1965   *The Satan Bug* (J. Sturges); *In Harm's Way* (Preminger); *Von Ryan's Express* (Robson); *A Patch of Blue* (Green); *Morituri* (*The Saboteur Code Name "Morituri"*) (Wicki); *The Agony and the Ecstasy* (Reed) (prologue only, d by Labella); *Our Man Flint* (Daniel Mann)
1966   *The Trouble with Angels* (Lupino); *Stagecoach* (Douglas); *The Blue Max* (Guillermin); *Seconds* (Frankenheimer); *The Sand Pebbles* (Wise); *Warning Shot* (Kulik)
1967   *In Like Flint* (Douglas); *Hour of the Gun* (J. Sturges); *The Flim-Flam Man* (*One Born Every Minute*) (Kershner); *Sebastian* (Greene); *Planet of the Apes* (Schaffner)
1968   *The Detective* (Douglas); *Bandolero!* (McLaglen); *100 Rifles* (Gries); *The Illustrated Man* (Smight)
1969   *The Most Dangerous Man in the World* (*The Chairman*) (Lee Thompson); *Justine* (Cukor); *Patton* (*Patton: Lust for Glory*) (Schaffner)
1970   *The Ballad of Cable Hogue* (Peckinpah); *The Magic Garden of Stanley Sweetheart* (Horn) (song); *Tora! Tora! Tora!*

(Fleischer, Masuda, and Fukasaku); *The Traveling Executioner* (Smight); *Rio Lobo* (Hawks); *The Mephisto Waltz* (Wendkos); *The Brotherhood of the Bell* (Wendkos)

1971   *Escape from the Planet of the Apes* (Taylor); *Wild Rovers* (Edwards); *The Last Run* (Fleischer); *A Step Out of Line* (McEveety); *The Homecoming* (Cook); *Do Not Fold, Spindle, or Mutilate* (Post); *The Cable Car Murder* (Thorpe)

1972   *The Culpepper Cattle Company* (Richards) (co); *The Other* (Mulligan); *Shamus* (Kulik); *Crawlspace* (Newland); *Pursuit* (Crichton); *The Man* (Sargent)

1973   *The Red Pony* (Totten); *Ace Eli and Rodger of the Skies* (Erman); *One Little Indian* (McEveety); *The Don Is Dead* (Fleischer); *Papillon* (Schaffner); *The Police Story* (*The Stake-Out*) (Graham); *Hawkins on Murder* (Taylor)

1974   **Chinatown** (Polanski); *Spys* (Kershner) (U.S. version only); *Ransom* (*The Terrorists*) (Wrede); *The Reincarnation of Peter Proud* (Lee Thompson); *Indict and Convict* (Sagal); *Winter Kill* (Taylor); *A Tree Grows in Brooklyn* (Hardy)

1975   *Breakout* (Gries); *The Wind and the Lion* (Milius); *Take a Hard Ride* (Margheriti); *Babe* (Kulik); *Breakheart Pass* (Gries); *A Girl Named Sooner* (Delbert Mann)

1976   *The Omen* (Donner); *Logan's Run* (Anderson); *High Velocity* (R. Kramer); *The Cassandra Crossing* (Cosmatos); *Islands in the Stream* (Schaffner)

1977   *Twilight's Last Gleaming* (Aldrich); *Coma* (Crichton); *MacArthur* (Sargent); *Damnation Alley* (Smight); *Capricorn One* (Hyams); *Contract on Cherry Street* (Graham)

1978   *Damien—Omen II* (Taylor); *The Swarm* (I. Allen); *The Boys from Brazil* (Schaffner); *Magic* (Attenborough); *The First Great Train Robbery* (*The Great Train Robbery*) (Crichton)

1979   *Alien* (Scott); *Players* (Harvey); *Cabo Blanco* (Lee Thompson); *Star Trek: The Motion Picture* (Wise)

1981   *Raggedy Man* (Fisk); *Inchon* (Young)

1982   *Night Crossing* (Delbert Mann); *Poltergeist* (Hooper); *The Challenge* (Frankenheimer); *The House on Sorority Row* (*House of Evil*) (Rosman) (co)

1983   *Psycho II* (Franklin); *Twilight Zone—The Movie* (Landis and others); *The Salamander* (Zinner); *Under Fire* (Spottiswoode)

1984   *Supergirl* (Szwarc); *Gremlins* (Dante); *Runaway* (Crichton); *Baby—Secret of the Lost Legend* (Norton); *The Lonely Guy* (Hiller)

1985   *King Solomon's Mines* (Lee Thompson); *Legend* (Scott); *Rambo: First Blood, Part II* (Cosmatos)

1986   *Hoosiers* (Anspaugh); *Link* (Franklin); *Explorers* (Dante); *Poltergeist II* (Gibson)

1987   *Extreme Prejudice* (Hill); *Innerspace* (Dante); *Lionheart* (Schaffner); *Allan Quatermain and the Lost City of Gold* (Nelson and Arnold)

1988   *Criminal Law* (Campbell); *Rambo III* (MacDonald); *Rent-a-Cop* (London)

1989   *The Burbs* (Dante); *Leviathan* (Cosmatos); *Star Trek V: The Final Frontier* (Shatner); *Warlock* (Miner)

1990   *The Russia House* (Schepisi); *Gremlins 2: The New Batch* (Dante); *Total Recall* (Verhoeven)

1991   *Not without My Daughter* (Gilbert); *Sleeping with the Enemy* (Ruben)

1992   *Basic Instinct* (Verhoeven); *Forever Young* (Miner); *Love Field* (Kaplan); *Medicine Man* (McTiernan); *Mom and Dad Save the World* (Beeman); *Mr. Baseball* (Schepisi)

1993   *Dennis the Menace* (Castle); *Malice* (H. Becker); *Matinee* (Dante); *Rudy* (Anspaugh); *Six Degrees of Separation* (Schepisi); *The Vanishing* (Sluizer)

1994   *The River Wild* (Hanson); *IQ* (Schepisi); *Gunmen* (Sarafian); *Angie* (Coolidge); *Bad Girls* (Kaplan); *Star Trek: The Next Generation—All Good Things* (Kolbe—series for TV); *The Shadow* (Mulcahy)

1995   *Star Trek: Voyager—Caretaker* (Kolbe—series for TV); *Star Trek: Voyager* (series for TV) (main title theme); *Legend* (Balaban and Bole—series for TV); *Congo* (Marshall); *First Knight* (Zucker); *Powder* (Salva)

1996   *City Hall* (Becker); *Executive Decision* (*Critical Decision*) (Baird); *Chain Reaction* (Davis); *The Ghost and the Darkness* (Hopkins); *Star Trek: First Contact* (Frakes)

1997   *Fierce Creatures* (Schepisi and Young); **L.A. Confidential** (Hanson); *Air Force One* (Petersen); *The Edge* (Tamahori); *Alien: Resurrection* (Jeunet)

1998   *Deep Rising* (Sommers); *U.S. Marshals* (Baird); *Mulan* (Bancroft and Cook—anim); *Small Soldiers* (Dante); *Star Trek: Insurrection* (Frakes)

1999   *The Mummy* (Sommers); *The 13th Warrior* (McTiernan); *The Haunting* (de Bont)

2000   *The Kid* (Turteltaub); *The Hollow Man* (Verhoeven)

Film as Music Director:

1969   *Joaquin Murieta* (Bellamy)

Publications

By GOLDSMITH: articles—

In *Knowing the Score*, by Irwin Bazelon, New York, 1975.
Cinema TV Today, 5 July 1975.
Films Illustrated (London), February 1976.
Interview with Elmer Bernstein, in *Film Music Notebook* (Calabasas, California), vol. 3, no. 1, 1977.
In *Film Score*, edited by Tony Thomas, South Brunswick, New Jersey, 1979.
Millimeter (New York), April 1979.
Films and Filming (London), May and June 1979.
Soundtrack! (Hollywood), Spring 1981.
Cinefantastique (New York), September/October 1982.
New Zealand Film Music Bulletin (Invercargill), August 1985.
Soundtrack! (Hollywood), vol. 6, no. 23, September 1987.
Interview with Vincent Jacquet-Françillon, in *Cue Sheet* (Hollywood), vol. 10, no. 3–4, 1993–1994.

On GOLDSMITH: articles—

Godfrey, Lionel, ''The Music Makers: Elmer Bernstein and Jerry Goldsmith,'' in *Films and Filming* (London), July 1966.
Focus on Film (London), May/August 1970.
Films in Review (New York), January 1972.
Thomas, Tony, in *Music for the Movies*, South Brunswick, New Jersey, 1973.
Ecran (Paris), September 1975.

Caps, John, in *Film Music Notebook* (Calabasas, California), vol. 2, no. 1, 1976.

Focus on Film (London), Summer/Autumn 1976.

Films in Review (New York), October 1976.

Maffet, James D., in *Film Music Notebook* (Calabasas, California), vol. 3, no. 1, 1977.

Cinema Papers (Melbourne), January 1977.

Films in Review (New York), November 1978.

Soundtrack! (Hollywood), April 1979.

Soundtrack! (Hollywood), October 1979.

Soundtrack! (Hollywood), January 1980.

Films in Review (New York), March 1980.

Score (Lelystad, Netherlands), March 1981.

Fistful of Soundtracks (London), November 1981.

Soundtrack! (Hollywood), December 1981.

Soundtrack! (Hollywood), June 1982.

Soundtrack! (Hollywood), December 1983.

Soundtrack! (Hollywood), vol. 4, no. 16, December 1985.

Séquences (Montreal), July 1986.

Soundtrack! (Hollywood), vol. 7, no. 28, December 1988.

Soundtrack! (Hollywood), vol. 11, June 1992.

Sequences, no. 164, May 1993.

Soundtrack! (Hollywood), June 1993.

Mancini, Henry, "Presentation of the SPFM Career Achievement Award to Jerry Goldsmith," in *Cue Sheet* (Hollywood), vol. 10, no. 3–4, 1993–1994.

Soundtrack! (Hollywood), June 1997.

Soundtrack! (Hollywood), September 1997.

Cahiers du Cinéma (Paris), December 1997.

Crowdus, Gregory, "Film Music Masters: Jerry Goldsmith," in *Cineaste* (New York), 1996.

Dutka, Elaine, "Cue the Composer: The Key to Jerry Goldsmith's Long and Prolific Career as a Composer of Film Music? 'I'm a Chameleon,' He Says," in *The Los Angeles Times*, 1 August 1999.

Woodard, Josef, "Goldsmith Hosts Night of Memorable Movie Themes," in *The Los Angeles Times*, 9 August 1999.

*   *   *

The career of Jerry Goldsmith is difficult to classify, either in cinematic or musical terms. One of the most prolific contemporary film composers, Goldsmith has provided scores for works in all genres and drawn on a wide range of musical styles, from the Latin chants provided in *The Omen* to the atonal approach of *Freud* and *Twilight's Last Gleaming* to the Copland-ish *Lonely Are the Brave* and the avant-garde effects created for *Planet of the Apes* and *Alien*. Goldsmith has demonstrated an ability to find the correct sound for each film but his employment of a vast number of musical styles has been more often innovative rather than merely imitative.

As one of a new generation of composers that began to emerge in the 1950s, Goldsmith not surprisingly displayed in his early work for film and television a familiarity with jazz and other contemporary idioms. Nevertheless, he has also demonstrated that he is equally comfortable with a more traditional symphonic approach, and thus he serves as a vital link between the film scoring techniques of the past and the practices of his peers. Unlike composers who have emphasized either discipline, Goldsmith, similar to Bernard Herrmann, has preferred to let the film dictate the musical approach rather than imposing a specific musical style onto the film, and this concern with finding the right approach to complement the image makes him in some respects more indicative of what a film composer should be than many of his colleagues who have shown through their scores the development of a recognizable style regardless of the subject matter.

In addition to the employment of a number of different styles, Goldsmith has also relied on selective instrumentation and use of the score in finding the appropriate sound for a given film. The score for *Seconds* played off piano against organ to match both the futuristic and lyrically nostalgic aspects of the story, while a specific ensemble was devised for *Chinatown* which employed several pianos and a solo trumpet. Goldsmith was not the original choice to score *Chinatown*. He was called in at the last minute to compose a new score in record time when the first composer's score was rejected. Goldsmith's score is so perfectly suited to the film's neo-noir mood, it is difficult to imagine the film scored any other way.

For *Planet of the Apes* Goldsmith chose to avoid the tendency in the science-fiction subjects toward electronic scoring by creating sound effects through avant-garde employment of a conventional orchestra augmented by percussion effects and devices such as the use of mixing bowls, and the result is an other-worldly sound reminiscent in places of the work of composers such as Bartok. Goldsmith has also been selective about where music is employed in films, providing a deliberately sparse (and consequently more effective) score for *Patton* and choosing not to provide music in *Coma* until halfway into the film.

The range of Goldsmith's work can be seen even in his identification with a single filmmaker such as Franklin J. Schaffner. The composer has provided a diversity of musical styles to match Schaffner's diverse number of subjects, from the aforementioned *Planet of the Apes* and the martial *Patton* score to the more lyrical *Islands in the Stream* and *Papillon*, the Viennese waltz for *The Boys from Brazil* to the elegant with a touch of strange *Lionheart*, Schaffner's ill-fated last film which was barely released. Yet, despite this variety many of Goldsmith's works contain trademark devices such as an employment of harsh glissandos during suspense scenes and driving passages founded on an abruptly syncopated style which are balanced off against melodic romantic themes. Although the latter tend at times, as in *Coma*, toward the maudlin. The latter themes are often recapitulated at the end of the film and many of the scores show a similarity of construction in this closing music with an abrupt punctuation of a few notes serving as the lead-in to the final swelling statement of the main thematic line.

While Goldsmith's early work was often for war films or contemporary espionage dramas, his recent output has often been for science-fiction subjects, the most popular contemporary genre. For many of these he has avoided repeating the approach of the *Apes* score and has instead sought out different but equally unique approaches, such as the use of horns to create a sense of isolation in *Alien*. Yet his prolific output has at times resulted in a sameness of approach and it is possible to detect repetition even in works that are seemingly unrelated. For example, a theme in *The Great Train Robbery* sounds like a modification and reorchestration of the waltz theme in *The Boys from Brazil* adapted to a new musical idiom. Nevertheless, most of Goldsmith's work reflects his dedication to the blending of sound and image and demonstrates the ability of film music to employ a variety of traditional approaches and even create some new ones.

Although he turned 70 in 1999, Jerry Goldsmith showed no signs of slowing down as the twenty-first century dawned. He scored two films (*The Kid* and *The Hollow Man*) scheduled for release in 2000, and then contracted for another (*The Shipping News*) due out in 2001.

In celebration of the composer's seventieth birthday, the Los Angeles Philharmonic performed an entire program devoted to his film scores. The performance drew a packed house to the Hollywood Bowl, possibly because of the evening's guest conductor — Jerry Goldsmith.

—Richard R. Ness, updated by John McCarty, further updated by Justin Gustainis

GOLDWYN, Samuel

Producer. **Nationality:** American. **Born:** Samuel Goldfisch in Warsaw, Poland, 27 August 1884; emigrated to the United States, 1897; naturalized, 1902. **Family:** Married 1) Blanche Lasky, 1910 (divorced 1919); 2) Frances Howard, 1925; son: the producer Samuel Goldwyn, Jr. **Career:** 1895—stayed with relatives in England and worked as blacksmith's helper; 1897—emigrated to the United States: worked as apprentice glovemaker, Gloversville, New York, and went to night school, then glove salesman; 1912—with his brother-in-law, Jesse L. Lasky, formed Jesse L. Lasky Feature Play Company, with Cecil B. De Mille as director (Goldwyn was treasurer); 1916—merged with Zukor's Famous Players (Goldwyn was chairman of the board); 1918—formed Goldwyn company with Edgar Selwyn; 1922—formed Samuel Goldwyn Productions, with no partners (his previous Selwyn company merged with Metro and Mayer companies to form Metro Goldwyn Mayer). **Awards:** Academy Award for *The Best Years of Our Lives*, 1946; Irving G. Thalberg

Samuel Goldwyn

Award, 1946; Jean Hersholt Humanitarian Award, 1957; U.S. Freedom Medal, 1971. **Died:** In Beverly Hills, California, 3 January 1974.

Films as Producer:

1923   *Potash and Perlmutter* (Badger)
1924   *The Eternal City* (Fitzmaurice); *Cytherea* (Fitzmaurice); *Tarnish* (Fitzmaurice); *In Hollywood with Potash and Perlmutter* (Green); **Greed** (von Stroheim) (co)
1925   *A Thief in Paradise* (Fitzmaurice); *His Supreme Moment* (Fitzmaurice); *The Dark Angel* (Fitzmaurice); *Stella Dallas* (H. King)
1926   *Ben-Hur* (Niblo) (co); *The Winning of Barbara Worth* (H. King); *Partners Again (With Potash and Perlmutter)* (H. King)
1927   *The Night of Love* (Fitzmaurice); *The Magic Flame* (H. King); *The Devil Dancer* (Niblo)
1928   *Two Lovers* (Niblo); *The Awakening* (Fleming)
1929   *The Rescue* (Brenon); *Bulldog Drummond* (Jones); *This Is Heaven* (Santell); *Condemned* (Ruggles)
1930   *Raffles* (D'Arrast and Fitzmaurice); *Whoopee!* (Freeland); *The Devil to Pay* (Fitzmaurice)
1931   *Street Scene* (K. Vidor); *One Heavenly Night* (Fitzmaurice); *Palmy Days* (Sutherland); *The Unholy Garden* (Fitzmaurice); *Arrowsmith* (Ford); *Tonight or Never* (LeRoy)
1932   *The Greeks Had a Word for Them* (V. Sherman); *Cynara* (K. Vidor); *The Kid from Spain* (McCarey)
1933   *Roman Scandals* (Tuttle); *The Masquerader* (Wallace)
1934   *Nana* (Arzner); *We Live Again* (Mamoulian); *Kid Millions* (Del Ruth)
1935   *The Wedding Night* (K. Vidor); *The Dark Angel* (Franklin); *Barbary Coast* (Hawks); *Splendor* (Nugent)
1936   *Strike Me Pink* (Taurog); *Dodsworth* (Wyler); *Come and Get It* (Hawks and Wyler); *These Three* (Wyler); *Beloved Enemy* (Potter)
1937   *Dead End* (Wyler); *Woman Chases Man* (Blystone); *Stella Dallas* (K. Vidor); *The Hurricane* (Ford and Heisler)
1938   *The Goldwyn Follies* (Marshall, and Potter uncredited); *The Adventures of Marco Polo* (Mayo, and Ford uncredited); *The Cowboy and the Lady* (Potter)
1939   *The Real Glory* (Hathaway); *Wuthering Heights* (Wyler); *They Shall Have Music (Ragged Angels)* (Mayo)
1940   *The Westerner* (Wyler); *Raffles* (Wood)
1941   **The Little Foxes** (Wyler); *Ball of Fire* (Hawks); *The Pride of the Yankees* (Wood)
1943   *The North Star (Armored Attack)* (Milestone); *They Got Me Covered* (Butler)
1944   *Up in Arms* (Nugent); *The Princess and the Pirate* (Butler)
1945   *Wonder Man* (Humberstone)
1946   *The Kid from Brooklyn* (McLeod); **The Best Years of Our Lives** (Wyler)
1947   *The Secret Life of Walter Mitty* (McLeod); *The Bishop's Wife* (Koster)
1948   *A Song Is Born* (Hawks); *Enchantment* (Reis)
1949   *Roseanna McCoy* (Reis); *My Foolish Heart* (Robson)
1950   *Edge of Doom* (Robson); *Our Very Own* (Miller)
1952   *Hans Christian Andersen* (C. Vidor); *I Want You* (Robson)
1955   *Guys and Dolls* (Mankiewicz)
1959   *Porgy and Bess* (Preminger)

Publications

By GOLDWYN: book—

Behind the Screen, New York, 1923.

By GOLDWYN: articles—

Sight and Sound (London), April-June 1953.
Kine Weekly (London), 13 September 1956.
Journal of Screen Producers Guild (Beverly Hills, California), December 1965.
American Film (Washington, D.C.), vol. 12, no. 10, September 1987.

On GOLDWYN: books—

Johnston, Alva, *The Great Goldwyn*, New York, 1937.
Griffith, Richard, *Samuel Goldwyn*, New York, 1956.
Crowthers, Bosley, *The Lion's Share: The Story of an Entertainment Empire*, New York, 1957.
Easton, Carol, *The Search for Samuel Goldwyn*, New York, 1976, 1989.
Marx, Arthur, *Goldwyn: A Biography of the Man Behind the Mask*, New York, 1976.
Marill, Alvin, H., *Samuel Goldwyn Presents*, South Brunswick, New Jersey, 1976.
Epstein, Lawrence J., *Samuel Goldwyn*, Boston, Massachusetts, 1981.
Freedland, Michael, *The Goldwyn Touch*, London, 1986.
Barnes, Jeremy, *Sam Goldwyn: Movie Mogul*, Englewood Cliffs, New Jersey, 1989.
Berg, A. Scott, *Goldwyn: A Biography*, New York, 1989; revised edition, 1998.

On GOLDWYN: articles—

Film (New York), November-December 1953.
Films and Filming (London), October 1956.
Zierold, Norman, in *The Moguls*, New York, 1969.
Films in Review (New York), December 1969, corrections in February 1970.
Positif (Paris), February 1976.
Cinématographe (Paris), May 1984.
Classic Images (Indiana, Pennsylvania), August 1984.
Film History, vol. 2, no. 2, June-July 1988.
Sarris, Andrew, "'We Are Dealing With Facts, Not Realities'," in *Film Comment* (New York), March-April 1989.
Greene, R., "The Big Picture," in *Boxoffice* (Chicago), August 1996.
Cousins, Russell, "Sanitizing Zola: Dorothy Arzner's Problematic Nana," in *Literature/Film Quarterly* (Salisbury), October 1996.

*   *   *

Samuel Goldwyn was one of the great independent producers during the heyday of the Hollywood studio system. Most of his films performed well at the box office, with critics, and at the Academy Awards.

Goldwyn's success was due, in part, to his genius for promoting his films and manipulating publicity about them. Perhaps more important to his success was his insistence that his films be well-crafted and of high quality—imbued, that is, with what became known as the Goldwyn Touch. Goldwyn's approach to movie-making was to buy the best available scripts, successful plays, and novels, and hire the best available writers, directors, and crews to bring them to the screen. The script for *These Three*, for example, was Lillian Hellman's adaptation of her Broadway hit play *The Children's Hour*; the director was William Wyler (with whom Goldwyn eventually collaborated on seven films, including their most successful film, *The Best Years of Our Lives*, which won seven Oscars); and the cinematographer was Gregg Toland, whose credits include most of the Wyler-Goldwyn collaborations, John Ford's *The Grapes of Wrath*, and Orson Wells's *Citizen Kane*, the film that established Toland's reputation as one of the greatest cinematographers in film history.

Goldwyn hated working with partners, so he usually financed his films himself, sparing no expense. For instance, Goldwyn paid Bette Davis $385,000—an exorbitant sum in 1940—to appear in *The Little Foxes*. And when halfway through the filming of *Nana*, Goldwyn decided that the rough cut lacked the Goldwyn Touch, he scrapped the whole production, throwing away the $411,000 that he had already spent on the film, and started all over with Dorothy Arzner replacing George Fitzmaurice as director.

Sam Goldwyn is remembered for his "Goldwynisms"—unintentionally humorous statements springing from Goldwyn's unorthodox way of thinking, such as, "Include me out," or "A verbal contract isn't worth the paper it's written on." He is remembered for his fierce independence and his desire to control every aspect of the production and marketing of his films, often to the dismay of his directors, stars, writers, and especially his partners. Most of all, he is remembered for his films and the quality that he brought to them—the Goldwyn Touch.

—Clyde Kelly Dunagan

GOLOVNYA, Anatoli

Cinematographer. **Nationality:** Russian. **Born:** Anatoli Dimitryevich Golovnya in Simferopol, Russia, 1900. **Education:** Attended the State Film School, Moscow, mid-1920s. **Family:** Married the photographer Tamara Lobova. **Career:** Entered films as camera assistant in mid-1920s; 1925—first film as cinematographer, *Chess Fever*; then worked almost exclusively on films of the director Vsevolod Pudovkin until 1950; 1934—began teaching at the Cinema Institute: became head of the camerawork department; also author of several books on photography. **Award:** People's Artist, 1935. **Died:** In 1982.

Films as Cinematographer:

1925   *Kirpichiki* (Obolenski and Doller) (asst); *Luch smerti* (*The Death Ray*) (Kuleshov) (asst); *Shakmatnaya goryachka* (*Chess Fever*) (Pudovkin)

1926   *Mekhanikha golovnovo mozga* (*Mechanics of the Brain*) (Pudovkin); **Mat** (*Mother*) (Pudovkin)

1927   **Konyets Sankt-Peterburge** (*The End of St. Petersburg*) (Pudovkin)

1928   **Potomok Chingis-khan** (*The Heir to Genghis Khan*; *Storm over Asia*) (Pudovkin); *Zhivoi trup* (*A Living Corpse*) (Otsep)

1929   *Chelovek iz restorana* (*The Man from the Restaurant*) (Protazanov)

1933   *Dezertir* (*Deserter*) (Pudovkin) (co)

1938   *Pobeda* (*Victory*) (Pudovkin and Doller)
1939   *Minin i Pozharsky* (Pudovkin and Doller) (co)
1941   *Suvorov* (Pudovkin and Doller) (co); *Pir v Girmunka* (*Feast at Zhirmunka*) (Pudovkin and Doller—for series *Fighting Film Albums*) (co)
1946   *Amiral Nakhimov* (*Admiral Nakhimov*) (Pudovkin) (co)
1950   *Yukovsky* (Pudovkin)

Publications

By GOLOVNYA: books—

Kompoziciya fotokadra [The Craft of the Cameraman], 1938.
Svet v iskusstve operatora [Light in the Cameraman's Art], Moscow, 1945.
The Screen Is My Palette (autobiography).

By GOLOVNYA: articles—

"Fundamentals of Camerawork," in *Sovietsky Ekran* (Moscow), 1 November 1927.
"On Soviet Film Art," in *Soviet Cinema*, edited by A.Y. Arosev, Moscow, 1935.
Soviet Film (Moscow), no. 12, 1968.

On GOLOVNYA: articles—

Sovietsky Ekran (Moscow), no. 12, 1959.
Filmkultura (Budapest), no. 7, 1961.
Soviet Film (Moscow), no. 11, 1970.
Iskusstvo Kino (Moscow), no. 2, 1975.
Soviet Film (Moscow), no. 2, 1975.
Iskusstvo Kino (Moscow), January 1983.

*   *   *

The work of Anatoli Golovnya will always be associated with the films of Pudovkin, whose close collaborator he was and for whom he worked almost exclusively. Before he joined Pudovkin's team he had worked for other directors or as assistant to the cameraman Levitsky. Golovnya photographed three great masterpieces of Pudovkin, *Mother*, *The End of St. Petersburg*, and *Storm over Asia*. His feeling for light and shade, the dramatic structure of the image, and his feeling for people made his contribution to these films a truly creative achievement. As Harry Alan Potamkin noted: "Golovnya's work in *The End of St. Petersburg* adds his name to the lists of the heroic in camera creation." He carried the plastic realism and the powerfully expressive vigour of painters like Surikov and Serov to the screen. In the Pudovkin films the style is essentially lyrical no matter how realistic the theme. His awareness of structure, his hypersensitive eye, and his acute intelligence gave shape and form to the imagery. Especially in *Storm over Asia* his virtuosity is particularly noticeable in the great and contrasting landscapes and in his portraits of both the actors and natural types that fill the film. From the first shots of the dissolving approach to the hut in the barren mountainside one's imagination is captured and held by the richness of the image. In *Yukovsky*, Pudovkin's last film, he had the opportunity to work in colour. He had a special interest in stereocinematography. As a writer on his special art he made a valuable contribution to the knowledge of film photography.

He upheld the cinema against the encroaches of theatricalism and literary impositions. "The main thing," he said, "is that the cinema be looked upon and conceived as an art." And of the camera: "the operator will certainly remainwhat he should be—the artist, the organiser of the visual material."

—Liam O'Leary

GOODRICH, Frances, and Albert HACKETT

GOODRICH. Writer. **Nationality:** American. **Born:** Belleville, New Jersey, 1891. **Education:** Attended Passaic Collegiate High School, graduated 1908; Vassar College, Poughkeepsie, New York, graduated 1912; New York School of Social Work, 1912–13. **Family:** Married 1) the actor Robert Ames, 1917 (divorced 1923); 2) the writer Henrik Willem Van Loon, 1927 (divorced 1930); 3) Albert Hackett, 1931. **Died:** Of cancer in New York City, 19 January 1984.

HACKETT. Writer. **Nationality:** American. **Born:** New York City, 16 February 1900. **Education:** Attended Professional Children's School, New York, 1914–16. **Died:** Of pneumonia 16 March 1995.

Both Goodrich and Hackett were actors: Goodrich made her stage debut in Massachusetts in 1913, and her Broadway debut in *Come Out of the Kitchen*, 1916; Hackett acted on stage and in films as a child;

Frances Goodrich and Albert Hackett

both acted in a Denver stock company, 1927; then collaborated on plays; 1933–39—writers for MGM, and for Paramount, 1943–46, and MGM again after 1948. **Awards:** Writers Guild Award for *Easter Parade*, 1948; *Father's Little Dividend*, 1951; *Seven Brides for Seven Brothers*, 1954; *The Diary of Anne Frank*, 1959; Pulitzer Prize (for drama) for *The Diary of Anne Frank*, 1956.

Films as Writers:

1933   *The Secret of Madame Blanche* (Brabin); *Penthouse* (*Crooks in Clover*) (Van Dyke)

1934   *Fugitive Lovers* (Boleslawsky) (co); ***The Thin Man*** (Van Dyke); *Hide-Out* (Van Dyke)

1935   *Naughty Marietta* (Van Dyke) (co); *Ah, Wilderness!* (Brown)

1936   *Rose Marie* (Van Dyke) (co); *Small Town Girl* (Wellman) (co); *After the Thin Man* (Van Dyke)

1937   *The Firefly* (Leonard)

1939   *Another Thin Man* (Van Dyke); *Society Lawyer* (Ludwig) (co)

1943   *Doctors at War* (Shumlin—short)

1944   *Lady in the Dark* (Leisen); *The Hitler Gang* (Farrow)

1946   *The Virginian* (Gilmore); ***It's a Wonderful Life*** (Capra) (co)

1948   *The Pirate* (Minnelli); *Summer Holiday* (Mamoulian); *Easter Parade* (Walters) (co)

1949   *In the Good Old Summertime* (Leonard) (co)

1950   *Father of the Bride* (Minnelli)

1951   *Father's Little Dividend* (Minnelli); *Too Young to Kiss* (Leonard)

1954   *Give a Girl a Break* (Donen); *Seven Brides for Seven Brothers* (Donen) (co); *The Long, Long Trailer* (Minnelli)

1956   *Gaby* (Bernhardt) (co)

1958   *A Certain Smile* (Negulesco)

1959   *The Diary of Anne Frank* (Stevens)

1962   *Five Finger Exercise* (Daniel Mann)

1980   *The Diary of Anne Frank* (Sagal)

Films as Actor (Hackett):

1919   *Come Out of the Kitchen* (Robertson); *Anne of Green Gables* (Taylor)

1921   *Molly O'* (Jones); *The Good-Bad Wife* (McCord)

1922   *The Country Flapper* (Jones); *The Darling of the Rich* (Adolfi); *A Woman's Woman* (Giblyn)

1930   *Whoopee!* (Freeland)

Publications

By GOODRICH and HACKETT: plays—

Up Pops the Devil, New York, 1933.
The Great Big Doorstep, Chicago, 1943.
The Diary of Anne Frank, New York, 1958.

On GOODRICH and HACKETT: articles—

Film Comment (New York), Winter 1970–71.
Films in Review (New York), October 1977.

Ahrlich, Evelyn, in *American Screenwriters*, edited by Robert E. Morsberger, Stephen O. Lesser, and Randall Clark, Detroit, Michigan, 1984.
Francke, Lizzie, ''*Father of the Bride*,'' in *Sight and Sound* (London), March 1992.
Obituary on Hackett, in *The Washington Post*, 19 March 1995.
Obituary on Hackett, in *Time*, 27 March 1995.
Obituary on Hackett, in *Variety* (New York), 3–9 April 1995.
Obituary on Hackett, in *Psychotronic Video* (Narrowsburg), no. 21, 1995.

*   *   *

Although the screenwriting team of Frances Goodrich and Albert Hackett received critical and popular acclaim for the 1959 adaptation of their Pulitzer Prize-winning stage play, *The Diary of Anne Frank*, most of their creative efforts were not ''serious'' works. Schooled in the sophisticated stage comedies of the late 1920s and early 1930s, Goodrich and Hackett adapted *The Thin Man* in 1934, and it is a work now as then considered to be the best of the cinema's detective comedies. They followed this exceptional adaptation with an excellent *After the Thin Man* and an effective *Another Thin Man*, in both of which they succeeded in translating the work of Dashiell Hammett to the screen while managing to maintain the quality of his stories. They were equally adept at musicals. In the 1930s they adapted two vehicles for Jeanette MacDonald and Nelson Eddy, *Naughty Marietta* and *Rose Marie*, reworking some of the stilted dialogue from the stage versions so that it was both more contemporary and more fluid. As well, the pair produced two splendid screen musicals—the flashy, colorful *The Pirate* in the late 1940s and the innovative *Seven Brides for Seven Brothers* in the mid-1950s.

Unusual in the couple's credits is Frank Capra's *It's a Wonderful Life*, a film that, in its warmth and humanity, seems more likely to have been the work of Robert Riskin, Capra's frequent collaborator, than that of the Hacketts. Critics now regard *It's a Wonderful Life* as an outstanding achievement—for its screenplay as well as for its execution. It was certainly a major film in Capra's career (coming ironically just when his fortunes were on the wane with the Hollywood establishment), and it is certainly the Hacketts's most significant contribution to film art.

Wonderful Life, *Anne Frank*, the subtleties of *The Thin Man*, and the fresh handling of plot and character in the designed-for-the-screen musicals, *The Pirate* and *Seven Brides*, all serve to suggest that Goodrich and Hackett still remain the most eclectic screenwriters that Hollywood has produced. Their scope has not yet been matched by any other team.

—Donald W. McCaffrey

GOOSSON, Stephen

Art Director. **Nationality:** American. **Born:** Grand Rapids, Michigan, 24 March 1893. **Education:** Attended Syracuse University. **Career:** Started as an art director in the 1921 silent films *The Love*

Light and *Little Lord Fauntleroy*. **Awards:** Academy Award, for *Lost Horizon*, 1937. **Died:** 1973.

Films as Art Director:

1921   *The Love Light*; *Little Lord Fauntleroy*
1922   *East Is West*; *The Eternal Flame*; *Oliver Twist*
1923   *The Hunchback of Notre Dame*
1924   *The Sea Hawk*
1927   *The Wreck of the Hesperus*
1928   *Skyscraper*; *Let 'Er Go Gallagher*; *Man-Made Woman*; *Midnight Madness*
1929   *The Trespasser* (E. Goulding); *Evangeline* (Carewe)
1930   *Are You There?* (MacFadden); *Fox Movietone Follies of 1930* (Stoloff); *Just Imagine* (D. Butler); *Oh, for a Man!* (MacFadden); *The Princess and the Plumber* (A. Korda and Blystone); *Such Men Are Dangerous* (K. Hawks)
1933   *Lady for a Day* (Capra)
1934   ***It Happened One Night*** (Capra); *One Night of Love* (Schertzinger)
1935   *The Black Room* (Neill); *She Couldn't Take It* (*Woman Tamer*) (Garnett); *She Married Her Boss* (La Cava); *Crime and Punishment* (von Sternberg)
1936   *The King Steps Out* (von Sternberg); *Pennies from Heaven* (McLeod); *Mr. Deeds Goes to Town* (Capra); *Theodora Goes Wild* (Boleslawski)
1937   *Girls Can Play* (Hillyer); *I'll Take Romance* (E. Griffith); *It's All Yours* (Nugent); *Lost Horizon* (Capra); *Paid to Dance* (*Hard to Handle*) (Coleman); *The Shadow* (Coleman); *When You're in Love* (Riskin); *The Awful Truth* (McCarey)
1938   *You Can't Take It with You* (Capra); *Holiday* (*Free to Live*) (Cukor); *Girls' School* (Brahm); *I Am the Law* (Hall); *Juvenile Court* (Lederman); *She Married an Artist* (Gering); *There's Always a Woman* (Hall); *Who Killed Gail Preston?* (Barsha)
1939   *Homicide Bureau* (Coleman)
1941   ***The Little Foxes*** (Wyler); *Meet John Doe* (Capra)
1943   *Cry Havoc* (Thorpe); *Swing Fever* (Whelan)
1944   *See Here, Private Hargrove* (Ruggles); *Together Again* (C. Vidor)
1945   *Tonight and Every Night* (Saville); *Counter-Attack* (*One against Seven*) (Z. Korda); *The Fighting Guardsman* (Levin); *Kiss and Tell* (Wallace); *She Wouldn't Say Yes* (Hall); *Snafu* (*Welcome Home*) (Moss); *A Thousand and One Nights* (A. Green); *Over 21* (C. Vidor)
1946   *Gallant Journey* (Wellman); *Gilda* (C. Vidor); *The Jolson Story* (A. Green); *Meet Me on Broadway* (Jason); *Mr. District Attorney* (Sinclair); *One Way to Love* (Enright); *Perilous Holiday* (E. Griffith); *Renegades* (G. Sherman); *The Return of Monte Cristo* (Levin); *Tars and Spars* (A. Green); *The Thrill of Brazil* (Simon); *The Walls Came Tumbling Down* (Mendes); *The Bandit of Sherwood Forest* (G. Sherman and Lewis)
1947   *Dead Reckoning* (Cromwell); *Down to Earth* (Hall); *Framed* (*Paula*) (Wallace); *Her Husband's Affairs* (Simon); *I Love Trouble* (Simon); *It Had to Be You* (Hartman and Maté);

Johnny O'Clock (Rossen); *The Swordsman* (J. Lewis); *The Corpse Came C.O.D.* (Levin); *The Guilt of Janet Ames* (Levin)
1948   *The Lady from Shanghai* (Welles); *The Black Arrow* (G. Douglas); *The Loves of Carmen* (C. Vidor); *The Man from Colorado* (Levin); *The Mating of Millie* (Levin); *Relentless* (G. Sherman); *The Return of October* (J. Lewis); *The Sign of the Ram* (J. Sturges); *To the Ends of the Earth* (Stevenson); *The Fuller Brush Man* (*That Man Mr. Jones*) (Simon); *The Gallant Blade* (Levin)

*   *   *

Stephen Goosson had a long and distinguished career as an art director in Hollywood. After graduating from Syracuse, Goosson was a practicing architect in Detroit when he entered the film business with David Selznick in 1919. Goosson worked for various studios during the silent era before finding a permanent home in 1930 at Columbia.

Goosson was supervising art director at Columbia when the small studio hit the jackpot in 1934 with *It Happened One Night*. Passed over by most major studios, the film bolstered Columbia's reputation and helped to make the studio a major player in the film industry. *It Happened One Night* was a small, unheard of romantic comedy starring Clark Gable and Claudette Colbert which became a commercial and critical success. With very little advertising or company push *It Happened One Night* went on to sweep the Academy Awards and cement Columbia's spot in the marketplace.

It Happened One Night firmly entrenched Goosson's position as Columbia's art director. He was associated with many of the studio's finest works of the 1930s and 1940s. These were Hollywood's ''golden years'' and Goosson was a busy man, working on 30 films in the years 1946 to 1948 alone. Goosson was an important figure at Columbia and worked with their top-notch directors of the era including Frank Capra and Orson Welles.

—Patrick J. Sauer

GREEN, Adolph

See **COMDEN, Betty, and Adolph GREEN**

GREEN, Johnny

Composer and Arranger. **Nationality:** American. **Born:** New York City, 10 October 1908; billed as John W. Green in early films. **Education:** Studied economics at Harvard University, Cambridge, Massachusetts, 1928. **Family:** Married 1) Betty Furness (divorced); 2) Bunny Waters, 1943; three daughters; 3) Bonnie (Green). **Career:** Bandleader and song writer; accompanist for Ethel Merman and Gertrude Lawrence; 1929—rehearsal pianist for Paramount; 1930—arranger and musical director; also composer for films; 1942—joined MGM as arranger/musical director; 1950–58—general music director, MGM; composer for TV, and concert hall conductor. **Awards:** Academy Award for *Easter Parade*, 1948; *An American in Paris*,

Johnny Green

1951; *The Merry Wives of Windsor Overture*, 1953; *West Side Story*, 1961; *Oliver!*, 1968. **Died:** In Beverly Hills, California, 15 May 1989.

Films as Arranger:

1930   *Leave It to Lester* (Cambria and Cozine) (+ song); *The Big Pond* (Henley); *Follow the Leader* (Taurog) (co); *Animal Crackers* (Heerman); *Heads Up* (Schertzinger); *Queen High* (Newmeyer); *The Sap from Syracuse* (Sutherland) (songs)

1931   *Secrets of a Secretary* (Abbott); *My Sin* (Abbott); *The Smiling Lieutenant* (Lubitsch)

1932   *Wayward* (Sloman); *The Wiser Sex* (Viertel)

1937   *Start Cheering* (Rogell)

1943   *Stage Door Canteen* (Borzage)

Films as Composer or Arranger/Director:

1944   *Broadway Rhythm* (Del Ruth); *Bathing Beauty* (Sidney)

1945   *Week-End at the Waldorf* (Leonard); *The Sailor Takes a Wife* (Whorf)

1946   *Easy to Wed* (Buzzell)

1947   *It Happened in Brooklyn* (Whorf); *Fiesta* (Thorpe); *Something in the Wind* (Pichel)

1948   *Easter Parade* (Walters); *Up in Central Park* (Walters)

1949   *The Inspector General* (Koster)

1950   *Toast of New Orleans* (Taurog); *Summer Stock* (Walters)

1951   *Royal Wedding* (Donen); *The Great Caruso* (Thorpe); ***An American in Paris*** (Minnelli); *Too Young to Kiss* (Leonard)

1952   *Because You're Mine* (Hall)

1954   *Brigadoon* (Minnelli); *Rhapsody* (C. Vidor)

1956   *High Society* (Walters)

1957   *Raintree Country* (Dmytryk)

1960   *Pepe* (Sidney)

1961   ***West Side Story*** (Wise)

1963   *Twilight of Honor* (Sagal); *Bye Bye Birdie* (Sidney)

1966   *Alvarez Kelly* (Dmytryk); *Johnny Tiger* (Wendkos)

1967   *The Busy Body* (Castle) (song)

1968   *Oliver!* (Reed)

1969   *They Shoot Horses, Don't They?* (Pollack) (+ assoc pr)

Publications

By GREEN: articles—

Down Beat, 22 August 1956.

''*Raintree County*,'' in *Film and TV Music* (New York), Fall-Winter 1957–58.

In *Hollywood Speaks! An Oral History*, by Mike Steen, New York, 1974.

Interview with Elmer Bernstein, in *Film Music Notebook* (Calabasas, California), vol. 2, no. 4, and vol. 3, no. 1, 1976–77.

Soundtrack! (Hollywood), vol. 9, no. 33, March 1990.

On GREEN: articles—

Thomas, Tony, in *Music for the Movies*, South Brunswick, New Jersey, 1973.

New Zealand Film Music Bulletin (Invercargill), November 1980.

Lacombe, Alain, in *Hollywood*, Paris, 1983.

Obituary in *Variety* (New York), 24 May 1989.

Obituary in *EPD Film* (Frankfurt), vol. 6, no. 7, July 1989.

*   *   *

A man who always conducted with a carnation in his buttonhole, the stylish Johnny Green enjoyed success as a song writer, a dance band leader, a symphonic conductor, a film composer, and the head of a major studio's music department. He won five Oscars as a music director and conductor, for *Easter Parade*, *An American in Paris*, *West Side Story*, *Oliver!*, and his MGM *Concert Hall* short-subject series.

Green graduated from Harvard University at the age of 19 with a degree in economics. At Harvard he was an arranger and conductor of the college band and dance orchestra, and it was at this time he wrote his first published song, ''Coquette.'' After graduation he dabbled with a career on Wall Street but gave it up when he was offered the job of Gertrude Lawrence's piano accompanist in late 1929. Soon after he wrote the song ''Body and Soul'' for her, an immediate hit which was incorporated in the Broadway revue *Three's a Crowd*, and his most famous composition. In 1930 Green started working as an arranger and conductor for Paramount at their Astoria, Long Island, studios, beginning with *The Big Pond*. He worked on a dozen films over the next two years, while at the same time taking jobs as an accompanist and song writer in the New York theater, including a stint as the conductor at Paramount's Brooklyn Theatre. This led to his being offered a job as orchestrator by Victor Young, then music director for the Atwater-Kent radio series, which in turn led to other radio assignments. Green enjoyed success with other songs, notably ''Out of Nowhere,'' ''I Cover the Waterfront,'' and ''You're Mine, You,'' and formed his own dance band. Some of his recordings, particularly those with Fred Astaire, would become collectors' items.

In 1942, while conducting the Rodgers and Hart musical *By Jupiter*, he was offered a position as a staff composer-arranger-conductor by MGM and assumed his duties in November of that year. The heyday of the great musicals was underway, and Green became a part of it, with time out to direct the music for two Deanna Durbin musicals at Universal (*Something in the Wind* and *Up in Central Park*) and write the score for Danny Kaye's *The Inspector General* at Warners. In 1950 he was signed by MGM as their general music director, which post he held for eight years, and during which time he wrote what he considered his *magnum opus*, the score for the epic *Raintree County*. During his lifetime he appeared with most of the major orchestras in the United States and Canada, and with conspicuous success at the Hollywood Bowl. Of all his musical activities, Green had a particular fondness for film scoring and conducting. On the value of film music, ''I think if you were to see a major film whose score you liked, and then saw the film without the score, you would find one of the major elements—and by major I mean almost as important as the photography—missing.''

—Tony Thomas

GRIMAULT, Paul

Animator. **Nationality:** French. **Born:** Neuilly-Sur-Seine, 23 March 1905. **Education:** Attended the Ecole des Arts Appliqués, Paris. **Career:** Scene painter for stage sets, and occasional actor on stage and in films; 1936–51—founding director, with André Surrat, *Les Gémeaux* production company; 1951—formed Les Films Paul Grimault for producing animated shorts, advertising films, and optical effects for films and television works. **Award:** Venice Festival Prize for *Le Petit Soldat*, 1948. **Died:** 29 March 1994.

Films as Animator:

1937   *Phénomènes électriques*
1938   *Le Messager de la lumière*
1939   *Gô chez les oiseaux* (revised version, *Les Passagers de la Grande Ourse*, 1941)
1942   *Le Marchand de notes*
1943   *L'Epouvantail*
1944   *Le Voleur de paratonnerres*
1946   *La Flute magique*
1947   *Le Petit Soldat*
1952   *Pierres oubliées*
1955   *Enrico cuisinier* (co—live-action)

1958   *La Faim du monde* (re-edited version for children, *Le Monde en raccourci*, 1975)
1969   *Le Diamant*
1973   *Le Chien Mélomane*
1980   *Le Roi et l'oiseau* (*The King and the Bird*) (incorporates footage from repudiated film *La Bergère et le ramoneur*, 1952)

Films as Actor:

1934   *L'Atalante* (Vigo); *L'Hôtel du libre échange* (M. Allégret)
1936   *Le Crime de Monsieur Lange* (*The Crime of Monsieur Lange*) (Renoir)
1953   *Les Vacances de M. Hulot* (*Mr. Hulot's Holiday*) (Tati)
1958   *Paris mange son pain* (P. Prévert); *Mon oncle* (Tati)

Other Films:

1961   *Cuba Si!* (Marker) (special effects); *Le Vrai Visage de Thérèse de Lisieux* (Agostini—short) (special effects)
1962   *Mourir à Madrid* (Rossif) (special effects); *Marcel, ta mère t'appelle* (Colombat) (pr)
1963   *La Foire aux cancres* (Daquin) (special effects); *Le Côte d'Adam* (Sengissen—short) (special effects); *Jacques Copeau* (Leenhardt—short) (special effects)
1964   *Les Temps morts* (Laloux) (pr)
1965   *La Demoiselle et le violoncelliste* (Laguionie) (pr)
1967   *L'Arche de Noé* (Laguionie) (pr)
1968   *La Tartelette* (Colombat) (pr)
1969   *Une Bombe par hasard* (Laguionie) (pr); *Calveras* (Colombat) (pr)
1973   *La Tête* (Bourget) (pr)
1974   *Un, deux, trois . . .* (Shaker) (pr)
1989   *La Table tournante* (d + co-sc + ro)

Publications

By GRIMAULT: articles—

Image et Son (Paris), December 1965.
Cinéma Français (Paris), no. 32, 1979.
Banc-Titre (Paris), March 1980.
Jeune Cinéma (Paris), July-August 1980.
Time Out (London), 19–25 July 1984.
Films (London), August 1984.
CinémAction (Courbevoie), April 1989.

On GRIMAULT: book—

Pagliano, Jean-Pierre, *Paul Grimault*, Paris, 1986.

On GRIMAULT: articles—

Chilo, M., in *Cinéma* (Paris), January 1957.
''Grimault Issue'' of *Image et Son* (Paris), April 1967.

Image et Son (Paris), March 1980.

Continental Film Review (London), April 1980.

Visions (Brussels), 15 January 1983.

CinémAction (Conde-sur-Noireau), no. 51, April 1989.

Sight and Sound (London), Autumn 1990.

Obituary, *Plateau*, vol. 15, no. 1, 1994.

Bref, no. 20, Spring 1994.

Télérama (Paris), 6 April 1994.

Film-dienst (Cologne), 26 April 1994.

Obituary, *Mensuel du Cinéma*, May 1994.

*   *   *

Paul Grimault's years of activity cover almost the whole period of French animation. He was fortunate to be associated, in his early days, with such outstanding artists as Marcel Carné, the abstractionist painter Max Ernst, and the famous French comedian Jacques Tati.

Grimault trained as a graphic designer, and in his early professional period he joined an advertising agency and was responsible for many short publicity films. He soon became a strong link between the glorious traditional French animation represented by Emil Cohl and previously by the magical cinematographic touch of Georges Meliès. He was certainly the most outstanding representative of the early period of French animation and was responsible for a new approach with a new look. This new look had a much richer visual content and was nearer to the quality of graphical fine art rather than a caricatured comic strip concept. This school of French animation was established immediately after the Second World War with such films as *Le Voleur de paratonnerres*, *La Flute magique*, and an extremely charming short film in 1947, *Le Petit Soldat*, based on the Hans Andersen fairy tale. After doing a number of commercial films, in 1973 he made *Le Chien Mélomane*, a short philosophical film about (as is so usual with many contemporary animators) the atomic bomb. By this time his style was established, and maintained by a new generation of young French artists, including Jean François Laguionie, Jacques Colombat, and Emil Bourget. In their visual style they follow closely Grimault's rich visualization of backgrounds and his conception of classical visual style.

Grimault's most notable achievement was the feature film *The King and the Bird*, which he finished in 1980. It was an instant success and he received a major national award for it, the Dulac Prize. His close collaboration with the outstanding French writer Jacques Prévert gave *The King and the Bird* a depth of content not usually seen in animated cartoons.

—John Halas

GROT, Anton

Art Director. Nationality: Polish. **Born:** Antocz Frantiszek Groszewski in Kelbasin, 18 January 1884; emigrated to the United States, 1909. **Education:** Studied illustration and design, Krakow School of Art and Technical High School, Konigsberg, Germany. **Career:** 1913–17—set designer for Lubin, Philadelphia; 1917–18—designer for Blaché; 1918–21—worked for Pathé; 1922—set designer for Fairbanks-Pickford unit at United Artists, Hollywood; 1922–27—set designer

for Cecil B. DeMille; 1927–48—set designer at Warner Bros.; after retirement, worked as painter. **Award:** Special Academy Award, 1940. **Died:** In Stanton, California, 21 March 1974.

Films as Art Director/Production Designer:

1913   *The Mouse and the Lion* (Brooks)

1916   *Arms and the Woman* (Fitzmaurice)

1917   *The Recoil* (Fitzmaurice); *The Iron Heart* (Fitzmaurice); *The Seven Pearls* (Mackenzie—serial)

1918   *The Naulahka* (Fitzmaurice); *Sylvia of the Secret Service* (Fitzmaurice)

1919   *Bound and Gagged* (Seitz—serial)

1920   *Pirate Gold* (Seitz—serial); *Velvet Fingers* (Seitz—serial)

1922   *Robin Hood* (Dwan) (co); *Tess of the Storm Country* (Robertson)

1924   *Dorothy Vernon of Haddon Hall* (Neilan); *The Thief of Bagdad* (Walsh) (co); *A Thief in Paradise* (Fitzmaurice)

1925   *Don Q, Son of Zorro* (Crisp) (co); *The Road to Yesterday* (DeMille) (co)

1926   *The Volga Boatman* (DeMille) (co); *Silence* (Julian); *Young April* (Crisp)

1927   *White Gold* (Howard); *Vanity* (Crisp); *The Little Adventuress* (*The Dover Road*) (W. De Mille); *The Country Doctor* (Julian); *The King of Kings* (DeMille) (co)

1928   *Stand and Deliver* (Crisp); *Hold 'em Yale* (*At Yale*) (E. Griffith); *The Blue Danube* (*Honour above All*) (Sloane); *Walking Back* (Julian); *A Ship Comes In* (*His Country*) (Howard); *The Godless Girl* (DeMille) (co); *The Barker* (Fitzmaurice); *Show Girl* (Santell); *Noah's Ark* (Curtiz)

1929   *Why Be Good?* (Seiter); *Smiling Irish Eyes* (Seiter); *The Man and the Moment* (Fitzmaurice); *Her Private Life* (A. Korda); *Footlights and Fools* (Seiter)

1930   *Lilies of the Field* (A. Korda); *Playing Around* (LeRoy); *No, No, Nanette* (Badger); *A Notorious Affair* (Bacon); *Song of the Flame* (Crosland); *Bright Lights* (Curtiz); *Top Speed* (LeRoy); *Outward Bound* (Milton); *Little Caesar* (LeRoy)

1931   *Body and Soul* (Santell); *Svengali* (Mayo); *Heartbreak* (Werker); *Honor of the Family* (Bacon); *The Mad Genius* (Curtiz); *Surrender* (Howard); *One Way Passage* (Garnett); *Big City Blues* (LeRoy)

1932   *The Hatchet Man* (*The Honourable Mr. Wong*) (Wellman); *Alias the Doctor* (Curtiz); *Two Seconds* (LeRoy); *Doctor X* (Curtiz); *The Match King* (Bretherton and Keighley); *Scarlet Dawn* (Dieterle); *Lawyer Man* (Dieterle); *20,000 Years in Sing Sing* (Curtiz)

1933   *Mystery of the Wax Museum* (Curtiz); *Grand Slam* (Dieterle); *The King's Vacation* (Adolfi); *Gold Diggers of 1933* (LeRoy); *Baby Face* (Green); *Ever in My Heart* (Mayo); *From Headquarters* (Dieterle); *Footlight Parade* (Bacon) (co); *Son of a Sailor* (Bacon); *Easy to Love* (Keighley)

1934   *Mandalay* (Curtiz); *Gambling Lady* (Mayo); *Upperworld* (Del Ruth); *He Was Her Man* (Bacon); *Dr. Monica* (Keighley); *The Firebird* (Dieterle); *Side Streets* (*Woman in Her Thirties*) (Green); *British Agent* (Curtiz); *Six Day Bike Rider* (Bacon); *The Secret Bride* (*Concealment*) (Dieterle); *Gold Diggers of 1935* (Berkeley)

1935   *Red Hot Tires* (*Racing Luck*) (Lederman) (co); *The Florentine Dagger* (Florey); *Traveling Saleslady* (Enright); *The Case of the Curious Bride* (Curtiz); *Stranded* (Borzage); *Broadway Gondolier* (Bacon); *Bright Lights* (*Funnyface*) (Berkeley); *Dr. Socrates* (Dieterle); *A Midsummer Night's Dream* (Reinhardt and Dieterle); *Captain Blood* (Curtiz)

1936   *The Golden Arrow* (Green); *The White Angel* (Dieterle); *Anthony Adverse* (LeRoy); *Stolen Holiday* (Curtiz); *Sing Me a Love Song* (*Come Up Smiling*) (Enright)

1937   *The Life of Emile Zola* (Dieterle); *Tovarich* (Litvak); *Confession* (May); *The Great Garrick* (Whale)

1938   *Fools for Scandal* (LeRoy); *Hard to Get* (Enright)

1939   *They Made Me a Criminal* (Berkeley); *Juarez* (Dieterle) (co); *The Private Lives of Elizabeth and Essex* (Curtiz)

1940   *The Sea Hawk* (Curtiz); *A Dispatch from Reuters* (*This Man Reuter*) (Dieterle)

1941   *The Sea Wolf* (Curtiz); *Affectionately Yours* (Bacon)

1943   *Thank Your Lucky Stars* (Butler) (co)

1944   *The Conspirators* (Negulesco)

1945   *Rhapsody in Blue* (Rapper) (co); **Mildred Pierce** (Curtiz)

1946   *My Reputation* (Bernhardt); *One More Tomorrow* (Godfrey); *Never Say Goodbye* (Kern); *Deception* (Rapper)

1947   *Nora Prentiss* (V. Sherman); *The Two Mrs. Carrolls* (Godfrey); *Possessed* (Bernhardt); *The Unsuspected* (Curtiz)

1948   *Romance on the High Seas* (*It's Magic*) (Curtiz); *June Bride* (Windust); *One Sunday Afternoon* (Walsh) (co); *Backfire* (*Somewhere in the City*) (V. Sherman)

Publications

On GROT: articles—

London Studio, December 1938.

Deschner, Donald, in *The Velvet Light Trap* (Madison, Wisconsin), Fall 1975.

In *The Art of Hollywood*, edited by John Hambley, London, 1979.

Positif, vol. 377, June 1992.

Webb, Michael, ''Designing Films: Anton Grot,'' in *Architectural Digest* (Los Angeles), April 1996.

*   *   *

Anton Grot's special Academy Award in 1940 for his invention of a ''ripple machine,'' which created weather and light effects on water, perhaps symbolizes his particular interest in the expressive qualities of light in motion pictures. Of all the major designers working in Hollywood in the 1930s, Grot was among those whose work was most strongly affected by European modernism in films and painting. The angular shadows and strong light-and-dark contrast found in *Little Caesar*, for example, help to establish the underworld context of the film. In the pressbook for *Doctor X* (a Technicolor film), Grot explained how he used heavy construction, low arches, dark colors, and shadows to create a mood of mystery and melodrama: ''We design a set that imitates as closely as possible a bird of prey about to swoop down upon its victim, trying to incorporate in the whole thing a sense of impending calamity, of overwhelming danger.'' Similar expressive qualities are found, particularly in scenes of danger or terror, in the melodramatic swashbucklers Grot designed, such as *Captain Blood*, *The Private Lives of Elizabeth and Essex*, and *The Sea Hawk*. In his designs for ''The Forgotten Man'' production number in *Gold Diggers of 1933*, Grot cast jagged shadows on the women who

sing of their forgotten men, and in the finale of the song, he silhouetted unemployed veterans marching ceaselessly over a machine-like series of curved bridges. Using traditional and natural forms freely in *A Midsummer Night's Dream*, Grot created such memorable images as the entrance of Oberon, king of the fairies, crowned with a spiky headdress, and wearing a sparkling black cloak that sweeps for many yards behind the horse on which he is riding.

Grot's use of stylistic qualities of 20th-century European art no doubt derived in part form his Polish background, yet this interest parallels that of contemporary American painters such as John Marin, Charles Burchfield, and Georgia O'Keeffe. Just as the abstract qualities found in the paintings of these artists is crucial to the success of their works, so, too, Grot's film designs can be seen as combinations of realistic details built upon abstract formal qualities, particularly those of light and shadow.

—Floyd W. Martin

GRUSIN, Dave

Composer. **Nationality:** American. **Born:** Littleton, Colorado, 26 June 1934; son of Henri (a violinist) and Rosabelle (a pianist) Grusin. **Education:** University of Colorado, B. Music (piano), 1956; graduate study at Manhattan School of Music, 1959–60. **Military Service:** U.S. Navy, involved with air operations, 1956–58. **Career:** Pianist, keyboardist, composer, conductor, arranger, and record producer. Worked and performed with Quincy Jones, beginning in early 1960s;

Dave Grusin

worked and performed with numerous artists, including Mel Torme, Peggy Lee, Ruth Price, Sergio Mendes, Tom Scott, Gerry Mulligan, Lee Ritenour, Sarah Vaughan, Carmen McRae, Jon Lucien, Roberta Flack, and Aretha Franklin; released over thirty albums, beginning with *Subways Are for Sleeping* (Epic, 1960); composer for over a dozen television series, including *The Virginian* (1962), *Gidget* (1965), *The Wild, Wild West* (1965), *Girl from U.N.C.L.E., The* (1966), *It Takes a Thief* (1968), *Maude* (1972), *Good Times* (1974), *Baretta* (1975), and *St. Elsewhere* (1982); conductor, *The Andy Williams Show*, 1963–1964; record producer, with Larry Rosen, beginning in 1976; owner, with Rosen, of GRP Records, Inc., 1983—; affiliated with N.Y./L.A. Dream Band, a septet of jazz-fusion artists; principal with N2K Inc. (record label), New York City. **Awards:** Grammy Award (with Paul Simon), Best Album or Original Instrumental Score for a Motion Picture or Television Special, for *The Graduate*, 1968; Academy Award, Best Original Score, for The *Milagro Beanfield War*, 1988; Grammy Award, Best Arrangement on an Instrumental, for "Suite from *The Milagro Beanfield War*" from *Migration* (album), 1989; Grammy Awards, Best Instrumental Arrangement Accompanying Vocals, for "My Funny Valentine" from *The Fabulous Baker Boys Motion Picture Soundtrack* (album) and Best Album of Original Instrumental Background Score Written for a Motion Picture or Television, for *The Fabulous Baker Boys Motion Picture Soundtrack*, 1989; Hollywood Discovery Award for Outstanding Achievement in Music in Film, Hollywood Film Festival, 1998; also winner of many other music awards, including several additional Grammy Awards, and recipient of honorary doctorates from University of California, Berkeley, 1988, and University of Colorado, 1989. **Office:** GRP Records, Inc., 555 West 57th St., New York, NY 10019. **Agent:** Gorfaine-Schwartz Agency, 3301 Barham Blvd., Suite 201, Los Angeles, CA 90068–1477, U.S.A.

Films as Composer:

1967   *Waterhole #3; Divorce American Style; The Graduate* (additional music); *The Scorpio Letters* (for TV)
1968   *The Heart Is a Lonely Hunter; Candy; Prescription: Murder* (*Columbo: Prescription Murder*) (for TV); *Where Were You When the Lights Went Out?*
1969   *Tell Them Willie Boy Is Here; The Mad Room; Generation* (*A Time for Caring; A Man Called Gannon; Winning*
1970   *Double Jeopardy* (for TV) (theme); *Halls of Anger; Adam at 6 A.M.; The Intruders* (for TV)
1971   *Deadly Dream* (for TV); *A Howling in the Woods* (for TV); *The Forgotten Man* (for TV); *The Gang That Couldn't Shoot Straight; Sarge* (*The Badge or the Cross*) (for TV); *The Pursuit of Happiness; Shootout*
1972   *Fuzz; The Family Rico* (for TV); *The Great Northfield, Minnesota Raid*
1973   *The Friends of Eddie Coyle*
1974   *The Midnight Man; The Nickel Ride; The Death Squad* (for TV)
1975   *The Trial of Chaplain Jensen* (for TV); *W.W. and the Dixie Dancekings; The Yakuza* (*Brotherhood of the Yakuza*; *Three Days of the Condor; Eric* (for TV)
1976   *Murder by Death; The Front*
1977   *The Goodbye Girl; Bobby Deerfield; Fire Sale; Mr. Billion* (*The Windfall*)
1978   *Heaven Can Wait*
1979   *The Champ; The Electric Horseman; . . . And Justice for All*

1980   *My Bodyguard*
1981   *Absence of Malice; On Golden Pond*
1982   *Tootsie; Author! Author!*
1984   *Falling in Love; Scandalous; The Little Drummer Girl; Racing with the Moon; The Pope of Greenwich Village*
1985   *The Goonies*
1986   *Lucas*
1987   *Ishtar*
1988   *The Milagro Beanfield War; Tequila Sunrise; Clara's Heart; This is America, Charlie Brown* (for TV)
1989   *The Fabulous Baker Boys; A Dry White Season*
1990   *Havana; The Bonfire of the Vanities*
1991   *For the Boys*
1993   *The Firm*
1995   *The Cure*
1996   *Mulholland Falls*
1997   *In the Gloaming* (for TV); *Hope* (for TV) (theme); *Selena*
1998   *Hope Floats*
1999   *Random Hearts*

Other Films:

1978   *The Wiz* (musician)
1984   *Falling in Love* (orchestrator)
1989   *The Fabulous Baker Boys* (musician)
1993   *The Firm* (performer)

Publications

By GRUSIN: articles—

Yagiyu, S., "A Conversation with Dave Grusin," interview in *Soundtrack* (Stanford, California), vol. 7, no. 27, September 1988.

On GRUSIN: articles—

Lander, David, "Grusin and Rosen of GRP, the Musician's Label," in *Audio* (Philadelphia), March 1988.
Yanow, Scott, "Dave Grusin: Scoring It Big," in *Down Beat* (Chicago), July 1989.
Pulliam, Becca, "Maintaining Standards," in *Down Beat* (Chicago), May 1992.
Tiegel, Eliot, "Scoring in Hollywood," in *Down Beat* (Chicago), October 1993.

*   *   *

Academy Award winner Dave Grusin has combined classical music training, jazz virtuosity, and a popular culture sensibility to become one of the most prolific composers of the late twentieth century. Educated at the University of Colorado, Grusin was a classical piano major who developed an affinity for jazz, and played with such visiting artists as Art Pepper and singer Anita O'Day.

After moving to New York to pursue an academic career, Grusin found a job touring behind Andy Williams as a pianist and arranger.

When he was asked to be Williams' musical director, Grusin moved to Hollywood to work on *The Andy Williams Show*. In 1964, Grusin left the popular program to score his first film, Norman Lear and Bud Yorkin's *Divorce American Style*. In 1967, Grusin was brought in to compose additional music for a film that became a hallmark of the 1960s, both musically and cinematically, *The Graduate*.

Grusin quickly rose to the ranks of one of Hollywood's premier and most prolific composers. By the time he received his first Oscar nomination in 1978 for *Heaven Can Wait*, he had worked on thirty films. The best of those were the result of his collaboration with Robert Redford, including *Tell Them Willie Boy is Here* (1969) and *Three Days of the Condor* (1975). In the latter, Grusin's jazz style shone through on the strength of Tom Scott's brilliant tenor saxophone. One of Grusin's personal favorites from this period was The *Heart is a Lonely Hunter* (1968), which featured an unforgettable love theme.

Grusin followed his 1978 Oscar nomination with another in 1979 for the tearjerker *The Champ*. During the 1980s, Grusin entered his most prolific period. He was nominated for three more Academy Awards for his scores for *On Golden Pond* (1981), *The Fabulous Baker Boys* (1989), and *The Milagro Beanfield War* (1988), for which he won the Oscar. Grusin was also nominated for Best Original Song for ''It Might Be You'' from *Tootsie* (1982). Other notable scores from this period include *The Goodbye Girl* (1977), *Bobby Deerfield* (1977), *Reds* (1981), and *Racing with the Moon* (1984). Grusin also continued his fruitful association with Redford, scoring most of the popular director's films.

The diversity of these films is mirrored by the wide range of Grusin's musical styles, tastes, and influences. In the jazzy score to *The Fabulous Baker Boys*, Grusin successfully mirrors the feel of the sexy standards performed by Michele Pfeiffer, while in The *Milagro Beanfield War*, Grusin's minimal use of music is offset by his lushly evocative themes conducted by John Scott with the Royal Philharmonic Orchestra.

Grusin's work from this period is also familiar to television audiences—he wrote the memorable theme songs for *Good Times*, *Maude*, *Baretta*, and *St. Elsewhere*.

During the 1990s, Grusin was nominated for two more Academy Awards for his scores for *Havana* and *The Firm*. And though his prolific output fell off somewhat, he continued to work on at least one film project a year throughout the decade.

Despite his cinematic successes, Grusin has remained true to his jazz roots. Highly respected in the jazz community, Grusin's successful recording and performing career has spanned three decades. He has won ten Grammy Awards, and collaborated with most of the world's major jazz talents.

Undoubtedly Grusin's strength as a film composer is his belief that he is at heart a great accompanist. He thinks of himself as writing music to accompany the visual and dramatic action of a movie. His scores can be broken down into two major styles: those influenced by jazz and the more intimate and sensitive orchestral scores redolent with strings. In both styles, Grusin never loses his gift for melody.

Though the Oscar and Grammy winner is certainly one of the most prolific and successful composers of the late twentieth century, it is his status as one of music's true Renaissance men that makes him unique among film composers, bringing with it the promise that each of his scores will take audiences into new areas of musical exploration.

—Victoria Price

GUERRA, Tonino

Writer. **Nationality:** Italian. **Born:** Antonio Guerra in Sant'Arcangelo, Romagna, 16 March 1920. **Education:** Degree in education. **Family:** Married Lora Iabloskina. **Career:** 1956—first script for film, *Uomini e Lupi*; also author of verse and fiction.

Films as Writer:

1956   *Uomini e lupi* (*Men and Wolves*) (De Santis)
1957   *Un ettaro di cielo* (Casadio)
1958   *Cesta duga godinu dana* (*La strada lunga un'anno*) (De Santis)
1959   **L'avventura** (Antonioni)
1960   *Le signore* (Vasile); *La garçonnière* (De Santis) **La notte** (*The Night*) (Antonioni); *Il carro armata dell'otto settembre* (Puccini)
1961   *L'assassino* (*The Lady Killer of Rome*) (Petri)
1962   *I giorni contati* (Petri); *L'eclisse* (*Eclipse*) (Antonioni)
1963   *La noia* (*The Empty Canvas*) (Damiani)
1964   *Gli invincibili sette* (*The Secret Seven*) (De Martino); *Il Deserto rosso* (*The Red Desert*) (Antonioni); ''Una donna dolce dolce'' ep. of *La Donna è una cosa meravigliosa* (Bolognini); *Le ore nude* (Vicario); *Matrimonio all'italiana* (*Marriage, Italian Style*) (De Sica); ''Una donna d'affari'' ep. of *Controsesso* (Castellani); *Saul e David* (*Saul and David*) (Baldi)
1965   *Casanova '70* (Monicelli); *I grandi condottieri* (Baldi); *La decima vittima* (*The Tenth Victim*) (Petri)
1966   **Blow-up** (Antonioni); ''Fata Armenia'' ep. of *Le fate* (*The Queens*) (Monicelli)
1967   *C'era una volta* (*More than a Miracle*) (Rosi); *Lo scatenato* (*Catch as Catch Can*) (Indovina); *L'occhio selvaggio* (*The Wild Eye*) (Cavara)
1968   *Un tranquillo posto di campagna* (*A Quiet Place in the Country*) (Petri); *Sissignore* (Tognazzi); *Amanti* (*A Place for Lovers*) (De Sica)
1969   *L'Invitata* (De Seta); *In Search of Gregory* (Wood)
1970   *I girasoli* (*Sunflower*) (De Sica); *Zabriskie Point* (Antonioni); *Tre nel mille* (Indovina); *Uomini contro* (Rosi); *Giochi particolari* (Indovina)
1971   *La supertestimone* (Giraldi)
1972   *Il caso Mattei* (*The Mattei Affair*) (Rosi); *Gli ordini sono ordini* (Giraldi); *Bianco, rosso, e . . .* (*White Sister*) (Lattuada)
1973   *Lucky Luciano* (Rosi)
1974   *Amarcord* (Fellini); *Dites-le avec les fleurs* (Grimblat)
1975   *Quaranta gradi all'ombra del lenzuolo* (Martino)
1976   *Cadaveri eccellenti* (*Illustrious Corpses*) (Rosi); *Caro Michele* (Monicelli)
1978   *Un Papillon sur l'épaule* (Deray); *Letti selvaggi* (Zampa)
1979   **Cristo si è fermato a Eboli** (*Christ Stopped at Eboli*) (Rosi); *Il mistero di Oberwald* (*The Oberwald Mystery*) (Antonioni)
1981   *La notte di San Lorenzo* (*The Night of San Lorenzo*) (P. & V. Taviani); *Tre fratelli* (Rosi)
1982   *Identificazione di una donna* (Antonioni)
1983   *E la nave va* (*And the Ship Sails On*) (Fellini); *Nostalghia* (Tarkovsky)
1984   *Carmen* (Rosi); **Kaos** (*Chaos*) (P. & V. Taviani)

1985 *Henry IV* (*Enrico IV*) (Bellocchio); *Taxidi sta kithira* (Angelopoulos)

1986 *Good Morning Babilonia* (*Hollywood Sunset*; *Good Morning Babylon*) (P. and V. Taviani); *Ginger e Fred* (Fellini); *O Melissokomos* (*The Beekeeper*) (Angelopoulos)

1987 *Cronaca di una morte annunciata* (*Chronicle of a Death Foretold*) (Rosi)

1988 *Topio stin omichli* (*Landscape in the Mist*; *Le Paysage dans le brouillard*; *Landschaft im Nebel*) (Angelopoulos); *Il frullo del passero* (*La femme de mes amours*) (Mingozzi)

1989 *Burro* (Sanchez); *Dimenticare Palermo* (*To Forget Palermo*; *Oublier Palerme*; *The Palermo Connection*) (Rosi)

1990 *Il sole anche di notte* (*Die Nachtsonne*; *The Sun Also Shines at Night*; *Nightsun*; *Il sole di notte*) (P. and V. Taviani); *Stanno tutti bene* (*Everybody's Fine*; *Ils vont tous bien*) (Tornatore)

1991 *Viaggio d'amore* (*Journey of Love*) (Fabbri); *To meteoro vima to Pelargou* (*Suspended Step of the Stork*; *Le Pas suspendu de la cicogne*; *Meteoro vima tou Pelargou*) (Angelopoulos); *La Domenica specialmente* (*Especially on Sunday*) (Tornatore)

1993 *The Petrified Garden* (Gitai)

1995 *To vlemma tou odyssea* (*Lo sguardo di Ulisse*; *Le regard d'Ulysse*) (Angelopoulos); *Al di là delle nuvole* (*Beyond the clouds*; *Par delà les nuages*) (Antonioni and Wenders)

1996 *La Tregua* (*The Truce*) (Rosi)

1997 *Tajna Marchello* (*Marcello's Secret*) (Naumov); *Porto Santo* (Vicente Jorge Silva)

1999 *Mia aiwniothta kai mia mera* (*Eternity and a Day*) (Angelopoulos); *Tierra del fuego* (Littin)

Publications

By GUERRA: books—

With others, *L'eclisse* and *La notte* (scripts) in *Screenplays by Michelangelo Antonioni*, New York, 1963.

L'equilibrio, Milan, 1967; as *Equilibrium*, London, 1969.

L'uomo parallelo, Milan, 1969.

With Antonioni and Elio Bartolini, *L'avventura* (script), New York, 1969.

I bu (*I buoi*), Milan, 1972.

With Federico Fellini, *Amarcord*, Milan 1973; as *Amarcord: Portrait of a Town*, London, 1974.

I cento uccelli, Milan, 1974.

Il polverone, Milan, 1978.

E' mel (*Il miele*), Rimini, 1981.

I guardatori della luna, Milan, 1981.

With Antonioni, *L'Aquilone: Una favola del nostro tempo*, Rimini, 1982.

Il Leone dalla barba bianca, Milan, 1983.

La pioggia tiepida, Milan, 1984.

La capanna . . . poema d'amore in dialetto santarcangiolese, Rimini, 1985.

With Gunter Roland, *Aufbruch in TroïsDorf*, Essen, 1992.

By GUERRA: articles—

Image et Son (Paris), December 1973.
Positif (Paris), February 1979.
Positif (Paris), October 1983.
Iskusstvo (Moscow), May 1985.
Positif (Paris), February 1986.
Positif (Paris), November 1988.
EPD Film (Frankfurt), vol. 7, no. 3, March 1990.
Kosmorama (Denmark), vol. 34, no. 206, 1993.
EPD Film (Frankfurt), vol. 10, no. 9, September 1993.
Avant-Scène Cinéma (Paris), February 1996.
Positif (Paris), February 1996.

On GUERRA: books—

Seminario popolare su Tonino Guerra e la poesia dialettale romagnola, Ravenna, 1976.
Tonino Guerra, Rimini, 1985.

On GUERRA: articles—

Film Guia, May 1975.
Film Dope, no. 22, March 1981.
Iskusstvo Kino (Moscow), May 1985.
Iskusstvo Kino (Moscow), No. 8, 1994.
Positif (Paris), February 1996.

*   *   *

Tonino Guerra first became creatively involved in cinema when he collaborated with Elio Petri and Giuseppe De Santis on the script of the latter's *Uomini e lupi* in 1956. Three years later he worked with Antonioni on *L'avventura*, beginning a remarkable partnership that was to stretch all the way through to *Identificazione di una donna* and *Al di là delle nuvole*. Before, however, one is tempted to read the bleakness and introversion of these films as a Guerra stylistic hallmark, it is worth noting that in 1967, with *C'era una volta*, he launched another series of incredibly fruitful collaborations, this time with Francesco Rosi, in such lucid works of "dramatic clarification" as *Il caso Mattei*, *Lucky Luciano*, and *Cadaveri eccellenti*. Before applying the label "political writer," though, one should bear in mind Guerra's remark that he considers the films of Fellini (with whom he worked on *Amarcord*, *E la nave va*, and *Ginger e Fred*) just as political as the seemingly more obvious examples. He has also enjoyed ongoing creative relationships with Elio Petri and the Taviani brothers, as well as working with Tarkovsky (*Nostalgia*), Angelopoulos (*Taxidi sta kithira*) and Bellocchio (*Henry IV*). Indeed, in terms of the Italian cinema at least, it might be easier to list the notable films on which he *hasn't* worked!

Guerra has stated that "I am different from all the filmmakers I've worked with, and I think that I've a different face for each of them." On the other hand this should not be taken as a denial of his own authorial role, and he is extremely critical of the low status customarily allotted to the writer in the Italian cinema. As he said in an interview: "in Italy, only the director counts. There are, of course, five or six author-directors who write their own scenarios, and what I'm saying here doesn't apply to them. But if, on the other hand, you think of the 240 films which are made here every year then it's absurd to talk only of their directors. . . . In my opinion, when it's a matter of a true 'auteur,' then the author of the film *is* the director. But in the case of the 240 films produced here each year the author, in most instances is the scenarist.''

Of course, Guerra is fortunate enough to have worked with all the author-directors, but it is also interesting to note that he actually considers his *poetry* the most important of his numerous accomplishments. As he stated in *Positif*: ''in my life I have attempted to be a poet. Being a scenarist is a secondary occupation. So every time a film project presents itself I look for a way of saying things through poetic suggestion. I try to suggest a poetic mode.'' If, however, his scenarios are full of poetry, ''everything I write—including the poems—is full of images. Writing is like the essence of the image. Everybody who reads invents their own images. But in cinema the director imposes his own choices; cinema is very possessive. I like films which succeed in making audiences work, films which, by appealing to their imaginations, give them the possibility to be creative. Books are a hundred thousand films at the same time, because each reader invents their own images.'' Hence, of course, his predilection for directors who ''always leave spaces open.'' Antonioni immediately springs to mind here rather than Rosi, and indeed Guerra has remarked that ''at the beginning there was a big difference between Rosi and me. He turned this limpid but sharp eye on reality. As I've always said, his shoes are so shiny they're like two violins; mine are rather less so.'' On the other hand, *Tre fratelli* is one of both director's and writer's most suggestive and resonant works, representing a particularly felicitous and productive director-writer match.

There's also a particularly close link here with Guerra's poetry, because, as he has pointed out ''what interested me here is this feeling of farewell—one of the fundamental themes of my poetry—farewell to the peasant world, to the peasant civilisation, this feeling of a way of life which we are in the process of losing.'' Guerra grew up in Sant'Arcangelo in Romagna (the region in which *Amarcord* is set) and his first publication was a book of poems in the local dialect, later followed by many others. It is possible to see a loose connection with Pasolini here, but there is none of the latter's rather dubious idealization of the peasantry, rather, a haunting sense of transience and irrevocable change.

Guerra's creative acts always communicate a sense of amazement, mystery, and fascination before the world. Nevertheless, his stories are rooted in Earth precisely because the peasant world has a common language that allows him to be at ease in environments as varied as Georgia, Greece, and Italy. These last years he has isolated himself in Pennabilli, a hill on the Adriatic side of the Appenines and he works only with those directors who continue to visit him. He has lately discovered the theater and writes short plays that he hopes some day to publish as a theatrical diary.

—Julian Petley, updated by Soon-Mi Peten

GUFFEY, Burnett

Cinematographer. **Nationality:** American. **Born:** Del Rio, Tennessee, 26 May 1905. **Education:** Attended school in Etowah, Tennessee. **Family:** Married; two daughters. **Career:** Worked as messenger boy in a bank then camera assistant for Fox in mid-1920s, and Famous Players-Lasky in late 1920s; 1944—first film as cinematographer, *Sailor's Holiday*; 1944–66—worked for Columbia; then freelance.

Awards: Academy Award for *From Here to Eternity*, 1953, and *Bonnie and Clyde*, 1967. **Died:** In Goleta, California, 29 May 1983.

Films as Cameraman:

1935   *Clive of India* (Boleslawsky); ***The Informer*** (Ford)
1939   *Framed* (Schuster)
1940   *Foreign Correspondent* (Hitchcock)
1941   *That Hamilton Woman* (*Lady Hamilton*) (A. Korda)
1944   *Cover Girl* (C. Vidor)

Films as Cinematographer:

1944   *Sailor's Holiday* (Berke); *The Soul of a Monster* (Jason); *U-Boat Prisoner* (*Dangerous Mists*) (Landers); *Kansas City Kitty* (Lord); *The Unwritten Code* (Rotsten); *Tahiti Nights* (Jason);
1945   *Eadie Was a Lady* (Dreifuss); *I Love a Mystery* (Levin); *Eve Knew Her Apples* (Jaswon); *The Fighting Guardsman* (Levin); *Blonde from Brooklyn* (Lord); *The Gay Senorita* (Dreifuss); *The Girl of the Limberlost* (M. Ferrer); *My Name Is Julia Ross* (Lewis)
1946   *Meet Me on Broadway* (Jason); *The Notorious Lone Wolf* (Lederman); *A Close Call for Boston Blackie* (*Lady of Mystery*) (Landers); *Night Editor* (*The Trespasser*) (Levin); *Gallant Journey* (Wellman); *So Dark the Night* (Lewis)
1947   *Johnny O'Clock* (Rossen); *Framed* (*Paula*) (Wallace)
1948   *To the Ends of the Earth* (Stevenson); *The Sign of the Ram* (J. Sturges); *The Gallant Blade* (Levin) (co)
1949   *Knock on Any Door* (Ray); *Undercover Man* (Lewis); *The Reckless Moment* (Ophüls); *And Baby Makes Three* (Levin)
1950   ***All the King's Men*** (Rossen); *Father Is a Bachelor* (Foster and Berlin); *Convicted* (Levin); ***In a Lonely Place*** (Ray); *Emergency Wedding* (*Jealousy*) (Buzzell)
1951   *Sirocco* (Bernhardt); *Two of a Kind* (Levin); *The Family Secret* (Levin); *Scandal Sheet* (*The Dark Page*) (Karlson); *Boots Malone* (Dieterle) (2nd unit)
1952   *The Sniper* (Dmytryk); *Assignment Paris* (Parrish) (co)
1953   ***From Here to Eternity*** (Zinnemann)
1954   *Human Desire* (F. Lang); *Private Hell 36* (Siegel); *The Bamboo Prison* (Seiler); *The Violent Men* (*Rough Company*) (Maté)
1955   *Tight Spot* (Karlson); *Count Three and Pray* (G. Sherman); *Three Stripes in the Sun* (*The Gentle Sergeant*) (Murphy); *Battle Stations* (Seiler)
1956   *The Harder They Fall* (Robson); *Storm Center* (Taradash); *Nightfall* (Tourneur)
1957   *The Strange One* (*End as a Man*) (Garfein); *The Brothers Rico* (Karlson); *Decision at Sundown* (Boetticher); *Not One Shall Die* (Rich)
1958   *The True Story of Lynn Stuart* (Seiler); *Screaming Mimi* (Oswald); *Me and the Colonel* (Glenville)
1959   *Gidget* (Wendkos); *They Came to Cordura* (Seigel); *Edge of Eternity* (Karlson); *Let No Man Write My Epitaph* (Leacock)
1961   *Cry for Happy* (Marshall); *Homicidal* (Castle); *Mr. Sardonicus* (Castle)

1962   *Birdman of Alcatraz* (Frankenheimer); *Kid Galahad* (Karlson)
1963   *Four for Texas* (Aldrich) (2nd unit)
1964   *Flight from Ashiya* (Anderson) (co); *Good Neighbor Sam* (Swift)
1965   *King Rat* (Forbes)
1966   *The Silencers* (Karlson); *How to Succeed in Business without Really Trying* (Swift)
1967   ***Bonnie and Clyde*** (Penn); *The Ambushers* (Levin) (co)
1968   *The Split* (Fleming)
1969   *Where It's At* (Kanin); *The Learning Tree* (Parks); *Some Kind of a Nut* (Kanin) (co); *The Madwoman of Chaillot* (Forbes) (co); *Suppose They Gave a War and Nobody Came* (Averback)
1970   *Halls of Anger* (Bogart); *The Steagle* (Sylbert); *The Great White Hope* (Ritt)

Publications

By GUFFEY: article—

"The Photography of *King Rat*," in *American Cinematographer* (Hollywood), December 1965.

On GUFFEY: articles—

Gavin, Arthur, on *They Came to Cordura* in *American Cinematographer* (Hollywood), March 1959.
Mitchell, George J., on *Hell to Eternity*, in *American Cinematographer* (Hollywood), July 1960.
Lightman, Herb A., on *Birdman of Alcatraz*, in *American Cinematographer* (Hollywood), June 1962.
On *Bonnie and Clyde*, in *American Cinematographer* (Hollywood), April 1967.
Monthly Film Bulletin (London), April 1971; August 1971; March 1972; April 1972.
Film Comment (New York), Summer 1972.
Focus on Film (London), no. 13, 1973.
Obituary in *Variety* (New York), 8 June 1983.
Screen International (London), 13–20 August 1983.
Obituary in *American Cinematographer* (Hollywood), November 1983.

*   *   *

Burnett Guffey's reputation and contributions to the art of cinematography rest not so much in what he did with the camera and lights, but in what he chose not to do. The major portion of Guffey's career behind the camera was spent deglamorizing the Hollywood film, a task that takes on mammoth proportions when one realizes that he was most active in the 1940s and 1950s. In a period when Cinemascope, spectacle, and lurid color were the rule, Guffey continued to work in black-and-white, stripping the romance from the world's most romantic form.

Although he was capable of achieving the slick commercial look of the more typical Hollywood film, Guffey's personal style led him to work primarily on rugged action and mystery pictures. For these movies he developed what has been characterized as "flat" photography, a functional rebuttal to the elaborate deep-focus cinematography of Gregg Toland. Using a simple, often single source of light, little or no fill light, and a minimum of camera movement, Guffey provided directors with a naturalistic, gritty look to complement hardboiled stories of criminals, convicts, and men at war. Even for his Academy Award-winning cinematography on *Bonnie and Clyde*, Guffey succeeded in subduing color, relying on worn hues to produce a common, dreary effect.

Set in the seedy world of boxing, *The Harder They Fall*, for which Guffey received an Academy Award nomination, stands as a typical example of his flat style. Making use of minimal contrast, Guffey emphasizes gray. Blacks flow into grays which flow into whites, giving the film a truly monotonal effect. Guffey's photography hides nothing, revealing the ugliness of the sport and the flaws of the people who cling to the edges of the ring. Much of the film takes place in the perpetual twilight of gyms and ill-lit hotel rooms and the glamor of professional sports is displaced with images that are harsh, often ugly. Though capable of depth, Guffey's compositions tend to emphasize flatness by placing people against walls or planes of like tone. The grey, monotonal quality of Guffey's work was ideally suited for stories that featured characters of ambiguous morality such as Bogart's gunrunner in *Sirocco*, the mobsters aiming for respectability in Phil Karlson's *The Brothers Rico*, and George Segal's P.O.W. camp racketeer in *King Rat*.

Guffey's tendency toward flat cinematography could be overridden by the potently baroque visuals of a director like Joseph H. Lewis in *My Name Is Julia Ross* and *So Dark the Night*. And there was always the danger of the flat cinematography being coupled with dull direction and the lackluster production design of a studio like Columbia to produce deadening visuals. Still, when combined with the proper story and strong direction, Burnett Guffey's flat cinematography provided an alternative aesthetic to the standard studio product.

—Eric Schaefer

GUILLEMOT, Agnès

Editor. **Nationality:** French. **Born:** Agnès Perche, in Roubaix, 1931. **Education:** Attended IDHEC, Paris, 1956–57. **Family:** Married the director Claude Guillemot. **Career:** 1956–57—editor for Télévision Canadienne (Télé-France); 1957–59—assistant editor at IDHEC; 1960—worked on TV news series, and then on series *L'Education sentimentale*, 1971, *L'Amour du métier*, 1972, *La Clé des champs*, 1973, and *Les Secrets de la Mer Rouge*, 1974; since 1980—teacher of film editing at IDHEC.

Films as Editor:

1953   *La Faute des autres* (Guez—short)
1955   *Walk into Paradise* (*L'Odyssée du Capitaine Steve*) (Robinson and Pagliero) (asst)
1958   *Vous n'avez rien contre la jeunesse* (Logereau—short); *Voyage en Boscavie* (Herman—short)
1959   *Voiles à Val* (Perol—short)
1960   *Le Gaz de Lacq* (Lanoe—short); *Thaumetopoea* (Enrico—short); *Un Steak trop cuit* (Moullet—short)
1961   *La Quille* (Herman—short); *Une Femme est une femme* (*A Woman Is a Woman*) (Godard)

1962   *Une Grosse Tête* (De Givray); **Vivre sa vie** (*My Life to Live*) (Godard); "Il Nuovo mondo" ep. of *Rogopag* (Godard)

1963   *Le Petit Soldat* (Godard—produced 1960); *Les Hommes de la Wahgi* (Villeminot—short); *Les Carabiniers* (Godard); **Le Mépris** (*Contempt*) (Godard); "Le Grand Escroc" ep. of *Les Plus Belles Escroqueries du monde* (*The Beautiful Swindlers*) (Godard); *Jérôme Bosch* (Weyergans—short); *Une Semaine en France* (C. Guillemot and Chambon—short)

1964   *Bande à part* (*Band of Outsiders*) (Godard); *Une Fille à la dérive* (Delsol); *Rues de Hong Kong* (C. Guillemot—short); *La Jonque* (C. Guillemot—short); *Les Tourbiers* (Weyergans—short); *De l'amour* (Aurel); *Une Femme mariée* (*The Married Woman*) (Godard) (co)

1965   **Alphaville** (*Une étrange aventure de Lemmy Caution*; *Alphaville: A Strange Adventure of Lemmy Caution*; *Tarzan versus I.B.M.*) (Godard)

1966   *Masculin-féminin* (*Masculine-Feminine*) (Godard); *Dialectique* (C. Guillemot—short); *Le Chien fou* (Matalon); *Nature morte* (C. Guillemot—short); *Made in U.S.A.* (Godard)

1967   "Anticipation" ep. of *Le Plus Vieux Métier du monde* (*The Oldest Profession*) (Godard); *La Chinoise* (Godard); **Week-end** (Godard)

1968   *Les Gauloises bleues* (Cournot); *Baises volés* (*Stolen Kisses*) (Truffaut); *One Plus One* (*Sympathy for the Devil*) (Godard); *La Trêve* (C. Guillemot)

1969   "L'amore" ep. of *Amore e rabbia* (*Vangelo '70*) (Godard); *La Sirène du Mississippi* (*Mississippi Mermaid*) (Truffaut); *L'Enfant sauvage* (*The Wild Child*) (Truffaut)

1970   *Domicile conjugal* (*Bed and Board*) (Truffaut)

1974   *L'Age tendre* (Laumet)

1975   *Le Grand Matin* (C. Guillemot—short); *Cousin cousine* (Tacchella)

1976   *Un Type comme moi ne devrait jamais mourir* (Vianey); *Le Pays bleu* (Tacchella)

1977   *Monsieur Badin* (Ceccaldi); *Jean de la lune* (Villiers); *Les Violons parfois* (Ronet)

1978   *Folies douces* (Ronet); *Le Concierge revient de suite* (Wyn)

1979   *Il y a longtemps que je t'aime* (Tacchella)

1983   *La Diagonale du fou* (*Dangerous Moves*) (Dembo)

1985   *Escalier C* (Tacchella)

1987   *La Brute* (C. Guillemot); *Fuegos* (C. Guillemot)

1988   *La Lumière du lac* (Comencini)

1990   *Un Week-End sur deux* (*Every Other Weekend*) (Nicole García)

1991   *Nord* (*North*) (Beauvois)

1994   *Le Fils préféré* (*The Favorite Son*) (Garcia)

1995   *N'oublie pas que tu vas mourir* (*Don't Forget That You're Going to Die*) (Beauvois)

1996   *Mémoires d'un jeune con* (Aurignac); *Parfait amour!* (Breillat)

1999   *Romance* (*Romance X*) (Breillat)

Publications

By GUILLEMOT: articles—

Cinématographe (Paris), March 1985.
Cahiers du Cinéma (Paris), November 1990.

On GUILLEMOT: articles—

Chaplin (Stockholm), December 1968.
Film Comment (New York), March/April 1977.

*   *   *

Agnès Guillemot's 45-year career places her as one of France's most important, respected, and influential editors. She teaches editing at IDHEC in Paris, edits television series, documentaries, and narrative features, and through the 1960s, established the basic editing style of modernist filmmaking, contemporary television commercials, and music videos. She began cutting film during the Nouvelle Vague period and remains strongly associated with that era.

As Jean-Luc Godard's favorite editor, Guillemot edited all of his films from 1961 to 1969, with the exceptions of *Pierrot le fou*, *Deux ou trois choses que je sais d'elle* (both edited by one of her former assistants, Françoise Collin), and *Le Gai Savoir*. Collaborating with Godard on 13 features and four episodes of compilation films, and having an assistant edit two others, she must share responsibility for the deconstructive narrative techniques and reflexive visual style usually credited to Godard. Although the similarity of the editing strategies in *Deux ou trois choses* and *Pierrot le fou* to all Godard's other films suggests the director's overriding influence, and Guillemot herself admits that an editor must embrace the personal rhythm of each director and not impose her own, Guillemot's reification of Godard's theories cannot be underestimated. By introducing a sense of musical rhythm and a disregard for spatial and temporal continuity, her work with Godard avoided the realist dictates of linear narrative and provided a locus for ideological analysis. This radicalizing of conventional editing eventually emerged as her most important legacy.

Within any one film, Guillemot's editing appears contradictory, or perhaps dialogic; in any case, her work seems, at first glance, an impossible melange of styles. She combines or juxtaposes the formal symmetry of long takes, the precise rigor of classical match-action editing and shot/reverse shot, the playfulness of reflexivity, and the spontaneity of jump cuts. These characteristics exactly demonstrate the musical and open narrative signature of the Nouvelle Vague. Guillemot cites her strongest work as *Une Femme est une femme*, with its interplay of words and music as in an opera, and *Les Carabiniers* for the crescendo of the postcard sequence. In *Alphaville*, she reinforces Godard's parody of American science fiction by employing standard editing techniques only to abandon them at moments of highest narrative expectation. In *Le Mépris*, she uses jump cuts sparingly as a metaphor for Camille's confused mind, ironically embedding them in a fluid pattern of graceful tracking shots. In *Masculin-féminin*, she plays off the symmetrical tension of the title to visually explore the energy of romance; initially, fast-paced jump cutting represents a new love, slowing to long takes as the romance dissolves. In *Weekend*, she summarizes her collaboration with Godard by fully exhibiting her varied and "contradictory" style of editing, a style perfectly suited for encapsulating Godard's "end of cinema."

Guillemot's late career allowed her to adapt radical Nouvelle Vague modernism for more mainstream cinema; as New Wave stylistics became accepted and standardized, she expanded the confining logic and limitations of classic linear narrative. She edited films for François Truffaut (including two of the Antoine Doinel series), Jean-Charles Tacchella (including the Oscar-nominated *Cousin cousine*), and Richard Dembo (the Academy Award-winning *La Diagonale du fou*). By comparing these films to her Godard period, one can easily see Guillemot's influence on contemporary film editing. Eschewing only the reflexivity of her Godard period, she employs the other techniques (especially visual and aural jump cuts) to stress spatial and temporal ellipses. Contained within classical match action and shot/reverse shot sequences and countered with long takes, these ellipses open up a narrative, regardless of how confining (*La Diagonale du fou*'s chess match) or how limited (*Cousin cousine*'s conventional love story) and offer the potential for social critique. Her editing on *La Lumière du lac* and *Un Week-End sur deux* accomplishes exactly this—expanding the parameters of linear narrative with humorous spontaneity, rhythmic pacing, and critical observations of modern society. She has also edited ten shorts and features by her husband Claude Guillemot, alternating between traditional documentary style and her Nouvelle Vague techniques.

Guillemot's New Wave cutting also influenced most contemporary film and television editing. Even though the link between her editing during the 1960s and today's television commercials and music videos loses its political edge, the continuation of her style in these formats seems incontrovertible (the 1989 Lee Jeans ads, particularly, acting as a direct homage). The formal symmetry of shot/reverse shot placed within long takes, invisible match-action editing alternating with jump cuts, a playful reflexivity, and loosely structured "nonnarratives" are now accepted as standard practice (almost every music video is edited this way). Like most historical avant-garde artists, her work seems much less radical today because of its wide appropriation. Nevertheless, Guillemot must be credited with modernizing editing during the 1960s, an accomplishment which continues to influence visual media today.

—Greg S. Faller

HACKETT, Albert

See **GOODRICH, Frances, and Albert HACKETT**

HAKIM, Raymond and Robert

Producers. **Nationality:** Egyptian. **Born:** Robert in Alexandria, 19 December 1907; Raymond in Alexandria, 23 August 1909. **Education:** Both brothers educated in France. **Career:** Both worked for Paramount in France; 1934—went into independent production; 1940—moved to Hollywood; 1950—returned to France; Robert went into distribution alone. **Died:** Raymond—in Deauville, 14 August 1980.

Films as Producers (selected list):

1937   *Pépé le Moko* (Duvivier)
1938   *La Bête Humaine* (Renoir)
1939   *Le Jour se lève* (Carné)
1945   *The Southerner* (Renoir) (co)
1947   *Her Husband's Affairs* (Simon); *The Long Night* (Litvak)
1949   *Without Honor* (Pichel)
1951   *The Blue Veil* (Bernhardt)
1952   *Casque d'or* (Becher)
1953   *Thérèse Raquin* (Carné)
1956   *The Hunchback of Notre Dame* (*Notre Dame of Paris*) (Delannoy)
1957   *Pot-bouille* (Duvivier)
1959   *A double tour* (*Web of Passion; Leda*) (Chabrol)
1960   *Plein Soleil* (Clément); *Les Bonnes Femmes* (Chabrol)
1962   *L'éclisse* (Antonioni); *Eva* (*Eve*) (Losey)
1963   *Chair de poule* (*Highway Pickup*) (Duvivier)
1964   *Weekend à Zuydcoote* (*Weekend at Dunkirk*) (Verneuil); *La Ronde* (Vadim)
1967   *Belle de jour* (Buñuel); *Isadora* (Reisz)
1968   *Heartbeat* (Cavalier)
1969   *The Loves of Isadora* (Reisz)
1976   *La Marge* (Borowczyk)

Publications

On HAKIM: article—

Obituary (Raymond), in *Variety* (New York), 3 September 1980.
Pawelczak, Andy, "Purple Noon," in *Films in Review*, September-October 1996.

*   *   *

After working for Paramount in Paris, the Egypt-born Hakim brothers became independent producers in 1934, financing Duvivier's *Pépé le Moko* and Renoir's *La Bête Humaine*. These sensational and discreetly salacious films by directors who, though well-established, were slightly out of the mainstream, established a strategy that would help the Hakims survive French cinema's most disastrous decades.

In 1940, they joined many colleagues (including Julien Duvivier and Jean Renoir) in fleeing to California. During World War II, the Hakims produced only *The Southerner*, a lean picture of sharecropper life, co-produced with David Loew. Renoir's film, which is unlike anything else the brothers ever backed, has all the marks of a project engineered by Hollywood to keep distinguished emigrés afloat.

The Hakims remained in America after the war but, of their three productions, only *The Long Night*, a remake of Marcel Carné's 1939 *Le Jour se lève*, with Henry Fonda replacing Jean Gabin, is notable, while the limp comedy *Heartbeat* effectively ended the Hollywood career of Jean-Pierre Aumont. The youngest Hakim, Andre, remained in America, where he married into the Zanuck family and became a producer for 20th Century-Fox, but in 1950, Robert and Raymond returned to France.

They financed Duvivier's *Pot-bouille* and the two films that launched Simone Signoret as a star, Becker's *Casque d'or* and Carné's *Thérèse Raquin*. However, intellectually out of sympathy with the *nouvelle vague* (and, moreover, committed to the *cinéma du papa* that most young directors reviled), the Hakims failed to imitate fellow independent producers Pierre Braunberger and Georges de Beauregard in backing the New Wave. Their only productions with the younger directors were Chabrol's *Les Bonnes Femmes* and his upper-class whodunit, *A double tour*. The latter, also known as *Web of Passion* and advertised with the graphic of a keyhole framing Bernadette Lafont in bikini underwear, was among the New Wave's first international commercial successes.

Throughout the 1960s, the Hakims seldom deviated from the style of film successful for them in the 1930s: star-driven melodramas with plenty of sex, and an international market built in. The recipe that launched Simone Signoret in *Casque d'or* proved equally serviceable for Alain Delon in René Clément's *Plein Soleil*, Roger Vadim's remake of *La Ronde*, Luis Buñuel's *Belle de jour* and Karel Reisz's *Isadora*. All shrewdly exploited the European cinema's reputation for sophisticated sensuality without surrendering totally to the mass market.

The Hakims's methods were not always popular. Attempting to make a BBC TV film on Isadora Duncan, Ken Russell found every available biography and memoir of the dancer bought up by the brothers to protect their 1969 production *The Loves of Isadora*. (Director Karel Reisz himself became disaffected when his film was shorn of 37 minutes for its U.S. release.) At the same time, François Truffaut, negotiating with the Hakims to film Cornell Woolrich's *Mississippi Mermaid*, quickly became deadlocked with them over casting. Truffaut wanted Jean-Paul Belmondo opposite Catherine Deneuve, but the brothers preferred Alan Bates or Alain Delon. After breaking off the deal, Truffaut discovered that the story rights belonged, not to the Hakims at all, but to 20th Century-Fox, from whom he purchased them to make *La Sirene du Mississippi*, with Belmondo and Deneuve. Such charges, however, should be weighed alongside the Hakims's impressive record. By putting their skills to work on behalf of great directors, they managed to make high-quality, bankable films.

—John Baxter

HALAS, John, and Joy BATCHELOR

HALAS. Animator. **Nationality:** Hungarian. **Born:** Janos Halasz in Budapest, 16 April 1912. **Family:** Married Joy Batchelor in late 1930s. **Career:** 1928–31—apprentice to George Pal; early 1930s—spent 18 months in Paris, returned to Budapest and taught at Atelier, graphic design school; 1934—opened first animation studio, Halas, Macskasi and Kassowitz; 1936—moved to England; 1970—elected president of International Council of Graphic Design Associations (ICOGRADA); 1975—president of International Animated Film Association (ASIFA); also chairman of the Federation of Film Societies; and contributing editor and film/TV correspondent to *Novum* (Munich); 1982—produced the world's first fully digitized film, *Dilemma*. **Died:** 21 January 1995.

BATCHELOR. Animator. **Nationality:** British. **Born:** Watford, Hertfordshire, England, 12 May 1914. **Career:** 1935—began working in films as artist; 1937—hired as designer and animator to work on *The Music Man*; 1973—retired but continued to act as adviser to animation students at International Film School, London. **Died:** 1991.

1940—Halas & Batchelor Cartoon Films formed; 1940–45—made numerous information and propaganda films for British government; 1951–54—produced only feature-length British cartoon, *Animal Farm*, based on George Orwell novel; 1968—Halas & Batchelor bought by Trident Television; Batchelor and Halas concentrated on individual projects working through their other company, Educational Film Centre; from 1968 to 1972 not responsible for films produced by Halas & Batchelor production company; 1974—Halas & Batchelor sold back to Halas after losing money for corporation.

Films as Directors:

1938   *The Music Man* (co-anim, Halas only d)
1940   *Train Trouble* (+ co-pr, anim); *Carnival in the Clothes Cupboard* (+ co-pr, co-des, co-anim)
1941   *Filling the Gap* (+ co-pr, co-sc, co-anim); *Dustbin Parade* (+ co-pr, co-sc, co-des, co-anim)
1942   *Digging for Victory* (+ co-pr, co-sc, co-anim; des: Batchelor)
1943   *Jungle Warfare* (+ co-pr, co-des, co-anim)
1944–45   *Handling Ships* (feature) (Halas only pr, co-d, des, anim)
1946   *Modern Guide to Health* (+ co-pr, co-des; sc: Batchelor); *Old Wives' Tales* (+ co-pr, co-des; sc: Batchelor)
1947   *First Line of Defence* (+ co-pr, co-sc); *This Is the Air Force* (+ co-pr, co-sc); *What's Cooking?* (+ co-pr, co-des; sc: Batchelor); *Dolly Put the Kettle On* (+ co-pr, co-des; sc: Batchelor)

1948   *Oxo Parade* (+ co-pr, co-des; sc: Batchelor); *Magic Canvas* (co-pr only; Halas: d, sc, co-des); *Water for Firefighting* (feature) (Halas only co-d); *Heave Away My Johnny* (+ co-pr, co-sc)
1949   *The Shoemaker and the Hatter* (+ co-pr, co-sc, co-des); *Submarine Control* (co-d with Privett and Crick; pr: Crick); *Fly about the House* (+ co-pr, co-des; sc: Batchelor)
1950   *Earth in Labour* (Halas only: d, co-pr, co-sc)
1951   *Moving Spirit* (Halas: co-d, co-pr; Batchelor: co-sc)
1952   *The Owl and the Pussycat* (stereoscopic) (Halas only: co-d, pr, co-sc); *Linear Accelerator*
1954   *Animal Farm* (feature, begun 1951) (+ co-pr, co-sc, co-des)
1956   *The World of Little Ig* (Halas: d, co-pr; Batchelor: sc, co-pr); *The Candlemaker* (Halas: co-d, pr; Batchelor: co-d, co-sc)
1957   *History of the Cinema* (Halas only: d, pr, co-sc, co-des); *Midsummer Nightmare* (only co-pr, co-sc; Halas: d, co-des)
1958   *The First Ninety-Nine* (co-pr only; Batchelor: d, co-sc); *The Christmas Visitor* (only co-pr, co-sc; Halas: d); *Dam the Delta* (+ Batchelor: sc); *Early Days of Communication* (Halas only: d, co-pr)
1959   *Man in Silence* (Halas only: co-d); *All Lit Up* (+ co-pr; Batchelor: sc); *Piping Hot* (+ co-pr; Batchelor: sc); *For Better for Worse* (+ co-pr; Batchelor: sc)
1960   *Wonder of Wool* (Halas only: d, pr)
1961   *Hamilton the Musical Elephant* (Halas only: d, pr, co-sc); *Hamilton in the Musical Festival* (Halas only: d, pr, co-sc)
1962   *Barnaby—Father Dear Father* (co-pr only; Halas: d, co-des); *Barnaby—Overdue Dues Blues* (co-pr only; Halas: d, co-des)
1963   *Automania 2000* (only co-pr, co-sc; Halas: d); *The Axe and the Lamp* (Halas only: d, pr)
1964   *Ruddigore* (feature) (co-pr only; Batchelor: d, sc)
1966   *ICOGRADA Congress* (live-action) (Halas only: d, pr, co-sc); *Dying for a Smoke* (Halas: d, pr; Batchelor: co-sc)
1967   *The Question* (Halas only: d, pr, co-sc); *The Colombo Plan* (co-pr only; Batchelor: d, sc); *The Commonwealth* (co-pr only; Batchelor: d, sc)
1968   *Bolly* (co-pr only; Batchelor: d, sc)
1969   *To Our Children's Children* (Halas only: d, pr, des, co-sc)
1970   *Short Tall Story* (co-pr only; Halas: d, co-sc); *The Five* (co-pr only; Batchelor: d, sc); *Wot Dot* (co-pr only; Batchelor: d, sc) *Flurina* (co-pr only; Halas: d, co-sc)
1971   *Children and Cars* (only co-pr, co-sc; Halas: d)
1973   *Contact* (+ Batchelor: co-sc; Halas: pr); *The Glorious Musketeers* (feature) (Halas only: d, pr, co-sc)
1974   *The Ass and the Stick* (Batchelor: d, co-sc; Halas: pr, co-sc); *Christmas Feast* (co-sc only; Halas: d, pr); *Carry on Milkmaids* (Batchelor: d, sc; Halas: pr)
1975   *How Not to Succeed in Business* (Halas only: d, pr, co-sc)
1976   *Skyrider* (Halas only: d, pr, co-sc)
1977   *Making It Move* (live-action) (Halas only: d, pr, co-sc)
1978   *Max and Moritz* (feature) (Halas only: d, co-pr, co-sc)
1979   *Ten for Survival* (Halas: d, co-pr; Batchelor: sc); *Autobahn* (Halas only: d, pr, co-sc)
1981   *The Figurehead* (+ pr); *First Steps* (Halas only: d)
1982   *Dilemma* (Halas only: d)
1983   *Players* (Halas only: d)
1984   *A New Vision: The Life and Work of Botticelli* (Halas only: d)
1985   *Toulouse-Lautrec* (Halas only: d); *Leonardo da Vinci* (Halas only: d)
1989   *Light of the World* (Halas only: d)

Charley Series—

1946–47   *Charley in the New Towns*; *Charley in the New Schools*;
          Charley in "Your Very Good Health"; *Charley in the New
          Mines*; *Charley Junior's Schooldays*; *Charley's March of
          Time* (+ co-pr, co-sc, co-des); *Robinson Charley* (+ co-pr,
          co-des)

Poet and Painter Series—

1951   Programme 1: *Twa Corbies*; *Spring and Winter*; Programme
       2: *Winter Garden*; *Sailor's Consolation*; *Check to Song*;
       Programme 3: *In Time of Pestilence*; *The Pythoness*;
       Programme 4: *John Gilpin* (Halas only: d, pr)

Popeye Series—

1955   *The Billionaire*; *Dog Done Dog Catcher*; *Matinee Idol*; *Model
       Muddle*; *Weight for Me*; *Potent Lotion*; *Which Is Witch?*
       (Halas only: co-d, pr)

Hatabales Series—

1960   *The Lion Tamer*; *Hairy Hercules*; *The Cultured Ape*; *The
       Insolent Matador*; *The Widow and the Pig*; *I Wanna Mink*
       (Halas only: co-d, pr)

Snip and Snap Series—

1960   *Bagpipes*; *Treasure of Ice Cake Island*; *Spring Song*; *Snakes
       and Ladders*; *In the Jungle*; *Lone World Sail*; *Thin Ice*;
       Magic Book; *Circus Star*; *Moonstruck*; *Snap and the Bean-
       stalk*; *Goodwill to All Dogs*; *In the Cellar*; *The Grand
       Concert*; *The Beggar's Uproar*; *The Birthday Cake*; *Snap
       Goes East*; *The Hungry Dog*; *Tog Dogs* (Halas only: co-d,
       pr, co-sc)

The Tales of Hoffnung Series—

1964   *Professor Ya-Ya's Memoirs* (Halas only: co-d, pr, co-sc); *The
       Maestro* (Halas only: co-d, pr, co-sc); *Birds Bees and
       Storks* (Halas only: d, pr, co-sc); *The Music Academy*
       (Halas only: co-d, pr, co-sc); *The Palm Court Orchestra*
       (Halas only: d, pr, co-sc)

The Carters of Greenwood English Language Teaching Series—

1964   12 films (Halas only: d, pr)

Martian in Moscow Russian Language Teaching Series—

1964   12 films (Halas only: d, pr)

Do Do Series—

1964   72 films (Halas only: d, pr)

*Les Aventures de la famile Carré French Language
Teaching* Series—

1964   12 films (Halas only: co-d, pr)

Classic Fairy Tales Series—

1966   6 films (Batchelor: d, sc; Halas and Batchelor: co-pr)

Lone Ranger Series—

1966–67   37 episodes (Halas only: co-d, co-pr, co-sc)

Tomfoolery Series—

1970   17 films (Halas only: d, pr, co-sc)

Masters of Animation Series—

1986–87   (Halas only)

Other Films:

1950   *As Old as the Hills* (Halas only: co-pr)
1952   *We've Come a Long Way* (Halas: co-pr; Batchelor: co-sc)
1953   *Power to Fly* (Halas: co-pr; Batchelor: co-sc)
1954   *Down a Long Way* (Halas: co-pr; Batchelor: co-sc); *The Sea*
       (Halas only: pr, sc)
1955   *Animal Vegetable Mineral* (Halas: co-pr; Batchelor: co-sc)
1956   *To Your Health* (Halas: pr; Batchelor: co-sc)
1958   *Speed the Plough* (Halas: co pr; Batchelor: co-sc)
1959   *How to Be a Hostess* (live action) (Halas: pr; Batchelor: sc);
       Energy Picture (Batchelor: sc; Halas & Batchelor: co-pr)
1960   *History of Inventions* (Halas only: co-pr, co-sc)
1961   *The Monster of Highgate Pond* (Halas: pr; Batchelor: sc); *The
       Guns of Navarone* (Foreman) (Halas only: des of excerpts)
1962   *The Showing Up of Larry the Lamb* (Halas only: pr)
1964   *The Tale of the Magician* (Halas only: pr); *Paying Bay*
       (Batchelor: co-sc; Halas & Batchelor: co-pr); *Follow That
       Car* (Batchelor: co-sc; Halas & Batchelor: co-pr)
1966   *Matrices* (Halas only: pr, co-sc); *Deadlock* (Halas only: pr,
       co-sc); *Flow Diagram* (Halas only: pr, co-sc); *Linear
       Programming* (Halas only: pr, co-sc)
1967   *What Is a Computer* (Halas only: co-pr, co-sc); *Girls Growing
       Up* (Halas only: pr, co-sc); *Mothers and Fathers* (Halas
       only: pr, co-sc)
1968   *Functions and Relations* (Halas only: pr, co-sc)
1969   *Measure of Man* (Halas only: pr, co-sc)
1970   *This Love Thing* (Halas only: pr, co-sc)
1971   *Football Freaks* (Halas only: pr, co-sc)
1973   *Children Making Cartoons* (live-action) (Halas only: pr,
       co-sc); *Making Music Together* (Halas only: pr, co-sc); *The
       Twelve Tasks of Asterix* (Watrin and Gruel) (animation in
       last reel only) (Halas only: pr, co-sc)
1974   *Kitchen Think* (Halas only: pr, co-sc); *Butterfly Ball* (Halas
       only: pr, co-sc)
1975   *Life Insurance Training Film* (excerpts) (Halas only: pr,
       co-sc)
1977   *Noah's Ark* (Halas only: pr, co-sc)

1979   *Bravo for Billy* (Halas only: co-pr, co-sc); *Dream Doll* (Halas only: co-pr, co-sc)
1980   *Bible Stories* (Halas only: pr, co-sc)

Foo-Foo Series—

1960   *The Scapegoat*; *The Gardener*; *The Birthday Treat*; *A Denture Adventure*; *A Misguided Tour*; *The Caddies*; *Burglar Catcher*; *The Art Lovers*; *The Three Mountaineers*; *Foo Foo's New Hat*; *The Big Race*; *The Treasure Hunt*; *The Magician*; *The Spy Train*; *Insured for Life*; *Automation Blues*; *The Beggar's Uproar*; *Sleeping Beauty*; *The Reward*; *The Dinner Date*; *Beauty Treatment*; *The Ski Resort*; *Lucky Street*; *The Stowaway*; *A Hunting We Will Go*; *The Pearl Divers*; *Foo Foo's Sleepless Night*; *The Salesman*; *Art for Art's Sake*; *The Dog Pound*; *The Hypnotist*; *Low Finance* (Halas only: pr)

Concept Films Series—

1961–69   200 films in areas of ''Biology,'' ''Science,'' and ''Maths'' (Halas only: pr)

The Tales of Hoffnung Series—

1964   *The Symphony Orchestra*; *The Vacuum Cleaner* (Halas only: pr, co-sc)

Evolution of Life—

1964   8 films (Halas only: pr, co-sc)

The Condition of Man Series—

1971   *Condition of Man*; *Quartet*; *Up*; *Let It Bleed*; *It Furthers One to Have Somewhere to Go*; *Xeroscopy* (Halas only: pr, co-sc)

The Addams Family Series—

1972   17 films (Halas only: pr, co-sc)

The Jackson Five Series—

1972   17 films (Halas only: pr, co-sc)

The Osmonds Series—

1973   17 films (Halas only: pr, co-sc)

Britain Series—

1973   *Animals*; *Sports*; *Roads* (Halas only: pr, co-sc—live-action)

Wilhelm Busch Album Series—

1978   13 films (Halas only: co-pr, co-sc)

Publications

By HALAS and BATCHELOR: books—

Archibald the Great, illustrations by Halas, London, 1937.
How to Cartoon for Amateur Films, London, 1951.
With Roger Manvell, *Technique of Film Animation*, London, 1959.
With Roger Manvell, *Design in Motion*, London, 1962.
With Walter Herdeg, *Film and Television Graphics*, London, 1967.
With Roger Manvell, *Art in Movement*, London, 1970.
Computer Animation, London, 1976.
Film Animation, Paris, 1976.
Visual Scripting, London, 1976.
Graphics in Motion, London, 1981.
Timing for Animation, London, 1981.
Masters of Animation, London, 1987.

By HALAS and BATCHELOR: articles—

''The Film Cartoonist,'' in *Working for the Films*, London, 1947.
''The Animated Film,'' in *Art and Industry* (London), July 1947.
''From Script to Screen,'' in *Art and Industry* (London), August 1947.
''Cartoon Films in Commerce,'' in *Art and Industry* (London), November 1947.
''The Approach to Cartoon Film Scriptwriting,'' in *This Film Business*, London, 1948.
''Introducing Hamilton . . . and Some of the People Who Gave Him Birth,'' in *Films and Filming* (London), June 1962.
''Talking with Halas and Batchelor,'' in *1000 Eyes* (New York), February 1976.
''The Way Forward,'' in *Film* (London), March 1979.
Plateau, vol. 5, no. 3, 1984.
Animatrix, no. 1, December 1984.
Animatrix, no. 2, November 1985.

On HALAS and BATCHELOR: book—

Manvell, Roger, *Art and Animation*, London, 1980.

On HALAS and BATCHELOR: articles—

''Halas and Batchelor: Profile of a Partnership,'' in *Film* (London), March 1955.
''Halas and Batchelor,'' in *International Film Guide*, London, 1965.
''Halas and Batchelor,'' in *Film* (London), Spring 1966.
Cineforum (Bergamo, Italy), vol. 23, no. 230, December 1983.
Plateau, vol. 5, no. 2, 1984.
Rothenberg, Robert S., ''Masters of Animation,'' in *USA Today Magazine*, July 1989.
New Orleans Review, vol. 18, no. 4, 1991.
Obituary for Batchelor, in *Variety* (New York), 27 May 1991.
Obituary for Batchelor, in *Animator* (Herts), October 1991.
Obituary for Halas, in *Film-Dienst* (Cologne), 31 January 1995.
Obituary for Halas, in *Film International* (Tehran), no. 3, 1995.

*   *   *

Halas and Batchelor, the distinguished animation studio, and film research and production center, was established in London in 1940. It was the result of the partnership (and subsequent marriage) of two artists, John Halas and Joy Batchelor. John Halas was educated in Budapest and Paris, and originally worked as an assistant to George Pal before establishing himself as an independent animator in 1934. In 1936 he came to England; while working on a cartoon film, *The Music Man*, he met Joy Batchelor, who entered films in 1935 as a commercial artist.

Their unit made its name during World War II for its imaginative and excellently designed government-sponsored cartoon propaganda and informational films, some 70 of which were produced between 1941 and 1945. They injected both wit and distinctive design into such forbidding subjects as saving scrap metal, turning them into a ballet of movement with the constant collaboration of two celebrated composers, Francis Chagrin and Matyas Seiber. Highly technical instructional films, for example, *Handling Ships* and the postwar *Water for Firefighting* and *Submarine Control*, extended their range and proved their capacity to match clarity of exposition with design in technological subjects. This was especially notable in the extensive series of informational films sponsored by British Petroleum on oil exploration and technology, such as *Moving Spirit*.

In the 1950s, Halas and Batchelor were able to expand their work yet further, producing films on purely artistic subjects, such as their *Poet and Painter* series (working with such artists as Henry Moore, Ronald Searle, and Mervyn Peake). The climax of this came with the feature cartoon version of George Orwell's *Animal Farm*, Britain's first full-length animated entertainment film. By now their London-based studio had become one of the largest in Western Europe, and the unit was capable of attracting international talent from Europe and America to supplement the work of such long-term resident animators as Harold Whitaker, Bob Privett, Digby Turpin, Vic Bevis, Tony Guy, and Brian Borthwick. The Canadian, Gerry Potterton, and the American, Philip Stapp, for example, directed their brilliant film on alcoholism, *To Your Health*, sponsored by the World Health Organization. Jack King supervised editing and sound, and supplemented the composition of innumerable original music scores by Chagrin, Seiber, and others with his own witty and tuneful compositions. The unit had from its start been distinguished for its sponsorship of fine scores; apart from Chagrin and Seiber (between them responsible for some 250 original compositions), contributing composers have included Benjamin Fraenkel, Tristram Cary, and John Dankworth.

Animal Farm, still perhaps the best-known internationally of Halas and Batchelor films, was sponsored in 1952 by the American producer, Louis de Rochemont; Orwell's fatalistic fable had been published in 1945. In a period when almost all cartoon films featuring animal characters were cutely comic, Orwell's novel demanded a serious approach to animal characterization. The 1,800 background drawings involved represented in somewhat stylized form a realistic farm setting, while the animals themselves were strongly developed as serious dramatic characters. Seiber wrote a powerful score, orchestrated for 36 instruments, and all the animals were voiced by a single, highly versatile actor, Maurice Denham. A controversial point was the provision of a somewhat uplifting end, in which it seemed the oppressed animals might be led to revolt against the police state established by the pigs, in place of Orwell's wholly negative view of a society irrevocably lost to any hope of democratic revival.

The economics of animation have always been precarious, and Halas and Batchelor primarily supported their unit by the mass production of commercials for television, the production of sponsored public relations films, films made in association with other production companies, and by sponsored entertainment series undertaken for television, such as the *Foo-Foo* cartoon series and the *Snip and Snap* series. The latter introduced paper sculpture animals, and both series, made in association with ABC-TV, enjoyed worldwide distribution.

Experimental work as early as the 1950s included stereoscopy (work with Norman McLaren for the 1951 Festival of Britain, and *The Owl and the Pussycat*); and advanced forms of film puppetry, with Alan Crock, in *The Figurehead*; work in New York (1953–54) for the original three-projection form of Cinerama; cooperation with the Czech stage presentation, *Living Screen*, combining the multi-projection of film in close synchronization with the live player on the stage; and the production from 1960 of some 200 8mm cassettes to illustrate through brief animation loops points in scientific and technological instruction linked directly to the textbook. Other subjects the studio pioneered were the first animated film version of a Gilbert and Sullivan opera, *Ruddigore*, *The Tales of Hoffnung*, a series co-sponsored with BBC-TV, and two animated series of language teaching films in Russian and French.

John Halas's interest in advanced forms of animation technology took him into computer animation in the early period of its development in the 1960s. The computer, once mastered as an ally, can cut costs as well as increase limitlessly the artistic propensities of the filmmaker. Halas's first production using the computer was a series of films on mathematics made in 1967; he originated his own computer language: HALAB. His later interests have included the investigation of hologram and laser techniques.

Looking back over the studio's 50 years' existence and its wide variety of prize-winning productions exemplifying many styles, from hand-drawn animation to computerized graphics, certain titles among others stand out as examples of their kind in the period of their production. For education, propaganda, and public relations: *Dustbin Parade*, *Fly about the House*, *As Old as the Hills*, *Down a Long Way*, *To Your Health*, *Wonder of Wool*, and *The Colombo Plan*; and as artistic works for entertainment: *Magic Canvas*, the *Poet and Painter* series, *The Owl and the Pussycat*, *The Figurehead*, *Animal Farm*, *History of the Cinema*, the *Snip and Snap* series, *Automania 2000* (the unit's record prize-winner), *The Tales of Hoffnung*, *Ruddigore*, *The Question*, *Butterfly Ball*, *Autobahn*, and *Dream Doll*. John Halas and Joy Batchelor will inevitably be linked with the history of the fuller development of international animation.

—Roger Manvell

HALL, Conrad

Cinematographer. **Nationality:** American. **Born:** Papeete, Tahiti, 1926; son of the writer James Norman Hall. **Education:** Studied journalism and film (under Slavko Vorkapich), University of Southern California, Los Angeles, graduated 1949. **Career:** 1949—founder, with Jack C. Couffer and Marvin R. Weinstein, Canyon Films to make advertising films and documentaries; also marketed Arriflex cameras; co-founder, Association of Film Craftsmen; 1956—first film as cinematographer, *Edge of Fury*; TV work includes series *Stoney Burke* and *The Outer Limits*, 1963; mid-1970s—formed Wexler-Hall Inc., with Haskell Wexler, to make commercials. **Awards:**

Conrad Hall

Academy Award, for *Butch Cassidy and the Sundance Kid*, 1969; British Academy Award, for *Butch Cassidy and the Sundance Kid*, 1970; Outstanding Achievement Award, American Society of Cinematographers, for *Tequila Sunrise*, 1988; Cognac Festival du Film Policier (France), award for Best Cinematography for *Jennifer 8*, 1993; Lifetime Achievement Award, American Society of Cinematographers, 1994; Camerimage Bronze Frog Award for *Searching for Bobby Fisher*, 1994; Camerimage Lifetime Achievement Award, 1995; National Society of Film Critics Award for Best Cinematography, for *American Beauty*, 1999; Academy Award and British Academy Award for Best Cinematography, for *American Beauty*, 2000.

Films as Cameraman:

1949   *Sea Theme* (co, + co-d, co-sc, co-ed—short)
1956   *Running Target* (*My Brother Down There*) (Weinstein) (uncredited, + co-sc)
1960   *The Adventure of Huckleberry Finn* (Curtiz); *Private Property* (Stevens); *The Gambler Wore a Gun* (Cahn)
1962   *Mutiny on the Bounty* (Milestone); *Pressure Point* (Cornfield)

Films as Cinematographer:

1956   *Edge of Fury* (Lerner and Gurney)
1965   *Fargo* (*The Wild Seed*) (Hutton); *Morituri* (*Saboteur Code Name "Morituri"*) (Wicki); *Incubus* (Stevens)

1966   *Harper* (*The Moving Target*) (Smight); *The Professionals* (R. Brooks)
1967   *Rogue's Gallery* (Horn); *Divorce American Style* (Yorkin); *Cool Hand Luke* (Rosenberg); *In Cold Blood* (R. Brooks)
1968   *Hell in the Pacific* (Boorman)
1969   *Butch Cassidy and the Sundance Kid* (Hill); *The Happy Ending* (R. Brooks); *Tell Them Willie Boy Is Here* (Polonsky)
1972   *Fat City* (Huston)
1973   *Electra Glide in Blue* (Guercio); *Catch My Soul* (McGoohan)
1974   *The Day of the Locust* (Schlesinger); *Smile* (Ritchie)
1975   *It Happened One Christmas* (Wrye)
1976   *Marathon Man* (Schlesinger)
1979   *The Rose* (Rydell) (co)
1987   *Black Widow* (Rafelson)
1988   *Tequila Sunrise* (Towne)
1991   *Class Action* (Apted)
1992   *Jennifer 8* (Robinson)
1993   *Searching for Bobby Fischer* (*Indecent Moves*) (Zaillian)
1994   *Love Affair* (Glenn Gordon Caron)
1998   *Without Limits* (Towne); *A Civil Action* (Zaillian)
1999   **American Beauty** (Mendes); *Sleepy Hollow* (Burton) (ph New York only)

Publications

By HALL: articles—

Film Quarterly (Berkeley, California), Spring 1971.
Dialogue on Film (Beverly Hills, California), October 1973.
Filmmakers Newsletter (Ward Hill, Massachusetts), November 1973.
"Photographing *The Day of the Locust*," in *American Cinematographer* (Hollywood), June 1975.
Millimeter (New York), July/August 1975.
Modern Photography (Cincinnati, Ohio), February and March 1976.
"The Cinematographer and the Theatre Feature Film," in *American Cinematographer* (Hollywood), August 1976.
In *The Art of the Cinematographer*, by Leonard Maltin, New York, 1978.
In *Masters of Light: Conversations with Contemporary Cinematographers*, by Dennis Schaefer and Larry Salvato, Berkeley, California, 1984.
American Cinematographer (Hollywood), January 1989.

On HALL: articles—

Lightman, Herb A., on *The Professionals* in *American Cinematographer* (Hollywood), February 1967.
On *Butch Cassidy and the Sundance Kid* in *American Cinematographer* (Hollywood), May 1970.
Film Comment (New York), Summer 1972.
Films and Filming (London), July 1972.
Ritchie, M., on *Smile* in *American Cinematographer* (Hollywood), October 1975.
Wilson, A., in *American Cinematographer* (Hollywood), October 1975.
Focus on Film (London), no. 13, 1973.
Cook, B., "Commercials: Another Kind of Filmmaking," in *American Film* (Washington, D.C.), October 1977.

McGilligan, P., in *Take One* (Montreal), no. 2, 1978.
Film Comment (New York), March/April 1987.
American Cinematographer (Hollywood), vol. 75, February 1994.
American Cinematographer (Hollywood), vol. 77, November 1996.
Ansen, David, "What 'American' Dream," in *Newsweek* (New York), 4 October 1999.
Daly, Steve, "Filmography," in *Entertainment Weekly* (New York), 8 October 1999.

*   *   *

When Conrad Hall returned to features in 1987 with Rafelson's *Black Widow*, after a self-imposed hiatus during which he established a production company with Haskell Wexler to make commercials, he was asked whether much had changed in the interim. "There are a few new time-saving innovations, but that's about it," he replied. "The real change is in the audience and the way the studios perceive it. Everything is geared toward people in their mid-twenties, and the prime ingredient in today's movies is violence. That puts me on the outside. I believe in the power of film to do good in the broadest sense of what that implies." The remark is particularly revealing, as is his citing of Boorman (*Hell in the Pacific*) and Richard Brooks (*The Professionals*, *In Cold Blood*, and *The Happy Ending*) as the directors with whom he has most enjoyed working.

Hall is clearly drawn towards directors with something to say— one might also cite Rosenberg (*Cool Hand Luke*), Polonsky (*Tell Them Willie Boy Is Here*), Huston (*Fat City*), Ritchie (*Smile*), and Schlesinger (*The Day of the Locust* and *Marathon Man*)—and it is altogether typical that the chief reason that he went into commercials was to buy himself time and freedom enough to be able to pursue screenwriting as a route into feature direction. In particular he hoped to be able to write and direct a film of Faulkner's "The Wild Palms," a long-cherished project still to see the light of day. As he himself put it "the sixties were very much alive, and I had given nothing to the new sensibilities and the new freedoms that were being staked out. I never threw a brick, I never marched, I never held a flower. I was getting better pictures, making more money, and having a wonderful time, while everyone else was struggling to change society. So, I thought, I'll stop my instrument. I went into retirement to write and to find films to direct that would influence society in a positive way." This is surely a trifle over-modest. As David Engelbach points out in *Millimeter*, "in the two years following *In Cold Blood*, Hall shot Stuart Rosenberg's best film *Cool Hand Luke* and John Boorman's strangely stylized adventure *Hell in the Pacific*. It was a period of genuine creative growth for American films and Hall was in the center of it. New directors had come along anxious to make critical, imaginative statements and eager to use the medium more imaginatively. During this period, every other interesting movie seemed to be shot by Conrad Hall."

For all his interest in using film as a social medium, Hall is not a cinematographer who tries to put a personal signature on all his films. As he once said "I don't think I have a style. I know I don't want one." Somewhat self-effacingly, Hall chooses the style to suit the material, as Engelbach suggests: "from the slick romanticism of *The Day of the Locust* to the hard-bitten realism of John Huston's *Fat City*, he has managed to portray and illuminate, through the visual atmosphere he imparts to a film, the psychological and emotional content of the material which often lies beneath the surface of the written script." If one is looking for stylistic signatures it is certainly possible to detect a preference for widescreen formats, and a gradual move away from the saturated colors which distinguish, for example, *The Professionals* and *Harper*. Or there is the more critical line adopted by *Take One* in its 1979 survey of contemporary cinematographers, which argued that "his work can be too immaculate, and his calculated artiness has helped to embalm such pictures as *In Cold Blood* and *Butch Cassidy*. At worst, there is too much sharpness in his imagery, too much deliberation, not enough involvement."

On the other hand, Hall's films can be taken separately and admired for their individual beauties—the soft pastels of *Smile*, the flashlight murder in *In Cold Blood*, or the rich tones of *Butch Cassidy*, which have been described by one critic as "alternately lyrical and foreboding." Equally sumptuous was *Day of the Locust*, which Hall describes as "a golden picture. I thought that this was a story that involved everything that was golden, not only the times but the money, the sunsets, the era and the idea of the moth drawn to the flame," that is, the losers lured towards destruction by their romantic dreams of fame and fortune. Rather than concentrate on the meagerness of the characters' actual lives Schlesinger and Hall decided that the look of the film should evoke their fantasies. As Hall himself explains: "Karen Black's character, when she's thinking about movies, always sees the glamorous aspect of it and always sees herself in it even though her life is nothing. So the visual approach was one that coincided with her dreams to make it more palatable for the audience. To me the best way to tell that story is to match the despair of it. But then again, if you did it that way, you'd have to somehow make despair palatable at the box office. I think that's possible." Possible or not, this is what Huston and Hall tried to do with *Fat City*, and what he also achieved with the environmental drama, *A Civil Action*. Talking about *Fat City*, Hall put it: "photographically speaking, I tried to make it real. I tried to make it the way it is. I tried not to make it look like a motion picture; I tried to make it look like a social study of down-and-out people rather than a slick way of looking at down-and-out people. I didn't want to beautify it in any way that would make it seem attractive. I made it abrasive; I tried to make the photography abrasive just as their lives were." Hall deliberately goes for an anonymous look to match the anonymity of the characters' lives, simply following the action as opposed to obviously adding anything to it. "If I could've hid the camera, it's what I would have done," adds Hall, a remarkable and revealing statement for one of Hollywood's top cameramen.

The look that Hall managed to create in *American Beauty* is another example of this idea. In a film narrated by a dead man telling the story of the events leading up to his death, the camera is of necessity hidden behind the point of view of the narrator; the integrity of the narrative depends on the integrity of the images through which it is expressed. Hall captures the superficial lives of the protagonists, emphasizing the garishness of the decorations in unsold houses, for example, or the unreal cleanliness of the expensive fabric on a sofa. Such attention to surfaces is contrasted with the strange beauty captured in the grainy video image of a plastic bag swirling in the wind. Hall won an Oscar for the cinematography in *American Beauty*, but his experience behind the camera also proved invaluable to first-time film director, Sam Mendes, who with characteristic openness, regularly asked him for advice on the practicalities of shooting a particular scene.

Hall elaborates in the 90-minute American Film Institute documentary *Visions of Light: The Art of Cinematography* on how his dogged pursuit of "the happy accident, the magic moment" has helped shape his 50-year career, and produced some of film history's most memorable images. His status as a cinematographer was officially recognized in 1994 when the American Society of Cinematographers honored him with its Lifetime Achievement Award.

—Julian Petley, updated by Denise Delorey,
further updated by Chris Routledge

HALLER, Ernest

Cinematographer. **Nationality:** American. **Born:** Los Angeles, California, 31 May 1896. **Career:** Worked as a bank clerk; 1914—actor for Biograph, then became cameraman in 1915; 1920—first film as cinematographer, *Love Is Everything*; 1925–51—worked mainly for First National (Warner Brothers), then freelance. **Awards:** Academy Award for *Gone with the Wind*, 1939. **Died:** In an automobile accident, 1970.

Films as Cinematographer:

1920 *Love Is Everything* (Bennett); *Neglected Wives* (B. King); *Yes or No* (Neill); *The Discarded Woman* (B. King); *Trumpet Island* (Terriss); *The Inner Voice* (Neill); *Dead Men Tell No Tales* (Terriss); *The Common Sin* (*For Your Daughter's Sake*) (B. King)

1921 *The Gilded Lily* (Leonard); *Such a Little Queen* (Fawcett); *Salvation Nell* (Webb); *Wife against Wife* (Bennett); *The Road to Arcady* (B. King); *The Iron Trail* (Neill)

1923 *The Ne'er-Do-Well* (Green); *Homeward Bound* (R. Ince); *Woman-Proof* (Green)

1924 *Pied Piper Malone* (Green); *Rough Ridin'* (Thorpe); *Empty Hearts* (Santell); *Three Keys* (Le Saint); *Parisian Nights* (Santell)

1925 *Any Woman* (H. King) (co); *High and Handsome* (*Winning His Stripes*) (Garson); *The New Commandment* (Higgin); *Bluebeard's Seven Wives* (Santell)

1926 *The Reckless Lady* (Higgin); *The Dancer of Paris* (Santell); *The Wilderness Woman* (Higgin); *Stacked Cards* (Eddy); *The Great Deception* (Higgin); *Hair Trigger Baxter* (Nelson); *The Prince of Tempters* (Mendes)

1927 *Convoy* (Boyle); *Broadway Nights* (Boyle); *Dance Music* (Halperin); *For the Love of Mike* (Capra); *French Dressing* (*Lessons for Wives*) (Dwan)

1928 *The Whip Woman* (Boyle); *Mad Hour* (Boyle); *Harold Teen* (LeRoy); *Wheel of Chance* (Santell); *Out of the Ruins* (Dillon); *Naughty Baby* (*Reckless Rosie*) (LeRoy)

1929 *Weary River* (Lloyd); *The House of Horror* (Christensen); *Drag* (*Parasites*) (Lloyd); *The Girl in the Glass Cage* (Dawson); *Dark Streets* (Lloyd); *Young Nowheres* (Lloyd); *Wedding Rings* (Beaudine)

1930 *Son of the Gods* (Lloyd); *A Notorious Affair* (Bacon); *The Dawn Patrol* (Hawks); *One Night at Susie's* (Dillon); *Sunny* (Seiter); *The Lash* (*Adios*) (Lloyd)

1931 *Millie* (Dillon); *Ten Cents a Dance* (L. Barrymore); *The Finger Points* (Dillon); *Chances* (Dwan); *I Like Your Nerve* (McGann); *Honor of the Family* (Bacon); *24 Hours* (*The Hours Between*) (Gering); *Compromised* (*We Three*) (Adolfi); *Girls about Town* (Cukor); *Blonde Crazy* (*Larceny Lane*) (Del Ruth)

1932 *The Woman from Monte Carlo* (Curtiz); *The Rich Are Always with Us* (Green); *Night after Night* (Mayo); *The Crash* (Dieterle); *Scarlet Dawn* (Dieterle)

1933 *King of the Jungle* (Marcin and Humberstone); *International House* (Sutherland); *The Emperor Jones* (Murphy); *Murders in the Zoo* (Sutherland); *The House on 56th Street* (Florey)

1934 *Easy to Love* (Keighley); *Journal of a Crime* (Keighley); *The Key* (Curtiz); *Merry Wives of Reno* (Humberstone); *Desirable* (Mayo); *British Agent* (Curtiz); *The Firebird* (Dieterle)

1935 *Age of Indiscretion* (Ludwig); *Mary Jane's Pa* (*Wanderlust*) (Keighley); *Captain Blood* (Curtiz); *Dangerous* (Green)

1936 *The Voice of Bugle Ann* (Thorpe); *Petticoat Fever* (Fitzmaurice); *Public Enemy's Wife* (*G-Man's Wife*) (Grinde); *Mountain Justice* (Curtiz); *The Captain's Kid* (Grinde); *The Great O'Malley* (Dieterle)

1937 *Call It a Day* (Mayo); *That Certain Woman* (Goulding); *The Great Garrick* (Whale)

1938 *Jezebel* (Wyler); *Four's a Crowd* (Curtiz); *Four Daughters* (Curtiz); *Brother Rat* (Keighley)

1939 *Dark Victory* (Goulding); *The Roaring Twenties* (Walsh); **Gone with the Wind** (Fleming); *Invisible Stripes* (Bacon)

1940 *It All Came True* (Seiler); *All This, and Heaven Too* (Litvak); *No Time for Comedy* (Keighley)

1941 *Honeymoon for Three* (Bacon); *Footsteps in the Dark* (Bacon); *Manpower* (Walsh); *The Bride Came C.O.D.* (Keighley); *Blues in the Night* (Litvak); *The Gay Parisian* (*Gaité Parisienne*) (Negulesco—short); *Spanish Fiesta* (*Capriccio Espagnol*) (Negulesco—short) (co)

1942 *In This Our Life* (Huston); *George Washington Slept Here* (Keighley)

1943 *Princess O'Rourke* (Krasna); *A Present with a Future* (V. Sherman—short)

1944 *Mrs. Skeffington* (V. Sherman); *The Doughgirls* (Kern)

1945 *Rhapsody in Blue* (Rapper) (co); **Mildred Pierce** (Curtiz); *Saratoga Trunk* (Wood)

1946 *Devotion* (Bernhardt); *A Stolen Life* (Bernhardt); *The Verdict* (Siegel); *Humoresque* (Negulesco); *Deception* (Rapper)

1947 *The Unfaithful* (V. Sherman)

1948 *My Girl Tisa* (Nugent); *Winter Meeting* (Windust)

1949 *My Dream Is Yours* (Curtiz) (co); *Always Leave Them Laughing* (Del Ruth); *Chain Lightning* (Heisler)

1950 *The Flame and the Arrow* (Tourneur); *Dallas* (Heisler)

1951 *Jim Thorpe—All American* (*Man of Bronze*) (Curtiz); *On Moonlight Bay* (Del Ruth); *Pictura: An Adventure in Art* (Dupont and others—compilation) (linking ph)

1952 *Monsoon* (Amateau); *Jhansi ri-rani* (*The Tiger and the Flame*) (Modi)

1954 *Carnival Story* (*Circus of Love*) (Neumann)

1955 *Magic Fire* (Dieterle); **Rebel without a Cause** (Ray)

1956 *The Come-On* (Birdwell); *Dakota Incident* (Foster); *The Cruel Tower* (Landers)

1957 *Men in War* (A. Mann); *The Young Don't Cry* (Werker); *Plunder Road* (Cornfield); *Hall on Devil's Island* (Nyby); *Back from the Dead* (Warren)

1958 *Hell's Five Hours* (Copeland); *God's Little Acre* (A. Mann); *Man of the West* (A. Mann); *Speed Crazy* (Hole)

Ernest Haller

1959   *The Miracle* (Rapper); *The Third Voice* (Cornfield)
1960   *Bob and the Pirates* (Gordon); *Why Must I Die?* (*Thirteen
        Steps to Death*) (Del Ruth); *Three Blondes in His Life*
        (Chooluck)
1961   *Chivato* (*Rebellion in Cuba*) (Gannaway); *Armored Com-
        mand* (Haskin); *Married Too Young* (*I Married Too Young*)
        (Moskov); *Fear No More* (Wiesen)
1962   *Pressure Point* (Cornfield); *Whatever Happened to Baby
        Jane?* (Aldrich)
1963   *Lilies of the Field* (Nelson)
1964   *Dead Ringer* (*Dead Image*) (Henreid)
1965   *The Restless Ones* (Ross)

Publications

By HALLER: article—

''The Future Cameraman,'' in *Breaking Into the Movies*, edited by
   Charles Reed Jones, New York, 1927.

On HALLER: articles—

Monthly Film Bulletin (London), November 1969.
Film Comment (New York), Summer 1972.
Focus on Film (London), no. 13, 1973.
Lovell, Glenn, ''*Gone With the Wind* (1998 Re-release of 1.33:1
   Aspect, with Digital Color Enhancements),'' in *Variety* (New
   York), 22 June 1998.

*   *   *

The longtime Hollywood cameraman Ernest Haller is probably
best known for his work on *Gone with the Wind*, for which he earned
his only Oscar. But his five nominations in fact tell more about his
reputation within Hollywood itself. Haller produced quality work for
45 years. He came into his own during the 1950s and was known
within industry circles for his expert location shooting.
   Haller's roots in the film business went back to Hollywood's
origins. After leaving high school, he began in 1914 with Biograph as
an actor, but switched to the camera department the following year.
His first work behind the camera came with an early serial, *The*

Hazards of Helen. He then moved his way up through the on-the-job training system which was then in force, and was credited for his first film as cinematographer in 1920. An Ernest Haller film would then appear every year until 1965.

At Warner Brothers during the early 1930s, work was fast and furious, and Haller helped grind films out at the rate of one every two months. Representative titles included Howard Hawks's *The Dawn Patrol* and Frank Lloyd's *Weary River*. But he worked on every possible genre, and did what he was told. By the late 1930s Ernest Haller had worked his way up to strictly A-budget feature films. He worked with all the major stars on the Warner lot, from Errol Flynn to Humphrey Bogart to James Cagney. If he had a specialty it was photographing the films of Bette Davis and Joan Crawford. Indeed he won an Oscar nomination for Davis's *Jezebel* and Crawford's *Mildred Pierce*. The latter film was one of the pioneering efforts in the early days of *film noir*.

With the coming of age of independent film production in the 1950s, Haller began to freelance like nearly all other cameramen. He formally left Warners in 1951 and worked on some poor films, and also on some of Hollywood's best. In the latter category we certainly must include *Rebel without a Cause*, directed by Nicholas Ray and a pioneering effort in CinemaScope, and *Man of the West* directed by Anthony Mann, a great director of westerns.

Yet despite his long association with Warners and other distinguished work, Haller will always best be remembered for his work behind the camera for *Gone with the Wind*. He was not David O. Selznick's original choice for cinematographer, and he started long after production was well underway, replacing Lee Garmes. Historians note that although Haller receives sole credit for the camerawork on the film (and received the film's Oscar for camerawork), Lee Garmes was responsible for most of the first hour of the picture. Yet certainly the bulk of *Gone with the Wind* is Haller's picture, and will always be noted as the most important color film made in Hollywood prior to the 1950s.

—Douglas Gomery

HAMBLING, Gerry

Editor. **Nationality:** British. **Born:** Gerald Hambling, 1926. **Career:** Began working as assistant to Ralph Kemplen; worked in late 1950s and 1960s on British comedies; worked eight years as editor in advertising, 1968–1976; Member of British Guild of Film Editors and American Cinema Editors Guild. **Awards:** British Academy of Film and Television Arts (BAFTA) Film Award for Best Editing, and British Guild of Editors Award for *Midnight Express*, 1979; British Guild of Editors Award for *Fame*, 1980; BAFTA Film Award for Best Editing, and American Cinema Editors (A.C.E.) Award for *Mississippi Burning*, 1990; BAFTA Film Award for Best Editing for *The Commitments*, 1992; American Cinema Editors Career Achievement Award, 1998.

Films as Editor:

1956   *Dry Rot* (Elvey)
1958   *The Whole Truth* (Guillermin)

1960   *The Bulldog Breed* (Asher); *The Poacher's Daughter* (*Sally's Irish Rogue*) (Pollock)
1961   *The Kitchen* (Hill)
1962   *She'll Have to Go* (*Maid for Murder*) (Asher)
1963   *A Stitch in Time* (Asher)
1965   *The Early Bird* (Asher); *The Intelligence Men* (*Spylarks*) (Asher)
1966   *Press for Time* (Asher); *That Riviera Touch* (Owen)
1967   *The Magnificent Two* (Owen)
1968   *The Adding Machine* (Epstein)
1976   *Bugsy Malone* (Parker)
1978   *Midnight Express* (Parker)
1980   *Fame* (Parker)
1981   *Heartaches* (Shebib)
1982   *Pink Floyd The Wall* (Parker); *Shoot the Moon* (Parker)
1984   *Another Country* (Kanievska); *Birdy* (Parker)
1985   *Invitation to the Wedding* (Brooks)
1986   *Absolute Beginners* (Temple)
1987   *Angel Heart* (Parker); *Leonard Part 6* (Weiland)
1988   *Mississippi Burning* (Parker)
1990   *Come See the Paradise* (Parker)
1991   *The Commitments* (Parker)
1992   *City of Joy* (*La Cité de la joie*) (Joffé)
1993   *In the Name of the Father* (Sheridan)
1994   *The Road to Wellville* (Parker)
1996   *Evita* (Parker); *White Squall* (Scott)
1997   *The Boxer* (Sheridan)
1998   *Talk of Angels* (Hamm)
1999   *Angela's Ashes* (Parker)

Other Films:

1961   *Left Right and Center* (Gilliat) (production designer)
1962   *Freud* (*Freud: The Secret Passion*) (Huston) (dubbing editor)
1963   *The Servant* (Losey) (sound editor)

Publications

On HAMBLING: articles—

O'Toole, Lawrence, Review of *The Commitments*, ''Uncommitted,'' in *Entertainment Weekly*, 15 May 1992.
Young, L.L., ''*Angela's Ashes*: The Novel, the Film, the Moviola,'' in *Cinemeditor* (Los Angeles), Fall 1999.

*   *   *

The film editing career of Gerry Hambling divides into two distinct periods, separated by eight years in which he worked as an editor of television commercials. During the 1950s and 1960s he worked with directors such as Robert Asher, editing archetypal British comedies, and sound editing for such notables as John Huston and Joseph Losey. Since the mid-1970s he has worked extensively with Alan Parker, adding his dynamic style to Parker's glossy visuals to create good-looking, high-impact movies such as *Mississippi*

Burning and *The Name of the Father*. But the real strength of their partnership has been in musical films such as *Bugsy Malone* and *Evita*, where their background in advertising is perhaps most evident.

Hambling began working as assistant to Ralph Kemplen, who eventually helped him through his first solo project in 1956, but it was working with Robert Asher that he had the first real successes of a career that has lasted more than fifty years. He worked with Asher on seven films, notably on the Norman Wisdom vehicles, *The Bulldog Breed*, and *A Stitch in Time*. The films had some success at the time, and are remembered, in the UK at least, with nostalgia for a gentler age, but their simple slapstick humour has limited appeal.

By the late 1960s, the British film industry was in crisis, and many filmmaking personnel, including Hambling, found themselves out of work. Hambling moved into advertising, where he edited commercials. The experience forced him to reconsider his approach to his craft, since commercials rely much more heavily on visual impact and editing to carry their message than film. It was through his work in advertising that Hambling met Alan Parker, with whom he began working in 1971, and whose first feature film, *Bugsy Malone* marks the beginning of the second phase in Hambling's film career. Hambling has edited all of Parker's films, and admires the director for his ability to produce just enough footage for the editor to cover a scene with very little going to waste.

The collaboration with Parker has ranged widely, from the musical *Bugsy Malone*, through the partly animated *Pink Floyd The Wall*, to the grim *Angel Heart* and the strange story of *The Road to Welville*. They have been particularly successful with musicals, Hambling's talent for creating the illusion of movement proving useful where musical performances appear in films such as *The Commitments*, which Lawrence O'Toole called "a great swim for the eyeballs." Perhaps because of their experience in advertising, Parker's slick and striking images combine well with Hambling's intuitive sense of pace and rhythm, for example in the otherwise problematic *Fame*, and in the much trailed, but poorly received *Evita*. Hambling's work on Julian Temple's *Absolute Beginners* is also indicative of his ability to find interest in what was little more than a feature length music video.

Hambling has worked with other directors than Parker, most notably with Jim Sheridan on *In the Name of the Father* and *The Boxer*. With both Parker and Sheridan he has been involved with projects that deal with the political and religious divisions of Northern Ireland, and his eye for narrative structures suits the demands of dark, tense films such as these and *Mississippi Burning*, Parker's film about racism in America's southern states. More recently, Hambling worked with Parker on his adaptation of Frank McCourt's biography, *Angela's Ashes*, a difficult film from a technical point of view in that it required three actors to play the different stages of McCourt's childhood. But the close relationship between Hambling and Parker means that their films are now more like true collaborations than the usual understanding between director and editor.

An unassuming man, who shies away from publicity and self-promotion, Hambling still works on two old-fashioned Moviola editing machines rather than learning new digital techniques. As the human pace of *Angela's Ashes* suggests, Hambling's instinct for what audiences enjoy and understand in the visual structures of a film is practically infallible. In an industry increasingly obsessed with technology and special effects, Hambling, as L.L. Young points out, "is the finest [editing] system money can buy."

—Chris Routledge

HAMLISCH, Marvin

Composer. **Nationality:** American. **Born:** New York, 2 June 1944. **Education:** Attended Queens College, New York. **Family:** Married Terre Blair, 1989. **Career:** 1968—began scoring films. **Awards:** Academy Award, for *The Sting*, 1973, and *The Way We Were*, 1973; Tony Award and Pulitzer Prize, for *A Chorus Line*, 1976.

Films as Composer:

1965 *Ski Party* (Rafkin) (song)
1968 *The Swimmer* (Perry)
1969 *The April Fools* (Simon); *Take the Money and Run* (W. Allen)
1970 *Flap* (*The Last Warrior*) (Reed); *Move* (Rosenberg)
1971 *Bananas* (W. Allen); *Kotch* (Lemmon); *Something Big* (McLaglen)
1972 *The Special London Bridge Special* (Winters); *Fat City* (Huston); *The War Between Men and Women* (Shavelson); *The World's Greatest Athlete* (Scheerer)
1973 *Save the Tiger* (Avildsen); *The Sting* (Hill); *The Way We Were* (Pollack)
1974 *The Prisoner of Second Avenue* (Simon)
1977 *The Spy Who Loved Me* (Gilbert)
1978 *Ice Castles* (Wrye); *Same Time, Next Year* (Mulligan)
1979 *Chapter Two* (Simon); *Starting Over* (Pakula)
1980 *The Absent-Minded Waiter* (Gottlieb); *Ordinary People* (Redford); *Seems Like Old Times* (Sandrich)

Marvin Hamlisch

1981   *The Devil and Max Devlin* (Stern); *The Fan* (Bianchi); *I Ought to Be in Pictures* (Ross); *Pennies from Heaven* (Ross)
1982   *Sophie's Choice* (Pakula)
1983   *Romantic Comedy* (Hiller)
1985   *A Chorus Line* (Attenborough); *D.A.R.Y.L.* (Wincer)
1987   *Shy People* (Konchalovsky); *Three Men and a Baby* (Nimoy)
1988   *Big* (Penny Marshall); *The January Man* (O'Connor); *Little Nikita* (Benjamin)
1989   *The Experts* (Thomas); *Shirley Valentine* (Gilbert); *Troop Beverly Hills* (Kanew)
1991   *Switched at Birth* (Hussein); *Frankie & Johnny* (G. Marshall)
1994   *Seasons of the Heart* (Grant—for TV)
1996   *Fairy Tales on Ice: Alice Through the Looking Glass* (for video); *Open Season* (Wuhl); *The Mirror Has Two Faces* (Streisand)

Publications

By HAMLISCH: article—

Screen International (London), no. 81, April 1977.

On HAMLISCH: articles—

Films and Filming (London), vol. 20, no. 9, June 1974.
Hollywood Reporter, vol. 238, no. 16, 26 September 1975.
Photoplay (New York), vol. 31, no. 6, June 1980.
Soundtrack! (Mechelen), June 1996.

*   *   *

A child prodigy, trained rigorously in classical music, Marvin Hamlisch discovered in his teens that playing piano concerts was not for him. Live performance made him too nervous. Instead, his talent took him in another direction. Hamlisch developed a love for popular music, especially show tunes. A fine ear enabled him to duplicate whatever he heard. ''I had no style of my own,'' he later confessed, ''Whatever I heard, I imitated.'' With his knowledge of music theory (particularly concepts of orchestration) and an affection for popular lyrics, Hamlisch decided on a career in show business.

One could hardly imagine a musician more suited to the composition of film music, a unique craft that demands acquaintance with a wide variety of musical styles, the ability to create simple yet attractive melodies which can be expressed and resolved in short phrases, and a familiarity with the tonalities and colors of different instruments. Film musicians also must be able to compose quickly, drawing on a repertoire of stock themes. Hamlisch proved, in a rather interesting way, that he could do this. After writing songs for such performers as Lesley Gore and Liza Minnelli, he was introduced by the latter to Buster Davis, a vocal arranger who gave him work on a number of Broadway productions, including *Funny Girl* and *Golden Rainbow*. Between assignments Hamlisch worked as a rehearsal pianist for *The Bell Telephone Hour* on television. One evening at a party he met movie producer Sam Spiegel, who was looking for someone to do the music for *The Swimmer* (eventually directed by Frank Perry). Hamlisch went home, wrote the theme music in three days, and got the job. Though not a complicated score, this music shows Hamlisch at his flexible best; its mournful, vaguely modern yet

expressive harmonies suit the failed antiromanticism of John Cheever's deranged hero and his impossible quest to re-create the past.

In many ways, the scoring done for his next assignment, Woody Allen's *Take the Money and Run*, is Hamlisch's most impressive. This is because Allen's postmodern pastiche offers a series of ironic and subversive comments on all aspects of cinematic traditionalism, including the emotional coloring and commentative functions of film music. Allen allows Hamlisch to foreground the presence of the scoring even as he asks him to poke fun at the traditional repertoire of musical colors. The result is a film that catalogs even as it makes fun of traditional method. To accompany the voice of God narrator, for example, Hamlisch composed an up-tempo, vaguely military theme, orchestrated with percussion, strings, and brass, which overstates its own seriousness. Similarly, romantic motifs, utilizing harp and piano, are too sweet and help send up the film's ironic concern with star-crossed lovers. Most interesting, perhaps, are the various ''action'' motifs Hamlisch creates, including one that's vaguely Jewish, with mazurka rhythms as well as a prominent clarinet and strings playing in a minor key.

No subsequent project, not even Allen's *Bananas*, has drawn on Hamlisch's many talents so extensively and profitably. The rest of his film work, however, is certainly varied and interesting. For George Roy Hill's *The Sting*, Hamlisch used a number of piano rag tunes by composer Scott Joplin to create a ''period'' musical atmosphere (actually the film is set during the Great Depression while Joplin's rags belong to an earlier era, but this historical inaccuracy does not spoil the audience's enjoyment). These compositions are somewhat complex harmonically, which meant that Hamlisch could not abstract short, flexible phrases to use as emotional color in dramatic scenes. Consequently, the Joplin rags are used almost exclusively during transitional passages and during action or montage sequences with no diegetic sound.

The Barbra Streisand/Robert Redford vehicle *The Way We Were*, though a very different project, also brought acclaim, awards, and financial success. The film's schmaltzy title tune, with lyrics by Marilyn and Alan Bergman, was initially rejected by Streisand as too simple musically, but her recording made the charts and won an Oscar for both lyricists and composer. This film is scored in a very traditional fashion with the title theme expressing a romantic emotional coloring associated, first, with the Streisand character and, second, with the film's overall nostalgic point of view. The theme assumes a number of different forms as it comments on moments of dramatic tension and emotion. As in the classic studio melodrama, the musical themes are an integral part of the drama, even though this is in no sense a musical film (Streisand does not ''perform''); hence the notion of a title theme subsequently accorded dramatic prominence is important. Hamlisch's work for the James Bond project *The Spy Who Loved Me* is similar; here his title theme is integrated with the already famous Bond signature theme, but, because the romantic elements of this film are emphasized more than in others of the same series, the lush naughtiness of Hamlisch's ''Nobody Does It Better'' is prominently featured as coloring in the many scenes between Roger Moore and Barbara Bach. Hamlisch's action themes, boldly orchestrated in the Bond film tradition, are also noteworthy.

Most of the other films in which Hamlisch was involved offered him less opportunity for creativity and made slighter demands on his compositional talents. For *Save the Tiger*, he reorchestrated as nondiegetic commentative music a number of 1940s swing tunes, particularly two by Benny Goodman; the effect is interesting, for the reorchestrations inevitably seem richer than their originals, which play diegetically throughout the film. This contrast between the diegetic and the nondiegetic musically embodies the functioning of memory as an idealized reconstruction of bygone pleasures. Trapped by a past he cannot relive, the protagonist is tortured by a nostalgia evoked but not satisfied by his scratchy records. Disappointingly, however, the film's nondiegetic themes play in only a limited number of scenes with no natural sound; hence the contrast between music as event and music as comment is never fully worked out. Employed on some Neil Simon vehicles (*The April Fools*, *The Prisoner of Second Avenue*, and *Chapter Two*), Hamlisch wrote effective "invisible" action scores without dominant themes or motifs. Other projects, such as *Seems Like Old Times*, required little more: a simple, dominant theme which could be orchestrated and colored for comic, action, and romantic scenes alike.

Hamlisch's career declined in the eighties; this was a reflex of new methods of scoring (most particularly, using a medley of already existing popular tunes with ready-made cultural associations or creating such a medley with the object of subsequent recording sales, as in Stigwood's *Saturday Night Fever*). Not all producers, however, have chosen music programs of this kind for their films. Hamlisch was thus able to create effectively unobtrusive background scoring for, among other similar projects, *Shirley Valentine*, *Three Men and a Baby*, and *Big*, three comedy dramas that traditionally benefit from this kind of musical treatment, where the themes are largely "unheard" but often contribute substantially to the creation of mood or meaning in a given scene. *A Chorus Line* offered Hamlisch the chance to adapt a Broadway musical for the screen; if the resulting film was less than successful, this could not be traced to his tasteful, if unflamboyant, rescoring. He has not worked much in the nineties, a period that has been dominated by big-budget action spectaculars that emphasize sound rather than music (e.g., *Terminator II*, *Twister*, *Waterworld*). With his considerable musical talents, Hamlisch, had he been active during the studios' classic period (1930–60) could well have equaled, perhaps surpassed the elaborate, occasionally symphonic work of music directors such as Max Steiner and Bernard Herrmann. In any event, his many credits and workmanlike, sometimes exceptional, scoring establish Hamlisch as the last and perhaps most talented in the line of traditional screen composers.

—R. Barton Palmer

HANNA, William, and Joseph BARBERA

HANNA. Animator. **Nationality:** American. **Born:** Melrose, New Mexico, 14 July, 1910. **Education:** Studied journalism at Compton Junior College in California. **Career:** Engineering/surveying assistant in California, 1929–1930; 1930—head of ink and paint department at Harmon-Ising Studio; 1933–1937—story editor, lyricist and director at Harmon-Ising, first animated film as director, *To Spring*, 1937; 1937—joined MGM's new in-house cartoon unit as director and writer: first animated film as director at MGM: *Blue Monday*, 1938.

BARBERA. Animator. **Nationality:** American. **Born:** New York City, 1911. **Education:** Attended the American Institute of Banking and the Art Students League in New York City, and Pratt Institute in Brooklyn. **Career:** Tax accountant, Irving Trust Bank, 1928–34, and

briefly cel painter and inker at Fleischer Studios; 1934—draftsman and animator at Van Beuren Studios; 1936—animator and storyboard editor at Paul Terry Studios; 1937—animator and story editor at MGM.

1938—Hanna and Barbera began collaborating as an animation team at MGM; 1940—*Puss Gets the Boot*, their first venture, marked the debut of Tom and Jerry; 1955—co-heads of MGM's cartoon unit, and producers of the *Tom and Jerry* series, until MGM closed the department in 1957; 1957—founded Hanna-Barbera Productions: first TV cartoon series, *The Ruff and Reddy Show;* first cinematic cartoon series from Hanna-Barbera Productions, *Loopy de Wolf;* 1959–65—television work includes primetime animated series *The Flintstones*, 1960–66, *Top Cat*, 1961–62; *The Jetsons*, 1962–63; *The Adventures of Jonny Quest*, 1964–65; 1965—daytime cartoon shows; and live-action and animated series and specials; produced film and home video features in full animation, live action or combined; 1967—named copresidents and codirectors of operations for the studio after its sale to Taft Broadcasting Company; 1978—*The Hanna-Barbera Happy Hour;* 1989—studio sold to Great American Broadcasting Company; 1990—collaborated as a producer/director team for the last time on *Jetsons: The Movie;* 1991—named cochairmen and cofounders of Hanna-Barbera Productions after its sale to Turner Broadcasting Company; 1994—made their acting debuts in *The Flintstones*. **Awards:** Tom and Jerry cartoon short subjects which received the Academy Award: *The Yankee Doodle Mouse*, 1943, *Mouse Trouble*, 1944, *Quiet Please!*, 1945, *The Cat Concerto*, 1947, *The Little Orphan*, 1949, *The Two Mouseketeers*, 1952, and *Johann Mouse*, 1953; Emmy Awards. *The Huckleberry Hound Show*, 1959; *Jack and the Beanstalk*, 1966; *The Last of the Curlews*, 1973; *The Runaways*, 1974; *The Gathering*, 1978; *The Smurfs*, 1982, 1983; and *The Last Halloween*, 1992; 1988—National Academy of Televison Arts and Sciences' Governors Award.

MGM Cartoon Shorts as Animation Directors/Writers (all Tom and Jerry, except those noted by *; "comp" indicates footage from earlier Tom and Jerry shorts):

1940	*Gallopin' Gals**; *Officer Pooch**; *Puss Gets the Boot*
1941	*The Goose Goes South**; *The Midnight Snack*; *The Night before Christmas*
1942	*The Bowling Alley-Cat*; *Dog Trouble*; *Fine Feathered Friend*; *Fraidy Cat*; *Puss 'n' Toots*
1943	*Baby Puss*; *The Lonesome Mouse*; *Sufferin' Cats!*; *The Yankee Doodle Mouse*
1944	*The Bodyguard*; *The Million Dollar Cat*; *Mouse Trouble*; *Puttin' on the Dog*; *The Zoot Cat*
1945	*Flirty Birdy*; *The Mouse Comes to Dinner*; *Mouse in Manhattan*; *Quiet Please!*; *Tea for Two*
1946	*The Milky Waif*; *Solid Serenade*; *Springtime for Thomas*; *Trap Happy*
1947	*The Cat Concerto*; *Cat Fishin'*; *Dr. Jekyll And Mr. Mouse*; *The Invisible Mouse*; *A Mouse in the House*; *Part Time Pal*; *Salt Water Tabby*
1948	*Kitty Foiled*; *Mouse Cleaning*; *Old Rockin' Chair Tom*; *Professor Tom*; *The Truce Hurts*
1949	*The Cat and the Mermouse*; *Hatch up Your Troubles*; *Heavenly Puss*; *Jerry's Diary* (comp); *The Little Orphan*; *Love That Pup*; *Polka-Dot Puss*; *Tennis Chumps*

(From left) Joseph Barbera, Gene Kelly, and William Hanna

1950   *Cueball Cat*; *The Framed Cat*; *Jerry and the Lion*; *Little Quacker*; *Safety Second*; *Saturday Evening Puss*; *Texas Tom*; *Tom and Jerry in the Hollywood Bowl*

1951   *Casanova Cat*; *Cat Napping*; *His Mouse Friday*; *Jerry and the Goldfish*; *Jerry's Cousin*; *Nit-Witty Kitty*; *Sleepy-Time Tom*; *Slicked-Up Pup*

1952   *Cruise Cat* (comp); *The Dog House*; *The Duck Doctor*; *Fit to Be Tied*; *The Flying Cat*; *Little Runaway*; *Push-Button Kitty*; *Smitten Kitten* (comp); *Triplet Trouble*; *The Two Mouseketeers*

1953   *Jerry and Jumbo*; *Johann Mouse*; *Just Ducky*; *Life with Tom* (comp); *The Missing Mouse*; *That's My Pup*; *Two Little Indians*

1954   *Baby Butch*; *Downhearted Duckling*; *Hic-Cup Pup*; *Little School Mouse*; *Mice Follies*; *Neapolitan Mouse*; *Pet Peeve*; *Posse Cat*; *Puppy Tale*; *Touché*; *Pussy Cat!*

1955   *Designs On Jerry*; *Good Will o Men** (CinemaScope remake of Hugh Harmon's 1939 cartoon short, *Peace on Earth*); *Mouse for Sale*; *Pecos Pest*; *Pup on a Picnic*; *Smarty Cat* (comp); *Southbound Duckling*; *That's My Mommy*; *Tom And Chérie*

1956   *Barbeque Brawl*; *Blue Cat Blues*; *Busy Buddies*; *Downbeat Bear*; *The Egg And Jerry* (CinemaScope remake of *Hatch Up Your Troubles*); *The Flying Sorceress*; *Give And Take**; *Muscle Beach Tom*; *Scat Cats**

1957   *Feedin' The Kiddie* (CinemaScope remake of *The Little Orphan*); *Mucho Mouse*; *One Droopy Knight**; *Timid Tabby*; *Tom's Photo Finish*; *Tops With Pops* (CinemaScope remake of *Love That Pup*)

1958   *Happy Go Ducky*; *Robin Hoodwinked*; *Royal Cat Nap*; *Tot Watchers*; *The Vanishing Duck*

Other MGM Films:

1938   *Blue Monday* (cartoon short; d—Hanna); *What a Lion!* (cartoon short; d—Hanna)

1945   *Anchors Aweigh* (d—Sidney) (ds—animated sequences)

1946   *Holiday in Mexico* (d—Sidney) (ds—animated sequences)

1949   *Neptune's Daughter* (d—Buzzell) (ds—animated sequences)

1952   *Dangerous When Wet* (d—Walters) (ds—animated sequences)

1956   *Invitation to the Dance* (d—Kelly) (ds—animated sequences)

Cartoon Shorts as Producers and Directors of Animation for Hanna-Barbera Productions (all featuring Loopy de Wolf):

1959   *Little Bo Bopped; Wolf Hounded*
1960   *Creepy Time Pal; The Do-Good Wolf; Here; Kiddie; Life With Loopy; No Biz Like Shoe Biz; Snoopy Loopy; A Tale of a Wolf*
1961   *Catch Meow; Count Down Clown; Child Sock-Cology; Fee Fie Foes; Happy Go Loopy; Kooky Loopy; Loopy's Hare-Do; This Is My Ducky Day; Two-Faced Wolf; Zoo Is Company*
1962   *Bearly Able; Beef for and After; Bungle Uncle; Bunnies Abundant; Chicken Fraca-See; Common Scents; Rancid Ransom; Slippery Slippers; Swash Buckled*
1963   *Bear Up!; Chicken-Hearted Wolf; Crook Who Cried Wolf; Drum-Sticked; A Fallible Fable; Habit Rabbit; Just a Wolf at Heart; Not in Nottingham; Sheep Stealers Anonymous; Whatcha Watchin'; Wolf in Sheep Dog's Clothing*
1964   *Bear Hug; Bear Knuckles; Elephantastic; Habit Troubles; Raggedy Rug; Trouble Bruin*
1965   *Big Mouse-Take; Crow's Fete; Horse Shoo; Pork Chop Fooey*

Feature-Length Theatrical Films:

1964   *Hey There, It's Yogi Bear*
1966   *A Man Called Flintstone*
1968   *Project X* (Castle) (ds—animated sequences)
1972   *Charlotte's Web* (Nichols and Takamoto) (prs)
1979   *C.H.O.M.P.S.* (Chaffey) (pr—Barbera; story—Barbera)
1982   *Heidi's Song* (Taylor) (prs; co-sc—Barbera)
1986   *GoBots: Battle of The Rock Lords* (Patterson)
1990   *Jetsons: The Movie*
1992   *Tom and Jerry: The Movie* (co-scs and creative consultants)
1993   *I Yabba-Dabba Do!; Hollyrock-a-Bye Baby*
1994   *The Flintstones* (Levant) (exec prs; creative consultants and ros)
1995   *Jonny Quest vs. the Cyber Insects* (exec prs)

Publications

By BARBERA: book—

My Life In 'Toons, Atlanta, 1994.

By HANNA and BARBERA: articles—

"The Sultans of Saturday Morning," an interview with G. Catsos, in *Filmfax* (Evanston), November/December 1995.

On HANNA and BARBERA: books—

Sennett, Ted, *The Art Of Hanna-Barbera*, New York, 1989.
Brion, Patrick, *Tom And Jerry: The Definitive Guide To Their Animated Adventures*, New York, 1990.
Cox, Stephen, *The Flintstones: A Modern Stone Age Phenomenon*, Atlanta, 1994.
Duncan, Jody, *The Flintstones: The Official Movie Book*, New York, 1994.

Hanna, William, *A Cast Of Friends*, Dallas, 1996.
Mallory, Michael, *Hanna-Barbera Cartoons*, Southport, 1998.

On BARBERA: articles—

Anton, Glenn, "Joe Barbera Speaks His Mind," in *Animator* (Springfield), Spring 1996.

*   *   *

The names of William Hanna and Joseph Barbera have become synonymous with television animation. From their earliest superstars, Huckleberry Hound and Yogi Bear, to the first prime-time cartoon series, *The Flintstones*, Hanna and Barbera are the biggest names in television animation, developing the largest cartoon mill in the world. The two men have come to represent the crank-'em-out-as-fast-as-you-can theory of television animation. Yet to their credit, Hanna and Barbera's creation of Tom and Jerry, the lovable cat and mouse, earned seven Academy Awards and 14 Oscar nominations. This was no small feat in the annals of theatrical animation.

Hanna and Barbera met at MGM, where both worked separately as animators before becoming involved on a project in 1938. Both men wanted to try their talents at directing, and were given the chance in 1940 on a cartoon about a cat and a mouse, *Puss Gets the Boot*. It was clear from this first cartoon that this was no ordinary cat and mouse, and the film was nominated for an Academy Award. Though the cat was named Jasper and the mouse's working, yet unmentioned, name was Jinx, this cartoon began the careers of Tom and Jerry. The *Tom and Jerry* series was consistently formulaic in content: Tom—frustrated, irate or arrogant—tried to exert his power and superiority over Jerry. Tom, with his blue body, yellow eyes and heavy black eyebrows, was clearly the instigator of the mayhem. Jerry, on the other hand, had a cherubic face, a happy-go-lucky personality, but also a devilish ingenuity that would retaliate against Tom's fury, giving the tabby his comeuppance in equal measure—and a dose more. While true adversaries by nature, Tom and Jerry also conveyed a sense that they needed and cared for one another, and this love-hate relationship endeared them to audiences.

As it worked out, the directing (Hanna) and writing (Barbera) became evenly divided between the two men. Because the series, unlike most cartoons, relied mainly on visual gags rather than witty dialog, it was much harder to keep up its consistency, and many of the early shorts were not always well timed; occasionally, too much effort was spent on ponderous pacing and setup of gags. By 1942, Tex Avery, with his surreal, frantic and irreverent style of humor, had joined MGM and, under his influence, the series achieved a refreshing and successfully artistic momentum, all within the same cat-and-mouse formula. Although Tom and Jerry never spoke a word of dialog (save for an utterance to punctuate a comic scene), their cartoons provided depth of character, valid story lines, brilliant gags, sprightly music, imaginative sound effects and exquisite animation. A great deal of time and thought went into developing personality traits and nuances for each animal. Their faces showed a wide range of expression and reaction to situations (it was Hanna who provided Tom's vocal shrieks of fright or pain), and their bodies appeared to be in a perpetual state of motion. They were *completely* animated characters.

Hanna and Barbera also contributed to the 1945 film, *Anchors Aweigh*. Its star, Gene Kelly, wanted to perform a dance number with a cartoon character. When Walt Disney declined the offer to provide the animation with Mickey Mouse, the job went to Hanna and Barbera, and would showcase MGM's mouse, Jerry (Tom appeared as a servant to Jerry.) To create the illusion of dancing with Jerry, Hanna and Barbera drew a detailed storyboard of the choreography Kelly devised. Kelly performed his part of the number alone, and his filmed dance was then rotoscoped, so Jerry's routine could be animated and synchronized, frame by frame, to Kelly's movements. Finally, the two images were matched within a single shot. The sequence remains a classic. Tom and Jerry were also featured in a 1952 musical, *Dangerous When Wet*, with its aquatic star, Esther Williams.

To keep Tom and Jerry fresh in the postwar era, new supporting characters were added. In *The Milky Waif*, Jerry's impulsive cousin Nibbles (later renamed Tuffy) was introduced. In *Little Quacker*, a raspy-voiced duckling made its debut, and later achieved fame as Yakky Doodle on the Yogi Bear television show. Hanna and Barbera also introduced a bulldog and his son, Butch and Pup (renamed Spike and Tyke afterwards), in *Love That Pup*. They later had their own short-lived series, and were finally metamorphosed into the more successful television characters of Augie Doggy and Doggie Daddy.

Like all the other cartoon studios, by the mid-1950s MGM began to find the cost of creating animation prohibitive, though the final Tom and Jerry cartoons created by Hanna and Barbera in 1955–1956—*That's My Mommy* and *Muscle Beach Tom*—were two of the very best. In 1957, after MGM shut down its cartoon unit, Hanna and Barbera joined the ranks of outstanding animators who went to television and founded Hanna-Barbera Productions. Their first series, *The Ruff and Reddy Show*, was only mildly successful, mainly because it was hindered by being integrated within a live show. In 1958, *The Huckleberry Hound Show*, their first totally animated series, was a huge hit with both adults and children, and it received the Emmy Award for Oustanding Children's Program in 1959. *Huckleberry Hound*'s acclaim spawned other successes such as *Yogi Bear, Quick Draw McGraw*, and the first animated prime-time series, *The Flinstones*. No two men were better prepared to pioneer, revolutionize and set the standards for television cartoon shows than Hanna and Barbera. Their adroit use of limited animation required far fewer individual drawings as a theatrical cartoon, and provided a more economical, less laborious yet very satisfying product. Hanna and Barbera also hired many of their old MGM colleagues and other seasoned professionals who were available after most Hollywood studios ceased making cartoons. And with their own impeccable filmmaking skills and business savvy, Hanna and Barbera dominated TV animation by delivering qualitative programs with audience appeal that were sought by networks and sponsors.

Throughout the 1960s, Hanna-Barbera Productions grew into an entertainment empire, reaping bonus revenues from merchandise licensing and product tie-ins, its own record label—and even its own theme park, Jellystone Park, in Ashland, New Hampshire. This expansion allowed them to experiment further, starting with full-length, animated features such as 1964's *Hey There, It's Yogi Bear*, and more ambitious television projects such as 1966's Emmy-winning *Jack and The Beanstalk*, a dazzling display of animation and live action starring Gene Kelly. During the era of James Bond and the Space Age, Hanna-Barbera focused on animated action-adventure and science-fantasy series, starting with 1964's *The Adventures Of Jonny Quest*, and reaching its zenith with *The Space Ghost* in 1966 and *The Herculoids* the year after, all of which had a comic-book-brought-to-life feel, and were immensely popular. Hanna-Barbera

Productions was sold to Taft Broadcasting in 1967; Hanna and Barbera were retained as copresidents and codirectors of operations.

But at the end of the 1960s, Hanna-Barbera had become a victim of its own success. Increased demand by networks for programming, more grueling schedules, escalating production costs, restrictive budgets, the departure of veteran artists and writers, and the rapidly changing tastes of its TV audience were taking their toll on the animation giant. Hanna-Barbera inevitably turned into a factory where quantity ruled, and creativity and quality suffered: formulas were repeated and, at times, unbearable to watch; characters began to lose individuality; cartoon pace slackened; and the artwork appeared shoddier. Through this phase, Hanna-Barbera prevailed with some hits such as *Scooby Doo, Where Are You?* in 1969, beginning the comedy-mystery-music TV cartoon genre.

In the 1970s, Hanna and Barbera reaffirmed their reputation as gifted storytellers, with highly successful ventures such as the animated feature, *Charlotte's Web* (1973), and Emmy-winning TV specials such as the *Last Of The Curlews* (1972) and the live-action yuletide tale, *The Gathering* (1977). Invariably, Hanna-Barbera was redefining itself as a producer of family entertainment. As for new cartoon shows, Hanna-Barbera not only created fresh characters, but also developed animated series adapted from live-action TV series, movies, comic strips and other sources, as well as reusing their tried-and-true stars in new vehicles. Capitalizing on current trends, and successfully reflecting them in its programs, was a key to Hanna-Barbera's mastery over increasingly fickle viewership.

Throughout the 1970s and 1980s, Hanna-Barbera underwent an impressive global expansion in order to efficiently handle its new theatrical and television productions and their international distribution. Hanna and Barbera also uncovered the possibilities in the new medium of home video, and from 1986–90, they created a series of outstanding animated features for video, *The Greatest Adventure: Stories from the Bible*. After 30 years of significant achievements and contributions to the television arts, the prolific pair were bestowed with the prestigious Governors Award at the 1988 Emmy Ceremonies. In 1989, the studio was acquired by Great American Broadcasting and, in turn, was sold to Turner Broadcasting Company in 1991; Hanna and Barbera stayed as cochairmen and cofounders. In 1990, they collaborated as an animation team for the last time on *Jetsons: The Movie*. In 1994, Hanna and Barbera made their screen debut as cavemen in the film, *The Flinstones*, and served as its co-executive producers. That same year, the industrious duo were named to the board of directors of the Cartoon Network, and also were inducted into the Television Academy Hall of Fame.

The impact Hanna and Barbera have made on the film and broadcasting industries is incalculable. They are visionaries who take their place alongside Walt Disney for daring innovation and reinvention of technique and style that elevates animation to an art form, and elicits the full spectrum of laughter and emotion from audiences universally. But it is television where Hanna and Barbera had their greatest exposure and influence. Though the entertainment value was at times uneven, their successes far outweighed the letdowns. Their triumphs in and over television established a familial connection that spans three generations, where parents and grandparents can relive the fun of old and new Hanna-Barbera cartoon friends—while watching along with their children, who are delighting in them for the first time on television or home video. And the tradition continues.

—Martin A. Gostanian

HARLAN, Russell

Cinematographer. **Nationality:** American. **Born:** Los Angeles, California, 16 September 1903. **Career:** 1924—laboratory assistant at Famous Players-Lasky; 1928–29—brief period as stand-in and stuntman for Gary Cooper; 1950s—much TV work. **Died:** 28 February 1974.

Films as Cinematographer:

1937   *North of the Rio Grande* (Watt); *Rustlers' Valley* (Watt); *Hopalong Rides Again* (Selander); *Texas Trail* (Selman)

1938   *Partners of the Plains* (Selander); *The Frontiersman* (Selander); *Heart of Arizona* (Selander); *Pride of the West* (Selander); *In Old Mexico* (Venturini); *The Mysterious Rider* (Selander)

1939   *Sunset Trail* (Selander); *Law of the Pampas* (Watt); *Silver on the Sage* (Selander); *Heritage of the Desert* (Selander); *The Renegade Trail* (Selander); *The Llano Kid* (Selander); *Range War* (Selander)

1940   *Santa Fe Marshall* (Selander); *Knights of the Range* (Selander); *The Showdown* (Bretherton); *The Light of Western Stars* (Selander); *Hidden Gold* (Selander); *Stagecoach War* (Selander); *Cherokee Strip* (*Fighting Marshall*) (Selander); *Three Men from Texas* (Selander)

1941   *Twilight on the Trail* (Bretherton); *Riders of the Timberline* (Selander); *Outlaws of the Desert* (Bretherton); *Secret of the Wastelands* (Abrahams); *Stick to Your Guns* (Selander); *Doomed Caravan* (Selander); *In Old Colorado* (Bretherton); *Border Vigilantes* (Abrahams); *The Round-Up* (Selander); *Pirates on Horseback* (Selander); *The Parson of Panamint* (McGann); *Wide Open Town* (Selander)

1942   *Tombstone, the Town Too Tough to Die* (McGann); *Leather Burners* (Henabery); *Hoppy Serves a Writ* (Archainbaud); *Undercover Man* (Selander); *Border Patrol* (Selander); *Silver Queen* (Bacon); *American Empire* (*My Son Alone*) (McGann); *Lost Canyon* (Selander)

1943   *Colt Comrades* (Selander); *Buckskin Frontier* (*The Iron Road*) (Selander); *The Kansan* (Archainbaud); *Bar Twenty* (Selander); *False Colors* (Achainbaud); *Riders of the Deadline* (Selander); *Tarzan's Desert Mystery* (Thiele) (co); *The Woman of the Town* (Archainbaud); *Texas Masquerade* (Archainbaud)

1944   *Lumberjack* (Selander); *Forty Thieves* (Selander); *Mystery Man* (Archainbaud)

1945   *A Walk in the Sun* (Milestone)

1947   *Ramrod* (de Toth); **Red River** (Hawks)

1948   *Four Faces West* (*They Passed This Way*) (Green); *Bad Men of Tombstone* (Neumann)

1949   **Gun Crazy** (*Deadly Is the Female*) (Lewis)

1950   *Guilty Bystander* (Lerner); *Tarzan and the Slave Girl* (Sholem); *The Kangaroo Kid* (Selander); *Southside 1–1000* (*Forgery*) (Ingster); *The Man Who Cheated Himself* (Feist)

1951   *The Thing from Another World* (*The Thing*) (Nyby)

1952   *The Big Sky* (Hawks); *The Ring* (Neumann); *Ruby Gentry* (Vidor)

1954   *Riot in Cell Block 11* (Siegel)

1955   *Blackboard Jungle* (Brooks); *The Last Hunt* (Brooks); *Land of the Pharaohs* (Hawks)

1956   *Lust for Life* (Minnelli) (co)

1957   *Witness for the Prosecution* (Wilder); *This Could Be the Night* (Wise); *Something of Value* (Brooks); *King Creole* (Curtiz)

1958   **Rio Bravo** (Hawks); *Run Silent, Run Deep* (Wise)

1959   *Operation Petticoat* (Edwards); *Day of the Outlaw* (de Toth)

1960   *Pollyanna* (Swift); *Hatari!* (Hawks); *Sunrise at Campobello* (Donehue)

1962   *The Spiral Road* (Mulligan); *To Kill a Mockingbird* (Mulligan)

1963   *Man's Favorite Sport?* (Hawks); *A Gathering of Eagles* (Delbert Mann)

1964   *Dear Heart* (Delbert Mann); *Quick, before It Melts* (Delbert Mann)

1965   *The Great Race* (Edwards)

1966   *Hawaii* (Hill); *Tobruk* (Hiller)

1969   *Darling Lili* (Edwards)

Publications

On HARLAN: articles—

Film Comment (New York), vol. 8, no. 2, Summer 1972.
Focus on Film (London) no. 13, 1973.

*   *   *

"This is pretty high on the hog for me," actor Bruce Cabot once commented of his accommodations at the Ritz in London while filming *Diamonds Are Forever*. "Location shooting usually means sitting in a tent outside Tombstone eating a box lunch with Duke Wayne." Likely to have been in the same tent, eating a similar meal, would be Russell Harlan, whose credentials in action cinema were as impeccable as those of Cabot and Wayne.

An ex-stuntman, Harlan began his cinematographic career with B-westerns, working often with veterans like Lloyd Bacon (on *Silver Queen*) and, on *The Parson of Panamint* and *American Empire* with William McGann, once Douglas Fairbanks's cameraman. Few men more frequently photographed Vasquez Rocks and the other desert settings beloved of B-westerns. Harlan, perhaps in reaction, developed a flinty black-and-white photographic style, shadowless and stark, that Lewis Milestone found ideal for *A Walk in the Sun*, his calculatedly unemotional picture of an American platoon trying to survive the last days of the war in Italy.

Two years later, Howard Hawks selected Harlan to shoot the seminal *Red River*, which created a bleak and unromantic picture of the west that had hardly been seen since the days of Thomas Ince and William S. Hart. Hawks was never a director of vistas and, in this, Harlan precisely echoed his vision. The dense, harsh lighting style for *Red River* was carried forward intact into Hawks's claustrophobic science fiction/horror film *The Thing* and then, almost immediately, into *The Big Sky*, a film that introduced a Hawksian intimacy into the spacious world of the pioneer fur trappers.

The Big Sky marked the high point of Harlan's relationship with Hawks. He later shot *Rio Bravo*, but that film is not especially distinguished photographically. He also did some additional shooting on the risible Egyptian epic *Land of the Pharaohs*, and was one of the dozen cameramen and scriptwriters who worked on the African comedy/drama *Hatari!* during the five years Hawks took to finish it. Harlan's best work at this time was with Richard Brooks. *Blackboard Jungle* exploited some of the hard-edged denseness of his work on

The Thing, and he imported the same edgy urban blackness into the color of *The Last Hunt*, a western which, like *The Big Sky*, reduced the drama and tragedy of westward expansion (in this case represented by two rival buffalo hunters) to the dimensions of personal conflict.

For many, Harlan's masterpiece, however, remains *Ruby Gentry*. King Vidor's feverish vision of the developing postwar South created a world where pillared mansions coexist with decaying swamps, raccoon hunting with Cadillacs, high fashion with dungarees. Even crawling through a mist-shrouded Edgar Allan Poe-like swamp to die in Charlton Heston's arms, Jennifer Jones demanded the high-style close-ups to which she'd become accustomed while working for David Selznick. Yet a film that might have been a dime-store mixture of conflicting styles is coherent and consistent, a copybook exercise in screen lighting.

—John Baxter

HARRISON, Joan

Screenwriter and Producer. **Nationality:** British. **Born:** Guildford, Surrey, England, 20 June 1909. **Education:** The Sorbonne, Paris; Oxford University, B.A. **Family:** Married the writer Eric Ambler, 1958. **Career:** Secretary; 1935—began working as Alfred Hitchcock's secretary; 1939—first film as writer for Hitchcock, *The Girl Was Young*; accompanied Hitchcock to the United States; 1944—first film as producer, *Phantom Lady*; 1953–64—producer of the TV series *Alfred Hitchcock Presents*; 1964—cofounder, Tarantula Productions. **Died:** 14 August 1994.

Films as Writer:

1937   *The Girl Was Young* (*Young and Innocent*) (Hitchcock)
1939   *Jamaica Inn* (Hitchcock)
1940   *Rebecca* (Hitchcock); *Foreign Correspondent* (Hitchcock)
1941   *Suspicion* (Hitchcock)
1942   *Saboteur* (Hitchcock)
1944   *Dark Waters* (de Toth)

Films as Producer:

1944   *Phantom Lady* (Siodmak) (+ co-sc)
1945   *Uncle Harry* (*The Strange Affair of Uncle Harry*) (Siodmak)
1946   *Nocturne* (Marin)
1947   *They Won't Believe Me* (Pichel); *Ride the Pink Horse* (Montgomery)
1949   *Once More, My Darling* (Montgomery)
1950   *Your Witness* (*Eye Witness*) (Montgomery); *Circle of Danger* (Tourneur)

Publications

By HARRISON: article—

Studio Review, November 1950.

On HARRISON: articles—

Chaplin (Stockholm), December 1968.
Obituary, in *Los Angeles Times*, section A, 24 August 1994.
Obituary, in *Boston Globe*, 25 August 1994.
Obituary, in *New York Times*, section D, 25 August 1994.
Obituary, in *Washington Post*, section D, 25 August 1994.
Obituary, in *Variety* (New York), 29 August 1994.
Obituary, in *Time*, vol. 144, 5 September 1994.
Current Biography, vol. 55, October 1994.
Obituary, in *Classic Images* (Muscatine), October 1994.

*   *   *

Those who think that there were no women producers in the old Hollywood studio system have perhaps never heard of the remarkable Joan Harrison. A wise woman who always made the most of her opportunities, the young Harrison took a job as secretary to Alfred Hitchcock, a reduction in salary and status from her former position in an advertising department of a London newspaper. (''I am probably the worst secretary Hitch ever had,'' she once told *Modern Screen* magazine.) Working for Hitchcock in the British film industry, she took her opportunity to invade every department, and learned all aspects of the business, so that when her opportunity to become a Hollywood producer came along, she was more than prepared. In

Joan Harrison

her eight years with Hitchcock, she collaborated with him on several of his best screenplays: *Rebecca*, *Foreign Correspondent*, *Suspicion*, and *Saboteur* among them. Ultimately she returned to work with him as the producer of his acclaimed TV series, *Alfred Hitchcock Presents*.

Harrison's mark was made in various types of crime films, particularly those which featured a woman in jeopardy. She had always been interested in criminal cases, and had followed many of England's more colorful examples through the courts of London. (She married the famous spy genre author Eric Ambler.) Her first film away from Hitchcock in Hollywood, as writer and associate producer, was *Dark Waters*, directed by Andre de Toth. It established the Harrison style in that it was a story about a young woman (Merle Oberon) caught in a *Gaslight* situation, being driven mad by a group of false relatives. Harrison's first feature as full producer was the much respected low-budget *film noir Phantom Lady*, directed by Robert Siodmak, starring Ella Raines as a fearless secretary bent on proving her boss did not actually murder his wife. These two excellent small pictures illustrate what would always be true of Harrison's work: she was a totally competent producer capable of making stylish mystery films from the woman's angle. They also illustrate a handicap she was never able to overcome in terms of critical acceptance. Having learned her lessons well from Hitchcock, she seemed forever destined to remain in his shadow. In addition, her solo productions are almost all directed by men like de Toth and Siodmak, who, like Hitchcock, are well-known for a personal vision. Thus, it was not only difficult to identify what might be her touch, but no one seemed willing to try to do so. Perhaps the outstanding thing that can be said for Harrison is that the films she produced were often complimented for "being in the Hitchcock tradition." This meant that she had learned her lessons from the master well, and that she *was* capable of putting that stamp on her movies. All of Harrison's films have these qualities in common: excellent women characters, who are frequently intrepid in their response to danger and death; a low-key, subtle suggestion of violence rather than overt blood and gore; and elegant production values, with handsome sets and modish costumes.

A thoughtful woman who always utilized what she had learned in her experience with Hitchcock, Harrison commented on what made an effective suspense thriller by saying, "There is a difference between violence and action. The two are not synonymous. This is a very important point to consider. Displayed violence, blow-by-blow account violence is irresponsible, unnecessary, and unworthy of creativity. Action, on the other hand, cannot be totally implied or merely suggested. For whodunits, no action is pretty bloody dull. Many persons equate in their minds action and violence. They speak of one when they mean the other. Each is an individual property, and suggested violence is much more interesting. I see no point in plunging a dagger in someone's chest and the viewer watching this unfold. One should see the dagger in the hand of the manipulator and then shift—the horror that results! This way is suspenseful and the audience gets involved."

Although her list of films is small, it displays subtle, tasteful suspense work in well-photographed, stylish films. It is also unique because few women achieved her status. Commenting on her unusual role as Hollywood's top female producer in the 1940s, Harrison remarked, "We women have to work twice as hard to be recognized in our own fields. But today there is more recognition of women's talents than ever before. Those women who want a career can certainly have one." The most obvious thing to say about Harrison's career is that what is remarkable about it is that it exists at all. Her work, however, is of a level of taste and intelligence that qualifies her

as something more than an oddity or a footnote, and certainly has earned her the right to be seen separately from, if not equal to, Alfred Hitchcock.

—Jeanine Basinger

HARRYHAUSEN, Ray

Special Effects Technician and Director. **Nationality:** American. **Born:** Los Angeles, California, 19 June 1920. **Education:** Attended Los Angeles City College. **Military Service:** Served in the Signal Corps during World War II. **Career:** Animator for Puppetoons series for George Pal in early 1940s; 1953—first film as special effects technician, *The Beast from 20,000 Fathoms*; developed model animation process Dynamation; 1955—began partnership with Charles H. Schneer; 1980s—retired. **Awards:** Gordon E. Sawyer Award for Technical Achievement, 1992.

Films as Director and Producer:

(shorts)

1946	*Mother Goose Presents Humpty Dumpty* (*Little Miss Muffet*; *Old Mother Hubbard*; *The Queen of Hearts*; *The Story Book Review*)
1949	*Story of Little Red Riding Hood*; *Mighty Joe Young* (Schoedsack) (asst)
1951	*The Story of Hansel and Gretel* (*Rapunzel*)
1953	*The Story of King Midas*

Films as Special Effects Technician:

1953	*The Beast from 20,000 Fathoms* (Lourié)
1955	*It Came from beneath the Sea* (Gordon); *The Animal World* (Allen)
1956	*Earth vs. the Flying Saucers* (Sears)
1957	*20 Million Miles to Earth* (Juran) (+ co-sc)
1958	*The Seventh Voyage of Sinbad* (Juran) (+ story)
1960	*The Three Worlds of Gulliver* (Sher)
1961	*Mysterious Island* (Endfield)
1963	*Jason and the Argonauts* (Chaffey) (+ assoc pr)
1964	*First Men in the Moon* (Juran)
1966	*One Million Years B.C.* (Chaffey)
1969	*The Valley of Gwangi* (O'Connolly) (+ assoc pr)
1973	*The Golden Voyage of Sinbad* (Hessler) (+ assoc pr)
1977	*Sinbad and the Eye of the Tiger* (Wanamaker) (+ assoc pr)
1981	*Clash of the Titans* (Davis) (+ co-pr)
1986	*The Puppetoon Movie* (Warren)

Film as Actor:

1985	*Spies Like Us* (Landis) (as Dr. Marston)
1994	*Beverly Hills Cop III* (Landis) (as Bar Patron)
1997	*Flesh and Blood* (Newsom) (as himself)
1998	*Mighty Joe Young* (Underwood) (as Gentleman at the Party)

Ray Harryhausen

Publications

By HARRYHAUSEN: book—

Film Fantasy Scrapbook, South Brunswick, New Jersey, 3 vols., 1974–81.

By HARRYHAUSEN: articles—

Kinoscope, vol. 3, no. 1, 1968.
L'Incroyable Cinéma (Salford, Warwickshire), Autumn 1971.
Cinema TV Today (London), 28 July 1973.
Film (London), October 1973.
Cinema Papers (Melbourne), January 1974.
Special Visual Effects, Spring 1974.
Millimeter (New York), April 1974.
Film Review (London), September 1975.
Horror Elite, September 1975.
Film Making, May 1976.
Filmmakers Newsletter (Ward Hill, Massachusetts), September 1977.
Cinefantastique (New York), Fall 1977.

Film Comment (New York), November/December 1977.
Ecran Fantastique (Paris), no. 12, 1980.
Starburst (London), no. 35, 1981.
Ecran Fantastique (Paris), no. 20, 1981.
American Cinematographer (Hollywood), June 1981.
American Film (Washington, D.C.), June 1981.
Cinefex (Riverside, California), July 1981.
Photoplay (London), October 1981.
Positif (Paris), December 1981.
Filmcritica (Rome), April 1982.
Cinema e Cinema (Bologna), January/March 1983.
Movie Maker (Hemel Hempstead, Hertfordshire), September 1983.
Revue du Cinéma (Brussels), May 1992.
Filmfax (Evanston), September-October 1995.

On HARRYHAUSEN: articles—

Midi-Minuit Fantastique (Paris), June 1963.
Cinéma (Paris), no. 113, 1967.
Photon (New York), no. 25, 1974.
Take One (Montreal), vol. 4, no. 8, 1974.

Cinefantastique (New York), Spring 1974.
In *The Saga of Special Effects*, by Ron Fry and Pamela Fourzon, Englewood Cliffs, New Jersey, 1977.
Vampir (Nuremberg), March 1977.
Starburst (London), no. 27, 1980.
Banc-Titre (Paris), January 1980.
Cahiers du Cinéma (Paris), November 1980.
Cinefantastique (New York), Winter 1980.
National Film Theatre Booklet (London), July 1981.
Cinefantastique (New York), Fall 1981.
Films in Review (New York), October 1981.
Cinefantastique (New York), December 1981.
Classic Images (Muscatine, Iowa), January 1984.
Movie Maker (Hemel Hempstead, Hertfordshire), March 1985.
American Cinematographer, vol. 73, 1992.
Entertainment Weekly (New York), 23 September 1994.
Outré (Evanston), vol. 1, no. 4, 1995.
Scarlet Street (Glen Rock), vol. 23, 1996.

* * *

From the 1950s until his retirement in the 1980s, Ray Harryhausen set the standards for stop-motion animation effects in film. Influenced as a child by Willis O'Brien's *King Kong*, Harryhausen contacted O'Brien in the late 1940s and worked with him on *Mighty Joe Young*, finally doing most of the animation for that production. He also worked with George Pal in the Puppetoons series of children's short films.

His big break came when he provided, for a minimal budget, the special effects for *The Beast from 20,000 Fathoms*. The rhedosaurus that attacked an amusement park was impressive, and it established Harryhausen's reputation. Three low-budget, black-and-white science-fiction films followed. In *It Came from beneath the Sea* Harryhausen created a giant octopus with five tentacles that attacked San Francisco and wrapped itself around the Golden Gate bridge; the fluid motion of the octopus and its integration with live-action shots made it a believable fantasy. This film was also Harryhausen's first collaboration with the producer Charles Schneer, a working relationship that lasted for a quarter of a century. Although the second of these films, *Earth vs. the Flying Saucers*, was made primarily to capitalize on the paranoia of the 1950s, Harryhausen's special effects brought some originality to what was otherwise a standard plot and mediocre characterization. In this film Harryhausen was challenged to make interesting an inanimate, virtually featureless, spaceship, and he succeeded in conveying menace while giving almost no views of the aliens. The opening sequence, when a flying saucer swoops down behind a car on a lonely desert highway is a classic example of alien paranoia. The most interesting of the three films is *20 Million Miles to Earth*, in which a Venusian Ymir grows rapidly and menaces the Italian countryside. Like King Kong in many ways, the Ymir is Harryhausen's most sympathetic monster. These early black-and-white films, even with their low budgets, often have a more unified plot and adult point of view than the later family films, which were technically more advanced but episodic. In his last strictly science-fiction film, *First Men in the Moon*, Harryhausen tackled the challenges of widescreen and color to bring H. G. Wells's period novel successfully to the screen. Willis O'Brien had made *The Lost World*, and Harryhausen also created prehistoric creatures for his heroes to battle in *Mysterious Island*, *One Million Years B.C.*, and *The Valley of*

Gwangi. *Gwangi* failed to be the box-office success that its creators expected from its unique combination of cowboys and dinosaurs.

Harryhausen's most popular films have been the "voyage" productions with Gulliver and Sinbad. All of these are episodic narratives with interchangeable plots in which the hero sets sail to aid a beautiful girl, right a wrong, or achieve some personal goal; but each film has outstanding examples of animation—the skeleton fight in *The Seventh Voyage of Sinbad*, the six-armed Kali of *The Golden Voyage of Sinbad*, the Minotaur or troglodyte in *Sinbad and the Eye of the Tiger*. Harryhausen focused on Greek mythology in two films, although mythological elements and figures show up in a number of other productions. With *Jason and the Argonauts* he came closest to capturing the power of myth; in the creaking movements of the statue Talos, in the attack of the harpies, and in Jason's fight with seven skeletons, he captures this sense of awful magic without reducing it to a child's point of view.

No one who works in science-fiction or fantasy films can escape the influence of Ray Harryhausen, and works as diverse as *Flesh Gordon* and *The Empire Strikes Back* draw upon techniques he perfected. Yet Harryhausen, for a number of reasons, has often been seen as a technician rather than as an artist. First, he has worked exclusively in the science-fiction/fantasy genres, an area considered unimportant by many film critics and scholars. Further, his biggest box-office successes have been directed toward children and have avoided the darker sides of fantasy that can enrich and give depth to the genre. Last, episodic scripts, often with banal dialogue and uninspired acting, have detracted from his special effects work. Yet Harryhausen's animation scenes are unique, and long after the weaker parts of the films have faded away, the best of them remain in the viewer's mind to exemplify a special kind of cinema magic.

—Leonard G. Heldreth

HASKIN, Byron

Cinematographer, Director, and Special Effects Photographer. **Nationality:** American. **Born:** Portland, Oregon, 22 April 1899. **Education:** Attended University of California at Berkeley. **Career:** Worked in advertising, and as cartoonist for the *San Francisco News*; 1919—assistant cameraman to Louis J. Selznick; 1927–32—worked in Britain; 1932—returned to the States, joined Warners as special effects photographer; 1937–45—head of special effects department at Warners; television work (as director) includes *Meet McGraw*. **Awards:** Academy Technical Award. **Died:** In California, 16 April 1984.

Films as Cinematographer:

1922   *Hurricane's Pal* (Holubar) (co); *The World's a Stage* (Campbell) (co); *Broken Chains* (Holubar)
1923   *Slander the Woman* (Holubar)
1924   *On Thin Ice* (St. Clair); *Bobbed Hair* (Crosland)
1925   *The Sea Beast* (Webb); *The Golden Cocoon* (Webb); *His Majesty, Bunker Bean* (Beaumont); *Where the Worst Begins* (McDermott)
1926   *Don Juan* (Crosland); *Across the Pacific* (Del Ruth); *Millionaires* (Raymaker); *When a Man Loves* (Crosland)
1927   *Wolf's Clothing* (Del Ruth)

1928   *Caught in the Fog* (Bretherton); *On Trial* (Mayo); *The Singing Fool* (Bacon)
1929   *The Redeeming Sin* (Bretherton); *The Madonna of Avenue A* (Curtiz); *The Glad Rag Doll* (Curtiz)
1930   *Deadline* (Hillyer)
1931   *The Guilty Generation*(Lee)
1934   *As the Earth Turns* (Green)
1935   *Side Streets* (*Woman in Her Thirties*); *Black Fury* (Curtiz); *Personal Maid's Secret* (Collins)
1936   *Colleen* (Green); *I Married a Doctor* (Mayo); *Stage Struck* (Berkeley); *Green Light* (Borzage)

Films as Special Effects Photographer:

1933   *20,000 Years in Sing Sing* (Curtiz)
1935   *A Midsummer's Nights Dream* (Reinhardt and Dieterle)
1937   *The Perfect Specimen* (Curtiz); *Submarine D-1* (Bacon) (co)
1939   *Dodge City* (Curtiz) (co); *Dust Be My Destiny* (Seiler); *The Roaring Twenties* (Walsh) (co); *The Private Lives of Elizabeth and Essex* (Curtiz) (co); *We Are Not Alone* (Goulding) (co); *Invisible Stripes* (Bacon)
1940   *The Fighting 69th* (Keighley) (co); *Brother Orchid* (Bacon) (co); *Castle on the Hudson* (*Years without Days*) (Litvak) (co); *It All Came True* (Seiler) (co); *'Till We Meet Again* (Goulding); *Torrid Zone* (Keighley) (co); *Flight Angels* (Seiler); *All This and Heaven Too* (Litvak) (co); *They Drive by Night* (*The Road to Frisco*) (Walsh) (co); *City for Conquest* (Litvak) (co); *The Sea Hawk* (Curtiz) (co); *Santa Fe Trail* (Curtiz) (co); *Knute Rockne—All American* (*A Modern Hero*); *Virginia City* (Curtiz)
1941   **High Sierra** (Walsh); *Dive Bomber* (Curtiz) (co); *Manpower* (Walsh) (co); *The Sea Wolf* (Curtiz) (co); *The Wagons Roll at Night* (Enright) (co); *The Bride Came C.O.D.* (Keighley) (co)
1942   *Captains of the Clouds*(Curtiz) (co); *In This Our Life* (Huston) (co); *Wings for the Eagle* (Bacon) (co); *Across the Pacific* (Huston) (co)
1943   *Truck Busters* (Eason); *Arsenic and Old Lace* (Capra) (co); *Mission to Moscow* (Curtiz); *Action in the North Atlantic* (Bacon)
1944   *Air Force* (Hawks)

Films as Director:

1927   *Matinee Ladies*; *Irish Hearts*; *Ginsberg the Great* (*The Broadway Kid*); *The Siren*
1947   *I Walk Alone*
1948   *Man Eater of Kumaon*
1949   *Too Late for Tears*
1950   *Treasure Island*; *Warpath*
1951   *Tarzan and the Jungle Queen* (*Tarzan's Peril*); *Silver City* (*High Vermilion*)
1952   *War of the Worlds*
1953   *His Majesty O'Keefe*; *The Naked Jungle*
1954   *Long John Silver*; *Sword of Vengeance* (—for TV); *Ship o' the Doom* (—for TV); *Conquest of Space*
1956   *The Boss*; *The First Texan*
1958   *From the Earth to the Moon*

1959   *Jet Over the Atlantic*; *The Little Savage*
1960   *September Storm*
1961   *Armored Command*
1962   *Captain Sinbad*
1964   *Robinson Crusoe on Mars*
1967   *The Power*

Publications

By HASKIN: book—

Byron Haskin: Interviewed by Joe Adamson, Metuchen, New Jersey, 1984, 1997.

By HASKIN: article—

Cinema Papers (Melbourne), no. 5, March-April 1975.

On HASKIN: articles—

Obituary in *Variety* (New York), 25 April 1984.
Obituary in *Hollywood Reporter*, vol. 281, no. 33, 23 April 1984.
American Cinematographer (Hollywood), vol. 65, no. 6, June 1984.
American Cinematographer (Hollywood), vol. 65, no. 10, October 1984.
Cineforum (Bergamo), vol. 31, no. 304, May 1991.
Nosferatu (San Sebastian), February 1994.
Reid's Film Index (Wyong, New South Wales), no. 24, 1996.

*   *   *

Although probably best known as the director of *War of the Worlds*, Byron Haskin made his greatest contributions to cinema as head of the special effects department at Warner Bros. from 1937 to 1945. He had joined Warners in 1932 as a special effects process photographer after a varied early career which included a stint as a newsreel cameraman for Pathé, and working as an assistant cameraman for Louis J. Selznick; he then progressed through the Metro and Goldwyn studios to become a leading cameraman at Warners, where John Barrymore requested him to work on films such as *Don Juan*, *The Sea Beast*, and *When a Man Loves*. He made his directorial debut in 1927 with the comedy drama *Matinee Ladies*, and shortly thereafter left for London to work for Herbert Wilcox as a production executive; in particular Wilcox wanted his help in introducing multiple-camera sound. Haskin found himself working on unlikely material such as adaptations of Aldwych farces and his recollections of the period suggest that he found English filmmaking methods almost impossibly crude and backward. Not surprisingly, he returned to the United States and to Warners in 1932.

Prior to his 1937 appointment Haskin worked on the special effects for Curtiz's *20,000 Years in Sing Sing* and the Reinhardt/Dieterle *A Midsummer Night's Dream*. As department head he supervised the special effects for virtually every Warner Bros. production for eight years, winning one technical Oscar and several nominations along the way. He worked on numerous films with Michael Curtiz, including *Dodge City*, *The Private Lives of Elizabeth and Essex*, *Virginia City*, *The Sea Hawk*, *The Sea Wolf*, and *Mission to Moscow* (in which he blended miniature trains, full-scale people, and glass shots in order to recreate Hamburg station), and also contributed to several films by Raoul Walsh, such as *The Roaring Twenties*, *They Drive by Night*, *High Sierra*, and *Manpower*. Other notable directors with whom he worked were Edmund Goulding (*We Are Not Alone*, *'Till We Meet Again*), John Huston (*In This Our Life*, *Across the Pacific*), and Frank Capra (*Arsenic and Old Lace*). Ever the innovator, Haskin invented and built a triple background projector which enabled him to film against anything up to a 5.4m screen (as opposed to the usual 1.82m one); meanwhile in Hawks's *Air Force* and Lloyd Bacon's *Action in the North Atlantic* he moved up from the conventional miniatures built on a scale of 1/4 inch to a foot to a one inch scale, abandoning the studio tank and shooting instead in Santa Barbara harbor.

In 1945 Hal Wallis, who had been in charge of production since the early thirties at Warners, left to set up in independent production and Haskin went with him as his production assistant. In 1947 Haskin returned to directing after a 20-year gap with *I Walk Alone*, an atmospheric and moody thriller starring Kirk Douglas, Burt Lancaster, and Wendell Cory. It would be impossible (and unnecessary) to seek out common themes in the films directed by Haskin over the next 20 years, given that he is much more a "*metteur en scène*" than a fully blown "auteur." However, without stretching a point, it is certainly possible to discern a markedly pictorial visual sense and a certain taste for the exotic—witness *Man Eater of Kumaon*, *Tarzan and the Jungle Queen*, *Treasure Island*, *Long John Silver*, *His Majesty O'Keefe*, *September Storm* (which tried to marry CinemaScope and 3-D), *Captain Sinbad*, and, of course, the famous *The Naked Jungle*, in which Charlton Heston's plantation is destroyed by soldier ants before eventually being wiped out in an apocalyptic flood.

This taste for the bizarre and the out-of-the-ordinary finds its fullest expression in Haskin's science-fiction films. In *War of the Worlds* (one of several very successful collaborations with George Pal) he consciously borrowed from Orson Welles's adaptation and transposed the story to a modern American setting in order to make it more frightening to a contemporary American audience. As he put it, the original is set "in the 1890s, out in the country, with vicars and old British gardener characters. The threat to humanity is an antiquated machine looking like a water tank tottering around the coutry on creaky legs, blowing whiffs of smoke and frightening a cast directly out of Agatha Christie." Unfortunately Haskin's latterday Americans are themselves barely credible, but nonetheless the film does conjure the sense of a terrifying and all-pervasive threat to normal daily life, and for the scenes of mass destruction Haskin drew quite consciously on his childhood memories of the 1906 San Francisco earthquake. *Conquest of Space* contains a curiously Oedipal subtext, while *Robinson Crusoe on Mars* remains one of the finest versions of this particular myth, the only problem being the silly title (Haskin wanted to call it *GPI Mars*, GPI standing for "Gravity Pull One.") The film, the director's personal favourite, was shot on the upper slopes of Death Valley with the skies matted in an orange-red colour, and engenders a convincing feeling of loneliness and isolation in a dead and inhospitable landscape. *Conquest of Space* has some impressive special effects but overall it is not a patch on *The Power*, Haskin's last feature film and one of his very best works which has a disturbing ability to communicate "the terror of a man who, step by inevitable step, has his own identity ripped from under him until finally he begins to doubt who the hell he is." Like Hitchcock or Lang, Haskin succeeds in creating here a wholly malign environment where everything mysteriously conspires to threaten the central character. As an evocation of imminent danger and sanity-shattering anomie *The Power* takes some beating and the overall effect is greatly enhanced by Miklos Rozsa's marvellous score which makes most atmospheric use of the cymbalon.

Some of Haskin's finest work in the science-fiction genre is to be found in his contributions to the TV series *The Outer Limits*. He directed six episodes in all, one of which, the Harlan Ellison-scripted *Demon with a Glass Hand*, is one of the high points of the whole series, although the other five are all noteworthy. He was also uncredited associate producer in charge of special effects for the series, and worked as an adviser on the pilot episode of *Star Trek*.

Byron Haskin's contribution to the cinema is probably best summed up by the obituary which appeared in *L'Ecran Fantastique* which stated that "he was not an auteur but a brilliant illustrator with the skills of a peerless technician, one of those self made men who have lifted the American cinema to an incomparable peak of technical achievement which has enabled it to take on subjects which would seem at first sight unrealisable."

—Julian Petley

HAVELOCK-ALLAN, (Sir) Anthony

Producer. **Nationality:** British. **Born:** Anthony James Allan Havelock-Allan (became baronet), in Darlington, England, 28 January 1904. **Education:** Attended Charterhouse school, and schools in Switzerland. **Family:** Married 1) the actress Valerie Hobson, 1939 (divorced 1952); two sons; 2) Maria Theresa Consuela Ruis de Villafranca, 1979. **Career:** 1924–29—artists and recording manager, Brunswick Gramophone Company, London, and Vox, Berlin; stockbroker, advertising representative, London, *Evening Standard;* in charge of entertainment, Ciro's Club London; 1933—entered films as casting director and producer's assistant; then head of production, British Paramount, 1935; 1938–40—producer for Pinebrook and Two Cities Films; 1942—cofounder, with David Lean and Ronald Neame, Cineguild, and producer or executive producer, 1942–47; 1949—formed Constellation Films; 1958—cofounder, British Home Entertainment. **Address:** c/o Lloyds Bank, Berkeley Square, London, W.1, England.

Films as Producer:

1935   *The Price of Wisdom* (Denham); *Key to Harmony* (Walker); *The Village Squire* (Denman); *Gentleman's Agreement* (Pearson); *School for Stars* (Pedelty); *Once a Thief* (Pearson); *Jubilee Widow* (Pearson); *Cross Currents* (Brunel); *The Mad Hatter* (Campbell); *Lucky Days* (Denham); *Checkmate* (Person); *Expert's Opinion* (Campbell)

1936   *Ticket of Leave* (Hankinson); *The Secret Voice* (Pearson); *The Belles of St. Clement's* (Campbell); *Love at Sea* (Brunel); *Two on a Doorstep* (Huntington); *Wednesday's Luck* (Pearson); *Playboy Adventure* (Kellino); *House Broken* (Hankinson); *Murder By Rope* (Pearson); *Grand Finale* (Campbell); *Show Flat* (Mainwaring); *The Scarab Murder Case* (Hankinson)

1937   *Cross My Heart* (Mainwaring); *Holiday's End* (Carstairs); *The Cavalier of the Streets* (French); *Museum Mystery* (Gulliver); *The Fatal Hour* (Pearson); *Night Ride* (Carstairs); *The Last Curtain* (Macdonald); *Mr. Smith Carries On*

Anthony Havelock-Allan

(Laurance); *Missing, Believed Married* (Carstairs); *Lancashire Luck* (Carstairs)

1938 *Incident in Shanghai* (Carstairs); *A Spot of Bother* (Macdonald); *Lightning Conductor* (Elvey); *This Man Is News* (Macdonald)

1939 *The Lambeth Walk* (de Courville); *Stolen Life* (Czinner); *The Silent Battle* (*Continental Express*) (Mason); *This Man in Paris* (Macdonald)

1941 *From the Four Corners* (+ d—doc)

1942 *Unpublished Story* (French) (+ co-sc); *In Which We Serve* (Coward and Lean)

1944 *This Happy Breed* (Lean) (co, + co-sc); *Blithe Spirit* (Lean) (+ co-sc)

1945 ***Brief Encounter*** (Lean) (co, + co-sc)

1946 ***Great Expectations*** (Lean) (co, + co-sc)

1947 *Take My Life* (Neame); *Blanche Fury* (M. Allegret)

1948 *Oliver Twist* (Lean) (co); *The Small Voice* (*Hideout*) (McDonell)

1949 *The Interrupted Journey* (Birt)

1950 *Shadow of the Eagle* (Salkow)

1952 *Never Take No for an Answer* (Cloche and Smart); *Meet Me Tonight* (*Tonight at 8:30*) (Pelissier)

1954 *The Young Lovers* (*Chance Meeting*) (Asquith)

1958 *Orders to Kill* (Asquith) (co)

1962 *The Quare Fellow* (Dreifuss)

1963 *An Evening with the Royal Ballet* (+ co-d)

1966 *Othello* (Burge) (co)

1967 *The Mikado* (Burge) (co)

1968 *Up the Junction* (Collinson) (co); *Romeo and Juliet* (Zeffirelli) (co)

1970 *Ryan's Daughter* (Lean)

Publications

By HAVELOCK-ALLAN: book—

With Noel Coward and David Lean, *Brief Encounter* (screenplay) in *Masterworks of the British Cinema*, London, 1974.

*   *   *

Anthony Havelock-Allan (like Anthony Asquith and John Knatchbull from titled families) decided not to follow the family tradition and pursue a career in the army, but instead with the Brunswick record company during the 1920s. His later job as the manager of cabaret entertainment at Ciro's Club in London led naturally into his first film assignment, to establish Jack Buchanan, then the leading British film star, in the American market.

Once he joined British Paramount as casting director, and later producer, he was destined to become one of the outstanding film producers of the Golden Age of British films. Besides introducing to the public such future stars as George Sanders, Margaret Rutherford, Wendy Hiller, Alistair Sim, and Vivien Leigh, by the early 1940s, he had produced such successful films as *This Man Is News*, *The Lambeth Walk*, *Unpublished Story*, and *This Man in Paris*. His two Noël Coward films, *In Which We Serve* and *This Happy Breed*, resulted in his forming Cineguild with David Lean and Ronald Neame, and he produced several other important British films under its auspices, including two additional Coward works (*Blithe Spirit* and *Brief Encounter*), and two films based on Dickens novels, *Great Expectations* and *Oliver Twist*.

Havelock-Allan has contributed his skill and experience as a producer to international organizations, including MGM, for such films as *Ryan's Daughter*, *Orders to Kill*, *Othello*, and *Romeo and Juliet*.

—John Halas

HAYASAKA, Fumio

Composer. **Nationality:** Japanese. **Born:** Sendai-City, 19 August 1914. **Education:** Attended Hokkai School; studied with Alexander Tcherepnin in Tokyo. **Career:** Organist at Yamahana Catholic Church, Sapporo; English teacher at Kosei and other schools; 1939—joined Toho company as composer; nonfilm music includes a piano concerto and Yukara suite; taught film scoring in a college: students include Masaru Sato and Toru Takemitsu. **Died:** Of tuberculosis, in Tokyo, 15 October 1955.

Films as Composer:

1939   *Ribon o musubu fujin* (*A Lady with a Ribbon*) (Yamamoto)
1940   *Kaigun bakugekitai* (*The Naval Bomber Fleet*) (Kimura); *Nyan-nyan-myan-hoi* (*Festival of Nyan-nyan-myan*) (Akutagawa); *Ina-bushi* (*The Ina Song*) (Kamei); *Kikansha C-57* (*Steam Locomotive C-57*) (Imaizumi); *Moyuru oozora* (*Flaming Sky*) (Abe); *Tabi yakusha* (*Traveling Actors*) (Naruse)
1941   *Shirasagi* (*Snowy Heron*) (Shimazu); *Gubijinso* (*Poppy*) (Nakagawa); *Shido monogatari* (*Instructive Story*) (Kumagai); *Wakai sensei* (*A Young Teacher*) (Sato)
1942   *Midori no daichi* (*The Green Earth*) (Shimazu); *Nankai no hanatabe* (*South Seas Bouquet*) (Abe); *Haha no chizu* (*Mother's Map*) (Shimazu); *Koharu kyogen* (*Koharu's Performance*) (Aoyagi)
1944   *Ano hata o ute* (*Fire the Flag!*) (Abe)
1945   *Nippon kengo-den* (*Great Swordsmen of Japan*) (Takizawa); *Kita no sannin* (*The Three Men of the North*) (Saeki)
1946   *Minshu no teki* (*An Enemy of the People*) (Imai)

1947   *Inochi aru kagiri* (*As Long as We Live*) (Kusuda); *Yottsu no koi no monogatari* (*Four Love Stories*) (Toyoda and others); *Chikagai 24-jikan* (*24 Hours in an Underground Market*) (Imai); *Kakedashi jidai* (*Tenderfoot Days*) (Saeki); *Ai yo hoshi to tomoni* (*Love, Live with the Stars*) (Abe); *Koisuru tsuma* (*A Wife in Love*) (Hagiwara); *Joyu* (*Actress*) (Kinugasa)
1948   *Hana hiraku* (*A Flower Blooms*) (Ichikawa); *Yoidore tenshi* (*Drunken Angel*) (Kurosawa); *Waga ai wa yama no kanata ni* (*My Love Is beyond the Mountain*) (Toyoda); *Ama no yugao* (*Evening Glory of Heaven*) (Abe); *Fuji sancho* (*The Summit of Mount Fuji*) (Saeki); *Ten no yugao* (*Moonflower of Heaven*) (Abe); *Ikiteiru gazo* (*Living Portrait*) (Chiba); *Niji o idaku shojo* (*A Virgin Who Embraces a Rainbow*) (Saeki)
1949   *Haru no tawamure* (*Spring Caprice*) (Yamamoto); *Nozomi naki ni arazu* (*Hope Is Not Dead Yet*) (Saeki); *Tobisuke boken ryoko* (*Tobisuke's Adventures*) (Nakagawa); *Nora inu* (*Stray Dog*) (Kurosawa)
1950   *Akatsuki no dasso* (*Escape at Dawn*) (Taniguchi); *Shikko yuyo* (*Reprieve*) (Saburi); *Shubun* (*Scandal*) (Kurosawa); *Sasame-yuki* (*The Makioka Sisters*) (Abe); **Rashomon** (Kurosawa); *Tsuma to onna kisha* (*Wife and Woman Journalist*) (Chiba); *Yuki Fujin ezu* (*A Picture of Madame Yuki*) (Mizoguchi); *Jodai no chokoku* (*Comical Sculpture*) (Mizuki—short)
1951   *Hakuchi* (*The Idiot*) (Kurosawa); *Nessa no byakuran* (*White Orchid of the Heating Desert*) (Kimura); *Oyu-sama* (*Miss Uyo*) (Mizoguchi); *Sono hito no na wa ienai* (*I Cannot Say That Person's Name*) (Sugie); *Musashino Fujin* (*Lady Musashin*) (Mizoguchi); *Shi no dangai* (*Death Cliff*) (Taniguchi); *Meshi* (*Repast*) (Naruse); *Bakuro ichidai* (*Life of a Horse Dealer*) (Kimura)
1952   *Dokoku* (*Wail*) (Saburi); **Ikiru** (*Living*) (Kurosawa); *Jinsei gekijo* (*Theatre of Life*) (Saburi)
1953   **Ugetsu monogatari** (*Ugetsu*) (Mizoguchi); *Sakai* (*Meeting Again*) (Kimura)
1954   *Hanran* (*Rebellion*) (Saburi); **Sansho dayu** (*Sansho the Bailiff*) (Mizoguchi); **Shichinin no samurai** (*Seven Samurai*) (Kurosawa); *Kimi shinitamau koto nakare* (*You Shouldn't Die*) (Maruyama); *Sen-hime* (*Lady Sen*) (Kimura); *Chikamatsu monogatari* (*A Story from Chikamatsu; Crucified Lovers*) (Mizoguchi); *Mitsuyu-sen* (*Smuggling Ship*) (Sugie)
1955   *Yokihi* (*The Princess Yan Kwei-fei*) (Mizoguchi); *Shin heike monogatari* (*New Tales of the Taira Clan*) (Mizoguchi); *Asunaro monogatari* (*Growing Up*) (Horikawa); *Ikomono no kiroku* (*Record of a Living Being; I Live in Fear*) (Kurosawa) (completed by Sato)

Publications

On HAYASAKA: article—

Chaplin (Stockholm), April-May 1965.

*   *   *

Fumio Hayasaka is among the most respected of Japanese composers. Beginning in the late 1930s he has worked for noted directors including Mikio Naruse, Yasujiro Shimazu, Tadashi Imai, Teinosuke Kinugasa, and Kon Ichikawa. However, he is most famous for his work for Kenji Mizoguchi and Akira Kurosawa.

Combining Japanese traditional instruments with Western instruments, Hayasaka wrote mysterious, stylized scores for Mizoguchi's *Ugetsu, Sansho the Bailiff,* and *A Story from Chikamatsu.* Interested in a wide variety of styles, he nonetheless sought to create a uniquely Japanese style of film music.

His collaboration with Kurosawa began in the late 1940s with *Drunken Angel,* and the two artists soon found each other indispensable. Their association continued in a spirit of mutual appreciation and respect until Hayasaka's death during the production of *Record of a Living Being* in 1955.

Kurosawa and Hayasaka both believed that film music should not always work to enhance the mood or the dramatic highlights of a scene, and that unexpected combinations of music and visual images would create more interesting effects. For instance, the lively spirit of the ''Cuckoo Waltz'' heard from a loudspeaker on a street in the black-market area starkly contrasts with the depressed psychological state of the hero of *Drunken Angel.* In *Stray Dog* the sound of a housewife practising piano is heard during the suspenseful confrontation of the criminal and the detective, and a children's song is heard in the scene of the criminal's arrest.

Hayasaka's bolero music for *Rashomon* is also uniquely effective. This theme music is used as a *leitmotif,* associated with the appearance of certain characters, and contrasts with the styles used in other scenes. Similarly, in *Seven Samurai* Hayasaka created powerful and emotional theme music for the samurai themselves, with more lyrical music used for the scenes of lovers and ominously rhythmical music for the battle scenes. The composer planned each of his scores by meticulously analyzing the structure and the mood of each scene. His constant experimentation, and his search to create a unique effect in each scene, won him wide acclaim.

—Kyoko Hirano

HAYES, John Michael

Writer. **Nationality:** American. **Born:** Worcester, Massachusetts, 11 May 1919. **Education:** Attended Massachusetts State College. **Family:** Married Mildred Hicks. **Career:** Newspaper and radio comedy writer in late 1930s and early 1940s: wrote for Lucille Ball's *My Favorite Husband, Suspense, The Adventures of Sam Spade,* and *Sweeney and March;* 1952—first film as writer, *Red Ball Express;* contract with Universal; 1954–57—writer for Alfred Hitchcock at Paramount: first film, *Rear Window;* 1957–64—writer at 20th Century-Fox, and after 1964 at Avco Embassy (several Harold Robbins adaptations). **Agent:** Ned Brown Agency, West Los Angeles, CA, U.S.A.

Films as Writer:

1952   *Red Ball Express* (Boetticher)
1953   *Thunder Bay* (A. Mann) (co); *Torch Song* (Walters) (co)
1954   *War Arrow* (Sherman); ***Rear Window*** (Hitchcock)
1955   *To Catch a Thief* (Hitchcock); *It's a Dog's Life* (Hoffman)

1956   *The Trouble with Harry* (Hitchcock); *The Man Who Knew Too Much* (Hitchcock) (co)
1957   *Peyton Place* (Robson)
1958   *The Matchmaker* (Anthony)
1959   *But Not for Me* (W. Lang)
1960   *Butterfield 8* (Daniel Mann) (co)
1961   *The Children's Hour* (Wyler)
1964   *The Chalk Garden* (Neame); *The Carpetbaggers* (Dmytryk); *Where Love Has Gone* (Dmytryk)
1965   *Harlow* (Douglas)
1966   *Judith* (Daniel Mann); *Nevada Smith* (Hathaway)
1975   *Nevada Smith* (Douglas)
1988   *Pancho Barnes* (Heffron—for TV)
1994   *Iron Will* (Haid) (co)

Publications

By HAYES: articles—

Film Comment (New York), Winter 1970–71.
In *Blueprint in Babylon,* by J. D. Marshall, Los Angeles, 1978.
Scarlet Street (Glen Rock), vol. 21, Winter 1996.
Scarlet Street (Glen Rock), vol. 22, 1996.

On HAYES: articles—

Carroll, Willard, in *American Screenwriters,* edited by Robert E. Morsberger, Stephen O. Lesser, and Randall Clark, Detroit, 1984.
Postscript (Commerce, Texas), vol. 9, nos. 1–2, Fall/Winter 1989–90.
Creative Screenwriting (Washington), Winter 1997.

*   *   *

Although John Michael Hayes will probably be best remembered for his association with Alfred Hitchcock in the middle 1950s, he also wrote a number of significant literary adaptations of such popular works as *Peyton Place, The Matchmaker, Butterfield 8, The Children's Hour,* and *The Carpetbaggers.* Hayes's total output has been small, but he has chosen his vehicles carefully and his work commands a healthy respect from the critical community as well as the professional film world.

After a brief stint as a radio dramatist on such shows as *Suspense, The Adventures of Sam Spade,* and the Lucille Ball comedy *My Favorite Husband,* Hayes broke into film writing in the early 1950s at Universal Studios scripting action films such as Anthony Mann's *Thunder Bay* and Budd Boetticher's *Red Ball Express* as well as star vehicles such as *Torch Song* for Joan Crawford and *War Arrow* for Jeff Chandler. Hayes's big break, however, came in 1954 when he moved to Paramount and began his partnership with Alfred Hitchcock.

The first movie they worked on was an immediate success and has been hailed as the quintessential Hitchcock film. *Rear Window* was taken from a story by Cornell Woolrich which Hayes expanded much in the same way that Evan Hunter would later extensively enlarge the Daphne du Maurier story of ''The Birds'' into another Hitchcock thriller. Hayes developed a female character Lisa Fremont, played by Grace Kelly, with whom the central character, L. B. Jefferies, played by James Stewart, could spar, and he also added a great deal of verbal byplay among the secondary characters of the nurse and the police-man, also missing in the original short story. The subtle sexual dance between the central figures literally played out against a backdrop of murder and suspense and highlighted many of Hitchcock's traditional themes in a contemporary, sophisticated setting. The multilayered screenplay which interweaves the tension of the murder plot with the indifferent personal relationship between the principals, and plays upon the voyeuristic preoccupations of the audience, is a tour de force of script writing and justly earned Hayes an Academy Award nomination.

Hayes created the same surface slickness, but with a more disarm-ingly romantic tone, in *To Catch a Thief,* his next film with Hitchcock. Partly because the star was Cary Grant rather than James Stewart, the film appears much lighter and more charming than *Rear Window.* Nevertheless, many of the same rather mordant attitudes towards relationships which darken the former film also shade the latter. In both cases the central female character, played to perfection by a stunningly beautiful Grace Kelly, proves to be not only a competent associate, full of pluck and daring, but also an alluring bait for a marriage entrapment the men appear to try to avoid. In both films murder, theft, marriage, and sex jockey for a proper arrangement, allowing the films to be too easily misread only as romantic comedies, the darker undertone carefully and safely hidden by the surface gloss and style. It is to the credit of the screenplay that Hayes was able to interrelate so carefully and skillfully the many tonal and stylistic layers which allow for multiple interpretations.

The next two Hitchcock/Hayes collaborations were neither as successful nor as interesting. *The Trouble with Harry,* a small-town murder/comedy, involved the constantly moving corpse of Harry as the various small-town figures tried to hide their own or others' culpability in Harry's demise. It is a one-joke idea, although still entertaining. The last film Hayes wrote for Hitchcock was a remake of *The Man Who Knew Too Much,* a film now best remembered for the wonderful and suspenseful set pieces, particularly the Albert Hall assassination attempt. In 1957 Hitchcock left Paramount and Hayes went to Twentieth Century-Fox where his only project was writing the script for *Peyton Place.* John Michael Hayes has been much praised for his adaptation of the Grace Metalious novel, bringing order and structure to what many felt was an unfilmable work. In retrospect, however, Hayes's screenplay seems less impressive. The original novel, although far too explicit sexually to be filmed without alterations, especially during the late 1950s, nevertheless was not a formless incoherent mess as many in Hollywood declared. The screen treatment, which became the basis for most of the later *Peyton Place* properties, greatly weakened the power and bite of the initial novel. Most of Grace Metalious's social commentary was smoothed out of recognition and the sharply feminist tone of the work was eliminated altogether. Hayes received another Academy Award nomina-tion for the job, and the film marked him as a writer able to handle sensitive material, especially of a sexual nature, which may account for his assignments on Lillian Hellman's *The Children's Hour,* John O'Hara's *Butterfield 8,* and Enid Bagnold's *The Chalk Garden.*

In the middle 1960s Hayes became an executive at Avco Embassy Pictures and began a series of adaptations of Harold Robbins novels: *The Carpetbaggers, Where Love Has Gone,* and *Nevada Smith.* Since the early 1970s, Hayes has written more for television, most of his screen work having gone unrealized, and he has remained at Avco as an executive. Perhaps, as one critic has remarked, the new Hollywood film does not lean toward the stylish craftsmanship which character-izes Hayes's best work. This may be so, but many observers feel that

his screenplays had been declining in quality since sometime in the late 1950s with the breakup of the Hitchcock partnership. Perhaps John Michael Hayes was one of those collaborative artists who was destined to do his finest work with a single director in a particu-lar period.

—Charles L. P. Silet

HEAD, Edith

Costume Designer. **Nationality:** American. **Born:** Edith Claire Posener in San Bernardino, California, 28 October 1897. **Education:** Attended elementary school in Redding, California to 1911; schools in Los Angeles; University of California, Berkeley; Stanford University; also attended classes at Otis Art Institute and Chouinard Art School, both in Los Angeles. **Family:** Married 1) Charles Head (divorced 1938); 2) the designer Wiard Ihnen, 1940 (died 1979). **Career:** French, Spanish, and art teacher at Bishop School for Girls, La Jolla, California, and at Hollywood School for Girls, 1923; 1924–27—sketch artist; 1927–38—assistant to Travis Banton; 1938–66—head of design, Paramount; then chief designer at Universal until her death; also designed for other studios, for stage shows, and for commercial companies; 1945–52—regular appearances on the radio show *Art Linkletter's House Party* (and on TV, 1952–69); 1949–51—lecturer, University of Southern California, Los Angeles (also in 1973); 1978—designed for the TV mini-series *Little Women.* **Awards:**

Edith Head (left)

Academy Award for *The Heiress*, 1949, *Samson and Delilah*, 1950, *All About Eve*, 1950, *A Place in the Sun*, 1951, *Roman Holiday*, 1953, *Sabrina*, 1954, *The Facts of Life*, 1960, and *The Sting*, 1973. **Died:** In Los Angeles, California, 26 October 1981.

Films as Costume Designer:

1924   *Peter Pan* (Brenon) (co)

1925   *The Golden Bed* (De Mille) (co); *The Wanderer* (Walsh) (co)

1926   *Mantrap* (Fleming)

1927   *Wings* (Wellman)

1929   *The Saturday Night Kid* (Sutherland) (co); *The Virginian* (Fleming); *The Wolf Song* (Fleming)

1930   *Along Came Youth* (Corrigan and McLeod); *Follow the Leader* (Taurog); *Only the Brave* (Tuttle); *The Santa Fe Trail* (Brower and Knopf)

1932   *The Big Broadcast of 1932* (Tuttle); *A Farewell to Arms* (Borzage) (co); *He Learned about Women* (Corrigan); *Hot Saturday* (Seiter); *Love Me Tonight* (Mamoulian); *The Sign of the Cross* (Banton) (co); *Two Kinds of Women* (W. De Mille); *Undercover Man* (Flood); *Wayward* (Sloman)

1933   *A Cradle Song* (Leisen) (co); *Crime of the Century* (Beaudine) (co); **Duck Soup** (McCarey); *Gambling Ship* (Gasnier and Marcin); *Hello, Everybody* (Seiter); *I'm No Angel* (Ruggles) (co); **She Done Him Wrong** (L. Sherman); *Sitting Pretty* (H. Brown); *Strictly Personal* (Murphy); *White Woman* (Walker) (co)

1934   *Ladies Should Listen* (Tuttle); *Little Miss Marker* (Hall); *Many Happy Returns* (McLeod); *The Notorious Sophie Lang* (Murphy) (co); *The Pursuit of Happiness* (Hall); *The Witching Hour* (Hathaway); *You Belong to Me* (Werker)

1935   *The Big Broadcast of 1936* (Taurog); *Car 99* (Barton); *The Crusades* (De Mille) (co); *Father Brown, Detective* (Sedgwick); *Four Hours to Kill* (Leisen); *The Glass Key* (Tuttle); *Here Comes Cookie* (McLeod); *Hold 'em, Yale* (Lanfield); *The Last Outpost* (Barton and Gasnier); *The Lives of a Bengal Lancer* (Hathaway) (co); *Man on the Flying Trapeze* (Bruckman); *Men without Names* (Murphy); *Mississippi* (Sutherland); *People Will Talk* (Santell); *Peter Ibbetson* (Hathaway); *Ruggles of Red Gap* (McCarey) (co); *Stolen Harmony* (Werker); *Two for Tonight* (Tuttle); *Wings in the Dark* (Flood)

1936   *The Accusing Finger* (Hogan); *The Big Broadcast of 1937* (Leisen); *Border Flight* (Lovering); *College Holiday* (Tuttle); *Collegiate* (Murphy); *Hollywood Boulevard* (Florey); *The Jungle Princess* (Thiele); *Lady Be Careful* (Reed); *The Milky Way* (McCarey); *Murder with Pictures* (Barton); *Poppy* (Sutherland); *The Return of Sophie Lang* (Archainbaud); *Rhythm on the Range* (Taurog); *Rose Bowl* (Barton); *The Texas Rangers* (K. Vidor); *Thirteen Hours by Air* (Leisen); *Three Cheers for Love* (McCarey); *Till We Meet Again* (Florey); *Too Many Parents* (McGowan); *Wedding Present* (Wallace); *Wives Never Know* (Nugent) (co); *Woman Trap* (Young)

1937   *Arizona Mahoney* (Hogan); *Artists and Models* (Walsh) (co); *The Barrier* (Selander); *Blonde Trouble* (Archainbaud); *Blossoms on Broadway* (Wallace); *Borderland* (Watt); *Born to the West* (Barton); *Bulldog Drummond Comes Back* (L. King); *Bulldog Drummond Escapes* (Hogan);

Bulldog Drummond's Revenge (L. King); *Clarence* (Archainbaud); *The Crime Nobody Saw* (Barton); *Daughter of Shanghai* (Florey); *A Doctor's Diary* (C. Vidor) (co); *Double or Nothing* (Reed); *Easy Living* (Leisen) (co); *Ebb Tide* (Hogan); *Exclusive* (Hall); *Forlorn River* (Barton); *Girl from Scotland Yard* (Vignola); *The Great Gambini* (C. Vidor); *Her Husband Lies* (Ludwig) (co); *Hideaway Girl* (Archainbaud); *Hills of Old Wyoming* (Watt); *Hold 'em, Navy* (Neumann); *Hopalong Rides Again* (Selander); *Hotel Haywire* (Archainbaud); *Interns Can't Take Money* (Santell); *John Meade's Woman* (Wallace) (co); *King of Gamblers* (Florey); *The Last Train from Madrid* (Hogan); *Let's Make a Million* (McCarey); *Love on Toast* (Dupont); *Make Way for Tomorrow* (McCarey); *Midnight Madonna* (Flood); *Mind Your Own Business* (McLeod); *Mountain Music* (Florey); *Murder Goes to College* (Riesner); *Night Club Scandal* (Murphy); *A Night of Mystery* (Dupont); *North of the Rio Grande* (Watt); *On Such a Night* (Dupont); *Outcast* (Florey); *Partners in Crime* (Murphy); *Partners of the Plains* (Selander); *Rustler's Valley* (Watt); *She Asked for It* (Kenton); *She's No Lady* (C. Vidor); *Sophie Lang Goes West* (Riesner) (co); *Souls at Sea* (Hathaway); *Texas Trail* (Selman); *This Way, Please* (Florey); *Thrill of a Lifetime* (Archainbaud); *Thunder Trail* (Barton); *True Confession* (Ruggles) (co); *Turn Off the Moon* (Seiter); *Waikiki Wedding* (Tuttle); *Wells Fargo* (Lloyd); *Wild Money* (L. King)

1938   *The Arkansas Traveler* (Santell); *Bar 20 Justice* (Selander); *Artists and Models Abroad* (Leisen) (co); *The Big Broadcast of 1938* (Leisen); *Booloo* (Elliott); *The Buccaneer* (De Mille); *Bulldog Drummond in Africa* (L. King); *Campus Confessions* (Archainbaud); *Bulldog Drummond's Peril* (Hogan); *Cassidy of Bar 20* (Selander); *Coconut Grove* (Santell); *College Swing* (Walsh); *Dangerous to Know* (Florey); *Doctor Rhythm* (Tuttle) (co); *The Frontiersman* (Selander); *Give Me a Sailor* (Nugent); *Heart of Arizona* (Selander); *Her Jungle Love* (Archainbaud); *Hunted Men* (L. King); *Illegal Traffic* (L. King); *In Old Mexico* (Venturini); *King of Alcatraz* (Florey); *Little Orphan Annie* (Holmes); *Men with Wings* (Wellman); *The Mysterious Rider* (Selander); *Pride of the West* (Selander); *Prison Farm* (L. King); *Professor Beware* (Nugent); *Ride a Crooked Mile* (Green); *Say It in French* (Stone); *Scandal Sheet* (Hogan); *Sing, You Sinners* (Ruggles); *Sons of the Legion* (Hogan); *Spawn of the North* (Hathaway); *Stolen Heaven* (Stone); *The Texans* (Hogan); *Thanks for the Memory* (Archainbaud); *Tip-Off Girls* (L. King); *Tom Sawyer, Detective* (L. King); *Touchdown Army* (Neumann); *Tropic Holiday* (Reed); *You and Me* (F. Lang)

1939   *All Women Have Secrets* (Neumann); *Arrest Bulldog Drummond* (Hogan); *Back Door to Heaven* (Howard); *The Beachcomber* (Pommer); *Beau Geste* (Wellman); *Boy Trouble* (Archainbaud); *Bulldog Drummond's Bride* (Hogan); *Café Society* (E. Griffith); *Bulldog Drummond's Secret Police* (Hogan); *The Cat and the Canary* (Nugent); *Death of a Champion* (Florey); *Disbarred* (Florey); *Disputed Passage* (Borzage); *Geronimo* (Sloane); *The Gracie Allen Murder Case* (Green); *Grand Jury Secrets* (Hogan); *The Great Victor Herbert* (Stone); *Heritage of the Desert* (Selander); *Honeymoon in Bali* (E. Griffith); *Hotel Imperial* (Florey); *Invitation to Happiness* (Ruggles);

Island of Lost Men (Neumann); *I'm from Missouri* (Reed); *King of Chinatown* (Grinde); *The Lady's from Kentucky* (Hall); *Law of the Pampas* (Watt); *The Llano Kid* (Venturini); *The Magnificent Fraud* (Florey); *Man about Town* (Sandrich); *Man of Conquest* (Nicholls) (co); *Midnight* (Leisen) (co); *Million Dollar Legs* (Grinde); *Never Say Die* (Nugent); *The Night of Nights* (Milestone); *Night Work* (Archainbaud); *$1,000 a Touchdown* (Hogan); *Our Leading Citizen* (Santell); *Our Neighbors, the Carters* (Murphy); *Paris Honeymoon* (Tuttle); *Persons in Hiding* (L. King); *Range War* (Selander); *The Renegade Trail* (Selander); *Rulers of the Sea* (Lloyd); *Silver on the Sage* (Selander); *Some Like It Hot* (Archainbaud); *The Star Maker* (Del Ruth); *St. Louis Blues* (Walsh); *Sudden Money* (Grinde); *The Sunset Trail* (Selander); *Television Spy* (Dmytryk); *This Man Is News* (McDonald); *Undercover Doctor* (L. King); *Union Pacific* (De Mille); *Unmarried* (Neumann); *What a Life* (Reed); *Zaza* (Cukor)

1940 *Adventure in Diamonds* (Fitzmaurice); *Arise, My Love* (Leisen) (co); *The Biscuit Eater* (Heisler); *Buck Benny Rides Again* (Sandrich); *The Cherokee Strip* (Selander); *Christmas in July* (P. Sturges); *Comin' round the Mountain* (Archainbaud); *Dancing on a Dime* (Santley); *Doctor Cyclops* (Schoedsack); *Emergency Squad* (Dmytryk); *The Farmer's Daughter* (Hogan); *French without Tears* (Asquith) (co); *Golden Gloves* (Dmytryk); *The Ghost Breakers* (Marshall); *The Great McGinty* (P. Sturges); *Hidden Gold* (Selander); *I Want a Divorce* (Murphy); *Knights of the Range* (Selander); *Light of Western Stars* (Selander); *The Light That Failed* (Wellman); *Love Thy Neighbor* (Sandrich); *Moon over Burma* (L. King); *Mystery Sea Raider* (Dmytryk); *A Night at Earl Carroll's* (Neumann); *Northwest Mounted Police* (De Mille) (co); *Opened by Mistake* (Archainbaud); *A Parole Fixer* (Florey); *The Quarterback* (Humberstone); *Queen of the Mob* (Hogan); *Rangers of Fortune* (Wood); *Remember the Night* (Leisen); *Rhythm on the River* (Schertzinger); *Road to Singapore* (Schertzinger); *Safari* (E. Griffith); *Santa Fe Marshall* (Selander); *Seventeen* (L. King); *The Showdown* (Bretherton); *Stagecoach War* (Selander); *Texas Rangers Ride Again* (Hogan); *Those Were the Days* (Reed); *Three Men from Texas* (Selander); *Typhoon* (L. King); *Untamed* (Archainbaud); *Victory* (Cromwell); *The Way of All Flesh* (L. King); *Women without Names* (Florey); *World in Flames* (Richard)

1941 *Aloma of the South Seas* (Santell); *Among the Living* (Heisler); *Bahama Passage* (E. Griffith); *Ball of Fire* (Hawks); *Birth of the Blues* (Schertzinger); *Border Vigilantes* (Abrahams); *Buy Me That Town* (Forde); *Caught in the Draft* (Butler); *Doomed Caravan* (Selander); *Flying Blind* (McDonald); *Forced Landing* (Wiles); *Glamour Boy* (Tetzlaff); *Henry Aldrich for President* (Bennett); *Here Comes Mr. Jordan* (Hall); *Hold Back the Dawn* (Leisen); *I Wanted Wings* (Leisen); *In Old Colorado* (Bretherton); *Kiss the Boys Goodbye* (Schertzinger); **The Lady Eve** (P. Sturges); *Las Vegas Nights* (Murphy); *Life with Henry* (Reed); *The Mad Doctor* (Whelan); *The Monster and the Girl* (Heisler); *New York Town* (C. Vidor); *The Night of January 16th* (Clemens); *Nothing But the Truth* (Nugent); *One Night in Lisbon* (E. Griffith); *The Parson of Panamint* (McGann); *Pirates on Horseback* (Selander); *Power Dive* (Hogan);

Reaching for the Sun (Wellman); *Road to Zanzibar* (Schertzinger); *Roundup* (Selander); *Secret of the Wastelands* (Abrahams); *Shepherd of the Hills* (Hathaway); *Skylark* (Sandrich) (co); **Sullivan's Travels** (P. Sturges); *Virginia* (E. Griffith); *There's a Magic in the Music* (Stone); *West Point Widow* (Siodmak); *Wide-Open Town* (Selander); *World Premiere* (Tetzlaff); *You Belong to Me* (Ruggles); *You're the One* (Murphy)

1942 *Are Husbands Necessary?* (Taurog); *Beyond the Blue Horizon* (Santell); *The Fleet's In* (Schertzinger); *The Gay Sisters* (Rapper) (co); *The Glass Key* (Heisler); *The Great Man's Lady* (Wellman); *Henry Aldrich, Editor* (Bennett); *Holiday Inn* (Sandrich); *I Married a Witch* (Clair); *The Lady Has Plans* (Lanfield); *Lucky Jordan* (Tuttle); *The Major and the Minor* (Wilder); *Mrs. Wiggs of the Cabbage Patch* (Murphy); *My Favorite Blonde* (Lanfield); *My Heart Belongs to Daddy* (Siodmak); *The Palm Beach Story* (P. Sturges) (co); *The Remarkable Andrew* (Heisler); *Road to Morocco* (Butler); *Star-Spangled Rhythm* (Marshall); *This Gun for Hire* (Tuttle); *Wake Island* (Farrow); *Young and Willing* (E. Griffith)

1943 *China* (Farrow); *The Crystal Bell* (Nugent); *Five Graves to Cairo* (Wilder); *Flesh and Fantasy* (Duvivier) (co); *For Whom the Bell Tolls* (Wood); *The Good Fellows* (Graham); *Happy Go Lucky* (Bernhardt); *Henry Aldrich Gets Glamour* (Bennett); *Hostages* (Tuttle); *Henry Aldrich Haunts a House* (Bennett); *Lady Bodyguard* (Clemens); *Lady of Burlesque* (Wellman) (co); *Let's Face It* (Lanfield); *Night Plane from Chungking* (Murphy); *No Time for Love* (Leisen) (co); *Riding High* (Marshall); *Salute for Three* (Murphy); *Tender Comrade* (Dmytryk) (co); *They Got Me Covered* (Butler) (co); *True to Life* (Marshall)

1944 *And Now Tomorrow* (Pichel); *And the Angels Sing* (Binyon); **Double Indemnity** (Wilder); *Going My Way* (McCarey); *The Great Moment* (P. Sturges); *Hail the Conquering Hero* (P. Sturges); *Henry Aldrich's Little Secret* (Bennett); *The Hitler Gang* (Farrow); *Here Come the Waves* (Sandrich); *The Hour before the Dawn* (Tuttle); *I Love a Soldier* (Sandrich); *I'll Be Seeing You* (Dieterle); *Lady in the Dark* (Leisen) (co); *The Man in Half Moon Street* (Murphy); *Ministry of Fear* (F. Lang); *The Miracle of Morgan's Creek* (P. Sturges); *National Barn Dance* (Bennett); *Rainbow Island* (Murphy); *Our Hearts Were Young and Gay* (Allen); *The Uninvited* (Allen); *Standing Room Only* (Lanfield); *Till We Meet Again* (Borzage); *You Can't Ration Love* (Fuller)

1945 *The Affairs of Susan* (Seiter); *The Bells of St. Mary's* (McCarey); *Bring on the Girls* (Lanfield); *Christmas in Connecticut* (Godfrey) (co); *Duffy's Tavern* (Walker) (co); *Hold That Blonde* (Marshall); *Incendiary Blonde* (Marshall); **The Lost Weekend** (Wilder); *Love Letters* (Dieterle); *Masquerade in Mexico* (Leisen); *A Medal for Benny* (Pichel); *Miss Susie Slagle's* (Berry) (co); *Murder He Says* (Marshall); *Out of This World* (Walker); *Road to Utopia* (Walker); *Salty O'Rourke* (Walsh); *The Stork Club* (Walker); *You Came Along* (Farrow)

1946 *The Blue Dahlia* (Marshall); *Blue Skies* (Heisler) (co); *The Bride Wore Boots* (Pichel); *Monsieur Beaucaire* (Marshall); *My Reputation* (Bernhardt) (co); **Notorious** (Hitchcock); *Our Hearts Were Growing Up* (Russell); *The Perfect*

379

Marriage (Allen); *The Strange Love of Martha Ivers* (Milestone); *To Each His Own* (Leisen); *The Virginian* (Gilmore); *The Well-Groomed Bride* (Lanfield)

1947 *Blaze of Noon* (Farrow); *Calcutta* (Farrow); *California* (Farrow) (co); *Cross My Heart* (Berry); *Cry Wolf* (Godfrey) (co); *Dear Ruth* (Russell); *Desert Fury* (Allen); *Easy Come, Easy Go* (Farrow); *I Walk Alone* (Haskin); *The Imperfect Wife* (Allen) (co); *My Favorite Brunette* (Nugent); *The Other Love* (de Toth) (co); *The Perils of Pauline* (Marshall); *Ramrod* (de Toth); *Road to Rio* (McLeod); *The Trouble with Women* (Lanfield); *The Two Mrs. Carrolls* (Godfrey) (co); *Variety Girl* (Marshall) (co); *Welcome Stranger* (Nugent); *Where There's Life* (Lanfield); *Wild Harvest* (Garnett)

1948 *The Accused* (Dieterle); *Arch of Triumph* (Milestone) (co); *Beyond Glory* (Farrow); *The Big Clock* (Farrow); *Dream Girl* (Leisen); *The Emperor Waltz* (Wilder) (co); *Enchantment* (Reis) (co); *A Foreign Affair* (Wilder); *Isn't It Romantic?* (McLeod); *June Bride* (Windust) (co); *Miss Tatlock's Millions* (Haydn); *My Own True Love* (Bennett); *The Night Has a Thousand Eyes* (Farrow); *Saigon* (Fenton); *Rachel and the Stranger* (Foster); *The Sainted Sisters* (Russell); *The Sealed Verdict* (Allen); *So Evil My Love* (Allen) (co); *Sorry, Wrong Number* (Litvak); *Whispering Smith* (Fenton) (co)

1949 *The Great Gatsby* (Nugent); *Beyond the Forest* (K. Vidor); *The Great Lover* (Hall); *The Heiress* (Wyler) (co); *Malaya* (Thorpe) (co); *Manhandled* (Foster); *My Foolish Heart* (Robson) (co); *My Friend Irma* (Marshall); *Red, Hot, and Blue* (Farrow); *Rope of Sand* (Dieterle); *Samson and Delilah* (De Mille) (co); *Song of Surrender* (Leisen)

1950 ***All about Eve*** (Mankiewicz) (co); *Copper Canyon* (Farrow) (co); *The Dark City* (Dieterle); *Fancy Pants* (Marshall); *The File on Thelma Jordan* (Siodmak); *The Furies* (A. Mann); *Let's Dance* (McLeod); *Mr. Music* (Haydn); *My Friend Irma Goes West* (Walker); *Paid in Full* (Dieterle); *No Man of Her Own* (Leisen); *Riding High* (Capra); *September Affair* (Dieterle); ***Sunset Boulevard*** (Wilder)

1951 *The Big Carnival* (Wilder); *Branded* (Maté); *Crosswinds* (Foster); *Darling, How Could You?* (Leisen); *Dear Brat* (Seiter); *Detective Story* (Wyler); *Here Comes the Groom* (Capra); *Hong Kong* (Foster); *The Last Outpost* (Foster); *The Lemon Drop Kid* (Lanfield); *My Favorite Spy* (McLeod); *Payment on Demand* (Bernhardt) (co); *Peking Express* (Dieterle); ***A Place in the Sun*** (Stevens); *Rhubarb* (Lubin); *Silver City* (Haskin); *The Stooge* (Taurog); *Submarine Command* (Farrow); *That's My Boy* (Walker); *When Worlds Collide* (Maté)

1952 *Aaron Slick from Punkin Crick* (Binyon); *Caribbean* (Ludwig); *Anything Can Happen* (Seaton); *Carrie* (Wyler); *Come Back, Little Sheba* (Daniel Mann); *Denver and Rio Grande* (Haskin); *The Greatest Show on Earth* (De Mille) (co); *Hurricane Smith* (Hopper); *Jumping Jacks* (Taurog); *Just for You* (Nugent) (co); *My Son John* (McCarey); *Red Mountain* (Dieterle); *Road to Bali* (Walker); *Ruby Gentry* (K. Vidor); *Sailor Beware* (Walker); *The Savage* (Marshall); *Somebody Loves Me* (Brecher); *Something to Live For* (Stevens); *Son of Paleface* (Tashlin); *This Is Dynamite* (Dieterle); *The Turning Point* (Dieterle)

1953 *Arrowhead* (Warren); *The Caddy* (Taurog); *Forever Female* (Rapper); *Here Come the Girls* (Binyon); *Houdini* (Marshall); *Jamaica Run* (Foster); *Little Boy Lost* (Seaton); *Off Limits* (Marshall); *Pleasure Island* (Hugh); *Pony Express* (Hopper); *Roman Holiday* (Wyler); *Sangaree* (Ludwig); *Scared Stiff* (Marshall); ***Shane*** (Stevens); *Stalag 17* (Wilder); *The Stars Are Singing* (Taurog); *Those Redheads from Seattle* (Foster); *Thunder in the East* (C. Vidor); *Tropic Zone* (Foster); *The Vanquished* (Ludwig); *War of the Worlds* (Haskin)

1954 *About Mrs. Leslie* (Daniel Mann); *Alaska Seas* (Hopper); *The Bridges at Toko-ri* (Robson); *The Country Girl* (Seaton); *Elephant Walk* (Dieterle); *Jivaro* (Ludwig); *Knock on Wood* (Panama and Frank); *Living It Up* (Taurog); *Money from Home* (Marshall); *Mr. Casanova* (McLeod); *The Naked Jungle* (Haskin); ***Rear Window*** (Hitchcock); *Red Garters* (Marshall) (co); *Sabrina* (Wilder); *Secret of the Incas* (Hopper); *Three-Ring Circus* (Pevney); *White Christmas* (Curtiz)

1955 *Artist and Models* (Tashlin); *Conquest of Space* (Haskin); *The Desperate Hours* (Wyler); *The Far Horizon* (Maté); *The Girl Rush* (Pirosh); *Hell's Island* (Karlson); *Lucy Gallant* (Parrish); *The Rose Tattoo* (Daniel Mann); *Run for Cover* (Ray); *The Seven Little Foys* (Shavelson); *Strategic Air Command* (A. Mann); *To Catch a Thief* (Hitchcock); *The Trouble with Harry* (Hitchcock); *You're Never Too Young* (Taurog)

1956 *Anything Goes* (Lewis); *The Birds and the Bees* (Taurog); *The Come-On* (Birdwell); *The Court Jester* (Panama and Frank) (co); *Hollywood or Bust* (Tashlin); *The Leather Saint* (Ganzer); *The Man Who Knew Too Much* (Hitchcock); *The Mountain* (Dmytryk); *Pardners* (Taurog); *The Proud and the Profane* (Seaton); *The Rainmaker* (Anthony); *The Scarlet Hour* (Curtiz); *The Search for Bridey Murphy* (Langley); *The Ten Commandments* (De Mille) (co); *That Certain Feeling* (Panama and Frank); *Three Violent People* (Maté)

1957 *Beau James* (Shavelson); *The Buster Keaton Story* (Sheldon); *The Delicate Delinquent* (McGuire); *The Devil's Hairpin* (Wilde); *Fear Strikes Out* (Mulligan); *Funny Face* (Donen) (co); *Gunfight at the O.K. Corral* (J. Sturges); *Hear Me Good* (McGuire); *The Joker Is Wild* (C. Vidor); *The Lonely Man* (Levin); *Loving You* (Kanter); *The Sad Sack* (Marshall); *Short Cut to Hell* (Cagney); *The Tin Star* (A. Mann); *Wild Is the Wind* (Cukor); *Witness for the Prosecution* (Wilder)

1958 *As Young as You Are* (Gerard); *The Buccaneer* (Quinn) (co); *The Geisha Boy* (Tashlin); *Hot Spell* (Daniel Mann); *Houseboat* (Shavelson); *Maracaibo* (Wilde); *I Married a Monster from Outer Space* (Fowler); *King Creole* (Curtiz); *The Matchmaker* (Anthony); *Me and the Colonel* (Glenville); *The Party Crashers* (Girard); *Rock-a-Bye Baby* (Tashlin); *Separate Tables* (Delbert Mann) (co); *St. Louis Blues* (Reisner); *Teacher's Pet* (Seton); ***Vertigo*** (Hitchcock)

1959 *Alias Jesse James* (McLeod); *The Black Orchid* (Ritt); *But Not for Me* (W. Lang); *Career* (Anthony); *The Hangman* (Curtiz); *Don't Give Up the Ship* (Taurog); *The Five Pennies* (Shavelson); *A Hole in the Head* (Capra); *The Jayhawkers* (Frank); *Last Train from Gun Hill* (J. Sturges); *That Kind of Woman* (Lumet); *Too Young for Love* (Girard); *The Trap* (Panama); *The Young Captives* (Kershner)

1960   *The Bellboy* (Lewis); *A Breath of Scandal* (Curtiz); *Cinderfella* (Tashlin); *The Facts of Life* (Frank) (co); *G.I. Blues* (Taurog); *Heller in Pink Tights* (Cukor); *It Started in Naples* (Shavelson); *Pepe* (Sidney); *The Rat Race* (Mulligan); *A Touch of Larceny* (Hamilton); *Visit to a Small Planet* (Taurog)

1961   *All in a Night's Work* (Anthony); *Blue Hawaii* (Taurog); **Breakfast at Tiffany's** (Edwards) (co); *The Errand Boy* (Lewis); *The Ladies' Man* (Lewis); *Love in a Goldfish Bowl* (Sher); *Mantrap* (O'Brien); *On the Double* (Shavelson); *The Pleasure of His Company* (Seaton); *Pocketful of Miracles* (Capra); *Summer and Smoke* (Glenville)

1962   *The Counterfeit Traitor* (Seaton); *Escape from Zahrain* (Neame); *A Girl Named Tamiko* (J. Sturges); *Girls! Girls! Girls!* (Taurog); *Hatari!* (Hawks); *It's Only Money* (Tashlin); **The Man Who Shot Liberty Valance** (Ford); *My Geisha* (Cardiff); *The Pigeon That Took Rome* (Shavelson); *Too Late Blues* (Cassavetes); *Who's Got the Action?* (Daniel Mann)

1963   **The Birds** (Hitchcock); *Come Blow Your Horn* (Yorkin); *Critic's Choice* (Weis); *Donovan's Reef* (Ford); *Fun in Acapulco* (Thorpe); *Hud* (Ritt); *I Could Go On Singing* (Neame); *My Six Loves* (Champion); *Love with the Proper Stranger* (Mulligan); *A New Kind of Love* (Shavelson) (co); *The Nutty Professor* (Lewis); *Papa's Delicate Condition* (Marshall); *Who's Been Sleeping in My Bed?* (Daniel Mann); *Who's Minding the Store?* (Tashlin); *Wives and Lovers* (Rich)

1964   *The Carpetbaggers* (Dmytryk); *The Disorderly Orderly* (Tashlin); *A House Is Not a Home* (Rouse); *Lady in a Cage* (Grauman); *Men's Favorite Sport?* (Hawks); *Marnie* (Hitchcock); *The Patsy* (Lewis); *Roustabout* (Rich); *Sex and the Single Girl* (Quine) (co); *Thirty-Six Hours* (Seaton); *What a Way to Go* (Lee Thompson) (co); *Where Love Has Gone* (Dmytryk)

1965   *Boeing, Boeing* (Rich); *The Family Jewels* (Lewis); *The Great Race* (Edwards) (co); *The Hallelujah Trail* (J. Sturges); *Harlow* (Douglas) (co); *Inside Daisy Clover* (Mulligan) (co); *John Goldfarb, Please Come Home* (Lee Thompson) (co); *Love Has Many Faces* (Singer); *Red Line 7000* (Hawks); *The Slender Thread* (Pollack); *The Sons of Katie Elder* (Hathaway); *Sylvia* (Douglas); *Who Has Seen the Wind?* (Sidney); *The Yellow Rolls-Royce* (Asquith) (co)

1966   *Assault on a Queen* (Donohue); *The Last of the Secret Agents* (Abbott); *Nevada Smith* (Hathaway); *Not with My Wife, You Don't!* (Panama); *The Oscar* (Rouse); *Paradise, Hawaiian Style* (Moore); *Penelope* (Hiller); *The Swinger* (Sidney); *This Property Is Condemned* (Pollack); *Torn Curtain* (Hitchcock); *Waco* (Springsteen)

1967   *Barefoot in the Park* (Saks); *The Caper of the Golden Bulls* (Rouse); *Chuka* (Douglas); *Easy Come, Easy Go* (Rich); *Hotel* (Quine) (co); *Warning Shot* (Kulik)

1968   *In Enemy Country* (Keller); *Madigan* (Siegel); *The Pink Jungle* (Delbert Mann); *The Secret War of Harry Frigg* (Smight); *What's So Bad about Feeling Good?* (Seaton)

1969   *Butch Cassidy and the Sundance Kid* (Hill); *Downhill Racer* (Ritchie); *Eye of the Cat* (Rich); *The Hellfighters* (McLaglen); *House of Cards* (Guillermin); *The Lost Man* (Arthur); *Sweet Charity* (Fosse); *Tell Them Willie Boy Is Here* (Polonsky); *Topaz* (Hitchcock); *Winning* (Goldstone)

1970   *Airport* (Seaton); *Colossus: The Forbin Project* (Sargent); *Myra Breckinridge* (Sarne) (co); *Skullduggery* (Douglas); *Story of a Woman* (Bercovici)

1971   *Red Sky at Morning* (Goldstone); *Sometimes a Great Notion* (Newman)

1972   *Hammersmith Is Out* (Ustinov); *Pete 'n' Tillie* (Ritt); *The Screaming Woman* (Smight)

1973   *Ash Wednesday* (Peerce); *A Doll's House* (Losey) (co); *Divorce His, Divorce Hers* (Hussein); *The Sting* (Hill); *The Don Is Dead* (Fleischer); *The Showdown* (Seaton); *The Life and Times of Judge Roy Bean* (Huston) (co)

1974   *Airport '75* (Smight)

1975   *The Great Waldo Pepper* (Hill); *Rooster Cogburn* (Miller); *The Man Who Would Be King* (Huston)

1976   *The Bluebird* (Cukor); *Family Plot* (Hitchcock); *Gable and Lombard* (Furie); *W. C. Fields and Me* (Hiller); *The Disappearance of Aimee* (Harvey)

1977   *Airport '77* (Hiller); *Sex and the Married Woman* (Arnold); *Sunshine Christmas* (Jordan)

1978   *The Big Fix* (Kagen); *Olly Olly Oxen Free* (Colla); *Sextette* (Hughes)

1979   *The Last Married Couple in America* (Cates)

1982   *Dead Men Don't Wear Plaid* (Reiner)

Publications

By HEAD: books—

With Jane Kesner Ardmore, *The Dress Doctor*, Boston, Massachusetts, 1959.
With Joe Hyams, *How to Dress for Success*, New York, 1967.
With Paddy Calistro, *Edith Head's Hollywood*, New York, 1983.

By HEAD: articles—

''A Costume Problem: From Shop to Stage to Screen,'' in *Hollywood Quarterly*, October 1946.
''Honesty in Today's Film Fashions,'' in *Show* (New York), 6 August 1970.
''Head on Fashion'' series in *Holiday* (New York), January-February 1973; July-August 1973; September-October 1974; November-December 1974; January-February 1975; March 1975; September-October 1975; March 1976.
In *Hollywood Speaks! An Oral History*, by Mike Steen, New York, 1974.
Inter/View (New York), January 1974.
Films Illustrated (London), September 1974.
Take One (Montreal), October 1976.
American Film (Washington, D.C.), May 1978.
Ciné Revue (Paris), 19 April 1979.

On HEAD: books—

Cjetti, David Chier, *Edith Head*, New York, 2000.

On HEAD: articles—

Films in Review (New York), February 1972.
In *Hollywood Costume Design*, by David Chierichetti, New York, 1976.

In *Costume Design in the Movies*, by Elizabeth Leese, New York, 1976.
In *In a Glamorous Fashion*, by W. Robert LaVine, New York, 1980.
Films (New York), May 1981.
Obituary, in *The Annual Obituary 1981*, New York, 1982.
The Velvet Light Trap (Madison, Wisconsin), no. 19, 1982.
Spoto, Donald, in *Architectural Digest*, vol. 49, April 1992.
Skrien (Amsterdam), October-November 1994.
Vanity Fair (New York), March 1998.

*   *   *

For many people, Edith Head and film costume design are synonymous. Other designers may have been more flamboyantly creative, or more consistently original, but no one did more to earn this art form popular recognition. Her guiding principle was that costume should support, rather than compete with, story and character development. Better than most, perhaps, she understood that clothing is not merely a matter of adornment, but a potent method of communication working in tandem with film's sound and other visual elements. Her longevity, her productivity, her frequent touches of genius, and her talent for self-promotion secured her a celebrity status rare among Hollywood's legions of production artists. Moviegoers have long remained oblivious to the identities of those who work in the shadow of the stars, but they seem to have found a place in their consciousness for this tiny, austere-looking woman who wove illusions out of beads and cloth.

Unlike most of her peers, Head entered film costuming without relevant training or experience. When Howard Greer, Paramount's chief designer, hired her as a sketch artist in 1923, she was a high school teacher of French and art looking for a way to supplement her income. She learned quickly, however, honing her skills by observing the masters at work. From Greer, she learned the value of attention to detail. From Travis Banton, another outstanding member of Paramount's design team, she learned how to fabricate the highest standards of glamor and elegance.

In her early years at the studio, Head mainly dressed minor characters and animals, and generated wardrobes for the countless B-pictures then in production. Gradually she progressed to creating costumes for stars with whom the senior designers lacked the time or inclination to work. Among her first major assignments were Clara Bow, Lupe Velez, and Mae West. Head became Paramount's chief designer in 1938, when Banton, who replaced Greer as head designer in 1927, left to start a couture business. She remained at the studio for another three decades, working with most of Hollywood's major actresses and some of its best-known actors. When Paramount was sold in 1967, she became chief designer at Universal, where she worked until her death.

During her career, which spanned nearly six decades, Head's productivity achieved legendary proportions. In 1940 alone, she supervised costumes for 47 films. She is estimated to have contributed to more than 1,000 movies during her lifetime. In terms of formal recognition, her record is equally staggering. She received 34 Academy Award nominations, of which eight resulted in an Oscar. Costume design did not become an Academy Award category until 1948. For the first 19 years in which this honor was given, Head was nominated at least once every year. Had the award been introduced earlier, she would surely have earned additional nominations for such distinctive creations as Dorothy Lamour's sarongs in *The Jungle Princess* or Barbara Stanwyck's Latin-inspired garments for *The Lady Eve*.

Much of her best work was executed in the 1950s, when glamor and high-fashion were the keynotes of costume design. Among the enduring images her designs helped promote were Grace Kelly's refined allure in *Rear Window* and *To Catch a Thief*, Elizabeth Taylor's incandescent sensuality in *A Place in the Sun*, Audrey Hepburn's chic individuality in *Sabrina*, Bette Davis's mature sophistication in *All about Eve*, and Gloria Swanson's anachronistic glamor in *Sunset Boulevard*. This was also an era in which Head's public visibility reached its zenith. Already a fashion magazine editor, columnist, and regular contributor to Art Linkletter's radio show *House Party*, Head now made frequent television appearances, acted as consultant for the Academy Awards show, and published her first book. The diversity of her activities helped to extend her influence well beyond the realm of motion pictures.

Perhaps her greatest asset was her adaptability. Entering the business when limitless spending permitted designers broad artistic license, she later had to adjust to the restrictions imposed by wartime shortages of luxury textiles and the government's L-85 ruling on the amount of materials which could be used in clothing manufacture. Following the return to glamor and clothing-as-special-effects during the 1950s, Head made yet another successful transition when the 1960s ushered in a new emphasis on realism.

Head was also able to adjust to widely varying ideas about her role among the directors with whom she worked. Attitudes ranged from Alfred Hitchcock and George Roy Hill's close involvement in design, to the laissez-faire approach of Joseph Mankiewicz. Describing herself on one occasion as "a better politician than costume designer," Head was expert at handling star temperament, preferring to yield ground on a neckline or dress length than engage in a battle of wills. The conservative, neutral-colored suits she perennially wore symbolized her willingness to suppress her individuality in the interests of her craft. With the exception of a dispute over whether she or Givenchy deserved the credit for Audrey Hepburn's famous bow-tied neckline in *Sabrina*, her career was unruffled by controversy.

Although she created a number of outstanding designs for period movies, most notably *The Heiress* and *Samson and Delilah*, she preferred to dress films with a contemporary theme, believing that they afforded more scope for originality. She also preferred to dress men rather than women, on the grounds that they were easier to deal with. One of her most effective wardrobes was the clothing worn by Robert Redford and Paul Newman in *The Sting*, in which her subtle use of accessories, especially hats, was brilliantly executed. Her designs, on occasion, set fashion trends, but she did not deliberately set out to influence what the public wore. She placed far more importance on enabling stars to assume their characters' identities. She also believed it essential to create designs which would not cause a movie to date prematurely. This preference for a middle-of-the-road approach dates from 1947, when Dior's "New Look" exploded onto the fashion scene, making Head's streamlined designs seem instantly outmoded.

Head's excellence as a designer was augmented by her keen understanding of the technical constraints within which she operated. She was acutely aware of the different requirements created by variations in lighting, sound, and color. She also believed in close collaboration with her fellow production artists. Although she worked in an industry in which honors and public recognition are focused on individual achievement, Head truly was a team player. She may have enjoyed the celebrity status earned by her television appearances and writing, but when it came to practicing her craft, aligning her skills with the needs of directors, cinematographers, art directors, and others is what mattered most. It was her capacity for partnership that helped her become one of Hollywood's preeminent production artists.

—Fiona Valentine

HECHT, Ben

Writer, Producer, and Director. **Nationality:** American. **Born:** New York City, 28 February 1893. **Education:** Attended Racine High School, Wisconsin. **Family:** Married 1) Marie Armstrong, 1915 (divorced 1925), one daughter; 2) Rose Caylor, 1925; one daughter. **Career:** Child violin prodigy and circus acrobat; 1910–14—staff member, Chicago *Journal*; 1914–18—reporter, correspondent in Berlin, 1918–19, and columnist, 1919–23, Chicago *News*; wrote first play in the mid-1910s, and first novel in 1921; 1923–25—founding editor, *Chicago Literary Times*; 1927—first film as writer, *Underworld*; 1934—formed production company with Charles MacArthur to write, produce, and direct their own films; 1940—began collaboration with Charles Lederer; 1948–51—boycotted by British exhibitors for his criticism of British policy in Palestine. **Awards:** Academy Awards for *Underworld*, 1928; *The Scoundrel*, 1935; Writers Guild Laurel Award, 1980. **Died:** Of a heart attack, 18 April 1964.

Ben Hecht

Films as Writer:

1927 *Underworld* (*Paying the Penalty*) (von Sternberg)
1928 *The Big Noise* (Dwan)
1929 *Unholy Night* (L. Barrymore); *Le Spectre vert* (*The Green Ghost*) (Feyder)
1930 *Roadhouse Nights* (*The River Inn*) (Henley); *The Great Gabbo* (Cruze)
1931 *The Unholy Garden* (Fitzmaurice)
1932 **Scarface—The Shame of a Nation** (Hawks)
1933 *Hallelujah, I'm a Bum* (*Hallelujah, I'm a Tramp; Lazy Bones*) (Milestone); *Turn Back the Clock* (Selwyn); *Design for Living* (Lubitsch)
1934 *Upper World* (Del Ruth); *Twentieth Century* (Hawks); *Crime without Passion* (+ co-d + co-pr); *Viva Villa!* (Conway)
1935 *Once in a Blue Moon* (+ co-d + co-pr); *The Scoundrel* (+ co-d + co-pr + ro); *Barbary Coast* (Hawks)
1936 *Soak the Rich* (+ co-d + co-pr + ro)
1938 *Nothing Sacred* (Wellman); *Goldwyn Follies* (Marshall)
1939 *Let Freedom Ring* (*Song of the West*) (Conway); *It's a Wonderful World* (Van Dyke); *Lady of the Tropics* (Conway); *Gunga Din* (Stevens) (+ ro); *Wuthering Heights* (Wyler); **Gone with the Wind** (Fleming) (dialogue)
1940 *Angels over Broadway* (+ co-d + pr + ro); *Comrade X* (K. Vidor)
1941 *Lydia* (Duvivier)
1942 *Tales of Manhattan* (Duvivier); *China Girl* (Hathaway) (+ pr); *The Black Swan* (H. King)
1945 *Spellbound* (Hitchcock); *Watchtower over Tomorrow* (Cromwell—short)
1946 *Specter of the Rose* (+ co-d + pr); **Notorious** (Hitchcock)
1947 *Her Husband's Affairs* (Simon); *Kiss of Death* (Hathaway); *Ride the Pink Horse* (Montgomery)
1948 *The Miracle of the Bells* (Pichel)
1950 *Whirlpool* (Preminger) (co-sc as Lester Bartow); *Where the Sidewalk Ends* (Preminger)
1952 *Actors and Sin* (+ co-d + pr + ro); *Monkey Business* (Hawks)
1954 *Light's Diamond Jubilee* (K. Vidor, Wellman and Taurog)
1955 *Ulisse* (*Ulysses*) (Camerini); *The Indian Fighter* (de Toth)
1956 *Miracle in the Rain* (Maté); *The Iron Petticoat* (Thomas)
1957 *Legend of the Lost* (Hathaway); *A Farewell to Arms* (C. Vidor)
1958 *Queen of Outer Space* (Bernds)
1959 *Hello Charlie* (Lanfield)
1964 *Circus World* (*The Magnificent Showman*) (Hathaway)

Films based on Hecht's writings:

1931 *The Front Page* (Milestone)
1934 *Shoot the Works* (Ruggles)
1935 *The Florentine Dagger* (Florey); *Spring Tonic* (Bruckman)
1939 *Some Like It Hot* (Archainbaud)
1940 **His Girl Friday** (Hawks)
1950 *Perfect Strangers* (Windust)
1959 **Some Like It Hot** (Wilder)
1969 *Chicago, Chicago* (Jewison)
1974 *The Front Page* (Wilder)
1986 *Je hais les acteurs* (Krawczyk)
1988 *Switching Channels* (Kotcheff)

Publications

By HECHT: plays—

With Maxwell Bodenheim, *The Master Poisoner*, New York, 1918.
With Kenneth Sawyer Goodman, *The Wonder Hat*, New York, 1920.
With Goodman, *The Hero of Santa Maria*, New York, 1920.
With Goodman, *The Hand of Siva*, New York, 1920.
Christmas Eve, New York, 1928.
With Charles MacArthur, *The Front Page*, New York, 1928.
With MacArthur, *Twentieth Century*, New York, 1932.
With Gene Fowler, *The Great Magoo*, New York, 1933.
With MacArthur, *Jumbo*, New York, 1935.
To Quito and Back, New York, 1937.
With MacArthur, *Ladies and Gentlemen*, New York, 1941.
With MacArthur, *Fun to Be Free*, New York, 1941.
We Will Never Die, New York, 1943.
With MacArthur, *Wuthering Heights* (script), in *Twenty Best Film Plays*, edited by John Gassner and Dudley Nichols, New York, 1946.
A Flag Is Born, New York, 1946.
With Angus MacPhail, *Spellbound* (script), in *Best Film Plays, 1945*, edited by John Gassner and Dudley Nichols, New York, 1946.
Hazel Flagg, New York, 1953.
Winkelberg, New York, 1958.

By HECHT: fiction—

Erik Dorn, New York, 1921.
Fantazius Mallare, Chicago, 1922.
A Thousand and One Afternoons in Chicago, Chicago, 1922.
Gargoyles, New York, 1922.
The Florentine Dagger, New York, 1923.
Humpty Dumpty, New York, 1924.
The Kingdom of Evil, Chicago, 1924.
With Bodenheim, *Cutie, A Warm Mamma*, Chicago, 1924.
Broken Necks, Chicago, 1926.
Count Bruga, New York, 1926.
A Jew in Love, New York, 1931.
The Champion from Far Away, New York, 1931.
Actor's Blood, New York, 1936.
A Book of Miracles, New York, 1939.
1001 Afternoons in New York, New York, 1941.
Miracle in the Rain, New York, 1943.
I Hate Actors!, New York, 1944, as *Hollywood Mystery!*, 1946.
Collected Stories, New York, 1945.
Concerning a Woman of Sin and Other Stories, New York, 1947.
The Cat That Jumped Out of the Story (for children), Philadelphia, Pennsylvania, 1947.
The Sensualists, New York, 1959.
In the Midst of Death, London, 1964.

By HECHT: other books—

A Guide for the Bedevilled, New York, 1944.
A Child of the Century (autobiography), New York, 1954.
Charlie: The Improbable Life and Times of Charles MacArthur, New York, 1957.
A Treasury of Ben Hecht, New York, 1959.
Perfidy, New York, 1961.

Gaily, Gaily (autobiography), New York, 1963.
Letters from Bohemia, New York, 1964.
Primack, Bret, editor, *The Ben Hecht Show: Impolitic Observations from the Freest Thinker of 1950s Television*, Jefferson, North Carolina, 1993.
Fifty Books That Are Books, Washington, 2000.

By HECHT: article—

"My Testimonial to the Movies," in *Theatre*, June 1929.

On HECHT: books—

Fetherling, Doug, *The Five Lives of Ben Hecht*, Toronto, 1977.
Martin, Jeffrey Brown, *Ben Hecht, Hollywood Screenwriter*, Ann Arbor, Michigan, 1985.
MacAdams, William, *Ben Hecht: A Biography*, New York, 1995.
Kovan, Florice W., *Rediscovering Ben Hecht: Selling the Celluloid Serpent*, Washington, 1999.

On HECHT: articles—

Photoplay (New York), October 1934.
Rains, Claude, in *Film Weekly* (London), 22 February 1935.
Houston, Penelope, in *Sight and Sound* (London), September 1951.
Bluestone, George, on *Wuthering Heights* in *Novels into Film*, Baltimore, Maryland, 1957.
Cinéma (Paris), June 1964.
Focus on Film (London), March-April 1970.
Fuller, Stephen, in *Film Comment* (New York), Winter 1970–71.
In *The Hollywood Screenwriters*, edited by Richard Corliss, New York, 1972.
National Film Theatre Booklet (London), April-May 1975.
Brown, Geoff, in *Sight and Sound* (London), Summer 1975.
Fuller, Stephen, in *Film Comment* (New York), January-February 1978.
Oakman, Elizabeth W., in *Twentieth-Century American Dramatists*, edited by John MacNicholas, Detroit, Michigan, 1981.
Skoop (Amsterdam), May-June 1981.
Clark, Randall, in *American Screenwriters*, edited by Robert E. Monberger, Stephen O. Lesser, and Randall Clark, Detroit, Michigan, 1984.
Télérama (Paris), 27 July-2 August 1985.
American Cinematographer (Hollywood), October 1985.
Klein, Andy, "Ben Hecht: The Man Behind the Legend," in *American Film*, November 1990.
Epstein, Joseph, "The Great Hack Genius," in *Commentary*, December 1990.
McGilligan, Patrick, "Ben Hecht: The Man Behind the Legend," in *Film Quarterly*, Fall 1991.
Brandlmeier, T., in *EPD Film* (Frankfurt), March 1993.
Slattery, W.J., "The Bindery," in *Audience* (Simi Valley), February-March 1996.

* * *

Ben Hecht is synonymous with the "Hollywood" film. He was one of the most prolific and sought-after screenwriters during the

1930s and 1940s, working in a variety of genres and with such notable directors as Howard Hawks, Alfred Hitchcock, and William Wyler.

Hecht first came into prominence as a screenwriter with his gangster story *Underworld* (directed by Josef von Sternberg). He further enhanced the development of the gangster genre with his script for the Howard Hawks classic *Scarface—The Shame of a Nation*. The material for these films and others, most strikingly *The Front Page*, can be traced back to his journalist days in Chicago. Hecht was only 16 when he began working as a reporter for the Chicago *Journal*. As a reporter, Hecht received a thorough education in the seamier side of human nature. He reported the foibles of the police, politicians, and gangsters in a colorful and cynical style—a style that would later emerge in his screenwriting.

During the early period in Chicago, Hecht was also developing his skills as a novelist and playwright. By 1922 he had published the first two of his many novels, *Erik Dorn* and *Gargoyles*. He was also involved in the bohemian life of the city. Charles MacArthur, a fellow reporter, and Hecht teamed up and worked in New York as successful playwrights. Their plays *The Front Page* and *Twentieth Century* were critical and financial successes and both were to become major motion pictures. There have been three screen versions of *The Front Page*. Lewis Milestone directed the first version in 1931.

Howard Hawks saw the film as a love story and changed the sex of the reporter, Hildy, from a man to a woman in *His Girl Friday*. The most recent version, directed by Billy Wilder in 1974, is the closest adaptation of the original play. *Twentieth Century*, also directed by Howard Hawks, became the prototype for the screwball comedy—a genre popular in the 1930s.

The collaborative efforts of Hecht and MacArthur were legendary in Hollywood, not only for their creative output (*Soak the Rich*, *Wuthering Heights*, and *Barbary Coast*) but also for their nonstop antics. Due to their quick success as screenwriters, Paramount awarded Hecht and MacArthur a four-film contract which guaranteed them full control over their work. Between 1934 and 1936, Hecht and MacArthur took over the Paramount Studios in Astoria, Long Island, and co-produced, co-directed, and co-wrote their own feature films. Their inspiration was to produce films that could compete with the European art films. All of the four films were financial failures, quickly ending their experiment in artistic autonomy. Of the films, only *Crime without Passion* and *The Scoundrel* received critical acclaim. These films, along with *Angels over Broadway*, the only film Hecht directed, produced, and wrote originally for the screen, reflected his preoccupation with German Expressionistic ideas that had also informed his earlier literary efforts. Hecht continued to work independently and with other writing partners, Charles Lederer, I. A. L. Diamond, and Gene Fowler, on film ideas. Although he never felt truly comfortable in Hollywood, his reputation as a quick and skilled screenwriter kept him involved in numerous film projects. He still pursued his literary career and considered it to be his more serious work. Critical success in the literary field eluded him while the film ideas he tossed out at an incredibly rapid rate were by contrast consistently well received.

With the advent of World War II, Hecht devoted considerable energies to protest the German slaughter of his fellow Jews. He also became an ardent Zionist and aligned himself with the Irgun Movement. Because of his strong attacks on the British position in Palestine, his films, although not dealing directly with this issue, were banned in Britain from 1949 to 1952. During this time, Hecht found it difficult to obtain work in Hollywood because the producers feared they would lose the British market. Until his death, Hecht remained active in a variety of fields, still working on occasional screenplays, writing articles and books, and even hosting his own television talk show in 1958.

Hecht's style at its best was a delicate balance between cynicism and sentimentalism. His heroes tended to embody his own anti-middle-class bias, preferring a life of rugged individualism over the bland comforts of conformity. His unique brand of rapid fire overlapping dialogue often served to unmask the quick-witted cynic as a surprisingly caring humanitarian. Film provided Hecht with a medium in which he could collaborate with like-minded individuals who shared his individualism, comradeship, and professionalism.

—Doreen Bartoni

HECKROTH, Hein

Designer. **Nationality:** German. **Born:** Giessen, 1897. **Education:** Studied art at Frankfurt, Munich, Dusseldorf, and Paris. **Career:** 1917—designed sets and costumes for the theatre and ballet; 1933—left Germany; prisoner in Australian Internment Camp during the Second World War. **Award:** Academy Award for *The Red Shoes*, 1948. **Died:** In 1970.

Films as Production Designer:

1946   *Caesar and Cleopatra* (Pascal)
1947   ***Black Narcissus*** (Powell and Pressburger) (+ costume design)
1948   ***The Red Shoes*** (Powell and Pressburger); *The Small Back Room* (Powell and Pressburger)
1950   *The Elusive Pimpernel* (*The Fighting Pimpernel*) (Powell and Pressburger); *Gone to Earth* (Powell and Pressburger)
1951   *The Tales of Hoffman* (Powell and Pressburger)
1953   *The Story of Gilbert and Sullivan* (*Gilbert and Sullivan*; *The Great Gilbert and Sullivan*) (Gilliat) (+ costume design)
1954   *Ludwig II—Glanz und Eland eines Königs* (Kautner)
1955   *The Sorceror's Apprentice* (Powell); *Oh . . . Rosalinda!* (Powell and Pressburger)
1957   *Robinson soll nicht sterben* (von Baky)
1964   *Herzog Blaubart's Burg* (*Bluebeard's Castle*) (Powell)
1966   *Torn Curtain* (Hitchcock)

Other Films:

1946   ***A Matter of Life and Death*** (*Stairway to Heaven*) (Powell and Pressburger) (costume design)
1956   *The Battle of the River Plate* (*Pursuit of the Graf Spee*) (Powell and Pressburger) (artistic adviser)
1962   *Die Dreigroschenoper* (*The Threepenny Opera*) (Staudte) (set and costume designer)

Publications

On HECKROTH: book—

Gibbon, Monk, *Heckroth and His Brush*, 1951.

Hein Heckroth

On HECKROTH: articles—

Bianco e Nero (Rome), vol. 13, no. 2, December 1952.
Obituary, in *Film and TV Technician*, vol. 36, no. 304, September 1970.
Film Dope (Nottingham), March 1982.
EPD Film (Frankfurt), July 1991.

*   *   *

Hein Heckroth belongs with the designers of *Caligari*, with Walt Disney, and William Cameron Menzies, as an auteur in production design whose creativity was in his day rarely appreciated. Moreover, his genius for fantasy, or at least fantastication, emerged when film theorists were preoccupied with literary qualities and realism.

He became known in German theatre in the 1920s for his startlingly modern theatre and opera designs at Essen (including three productions of *Tales of Hoffman*). In 1924 he cofounded Kurt Jooss's first ballet company, later designing Jooss's biggest success, *The Green Table* (1932), a highly stylised piece about disarmament conferences. Its bold, simple design, with lightweight masks and stylised splashes of paint, provoked the exchange: "How could you get the chairs away so quickly from the table?"—"There were no chairs"; "How could you change the diagonal road so quickly?"—"There was no road." The "sense of presence" came not through illusionism (the idiom was satirical-expressionist), but through the integration of Jooss's nonclassical choreography with Heckroth's characteristic style—colour-schemes intricate yet strong, forms suggestive of several things, sumptuous textures and cursive lines—a sort of theatrical *fauvism*. Nazism and the war dislocated Heckroth's career, but after the war Powell's usual art designer, Alfred Junge, set him designing the costumes for *A Matter of Life and Death* and *Black Narcissus*. At this time Powell's interests were evolving away from Junge's large, solid, heavy sets, and he recognised Heckroth as the ideal collaborator for the *The Red Shoes* ballet, with its "dream-kaleidoscope" of settings, styles, and soul states. As for *Tales of Hoffman*, its air of extravagant opulence came not from enormous expense but from swift assemblages of painted flats, drapes, objects as vivid as unsubstantial, and strong yet intricate clashing of hues and styles. The effect is of a fluid, chamelonic romanticism, a joy in eclectic clash-and-splash, in spasm, sensuality, and parade; exploring extreme soul states, bu with joyously sceptical excess. Just as the film half-fuses, half-juxtaposes, opera and ballet, filmed theatre and pure cinema, so the design concept conglomerates innumerable styles and motifs—the third tale alone calls on the Swiss Romantic painter Arnold Boecklin, Méliès, *Caligari*, and *Nosferatu*, to cite only the central references. Overall, the film's salmagundi of Expressionism, Bavarian barococo, Festival of Britain cheeriness, early Romanticism, Gothickry, Baudelairean decadence, and even Bauhaus streamline, is as joyously artificial as Disney's *Fantasia*.

Two more conventional films, *The Small Back Room* and *Gone to Earth*, owed less to some obviously ''delirious'' motifs—a gigantic whisky bottle, hobgoblinish rocks—than to Heckroth's feverish heightening of everyday atmospheres. Heckroth, rather than Powell, was initiator and auteur of two short essays, for German TV, in ''fantasticated theatre,'' *The Sorcerer's Apprentice* and *Bluebeard's Castle*, the latter achieving a crystalline simplicity.

Though a man of the theatre, at home in 3-D design for human movement, Heckroth deeply delighted in film design as ''paintings in motion.'' He was one of the very few designers capable of following Powell's interest in films as ''visual music,'' programmed, like cartoons, to preexisting musical scores. It's arguable that from *The Red Shoes* until the failure of *Oh, Rosalinda!*, Heckroth succeeded Pressburger as Powell's creative soulmate. *The Red Shoes Ballet Sketches*, which assembles Heckroth's storyboard, under the music, into a film, was Powell's tribute to his designer; as a film without motion, but richly suggestive of it, it precedes by 15 years Marker's better-known *La Jetée*.

—Raymond Durgnat

HELLER, Otto

Cinematographer. **Nationality:** British. **Born:** Prague, 3 September 1896; became British citizen 1945. **Military Service:** 1916—made first film (of Emperor Franz Josef's funeral procession) while in Austrian army; 1940—joined Czech airforce and settled permanently in Britain. **Career:** While still in teens, worked as a cinema usher and projectionist in Prague; 1918—became professional cameraman; 1928–30—cinematographer in Czechoslovakia and Germany; 1930–35—worked in Germany. **Award:** British Academy Award for *The Ipcress File*, 1965. **Died:** In London, 17 February 1970.

Films as Cinematographer:

1918   *Československý ježíšek* (*Small Czechoslovak Icon*) (Branald) (co)

1919   *Alois vyhrál los* (*Alois Won a Prize*) (Branald) (co); *Vzteklý ženich* (*The Mad Bridegroom*) (Lamač) (co); *Probuzené svedomí* (*Roman lásky a pomsty*; *The Awakened Conscience*; *Story of Love and Revenge*) (Zdráhal); *Palimpest* (Jencik); *Záhadný případ* (*The Strange Case*) (Marten); *Krasavice Ka a* (*Beautiful Katya*) (Binovec)

1920   *Dráteníček* (*The Little Tinker*) (Šimek); *Komediantka* (*The Comedienne*) (Rovenský); *Odplata* (*Retaliation*) (Winter); *Plameny života* (*Ráj a peklo bohemy*; *The Flames of Life*; *Heaven and Hell of Bohemia*) (Binovec) (co); *Zpev zlata* (*Song of Gold*) (Kolar); *Za svobudu národa* (*For the Fredom of the People*) (Binovec) (co)

1921   *Nad propastí* (*Above the Abyss*) (Majer); *Příchozí z temnot* (*Arrival from the Dark*; *Redivivus*) (Kolar) (co); *Otrávené svetlo* (*Poisoned Light*) (Kolar); *Trny a kveti* (*Žabec*; *Thorns and Flowers*; *A Lass*) (Pištek); *Cesty k výšinam* (*Way to the Heights*) (Sotek); *Moderní Magdalena* (Orlicky and Kolar); *Kríž u potoka* (*The Cross by the Brook*) (Kolar); *Stíny* (*Záhada Noci*; *Shadows*; *Mystery of the Night*) (Pražský); *Manželé paní Mileny* (*Navrat mrtvého*; *Pyrrhovo vítezství*; *Madame Milena's Husbands*; *Dead Man's Return*; *Pyhrric Victory*) (Majer)

1922   *Harémy kouzla zbavené* (*Maharadžovo potešení*; *Harems Devoid of Magic*; *The Maharajah's Pleasures*) (Anton) (+ ro); *Jejich svatební noc* (*Their Bridal Night*) (Leopold); *Mrtví žijí* (*The Dead Live*) (Kolar); *Poslední polibek* (*The Last Kiss*) (Anton); *Proudy* (*Proudem stržna*; *Streams*; *Carried Away by the Current*) (Pistek); *Koryatovič* (*Zacearovaný klíček karpatsky*; *A Spell on the Carpathian Key*) (Rust-Rozvoda); *Proč se nesmeješ* (*Why Aren't You Laughing?*) (Piala)

1923   *Tu Ten Kámen* (*Tutankhamen*; *How to Have Love Flame on the Spot, even for the Deceased*) (Anton); *Muž bez srdce* (*Man without a Heart*) (Horňák and Koebner); *Únos bankére Fuxe* (*The Kidnapping of Banker Fuxe*) (Anton) (co); *Za opunu smrti* (*The Miraculous Doctor*) (Futurista)

1924   *Bílý Ráj* (*The White Paradise*) (Lamač); *Chytte ho!* (*Lupič nešika*; *Catch Him!*; *The Clumsy Robber*) (Lamač)

1925   *Píseň života* (*Song of Life*) (Krňanský); *Vdavky Nanynky Kulichovy* (*Marriage of Nanynky Kulickova*) (Krňanský); *Syn hor* (*Son of the Mountains*) (Slavínsky) (+ ro); *Lucerna* (*The Lantern*) (co); *Josef Kajetán Tyl* (Innemann)

1926   *Dobry voják Švejk* (*The Good Soldier Svejk*) (Lamač); *Hrabenka z Podskalí* (*Countess from Podskali*) (Lamač); *Příběh jednoho dne* (*Story of One Day*) (Krňanský); *Falešná kočička* (*The False Kitten*) (Innemann); *Švejk na fronte* (*Svejk at the Front*) (Lamač); *Lásky Kaňenky Strnadové* (*Loves of Kacenky Strnadova*) (Innemann); *Aniceko, vrate se!* (*Tulák*; *Anicka, Come Back!*; *Vagabond*) (Pištek)

1927   *Pantáta Bezoušek* (*Old Man Bezouska*) (Lamač); *Loupezeníci na Chlumu* (*Robbers on the Hill*) (Hajjsky) (co); *Kreutzerova sonáta* (*Kreutzer Sonata*) (Machatý); *Werther* (*Utrpení mladé lásky*; *Sorrows of Young Love*) (Hajsky); *Kvet ze Šumavy* (*Flowers from the Sumava*) (Lamač); *Kilenky starého kriminálníka* (*Loves of an Old Criminal*) (Innemann); *Sladká Josefínka* (*Sweet Little Josefina*) (Lamač); *Saxophon-Susi* (Lamač)

1928   *Dcery Eviny* (*A Married Daughter*, *Eve's Daughters*) (Lamač); *Evas Töchter* (Lamač); *Der erste Kuss* (Lamač); *Kedlubnový kavalír v ráji* (*A Gentleman in Paradise*) (Bondy)

1929   *Známosti z ulice* (*Acquaintances of the Street*) (Medeotti-Boháč); *Hřích* (*The Sin*) (Lamač); *Páter Vojtech* (*Father Vojtech*) (Frič); *Sündig und Süss* (Lamač); *Das Mädel mit der Peitsche* (Lamač); *Adjunkt Vrba* (Krňanský); *Die Kaviarprinzessin* (Lamač)

1930   *Starý hřích* (*The Old Sin*) (Krňanský); *Svatý Václav* (Kolár) (co); *Pradlenka Jeho Jasnosti* (*Her Highness' Young Washerwoman*) (Sauer); *Das Mädel aus U.S.A.* (Lamač); *Erzehog Otto und das Wäschermadel* (*Wiener Herzen*) (Sauer); *Eine Freundin so goldig wie Du* (Lamač); *Das Kabinett des Dr. Larifari* (Wohlmuth) (co); *Die von Rummelplatz*

(Lamač) (co); *Der falsche Feldmarschall* (*Der K und
K Feldermarschall*) (Lamač)

1931   *Monsieur Le Maréchal* (Lamač); *Die Privatsekretärin* (Thiele)
(co); *On a jeho sestra* (*He and His Sister*) (Lamač and
Frič); *Er und seine Schwester* (Lamač); *Dactylo* (Thiele)
(co); *Le Chauve-souris* (Lamač and Billon); *Die Fledermaus* (Lamač); *Der Zinker* (Lamač and Frič); *To neznáte
Hadimršku* (*So Nobody Knows Hadimrsku*) (Lamač and
Frič) (+ ro); *Mamsell Nitouche* (Lamač); *Une Nuit au
paradis* (Lamač and Frič)

1932   *Wehe, wenn er losgelassen* (*Unter Geschäftsaufsich*) (Lamač
and Frič); *Anton Špelec, ostrostřelec* (*Anton Spelec, Sharpshooter*) (Frič); *Funebrák* (*Funeral Attendant*; *What a Funeral*) (Lamač) (co); *Kantor Ideál* (*Ideal Teacher*) (Fric);
Die grausame Freundin (Lamač); *Faut-il les marier?* (Lamač
and Billon); *Lelíček ve službách Sherlocka Holmes* (*Lelicek
in the Service of Sherlock Holmes*) (Lamač); *Le Roi bis*
(Beaudoin) (co); *Před maturitou* (*Before Matriculation*)
(Vanceura and Innemann); *Der Hexer* (Lamač); *Baby*
(Lamač); *Kiki* (Lamač); *Zapadlí vlastenci* (*Forgotten Patriots*) (Krňanský)

1933   *La Fille du régiment* (Lamač and Billon); *Die Regimentstochter*
(Lamač and Zerlett) (co); *Betragen ungenuend* (Frič);
Dobrý tramp Bernasek (*Good Tramp Bernasek*) (Lamač);
Jindra, hrabenka Ostrovínová (*Jindra, Countess Ostrovin*)
(Lamač); *Jsem devče s čertem v tele* (*The Girl with the
Devil in Her*) (Anton) (co); *Fräulein Hoffmanns Erzählungen*
(Lamač) (co); *Pobočník jeho výsosti* (*His Highness' Adju-
tant*) (Frič); *Der Adjutant seiner Hoheit* (Frič); *Prodaná
nevesta* (*The Bartered Bride*) (Kvapil, Innemann and Pollert);
S vyloučenim veřejnosti (*Behind Closed Doors*) (Frič)
(+ ro); *Das verliebte Hotel* (Lamač) (co)

1934   *Anita v Ráji* (*Anita in Paradise*) (Sviták); *Hej rup!* (*Heave
Ho!*) (Frič); *Nezlobte dedečka* (*Don't Make Grandfather
Angry*) (Lamač); *Die vertauschte Braut* (Lamač) (co);
L'Amour en cage (Lamač and de Limur); *Karneval und
Liebe* (Lamač) (co); *Klein Dorrit* (Lamač) (co); *Zena, která
ví, co chce* (*The Woman Who Knows What She Wants*)
(Binovec) (co); *Tři kroky od tela* (*Three Steps Away from
Me*) (Innemann); *Polenblut* (Lamač); *Polská krev* (*Polish
Blood*) (Lamač)

1935   *A Život jde dál* (*And Life Goes On*) (Junghans); *Bařbora rádí*
(*Angry Barbara*) (Cikán); *Bezdetná* (*Childless*) (Krňanský);
Knock Out; *Ein junges Mädchen—ein junger Mann* (Lamač
and Zerlett); *Grossreinemachen* (Lamač) (co); *Jedenácté
preikazání* (*The Eleventh Commandment*) (Frič)

1936   *Jízdní hlídka* (*The Horse Patrol*) (Binovec) (co); *Na ty louce
zeleny* (*On the Green Meadow*) (Lamač); *Port Arthur*
(Farkas) (co); *Ulička v Ráji* (*An Alley in Paradise*; *Crumbs
for the Poor*) (Frič); *Uličnice* (*Gamine*; *Street Urchin*)
(Slavínský) (co); *The Amazing Quest of Ernest Bliss* (*Romance and Riches*) (Zeisler)

1937   *Litomyšl* (+ co-d with Pecenka); *Secret Lives* (*I Married
a Spy*) (Greville); *The High Command* (Dickinson); *Bílá
nemoc* (*The White Scourge*) (Haas); *Devčata, nedejte se!*
(*Don't Give In, Girls!*) (Haas); *Mademoiselle Docteur*
(*Under Secret Orders*) (Greville); *Svet patří nám* (*The
World Belongs to Us*) (Frič); *Duvod k rozvodu* (*Cause for
Divorce*) (Lamač); *Filosofská historie* (*Philosophical Story*)
(Vávra); *Karel Hynek Mácha* (Molas) (co)

1938   *Ducháček to zaridi* (*Duchacek Will See to It*) (Lamač); *Krok
do tmy* (*A Step to Darkness*) (Frič); *Slávko, nedej se!*
(*Slavka, Don't Give In!*) (Lamač) (co); *Treti zvoneni* (*The
Third Bell*) (Sviták); *Vertig Jaren* (*Forty Years*) (Greville)

1939   *Le Grand Élan* (Christian-Jaque) (co); *L'Enfer des anges*
(Christian-Jaque) (co); *Menaces* (Greville) (co)

1940   *De Mayerling á Sarajevo* (Max Ophuls); *L'Empreinte de Dieu*
(Moguy); *Soyez les bienvenus* (de Baroncelli); *Vingt-quatre
heures de perm'* (Cloche)

1942   *Alibi* (Hurst); *Tomorrow We Live* (*At Dawn We Die*) (King);
The Night Invader (Mason)

1943   *The Dark Tower* (Harlow); *They Met in the Dark* (Lamač);
The Hundred Pound Window (Hurst); *Candlelight in Algeria* (King)

1944   *One Exciting Night* (*You Can't Do without Love*) (Forde); *Mr.
Emmanuel* (French); *Flight from Folly* (Mason)

1945   *I Live in Grosvenor Square* (*A Yankee in London*) (Wilcox);
Gaiety George (*Showtime*) (King); *Night Boat to Dublin*
(Huntington)

1947   *They Made Me a Fugitive* (*I Became a Criminal*) (Cavalcanti);
Temptation Harbour (Comfort)

1948   *Bond Street* (Parry); *Noose* (*The Silk Noose*) (Greville); *The
Queen of Spades* (Dickinson); *The Last Days of Dolwyn*
(*Woman of Dolwyn*) (Williams)

1949   *Now Barabbas Was a Robber . . .* (*Now Barabbas*) (Parry);
Three Men and a Girl (Parry)

1950   *The Woman with No Name* (*Her Panelled Door*) (Vajda and
O'Ferrall); *I'll Get You for This* (*Lucky Nick Cain*) (Newman)

1951   *Flesh and Blood* (Kimmins); *Never Take No for an Answer*
(Cloche and Smart)

1952   *The Crimson Pirate* (Siodmak); *The Man Who Watched
Trains Go By* (*The Paris Express*) (French)

1953   *The Square Ring* (Dearden); *His Majesty O'Keefe* (Haskin)

1954   *The Rainbow Jacket* (Dearden); *The Divided Heart* (Crichton)

1955   *The Ladykillers* (Mackendrick); *Richard III* (Olivier)

1956   *Who Done It?* (Dearden); *Child in the House* (de Latour);
Circus Friends (Thomas); *The Passionate Stranger* (*A
Novel Affair*) (Muriel Box); *Kings and Queens* (Czinner)

1957   *The Silent Enemy* (Fairchild); *The Truth about Women* (Muriel
Box); *The Vicious Circle* (*The Circle*) (Thomas); *Manuela*
(*Stowaway Girl*) (Hamilton)

1958   *The Duke Wore Jeans* (Thomas); *The Sheriff of Fractured Jaw*
(Walsh); *Hello London* (Smith)

1959   *Ferry to Hong Kong* (Gilbert); *The Rough and the Smooth*
(*Portrait of a Sinner*) (Siodmak); *A Dog of Flanders*
(Clark); ***Peeping Tom*** (Powell)

1960   *The Singer Not the Song* (Baker); *An heiligen Wassern*
(Weidenmann)

1961   *The Big Show* (Clark); ***Victim*** (Dearden); *Light in the
Piazza* (Gren)

1962   *Tiara Tahiti* (Kotcheff); *Life for Ruth* (*Walk in the Shadow*)
(Dearden); *We Joined the Navy* (Toye)

1963   *West 11* (Winner); *What a Crazy World* (Carreras)

1964   *Woman of Straw* (Dearden); *The Curse of the Mummy's Tomb*
(Carreras); *A Gift for Love* (de Latour); *Masquerade*
(Dearden)

1965   *The Ipcress File* (Furie); *Alfie* (Gilbert)

1966   *That Riviera Touch* (Owen); *Funeral in Berlin* (Hamilton)

1967   *The Naked Runner* (Furie); *I'll Never Forget What's 'is Name*
(Winner); *Don't Raise the Bridge, Lower the River* (Paris)

1968   *Duffy* (Parrish)
1969   *Can Heironymus Merkin Ever Forget Mercy Humppe and
        Find True Happiness?* (Newley); *Bloomfield* (*The Hero*)
        (Harris); *In Search of Gregory* (Peter Wood)

Publications

On HELLER: articles—

Film a Doba (Prague), vol. 11, no. 769–771, 1959.
Obituary in *Today's Cinema*, no. 9781, 20 February 1970.
Focus on Film (London), no. 13, 1973.
Film Dope (Nottingham), March 1982.

*   *   *

Otto Heller is one of the many distinguished cameramen to have
come from the Czechoslovak region (others include Freund, Planer,
Ondricek, Kucera, Stallich, and Vich). His output is extremely wide-
ranging and prolific: credited with over 250 films, he worked in
Czechoslovakia, Austria, Germany, Holland, France, and England.

Heller's career began in earnest in 1918, after he filmed the
triumphal entry into Prague of the founder President of Czechoslovakia, Thomas Garrigue Masaryk. He contributed to many of the most
famous Czech films, Machatý's *Kreutzer Sonata*, Innemann's *Pred
maturitou*, and the films of Voscovec and Fric—*Hej rup!* and *Svet
patří nám*. He was especially associated with the films of Anny Ondra
and her husband Karl Lamač with whom he worked in many countries. Ironically, he was not appreciated as he should have been in his
native country and was often teamed with another cameraman.

He extended his experience in Germany, and in the *Berlin Film
Lexicon* of 1931 he is said to be esteemed for his technical knowledge
and refined taste, and capable of producing striking effects for any
subject. His exile to England in 1935 gave him the opportunity of
filming a wide range of subjects by many different directors, but
perhaps his greatest achievement was the exquisite work he did on
Thorold Dickinson's *Queen of Spades*, where Oliver Messel's superb
sets were seen at their best through Heller's creative lens. In 1955, he
filmed Mackendrick's *The Ladykillers* and Olivier's *Richard III*. His
technical knowledge and expertise in colour extended his previous
success in black-and-white photography.

—Liam O'Leary

HENRY, Buck

Writer and Actor. **Nationality:** American. **Born:** Buck Henry
Zuckerman in New York City, 9 December 1930; son of the actress
Ruth Taylor. **Education:** Attended Harvard Military Academy; Choate
School; Dartmouth College, Hanover, New Hampshire, graduated.
Military Service: U.S. Army (in 7th Army Repertory Company),
1952–54. **Career:** Stage and TV actor in New York; writer for Steve
Allen and Garry Moore TV shows, Hollywood; 1963—first film as
writer, *The Troublemaker*; 1964–65—writer and performer, *That

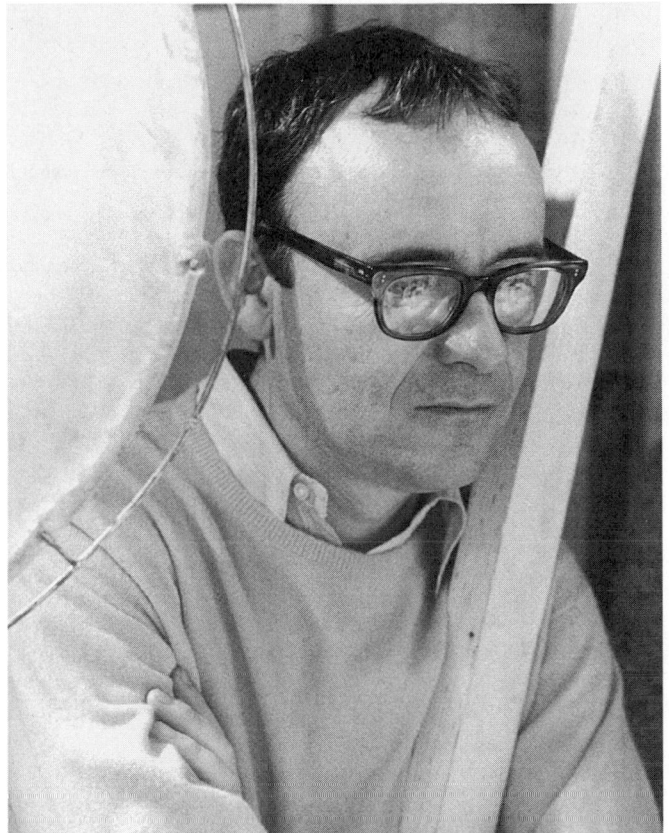

Buck Henry

Was the Week that Was; 1965–70—writer, TV series *Get Smart*;
1970s—appeared regularly on *Saturday Night Live*. **Awards:** British
Academy Award and Writers Guild Award, for *The Graduate*, 1968.
Agent: William Morris Agency, 151 El Camino Drive, Beverly Hills,
CA 90212, U.S.A.

Films as Writer:

1964   *The Troublemaker* (Flicker) (+ ro)
1968   ***The Graduate*** (Nichols) (+ ro); *Candy* (Marquand)
1970   *Catch-22* (Nichols) (+ ro); *The Owl and the Pussycat* (Ross)
1972   *What's Up, Doc?* (Bogdanovich)
1973   *The Day of the Dolphin* (Nichols)
1980   *First Family* (+ d, ro)
1984   *Protocol* (Ross)
1995   *To Die For* (Van Sant) (+ ro)
2000   *Town and Country* (Chelsom) (co)

Films as Actor:

1971   *Taking Off* (Forman) (as Larry Tyne); *Is There Sex after Death*
        (J. & A. Abel)
1976   *The Man Who Fell to Earth* (Roeg) (as Oliver Farnsworth)
1978   *Old Boyfriends* (Tewkesbury) (as Art Kopple); *Heaven Can
        Wait* (Beatty) (as the Escort, + co-d)

1979   *The Absent-Minded Waiter* (Gottlieb—short)
1980   *Gloria* (Cassavetes) (as Jack Dawn)
1982   *Eating Raoul* (Bartel) (as Mr. Leech)
1987   *Aria* (Temple) (as Mr. Preston)
1989   *Rude Awakening* (Russo) (as Lloyd)
1990   *Aunt Julia and the Scriptwriter* (*Tune in Tomorrow*) (Amiel)
       (as Fr. Serafim)
1991   *Defending Your Life* (Albert Brooks) (as Dick Stanley)
1992   **The Player** (Altman); *The Linguini Incident* (R. Shepard)
       (as Cecil)
1993   *Short Cuts* (Altman) (as Gordon Johnson); *Grumpy Old Men*
       (Petrie) (as Elliott Snyder); *Even Cowgirls Get the Blues*
       (Van Sant)
1997   *The Real Blonde* (DiCillo) (as Dr. Leuter)
1998   *The Story of X* (doc for Video) (as Host); *1999* (Davis) (as Mr.
       Goldman); *I'm Losing You* (Wagner) (as Philip Dragom)
1999   *Curtain Call* (Yates) (as Charles Van Allsburg); *Breakfast of
       Champions* (Rudolph) (as Fred T. Barry)
2000   *Famous* (as himself)

Publications

By HENRY: articles—

Films Illustrated (London), May 1976.
Sight and Sound (London), Summer 1976.
Film Comment, September 1993.
Fade In (Beverly Hills), vol. 1, no. 2, 1995.
Scenario (Rockville), vol. 2, no. 2, Summer 1996.

On HENRY: articles—

Focus on Film (London), Summer 1972.
American Film (Washington, D.C.), December 1980.
Film Comment (New York), September-October 1993.

*   *   *

Buck Henry is probably better known as an actor and comedian than as a screenwriter. In his screenplays, Henry shows an intellectual and often biting satirical wit. He takes on the contemporary human condition and allows the viewer to see and often laugh at the incongruities of life. His characters, however silly they act at times, are vulnerable and therefore human.

Henry began his career writing for television, including *The Steve Allen Show*, *That Was the Week that Was*, and numerous television comedians. He and Mel Brooks created the popular comedy spy spoof *Get Smart*, which ran on television for five years. Henry was story editor and won an Emmy Award for the series. The hero, Maxwell Smart, was a bumbling spy who, although seemingly naive and unaware of the forces at work around him, battled the evil organization K.A.O.S. and triumphed. The idea of an innocent person gaining wisdom and triumphing over chaos—"getting smart"—is a frame of reference that can be applied to Buck Henry's wildly satiric and often bittersweet screenplays. Many major film characters learn from their experiences, but in a Henry script the characters are often so unaware and confused that the gaining of insight is truly monumental.

His first film script, *The Troublemaker*, which he wrote with director Theodore Flicker, is about an honest country fellow who comes to New York to open a coffeehouse but first must pay off officials for licenses. The film stars actors from the improvisational group The Premise, which Henry joined in 1960. Although the satire is funny, the film lacks a tight structure due to the many improvisations.

Henry's next script, based on the novel by Charles Webb, was *The Graduate*, which he wrote with Calder Willingham. This film was the first of three Henry would write for director Mike Nichols, who undoubtedly did the finest interpretations of Henry's material. *The Graduate* is the story of Benjamin (Dustin Hoffman) who, although a whiz at college in both studies and athletics, appears zombielike to his parents and their friends, who have different values. Wonderfully satiric lines carry the innocent Benjamin through his affair with Mrs. Robinson (Anne Bancroft) until he gains real knowledge and decides on his own set of values. Having fallen in love with Mrs. Robinson's daughter Elaine (Katharine Ross), he overcomes all odds and rescues her at the church just before she weds a medical student. In the bittersweet ending, Benjamin and Elaine, finally together on a bus, say nothing to each other while Simon and Garfunkel's "The Sound of Silence" is heard on the soundtrack. The implied question is whether Benjamin and Elaine can really escape becoming like their parents. Few American films have enjoyed the immediate financial and critical success of *The Graduate*. It was a watershed film for those young people who were concerned about the values of a materialistic, plastic society.

Henry's next script was *Candy*, directed by Christian Marquand. Again, loss of innocence is a theme. The heroine (Ewa Aulin) is a teenager who encounters various odd characters in her search for wisdom. The novel was a parody of pornographic novels, which sadly did not translate well to the screen.

His next screenplay, his second for director Mike Nichols, was an adaptation of Joseph Heller's novel *Catch-22*. The innocent in this film is Yossarian (Alan Arkin), a bombardier in World War II, who perceives war and his military life as insane. The film becomes Yossarian's dream (actually a series of dream sequences) during which, as in psychoanalysis, more and more is revealed. Yossarian eventually gains insight and is able to make a decision about what to do. The lines are wonderfully funny, yet behind the humor is also the revelation of the horror of war itself. The circular construction of the script is brilliant.

Henry's next script, *The Owl and the Pussycat*, was adapted from a play by Bill Manhoff and directed by Herbert Ross. The film is about trying to get in touch with reality. An innocent aspiring writer-book salesman, Felix Sherman (George Segal) meets aspiring actress-hooker (Barbra Streisand) and through a series of comic situations, both learn that it is important to be themselves, to be real. A similar structure can be found in Henry's next work for director Peter Bogdanovich, *What's Up, Doc?* Henry did the final rewrite on Robert Benton and David Newman's screenplay, developed from a story by Bogdanovich. In this tribute to screwball comedies of the 1930s, unconventional student Judy Maxwell (Barbra Streisand) liberates conventional professor Dr. Howard Bannister (Ryan O'Neal) from a closed, boring life. The innocent professor, through a series of comic situations, comes to an understanding of both love and freedom.

In his third script for Mike Nichols, *The Day of the Dolphin*, Henry turns from comedy to drama. This time the innocents are two dolphins, Alpha and Beta, who are taught to speak English by marine biologist Dr. Jake Terrell (George C. Scott). Terrell himself is innocent too, as he does not consider all the implications of his work until the dolphins are stolen by men who plan to use them to blow up the yacht of the president of the United States. The dolphins escape and the attempted assassination is foiled. But the tremendously sad and difficult ending, where Terrell tells the dolphins to return to the sea and speak to no one again, and where he waits, wiser yet doomed, for the assassins to return to destroy him and all the evidence, made this film difficult for audiences who may have wanted a happy "Lassie"-type animal picture.

In 1978, Henry and Warren Beatty directed *Heaven Can Wait*, a remake of *Here Comes Mr. Jordan* (1941). Although Henry is not given writing credit, he probably contributed to the script by Beatty and Elaine May, which is about a football player, prematurely killed, who returns in a murdered millionaire's body. The innocent football player, Joe Pendleton (Beatty), gains wisdom quickly enough, and in hilarious scenes runs the millionaire's company ethically, harasses the murderers relentlessly, and finds true love.

Henry then wrote and directed *First Family*, about wacky U.S. President Manfred Link (Bob Newhart), his alcoholic wife (Madeline Kahn), nymphomaniac daughter (Gilda Radner), and various nutty staff members. President Link is trying to establish diplomatic relations (a link?) with the emerging African nation Upper Gorm, and this provides a showcase for many wild verbal and visual gags. In *First Family*, Henry satirizes high government officials of the United States and the mythical African country, but offers no solutions to their antics.

Henry does offer a solution in his next film, the second for director Herbert Ross, *Protocol*. Basing his script on a story by Charles Shyer, Nancy Meyers, and Harvey Miller, Henry makes the point that the people are responsible if their leaders are bunglers and that the people need to get involved in every phase of political life, from voting to holding elective office. The film satirizes not only politics but also contemporary media. It continues Henry's theme of an innocent gaining wisdom. An uncorrupted Washington cocktail waitress, Sunny Davis (Goldie Hawn), saves an emir from assassination. Immediately she becomes the darling of the media and also of the emir, who wants her as his bride. Seeing the opportunity to exchange her for a military base in the emir's mythical Middle Eastern country, members of the government make her a protocol officer to cover up their real motivation. Davis becomes aware of the plan, and through some very funny situations not only sets matters right but also finally runs for political office herself. She will now help make the system better. The film contains a positive message as well as being very funny. After *Protocol*, Henry continued to be very versatile. He acted in films and on the stage, wrote articles, and did other related work.

In 1995, he wrote the script for *To Die For*, based on the book by Joyce Maynard (a work of fiction suggested by a real murder) and directed by Gus Van Sant. In this complex, important, and satiric look at celebrity status, television, and contemporary society, there are many humorous moments, but underlying theme is true horror. The main character, Suzanne Stone (Nicole Kidman), like a "stone," has no feelings for others. She is captivated by television and will do anything to promote her rising career as a television news star, including manipulating a high school student and his friends to murder her husband, Larry Maretto (Matt Dillon), whom she sees as standing in her way. The form of the film is appropriate for the content. The narrative is fused with television techniques and imagery, and scenes are often fragmented and not necessarily in order. For example, there are television-like interviews, including one with Larry's sister Janice (Illeana Douglas) talking directly into the camera, with cuts to scenes illustrating her comments. And when Suzanne makes a videotape of her students, there are cuts from this to images on the tape itself. Continuing Henry's theme of people losing innocence and gaining wisdom, most people around Suzanne do "wise up" to her. But for some, including, ironically, Suzanne herself, wisdom comes too late, or not at all.

Buck Henry remains one of America's leading satirical screenwriters. Through his wit and insight, the viewer gains wisdom. He is an example of an "auteur" screenwriter, as his scripts all seem to be variations on a theme—his characters "get smart."

—H. Wayne Schuth

HENSON, Jim

Animator, Puppeteer, Director, and Producer. **Nationality:** American. **Born:** James Maury Henson in Greenville, Mississippi, 24 September 1936. **Education:** Studied theater arts, University of Maryland. **Family:** Married partner in puppetry Jane Nebel, 1959, children: Lisa, Cheryl, Brian, John, and Heather. **Career:** 1954— while still attending high school in Washington, D.C. worked as puppeteer on local TV show; while in college, produced regular five-minute TV puppet show, *Sam and Friends*, whose characters evolved into the Muppets; 1960s—Muppets featured on *Steve Allen Show, Ed Sullivan Show* and other prime-time programs, becoming a cult; 1965—short film *Timepiece* nominated for Academy Award; 1969— *Sesame Street* launched on PBS network, subsequently shown in 80 countries, winning numerous Emmys and a Peabody Award; 1976— *The Muppet Show* launched with backing from UK TV mogul Lord Grade, winning three Emmys and seen in 100 countries by an estimated 235 million viewers; 1979—set up Jim Henson's Creature Shop in London; made first feature film, *The Muppet Movie*; 1981— film-directing debut with *The Great Muppet Caper*; 1982—first all-animatronic feature, *The Dark Crystal*. **Awards:** Local Emmy, 1958. **Died:** Of streptococcal pneumonia, in New York City, 16 May 1990.

Films as Animator/Puppeteer:

1965 *Timepiece* (short) (+ d)
1968 *Hey Cinderella* (+ d)
1970 *Number Twelve Rocks* (short) (+ d)
1971 *Frog Prince* (+ d)
1979 *The Muppet Movie* (Frawley) (+ pr, ro)
1981 *The Great Muppet Caper* (+ d, pr, ro)
1982 *The Dark Crystal* (+ co-d with Oz, co-pr, co-sc)
1984 *The Muppets Take Manhattan* (Oz) (+ pr, ro)
1986 *Labyrinth* (+ d, co-sc)

Jim Henson

Other Films:

1985   *Into the Night* (Landis) (ro as man on phone); *Dreamchild*
        (Millar) (creature des)
1989   *The Bear* (Annaud) (creature des)
1990   *Teenage Mutant Ninja Turtles* (Barron) (creature des); *The
        Witches* (Roeg) (creature des, co-pr)

Publications

By HENSON: article—

Interview in *American Film* (Washington, D.C.), November 1989.

On HENSON: books—

Finch, Christopher, *Of Muppets and Men*, New York, 1981.
Froud, Brian, *The World of the Dark Crystal*, New York, 1982.
Finch, Christopher, *The Making of the Dark Crystal*, New York, 1983.

Finch, Christopher, *Jim Henson the Works: The Art, the Magic, the
    Imagination*, New York, 1993.
St. Pierre, Stephanie, *The Story of Jim Henson: Creator of "The
    Muppets,"* Milwaukee, 1997.
Bacon, Matt, *No Strings Attached: The Inside Story of Jim Henson's
    Creature Factory*, New York, 1997.
Canizares, Susan, *Meet Jim Henson*, New York, 1999.
Minghella, Anthony, *Jim Henson's Storyteller*, New York, 1999.

On HENSON: articles—

Skow, John, "Those Marvellous Muppets," in *Time* (New York), 25
    December 1978.
American Cinematographer (Hollywood), July 1979.
Magid, Ron, "Goblin World Created for *Labyrinth*," in *American
    Cinematographer* (Hollywood), August 1986.
Wells, Theresa, "Henson: From Muppets to 'Storyteller,'" in *Holly-
    wood Reporter*, 30 January 1987.
Prady, Bill, "Jim Henson," in *Rolling Stone* (New York), 28 June 1990.
Owen, David, "Looking out for Kermit," in *New Yorker*, 16
    August 1993.

Johnson, Richard, ''Muppet Master,'' in *Radio Times* (London), 8 July 1995.

''Jim Henson 40th Anniversary,'' special issue of *Variety* (New York), 11 December 1995.

Ecran Fantastique (Paris), June 1996.

Collins, James, ''Jim Henson,'' in *Time*, 8 June 1998.

''Jim Henson: A Gentle Genius Changed Forever the Way America Looks at Talking Frogs—and Children's Television,'' in *People Weekly*, 15 March 1999.

* * *

As a child, Jim Henson devised his first puppets by cutting bits of cloth from a discarded coat of his mother's. When he made his television debut, on a local station in Washington, D.C., his puppet was an old green sock with his hand inside it. Though he was to pioneer a revolution in puppeteering through such intricate and subtle techniques as animatronics and computer-generated imaging (CGI), something of the same basic simplicity always remained at the heart of Henson's creations. Kermit the frog, his most famous character, was visibly close kin to that old green sock. Henson could stick two eyes on a lump of wood and the thing would take on a life and personality of its own.

It was this mix of simplicity and sophistication that fueled the success of the Muppets, Henson's best-known creations. Both the educationally oriented *Sesame Street* and its successor, *The Muppet Show* appealed to children and adults alike because, although the shows' outlook on the world (which was also Henson's outlook) was essentially benevolent, it was never sugary or sentimental. As well as the engagingly laid-back humor, there was an underlying anarchy to the Muppets; characters could be spiky, grotesque, malicious, even tragic. Fozzie Bear was an unstable depressive; Miss Piggy was a monster of vanity, all the funnier for recalling so many human showbiz counterparts; Rowlf the jazz-pianist dog was clearly high on something more potent than lemonade; and melancholy lurked behind Kermit's perky resilience. When he sang, ''It's Not Easy Being Green'' (voiced, as Kermit always was, by Henson himself), it was with a heartbreaking and universal sadness.

Like most acts originally conceived for television, the Muppets never worked quite so well on the big screen. Henson himself masterminded the first three Muppet films (there have been two more since his death), but despite his direct input the need to sustain a feature-length plot and the loss of the enclosed, backstage music-hall world of the television show left the characters feeling overextended and adrift, and the films rarely attained the same level of exuberant irreverence. Their chief value lay in the opportunities they afforded Henson to exercise his creative ingenuity and stretch his technique—such as the famous scene in *The Great Muppet Caper* where Kermit and Miss Piggy ride (real) bicycles around each other in Hyde Park.

Even more ambitious in terms of sheer technique were Henson's two excursions into the realm of semi-adult fantasy, *The Dark Crystal* and *Labyrinth*. In these films he seized every chance to extend the boundaries of animatronics, his technique of remote-controlling puppet figures via multiple electronic impulses—thus allowing a far wider range of emotions to be expressed than could ever be achieved through traditional puppeteering. But in both films the technique, dazzling as it was, and Henson's evident delight in the minutiae of his blinking, twitching creatures, tended to swamp the already fairly thin story lines.

Had Henson not died suddenly at age 53, he would almost certainly have found ways of reconciling sophistication with simplicity, of rendering his increasingly complex techniques unobtrusive and placing them at the service of a strong, clear story line. Five years after his death the company he founded, Jim Henson Productions, succeeded in producing just such a film, *Babe*—and reaped the reward both critically and at the box office. As *Babe* shows, Henson's legacy is twofold: through Henson Productions, now headed by his son Brian and resurgent from the trauma of its founder's death; and in wider terms through his achievement in advancing puppet-animation technique into areas of complexity undreamt of when he started out armed only with humor, ingenuity, and a green sock.

—Philip Kemp

HERLTH, Robert

Art Director. **Nationality:** German. **Born:** Robert Paul Fritz Herlth in Wriezen an der Oder, 2 May 1893. **Education:** Attended High School for Fine Arts, Berlin, 1912–14; Staatliche Kunstegewerbeschule, Berlin, 1919–20. **Military Service:** 1914–18—served in the German army. **Family:** Brother of the designer Kurt Herlth. **Career:** 1916–18—first theatre designs for army theatre, Wilna, with Herman Warm; 1922–36—film designer, often with Walter Röhrig, for UFA; 1937–39—designed for Tobis; 1939–45—designed for Terra; 1946–47—designed for Ulenspiegel; 1947–49—designed for Columbia, Rome; 1949–50—designed for Kamera; 1950–62—freelance film and stage designer. **Died:** In Munich, 6 January 1962.

Films as Art Director:

1920   *Das Lachende Grauen* (Meinert); *Das Geheimnis von Bombay* (Holz); *Die Toteninsel* (Froelich); *Irrende Seelen* (Froelich)

1921   *Schloss Vogelöd* (Murnau); *Satansketten* (Lasko); *Der müde Tod* (*Between Two Worlds*; *Destiny*) (Lang); *Das Speil mit dem Feuer* (Wiene and Kroll); *Die Intriguen der Madame de la Pommeraye* (Wendhausen)

1922   *Der Taugenichts* (Froelich); *Der Graf von Essex* (Felner); *Pariserinnen* (Lasko); *Fräulein Julie* (*Miss Julie*) (Basch); *Luise Millerin* (Froelich)

1923   *Der Schatz* (*The Treasure*) (Pabst)

1924   *Komödie des Herzens* (Gliese); ***Der letzte Mann*** (*The Last Laugh*) (Murnau)

1925   *Zur Chronik von Grieshuus* (*At the Grey House*) (von Gerlach); *Tartüff* (*Tartuffe*) (Murnau)

1926   *Faust* (Murnau)

1927   *Luther* (Kyser)

1928   *Looping the Loop* (Robison); *Rutschbahn* (Eichberg)

1929   *Die wunderbare Lüge der Nina Petrowna* (*The Wonderful Lie of Nina Petrovna*) (Schwarz); *Asphalt* (May); *Manolescu* (Tourjansky); *The Informer* (Robison)

1930   *Der unsterbliche Lump* (Ucicky); *Hokuspokus* (*Hocus pocus*) (Ucicky); *Rosenmontag* (Steinhoff); *Ein Burschenlied aus Heidelberg* (Hartl); *Das Flötenkonzert von Sanssouci* (Ucicky); *Der Mann, der seinen Mörder sucht* (Siodmak)

1931   *Der falsche Ehemann* (Guter); *Nie wieder Liebe* (Litvak); *Im Genheimdienst* (Ucicky); *Der kleine Seitensprung* (Schünzel); *Der Kongress tanzt* (*The Congress Dances*) (Charell); *Yorck* (Ucicky)

1932   *Die Gräfin von Monte Cristo* (Hartl); *Mensch ohne Namen* (*Man without a Name*) (Ucicky); *Der Schwarze Husar* (*The Black Hussar*) (Lamprecht)

1933   *Morgenrot* (Ucicky); *Ich und die Kaiserin* (*The Only Girl*) (Hollaender); *Saison in Kairo* (Schünzel); *Walzerkrieg* (*Waltz Time in Vienna*) (Berger); *Flüchtlinge* (Ucicky)

1934   *Die Csardasfürstin* (Jacoby); *Der junge Baron Neuhaus* (Ucicky); *Prinzessin Turandot* (Lamprecht)

1935   *Frischer Wind aus Kanada* (Kenter and Holder); *Barcarole* (Lamprecht); *Das Mädchen Johanna* (Ucicky); *Amphitryon* (Schünz el); *Königswaltzer* (Maisch)

1936   *Hans im Glück* (+ d + sc); *Savoy-Hotel 217* (Ucicky); *Unter heissem Himmel* (Ucicky)

1937   *Der Herrscher* (*The Ruler*) (Harlan); *Der zerbrochene Krug* (Ucicky); *Der Maulkorb* (Engel)

1938   **Olympia** (Riefenstahl); *Der Spieler* (Lamprecht)

1939   *Morgen werde ich verhaftet* (Stroux); *Maria Ilona* (von Bolvary); *Opernball* (von Bolvary)

1940   *Kleider machen Leute* (Kütner); *Rosen in Tirol* (von Bolvary)

1941   *Die schwedische Nachtigall* (Brauer)

1942   *Andreas Schlüter* (Maisch)

1943   *Wenn die Sonne weider scheint* (Barlog); *Ein Mann mit Grundsaltzen?* (von Bolvary)

1944   *Melusine* (Steinhoff)

1946   *Die Fledermaus* (von Bolvary)

1947   *Zwischen gestern und morgen* (Braun); *Film ohne Titel* (*Film without Title*) (Jugert)

1949   *La leggenda di Faust* (Gallone); *Verspieltes Leben* (Meisel); *1 x 1 der Ehe* (Jugert); *Geliebter Lügner* (Schweikart)

1950   *Kein Engel ist so rein* (Weiss); *Das Doppelte Lottchen* (von Baky); *Dämonische Liebe* (*Der Teufel führt Regie*) (Meisel)

1951   *Dr. Holl* (Hansen); *Das weisse Abenteuer* (Rabenalt)

1952   *Herz der Welt* (Braun); *Hinter Kostermann* (Reinl); *Die Försterchristl* (Rabenalt); *Der grosse Zapfeinstreich* (Hurdalek); *Alraune* (Rab enalt); *Im weissen Rössl* (Forst); *Der Kaplan von San Lorenzo* (Ucicky)

1953   *Das Dorf unter Himmel* (Häussler); *Musik bei Nacht* (Hoffmann); *Die geschiendene Frau* (Jacoby); *Hochzeitglocken* (Wildhagen)

1954   *Sauerbruch—Das war mein Leben* (Hansen); *Das fliegende Klassenzimmer* (Hoffman); *Der letzte Sommer* (Braun); *Geliebte Feindin* (Hansen)

1955   *Solang' es hübsche Mädchen gibt* (Rabenalt); *Hanussen* (Fischer and Marischka); *Der letzte Mann* (Braun); *Teufel in Seide* (*Devil in Silk*) (Hansen); *Regine* (Braun)

1956   *Magic Fire* (Dieterle); *Heute heiratet mein Mann* (Hoffmann); *Die Trapp-Familie* (Liebeneiner); *Heisse Ernte* (König)

1957   *Die Letzten werden die Ersten sein* (Hansen); *Bekenntnisse des Hochstaplers Felix Krull* (*The Confessions of Felix Krull*) (Hoffmann); *. . . und führe uns nicht in Versuchung* (Hansen); *Das Wirtshaus im Spessart* (*The Spessart Inn*) (Hoffmann)

1958   *Taiga* (Liebeneiner); *Auferstehung* (*Resurrection*) (Hansen); *Die Trapp-Familie in Amerika* (Liebeneiner) (condensed version of two Trapp Family films released as *The Trapp*

Family, 1958); *Ein gewisser Judas* (Werner); *Dorothea Angermann* (Siodmak)

1959   *Das schöne Abenteuer* (Hoffmann); *Buddenbrooks* (Weidenmann—2 parts); *Ein Tag, der nie zu Ende geht* (Wirth)

1960   *Eine Frau fürs ganze Leben* (Liebeneiner); *Gustav Adolfs Page* (Hansen)

1961   *Die Auster und die Perle* (Schnell)

1962   *Jack Mortimer* (Kahlmann)

1963   *Herr und Hund* (van den Berg); *In einer Fremden Stadt* (Hess); *Zum Tee bei Dr. Borsig* (Hess); *Millionär für 3 Tage* (Sedlmayer)

Publications

By HERLTH: book—

Filmarchitektur, Munich, 1965.

By HERLTH: articles—

''With Murnau on the Set,'' in *Murnau*, by Lotte H. Eisner, Paris, 1964, London, 1973.
Contracampo (Madrid), no. 38, Winter 1985.

On HERLTH: articles—

Kaul, Walter, in *Schöpferische Filmarchitektur*, Berlin, 1971.
Retro (Munich), May-June 1981.
Richter, Arno, in *Cinématographe* (Paris), February 1982.
Skrien (Amsterdam), February-March 1990.
Film-Dienst (Cologne), 25 May 1993.

*   *   *

If the pinnacle of German art direction occurred from the late 1910s through the early 1930s, then Robert Herlth, Walter Röhrig, and Hermann Warm represented that period's preeminent set designers. They fully visualized the distorted Expressionist film style as well as the more naturalistic *Kammerspiel*. Together they were responsible for the impressive UFA films by such important directors as Fritz Lang, Gustav Ucicky, Gerhard Lamprecht, Reinhold Schünzel, and F.W. Murnau.

Though he worked within the Expressionistic mode, Herlth's designs were not as severe as Röhrig's and Warm's, especially when compared to their extreme *The Cabinet of Dr. Caligari*. Herlth seemed more interested in exploiting the liberating romantic potentials of the movement's visual *Helldunkel* then its claustrophobic psychoses. His collaboration with Murnau and Röhrig on *Der letzte Mann*, *Tartuffe* and *Faust* demonstrates this direction. They modified Expressionism by pushing beyond its strict borders towards a naturalism that ironically permitted more fantasy and psychological investigation. As large baroque sets became simpler and sparser, camera stasis yielded to camera action. Instead of designing ''expressive'' spaces that limited action and camera movement and into which an actor was placed and frequently dwarfed, Herlth and Röhrig provided psychological impetus for movement based on locations suggested by an actor's situation. Herlth said that they attempted to adapt the space to the actor; the set could function only when the actor filled and controlled the space. Under these circumstances, the "moving camera," or *Entfesselte Kamera* as it was originally known, was born during the filming of *Der letzte Mann*. Karl Freund's incessantly moving camera perfectly complemented the interior psychology and dreams of the film as expressed by the art direction and narrative.

Herlth, Röhrig, Murnau, and Freund continued this experimentation in *Tartuffe*, by suggesting a historical era through evocative yet partial sets, and in the definitive screen version of *Faust* (Freund was replaced by Carl Hoffmann), by adopting unusual point-of-view shots, for example, Mephisto soaring over an expansive miniature landscape.

Herlth and Röhrig settled down to much less adventurous careers after Murnau's untimely death. Both worked during the period of the Third Reich, their *Kammerspiel* style giving way to social realism in the guise of propaganda. Herlth collaborated with Leni Riefenstahl for the visual strategies of the epic *Olympia*. After the war, Herlth was a prolific designer for routine studio productions and television until the early 1960s.

—Greg S. Faller

HERRERA, Jorge

Cinematographer. **Nationality:** Cuban. **Career:** Cameraman, Cuban Film Institute; 1966—first film as cinematographer. **Died:** In November 1981.

Films as Cinematographer:

1966   *La salación* (Gómez); *Manuela* (Solás)
1968   *Lucía* (Solás)
1969   **La primera carga al machete** (*The First Charge of the Machete*) (Gómez)
1971   *Las dias del agua* (Gómez)
1975   *Cantata de Chile* (Solás)
1981   **Alsino y el condor** (*Alsino and the Condor*) (Littin)

Publications

By HERRERA: articles—

"Apuntes sobre la fotografía de *La primera carga al machete*," in *Cine Cubano* (Havana), May-August 1969.
Cinema 2002 (Madrid), March-April 1980.

On HERRERA: articles—

Littin, Miguel, "Recado a Jorge," in *Cine Cubano* (Havana), no. 102, 1982.
In *The Cuban Image: Cinema and Cultural Politics in Cuba*, by Michael Chanan, London, 1985.

*   *   *

Best known for the expressive realism of his cinematography in *Lucía* and *The First Charge of the Machete*, Jorge Herrera was at one

with the revolutionary cultural effervescence of the late 1960s in Cuba. An outstanding cameraman of the Cuban Film Institute (Instituto Cubano de Arte e Industria Cinematográfica)—and one of the most creative in Latin America—Herrera argued that the most important role of the camera was to make images live with their greatest intensity. Thus, he felt that cinematography should be expressive rather than naturalist, penetrating into reality to decipher it, rather than remaining at the surface of things, with a mere reflection of nature. He perceived the camera as a participant in film: not just watching, but inciting, stimulating, and impelling the action.

For Herrera, the hand-held camera was the means to achieve his cinematographic goals. He stated: "The hand-held camera is more human, more authentic, and more intimate. It implies freshness, spontaneity, and improvisation; it lives, feels, loves, and hates. It also provides the actors with greater liberty of action, helping them to feel themselves as human beings and not just actors." Herrera felt that this technique led away from the artificial sense of films produced with enormously complicated apparatus for lighting, set decoration, and cameras, and moved toward a light, agile cinema more suited to Cuban reality and, obviously, greatly influenced by the Cuban tradition of documentary film.

However, if Herrera's use of the hand-held camera was a step beyond the traditional cinematography of Hollywood, his style must also be differentiated from other forms which employ this technique. For example, in contrast to the casual, personal aesthetic of the French New Wave, where the hand-held camera emphasizes the fact of the auteur, Herrera's style stressed collectivity and the reality of revolutionary struggle. Here, however, it is important to note that Herrera was not searching for a realist aesthetic, but attempting to convey a certain attitude toward reality. Thus, Herrera also goes beyond what might be described as the television news style of on-the-spot reportage. He accomplishes this, first of all, by having the camera participate in the action, demonstrating that everyone is involved, even those who attempt to remain calmly on the sidelines reporting on the occurrence.

Herrera's most important contribution to world cinema, though, is the manner in which he demolishes the classic dichotomy of realism and expressionism in the battle sequence of *The First Charge of the Machete*. There, the hand-held camera initially appears to effect the characteristic form of modern realism, reproducing the sensation of television's live coverage of events. However, as the sequence evolves and the battle heightens, Herrera's camera begins to career wildly, taking on the frenzy of the hand-to-hand combat; combined with an extreme high-contrast film, this produces a screen image which at times is little more than a swirling mass of abstract patterns. The poles of realism and expressionism are joined in this paean to revolutionary struggle in the field and with the camera, resulting in the simultaneous distancing and sensuous identification for which the cinema of Cuba has been justifiably praised.

—John Mraz

HERRMANN, Bernard

Composer. **Nationality:** American. **Born:** New York City, 29 June 1911. **Education:** Attended DeWitt Clinton High School and New York University; studied with Philip James, Bernard Wagenaar, and

Albert Stoessel at Juilliard Graduate School, New York. **Family:** Married the writer Lucille Fletcher, 1939 (divorced). **Career:** 1931— organized New Chamber Orchestra; 1934–59—worked for CBS, as conductor, and composer (including music for Welles's *Mercury Theater Playhouse*), and, from 1940, chief conductor of the CBS Symphony Orchestra; also composer of orchestra and stage works; 1941—first score for film, *Citizen Kane*; also composer for TV. **Awards:** Academy Award, for *All that Money Can Buy*, 1941; British Academy Award, for *Taxi Driver*, 1976. **Died:** 24 December 1975.

Films as Composer:

1941   *Citizen Kane* (Welles); *All that Money Can Buy* (*The Devil and Daniel Webster*; *Here Is a Man*; *Daniel and the Devil*) (Dieterle)
1942   *The Magnificent Ambersons* (Welles) (co)
1943   *Jane Eyre* (Stevenson)
1945   *Hangover Square* (Brahm)
1946   *Anna and the King of Siam* (Cromwell)
1947   *The Ghost and Mrs. Muir* (Mankiewicz)
1948   *Portrait of Jennie* (*Jennie*) (Dieterle) (song)
1951   *The Day the Earth Stood Still* (Wise); *On Dangerous Ground* (Ray)
1952   *Five Fingers* (Mankiewicz); *The Snows of Kilimanjaro* (H. King)
1953   *White Witch Doctor* (Hathaway); *Beneath the 12-Mile Reef* (Webb); *King of the Khyber Rifles* (H. King)
1954   *Garden of Evil* (Hathaway); *The Egyptian* (Curtiz) (co); *Prince of Players* (Dunne); *The Trouble with Harry* (Hitchcock)
1955   *The Kentuckian* (Lancaster); *The Man Who Knew Too Much* (Hitchcock) (+ bit ro)
1956   *The Man in the Gray Flannel Suit* (Johnson); *The Wrong Man* (Hitchcock)
1957   *A Hatful of Rain* (Zinnemann); *Williamsburg*: *The Story of a Patriot* (Seaton—short)
1958   *Vertigo* (Hitchcock); *The Naked and the Dead* (Walsh); *The Seventh Voyage of Sinbad* (Juran)
1959   *North by Northwest* (Hitchcock); *Blue Denim* (*Blue Jeans*) (Dunne); *Journey to the Center of the Earth* (Levin)
1960   *Psycho* (Hitchcock); *The Three Worlds of Gulliver* (Sher)
1961   *Mysterious Island* (Endfield); *Cape Fear* (Lee Thompson); *Tender Is the Night* (H. King)
1963   *Jason and the Argonauts* (Chaffey); *The Birds* (Hitchcock) (consultant)
1964   *Marnie* (Hitchcock); *Joy in the Morning* (Segal)
1966   *Fahrenheit 451* (Truffaut)
1967   *La Mariée était en noir* (*The Bride Wore Black*) (Truffaut)
1968   *Twisted Nerve* (R. Boulting); *Companion in Nightmare* (Lloyd); *Bitka na Neretvi* (*Battle of Neretva*) (Bulajic—English version)
1970   *The Night Digger* (*The Road Builder*) (Reid)
1972   *Endless Night* (Gilliat); *Sisters* (*Blood Sisters*) (De Palma)
1973   *It's Alive* (Cohen)
1975   *Obsession* (De Palma)
1976   *Taxi Driver* (Scorsese)

Posthumous Films:

1978   *It Lives Again* (Cohen)
1987   *It's Alive III: Island of the Alive* (Cohen)
1991   *Cape Fear* (Scorsese) (arranged by Elmer Bernstein)

Publications

By HERRMANN: articles—

''From Soundtrack to Disc,'' in *Saturday Review of Literature* (New York), 27 September 1947.
Sight and Sound (London), Winter 1971–72.
In *Knowing the Score*, by Irwin Baselon, New York, 1975.
In *Film Score*, edited by Tony Thomas, South Brunswick, New Jersey, 1979.
In *Sound and the Cinema*, edited by Evan Cameron, Pleasantville, New York, 1980.

On HERRMANN: books—

Bruce, Graham, *Bernard Herrmann: Film Music and Narrative*, Ann Arbor, Michigan, 1985.
Smith, Stephen C., *A Heart at Fire's Center: The Life and Music of Bernard Herrmann*, Berkeley, California, 1991.
Kalinak, Kathryn, *Settling the Score: Music and the Classical Hollywood Film*, Madison, Wisconsin, 1992.
Brown, Royal S., *Overtones and Undertones: Reading Film Music*, Berkeley, California, 1994.

On HERRMANN: articles—

Cook, Page, in *Films in Review* (New York), August/September 1967.
Films in Review (New York), June/July 1970.
Monthly Film Bulletin (London), November 1970, corrections in November 1972.
Special Visual Effects, Summer 1972.
National Film Theatre Booklet (London), June/July 1972.
Thomas, Tony, in *Music for the Movies*, South Brunswick, New Jersey, 1973.
Dirigido por . . . (Barcelona), March 1974.
Steiner, Fred, in *Film Music Notebook* (Calabasas, California), Fall 1974.
Films in Review (New York), October 1974.
Ecran (Paris), September 1975.
Photon (New York), no. 27, 1976.
De Palma, Brian, in *Take One* (Montreal), vol. 5, no. 2, 1976.
Films in Review (New York), January 1976.
Skoop (Amsterdam), February 1976.
Film Français (Paris), 6 February 1976.
Films in Review (New York), March 1976.
Cinema Papers (Melbourne), March/April 1976.
Films in Review (New York), April 1976.
Focus on Film (London), Summer/Autumn 1976.
Broeck, John, ''Music of the Fears,'' in *Film Comment* (New York), September/October 1976.

Palmer, Christopher, in *Monthly Film Bulletin* (London), October 1976, corrections in January 1980.

Positif (Paris), November 1976.

Maffet, James D., in *Film Music Notebook* (Calabasas, California), vol. 3, no. 1, 1977.

Film Music Notebook (Calabasas, California), vol. 3, no. 2, 1977.

Films Illustrated (London), April 1977.

Ecran Fantastique (Paris), no. 3, 1978.

Classic Film/Video Images, July 1980.

Soundtrack! (Hollywood), Spring 1981.

Filmcritica (Rome), June 1981.

Filmusic (Leeds), 1982.

Cinema Journal (Evanston, Illinois), Spring 1982.

Lacombe, Alain, in *Hollywood*, Paris, 1983.

Soundtrack! (Hollywood), September 1985.

Soundtrack! (Hollywood), vol. 5, no. 18, June 1986.

Soundtrack! (Hollywood), vol. 5, no. 19, September 1986.

Kalinak, K., "The Text of Music: A Study of *The Magnificent Ambersons*," in *Cinema Journal* (Champaign, Illinois), Summer 1988.

Palmer, Christopher, in *The Composer in Hollywood*, 1990.

Chanan, Michael, "American Rhapsodies," in *Sight & Sound* (London), November 1991.

Fischer, D., "Bernard Herrmann," in *Soundtrack* (Mechelen), September 1992.

Pool, Jeannie, "Music for the Movies: Bernard Herrmann: An Interview with Director Joshua Waletzky and Composer David Raskin," in *Cue Sheet* (Hollywood), Spring 1993–1994.

Landrot, Marine, "La musique qui tue," in *Télérama* (Paris), 1 December 1993.

Doherty, Jim, "Concert Works," in *Soundtrack* (Mechelen), June 1994.

*   *   *

Surely no film scores have inspired so many passionate admirers or so much detailed analysis as have those of Bernard Herrmann. Even the general public, asked to cite memorable "movie music," may think not only of tunes such as the title theme of *Gone with the Wind* (Max Steiner) or *Breakfast at Tiffany's* "Moon River" (Henry Mancini) but of the violin shrieks of Herrmann's *Psycho* score (or turning to television, his *Twilight Zone* theme). Arriving on the film scene to score Orson Welles's *Citizen Kane*, and reaching his greatest fame working for Alfred Hitchcock—a collaboration which produced in a row three of the director's and the composer's finest achievements, *Vertigo*, *North by Northwest*, and *Psycho*—the famously cantankerous Herrmann achieved little public recognition among his peers: he did receive an Oscar in 1941 but only two other nominations (in 1941 and 1946) until two more posthumous ones in 1976. Still, he was championed in his later years by a younger generation of major directors—François Truffaut, Brian De Palma, Martin Scorsese—and is now one of the few composers of film music to be the subject of full-length book treatments (a biography and a critical study of his work).

Herrmann's first notes of music for the cinema—the portentous opening of *Citizen Kane*—already offer many characteristics of the Herrmann style: unusual orchestrations (e.g., low winds, vibraphone); unresolved chords that are not simply suspenseful in some melodramatic way but also create a brooding sense of time suspended; and melodic fragments (or what Graham Bruce calls cellular units rather than lengthier leitmotifs) that will later be developed. Herrmann worked closely with Welles on the project, rather than being brought in only on postproduction. Thus the two were able to achieve some virtuoso fusions of music and drama, as in the breakfast montage portraying the collapse of Kane's first marriage, in which the editing is done to match Herrmann's theme-and-variations, and in the opera-house scene, with Herrmann's French aria à la Massenet providing music that Susan is ill-equipped to sing, as well as a grandiosity that seems to mock Kane's ambitions.

A later 1940s score, one of Herrmann's personal favorites, for *The Ghost and Mrs. Muir*, is superficially closer to standard Hollywood practice, but it too is suggestive of Herrmann's qualities as a whole. Mrs. Muir's first visit to the haunted cottage is scored with music that is, as one would expect, suspenseful, but again not crassly melodramatic or spooky: indeed, much of it is rather tender (befitting a wistful supernatural romance, as the film turns out to be), if not downright yearning. It is not melodic in the usual sense (such as, say, the tune for *Laura*), but its curious harmonic suspensions keep *us* in a state of suspension. The technique is essentially the same in Herrmann's score a few years later for *The Day the Earth Stood Still*, except of course for the electronic instruments giving a greater eeriness to that science fiction film. And we are not far from the moody music for investigative scenes in *The Man Who Knew Too Much* and *Vertigo*.

Herrmann worked in fewer genres than the majority of Hollywood veterans: chiefly dramas of suspense (including no less than eight about demented killers, and as many again about haunted or driven men) and more boisterous action-adventure tales, including a fantasy series beginning with *The Seventh Voyage of Sinbad*. But there are consistencies in his style, beginning with a special attention to orchestration. Unlike most Hollywood composers (if one may use a term he detested), Herrmann always did his own orchestrations—one reason he was less prolific than many. There are characteristic Herrmann sounds and favorite instruments, e.g., clarinets in low register, French horns (nine used for the manhunt in *On Dangerous Ground*), and harps (again nine solo parts in *Beneath the 12-Mile Reef*). But equally characteristic is his experimentation with unusual sounds: the sonic palette reduced to strings for *Psycho*, no strings in *Journey to the Center of the Earth*, the contrabassoon-like serpent in *White Witch Doctor*. (For *The Birds*, he composed no music at all, but worked closely with Hitchcock to integrate electronic renditions of bird sounds into the drama.)

He is hardly the only composer, classical or popular, to use seventh chords extensively for a mood of suspense, tension, or irresolution; but few have used such unresolved chords as such a basic principle of musical organization, as studies of Herrmann's Hitchcock scores have demonstrated. Passages in Herrmann scores certainly hark back to classical music: the scene in *Vertigo* of Scottie waiting to see Judy transformed back into his lost Madeleine virtually quotes from Wagner's *Tristan und Isolde*, and echoes of Ravel, Elgar, even Tchaikovsky (the love theme of *North by Northwest*), and others are common enough. Yet his particular choices of melodic fragments, harmonies, and orchestrations, all combined, make Herrmann one of the most readily identifiable of all soundtrack composers.

If one were to single out a Herrmann score as the composer's supreme achievement, a major contender would be the one for

Vertigo. Unforgettably passionate and yearning, sometimes night-marish and other times coolly eerie, the music drenches the San Francisco Bay Area setting in varied moods and seems the very essence of the protagonist's obsessive love. But one could make a case for several others, including the score for *Psycho*, alternately conveying frantic desperation and a state of being frozen in time, or even the exuberant, witty *North by Northwest.* Herrmann may not have been responsible for a measurable "40 percent" of the success of Hitchcock's films, as the composer liked to boast, but his contributions to those films' astonishing sense of seamless artistic wholeness are incalculable.

Dismissed by Hitchcock in a disagreement over the soundtrack for *Torn Curtain,* Herrmann found himself less in demand in a world where pop or rock scores, with their lucrative soundtrack recording possibilities, were becoming the norm. One regrets that the composer did not live into an era, signaled by John Williams's work for Steven Spielberg and George Lucas, when the orchestral score was again in high repute; but at least he did end his career with work for major films by De Palma and Scorsese. Perhaps the most fitting tribute to the composer, beyond the books devoted to him and his work, has been Scorsese's splendidly prominent use of Herrmann's 1961 score for *Cape Fear* in his 1991 remake.

—Joseph Milicia

HOCH, Winton C.

Cinematographer. **Nationality:** American. **Born:** Iowa, 1907. **Education:** Attended California Institute of Technology, B.A. in physics, 1931. **Military Service:** 1941–44—served in the photographic science laboratory of the United States Navy: filmed top-secret material, including Los Alamos. **Career:** 1931–34—research physicist; 1934—joined Technicolor Corporation: lens technician, helped develop 3-color film system; contracted to C.V. Whitney Productions after the war; TV work includes the series *Lost in Space,* 1965, and *Voyage to the Bottom of the Sea* series. 1979—President, American Society of Cinematographers. **Awards:** Technical Academy Award, 1939, and award for *Joan of Arc,* 1948; *She Wore a Yellow Ribbon,* 1949; *The Quiet Man,* 1952. **Died:** Santa Monica, California, 20 March 1979.

Films as Cinematographer (Shorts directed by Fitzpatrick):

1936   *St. Helena and Its Man of Destiny; Colorful Islands—Madagascar and Seychelles; Picturesque South Africa*
1937   *India on Parade; Colorful Bombay; Glimpses of Java and Ceylon; Serene Siam; Glimpses of Peru; Stockholm, Pride of Sweden; Chile, Land of Charm; Land of the Incas*
1938   *Glimpse of Austria; Glimpses of New Brunswick; Beautiful Budapest; Rural Sweden; Czechoslovakia on Parade*
1939   *Rural Hungary*
1944   *Over the Andes*

Other Films as Cinematographer (Shorts):

1935   *Beautiful Banff and Lake Louise* (Sharpe)
1937   *Rocky Mountain Grandeur* (Smith)

Winton C. Hoch

1938   *Natural Wonders of the West* (Smith)
1947   *Carbon Arc Projection* (Wright)
1960   *A Light in Nature* (Orrom) (co)

Films as Cinematographer (Features):

1940   *Dr. Cyclops* (Schoedsack) (assoc)
1941   *The Reluctant Dragon* (Werker) (co); *Memories of Europe* (Fitzpatrick—compilation); *Dive Bomber* (Curtiz) (co)
1942   *Captains of the Clouds* (Curtiz) (co)
1947   *Melody Time* (Geronimi) (co); *Tap Roots* (Marshall) (co); *So Dear to My Heart* (Schuster) (co); *Joan of Arc* (Fleming) (co); *Three Godfathers* (Ford) (co); *Tulsa* (Heisler)
1949   *She Wore a Yellow Ribbon* (Ford); *The Sundowners* (*Thunder in the Dust*) (Templeton)
1951   *Halls of Montezuma* (Milestone) (co); *Bird of Paradise* (Daves)
1952   *The Quiet Man* (Ford); *The Redhead from Wyoming* (Sholem)
1953   *Salome* (Dieterle) (co); *Return to Paradise* (Robson)
1955   *Mister Roberts* (Ford and LeRoy)
1956   ***The Searchers*** (Ford)
1957   *The Missouri Traveler* (Hopper); *Jet Pilot* (von Sternberg—produced 1970); *The Young Land* (Tetzlaff) (co)
1959   *Darby O'Gill and the Little People* (Stevenson); *The Big Circus* (Newman)
1960   *The Lost World* (Allen)
1961   *Voyage to the Bottom of the Sea* (Allen)

1962 *Sergeants Three* (J. Sturges); *Five Weeks in a Balloon* (Allen)
1964 *Robinson Crusoe on Mars* (Haskin)
1968 *The Green Berets* (Wayne and Kellogg)
1972 *Necromancy* (Gordon)

Publications

By HOCH: article—

On *The Green Berets* in *American Cinematographer* (Hollywood),
   September 1968.

On HOCH: articles—

Black, Hilda, on *Return to Paradise* in *American Cinematographer*
   (Hollywood), April 1953.
Loring, Charles, on *Robinson Crusoe on Mars* in *American Cinema-
   tographer* (Hollywood), March 1964.
Film Comment (New York), Summer 1972.
Focus on Film (London), no. 13, 1973.
"A.S.C. Mourns the Passing of its President Winton C. Hoch," in
   American Cinematographer (Hollywood), May 1979.
McBride, Joseph, in *Film Comment* (New York), November-Decem-
   ber 1979.
Film Dope (Nottingham), March 1982.
Gallagher, V., in *American Classic Screen* (Shawnee Mission, Kan-
   sas), no. 1, 1982.

*   *   *

In the written history of film thus far, John Ford has tended to get
credit for most of Winton C. Hoch's accomplishments. Articles and
books are churned out that praise Ford's "eye for color" and "visual
sense." These attributes he undoubtedly had, but it was Hoch's "eye
for color"—and his peerless technical expertise at putting that eye at
the service of Ford's pictorial and narrative concerns—that impart
such rare visual beauty to *She Wore a Yellow Ribbon*, *The Quiet Man*,
and *The Searchers*.

Hoch never shot a film in black-and-white. His years of experience as a technician in the Technicolor laboratories gave him a unique
perspective in the uses and possibilities of color cinematography. He
began his career as "co-cinematographer" (actually a Technicolor
consultant) on films like *Dr. Cyclops*, *Dive Bomber*, *Captains of the
Clouds*, and *Joan of Arc*. Though ace cinematographers such as Bert
Glennon and Sol Polito were none too happy with Hoch's co-credit on
these films, (he shared an Oscar with Joseph Valentine and William
Skall for *Joan of Arc*), Hoch quickly gained the experience needed to
become a director of photography himself.

Hoch, throughout his thirty-year career, supplied sumptuous color
images to films as diverse as the exotic *Bird of Paradise*, the delirious
Jet Pilot, and the fanciful and imaginative *Five Weeks in a Balloon*
and *Robinson Crusoe on Mars*. But his five pictures for John Ford
remain the backbone of his work. In *Three Godfathers*, *She Wore
a Yellow Ribbon* (for which he won his only solo Oscar), *The Quiet
Man*, *Mister Roberts*, and *The Searchers*, Hoch provided the director

with some of his most elegant and striking images. *Mister Roberts*
boasts admirable use of the CinemaScope frame. The film also
contains one of Hoch's favorite shots: the dawn-lit panorama of the
fleet which appears under the film's title. Hoch later told an interviewer that the shot was "almost hypnotic."

The Quiet Man is among the loveliest of Ford's films. Hoch
suffuses the screen with dewy, pastel greens. Of course, nature also
had its hand in that striking visual quality; virtually the entire film was
shot in an overcast—usually rainy—Irish countryside.

The three westerns were shot on Ford's favorite location—
Monument Valley, a spot which has proved unusually receptive to
any number of visual approaches. Monument Valley is a poignant
and mythic locale; Winton Hoch—perhaps more than any other
cinematographer—was responsible for capturing its unworldly beauty in
Technicolor that was by turns stark, luscious, symbolic, and rousing.
Hoch's seasoned eye saw the links between the red of blood and clay
and the blue of sky and cavalry uniform. Monument Valley, through
Hoch's lens, could be flag, desert, hellish void, nourishing Eden.

In the 1960s, Hoch worked often with producer Irwin Allen and
proved adept at visualizing the fantastic in *The Lost World*, *Voyage to
the Bottom of the Sea*, *Five Weeks in a Balloon*, and Allen's TV show
The Time Tunnel. Hoch also worked on the much-reviled *The Green
Berets* but even his formidable technique was unable to convince the
viewer that Georgia was Vietnam.

It's one of the peculiarities of our age that audiences "demand"
color in films today yet apparently care nothing about the quality of
that color. But no matter how prosaic today's cinematographers
become, no matter what harm is wrought with the horror of
"colorization," Hoch's brilliant use of the medium should stand
forever at the art's highest plane.

—Frank Thompson

HOFFENSTEIN, Samuel

Writer. **Nationality:** American. **Born:** Samuel Goodman Hoffenstein
in Lithuania, 8 October 1890; emigrated to the United States with his
parents, 1894. **Education:** Attended Lafayette College, Easton, Pennsylvania, Ph.B. 1911. **Family:** Married Edith Morgan, 1927. **Career:**
1911–12—staff writer, Wilkes-Barre *Times Leader*, Pennsylvania,
then reporter, 1912, special writer, 1913, and drama critic, 1914–15,
New York *Sun*; 1916—first of several volumes of light verse;
1916–27—press agent for the theater producer Al Woods; 1923–25—
columnist ("The Dome"), New York *Tribune*; 1931—first film as
writer, *An American Tragedy*; 1932—coauthor of the play *Gay
Divorcee*. **Died:** Of a heart attack, 6 October 1947.

Films as Cowriter:

1931 *An American Tragedy* (von Sternberg); *Once a Lady* (McClintic)
1932 **Dr. Jekyll and Mr. Hyde** (Mamoulian); *Love Me Tonight*
      (Mamoulian); *Sinners in the Sun* (Hall)
1933 *Song of Songs* (Mamoulian); *White Woman* (Walker)

1934   *All Men Are Enemies* (Fitzmaurice); *Change of Heart* (Blystone); *The Fountain* (Cromwell); *Wharf Angel* (Menzies and Somnes); *Marie Galante* (H. King); *The Gay Divorcee* (Sandrich)

1935   *Enchanted April* (Beaumont); *Paris in Spring* (Milestone)

1936   *Desire* (Borzage); *Voice of Bugle Ann* (Thorpe); *Piccadilly Jim* (Leonard)

1937   *Conquest* (Brown)

1938   *The Great Waltz* (Duvivier)

1939   *Bridal Suite* (Thiele)

1941   *Lydia* (Duvivier)

1942   *The Loves of Edgar Allan Poe* (Lachman); *Tales of Manhattan* (Duvivier)

1943   *Flesh and Fantasy* (Duvivier); *His Butler's Sister* (Borzage); *The Phantom of the Opera* (Lubin)

1944   *Laura* (Preminger)

1946   *Cluny Brown* (Lubitsch); *Sentimental Journey* (W. Lang)

1947   *Carnival in Costa Rica* (Ratoff)

1948   *Give My Regards to Broadway* (Bacon)

Publications

By HOFFENSTEIN: books—

Life Sings a Song (verse), New York, 1916.

(Editor), *The Broadway Anthology*, New York, 1917.

Poems in Praise of Practically Nothing, New York, 1928.

Year In, You're Out (verse), New York, 1930.

Pencil in the Air (verse), New York, 1947.

With Percy Heath, *Dr. Jekyll and Mr. Hyde* (screenplay), edited by Richard Anobile, New York, 1976.

On HOFFENSTEIN: articles—

Monthly Film Bulletin (London), February 1976.

Wermuth, Paul C., in *American Humorists 1900–1950*, edited by Stanley Trachtenberg, Detroit, Michigan, 1982.

*   *   *

The poet Samuel Hoffenstein took to screenwriting during the last 14 years of his life. His musical ability and sublime gift for working ethereal elements into a story line meshed well with the lavish film productions on which he worked during the 1930s and 1940s.

Hoffenstein and the director Rouben Mamoulian began an exemplary working relationship in the highly successful *Dr. Jekyll and Mr. Hyde*, which starred Fredric March. Regarded as the best screen version of the Robert Louis Stevenson novel, in which a doctor creates a potion that reflects the lower elements of his soul, this early talkie explored the use of sound effects and music to heighten tension. The musical background of both writer and director, and Mamoulian's insistence on cinematic expression, resulted in a florid masterpiece.

Love Me Tonight incorporates the best of Hoffenstein's talents in music, song, and storytelling. Mamoulian got Richard Rodgers and Lorenz Hart to create the songs first, and built them around a story idea he got from Leopold Marchand. After this stage, the screenwriters were engaged to bridge these musical sequences in a smooth, uninterrupted narrative flow. "Isn't It Romantic?" introduces the tailor (Maurice Chevalier), the Count, the Viscount and all the main characters as each, by design, picks up a thread of the song until it reaches a chateau where it is given the crowning trill by a princess (Jeanette MacDonald). It gives the effect of a love song consummated by two people who are destined to meet.

Hoffenstein and Kenneth Webb did the musical adaptation to *The Gay Divorcee*, the first picture to star Astaire and Rogers. They did a number of variations on "The Continental," changing the tempo to Latin, waltz time, and jazz. It was the first song to win an Academy Award.

The Phantom of the Opera, written with Erich Taylor, tried to recreate the success of *Dr. Jekyll and Mr. Hyde* and brought it off in some stretches. A stubborn attention to its singing star (Nelson Eddy) detracted from a splendid array of catacombs and a stylish, masterful performance by Claude Rains as the tortured Phantom.

With *His Butler's Sister*, a Deanna Durbin vehicle, Hoffenstein began working with Betty Reinhardt and they established themselves as a writing team thereafter. *Laura* is an elegant *film noir*, based on the novel and play by Vera Caspary. The drama managed to encompass the darkest sides of its players in a sophisticated setting as a hired detective (Dana Andrews) comes on the scene to investigate a young woman's murder. Laura (Gene Tierney), believed to be the victim, reappears and becomes a suspect. *Laura* was relegated to the B-picture unit at Fox, where the producer Otto Preminger and the writer Jay Dratler worked on the script. Preminger got supervisor Bryan Foy's permission to hire Hoffenstein and Reinhardt to work on it. The revised script moved the picture up to A status, and Zanuck took over the supervision. The new treatment told the story from two viewpoints. Hoffenstein practically created the character of Waldo Lydecker, the acid-tongued columnist whose narration guides the first half of the picture. The second half was told from the viewpoint of the detective, who falls in love with Laura's portrait, a haunting image of her mystery. The scene in which the detective dozes in a chair and suddenly the woman in the portrait appears before him is one of the most poetic images in movie history. *Laura* was to be directed by Rouben Mamoulian, but Preminger took over the shooting. One of the most enduring accomplishments of this film is the brittle wit and almost detached romance injected throughout, in an atmosphere where, as Vincent Price puts it, "I can afford a blemish on my character, but not on my clothes."

Leslie Halliwell describes *Sentimental Journey* as "Hollywood's most incredible three-handkerchief picture; nicely made, but who'd dare write it?" It was Hoffenstein and Reinhardt who adapted the Nelia Gardner White story about an orphan adopted by a dying actress. The actress dies of a heart condition, leaving the child to look after the widowed husband. In one scene, the child makes an otherworldly contact with the actress to soothe the grieving husband. "It's the weeper of all weepers," declared *Variety*. *Sentimental Journey* was made into hash by critics, but pictures like this defy criticism. It was a phenomenal success at the box office.

Ernst Lubitsch supervised the production of the Marlene Dietrich-Gary Cooper comedy *Desire*, for which Hoffenstein provided material. The film *Cluny Brown* was a slight but very enjoyable tale about a stuffy English family who play host to a dreamy-souled plumber's niece. The family prides itself on being better than others and is a bit too particular about speech and manners. Hoffenstein and Reinhardt fashion them as a close-knit and ultimately endearing lot, though not the kind of folks you'd want your niece to marry. Lubitsch, in the last film he completed as director got the best out of this largely British ensemble.

—Rob Pinsel

HOFFMANN, Carl

Cinematographer. **Nationality:** German. **Born:** Neisse an der Wobert, Germany (now Nysa, Poland), 9 June 1881. **Family:** Son: the director and producer Kurt Hoffmann. **Career:** 1908—entered films as cameraman with Decla (many early films are unknown); 1928—directed first film, *Der geheimnisvolle Spiegel*. **Died:** In 1947.

Films as Cinematographer:

1913   *Fiesko*
1914   *Irrfahrt ins Glück* (Hamburger)
1916   *Friedrich Werders Sendung* (Rippert); *Homunculus* (Rippert—serial); *Das Tagebuch des Dr. Hart* (Leni)
1917   *Das Buch des Lasters* (Rippert); *Das Defizit* (Neuss); *Die Fremde* (Rippert); *Die Konigstochter von Travankore* (Rippert); *Das Mädel von Nebenan* (Rippert); *Hilda Warren und der Tod* (May) (co); *Die Hochzeit in Ekzentrik Klub* (*The Wedding in the Eccentric Club*) (May)
1918   *Die Krone des Lebens* (Rippert); *Das Lied der Mutter* (Neuss); *Der Weg, der qur Verdammnis führt* (Rippert)
1919   *Der Hirt von Maria Schnee* (Raffay); *Johannestraum* (Justitz); *Der Herr der Liebe* (F. Lang); *Der Knabe in Blau* (*The Boy in Blue*) (Murnau); *Prinz Kuckuck* (Leni); *Die Frau mit den Orchiden* (*The Woman with the Orchid*) (Rippert); *Unheimliche Geschichten* (Oswald); *Wahnsinn* (Veidt); *Hara-Kiri* (F. Lang); *Halbblut* (*Half Caste*) (F. Lang); *Die Pest in Florenz* (Rippert)
1920   *Eine Frau mit Vergangenheit* (Ziener); *Der Graf von Cagliostro* (Schünzel); *Das Haus zum Mond* (Martin); *Das Herz vom Hochland* (Oberländer); *Der Januskopf* (*Janus-Faced*) (Murnau) (co); *Kurfürstendamm* (Oswald); *Patience* (Leni); *Der Reigen* (Oswald); *Sehnsucht* (Murnau); *Störtebeker* (Wendt); *Uriel Acosta* (Wendt); *Von Morgens bis Mitternachts* (Martin)
1921   *Nachtgestalten* (Oswald); *Der Erbe der Van Diemen* (Ziener); *Der Flug in den Tod* (Ziener); *Der Herr der Bestien* (Wendt); *Die Intriguen der Madame de la Pommeraye* (Wendhausen); *Lady Hamilton* (Oswald); *Landstrasse und Gross-stadt* (Wilhelm); *Der Liebling der Frauen* (Wilhelm); *Die Tigerin* (Wendt); *Die Schreckensnacht in der Menagerie* (Wendt); *Unter Räubern und Bestien* (Wendt); *Fiesco* (*Die Verschwörung zu Genua*) (Leni)
1922   **Dr. Mabuse, der Spieler** (*Dr. Mabuse, the Gambler*) (F. Lang—2 parts)

1923   *Der steinerne Reiter* (Wendhausen)
1924   *Die Andere* (Lamprecht); **Die Nibelungen** (F. Lang—2 parts) (co)
1925   *Blitzzug der Liebe* (Guter); *Die Frau mit dem schlechten Ruf* (Christensen)
1926   *Faust* (Murnau)
1927   *Die Fraungasse von Algier* (Hoffman-Harnisch); *Jugendrausch* (Asagaroff); *Die sieben Töchter der Frau Gyurkovics* (Hylten-Cavallius)
1928   *Der geheimnisvolle Spiegel* (+ co-d); *Looping the Loop* (Robison); *Ungarische Rhapsodie* (*Hungarian Rhapsody*) (Schwarz)
1929   *Die wunderbare Lüge der Nina Petrowna* (*The Wonderful Lie of Nina Petrovna*) (Schwarz); *Manolescu* (Tourjansky)
1930   *Ein Burschenlied aus Heidelberg* (Hartl); *Der Tiger* (Meyer); *Das Flötenkonzert von Sanssouci* (Ucicky); *Hokuspokus* (*Hocuspocus*) (Ucicky); *Der unsterbliche Lump* (Ucicky)
1931   *Der falsche Ehemann* (Guter); *In Geheimdienst* (Ucicky); *York* (Ucicky); *Der Kongress tanzt* (*The Congress Dances*) (Charell)
1932   *Mensch ohne Namen* (Ucicky); *Der weisse Dämon* (Gerron); *Wie sag ich's meinem Mann* (Schünzel)
1933   *Inge und die Millionen* (Engel); *Morgenrot* (Ucicky); *Saison in Kairo* (Schünzel); *Der Tunnel* (Bernhardt); *Walzerkrieg* (*Waltz War*) (Berger)
1934   *Die Czardasfürstin* (Jacoby); *Peer Gynt* (Wendhausen)
1939   *Befriete Hände* (Schweikart); *Der Florentiner Hut* (Liebeneiner); *Gold in New Frisco* (Verhoeven); *Ich bin Sebastian Ott* (Forst and Becker)
1940   *Das Fräulein von Barnhelm* (Schweikart); *Golowin geht durch die Stadt* (Stemmle); *Das Mädchen von Fanö* (Schweikart)
1941   *Alarmstufe V* (Lippl)
1942   *Symphonie eines Lebens* (Bertram) (co); *Zwei in einder grosser Stadt* (von Collande)
1945   *Via Mala* (von Baky)

Films as Director:

1934   *Viktoria*; *Die lustigen Weiber*
1938   *Ab Mitternacht*

Publications

By HOFFMANN: article—

''The 'Unchained' Camera,'' in *The Picturegoer's Who's Who and Encylopaedia*, London, 1933.

On HOFFMANN: articles—

Focus on Film (London), no. 13, 1973.
Filme (Berlin), May/June 1981.

*   *   *

Carl Hoffmann was one of the leading German cinematographers of the 1910s and 1920s, working for such directors as Leni, May, Murnau, Oswald, Veidt, Wilhelm, Fritz Lang, and Robison. Many of the films he worked on are masterpieces of the Expressionist movement, and Hoffmann became a master of the style—the control of light and dark, the odd juxtapositioning of objects and figures, the slightly out-of-kilter or dizzying effects. There is a marvelous use of these techniques in Murnau's *Faust*, a story entirely appropriate to the expressionistic mood; he is most effective in arranging the dark-light contrasts as they change around the character of Mephistopheles, and in the soaring camera when Faust is shown the world he can gain by selling his soul. But his masterpiece is perhaps in Lang's *Dr. Mabuse, the Gambler*, for which Hoffmann's camerawork is generally recognized as perfect. Besides the obvious lighting and camera effects, Hoffmann uses chiaroscuro lighting, irising effects, and double, triple, and quadruple exposures; the film is full of wonderful moments such as the count wandering through his twilit mansion with a candelabra. Hoffmann's later works were more conventional, and he made comedies and musicals into the Nazi period.

HONEGGER, Arthur

Composer. **Nationality:** Swiss. **Born:** Le Havre, France, of Swiss parents, 10 March 1892. **Education:** Studied harmony with R. C. Martin and the violin with Capet, Paris; Zurich Conservatory, two years; Paris Conservatory under Gédalge, Widor, and d'Indy. **Military Service:** Swiss military service, 1914–15. **Family:** Married the composer and pianist Andrée Vaurabourg. **Career:** Composer of works for the stage (ballets and operas, incidental music for stage plays), as well as orchestra and choral works; associated with the group Les Six; 1923—composed works to accompany silent film *La Roue*; 1930—score for first film, *La Fin du monde*. **Died:** In Paris, 27 November 1955.

Films as Composer of Accompaniment Music:

1923   *La Roue* (Gance); *Faits divers* (Autant-Lara—short)
1926   ***Napoléon*** (Gance)
1927   *Maldone* (Grémillon) (co)

Films as Composer:

1930   *La Fin du monde* (Gance) (co)
1934   *L'Idée* (Bartosch—short); *Cessez le feu* (de Baroncelli) (co);
         Les Misérables (Bernard—2 parts); *Rapt* (Kirsanoff) (co);
         Le Roi de Camargue (de Baroncelli) (co); *Angèle* (Pagnol)
1935   *Crime et châtiment* (Chenal); *L'Equipage* (Litvak) (co); *Der
         Dämon des Himalaya* (Dyhrenfurth)
1936   *Anne-Marie* (Bernard) (co); *Mayerling* (Litvak) (co); *Les
         Mutinés de l'Elseneur* (Chenal); *Nitchevo* (de Baroncelli)
         (co); *Visages de France* (Kirsanoff) (co)
1937   *La Citadelle du silence* (L'Herbier) (co); *Liberté* (Kemm)
         (co); *Mademoiselle Docteur (Salonique, nid d'espions)*
         (Pabst) (co); *Marthe Richard au service de la France*
         (Bernard); *Miarka, la fille à l'ourse* (Choux) (co); *Passeurs
         d'hommes* (Jayet) (co); *Regain* (Pagnol)
1938   *Les Bâtisseurs* (Epstein) (co); *Pygmalion* (Asquith and Howard)
1939   *Cavalcade d'amour* (Bernard); *Le Déserteur (Je t'attendrai)*
         (Moguy) (co); *Farinet, oder das falsche Geld (L'Or dans la
         montagne; Farinet, ou la fausse monnaie; Faux monnayeurs)*
         (Haufler); *Les Musiciens du ciel* (Lacombe) (co)
1942   *Le Capitaine Fracasse* (Gance); *Huit hommes dans un château*
         (Pottier) (co); *Le Journal tombe à cinq heures* (Lacombe)
1943   *Mermoz* (Cuny); *Secrets* (Blanchar); *Un Seul Amour* (Blanchar);
         La Boxe de la France (Ganier-Raymond); *Les Antiquités de
         l'Asie occidentale* (Membrin—short); *Callisto* (Marty—
         short) (co)
1945   *Les Démons de l'auge* (Y. Allégret) (co); *Un Ami viendra ce
         soir* (Bernard)
1946   *Un Revenant (A Lover's Return)* (Christian-Jaque) (+ ro)
1947   *Le Village perdu* (Strengel)
1950   *Bourdelle* (Lucot—short)
1951   *Paul Claudel* (Gillet—short); *La Tour de Babel* (Rony) (co)

Publications

By HONEGGER: books—

Incantation aux fossiles, Lausanne, 1948.
Je suis compositeur, Paris, 1951, as *I Am a Composer*, New York, 1966.

Arthur Honegger

On HONEGGER: books—

Tappolet, W., *Arthur Honegger*, Zurich, 1933, rev. ed., 1954.
Claudel, Paul and others, *Arthur Honegger*, Paris, 1943.
Bruyr, J., *Honegger*, Paris, 1947.
Dellany, Marcel, *Honegger*, Paris, 1953.
Landowski, M., *Honegger*, Paris, 1957.
Gauthier, A., *Arthur Honegger*, London, 1957.
Guilbert, Y., *Honegger*, Paris, 1959.
Spratt, Geoffrey K., *The Music of Arthur Honegger*, Cork, 1987.
Halbreich, Harry, *Arthur Honegger*, Portland, 1999.

On HONEGGER: articles—

Cinema (Rome), 15 March 1951.
Cinéma (Paris), December 1955.
Colpi, Henri, in *Défense et illustration de la musique dans le film*, Lyon, 1964.
Porcile, François, in *Présence de la musique à l'écran*, Paris, 1969.
Lacombe, Alain, and Claude Rocle, in *La Musique du film*, Paris, 1979.
Film Dope (Nottingham), November 1982.

*   *   *

Arthur Honegger first achieved fame as a member of "Les Six," the group of composers impulsively yoked together in 1917 by Jean Cocteau to create anti-Romantic, "quintessentially French" music. But Honegger's pensive, serious-minded outlook found little in common with the nose-thumbing frivolities of Poulenc and Milhaud, and he soon seceded from the group. In his film music, too, he always responded most intensely to subjects of a tragic or exalted stamp. Faced with lighter material his work, though never less than craftsmanlike, could become what he once dismissively described all film scores as, "music that one forgets." At its best, though, Honegger's film music is powerful, imaginatively scored, and anything but forgettable.

Like so much of the music composed for the silent cinema, Honegger's earliest film scores have either been lost or survive only in fragmentary form. Of his first score, for Abel Gance's railway melodrama *La Roue*, only the overture still exists. As well as providing—with its motoric rhythms—an early example of Honegger's lifelong fascination with trains (his famous symphonic poem "Pacific 231" would follow a year later), it shows him responding to the pulsating intensity of Gance's conception. His score for Gance's grandiose epic, *Napoléon*, survives as no more than a few episodes in the composer's autograph; Honegger himself stormed out before the premiere, infuriated by the director's obsessive last-minute reediting. But one passage, depicting the swelling fervor of the revolution, anticipates a polyphonic device he favored in his symphonies: over a low, brooding theme on brass and low woodwind, two revolutionary songs ("Ça ira" and "La Carmagnole") are counterpointed, rising to a frenzied climax.

Unimpressed by the sound quality of early talkies, Honegger composed little film music in the early thirties. But by 1934, with recording and reproduction techniques rapidly improving, he had regained interest in the medium and that year alone composed five scores, remarkable in their diversity. For Berthold Bartosch's animated satire *L'Idée*, Honegger set the remote, ethereal tones of the *ondes martenot* (representing the eponymous Idea in all its purity) against a restless, urban-jazz tinged ensemble dominated by trombone, trumpet, and alto sax that hinted at the influence of Kurt Weill. *Rapt*, like *Farinet, oder das falsche Geld* five years later, was adapted from a novel by the Swiss writer Ramuz; both scores recall the composer's own Swiss background, evoking the mountain landscapes of the Valais with striding, folklike motifs of elemental dignity. Raymond Bernard's three-part version of Hugo's *Les Misérables* brought out the lyrical, romantic side of Honegger's nature with a score that rises to stirring pathos with the death of Jean Valjean and erupts in fury for the uprising of the urban poor.

Over the next ten years, until ill health curtailed his activities, Honegger composed virtually all his most original film scores. Regrettably, they were rarely destined for films of great distinction. *Le Capitaine Fracasse* reunited him with Abel Gance, but it was a minor work in Gance's declining career; even so, Honegger entered with gusto into the film's swaggering spirit. His score for *Crime et châtiment* did far more justice to Dostoyevsky than anything else in Pierre Chénal's stilted adaptation; somber and atmospheric, it set obsessive ostinato figures and canonlike themes roaming about each other to suggest Raskolnikov's tormented mind and the quiet doggedness of the implacable Inspector Porfiry.

Three of Honegger's most exceptional scores were composed for films now largely, or entirely, forgotten. His music for *Der Dämon des Himalaya*, highly chromatic and audaciously scored, underlines the way that mountains and high places always brought out his most personal responses. "Le Grand Barrage," a three-minute fragment from 1942 evidently intended to accompany newsreel footage of the building of a dam, conjures up in its brief span a vivid picture of enraged, rushing waters. Even more dramatic is the score for Louis Cuny's *Mermoz*, a biopic about a celebrated French aviator. Honegger's music, dissonant and tumultuous, allotting prominent roles to high woodwind, saxophone, and percussion, recreates the trepidation and hypnotic strangeness of the pioneer airman's world.

Had Honegger been able to work with major filmmakers at the height of their powers, his reputation as a film composer would almost certainly stand far higher. Until recently, most of his finest film scores have lain buried in obscure movies and primitive, crackly sound-tracks. Their emergence on compact disc offers the opportunity to reevaluate his contribution to the genre, and to do it belated justice.

—Philip Kemp

HORNBECK, William

Editor. **Nationality:** American. **Born:** Los Angeles, California, 23 August 1901. **Military Service:** Served in the Pictorial Service of the Signal Corps (edited the *Why We Fight* series): Lt. Colonel. **Career:** Lab assistant at Keystone studio, eventually supervising editor of Sennett comedies; 1934–40—in charge of editing for Korda films in England; 1946—assistant to vice-president in charge of studio operations at Republic; 1960—supervisor of editorial operations, and, in

1966, vice-president, Universal; 1976—retired. **Award:** Academy Award for *A Place in the Sun*, 1951. **Died:** In Ventura, California, 11 October 1983.

Films as Assistant Editor:

1921   *A Small Town Idol* (Kenton); *Molly O'* (Jones)
1922   *The Crossroads of New York* (*For Love or Money*) (Jones); *Susanna* (Jones)
1923   *The Shriek of Araby* (Jones)

Films as Editor (Features):

1921   *Home Talent* (Sennett) (co)
1923   *The Extra Girl* (Jones)
1927   *His First Flame* (Edwards)
1928   *The Good-Bye Kiss* (Sennett)
1930   *Midnight Daddies* (Sennett)
1932   *Hypnotized* (Sennett) (co)
1935   *The Scarlet Pimpernel* (Young)
1941   *Lydia* (Duvivier)
1946   *It's a Wonderful Life* (Capra)
1947   *Singapore* (Brahm); *Magic Town* (Wellman) (montages)
1948   *State of the Union* (*The World and His Wife*) (Capra)
1949   *The Heiress* (Wyler)
1950   *Riding High* (Capra)
1951   *A Place in the Sun* (Stevens); *Something to Live For* (Stevens) (co)
1953   *Shane* (Stevens) (co); *Act of Love* (Litvak)
1954   *The Barefoot Contessa* (Mankiewicz)
1955   *The Girl Rush* (Pirosh)
1956   *Giant* (Stevens)
1957   *The Quiet American* (Mankiewicz)
1958   *I Want to Live!* (Wise)
1959   *A Hole in the Head* (Capra)

Films as Editor (Shorts):

1926   *Saturday Afternoon* (Edwards); *Soldier Man* (Edwards)
1928   *Run, Girl, Run* (Goulding); *Love at First Flight* (Cline); *The Swim Princess* (Goulding); *Smith's Army Life* (Goulding); *Smith's Holiday* (Goulding); *Smith's Farm Days* (Whitman); *Smith's Restaurant* (Whitman); *His Unlucky Night* (Edwards); *Taxi for Two* (Lord); *Caught in the Kitchen* (Whitman); *A Dumb Waiter* (Edwards); *Motor Boat Mamas* (Edwards); *A Taxi Scandal* (Lord); *Hubby's Latest Alibi* (Whitman); *A Jim Jam Janitor* (Edwards); *The Burglar* (Whitman); *Hubby's Week End Trip* (Edwards); *Taxi Beauties* (Lord); *His New Stenographer* (Whitman); *Clunked on the Corner* (Edwards); *Smith's Boby's Birthday* (Whitman)
1929   *Uncle Tom* (Whitman); *Taxi Spooks* (Lord); *Button My Back* (Whitman); *Ladies Must Eat* (Edwards); *Foolish Husbands*

(Whitman); *The Rodeo* (Goulding); *Matchmaking Mamma* (Edwards); *Taxi Dolls* (Lord); *Pink Pajamas* (Whitman); *The Night Watchman's Mistake* (Edwards); *The New Aunt* (Rodney); *The Old Barn* (Sennett); *A Close Shave* (Edwards); *Motoring Mamas* (Whitman); *Don't Get Jealous* (Whitman); *Caught in a Taxi* (Lord)
1931   *I Surrender Dear* (Sennett); *One More Chance* (Sennett)
1932   *Dream House* (Lord); *Billboard Girl* (Pearce)

Films as Supervisor:

1935   *Sanders of the River* (Z. Korda); *Moscow Nights* (*I Stand Condemned*) (Asquith); *The Ghost Goes West* (Clair); *Things to Come* (Menzies)
1936   *Forget-Me-Not* (*Forever Yours*) (Z. Korda); *The Man Who Could Work Miracles* (Mendes); *Rembrandt* (A. Korda); *Men Are Not Gods* (Saville)
1937   *Dark Journey* (Saville); *Elephant Boy* (Flaherty and Z. Korda); *Storm in a Teacup* (Saville and Dalrymple); *Knight without Armour* (Feyder); *The Return of the Scarlet Pimpernel* (Schwarz); *Paradise for Two* (*The Gaiety Girls*) (Freeland); *Over the Moon* (Freeland); *21 Days* (*The First and the Last*; *21 Days Together*) (Dean)
1938   *The Divorce of Lady X* (Whelan); *The Drum* (*Drums*) (Z. Korda); *Prison without Bars* (Hurst)
1939   *Q Planes* (*Clouds over Europe*) (Whelan); *The Revel Son* (Brunel); *The Spy in Black* (*U-Boat 29*) (Powell); *The Four Feathers* (Z. Korda); *The Lion Has Wings* (Powell, Hurst, and Brunel)
1940   *The Thief of Bagdad* (Berger, Whelan, and Powell)
1941   *That Hamilton Woman* (*Lady Hamilton*) (A. Korda)
1942   *Jungle Book* (*Rudyard Kipling's Jungle Book*) (Z. Korda); *Prelude to War* (Capra); *The Nazis Strike* (Capra and Litvak—short in *Why We Fight* series)
1943   *Divide and Conquer* (Capra and Litvak—short in *Why We Fight* series); *The Battle of Britain* (Veiller—short in *Why We Fight* series); *Know Your Ally: Britain* (Veiller); *Tunisian Victory* (Capra and R. Boulting)
1944   *The Battle of Russia* (Litvak) (co); *The Battle of China* (Capra and Litvak) (co)
1945   *War Comes to America* (Litvak); *Two Down and One to Go!* (Capra—short)

Film as Editorial Consultant:

1959   *Suddenly, Last Summer* (Mankiewicz)

Publications

By HORNBECK: articles—

The Velvet Light Trap (Madison, Wisconsin), Summer 1983.
American Cinematographer (Hollywood), Summer-Fall 1983.

On HORNBECK: articles—

Film Comment (New York), March-April 1977.
Film Dope (Nottingham), November 1982.
Obituary in *Variety* (New York), 19 October 1983.
The Annual Obituary 1983, Chicago, 1984.
American Film (Washington, D.C.), December 1985.

*   *   *

Frank Capra called William Hornbeck "the greatest film editor in the history of motion pictures," and in a 1977 poll 100 of his peers named Hornbeck the best editor in the film industry, two great compliments for a man relatively unknown to most filmgoers. In a tribute to Hornbeck after his death, the Academy of Motion Picture Arts and Sciences distributed a program note that said, "If William Hornbeck had been anything other than a film editor, he would have been proclaimed by the world at large to be what his associates always knew him to be—a true Hollywood legend." Although the general public is not familiar with his name and few film books refer to him, he was unquestionably one of the true pioneers of his chosen field of film editing.

Hornbeck's career is remarkable for its influence and longevity. He began at the bottom as a winder of film when hardly more than a child, and worked up the ladder of the business slowly and thoroughly, learning every phase of film cutting. He became the head of the Mack Sennett department before he was even 20 years old, cutting 52 comedies a year. In the 1930s he was head editor for Alexander Korda in England, in charge of such famous films as *The Scarlet Pimpernel*, *The Ghost Goes West*, *That Hamilton Woman*, and *The Thief of Bagdad*. (His influence in those years comes not only from these classic films, but also from his teaching such men as David Lean the art of film cutting.) In the 1940s he assumed the responsibility for editing the famed Second World War *Why We Fight* series, and followed that decade with an Oscar-winning career editing such film classics as *A Place in the Sun*, *Giant*, *The Heiress*, *It's a Wonderful Life*, *The Barefoot Contessa*, *Shane*, and *I Want to Live!* His final years were spent as an executive at Universal Pictures in the 1960s, where he remained until his retirement in 1976. Although he did not take screen credit, he polished and completed many successful Universal films during that period, among them *Topaz*, *American Graffiti*, and *Earthquake*.

Taken as a whole, Hornbeck's career is like a miniature history of the motion picture. His remarkable range of experience on shorts, documentaries, and features of all types turned him into a consummate craftsman—a man who understood film and its communicative process perhaps better than anyone else.

The Hornbeck style was eclectic and flexible. ("If you had rules for editing," he said, "you could put it in a book and anyone could become an editor.") His editing technique is simple: it serves its story, and the intent of the director, according to what is most appropriate; it is superbly crafted; it is humanistic in tone. Two films Hornbeck cut for George Stevens, *Shane* and *A Place in the Sun*, illustrate these tendencies. In two films made within a short time span, Hornbeck used two entirely different styles. In *Shane*, during a lengthy fight in a saloon, the story presents the fascinated young boy (Brandon DeWilde) watching his hero, Alan Ladd, defeat the badmen. The action of the fight is cut so that the audience is returned several times to the sight of DeWilde watching the fight. Since the response of the boy to the gunfighter hero is one of the basic thematic concerns of the film, rapidly cutting him into the dynamic action of the saloon fight maintains the integrity of the fight but also grounds it firmly in the point of view of the child. Later in the same film, DeWilde "participates" in the final gunfight by warning the hero at a crucial moment. Hornbeck's cutting on sound (the cry of the boy's warning) again effectively illustrates the point of the boy's desire not only to watch the hero, but to *be* the hero. A hard punch on a villain's jaw by Alan Ladd is followed by a cut to the boy crunching down hard on a candy stick. The crack of the candy replaces the sound of the jaw punch, and again unites action to thematic purpose. (These masterful examples of Hornbeck's work were chosen by the Academy of Motion Picture Arts and Sciences to illustrate the technique of editing at one of their annual Oscar shows.)

On the other hand, Hornbeck's Oscar-winning film *A Place in the Sun* shows a totally different approach, one appropriate to that film's romantic and passionate nature. Instead of rapid cutting, Hornbeck uses slow dissolves, in which the intense close-ups of the very beautiful Elizabeth Taylor and Montgomery Clift attempt to express their love for one another. Eerie cries of loons overlap many images, as Hornbeck helped Stevens create a mannered but exquisitely emotional viewing experience.

A true pioneer and a major international influence on film editing, Hornbeck and his work should be remembered for its quality and influence, as well as for his contribution in terms of training a whole generation of young editors in both England and America.

—Jeanine Basinger

HORNER, Harry

Art Director. **Nationality:** American. **Born:** Holicz, Austria-Hungary, 24 July 1910; emigrated to the United States, 1935; naturalized, 1938. **Education:** Studied architecture, University of Vienna, graduated 1934; also studied at Max Reinhardt's Seminary for Drama and Stage Direction, Vienna; studied costume design under Professor Roller. **Military Service:** Served in the United States Army Air Force, 1942–44. **Family:** Married 1) Betty Pfaelzer, 1938 (died 1950); 2) Joan Fraenkel, 1952; sons: James, Christopher, and Antony. **Career:** Actor and designer for Reinhardt's Viennese company, 1934–35, and with Reinhardt in the United States, then art director, and film director, in Hollywood; also stage designer in Europe and the United States; also TV designer, and director of *Reader's Digest* series, and episodes of other series. **Awards:** Academy Awards for *The Heiress*, 1949; *The Hustler*, 1961. **Died:** 7 December 1994.

Films as Art Director:

1940 *Our Town* (Wood) (co)
1941 ***The Little Foxes*** (Wyler) (co)
1943 *Tarzan Triumphs* (Thiele); *Stage Door Canteen* (Borzage)

1944   *Winged Victory* (Cukor) (co); *A Double Life* (Cukor)
1949   *The Heiress* (Wyler)
1950   *Tarzan and the Slave Girl* (Sholem); *Outrage* (Lupino); *Born
         Yesterday* (Cukor)
1951   *He Ran All the Way* (Berry)
1952   *Androcles and the Lion* (Erskine)
1958   *Separate Tables* (Delbert Mann) (+ 2nd unit d)
1959   *The Wonderful Country* (Parrish)
1961   **The Hustler** (Rossen)
1964   *The Luck of Ginger Coffey* (Kershner)
1969   *They Shoot Horses, Don't They?* (Pollack)
1971   *Who Is Harry Kellerman and Why Is He Saying Those
         Terrible Things about Me?* (Grobard)
1972   *Up the Sandbox* (Kershner)
1975   *The Black Bird* (Giler)
1976   *Harry and Walter Go to New York* (Rydell)
1977   *Audrey Rose* (Wise)
1978   *The Driver* (Hill); *Moment by Moment* (Wagner)
1979   *Strangers: The Story of a Mother and Daughter* (Katselas)
1980   *The Jazz Singer* (Fleischer and Furie)

Films as Director:

1952   *Red Planet Mars*; *The Marrying Kind* (Cukor) (2nd unit);
         Beware My Lovely
1953   *Vicki*; *New Faces*
1954   *A Life in the Balance*
1956   *Man from Del Rio*; *The Wild Party*

Publications

By HORNER: articles—

Theatre Arts (New York), December 1947.
''Designing *The Heiress*,'' in *Hollywood Quarterly*, Fall 1950.
American Film (Washington, D.C.), February 1977
Cinématographe (Paris), February 1982.

On HORNER: articles—

Film Dope (Nottingham), November 1982.
Comuzio, E., ''Harry Horner,'' in *Cineforum*, no. 31, May 1991.
Obituary in *The New York Times*, 8 December 1994.
Obituary in *Variety* (New York), 12 December 1994.
Obituary in *EPD Film* (Frankfurt), February 1995.

                    *   *   *

Harry Horner was born in Czechoslovakia in 1910 with an Austrian-Jewish background. At the University of Vienna, he began his studies in architecture. A well-educated and literate man, Horner grew increasingly interested in the theater. He began working as an actor and studied stage design under the theatrical producer Max Reinhardt. Horner also studied costume design.

In 1935 Horner emigrated to the U.S., and became a leading designer of opera productions and Broadway plays. When he finally began his film career he was to work with some of Hollywood's very best directors including William Wyler and George Cukor.

In his first film, *Our Town*, Horner apprenticed under the tutelage of that great Hollywood production designer William Cameron Menzies (best known to the American public for his extensive contributions to the movie *Gone with the Wind*). Horner created drawing after drawing illustrating the individual and detailed lives of the townspeople. It became a living Norman Rockwell illustration, an appropriate vision for this folksy Thornton Wilder tale of smalltown life.

Horner began his work on a picture by doing extensive research, concentrating on spatial necessities and those objects essential to the plot. Constant drawings and plans were made before the actual blueprints for construction will be drawn. Horner provided his director and cameraman with continuity sketches of the entire picture from start to finish, from the very first close-up to that last distant long shot. These were used as a visual script for the picture by the cameraman and director. Throughout shooting Horner stayed on the set to make sure the lighting of spaces and the shooting of the performances were harmoniously integrated with his designs.

Historical films such as *The Heiress* required intensive investigation of the different periods involved and for this picture Horner accumulated three notebooks full of photographs filled with historically accurate details. He used these only as a starting point. His own designs were created specifically to highlight certain dramatic elements present in the story. Even such contemporary films as *The Hustler* demanded hours of Horner's research. He traveled from poolroom to poolroom searching for just the right touches for the story, and even toured college co-ed apartments to get a sense of how Eddie's girlfriend might live. As a result, his sets gave the feel of real people, their habits and ways of life. Horner gave characters an unstated third dimension.

Horner expressed great interest in character development and uses this as a pre-condition in his design. In *The Little Foxes*, the sets were designed around Regina, a dominant and demonic character filled with greed and a lust for material pleasures. At one point she stands in front of a piece of furniture that actually gives her devil's horns! That this was indeed Horner's intent can be proved by referring to his still intact continuity sketches.

In *The Heiress*, the house shows both Dr. Sloper's dominance over his daughter, Catherine, and his bitter grief over his wife's death. Sloper was portrayed both as master of the house, in a position of kingly power, and as a dark figure shown in the shadows of his gothic study. Catherine was an awkward helpless prisoner. Horner vividly illustrates this when he encloses her in the cagelike staircase. Latticed wallpaper further reinforced the image. As her character later gained strength, her manner of presentation changes. Horner surrounded Morris, Catherine's fortune-hunting suitor, with seductive details— highly polished mahogany, shimmering crystal, gleaming silverware. This represented Morris's elusive dreams of material wealth.

In *The Heiress* Horner gave such a clear explanation of the house's complex spaces (one even perceived a sense of four enclosing walls if one pays attention from scene to scene) that it can easily be reconstructed.

Horner expressed moments of emotional intensity with an expressionist style filled with high contrast lighting and extreme angles.

This is true in *The Heiress* and many of his other films. In *A Double Life* he used this style to indicate the character's growing madness.

Horner worked on several comedies. His exaggerated, out-of-scale Baroque hotel room in *Born Yesterday* showed the bad taste in a humorous manner as the gangster awkwardly tries to express his wealth and power. *Who Is Harry Kellerman and Why Is He Saying Those Terrible Things About Me?* is a black comedy, and Horner's use of cold, impersonal interiors express the anti-hero's sense of loneliness and alienation. Horner's use of the outrageous and surreal gives the film an existential absurdity.

Horner approached his films as a visual author, retelling a story through its images. He used every tool at his command, from studious researching of the past to personal odysseys into aspects of contemporary life. Horner applied the knowledge and techniques found in centuries of art history, the technical virtuosity of an architectural background, and his own insights on the human condition. Horner's finest films revealed the motion picture as the powerful art form it can be.

—Edith C. Lee

HOUSEMAN, John

Producer and Actor. **Nationality:** American. **Born:** Jacques Haussmann in Bucharest, Romania, 22 September 1902; emigrated to the United States, 1925; naturalized, 1943. **Education:** Attended Clifton College, Bristol, England, 1911–18. **Family:** Married 1) the actress Zita Johan, 1929 (divorced 1932); 2) Joan Courtney, 1950; sons: John and Charles. **Career:** 1921—apprentice in wheat brokerage firm, London; 1925—representative of Continental Grain Corporation, New York; 1929–30—director, Oceanic Grain Corporation; stage director and producer since the 1930s (*Four Saints in Three Acts*, 1934; *Hamlet*, 1936; *King Lear*, 1951; *Clarence Darrow*, 1974; and operas *Othello*, 1963; *Tosca*, 1965; and *Macbeth*, 1973); 1935—head of Negro Theatre Project (part of Works Progress Authority): produced *Negro Macbeth* and other plays; 1937–41—co-founder, and writer and producer for Mercury Theatre, with Orson Welles; 1937–38—associate professor, Vassar College, Poughkeepsie, New York; 1941—vice-president, David O. Selznick Productions; 1941–43—overseas radio programmer, Office of War Information; 1943–46—film producer, Paramount; 1947—founded Hollywood Film Society; 1947–49—producer at RKO; 1949—founded Media Productions; 1950–56—producer at MGM; 1956–59—producer, CBS-TV, including *Seven Lively Arts* series, 1958–59; 1956–69—artistic director, American Shakespeare Festival, Stratford, Connecticut; 1959–63—director, professional theatre group, University of California, Los Angeles; 1963—first film acting role, in *Seven Days in May*; 1967—director, Drama Division, Juilliard School, New York; 1967–69—producing director, A.P.A. Repetory Company, Phoenix Theatre, 1969–70, and City Center Acting Company, 1972–75; 1971–72—Cockefair Professor, University of Missouri, Kansas City; 1976—acted in TV mini-series *Captains and the Kings*, and in *Washington behind Closed Doors*, 1977, *Aspen*, 1977, *The French Atlantic Affair*, 1979, *Marco Polo*, 1982, *The Winds of War* 1983, and *A.D.*, 1986. **Awards:** Best Supporting Actor Academy Award for *The Paper Chase*, 1973. **Died:** 31 October 1988.

John Houseman

Films as Producer:

1945   *First Tuesday in November* (Berry—short); *The Unseen* (Allen) (assoc); *The Blue Dahlia* (Marshall)

1946   *Miss Susie Slagle's* (Berry) (assoc)

1948   ***Letter from an Unknown Woman*** (Ophüls); ***They Live by Night*** (*The Twisted Road; Your Red Wagon*) (Ray)

1950   *The Company She Keeps* (Cromwell)

1951   *On Dangerous Ground* (Ray)

1952   *Holiday for Sinners* (Mayer); *The Bad and the Beautiful* (Minnelli)

1953   *Julius Caesar* (Mankiewicz); *Executive Suite* (Wise); *Her Twelve Men* (Leonard)

1955   *Moonfleet* (F. Lang); *The Cobweb* (Minnelli)

1956   *Lust for Life* (Minnelli)

1962   *All Fall Down* (Frankenheimer); *Two Weeks in Another Town* (Minnelli)

1963   *In the Cool of the Day* (Stevens)

1964   *Voyage to America* (Jackson—short) (+ sc)

1966   *This Property Is Condemned* (Pollack)

1980   *Gideon's Trumpet* (Collins) (exec, + ro)

1983   *Choices of the Heart* (Sargent) (co-exec)

Films as Actor:

1963   *Seven Days in May* (Frankenheimer)

1973   *The Paper Chase* (Bridges)

1975   *Rollerball* (Jewison); *Three Days of the Condor* (Pollack);
      Fear on Trial (Johnson)

1976   *St. Ives* (Lee Thompson); *Circle* (Seidelman); *Six Characters
      in Search of an Author* (Keach); *Truman at Potsdam*
      (Schaefer); *Hazard's People* (Szwarc)

1978   *Old Boyfriends* (Tewkesbury); *The Cheap Detective* (Moore);
      The Paper Chase (Hardy)

1979   *The Fog* (Carpenter); *The Last Convertible* (Trikonis, Swerling,
      and Hayers)

1980   *Wholly Moses!* (Weis); *My Bodyguard* (Bill); *A Christmas
      without Snow* (Korty); *The Babysitter* (Medak)

1981   *Ghost Story* (Irvin)

1982   *Bells* (*Murder By Phone*) (Anderson)

1984   *The Good Fight: The Abraham Lincoln Brigade in the Span-
      ish Civil War*

1985   *A.D.* (Cooper—for TV)

1988   *Gore Vidal's Lincoln* (Johnson—for TV); *Another Woman*
      (Allen); *The Naked Gun* (Zucker); *Scrooged* (Donner)

Publications

By HOUSEMAN: books—

With Jack Landau, *The American Shakespeare Festival: The Birth of
a Theatre*, New York, 1959.

Run-through: A Memoir, New York, 1972.

Front and Center, New York, 1979.

Final Dress, New York, 1984.

*Entertainers and the Entertained: Essays on Theatre, Film, and
Television*, New York, 1986.

Unfinished Business, New York, 1986.

By HOUSEMAN: articles—

''Hollywood Faces the Fifties,'' in *Harper's* (New York), April and
May 1950.

''How—and What—Does a Movie Communicate,'' in *Quarterly of
Film, Radio, and Television* (Berkeley, California), Spring 1956.

Interview with Penelope Houston, in *Sight and Sound* (London),
Autumn 1962.

Film Comment (New York), March-April 1975.

Millimeter (New York), June 1975.

Sight and Sound (London), Autumn 1986.

On HOUSEMAN: articles—

The Christian Science Monitor, 16 December 1952.

''Ten Stars at Work on *Executive Suite*,'' in *The Christian Science
Monitor*, 10 November 1953.

''John Houseman on the Video Front: A Producer's Day at *Playhouse
'90*,'' in *The Christian Science Monitor*, 23 December 1958.

National Film Theatre booklet (London), April-May 1973.

Cinématographe (Paris), May 1984.

Obituary, in *Variety* (New York), 2 November 1988.

Cahiers du Cinéma (Paris), no. 414, December 1988.

*   *   *

In terms of versatility, scope, and intensity of achievement, John Houseman's was one of the most extraordinary careers in the history of American drama. Theatrical director and producer in New York (and later in Los Angeles and Stratford, Connecticut), motion picture and television producer in Hollywood, he gained popular fame near the end of his life as an actor in films, TV, and commercials and as the author of a best-selling three-volume autobiography comparable in its irony and cultural awareness to *The Education of Henry Adams*. Infused into these various intersecting activities were qualities of resolute zest and magisterial charm.

His French father died when he was 15. After leaving school, he found his mother's finances in such poor shape that he turned down a prestigious scholarship at Trinity College, Oxford. He was then shipped off to Argentina, where a family friend trained him in grain marketing. He pursued this in England and the U.S. for eight years with increasing success, then was wiped out by the 1929 stock market crash. Responding to his own yearning for creative outlets, Houseman wrote and translated plays, but had indifferent luck until Virgil Thomson offered him in 1934 the chance to direct an experimental Gertrude Stein opera for which he had written the music, *Four Saints in Three Acts*. Houseman used black actors in the production, and when a Federal Theater for blacks was proposed as a WPA relief project, he was named head of it. By 1937, he and Orson Welles were running something called the Mercury Theatre, whose controversial and popular productions ranged from a modern-dress version of *Julius Caesar* to the shocking newsreel-style radio version of H. G. Wells' *The War of the Worlds*, which caused thousands of listeners to believe Martians had landed.

This scandal carried both of them to Hollywood. After various false starts at RKO, Welles persuaded Houseman to work with Herman Mankiewicz in developing a script which became *Citizen Kane*—a writing-editing feat that was long one of the best-kept secrets in Hollywood history. After Pearl Harbor, Houseman resigned from David O. Selznick Productions to work for the U.S. government as head of radio for the Office of War Information in New York City. Toward the end of the war he produced his first film, also for the OWI, a documentary on the voting booth called *First Tuesday in November*.

Soon after, he was back on the west coast, switching to the opposite side of the spectrum with a Raymond Chandler *film noir*, *The Blue Dahlia*. In 1952 he was able to carry off a movie about movie making; *The Bad and the Beautiful* won several Oscars and established him at MGM and in Hollywood as someone who knew the ropes. In this film, as in his other collaborations with Vincente Minnelli (*The Cobweb*, *Lust for Life*, *Two Weeks in Another Town*), Houseman's taste and toughness were dominant. The black-and-white *Julius Caesar* drew on his Shakespearean expertise in a way Joseph Mankiewicz could not match. *Executive Suite*, one of the rare films actually dealing with American business practices, prompted an assessment by a *Christian Science Monitor* interviewer, which Houseman accepted, that he was deeply interested in the uses of power—in business, in Roman history, and in Hollywood.

He was unable to apply any of the levers of power at Metro, however, after the departure of former writer Dore Schary as head of production. Instead, Houseman turned his talents to television, producing (at CBS) a series called *The Seven Lively Arts* based on the Gilbert Seldes book and several 90-minute shows on that last great effort of TV drama, *Playhouse 90*.

Then, as before, he went back to the stage, as director or producer, on Broadway and in regional centers. In bewildering succession—and sometimes simultaneously—he ran the Shakespeare Festival in Connecticut and a professional theater at UCLA, and directed the first actors' training program at the Juilliard School (1967–76), inventing the Acting Company for its graduates, which continues to tour the country.

Houseman also entered upon his final career as an actor, notably as the crusty law professor in *The Paper Chase*, a movie and a TV series. The role was not unlike the man, some associates felt, but perhaps this was his prerogative as a master of several languages, a wide-ranging reader and traveler, and one of the most cultivated men ever to bear the title of producer in Hollywood.

—Richard Dyer MacCann

HOWARD, Sidney

Writer. **Nationality:** American. **Born:** Sidney Coe Howard in Oakland, California, 26 June 1891. **Education:** Attended the University of California, Berkeley, B.A. 1915; studied with George Pierce Baker

Sidney Howard

at Harvard University, Cambridge, Massachusetts, 1915–16. **Family:** Married 1) the actress Clare Jenness Eames, 1922 (divorced 1930); one daughter; 2) Leopoldine Blaine Damrosch, 1931; one daughter and one son. **Career:** Served in the American Ambulance Corps, and later in the Army Air Corps during World War I: Captain; 1919–22—member of the editorial staff, and literary editor, 1922, *Life* magazine; 1921—first play produced, *Swords*; 1929—first film as writer, *Bulldog Drummond*; 1938—founder, with S.N. Behrman and others, Playwrights Company. **Awards:** Pulitzer Prize for play *They Knew What They Wanted*, 1925; Academy Award for *Gone with the Wind*, 1939. **Member:** American Academy. **Died:** In a farm accident, in Tyringham, Massachusetts, 23 August 1939.

Films as Writer:

1929   *Bulldog Drummond* (Jones) (co); *Condemned* (Ruggles)
1930   *Raffles* (D'Arrast); *One Heavenly Night* (Fitzmaurice); *A Lady to Love* (Sjöström) (co)
1931   *Arrowsmith* (Ford) (co)
1932   *The Greeks Had a Word for Them* (L. Sherman) (co)
1936   *Dodsworth* (Wyler)
1939   **Gone with the Wind** (Fleming)
1940   *Raffles* (Wood) (co)

Publications

By HOWARD: plays—

Swords, New York, 1921.
Casanova, New York, 1924.
They Knew What They Wanted, New York, 1925.
Lucky Sam McCarver, New York, 1926.
Ned McCobb's Daughter, New York, 1926.
The Silver Cord, New York, 1927.
Olympia, New York, 1928.
Half Gods, New York, 1930.
The Late Christopher Bean, New York, 1933.
Alien Corn, New York, 1933.
Dodsworth, New York, 1934.
Yellow Jack, New York, 1934.
Paths of Glory, New York, 1935.
The Ghost of Yankee Doodle, New York, 1938.
One, Two, Three, New York, 1952.
Madam, Will You Walk?, New York, 1955.
Lute Song, Chicago, 1955.

By HOWARD: other books—

The Labor Spy (nonfiction), New York, 1921.
With John Hearley, *Professional Patriots* (nonfiction), New York, 1927.
Gone with the Wind (screenplay), edited by Richard Harwell, New York, 1980.

By HOWARD: article—

''The Story Gets a Treatment,'' in *We Make the Movies*, edited by Nancy Naumburg, New York, 1937.

On HOWARD: book—

White, Sydney H., *Sidney Howard*, Manchester, 1977.

On HOWARD: articles—

Theatre Arts (New York), February 1957.
Sorelle, Cynthia M., in *Twentieth-Century American Dramatists*, edited by John MacNicholas, Detroit, Michigan, 1981.
Yeck, Joanne, in *American Screenwriters*, edited by Robert E. Morsberger, Stephen O. Lesser, and Randall Clark, Detroit, Michigan, 1984.
Finkle, D., ''Tara! Tara! Tara!'' in *New York Times*, 10 December 1989.

* * *

If Sidney Howard had written only the screenplay for *Gone with the Wind*, he would have earned his place in film history. But in addition to writing America's most popular movie, Howard's talents helped bring prestige and dignity to some of the best films of the 1930s.

Born in California in 1891, Sidney Howard began writing at the age of nineteen when he was confined in a Swiss sanatorium for tuberculosis. He graduated from Berkeley, studied English literature at Harvard, served as an ambulance driver and flyer during the World War I, then went to work as a journalist, contributing to such magazines as *Colliers*, *The New Republic*, and *Hearst's International*. His war experience had made a realist of Howard. This realism, combined with a strong social conscience, was reflected in his articles and eventually in his plays. In the mid-1920s, he gained national prominence as a dramatist with a series of Broadway successes, including the Pulitzer Prize-winning *They Knew What They Wanted*.

When the movies began to talk in 1927, Hollywood's producers combed New York for playwrights interested in writing for the screen. Lured by the promise of riches and the challenge of a new form, Howard was one of the first wave of notable New York writers to head west. He went to work for Samuel Goldwyn, Hollywood's most illustrious independent producer, who appreciated Howard's refined sensibilities.

Howard recognized that early sound films had suffered from too much talk. He acknowledged the power of silence and respected the impact of visual movement. Unlike many screenwriters, who are married to their words, Howard believed that a screenwriter should provide the director with ''rhythms and ideas.''

When Howard went to work for Goldwyn the producer's top star was Ronald Colman. Goldwyn was eager to maintain Colman's box office power and assigned Howard to the actor's first three talking pictures, *Bulldog Drummond*, *Condemned*, and *Raffles*. Colman's exquisite voice and Howard's sophisticated dialogue turned out to be a winning team, both at the box office and with the critics. *Bulldog Drummond* was so successful that Goldwyn produced a sequel, *Bulldog Drummond Strikes Back*, and Paramount eventually serialized it in the late 1930s featuring John Barrymore as the highly articulate adventurer. *Raffles*, the gentleman thief, proved durable as well; Goldwyn remade the film in 1940 with David Niven. Howard is credited along with fellow playwright John Van Druten. In these three distinctly different scripts, Howard proved his versatility. He could provide an abundance of witty, staccato dialogue when it was called for and could be equally economical when action was required.

Howard's comedic adaptations of Louis Bromfield's *One Heavenly Night*, which blended light satire with musical numbers, and Zoë Akins's racy *The Greeks Had a Word for It*, retitled *The Greeks Had a Word for Them*, were less successful. Although his dialogue was aptly sophisticated, his strength lay in more realistic material.

Of the Goldwyn films, Howard's adaptations of two Sinclair Lewis novels, *Arrowsmith* and *Dodsworth*, were his most notable works. *Arrowsmith* was hailed as one of the decade's first serious message pictures, named by the *New York Times* as one of the ''Ten Best of 1931,'' and garnered four Academy Award nominations, including Best Picture and Best Screen Adaptation. *Dodsworth*, which he had successfully dramatized for the New York theater two years before, also remains highly regarded. It received eight Academy nominations; again, the screenwriter was honored. The following year Howard attempted a third Lewis property, *It Can't Happen Here* (1935). The political content, however, was unacceptable to Hollywood's censors; it went unproduced.

Howard wrote only two scripts which were not produced by Goldwyn. In 1930, he adapted his own play *They Knew What They Wanted* for MGM. Called *A Lady to Love*, it was the second screen version of his play. The silent film, retitled *Secret Hour*, starred vamp Pola Negri and Jean Hersholt as the lovable Italian vintner. In 1940, RKO made a third attempt to recreate the impact of Howard's play, but was unable to retain its honest portrayal of adultery under the prevailing censorship.

Howard's last screenplay, *Gone with the Wind*, was an outstanding achievement. His reduction of Margaret Mitchell's 1,037 page epic of the old South to a manageable screenplay was a herculean task. His initial submission, though still over long, was faithful to the spirit of the book despite its extensive condensation of material. When Howard refused to leave New England to continue rewrites, producer David O. Selznick replaced him with a series of writers including Ben Hecht, John Van Druten, F. Scott Fitzgerald, Oliver H.P. Garrett, and Charles MacArthur. Despite the multiplicity of contributors, the final script was remarkably close to Howard's 1936 draft, resulting in a single credit and a posthumously awarded Oscar for Best Screenplay. Howard had died tragically a few months before the awards at the age of forty-eight, crushed by a tractor on his farm in Tyringham, Massachusetts.

In the published preface to his play *Lucky Sam McCarver* Howard wrote, ''The novelist prefers writing to anything; the dramatist prefers acting to anything. The drama does not spring from a literary impulse but from a love of the brave, ephemeral, beautiful art of acting.'' Howard's respect for talking pictures combined with his sincere love of acting unquestionably advanced the art of filmmaking in the 1930s.

—Joanne L. Yeck

HOWE, James Wong

Cinematographer. **Nationality:** American. **Born:** Wong Tung Jim in Kwantung, China, 28 August 1899; emigrated to the United States, 1904; credited early in his career as James or Jimmie Howe. **Family:** Married the writer Sanora Babb. **Career:** Farm laborer, professional boxer, delivery boy; 1917—janitor, then camera assistant, Lasky Studios; 1922—first film as cinematographer, *Drums of Fate*; 1954—directed first film, *Go Man Go*; some TV and commercial photography in the 1960s. **Awards:** Academy Award for *The Rose Tattoo*, 1955, and *Hud*, 1963. **Died:** 12 July 1976.

Films as Assistant Cameraman:

1919   *Puppy Love* (Neill); *For Better, For Worse* (W. De Mille); *Told in the Hills* (Melford); *Male and Female* (C. De Mille)
1921   *Everything for Sale* (O'Connor)
1922   *The Woman Who Walked Alone* (Melford); *The Sired Call* (Willat); *Burning Sands* (*The Dweller in the Desert*) (Melford)

Films as Cinematographer:

1922   *Drums of Fate* (*Drums of Destiny*) (Maigne)
1923   *The Trail of the Lonesome Pine* (Maigne); *To the Last Man* (Fleming) (co); *The Woman with Four Faces* (Brenon); *The Spanish Dancer* (Brenon); *The Call of the Canyon* (Fleming)
1924   *The Breaking Point* (Brenon); *The Side Show of Life* (Brenon); *The Alaskan* (Brenon); *Peter Pan* (Brenon)
1925   *The Charmer* (Olcott); *Not So Long Ago* (Olcott); *The King on Main Street* (Bell); *The Best People* (Olcott)
1926   *The Song and Dance Man* (Brenon); *Sea Horses* (Dwan); *Padlocked* (Dwan); *Mantrap* (Fleming)
1927   *The Rough Riders* (*The Trumpet Call*) (Fleming); *Sorrell and Son* (Brenon)
1928   *Laugh, Clown, Laugh* (Brenon); *The Perfect Crime* (Glennon); *Four Walls* (Nigh)
1929   *Desert Nights* (*Thirst*) (Nigh)
1930   *Today* (Nigh); *The Criminal Code* (Hawks) (co)
1931   *Transatlantic* (Howard); *The Spider* (McKenna and Menzies); *The Yellow Ticket* (*The Yellow Passport*) (Walsh); *Surrender* (Howard); *Dance Team* (Lanfield)
1932   *After Tomorrow* (Borzage); *Amateur Daddy* (Blystone); *Man about Town* (Dillon); *Chandu the Magician* (Varnel and Mensies)
1933   *Hello, Sister!* (*Walking down Broadway*) (von Stroheim and Walsh); *The Power and the Glory* (*Power and Glory*) (Howard); *Beauty for Sale* (*Beauty*) (Boleslawsky)
1934   *The Show-Off* (Reisner); *Viva Villa!* (Conway) (co); *Manhattan Melodrama* (Van Dyke); *Hollywood Party* (Dwan and others); **The Thin Man** (Van Dyke); *Stamboul Quest* (Wood); *Have a Heart* (Butler); *Biography of a Bachelor Girl* (Griffith)
1935   *The Night Is Young* (Murphy); *Mark of the Vampire* (Browning); *The Flame Within* (Goulding); *O'Shaughnessy's Boy* (Boleslawsky); *Whipsaw* (Wood)

1936   *Three Live Ghosts* (Humberstone) (co); *Fire over England* (Howard)
1937   *Farewell Again* (*Troopship*) (Whelan); *Under the Red Robe* (Sjöström) (co); *The Prisoner of Zenda* (Cromwell)
1938   *The Adventures of Tom Sawyer* (Taurog) (co); *Algiers* (Cromwell); *Comet over Broadway* (Berkeley)
1939   *They Made Me a Criminal* (Berkeley); *The Oklahoma Kid* (Bacon); *Daughters Courageous* (Curtiz); *Dust Be My Destiny* (Seiler); *On Your Toes* (Enright)
1940   *Abe Lincoln in Illinois* (*Spirit of the People*) (Cromwell); *The Story of Dr. Ehrlich's Magic Bullet* (*Dr. Ehrlich's Magic Bullet*) (Dieterle); *Saturday's Children* (V. Sherman); *Torrid Zone* (Keighley); *City for Conquest* (Litvak) (co); *A Dispatch from Reuters* (*This Man Reuter*) (Dieterle)
1941   *The Strawberry Blonde* (Walsh); *Shining Victory* (Rapper); *Navy Blues* (Bacon) (co); *Out of the Fog* (Litvak)
1942   *Kings Row* (Wood); *Yankee Doodle Dandy* (Curtiz)
1943   *Air Force* (Hawks); *Hangmen Also Die!* (F. Lang); *The Hard Way* (V. Sherman); *The North Star* (Milestone)
1944   *Passage to Marseilles* (Curtiz)
1945   *Objective Burma!* (Walsh); *Counter-Attack* (*One Against Seven*) (Z. Korda); *Confidential Agent* (Shumlin); *Danger Signal* (Florey)
1946   *My Reputation* (Bernhardt)
1947   *Nora Prentiss* (V. Sherman); *Pursued* (Walsh); *Body and Soul* (Rossen)
1948   *Mr. Blandings Builds His Dream House* (Potter); *The Time of Your Life* (Potter)
1950   *The Baron of Arizona* (Fuller); *The Eagle and the Hawk* (Foster); *Tripoli* (Price)
1951   *The Brave Bulls* (Rossen) (co); *He Ran All the Way* (Berry); *Behave Yourself* (Beck); *The Lady Says "No"* (Ross)
1952   *The Fighter* (Kline); *Come Back, Little Sheba* (Daniel Mann)
1953   *Main Street to Broadway* (Garnett); *Jennifer* (Newton)
1955   *The Rose Tattoo* (Daniel Mann); *Picnic* (Logan)
1956   *Death of a Scoundrel* (Martin)
1957   *Drango* (Bartlett and Bricken); **The Sweet Smell of Success** (Mackendrick)
1958   *The Old Man and the Sea* (J. Sturges); *Bell, Book, and Candle* (Quine)
1959   *The Last Angry Man* (Daniel Mann); *The Story on Page One* (Odets)
1960   *Tess of the Storm Country* (Guilfoyle); *Song without End* (C. Vidor and Cukor) (co)
1962   *Hud* (Ritt)
1964   *The Outrage* (Ritt)
1965   *The Glory Guys* (Laven)
1966   *This Property Is Condemned* (Pollack); *Seconds* (Frankenheimer); *Hombre* (Ritt)
1968   *The Heart Is a Lonely Hunter* (Miller)
1969   *Blood Kin* (*The Last of the Mobile Hot-Shots*) (Lumet); *The Molly Maguires* (Ritt)
1974   *Funny Lady* (Ross)

Films as Director:

1954   *Go Man Go*
1955   *Dong Kingman* (*The World of Dong Kingman*) (+ pr—short)
1958   *Invisible Avenger* (co)

411

James Wong Howe

Publications

By HOWE: articles—

"Lightning," in *Cinematographic Annual 1931*, Hollywood 1931.
"Reactions on Making His First Color Productions," in *American Cinematographer* (Hollywood), October 1937.
"The Cameraman Talks Back," in *Screen Writer*, October 1945.
On *The Glory Boys*, in *American Cinematographer* (Hollywood), August 1965.
Sight and Sound (London), Autumn 1967.
In *Sources of Light*, edited by Charles Higham, London, 1970.
Filmmakers Newsletter (Ward Hill, Massachusetts), February 1973.
On *Funny Lady*, in *American Cinematographer* (Hollywood), September 1976.
Image (Rochester, New York), no. 1, 1977.

On HOWE: book—

Rainsberger, Todd, *James Wong Howe, Cinematographer*, San Diego, California, 1981.

On HOWE: articles—

Crichton, K., in *Collier's* (New York), 12 June 1937.
Jacobs, Jack, in *Films in Review* (New York), April 1961.
Lightman, Herb A., on *Hud* in *American Cinematographer* (Hollywood), July 1963.
Lightman, Herb A., on *The Outrage* in *American Cinematographer* (Hollywood), April 1964.
Lightman, Herb A., on *The Molly Maguires* in *American Cinematographer* (Hollywood), April 1970.
Eyman, W.S., in *Take One* (Montreal), March-April 1972.
Film Comment (New York), Summer 1972.
Focus on Film (London), no. 13, 1973.
Lawrence, R., in *Today's Filmmaker* (Hempstead, New York), no. 4, 1974.
Kaye, A., and P.J. Smith, in *American Cinematographer* (Hollywood), February 1974.
Stein, R., in *Audience* (New York), December 1974.
Gillet, John, in *Sight and Sound* (London), Autumn 1976.·
Parrish, Robert, in *Focus on Film* (London), November 1976.
Gerely, A., in *Film und Ton* (Munich), October 1977.

Parrish, Robert, in *American Film* (Washington, D.C.), April 1986.
Eyman, Scott, in *Five American Cinematographers*, London, 1987.

*   *   *

Despite the fact that the motion-picture camera is the mechanical means by which films actually come to be, the role of the cameraman, or director of photography, or cinematographer, is often overlooked in assessing a movie's value. James Wong Howe is one of the few cinematographers to receive any individual recognition before the 1970s, two others being Billy Bitzer and Karl Freund. Howe's lengthy career spans more than five decades. He earned a reputation as one of the most innovative cameramen, always eager to experiment, and one of the professional craftsmen who was responsible for the "look" of the Warner Brothers product with the 26 pictures he photographed at that studio between 1938 and 1947.

A Chinese immigrant interested in athletics and boxing, Howe landed a job as assistant to Alvin Wyckoff, Cecil B. De Mille's photographer. He learned the rudiments of photography from Wyckoff, convinced Mary Miles Minter to allow him to take some publicity shots of her, and as a result she requested he photograph her in *Drums of Fate* and *The Trail of the Lonesome Pine* in 1922–23. His use of low-key lighting to emphasize fantasy in Betty Bronson's *Peter Pan* enhanced his reputation, as did his realistic lighting for *Laugh, Clown, Laugh*, starring Lon Chaney. When the arrival of sound threw Hollywood studios into turmoil, Howe took time off to visit his homeland. Upon his return he had difficulty finding work because producers explained they needed photographers who *understood* sound.

Howard Hawks broke the ice by hiring him to shoot *The Criminal Code*, which earned him a two-year contract at Fox, where his best film was *The Power and the Glory*, directed by Preston Sturges and filmed in straightforward, newsreel style. Howe went to MGM in 1933 where his films included *Viva Villa!*, *The Thin Man*, and *Whipsaw*. He became bored at MGM, and, after shooting the color tests of Marlene Dietrich for *The Garden of Allah* for David O. Selznick, went to England where he photographed *Fire over England*, then returned to the US to do some of his finest work in Selznick's *The Prisoner of Zenda*. That film cast Ronald Colman in dual roles and is famous for the scene in which Colman shakes hands with himself. Howe explained, "Split screen was used, of course, but not the usual straight line split. I placed a three-by-four-foot optical glass three feet in front of the camera. Ronald Colman shook hands with a double. The double's head and shoulders were matted out with masking tape on the glass. The scene was photographed, the camera shutter was closed, and the film was wound backward to the beginning of the scene. We then masked out everything but Colman's head and shoulders and re-photographed the scene. This required great accuracy on the part of everyone involved, especially on Ronald Colman's part as he spoke and reacted to himself. We did all this 14 times. The third try was the best."

Following that success, he shot his first color film, also for Selznick, *The Adventures of Tom Sawyer*. "A splash of red or blue in the background of a color picture can distract audience attention in the same way a strong highlight does in monochrome," explained Howe. "In *The Adventures of Tom Sawyer* I tried to subordinate background color and to confine the major coloring of any scene to the players. This is not as difficult as it sounds, and it worked out successfully." Howe followed *Sawyer* with the atmospheric black-and-white *Algiers*. Howe recalled that Hedy Lamarr, in her first US film, "was bewildered and possessed of all the physical defects the average girl has on

her arrival at the film factories." His success in transforming her into a glamor girl earned him a contract with Warner Brothers, where, in a ten-year period, he photographed 36 films. Howe's realistic style was a perfect match for the hard-hitting Warner Brothers product. These films include a sepia-toned *The Oklahoma Kid*, *Dr. Ehrlich's Magic Bullet*, *Kings Row*, *Yankee Doodle Dandy*, and *Body and Soul*.

During the 1950s and 1960s Howe freelanced, doing his most memorable work—*Come Back, Little Sheba*, *Picnic*, *The Rose Tattoo* (for which he received his first Oscar), *The Sweet Smell of Success*, and *The Old Man and the Sea*. His sense of dramatic realism was in full evidence in *Hud*, which earned him a second Oscar, and, to many, his best work was his innovative, distorting, wide-angle photography for John Frankenheimer's *Seconds*.

—Ronald Bowers

HUBLEY, John

Animator. Nationality: American. **Born:** Marinette, Wisconsin, 21 May 1914. **Education:** Attended the Art Center, Los Angeles. **Military Srvice:** 1943–45—worked on training films for United States Air Force. **Family:** Married the editor Faith Elliot, 1955. **Career:** 1935–41—worked as assistant animator, Walt Disney; 1941–43—worked for Screen Gems unit of Columbia; 1946–52—animation director, United Productions of America (UPA); initiated TV series *Dusty of the Circus*; 1954—formed Storyboard Productions, and Hubley Studio, 1965: later television work includes credits designs, specials, and series including *Sesame Street* and *Everybody Rides the Carousel*. **Awards:** Academy Awards for *Moonbird*, 1959; *The Hole*, 1962; *Herb Alpert and the Tijuana Brass Double Feature*, 1966. **Died:** 23 February 1977.

Films as Director:

1940   *Old Blackout Joe* (co); *The Dumbconscious Mind* (co); *King Midas, Junior* (co)
1943   *The Vitamin G-Man* (co); *Prof. Small and Mr. Tall* (co); *He Can't Make It Stick* (co)
1944   *Position Firing* (co); *Operation of the K-13 Gunsight* (co)
1945   *Tuesday in November* (Berry) (animation sequences)
1946   *Flat Hatting*
1947   *Human Growth* (Lerner) (animation sequences)
1948   *Robin Hoodlum*; *The Magic Fluke*
1949   *Mr. Magoo*; *The Ragtime Bear*; *Punchy De Leon*
1950   *Spellbound Hound*; *Trouble Indemnity*; *Barefaced Flatfoot*
1951   *Fuddy Duddy Buddy*; *Rooty Toot Toot*
1952   *The Four Poster* (Reis) (animation sequences)
1957   *The Adventures of* *; *Date with Dizzy*
1958   *The Tender Game*; *Harlem Wednesday*
1959   *Moonbird*
1960   *Children of the Sun*
1961   *Of Stars and Men*
1962   *The Hole*; *Horses and Their Ancestors*; *Man and His Tools*
1964   *The Hat*
1966   *Herb Alpert and the Tijuana Brass Double Feature*; *Urbanissimo*; *The Year of the Horse* (Sunasky) (animation sequences)

1967   *The Cruise*
1968   *Zuckerkandl!*; *Windy Day*
1969   *Of Men and Demons*
1970   *Eggs*
1973   *Cockaboody*; *Upkeep*
1974   *Voyage to Next*
1975   *People, People, People*

Other Films:

1940   "The Rite of Spring" sequence of *Fantasia* (Grant and
        Sharpsteen) (co); *Pinocchio* (Sharpsteen and Luske)
        (co-art-d)
1942   *Bambi* (Hand) (co-art-d)
1944   *Hell-Bent for Election* (Jones) (co-sc, uncredited)
1946   *Brotherhood of Man* (Cannon) (co-sc + des)
1951   *M* (Losey) (co-des); *Georgie and the Dragon* (Cannon) (co-sc
        + des); *Grizzly Golfer* (Burness) (pr); *Sloppy Jalopy*
        (Burness) (pr)
1953   *Heritage* (Moore) (sc)
1968   *Uptight* (Dassin) (title des)

Publications

By HUBLEY: articles—

With Zachary Schwartz, "Animation Learns a New Language," in
    Hollywood Quarterly, July 1946.
With others, "*Brotherhood of Man*; a Script," in *Hollywood Quar-*
    terly, July 1946.

On HUBLEY: articles—

Korty, J., "Of Stars and Men," in *Film Quarterly*, (Berkeley,
    California), vol. 15, no. 4, 1962.
Martin, A., in *Cinéma* (Paris), no. 98, 1965.
Image et Son (Paris), July 1967.
Archibald, Lewis, in *Film Library Quarterly* (New York), Spring 1970.
Cinéma (Paris), January 1975.
National Film Theatre booklet (London), November 1976.
Millimeter (New York), February 1977.
Ecran (Paris), May 1977.
Lenburg, Jeff, in *The Great Cartoon Directors*, London, 1983.
Roudevitch, Michel, in *Cinémaction* (Courbevoie), April 1989.
Lane, B.K., "Animation That Reaches Realms Beyond Disney," in
    New York Times, 4 April 1993.
Kim, D.D., "The Hubley Film Festival," in *Village Voice* (New
    York), 13 April 1993.
Dauphin, G., "'The Hubley Studio: A Home for Animation'," in
    Village Voice (New York), 23 December 1997.

*   *   *

John Hubley, a remarkable animator by any standards, is noted not
only for creating a new and important image in the animated film, but
also for being the basic influence on a whole new genre in world
animation. Having studied at the Los Angeles Art Center, Hubley
joined the Disney studio as assistant director, tracing and painting the
backgrounds, and soon progressing to layouts on Disney's first full-
length cartoon, *Snow White and the Seven Dwarfs*. He was then
promoted to full art director (or layout man) and worked on the
"Earth Settling" segment from "The Rite of Spring" sequence and
painting backgrounds for "The Sorcerer's Apprentice" sequence in
Fantasia.

In 1942 Hubley left Disney to work under the legendary Dave
Fleischer at Columbia's Screen Gems, where he co-directed a number
of short cartoons with the animator Paul Sommer. These show the
early roots of the Hubley influence through the use of crisp, sharp
lines with bold, bright colors in the background as well as in the
characters.

During the Second World War years, while Hubley was making
training films in the Air Corps, a group of Disney drop-outs and
refugees were forming their own company, United Productions of
America, and had started producing sponsored cartoons. *Hell-Bent
for Election* was the big turning point in many ways. This 16-minute
short was made for the 1944 Roosevelt presidential campaign mostly
by moonlighting animators, so dedicated to the cause that they made it
for free. The graphic design and bright coloring were light years away
from what cinema audiences were used to, and the film was to set the
standard which other studios would try to match. Hubley was hired as
UPA's creative head, and when the producer Stephen Bosustow
bought UPA outright from his original partners, Hubley joined him as
studio boss. When a contract was signed with Columbia to make
a series of theatrical entertainment cartoons, Hubley came into his
element, and created his most popular character, a near-sighted old
grouch who saw only what he wanted to see, Mister Magoo.

Hubley left UPA in 1952 and formed Storyboard Productions. It
specialized in television commercials, though Hubley (and his wife
Faith, now his partner) intended to make at least one serious film
a year. The first was *The Adventures of *, commissioned by the
Guggenheim Museum. Since the film concerns the need by the old for
the vision of the young, the style is that of the crayon drawings of
a child, double-exposed over rendered backgrounds. The success of
*The Adventures of * was phenomenal, and was followed by experi-
ments with water color on wax, spraying cells, and many other
techniques exploring the Hubley's own artistry. The Hubley cartoons
are not only intended to entertain, but often to make a serious point, be
it about pollution, over-population, world peace, or the atomic bomb.
They are always refreshing.

The final years of Hubley's creative life were taken up with
initiating the feature *Watership Down*. Although he was fired by the
producer and all his work scrapped, the prologue looks decidedly
Hubley-esque and more than a cut above the rest of the film. He was
storyboarding a 26-minute TV special of Garry Trudeau's comic strip
Doonesbury when he died while undergoing heart surgery. His wife
Faith completed it, and has been carrying on the good work ever since.

—Graham Webb

HUNTE, Otto

Designer. **Nationality:** German. **Career:** 1910s—experimental artist
based in Munich, designed sets for Lang and Von Harbou; 1930s—
continued working in Germany during the War; 1945–60—remained
in Germany. **Died:** In Berlin, 1960.

Films as Art Director/ Production Designer (selected list):

1919   *Das Kabinett des Dr. Caligari* (*The Cabinet of Dr. Caligari*)
           (Wiene); *Madame Dubarry* (Lubitsch)
1920   *Das Indische Grabmal* (May); *Die Herrin der Welt* (May)
1922   *Dr. Mabuse, der Spieler* (*Dr. Mabuse the Gambler*) (Lang) (co)
1924   *Die Nibelungen* (*The Nibelungen Saga*) (Lang)
1926   *Metropolis* (Lang)
1927   *Die Liebe der Jeanne Ney* (Pabst)
1929   *Frau im Mond* (*The Girl in the Moon*) (Lang)
1930   *Der blaue Engel* (*The Blue Angel*) (von Sternberg)
1933   *Das Testament des Dr. Mabuse* (Lang) (co)
1940   *Jud Süss* (Harlan)
1946   *Die Mörder sind unter uns* (Staudte)

Publications

On HUNTE: articles—

Codelli, L., in *Griffithiana* (Gemona, Italy), September 1996.
Marsilius, Hans Jörg, in *Film-Dienst* (Cologne), 22 October 1996.
Journal of Film Preservation (Brussels), November 1996.

*   *   *

After the monumental Italian spectacles of the early 20th century, and D.W. Griffith's epics, a new film phenomenon appeared which carried cinema to new heights. The striking decors of *The Cabinet of Dr. Caligari* and Lubitsch's *Madame Dubarry*, both made in 1919, helped the German cinema to break through the barrier of political prejudice built up against it by the Allied nations after the First World War. The technical and artistic superiority of German studio craftsmanship, as well as Expressionism, then a powerful force in German art, and the considerable influence of Reinhardt's theatre, were ultimately to influence film production worldwide.

Otto Hunte, who began his career as an artist in a Munich experimental group, was certainly an outstanding contributor to the success of the German film industry in the 1920s. However, because the success of the Golden Age of German film relied on close cooperation between directors, designers, and cameramen, it becomes a little difficult to sort out the different functions of separate individuals. Where several artists worked together, as in the case of Hunte, Vollbrecht and others, records do not always reveal who did what. Hunte often shared credits with Jacoby-Boy, Kettelhut, Stahl Urach, and Emil Hasler.

It is clear, however, that Hunte was Lang's major designer, bringing his experience as a painter to the director's architectural background. He created the great landscapes of *Die Nibelungen*, the futuristic constructions of *Metropolis* and *The Girl in the Moon*, and the seedy coulisses of the *Mabuse* films. Often it was Hunte who interpreted the ideas of Lang and his scriptwriter wife Thea Von Harbou, leaving much of the actual construction to his assistant Vollbrecht, who then made his own personal contributions to the films—for example, in the dragon sequence of *Die Nibelungen*.

Hunte's studio-based art was very much a characteristic of the German cinema. The forests of *Siegfried*, the first episode of *Die Nibelungen*, were studio forests, artificially created, and the set pieces of the cathedral steps and Gunthur's castle were solid studio constructions. What made these films so outstanding was the perfect coordination of many diverse elements, fused together by the tyrannous energy of Lang.

The designer did not work solely for Lang. Von Harbou had associations with Robert Dineson, the Danish director working in Berlin, and Joe May. Hunte worked with them both, designing for the latter *Das Indische Grabmal* and *Die Herrin der Welt*. He showed a very different style from his work with Lang in Pabst's *Liebe der Jeanne Ney*, and in 1930, he worked on Sternberg's *Der blaue Engel*.

After Lang's escape to exile, Hunte remained in Germany, working with Von Harbou on many of her films and even designing the notoriously anti-semitic *Jud Süss*. After the war, however, he was equally amenable to working with Wolfgang Staudte on the impressive anti-Nazi film, *Die Mörder sind unter uns* for the East German DEFA company. He continued working until his death in 1960.

—Liam O'Leary

HUNTER, Ross

Producer. **Nationality:** American. **Born:** Martin Fuss in Cleveland, Ohio, 6 May 1916. **Education:** Attended Western Reserve University, Cleveland, M.A. **Career:** 1942–43—schoolteacher, Cleveland; 1944–47—actor, Columbia, then teacher and stage producer and director; 1951—associate producer, then producer for Universal,

Ross Hunter

Columbia, and Paramount; also producer of TV mini-series *Arthur Hailey's The Moneychangers*, 1976, and *The Best Place to Be*, 1979. **Died:** Of lymphoma; in Century City, California, 10 March 1996.

Films as Associate Producer:

1951   *Flame of Araby* (Lamont)
1952   *Steel Town* (G. Sherman); *Battle at Apache Pass* (G. Sherman)

Films as Producer:

1953   *Take Me to Town* (Sirk); *All I Desire* (Sirk); *Tumbleweeds* (Juran); *Taza, Son of Cochise* (Sirk)
1954   *Magnificent Obsession* (Sirk); *Naked Alibi* (Hopper); *The Yellow Mountain* (Hibbs); *One Desire* (Hopper)
1955   *The Spoilers* (Hibbs); *Captain Lightfoot* (Sirk); *There's Always Tomorrow* (Sirk)
1956   ***All that Heaven Allows*** (Sirk)
1957   *Battle Hymn* (Sirk); *Tammy and the Bachelor* (Tammy) (Pevney); *My Man Godfrey* (Koster); *Interlude* (Sirk)
1958   *This Happy Feeling* (Edwards); *Stranger in My Arms* (Käutner); *The Restless Years* (*The Wonderful Years*) (Käutner)
1959   *Imitation of Life* (Sirk); *Pillow Talk* (Gordon) (co)
1960   *Portrait in Black* (Gordon); *Midnight Lace* (Miller) (co)
1961   *Back Street* (Miller); *Tammy Tell Me True* (Keller); *Flower Drum Song* (Koster)
1962   *If a Man Answers* (Levin)
1963   *The Thrill of It All* (Jewison) (co); *Tammy and the Doctor* (Keller)
1964   *The Chalk Garden* (Neame); *I'd Rather Be Rich* (Smight)
1965   *The Art of Love* (Jewison)
1966   *Madame X* (Rich); *The Pad . . . and How to Use It* (Hutton)
1967   *Rose* (Rich) (exec); *Thoroughly Modern Millie* (Hill)
1970   *Airport* (Seaton and Hathaway)
1972   *Lost Horizon* (Jarrott)
1975   *The Lives of Jenny Dolan* (Jameson) (exec)
1978   *Suddenly, Love* (Margolin) (co); *A Family Upside Down* (Rich—for TV) (co)

Films as Actor:

1944   *Louisiana Hayride* (Barton) (as Gordon Pearson)
1945   *A Guy, a Gal, and a Pal* (Boetticher) (as Jimmy Jones)
1946   *Hit the Hay* (Lord) (as Ted Barton); *Sweetheart of Sigma Chi* (Bernhard) (as Ted Sloan)

Publications

By HUNTER: articles—

Sight and Sound (London), Summer 1963.
"Magnificent Obsessions," in *American Film* (Washington, D.C.), April 1988.

On HUNTER: articles—

Daily Cinema (London), 21 August 1967.
Greater Amusements, December 1967.
Castell, David, in *Films Illustrated* (London), April 1973.
Show (New York), September 1973.
Movieline (Escondido), vol. 3, September 1991.
Obituary, in *Variety* (New York), 18–24 March 1996.
Obituary, in *Classic Images* (Muscatine), May 1996.

* * *

Ross Hunter's career has certain parallels to that of George Cukor, who was often called a "woman's director." In Hunter's case, he was (after an inauspicious acting career) a "woman's producer": the dramatic focus of many of his most successful films was a woman's quest for romantic love. Additionally, his most typical films were soap operas and comedies (as opposed to noirish crime dramas, Westerns, or war films), genres always held by the critical establishment to be of special interest to women.

In many of Hunter's best efforts as producer, the specifics of the scenario are transcended by sheer production values. Douglas Sirk has generally been given credit for the melodramas made with Hunter, but if it is the producer's job to actually produce and assemble the variety of elements, Hunter must certainly be acknowledged for that particular confluence which appeared so significantly and expressively in *Magnificent Obsession*, *All that Heaven Allows*, *Battle Hymn*, and *Imitation of Life* (along with such similarly themed non-Sirk melodramas as *Portrait in Black* and *Back Street*). Indeed, it is not far-fetched to see in Hunter, with his preoccupation with style, the roots of Fassbinder's brand of New German Cinema.

Some of the most successful of Hunter's films starred his friend Rock Hudson. Perhaps Hunter's most interesting non-Sirk film, also featuring Hudson, is *Pillow Talk*, a socially and politically schizophrenic comedy. On one hand, the film openly deals with sex and presents the kind of liberated career woman not to be found on screen since World War II. Yet at the same time, the scenario depicts a repressed sexuality and an almost anachronistic obsession with female virginity. Hunter's association with Doris Day, Hudson's *Pillow Talk* co-star, continued with the suspense melodrama *Midnight Lace* and the comedy *The Thrill of It All*. He also produced a series of comedies with Debbie Reynolds, including *Tammy and the Bachelor*, and a "Tammy" sequel, *Tammy Tell Me True*, starring Sandra Dee. Along with Day, these two actresses celebrated the type of idealized 1950s/early-1960s celluloid virginity which was then expected of "good" girls but which today is laughably outdated.

It must be pointed out as well the tremendous irony of Rock Hudson, whose homosexuality was to remain publicly closeted for most of his lifetime, appearing in *Pillow Talk* as a character whose pretended fear of homosexuality is a way of "getting girls." Although a bright, sophisticated, and stylish comedy for its time, *Pillow Talk* thus becomes on another level an unusually vile and hypocritical work.

The commercial climax of Hunter's career was undoubtedly *Airport*, based on the Arthur Hailey best-seller: an unashamedly old-fashioned (for 1970) thriller which combined Academy Award-winning actors with soap opera, suspense, and production values. The result was one of the most commercially successful films of its time, spawning a spate of sequels and other similar "disaster" spectaculars.

Hunter's sensibility, his interest in style, production values, and good taste, had the tendency to descend into kitsch or camp if not controlled by a strong director such as Sirk. The potential capstone of his career, the musical version of *Lost Horizon*, was a fiasco in almost all areas. It was deadened by the tasteful if dull casting of Liv Ullmann and Peter Finch, as well as by undistinguished music by Burt Bacharach. Its story, production values, and old-fashioned Holly-wood sensibility doomed the film and—in the midst of the Vietnam War, the sexual revolution, and the increasingly youthful age of the typical moviegoer—made Hunter himself an anachronism. Even though he never officially retired, he remained mostly inactive during the almost two decades before his death in 1996.

—Charles Derry, updated by Rob Edelman

IBERT, Jacques

Composer. **Nationality:** French. **Born:** Jacques-François Antoine Ibert in Paris, 15 August 1890. **Education:** Attended Rollin College; musical studies under Pessard and Fauré at Paris Conservatory, 1910–14. **Career:** Composer of stage works (operas and ballets) as well as works for orchestra; 1931—first film score, *S.O.S. Foch*; 1937–40 and 1946–60—director, Academy of France in Rome. **Died:** 5 February 1962.

Films as Composer:

1931 *S.O.S. Foch* (Arroy—short); *Les Cinq gentlemen maudits* (Duvivier)

1933 *Don Quichotte* (*Don Quixote*) (Pabst); *Les Deux Orphelines* (M. Tourneur) (co)

1934 *Maternité* (Choux)

1935 *Justin de Marseille* (M. Tourneur) (co); *Golgotha* (Duvivier)

1936 *Koenigsmark* (*Crimson Dynasty*) (M. Tourneur); *Le Coupable* (Bernard); *L'Homme de nulle part* (Chenal); *Anne-Marie* (Bernard) (co); *Courrier sud* (Billon) (co); *Branle-bas de combat* (Lallier—short); *Paris* (Choux)

1937 *Feu!* (de Baroncelli)

1938 *Le Patriote* (M. Tourneur); *La Maison du Maltais* (Chenal) (co), *Le Héros de la Marne* (Hugon); *Thérèse Martin* (de Canonge)

1939 *La Charette fantôme* (*The Phantom Carriage*) (Duvivier); *Le Père Lebonnard* (*Papa Lebonnard*) (de Limur); *Angelica* (Choux)

1940 *La Comédie du bonheur* (L'Herbier)

1942 *Félicie Nanteuil* (*Histoire comique*) (M. Allégret)

1943 *Les Petites du Quai aux Fleurs* (M. Allégret)

1945 *Le Père Serge* (Gasnier-Raymond)

1946 *L'Affaire du collier de la reine* (*The Queen's Necklace*) (L'Herbier); *Panique* (Duvivier)

1947 *Lyautey, bâtisseur d'empire* (Lucot—short)

1948 *Macbeth* (Welles)

1952 *Equilibre* (Mansart); *From Doric to Gothic* (Gillet—short)

1954 "Circus" ep. of *Invitation to the Dance* (Kelly)

1955 *Marianne de ma jeunesse* (Duvivier)

Publications

On IBERT: books—

Feschotte, J., *Jacques Ibert*, Paris, 1958.
Michel, G., *Jacques Ibert*, Paris, 1968.

On IBERT: articles—

Colpi, Henri, in *Défense et illustration de la musique dans le film*, Lyon, 1964.
Porcile, François, in *Présence de la musique à l'écran*, Paris, 1969.
Lacombe, Alain, and Claude Rocle, in *La Musique du film*, Paris, 1979.
Film Dope (Nottingham), January 1983.

* * *

Jacques Ibert's reputation as a lightweight composer of witty frivolities—a kind of ex officio member of "Les Six"—does him a lot less than justice. The ebullient high spirits of his best-known works such as the parodistic "Divertissement," though typical of one aspect of him, have come to eclipse the darker, more complex elements in his music. For Ibert was also the composer of the somber symphonic poem "Ballade de la geôle de Reading," inspired by Oscar Wilde's poem, and the nightmarish "Chant de folie." And this "shadow side" of Ibert's musical personality emerges too in his film music, as in the scores he wrote for Duvivier's *Golgotha* and Welles's *Macbeth*.

Like others of his generation, Ibert developed his love of cinema during the silent era, and for a time earned his living (as did Shostakovich) playing piano in movie houses. The "Divertissement," composed as incidental music for a staging of the same Labiche farce, *Un chapeau de paille d'Italie*, that René Clair used as basis for his film, could well stand as a tribute to silent film comedy. The finale, with its frenetic percussion and massed police whistles, immediately evokes the world of Chaplin, Keaton, and the Keystone cops, and even allows the trumpet to mimic one of Chaplin's skidding, one-legged about-turns. Indeed, though not written as a film score, Ibert's music was subsequently used to accompany Clair's film, an oblique acknowledgment of its essentially cinematic spirit.

Proudly eclectic, Ibert always disdained schools of composition. "All systems are valid," he maintained, "so long as one derives music from them." In his film music, as in his concert and chamber works, he was happy to incorporate elements from whatever style or culture seemed appropriate to the job in hand. For his first feature film as composer, Duvivier's *Les Cinq gentlemen maudits*, he matched the North African story line by working Moroccan chants and animal cries into the score. It was for another film directed by Duvivier, the biblical epic *Golgotha*, that Ibert composed one of his most expressive scores of the 1930s drawing on elements of Gregorian chant, Handelian chorales, sinuous oriental melodies and the traditional theme of the "Dies Irae." For the climax, the crucifixion itself, he unleashed a tour de force of orchestral sonorities, with brass and rattling percussion vying for supremacy, culminating in a sepulchral march with the *ondes martenot* wailing desolately above it like a grief-stricken voice.

Expert at adapting his own characteristic tone to a wide range of idioms, Ibert was the ideal composer to provide evocative orchestral color for films set in exotic times or places—whether in the Sahara (*Courrier sud*), in dynastic Ruritanian Europe (*Koenigsmark*), or even in the other world (*La Charrette fantôme*). When the ailing Maurice Ravel was unable to meet the deadline, Ibert stepped in to craft elegant Spanish pastiche for Pabst's *Don Quichotte*.

Hollywood never tempted Ibert, for whom the idea of entrusting his orchestration to some studio hack would have been anathema, and only twice did he stray outside French cinema. For the "Circus" episode of Gene Kelly's *Invitation to the Dance* he provided a ballet score full of whirlwind rhythms and darting fantasy. But his finest and most original film music was inspired by Orson Welles's idiosyncratic version of *Macbeth*, filmed amid the papier-mâché sets and dry ice of the cut-price Republic studios. In place of conventional Shakespearean grandeur, Ibert set out to evoke the play's eerie atmosphere through grotesque, prowling dissonances, outlandish scoring—including celesta, tabor, and Chinese gongs—and such disquieting effects as a wordless "breathing chorus" like a host of unquiet spirits. An insidious march on high woodwind and snare drum acts as ominous leitmotiv (accompanied at one point by an ensemble of out-of-tune bagpipes), and Banquo's ghost is heralded by a lurching bass-tuba backed by gurgles from the double-bassoon. Regrettably, much of the subtlety of Ibert's score was lost in the murk of Republic's garbled soundtrack; had it been better presented, it might well have put paid to the dismissive view of him as a skilled but conventional composer.

—Philip Kemp

INCE, Thomas H.

Producer and Director. **Nationality:** American. **Born:** Thomas Harper Ince in Newport, Rhode Island, 6 November 1882. **Family:** Son of the comedian John E. Ince; brother of the directors John and Ralph Ince; married Elinor Kershaw, 1907. **Career:** Child actor: stage debut at age 6, and toured in vaudeville and legitimate stage plays, and also acted in some films; 1910–11—director, Independent Motion Pictures (IMP): directed some films with Mary Pickford; 1911–15—producer and director, New York Motion Pictures: set up Hollywood studio, and hired directors Francis Ford, William S. Hart (also actor), Reginald Barker, Jack Conway, Fred Niblo, and Frank Borzage; 1915–17—Director-General of the consolidated company Triangle; 1918—formed his own production company, and in 1919 member of Associated Producers, Inc.: this merged with First National, 1922. **Died:** In Beverly Hills, California, 19 November 1924.

Films as Director (selected list):

1910   *Little Nell's Tobacco* (+ sc)
1911   *Their First Misunderstanding* (co); *The Dream* (co); *Maid or Man*; *Her Darkest Hour*; *Artful Kate*; *A Manly Man*; *The Message in the Bottle*; *The Fisher-Maid*; *In Old Madrid*; *Sweet Memories of Yesterday*; *For Her Brother's Sake* (co); *Behind the Stockade* (co); *In the Sultan's Garden*; *The Aggressor* (co); *The New Cowboy*; *The Winning of Wonega*
1912   *The Crisis*; *Across the Plains* (+ co-sc); *The Indian Massacre*; *The Battle of the Red Men*; *The Deserter*; *Lieutenant's Last*

Thomas H. Ince

Fight; *The Hidden Trail*; *On the Firing Line*; *War on the Plains* (*Across the Plains*) (+ co-sc); *Custer's Last Raid* (co); *The Colonel's Ward*; *When Lee Surrenders*; *The Invaders* (co); *A Double Reward*; *The Law of the West*
1913   *The Mosaic Law*; *A Shadow of the Past*; *With Lee in Virginia*; *Bread Cast upon the Water*; *The Drummer of the Eighth*; *The Boomerang*; *The Battle of Gettysburg* (co); *The Seal of Silence*; *Days of '49*
1914   *Love's Sacrifice* (co); *A Relic of Old Japan*; *One of the Discard* (co); *The Golden Goose* (co); *The Last of the Line*

Films as Producer:

1912   *The Clod*; *His Nemesis*; *A Mexican Tragedy*; *For Freedom of Cuba*; *A Doctor's Trouble* (Balshofer); *The Sergeant's Boy* (Barker); *The Vengeance of Fate* (Giblyn); *The Massacre of Sante Fe Trail* (Montgomery); *Sundered Ties* (F. Ford); *His Better Self* (Balshofer); *An Indian Legend* (Giblyn); *The Sheriff's Adopted Child* (Morty); *For the Honor of the 7th* (Barker); *Mary of the Mines* (Morty and Balshofer); *On Secret Service* (Edwards); *The Altar of Death* (West); *The Civilian* (Balshofer); *The Ball Player and the Bandit* (F. Ford); *His Squaw* (Giblyn); *Blood Will Tell* (Edwards); *His Sense of Duty* (Barker); *The Dead Pays* (West); *The Great Sacrifice* (West)
1913   *In the Ranks* (F. Ford); *A Blue Grass Romance* (Giblyn); *The Little Turncoat* (Balshofer); *The Favorite Son* (F. Ford);

The Counterfeiter (West); *The Sharpshooter* (Giblyn); *A Frontier Wife* (F. Ford); *The Iconoclast* (West); *The Pride of the South* (King); *Texas Kelly at Bay* (F. Ford); *The Grey Sentinel* (King); *A Southern Cinderella* (King); *A Slave's Devotion* (Giblyn); *An Indian's Gratitude* (Morty); *Banzai* (Giblyn); *Old Mammy's Secret Code* (Giblyn); *The House of Bondage* (West); *An Orphan of the War* (F. Ford); *The Flame in the Ashes* (Morty); *The Quakeress* (West); *The Green Shadow* (Giblyn); *The Land of Dead Things* (Morty); *The Greenhorn* (Giblyn); *The Witch of Salem* (West); *The Claim Jumper* (Morty); *The Maelstrom* (Morty); *The Belle of Yorktown* (F. Ford); *The Sign of the Snake* (Giblyn); *The Revelation* (Balshofer); *The Long Portage* (Montgomery and Conway); *Devotion* (Clifford); *Her Legacy* (Balshofer); *The Pitfall* (Giblyn); *Harvest of Sin* (Edwards); *A Military Judas* (Hunt)

1914   *The Ambassador's Envoy*; *The Harp of Tara* (West); *Romance of Sunshine Alley* (Miller); *For Her Brother's Sake* (Hunt); *A New England Idyll* (Edwards); *Divorce* (West); *O Mimi San* (Miller); *Repaid* (Edwards); *The Play's the Thing* (Sidney); *The Courtship of O San* (Miller); *The Adventures of Shorty* (F. Ford); *The Bell of Austi* (West); *Desert Gold* (Sidney); *The Squire's Son* (West); *The Geisha* (West); *Love vs. Duty* (Edwards); *Breed o' the North* (Edwards); *The Embezzler* (Osborn); *The Wrath of the Gods* (*The Destruction of Sakura Jim*) (Barker and West); *His Hour of Manhood* (Barker or Chatterton); *The Curse of Humanity* (Sidney); *The Final Reckoning* (Edwards); *The City* (West); *An Eleventh Hour Reformation* (Edwards); *The Gangsters and the Girl* (Sidney); *The Winning of Denise* (Edwards); *The Typhoon* (Barker); *The Worth of a Life* (Sidney); *Fortunes of War* (Hunt); *The Panther* (Edwards); *The Vigil* (Osborn)

1915   *On the Night Stage* (Barker) (+ co-sc); *The Alien* (+ d); *The Face on the Ceiling* (Edwards); *A Flower in the Desert* (Miller); *The Italian* (Barker); *Mother Hulda* (West); *The City of Darkness* (Barker); *The Iron Strain* (Barker); *The Coward* (Barker); *The Golden Claw* (Barker); *Matrimony* (Sidney); *The Winged Idol* (Edwards ?); *Aloha Oe* (Hamilton ?); *The Painted Soul* (Sidney)

1916   *Peggy* (Giblyn); *The Dividend* (Edwards); *Moral Fabric* (West); *The Deserter* (Edwards); *Civilization* (West and others); *Home* (Miller); *Plain Jane* (Miller); *Lieut. Danny, U.S.A.* (Hamilton)

1917   *Paddy O'Hara* (West); *Back of the Man* (Barker); *The Pinch Hitter* (Schertzinger); *Paws of the Bear* (Willat); *Happiness* (Storm); *Princess of the Dark* (Niblo); *The Dark Road* (Geffron)

1918   *Those Who Pay* (West); *Playing the Game* (Schertzinger); *The Vamp* (Storm); *When Do We Eat?* (Hart); *String Beans* (Schertzinger); *The Midnight Patrol* (Willat); *The Narrow Trail* (Hillyer)

1919   *The Sherriff's Son* (Schertzinger); *The Homebreaker* (Schertzinger); *The Busher* (Storm); *Wagon Tracks* (Hillyer); *Behind the Door* (Willat); *The Woman in the Suitcase* (Niblo); *Alarm Clock Andy* (Storm)

1920   *Silk Hosiery* (Niblo)

1921   *Lying Lips* (Wray); *Beau Revel* (Wray); *Hail the Woman* (Wray)
1922   *Lorna Doone* (Torneur)
1923   *Human Wreckage* (Wray); *Anna Christie* (Wray)
1924   *Barbara Frietchie* (*Love of a Patriot*) (Hillyer)
1925   *Enticement* (Archainbaud); *Percy* (*Mother's Boy*) (Neill); *Playing with Souls* (R. Ince)

Films as Actor:

1906   *Seven Ages of Man*
1908   *Richard III* (Ranous); *Macbeth*
1909   *The Cardinal's Conspiracy* (Griffith and Powell)
1910   *The Englishman and the Girl* ; *His New Lid* (Powell)

Publications

By INCE: articles—

"Drama and the Screen," in *Photoplay* (New York), September 1916.
"What Does the Public Want?," in *Photoplay* (New York), January 1917.
"The Undergraduate and the Scenario," in *Bookman*, June 1918.
"Your Opportunity in Motion Pictures," in *Opportunities in the Motion Picture Industry*, Los Angeles, California, 1922.

On INCE: books—

Mitry, Jean, *T.H. Ince, maître du cinéma*, Paris, 1956.
Lahue, H. Karlton, *Dreams for Sale: The Rise and Fall of the Triangle Film Corporation*, New York, 1971.
Daggett, Dennis Lee, *The House That Ince Built*, Glendale, California, 1980.

On INCE: articles—

Carr, Harry C., in *Photoplay* (New York), July 1915.
Milne, Peter, "The Method of Thomas H. Ince," and "Directors Schooled by Ince," in *Motion Picture Directing*, New York, 1922.
Cahiers du Cinéma (Paris), January 1953.
Cahiers du Cinéma (Paris), February 1953.
Cahiers du Cinéma (Paris), March 1953.
Everson, William K., in *Cinemage* (New York), June 1955.
Image (Rochester, New York), May 1956.
Mitchell, George, in *Films in Review* (New York), October 1960, corrections in November 1960.
In *Spellbound in Darkness*, edited by George C. Pratt, Rochester, New York, 1966.
Silent Picture (London), Spring 1972.
Cinema Journal (Evanston, Illinois), Spring 1979.
Mitry, Jean, in *Cinema Journal* (Evanston, Illinois), Winter 1983.
Cinématographe (Paris), January 1985.
Bianco e Nero (Rome), January-March 1985.
Cinema e Cinema (Bologna), January-April 1985.

Positif (Paris), April 1985.

Griffithiana (Gemona, Italy), September 1986.

Dyer MacCann, Richard, in *The First Filmmakers*, London, 1989.

Wanamaker, M., "Thomas Ince's Dias Dorados: Spanish Style Grandeur for a Pioneer Producer," in *Architectural Digest* (Los Angeles), April 1994.

Dumaux, S., "King Baggot and the Mystery of *The Lost Mirror*," in *Classic Images* (Muscatine), November 1997.

* * *

Thomas H. Ince's contribution to film history is perhaps easy to define but hard to evaluate. Much of the attention he has received in recent years has come from European critics who have given him credit for the direction of Ince productions. These were actually undertaken by others, but because of Ince's showman instincts he put his name as director to all his productions through the mid-1910s, and today it is a far from easy task to assign credit. Critical praise for Ince has also come from left-wing historians anxious to find a suitable recipient for the praise which rightfully belongs to the politically unacceptable D. W. Griffith.

After a lengthy and successful stage career, Ince came to films initially as a director, and from all accounts, a not very good one (particularly if Mary Pickford is to be believed). After joining the New York Motion Picture Company, Ince embarked on a production career which was to keep him a prominent member of the film community until his death. He was a great organizer and entrepreneur, who understood the value of detailed shooting scripts and production schedules at a time when the industry was very undisciplined. Between 1911 and 1913, he produced some superb, realistic westerns, the most important of which is *War on the Plains*, starring Ethel Grandin and Francis Ford (who, with E. H. Allen, was probably responsible for most if not all of the direction of this and other Ince westerns). As William K. Everson has noted, "Ince was a showman, a routine director, and a mediocre editor," but his early films had a popular and down-to-earth appeal, lacking in the work of many of his contemporaries.

Ince was also a sound recognizer of talent: witness his signing of cowboy star William S. Hart and bucolic actor Charles Ray, both of whom enjoyed long careers under contract to the producer. Ince deserves credit for making Frank Borzage a director, and for the production of a number of exquisite Japanese idylls starring Sessue Hayakawa and his wife Tsuru Aoki.

Civilization was Ince's last great production, a somewhat sorry allegorical plea for pacifism, and for the next eight years Ince seemed content to turn out program pictures starring the likes of Enid Markey, Enid Bennett, and William Desmond. He does, however, deserve credit for discovering popular romantic comedian Douglas McLean in the late 1910s and for producing the first screen version of a Eugene O'Neill play, *Anna Christie*, which was highly regarded in its day and contains one of the best performances by its star, Blanche Sweet.

Ince died shortly after being taken ill on board William Randolph Hearst's yacht, and his death has been the subject of much innuendo and gossip. Indeed, sadly the "mysterious" circumstances surrounding Ince's death seem to hold more interest for students and scholars than the man's extraordinarily long and profitable career.

—Anthony Slide

IRENE

Costume Designer. **Nationality:** American. **Born:** Irene Lentz in Montana, 1901. **Family:** Married the screenwriter Elliot Gibbons. **Career:** 1932—first costume designs for film, *The Animal Kingdom*; 1942–50—chief designer for MGM; 1950—formed own design manufacturing company, with some freelance film work in early 1960s. **Died:** (Suicide) in Hollywood, 15 November 1962.

Films as Costume Designer:

1932   *The Animal Kingdom* (Griffith) (co)

1933   *Goldie Gets Along* (St. Clair); *Flying Down to Rio* (Freeland) (co)

1936   *The Unguarded Hour* (Wood)

1937   *Vogues of 1938* (Cummings) (co)

1938   *Algiers* (Cromwell); *Merrily We Live* (McLeod) (co); *There Goes My Heart* (McLeod); *Trade Winds* (Garnett) (co); *Vivacious Lady* (Stevens) (co); *You Can't Take It with You* (Capra) (co); *Blockade* (Dieterle)

1939   *Bachelor Mother* (Kanin); *Eternally Yours* (Garnett); *Intermezzo* (Ratoff); *Topper Takes a Trip* (McLeod); *Midnight* (Leisen) (co); *The Housekeeper's Daughter* (Roach)

1940   *Arise My Love* (Leisen) (co); *Lucky Partners* (Milestone) (co); *Seven Sinners* (Garnett) (co); *The House Across the Bay* (Mayo)

Irene

1941   *That Uncertain Feeling* (Lubitsch); *Skylark* (Sandrich) (co); *Sundown* (Hathaway) (co); *Escape to Glory* (*Submarine Zone*) (Brahm); *Bedtime Story* (Hall)

1942   *The Lady Is Willing* (Leisen); *The Palm Beach Story* (P. Sturges); *The Talk of the Town* (Stevens); *They All Kissed the Bride* (Hall); *To Be or Not to Be* (Lubitsch) (co); *Twin Beds* (Whelan) (co); *Take a Letter, Darling* (*The Green Eyed Woman*) (Leisen) (co); *Reunion in France* (*Mademoiselle France*) (Dassin); *You Were Never Lovelier* (Seiter); *Three Hearts for Julia* (Thorpe)

1943   *Song of Russia* (Ratoff); *The Heavenly Body* (Hall); *Cry Havoc* (Thorpe); *Lost Angel* (Rowland); *The Youngest Profession* (Buzzell); *Above Suspicion* (Thorpe); *Thousands Cheer* (Sidney); *Slightly Dangerous* (Ruggles); *The Human Comedy* (Brown); *The Man from Down Under* (Leonard); *Dr. Gillespie's Criminal Case* (Goldbeck); *Whistling in Brooklyn* (Simon); *Cabin in the Sky* (Minnelli) (co); *Assignment in Britanny* (Conway) (co); *Du Barry Was a Lady* (Del Ruth) (co); *Swing Shift Maisie* (*The Girl in Overalls*) (McLeod); *Best Foot Forward* (Buzzell) (co); *Girl Crazy* (Taurog) (co); *Madame Curie* (LeRoy) (co); *No Time for Love* (Leisen) (co); *Broadway Rhythm* (Del Ruth) (co)

1944   *Between Two Women* (Goldbeck); *The Seventh Cross* (Zinnemann); *Two Girls and a Sailor* (Thorpe); *An American Romance* (K. Vidor); *Nothing but Trouble* (Taylor); *Andy Hardy's Blonde Trouble* (Seitz); *A Guy Named Joe* (Fleming); *See Here, Private Hargrove* (Ruggles); *Maisie Goes to Reno* (Beaumont); *Kismet* (Dieterle); *Mrs. Parkington* (Garnett) (co); *The White Cliffs of Dover* (Brown) (co); *Meet the People* (Riesner) (co); *Two Girls and a Sailor* (Thorpe) (co); *Bathing Beauty* (Sidney) (co); *Gaslight* (*Murder in Thornton Square*) (Cukor) (co); *Three Men in White* (Goldbeck); *The Thin Man Goes Home* (Thorpe) (co); *Marriage Is a Private Affair* (Leonard) (co); **Meet Me in St. Louis** (Minnelli) (co); *Blonde Fever* (Whorf); *Thirty Seconds over Tokyo* (LeRoy) (co); *Music for Millions* (Koster) (co)

1945   **The Picture of Dorian Gray** (Lewin) (co); *Adventure* (Fleming); *The Sailor Takes a Wife* (Whorf) (co); *Weekend at the Waldorf* (Leonard) (co); *National Velvet* (Brown) (co); *This Man's Navy* (Wellman) (co); *Keep Your Powder Dry* (Buzzell) (co); *Anchors Aweigh* (Sidney) (co); *The Clock* (*Under the Clock*) (Minnelli) (co); *Without Love* (Bucquet) (co); *Son of Lassie* (Simon); *Valley of Decision* (Garnett) (co); *Thrill of a Romance* (Thorpe) (co); *Twice Blessed* (Beaumont) (co); *The Hidden Eye* (Whorf) (co); *Our Vines Have Tender Grapes* (Rowland) (co); *Abbott and Costello in Hollywood* (Simon) (co); *Dangerous Partners* (Cahn) (co); *She Went to the Races* (Goldbeck); *Yolanda and the Thief* (Minnelli) (co); *What Next Corporal Hargrove?* (Thorpe); *Up Goes Maisie* (*Up She Goes*) (Beaumont)

1946   *Bad Bascomb* (Simon); *Easy to Wed* (Buzzell) (co); *Holiday in Mexico* (Sidney) (co); *Undercurrent* (Minnelli); *Two Smart People* (Dassin) (co); *Courage of Lassie* (Wilcox); *Boys' Ranch* (Rowland); *The Lady in the Lake* (Montgomery) (co); *Love Laughs at Andy Hardy* (Goldbeck); *The Secret Heart* (Leonard) (co); *No Leave No Love* (Martin); *The Green Years* (Saville) (co); *Faithful in My Fashion* (Salkow) (co); *The Postman Always Rings Twice* (Garnett) (co); *Little*

Mister Jim (Zinnemann) (co); *Three Wise Fools* (Buzzell) (co); *The Dark Mirror* (Siodmak); *Undercurrent* (Minnelli); *My Brother Talks to Horses* (Zinneman) (co); *The Mighty McGurk* (Waters) (co); *Till the Clouds Roll By* (Whorf) (co); *The Yearling* (Brown) (co); *The Harvey Girls* (Sidney)

1947   *Summer Holiday* (Mamoulian); *Fiesta* (Thorpe) (co); *This Time for Keeps* (Thorpe) (co); *The Arnelo Affair* (Obeler); *The Beginning of the End* (Taurog); *Undercover Maisie* (Beaumont); *Dark Delusion* (Goldbeck); *High Barbaree* (Conway); *Desire Me* (Cukor and others—uncredited); *The Hucksters* (Conway); *Cynthia* (*The Full Rich Life*) (Leonard); *Merton of the Movies* (Alton) (co); *Living in a Big Way* (La Cava) (co); *Song of Love* (Franklin and Marion) (co); *The Romance of Rosy Ridge* (Rowland) (co); *Song of the Thin Man* (Buzzell) (co); *The Unfinished Dance* (Koster) (co); *Green Dolphin Street* (Saville) (co); *10th Avenue Angel* (Rowland); *If Winter Comes* (Saville)

1948   *Three Daring Daughters* (Wilcox); *State of the Union* (Capra); *Easter Parade* (Walters) (co); *Cass Timberlane* (Sidney); *Julia Misbehaves* (Conway); *On an Island with You* (Thorpe); *B.F.'s Daughter* (Leonard)

1949   *The Bribe* (Leonard); *The Great Sinner* (Siodmak) (co); *Neptune's Daughter* (Buzzell); *Malaya* (Thorpe) (co); *The Barkleys of Broadway* (Walters); *In the Good Old Summertime* (Leonard) (co); *The Sun Comes Up* (Thorpe); *The Shadow on the Wall* (Jackson); *The Scene of the Crime* (Rowland); *Please Believe Me* (Taurog)

1950   *Key to the City* (Sidney)

1960   *Midnight Lace* (Miller)

1962   *Lover Come Back* (Delbert Mann)

1963   *A Gathering of Eagles* (Delbert Mann)

Film as Actor:

1922   *A Tailor Made Man* (De Grasse)

Publications

On IRENE: articles—

Chierichetti, David, in *Hollywood Costume Design*, New York, 1976.
Leese, Elizabeth, in *Costume Design in the Movies*, New York, 1976.
LaVine, Robert, in *In a Glamorous Fashion*, New York, 1980.

*   *   *

Irene's first work in Hollywood was as a movie extra, but after studying at the Wolfe School of Design, she opened a dress shop at U.C.L.A., which attracted the likes of Lupe Velez and Dolores Del Rio. The actresses loved Irene's elegant evening gowns and gladly recommended her to their celebrity friends. Following a trip to Europe, where she studied the couturier collections in search of inspiration, Irene opened an even larger boutique, catering to scores of Hollywood starlets. Her reputation soon landed her a position as head of Bullock's Wilshire Custom Salon, during which time she often received commissions to dress clients such as Ginger Rogers,

Myrna Loy, Rosalind Russell, Irene Dunne, and Claudette Colbert for their film roles. Her designs leant the actresses the level of taste and sophistication they sought to exude, both privately and on screen, and, in turn, the starlets were willing to champion Irene's work in film. By 1942, Irene had signed a seven-year contract with MGM to be Adrian's successor as executive designer

Irene's film specialty was an extension of her boutique work—the fabulous evening gown. Her soufflé gowns were soft and classic, draped elegantly, and clinging in such a way as to accentuate the flowing lines of the women she dressed. Those women were often likened to moving sculptures, and are best represented by Claudette Colbert in *The Palm Beach Story* and Rita Hayworth in *You Were Never Lovelier*. She was not limited to one style, though. Among her most famous works was Lana Turner's midriff blouse/turban/hot pants ensemble from *The Postman Always Rings Twice*. Irene was one of the most prolific designers in the screwball comedy genre. She dressed the actresses in confident-yet-feminine outfits that the strong female characters in these films begged for, such as with Carole Lombard in *Mr. and Mrs. Smith* and Claudette Colbert in *Midnight*. In addition, Irene perfected the sensible career gal look, which she favored for herself. Her suits were worn with flair by Rosalind Russell in *Take A Letter Darling* and Joan Crawford in *They All Kissed The Bride*.

Unfortunately, Irene's costumes had a reputation for being quite costly. A custom-tailored Irene gown sold for double what a Paris original of equal quality did, and her film designs were often just as extravagant. One failed outlandish outfit for *Kismet* had Marlene Dietrich wearing pants made entirely of hundreds of tiny gold chains, a creation that fell apart once Dietrich began performing in them. The mistake raised the ire of Irene's boss, Louis B. Mayer, who felt his executive designer wasted too much money. Irene's penchant for costly designs is very apparent in her period dresses. Because she was not comfortable with historical costumes, her designs were as indicative of the times Irene lived as of the times they were meant to depict. *Meet Me In St. Louis*, which took place in 1903, featured waltz length skirts, which were very popular in the 40s, and a striped dress which capitalized on a favored pattern of the decade. The *Great Sinner*, which took place in Germany in the 1800s, featured elegant gowns in popular 1940s soft fabrics, not the stiff silk used in the era. Period pictures dressed by Irene (such as the Oscar nominated *Mrs. Parkington*) were noted for their asymmetrical rayon crepe gowns draped with layered chiffon and other couture fabrics, resembling creations out of her own boutiques. But what Irene lacked in authenticity, she more than made up for in beauty. For *The Pirate*, because there were no records of dress styles in the West Indies in 1830, Irene created an original look based on European fashion of that time. While such films have created the negative notion of Irene's "fashion pictures," it is largely due to her sharp inventiveness in costuming, rather than a reliance on painstaking recreation.

Obviously suited for more personal and singular design work, and convinced her stint with MGM had been a mistake, Irene left the field of costume design almost completely in 1949, preferring to devote her full attentions to her boutiques, which she launched in 1947. She was lured back on a few occasions, most notably to dress Doris Day in a couple of films in the 1950s. In *Midnight Lace*, Irene created a very popular and memorable black lace negligee for Day to wear, which earned her an Academy Award nomination. In *Lover Come Back*, Irene furthered Day's cheerleader chic image with more white hats, dresses, and gloves, as well as favorable use of furs. Her last film, *A*

Gathering Of Eagles, was completed shortly before her suicide in 1962. By the time Irene leapt from the Knickerbocker Hotel, the era of glamour which she had helped clothe so immaculately was long gone.

—John E. Mitchell

IVANOV-VANO, Ivan

Animator. **Nationality:** Russian. **Born:** Moscow, 8 February 1900. **Career:** Animator from 1923, and independent director from 1927. **Died:** March 1987.

Films as Animator:

1927	*Senka the African*
1934	*The Czar Durandai*
1938	*The Three Musketeers*
1947	*The Little Humpbacked Horse*
1952	*The Snow Maiden*
1953	*The Tale of a Dead Princess*
1955	*The Brave Hare*
1957	*Once Upon a Time*
1963	*The Seasons*
1964	*The Mechanical Flea*; *The Left Hander*
1966	*Go to Nowhere*
1968	*Legend of a Cruel Giant*
1971	*Battle under the Walls of Kerchenetz* (co)

Publications

By IVANOV-VANO: articles—

Soviet Film (Moscow), no. 5, 1977.
Film a Doba (Prague), vol. 33, no. 11, November 1987.

On IVANOV-VANO: articles—

Iskusstvo Kino (Moscow), no. 2, 1975.
Iskusstvo Kino (Moscow), April 1980.
Iskusstvo Kino (Moscow), September 1985.
Film en Televisie + Video (Brussels), December 1986.
Obituary, in *Iskusstvo Kino* (Moscow), July 1987.

*   *   *

Ivan Ivanov-Vano was one of the founders of Soviet animation, beginning his work in 1923, and his contribution to the totality of Russian animated art has been appreciated all over the world. His first effort as an independent director was in 1927, and from that time forward he was in the forefront of technical and artistic developments in the medium in Russia. At the start his style was perhaps too advanced, but the market caught up with him to such an extent that he was called the Russian Disney. The similarity may lie in the fact that he recognized that audience appeal is an essential element for success. He often changed his style, trying new ways to make films with new techniques to add interest. Most of his subjects were based on traditional Russian tales, using an extremely rich supply of local poetry, folk tales, embroideries, carvings, and architecture. Other similarities between him and Disney were in the scale of production. They were big, with no shortcuts, full of spectacular effects, and totally absorb the audience's attention. But the parallel ended here. Disney stories, which as a rule were based on old German and British folk tales, were diluted to please a general audience. Although Ivanov-Vano did please his audience, he made fewer compromises and retained a purer sense of poetry and aesthetic concepts. One feels that he really satisfied himself before satisfying his audience.

Out of his wide range of subjects in over 50 years of animated film direction, *The Tale of a Dead Princess*, *The Little Humpbacked Horse*, *The Snow Maiden* (based on Ostrovsky's play), and *Once Upon a Time* are perhaps the most distinguished. *The Seasons*, based on Tchaikovsky's music, is an imaginative and colourful interpretation of the Russian landscape. But the most powerful and best-designed of his films is *Battle under the Walls of Kerchenetz*, based on Rimsky-Korsakov's opera *The Legend of the Invisible Town of Kitezh*. The film is a fusion of old Russian icons, with their brilliant transparent colour and elegant design, and the rhythm of music, making excellent use of time and space and the dynamic aspects of film cutting. In contrast, after the battle, the peasants return home to revive their land, in a sequence which has a sense of lyricism which is quite outstanding in colour treatment and poetic mood. Yuri Norstein, a young filmmaker and disciple of Ivanov-Vano, codirected this film and has since made his way independently.

—John Halas

IWERKS, Ub

Animator and Special Effects Technician. **Nationality:** American. **Born:** Ubbe Ert Iwerks in Kansas City, Missouri, 24 March 1901. **Education:** Attended Ashland Grammar School, Kansas City, to age 13. **Career:** Worked for a bank; 1919–20—worked for commercial art firm; 1920–23—formed two artwork companies with Walt Disney, both of which failed; 1923–30—joined Disney's successful company in Hollywood as an animator; 1930–36—directed his own Ub Iwerks Studio, releasing through MGM; 1937–40—worked for Columbia and Warner Brothers; 1941—reconciled with Disney, and became special effects director; also designed several Disneyland attractions. **Awards:** Academy Technical Award, 1959, 1964. **Died:** 7 July 1971.

Films as Animator:

1928   *The Gallopin' Gaucho*; **Steamboat Willie**
1929   *Plane Crazy*; *The Barn Dance*; *The Opry House*; *When the Cat's Away*; *The Skeleton Dance*; *The Barnyard Battle*; *The Plow Boy*; *The Karnival Kid*; *Mickey's Follies*; *El Terrible Toreador*; *Mickey's Choo-Choo*; *Springtime*; *The Jazz Fool*; *Hell's Bells*; *Jungle Rhythm*; *The Haunted House*
1930   *Summer, Autumn*

1931   *Fiddlesticks*; *Flying Fists*; *The Village Barber*; *The Coocoo Murder Case*; *Puddle Pranks*; *Laughing Gas*; *Ragtime Romeo*; *Little Orphan Willie*; *The Village Smitty*; *The Soup Song*; *Movie Mad*; *The New Car*
1932   *Jail Birds*; *Africa Squeaks*; *The Village Specialist*; *What a Life*; *The Milkman*; *Fire! Fire!*; *Spooks*; *Puppy Love*; *Stormy Seas*; *School Days*; *The Bully*; *The Office Boy*; *Room Runners*; *Circus*; *The Goal Rush*; *The Phony Express*; *The Toy Parade*; *The Music Lesson*; *Nurse Maid*
1933   *Funny Face*; *Technocracked*; *Bulloney*; *A Chinaman's Chance*; *Pale-Face*; *The Soda Squirt*; *Play Ball*; *Jack and the Beanstalk*; *Spite Flight*; *Stratos-Fear*
1934   *Davy Jones' Locker*; *Hell's Fire* (Vulcan Entertains); *The Little Red Hen*; *Robin Hood, Jr.*; *Insultin' the Sultan*; *The Brave Tin Soldier*; *Reducing Creme*; *Rasslin' Round*; *Puss in Boots*; *The Cave Man*; *The Queen of Hearts*; *Jungle Jitters*; *Aladdin and the Wonderful Lamp*; *A Good Scout*; *Viva Willie*; *The Headless Horseman*; *The Valiant Tailor*; *Don Quixote*; *Jack Frost*
1935   *Little Black Sambo*; *Bremen Town Musicians*; *Old Mother Hubbard*; *Mary's Little Lamb*; *Summertime*; *Sinbad the Sailor*; *The Three Bears*; *Balloonland* (The Pincushion Man); *Simple Simon*; *Humpty Dumpty*; *See How They Won*
1936   *Ali Baba*; *Tom Thumb*; *Dick Whittington's Cat*; *Little Boy Blue*; *Happy Days*; *Leave It to John*; *Two Lazy Crows*
1937   *Skeleton Frolic*; *Merry Mannequins*; *The Foxy Pup*; *Porky and Gabby*; *Porky's Super Service*
1938   *The Horse on the Merry-Go-Round*; *Snowtime*; *The Frog Pond*; *Midnight Frolics*
1939   *The Gorilla Hunt*; *Nell's Yells*; *Crop Chasers*
1940   *Blackboard Revue*; *The Egg Hunt*; *Ye Olde Swap Shoppe*; *The Wise Owl*
1941   *Stop That Tank*

Films as Special Effects Technician:

1941   *The Reluctant Dragon* (Werker and others)
1944   *The Three Caballeros* (Ferguson)
1946   *Make Mine Music* (Kinney and others); *Song of the South* (Foster)
1947   *Fun and Fancy Free* (Kinney and others)
1948   *Melody Time* (Luske and others)
1949   *Ichabod and Mr. Toad* (Kinney, Algar, and Geronimi); *Cinderella* (Jackson, Luske, and Geronimi)
1953   *The Living Desert* (Algar)
1954   *The Vanishing Prairie* (Algar); *20,000 Leagues under the Sea* (Fleischer)
1955   *Lady and the Tramp* (Luske, Geronimi, and Jackson); *The African Lion* (Algar)
1956   *Secrets of Life* (Algar); *Westward Ho the Wagons!* (Beaudine)
1957   *Lapland* (Sharpsteen); *Johnny Tremain* (Stevenson); *Perri* (Kenworthy and Wright)
1958   *White Wilderness* (Algar); *Sleeping Beauty* (Geronimi)
1959   *Toby Tyler, or Ten Weeks with a Circus* (Barton); *Jungle Cat* (Algar)
1960   *Pollyanna* (Swift); *Ten Who Dared* (Beaudine); *One Hundred and One Dalmations* (Reitherman, Luske, and Geronimi)
1961   *The Parent Trap* (Swift)
1963   **The Birds** (Hitchcock); *The Three Lives of Thomasina* (Chaffey)

Publications

On IWERKS: book—

Holliss, Richard, and Brian Sibley, *Walt Disney's Mickey Mouse: His Life and Times*, New York, 1986.

On IWERKS: articles—

Film Fan Monthly, January 1968.
Brosnan, John, in *Movie Magic*, New York, 1974.
The Velvet Light Trap (Madison, Wisconsin), Spring 1978.
Maltin, Leonard, in *Of Mice and Magic*, New York, 1980.
Lenburg, Jeff, in *The Great Cartoon Directors*, London, 1983.
Banc-Titre (Paris), September 1983.
Classic Images (Muscatine, Iowa), August 1984.
Griffithiana (Gemona, Italy), December 1986.
Dobbs, G. Michael, "Cartoons That Time Forgot Series," in *Video Watchdog* (Cincinnati), September-October 1993.
Hogan, D. J., "Cartoons That Time Forgot—The UB Iwerks Collection: Things That Go Bump in the Night," in *Filmfax* (Evanston), February-March 1994.
Reid, J.H., "*Tom Thumb*," in *Reid's Film Index* (Wyong, New South Wales), no. 27, 1996.
Kaufman, J.B., "The Transcontinental Making of *The Barn Dance*," in *Animation Journal* (Orange), vol. 5, no. 2, 1997.

*   *   *

Along with Tex Avery, Ub Iwerks is certainly one of the most neglected artists who worked in the field of classical animation. Long associated with the animator Walt Disney, Iwerks never received the public or critical acclaim which rightfully should have been his, simply because, unlike Disney, Iwerks was an animator first, and a businessman second.

Iwerks met up with Disney in Kansas City, Missouri, in 1919, while both were working at a small commercial art house. In 1920, Iwerks and Disney left that company to try their luck as an independent organization, but they met with little success. Disney struck out on his own, and soon had a prosperous studio in Los Angeles. In 1923 Disney asked Iwerks to rejoin him and assist in animating his early live action/cartoon series, *Alice in Cartoonland*. This led to the first Mickey Mouse cartoons, including the silent *Plane Crazy* and the ground-breaking *Steamboat Willie* (the first theatrical cartoon with a synchronized sound track). Iwerks was credited on these productions with a "Drawn by" logo, and indeed, Iwerks's animation of these early Disney cartoons makes them fresh, imaginative, and funny, characteristics that Disney's later assembly-line style would almost totally obliterate.

P.A. Powers, an independent producer, offered Iwerks the chance to set up his own shop, and, much to Disney's chagrin, Iwerks accepted the offer. The move proved a milestone in Iwerks's career: he was given the chance to create his own cartoons, which were far more sophisticated and faster-paced than the Mickey Mouse cartoons. But Powers simply lacked the financial base to adequately launch the Iwerks studio, and although Iwerks created a series of excellent cartoons in the *Flip the Frog* series (1931–33) and some good, if unremarkable, entries in the *Willie Whopper* series (1933–34), the public was clearly not ready for Iwerks's advanced attempts at comic animation.

Flip the Frog, as he evolved into a mature character in such films as *The Goal Rush*, *What a Life*, *The Phony Express*, *The Coocoo Murder Case*, *Technocracked*, *Movie Mad*, and many others, displayed a cheerfully cynical, almost nihilistic attitude toward the world he inhabited. Iwerks packed the *Flip* cartoons with non-stop action, surrealist sight gags, decidedly adult *double entendre* jokes (many with frankly sexual overtones), and episodes of unprovoked violence which Disney would never have tolerated. Flip was far from the cuddly world of Mickey Mouse, and he made no attempt to cater to mainstream sensibilities. In many ways, Flip was much like Chaplin's tramp: abused, rejected, unlucky in love, triumphing only occasionally, and then usually through devious means. Many of the gags in the *Flip* cartoons still bring a gasp from contemporary audiences. In *The Goal Rush*, for example, a flute player in a marching band is summarily shot by the band-leader when he proves unable to play in key. In *The Coocoo Murder Case*, Iwerks displays his surrealist bent in a sequence near the end of the cartoon where Flip comes face to face with the Grim Reaper. Attempting to escape Death's clutches, Flip runs frantically down a hallway, opening one door after another in blind panic, until the hallway finally ends in a black pit. After a split second's hesitation, Flip dives into oblivion, and the cartoon ends in complete darkness. In all of the *Flip* cartoons, Iwerks's protagonist emerges as a real and delightfully complex character, in sharp contrast to the one-dimensional "antics" of the Disney stable, or the early Harman-Ising cartoons, with their cuddly mice and singing squirrels. But the humor was simply over most people's heads, and after a half-hearted attempt in the *Willie Whopper* series to play down to his presumably juvenile audience (the best *Willie Whopper* cartoon being *Spite Flight*), Iwerks went back to Disney, hat in hand. Disney took him back. He was too good a businessman to ignore Iwerks's value as an animator, but on a personal level he apparently never forgave Iwerks for his abortive bid for creative independence.

Iwerks took over the function of animation special effects supervisor full time. He worked extensively on Disney's multiplane camera, which lent a remarkable sense of depth to animated scenes (the camera was used spectacularly in the opening shot of Disney's *Pinocchio*). In the early 1960s perfected a method of transferring pencil drawings used in animation directly to plastic transparencies, or "cels," using a Xerox process. This advance eliminated the "inking" stage, where pencil drawings are traced in ink on the cels, and later gave such Disney features as *One Hundred and One Dalmations* a freshness and flexibility in characters' movements that was hitherto unattainable. Iwerks also worked to improve the "blue matte" process, which Disney used to combine live action with animation in many of his 1960s films. Alfred Hitchcock borrowed Iwerks from Disney to supervise the special effects in his 1963 production of *The Birds*.

Iwerks won two Academy Awards, in 1959 and 1964, for his accomplishments as an animator, and for the many innovative techniques he brought to the art form. By all accounts, he was much liked and respected within the industry and generally regarded as the supreme technical innovator of his day in the animation field. However, his skill remained an industry secret, and when he died in 1971 the obituaries, except in *Variety*, were brief. Iwerks certainly deserved better than that, not only for his own remarkably wry sense of humor as displayed in the *Flip* films, but also as the man who really brought Mickey Mouse to life. Without Iwerks, the Disney story would probably be quite different.

—Wheeler Winston Dixon

JAENZON, Julius

Cinematographer and Director. **Pseudonym:** Also used the pseudonym J. Julius. **Nationality:** Swedish. **Born:** Gothenborg, 1885. **Family:** Brother of the cinematographer Henryk Jaenzon. **Career:** Documentary photographer; 1910—joined Svenska Biografteatern as photographer for Charles Magnusson; from 1912—associated with the directors Stiller and Sjöström; instructor at Svensk Filmindustri for several decades. **Died:** In 1961.

Films as Cinematographer:

1907   *Report from the United States on President Theodore Roosevelt*
1908   *Fiskelivets favor*
1910   *Regina von Emmertiz och Gustav II Adolf* (Linden)
1911   *Bröllopet på Ulfåsa* (*The Wedding at Ulfåsa*); *Järnbäraren* (*Iron-Carrier*) (Linden); *Opiumhulan* (*Opium Den*) (+ d)
1912   *Två Svenska emigranters aventyr i Amerika* (*The Adventures of Two Swedish Emigrants in America*) (+ d); *Fabror Johannes ankomst till Stockholm* (*Uncle John's Arrival in Stockholm*) (+ d); *Mor och dotter* (*Mother and Daughter*) (Stiller); *Laban Petterqvist tränär för Olympiska spelen* (*Laban Peterqvist Training for the Olympic Games*); *Samhallets dom* (*The Justice of Society*) (+ d); *Kolingens galoscher* (*The Vagabond's Galoshes*) (+ co-d); *De svarta makerna* (*The Black Masks*) (Stiller); *Vampyren* (*Vampire*) (Stiller); *Barnet* (*The Child*) (Stiller); *Branningar, eller Stulen lycka* (*Breakers, or Stolen Happiness*) (+ d); *Detgröna halsbandet* (*The Green Necklace*) (Magnusson); *Trädgårdsmästaren* (*The Gardener*) (Sjöström); *I livets var, eller Forsta alskarinnan* (*In the Spring of Life, or His First Love*) (Garbagny); *Agaton och Fina* (*Agaton and Fina*) (+ d)
1913   *Aktenskapsbrydån* (*The Marriage Agency*) (Sjöström); *Livets konflikter* (*Conflicts of Life*) (Stiller and Sjöström); *Gransfolken* (*The Border Feud*) (Stiller); *Löjen och tårar* (*Ridicule and Tears*) (Sjöström); *När kärleken dödar* (*When Love Kills*) (Stiller); *När larmklockan ljuder* (*When the Alarm Bell Rings*) (Stiller); *Lady Marions Sommarflirt* (*Lady Marion's Summer Flirt*) (Sjöström); *Mannekängen* (*The Model*) (Stiller); *Blodets röst* (*Voice of the Blood*) (Sjöström); *På livets ödesvägar* (*The Smugglers*) (Stiller); *Bröderna* (*Brothers*) (Stiller); *Miraklet* (*The Miracle*) (Sjöström)
1914   *Prästen* (*The Priest*) (Sjöström); *Kammarjunkaren* (*The Chamberlain*) (Stiller); *Högfjället dotter* (*Daughter of the Mountains*) (Sjöström); *När konstnärer älska* (*When Artists Love*) (Stiller); *Det röda tornet* (*The Master*) (Stiller); *Stormfågeln* (*The Stormy Petrel*) (Stiller); *Skottet* (*The*

Shot) (Stiller); *Kärlek starkare än hat* (*Love Stronger Than Hatred*) (Sjöström)
1915   *Hans hustrus förflutna* (*His Wife's Past*) (Stiller); *Dolken* (*The Dagger*) (Stiller); *Strejken* (*Strike*) (Sjöström); *Högsta vinsten* (*The First Prize*); *Judaspengar* (*Judas Money*) (Sjöström); *Mästerjuven* (*The Son of Fate*) (Stiller); *Madame de Thèbes* (Stiller)
1916   *Kärlek och journalistik* (*Love and the Journalist*) (Stiller); *Vingarne* (*The Wings*) (Stiller); *Balettprimadonnan* (*Anjuta, the Dancer*) (Stiller); *Landshövdingens döttrar* (*The Governor's Daughters*) (Sjöström); *Rosen på Tistelön* (*The Rose of Thistle Island*) (Sjöström); *Therese* (Sjöström)
1917   *Terje vigen* (*A Man There Was*) (Sjöström); *Alexander den Store* (*Alexander the Great*) (Stiller); *Dodskyssen* (*Kiss of Death*) (Sjöström)
1918   *Berg-Ejvind och hans hustru* (*The Outlaw and His Wife*) (Sjöström); *Sången om den eldröda blomman* (*Song of the Scarlet Flower*) (Stiller)
1919   *Ingmarsönerna* (*Sons of Ingmar*) (Sjöström—2 parts); **Herr Arnes pengar** (*Sir Arne's Treasure*) (Stiller)
1920   *Dunungen* (*The Downey Girl*) (Hedqvist); *Mästerman* (*Master Samuel*) (Sjöström)
1921   *Körkarlen* (*The Phantom Carriage*) (Sjöström)
1922   *Vem dömer* (*Love's Crucible*) (Sjöström); *Gunnar Hedes saga* (*Gunnar Hede's Saga*) (Stiller)
1923   **Gösta Berlings saga** (*The Story of Gösta Berling*) (Stiller); *Karusellen* (Buchowetzki); *Eld ombord* (*The Tragic Ship*) (Sjöström)
1924   *Livet på landet* (*Life in the Country*); *Två konungar* (*Two Kings*)
1925   *Ingmarsarvet* (*The Ingmar Inheritance*) (Molander); *Till Osterland* (*To the Orient*) (Molander)
1926   *Hon den enda* (*She's the Only One*) (Molander); *Hans engelska fru* (*His English Wife*) (Molander)
1927   *Förseglade läppar* (*Sealed Lips*) (Molander)
1928   *Parisiskor* (*Women of Paris*) (Molander); *Synd* (*Sin*) (Molander)
1929   *Hjärtats triumpf* (*Triumph of the Heart*) (Molander); *Säg det i toner* (*Say It with Music*) (+ co-d)
1930   *Ulla, min Ulla* (*Ulla, My Ulla*) (+ d); *För hennes skull* (*For Her Sake*); *Charlotte Löwenskjöld* (Molander); *Fridas visor* (*Frida's Songs*) (Molander); *Markurells i Wadköping* (Sjöström); *Svärmor kommer* (*Mother-in-Law Is Coming*); *Sten Stensson Stéen fran Eslöv på nya äventyr* (*Sten Stensson Stéen from Eslöv on New Adventures*)
1932   *Kärlek och kassabrist* (*Love and Deficit*) (Molander)
1933   *Vad veta val männen?* (*What Do Men Know?*) (Adolphson); *Giftasvuxnar döttrar* (*Marriageable Daughters*) (Wallén); *Tva man om en änka* (*Two Men and a Widow*); *Kungliga Johansson* (*Royal Johansson*)
1934   *Sången om den eldröda blomman* (*Song of the Scarlet Flower*) (Molander)

1935   *Smålänningar* (*People of Småland*) (Rodin); *Brannigar* (*Ocean Breakers*) (Johansson); *Aktenskapsleken* (*The Marriage Game*); *Bröllopsresan* (*The Honeymoon Trip*) (Molander)

1936   *Johan Ulfstjerna* (Edgren); *Samvetsomma Adolf* (*Conscientious Adolf*) (Wallén); *Aventyret* (*Adventure*) (Branner)

1937   *Sara lär sig folkvett* (*Sara Learns Manners*) (Molander); *Klart till drabbning* (*Clear the Decks for Action*) (Adolphson); *Vi går landsvagen* (*Walking along the Main Road*) (Wallén); *Pappas pojke* (*A Rich Man's Son*) (Martin)

1939   *Emilie Högqvist* (Molander); *Stora famnen* (*A Big Hug*) (Henrikson); *Valfångare* (*Whalers*) (Henrikson) (co)

1940   *Den ljusnande frantis* (*Bright Prospects*) (Molander); *En, men ett lejon* (*One, But a Lion*) (Molander)

1941   *Göranssons pojke* (*Göransson's Boy*) (Hildebrand); *Löjtnantshjärtan* (*Hearts of Lieutenants*)

1943   *Katrina* (Edgren)

1945   *Jolanta—den gäckande suggan* (*Jolanta—the Elusive Sow*) (Molander)

1948   *Life at Forsbyholm*

Publications

On JAENZON: articles—

Chaplin (Stockholm), vol. 15, no. 5, 1973.

*   *   *

The English film critic Caroline Lejeune, in an assessment of the early Swedish cinema, noted the sense of reality given by the feeling of texture in objects and clothing and the awareness of landscape. It is obvious that Sjöström and Stiller, the masters of this great period of Scandinavian cinema, owed much to the technical and artistic skills of their cameramen, the principal of whom was Julius Jaenzon.

Jaenzon had joined Svenska Biograf in 1910 and had photographed many films before he met Sjöström and Stiller. As Sjöström acted in many of his own films, he must have relied a great deal on the collaboration of his cameraman. Jaenzon's association with Sjöström goes back to 1912 when he filmed *The Gardener*, and he worked with Stiller on *Mother and Daughter* and *The Black Masks* in the same year. These proved to be fruitful collaborations. Jaenzon's work on Sjöström's *A Man There Was* and his *The Outlaw and His Wife* are characteristic of his work which created an identifiable Scandinavian film style, and won for it a universal appreciation in its time. The brilliant sequence of the capture of Terje by the British gunboat in the former, with its unforgettable image of the sinking rowboat, laden with grain for the starving people, and, in *The Outlaw and His Wife*, the stark landscapes, contrasting with the frozen clothing of the doomed lovers, are some of the screen's great achievements. The sombre feeling of these films owed much to Jaenzon. In Stiller's *Sir Arne's Treasure* the primitive mediaeval ambience is superbly conveyed. The mercenary soldiers move through snowy landscapes, and one can almost feel their clothing touching the skin. The perception of the viewer is conditioned by the sensitive lens of a great cameraman. The visual virtuosity of Sjöström's *The Phantom Carriage* represents Jaenzon's most spectacular use of the camera with its ghostly images and superimpositions. In the same director's *Love's Crucible*, the pictorial quality of this mediaeval tale is very striking. Stiller used him to film his epic *The Story of Gösta Berling*, originally a two-part

film. The range of Jaenzon's work is remarkable. In the exciting sequence of the sled chased across the frozen lake by wolves, or the lovely visions of Garbo in her first great success, and the cavaliers of Ekeby in their revels, the beauty of Jaenzon's work is unmistakable. One remembers the blazing eyes of Lars Hanson as he denounces his parishoners from the pulpit or the two lonely figures of Margarita Samzelius and her old mother pushing the great wooden levers of the old mill while no words pass between them.

He continued to serve these two directors until their departure for Hollywood in the mid-1920s, thereby presenting an image of Sweden to the world. With the coming of sound, he was codirector with Edvin Adolphson of the first popular Swedish musical film *Say It with Music*. He was to film his old Master Sjöström in *Markurells i Wadköping* and photograph for Gustav Molander the second version of *Song of the Scarlet Flower* which he had already brilliantly filmed for Stiller in 1918.

—Liam O'Leary

JARRE, Maurice

Composer. **Nationality:** French. **Born:** Maurice Alexis Jarre in Lyon, 13 September 1924. **Education:** Attended University of Lyon and the Sorbonne, Paris, as engineering student; then studied under Honegger and Félix Passerone at Paris Conservatory. **Military Service:** French Army during World War II. **Family:** One son, the

Maurice Jarre

composer Jean-Michel Jarre, from first marriage; married 2) the actress Dany Saval, 1965 (divorced), one daughter; 3) Laura Devon, 1967; 4) Khong Fui Fong, 1984. **Career:** Timpanist in the navy band La Musique des Equipages de la Flotte, and with radio orchestras; percussionist with Renaud-Barrault Theatre Company, under Pierre Boulez, 1940s, and musical director for the Théâtre National Populaire, 1950s, writing incidental music for many plays; 1951—first score for film, *Hôtel des Invalides*; has also composed orchestra music, and for TV, including the mini-series *Jesus of Nazareth*, 1977, *Mourning Becomes Electra*, 1978, and *Shogun*, 1980. **Awards:** Academy Award, for *Lawrence of Arabia*, 1962, *Doctor Zhivago*, 1965, and *A Passage to India*, 1984; British Academy Award, for *Witness*, 1985, and *Dead Poets Society*, 1989; Special César award, 1985.

Films as Composer:

1951 *Hôtel des Invalides* (Franju—short)
1953 *Le Voyage d'Abdallah* (Régnier—short)
1954 *L'Universe d'Utrillo* (Régnier—short)
1955 *Le Grand Silence* (Gout—short)
1956 *Le Théâtre National Populaire* (Franju—short); *Sur le pont d'Avignon* (Franju—short); *Toute la mémoire du monde* (Resnais—short)
1957 *Bravo Alpha* (Venard—short); *Le Bel Indifférent* (Demy—short)
1958 *La Génération du désert* (Stéphane—short); *Le Grand Oeuvre* (Zuber—short); *Donne-moi la main* (Blanc—short); *La Tête contre les murs* (*The Keepers*) (Franju)
1959 *Vous n'avez rien à déclarer?* (Duhour); *Chronique provinciale* (Rappeneau—short); *La Bête a l'affût* (Chenal); *Les Drageurs* (Mocky); *Les Étoiles de Midi* (Ichac); *La Corde raide* (Dudrumet); *La Main chaude* (Oury)
1960 *Vel' d'hiv'* (Blanc and Rossif—short); *Recours en grace* (Benedek); *Malrif, aigle royal* (Hessens—short); *Le Tapis volant* (Mambouch and Stéphane—short); **Les Yeux sans visage** (*The Horror Chamber of Dr. Faustus*) (Franju); *Crack in the Mirror* (Fleischer); *The Big Gamble* (Fleischer); *Le Puits aux trois vérités* (Franju); *Le Président* (Verneuil)
1961 *Le Soleil dans l'oeil* (Bourdon); *Pleins feux sur l'assassin* (Franju); *Le Temps du ghetto* (*The Witnesses*) (Rossif); *Amours célèbres* (Boisrond); *Cybèle, ou les dimanches de Ville d'Avray* (*Sundays and Cybele*) (Bourguignon)
1962 *The Longest Day* (Annakin, Marton, and Wicki); **Thérèse Desqueyroux** (*Thérèse*) (Franju); *Ton ombre est la mienne* (Michel); *L'Oiseau de paradis* (Camus); *Mourir à Madrid* (*To Die in Madrid*) (Rossif); **Lawrence of Arabia** (Lean); *Les Oliviers de la justice* (*The Olive Trees of Justice*) (Blue); *Présence d'Albert Camus* (Régnier—short)
1963 *Les Travestis du diable* (de Bravura—short); *Mort, où est ta victoire?* (Bromberger); *Les Animaux* (Rossif); *Judex* (Franju); *Pour l'Espagne* (Rossif—short); *Un Roi sans divertissement* (Leterrier)
1964 *Behold a Pale Horse* (Zinnemann); *The Train* (Frankenheimer); *Week-end à Zuydcoote* (Verneuil)
1965 *The Collector* (Wyler); *Doctor Zhivago* (Lean); *Encore Paris* (Rossif—short)
1966 *Paris brûle-t-il?* (*Is Paris Burning?*) (Clément); *Gambit* (Neame); *Grand Prix* (Frankenheimer); *The Professionals* (R. Brooks); *The Night of the Generals* (Litvak)
1967 *Barbarella* (Vadim)

1968 *The Fixer* (Frankenheimer); *5 Card Stud* (Hathaway); *Isadora* (*The Loves of Isadora*) (Reisz); *Villa Rides* (Kulik); *The Extraordinary Seaman* (Frankenheimer)
1969 *La caduta degli dei* (*The Damned*) (Visconti); *The Only Game in Town* (Stevens); *Topaz* (Hitchcock); *Broceliande* (Hacquard—short)
1970 *El Condor* (Guillermin); *Ryan's Daughter* (Lean); *Plaza Suite* (Hiller)
1971 *Una stagione all'inferno* (N. Risi); *Soleil rouge* (*Red Sun*) (Young)
1972 *The Effect of Gamma Rays on Man-in-the-Moon Marigolds* (Newman); *Pope Joan* (Anderson); *The Life and Times of Judge Roy Bean* (Huston)
1973 *Ash Wednesday* (Peerce); *The Mackintosh Man* (Huston); *The Island at the Top of the World* (Stevenson); *Airborne* (short); *Mrs. Uschyck* (Quinn—short)
1974 *Grandeur nature* (*Life Size*) (Berlanga)
1975 *Mandingo* (Fleischer); *Great Expectations* (Hardy); *The Man Who Would Be King* (Huston); *Posse* (Douglas); *Mr. Sycamore* (Kohner); *The Silence* (Hardy)
1976 *Mohammad, Messenger of God* (Akkad); *The Last Tycoon* (Kazan); *Shout at the Devil* (Hunt)
1977 *Lorenzaccio* (Carrière); *March or Die* (Richards); *The Prince and the Pauper* (*Crossed Swords*) (Fleischer)
1978 *Two Solitudes* (Chetwynd); *Mon royaume pour un cheval* (Bourguignon); *Der Magier* (*The Magician of Lublin*) (Golan); *The Users* (Hardy); *Ishi, the Last of His Tribe* (Miller)
1979 *Winter Kills* (Richert); **Die Blechtrommel** (*The Tin Drum*) (Schlöndorff); *The American Success Company* (*Success*; *American Success*) (Richert); *The Black Marble* (H. Becker)
1980 *The Last Flight of Noah's Ark* (Jarrott); *Lion of the Desert* (Akkad); *Resurrection* (Petrie); *Enola Gay: The Men, the Mission, the Atomic Bomb* (Rich)
1981 *Die Fälschung* (*Circle of Deceit*) (Schlöndorff); *Taps* (H. Becker); *Chu Chu and the Philly Flush* (Rich)
1982 *Don't Cry, It's Only Thunder* (Werner); *Coming Out of the Ice* (Hussein); *Firefox* (Eastwood); *Young Doctors in Love* (G. Marshall); *The Year of Living Dangerously* (Weir)
1984 *A Passage to India* (Lean); *Dreamscape* (Ruben); *The Sky's No Limit* (Rich); *Top Secret!* (Abrahams and D. & J. Zucker); *Samson and Delilah* (Philips)
1985 *Witness* (Weir); *The Bride* (Roddam); *Mad Max: Beyond Thunderdome* (Miller)
1986 *The Mosquito Coast* (Weir); *Solarbabies* (Johnson); *Tai-Pan* (Duke)
1987 *Fatal Attraction* (Lyne); *Gaby—A True Story* (Mandoki); *Julia and Julia* (Del Monte); *No Way Out* (Donaldson); *Shuto Shoshitsu* (*Tokyo Blackout*) (Masuda)
1988 *Buster* (Green); *Distant Thunder* (Rosenthal); *Gorillas in the Mist* (Apted); *Moon over Parador* (Mazursky); *Le Palanquin des larmes* (Dorfmann)
1989 *Chances Are* (Ardolino); *Dead Poets Society* (Weir); *Enemies, a Love Story* (Mazursky); *Prancer* (Hancock)
1990 *Jacob's Ladder* (Lyne); *After Dark, My Sweet* (Foley); *Ghost* (Zucker); *Solar Crisis* (Sarafian); *Almost an Angel* (Cornell)
1991 *Fires Within* (G. Armstrong); *Only the Lonely* (Columbus)
1992 *Wildfire* (Z. King—produced in 1986); *School Ties* (Mandel)
1993 *Fearless* (Weir); *Mr. Jones* (Figgis); *Shadow of the Wolf* (*Agaguk*) (Dorfmann)

1995   *A Walk in the Clouds* (Arau)
1996   *The Sunchaser* (Cimino)
1997   *Le Jour et la nuit* (*Day and Night*) (Lévy)
1999   *Sunshine* (Szabó)
2000   *I Dreamed of Africa*

Publications

By JARRE: articles—

Chaplin (Stockholm), no. 28, 1962.
Image et Son (Paris), no. 163, 1963.
Cinema (Los Angeles), July 1966.
Film Review (London), November 1976.
Soundtrack! (Hollywood), April 1979.
Soundtrack! (Hollywood), December 1984.
Soundtrack! (Hollywood), March 1985.
Revue du Cinéma (Paris), no. 417, June 1986.
Sequences (Haute-Ville) January 1993.
Cue Sheet (Hollywood), vol. 11, no. 3, 1995.
Scoundtrack! (Mechelen), December 1996.

On JARRE: articles—

Image et Son (Paris), no. 184, 1965.
Films in Review (New York), October 1972.
Ecran (Paris), September 1975.
Score (Lelystad, Netherlands), February 1978.
Soundtrack! (Hollywood), Fall 1980.
Séquences (Montreal), July 1985.
Soundtrack! (Hollywood), June 1991.
Séquences (Montreal), January 1993.
EPD Film (Franfurt/Main), June 1993.
Cahiers du Cinéma (Paris), 1995.
Soundtrack! (Mechelen), December 1996.
Variety (New York), 30 August 1999.

*   *   *

Maurice Jarre, who began scoring films during the 1950s, had studied under the composer Arthur Honegger, best known for his programmatic works—a train speeding along a track and a rugby game. Jarre inherited his teacher's appreciation of the evocative and descriptive capacities of music, certainly a useful legacy for enhancing the filmic experience. Drawing upon an even deeper vein in the French musical tradition, Jarre shares with Bizet and Debussy the ability to adapt exotic elements from other cultures into his own musical fabric. His range of applying these traditions is equally wide. Jarre's film scores fall into the two most contrastive groups possible: those where his music constantly impresses itself upon the ordinary members of the audience and those where the music is below their level of consciousness.

For the first group, Jarre pulls out all the stops in his orchestral, harmonic, and exotic borrowings. The most famous among these are his award-winning scores for David Lean's spectacles. Overwrought music perfectly matches the overblown visuals—and yet, one cannot deny to the total effect a certain admiration. In *Lawrence of Arabia*,

Jarre employs strings in tremolo and in wide-spaced voice lines to suggest the vast, open waste of the Arabian desert baking in the sun, and he tries to re-create the effects of Arabic music with heavy chromaticism. In *Doctor Zhivago*, he similarly employs open intervals to suggest the extensive steppes and wastes of Siberia. He exploits Russian Orthodox liturgical modes and derives inspiration from the great nineteenth-century Russian composers; however, sometimes he draws on their more saccharine violin style for his love scenes. His music for the Karel Reisz's *Isadora* sounds disconcertingly like that for *Doctor Zhivago*, and—of particular danger when inspiration is lacking—it falls even more deeply than the Lean scores into those 1930s paradigms that Korngold, Steiner, and Herrmann created. *Passage to India*, on the other hand, succeeds. Perhaps, the inspiration of Indian music returned to him some of his former strength. Be that as it may, his still old-fashioned score fits this anachronistically shot epic—with outdoor night-scenes shot in the studio.

While continuing to draw on a wide musical background and resulting vocabulary, Jarre has moved in the direction of more austerity and down below the level of consciousness. He works in touches, rich and evocative, but still touches. Sometimes, natural or human sounds are either suggested or actually employed to such an extent that one is not able to determine where the composer's contributions end and the sound-effects editor's begin. When the music is assertive, it is the music of other composers chosen for the moment, or it derives from some local or exotic source—this last can lead into some fine inventive veins. In *Taps*, he not only uses the actual theme suggested in the title to great effect, but, for really highly charged moments, he has a brass choir playing fragments of the theme in a closely knit polyphonic texture, bearing an uncanny resemblance to Wagner's "Rhine Journey" music for *The Twilight of the Gods*; however, the subtlety of applying the motif is Jarre's and had nothing to do with the German's heavy-handed reiterations. *Mad Max: Beyond Thunderdome* also has a few touches of conventional orchestra instruments that have a Wagnerian feel.

Jarre shows himself quite able to employ synthesized music in his score for Peter Weir's *The Year of Living Dangerously* (supplemented by music in this vein by Vangelis). Jarre's quiet eerie dissonance is apt accompaniment for the walk through the Jakarta (Manila) slums of Billy (Linda Hunt) and Guy (Mel Gibson). This music is created by muted percussive instruments and a sense of muted strings from a synthesizer, composed by Jarre and programmed by Andrew Thomas Wilson. The tonality for the music of this slum scene and other darker moments of the film seems to be based on a whole-tone scale, so much favored by Debussy; it is an amorphous, mysterious scale. Jarre, however, bases most of his film music on another scale loved by Debussy: it is, appropriate to the setting, a five-tone or pentatonic scale—that of most far-Eastern music.

As with Lean, Weir has discovered an ideal collaborator in Jarre—but the change from the one to the other offers a significant metamorphosis. As if to match the neocolonial aura that plays about Lean's films, Jarre has given us exotic embellishments. However, for Weir's truly postcolonial efforts, Jarre has made every effort to use real instruments. While his music for Lean often seems to be what Edward Said would label "Orientalism" or a sort of Westernized Eastern decorative pastiche, Jarre really dug into the Indonesian musical traditions. He went for what in 1982 were relatively untapped sources for inspiration: the ceremonial music of Java and the temple music of Bali. Weir has always advocated periodic dunkings of Westerners in alternative cultures. C. H. Koch, the author of the novel on which

Dangerously is based, has repeated denied that Australians are Western, but really as much a part of Southeast Asia as Indonesia—at least, in potential and prospect. Further, Jarre uses the traditional Javanese gamelan, which translates as "orchestra" consisting of drums, gongs, and a stringed instrument. The actual gamelan players for the film were from the Department of Music of Sydney University. The sprightly, cheerful music that accompanies Billy and Guy's first moments of journalistic camaraderie consists of a gamelan accompaniment that moves at the fast tempo most characteristic of the style. But for quieter moments—such as the symbolically important moments when Billy shows Guy the *wayang* puppets or Guy searches for his news story along a highway snaking through emerald rice paddies—Jarre has slowed down the tempo. Another sign of Jarre's postcolonialism is that what is good for Indonesia is also good for the United States. In *Dead Poets Society*, Jarre uses the dulcimer to accompany shots of the Delaware countryside and bagpipes to fit the Anglo-Scotch pretensions of the Eastern prep-school where the film is set (St. Andrews); both instruments recur in the closing-credits music.

There is one outstanding aspect of the Jarre and Weir collaboration that, while it goes beyond the perimeters usually set for judging a film composer, is resonant in its capacity to reveal the psychology of the characters and touch that of the audience: the music chosen from the canonical or classic masterpieces. Their approach is a compromise between an original orchestral score employed throughout and the use of massive portions of the classics—the approach one usually associates with Stanley Kubrick. For *Year of Living Dangerously*, Jarre leaves the lushness of orchestration, as it were, up to Richard Strauss, whose "September" from his *Four Last Songs* plays—appearing diagetically, as if Billy is playing a recording—at moments of great psychological tension for Guy and especially for Billy. The old-fashioned music of the autumnal glow in European culture and imperialism is juxtaposed with the vitality and freshness of the music of the Third World. Music from an album suite by Vangelis was chosen for the lovers' dangerous post-curfew ride to a night of love. For *Dead Poets Society*, Beethoven—again introduced diagetically, as if played on a phonograph by the teacher hero (Robin Williams)—matches the dynamic self-assertion that is advocated by this teacher. An almost nonexistent original score for *Fearless* is supplemented by fragments from music of Penderecki and culminated by an impressive selection from that of Gorecki.

—Rodney Farnsworth

JARRICO, Paul

Writer. **Nationality:** American. **Born:** Israel Shapiro in Los Angeles, 12 January 1915. **Family:** Married writer-editor Sylvia Gussin (divorced); married Lia Benedetti; son: Bill Jarrico. **Education:** A.B., University of Southern California, 1936. **Military Service:** Served in the United States Merchant Marine, 1943; served in the United States Navy, 1945–46; **Career:** Joined the National Student League and Young Communist League, 1930s; joined the Communist Party; began writing B-film scripts for Columbia Pictures, 1937; made his A-film breakthrough with his script for *Tom, Dick and Harry*, 1941; refused to testify before the House UnAmerican Activities Committee, and was blacklisted, 1952; produced *Salt of the Earth*, made with other Hollywood blacklistees, 1953; worked as a television writer on

such series as *The Phil Silvers Show* and *The Defenders*, mid-1950s-early 1960s; left the United States for Europe, where he worked for the following two decades, 1958; returned to the United States and eventually wrote a play, *Leonardo*, and taught film at the University of California, Santa Barbara (where he was Regents Lecturer and visiting assistant professor of writing), 1977–87; served as executive story editor of the TV series *Call to Glory* and *Fortune Dane*, 1984–86. **Awards:** Academy Award nomination, Best Original Screenplay, for *Tom, Dick and Harry*, 1941; Lt. Robert Meltzer Award, 1999 (awarded posthumously). **Died:** In an auto accident, while driving from Beverly Hills to his home in Ojai, California, 28 October 1997.

Films as Screenwriter:

1938   *Little Adventuress* (Lederman) (co-story only); *No Time to Marry* (Lachman) (also story); *I Am the Law* (Hall) (contributed to script)

1939   *Beauty for the Asking* (Tryon) (co-sc)

1941   *Tom, Dick and Harry* (Kanin) (also story); *The Face Behind the Mask* (Florey) (co-sc); *Men of the Timberland* (Rawlins) (story only)

1943   *Thousands Cheer* (Sidney) (co-sc and story); *Song of Russia* (Ratoff) (co-sc)

1946   *Little Giant* (Seiter) (co-sc)

1948   *The Search* (Zinnemann) (co-sc)

1949   *Not Wanted* (Clifton, Lupino) (co-sc)

1950   *The White Tower* (Tetzlaff)

1952   *The Las Vegas Story* (Stevenson) (co-sc, originally uncredited)

1957   *The Girl Most Likely* (Leisen) (story and co-sc, originally uncredited)

1960   *5 Branded Women* (Ritt) (co-sc, originally uncredited)

1961   *All Night Long* (Dearden) (co-sc, billed as Peter Achilles)

1965   *Treasure of the Aztecs* (Siodmak) (uncredited)

1966   *Wer Kennet Jonny R?* (*Who Killed Johnny Ringo*) (Madrid) (co-sc; as Peter Achilles)

1968   *Le Rouble a Deux Faces* (*The Day The Hot Line Got Hot*) (Perier)

1975   *Sarajevsky Atentat* (*The Day That Shook the World*; *Assassination at Sarajevo*) (Bulajic) (co-sc)

1988   *Messenger of Death* (Thompson)

1992   *Stalin* (Passer—for TV) (uncredited rewrite)

Other Films:

1950   *The Hollywood Ten* (short) (doc) (pr)

1953   *Salt of the Earth* (Biberman) (pr)

1987   *Legacy of the Hollywood Blacklist* (Chaikin) (doc) (creative consultant)

Publications

By JARRICO: articles—

"A True-Blue Red in Hollywood: An Interview With Paul Jarrico," interview with Patrick McGilligan, in *Cineaste* (New York), no. 1, 1997.

On JARRICO: articles—

"Reunion Recalls Movie on Hispanic Strikers Made at Time of Film Blacklist," in *New York Times*, 3 May 1982.

Kernan, Lisa, "'Keep Marching, Sisters': The Second Generation Looks at *Salt of the Earth*," in *Nuestro*, vol. 9, May 1985.

Goldstein, Patrick, and Fred Alvarez, "Blacklisted Writer Dies after Long-awaited Triumph," in *Los Angeles Times*, 30 October 1997.

"Paul Jarrico, 82, Blacklisted Screenwriter" (obituary), in *New York Times*, 30 October 1997.

"Blacklisted Screenwriter Is Honored, Then Dies," in *Newsday* (Melville, New York), 30 October 1997.

Vosburgh, Dick, "Obituary: Paul Jarrico," in *Independent* (London), 5 November 1997.

Ybarra, Michael, "The Real Story of the Hollywood Ten: Blacklist Whitewash," in *New Republic* (Washington, D.C.), 5 January 1998.

* * *

Paul Jarrico's career is inextricably linked to the Hollywood blacklist—and to spirit and daring with which he responded to the post-World War II House UnAmerican Activities Committee (HUAC) witchhunt. Back in the early 1950s, when he was called to testify before HUAC, Jarrico took the Fifth Amendment. Not only did he recoil at naming names before the committee but challenged the very nature of HUAC when he declared, in his testimony, "I should be happy to help this committee uncover subversion, but one man's subversion is another man's patriotism. I consider the activities of this committee subversive of the American Constitution." He added, "I believe this country was founded on the doctrine of freedom, the right of a man to advocate anything he wishes—advocate it, agitate for it, organize for it, attempt to win a majority for it. And I think that any committee that intimidates people, that makes it impossible for people to express their opinions freely, is subverting the basic doctrine of the United States and its constitution."

Because of the blacklist, Jarrico's work as a screenwriter is a footnote to his career. Yet even before he was expunged from Hollywood, his screen output was markedly uneven. His best film by far is *Tom, Dick and Harry*, a romantic comedy about a telephone operator who is determined to marry for money but ends up with the man she truly loves, an idealistic garage mechanic. After entering the industry and toiling on several B-film scripts, *Tom, Dick and Harry* brought Jarrico to the A-list forefront and earned him an Academy Award nomination. Otherwise his pre-blacklist credits are a hodge-podge of features, ranging from the Abbott and Costello comedy *Little Giant* and the Gene Kelly-Kathryn Grayson musical *Thousands Cheer* to *Song of Russia*, about an American orchestra conductor's love affair with a Russian musician. He also co-scripted *The Search*, a penetrating drama about a young Czechoslovakian concentration camp survivor who is looked after by an American GI while his mother searches the prison camps for him. Jarrico's work here is overshadowed by the contributions of others, and the controversy surrounding star Montgomery Clift's rewriting and improvising his lines.

Jarrico admittedly was far-left-of-center; he was a member of the Communist Party, joining in 1937 and remaining on its rolls until the 1950s. According to film historian Larry Ceplair, in the late 1930s the "younger screenwriters—Richard Collins, Budd Schulberg, Ring Lardner, Jr., and Paul Jarrico, among others" formed "a special (party) branch, one in which they could explore how to communicate their radical political and social ideas in scripts and where they could discuss revolutionary theories and techniques of moviemaking. The men and women in this branch. . . fiercely debated their creative role within the Hollywood movie industry." Yet can it be said that Jarrico's politics subverted the content of his scripts, rendering a film like *Song of Russia* little more than sly communist propaganda? The film's plot is "pro-Russia," to be sure. In his "friendly" testimony before HUAC, Robert Taylor (who played the conductor) declared that he believed *Song of Russia* to be "distastefully Communistic" and "favoring Russian ideologies, institutions, and ways of life." On the other hand, is *Song of Russia* innocently supportive of Russia in the same way that *Mrs. Miniver* is pro-British? After all, the film was made when the United States and Russia were allies, struggling for survival against a common Axis enemy.

Similarly, is *Tom, Dick and Harry* an anti-capitalist diatribe because its heroine rejects Tom and Dick—the first an "ambitious capitalist" and the second a wealthy man—for Harry, a worker-of-the-world? Or is it simply a cleverly plotted romantic comedy in which the heroine opts for true love rather than materialistic comfort?

Conspiracy theorists might find hidden meaning in *Beauty for the Asking*, one of Jarrico's B-films, because it is the story of a money-hungry man who rejects a working woman but comes squirming back after she invents a beauty cream. Another Jarrico B film is *The Face Behind the Mask*, in which a law-abiding Hungarian immigrant turns to crime when he cannot find employment after being disfigured during a hotel fire. Is this film an innocent entertainment, or is it loaded with left-wing propaganda because it is the story of a man who is denied a livelihood because he is "different"? One can view *The Face Behind the Mask, Beauty for the Asking, Song of Russia*, and *Tom, Dick and Harry* decades after their release, and render an opinion.

In the 1940s, Jarrico and his colleague Richard Collins collaborated on the scripts for *Thousands Cheer, Little Giant*, and the notorious *Song of Russia*. By the early 1950s, now-former co-writers had become public enemies, denouncing and accusing one another in a highly politicized arena. In April 1952, Collins "named names" before HUAC, testifying that Jarrico and others-including Schulberg, Robert Rossen, Lardner, Jr., Frank Tuttle, Waldo Salt, Abraham Polonsky—were card-carrying Communists. The following month, Schulberg named Jarrico, Salt, Lardner, and others as Communist Party members. Yet unlike Collins and Schulberg, Jarrico valued moral principle over blowing with the shifting winds and refused to kowtow to the HUAC.

Even before his testimony, Jarrico reportedly knew he was going to be blacklisted. At the time, he was under contract to RKO, and found that he was barred from the lot on the morning he was served his HUAC subpoena. As reported in the 7 April 1952 *New York Times*, Howard Hughes, the studio's principal stockholder and managing director, refused to give Jarrico "screen credit on a movie." The film in question was *The Las Vegas Story*, and this development resulted in a breach of contract accusation against RKO, filed by the Screen Writers Guild. By contract, the Guild had the authority to determine the writing credits on a film. Yet at the time, Jarrico's name was not restored to the film's credits.

Jarrico was anything but passive in his response to his blacklisting. He was one of 23 film workers who in 1953 filed a $51,750,000 lawsuit in the California State Supreme Court, charging that they had been barred from working in Hollywood. The following year, it was ruled that the motion picture industry had the right to blacklist employees who had refused to testify before HUAC. Meanwhile,

Jarrico and fellow blacklistees Michael Wilson (who was his brother-in-law) and Herbert Biberman set out to make *Salt of the Earth*, the celebrated drama about striking Mexican-American zinc miners—and the only independent film made by blacklisted Hollywood talent. *Salt of the Earth* is an extraordinary film, a hard-hitting exploration of class and sexual struggle in the United States. The efforts to prevent *Salt of the Earth* from being produced and, then, distributed, are legendary.

In the late 1950s Jarrico moved to Europe, where he lived and worked for two decades. The first of the relatively few movie scripts he wrote were credited to a pseudonym, ''Peter Achilles.'' All, though, were artistically underwhelming. His final credit is 1988's *Messenger of Death*, an unexceptional Charles Bronson mystery thriller. Jarrico's later years are distinguished not by any script he authored, but by his remaining at the forefront of the battle to restore the screen credits of blacklisted artists. He even requested that his name be withheld from his work until all others had their credits restored.

On 27 October 1997, the Screen Actors Guild, the Directors Guild of America, the Writers Guild of America, and the American Federation of Television and Radio Artists produced ''Hollywood Remembers the Blacklist,'' an event commemorating the 50th anniversary of the citing of the Hollywood Ten for contempt of Congress for refusing to divulge their political associations during their HUAC testimony. The evening featured dramatic presentations recreating incidents from the era, with Kevin Spacey portraying Jarrico. The 82-year-old screenwriter was present and he and fellow blacklistee Ring Lardner, Jr., won standing ovations after recalling the toll of the times, and how they were driven from the industry they loved by the blacklist. Sadly, Jarrico was killed in an automobile accident the following day, while returning from the event to his home in Ojai, California.

In July 1998, nine months after his death, the Writers Guild of America restored credit on four films Jarrico had scripted during his blacklist years: *The Las Vegas Story*, *The Girl Most Likely* (a remake of *Tom, Dick and Harry*), *5 Branded Women*, and *All Night Long*.

—Rob Edelman

JAUBERT, Maurice

Composer. **Nationality:** French. **Born:** Nice, 3 January 1900. **Education:** Attended Lycée Masséna and Nice Conservatory; studied law at the Sorbonne, Paris; studied music with Albert Groz. **Military Service:** 1920–22; 1939—recalled into the army, and killed in action. **Family:** Married the singer Marthe Bréga. **Career:** Practiced law briefly, then music director for Pleyela Records, 1925, and music director for Pathé-Natan Studios, 1930–35; also composed music for orchestra and for stage works. **Died:** In Azerailles, 19 June 1940.

Films as Composer:

1929 *Die wünderbare Lüge der Nina Petrowna* (Schwarz) (French accompaniment)
1930 *Le Hyas* (Painlevé—short); *Le Petit Chaperon rouge* (Cavalcanti); *Caprelles et pantopodes* (Painlevé—short) (co)
1931 *Au pays du scalp* (de Wavrin); *Le Bernard-l'hermite* (Painlevé—short); *Ostende, reine de plages* (Storck—short)

1932 *L'Affaire est dans le sac* (*It's in the Bag*) (Prévert—short); *La Vie d'un fleuve: La Seine* (Lods—short); *Quatorze Juillet* (Clair)
1933 ***Zéro de conduite*** (Vigo—short); *Trois vies et une corde* (Storck—short); ***L'Atalante*** (Vigo)
1934 *Obsession* (*L'Homme mystérieux*) (M. Tourneur—short) (co); *Le Dernier Milliardaire* (Clair); *En Crète sans les dieux* (Leenhardt and Zuber—short)
1935 *L'Ile de Pâques* (Fernhout—short) (+ narrator); *Barbe-Bleue* (Painlevé and Bertrand—short); *Trois-mâts ''Mercator''* (Fernhout—short)
1936 *Mayerling* (Litvak) (co); *Regards sur la Belgique ancienne* (Storck—short)
1937 *Un Carnet de bal* (Duvivier); *We Live in Two Worlds* (Cavalcanti—short); *Drôle de drame* (*Bizarre Bizarre*) (Carné); *Les Maisons de la misère* (Storck—short)
1938 *Les Filles du Rhône* (Paulin); ***Le Quai des brumes*** (*Port of Shadows*) (Carné); *Altitude 3.200* (*Nous les jeunes*) (Benoît-Lévy and Epstein); *Lumières de Paris* (Pottier) (uncredited, + ro); *Eau-vive* (Epstein—short); *Hôtel du nord* (Carné); *L'Esclave blanche* (Sorkin) (co); *La Fin du jour* (Duvivier)
1939 ***Le Jour se lève*** (*Daybreak*) (Carné)
1940 *Violons d'Ingres* (Brunius—short); *Village dans Paris: Montmartre* (Harts— short)
1945 *Solutions françaises* (Painlevé—short) (produced 1939)

Films as Music Director:

1932 *Poil de carotte* (Duvivier); *Der Traumende Mund* (*Dreaming Lips*) (Czinner) (+ ro); *Mirages de Paris* (Ozep)
1933 *Le Petit Roi* (Duvivier)
1934 *Les Misérables* (Bernard—3 parts); *Sapho* (Perret); *Sans famille* (M. Allégret); *Les Nuits moscovites* (Granowsky)
1935 *La Vie parisienne* (Siodmak); *L'Equipage* (Lit vak); *Terre d'amour* (Cloche—short)
1939 *Nuit de décembre* (Bernhardt) (+ ro)

Film as Consultant:

1937 *Ces dames aux chapeaux verts* (Cloche)

Films Using Precomposed Music by Jaubert:

1971 *L'Histoire d'Adèle H.* (Truffaut)
1976 *L'Argent de poche* (Truffaut)
1977 *L'Homme qui aimait les femmes* (Truffaut)
1978 *La Chambre verte* (Truffaut)
1985 *Le Temps détruit: lettres d'une guerre 1939–40* (Beuchot)

Publications

By JAUBERT: article—

''Music on the Screen,'' in *Footnotes to the Film*, edited by Charles Davy, London, 1937.

On JAUBERT: book—

Porcile, François, *Maurice Jaubert, musicien populaire ou maudit?*, Paris, 1971.

On JAUBERT: articles—

"Jaubert Issue" of *Information Musicale* (Paris), 4 June 1943.
Sight and Sound (London), Autumn 1947.
Cinématographie Française (Paris), no. 1473, June 1952.
"Hommage à Maurice Jaubert" (Montréal: La Cinémathèque Canadienne), April 1967.
Film Français (Paris), no. 1592, September 1975.
Avant-Scène du Cinéma (Paris), no. 165, January 1976.
Image et Son (Paris), no. 327, April 1978; no. 461, June 1990.
Rivista del Cinematografo (Rome), vol. 54, no. 11, November 1981.
Film Dope, no. 27, July 1983.
Catherine A Surowiec, "Maurice Jaubert: Poet of Music," in *Rediscovering French Film*, edited by Mary Lea Bandy, New York, 1983.
Cahiers du Cinéma (Paris), no. 393, March 1987.
Revue du Cinéma (Paris), no. 461, June 1990.
Time, 12 November 1990.
Positif (Paris), no. 359, January 1991.
Kosovsky, B., "Musique de films de Marcel Carne," in *Film Score Monthly* (Los Angeles), April 1994.
Cahiers du Cinéma (Paris), Hors Serie, 1995.
Film en Télévisie (Brussels), no. 458, January 1996.

*　　*　　*

Initially destined to become a partner in his father's law firm, Maurice Jaubert rejected this conventional opening to pursue a less predictable career in music. After early studies at the Nice Conservatory, he pursued his musical education under Albert Groz in Paris and came into contact with future leading composers of his generation: Georges Auric and Arthur Honneger. In the course of the 1920s, as film moved from the silent to the sound era, Jaubert gained important experience both of the music industry and as a music critic and composer. As director of the perforated sheet music company Pleyela, he came to know Jean Grémillon and Maurice Ravel, whilst as music critic for *Esprit*, he began to formulate, under the pseudonym Maurice Gineste, an aesthetic of film music.

His initial experience with silent film was the selection of suitable music to accompany the images, notably for Renoir's *Nana* (1926) and Grémillon's *Maldone* (1927). Meanwhile, his own creative talents found expression in commissions for the theatre, *Le Magicien Prodigieux* (1925), *Terminus* (1928), and for Falconneti in the cabaret *Attractions* (1928). These excursions into other art forms further developed his conception of how music should eventually become part of film, not simply as a pleonastic accompaniment, but as an integral part of the film's dynamics.

In the following decade, successive scores marked out his immense contribution to the now rapidly evolving sound cinema. After providing music for shorts by Jean Painlevé, notably *Caparelles et pantopodes* (1930) which drew on themes by Scarlatti, and *Le Bernard-l'hermite* (1931) using themes by Bellini, Jaubert produced some of his finest original compositions for René Clair, Jean Vigo, and, in the darker late 1930s, for Marcel Carné.

The music for Clair's films demonstrated the composer's gift for underpinning the director's message. In the bittersweet *Quatorze*

Juillet (1932), the theme song "A Paris dans chaque faubourg" (composed by Grémillon, but developed by Jaubert) captured the poignancy of transient happiness and rapidly became a popular success, while for the heavily satirical *Le Dernier Millionaire* (1934), telling of the marriage of a megalomaniac financier to a bankrupt princess, the pomposity of the court is deflated by a clever burlesque of the national anthem.

With Vigo, Jaubert achieved a particularly fruitful partnership. His highly inventive score for *Zéro de Conduite* (1933) echoed in musical terms the subversive thrust of Vigo's iconoclastic images. In the dream-like sequence of schoolboy rebellion, for example, Jaubert experimented by inverting his original score to achieve a suitably surrealist soundtrack. Perhaps the more potent success of the partnership, however, came with *L'Atalante* (1933), where again Vigo experimented with dream sequences and the depiction of affective memory. In a highly evocative score characterized by simple themes and pulsating rhythms imitating the boat's engine, Jaubert created a rare poetic lyricism to match Vigo's erotic vision. Particularly powerful elements include Jules's rendering of "Le Chant des mariniers" on his accordion and the use of the composer's preferred solo instrument, the alto saxophone, in scenes of tender intimacy.

Jaubert's ability to conjure up atmosphere was again a key element in the success of Duvivier's *Un Carnet de bal* (1937), where the haunting melancholy of the composer's *valse grise* (inspired by Sibelius' *Valse triste*), provided the all-pervading tone of nostalgia essential to the widow's recollections. An elegiac, increasingly fatalistic mood is also central to Carné's films at the close of the decade: *Le Quai des brumes* (1938), *Hôtel du nord* (1938), and *Le jour se lève* (1939). The celebrated poetic realism of these films is frequently defined in terms of visual style alone, thereby failing to give sufficient recognition to Jaubert's music as a vital ingredient in the creation of the characteristic mood. The downbeat seediness permeating *Hôtel du nord*, the doom-laden atmosphere of *Le Quai des brumes* or the fatalistic mood of *Le Jour se lève* are all derived in no small degree from the suggestive scores composed to encapsulate precisely these values.

Reflecting on the role of the film composer in *Footnotes to the Film*, Jaubert was adamant that music should not be used simply "to annotate the action." For him, music should be used sparingly rather than as a continuous background accompaniment, and deployed to its maximum effect to suggest subjective states "when the image escapes from strict realism and calls for the poetic extension of music."

Resourceful and innovative, Jaubert preferred to develop scores around strong melodies with frequently unconventional harmonies. His intimate understanding of the film medium, with his sensitivity to the internal rhythms of the image structure, combined with a creative talent which is rare amongst film composers. In that sadly single decade of the 1930s, Jaubert achieved an outstanding position as a film composer, providing leading directors with some 38 scores, both for short- and feature-length productions. Neither did his involvement stop at composition, for as Director of Music at the Pathé-Nathan studios between 1930–35, he conducted several musical scores for the studios' films and on two occasions actually appeared in the role of a conductor, in *Mélo* (1932) and *Nuit de décembre* (1939). Although essentially a composer for the French cinema, Jaubert was tempted to work briefly in London, where he scored films for the celebrated GPO film unit, most notably Cavalcanti's *We Live in Two Worlds* (1937).

The most fitting homage to Jaubert's enduring qualities came from François Truffaut when, for four of his films (*L'Histoire d'Adèle*

H. [1971], *L'Argent de poche* [1976], *L'Homme qui aimait les femmes* [1977], *La Chambre verte* [1978]), he chose to use the composer's music, and compositions which had not initially been written for the screen. Thus in *L'Histoire d'Adèle H.*, Truffaut draws on orchestral compositions (*Suite française* from 1932 and *Sonata à due* from 1936), as well as music originally composed for Giraudoux's *La Guerre de Troie n'aura pas lieu* (1935). Few film composers can have advanced further the recognition of music as a discrete and integral component of film aesthetics, either by their compositions or by their theoretical writings, than Maurice Jaubert.

—R. F. Cousins

JEAKINS, Dorothy

Costume Designer. **Nationality:** American. **Born:** California, 1914. **Education:** Attended Otis Art Institute. **Career:** Stage and TV designer; 1948—first film as costume designer, *Joan of Arc*. **Awards:** Academy Awards for *Joan of Arc*, 1948; *Samson and Delilah*, 1950; *The Night of the Iguana*, 1964. **Died:** 21 November 1995.

Films as Costume Designer:

1948   *Joan of Arc* (Fleming) (co)
1949   *Samson and Delilah* (DeMille) (co)
1952   *Belles on Their Toes* (Levin); *The Big Sky* (Hawks); *The Greatest Show on Earth* (DeMille) (co); *Les Misérables* (Milestone); *Lure of the Wilderness* (Negulesco); *My Cousin Rachel* (Koster); *The Outcasts of Poker Flat* (Newman); *Stars and Stripes Forever* (Koster); *Treasure of the Golden Condor* (Daves)
1953   *Beneath the Twelve Mile Reef* (Webb); *City of Bad Men* (Jones); *Inferno* (Baker); *The Kid from Left Field* (Jones); *Niagara* (Hathaway); *Titanic* (Negulesco); *White Witch Doctor* (Hathaway)
1954   *Three Coins in the Fountain* (Negulesco)
1956   *Friendly Persuasion* (Wyler)
1957   *The Ten Commandments* (DeMille) (co)
1958   *South Pacific* (Logan)
1959   *Green Mansions* (M. Ferrer)
1960   *Elmer Gantry* (R. Brooks); *Let's Make Love* (Cukor); *The Unforgiven* (Huston)
1961   *The Children's Hour* (Wyler)
1962   *All Fall Down* (Frankenheimer); *The Music Man* (da Costa)
1964   *The Best Man* (Schaffner); *Ensign Pulver* (Logan); *The Night of the Iguana* (Huston)
1965   *The Fool Killer* (Gonzalez); *The Sound of Music* (Wise)
1966   *Any Wednesday* (Miller); *Hawaii* (Hill); *Violent Journey*
1967   *The Flim-Flam Man* (Kershner); *Reflections in a Golden Eye* (Huston)
1968   *Finian's Rainbow* (Coppola); *The Fixer* (Frankenheimer); *The Stalking Moon* (Mulligan)
1969   *True Grit* (Hathaway)
1970   *Little Big Man* (Penn); *The Molly Maguires* (Ritt)
1972   *Fat City* (Huston); *Fuzz* (Colla)
1973   *The Iceman Cometh* (Frankenheimer)

1974   *Young Frankenstein* (M. Brooks)
1975   *The Hindenburg* (Wise)
1977   *Audrey Rose* (Wise)
1978   *The Betsy* (Petrie)
1981   *The Postman Always Rings Twice* (Rafelson); *On Golden Pond* (Rydell)
1987   **The Dead** (*The Dubliners*) (Huston)

Publications

On JEAKINS: articles—

Chierichetti, David, in *Hollywood Costume Design*, New York, 1976.
Obituary in *The Los Angeles Times*, 28 November 1995.
Obituary in *Variety* (New York), 4–10 December 1995; 11–17 December 1995.
Obituary in *Classic Images* (Muscatine), February 1996.
Obituary in *TCI*, February 1996.

*   *   *

Dorothy Jeakins was abandoned by her natural parents for unknown reasons, and she had an unhappy childhood. She lived with a foster mother who frequently whipped her and threatened to send her to reform school. Often left alone, she would roam the streets of Los Angeles as a young child and ask people for free food and clothes. She called it a "Dickensian existence." She has described herself as "pathologically shy and neurotically modest," but very secure in her sense of taste and style, with the "sensitive soul of an artist." Perhaps as a result of her shyness, virtually nothing has been written about Jeakins or her impressive film credits.

At Fairfax High School she found plays to be a "sweet escape into fantasy." Encouraged into drama by sympathetic teachers, she discovered her vocation when she visited a costume house and found a means of interpreting the plays she loved through costume. She attended Otis Art Institute on a scholarship and continued to frequent the public library to read and illustrate the characters of plays.

She worked for the WPA at the age of 19 during the Depression, and then moved on to Disney studios as an illustrator for $16 a week until a strike left her unemployed. She next became an illustrator of fashion layouts for I. Magnin's advertising department. Eventually a studio art director saw her sketches and hired her as an assistant designer for *Joan of Arc*, her first major film for which she won her first Oscar. (She had also been an assistant to the designer Ernst Dryden for *Dr. Rhythm*, 1938.)

Jeakins has an impressive number of credits, almost equally divided between the theater and motion pictures. Some plays she designed for on Broadway, she later designed as films, including *South Pacific* and *The Sound of Music*.

Jeakins's noted specialty is for ethnic and period costumes, as well as her use of color. With each film Jeakins considered how she could use costume in a new way, and when searching for inspiration for the color scheme considered such natural elements as "wet stones or peonies or pullet-eggs beige and white or Chinese-coolie blues." The designer Edith Head once commented that Jeakins had a particularly good eye for color. On a separate occasion, Jeakins said candidly of Edith Head that "her work is extremely mediocre . . . but Edith deserves a lot of credit for hanging in there." Jeakins was also budget-conscious when she worked on films and made elegant costumes with inexpensive muslin. As a designer, she said of herself, ''I'm dependable, experienced, organized, aesthetic, creative.''

—Susan Perez Prichard

JEANSON, Henri

Writer. **Nationality:** French. **Born:** Henri Jules Jeanson in Paris, 6 March 1900. **Career:** Actor, journalist, film critic, and playwright: plays produced include *Toi que j'ai tant aimée*, 1928, *Amis comme avant*, 1929, *Aveux spontanés*, 1930, *Pas de taille* (with C.-A. Puget) 1930, *Tout va bien*, 1931, *Parole d'honneur*, 1934; early 1930s—scenarist for Paramount di Joinville: 1932—first film script, for *Le Jugement de minuit*; 1950—directed the film *Lady Paname*; 1951—wrote libretto for musical work by Tailleferre, *Il était un petit navire*. **Died:** In Honfleur, 6 November 1970.

Films as Writer:

1932   *Le Jugement de minuit* (Esway)
1933   *Les Aventures du roi Pausole* (Granowsky); *La Dame de chez Maxim's* (A. Korda); *Bach Millionnaire* (Wulschleger); *Mariage à responsabilité limitée* (de Limut)
1934   *Sidonie Panache* (Wulschleger)
1935   *Marchand d'amour* (Gréville)
1936   *Mister Flow* (*Compliments of Mr. Flow*) (Siodmak); *Le Chemin de Rio* (Siodmak)
1937   **Pépé le Moko** (Duvivier); *Un Carnet de bal* (Duvivier); *Le Mensonge de Nina Petrowna* (*The Lie of Nina Petrovna*) (Tourjansky); *Prison sans barreaux* (Moguy); *Les Rois du sport* (Colombier)
1938   *Entrée des artistes* (*The Curtain Rises*) (M. Allégret); *Le Patriote* (*The Mad Emperor*) (Tourneur); *Hôtel du nord* (Carné); *Le Drame de Shanghaï* (Pabst); *Tarakanowa* (Ozep)
1942   *La Nuit fantastique* (L'Herbier)
1943   *L'Honorable Catherine* L'Herbier)
1944   *Florence est folle* (Lacombe)
1945   *Carmen* (Christian-Jaque—produced 1943); *Boule de suif* (*Angel and Sinner*) (Christian-Jaque); *Farandole* (Zwoboda); *Le Jugement dernier* (Chanas)
1946   *Un Revenant* (*A Lover's Return*) (Christian-Jaque)
1947   *Les Maudits* (*The Damned*) (Clément); *Carré de valets* (Berthomieu); *Copie conforme* (Dréville); *La Taverne du poisson couronné* (Chanas)
1948   *Les Amoureux sont seuls au monde* (*Monelle*) (Decoin); *La Vie en rose* (*Loves of Colette*) (Faurez); *Aux yeux du souvenir* (*Souvenir*) (Delannoy); *Scandale* (Le Hénaff)
1949   *Au royaume des cieux* (*The Sinners*) (Duvivier); *Entre onze heures et minuit* (Decoin)
1950   *Lady Paname* (+ d); *Souvenirs perdus* (Christian-Jaque); *Meurtres* (*Three Sinners*) (Pottier)
1951   *Le Garçon sauvage* (*Savage Triangle*) (Delannoy); *Fanfan la Tulipe* (*Fanfan the Tulip*) (Christian-Jaque); *Identité judiciaire*

(Bromberger); *Barbe-Bleue* (Christian-Jaque); *L'Homme de ma vie* (Lefranc)
1952   *La Minute de verité* (*The Moment of Truth*) (Delannoy); *La Fête à Henriette* (*Holiday for Henrietta*) (Duvivier)
1953   ''Lysistrata'' ep. of *Destinées* (*Daughters of Destiny*) (Christian-Jaque)
1954   *Madame Du Barry* (Christian-Jaque)
1955   *Nana* (Christian-Jaque); *Marguerite de la nuit* (Autant-Lara)
1957   *Pot-Bouille* (Duvivier)
1958   *Montparnasse 19* (*Modigliani of Montparnasse*) (Becker); *Maxime* (Verneuil); *Marie-Octobre* (Duvivier); *Guinguette* (Delannoy)
1959   *La Vache et le prisonnier* (*The Cow and I*) (Verneuil)
1961   *Vive Henri IV, vive l'amour* (Autant-Lara); *Le Puits aux trois verités* (*Three Faces of Sin*) (Villiers); *Madame Sans-Gêne* (*Madame*) (Christian-Jaque)
1962   *Le Crime ne paie pas* (*Crime Does Not Pay*) (Oury); *Le Diable et les dix commandements* (*The Devil and the Ten Commandments*) (Duvivier)
1963   *La Glaive et la balance* (*Two Are Guilty*) (Cayette); *Les Bonnes Causes* (*Don't Tempt the Devil*) (Christian-Jaque)
1964   *Le Repas des fauves* (Christian-Jaque)
1965   *Le Majordôme* (Delannoy)
1966   *Paris au mois d'août* (*Paris in the Month of August*) (Granier-Deferre)

Film as Dialogue Supervisor:

1938   *Gargousse* (Wulschleger)

Publications

By JEANSON: books—

With J. Galtier-Boissière, *Scandales de la IVe* (play), Paris, 1955.
With others, *Radio-télé* (play), Paris, 1963.
Mots, propos, aphorismes, Paris, 1971.
70 ans d'adolescence, edited by Joelle Jouillié and Pierre Serval, Paris, 1971.
With others, *Pépé le Moko* (script) in *Avant-Scène* (Paris), 1 June 1981.

By JEANSON: article—

Image et Son (Paris), March 1968.

On JEANSON: articles—

Cinémonde (Paris), 20 February 1953.
Cinémonde (Paris), 30 June 1959.
Skrien (Amsterdam), March 1979.
Positif (Paris), November 1993.
French Review, March 1996.
Positif (Paris), November 1996.
Sight and Sound (London), March 1999.

*   *   *

Henri Jeanson is the author of some of the most famous, most quoted dialogues of French cinema. It is he who wrote the unforgettable exchanges between Arletty and Louis Jouvet in Carné's *Hôtel du nord*, concise and brilliantly witty, and those for Marc Allégret's *Entrée des artistes*, equally humorous as delivered by Jouvet in his characteristically dry tone of understatement.

Indeed, Jeanson's dialogues were most successful when specifically written for performers whom he knew well and whose talents he appreciated. This was how he preferred to work and was especially true for Louis Jouvet, for whom he wrote the dialogues for some 10 films (including Siodmak's *Mister Flow*, Duvivier's *Un Carnet de bal*, and Christian-Jaque's *Un Revenant*). But if the relationship of dialogue to the accent and presence of an actor or actress contributes to its success (one thinks not only of Jouvet, but of Arletty in *Hôtel du nord* squalling in her inimitable Parisian accent, "Atmosphère, atmosphère! Non, mais est-ce que j'ai une gueule d'atmosphère?"), it is also at the heart of the weakness of many of the films on which Jeanson worked. *Entrée des artistes*, for example, although studded with some brilliantly witty dialogue and an outstanding performance by Jouvet, lacks any real consistent depth, and the awkwardly presented and overstated moral conclusion shows the film up as little more than a vehicle for the talents of both Jouvet and Jeanson. Ultimately, Jeanson's preoccupation with writing for performers meant that he often failed to write for *characters*. Behind the dazzling dialogues there is often neither substance nor development. Jeanson's ability to tell a story falls short of his ability to be comic, and he is often guilty of allowing his taste for witty rhetoric to dominate the less ostentatious task of good narrative construction. Consequently, the films on which Jeanson worked are usually memorable for certain scenes or dialogues rather than any more profound moral or philosophical vision or poetry of the quality of the screenwriting of Jacques Prévert. In *Entrée des artistes*, for example, one remembers Jouvet's visit to the laundry run by the parents of one of his pupils, and some of the exchanges with these pupils. In *Pépé le Moko*, one remembers the death of the informer, Charpin, and the scene in which Jean Gabin and Mireille Balin reminisce and love each other through their memories of Paris. In *Hôtel du nord*, the shrill exasperation of Arletty rebounding against the placid resignation of Jouvet is one of the most quoted passages of French cinema of the 1930s. Jeanson's writing is best suited to the deliberately fragmented narrative of *Un Carnet de bal*, a film composed of seven sketches united by one common character.

Considering the true author of a film to be the dialogue writer, Jeanson staunchly opposed both the notion of filmmaking as team work and the director as "auteur," seeing the latter as little more than a functional artisan. This apparent lack of respect for directors (he once described Marcel Carné as just "one of Prévert's thousand and one little inventions") meant that Jeanson never established such long-lasting creative collaborations as those of Carné and Prévert or Autant-Lara with Aurenche and Bost. Rather, Jeanson worked for a variety of directors, often supplying the dialogues for scenarios written by other screenwriters. For Christian-Jaque, for example, Jeanson wrote the dialogues for *Carmen* for a scenario by Charles Spaak and Jacques Viot; those for *Boule de suif* for a scenario by Louis d'Hée; and those for René Clément's *Les Maudits* were written for a scenario by Jacques Companeez and Alexandroff. Having made something of a speciality out of supplying dialogues for scenarios prepared by others, Jeanson's work lacks any real thematic coherence, and he worked on films as different as L'Herbier's burlesque comedy *L'Honorable Catherine*, Clément's drama *Les Maudits*, and Duvivier's melodramatic romance set in a girl's boarding school, *Au royaume des cieux*. His best work, however, is for films in which he wrote the scenario himself, as in the case of *Pépé le Moko* and *Un Revenant*, or actively collaborated in its writing, as for *Hôtel du nord* (written with Jean Aurenche).

Apart from his writing for film, Jeanson wrote a number of plays and worked throughout his life as a journalist, writing polemical articles for newspapers such as *Bonsoir*, *L'Oeuvre*, *L'Aurore*, and *Le Canard Enchaîné*. Like many of his films, Jeanson's journalism relied on his irrepressible wit, but its caustic irreverence often got him into trouble with those whom he delighted in attacking. He was an editor of the *Ciné-Liberté* journal in 1936 and worked alongside Jean Renoir on the fund-raising for *La Marseillaise*. He later considered Renoir to be guilty of political opportunism during the war and refers to him in his memoirs as "Jean Renoir, ou la grand désillusion." Perhaps symptomatic of his ability to offend everyone, Jeanson was both imprisoned by the Germans during World War II and then accused at the Liberation of "favouring enemy plans." After the war, his newspaper articles lost nothing of their ferocity. In the late 1950s and early 1960s, he regularly selected the New Wave critics and filmmakers for attack. François Truffaut's own brand of iconoclastic yet incisive criticism made him a particularly frequent target for Jeanson. And it was precisely the generation of New Wave directors which revolted against and then swept aside the sort of dialogue-centered filmmaking which Jeanson had always advocated and had clearly shown in the one film that he directed himself, *Lady Paname*.

—Richard Alwyn

JENKINS, George

Art Director. **Nationality:** American. **Born:** Baltimore, Maryland, 19 November 1908. **Education:** Studied architecture at the University of Pennsylvania, Philadelphia, 1931. **Family:** Married Phyllis Adams, 1955; one daughter by a previous marriage, and one stepdaughter. **Career:** Interior designer and engineer; 1937–41—assistant to the stage designer Jo Mielziner; 1943—first Broadway play as stage designer, *Early to Bed*, followed by a series of plays including *I Remember Mama*, *Lost in the Stars*, *The Bad Seed*, and *The Miracle Worker*; 1946—first film as art director, *The Best Years of Our Lives*; 1953–54—worked for TV; art director in charge of color, CBS; consultant in theater, University of Pennsylvania; 1985–88, professor of motion picture design, University of California, Los Angeles. **Awards:** Academy Award, for *All the President's Men*, 1976.

Films as Art Director:

1946   *The Best Years of Our Lives* (Wyler)
1947   *The Secret Life of Walter Mitty* (McLeod); *The Bishop's Wife* (Koster)
1948   *A Song Is Born* (Hawks); *Enchantment* (Reis)
1949   *Little Women* (LeRoy) (uncredited); *Roseanna McCoy* (Reis)

1950 *At War with the Army* (Walker)
1952 *The San Francisco Story* (Parrish)
1953 *Monsoon* (Amateau)
1962 *The Miracle Worker* (A. Penn) (co)
1965 *Mickey One* (A. Penn)
1967 *Up the Down Staircase* (Mulligan); *Wait until Dark* (Young)
1968 *No Way to Treat a Lady* (Smight); *The Subject Was Roses* (Grosbard)
1969 *Me, Natalie* (Coe)
1970 *The Angel Levine* (Kadar)
1971 *The Pursuit of Happiness* (Mulligan); **Klute** (Pakula)
1972 *1776* (Hunt)
1973 *The Paper Chase* (Bridges)
1974 *The Parallax View* (Pakula)
1975 *Funny Lady* (Ross); *Night Moves* (A. Penn)
1976 *All the President's Men* (Pakula)
1978 *Comes a Horseman* (Bridges); *The China Syndrome* (Bridges)
1979 *Starting Over* (Pakula)
1980 *Power* (Shear)
1981 *Rollover* (Pakula); *The Postman Always Rings Twice* (Rafelson)
1982 *Sophie's Choice* (Pakula)
1984 *The Dollmaker* (Petrie—for TV)
1986 *Dream Lover* (Pakula)
1987 *Orphans* (Pakula)
1989 *See You in the Morning* (Pakula)
1990 *Presumed Innocent* (Pakula)

Publications

By JENKINS: article—

Film Comment (New York), May/June 1978.

On JENKINS: article—

Skoop, August-September 1976.

*   *   *

During a 45-year career that began with the prestigious *The Best Years of Our Lives*, George Jenkins specialized in creating environments which define "realism." This "realism" most obviously manifests itself in the numerous sets which reflect actual locations: Louisa May Alcott's childhood home for *Little Women*, the fifth-floor newsroom of the *Washington Post* for *All the President's Men*, and a Harvard law classroom for *The Paper Chase*. Less obviously, but just as convincingly, Jenkins could recreate a lost or fictional setting by combining various sources of information: visiting many small newspapers for *The Parallax View*, locating a Victorian house that resembled Helen Keller's home in Georgia for *The Miracle Worker*, adapting the layouts of several nuclear power plant control rooms for *The China Syndrome* (which earned him an Academy Award nomination), and condensing World War II concentration camp photographs for *Sophie's Choice*. Whatever the situation, his designs concretely visualize and authenticate a film's space and time.

Although best known for transforming the everyday into a gritty screen equivalent, Jenkins also successfully accomplished more colorful or idiosyncratic works. While still sharply delineating a film's setting and always matching design to story, he also moved the "real" into purely cinematic style. Jenkins created the bright musical worlds of *1776* and *Funny Lady*; the cool, sleek urban settings of *Rollover* and *Power*; the claustrophobic working-class homes of *The Subject Was Roses* and *The Postman Always Rings Twice*; and the dark, frightening visions of *Wait until Dark* and *No Way to Treat a Lady*. Two of the three films he designed for Arthur Penn best demonstrate this facet of his talent. *Mickey One* established and maintained the black-and-white location of a surrealistic city, continually threatening to disappear into the dark and fog of a nightmare. Jenkins said it was an opportunity to do sets where there really weren't any sets at all. *Night Moves* employed vivid primary colors to transform the apparently tedious detective work of the protagonist into an interior reevaluation of his life. The film's colors are not necessarily symbolic, but their placement in an otherwise dreary environment generates a disturbing space of doubt and confusion. More recently, *Presumed Innocent*'s courtroom and law offices seem almost banal, but their darkness and heavy furnishings generate an ominous claustrophobia that perfectly reflects Rusty Savage's predicament.

Jenkins prided himself on his thorough research, precision, and an exacting use of props and set decorations. For example, he shipped three months of news-desk paperwork from the *Washington Post* to Hollywood for *All the President's Men*. This fastidious attention to detail rewarded him with an Oscar. Jenkins also firmly believed in filmmaking as a collaborative art, consulting with director, actor, and cinematographer before drafting a final design. This attitude explains why he designed ten films for Alan J. Pakula, a director known for cinematic "texture" (on all levels). In a similar (and typical) manner, Jenkins worked closely with Jane Fonda on *Klute* as she decided which props of her character's apartment she would use. Acutely aware that his sets must pass through the eyes of the cinematographer, he designed with the cinematographer in mind. The first to construct sets of normal size and perspective, he removed some of the cinematographer's bothersome responsibilities.

Jenkins worked with many first-level cinematographers: Gregg Toland (*The Best Years of Our Lives*), Charles Lang (*Wait until Dark*), Nestor Almendros (*Sophie's Choice*), Ghislain Cloquet (*Mickey One*), and Sven Nykvist (*Starting Over*, *The Postman Always Rings Twice*, and *Dream Lover*). His six collaborations with Gordon Willis (*Klute*, *The Paper Chase*, *The Parallax View*, *All the President's Men*, *Comes a Horseman*, and *Presumed Innocent*) proved to be amongst his (and Willis's) finest works.

—Greg S. Faller

JENNINGS, Talbot

Writer. **Nationality:** American. **Born:** Shoshone, Idaho, 1905 (some sources give 1895). **Education:** Attended Harvard University, Cambridge, Massachusetts, M.A.; Yale Drama School, New Haven,

Connecticut. **Career:** Author of plays *No More Frontier*, 1931, and *This Side of Idolatry*, 1933; 1935—first film as writer, *Mutiny on the Bounty*. **Died:** Of cancer in East Glacier Park, Montana, 30 May 1985.

Films as Writer:

1934   *We Live Again* (Mamoulian) (uncredited)
1935   *Mutiny on the Bounty* (Lloyd)
1936   *Romeo and Juliet* (Cukor)
1937   *The Good Earth* (Franklin)
1938   *Spawn of the North* (Hathaway); *Marie Antoinette* (Van Dyke)
1939   *Rulers of the Sea* (Lloyd)
1940   *Northwest Passage* (K. Vidor); *Edison the Man* (Brown)
1941   *So Ends Our Night* (Cromwell)
1944   *Frenchman's Creek* (Leisen)
1946   *Anna and the King of Siam* (Cromwell)
1950   *The Black Rose* (Hathaway)
1951   *Across the Wide Missouri* (Wellman)
1953   *Knights of the Round Table* (Thorpe)
1955   *Escape to Burma* (Dwan); *Pearl of the South Pacific* (Dwan); *Untamed* (H. King)
1957   *Gunsight Ridge* (Lyon)
1959   *The Naked Maja* (Koster)
1965   *The Sons of Katie Elder* (Hathaway)

Publications

By JENNINGS: books—

No More Frontier (play), New York, 1931.
The Light upon the Mountains, music by Hall McIntyre Macklin, Moscow, Idaho, 1939.

On JENNINGS: articles—

Obituary, in *Variety* (New York), 12 June 1985.

*   *   *

Talbot Jennings was one of Hollywood's most intelligent screenwriters, a protégé of Irving Thalberg who enjoyed a profitable career on prestigious films. Jennings specialized in historical drama and worked on the screenplays for some of the best in the genre, such as *Mutiny on the Bounty*, *Northwest Passage*, and *Rulers of the Sea*. He was also skilled at adaptation, as witness *Bounty*, *Romeo and Juliet*, *The Good Earth*, and *Anna and the King of Siam*.

At MGM, Thalberg chose Jennings to script his personal productions, a heady debut for a 30-year-old playwright. *Mutiny on the Bounty* was designed as Metro's roadshow epic for 1935, based on the Charles Nordhoff and Norman Hall novel inspired by the 1787 mutiny on board the *H.M.S. Bounty*. Carey Wilson and John Farrow had already written an unsatisfactory adaptation when Jennings was assigned to work with director Frank Lloyd on an acceptable draft.

The veteran screenwriter Jules Furthman was brought in to work with the neophyte Jennings and the pair was further aided by the humorist Allen Rivkin. The Oscar-nominated screenplay was ultimately credited on screen to Jennings, Furthman, and Wilson. The film won a Best Picture Oscar, and has become a perennial with its drama between Fletcher Christian (Clark Gable) and the martinet Captain Bligh (Charles Laughton), martial justice, and survival at sea, inspiring two remakes (in 1962 and 1984).

Thalberg loaned Jennings to Samuel Goldwyn for an uncredited polish of Preston Sturges's adaptation of Tolstoy's *Resurrection* (released as *We Live Again*), to be followed by a solo job of adapting Shakespeare's *Romeo and Juliet*. It was a formidable task, but Jennings retained the best of the play's narrative, and remained faithful to the dialogue. While Norma Shearer and Leslie Howard were much older than the playwright intended, George Cukor directed with great taste, and Jennings's work is certainly the best adaptation of Shakespeare in Hollywood history.

Jennings also contributed to two of Thalberg's last productions, *The Good Earth*, based on Pearl Buck's novel, and *Marie Antoinette*. His primary chore on *The Good Earth* was on the script's structure, while the predominant feminine focus on the material was provided by Tess Slesinger and Claudine West. He worked uncredited (along with F. Scott Fitzgerald) on *Marie Antoinette*, a sprawling showcase for Norma Shearer.

After Thalberg's death, Jennings signed with Paramount at the behest of *The Good Earth*'s coproducer, Albert Lewin. He was reunited with Jules Furthman for *Spawn of the North*, an extravagant adventure set in Alaska detailing the salmon wars between Russians and Americans. Jennings coauthored an original, *Rulers of the Sea*, with Frank Cavett and Richard Collins, then scripted the film for *Bounty* director Frank Lloyd. The result was a superior drama about the first steamship to make the Atlantic crossing.

Jennings returned to Metro to write two of Spencer Tracy's finest vehicles, King Vidor's *Northwest Passage* (with Laurence Stallings) and *Edison the Man* (with Bradbury Foote). *Northwest Passage* was based on the Kenneth Roberts novel about Roger's Rangers, the intrepid scouts of the French and Indian War. The film is a model of historical adventure, with stunning action setpieces such as the raid on the Abenaki village, and the trek through the wilderness balanced with superb characterization and period flavor. *Edison the Man* is one of the best film biographies, a sincere drama that succeeded in humanizing the legendary inventor.

Jennings freelanced throughout the rest of his career. He adapted Erich Maria Remarque's novel *Flotsam*, one of his few contemporary scripts. Filmed as *So Ends Our Night*, it was a powerful tale about refugees from Nazi Germany. Other adaptations during the mid-1940s included a nonmusical version of Margaret Landon's book *Anna and the King of Siam* (later popularized as *The King and I*), and the lush romantic drama *Frenchman's Creek*, from the Daphne du Maurier novel about the love between a Lady (Joan Fontaine) and a pirate (Arturo de Cordova). Jennings dealt with the middle ages in Henry Hathaway's *The Black Rose*, based on Thomas Costain's novel, and *Knights of the Round Table* (coscripted with Jan Lustig and Noel Langley), from Books VI and XI of Sir Thomas Malory's epic poem *Le Morte d'Arthur*, directed by Richard Thorpe as a follow-up to *Ivanhoe*.

Jennings ended his career writing the stories for *The Naked Maja*, a disappointing account of the love affair between the Spanish painter

439

Goya and the Duchess of Alba, and the rousing John Wayne western *The Sons of Katie Elder*, a revenge story directed by Hathaway with great vigor. Jennings was something of a rarity among Hollywood screenwriters in that his period pictures were much more realistic than most, his dialogue rarely florid or anachronistic. Throughout his career he adhered to a seasoned formula of integrating romance, action, and history, bound together by his unerring sense of narrative.

—John A. Gallagher

JHABVALA, Ruth Prawer

Writer. **Nationality:** American. **Born:** Cologne, Germany, of Polish parents, 7 May 1927; emigrated to England as a refugee, 1939; naturalized, 1948; became U.S. citizen, 1986. **Education:** Attended Hendon County School, London; Queen Mary College, University of London, M.A. in English literature 1951. **Family:** Married Cyrus Jhabvala, 1951, three daughters. **Career:** Lived in India, 1951–75; published her first novel, *To Whom She Will*, 1955; began her association with producer Ismail Merchant and director James Ivory, by scripting *The Householder*, 1963; moved to New York, 1975. **Awards:** Booker Prize, 1975; Best Adapted Screenplay British Academy Award, for *Heat and Dust*, 1983; Best Screenplay Based on Material from Another Medium Academy Award, Writers Guild of America Best Screenplay Based on Material from Another Medium, for *A Room with a View*, 1986; New York Film Critics Circle Best Screenplay, for *Mr. and Mrs. Bridge*, 1990; Best Screenplay Based on Material from Another Medium Academy Award, for *Howards End*, 1992; Writers Guild of America Laurel Award for Screenwriting Achievement, 1994; Writers Award Gotham Award, 1997. **Address:** 400 East 52nd Street, New York, NY 10022, U.S.A.

Films as Writer for Director James Ivory:

1963　*The Householder*
1965　*Shakespeare Wallah*
1968　*The Guru*
1970　*Bombay Talkie*
1975　*Autobiography of a Princess* (co)
1977　*Roseland*
1978　*Hullabaloo over Georgie and Bonnie's Pictures*
1979　*The Europeans*
1980　*Jane Austen in Manhattan*
1981　*Quartet*
1983　*Heat and Dust*
1984　*The Bostonians*
1986　*A Room with a View*
1990　*Mr. and Mrs. Bridge*
1992　**Howards End**
1993　*The Remains of the Day*
1995　*Jefferson in Paris*
1996　*Surviving Picasso*
1998　*A Soldier's Daughter Never Cries* (co-sc)
2000　*The Golden Bowl*

Other Films as Writer:

1982　*The Courtesans of Bombay* (Merchant) (doc)
1988　*Madame Sousatska* (Schlesinger) (co-sc)

Publications

By JHABVALA: fiction—

To Whom She Will, London, 1955, as *Amrita*, New York, 1956.
The Nature of Passion, London, 1956.
Esmond in India, London, 1958.
The Householder, London, 1960.
Get Ready for Battle, London, 1962.
Like Birds, Like Fishes and Other Stories, London, 1963.
A Backward Place, London, 1965.
A Stronger Climate: Nine Stories, London, 1968.
An Experience of India, London, 1971.
A New Dominion, London, 1972, as *Travelers*, New York, 1973.
Heat and Dust, London, 1975.
How I Became a Holy Mother and Other Stories, London, 1976.
In Search of Love and Beauty, London, 1983.
Out of India: Selected Stories, New York, 1986.
Three Continents, London, 1987.
Poet and Dancer, London, 1993.
Shards of Memory, London, 1995.
East into Upper East: Plain Tales from New York and New Delhi, Washington, D.C., 1998.
Travelers, Washington, D.C., 1999.

By JHABVALA: other books—

Meet Yourself at the Doctor (nonfiction), London, 1949.
Shakespeare Wallah (screenplay), London, 1973.
Autobiography of a Princess (screenplay), London, 1975.

By JHABVALA: articles—

Sight and Sound (London), Winter 1978–79.
Interview (New York), December 1983.

On JHABVALA: books—

Williams, H. M., *The Fiction of Ruth Prawer Jhabvala*, Calcutta, 1973.
Shahane, Vasant A., *Ruth Prawer Jhabvala*, New Delhi, 1976.
Gooneratne, Yasmine, *Silence, Exile, and Cunning: The Fiction of Ruth Prawer Jhabvala*, New Delhi, 1983.
Pym, John, *The Wandering Company*, London, 1983.
Sucher, Laurie, *The Fiction of Ruth Prawer Jhabvala*, London, 1989.
Bailur, Jayanti, *Ruth Prawer Jhabvala: Fiction & Film*, 1992.
Chakravarti, Aruna, *Ruth Prawer Jhabvala: A Study in Empathy & Exile*, Delhi, 1998.

On JHABVALA: articles—

"*Quartet* Issue" of *Avant-Scène* (Paris), 1 October 1981.
Film Dope (Nottingham), July 1983.

Ruth Prawer Jhabvala

Firstenberg, J., "A Class Act Turns Twenty-Five," in *American Film*, September 1987.

Variety (New York), 28 October/3 November, 1996.

Yunis, Alia, "Ruth Prawer Jhabvala: Writer With a View," in *Script* (Baldwin, Maryland), vol. 5, no. 6, 1996.

*   *   *

Since the 1960s, Ruth Prawer Jhabvala has enjoyed a unique position among screenwriters as one of the principal collaborators in Merchant Ivory Productions, the independent film company headed by the Indian producer Ismail Merchant and the American director James Ivory. Jhabvala has supplied the scripts for a majority of the company's productions, in a happy blend of narrative styles and thematic concerns that has proven so seamless it is often difficult to tell where the writer's influence ends and the filmmaker's begins.

Jhabvala was born in Germany and emigrated with her parents to England in 1939. She later married the architect Cyrus Jhabvala and moved with him to India, where she lived for 24 years. (She eventually was to divide her time between India and New York City.) Her life in India became the source of many of her richest earliest

works, and fostered within her a fascination with the country that she shares with Ivory. Beginning with *The Householder*, an adaptation of one of her own novels, Jhabvala wrote a series of films for Merchant Ivory Productions which helped establish both the company itself and James Ivory's reputation as a director. All of these films are set in India and deal with cultural clashes of one kind or another, a theme that would become a hallmark of the company's output. The best known of the group, *Shakespeare Wallah*, follows the fortunes of a British touring theatrical company, sadly out of place in modern India yet determined to hang on to their traditional way of life. Conflicts between East and West, tradition and change, or simply different strata of the same society recur throughout the Jhabvala-Ivory collaborations, with the stories' characters trying—and often failing—to reconcile themselves to their differences in culture and class.

Ivory's films are exquisite, leisurely portraits of minutely observed people and places, and Jhabvala's screenplays lend themselves admirably to the director's style. Subtle nuances of dialogue reveal shifts in a character's thoughts or emotions, while the story is allowed to unfold through delicately sketched character interaction rather than dynamic physical activity. The themes that mark the team's earliest films were applied on a more diverse scale in their collaborations between the mid-1970s and mid-1980s, with *The Europeans*, adapted from Henry James's novel, exploring the conflicts between British and American culture; *The Bostonians*, again adapted from James, examining the problematic interplay between men and women; and *Roseland* depicting the gulf between reality and imagination in its stories of the people who frequent an outmoded New York ballroom. *Autobiography of a Princess* and *Heat and Dust* find Jhabvala and Ivory returning again to the Anglo-Indian cultural conflict, with a particular emphasis on the differences between present-day India and the India of the British Raj.

Merchant-Ivory's 1986 adaptation of E. M. Forster's *A Room with a View* introduced new audiences to the style of filmmaking that had won them a hitherto select—but devoted—following. Its story of a young Englishwoman's emotional and sexual awakening in the face of the beauty and passion of Florence was ideally suited to Ivory's and Jhabvala's long-standing concerns. The latter's witty, literate script is alive with carefully shaded characterizations. The same can be said for *Howards End*, also based on Forster, which explores class distinctions in 1910 England (and is considered the penultimate Merchant-Ivory-Jhabvala collaboration); and *The Remains of the Day*, adapted from Kazuo Ishiguro's novel, about an efficient, mindlessly selfless professional servant, in which most of the narrative occurs between the world wars. Less successful (but no less ambitious) were *Mr. and Mrs. Bridge* (about the manner in which the passage of time affects a Midwestern couple); *Jefferson in Paris* (chronicling Thomas Jefferson's experiences while serving as the U.S. ambassador to France); and *Surviving Picasso* (the based-on-fact account of Francoise Gilot, a young artist who becomes the lover of an egotistical, womanizing Pablo Picasso). Jhabvala's final Merchant-Ivory film of the 1990s, *A Soldier's Daughter Never Cries*, is an improvement over their most recent collaborations. Based on the autobiographical novel by Kaylie (daughter of James) Jones, it is the heartfelt, though somewhat episodic, account of a famed expatriate novelist and his familial bonds. Despite its flaws, *A Soldier's Daughter Never Cries* is a rarity in contemporary cinema in that it offers a portrait of a loving, non-dysfunctional family.

In the 1990s, the ever-thinning line between Hollywood and the world of independent cinema may be best symbolized by Merchant-Ivory's inking a three-film pact with the Walt Disney Company. Nonetheless, despite their artistic lapses, Merchant-Ivory—and Jhabvala—have sustained the conviction that the tradition of the intelligent, thoughtful film, brimming with observations on the complexities of human nature—a conviction that seems so out of place in contemporary Hollywood—remains safe and alive in their hands.

—Janet Lorenz, updated by Rob Edelman

JOHNSON, Nunnally

Writer, Producer, and Director. **Nationality:** American. **Born:** James Nunnally Johnson in Columbus, Georgia, 5 December 1897. **Education:** Attended Columbus High School. **Family:** Married 1) Alice Love Mason, 1919 (divorced); one daughter; 2) Marion Byrnes, 1927 (divorced); one daughter; 3) Dorris Bowden, 1940; two daughters and one son. **Career:** 1915–16—newspaper reporter in Columbus and Savannah; 1916–18—served in the Mexican Border Service of the United States Army; 1918–19—reporter, New York *Tribune*, then reporter and columnist, Brooklyn *Eagle*, and columnist and writer for New York *Herald-Tribune* and *Saturday Evening Post*; 1933—writer for Paramount; 1934–43—writer and producer-director for 20th Century-Fox; 1943–48—worked at International Pictures; 1948–59—returned to 20th Century-Fox; freelance writer after 1960. **Awards:** Writers Guild Laurel Award, 1958. **Died:** 25 March 1977.

Films as Writer:

1931   *It Ought to Be a Crime* (A. Ray—short); *Mlle. Irene the Great* (Cline—short)
1932   *Twenty Horses* (A. Ray—short)
1933   *A Bedtime Story* (Taurog); *Mama Loves Papa* (McLeod); *The House of Rothschild* (Werker)
1934   *Moulin Rouge* (Lanfield); *Bulldog Drummond Strikes Back* (Del Ruth)
1935   *Baby Face Harrington* (Walsh); *Thanks a Million* (Del Ruth)
1936   *The Prisoner of Shark Island* (Ford); *Banjo on My Knee* (Cromwell)
1941   *Tobacco Road* (Ford)
1944   *The Keys of the Kingdom* (Stahl) (co)
1945   *Along Came Jones* (Heisler)
1951   *The Long Dark Hall* (Bushell and Beck)
1952   ''The Ransom of Red Chief'' ep. of *O. Henry's Full House* (*Full House*) (Hawks)
1959   *Flaming Star* (Siegel) (co)
1962   *Mr. Hobbs Takes a Vacation* (Koster)
1963   *Take Her, She's Mine* (Koster)
1964   *The World of Henry Orient* (Hill) (co)
1967   *The Dirty Dozen* (Aldrich) (co)

Films as Associate Producer:

1936   *The Country Doctor* (H. King); *The Road to Glory* (Hawks); *Dimples* (Seiter); *Cardinal Richelieu* (Lee)
1937   *Nancy Steele Is Missing* (Marshall); *Cafe Metropole* (E. Griffith); *Slave Ship* (Garnett); *Love under Fire* (Marshall)
1940   *I Was an Adventuress* (Ratoff)
1950   *The Gunfighter* (H. King)

Films as Producer and Writer:

1935   *The Man Who Broke the Bank at Monte Carlo* (Roberts) (assoc pr)
1939   *Jesse James* (H. King) (assoc pr); *Wife, Husband, and Friend* (Ratoff) (assoc pr); *Rose of Washington Square* (Ratoff) (assoc pr)
1940   ***The Grapes of Wrath*** (Ford) (assoc pr); *Chad Hanna* (H. King) (assoc pr)
1942   *Roxie Hart* (Wellman); *The Pied Piper* (Pichel); *Life Begins at Eight-Thirty* (*The Light of Heart*) (Pichel)

1943   *The Moon Is Down* (Pichel); *Holy Matrimony* (Stahl)
1944   *Casanova Brown* (Wood); *The Woman in the Window* (F. Lang)
1946   *The Dark Mirror* (Siodmak)
1947   *The Senator Was Indiscreet* (*Mr. Ashton Was Indiscreet*)
        (Kaufman)
1948   *Mr. Peabody and the Mermaid* (Pichel)
1949   *Everybody Does It* (Goulding)
1950   *Three Came Home* (Negulesco); *The Mudlark* (Negulesco)
1951   *The Desert Fox* (*The Story of Rommel*) (Hathaway)
1952   *Phone Call from a Stranger* (Negulesco); *We're Not Married*
        (Goulding); *My Cousin Rachel* (Koster)
1953   *How to Marry a Millionaire* (Negulesco)

Films as Writer and Director:

1954   *Night People*; *Black Widow* (+ pr)
1955   *How to Be Very, Very Popular* (+ pr)
1956   *The Man in the Gray Flannel Suit*
1957   *Oh, Men! Oh, Women!* (+ pr); *The Three Faces of Eve* (+ pr)
1959   *The Man Who Understood Women* (+ pr)
1960   *The Angel Wore Red*

Publications

By JOHNSON: books—

There Ought to Be a Law, and Other Stories, New York, 1931.
The Grapes of Wrath (script), in *Twenty Best Film Plays*, edited by
    John Gassner and Dudley Nichols, New York, 1943.
The Letters of Nunnally Johnson, edited by Dorris Johnson and Ellen
    Leventhal, New York, 1981.

By JOHNSON: article—

"The Long and Short of It," in *Films and Filming* (London),
    June 1957.

On JOHNSON: books—

French, Warren, *Filmguide to the Grapes of Wrath*, Bloomington,
    Indiana, 1973.
Flashback: Nora Johnson on Nunnally Johnson, New York, 1979.
Stempel, Tom, *Screenwriter: The Life and Times of Nunnally John-
    son*, San Diego, California, 1980.
Hulse, Ed, *The Films of Betty Grable*, Burbank, 1995.

On JOHNSON: articles—

Bluestone, George, on *The Grapes of Wrath* in *Movies into Film*,
    Baltimore, Maryland, 1957.
Kino Lehti (Helsinki), no. 1, 1969.
Corliss, Richard, in *Talking Pictures*, Woodstock, New York, 1974.
Obituary in *New York Times*, 27 March 1977.

Obituary in *Variety* (New York), 30 March 1977.
Obituary in *Boxoffice* (Chicago), 11 April 1977.
Obituary in *Cinéma 72* (Paris), May 1977.
Film Dope (Nottingham), December 1983.
Bohn, Thomas, in *American Screenwriters*, edited by Robert E.
    Morsberger, Stephen O. Lesser, and Randall Clark, Detroit, Michi-
    gan, 1984.
Cineforum, no. 313, April 1992.
"*How to Be Very, Very Popular!*" in *Reid's Film Index* (Wyong,
    New South Wales), no. 17, 1995.
Bisplinghoff, G.D., and C.J. Slingo, "Eve in Calcutta: The Indianization
    of a Movie Madwoman," in *Asian Cinema* (Drexel Hill), no. 1, 1997.

*   *   *

Like most writers, Nunnally Johnson desired complete control over his work. Unlike most writers in Hollywood, he got it. He accomplished this by producing and, later, by directing his own screenplays. Johnson's true talent was in writing, however, and it was in this capacity that he made his greatest contribution to the cinema.

In his dramatic work, Johnson portrayed characters that were faced with obstacles which they had to overcome to survive. Some were imprisoned (*The Prisoner of Shark Island*, *Three Came Home*), others were threatened with death (*Jesse James*, *The Grapes of Wrath*, *Flaming Star*, *The Desert Fox*), and still others faced mid-life crises (*Phone Call from a Stranger*, *The Man in the Gray Flannel Suit*) or mental problems (*The Three Faces of Eve*, *The Dark Mirror*). On the lighter side, Johnson's comedies involved characters, such as Roxie in *Roxie Hart*, facing imprisonment, the three women in *How to Marry a Millionaire* facing the dreaded single life with no money, the senator in *The Senator Was Indiscreet* threatened with scandal, and bored husbands flirting with adultery in *The Woman in the Window* and *Mr. Peabody and the Mermaid*.

The characters themselves were much more interesting than the traumas that they encountered, however, because Johnson was fasci-nated with good and evil and the ambiguities of life. Many of his "villains" were not entirely evil—they were doing jobs they felt were right, or that circumstances forced them to do. The "enemy" was a human being, whether Japanese (*Three Came Home*), Indian (*Flaming Star*), Russian (*Night People*), or Nazi (*The Desert Fox*). The trait that most of Johnson's characters shared and which made them more human was their love of family, and particularly their adoration for their children. They judged themselves by their success or failure as parents. Colonel Suga, head of the brutal prison camp in *Three Came Home*, tenderly describes his children to Mrs. Keith, and General Rommel is heartbroken knowing that he is seeing his son for the last time at the end of *The Desert Fox*. Jesse James gives up robbery (which he is prodded into doing because of his mother's murder) to take care of his beloved son, and Dr. Mudd, who set John Wilkes Booth's leg by circumstance, is equally devoted to his family in *The Prisoner of Shark Island*.

Johnson's fascination with good and evil traits was demonstrated further in *The Dark Mirror* with twins—one good and one evil. This duality was explored again in *My Cousin Rachel* (both films starred Olivia de Havilland) in which the main character at times seemed quite capable of murder and, at other times, was a kind, caring woman. One step beyond this premise was Eve in *The Three Faces of Eve*. Eve was inhabited by three personalities—the first, repressed and dowdy, the second, noisy and uninhibited, and the third, calm and stable.

Nunnally Johnson was, above all, an optimistic writer: he believed in the basic goodness of humanity despite its faults, and that eventually good would triumph over evil. Even his doomed characters, such as Rommel in *The Desert Fox*, Tom Joad in *The Grapes of Wrath*, Pacer Burton in *Flaming Star*, and Jesse in *Jesse James*, all leave behind a family who will carry on and attempt to achieve what they could not: to make a better world or, at least, gain an understanding and an acceptance of others, no matter how different from themselves.

—Alexa L. Foreman

JONES, Chuck

Animator. **Nationality:** American. **Born:** Spokane, Washington, 21 September 1912. **Education:** Attended Chouinard Art Institute, Los Angeles. **Family:** Married Dorothy Webster (deceased). **Career:** Early 1930s—worked at various animation studios in variety of capacities, including for Charles Mintz at Screen Gems, Ub Iwerks at Flip the Frog Productions, and for Walter Lantz; about 1935—joined Warner Bros. as animator; worked under Ub Iwerks, Robert Clampett, and Tex Avery; 1938–62—cartoon director for Warners; 1955—four months at Disney Studios, then returned to Warners; 1963–67—directed for MGM; 1970-on—directed and produced television specials. **Awards:** Academy Award, for *For Scent-imental Reasons*, 1949; *So Much for So Little*, 1949; *The Dot and the Line*, 1965; Peabody Award, for *Horton Hears a Who*, 1971; L.A. Critics' Award, for life achievement, 1990; Academy Award, for life achievement, 1995.

Films as Director at Warner Bros.:

1938   *Night Watchman; Dog Gone Modern*
1939   *Robin Hood Makes Good; Presto Change-O; Daffy Duck and the Dinosaur; Naughty but Mice; Old Glory; Snowman's Land; Little Brother Rat; Little Lion Hunter; The Good Egg; Sniffles and the Bookworm; Curious Puppy*
1940   *Mighty Hunters; Elmer's Candid Camera; Sniffles Takes a Trip; Tom Thumb in Trouble; The Egg Collector; Ghost Wanted; Good Night Elmer; Bedtime for Sniffles; Sniffles Bells the Cat*
1941   *Toy Trouble; The Wacky Worm; Inki and the Lion; Snow Time for Comedy; Joe Glow the Firefly; Brave Little Bat; Saddle Silly; The Bird Came C.O.D.; Porky's Ant; Conrad the Sailor; Porky's Prize Pony; Dog Tired; The Draft Horse; Hold the Lion, Please; Porky's Midnight Matinee*
1942   *The Squawkin' Hawk; Fox Pop; My Favorite Duck; To Duck or Not to Duck; The Dover Boys; Case of the Missing Hare; Porky's Cafe*
1943   *Flop Goes the Weasel; Super Rabbit; The Unbearable Bear; The Aristo Cat; Wackiki Wabbit; Fin 'n Catty; Inki and the Mynah Bird*
1944   *Tom Turk and Daffy; Angel Puss; From Hand to Mouse; The Odor-able Kitty; Bugs Bunny and the Three Bears; The Weakly Reporter; Lost and Foundling*
1945   *Trap Happy Porky; Hare Conditioned; Hare Tonic; Hush My Mouse; Fresh Airedale; Quentin Quail; Hair Raising Hare; The Eager Beaver*

1946   *Roughly Squeaking; Scenti-Mental over You; Fair and Wormer; A Feather in His Hare*
1947   *Little Orphan Airedale; What's Brewin' Bruin; House Hunting Mice; Haredevil Hare; Inki at the Circus; A Pest in the House; Rabbit Punch*
1948   *You Were Never Duckier; Mississippi Hare; Mouse Wreckers; Scaredy Cat; My Bunny Lies over the Sea; Awful Orphan; The Bee-Deviled Bruin; Daffy Dilly; Long-Haired Hare*
1949   *Frigid Hare; Rabbit Hood; Often an Orphan; Fast and Furryous; For Scent-imental Reasons; Bear Feat; Homeless Hare; So Much for So Little*
1950   *The Hypo-Chondri-Cat; Dog Gone South; The Scarlet Pumpernickel; Eight-Ball Bunny; The Ducksters; Rabbit of Seville; Caveman Inki*
1951   *Two's a Crowd; A Hound for Trouble; Rabbit Fire; Chow Hound; The Wearing of the Grin; A Bear for Punishment; Bunny Hugged; Scent-Imental Romeo; Cheese Chasers; Drip-Along Daffy*
1952   *Operation Rabbit; Water, Water Every Hare; The Hasty Hare; Mousewarming; Don't Give Up the Sheep; Feed the Kitty; Little Beau Pepe; Beep Beep; Going! Going! Gosh!; Terrier Stricken; Rabbit Seasoning; Kiss Me Cat*
1953   *Forward March Hare; Wild over You; Bully for Bugs; Duck Amuck; Much Ado about Nutting; Duck Dodgers in the 24 1/2th Century; Zipping Along; Feline Frame-Up*
1954   *Punch Trunk; From A to ZZZZ; Bewitched Bunny; Duck! Rabbit! Duck!; No Barking; Stop, Look, and Hasten!; Sheep Ahoy; My Little Duckaroo*
1955   *The Cat's Bah; Claws for Alarm; Lumber Jack Rabbit (in 3-D); Ready, Set, Zoom!; Rabbit Rampage; Double or Mutton; Baby Buggy Bunny; Beanstalk Bunny; Past Performance; Jumpin' Jupiter; Guided Muscle; Knight-Mare Hare*
1956   *Two Scents' Worth; One Froggy Evening; Bug's Bonnets; Rocket Squad; Heaven Scent; Rocket-Bye Baby; Gee Whizzz; Barbary Coast Bunny*
1957   *Deduce You Say; There They Go-Go-Go!; Scrambled Aches; Go Fly a Kit; Steal Wool; Zoom and Bored; To Hare Is Human; Ali Baba Bunny; Boyhood Daze; What's Opera, Doc?; Touché and Go*
1983   *Daffy Duck's Movie: Fantastic Island*
1986   *Porky Pig in Hollywood*
1990   *Merrie Melodies: Starring Bugs Bunny and Friends*
1995   *Another Froggy Evening (+ pr); That's Warner Bros!*
1996   *From Hare to Eternity (+ pr); The Bugs n' Daffy Show; Superior Duck*

Films as Writer and Director at Warner Bros.:

1958   *Hare-Way to the Stars; Hook, Line, and Stinker; Robin Hood Daffy; Whoa, Begone!; To Itch His Own*
1959   *Baton Bunny; Hot Rod and Reel; Cat Feud; Hip Hip—Hurry!; Really Scent*
1960   *Fastest with the Mostest; Who Scent You?; Rabbit's Feat; Wild about Hurry*
1961   *High Note; Hopalong Casualty; The Abominable Snow Rabbit; Scent of the Matterhorn; Lickety Splat; Zip 'n Snort; The Mouse on 57th Street; Compressed Hare*
1962   *Louvre Come Back to Me; Beep Prepared; A Sheep in the Deep; Nelly's Folly; Zoom at the Top*

Chuck Jones

1963   *Martian thru Georgia*; *Now Hear This*; *Hare-Breadth Hurry*;
        I Was a Teenage Thumb; *Woolen under Where*
1994   *Chariots of Fur* (+ pr)

Films as Director of Tom and Jerry Cartoons for MGM:

1963   *Penthouse Mouse*
1964   *The Cat Above and the Mouse Below*; *Is There a Doctor in the
        Mouse*; *Much Ado about Mousing*; *Snowbody Loves Me*;
        Unshrinkable Jerry Mouse
1965   *Ah Sweet Mouse-Story of Life*; *Bad Day at Cat Rock*; *Brothers
        Carry Mouse Off*; *Haunted Mouse*; *I'm Just Wild about
        Jerry*; *Of Feline Bondage*; *Year of the Mouse*; *Cat's Me-
        Ouch*
1966   *Duel Personality*; *Jerry Jerry Quite Contrary*; *Love Me, Love
        My Mouse* (with Ben Washam)
1967   *Cat and Duplicat*

Other Films as Director:

1965   *The Dot and the Line*
1967   *The Bear that Wasn't*

1970   *How the Grinch Stole Christmas* (for TV)
1971   *The Phantom Toll Booth* (with Livitow); *Horton Hears a Who*
        (for TV); *The Pogo Special Birthday Special* (for TV);
        The Cricket in Times Square (for TV); *A Very Merry
        Cricket* (for TV)
1974   *Yankee Doodle Cricket*
1975   *Riki-Tiki-Tavy*
1979   *The Great American Bugs Bunny-Road Runner Chase* (+ pr, sc)
1981   *Uncensored Cartoons*

Other Films:

1962   *Gay Purr-ee* (Levitow) (story)
1971   *Christmas Carol* (exec pr) (TV special)
1982   *Bugs Bunny's Third Movie* (Detiege, Art Davis, and Perez)
        (animator)
1984   *Gremlins* (Dante) (animator)
1987   *Innerspace* (Dante) (animator)
1988   *Daffy Duck's Quackbusters* (Ford) (sequenced); *Who Framed
        Roger Rabbit* (Zemeckis) (anim consultant)
1990   *Gremlins 2: The New Batch* (Dante) (animator)
1992   *Stay Tuned* (Hyams) (anim dir)
1993   *Mrs. Doubtfire* (Columbus) (anim dir)

1995 *Four Rooms* (Anders, Rockwell, Rodriguez, Tarantino) (creative consultant)
1999 *Roughnecks: The Starship Troopers Chronicles* (Berkeley, Caldwell, Hartman, Liu, Oliva, Paden, Song—series for TV) (character designer)

Publications

By JONES: books—

Chuck Amuck, New York, 1989.
Chuck Jones' Peter & the Wolf, New York, 1994.

By JONES: articles—

"The Road Runner and Other Characters," interview with R. Benayoun, in *Cinema Journal* (Evanston, Illinois), Spring 1969.
Interview with M. Barrier, in *Funnyworld* (New York), Spring 1971.
Interview with J. Colombat, in *Image et Son* (Paris), January 1972.
"The Hollywood Cartoon," interview with J. Canemaker, in *Filmmakers Newsletter* (Ward Hill, Massachusetts), April 1974.
"Animation Is a Gift Word," in *AFI Report* (Washington, D.C.), Summer 1974.
Interview with G. Ford and R. Thompson, in *Film Comment* (New York), January/February 1975.
"L'Animation, un art nu," in *Positif* (Paris), February 1975.
"Cel Washer: 'Kid-vid' Is a Dirty Word," in *Take One* (Montreal), no. 4, 1976.
Interview with J. Rubin, in *Classic Film Collector* (Muscatine, Iowa), Summer 1976.
"Friz Freleng and How I Grew," in *Millimeter* (New York), November 1976.
"Chuck Jones Interviewed," with Joe Adamson, in *The American Animated Cartoon*, edited by Gerald and Danny Peary, New York, 1980.
Revue du Cinéma (Paris), no. 465, November 1990.
"A Master of Animated Art: Chuck Jones," an interview with Gregory J. M. Catsos, in *Filmfax* (Evanston), August-September 1992.
"The Return of Duck Dodgers. Sequel to the Cartoon Classic," in *Outré* (Evanston), no. 7, 1997.

On JONES: books—

Maltin, Leonard, *Of Mice and Magic*, New York, 1980.
Kenner, Hugh, *Chuck Jones: A Flurry of Drawings*, Berkeley, California, 1994.

On JONES: articles—

Thompson, R., "*Duck Amuck*," in *Film Comment* (New York), January/February 1975.
Cohen, M. S., "Looney Tunes and Merrie Melodies," in *Velvet Light Trap* (Madison, Wisconsin), Autumn 1975.
Ward, A., "Master Animator Chuck Jones: The Movement's the Thing," in *New York Times*, 7 October 1979.

Thompson, Richard, "Meep Meep!," and "Pronoun Trouble," in *The American Animated Cartoon*, edited by Gerald and Danny Peary, New York, 1980.
Cahiers du Cinéma (Paris), December 1982.
Plateau, vol. 7, no. 4, 1986.
CinémAction (Conde-sur-Noireau), April 1989.
Cahiers du Cinéma (Paris), September 1990.
O'Brien, Ken, "Chuck Jones and MGM: Reevaluating Tom and Jerry," in *Animation Journal* (Irvine), vol. 1, Fall 1996.
Williams, David R., "The Mouse that Chuck Built," in *Animation Journal* (Irvine), vol. 2, Spring 1997.

*   *   *

During a career of nearly 60 years (and still going strong) in cartoon animation, Chuck Jones has created more than 240 animated films. His most famous work was done at Warner Brothers where from 1938 to 1962 he directed such "stars" as Bugs Bunny, Daffy Duck, and Porky Pig. Although many different animators worked with these characters, Jones developed his own particular style of animation that set his cartoons apart from the others.

Part of that style has to do with the development of his characters, who have very strong personalities. For example, Pepe LePew is an ever-confident Casanova. No matter how many times he is pushed off the road to romance, he remains undaunted in his attempts to pursue his heart's "true love." Daffy Duck, on the other hand, is a self-centered egotist. He is always looking out for "number one", and he must, above all, maintain his dignity. By using such strong characters in his films, Jones creates humor not out of what is happening to the character, but from how the character reacts to what is happening. For example, the Roadrunner series (one of Jones's own creations) relies on character reaction throughout the story. Whenever Wile E. Coyote finds that he is about to go over the edge of a cliff, he remains in mid-air, looks down, realizes his predicament, gulps, looks to the audience for sympathy, and then falls. The humor is not in his falling, but in the way Wile E. Coyote reacts to his situation.

Another characteristic found in many of Jones's cartoons is his distinctive use of the medium. It is not uncommon to find references to the techniques of animation in his films. The most obvious example of Jones's self-reflexivity in a cartoon is *Duck Amuck*. In this film Daffy Duck is plagued by the animator who, in a series of gags, erases Daffy, gives him the wrong voice, rolls the picture, collapses the frame line, and finally blows up Daffy by drawing in a bomb. Another of Jones's cartoons that is filled with in-jokes is the Oscar-winning *What's Opera, Doc?* In this cartoon (which can be viewed as a parody of Disney's *Fantasia*), Bugs Bunny and Elmer Fudd continue to play their roles of the hunter and hunted, but as "actors" within the very formal structure of a Wagnerian opera. It is the only cartoon in which Bugs "dies," but, as he says while the camera irises out, "What did you expect in an opera, a happy ending?" *One Froggy Evening*, a comic parable on the lure of fame and riches in which a man finds a singing frog and sees dollar signs but loses everything because the frog will perform only for him, is one of Jones's most memorable creations.

Another distinctive trait that can be found in Jones's cartoons is his sense of comic timing. Whereas some cartoon directors pile gag upon gag at a frantic pace, Jones often uses pauses within his gags. For example, when Wile E. Coyote fell from a cliff, the overhead point of view would show him getting smaller and smaller until he was invisible, and a few frames later a puff of smoke could be seen where he crashed. Jones knew exactly how many frames it would take to create the right amount of tension before Wile E. Coyote actually hit the ground. It was a piece of timing he had to teach all of his animators on the Roadrunner series.

With the closing of the studio cartoon departments, Jones moved his animation talents into television and feature-length production. His more recent work has proven to be very popular with audiences. Now viewed as the craft's elder statesman, he has been paid homage to by a generation of admirers, including such as directors Steven Spielberg and Joe Dante, who not only acknowledge Jones's influence on the slam-bang style of their own work, but frequently give him cameos in their films. He continues as well to lend his innovative hand to advances in the art of animation such as the groundbreaking *Who Killed Roger Rabbit?*, which seamlessly mixed live action with cartoon images. The Academy of Motion Picture Arts and Sciences honored Jones with a special life achievement award in 1995 for the enduring appeal of his work, which shows no signs of age.

—Linda Obalil, updated by John McCarty

JONES, Quincy

Composer and Producer. **Nationality:** American. **Born:** Quincy Delight Jones, Jr., in Chicago, Illinois, 14 March 1933. **Education:** Attended Seattle University, Washington; Berklee School of Music, Boston; also studied with Boulanger and Messiaen in Paris. **Family:**

Quincy Jones

Married 1) Jeri Caldwell, 1957 (divorced 1966); 2) Ulla Anderson, 1967 (divorced 1974); 3) the actress Peggy Lipton, 1974 (divorced 1990); seven children in all. **Career:** 1950–53—trumpeter and arranger for Lionel Hampton; then freelance arranger for Ray Anthony, Count Basie, Sarah Vaughan, and Peggy Lee; 1956—musical director, Dizzy Gillespie's orchestra; arranger for Barclay Discs, Paris; 1961—music director, then vice president, 1964, Mercury Records; composer of instrumental works, and for TV series *Hey Landlord*, 1966–67, *The Bill Cosby Show*, 1969, and *Sanford & Son*, 1972–77, and for the mini-series *Roots*, 1976; 1990s—executive producer of TV series *The Fresh Prince of Bel Air*, *The Jesse Jackson Show*, *In the House*, *Mad TV*. **Awards:** Jean Hersholt Humanitarian Award, 1994. **Agent:** Rogers and Cowan Inc., 1888 Century Park East, Los Angeles, CA 90067–7007, U.S.A.

Films as Composer:

1960   *Pojken i trädet* (*The Boy in the Tree*) (Sucksdorff)
1964   *The Pawnbroker* (Lumet); *Mirage* (Dymtryk)
1965   *Made in Paris* (Sagal) (songs); *The Slender Thread* (Pollack)
1966   *Walk Don't Run* (Walters); *The Deadly Affair* (Lumet); *Enter Laughing* (C. Reiner)
1967   *Banning* (Winston); *In Cold Blood* (R. Brooks); *In the Heat of the Night* (Jewison); *Ironside* (Goldstone—for TV)
1968   *A Dandy in Aspic* (A. Mann); *Jigsaw* (Goldstone); *The Counterfeit Killer* (Leytes); *For Love of Ivy* (Daniel Mann); *The Split* (Fleming); *The Hell with Heroes* (Sargent); *MacKenna's Gold* (Lee Thompson); *Split Second to an Epitaph* (Horn)
1969   *The Italian Job* (Collinson); *The Lost Man* (Aurthur); *Bob and Carol and Ted and Alice* (Mazursky); *Cactus Flower* (Saks); *John and Mary* (Yates); *The Out-of-Towners* (Hiller); *Blood Kin* (*The Last of the Mobile Hot-Shots*) (Lumet)
1970   *They Call Me MISTER Tibbs!* (Douglas); *Eggs* (Hubley—short); *Of Men and Demons* (J. & F. Hubley short); *Up Your Teddy Bear* (*The Toy Grabbers*) (Joslyn); *Brother John* (Goldstone)
1971   *The Anderson Tapes* (Lumet); *Honky* (Graham); *$* (*The Heist*) (R. Brooks)
1972   *The Hot Rock* (*How to Steal a Diamond in Four Uneasy Lessons*) (Yates); *The New Centurions* (*Precinct 45 Los Angeles Police*) (Fleischer); *The Getaway* (Peckinpah); *Killer by Night* (McEveety)
1976   *Mother, Jugs, and Speed* (Yates) (songs)
1985   *Portrait of an Album* (+ d); *Fast Forward* (Poitier); *Lost in America* (Albert Brooks) (song); *The Slugger's Wife* (Ashby); ***The Color Purple*** (Spielberg) (+ co-pr)
1988   *Heart and Soul* (Pasquin) (+ co-exec pr)
1990   *Listen Up: The Lives of Quincy Jones* (Weissbrod—doc) (+ ro)

Films as Music Director:

1971   *Man and Boy* (Swackhamer)
1972   *Come Back Charleston Blue* (Warren) (+ song)
1978   *The Wiz* (Lumet) (+ songs)
1985   *The Slugger's Wife* (Ashby) (exec music pr); *Fast Forward* (exec mus pr)

Publications

By JONES: articles—

Vanity Fair (New York), July 1996.

On JONES: books—

Horricks, Raymond, *Quincy Jones*, New York, 1986.
Cuellar, Carol, *Quincy Jones: Q's Jook Joint*, Miami, 1996.
Kallen, Stuart A., *Quincy Jones*, Edina, 1996.
Kavanaugh, Lee H., *Quincy Jones: Musician, Composer, Producer*, Berkeley Heights, 1998.

On JONES: articles—

Cinestudio (Madrid), April 1973.
Dirigido por . . . (Barcelona), September 1974.
Ecran (Paris), September 1975.
Film Dope (Nottingham), no. 28, December 1983.
Film Score Monthly (Los Angeles), July 1996.
Variety (New York), 18 November 1996.
Jet, 31 May 1999.

*   *   *

With the incorporation of jazz and pop styles into film music in the 1950s and 1960s, it was inevitable that composers from such backgrounds would be commissioned to compose film scores. Quincy Jones's experience as an arranger, composer, and performer made him particularly adept at matching the disciplines of these styles to the demands of the medium.

Jones has brought to film music a range of influences from Latin stylings to American blues. Such influences are apparent in his first major score, for Sidney Lumet's *The Pawnbroker*. The urban realism of Lumet's film is balanced by equally authentic musical accompaniment, showing not only Jones's facility with jazz, but also with Puerto Rican and other ethnic musical idioms. Jones's handling of these elements led to his scoring a number of crime films and social dramas with contemporary urban settings. In many of these works, he combined modern rhythms with melodic pop themes reminiscent of the work of Henry Mancini.

This approach made Jones a natural choice for contemporary directors seeking a "new" sound. The score for Norman Jewison's *In the Heat of the Night* employs bluegrass and blues elements appropriate to its Southern setting while Jones's music for Richard Brooks's *In Cold Blood* incorporates unusual percussive effects, throbbing bass lines, and even a use of bottles at one point. Jones has also continued to work on and off for Lumet, serving as arranger and conductor for the filmmaker's production of *The Wiz*, adapted from William F. Brown and Charlie Smalls's hit Broadway musical. Jones gained further recognition in the motion picture industry as one of the producers and the musical coordinator for Steven Spielberg's *The Color Purple*. Assembling a team of composers, orchestrators, and musicians, Jones constructed a score that combines a broad spectrum of musical influences, from African rhythms to jazz and blues. The music also contains more traditional approaches to film scoring, as in a lyrical symphonic theme which bears in its principal woodwind line a resemblance to Georges Delerue's main theme for *Our Mother's House*. Above all, Jones's work for *The Color Purple* demonstrates

his ability not only to handle a variety of musical styles but also his influence as a producer.

The Color Purple aside, from the mid-1970s on Jones became less active in films, turning his attention more to arranging and conducting and, in particular, to his film and television production company, Quincy Jones Entertainment. He also established his own broadcasting company to acquire television and radio properties. And in recent years he has become an elder statesman among American (and even more specifically, African-American) composers/arrangers/music producers. In 1990, he was the subject of a documentary/homage, *Listen Up: The Lives of Quincy Jones*, a portrait in words, music, and images in which his "genius" is acknowledged by a diverse group of celebrities, from Dizzy Gillespie to Ice T, Miles Davis to Frank Sinatra, Barbra Streisand to Big Daddy Kane.

—Richard R. Ness, updated by Rob Edelman

JUNGE, Alfred

Art Director. **Nationality:** German. **Born:** Görlitz, 29 January 1886. **Education:** Studied in Germany and Italy. **Career:** Joined Görlitz City Theatre at age 18 as actor/factotum; then designed sets for Berlin State Opera and State Theatre; 1920—joined UFA as art director; 1928—worked for Dupont in England, and briefly in France; then settled in England: late 1940s—head of MGM British studios. **Award:** Academy Award for *Black Narcissus*, 1947. **Died:** In 1964.

Films as Art Director:

1921   *Hintertreppe (Backstairs)* (Jessner)
1923   *Die grüne Manuela (The Green Manuela)* (Dupont) (co); *Das alte Gesetz (The Ancient Law; Baruch)* (Dupont) (co)
1924   *Das Wachsfigurenkabinett (Waxworks)* (Leni) (uncredited); *Mensch gegen Mensch* (Steinhoff) (co); *Der Mann um Mitternacht* (Holger-Madsen)
1925   *Die Kleine aus der Kongektion (Gross-stadtkavaliere)* (Neff); *Athleten* (Zelnik); *Sündelbabel* (David); *Ein Lebenskünstler* (Holger-Madsen); *Der vertauschte Braut* (Wilhelm); *Der Kampfgegen Berlin* (Reichmann)
1926   *Spitzen (Der Ei des Fürsten Ulrich)* (Holger-Madsen); *Brennende Grenze* (Waschneck); *Liebeshandel* (Speyer)
1927   *Die Tragödie eines Verlorenen* (Steinhoff); *Da hält die Welt den Aten an (Maquillage)* (Basch) (co); *Mata Hari (Die rote Tanzerin)* (Feher); *Regine, die Tragödie einer Frau* (Waschneck)
1928   *Die Carmen von St. Pauli* (Waschneck); *Moulin Rouge* (Dupont); *Piccadilly* (Dupont)
1929   *Der Günstling von Schönbrunn* (Waschneck and Reichmann); *Ich lebe für dich (Triumph des Lebens)* (Dieterle); *Die Drei um Edith* (Waschneck)
1930   *Two Worlds* (Dupont); *Cape Forlorn (The Love Storm)* (Dupont)
1931   *Salto mortale (The Circus of Sin)* (Dupont); *Marius* (A. Korda); *Die Nächte von Port Said* (Mittler)
1932   *Teilnehmer antwortet nicht* (Katscher and Sorkin); *Acht Mädels im Boot* (Waschneck); *After the Ball* (Rosmer); *Service for*

Ladies (*Reserved for Ladies*) (A. Korda); *The Midshipman* (de Courville); **Fanny** (Allégret)

1933 *The Good Companions* (Saville); *Sleeping Car* (Litvak); *Waltz Time* (Thiele); *Orders Is Orders* (Forde); *Britannia of Billingsgate* (Hill); *The Ghoul* (Hunter); *I Was a Spy* (Saville); *The Fire Raisers* (Powell); *Just Smith* (Walls); *Channel Crossing* (Rosmer); *A Cuckoo in the Nest* (Walls); *Friday the Thirteenth* (Saville) (co); *Turkey Time* (Walls); *Waltzes from Vienna* (*Strauss's Great Waltz*) (Hitchcock)

1934 *Jack Ahoy!* (Forde); *Red Ensign* (*Strike!*) (Powell); *The Night of the Party* (*The Murder Party*) (Powell); *Evergreen* (Saville); *A Cup of Kindness* (Walls); *Wild Boy* (de Courville); *My Song for You* (Elvey); *Little Friend* (Viertel); *Evensong* (Saville); *Jew Süss* (*Power*) (Mendes); *Lady in Danger* (Walls); *Road House* (Elvey); *The Iron Duke* (Saville); *Dirty Work* (Walls); *The Man Who Knew Too Much* (Hitchcock)

1935 *Bulldog Jack* (Forde); *The Clairvoyant* (Elvey); *Brown on Revolution* (*Forever England*; *Born for Glory*) (Forde); *Me and Marlborough* (Saville); *Car of Dreams* (Cutts and Melford); *The Guv'nor* (*Mister Hobo*) (Rosmer)

1936 *It's Love Again* (Saville); *His Lordship* (Mason); *Everything Is Thunder* (Rosmer); **Cesar** (Pagnol)

1937 *Head over Heels* (Hale); *King Solomon's Mines* (Stevenson); *Gangway* (Hale); *Young and Innocent* (*The Girl Was Young*) (Hitchcock)

1938 *Sailing Along* (Hale); *Climbing High* (Reed); *The Citadel* (K. Vidor) (co)

1939 *The Mind of Mr. Reeder* (Raymond); *Goodbye, Mr. Chips* (Wood)

1940 *Contraband* (Powell) (co); *Gaslight* (*Angel Street*) (Dickinson) (supervisor); *Busman's Honeymoon* (*Haunted Honeymoon*) (Woods)

1941 *He Found a Star* (Carstairs)

1942 **The Life and Death of Colonel Blimp** (*Colonel Blimp*) (Powell and Pressburger)

1943 *The Silver Fleet* (Sewell and Wellesley); *The Volunteer* (Powell and Pressburger—short)

1944 *A Canterbury Tale* (Powell and Pressburger)

1945 *I Know Where I'm Going!* (Powell and Pressburger)

1946 **A Matter of Life and Death** (*Stairway to Heaven*) (Powell and Pressburger)

1947 **Black Narcissus** (Powell and Pressburger)

1948 *Edward, My Son* (Cukor)

1949 *Conspirator* (Saville)

1950 *The Miniver Story* (Potter)

1951 *Calling Bulldog Drummond* (Saville); *Ivanhoe* (Thorpe)

1952 *The Hour of 13* (French); *Time Bomb* (*Terror on a Train*) (Tetzlaff)

1953 *Never Let Me Go* (Daves); *Mogambo* (Ford); *Knights of the Round Table* (Thorpe) (co)

1954 *The Flame and the Flesh* (Brooks); *Betrayed* (Reinhardt); *Seagulls over Sorrento* (*Crest of the Wave*) (J. & R. Boulting); *Beau Brummell* (Bernhardt); *Bedevilled* (Leisen); *Invitation to the Dance* (Kelly) (co)

1955 *That Lady* (Young) (uncredited); *The Adventures of Quentin Durward* (*Quentin Durward*) (Thorpe)

1956 *The Barretts of Wimpole Street* (Franklin)

1957 *A Farewell to Arms* (C. Vidor)

Publications

By JUNGE: article—

''The Art Director and His Work,'' in *Artist* (London), May-June 1944.

On JUNGE: articles—

Carrick, Edward, in *Art and Design in the British Film*, London, 1948. *Film Dope* (Nottingham), December 1983.

* * *

Before settling in England permanently in 1932, set designer Alfred Junge had established a reputation through his work in German cinema for superb technical skill. His background as a painter, costume designer, lighting technician, and set builder in theater and, later, as a designer for UFA and other German film companies had given him an excellent, broad background on which he based a wide interpretation of the importance and influence of design in film art. Junge's vast output of work for various British film companies after 1932 and, in particular, his work for MGM rested on his considerable managerial skill in overseeing the many complex and interrelated aspects of the film's appearance.

Junge's personal artistic flair is apparent in his set design drawings, often done in wash, which show a draftsmanship of great delicacy and charm. His drawing style was fluid and immediate and yet had a sparseness of composition and an atmospheric lightness. This economy of means, using a few carefully selected details to convey an appropriate atmosphere, was translated directly to the screen in Junge's best work, such as the staircase setting used in *A Matter of Life and Death*. Here, an essentially fantastic narrative is given credibility by a setting which is at once ephemeral in its spatial relations and highly concrete in its structure and detailing.

During the 1930s, Junge was in charge of all art direction for Michael Balcon at his Lime Grove Studios in Shepherds Bush. There, he became the first supervising art director in the British film industry. Junge worked on Hitchcock's *Young and Innocent*, *Waltzes from Vienna*, and his first version of *The Man Who Knew Too Much*, but met with only mixed success. Junge's greatest collaboration was with Michael Powell and Emeric Pressburger. Beginning with *The Life and Death of Colonel Blimp*, Junge's work for Powell and Pressburger generated some of the most memorable images of England and Empire. In *Goodbye, Mr. Chips*, directed by Sam Wood, Junge used combinations of some of the largest sets built for a British film up to that time with glass shots to evoke what is still a standard view of English public school life. Junge's versatility is apparent in *Black Narcissus*, which won an Academy Award for both Art Direction and Set Decoration. In this film Junge convincingly recreated the exotic interiors and exteriors of an Indian palace, all in the studio, and in the new medium of Technicolor.

Junge had worked with color since *Colonel Blimp*, the first British color film. But it was with *A Matter of Life and Death* that color became a mature tool in the exploration of the poetic potential of a narrative. Junge was required to produce sets in black-and-white for the hereafter sequences and color to describe the world of the living. Thus, design in color became an essential element in the fabric of the film.

From his early work under the direction of Dupont through his Hitchcock films, the collaboration with Powell and Pressburger, and, ultimately, his direction of MGM's art department throughout the 1950s, Junge contributed substantially to establishing the importance of design in British cinema. Throughout his career, he strongly supported the recognition of set design as an artistic rather than a technical element of film.

—Gregory Votolato

JUSTIN, George

Producer and Production Executive. **Nationality:** American. **Born:** New York, New York, 7 July 1916. **Education:** City College of New York, B.S.S. **Family:** Married Valerie Sharaf, 1955; one daughter: Andrea Boggs (nee Justin). **Military Service:** U.S. Army Signal Corps, 1942–1946; cameraman on training films, including films on prisoners of war, glider planes, and pontoon bridges. **Career:** Test director for director George Cukor on casting for *Gone with the Wind*, 1937; cameraman and/or director on documentary and industrial films shot in the U.S. and abroad for Church World Service, International Film Foundation, and Southern Film Service, 1946–1953; instructor, New Institute for Film, Brooklyn, New York, 1951–1955; production manager, production supervisor, associate producer, and producer on television series and films/film pilots for television, including *The Doctors, Ella Raines, Registered Nurse, You Are There, The Defenders*, and *Espionage*, 1953–1962; New York–based production manager, production supervisor, associate producer, and producer on feature length motion pictures, 1954–1972; director, television series, *Top Secret*, 1955; co-producer (with Leo Kerz and Harry Belafonte), *Moonbirds*, a play by Marcel Ayme, on Broadway, 1959; Vice President, Production Management, Paramount Pictures, 1972–1975; associate producer, production supervisor, and trouble shooter on motion picture features, 1976–1978; executive production manager, Orion Pictures, supervising all film production world wide, 1979–1981; vice president, MGM, then senior vice president, production management, MGM/UA, 1981–1983; production manager, feature and television motion pictures, 1983–1989. **Address:** 85 Suffolk St., Sag Harbor, New York 1193-3434, U.S.A.

Films as Producer or Production Executive:

1954   *On the Waterfront* (Kazan) (pr manager)
1957   *A Face in the Crowd* (Kazan) (pr manager); *12 Angry Men* (Lumet) (assoc pr)
1958   *Wind Across the Everglades* (Ray) (pr manager); *The Goddess* (Cromwell) (pr supervisor)
1959   *The Fugitive Kind* (Lumet) (assoc pr); *Happy Anniversary* (Miller) (assoc pr); *Middle of the Night* (Mann) (pr); *The Defenders* (Powell—for TV) (pr)
1961   *The Young Doctors* (Karlson) (pr manager); *Something Wild* (Garfein) (pr)
1962   *Long Day's Journey Into Night* (Lumet) (pr manager)
1963   *Espionage* (Powell—13 films for TV) (pr)
1965   *Inside Daisy Clover* (Mulligan) (pr manager)
1967   *Up the Down Staircase* (Mulligan) (pr manager); *The Graduate* (Nichols) (pr supervisor); *The Tiger Makes Out* (Hiller) (pr)

1968   *The Night They Raided Minsky's* (*The Night They Invented Striptease*) (Friedkin) (pr manager)
1970   *The Owl and the Pussycat* (Ross) (pr supervisor + assoc pr); *The Possession of Joel Delaney* (Hussein) (pr supervisor)
1971   *The Anderson Tapes* (Lumet) (assoc pr + ro as waiter/double agent)
1976   *Marathon Man* (Schlesinger) (pr manager + assoc pr)
1977   *The Deep* (Yates) (pr manager + assoc pr)
1978   *The Eyes of Laura Mars* (Kershner) (pr exec)
1981   *Rollover* (Pakula) (pr exec); *Wolfen* (Wadleigh) (pr exec)
1984   *No Small Affair* (Schatzberg) (exec pr)
1985   *Murphy's Romance* (Ritt—for TV) (assoc pr)
1986   *Dreams of Gold: The Mel Fisher Story* (Goldstone—for TV) (pr manager)
1987   *Deadly Illusion* (*Love You to Death*) (Cohen & Tannen) (pr manager)
1990   *Incident at Lincoln Bluff* (*The Incident*) (Sargent) (pr exec)
1994   *Star Struck* (Drake—for TV) (unit pr manager)

Other Films:

1974   *Chinatown* (ro as barber)
1975   *Shampoo* (ro as producer)

Publications

On JUSTIN: articles—

Zunser, Jesse, "Hollywood-On-Hudson," in *Cue*, 29 August 1959.
Pitman, Jack, "NY Production Helping & Hurting," in *Variety*, 1 November 1961.
Thompson, Howard, "George Justin: Local Movie Man On Our Town," in *New York Times*, 26 November 1961.
"George Justin Gets PAR Veepee Stripes," in *Variety*, 28 March 1973.
"Orion Gives Justin His Veepee Stripes," in *Variety*, 31 March 1980.
"Justin VP Production Management at MGM," in *The Hollywood Reporter*, 11 August 1981.

*   *   *

George Justin played a key role in the ferment that was New York based filmmaking in the 1950s and 1960s. Justin was one of a number of figures who emerged out of the industrial and documentary film background that WWII had fostered and into an era of new possibilities in the New York of the early 1950s, which could be defined by its differences from the industrial conditions of the Hollywood studios, whose empires were declining. When directors like Elia Kazan, at the peak of his prestige but estranged from Hollywood, and up-and-coming Sidney Lumet turned to New York City as a possible production base, they found an array of talent and enthusiasm among individuals who had learned their crafts abroad (cinematographers Boris Kaufman and Eugen Schüfftan, for example), in the field of documentary and news, in radio and theater, and in the open, inventive atmosphere of the new medium of television production.

As production manager, supervisor, associate producer, and producer, Justin corralled much of this talent into a so-called "first team"—crews that lent a spirit of independence, energy, and innovation to watershed films like *On the Waterfront, 12 Angry Men*, and

The Goddess. Justin developed a reputation for assembling crews of consummate professionals and keeping films on schedule and budget with good-spirited control. The soundstages on which productions he supervised were shot were hung with his banner, ''Keep 'em in the East,'' rallying for the New York cause. His daily call sheets, ''Letters to the Troops,'' reflected his gift for management through a refined combination of discipline, organization, and humor. Many films for television were made in the same crucible as features during the ''golden age of television.'' Justin worked on a number of those productions, too, in New York (e.g. *The Doctors, You Are There, The Defenders*) and in Europe (*Espionage*), with prominent directors including Lumet and Michael Powell.

Justin's reputation garnered him offers from Los Angeles and he became part of the so-called Hollywood Renaissance as Vice President for Production Management at Paramount. During Justin's Justin's tenure there (1972–1975), Paramount released, among many other films, Francis Ford Coppola's *The Conversation* and *The Godfather*, Robert Altman's *Nashville*, Peter Bogdonavich's *Paper Moon*, Woody Allen's *Play it Again, Sam*, and Roman Polanski's

Chinatown, in the last of which Justin appeared as the gravelly voiced barber who tells an off-color joke to Jake Gittes (Jack Nicholson). One of Justin's other notable appearances as an actor was rather a bit of type-casting: he played a producer in *Shampoo* (1975). From 1976 to 1978 Justin worked as associate producer on films in production and development at Columbia Pictures, then worked as Executive Production Manager at Orion Pictures, supervising worldwide productions. Justin's last studio affiliation was with MGM, for which he served as Vice President, then was promoted to Senior Vice President, Production Management for worldwide production for MGM/UA. Justin, who loved working on location and never tired of the creative energy of the movie set, left the desks of executive office buildings to resume, in 1983, freelance work in production management. Though not a household name, his will remain indelibly attached to the slew of powerful New York films that he ''enabled'' in the first two decades of his career.

—Susan Felleman

K

KAHN, Gus

Lyricist. **Nationality:** Russian. **Born:** Koblenz, Germany, 6 November, 1886. **Career:** Vaudeville; Tin Pan Alley; Broadway; 1927–1930—served on the board of directors of ASCAP (American Society of Composers, Authors and Publishers); 1933—began working in the film industry as lyricist. **Award:** Academy Award for *One Night of Love*, 1934. **Died:** Of a heart attack, in California, 8 October 1941.

Films as Lyricist:

1927	*The Jazz Singer* (Crosland)
1928	*Hit of the Show*
1930	*Whoopee!* (Freeland)
1932	*Big City Blues* (LeRoy)
1933	*Flying Down to Rio* (Freeland); *Storm at Daybreak* (Boleslawski)
1934	*Bottoms Up* (Butler); *Caravan* (Charell); *Hollywood Party*; *Kid Millions* (Del Ruth); *The Merry Widow* (*The Lady Dances*) (Lubitsch); *One Night of Love* (Schertzinger); *Stingaree* (Wellman)
1935	*Escapade* (Leonard); *Love Me Forever* (Schertzinger); *Naughty Marietta* (Van Dyke); *Reckless* (Fleming); *Thanks a Million* (Del Ruth)
1936	*Let's Sing Again*; *Rose Marie* (*Indian Love Call*) (Van Dyke); *San Francisco* (Van Dyke); *Three Smart Girls* (Koster)
1937	*Captains Courageous* (Fleming); *A Day at the Races* (Wood); *The Firefly* (Leonard); *Music for Madame* (Blystone)
1938	*Everybody Sing* (Marin); *The Girl of the Golden West* (Leonard)
1939	*Balalaika* (Schunzel); *Broadway Serenade* (Leonard); *Honolulu* (Buzzell); *Let Freedom Ring* (Conway)
1940	*Bitter Sweet* (Van Dyke); *Go West* (*Marx Brothers Go West*) (Buzzell); *Lillian Russell* (Cummings); *Spring Parade* (Koster)
1941	*The Chocolate Soldier* (Del Ruth); *Ziegfeld Girl* (Leonard)
1944	*Broadway Rhythm* (Del Ruth); *Show Business* (Marin)

*   *   *

When the film industry learned to talk, it was evident it would also have to sing. While technicians struggled with the technology of sound recording, recruiters turned frantically to Broadway for talent; Irving Berlin, Busby Berkeley, Al Jolson, Fanny Brice, the Gershwins, and many others were obtained to give voice and form to the musical motion picture. The frenzy that ensued has never been fully documented by film historians, and one such talent overlooked during the period was lyricist Gus Kahn. Working initially in Tin Pan Alley and later on Broadway, Kahn entered the industry in 1933. For eight years, until his death in 1941, he worked prolifically as lyricist for many of the major studios. Spanning the 1920s and 1930s, his work expressed both the capricious energy of the Jazz Age and the forlorn escapism of the Depression. Though he remained largely unknown to the public, his lyrics were linked to many of the great musical talents of the era, most notably Al Jolson, Eddie Cantor and Jeanette McDonald.

A native of Koblenz, Germany, Gus Kahn emigrated to the United States with his family in 1890. His career as lyricist began in earnest with the success of "I Wish I Had a Girl," written in 1908 with composer (and future wife) Grace LeBoy. In 1915, he wrote the hit song "Memories" with Egbert van Alstyne, and later in 1921, they provided "Pretty Baby," for Al Jolson. Shortly afterwards, Kahn moved to New York and began a productive partnership with composer Walter Donaldson, releasing such hit songs as "Carolina in the Morning," "Yes Sir, That's My Baby," and "My Sweetie Turned Me Down." In 1927, in *The Jazz Singer*, Kahn's lyrics to the peppy, effervescent "Toot, Toot Tootsie" ("Watch for the mail / I'll never fail / If you don't get a letter / Then you'll know I'm in jail") were given wonderful treatment by Al Jolson's high-energy vocalizations.

In 1928 Kahn and Donaldson wrote *Whoopee!*, their only score for Broadway. Produced by Flo Ziegfeld and starring comedian Eddie Cantor, the play was an immediate box office success. It ran for 379 performances and launched Cantor's career. Most notable are Kahn's lyrics to the title song: "The Choir sings 'Here comes the Bride' / Another victim is by her side / He's lost his reason / Cause it's the season / For makin' whoopee"—a sly, witty little number made famous by Cantor's dead-pan delivery. In 1930 MGM produced the film version with replacement songs from Kahn and Donaldson, including the memorable "My Baby Just Cares for Me." Cantor repeated his role. The film's music numbers were choreographed by Busby Berkeley (his first for Hollywood), and the entire project was shot in the early 2-color Technicolor process. A static and stilted film, the energy—what there is of it—is derived largely from the music.

Despite the growing relationship between Broadway and the film industry, Kahn, out of reticence, remained distant from Hollywood. However in the early 1930s a combination of financial need and ill health brought Kahn to California. And it was here, in 1933, that he undertook full-time employment in the industry. His first project was *Flying Down to Rio* (1933), notable for the first-ever pairing of Fred Astaire and Ginger Rogers. Kahn provided lyrics for the title song, "Orchids in the Moonlight," and the energetic "Carioca."

He resumed his collaboration with Donaldson for the Eddie Cantor vehicle *Kid Millions* (1934), writing the suitably loud "An Earful of Music" for Ethel Merman and Cantor's hopeful, anti-Depression hit "When My Ship Comes In." Released at the height of the recession, "When My Ship Comes In" was indicative of Hollywood's attempt to distract audiences with fancy: "I'll buy out every ice-cream factory / So all the kids can come and get in free / And I'll throw all the spinach in the sea / When my ship comes in.''

During his stay in Hollywood, Kahn had many collaborators; he worked with such composers as Vincent Youmans, Bronislaw Kaper, Sigmund Romberg and Jerome Kern, and penned lyrics for the Marx Brothers, Maurice Chevalier, Nelson Eddy, Dick Powell and Jeanette McDonald. It was for McDonald (with Kaper as composer) that he wrote ''San Francisco,'' the title song to the 1936 film which has since become the unofficial anthem of the city.

Though many of Kahn's lyrics are noted for their comic vibrancy, he was also a proficient writer of romantic operetta songs. In 1934, Kahn's delicious, whimsical score for *One Night of Love*, a film for which he provided thematic music and title song, earned him his only Academy Award. He wrote the lovely lyrics to Jeanette McDonald's ''Tonight Will Teach Me to Forget'' number from Lubitsch's *The Merry Widow* and worked on several other MGM operettas, including *Naughty Marietta* (1935), *Rose Marie* (1936) and *The Firefly* (1937).

In 1941 Kahn died suddenly of a heart attack. A consummate lyricist, his death marked the end of one of the busiest and most productive careers in popular songwriting. In 1952 MGM produced *I'll See You in My Dreams*, a biopic based on Kahn's life, with Danny Thomas as Kahn, Doris Day as LeBoy, and Michael Curtiz directing. Featuring many of Kahn's greatest songs, the film traced the inimitable success of a man who conveyed in popular, colloquial terms the simple (and oftentimes humorous) feelings of love, patriotism and the desire for something better.

—Peter Flynn

KAMINSKI, Janusz

Cinematographer. **Nationality:** Polish. **Born:** Ziembice, Poland, 27 June 1959; moved to U.S., 1981. **Education:** Columbia College, B.A., 1987; American Film Institute, Cinematography Fellow. **Family:** Married actress Holly Hunter, 1995. **Career:** Debut as cinematographer at AFI, *Lisa*, 1988; began association with Steven Spielberg when hired to work on *Class of '61*, TV movie, 1990; earned international acclaim for work on *Schindler's List*, 1993; directorial debut, *Lost Souls*, 1999. **Awards:** Line Eagel Award, Illinois Film Festival, for *Lisa*, 1988; Academy Award for Best Cinematography, National Society of Film Critics Award for Best Cinematography, New York Film Critics Circle Award for Best Cinematography, Los Angeles Film Critics Award for Best Cinematography, BAFTA Award (UK) for Best Cinematography, British Society of Cinematographers Award for Best Cinematography, and Chicago Film Critics Association Award for Best Cinematography, all for *Schindler's List*, 1993; Golden Satellite Award for Best Cinematography, for *Amistad*, 1997; Academy Award for Best Cinematography, Boston Society of Film Critics Award for Best Cinematography, Los Angeles Film Critics Award for Best Cinematography, and Florida Film Critics Circle Award for Best Cinematography, for *Saving Private Ryan*, 1998. **Address:** c/o American Society of Cinematographers, P.O. Box 2230, Hollywood, CA 90078, U.S.A.

Janusz Kaminski

Films as Cinematographer:

1990   *The Rain Killer* (Stein); *The Terror Within II* (Stevens)
1991   *Pyrates* (Stern); *Cool As Ice* (Kellogg); *Wildflower* (Keaton—for TV)
1992   *Trouble Bound* (Reiner); *Killer Instinct* (Clark and Stein); *Class of '61* (Hoblit—for TV)
1993   *Schindler's List* (Spielberg); *Adventures of Huck Finn* (Sommers)
1994   *Tall Tale* (Checkik); *Little Giants* (Dunham)
1995   *How to Make an American Quilt* (Moorhouse)
1996   *Jerry Maguire* (Crowe); *Amistad* (Spielberg)
1997   *The Lost World: Jurassic Park II* (Spielberg)
1998   *Saving Private Ryan* (Spielberg)
2001   *A. I.*; *Memoirs of a Geisha*

Other Films:

1990   *Watchers II* (Notz) (second ph)
1990   *To Die Standing* (Morneau) (second ph)
1991   *One False Move* (Franklin) (second ph)

1998   *Armageddon* (Bay) (second ph)
2000   *Lost Souls* (d)

Publications

On KAMINSKI: articles—

"Schindler's List," in *American Cinematographer* (Hollywood), January 1994.
"Chase, Crush and Devour," in *American Cinematographer* (Hollywood), June 1997.
Probst, Christopher, "The Last Great War," in *American Cinematographer* (Hollywood), August, 1998.

*   *   *

Janusz Kaminski became an international sensation for his work on Steven Spielberg's 1993 Nazi Holocaust tale, *Schindler's List*. The film earned Kaminski seven awards for Best Cinematography, including his first Academy Award. The two men met in 1990, after Spielberg saw Kaminski's work in Diane Keaton's television movie *Wildflower* and hired him to shoot *Class of '61*. Since that time, the successful collaboration between director Spielberg and cinematographer Kaminski has produced four major motion pictures, two highly honored.

A native of Poland, Kaminski moved to the United States in 1981 and began his education at Columbia College in Chicago, where he received his B.A. in film in 1987. His skills led him to Los Angeles, where he was granted a position as a Cinematography Fellow at the prestigious American Film Institute. From the beginning, Kaminski's cinematography was lauded. His debut work, *Lisa* (1988), won the Line Eagel Award at the Illinois Film Festival. A year later, his association with Spielberg began.

While not new to the role of director of photography (having shot seven films by 1993), the experience garnered on *Class of '61* was obviously pivotal in Kaminski's career. The following year, the enormously successful *Schindler's List* was released. It was immediately acclaimed for its elegant black and white photography. Kaminski used a high speed film stock to create a look which was reminiscent of documentary work, thus enhancing the feeling of realness in the film. The cinematography in *Schindler's List* was intensely fine-grained, had great detail, and seemed archival rather than concocted.

He worked on five more films before he collaborated again with Spielberg in 1997's *Amistad*. This film, and the one that followed, Spielberg's *The Lost World: Jurassic Park II*, were less successful, both critically and at the box office. When Spielberg turned again to the World War II era as a setting, he brought Kaminski into the project. *Saving Private Ryan* (1998) explored the invasion of Normandy in a way that no film had done before. The two men studied original film shot by the Army Signal Corps as well as combat photographs from the era to develop an accurate depiction of the 1944 battle. Kaminski used several experimental techniques which are rarely seen in narrative film.

To re-create the essence of the battle and the style of filmmaking done in combat situations, Kaminski first located some old lenses from the era. He had Panavision remove the coatings on them to replicate the way light was transmitted in the 1940s. This weathering of the lenses made light bounce around inside the barrels, causing flares and automatically diffusing the light. The result was images that seemed foggy rather than the clear transmission we are used to today. A combination of coated Ultraspeeds and these deteriorated lenses was used in the film. This technique, coupled with an aggressive use of a variety of frame rates to create slow and fast motion, brought the gritty look of battle to the images photographed.

In addition to these experiments, Kaminski also made use of the camera's shutter to best capture the battle scenes. The crew frequently shot with the shutter set at 45 or 90 degrees to change the appearance of motion in the image. This meant that the explosions shot with a 45 degree shutter seemed hyper-realistic; individual grains of sand seem to fly at the lens and minute details are extremely apparent. Kaminski also employed an out-of sync shutter to create the strange effect of light streaks in the film in some scenes. The film earned Kaminski four major awards for best cinematography.

Kaminski is obviously a gifted artist with a great interest in using experimental techniques to create highly specialized concepts in his photography.

—Tammy Kinsey

KANIN, Garson

Writer and Director. **Nationality:** American. **Born:** Rochester, New York, 24 November 1912. **Education:** Left school at age 15; later attended the American Academy of Dramatic Arts, New York. **Military Service:** U.S. Army Signal Corps, 1941–42: private; served in the Air Force, 1942–43, and the Office of Strategic Services, 1943–45; captain, on staff of SHAEF (European Theater Operations); made documentaries for the Office of Emergency Management. **Family:** Married the actress and writer Ruth Gordon, 1942 (died 1985). **Career:** 1929–32—jazz musician, Western Union messenger, stock boy and advertising proofreader at Macy's, New York; burlesque comedian, and summer camp social director; 1933—Broadway debut as actor; 1935–37—assistant to the Broadway director George Abbott; then freelance producer and director for the stage; 1938–41—director, RKO: first film, *A Man to Remember*; 1946—first play produced, *Born Yesterday*; 1947—first of several screenplays in collaboration with Ruth Gordon, *A Double Life*; 1955—first novel published, *Do Re Mi*; 1967—formed Kanin Productions; also wrote for TV. **Awards:** Academy Award, for *The True Glory*, 1945. **Died:** Of heart failure, 13 March 1999, in New York, NY.

Films as Director:

1938   *A Man to Remember*; *Next Time I Marry*
1939   *The Great Man Votes*; *Bachelor Mother* (+ ro)
1940   *My Favorite Wife*; *They Knew What They Wanted*
1941   *Tom, Dick, and Harry*
1942   *Night Shift* (doc); *Ring of Steel* (doc); *Fellow Americans* (doc)

Garson Kanin (center) with Ruth Gordon and Ronald Colman

1943   *German Manpower* (doc)
1944   *Night Stripes* (doc); *A Salute to France* (co-d with Renoir—
            doc); *Battle Stations* (doc)
1945   *The True Glory* (co-d with Reed—doc)
1946   *Salute to France* (co-d with Renoir)

Films as Writer:

1946   *From This Day Forward* (Berry)
1947   *A Double Life* (Cukor) (with Ruth Gordon)
1949   ***Adam's Rib*** (Cukor) (with Ruth Gordon)
1952   *The Marrying Kind* (Cukor) (with Ruth Gordon); *Pat and
            Mike* (Cukor) (with Ruth Gordon)
1953   *It Should Happen to You* (Cukor)
1956   *Born Yesterday* (+ co-d)
1960   *The Rat Race* (Mulligan); *High Time* (Edwards)
1964   *An Eye on Emily* (+ d)
1968   *Where It's At* (+ d)
1969   *Some Kind of Nut* (+ d)

1980   *Hardhat and Legs* (Philips—for TV); *The Year's Blonde*
            (Erman—for TV); *The Scarlett O'Hara War* (Erman—for
            TV); *The Silent Lovers* (Erman—for TV)
1993   *Born Yesterday* (Mandoki) (co-sc)

Films Based on Kanin's Writings:

1956   *The Girl Can't Help It* (Tashlin)
1961   *The Right Approach* (Butler)

Publications

By KANIN: plays—

Born Yesterday, New York, 1946.
The Smile of the World, New York, 1949.

Fledermaus, New York, 1950.
The Rat Race, New York, 1950.
The Live Wire, New York, 1951.
A Gift of Time, New York, 1962.
Come On Strong, New York, 1964.

By KANIN: fiction—

Do Re Mi, New York, 1955.
Blow Up a Storm, New York, 1959.
The Rat Race, New York, 1960.
A Cast of Characters, New York, 1969.
Where It's At, New York, 1969.
A Thousand Summers, New York, 1973.
One Hell of an Actor, New York, 1976.
Smash, New York, 1980.
Cordelia?, New York, 1982.

By KANIN: other books—

Remembering Mr. Maugham, New York, 1966.
Tracy and Hepburn (nonfiction), New York, 1971.
With Ruth Gordon, *Adam's Rib* (script), New York, 1972.
Hollywood (nonfiction), New York, 1974.
It Takes a Long Time to Become Young, New York, 1978.
Together Again, New York, 1981.

By KANIN: articles—

Interview with Penelope Houston and John Gillett, in *Sight and Sound* (London), Summer 1972.
Focus on Film (London), Spring 1974.
Film Comment (New York), July/August 1978.

On KANIN: book—

Krautz, Alfred, *Encyclopedia of Film Directors in the United States & Europe: Comedy Films to 1991*, Munchen, 1993.

On KANIN: articles—

Houston, Penelope, "Cukor and the Kanins," in *Sight and Sound* (London), Spring 1955.
Films in Review (New York), December 1964.
Film Comment (New York), Winter 1970–71.
National Film Theatre Booklet (London), April/May 1972.
Monthly Film Bulletin (London), September 1972, additions in January and February 1973.
Films in Review (New York), November 1974.
American Film (Washington, D.C.), March 1976.
Film Dope (Nottingham), March 1984.
Architectural Digest (Los Angeles), April 1990.
Iskusstvo Kino (Moscow), May 1994.
Obituary, in *Variety* (New York), 22 March 1999.
Obituary, in *Opera News*, July 1999.

*   *   *

Garson Kanin appears in this volume principally for his work as a screenwriter, but his contributions to American popular arts and letters, a number of them uncredited, were in a variety of genres and forums. He acted on the stage and in radio and wrote and directed for stage, screen, and television. He published novels, biographies, memoirs, and an extensive array of short fiction in magazines that run the gamut from *Atlantic Monthly* to *Penthouse*. As an actor in the 1930s, he appeared in several Broadway plays and in radio roles on programs ranging from the high-toned *March of Time* and *Theatre Guild on the Air* to the soap operatic *Aunt Jennie's Real Life Stories* and *The Goldbergs*.

Influenced by his work as production assistant to the legendary Broadway director George Abbott, Kanin began to direct plays in New York, mostly road company versions of Abbott productions. He joined Samuel Goldwyn's production staff in 1937, an inauspicious association that lasted only a year, but which led to a contract with RKO, where between 1938 and 1941 he directed seven pictures featuring such major stars as Ginger Rogers (*Bachelor Mother* and *Tom, Dick, and Harry*), Cary Grant and Irene Dunne (*My Favorite Wife*), and Carole Lombard and Charles Laughton (*They Knew What They Wanted*). Kanin also directed a group of films for the war effort after being drafted into the army. One of them, *The True Glory*, won an Oscar as best documentary for 1945.

Although he had made uncredited contributions to the screenplays for *Bachelor Mother*, which he directed, the Hepburn-Tracy *Woman of the Year*, and Jean Arthur's *The More the Merrier* Kanin was known primarily as a director until he wrote (and also directed) the Broadway play *Born Yesterday* (1946)—and until he and his wife, actress-writer Ruth Gordon, collaborated on a series of four memorable screenplays. Those screenplays are certain to stand as the pair's enduring legacy to American film. Two of them—*Adam's Rib* and *Pat and Mike*—were written for Katharine Hepburn and Spencer Tracy, whose contrasting elegance and gruffness provide the comic center around which each script's situations and dialogue sparkle. Both films (such as the two other Kanin Gordon scripts, *A Double Life* and *The Marrying Kind*) were directed by George Cukor and in them Cukor, Kanin, Gordon, Tracy, and Hepburn Americanized the Restoration comedy of manners.

Kanin boasts that neither he nor his late wife was "ever employed as a screenwriter for so much as a day by any studio in Hollywood," ever aware that a Hollywood contract "was the closest form of slavery in our time." Their scripts were therefore written on speculation in the east, and then offered for sale. "Some, we sold."

—Mark W. Estrin

KAPER, Bronislau

Composer. **Nationality:** Polish. **Born:** Warsaw, 5 February 1902; given name also spelled Bronislaw. **Education:** Attended Warsaw Conservatory. **Career:** Composer and pianist in Warsaw, Berlin, Vienna, London, and Paris; 1930—scored first of several German films; 1933—left Germany with rise of Nazis, and went via France to the U.S.A.; 1935—worked in Hollywood, often with lyricist Gus Cahn; 1940—began long-term contract with MGM. **Award:** Academy Award for *Lili*, 1953. **Died:** 25 April 1983.

Films as Composer:

1930 *Der Korvettenkapitän* (Walther-Fein) (co); *Alraune* (Oswald)
1931 *Die grosse Attraktion* (Reichmann)
1932 *Melodie der Liebe* (Jacoby); *Es wird schon wieder besser* (Gerron); *Ein toller Einfall* (Gerron); *Hochzeitsreise zu Dritt* (Schmidt)
1933 *Ein Lied für Dich* (May); *Heut' kommt's drauf an* (Gerron); *Madame wünscht keine Kinder* (Steinhoff)
1934 *On a volé un homme* (Ophüls) (co)
1935 *Escapade* (Leonard) (co); *The Perfect Gentleman* (Whelan); *Mutiny on the Bounty* (Lloyd); *The Last of the Pagans* (Thorpe); *A Night at the Opera* (Wood) (songs); *San Francisco* (Van Dyke) (song)
1937 *Three Smart Girls* (Koster); *A Day at the Races* (Wood) (songs)
1938 *Everybody Sing* (Marin)
1940 *Lilian Russell* (Cummings) (songs); *I Take This Woman* (Van Dyke); *The Mortal Storm* (Borzage); *The Captain Is a Lady* (Sinclair); *We Who Are Young* (Bucquet); *Dulcy* (Simon); *Comrade X* (K. Vidor)
1941 *Go West* (Buzzell); *Blonde Inspiration* (Berkeley); *Rage in Heaven* (Van Dyke); *I'll Wait for You* (Sinclair); *Barnacle Bill* (Thorpe); *Whistling in the Dark* (Simon); *Dr. Kildare's Wedding Day* (Bucquet); *When Ladies Meet* (Leonard); *The Chocolate Soldier* (Del Ruth) (co); *Johnny Eager* (LeRoy); *H.M. Pulham, Esquire* (K. Vidor); *A Woman's Face* (Cukor); *Two-Faced Woman* (Cukor)
1942 *We Were Dancing* (Leonard); *Crossroads* (Conway); *Fingers at the Window* (Lederer); *The Affairs of Martha* (Dassin); *Somewhere I'll Find You* (Ruggles); *A Yank at Eton* (Taurog); *White Cargo* (Thorpe)
1943 *Slightly Dangerous* (Ruggles); *Above Suspicion* (Thorpe); *Bataan* (Garnett); *The Cross of Lorraine* (Garnett); *The Heavenly Body* (Hall); *Keeper of the Flame* (Cukor)
1944 *Marriage Is a Private Affair* (Leonard); *Mrs. Parkington* (Garnett); *Gaslight* (Cukor)
1945 *Without Love* (Bucquet); *Bewitched* (Oboler); *Our Vines Have Tender Grapes* (Rowland)
1946 *The Stranger* (Welles); *Three Wise Fools* (K. Vidor); *Courage of Lassie* (Wilcox); *The Secret Heart* (Leonard)
1947 *Cynthia* (*The Rich Full Life*) (Leonard); *Green Dolphin Street* (Saville); *Song of Love* (Brown)
1948 *B.F.'s Daughter* (Leonard); *Homecoming* (LeRoy); *The Secret Land* (doc); *High Wall* (Bernhardt); *Act of Violence* (Zinnemann)
1949 *The Secret Garden* (Wilcox); *That Forsyte Woman* (*The Forsyte Saga*) (Bennett); *Malaya* (Thorpe); *Key to the City* (Sidney); *The Great Sinner* (Siodmak)
1950 *The Skipper Surprised His Wife* (Nugent); *To Please a Lady* (Brown); *Grounds for Marriage* (Leonard); *Three Guys Named Mike* (Walters); *Mr. Imperium* (Hartman); *A Life of Her Own* (Cukor)
1951 *Too Young to Kiss* (Leonard); *Shadow in the Sky* (Wilcox); *Invitation* (Reinhardt); *The Red Badge of Courage* (Huston); *It's Big Country* (Weis and others)
1952 *The Wild North* (Marton)
1953 *The Actress* (Cukor); *Lili* (Walters); *The Naked Spur* (A. Mann); *Ride, Vaquero!* (Farrow); *Saadia* (Lewin); *Her Twelve Men* (Leonard)
1954 *Them!* (Douglas)
1955 *The Prodigal* (Thorpe); *Forever, Darling* (Hall); *Quentin Durward* (*The Adventures of Quentin Durward*) (Thorpe); *The Glass Slipper* (Walters)
1956 *The Swan* (C. Vidor); *The Power and the Prize* (Koster); *Somebody Up There Likes Me* (Wise); *The Barretts of Wimpole Street* (Franklin)
1957 *Jet Pilot* (Von Sternberg—produced 1950); *Don't Go Near the Water* (Walters)
1958 *Auntie Mame* (Da Costa); *The Scapegoat* (Hamer); *The Brothers Karamazov* (Brooks)
1959 *Green Mansions* (M. Ferrer); *Home from the Hill* (Minnelli)
1960 *The Angel Wore Red* (Johnson); *Butterfield 8* (Daniel Mann)
1961 *Ada* (Daniel Mann); *Two Loves* (Walters)
1962 *Mutiny on the Bounty* (Milestone)
1964 *Kisses for My President* (Bernhardt)
1965 *Lord Jim* (Brooks)
1967 *Tobruk* (Hiller); *The Way West* (McLaglen)
1968 *Counterpoint* (Nelson); *A Flea in Her Ear* (Charon)

Publications

By KAPER: articles—

Film Music Notebook (Calabasas, California), vol. 4, no. 2, 1978.
In *Film Score*, edited by Tony Thomas, South Brunswick, New Jersey, 1979.

On KAPER: articles—

Thomas, Tony, in *Music for the Movies*, South Brunswick, New Jersey, 1973.
Rivista del Cinematografo (Rome), May 1980.
Obituary, in *Variety* (New York), 4 May 1983.
Films in Review (New York), June-July 1983.
Lacombe, Alain, in *Hollywood*, Paris, 1983.
New Zealand Film Music Bulletin (Invercargill), August 1983.
Films in Review (New York), January 1989.

*   *   *

MGM's contribution to the history of film music is a large one, and the composer who spent more time with that studio than any other was Bronislau Kaper. His 26-year tenure began with the hit title song for *San Francisco* in 1936 and ended with the writing of his most ambitious score, for *Mutiny on the Bounty*, in 1962. In between came the writing of music for all manner of films but with a particular talent for deftly comedic, romantic scoring, of which his Oscar-winning *Lili*, *The Glass Slipper*, *The Swan*, and *Auntie Mame* are conspicuous examples.

Born in Warsaw in 1902, Kaper discovered an affinity with the piano at the age of seven. It was found that he could play even without instruction. Formal musical education followed and Kaper graduated from the Chopin Music School, having studied theory and composition as well as the piano. He went to Berlin to further his education and took jobs as a cabaret pianist in order to support himself. It was a time of burgeoning theatrical activity in Berlin, and Kaper became more and more a part of it as he discovered his facility for making arrangements and writing songs. With the arrival of sound on film he moved into the arranging of scores for musicals and established a solid reputation. In 1933 Kaper moved to Paris to do similar work for French film musicals. In the summer of 1935 Louis B. Mayer vacationed in Europe and heard the song on the radio everywhere. He traced the composer and invited him to his hotel in Paris. Kaper was thereupon offered an MGM contract and arrived in Los Angeles in early 1936.

For the first four years he was limited to the duties of a song writer and arranger of musicals, but his insistence on being given the opportunity to write dramatic underscoring resulted in *I Take This Woman* in 1940. It was followed by more than a hundred scores during the remainder of his years in film composition. Despite the association with romantic film fare, Kaper, again through his own insistence, proved his ability with darkly serious material, such as *Gaslight*, *The Red Badge of Courage*, *Them!*, and *Lord Jim*. Among his biggest commercial successes, in addition to *Lili*, were the themes from *Green Dolphin Street*, *Invitation*, and the title music for the long-running television series *The F.B.I.*

A man noted for his wit and charm, Kaper was active in the musical life of Los Angeles as a member of the board of the Philharmonic Orchestra. Although he never performed in public, his ability as a pianist, with music that ranged from his own to the sonatas of Clementi, was appreciated by the guests in his home. When asked if he felt that after writing film music for more than 40 years, everything had been said and done, he replied, "No. If you're excited by something, you'll come up with new ideas. How many women have you known in your life? Then along comes another and you love her. It's the same with film. All you need are a few little things and off you go again. If I were bothered by the clichés of the past, I couldn't live. Not just music. Life is also full of clichés. Don't fall for them."

—Tony Thomas

KÄSTNER, Erich

Writer. **Nationality:** German. **Born:** Dresden, Saxony, Germany, 23 February 1899. **Education:** Attended *Lehrerseminar* (teacher training school) in Dresden; attended König-Georg-Gymnasium (grammar school) in Dresden after World War I; won a scholarship to Leipzig University; awarded a doctorate for a dissertation written in French on Frederick II and German literature, 1925. **Military Service:** Served in Army during World War I. **Family:** Partner, Luiselotte Enderle, from 1939. **Career:** Published poems in *Dichtungen Leipziger Studenten* (*Poems by Leipzig Students*), 1920; worked as a bookkeeper and wrote journalism and advertising copy in 1920s; wrote extensively for the journal *Die Weltbühne*; published several novels and collections of poetry during 1930s; refused to leave Nazi Germany during World War II, and witnessed the burning of his own books on 10 May 1933; twice arrested by Gestapo and questioned about his writing; books published in Switzerland from 1933; edited magazine section of *Die neue Zeitung* (Munich newspaper), 1945–47; founded *Pinguin* (children's magazine); President of West German PEN Writers' Organization, 1952–62; cultural adviser for Munich Olympics, 1972. **Awards:** Federal Film Prize (Germany), for *Das Doppelte Lottchen*, 1950. **Died:** In Munich, Germany, 29 July 1974.

Films as Writer:

1931 *Dann schon lieber Lebertran* (*I'd Rather Have Cold Liver Oil*) (Ophüls) (co-screenwriter and story); *Emil und die Detektive* (*Emil and the Detectives*) (Lamprecht) (novel, credited as Berthold Bürger); *Die Koffer des Herrn O.F.* (*Build and Marry*, *The Thirteen Trunks of Mr. O.F.*, *The Trunks of Mr. O.F.*) (Granowsky) (lyricist)

1935 *Emil and the Detectives* (Rosmer) (novel, *Emil und die Detective*)

1936 *Stackars miljonärer* (Arvedon and Ibsen) (novel *Drei Männer im Schnee*)

1938 *Paradise for Three* (*Romance for Three*) (Buzzell) (novel *Drei Männer im Schnee*, credited as Erich Kaestner)

1943 *Münchhausen* (*The Adventures of Baron Munchausen* [USA], *Baron Munchhausen*, *The Extraordinary Adventures of Baron Muenchhausen*) (von Baky) (novel and screenplay, credited as Berthold Bürger); *Der Kleine Grenzverkehr* (Deppe) (novel)

1950 *Das Doppelte Lottchen* (*Two Times Lotte* [USA]) (von Baky) (novel, screenplay, and role as speaker)

1953 *Pünktchen und Anton* (Engel) (story); *Twice Upon a Time* (Pressburger) (novel *Das Doppelte Lottchen*)

1954 *Das Fliegende Klassenzimmer* (*The Flying Classroom* [USA]) (Hoffman) (novel and screenplay, credited as Berthold Bürger); *Emil und die Detektive* (Stemmle) (novel, credited as Berthold Bürger)

1955 *Drei Männer im Schnee* (Hoffman) (novel, credited as Berthold Bürger)

1957 *Salzburger Geschichten* (Hoffman) (novel and co-screenwriter)

1961 *The Parent Trap* (Swift) (novel *Das Doppelte Lottchen*, credited as Berthold Bürger)

1964 *Emil and the Detectives* (Tewkbury) (novel, *Emil und die Detektive*, credited as Berthold Bürger)

1969 *Konferenz der Tiere* (Linda) (novel, credited as Berthold Bürger)

1973 *Das Fliegende Klassenzimmer* (Jacobs) (novel, credited as Berthold Bürger)

1980 *Fabian* (Gremm) (novel)

1989 *Die Verschwundene Miniatur* (Loebner—for TV) (novel); *Parent Trap III* (*Parent Trap IV: Hawaiian Honeymoon*) (Miller—for TV) (novel, *Das Doppelte Lottchen*)

1993 *Charlie & Louise—Das Doppelte Lottchen* (Vilsmaier) (novel, *Das Doppelt Lottchen*)

1998 *The Parent Trap* (Meyers) (novel, *Das Doppelte Lottchen*)

1999 *Pünktchen und Anton* (*Annaluise and Anton* [USA]) (Link) (novel)

Publications:

By KÄSTNER: books—

Emil und die Detektive, Berlin, 1928 (as *Emil and the Detectives*, London, 1931, 1959).

Fabian, Die Geschichte eines Moralisten, Berlin, 1931 (as *Fabian, the Tale of a Moralist*, London, 1932).

Pünktchen und Anton, Berlin, 1931 (as *Annaluise and Anton*, London, 1932).

Emil und die drie Zwillinge, Zurich, 1934 (as *Emil and the Three Twins*, London, 1935, 1970).
Drei Männer im Schnee, Zurich, 1934 (as *Three Men in the Snow*, London, 1935).
Das Fliegende Klassenzimmer, Zurich, 1934 (as *The Flying Classroom*, London, 1934, 1967).
Die veschwundene Miniature, Zurich, 1935 (as *The Missing Miniature*, London, 1936).
Der kleine Grenzverkehr, Zurich, 1938.

On KÄSTNER: books—

Winkelmann, J., *Social Criticism in the Early Works of Erich Kästner*, Columbia, 1953.
Kästner, Erich, and Luiselotte Enderle, *Erich Kästner, Life and Work* (texts for an exhibition arranged by the Goethe-Institut, Munich), Munich, 1964.
Beutler, K., *Erich Kästner*, Berlin, 1967.
Last, R.W., *Erich Kästner*, London, 1974.

On KÄSTNER: articles—

Wiley, R.A., "The Role of the Mother in Five Pre-War Editions of Erich Kästner's Works," in *German Quarterly* (Philadelphia), 1953.
Christensen, Peter G., "The Representation of the Late Eighteenth Century in the Von Baky/Kästner *Baron Munchhausen*: The Old Regime and its Links to the Third Reich," in *German Life and Letters* (Oxford), October 1990.
Schwarzbaum, Lisa, "Girls of Wisdom," (review of *The Parent Trap*) in *Entertainment Weekly* (New York), 7 August 1998.
Murray, Giala, review of *The Parent Trap* in *Empire* (London), July 1999.

On KÄSTNER: film—

Das Große Erich Kästner Festival, 1999.

*   *   *

Best known as a writer of children's fiction, Erich Kästner was also an acclaimed poet, journalist, and the editor of several newspapers and journals. His novels have been adapted many times for the cinema in Germany and the United States, but his contribution to filmmaking also extends to work as a screenwriter and lyricist. In 1950, he even performed as the narrator of an adaptation of his novel, *Das Doppelte Lottchen*. Kästner's experiences at school and as a conscript during World War I left him antagonistic to authority and convention. His children's stories, such as *Emil und die Detektive*, in which a child bypasses the police in order to apprehend a thief, reflect his suspicion that humanity is not well served by the law and the government.

Against the advice of his friends, many of whom fled the country when Adolf Hitler and his Nazi party came to power in 1933, Kästner chose to remain in Germany, where he witnessed the burning of his books along with the works of Brecht, Joyce, and Heinrich Mann. Kästner's work was considered threatening to the Nazi cause because of its emphasis on common humanity over the artificial structures of state and government. He was twice apprehended by the Gestapo, but

Kästner continued to work, publishing novels from Zurich, Switzerland, rather than Berlin. Metro-Goldwyn-Mayer bought the film rights to several of his novels during this time. In 1942, he was even asked by Goebbels to write the script for a film, although the Nazi government refused to allow his name to appear on the credits. By way of commenting on this restriction, Kästner adopted the pseudonym of Berthold Bürger, a combination of the first name of dramatist Berthold Brecht, and the German word for "citizen." Kästner apparently suggested the life of Baron Munchhausen as the film's subject on the grounds that the "commission has come from the world's greatest liar—why not do a film about his closest competitor."

Münchhausen, directed by Josef Von Baky, was made in honor of the twenty-fifth anniversary of the famous German studio, UFA. It was filmed in Agfacolor, and contains elaborate special effects and trick photography. The luxurious banquet and street procession scenes seem all the more remarkable when it is remembered that the film was made during war-time. Kästner's script tells the involved story of Baron Münchhausen and his various adventures, including being shot on a cannonball, numerous duels, and a balloon that travels to the moon. In its original length the film ran to almost two and a half hours, but was finally reduced by about an hour. Overall the film is a great technical achievement, although the color process now seems rather crude.

Although *Münchhausen* was a great success, Kästner was soon banned from writing altogether, and it is perhaps because of this enforced silence that his greatest contribution to film is through adaptations of his novels. In particular *Emil und die Detektive* and *Das Doppelte Lottchen* continue to be of interest to filmmakers, having been filmed four and six times respectively on both sides of the Atlantic. Disney in particular picked up on the charming simplicity of Kästner's stories, producing *The Parent Trap* (based on *Das Doppelte Lottchen*) and *Emil and the Detectives* within a few years of each other in the early 1960s. More recently, in 1998, *The Parent Trap* was filmed again by Disney, and the result is if anything an improvement on the 1961 production, with a slick cast, including Dennis Quaid, Natasha Richardson, and Lindsay Lohan, carrying the breezy humour with ease. *Emil und die Detektive* has been less well served by later remakes, but Gerhard Lamprecht's 1931 adaptation of the novel is perhaps the best of the many films adapted from Kästner's work. With a script by a young Billy Wilder, this German film successfully transfers the innocent humour of the novel to the screen without seeming contrived.

Despite his reputation as a writer for children, Kästner also produced adult novels, including *Fabian*, which was adapted for the screen in 1980. Sometimes read as an archetypal existential novel, *Fabian* tells the story of a young man whose cynical view of German society leads him into a series of adulterous affairs and finally accidental death while trying to save a child from drowning. The novel's cold tone presents special difficulties for the filmmaker, and despite high production values, Wolf Gremm's adaptation is not a great success. *Drei Männer im Schnee* has similarly suffered, with its satirical edge blunted by the possibilities it offers for romantic comedy.

A prolific writer, Kästner had a practical approach to life, and seems not to have been concerned that his career as a scriptwriter should have been so quickly curtailed. The enduring success of his novels and stories in movies for adults and children is a testament to the power of his imaginative vision. It is disappointing that so many adaptations of his work have been inclined towards the sentimental, since Kästner's fiction itself conspicuously avoids romanticising human relationships.

—Chris Routledge

KAUFMAN, Boris

Cinematographer. **Nationality:** Polish. **Born:** Bialystok, 24 August 1906; **Education:** Studied at the Sorbonne, Paris. **Military Service:** 1939–41—served in the French infantry. **Family:** Brother of the directors Dziga Vertov (born Denis Kaufman) and Mikhail Kaufman; married; one son. **Career:** Left Soviet Union in early 1920s;1928— first film as cinematographer, *Champs-Elysées*; after the German occupation began, moved to New York; 1942–43—worked for National Film Board of Canada; worked for Office of War Information, New York; mid-1950s—first U.S. features as cinematographer. **Award:** Academy Award for *On the Waterfront*, 1954. **Died:** In New York City, 24 June 1980.

Films as Cinematographer (Shorts):

1928   *Champs-Elysées* (Lods); *La Marche des machines* (Deslaw); *Vingt-quatre heures en trente minutes* (Lods)
1929   *Les Halles* (Galitzine) (co)

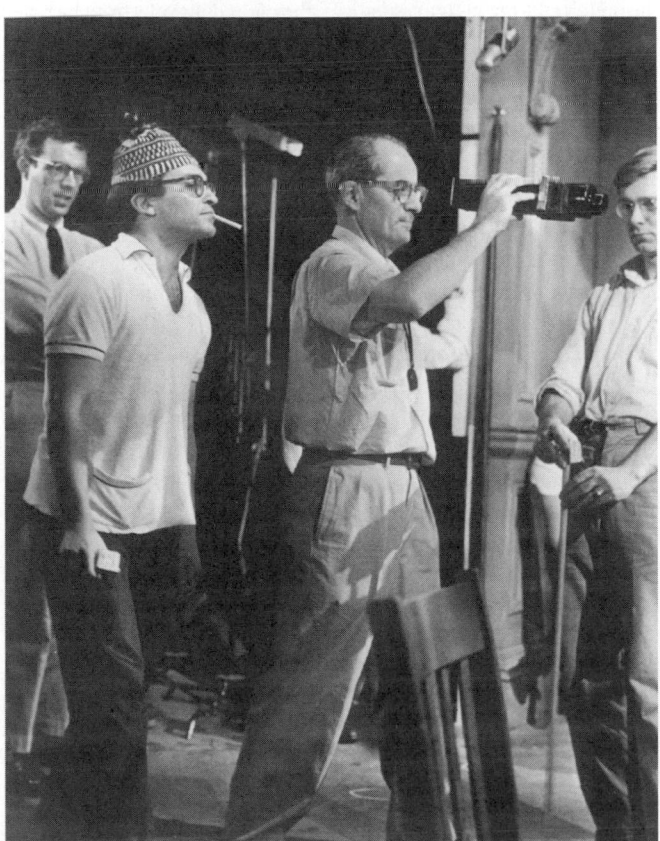

Boris Kaufman (left) with Sidney Lumet

1930   *A propos de Nice* (Vigo)
1932   *La Vie d'un fleuve: La Seine* (Lods); *Le Mile de Jules Ladoumègue* (Lods); *Traveaux du tunnel sous l'Escaut* (Storck) (co)
1933   *Zéro de conduite* (Vigo)
1945   *A Better Tomorrow* (Hackenschmied); *Toscanini, Hymn of the Nations* (Hackenschmied) (co); *Capital Story* (Rodakiewicz); *The Southwest* (*Land of Enchantment: Southwest U.S.A.*) (Rodakiewicz)
1946   *Journey into Medicine* (W. Van Dyke)
1948   *Terribly Talented* (Hackenschmied); *Osmosis* (W. Van Dyke)
1949   *The Lambertville Story*
1950   *Preface to a Life* (Resnick); *The Tanglewood Story* (*Tanglewood, Music School and Music Festival*) (Maddison)
1951   *The Gentleman in Room 6* (Hackenschmied)
1953   *And the Earth Shall Give Back Life* (Jurgens)
1954   *Within Man's Power* (Webster); *Amazing What Color Can Do*
1955   *A Family Affair* (Jacoby)
1958   *Home Again* (Jacoby)
1965   *Film* (Schneider)

Films as Cinematographer (Features):

1933   *Le Chemin du bonheur* (Mamy)
1934   *L'Atalante* (Vigo) (co); *Le Père Lampion* (Christian-Jaque); *Zouzou* (M. Allegret)
1935   *Lucrèce Borgia* (Gance) (co)
1936   *L'Homme sans coeur* (Joannon); *Oeil-du Lynx, détective* (Ducis); *On ne roule pas Antoinette* (Madeux); *Quand minuit sonnera* (Joannon) (co)
1937   *Cinderella* (Caron); *Etes-vous jalouse?* (Chomette); *Les Hommes sans nom* (Vallée) (co)
1938   *Fort-Dolorès* (Le Hénaff); *Les Gaités de l'exposition* (Hajos)
1939   *Sérénade* (Boyer) (co); *Le Veau gras* (de Poligny) (co)
1952   *Leonardo da Vinci* (Emmer) (co)
1954   *Garden of Eden* (Nosseck); *On the Waterfront* (Kazan)
1956   *Crowded Paradise* (Pressburger); *Baby Doll* (Kazan); *Twelve Angry Men* (Lumet); *Patterns* (*Patterns of Power*) (Cook)
1959   *That Kind of Woman* (Lumet); *The Fugitive Kind* (Lumet)
1961   *Splendor in the Grass* (Kazan)
1962   *Long Day's Journey into Night* (Lumet)
1963   *All the Way Home* (Segal); *Gone Are the Days!* (*Purlie Victorious*; *The Man from C.O.T.T.O.N.*) (Webster)
1964   *The World of Henry Orient* (Hill) (co); *The Pawnbroker* (Lumet)
1966   *The Group* (Lumet)
1967   *Bye Bye Braverman* (Lumet)
1968   *Uptight* (Dassin); *The Brotherhood* (Ritt)
1969   *Tell Me That You Love Me, Junie Moon* (Preminger)

Publications

By KAUFMAN: articles—

Film Culture (New York), Summer 1955.
On *Twelve Angry Men* in *American Cinematographer* (Hollywood), December 1956.

On *Baby Doll* in *American Cinematographer* (Hollywood), February 1957.
Cahiers du Cinéma (Paris), January 1982.

On KAUFMAN: articles—

Foster, Frederick, on *The Fugitive Kind* in *American Cinematographer* (Hollywood), June 1960.
Monthly Film Bulletin (London), 1962.
Film Comment (New York), Summer 1972.
Focus on Film (London), no. 13, 1973.
Cinéma (Paris), July-August 1973.
Obituary, *New York Times*, 27 June 1980.
Obituary, *The Annual Obituary 1980*, New York, 1981.
Film Dope (Nottingham), March 1984.

*   *   *

In his 45-year-long career, Boris Kaufman filmed newsreels, avant-garde films, documentaries, industrials, TV commercials, and feature films, winning an Academy Award for black-and-white cinematography in 1954 (*On the Waterfront*) and maintaining lengthy collaborations with three notable movie directors—Jean Vigo, Elia Kazan, and Sidney Lumet.

Kaufman was the youngest of three brothers who themselves are a noteworthy trio. Denis, the older, became world-famous as Dziga Vertov (*Kino-Eye, Kino-Pravda, The Man with the Movie Camera*); Mikhail, the middle brother, was chief cameraman on many of Denis's films and on his own documentary films as well. While Denis and Mikhail remained in Moscow at the end of the First World War, Boris went on to Paris to study poetry and philosophy. Inspired by letters from Denis, who wrote him that the camera was "the chief instrument of filmmaking" and that "only by discovering its secrets could one realize the full potential of the new art of cinema," Boris attended a small technical school in Paris where he learned the rudiments of operating a motion picture camera. His first assignments were on reportage and documentary "pictures" (as he called them, using the Hollywood term— although he never worked in Hollywood).

In 1928 Kaufman filmed Eugene Deslav's *La Marche des machines*, which began as a routine assignment covering a technological exposition but which led Kaufman into an abstract study of mechanical movements. The film was shown in a Paris art theater, without Kaufman's credit, as he was violently opposed to its editing. This seems to have been the only time he refused credit on a film—even a nudist film he shot many years later in Florida had his name on it.

After filming other experimental films, Kaufman was invited by Jean Vigo to work with him on *A propos de Nice*, a short, shocking satire on upper- and middle-class lifestyles in that resort city. Kaufman used a Kinamo (one of the first hand-held 35mm cameras, which his brother Denis had brought him in 1927) "to get rid of the tripod, to be more flexible, and to avoid being noticed by the people we were filming."

Their second film, *Zéro de conduite*, was shot in 16 1/2 days— seven in a Paris studio for the interiors, then nine-and-a-half in a school in suburban St. Cloud. The shooting ratio was two or three to one, which was all they could afford. For the sound shooting Kaufman used a Debry camera, and for more flexibility, the little Kinamo. Their final film, *L'Atalante*, was shot on a barge on the canals around Paris in late fall and winter, in bitter cold. Vigo's frail health gave out completely, just as the filming was finished; his death soon afterwards, at age 29, ended their close personal friendship, as well as the avant-garde phase of Kaufman's career. The Vigo-Kaufman collaboration lasted only five years, but was one of the most creative and memorable in film history, ranking perhaps with Griffith and Bitzer and Eisenstein and Tisse.

In the middle and late 1930s, Kaufman worked as staff cameraman at Paramount's Paris studio, where he began learning English, and on numerous European features, little known today. In the Second World War he was drafted into the army as a French citizen, and, when France fell, escaped to the United States with his wife and their son. For the remaining war years, he worked at the National Film Board of Canada in Ottawa and at the Office of War Information in New York. As documentary assignments grew scarcer and less challenging, he began shooting industrial films—and those new one-minute oddities called TV commercials. He longed to return to feature dramatic films, but Hollywood was out of the question.

When Kaufman heard that Elia Kazan was going to shoot *On the Waterfront* in New Jersey, he wanted to show him *L'Atalante*, but could not find a print in the United States. He showed two of his American documentaries instead, and got the job anyway, beginning the second of his three important collaborations. After filming on the docks and rooftops, Kazan gave Kaufman the choice of filming the interiors in a studio or on location. Later, Kaufman said that while studio shooting would have been easier, especially in dead of winter, he preferred "the patina of reality" they found in waterfront bars and sixth-floor tenements. Kaufman won the 1954 Academy Award for black-and-white cinematography (the writer Budd Schulberg, the art director Richard Day, and Kazan also won Oscars). "I drew upon my experience, I developed ways to apply precise lighting on location, which is not easy. By precision lighting I mean lighting that has a meaning. Of course, the only meaning of lighting is to reveal the inner expression of the face or the mood of a place." *Baby Doll*, filmed for Kazan under difficult conditions in Mississippi, brought Kaufman a 1955 Oscar nomination. Meanwhile, Kaufman was thought by some producers to be "slow." Kazan may have had this in his mind when he wrote, after Boris's death, for a tribute at the Museum of Modern Art: "Poetry, as everyone knows who's tried it, takes a little longer. He didn't hurry his pace, become careless, diminish his devotion."

Kaufman's third major collaboration was in 1956 with *Twelve Angry Men*, Sidney Lumet's first film, based on a television play he had directed. They worked together off and on for some ten years. Lumet considers *Long Day's Journey into Night* their "closest and most successful collaboration" (and at one time, called it his own favorite production). In later years, Kaufman worked with Jules Dassin, Martin Ritt, Otto Preminger and others. He retired in 1972.

It was Kaufman's increasing burden, especially later in his career, that he often knew and cared more about the "pictures" he worked on than their directors did. Nothing, of course, could equal the first great collaboration with Vigo, when they were young. "I had no second thoughts about risks involved," Kaufman later recalled. "When you carry a bigger responsibility in a larger picture, you have to be conscious of many things—and you discipline yourself just to survive in available conditions. . . . This art form has to survive in very materialistic and utilitarian conditions, which is not easy.'' No one ever accused Boris Kaufman of taking the easy way.

—Cecile Starr

KIDD, Michael

Choreographer. **Nationality:** American. **Born:** Milton Greenwald in Brooklyn, New York, 12 August 1919. **Education:** Attended New Utrecht High School, Brooklyn, graduated 1936; studied chemical engineering, City College of New York, 1936–37; attended School of American Ballet, 1937–39. **Family:** Married 1) the dancer Mary Heater, 1940, two daughters; 2) Shelah Hackett, one daughter, one son. **Career:** Copyboy on New York *Daily Mirror*; dance photographer; 1941–42—dancer for Eugene Loring's Dance Players, and for Ballet Theatre, 1942–47; 1952—first choreography for film, *Where's Charley*.

Films as Choreographer:

1952   *Where's Charley* (Butler)
1953   **The Band Wagon** (Minnelli); *Knock on Wood* (Panama and Frank)
1954   *Seven Brides for Seven Brothers* (Donen)
1955   *Guys and Dolls* (Mankiewicz)
1958   *Merry Andrew* (+ d)
1968   *Star!* (Wise)
1969   *Hello, Dolly!* (Kelly)
1976   *Peter Pan* (Hemion)
1978   *Movie Movie* (Donen) (+ ro)

Other Films:

1955   *It's Always Fair Weather* (Kelly and Donen) (ro)
1956   *Your Key to the Future* (d—short)
1974   *Smile* (Ritchie) (ro)
1978   *Actor* (Lloyd) (ro)
1989   *Skin Deep* (Edwards) (ro)
1997   *The Making of Seven Brides for Seven Brothers* (Benson—doc for TV) (ro)

Publications

By KIDD: articles—

''The Camera and the Dance,'' in *Films and Filming* (London), January 1956.
Cahiers du Cinéma (Paris), April 1957.
Positif (Paris), July-August 1997.

On KIDD: articles—

Film Dope (Nottingham), September 1984.
Variety (New York), 3 March 1997.

*   *   *

Throughout the 1950s, Michael Kidd ricocheted repeatedly between Broadway and Hollywood, enlivening the American musical with his fanciful and unabashedly energetic choreography. Yet, despite the conspicuous contributions that Kidd made to both the stage and screen musical during that decade, particularly at MGM, the tremendous success of his work on Broadway (Kidd received four of his five Tony Awards for productions he choreographed in the 1950s) has long overshadowed his role in revitalizing the Hollywood musical.

Although Kidd's style of choreography—a heady blend of ballet, acrobatics, and folk, jazz, and modern dance—was undoubtedly influenced by the training he received in the late 1930s when the American dance, itself a powerful mixture of various dance forms, was born, his work has been too consistently singular to be considered a clever variation on some grand theme. With the 1945 premiere of his first choreographed piece, *On Stage!*, which he performed, Kidd established himself as a distinctive choreographer, one capable of creating inventive and visually arresting dances. Of even greater importance to Broadway and Hollywood, *On Stage!* revealed Kidd's talent for using dance to communicate with and entertain an audience.

Nowhere is Kidd's choreography for the motion picture better displayed than in a handsome trio of MGM musicals: Vincente Minnelli's *The Band Wagon*, Stanley Donen's *Seven Brides for Seven Brothers*, and Joseph L. Mankiewicz's *Guys and Dolls*. The versatility of Kidd's dance compositions is manifest in *The Band Wagon*, which boasts such disparate musical numbers as the thematic ''That's Entertainment,'' with its music-hall exuberance, and ''Girl Hunt,'' the sleek and steamy satire that ends the picture. In *Seven Brides for Seven Brothers*, Kidd celebrated the dancer as artist and athlete through a broad and colorful palette of spectacular dance numbers, represented best by the unforgettable barn-raising ballet. By recreating the dance routines he composed for the 1950 stage production of *Guys and Dolls*, Kidd provided the film version of Damon Runyon's story with its full-blown vitality and metropolitan rhythm.

During his association with MGM in the 1950s, Kidd also made his on-screen debut in Gene Kelly and Stanley Donen's *It's Always Fair Weather*. Describing Kidd's performance as ex-soldier/hot-dog stand proprietor Angie Valentine for the *New York Times*, the critic Bosley Crowther noted the naturalness and agreeableness of Kidd's acting, which was ''somewhat in the style of Frank Sinatra,'' adding ''and—needless to say—he can dance.'' Before leaving MGM and Hollywood near the end of the decade, Kidd, who had recently directed and co-produced *Li'l Abner* on Broadway, completed his sole directorial effort in film, *Merry Andrew*.

In the 1960s and 1970s Kidd concentrated on choreographing, directing, and occasionally co-producing a number of Broadway productions—*Wildcat*, *Skyscraper*, *The Rothschilds*—though not to the exclusion of working in film. Kidd rejoined director Gene Kelly in 1969 to choreograph *Hello, Dolly!*, whose excessive budget provoked Pauline Kael to decry in *The New Yorker* nearly everything about the movie, including its ''asexual and unromantic'' dancing, an assessment that was countered by several other film critics (*Time*'s critic,

Michael Kidd

for example, thought Kidd's dances "blithe and sumptuous"). In 1975 Kidd again performed on-screen in Michael Ritchie's satirical *Smile*, playing with charm and a touch of irony a Hollywood choreographer hired to stage a small-town beauty pageant.

—Nancy Jane Johnston

KOCH, Howard W.

Writer and Producer. **Nationality:** American. **Born:** New York City, 12 December 1902. **Education:** Attended St. Stephen's College (now Bard College), Annandale-on-Hudson, B.A. 1922; Columbia Law School, New York, LL.B. 1925. **Family:** Married 2) Anne Green, 1944; three children. **Career:** 1926–37—practiced law in Hartsdale, New York, and writer: first play produced, 1929, *Great Scott!* (later plays include *Give Us This Day*, 1933, *The Lonely Man*, 1937, *In Time to Come*, with John Huston, 1940, and *Dead Letters*, 1971); 1938—joined Orson Welles's Mercury Theatre Company, and wrote script

for the radio play *War of the Worlds*; 1939–46—contract writer, Warner Bros.: first film as writer, *The Sea Hawk*, 1940; 1947—beginning of House Un-American Activities Committee investigation of Koch, and eventually blacklisted in 1951; 1952–56—worked in England, using the pseudonym Peter Howard. **Award:** Academy Award for *Casablanca*, 1943. **Died:** 17 August 1995.

Films as Writer:

1940   *The Sea Hawk* (Curtiz); *The Letter* (Wyler); *Virginia City* (Curtiz) (uncredited)
1941   *Shining Victory* (Rapper); *Sergeant York* (Hawks)
1942   *In This Our Life* (Huston); **Casablanca** (Curtiz)
1943   *Mission to Moscow* (Curtiz)
1944   *In Our Time* (Sherman)
1945   *Rhapsody in Blue* (Rapper); *Tuesday in November* (Berry—short)
1946   *Three Strangers* (Negulesco); **The Best Years of Our Lives** (Wyler) (uncredited)
1948   **Letter from an Unknown Woman** (Ophüls)

464

1950   *No Sad Songs for Me* (Maté)
1951   *The Thirteenth Letter* (Preminger)
1956   *The Intimate Stranger* (*Finger of Guilt*) (Losey) (as Peter Howard)
1961   *The Greengage Summer* (*Loss of Innocence*) (Gilbert)
1962   *The War Lover* (Leacock)
1964   *633 Squadron* (Grauman)
1967   *The Fox* (Rydell) (+ assoc pr)
1974   *The Woman of Otowi Crossing* (Daniel Mann)

Other Films:

1949   *Border Incident* (Mann) (asst d)
1955   *Fort Yuma* (Selander) (pr)
1962   *The Manchurian Candidate* (Frankenheimer) (exec pr)

Publications

By KOCH: books—

With John Huston, *In Time to Come* (play), New York, 1942.
With Julius J. and Philip G. Epstein, *Casablanca* (script), in *The Best Film Plays of 1943–44*, edited by John Gassner and Dudley Nichols, New York, 1945.
The Panic Broadcast, Boston, Massachusetts, 1970.
Casablanca, Script and Legend, Woodstock, New York, 1973.
As Time Goes By (autobiography), New York, 1978.

By KOCH: articles—

"A Playwright Looks at the 'Filmwright,'" in *Sight and Sound* (London), July 1950.
"Script to Screen with Max Ophüls," in *The Hollywood Screenwriter*, edited by Richard Corliss, New York, 1972.
Letter in *American Film* (Washington, D.C.), February 1978.
Film Comment (New York), July-August 1978.

On KOCH: book—

Anobile, Richard J., (ed.), *Michael Curtiz's Casablanca*, New York, 1974.

On KOCH: articles—

Présence du Cinéma (Paris), June 1962.
Film Comment (New York), May-June 1973.
Culbert, David, on *Mission to Moscow* in *American History/American Film*, edited by John E. O'Connor and Martin A. Jackson, New York, 1979.
Rogers, Michael, "*Casablanca*: Script and Legend," in *Library Journal*, 1 November 1992.
Gillman, Michael, "Howard Koch: You Must Remember This," in *Library Journal*, 1 September 1993.

Howard W. Koch

Hoffman, Preston, "*The War of the Worlds*—Fiftieth Anniversary Production," in *Wilson Literary Bulletin*, September 1994.
Gussow, M., Obituary, in *The New York Times*, 18 August 1995.
Obituary, in *Variety* (New York), 21 August 1995.
Obituary, in *Facts on File*, 24 August 1995.
Obituary, in *Economist*, 26 August 1995.
Obituary, in *Time*, 28 August 1995.

*   *   *

Although he was responsible for writing a number of distinguished film scripts for Warner Bros. in the 1940s and for Columbia in the 1950s and 1960s, Howard Koch will probably best be remembered for contributing the marvelous dialogue to *Casablanca* which he coscripted with Julius and Philip Epstein in 1943. It is to his credit that the dialogue for this relatively low-budget, war-time melodrama still resonates today with wit and charm. In part, of course, it is the quality of the cast which is responsible for such timelessness, an embarrassing number of fine character actors (as one critic has described it) deliver the lines with style and control: Bogart is perfect as Rick as is Bergman as Ilse and so on. But it was Howard Koch, still a relative newcomer to film writing, who crafted the movie into one of cinema's rare and privileged films.

Koch himself arrived in Hollywood in the late 1930s in a privileged position as he followed Orson Welles to the coast on the heels of the Halloween broadcast, *War of the Worlds*, which he wrote for the Mercury Theatre. He was cautious in his choice of screen assignments, and produced, in the three short years before *Casablanca*, scripts of high literary and artistic merit. He wrote the swashbuckler *The Sea Hawk*, not as just another adventure film written to formula but as a thoughtful historical romance with thematic connections to the current events taking place in Europe with the rise of Adolph Hitler. He followed *The Sea Hawk* with a literary adaptation of Somerset Maugham's play, *The Letter*, which under Koch's tutelage became more than just a star vehicle for Bette Davis who was picked to act the role of Leslie Crosby, the neglected wife of the English planter. Although melodramatic, *The Letter* crackles with good dialogue and marked Koch as not only a fine adaptator but a fine screen craftsman as well. The next two films he wrote were also melodramas, *Shining Victory*, a play by A.J. Cronin which Koch adapted with Anne Froelich, and Ellen Glasgow's *In This Our Life* which he cowrote with John Huston as an uncredited collaborator. He had worked once before with Huston on *Sergeant York*, a film about a pacifist farmer who overcomes his objections to killing and becomes the most decorated hero of the First World War. Although the assignment created political problems for Koch, he had an opportunity to work with Howard Hawks who directed the film. In spite of the film's obviously propagandistic tone, Koch and Huston were nominated for an Academy Award.

Koch was brought in to work on his next project after it had been abandoned by the Epstein brothers. *Casablanca* was a film which took ample advantage of Koch's idealism and political leanings and avoided the cloying patriotism of *Sergeant York* while nevertheless supplying a pro-war, pro-ally message. *Casablanca* retains the correct mixture of romanticism and cynicism to remain perennially fresh and contemporary. Koch's handling of the film's political contents earned him an assignment on *Mission to Moscow*, based on Ambassador Joseph Davies's book and already begun by Erskine Caldwell. The film is now a political embarrassment because of its favorable portrait of Joseph Stalin, who comes across as a lovable Uncle Joe, and it also was one of the sources for Koch's blacklisting as the film was seen as subversive in a cold war perspective. Koch wrote three more films for Warner Bros.: *In Our Time*, with Ellis St. Joseph, *Rhapsody in Blue*, with Elliot Paul and later Clifford Odets, and *Three Strangers*, with John Huston. All three scripts show evidence of Koch's skill with dialogue.

In 1947, in an appearance before the House Un-American Activities Committee, Jack Warner denied that any Warner films contained communist propaganda and mentioned Koch among others as a writer he had fired for his political leanings. Koch was called before the committee to deny Warner's allegations, and, although he proved his point, he was "graylisted" for his support of the political left in Hollywood. Koch lost jobs because of his listing and wrote very little that was produced during the 1950s. One notable exception was *Letter from an Unknown Woman*, written for Max Ophüls. It is a fine film and captures the ambience of Vienna in the same way *Casablanca* did for the city of its title. Following *The Thirteenth Letter*, which Koch did for Otto Preminger, he was officially blacklisted and left Hollywood for Woodstock, New York, and later for Europe.

In 1961 Koch's name was finally removed from the blacklist after a lengthy legal battle and he was allowed to work again. The writing he did on *The Greengage Summer*, *The War Lover*, and *633 Squadron* was undistinguished although workmanlike; in the case of *633 Squadron*, written mostly by James Clavell, Koch was brought in as a script doctor and cannot be held responsible for the rather lackluster script.

Koch's scripting job on *The Fox*, an adaptation of the D.H. Lawrence short novel, became distorted beyond recognition, so much so that Koch took the script to the Writers Guild for arbitration but lost. The final film owes little to Lawrence or to Howard Koch.

Koch's career, like so many others' disrupted by the era of blacklisting, never recovered from the period of enforced absence from motion-picture writing. Hollywood changed radically during the 1950s, and those who were kept out of the studios during that period seem not to have made a transition after the blacklisting was lifted. The case of Howard Koch is particularly saddening because his obvious talent as a screenwriter was thrown away for the sake of political expediency, and in the process the screen lost one of its most skilled artists.

—Charles L. P. Silet

KOLOWRAT-KRAKOWSKY, Count "Sascha" Alexander

Producer. **Nationality:** Austrian. **Born:** Count Alexander Joseph Kolowrat-Krakowsky in Glenridge, New York, 29 January 1886; son of Count Leopold Kolowrat and Nadine Baroness von Huppmann-Valbella. **Education:** Attended the Kalksburg Gymnasium, near Vienna, 1896–1906. **Military Service:** One year voluntary service in the exclusive feudal Thirteenth Dragoons, 1907–08. **Family:** Married the Russian émigré Sophia Nikolajewna Princess Troubetzkoy, 30 April 1923 in Vienna. **Career:** Inherited the vast Bohemian family estates, including a palace in Prague and one in Vienna, as well as 21 churches, 1910; began Sascha film company at his castle in Pfraumberg, Bohemia, 1910; opened Sascha film company in Vienna, 1914; served as officer in the imperial automobile corps, 1914; head of the film branch of the imperial War Press Service; 1915; film company becomes Sascha-Messter film company, and began construction of new studio in Sievering, 1916; Sascha film becomes a stock company, 1918; president of film company until his death, 1918–1927. Constructed with Porsche sen. in Wiener Neustadt, Lower Austria, the Sascha Daimler car, after war ended in 1918. **Award:** Award of the *Internationale Kino-Ausstellung*, Vienna, 1912. **Died:** Of Cancer, in Sanatorim Loew, Vienna, on 4 December 1927.

Films as Producer:

For many early films the director is not known. Early attempts at filmmaking included short travelogues and documentaries: *Die Gewinnung des Eisens am steirischen Erzberg (Mining on Erzberg), Burg Kreutzenstein (Castle Kreutzenstein); Die Dolomiten (The Dolomites); Der Gardasee (Lake Garda); Der Stapellauf der Dreadnought Tegetthoff (The Launch of the Battleship Tegetthoff); Im Auto durch die österreichischen Alpen (By Car through the Austrian Alps).*

Early attempts at comedies, which were never shown publicly: *Pampulik hat Hunger (P. Is Hungry); Pampulik kriegt ein Kind (P. Is Pregnant); Pampulik als Affe (P. as a Monkey)*, all of them with Max Pallenberg.

1912   *Onkel Cocl am Gänsehäufel* (*Uncle Cocl at the Gänsehäufel Swimming Pool*); *Cocl als Säugling* (*Cocl as Baby*); *Kaiser Joseph II* (*Emperor Joseph II*) (Kolowrat and J.H. Groß)

1913   *Cocl geht zum Maskenball* (*Cocl Goes to the Masked Ball*) (Zeitlinger); *Die Feuerprobe* (*Test by Fire*); *Wie aus Cocl Asta Pilsen wurde* (*How Cocl Became Asta Pilsen*); *Der Millionenonkel* (*The Millionaire Uncle*) (Marischka)

1914   *Augustin auf Brautschau* (*Augustin Looks for a Bride*); *Cocl als Hausherr* (*Cocl as the Master of the House*); *Onkel Cocls Klassenlos* (*Uncle Cocl's Lottery Ticket*); *Durch Verrat zum Sieg* (*Through Treason to Victory*); *Siegreich durch Serbien* (*Victorious through Serbia*) (exact year unknown)

1916   *Wien im Krieg* (*Vienna at War*); *Sami der Seefahrer* (*Sami the Seafarer*); *Die Verteidigung der Karpaten* (*The Defense of the Carpathians*)

1917   *Der Nörgler* (*The Grumbler*); *Der Viererzug* (*Team of Four*) (Wilhelm); *Er muß sie haben* (*He Must Have Her*) (Hahn); *Das schwindende Herz* (*The Disappearing Heart*); *Der Brief einer Toten* (*Letter from a Dead Woman*) (Freissler), *Wenn die Liebe auf den Hund kommt* (*When Love Fades*); *Um ein Weib* (*For a Woman*) (Ernst and Hubert Marischka); *Licht und Finsternis* (*Light and Darkness*); *Frank Boyers Diener* (*Frank Boyer's Servant*) (Wiene); *Der Mann mit der Maske* (*The Man with the Mask*); *Der Diebstahl* (*The Theft*) (R. Löwenstein); *Der gewonnene Prozeß* (*Victory in Court*); *Die goldene Wehr* (*The Golden Shield*) (Stein), *Die feldgraue Krone* (*The Gray Crown*); *Wir und die andern* (*We and the Others*) (Rob); *Der sichere Weg zum Frieden* (*The Sure Way to Peace*) (Rob); *Was die Liebe vermag* (*What Love Can Do*) (Freissler); *Er rächt seine Schwiegermutter* (*He Revenges His Mother-in-Law*); *Dem Frieden entgegen* (*Towards Peace*) (K. Wiene); *Der Gewissenswurm* (*A Guilty Conscience*) (Theyer); *Herrn Zabladies seltsamer Traum* (*The Strange Dream of Mr. Zabladie*); *Das Nachtlager von Mischli-Michloch* (*The Camp of Mischli-Mischloch*) (Freissler)

1918   *Der Märtyrer seines Herzens* (*The Martyr of His Heart*) (Jistitz); *Das neue Leben* (*The New Life*); *Fred Roll*, parts I and II (Ernst Marischka); *Das andere Ich* (*The Other Self*) (Freissler); *Don Juans letztes Abenteuer* (*Don Juan's Last Adventure*); *Der letzte Erbe von Lassa* (*The Last Heir of Lassa*) (Konrad Wiene); *Das Haus ohne Lachen* (*House without Laughter*) (K. Wiene); *Am Tor des Lebens* (*At the Gate of Life*) (Wiene)

1919   *Der Umweg zur Ehe* (*Detour to Marriage*) (K. Wiene); *Die Spinne* (*The Spider*) (K. Wiene); *Zwei Welten* (*Two Worlds*) (Wiene); *Der Einbrecher im Frack*, parts I and II (*The Thief in Tuxedo*) (Ralph); *In letzter Stunde* (*At the Last Minute*) (Freissler); *Ein gefährliches Spiel* (*A Dangerous Game*) (Freissler); *Die Dame mit den schwarzen Handschuhen* (*The Lady with the Black Gloves*) (Kertész)

1920   *Der Stern von Damaskus* (*Star of Damaskus*) (Kertész); *Die Gottesgeissel* (*God's Punishment*) (Kertész); *Die Dame mit den Sonnenblumen* (*The Lady with the Sunflowers*) (Kertész); *Prinz und Bettelknabe* (*The Prince and the Pauper*) (Korda)

1921   *Mrs. Tutti Frutti* (Kertész); *Cherchez la femme* (Kertész); *Dorothys Bekenntnis* (*Dorothy's Confession*) (Kertész); *Wege des Schreckens* (*Roads of Horror*) (Kertész)

1922   *Herren der Meere* (*Masters of the Sea*) (Korda); *Eine versunkene Welt* (*A Sunken World*) (Korda); *Der Ausflug in die Seligkeit* (*The Trip to Bliss*) (Freissler); *Zigeunerliebe* (*Gypsy Love*) (Walsh); *Serge Panine* (Maudru); *Sodom and Gomorrha* (*Moon of Israel*) (Kertész)

1923   *Kinder der Revolution* (*Children of the Revolution*) (Theyer); *Die Lawine* (*The Avalanche*) (Kertész); *Das Rumpelstilzchen* (*Rumpelstiltskin*) (Desider Kertész); *Fräulein Frau* (*Miss Mrs.*) (Theyer); *Der junge Medardus* (*The Young Medardus*) (Kertész); *Namenlos* (*Without a Name*) (Kertész)

1924   *Harun al Raschid* (Kertész); *Wenn du noch eine Mutter hast* (*If You Still Have a Mother*) (Desider Gardener-Kertész); *Jedermanns Weib* (*Everyman's Woman*) (Korda); *Die Sklavenkönigin* (*The Slave Queen*) (Kertész)

1925   *Salammbo* (Maradon); *Die Rache des Pharao* (*Pharao's Revenge*) (Theyer); *Das Spielzeug von Paris* (*The Toy of Paris*) (Kertész)

1926   *Fiaker Nr. 13* (Kertész); *Der goldene Schmetterling* (*The Golden Butterfly*) (Kertész); *Die Pratermizzi* (*Prater Girl*) (Kolowrat and his staff)

1927   *Tingel Tangel* (Ucicky); *Die Beichte des Feldkuraten* (*The Confession of a Military Priest*) (Löwenstein); *Café Electric* (Ucicky)

During World War I, Kolowrat produced a newsreel: *Österreichischer Kino-Wochenbericht vom nördlichen und südlichen Kriegsschauplatz* (*Austrian Weekly Newsreel from The Northern and Southern Battle fronts*), later *Sascha-Kriegswochenbericht* (*Sascha's Weekly Report*).

War documentaries include: *Heldenkampf in Schnee und Eis* (*Heroic Battle in Snow and Ice*); *Die zehnte Isonzoschlacht* (*The Tenth Isonzo Battle*).

Publications

On KOLOWRAT: books—

Porges, Friedrich, *Schatten erobern die Welt*, Basel, 1946.

Sascha-Film, ed., *Dreißig Jahre Sascha-Film*, Vienna, 1948.

Gesek, Ludwig, *Gestalter der Filmkunst. Von Asta Nielsen bis Walt Disney*, Vienna, 1948.

Hübl, Ingrid Maria, Sascha Kolowrat. *Ein Beitrag zur Geschichte der österreichischen Kinematographie*, unpublished manuscript, Filmarchiv Austria, 1950.

Festschrift der Sascha-Film Gesellschaft m.b.H. Wien, Vienna, 1957.

Herle, Roman, *Die 9. Seligkeit. Licht und Dunkel des Films*, Vienna, 1962.

Guha, Wilhelm, *Die Geschichte eines österreichischen Filmunternehmens: Von der Sascha-Film-Fabrik in Böhmen zur Wien-Film*, unpublished manuscript, Filmarchiv Austria, Vienna, 1975.

Österreichisches Filmarchiv, ed., *Materialien zu Sascha Kolowrat*, Vienna, 1987.

Fritz, Walter, and Margit Zarahdnik, *Erinnerungen an Graf Sascha Kolowrat*. Bound typescript. Vienna, 1992.

Steiner, Gertraud, *Traumfabrik Rosenhügel. Filmstadt Wien/Wien-Film/Tobis-Sascha/Vita-Film*. Vienna, 1997.

On KOLOWRAT: articles—

Krenn, Günter, ''Der bewegte Mensch—Sascha Kolowrat,'' in *Elektrische Schatten. Beiträge zur österreichischen Stummfilmgeschichte*, edited by Francesco Bono, Paolo Caneppele, and Günter Krenn, Vienna, 1999.

*   *   *

The ''film count,'' one of the most flamboyant personalities ever to work in film, had been preceded by Anton and Louise Kolm as professional filmmakers in the Austro-Hungarian monarchy, but Alexander Kolowrat was the one to found the larger and lasting firm. ''Sascha,'' as his friends called him, was descended from old Bohemian aristocracy. With the fortune he inherited upon his father's death in 1910, he was financially able to indulge his passion for the new art. His wealth and title also gave him useful high ranking contacts in his own country and abroad. He could travel at will on business and pleasure trips to Paris and New York to stay abreast of the newest developments in film technology and distribution.

Kolowrat was born in the United States in Glenridge, New York, where his father spent a few years in exile for killing Prince Auersperg in a duel of honor. The family soon returned to the monarchy. From early youth on Sascha was fascinated by technical matters, even working at the Laurin and Klement car factory. He was a daredevil, who won motorcycle races as a student and was a regular participant in the Semmering mountain race car competition. He was one of the earliest Austrian pilots and the first balloonist. His parties at the Viennese Sacher hotel were legendary, and in spite of his corpulence the young count was a dashing and charming man with an eye for beautiful women.

Upon seeing his first film in 1909 at the Pathé Brothers in Paris, he knew he had found his mission in life. Film enabled him to combine all of his passions: technology, adventurous travel, and women. He especially indulged his appetite for beautiful women by regularly inviting them to his studio for screen tests.

In 1910 he founded the ''Sascha-Filmfabrik in Pfraumberg in Bohemia,'' and after two years of experimenting he showed a film in 1912 about mining iron at Styrian Erzberg mountain. He produced a number of travelogues before he attempted feature films. In one of his castles, Gross-Meierhöfen near Pfraumberg in Bohemia, he installed a makeshift workshop for film developing. When he found that he had to be closer to the market, he moved to a studio in Biberstrasse in the center of Vienna in 1912. In 1913 he achieved his first big success with *Der Millionenonkel*. This film featured the famous Alexander Girardi performing scenes from his most famous operetta roles.

Kolowrat hired a stellar professional team: Oskar Berka, the head of his laboratory; Karl Freund, later the famous cinematographer; and the cameraman Hans Theyer, who had learned his craft with Pathé in Paris. In 1916 Theyer helped Kolowrat set up the first free-standing film studio in Austria. Kolowrat had bought the iron structure of an airplane hangar in Germany and rebuilt it, covered with glass for maximum light, in the quaint, wine-growing Viennese suburb of Sievering.

The First World War marked the turning point of the business. The exclusion of competitors, mainly the French, propelled the Sascha company into a thriving business. Kolowrat's influential contacts made possible his appointment as director of the film section of the military press service. As director, his authority enabled him to gather many of his trusted coworkers, among them Theyer, Karl Hartl, Gustav Ucicky, and Fritz Freissler. In October 1914 the Sascha company received permission to produce a weekly war newsreel, *Sascha-Kriegswoche*. An even bigger coup was his gaining the exclusive right to film the funeral of Emperor Franz Joseph in November 1916. By working around the clock, Kolowrat and his staff produced 255 copies within three days and nights, to be distributed to every corner of the monarchy. By the end of the war, the Sascha company had turned out approximately 300 films. The satirist Karl Kraus attacked Kolowrat in his monumental play *Die letzten Tage der Menschheit* as a war profiteer.

In 1916 the Sascha company formed a partnership with Messter-Film in Berlin. In 1918 the German UFA took over Messter-Film, thus becoming a shareholder in Sascha. In 1918 Sascha-Film merged with the Viennese distributing firm Philipp and Pressburger to form Sascha-Filmindustrie AG. The company established headquarters at Siebensterngasse 31 in the seventh district of Vienna, where it operated for many decades.

The end of the Austro-Hungarian monarchy in 1918 meant the loss of markets for Sascha. To seek new opportunities and learn the latest developments in the film business, Kolowrat made two trips to the United States in 1919 and 1920 as president of the company, accompanied on the second visit by Arnold Pressburger, Director General of Sascha-Film. They were able to engage the Herz Film Corporation as a distributor of Sascha Films in the United States. At the same time, they contracted to represent Paramount Pictures in Austria. Greatly impressed by D.W. Griffiths' *Intolerance* (1916), Kolowrat produced costly spectaculars for the world market: *Sodom and Gomorrha* in 1922, the bizarre climax of Austrian silent film, and *Die Sklavenkönigin* in 1924, both directed by Michael Kertész, a Hungarian who worked for Kolowrat for several years. In 1926, under the name Michael Curtiz, he began an extremely successful career in Hollywood, directing *Casablanca* in 1942.

Kolowrat also teamed up with other Hungarians in the early 1920s. Alexander Korda and his wife, the silent film star Maria Corda, who worked for him briefly before they moved to Berlin and later to Hollywood. Ultimately Korda found his niche as a major producer in England. He achieved Sascha-Film's first international success with *Prinz und Bettelknabe* (The Prince and the Pauper) in 1920, a film based on Mark Twain's novel.

The last costly production was *Der junge Medardus*, a film based on Arthur Schnitzler's drama. The film, which was set in the Napoleonic wars in 1809 in Vienna, was also directed by Michael Kertesz. By the middle of the 1920s the economic crisis had put an end to lavish spectaculars in Austria. A less expensive production, but a film depicting the effects of the depression and similar in style to G.W. Pabst's *Die freudlose Gasse* (1925), was *Café Elektric* (1927), which introduced the future stars Willi Forst and Marlene Dietrich. Kolowrat became seriously ill during this production which proved to be his last film. He died of cancer on 4 December 1927 at the age of 42 in Vienna. With his energy, charisma, contacts, and money he had brought Austrian film to international recognition. In the years after his death, his film company fell on hard times, but the legacy of this remarkable film pioneer—with his 140 feature films of various lengths between 1911 and 1927—and his company have endured.

—Gertraud Steiner Daviau

KORDA, (Sir) Alexander

Producer and Director. **Nationality:** British. **Born:** Sándor László Kellner in Túrkeve, Hungary, 16 September 1893; became British Citizen 1936. Brother of the production designer Vincent Korda and the director Zoltan Korda. **Education:** Attended Jewish School in Túrkeve. **Family:** Married 1) the actress María Farkas (divorced 1930); 2) the actress Merle Oberon, 1939 (divorced 1945); 3) Alexandra Boycun, 1953. **Career:** Newspaper reporter in Budapest; secretary and assistant at Ungerleider Projectograph Distribution Company; 1914—exempted from military service on health grounds, directed educational films and others; 1917—bought Corvin Production Company and built studio in Budapest; 1919—escaped to Vienna after overthrow of the Béla Kun regime in Hungary, and began collaboration with Lajos Biro; formed Korda Productions with Maria Corda; 1927—signed contract with First National in Hollywood; 1930—contract with Fox cancelled after one film, went to Paris with Biro; 1931—signed contract with Paramount-British in London; 1932—formed London Film Productions, making "quota quickies"; *The Private Life of Henry VIII* brought international fame and long-term contract with United Artists; 1935—became partner in United Artists; 1939—established Alexander Korda Productions; 1940—went to U.S., formed production companies Romaine Film Productions and Gloria Pictures; 1944—left United Artists; 1946—took control of British Lion Distribution; took over Regina Productions in France with Marcel Carné, René Clair and Julien Duvivier; formed Tricolore Films to distribute films in the US; took over Shepperton Studios;

1949—withdrew from British Lion and announced the removal of his name from the credits on his productions; 1955—formed London Films Television Company, which was liquidated upon his deth and before any programmes were made; 1943—knighted. **Died:** In 1956.

Films as Producer:

1917   *A csikós* (*The Horseherder*) (Pásztory); *A peleskei notárius* (*The Notary*) (Pásztory); *Piros bugyelláris* (*The Crimson Notebook*); *A riporterkirály* (*The King of Reporters*) (Pásztory); *A ketlekü asszony* (*The Woman in Two Minds*)

1918   *Károly Bakák* (Z. Korda and Pásztory); *A testör* (*The Guardsman*) (Antalffy); *A kis lord* (*The Little Lord*) (Antalffy)

1932   *Men of Tomorrow* (Sagan and Z. Korda); *That Night in London* (*Overnight*) (Lee); *Strange Evidence* (Milton)

1933   *Counsel's Opinion* (Dwan); *Cash* (*For Love or Money*) (Z. Korda)

1934   *Catherine the Great* (*The Rise of Catherine the Great*) (Czinner); *The Private Life of the Gannets* (Huxley)

1935   *Sanders of the River* (*Bosambo*) (Z. Korda); *Wharves and Strays* (Browne); *Moscow Nights* (*I Stand Condemned*) (Asquith); *The Ghost Goes West* (Clair); ***Things to Come*** (Menzies)

1936   *Fire over England* (Howard); *The Man Who Could Work Miracles* (Mendes); *Men Are Not Gods* (Reisch); *Miss Bracegirdle Does Her Duty* (Garmes); *Forget-Me-Not* (*Forever Yours*) (Z. Korda); *Fox Hunt* (Gross and Hoppin)

1937   *Dark Journey* (Saville); *Elephant Boy* (Flaherty and Z. Korda); *Farewell Again* (*Troopship*) (Whelan); *Action for Slander* (Whelan); *Knight without Armour* (Feyder); *The Squeaker* (*Murder on Diamond Row*) (Howard); *The Return of the Scarlet Pimpernel* (Schwartz); *Paradise for Two* (*The Gaiety Girls*) (Freeland); *Over the Moon* (Freeland); *21 Days* (*21 Days Together*; *The First and the Last*) (Dean)

1938   *Prison without Bars* (Hurst); *The Challenge* (Rosmer); *The Drum* (*Drums*) (Z. Korda); *South Riding* (Saville); *The Divorce of Lady X* (Whelan)

1939   *Q Planes* (*Clouds over Europe*) (Whelan); *The Rebel Son* (Granovsky and Brunel); *The Spy in Black* (*U-Boat 29*) (Powell); *The Four Feathers* (Z. Korda); *The Lion Has Wings* (Powell, Hurst and Brunel)

1940   *The Conquest of the Air* (Z. Korda, Esway, Taylor, Shaw, Saunders and Menzies); *The Thief of Bagdad* (Berger, Powell and Whelan); *Old Bill and Son* (Dalrymple)

1941   *Lydia* (Duvivier); *New Wine* (Schunzel)

1942   *To Be or Not To Be* (Lubitsch); *Jungle Book* (Z. Korda)

1943   *The Biter Bit*

1946   *The Shop at Sly Corner* (*The Code of Scotland Yard*) (King)

1947   *A Man about the House* (Arliss); *Mine Own Executioner* (Kimmins); *Night Beat* (Huth); *Anna Karenina* (Duvivier); *Les Dessous des cartes* (Cayatte)

1948   *The Fallen Idol* (Reed); *The Winslow Boy* (Asquith); *Bonnie Prince Charlie* (Kimmins); *The Small Back Room* (Powell and Pressburger); *The Last Days of Dolwyn* (*Woman of Dolwyn*) (Williams)

1949   *Saints and Sinners* (Arliss); *That Dangerous Age* (*If This Be Sin*) (Ratoff); *Interrupted Journey* (Birt); ***The Third Man*** (Reed); *The Cure for Love* (Donat); *The Angel with the Trumpet* (Bushell)

Alexander Korda

469

1950 *State Secret (The Great Man Hunt)* (Gilliat); *The Happiest Days of Your Life* (Launder); *My Daughter Joy (Operation X)* (Ratoff); *The Wooden Horse* (Lee); *Seven Days to Noon* (Boulting); *Gone to Earth* (Powell and Pressburger); *The Bridge of Time* (Eday and Boothby); *The Wonder Kid* (Hartel)

1951 *Flesh and Blood* (Kimmins); *The Tales of Hoffman* (Powell and Pressburger); *Lady Godiva Rides Again* (Launder); *Mr. Denning Drives North* (Kimmins); *Outcast of the Islands* (Reed); *Cry, the Beloved Country (African Fury)* (Z. Korda)

1952 *Home at Seven (Murder on Monday)* (Richardson); *Who Goes There! (The Passionate Century)* (Kimmins); *Edinburgh* (Eady); *The Road to Canterbury* (Eady); *The Sound Barrier (Breaking the Sound Barrier)* (Lean); *The Holly and the Ivy* (O'Ferrall); *The Lost Hours (The Big Frame)* (Macdonald); *Folly to Be Wise* (Launder); *The Ringer* (Hamilton)

1953 *Twice upon a Time* (Pressburger); *The Man Between* (Reed); *The Heart of the Matter* (O'Ferrall); *Hobson's Choice* (Lean); *Three Cases of Murder* (Toye, Eady, and O'Ferrall); *The Captain's Paradise* (Kimmins); *The Story of Gilbert and Sullivan (Gilbert and Sullivan; The Great Gilbert and Sullivan)* (Gilliat)

1954 *Devil Girl from Mars* (Macdonald); *The Green Scarf* (O'Ferrall); *A Kid for Two Farthings* (Reed); *The Constant Husband* (Gilliat); *The Man Who Loved Redheads* (French); *Aunt Clara* (Kimmins); *The Teckman Mystery* (Toye); *The Belles of St. Trinian's* (Launder)

1955 *Raising a Riot* (Toye); *Summer Madness (Summertime)* (Lean); *The Deep Blue Sea* (Litvak); *Storm over the Nile* (Z. Korda and Young); *Richard III* (Olivier); *The Man Who Never Was* (Neame); *I Am a Camera* (Cornelius)

1956 *Smiley* (Kimmins)

Films as Director:

1914 *A becsapott újságíró (The Duped Journalist)*

1915 *Tutyu és Totyo (Tutyu and Totyo)*; *Lyon Lea (Lea Lyon)* (with Pásztory); *A tiszti kardbojt (The Officer's Swordknot)* (+ sc)

1916 *Mágnás Miska (Miska the Magnate)*; *A nevtö Szaszkia (The Laughing Saskia)*; *Vergödö szívek (Struggling Hearts)*; *Ciklámen (Cyclamen)*; *Fehér éjszakák (White Nights; Fedora)* (+ sc); *A nagymama (The Grandmother)* (+ sc); *Mesék az írógépröl (Tales of the Typewriter)* (+ sc); *A ketszívü férfi (The Man with Two Hearts)*; *Az egymillió fontos bankó (The Million Pound Note)*

1917 *A gólyakalifa (The Stork Caliph)*; *Mágia (Magic)*; *Harrison es Barrison (Harrison and Barrison)*; *Faun*

1918 *Az aranyember (The Man with the Golden Touch)*; *Mary Ann*

1919 *Ave Caesar!*; *Fehér Rosza (White Rose)*; *Yamata*; *Se ki, se be (Neither in Nor Out)*; *A 111-es (No. 111)*

1920 *Seine Majestat das Bettelkind (Prinz und Bettelknabe)*

1922 *Herren der Meere*; *Eine versunkene Welt (Die Tragödie eines verschollenen Fürstensohnes)*; *Samson und Delila (Der Roman einer Opernsängerin)* (+ co-sc)

1923 *Das Unbekannte Morgen* (+ co-sc)

1924 *Jedermanns Frau (Jedermanns Weib)*; *Tragodie im Haus Habsburg (Das Drama von Mayerling; Der Prinz der Legende)*

1925 *Der Tänzer Meiner Frau*

1926 *Eine Dubarry Von Heute*

1927 *The Stolen Bride*; *The Private Life of Helen of Troy*

1928 *The Yellow Lily*; *The Night Watch*

1929 *Love and the Devil*; *Her Private Life*; *The Squall*

1930 *Lilies of the Field*; *The Princess and the Plumber*; *Women Everywhere*

1931 *Rive Gauche*; *Marius (Zum Goldenen Anker)*

1932 *Service for Ladies (Reserved for Ladies)*

1933 *Wedding Rehearsal*; **The Private Life of Henry VIII**; *The Girl from Maxim's*

1934 *The Private Life of Don Juan*

1936 *Rembrandt*

1941 *That Hamilton Woman (Lady Hamilton)*

1945 *Perfect Strangers (Vacation from Marriage)*

1947 *An Ideal Husband*

Publications

By KORDA: articles—

Photoplay (New York), vol. 32, no. 6, November 1927.
Picturegoer, vol. 3, no. 154, May 1934.
Film Weekly, vol. 19, no. 456, 10 July 1937.

On KORDA: books—

Tabori, Paul, *Alexander Korda*, London, 1959.
Kulik, Karol, *Alexander Korda—the Man Who Could Work Miracles*, London, 1975.
Korda, Michael, *Charmed Lives* (autobiography), 1979.
Stockham, Martin, *The Korda Collection: Alexander Korda's Film Classics*, Secaucus, New Jersey, 1993.
Frayling, Christopher, *Things to Come*, London, 1995.

On KORDA: articles—

Picturegoer, vol. 5, no. 243, 18 January 1936.
Sight and Sound Supplement: Films of 1951 (London), 1951.
Sight and Sound (London), Spring 1956.
Quarterly Journal of Film, Radio and Television, vol. 11, no. 3, Spring 1957.
Screen (London), vol. 13, no. 2, Summer 1972 + filmo.
National Film Theatre booklet (London), February-March 1976.
Australian Journal of Screen Theory, no. 5–6, January-July 1979.
Films and Filming (London), no. 346, July 1983.
Film Dope (London), no. 31, January 1985 + filmo.
Historical Journal Of Film, Radio and Television (Abingdon), vol. 6, no. 2, October 1986.
Sight and Sound (London), vol. 55, no. 2, Spring 1986.
Watson, G., in *Variety*, 28 September 1992.
De Toth, A., in *Positif*, September 1993.
Schiff, Morty, ''*Marius*,'' in *Cineaste* (New York), Winter 1993.
Ringer, Paula, ''Alexander Korda: Producer, Director Propogandist,'' in *Classic Images* (Muscatine), May 1995.
Fischer, Dennis, ''A World of Childhood Delights: *The Thief of Baghdad*,'' in *Filmfax* (Evanston), April-May 1997.

Wilinsky, Barbara, "First and Finest: British Films on U.S. Television in the Late 1940s," in *Velvet Light Trap* (Austin), Fall 1997.

Wollen, Peter, "The Vienna Project: *The Third Man* to be Re-released," in *Sight and Sound* (London), July 1999.

*　　*　　*

After the last and greatest of the financial crises that punctuated his career, Alexander Korda was obliged to relinquish the chairmanship of his production company, British Lion. Rather tactlessly, the government receiver asked him to recommend a suitable successor. Korda considered, but failed to come up with any suggestions. "You see," he explained urbanely, "I don't grow on trees."

Irreplaceable Korda certainly was. When, in 1933, with the audacious and unexpected success of *The Private Life of Henry VIII*, he erupted on to the international scene, the staid British movie industry had never experienced anyone like him: a mogul on the grand scale, flamboyant, lavish, autocratic, and infinitely ambitious. Since his death in 1956, no other British producer has come within a mile of replacing him.

Cosmopolitan and cultured, Korda never took to the parochial world of Hollywood ("it was like Siberia"), but he readily absorbed the blockbuster mentality. "I can't afford to make cheap pictures," he observed once. Though in fact quite capable of making small-scale, intimate films (*Rembrandt*, *Perfect Strangers*), he instinctively gravitated towards grand themes, epic tales of history and heroism which were given the full spectacular treatment. At all times, even when money was short, he believed in thinking big. The finest and most expensive personnel were hired. Prestigious names such as Churchill and H.G. Wells were drafted in to write scripts. Denham, founded on the strength of *Henry VIII*, was the first British film studio built on a Hollywood scale.

Although Korda was also a director, his achievements in this field were rarely more than competent, and he often admitted to finding directing work dull. His real talent was as an impresario, inspiring others with his own glittering, slightly cockeyed vision. Teamwork was never his style ("you can work *for* Korda, but not *with* him," a colleague noted), but he knew how to flatter. Actors, writers, and directors—including the prickly von Sternberg—were disarmed by his professional understanding of their problems. To Britain, his adopted country, he offered a shrewdly inflated version of the national myth, Kiplingesque sagas subtly leavened with sophisticated Hungarian irreverence. His pre-war "Empire trilogy" (*Sanders of the River*, *The Drum*, *The Four Feathers*) make embarrassing viewing today, but in the 1930s provided reassurance to an insecure nation—as did *Fire over England*, with its ringing patriotic defiance of potential invaders.

During the war Korda continued in heroic vein with *Lady Hamilton*—"propaganda with a very thick coating of sugar," in his own estimation, but Churchill's favourite film. As post-war tastes changed, his penchant for high period style betrayed him: both *Bonnie Prince Charlie* and *Anna Karenina* fell woefully flat. The greatest success of his later years was *The Third Man*—romanticism still, but of the dark, downbeat variety. Not that failure ever narrowed the scope of his ambition. Among his final projects were a remake of *The Four Feathers* (*Storm over the Nile*) and Laurence Olivier's *Richard III*.

Korda's greatest asset as a producer was his legendary charm. He was, recalled the actor Jack Hawkins, "a man to whom it was impossible to say no," and hard-headed businessmen melted into compliance in his presence. The Prudential Assurance Company, belying its name, was beguiled into financing Denham, and watched helplessly as £2m (of pre-1939 money) vanished beyond recall. "His engaging personality and charm of manner must be resisted. His financial sense is non-existent and his promises (even when they are sincere) worthless," reported a Prudential executive—but by then it was far too late. Yet even after this debacle, when Korda's profligacy was public knowledge, he could coolly appropriate £1m from MGM to re-establish himself in London after the Second World War. Later still the British Government was persuaded to pour a further £2m into the ravenous jaws of British Lion.

It would be wrong to dismiss Korda as little more than a glorified con man. True, he could be accused of making rootless, international films lacking in any indigenous style, and of inducing delusions of grandeur among other British producers (most notably J. Arthur Rank). He was largely, if not entirely, responsible for making cinema such a suspect investment that the British movie industry has remained chronically underfunded to this day. On all these counts, the downfall of a company like Goldcrest can be traced directly back to Korda's disastrous precedent.

But against that, he brought to British cinema qualities it badly needed: vitality, imagination, sophistication, and style. At their best, there is an ebullience of conception about Korda's films for which he himself (always a great initiator of projects) deserves full credit. The generosity of his nature and the excitement engendered by his presence, inspired everyone who came into contact with him. Ralph Richardson spoke of the "gleam of light from the steel of his personality that gave one courage." A prestigious array of actors—Richardson, Charles Laughton, Olivier, Leslie Howard, Vivien Leigh, Merle Oberon—owed their screen careers to his encouragement, and it was his flair for teaming that introduced Graham Greene to Carol Reed, and Michael Powell to Emeric Pressburger. Without Korda, the British film industry might well have been a more soundly-based structure, but it would have been a duller one, too.

—Philip Kemp

KORDA, Vincent

Art Director. **Nationality:** British. **Born:** Vincze Kellner in Pusztaturpaszto, Hungary, 1897; brother of the directors Alexander and Zoltan Korda; emigrated to Britain, 1932; naturalized 1938. **Education:** Attended schools in Túrkeve, Kecskemet, and Budapest until 1909; studied at the College of Industrial Art, Budapest, 1910–12; also apprentice in an architect's office, Budapest, 1910–12; studied painting and drawing under Belya Avanyi Grunwald, Kecskemet art colony, 1912–15; also studied painting in Vienna, Florence, and Paris, 1919–25. **Family:** Married the actress Gertrude Musgrove, 1933 (divorced 1942); son: the writer Michael Korda. **Career:** 1916–18—served in Hungarian army; then painter in Hungary and Paris; 1932–45—art director, London Films, and later for British Lion Films, 1946–54. **Awards:** Academy Award for *The Thief of Bagdad*, 1940. **Died:** In London, 5 January 1979.

Vincent Korda

Films as Art Director/Production Designer:

1931 *Marius* (A. Korda)
1932 *Men of Tomorrow* (Sagan and Z. Korda); *Fanny* (Allégret)
1933 *Wedding Rehearsal* (A. Korda) (co); *The Private Life of Henry VIII* (A. Korda); *The Girl from Maxim's* (A. Korda)
1934 *Catherine the Great* (*The Rise of Catherine the Great*) (Czinner); *The Private Life of Don Juan* (A. Korda)
1935 *The Scarlet Pimpernel* (Young); *The Ghost Goes West* (Clair); *Sanders of the River* (*Bosambo*) (Z. Korda); *Moscow Nights* (*I Stand Condemned*) (Asquith); *Things to Come* (Menzies)
1936 *The Man Who Could Work Miracles* (Mendes); *Rembrandt* (A. Korda); *Men Are Not Gods* (Reisch); *Cesar* (Pagnol)
1937 *Elephant Boy* (Flaherty and Z. Korda); *I, Claudius* (von Sternberg—unfinished); *The Squeaker* (*Murder on Diamond Row*) (Howard); *Over the Moon* (Freeland); *21 Days* (*The First and the Last; 21 Days Together*) (Dean)
1938 *The Drum* (*Drums*) (Z. Korda)
1939 *The Lion Has Wings* (Powell, Hurst, and Brunel)
1940 *The Conquest of the Air* (Z. Korda and others) (co); *The Thief of Bagdad* (Berger, Powell, and Whelan); *Old Bill and Son* (Dalrymple)
1941 *Major Barbara* (Pascal) (co); *Lydia* (Duvivier); *That Hamilton Woman* (*Lady Hamilton*) (A. Korda)
1942 *To Be or Not To Be* (Lubtisch); *Jungle Book* (*Rudyard Kipling's Jungle Book*) (Z. Korda)
1945 *Perfect Strangers* (*Vacation from Marriage*) (A. Korda)

1947 *An Ideal Husband* (A. Korda)
1948 *The Fallen Idol* (Reed); *Bonnie Prince Charlie* (Kimmins) (co)
1949 **The Third Man** (Reed)
1950 **Miracolo a Milano** (*Miracle in Milan*) (De Sica) (uncredited)
1951 *Outcast of the Islands* (Reed)
1952 *Home at Seven* (*Murder on Monday*) (Richardson); *The Sound Barrier* (*Breaking the Sound Barrier*) (Lean); *The Holly and the Ivy* (O'Ferrall) (co)
1954 *Malaga* (*Fire over Africa*) (Sale) (co)
1955 *Summer Madness* (*Summertime*) (Lean); *The Deep Blue Sea* (Litvak)
1960 *Scent of Mystery* (*Holiday in Spain*) (Cardiff)
1962 *The Longest Day* (Annakin, Marton, and Wicki) (co)
1964 *The Yellow Rolls-Royce* (Asquith) (co)
1971 *Nicholas and Alexandra* (Schaffner) (uncredited)

Films as Supervisor:

1937 *Action for Slander* (Whelan); *Paradise for Two* (*The Gaiety Girls*) (Freeland)
1938 *The Challenge* (Rosmer); *Prison without Bars* (Hurst)
1939 *Q Planes* (*Clouds over Europe*) (Whelan); *The Spy in Black* (*U-Boat 29*) (Powell)

Publications

By KORDA: article—

''The Artist and the Film,'' in *Sight and Sound* (London), Spring 1934.

On KORDA: books—

Kulik, Karol, *Alexander Korda*, London, 1975.
Korda, Michael, *Charmed Lives* (autobiography), London, 1979.

On KORDA: articles—

Picturegoer (London), 17 August 1935.
Myerscough-Walker, R., in *Stage and Film Decor*, London, 1940.
Carrick, Edward, in *Art and Design in the British Film*, London, 1948.
Film Dope (Nottingham), January 1985.

*   *   *

Vincent Korda, who took charge of the art department at Denham Film studios in the 1930s, brought to art direction there a quality far higher than that of the average designer in either theatre or film. His period as a painter in France made an imprint on both his personal set designs and those produced under his charge in the studio, while his strongly persuasive character and impatience dominated the work of those around him, from his fellow designers to carpenters and decorators who carried out the finished sets.

The ideal situation in set design is a cooperative, integrated effort between the film director, the cameraman, and the designer. In many instances, the role of the latter has been considered unimportant, but Korda never allowed this to happen. If anything, his art direction, with his strong personality, dominated the production. On the other hand, he insisted on emphasizing the director's ideas and the cameraman's artistic and technical potential. Consequently, the end result was almost always satisfactory, well above average. Even when the film itself failed to gain acceptance, the set design received acclaim.

Such was the case with the film *Things to Come*, one of the first science-fiction subjects brought to the screen by Denham Studios in 1935. The sets stunned with their functional, Bauhaus interiors and immensely distorted perspectives of exteriors. Korda pioneered the use of models for trick effects for this production, accentuating distances, and avoiding the flat, direct appearance of ordinary, dull reality.

Possibly his most memorable designs were the sets for the film *Rembrandt*, made in 1936. As a former painter, he found a remarkable sympathy with Rembrandt and succeeded in recreating the background and atmosphere of the subject. His knowledge of architecture, combined with his pictorial sense and attention to minute detail, as well as—for a change—the money lavished on this production, resulted in one of the most satisfying achievements in the history of set design.

Korda's approach differed from Hollywood's. Instead of lavishing money on sets which did not reflect their cost on the screen, he spent little but made the sets look expensive. He strove frequently to save money and, with it, valuable time. He made his team work throughout the night on the production of *The Private Life of Henry VIII*, re-using many props to turn a bedroom into a banquet hall ready for the cameras the following morning. The next night, he turned the same set back into a reception room. He even saved (as his son maintains) the reusable nails and pasteboard structures to be used in another production. The success of this film included comments to the effect that no other film resembled such classic "Englishness" as *Henry VIII*.

He succeeded in applying his sense of period style in other films such as the unfinished *I, Claudius*, *That Hamilton Woman*, and *The Thief of Bagdad*, although the latter also demanded huge sets which proved to be almost beyond the technical resources of the British film industry at that time. In spite of his personal dislike of the style of the production, it won him an Oscar for art direction. Another production of great distinction was *The Drum*, which once again gave proof of his unique sense of pictorial style, his talent for establishing the right atmosphere, and his technical perfection. Korda is one of the most imaginative art directors the film medium has had.

—John Halas

KORNGOLD, Erich Wolfgang

Composer. **Nationality:** American. **Born:** Brno (now Czechoslovakia), 29 May 1897; son of the music critic Julius Korngold; became American citizen, 1943. **Family:** Married Luzi von Sonnenthal, 1924; two sons. **Career:** Precocious musical talent: early stage works performed successfully in Vienna; served in Austrian army as musical

Erich Wolfgang Korngold

director of his regiment; 1919–22—conductor at Hamburg Opera House; taught opera and composition at Vienna City Academy from 1927; 1934—accompanied Max Reinhardt to Hollywood for production of *A Midsummer Night's Dream* on stage (and did film version, 1935); worked for Paramount and MGM as film composer; 1949–51—worked in Vienna. **Awards:** Academy Award for *Anthony Adverse*, 1936, *The Adventures of Robin Hood*, 1938. **Died:** In Hollywood, California, 29 November 1957.

Films as Composer:

1936   *Rose of the Rancho* (Gering) (song); *Give Us This Night* (Hall); *Anthony Adverse* (LeRoy); *Hearts Divided* (Borzage) (co; uncredited)
1937   *The Prince and the Pauper* (Keighley); *Another Dawn* (Dieterle)
1938   **The Adventures of Robin Hood** (Curtiz and Keighley) (+ music for trailer)
1939   *Juarez* (Dieterle); *The Private Lives of Elizabeth and Essex* (Curtiz)
1940   *The Sea Hawk* (Curtiz)
1941   *The Sea Wolf* (Curtiz)
1942   *Kings Row* (Wood)
1943   *The Constant Nymph* (Goulding)
1944   *Between Two Worlds* (Blatt)
1946   *Devotion* (Bernardt—produced 1943) (+ bit ro); *Of Human Bondage* (Goulding)
1947   *Deception* (Rapper); *Escape Me Never* (Godfrey)

Films as Arranger:

1935   *A Midsummer Night's Dream* (Reinhardt and Dieterle); *Captain Blood* (Curtiz)
1936   *The Green Pastures* (Connelly and Keighley) (co—uncredited)
1955   *Magic Fire* (Dieterle) (+ ro)

Publications

By KORNGOLD: article—

In *Film Score*, edited by Tony Thomas, South Brunswick, New Jersey, 1979.

On KORNGOLD: books—

Hoffmann, R. S., *Erich Wolfgang Korngold*, Vienna, 1922.
Korngold, Julius, *Child Prodigy*, New York, 1945.
Korngold, Luzi, *Erich Wolfgang Korngold*, Vienna, 1967.
Carroll, Brendan G., *Erich Wolfgang Korngold*, Paisley, Scotland, 1984.
Carroll, Brendan G., *Erich Korngold 1897–1957: His Life and Works*, Paisley, Scotland, 1987, 1989.
Duchen, Jessica, *Erich Wolfgang Korngold*, New York, 1996.

On KORNGOLD: articles—

Films in Review (New York), March 1962.
Thomas, Anthony, in *Films in Review* (New York), February 1965.
Behlmer, Rudy, in *Films in Review* (New York), February 1967.
Films and Filming (London), March 1972, corrections in April 1973.
Thomas, Tony, in *Music for the Movies*, South Brunswick, New Jersey, 1973.
International Film Collector, February 1973.
Dale, S. S., in *The Strand* (London), August 1976.
Positif (Paris), November 1976.
24 Images (Longueuil, Quebec), September 1981.
Rivista del Cinematografo (Rome), November 1981.
Lacombe, Alain, in *Hollywood*, Paris, 1983.
Films in Review (New York), May 1989.
Palmer, Christopher, in *The Composer in Hollywood*, New York, 1990.
Walsh, M., "From High Art to Hollywood," in *Time*, 28 June 1993.
Brown, Royal S., "Film Music: The Good, the Bad, and the Ugly," in *Cineaste* (New York), Winter-Spring 1995.
Teachout, Terry, "I Heard it at the Movies," in *Commentary*, November 1996.
Deutsch, D.C., "The Warner Bros. Years," in *Soundtrack* (Mechelen), March 1997.
Faulkner, Dewey, "Erich Wolfgang Korngold: The Warner Bros. Years," in *Yale Review*, July 1997.
Classic Images (Muscatine), March 1998.
James, Jamie, "Songs by Korngold, Mahler, and Alma Schindler-Mahler," in *Stereo Review*, April 1998.
Carroll, Brendan, "From Around the World: Trier, Germany," in *Opera News*, November 1999.

*   *   *

Of the many Austrian and German talents who migrated to America because of the Nazi regime, Erich Wolfgang Korngold rates among the most important and influential. He was the first composer of international stature to sign a contract with a Hollywood studio. Born in Brno, Czechoslovakia, the son of Julius Korngold, one of the most powerful music critics of the time, the boy was a prodigy of astonishing talent, writing piano and chamber pieces while still a child and enjoying success with his pantomime-ballet *Der Schneemann* at the age of 11. A year later his piano trio received performances by top musicians, as did all the following works, with much comment on how a boy could write music of such complexity and maturity. Korngold was 18 when his two one-act operas, *Der Ring des Polykrates* and *Violanta*, were staged, and 23 when *Die tote Stadt*, one of the few greatly successful operas of the 20th century, had its first performance. He followed it with other works, including two more operas, but he never again matched the success of *Die tote Stadt*. In 1929 he began an association with the famous director and producer Max Reinhardt, for whom he rescored a number of operettas by Johann Strauss, Jr., Leo Fall, and Jacques Offenbach. Their biggest success was a restructured version of *Die Fledermaus*, titled *Rosalinda*.

In 1934 Reinhardt was signed by Warner Bros. to film his celebrated staging of Shakespeare's *A Midsummer Night's Dream* and he brought Korngold with him to arrange, expand, and conduct the music Mendelssohn had written in 1827. The film fared better with the critics than the public, but Korngold had made an impression on the film community. He was brought back from Vienna in 1936 to write, with lyricist Oscar Hammerstein II the score for Paramount's quickly forgotten musical *Give Us This Night*, but while doing it he was asked by Warners to score their production of *Captain Blood*, starring the newcomer Errol Flynn. The film made a vivid impact, particularly the richly textured, lilting score. Korngold won an Oscar with his next score, *Anthony Adverse*, and another two years later with *The Adventures of Robin Hood*.

By now it was impossible to return to Vienna and he settled in the Toluca Lake district of North Hollywood, within walking distance of the Warners studios. Of his other scores, *The Private Life of Elizabeth and Essex* and *The Sea Hawk* were also nominated for Oscars. Korngold worked on only 20 films, and ceased scoring them in 1946 to return to absolute music. Being referred to as a film composer had become a little bothersome to him and he also felt the films being offered him were of lesser quality. At the beginning he felt excited by the possibilities of bringing music to vast audiences but with time he felt disillusioned. "A film composer's immortality lasts from the recording stage to the dubbing room." He died in 1957, believing that both his serious works and his film scores had been largely forgotten. Sadly he never lived to see the resurgence of interest in both, with recordings and performance of most of his best works, and the acknowledgment of his place in the history of film composition.

—Tony Thomas

KOSMA, Joseph

Composer. **Pseudonym:** Used pseudonym Georges Mouqué during World War II. **Nationality:** French. **Born:** Jozsef Kozma in Budapest, Hungary, 22 October 1905; naturalized French citizen, 1949. **Education:** Attended Budapest Academy of Music, and studied in Berlin. **Career:** Composed incidental music for plays, operas, and ballets; 1929—first film score, in Hungary; 1933—settled in Paris.

Award: Cannes Festival Prize for *Juliette, ou la clé des songes*, 1951.
Died: Paris, 7 August 1969.

Films as Composer:

1929   *Elet, hal l, szerelem* (*Eternal Love*) (Lázar)
1934   *La Pêche à la baleine* (Bunin—short)
1935   *La Marche de la faim* (Daniel—short); **Le Crime de Monsieur Lange** (*The Crime of Monsieur Lange*) (Renoir) (song)
1936   *Jenny* (Carné) (co, + ro)
1937   **La Grande Illusion** (*Grand Illusion*) (Renoir); *Le Temps des cérises* (Le Chanois)
1938   *La Goualeuse* (Rivers) (co); **La Bête humaine** (*The Human Beast*) (Renoir)
1941   *Le Soleil a toujours raison* (Billon) (song); *Une Femme dans la nuit* (Gréville)
1942   *Les Visiteurs du soir* (*The Devil's Envoy*) (Carné) (songs)
1943   *Adieu Leonard* (P. Prévert)
1945   **Les Enfants du paradis** (*Children of Paradise*) (co, + song)
1946   *Messieurs Ludovic* (Le Chanois); *Pétrus* (M. Allégret); *Les Portes de la nuit* (*Gates of the Night*) (Carné); *Les Chouans* (Calef); *L'Arche de Noë* (Jacques); *L'Amour autour de la maison* (de Hcrain); *Voyage-surprise* (P. Prévert); *Aubervilliers* (Lotar—short); *L'Homme* (Margaritis—short); **Une Partie de campagne** (*A Day in the Country*) (Renoir—produced 1936)
1947   *Bethsabée* (Moguy); *Le Petit Soldat* (Grimault—short); *La Dame d'onze heures* (Devaivre)
1948   *Le Carrefour des passion* (Giannini); *D'homme à hommes* (*Man to Men*) (Christian-Jaque); *Bagarres* (Calef); *L'Ecole buissonniSre* (Le Chanois); *Les Amants de Vérone* (*The Lovers of Verona*) (Cayatte); *Le Paradis des pilotes perdus* (Lampin); *Hans le marin* (Villiers); *France, nouvelle patrie* (Deleule—short); **Le Sang des bêtes** (Franju—short)
1949   *Les Eaux troublés* (Calef); *Au grand balcon* (Decoin); *La Ferme des sept péchés* (Devaivre); *La Marie du port* (Carné); *Le Jugement de Dieu* (Bernard); *La Belle que voilà* (Le Chanois)
1950   *Vendetta en Camargue* (Devaivre); *Trois télégrammes* (Decoin); *Souvenirs perdus* (Christian-Jaque); *Ombre et lumière* (Calef); *Sans laisser d'adresse* (Le Chanois); *Black Jack* (Duvivier); *L'Inconnue de Montréal* (*Son Copain; Fugitive from Montreal*) (Devaivre); *Dans la vie tout s'arrange* (Cravenne); *Champions juniors* (Blondy—short) (co); *En passant par la Lorraine* (Franju—short)
1951   *Juliette, ou la clé des songes* (Carné); *Un Grand Patron* (Ciampi); *Parigi è sempre Parigi* (Emmer); *Le Cap de l'Espérance* (Bernard); *Les Loups chassent la nuit* (Borderie); *Dupont-Barbès* (Lepage); *The Green Glove* (Maté); *Agence matrimoniale* (Le Chanois); *Les Anonymes du ciel* (Devaivre—short); *Le Canard aux cérises* (de Roubaix—short); *La Commune de Paris* (Menegoz—short); *Isabelle* (Gout—short); *Festival acrobatique* (Devaivre—short); *Mon ami Pierre* (Neurisse and Félix—short); *Si toutes les villes du monde . . .* (Freedland—short)
1952   *La Bergère et le ramoneur* (Grimault); *Opération Magali* (Kish); *Le Rideau rouge* (Barsacq); *Torticola contra Frankensberg* (Paviot—short)

1953   *Innocents in Paris* (Parry); *Les Enfants de l'amour* (Moguy); *Alerte au sud* (Devaivre); *Les Fruits Sauvages* (Bromberger); *Le Cigale et la fourmi* (Image—short); *François le rhinocéros* (Alexandre—short); *Le Loup et l'agneau* (Image—short); *Lumière et l'invention du cinématographe* (*Louis Lumière*) (Paviot—short)
1954   *Le Port du désir* (Gréville); *Huis clos* (*No Exit*) (Audry); *Fantaisie d'un jour* (Cardinal); *Les Evadés* (Le Chanois); *Pas de souris dans le bizness* (Lepage); *Les Chiffonniers d'Emmaüs* (DarSne); *A Paris . . . un jeudi* (Gout—short); *Le Village magique* (Le Chanois); *Ma Jeannette et mes copains* (Gout—short)
1955   *M'sieur la Caille* (Pergament); *Cela s'appelle l'aurore* (Buñuel); *Pas de pitié pour les caves* (Lepage); *Goubbiah* (DarSne); *Des gens sans importance* (Verneuil); *Chagall* (Hessens—short); *L'Amant de Lady Chatterley* (*Lady Chatterley's Lover*) (M. Allégret); *Maigret dirige l'enquête* (Cordier); *Le Devoir de Zouzou* (Vidal—short); *Un Grain de bon sens* (Image—short); *Guillaume Apollinaire* (*Je m'appellerai Guillaume Apollinaire*) (Prouteau—short); *Le Sixième Jour* (Huisman—short); *Tindous* (Devaivre—short); *La Tapisserie au XXe siècle* (Demain—short); *Le Trésor d'Ostende* (Stock—short); *Zut, chien des rues* (d'Artec—short)
1956   *Calle Mayor* (Bardem); *Le Quai des illusions* (Couzinet); *Le Long des trottoirs* (Moguy); *Soupçons* (Billon); *Eléna et les hommes* (*Paris Does Strange Things*) (Renoir); *Je reviendrai à Kandara* (Vicas); *Le Cas du Docteur Laurent* (Le Chanois); *L'Inspecteur aime la bagarre* (Devaivre)
1957   *Les Louves* (Saslavsky); *Trois jours à vivre* (Grangier); *Un Certain M. Jo* (Jolivet); *Tamungo* (Berry)
1958   *La Chatte* (*The Cat*) (Decoin); *The Doctor's Dilemma* (Asquith); *G.S.O.* (Menegoz—short); *Magie du diamant* (Roos—short)
1959   *Le Testament du Docteur Cordelier* (Renoir); *Le Déjeuner sur l'herbe* (*Picnic on the Grass*) (Renoir); *La Chatte sort ses griffes* (Decoin); *La Cocotte d'azur* (Varda—short)
1960   *Katya* (*The Magnificent Sinner*) (Siodmak); *Le Huitième Jour* (Hanoun); *Crésus* (Giono); ''L'Enfance'' ep. of *La Française et l'amour* (*Love and the Frenchwoman*) (Decoin); *Le Grand Erg oriental* (Jacques—short); *Neuf étages tout acier* (Wronecki—short); (co); *Quand midi sonne par la France* (Sirkis—short); *Teiva, enfant des îles* (Mazière—short)
1961   *Le Pavé de Paris* (Decoin); *Snobs!* (Mocky); *Le Trésor des hommes bleus* (Agabra); *Accident* (Daninos—short); *Les Hommes veulent vivre* (Moguy); *Henri Matisse, ou le talent du bonheur* (Marcel Ophüls—short)
1962   *La Caporal epinglé* (*The Elusive Corporal*) (Renoir); *Lemmy pour les dames* (Borderie); *La Poupée* (*He, She, or It*) (Baratier) (co); *A fleur de peau* (Bernard-Aubert); *La Salamandre d'or* (Regamy); *In the French Style* (Parrish)
1963   *Un Dr"le de paroissien* (*Thank Heaven for Small Favors*) (Mocky); *A l'aube du troisième jour* (*Les Moutons de Praxos*) (Bernard-Aubert) (co)
1966   *Un Soir à Tibériade* (Bromberger); *Fruits amers* (*Soledad*) (Audry)
1970   ''Le Cireuse électrique'' ep. of *Le Petit Théâtre de Jean Renoir* (*The Little Theatre of Jean Renoir*) (Renoir)

Films as Co-Arranger:

1938   *La Marseillaise* (Renoir)
1939   *La Règle du jeu* (*Rules of the Game*) (Renoir)

Publications

By KOSMA: article—

Image et Son (Paris), December 1965.

On KOSMA: article—

Unifrance Film (Paris), November 1951.
Film Dope (Nottingham), January 1985.
Glayman, Claude, "Kosma: Chansons + Baptiste," in *UNESCO Courier*, July 1991.
Kosovsky, B., in *Film Score Monthly* (Los Angeles), April 1994.

*   *   *

If Joseph Kosma is generally remembered for his "literary" songs, written in collaboration with Jacques Prévert, he was also one of France's finest composers of film music, working on over a hundred films. Throughout his career, whether setting to music the poetry of Jacques Prévert, Robert Desnos, Raymond Queneau, or Jean-Paul Sartre, or collaborating on the films of Jean Renoir, Pierre Prévert, Marcel Carné, or Paul Grimault, or composing ballet music or operas, Kosma wrote music identifiable by its popular accessibility. Rather than a commercial decision, the popular nature of Kosma's work reflects an ideological stance which held music as a means of communication with the people, he constantly succeeded in producing an "engaged" music that was free from potentially alienating intellectual forms.

Born in Hungary, Kosma first studied at the Budapest Academy of Music and, before accepting a scholarship to study in Berlin in 1929, he wrote his first score, for one of the earliest Hungarian sound films, Lajos Lázar's *Eternal Love*. In Berlin he met, and was considerably influenced by, Bertolt Brecht, Kurt Weill, and Hanns Eisler, but in 1933 Hitler's accession to power forced Kosma to leave for Paris where he settled and took French citizenship in 1949.

Despite this international background, Kosma soon became the favoured composer of Jean Renoir, thus contributing to some of the most quintessentially French of French films. Having composed the score for I.M. Daniel's fictional appeal for worker solidarity, *La Marche de la faim*, in which the influence of Eisler and Weill is clear, he embarked on his collaboration with Renoir by composing the song, "Au jour le jour, à la nuit la nuit" for *Le Crime de Monsieur Lange*. There followed Carné's first feature film, *Jenny*, in which Kosma also played the role of a pianist, scripted by his life-long friend and colleague Jacques Prévert. But while the high moments of the poetic realism of the films of Carné involved compositions by Maurice Jaubert, Kosma continued to work with Renoir on some of his most celebrated prewar films: *La Grande Illusion*, *La Marseillaise*, *La Bête humaine*, and *La Règle du jeu*. His vigorous opening "symphonie du rail" for *La Bête humaine* has been compared to that composed by Honegger for Abel Gance's *La Roue*, and is in marked contrast to the gentle and melodious score for the unfinished *Une Partie de campagne*. But in both cases, the music perfectly complements the visual style of

Renoir, demonstrating Kosma's belief that the successful composition of film scores involved the discreet relationship of the music to both the subject of the film and the atmosphere created visually by the director. Hence he always preferred to compose his scores from the shot material rather than from the scenario.

During the war, working under the name Georges Mouqué, Kosma resumed his collaboration with Marcel Carné and Jacques Prévert (together with Alexandre Trauner, also working clandestinely). He wrote two songs for *Les Visiteurs du soir* and the mime sequence for *Les Enfants du paradis* which was so successful that it entered Jean-Louis Barrault's own repertoire as the ballet *Baptiste*. Immediately after the war the same team produced *Les Portes de la nuit*, including the tenderly romantic song, "Les Enfants qui s'aiment." Kosma's postwar career is prolific and varied. He collaborated with "quality" directors such as André Cayatte (the grandiose oratorio at the end of *Les Amants de Vérone*) and Henri Decoin (the classical overture of *Au grand balcon*), but he also wrote music for the animated films of Paul Grimault and Jean Image, the documentaries of Eli Lotar, Georges Franju, and Robert Ménégoz, and the postwar French films of Renoir (including, for example, the "Air des Bohémiens" in *Eléna et les hommes*).

In 1951, Kosma was awarded the Cannes Film Festival's prize for the best musical score for *Juliette, ou la clé des songes*, a somewhat mediocre fantasy directed by Carné. But Kosma's music excels less in such a fantasy world as in the precise location of popular Paris, the working-class districts into which he injects a degree of poetic pathos—such as in the plaintive opening of *Le Sang des bêtes* or, with recourse to song, the gentle revolt of Prévert's verse in Lotar's *Aubervilliers*.

Towards the end of his life, Kosma concentrated less on film music than on opera and lyrical theatre, always as a means of communication with the people. His oratorio *Les Canuts*, inspired by the revolt of the oppressed silk weavers of Lyon in 1831, is typical of Kosma's wish to apply his classical training to the service of the masses; in *Les Canuts*, there are no virtuoso solo parts, but a choral mass represents an impressive and powerful working class.

Although Kosma did compose purely instrumental pieces such as his "Suite languedocienne" and "Sonatine pour violon," his music was at its best when in conjunction with images or verse. His name will remain associated not only with the films of Renoir and Carné but with the heyday of postwar Saint German-des-Prés and the voices of Juliette Greco and Yves Montand singing his settings for the poetry of Jacques Prévert: the supple melodies of the melancholic "Autumn Leaves" and "Les enfants qui s'aiment" and the lyrical realism of "Barbara" have ensured these songs a permanent place in French culture.

—Richard Alwyn

KOVACS, Laszlo

Cinematographer. **Nationality:** American (naturalised, 1963). **Born:** Budapest, 14 May 1933; credited as Leslie Kovacs on early films. **Education:** Attended Budapest Film School, graduated with an M.A. 1956. **Family:** One son, Imre, one daughter, Julia. **Career:** 1956— escaped to Austria during Hungarian Revolution with the photographer Vilmos Zsigmond, then to the United States, 1957; worked as still photographer and in TV laboratory; first U.S. film credits in mid-1960s; freelance cinematographer for motion pictures and commercials; lecturer at various film schools; member of Academy of Motion Picture Arts and Sciences; member of American Society of Cinematographers. **Awards:** Camerimage Lifetime Achievement Award, 1998; Hawaii International Film Festival Cinematography Award, for body of work, 1998; Worldfest Flagstaff Lifetime Achievement Award, 1999. **Address:** Mirisch Agency Ste 700, 10100 Santa Monica Boulevard, Los Angeles, CA 90067, U.S.A.

Films as Cinematographer:

1957   *Hungarn in Flammen (Revolt in Hungary)* (Erdelyi—doc) (co)
1965   *The Nasty Rabbit (Spies A-Go-Go)* (James Landis) (asst, + ro); *Mark of the Gun* (Compo); *The Notorious Fanny Hill* (Stootsberry)
1967   *Hell's Angels on Wheels* (Rush); *Mondo Mod* (Perry) (co); *A Man Called Dagger* (Rush); *Targets* (Bogdanovich); *Blood of Dracula's Castle* (Adamson); *Rebel Rousers* (Cohen)
1968   *Single Room Furnished* (Cimber); *Psych-Out* (Rush); *The Savage Seven* (Rush); *Hell's Blood Devils* (Adamson—re-edited version: *Smashing the Crime Syndicate*); *Mark of the Gun*
1969   *That Cold Day in the Park* (Altman); **Easy Rider** (Hopper); *A Day with the Boys* (Gulager—short)
1970   *Getting Straight* (Rush); **Five Easy Pieces** (Rafelson); *Alex in Wonderland* (Mazursky); *The Marriage of a Young Stockbroker* (Turman)
1971   *The Last Movie* (Hopper); *Directed by John Ford* (Bogdanovich—short); *A Reflection of Fear* (Fraker); *The Last Picture Show* (Bogdanovich)
1972   *Pocket Money* (Rosenberg); *What's Up, Doc?* (Bogdanovich); *The King of Marvin Gardens* (Rafelson); *Steelyard Blues* (Myerson) (co)
1973   *Slither* (Zieff); *Paper Moon* (Bogdanovich)
1974   *Huckleberry Finn* (Lee Thompson); *For Pete's Sake* (Yates); *Freebie and the Bean* (Rush)
1975   *Shampoo* (Ashby); *At Long Last Love* (Bogdanovich)
1976   *Baby Blue Marine* (Hancock); *Harry and Walter Go to New York* (Rydell); *Nickelodeon* (Bogdanovich); *Family* (Rydell)
1977   *New York, New York* (Scorsese); **Close Encounters of the Third Kind** (Spielberg) (co)
1978   *F.I.S.T.* (Jewison); *Paradise Alley* (Stallone); *The Last Waltz* (Scorsese) (co)
1979   *Butch and Sundance: The Early Days* (Lester); *The Runner Stumbles* (Kramer); *Heart Beat* (Byrum); *The Rose* (Rydell) (co)
1980   *Inside Moves* (R. Donner)
1981   *The Legend of the Lone Ranger* (Fraker)
1982   *Frances* (Clifford); *The Toy* (R. Donner)
1984   *Crackers* (Malle); *Ghostbusters* (Reitman)
1985   *Mask* (Bogdanovich)
1986   *Legal Eagles* (Reitman)
1988   *Little Nikita* (Benjamin)
1989   *Say Anything . . .* (Crowe)
1991   *Shattered (The Plastic Nightmare)* (Petersen)
1992   *Radio Flyer* (R. Donner); *Ruby Cairo (Deception)* (Clifford)
1993   *Sliver* (Noyce) (co)
1994   *The Next Karate Kid* (Cain); *The Scout* (Ritchie)
1995   *Copycat* (Amiel); *Free Willy 2: The Adventure Home* (Little)
1996   *Multiplicity* (Ramis)
1997   *My Best Friend's Wedding* (Hogan)
1998   *Jack Frost* (Miller)
2000   *Return to Me* (Hunt); *Miss Congeniality*

Other Films:

1964   *The Time Travelers* (Melchior) (cam)
1971   *The American Dreamer* (Carson and Schiller)
1992   *Visions of Light* (as Laszlo Kovacs)

Publications

By KOVACS: articles—

Dialogue on Film (Beverly Hills, California), October 1974.
On *F.I.S.T.* in *American Cinematographer* (Hollywood), February 1978.
Filmmakers Newsletter (Ward Hill, Massachusetts), July 1978.
American Film (Washington, D.C.), June 1979.
On *The Runner Stumbles* in *American Cinematographer* (Hollywood), November 1979.
On *The Legend of the Lone Ranger* in *American Cinematographer* (Hollywood), July 1981.
In *Masters of Light: Conversations with Contemporary Cinematographers*, by Dennis Schaefer and Larry Salvato, Berkeley, California, 1984.
Ecran Fantastique (Paris), December 1984.
Filmkultura (Budapest), vol. 25, no. 6, 1989.
"Multiple Keatons Add Up to a New Challenge for a DP of Many Faces," in *Lighting Dimensions* (Los Angeles), 1 June 1996.

On KOVACS: articles—

Mitchell, George J., in *Take One* (Montreal), July/August 1970.
Focus on Film (London), no. 13, 1973.
McNicoll, D., in *Cinema Canada* (Montreal), October/November 1979.
Films and Filming (London), May 1980.
Goodwin, M., in *Moving Image* (San Francisco), March/April 1982.
Patterson, R., on *Frances* in *American Cinematographer* (Hollywood), March 1983.
McCarthy, T., in *Film Comment* (New York), March/April 1984.
Lofficier, Randy, in *American Cinematographer* (Hollywood), June 1984.

*   *   *

Born in Hungary, Laszlo Kovacs—sometimes billed early in his career as Leslie Kovacs or Art Radford—escaped to the West along with Vilmos Zsigmond, with whom he collaborated on a documentary about the 1956 Hungarian uprising and, later, *Close Encounters of the Third Kind*. It appears to have been a total coincidence that his name was used by Jean-Paul Belmondo as an alias in *A Bout de Souffle*, but this did give rise to the speculation—when he worked with movie buff Peter Bogdanovich on *Targets* and the documentary *Directed by John Ford*—that Bogdanovich was functioning as his own director of photography and assuming an in-joke pseudonym. Like Zsigmond, although to a lesser extent, Kovacs cut his teeth on marginal exploitation movies, such as *The Notorious Fanny Hill*. In his case, however, the transition from drive-in underground to the mainstream was fairly straightforward and represented no particular change of style. Kovacs's first attention-getting credit was for *Easy Rider*, which was an obvious extension of his work on the late 1960s cycle of biker exploitation movies, especially *The Savage Seven* and *Hell's Angels on Wheels*. These were directed by Richard Rush, with whom Kovacs also worked on *Psych-Out*, a freeform hippie odyssey with Jack Nicholson that prefigured many of the countercultural aspects of Dennis Hopper's movie and also the kind of subculture seaminess Kovacs would explore with Nicholson and Bob Rafelson in *Five Easy Pieces* and *The King of Marvin Gardens*.

The most lasting associations of Kovacs's career—with Rush, Bogdanovich, and *Easy Rider* associate Rafelson—come from this period, when a group of filmmakers loosely clustered around Roger Corman and American International Pictures, spun off the stuff of youth exploitation—bikes, drugs, drop-outs—into the 1970s "road movie" and the kinetic psychedelia of Hollywood's flirtation with pop art. The photographic hallmarks of Kovacs's work are images of rebel youths—Hopper, Nicholson, Peter Fonda—with their hair long and beards unshaven, perched on gleaming bikes and traveling through the dusty western roads that had replaced the trails ridden by Hopalong Cassidy or John Ford's heroes. The psychedelic aspect led to various attempts to simulate drug-induced altered states of perception, and Kovacs shot, in *Easy Rider* and *Psych-Out*, more than his share of flashing lights, bleary wanderings, and cut-to-the-rhythm-of-the-rock-soundtrack freak-outs. This specialty found him yoked to such commercially disastrous ventures as Robert Altman's psychodrama *That Cold Day in the Park*, Rush's (not as embarrassing as most of its genre) "campus revolt" picture *Getting Straight*, Hopper's willful *The Last Movie*, and Paul Mazursky's cool-hippie *Alex in Wonderland*. It also allowed him to demonstrate a growing mastery of a visual technique that was at once loose enough to allow for the druggy improvisation of Hopper but formally neat enough to suggest the old Hollywood virtues Bogdanovich was aspiring to in *Targets*.

In the 1970s, Kovacs stuck by Bogdanovich, making the black-and-white images of *The Last Picture Show* and *Paper Moon* work, turning in a perfectly acceptable simulation of Ross Hunter gloss for *What's Up, Doc?*, and filming black-and-white-in-color for the bizarre but increasingly impressive *At Long Last Love*. He was at a loss, however, with the prettified nostalgia of *Nickelodeon* and later failed to make *Mask*, with its bikers and deformed hero, look like anything as interesting as *Hell's Angels on Wheels*. The association also spilled over into shooting dud imitations of the genre trifles Bogdanovich usually managed to pull off, resulting in such credits as *For Pete's Sake* and *Harry and Walter Go to New York*.

Kovacs was becoming the photographic master of the roadside movie through his work for Rafelson, in *Five Easy Pieces* and *The King of Marvin Gardens*, which mix tatty observation with a wry romantic pessimism, and found that this experience, plus all those hog-straddling Hell's Angel movies, equipped him for road movies as varied as Stuart Rosenberg's modern Western *Pocket Money*, Howard Zieff's seductive comic-caper *Slither*, Richard Rush's car-crash cop comedy *Freebie and the Bean*, Hal Ashby's Beverly Hills road movie *Shampoo*, and Spielberg's magical American odyssey, *Close Encounters*. Cars and motorbikes crop up constantly, and Kovacs has become adept at shooting scenes in diners and lay-bys, frequently catching some unexpected slice of Americana in the background.

His affinity for the landscape of the west, demonstrated in *Easy Rider*, *The Last Picture Show*, *Pocket Money*, and *Close Encounters*, was disappointingly betrayed by his only real Western credit, the lamentable *The Legend of the Lone Ranger*. Throughout the 1970s, Kovacs was on-call for major Hollywood figures, following Martin Scorsese from the glittering, hard-edged 1940s feel of *New York, New York* to the aptly AIP-ish fuzziness of *The Last Waltz*. He even formed an association with Sylvester Stallone—like Scorsese, another Corman graduate—on the star's ambitious but inconsistent post-*Rocky* attempts to be a blue-collar artist in *F.I.S.T.* and *Paradise Alley*. Kovacs later found himself involved with such self-consciously "sincere" works as *The Runner Stumbles* and *Frances* but, unlike the more prettifying Zsigmond, he has never really become "respectable" enough for Academy Award consideration. Like Rafelson, Bogdanovich, Rush, and Hopper, Kovacs is essentially a 1970s talent, and his major works are all clustered around the beginning of that decade. Despite his contribution to *Close Encounters*, he never quite got the knack for the large-scale fantasies which predominated in the 1980s, taking Hollywood away from the rough-edged observation in which he specialized. Considering his work on *Ghostbusters*, a mainly successful entertainment, one is struck by how drab the film *looks*, as if Kovacs had been ordered not to let his visual imagination swamp the special effects or the wisecracks, and it is notable that he was the only major contributor to this box-office hit who was not involved in he equally anonymous-looking *Ghostbusters 2*.

In the early 1990s, Kovacs was reduced to shaky assignments such as *Ruby Cairo* and *The Next Karate Kid*, while in the second half of the decade he fared a little better with lightweight comedies such as *My Best Friend's Wedding*, *Jack Frost*, and *Return to Me*. Although Kovacs provided a steadying influence on these films, there are few signs in them of the cinematic quality and style with which he made his name in the 1970s. The current trend in Hollywood seems to be for movies with strong narratives, driven home with special effects. In such a climate, cinematographers like Kovacs, who excel at observational, descriptive filmmaking, have few opportunities to show off their skills. In the 1990s, only the flop *Radio Flyer* contained elements reminiscent of Kovacs' great days.

—Kim Newman, updated by Chris Routledge

KRÄLY, Hanns

Writer. **Nationality:** German. **Born:** 1885; sometimes credited as Hans Kraly in the United States. **Career:** Stage and film actor; 1912—first film as writer, *Die Kinder des Generals*, the first of several films for Urban Gad; 1916—first of many films for Ernst Lubitsch, *Schuhpalast Pinkus*; 1923—accompanied Lubitsch to Hollywood, and continued to write until 1943. **Award:** Academy Award for *The Patriot*, 1928–29. **Died:** In Los Angeles, California, 11 November 1950.

Films as Writer:

1912   *Die Kinder des Generals* (Gad)
1913   *Engelein* (Gad); *Die Filmprimadonna* (Gad)

1914	*Das Feuer* (Gad); *Die ewige Nacht* (Gad); *Weisse Rosen* (Gad)
1916	*Schuhpalast Pinkus* (Lubitsch)
1917	*Der Blusen König* (Lubitsch); *Eine Walternacht* (Kaden)
1918	*Die Augen der Mummie Mâ* (*The Eyes of the Mummy*) (Lubitsch); *Carmen* (*Gypsy Blood*) (Lubitsch); *Das Mädel vom Ballett* (Lubitsch); *Der gelbe Schein* (Janson and Illes); *Der Prozess Hauers* (Zeyn); *Die drei van Hells* (Brenkin)
1919	*Meine Frau, die Filmschauspielerin* (Lubitsch); *Comtesse Doddy* (Jacoby); *Die Austerprinzessin* (*The Oyster Princess*) (Lubitsch); *Das Rosa Trikot* (Lasko); *Madame Du Barry* (*Passion*) (Lubitsch); *Die Fahrt ins Blaue* (Biebrach); *Die Puppe* (*The Doll*) (Lubitsch); *Monica Vogelsang* (Biebrach); *Rausch* (Lubitsch)
1920	*Sumurun* (*One Arabian Night*) (Lubitsch); *Arme Violetta* (Stein); *Anne Boleyn* (*Deception*) (Lubitsch); *Kohlhiessels Töchter* (Lubitsch); *Romeo and Juliet im Schnee* (Lubitsch)
1921	*Die Bergkatze* (*The Wildcat*) (Lubitsch)
1922	*Das Weib des Pharao* (*The Loves of Pharoah*) (Lubitsch)
1923	*Alles für Geld* (*Fortune's Fool*) (Schünzel); *Die Flamme* (*Montmartre*) (Lubitsch); *Boheme* (Righelli); *Rosita* (Lubitsch); *Das Paradies im Schnee* (Jacoby); *Black Oxen* (Lloyd)
1924	*Komödianten des Lebens* (Jacoby); *Three Women* (Lubitsch); *Forbidden Paradise* (Lubitsch); *Her Night of Promise* (Franklin)
1925	*The Eagle* (Brown); *His Sister from Paris* (Franklin); *Kiss Me Again* (Lubitsch)
1926	*So This Is Paris* (Lubitsch); *The Duchess of Buffalo* (Franklin); *Kiki* (Brown)
1927	*Quality Street* (Franklin); *The Student Prince in Old Heidelberg* (Lubitsch)
1928	*The Patriot* (Lubitsch); *The Garden of Eden* (Milestone)
1929	*Eternal Love* (Lubitsch); *Betrayal* (Milestone); *The Last of Mrs. Cheyney* (Franklin); *The Kiss* (Feyder); *Wild Orchids* (Franklin); *Devil-May-Care* (Franklin)
1930	*Lady of Scandal* (Franklin); *A Lady's Morals* (Franklin); *Die Sehnsucht jeder Frau* (Sjöström—German version of *A Lady to Love*)
1931	*Private Lives* (Franklin)
1933	*My Lips Betray* (Blystone); *By Candlelight* (Blystone)
1935	*Broadway Gondolier* (Bacon)
1937	*One Hundred Men and a Girl* (Koster)
1939	*Broadway Serenade* (Leonard)
1941	*It Started with Eve* (Koster); *West Point Widow* (Siodmak)
1942	*The Mad Ghoul* (Hogan)

* * *

While still a teenage actor in Berlin before the Second World War, Hanns Kräly wrote for the burgeoning German cinema. After his scripts for Danish director Urban Gad's *Die Kinder des Generals*, *Engelein*, and *Die Filmprimadonna* had done much to make Gad's wife Asta Nielsen a star, Kräly was approached by Ernst Lubitsch, another ex-actor with ambitions to direct, and even younger than himself. Lubitsch filmed Kräly's *Schuhpalast Pinkus* in 1916. In 1918, both men joined Paul Davidson's tiny Union-Film A. G., where Kräly became Lubitsch's *dramaturg*, editing, adapting, and coscripting almost all the satires and comedies that built the director's reputation.

Kräly and Lubitsch satirized the American *nouveau riche* in *Die Austerprinzessin*, made an adaptation of E. T. A. Hoffmann's fable of an inventor's daughter masquerading as a robot as *Die Puppe*, and filmed *Sumurun*, the Arabian Nights pantomime/ballet in which Max Reinhardt launched Pola Negri. In *Die Augen der Mummie Mâ*, Emil Jannings played a religious visionary pursuing Negri around the world. Its success sparked the Negri/Jannings historical romances which made them Europe's biggest stars.

Cleverly manipulating literature and history, Kräly turned Anne Boleyn, Dubarry, and Carmen into archetypal Negri women—trashy, treacherous, irresistible. Intrigued in particular by *Passion*, Lubitsch and Kräly's version of the Dubarry story, Mary Pickford invited Lubitsch to America in 1922, and Kräly soon joined him. Asked to destroy forever Pickford's coy image, the partners, with Edward Knoblock, adapted a nineteenth-century Spanish romance into the Negri-esque story of a street girl who catches a king's eye. Tough Berlin humour fills *Rosita*. A scented handkerchief handed around her family is sniffed by everyone but a kid brother, who blows his nose on it, while, in a carnival scene, a girl whose lover has just been stabbed releases his corpse to embrace the killer with equal passion. Horrified, Pickford shelved *Rosita*, but Lubitsch and his team flourished.

Kräly wrote Negri's first American film, *Forbidden Paradise*, and followed it up with a version of *The Student Prince* with Ramon Novarro and Norma Shearer. Both films sparkled with the visual *double entendres* that Hollywood (with no resistance from the director) now called "Lubitsch Touches." Kräly's contribution was seldom mentioned, despite the evidence of his scripts for *The Eagle*, a Russian comedy romance with Valentino, and *The Garden of Eden*, a romp through Hapsburg high life and low morals with Corinne Griffith as an ambitious actress on the loose among the Austro-Hungarian aristocracy. Both are as witty and sophisticated as anything by Lubitsch, yet they were directed by Clarence Brown and Lewis Milestone, respectively. Kräly also wrote *The Kiss* and *Wild Orchids* for Garbo, but Hollywood continued to credit Lubitsch alone with real genius.

Inevitably, the partnership ended. *Eternal Love*, in 1929, was their last film together. To be "liquidated by Lubitsch," as Josef von Sternberg put it, was no novelty, and it was Kräly's turn in 1931. The two men had a famous fist fight over a real or fancied affair with Lubitsch's wife, from which the writer emerged effectively blacklisted. Ernest Vajda and Samson Raphaelson supplanted him on Lubitsch's sound films. Kräly went on to adapt *Private Lives* at MGM, and wrote the Deanna Durbin vehicle *One Hundred Men and a Girl*, but his credits dwindled. His last script, for a cheap horror film, was a squalid end to a distinguished, yet blighted career.

—John Baxter

KRASKER, Robert

Cinematographer. **Nationality:** Australian. **Born:** Perth, Western Australia, 12 August 1913. **Education:** Attended Photohandler Schule, Dresden, and art school, Paris. **Career:** Assistant at Paramount Studios, Paris; 1932—assistant to Georges Périnal at London Films,

Robert Krasker

England; 1943—first film as cinematographer, *The Lamp Still Burns*. **Award:** Academy Award for *The Third Man*, 1950. **Died:** 16 August 1981.

Films as Cameraman:

1934   *Catherine the Great* (*The Rise of Catherine the Great*) (Czinner); *The Private Life of Don Juan* (A. Korda)
1935   *Things to Come* (Menzies)
1936   *Forget-Me-Not* (*Forever Yours*) (Z. Korda); *Rembrandt* (A. Korda); *Men Are Not Gods* (Reisch); *The Man Who Could Work Miracles* (Mendes)
1937   *I, Claudius* (von Sternberg—unfinished); *The Squeaker* (*Murder on Diamond Row*) (Howard)
1938   *The Drum* (*Drums*) (Z. Korda); *The Challenge* (Rosmer)
1939   *The Four Feathers* (Z. Korda)
1940   *The Thief of Bagdad* (Berger, Powell, and Whelan)
1941   *Dangerous Moonlight* (*Suicide Squadron*) (Hurst)
1942   *Rose of Tralee* (Burger); *One of Our Aircraft Is Missing* (Powell and Pressburger)

Films as Cinematographer:

1943   *The Lamp Still Burns* (Elvey); *The Gentle Sex* (Howard); *The Saint Meets the Tiger* (Stein)
1944   **Henry V** (Olivier)
1945   **Brief Encounter** (Lean); *Caesar and Cleopatra* (Pascal) (co)
1947   **Odd Man Out** (Reed); *Uncle Silas* (*The Inheritance*) (Frank)
1948   *Bonnie Prince Charlie* (Kimmins)
1949   **The Third Man** (Reed); *The Angel with the Trumpet* (Bushell)
1950   *State Secret* (*The Great Manhunt*) (Gilliat); *The Wonder Kid* (Hartl) (co)
1951   *Cry, the Beloved Country* (*African Fury*) (Z. Korda); *Another Man's Poison* (Rapper)
1953   *Never Let Me Go* (Daves); *Malta Story* (Hurst)
1954   *Romeo and Juliet* (Castellani); *Senso* (*The Wanton Countess*) (Visconti)
1955   *That Lady* (Young); *Alexander the Great* (Rossen)
1956   *Trapeze* (Reed); *The Rising of the Moon* (Ford)
1957   *The Story of Esther Costello* (Miller)
1958   *The Quiet American* (Mankiewicz); *Behind the Mask* (Hurst); *The Doctor's Dilemma* (Asquith)

1959	*Libel* (Asquith)

1959 *Libel* (Asquith)
1960 *The Criminal* (*The Concrete Jungle*) (Losey); *Romanoff and Juliet* (Ustinov)
1961 *El Cid* (A. Mann)
1962 *Guns of Darkness* (Asquith); *Billy Budd* (Ustinov)
1963 *The Running Man* (Reed)
1964 *The Fall of the Roman Empire* (A. Mann)
1965 *The Collector* (Wyler) (co)
1966 *The Trap* (Hayers)
1976 *Red* (Frank—short)
1980 *Cry Wolf* (Burzynski—short)

Publications

On KRASKER: articles—

Lightman, Fred A., on *El Cid* in *American Cinematographer* (Hollywood), January 1962.
Monthly Film Bulletin (London), December 1972.
Focus on Film (London), no. 13, 1973.
Obituary in *Films & Filming*, November 1981.
Filme (Berlin), November-December 1981.
The Annual Obituary 1981, New York, 1982.
Film Dope (Nottingham), March 1985.
Murray, S., in *Cinema Papers* (Fitzroy), April 1997.

*   *   *

Robert Krasker began his film career as a cameraman by serving an "apprenticeship" with Georges Périnal at London Films, where he worked on several films directed by Zoltan and Alexander Korda. His work on *The Drum* and *The Four Feathers* (the location shooting in the Sudan produced footage used in films made 20 years later) gave him the experience he would use in the later epic films *El Cid* and *The Fall of the Roman Empire*, both directed by Mann. Work on the abortive *I, Claudius* and *Rembrandt* also stood him in good stead for Olivier's *Henry V*, which expressionistically merges theatre and film in the opening sequence. Although he lacked experience in Technicolor, Krasker achieved some stunning shots, among them the scene before Agincourt, which critic James Agee described as a "crepuscular shot of the doomed and exhausted English as they withdraw along a sunset stream to encamp for the night." Krasker was equally adept at achieving claustrophobic effects, as in *Brief Encounter* and *The Criminal*, in which he used mirrors to double the size of the set.

Although he worked repeatedly with the same directors, Krasker's most productive collaboration seems to have been with Carol Reed. Robert Moss has written that Krasker was "one of the few men whose patient craftsmanship and innovative ideas matched Reed's." In *The Third Man* Krasker captured in black-and-white the gloomy, corrupt decadence of postwar Vienna, where everything was for sale. Using oblique camera angles, he suggested a distorted world in which buildings loom over characters who seem isolated and vulnerable within the frame. Using shadows he distorted size, as he did with the balloon man, and juxtaposed appearance and reality. The initial appearance of Harry Lime, his lighted face surrounded ominously by blackness, the maze-like sewer sequence mirroring the above-ground moral ambiguity and "waste," and the shot of Lime's fingers sticking up through the sewer drain—these shots were symbolic as well as representational. Even the concluding long take of Anna walking past the waiting Harry Martin comments not only on her rejection of him, but, in its focus on the seemingly endless and almost empty road, also commented on Martin's empty and isolated life.

Krasker's color cinematography for Mann's *El Cid* was remarkable not only for its fluid long takes, but also for pushing the barriers of color photography to their limits. He shot at dusk and dawn and achieved remarkable results. The most striking shot was the resplendent white image of the dead Cid whose armored brilliance cinematically transports him from history to legend as he emerges from the gates of the city. Not even Krasker's cinematography could salvage Mann's later epic, *The Fall of the Roman Empire*, a talky, ponderous film, but the film bears the Krasker signature: fluid camera work, long takes, interesting compositions (the Z-shaped procession which begins and ends the film), and the symbolic shot (the tracking camera moves from behind Aurelius's funeral pyre to the crowd and then to the storm clouds over the mountains, thereby linking cause and effect).

In Wyler's *The Collector* and Visconti's *Senso*, Krasker shared the credit but in each case the results were excellent. Visconti actually worked with three photographers, each of which had his own tonality, though all three were related to the styles of 19th-century painting. The film, which blends art, (in this case opera), with life, has been cited for Krasker's *tour de force* opening sequence, which featured diffuse lighting. In *The Collector* Krasker shot the exterior shots on location, while Robert Surtees was responsible for the interior studio shooting, but the division of labor produces a visual balance between the exterior greens and blues of freedom and the interior yellows, browns, and oranges associated with captivity. Krasker also shot the stalking sequence in which the victim is caught in the "frame" of her pursuer's rear-view mirror.

In both black-and-white and in color films Krasker was a daring innovator, a master of different cinematic styles, and an expert at lighting. Using the camera, he not only rendered reality, but interpreted it for the audience.

—Thomas L. Erskine

KRASNA, Norman

Writer and Producer. **Nationality:** American. **Born:** Queens, New York City, 7 November 1909. **Education:** Attended Columbia University and St. John's University Law School, New York, 1928. **Military Service:** 1943–45—served with the United States Army Air Force motion-picture unit. **Family:** Married 1) Ruth Frazee, 1940 (divorced 1950); 2) Erle Galbraith Jolson, 1951. **Career:** 1928–29—copyboy and assistant to drama editor, *New York World*; 1929–30—drama critic, *New York Evening Graphic*; 1930–31—staff member, *Exhibitors Herald-World*; 1931—first play produced, *Louder, Please*; 1932–37—writer for Columbia: first film as writer, *Hollywood Speaks*; 1937–42—writer and producer, MGM, and at Warner Bros., 1942; 1950–52—director, with Jerry Wald, Wald-Krasna Productions; then freelance writer. **Awards:** Academy Award for *Princess O'Rourke*, 1943; Writers Guild Laurel Award, 1959. **Died:** In Los Angeles, California, 1 November 1984.

Norman Krasna (left) with Eddie Buzzell

Films as Writer:

1932 *Hollywood Speaks* (Buzzell); *That's My Boy* (Neill)
1933 *So This is Africa* (Cline); *Parole Girl* (Cline); *Love, Honor, and Oh Baby!* (Buzzell); *Meet the Baron* (W. Lang)
1934 *The Richest Girl in the World* (W. Lang)
1935 *Romance in Manhattan* (Roberts); *Four Hours to Kill* (Leisen); *Hands across the Table* (Leisen)
1936 *Wife vs. Secretary* (Brown); *Fury* (F. Lang)
1937 *The King and the Chorus Girl* (*Romance Is Sacred*) (LeRoy); *As Good As Married* (Buzzell); *Big City* (Borzage) (+ pr)
1938 *The First Hundred Years* (Thorpe) (+ pr); *You and Me* (F. Lang)
1939 *Bachelor Mother* (Kanin)
1940 *It's a Date* (Seiter)
1941 *Mr. and Mrs. Smith* (Hitchcock); *The Devil and Miss Jones* (Wood); *The Flame of New Orleans* (Clair); *It Started with Eve* (Koster)
1943 *Princess O'Rourke* (+ d)
1944 *Bride by Mistake* (Wallace); *Practically Yours* (Leisen)
1949 *The Big Hangover* (+ d + pr)
1954 *White Christmas* (Curtiz)
1956 *Bundle of Joy* (Taurog); *The Ambassador's Daughter* (+ d + pr)
1958 *Indiscreet* (Donen)
1959 *Who Was That Lady?* (Sidney) (+ pr)
1960 *Let's Make Love* (Cukor)
1961 *My Geisha* (Cardiff)

1963 *Sunday in New York* (Tewksbury)
1964 *I'd Rather Be Rich* (Smight)

Films as Producer:

1938 *Three Loves Has Nancy* (Thorpe)
1951 *Behave Yourself* (Beck); *The Blue Veil* (Bernhardt)
1952 *Clash By Night* (F. Lang); *The Lusty Men* (Ray)

Films based on Krasna's writings:

1947 *Dear Ruth* (Russell)
1949 *John Loves Mary* (Butler)
1950 *Dear Wife* (Haydn)
1951 *Dear Brat* (Seiter)

Publications

By KRASNA: plays—

Louder, Please, New York, 1932.
Small Miracle, New York, 1935.
Bachelor Mother (script), in *The Best Pictures 1939–1940*, New York, 1940.
Fury (script), in *Twenty Best Film Plays*, edited by John Gassner and Dudley Nichols, New York, 1943.
Dear Ruth, New York, 1945.
John Loves Mary, New York, 1947.
With Groucho Marx, *Time for Elizabeth*, New York, 1949.
Kind Sir, New York, 1954.
Who Was That Lady I Saw You With?, New York, 1958.
Sunday in New York, New York, 1962.
Love in E-Flat, New York, 1967.
Watch the Birdie!, New York, 1969.
Bunny, New York, 1970.

By KRASNA: articles—

In *The Hollywood Screenwriter*, edited by Richard Corliss, New York, 1972.
Sight and Sound (London), Autumn 1985.

On KRASNA: articles—

Atkins, Irene, in *American Screenwriters*, edited by Robert E. Morsberger, Stephen O. Lesser, and Randall Clark, Detroit, Michigan, 1984.
Obituary in *Variety* (New York), 7 November 1984.
The Annual Obituary 1984, Chicago 1985.
Film Dope (Nottingham), March 1985.
''*The Ambassador's Daughter*,'' in *Reid's Film Index* (Wyong, New South Wales), no. 25, 1996.

*   *   *

When Hollywood producers of the 1940s demanded ''sophisticated Broadway comedy,'' they usually meant Norman Krasna.

A New York film and drama critic whose screenwriting career paralleled his other as playwright, Krasna was well placed in the early 1930s to merchandise Broadway's less louche plots to a film industry flirting with sophistication.

His specialty, the farce of misunderstanding and mistaken identity, imported from Europe a generation before and found, over decades, to be largely actor-proof, was a gift to Hollywood's lighter comedians. Miriam Hopkins could hardly fail in *The Richest Girl in the World*, testing suitors by posing as her own secretary, nor could Ginger Rogers flop as the shopgirl who inherits a baby in *Bachelor Mother*.

Cecil Parker's comment of Ingrid Bergman in *Indiscreet*, "There is no sincerity like a woman telling a lie," captures perfectly Krasna's relish for duplicity. His women pretend to be mothers (*Bachelor Mother*, *It's a Date*—and the latter's remake *Nancy Goes to Rio*) or elder sisters (*Dear Ruth*). A *demimondaine* pretends virtue in *Flame of New Orleans*, while a virginal Jane Fonda in *Sunday in New York* claims experience. Shirley MacLaine in *My Geisha* pretends to be Japanese. Millionaire store owner Charles Coburn in *The Devil and Miss Jones* pretends to be poor.

Marriage was a frequent Krasna playground. His men marry to win American citizenship for a friend's girl (*John Loves Mary*) or, as in *Mr. and Mrs. Smith*, think they are married but find they are not. Cary Grant in *Indiscreet* invents a wife to avoid entanglements, and in *Who Was That Lady?*, Tony Curtis hides extramarital affairs by pretending to be a spy.

Intermittently active as both producer and director, Krasna never caught fire as either. His production company, Monovale, founded in 1950, made little splash, and his sole Academy Award, for *Princess O'Rourke* in 1943, was not for direction but for the film's script. However, he enjoyed a revival as a writer in the new sexual climate of the 1960s. Slick and suggestive, *Let's Make Love, Sunday in New York*, and especially *Who Was That Lady?*, a domestic comedy crossed with espionage spoof, offered sturdy vehicles to minor comedians like Dean Martin, Yves Montand, and Jane Fonda.

Throughout his career, studios habitually allocated his scripts to the second string, robbing Krasna of much association with great directors, but it is debatable whether he could have risen to the challenge. Working with a Krasna plot in *Mr. and Mrs. Smith*, Hitchcock made one of his weakest films. In *Fury*, the writer did, it is true, flesh out a four-page outline into a screenplay the *New York Times'* Frank Nugent called "elemental in its simplicity . . . yet an encyclopedia of lynch law," but since his collaborators were Fritz Lang and veteran crime movie writer Bartlett Cormack, credit is difficult to allocate. Of the Krasna films by great directors, only *Flame of New Orleans* achieved any synthesis of dialogue and style, with accomplished farceurs like Mischa Auer bouncing the lines off the languorously impassive Dietrich. Ironically, however, the film, forced on Hollywood newcomer René Clair, was one the director disliked intensely.

—John Baxter

KRASNER, Milton

Cinematographer. **Nationality:** American. **Born:** Philadelphia, Pennsylvania, 1901; sometimes credited as Milton R. Krasner. **Career:** Joined Vitagraph in New York as laboratory worker, then assistant editor; camera assistant and second cameraman for various studios in Hollywood in the 1920s; 1933—first film as cinematographer, *Strictly Personal*; TV work includes the series *Macmillan and Wife* and *Macmillan*, 1971–76. **Award:** Academy Award for *Three Coins in the Fountain*, 1954. **Died:** Of heart failure, in Los Angeles, California, 16 July 1988.

Films as Cinematographer:

1933 *Strictly Personal* (Murphy); *I Love That Man* (H. Brown); *Golden Harvest* (Murphy); *Sitting Pretty* (H. Brown)

1934 *She Made Her Bed* (Murphy); *Private Scandal* (Murphy); *The Great Flirtation* (Murphy); *Paris Interlude* (Marin); *Death on the Diamond* (Sedgwick)

1935 *Women Must Dress* (Barker); *Great God Gold* (Lubin); *Honeymoon Limited* (Lubin); *Hold 'em Yale* (*Uniform Lovers*) (Lanfield); *Murder in the Fleet* (Sedgwick); *Cheers of the Crowd* (Moore) (co); *The Virginia Judge* (Sedgwick); *Forbidden Heaven* (Barker); *The Great Impersonation* (Crosland)

1936 *Arbor Day* (Newmeyer—short); *Laughing Irish Eyes* (Santley) (co); *Crash Donovan* (Nigh); *Yellowstone* (Lubin); *The Girl on the Front Page* (Beaumont); *Mister Cinderella* (Sedgwick); *Love Letters of a Star* (Foster and Carruth); *Mysterious Crossing* (Lubin)

1937 *She's Dangerous* (Foster and Carruth); *We Have Our Moments* (Werker); *Oh, Doctor* (McCarey); *Love in a Bungalow* (McCarey); *The Lady Fights Back* (Carruth); *There Goes the Groom* (Santley); *A Girl with Ideas* (Simon); *Prescription for Romance* (Simon)

1938 *The Jury's Secret* (Sloman); *Midnight Intruder* (Lubin); *The Crime of Dr. Hallett* (Simon); *The Nurse from Brooklyn* (Simon); *The Devil's Party* (McCarey); *The Missing Guest* (Rawlins); *The Storm* (Young); *Newsboys Home* (Young)

1939 *You Can't Cheat an Honest Man* (Marshall); *The Family Next Door* (Santley); *The House of Fear* (May); *I Stole a Million* (Tuttle); *Missing Evidence* (Rosen); *Little Accident* (Lamont); *The Man from Montreal* (Cabanne)

1940 *The Invisible Man Returns* (May); *Oh, Johnny, How You Can Love!* (Lamont); *Zanzibar* (Schuster); *The House of the Seven Gables* (May); *Ski Patrol* (Landers); *Sandy Is a Lady* (Lamont); *Private Affairs* (Rogell); *Hired Wife* (Seiter); *Diamond Frontier* (Schuster); *The Bank Dick* (*The Bank Detective*) (Cline); *Trail of the Vigilantes* (Dwan) (co); *Beat Me Daddy, Eight to the Bar!* (Ceballos—short)

1941 *Buck Privates* (*Rookies*) (Lubin); *The Lady from Cheyenne* (Lloyd); *Too Many Blondes* (Freeland); *Bachelor Daddy* (Young); *This Woman Is Mine* (Lloyd); *Paris Calling* (Marin)

1942 *Swing Frolic* (Ceballos—short); *The Ghost of Frankenstein* (Kenton) (co); *A Gentleman after Dark* (Marin); *The Spoilers* (Enright); *Pardon My Sarong* (Kenton); *Men of Texas* (*Men of Destiny*) (Enright); *Arabian Nights* (Rawlins) (co)

1943 *Two Tickets to London* (Marin); *We've Never Been Licked* (*Texas to Tokyo*) (Rawlins); *The Mad Ghoul* (Hogan); *So's Your Uncle* (Yarborough) (co); *Gung Ho!* (Enright)

1944 *Hat Check Honey* (Cline); *The Invisible Man's Revenge* (Beebe); *The Woman in the Window* (F. Lang)

1945 *Delightfully Dangerous* (Lubin); *Along Came Jones* (Heisler); *Scarlet Street* (F. Lang)

1946 *Without Reservations* (LeRoy); *The Dark Mirror* (Siodmak)

1947 *The Farmer's Daughter* (Potter); *The Egg and I* (Erskine); *Something in the Wind* (Pichel); *A Double Life* (Cukor)

1948 *Up in Central Park* (Seiter); *The Saxon Charm* (Binyon); *The Accused* (Dieterle)

1949 *The Set-Up* (Wise); *House of Strangers* (Mankiewicz); *Holiday Affair* (Hartman)

1950 *Three Came Home* (Negulesco); *No Way Out* (Mankiewicz); **All about Eve** (Mankiewicz); *Rawhide* (Hathaway)

1951 *I Can Get It for You Wholesale* (*This Is My Affair*) (Gordon); *Half Angel* (Sale); *People Will Talk* (Mankiewicz); *The Model and the Marriage Broker* (Cukor)

1952 *Dreamboat* (Binyon); *Phone Call from a Stranger* (Negulesco); *Deadline U.S.A.* (*Deadline*) (Brooks); "The Ransom of Red Chief" ep. of *O. Henry's Full House* (*Full House*) (Hawks); *Monkey Business* (Hawks)

1953 *Taxi* (Ratoff); *Dream Wife* (Sheldon); *Vicki* (Horner)

1954 *Roger Wagner Chorale* (O. Lang—short); *Garden of Evil* (Hathaway); *Three Coins in the Fountain* (Negulesco); *Demetrius and the Gladiators* (Daves); *Desirée* (Koster)

1955 *The Seven Year Itch* (Wilder); *How to Be Very, Very Popular* (Johnson); *The Girl in the Red Velvet Swing* (Fleischer); *The Rains of Ranchipur* (Negulesco)

1956 *23 Paces to Baker Street* (Hathaway); *Bus Stop* (Logan)

1957 *Boy on a Dolphin* (Negulesco); *An Affair to Remember* (McCarey); *Kiss Them for Me* (Donen)

1958 *The Gift of Love* (Negulesco); *A Certain Smile* (Negulesco)

1959 *The Remarkable Mr. Pennypacker* (Levin); *Count Your Blessings* (Negulesco) (co); *The Man Who Understood Women* (Johnson)

1960 *Bells Are Ringing* (Minnelli); *Go Naked in the World* (MacDougall); *Home from the Hill* (Minnelli)

1961 *King of Kings* (Ray) (co); *Sweet Bird of Youth* (Brooks)

1962 *The Four Horsemen of the Apocalypse* (Minnelli); *Two Weeks in Another Town* (Minnelli); *How the West Was Won* (Hathaway, Marshall, and Ford) (co)

1963 *The Courtship of Eddie's Father* (Minnelli); *A Ticklish Affair* (Sidney); *Love with the Proper Stranger* (Mulligan); *Advance to the Rear* (*Company of Cowards*) (Marshall)

1964 *Looking for Love* (Weis); *Fate Is the Hunter* (Nelson); *Goodbye Charlie* (Minnelli)

1965 *The Sandpiper* (Minnelli); *Red Line 7000* (Hawks); *Made in Paris* (Sagal); *The Singing Nun* (Koster)

1966 *The Venetian Affair* (J. Thorpe); *Hurry Sundown* (Preminger) (co)

1967 *The Ballad of Josie* (McLaglen); *Don't Just Stand There* (Winston); *The St. Valentine's Day Massacre* (Corman)

1968 *The Sterile Cuckoo* (*Pookie*) (Pakula); *Beneath the Planet of the Apes* (Post)

Films as Cameraman:

1932 *A Woman Commands*; *Is My Face Red* (Seiter); *Ride Him Cowboy* (*The Hawk*) (Allen); *70,000 Witnesses* (Murphy)

Publications

By KRASNER: articles—

On *The Sandpiper* in *American Cinematographer* (Hollywood), July 1965.

Seminar with Robert Wise in *American Cinematographer* (Hollywood), March 1980.

In *Backstory: Interviews with Screenwriters of the Golden Age*, edited by Pat McGilligan, Berkeley, California, 1986.

On KRASNER: articles—

Allen, Leigh, on *All about Eve* in *American Cinematographer* (Hollywood), January 1951.

Balter, Allan, in *American Cinematographer* (Hollywood), December 1955.

Rowan, Arthur, on *Boy on a Dolphin* in *American Cinematographer* (Hollywood), May 1957.

Lightman, Herb A., on *The St. Valentine's Day Massacre* in *American Cinematographer* (Hollywood), October 1967.

Film Comment (New York), Summer 1972.

Focus on Film (London), no. 13, 1973.

Kimble, G., on *How the West Was Won* in *American Cinematographer* (Hollywood), October 1983.

Turner, George, in *American Cinematographer* (Hollywood), September 1986.

Obituary in *Variety* (New York), 20 July 1988.

Obituary in *American Cinematographer* (Hollywood), September 1988.

Obituary in *EPD Film* (Frankfurt), vol. 5, no. 10, October 1988.

*   *   *

Milton Krasner's film career, spanning the years 1919 to 1975, illustrates two fundamental aspects of the life of a craftsman in Hollywood's Golden Age. First, the long and arduous (some, wistfully, would say luxurious) apprenticeship of the young technician. Second, the extreme diversity possible even within a segregated crafts system. Krasner, as an example, worked in black-and-white and color, standard format and widescreen, in a variety of genres, for a multitude of directors, at all the major studios. Indeed, Krasner's career is of such breadth that his development as a cinematographer in many ways parallels the maturation of the art itself, as well as the manner in which the studio system of production appropriated that art.

Krasner began his career in the lab (and for a brief stint, in the cutting room) at the Vitagraph Studios in Brooklyn. From that position, he graduated to assistant cameraman, loading and unloading magazines, working the slate, and carrying gear. Moving to California in the early 1920s, Krasner worked on Broncho Billy Anderson westerns, Johnny Hines comedies for First National, and, most significantly, with Sol Polito on Harry Carey westerns at Pathé. At Universal, beginning in 1927, he worked with the crack team of Polito and Ted McCord on Ken Maynard westerns for several years.

By the time of Krasner's first credit as director of photography, he had worked at nearly every studio in Hollywood, major and minor, and had assisted such cinematographers as McCord, Polito, Billy Bitzer, Lee Garmes, Lucien Andriot, Hal Mohr, and Joseph Walker. If there is a difficulty in detecting a "Krasner style" in his later work, perhaps this is due to the multiplicity of influences bearing on him during his long apprenticeship.

By late 1935, Krasner was located at Universal Studios, and between 1937 and 1944, made 54 films. The budgets were low, but his competence and craftsmanship gained a name in the industry.

The 1940s were the breakthrough period for Krasner. His long apprenticeship ended, he could finally work at a slower pace on the black-and-white horror and crime features he was increasingly specializing in, as well as begin work in other genres. His most important assignment in this respect was the Technicolor *Arabian Nights*, an Ali Baba-esque epic for which he and his two co-cinematographers received an Academy Award nomination. But Krasner's best work in this period, and the work which gained him the greatest notoriety, were the two films done under director Fritz Lang, *The Woman in the Window* and *Scarlet Street*. The films remain two of Krasner's most dramatic creations, and feature some of the most characteristic imagery in the *film noir* canon. *The Woman in the Window*'s lush, modern apartment set, in which much of the film's action takes place, is imbued with a rich range of gray tones by Krasner, giving the set an air of complexity and suspense. Krasner's camera moves effortlessly from one set-up to another. Though not then noted for dramatic treatment of interior space, Krasner here shows an excellent story sense. The exterior of the apartment building, on the other hand, is a triumph, and the image of a rain-soaked street (shot in the Goldwyn lot), its deserted brownstone fronts receding in geometric regularity into deep space, has become an icon of the genre. *Scarlet Street* played to the cinematographer's strength. The backlot street scene of this film (which in structure and plot is virtually identical to *Woman in the Window*), is expanded into an entire sequence. Krasner's work, this time on the Universal backlot, has a rare (for him) expressionist flavor. Edward G. Robinson, a timid bank clerk, witnesses a mock fight between Joan Bennett and her scheming boyfriend, Dan Duryea. Charaters in both films, moreover, move from interior to exterior space within the same sequences, and exterior space is constantly alluded to through open windows and doorways. Soundstage-shot, false exteriors and backlot streets give these films a Baroque style all their own. Lotte Eisner, writing about *The Woman in the Window*, noted the remarkable effect of *noir* stylistics combined with Krasner's subtle exploration of cinematic space in the film's most dramatic scene, the murder of an intruder: ''As a new taxi drives up outside the apartment building, rain is pouring down. It is the kind of rain that produces an unnerving insecurity and hints at potential catastrophe. Horror and brutality are about to invade the cool, civilized interior of the luxury apartment.''

Increasingly lightweight, even hand-held cameras, faster film stocks, and improvements in set design (such as the use of ''wild'' walls, removable during a tracking motion) abetted Krasner's natural abilities in the late 1940s. He was drawn more and more, as was the case with colleagues such as Franz Planer, to storyboarding sequences early in the production process. This sophistication was responsible for the look of one of Krasner's great accomplishments, *The Set-Up*. This brilliant, low-budget fight film is played in real time, on sets whose spatial relationship to one another is an integral part of the story. Krasner used three cameras for the fight sequences, including a hand-held camera used in the ring. The director, Robert Wise, an experienced editor (he had cut both *Citizen Kane* and *The Magnificent Ambersons*), cut this sequence himself, and the combined efforts of Krasner and Wise make the extended sequence (it takes up roughly one sixth of the film) one of the best of its kind, in a genre (the fight film) noted for its remarkable camerawork. The rest of the film is a cameraman's soliloquy. There are low-angle expressionist shots of distorted, screaming faces of bloodthirsty fans in extreme close-up, long, arching tracks-in across streets, multiple set-ups in tiny interior spaces. The film even throws in a bit of location footage, as well: in an emotive moment, the hero's wife tears up a ticket to the fight and scatters it over trolley tracks. With this fillip, Krasner demonstrates facility with every major cinematographic device in one 72-minute, low-budget film.

Krasner's other work at RKO in this period, notably *Holiday Affair*, also demonstrated an increased technical skill, particularly with miniatures. RKO's special effects department was known as the best in the industry at this time, and Krasner's exposure to RKO's matte painters, lab technicians, and miniature builders might be said to constitute the last part of his lengthy, productive apprenticeship in the motion picture industry.

In 1949, Krasner began a fruitful relationship with the writer-director-producer Joseph Mankiewicz, and an even longer relationship with 20th Century-Fox. After working on two thrillers with Mankiewicz, *House of Strangers* and *No Way Out*, Krasner was chosen to photograph *All about Eve*, an extremely theatrical and carefully blocked story of shifting allegiances and loyalties in the world of the theater. Krasner literalized this motif through his use of exclusionary framing, staging within the frame, and subtle manipulation of the film's basic shot scale, the medium shot. Krasner's camera gently narrates *All about Eve*, operating in parallel but muted fashion to Mankiewicz's shrill, talky screenplay.

The 1950s and 1960s saw Krasner, now among the upper ranks of Hollywood cinematographers, attain the role of full collaborator on major projects. As the industry changed, Krasner also changed with apparent ease. He adapted well to huge budgets, European locales, different color processes, and widescreen formats. Krasner shot the second film in CinemaScope, *Demetrius and the Gladiators*, and won an Academy Award for his color and location work on *Three Coins in the Fountain*. Krasner demonstrated a certain ability to work in the more expensive, cumbersome, widescreen processes, and he was a natural choice to serve with Charles Lang, William Daniels, and Joseph La Shelle on one of only two features fully produced in Cinerama, *How the West Was Won*. Krasner shot the entire last section of the film, ''The Outlaws'' (for which Henry Hathaway has claimed most of the directing credit) and many scenes in the rest of the film. The cinematographers found the Cinerama system daunting: because of the separate optical targets of the three-in-one camera format, three vanishing points could potentially appear on screen, and, though synchronized, the edges of each camera's field had to be carefully ''blended'' through skillful placement of trees and other vertical set elements, while cameramen had to be equally careful not to let a horizontal element stray across the ''blend line.'' Moreover, cameras couldn't be tilted or panned during a scene. In fact, to compensate for the distortion, actors at the edges of the Cinerama image had to stand *behind* actors near the center of the image in order to be seen on the same depth plane. Krasner's section is the one least demanding the Cinerama treatment, and is as visually rich as any of his work in this period—quite an accomplishment, given the limitations of the format.

With *The St. Valentine's Day Massacre*, Krasner came full circle. Shooting mostly on a backlot dressed to look like 1920s Chicago, Krasner found himself advising the young Roger Corman how to get the feel of classical black-and-white photography on color stock. Corman found Krasner's ability to combine interior and exterior shooting in the same sequence especially important to the dramatic needs of the story. Parts of the film were shot in ''documentary style,'' and the entire film was done in a modified widescreen process (Panavision). The film was carefully storyboarded, but a sequence depicting an argument between two characters was improvised with hand-held work. Thus Krasner reviewed techniques and specific skills learned in 45 years of work.

Milton Krasner's career in the movies is a testament to an ethic of patience, an industry's willingness to nurture talent, and the extraordinary variety of ways that talent was allowed to express itself when finally it did come to fruition.

—Kevin Jack Hagopian

KUREISHI, Hanif

Writer. **Nationality:** British. **Born:** London, 5 December 1954; son of Rafiushan Kureishi and Audrey Buss. **Education:** Degree in Philosophy from King's College, London. **Family:** Former partner, Tracey Scoffield; children: twin sons, born 1994. **Career:** First play, *Soaking the Heat*, at Royal Court Theatre Upstairs, 1976; several plays produced in London during 1970s and 1980s; Writer in Residence at Royal Court Theatre, 1982; first screenplay, *My Beautiful Laundrette* nominated for Oscar for Best Writing and BAFTA Best Screenplay Award; *The Buddha of Suburbia* produced as BBC-TV mini-series, 1993; British Independent Film Awards nomination for *My Son the Fanatic*; continues to work in theatre, writing short stories and novels. **Awards:** George Divine Drama Award, for *Outskirts* (play); Whitbread Award, for *The Buddha of Suburbia* (novel); National Society of Film Critics Award for Best Screenplay and New York Film Critics Circle Awards Award, for Best Screenplay, for *My Beautiful Laundrette*, 1986. **Agent:** Stephen Durbridge, The Agency, 24, Pottery Lane, Holland Park, London W11 4LZ, England.

Films as Writer:

1985   *My Beautiful Laundrette* (Frears —originally for TV) (+ sc)
1987   *Sammy and Rosie Get Laid* (Frears) (+ sc)
1991   *London Kills Me* (+ d, sc)
1998   *My Son the Fanatic* (Prasad) (+ sc)
1999   *Mauvaise passe* (*The Escort*; *The Wrong Blonde*) (Blanc)
2000   *Intimacy*

Publications:

By KUREISHI: books—

The Buddha of Suburbia, London, 1990.
The Black Album, London, 1995.
The Faber Book of Pop, edited with John Savage, London, 1995.
Intimacy, London, 1998.
Love in a Blue Time (short story collection), London, 1997.
Midnight All Day (short story collection), London, 1999.

By KUREISHI: articles—

''Hanif Kureishi on London,'' Interview in *Critical Quarterly*, Fall 1999.

On KUREISHI: books—

Kaleta, Kenneth, C., *Hanif Kureishi: Postcolonial Storyteller*, Austin, Texas, 1997.

On KUREISHI: articles—

Mody, Anjali, ''Hanif's Story: Too Intimate for Words,'' in *The Indian Express* (Bombay), 11 May 1998.
Dawson, Tom, Review of *My Son the Fanatic*, in *Total Film* (London), June 1998.
Richards, Terry, Review of *My Son the Fanatic*, in *Film Review* (London), June 1998.

*   *   *

A controversial novelist, playwright, and screenwriter, Hanif Kureishi is an outspoken commentator on multiculturalism in the United Kingdom. His fictional works explore in graphic terms the experiences of British Asians, and his work as a screenwriter and a novelist has been praised on both sides of the Atlantic, suggesting that the views of ethnic differences expressed in films such as *My Beautiful Laundrette* and *Sammy and Rosie Get Laid*, are recognisable beyond their London setting. Kureishi is known for his left-wing politics, sharp humour, and uncompromising views on literary production.

Kureishi had his first play produced professionally in 1976, but it is as a screenwriter and more recently a novelist that he has reached his widest audience. The plots of Kureishi's films tend to revolve around the problems encountered when immigrant families find that their culture is at odds with the traditions and moral structures of their adopted country. His first screenplay, *My Beautiful Laundrette*, for which he received an Oscar nomination, and which became something of a cult movie in the gay community in Britain in the late 1980s, tells the story of two young men, one working-class white, one Pakistani, as they try to run a laundrette. While the relationship between the two seems at first not to be affected by the differences in their backgrounds, their expectations of the venture could not be more different. While Johnny sees the laundrette as a way of salvaging his life and regaining some self-respect, Omar finds himself attracted to Johnny, rebelling against his father's demands that he marry an upper-class Pakistani girl, and looking on the business as his ticket to wealth and respectability.

Directed by Stephen Frears, *My Beautiful Laundrette* was a remarkable start to Kureishi's movie career, and his second collaboration with the director, *Sammy and Rosie Get Laid*, is no less impressive. Also featuring a domineering and conservative father figure, the second film's most inventive twist is having the father return from India lamenting the loss of the British culture he used to know. It has become a hallmark of Kureishi's work to overturn conventional views of immigrant families, in this case showing the reactionary father to be more ''British'' than the British themselves.

After winning the Whitbread prize for his first novel, *The Buddha of Suburbia*, Kureishi returned to filmmaking with *London Kills Me*, his directorial debut. Set among the low-lifes and drug addicts on the streets of London, the film predates *Trainspotting* by five years, but is far less rewarding either as a voyeuristic spectacle, or as an insight into the lives of the characters. Unlike *Trainspotting*, which offers up heroin addiction as an Existential choice of some magnitude, here the horrors of the streets are more easily escaped, and therefore seem more trivial.

While *London Kills Me* seemed rather an aimless movie, Kureishi's adaptation of his novel *The Buddha of Suburbia* as a four-part TV mini-series was a welcome return to form. It was also a return to the themes of his earlier work for the big screen, being the story of the decline into drugs and delinquency of the son of a respectable Pakistani family in London. *My Son the Fanatic*, directed by Udayan Prasad failed to make such an impact on critics and award committees as Kureishi's early films. Tending towards the sentimental in its portrayal of Parvez, a hard-working taxi driver who gradually transforms into a friendly pimp, *My Son the Fanatic* lacks the intensity and pace of *My Beautiful Laundrette* and *Samie and Rosie*. Yet it is an engrossing movie, reversing the stereotype to cast the older members of a British Asian family as liberal and open to new ideas, while the younger generation embrace religious fundamentalism.

Kureishi's films and writing projects have often placed him in conflict with his family and with the British Asian community whose problems his work explores. Yet his stories have gone some way towards making that community more visible in the British media. Many of the inversions of stereotypes that made *My Beautiful Laundrette* so unusual in the 1980s, have become staples of British Asian humour in the year 2000, to the point that a hit British TV comedy show *Goodness Gracious Me* bases its sketches on the kinds of racial inversions that seemed shocking in 1985. Kureishi's latest outing as a screenwriter, *Mauvaise passe*, teams him up with director Michel Blanc, and French star Daniel Auteuil.

—Chris Routledge

KURI, Yoji

Animator. **Nationality:** Japanese. **Born:** Hideo Kurihara in Fukui, 9 April 1928. **Education:** Studied at the Bunka Gakuen Art School, Tokyo. **Career:** Newspaper cartoonist, painter, and designer: worked for the animation studios Toei Doga and Mushi before setting up his own independent studio in late 1950s.

Films as Animator (selected list):

1960   *Fashion*
1961   *Stamp Fantasia; Human Zoo; Here and There*
1963   *Locus; Love; The Chair; The Face; Discovery of Zero*
1964   *Man, Woman, and Dog; Aos*
1965   *The Man Next Door; Samurai; The Window*
1966   *Little Murmurs; Au Fou!*
1967   *The Room; The Flower*
1968   *Two Grilled Fish; Crazy World; Concerto in X Minor*
1969   *Imagination; Little Island*
1970   *The Bathroom; Pop*
1972   *Fantasy for Piano; The Midnight Parasites*
1973   *Imus*
1977   *Monga*
1978   *Vanish*
1980   *Love*

Publications

By KURI: articles—

''Made in Japan,'' in *Annecy Festival* catalogue, 1965.
Le Technicien du Film (Paris), July-August 1977.

On KURI: articles—

Film (London), Winter 1964.
Anderson, W., in *Chaplin* (Stockholm), no. 63, 1966.
Films and Filming (London), March 1966.
Image et Son (Paris), November 1967.
Film a Doba (Prague), no. 9, 1968.
Cinéma (Paris), January 1968.
Cinema TV Digest, Winter 1970–71.
Sambonet, L., in *Comics*, no. 5, 1972.
Kinoisskustvo (Sofia), vol. 39, no. 5, 1984.
Positif (Paris), April 1994.

*   *   *

The contemporary Japanese animator Yoji Kuri has enjoyed the most successful international career of all the many independent Japanese animators whose work stands in contradistinction to the more elaborate, more collaborative, and more commercial productions from such industrial giants as the Toei and Toho studios. As such, Kuri constitutes a fine example of the Japanese experimental film artist, being in a sense an Asian analogue to such animators as the American Robert Breer.

Kuri's early years were spent as a cartoonist, but by 1960 he had established a small independent studio which centered upon a solitary 35mm animation camera. In the following year he completed *Human Zoo*, which won the Bronze Medal at the Venice Film Festival in 1962. As the film-scholar Millie Paul suggests, it was this award that truly launched his career. The brief animated work that followed— such as the erotic *Aos*, the abstract *Locus*, the educational *Discovery of Zero*—allowed him to develop his reputation and style. The 1967 film *The Room* (which grew out of one of Kuri's flip-books) provides some insights into that style, and the structures which came to mark his acollaborative, independent animation through the 1960s and 1970s.

The Room is precisely five minutes long and is made up of 19 brief tableau units, each of which is largely confined to the rather surreal space of a stark and simple line drawing of an empty ''room.'' Such simple, black-and-white line drawings are typical of Kuri's style, not unlike that of the American cartoonist James Thurber. Further, while *The Room* was shot—frame by frame, in an admixture of animated cels and cut-outs—on color stock, rarely does color appear in the film (and only then to heighten an effect or to underscore a mood). Tableau One provides the film's titles, which appear within the room's simple space. What follows are 18 disparate tableaux with almost no narrative causality or continuity between them. Each tableau itself is distinctly marked by often bizarre metamorphic transformations.

In Tableau Two, for example, two feet emerge from the room's right and left walls, then feet metamorphose into a bird which flies around the room. Such metamorphic transformations—where one figure seems almost to ''melt'' and then reform into a very different figure, linked to the first only by subtle topologic similarities—are one of Kuri's stylistic and structural hallmarks. *The Room* is replete with them, having more than 40. In lieu of more traditional (and commercial) narrative linkings between images, these metamorphoses underscore far more associational (and thematic) unities which bond Kuri's rapidly paced exchanges of mise en scène. *The Room*, like most of Kuri's work, is for adult audiences, and such themes as the conflict between the sexes, the violence of war, and bureaucratic boredom, predominate. But perhaps even more predominant is Kuri's artistic insistence upon graphic similarities: comparisons and contrasts of tones, lines, and forms which continue to reiterate the essential (etymological) meaning of our Western term ''aesthetic'' as ''a study of sensation/perception.''

Not only for *The Room* but for all of Kuri's extensive production (which likely exceeds 400 films, many unreleased, many others international prize winners), one must keep in mind Kuri's total control as an independent artist. All funding, conception, scripting, graphics, shooting, sound, editing, and even distribution are—in the main—from his hand. As a result, Kuri's films, such as *The Room*, are very personal, yet remarkably international, partly due to his penchant for soundtracks which avoid spoken language and which instead consist of an ''international language'' of sound effects and/or music.

Kuri's total artistic production is very varied. He began his creative life as a cartoonist and continues such work today. He continues to fashion flip-books, kinetic sculptures, paintings and drawings, and cut-out compositions. He is probably the best-known Japanese independent both in his own country and throughout the world. His satire and sexuality, his caricature and metamorphoses, and (perhaps above all) his post-Hiroshima ''black humor'' all bond together with an experimental willingness to explore various animation media. The result is seriously funny adult fare, at once popular and yet ''theoretical'' enough for the connoisseur and magically international in its appeal. He is a consummate, exemplary independent artist who is constantly and consistently creative.

—Edward S. Small

LAEMMLE, Carl, Sr., and Carl, Jr.

CARL, SR. Producer. **Nationality:** American. **Born:** Laupheim, Germany, 17 January 1867, family emigrated to the United States in 1884. **Education:** Attended schools in Laupheim. **Family:** Married Recha Stern, 1898; two children including the producer Carl, Jr. **Career:** Newsboy, salesman and bookkeeper; 1906—opened Whitefront Theatre nickelodeon in Chicago; 1909—defied the Motion Picture Patents Trust and went into production with his Independent Moving Picture Company; 1912—formed Universal Productions; 1914— company moved to lot outside Hollywood. **Died:** In Beverly Hills, California, 24 September 1939.

CARL, JR. Producer. **Nationality:** American. **Born:** Chicago, Illinois, 28 April 1908. **Education:** Attended Clark School, Chicago. **Career:** Supervisor of short subjects at Universal while still in his teens; 1927—began supervising Universal's feature films; 1928—associate producer; 1929—in charge of company's total film production; 1936—Universal sold to outside investors and Laemmle, Jr.

Carl Laemmle, Sr. and Carl Laemmle, Jr.

forced to resign; 1936–37—producer at MGM, but made no films. **Award:** Academy Award for *All Quiet on the Western Front*, 1930. **Died:** Of a stroke, in Los Angeles, California, in 1979.

Films as Producer (Carl, Sr.):

1921   *Cheated Hearts* (Henley); *Colorado* (Eason); *The Conflict* (Paton); *Danger Ahead* (Sturgeon); *The Dangerous Moment* (De Sano); *Desperate Trails* (Ford); *False Kisses* (Scardon); *The Cat* (Dawn)

1922   *The Altar Stairs* (Hillyer); *Another Man's Shoes* (Conway); *Broad Daylight* (Cummings); *Caught Bluffing* (Hillyer); *Confidence* (Pollard); *A Dangerous Game* (Baggot); *Don't Get Personal* (Badger); *Don't Shoot* (Conway); *The Flaming Hour* (Sedgwick); *The Flirt* (Henley); **Foolish Wives** (von Stroheim); *Forsaking All Others* (Chautard)

1923   *The Flame of Life* (Henley); *Burning Words* (Paton); *Crossed Wires* (Baggot); *Don Quickshot of the Rio Grande* (Marshall); *Double Dealing* (Lehrman); *Drifting* (Browning); *The First Degree* (Sedgwick)

1924   *Fools Highway* (Cummings); *Butterfly* (Brown); *Excitement* (Hill); *The Family Secret* (Seiter); *The Fast Worker* (Sciter); *The Fighting American* (Forman); *The Gaiety Girl* (Baggot)

1925   *Daring Days* (O'Brien); *The Demon* (Smith); *Fifth Avenue Models* (Gade); **Phantom of the Opera** (Julian)

1926   *The Buckaroo Kid* (Reynolds); *Bucking the Truth* (Morante); *Down the Stretch* (Baggot); *The Escape* (Morante); *The Fighting Peacemaker* (Smith); *Butterflies in the Rain* (Sloman)

1927   *Back to God's Country* (Willat); *Beware of Widows* (Ruggles); *Blazing Days* (Wyler); *The Border Cavalier* (Wyler); *The Broncho Buster* (Ernst Laemmle); *Call of the Heart* (F. Ford); *The Cat and the Canary* (Leni); *Cheating Cheaters* (Edward Laemmle); *The Cheerful Fraud* (Seiter); *The Chinese Parrot* (Leni); *The Claw* (Olcott); *The Denver Dude* (Eason); *Desert Dust* (Wyler); *Fangs of Destiny* (Paton); *Fast and Furious* (Brown); *The Fighting Three* (Rogell); *The Four-Footed Ranger* (Paton); *The Fourflusher* (Ruggles); *The Fourth Commandment* (Johnson); *Galloping Fury* (Eason)

1928   *Arizona Cyclone* (Lewis); *Buck Privates* (M. Brown); *The Clean-Up Man* (Taylor); *The Cohens and Kellys in Paris* (Beaudine); *The Count of Ten* (Flood); *The Fearless Rider* (Lewis)

1929   *Come Across* (Taylor); *Courtin' Wildcats* (Storm)

1930   *Captain of the Guard* (Robertson); *The Cat Creeps* (Julian); *The Climax* (Hoffman); *The Cohens and Kellys in Scotland* (Craft); *The Concentratin' Kid* (Rosson); *The Czar of Broadway* (Craft); *Dames Ahoy!* (Craft); *East is West*

(Bell); *Embarrassing Moments* (Craft); *The Fighting Legion*
(Harry Joe Brown)

Films as Producer (Carl, Jr.):

1923   *The Love Brand* (Paton)
1927   *The Irresistible Lover* (Beaudine)
1928   *The Last Warning* (Leni); *We Americans* (Sloman); *Lonesome* (Fejos)
1929   *Broadway* (Fejos); *College Love* (Ross); *The Last Performance* (Fejos)
1930   ***All Quiet on the Western Front*** (Milestone); *The King of Jazz* (Anderson); *A Lady Surrenders* (Stahl); *The Boudoir Diplomat* (St. Clair)
1931   *The Spirit of Notre Dame* (Mack); ***Dracula*** (Browning); ***Frankenstein*** (Whale); *Waterloo Bridge* (Whale); *The Bad Sister* (Henley)
1932   *Back Street* (Stahl); *Murders in the Rue Morgue* (Florey); *Once in a Lifetime* (Mack); *Air Mail* (Ford); *The Old Dark House* (Whale)
1933   *Only Yesterday* (Stahl); *Out All Night* (Taylor); *The Invisible Man* (Whale); *Don't Bet on Love* (Roth); *The Mummy* (Freund)
1934   *Imitation of Life* (Stahl); *The Countess of Monte Cristo* (Freund); *By Candlelight* (Whale); *Glamour* (Wyler); *Little Man, What Now?* (Borzage); *One More River* (Whale)
1935   *The Good Fairy* (Wyler); *The Bride of Frankenstein* (Whale); *Night Life of the Gods* (L. Sherman); *Remember Last Night* (Whale)
1936   *Show Boat* (Whale)

Publications

By LAEMMLE (Sr.): articles—

"Mes débuts dans le cinéma," in *Anthologie du cinéma*, edited by Marcel Lapierre, Paris, 1946.
"This Business of Motion Pictures," in *Film History* (Bristol), vol. 3, no. 1, 1989.

On LAEMMLE (Sr.): books—

Gordon, R., *Carl Laemmle & Universal Pictures: A Tribute*, New York, 1976.
Drinkwater, John, *The Life and Adventures of Carl Laemmle*, London, 1931, 1978.
Gabler, Neal, *An Empire of Their Own: How the Jews Invented Hollywood*, New York, 1988.

On LAEMMLE (Sr.): articles—

Film Weekly, vol. 5, no. 137, 30 May 1931.
Film Weekly, vol. 12, no. 311, 28 September 1934.
Motion Picture Herald, vol. 136, no. 14, 30 September 1939.
Zierold, Norman, in *The Hollywood Tycoons*, London, 1969.
Classic Images (Muscatine, Iowa), January 1983.

Simmons, Jerold, "Film and International Politics: the Banning of *All Quiet on the Western Front* in Germany and Austria, 1930–1931," in *Historian*, November 1989.
Everschor, Franz, in *Film-Dienst* (Cologne), 4 August 1992.

*   *   *

Carl Laemmle, Sr., founded one of the major Hollywood studios, Universal Pictures. His life was a true "rags to riches" tale. He had made his way to the United States from Germany three decades before the movie industry was created. In 1906, at age 39, he opened a nickelodeon in Chicago. Once he had fought off takeover attempts by the Motion Pictures Patents Trust, Laemmle, Sr. began to expand his operations into filmmaking. He moved to Hollywood and built Universal City Studios in 1915.

During the late 1910s and early 1920s Universal City Studios functioned as the largest, most modern moviemaking operation in the world. But while Famous Players-Lasky moved up to number one in the industry by signing top stars and expanding its feature film budgets, Laemmle maintained a conservative business posture. He continued doing what had worked so well in the past, making low-budget formula films. Indeed the studio became famous as a place for developing such talents as director John Ford and studio executive Irving Thalberg, and then losing them to the more prosperous Paramount Pictures and Metro-Goldwyn-Mayer.

With the coming of the Great Depression and the attendant economy drives required, Universal was able only to play a marginal role during the lucrative Studio Era, producing low-budget films, including such horror classics as *Dracula*, *The Mummy*, *The Invisible Man*, and *The Bride of Frankenstein*. Universal Pictures never did obtain much power or prestige, but Laemmle, Sr., was able to set up his son in the business. Someone in Hollywood once noted that, contrary to what Ernest Hemingway wrote, in Lotus land it was "the *son* also rises." That cynic must have had Carl Laemmle, Jr., in mind.

By 1929 Carl Laemmle, Jr., was in charge of all film production at a major Hollywood studio. His only line experience had been as a writer of a popular series of two-reel comedies, *The Collegians*, for Universal in the mid-1920s. Since his father owned and operated the company, Carl, Jr., in 1927, at age 19, was suddenly supervising feature films. One year later he was appointed an associate producer and in that capacity produced the flamboyant screen version of *Broadway*, a spectacle meant to outdo all talkie spectacles that had come before.

The Great Depression severely limited what Laemmle, Jr., could do. Still, despite the fact the company immediately went into the red and would be sold to outside investors seven years later, Laemmle never looked back. Indeed at first he did make a splash. He invested considerable resources in *All Quiet on the Western Front*, a daring pacifist tale told from the German point of view. The picture won the Oscar for best picture in 1930, and brought respectability to a studio best known for its low-budget dramas and B-westerns.

But Laemmle could not afford to spend more than one million dollars for every film, regardless of how much prestige it bought the family company. Gradually he moved Universal more and more into the red. Eventually, despite all Laemmle, Sr.'s efforts, he could not get out from under mounting debts and in March 1936 sold Universal to a group of rich eastern bankers. Laemmle, Jr., politely retired, just as his last major effort, a film version of *Show Boat*, was being released. Laemmle, Sr., retired to become an elder statesman of the film business; Laemmle, Jr., not yet 30, would live in quiet obscurity for four more decades, making no more contributions to the motion picture business.

—Douglas Gomery

LAI, Francis

Composer. **Nationality:** French. **Born:** Francis Albert Lai in Nice, 26 April 1932. **Education:** Attended Lycée Saint-Philippe, Nice. **Family:** Married Dagmar Pütz, 1968; two sons, one daughter. **Career:** 1950—orchestra musician; then accompanist for Claude Goaty, 1955, Edith Piaf, 1960–63, and Mireille Mathieu, 1965; composer of songs for Piaf, Gréco, Montand, and others; 1966—first film score, for *A Man and a Woman*, the first of many films for Lelouch; also composer for radio and TV. **Awards:** Academy Award, for *Love Story*, 1970.

Films as Composer:

1966   *Un Homme et une femme* (*A Man and a Woman*) (Lelouch); *Masculin-Féminin* (*Masculine-Feminine*) (Godard) (co)

1967   *La Louve solitaire* (Logereau); *The Bobo* (Parrish); *Mon amour, mon amour* (Trintignant); *Le Soleil des voyous* (*Action Man*; *Leather and Nylon*) (Delannoy); *I'll Never Forget What's 'is Name* (Winner); *Vivre pour vivre* (*Live for Life*) (Lelouch)

1968   *Mayerling* (Young); *Treize jours en France* (Grenoble) (Lelouch and Reichenbach—doc)

1969   *La Vie, l'amour, la mort* (*Life, Love, Death*) (Lelouch); *Three into Two Won't Go* (Hall); *Hannibal Brooks* (Winner); *House of Cards* (Guillermin); *La Modification* (Worms); *Un Homme qui me plaît* (*Love Is a Funny Thing*) (Lelouch); *Le Passager de la pluie* (*Rider on the Rain*) (Clément)

1970   *Du soleil plein les yeux* (Boisrond); *Madly* (Kahane); *Le Voyou* (*The Crook*) (Lelouch); *The Games* (Winner); *Dans la poussière du soleil* (Balducci); *Hello-Goodbye* (Negulesco); *Love Story* (Hiller); *Berlin Affair* (Rich)

1971   *Smic, Smac, Smoc* (Lelouch) (+ ro); *Le Petit Matin* (Albicocco); *L'Odeur des fauves* (Balducci); *Les Pétroleuses* (*The Legend of Frenchie King*; *The Petroleum Girls*) (Christian-Jaque)

1972   *Le Petit Poucet* (Boisrond); *Les Hommes* (Vigne); *L'Aventure c'est l'aventure* (*Money Money Money*) (Lelouch); *La Course du lièvre à travers les champs* (*And Hope to Die*) (Clément)

1973   *Un Homme libre* (*A Free Man*) (Muller); *La Bonne Année* (*Happy New Year*) (Lelouch)

1974   *Child under a Leaf* (Broomfield); *La Ronde* (*Le Baiser*) (Schenk); *The Sex Symbol* (Rich) (co); *Toute une vie* (*And Now My Love*; *A Lifetime*) (Lelouch); *Par le sang des autres* (*With the Blood of Others*) (Simenon); *Un Amour de pluie* (*Loving in the Rain*) (Brialy); *A Visit to a Chief's Son* (Johnson); *Emmanuelle* (Jaeckin)

1975   *Le Chat et la souris* (*Cat and Mouse*) (Lelouch); *Le Baby-Sitter* (Clément); *Mariage* (Lelouch); *Emmanuelle II: L'Anti-vierge* (*Emmanuelle II: Joys of a Woman*) (Giacobetti)

1976   *Le Bon et les méchants* (*The Good and the Bad*) (Lelouch); *Si c'était à refaire* (*A Second Chance*) (Lelouch); *Le Corps de mon ennemi* (*The Body of My Enemy*) (Verneuil)

1977   *Anima persa* (Risi); *Bilitis* (Hamilton); *Un Autre Homme, une autre chance* (*Another Man, Another Chance*) (Lelouch); *Nido de viudas* (*Widows' Nest*) (Navarro)

1978   *International Velvet* (Forbes); *Robert et Robert* (Lelouch); *Oliver's Story* (Korty); *Passion Flower Hotel* (Farwagi); *Les Ringards* (*The Small Timers*) (Pouret)

1979   *A nous deux* (*Us Two*) (Lelouch)

1981   *Les Uns et les autres* (*Bolero*; *Within Memory*) (Lelouch); *Madame Claude 2* (*Intimate Moments*) (Mimet); *Beyond the Reef* (Clarke)

1982   *Salut la puce* (Balducci)

1983   *Edith et Marcel* (*Edith and Marcel*) (Lelouch); *Canicule* (*Dogsday*) (Boisset)

1984   *Les Ripoux* (*My New Partner*; *Le Cop*) (Zidi); *J'ai recontré le Père Noel* (*Here Comes Santa Claus*) (Gion)

1985   *Marie* (Donaldson)

1986   *Association de malfaiteurs* (Zidi); *Un Homme et une femme: vingt ans déjà* (*A Man and a Woman: 20 Years Later*) (Lelouch)

1987   *Attention Bandits* (*Bandits*) (Lelouch); *Oci ciornie* (*Dark Eyes*) (Mikhalkov)

1988   *Bernadette* (Delannoy); *Itinéraire d'un enfant gaté* (Lelouch); *Les Pyramides bleues* (Dombasle)

1989   *Der Aten*; *Earth Girls Are Easy* (Temple) (song); *Trop belle pour toi* (*Too Beautiful for You*) (Blier)

1990   *Il y a des jours . . . et des lunes* (*There Were Days . . . and Moons*) (Lelouch) (co); *Provincial* (Gion); *Ripoux contre Ripoux* (*My New Partner II*; *Le Cop 2*) (Zidi)

1991   *Les Cléfs du paradis* (DeBroca); *La Belle Histoire* (Lelouch)

1992   *Tolgo il disturbo* (Risi); *L'inconnu dans la maison* (Lautner)

1993   *Tout ça pour ça* (Lelouch)

1994   *Le voleur at la menteuse* (Boujenah)

1995   *Les Misérables* (Lelouch)

1996   *Hommes, femmes, mode d'emploi* (*Men, Women: A User's Manual*)

1997   *My Best Friend's Wedding* (Hogan)

2000   *Une pour toutes* (*One 4 All*) (Lelouch)

Publications

By LAI: article—

Film Français (Paris), 16 January 1981.
CinémAction (Conde-sur-Noireau), September 1990.

On LAI: articles—

Ecran (Paris), September 1975.
Film Français (Paris), 3 February 1978.
Film Français (Paris), 2 February 1979.
Score (Lelystad, Netherlands), December 1980.
Lelouch, Claude, in *Sight and Sound* (London), Summer 1983.

*   *   *

Francis Lai's first movie credits were for *Masculine-Feminine* and *A Man and a Woman*, both released in 1966. Lai's participation in *Masculine-Feminine* went almost unnoticed, but his score for *A Man*

Francis Lai (right)

and a Woman made him an internationally prominent film composer. *A Man and a Woman* brought honors and recognition to both the director Claude Lelouch (Grand Prize at Cannes, two Academy Awards) and composer Lai (gold record, many versions of the theme song).

The music of *A Man and a Woman* is simple, lyrical, and sentimental. Lai's songs and Pierre Barouh's lyrics are often charming. But the original aspect of this score lies in the combination of music and image. Music in *A Man and a Woman* often has an importance at least equal to the images. Music provides emotion, tempo, and movement, while Lelouch's swooping camera and rapid montage add impressionistic details. This is especially true of the film's last half hour, where Lelouch and Lai present several fine songs-with-montage and very few dialogue scenes. In contemporary terms, one could describe the concluding half hour as a suite of music videos. The integration of image and score in *A Man and a Woman* was widely copied in the 1960s and 1970s.

Lai and Lelouch collaborated on a number of films. Their working method was unusual. Lai would write the main themes for a film after discussions with the director, but *before* production. The music then served as a guide for filming and editing. Writing music before rather than after production makes the composer much more of a creative partner to the writer and director than is normally the case.

The Lai-Lelouch collaborations are surprisingly diverse. *Live for Life* and *Love Is a Funny Thing* have sentimental scores and montage sequences on the model of *A Man and a Woman*. *Treize jours en France*, a documentary of the Winter Olympics of 1968, has a lovely score of four interwoven songs which pulls together the sometimes scattered images. The score of *The Crook* consists mainly of one brash pop song fragmented and repeated in various ways. In *Smic, Smac, Smoc*, Lai appears on camera as a blind accordionist to play the film's theme song. *The Good and the Bad*, set in the 1940s, has an interesting period score, with Lai quoting liberally from Glenn Miller. *And Now My Love* and *Les Uns et les autres*, both ambitious generational sagas, use music and image to evoke a number of historical periods. *And Now My Love*'s amalgam of Lai originals, Gilbert Bécaud vocals, and American and French pop tunes is more successful than the even more eclectic mix (''Bolero,'' Beethoven, Glenn Miller, Francis Lai, Michel Legrand) of *Les Uns et les autres*.

Aside from his work with Lelouch, Lai is best-known for his Academy Award-winning score for *Love Story*. The sad, sentimental theme for that film has become a pop standard, and he went on to write another strong theme for *Oliver's Story*, the sequel. Lai's other credits include the haunting music for *Rider on the Rain* and the very sentimental score for *International Velvet*. He has worked extensively in France, England, and the United States, and he has composed for everything from historical epics to soft-core pornography.

Lai's great strength is his ability to shape a score to the needs of a particular film. Although he is one of Muzak's favorite composers—half a dozen of his songs can be heard at the local supermarket or dentist's office—he is also a competent craftsman of film music, with several fine scores to his credit.

—Peter Lev

LANCI, Giuseppe ("Beppe")

Cinematographer. **Nationality:** Italian. **Born:** Rome, 1942. **Education:** Institute of Art, then Rome's Centro Sperimentale di Cinematografia. **Career:** Mid-1960s—entered film industry as an apprentice cameraman; by the 1970s, had become one of Europe's most noted cinematographers, working on films with a number of European luminaries.

Films as Cinematographer:

1978   *Maternale*
1980   *Salto nel Vuoto* (*Leap into the Void*) (Bellochio); *Confusione* (Natoli)
1982   *Gli occhi, la bocca* (*The Eyes, the Mouth*) (Bellochio); *Piso Piselli* (*Swee' Pea*) (Delmonte)
1983   *Nostalghia* (*Nostalgi*) (Tarkovsky); *Stelle emigranti* (Mazeni—for TV)
1984   *Enrico IV* (*Henry IV*) (Bellochio); *Kaos* (*Chaos*) (P. and V. Taviani)
1985   *Un Complicato intrigo di Bonne vicoli e delitti* (*Camorra*) (Wertmüller)
1986   *Good Morning Babilonia* (*Good Morning, Babylon*) (P. and V. Taviani); *Il Diavolo in Corpo* (*Devil in the Flesh*) (Bellochio); *La Venexiana* (*The Venetian Woman*) (Bolognini); *Every Time We Say Goodbye* (Mizrahi)
1987   *Havinck* (Weisz)
1988   *Paure e Amore* (*Three Sisters*; *Love and Fear*) (Von Trotta); *Zoo*; *La Visione del Sabba* (*The Sabbath*) (Bellocchio)
1989   *Francesco* (*St. Francis of Assisi*) (Cavani); *Il Prete bello* (*The Handsome Priest*); *Palombella rossa* (Moretti)
1990   *La-Baule-Les-Pins* (*C'est la Vie*) (Kurys); *Il Sole anche di notte* (*Night Sun*) (P. and V. Taviani)
1991   *Johnny Stecchino* (*Johnny Toothpick*) (Benigni)
1992   *Fiorile* (*Wild Flower*) (P. and V. Taviani); *La Villa del venerdi* (*Husbands and Lovers*) (Bolognini); *Tra due risvegli* (Fago)
1994   *The Conviction* (Bellochio); *Caro Diario* (*Dear Diary*) (Moretti); *Con gli occhi chiusi* (*With Closed Eyes*) (Archibugi)
1996   *Compagna di viaggio* (Del Monte); *Le Affinita elettive* (*The Elective Affinities*) (P. and V. Taviani)
1997   *Santostefano* (Pasquini); *Il Principe di Homburg* (*The Prince of Homburg*) (Bellochio)
1998   *I Piccoli maestri* (*Little Teachers*) (Luchetti); *Oscar per due* (Farina—for TV); *Aprile* (Moretti); *Tu ridi* (*You Laugh*) (Paolo Taviani and Vittorio Taviani)
1999   *La Balia* (*The Nanny*; *The Wet Nurse*) (Bellochio)

Publications

On LANCI: article—

"Italian cinematographers: le nuove tendenze," in *Cineforum*, July/August 1983.

*   *   *

Italian cinematographer Giuseppe Lanci's gift with the camera has kept him in the esteemed company of such landmark European directors as Lina Wertmüller, Paolo and Vittorio Taviani, and most frequently with Marco Bellochio during a career that spans three decades. Whether it is the lush, romantic style his vision has brought to such Taviani films as *Good Morning Babilonia* or the overheated visuals that suit the melodramas of Bellochio's work, Lanci has proven to be an artist with the camera.

Lanci studied cinematography at Rome's noted Centro Sperimentale, which Bellochio also attended. The two seem to have been meant for each other cinematically so aptly has Lanci's work complemented Bellochio's directing since *Leap into the Void*. Their *Devil in the Flesh* perhaps gained the most attention when it created international controversy due to a scene of oral sex. Nevertheless, its portrait of obsession leading to madness was far more noteworthy and greatly heightened by the cinematographer's contribution.

Although a number of the films Lanci has worked on have gained both critical and popular acclaim, it seems a little ironic that Lanci gained his greatest commercial success with *Johnny Stecchino*—made with actor, director, and co-writer Roberto Benigni—a simple comedy of gangsters and mistaken identity; it went on to become the highest grossing film ever to play in Italy.

It is understandable that Lanci has been chosen as cinematographer by many of Europe's noted and often most controversial directors, including Lina Wertmüller and Diane Kurys, given his fluid camera and provocative use of lighting and color to underline the mood of the scene. Lanci entered the 2000s as one of Europe's leading cinematographers.

—Allen Grant Richards

LANG, Charles B.

Cinematographer. **Nationality:** American. **Born:** Charles Bryant Lang, Jr., in Bluff, Utah, 27 March 1902. **Education:** Attended Lincoln High School, Los Angeles; studied law briefly, University of Southern California, Los Angeles. **Career:** 1919–22—laboratory assistant, then assistant cameraman, Realart Studio; still photographer, Preferred Picture Corporation, then with Paramount from mid-1920s until 1951 (director of photography, 1929–51), then freelance.

Awards: Academy Award, for *A Farewell to Arms*, 1932–33; Life Achievement Award, Society of American Cinematographers, 1991. **Died:** Of pneumonia, in Santa Monica, California, 3 April 1998.

Films as Cinematographer:

1927   *Ritzy* (Rosson)

1928   *The Shopworn Angel* (Wallace)

1929   *Innocents of Paris* (Wallace); *Half-Way to Heaven* (Abbott) (co)

1930   *Behind the Make-Up* (Milton); *Seven Days Leave* (*Medals*) (Wallace); *Street of Chance* (Cromwell); *Sarah and Son* (Arzner); *For the Defense* (Cromwell); *The Light of Western Stars* (Brower and Knopf); *Shadow of the Law* (Gasnier); *Anybody's Woman* (Arzner); *Tom Sawyer* (Cromwell); *The Right to Love* (Wallace)

1931   *Unfaithful* (Cromwell); *The Vice Squad* (Cromwell); *Caught* (Sloman); *Forbidden Adventure* (*Newly Rich*) (Taurog); *The Magnificent Life* (Viertel); *Once a Lady* (McClintic)

1932   *No One Man* (Corrigan); *Tomorrow and Tomorrow* (Wallace); *Thunder Below* (Wallace); *Devil and the Deep* (Gering); *He Learned about Women* (Corrigan); *A Farewell to Arms* (Borzage)

1933   ***She Done Him Wrong*** (L. Sherman); *A Bedtime Story* (Taurog); *Gambling Ship* (Gasnier and Marcin); *The Way to Love* (Taurog); *Cradle Song* (Leisen)

1934   *Death Takes a Holiday* (Leisen); *We're Not Dressing* (Taurog); *She Loves Me Not* (Nugent); *Mrs. Wiggs of the Cabbage Patch* (Taurog)

1935   *The Lives of a Bengal Lancer* (Hathaway); *Mississippi* (Sutherland); *Peter Ibbetson* (Hathaway)

1936   *Desire* (Borzage)

1937   *Souls at Sea* (Hathaway) (co); *Angel* (Lubitsch); *Tovarich* (Litvak)

1938   *Doctor Rhythm* (Tuttle); *You and Me* (F. Lang); *Spawn of the North* (Hathaway)

1939   *Zaza* (Cukor); *Midnight* (Leisen); *The Gracie Allen Murder Case* (Green); *The Cat and the Canary* (Nugent)

1940   *Women without Names* (Florey); *Adventure in Diamonds* (Fitzmaurice); *Buck Benny Rides Again* (Sandrich); *Dancing on a Dime* (Santley); *The Ghost Breakers* (Marshall); *Arise, My Love* (Leisen)

1941   *The Shepherd of the Hills* (Hathaway); *Nothing but the Truth* (Nugent); *Sundown* (Hathaway); *Skylark* (Sandrich); *The Lady Has Plans* (Lanfield)

1942   *Are Husbands Necessary?* (Taurog); *The Forest Rangers* (Marshall) (co)

1943   *So Proudly We Hail* (Sandrich); *True to Life* (Marshall); *The Uninvited* (L. Allen); *No Time for Love* (Leisen)

1944   *Standing Room Only* (Lanfield); *I Love a Soldier* (Sandrich); *Practically Yours* (Leisen); *Here Comes the Waves* (Sandrich)

1945   *The Stork Club* (Walker)

1946   *Miss Susie Slagle's* (Berry); *Blue Skies* (Heisler) (co); *Cross My Heart* (Berry)

1947   *Desert Fury* (L. Allen) (co); *The Ghost and Mrs. Muir* (Mankiewicz); *Where There's Life* (Lanfield)

1948   *A Foreign Affair* (Wilder); *Miss Tatlock's Millions* (Haydn); *My Own True Love* (Bennett)

1949   *Rope of Sand* (Dieterle); *The Great Lover* (Hall)

1950   *Fancy Pants* (Marshall); *Copper Canyon* (Farrow); *Branded* (Maté); *September Affair* (Dieterle); *The Mating Season* (Leisen)

1951   *Ace in the Hole* (*The Big Carnival*) (Wilder); *Peking Express* (Dieterle); *Mr. Belvedere Rings the Bell* (Koster) (co); *Red Mountain* (Dieterle); *Aaron Slick from Punkin Crick* (*Marshmallow Moon*) (Binyon)

1952   *The Atomic City* (Hopper); *Sudden Fear* (Miller)

1953   *Salome* (Dieterle); ***The Big Heat*** (F. Lang); *It Should Happen to You* (Cukor)

1954   *Sabrina* (*Sabrina Fair*) (Wilder); *Phffft!* (Robson)

1955   *The Man from Laramie* (A. Mann); *Female on the Beach* (Pevney); *Queen Bee* (MacDougall)

1956   *Autumn Leaves* (Aldrich); *The Solid Gold Cadillac* (Quine); *The Rainmaker* (Anthony); *Gunfight at the O.K. Corral* (J. Sturges)

1957   *Loving You* (Kanter); *Wild Is the Wind* (Cukor) (co)

1958   *The Matchmaker* (Anthony); *Separate Tables* (Delbert Mann); *Last Train from Gun Hill* (J. Sturges)

1959   ***Some Like It Hot*** (Wilder)

1960   *Strangers When We Meet* (Quine); *The Magnificent Seven* (J. Sturges); *The Facts of Life* (Frank); *One-Eyed Jacks* (Brando)

1961   *Blue Hawaii* (Taurog); *Summer and Smoke* (Glenville)

1962   *A Girl Named Tamiko* (J. Sturges); *How the West Was Won* (Hathaway, Marshall, and Ford) (co)

1963   *Critic's Choice* (Weis); *The Wheeler Dealers* (*Separate Beds*) (Hiller); *Charade* (Donen); *Paris When It Sizzles* (Quine)

1964   *Father Goose* (Nelson); *Sex and the Single Girl* (Quine)

1965   *Inside Daisy Clover* (Mulligan)

1966   *How to Steal a Million* (Wyler); *Not with My Wife, You Don't!* (Panama)

1967   *Hotel* (Quine); *The Flim-Flam Man* (*One Born Every Minute*) (Kershner); *Wait until Dark* (Young)

1968   *A Flea in Her Ear* (Charon); *The Stalking Moon* (Mulligan)

1969   *How to Commit Marriage* (Panama); *Bob and Carol and Ted and Alice* (Mazursky); *Cactus Flower* (Saks); *A Walk in the Spring Rain* (Green)

1970   *Doctors' Wives* (Schaefner)

1971   *The Love Machine* (Haley)

1972   *Butterflies Are Free* (Katselas)

1973   *Forty Carats* (Katselas)

Other Films:

1923   *Are You a Failure?* (Forman) (asst); *The Virginian* (Forman) (asst)

1925   *The Golden Princess* (Badger) (asst)

1926   *The Night Patrol* (Smith) (2nd cam)

1992   *Visions of Light: The Art of Cinematography* (Glassman and McCarthy) (as himself)

Publications

By LANG: articles—

''Some Thoughts on Low-Key Lighting,'' in *American Cinematographer* (Hollywood), August 1994.

On LANG: articles—

Wayne, Palma, in *Saturday Evening Post* (Philadelphia), 22 July 1933.

Rowan, Arthur, on *Gunfight at the O.K. Corral* in *American Cinematographer* (Hollywood), July 1957.

Gavin, Arthur, on *Wild Is the Wind* in *American Cinematographer* (Hollywood), January 1958.

Lightman, Herb A., on *Last Train from Gun Hill* in *American Cinematographer* (Hollywood), September 1959.

Scot, Darrin, in *American Cinematographer* (Hollywood), December 1961.

Lightman, Herb A., on *Charade* in *American Cinematographer* (Hollywood), May 1964.

Films in Review (New York), October 1970.

Film Comment (New York), Summer 1972.

Focus on Film (London), no. 13, 1973.

American Cinematographer (Hollywood), March 1974.

American Cinematographer (Hollywood), August 1975.

American Cinematographer (Hollywood), December 1990.

Obituary, in *Variety* (New York), 27 April 1998.

*   *   *

One of Hollywood's most famous cinematographers, Charles B. Lang labored long and hard in the Golden Age of Hollywood, receiving credit on more than 150 feature films. When the roster of the great camera operators in Hollywood history is drawn up, Charles B. Lang will belong in the top ten. His style is most closely associated with his romantic black-and-white technique, awash with translucent light, which emerged in the 1930s with such films as *A Farewell to Arms*, *Desire*, and *Angel*. Yet, like all the cinematographers of his era, he worked on films from all genres, in all visual styles.

Cinematographers, like all Hollywood employees during the 1930s and 1940s, were signed to long-term, binding contracts. Thus the bulk of their work was associated with one studio. Charles B. Lang toiled for Paramount Pictures from 1929 to 1951, almost the complete length of the Golden Age of the Hollywood studio system. As such he fulfilled his promise as a cinematographer early on, since Paramount, then under the influence of Ernst Lubitsch and Josef von Sternberg, was the home of great photographers of black-and-white cinema.

But as required by changing studio personnel and dictates, Lang adapted to the harsher film noir style of the 1940s. *The Big Heat*, directed by Fritz Lang in 1953, remains one of the most important examples of the late film noir period. It creates a beauty in the American suburbs and contrasts the jagged edges of the changing American urbanscape. *The Big Heat* represents an example of black-and-white cinematography at its best. The film would have been far poorer without Lang's work. Finally there have been his color films. Here Lang moved outdoors to film such Westerns as *Gunfight at the O.K. Corral* and *One-Eyed Jacks*. Again he adapted to a changing Hollywood; he produced many beautiful color motion pictures.

The quality of Lang's work was recognized by his peers. He was among the most honored of Hollywood's cameramen. He won his first Academy Award for cinematography in 1933 with *A Farewell to Arms*, and was nominated no less than 16 times for films which included *The Right to Love*; *Arise, My Love*; *So Proudly We Hail*; *The Ghost and Mrs. Muir*; *A Foreign Affair*; *Sudden Fear*; and *Some Like It Hot*.

As part of the Hollywood system from 1922 to 1973, Lang worked on many a mediocre film. But his name on the credits of any film usually guaranteed an interesting visual effort. His greatest work created a complexity of visual delight that students of film will continue to appreciate far off into the future. This is especially true for his work with the directors Billy Wilder and Fritz Lang.

—Douglas Gomery

LANSING, Sherry

Nationality: American. **Born:** Sherry Lee Lansing in Chicago, 31 July 1944. **Family:** Married to film director William Friedkin. **Education:** B.S. in theatre, summa cum laude, Northwestern University, 1966. **Career:** Began teaching high school math, English, and drama in Watts and East Los Angeles, 1966; pursued a modeling career, working for Max Factor and Alberto-Culver, 1969; had supporting parts in the films *Loving* and *Rio Lobo*, hired as executive story editor at Wagner International, 1970; hired as executive in charge of West Coast development at Talent Associates, 1974; hired as story editor at MGM, 1975; promoted to vice president, creative affairs, at MGM; named vice president, production, at Columbia Pictures, 1977; promoted to Columbia senior vice president, 1978; named president of 20th-Century Fox, 1980; formed Jaffe-Lansing Productions, an independent production company, with Stanley R. Jaffe; established a five-year relationship with Paramount Pictures, 1983; extended relationship with Paramount Pictures, 1987; became Chair and CEO of Paramount Pictures Motion Picture Group, 1992.

Sherry Lansing

Address: c/o Paramount Pictures Corp., 5555 Melrose Avenue, Los Angeles, California 90038–3197 U.S.A.

Films as Producer/Co-Producer/Co-Executive Producer:

1984   *Firstborn* (Apted); *Racing with the Moon* (Benjamin)
1987   *Fatal Attraction* (Lyne); *When the Time Comes* (Erman—for TV)
1988   *The Accused* (Kaplan)
1989   *Black Rain* (Scott)
1992   *School Ties* (Mandel)
1993   *Indecent Proposal* (Lyne)

Other Films:

1970   *Loving* (Kershner) (ro); *Rio Lobo* (Hawks) (ro)

Publications

By LANSING: articles—

"Actress' Life Is a Bore; Lansing Now MGM V.P.," interview in *Variety* (New York), 13 April 1977.
"At the Movies," interview with J. Maslin, in *New York Times*, 23 March 1984.
"Sherry Lansing: an interview," interview with C. Krista, in *Films in Review* (New York), November 1984.

On LANSING: articles—

"Sherry Lansing Takes Post as Col. Production V-P," in *Box Office* (Los Angeles), 7 November 1977.
"Sherry Lansing Enjoys More Film Corp. Rank than Ever Given Woman," in *Variety* (New York), 27 September 1978.
"Chasman and Lansing New Col. Senior V-Ps," in *Box Office* (Los Angeles), 21 August 1978.
"Boone Ankles Fox; Lansing Quits Col," in *Variety* (New York), 5 December 1979.
"Sherry Lansing Cues Chasman Elevation on Columbia Staff," in *Variety* (New York), 12 December 1979.
"Sherry Lansing New Prod. Chief at Fox; First Woman to Assume Job," in *Variety* (New York), 2 January 1980.
Harmetz, A., "Sherry Lansing, Former Model, Named Head of Fox Productions," in *New York Times*, 2 January 1980.
"Woman First to Reach Studio President's Rank," in *Box Office* (Los Angeles), 7 January 1980.
Harmetz, A., "Sherry Lansing and 2 Hollywood Hits," in *New York Times*, 7 February 1980.
Schulberg, B., "What Makes Hollywood Run Now?," in *New York Times*, 27 April 1980.
Current Biography (New York), 1981.
Daniell, T., "15 Fox Starts Ahead of an Iffy Strike," in *Variety* (New York), 18 February 1981.
Kaminsky, B., "Fox's Lansing Slates Ten New Productions for 1982," in *Film Journal* (New York), 21 December 1981.
Klain, S., "Brandeis' Tribute to Lansing Cues Droll Davis-Hirschfeld Sparring," in *Variety* (New York), 30 June 1982.

"Sherry Lansing's Fox Deal Extended for Indefinite Term," in *Variety* (New York), 21 July 1982.
Harmetz, A., "How a Hollywood Rumor Was Born, Flourished and Died," in *New York Times*, 12 December 1982.
Harmetz, A., "Sherry Lansing Resigns as Fox Production Chief," in *New York Times*, 21 December 1982
Harwood, J., "Lansing Trots from Fox Studio Niche; Has Job, Won't Elaborate," in *Variety* (New York), 22 December 1982.
Nicholson, T., "Business: Lansing's Farewell to Fox," in *Newsweek* (New York), 3 January 1983.
"Lansing, Jaffe Form Own Feature Shop, 5-year Marriage to Par.," in *Variety* (New York), 5 January 1983.
Farber, S., "Script to Screen: A Rocky Path," in *New York Times*, 6 November 1983.
"Business Update: Sherry Lansing's New Role in Movies," in *New York Times*, 6 November 1983.
"Jaffe and Lansing Extend Par pact," in *Variety* (New York), 30 September 1987.
Mass, R., "The Mirror Cracked: The Career Woman in a Trio of Lansing Films," in *Film Criticism* (Meadville, Pennsylvania), no. 2, 1988.
Vincenzi, L., "Motion Pictures: Stanley R. Jaffe and Sherry Lansing," in *Millimeter* (Cleveland, Ohio), January 1988.
Phillips, L., "Cameos: Sherry Lansing," in *Premiere* (New York), October 1988.
Beller, M., "Producer Sherry Lansing: Class Act in a Nasty Business," in *Life* (New York), 10 April 1989.
Matthews, T., "Weathering *Black Rain*," in *Box Office* (Los Angeles), 11 September 1989.
Hall, C., "Sherry Lansing: Living on Hollywood's Front Lines," in *Newsday* (Melville, New York), 23 September 1992.
Meisel, M., "A New Era Begins for Sherry Lansing," in *Film Journal* (New York), October/November 1992.
Wechsler, P., "Succeeding Tartikoff in Top Post: Paramount Taps Sherry Lansing," in *Newsday*, 5 November 1992.
Fabricant, G., "Sherry Lansing Is Named to Head Paramount," in *New York Times*, 5 November 1992.
Marx, A., and B. Lowry, "Lansing Ascends at Paramount," in *Variety* (New York), 9 November 1992.
Bart, P., "Queen of the Mountain," in *Variety* (New York), 26 July 1993.
Weinraub. B., "Hollywood Takes Bidding War in Stride (for Now)," in *New York Times*, 1 October 1993.
Conant, J., "Sherry Lansing (Chairwoman of Paramount Pictures' Motion Picture Group)," in *Harper's Bazaar* (New York), 1 January 1994.
Sellers, P., "The 50 Most Powerful Women in American Business," in *Fortune* (New York), 12 October 1998.
Kit, Z., "Women in Entertainment—The Power," in *Hollywood Reporter*, December 1999.

*   *   *

The career of Hollywood producer/executive Sherry Lansing, and her impact on the motion picture industry, is concisely summarized in a series of headlines of news articles chronicling her career:

1977: "Sherry Lansing Takes Post as Col. Production V-P"
1978: "Sherry Lansing Enjoys More Film Corp. Rank than Ever Given Woman"

1979: ''Boone Ankles Fox; Lansing Quits Col''
1980: ''Sherry Lansing New Prod. Chief at Fox; First Woman to Assume Job''
1981: ''Fox's Lansing Slates Ten New Productions for 1982''
1982: ''Sherry Lansing's Fox Deal Extended for Indefinite Term''
1982: ''Sherry Lansing Resigns as Fox Production Chief''
1983: ''Lansing, Jaffe Form Own Feature Shop, 5-year Marriage to Par.''
1987: ''Jaffe and Lansing Extend Par Pact.''
1992: ''Sherry Lansing Is Named to Head Paramount''
1998: ''The 50 Most Powerful Women in American Business''

Then there is the 1989 headline that offers insight into Lansing's Hollywood staying power: ''Producer Sherry Lansing: Class Act in a Nasty Business.''

Such headlines not only mirror Lansing's rise among Hollywood's power elite, but reflect on the chess-and-checkers nature of employment in the motion picture industry's upper echelons. In Hollywood, nothing is forever; Monday's hot story is Wednesday's old news. One year, you make headlines for signing on at a studio and announcing big plans for future productions. The next year, you have already left (or, in *Variety* lingo, ''ankled'') that studio and have resurfaced elsewhere. In this regard, Lansing is no different from any one of a score of studio ''suits.'' What makes her stand out is her status as the first woman to earn and enjoy the power of a high-level motion picture industry decisionmaker.

Lansing's career is analogous to that of Jackie Robinson, the Hall of Fame ballplayer who broke the major league baseball color line. Robinson's signing by Branch Rickey to play for the Brooklyn Dodgers is an event than transcends sports. It is one of a number of occurrences—others include the integration of the American military and Brown vs. Board of Education—which signaled the stirrings of the civil rights movement. Had Robinson not been of exemplary character, and had he not shone on the ballfield, he might have indefinitely set back the cause of his race. Similarly, Lansing's career path and accomplishments are outgrowths of another 20th-century social movement: late 1960s and early 1970s feminism. Her know-how as a decisionmaker and knack for surviving and thriving in the all-male club of Hollywood executives allowed her to open the door to future female powerbrokers.

Lansing entered the entertainment industry as a model and actress. After playing supporting roles in two films released in 1970—*Loving*, Irvin Kershner's suburban-marriage-in-crisis drama, and *Rio Lobo*, a Howard Hawks-John Wayne Western—she abandoned performing for a career behind the camera. She steadily rose from story editor to production executive to studio president to independent producer to, finally, Paramount Pictures Chair and CEO. As an independent producer, Lansing's most typical films spotlight contemporary sexual politics and manipulative, incendiary relationships between men and women. Among the characters in her films are a loutish man who abuses a women (*Firstborn*); a psychotic woman who becomes unhinged when she thinks she has been exploited by a man (*Fatal Attraction*); a woman who is gang-raped, and demands her day in court (*The Accused*); and a wealthy man who offers a poor couple $1-million to spend one evening in the arms of the wife (*Indecent Proposal*). Even more significant, however, are the films made under Lansing's aegis as a studio executive. These range from *The China Syndrome* and *Kramer vs. Kramer*, two of the most highly regarded Hollywood films of the late 1970s, produced when Lansing was at Columbia Pictures, through such 1990s Academy Award-winning

Paramount Pictures mega-hits as *Forrest Gump* and *Titanic*. For years, Lansing regularly has been among the highest-ranking women listed on the various polls of ''100 most powerful people in Hollywood.'' Given the worldwide popularity of the American motion picture industry, Lansing's authority is international in scope. In 1996, *The Australian* magazine ranked her Number 37 on its list of ''100 Most Powerful Women in the World.''

—Rob Edelman

LANTZ, Walter

Animator. **Nationality:** American. **Born:** New Rochelle, New York, 27 April 1900. **Education:** Attended the Arts Student League, New York. **Family:** Married 1) Doris Hollister (divorced 1940), 2) the actress Grace Stafford, 1940 (died 1992). **Career:** 1915–16—office boy, *New York American*; also cartoonist; 1916–18—camera assistant and animator on Hearst cartoon films, Cosmopolitan: worked on *Jerry on the Job* series; 1918–21—animator, Barre-Bowers Studio: worked on *Mutt and Jeff* cartoons; 1921–27—worked at Bray Studios: first animated film as director, *Col. Heezaliar's Forbidden Fruit*, 1924; 1927–29—gag writer, Mack Sennett studio; 1929–36—director at Universal; 1936–73—independent producer; directed only a few films after 1942; work for TV includes the series *The Woody Woodpecker Show*, 1957–66. **Awards:** Academy Award for *The*

Walter Lantz

Merry Old Soul, 1933; Special Academy Award, 1978. **Died:** Of heart failure, in Burbank, California, 22 March 1994.

Films as Director of Animation:

1924   *Col. Heezaliar's Forbidden Fruit; African Jungle; Col. Heezaliar's Ancestors; Sky Pilot; Col. Heezaliar's Vacation; Col. Heezaliar's Knighthood; Horse Play; The Magic Lamp; The Giant Killer; The Pied Piper*

1925   *Little Red Riding Hood; Lyin' Tamer; The House That Dinky Built; Cinderella; Peter Pan Handled; Magic Carpet; Robinson Crusoe; Three Bears; Just Spooks; Dinky Doodle in the Circus (Dinky Doodle in the Restaurant)*

1926   *Dinky Doodle in Lost and Found (Dinky Doodle in Uncle Tom's Cabin; Dinky Doodle in the Arctic; Dinky Doodle in Egypt; Dinky Doodle in the Wild West; Dinky Doodle and the Little Orphan; Dinky Doodle in the Army); The Pelican's Bill; Dinky Doodle's Bed Time Story; Cat's Whiskers; The Mule's Disposition; The Pig's Curly Tail; For the Love 'o Pete; Pete's Haunted House (Party); The Tail of the Monkey*

1927   *Dog Gone It; Cat's Nine Lives; Hyena's Laugh; Puppy Express; Petering Out; S'matter, Pete?; Lunch Hound; Jingle Bells*

1929   *Ozzie of the Circus; Stage Stunt; Stripes and Stars; Wicked West; Nuts and Jolts; Ice Man's Luck; Wear Willies; Jungle Jingles; Saucy Sausages; Race Riot; Oil's Well; Permanent Wave; Cold Turkey; Amature Nite; Hurdy Gurdy; Nutty Notes*

1930   *Chile con Carmen; Kisses and Kurses; Broadway Folly; Bowery Bimboes; Bowling Bimboes; Tramping Tramps; The Hash Shop; The Prison Panic; Hot for Hollywood; Hell's Heels; My Pal Paul; Not So Quiet; Spooks; Hen Fruit; Cold Feet; Snappy Salesman; The Singing Sap; The Detective; The Fowl Ball; The Navy; Mexico; Africa; Alaska; Mars*

1931   *China; College; Shipwrecked; The Farmer; The Fireman; Sunny South; The Country School; The Band Master; North Woods; The Stone Age; Radio Rhythm; Kentucky Bells; Hot Feet; The Hunter; Wonderland; The Hare Mail; The Fisherman; The Clown*

1932   *Mechanical Man; Grandma's Pet; Wins Out; Beau and Arrows; Making Good; Let's Eat; The Winged Horse; To the Rescue; Cat Nipped; A Wet Knight; A Jungle Jumble; Day Nurse; The Athlete; The Busy Barber; The Butcher Boy; Carnival Capers; The Crowded Snores; The Underdog; Wild and Woolly; Cats and Dogs; The Teacher's Pests*

1933   *Merry Dog; The Plumber; The Terrible Troubadour; The Shriek; The Lumber Chumps; Going to Blazes; Beau Beste; Nature's Workshop; Ham and Eggs; Pin Feathers; Confidence; Hot and Cold; King Klunk; Five and Dime; They Done Him Right; The Zoo; The Merry Old Soul; Parking Space*

1934   *Chicken Reel; The Candy House; The Country Fair; The Toy Shoppe; Wolf! Wolf!; The Ginger Bread Boy; Annie Moved Away; Goldielocks and the Three Bears; The Wax Works;*

William Tell; Chris Columbus, Jr.; The Dizzy Dwarf; Ye Happy Pilgrims; Jolly Little Elves; The Sky Larks; Spring in the Park; Toyland Premiere

1935   *Robinson Crusoe Isle; The Hillbilly; Two Little Lambs; Do a Good Deed; Candy Lamb; Elmer the Great Dane; Springtime Serenade; Towne Hall Follies; At Your Service; Three Lazy Mice; Bronco Buster; Amateur Broadcast; The Quail Hunt; The Fox and the Rabbit; Monkey Wretches; The Case of the Lost Sheep; Doctor Oswald*

1936   *Soft Ball Game; Alaska Sweepstakes; Slumberland Express; Beauty Shoppe; Barnyard Five; Fun House; Farming Fools; Battle Royal; Music Hath Charms; Kiddie Review; Beach Combers; Night Life of the Bugs; The Puppet Show; Unpopular Mechanic; Turkey Dinner; Gopher Trouble; Knights for a Day*

1937   *The Golfers; House of Magic; Everybody Sings; The Big Race; Duck Hunt; Lumber Camp; The Birthday Party; Steel Workers; Trailer Thrills; The Stevedores; The Wily Weasel; Countr y Store; The Playful Pup; Fireman's Picnic; Rest Resort; Ostrich Feathers; Air Express; Lovesick; The Keeper of the Lions; The Mechanical Handy Man; Football Fever; The Mysterious Jug; The Dumb Cluck*

1938   *Yokel Boy Makes Good*

1940   *Crazy House; Knock, Knock; Syncopated Sioux*

1941   *Fair Today; Scrub Me Mama with a Boogie Beat; Hysterical High Spots in American History; Dizzy Kitty; Salt Water Daffy; Woody Woodpecker; The Screwdriver; The Boogie Woogie Bugle Boy of Company B; Man's Best Friend; Pantry Panic; $21.00 a Day Once a Month*

1942   *Hollywood Matador; The Hams That Couldn't Be Cured; Mother Goose on the Loose; Goodbye Mr. Moth*

1951   *Wicket Wacky; Slingshot 67/8; Redwood Sap; Woody Woodpecker Polka; Destination Meatball*

1952   *Born to Peck; Stage Hoax; Woodpecker in the Rough; Scalp Treatment; The Great Who Dood It*

1960   *Bats in the Belfry* (+ pr); *Coca Cola Cartoons*

1989   *Poet and Peasant*

Publications

By LANTZ: articles—

''Let's Try Animation,'' in *American Cinematographer* (Hollywood), September 1934.
Films and Filming (London), July 1965.
Griffithiana (Gemona, Italy), December 1986.
''Woodpeckers, Rabbits and Pandas—Oh My!'' an interview with Frank Cali, in *Outré* (Evanston), no. 6, 1996.

On LANTZ: book—

Adamson, Joe, *The Walter Lantz Story*, New York, 1985.

On LANTZ: articles—

Films and Filming (London), April 1971.
American Cinematographer (Hollywood), Fall 1971.

Maltin, Leonard, in *Of Mice and Magic*, New York, 1980.

Lenburg, Jeff, in *The Great Cartoon Directors*, London, 1983.

Obituary, in *The New York Times*, 23 March 1994.

Obituary, in *Variety* (New York), 28 March 1994.

Obituary, in *Time*, 4 April 1994.

Cali, F., "June Foray," in *Outré* (Evanston), vol. 1, no. 6, 1996.

*   *   *

Although his obituary in *Variety* called him one of the most successful and durable animation producers of all time, "Nice guys finish last" can truly be said about Walter Lantz. Lantz was the last major producer of theatrical cartoon shorts, closing shop in 1973 after 45 years in the business. Because of his pleasant personality Lantz never raided other cartoon studios for talent. And yet some of the biggest names in the business had worked for him. Tex Avery, Jack Hannah, and Hugh Harman were just three of the talents who had entered his studio over the years. Lantz was a sound businessman and produced cartoons on a budget, though he didn't skimp on his cartoon production.

Lantz began his career as an animator, and got his big break at Universal Studios where he took over the Walt Disney creation of Oswald the Lucky Rabbit. He made history when he and his partner Bill Nolan completed the first Technicolor cartoon. The five-minute opening sequence of Universal's multimillion dollar musical *The King of Jazz* was a jaunty musical number featuring Whiteman vocalist Bing Crosby. In 1935 Lantz went on to become an independent producer giving distribution rights to Universal. He was still using the character of Oswald the Rabbit, but realized that if his studio were to succeed he needed to introduce new characters. After a series of unsuccessful character creations, Lantz tried looking for animals that had never been used in cartoons before. One of Lantz's studio personnel, Alex Lovy, had come up with Andy Panda, who was to become one of Lantz's most successful characters. At first Andy starred with his thick-witted, lumbering father whom Andy always managed to get into trouble. As the series progressed Andy grew older, and the father/son story lines were dropped. In 1940 Ben "Bugs" Hardaway joined the studios. Hardaway had recently left Warner Bros. where he created such superstar notables as Daffy Duck and Bugs Bunny. His goal was to create a similar character for Lantz. He decided that the father/son pandas would provide the perfect introduction to Woody Woodpecker. Woody made his debut in *Knock, Knock* as a rapscallion woodpecker. Andy and Pop make every effort to get rid of the annoying woodpecker, but like Daffy and Bugs he outsmarts them, at every turn getting the better of the situation. It was in this cartoon that Woody's infamous laugh—"ha-ha-ha-HA-ha"—was heard for the first time. Initially Woody was a rather ugly, grotesque-looking character. Over the years that changed as Woody became more likeable and easygoing. But in those early years Woody was an extremely daffy lunatic. He was unlike other Lantz characters in almost every way, often violent and excessively active. Lantz directed most of the early Woody films in an almost frenetic pace. They can easily be differentiated from the evenly paced work of Alex Lovy. Lovy left the studio in 1942 and Lantz had to find someone to take his place. That person was James "Shamus" Culhane. He took on the Woody Woodpecker character and continued in the frantic manner of Lantz with his first Woody cartoon, *The Barber of Seville*. Culhane continued directing Woody Woodpecker cartoons with a similar brand of violent humor usually found in Tex Avery cartoons.

After the Second World War, Lantz and his studio went through some rather hard times and he had to close down for over a year. When he finally reopened, he had to be more cost-conscious than ever. To save money, Lantz went back to directing, produced only Woody Woodpecker cartoons, and hired his wife to become the voice of Woody Woodpecker. After producing several cartoons in 1951–52, Lantz was once again able to expand his operation and increase cartoon production. In 1954 Tex Avery returned to the Lantz studios and provided a needed shot in the arm. Despite the poor quality of animation, Avery's first cartoon for Lantz, *Crazy Mixed-Up Pup* was nominated for an Academy Award. Avery went on to feature a new character originally created by Alex Lovy, *Chilly Willy*, a penguin who desired nothing more than a warm climate. In *The Legend of Rockabye Point* Avery earned another Academy Award nomination. Avery soon left the studio over salary negotiations, but his influence had already seeped into the studio. When Avery left, Lovy once again returned to the studio.

In 1957 Lantz began to eye television as a possible outlet for his cartoons. Jack Hannah joined the studio and began working on *The Woody Woodpecker Show*, which combined previous theatrical re-leases with newly animated sequences and live-action shots featuring Lantz himself. Woody would introduce him by saying, "Here's my boss, Walter Lantz." This segment of the show explained the process of how cartoons are created, first for television and cartoon animation. These early television programs helped Lantz to continue producing cartoons for theatrical release, although higher costs reduced the amount of animation—fewer cels per second. Chilly Willy and Woody Woodpecker remained his most popular cartoons. They lasted until Lantz retired, unable to recoup production costs quickly.

In 1979 the Motion Picture Academy honored Lantz and his contribution to the field of animation. Lantz responded by having Woody Woodpecker accept the award with him. Lantz may not be as revered as Disney but he produced satisfying cartoons, provided the world with one of the most interesting characters in Woody Woodpecker, and remained a most dedicated cartoon animator. If anyone truly loved his craft, it was Walter Lantz.

—Maryann Oshana, updated by Denise Delorey

LARDNER, Ring Jr.

Writer. **Nationality:** American. **Born:** Ringgold Wilmer Lardner, Jr., in Chicago, Illinois, 19 August 1915; son of the satirical writer Ring Lardner. **Education:** Attended Great Neck Preparatory School; Phillips Academy; Princeton University, New Jersey, two years. **Family:** Married 1) Silvia Schulman, 1937 (divorced 1943), two children; 2) the actress Frances Chaney, 1946, one son. **Career:** 1935—journalist, New York *Daily Mirror*; 1936–41—worked for Selznick International, Warner Bros., RKO, and Republic; first film as writer, *Meet Dr. Christian*, 1940; then contracts with MGM and 20th Century-Fox; 1947—beginning of House Un-American Activities Committee investigation of Lardner: served a nine-month sentence for contempt of Congress, 1950–51, and blacklisted; worked on British TV series *The Adventures of Robin Hood* and *Sir Lancelot*,

Ring Lardner, Jr.

and used pseudonyms Oliver Skeyne and Philip Rush (credited as Ring Lardner only after 1965); 1964—co-author of the musical play *Foxy*. **Awards:** Academy Award, for *Woman of the Year*, 1942; Academy Award and Writers Guild Award, for *M*A*S*H*, 1970. **Agent:** Jim Preminger Agency, Los Angeles, California, U.S.A.

Films as Writer:

1940   *Meet Dr. Christian* (Vorhaus); *The Courageous Dr. Christian* (Vorhaus)
1941   *Arkansas Judge* (*False Witness*) (McDonald) (co)
1942   *Woman of the Year* (Stevens)
1943   *The Cross of Lorraine* (Garnett)
1944   *Tomorrow the World* (Fenton); *Laura* (Preminger) (uncredited)
1946   *Cloak and Dagger* (F. Lang); *Brotherhood of Man* (Cannon—short)
1947   *Forever Amber* (Preminger)
1948   *The Forbidden Street* (*Britannia Mews*) (Negulesco); *Four Days Leave* (*Swiss Tour*) (Lindtberg) (co)
1950   *The Hollywood Ten* (Berry—short)
1951   *The Big Night* (Losey)
1958   *Virgin Island* (Jackson); *A Breath of Scandal* (Curtiz) (co)
1965   *The Cincinnati Kid* (Jewison)
1970   *M*A*S*H* (Altman)
1971   *La mortadella* (*Lady Liberty*) (Monicelli) (co)
1977   *The Greatest* (Gries)
1978   *Semi-Tough* (uncredited)

Film as Actor:

1988   *My Name Is Bertolt Brecht—Exile in U.S.A.* (Bunge)

Publications

By LARDNER: books—

The Ecstasy of Owen Muir (novel), New York, 1954.
The Lardners: My Family Remembered, New York, 1976.
All for Love (novel), New York, 1985.

By LARDNER: articles—

In *The Hollywood Screenwriter*, edited by Richard Corliss, New York, 1972.
Cine Cubano (Havana), no. 98, 1980.
Film Comment (New York), September/October 1988.

On LARDNER: articles—

Olin, Joyce, in *American Screenwriters*, edited by Robert E. Morsberger, Stephen O. Lesser, and Randall Clark, Detroit, 1984.
Filmnews, April 1991.
Robb, D., "Naming the Right Names: Amending the Hollywood Blacklist," in *The Journal: Writer's Guild of America, West* (Los Angeles), November 1996.
U.S. News & World Report, 3 November 1997.
Free Inquiry, vol. 18, no. 3, Summer 1998.

*   *   *

Ring Lardner, Jr., had a spotty career as a writer for films. Richard Corliss described it as perhaps the most frustrating of any major screenwriter in Hollywood. He began his film work at Selznick International Pictures in 1936, where he wrote the ending of *A Star Is Born* with Budd Schulberg and married Selznick's secretary Silvia Schulman. He soon moved to Warner Bros., however, because of the lack of other opportunities with Selznick. But here, too, he failed to establish himself as a screenwriter of notice, and in the fall of 1938 he moved again, this time to RKO where he finally received his first screen credits in 1940 for two run-of-the-mill film adaptations of Jean Hersholt's *Dr. Christian* radio series.

Lardner's big break finally came when, before being inducted into the army, Garson Kanin, who had been directing at RKO, turned over an idea for a Katharine Hepburn film to his brother, Michael, and Lardner. The two young screenwriters did a 90-page treatment for a film, later to be titled *Woman of the Year*, and sent it to Hepburn. She directed it to Louis B. Mayer and negotiated a contract for them. The movie became the first of the nine Tracy–Hepburn films and garnered an Academy Award for best screenplay. It proved to be the first of a run of successes for Lardner during the 1940s, including Tay Garnett's *The Cross of Lorraine*, Fritz Lang's *Cloak and Dagger*, Otto Preminger's *Forever Amber*, and Jean Negulesco's *Forbidden Street*.

But in 1947 Lardner's career was suddenly halted when he was blacklisted for his leftist political activities. Until 1963, Lardner was reduced to writing anonymously for British and American television dramas with an occasional unsigned film script. He would later say of this time that it probably did him some good to be removed from the temptations of writing for the screen and southern California. During his years on the blacklist, Lardner wrote a novel, *The Ecstasy of Owen Muir* (1954). Nonetheless, his movie career was spectacularly resurrected in 1970 when he won both an Academy Award and the Writers Guild Award for his screenplay for Robert Altman's *M*A*S*H*. But since that triumph Lardner has spent less time working on screenplays and more time on fiction and journalism.

Lardner and Kanin's *Woman of the Year* proved the ideal Hepburn vehicle because it deals with sex roles and the difficulty of keeping private and professional lives separate. Tracy's maleness and Hepburn's femininity are both so assured that the reversal of roles is accomplished within the film as the two newspaper employees, a sportswriter and political correspondent, are able to put together a far-from-conventional marriage. Although the film finally comes down on the side of convention and Sam Craig (Tracy), it is clear that Tess Harding (Hepburn) will remain an independent woman, but one who can manage both career and home.

The screen work Lardner did between winning his Academy Award and his blacklisting reflected his leftist activities, which had begun as early as 1937 when he attended a Marxist study group with Budd and Virginia Schulberg. Lardner spent the middle 1940s scripting a number of politically committed films. After doing some uncredited rewriting on Otto Preminger's *Laura* and Robert Z. Leonard's *Marriage Is a Private Affair*, Lardner wrote *The Cross of Lorraine* which dealt with French capitulation to the Nazis but ended with a restatement of a commitment to fight for a free France, and *Tomorrow the World*, which was adapted from a Broadway play and traces the activities of a German youth who was brought to the Midwest by his father's brother after his parents perish in a concentration camp. The boy believes fervently in the Nazi cause and tries to spread anti-Semitism and steal war documents from his uncle. Finally, Lardner worked with Fritz Lang on a melodramatic spy film about the OSS called *Cloak and Dagger*. Although the scripts for these films are far from distinguished, they do reflect Lardner's political leanings.

Lardner's last two films before his blacklisting were for Otto Preminger at Twentieth Century-Fox, and were both costume dramas. First, he was hired to work on Michael Dunn's script for *Forever Amber* and then to adapt Margery Sharp's *Britannia Mews* into the film *The Forbidden Street*, another melodrama depicting the clash between classes brought on by marriage between the upper and lower orders.

Summoned before the House Un-American Activities Committee (HUAC) in 1947, Lardner was questioned about his political values and uttered his famous retort that he could answer but that he would hate himself in the morning. He was jailed for contempt of Congress for his silent resistance and for refusing to name names and served nine months of a one-year sentence at the Federal Corrections Institution in Danbury, Connecticut. For the next ten years Lardner wrote uncredited material for television and the movies, often abroad, including work on Joseph Losey's *The Big Night* (1951). In 1963 Sam Peckinpah hired Lardner to adapt Richard Jessup's novel *The Cincinnati Kid* for the screen. Although both Peckinpah and Lardner were eventually fired from the project—Norman Jewison subsequently directed the film and Terry Southern rewrote it—Lardner was credited for the script when the movie was released in 1965, thereby breaking his long exile from the movies.

Lardner received his second Academy Award and revived his career as a screenwriter with his work on *M*A*S*H*, directed by Robert Altman. The script was only partially based on the novel by a former Army surgeon writing under the pseudonym of Richard Hooker. The film has been widely criticized for its violence and antifeminist tone, especially in handling the major female character, ''Hot Lips'' Houlihan. Much has also been made of the film's antiwar message delivered via the violence and sadism of the central characters. The film's message seemed to say the only way to remain sane during wartime is to go *in*sane. The film and its attitude towards its characters and the war continues to create controversy, but it restored Lardner to a position of eminence in the film world. Nevertheless, it was a position which failed to inspire him to throw himself exclusively back into script writing.

Lardner's career in the movies has been described as one of the most frustrating of any of the major screenwriting talents which came out of the Hollywood system. So, perhaps, it is understandable that in spite of his reclaimed fame he would remain leery of an industry which shut him out so completely during the years of his blacklisting. Now, although he still works on movie projects, he also continues to devote time to television and journalism as well.

—Charles L. P. Silet

LA SHELLE, Joseph

Cinematographer and cameraman. **Nationality:** American. **Born:** Los Angeles, California, 1905 (some sources say 1900); sometimes credited as Joseph W. La Shelle. **Education:** Trained as electrical engineer. **Career:** 1923—joined Lasky Studios as laboratory assistant, then superintendent of printing room at Paramount, and assistant cameraman: assistant to Charles G. Clarke in late 1920s, and to Arthur Miller at Pathé and Fox during 1930s; 1943—first film as cinematographer, *Happy Land*. **Award:** Academy Award for *Laura*, 1944. **Died:** In San Diego, California, 20 August 1989.

Films as Cameraman:

1926   *Rocking Moon* (Melford); *Whispering Smith* (Melford); *The Flame of the Yukon* (Melford)
1929   *The Pagan* (Van Dyke)
1931   *The Painted Desert* (Higgin)
1934   *The White Parade* (Cummings)
1935   *The Little Colonel* (Butler); *It's a Small World* (Cummings)
1938   *The Baroness and the Butler* (W. Lang)
1940   *Brigham Young—Frontiersman* (Hathaway)
1941   *Tobacco Road* (Ford); *How Green Was My Valley* (Ford)
1943   *The Song of Bernadette* (H. King)

Films as Cinematographer:

1943   *Happy Land* (Pichel)
1944   *Bermuda Mystery* (Stoloff); *The Eve of St. Mark* (Stahl); *Take It or Leave It* (Stoloff); *Laura* (Preminger)
1945   *Hangover Square* (Brahm); *A Bell for Adano* (H. King); *Fallen Angel* (Preminger)
1946   *Doll Face* (*Come Back to Me*) (Seiler); *Cluny Brown* (Lubitsch); *Claudia and David* (W. Lang)

1947   *The Late George Apley* (Mankiewicz); *The Foxes of Harrow* (Stahl)
1948   *Deep Waters* (H. King); *The Luck of the Irish* (Koster); *Road House* (Negulesco)
1949   *The Fan* (*Lady Windermere's Fan*) (Preminger); *Come to the Stable* (Koster); *Everybody Does It* (Goulding)
1950   *Mother Didn't Tell Me* (Binyon); *Under My Skin* (Negulesco); *Where the Sidewalk Ends* (Preminger); *Mr. 880* (Goulding); *The Jackpot* (W. Lang)
1951   *The Guy Who Came Back* (Newman); *The Thirteenth Letter* (Preminger); *Mr. Belvedere Rings the Bell* (Koster) (co); *Elopement* (Koster)
1952   *The Outcasts of Poker Flat* (Newman); *Les Miserables* (Milestone); *My Cousin Rachel* (Koster); *Something for the Birds* (Wise)
1953   *Dangerous Crossing* (Newman); *Mister Scoutmaster* (Levin)
1954   *Tournament of Roses* (O. Lang—short); *River of No Return* (Preminger); *The First Piano Quartet* (O. Lang—short); *Movie Stunt Pilot* (O. Lang—short); *Piano Encores* (O. Lang—short); *Jet Carrier* (O. Lang—short); *Marty* (Delbert Mann)
1955   *Storm Fear* (Wilde); *The Conqueror* (Powell) (co)
1956   *Our Miss Brooks* (Lewis); *Run for the Sun* (R. Boulting); *Crime of Passion* (Oswald); *Fury at Showdown* (Oswald); *The Bachelor Party* (Delbert Mann)
1957   *I Was a Teenage Werewolf* (Fowler); *The Fuzzy Pink Nightgown* (Taurog); *The Abductors* (McLaglen); *No Down Payment* (Ritt)
1958   *The Long Hot Summer* (Ritt); *The Naked and the Dead* (Walsh)
1959   *Career* (Anthony)
1960   ***The Apartment*** (Wilder); *All in a Night's Work* (Anthony)
1961   *The Honeymoon Machine* (Thorpe); *The Outsider* (Delbert Mann)
1962   *A Child Is Waiting* (Cassavetes); *How the West Was Won* (Hathaway, Marshall, and Ford) (co)
1963   *Irma La Douce* (Wilder); *Wild and Wonderful* (Anderson)
1964   *Kiss Me, Stupid* (Wilder)
1965   *Seven Women* (Ford); *The Chase* (Penn)
1966   *The Fortune Cookie* (*Meet Whiplash Willie*) (Wilder)
1967   *Barefoot in the Park* (Saks); *Kona Coast* (Johnson)
1969   *U.M.C.* (*Operation Heartbeat*) (Sagal); *80 Steps to Jonah* (Oswald)

Publications

By LA SHELLE: article—

"Cukoloris: Set Lighting's Most Versatile Tool," in *American Cinematographer* (Hollywood), July 1984.

On LA SHELLE: articles—

Lightman, Herb A., on *My Cousin Rachel* in *American Cinematographer* (Hollywood), February 1953.
Film Comment (New York), Summer 1972.
Focus on Film (London), no. 13, 1973.
Kimble, G., on *How the West Was Won* in *American Cinematographer* (Hollywood), October 1983.
Film Dope (Nottingham), November 1985.

Obituary in *Variety* (New York), 30 August 1989.
Obituary in *American Cinematographer* (Hollywood), October 1989.

*   *   *

During a long career extending from 1924 through 1969, Joseph La Shelle earned a reputation as one of Hollywood's foremost practitioners of stylistic and literate cinematography through his work on such milestones as *Laura*, *My Cousin Rachel*, *The Naked and the Dead*, and *The Apartment*. In particular, he excelled at the difficult art of successfully transferring works initially conceived for other media to the screen by experimenting with angles and lighting to imbue them with a fresh perspective.

In *Laura*, which was taken from the stage, he overcame a script that called for no exterior shots other than one or two designed exclusively for studio sets. Through sheer artistry, he managed to convey a world of café society, expensive restaurants, and ornate Park Avenue apartments with few viewers noticing the absence of city streets and country parks. For this achievement, he received an Academy Award. However, his achievement is equally apparent on such other adaptations from the stage as *The Long Hot Summer* and *Barefoot in the Park*.

La Shelle started in films as a lab assistant in 1923 following his graduation from high school. He worked his way up to become head of the film laboratory at Lasky's by 1925 but deserted it for a job behind the camera a year later. After a variety of photographic assignments at the Metropolitan Studios and at the Cecil B. DeMille lot, he became a camera operator for the prominent cinematographer Arthur Miller, a position he held until 1943. During this period he achieved particular recognition for his work on John Ford's *How Green Was My Valley* and Henry King's *The Song of Bernadette*. After the latter film, he graduated to the rank of cinematographer and won the Academy Award for *Laura* a year later.

During a distinguished career, he was recognized as being equally adept in both black-and-white and color cinematography and was similarly "at home" with intimate comedy-dramas (*The Apartment*) or sprawling outdoor panoramas (*How the West Was Won*). He received 15 Academy Award nominations, making him one of the most critically acclaimed artists, regardless of category, in motion picture history.

—Stephen L. Hanson

LASKY, Jesse L.

Producer. **Nationality:** American. **Born:** Jesse Louis Lasky in San Jose, California, 13 September 1880. **Education:** Attended San Jose High School. **Family:** Married Bessie Ginzberg, 1909; sons: the writer Jesse L. Lasky, Jr., and William Raymond; daughter: Bessie Dorothy. **Career:** 1897–98—reporter, *San Francisco Post*; 1898–1900—cornetist in San Francisco theatre; 1900—joined Alaska gold rush, then cornet player in Honolulu; for the next 10 years in duo act with his sister Blanche in vaudeville, and promoter and impresario: produced Cecil B. DeMille's operetta *California*, 1912; 1913—cofounder, with Samuel Goldfisch (later Goldwyn; his brother-in-law) and DeMille, Jesse L. Lasky Feature Play Company: served as president: first film, the feature-length *The Squaw Man*, was big hit; 1916—merged with Adolph Zukor's Famous Players to form Famous

Jesse L. Lasky (left)

Players-Lasky, eventually Paramount; 1932—ousted from his executive post, and became independent producer, for Fox, Warner Bros., and RKO; 1935—formed short-lived partnership with Mary Pickford, Pickford-Lasky Company; 1938–40—produced radio talent show *Gateway to Hollywood*; 1945—formed Jesse L. Lasky Productions; mid-1950s—returned to Paramount, but died before first production was begun. **Died:** In Beverly Hills, California, 13 January 1958.

Films as Producer (Selected List):

1923   *The Covered Wagon* (Cruze)
1927   *Underworld* (Von Sternberg)
1933   *Berkeley Square* (Lloyd); *The Power and the Glory* (Howard);
        Zoo in Budapest (Lee)
1934   *As Husbands Go* (MacFadden); *Grand Canary* (Cummings);
        Springtime for Henry (Tuttle); *Coming Out Party* (Blystone);
        The White Parade (Cummings); *I Am Suzanne* (Lee)
1935   *Here's to Romance* (Green); *Helldorado* (Cruze); *Redheads*
        on Parade (McLeod); *The Gay Deception* (Wyler)
1936   *One Rainy Afternoon* (Lee); *The Gay Desperado* (Mamoulian)
1937   *Music for Madame* (Blystone); *Hitting a New High* (Walsh)
1941   *Sergeant York* (Hawks)
1944   *The Adventures of Mark Twain* (Rapper)
1945   *Rhapsody in Blue* (Rapper)
1946   *Without Reservations* (LeRoy)
1948   *The Miracle of the Bells* (Pichel)

Publications

By LASKY: book—

With Don Weldon, *I Blow My Own Horn*, New York, 1957.

By LASKY: articles—

"Production Problems," in *The Story of the Films as Told by Leaders of the Industry*, New York, 1927.
"Hearing Things in the Dark," in *Collier's* (New York), 25 May 1929.

On LASKY: articles—

Current Biography 1947, New York, 1947.
Cinéma (Paris), March 1958.
Zierold, Norman, in *The Moguls*, New York, 1969.
National Film Theatre booklet (London), September 1980.
Cinématographe (Paris), May 1984.
In *The First Tycoons*, edited by Richard Dyer MacCann, London, 1987.
Higashi, S., "Cecil B. DeMille and the Lasky Company," in *Film & History*, no. 4, 1990.
Lasky, B., "*Zoo in Budapest*: Lasky's Poetic Redemption," in *American Cinematographer* (Hollywood), April 1995.
Berg, A. Scott, "Jesse Lasky," in *Architectural Digest* (Los Angeles), April 1996.

*   *   *

Jesse L. Lasky, along with Cecil B. DeMille and Samuel Goldwyn, was literally one of the three founding fathers of Hollywood. In the words of his son, Jesse, Jr., he was "a gentle man who was more interested in the creative than the commercial aspect of film." As first president of the Jesse L. Lasky Feature Play Company, then first vice-president in charge of production of Famous Players-Lasky (the precursor of Paramount), Lasky was one of the movies' preeminent moguls. His roller-coaster success story is synonymous with the history of Hollywood.

His first upstart company purchased the rights to Edwin Milton Royle's play, *The Squaw Man* for $15,000 and hired the Broadway matinee idol Dustin Farnum to star. Rather than film the picture in nearby Fort Lee, New Jersey, they opted for the authenticity of the real west, and sent DeMille, Farnum, and the crew to Flagstaff, Arizona, because it *sounded* at once authentic and romantic. Upon arrival in Flagstaff, the green New Yorkers found the town in the midst of a cattlemen-sheepmen war. They traveled further west where DeMille shot off the following wire to Lasky: "Flagstaff no good for our purpose. Have proceeded to California. Want authority to rent barn in place called Hollywood for seventy-five dollars a month. Regards to Sam. Cecil." And so in January 1914 the motion picture industry arrived in Hollywood with "one barn, one truck and one camera."

The Squaw Man, the first large-scale western, was a huge success, and the company moved its business west where Lasky prided himself in attracting writers to his company because he believed "the play was the thing." Economical vicissitudes forced the company to merge with Adolph Zukor's Famous Players in 1915. Famous Players-Lasky had Zukor as president, Lasky as first vice-president in charge of production, Goldwyn as chairman, and DeMille as director-general. Zukor believed in stars and that is the direction the new company pursued. Subsequent mergers eventually resulted in the creation of the Paramount Famous Lasky Corporation (1917) and the Paramount Publix Corporation (1930). These mergers helped Lasky amass a $12 million fortune and have his name listed as "presenter" of over 350 films. This prolific period saw Paramount present such talent as Valentino, Lubitsch, von Sternberg, Dietrich, Pickford, and Chevalier.

However, gradually it was Zukor's name as presenter, and in 1932 the Depression brought what Lasky, Jr., describes as "a revolution of power" in which the senior Lasky was ousted by the obvious machinations of his personal assistant, "a ruthless little bastard named Manny Cohen." Lasky suffered bankruptcy but managed to organize J.L. Lasky Productions via a distribution deal with Fox. These independent productions included *Zoo in Budapest* and *Berkeley Square*. In 1935, he created Pickford-Lasky Productions with Mary Pickford and supervised *One Rainy Afternoon* and *The Gay Desperado*. He joined RKO in 1937 and produced a radio show called *Gateway to Hollywood*, then moved over to Warners producing such films as *Sergeant York*, *The Adventures of Mark Twain*, and *Rhapsody in Blue*. The amiable and well-liked Lasky was never able to regain the prominent position he had once held. Heavily in debt to the IRS, he was in the midst of production plans with Goldwyn and DeMille for a film called *The Big Brass Band* when he died in 1958.

His son says, "When the success and fortune go, many people have nothing to turn to except suicide. Curiously, my father turned to metaphysical philosophy. I think he must have learned about it from my mother most likely by osmosis. She was attuned to that kind of sensitivity while he never appeared to be so."

—Ronald Bowers

LASSALLY, Walter

Cinematographer. **Nationality:** German. **Born:** Berlin, 18 December 1926; emigrated to England, 1939; used the pseudonym John Walters on some early films. **Career:** Clapper boy for Riverside Studios; 1946—directed first film, *Smith, Our Friend*; 1950—first film as cinematographer, *Every Five Minutes*; TV work includes the series *The Commanding Sea*, 1981. **Awards:** Academy Award for *Zorba the Greek*, 1964.

Films as Cinematographer:

(shorts)

1950   *Every Five Minutes* (M. Anderson)
1951   *From Plan into Action* (Alexander) (co); *Forward a Century* (Napier-Bell) (co)
1952   *Festival* (York); *At Whose Door?* (Napier-Bell); *We Who Are Young* (Simmons); *The Pleasure Garden* (Broughton); *Three Installations* (L. Anderson); *Wakefield Express* (L. Anderson)
1953   *Power Signal Lineman* (M. Anderson); *High Speed*; *Sunday by the Sea* (Simmons); *One Great Vision* (Simmons); *Thursday's Children* (L. Anderson and Brenton)

1954   *Bow Bells* (Simmons); *Friend of the Family* (Thomson)
1955   *Green and Pleasant Land* (L. Anderson); *Henry* (L. Anderson); *Continuous Observation* (Thomson); *The Children Upstairs* (L. Anderson); *A Hundred Thousand Children* (L. Anderson); *Foot and Mouth* (L. Anderson)
1956   *Together* (Mazzetti) (co); *The Brighton Story* (Wilcox); *The Gentle Corsican* (Simmons); *Momma Don't Allow* (Reisz and Richardson); *Return from the Sun* (Casparius); *Simon* (Zadek); *The Simpson and Godlee Story* (Casparius); *Children's Corner* (*Day Nursing*) (+ ed, co-d with Nadelmann)
1957   *Every Day Except Christmas* (L. Anderson); *A River Speaks* (Casparius); *Ten Bridges* (Luke); *George Bernard Shaw* (Shaw-Ashton); *A Sculptor's Landscape* (Read)
1958   *Blue Peter* (Fernhout); *A.B.C.* (*Aruba, Bonaire, Curazao*) (Fernhout); *Alone with the Monsters* (Nour); *A Song for Prince Charlie* (O'Leary)
1959   *Refuge England* (Vas); *Enquiry into General Practice* (Dickson)
1960   *Midsummer Music* (Swift)
1961   *Let My People Go* (Krish); *Why Bri?* (Napier-Bell) (co); *London University* (Napier-Bell) (co)
1964   *The Peaches* (Gill); *Lila* (Raggett) (co); *Dublin through Different Eyes* (Carr)
1965   *Mao le veut*; *Dan* (+ pr, co-d with Campbell); *The Greeks* (+ pr, co-d with Campbell)
1967   *Labyrinth* (Kroiter, Low, and O'Connor)
1970   *Henry Moore at the Tate Gallery* (+ co-d with Sylvester)
1971   *Can Horses Sing?* (Sussex); *Bilocation* (*Within Hail*) (Cornu); *Paris Restaurants* (Sher)
1974   *Carved in Ivory* (Gill); *W.S.P.* (J. Anderson)
1976   *Ernst Fuchs* (Jasny)

(features)

1954   *The Passing Stranger* (Arnold)
1955   *To koritsi me ta mavra* (*A Girl in Black*) (Cacoyannis); *Another Sky* (Lambert)
1957   *To teleftaio psemma* (*A Matter of Dignity*) (Cacoyannis)
1958   *We Are the Lambeth Boys* (Reisz); *Jago hua savera* (*Day Shall Dawn*) (Kardar) (co)
1959   *As Dark as the Night* (Young)
1960   *Beat Girl* (*Wild for Kicks*) (Greville); *Maddalena* (Dimopoulos); *Eroica* (*Our Last Spring*) (Cacoyannis); *Aliki sto naftiko* (*Aliki in the Navy*) (Sakellarios)
1961   *Electra* (Cacoyannis); *I Liza kai i alli* (*Liza and Her Double*) (Dimopoulos); *A Taste of Honey* (Richardson)
1962   *The Loneliness of the Long Distance Runner* (Richardson)
1963   **Tom Jones** (Richardson)
1964   *Psyche 63* (Singer); *Zorba the Greek* (Cacoyannis)
1966   *Assignment Skybolt* (Tallas)
1967   *The Day the Fish Came Out* (Cacoyannis); *Oedipus the King* (Saville)
1968   *The Adding Machine* (Epstein); *Joanna* (Sarne); *Three into Two Won't Go* (Hall); *Anichti epistoli* (*Open Letter*) (Stambolopoulos); *Olimpiada en Mexico* (*The Olympics in Mexico*) (Isaac); *Battleship Potemkin Survivor* (Montaldi—for TV)

Walter Lassally

1969 *Twinky* (*Lola*) (Donner)

1970 *Something for Everyone* (*Black Flowers for the Bride*) (Prince)

1971 *To Kill a Clown* (Bloomfield)

1972 *Adventures of a Brown Man in Search of Civilisation* (Ivory); *Savages* (Ivory); *Gun before Butter* (Zadek)

1973 ''The Highest'' ep. of *Visions of Eight* (Penn); *Happy Mother's Day . . . Love George* (McGavin); *The Seaweed Children* (*Malachi's Cove*) (Herbert)

1974 *The Wild Party* (Ivory); *Après le vent des sables* (*The Web*) (Zaccai); *Henry Cotton: This Game of Golf* (Raeburn); *The World of Sam Smith* (Zetterling)

1975 *Autobiography of a Princess* (Ivory); *Ansichten eines Clowns* (*The Clown*) (Jasny); *Requiem for a Village* (Gladwell) (co); *In the Beginning* (Gill)

1976 *Pleasantville* (Locker and Polon); *Fluchtversuch* (*I vo*) (Jasny)

1977 *Shenanigans* (*The Great Georgia Bank Hoax*; *The Great Bank Hoax*) (Jacoby); *Morgensterne*; *The Blood of Hussain* (Dehlavi)

1978 *Hullabaloo over Georgie and Bonnie's Pictures* (Ivory); *Too Far to Go* (Cook); *Die Frau gegenüber* (*The Woman across the Way*) (Noever)

1979 *Something Short of Paradise* (Helpern)

1980 *The Pilot* (Richardson); *Der Preis fürs Überleben* (*The Price of Survival*) (Noever); *Life on the Mississippi* (Hunt); *Gauguin the Savage* (Cook)

1981 *Memoirs of a Survivor* (Gladwell); *Engel aus Eisen* (*The Iron Angel*) (Brasch); *The Private History of a Campaign that Failed* (Hunt); *The Mysterious Stranger* (Hunt)

1982 *Heat and Dust* (Ivory); *Tuxedo Warrior* (Sinclair); *Mystery at Fire Island* (Fuest)

1983 *Private School* (Black); *The Case of Marcel Duchamp* (Rowan); *Pudd'nhead Wilson* (Bridges)

1984 *The Bostonians* (Ivory); *Children in the Crossfire* (Schaefer) (co); *The Bengal Lancers* (Weeks)

1985 *Adventures of Huckleberry Finn* (Hunt); *Stone Pillow* (Schaefer—for TV); *Mrs. Delafield Wants to Marry* (Schaefer—for TV)

1987 *Indian Summer* (Forder)

1988 *The Perfect Murder* (Hai); *The Deceivers* (Meyer)

1989 *Fragments of Isabella* (O' Leary); *Kamilla og tyven II*

1991 *The Ballad of the Sad Café* (Callow)

1992 *The Man Upstairs* (Schaefer—for TV)

Other Films:

1946   *Smith, Our Friend* (co-d with York—short, + co-pr)
1947   *Dancing with Crime* (Carstairs—short) (asst ph); *This Was
            a Woman* (Whelan—short) (asst ph)
1948   *What's in a Number* (Krish—short) (asst ph); *Things Happen
            at Night* (Searle—short) (asst ph)
1950   *Night and the City* (Dassin—short) (asst ph)
1953   *House of Blackmail* (Elvey) (asst ed)

Publications

By LASSALLY: book—

Itinerant Cameraman, London, 1987.

By LASSALLY: articles—

"Subjective Cinema: An Analysis of the MGM Film *Lady in the
    Lake*," in *Film Industry*, April 1947.
With Richard Kohler, "The Big Screens," in *Sight and Sound*
    (London), January/March 1955.
Sight and Sound (London), Summer 1956.
"The Dead Hand," in *Sight and Sound* (London), Summer 1960.
Film (London), no. 37, 1963.
Sight and Sound (London), Summer 1965.
Film (London), no. 51, Spring 1968.
Journal of the University Film Association (Carbondale, Illinois), vol.
    26, no. 4, 1974.
American Cinematographer (Hollywood), February 1975.
Deutsche Kameramann (Munich), April/May 1976.
Sight and Sound (London), Spring 1980.
On *Heat and Dust* in *American Cinematographer* (Hollywood),
    January 1984.
"Ford Fever," in *Sight and Sound* (London), November 1992.
Jeune Cinéma, no. 224, October 1993.
"Of Guilds and Unions and Long Hours," in *Eyepiece* (Greenford),
    vol. 17, no. 1, 1996.
"Call For a New Standard Format," in *Eyepiece* (Greenford), vol. 17,
    no. 2, 1996.
"Desert Island Flicks," in *Eyepiece* (Greenford), vol. 17, no. 4, 1996.

On LASSALLY: articles—

Films and Filming (London), December 1954.
Focus on Film (London), no. 13, 1973.
On *Heat and Dust* in *Film* (London), April/May 1984.
Film Dope (Nottingham), November 1985.
Baker, Rick, "Rockport Lighting Seminar: Walter Lassally, BSC,"
    in *American Cinematographer* (Hollywood), November 1989.

*   *   *

The evolution of Walter Lassally from clapperboy to lighting
cameraman with a world reputation makes a fascinating story. His

father was an industrial filmmaker in Berlin and his mother was of
Polish origin. Fleeing from the Nazi menace in 1939, his father set up
a one-man film unit in London, so film was in Lassally's blood.
Cutting short his science studies, he took up the job of clapperboy in
the Riverside studios where he found that theory and practice did not
run hand-in-hand. A young man with high ideals, his experience in the
film industry fell short of these. When the studio went bankrupt he
began freelancing. Around this time (1954), the *Sequence* magazine
group was absorbed into the British Film Institute and there was
a ferment of ideas in this quarter where the young Lassally met people
such as Lindsay Anderson, Gavin Lambert, and Karel Reisz. It was
among this group that the British Free Cinema Movement was born,
and Lassally photographed many of their films. They tried to illuminate the life about them and break away from the stereotyped view of
the commercial cinema. In 1954 he got his first major lighting camera
job on a feature film, Gavin Lambert's beautiful, if neglected,
Another Sky, shot on location in Morocco. The young film buff now
chose the more adventurous path of the independent, low-budget film,
open to a personal and creative approach. As he said himself:
"Atmospheric photography is still one of my criteria when I decide
what projects to accept." It has been for him a gratifying choice as he
has worked with such directors as Karel Reisz, Tony Richardson,
Lindsay Anderson, Michael Cacoyannis, James Ivory, and Arthur
Penn. He has an international awareness of cinema and he deplores
the narrow chauvinistic approach of many national film industries.

While his film style is straightforward, he has not hesitated to
break the conventions on occasion, as in *Tom Jones*, directed by Tony
Richardson, and in his mixture of color, sepia, and black and white in
James Ivory's *Savages*. Lassally is especially at home with natural
settings, and shot the first British film to be filmed totally on location,
A Taste of Honey, also directed by Richardson. Nearly 30 years later,
Lassally's filming of *The Perfect Murder*, shot on location in Bom-
bay, received critical praise, as did his work on *The Ballad of the Sad
Café*, in which he used filters to create stark Edward Hopper-like
lighting effects.

In 1964 he won an Academy Award for his photography of *Zorba
the Greek* directed by Cacoyannis, thereby setting a seal on a career
that was further added to by the films he made for James Ivory,
including *Heat and Dust*. Lassally, whose *Itinerant Cameraman* is an
autobiography crammed with technical knowledge and observations
about film, is a cinematographer who writes about his craft. His
beliefs have led him to work primarily on quality intellectual films
and adaptations, rather than on Hollywood blockbuster spectacles.

—Liam O'Leary, updated by Thomas L. Erskine

LASZLO, Ernest

Cinematographer. **Nationality:** Hungarian. **Born:** Budapest, 1896
(or 1906). **Career:** 1926—emigrated to the United States; cameraman and occasional cinematographer during late 1920s and 1930s,
mainly for Paramount; cinematographer from mid-1940s; 1972–74—
President, American Society of Cinematographers. **Award:** Academy Award for *Ship of Fools*, 1965. **Died:** In Woodland Hills,
California, 6 January 1984.

Films as Cinematographer:

1928   *The Pace That Kills* (Parker); *Linda* (*Mrs. Wallace Reid*) (co)

1929   *The White Outlaw* (Horner); *Street Corners* (Birdwell)

1930   *The Primrose Path* (O'Connor) (co)

1944   *The Hitler Gang* (Farrow)

1946   *Two Years Before the Mast* (Farrow)

1947   *Dear Ruth* (Russell); *Road to Rio* (McLeod); *A Miracle Can Happen* (*On Our Merry Way*) (K. Vidor and Fenton) (co)

1948   *Lulu Belle* (Fenton); *The Girl from Manhattan* (Green); *Let's Live a Little* (Wallace); *Impact* (Lubin)

1949   *The Lucky Stiff* (Foster); *Cover-Up* (Green); *Manhandled* (Foster); *The Big Wheel* (Ludwig); *D.O.A.* (Maté)

1950   *Riding High* (Capra) (co); *The Jackie Robinson Story* (Green); *When I Grow Up* (Kanin)

1951   *M* (Losey); *The Well* (Popkin and Rouse); *Mutiny* (Dmytryk)

1952   *The First Time* (Tashlin); *The Trio: Rubenstein, Heifetz, and Piatigorsky* (*Million Dollar Trio*) (Dassin); *Three for Bedroom "C"* (Bren); *The Lady in the Iron Mask* (Murphy); *The Star* (Walker); *Stalag 17* (Wilder); *The Steel Trap* (Stone)

1953   *Scared Stiff* (Marshall); *The Moon Is Blue* (Preminger); *Houdini* (Marshall); *The Naked Jungle* (Haskin)

1954   *Apache* (Aldrich); *About Mrs. Leslie* (Daniel Mann); *Vera Cruz* (Aldrich)

1955   ***Kiss Me Deadly*** (Aldrich); *The Kentuckian* (Lancaster); *The Big Knife* (Aldrich)

1956   *While the City Sleeps* (F. Lang); *Bandido* (Fleischer)

1957   *Omar Khayyam* (*The Loves of Omar Khayyam*) (Dieterle); *Valerie* (Oswald); *Gunsight Ridge* (Lyon)

1958   *Attack of the Puppet People* (*Six Inches Tall*) (Gordon); *The Space Children* (Gordon); *The Restless Years* (*The Wonderful Years*) (Kautner); *Ten Seconds to Hell* (Aldrich)

1960   *Inherit the Wind* (Kramer); *Tormented* (Gordon)

1961   *The Last Sunset* (Aldrich); *Judgment at Nuremberg* (Kramer)

1963   *It's a Mad, Mad, Mad, Mad World* (Kramer); *Four for Texas* (Aldrich); *One Man's Way* (Sanders)

1964   *Baby the Rain Must Fall* (Mulligan)

1965   *Ship of Fools* (Kramer)

1966   *Fantastic Voyage* (Fleischer)

1967   *Luv* (Donner)

1968   *Star* (Wise); *The First Time* (*You Don't Need Pajamas at Rosie's*) (Neilson)

1969   *Daddy's Gone A-Hunting* (Robson); *Airport* (Seaton)

1972   *Showdown* (Seaton)

1974   *That's Entertainment!* (Haley) (co)

1976   *Logan's Run* (Anderson); *The Domino Principle* (*The Domino Killings*) (Kramer) (co)

Films as Cameraman:

1927   *Tongues of Scandal* (Clements)

1931   *Rich Man's Folly* (Cromwell)

1932   *The Miracle Man* (McLeod); *The Phantom President* (Taurog)

1935   *The Case of the Curious Bride* (Curtiz)

1941   *Hold Back the Dawn* (Leisen)

1942   *The Major and the Minor* (Wilder)

Publications

By LASZLO: articles—

American Cinematographer (Hollywood), June 1976.

"Speaking of Film," in *Business and Home TV Screen* (New York), March 1978.

On LASZLO: articles—

Rowan, Arthur, on *The Steel Trap* in *American Cinematographer* (Hollywood), November 1952.

On *It's a Mad, Mad, Mad, Mad World* in *American Cinematographer* (Hollywood), December 1963.

American Cinematographer (Hollywood), January 1965.

On *Fantastic Voyage* in *American Cinematographer* (Hollywood), February 1966.

Land, Kevin, on *Star* in *American Cinematographer* (Hollywood), March 1969.

Film Comment (New York), Summer 1972.

Focus on Film (London), no. 13, 1973.

Obituary in *Variety* (New York), 18 January 1984.

Obituary in *American Cinematographer* (Hollywood), March 1984.

Film Dope (Nottingham), November 1985.

*   *   *

A superior craftsman and technician, Ernest Laszlo belonged to a generation of cameramen trained by the master cinematographers of the silent era. He became a director of photography towards the end of the traditional Hollywood studio system, and tended to work with strong directors who brought a new realism to the commercial American cinema. Robert Aldrich, Otto Preminger, Billy Wilder, Fritz Lang, and Stanley Kramer generally functioned as their own bosses, on the set if not in the final edit, and they dealt with reality in their films rather than Hollywood fantasy. Laszlo painted their naturalistic visions on celluloid with dramatic lighting and a detached eye. He possessed an almost Germanic style, influenced in part by the German cinema of the 1920s, and throughout his career was rarely required to shoot romantically pretty pictures.

Like William Clothier and Russel Harlan, Laszlo was an assistant cameraman on William Wellman's aviation classic *Wings*, part of an army of cinematographers under the supervision of Harry Perry. Laszlo participated on the aerial photography, and also worked on the celebrated Folies Bergère tracking shot. He was an assistant on another aerial epic, Howard Hughes's *Hell's Angels*, along with such talented cameramen as Edward Snyder, Paul Ivano, and Henry Cronjager, with camera crew again headed by Harry Perry. Laszlo photographed a few low-budget B-movies, and some comedy shorts for Al Christie, then joined Paramount as a camera operator. He operated for cinematographers Karl Struss, David Abel, Charles Lang, and Leo Tover through the 1930s, and was finally promoted to director of photography by the director John Farrow on *The Hitler Gang* and *Two Years Before the Mast*. They are dark, brooding, atmospheric films, and earned Laszlo recognition for his mastery of low-key lighting. He introduced a new style of cinematography at

Paramount. By eliminating most of the fill light, he achieved a more realistic look instead of the usual soft, glossy Paramount visuals.

Laszlo carried his style over to some of the most memorable *films noirs. D.O.A.*, directed by the former cameraman Rudolph Maté, is a fine example, the seedy underworld perfectly captured by Laszlo's *chiaroscuro* lighting and fluid camera. Joseph Losey's *M*, a remake of the Fritz Lang classic, was also effectively photographed, following the outline of the original but updated to reflect the paranoia of the early 1950s through dark tones. *Manhandled*, directed by Lewis Foster, contains a fascinating expressionistic dream sequence that overshadows the mediocre film.

Billy Wilder's *Stalag 17* was treated in a realistic manner, its story of a German prison camp during the Second World War evoked with stark Laszlo cinematography. Again, the low-key lighting and the documentary style were uncommon in major studio Hollywood at the time, and the film's success proved that movies did not have to be candy-coated to work with audiences. For Fritz Lang, Laszlo shot the thriller *While the City Sleeps*, and gave the lurid tale a more subtle lighting to downplay the seamy material.

Laszlo had a productive relationship with Robert Aldrich, photographing the westerns *Apache, Vera Cruz, The Last Sunset*, and *Four for Texas*, all in color, and the black-and-white dramas *Kiss Me Deadly, The Big Knife*, and *Ten Seconds to Hell. Apache* and *Vera Cruz* used beautiful locations and reveal a strong sense of landscape; *The Last Sunset* is equally effective although a modern-day western, but *Four for Texas* is disappointing Rat Pack hijinks. *Kiss Me Deadly* and *The Big Knife* are brilliantly photographed, cynical, latter-day noir. Laszlo cited *Kiss Me Deadly* as his best black-and-white work, with its reliance on actual locations.

Laszlo also contributed outstanding black-and-white photography to Stanley Kramer's *Inherit the Wind, Judgment at Nuremberg*, and *Ship of Fools*. Each has a claustrophobic setting (courtrooms and an ocean liner), and Laszlo was called upon to make great use of close-ups to accentuate the drama. The Kramer films are presented in a documentary-like fashion, with Laszlo utilizing deep grays and blacks in keeping with the somber dramatics.

Ernest Laszlo helped bring realism to the American cinema through his naturalistic cinematography, breaking down the barriers imposed by the glamour-conscious studios of the 1940s. He was fortunate to work with directors willing to suspend the usual high-key lighting effects in order to create genuine settings, and fused a new and practical form of photography for motion pictures.

—John A. Gallagher

LATHROP, Philip H.

Cinematographer. **Nationality:** American. **Born:** 22 October 1916. **Family:** Married Betty Jo Lathrop. **Career:** Camera operator and cinematographer, from 1948. **Awards:** American Society of Cinematographers Award, Outstanding Achievement in Cinematography in Movies of the Week/Pilots for *Little Girl Lost*, 1989, Lifetime Achievement Award, American Society of Cinematographers, 1992. **Died:** 12 April 1995.

Films as Cinematographer:

1958   *Wild Heritage* (Haas); *Perfect Furlough* (*Strictly for Pleasure*) (Edwards); *The Monster of Piedras Blancas* (Berwick); *Money, Women and Guns* (Bartlett); *Live Fast, Die Young* (Henreid); *Girls on the Loose* (Henreid); *The Saga of Hemp Brown* (Carlson)

1959   *Cry Tough* (Stanley)

1961   *The Private Lives of Adam and Eve* (Rooney and Zugsmith)

1962   *Experiment in Terror* (*The Grip of Fear*) (Edwards); *Days of Wine and Roses* (Edwards); *Lonely Are the Brave* (*Last Hero*) (credited as Philip Lathrop) (Miller)

1963   *The Pink Panther* (credited as Philip Lathrop) (Edwards); *Twilight of Honor* (*The Charge Is Murder*) (credited as Philip Lathrop) (Sagal); *Dime with a Halo* (Sagal); *Soldier in the Rain* (Nelson)

1964   *36 Hours* (Seaton); *The Americanization of Emily* (*Emily*) (Hiller)

1965   *Girl Happy* (Sagal); *Never Too Late* (Yorkin); *The Cincinnati Kid* (Jewison)

1966   *What Did You Do in the War, Daddy?* (Edwards)

1967   *Gunn* (Edwards); *The Happening* (Silverstein); *Point Blank* (Boorman); *Don't Make Waves* (Mackendrick)

1968   *I Love You, Alice B. Toklas!* (*Kiss My Butterfly*) (Averback); *Finian's Rainbow* (Coppola)

1969   *The Gypsy Moths* (credited as Philip Lathrop) (Frankenheimer); *The Illustrated Man* (Smight); *They Shoot Horses, Don't They?* (Pollack)

1970   *The Traveling Executioner* (credited as Philip Lathrop) (Smight); *Rabbit, Run* (Smight); *The Hawaiians* (*Master of the Islands*) (Gries)

1971   *Wild Rovers* (credited as Philip Lathrop) (Edwards)

1972   *Portnoy's Complaint* (credited as Philip Lathrop) (Lehman); *Every Little Crook and Nanny* (Howard)

1973   *The Thief Who Came to Dinner* (Yorkin); *Lolly-Madonna XXX* (*The Lolly Madonna War*) (Sarafian)

1974   *Together Brothers* (Graham); *The Prisoner of Second Avenue* (Frank); *Mame* (Saks); *Airport 1975* (credited as Philip Lathrop) (Smight); *Earthquake* (Robson)

1975   *Hard Times* (*The Streetfighter*) (Hill); *The Black Bird* (Giles); *The Killer Elite* (Peckinpah) (credited as Philip Lathrop)

1976   *Swashbuckler* (*Scarlet Buccaneer*) (Goldstone)

1977   *Captains Courageous* (credited as Philip Lathrop) (Hart—for TV); *Never Con a Killer* (*The Feather & Father Gang*) (Kulik—for TV); *Airport '77* (credited as Philip Lathrop) (Jameson)

1978   *The Driver* (Hill); *A Different Story* (Aaron)

1979   *Moment by Moment* (Wagner); *Foolin' Around* (Heffron); *The Concorde: Airport '79* (*Airport '79*; *Airport '80: The Concorde*; *The Concorde Affair*; *The Concorde*; *S.O.S. Concorde*) (Rich)

1980   *Little Miss Marker* (Bernstein); *A Change of Seasons* (Lang); *Loving Couples* (Smight)

1981   *All Night Long* (Tramont)

1982   *Jekyll & Hyde. . . Together Again* (Belson); *Hammett* (Wenders); *Class Reunion* (*National Lampoon's Class Reunion*) (Miller)

1985   *Between the Darkness and the Dawn* (Levin—for TV); *Love on the Run* (Trikonis—for TV); *Malice in Wonderland*

(Trikonis—for TV); *Picking Up the Pieces* (Wendkos—for TV)
1986   *Deadly Friend* (Craven)
1987   *Ray's Male Heterosexual Dance Hall* (Gordon)
1988   *Little Girl Lost* (Miller—for TV)

Other Films:

1948   *All My Sons* (Reis) (camera operator)
1958   *Touch of Evil* (Welles) (camera operator)
1965   *In Harm's Way* (Preminger) (director of photography: second unit)
1992   *Visions of Light* (*Visions of Light: The Art of Cinematography*) (Glassman, McCarthy, Samuels) (committee member: ASC education, ro as Philip Lathrop)

Publications:

On LATHROP: articles—

Obituary in *American Cinematographer* (Hollywood), June 1995.
French, Philip, "The Week in Reviews: Rerelease of the Week: *Point Blank*: Perfect Crime," in *The Observer* (London), 21 June 1998.

On LATHROP: film—

Visions of Light, directed by Glassman, McCarthy, and Samuels, 1992.

*   *   *

Philip H. Lathrop began his career as camera operator on the Irving Reis film *All My Sons*, working with cinematographer Russell Metty as he did ten years later on Orson Welles's *A Touch of Evil*. The two pictures, in particular the film which marked Welles's return to Hollywood in 1958, proved a valuable training ground for Lathrop, whose own career as a director of photography took off in the same year. In his long career, Lathrop developed a reputation for his detailed approach to lighting and camera placement, and for his skill with widescreen technology in beautifully photographed films such as Blake Edwards's *The Pink Panther*. Lathrop worked several times with Edwards, and the reliable, though not always very inspiring films on which they collaborated are notable for the quality of their photography.

With the exception of films such as *The Driver*, and *Hammett*, a stylized detective story loosely based on the life of writer Dashiell Hammett, Lathrop's most impressive work as a cinematographer came in the 1960s. His particular visual style seemed to epitomize the times, giving a glossy, dense feel to tough films like John Boorman's excellent thriller, *Point Blank*, and a dreamy atmosphere to strange comic offerings like *The Americanization of Emily*, for which he received an Oscar nomination. *The Cincinnati Kid*, which stars Edward G. Robinson and Steve McQueen as opposing poker players "The Man," and "The Kid," displays Lathrop's skills at their best, creating a shiny, disconcerting surface to the images that is not unlike the "Photorealist" paintings that became popular at the same time. Ten years later, Lathrop's style gave an air of quality to films at the end of their era, such as Sam Pekinpah's *The Killer Elite*. Lathrop went on to be involved in several well-regarded projects, such as the

1969 adaptation of Horace McCoy's bleak existentialist novel, *They Shoot Horses, Don't They?*, yet in the 1970s most of his work was on films that have since come to embody Hollywood's shortcomings in that period. Commercial movies such as the *Airport* series of films, and disaster movies such as *Earthquake* (for which Lathrop received his second Oscar nomination) almost became parodies of themselves with their ever more improbable story lines and predictable dramatic twists. In *Class Reunion*, Lathrop's photography helps sustain the viewer's interest in an otherwise thin parody of high school horror movies.

Lathrop's talent was largely stifled by the demands of the studios in the 1970s, and opportunities for outstanding photography became increasingly limited. Yet despite the overall weakness of the commercial projects he was involved with later in his career, Lathrop's work remained of a high standard, often rescuing films with little else to recommend them. When German director Wim Wenders partially succeeded in resisting the influence of Francis Ford Coppola's Zoetrope studio during the making of *Hammett*, Lathrop was allowed to shine: as a cinematographer he remained capable of producing extraordinary images. Although he ended his career with a series of limp TV movies, Lathrop will be remembered for his contribution to the "look" of Hollywood cinema in the 1960s.

—Chris Routledge

LEDERER, Charles

Writer. **Nationality:** American. **Born:** New York City, 31 December 1910; raised by his aunt, the actress Marion Davies. **Education:** Attended the University of California, Berkeley, graduated. **Family:** Married 1) Virginia Bell, 1940 (divorced); 2) the actress Anne Shirley, 1949. **Career:** Journalist; 1929—began association with Ben Hecht, and collaborated with him over the years; 1931—first film as writer, *The Front Page*; then writer for Paramount, and MGM; freelance writer after 1944; 1953—wrote and produced the musical *Kismet*. **Died:** 5 March 1976.

Films as Writer:

1931   *The Front Page* (Milestone)
1932   *Cock of the Air* (Buckingham)
1937   *Double or Nothing* (Reed); *Mountain Music* (Florey)
1939   *Broadway Serenade* (Leonard); *Within the Law* (Machary)
1940   **His Girl Friday** (Hawks); *Comrade X* (K. Vidor); *I Love You Again* (Van Dyke)
1941   *Love Crazy* (Conway)
1943   *Slightly Dangerous* (Ruggles); *The Youngest Profession* (Buzzel)
1947   *Kiss of Death* (Hathaway); *Ride the Pink Horse* (Montgomery); *Her Husband's Affairs* (Simon)
1949   *I Was a Male War Bride* (Hawks); *Red, Hot and Blue* (Farrow)
1950   *Wabash Avenue* (Koster)
1951   *The Thing* (Nyby)
1952   *Fearless Fagan* (Donen); *Monkey Business* (Hawks)
1953   *Gentlemen Prefer Blondes* (Hawks)
1955   *Kismet* (Minnelli)
1956   *Gaby* (Bernhardt)

1957   *The Spirit of St. Louis* (Wilder); *Tip on a Dead Jockey*
        (Thorpe)
1959   *Never Steal Anything Small* (+ d); *It Started with a Kiss*
        (Marshall)
1960   *Can-Can* (W. Lang); *Ocean's 11* (Milestone)
1962   *Follow That Dream* (Douglas); *Mutiny on the Bounty*
        (Milestone)
1964   *A Global Affair* (Arnold)

Films as Director:

1942   *Fingers at the Window*
1951   *On the Loose*

Publications

By LEDERER: book—

With Luther Davis, *Kismet* (play), New York, 1954.

On LEDERER: articles—

Film Comment (New York), Winter 1970–71.
Cinéma 72 (Paris), May 1976.
Films and Filming (London), June 1983.
Levine, Scott, in *American Screenwriters*, edited by Robert E.
    Morsberger, Stephen O. Lesser, and Randall Clark, Detroit, Michi-
    gan, 1984.
Film Dope (Nottingham), March 1986.
''*On the Loose,*'' in *Reid's Film Index* (Wyong), no. 9, 1992.
''*Never Steal Anything Small,*'' in *Reid's Film Index* (Wyong), no.
    12, 1993.

*   *   *

Charles Lederer is probably best known for his adaptations,
especially of comic material, in collaboration with such notable
Hollywood writers as Ben Hecht, I.A.L. Diamond, George
Oppenheimer, and Albert Hackett. It was Ben Hecht who first
introduced Lederer to screenwriting when he hired him as a young
man to contribute uncredited material for the original screen version
of the Hecht-Charles MacArthur play *The Front Page*. It was an
experience Lederer would find valuable later when he worked on *His
Girl Friday* for Howard Hawks, in which he recast the central
characters of the play as ex-marrieds, husband and wife, thereby
turning the earlier drama into a screwball comedy.

Although Lederer's career spanned some 30 years in Hollywood,
his employment was often sporadic. He went for periods without
writing for the screen, and when he was working, his scripts were
often uneven. His best efforts were done in collaboration with Hecht
or under the tutelage of Hawks, who hired Lederer on a number of
occasions. The Hecht-Lederer scripts include two *films noirs*, *Kiss of
Death* directed by Henry Hathaway and *Ride the Pink Horse* directed
by Robert Montgomery, and Howard Hawks's *Monkey Business*,

written with I.A.L. Diamond. These films possess a wit and style
worthy of the best Hollywood writing. On his own, however, with the
exception of the work with Hawks, Lederer's scripts often only
achieved the level of the work-a-day quality of studio assembly-line
products. And after *The Spirit of St. Louis*, on which he labored
unsuccessfully with Billy Wilder, Lederer did little more than turn out
star vehicles for such celebrities as Frank Sinatra, Elvis Presley, and
Bob Hope. Even the screen version of Lederer's highly popular
musical *Kismet*, which he coauthored with Luther Davis, failed to
achieve much success as a film.

Lederer's long-term association with Hawks produced notably
different results and may well have provided the screenwriter with the
best projects of his career. Certainly Lederer's solo work on *His Girl
Friday*, *The Thing*, and *Gentlemen Prefer Blondes* produced the best-
remembered of his scripts and did much to establish his reputation
after his early years in the business. The screenplays for these films
reflect Lederer's genuine talent for adapting non-film materials to the
requirements of the screen. Given the right material and the right
director, Lederer obviously was able to produce first-rate writing.
That he did not do so more often speaks more to the requirements and
limitations of the studio system than to any inherent deficiency on
Lederer's part.

—Charles L.P. Silet

LEGRAND, Michel

Composer. **Nationality:** French. **Born:** Paris, 24 February 1932; son
of the musician Raymond Legrand. **Education:** Attended the Paris
Conservatory, 1943–50: studied with Henri Chaland and Boulanger.
Family: Married Christine Bouchard, 1958, two sons, one daughter.
Career: Band leader, light music arranger, and conductor for Maurice Chevalier; 1955—first full-length film score, *Les Amants du
Tage*; also composer for TV mini-series *A Woman Called Golda*,
1982, and *The Jesse Owens Story*, 1984. **Awards:** Academy Award,
for song ''The Windmills of Your Mind,'' 1968, *Summer of '42*,
1971, and *Yentl*, 1983; British Academy Award, for *Summer of '42*,
1971; inducted into Songwriters Hall of Fame, 1990.

Films as Composer:

1953   *Beau fixe* (Loew—short)
1955   *Les Amants du Tage* (*Lovers' Net*) (Verneuil)
1957   *Le Triporteur* (Pinoteau); *Raffles sur la ville* (Chenal)
1958   *Charmants garçons* (Decoin)
1960   *Chien de pique* (Y. Allégret); *Terrain vague* (Carné); *Les
        Portes claquent* (Poitrenaud and Fermaud); *L'Amérique
        insolite* (*L'Amérique vue par un français*) (Reichenbach)
1961   *Lola* (Demy); *Cause toujours mon lapin* (Roitfeld); *Le Cave
        se rebiffe* (*The Counterfeiters of Paris*) (Grangier) (co);
        Une Femme est une femme (*A Woman Is a Woman*)
        (Godard); *Me faire ça à moi* (Grimblatt)
1962   *Une Grosse Tête* (de Givray); ***Cléo de 5 à 7*** (*Cleo from 5 to 7*)
        (Varda) (co); ''Envie'' ep. of *Les Sept Péchés capitaux*

Michel Legrand

(*Seven Capital Sins*) (Molinaro); **Vivre sa vie** (*My Life to Live*) (Godard); *Eva* (Losey); *Le Coeur battant* (*The French Game*) (Doniol-Valcroze); *Comme un poisson dans l'eau* (Michel); *L'Empire de la nuit* (Grimblat)

1963   *Love Is a Ball* (Swift); *Les Amoureux du France* (Gimblat); *La Baie des anges* (*Bay of the Angels*) (Demy); *Le Gentleman d'Epsom* (Grangier); **Le Joli Mai** (Marker)

1964   *Les Parapluies de Cherbourg* (*The Umbrellas of Cherbourg*) (Demy); *Bande à part* (*Band of Outsiders*) (Godard); *Une Ravissante Idiote* (*Ravishing Idiot*) (Molinaro)

1965   *Monnaie de singe* (Robert); *L'Or et le plomb* (Cuniot); *Qui êtes vous, Polly Magoo* (Klein); *Quand passent les faisans* (Molinaro)

1966   *La Vie de château* (*A Matter of Resistance*) (Rappeneau); *Tendre voyou* (*Tender Scoundrel*) (Jean Becker)

1967   *Les Demoiselles de Rochefort* (*The Young Girls of Rochefort*) (Demy); *L'Homme à la Buick* (Grangier); *Pretty Polly* (*A Matter of Innocence*) (Green); *Le Plus Vieux Métier du monde* (*The Oldest Profession*) (de Broca and others)

1968   *How to Save a Marriage—and Ruin Your Life* (Cook); *Sweet November* (Miller); *Play Dirty* (De Toth); *The Thomas Crown Affair* (Jewison); *Ice Station Zebra* (J. Sturges)

1969   *Castle Keep* (Pollack); *The Happy Ending* (R. Brooks); *La Piscine* (*The Swimming Pool*) (Deray)

1970   *Pieces of Dreams* (Haller); *Wuthering Heights* (Fuest); *The Lady in the Car with Glasses and a Gun* (Litvak); *The Plastic Dome of Norma Jean* (Compton); *Le Décharge* (Deray); *Les Mariés de l'an II* (Rappeneau)

1971   *Peau d'âne* (*Donkey Skin*) (Demy); *Summer of '42* (Mulligan); *Le Mans* (Katzin); *Brian's Song* (Kulik—for TV); *The Go-Between* (Losey); *A Time for Loving* (Miles); *Un Peu de soleil dans l'eau froide* (Deray); *La Poudre d'escampette* (*French Leave*) (de Broca)

1972   *One Is a Lonely Number* (Stuart); *The Picasso Summer* (Sallin); *Barbe-Bleue* (*Bluebeard*) (Dmytryk); *Portnoy's Complaint* (Lehman); *Les Feux de la chandeleur* (*Hearth Fires*) (Korber); *La Vieille Fille* (*The Old Maid*) (Blanc); *Lady Sings the Blues* (Furie); *Pas folle la guêpe* (Delannoy)

1973   *A Bequest to the Nation* (*The Nelson Affair*) (Jones); *Un Homme est mort* (*A Man Is Dead*) (Deray); *Impossible Object* (Frankenheimer); *A Doll's House* (Losey); *L'Evenement le plus important depuis que l'homme a marché sur la lune* (*A Slightly Pregnant Man*) (Demy); *The Adventures of Don Quixote* (Rakoff); *40 Carats* (Katselas); *Cops and Robbers* (Avakian); *Breezy* (Eastwood); *Le Gang des otages* (Molinaro)

1974   *The Three Musketeers* (Lester); *It's Good to Be Alive* (Landon—for TV); *Our Time* (*Death of Her Innocence*) (Hyams)

1975   *F for Fake* (Welles); *La Sauvage* (*The Savage*) (Rappeneau); *Sheila Levine Is Dead and Living in New York* (Furie)

1976   *Gable and Lombard* (Furie); *Gulliver's Travels* (Hunt); *La Flûte à six schtroumpfs* (*The Smurfs and the Magic Flute*) (Peyo or Dutillieu); *Jalousie 1976* (*Le Voyage de noces*; *The Honeymoon Trip*) (Trintignant); *Ode to Billy Joe* (Baer)

1977   *The Other Side of Midnight* (Jarrott); *Hinotori* (Ichikawa)

1978   *Les Routes du sud* (Losey); *Lady Oscar* (Demy); *On peut le dire sans se fâcher!* (*La Belle Emmerdeuse*; *One Can Say It without Getting Angry*; *The Beautiful Nuisance*) (Coggio); *Mon premier amour* (Chouraqui); *Michel's Mixed Up Bird* (+ co-sc, d, ro)

1979   *Blind Love* (+ d); *Je vous ferai aimer la vie* (Korber); *The Fabulous Adventures of the Legendary Baron Munchausen* (Image)

1980   *Falling in Love Again* (Paul); *The Hunter* (Kulik); *Melvin and Howard* (Demme)

1981   *Atlantic City* (Malle)

1982   *Le Cadeau* (*The Gift*) (M. Lang); *Best Friends* (Jewison); *Qu'est-ce qui fait courir David?* (*What Makes David Run?*) (Chouraqui)

1983   *Eine Liebe in Deutschland* (*A Love in Germany*) (Wajda); *Never Say Never Again* (Kershner); *Yentl* (Streisand)

1984   *Train d'enfer* (Hanin); *Paroles et musique* (Chouraqui); *Slapstick of Another Kind* (Paul)

1985   *Palace* (Molinaro); *Parking* (Demy); *Partir, revenir* (*Going and Coming Back*) (Lelouch); *Secret Places* (Barron); *Micki and Maude* (Edwards) (song)

1987   *Club de rencontres* (M. Lang); *Spirale* (Frank); *The Jeweller's Shop* (*La Boutique de l'Orfèvre*; *The Goldsmith's Shop*) (Anderson)

1988   *Switching Channels* (Kotcheff)

1989   *Cinq jours en juin* (*Five Days in June*) (+ d, sc); *Grand Piano* (Coulson) (+ ro); *As Summer Dies* (*As Summers Die*) (Tramont)

1990   *Gaspard et Robinson* (Gatlif); *Eternity* (Paul)

1991   *Dingo* (DeHeer)

511

1992 *Fate* (Paul)
1993 *Les Demoiselles ont eu 25 Ans* (*The Young Girls Turn 25*) (Varda); *The Pickle* (Mazursky)
1994 *Ready to Wear* (*Prêt-à-Porter*) (Altman)
1995 *Les Enfants de lumière* (Asseo and others); *Les Misérables* (Lelouch); *Die Schelme von Schelm* (*Aaron's Magic Village*) (Benousilio and Kaminski)
1996 *Le Monde est un grand chien* (Kaminski); *The Ring* (Armand Mastroianni—for TV)
1998 *Madeline* (von Scherler Mayer)
1999 *Doggy Bag* (Comtet); *La Bûche* (*Season's Beatings*) (Thompson)
2000 *La Bicyclette bleue* (for TV)

Publications

By LEGRAND: articles—

Radio Times (London), 24 February-2 March 1979.
Film Français (Paris), 16 January 1981.
Cinéma (Paris), July/August 1981.
Cahiers du Cinéma (Paris), no. 438, December 1990.

On LEGRAND: articles—

Film Français (Paris), 2 February 1979.
Soundtrack! (Hollywood), December 1983.
Film Français (Paris), 1 March 1985.
Film Dope (Nottingham), March 1986.
Down Beat, January 1990.
Architectural Digest (Los Angeles), July 1997.
Billboard, 9 May 1998.
Sweeney, Phil, "The Man Who Always Knew the Score," in *The Independent* (London), 27 September 1999.

*   *   *

Michel Legrand's ability to write melodic themes that could be successfully marketed beyond the films for which they were written made him a popular favorite of studios seeking "hit" songs. Although Legrand was in demand for contemporary subjects, he also began in the early 1970s to score lyrical period works. While many of his works showed a facility with jazz, the period pieces also demonstrated a background in a variety of musical styles.

Legrand scored a number of French films, including works by Jean-Luc Godard beginning in the mid-1950s, but he gained international attention with his scores for the ambitious homages to Hollywood musicals created by Jacques Demy. *The Umbrellas of Cherbourg* and *The Young Girls of Rochefort* provided Legrand with an opportunity to write extended scores based on recurring themes and showed his ability to create memorable light popular tunes. Although his association with Demy continued on subsequent films, they have not been on the same grand scale.

Legrand's score for *The Thomas Crown Affair* began an association with the lyricists Alan and Marilyn Bergman, with whom the

composer collaborated on a number of projects ranging from *Wuthering Heights* to more recent films such as *Best Friends* and the song score for *Yentl*. The use of a central theme song has at times led to a tendency toward monothematic scoring with the results being more redundancy than variation. Somewhat more varied have been the composer's scores for period works such as *The Three Musketeers* in which Legrand has been able to apply his light flowing melodic approach to a greater variety of styles.

Legrand's song writing skills have at times led to his being selected for projects for which his style is not wholly suited. Despite his background in jazz, his overly romantic approach did not always mesh well with the songs in the Billie Holiday biography, *Lady Sings the Blues*, particularly when the score swells lushly during a heroin-shooting scene. The 1960s-style Latin beat provided for scenes in *Never Say Never Again* may have been appropriate on some level to the nostalgic feeling the character of James Bond creates, but it did little to enhance the dramatic action of the film.

Legrand continues to be as prolific as ever. In 1989 he directed *Five Days in June*, an autobiographical story of the teenaged Legrand's love affair with a woman twice his age. He composed the music for, and acted in the film *The Young Girls Turn 25*. In 1994, Legrand provided the score for *Ready to Wear*, a movie exposing what goes on behind the scenes at the Paris fashion shows. Since then, he has composed music for several other films: *Les Misérables*, *Les Enfants de lumière*, and *Le Monde est un grand chien*.

With the move toward more and more contemporary sounds in films as an attempt to keep up with changing musical styles, Legrand's own brand of pop music, once very much in vogue, now seems somewhat outdated. Not surprisingly his most successful work of late has been for noncontemporary subjects which require a more gentle lyricism. As with many of his contemporaries who were in demand in the 1960s and early 1970s, Legrand has found it necessary to modify his approach, and ironically the move has been back toward the more traditional symphonic style for which artists such as himself were originally intended as an alternative. As the twentieth century became the twenty-first, Legrand was devoting most of his professional efforts to writing music for the stage and did very little composing for films.

—Richard R. Ness, updated by Justin Gustainis

LEHMAN, Ernest

Writer, Producer, and Director. **Born:** Ernest Paul Lehman, New York City, 1920. **Education:** Studied creative writing at City College of New York. **Family:** Married Jacqueline, children: Roger, Alan. **Career:** Became copy editor of Wall Street financial journal, then briefly freelance short-story writer, before working as publicity writer for *Hollywood Reporter* columnist; 1953—invited to Hollywood to script first film, *Executive Suite*; 1960—nominated for Best Screenplay Academy Award for *North by Northwest*; 1962—nominated for Best Screenplay Academy Award for *West Side Story*; 1966—produced first film, *Who's Afraid of Virginia Woolf?*; 1972—made directorial debut, *Portnoy's Complaint*; 1977—published first novel,

Ernest Lehman (right) with Richard Benjamin

The French Atlantic Affair; elected president of the Writers Guild of America, in the 1980s.

Films as Writer:

1954 *Executive Suite* (Wise); *Sabrina* (Wilder)
1956 *Somebody Up There Likes Me* (Wise); *The King and I* (W. Lang)
1957 **Sweet Smell of Success** (Mackendrick) (co-sc, story)
1959 **North by Northwest** (Hitchcock)
1960 *From the Terrace* (Robson)
1961 **West Side Story** (Wise)
1963 *The Prize* (Robson)
1965 *The Sound of Music* (Wise)
1966 *Who's Afraid of Virginia Woolf?* (Nichols) (+ pr, ro as extra)
1969 *Hello Dolly!* (Kelly) (+ pr)
1972 *Portnoy's Complaint* (+ d, pr)
1976 *Family Plot* (Hitchcock)
1977 **Black Sunday** (Frankenheimer) (co-sc)

1979 *The French Atlantic Affair* (Heyes—mini for TV) (co-sc)
1995 *Sabrina* (Pollack) (co-sc)

Other Films:

1948 *The Inside Story* (Dwan) (story)

Publications

By LEHMAN: books—

The Comedian and Other Stories (fiction), New York, 1957.
Sweet Smell of Success and Other Stories (fiction), New York, 1957.
North by Northwest (screenplay), New York 1973.
The French Atlantic Affair (fiction), New York, 1977.
Screening Sickness and Other Tales of Tinsel Town (collected articles), New York, 1982.
Farewell Performance (fiction), New York, 1982.

By LEHMAN: articles—

"Dialogue on Film," interview with James Powers and audience, in *American Film* (Washington, D.C.), October 1976.

"Nobody *Tries* to Make a *Bad* Picture," in *American Film* (Washington, D.C.), March 1978.

"He Who Gets Hitched," in *American Film* (Washington, D.C.), May 1978.

"Ernest Lehman Remembers," interview with James Bawden, in *Classic Images* (Muscatine, Iowa), October 1994.

"Back Story," in *Fade In* (Beverly Hills), vol. 2, no. 3, 1996.

"North by Northwest/Writing North by North-west," in *Scenario* (Rockville), vol. 3, no. 1, Spring 1997.

On LEHMAN: books—

Newquist, Roy, *Showcase*, New York, 1966.

Corliss, Richard, *Talking Pictures*, Woodstock, New York, 1974.

Ernest Lehman: An American Film Institute Seminar on His Work, Glen Rock, New Jersey, 1977

Brady, John, *The Craft of the Screenwriter*, New York, 1981.

Engel, Joel, *Screenwriters on Screenwriting*, New York, 1995.

On LEHMAN: articles—

Madsen, Axel, "Who's Afraid of Alfred Hitchcock?," in *Sight and Sound* (London), Winter 1967/68.

Billington, Michael, "From *Dolly* to *Portnoy*," in *Times* (London), 30 December 1969.

Canby, Vincent, "Here's to Hollywood's Downtrodden Writers," in *New York Times*, 30 October 1983.

"Lehman, Ernest," in *Dictionary of Literary Biography*, Volume 44: *American Screenwriters, Second Series*, Detroit, 1986, 157–65.

*   *   *

Given that Ernest Lehman has scripted some of the most Oscar-laden films ever made, it comes as something of a surprise to realize that he has never won an Academy Award for Best Screenplay— several nominations, but no Oscar. Lehman himself might well, with a rueful shrug, adduce the fact as further evidence for the persistent undervaluing of the writer's contribution to any movie, good or bad. "I've spent the best years of my life trying to convince movie critics . . . that if a film is any good, it was probably well written, and that if it was a stinker, it was probably due to a bad screenplay, but I couldn't even make a *dent*."

Not that Lehman, intelligent and ironic, has ever been one to make grandiose claims. "I don't take writing as seriously as some writers would, or should," he says, and refuses to regard screenwriting as an "art": "When it works it's skill and craft and some unconscious ability." Lehman's own skill and craft have never been in doubt; the opening of his very first film as screenwriter, *Executive Suite*, could stand as a textbook model of classic exposition, lucid and economical. What is more disputable is whether that skill and craft—and ability— have been exploited to anywhere near their full potential.

Of Lehman's relatively brief filmography as screenwriter only one, *North by Northwest*, is an original. All the rest are adaptations, from novels or the stage—although in some cases, such as *The Prize*, the script might almost qualify as an original, so thoroughly was the source material reworked. (In *Sweet Smell of Success* Lehman, was

working from his own novella, and the plot structure is entirely his, but after he quit the production the dialogue was rewritten almost in toto by Clifford Odets.) Furthermore, four of his films were adaptations not just of plays, but of Broadway musicals (*The King and I*, *West Side Story*, *The Sound of Music*, and *Hello Dolly!*), a genre always liable to incite critical condescension.

In *Talking Pictures* Richard Corliss, mocking Lehman as "Curator-in-Chief of the Hollywood Museum of High-Priced Broadway Properties," suggested that these "close adaptations . . . strike Lehman's admirers as acts of treason against his considerable talent." Lehman would dispute the closeness no less than the treason. In the case of *Sound of Music*, he points out that much of the film's dramatic structure, including the famous airborne opening, was his creation alone. "I saw the Broadway show, and it consisted of lead-ins to the next number. No story." Even with *West Side Story*, where the original had a far stronger plot, Lehman extensively restructured the play to bring out its social emphasis. "I rearranged it quite a bit to keep the dramatic line very clean, and I moved around musical numbers."

When it comes to adapting novels, Lehman argues that the writer's contribution to the finished movie is yet more crucial—and no less generally undervalued. "There are a million decisions made by the screenwriter. . . . He's the one who looks at a sequence . . . and decides: *It won't work in the movie*. We'll have to forget it. Or change it from a ship to a plane. The director doesn't say, 'Let's shoot the scene in a plane instead of a boat.' No, it's written. It's *written*." Corliss's contemptuous phrase, "a mere service-station attendant of other writers' vehicles," seems singularly inapt in view of Lehman's shrewdly gauged treatment of Albee's *Who's Afraid of Virginia Woolf?*, and his elegant transmutation of Victor Canning's novel *The Rainbird Pattern* into Hitchcock's final movie, *Family Plot*.

All the more puzzling, then, that a writer with such an evident instinct for screenwriting should number only one original screenplay among his credits—especially when that one is so outstanding. Lehman's script for *North by Northwest* has a good claim to be the finest ever written for a Hitchcock film. Witty, literate, well-paced, and stylish, it deftly captures the sly mix of terror and teasing humor that typifies Hitchcock's cinema at its best, while still lightly sketching in a serious subtext: the regeneration of an empty, selfish man. Yet for all its clear and satisfying structure, the writing of it caused Lehman continual agony. "I recall having tried to quit the picture a dozen times. . . . I never knew what the hell I was going to write next." Rather than face that agony again, he preferred to divert into producing, and once even disastrously into directing (the ill-starred *Portnoy's Complaint*), before quitting screenwriting for good. *North by Northwest*, regrettably, seems destined to remain unique in his output.

—Philip Kemp

LeMAIRE, Charles

Costume Designer. **Nationality:** American. **Born:** Chicago, Illinois *c.* 1897. **Family:** Married. **Career:** Vaudeville actor; designer for Andre-Sherri, New York; then designed for many Broadway shows in the 1920s; 1943–49—designer, 20th Century-Fox; then opened his own salon; 1962—retired to paint: several shows of paintings. **Awards:** Academy Award for *All about Eve*, 1950; *The Robe*, 1953; *Love Is* *a Many Splendored Thing*, 1955. **Died:** In Palm Springs, California, 8 June 1985.

Films as Costume Designer:

1925   *Heart of a Siren* (Rosen)

1929   *The Cocoanuts* (Santley and Florey)

1933   *Take a Chance* (Schwab, Brice, and De Sylva)

1934   *George White's Scandals* (Freeland)

1935   *Scandals* (White)

1941   *The Men in Her Life* (Ratoff) (co)

1946   *Strange Triangle* (McCarey); *The Razor's Edge* (Goulding) (co); *Boomerang* (Kazan) (co)

1947   *Captain from Castile* (H. King); *Kiss of Death* (Hathaway); *The Home Stretch* (Humberstone) (co); *Moss Rose* (Ratoff) (co); *Miracle on 34th Street* (*The Big Heart*) (Seaton) (co); *The Ghost and Mrs. Muir* (Mankiewicz) (co); *I Wonder Who's Kissing Her Now* (Bacon) (co); *Thunder in the Valley* (*Bob, Son of Battle*) (L. King) (co); *Mother Wore Tights* (W. Lang) (co); *Nightmare Alley* (Goulding) (co); *The Foxes of Harrow* (Stahl) (co); *Forever Amber* (Preminger) (co); *Daisy Kenyon* (Preminger); *Gentleman's Agreement* (Kazan) (co); *Call Northside 777* (Hathaway) (co); *Sitting Pretty* (W. Lang) (co)

1948   *Escape* (Mankiewicz); *Deep Waters* (H. King); *Yellow Sky* (Wellman); *Scudda Hoo! Scudda Hay!* (*Summer Lightning*) (Herbert) (co); *Green Grass of Wyoming* (L. King) (co); *Deep Waters* (H. King); *Give My Regards* (Bacon) (co); *The Iron Curtain* (Wellman) (co); *Unfaithfully Yours* (P. Sturges) (co); *The Street with No Name* (Keighley) (co); *The Walls of Jericho* (Stahl) (co); *Cry of the City* (Siodmak) (co); *Apartment for Peggy* (Seaton) (co); *Road House* (Negulesco) (co); *The Luck of the Irish* (Koster) (co); *The Snake Pit* (Litvak) (co); *That Lady in Ermine* (Lubitsch) (co); *That Wonderful Urge* (Sinclair) (co); *Chicken Every Sunday* (Seaton); *When My Baby Smiles at Me* (W. Lang) (co); *You Were Meant for Me* (Bacon) (co)

1949   *Down to the Sea in Ships* (Hathaway); *House of Strangers* (Mankiewicz); *Pinky* (Kazan); *Come to the Stable* (Koster); *A Letter to Three Wives* (Mankiewicz); *The Fan* (*Lady Windermere's Fan*) (Preminger) (co); *Mr. Belvedere Goes to College* (Nugent) (co); *It Happens Every Spring* (Bacon) (co); *You're My Everything* (W. Lang); *Everybody Does It* (Goulding) (co); *Thieves' Highway* (Dassin); *Oh, You Beautiful Doll* (Stahl); *Dancing in the Dark* (Reis) (co); *Whirlpool* (Preminger) (co)

1950   ***All about Eve*** (Mankiewicz) (co); *For Heaven's Sake* (Seaton); *My Blue Heaven* (Koster); *Three Came Home* (Negulesco); *Under My Skin* (Negulesco); *Wabash Avenue* (Koster); *Halls of Montezuma* (Milestone); *Mother Didn't Tell Me* (Binyon) (co); *When Willie Comes Marching Home* (Ford) (co); *Cheaper By the Dozen* (W. Lang) (co); *The Gunfighter* (H. King) (co); *Ticket to Tomahawk* (Sale) (co); *Panic in the Streets* (Kazan) (co); *Stella* (Binyon) (co); *Where the Sidewalk Ends* (Preminger) (co); *Mr. 880* (Goulding) (co); *No Way Out* (Mankiewicz) (co); *I'll Get By* (Sale) (co); *Two Flags West* (Wise) (co); *The Jackpot* (W. Lang) (co); *Rawhide* (Hathaway) (co); *American Guerilla in the Philippines* (*I Shall Return*) (F. Lang) (co);

The Thirteenth Letter (Preminger) (co); *I Can Get It for You Wholesale* (*This Is My Affair*) (Gordon)

1951   *Call Me Mister* (Bacon); *Elopement* (Koster); *The Frogmen* (Bacon); *Golden Girl* (Bacon); *People Will Talk* (Mankiewicz); *You're in the Navy Now* (Hathaway); *Bird of Paradise* (Daves) (co); *I'd Climb the Highest Mountain* (H. King) (co); *Follow the Sun* (Lanfield) (co); *Fourteen Hours* (Hathaway) (co); *The House on Telegraph Hill* (Wise) (co); *On the Riviera* (W. Lang) (co); *The Guy Who Came Back* (Newman) (co); *Secret of Convict Lake* (Gordon) (co); *Take Care of My Little Girl* (Negulesco) (co); *Mr. Belvedere Rings the Bell* (Koster) (co); *Meet Me after the Show* (Sale) (co); *David and Bathsheba* (H. King) (co); *The Day the Earth Stood Still* (Wise) (co); *Love Nest* (Newman) (co); *Let's Make It Legal* (Sale) (co); *Anne of the Indies* (Tourneur) (co); *Fixed Bayonet* (Fuller); *The Model and the Marriage Broker* (Cukor) (co)

1952   *The Bloodhounds of Broadway* (Jones); *Five Fingers* (Mankiewicz); *My Pal Gus* (Parrish); *My Wife's Best Friend* (Sale); *The Snows of Kilimanjaro* (H. King); *With a Song in My Heart* (W. Lang); *As Young as You Feel* (Jones) (co); *Viva Zapata!* (Kazan) (co); *Red Skies of Montana* (Newman) (co); *Return of the Texan* (Daves) (co); *The Pride of St. Louis* (Jones) (co); *Deadline, U.S.A.* (*Deadline*) (Brooks) (co); *Belles on Their Toes* (Levin) (co); *Les Miserables* (Milestone) (co); *Outcasts of Poker Flat* (Newman) (co); *Lydia Bailey* (Negulesco) (co); *Wait 'til the Sun Shines, Nellie* (H. King) (co); *The Girl Next Door* (Sale) (co); *We're Not Married* (Goulding) (co); *Dreamboat* (Binyon) (co); *Don't Bother to Knock* (Baker) (co); *What Price Glory* (Ford) (co); *Lure of the Wilderness* (Negulesco) (co); *O. Henry's Full House* (*Full House*) (Koster and others) (co); *Monkey Business* (Hawks) (co); *Night without Sleep* (Baker) (co); *Something or the Birds* (Wise) (co); *Destination Gobi* (Wise); *Way of a Gaucho* (Tourneur) (co); *Stars and Stripes Forever* (*Marching Along*) (Koster) (co); *My Cousin Rachel* (Koster) (co); *The President's Lady* (Levin) (co); *Down among the Sheltering Palms* (Goulding) (co)

1953   *A Blueprint for Murder* (Stone); *The Desert Rats* (Wise); *The Robe* (Koster) (co); *Taxi* (Ratoff) (co); *Niagara* (Hathaway) (co); *Treasure of the Golden Condor* (Daves) (co); *The Silver Whip* (Jones) (co); *Tonight We Sing* (Leisen) (co); *The Farmer Takes a Wife* (Levin) (co); *The Siege at Red River* (Maté) (co); *Titanic* (Negulesco) (co); *Man on a Tightrope* (Kazan) (co); *Powder River* (L. King) (co); *Pickup on South Street* (Fuller) (co); *City of Bad Men* (Jones) (co); *Gentlemen Prefer Blondes* (Hawks) (co); *White Witch Doctor* (Hathaway) (co); *Dangerous Crossing* (Newman) (co); *Inferno* (Baker) (co); *Mr. Scoutmaster* (Levin) (co); *The Kid from Left Field* (Jones) (co); *How to Marry a Millionaire* (Negulesco); *King of the Kyber Rifles* (H. King) (co); *Beneath the Twelve Mile Reef* (Webb) (co); *Three Young Texans* (Levin) (co); *Man in the Attic* (Fregonese) (co)

1954   *Demetrius and the Gladiators* (Daves); *The Egyptian* (Curtiz); *Prince Valiant* (Hathaway); *Woman's World* (Negulesco); *Night People* (Johnson) (co); *Hell and High Water* (Fuller) (co); *River of No Return* (Preminger) (co); *Three Coins in the Fountain* (Negulesco) (co); *Broken Lance* (Dmytryk) (co); *Garden of Evil* (Negulesco) (co); *The Black Widow* (Johnson) (co); *Desiree* (Koster) (co); *Prince of Players* (Dunne) (co); *There's No Business Like Show Business* (W. Lang) (co)

1955   *The Girl in the Red Velvet Swing* (Fleischer); *Yacht on the High Seas* (Post); *Love Is a Many Splendored Thing* (H. King) (co); *Soldier of Fortune* (Dmytryk); *The View from Pompey's Head* (Dunne); *Violent Saturday* (Fleischer) (co); *Daddy Long Legs* (Negulesco) (co); *The Seven Year Itch* (Wilder) (co); *The Virgin Queen* (Koster) (co); *House of Bamboo* (Fuller); *How to Be Very, Very Popular* (Johnson) (co); *The Left Hand of God* (Dmytryk) (co); *The Tall Men* (Walsh) (co); *Seven Cities of Gold* (Webb) (co); *The Rains of Ranchipur* (Negulesco) (co); *The Lieutenant Wore Skirts* (Tashlin) (co)

1956   *The Bottom of the Bottle* (*Beyond the River*) (Hathaway) (co); *On the Threshold of Space* (Webb); *The Revolt of Mamie Stover* (Walsh) (co); *The Best Things in Life Are Free* (Curtiz); *D-Day, the Sixth of June* (Koster); *The Girl Can't Help It* (Tashlin); *Hilda Crane* (Dunne); *The Man in the Gray Flannel Suit* (Johnson); *Twenty Three Paces to Baker Street* (Hathaway) (co); *The Proud Ones* (Webb) (co); *Bus Stop* (Logan) (co); *Bigger Than Life* (Ray) (co); *The Last Wagon* (Daves) (co); *Between Heaven and Hell* (Fleischer) (co); *Teenage Rebel* (Goulding) (co)

1957   *An Affair to Remember* (McCarey); *Kiss Them for Me* (Donen); *Oh Men! Oh Women!* (Johnson); *Stopover Tokyo* (Breen); *The Sun Also Rises* (H. King) (co); *Will Success Spoil Rock Hunter?* (Tashlin); *Top Secret Affair* (*Their Secret Affair*) (Tashlin); *Three Brave Men* (Dunne) (co); *The Way to the Gold* (Webb) (co); *The Wayward Bus* (Vicas) (co); *The Desk Set* (*His Other Woman*) (W. Lang); *A Hatful of Rain* (Zinnemann) (co); *Bernardine* (Levin) (co); *Three Faces of Eve* (Johnson) (co); *No Down Payment* (Ritt) (co); *Forty Guns* (Fuller) (co); *April Love* (Levin) (co); *The Enemy Below* (Powell)

1958   *The Barbarian and the Geisha* (Huston); *The Bravados* (H. King); *The Gift of Love* (Negulesco); *The Hunters* (D. Powell); *Mardi Gras* (Goulding); *A Nice Little Bank That Should Be Robbed* (Levin); *Ten North Frederick* (Dunne); *The Young Lions* (Dmytryk) (co); *The Long Hot Summer* (Ritt) (co); *The Fly* (Neumann) (co); *From Hell to Texas* (*Manhunt*) (Hathaway) (co); *In Love and War* (Dunne) (co); *These Thousand Hills* (Fleischer); *The Fiend Who Walked the West* (Douglas) (co)

1959   *Compulsion* (Fleischer) (co); *Thunder in the Sun* (Rouse); *Rally 'round the Flag, Boys* (McCarey); *The Remarkable Mr. Pennypacker* (Levin) (co); *Warlock* (Dmytryk); *A Woman Obsessed* (Hathaway); *The Diary of Anne Frank* (Stevens) (co); *Say One for Me* (Tashlin) (co)

1960   *The Marriage-Go-Round* (W. Lang)

1962   *Walk on the Wild Side* (Dmytryk)

Publications

On LeMAIRE: articles—

Chierchetti, David, in *Hollywood Costume Design*, New York, 1976.
Leese, Elizabeth, in *Costume Design in the Movies*, New York, 1976.

Obituary in *Variety* (New York), 12 June 1985.
Obituary in *Time*, 24 June 1985.

*   *   *

It is no surprise that Charles LeMaire was wardrobe director at 20th Century-Fox from 1943 to 1959, during the flamboyant years of the Technicolor musical. The studio, once referred to as "more hysterical than historical," used an approach in their costuming which dealt more in stereotypes than research, a virtual burlesque of genuine styles. LeMaire's background of showy theatrical flash suited the studio far better than a Chanel would.

LeMaire was born in Chicago, and started out as vaudeville actor and song plugger. In New York, after a year on the circuit, he became a shopper for the couture house of Antoinette Sherri. This sparked a new career direction for LeMaire. He began designing on- and off-stage costumes for many Broadway stars and in 1919 received his first major commission: to design for the Ziegfeld Follies. From 1919 to 1926, he designed for a string of Hammerstein operettas. He also worked for George White's *Scandals*, Earl Carroll's *Vanities*, and Irving Berlin's *Music Box Revue*. He became head designer at Brooks Costume firm from 1924 to 1929. LeMaire continued to work freelance and in 1931 opened his own firm: LeMaire Studio Design. His many projects included a spectacular for John Ringling North's circus.

After leaving the Army in 1943, LeMaire began at 20th Century-Fox, as executive designer and director of wardrobe, where he specialized in Betty Grable movies. His concepts for the star are mindlessly glamorous and visually stunning: Grable was decorated as baroque cheesecake, iced with sequins, and quivering with feathers. Designs for Grable were neither history nor fashion. They were basically showgirl costumes, created to emphasize Grable's sexy legs. Her historical movies were nothing to assign to a social studies class (except, perhaps, one studying postwar Americana). They were mostly nightclub images of the past, and her costumes could serve as precursors to the "Vegas" look.

It must be emphasized, however, that as crass as these costumes seem they were appropriate to the image of the actress they featured. Grable was not a Joan Crawford, with Crawford's innate sense of style, crawling her way to the top. When Adrian dressed Crawford as economically disadvantaged in *Dancing Lady* and *The Women*, she still had more class than anyone in the audience. Nor had Grable the continental class and mystery of a Dietrich. Travis Banton's interpretation of rags in Dietrich's *Blonde Venus* was more aesthetic than a Clifford Still painting.

LeMaire teaming up with Grable was cinematically correct. Grable played the spunky, sexy, American-girl-next-door fantasy. Like a lot of her audience, she was probably from a lower-class immigrant-parent background with a fashion code which ruled that more was better. No doubt she had a multitude of fans who agreed.

LeMaire is credited with an enormous filmography. Dealing with his works is as difficult as trying to pin down the credits of MGM's head art director Cedric Gibbons. Did LeMaire actually contribute to any of these projects? Did he merely approve them? In any case, because of his status at Fox, his credits are linked with such other artists as Rene Hubert, Kay Nelson, Bonnie Cashin, Travilla, Edith Head, Renie, Edward Stevenson, Orry-Kelly, Oleg Cassini, Dorothy Jeakins, Eleanor Behm, Perkins Bailey, Mario Vanarelli, Ursula Maes, Miles White, Mary Wills, Yvonne Wood, Helen Rose, Adele Palmer, Leah Rohes, and Adele Balkan.

Perhaps LeMaire's greatest contribution to the history of American film (aside from his assistance in creating Grable as an ultimate American legend) was his help in establishing a category for the costumer among the many Academy Awards. It is hard to believe that before this time no such recognition was given. The Academy, in turn, was good to LeMaire, though there is some controversy amid his honors. He shared his Oscar for *All about Eve* with his good friend Edith Head. Head explained that because she really wanted to do Davis's costumes for *All about Eve* and LeMaire was very busy with other projects, he agreed to this arrangement. Head stated that LeMaire had already done the other costumes for Anne Baxter, Celeste Holm, Thelma Ritter, Barbara Bates, and Marilyn Monroe. However, the only costumes one remembers are Head's and some sources on the picture seem to question LeMaire's authorship on the others. As for LeMaire's award for *Love Is a Many Splendored Thing*, Head claimed that he really didn't deserve his Oscar, that the costumes were ''blah,'' and could have been bought off the rack in Hong Kong. In addition to these dubious distinctions, LeMaire won an Academy Award jointly with Emile Santiago for the biblical extravaganza *The Robe*.

LeMaire left the studio in 1959 and worked freelance and in the wholesale dress business. He was among the many major designers leaving the industry as the age of the hollywood costume designer rapidly faded to memory.

—Edith C. Lee

LENICA, Jan

Animator and director. **Nationality:** French. **Born:** Poznan, Poland, 4 January 1928; became French citizen. **Education:** Educated in architectural engineering, Polytechnic, Warsaw, until 1952. **Family:** Married Merja Alanen, 1969, children: Anneli and Maia. **Career:** 1945—published humorous and satirical drawings; 1948—first one man show, Warsaw; 1950—began designing posters; 1957—began collaboration with Walerian Borowczyk; 1958—left Poland to work in France; 1960s—poster designs featured in numerous international exhibitions; 1963—left France for West Germany; 1990s—professor of graphic design, Hochschule der Künste, Berlin. **Awards:** Polish Film Critics Prize for *Once upon a Time . . .*, 1957; Golden Dragon, Cracow, and Polish Film Critics Prize, for *New Janko the Musician*, 1960; Golden Dragon, Cracow, for *Labyrinth*, 1962; Grand Prix, Oberhausen Festival, for *A*, 1964; Golden Lion, Venice Festival, for *Woman the Flower*, 1965.

Films as Director and Animator:

1957　*Był sobie raz . . . (Once upon a Time . . .)* (with Walerian Borowczyk); *Nagrodzone uczucie (Love Required)* (with Borowczyk); *Strip-Tease* (with Borowczyk—under 3 min)
1958　*Dom (The House)* (with Borowczyk); *Sztandar młodych (Banner of Youth)* (with Borowczyk—under 3 min)
1959　*Monsieur Tête (Mr. Head)* (with Borowczyk)
1960　*Nowy Janko muzykant (New Janko the Musician)*
1961　*Italia 61 (Italy 61)* (with W. Zamecznik—under 3 min, film lost)
1962　*Labirynt (Labyrinth)*

1963　*Die Nashörner (Rhinoceroses)*
1964　*A*
1965　*La Femme-Fleur (Woman the Flower)*
1966　*Weg zum Nachbarn* (under 3 min; for Oberhausen Festival)
1969　*Adam II (Adam 2)*; *Stilleben (Still Life)*
1970　*Nature morte*
1972　*Fantorro, le dernier justicier (Fantorro, the Last Just Man)*
1973　*Life Size* (under 3 min)
1974　*Landscape*
1976　*Ubu Roi (King Ubu)*
1979　*Ubu et la Grande Gidouille (Ubu and the Great Gidouille)*

Films as Animator:

(trailers)

1964　*Cul-de-sac* (Polanski)
1972　*Quatre Mouches de velours gris*; *César et Rosalie* (Sautet)
1973　*Le Petit Poucet* (Boisrond)
1975　*Das kleine Fernsehspiel*

Publications

By LENICA: books—

Plakat Tadeusza Trepkowskiego, Warsaw, 1958.
With Alfred Sauvy, *Population Explosion*, New York, 1962.
Monsieur Tête, text by Eugène Ionesco, Munich, 1970.

By LENICA: article—

Animafilm, April/June 1980.

On LENICA: books—

Kauzyński, Zygmunt, *Jan Lenica*, Warsaw, 1963.
Kristahn, Heinz-Jürgen, editor, *Das polnische Plakat von 1892 bis heute*, Berlin, 1981.
Kristahn, Heinz-Jürgen, editor, *Jan Lenica*, Berlin, 1981.

On LENICA: articles—

''Jan Lenica,'' in *Film* (London), Summer 1963.
''Animation Quartet,'' in *International Film Guide* (London), 1966.
''Artist and Animator,'' in *Film* (London), Spring 1972.
''Jan Lenica,'' in *Polish Film Polonaise* (Warsaw), no. 5, 1976.
Cornand, A., ''Le Festival d'Annecy et les rencontres internationales du cinéma d'animation,'' in *Image et Son* (Paris), January 1977.
Bassan, R., ''L'Enfer tranquille de Jan Lenica,'' in *Image et Son* (Paris), July-August 1980.
Film Quarterly, vol. 45, no. 4, 1992.

*　　*　　*

Jan Lenica's checkered career has encompassed excursions into music, architecture, poster-making, costume design, children's book illustration, and all aspects of filmmaking. It is, however, for his animation that he is best known, particularly his collage and "cut-out" films, which have their roots in the art of Max Ernst and John Heartfield. The films have influenced the work of Jan Švankmajer and Terry Gilliam.

In the 1950s, his films with Walerian Borowczyk led an aesthetic revolution in Poland that sent reverberations all over the Eastern European animation scene. Before Lenica entered the scene, Polish animation consisted mainly of American-influenced character animation, over which the shadow of Walt Disney lugubriously hung, sometimes with vaguely political overtones on the fringe. Lenica and Borowczyk moved the avant-garde into the mainstream. They attempted to forge a new experimental cinema that would coalesce contemporary artistic practices such as abstraction, collage, and satirical surrealism without jettisoning commitment to the Marxist concepts of artistic integration of form and content and art for the masses. Often their films deal with alienation in a modern world, and the challenge of the detritus of history, figured in their use of old newspaper and postcards and the ironic confrontation with the "Great Masters" of painting which consume the protagonist of *Once upon a Time . . . .* In *The House*, a wide range of techniques illustrate a strange mechanical rite. The rough simplicity of their materials in these films conveys simultaneously the menace of an absurd disordered universe, and an affecting artlessness of execution.

The films Lenica made on his own, like Borowczyk's later work, are even more preoccupied with the grotesque, though Lenica's are more concerned with the confrontation of innocent Everymen and modern Candides, with a hellish world of threatening technology—violent, unpredictable, and self-referential. In this, they are reminiscent of the work of contemporaneous literary figures, such as Beckett, Ionesco, Jarry, and the newly rediscovered Kafka, and belie an interest in the Existentialism which was then all the rage in Paris, where Lenica moved in 1958. *Monsieur Tête* and *Rhinoceroses* are some of his most self-consciously literary works, though still in the style of *The House. Labyrinth*, with its butterfly-men and giant reptiles, depicts a nightmare world of misbegotten genetic experiments, yet the beauty of some of the surreal creations depicted in it suggest a visionary and fantastic view as much as that of a pessimistic dystopian. The triumph of the beleaguered office worker in *Adam II* (1969) pointed to a resurgent optimism in Lenica's work. It can be read also as an allegory of the artist under communism, a theme more ambiguously rendered by the Estonian animator, Pritt Pjarn, in his masterful *Hotel E* (1991). One troubling aspect of Lenica's work remains the presence of a certain latent misogyny, particularly evinced by *Nature morte*, that is somewhat reminiscent of his compatriot Roman Polanski, for whom he designed the British film posters for *Repulsion* and *Cul-de-sac*.

During the 1970s, Lenica's animated output was considerably reduced as he became more interested in teaching and costume and theater design. *Ubu Roi*, his adaptation of Jarry's play, marked a significant departure from the best-known work of his early career, with its hand-drawn images and more static quality. Jarry's text, however, was attractive to Lenica due to its emphasis on the grotesque and the satirical, which complemented Lenica's earliest interest in caricature. He said in an interview that, "The art of animation is stretched between two extremes. On the one side there is Walt Disney with his enormous popularity and resonance with viewers, and on the other there are quests, experiments, interesting as they are, but separated from audiences. I would like to bring these two extremes closer together, to find a golden mean for them, that is to win viewers on the one hand, while not losing anything of what is my own style. *Ubu* is precisely the outcome of this striving." The reconciliation of extremes is a concern which pervades his work as a whole.

—Leslie Felperin Sharman

LEVEN, Boris

Art Director. **Nationality:** American. **Born:** Moscow, Russia, 13 August 1912; emigrated to the United States, 1927: naturalized, 1938. **Education:** Studied architecture at the University of Southern California, Los Angeles, 1927–32, B.Arch. 1932; attended Beaux Art Institute of Design, New York, 1932–33, Certificate-Beaux Art 1933. **Family:** Married Vera Gloushkoff, 1948. **Career:** 1933–35—designer, Paramount, then designer and art director for Samuel Goldwyn; 1936, Major; 1936, 20th Century-Fox; 1937–38, 1941–42, 1945–46, and Universal; 1947–48, then freelance; also artist. **Awards:** Academy Award for *West Side Story*, 1961. **Died:** 18 October 1986.

Films as Art Director:

1938   *Alexander's Ragtime Band* (H. King); *Just around the Corner* (Cummings)
1940   *Second Chorus* (Potter)
1941   *The Shanghai Gesture* (von Sternberg)
1942   *Tales of Manhattan* (Duvivier); *Life Begins at 8:30* (Pichel)
1943   *Hello, Frisco, Hello* (Humberstone)
1945   *Doll Face* (Seiler)
1946   *Home Sweet Homicide* (Bacon); *Shock* (Werker)
1947   *The Shocking Miss Pilgrim* (Seaton); *I Wonder Who's Kissing Her Now* (Bacon); *The Senator Was Indiscreet* (Kaufman)
1948   *Mr. Peabody and the Mermaid* (Pichel)
1949   *Criss Cross* (Siodmak); *The Lovable Cheat* (Oswald); *Search for Danger* (Bernhard); *House by the River* (F. Lang)
1950   *Woman on the Run* (Foster); *Quicksand* (Pichel); *Dakota Lil* (Selander); *Destination Murder* (Cahn); *Once a Thief* (W. Wilder)
1951   *The Second Woman* (Kern); *The Prowler* (Losey); *A Millionaire for Christie* (Marshall); *Two Dollar Bettor* (Cahn); *The Basketball Fix* (Feist)
1952   *Sudden Fear* (Miller); *Rose of Cimarron* (Keller)
1953   *The Star* (Heisler); *Invaders from Mars* (Menzies); *Donovan's Brain* (Fiest)
1954   *The Long Wait* (Saville)
1955   *The Silver Chalice* (Saville)
1956   **Giant** (Stevens)
1957   *Courage of Black Beauty* (Schuster); *My Gun Is Quick* (White and Victor); *Zero Hour* (Bartlett)
1959   *Anatomy of a Murder* (Preminger); *Thunder in the Sun* (Rouse)
1960   *September Storm* (Haskin)
1961   **West Side Story** (Wise)
1962   *Two for the Seesaw* (Wise)
1964   *Strait-Jacket* (Castle)
1965   *The Sound of Music* (Wise)
1966   *The Sand Pebbles* (Wise)
1968   *Star!* (Wise)

1969   *A Dream of Kings* (Daniel Mann)
1971   *The Andromeda Strain* (Wise); *Happy Birthday Wanda June*
            (Robson)
1972   *The New Centurions* (Fleischer)
1973   *Jonathan Livingston Seagull* (Bartlett)
1974   *Reflections of Murder* (Badham); *Shanks* (Castle)
1975   *Mandingo* (Fleischer)
1977   *New York, New York* (Scorsese)
1978   *The Last Waltz* (Scorsese); *Matilda* (Daniel Mann)
1983   *The King of Comedy* (Scorsese)
1985   *Fletch* (Ritchie)
1986   *Wildcats* (Ritchie)

Publications

By LEVEN: articles—

Film Index (Mosman Bay, New South Wales), no. 15, 1973.
Film Comment (New York), May-June 1978.

On LEVEN: articles—

Kaplan, Mike, in *Today's Film Maker* (Hempstead, New York),
    August 1971.
Film Dope (Nottingham), September 1986.
Obituary in *Variety* (New York), 22 October 1986.

*   *   *

Boris Leven has been described by the critic Carrie Rickey as one of the progenitors of theatrical realism in American art direction. Theatrical realism, as Rickey describes it, is an art directional style in which the realism of the world as we normally encounter it is couched against a reconstructed realism which only ostensibly disguises its manufactured qualities.

Leven studied at the Institute of Design and the University of Southern California Architecture School. His first credited film, *Alexander's Ragtime Band*, utilized more than 85 sets and was one of the first large-budget musicals to use a series of period sets as a backdrop for a progression of popular songs. Leven also designed *Hello, Frisco, Hello*, another of this genre for 20th Century-Fox.

Giant, directed by George Stevens, is arguably Leven's most significant work of the 1950s. Among the numerous sets, the Victorian home, which he designed to sit isolated in an expanse of prairie, carries the emotional chill of an Edward Hopper painting. Contemporary reviews of this film concurred that the thematic basis of the story, the social constructions of wealth and power, were borne out by the visual aspects of the film. Sets including the opulent railway coach and immense family home carry the sense of materialism and conspicuous consumption that contrast directly with the rugged Texas environment.

Rickey isolates the Academy Award-winning *West Side Story* as probably the first film in which the contrast between the real and the deliberately unreal was maintained throughout the course of the movie. The heavily stylized visual sensibilities are conveyed through dynamic camera angles, abrupt cuts, and sets which range from location shots of New York streets, to areas such as the gym/dance

hall and the tenement rooftop which are patently false and maintain ties to the original, more abstract stage production.

Working again with *West Side Story* director Robert Wise in *The Sound of Music*, Leven relied much more heavily on Salzburg location shots which offered the necessary air of authenticity to this script based on the lives of the Trapp family singers. Only certain sets, such as the terrace where the oldest daughter dances with her boyfriend, offer a light sense of contrivance which refers back to the original stage production and allow a segue between some of the lighter musical numbers and the dramatic action.

Of his later work, *Mandingo* offers an example of Leven's mastery of accurately-based historical settings, while *New York, New York* sought in Leven's words a "totally false, totally Forties Hollywood" look. This film succeeds in visually comparing Hollywood stereotypes of New York City, one of glamor and sophistication and the other of crowds of energetic urbanites. These films illustrate Leven's adeptness at recreating period settings as well as his skill in fabricating sensational environments that correspond more completely to emotional and thematic demands.

—Giselle Atterberry

LEVIEN, Sonya

Writer. **Nationality:** American. **Born:** near Moscow, Russia, 25 December 1888; emigrated to the United States with her parents when she was a child. **Education:** Attended New York University, law degree. **Family:** Married the writer Carl Hovey, 1917; two children. **Career:** Practiced law briefly; 1916–20—staff member, *Woman's Journal* and *Metropolitan* magazines; 1919—first film writing credit, *Who Will Marry Me?*; 1929–41—writer for 20th Century-Fox, and for MGM, 1941–56. **Award:** Academy Award for *Interrupted Melody*, 1955. **Died:** Of cancer, in Hollywood, California, 19 March 1960.

Films as Writer:

1919   *Who Will Marry Me?* (Powell)
1921   *Cheated Love* (Baggot); *First Love* (Campbell)
1922   *The Top of New York* (Taylor); *Pink Gods* (Stanlaws)
1923   *The Snow Bride* (Kolker); *The Exciters* (Campbell)
1925   *Salome of the Tenements* (Olcott)
1926   *The Love Toy* (Kenton); *Christine of the Big Tops* (Mayo)
1927   *The Princess from Hoboken* (Dale); *The Heart Thief*
            (Chrisander); *A Harp in Hock* (Hoffman)
1928   *A Ship Comes In* (Howard); *The Power of the Press* (Capra);
            Behind That Curtain (Cummings); *The Younger Genera-*
            tion (Capra); *Trial Marriage* (Kenton); *Lucky Star* (Borzage);
            They Had to See Paris (Borzage); *South Sea Rose* (Dwan);
            Frozen Justice (Dwan)
1930   *Song o' My Heart* (Borzage); *So This Is London* (Blystone);
            The Brat (Ford); *Surrender* (Howard)
1932   *She Wanted a Millionaire* (Blystone); *After Tomorrow* (Borzage)
1933   *State Fair* (H. King); *Warrior's Husband* (W. Lang); *Berkeley*
            Square (Lloyd); *Mr. Skitch* (Cruze)
1934   *Change of Heart* (Blystone); *The White Parade* (Cummings)
1935   *Here's to Romance* (Green); *Navy Wife* (Dwan)

1936   *The Country Doctor* (H. King); *Reunion* (Taurog)
1938   *In Old Chicago* (H. King); *Kidnapped* (Werker); *Four Men and a Prayer* (Ford)
1939   *Drums Along the Mohawk* (Ford); *The Hunchback of Notre Dame* (Dieterle)
1941   *Ziegfeld Girl* (Leonard)
1943   *The Amazing Mrs. Holliday* (Manning); *Rhapsody in Blue* (Rapper); *State Fair* (W. Lang)
1946   *The Green Years* (Saville); *The Valley of Decision* (Garnett); *Ziegfeld Follies* (Minnelli)
1947   *Cass Timberlane* (Sidney)
1948   *Three Darling Daughters* (Wilcox)
1951   *The Great Caruso* (Thorpe)
1952   *The Merry Widow* (Bernhardt)
1954   *The Student Prince* (Thorpe)
1955   *Hit the Deck* (Rowland); *Interrupted Melody* (Bernhardt); *Oklahoma!* (Zinnemann); *Bhowani Junction* (Cukor)
1957   *Jeanne Eagels* (Sidney)
1960   *Pepe* (Sidney)

Films as Cowriter with S. N. Behrman:

1930   *Lightnin'* (H. King); *Liliom* (Borzage)
1931   *Delicious* (Butler); *Daddy Long Legs* (Santell)
1932   *Rebecca of Sunnybrook Farm* (Santell); *Tess of the Storm Country* (Santell)
1933   *Cavalcade* (Lloyd)
1934   *As Husbands Go* (MacFadden)
1935   *Anna Karenina* (Brown)
1938   *The Cowboy and the Lady* (Potter)
1951   *Quo Vadis* (LeRoy)

Publications

On LEVIEN: book—

Ceplair, Larry, *A Great Lady: A Life of the Screenwriter Sonya Levien*, Lanham, MD, Scarecrow Press, 1996.

On LEVIEN: articles—

Film Comment (New York), Winter 1970–71.
Hurwitz, Edith, in *American Screenwriters*, 2nd series, edited by Randall Clark, Detroit, Michigan, 1986.
Rosenbloom, Nancy J., "In Defense of the Moving Pictures: the People's Institute, the National Board of Censorship and the Problem of Leisure in Urban America," in *American Studies*, Fall 1992.
McCreadie, Marsha, "Pioneers (Part Two)," in *Films in Review* (New York), January-February 1995.

*   *   *

Throughout the golden era of the Hollywood studio system, Sonya Levien wrote enough screenplays (sometimes as many as five per year) to qualify her as a guaranteed professional name, but on most of her films she shared the writing credit, so that identifying her personal trademarks becomes difficult. However, despite a minimum of biographical knowledge and no opportunity to examine the evolution of any single screenplay she worked on, it is still possible to assume three primary characteristics to her career: a strong tendency toward coauthorship, a talent for adaptation, and a flair for creating women characters who are intelligent, noble, and independent, but who are also searching to define their particular roles in life.

When Levien was paired with an established male author, it seems possible to assume she was hired to represent the feminine point of view, and to enhance the female characters. For instance, she was paired more than once with such different writers as S. N. Behrman, Lamar Trotti, and William Ludwig. As might be expected, the Behrman films are sophisticated comedies, the Trotti are prestige productions of an epic scale, and the Ludwig are musical adaptations. Since in all three cases she is working with an established writer with a personal style, her contribution is an enrichment of the leading female roles. The best example is probably the Trotti-Levien adaptation of *Drums along the Mohawk*, in which the central role of Lana, played by Claudette Colbert, is a classic example of the pioneer wife, feminine and attractive, but strong enough to survive the dangers and hardships presented in the story line.

Levien's association with what were termed "quality" projects led her to work on many adaptations of novels, plays, and musicals. One of her most successful solo efforts was her adaptation of Sinclair Lewis's *Cass Timberlane*, in which the plot was restructured to reflect the postwar era in which it was released by including a character who sold faulty war materials for profit. Her skill at updating projects is also reflected in the three versions of *State Fair* she worked on, as well as in her refurbishing of such older musicals as *The Merry Widow* and *The Student Prince*. In all cases, she maintains the essential characters and overall ambience of the original, while removing outdated attitudes, particularly toward women and sex.

Given the number of collaborations Levien was involved in, it is difficult to identify exactly what she might have contributed to a specific characterization. Nevertheless, it is obvious that the assignments she was given—and took—are frequently stories about women. It must have been assumed that her name and her talent enhanced a project that would feature a leading actress. Thus, her work for Greer Garson in *The Valley of Decision*, and Eleanor Parker in *Interrupted Melody*, created strong roles for which both actresses were nominated for Oscars. In addition, such sex symbols as Lana Turner, Ava Gardner, and Kim Novak found parts which stretched their reputations and abilities in *Cass Timberlane* and *Ziegfeld Follies*, *Bhowani Junction* and *Jeanne Eagels*, respectively. The difficulty of untangling "who is responsible for what" in Sonya Levien's prolific and successful career points to the problems of historical research, and illustrates how much is yet to be learned about many of Hollywood's most influential writers.

—Jeanine Basinger

LEVINE, Joseph E.

Producer. **Nationality:** American. **Born:** Joseph Edward Levine in Boston, Massachusetts, 9 September 1905. **Career:** 1940s—exhibitor of foreign films; 1960s—moved into production. **Died:** In Greenwich, Connecticut, 21 July 1987.

Joseph E. Levine

Films as Producer/Executive Producer:

1955 *Attila*
1960 *La ciociara* (*Two Women*) (De Sica)
1963 *The Carpetbaggers* (Dmytryk); *La Noia* (*The Empty Canvas*) (Damiani); *Otto e mezzo* (*8 1/2*) (Fellini); *Le Mépris* (*Contempt*) (Godard)
1964 *Where Love Has Gone* (Dmytryk); *Matrimonio all'Italiana* (*Marriage—Italian Style*) (De Sica)
1965 *Harlow* (Douglas); *Sands of the Kalahari* (Endfield); *Casanova '70* (Monicelli); *The Oscar* (Rouse); *La decima vittima* (*Tenth Victim*) (Petrie); *Nevada Smith* (Hathaway)
1966 *The Idol* (Petrie); *The Spy with a Cold Nose* (Petrie); *The Caper of the Golden Bulls* (*Carnival of Thieves*) (Rouse); *A Man Called Adam* (Penn)
1967 *Robbery* (Yates); *Woman Times Seven* (*Sept fois femme*) (De Sica); *The Graduate* (Nichols); *The Producers* (Brooks)
1968 *The Lion in Winter* (Harvey)
1969 *I girasoli* (De Sica); *La Piscine* (Deray); *Stiletto* (Kowalski)
1970 *The Adventurers* (Gilbert); *The Ski Bum* (Clark)
1971 *Carnal Knowledge* (Nichols)
1972 *Rivals* (Shah)
1973 *Hurry Up, Or I'll Be Thirty* (Jacoby); *Interval* (Mann); *The Day of the Dolphin* (Nichols)
1975 *Paper Tiger* (Annakin)
1977 *A Bridge Too Far* (Attenborough)
1978 *Magic* (Attenborough)
1981 *Tattoo* (B. Brooks)

Publications

On LEVINE: articles—

Cinema (Hollywood), vol. 1, no. 3, Fall 1963.
In *Filmmakers on Filmmaking*, edited by Joseph McBride, Los Angeles, 1983.
Obituary in *Variety* (New York), 5 August 1987.
Obituary in *Classic Images* (Muscatine, Iowa), no. 147, September 1987.
Obituary in *Films and Filming* (London), no. 396, September 1987.
Schlossberg, J., "Remembering Joe E. Levine," in *Variety* (New York), 28 October-3 November 1996.

*   *   *

No Hollywood figure of the 1960s better represented the free-wheeling, independent motion picture producer than Joseph E. Levine. As the studio system of the 1930s and 1940s, with its complete domination of all phases of production, distribution, and exhibition, gave way to a system of independent producers feeding distributor studios, the Paramounts, Warners, and Columbias came to rely on entrepreneurs to feed their distribution needs. Joseph E. Levine was responsible for a number of high-grossing films of the 1960s including *The Carpetbaggers*, *Harlow*, *The Oscar*, *The Producers*, and *The Graduate*.

Levine began his career on the fringe of a film industry then dominated by Hollywood, as an exhibitor in New England during the 1930s. His first theatre was in New Haven, Connecticut. After the Second World War, he saw a gap in the system and began to import films for placement into the growing number of art theaters. His chief supply ground was Italy and its widely respected neorealist films. In time he would import such noted Italian films as *Divorce—Italian Style*, *Two Women*, and *81/2*.

But fame and power for Joseph E. Levine came from an altogether different type of film. In 1959 he established Embassy Pictures Corporation, and in a notoriously extravagant publicity campaign, began to put spectacles such as *Hercules*, starring American muscleman Steve Reeves, into theaters desperate for a product for the new teenage audiences. The cost of *Hercules* was half the price of a Hollywood spectacle because it was made in Italy and then dubbed into English. As a result of matching audience, publicity, and lower costs, *Hercules* grossed more than $20 million on a cost of only a couple of million.

Levine was on a roll. He signed to work with Paramount, and in 1963, he produced *The Carpetbaggers*, starring George Peppard, Alan Ladd, and Carroll Baker. This was the studio with its biggest hit in a decade. Although, as with *Hercules*, newspaper reviewers found the film camp at best and trash at worst, *The Carpetbaggers* was only surpassed at the box office by two other films during 1964.

In the late 1960s Levine hit his peak. He formed his own company, Avco Embassy, and in 1967 turned out *The Graduate*, a film that cost less than $3 million to make, but grossed in excess of $100 million and set off the era of the youth-oriented blockbuster film. Levine had taken a big chance. Director Mike Nichols had only directed *Who's Afraid of Virginia Woolf?*; Dustin Hoffman had only made low-budget films and TV advertisements. By the time all the dollars had been counted, *The Graduate* had finished as the top box-office attraction of 1967 and was then ranked third, to *Gone with the Wind* and *The Sound of Music*, on *Variety*'s list of all-time box-office champions.

But Levine could not sustain his success into the 1970s. In 1974 he ended his participation in Avco Embassy. Films such as *Carnal Knowledge* and *The Day of the Dolphin* did little to advance his career. *A Bridge Too Far* in 1977 was Levine's swansong as a major producer. A new breed of independent producers, baby boom era movie brats such as Steven Spielberg and George Lucas, had captured the day.

—Douglas Gomery

LEWTON, Val

Producer. **Nationality:** American. **Born:** Vladimir Ivan Leventon in Yalta, Russia, 7 May 1904; emigrated to the United States at age seven. **Education:** Attended Columbia University, New York. **Family:** Nephew of the actress Alla Nazimova. Married Ruth (Lewton); one daughter, one son. **Career:** Writer: novels published under his own name and as Carlos Keith, Cosmo Forbes, and Herbert Kerkow; worked in MGM publicity department; 1933–42 —editorial assistant to David O. Selznick; also wrote radio scripts (*The Luck of Joan Christopher*, 1933); 1942—in charge of low-budget RKO production unit. **Died:** Of heart attack, in Hollywood, California, 14 March 1951.

Val Lewton

Films as Producer:

1942   *Cat People* (J. Tourneur)
1943   *I Walked with a Zombie* (J. Tourneur); *The Leopard Man* (J. Tourneur); *The Seventh Man* (Robson); *The Ghost Ship* (Robson)
1944   *Mademoiselle Fifi* (Wise); *Youth Runs Wild* (Robson); *The Curse of the Cat People* (Wise and von Fritsch)
1945   *The Body Snatcher* (Wise); *Isle of the Dead* (Robson)
1946   *Bedlam* (Robson)
1949   *My Own True Love* (Bennett)
1950   *Please Believe Me* (Taurog)
1951   *Apache Drums* (Fregonese)

Publications

By LEWTON: fiction—

Improved Road, Edinburgh, 1925.
The Cossack Sword, Edinburgh, 1926, as *Rape of Glory*, New York, 1931, as *Sword of the Cossack*, London, 1932.
The Theatre of Casanova, New York, 1927.
The Women of Casanova, New York, 1927.
Manual and History of Cosmetics, New York, 1930.
The Fateful Star Murder, New York, 1931.
The Unemployed Working Girl in the Present Crisis, New York, 1931.
No Bed of Her Own, New York, 1932.
Where the Cobra Sings, New York, 1932.
4 Wives, New York, 1932.
Yearly Lease, New York, 1932.
A Laughing Woman, New York, 1933.
This Fool, Passion, New York, 1934.

By LEWTON: other books—

Panther Skin and Grapes (verse), London, 1923.
The Green Flag of Jehad (nonfiction), New York, 1926.
The Rogue Song (novelization of screenplay), New York, 1930.
Rasputin and the Empress (novelization of screenplay), New York, 1933.

On LEWTON: books—

Siegel, Joel, *Val Lewton: The Reality of Terror*, London, 1972.
Telotte, J.P., *Dreams of Darkness: Fantasy and the Films of Val Lewton*, Urbana, Illinois, 1985.
Bansak, Edmund G., *Fearing the Dark: The Val Lewton Career*, Jefferson, North Carolina, 1995.

On LEWTON: articles—

Sight and Sound (London), May 1951.
Bodeen, DeWitt, in *Films in Review* (New York), April 1963.
Sight and Sound (London), Winter 1965–66.
Cinema (Los Angeles), March 1966.
Photon (New York), no. 1, 1969.
Films in Review (New York), March 1970.
Focus on Film (London), Winter 1972.
National Film Theatre booklet (London), July-September 1973.

Action (Los Angeles), January-February 1976.

Monthly Film Bulletin (London), July 1981.

Literature/Film Quarterly (Salisbury, Maryland), vol. 10, no. 1, 1982.

Post Script (Jacksonville, Florida), Winter 1982.

American Classic Screen (Shawnee Mission, Kansas), May-June 1983.

Cinématographe (Paris), May 1984.

Filmcritica (Florence), vol. 35, no. 348–349, October-November 1984.

Classic Images (Indiana, Pennsylvania), January 1985.

In *Aspects of Fantasy*, edited by William Coyle, Westport, Connecticut, 1986.

In *Forms of the Fantastic*, edited by Jan Hokenson and Howard Pearce, Westport, Connecticut, 1986.

Cineforum, vol. 31, no. 304, 1991.

Midnight Marquee, no. 44, Summer 1992.

Washington Post, section D, 30 January 1993.

New York Times, section C, 2 July 1993.

Village Voice, vol. 38, 6 July 1993.

Saada, Nicolas, "Universal Contre RKO," in *Cahiers du Cinéma* (Paris), April 1994.

Brunas, M., "The Cat Behind the Door!" in *Scarlet Street* (Glen Rock), Fall 1995.

Fischer, D., in *Cinefantastique* (Forest Park), no. 6, 1996.

Ambrogio, A., "What if *The Uninvited* Had Haunted Universal or RKO?" in *Midnight Marquee* (Baltimore), Spring 1997.

Newman, Kim, "Bring Back the Cat: *Cat People*," in *Sight and Sound* (London), November 1999.

* * *

A minor novelist and story editor for David O. Selznick, Val Lewton joined RKO Studios in 1942 to form a "horror" unit, producing low-budget films to compete with Universal's successful monster series. Gathering about him young but talented directors like Jacques Tourneur, Mark Robson, and Robert Wise, and writers like DeWitt Bodeen and Ardel Wray, Lewton put together a production group that turned out a string of critically acclaimed and financially successful films between 1942 and 1946. More than simply the producer for this group, Lewton served as a kind of creative centerpiece, overseeing every project, and contributing his considerable skills as a writer and judge of what is cinematic.

While forced to work within a number of severe limitations, Lewton did find substantial room for creativity within the horror/fantasy format. The budgets for his films typically ran to $150,000 and the shooting schedules to approximately 28 days. Whenever possible, standing sets were used and RKO contract players employed. And since the films were slated for double bills, running time seldom exceeded 75 minutes. Given these conditions, along with studio-assigned, audience-tested titles, Lewton and his coworkers were generally free of front-office interference in the design and shooting of their films. Thus when faced with an assigned title like *I Walked with a Zombie*, they could essentially discard the original magazine piece on which the film was to be based and instead adapt *Jane Eyre* to a West Indies setting, or even create a thoughtful study of childhood anxiety and fantasy out of *The Curse of the Cat People*. That such creative developments were largely Lewton's own doing is attested to by his coworkers on the horror unit. Not only did he often initiate specific projects, but, as his secretary notes, for each screenplay "the last draft was always his."

What is probably most distinctive about the nine fantasy films and two melodramas Lewton produced between 1942 and 1946, though,

is their visual style. While most horror films of the period, and especially the Universal series, emphasized horrific *appearances*—wolfmen and Frankenstein monsters in exotic locales—Lewton's productions capitalized on limitation by employing suggestion, leaving portions of every shot in shadow and inviting viewers to populate the screen with whatever terrors they might imagine. As he described his guiding strategy, "If you make the screen dark enough, the mind's eye will read anything into it you want! We're great ones for dark patches." Through the strategic placement of shadows and sharp editing, viewers could thus be primed to expect an attacking panther in *Cat People*, even though nothing more than a bus appears, or to interpret a tumbleweed as a leopard in *The Leopard Man*.

This emphasis on "dark patches" represents more than just a stylistic trait, though. It points to Lewton's consistent concern with how we see and understand the world around us. Throughout the Lewton films, after all, there are characters who suffer, or cause suffering for others, because they have such a narrow perspective, one determined by their rational biases or, as with *Cat People*'s protagonist, their superstitious beliefs—in effect, because of certain "dark patches" within their psyches. What Lewton apparently realized is that the greatest terrors are not necessarily in our environment, but in the mind, which in turn represses our fears or projects them onto others, thereby filling the surrounding world with horrors of our own devising. Thus the play of shadows, of light and dark in these films is not simply atmospheric. If monsters do show up in them, they take in their true shape from a basic human inability to dispel the darkness inside us, or from our failure to accept those ambiguities that characterize the human world. For this reason, the Lewton films often employ unlikely, even unconventional, threatening figures, such as an anthropologist in *The Leopard Man* and a doctor in *The Body Snatcher*. Such figures of authority gone mad underscore the very fragile nature of the world we construct for ourselves.

Removed from this fantasy formula and paired with less talented directors, Lewton was not as successful. After leaving RKO to work as an independent writer and producer, he turned out only three films, none of which earned the critical praise of his earlier movies. It is that early work, and particularly the fantasy films, that would influence filmmakers like Alfred Hitchcock and Brian De Palma, and would prompt James Agee to praise the "gentle, pleasing, resourceful kind of talent" that Lewton brought to the movie industry.

—J. P. Telotte

LHOMME, Pierre

Cinematographer. **Nationality:** French. **Born:** Boulogne-sur-Seine, 5 April 1930. **Education:** French public school through lycée; studied at the École Normale des Ponts et des Chaussées (technical school for civil engineering). **Career:** Worked as an assistant cameraman; 1961—works on *Saint Tropez Blues*; 1963—receives acclaim for his work on *Le Joli mai*; 1990—receives critical acclaim for his work on *Cyrano de Bergerac*. **Awards:** Cannes Film Festival, Technical Grand Prize, for *Cyrano de Bergerac*, 1990; French Academy of Film Arts Award, Best Cinematography, for *Cyrano de Bergerac*, 1991; British Society of Cinematographers, Best Cinematography Award, for *Cyrano de Bergerac*, 1992; British Academy of Film and Television Award, Best Cinematography, for *Cyrano de Bergerac*, 1992.

Films as Cinematographer:

1961   *Saint Tropez Blues* (Moussy); *Le Combat dans l'île* (Cavalier, Malle)

1963   *Le Joli mai* (Marker)

1965   *La Vie de château* (*Gracious Living*) (Rappeneau); *Le Mistral* (Ivens)

1966   *Le Roi de coeur* (de Broca)

1967   *Mise à sac* (Cavalier); *Coplan sauve sa peau* (*Devil's Garden*) (Boisset); *Le Plus vieux métier du monde* (*The Oldest Profession in the World*) (Autant-Lara, Bolognini)

1968   *À bientôt j'espère* (Marker); *Le Dernier homme* (*The Last Man*) (Bitsch); *La Chamade* (Cavalier)

1969   *La Coqueluche* (Arrighi); *L'Armée des ombres* (*Army In the Shadows*) (Melville); *Mister Freedom* (Klein)

1971   *La Vieille fille* (Blance); *Someone Behind the Door* (Gessner); *Quatre nuits d'un rêveur* (*Four Nights of a Dreamer*) (Bresson)

1973   *La Maman et la putain* (*The Mother and the Whore*) (Eustache); *Je sais rien mais je dirai tout* (Richard); *Le Sex Shop* (Berri)

1974   *Sweet Movie* (Makavejev); *La Solitude du chanteur de fond* (*The Loneliness of the Long Distance Singer*) (Marker); *La Chair de l'orchidée* (*Flesh of the Orchid*) (Chéreau)

1975   *Le Sauvage* (*The Savage*) (Rappeneau); *Die Große Ekstase* (Berry)

1977   *Une sale histoire* (Eustache); *Les Enfants du placard* (Jacquot); *Dîtes-lui que je l'aime* (*This Sweet Sickness*) (Miller)

1978   *L'État sauvage* (*The Savage State*) (Girod); *Judith Therpauve* (Chéreau)

1979   *Retour à la bien-aimée* (Adam)

1981   *Tout feu, tout flamme* (*All Fired Up*) (Rappeneau); *Quartet* (Ivory)

1983   *Mortelle randonnée* (*Deadly Run*) (Miller); *Le Grand carnaval* (Arcady)

1985   *Urgence* (Behrat)

1986   *My Little Girl* (Kaisernan); *Champagne amer* (*Secret Obsession*) (Behi, Vart)

1987   *Maurice* (Ivory)

1988   *Baptême* (Feret); *Camille Claudel* (Nuytten)

1990   *Cyrano de Bergerac* (Rappeneau)

1991   *Homo Faber* (*Voyager*) (Shclöndorff)

1992   *Promenades d'été* (*Summer Strolls*) (Feret)

1993   *Toxic Affair* (Esposito)

1994   *Dieu que les femmes sont amoureuses* (*Oh God, Women Are So Loving*) (Clément)

1995   *Jefferson in Paris* (Ivory)

1996   *Mon homme* (*My Man*) (Blier); *Anna Oz* (Rochant)

1997   *Les Palmes de M. Schutz* (Pinoteau)

1998   *Voleur de vie* (*Stolen Life*) (Angelo)

1999   *Cotton Mary* (Merchant)

*   *   *

Although he remains virtually unknown and although he has escaped critical attention, cinematographer Pierre Lhomme has had a long and distinguished career, working with some of the most highly acclaimed directors and filmmakers of the modern era, including Jean-Pierre Melville, Robert Bresson, and Volker Schlöndorff. Lhomme worked on *Saint Tropez Blues* in 1961, but his first landmark film was Chris Marker's *Le Joli mai*, filmed in 1963. This film, a presentation of Paris in the early 1960s, is a documentary which captures the pulse of an international capital in the throes of (post)modernization. Lhomme's cinematography focuses on the people, the action, the movement of the time, and gives the film the high-realism necessary for such a socially real motion picture. The collaboration between Lhomme and Marker was such a success that the two worked together again on Marker's 1968 film, *À bientôt j'espère* and his 1974 film, *La Solitude du chanteur de fond* (*The Loneliness of the Long Distance Singer*).

Apart from his early work with Marker, Lhomme has also cultivated two other long-standing collaborative relationships, the first with French filmmaker Jean-Paul Rappeneau, and the second with Ismaël Merchant and James Ivory. Lhomme first worked with Rappeneau in 1965 on the film *La Vie de château* (*Gracious Living*), a comedy set during the German occupation of France. Subsequently, the two collaborated on *Le Sauvage* (*The Savage*) in 1975, and *Tout feu, tout flamme* (*All Fired Up*) in 1981. By far the most well known and most acclaimed film produced by the team Rappeneau-Lhomme, however, was 1990s *Cyrano de Bergerac*, an adaption of Rostand's play by the same name. With *Cyrano*, Lhomme reveals his expert ability to film historical drama. The camera in Cyrano captures all of the detail worked into the setting and costume of the film—the details of fabric, the dim, interior lighting, the grit and grime of battle. There is also a concentrated use of close-up, which serves to remind the viewer that this film was based upon a play. The closely framed shots of Cyrano, Roxanne, and others replicate the more intimate viewing experience of the theater, while the panoramics point to the specific possibilities of cinema. Lhomme's work on *Cyrano* earned him several prestigious awards, including a César and a BAFTA award. To date, it remains his most critically acclaimed piece of work.

Lhomme's work with Merchant and Ivory dates to his work on the 1981 film *Quartet*. This film also reveals Lhomme's talent for historical drama. Here the setting is 1920s Paris, and the details of the period are richly captured in Lhomme's shots of smoky nightclubs and upper middle class apartments. Lhomme has gone on to make three other films with Merchant and Ivory, including *Maurice* (1987), *Jefferson in Paris* (1995), and *Cotton Mary* (1999). All three, also historical dramas, illustrate Lhomme's attention to detail in his filming of costume and setting, and his talent for recreating the ambiance of any particular country at any particular moment in time.

In addition to such collaborative endeavors, Lhomme has contributed to the work of other directors with whom he has worked only once. His cinematography in Robert Bresson's 1971 film, *Quatre nuits d'un rêveur* (*Four Nights of a Dreamer*) for example, adequately captures the sober, ascetic, almost dream-like hyper-realism so characteristic of Bresson's work. The film, based on a short story by Dostoyevsky, recounts four days in the life of a young man and his encounter with a young woman on a bridge. Bresson turns the story into a meditation on youth, and Lhomme contributes to this an elegant simplicity that focuses the spectator on the act of looking—looking at youth, looking at life.

Another particularly good example of Lhomme's ability to capture light, emotion, and the feel of an age is his work on Bruno Nuytten's *Camille Claudel* (1988). The film, based on the life of sculptor Camille Claudel, is striking for its whiteness, the white of plaster cast, of Parisian sunlight, of canvas, and Lhomme's camera work emphasizes this whiteness without blinding the spectator. Furthermore, his presentation of Isabelle Adjani in the role of Camille works to show the torment and emotion of the volatile female artist, trapped in a man's world.

Lhomme's films span several eras of modern filmmaking, from the New Wave to the Postmodern, from documentary to comedy to drama. The fact that he has worked on so many films, and with so many renowned filmmakers is, perhaps, an even greater testament to his talent as a cinematographer than the awards he has received.

—Dayna Oscherwitz

LITTLETON, Carol

Editor. **Nationality:** American. **Born:** Oklahoma, c.1948. **Education:** Attended University of Oklahoma. **Family:** Married the cinematographer John Bailey. **Career:** 1972–77—owned company which made commercial ad spots; 1977—began as editor with director Karen Arthur on *Legacy*, followed by Arthur's *The Mafu Cage* in 1978 before her first major commercial release with 1979's *French Postcards*; 1982—Oscar nomination for editing Steven Spielberg's *E.T.—The Extraterrestrial*; 1987—elected president of Editors Guild Local 776 (West Coast).

Films as Editor:

1977 *Legacy* (Arthur)
1978 *The Mafu Cage (My Sister, My Love)* (Arthur)
1979 *French Postcards* (Huyck)
1980 *Roadie* (Rudolph)
1981 *Body Heat* (Kasdan)
1982 ***E.T.—The Extraterrestrial*** (Spielberg)
1983 *The Big Chill* (Kasdan)
1984 *Places in the Heart* (Benton)
1985 *Silverado* (Kasdan)
1986 *Brighton Beach Memoirs* (Saks)
1987 *Swimming to Cambodia* (Demme)
1988 *Vibes* (Kwapis); *The Accidental Tourist* (Kasdan)
1990 *White Palace* (Mandoki)
1991 *The Search for Signs of Intelligent Life in the Universe* (Bailey); *Grand Canyon* (Kasdan)
1993 *Benny & Joon* (Chechik)
1994 *China Moon* (Bailey) (co); *Wyatt Earp* (Kasdan)
1996 *Diabolique* (Chechik)
1998 *Twilight* (Benton); *Beloved* (Jonathan Demme)
1999 *Mumford* (Kasdan); *Tuesdays with Morrie* (Mick Jackson—for TV)

Publications

On LITTLETON: books—

Oldham, Gabriella, *First Cut: Conversations with Film Editors*, 1992.

On LITTLETON: articles—

"Close-ups: Off-Screen Romance," in *Millimeter*, February 1986.
"The Art of Light and Rhythm," in *American Cinematographer* (Hollywood), May 1987.

Travers, Peter, "Twilight," *Rolling Stone*, March 1997.
Van Schaick, A., "Women on the Cutting Edge," in *Moviemaker* (Pasadena), May/June/July 1997.

*   *   *

Editor Carol Littleton's music training is evident in the lyrical images that open *Places in the Heart*. Pictures of people populating a dustbowl town during the Great Depression may epitomize her work, a gentle evocation of humanity undergoing some emotionally trying struggle of common rather than Herculean tests.

Her greatest achievements in structuring film images seem to fall into quiet, understated imagery. Even with the fantastical elements of *E.T.*, for which she received an Academy Award nomination for her editing, Littleton emphasized the simple magic of the friendship between the boy, Elliott, and his alien visitor in a manner suitable to François Truffaut. While it may have been an unlikely approach to science-fiction fantasy, it surely had much to do with why audiences responded to the fable. Even hardened audiences warmed to this sentimental and charming story.

With frequent collaborator Lawrence Kasdan, Littleton has helped bring warmth to *The Accidental Tourist* and the entertaining *The Big Chill*, two of his successes. The stylish *Body Heat*, revisiting Hollywood's film noir, brought imitation after imitation, perhaps including Littleton's own collaboration with her husband, cinematographer John Bailey, in his foray as director with *China Moon*. Kasdan and Littleton also worked together on two Westerns, *Silverado* and *Wyatt Earp*, the former a superficial homage to childhood oaters and the latter windy, dry, and far too long.

Littleton has said that simplicity is the key and that, while many editors have great technical knowledge, those that "can make a film purely emotional at the same time" are rarer. And in fact Littleton's best work seems simple on the surface but has an underlying emotional core that strikes a real note for audiences. Friendship could be said to be at the heart of *E.T.*, *Places in the Heart*, and most of her work with director Kasdan and this is some of her most successful work artistically.

Even in the less-pleasing films Littleton has edited, such as *Vibes*, *Brighton Beach Memoirs* and the remake of *Diabolique*, critics take note of the assistance that she has given the work. The film may not be good, but Littleton as editor has helped make it a little better.

The editor's role is unspecific and anonymous, according to Littleton; it is much like that of a symphony conductor who pulls diverse elements together in an attempt to make a cohesive whole. Her best work seems to emphasize affection and humanity that is clearly heartfelt.

—Allen Grant Richards

LOEW, Marcus

Executive. **Nationality:** American. **Born:** New York City, 7 May 1870. **Education:** Left school at age six to sell newspapers. **Family:** Married Caroline, 1894; twin sons: David and Arthur. **Career:** Worked as a salesman and a furrier; formed People's Vaudeville Company to produce variety shows in New York City and environs,

Marcus Loew

1904; founded Loew's Theatrical Enterprises, New York City, 1910, which is reorganized as Loew's, Inc., 1919; acquired Metro Pictures Corporation, Hollywood, 1919; opened 3500-seat flagship Loew's State Theater in Times Square, New York City, 1921; acquired Goldwyn Pictures Corporation and Louis B. Mayer Productions, 1924, which are merged with Metro to create Metro-Goldwyn-Mayer (MGM); retired, 1926. **Died:** In Long Island, New York, 5 September 1927.

Publications

On LOEW: books—

Irwin, Will, *The House that Shadows Built: The Story of Adolph Zukor and His Circle*, Garden City, New York, 1928.
Crowther, Bosley, *The Lion's Share: The Story of an Entertainment Empire*, New York, 1957.
Sobel, Robert, *The Entrepreneurs: Explorations within the American Business Tradition*, New York, 1974.
Gomery, Douglas, *The Hollywood Studio System*, New York, 1986.
Gabler, Neal, *An Empire of Their Own: How the Jews Invented Hollywood*, New York, 1988.
Schatz, Thomas, *The Genius of the System*, New York, 1988.
Hay, Peter, with Woolsey Ackerman, *MGM-When the Lion Roars*, Atlanta, 1991.

*   *   *

Executive Marcus Loew was the founder of Loew's, Inc., a huge entertainment company which grew from a New York City theater circuit presenting vaudeville and early moving pictures into one of Hollywood's most successful integrated film corporations. Metro-Goldwyn-Mayer, the grandest of studios during Hollywood's Golden Age, was in reality only the production arm of this powerful firm. Like all vintage Hollywood businesses, Loew's, Inc. was an oligopoly which produced, distributed, and exhibited movies during what is now known as Hollywood's studio era, a period running roughly from the silent era of the 1920s through the 1950s.

Like the other major film corporations of the era, Loew's was also a bi-coastal enterprise in which the Hollywood production (or "creative") branch was carefully monitored and financially controlled by the New York/east coast executive branch. As the president of Loew's, Inc., Marcus Loew himself was never actively involved in the making of motion pictures, but instead hired and supervised film creators from the company's corporate offices in New York City. At the same time, he built up a nationwide chain of theaters which were as essential a part of this interlocking system as the studio production unit. Loew never lived in Hollywood, preferring instead to reside in his palatial mansion by the sea in Glen Cove, Long Island.

Loew was born to emigrant parents on Manhattan's Lower East Side in 1870. His father was a Viennese waiter, and his mother a German widow. Like many future moguls, Loew had an impoverished childhood, and quit school to work while still a young child. After a variety of unsuccessful pursuits, primarily in the garment industry, Loew developed a relationship with another future mogul, Adolph Zukor, whom he had met during an unsuccessful stint in the fur trade. Zukor, a Jewish emigrant from a small village in Hungary, would later build Paramount Pictures, and it was through him that Marcus Loew first became involved in the entertainment business, investing in several Zukor ventures, including several lucrative penny arcades in New York City.

With an actor friend, David Warfield, Loew formed his own People's Vaudeville Company in 1904. People's first venture was a Manhattan amusement arcade, and within months they opened four more in New York City, with a fifth in Cincinnati, Ohio. While in Cincinnati, Loew witnessed an early exhibition of moving pictures, and was impressed by the audiences it attracted. He installed a 110-seat theater above his Penny Hippodrome in Cincinnati, which opened to huge crowds. Loew soon converted all of his arcades into theaters which offered affordable variety shows of vaudeville and early moving pictures. Gradually expanding his business in New York and environs, Loew was finally established in the entertainment industry.

By 1910 Loew's theatrical empire had expanded along the east coast, and Loew's Consolidated Entertainment was incorporated with one of Loew's early managers, Nicholas Schenck, as secretary-treasurer. With World War I, the focus of the American entertainment business shifted from vaudeville to movies. Loew's Consolidated was still geared only for motion picutre exhibition, and Loew only gradually realized that like the other integrated majors (such as Famous Players-Lassky and First National), he needed to expand into the production and distribution of films. In 1919 Loew purchased Metro Pictures Corporation, which had been formed in 1915 to produce and market the films of five small Hollywood production companies. The acquisition motivated the birth of the new and reorganized Loew's, Inc., which moved Loew into the motion picture business in earnest. In 1921 Metro's *The Four Horsemen of the Apocalypse*, starring Rudolph Valentino, became a huge hit.

In 1924 Loew's further expanded his Hollywood empire by acquiring the foundering Goldwyn Pictures Corporation and Louis B. Mayer Productions. This key deal included the large Goldwyn studios in Culver City, and a supervisory production team which included Mayer himself and the 24-year-old Hollywood production wonderboy, Irving G. Thalberg. Thus a new and major Loew's subsidiary, Metro-Goldwyn-Mayer (MGM), was created on May 17, 1924. With Goldwyn Pictures had come a small chain of theaters, including another Times Square property, the Capitol, but the prime incentive was the Goldwyn production facility itself. The Culver City studio had been built around 1915 as Triangle Pictures by pioneering film-maker Thomas Ince and included 45 acres of self-contained production facilities. As MGM this complex of soundstages and backlots would expand throughout the next two decades into one of the greatest and most lavish production units of the studio era.

But Loew would not live to see the great organization he created expand to its full potential. Loew died in 1927, a year after the release of the second of his company's hits, the silent version of *Ben Hur*, and two years after MGM's first major production, King Vidor's *The Big Parade*, had grossed over $5 million. Loew was the first of the pioneering moguls to pass away, and one of the most respected and well-loved in this early phase of the industry. He left behind an estate estimated at over $30 million.

Loew's, Inc., and MGM persisted as major players in the history of American film after Loew's death. Nicholas Schenck succeeded Loew as president of the company from 1927 to 1955. A short-lived merger instigated by William Fox created Fox-Loew's from 1928 until 1930, but the largest entertainment conglomerate up to that point in history was soon broken up by early government anti-trust action. In Hollywood, Mayer and Thalberg honed MGM into the most financially and artistically successful studio of the Great Depression, while Schenck and Mayer continued to supervise production into the 1950s. Loew's son, Arthur, supervised the company's extensive overseas expansion, and acted as president for one year in 1955 after Schenck's retirement. After the monopolistic production/exhibition system was finally disbanded by government trust busting in the late 1940s and most of Loew's theaters were razed, MGM like the other troubled Hollywood studios survived into the 1960s with varying degrees of success. In 1969 Loew's sold off its famous Culver City MGM backlots, and the artifacts of Loew's most famous creation went on the auction block. What remains of the original MGM studio is now Sony Pictures, and Loew's west coast flagship theater, Loew's State, still stands on Broadway in the historic but now sadly decaying old downtown of Los Angeles. .

—Ross Care

LOOS, Anita

Writer and Producer. **Nationality:** American. **Born:** Corinne Anita Loos in Sissons (now Mount Shasta), California, 26 April 1888. **Education:** Attended schools in San Francisco and San Diego. **Family:** Married 1) Frank Pallma, Jr., 1915 (divorced 1915); 2) the director and writer John Emerson, 1920 (died 1956); one adopted daughter. **Career:** Child actress briefly; 1912—first film as writer, *The New York Hat*, followed by a large number of films for D.W. Griffith; 1916—collaborator with Emerson, and coproducer with

Anita Loos

Emerson from 1919; 1925—published the novel *Gentlemen Prefer Blondes* (play version, 1926, film version, 1928); other plays include *The Whole Town's Talking*, *The Fall of Eve*, *The Social Register*, *Happy Birthday*, *Gigi*, *The Amazing Adèle*, *Chéri*, *Gogo Love You*; 1963—one-woman show, *An Evening of Theatrical Reminiscences*. **Died:** In New York City, 18 August 1981.

Films as Writer:

1912 *The New York Hat* (Griffith)

1913 *The Power of the Camera*; *The Telephone Girl and the Lady* (Griffith—short); *A Horse on Bill* (Powell); *The Hicksville Epicure* (Henderson); *Highbrow Love* (O'Sullivan); *Pa Says* (Powell); *The Widow's Kids* (Powell); *The Lady in Black*; *His Hoodoo* (Powell); *A Fallen Hero* (Powell); *A Cure for Suffragettes* (Kirkwood); *The Suicide Pact* (Powell); *Bink's Vacation* (*Bink Runs Away*); *How the Day Was Saved* (Powell); *The Wedding Gown* (Powell); *Gentleman or Thief*; *For Her Father's Sins* (O'Brien); *A Narrow Escape*; *The Mother*; *The Lady and the Mouse* (short); *The Mistake* (short)

1914 *Hickville's Finest*; *His Awful Vengeance*; *The Saving Grace* (Cabanne); *A Bunch of Flowers*; *When a Woman Guides*; *The Road to Plaindale*; *The Saving Presence*; *The Meal Ticket*; *The Suffering of Susan*; *Nearly a Burglar's Bride*; *Some Bull's Daughter*; *The Fatal Dress Suit*; *The Girl in the Shack*; *The Stolen Masterpiece* (Pollard); *A Corner in Hats*;

The Million Dollar Bride; *A Flurry in Art*; *Billy's Rival (Izzy and His Rival)* (Taylor—short); *The Last Drink of Whiskey* (Dillon); *Nell's Eugenic Wedding*; *The White Slave Catchers*; *The Deceiver* (Dillon); *How to Keep a Husband*; *The Gangsters of New York* (short); *The Hunchback*; *A Lesson in Mechanics*

1915   *The Deacon's Whiskers* (Dillon); *The Tear on the Page*; *Pennington's Choice* (Lund); *Sympathy Sal*; *Mixed Values* (Dillon); *The Fatal Finger Prints* (Dillon); *Lord Chumley*; *The Sisters* (short); *A Ten-Cent Adventure* (short); *When the Road Parts* (short); *Double Trouble*; *The Lost House*

1916   *The Little Liar* (Ingraham); *A Corner in Cotton* (Balshofer); **Intolerance** (Griffith); *Macbeth* (Emerson); *Stranded* (Ingraham); *Wild Girl of the Sierras* (Powell); *A Calico Vampire*; *Laundry Liz*; *The French Milliner*; *The Wharf Rat* (Withey); *The Half-Breed* (Dwan); *American Aristocracy* (Ingraham); *A Daughter of the Poor*

1917   *Wild and Woolly* (Emerson); *Down to Earth* (Emerson); *The Deadly Glass of Beer*

1927   *Stranded* (Rosen); *Publicity Madness* (Ray)

1932   *Red-Headed Woman* (Conway); *Blondie of the Follies* (Goulding)

1933   *The Barbarian* (Wood); *Hold Your Man* (Wood); *Midnight Mary* (Wellman)

1934   *Biography of a Bachelor Girl* (E. Griffith); *The Merry Widow* (uncredited)

1936   *Riffraff* (Rubin); *San Francisco* (Van Dyke)

1937   *Mama Steps Out* (Seita); *Saratoga* (Conway)

1939   **The Women** (Cukor)

1940   *Susan and God (The Gay Mrs. Trexel)* (Cukor)

1941   *They Met in Bombay* (Brown); *Blossoms in the Dust* (LeRoy); *When Ladies Meet* (Leonard)

1942   *I Married an Angel* (Van Dyke)

Films as Cowriter with John Emerson:

1916   *His Picture in the Papers* (Emerson); *Manhattan Madness* (Powell); *The Matrimaniac* (Powell); *The Social Secretary* (Emerson)

1917   *In Again, Out Again* (Emerson); *Reaching for the Moon* (Emerson); *The Americano* (Emerson)

1918   *Let's Get a Divorce* (Giblyn); *Hit-the-Trail Holliday* (Neilan); *Come On In* (Emerson); *Good-bye-Bill* (Emerson)

1919   *Oh, You Women!* (Emerson); *The Isle of Conquest* (Jose); *Under the Top* (Crisp); *Getting Mary Married* (Dwan) (+ co-pr); *A Temperamental Wife* (Emerson) (+ co-pr); *A Virtuous Vamp* (Kirkland) (+ co-pr)

1920   *In Search of a Sinner* (Kirkland) (+ co-pr); *The Perfect Woman* (Kirkland); *The Love Expert* (Kirkland); *Two Weeks* (Franklin); *The Branded Woman* (Parker)

1921   *Dangerous Business* (Neill); *Mama's Affair* (Fleming); *A Woman's Place* (Fleming)

1922   *Polly of the Follies* (Emerson); *Red Hot Romance* (Fleming) (+ co-pr)

1923   *Dulcy* (Franklin)

1924   *Three Miles Out* (Willat)

1925   *Learning to Love* (Franklin)

1928   *Gentlemen Prefer Blondes* (St. Clair)

1929   *The Fall of Eve* (Strayer)

1931   *The Struggle* (Griffith)

1934   *The Girl from Missouri* (Conway)

Films based on Loos's Writings:

1926   *The Whole Town's Talking* (Edward Laemmle)

1931   *Ex-Bad Boy* (Moore)

1934   *The Social Register* (Neilan)

1953   *Gentlemen Prefer Blondes* (Hawks)

1955   *Gentlemen Marry Brunettes* (Sale)

Publications

By LOOS: fiction—

Gentlemen Prefer Blondes, New York, 1925 (play version, with John Emerson, New York, 1926).
But Gentlemen Marry Brunettes, New York, 1928.
A Mouse Is Born, New York, 1951.
No Mother to Guide Her, New York, 1961.

By LOOS: other books—

With John Emerson, *How to Write Photoplays* (includes script *The Love Expert*), New York, 1920.
With John Emerson, *Breaking into the Movies* (includes script *Red Hot Romance*), New York, 1921.
With John Emerson, *The Whole Town's Talking* (play), New York, 1925.
With Jane Murfin, *The Women* (script), in *Twenty Best Film Plays*, edited by John Gassner and Dudley Nichols, New York, 1943.
Happy Birthday (play), New York, 1947.
Gigi (play), New York, 1952.
With D.W. Griffith, *Intolerance* (script), New York, 1955.
A Girl Like I (autobiography), New York, 1966.
The King's Mare (play), London, 1967.
With Helen Hayes, *Twice over Lightly: New York Then and Now*, New York, 1972.
Kiss Hollywood Good-by, New York, 1974.
Cast of Thousands, New York, 1977.
The Talmadge Girls: A Memoir, New York, 1978.
San Francisco (script), edited by Matthew J. Bruccoli, Carbondale, Illinois, 1979.
Fate Keeps on Happening: Adventures of Lorelei Lee and Other Writings, edited by Ray P. Corsini, New York, 1984.

By LOOS: articles—

Close Up (London), April 1928.
Inter/View (New York), July 1972.

On LOOS: book—

Casey, Gary, *Anita Loos: A Biography*, New York, 1988.
Douglas, George H., *Women of the Twenties*, Dallas, 1989.

On LOOS: articles—

Schmidt, Karl, "The Handwriting on the Screen," in *Everybody's* (New York), May 1917.
Carey, Gary, in *The Hollywood Screenwriter*, edited by Richard Corliss, New York, 1972.
Cinema (Beverly Hills), no. 35, 1976.
Quarterly Journal of the Library of Congress (Washington, D.C.), Summer-Fall 1980.
Grant, Thomas, in *American Humorists 1800–1950*, edited by Stanley Trachtenberg, Detroit, Michigan, 1982.
Obituary, *The Annual Obituary 1981*, New York, 1982.
Yeck, Joanne, in *American Screenwriters*, edited by Robert E. Morsberger, Stephen O. Lesser, and Randall Clark, Detroit, Michigan, 1984.
Goldhurst, W. "Regeneration Through Disaster: San Francisco," in *Post Script* (Commerce), Winter 1985.
Film Dope (Nottingham), February 1987.
McCreadie, Marsha, "Pioneers (Part Two)," in *Films in Review* (New York), January-February 1995.
Lutes, Jean Marie, "Authoring *Gentlemen Prefer Blondes*: Mass-market Beauty Culture and the Makeup of Writers (Anita Loos' International Bestseller *Gentlemen Prefer Blondes*)," in *Prospects*, vol. 23, Annual 1998.

* * *

At the early age of 16, Anita Loos began her career in films by scripting over 100 scenarios for D.W. Griffith's Biograph Company. She is credited with writing the subtitles for *Intolerance* (1916), and is regarded as one of the first screenwriters to employ intertitles to silent films. Although she wrote serious plots for silent films (*Wild Girl of the Sierras* and *Stranded*), her early success came as a satirist of everyday events. Indeed, her original use of intertitles provided her with the opportunity to let loose with her wise-cracks that teased the picture. She was also proficient in slapstick comedy and wrote a number of half-reels featuring the Keystone Kops.

It was Loos, with her husband the director John Emerson (who assumed much of the credit for her creative endeavors) who first realized that Douglas Fairbanks's acrobatics were an extension of his effervescent personality. Loos, Emerson, and Fairbanks worked as a unit in Griffith's company and parlayed Fairbanks's natural athletic ability into swashbuckling adventure roles. Never missing a chance for satire, Loos (the "O'Henrietta of the Screen") parodied not only the *nouveau riche* American industrialist but also Fairbanks's own star persona in *American Aristocracy*. The scenario for the film is typical of Loos's humor: Fairbanks foils a buccaneer who is sending powder to Mexico in the guise of malted milk and as the result of his adventurous exploits wins the heart of a hatpin king's daughter. In pursuit of the villain, Fairbanks vaults a dozen walls and fences. He readies himself to leap at a window ten feet above the ground when he suddenly decides to take the easy way out and opens a basement window, climbing in the building like an ordinary mortal. Loos wrote other humorous films which firmly established Fairbanks as a major leading man of the American screen. Americans' love of publicity was ridiculed in *His Picture in the Papers* and pacifics was satirized in *In Again, Out Again*.

Loos left the Griffith studio in 1925 and moved east with her husband. During her brief "retirement" from the film colony, she wrote the durable story of Lorelei Lee, *Gentlemen Prefer Blondes*.

The story was quite successful as a novel, broadway musical, and film. Loos and Herman J. Mankiewicz cowrote the intertitles for the original silent film version directed by Mal St. Clair in 1928. Howard Hawks's *Gentlemen Prefer Blondes* (1953) was an adaptation of the stage play and featured Marilyn Monroe as Lorelei and Jane Russell as her dark-haired girlfriend. Through the perils of Lorelei, the amoral and dim-witted young blond from Little Rock, Loos poked fun at male-female relationships. The blonde's flirtations and the gullible millionaires who surrounded her provided Loos with rich material gleefully to expose the merchandising of sexuality.

Loos returned to Hollywood and worked for MGM during the Irving Thalberg reign. She took over the writing duties from F. Scott Fitzgerald on the Harlow vehicle *Red-Headed Woman*. She also wrote *Hold Your Man* starring Harlow and Clark Gable. Gable, Jeanette MacDonald, and Spencer Tracy were featured in the Loos script for *San Francisco*. This large-scale Hollywood soap opera evolved around San Francisco at the time of the great earthquake. Loos and the veteran MGM scriptwriter Jane Murfin adapted Clare Booth Luce's venomous comedy *The Women* to the screen; it featured an all-woman cast including Norma Shearer, Rosalind Russell, Paulette Goddard, and Joan Crawford.

—Doreen Bartoni

LOQUASTO, Santo

Production Designer and Costume Designer. **Nationality:** American. **Born:** Wilkes-Barre, Pennsylvania, 26 July 1944. **Education:** Received B.A. from King's College in Pennsylvania; attended Yale School of Drama, majoring in design, 1969. **Career:** Worked in regional theater, late 1960s; worked as set designer for Broadway and off-Broadway productions, 1970 to the present; worked as set designer for opera, including the San Diego Opera, Opera Society of Washington, and San Francisco Spring Opera, 1970s; worked as costume and set designer for contemporary choreographers such as Mark Morris, Twyla Tharp, and Paul Taylor, 1970s-80s; began working as a costume designer and production designer for films, 1975. **Awards:** Tony Award for Costume Design, for *The Cherry Orchard*, 1977; Best Production Design British Academy Award, for *Radio Days*, 1987; Tony Award for Costume Design, for *Grand Hotel*, 1990.

Films as Costume Designer:

1978　*Sammy Stops the World* (Shapiro)
1980　*Simon* (Brickman); *Stardust Memories* (W. Allen)
1982　*A Midsummer's Night Sex Comedy* (W. Allen)
1983　*Zelig* (W. Allen)
1985　*Desperately Seeking Susan* (Seidelman)

Films as Production Designer:

1975　*Rancho Deluxe* (Perry)
1981　*The Fan* (Bianchi); *So Fine* (A. Bergman)
1984　*Falling in Love* (Grosbard)
1985　*Desperately Seeking Susan* (S. Seidelman) (+ costume designer)
1987　*Radio Days* (W. Allen); *September* (W. Allen)

1988	*Big* (P. Marshall); *Bright Lights, Big City* (J. Bridges); *Another Woman* (W. Allen)
1989	''Oedipus Wrecks'' ep. of *New York Stories* (W. Allen); *She-Devil* (S. Seidelman); *Crimes and Misdemeanors* (W. Allen)
1990	*Alice* (W. Allen)
1992	*Shadows and Fog* (W. Allen); *Husbands and Wives* (W. Allen)
1993	*Manhattan Murder Mystery* (W. Allen)
1994	*Bullets over Broadway* (W. Allen)
1995	*Mighty Aphrodite* (W. Allen)
1996	*Everyone Says I Love You* (W. Allen)
1997	*Deconstructing Harry* (W. Allen)
1998	*Celebrity* (W. Allen)
1999	*Sweet and Lowdown* (W. Allen)
2000	*Small Time Crooks* (W. Allen)

Publications

On LOQUASTO: articles—

Seebohm, Caroline, ''Everybody but Santo Loquasto Thinks He Is the Wizard of Sets,'' in *Connoisseur* (New York), July 1986.

Hickox, Fayette, ''Set Design: Santo Loquasto,'' in *Interview* (New York), September 1987.

Smith, Wendy, ''Cameos: Santo Loquasto, Set Designer,'' in *Premiere* (New York), December 1988.

Albrecht, Donald, ''Cinema Paranoia,'' in *Metropolitan Home*, November 1991.

Pinsker, Beth, ''Woody's Point (of View) Man,'' in *Entertainment Weekly* (New York), 9 December 1994.

Oppenheimer, Jean, ''Team Woody Fires *Bullets over Broadway*,'' in *American Cinematographer* (Hollywood), February 1995.

Berman, Avis, ''Setting the Scene: Production Designers' Cinematic Sources in New York, Los Angeles and Budapest,'' in *Architectural Digest* (Los Angeles), April 1998.

*   *   *

Santo Loquasto is one of the most imaginative and sought-after production designers for stage and screen. The hallmark of his work is his attention to all details no matter how large or how small and his ability to capture the mood of a script by the establishment of a physical context.

What has come to be recognized as ''The Loquasto Style'' was introduced to Hollywood in 1980 when Loquasto served as costume designer on the Marshall Brickman film *Simon*. But it is with his work with director Woody Allen that he began to take on the challenge of making the physical elements of a film operate on the same level as the emotional ones. Starting as a costume designer on Allen's early work, culminating in *Zelig* for which he received an Academy Award nomination, he graduated to the role of production designer on Allen's 1987 *Radio Days*. According to Allen, ''What distinguishes Santo is his degree of inspiration.'' Unlike other designers, he does not simply do the job but brings an exceptional level of creativity to it. Loquasto interprets his role of a production designer as being responsible for everything that the camera sees other than the actors. He credits his primary influences as being the films of Hollywood's classic years, particularly the films of Fred Astaire. He feels that these films incorporate such vital elements as pattern, sculpture, and illusion into a very definite sense of style. Another influence on Loquasto is the work of cinematographer Gordon Willis with whom he collaborated on the film *Bright Lights, Big City*. For this film Willis took the ''hip'' personal style of the main character and reinforced it through the physical and visual elements of the setting. Through this experience, Loquasto developed the belief that scenery can subtly convey real stature and emotion, without intruding on the story itself.

The diverse group of films Woody Allen has directed in the 1980s and 1990s has provided an opportunity for Loquasto to display his own creative talents in a multiplicity of settings. His sets have embodied the periods from the 1920s to the 1990s, yet they share one unifying characteristic: all display the many faces of New York City. Loquasto has used various aspects of New York to create a World War II ambiance for *Radio Days*; an FAO Schwarz fantasyland for director Penny Marshall's *Big*; a yuppiefied Manhattan for James Bridges' *Bright Lights, Big City*; silk-stocking and net-stocking Manhattan for *Mighty Aphrodite*; a period literary vision for *Bullets Over Broadway*; contemporary literary Manhattan and attractive suburbia for *Deconstructing Harry*; upper East Side upper-middle-class Manhattan for *Manhattan Murder Mystery*; gentrified Manhattan for *Everyone Says I Love You*; a more funky, freewheeling downtown for Susan Seidelman's *Desperately Seeking Susan*; and an array of New York uptown and downtown environs and outer-borough ambience for *Celebrity*. But Loquasto is equally adept at designing a non-New York film. *Sweet and Lowdown*, set in the 1930s, may be the rare Woody Allen feature with an outside-the-city storyline, yet Loquasto richly evokes a believably authentic time and place.

In preparing for a film, Loquasto compiles background information on all the principal characters. He then creates environments that would be compatible with the personality of each and imbues them with a sense of complete reality. As a production designer, he works to create a mood for the film but he instinctively understands the truly collaborative nature of film work. In his view, the power of the film is ultimately in the hands of the director and cinematographer. Yet, Loquasto believes that he can give the cinematographer the raw materials—tonality, visual character information, and the physical composition of the settings even though the final decisions are not in his hands. Nonetheless, because he has collaborated over and over with Woody Allen and Carlo Di Palma (the cinematographer of the majority of Allen's films he has designed), Loquasto has a sense of their design requirements and can almost instinctively provide them with the ''look'' they need.

Loquasto considers his forte to be period stories and particularly enjoys the opportunity to go into what he terms ''real spaces.'' For example, in *Radio Days*, he found a small Hebrew school on New York's Attorney Street which had a crumbling brick facade that worked perfectly to convey an old-world feeling. For the Dianne Weist character in *Bullets over Broadway*, an apartment setting was needed that did not include views of the Empire State Building or the Chrysler Building—no small requirement when the financial status of the character and the available buildings in her price range were taken into consideration. As a result of his never-ending travels around the city, Loquasto found an ideal apartment in lower Manhattan that both reflected the character's personality and status and maintained the ''period'' feel of the rest of the film. What is interesting about using actual locations, Loquasto reflects, ''is how much further visually many of the places are decorated than I would have taken them, the sort of thing you would never do yourself because you think, 'well, this is too much.' ''

On his period films, Allen prefers to employ a brighter color palette than on his contemporary works. For *Radio Days* which portrays New York in the 1940s, Loquasto designed vibrant greens, yellows, and oranges mixed with bold period patterns. In *Bullets over Broadway*, he switched to bright reds and yellows to vividly depict a literary world of the city a decade earlier, populated by gangsters, molls, and pretentious theater types. Both films were bathed in a golden hue because Allen and Di Palma insist that this type of lighting works best for period pieces and provides added texture to the characters who inhabit this world.

Loquasto admits that working on Allen's films requires a great deal of spontaneity and ''on the spot'' creativity because the scripts are not always completely fleshed out. A significant example is the 1992 *Shadows and Fog*. The script, which recounts the story of a night-stalking strangler who terrorizes a city, provided no description of the various locations. As Loquasto began to prepare for the film, there were only two pieces of information that the production designer could count on. The first was that the story took place around the general time of World War I in an imaginary Eastern European city, and the second was that Allen wanted a place that was full of anxiety and paranoia.

Loquasto began with a scaled-down model of what he thought the city would resemble but Allen was not happy with it. Finally, the designer put together a full-scale city complete with a flowing river and crumbling Gothic church. The finished product consisted of winding streets, jagged rooftops, and leaning facades to give physical form to the disorientation of the main character.

A second challenge was the fact that the film was to be shot in black and white, which raised issues of color and contrast. If the actual colors of the sets were too close in value, they would wipe each other out. The sets, props, and costumes were tested both individually and in relation to each other to ensure that the proper contrasts were achieved in the finished film.

In the final analysis, Loquasto's strength is his close attention to the small details of setting and decor which, while only a small aspect of what the camera sees, can make or break a film in terms of mood and character development. In *Shadows and Fog*, these details consisted of worn stone stoops, wrought-iron grills, and appropriately weathered signs. For *Bright Lights, Big City*, the details consisted of such things as old school notebooks and a Dartmouth sweatshirt lying on the floor. Although there is every chance that these items might not be picked up in the camera sweep, Loquasto must create total reality for every period that he is asked to re-create. Because he is able to think small, his collaborators such as Allen and Di Palma can weave their grand designs.

—Sandra Garcia-Myers, updated by Rob Edelman

LOUIS, Jean

Costume Designer. **Nationality:** French. **Born:** Jean Louis Berthault in Paris, France, 5 October 1907. **Family:** Married 1) Loretta Young, 1993. **Career:** Studied Decorative Arts, Paris; moved to New York in early 1930s; worked for Hattie Carnegie's fashion for seven years; named head designer of Columbia Pictures in Hollywood in 1943; moved to Universal in 1958; in 1961, became free-lance designer for films and began ready-to-wear fashion business. **Award:** Academy

Jean Louis

Award for *The Solid Gold Cadillac.* **Died:** In Palm Springs, California, 20 April 1997.

Films as Costume Designer

1944   *Together Again* (Vidor)

1945   *Kiss and Tell* (Wallace); *Over 21* (Hall); *Tonight and Every Night* (Saville); *Thousand and One Nights* (Green)

1946   ***Gilda*** (Vidor); *Mr. District Attorney* (Morgan); *One Way to Love* (Enright); *The Thrill of Brazil* (Sylvan Simon); *Tomorrow is Forever* (Pichel); *The Jolson Story* (Green)

1947   *Down to Earth* (Hall); *Dead Reckoning* (Cromwell); *Johnny O'Clock* (Rosen)

1948   *The Lady from Shanghai* (Welles); *The Loves of Carmen* (Vidor); *Ladies of the Chorus* (Karlson)

1949   *Johnny Allegro* (Tetzlaff); *Jolson Sings Again* (Levin); *Knock on Any Door* (Ray); *Shockproof* (Sirk); *Miss Grant Takes Richmond* (Bacon); *Tokyo Joe* (Heisler)

1950   *In a Lonely Place* (Ray); *The Walking Hills* (Sturges); *We Were Strangers* (Huston); *A Woman of Distinction* (Buzzell)

1951   *Born Yesterday* (Cukor)

1952   *The Marrying Kind* (Cukor); *Affair in Trinidad* (Sherman); *Scandal Sheet* (Karlson)

1953   ***The Big Heat*** (Lang); *Miss Sadie Thompson* (Bernhardt); ***From Here to Eternity*** (Zinneman); *Salome* (Dieterle)

1954   *Phfft!* (Robson); *It Should Happen to You* (Cukor); ***A Star is Born*** (Cukor)

1955   *Picnic* (Logan); *Queen Bee* (MacDougall); *Three for the Show* (Potter)

1956   *The Eddy Duchin Story* (Sidney); *You Can't Run Away From It* (Powell); *The Solid Gold Cadillac* (Quine); *Autumn Leaves* (Aldrich) *The Revolt of Mamie Stover* (Walsh)

1957   *Jeanne Eagels* (Sidney); *The Garment Jungle* (Aldrich/Sherman); *The Brothers Rico* (Karlson); *The Story of Esther Costello* (Miller); *Pal Joey* (Sidney); *3:10 to Yuma* (Daves)

1958   *Bell, Book and Candle* (Quine)

1959   *Pillow Talk* (Gordon); *The Last Angry Man* (Mann); *Imitation of Life* (Sirk); *They Came to Cordura* (Rossen); *Suddenly Last Summer* (Mankiewicz)

1960   *Strangers When We Meet* (Quine); *Who Was That Lady* (Sidney)

1961   *Back Street* (Stevenson); *Judgment at Nuremberg* (Kramer)

1962   *If a Man Answers* (Levin)

1963   *For Love of Money* (Gordon); *The Thrill of It All* (Jewison)

1964   *Send Me No Flowers* (Jewison)

1965   *Mirage*; *Ship of Fools* (Dmytryk); *Bus Riley's Back in Town* (Kramer)

1966   *Madame X* (Rich); *Gambit* (Neame)

1966   *Guess Who's Coming to Dinner* (Kramer); *Thoroughly Modern Millie* (Hill)

1968   *P.J.* (Guillermin); *To Hell with Heroes* (Sargent)

1969   *House of Cards* (Guillermin)

1970   *Waterloo* (Bondarchuk)

1973   *Lost Horizon* (Jarrott); *Forty Carats* (Katselas)

Publications

By LOUIS: articles—

Screenland (Hollywood), December 1949.

On LOUIS: articles—

Movieland (Hollywood), February 1945.
Life (Chicago), 4 February 1946.
Motion Picture (New York), November 1947.
Movieland (Hollywoood), December 1947.
Photoplay (London), September 1950.
Photoplay (London), January 1952.
Photoplay, May 1952.
Motion Picture Costumes, 1960.
New York Times, 17 October 1967.
Los Angeles Times West Magazine, 7 November 1971.
New York Times, 15 March 1973.
Los Angeles Times, section 4, 29 August 1973.
Los Angeles Herald-Examiner, section F, 17 February 1974.
Los Angeles Times, section 4, 21 February 1974.
Films in Review (New York), June-July 1975.
World of Fashion, 1976.
Los Angeles Times, fashion 78, 27 October 1978.
People Weekly (Chicago), vol. 27, 9 February 1987.
Obituary, in *EPD Film* (Frankfurt/Main), June 1997.
Obituary, in *Variety* (New York), April 28, 1997.

*   *   *

Jean Louis is most often associated with the famous black satin gown he designed for Rita Hayworth in *Gilda*. Indeed, Louis will be forever linked with the glamour of Hayworth, as he designed most of her gowns and costumes when she was at the peak of her career. While it is Hayworth who is most associated with Louis, his career break came from Irene Dunne, who was responsible for his contract at Columbia Pictures. Dunne first noticed Louis at Hattie Carnegie's fashion house in New York. She was so impressed with his work that she asked Columbia Studio head Harry Cohn to recruit Louis for her next movie, *Together Again*, thus beginning Louis' 13-year association with Columbia Pictures.

He moved to Universal Studios in 1958 and worked with Ross Hunter on a number of films. He later free-lanced while building a ready-to-wear fashion business. He was nominated for ten Academy Awards, winning one for *The Solid Gold Cadillac*. Although later in his career Louis would lament that Columbia had no big stars except Hayworth, he could count Doris Day, Joan Crawford, Kim Novak, Claudette Colbert, Lana Turner, Deborah Kerr, Elizabeth Taylor and Marilyn Monroe among the stars for whom he designed. Louis was also able to design costumes for a wide range of stories. There were westerns like *Walking Hills* and period pieces like *Salome* and *Thoroughly Modern Millie*, but the majority of the films were modern.

Contemporary films were a special challenge, since movie costumes influenced fashion trends. Consequently, the designs had to be in the front line of fashion and the strapless gown is a good example of this. While the strapless gown was used by designer Travis Banton two years before, it did not catch the imagination of the public until Louis designed it. Using the portrait of Mrs. X by John Singer Sargent as inspiration, Louis sheathed Hayworth in black satin. He not only created the look that would make Rita Hayworth a star and the dream girl of men all over the world, but also launched the strapless gown as a fashion statement that would last for decades. The strapless gown became the trademark of the Louis-Hayworth association, and Louis would use the same design idea in later films.

The *Gilda* gown was not only a design marvel, but something of a technical feat as well. It had to be built to stay put while Hayworth sang and danced and its construction demonstrates Louis' ability to engineer costumes as well as design them. He would later engineer the costume for Hayworth's *Salome* dance as well as the famous "see thru" gown that Marlene Dietrich used for her Las Vegas show. Louis constructed the *Gilda* gown by creating a harness. Plastic was molded around the top of the dress and three stays were used under the bust, one in the center and one on each side. For *Salome*'s strip tease, Louis designed an innovative plastic body stocking, so that Hayworth could appear to be nude under the multicolored semitransparent veils. The body suit would also be used under the Dietrich gown. Dietrich wanted a gown that appeared to be transparent with strategically placed beads. Jean Louis made the dress in thin chiffon; the skin-tight body suit was the secret to the "see through" look.

In contrast to these engineered costumes, Louis also designed clothes that would move with the body. While his designs would begin with the role, he would also incorporate his impressions of the body and the personality of the star he was designing for as well. For example, he felt that suits would not go well on Hayworth. For Rosalind Russell, suits were an ideal choice. For Doris Day in *Pillow Talk*, he successfully gauged her character, her figure and her personality to create costumes that would change her image of virginal heroine by revealing her sexuality.

While Louis endeavored to incorporate his design philosophy into all of his work, the studio would sometimes demand certain trends and looks. When the busty look was popular during the forties, Louis was obliged to use corsets and pads for his less-endowed actresses although he felt that designs of this sort were very constricting for the actresses. Following trends could also cause problems when the fashion scene influenced movie costumes, because films were often released a year or more after filming. Louis cites a bad experience when Joan Fontaine wanted to use a Christian Dior look for her costumes. When the movie was released a year later, the look was no longer in fashion and Louis felt the costumes were a catastrophe. But trends when used well could enhance the development of character. In *Thoroughly Modern Millie*, Louis used the fashions of the 1920s flapper girl to show an evolution in Julie Andrews' character. She begins by arriving in New York dressed as a provincial country girl. As she walks by the city's fashionable shops, she notices the straight flapper dresses and the long beads that the mannequins are wearing. Comparing the clothes she is wearing to these, Andrews enters a store and comes out wearing a new dress and beads, modernized and thus transformed.

Louis made a career of keeping a step ahead of fashion, working with actresses as well as characters and using the latest technology to meet design challenges to produce sumptuous gowns, gorgeous costumes and trend-setting fashions. He was able to turn his experience into a ready-to-wear line which was well received in New York and Los Angeles. The styles of his last film, *The Lost Horizon*, started a trend that influenced jewelry and clothes. Ironically, the caftan, a loose, figure-hiding gown, was particularly popular. This from the designer who launched the famous form-fitting strapless evening dress!

—Renee Ward

LOURIÉ, Eugène

Art Director. **Nationality:** Russian. **Born:** Kharkov, 1905. **Career:** Painter and ballet set designer in Paris after 1921; assistant on films in the late 1920s and early 1930s; 1934—first film designs, for *La Porteuse de pain*; 1943—first film in Hollywood, *Three Russian Girls*; 1953—directed first film, *The Beast from 20,000 Fathoms*; designed the TV series *Kung Fu*, 1973–75, and others. **Died:** From heart failure, in California, 26 May 1991.

Films as Assistant Art Director:

1927　*Napoléon* (Gance)
1931　*Un Coup de téléphone* (Lacombe)
1933　*Madame Bovary* (Renoir)

Films as Art Director:

1934　*La Porteuse de pain* (Sti); *Le Bossu* (Sti); *Jeanne* (Tourjansky)
1935　*Les Yeux Noirs* (Tourjansky); *Quand la vie était belle* (Sti); *La Petite Sauvage* (de Limur); *Le Bébé de l'escadron* (Sti); *Crime et châtiment* (Chenal)
1936　*Sous les yeux d'occident* (Razumov) (M. Allégret); *Baccara* (Mirande); *Les Hommes nouveaux* (L'Herbier); *Le Grand*

Refrain (Siodmak); *Aventure à Paris* (M. Allégret); *Les Bas-fonds* (*The Lower Depths*) (Renoir)
1937　*La Grande Illusion* (*Grand Illusion*) (Renoir); *L'Alibi* (Chenal) (co); *Le Messager* (Rouleau); *Nuits de feu* (L'Herbier) (co)
1938　*La Bête humaine* (*The Human Beast*) (Renoir); *Ramuntcho* (Barberis); *L'Affaire Lafarge* (Chenal) (co); *Werther* (Ophüls) (co); *La Tragédie impériale* (*Rasputin*) (L'Herbier); *Le Paradis de Satan* (de Gandera); *Les Nouveaux Riches* (Berthomieu); *La Règle du jeu* (*The Rules of the Game*) (Renoir) (co)
1939　*Sans lendemain* (Ophüls); *L'Or du Cristobal* (Becker)
1940　*Une Fause Alerte* (de Baroncelli); *Air pur* (Clair—unfinished)
1943　*Three Russian Girls* (Ozep); *This Land Is Mine* (Renoir); *Sahara* (Z. Korda)
1944　*The Imposter* (Duvivier); *In Society* (Yarbrough); *The House of Fear* (Neill)
1945　*Uncle Harry* (*The Strange Affair of Uncle Harry*; *The Zero Murder Case*) (Siodmak); *The Southerner* (Renoir)
1946　*The Diary of a Chambermaid* (Renoir)
1947　*The Long Night* (Litvak); *The Song of Scheherazade* (Reisch)
1948　*A Woman's Vengeance* (Z. Korda)
1951　*The River* (Renoir); *The Adventures of Captain Fabian* (Marshall)
1952　*Limelight* (Chaplin)
1953　*The Diamond Queen* (Brahm)
1954　*So This Is Paris* (Quine)
1961　*Confessions of an Opium Eater* (Zugsmith)
1962　*Shock Corridor* (Fuller); *The Strangler* (Topper); *Flight from Ashiya* (Anderson)
1963　*The Naked Kiss* (Fuller)
1964　*Bikini Paradise* (Tallas)
1965　*A Crack in the World* (Marton) (+ special effects); *Battle of the Bulge* (Annakin) (+ special effects)
1966　*Custer of the West* (Siodmak) (+ special effects)
1969　*Krakatoa, East of Java* (Kowalski) (+ special effects); *Royal Hunt of the Sun* (Lerner) (+ special effects)
1971　*Eliza's Horoscope* (Sheppard); *Death Takes a Holiday* (Butler)
1972　*The Delphi Bureau* (Wendkos); *What's the Matter with Helen?* (Harrington); *Kung Fu* (Thorp); *Haunts of the Very Rich* (Wendkos)
1973　*What Are Best Friends For?* (Sandrich)
1975　*Carola* (Lloyd); *Burnt Offerings* (Curtiss)
1976　*Philemon* (Lloyd); *Time Travelers* (Singer)
1978　*Lacy and the Mississippi Queen* (Butler); *An Enemy of the People* (Schaeffer)
1979　*Supertrain* (Curtiss) (+ special effects)
1980　*Bronco Billy* (Eastwood); *Freebie and the Bean* (Auerback)

Other Films:

1953　*The Beast from 20,000 Fathoms* (d)
1954　*Napoleon* (Guitry) (2nd unit d)
1955　*Si Paris nous était conté* (Guitry) (2nd unit d)
1957　*The Colossus of New York* (d)
1958　*The Giant Behemoth* (d)
1961　*Gorgo* (d); *Back Street* (Miller) (2nd unit d)
1962　*That Touch of Mink* (Delbert Mann) (2nd unit d)
1980　*A Whale for the Killing* (consultant)
1983　*Breathless* (McBride) (ro)

Publications

By LOURIÉ: book—

My Work in Films, New York, 1985.

By LOURIÉ: articles—

Film Comment (New York), May-June 1978.
American Film (Washington, D.C.), January-February 1985.

On LOURIÉ: articles—

Films and Filming (London), February 1960.
Films and Filming (London), December 1961.
Monthly Film Bulletin (London), January 1972.
Film Dope (Nottingham), February 1987.
Positif (Paris), July-August 1988.
Obituary in *Variety* (New York), 3 June 1991.
Della Casa, S., in *Cineforum*, no. 306, July/August 1991.
Schactman, K., "*Gorgo,*" in *Scarlet Street*, Spring 1992.

* * *

While best known as one of Jean Renoir's main collaborators—he was production designer on eight of the director's films—Eugène Lourié's credits include production design for TV and stage, second unit direction for film, and special effects direction for both TV and film, as well as the direction of four feature films and three TV projects. While his undisputed masterpieces are his designs for Renoir's *Grand Illusion* and *The Rules of the Game*, many of his other achievements are of note.

An avid cinema fan since his childhood days in czarist Russia, Lourié began his career in the cinema as a red guard drunk with power in an anti-communist film entitled *Black Crows*. Later, after escaping to Turkey with his family, Lourié worked as an illustrator of movie posters before arriving in his ultimate destination—Paris—where he began as a scenery painter on Ivan Mozhukin's *Le Brasier ardent*. Then, after working briefly as a costume designer, Lourié abandoned his plans to study painting and became a full-time production designer for film.

Lourié's association with Renoir began early in his career, when Alexander Kamenka, the head of Albatross Pictures—originally a Russian company—began planning a film of Maxim Gorky's famous stage play *The Lower Depths*. From a list of prospective directors, Lourié recommended Renoir. Their shared notion of elevating the Russian play to reflect a universality began a collaboration which flourished while Renoir moved from France to Hollywood and then to India.

In his autobiography, *My Work in Films*, Lourié discussed his work on six of the eight Renoir films. Early in his discussion of *Grand Illusion*, he states that "Renoir preferred shooting under the controlled conditions of a stage. He was convinced, as was I, that studio sets could be more dramatically expressive and fit the story better than some actual locations." Throughout the book, he confirmed the positive benefits of working with Renoir, particularly the collaborative spirit which Renoir developed with all members of his cast and crew: "Renoir knew how important his collaborators were to his work, and being a truly great director, he did not deny their influence but tried to assimilate it to reinforce his own point of view."

That collaborative spirit influenced Lourié's work aesthetic: the plans for the *Grand Illusion* set occupied by Erich von Stroheim's character were worked out in collaboration with the actor. When von Stroheim was planning *The Iron Crown*—his unrealized film of the fall of the Austrian empire—he asked Lourié to design it.

Renoir's allowance for collaborative freedom found its greatest result in *The Rules of the Game*. On that film, Lourié created the perfect atmosphere to reflect Renoir's vision of a society dancing on the edge of a volcano. In typical style, Renoir's final vision of character action was developed after seeing Lourié's finished sets. In designing the set, Lourié adhered to an aesthetic sensibility he shared with Renoir: uncluttered, light-colored sets which provide perfect backgrounds for the silhouetted movement of actors. Like Renoir, Lourié preferred not to obscure the movement of performers, but to heighten them.

Among Lourié's other outstanding production designs are the sets for Max Ophüls's *Werther* and Charlie Chaplin's *Limelight*. On the former, Lourié claimed he developed an appreciation for the close affinity between production design and musical expression. On *Limelight*, Lourié's approach was that of his work with Renoir: he designed sets which allowed for the foregrounding of the players' actions.

In the 1950s Lourié began designing and directing films with more expansive settings, notably science fiction and war films which involved a foregrounding of set design and the use of miniatures. Among his most impressive contributions to 1960s cinema was his set for Sam Fuller's *Shock Corridor*, a stark set which perfectly reflects the growing psychological tension and deterioration of the hospital inmates.

Lourié was still active into the 1980s. In 1980 he served as production designer on Clint Eastwood's *Bronco Billy*, while in 1983 he returned to the other side of the cameras as Dr. Boudreaux in Jim McBride's remake of Jean-Luc Godard's *Breathless*.

—Doug Tomlinson

LUNDGREN, P. A.

Art Director and Production Designer. **Nationality:** Swedish. **Born:** Per Axel Lundgren in Vastra Harg, Sweden, 1911. **Career:** Worked with Swedish directors, mainly Ingmar Bergman.

Films as Art Director and Production Designer:

1944   *A Day Shall Dawn*
1946   *It Rains On Our Love*
1948   *Musik i mörker* (*Music in Darkness*; *Night Is My Future*) (Bergman)
1949   *Fängelse* (*Prison*; *The Devils Wanton*) (Bergman)
1953   *Sommaren med Monika* (*Monika*; *Summer with Monika*) (Bergman)
1954   *En lektion i kärlek* (*A Lesson in Love*) (Bergman)
1955   **Sommarnattens leende** (*Smiles of a Summer Night*) (Bergman)
1956   *Song of the Scarlet Flower*; **Det sjunde inseglet** (*The Seventh Seal*) (Bergman)

1958	*Ansiktet* (*The Magician*) (Bergman)
1960	*Jungfrukällen* (*The Virgin Spring*) (Bergman); *Djävulens öga* (*The Devil's Eye*) (Bergman)
1961	*Såsom i en spegel* (*Through a Glass Darkly*) (Bergman); *Pleasure Garden*
1962	*The Swedish Mistress*
1963	*Nattvardsgästerna* (*Winter Light* (Bergman); **Tystnaden** (*The Silence*) (Bergman)
1964	*491*; *För att inte tala om alla dessa kvinnor* (*All These Women*; *Now about These Women*) (Bergman)
1966	*Syskonbädd 1782* (*My Sister My Love*)
1967	*Hagbard and Signe/The Red Mantle*; *Stimulantia* (co)
1968	*Skammen* (*Shame*) (Bergman)
1969	*En Passion* (*The Passion of Anna*) (Bergman)
1971	*The Emigrants* (Troell)
1973	*The New Land*
1977	*The American Dream* (Abrahamsen) (+ co pr)
1980	*Barna från Blåsjöfjället* (Sima)

Films as Production Designer:

1944	*Excellensen*; *Flickan och djävulen*; *Mitt folk är icke ditt*; *Vi behöver varann*
1946	*Ödemarksprästen*
1947	*Skepp till India land* (*Frustration*); *Livet i Finnskogarna*
1948	*Främmande hamn*; *Hammarforsens brus*; *Lars Hård*; *Marknadsafton*
1949	*Bohus bataljon*; *Lång-Lasse i Delsbo*; *Havets son* (*Son of the Sea*); *Gatan*; *Hin och smålänningen*
1950	*När kärleken kom till byn*
1951	*Poker*; *Spöke på semester*; *Motorkavaljerer*
1952	*När syrenerna blomma*
1953	*Glasberget* (*Unmarried*)
1955	*Ljuset från Lund*; *Enhörningen* (*The Unicorn*); *Våld*
1956	*Den Hårda leken*; *Ratataa* (*The Staffan Stolle Story*); *Sjunde himlen*
1957	*Sommarnöje sökes*; *Far till sol och vår*
1958	*Flottans överman*
1959	*Himmel och pannkaka*
1960	*På en bänk i en park*; *Kärlekens decimaler*; *Bara en kypare* (*Only a Waiter*)
1961	*Briggen Tre Liljor*; *Stöten*
1962	*Chans* (*Just Once More*)
1964	*Svenska bilder*
1965	*. . . för vänskaps skull. . .*
1967	*Människor möts och ljuv musik uppstår i hjärtat* (*People Meet and Sweet Music Fills the Air*)
1970	*Rötmånad* (*Dog Days*); *The Night Visitor* (*Salem Come to Supper*)
1971	*Lockfågeln* (*The Decoy*); *Beröringen* (*The Touch*)
1973	*Smutsiga fingrar* (*Dirty Fingers*)
1974	*Jorden runt med Fanny Hill* (*Around the World with Fanny Hill*); *En Handfull kärlek* (*A Handful of Love*)
1976	*Mina drömmars stad*
1977	*Bröderna Lejonhjärta* (mini-series—for TV)
1979	*Den Åttonde dagen*

*   *   *

Though often overlooked, art directors bring much to a film's look and overall feel. Lundgren's sets are almost as much a part of a film as the actors; his carefully chosen locations add a valuable component to the story.

Throughout Lundgren's career, he has been most often been recognized for his work with Swedish director Ingmar Bergman. The two have collaborated on many films, including *Smiles of a Summer Night*, *The Seventh Seal*, *The Magician*, *The Virgin Spring*, *The Devil's Eye*, *Through a Glass Darkly*, *Winter Light*, *The Silence* and *Shame*. While Bergman's films are often microscopic views of dramatic relationships, the background plays a crucial role in telling his stories. In *The Seventh Seal*, Lundgren provided Bergman with the perfect setting to tell the story of a 14th-century knight playing chess with Death. The opening shot of waves lapping the rocky beach as the knight, Max Von Sydow, lies beaten on the shore sets the mood for the entire film. Lundgren's stark, bare visuals allow us to understand the bleakness of life and the challenge of a game with Death when there is nothing left to lose. As the film continues, the man is left alone with nature, where he must fend for himself. Bergman's wide shots coupled with Lundgren's scenery make *The Seventh Seal* what Roger Ebert refers to as "one of Bergman's most visual films."

While Lundgren did not work exclusively with Bergman, he did work mainly with Swedish directors. In 1977 he coproduced *The American Dream* while acting as production designer.

—Robert Dixter

LYE, Len

Animator. **Nationality:** New Zealander. **Born:** Christchurch, 5 July 1901; became citizen of the United States, 1950. **Education:** Attended Wellington Technical College; Canterbury College of Fine Arts. **Career:** 1921—assistant for Australian film company; made first hand-painted film; 1926—came to England, worked as stage hand, Lyric Theatre, London; 1927—began first animated film with support of the London Film Society; 1931—property boy at Wembley Studio; 1933—resumed experiments with "direct film": drawing and painting on celluloid; 1935—began sporadic association with G.P.O. Film Unit under John Grierson; 1940–44—worked on wartime propaganda films; 1944—went to U.S. to work on *March of Time* series; 1958—devoted attention to kinetic sculpture. **Died:** In Warwick, Rhode Island, 15 May 1980.

Films as Director, Writer and Animator (Shorts):

1921	Untitled handmade films, Australia
1929	*Tusalava* (begun 1927)
1933	*Experimental Animation: Peanut Vendor* (not completed)
1935	*A Color Box* (*Colour Box*); *Kaleidoscope*
1936	*The Birth of a Robot* (puppet animation); *Rainbow Dance*
1937	*Trade Tattoo* (*In Time with Industry*)
1938	*N or NW* (*N. or N.W. North or North West*) (live action); *Colour Flight*
1939	*Swinging the Lambeth Walk*
1940	*Musical Poster No.1*; *Profile of Britain* (*March of Time* Series) (live action)

1941   *When the Pie Was Opened* (live action); *Newspaper Train* (live action)
1942   *Work Party* (live action); *Kill or Be Killed* (live action); *German Calling* (live action)
1943   *Planned Crops* (live action)
1944   *Cameramen at War* (live action)
1944–51   *March of Time* (Series: 7 films)
1952   *Fox Chase* (live action)
1953   *Color Cry* (handmade); *Rhythm* (handmade)
1957   *Free Radicals* (handmade)
1961–66   *Particles in Space* (handmade)
1980   *Tal Farlow* (handmade)

Publications

By LYE: books—

No Trouble, Majorca, 1930.
Figures of Motion, Auckland, New Zealand, 1982.

By LYE: articles—

"Colour and the Box Office," in *Life and Letters Today*, September 1935.
"Experiment in Colour," in *World Film News*, December 1936.
"Television: New Axes to Grind," in *Sight and Sound* (London), Summer 1939.
"The Man Who Was Colour Blind," in *Sight and Sound* (London), Spring 1940.
"On the End of Audiences," in *Film Culture* (New York), Summer 1961.
"Is Film Art?," in *Film Culture* (New York), no.29, 1963.
"Len Lye Speaks at the Film Makers Cinematheque," in *Film Culture* (New York), Spring 1967.
"Len Lye—Composer of Motion," interview with J. Kennedy, in *Millimeter* (New York), February 1977.
Cinemanews (San Francisco), no. 2–4, 1979.
"Len Lye: Some Unpublished Writings," in *Film Library Quarterly* (New York), 1981.

On LYE: book—

Russett, Robert, and Cecile Starr, *Experimental Animation*, New York, 1976.

On LYE: articles—

Blakeston, Oswell, "Len Lye Visuals," in *Architectural Review* (London), July 1932.
Cavalcanti, Alberto, "Presenting Len Lye," in *Sight and Sound* (London), Winter 1947–48.
Breslin, James, "My Best Films Will Never Be Made," in *The Village Voice* (New York), 28 May 1958.
"Forms in Air: Tangibles," in *Time* (New York), 24 August 1959.
Dandignac, P., "Visionary Art of Len Lye," in *Craft Horizons* (New York), May 1961.
"Timehenge," in *Newsweek* (New York), 22 March 1965.
Mancis, A., and W. Van Dyke, "Artist as Filmmaker," in *Art in America* (New York), July 1966.

Curnow, W., "Len Lye and *Tusalava*," in *Cantrill's Filmnotes* (Melbourne), February 1979.
Horrocks, R., "Len Lye's Figures of Motion," in *Cantrill's Filmnotes* (Melbourne), November 1979.
Obituary in *New York Times*, 16 May 1980.
Obituary in *Variety* (New York), 21 May 1980.
"The Len Lye Lists," in *Bulletin of New Zealand Art History*, 1980.
"Len Lye, 1901–1980," in *Cantrill's Filmnotes* (Melbourne), August 1980.
Obituary in *Plateau*, vol. 2, no. 2, 1981.
Sight and Sound (London), Winter 1987–88.
O'Pray, Michael, "Mixes," in *Sight & Sound* (London), July 1991.

*   *   *

Until fairly recently, it was no exaggeration to state that Len Lye was all that New Zealand had contributed to international cinema. An artist—equally at home with painting or sculpture—Lye was the progenitor of experimental cinema, yet, at the same time, was willing to work within a more mainstream cinema unlike so many of his successors. Lye's closest equivalent in contemporary cinema was Norman McLaren, who continued the technique of drawing directly on film which was created by Lye in the early 1930s.

Lye came to London in the 1920s and there made his first attempt at experimental filmmaking with *Tusalava*, which tried to merge elements of European modern art with the primitive art which he had experienced in the South Sea Islands. It was not until 1935 that Lye was able to complete another film, and that was his revolutionary *Colour Box*, for which he painted directly on the film. John Grierson's G.P.O. Film Unit sponsored the production, and Grierson hired Lye to work for his organization. Here Lye experimented with the use of color—in this instance, Gasparcolor—and with puppet animation, creating the highly praised *The Birth of a Robot*. What is perhaps most extraordinary about Lye's work at this time is that he took mundane subjects handed to him by the Unit, which was established to create short propaganda films for the British mail service, and transformed them into surrealistic exercises. Nowhere is this more apparent than in *N. or N.W.*, which warns its audience of the danger in incorrectly addressing envelopes through a series of bizarre close-ups and superimpositions.

During the Second World War, Lye's films were more realistic in content, as he worked for the British Ministry of Information. Most were live action, although in *When the Pie Was Opened*, he combines live action and animation to present a wartime recipe for vegetable pie. All those films support Cavalcanti's claim that "Len Lye could be described in the history of British cinema by one word—Experiment."

Coming to the United States in 1944, Lye put his experimental filmmaking behind him and settled down to creating live-action documentaries, initially for *March of Time*. He returned briefly to experimental filmmaking in the 1950s with *Color Cry*, based on a method of "shadow casting" created by Man Ray, and *Free Radicals* and *Particles in Space*, in both of which the images were scratched on the film. Lye eventually seemed to lose interest in film, becoming more involved in movable and kinetic sculpture. In the *New York Times*, Grace Glueck described him thus, "Bald as an egg, with a pointed goatee, Len Lye was a sprightly man who, despite his fascination with technology, referred to himself as 'an old-brain guy who can't even drive a car'."

The most important period in Len Lye's filmmaking career was when he worked in Britain for the G.P.O. and the Ministry of Information. As Dave Curtis has written in *Experimental Cinema*, ''Len Lye is one of the few significant figures in British cinema between the wars. He is as important to personal (informal) animation as Griffith is to the traditional narrative film.''

—Anthony Slide

M

MacARTHUR, Charles

Writer, Producer, and Director. **Nationality:** American. **Born:** Charles Gordon MacArthur in Scranton, Pennsylvania, 5 November 1895. **Education:** Attended Wilson Memorial Academy, Nyack, New York. **Military Service:** 1916—served as a trooper in the 1st Illinois Cavalry on the Mexican Border, and as a Private in the 149th Field Artillery, 1917–19. **Family:** Married 1) Carol Frink (divorced); 2) the actress Helen Hayes, 1928; one daughter and one son, the actor James MacArthur. **Career:** 1914–16—reporter, City News Bureau, *Herald and Examiner*, and *Tribune*, all Chicago; 1921–23—journalist, New York *American*; 1924—special writer, *Hearst's International Magazine*; 1926—first play produced, *My Lulu Belle*; 1928—began collaboration with Ben Hecht, on play *The Front Page*; 1930—first film as writer; 1934—formed production company with Hecht to write, produce, and direct their own films; 1942–45—Assistant to the Chief of the Chemical Warfare Service; Lt. Colonel. **Awards:** Academy Award for *The Scoundrel*, 1935. **Died:** 21 April 1956.

Charles MacArthur

Films as Writer:

1930   *The Girl Said No* (Wood); *The King of Jazz* (Anderson); *Billy the Kid* (K. Vidor); *Way for a Sailor* (Wood)
1931   *Paid* (Wood); *The Unholy Garden* (Fitzmaurice); *The Sin of Madelon Claudet* (*The Lullaby*) (Selwyn); *The New Adventures of Get-Rich-Quick Wallingford* (Wood)
1932   *Rasputin and the Empress* (Boleslawsky)
1940   *I Take This Woman* (Van Dyke)
1947   *The Senator Was Indiscreet* (Kaufman)
1948   *Lulu Belle* (Fenton)

Films as Cowriter with Ben Hecht:

1934   *Twentieth Century* (Hawks); *Crime without Passion* (+ co-d+ co pr)
1935   *Once In a Blue Moon* (+ co-d + co-pr); *The Scoundrel* (+ co-d + co-pr)
1936   *Soak the Rich* (+ co-d + co-pr)
1939   *Gunga Din* (Stevens); *Wuthering Heights* (Wyler)

Publications

By MacARTHUR: plays—

My Lulu Belle, New York, 1925.
With Ben Hecht, *The Front Page*, New York, 1928.
With Hecht, *Twentieth Century*, New York, 1932.
With Hecht, *Jumbo*, New York, 1935.
With Hecht, *Fun to Be Free*, New York, 1941.
With Hecht, *Wuthering Heights* (script), in *Twenty Best Film Plays*, edited by John Gassner and Dudley Nichols, New York, 1943.
Stage Works, Tallahassee, Florida, 1974.

By MacARTHUR: other books—

A Bug's-Eye View of the War (nonfiction), Oak Park, Illinois, 1919.
War Bugs (nonfiction), New York, 1929

On MacARTHUR: books—

Hecht, Ben, *Charlie: The Improbable Life and Times of Charles MacArthur*, New York, 1957.
Robbins, J., *Front Page Marriage: Helen Hayes and Charles MacArthur*, New York, 1982.

On MacARTHUR: articles—

Film Comment (New York), Winter 1970–71.
National Film Theatre booklet (London), April-May 1975.
Sight and Sound (London), Summer 1975.
Film Dope (Nottingham), June 1987.
''*The Scoundrel*,'' in *Reid's Film Index*, no. 3, 1989.
''*Crime Without Passion*,'' in *Reid's Film Index*, no. 6, 1991.

* * *

Charles MacArthur is best known for his collaborations with Ben Hecht, yet his contributions to the Hollywood era proved him an exemplary crafter of what Howard Hawks referred to as ''three cushion dialogue.'' He created sophisticated banter which could bounce gaily about a ticklish subject yet pocket a message usually left to cruder forms of innuendo. He participated in the artistic cross-fertilization of the movie-mills and the New York theatrical dynasty, bringing to each a sensibility of impertinent perfectionism.

After his immensely successful collaboration with Hecht, *The Front Page*, left a permanent mark on Broadway, MacArthur went to work for MGM as a dialogue writer on such early talkies as *Way for a Sailor* and *Billy the Kid*. His first complete script, *The Sin of Madelon Claudet*, provided his wife Helen Hayes with her first film role and an Academy Award for best actress.

Samuel Goldwyn, always in search of a great script, bought the Hecht/MacArthur team for the first of their eventual nine film collaborations. The result was *The Unholy Garden*, which failed critically and financially in spite of much witty dialogue and the magnetic presence of the stars Ronald Colman and Fay Wray. In the mid-1930s Paramount financed MacArthur and Hecht to produce and direct four feature films, most notably *The Scoundrel*. This film won an Academy Award for best original story and discovered an audience hungry for their Baroque style of dark humor and crisp naturalism.

While MacArthur's second billing to Hecht was originally determined (according to Hecht) by a flip of a coin, he nonetheless played the sidekick role well, acting as model, muse, and editor for Hecht's wildly erratic genius. Much of the sparkling repartee found in their films was but a replay of conversations between these old friends.

The occasional sentimentality of MacArthur's own scripts reveals a central ambiguity of his personality: he was a reverent iconoclast. In Hecht's words, ''He believed in all the conventions he flouted. He broke laws but he never took sides against them.'' At the same time MacArthur brought his own personal charm and his objectivity toward human folly and pomposity to all his best work.

—Rick Broussard

MacGOWAN, Kenneth

Producer. **Nationality:** American. **Born:** Winthrop, Massachusetts, 30 November 1888. **Education:** Attended Harvard University, Cambridge, Massachusetts, graduated 1911. **Career:** 1910–25—drama critic; stage producer with Eugene O'Neill's Provincetown Playhouse, New York; story editor for RKO, then producer for RKO, 1932–35, Fox, 1935–44, and for other studios until 1947; then head of Department of Theater Arts, University of California, Los Angeles. **Died:** In Los Angeles, California, 27 April 1963.

Films as Producer/Associate Producer:

1932   *The Penguin Pool Murder* (Archainbaud)
1933   *Topaze* (D'Arrast); *Double Harness* (Cromwell); *Little Women* (Cukor); *The Great Jasper* (Ruben); *Rafter Romance* (Seiter); *If I Were Free* (Nugent)
1934   *La Cucaracha* (Corrigan—short); *Anne of Green Gables* (Nicholls); *Murder on the Blackboard* (Archainbaud); *Long Lost Father* (Schoedsack); *Finishing School* (Tuchock and Nicholls); *Hat, Coat, and Glove* (Miner); *Wednesday's Child* (Robertson)
1935   ***Becky Sharp*** (Mamoulian); *King of Burlesque* (Lanfield); *Jalna* (Cromwell); *The Return of Peter Grimm* (Nicholls); *Half Angel* (Lanfield); *Murder on a Honeymoon* (Corrigan); *Enchanted April* (Beaumont)
1936   *Lloyds of London* (H. King); *To Mary—with Love* (Cromwell); *Sins of Man* (Brower and Ratoff)
1937   *This Is My Affair* (Seiter); *Wake Up and Live* (Lanfield); *Love and Hisses* (Lanfield)
1938   *Four Men and a Prayer* (Ford); *In Old Chicago* (H. King); *Kentucky Moonshine* (Butler); *Kidnapped* (Werker); *I'll Give a Million* (W. Lang)
1939   ***Young Mr. Lincoln*** (Ford); *Stanley and Livingstone* (H. King); *Swanee River* (Lanfield); *The Return of the Cisco Kid* (Leeds); *The Story of Alexander Graham Bell* (Cummings); *Susannah of the Mounties* (Seiter)
1940   *Brigham Young—Frontiersman* (Hathaway); *Star Dust* (W. Lang); *The Return of Frank James* (F. Lang); *Tin Pan Alley* (W. Lang)
1941   *Hudson's Bay* (Pichel); *Man Hunt* (F. Lang); *The Great American Broadcast* (Mayo); *Belle Starr* (Cummings)
1943   *Happy Land* (Pichel)
1944   *Lifeboat* (Hitchcock); *Jane Eyre* (Stevenson)
1947   *Easy Come, Easy Go* (Farrow)

Publications

By MacGOWAN: books—

The Theater of Tomorrow, New York, 1921.
With Robert Edmond Jones, *Continental Stagecraft*, New York, 1922.
With Herman Rosse, *Masks and Demons*, New York, 1923.
Footlights across America, New York, 1929.
With G. V. Hamilton, *What Is Wrong with Marriage*, New York, 1929.
Early Man in the New World, New York, 1950.
A Primer of Playwriting, New York, 1951.
With others, *Theatrer Pictorial*, New York, 1953.
With William Welnitz, *The Living Stage*, New York, 1955.
Behind the Screen: The History and Techniques of the Motion Picture, New York, 1965.

By MacGOWAN: articles—

''Seeing the News by Film,'' in *Collier's* (New York), 1 April 1916.
''Beyond the Screen,'' in *Seven Arts* (New York), December 1916.
''Cross-Roads of Screen and Stage,'' in *Seven Arts* (New York), April 1917.

"As the Movies Mend," in *Seven Arts* (New York), September 1917.
"On the Screen," in *New Republic* (New York), 15 September 1917.
"The March of the Photoplay," in *Motion Picture Classic* (New York), May 1919.
"George Loane Tucker—Miracle Man," in *Motion Picture Classic* (New York), December 1919.
"Artistic Future of the Movies," in *North American Review* (New York), February 1921.
"The Coming of Sound to the Screen," in *Quarterly of Film, Radio, and Television* (Berkeley, California), Winter 1955.
"When the Talkies Came to Hollywood" in *Quarterly of Film, Radio, and Television* (Berkeley, California), Spring 1956.

On MacGOWAN: book—

Bloom, Thomas Alan, *Kenneth MacGowan and the Aesthetic Paradigm for the New Stagecraft in America*, New York, P. Lang, 1994, 1997.

On MacGOWAN: articles—

Dickson, Robert G., in *Films in Review* (New York), October 1963.
Chansky, Dorothy, "Kenneth Macgowan and the Aesthetic Paradigm for the New Stagecraft in America," in *Theatre Survey*, May 1998.

* * *

Kenneth MacGowan was a creative motion picture producer, film scholar, and teacher. The 50 films for which he was responsible include two milestones in the use of three-color Technicolor, and his ten years at 20th Century-Fox resulted in his being regarded as an expert in historical biographies.

A New Englander and Harvard graduate, MacGowan was the entertainment editor of the Philadelphia *Evening Ledger*, publicity director for Goldwyn Pictures, and drama critic for the New York *Globe*. More importantly, in 1924 he was named director of the revamped Provincetown Playhouse, the two associate directors being the playwright Eugene O'Neill and the scenic designer Robert Edmund Jones. That trio's productions of O'Neill's *All God's Chillun Got Wings*, *Desire under the Elms*, and *The Emperor Jones* were revolutionary in theater history. By 1926 financial setbacks forced MacGowan into play production outside Provincetown Playhouse, and he was eventually hired by David O. Selznick—at the suggestion of director Irving Pichel—as story editor at RKO. He went from story editor to producer, his first important production being the charming *Topaze* starring John Barrymore and Myrna Loy, followed by the highly successful and enduring *Little Women*. He then produced *La Cucaracha*, the first live-action film in three-color Technicolor for which he hired Robert Edmund Jones to "design Light." That led to his technically innovative Technicolor production of *Becky Sharp*, directed by Rouben Mamoulian.

Following disagreements with RKO, MacGowan joined the newly formed 20th Century-Fox in 1935 where his assignments ran the gamut of Fox's output from musicals to basic programmers. With the success of *Lloyds of London* in 1936, he was handed many of Fox's biographical features, including *In Old Chicago*. Darryl F. Zanuck suggested that story as a result of MGM's success with *San Francisco*. The film's famous Chicago fire sequence remains a landmark

in special effects. Subsequently, MacGowan produced *The Story of Alexander Graham Bell*, *Stanley and Livingstone*, *Brigham Young—Frontiersman*, and *Tin Pan Alley*. MacGowan's favorite film was *Happy Land*, a piece of Americana about "the effects of World War II on a typical American Family." He was instrumental in arranging for John Steinbeck to flesh out Alfred Hitchcock's nucleus of an idea for *Lifeboat*, one of the director's more unusual and interesting films. MacGowan ended his association with Fox in 1944 with *Jane Eyre*, but was one of numerous producers on that project.

After producing *Easy Come, Easy Go* for Paramount in 1947, he left the motion picture business to join UCLA, where he was responsible for organizing one of the best university theater departments in the country. That university's theater building is now named after him, and shortly before his death he completed work on his unique and lasting book, *Behind the Screen: The History and Techniques of the Motion Picture*.

—Ronald Bowers

MACPHERSON, Jeanie

Writer, Director, and Actress. **Nationality:** American. **Born:** Boston, Massachusetts, in 1884. **Education:** Attended Mademoiselle DeJacque's School, Paris. **Career:** 1907–14—stage and film actress: member of the chorus, Chicago Opera House, film debut in *Mr. Jones at the Ball*, 1908, and in road companies of *Cleopatra* and *Strongheart* and on Broadway in *Havana*; 1912—directed and appeared in new version of lost film, *The Tarantula*; 1915—began long association with Cecil B. De Mille. **Died:** Of cancer, 26 August 1946.

Films as Writer for Cecil B. De Mille:

1915 *The Unafraid*; *The Captive* (+ ro); *Chimmie Fadden Out West*; *The Golden Chance*
1916 *Maria Rosa*; *Temptation*; *The Trail of the Lonesome Pine*; *The Heart of Nora Flynn*; *The Dream Girl*
1917 *Joan the Woman*; *A Romance of the Redwoods*; *The Little American*; *The Woman God Forgot*; *The Devil Stone*
1918 *The Whispering Chorus*; *Old Wives for New*
1919 *Don't Change Your Husband*; *For Better, for Worse*; *Male and Female*
1920 *Something to Think About*
1921 *Forbidden Fruit*; *The Affairs of Anatol*
1922 *Saturday Night*; *Manslaughter*
1923 *Adam's Rib*; *The Ten Commandments*
1924 *Triumph*
1925 *The Golden Bed*; *The Road to Yesterday*
1927 *The King of Kings*
1929 *The Godless Girl*; *Dynamite*
1930 *Madam Satan*
1935 *The Crusades*
1937 *The Plainsman*
1938 *The Buccaneer*
1939 *Land of Liberty* (doc); *Union Pacific*
1940 *North West Mounted Police*
1944 *The Story of Dr. Wassel*

Other Films as Writer:

1912   *The Tarantula* (+ d + ro)
1914   *The Ghost Breaker* (+ d)
1926   *Red Dice* (Howard); *Young April* (Crisp)
1933   *Fra Diavolo* (*The Devil's Brother*) (Roach)

Films as Actress for D.W. Griffith:

1908   *Mr. Jones at the Ball*
1909   *Mrs. Jones Entertains*; *A Corner in Wheat*
1910   *Winning Back His Love*
1911   *The Spanish Gypsy*; *Fisher Folks*; *Enoch Arden*
1914   *The Desert's Sting* (d unknown)

Films as Actress for Cecil B. De Mille:

1914   *Rose of the Rancho*
1915   *The Girl of the Golden West*; *Carmen*

Publications

By MACPHERSON: articles—

"Development of Photodramatic Writing," in *Moving Picture World*, 21 July 1917.
"Functions of the Continuity Writer," in *Opportunities in the Motion Picture Industry*, Los Angeles, 1922.
"The Subtitle: Friend and Foe," in *Motion Picture Director* (Hollywood), November 1926.
"Development of Photodramatic Writing," in *Film History* (London), no. 3, 1997.

On MACPHERSON: articles—

Cinema (Beverly Hills, California), no. 35, 1976.
Foreman, Alexa L., in *American Screenwriters, 2nd series*, edited by Randall Clark, Detroit, Michigan, 1986.
McCreadie, Marsha, "Pioneers (Part Two)," in *Films in Review* (New York), January-February 1995.
Kino (Sophia), no. 4, 1995.

*   *   *

Jeanie Macpherson was not a screenwriter when she was introduced to Cecil B. De Mille. She had been a director at Universal at one time, but when she met De Mille she was concentrating on acting. Due to her dark features, however, she was being typecast as either a gypsy or a Spaniard. Macpherson was cast by De Mille to act in a few of his features (*Rose of the Rancho*, *The Girl of the Golden West*, *Carmen*, and *The Captive*—the last of which she also wrote) before she decided to turn exclusively to screenwriting. There was mutual attraction between Macpherson and De Mille from the start: she loved the challenge of working with a hard-driving perfectionist; he was drawn

to her spirit and courage. It was a partnership that would last over 25 years.

Macpherson and De Mille held a common belief that would be the basis for every screenplay on which they collaborated: they despised weakness in men and women. In Macpherson's scripts, weak men were taken advantage of and degraded, and weak women were shallow, gold-digging, and destructive creatures who went from one rich man to the next. The screenwriter believed that men and women could learn from experience, however, and change weak or evil ways, and she demonstrated this in her early social dramas. Both Macpherson and De Mille celebrated the hero and the heroine—biblical, historical, or fictional—and praised their courage and perseverance.

Macpherson's strength was writing historical dramas. When she began her work for De Mille, she assisted the director in writing features for Geraldine Farrar, the operatic star, including *Maria Rosa*, *Temptation*, and *Joan the Woman*. This last was based on the life of Joan of Arc. While De Mille created the huge frame around the French girl's life with his grandiose settings and hundreds of extras, Macpherson fashioned a human drama with which the audience could identify. Thus, while Joan was part of a spectacular event, upon a closer look she was seen as a frightened young girl driven by her spiritual beliefs. The title, Macpherson's idea, emphasized the view of Joan as a human being rather than an indestructible saint. This same viewpoint was used in the De Mille epic *The King of Kings*. Based on the life of Jesus Christ, the film portrayed Mary Magdalene as a woman who was not evil but misguided, and Jesus as a virile and strong man.

By the Roaring Twenties, Macpherson had begun writing contemporary drama rather than historical projects. The liberal moral climate gave rise to the flapper, the sexually aware young woman who rejected conventional mores. Some of the best films De Mille and Macpherson created were responses to America's change in mood and fashion: *Old Wives for New*, *Don't Change Your Husband*, *Male and Female*, *The Affairs of Anatol*, *Manslaughter*, and *Adam's Rib*. *Male and Female*, an update of the play *The Admirable Crichton*, introduced a new element into Macpherson's screenplays: the blending together of past and present stories. Macpherson interweaved episodes from history and the Bible into modern dramas to demonstrate moral lessons. These lessons warned audiences of the excesses of the 1920s and what the future would hold if the warnings were not heeded. Flashbacks were used as lessons, such as the prologue to *The Ten Commandments* which concerned Moses and the story of the commandments (this version of *Ten Commandments* had a modern-day plot). *Male and Female* contained a flashback to Babylon; *Manslaughter* to ancient Rome; *Adam's Rib* to prehistoric times; *Triumph* to Romeo and Juliet; and *The Road to Yesterday* to 17th-century England. These screenplays offered audiences not only an admonishment for their money, but also the attraction of seeing stars in the period costumes that each flashback required.

In 1933, while De Mille was busy with other projects, Macpherson wrote the screenplay for *Fra Diavolo* for Laurel and Hardy, before rejoining the director for several films celebrating heroes: King Richard the Lionhearted in *The Crusades*, Wild Bill Hickok in *The Plainsman*, Jean Lafitte in *The Buccaneer*, the men who started the transcontinental railroad in *Union Pacific*, Canadian Mounties in *North West Mounted Police*, and Dr. Corydon E. Wassell in *The Story of Dr. Wassell*. In 1939, she coauthored and narrated the De Mille film *Land of Liberty*, a historical look at America for the New York World's Fair. These last research and writing projects were done mostly without credit. Before she could finish her research work on

Unconquered for De Mille, Macpherson died of cancer in 1946. Her screenplays had gone full circle from the early escapist and historical films to realistic and social dramas and back to escapist and historical pictures again.

—Alexa L. Foreman

MADDOW, Ben

Writer and director and producer. **Pseudonyms:** Used pseudonyms David Wolff and David Forrest in early documentary films. **Nationality:** American. **Born:** Passaic, New Jersey, 1909; **Education:** Attended Columbia University, New York, graduated 1930. **Military Service:** 1945–47—served in the United States Army Air Corps motion picture unit. **Career:** 1930–35—worked as hospital orderly and social worker; also a writer; 1935—first film as writer, the documentary *Harbor Scenes*; 1935–42—cofounding writer, Nykino (later Frontier Films); wrote commentary for the newsreel series *The World Today*; 1947—first fiction film as writer, *Framed*; 1952–60—blacklisted because of his leftish background; worked (uncredited) on several screenplays, often with Philip Yordan; 1960—codirected *The Savage Eye*; 1980s—TV work included scripts for *The Untouchables*. **Died:** October 1992.

Films as Writer (Documentaries):

1935 *Harbor Scenes* (Steiner)
1937 *Heart of Spain* (Klein and Karpathi); *China Strikes Back* (Dunham); *People of the Cumberland* (Meyers)
1938 *Return to Life* (Kline and Cartier-Bresson)
1939 *The History and Romance of Transportation* (Meyers and Berman)
1940 *United Action* (Berman); *White Flood* (Meyers and Berman); *Tall Tales* (Van Dyke); *Valley Town* (Van Dyke)
1941 *A Place to Live* (Bobker); *Here Is Tomorrow* (Kerkow)
1942 *Native Land* (Hurwitz and Strand); *The Bridge* (Van Dyke) (+ co-d); *Pacific Northwest* (Van Dyke)
1948 *The Photographer* (Van Dyke)
1951 *The Steps of Age* (+ d)
1953 *The Stairs* (+ d)

Films as Writer (Features):

1947 *Framed* (*Paula*) (Wallace)
1948 *Kiss the Blood Off My Hands* (*Blood on My Hands*) (Foster); *The Man from Colorado* (Levin)
1949 *Intruder in the Dust* (Brown)
1950 **The Asphalt Jungle** (Huston)
1952 *Shadow in the Sky* (Wilcox)
1954 **Johnny Guitar** (Ray) (uncredited); *The Naked Jungle* (Haskin) (uncredited)
1957 *Men in War* (A. Mann) (uncredited)
1958 *God's Little Acre* (A. Mann)
1960 *The Savage Eye* (+ co-pr + co-d); *The Unforgiven* (Huston)
1961 *Two Loves* (Walters)

1963 *The Balcony* (Strick); *An Affair of the Skin* (+ d—reedited version, as *Love As Disorder* , 1971)
1967 *The Way West* (McLaglen)
1969 *The Chairman* (Thompson); *The Secret of Santa Vittoria* (Kramer)
1970 *Storm of Strangers* (+ pr + d)
1971 *The Mephisto Waltz* (Wendkos)

Publications

By MADDOW: books—

44 Gravel Street (novel), Boston, Massachusetts, 1952.
The Great Right Horn of the Ram (play), New York, 1967.
Edward Weston (biography), New York, 1973, revised edition 1979.
Faces: A History of Portrait Photography from 1820 to the Present, New York, 1977.
A Sunday between Wars: The Course of American Life from 1865 to 1917, New York, 1979.
With John Huston, *The Asphalt Jungle* (script), edited by Matthew J. Bruccoli, Carbondale, Illinois, 1980.
The Photography of Max Yavno, Berkeley, California, 1981.
With Marketa Luskacovas, *Aperture, no. 92*, New York, 1983.
A False Autobiography: Poems, 1940–1990, Carmel, 1991.

By MADDOW: articles—

''Film into Poem,'' in *New Theatre*, November 1936.
''The Writer's Function in Documentary Film,'' in *Proceedings of the Writers' Congress, Los Angeles, 1943*, Berkeley, California, 1944.
''Eisenstein and the Historical Film,'' in *Hollywood Quarterly*, October 1945.
In *The Hollywood Screenwriter*, edited by Richard Corliss, New York, 1972.
Action (Los Angeles), January-February 1975.
Film Comment (New York), March-April 1980.

On MADDOW: books—

Fadiman, Regina K., *Faulkner's ''Intruder in the Dust'': Novel into Film*, Knoxville, Tennessee, 1978.
Alexander, William, *Film on the Left*, Princeton, New Jersey, 1981.

On MADDOW: articles—

Fields, Verna, in *American Film* (Washington, D.C.), June 1976.
Hagan, John, in *American Screenwriters, 2nd series*, edited by Randall Clark, Detroit, Michigan, 1986.
Film Dope (Nottingham), December 1987.
Sight and Sound (London), Summer 1989.
McGilligan, Patrick, ''Ben Maddow: The Invisible Man,'' in *Sight and Sound* (London), Summer 1989.
Obituary in *New York Times*, vol. 142, 14 October 1992.
Obituary in *Variety*, vol. 348, 19 October 1992.
Obituary in *Time*, vol. 140, 26 October 1992.
Obituary in *Time*, 26 October 1992.

Obituary in *Classic Images*, no. 209, November 1992.
Obituary in *Film en Televisie + Video*, no. 427, December 1992.
Kemp, Philip, "'The Story of All Wars': Anthony Mann's Men in
    War," in *Film Comment* (New York), July-August 1996.

*   *   *

Ben Maddow spent much of his screenwriting career working
without credit or under a pseudonym, and on commercial projects
over which he maintained little control. Despite this, he gained
a reputation in both independent and popular cinema as a socially
concerned artist. Maddow's involvement with film began in 1935
when he answered an advertisement placed by the celebrated still
photographer Ralph Steiner who was seeking a poet to write narration
for his film *Harbor Scenes*. Maddow, who had begun to have his
poetry published in small literary journals, found that his words came
to life when combined with the film's images. Through Steiner, he
met a number of photographers and developed the aesthetic concern
with photography which would play a large role in much of his later
film work.

Maddow joined Steiner and other leftist artists to form Nykino, an
informal organization devoted to making films that promoted social
awareness and the interests of the working class. Nykino was succeeded by Frontier Films which Maddow participated in as a writer of
narration and commentary under the pseudonym David Wolff. (Pseudonyms were used by a number of artists at this time since their
government-subsidized jobs prohibited their taking on outside employment.) The members of Frontier Films were influenced by the
popular *March of Time* series which combined staged scenes and
documentary footage. At the same time, they wished to deal with
social problems in a more politically and stylistically radical fashion
by presenting stories about individuals which would provide a configuration and illumination of the class struggle in American society.
As Maddow expressed it, the documentary director, writer, and
cameraman should work as a team, with the writer looking "constantly for ideas in their specific personal forms" but linked by "a
hard, invariable core of essential truth." He felt that any method—
individual stories, animation, reenactment, candid material—could
be utilized in expressing these ideas.

Maddow admired *The March of Time*'s use of offscreen narration
and thought that this procedure might be used further to achieve a new
form of cinema, the "cine-poem," in which a continuous voice would
serve as a "sort of ground-bass to the images on screen." Freed from
any fixed temporal continuity, a film could "encompass modern
events, their violent compressions and simultaneities," by selecting
and presenting actions which, when linked, would delineate larger
social issues. As an alternative to *The March of Time*'s practice of
writing the narration first and then fitting the image to it, Maddow
proposed that the writer finish a few minutes of narration, then read it
aloud and watch the film on the movieola, going back over it
repeatedly—experimenting with how words could be arranged to
correspond to the movement of the image on screen and with how
they could be used to accentuate or conceal a detail, retard or increase
the tempo. He felt, however, that the result must always be the same:
to combine words and images to form a single indivisible impression.

When Frontier Films disbanded, Maddow went to South America
to work on *The Bridge*, a documentary about trade problems faced by
that continent. Upon his return to the United States, he was drafted
and served in the Army Air Force's Hollywood Motion Picture
Bureau. During this period, he wrote a screen treatment titled *Death*

and Mathematics which, while never filmed, reflects the concerns
raised in Maddow's previous writings on film and anticipates the
complex, eclectic style of many of the later films over which he
maintained control. *Death and Mathematics* concerns a science
teacher who returned wounded from the war and is scheduled to teach
a university course in nuclear physics, but is uncertain whether to
mention atomic energy's destructive possibilities. His voice is heard
intermittently on the soundtrack over screen images which are at
times seen from his viewpoint and at other times from a sort of
omniscient perspective. Close-ups, commentary, photographs, animation, stock footage, and staged scenes are all used to fuse the
personal and educational aspects of the film.

After leaving the Army, Maddow wrote screenplays for several
Hollywood studios. *Intruder in the Dust*, his adaptation of William
Faulkner's novel about racial prejudice, was his first major achievement as a Hollywood screenwriter. The complexity of Faulkner's plot
and the movement of the narrative back and forth in time led Maddow
to simplify story details and to reorganize the narrative's temporal
structure. After this, he worked with John Huston on the screenplay of
The Asphalt Jungle, a study of the criminal mind. Maddow's script for
Shadow in the Sky dealt with difficulties faced by a war veteran upon
his release from a mental hospital. *The Steps of Age* and *The Stairs*,
two documentaries made by Maddow outside the studio system,
concerned the issues of aging and mental health. During the Hollywood blacklist, Maddow worked without credit on several scripts. He
went on to write for a number of television drama series and resumed
screenwriting under his name with Huston's *The Unforgiven*, a study
of racial strife in Texas shortly after the American Civil War.

Maddow's next film was *The Savage Eye*, on which he worked
intimately with Joseph Strick and Sidney Meyers. It concerned
a recently divorced woman, adrift and traveling alone through Los
Angeles. As she converses offscreen with what seems to be an inner
voice guiding her through the agony of realization, a series of
disparate images is seen. Maddow has claimed that *The Savage Eye*
was imitated widely by American and European filmmakers. One can
see how, in its study of a woman whose marital problems have
estranged her from the world, it anticipated, if not influenced, such
films as *The Misfits, Red Desert*, and *Juliet of the Spirits*. Maddow
and Strick again worked together on a film of Jean Genet's *The
Balcony*, with the play's "house of illusions" setting changed from
a brothel to a converted movie soundstage.

Certain motifs recur in Maddow's work whether it be independent
or commissioned, original or an adaptation. In his screenplay for *Two
Loves*, derived from Sylvia Ashton-Warner's novel *Spinster*, the
themes of emotional inhibition, postwar trauma, and cultural clashes
are again addressed. In *An Affair of the Skin*, written and directed by
Maddow, a woman spurns, yet yearns for, affection. Maddow felt that
this story of romantic entanglements as seen through the eyes of
a black woman photographer had been rushed for financial reasons.
Ten years later, he reedited and released it again under the title *Love
As Disorder*. An offscreen narration by the photographer was added
to establish her as an observer: a participant in the action but also
a caustic chronicler of it. As in much of Maddow's work, inner
disorder is seen against a background of social unrest as described in
a highly imagistic manner by a person who has both emotional
involvement and critical detachment.

In *The Chairman*, the United States and the Soviet Union are
forced into an uneasy alliance against Red China which has discovered an enzyme which makes great agricultural development possible. A parallel is drawn in the film between the American General

Shelby, willing to sacrifice his and others' lives for the sake of his country, and the Chinese Chairman who believes that an individual's fate is unimportant in the struggle for the progress of the masses. The fanatical Shelby resembles the men warped by war in earlier Maddow films. His glasses, with one lens tinted black, recall the black eye patch worn by the war veteran in *Death and Mathematics*. In both instances, the dark eye covering serves to suggest a psychological as well as physical injury. Like *Death and Mathematics*, which made the point that Fascism's worst crime was that it forced democracy to pervert science for wartime purposes, *The Chairman* holds up to criticism two opposing ideologies. Again in Maddow's work, social deficiencies are seen in microcosm in the individual's search for emotional fulfillment. The General, who shows no interest in the death of a scientist's wife, and the Chairman, who believes that individual love is less important than love of the masses, are contrasted with the scientist, whose wish to use the enzyme for the international alleviation of poverty coincides with his search for personal happiness.

Maddow's most notable film in the 1970s was his independent production *Storm of Strangers* which depicts how, for turn-of-the-century immigrants living in New York's Lower East Side slums, "It was better to be an uptown horse than a downtown Jew." For the film, Maddow devised a new, less expensive method of scanning photographs to approximate the way the eye scans an image, so that the camera movement would be as personalized as the first-person narration. Here too one finds Maddow combining precise visual imagery with ornate offscreen language in a purely cinematic attempt to deal with individual lives and the larger social issues which they delineate.

—John Hagan

MAGNUSSON, Charles

Producer and director. **Nationality:** Swedish. **Born:** Göteborg, 26 January 1878. **Career:** Professional photographer from 1894; 1905—newsreel cameraman; 1907—founded Swedish Cinematographic Society; 1909—named director of first Swedish studio, Svenska Biografteatern: first film, *Varmlanningarne*; located in Kristianstad until 1911, then in Stockholm; 1912—hired Stiller and Sjöström as directors; 1919–28—production chief of Svensk Filmindustri. **Died:** In Stockholm, 18 January 1948.

Films as Producer:

1909   *Varmlanningarne* (Engdahl) (+ sc); *Spiskroksvalsen* (+ d); *Sjörövaren* (+ d); *Fiskarvals från Bohuslän* (+ d); *När jag var Prins Utav Arkadien* (+ d); *Nattmarschen i Sankt Eriks Gränd* (+ d); *Minnen fran Bostonklubben* (*Memories from the Boston Club*) (+ d + sc); *Brollopet pa Ulfasa* (Engdahl) (+ sc); *Fanrik Stals Sagner* (Engdahl) (+ sc)

1910   *Faderulla, ur Göteborgssystemet I ...* (+ d); *Pick Me Up, ur Flickorna Jackson* (+ d); *Nu gar jag till Maxim* (+ d); *Entres angen, ur Dollarprinsessan* (+ d); *Urfeus i underjorden* (*Orpheus in the Underworld*) (+ d + sc)

1911   *Järnbäraren* (*Iron-Carrier*) (Linden); *Sjömansdansen* (+ d); *Amuletten* (*The Talisman*) (+ d)

1912   *Det gröna halsbandet* (*The Green Necklace*) (+ d); *Samhallets dom* (*The Justice of Society*) (Jaenzon) (+ sc); *Kolingens galoscher* (Jaenzon) (+ sc); *Tva Svenska emigranters aventyr i Amerika* (*The Adventures of Two Swedish Emigrants in America*) (Jaenzon) (+ sc); *Branningar, eller Stulen lycka* (Jaenzon) (+ sc); *De svarta maskerna* (*The Black Masks*) (Stiller); *Dodshoppet farn circkuskupolen* (af Klercker); *Mor och dotter* (*Mother and Daughter*) (Stiller); *Trädgardsmästaren* (*The Gardener*) (Sjöström); *Ett hemligt giftermäl* (*A Secret Marriage*) (Sjöström); *I livets vår, eller Forsta alskarinnan* (*In the Spring of Life, or His First Love*) (Garbagny); *Den tryanniske fästmannen* (*The Tyrannical Fiancee*) (Stiller); *Skandalen* (*Scandal*) (af Klercker); *Vampyren* (*Vampire*) (Stiller); *En sommarsaga* (*A Summer Tale*) (Sjöström); *Barnet* (*The Child*) (Stiller)

1913   *Löjen och tårar* (*Ridicule and Tears*) (Sjöström); *När kärleken dödar* (*When Love Kills*) (Stiller); *Lady Marions sommarflirt* (*Lady Marion's Summer Flirtation*) (Sjöström); *Ingeborg Holm* (*Give Us This Day*) (Sjöström); *Gränsfolken* (*The Border Feud*) (Stiller); *Miraklet* (*The Miracle*) (Sjöström); *Halvblod* (*Halfbreed*) (Sjöström)

1914   *Prästen* (*The Priest*) (Sjöström); *Strejken* (*Strike*) (Sjöström); *Stormfågeln* (*The Stormy Petrel*) (Stiller); *Gatans barn* (*Children of the Street*) (Sjöström); *Det roda tornet* (*The Master*) (Stiller); *Högfjällets dotter* (*Daughter of the Mountains*) (Sjöström)

1915   *Madame de Thèbes* (Stiller); *Hans bröllopsnatt* (*His Wedding Night*) (Stiller)

1916   *Rösen på Tistelön* (*The Rose of Thistle Island*) (Sjöström); *Karlek och journalistik* (*Love and the Journalist*) (Stiller); *Vingarna* (*The Wings*) (Stiller); *Therese* (Sjöström); *Den levande mumien* (*The Living Mummy*) (F. Magnusson); *Vem Skot?* (Tallroth); *Balettprimadonnan* (*Anjuta, the Dancer*) (Stiller)

1917   *Terje vigen* (*A Man There Was*) (Sjöström); *Thomas Graals bästa film* (*Thomas Graal's Best Picture*) (Stiller)

1918   *Tösen från stormyrtorpet* (*The Lass from the Stormy Croft*) (Sjöström); *Berg-Ejvind och hans hustru* (*The Outlaw and His Wife*) (Sjöström); *Thomas Graals bästa barn* (*Thomas Graal's Best Child*) (Stiller); *Sången om den eldröda blomman* (*Song of the Scarlet Flower*) (Stiller)

1919   *Ingmarssonerna* (*Sons of Ingmar*) (Stiller—2 parts); *Dunungen* (*The Downey Girl*) (Hedqvist); *Herr Arnes pengar* (*Sir Arne's Treasure*) (Stiller); *Hans nåds testamente* (*The Will of His Grace*) (Sjöström); *Fiskebyn* (*The Fishing Village*) (Stiller)

1920   *Klostret it sendomir* (*The Monastery of Sendomir*) (Sjöström); *Karin Ingmarsdotter* (*Karin, Daughter of Ingmar*) (Sjöström); *Mästerman* (*Master Samuel*) (Sjöström); *Prästänkan* (*The Parson's Widow*) (Dreyer); *Guyrkoviscarna* (Brunius); *Familjens traditioner* (Carlsten); *Carolina Rediviva* (Hedqvist); *Erotikon* (Stiller); *Johan* (Stiller)

1921   *Körkarlen* (*The Phantom Chariot*) (Sjöström); *Vallfarten till Kevlar* (*Pilgrimage to Kevlar*) (Hedqvist); *Kvarnen* (Brunius); *Hogre andamal* (Carlsten); *De landsflyktiga* (*The Exiles*) (Stiller); *En vildfagel* (Brunius)

1922   *Vem dömer?* (*Love's Crucible*) (Sjöström); *Det omrigade huset* (*The Surrounded House*) (Sjöström); *Gunnar Hedes Saga* (*Gunnar Hede's Saga*) (Stiller)

1923 *Eld ombord* (*The Tragic Ship*) (Sjöström); *Harda viljor*
      (Brunius); *Johan Ulfstjerna* (Brunius); *Mälarpirater* (*Pi-
      rates on Lake Mälar*) (Molander); *Karusellen* (Buchowetzki);
      Boman på utstallningen (Brunius); *Gösta Berlings Saga*
      (*Gösta Berling's Saga*) (Stiller—2 parts)
1924 *En piga blad pigor* (Brunius)
1925 *Ingmarsarvet* (*The Ingmar Inheritance*) (Molander)
1926 *Till Osterland* (*To the Orient*) (Molander)

Publications

On MAGNUSSON: articles—

Waldekranz, Rune, "Un produttore, una cinematografia," in *Bianco
  e Nero* (Rome), July 1960.
Lutro, D., "Da spillefilmen fikk sitt gjennombrudd," in *Film & Kino*
  (Oslo), March 1979.

                    *   *   *

The Swedish cinema and its early silent masterpieces were largely
due to the vision and talent of Charles Magnusson. His knowledge of
the technical side of filmmaking (he was a newsreel cameraman) as
well as the aesthetics of recording images and controlling performances (he was also a director) made him an ideal producer. His artistic
ambitions consciously strove to lend cultural respectability to the
movies. Believing that the short farces which dominated the early
cinema only exploited the film medium for financial gain, he encouraged his directors to attempt themes of complexity and sophistication.
During the period he served as director of Svenska Biografteatern,
Magnusson led Sweden to the forefront of world cinema.

One of the many striking characteristics of Swedish silent films is
their spectacular use of outdoor settings. Magnusson eschewed the
use of studio sets, voicing an opinion that natural locations induced
other qualities. His films embody a lyricism previously untapped by
the cinema and create a drama between the characters and nature
which evolves into a mystical relationship. Taking the actors out of
the studio also resulted in another important development: a restraint
and realism of performance. Magnusson laid the foundations of
a non-theatrical style, in which nature, history, and reality were an
essential part, that still influences cinema today. He also initiated the
development of longer narrative films based on fine literature and
epic folk tales. By obtaining the rights to all of Selma Lagerlöf's work
(the greatest of Swedish storytellers) and adapting many of Henrik
Ibsen's plays, he provided a source of rich material for the studio to
use, material which echoed his interest in nature and Swedish history.

Magnusson firmly centered himself as controlling force of the
Swedish film industry, yet he was not dictatorial. He allowed his
directors a freedom uncommon for that period. He once commented
that "the film producer must be supreme ruler. He alone decides . . .
but after he has given the starting signal, he should leave the director
in peace. If the director is unworthy of this confidence, he is not fit to
be director." The films of Mauritz Stiller and Victor Sjöström, which
represent many milestones in the history of cinema, justified
Magnusson's faith in them.

Besides his work as a producer, Magnusson was active in many
other related fields. He experimented with a stereoscopic film process
and instigated the reorganization of the film censorship board. A social reformer, he used his films to make viewers aware of society's

inadequacies and injustices. These films were rarely didactic because
he realized the importance of interest and the role of identification.
Magnusson said that "the action is the picture's Alpha and Omega. It
should . . . give opportunities for intensely exciting and interesting
situations." His productions during the golden age of Swedish
cinema make this tenet crystal clear.

—Greg S. Faller

MAINWARING, Daniel

Writer. **Pseudonyms:** early 1930s and late 1940s—novelist (under pseudonym Geoffrey Homes); early 1940s through 1960s—
screenwriter (under given name and Geoffrey Homes pseudonym).
Nationality: American. **Born:** Oakland, California, 27 February
1902. **Education:** University of Fresno, California. **Career:** 1920s
and early 1930s—private detective, newspaper reporter, *San Francisco Chronicle*, writer in Warner Bros. publicity department.
Died: 1977.

Films as Writer:

1943 *Secrets of the Underground* (Morgan) (co-sc, as
      Geoffrey Homes)
1944 *Dangerous Passage* (Berke)
1945 *Scared Stiff* (McDonald) (co-sc); *They Made Me a Killer*
      (Thomas) (co-sc)
1946 *Swamp Fire* (Pine) (+ story); *Hot Cargo* (Landers); *Tokyo
      Rose* (Landers)
1947 *Big Town* (Thomas) (as Geoffrey Homes, also radio pro-
      gram); *Out of the Past* (Tourneur) (as Geoffrey Homes,
      also novel)
1948 *Big Town Scandal* (Thomas) (co-sc, as Geoffrey Homes, also
      radio program)
1949 *Roughshod* (Robson) (co-sc); *The Big Steal* (Siegel) (co-sc, as
      Geoffrey Homes)
1950 *The Lawless* (Losey) (as Geoffrey Homes, also novel); *The
      Eagle and the Hawk* (Foster) (co-sc)
1951 *The Last Outpost* (Foster) (co-sc, as Geoffrey Homes)
1952 *This Woman Is Dangerous* (Feist) (co-sc, as Geoffrey Homes);
      Bugles in the Afternoon (Rowland) (co-sc, as
      Geoffrey Homes)
1953 *Powder River* (King) (co-sc, as Geoffrey Homes); *The Hitch-
      Hiker* (Lupino) (co-sc, uncredited); *Those Redheads from
      Seattle* (Foster)
1954 *The Desperado* (Carr) (as Geoffrey Homes); *Black Horse
      Canyon* (Hibbs); *Southwest Passage* (Nazarro) (co-sc);
      Alaska Seas (Hopper) (co-sc, as Geoffrey Homes)
1955 *Tormenta* (Acebal/Guillermin) (co-sc + story, as Geoffrey
      Homes); *The Phenix City Story* (Karlson) (co-sc); *A Bullet
      for Joey* (Allen) (co-sc, as Geoffrey Homes); *An Annapolis
      Story* (Siegel) (co-sc, as Geoffrey Homes)
1956 *Invasion of the Body Snatchers* (Siegel)
1957 *Baby Face Nelson* (Siegel) (co-sc)
1958 *Space Master X-7* (Bernds) (co-sc); *The Gun Runners* (Siegel);
      Cole Younger, Gunfighter (Springsteen)
1960 *Walk Like a Dragon* (Clavell) (co-sc)

1961   *The Minotaur* (Amadio) (co-sc); *The George Raft Story* (Newman) (co-sc); *Atlantis, The Lost Continent* (Pal); *The Revolt of the Slaves* (Malasomma) (co-sc)
1964   *The Woman Who Wouldn't Die* (Hessler)
1965   *Convict Stage* (Selander)

Other Films:

1941   *No Hands on the Clock* (McDonald) (novel)
1944   *Crime by Night* (Clemens) (novel)
1947   *Big Town after Dark* (Thomas) (radio program)
1951   *The Tall Target* (Mann) (story, as Geoffrey Homes); *Road-block* (Daniels) (story, as Geoffrey Homes)
1984   *Against All Odds* (Hackford) (novel)

*   *   *

Considering that the *film noir* masterpiece *Out of the Past* and the prototypical close encounter of the third kind science-fiction thriller *Invasion of the Body Snatchers* continue to cast giant shadows over their respective genres and influence filmmakers to this day, it is ironic that the name of their screenwriter is all but forgotten. This may be because the former was written under a pseudonym and the latter under the writer's given name. This gives the impression that these works were scribed by different individuals. As a result, in most discussions of screenwriters who have left their mark on cinema history, Daniel Mainwaring—who left his mark with not just one but *two* seminal films—seldom comes up.

Mainwaring began his writing career as a newspaper reporter for the *San Francisco Chronicle*, where he drew upon previous experience as a private detective to cover the city's crime and other beats for almost a decade before shifting to detective fiction during the golden age of the pulps. Influenced by the hard-boiled school of writers like Dashiell Hammett (who'd also used firsthand experience as a private eye to give his thrillers a sense of authenticity), Mainwaring published his first crime novel, *One Against the Earth*, in 1933 under his real name. Thereafter, the prolific author used the pseudonym Geoffrey Homes on all of his novels and most of his screenplays as well.

He produced a series of crime novels—boasting such pulpish titles *The Doctor Died at Dusk, The Man Who Didn't Exist*, and *Then There Were Three*—which featured the recurring character of reporter-turned-private eye Robin Bishop. Mainwaring set Bishop apart from other fictional sleuths of the time by making him less hard-boiled and less susceptible to the charms of every femme fatale who comes because he has a wife. The author retired Bishop after five books to launch a new, more hard-boiled detective hero, Humphrey Campbell, in 1938. Campbell appeared in four books before being phased out by a final series character, the Mexican Indian sleuth Jose Manuel Madero, who debuted in *The Street of the Crying Woman*, then disappeared after one more outing.

Mainwaring also turned out several thrillers with no recurring character. The most notable of them was also his biggest bestseller and final book, *Build My Gallows High*. Published in 1946, it became, under the direction of Jacques Tourneur, the definitive *film noir* a year later as *Out of the Past*. It was remade in 1984 as *Against All Odds*. Despite the popularity they enjoyed in their day, none of Mainwaring's Geoffrey Homes books are currently in print, and thus ripe for rediscovery.

A stint as a publicist at Warner Brothers (where he met an aspiring director named Don Siegel who was then working as an editor in Warners montage department) gave Mainwaring an insider's look at the movies. He used his knowledge of Hollywood as background for his 1943 thriller *The Hill of the Terrified Monk*. Mainwaring's studio work as a publicist also opened doors for him as a screenwriter. He adapted his novel *Forty Whacks* to the screen for Warner Brothers as *Crime by Night* in 1944, but it was his crackling adaptation of *Build My Gallows High* into *Out of the Past* for RKO that enabled him to turn his back on novels and pursue a screenwriting career full time.

Mainwaring hooked up with his old pal Don Siegel (by then a director) on *The Big Steal*, a chase melodrama set in Mexico that was made by RKO to capitalize on the success of *Out of the Past* by re-teaming its two stars, Robert Mitchum and Jane Greer with the same writer. Mainwaring and Siegel collaborated four more times. Their biggest success together was *Invasion of the Body Snatchers*, a science-fiction parable about desensitization and loss of identity that made the word "pod" part of the American vocabulary. The archetypal alien invasion flick, it has been remade twice and ripped off countless times.

They also had a notable success as a team a year later with *Baby Face Nelson*, a top-notch period gangster film that earned Mickey Rooney the French equivalent of the Oscar for his incendiary performance in the title role. Of this now largely forgotten but also influential Siegel/Mainwaring collaboration, Siegel biographer Stuart M. Kaminsky writes, "It started a genre of psychological gangster films culminating in . . . Arthur Penn's *Bonnie and Clyde*."

—John McCarty

MAMET, David

Writer and director and actor. **Nationality:** American. **Born:** Chicago, Illinois, 30 November 1947. **Education:** Studied acting at the Neighborhood Playhouse, 1968–69; Goddard College, B.A. (English), 1969. **Family:** Married 1) Lindsay Crouse (an actress), 21 December 1977 (divorced); children: Willa, Zosia; 2) married Rebecca Pidgeon (an actress, singer, and songwriter), 22 September 1991; children: Clara. **Career:** Worked as a busboy, Second City Theatre, Chicago, a stagehand, Hull House Theatre, Chicago, and as factory worker, real estate agent, window washer, office cleaner, taxi driver, truck driver, short order cook, and salesperson; actor in New England summer theatre productions, 1969; special lecturer in drama, Marlboro College, Marlboro, Vermont, 1970; artist-in-residence and instructor in drama, Goddard College, Plainfield, Vermont, 1971–73; founding member and artistic director, St. Nicholas Company, Plainfield, Vermont, 1972; founder (with others), 1973, artistic director, 1973–76, member of the board of directors, beginning in 1973, St. Nicholas Theatre Company, Chicago; faculty member, Illinois Arts Council, Chicago, 1974; contributing editor, *Oui*, 1975–76; visiting lecturer, University of Chicago, Chicago, 1975–76 and 1979; teaching fellow at the School of Drama, Yale University, New Haven, Connecticut, 1976–77; associate artistic director, 1978–79, playwright-in-residence, 1978–84, Goodman Theatre, Chicago; visiting lecturer at the Tisch School of the Arts, 1981, founder of the Atlantic Theatre Company, 1988, and chair of the Atlantic Theatre Company board of

David Mamet with Rebecca Pidgeon

directors, New York University, New York City; associate director, New Theatre Company, Chicago, beginning in 1985; associate professor of film, Columbia University, New York City, 1988; Dinglefest Theatre, Kansas State University, Manhattan, Kansas, founder (with others). **Awards:** Golden Osella, Venice Film Festival, best original screenplay, and Pasinetti Award, Venice Film Festival, best film, for *House of Games*, 1987; also winner of numerous theatre and literary awards. **Agent:** Howard Rosenstone, Rosenstone/Wender, 3 East 48th Street, New York, NY 10017, U.S.A.

Films as Writer:

1979   *A Life in the Theater* (Browning, Gutierrez—for TV)
1981   *The Postman Always Rings Twice* (Rafelson)
1982   *The Verdict* (1982)
1986   *About Last Night. . .* (Zwick) (from his play *Sexual Perversity in Chicago*)
1987   *The Untouchables* (De Palma); *House of Games* (+ d)
1988   *Things Change* (+ d)
1989   *We're No Angels* (Jordan)

1991   *Uncle Vanya* (Mosher—for TV) (translation); *Homicide* (+ d)
1992   *Glengarry Glen Ross* (Foley); *Hoffa* (DeVito) (+ assoc pr); *The Water Engine* (Schachter—for TV) (+ ro)
1993   *Rising Sun* (Kaufman) (uncredited); *A Life in the Theater* (Mosher—for TV) (+ exec pr)
1994   *Texan* (Williams—for TV); *Oleanna* (+ d); *Vanya on 42nd Street* (Malle)
1996   *American Buffalo* (Corrente)
1997   *The Spanish Prisoner* (+ d); *Wag the Dog* (Levinson); *The Edge* (Tamahori)
1998   *Ronin* (Frankenheimer) (as Richard Weisz)
1999   *Lansky* (McNaughton) (for TV) (+ exec pr); *The Winslow Boy* (+ d)
2000   *Lakeboat* (Mantegna); *Whistle* (Lumet); *State and Main* (+ d)

Films as Actor:

1984   *Sanford Meisner: The American Theatre's Best Kept Secret* (Doob) (as Himself)
1986   *Black Widow* (Rafelson) (as Herb)

Publications

By MAMET: books (nonfiction)—

On Directing Film, New York, 1991.
Cabin: Reminiscence and Diversions, New York, 1992.
A Whore's Profession: Notes and Essays, London and Boston, 1994.
Jafsie and John Henry: Essays, New York, 1999.
On Acting, New York, 1999.

By MAMET: articles—

"I Lost It at the Movies," interview with P. Biskind, in *American Film* (Farmingdale, New York), vol. 12, no. 8, June 1987.
Interview in *Time Out* (London), 12 August 1998.
Interview in *Sight and Sound* (London), vol. 8, no. 10, October 1998.
Interview in *Interview* (New York), April 1998.
"The Spanish Prisoner" and "Writing and Directing The Spanish Prisoner," in *Scenario* (Rockville, Maryland), vol. 4, no. 1, 1998.

On MAMET: books—

Bigsby, C. W. E., *David Mamet*, London, 1985.
Carroll, Dennis, *David Mamet*, New York, 1987.
Dean, Anne, *David Mamet: Language as Dramatic Action*, Rutherford, New Jersey, and London, 1990.
Trussler, Simon, Malcolm Page, and Steven Dykes, *File on Mamet*, New York, 1991.
Brewer, Gay, *David Mamet and Film: Illusion/Disillusion in a Wounded Land*, Jefferson, North Carolina, 1993.
McDonough, Carla J., *Staging Masculinity: Male Identity in Contemporary American Drama*, Jefferson, North Carolina, 1997.
Kane, Leslie, *Weasels and Wisemen: Ethics and Ethnicity in the Work of David Mamet*, New York, 1999.

On MAMET: articles—

"David Mamet," in *Film Dope* (Nottingham), no. 38, December 1987.
Weinberger, M., and others, "Engrenages," in *Cinéma 87/88* (Paris), no. 427, 3 February 1988.
Hoberman, J., "Identity Parade," in *Sight and Sound* (London), vol. 1, no. 7, November 1991.
Brewer, G., "Studied Simplicity," in *Literature/Film Quarterly* (Salisbury, Maryland), vol. 20, no. 2, April 1992.
Fisher, Bob, "Minting a Screen Version of *American Buffalo*," in *American Cinematographer* (Hollywood), vol. 77, no. 2, February 1996.
Hudgins, Christopher, "Lolita 1995: The Four Filmscripts," in *Literature/Film Quarterly* (Salisbury, Maryland), vol. 25, no. 1, January 1997.
Rosenbaum, J., "Mamet and Hitchcock: The Men Who Knew Too Much," in *Scenario* (Rockville, Maryland), vol. 4, no. 1, 1998.

*   *   *

From stage playwright to screenwriter is a common enough jump, but relatively few playwrights have gone on to become directors. And none, with the exception of Marcel Pagnol, has done so as successfully as David Mamet. Like Pagnol, Mamet has been able to use his theatrical prestige to resist crass commercial pressures. His films as writer-director are unmistakably personal, made without interference or compromise. The same hasn't always been true of his scripts for other directors, as he readily acknowledges in *On Directing Films*: "Working as a screenwriter-for-hire, one is in the employ not of the eventual consumers (the audience, whose interests the honest writer must have at heart), but of speculators, whose ambition . . . is not to please the eventual consumer, but to extort from him as much money as possible."

Nonetheless, clear thematic preoccupations run through all his film work, whether as writer or as director. The characters that fascinate him are those on the precarious margins of society: con-men, salesmen and hucksters, cops and petty criminals. He is concerned with the codes these fringe people live by, and those they break. Matters of trust and betrayal, illusion and deception, confidence bestowed and confidence betrayed, loom large in his work. Along with these codes goes the jargon: in his films as in his plays, Mamet is famous for the speed and ferocity of his dialogue, the obsessive, almost ritualistic repetitions of words and phrases. Underlying all this is a despairing sense of the corruption of the American Dream, the busted illusion of the pursuit of happiness that haunts a sour, wounded society. In his own typically eloquent words, "My characters are trapped in the destructive folds of the public myths on my country." His first script was for Bob Rafelson's version of James M. Cain's classic pulp *The Postman Always Rings Twice*—the definitive portrait of the footloose American go-getter as bum, sexual opportunist, conspirator and killer.

According to Mamet's own account, he "saw the craft of directing as the joyful extension of screenwriting." But he also followed a well-established tradition of eminent writer-directors (Billy Wilder, Preston Sturges, Joseph Mankiewicz, et al), in taking up direction partly in order to protect his own writing. His directorial debut, *House of Games*, followed closely on the travesty of his play *Sexual Perversity in Chicago* being filmed (not to his script) as *About Last Night* (1986). In that same writer-director tradition, Mamet tends to be matter-of-fact to the point of dismissiveness about his own cinematic technique, disclaiming any pretensions to being an auteur. The director's job, he maintains, "is the work of constructing the shot list from the screenplay. The work on the set is nothing. All you have to do on the set is stay awake, follow your plans, help the actors be simple, and keep your sense of humour. The film is directed in the making of the shot list. . . . It is the plan that makes the movie."

"The plan" in more senses than one. In Mamet's films—many of those he has directed, and several that he has written—the action is often set up to deceive the audience, a visual sleight of hand paralleling the scam that's being worked on the characters. In *House of Games* and *The Spanish Prisoner* (itself named after a classic con routine), the rug is repeatedly pulled out from under us; just as we think we know what is going on, Mamet reveals a further layer of deception. In *Homicide* we are led to believe that Joe Mantegna's cop is uncovering a vast anti-Semitic conspiracy, until a supposed Nazi slogan proves to be a brand of pigeon-feed and the whole miasma of suspicion dissolves into nothingness. (Or maybe not, since the film leaves it possible that this revelation is itself just another trick.) Sometimes Mamet enjoys letting us in on the act, as in *Things Change*, or in his tour de force political satire *Wag the Dog* where—as if in ironic homage to Baudrillard—a whole war is faked up to hoax the public. Though even here, when we have watched the entire scam being devised, the denouement reveals other dimensions that we were not aware of. Referring to *The Spanish Prisoner* Mamet oberved: "I

549

don't feel like I created this script—I feel like I've solved it. It's like a magic trick. You have to give people information, but in such a way that they don't realise it is information.''

Adapting his own stage work for the screen (as in *Oleanna*, which he directed, or *American Buffalo* and *Glengarry Glen Ross*, which he didn't), Mamet simplifies it without losing its pungent flavour, cutting down on the repetitions and truculent non-sequiturs of the original. ''You're basically trying to make up pictures and you only resort to dialogue when you can't make up the perfect picture. . . . The main message is being carried to the audience not by what people say or by how they say it, but by what the camera is doing.'' Not that the camera, in his view, should do very much: he believes in ''let[ting] the cut tell the story,'' and adds that ''fantastic cinematography has been the death of American film.'' He may well have been thinking of *The Untouchables*, where Brian De Palma's showy direction jarred with Mamet's taut dialogue. Despite his own outspoken distaste for Hollywood (''Hell with valet parking'') and the movie industry, Mamet seems increasingly at ease with filmmaking. In recent years he has shown himself ever more inclined to direct his own scripts—and to adapt and direct the work of other playwrights he admires, such as Terence Rattigan and Samuel Beckett. In the register of Mamet's career his status as screenwriter and director may never rival his towering acclaim as a playwright, but it looks set to run it a very respectable second.

—Philip Kemp

MANCINI, Henry

Composer and music director. **Nationality:** American. **Born:** Enrico Nicola Mancini in Cleveland, Ohio, 16 April 1924. **Education:** Studied flute and piano as a child; attended Juilliard School, New York; also studied with Knek, Castelnuovo-Tedesco, and Senrey. **Military Service:** During World War II. **Family:** Married Virginia O'Connor, 1947, one son and twin daughters. **Career:** Arranger and pianist with Glenn Miller Orchestra and other bands; 1952–58—arranger, orchestrator, and composer for Universal; also song composer, and composer for TV, including the mini-series *Arthur Hailey's The Moneychangers*, 1976, *The Best Place to Be*, 1979, and *The Thorn Birds*, 1983. **Awards:** Academy Award, for *Breakfast at Tiffany's* and song ''Moon River,'' 1961, the song ''Days of Wine and Roses,'' *Day of Wine and Roses*, 1962, and *Victor/Victoria*, 1982. **Died:** Of liver and pancreatic cancer, in Los Angeles, 14 June 1994.

Films as Composer:

1954   *Creature from the Black Lagoon* (Arnold); *Six Bridges to Cross* (Pevney) (song); *Four Guns to the Border* (Carlson)
1955   *The Private War of Major Benson* (Hopper); *Tarantula* (Arnold); *This Island Earth* (J. Newman)
1956   *The Creature Walks among Us* (Sherwood); *Congo Crossing* (Pevney); *Rock, Pretty Baby* (Bartlett)
1957   *Man Afraid* (Keller); *The Big Beat* (Cowan)
1958   *Damn Citizen* (Gordon); *Flood Tide* (Biberman); *Summer Love* (Haas); **Touch of Evil** (Welles); *Voice in the Mirror* (Keller)
1960   *High Time* (Edwards)

Henry Mancini

1961   *The Second Time Around* (Sherman) (song); *The Great Imposter* (Burks); *Bachelor in Paradise* (Arnold); **Breakfast at Tiffany's** (Edwards); *Hatari!* (Hawks)
1962   *Experiment in Terror* (*The Grip of Fear*) (Edwards); *Mr. Hobbs Takes a Vacation* (Koster); *Days of Wine and Roses* (Edwards)
1963   *Charade* (Donen); *Soldier in the Rain* (Nelson)
1964   *Man's Favorite Sport?* (Hawks); *The Pink Panther* (Edwards); *A Shot in the Dark* (Edwards); *The Killers* (Siegel)
1965   *Dear Heart* (Delbert Mann); *The Great Race* (Edwards)
1966   *Moment to Moment* (LeRoy); *Arabesque* (Donen); *What Did You Do in the War, Daddy?* (Edwards); *Two for the Road* (Donen)
1967   *Gunn* (Edwards); *Wait until Dark* (Young)
1968   *The Party* (Edwards)
1969   *Me, Natalie* (Coe); *Gaily, Gaily* (*Chicago, Chicago*) (Jewison)
1970   *The Molly Maguires* (Ritt); *Darling Lili* (Edwards); *The Hawaiians* (Gries); *I girasoli* (*Sunflower*) (De Sica)
1971   *Sometimes a Great Notion* (*Never Give an Inch*) (P. Newman); *The Night Visitor* (*Salem Came to Supper*) (Benedek)
1973   *Oklahoma Crude* (Kramer); *Visions of Eight* (Lelouch and others); *The Thief Who Came to Dinner* (Yorkin)
1974   *That's Entertainment!* (Haley) (additional music); *99 and 44/100% Dead* (*Call Harry Crown*) (Frankenheimer); *The White Dawn* (Kaufman); *The Girl from Petrovka* (Miller); *Once Is Not Enough* (Green)
1975   *The Return of the Pink Panther* (Edwards); *The Blue Knight* (Lee Thompson—for TV); *The Great Waldo Pepper* (Hill)

1976   *W. C. Fields and Me* (Hiller); *Alex and the Gypsy* (Korty); *Silver Streak* (Hiller); *The Pink Panther Strikes Again* (Edwards)

1978   *House Calls* (Zieff); *Revenge of the Pink Panther* (Edwards); *Who Is Killing the Great Chefs of Europe?* (*Too Many Chefs*) (Kotcheff); *A Family Upside Down* (Rich)

1979   *Nightwing* (Hiller); *The Great Event* (Zieff); *The Prisoner of Zenda* (Quine); *10* (Edwards)

1980   *Little Miss Marker* (Bernstein)

1981   *S.O.B.* (Edwards); *Condorman* (Jarrott); *The Shadow Box* (P. Newman); *Back Roads* (Ritt); *Mommie Dearest* (Perry)

1982   *Trail of the Pink Panther* (Edwards); *Victor/Victoria* (Edwards)

1983   *Curse of the Pink Panther* (Edwards); *Second Thoughts* (Turman); *Better Late than Never* (Forbes); *The Man Who Loved Women* (Edwards)

1984   *Angela* (Sagal); *Harry & Son* (P. Newman)

1985   *That's Dancing!* (Haley); *Lifeforce* (Hooper); *Santa Claus: The Movie* (Szwarc)

1986   *The Great Mouse Detective* (Musker and others); *A Fine Mess* (Edwards); *That's Life!* (Edwards)

1987   *Blind Date* (Edwards); *The Glass Menagerie* (P. Newman); *Heaven* (D. Keaton) (songs); *No Man's Land* (Werner) (song)

1988   *Heavy Petting* (Benz); *Permanent Record* (M. Silver) (song); *Physical Evidence* (M. Crichton); *The Presidio* (Hyams) (song); *Sunset* (Edwards); *Without a Clue* (Eberhardt)

1989   *Fear* (O'Bannon—for TV); *Born on the Fourth of July* (O. Stone) (song); *Mother, Mother* (short) (song); *Welcome Home* (Schaffner); *Days of Thunder* (T. Scott)

1990   *Tom and Jerry: The Movie* (Roman) (co); *Ghost Dad* (Poitier)

1991   *Switch* (Edwards); *Never Forget* (Sargent—for TV)

1993   *Married to It* (Hiller); *Son of the Pink Panther* (Edwards)

Other Films:

1954   *The Glenn Miller Story* (A. Mann) (mus d)

1956   *The Benny Goodman Story* (Davies) (arranger)

1974   *The Sex Symbol* (Rich) (mus d)

Publications

By MANCINI: books—

Sounds and Scores, Northridge Music, 1962.
Did They Mention the Music?, New York, 1989.
The New Henry Mancini Songbook, Totowa, 1994.

By MANCINI: articles—

Cinema (Los Angeles), July 1966.
Action (Los Angeles), November/December 1971.
Dialogue on Film (Beverly Hills, California), January 1974.
Photoplay (London), October 1974.
Soundtrack! (Hollywood), May 1977.
Interview with Elmer Bernstein, in *Film Music Notebook* (Calabasas, California), vol. 4, no. 1, 1978.
In *Film Score*, edited by Tony Thomas, South Brunswick, New Jersey, 1979.

Millimeter (New York), June 1979.
Photoplay (London), May 1983.
Soundtrack! (Hollywood), vol. 7, no. 26, 1988.

On MANCINI: articles—

Focus on Film (London), March/April 1970.
Thomas, Tony, in *Music for the Movies*, South Brunswick, New Jersey, 1973.
Dirigido por . . . (Barcelona), January 1974.
Films in Review (New York), September 1975.
Ecran (Paris), September 1975.
Caps, John, in *Film Music Notebook* (Calabasas, California), vol. 3, no. 2, 1977.
24 Images (Longueuil, Quebec), September/October 1980.
Fistful of Soundtracks (London), October 1980.
Fistful of Soundtracks (London), May 1981.
Soundtrack! (Hollywood), March 1982.
Films (London), October 1982.
Avant-Scène (Paris), January/February 1986.
Soundtrack! (Hollywood), vol. 9, no. 34, June 1990.
Obituary in *Current Biography*, August 1994.
Obituary in *Down Beat*, September 1994.
Obituary in *Soundtrack*, December 1994.
Scheurer, Timothy E., "Henry Mancini: An Appreciation and Appraisal," in *Journal of Popular Film and Television* (Washington, D.C.), Spring 1996.
Boyd, Herb, "A Tribute to Henry Mancini," in *Down Beat*, June 1996.
McKone, G., "Henry Mancini," in *Film Score Monthly* (Los Angeles), no. 5, 1997.

*   *   *

The composer who made the most important stylistic change in American film music in the late 1950s was Henry Mancini. Using the more modern techniques of the recording industry rather than the by-then outmoded ones of the film studios, and with smaller orchestras and different instrumental groupings, Mancini brought a new awareness to scoring, particularly in the case of the television series *Peter Gunn.*

Mancini was the son of Italian immigrants and grew up in West Aliquippa, Pennsylvania, where his steelworker father was a member of the town band, The Sons of Italy. The boy was started on the piccolo at the age of eight and sent to teachers, of whom the most important was Max Adkins, the conductor of the Stanley Theater in Pittsburgh. Through Adkins, Mancini went straight from high school graduation in 1942 to the Juilliard School of Music in New York. After one year of study he was called to military service, returning to civilian life in 1946, when he was hired as a pianist and arranger with Tex Beneke's newly formed Glenn Miller Orchestra.

In 1952 Mancini was asked to arrange the music for a short subject at Universal. Head of music, Joseph Gershenson, then hired him to do some arrangements for Abbott and Costello's *Lost in Africa*. A contract followed and Mancini spent the next six years adapting library music, orchestrating, and scoring all manner of movies. His dance-band background proved invaluable in being assigned *The Glenn Miller Story* and *The Benny Goodman Story*. Among the many people impressed by Mancini's score for the Orson Welles classic *Touch of*

Evil was Blake Edwards, who hired him to write the ground breaking, jazz-influenced score for *Peter Gunn*. Its success began an association with Edwards that resulted in the scores for *Breakfast at Tiffany's*, which included the song "Moon River" (written with lyricist Johnny Mercer), with Oscars for both the score and the song; *Days of Wine and Roses* (also working with Mercer and winning another best song Oscar); *The Pink Panther* and its sequels; *The Great Race*; *10*; *S.O.B.*; and *Victor/Victoria*, which brought him an Oscar for best original song score. Mancini's film composing ran the gamut of genres. His scary music for *Experiment in Terror* (another Edwards-directed feature) and *Wait until Dark*, the poignant *The Molly Maguires*, and the chilling, unsettling music for *The White Dawn* are as much Mancini as the amusing music for *Hatari!* and *The Great Waldo Pepper*.

Additionally, he was able to employ the lighter and serious sides of his composing talents with equal effectiveness as a popular recording and performing artist, in the process winning a far greater public identity than most of his colleagues. He recorded more than 90 record albums, ranging in scope from jazz to classical-pop to big band, and each year averaged 50 concert performance dates.

Mancini was a much-loved, much-honored figure who won a total of 18 Oscar nominations (beginning in 1954, for *The Glenn Miller Story*) and an astounding 72 Grammy Award nominations (including 20 wins, beginning in 1958 with an "album of the year" prize for *Peter Gunn*). His final credit, prior to his death in 1994: composing for the Broadway musical version of *Victor/Victoria*, directed by Blake Edwards and starring Julie Andrews.

On the art of scoring Mancini said, "One thing I have learned is that good music can improve a fine film but it can never make a bad film good. Another is to recognize those parts of a film which are better off without music. We composers are not magicians. We write music. We are one of the elements that go into the making of a final piece of work. When it works and when we feel we've made a contribution, it's a great source of satisfaction."

—Tony Thomas, updated by Rob Edelman

MANDEL, Johnny

Composer. **Nationality:** American. **Born:** New York, New York, 23 November 1925. **Education:** Studied symphonic music at Manhattan School of Music and Julliard School of Music. **Career:** Discovered he had perfect pitch when he was five; began writing big band arrangements at age 12; played in swing bands at age 16; after graduation worked with violinist Joe Venuti; arranged, wrote, and performed (generally on trombone and trumpet) with Alvino Rey, Artie Shaw, Jimmy Dorsey, Buddy Rich, Elliott Lawrence, and the Henry Jerome Orchestra, 1940s and 1950s; radio and television work, including *Your Show of Shows*. Joined Count Basie Orchestra; session work with Frank Sinatra, Tony Bennett, Chet Baker, Paggy Lee, Anita O'Day, Maynard Ferguson, Mel Torme, and Andy Williams, Los Angeles; turned from playing to composing music, late 1950s; began scoring films with *I Want to Live*, 1958; composed music for the TV series *Banyon*, 1972, *M*A*S*H*, 1972, "One for the Road" episode of *Amazing Stories*, 1985. **Awards:** Academy Award, Best Song, for "The Shadow of Your Smile," and Grammy Award, Best

Original Score Written for a Motion Picture or Television Show, for *The Sandpiper*, 1966; ASCAP Henry Mancini Award, 1997.

Films as Composer:

1958 *I Want to Live* (Thomas) (billed as John Mandel)
1960 *The Third Voice* (Cornfield); *The Lawbreakers* (Newman)
1963 *Drums of Africa* (Clark)
1964 *The Americanization of Emily* (*Emily*) (Hiller)
1965 *The Sandpiper* (Minnelli)
1966 *An American Dream* (*See You in Hell, Darling*) (Gist); *Harper* (Smight); *The Russians Are Coming, The Russians Are Coming* (Jewison)
1967 *Code Name: Heraclitus* (Goldstone—for TV); *Point Blank* (Boorman)
1968 *Pretty Poison* (Black)
1969 *That Cold Day in the Park* (Altman); *Some Kind of Nut* (Kanin); *Heaven with a Gun* (Katzin)
1970 *The Man Who Had Power Over Women* (Krish); *M*A*S*H* (Altman)
1971 *The Trackers* (*No Trumpets, No Drums*) (Bellamy—for TV)
1972 *Molly and Lawless John* (Nelson); *Journey Through Rosebud* (Gries)
1973 *Summer Wishes, Winter Dreams* (Cates); *The Last Detail* (Ashby)
1974 *W* (*I Want Her Dead*) (Quine)
1975 *Escape to Witch Mountain* (Hough); *The Turning Point of Jim Malloy* (*Gibbsville: The Turning Point of Jim Malloy*) (Gilroy—for TV)
1976 *The Sailor Who Fell from Grace with the Sea* (Carlino)
1977 *Freaky Friday* (Nelson)
1979 *Being There* (*Chance*) (Ashby); *Agatha* (Apted)
1980 *Baltimore Bullet* (Ellis Miller); *Caddyshack* (Ramis)
1981 *Evita Peron* (Chomsky—for TV)
1982 *The Verdict* (Lumet); *Soup for One* (Kaufer) (additional music); *Deathtrap* (Lumet); *Lookin' to Get Out* (Ashby)
1983 *Staying Alive* (Stallone) (additional music)
1985 *A Letter to Three Wives* (Elikann—for TV);
1987 *Foxfire* (Taylor—for TV); *Assault and Matrimony* (Frawley—for TV)
1989 *Brenda Starr* (Ellis Miller); *Single Women, Married Men* (Havinga—for TV)
1990 *Kaleidoscope* (Taylor—for TV)

Other Films:

1994 *A Great Day in Harlem* (Bach) (music consultant)

Publications:

By MANDEL: articles—

"Themes in the Key of Mandel," interview with Jem Aswad, on *ASCAP Film and TV Legends*, http://www.ascap.com/filmtv/mandel.html, April 1997.

On MANDEL: articles—

McGilligan, Patrick, liner notes to *I Want To Live* (originally released 1958), Rykodisc, 1999.

*   *   *

Composer/arranger/instrumentalist Johnny Mandel came into film scoring and Hollywood songwriting after a long and successful career playing and arranging jazz and big band music. Like Henry Mancini, Mandel was one of Hollywood's last true links to the classic American pop era of big band, swing, and bebop.

Mandel's musical education began at age 5 when his musical family discovered he had perfect pitch. Piano lessons followed but the young Mandel soon found his true calling in the brass family of instruments: first on trumpet and later trombone. By age 12 he was writing big band arrangements, and by 16 was performing in bands in Catskill Mountain resorts.

During the prime big band era, Mandel got the kind of thorough working musical education impossible to achieve today. "A lot of the people I came up with—Stan Getz, Zoot Sims, Miles Davis—were out on the road from when we were 16 and 17 years old. I did it for ten years, one-nighters all down the line. You can't learn this, you have to live it. We were very lucky because we had bands to play in. That's how you learn," Mandel remembered in an ASCAP interview.

Mandel's road work included performing with Alvino Rey, Artie Shaw, and Count Basie, among many others. With the decline of the big bands, Mandel began writing for radio and television in 1949, and by 1954 had settled in Los Angeles, doing session recording work, and concentrating on writing and arranging. His first film work was as an uncredited arranger for the 1955 Martin/Lewis film, *You're Never Too Young*. Mandel's career in actual film scoring commenced in 1958 with an innovative jazz score for *I Want To Live*, Robert Wise's grimly realistic crime drama about playgirl/convicted murderess Barbara Graham and her eventual execution in the San Quentin gas chamber. Mandel commented: "I felt totally at home doing movies because I'd done everything else first. I'd worked Vegas shows and in television with Sid Caesar's *Your Show of Shows* where you had to write visual cues, where you were catching dance accents and marrying music to sight cues. And I'd done some radio drama in the late '40s and early '50s, so I'd learned to write to the second hand. Movies combine all of those things, so I realized—very late!—that I already knew how to do it."

Fortunately, Mandel broke into film scoring in a cinematic era that was ideally suited to his talents. The old order studio system, with its wall-to-wall symphonic orchestral scores, had crumbled by the late 1950s, and a new mode of film music, based on pop and jazz idioms, was quickly emerging.

Though jazz had been fused with orchestral scoring in several previous Hollywood films—most notably Alex North's landmark 1951 score for *A Streetcar Named Desire*, and Elmer Bernstein's *The Man With the Golden Arm* in 1955—*I Want To Live* was the first film to be completely scored in an authentic jazz mode. The real life Graham had been a fan of saxophonist Gerry Mulligan, who was at the height of his popularity in the late 1950s. Mulligan and his combo appear in the opening club scene, and perform all the source music in the film.

The underscoring was also based on 1950s jazz styles, utilizing unusual instruments and conventional ones employed in extreme ranges such as the piccolo heard in an uncharacteristic low register in the execution cue. Mandel placed an emphasis on jazz drumming and exotic percussion for the suspense cues, sometimes employing several jazz percussionists. Two original soundtracks albums were released by United Artists Records at the time of the film's release, one featuring the source music played by Mulligan's combo, and the other including the more expansive, big band influenced underscoring. In the digital era, both albums were combined on a Rykodisc CD which included extensive liner notes on both the film and Mandel's unique score.

By the late 1950s, pop/jazz scores such as *I Want To Live* and Henry Mancini's *Touch of Evil* and *Breakfast At Tiffany's* were increasingly in demand. They were commercially successful, often producing both lucrative popular songs and soundtrack LPs, which meant both royalties and free promotion for the film. Mandel himself had several pop song successes, and a string of original soundtracks albums during the late 1950s and early 1960s.

After three small features, Mandel scored two major films, both of which produced successful theme songs. *The Americanization of Emily*, an off-beat comedy-drama about a less than heroic American soldier in World War II England, produced the hit "Emily," with lyrics by Johnny Mercer. Even more successful was a tune written for *The Sandpiper*, a project chiefly motivated by the then-much publicized coupling of Elizabeth Taylor and Richard Burton. Today the film is primarily remembered for Mandel's ballad, "The Shadow Of Your Smile." With lyrics by Paul Frances Webster, the lyrical melody with a contemporary bossa nova beat became one of the most recorded film songs of the decade, and won an Academy Award for Best Song in 1965.

Mandel followed *Sandpiper* with *An American Dream*, a watered-down version of the Norman Mailer novel, which nonetheless introduced another sensitive jazz ballad, "A Time for Love" ("A Time For Love" was again nominated for an Academy Award, but lost to "Born Free.") These popular successes led to Mandel scoring a number of 1960s "New Hollywood" classics, among them *Harper*, *Point Blank*, *Pretty Poison*, and *That Cold Day in the Park*. In 1970 he hit commercial gold again with his score for Robert Altman's *M*A*S*H*, which produced the hit "Suicide Is Painless" (also known as "Theme from M*A*S*H"). Mandel also scored the TV series based on the film.

Along with *The Last Detail* in 1973, *M*A*S*H* was the last film of consequence that Mandel scored, moving on as he did to Disney live-action features (*Escape to Witch Mountain*, *Freaky Friday*), and a mixed bag of comedies (*Caddyshack*), TV movies, and the occasional major feature (*Deathtrap*, *Brenda Starr*). Mandel's last score was for a TV movie of Danielle Steel's *Kaleidoscope* in 1990.

In spite of his prolific film work, Mandel considered himself primarily a jazz musician, and during the 1990s, he returned to his arranging roots with arrangements for a variety of major recording artists, including Michael Jackson, Quincy Jones, and Barbra Streisand, as well as producing his own solo albums. In addition to his Academy Award and two nominations, Mandel has won four Grammys, and in 1997 was awarded ASCAP's prestigious Henry Mancini Award.

—Ross Care

MANDELL, Daniel

Editor. **Nationality:** American. **Born:** New York, in 1895. **Career:** Vaudeville acrobat until war injury ended his career; 1920—film editor: first film, *The Match Breaker*; then worked for Samuel Goldwyn, 24 years; retired in 1966. **Awards:** Academy Award for *The Pride of the Yankees*, 1942, *The Best Years of Our Lives*, 1946, and *The Apartment*, 1960. **Died:** In California, 8 June 1987.

Films as Editor:

1921 *The Match Breaker* (Fitzgerald); **Foolish Wives** (von Stroheim)
1923 *Lady of Quality* (Henley)
1924 *The Turmoil* (Henley)
1925 *California Straight Ahead* (Pollard)
1927 *Uncle Tom's Cabin* (Pollard) (co)
1928 *Love Me and the World Is Mine* (Dupont) (co)
1929 *Man, Woman, and Wife* (E. Laemmle); *Melody Lane* (Hill); *Show Boat* (Pollard) (co); *Silks and Saddles* (Hill); *Tonight at Twelve* (Pollard)
1930 *Holiday* (E. Griffith); *Sin Takes a Holiday* (Stein); *Swing High* (Santley); *Undertow* (Pollard)
1931 *Beyond Victory* (Robertson); *Devotion* (Milton); *Rebound* (E. Griffith)
1932 *The Animal Kingdom* (E. Griffith); *A Woman Commands* (Stein)
1932–33 Six comedy shorts
1933 *Counsellor-at-Law* (Wyler); *Emergency Call* (Cahn)
1934 *Embarrassing Moments* (E. Laemmle); *I'll Tell the World* (Sedgwick); *Love Birds* (Seiter); *Wake Up and Dream* (Neumann)
1935 *Diamond Jim* (Sutherland); *The Good Fairy* (Wyler); *His Night Out* (Nigh); *King Solomon of Broadway* (Crosland)
1936 *Dodsworth* (Wyler); *These Three* (Wyler)
1937 *Dead End* (Wyler); *Woman Chases Man* (Blystone); *You Only Live Once* (F. Lang)
1939 *The Real Glory* (Hathaway); *Wuthering Heights* (Wyler)
1940 *The Westerner* (Wyler)
1941 *Ball of Fire* (Hawks); **The Little Foxes** (Wyler); *Meet John Doe* (Capra)
1942 *The Pride of the Yankees* (Wood); *They Got Me Covered* (Butler)
1943 *The North Star* (Milestone)
1944 *Arsenic and Old Lace* (Capra) (co); *The Princess and the Pirate* (Butler); *Up in Arms* (Nugent)
1945 *Wonder Man* (Humberstone)
1946 **The Best Years of Our Lives** (Wyler); *The Kid from Brooklyn* (McLeod)
1948 *Enchantment* (Reis); *A Song Is Born* (Hawks)
1949 *My Foolish Heart* (Robson); *Roseanna McCoy* (Reis)
1950 *Edge of Doom* (Robson)
1951 *I Want You* (Robson); *A Millionaire for Christy* (Marshall); *Valentino* (Allen)
1952 *Hans Christian Andersen* (C. Vidor)
1953 *Return to Paradise* (Robson)
1955 *Guys and Dolls* (Mankiewicz)
1956 *The Sharkfighters* (Hopper)
1957 *Witness for the Prosecution* (Wilder)
1959 *Porgy and Bess* (Preminger)
1960 **The Apartment** (Wilder)
1961 *One, Two, Three* (Wilder)
1963 *Irma La Douce* (Wilder)
1964 *Kiss Me, Stupid* (Wilder)
1966 *The Fortune Cookie* (Wilder)

Publications

On MANDELL: articles—

Film Comment (New York), March-April 1977.
''Daniel Mandell, Won 3 Film Editing Oscars,'' in *New York Times*, 13 June 1987.

*   *   *

The greatest accomplishment of a good editor is, ironically, that the audience is totally unaware of his or her work. Unlike actors, art directors, or cinematographers, whose work is placed before the viewer on a platter, the editor must interpret, dissect, and anticipate the product to make the average filmgoer completely oblivious to his or her efforts on the picture.

This was perhaps more evident in the days before quick action and special effects were so lavish on the screen and is characteristic of the work of the veteran editor Daniel Mandell. Mandell, who flourished within the studio system of the 1930s and 1940s, had the ability to anticipate what would look good to an audience and cull that product out of the mass of scenes, shots, and directives given to him. According to interviews with Mandell, his early training in vaudeville made him very sensitive to timing and the ways in which audiences react.

His editing career began with assistant ''cutter'' jobs at Metro, then, during the 1920s and early 1930s, he went from studio to studio working on some noteworthy films, including Erich von Stroheim's *Foolish Wives*, until he settled in at the Samuel Goldwyn studios. There he worked until well into the 1950s and was head editor of a number of the high-budget Goldwyn productions.

His specialty was the serious film such as *These Three*, *Dodsworth*, and *Wuthering Heights* in which his sensitive editing helped to pace the strong stories. Mandell won an Oscar for his editing of *The Pride of the Yankees*, an adept combination of action, intimate drama, and montage which, though somewhat maudlin, nevertheless is touching and well paced. His second Oscar, again for Goldwyn, was for the magnificent work he did on *The Best Years of Our Lives*. Although the film was an almost actionless drama, the superb editing of the climactic sequence at the deserted airfield was an outstanding achievement. It still stands up well against the more modern, technologically advanced work of films like the *Terminator* series in which technique dominates artistry.

Perhaps Mandell's greatest asset was his subtlety. This was evident again in 1960 when he won his third award for Billy Wilder's *The Apartment*, a small, black-and-white drama which proved that, after a number of years of the Oscar going to lavish color productions like *Ben-Hur*, sensitivity could still count. It was, in fact, one of only two films (the other being *Z*), that was neither color nor large-budget spectacular to win the best editing Oscar in the last 45 years.

—Patricia King Hanson

MANKIEWICZ, Herman

Writer and Producer. **Nationality:** American. **Born:** Herman Jacob Mankiewicz in New York City, 7 November 1897; brother of the writer and director Joseph Mankiewicz. **Education:** Attended Columbia University, New York, graduated; University of Berlin. **Family:** Married Shulamith Sara Aronson, 1920; one son, the writer Don M. Mankiewicz. **Career:** 1918—served in the United States Marine Corps; then worked in Europe for the Red Cross Press Service, as publicity manager for Isadora Duncan, and Berlin correspondent for the Chicago *Tribune*; 1922–26—assistant drama editor, *New York Times*; 1926—first film as writer, *The Road to Mandalay*, followed in the next dozen years by many films as writer, often as title writer (through the end of the silent period) and script doctor (often uncredited); 1930–32—produced four films, including two Marx Brothers comedies; 1939—began association with the director Orson Welles. **Awards:** Academy Award for *Citizen Kane*, 1941. **Died:** 5 March 1953.

Herman Mankiewicz

Films as Writer:

1926   *The Road to Mandalay* (Browning); *Stranded in Paris* (Rosson)
1927   *Fashions for Women* (Arzner); *A Gentleman of Paris* (D'Arrast); *Figures Don't Lie* (Sutherland); *The Spotlight* (Tuttle); *The City Gone Wild* (Cruze); *The Gay Defender* (La Cava); *Honeymoon Hate* (Reed)
1928   *Two Flaming Youths* (Waters); *Gentlemen Prefer Blondes* (St. Clair); *The Last Command* (von Sternberg); *Love and Learn* (Tuttle); *A Night of Mystery* (Mendes); *Abie's Irish Rose* (Fleming); *Something Always Happens* (Tuttle); *His Tiger Lady* (Henley); *The Drag Net* (von Sternberg); *The Magnificent Flirt* (D'Arrast); *The Big Killing* (Jones); *The Water Hole* (Jones); *The Mating Call* (Cruze); *Avalanche* (Brower); *The Barker* (Fitzmaurice); *Three Weekends* (Badger); *What a Night!* (Sutherland)
1929   *Marquis Preferred* (Tuttle); *The Canary Murder Case* (St. Clair); *The Dummy* (Milton); *The Man I Love* (Wellman); *Thunderbolt* (von Sternberg)
1930   *Men Are Like That* (Tuttle); *The Love Doctor* (Brown); *The Mighty* (Cromwell); *Honey* (Ruggles); *Ladies Love Brutes* (Lee); *Love among the Millionaires* (Tuttle); *The Vagabond King* (Berger); *True to the Navy* (Tuttle)
1931   *The Royal Family of Broadway* (Cukor and Gardner); *Man of the World* (Wallace); *Ladies' Man* (Mendes)
1932   *The Lost Squadron* (Archainbaud); *Dancers in the Dark* (Burton); *Girl Crazy* (Seiter)
1933   *Another Language* (E. Griffith); *Dinner at Eight* (Cukor); *Meet the Baron* (W. Lang)
1934   *The Show-Off* (Reisner); *Stamboul Quest* (Wood)
1935   *After Office Hours* (Leonard); *Escapade* (Leonard)
1937   *John Meade's Woman* (Wallace); *My Dear Miss Aldrich* (Seitz)
1939   *It's a Wonderful World* (Van Dyke)
1941   *Keeping Company* (Simon); **Citizen Kane** (Welles); *Rise and Shine* (Dwan)
1942   *Pride of the Yankees* (Wood)
1943   *Stand By for Action* (Leonard)
1944   *Christmas Holiday* (Siodmak)
1945   *The Enchanted Cottage* (Cromwell); *The Spanish Main* (Borzage)
1949   *A Woman's Secret* (Ray)
1952   *The Pride of St. Louis* (Jones)

Films as Producer:

1930   *Laughter* (D'Arrast)
1931   *Monkey Business* (McLeod)
1932   *Horse Feathers* (McLeod); *Million Dollar Legs* (Cline)
1933   **Duck Soup** (McCarey)

Publications

By MANKIEWICZ: book—

With Orson Welles, *Citizen Kane* (script) in *The Citizen Kane Book*, by Pauline Kael, Boston, Massachusetts, 1971.

On MANKIEWICZ: books—

Meryman, Richard, *Mank: The Wit, World, and Life of Herman Mankiewicz*, New York, 1978.
Carringer, Robert L., *The Making of Citizen Kane*, Berkeley, California, 1985.

On MANKIEWICZ: articles—

Film Comment (New York), Winter 1970–71.
Ciment, Michel, "Ouragans autour de Kane," in *Positif* (Paris), March 1975.
Kilbourne, Don, in *American Screenwriters*, edited by Robert E. Morsberger, Stephen O. Lesser, and Randall Clark, Detroit, Michigan, 1984.
Film Comment (New York), July-August 1984.
Films in Review (New York), October-November 1984.
Film Dope (Nottingham), December 1987.
Turan, Kenneth, "The Brothers Mankiewicz: A Gold Touch," in the *Los Angeles Times*, 8 July 1993.

*   *   *

Lillian Gish once exclaimed, "Yes, Orson Welles is a genius, a genius at self-promotion." That genius for self-promotion, his many talents notwithstanding, was largely responsible for Welles receiving and accepting *all* credit for the screenplay to *Citizen Kane*. Despite Welles's statement that "the writer should have the first and last word in filmmaking, the only better alternatives being the writer-director, but with the stress on the first word," he perpetuated the myth that he was solely responsible for the creation of *Kane*, with utter disregard for the fact that he shared screen credit and the Academy Award with Herman Mankiewicz. Critics and film historians went along with this injustice until 1971 when Pauline Kael exploded the misconception with her controversial essay "Raising Kane," wherein she set the record straight as to Mankiewicz being the primary contributor to the screenplay. Offensive as this premise was to the auteurists and possibly to Welles, Mankiewicz's contribution to *Kane* is now an accepted fact, so much so that writers like Richard Corliss can confidently state that "Herman Mankiewicz wrote *Citizen Kane* with only nominal assistance from Orson Welles."

Why had Mankiewicz's contribution been so ignored for three decades? The two chief reasons were the ego of Orson Welles and the ego of Herman Mankiewicz. Welles's complicity is easy to understand, but who *was* Herman Mankiewicz? This elder brother of Joseph was a bright, acerbic, hard-drinking *bon vivant* who began his writing career as a Berlin correspondent for the Chicago *Tribune* and went on to become a second-string drama editor for the *New York Times* and a frequent contributor to *The New Yorker*. He was a familiar face to the Algonquin Round Table set, and Ben Hecht dubbed him "The Central Park West Voltaire." When he went to Hollywood in 1926, he was accused of selling out, but the money was alluring and Mankiewicz had a strong self-destructive and undisciplined streak in him. Screenwriting enhanced his lifestyle, and if one looks at the forty-odd films to which he contributed, there are few

clues to foreshadow the excellence of *Citizen Kane*. A number of his screenplays did carry the reporter/newspaper theme—a milieu he knew very well—and a number of others revealed the wit for which he was well known. The best film for which he received credit was *Dinner at Eight*, which he wrote in collaboration with Frances Marion. His best writing seems to be for those films on which he was executive producer and for which he took no writing credit— *Laughter*, *Monkey Business*, *Horse Feathers*, *Million Dollar Legs*, and *Duck Soup*.

Mankiewicz was a friend of both William Randolph Hearst and Marion Davies, and his depiction of them in the *Kane* script was considered the betrayal of friendship by an alcoholic loser. But personal vendetta aside, Mankiewicz's script is a masterful dissection of power and the fall from grace, and his contribution cannot be overlooked. With that balance in mind, it is fair to concede that while Mankiewicz did write the script, it was Welles's sense of the baroque, his irony, and his entrepreneurial audacity which makes *Citizen Kane* great cinema.

Mankiewicz's own assessment of screenwriting (circa 1935), while somewhat flippant, is probably closer to the truth than most practitioners would like to admit: "You don't really need to be a writer, in the accepted sense of the word, to write for pictures. Some of the best scenario writers in Hollywood can't write at all. They simply have a flair for ideas, for situations; these, in turn, suggest bits of business; then they tie dialogue onto the business, or hire someone to do it for them. . . . In the movies, for the most part, there is no such thing as individual creation. No one person makes a picture. It is the blend of the work from five to fifteen people—each one of whom is boss of his particular field, each one of whom has to be satisfied. And if it takes ten writers to satisfy the real bosses, what difference does it make, as long as the picture is good." A far cry from Welles, who once pompously opined: "Theatre is a collective experience; cinema is the work of one single person."

—Ronald Bowers

MARION, Frances

Writer, director, and actress and editor. **Nationality:** American. **Born:** Frances Marion Owens in San Francisco, California, 18 November 1890. **Education:** Attended Hamilton Grammar School; St. Margaret's Hall; University of California, Berkeley. **Family:** Married 1) Wesley De Lappé, 1907 (divorced 1909); 2) Robert Pike, 1910; 3) Fred Thomson (died 1928); two sons; 4) George William Hill, 1930 (divorced 1931). **Career:** 1909—reporter, San Francisco *Examiner*; then commercial artist, advertising designer, model, and poster painter for Oliver Morosco's Theatre; 1914—assistant to Lois Weber; 1915–17—writer for World Company Films (association with Mary Pickford), and Paramount; 1918–19—war correspondent in France; after 1920, wrote for Hearst's Cosmopolitan Studios, MGM, and Columbia; 1925—first novel published; 1940—retired from screenwriting; taught scriptwriting at the University of Southern California, Los Angeles. **Awards:** Academy Award for *The Big House*, 1930 and *The Champ*, 1932. **Died:** 12 May 1973.

Frances Marion

Films as Writer, Actress, and Editor/Assistant Editor to Lois Weber:

1914   *False Colors*; *Hypocrites*; *It's No Laughing Matter*; *Like Most Wives*; *Traitor*
1915   *Sunshine Molly*

Films as Writer:

1915   *Camille* (Capellani); *'Twas Ever Thus* (Janis) (+ ro); *Nearly a Lady* (Janis) (+ ro)
1916   *The Foundling* (O'Brien); *The Yellow Passport* (August); *Then I'll Come Back to You* (Irving); *The Social Highwayman* (August); *The Feast of Life* (Capellani); *Tangled Fates* (Vale); *La Vie de Bohème* (Capellani); *The Crucial Test* (J. Ince and Thornby); *A Woman's Way* (O'Neil); *The Summer Girl* (August); *Friday, the 13th* (Chautard); *The Revolt* (O'Neil); *The Hidden Scar* (O'Neil); *The Gilded Cage* (Knoles); *Bought and Paid For* (Knoles); *All Man* (Chautard); *The Rise of Susan* (S.E. Taylor); *On Dangerous Ground* (Thornby)

1917   *A Woman Alone* (Davenport); *Tillie Wakes Up* (Davenport); *The Hungry Heart* (Chautard); *A Square Deal* (Knoles); *A Girl's Folly* (Tourneur); *The Web of Desire* (Chautard); *A Poor Little Rich Girl* (Tourneur); *As Man Made Her* (Archainbaud); *The Social Leper* (Knoles); *Forget-Me-Not* (Chautard); *Darkest Russia* (Vale); *The Crimson Dove* (Fielding); *The Stolen Paradise* (Knoles); *The Divorce Game* (Vale); *The Beloved Adventuress* (Brady and Cowl); *The Amazons* (Kaufman); *Rebecca of Sunnybrook Farm* (Neilan); *A Little Princess* (Neilan)

1918   *Stella Maris* (Neilan); *Amarilly of Clothes-Line Alley* (Neilan); *M'Liss* (Neilan); *How Could You, Jean?* (W. Taylor); *The City of Dim Faces* (Melford); *Johanna Enlists* (W. Taylor); *He Comes Up Smiling* (Dwan); *The Temple of Dusk* (Young); *The Goat* (Crisp)

1919   *Captain Kidd, Jr.* (W. Taylor); *The Misleading Widow* (Robertson); *Anne of Green Gables* (W. Taylor); *A Regular Girl* (Young)

1920   *The Cinema Murder* (Baker); *Pollyanna* (Powell); *Humor-esque* (Borzage); *The Flapper* (Crosland); *The Restless Sex* (Leonard and d'Usseau); *The World and His Wife* (Vignola)

1921   *Just around the Corner* (+ d); *The Love Light* (+ d); *Straight Is the Way* (Vignola)

1922   *Back Pay* (Borzage); *The Primitive Lover* (Franklin); *Sonny* (King); *East Is West* (Franklin); *Minnie* (Nielan and Urson)

1923   *The Voice from the Minaret* (Lloyd); *The Famous Mrs. Fair* (Niblo); *The Nth Commandment* (Borzage) (+ artistic supervisor); *Within the Law* (Lloyd); *The Love Piker* (Hopper); *Potash and Perlmutter* (Badger); *The French Doll* (Leonard)

1924   *The Song of Love* (Franklin) (+ co-ed); *Through the Dark* (Hill); *Abraham Lincoln* (Rosen); *Secrets* (Borzage); *Cytherea* (Fitzmaurice); *Tarnish* (Fitzmaurice); *In Hollywood with Potash and Perlmutter* (Green); *Sundown* (Trimble and Hoyt)

1925   *A Thief in Paradise* (Fitzmaurice); *The Lady* (Borzage); *The Flaming Forties* (Forman); *His Supreme Moment* (Fitzmaurice); *Zander the Great* (Hill); *Lightnin'* (Ford); *Graustark* (Buchowetzki); *The Dark Angel* (Fitzmaurice); *Lazy Bones* (Borzage); *Thank You* (Ford); *Simon the Jester* (Melford) (+ pr); *Stella Dallas* (H. King)

1926   *The First Year* (Borzage); *Partners Again* (H. King); *Paris at Midnight* (Hopper) (+ pr); *The Son of the Sheik* (Fitzmaurice); *The Scarlet Letter* (Sjöström); *The Winning of Barbara Worth* (H. King)

1927   *The Red Mill* (Goodrich); *The Callahans and the Murphys* (Hill); *Madame Pompadour* (Wilcox); *Love* (Goulding)

1928   *Bringing Up Father* (Conway); *The Cossacks* (Hill); *Excess Baggage* (Cruze); **The Wind** (Sjöström); *The Awakening* (Fleming); *The Masks of the Devil* (Sjöström)

1929   *Their Own Desire* (Hopper and Forbes)

1930   *Anna Christie* (Brown); *The Rogue Song* (L. Barrymore); *The Big House* (Hill); *Let Us Be Gay* (Leonard); *Good News* (Grinde and MacGregor); *Min and Bill* (Hill); *Wu Li Chang* (Grinde)

1931   *The Secret Six* (Hill); *The Champ* (Vidor)

1932   *Emma* (Brown); *Blondie of the Follies* (Goulding); *Cynara* (Vidor)

1933   *Secrets* (Borzage); *Peg o' My Heart* (Leonard); *Dinner at Eight* (Cukor); *The Prizefighter and the Lady* (Van Dyke); *Going Hollywood* (Walsh)

1935   *Riffraff* (Ruben)

1937   **Camille** (Cukor); *Love from a Stranger* (Lee); *Knight without Armour* (Feyder)

1940   *Green Hell* (Whale)

Films as Actress:

1915   *Caprices of Kitty* (Janis); *Betty in Search of a Thrill* (Janis); *A Girl of Yesterday* (Dwan); *City Vamp*; *The Wild Girl from the Hills*; *Captain Courtesy* (stunt double)

Publications

By MARION: books—

Minnie Flynn (novel), New York, 1925.
The Scarlet Letter (script) in *Motion Picture Continuities*, by Frances Patterson, New York, 1929.
The Cup of Life (play) in *Hollywood Plays*, edited by Kenyon Nicholson, New York, 1930.
The Secret Six (novel), New York, 1931.
Valley People (novel), New York, 1935.
How to Write and Sell Film Stories (nonfiction), New York, 1937.
Molly, Bless Her (novel), New York, 1937.
Westward the Dream (novel), New York, 1948.
The Powder Keg (novel), Boston, Massachusetts, 1954.
Off with Their Heads! (autobiography), New York, 1972.

By MARION: articles—

Film Weekly (London), 10 November 1935.
"Scenario Writing," in *Behind the Screen*, edited by Stephen Watts, London, 1938.

On MARION: articles—

Tully, Jim, in *Vanity Fair* (New York), January 1927.
Bodeen, Dewitt, in *Films in Review* (New York), February and March 1969, additions in April 1969 and August-September 1973.
Film Comment (New York), Winter 1970–71.
Bodeen, Dewitt, in *More from Hollywood*, South Brunswick, New Jersey, 1977.
Olin, Joyce, in *American Screenwriters, 2nd series*, edited by Randall Clark, Detroit, Michigan, 1986.
Berg, A. Scott, "Frances Marion: A Mediterranean Villa for the Oscar-winning Writer of *The Champ*," in *Architectural Digest* (Los Angeles), April 1990.
Beauchamp, Cari, "Frances Marion: 'Writing on the Sand with the Wind Blowing,'" in *Creative Screenwriting* (Washington, D.C.), Fall 1994.
McCreadie, Marsha, "Pioneers (Early Women Film Script Writers)," in *Films in Review* (New York), November-December 1994.
Basinger, Jeanine, "The Women Who Write the Movies: From Frances Marion to Nora Ephron," in *Historical Journal of Film, Radio and Television* (Abingdon), June 1996.
Beauchamp, Cari, "*The Big House*," in *Creative Screenwriting* (Washington, D.C.), Winter 1996.
Taubin, A., "Frances Marion and Her Circle," in *Village Voice* (New York), 24 June 1997.

*   *   *

Generally ranked with the leading screenwriters of all time, Frances Marion had more than 130 screen credits during her 25-year career, spanning the years 1915 to 1940, from the rise of the star-laden silent features to the height of the Golden Age of talkies. Her work encompasses such diversities as the 1915 *Camille* starring Clara Kimball Young and the 1937 Garbo version, *A Poor Little Rich Girl* with Mary Pickford in 1917 and *Riffraff* with Jean Harlow in 1935; but she was best known for her "four-handkerchief" pictures (*Stella*

Dallas, *The Champ*) and high dramas (*The Big House*, *Dinner at Eight*).

Marion arrived in Los Angeles from San Francisco in 1913 at age 23, twice married and divorced, talented and ambitious, having already worked as a journalist, artist's and photographer's model, commercial artist/illustrator, and writer of published stories and verse. She got into film work under a system that today would be called "networking," when her close friend Adela Rogers St. Johns introduced her to director-producer-writer Lois Weber, who took Marion into Bosworth studios as her protégée, doing a little bit of everything—acting, writing, cutting, publicity. There Marion met actor Owen Moore who introduced her to his wife, Mary Pickford. Marion and Pickford became and remained the best of friends, and frequent colleagues, for life.

If that sounds like the start of a heartwarming movie script, one could add other similar episodes. Friendship was one of Marion's special talents, so when Lois Weber died penniless and forgotten after a significant career, it was Marion who, at the peak of her own fame and fortune, arranged and paid for Weber's funeral. When Marie Dressler, another old friend, couldn't get work on stage or screen, Marion revitalized her career with lively hand-tailored scripts—and helped get her cast as Marthy in *Anna Christie* which Marion had also scripted. After that, there was no stopping Dressler, who consulted Marion at every turn. Among other close friends for whom Marion wrote scripts were Alice Brady, Elsie Janis, Billie Burke, and Marion Davies. She also wrote vehicles for Ronald Coleman, Rudolph Valentino, John Gilbert, and Wallace Beery, and helped discover Gary Cooper and Clark Gable.

Although by tradition Hollywood writers usually travel in their own circles, Marion also had many good friends among producers: William A. Brady, who gave her a writing contract at $200 a week in 1917; William Randolph Hearst, who let her direct her first film, *Just around the Corner*, in 1921; Joe Kennedy, who encouraged her third husband, the ex-chaplain and college athlete Fred Thomson, to star in westerns; Samuel Goldwyn, her favorite producer, who called her his favorite scriptwriter; Irving Thalberg, who over several years sought her advice on production problems and on other writers' scripts.

What distinguished Marion's scripts, according to DeWitt Bodeen (who researched and interviewed Marion in her later life), were her original characters with their dramatic but genuinely human conflicts, and her eye-minded stories, written always with the camera in mind. Her screenplays *moved*, and could be *acted*, Bodeen wrote. As one of the few scriptwriters who made a successful transition from silent films to talkies, Marion often wrote sequences without any dialogue, relying on pantomime (and the especially expressive faces of Garbo, Beery, and Dressler) to reach audiences more effectively than words could.

Soon after Marion started a long-term $3,500-a-week contract at MGM, as one of Hollywood's highest paid scriptwriters, tragedy came into her life: her husband died suddenly of tetanus, leaving their two young sons for her to raise alone. A later short-lived marriage to George W. Hill, a director-friend, was followed by his suicide a few years after their divorce. Already feeling vulnerable, as screenwriting was being handled more and more on an assembly-line basis, Marion decided that she would have to be a writer-director or writer-producer to maintain the integrity of her scripts.

She had already tried directing and it seemed to go nowhere. Following her first effort for Hearst in 1921, Marion had directed

Mary Pickford in *The Love Light*. A few years later, when the film's director was too ill to work, Marion had finished directing her own script for *The Song of Love*, a Norma Talmadge production. But her efforts to produce her own scripts in the late 1930s and 1940s never got off the ground. She turned instead to magazine stories and serials. Her book *How to Write and Sell Film Stories* emphasizes visual over verbal communication, stresses simplicity and detail, colorful personalities, and everyday emotions. Her later book of reminiscences, *Off with Their Heads!*, tells more about her friends than about herself. She mentions merely in passing that she directed three films but writes nothing about her experiences or why she stopped.

—Cecile Starr

MARSHALL, Frank

Producer and Director. **Nationality:** American. **Born:** Los Angeles, 13 September 1946. **Education:** Attended University of California, Los Angeles, as political science major. **Family:** Married the producer Kathleen Kennedy. **Career:** Protégé of Peter Bogdanovich, working on his production crew and serving as an assistant on *Targets*, 1968, location manager on *The Last Picture Show*, 1971, and *What's Up, Doc?*, 1972; line producer on Orson Welles's *The Other Side of the Wind* (unreleased); 1981—began collaboration with Steven Spielberg as a producer for *Raiders of the Lost Ark*; 1982— with Spielberg and Kathleen Kennedy, formed production company,

Frank Marshall

Amblin Entertainment. **Awards:** ShoWest Award, Producer of the Year, 1982. **Address:** Kennedy-Marshall Co., 1351 4th Street, 4th Floor, Santa Monica, California 90401–1337, U.S.A.

Films as Producer:

1973   *Paper Moon* (Bogdanovich) (asst)
1974   *Daisy Miller* (Bogdanovich) (asst)
1975   *At Long Last Love* (Bogdanovich) (asst)
1976   *Nickelodeon* (Bogdanovich) (asst)
1978   *The Last Waltz* (Scorsese—doc) (line pr); *The Driver* (W. Hill)
1979   *The Warriors* (W. Hill) (exec)
1981   ***Raiders of the Lost Ark*** (Spielberg) (+ ro as pilot)
1982   *Poltergeist* (Hooper) (co)
1983   *Twilight Zone—The Movie* (Landis, Spielberg, and Dante) (exec)
1984   *Indiana Jones and the Temple of Doom* (Spielberg) (co-exec); *Gremlins* (Dante) (co-exec)
1985   *Fandango* (K. Reynolds) (co-exec); *The Goonies* (R. Donner) (co-exec); *Back to the Future* (Zemeckis) (co-exec); *Young Sherlock Holmes* (Levinson) (co-exec); *The Color Purple* (Spielberg) (co)
1986   *An American Tail* (Bluth—animation) (co-exec); *The Money Pit* (Benjamin) (co)
1987   *Innerspace* (Dante) (co-exec); **batteries not included* (M. Robbins) (co-exec); *Empire of the Sun* (Spielberg) (co)
1988   *Who Framed Roger Rabbit?* (Zemeckis) (co); *The Land before Time* (Bluth—animation) (co-exec)
1989   *Indiana Jones & the Last Crusade* (Spielberg) (co-exec); *Dad* (Goldberg) (co-exec); *Back to the Future Part II* (Zemeckis) (co-exec); *Always* (Spielberg) (co)
1990   *Back to the Future Part III* (Zemeckis) (co-exec); *Gremlins II* (Dante) (co-exec); *Joe Versus the Volcano* (Shanley) (co-exec)
1991   *Cape Fear* (Scorsese) (co-exec); *Hook* (Spielberg) (co); *An American Tail: Fievel Goes West* (Nibbelink and Wells—animation) (co-exec)
1992   *Noises Off* (Bogdanovich)
1993   *Swing Kids* (Carter) (co-exec); *A Far Off Place* (Salomon) (co-exec); *We're Back! A Dinosaur's Story* (D. & R. Zondag, Nibbelink, and Wells—animation) (co-exec)
1994   *Milk Money* (Benjamin) (co)
1995   *The Indian in the Cupboard* (Oz) (co)
1999   *Olympic Glory* (Merrill) (co-prod); *The Sixth Sense* (Shyamalan); *Snow Falling on Cedars* (Hicks) (+ 2nd unit director); *A Map of the World* (Elliott); *Sports Pages* (series)

Films as Director:

1990   *Arachnophobia* (+ co-exec pr); *Tummy Trouble* (live-action only, short); *Rollercoaster Rabbit* (live-action only, short)
1993   *Alive*
1995   *Congo* (+ co-exec pr)

Publications

On MARSHALL: articles—

Wells, J., ''Producer Frank Marshall on Poltergeist,'' in *Film Journal*, 24 May 1982.
Chase, Donald, ''Frank Marshall and Kathleen Kennedy: Executive Producers Back to the Future,'' in *Millimeter*, December 1985.
McDonagh, Maitland, ''Paramount Gears Up for Final *Indiana Jones*,'' in *Film Journal*, May 1989.
Avins, Mimi, ''Director Frank Marshall Sets Up a Superspider's Revenge in *Arachnophobia*,'' in *Premiere* (New York), July 1990.
Spotnitz, F., ''Frank Marshall, the Amblin Producer Finds His Stride in the Director's Chair,'' in *American Film* (Washington, D.C.), March 1991.
Avins, Mimi, ''Shot by Shot: Alive,'' in *Premiere* (New York), 1 March 1993.
Clark, John, ''Hollywood and Vines: *Congo* Serves Up Old-Fashioned Jungle Adventure with New Fangled Special Effects,'' in *Premiere* (New York), July 1995.
Fischer, Dennis, ''Congo,'' in *Cinefantastique* (New York), 1 August 1995.
Ojumu, Akin, ''When They Talk, Spielberg Listens,'' in *The Observer* (London), 23 April 2000.

*   *   *

Frank Marshall is one of the most respected filmmakers working in the film industry today. Though perhaps best known for his hugely successful collaborations with producer Kathleen Kennedy and director Steven Spielberg, Marshall started out as a protégé of Peter Bogdanovich and gained valuable experience through collaborations with such legends as Orson Welles, Martin Scorsese, and George Lucas.

All of these directors were unabashed film buffs who imbued Marshall with a certain sentimentality for things past and a desire to entertain audiences the same way that they had been entertained by the great films of yesteryear. These traits show clearly in his own initial directorial efforts, particularly *Arachnophobia* and *Congo*, which hearken back to such great sci-fi classics as *Tarantula* (1955) and *King Kong* (1933) and feature strong story lines at a rudimentary level and depend on technical craftsmanship and strong special effects to captivate the audience.

Marshall's career appears to reflect three significant turning points in an evolution from apprentice to producer and ultimately to producer/director. As a political science student at the University of California, Los Angeles, in the late 1960s, he had a chance introduction to the film historian Peter Bogdanovich who was about to make his directorial-debut film *Targets*, financed by Roger Corman. The minuscule budget meant Marshall was involved in all aspects of making the film. He later said this experience was the best introduction to the film industry.

Working with the always cash-poor Bogdanovich gave Marshall insights into the difficulties inherent in the film business and allowed him to develop a sense of what he saw as his primary function as a producer. To Marshall, the producer is the person who serves as a direct line to the director and his needs, and it is the producer's job to fulfill those needs. In this view, the finished film should reflect the creative vision of the director and not the producer.

The Bogdanovich-Marshall pairing included some of the director's most successful films including *The Last Picture Show*, *Paper*

Moon, and *What's Up Doc?*, but it was the producer's work on the less successful *Daisy Miller* that led to another turning point in Marshall's professional development. Steven Spielberg was in Europe promoting his film *Duel* and dropped by the studio to have lunch with Bogdanovich when Marshall came in to ask his director about a problem on the set. Marshall later learned that Spielberg was impressed with the way that he handled himself and was the type of person Spielberg wanted working with him. He wanted a producer who could ''take care of things on the set.'' Five years later, when George Lucas asked Spielberg who he wanted as producer for *Raiders of the Lost Ark*, Spielberg's response was: ''See if that guy Frank Marshall is available.'' Marshall was and a long association with one of the most successful directors in the history of film was begun.

The producer and director, joined by Marshall's future wife Kathleen Kennedy, formed Amblin Entertainment Company in 1982. According to Marshall, the main criteria behind the films ''greenlighted'' into production for Amblin was story content. The most important factor to him was that the film tell a good story—one that he would like to see himself. Just as he would come to emphasize in his directorial efforts, he looked for films that reminded him of the matinee films of his youth. Such films as *Back to the Future*, *Poltergeist*, *E.T.—The Extra-Terrestrial*, and *Hook* have timeless themes and are demographically perfect for capturing the widest possible audience—the 13-to-25 age group. Nevertheless, a number of Marshall's productions, including *The Color Purple*, *Empire of the Sun*, and *Always*, while less successful financially than other Amblin films, reflected strong story lines aimed at adult audiences. Marshall and Spielberg were not afraid to deal with less-commercial material if solid story content was there.

Although Amblin has become identified in the popular mind as being virtually synonymous with Steven Spielberg, Marshall and his co-producer Kennedy exercised considerable influence on the director's choice of projects and exercised control over the broad range of corporate output. Within the company, if Spielberg was directing, Marshall and Kennedy were always the producers. If other directors were doing Amblin projects, the two would either co-produce or executive produce depending on the work load within the company. This versatility allowed Amblin to produce a phenomenal output in its relatively short existence.

The association with Spielberg provided a third turning point in Marshall's evolution as a producer and director. First, working on ''A'' projects with some of the most talented people in the business gave the producer an opportunity to hone his skills at the highest level. His strength lies in the day-to-day details of production. As Spielberg has noted, Marshall is an ''on the set'' producer who employs a hands-on approach and likes to keep his crews as small as possible. He also prefers to work with the same group of people again and again because he considers communication behind the camera to be the most important aspect of making things run smoothly. His people are now so familiar with his style that they can anticipate many of his techniques to support his director.

Second, while keeping up with his production duties in the late 1980s, Marshall took advantage of his association with Spielberg to learn the craft of directing. As a second-unit director on the famous director's recent films, he prepared himself for a 1990 directorial debut on *Arachnophobia*. Although the light horror film may not have been the aspiring director's first choice, it was a green-lighted project, ready to go, and he jumped at it. The project was unique in that it allowed Marshall to utilize both his producer and directorial skills. Having been a producer, Marshall understood the importance of combining the creative with the business aspects of making a film. Indeed, from a producer's point of view, a film about killer spiders terrorizing the Midwest was a tough sell. The original draft of the screenplay was stark horror with no letup. At least in Spielberg's *Jaws* (1973), audiences knew that the danger only lurked in the water. On land, you were safe. Here, there was no shelter; spiders could be lurking anywhere, even in your popcorn.

As a director who knew that his audience was composed of people with conflicting views of spiders, Marshall was able to leaven the terror through the device of a comic exterminator played by John Goodman who broke the tension in some of the story's climactic scenes. This provided a ''word of mouth'' that would intrigue both horror fans and John Goodman fans. This combination of producer and directorial psychologies has contributed to the success of Marshall's subsequent directorial efforts *Alive* and *Congo*.

The year 1999 was busy for Marshall, with four projects coming to completion and release. The Bruce Willis vehicle *The Sixth Sense* turned out to be the most successful of these, continuing Marshall's involvement with projects reminiscent of cinema past: the child Cole Sear's troubling declaration that ''I see dead people'' might easily have come from *The Exorcist*, for example. Other films of that year, such as *Snow Falling on Cedars* and *A Map of the World*, deal with the more adult themes of love and loss. *Olympic Glory* is a well-meaning but overly sentimental documentary, filmed in the large IMAX format, about the 1998 Winter Olympics in Nagano, Japan. *Olympic Glory* nevertheless deserves a look if only to experience the ski-jump projected on the IMAX screen.

Marshall, having the choice of either directing or producing films, has the responsibility of having to make the decisions on all of the creative aspects of, a film he is directing while in the producer role, he likes being the support system for the film and keeping the momentum going on the set. For example, early in his producing career, to keep spirits up on one particularly difficult shoot, Marshall put on a magic show starring himself as Dr. Fantasy. This magic show has now become a tradition on all Marshall productions. This is indicative of the producer/director's philosophy of filmmaking. For him, making films is like putting on one big expensive magic show and he plans to keep on pulling films out of his hat for a long time to come.

—Sandra Garcia-Myers, updated by Chris Routledge

MATÉ, Rudolph

Cinematographer and Director and Producer. **Nationality:** Hungarian. **Born:** Rudolf Matheh in Cracow, Poland, 21 January 1898. **Education:** Attended University of Budapest. **Career:** Assistant cameraman for Alexander Korda in Budapest; then worked in Vienna and Berlin (apprentice to Karl Freund, assistant to Erich Pommer), and in France; 1935—emigrated to Hollywood; 1948—directed first film; TV work includes *The Loretta Young Show*. **Died:** 27 October 1964.

Films as Cinematographer:

1923   *Der Kaufmann von Venedig* (Felner)
1924   *Michael* (Dreyer) (co)

1926 *Die Hochstaplerin*
1928 **La Passion de Jeanne d'Arc** (*The Passion of Joan of Arc*) (Dreyer)
1929 *Le Manque de mémoire* (Chomette)
1930 *Prix de beauté* (Genina)
1931 *La Couturière de Linevile* (Lachman); *Le Monsieur de minuit* (Lachman); *Le Roi de Camembert* (Mourre)
1932 *La Belle Marinière* (Lachman); *Monsieur Albert* (Anton); **Vampyr** (*The Dream of Allan Gray*) (Dreyer)
1933 *Paprika* (de Limur); *Les Aventures du Roi Pansole* (Granowsky); *La Mille-et-Deuxième Nuit* (Wolkoff); *Une Femme au volant* (Gerron and Billon); *Dans les rues* (Trivas)
1934 *Le Dernier Milliardaire* (Clair); *Liliom* (Lang)
1935 *Dante's Inferno* (Lachman); *Dressed to Thrill* (Lachman); *Metropolitan* (Boleslawsky); *Beauty's Daughter* (Dwan) (co); *Professional Soldier* (Garnett)
1936 *Charlie Chan's Secret* (Wiles); *Message to Garcia* (Marshall); *Our Relations* (Lachman); *Dodsworth* (Wyler); *Come and Get It* (Wyler and Hawks) (co)
1937 *Outcast* (Florey); *Stella Dallas* (K. Vidor); *The Adventures of Marco Polo* (Mayo)
1938 *Blockade* (Dieterle); *Youth Takes a Fling* (Mayo); *Tradewinds* (Garnett)
1939 *Love Affair* (McCarey); *The Real Glory* (Hathaway)
1940 *My Favorite Wife* (McCarey); *Foreign Correspondent* (Hitchcock); *Seven Sinners* (Garnett)
1941 *Lady Hamilton* (*That Hamilton Woman*) (A. Korda); *Flame of New Orleans* (Clair)
1942 *To Be or Not to Be* (Lubitsch); *It Started with Eve* (Koster); *The Pride of the Yankees* (Wood)
1943 *They Got Me Covered* (Butler); *Sahara* (Z. Korda)
1944 *Address Unknown* (Menzies); *Cover Girl* (C. Vidor) (co)
1945 *Tonight and Every Night* (C. Vidor)
1946 **Gilda** (C. Vidor)
1947 *Down to Earth* (Hall); *It Had to Be You* (+ co-d)

Films as Director:

1948 *The Dark Past*
1950 *D.O.A.*; *Branded*; *No Sad Songs for Me*; *Union Station*
1951 *The Prince Who Was a Thief*; *When Worlds Collide*
1952 *The Green Glove*; *Paula*; *Sally and Saint Anne*; *Mississippi Gambler*
1953 *Second Chance*; *Forbidden*; *The Siege of Red River*
1954 *The Black Shield of Falworth*
1955 *The Violent Men*; *The Far Horizons*
1956 *Miracle in the Rain*; *Rawhide Years*; *Port Afrique*; *Three Violent People*
1958 *The Deep Six*; *Serenade einer grossen Liebe* (*For the First Time*)
1960 *Revak, lo schiavo di Cartagine* (*The Barbarians*) (+ pr); *The Immaculate Road*; *Il dominatore dei sette mari* (*Seven Seas to Calais*) (co-d)
1961 *The Lion of Sparta* (*The Three Hundred Spartans*) (+ pr)
1962 *Aliki* (*Aliki, My Love*) (+ co-pr)

Film as Producer:

1948 *The Return of October* (Lewis)

Publications

By MATÉ: articles—

Films and Filming (London), November 1955.
Nosferatu (San Sebastian), February 1994.

On MATÉ: articles—

Kine (London), 24 November 1955.
Luft, Herbert, in *Films in Review* (New York), October 1964.
Film Ideal (Madrid), 1 July 1965.
Kino Lehti (Helsinki), no. 2, 1970.
Film Comment (New York), Summer 1972.
Focus on Film (London), no. 13, 1973.
Film Dope (Nottingham), March 1989.
Liberti, F., and L. Franco, "Rudolph Maté," in *Cineforum*, no. 31, May 1991.
"The Dark Past," in *Reid's Film Index* (Wyong), no. 15, 1995.
"When Worlds Collide," in *Midnight Marquee* (Baltimore), no. 48, Winter 1995.

*   *   *

Rudolph Maté was a great cameraman whose film career divided neatly into three parts. In the first, he worked in Europe on major films such as Carl Theodor Dreyer's *The Passion of Joan of Arc* and René Clair's *Le Dernier Milliardaire*. He then came to Hollywood in 1935 and worked as a cameraman, earning five consecutive Academy Award nominations between 1940 and 1944. In the third phase, Maté switched to directing, principally of B-films in Hollywood, from 1947 until his death in 1964. Thus most historians see his as a career continually in decline, from the heights of the European art film of the 1920s to the schlock B-film of Hollywood in the 1950s.

In 1919 Maté set off on a remarkable 15-year career as a cinematographer in Europe. Alexander Korda gave him the needed break; Carl Theodor Dreyer guaranteed him a place in film history by having him photograph *The Passion of Joan of Arc* and *Vampyr*. It is not clear, however, how much Maté contributed to those films other than following Dreyer's orders. The remainder of his career would indicate that Dreyer offered the vision and Maté executed the orders.

In 1935 Maté left Nazi Germany for the United States. William Wyler gave him his break in Hollywood by hiring him to photograph *Dodsworth* and *Come and Get It* in 1936. It took Maté little time to reach the list of top Hollywood cinematographers. In 1940 he reached his peak by working as the director of photography for Hitchcock's *Foreign Correspondent*. For this fine film Maté earned an Oscar nomination for cinematography in black-and-white. He then earned nominations for *That Hamilton Woman*, *The Pride of the Yankees*, *Sahara*, and *Cover Girl*.

After the Second World War, Maté got the itch to work on his own films and began to direct, at times even produce, features. In 1947 he entered this third phase of his career with his directorial debut: *It Had to Be You*, completed when Maté was 49 years old. He worked for a number of Hollywood studios until 1958, and then tried his luck with several European productions such as *The 300 Spartans*, released by 20th Century-Fox. He also directed 20 episodes of *The Loretta Young Show* TV series in the late 1950s.

There were some gems in the 29 feature films Maté directed. *D.O.A.*, starring Edmund O'Brien, would seem to be Maté's finest directorial effort, a classic *film noir*. *When Worlds Collide* succeeds on the level of spectacular effects. But except for those two, critics seem to agree that Maté's directorial career is dotted with third-rate westerns and dramas. It is his career as a cinematographer for others which has secured Rudolph Maté's place in the history of film.

—Douglas Gomery

MATHIESON, Muir

Music Director and actor. **Nationality:** British. **Born:** Stirling, Scotland, 24 January 1911. **Education:** Attended Stirling High School (conductor of the boys orchestra at age 13); Royal College of Music, London. **Career:** 1931—music director for Korda's London Films: introduced leading UK composers to film music writing (e.g., Bliss, Vaughan-Williams, Bax, Walton, Ireland); 1940–45—music director for government film units; after the war, music director for Rank Organisation; also orchestra conductor, and for opera and ballet. **Died:** In Oxford, 2 August 1975.

Films as Music Director (selected list):

1934   *The Private Life of Don Juan* (A. Korda); *Catherine the Great* (Czinner)
1935   *The Scarlet Pimpernel* (Young); *The Ghost Goes West* (Clair)
1936   **Things to Come** (Menzies)
1937   *Q Planes* (*Clouds over Europe*) (Whelan)
1940   *Contraband* (*Blackout*) (Powell); *The Thief of Baghdad* (Powell, Berger, and Whelan)
1941   *Dangerous Moonlight* (Hurst); *49th Parallel* (Powell)
1942   *The First of the Few* (Howard)
1943   **Fires Were Started** (*I Was a Fireman*) (Jennings)
1944   *The Way Ahead* (Reed)
1945   *The Rake's Progress* (Gilliat); **Brief Encounter** (Lean); **Henry V** (Olivier); *A Diary for Timothy* (Jennings) (conductor)
1946   *The Seventh Veil* (Bennett); *Caesar and Cleopatra* (Pascal); *Instruments of the Orchestra* (+ d)
1947   *Odd Man Out* (Reed); *The Woman in the Hall* (Lee); *Green for Danger* (Gilliat); *Dear Murderer* (Crabtree)
1948   *Oliver Twist* (Lean); *Hamlet* (Olivier)
1949   *Christopher Columbus* (MacDonald)
1950   *Waterfront* (*Waterfront Women*) (Anderson); *The Miniver Story* (Potter); *The Black Rose* (Hathaway)
1952   *Who Goes There* (*The Passionate Sentry*) (Kimmins); *The Crimson Pirate* (Siodmak)
1953   *Sailor of the King* (R. Boulting)
1954   *The Sea Shall Not Have Them* (Gilbert); *Three Cases of Murder* (Toye); *Father Brown* (Hamer)
1955   *I Am a Camera* (Cornelius); *The Intruder* (Hamilton)
1956   *The Man Who Never Was* (Neame)
1957   *After the Ball* (Bennett)
1958   **Vertigo** (Hitchcock); *Sea of Sand* (*Desert Patrol*) (Green)

1959   *Ferry to Hong Kong* (Gilbert); *The Rough and the Smooth* (*Portrait of a Sinner*) (Siodmak); *The Savage Innocents* (Ray)
1960   *Macbeth* (Schaefer); *Circus of Horrors* (Hayers)
1961   *The Naked Edge* (Anderson); *The Canadians* (Kennedy)
1962   *H.M.S. Defiant* (*Damn the Defiant!*) (Gilbert); *The Devil Never Sleeps* (*Satan Never Sleeps*) (McCarey); *Only Two Can Play* (Gilliat); *The L-Shaped Room* (Forbes); *Waltz of the Toreadors* (*The Amorous General*) (Guillermin); *The War Lover* (Leacock)
1963   *The Running Man* (Reed); *The Mind Benders* (Dearden)
1964   *Becket* (Glenville); *Woman of Straw* (Dearden)
1965   *Lord Jim* (Brooks); *Genghis Khan* (Levin)
1968   *Shalako* (Dmytryk)
1970   *You Can't Win 'em All* (Collinson)

Film as Actor:

1951   *The Magic Box* (J. Boulting)

Publications

By MATHIESON: articles—

"Aspects of Film Music," in *Tempo* (London), no. 9, 1944.
Cinema and Theatre Construction, September 1947.
"Developments in Film Music," in *Penguin Film Review* (London), October 1947.
"Music for Crown," in *Hollywood Quarterly*, Spring 1948.

On MATHIESON: article—

Picturegoer (London), 8 October 1947.
Obituary in *Variety* (New York), 6 August 1975.

*   *   *

Muir Mathieson, as music director and conductor of British film scores for both feature films and documentaries, became the single most influential name in British film music. His career began as early as 1931, when, aged 20, he became assistant director of music at Alexander Korda's Denham Studios, and extended into the 1970s. He received his first credit as music director for Korda's *The Private Life of Don Juan*, scored by Mischa Spoliansky. After the Second World War, he became music director for the Rank Organisation.

Mathieson was to initiate and conduct some thousand film scores, and introduce such eminent composers as Arthur Bliss, Vaughan Williams, Arnold Bax, William Walton, and Malcolm Arnold to the composition of orchestral scores for films. He had studied conducting and composition at the Royal College of Music, and conducted while still a teenager. Throughout his career in films he also conducted in concert halls in Britain and overseas, and pioneered the presentation of film music as BBC broadcasts. He established that British films at their best should have music of the highest quality, specially commissioned and composed as an integral part of a film's creative process. This was early evident in Bliss's distinguished score for Korda's production of H.G. Wells's film *Things to Come* in the mid-1930s.

Muir Mathieson (center) with (from left) Elmer Bernstein, Henry Mancini, Ron Goodwin, and James Mason

''The music is a part of the constructive scheme of the film,'' Wells had written. ''Sound sequences and picture sequences were closely interwoven. This Bliss music . . . is part of the design.'' Bliss's impressionistic score was subsequently developed as an orchestral suite for the concert hall, and issued on a set of gramophone recordings.

In this way, as in so many others, Mathieson proved an indefatigable, extrovert, and enthusiastic pioneer. This enthusiasm spread to the composers themselves, inspiring Vaughan Williams to claim in his seventies that he believed ''the film contains potentialities for the combination of all the arts such as Wagner never dreamed of.'' He held working for films to be a splendid discipline in which he was, in effect, being trained by Mathieson, like many other distinguished composers.

At the same time, Mathieson regarded American studio composers and musicians as technically more advanced than the British. Writing in 1947 he acknowledged, ''the American composer has turned himself more thoroughly into a music dramatist than the British.'' He instanced Bernard Herrmann's brilliantly integrated score for Orson Welles's *Citizen Kane*. Among the many notable earlier scores Mathieson was to commission and conduct (usually

with the London Symphony Orchestra) were those by Arnold Bax for David Lean's *Oliver Twist* and by William Walton for Laurence Olivier's *Henry V*. During the war years and subsequently, Mathieson originated and conducted many scores for documentary, and he himself directed the film of Benjamin Britten's composition *Instruments of the Orchestra*, which featured the London Symphony Orchestra conducted by Malcolm Sargent.

A list of Mathieson's credits as music director reads like a history of the British films from the 1930s to the 1960s. His views are fully recorded in John Huntley's pioneer book, *British Film Music* (1947), and elaborated further in Roger Manvell and John Huntley's *The Technique of Film Music* (1957, revised and enlarged along with Richard Arnell and Peter Day in 1975), of which Mathieson was one of the advisory editors. In this he states: ''All that remains is for it to be unreservedly recognized that music, having a form of its own, has ways of doing its appointed task in films with distinction, judged purely as music, and with subtlety, judged as a part of a whole film. It must be accepted not as a decoration or a filler of gaps in the plaster, but as a part of the architecture.''

—Roger Manvell

MATHIS, June

Writer. **Nationality:** American. **Born:** Leadville, Colorado, 1892. **Career:** 1910–16—stage and vaudeville actress; 1918—hired at Metro as writer; 1919—appointed head of script department; associated with the performers Nazimova, Valentino, and Colleen Moore, and the director Rex Ingram during the next few years; 1923—edited von Stroheim's *Greed* down from 18 to 10 reels. **Died:** In New York City, 27 July 1927.

Films as Writer:

1918   *To Hell with the Kaiser* (Irving); *An Eye for an Eye* (Capellani)
1919   *Out of the Fog* (Capellani); *The Red Lantern* (Capellani); *The Brat* (Blaché)
1920   *Old Lady 31* (J. Ince); *Hearts Are Trumps*; *Polly with a Past* (De Cordova)
1921   **The Four Horsemen of the Apocalypse** (Ingram); *The Conquering Power* (Ingram); *A Trip to Paradise* (Karger); *Camille* (Smallwood); *The Idle Rich* (Karger)
1922   *Turn to the Right* (Ingram); *Kisses* (Karger); *Hate* (Karger); *Blood and Sand* (Niblo); *The Young Rajah* (Rosen)
1923   *Three Wise Fools* (K. Vidor); *The Spanish Dancer* (Brenon); *In the Palace of the King* (Flynn); **Greed** (von Stroheim) (re-write, re-edit)
1925   *Sally* (Green); *The Desert Flower* (Cummings); *Classified* (Santell); *We Moderns* (Dillon)
1926   *Ben-Hur* (Niblo); *Irene* (Green); *The Greater Glory* (Rehfeld); *The Masked Woman* (Balboni); *The Magic Flame* (H. King)

Publications

By MATHIS: book

Greed, edited by Joel W. Finler, London, 1972.

By MATHIS: article—

"Tapping the Thought Wireless," in *Moving Picture World*, 21 July 1917.

On MATHIS: articles—

Photoplay (New York), October 1926.
Cinema (Beverly Hills, California), no. 35, 1976.
Slater, Thomas, in *American Screenwriters, 2nd series*, edited by Randall Clark, Detroit, Michigan, 1986.
McCreadie, Marsha, "Pioneers (Early Women Film Script Writers)," in *Films in Review* (New York), November-December 1994.
Slater, Thomas J., "June Mathis: A Woman Who Spoke Through Silents," in *Griffithiana* (Gemona, Italy), May 1995.
Slater, Thomas J., "June Mathis's *Classified*: One Woman's Response to Modernism," in *Journal of Film and Video* (Atlanta), Summer 1998.

*   *   *

June Mathis

June Mathis in her short but brilliant career (she died in her mid-thirties) was one of the most influential women in Hollywood production during the silent film era, becoming chief of Metro's script department in 1919 when she was only 27. Her family had a background in the theatre, and she had already begun to write for the theatre when she secured a job with Metro as scenario-writer in 1918. She was immediately responsible for scripting a range of films with titles such as *To Hell with the Kaiser*, *An Eye for an Eye*, *Hearts Are Trumps*, and *Polly with a Past*. This initial work culminated in her notable adaptation of the famous war novel by Vincente Blasco Ibánez, *The Four Horsemen of the Apocalypse*. By this stage, she was influential enough to succeed in her insistence with Metro on the appointment of her young friend Rex Ingram (aged 29) as the film's director, though his postwar reputation rested only on the direction of a few minor features, and on the casting of Rudolph Valentino (then only a bit player) as the star, so establishing his meteoric career (like hers, to be only too short) as the embodiment of the erotic imaginings of the mass international female film-going public. Mathis went on to script and supervise a range of Valentino's subjects, including *Camille*, *Blood and Sand*, and *The Young Rajah*.

Mathis had by now extended her status in the studios to that of an associate producer. She assumed a similar responsibility of scripting and cutting (then often a producer's prerogative) over a considerable range of films. According to Lewis Jacobs, in his authoritative book *The Rise of the American Film*, she was the "most esteemed scenarist in Hollywood;" her strength lay in careful pre-preparation of the shooting script along with the director, cutting out waste in production while at the same time sharpening narrative continuity. She became in effect head, or one of the heads, of the Metro and Samuel Goldwyn units, and joined with other youthful women writers (such as Anita Loos and Bess Meredyth) in establishing the importance of the basic screenplay scenario in silent American film. It was she who was in good measure responsible for persuading Metro-Goldwyn to agree to sponsor Erich von Stroheim's celebrated film *Greed*. She became notorious among film devotees, who see the company she represented as ''betraying'' one of the greatest artists of silent cinema, and all but destroying one of its potentially greatest films. *Greed*, as initially shot and assembled by Stroheim, ran to 42 reels (ten hours), following every detail of Frank Norris's novel *McTeague*. Stroheim himself reduced this to 24 reels (six hours), hoping the film could then be screened with intermissions in two successive evenings. But Metro-Goldwyn-Mayer (as the company had now become) demanded more drastic cutting. At Stroheim's request, his close friend Rex Ingram reduced it to 18 reels (4.5 hours). But Mathis was instructed to reduce the film without consultation with Stroheim to ten reels (2.5 hours), which she undertook with the aid of a routine cutter, Joseph W. Farnham, ''on whose mind was nothing but a hat,'' as Stroheim put it. The exact nature of this drastic cutting of an overlong masterpiece of realistic, psychological cinema is detailed by Joel W. Finler in his edition of Stroheim's full-scale original script *Greed*.

Mathis went on to script and supervise the adaptation of the epic *Ben-Hur* for Goldwyn, finally after much trouble directed by Fred Niblo and starring Francis X. Bushman and Ramon Novarro. Mathis, however, was withdrawn from the film by MGM while on location in Italy, but in any case she disowned what had initially been shot by the film's first director, Charles Brabin, whom she had chosen. Her final films included *Irene* for Colleen Moore and *The Magic Flame* with Ronald Colman and Vilma Banky. She died suddenly in 1927.

—Roger Manvell

MATRAS, Christian

Cinematographer and Director. **Nationality:** French. **Born:** Valence, 29 December 1903. **Career:** Newsreel photographer; late 1920s—worked on short films as photographer and director; from early 1930s—cinematographer on feature films. **Died:** 4 May 1977.

Films as Cinematographer:

1926   *De Babord à Tribord* (+ d)
1927   *Maldone* (Grémillon)
1930   *Eperon d'or* (+ d)
1931   *Sous la terre* (+ d)
1932   *Au fil de l'eau* (+ d); *Le Billet de mille* (Didier)
1933   *La Chatelaine du Liban* (Epstein); *Le Paqueboat Tenacity* (Duvivier); *L'Or des mers* (Epstein)
1934   *L'Affaire Coquelet* (Gourguet); *La Maison dans la dune* (Billon); *Le Scandale* (L'Herbier)
1935   *Maternité* (Choux)
1936   *L'Argent* (Billon); *Les Mutinés de l'Elseneur* (Chenal); *Les Réprouvés* (Severac)
1937   *Le Chanteur de minuit* (Joannon); **La Grande Illusion** (*Grand Illusion*) (Renoir); *Prison sans barreaux* (Moguy)

1938   *Café de Paris* (Mirande and Lacombe); *La fin du jour* (*The End of Day*) (Duvivier); *Entrée des artistes* (*The Curtain Rises*) (M. Allégret); *Je chante* (Stengel); *Légions d'honneur* (Gleize); *La Piste du sud* (Billon)
1939   *Le Dernier Tournant* (Chenal); *Le Duel* (Fresnay); *Paradise perdu* (Gance)
1940   *La Nuit merveilleuse* (Paulin)
1941   *Le Briseur de chaines* (Daniel-Norman); *La Duchesse de Langeais* (de Baroncelli); *Paradise en sept nuits* (M. Allégret); *Romance de Paris* (Boyer)
1942   *Pontcarral, Colonel d'empire* (Delannoy); *La Loi du printemps* (Daniel-Norman); *Mahlia la métisse* (Kapps); *Secrets* (Blanchar)
1943   *L'Escalier sans fin* (Lacombe); *Lucrèce* (Joannon); *Un Seul Amour* (Blanchar); *Le Voyageur sans bagages* (Anouilh)
1944   *Le Bossu* (Delannoy); *Mademoiselle X* (Billon)
1945   *Boule de suif* (*Angel and Sinner*) (Christian-Jaque); *L'Idiot* (*The Idiot*) (Lampin); *Tant que je vivrai* (de Baroncelli)
1946   *Il suffit d'une fois* (Felix)
1947   *Le Beau Voyage* (Cuny); *Eternel conflit* (Lampin); *L'Aigle à deux têtes* (*The Eagle with Two Heads*) (Cocteau); *La Révoltée* (*Stolen Affections*) (L'Herbier); *Les Jeux sont faits* (*The Chips Are Down*) (Delannoy)
1948   *D'homme à hommes* (*Man to Men*) (Christian-Jaque); *Tous les chemins mènent à Rome* (Boyer)
1949   *Singoalla* (*The Wind Is My Lover*) (Christian-Jaque)
1950   *La Valse de Paris* (*The Paris Waltz*) (Achard); **La Ronde** (Ophüls); *Souvenirs perdus* (Christian-Jaque)
1951   *Barbe-Bleue* (*Bluebeard*) (Christian-Jaque); *Olivia* (Audry); *Fanfan la Tulipe* (*Fanfan the Tulip*) (Christian-Jaque)
1952   *Adorables créatures* (*Adorable Creatures*) (Christian-Jaque); *Violettes impériales* (Pottier); *Destinées* (*Daughters of Destiny*) (Christian-Jaque); *Lucrèce Borgia* (*Sins of the Borgias*) (Christian-Jaque); *Le Plaisir* (Ophüls) (co)
1953   **Madame de . . .** (*The Earrings of Madame de . . .*) (Ophüls); *Secrets d'alcove* (Delannoy)
1954   *Madame Du Barry* (Christian-Jaque); *Nana* (Christian-Jaque)
1955   **Lola Montès** (*Lola*) (Ophüls); *Les Espions* (Clouzot)
1956   *Die Abenteuer des Till Ulenspiegel* (*The Adventures of Till Eulenspiegel*) (Philipe and Ivens); *Oeil pour oeil* (*An Eye for an Eye*) (Cayatte); *Rencontre à Paris* (Lampin)
1957   *Les Carnets du Major Thompson* (*The French, They Are a Funny Race*) (P. Sturges); *Une Manche et la belle* (Verneuil)
1958   *Christine* (Gaspard-Huit); *Montparnasse 19* (*Modigliani of Montparnasse*) (Becker); *Maxime* (Verneuil)
1959   *La Belle et l'empereur* (von Ambesser); *La Bête a l'affût* (Chenal); *Le Chemin des écoliers* (Boisrond); *Pourquoi viens-tu si tard?* (Decoin); *Vers l'extase* (Wheeler)
1960   *Les Magiciennes* (*Double Deception*) (Friedman); *Ma femme est une panthère* (Bailly)
1961   *Paris Blues* (Ritt); *Le Jeu de la verité* (Hossein); *Les Lions sont lâchés* (Verneuil)
1962   *Le Crime ne paie pas* (*Crime Does Not Pay*) (Oury); *Le Coeur Battant* (*The French Game*) (Doniol-Valcroze); **Thérèse Desqueyroux** (*Thérèse*) (Franju); *Cartouche* (de Broca); *Coup de bambou* (Boyer); *Virginie* (Boyer)
1963   *Shéhérazade* (*Scheherazade*) (Gaspard-Huit) (co)
1964   *Les Amitiés particulières* (*This Special Friendship*) (Delannoy)
1965   *Les Fêtes galantes* (Clair)

1967   *Sept fois femme* (*Woman Times Seven*) (De Sica); *Más allá de las montañas* (*The Desperate Ones*; *Beyond the Mountains*) (Ramati)
1968   *Les Oiseaux vont mourir au Perou* (*Birds in Peru*) (Gary)
1969   *La Voie lactée* (*The Milky Way*) (Buñuel)
1970   *Le Bal du Comte d'Orgel* (M. Allégret)
1971   *Variétés* (Bardem)
1972   *Pas folle la guepe* (Delannoy)

Publications

On MATRAS: articles—

Cinéma (Paris), December 1972.
Focus on Film (London), no. 13, 1973.
Le Technicien du Film (Paris), May-June 1977.
Film Français (Paris), 10 June 1977.
Cinéma (Paris), August-September 1977.
Film Dope (Nottingham), March 1989.

*   *   *

At the beginning of his career, Christian Matras quickly established a reputation as a solid technician and an expert in creating decorative and psychological ambiences which testify to his range of taste. During his career, he adapted to developing techniques, as well as to the demands of varied directors. In more than 80 films, he worked with the biggest names in French cinema: Jean Renoir, Jean Cocteau, Jacques Becker and, most significantly, Max Ophüls.

Using his early training as a newsreel photographer, Matras successfully applied the technique of plain observation to feature films in the '30s. His documentary style was put to good use in Renoir's *La Grande Illusion*, a study of war. Renoir chose to tell his story of the dry rot of inaction, not on the battlefield, but behind the lines in a prison camp. It is a story of complex themes often revealed through camera movements.

This technique would typify Matras' work prior to World War II. During this period, it was careful, painstakingly detailed, and intelligent, almost to the point of coldness. After World War II, his documentary style gave way to dazzling, flowing camera movements. Matras adapted well to color filming; his *Barbe Bleu* was considered the first successful French film in color.

However, it is his work with Max Ophüls for which Matras is best known. Ophüls' films demanded complex camera work—long elaborate takes with flowing camera movements. Brilliant camera use became the director's trademark; without the fluid, impressionistic skill of Matras, Ophüls would not be as highly regarded as he is. In *La Ronde*, Matras' first collaboration with Ophüls, Matras used sweeping camera work that would develop into the camera choreography used in *Lola Montes*. This film was the most expensive European production ever made at that time, and one of the first to use CinemaScope. Ophüls disliked CinemaScope, which he felt made proportions crushingly flat. He altered perspectives by affixing black velvet maskings to the camera.

The filming of *Lola Montes* is the epitome of Matras' craftsmanship and technique. For example, in the circus scenes, Ophüls was more interested in the audience than the main action. For this, Matras

uses 360 degree camera shots. Some scenes were conceived and written to constitute dynamic walkthroughs, and the camera stays with the characters, persistent and unshakeable as it stalks and prowls with them. Matras' virtuoso camera movement makes the landscape and architecture seem to move.

The Earrings of Madame. . . . also contained fabulous photography. The story would be tedious if not for Matras' fluid camera, which juxtaposes intimate and dramatic shots to reveal theme and character. Lean camera work balances against the lush setting in which events unfold. Ophüls relied on continuous flow as opposed to collisions between shots for his storytelling, and long tracks are used not only to convey action, but to convey shifts of mood, the evolution of time, and plot development. At the heart of the film is the ball scene. The couple dances round and round through one elegant ballroom after another, and the camera stays with them recording their changing feelings as the mood of frivolity recedes. A long continuous take follows the servant as he moves from light to light, extinguishing each until he finally blankets the scene in darkness when he covers the harp.

Matras' last collaboration with Ophüls was *Le Plaisir* made in 1955. Matras continued to work in films until the 1970s, although this later work would not attract the same critical attention as his films with Ophüls.

—Renee Ward

MAYER, Carl

Writer. **Nationality:** Austrian. **Born:** Graz, 20 February 1894. **Career:** Sold barometers, portrait sketcher, stage actor; 1920—first script for film, *Das Kabinett des Dr. Caligari*; 1927–30— lived in the United States; 1931—emigrated to England. **Died:** In London, 1 July 1944.

Films as Writer:

1920   ***Das Kabinett des Dr. Caligari*** (*The Cabinet of Dr. Caligari*) (Wiene); *Johannes Goth* (Gerhardt); *Der Bucklige und die Tänzerin* (*The Hunchback and the Dancer*) (Murnau); *Genuine: Die Tragödie eines seltsamen Hauses* (Wiene); *Der Dummkopf* (*The Idiot*) (Pick)
1921   *Verlogene Moral* (*Brandherd*) (Kobe); *Der Gang in die Nacht* (*Journey into the Night*) (Murnau); *Schloss Vogelöd* (*The Haunted Castle*) (Murnau); *Scherben* (*Shattered*) (Pick); *Grausige Nächte* (Pick); *Die Hintertreppe* (*Backstairs*) (Jessner and Leni)
1922   *Vanina* (von Gerlach)
1923   *Erdgeist* (Jessner); *Der Puppenmacher von Kiang-Ning* (Wiene); *Sylvester: Tragödie einer Nacht* (*New Year's Eve*) (Pick)
1924   ***Der Letzte Mann*** (*The Last Laugh*) (Murnau)
1926   *Tartüff* (*Tartuffe*) (Murnau)
1927   ***Berlin—die Symphonie einer Grosstadt*** (*Berlin—Symphony of a Big City*) (Ruttmann); ***Sunrise*** (Murnau)
1929   *Four Devils* (Murnau)

1931   *Ariane* (Czinner)
1932   *Der Träumende Munde* (*Dreaming Lips*) (Czinner)
1937   *Dreaming Lips* (Czinner) (English language remake)
1938   *Pygmalion* (Berger)
1940   *Major Barbara* (Pascal); *The Fourth Estate* (Rotha)
1942   *World of Plenty* (Rotha)

Publications

By MAYER: books—

(Editor) *Innsbrucker Theater-Almanach*, Innsbruck, 1914.
Sylvester: Ein Lichtspiel, Potsdam, 1924.
Sonnenaufgang (script of *Sunrise*), Wiesbaden, 1971.
With Hans Janowitz, *The Cabinet of Dr. Caligari* (script), New
    York, 1972.

By MAYER: articles—

World Film News, September 1938.
Sight and Sound (London), Winter 1938–39.

On MAYER: books—

Tribute to Carl Mayer (pamphlet), 1947.
Hempel, Rolf, *Carl Mayer: Ein Autor schreibt mit der Kamera*,
    Berlin, 1968.
Kasten, Jurgen, *Carl Mayer, Filmpoet: Ein Drehbuchautor schreibt
    Filmgeschichte*, Berlin, Vistas Verlag, 1994.

On MAYER: articles—

Wilhelm, Wolfgang, in *Sight and Sound* (London), July 1944.
Revue du Cinéma (Morges, Switzerland), Spring 1947.
Daugherty, Frank, in *Films in Review* (New York), March 1953.
Luft, Herbert G., ''Notes on the World and Work of Carl Mayer,'' in
    Quarterly of Film, Radio, and Television (Berkeley, California),
    Summer 1954.
Filmkunst (Vienna), no. 39, 1963.
Film Culture (New York), Summer 1965.
Bianco e Nero (Rome), July-August 1968.
Cinema Journal (Evanston, Illinois), Fall 1968.
Luft, Herbert G., ''Carl Mayer, Screen Author,'' in *Film Quarterly*
    (Berkeley, California), Fall 1968.
Bianco e Nero (Rome), September-October 1968.
Bianco e Nero (Rome), November-December 1968.
Films in Review (New York), November 1972, additions in May 1973.
Monthly Film Bulletin (London), June 1979.
Film Dope (Nottingham), March 1989.
Cinema & Cinema, September-December 1991.
Kosmorama (Copenhagen), Spring 1995.

*   *   *

An Austrian Jewish screenwriter of great imagination, Carl Mayer
was thrown out on the streets at an early age along with his younger

brothers by their father, an inveterate gambler who was on the point of
killing himself. This began a period of adolescent stress and deprivation that was deeply to colour Mayer's outlook and darken the nature
of the subject matter he chose for his outstanding work for the German
silent cinema. He had to undergo psychiatric treatment for a while
when his mind was considered unbalanced. At first an actor and
painter during the First World War, Mayer turned to writing when he
collaborated with a young Czech ex-army officer, Hans Janowitz, on
the basic script for the German Expressionist film *The Cabinet of Dr.
Caligari*—the full story behind this collaboration being revealed first
by Siegfried Kracauer in his book *From Caligari to Hitler*. The antiauthoritarian theme of the film (as intended by these young pacifist
writers) was entirely discarded as the subject passed through Erich
Pommer's studio. It became rather a psychological melodrama, much
discussed internationally for its Expressionistic settings and remarkable stylized acting by Werner Krauss and Conrad Veidt. Mayer's
name was established as a promising screenwriter and he was
commissioned to write Robert Wiene's subsequent film, *Genuine* (the
name of a seductive Oriental princess who avenges herself on the
male sex which ill-uses her), a film made in a similar, Expressionistic
manner but with less lasting success.

Mayer, however, put his creative roots down in film. He realized
that the darkened world of the cinema with its black-and-white
photographic values and its potential intimacy of approach to concentrated, emotionalized characterization offered a new form of wholly
visual, psychological drama that appealed to his deepening awareness. While working with great artistic success for Arthur von
Gerlach on *Vanina* and for Lupu Pick on *Shattered*, a dark and
symbolistic psychological film made without the verbal intrusion of
captions representing either narrative or dialogue, and on *Sylvester*,
which Mayer called a ''light-play'' (*ein Lichtspiel*), alluding not only
to its black-and-white images, but to the light and shadow it revealed
in a man's soul, Mayer was discovering a branch of intimate, haunted
drama for film that became known as the *Kammerspiel* (chamber-
drama), a term originating from the great theatre director Max
Reinhardt's promotion of intimate live theatre. Mayer was to discover
his closest interpreter of this genre in F.W. Murnau, most notably in
their later films, the German *The Last Laugh* and the American
Sunrise.

Mayer's great gift to cinema was to conceive the written script as
closely as possible in detailed visual terms, the result often of an
advance collaboration with director and cameraman alike (notably
Murnau and Karl Freund), writing in an abrupt, expressionist style of
poetic prose. Many of Mayer's scripts (especially for Murnau)
survive and can be found quoted by Lotte Eisner in her invaluable
books *Murnau* and *The Haunted Screen*. Mayer was always deeply
concerned with the camera and its potential movements, whereas
Murnau (for all his strength in handling actors) rarely looked through
the viewfinder. For Mayer the camera was like another actor participating directly in the action. As we have seen, he also resented the
intrusive captioning between shots characteristic of the conventional
silent film. The narrative continuity rested entirely on the images, on
mimed action, and on facial and bodily expression.

However, after *Battleship Potemkin* came to Berlin astonishing
audiences and filmmakers alike, Mayer's intense preoccupation with
the psychological unbalance of his characters began to accommodate
the much more naturalistic approach to subject matter represented by
the new Soviet directors. Mayer, with his already marked social-
sociological interests, was among those ready to be influenced, and

The Last Laugh (with its theme of a hotel hall-porter obsessed by the class distinction given him by his grand uniform) shows a definite socially realistic interest.

When Murnau left for Hollywood in 1926, Mayer refused to go with him, preferring to write for him in Germany. Murnau's first American film, *Sunrise*, was adapted by Mayer from one of Sudermann's stories, *The Journey to Tilsit*. Robert Sherwood considered the result at the time, "the most important picture in the history of the movies." Mayer's last script for Murnau was to be *Four Devils*, a psychological study of acrobats in a circus setting but with a happy ending imposed by Hollywood. Mayer, still in Berlin, and preoccupied now with new concepts of realism, began to work on a documentary study of life in Berlin. This was to become Walter Ruttmann's city-symphony film *Berlin*, which Mayer disowned because his basic idea—the rhythm of human life in a great city—was sacrificed in order to feature the purely plastic visual rhythms of movement observed by the camera and developed through the fluidity of skilled editing.

With the coming of sound, Mayer's next continuous association was with Paul Czinner and his wife, Elizabeth Bergner, who played the lead in both films Mayer initially scripted for her husband—*Ariane* and *Dreaming Lips*. The latter was remade by the three of them in England in 1937.

Faced with the rise of Nazism in Germany, Mayer emigrated to England in 1932, where he established a close relationship with Paul Rotha, the rising young documentary director and film historian. In England Mayer acted as script consultant to Czinner (who was also in London) and many others, including Rotha, though the only credits he appears to have received were for two of Rotha's films.

Mayer died in London of cancer in 1944; his plans for films of his own (including one on the city of London, to be what *Berlin* should have been, in his view) never realized. Although several of his scripts, as we have seen, survive, only two have been published. Mayer published no literary work. Yet he remains one of the great creative names in early cinema.

—Roger Manvell

MAYER, Louis B.

Producer. **Nationality:** American. **Born:** Eliezer Mayer in Minsk, Russia, 4 July 1885; family emigrated to New Brunswick, Canada, 1888. **Family:** Married 1) Margaret Schenberg, 1904 (marriage dissolved), two daughters; 2) Lorena Danker, 1948. **Career:** Helped in father's scrap business; 1904—moved to Boston, Massachusetts, to set up his own scrap business; became nickelodeon manager; 1915—moved into distribution; 1917—formed the independent Mayer Production Company in New York; 1920—opened studios in Hollywood; 1923—hired Irving Thalberg as vice president and production assistant; 1924—vice president in charge of production and general manager of the newly formed Metro-Goldwyn-Mayer Productions with Loew and Sam Goldwyn; Thalberg became supervisor of individual film production, Mayer took charge of the west coast operation; 1931–36—president of the Motion Pictures Producers Association; 1951—left MGM. **Awards:** Special Academy Award, for "distinguished service to the Motion Picture industry," 1950. **Died:** In Hollywood, California, 29 October 1957.

Louis B. Mayer

Films as Executive Producer for MGM (selected list):

1924   *Greed* (von Stroheim); *Bread* (Schertzinger); *Sinners in Silk* (Henley); *The Arab* (Ingram); *He Who Gets Slapped* (Sjöström); *His Hour* (K. Vidor); *The Navigator* (Keaton and Crisp); **Sherlock, Jr.** (Keaton)

1925   *Ben-Hur* (Niblo); *Cheaper to Marry* (Leonard); *Confessions of a Queen* (Sjöström); *Daddy's Gone A-Hunting* (Borzage); *The Denial* (*The Square Peg*) (Henley); *The Dixie Handicap* (Barker); *Excuse Me* (Goulding); *Fine Clothes* (*Fashions for Men*) (Stahl); *The Great Divide* (Barker); *Mare Nostrum* (Ingram); **The Big Parade** (K. Vidor); **The Merry Widow** (von Stroheim); *The Snob*; *Sally, Irene and Mary* (Goulding); *The Torrent* (Bell); *The Temptress* (Stiller and Niblo); *Brown of Harvard* (Conway); *La Bohème* (K. Vidor); *Go West* (Keaton); *Seven Chances* (Keaton); *The Tower of Lies* (Sjöström); *The Monster* (West); *The Unholy Three* (Conway); *The Masked Bride* (Cabanne)

1926   *Flesh and the Devil* (Brown); *The Magician* (Ingram); *The Scarlet Letter* (Sjöströmm); *The Enemy* (Niblo); *Blarney* (de Sano); *Valencia* (Buchowetski); *Twelve Miles Out* (Conway); *The Road to Mandalay* (Browning); *The Waning Sex* (Leonard); *Paris* (Goulding); *The Barrier* (Hill); *Bardelys the Magnificent* (K. Vidor); *Upstage* (Bell); *The Black Bird* (Browning)

1927   *The Garden of Allah* (Ingram); *Tess of the D'Urbervilles* (Neilan); *This Sporting Genius* (Neilan); *The Great Love* (Neilan); *White Shadows in the South Seas* (Van Dyke);

The Crowd (K. Vidor); *The Student Prince* (Lubitsch); *Mr. Wu* (Nigh); *London After Midnight (The Hypnotist)* (Browning); *Mockery* (Christensen); *The Taxi Dancer* (Millarde); *Love* (Goulding); *The Unknown* (Browning)

1928   *The Wind* (Sjöström); *Our Dancing Daughters* (Beaumont); *Voice of the City* (Mack); *The Divorcee* (Leonard); *Let Us Be Gay* (Leonard); *The Kiss* (Feyder); *Broadway Melody* (Beaumont); *The Trial of Mary Dugan* (Veiller); *Wickedness Preferred* (Henley); *The Mysterious Lady* (Niblo); *A Lady of Chance* (Leonard); *Across to Singapore* (Nigh); *The Cameraman* (Sedgwick); *The Actress* (Cukor); *A Woman of Affairs* (Brown); *The Divine Woman* (Sjöström)

1929   *Anna Christie* (Brown); *The Big House* (Hill); *His Glorious Night* (Barrymore); *Redemption* (Niblo); **Hallelujah** (K. Vidor); *The Mysterious Island* (Tourneur and Hubbard); *Hollywood Revue of 1929* (Reisner); *Alias Jimmy Valentine* (Conway); *The Trail of '98* (Brown); *Our Modern Maidens* (Conway); *Thunder* (Nigh); *Untamed* (Conway); *Dynamite* (DeMille)

1930   *Min and Bill* (Hill); *Paid* (Wood); *A Free Soul* (Brown); *The Easiest Way* (Conway); *Way for a Sailor* (Wood); *Those Three French Girls* (Beaumont); *A Lady's Morals* (Franklin); *Susan Lenox, Her Fall and Rise* (Leonard); *Men of the North* (Roach); *Billy the Kid* (K. Vidor); *Madam Satan* (DeMille); *The Sin of Madelon Claudet* (Selwyn); *Trader Horn* (Van Dyke); *Romance* (Brown); *Paid* (Wood); *The Unholy Three* (Conway); *The Rogue Song* (Barrymore); *Good News* (Grindé)

1931   *The Champ* (K. Vidor); *Possessed* (Brown); *As You Desire Me* (Fitzmaurice); *The Guardsman* (Franklin); *Private Lives* (Franklin); *Red-Headed Woman* (Conway); **Freaks** (Browning); *Tarzan the Ape Man* (Van Dyke); *The Wet Parade* (Fleming); *Come Clean* (Horne); *Inspiration* (Brown); *Mata Hari* (Fitzmaurice); *A Free Soul* (Brown); *The Squaw Man* (DeMille); *The Man in Possession* (Wood); *Dr. Jekyll and Mr. Hyde* (Mamoulian); *New Moon* (Leonard); *The Secret Six* (Hill)

1932   *Rasputin and the Empress* (Boleslawsky); *Red Dust* (Fleming); *Grand Hotel* (Goulding); *Gabriel over the White House* (La Cava); *Strange Interlude* (Leonard); *Smilin' Through* (Franklin); **The Music Box** (Parrott)

1933   *Tugboat Annie* (LeRoy); *Treasure Island* (Fleming); *Manhattan Melodrama* (Van Dyke); **The Thin Man** (Van Dyke); *Queen Christina* (Mamoulian); *Dancing Lady* (Leonard); *Night Flight* (Brown); *Dinner at Eight* (Cukor); *Eskimo* (Van Dyke); *When Ladies Meet* (Beaumont); *The Barbarian (A Night in Cairo)* (Wood); *Hold Your Man* (Wood); *Bombshell* (Fleming)

1934   *David Copperfield* (Cukor); *Merry Widow* (Lubitsch); *Mutiny on the Bounty* (Lloyd); *The Barretts of Wimpole Street* (Franklin); *A Wicked Woman* (Brabin); *The Show-Off* (Riesner); *Sadie McKee* (Brown); *Chained* (Brown); *The Painted Veil* (Boleslawsky); *Tarzan and His Mate* (Gibbons); *Riptide* (Goulding); *Viva Villa!* (Conway)

1935   *China Seas* (Garnett); *A Tale of Two Cities* (Conway); *San Francisco* (Van Dyke); *Anna Karenina* (Brown); **A Night at the Opera** (Wood); *Libeled Lady* (Conway); *Rendezvous* (Howard); *Whipsaw* (Wood); *No More Ladies* (E. Griffith and Cukor); *Ah Wilderness* (Brown)

1936   *The Great Ziegfeld* (Leonard); *Romeo and Juliet* (Cukor); *The Good Earth* (Franklin); *The Broadway Melody of 1936* (Del Ruth); *Naughty Marietta* (Van Dyke); *Born to Dance* (Del Ruth); *Rose Marie* (Van Dyke); *Fury* (Lang); *After the Thin Man* (Van Dyke); *Tarzan Escapes* (Thorpe)

1937   **Camille** (Cukor); *Captains Courageous* (Fleming); *Night Must Fall* (Thorpe); *A Family Affair* (Seitz); *The Last of Mrs. Cheyney* (Boleslawsky); *Parnell* (Stahl); *The Broadway Melody of 1938* (Del Ruth); *Thoroughbreds Don't Cry* (Green); *Rosalie* (Van Dyke); *Maytime* (Leonard); *The Firefly* (Leonard); *A Day at the Races* (Wood)

1938   *Sweethearts* (Van Dyke); *Young Doctor Kildare* (Bucquet); *Boys Town* (Taurog); *Mannequin* (Borzage); *Test Pilot* (Fleming); *Three Comrades* (Borzage); *The Crowd Roars* (Thorpe); *A Yank at Oxford* (Conway); *The Citadel* (K. Vidor); *Marie Antoinette* (Van Dyke)

1939   *Goodbye, Mr. Chips* (Ross); **Ninotchka** (Lubitsch); *The Adventures of Huckleberry Finn* (Thorpe); **The Wizard of Oz** (Fleming); **Gone with the Wind** (Fleming); **The Women** (Cukor)

1940   *Strike Up the Band* (Berkeley); *Pride and Prejudice* (Leonard); *Little Nellie Kelly* (Taurog); *The Broadway Melody of 1940* (Taurog); *Northwest Passage* (K. Vidor); *Edison the Man* (Brown); *Boom Town* (Conway); *Waterloo Bridge* (LeRoy); **The Philadelphia Story** (Cukor); *Comrade X* (K. Vidor); *Strange Cargo* (Borzage); *I Love You Again* (Van Dyke); *Escape* (LeRoy)

1941   *Billy the Kid* (Miller); *Two Faced Woman* (Cukor); *A Woman's Face* (Cukor); *Dr. Jekyll and Mr. Hyde* (Fleming); *Blossoms in the Dust* (LeRoy); *Smilin' Through* (Borzage); *The Chocolate Soldier* (Del Ruth); *Babes on Broadway* (Berkeley); *Lady Be Good* (McLeod); *Ziegfeld Girl* (Leonard)

1942   **Mrs. Miniver** (Wyler); *Woman of the Year* (Stevens); *Keeper of the Flame* (Cukor); *Her Cardboard Lover* (Cukor); *I Married an Angel* (Van Dyke); *Tarzan's New York Adventure* (Thorpe); *White Cargo* (Thorpe); *Johnny Eager* (LeRoy); *Me and My Gal (Pier 13)* (Walsh); *Random Harvest* (LeRoy)

1943   *Above Suspicion* (Thorpe); *Madame Curie* (LeRoy); *Bataan* (Garnett); *Stand by for Action (Cargo of Innocents)* (Leonard); *A Guy Named Joe* (Fleming); *Lassie Come Home* (Wilcox); *The Heavenly Body* (Hall); *Cabin in the Sky* (Minnelli); *Girl Crazy (When the Girls Meet the Boys)* (Taurog); *Thousands Cheer* (Sidney)

1944   **Meet Me in St. Louis** (Minnelli); *Broadway Rhythm* (Del Ruth); *Bathing Beauty* (Sidney); *The Seventh Cross* (Zinnemann); *Thirty Seconds over Tokyo* (LeRoy); *The White Cliffs of Dover* (Brown); *Mrs. Parkington* (Garnett)

1945   *Anchors Aweigh* (Sidney); *The Valley of Decision* (Garnett); *Adventure* (Fleming); *The Clock (Under the Clock)* (Minnelli); *National Velvet* (Brown); *Son of Lassie* (Simon); *They Were Expendable* (Ford); **The Picture of Dorian Gray** (Lewin)

1946   *The Yearling* (Brown); *The Harvey Girls* (Sidney); *Till the Clouds Roll By* (Whorf); *Ziegfeld Follies* (Minnelli); *The Postman Always Rings Twice* (Garnett); *Lady in the Lake* (Montgomery)

1947   *The Hucksters* (Conway); *Homecoming* (LeRoy); *Sea of Grass* (Kazan); *Cass Timberlane* (Sidney); *High Wall* (Bernhardt); *Good News* (Walters); *Song of Love* (Brown);

Merton of the Movies (Alton); *Green Dolphin Street* (Saville); *Fiesta* (Thorpe); *The Unfinished Dance* (Koster); *Cynthia (The Rich Full Life)* (Leonard)

1948   *Easter Parade* (Walters); *The Pirate* (Minnelli); *Words and Music* (Taurog); *Summer Holiday* (Mamoulian); *On an Island with You* (Thorpe); *Luxury Liner* (Whorf); *Command Decision* (Wood); *State of the Union* (Capra); *The Search* (Zinnemann)

1949   ***On the Town*** (Donen and Kelly); *Take Me Out to the Ball Game* (*Everybody's Changing*) (Berkeley); *The Barkleys of Broadway* (Walters); *Intruder in the Dust* (Brown); ***Adam's Rib*** (Cukor); *Neptune's Daughter* (Buzzell); *That Midnight Kiss* (Taurog); *Any Number Can Play* (LeRoy); *Little Women* (LeRoy)

1950   *Father of the Bride* (Minnelli); *Annie Get Your Gun* (Sidney); *Three Little Words* (Thorpe); *Summer Stock* (*If You Feel Like Singing*); *The Toast of New Orleans* (Taurog); *Two Weeks with Love* (Rowland); *Duchess of Idaho* (Leonard); *King Solomon's Mines* (Bennett); *To Please a Lady* (Brown); *The Miniver Story* (Potter); *A Life of Her Own* (Cukor); *Devil's Doorway* (A. Mann); ***The Asphalt Jungle*** (Huston); *Crisis* (R. Brooks); *Mystery Street* (J. Sturges); *Right Cross* (J. Sturges); *The Next Voice You Hear* (Wellmann)

Other Films as Producer:

1917   *The Great Secret* (Cabanne—serial)

1919   *Human Desire* (North); *Virtuous Wives*; *In Old Kentucky* (Neilan); *Midnight Romance*; *Mary Regan*

1920   *Harriet and the Piper* (Bracken); *The Inferior Sex*

1921   *The Child Thou Gavest Me* (*Retribution*) (Stahl); *Her Mad Bargain* (Carewe); *The Invisible Fear* (Carewe); *Playthings of Destiny* (Carewe); *Sowing the Wind* (Carewe)

1922   *The Dangerous Age* (Stahl); *One Clear Call* (Stahl); *The Song of Life* (Stahl); *Her Kingdom of Desire* (Neilan)

1923   *The Famous Mrs. Fair* (Niblo); *The Eternal Struggle* (*The Man Thou Gavest Me*; *The Master of Woman*) (Barker); *Hearts Aflame* (Barker); *Pleasure Mad* (Barker); *Strangers of the Night* (Niblo); *The Wanters* (Stahl)

1924   *Thy Name Is Woman* (Niblo)

Publications

On MAYER: books—

Ross, Lillian, *Picture*, New York, 1952.

Crowther, Bosley, *Hollywood Rajah*, New York, 1960.

Marx, Sam, *Mayer and Thalberg: The Make-Believe Saints*, London, 1975.

Eames, John Douglas, *The MGM Story*, New York, 1976.

Carey, Gary, *All the Stars in Heaven*, London, 1981.

Gabler, Neal, *An Empire of Their Own: How the Jews Invented Hollywood*, New York, 1988.

Brownstein, Ronald, *The Powder and the Glitter*, New York, 1990.

Altman, Diana, *Hollywood East: Louis B. Mayer & the Origins of the Studio System*, Carol Publishing, 1992.

Higham, Charles, *Merchant of Dreams: Louis B. Mayer, M.G.M. & the Secret Hollywood*, New York, 1994.

Tygiel, Jules, *The Great Los Angeles Swindle: Oil, Stocks & Scandal During the Roaring Twenties*, Collingdale, 1998.

On MAYER: articles—

Photoplay (New York), vol. 44, no. 3, August 1933.

Theater Arts, vol. 35, no. 9, September 1951.

Sight and Sound (London), vol. 22, no. 4, April/June 1953.

Obituary in *Times* (London), 30 October 1957.

Obituary in *Motion Picture Herald*, vol. 209, no. 5, 2 November 1957.

Time (New York), 4 April 1960.

Sight and Sound (London), vol. 45, no. 3, Summer 1976.

Giles, D., "The Ghost of Thalberg: MGM 1946–1951," in *Velvet Light Trap* (Austin), Spring 1978.

Berg, A. Scott, "Louis B. Mayer: MGM's Archetypal Studio Head at Home," in *Architectural Digest* (Los Angeles), April 1990.

Film and TV Technician, no. 544, February 1991.

Thompson, David, "Merchant of Dreams: Louis B. Mayer, MGM and the Secret Hollywood," in *New Republic*, 12 April 1993.

Rickman, Gregg, "Hollywood East: Louis B. Mayer and the Origins of the Studio System," in *Film Quarterly* (Berkeley), Summer 1993.

Gordon, Alex, "J for Jewish: Motion Pictures with Jewish Connections," in *Sight and Sound* (London), March 1997.

Niderost, E., "The Ultimate Mogul: Louis B. Mayer," in *Classic Images* (Muscatine), May 1997.

Schulberg, Budd, "Lion of Hollywood—Louis B. Mayer," in *Time*, 7 December 1998.

*   *   *

Metro-Goldwyn-Mayer, with its internationally famous symbol of a roaring "Leo the Lion," surely represented the most famous of the Hollywood studios of the 1930s and 1940s. The studio executive in charge of the 52 feature films and hundreds of short subjects that emerged annually from that filmmaking empire was Louis B. Mayer. During those glorious years MGM had a complete movie factory with 27 sound stages on a 168-acre Culver City, California lot. MGM's laboratories could process 150,000 feet of film each day, and its property rooms contained more than 15,000 items to be used in movie after movie. It fed the films produced directly to Loew's theaters, its parent company.

MGM's method of film production reflected Mayer's conservative business philosophy. During the Great Depression, the studio publicly projected an image as the Tiffany of studios: a high class, elegant operation. Greta Garbo and Norma Shearer headlined in a series of high-gloss, sophisticated melodramas, guaranteed to project positively with even the most jaded movie fan.

But Mayer covered all his bets, making a wide variety of feature films, many of which we would hardly classify as "high class." Consider that in MGM's best years, the early 1930s, the studio's star who most often was ranked highest in popularity polls was none other than 61-year-old, gruff Marie Dressler. Dressler played an older woman with a heart of gold in *Min and Bill* and *Tugboat Annie*, two hits of the period, and brought MGM far more money than Garbo or Shearer.

Indeed Mayer's MGM studio-factory employed a vast array of stars. In the 1930s, he set up a series of *Tarzan* jungle adventures with

Johnny Weissmuller, slapstick comedies with Stan Laurel and Oliver Hardy, and the satire and burlesque of the Marx Brothers in *A Night at the Opera* and *A Day at the Races*. Year-in, year-out through the two decades of the Golden Age of Hollywood, Clark Gable and Spencer Tracy represented Mayer's most long-lived stars, two rugged males essaying roles which many took to define the ideal American male.

During the 1940s, Mayer went on to sponsor a certain glossy brand of Technicolor musical. *Meet Me in St. Louis* (1944) with Judy Garland (and directed by her then husband Vincente Minnelli), *Easter Parade* with Garland and Fred Astaire, and the innovative *On the Town*, starring Gene Kelly and co-directed by Kelly and Stanley Donen, offered widely engaging films, and attracted large audiences. But Technicolor musicals cost a great deal, and thus never did make much in the way of pure profit. In the 1940s Mayer contributed more to the Loew's bottom line with the low-budget B *Dr. Kildare* and *Hardy* family series. *Our Gang* comedy shorts also made millions for Loew's. In the 1940s the studio also developed the popular *Tom and Jerry* cartoon series.

Mayer prospered during the 1930s and into 1940s. Nonetheless, while larger than life to the moviegoing public on a daily basis and from a purely business perspective, he always knew he worked for a division of a larger multinational corporate enterprise, Loew's, Inc. Loew's management, led by Nicholas M. Schenck who was based in New York City, had hired Mayer as part of the 1924 merger that had created Metro-Goldwyn-Mayer. Indeed, prior to the merger, Mayer had produced his own films, a corpus now long forgotten.

Schenck kept Mayer as MGM studio chief as long as Mayer did well. But with the arid days of the late 1940s and into the television era of the 1950s, MGM began a financial slide downhill. Mayer was blamed for the red ink, and as an employee, not top executive, was blamed for the debacle and summarily kicked out. Mayer thus did not end his career at MGM but working for a rival, helping Cinerama crack the widescreen movie market during the 1950s.

—Douglas Gomery

McALPINE, Donald

Cinematographer. **Nationality:** Australian. **Born:** 1934. **Career:** Nominated for Australian Film Institute Awards for Best Achievement in Cinematography for *Wu ting*, 1981 and *The Fringe Dwellers*, 1986; nominated for Golden Satellite Award for Outstanding Cinematography and British Academy Award (BAFTA) for Best Cinematography for *Romeo + Juliette*. **Awards:** Australian Film Institute, Awards for Best Achievement in Cinematography for *My Brilliant Career*, 1979, and *Breaker Morant*, 1980; Australian Cinematographers Society, Cinematographer of the Year, 1981, Award of Distinction, 1997.

Films as Cinematographer:

1972   *The Adventures of Barry McKenzie* (Beresford)
1974   *Barry Mackenzie Holds His Own* (Beresford)
1976   *Don's Party* (Beresford) (as Don McAlpine)
1977   *The Getting of Wisdom* (Beresford)
1978   *Patrick* (Franklin)

1979   *The Journalist* (Thornhill); *Money Movers* (Beresford); *The Odd Angry Shot* (Jeffrey); *My Brilliant Career* (Armstrong)
1980   *The Earthling* (Collinson) (as Don McAlpine); *Breaker Morant* (Beresford); *The Club* (*Players*) (Beresford)
1981   *Puberty Blues* (Beresford)
1982   *Tempest* (Mazursky); *Don't Cry, It's Only Thunder* (Werner)
1983   *Now and Forever* (Carr); *Blue Skies Again* (Michaels)
1984   *Moscow on the Hudson* (Mazursky); *Harry and Son* (Newman)
1985   *My Man Adam* (Simon); *King David* (Beresford)
1986   *The Fringe Dwellers* (Beresford); *Down and Out in Beverly Hills* (Mazursky)
1987   *Orphans* (Mullan); *Predator* (McTiernan)
1988   *Moon Over Parador* (Mazursky)
1989   *See You in the Morning* (Pakula); *Parenthood* (Howard)
1990   *Stanley & Iris* (Ritt)
1991   *Career Opportunities* (*One Wild Night*) (Gordon); *The Hard Way* (Badham)
1992   *Medicine Man* (McTiernan); *Patriot Games* (Noyce) (as Donald M. McAlpine)
1993   *Mrs. Doubtfire* (Columbus); *The Man without a Face* (Gibson) (as Donald M. McAlpine)
1994   *Clear and Present Danger* (Noyce)
1995   *Nine Months* (Columbus)
1996   *Romeo+Juliet* (*Romeo and Juliet*; *William Shakespeare's Romeo+Juliet*) (Luhrman) (as Donald M. McAlpine)
1997   *The Edge* (Tamahori) (as Donald M. McAlpine) (A.S.C.) (+sc)
1998   *Stepmom* (Columbus) (as Donald M. McAlpine)

Publications:

By McALPINE: articles—

Magid, R., "Playing for Keeps: *Patriot Games*," interview in *American Cinematographer* (Hollywood), vol. 73, no. 6, 1992.

On McALPINE: books—

McFarlane, Brian, *Australian Cinema 1970–1985*, London, 1987.

*   *   *

An important figure in the development of the new Australian cinema in the late 1970s, Donald McAlpine has gone on to become an influential figure in Hollywood. He worked as cinematographer on some of the most successful films of the 1990s. His collaboration with Australian director Bruce Beresford began in the early 1970s with the slapstick "Barry MacKenzie" films, but went on to create some of the key films in which Australian filmmakers began to explore Australia's emergence as a nation (roughly between 1890 and 1920). His more recent Hollywood output has been less consequential, but McAlpine works to a consistently high standard, whether it is on a gritty thriller, such as *Clear and Present Danger*, or a comic romp like *Mrs. Doubtfire*. The beginning of McAlpine's career coincided with a revival in Australian cinema from which emerged some of the most talented filmmakers of their generation. The cinematographer has worked with several of the key directors of this revival, including Gillian Armstrong, but his collaboration with Beresford, with whom he has worked on many film projects, has proved the most productive. Films such as *Breaker Morant*, which dramatizes an episode in the

Boer war in which Australian officers were court-martialled for killing prisoners take a polemical approach to British imperialism. Brian McFarlane argues that although detailed, the film's approach to historical fact is heavily influenced by contemporary Australian attitudes to the influence of British authority. Nevertheless, McFarlane praises McAlpine's use of the camera to "underline the drama."

The same may also be said of an earlier film, *The Getting of Wisdom*, which, in common with many Australian films of the time, is based on work by a notable Australian writer, Ethel Lindesay Richardson. More successfully, the Armstrong/McAlpine partnership was responsible for *My Brilliant Career*, another adaptation of a work by Australian woman writer. While both films are impressive in their recreation of the period, McFarlane points out that Armstrong's film is more successful in using the 1890s setting to make points about 1970s feminism and Australian nationalism. Both films tell the stories of young women emerging as artists in their own right but, helped by McAlpine's camerawork, the later film is altogether more confident about presenting Sybylla Melvyn's rebellious struggle for autonomy as analogous to Australia's growing confidence in itself as a nation.

Since the mid-1980s, McAlpine's career has centred on Hollywood. Some of his most impressive work has been on tough thrillers, such as *Patriot Games* and its sequel *Clear and Present Danger*, (both of which were directed by Australian director Phillip Noyce), in which McAlpine's skill with positioning the camera enhance the sense of narrowing possibilities. It was on these films that McAlpine became involved with the development of computer generated images (CGI), and many of the skills that enhance these films are on show in John Badham's comedy *The Hard Way*, in which an actor joins a cop in the hunt for a serial killer.

The hit of 1996, *Romeo+Juliet* set Shakespeare's play in "Verona Beach," California, and has been praised for the tongue-in-cheek inventiveness of its updating of the text (for example, handguns made by the "Sword" gun company). The film features rapid editing and swooping tracking shots that create a tension and sense of space that is all but impossible to achieve in the live theatre. McAlpine's ability to use camera positioning to capture not only the action but also the context for the action is undoubtedly one of the many reasons for the film's success.

Yet despite being so well suited to the demands of the thriller, perhaps McAlpine's most productive Hollywood collaboration has been with director Chris Columbus, famous for romantic comedies and sentimental dramas. Their first project together was on the Robin Williams vehicle, *Mrs. Doubtfire*, is reminiscent in many ways of McAlpine's earlier film, *Parenthood*, in which three generations of sons and fathers try to understand their relationships to one another. The small-scale settings for these films allow characters to dominate scenes with often hilarious results, and are ideal for Williams's slapstick style in the later film. In *Mrs. Doubtfire* McAlpine photographs the manly frame of Williams posing as a female housekeeper in such a way as to keep the audience in on the joke while leaving the impersonation convincing enough in the context of the film. More recent and less successful collaborations with Columbus have produced the flop *Nine Months* and *Stepmom*, a mediocre family drama which overuses the sentimental possibilities of terminal illness.

McAlpine's beginnings in the revival in Australian cinema at the end of the 1970s are now largely eclipsed by his success with more popular Hollywood offerings. Yet it was in the earlier period that McAlpine both developed his perceptive style and produced most of his best work. With the exceptions of the *Patriot Games* films, and *Romeo+Juliet*, a virtuoso piece of camerawork, McAlpine has rarely

had the opportunity to show off the extent of his abilities in the 1990s. While his work on a succession of Hollywood comedies and dramas has always been slick and proficient, it is for his work in Australia that his career will be most favourably assessed.

—Chris Routledge

McCAY, Winsor

Animator. **Nationality:** American. **Born:** Winsor Zenis McCay in Spring Lake, Michigan, 26 September 1871. **Education:** Attended Ypsilanti Normal School, Michigan. **Family:** Married Maud Defore, 1891; children: Robert and Marion. **Career:** Before 1889—worked for poster firm, Chicago; 1891—scenic artist, Vine Street Dime Museum, Cincinnati, Ohio; 1898—reporter for Cincinnati *Commercial Tribune*, and later for *Enquirer*; 1903—drawings in strip form parodying Kipling's *Just So Stories* attracted attention of James Gordon Bennett, Jr., of *New York Herald*; hired to draw for New York *Evening Telegram*; created strip *Dreams of a Rarebit Fiend* using pseudonym "Silas"; began comic strips for *Herald*; 1905—created *Little Nemo in Slumberland*; 1906—began giving chalk talks on vaudeville circuit; 1908—successful Broadway musical based on *Little Nemo*; 1909—introduced to cartoon animation by J. Stuart Blackton; began work on *Little Nemo*, first cartoon; 1911—premiered *Little Nemo* in vaudeville act; 1914—used *Gertie the Dinosaur* as part of vaudeville act; 1918—premiere of *The Sinking of the Lusitania*, probably first cartoon feature. **Died:** In 1934.

Films as Director, Writer and Animator:

1909   *Little Nemo* (short)
1911   *Winsor McCay*
1912   *How a Mosquito Operates* (*The Story of a Mosquito*) (short)
1914   **Gertie the Dinosaur** (**Gertie the Trained Dinosaur**) (short)
1916   *Winsor McCay and His Jersey Skeeters*
1918   *The Sinking of the Lusitania*
1918–21   *The Centaurs* (short); *Flip's Circus* (short); *Gertie on Tour* (short)
1921   *Dreams of a Rarebit Fiend* Series; *The Pet*; *Bug Vaudeville*; *Flying House* (shorts) (co-d with son Robert McCay)

Publications

On McCAY: book—

Canemaker, John, *Winsor McCay: His Life and Art*, New York, 1987.

On McCAY: articles—

Canemaker, J., "Winsor McCay," in *Film Comment* (New York), January-February 1975.
Canemaker, J., "The Birth of Animation," in *Millimeter* (New York), April 1975.
Cornand, A., "Le Festival d'Annecy et les Rencontres internationales du cinéma d'animation," in *Image et Son* (Paris), January 1977.
Positif (Paris), no. 355, September 1990.

Winsor McCay (right)

Marschall, R., ''Masters of Comic Strip Art,'' in *American History Illustrated*, March-April 1990.

Parsons, Scott, ''Animation Legend: Winsor McCay,'' in *Library Journal*, 15 September 1994.

Blonder, R., ''Mosquitoes, Dinosaurs, and the Image-ination,'' in *Animatrix* (Los Angeles), no. 8, 1994–1995.

Filmvilag (Budapest), no. 8, 1996.

Blackmore, Tim, ''McCay's Mechanical Muse: Engineering Comic-Strip Dreams,'' in *Journal of Popular Culture*, Summer 1998.

*   *   *

Winsor McCay is generally regarded as the first American auteur of animation. Although not the first to experiment with animated films, McCay achieved artistic and technical heights that established animation as a viable form and that set ground rules for a style of pictorial illusionism and closed figurative forms in American animated cartoons.

McCay studied art and worked as an illustrator and sign painter before settling down in 1889 as a newspaper cartoonist in Cincinnati. His success as a cartoonist led him to move in 1903 to the New York *Evening Telegram*. There he worked as a staff illustrator and developed the comic strips that brought him international fame.

During the next several years, McCay created such comic strips as *Hungry Henrietta*, *Little Sammy Sneeze*, *Dream of the Rarebit Fiend*, *Pilgram's Progress*, and his most famous work, *Little Nemo in Slumberland*. *Little Nemo*, which ran from 1905 to 1911, is the pinnacle of comic strip art in the first decade of the 20th century. It displays an unparalleled application of Art Nouveau graphic style, translating sinewy, irregular forms and rhythms into a delightfully decorative comic strip design. The strips related the fantastic adventures which befell the child Little Nemo, who always woke up in the last panel of the comic strip.

Sometime about 1909, McCay set to work on making an animated film of *Little Nemo in Slumberland*. (He credits his son's interest in flip books as the source of inspiration for his cinematic experiment.) After drawing and hand-coloring more than 4,000 detailed images on rice paper, McCay employed his animated film in his vaudeville act while Vitagraph, the company that shot and produced the film, simultaneously announced its release of *Little Nemo*. The animation did not employ a story but rather showed the characters of the comic strip continuously moving, stretching, flipping, and metamorphosing.

McCay used foreshortening and exact perspective to create depth and an illusionistic sense of space even without the aid of any background. The animation sequence is framed by a live-action story in which McCay's friends scoff at the idea that he can make moving pictures and then congratulate him when he succeeds.

The advertisements and the prologue for the film stressed the monumental amount of labor and time required to do the drawings. McCay promoted and flaunted not only his role as an artist but the animator's "trade secrets." Throughout his career, McCay emphasized the revelation of the mechanics and process of animation, a self-reflexive approach that grew naturally out of the way he self-consciously undermined conventions of comic strip art and constantly called attention to the form itself.

McCay made his second animated cartoon in 1911–12. *How a Mosquito Operates* relies on a simpler, less intricately graphic style in order to tell the story of a large mosquito's encounter with a sleeping victim. Two years later, McCay completed the animated film for which he is most famous, *Gertie the Dinosaur*. Like his previous two films, McCay incorporated the cartoon into his vaudeville act and, like *Little Nemo*, Gertie's animation is framed by a live-action sequence. But in *Gertie*, McCay combined the lessons of his earlier two films in order to create a character who is animation's first cartoon personality.

After *Gertie the Dinosaur*, McCay continued doing other animated cartoons but began utilizing celluloid (instead of rice paper) and stationary backgrounds that did not have to be redrawn for every frame. He also devised a system of attaching pre-punched sheets to pegs so that he could eliminate the slight shifting that occurred from drawing to drawing. His discovery represents the first instance of peg registration, a technique commonly employed in modern animation.

Although McCay's later cartoons were popular and praised for their naturalness (*Centaurs* and *Sinking of the Lusitania*), McCay's elaborate full animation proved too time-consuming and costly to inspire others, more concerned with production, to adhere to his high standards. Neither a full-time animator nor part of a movie studio, McCay was free to pursue his own ends. His success is due to his ability to translate graphic style to animation as well as to his gregarious showmanship.

McCay stopped making animated films in 1921, and by the time he died of a cerebral hemorrhage in 1934, his contribution as an animator was almost forgotten. Only in the 1960s was McCay rediscovered as an American artist. In 1966, New York's Metropolitan Museum sponsored an exhibit of his work.

—Lauren Rabinovitz

McCORD, Ted

Cinematographer. **Nationality:** American. **Born:** Sullivan County, Indiana, 1898; sometimes credited as T. F. McCord. **Military Service:** Served as captain in the United States Army during World War II: with the first group of Americans to enter Berlin (photographed Hitler's chancellory). **Career:** 1917—camera assistant, Bosworth Studios; 1921—first film as cinematographer, *Sacred and Profane Love*; did much later work for Warner Bros. **Died:** 19 January 1976.

Films as Cinematographer:

1921   *Sacred and Profane Love* (Taylor) (co)
1924   *Flirting with Love* (Dillon); *For Sale* (Archainbaud); *So Big* (Brabin)
1925   *The Pace That Thrills* (Campbell); *The Desert Flower* (Cummings); *Sally* (Green); *We Moderns* (Dillon)
1926   *Irene* (Green)
1927   *The Valley of the Giants* (Brabin)
1928   *The Code of the Scarlet* (H. Brown); *The Crash* (Cline); *The Upland Rider* (Rogell); *The Canyon of Adventure* (Rogell); *The Phantom City* (Rogell)
1929   *The Wagon Master* (H. Brown); *The Royal Rider* (H. Brown); *Senor Americano* (H. Brown)
1930   *The Fighting Legion* (H. Brown); *The Dawn Trail* (Cabanne); *The Lone Rider* (L. King); *Mountain Justice* (H. Brown); *Sons of the Saddle* (H. Brown); *Lucky Larkin* (H. Brown); *Parade of the West* (H. Brown); *Song of the Caballero* (H. Brown); *Men without Law* (L. King); *Shadow Ranch* (L. King)
1931   *Desert Vengeance* (L. King); *Freighters of Destiny* (Allen); *Sundown Trail* (Hill)
1932   *Carnival Boat* (Rogell); *The Big Stampede* (Wright); *Beyond the Rockies* (Allen); *The Saddle Buster* (Allen); *Hell-Fire Austin* (Sheldon) (co); *Ride Him, Cowboy!* (Allen); *False Faces* (L. Sherman) (co)
1933   *The Man from Monterey* (Wright); *Fiddling' Buckaroo* (Maynard); *Somewhere in Sonora* (Wright); *The Telegraph Trail* (Wright); *King of the Arena* (James); *Strawberry Roan* (James)
1934   *Gun Justice* (James); *The Trail Drive* (James); *Wheels of Destiny* (James); *Fugitive Road* (Strayer); *Smoking Guns* (James); *Rocky Rhodes* (Raboch); *When a Man Sees Red* (James)
1935   *The Rainmakers* (Guiol); *Stone of River Creek* (Grinde)
1936   *Feud of the West* (Fraser); *Trailin' West* (Smith)
1937   *Fugitive in the Sky* (Grinde) (co); *Guns of the Pecos* (Smith)
1938   *Sergeant Murphy* (Eason); *The Daredevil Drivers* (Eason)
1939   *Secret Service of the Air* (Smith); *Code of the Secret Service* (Smith); *Pride of Bluegrass* (McGann); *Cowboy Quarterback* (Smith)
1940   *Ladies Must Live* (Smith); *Calling All Husbands* (Smith); *Murder in the Air* (Seiler); *Father Is a Prince* (Smith)
1941   *The Case of the Black Parrot* (Smith); *Nine Lives Are Not Enough* (Sutherland); *She Couldn't Say No* (Clemens); *Singapore Woman* (Negulesco); *Knockout* (Clemens); *Highway West* (McGann); *Bullets for O'Hara* (Howard)
1942   *Wild Bill Hickok Rides* (Enright); *Murder in the Big House* (Eason); *Bullet Scars* (Lederman); *I Was Framed* (Lederman)
1943   *Action in the North Atlantic* (Bacon)
1947   *Deep Valley* (Negulesco); *That Way with Women* (de Cordova)
1948   **The Treasure of the Sierra Madre** (Huston); *Johnny Belinda* (Negulesco); *June Bride* (Windust); *Smart Girls Don't Talk* (Bare)
1949   *Flamingo Road* (Curtiz); *The Lady Takes a Sailor* (Curtiz)
1950   *The Damned Don't Cry* (V. Sherman); *Young Man with a Horn* (Curtiz); *The Breaking Point* (Curtiz); *Rocky Mountain* (Keighley)
1951   *Goodbye My Fancy* (V. Sherman); *Force of Arms* (Curtiz); *I'll See You in My Dreams* (Curtiz); *Starlift* (Del Ruth)

1952 *This Woman Is Dangerous* (Feist); *Operation Secret* (Seiler);
      Cattle Town (Smith); *Stop, You're Killing Me!* (Del Ruth)
1953 *South Sea Woman* (Lubin)
1954 *Young at Heart* (Douglas)
1955 **East of Eden** (Kazan); *I Died a Thousand Times* (Heisler)
1956 *The Girl He Left Behind* (Butler); *The Burning Hills* (Heisler)
1957 *The Helen Morgan Story* (Curtiz)
1958 *The Proud Rebel* (Curtiz)
1959 *The Hanging Tree* (Daves)
1960 *The Adventures of Huckleberry Finn* (Curtiz); *Private Prop-
      erty* (L. Stevens)
1962 *Hero's Island* (L. Stevens); *Two for the Seesaw* (Wise); *War
      Hunt* (Sanders)
1965 *The Sound of Music* (Wise)
1966 *A Fine Madness* (Kershner)

Publications

On McCORD: articles—

Obituary in *Variety* (New York), 28 January 1976.
Obituary in *Cinema 76* (Paris), April 1976.
Giddins, Gary, "*Young Man with a Horn*," in *American Film*,
   April 1991.

*   *   *

The veteran cinematographer Ted McCord worked in the American film industry for a remarkable six decades, from the 1910s through the 1960s. As such he toiled on many a big-budget silent film such as First National's *Sally* and was behind the camera for the major blockbuster of the 1960s, 20th Century-Fox's *The Sound of Music*. But remarkably he never won an Academy Award, though he received three nominations for *Johnny Belinda*, *Two for the Seesaw*, and *The Sound of Music*. McCord was considered a good craftsman, not a great artist.

He was most praised for his complex use of lighting. McCord attributed his use of deep shadows to his interest in the paintings of Rembrandt and the cinematography of the great Gregg Toland. This was particularly apparent in such sequences as the "Climb Every Mountain" number in *The Sound of Music* and the brothel hallway footage in *East of Eden*.

Like many who entered the industry in the 1910s, McCord had no formal training in photography or aesthetics. Rather he learned on the job. He began in a film laboratory and took his training under James Van Trees at the old Hobart Bosworth Studio. He then moved on to film dozens of B- westerns. He was able to move to a major studio only as the Second World War sent many a younger cinematographer to battle and thus opened up positions in Hollywood.

Many of the great cameramen of the studio era took long tenures at one studio. For McCord that was Warner Bros. He worked on many of the studio's most famous and profitable films of the 1940s, including *The Treasure of the Sierra Madre*, *Action in the North Atlantic*, and *Flamingo Road*. Few of these are remembered as classics, but all were interesting visual artifacts. This is the portion of his career for which McCord will probably be most remembered.

He was also a generous benefactor to younger cameramen. Conrad Hall, cinematographer on such films as *Cool Hand Luke*, tells all interviewers that it was McCord who opened up the system for him

and other aspiring cinematographers of the 1960s. McCord was a self-confident "old pro." He was not set in his ways, but willing to help a new generation learn from the great craftsmen of the past.

—Douglas Gomery

McKIMSON, Robert

Animator. **Nationality:** American. **Born:** Denver, Colorado, 1910. **Career:** 1928—worked briefly for Walt Disney and the Romer Grey studio; joined the Harman-Ising studio, and remained with the unit at Warner Bros. until 1963; 1963–76—worked for DePatie-Freleng Enterprises: television work includes series *The Famous Adventures of Mr. Magoo*, *The Bugs Bunny Show*, *Super President*, *The Oddball Couple*, *Baggy Pants and the Nitwits*, and *Bailey's Comets*. **Died:** In 1976.

Films as Director of Animation (selected list):

1946 *Daffy Doodles*; *Hollywood Canine Canteen*; *Acrobatty Bunny*;
      Walky Talky Hawky; *The Mousemerized Cat*; *One Meat
      Brawl*
1947 *Birth of a Notion*; *Hobo Bobo*; *Crowing Pains*; *Horsefly Fleas*
1948 *Daffy Duck Slept Here*; *Hop, Look, and Listen*; *Easter Yeggs*;
      Gorilla My Dreams; *The Shell-Shocked Egg*; *The Upstand-
      ing Sitter*; *The Foghorn Leghorn*; *Hot-Cross Bunny*; *A Lad
      in His Lamp*; *Hurdy Gurdy Hare*
1949 *Paying the Piper*; *Daffy Duck Hunt*; *Rebel Rabbit*; *The
      Greyhounded Hare*; *The Windblown Hare*; *Swallow the
      Leader*; *A Ham in a Role*; *Boobs in the Woods*
1950 *Strife with Father*; *The Leghorn Blows at Midnight*; *An Egg
      Scramble*; *What's Up Doc?*; *It's Hummer Time*; *Hillbilly
      Hare*; *A Fractured Leghorn*; *Pop 'im Pop*; *The Bushy Hare*;
      Dog Collared
1951 *A Fox in a Fix*; *Corn Plastered*; *Early to Bet*; *French Rarebit*;
      Leghorn Swoggled; *Lovelorn Leghorn*; *Sleepytime Pos-
      sum*; *Big Top Bunny*; *The Prize Pest*; *Here We Go*
1952 *Who's Kitten Who?*; *Thumb Fun*; *Kiddin' the Kitten*; *Sock-a-
      Doodle Do*; *The Turn-Tail Wolf*; *The Oily Hare*; *Hoppy Go
      Lucky*; *The Egg-cited Rooster*; *The Super Snooper*; *Rab-
      bit's Kin*; *Fool Coverage*
1953 *Upswept Hare*; *A Peck o'Trouble*; *Muscle Tussle*; *There Auto
      Be a Law*; *Plop Goes the Weasel*; *Cat-Tails for Two*; *Easy
      Peckin's*; *Of Rice and Hen*; *Cats A-Weigh*
1954 *Wild Wife*; *Design for Leaving*; *Bell Hoppy*; *No Parking Hare*;
      Little Boy Boo; *Devil May Hare*; *The Oily American*; *Gone
      Batty*; *Quack Shot*
1955 *Feather Dusted*; *All Fowled Up*; *Lighthouse Mouse*; *The Hole
      Ideal Dime to Retire*
1956 *Too Hop to Handle*; *Weasel Stop*; *The High and the Flighty*;
      Mixed Master; *The Unexpected Pest*; *Stupor Duck*; *Half-
      Fare Hare*; *Raw! Raw! Rooster*; *The Slap-Happy Mouse*;
      Wideo Wabbit; *The Honeymousers*
1957 *Bedevilled Rabbit*; *Cheese It, the Cat!*; *Fox Terror*; *Boston
      Quackie*; *Ducking the Devil*; *Mouse-taken Identity*; *Rabbit
      Romeo*

1958	*Don't Axe Me*; *Tortilla Flaps*; *Feather Bluster*; *Now Hare This*; *Dog Tales*; *Weasel While You Work*; *Pre-hysterical Hare*; *Gopher Broke*
1959	*Mouse-placed Kitten*; *China Jones*; *The Mouse That Jack Built*; *A Mutt in a Rut*; *Backwoods Bunny*; *Bonanza Bunny*; *A Broken Leghorn*; *People Are Bunny*
1960	*West of the Pesos*; *Wild, Wild World*; *Crockett Doodle-Do*; *Mice Follies*; *The Dixie Fryer*; *Doggone People*
1961	*Cannery Woe*; *Hoppy Daze*; *Strangled Eggs*; *Birds of a Father*; *Daffy's Inn Trouble*; *What's My Lion?*
1962	*Wet Hare*; *Fish 'n Slips*; *Bill of Hare*; *The Slick Chick*; *Mother Was a Rooster*; *Good Noose*
1963	*Fast Buck Duck*; *The Million-hare*; *Banty Raids*; *Aqua Duck*; *Claws in the Lease*; *A Message to Gracias*
1964	*The Incredible Mr. Limpet* (Lubin) (animation sequences); *Bartholomew vs. the Wheel*; *Freudy Cat*; *Dr. Devil and Mr. Hare*; *False Hare*
1965	*Moby Duck*; *Assault and Peppered*; *Well Worn Daffy*; *Suppressed Duck*; *Rushing Roulette*; *Tease for Two*; *Chili con Corny*; *Go Go Amigo*
1966	*The Astroduck*; *Mucho Locos*; *Mexican Mousepiece*; *Daffy Rents*; *A-Haunting We Will Go*; *Snow Excuse*; *A Squeak in the Deep*; *Feather Finger*; *Swing Ding Amigo*; *Sugar and Spies*; *A Taste of Catnip*; *Cock-a-Doodle Deaux Deaux*
1967	*Daffy's Dinner*; *Sacré Bleu Cross*; *Le Quiet Squad*
1968	*Bunny and Claude*; *The Fistic Mystic*
1969	*The Great Carrot Train Robbery*; *Rabbit Stew and Rabbits Too*; *Shamrock and Roll*; *Bugged by a Bee*; *Injun Trouble*
1973	*Fowl Play*
1975	*Pink Davinci*; *It's Pink But Is It Mink?*
1976	*Mystic Pink*; *The Pink Pro*; *Sherlock Pink*

Publications

On McKIMSON: articles—

"The Dixie Fryer," in *Reid's Film Index*, no. 27, 1996.
"Feather Duster," in *Reid's Film Index*, no. 27, 1996.
"French Rarebit," in *Reid's Film Index*, no. 27, 1996.
"A Mutt in a Rutt," in *Reid's Film Index*, no. 27, 1996.
"One Meat Brawl," in *Reid's Film Index*, no. 27, 1996.
"Pop 'Im Pop!" in *Reid's Film Index*, no. 27, 1996.

*   *   *

The cartoon director Robert McKimson is best known for his successful contributions to animation history by creating the mindlessly destructive beast known as The Tasmanian Devil and the voluble rooster, Foghorn Leghorn.

In the early 1930s, individual animator's work, such as McKimson's, was almost indistinguishable, although most animators see this period as a great training ground for their later careers. Hugh Harman and Rudolf Ising's main character was Bosko, who had as many adventures as his counterpart Mickey Mouse. The humor was as broad as the artwork, and, when Harman and Ising sold out to Leon Schlesinger, McKimson found himself animating on a new, but similar, character named Buddy. During these early years, McKimson animated for some of the best directors: Jack King, Friz Freleng, Chuck Jones, Tex

Avery, Frank Tashlin, and finally Bob Clampett, a very good foundation for any director. Some of his most notable animation occurs in many of Clampett's works, in particular Bugs Bunny appearing as a ballerina in *A Corny Concerto* or Bugs's death scene in *The Old Grey Hare*. Although a great deal of the characterization of Bugs Bunny must go to Tex Avery, McKimson did design and draw the first model sheets while with Avery's unit. McKimson, who had shunned being promoted to director for seven years for the simple reason that he was "still learning," made his first film as animation director in 1946. The third cartoon he made featured his most popular character, the bombastic, blowhard rooster, Foghorn Leghorn, based on two radio characters; one, the hard-of-hearing Sheriff from *Blue Monday Jamboree*; the other, Kenny Delmar's overbearing creation Senator Cloghorn from the *Fred Allen Show*. Raucous, noisy, and a total pain-in-the-neck, Leghorn would spend entire cartoons relieving the boredom down on the farm by irritating all and sundry, especially the luckless watchdog, with his ceaseless talking, tricks, and gadgets to upset many an applecart. Occasionally he would join forces with a weasel to help him catch the chicks that the dog was guarding.

Often criticized for using too much dialogue and not enough action, McKimson soon rectified matters by creating the fast-paced speed demon, Speedy Gonzales, and a bizarre horned, whirling-dervish of a beast who tore through mountains as though they were lumps of cake, eating everything in sight—the Tasmanian Devil. The producer Eddie Selzer disliked the character so much that he ordered McKimson to put a stop to it. He was mercifully overridden by his boss, Jack Warner, who wanted to see more of the unsightly beast.

McKimson's style is very much his own, more restrained than his contemporaries Clampett and Avery, and very much attuned to radio and television parodies. Apart from his own characters, he worked best with characters he knew and had helped develop. Bugs Bunny teamed with Daffy Duck worked extremely well, as did Sylvester and his prig of a son. The culmination of his passion for radio and TV came when Jack Benny and his cast agreed to appear in McKimson's parody *The Mouse That Jack Built* for just the cost of a print of the cartoon.

When Warners finally closed its doors on cartoons, McKimson floundered around until he rejoined his former associate Friz Freleng, who had formed his own company, DePatie-Freleng Enterprises, and was making a series of new cartoons for none other than Warners. This was the beginning of the unfortunate era of cheap and quick cartoons. McKimson was never happy with what he was given to do at DFE, but tried to do his best on a shoestring budget in the quickest possible time. His final years with DFE were spent toying with commercials and TV episodes, so that, ironically, the medium he had enjoyed ribbing so mercilessly in the 1950s had now got its revenge and had the last laugh.

—Graham Webb

McLAREN, Norman

Animator. **Nationality:** Scottish. **Born:** Stirling, 11 April 1914. **Education:** Attended Stirling public schools; Glasgow School of Art. **Career:** 1934—while a student at Glasgow School of Art made

Norman McLaren

antiwar film with animated sequence which won first prize, Scottish Film Festival; 1936—after graduation hired by John Grierson at General Post Office Film Unit; 1936–38—worked on live-action documentaries; 1938—made first professional animated film *Love on the Wing*; first example of his drawing-directly-on-film technique; 1939–41—worked in New York independently, and for company producing publicity shorts and Museum of Non-Objective Art; 1941—hired by Grierson at Canada's National Film Board to set up animation department; 1949—began long collaboration with Evelyn Lambert on *Begone Dull Care*; 1952—for antiwar film *Neighbors* developed process of animating film of live actors called "pixillation." **Award:** Academy Award for *Neighbors*, 1952. **Died:** 1987.

Films as Director:

1934–35   *Hand Painted Abstraction*; *Seven Till Five*; *Camera Makes Woopee*; *Colour Cocktail*
1936–37   *Hell Unlimited*; *The Defense of Madrid*
1937–39   (For GPO Film Unit, London) *Book Bargain*; *News for the Navy*; *Many a Pickle*; *Love on the Wing*

1939   (For Film Center, London) *The Obedient Flame*
1939–41   (For Museum of Non-Objective Art, New York) *Dots**; *Scherzo*; *Loops**; *Rumba* (lost); *Stars and Stripes**; *Boogie Doodle**

(For National Film Board of Canada)

1941   *Mail Early*; *V for Victory*
1942   *Five for Four*; *Hen Hop**
1943   *Dollar Dance*
1944   *C'est l'aviron*; *Keep Your Mouth Shut*
1945   *La Haut sur ces montagnes*
1946   *A Little Phantasy*; *Hoppity Pop**
1947   *Fiddle-de-dee**; *Poulette grise*
1948–52   *A Phantasy*
1949   *Begone Dull Care**
1950–51   *Around Is Around*; *Now Is the Time*
1952   *Neighbors (Les Voisins)*** (+ mus); *Two Bagatelles*** (+ mus)
1954–55   *Blinkity Blank**
1956   *Rythmetic* (+ mus)
1957   *A Chairy Tale (Il était une chaise)***

1958 *Le Merle*
1959 *Serenal**; *Short and Suite**; *Mail Early for Christmas*; *The Wonderful World of Jack Paar* (for TV) (credit sequence only)
1960 *Lignes verticales (Lines-Vertical)**; *Opening Speech (Discours de bienvenue de McLaren)***
1961 *New York Lightboard*
1962 *Lignes horizontales (Lines-Horizontal)**
1963 *Caprice de Noël (Christmas Crackers)*** (credit sequence and intertitles only)
1964 *Canon***
1965 *Mosaic (Mosaïque)** (+ mus)
1967 *Pas de deux* (live action)
1969 *Sphères (Spheres)*
1971 *Synchromy*
1972 *Ballet adagio*
1973 *L'Écran d'épingles* (co-d with Alexeieff and Parker) (documentary)
1976–78 *Le Mouvement image par image* (series of 5 animation instruction films)
1981–83 *Narcissus* (live action)

* films without camera (direct drawing, engraving, or painting on film)

** "pixillation"

Publications

By McLAREN: books—

The Drawings of Norman McLaren, Montreal, 1975.
Norman McLaren on the Creative Process, edited by Donald McWilliams, Montreal, 1991.

By McLAREN: articles—

"L'Animation stéréographique," in *Cahiers du Cinéma* (Paris), July-August 1952.
"Notes on Animated Sound," in *Quarterly of Film, Radio, and Television* (Berkeley, California), Spring 1953.
Cahiers du Cinéma (Paris), December 1955.
"L'Écran et le pinceau," in *Séquences* (Montreal), December 1955.
"Making Films on Small Budgets," in *Film* (London), December 1955.
Interview, in special animation issue of *Cinéma* (Paris), January 1957.
Séquences (Montreal), October 1965.
"The Synthesis of Artificial Movements in Motion Picture Projection," with Guy Glover, in *Film Culture* (New York), no. 48–49, 1970.
Film Library Quarterly (New York), Spring 1970.
"Où va l'animation?," in *Ecran* (Paris), January 1973.
"Rhythm 'n Truths," interview with D. Elley, in *Films and Filming* (London), June 1974.
"A Dictionary of Movement," interview with M. Magistros and G. Munro, in *Wide Angle* (Athens, Ohio), v. 3, no. 4, 1980.

On McLAREN: books—

Forsyth, Hardy, *Dots and Loops: The Story of a Scottish Film Cartoonist*, Edinburgh, 1951.
Norman McLaren, La Cinémathèque québécoise, Montreal, 1965.
Collins, Maynard, *Norman McLaren*, Canadian Film Institute, 1975.
Russett, Robert, and Cecile Starr, *Experimental Animation*, New York, 1976.
Bakedano, Jose J., *Norman McLaren*, Bilbao, 1987.

On McLAREN: articles—

"Hen Tracks on Sound Tracks," in *Popular Mechanics*, April 1949.
Queval, Jean, "Norman McLaren ou le cinéma du VVIe siècle," in *Cahiers du Cinéma* (Paris), October-November 1951.
"Movies without a Camera, Music without Instruments," in *Theatre Arts* (New York), October 1952.
Jordan, William, "Norman McLaren: His Career and Techniques," in *Quarterly of Film, Radio and Television* (Berkeley, California), Fall 1953.
Special animation issue of *Cinéma* (Paris), January 1957.
Martin, André, "Le Cinéma de deux mains," in 2 parts, in *Cahiers du Cinéma* (Paris), January and February 1958.
Martin, André, "Mystère d'un cinéma instrumental," in 3 parts, in *Cahiers du Cinéma* (Paris), February, March and April 1958.
D'Yvoire, Jean, "Les Démons de McLaren," in *Radio-Cinéma-Télévision* (Paris), 29 June 1958.
Mekas, Adolfas, "The Second Story—Honoring the Only Canadian Artist," in *Film Culture* (New York), Summer 1962.
Weinberg, Gretchen, "Mc et Moi," in *Film Culture* (New York), Summer 1962.
"The Craft of Norman McLaren," in *Film Quarterly* (Berkeley, California), Winter 1962–63.
Egly, Max, "Klee, Steinberg, McLaren," in *Image et Son* (Paris), March 1965.
Cutler, May, "The Unique Genius of Norman McLaren," in *Canadian Art*, May-June 1965.
Vinet, Pierre, "Multi-McLaren," in *Take One* (Montreal), September-October 1966.
Burns, Dan, "Pixillation," in *Film Quarterly* (Berkeley, California), Fall 1968.
"The Career of Norman McLaren," in *Cinema Canada* (Montreal), August-September 1973.
Elley, D., "Rhythm 'n Truths," in *Films and Filming* (London), June 1974.
"Norman McLaren au fil de ses films," in special McLaren issue of *Séquences* (Montreal), October 1975.
Revue de la Cinémathèque (Montreal), February-April 1990.
Bassan, R., "Trois films de Norman McLaren," in *Bref*, no. 10, Autumn 1991.
Ciment, G., "Voyage à l'interieur d'un crane," in *Positif*, no. 371, January 1992.
Werner, L., "Spontaneous Frames of Movement," in *Americas*, September-October 1993.
Chevassu, F., "Hommage à Norman McLaren," in *Mensuel*, no. 11, November 1993.
Clark, Jeff, "Selected Films: Norman McLaren," in *Library Journal*, 15 March 1994.

Felperin, Leslie, "A: Animation," in *Sight and Sound* (London), June 1996.

Robinson, C., "Norman McLaren: A Tribute," in *Take One* (Toronto), Summer 1997.

* * *

Norman McLaren was one of the great polymaths of animation and filmmaking. Although many independent and experimental animators can, and do, work with a range of different techniques, few have explored the breadth of possibilities with such thoroughness and expertise as McLaren. Cel animation, animation with paper cutouts, pastels, paint, three-dimensional objects, "pixillated" human beings, the light board at Times Square, and even "animation without a camera" are just some of the methods he used in his nearly fifty-year-long career. In addition, he also painted and drew, wrote extensively about animation, collaborated with and inspired many other artists (including John Grierson, Benny Goodman, Oscar Peterson, Evelyn Lambert, Rene Jodoin, George Dunning, Alexander Alexeieff and Claire Parker, and Ravi Shankar, to name but a few), developed sophisticated optical printing techniques for live-action film, and is said to have invented the "travelling zoom" shot which inspired the "portal" sequence in Stanley Kubrick's *2001: A Space Odyssey*. Nonetheless, though his technical accomplishments and aesthetic achievements have profoundly influenced animators all over the world, he often maintained that his films' primary function was to convey his own feelings and to elicit an emotional response in his viewers. Towards the end of his life he said, "I just would like to be remembered for having made some films which have touched people greatly or melted them or moved them in some way or excited them."

Although the body of his work is heterogeneous, eclectic, and resistant to totalizing characterization, its single, unifying concern is the representation of movement. Indeed, he is said to have described animation itself as not the art of moving drawings, but of drawing movement. His later interest in dance, and ballet especially, is thus not an aberration from his animated work, but contiguous with it, as *Pas de deux* (1967) demonstrates. In an interview with Maynard Collins, McLaren revealingly notes that even when listening to music, which is so integral to his work, "I see movement, rather than specific images. . . . Movement is my basic language."

The most intriguing films in which McLaren articulates this "language" of movement are the "cameraless" and abstract ones he made while working independently and for the National Film Board of Canada where he headed their animation department. Some of these depict recognizable figures and imagery, like *Dollar Dance* (1943) and *Hen Hop* (1942) (of the latter, Picasso is said to have proclaimed "At last, something new in the art of drawing!"). Others veer in the direction of total abstraction and consist of flickering patterns of colour, line, and form, like *Begone Dull Care* (1949). This last is probably one of his best known cameraless films, made with Evelyn Lambert, his longtime collaborator, and scored by Oscar Peterson. It consists of a rich jumble of jiving squiggles and blobs rendered by washes of dyes that were etched, scratched and variously textured by a number of materials, including Lambert's fortuitous and accidental discovery of dust. Some of McLaren's abstract films consist of elaborations on a single geometrical theme or figure taken to their furthest logical extreme, like *Lines-Vertical* (1960), *Lines-Horizontal* (1962), *Dots* and *Loops* (1940), and *Mosaic* (1965). This aspect of his *oeuvre* owes a considerable artistic debt to Oscar Fischinger.

McLaren's reputation as a sort of abstract expressionist of film has tended to occlude recognition of the overtly political films he made throughout his life. It was, after all, the powerful antiwar film he made as an art student at Glasgow's School of Art, *Hell Unlimited* (1936), that launched his professional career and gained him entry to the G.P.O. Film Unit in the 1930s, leading to his work on *The Defense of Madrid* (1937) with Ivor Montague. Some of the "propaganda" films—*Stars and Stripes* (1941), *Mail Early* (1941), and *V for Victory* (1941)—he made in America during the Second World War may seem facile now, and perhaps mere excuses for formalist experiment, but *Neighbors* (1952) an allegory of war with two "pixillated" men fighting to the death over a flower, manages to synthesize emotive content with technical innovation. *Neighbors* eschews intellectual proselytizing and makes its pacifist point with admirable economy of expression. Its clarity has won it a place in many a school film library, an appropriate place for a man who was as much an educator, literally and figuratively, as he was an animated film maker.

—Leslie Felperin Sharman

MEERSON, Lazare

Art Director. **Nationality:** Russian. **Born:** 1900. **Career:** Left Russia in wake of the revolution, lived in Germany, then settled in France in 1924; 1936–38—worked in England. **Died:** In London, June 1938.

Films as Art Director:

1925   *Feu Mathias Pascal* (*The Late Mathias Pascal*) (L'Herbier) (asst); *Le Nègre blanc* (Rimsky and Wulschleger); *Gribiche* (*Mother of Mine*) (Feyder); *Les Aventures de Robert Macaire* (Epstein)

1926   *Carmen* (Feyder); *La Proie du vent* (Clair) (co)

1927   *Un Chapeau de paille d'Italie* (*An Italian Straw Hat*) (Clair); *Le Chasseur de chez Maxim's* (Rimsky and Lion)

1928   *Cagliostro* (Oswald); *Les Deux Timides* (Clair); *L'Argent* (L'Herbier) (co); *Souris d'hôtel* (Millar); *Les Nouveaux Messieurs* (*The New Gentlemen*) (Feyder); *La Comtesse Maria* (Perojo)

1929   *Le Requin* (Chomette)

1930   *L'Etrangère* (Ravel); *Jean de la Lune* (Choux); *David Golder* (Duvivier); *Sous les toits de Paris* (*Under the Roofs of Paris*) (Clair); *Le Mystère de la chambre jaune* (L'Herbier)

1931   *La Fin du monde* (Gance); *Le Million* (Clair); *Les Cinq Gentlemen maudits* (Duvivier); *Le Monsieur de minuit* (Lachman); *Der Ball* (Thiele); *A nous la liberté* (Clair); *Prisonnier de mon coeur* (Tarride); *Un Coup de téléphone* (Lacombe) (co); *Le parfum de la dame en soie* (L'Herbier)

1932   *La Femme en homme* (Genina); *Conduisez-moi madame* (Selpin); *La Femme nue* (Paulin); *Le Quatorze juillet* (Clair); *Il a été perdu une mariée* (Joannon)

1933   *Ciboulette* (Autant-Lara); *La Femme invisible* (Lacombe); *L'Ange gardien* (Choux); *Primerose* (Guissart); *Amok* (Ozep)

1934   *Lac-aux-Dames* (M. Allégret); *Le Grand Jeu* (Feyder); *La Banque Nemo* (Viel and Choux); *Poliche* (Gance); *L'Hôtel du libre-échange* (M. Allégret); *Zouzou* (M. Allégret)

1935   *Pension Mimosas* (Feyder); *Justin de Marseille* (Tourneur); *Princesse Tam-Tam* (Gréville) (co); *Les Beaux Jours* (M. Allégret); **La Kermesse héroïque** (*Carnival in Flanders*) (Feyder)
1936   *As You Like It* (Czinner); *Fire over England* (Howard)
1937   *Knight without Armour* (Feyder); *The Scarlet Pimpernel* (Schwartz); *South Riding* (Saville); *The Divorce of Lady X* (Whelan); *Break the News* (Clair)
1938   *The Citadel* (K. Vidor)

Publications

On MEERSON: articles—

Jourdan, R., ''Le Style Clair-Meerson,'' in *La Revue du Cinéma* (Paris), no. 27, 1931.
Sight and Sound (London), Summer 1938.
Bandini, B., in *Cinema* (Rome), no. 130, 1941.
Barsacq, Léon, ''Le Décor de Lazare Meerson,'' in *Jacques Feyder*, Brussels, 1949.
Ciment, Michel, and I. Jordan, in *Positif* (Paris), October 1979.
Cavalcanti, Alberto, in *Cinématographe* (Paris), March 1982.
Film Dope (Nottingham), March 1989.
Ficat, C., in *Cinémathèque* (Paris), May 1992.

*   *   *

A gifted artist and student of architecture, Lazare Meerson left Russia after the October Revolution to work first in Germany before settling in France. Influenced both by Russian constructivist theory and the Expressionist movement of the Berlin studios, he brought to Paris creative talent, experience, and artistic skills which were to make him the most influential set designer of his generation. His association with Alexander Kamenka, a fellow Russian emigré and director of the Société des Films Albatros at the Montreuil Studios, resulted in a successful collaboration with several leading directors, notably Jacques Feyder, Marcel L'Herbier, and René Clair. Already the group of expatriate Russian filmmakers at Montreuil had encouraged the rejection of conventional theatrical *trompe l'oeil* painted scenery in favour of more substantial architecturally conceived sets built from natural materials in order to create greater authenticity. Their achievements led to a new perception of the designer's role in the production of mood and meaning in film, and henceforth they were invited to work more closely with the director to express in plastic terms the essential tenor of the film narrative. In this conducive environment, Meerson's talents flourished and his influence grew, but he modestly argued that his sets were there simply to discretely serve a film's action and not to impose upon it: subject matter, the quality of the acting, and *mise en scène* should remain the prime considerations. The value of set design, he maintained, lay in the atmosphere it could generate to inspire actors and director alike as they worked towards their artistic statement.

Meerson's long association with Feyder began in the mid-1920s with *Gribiche*, for which he created spacious, yet deliberately uninviting sets to epitomize a wealthy American's luxurious modern apartment. A studied attention to detail and mood soon became his trademark. For *Carmen* he evoked the character of the lovers' café in Seville with meticulously observed architectural features; for *Les Nouveaux Messieurs* a spectacularly detailed studio reconstruction of the Chamber of Deputies was undertaken, and for *Le Grand Jeu* the representation of the colonial garrison and its mess was similarly impressive in its authentic feel. The powerfully realist decors of *Pension Mimosas* with an atmospheric rendering of low gambling dives and the eponymous boarding house confirmed Meerson's adherence to poetic realism. However, it was with *La Kermesse héroïque*, perhaps France's most successful historical film, that Meerson's work with Feyder achieved new heights. The studio reconstruction of a 17th-century Flemish town, complete with canals and natural vegetation, brilliantly recreates the tone and perspectives of Dutch and Flemish paintings of the period.

For L'Herbier, Meerson initially worked as an assistant to Cavalcanti on the decors for *Feu Mathias Pascal*. Here memorable cluttered sets conveyed the closed and claustrophobic world of French provincial society, while a dramatically counterpointed Rome apartment building characterized by large, unadorned rooms signalled a new mood of liberation. The hallmark of his designs for L'Herbier's version of Zola's *L'Argent* was a series of spectacularly grandiose sets. Working in collaboration with Léon Barsacq, he constructed a magnificent bank interior, a huge banqueting hall, a restaurant, and opulent private chambers which included a circular room representing the globe. All were to serve as visual metaphors for money's power and universal influence.

Meerson's association with René Clair began when he worked with Bruni on the imaginative sets for the mysterious castle in *La Proie du vent*. His subsequent designs mirror the director's concern with social issues or social satire. For *Un Chapeau de paille d'Italie* he reproduced in consummate ironical detail the decorative Henri II style of furnishing so favoured by the French middle classes of the *Belle Epoque*, while for *Les Deux Timides* the life-style of two lawyers is differentiated through objects which acquire narrative significance such as an old sewing machine or a collection of less than comfortable chairs. The authenticity of the central Court Room scenes derives from minutely observed detail carefully reproduced in the studio sets. With the advent of sound, Meerson accompanied Clair to the Tobis studios where, for the next four films he collaborated successfully with the cameraman Georges Périnal. For Clair's first sound film, *Sous les toits de Paris*, both exteriors and interiors were studio-built, with Meerson ingeniously using parts of the Tobis buildings themselves for his sets. The stylized decors, realist in mode but imbued with an air of romantic nostalgia, conferred on his representation of the working-class districts of the city a poetic quality which initially confounded audiences accustomed to the authenticity of location shooting. However, the carefully crafted sets with their evocative rooftops, chimneys, narrow streets, and cafés were soon to be critically acclaimed. Similar stylizations were employed for both *Le Quatorze juillet* with its flag-bedecked streets and its false perspectives, notably the magnificent flight of steps, and *Le Million*, a comedy about a lost lottery ticket, which involves a chase across the rooftops of the city, once again immediately identifiable as Paris, but a Paris charmed by the air of joyful fantasy which characterizes the film's mood. The dreamlike quality was in part achieved through an innovative use of tulle in the set construction. For *A nous la liberté*, a left-wing satire of big business and mass production methods, comparisons are established between factory and prison. Here the cold, futuristic sets with parodistic allusions to Art Deco, express through their disturbing proportions the dehumanizing nature of the factory process and the pursuit of profit.

Tempted by Alexander Korda to join his London Film Productions at the superbly appointed Denham studios, Meerson moved to England, where he worked until his sadly premature death. Although a number of worthy films resulted, none matched the quality of his French productions. Among the more memorable sets of this period were an impressive castle complete with black mirror floors for Czinner's *As You Like It*, the deserted Russian station for Feyder's *Knight without Armour*, and, working for the only time for a film in colour, the London barrister's flat which is at the centre of Whelan's comedy *The Divorce of Lady X*.

Meerson's contribution to the evolution of film set design can hardly be overstated. His personal style, shaped out of his own artistic talent and the influences of his Russian formation and the experience of Berlin, encouraged several developments in the cinema including that of poetic realism. His use of natural materials in set construction, his meticulous studio recreations and finely worked false perspectives, reinforced by his exacting personal supervision of the work at every stage, ensured new standards for the art of film decor. His stylized evocations of the poorer quarters of Paris broke new ground, while his frequently enormous sets opened up new opportunities for cameramen and experiments in the evocative play of lighting. The work of many designers, particularly that of Trauner, Douy, and Wakhévitch, testifies to his seminal influence.

—R. F. Cousins

MENGES, Chris

Cinematographer and Director. **Nationality:** British. **Born:** Herefordshire, England, 1940. **Family:** Married the sound technician Judy Freeman. **Career:** 1958–60—apprentice to director Alan Forbes; 1961—camera assistant to Brian Probyn; 1963—cameraman on Granada TV's *World in Action* documentary series. **Awards:** Academy Award, for *The Killing Fields*, 1984, and *The Mission*, 1986. **Agent:** Leading Artists, 455 N. Bedford Drive, Beverly Hills, CA 90210, U.S.A.

Films as Camera Operator:

1959   *No Place to Hide* (Forbes and Knight) (camera assistant)
1962   *The Saturday Men* (Fletcher) (camera assistant)
1967   *Poor Cow* (Loach)
1968   *If . . .* (L. Anderson)

Films as Cinematographer:

1962   *The War Game* (Zetterling) (co)
1964   *The Opium Trail* (Cowell—for TV)
1967   *In Search of Opportunity* (Hassan)
1968   *Beyond the Tropopause* (Hassan); *Abel Gance, the Charm of Dynamite* (Brownlow—for TV)
1969   *Wild and Free—Twice Daily* (+ d—for TV); *Solo* (Misha Donat); *Kes* (Loach)

1970   *Loving Memory* (Scott); *The Tribe that Hides from Man* (Cowell—for TV) (co)
1971   *After a Lifetime* (Loach—for TV); *Talk about Work* (Loach); *Gumshoe* (Frears); *Black Beauty* (Hill)
1974   *The Opium Warlords* (Cowell—for TV)
1975   *To Be Seven in Belfast* (Sheppard—for TV); *Chicago Streets* (Cokliss—for TV)
1976   *Busker* (Pearce—for TV)
1979   *Auditions* (Loach—for TV); *Bloody Kids* (Frears—for TV); *Black Jack* (Loach); *Before the Monsoon* (Grigsby—for TV)
1980   *The Gamekeeper* (Loach—for TV) (co); **The Empire Strikes Back** (Kershner) (2nd unit cinematographer); *Babylon* (Rosso)
1981   *A Sense of Freedom* (Mackenzie—for TV); *East 103rd Street* (+ d, pr); *Couples and Robbers* (Peploe); *Battletruck* (Cokliss); *Looks and Smiles* (Loach)
1982   *Angel* (Jordan); *Made in Britain* (Clarke—for TV); *Walter* (Frears—for TV)
1983   *Local Hero* (Forsyth); *Rhino* (Howell—for TV); *Walter and June* (Frears—for TV)
1984   *The Killing Fields* (Joffé); *Comfort and Joy* (Forsyth); *Winter Flight* (Battersby—for TV)
1985   *Marie* (Donaldson); *Which Side Are You On?* (Loach—for TV)
1986   *Fatherland—Singing the Blues in Red* (Loach); *High Season* (Peploe); *The Mission* (Joffé)
1987   *Shy People* (Konchalovsky); *High Season* (Peploe)
1996   *Michael Collins* (Jordan)
1997   *The Boxer* (Sheridan)
2000   *The Pledge*

Films as Director:

1971   *A Completely Different Way of Life* (for TV)
1973   *Radical Lawyer* (for TV)
1975   *A Family Doctor* (for TV)
1978   *Fly on the Wall* (for TV)
1987   *A World Apart*
1990   *CrissCross*
1994   *Second Best*
1999   *The Lost Son*

Publications

By MENGES: articles—

Stills (London), no. 6, May/June 1983.
American Cinematographer (Hollywood), February 1987.
In Camera (Hemel Hempstead, Hertfordshire), Spring 1988.
Positif (Paris), October 1988.

On MENGES: articles—

Sight and Sound (London), vol. 47, no. 2, Spring 1978.
Stills (London), no. 27, May/June 1986.

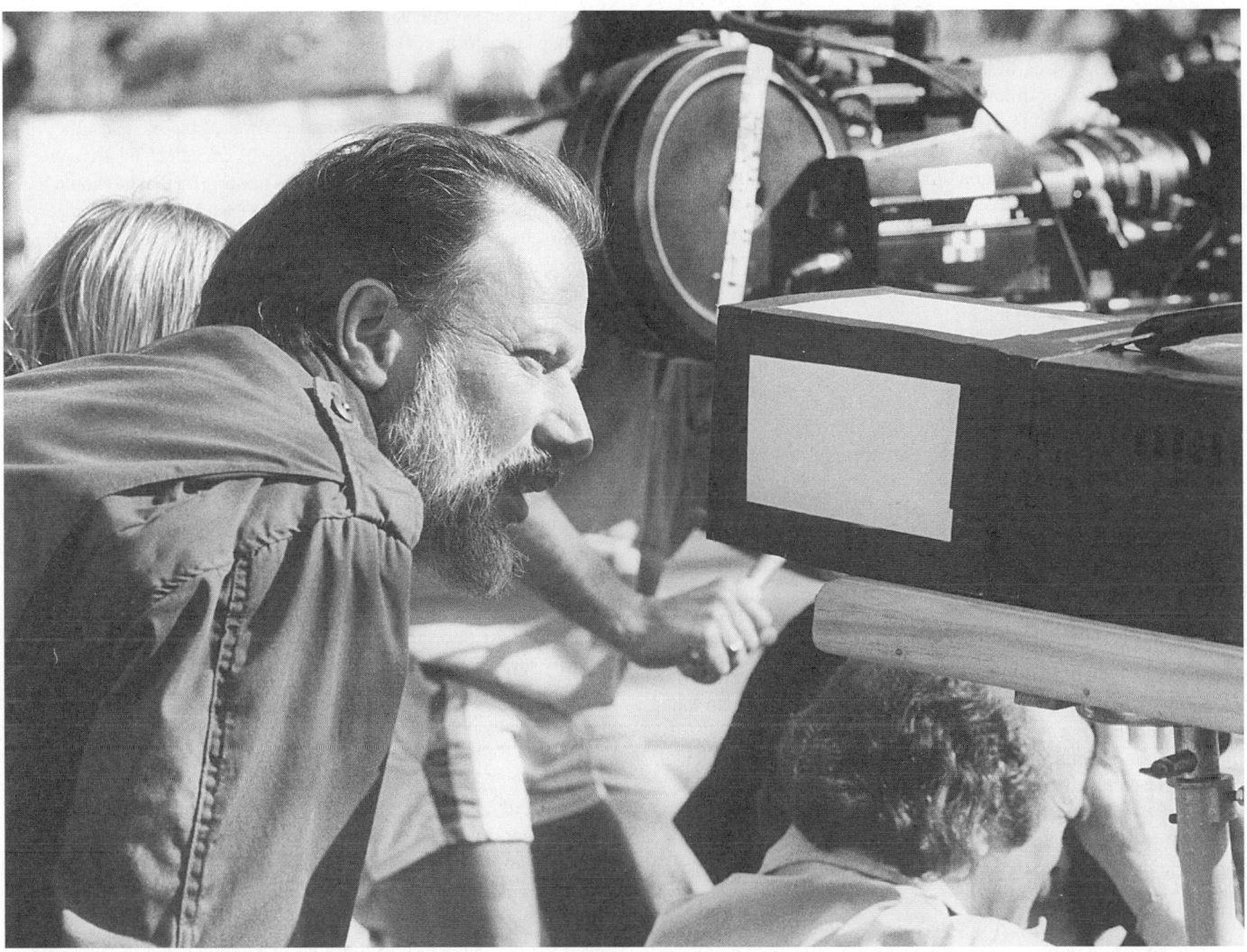

Chris Menges

Film Comment (New York), vol. 24, no. 2, March/April 1988.
Films and Filming (London), no. 407, August 1988.
Film Comment (New York), vol. 25, no. 5, September/October 1989.
Oppenheimer, J., ''Revolutionary Images,'' in *American Cinematographer* (Hollywood), October 1996.

*   *   *

In the 1980s, Chris Menges became well-known as the Oscar-winning cinematographer of *The Killing Fields* and *The Mission*, and the director of *A World Apart*. But like so many British cinema ''names'' of the decade, Menges had enjoyed a long and distinguished career in television in the 1960s and 1970s. He built up a considerable and consistent body of work with two key directors in particular: Kenneth Loach and Stephen Frears. He also shot numerous editions of the trailblazing Granada documentary series *World in Action*, in which he found himself working under perilous conditions in some of the world's worst trouble spots. And he was the cameraman on such major contributions to the documentary genre as Mike Grigsby's *Before the Monsoon* and three remarkable films by Adrian Cowell: *The Opium Trail*, *The Opium Warlords*, and *The Tribe that*

Hides from Man. In the cinema, Menges started as a camera operator on Lindsay Anderson's *If . . .* and Loach's *Poor Cow*. Since then he has made features with both Frears and Loach, and worked on such notable British films as *Radio On*, *Babylon*, *Angel*, and *Local Hero*.

Clearly, variety is one of Menges's hallmarks. As Michael Goldfarb wrote in *The Guardian*, ''He has a sensitive eye for capturing a setting, whether it is the lingering, silver-blue light of a summer evening in Scotland's Western Isles, as in *Local Hero*, the tropical pastel salmons and greens of *The Killing Fields* and *The Mission*, or the sooty, fog-encrusted light of our own latitude in *Fatherland*.''

This stylistic variety is a crucial ingredient of Menges's working philosophy. As he put it in a revealing interview with John Wyver in *Stills*, ''My personality is not ever to fight for a style. My feeling about all work is, it's not about style, but about what it's trying to say, what it's worth. The actual style should be an integrated part of the whole. . . . What are you interested in? What do you care about? That's the only message.'' In the same interview, he traced a continuity in the work of those with whom he had most enjoyed collaborating: ''The idea that life is a real joy, but that the world we live in is a real struggle; that over the centuries man has learnt to be very unjust, and that it's just not good enough any more. So I've worked with people who tried to encompass a feeling and understanding about what life could and should be about.''

One of Menges's earliest experiences was working with the American independent filmmaker Alan Forbes on a film about London's buskers. From Forbes, and from seeing the hugely influential work of Dennis Mitchell, Menges came to realize the importance of simply letting people speak on film. Indeed, what counts above all else for him is people and what they have to say. But equally importantly, he also took the advice of Canadian documentarist Alan King, who told him that ''it doesn't matter if the person you're filming is not talking. Sometimes the person listening is more interesting than the person talking.''

Ken Loach, with whom Menges first worked as a feature cameraman, is still the director whom he most admires. It is hardly difficult to see why this should have been such a successful and fruitful partnership, since both men care passionately about their subjects, and both share similarly democratic attitudes to the people they film, be they actors or the subjects of a documentary. Menges played a crucial role in achieving the remarkable feeling of spontaneity in Loach's films. As Loach himself declared to Stephen Peet, in an article in *Eyepiece*, ''His feeling for light is related to his feeling for people. Because he has a warm appreciation of people he then finds a light that is sympathetic to them and doesn't intrude on them.'' In one of his earliest interviews, Menges described his way of working in a fashion which recalls Loach: ''I like it when the circumstances dictate what I as a cameraman focus on. I go into a room and sit there and think about it and listen and talk and feel it all. When obviously the moment's come, I pick up the camera and let everybody there dictate, to some extent, how it's going to be done. They get on with their own business.''

While working on *The Killing Fields* with director Roland Joffé, Menges hoped to capture the very feeling of authentic war conditions, ''the *instinct* of how the actual physical locations felt,'' and decided to go for a ''cruddy, grainy, ill-mannered and vital'' look. Joffé chose him for the job mainly on the strength of his work on *The Opium Warlords*. After seeing *The Killing Fields*, it comes as absolutely no surprise to discover that the photographer Cartier-Bresson has been an enormous influence on Menges, for the work of both men is characterized by those all-revealing ''decisive moments'' seized from the flux of action, moments which are also found in the early films of Raoul Coutard, another cinematographer much admired by Menges.

The Killing Fields is a film that effectively counterpoints expansive and often extremely beautiful landscapes with the claustrophobic inner dramas taking place within them. If anything, *The Mission* (for which Menges also worked as Joffé's cinematographer) is packed with even more contrasts, from intimate close-ups to vast vistas, interior and exterior sets, and locations and battles on both land and water, making it a considerable challenge for director and cinematographer alike. The feel is far less documentary than in *The Killing Fields*, and Menges himself has described it as ''operatic,'' a means of telling the story that ''encompassed its grandness and also its simplicity.'' Menges and Joffé looked at Spanish paintings from the eighteenth century, the time in which the film is set, to glean a feeling of what it was like to live during this period, and in particular to see what kind of light was shed by the oil-wick lamps of the time. They also devised a scheme in which certain scenes were coded in particular colors according to the emotional feel of the scene and its

place in the overall narrative. But however complex the filming, Menges and Joffé still manage to give the actors the freedom and space they need. Witness the fight scene between Robert De Niro and Aidan Quinn, where the camera never intrudes or causes complications, thus never detracting from the power of the scene itself.

Given the combination of Menges's empathy and tremendous concern for subject matter, it comes as no surprise that he should have chosen such a weighty subject as South Africa for his first feature film as director, *A World Apart*. It is a humanistic, deeply personal, and politically savvy drama about Molly Roth (Jodhi May), a girlish 13 year old whose parents are virulent antiapartheid activists. Her father, Gus, is wanted by the authorities and has gone into hiding. Her mother, Diana (Barbara Hershey), is so passionately committed to the cause that she disregards her family and neglects to directly communicate with Molly. In this regard, *A World Apart* is as much an intimate family drama as it is a portrait of the apartheid regime. As Menges has said about the excellent performances in the film, ''The directing was knowing when to shut up and keeping the technical side to a minimum.''

Of course, the film's feeling for its characters' plight under apartheid is a crucial aspect of its politics. Significantly, *A World Apart* is set in 1963, the year in which Menges first worked on *World in Action*. At that time, he even visited South Africa to cover the events surrounding the arrest of the leaders of the African National Congress and the imposition of the infamous 90-day detention act—which, within the scenario of *A World Apart*, is employed to incarcerate Diana Roth.

Menges's follow-up feature, *CrissCross*, was less successful dramatically, but involves a similar theme to that in *A World Apart*: the manner in which a child is affected by a parent whose priorities are dictated by events outside the family circle. Here, he tells the story of an alienated 12-year-old boy whose Vietnam veteran father had abandoned the family years before. Ironically, in *Second Best*, his next feature, Menges tells the story of an adult eager to embrace the responsibilities of parenthood: a reserved, unmarried fortysomething Welsh postmaster who becomes determined to adopt an intensely troubled ten-year-old boy.

In 1985, Menges gave an interview, published in *American Cinematographer*, in which he summarized his personal, political and creative philosophies: ''You do things that make you grow and make you learn, and I've always been interested in things that teach me something. That's where the politics comes in—[it's all about] learning and caring.''

—Julian Petley, updated by Rob Edelman

MENKEN, Alan

Composer. **Nationality:** American. **Born:** New Rochelle, New York, 22 July 1949. **Education:** New York University; Lehman Engel Musical Theatre Workshop. **Family:** Married to Janis, two children. **Career:** Contemplated a medical career before following his earliest ambition to be a musician and composer; performed in local clubs, as well as composing and writing advertising jingles during the mid

Alan Menken

1970s; worked on several musicals, made his off-Broadway debut in 1979, his first teaming with Howard Ashman, on *God Bless You, Mr. Rosewater*; 1986—*Little Shop of Horrors*, also with Ashman, marked his movie debut; 1989—first worked with Ashman for Disney on *The Little Mermaid*; 1993—reworked *Beauty and the Beast* for Broadway; 1994—debuted a new musical of Dickens' *A Christmas Carol* on Broadway; adapted Broadway style to various musical demands of Disney's most commercially successful films throughout the 1980s and 1990s. **Awards:** Academy Awards, *The Little Mermaid*, 1989; *Beauty and the Beast*, 1991; *Aladdin*, 1992; *Pocahontas*, 1995. Golden Globe Awards, *The Little Mermaid*, 1989; *Beauty and the Beast*, 1991; Aladdin, 1992; *Pocahontas*, 1995. Grammy Awards, *The Little Mermaid*, 1989; *Beauty and the Beast*, 1991; *Aladdin*, 1992; *Pocahontas*, 1995. New York Drama Critic's Award, The Drama Desk Award, the Outer Critic's Circle Award, The London Evening Standard Award for Best Musical for *Little Shop of Horrors*, 1986. BMI Career Achievement Award; Tony and Drama Desk Award for *Beauty and the Beast*, 1993; Razzie awards for Worst Original Song for *Newsies*, 1993, and *Rocky v*, 1991. **Address:** The Schukat Company, 340 West 55th Street, Apt. 1A, NY 10019–3744, U.S.A.

Films as Composer:

1986   *Little Shop of Horrors* (Oz)
1989   *The Little Mermaid* (Musker/Clements)
1990   *Rocky V* (song only—Avildsen)
1991   *Beauty and the Beast* (Trousdale/Wise)
1992   *Newsies* (Ortega); *Aladdin* (Musker/Clements); *Home Alone 2* (song only—Columbus)
1993   *Life with Mikey* (Lapine)
1995   *Pocahontas* (Gabrie/Goldberg)
1996   *The Hunchback of Notre Dame* (Trousdale/Wise)
1997   *Hercules* (Trousdale and Wise)

Publications

On MENKEN: articles—

The Hollywood Reporter (Hollywood), July 1991.
Teitelbaum, Sheldon, "Disney's Aladdin," in *Cinefantastique* (New York), 1 December 1992.

Williamson, Kim, "Plus: Making Music With Alan Menken," in *Boxoffice* (Kansas City), 1 June 1995.

Soundtrack (London), March 1996.

Spaeth, Jeanne, "Alan Menken on Music's Many Forms," in *Music Educator's Journal* (Reston, Virginia), 1 November 1997

*   *   *

A graduate of the New York musical theatre, Alan Menken has benefitted from a financially and creatively fruitful association with the Walt Disney Studios. Reaching a peak of creativity at a time when the studio's lumbering animation division finally kicked into life again, Menken has composed some memorable music for films that are essentially the last musical outpost of modern Hollywood.

In a well-worn route to musical success, Menken performed in clubs and even contributed advertising jingles before he met his first significant collaborator, lyricist Howard Ashman. With Ashman Menken wrote *God Bless You, Mr. Rosewater*, which met with some success when it opened off-Broadway. He remained devoted to the New York stage, providing music for theatre workshops, from the rock musical *Battle of the Giants* (*Atina: Evil Queen of the Galaxy*), to the more traditional *Real Life Funnies*, as well as countless reviews.

Teamed with Ashman once again, Menken achieved his first feature film success on *Little Shop of Horrors*, providing vibrant and larger-than-life music for Ashman's aggressively witty lyrics. For their efforts Menken and Ashman received several awards, as well as an Oscar nomination for the song "Mean Green Mother from Outer Space."

Further forays into the theatre, such as *The Apprenticeship of Duddy Kravitz*, were truncated by the beginning of his association with Disney. Hired to write the songs for *The Little Mermaid*, based on a Hans Christian Andersen story, Menken and Ashman came up with a selection that brought the film alive and carried the drama instead of simply interrupting it.

Inspired by the calypso tradition, the songs allowed for Ashman's typically witty and irreverent verbal gymnastics and became an integral part of the film's success, returning Disney to the forefront of musical films at a time when the genre was redundant. Menken and Ashman had succeeded where others had failed by finding a fine balance of catchy, amusing songs that offered insight into the characters' innermost thoughts. Other films had simply treated characters like marketing opportunities for the spin-off album.

Modern cinema audiences had proved wary of musicals, unwilling or unable to suspend their disbelief long enough for a song break within a comedy or a drama. Disbelief is so much more easily suspended when applied to an animated film where reality is stylised. Menken and Ashman consolidated their success with *Beauty and the Beast*, writing a collection of folksy, funny, traditional-sounding ballads—songs reminiscent of the contemporary American musical theatre.

Menken's working relationship with Howard Ashman was by no means exclusive; indeed, he recharged his creative batteries by working with many other lyricists, notably Jack Feldman on the schmaltzy "My Christmas Tree" in *Home Alone 2* and on the ill-judged but brave live-action musical *Newsies*. Unfazed by occasional disappointments, Menken worked on scoring television miniseries and contributing a song to *Rocky V* in collaboration with Elton John. He returned to Disney to work on *Aladdin*, and with Ashman wrote some of the most memorable songs of his career, in spite of Ashman's failing health and eventual death during production. Hurriedly teamed

with Tim Rice, a British lyricist from a similarly theatrical tradition, Menken was sensitive to his new collaborator and his very different way of working. Together they came up with the remainder of the songs, including the Oscar-winning number "A Whole New World."

Such was the success of Disney's animated output that the studio decided the musicals should play on Broadway. Menken was the man responsible for adding songs, tweaking existing numbers and ensuring everything was in order musically. *Beauty and the Beast* subsequently opened to great acclaim.

Menken's niche at Disney has proved every bit as comfortable and familiar as the podium from which he annually collects his Academy Award. His precocious talents and prodigious output have dominated the Best Song category for several years.

Menken has continued to produce varied, good quality music with whomever he has been assigned to work. Broadway lyricist Stephen Schwartz worked with him on *Pocahontas* and *The Hunchback of Notre Dame*, while David Zippel was his collaborator on *Hercules*. Menken is happiest being involved in the collaborative process, which at Disney means that the songwriters are amongst the various talents involved in the earliest stages of story discussions. With the exhaustive 3-to-5-year production schedule that an animated film typically requires, this also allows more time for the songwriter and lyricist to produce exactly the right songs for the plot as it unfolds.

Given the contrasting nature of the projects, and Menken's own ability to mimic so many musical traditions and styles, there hardly seems a repeated note in his work. He admits that the challenge to produce something different invigorates him, and that is certainly the case with the relentlessly pounding beat of "Savages" in *Pocahontas*, and the over-the-top genie number "You Ain't Never Had a Friend Like Me" in *Aladdin*. Because of the scale of the success of Disney's output in the 1980s and 1990s, Menken's music has become familiar to audiences beyond cinema. An indication of his wider success is the popularity of ice-dance adaptations of Disney movies such as *Beauty and the Beast* and *Aladdin*. In these live concerts, several of which have been recorded for TV and video, Menken's music is the backdrop for ice skating displays. Most recently, the skater Michelle Kwan starred in a performance entitled *Michelle Kwan Skates to Disney's Greatest Hits*, in which many of the musical numbers were composed by Menken. For *Hercules*, Disney's animated epic of 1997, Menken's music had to match the scale of the movie and its subject. True to form, he managed to come up with spectacular tunes to match the images on the screen.

These numbers and the hundreds of others like them are typically memorable, typically successful, and, by their impact and individualism, typically Menken.

—Anwar Brett, updated by Chris Routledge

MENZIES, William Cameron

Art Director and Director. **Nationality:** American. **Born:** William Howe Cameron Menzies in New Haven, Connecticut, 29 July 1896. **Education:** Attended Yale University, New Haven, Connecticut; University of Edinburgh; Art Students League, New York. **Military Service:** Served in the United States Army during World War I. **Family:** Married Mignon (Menzies); daughters: Jane and Suzanne.

Career: 1920–22—worked in special effects and design, Famous Players-Lasky, London and New York; from 1923—art director for independent and major studios, and director from 1931. **Awards:** Academy Awards for *The Dove* and *The Tempest* (one award), 1928, and *Gone with the Wind*, 1939; Special Academy Award, 1939. **Died:** In Hollywood, California, 5 March 1957.

Films as Art Director:

1918   *The Naulahka* (Fitzmaurice) (co); *Innocent* (Fitzmaurice)
1919   *The Witness for the Defense* (Fitzmaurice); *A Society Exile* (Fitzmaurice)
1920   *The Deep Purple* (Walsh)
1921   *The Oath* (Walsh); *Serenade* (Walsh); *The Three Musketeers* (Niblo) (co)
1922   *Kindred of the Dust* (Walsh); *Robin Hood* (Dwan) (co)
1923   *Rosita* (Lubitsch)
1924   *The Thief of Bagdad* (Walsh) (co)
1925   *The Lady* (Borzage); *Her Sister from Paris* (Franklin); *The Eagle* (Brown); *Cobra* (Henabery); *What Price Beauty* (Buckingham); *Graustark* (Buchowetzki); *The Dark Angel* (Fitzmaurice);
1926   *The Wanderer* (Walsh) (co); *Kiki* (Brown); *The Bat* (West); *The Son of the Sheik* (Fitzmaurice); *Fig Leaves* (Hawks)
1927   *The Beloved Rogue* (Crosland); *Camille* (Niblo); *Two Arabian Knights* (Milestone); *Sorrell and Son* (Brenon) (co); *The Dove* (West)
1928   *Sadie Thompson* (Walsh); *Drums of Love* (Griffith); *The Garden of Eden* (Milestone); *The Tempest* (Taylor); *The Woman Disputed* (H. King and Taylor); *The Loves of Zero* (Florey); *The Awakening* (Fleming)
1929   *The Iron Mask* (Dwan) (co); *The Rescue* (Brenon); *Lady of the Pavements* (Griffith); *Alibi* (West); *Coquette* (Taylor); *Three Live Ghosts* (Freeland); *The Locked Door* (Fitzmaurice); *Bulldog Drummond* (Jones); *Condemned* (Ruggles); *The Taming of the Shrew* (Taylor) (co); *New York Nights* (Milestone)
1930   *Abraham Lincoln* (Griffith) (co); *The Bad One* (Fitzmaurice) (co); *Be Yourself* (Freeland) (co); *The Lottery Bride* (Stein) (co); *Dubarry, Woman of Passion* (Taylor) (co); *Lummox* (Brenon) (co); *One Romantic Night* (Stein) (co); *Puttin' on the Ritz* (Sloman) (co); *Raffles* (D'Arrast and Fitzmaurice) (co)
1931   *Reaching for the Moon* (Goulding); *Always Goodbye* (+ co-d)
1933   *Trick for Trick* (McFadden); *Alice in Wonderland* (McLeod) (co, + co-sc); *Cavalcade* (Lloyd) (co)
1936   ***Things to Come*** (co, + d)
1938   *The Adventures of Tom Sawyer* (Taurog) (co); *The Young in Heart* (Wallace) (co); *Intermezzo* (Ratoff) (co); *Made for Each Other* (Cromwell) (co)
1939   ***Gone with the Wind*** (Fleming) (co)
1940   *Foreign Correspondent* (Hitchcock) (co); *Our Town* (Wood) (co); *The Thief of Bagdad* (Berger, Powell, and Whelan) (co)
1941   *Kings Row* (Wood) (co); *So Ends Our Night* (Cromwell) (co); *The Devil and Miss Jones* (Wood)
1942   *The Pride of the Yankees* (Wood) (co)
1943   *Mr. Lucky* (Potter) (co); *The North Star* (Milestone) (co); *For Whom the Bell Tolls* (Wood) (co)

1944   *Address Unknown* (+ pr + d)
1947   *Ivy* (+ co-pr)
1948   *Arch of Triumph* (Milestone)
1951   *Drums in the Deep South* (+ d); *The Whip Hand* (+ d)
1953   *Invader from Mars* (co, + d); *The Maze* (co, + d)

Other Films:

1931   *Almost Married* (co-d); *Chandu the Magician* (co-d)
1933   *I Loved You Wednesday* (co-d)
1934   *Wharf Angel* (co-d)
1937   *The Green Cockatoo* (*Four Dark Hours*; *Race Gang*) (d)
1940   *Conquest of the Air* (co-d)
1946   *Duel in the Sun* (K. Vidor) (uncredited co-d)
1949   *Reign of Terror* (*The Black Book*) (A. Mann) (pr)
1956   *Around the World in 80 Days* (Anderson) (assoc pr)

Publications

By MENZIES: articles—

"Cinema Design," in *Theatre Arts* (New York), September 1929.
"Pictorial Beauty in the Photoplay," in *Cinematographic Annual 1930*, Hollywood, 1930.
Film Weekly (London), 5 April 1935.

On MENZIES: articles—

"Layout for *Bulldog Drummond*," in *Creative Art* (New York), October 1929.
Gordon, Jan and Cora, in *Star-Dust in Hollywood*, London, 1930.
Picturegoer (London), 16 September 1939.
Kino Lehti (Helsinki), no. 3, 1970.
Film Index (Mosman Bay, New South Wales), no. 14, 1972.
Brosnan, John, in *Movie Magic*, New York, 1974.
Monthly Film Bulletin (London), October 1975, corrections December 1975 and March 1976.
In *The Art of Hollywood*, edited by John Hambley, London, 1979.
Cinématographe (Paris), February 1982.
Film History (New York), vol. 3, no. 2, 1989.
Liberti, F., and L. Franco, "William Cameron Menzies," in *Cineforum*, no. 31, July/August 1991.
Vertrees, A. D., "Reconstructing the 'Script in Sketch Form'," in *Film & History*, no. 3, 1989.
Film Dope (Nottingham), October 1989.
Nosferatu (San Sebastian), February 1994.
Webb, M., "Designing Films: William Cameron Menzies," in *Architectural Digest*, April 1994.
Lovell, Glenn, "*Gone With the Wind* (1998 Re-release of 1.33:1 Aspect, with Digital Color Enhancements)," in *Variety* (New York), 22 June 1998.

*   *   *

If there is one person who did more than any other to show the importance of art direction in filmmaking, it was William Cameron Menzies. For *Gone with the Wind*, David Selznick wanted Menzies to be involved early in the preparatory stages because he knew Menzies would plan the whole film on paper. He also wanted the art director to prepare continuity sketches showing lighting and camera angles and to handle the montage sequences. For undertaking these tasks, Menzies was then given the title "production designer," while Lyle Wheeler, who handled the more traditional aspects of set and costume design, was called "art director." Menzies also directed about ten percent of *Gone with the Wind*, including the Atlanta fire scene, and thus was one of four directors who ultimately directed parts of the film. That the film was a success despite having had so many directors must be attributed in large part to the unity provided by Menzies's design program.

Menzies typically used jagged shapes on railings or fences during scenes of tension or heightened, negative emotions. He was, however, eclectic in his style, drawing inspiration from a variety of sources. Illustrations of fantasy, such as those by Maxfield Parrish or Kay Nielson, inspired the designs for Douglas Fairbanks's *The Thief of Bagdad*, while German Expressionist films inspired the appearance of *The Beloved Rogue*. Menzies was also aware of the tradition of careful film design in Hollywood itself, notably in the films of D.W. Griffith. In an article written in 1929, Menzies said that movies required built sets with a simplified design, for the eye could see any one scene for only a short time. He believed the designer's job was to create a broad design of lines and values to which was then applied the realism of architecture, figures, and properties. By expressing this relationship between details and an underlying structure, Menzies's art can be seen to parallel American paintings of the period, specifically those by artists such as Charles Sheeler or Edward Hopper who apply some realistic details to a carefully organized composition. Menzies undoubtedly was an important figure in solidifying the position of the art director or production designer in Hollywood. His influence is found in many films that display designs with carefully controlled atmosphere, texture, color, and composition.

—Floyd W. Martin

Johnny Mercer

MERCER, Johnny

Lyricist. **Nationality:** American. **Born:** John H. Mercer in Savannah, Georgia, 18 November 1909. **Education:** Attended Woodbury Forest School, Orange, Virginia. **Family:** Married Ginger Meehan, children: one daughter, one son. **Career:** 1927–29—stage actor; then band vocalist; lyricist for Jerome Kern, Hoagy Carmichael, Harold Arlen, Henry Mancini, and others; 1933—lyrics for first film, *College Coach*; co-founder, Capitol Records. **Awards:** Academy Award, for songs "On the Atchison, Topeka, and the Santa Fe," 1946, "In the Cool Cool Cool of the Evening," 1951, "Moon River," 1961, and "Days of Wine and Roses," 1962. **Died:** 27 June 1976.

Films as Lyricist:

1933   *College Coach* (Wellman); *The Good Companions* (Saville) (co)
1935   *Old Man Rhythm* (Ludwig) (+ ro); *To Beat the Band* (Stoloff) (+ ro)
1936   *Rhythm on the Range* (Taurog)

1937   *Varsity Show* (Keighley); *Ready, Willing, and Able* (Enright); *The Singing Marine* (Enright); *Hollywood Hotel* (Berkeley)
1938   *Gold Diggers in Paris* (Enright); *Going Places* (Enright); *Hard to Get* (Enright); *Cowboy from Brooklyn* (Bacon); *Garden of the Moon* (Berkeley)
1939   *Naughty But Nice* (Enright); *Wings of the Navy* (Bacon)
1940   *You'll Find Out* (Butler)
1941   *Second Chorus* (Potter); *Blues in the Night* (Litvak); *Let's Make Music* (Goodwins); *You're the One* (Murphy); *Navy Blues* (Bacon); *Birth of the Blues* (Schertzinger)
1942   *The Fleet's In* (Schertzinger); *Star Spangled Rhythm* (Marshall); *You Were Never Lovelier* (Seiter); *All through the Night* (Sherman); *Captains of the Clouds* (Curtiz); *They Got Me Covered* (Butler)
1943   *The Sky's the Limit* (Griffith); *True to Life* (Marshall)
1944   *Here Come the Waves* (Sandrich); *To Have and Have Not* (Hawks)
1945   *Out of This World* (Walker); *Her Highness and the Bellboy* (Thorpe)
1946   *The Harvey Girls* (Sidney); *Centennial Summer* (Preminger)
1947   *Dear Ruth* (Russell)
1948   *Mr. Peabody and the Mermaid* (Pichel)
1949   *Make Believe Ballroom* (Santley); *Always Leave Them Laughing* (Del Ruth)

1950   *The Petty Girl* (Levin)
1951   *Here Comes the Groom* (Capra); *My Favorite Spy* (McLeod);
            The Belle of New York (Walters)
1953   *Dangerous When Wet* (Walters); *Everything I Have Is Yours*
            (Leonard); *Those Redheads from Seattle* (Foster); *Seven
            Brides for Seven Brothers* (Donen)
1954   *Timberjack* (Kane)
1955   *Daddy Long Legs* (Negulesco) (+ composer); *I'll Cry Tomor-
            row* (Daniel Mann)
1956   *You Can't Run Away from It* (Powell); *Spring Reunion*
            (Pirosh)
1957   *Bernardine* (Levin) (+ composer); *Missouri Traveler* (Hopper)
1958   *Merry Andrew* (Kidd); *Love in the Afternoon* (Wilder)
1959   *Li'l Abner* (Frank)
1960   *Facts of Life* (Frank)
1961   **Breakfast at Tiffany's** (Edwards); *Hatari!* (Hawks)
1962   *Days of Wine and Roses* (Edwards); *Mr. Hobbs Takes a Vaca-
            tion* (Koster)
1963   *Charade* (Donen); *Love with the Proper Stranger* (Mulligan);
            How the West Was Won (Ford, Marshall, and Hathaway)
1964   *The Americanization of Emily* (Hiller); *The Pink Panther*
            (Edwards); *Man's Favorite Sport?* (Hawks)
1965   *The Great Race* (Edwards); *Johnny Tiger* (Wendkos)
1966   *Not with My Wife, You Don't!* (Panama); *Alvarez Kelly*
            (Dmytryk); *Moment to Moment* (LeRoy); *A Big Hand for
            the Little Lady* (Cook)
1967   *Barefoot in the Park* (Saks); *Rosie* (Rich)
1970   *Darling Lili* (Edwards)
1971   *Kotch* (Lemmon)
1973   *Robin Hood* (Reitherman); *The Long Goodbye* (Altman)

Publications

On MERCER: book—

Bach, Bob, and Ginger Mercer, editors, *Our Huckleberry Friend: The
    Life, Times, and Lyrics of Johnny Mercer*, Secaucus, New Jer-
    sey, 1982.

On MERCER: articles—

Lees, Gene, in *American Film* (Washington, D.C.), December/Janu-
    ary 1978.
Craig, Warren, in *The Great Songwriters of Hollywood*, San
    Diego, 1980.
Albertson, Chris, "The Lyrics of Johnny Mercer," in *Stereo Review*,
    June 1988.
Zinsser, William, "From Natchez to Mobile, From Memphis to St.
    Joe: Songwriters Hoagy Carmichael, Harold Arlen and Johnny
    Mercer," in *American Scholar*, Spring 1994.
Macnie, Jim, "On *Midnight* Soundtrack, Mercer Is Man of the
    Hour," in *Billboard*, 6 December 1997.

*   *   *

When the American film business converted to sound movies in
the late twenties, an important motive for this sweeping technological

and institutional change was economic. Though films had been silent,
theaters had not; an important element in the attractiveness of the
"picture palaces" built in the first two decades of the studio period
was that they had not just screens, but stages, orchestra pits, and
elaborate organs, all of which produced music to please the paying
customers. Sound film not only enabled the films themselves to talk;
it allowed them to make music as well, replacing the expensive live
musicians who had previously provided it.

It was this change that permitted a number of experienced lyricists
and composers to leave Broadway for California, lured by the
promise of large salaries and steady work. The list of Broadway
notables who began film work in the early thirties includes Ralph
Rainger, Dorothy Fields, Jimmy McHugh, Mack Gordon, Richard
Whiting, and Al Dubin. And there was also Johnny Mercer, a lyricist
who had worked on stage productions with such notables as Jerome
Kern and had written songs for Paul Whiteman's band. Taking
advantage of the boom in film music work, he was able to launch
a Hollywood career that would endure for four decades. In the thirties
and forties, Mercer's talents were in demand to write songs not only
for those films in which vocal performance was of predominant
importance (the genre that would, on the analogy of similar productions on Broadway, be known as "musicals"), but also to write
numerous songs for films that featured one or at most several vocal
performances that provided moments of musical entertainment that
interrupted what was otherwise a dramatic or comedic narrative.
Though they often led to the sale of lyric sheets, the majority of these
songs achieved no enduring popularity outside the films in which they
were performed, and these were largely forgettable themselves: not
prestige productions but ordinary films that were a part of Hollywood's vast output during the decade. For *Varsity Show*, for example,
Mercer penned no fewer than ten songs, including "On with the
Dance," "Little Fraternity Pin," and "We're Working Our Way
through College." The work was varied and steady. Occasionally,
Mercer got the opportunity to do title-song work for prestige productions; a good example is his "Jezebel" for the Warners's Civil War
epic of the same name. These songs were often more recognized,
notably the title song for *Blues in the Night*, which received an Oscar
nomination.

In fact, during the forties it became more common to market a film
through its title song. Mercer wrote the title theme for *Laura*, for
example, after the movie was released; the nondiegetic music in the
film itself is wordless. Mercer also did important title work for *I'll Cry
Tomorrow*, *Love in the Afternoon*, *Bernardine*, *Days of Wine and
Roses*, and, of course, most famously, *Breakfast at Tiffany's*, whose
"Moon River" became his signature song. In the fifties and sixties,
demand for film lyrics lessened as Hollywood began to depend more
exclusively on already successful Broadway productions as source
material for film musicals. At the same time, dramatic films and
comedies of the period depended less on the "performance moments" that required the lyric inventiveness of a commercial composer such as Mercer. Because he was never much of a success on
Broadway, despite several attempts, and because he never formed
a long-term partnership with a music composer, Mercer has undoubtedly received less than a fair share of credit for contributions to
American popular music, especially of the Hollywood variety. His
many songs, however, some of which have become standards, decisively shaped the character of the American cinema during the studio
period, which without him would have lacked the joyful humor of
"The Square of the Hypoteneuse" (*Merry Andrew*) and the poignant

romanticism of ''Moment to Moment'' (from the film of the same name), among many other examples.

—R. Barton Palmer

MERCHANT, Ismail

Producer and Director. **Nationality:** Indian. **Born:** Ismail Noormohamed Abdul Rehman in Bombay, 25 December 1936. **Education:** Attended St. Xavier's College, Bombay, arts degree; New York University, M.A. in business administration. **Career:** Worked at United Nations and in advertising agency; 1960—produced short film, *The Creation of Woman*, nominated for Academy Award; 1961—met director James Ivory and novelist Ruth Prawer Jhabvala, formed Merchant-Ivory Productions; 1963—produced first MIP film, *The Householder*; 1972—produced first U.S. film, *Savages*; 1974—made directorial debut with short, *Mahatma and the Mad Boy*; 1983—first feature-length film as director, *The Courtesans of Bombay*.

Films as Producer

(all directed by James Ivory unless otherwise noted)

1960   *The Creation of Woman* (Schwep) (short)
1963   *Gharbar* (*The Householder*)

Ismail Merchant

1965   *Shakespeare Wallah* (+ ro as theater manager)
1968   *The Guru* (+ ro as compere)
1970   *Bombay Talkie* (+ ro as film producer)
1971   *Adventures of a Brown Man in Search of Civilisation* (doc)
1972   *Savages*
1973   *Helen, Queen of the Nautch Girls* (Korner) (doc short)
1974   *Mahatma and the Mad Boy* (+ d) (doc short); *The Wild Party*
1975   *Autobiography of a Princess*
1976   *Sweet Sounds* (Robbins) (doc short)
1977   *Roseland*
1979   *Hullabaloo over Georgie and Bonnie's Pictures* (+ ro as extra); *The Europeans*
1980   *Jane Austen in Manhattan*
1981   *Quartet*
1983   *Heat and Dust* (+ ro as peasant); *The Courtesans of Bombay* (doc) (+ d, co-sc)
1984   *The Bostonians*
1985   ***A Room with a View***
1986   *My Little Girl* (Kaiserman)
1987   *Maurice*
1988   *The Deceivers* (Meyer); *The Perfect Murder* (Hai)
1989   *Slaves of New York* (+ ro as extra)
1990   *Mr. and Mrs. Bridge*
1991   *The Ballad of the Sad Café* (Callow); *Second Daughter* (Kaiserman)
1992   ***Howards End***
1993   *The Remains of the Day*; *In Custody* (+ d)
1994   *Street Musicians of Bombay* (Robbins)
1995   *Jefferson in Paris* (+ ro as Tipoo Sultan's Ambassador); *The Feast of July* (Menaul); *Lumière et compagnie* (Moon)
1996   *Surviving Picasso*; *Propritaire* (*The Proprietor*) (+ dir)
1997   *Side Streets* (Gerber) (exec)
1998   *A Soldier's Daughter Never Cries*
1999   *Cotton Mary* (+ dir)
2000   *The Golden Mary* (*La Coupe d'Or*)

Publications

By MERCHANT: books—

Ismail Merchant's Indian Cuisine (cookbook), New York, 1986.
Hullaballoo in Old Jaypore: The Making of The Deceivers, London, 1988.

By MERCHANT: articles—

Interview with Jaz Mohan, Basu Chatterji, and Arun Kaul, in *Close-Up* (Bombay), October/December 1968.
Interview with Amena Meer, in *Interview* (New York), April 1994.
''The Maker of Dreams,'' interview with Shahrukh Husain, in *Index on Censorship* (London), 1995.

On MERCHANT: books—

Pym, John, *Wandering Company: Twenty-one Years of Merchant Ivory Films*, London/New York, 1983.
Long, Robert Emmet, *The Films of Merchant Ivory*, New York, 1991.

On MERCHANT: articles—

Gillett, John, "Merchant-Ivory," in *Sight and Sound* (London), Spring 1973.

Gillett, John, "A Princess in London," in *Sight and Sound* (London), Summer 1974.

Arora, Nina, "The Dream Merchant from New York," in *Film World* (Bombay), February 1976.

Watts, Janet, "Three's Company," in *Observer* (London), 17 June 1979.

Bergson, Phillip, "The Producer," in *What's On in London*, 27 January 1983.

Malcolm, Derek, "The Wizard behind the Ivory Trade," in *The Guardian* (London), 3 February 1983.

Newman, Charles, "Ismail Merchant: Snowballs to Eskimos," in *AIP & Co* (London), July 1984.

Fistenberg, P., "A Class Act Turns Twenty-Five," in *American Film* (Washington, D.C.), September 1987.

Callow, Simon, "Pair Excellence," in *Evening Standard* (London), 12 March 1992.

Dalrymple, William, "Star of India," in *Sunday Times Magazine* (London), 5 June 1994.

Naughton, John, "Profile," in *Empire* (London), July 1994.

Giovannini, Joseph, and Marina Faust, "Ismail Merchant," in *Architectural Digest* (Los Angeles), April 1996.

"Collective Works of the Merchant Ivory Troika," in *Variety* (New York), September 30-November 3 1996.

Kemp, P., "In a Family Way," in *Variety* (New York), October 28-November 3 1996.

Roberts, J., "A Duo With a View," in *Variety* (New York), October 28-November 3 1996.

*   *   *

The 35-year producer-director partnership of Ismail Merchant and James Ivory is now officially enshrined in the Guinness Book of Records as the longest collaboration in the history of cinema. To their two names should be joined that of the novelist Ruth Prawer Jhabvala, scriptwriter on most of their films. The reason for the partnership's endurance, it is generally agreed, lies in an exceptionally happy balance of similarities and contrasts between its members. All three, despite their very different backgrounds, share cultured, cosmopolitan sensibilities; but while Ivory and Jhabvala are quiet and self-effacing, with nothing of the huckster about them, Merchant is outgoing, energetic, charming, and irresistibly persuasive.

It was not until their 15th feature together, *A Room with a View*, that Merchant-Ivory went securely into profit, but that never deterred Merchant in his tireless quest for finance. "If you have enthusiasm, and a sincere belief in what you are doing," he declares, "money is no problem." A colleague of his (quoted by Robert Emmet Long) describes him as "like an elephant outside the financier's door. You can see him through the glass, you cannot shift him, he won't go away, he is very patient, and there is always the chance that he will come crashing in."

To be an independent producer, Merchant has observed, "you have to be a master of survival." If Merchant-Ivory has not only survived, but remained staunchly independent, it is due largely to Merchant's negotiating acumen and business training. Few producers are as well qualified to see through the industry's notoriously baroque accounting practices. "Strange charges are applied to your film's earnings," he notes. "Executives buy suits from Armani and charge them to your quarterly report. You have to have an eagle's-eye watch on them all the time." He keeps an equally close eye on the company's own accounts: Merchant-Ivory productions are famous for their tight budgeting and for looking a lot more expensive than they are. Major stars are cajoled into working for well below their normal asking rate, and valuable props are borrowed rather than bought—often for free.

Thanks to these shrewd financial tactics, Merchant-Ivory has maintained an independence of operation rare for a company of such modest size. Remarkably few projects have had to be aborted for want of finance, and almost all—especially since the worldwide success of *A Room with a View*—have enjoyed wide international release through major distribution networks. Yet the company has kept Hollywood safely at arm's-length, retaining control over subject, script, casting, and final cut. Pressures to go down-market, to embark on more crowd-pleasing ventures, have been resisted. All these achievements can be credited almost entirely to Merchant.

Still, those who criticize Merchant-Ivory for making (in the director Alan Parker's dismissive phrase) "Laura Ashley films" might well retort that an excursion or two down-market might not be a bad thing. Certainly the company has increasingly tended to concentrate on literary-based "heritage cinema," partly no doubt because audience response to their occasional forays into more robust territory—*Savages, The Wild Party, Slaves of New York*—has been less than enthusiastic. But while even Merchant-Ivory's strongest admirers have detected something slightly airless about such latter-day offerings as *Jefferson in Paris*, there is no evidence that this tendency has stemmed from specifically financial pressure being brought to bear by Merchant.

It may be a sign of restlessness that in recent years Merchant has begun to branch out: into directing on his own account, and into producing films directed by people other than Ivory. As yet, he has not ranged too far afield. The other directors have mainly been members of the Merchant-Ivory team such as Connie Kaiserman, associate producer on many of their productions, and regular actors in their films such as Simon Callow. Merchant's own directorial efforts, clearly much influenced by Ivory, have aroused little excitement. The partnership with Ivory and Jhabvala seems likely to remain his chief commitment; understandably so, providing as it does the ideal vehicle to fulfill his lifelong passion "to make movies, and movies of substance and quality." At the end of the '90s, his most noteworthy production, once again teamed with Ivory and Jhabvala, has been *A Soldier's Daughter Never Cries*. This finely detailed character study of an unusual multicultural family consisting of a writer, his glamorous wife, and their two children, one of whom is adopted, depends on carefully modulated performances and excellent dialogue. Abjuring plot, in the tradition of Merchant/Ivory/Jhabvala classics such as *Heat and Dust*, the film offers a string of finely observed moments, the undramatic crises and recognitions that reveal the inner workings of the those who live together as intimate strangers. The critical, if not box office success of the film demonstrates that Merchant continues to offer meaningful high-culture alternatives to the limited formulas, conventions, and erotic appeals of Hollywood cinema.

—Philip Kemp, updated by R. Barton Palmer

MESSMER, Otto

Animator. **Nationality:** American. **Born:** New Jersey, 16 August 1892. **Family:** Married; two children. **Career:** Painted backdrops for a theater company; 1913—painted backcloths at Universal Studios; 1915—made his first animated film, *Motor Mat* (unreleased); 1919—developed the character of Felix the Cat at Pat Sullivan's New York Studios. **Died:** Of a heart attack in Newark, New Jersey, 28 October 1983.

Films as Animator (selected list):

1915   *Motor Mat* (unreleased); *The Travels of Teddy*
1916   *Felix Gets It Wrong; Felix on the Job*
1917   *Them Were the Happy Days*
1919   *Feline Follies* series; *Musical Mews*
1922   *Felix Saves the Day; Felix at the Fair; Felix Makes Good; Felix All at Sea; Felix in Love; Felix in the Swim; Felix Finds a Way; Felix Gets Revenge; Felix Wakes Up; Felix Minds the Kid; Felix Turns the Tide; Felix on the Trail; Felix Lends a Hand; Felix Gets Left; Felix in the Bone Age*
1923   *Felix the Ghost Breaker; Felix Wins Out; Felix Tries for Treasure; Felix Revolts; Felix Calms His Conscience; Felix the Globe Trotter; Felix Gets Broadcasted; Felix Strikes It Rich; Felix in Hollywood; Felix in Fairyland; Felix Laughs Last; Felix Fills a Shortage; Felix the Goat Getter; Felix Goes A-Hunting*
1924   *Felix Loses Out; Felix Hits the Hipps; Felix Crosses the Crooks; Felix Tries to Rest; Felix Punches the Pole; Felix Puts It Over; Felix, Friend in Need; Felix Baffled By Banjos; Felix All Balled Up; Felix Goes West; Felix Finds Out; Felix Brings Home the Bacon; Felix Finishes First; Felix Goes Hungry; Felix Out of Luck; Felix Gets the Can; Felix Dopes It Out*
1925   *Felix Wins and Loses; Felix All Puzzled; Felix Follows the Swallows; Felix Rests in Peace; Felix the Cat Busts into Business; Felix the Cat Trips Through Toyland; Felix Trifles with Time; Felix the Cat on the Farm; Felix the Cat on the Job; Felix the Cat in the Cold; Felix the Cat in Eats Are West; Felix the Cat Tries the Trades; Felix the Cat in At the Rainbows End; Felix the Cat Kept Walking*
1926   *Felix the Cat Spots the Spooks; Felix the Cat Flirts with Fate; Felix the Cat in Blunderland; Felix Fans the Flames; Felix the Cat Laughs It Off; Felix the Cat Weathers the Weather; Felix the Cat Uses His Head; Felix the Cat Misses the Cue; Felix the Cat Braves the Briny; Felix the Cat in A Tale of Two Kitties; Felix Scoots through Scotland; Felix the Cat Rings the Ringer; Felix the Cat in School Daze; Felix the Cat Seeks Solitude; Felix the Cat Misses His Swiss; Felix the Cat in Gym Gems; Felix the Cat in Two Lips Time; Felix the Cat in Scrambled Eggs; Felix the Cat Shatters the Sheik; Felix the Cat Hunts the Hunter; Felix the Cat in Land O'Fancy; Felix the Cat Busts a Bubble; Felix the Cat in Reverse English; Felix the Cat Trumps the Ace; Felix the Cat Collars the Button; Felix the Cat in Zoo Logic*
1927   *Felix the Cat Dines and Pines; Felix the Cat in Pedigreedy; Felix the Cat in Icy Eyes; Felix the Cat in Stars and Stripes;*

Felix the Cat Sees 'Em in Season; Felix the Cat in Barn Yarns; Felix the Cat in Germ Mania; Felix the Cat in Sax Appeal; Felix the Cat in Eye Jinks; Felix the Cat as Romeeow; Felix the Cat Ducks His Duty; Felix the Cat in Dough-Nutty; Felix the Cat in ''Loco'' Motive; Felix the Cat in Art for Hearts Sake; Felix the Cat in the Travel-Hog; Felix the Cat, Jack of All Trades; Felix the Cat in The Non-Stop Fright; Felix the Cat in Wise Guise; Felix the Cat in Film Flam Films; Felix the Cat Switches Witches; Felix the Cat in No Fuelin'; Felix the Cat in Daze and Knights; Felix the Cat in Uncle Tom's Crabbin'; Felix the Cat in Whys and Otherwhys; Felix the Cat Hits the Deck; Felix the Cat Behind in Front
1928   *Felix the Cat in the Smoke Scream; Felix the Cat in Draggin' the Dragon; Felix the Cat in the Oily Bird; Felix the Cat in Ohm Sweet Ohm; Felix the Cat in Japanicky; Felix the Cat in Polly-tics; Felix the Cat in Comicalamities; Felix the Cat in Sure-Locked Homes; Felix the Cat in Eskimotive; Felix the Cat in Arabiantics; Felix the Cat in In and Out-Laws; Felix the Cat in Outdoor Indore; Felix the Cat in Futuritzy; Felix the Cat in Astronomeows; Felix the Cat in Jungle Bungles; Felix the Cat in the Last Life*
1930   *Felix the Cat in False Vases; Felix the Cat Woos Whoopee; Felix the Cat in April Maze; Felix the Cat in Oceanantics; Felix the Cat in Skulls and Sculls; Felix the Cat in Forty Winks; Felix the Cat in Tee-Time; Hootchy Kootchy Parlais Vous; Felix in Love*
1936   *Felix the Cat and the Goose That Laid the Golden Egg; Neptune Nonsense; Bold King Cole*

Publications

By MESSMER: article—

Segnocinema (Vicenza), vol. 5, no. 18, May 1985.

On MESSMER: book—

Canemaker, John, *Felix: The Twisted Tale of the World's Most Famous Cat*, New York, 1991.

On MESSMER: articles—

Millimeter (New York), vol. 4, no. 9, September 1976.
Crafton, Donald, in *Before Mickey: The Animated Film 1898–1928*, Cambridge, Massachusetts, 1982.
Obituary in *New York Times*, 29 October 1983.
Obituary in *Film Français* (Paris), 11 November 1983.
Obituary in *Cine-Revue* (Paris), vol. 63, no. 46, 17 November 1983.
Griffithiana (Gemona), vol. 8, no. 22–23, May 1985.
''The Advertising Pioneers: The Search for the Creator of That First Animated TV Commercial,'' in *Animation Magazine*, May-June 1991.
Tom, Patricia Vettel, ''Felix the Cat as Modern Trickster,'' in *American Art*, Spring 1996.
Barrett, Michael, ''Presenting Felix the Cat: The Otto Messmer Classics, vols. 1–2,'' in *Library Journal*, 15 October 1996.

On MESSMER: film—

Otto Messmer and Felix the Cat, 1977.

* * *

Animation's history, is peopled by innumerable men and women whose labors have been effaced by prominently displayed names, like Walt Disney or Leon Schlesinger, producers who may have contributed in varying degrees to the overall direction and management of cartoons, but who in fact usually had little to do with the actual work of animation. Such is the case with animation's first international "star," Felix the Cat, for whom the credit was stolen by the producer and cartoonist Pat Sullivan from the famous feline's director and *real* progenitor, Otto Messmer. Sullivan also reaped most of the profits and neglected to leave Messmer the rights to the character in his will, as promised before he died. Now, due to the efforts of film scholars, Messmer is recognized as one of the most talented screen cartoonists of the silent era, acclaimed especially for his inventive and influential gags, his expressive handling of form, and his contribution to the overall craft of character animation.

Born and bred in New Jersey from immigrant German-Catholic stock, Messmer was fascinated from an early age by films, then only an evolving art form, and drawn cartoons. He took an art correspondence course, attended the Thomas School of Art in New York City, and published several cartoons in the *New York World*'s Sunday supplement *Fun* that are of note for their dynamic sense of movement and use of visualized puns, a staple element of the filmic cartoon. After viewing the works of Winsor McCay, Emile Cohl, and other early animators, Messmer was inspired to produce his own film, *Motor Mat* (c. 1915, never released) on a homemade animation drawing board built for him by his father. Motor Mat, a motoring fanatic, shared with the later Felix a convenient aptitude for transforming objects around him, like smoke rings into tires. Unaware of either Bray's cel system or Barré's peg system, Messmer made this test film on cumbersome cardboard and photographed it on hired equipment at the Universal studio. Hy Mayer, then a well-known cartoonist, offered Messmer work on *The Travels of Teddy*, an animated cartoon based on Teddy Roosevelt, and from this experience he learned the shortcuts and techniques for production. He was next hired by Sullivan to work in his small animation studio, and collaborated on two series, one based on Sullivan's *Sammy Johnsin* strip, and one based on Charlie Chaplin. Messmer gradually assumed more responsibility for production with Sullivan concentrating on the financial management and promotional part of the business. Relations were briefly suspended for three years while Messmer served on the French Front and Sullivan served time in gaol for the rape of a minor. Reunited with Sullivan in 1919, Messmer designed *Feline Follies* for *Paramount Screen Magazine*, starring a Felix prototype called Mater Tom, and from that, spurred by increasing popularity, evolved Felix, named so in the third film after the suggestion of Mr. King of Paramount, deriving its etymological roots from "feline" and "felicity," equalling "good luck cat." Felix's reputation for good luck inspired the apocryphal story that a stuffed effigy of him accompanied Lindbergh on his solo Atlantic flight. He did, however, bring Messmer and Sullivan a substantial portion of luck until his demise with the advent of sound films in the late 1920s.

As the series' popularity grew, a litter of false felines and pretenders of other species populated the cartoon world, but only the Fleischer's *Out of the Inkwell* series and Paul Terry's *Aesop's Fables* could compete in popularity. Despite Sullivan's self-promotion in the press, many in the animation industry knew that Messmer was the real pen behind the camera. Just after the release of *Steamboat Willie*, Walt Disney offered him a job at his new studio, but Messmer, attached to his east coast roots, declined, mistakenly assuming that Felix would run forever.

The rejection bears a certain symbolic dimension; for while Disney's works moved towards greater mimetic realism, through the use of various technologies—sound, technicolor, the multiplane camera—the silent, black-and-white, plainer *Felix* cartoons have an austere, almost abstract quality that make them in some ways more striking than Disney's dated pyrotechnics. In its graphic simplicity, Messmer's work could be usefully compared with Norman McLaren's, in which the fluid rendering of movement rather than figurative verisimilitude is favored. Above all, Messmer's true gift was for characterization. Felix's gestures, expressions, his famous walk, and even his intertitled speech patterns, modelled on Messmer's own, were distinctive and endearing. Unlike his creator, Felix led a far more exciting and adventurous life, his personality adapting subtly to suit the situation, be it falling in love, travelling through the Arctic, or Fairyland, or Time, playing the devoted father or the denizen of the speakeasy, or, like Messmer, fighting on the warfront. Felix's plasticity, his ability to eschew the laws of physics and exploit to the fullest his cartoonal powers, had a profound effect on the medium which, with the exceptions of Cohl and McCay, had hitherto tended to cling to the raft of realism and model itself on the slapstick of live-action cinema, rather than realizing its own potential for excess, for making the impossible corporeal.

After Sullivan died, Messmer remained on the east coast, illustrating the *Felix* comics, occasionally contributing to animated cartoons for Famous Studios, and doing the animation for the well-known electric billboards on Times Square which eminently suited his talent for working with black-and-white silhouettes, which he also put to use for the first animated commercials on television for Botany Mills Ties. Although an obscure figure until scholars like Crafton, Canemaker, and Cohen uncovered material about him in the late 1970s and 1980s, Messmer died at the age of 91 with his reputation rightly restored. Felix, of course lived on, in several new films, and on a thousand tee-shirts and coffee mugs.

—Leslie Felperin Sharman

MESSTER, Oskar

Producer and Director. **Nationality:** German. **Born:** Oskar Eduard Messter in Berlin, 22 November 1866. **Family:** Married Antonie (Messter). **Career:** Worked in his father's optical plant, later a director; 1896—formed film company, and produced many short films from 1897, and a weekly newsreel (*Messter-Woche*) from 1914; over the years developed various motion picture processes and appliances (Germans claim he invented the Maltese Cross—a mechanism to allow individual frames to be quickly projected); also credited with the close-up as early as 1897; manufactured film equipment; 1917—his company absorbed by UFA. **Died:** In Leitenbauernhof, 6 December 1943.

Films as Producer:

1897?   *Die Sone*
1897   *Rapunzel*; *Gestärtes Rendez-vous* (+ d)
1898   *Gemütlich beim Kaffee* (+ d)
1900   *Rückkehr der Truppen von der Frühlingsparade* (+ d)
1902   *Salome* (+ d)
1903   *Auf der Radrennbahn* (+ d)
1906   *Apachentanz* (Porten); *Fra Diavolo*
1907   *Lohengrin*; *Meissner Porzellan* (Porten)
1908   *Desdemona*; *Tief in Böhmerwald* ; *Wiegenlied* (Porten)
1909   *Andreas Hofer* (Biebrach); *Das Liebesglück einer Blinden*
        (The Love of the Blind Girl) (Biebrach)
1910   *Verkannt* (+ d); *Der Kinderarzt* (Stark)
1911   *Mütter, verzaget nicht!* (Gärtner); *Adressatin verstorben* (Stark);
        Die Blinde (Stark); *Der Eindringling* (Stark); *Das gefährliche*
        Alter (Stark); *Die Magd* (Stark); *Ein Schwere Opfer* (Stark);
        Zwei Frauen (Stark); *Zu spät* (Froelich)
1912   *Die Rache ist mein* ; *Des Pfarrers Töchterlein* (Biebrach);
        Richard Wagner (Froelich); *Feenhände* (Stark); *Gefangene*
        Seelen (Stark); *Der Kuss des Fürsten* (Stark); *Die Nacht des*
        Grauens (Stark); *Schatten des Meeres* (Stark)
1913   *Ungarische Rhapsodie (Hungarian Rhapsody)* (Biebrach);
        Eva (Stark); *Gräfin Küchenfee* (Biebrach); *Die grosse*
        Sünderin (Biebrach); *Heroismus einer Französin* (Biebrach);
        Schuldig (Oberländer); *Um Haaresbreite* (Biebrach); *Das*
        Tal des Lebens (Biebrach)
1914   *Abseits vom Glück* (Biebrach); *Alexandra* (Biebrach); *Das*
        Ende vom Lied (Biebrach); *Nordlandrose* (Biebrach); *Tirol*
        in Waffen (Biebrach and Froelich)
1915   *Frau Eva (Arme Eva)* (Wiene); *Auf der Alm da gibt's ka Sünd*
        (Biebrach); *Claudi vom Geisterhof* (Biebrach); *Der Schirm*
        mit dem Schwan (Froelich); *Ein Euberfall in Feindesland*
        (Biebrach)
1916   *Die Ehe der Luise Rohrbach* (Biebrach); *Der Liebesbrief*
        der Königin (Wiene); *Der Mann im Spiegel* (Wiene);
        Problematische Naturen (Oberländer); *Der Sekretär der*
        Königin (Wiene); *Das Wandernde Licht* (Wiene)
1917   *Die Dame, der Teufel, und die Probiermamsell* (Biebrach);
        Die Faust des Riesen (Biebrach); *Die Kunst zu heiraten*
        (Larsen)
1918   *Die blaue Laterne* (Biebrach); *Maskenfest der Liebe* (Biebrach);
        Odysseus' Heimkehr (Biebrach); *Der Mann mit den sieben*
        Masken (Larsen)
1919   *Die rollende Kugel* (Biebrach)
1920   *Anna Boleyn (Deception)* (Lubitsch); *Die goldene Krone*
        (Halm); *Die Tarantel* (Biebrach)
1921   *Der Stier von Olivera* (Buchowetzki)
1923   *Tatjana* (Dineson)
1924   *Gehetzte Menschen* (Schönfelder)

Publications

By MESSTER: book—

Mein Weg mit dem Film, Berlin, 1936.

On MESSTER: book—

Narath, Albert, *Oskar Messter*, Berlin, 1966.

On MESSTER: article—

Narath, Albert, in *Journal of the SMPTE* (New York), October 1960.
Baer, Volker, "Ein Mann der ersten Stunde," in *Film-Dienst* (Cologne), 20 December 1994.
Kintop, no. 3, 1994.
Horak, Jan-Christopher, "100 Jahre Kino-Oskar Messter: Filmpionier der Kaiserzeit KINtop Schriften 2," in *Historical Journal of Radio and Television*, October 1995.

*   *   *

Remembered today both as the inventor of the Maltese Cross (a small device still in use which allows film to move intermittently through a projector) and as the pioneering patriarch of German cinema, Oskar Messter exerted more influence on the early German film industry than any other individual before the First World War. Although the hundreds of films he produced, directed, scripted, shot, cast, and exhibited had little artistic impact on either his contemporaries or Expressionist successors, Messter's constant attempts at innovation and experimentation in film manufacture, production, and exhibition refined the medium itself and enabled Germany to develop a full-fledged film industry and studio system.

From the earliest days in his father's optical plant and throughout his career, Messter demonstrated a fascination and keen facility for the technical processes of motion pictures. His constant invention, refinement, and subsequent marketing of new projection systems, film stocks, movie cameras, and processors laid the foundation for the German film equipment industry, and made both film production and exhibition more practical.

Not content merely to design and manufacture motion picture apparatus, Messter began to produce and show his own short films almost as quickly as the technology was available to him. The earliest Messter films varied greatly in content, but a typical program consisted of a series of short actualities, sports footage, street scenes, comic sketches, cabaret acts, and an occasional squib of animation. The quality of these turn-of-the-century works was primitive, though apparently an improvement on the technically crude, often pornographic, German films being exhibited at tent shows and nickelodeons. By building his own studio (the first in Germany) and becoming the first filmmaker ever to use artificial lighting, Messter was able to produce a remarkable number and variety of films while the medium itself was still in its infancy. His actuality and documentary pictures were demanded internationally and eventually were consolidated into a newsreel program, *Messter-Week*, that continued in production for many years (although government interests were so closely served that often staged propaganda pieces replaced authentic footage). In the area of entertainment films, Messter tended to produce rather wooden costume dramas and static adaptations of literary, theatrical, and historical works. Many of Germany's leading stage talents appeared in these productions at some point, but under Messter none reached the artistic levels they realized in the employ of his rival company, Paul Davidson's Projection-A.G. Union. Messter's dramas, comedies, thrillers, and serials were popular in their day, but none matched the achievement of Davidson's productions with Max

Reinhardt, Ernst Lubitsch, and other talents who would rise to international fame in the 1920s.

But, although his films never developed a memorable style or artistic power, Messter's efforts in the film world remained noteworthy and popular because of his penchant for innovation and experimentation. Often his technical experiments yielded film techniques that benefited the scientific community, if not the movie-going public. His demonstrations of slow motion, microscopic, and time lapse photography, for example, offered the world new ways of seeing, while they also were applied to the production of diverting little "trick films." Later in his career, Messter was called upon to make much more serious use of his film skills as he developed a number of technical military applications for the motion picture in the service of the German armed services. (Messter's allegiance to the fatherland continued into the Nazi period—his ideological association no doubt accounts for his being left behind by Germany's artistic avant garde, most of whom disassociated themselves from the government during both World Wars.)

Other technical innovations by Messter led to more popular successes in his film production. Most notably, his attempts to design a reliable sound system for motion pictures created interest in his company's work and spurred on sound experimenters abroad. Using his crudely synchronized "biophon" system, Messter produced operettas, short films starring music-hall performers, and dramatic pieces. By 1904 (after his popular demonstration of English language talkies at the St. Louis World's Fair), his company offered 120 sound films, and by 1913, some 500 theaters were equipped with Biophon. The system ultimately proved inadequate, but Messter's films whetted the public's appetite for sound. His later experiments with sound-on-disc talkies proved less innovative and became obsolete with the invention of sound-on-film systems. Other Messter experiments also sought color and three-dimensional processes film. But patents were not forthcoming, and such color and dimensional films as he was able to produce remained nothing more than minor novelties.

However, not all of Messter's contributions to the film industry were purely technical. Just as he was among the earliest producers of newsreels, scientific films, and sound films, Messter also began producing longer narratives and eventually feature-length movies before such became standard fare for the film industry. Even more importantly, Messter the studio executive realized the value of the movie star as early as anyone in the industry. With the debut of his film *The Love of the Blind Girl*, the unknown "Messter Girl" in the title role became enormously popular among moviegoers. Messter recognized the mass appeal that the girl, Henny Porten, possessed and so presented her name and face to the public with a large publicity campaign. Because Henny Porten rose to fame at the same time as Denmark's Asta Nielsen and America's Florence Lawrence, Messter must be given credit for helping to invent the star system as we know it today.

Finally, other attempts by Messter to utilize film—such as his circa 1897 home sales catalogue of movies and equipment, and his production of "conductor films" (photographing noted maestros so that orchestras could later be led by a filmed baton)—which stand today as mere cinematic curios, added to the overall strength of the pioneering producer's work. Certainly no single film from his multitude of productions stands out for its historic or artistic achievement, and in fact most Messter films, even though they represent the best of the early German cinema, pale in comparison to the lively works of other primitive era filmmakers such as Lumière, Méliès, Edison, or Porter. But the cumulative effect of Messter's films was to create and enliven both a film audience and a filmmaking community in Germany, while the contribution of technical achievement was to help refine the medium itself.

—Dan Streible

METTY, Russell

Cinematographer. **Nationality:** American. **Born:** Los Angeles, California, in 1906. **Career:** 1925—worked in camera department of Paramount Studios; 1929—joined RKO, where became Director of Photography. Television work during the 1970s includes episodes of *The Waltons, Columbo,* and *Rich Man, Poor Man.* **Award:** Academy Award for *Spartacus,* 1960. **Died:** In 1978.

Films as Cinematographer:

1935   *West of the Pecos* (Rosen)
1936   *Night Waitress* (Landers)
1937   *They Wanted to Marry* (Landers); *Behind the Headlines* (Rosen); *Edgar and Goliath* (Goodwins); *Forty Naughty Girls* (Cline); *You Can't Beat Love* (Cabanne); *Annapolis Salute (Salute to Romance)* (Cabanne)
1938   *The Dummy Owner* (Yarborough); *Ears of Experience* (Goodwins); ***Bringing Up Baby*** (Hawks); *Mr. Doodle Kicks Off* (Goodwins); *Annabel Takes a Tour* (Landers); *Stage Fright* (Roberts); *The Affairs of Annabel* (Stoloff); *Next Time I Marry* (Kanin); *The Sunset Trail* (Selander)
1939   *The Great Man Votes* (Kanin); *The Girl and the Gambler* (Landers); *The Spellbinder* (Hively); *Three Sons* (Hively); *That's Right, You're Wrong* (Butler); *Everything's on Ice* (Kenton)
1940   *Scrappily Married* (Ripley); *Irene* (Wilcox); *Curtain Call* (Woodruff); ***Dance, Girl, Dance*** (Arzner); *No, No, Nanette* (Wilcox); *Sunk By the Census* (D'Arcy)
1941   *A Girl, a Guy and a Gob* (Wallace); *Sunny* (Wilcox); *Weekend for Three* (Reis); *Four Jacks and a Jill* (Hively)
1942   *Joan of Paris* (Stevenson); *Dear! Deer!* (Holmes); *Army Surgeon* (Sutherland); *The Falcon's Brother* (Logan); *The Big Street* (Reis); *Mexican Spitfire Sees a Ghost* (Goodwins); *Framing Father* (Roberts)
1943   *Hitler's Children* (Dmytryk); *Double Up* (Holmes); *Forever and a Day* (Clair, Goulding, Hardwicke, Lloyd, Saville, Stephenson, and Wilcox); *Behind the Rising Sun* (Dmytryk); *Tender Comrade* (Dmytryk); *Around the World* (Dwan); *Not on My Account* (Roberts); *The Sky's the Limit* (E. Griffith)
1944   *Seven Days Ashore* (Auer); *Music in Manhattan* (Auer); *Triple Trouble* (D'Arcy); *The Master Race* (Bibberman); *It's in the Bag* (Wallace)
1945   *Betrayal from the East* (Berke); *The Story of GI Joe* (Wellman); *Pardon My Past* (Fenton); *Breakfast in Hollywood (The Madhatter)* (Schuster)
1946   *The Stranger* (Welles); *The Perfect Marriage* (Allen); *The Private Affairs of Bel Ami* (Lewin); *Whistle Stop* (Moguy)

1947   *Ivy* (Wood); *Ride the Pink Horse* (Montgomery); *A Woman's Vengeance* (Zoltan Korda); *Arch of Triumph* (Milestone)

1948   *All My Sons* (Reis); *Mr. Peabody and the Mermaid* (Pichel); *Kiss the Blood Off My Hands* (*Blood on My Hands*) (Foster); *You Gotta Stay Happy* (Potter)

1949   *The Lady Gambles* (Gordon); *Bagdad* (Lamont); *Curtain Call at Cactus Creek* (Lamont); *We Were Strangers* (Huston)

1950   *Buccaneer's Girl* (de Cordova); *Sierra* (Green); *Peggy* (de Cordova); *The Desert Hawk* (de Cordova); *Wyoming Mail* (Le Borg); *Katie Did It* (de Cordova)

1951   *Upfront* (Hall); *Little Eygpt* (*Chicago Masquerade*) (de Cordova); *The Treasure of Lost Canyon* (Tetzlaff); *The Golden Horde* (Sherman); *The Raging Tide* (Sherman); *Flame of Araby* (Lamont)

1952   *Scarlet Angel* (Salkow); *The World in His Arms* (Walsh); *Against All Flags* (Sherman); *Because of You* (Pevney); *Yankee Buccaneer* (de Cordova)

1953   *The Bond between Us* (Cowan); *Seminole* (Boetticher); *It Happens Every Thursday* (Pevney); *The Man from the Alamo* (Boetticher); *Take Me to Town* (Sirk); *Tumbleweed* (Juran)

1954   *Magnificent Obsession* (Sirk); *Naked Alibi* (Hopper); *Four Guns to the Border* (Carlson); *Sign of the Pagan* (Sirk)

1955   *Crashout* (Foster); *Man without a Star* (King Vidor); *Cult of the Cobra* (Lyon); *There's Always Tomorrow* (Sirk); ***All That Heaven Allows*** (Sirk); *The Man from Bitteridge* (Arnold); *Miracle in the Rain* (Mate)

1956   *Congo Crossing*; ***Written on the Wind*** (Sirk)

1957   *Battle Hymn* (Sirk); *Mr. Cory* (Edwards); *Man Afraid* (Keller); *The Midnight Story* (*Appointment with a Shadow*) (Pevney); *The Female Animal* (Keller)

1958   ***Touch of Evil*** (Welles); *The Thing That Couldn't Die* (Cohen); *A Time to Love and a Time to Die* (Sirk); *Step Down to Terror* (*The Silent Stranger*) (Keller); *Monster on the Campus* (Arnold)

1959   *Imitation of Life* (Sirk); *This Earth Is Mine* (King) (co); *Platinum High School* (*Rich, Young and Deadly*) (Haas)

1960   *Portrait in Black* (Gordon); *Spartacus* (Kubrick); *Midnight Lace* (Miller)

1961   *The Misfits* (Huston); *Flower Drum Song* (Koster); *By Love Possessed* (Sturges)

1962   *If a Man Answers* (Levin); *The Interns* (Swift); *That Touch of Mink* (Mann)

1963   *The Thrill of It All* (Jewison); *Tammy and the Doctor* (Keller); *Captain Newman* (Miller)

1964   *I'd Rather Be Rich* (Smight)

1965   *The Warlord* (Schaffner); *The Art of Love* (Jewinson); *Bus Riley's Back in Town* (Hart); *Madam X* (Rich)

1966   *Texas across the River* (Gordon)

1967   *Thoroughly Modern Millie* (Hill); *The Secret War of Harry Frigg* (Smight); *Counterpoint* (Nelson); *Rough Night in Jericho* (Laven)

1968   *The Pink Jungle* (Delbert Mann); *Madigan* (Siegel)

1969   *Eye of the Cat* (Rich) (co); *Change of Habit* (Graham)

1970   *How Do I Love Thee?* (Gordon); *Tribes* (*The Soldier Who Declared Peace*) (Sargent—for TV)

1971   *The Omega Man* (Sagal)

1972   *Ben* (Karlson); *Cancel My Reservation* (Bogart)

1974   *That's Entertainment!* (Haley) (co)

Publications

On METTY: articles—

Film Comment (New York), vol. 8, no.2, Summer 1972.
Focus on Film (London), Special Cinematography Issue, no. 13, 1973.
Film Dope (London), no. 42, October 1989 + filmo.
Michigan Quarterly Review, no. 4, 1995.
New Republic, 28 September 1998.

*   *   *

Despite Russell Metty's outstanding black-and-white photography for films like *The Stranger*, *Ivy*, *Touch of Evil*, and *The Misfits*, it is with the glistening color of his work for Douglas Sirk at Universal-International that his name remains principally identified. When he and Sirk teamed up for the first time to make *Take Me to Town*, it was the fruit of a determined effort on Sirk's part to get him: "He was very expensive, and very much in demand, but I finally succeeded. We always agreed about everything: we had just the same way of seeing things, and we had a great time working together." Equally impressed was Charlton Heston, who later described Metty as "unquestionably one of the great cameramen. He is nearly the *only* one of them who is also fast. Most of the time you hear things like 'Do you want it fast, or do you want it good?' With Russ you got both." To a relatively humble outfit like Universal, Metty was an especially valuable asset, since the box-office potential of their carefully budgeted little pictures usually owed more to their visual qualities than to their plots, and perhaps even their stars. Sirk himself said that he felt color "very essential to this type of picture to give it the necessary warmth and glow and commercially, to add box-office power to their rather second-rate star value."

Ironically, prior to his arrival at Universal during the mid-forties, Metty's sole contact with Technicolor seems to have consisted of the "Alice Blue Gown" sequence in *Irene*; but he was soon to be set to work on a sizable proportion of the stream of inexpensive action and adventure films in Technicolor with which the studio was attempting, by the early fifties, to free itself of its financial dependence upon its Abbott & Costello, Ma and Pa Kettle, and Francis the Mule comedies. By the end of the decade, when permitted the sort of resources lavished upon the $12,000,000 *Spartacus* (Universal's most expensive picture to date), Metty's Technirama photography had little difficulty in collecting the 1960 Academy Award for color photography.

But his work in color was only half the story. Metty would take whatever Universal pushed his way, moving swiftly from genre to genre, from high to low budgets, from color to black and white, from widescreen to standard, and back again. For example, 1958 saw Metty's name on five Universal releases. In addition to the latest collaboration with Sirk (*A Time to Love and a Time to Die*), in CinemaScope and Eastmancolor, there were four black-and-white programmers intended for double bills: *Step Down to Terror*, which was a quickie remake of *Shadow of a Doubt*; *The Thing That Couldn't Die*, and *Monster on the Campus*, titles that speak for themselves; and *Touch of Evil*. During his European exile, Orson Welles had sorely missed the superior facilities and technicians which only Hollywood could provide, and reunited with Metty he marked the occasion by opening *Touch of Evil* with one of the most spectacular crane shots ever filmed (copied in *Absolute Beginners* and various pop videos). The film abounds in classic *film noir* set pieces, but equally impressive are less showy moments, such as the glacial deep-focus of the brief scene in the hall of records, or the dusty, sun-bleached exteriors for which Venice, California, masqueraded as the dismal little Mexican border town of Los Robles. During a later location shoot, in Nevada for *The Misfits* (for which Metty had been loaned to United Artists), John Huston must have been grateful indeed for Metty's level-headed professionalism as Huston grappled with that film's painful gestation.

During the 1960s Metty's assignments continued to veer between cheerful trivia like *Tammy and the Doctor* and genuine challenges like *The Warlord*, but his behavior during the making of *Madigan* suggests that he no longer felt the same involvement in his work; Don Siegel was to recall that he "did not seem particularly interested in the movie" and had needed prodding to perform reluctantly as basic a task as shining additional light through a window on which the blind had just been raised. Logically enough he was now to become increasingly busy with Universal TV series such as *Columbo* (where his directors included a fledgling Steven Spielberg), still a valuable asset to his employers, no doubt, but probably more for his speed than for his imagination.

—Richard Chatten

METZNER, Ernö

Art Director and Director. **Nationality:** Hungarian. **Born:** 25 February 1892. **Education:** Attended the Academy of Fine Arts, Budapest. **Family:** Married the actress Grace Chiang. **Career:** Art director on films in Germany from 1920: first film as art director, *Sumurun*; 1927–29—directed and designed several films; 1933—left Germany with the rise of the Nazis, and worked in the United Kingdom and the United States. **Died:** In 1953.

Films as Art Director:

1920   *Sumurun* (*One Arabian Night*) (Lubitsch)
1921   *Das Weib des Pharao* (*The Loves of Pharaoh*) (Lubitsch)
1921–23   *Fridericus Rex* (von Cserepy—4 parts)
1922   *Fra Diavolo* (Lange); *Don Juan* (Heine and Land); *Salome* (Wiene) (+ co-d)
1923   *Alt-Heidelberg* (Behrendt); *I.N.R.I.* (Wiene)
1924   *Arabella* (Grune); *Ein Sommernachstraum* (*A Midsummer Night's Dream*) (Neumann)
1926   *Geheimnisse einer Seele* (*Secrets of a Soul*) (Pabst)
1927   *Man steigt nach* (+ d + co-sc)
1928   *Uberfall* (*Accident*) (+ d, ph); *Hotel Geheimnisse* (Feger); *Mikosch rückt ein* (Randolf); *Freie Fahrt* (+ d); *Dein Schicksal* (Lohmann); *In Anfang war das Wort* (+ d)
1929   *Das Tagebuch einer Verlorenen* (*Diary of a Lost Girl*) (Pabst); *Die weisse Hölle von Piz Palü* (*The White Hell of Piz Palü*) (Pabst and Fanck)
1930   *Westfront 1918* (*Comrades of 1918*) (Pabst); *Zwei Krawatten* (Basch-Weichert); *Die Firma heiratet* (Wilhelm); *Fra Diavolo* (Bonnard)
1931   ***Kameradschaft*** (*Comradeship*) (Pabst); *Eine Nacht im Grandhotel* (Neufeld); *Der unbekannte Gast* (Emo)
1932   *L'Atlantide* (*Die Herrin von Atlantis*) (Pabst); *Ein bisschen Liebe für dich* (Neufeld); *Skandal in der Parkstrasse* (Wenzler); *Zigeuner der Nacht* (Schwarz)
1933   *Das Meer ruft* (Hinrich); *Der Läufer von Marathon* (*The Marathon Runner*) (Dupont)
1934   *Du haut en bas* (Pabst); *Princess Charming* (Elvey); *Chu-Chin-Chow* (Forde)
1935   *The Tunnel* (Elvey); *The Robber Symphony* (Feher)
1936   *Seven Sinners* (de Courville); *Strangers on Honeymoon* (de Courville)
1937   *Take My Tip* (Mason)
1944   *It Happened Tomorrow* (Clair)
1947   *The Macomber Affair* (Z. Korda)

Other Films:

1921   *Stier von Olivera* (Buchowetzki) (costumes); *Fiesco* (*Die Verschwöhrung zu Genua*) (Leni) (costumes)
1922   *Sein ist das Gericht* (Lange) (costumes)
1923   *Schlagende Wetter* (Grune) (costumes)
1925   *Der Leibgardist* (*Der Gardeoffizier*) (Wiene) (costumes)
1929   *Achtung! Liebe-Lebensgefahr!* (d—revised sound version, *Rivalen im Weltrekord*, 1930)
1930   *Revolte im Erziehungshaus* (co-d)

Publications

By METZNER: articles—

"Defence of *Uberfall*," in *Close Up* (London), March 1929.
"A Mining Film," in *Close Up* (London), March 1932.
"On the Sets for the Film *Atlantis*," in *Close Up* (London), September 1932.
"The Travelling Camera," in *Close Up* (London), June 1933.

On METZNER: articles—

Close Up (London), February 1929.
Close Up (London), April 1929.
Close Up (London), May, 1929.
Close Up (London), October 1929.
Blakeston, Oswell, on *Uberfall* in *Film Weekly* (London), 21 October 1929.
Film Dope (Nottingham), October 1989.

*   *   *

The contribution of Hungary to world cinema has been considerable—writers, actors, cameramen, and critics. Ernö Metzner is a Hungarian whose best work was done outside his homeland. In Germany, from 1920 to his enforced exile in 1933, he achieved distinction as a film designer as well as a director of films of great originality, experimental in spirit and strongly imbued with social comment.

He worked for Lubitsch on the spectacular *Sumurun* and designed some of the costumes for *Das Weib des Pharao*. For von Cserepy's mammoth four-part epic *Fridericus Rex*, he was codesigner. While he had wide experience with the films of Paul Leni, Karl Grune, Robert

Wiene, Hans Behrendt, and Friedrich Feher, it was with G.W. Pabst that he realised his best work. He designed the fantastic and complex settings for *Geheimnisse einer Seele*, a psychoanalytical drama supervised by Dr. Hans Sachs, a colleague of Freud. The distorted images of mental breakdown required a special type of setting specially related to camera effects.

From 1927 to 1929, he took up directing, which also included design and camerawork. The most famous of the films from this period was *Uberfall*, the adventures of a man who finds a gold coin in the street and is pursued by thugs who beat him up. This was virtuoso filming, using all the creative devices of the camera lens, including distortion effects. The film became a *cause célèbre* when the German censor banned it on the grounds of brutality, a decision that seemed rather ridiculous even in its time. He also made *Freie Fahrt* for the Social Democratic Party, a film very much influenced by the Russian films then popular in Berlin. In these films he featured his wife, Grace Chiang, and the famous still photographer Hans Casparius.

Again he worked for Pabst on *Das Tagebuch einer Verlorenen* which featured Louise Brooks and on *Die weisse Hölle von Piz Palü* in which Pabst shared direction with Dr. Arnold Fanck.

With the coming of the sound film and its inhibiting effect on the visuals and camera work, Metzner magnificently overcame these problems in three films for Pabst. In *Westfront 1918* he designed for the moving camera in the war scenes, while in *Kameradschaft*, his studio construction of a mine was completely functional, allowing mobility of camera in a narrow space and achieving the most extreme realism in the visual action. The collapse of the mine tunnels during an explosion, the claustrophobic feeling of being trapped, the texture and tactile image of the mine guaranteed a unique involvement of the spectator. On the other hand, his design for *Die Herrin von Atlantis* embraced pure fantasy, and Metzner carefully selected material which would reinforce the illusion of an underground city in the desert. His sensitive awareness of the needs of the movie camera was remarkable, derived perhaps from his experience as a total filmmaker. His feeling for abstraction changed to accommodate the realism of his work for Pabst. He was to work on one more film for Pabst—*Du haut en bas*—when he was an exile in France, a refugee from the Nazi persecution of the Jews.

In England he worked on a series of minor films, but in 1935 he designed Friedrich Feher's delightful fantasy *The Robber Symphony*. (He had worked with Feher previously in Berlin on *Hotel Geheimnisse*.) Visually *The Robber Symphony* was a delight to watch and provided Metzner with the opportunity for his imaginative skills. In the early 1940s, he found himself in Hollywood where he does not seem to have had much success, although he worked with both René Clair and Zoltan Korda.

—Liam O'Leary

MILHAUD, Darius

Composer. **Nationality:** French. **Born:** Aix-en-Provence, 1892; moved to the United States in 1940. **Family:** Married his cousin, Madeleine Milhaud, who wrote the libretti for many of his operas. **Education:** Attended Lycée Mignet, 1902–09, Conservatoire Nationale de Musique, Paris, 1909–14. **Career:** 1909–14—played violin in student orchestra under the direction of Paul Dukas; 1920s-1930s—toured as composer until stricken by arthritis; 1947—Professor of Composition at the

Darius Milhaud

Conservatoire in Paris, also taught at Mills College, California, and the Music School of Aspen, Colorado; 1971—retired and moved to Geneva. **Died:** In 1974.

Films as Composer:

1923	*L'Inhumaine* (L'Herbier)
1929	*La Petite Lilie* (Cavalcanti)
1933	*Hallo Everybody* (Richter)
1934	*Madame Bovary* (Renoir); *L'Hippocampe* (Painlevé); *Tartarin de Tarascon* (Bernard)
1935	*Voix d'enfants* (Reynaud)
1936	*The Beloved Vagabond* (Bernhardt)
1937	*Vom Blitz zum Fernsehbild* (*La Conquête du ciel*) (Richter); *La Citadelle du silence* (L'Herbier); *Mollenard* (*Capitaine Corsaire*) (Siodmak)
1938	*La Tragédie impériale* (L'Herbier)
1939	*Les Otages* (Bernard); *The Islanders* (Harvey); *L'Espoir* (*Sierra de Teruel*) (Malraux); *Cavalcade d'amour* (Bernard) (co); *Gulf Stream* (Alexeleff)
1946	*The Private Affairs of Bel-Ami* (Lewin); ''Ruth, Roses and Revolver'' ep. of *Dreams That Money Can Buy* (Richter)
1949	*Paul Gauguin* (Resnais)
1950	*La Vie commence demain* (Védrès)
1954	*Ils étaient tous des volontaires* (Villiers); *Un Monde perdu* (Lorenzi—for TV) (co)
1959	*Rentrée des classes* (Rozier)

1963 *Peintres françaises d'aujourd'hui—Edouard Pignon* (Bourniquel and Suzuki)
1969 *Vézélay* (Vitaly); *Dieu a choisi Paris* (Prouteau and Arthuys)
1973 *Les Mariés de la Tour Eiffel* (Averty—for TV)

Publications

By MILHAUD: books—

Études, Paris, 1927.
Notes sans musique (autobiography), Paris, 1949.
Ma vie heureuse (autobiography), Paris, 1974; as *My Happy Life*, translated by Donald Evans and Christopher Palmer, London, M. Boyars, 1994.

On MILHAUD: book—

Callaer, Paul, and Jane Hahfield, *Darius Milhaud*, London, 1988.
Mawer, Deborah, *Darius Milhaud: Modality & Structure in Music of the 1920s*, Brookfeild, 1997.

On MILHAUD: articles—

Theatre Arts, vol. 31, no. 9, September 1947.
Film Dope (London), no. 43, January 1990.
Smith, Richard Langham, "Darius Milhaud," in *Music & Letter*, February 1990.
Wentzel, Wayne C., in *Notes*, March 1992.
Thiel, Wolfgang, in *Film-Dienst* (Cologne), 18 August 1992.
Monaghan, Peter, "An Idiosyncratic Composer Explores the Sonic Mystery of the World," in *Chronicle of Higher Education*, 19 April 1996.
Teachout, Terry, "Modernism with a Smile: Composers Darius Milhaud and Francis Poulenc," in *Commentary*, April 1998.

On MILHAUD: film—

A Visit with Darius Milhaud, 1955.

*   *   *

Darius Milhaud was one of the most prolific composers of the century, with a final tally of well over 400 opus numbers taking in every major musical form. It is not surprising that, along with everything else, he composed a good deal of film music. Indeed it would have been more surprising if he had not, given his lifelong love of the cinema. His first major success, the 1919 Surrealist ballet *Le Boeuf sur le toit*, was originally subtitled a *Cinéma-symphonie*, "suitable for an accompaniment to one of Charlie Chaplin's films."

Milhaud supplied music for some 25 films, starting out in the silent era with a score to accompany Marcel L'Herbier's avant-garde melodrama *L'Inhumaine*. The music is lost, but it is reputed to have matched the film's abrupt, expressionist rhythm, climaxing—for a scene where the hero resurrects his dead love in a futuristic laboratory—in a bravura cadenza scored solely for percussion instruments.

Audacious and (at least in his younger years) impudently iconoclastic, Milhaud relished experimentation for its own sake. He was one of the first to co-opt cinema into opera; his *Christophe Colombe* uses a backdrop movie screen to convey the thoughts of his characters, or to extend the action "into an inner universe opening out from our own." Even when his stance had become less outrageous, he retained a penchant for the avant-garde, and provided some suitably spiky music for the Man Ray section of Hans Richter's self-consciously Surrealist *Dreams That Money Can Buy*.

Milhaud's own musical idiom was nothing if not eclectic. He admired Debussy and Mussorgsky (and detested Wagner), but happily threw in elements of whatever took his fancy—jazz, Brazilian dance rhythms, the medieval troubadour songs of his native Provence. Rather than cast his music in a predetermined style, he preferred to adopt whatever forms and materials seemed appropriate to the given task. This adaptability, together with his fluency (he once defined inspiration as "the amount of ink in my pen"), should have made him an ideal film composer. But his relationship with the movie industry remained oddly uneasy. He believed that his "symphonic" style aroused mistrust among filmmakers, recalling in his memoirs a "rather inquisitorial visit" from Renoir while he was composing the score for *Madame Bovary*.

This, coupled with a perhaps inadvertent tendency to write down to movie audiences—he felt that film music must "remain modest . . . be extremely simple"—may explain why Milhaud's film scores are mostly less distinguished than might be expected from a composer of his stature. He was at his best with straightforward, light-hearted subjects such as Raymond Bernard's *Cavalcade d'amour*, a look at love during three periods of history. Each section of the film used a different composer: Milhaud chose the Middle Ages, and produced a fresh, transparent score, whose chamber-music textures breathed Mediterranean sunshine. He later adapted it into a suite for wind quintet, entitled *La Cheminée du Roi René*.

If offered a subject which genuinely engaged his emotions, Milhaud could still come up with film music that belied his reputation for elegant frivolity. André Malraux's only film, the stark Spanish Civil War drama *L'Espoir*, has no music until the final reel, when a long procession of villagers winds down a mountainside carrying the bodies of dead Republican airmen. For this wordless sequence, Milhaud supplied an 11-minute passage of sustained and sombre nobility. This too was adapted for concert use, as the *Cortège funèbre*.

Although Milhaud spent much of his later life in America, he was loath to work in Hollywood, disliking the system of handing over the composer's short score to professional orchestrators "who churn out on a commercial scale musical pathos *à la* Wagner or Tchaikovsky." The one Hollywood assignment he did accept was *The Private Affairs of Bel-Ami*, scripted (after Maupassant) and directed by Albert Lewin—"a highly cultured man," Milhaud noted, "and what is even rarer in those circles, genuinely modest." Lewin allowed Milhaud not only to orchestrate his own music, but to conduct it and sit in on the mixing sessions. The result was a score that vividly evoked the Paris of the Belle Epoque, but without the usual wash of romantic nostalgia. This, Milhaud's strutting themes and jaunty brass writing suggested, was a society whose glittering facade concealed callousness and rampant ambition—a vision entirely in keeping with Maupassant's cynical tale of a cad on the make.

—Philip Kemp

MILLER, Arthur C.

Cinematographer. **Nationality:** American. **Born:** Roslyn, New York, 8 July 1895. **Career:** Bit player and camera assistant from age 13; then assistant cameraman and laboratory technician for Edwin S. Porter (cameraman on *The Perils of Pauline*, 1914); 1915–25—worked almost exclusively with the director George Fitzmaurice; then later worked with 20th Century-Fox; 1951—retired; then President, American Society of Cinematographers. **Awards:** Academy Award for *How Green Was My Valley*, 1941; *The Song of Bernadette*, 1943; *Anna and the King of Siam*, 1946. **Died:** In 1970.

Films as Cinematographer for Fitzmaurice:

1915   *At Bay*
1916   *New York*; *Fifth Avenue*; *Big Jim Garrity*; *Arms and the Woman*; *Romantic Journey*
1917   *Hunting of the Hawk*; *Recoil*; *The Iron Heart*; *The Mark of Cain*; *Sylvia of the Secret Service*
1918   *The Hillcrest Mystery*; *The Naulahka*; *A Japanese Nightingale*; *The Narrow Path*
1919   *Counterfeit*; *Common Clay*; *The Cry of the Weak*; *The Profiteers*; *Witness for the Defense*; *Avalanche*; *Our Better Selves*; *A Society Exile*
1920   *On with the Dance*; *The Right to Love*; *Idols of Clay*
1921   *Paying the Piper*; *Experience*; *Forever*
1922   *Kick In*; *The Man from Home*; *Three Live Ghosts*; *To Have and to Hold*
1923   *Bella Donna*; *The Cheat*; *The Eternal City*
1924   *Cytherea*; *Tarnish* (co)
1925   *A Thief in Paradise*; *His Supreme Moment*

Other Films as Cinematographer:

1914   *The Perils of Pauline* (Gasnier—serial) (cam)
1917   *Vengeance Is Mine* (Crane); *Stranded in Arcady* (Crane)
1918   *Convict 993* (Parke)
1920   *His House in Order* (H. Ford); *Lady Rose's Daughter* (H. King)
1924   *In Hollywood with Potash and Perlmutter* (Green) (co)
1925   *The Coming of Amos* (Sloane)
1926   *Made for Love* (Sloane); *The Clinging Vine* (Sloane); *Eve's Leaves* (Sloane); *For Alimony Only* (W. De Mille); *The Volga Boatman* (C. DeMille) (co)
1927   *The Angel of Broadway* (Weber); *The Fighting Eagle* (Crisp); *Nobody's Widow* (Crisp); *Vanity* (Crisp)
1928   *Annapolis* (Cabanne); *Blue Danube* (Sloane); *The Cop* (Crisp); *Hold 'em Yale* (Griffith); *The Spieler* (Garnett)
1929   *Bellamy Trial* (Bell); *Big News* (La Cava); *The Flying Fool* (Garnett); *His First Command* (La Cava) (co); *Oh, Yeah!* (Garnett); *Sailor's Holiday* (Newmeyer); *Strange Cargo* (Glazer and Gregor)
1930   *The Lady of Scandal* (Franklin) (co); *Officer O'Brien* (Garnett); *See American Thirst* (Craft) (co); *The Truth about Youth* (Seiter); *Behind the Make-Up* (Bell); *Father's Son* (Beaudine)
1931   *Bad Company* (Garnett)

1932   *Panama Flo* (Murphy); *Big Shot* (Murphy); *Young Bride* (Seiter); *Breach of Promise* (Stein); *Me and My Gal* (Walsh); *Okay, America* (Garnett)
1933   *Sailor's Luck* (Walsh); *Hold Me Tight* (Butler); *The Man Who Dared* (MacFadden); *The Last Trail* (Tinling); *The Mad Game* (Cummings); *My Weakness* (Butler)
1934   *Bottoms Up* (Butler); *Ever Since Eve* (Marshall); *Handy Andy* (Butler); *Love Time* (Tinling); *The White Parade* (Cummings); *Bright Eyes* (Butler)
1935   *The Little Colonel* (Butler); *It's a Small World* (Cummings); *Black Sheep* (Dwan); *Welcome Home* (Tinling); *Paddy O'Day* (Seiler)
1936   *White Fang* (Butler); *36 Hours to Kill* (Forde); *Pigskin Parade* (Butler); *Stowaway* (Seiter)
1937   *Wee Willie Winkie* (Ford); *Heidi* (Dwan)
1938   *The Baroness and the Butler* (W. Lang); *Rebecca of Sunnybrook Farm* (Dwan); *Little Miss Broadway* (Cummings); *Submarine Patrol* (Ford)
1939   *The Little Princess* (W. Lang) (co); *Susannah of the Mounties* (Seiter); *Here I Am a Stranger* (Del Ruth); *The Rains Came* (Brown); *Young Mr. Lincoln* (Ford)
1940   *The Blue Bird* (W. Lang) (co); *Johnny Appollo* (Hathaway); *On Their Own* (Brower); *The Mark of Zorro* (Mamoulian); *Brigham Young—Frontiersman* (Hathaway)
1941   *Tobacco Road* (Ford); *Man Hunt* (F. Lang); *The Men in Her Life* (Ratoff) (co); *How Green Was My Valley* (Ford)
1942   *This Above All* (Litvak); *Iceland* (Humberstone)
1943   *The Moon Is Down* (Pichel); *The Immortal Sergeant* (Stahl) (co); *The Ox-Bow Incident* (Wellman); *The Song of Bernadette* (H. King)
1944   *The Purple Heart* (Milestone); *The Keys of the Kingdom* (Stahl)
1945   *A Royal Scandal* (Preminger and Lubitsch)
1946   *Dragonwyck* (Mankiewicz); *Anna and the King of Siam* (Cromwell); *The Razor's Edge* (Goulding)
1947   *Gentleman's Agreement* (Kazan)
1948   *The Walls of Jericho* (Stahl)
1949   *A Letter to Three Wives* (Mankiewicz)
1950   *Whirlpool* (Preminger); *The Gunfighter* (H. King)
1951   *The Prowler* (Losey)

Publications

By MILLER: books—

With John V. Mascelli, *American Cinematographer Manual*, Hollywood, 1960.
With Fred J. Balsofer, *One Reel a Week*, Berkeley, California, 1967.

By MILLER: articles—

American Cinematographer (Hollywood), January 1953.
''Motion Picture Set Lighting,'' in *American Cinematographer* (Hollywood), April 1961.
'''Natural' Lighting for Interior Sets,'' in *American Cinematographer* (Hollywood), September 1966.
In *Sources of Light*, edited by Charles Higham, London, 1970.

In *The Art of the Cinematographer*, edited by Leonard Maltin, New York, 1978.

''*How Green Was My Valley*,'' an interview with G. J. Mitchell, in *American Cinematographer* (Hollywood), September 1991.

On MILLER: articles—

American Cinematographer (Hollywood), May 1954.
Critisch Filmforum (The Hague), no. 1, 1969.
American Cinematographer (Hollywood), August 1970.
Films in Review (New York), October 1970.
Focus on Film (London), no. 13, 1973.
Film Dope (Nottingham), January 1990.

* * *

Arthur C. Miller prided himself on hard, brittle images, with deep shadows and brilliant highlights. To achieve these highlights, Miller went to great lengths, even to the point of oiling the furniture and other woodwork. He was more than a realist—he was a superrealist. His desire to achieve high glossiness and intense coloration resembles the approach of the painter Richard Estes.

Miller began working in films when the industry was in New York. Most of the films he made during the 1920s were done with George Fitzmaurice, who allowed Miller some experimental leeway. The cinematographer filmed a scene in the early morning fog, for example, for *Peter Ibbetson*. He had a rather stormy confrontation, however, in making *The Volga Boatman* with Cecil B. DeMille; Miller expected a free hand in the lighting and photographing.

During the 1930s, Miller became Shirley Temple's cameraman—in the way that William Daniels was Greta Garbo's and Lee Garmes was Marlene Dietrich's. As did these cameramen, he developed the most effective lighting for his star, backlighting Temple's golden hair so as to create an aureole. Sometimes, he lit her in high key for one shot and lit the actor to whom she was talking in low key. In 1943 Miller used similar quasimystical effects in *The Song of Bernadette*.

While filming Temple in *Wee Willie Winkie*, Miller had a chance to work with the man who was to become his favorite director, John Ford. The cameraman found a director who was highly professional at his job and did not bother Miller in his: Ford left the details of cinematography up to the cameraman. In 1941 Miller and Ford joined forces on *Tobacco Road* and *How Green Was My Valley*. Miller never did a western with Ford; however, his photography for Wellman's *The Ox-Bow Incident* is interesting because it was a western that was filmed entirely in the studio. The lighting gives the impression of its taking place in the course of one day—from sunset to sunrise.

—Rodney Farnsworth

MILLER, Seton I.

Writer and Producer. **Nationality:** American. **Born:** Chehalis, Washington, 2 May 1902. **Education:** Attended Yale University, New Haven, Connecticut, graduated. **Family:** Married 1) Bonita-Jessie Nichols, 1927; children: one son and one daughter; 2) Ann Marie White, 1944; children: one daughter. **Career:** 1926—technical adviser and actor, MGM; 1927—first film as writer, *Paid to Love*, first of several films for Howard Hawks; 1945—first film as producer,

Ministry of Fear. **Award:** Academy Award for *Here Comes Mr. Jordan*, 1941. **Died:** 29 May 1974.

Films as Writer:

1927 *Paid to Love* (Hawks); *Two Girls Wanted* (Green); *High School Hero* (Butler); *Wolf Fangs* (Seiler)
1928 *A Girl in Every Port* (Hawks); *Fazil* (Hawks); *The Cowboy Kid* (Carruth); *The Girl-Shy Cowboy* (Hough); *The Air Circus* (Hawks, Seiler, and Judels)
1929 *The Far Call* (Dwan)
1930 *The Lone Star Ranger* (Erickson and Van Buren); *Harmony at Home* (MacFadden); *The Dawn Patrol* (Hawks); *Today* (Nigh)
1931 *The Criminal Code* (Hawks)
1932 *Scarface* (Hawks); *The Crowd Roars* (Hawks); *If I Had a Million* (Cruze and others); *The Last Mile* (Bischoff)
1933 *Eagle and the Hawk* (Walker)
1934 *Charlie Chan's Courage* (Hadden)
1935 *G-Men* (Keighley); *Frisco Kid* (Bacon); *It Happened in New York* (Crosland)
1936 *The Leathernecks Have Landed* (Bretherton); *Bullets or Ballots* (Keighley) (Bacon); *Back in Circulation* (Enright)
1938 **The Adventures of Robin Hood** (Keighley and Curtiz); *Penitentiary* (Brahm); *Valley of the Giants* (Keighley); *The Dawn Patrol* (Goulding)
1940 *Castle on the Hudson* (Litvak); *The Sea Hawk* (Curtiz)
1941 *Here Comes Mr. Jordan* (Hall); *This Woman Is Mine* (Lloyd)
1942 *The Black Swan* (H. King); *My Gal Sal* (Cummings)
1947 *Singapore* (Brahm)
1953 *The Mississippi Gambler* (Maté)
1954 *The Shanghai Story* (Lloyd); *Bengal Brigade* (Benedek)
1957 *Istanbul* (Pevney)
1959 *The Last Mile* (Koch)

Films as Producer and Writer:

1945 *Ministry of Fear* (F. Lang)
1946 *Two Years Before the Mast* (Farrow)
1947 *Calcutta* (Farrow)
1948 *Fighter Squadron* (Walsh)
1951 *Queen for a Day* (Lubin) (co-pr)

Film as Producer:

1947 *California* (Farrow)

Publications

On MILLER: articles—

Présence du Cinéma (Paris), June 1962.
Film Comment (New York), Winter 1970–71.

* * *

Seton I. Miller was one of Hollywood's finest action writers, with a flair for taut dialogue, well-drawn characters, and solid construction. As Howard Hawks's screenwriter on seven of the director's early efforts, Miller collaborated on the formation of the Hawksian cinema, yet like that of many of Hollywood's unsung craftsmen, Miller's reputation has been obscured by the high critical profile of the auteur director. *A Girl in Every Port*, *The Dawn Patrol*, and *Scarface* are among Hawks's most accomplished achievements; Miller's name is scarcely mentioned in the many volumes on Hawks. At Warners in the 1930s, Miller was responsible for scripting one of the best Cagney movies, *G-Men*, and a superior Edward G. Robinson vehicle, *Bullets or Ballots*, and, similarly, coauthored such Errol Flynn films as *The Adventures of Robin Hood*, *The Dawn Patrol* remake, and *The Sea Hawk*. Miller was plagued by the vagaries of the studio system, corporate policies that saw multiple writers reworking each other's material, and debates over proper screen credit; ultimately, he became a producer to protect his work.

Miller had a curious entry into pictures. A Yale graduate, he was transported to MGM as an actor and technical advisor on the collegiate tale *Brown of Harvard*. He did not find histrionics to his liking, and made the move from thespian to author with the help of a bright young Fox director, Howard Hawks. The pair became close friends, and Miller stayed in Hollywood as Hawks's scenarist. Their first picture together, *Paid to Love*, was a contractual obligation for Hawks, and the clichéd story about a prince and a nightclub entertainer, coscripted by William Conselman, was not fondly recalled by the director. The same is true of *Fazil*, adapted by Miller and Philip Klein from a play by Pierre Frondaie about a Frenchwoman and an Arab shiek.

A Girl in Every Port is one of the triumphs of the late silent era, written by Miller from a Hawks idea. A raucous, delightful comedy, the film is blessed with Louise Brooks's inimitable presence as the object of Victor McLaglen and Robert Armstrong's rowdy affections. The ribaldry is offset by the McLaglen and Armstrong relationship, a rivalry turned to friendship that would become a staple Hawks ingredient. Hawks called *A Girl in Every Port* "a love story between two men" in a 1962 interview with Peter Bogdanovich. *The Air Circus* was caught in the transition from silence to sound; Hawks directed a scenario by Miller and Norman McLeod about a young man learning to fly, then dialogue sequences written by Hugh Herbert were added after the fact. Hawks withdrew from the project and Lewis Seiler directed the additional footage.

The Hawks and Miller partnership flowered with the Warner Bros. production of *The Dawn Patrol*. John Monk Saunders provided the story, "Flight Commander," which, like *Wings*, was based on his own experiences as a First World War aviator. Hawks shared screenwriting credit with Miller and Dan Totheroh, and injected the picture with a creative use of dialogue that would become a trademark. Hawks did not really come into his own until the advent of talking pictures, but unlike many early sound movies, the dialogue in *The Dawn Patrol* is sparse yet flavorful; as Gerald Mast writes in *Howard Hawks, Storyteller* it "seemed restrained, natural, underplayed, understated." As he would do with John Wayne and Montgomery Clift in *Red River*, and Katharine Hepburn and Cary Grant in *Bringing Up Baby*, Hawks gained great effect from contrasting character types in *The Dawn Patrol*, in this case the war-hardened cynicism of Richard Barthelmess with the youthful enthusiasm of Douglas Fairbanks, Jr. *The Dawn Patrol* was a great success, and eight years later Warners had Miller rewrite the original script as

a vehicle for Errol Flynn and Basil Rathbone. This consisted primarily of rewriting dialogue to fit the new players, a chore Miller did with director Edmund Goulding, but the remake followed the Hawks original very closely. With the Second World War looming, the second *Dawn Patrol* was especially timely with its pacifistic script, and also succeeded at the box office.

Andrew Sarris called *Scarface* "Hawks' greatest film, with the bloodiest and most brutal of the gangster films which embellished the American cinema of the early 1930s," and the film retains its power sixty years later. Inspired by the Al Capone saga, influenced by the villainous medieval Borgia family, the story was developed by Hawks with a stellar writing crew—a novel by Armitage Trail supplied the title and a smattering of plot; Seton Miller, John Lee Mahin, and W.R. Burnett wrote the first draft; Hawks and Ben Hecht did the final screenplay in a reported 11 days. It is hard to gauge Miller's exact contribution; as with the other Hawks pictures, it is likely he was the director's earliest sounding board on the project, and was involved in the script's construction. *Scarface* was made in 1930, but held up for release by the censors for two years; in the meantime, Hawks took Miller with him to Columbia for *The Criminal Code*, and back to Warners for *The Crowd Roars*.

Based on a play by Martin Flavin, *The Criminal Code* is one of the best prison pictures, with a sense of reality that Hawks and Miller gleaned from interviews with actual convicts. Miller did a first draft for Hawks on the director's original story *The Crowd Roars*; subsequent versions were scripted by Kubec Glasmon and John Bright, and Niven Busch worked on revisions during the shooting. Set against the world of race-car drivers, *The Crowd Roars* is quintessential Hawks, dealing with rivalry and camaraderie between professionals; tough characters, both male and female, abound in the film, drawn with depth and sensitivity.

After *The Crowd Roars*, Miller stayed at Warners to become a staff writer, and, unfortunately, never wrote another produced film for Hawks. When Warners brass wanted a new image for James Cagney, who had starred in *The Crowd Roars*, they called upon Miller to fashion the screenplay for *G-Men*, based on *Public Enemy No. 1* by Gregory Rogers. Cagney scored as the FBI agent Brick Davis in a brisk action drama. Miller teamed again with *G-Men* director William Keighley on *Bullets or Ballots*, which also cast a screen bad guy, Edward G. Robinson, on the right side of the law, as an undercover cop busting a crime syndicate. The box-office response to *G-Men* and *Bullets or Ballots* was high, and *Kid Galahad*, another solo writing credit for Miller, topped even these in popularity. Michael Curtiz's film is among the best prizefighting pictures ever produced, remade twice, and memorable for Miller's fast and furious narrative and wisecracking dialogue.

Warners rewarded Miller with an assignment on their epic *The Adventures of Robin Hood* with Errol Flynn. Norman Reilly Raine had completed a draft and revision before Miller was brought in to collaborate. The result is a model screenplay, directed by Curtiz and Keighley, blending dashing adventure, humor, believable dialogue, and even a plea against intolerance. A follow-up Flynn vehicle, *The Sea Hawk*, hastened Miller's departure from Warner Bros. The writer completed a total revamping of the Rafael Sabatini novel, calling it *Beggars of the Sea*; Warners assured him he would complete the job, then called in first Milton Krims, then Howard Koch, to rewrite Miller. The experience, quite common at the time, rankled Miller, and he left to freelance his services.

Miller went to Columbia, where he and Sidney Buchman won an Oscar for their adaptation of Harry Segall's play *Here Comes Mr.*

Jordan, a mirthful comedy fantasy about a punch-drunk prizefighter (Robert Montgomery) who is killed and sent back to earth. The screenwriters expanded the confines of the original play, and Alexander Hall directed the wonderful material with great skill. Miller collaborated with Ben Hecht on a Tyrone Power swashbuckler at 20th Century-Fox, *The Black Swan*; the writers played up the tongue-in-cheek humor of the Sabatini pirate story, discarding most of the novel's florid dialogue.

Fulfilling a long-standing ambition, Miller signed a producing contract at Paramount in 1943. His first and best film as writer-producer was Fritz Lang's *Ministry of Fear*, adapted from Graham Greene's spy thriller. It has some nice moments of suspense, but is a lesser Lang film; he and Miller disagreed on the script, and theirs was not a happy relationship. Miller had a more pleasant association with John Farrow on *Two Years before the Mast*, *California*, and *Calcutta*; unfortunately the pictures are routine. Raoul Walsh's *Fighter Squadron*, a Second World War drama produced by Miller and cowritten with Martin Rackin, contained action sequences worthy of Miller's previous work.

Miller's career as a producer was rather an anticlimax to his years as a major screenwriter. Paradoxically, Miller seemed to create his best work under strong filmmakers like Howard Hawks and Warners production head Hal Wallis. His place in American film history is secure with contributions on *A Girl in Every Port* and *Here Comes Mr. Jordan*, which reflect his subtle comedic talent, and his more characteristic action pictures like *The Dawn Patrol*, *Scarface*, *G-Men*, and *The Adventures of Robin Hood*.

—John A. Gallagher

MILLER, Virgil

Cinematographer. **Nationality:** American. **Born:** Coffeen, Illinois, 20 December 1887. **Education:** Studied electrical engineering at Kansas State University, Manhattan, B.S. **Career:** Teacher; 1913–15—gaffer, then cameraman, 1915–26, Universal; then worked for Warner Bros., Paramount, seven years, David O. Selznick, and 20th Century-Fox; mid-1940s—photographed 62 of James Fitzpatrick's *Travel Talks* documentary series; TV work includes *You Bet Your Life* and *Do You Trust Your Wife* series, 1950s. **Died:** 5 October 1974.

Films as Cinematographer:

1921   *The Big Adventure* (Eason); *Cheated Hearts* (Henley); *Colorado* (Eason); *Luring Lips* (Baggot); *Red Courage* (Eason); *Sure Fire* (Ford)

1922   *The Black Bag* (Paton); *Don't Shoot* (Conway); *The Lone Hand* (Eason); *The Man under Cover* (Browning); *Ridin' Wild* (Ross); *The Scrapper* (Henley); *The Trap* (Thornby)

1923   *Blinky* (Sedgwick); *The Flame of Life* (Henley); *The Gentleman from America* (Sedgwick); *Kindled Courage* (Worthington); *Nobody's Bridge* (H. Blanché); *Out of Luck* (Sedgwick); *The Ramblin' Kid* (Sedgwick); *The Scarlet Car* (Paton); *Shootin' for Love* (Sedgwick); *Single Handed* (Sedgwick); *The Thrill Chaser* (Sedgwick)

1924   *Broadway or Bust* (Sedgwick); *40-Horse Hawkins* (Sedgwick); *Hit and Run* (Sedgwick); *Hook and Ladder* (Sedgwick); *Ride for Your Life* (Sedgwick); *The Ridin' Kid from Powder River* (Sedgwick); *The Sawdust Trail* (Sedgwick)

1925   *The Hurricane Kid* (Sedgwick); *Let 'er Buck* (Sedgwick); *Lorraine of the Lions* (Sedgwick); **The Phantom of the Opera** (Julian); *Ridin' Wild* (De La Mothe) (co); *The Saddle Hawk* (Sedgwick)

1926   *Broken Hearts of Hollywood* (Bacon); *The Flaming Frontier* (Sedgwick); *Private Izzy Murphy* (Bacon); *The Runaway Express* (Bacon); *Under Western Skies* (Bacon)

1927   *Finger Prints* (Bacon); *The Gay Old Bird* (Raymaker); *Irish Hearts* (Haskin)

1928   *Alex the Great* (Murphy); *Captain Careless* (Storm); *The Count of Ten* (Flood); *Finders Keepers* (Ruggles); *Gang War* (Glennon); *Guardians of the Wild* (MacRae); *Headin' for Danger* (Bradbury); *Sally's Shoulders* (Shores); *Stores and Blondes* (Murphy); *The Two Outlaws* (MacRae); *Young Whirlwind* (L. King)

1929   *The Amazing Vagabond* (Fox); *Come and Get It* (Fox); *Laughing at Death* (Fox); *The Little Savage* (L. King); *Pals of the Prairie* (L. King); *The Vagabond Club* (L. King); *The Woman I Love* (Melford)

1935   *Drift Fence* (Lovering)

1936   *The Garden of Allah* (Boleslawsky); *Little Lord Fauntleroy* (Cromwell)

1937   *Find the Witness* (Selman); *Charlie Chan at the Olympics* (Humberstone); *The Slave Ship* (Garnett); *Danger, Love at Work* (Preminger); *Thank You, Mr. Moto* (Foster)

1938   *Walking down Broadway* (Foster); *Mr. Moto Takes a Chance* (Foster); *Time Out for Murder* (Humberstone); *Inside Story* (Cortez)

1939   *Mr. Moto's Last Warning* (Foster); *Chasing Danger* (Cortez); *Charlie Chan in Reno* (Foster); *Charlie Chan at Treasure Island* (Foster); *Charlie Chan in the City of Darkness* (Leeds); *The Honeymoon's Over* (Forde)

1940   *The Man Who Wouldn't Talk* (Burton); *Charlie Chan in Panama* (Foster); *Charlie Chan's Murder Cruise* (Forde); *Pier 13* (Forde); *Manhattan Heartbeat* (Burton); *Charlie Chan at the Wax Museum* (Shores); *Murder over New York* (Lachman)

1941   *Ride, Kelly, Ride* (Foster); *Scotland Yard* (Foster); *Man at Large* (Forde); *My Life with Caroline* (Milestone); *Private Nurse* (Burton); *Small Town Deb* (Schuster)

1942   *Who Is Hope Schuyler?* (Loring); *Castle in the Desert* (Lachman); *Right to the Heart* (Forde); *Berlin Correspondent* (Forde); *Dr. Renault's Secret* (Lachman)

1943   *Calling Dr. Death* (Le Borg)

1944   *Weird Woman* (Le Borg); *The Pearl of Death* (Neill)

1945   *The House of Fear* (Neill); *The Woman in Green* (Neill); *The Falcon in San Francisco* (Lewis)

1946   *The Michigan Kid* (Taylor)

1947   *The Big Fix* (Flood); *The Red Stallion* (Selander); *The Vigilante's Return* (Taylor)

1948   *Street Corner* (Kelley)

1952   *Navajo* (Bartlett)

1953   *Murder without Tears* (Beaudine); *Crazylegs* (Lyon); *Miss Robinson Crusoe* (Frenke)

1955   *Unchained* (Bartlett)

Publications

By MILLER: articles—

American Film (Washington, DC), July-August 1987.
American Cinematographer (Hollywood), September 1991.

On MILLER: article—

Birchard, Robert C., in *American Cinematographer* (Hollywood), May 1983.
Obituary in *Variety* (New York), 16 October 1974.

*   *   *

Virgil Miller, a pioneer in the film industry in lighting and cinematography, began his long career at Universal around 1913. He was hired by Universal head Carl Laemmle to establish an electrical lighting department because the studio was considering the use of artificial light to supplement the natural sunshine the industry had depended on since it moved to California. Neither Laemmle nor Miller realized the ultimate impact such a decision would have on filmmaking, for with the introduction of artificial lighting came the means to create a specific atmosphere and the ability to manipulate the look, and therefore the meaning, of a scene.

Miller began the new department by assembling small lighting packages of spots and small packages of broads, which produce a large area of soft, diffused light. He was then put in charge of teaching the other photographers about electrical lighting. Miller also became Universal's powder and explosives expert, a job which entailed small effects such as a glass exploding in a character's hand as though it had been shot out.

Miller's interests also extended to cinematography, and in 1915 he was put in charge of the camera department. Constantly experimenting with both lighting and photography, Miller soon gained a reputation for his "tricks." For example, he perfected a process shot where a dancer seemed to cavort in and around a champagne glass. In another film, a western, he was able to match a shot of three covered wagons to make it look as though there were twelve covered wagons. The director Elmer Clifton was so impressed with the tricks that he consistently requested Miller to be his cinematographer. Miller was also Lon Chaney, Sr.'s favorite cameraman.

Eventually, this talented cinematographer was employed by almost all of the major studios. In 1926, he began working at Warner Brothers. Soon after, he joined Paramount, where he was in charge of their camera department for over seven years. He also worked for David O. Selznick's studios, where he enjoyed the position of "superintendent of photography," which meant he was consulted about the cinematography on every film.

With his work as a cinematographer on some of the Charlie Chan and Mr. Moto mysteries, Miller became associated with a particular atmospheric style. The use of heavy, dark shadows and the sharp contrasts of light and dark helped to create a sinister or eerie effect, which has always been a code for mystery and horror films. When director Roy William Neill of Universal began the Sherlock Holmes film *The Pearl of Death*, he requested the services of Miller to create this moody effect. Miller found himself again employed at Universal.

Miller's final long-standing job was as the head cinematographer on Groucho Marx's television game show, *You Bet Your Life*. Though perhaps not as creative or significant as his film work, the job still had its interesting problems. Marx had poor eyesight and was sensitive to the large amount of light necessary for a television program. Miller had to adjust the light so as not to hurt Marx's eyes, yet still have enough to light the set. In addition, Miller had to find the exact spot for the camera so that light was not reflected in Marx's glasses. After six years with *You Bet Your Life*, Miller retired.

In 1953 Miller was nominated for an Academy Award for *Navajo*, which had an all-Indian cast. Though Miller was quite proud of *Navajo* and his nomination, the film, like its cinematographer, remains relatively unknown. Miller's filmography does not include many prestigious projects, yet he is an important historical figure for his pioneering work at Universal in setting up one of the first electrical lighting departments in Hollywood, and for his experiments in lighting effects and trick photography.

—Susan Doll

MINDADZE, Aleksandr

Writer. **Nationality:** Russian-Georgian. **Born:** Moscow, Soviet Union (now Russia), 28 April 1949. **Education:** Studied screenwriting at VGIK in Moscow. **Awards:** President of the Italian Senate's Gold Medal, Venice Film Festival, for *Plyumbum, ili opasnaya igra*, 1987; Alfred Bauer Award, Berlin International Film Festival, for *Sluga*, 1989; Silver Berlin Bear, Berlin International Film Festival, for *Pyesa dlia passazhira*, 1995; Nika Award for Best Script, for *Vremya tantsora*, 1998; Swissair/Crossair Special Prize, Locarno International Film Festival, for *Vremya tantsora*, 1998.

Films as Writer:

1976   *Vesyonnij prizyv* (*Spring Call*) (Pavel Lyubimov); *Slovo dlia zashchity* (*A Speech for the Defence*) (Vadim Abdrashitov)
1978   *Povorot* (*The Turning Point*) (Abdrashitov)
1980   *Okhota na lis* (*A Fox Hunt*) (Abdrashitov)
1982   *Ostanovilsya poyezd* (*The Train Stopped*) (Abdrashitov)
1984   *Parad planet* (*Parade of the Planets*) (Abdrashitov)
1986   *Plyumbum, ili opasnaya igra* (*Plumbum, or Dangerous Game*) (Abdrashitov)
1988   *Sluga* (*The Servant*) (Abdrashitov)
1991   *Armavir* (Abdrashitov)
1995   *Pyesa dlia passazhira* (*A Play for a Passenger*) (Abdrashitov)
1998   *Vremya tantsora* (*Time of the Dancer*) (Abdrashitov)

Publications:

On MINDADZE: books—

Galichenko, Nicholas, *Glasnost: Soviet Cinema Responds*, Austin, Texas, 1991.

*   *   *

A scrutiny of Aleksandr Mindadze's screenwriting work reveals a well-founded gloomy and pessimist world view. He has taken the challenging task of unearthing people's existential insecurities and uncovering displeasing and ominous features of social behavior. His work is the exact opposite of entertainment filmmaking, as he has cast aside any idealist illusions about human nature. He is particularly skilled in developing cerebral plots and unpleasant characters. It is for these features of his work that he enjoys the specific position of a highly respected maverick in Russian filmmaking.

With only one exception, the comedy *Vesyonnij prizyv* (1976), which he scripted for director Pavel Lyubimov, Mindadze's work is closely connected with director Vadim Abdrashitov. It is a screenwriter-director partnership which mirrors other established creative teams such as Eldar Ryazanov and Edvard Braginski in Russia, and Krzysztof Kieslowski and Krzysztof Piesiewicz in Poland.

Mindadze comes from a film family: his father was well-established scriptwriter Anatoli Grebnev. He studied screenwriting at VGIK and met Vadim Abdrashitov in the mid-1970s. Abdrashitov had also studied at VGIK in Mikhail Romm's director's class. Since that meeting, Mindadze and Abdrashitov have worked exclusively with each other, forming a team which collaborates so closely that it is not possible to determine what precisely is their individual input, although the scripts to Abdrashitov's films are regularly credited solely to Mindadze. According to film scholar Nicholas Galichenko, Mindadze and Abdrashitov have established themselves as "leading exponents of the rationalist trend in Soviet cinema, specializing in pictures that provoke viewers by exposing public and social problems." They have displayed a preference for simple plot-lines which evolve around subtle ethical conundrums, often exposing social sores and moral transgressions rarely approached by other filmmakers.

It is notable that Abdrashitov and Mindadze began their work at a time when the "cinema of moral anxiety" developed as a leading East European trend, and their early work can be described as a Russian extension of this otherwise more East Central European direction. Moral problems are in the center of their first collaboration, *Slovo dlia zashchity* (1976). In *Povorot* (1978), a husband and wife representing an ordinary Soviet couple knock down an old woman by accident while making a turn. The film focuses on the aftermath of the incident, showing the couple's apprehensive reaction. Unprepared to face the consequences, they try to bribe witnesses, and as a result grow estranged from each other.

Fantasy and magical realist elements have often been used by Mindadze and Abdrashitov, most notably *Okhota na lis* (1980) and *Parade of Planets* (1984). In the first film, some of the characters wear futuristic headsets and engage in an elaborate ritualistic game; in the latter the protagonists are drawn in symbolic maneuvers and fantastic journeys through time and space. The selective use of sci-fi elements is a device which enables Mindadze and Abdrashitov to appeal to the intellect rather than to the emotions of the audience.

The moral investigations of Abdrashitov and Mindadze preceded perestroika by several years. In the early 1980s they were already making films in the spirit of perestroika—strongly critical of serious moral and social problems. An example is *Ostanovilsya poyezd* (1982). The plot evolves around an investigator and a journalist, both investigating the same train crash, their inquiries impeded by the sluggishly indolent authorities and the meandering evasiveness of the locals, resulting in diverging interpretations of what really happened. The film is a unique investigation of epistemological riddles revealed in the dialectical relationship of categories like truth, conformity, and expostulation. It is a commentary on the existential reluctance of people to admit and therefore face unwanted realities.

The features which Abdrashitov and Mindadze made during perestroika proper (the second part of the 1980s) focused on issues of conformity and twisted morals. Their *Plyumbum* (1986), a film which depicted a reprehensibly amoral adolescent protagonist, caused a controversy, as critics read the portrayal of this allegorical "test-tube monster" as a sweeping generalization of the troubled status of Soviet society. The corrupt morals of the younger generation were also the subject matter of Abdrashitov and Mindadze's other perestroika film, *Sluga* (1988).

Abdrashitov is a Tatar by ethnic background, and Mindadze is half-Georgian. This may partially explain the team's interest in the traditional mores of the South of Russia and the former Soviet republics of the Caucasus. Their *Armavir* (1991) was set in the South of Russia. So was *Vremya Tantsora* (1998), the action of which takes place in an unnamed region in the South, with the clearly visible snowy peaks of the Caucasus in the background. The setting is contemporary but the story evolves around interpersonal rivalries, raising questions about the essence of cruelty, and juxtaposing ritualistic dancing to ritualistic violence, all this making the film yet another existential allegory.

—Dina Iordanova

MIRISCH, Walter

Producer. **Nationality:** American. **Born:** Walter Mortimer Mirisch in New York City, 8 November 1921. **Education:** Attended City College of New York; University of Wisconsin, Madison, B.A. 1942;

Walter Mirisch

Harvard Business School, Cambridge, Massachusetts, I.A. 1943. **Family:** Married Patricia Kahan, 1947, children: one daughter, two sons. **Career:** 1938–40—Skouras Theatres, and with Oriental Theatre Corporation, 1940–42, while in college; 1945—producer, Monogram; 1951—executive producer, Allied Artists; 1957—co-founder, with Marvin and Harold Mirisch, Mirisch Company: served as vice president in charge of production; 1973–77—president, Motion Picture Academy; 1998–99—executive producer, *The Magnificent Seven*, television series. **Awards:** Academy Award, for *In the Heat of the Night*, 1967; Irving G. Thalberg Award, 1977; Jean Hersholt Humanitarian Award, 1982. **Address:** The Mirisch Corporation, 100 Universal City Plaza, Universal City, CA 91608, U.S.A.

Films as Producer (selected list):

1947   *Fall Guy* (Le Borg)
1948   *I Wouldn't Be in Your Shoes* (Nigh)
1949   *Bomba the Jungle Boy* (Beebe)
1950   *The Hidden City* (*Bomba and the Hidden City*) (Beebe); *The Lost Volcano* (Beebe); *Bomba on Panther Island* (Beebe); *County Fair* (Beaudine)
1951   *Flight to Mars* (Selander); *Cavalry Scout* (Selander); *Elephant Stampede* (*Bomba and the Elephant Stampede*) (Beebe); *Rodeo* (Beaudine); *Fort Osage* (Selander)
1962   *Hiawatha* (Neumann); *Wild Stallion* (Collins); *The Lion Hunters* (*Bomba and the Lion Hunters*) (Beebe); *Flat Top* (Selander); *Bomba and the Jungle Girl* (Beebe); *African Treasure* (*Bomba and the African Treasure*) (Beebe)
1953   *The Maze* (Menzies) (exec)
1955   *An Annapolis Story* (*The Blue and the Gold*) (Siegel); *The Dark Avengers* (*The Warriors*) (Levin); *Wichita* (J. Tourneur)
1956   *The First Texan* (Haskin)
1957   *The Oklahoman* (Lyon); *The Tall Stranger* (Carr)
1958   *Man of the West* (A. Mann); *Fort Massacre* (Newman); *The Man in the Net* (Curtiz); *The Gunfight at Dodge City* (Newman)
1959   *The Horse Soldiers* (Ford); *Cast a Long Shadow* (Carr); **Some Like It Hot** (Wilder)
1960   *The Magnificent Seven* (J. Sturges); **The Apartment** (Wilder)
1961   **West Side Story** (Wise and Robbins) (exec); *By Love Possessed* (J. Sturges); *One, Two, Three* (Wilder)
1962   *Two for the Seesaw* (Wise); *The Great Escape* (Sturges)
1963   *Toys in the Attic* (Hill); *The Pink Panther* (Edwards)
1966   *Hawaii* (Hill)
1967   *In the Heat of the Night* (Jewison); *Fitzwilly* (Delbert Mann)
1969   *Sinful Davy* (Huston) (exec); *Some Kind of Nut* (Kanin)
1970   *Halls of Anger* (Bogart) (exec); *The Hawaiians* (Gries); *They Call Me MISTER Tibbs!* (Douglas) (exec)
1971   *The Organization* (Medford)
1972   *Scorpio* (Winner)
1974   *The Spikes Gang* (Fleischer); *Mr. Majestyk* (Fleischer)
1976   *Midway* (Smight)
1978   *Gray Lady Down* (Greene)
1979   *Same Time Next Year* (Mulligan); *The Prisoner of Zenda* (Quine); *Dracula* (Badham) (co)
1983   *Romantic Comedy* (Hiller) (co)
1993   *Trouble Shooters: Trapped Beneath the Earth* (May—for TV) (exec)
1996   *A Case for Life* (Laneuville—for TV)

Publications

By MIRISCH: articles—

Films and Filming (London), March 1972.
Screen International (London), 29 January 1977.

On MIRISCH: articles—

Film Daily, 28 October 1952.
Film Daily, 19 April 1968.

*   *   *

The enterprise and enthusiasm of Walter Mirisch carried his company, The Mirisch Corporation (which he formed with his brothers, Harold and Marvin), through an unprecedented commercial and critical success from its inception in 1957 throughout its heyday in the 1960s and early 1970s. His record as an independent producer is outstanding both as an Oscar winner and as a box-office champion.

Mirisch's background is an excellent illustration of the experience needed to become a successful producer. His entry into the motion-picture business came at the bottom level—as an usher in a New Jersey movie house. To this he added a solid education at the Harvard Business School and six years as one of the youngest men in film history ever to become an executive producer at an important studio (Allied Artists). Mirisch consistently and thoroughly learned the business from the ground up. When he ultimately formed his own company, he had been either a consumer, exhibitor, distributor, or producer of motion pictures nearly all his life.

Mirisch's career is of particular historical interest in that he represents both the old and new Hollywood. Although he began independent production just when the old studio system began its final decline and Hollywood was facing its more difficult days, his company succeeded. His level of education and independent production status are those associated with the days that followed the final collapse of the old system, but his ability to spot films that would appeal to a wide audience links him to the common touch associated with the old moguls of the 1930s and 1940s.

With Walter as chief of production, the Mirisch brothers demonstrated the qualities that made Hollywood what it was in its golden years: courage, independence, taste, and just enough craziness to put it all together and sell it. In order to do this, Mirisch aggressively courted the very best film directors (Ford, Wilder, Edwards, and Wise) and gave them well-written scripts and a first-rate production team. Then he left them alone to do what they did best—make good movies. The Mirisch Company was a well-organized group. It handled all behind-the-scenes business matters with skill, allowing the filmmakers to concentrate on only the film itself. In short, Mirisch accomplished what many today dream of: he ran his business with the efficiency of the old studios, but with the flexibility and daring of an independent unit. The company took the risk, and took it in a wide range of types of films. "We try to make movies that have mass appeal, yet are first-rate artistically and state a meaningful theme," said Mirisch.

The hallmark of the films made under the Mirisch banner is the ability to combine high-quality projects (which could win Oscars) with audience appeal. His work is a bright spot for American moviemaking during the 1960s, as his taste, imagination, and good business sense brought out a remarkable string of respected classics:

Billy Wilder's *Some Like It Hot*; *The Apartment*; *One, Two, Three* (and more); Robert Wise's *West Side Story*; Blake Edwards's *The Pink Panther*; Norman Jewison's *In the Heat of the Night* (for which he won the Oscar); and John Sturges's *The Great Escape*. Mirisch did not follow trends. He made unique projects that were themselves trendsetters, such as *The Pink Panther*, or were too unusual to be imitated, such as his remarkable string of productions from his long association with Wilder.

Mirisch is an example of a type that is more often associated with the late 1970s and early 1980s—the lifelong movie fan who enters the business. Nevertheless, instead of ravaging old movies for plots and remaking the classics, Mirisch signed up the people he had long admired and gave them the opportunity to make films. "To me, good taste means good taste in terms of writing, directing, acting, scoring, editing, and all the other phases of the picture business," said Mirisch, who saw the producer's role as helping the collaborative process to work smoothly. In private life Mirisch is known as a man who is dedicated to worthwhile charities and projects which further the appreciation of American movies. He has received the Irving Thalberg Award and Producer of the Year Award, among many others, and has served as a trustee of the American Film Institute, Filmax, and the Motion Picture Academy. He also as served four terms as president of the latter. Mirisch sums up his outstanding career as an independent producer by saying: "Since my early boyhood, I have been having a love affair with films, and it has been my great good fortune to spend most of my adult life in active pursuit of that affair. My ardor has never cooled, and I trust it never will."

—Jeanine Basinger

MITRA, Subrata

Cinematographer. **Nationality:** Indian. **Born:** Calcutta, 12 October 1930. **Education:** Trained in science. **Career:** 1950—assisted Jean Renoir on film *The River*; 1955—first film as cinematographer, *Pather Panchali*, first of several films for Satyajit Ray; 1963—first of several films for James Ivory, *The Householder*; visiting professor, Film and Television Institute. **Awards:** Padma Shri (awarded by the President of India), 1985.

Films as Cinematographer:

1955	*Pather Panchali* (*Father Panchali*) (Ray)
1956	*Aparajito* (*The Unvanquished*) (Ray)
1957	*Parash Pather* (Ray)
1958	*Jalsaghar* (*The Music Room*) (Ray)
1959	*Apur Sansar* (*The World of Apu*) (Ray)
1960	*Devi* (*The Goddess*) (Ray)
1962	*Kanchanganga* (Ray)
1963	*Mahangar* (*The Big City*) (Ray); *The Householder* (Ivory)
1964	*Charulata* (*The Lonely Wife*) (Ray)
1965	*Akash Kusum* (*Up in the Clouds*) (M. Sen); *Shakespeare Wallah* (Ivory)
1966	*Nayak* (*The Hero*) (Ray)
1968	*The Guru* (Ivory)
1970	*Bombay Talkie* (Ivory)
1986	*New Delhi Times* (Sharma)

Publications

By MITRA: article—

Montage, July 1966.

On MITRA: article—

Owen, Derek, "1159 Subrata Mitra," in *Film Dope* (Nottingham), March 1990.

* * *

Subrata Mitra is usually associated with Satyajit Ray's films, of which he worked as cinematographer on as many as ten from *Pather Panchali* to *Nayak*, spanning about 14 years. They parted ways in 1967, probably due to Ray's desire to control all aspects of filmmaking. Mitra has since directed photography on four outstanding Indo-American films, James Ivory's *The Householder*, *Shakespeare Wallah*, *Bombay Talkie*, and *The Guru*. But it was Ray who elevated him from an amateur still photographer to an ace director of photography in *Pather Panchali*, which remains the most lyrical of his works. To help create an illusion of reality by naturalistic illumination, he introduced "bounced" lighting in Ray's *Aparajito* by such a simple and inexpensive device as a white outstretched cloth, which achieved a soft shadowless diffusion. In the early 1960s, while shooting Ray's *Devi* and *Kanchanganga* he dispensed with bounced lighting and developed instead a soft light system in *Charulata* to achieve the same quality. In Ray's films of the 1950s, he developed the Arriflex-Nagra combination, for image and sound, respectively, which later became the standard film equipment in India. He also pioneered the use of halogen lights for shooting *The Guru*.

Mitra does not believe, however, that the excellence of a film is "terribly dependent" on its technical quality, because "it is not the lens in the camera that really matters but the eye at the other side of it." This faith in the supremacy of the artist over his artefact has been borne out amply in many of his films. His use of dolly shots, e.g., in the sequence of Durga's death in a stormy night (*Pather Panchali*), of varying cinema angles with limited number of cameras, e.g., in photographing the *ghats* of Varanasi in *Aparajito*, and the jerky camera movement in *New Delhi Times*, will remain examples of excellent cinematography by any standard. Official recognition came very late to this self-schooled wizard of Indian cinematography. Additionally, his competence in playing the sitar was used by Renoir in a solo piece for the title music of *The River*, and by Ray for composing additional sitar pieces in *Pather Panchali*.

—Bibekananda Ray

MIYAGAWA, Kazuo

Cinematographer. **Nationality:** Japanese. **Born:** Kyoto City, 25 February 1908. **Education:** Studied Japanese ink painting. **Career:** 1926–30—worked in Nikkatsu Kyoto Studio laboratory; 1930—became assistant cameraman in same studio; 1935—first film as cinematographer, *Ochiyo's Umbrella*; taught at Osaka Art College.

Awards: Japanese Academy Award, for *Banished Orin*, 1977, and *MacArthur's Children*, 1984; Imperial Order of Culture, 1978; special tribute and retrospective screenings, American Academy of Motion Picture Arts and Sciences, 1981. **Died:** 7 August 1999, in Tokyo, Japan, of kidney failure.

Films as Cinematographer:

1935   *Ochiyo-gasa* (*Ochiyo's Umbrella*) (Ozaki); *Komoriuta Bushu-dako* (*Lullaby Bushu's Kite*) (Miyata); *Senjin* (*Battle Dust*) (Ogata)

1936   *Ittouryu shinan* (*The Teaching of the Ittou Style*) (Ishibashi); *Gokuraku hanayome-juku* (*The Paradise Bride's School*) (Ogata); *Onshuh junreiuta* (*Pilgrimage Song of Grace and Grudge*) (Kumita)

1937   *Ochiyo toshigoro* (*The Prime of Ochiyo's Life*) (Suganuma); *Hiryuh no ken* (*Sword of Flying Dragon*) (Inagaki)

1938   *Muhoumono Ginpei* (*Ginpei the Outlaw*) (Inagaki); *Kurama Tengu: Kakubei-jishi no maki* (*Kurama Tengu: The Book of Kakubei's Lion Club*) (Makin and Matsuda); *Shusse Taikou-ki* (*Toyotomi's Record of Promotion*) (Inagaki); *Yami no Kageboushi* (*Shadow of Darkness*) (Inagaki); *Jigoku no mushi* (*Hell's Worm*) (Inagaki); *Mazou* (*Magic Statue*) (Inagaki)

1939   *Ibaragi Ukon* (Inagaki); *Kesa to Moritou* (*Kesa and Moritou*) (Makino); *Sonnou sonjuku* (*Village School of Emperor Supporters*) (Inagaki); *Rougoku no hanayome* (*Prison Bride*) (Arai) (2 parts); *Gaou utaggasen* (*The Geese and Ducks' Singing Contest*) (Makino)

1940   *Miyamoto Musashi* (Ingawa—3 parts); *Shinrei Jakouneko* (Arai—2 parts)

1941   *Kurama Tengu: Satsuma no misshi* (*Kurama Tengu: Secret Agent from Satsuma*) (Suganuma)

1942   *Mampou hattenshi: Umi no gouzoku* (*The Development History of the Southern Sea: Tribes of the Ocean*) (Arai)

1943   *Muhoumatsu no issho* (*The Rickshaw Man*; *The Life of Reckless Matsu*) (Inagaki)

1944   *Dohyou matsuri* (*Sumo Festival*) (Marune); *Kodachi o tsukau onna* (*A Woman Using a Small Sword*) (Marune); *Kakute kamikaze wa fuku* (*Thus the Divine Wind Arrives*) (Matsuda and Tateoka)

1945   *Toukai Suiko-den* (*Toukai's Suiko Story*) (Ito); *Siago no jouitou* (*The Last Party of Chauvinists*) (Inagaki)

1946   *Tobira o hiraku onna* (*The Woman Opening the Door*) (Kimura); *Tebukuro o nugasu otoko* (*The Man Taking Off His Gloves*) (Mori); *Yari-odori gojusan-tsugi* (*Spear Dance of 53 Stations*) (Mori); *Soushi gekijou* (*Political Theatre*) (Inagaki)

1947   *Akuma no kanpai* (*Devil's Toast*) (Marune)

1948   *Te o tsunaqu kora* (*Children Hand in Hand*) (Inagaki); *Koushoku gonin onna* (*Saikaku's Five Women*) (Nobuchi); *Otoko o sabaku onna* (*A Woman Who Convicts Men*) (Sasaki); *Sonoyo no bouken* (*That Night Adventure*) (Yasuda); *Kuroun kaidou* (*A Line of Black Clouds*) (Matsuda and Mori)

1949   *Niizuma kaigi* (*New Wives' Conference*) (Chiba); *Yuhrei ressha* (*Ghost Train*) (Nobuchi); *Onna goroshi abura jigoku* (*Oil Hell of Killing Women*) (Nobuchi)

1949–50   *Hebihime douchuh* (*Princess Snake's Travels*) (Kimura and Marine—2 parts)

1950   *Ai no sanga* (*Mountain and River of Love*) (Koishi); *Jougasaki no ame* (*Jougasaki's Rain*) (Tanaka); **Rashomon** (Kurosawa)

1951   *Kenran taru satsujin* (*Brilliant Murder*) (Kado); *Oyu-sama* (*Miss Oyu*) (Mizoguchi); *Omagatsuji no ketto* (*Omagatsuji's Duel*) (Mori)

1952   *Nishijin no shimai* (*Sisters of Nishijin*) (Yoshimura); *Taki no shiraito* (*Water Magician, or The White Thread of the Waterfall*) (Nobuchi); *Sutobi kago* (*Express Sedan*) (Makino)

1953   *Senba-zuru* (*A Thousand Cranes*) (Yoshimura); **Ugetsu monogatari** (*Ugetsu*; *Tales of a Pale and Mysterious Moon after the Rain*) (Mizoguchi); *Yukubo* (*Desire*) (Yoshimura); *Gion bayashi* (*Gion Festival Music*) (Mizoguchi)

1954   **Sansho dayu** (*Sansho the Bailiff*) (Mizoguchi); *Uwasa no onna* (*The Woman of the Rumor*) (Mizoguchi); *Chikamatsu monogatari* (*A Story from Chikamatsu*) (Mizoguchi)

1955   *Jinanbou garasu* (*Second Son Crow*) (Hirotsu); *Tenka o nerau bishounen* (*Handsome Boy Trying to Rule the World*) (Arai); *Shin Heike monogatari* (*New Tales of the Taira Clan*) (Mizoguchi); *Baku wa Toukichiroh* (*I Am Tokichiro*) (Mori)

1956   **Akasen chitai** (*Street of Shame*) (Mizoguchi); *Yoru no kawa* (*Night River*) (Yoshimura); *Shin Heike monogatari: Shizuka to Yoshitsune* (*New Tale of Genji: Shuzuka and Yoshitsune*)

1957   *Suzaku-mon* (*Suzaku Gate*) (Mori); *Yoru no cho* (*Night Butterflies*) (Yoshimura); *Meido no kaoyaku* (*Hell's Boss*) (Murayama)

1958   *Tsukihime keizu* (*The Origin of Princess Moon*) (Watanabe); *Akadou Suzunosuke* (Mori); *Enjo* (*Conflagration*) (Ichikawa); *Benten kozou* (*Benten Boy*) (Ito)

1959   *Onna to kauzoku* (*Woman and Pirates*) (Ito); *Kagi* (*Odd Obsession*) (Ichikawa); *Ukigusa* (*Floating Weeds*; *The Duckweed Story*; *Drifting Weeds*) (Ozu)

1960   ''Koi o wasureta onna'' (''The Woman Who Forgot Love'') ep. of *Jokei* (*Women's Scroll*) (Yoshimura); *Bonchi* (*Young Lord*) (Ichikawa); *Kirare Yosaburou* (*Slashed Yosaburo*) (Ito); *Ototo* (*Her Brother*) (Ichikawa); *Yojimbo* (*The Bodyguard*) (Kurosawa)

1961   *Konki* (*Marriage Time*) (Yoshimura); *Kutsukake Tokojiro* (*Tokojiro of Katsukake*) (Ikehiro); *Akumyo* (*Bad Names*) (Tanaka—2 parts)

1962   *Hakai* (*The Outcast*) (Ichikawa)

1963   *Daisan no Akumyo* (*The Third Bad Name*) (Tanaka); *Jokei kazoku* (*Women Family*) (Misumi); *Zouhei monogatari* (*Low-Rank Soldiers*) (Ikehiro); *Echizen take ningyo* (*Bamboo Doll of Echizen*) (Yoshimura)

1964   *Zatouichi senryo kubi* (*Zatoichi: A Thousand Dollar Price on His Head*) (Ikehiro); *Zenin no odori* (*The Money Dance*) (Ichikawa); *Suruga yuhkyou-den: Yabure takka* (*Gamblers' Story of Saruga: Broken Iron Fire*) (Tanaka)

1965   *Akai shuriken* (*Red Throwing Knives*) (Tanaka); **Tokyo Orimpikku** (*Tokyo Olympiad*) (Ichikawa and others); *Akumyo niwaka* (*Suddenly Bad Names*) (Tanaka); *Akumyo muteki* (*Invincible Bad Names*) (Tanaka)

1966   *Irezumi* (*Tattoo*) (Masumura); *Akumyo zakura* (*Bad Names' Cherry Blossoms*) (Tanaka); *Zatouichi no uta ga kikoeru* (*Zatouichi's Song Is Heard*) (Tanaka)

1967   *Chiisana tobosha* (*The Little Runaway*) (Kinugasa and Bocharov); *Aru koroshiya* (*A Murderer*) (Masumura); *Zatouichi rouyaburi* (*Zatouichi Breaking Out of Prison*)

(Yamamoto); *Aru koroshiya no kagi* (*Key of a Murderer*) (Mori)

1968 *Tomuraishi tachi* (*Undertakers*) (Misumi); *Koudoukan hamonjou* (*Judo School Expulsion Letter*) (Inoue); *Zatouichi hatashijou* (*Zatouichi Challenge Letter*) (Yasuda)

1969 *Shutsugoku yonjuhachi jikan* (*48-Hour Prison Break*) (Mori); *Shirikurae Magoichi* (*The Magoichi Saga*) (Misumi); *Koroshiya o barase* (*Kill the Killer*) (Ikehiro); *Ono no sumu yakata* (*Devil's Temple*) (Misumi); *Shiriboe Sonichi* (*Barking-Donkey Sonichi*) (Misumi)

1970 *Zatouichi to Yojimbo* (*Zatouichi Meets Yojimbo*) (Okamoto); *Zatouichi abare himatsuri* (*Zatouichi: Wild Fire Festival*) (Misumi)

1971 *Chinmoku* (*Silence*) (Shinoda)

1972 *Mushukunin Mikoshin no Joukichi* (*Outlaw Joukichi of Mikoshin*) (Ikehiro—2 parts); *Kozure ohkami* (*Wolf with Child*) (Saito)

1973 *Goyoukiba: Kamisori Hanzo jigokuzeme* (*Police Fang: Razor Hanzo's Torture in Hell*) (Masumura)

1974 *Akumyo nawabari arashi* (*Bad Names' Breaking of Territories*) (Masumura)

1976 *Yoba* (*The Old Woman Ghost*) (Imai)

1977 *Hanare goze Orin* (*Banished Orin*) (Shinoda)

1980 *Kagemusha* (*The Shadow Warrior; The Double*) (Kurosawa); *Akuma-to* (*Devil's Island*) (Shinoda)

1981 *Sonezaki shinjuh* (*Double Suicide of Sonezaki*) (Kurisaki)

1984 *Setouchi shounen yakyu-dan* (*MacArthur's Children*) (Shinoda)

1985 *Yari no Gonza* (*Gonza the Spearman*) (Shinoda)

1989 *Maihime* (*The Dancer*) (Shinoda) (co)

Publications

By MIYAGAWA: articles—

Sight and Sound (London), Summer 1979.
"Kazuo Miyagawa: Japan's Master Cinematographer," interview with Rob Edelman, in *Films in Review* (New York), June/July 1981.

On MIYAGAWA: articles—

American Cinematographer (Hollywood), May 1981.
Film Dope (Nottingham), March 1990.
Post Script, vol. 11, no. 1, 1991.
Obituary in *Variety* (New York), 16 August 1999.

*   *   *

Kazuo Miyagawa was, quite simply, Japan's preeminent cinematographer. Commencing in the 1930s, he worked with some of his country's foremost directors, including Kenji Mizoguchi, Yasujiro Ozu, Akira Kurosawa, Kon Ichikawa, Daisuke Ito, Hiroshi Inagaki, and Masahiro Shinoda, and his credits include some of the all time greatest Japanese films, including *Rashomon, Ugetsu, Sansho the Bailiff, Street of Shame, Yojimbo, Floating Weeds, Odd Obsession*, and *Kagemusha*.

Beginning his study of cinematography in 1926, after several years as an art student, Miyagawa was particularly impressed by the high-contrast lighting used in the German expressionist films of the era. Starting as a focus puller and assistant cameraman at the Nikkatsu Kyoto Studio laboratory, Miyagawa utilized his knowledge of film chemistry to experiment with the composition of film stock and the degree of exposure before shooting. Thus, he was able to determine the optimum exposure despite the varied physical conditions of location shooting; in fact, he did not even work with a light meter until *Rashomon*, in 1950.

Between 1935 and 1943, Miyagawa was in charge of second-unit photography and special effects at the Nikkatsu Studio. His first great success as chief cinematographer came in 1943, with his work on Hiroshi Inagaki's *The Rickshaw Man*, in which his ambitious camerawork captures the vivid images of the life of a rough but straightforward rickshaw man in a small city, using montage to recreate the flow of time. While he has attributed his success to the traditionally high standards of the studio's cinematographers and camera mechanics—"Working in the film lab taught me the basics, the fundamental part of making pictures," he once explained—he also noted, "It was my training in [Japanese] ink painting that really taught me how to see."

Indeed, it was Miyagawa's early study of this art form that gave him the understanding of subtle shadings which was evident in his black-and-white films. His fluid camera movements, particularly the long takes in Mizoguchi's films, demonstrate his knowledge of the Japanese traditional *emakinomo* scroll painting style. In order to satisfy Mizoguchi's demand to draw out the tense moments of highly dramatic performances, Miyagawa conceived the technique of suspenseful long takes, which capture highly dramatic performances without interruptions. He used many crane shots to create the mysterious atmosphere of *Ugetsu* and the romantic escape scenes of *A Story from Chikamatsu*. Long and complicated pannings such as those of the garden scene and the last scene of *Ugetsu* and the ending of *Sansho the Bailiff* are breathtakingly inventive. Further, in the latter film, he experimented with shooting the entire film in counter-light, to create the cold image suggested by the subject of slavery.

Miyagawa also contributed his dynamic camera style to Kurosawa's work. Utilizing the light reflecting directly on a mirror, he captured in bright summer daylight the surging emotions of the characters of *Rashomon*. The image of sunlight flickering behind the trees became legendary. In *Yojimbo* Miyagawa used telephoto lenses to successfully convey the powerful images of swordplay in the swirling dust. He also used telephoto lenses effectively in Ichikawa's *Tokyo Olympiad* to capture the poetic moments of physical movement, often in combination with slow motion. Miyagawa's bold use of the CinemaScope screen is evident in other successful films of Ichikawa. Particularly important was Miyagawa's technique of inventing the "silver tone" in the chemical process to create a greenish-gray tone, appropriate for the turn-of-the-century atmosphere of *Her Brother*.

Miyagawa's sensitive and ingenious approach to the specific tones of each of his color films is evident in his work for Ozu, Ito, Shinoda, Kouzaburo Yoshimura, Masuzo Yasumura, and others. He studied each type of film stock for specific color effects according to the subject. For *Floating Weeds*, the only Ozu film on which Miyagawa worked, he used a light color scheme to recreate the atmosphere of a town in southern Japan. The tension of the scene of a hard rainstorm under which a couple quarrels from opposite sides of a street was accentuated by Miyagawa's usage of a large light source with the dripping water captured in counter-light. The combination of bold colors and lyrical night scenes of Kyoto in Yoshimura's *Night River*, the recreation of the world of Kabuki and the bright-colored woodprints in Ito's *Benten Boy* and Masumura's *Tattoo*, the magnificent land-scape colors in Shinoda's *Silence* and *Banished Orin*, and the dazzling color spectacle of Kurosawa's *Kagemusha* are other highly acclaimed examples of Miyagawa's skill.

The cinematographer was employed by the same studio between 1926 and 1971, working elsewhere only twice: on *Yojimbo*, shot at the Toho Studio; and *Tokyo Olympiad*, produced independently. Before his death, his more notable credits were *Kagemusha*, and Shinoda's *Gonza the Spearman* and *MacArthur's Children*. He remained professionally active into his eighties. ''A director and cameraman are like husband and wife,'' Miyagawa once declared. ''Even though they may fight, all their films are their offspring.'' He added, proudly, ''I am a cinematographer. I've never had any ambition to become a director. A film is not one individual's method of personal expression but a matter of teamwork, a cooperative venture.''

—Kyoko Hirano, updated by Rob Edelman

MNOUCHKINE, Alexandre

Producer. **Nationality:** Russian and French. **Born:** Leningrad, USSR, 10 February 1908. Took French citizenship in 1930. **Family:** Married 1) June Hannen; two daughters, Ariane and Joelle; 2) actress Simone Renant. **Career:** 1932—administrator at Majestic films; 1938—first film as producer *Alerte en Méditerranée* (Léo Joannon); 1945—founded with Georges Dancigers and Francis Cosne Les Films Ariane, named after his daughter; 1986—Films Ariane acquired by Cora-Reveillon group, which in 1988 becomes Les Editions Mondiales Révcom; 1987—appeared as Pattos in *Cronaca di una morte annunciata*; 1989—elected president of the Académie des arts et technique du cinéma. **Awards:** Academy Awards, *Préparez vos Mouchoirs*, 1977, *Cinema Paradiso*, 1989; Cesar Award, *La Balance*, 1982. **Died:** In Paris, 3 April 1993.

Films as Producer or Coproducer:

1938   *Alerte en Méditerranée* (*S.O.S. Mediterranean*) (Joannon)
1939   *L'Emigrante* (Joannon)
1945   *Tant que je vivrai* (de Baroncelli)
1946   *Le Destin s'amuse* (Reinert)
1947   *Non coupable* (Décoin); *Les Condamnés* (Lacombe)
1948   *L'Aigle a deux têtes* (*Eagle with Two Heads*) (Cocteau); *Bal Cupidon* (Sauvajon)
1949   *Les Parents terribles* (*The Storm Within*) (Jean Cocteau); *Julie de Carneilhan* (Manuel); *Mon ami Sainfoin* (Sauvajon)
1950   *L'Homme de joie* (Grangier); *L'Amant de paille* (Grangier)
1951   *Le Cap de l'Espérance* (Bernard)
1952   *Fanfan la Tulipe* (*Fearless Little Soldier*) (Christian-Jaque)
1953   *Lucrèce Borgia* (*Lucrezia Borgia*) (Christian-Jaque); *Viaggio in Italia* (*L'Amour est le plus fort*; *Journey to Italy*) (Rossellini)
1954   *Madame du Barry* (Christian-Jaque)
1955   *La Madelon* (Boyer)
1956   *Le Retour de Don Camillo* (Duvivier); *Si tous les gars du monde* (*Race for Life*) (Christian-Jaque)

1957   *Une Parisienne* (Michel Boisrond); *Les Aventures de Till l'Espiègle* (*The Bold Adventure*) (Philipe); *Club de femmes* (Habib)
1958   *La Loi, c'est la loi* (Christian-Jaque)
1959   *Babette s'en va-t-en guerre* (*Babette Goes to War*) (Christian-Jaque); *Rue des prairies* (de la Patellière)
1960   *I Delfini* (Maselli); *Fantasma a Roma* (*Les Joyeux Fantômes*) (Pietrangeli)
1961   *L'Amant de cinq jours* (*The Five-Day Lover*) (de Broca); *Cartouche* (*Swords of Blood*) (de Broca); *Jessica* (*La Sage femme, le curé et le bon Dieu*) (Negulesco); *Arrivano i Titani* (*Les Titans*) (Tessari)
1963   *Mare Matto* (Castellani)
1964   *L'Homme de Rio* (*L'Uomo di Rio*; *The Man from Rio*) (de Broca); *The Train* (Frankenheimer)
1965   *Les Tribulations d'un Chinois en Chine* (*Up to His Ears*) (de Broca)
1967   *Vivre pour Vivre* (*Live for Life*) (Lelouch); *Mise à sac* (*Pillaged*) (Alain Cavalier)
1968   *La Vie, l'amour, la mort* (*Love, Life, Death*) (Lelouch); *Les Gauloises bleues* (Cournot); *La Chamade* (*Heartbeat*) (Cavalier); *Une Infinie tendresse* (Jallaud)
1969   *L'Américain* (Bozzuffi); *Un Homme qui me plaît* (*Love Is a Funny Thing*) (Lelouch)
1970   *Le Voyou* (*The Crook*; *Storia di una Canaglia*) (Lelouch); *La Poudre d'escampette* (*Touch and Go*) (de Broca)
1972   *Chère Louise* (*Louise*) (de Broca); *L'Aventure, c'est l'aventure* (Lelouch)
1973   *Le Magnifique* (*How to Destroy the Reputation of the Greatest Secret Agent*) (de Broca); *1789* (Ariane Mnouchkine); *L'Emmerdeur* (*The Pain in the Neck*) (Molinaro)
1974   *Stavisky* (Resnais); *Vous ne l'emporterez pas au paradis* (Dupont-Midy)
1975   *L'Incorrigible* (de Broca); *Monsieur Albert* (Renard); *Adieu Poulet* (*So Long Copper*) (Granier-Deferre)
1977   *Tendre Poulet* (*Dear Detective*) (de Broca); *Un Autre homme et une autre chance* (*Simon et Sarah*) (Lelouch)
1978   *Préparez vos mouchoirs* (*Get out Your Handkerchiefs*) (Blier); *Le Cavaleur* (*The Skirt Chaser*) (de Broca); *L'Homme en colère* (Pinoteau)
1979   *On a volé la cuisse de Jupiter* (de Broca); *Cappotto di astrakan* (*The Persian Lamb Coat*) (Vicario)
1981   *Le Professionnel* (Lautner); *Psy* (de Broca); *Garde à vue* (*Under Suspicion*) (Miller); *T'empêches tout le monde de dormir* (Lauzier)
1982   *La Balance* (*The Nark*) (Swaim); *Pauline à la plage* (Rohmer)
1983   *Le Marginal* (*The Outsider*) (Deray); *La Vie est un roman* (*Life Is a Bed of Roses*) (Resnais)
1984   *L'Amour à mort* (Resnais); *Les Nuits de pleine lune* (*Full Moon in Paris*) (Rohmer); *Staline* (Aurel)
1985   *Hold-up* (Arcady); *Tranches de vie* (Leterrier)
1986   *Der Name der Rose* (*The Name of the Rose*) (Annaud); *Ginger e Fred* (Fellini); *Rue du départ* (Gatlif)
1987   *Cronaca di una morte annunciata* (*Chronicle of a Death Foretold*) (Rossi) (+ role as Pattos); *Dernier Eté à Tanger* (Acardy); *Exploits d'un jeune Don Juan* (Mingozza); *Famiglia* (Ettore Scola); *Flag* (Santi); *Les Fous de Bassan* (*In the Shadow of the Wind*) (Yves Simoneau); *Giono Prima* (*Control*) (Montaldo); *Ennemis intimes* (Amar); *Oeil au beurre noir* (Meynard)

1989 *Nuovo cinema paradiso* (*Cinema Paradiso*) (Tornatore); *La Revolution française: Les années lumiere* (co; Enrico and Heffron); *L'Ami retrouvé* (Schatzberg); *Vanille Française* (Oury); *Ague di Primavera* (*Torrents of Spring*) (Skolimowski)

1990 *Au Bonheur des chiens* (Tessori)

1991 *Afraid of the Dark* (Peploe); *Rue Saint Sulpice* (Lewin); *Impromptu* (Lapine)

1992 *Becoming Colette* (Huston); *Rey Pasmado* (*The King Struck Dumb*) (Uribe); *Map of the Human Heart* (Ward); *Sarafina!* (Roodt)

1993 *Nuit Sacrée* (Klotz); *A l'Heure ou les grandes fauves vont boire* (*When the Jungle Cats Go to Drink*) (Jolivet); *Ruptures* (Citti); *Una Pura Formalita* (*Une simple formalité*; *A Simple Formality*) (Tornatore)

1994 *Prince of Jutland* (Axel); *Le Colonel Chabert* (Angelo); *La Prédiction* (Ryazanov)

Publications

By MNOUCHKINE: articles—

Film Français (Paris), no. 1837, December 1980; no. 1976, January 1984; no. 2000, August 1984; no. 2292, April 1990.
Cinématographe (Paris), no. 100, May 1984.
Première (Paris), no. 145, April 1989.

On MNOUCHKINE: articles—

Cinéma Français (Paris), no. 10, 1977.
Film Français (Paris), no. 1843, January 1981; no. 2449, April 1993; nos. 2453/4, May 1993.
Cinéma, no. 293, May, 1983.
"Alexandre Mnouchkine and Georges Dancigers," in *Les Producteurs* (Paris), 1986,
Mills, Nancy, "Lights, Action, Revolution," in *American Film*, October 1989.
Screen International, no. 904, April 1993.
Obituary in *New York Times*, 7 April 1993.
Obituary in *Variety* (New York), 12 April 1993.
Facts on File, 15 April 1993.
Classic Images, no. 215, May 1993.
Studio Magazine, no. 73, May 1993.

*   *   *

After fleeing to Paris from Stalinist Russia, Alexandre Mnouchkine took French citizenship and found work as a props man with René Clair. By 1932, his boundless enthusiasm for filmmaking and organizational skills saw him installed as administrator at Majestic films, and by 1938, he had gained his first production credits for Léo Joannon's action-packed sea drama, *Alerte en Mediterranée*. With the relaunch of French filmmaking after the Occupation, Mnouchkine joined with fellow emigré Georges Dancigers and Francis Cosne to create Les Films Ariane which remained an influential force in French film production for over forty years.

As chief executive of Ariane, Mnouchkine has been identified with over one hundred films, though his individual production credits are considerably fewer. In practice he and Dancigers worked closely together, and although occasionally one or the other took sole responsibility for a given film, they were more often than not coproducers. As a relatively small company, Ariane was frequently involved in coproductions, largely in France and in Italy, but also in Canada, notably for Claude Pinoteau's *L'Homme en colère* (1978), Alexandre Arcady's *Hold-up* (1985) and Yves Simoneau's *Les Fous de Bassan* (1987). In those instances where Ariane was the moving force, Mnouchkine and Dancigers committed themselves completely to the production, from the script to the publicity launch.

Although recognizing the undoubted value of stars to a film's success, their prime consideration was always a quality scenario. Rather than deal with ready-made scripts, they invited treatment of a given subject and were prepared not only to invest considerable sums in these commissions, but also to abandon a film at the shooting stage if they were unhappy. Though there were failures, the impressive list of successes reflects their shrewd judgement of public taste, their instinct for a good script, and their insistence that quality should never be compromised. Over the years an array of directors and stars enhanced their own careers in films either produced, coproduced or in part financed by the Ariane Company: the names of Jean Cocteau, Philippe de Broca, Julien Duvivier, Claude Lelouch, Claude Miller, Bob Swain, Alain Resnais, Eric Rohmer, Edouard Molinaro or Bertrand Blier testify to the rich diversity amongst directors, while an equally impressive roll-call of stars includes Gérard Philipe, Fernandel, Jean Gabin, Gérard Depardieu, Jean-Paul Belmondo, Michel Piccoli, Philipe Noiret, Michel Simon, Lina Ventura, Brigitte Bardot, Annie Girardot, Catherine Deneuve, Gina Lollobrigida and Martine Carol.

The early link with Cocteau was a fortunate beginning: Dancigers produced *L'Aigle à deux têtes* (1948) and Mnouchkine and Cosne, *Les Parents terribles* (1949). The fifties brought comedies with Gilles Grangier (*L'Homme de joie*, 1950, and *L'Amant de paille*, 1950) and Julien Duvivier (*Le Retour de Don Camillo*, 1956), while Gérard Philipe was given the opportunity to direct himself as the swashbuckling hero of *Les Aventures de Till l'Espiègle* (1957). However, the most fruitful association in this decade came with Christian-Jaque for whom Mnouchkine and Dancigers produced a series of popular romantic adventures. The first was the hugely successful *Fanfan la Tulipe* (1952), which brought together Gérard Philipe and Gina Lollobrigida in the first of many Franco-Italian coproductions. Equally colourful period costume dramas followed in which Jaque displayed his wife Martine Carol as the lead in *Lucrèce Borgia* (1953) and *Madame du Barry* (1954). After *Si Tous les gars du monde* (1956), a dramatic story scripted by Henri Clouzot about a stricken fishing boat, Jaque returned to more typical territory with lightweight vehicles for Fernandel (*La Loi, c'est la loi*, 1958) and Brigitte Bardot (*Babette s'en va-t-en guerre*, 1959).

The cost-cutting production methods of the New Wave movement left Mnouchkine and Dancigers unmoved. In the sixties and seventies their instincts proved correct with box-office successes directed by Philippe de Broca and Claude Lelouch. They kept faith with de Broca after the failed romantic comedy *L'Amant de cinq jours* (1961) and went on to produce a series of highly popular, often tongue-in-cheek, action films set in exotic locations, in which Jean-Paul Belmondo teamed up with attractive female co-stars: Claudia Cardinale in *Cartouche* (1961); Françoise Dorléac in *L'Homme de Rio* (1964); Ursula Andress in *Les Tribulations d'un Chinois en Chine* (1965) and in 1975 with Geneviève Bujold for *L'Incorrigible*. Under the Ariane umbrella, de Broca also directed the desert war drama, *La Poudre d'escampette* (1970) with Michel Piccoli; the sentimental *Chère Louise* (1972) with Jeanne Moreau; and romantic comedies starring

Annie Girardot and Philippe Noiret: *Tendre Poulet* (1977) and *On a volé la cuisse de Jupiter* (1979), while in *Le Cavaleur* (1978) Girardot was joined by Danielle Darrieux. The final de Broca/Ariane production was a gentle satire on group psychotherapy, *Psy* (1981).

The association with Lelouch brought romantic dramas which were essentially thematic variations on *Un homme et une femme*, largely differentiated by their locations and leading players. In *Vivre pour vivre* (1967), political and emotional involvements tested Yves Montand and Annie Girardot; in *Un Homme qui me plaît* (1969), Girardot and Belmondo enjoyed a chance encounter in America; in *Un Autre homme, une autre chance* (1977), James Caan and Geneviève Bujold starred in a virtual remake of *Un Homme et une femme* given an American setting. Other films included the portrait of a murderer (*La Vie, l'amour, la mort*, 1968); a gangster film with Lino Ventura (*L'Aventure, c'est l'aventure*, 1972) and Jean-Louis Trintignant as a crooked lawyer in *Le Voyou* (1977). The decade also saw the production of Resnais' political drama *Stavisky* (1974), Blier's Oscar-winning comedy *Préparez vos mouchoirs* (1978) with Gérard Depardieu as the husband seeking ways to dispel his wife's depression, and a filmed performance of Ariane Mnouchkine's documentary play *1789*.

Among the more notable films in the eighties, were Claude Miller's taut psychological thriller *Garde à vue* (1981), Bob Swain's award-winning Parisian gangster story, *La Balance* (1982), and Jacques Deray's *Le Marginal* (1983) with Belmondo as the tough detective investigating drug dealers.

Although largely associated with popular entertainment films, Ariane's support for more highbrow productions is evidenced by the company's backing for Alain Resnais' *Stavisky* (1974), *La Vie est un roman* (1983) and *L'Amour à mort* (1984), and for Eric Rohmer's *Pauline à la plage* (1982) and *Les Nuits de pleine lune* (1984).

After suffering a serious heart attack in 1981, Mnouchkine resigned as head of Ariane, but continued as a producer and production adviser. His final credits included Jean-Jacque Annaud's fourteenth-century mystery thriller *Der Name der rose* (1986), the historical reconstruction *La Revolution française* (1989), Guiseppe Tornatore's nostalgic *Cinema paradiso* (1989), Eldar Ryazanov's tale of fortune-telling, *La Prédiction* (1994), while his Russian location experience served Yves Angelo for *Le Colonel Chabert* (1994). It was during the shooting of Tornatore's thriller *Una pura formalita* (1993) that "Sania," as Alexandre Mnouchkine was affectionately known, suffered his fatal illness. His life-long partner, Georges Dancigers, survived him by barely seven months, but their joint Ariane legacy leaves a lasting monument of well-produced films.

—R. F. Cousins

MOHR, Hal

Cinematographer. **Nationality:** American. **Born:** San Francisco, California, 2 August 1894. **Military Service:** 1917–18—in photography section of US Army. **Family:** Married the actress Evelyn Venable, 1934. **Career:** Part-time film inspector and winder while still at school; 1909—freelance cameraman and photographer's assistant; 1913—filmed newsreels for the California Motion Picture Corporation; 1915—film cutter at Universal Studios; 1920s—documentary filmmaker in Hollywood. Television work from the mid-1950s includes episodes of *Life with Father*, *The Barbara Stanwyck*

Show, and *That's My Boy*. **Awards:** Academy Award for *A Midsummer Night's Dream*, 1935; *The Phantom of the Opera*, 1943. **Died:** In 1974.

Films as Cinematographer:

1914   *Salomy Jane* (Henderson); *Money* (Keane) (+ co-ed)

1918   *Restitution* (*God's Tomorrow*; *By Super Strategy*; *The Conquering Christ*) (Gaye) (co); *The Big Idea* (+ d—short)

1920   *The Golden Trail* (Hersholt and Moomaw) (co); *The Deceiver* (Hersholt and Moomaw)

1921   **The Four Horsemen of the Apocalypse** (Ingram); *The Unfoldment* (Kern and MacQuarrie) (co)

1922   *Watch Him Step* (Nelson)

1923   *Bag and Baggage* (Fox)

1924   *A Woman Who Sinned* (Fox) (co); *Vanity's Price* (*This House of Vanity*) (Neill)

1925   *Little Annie Rooney* (Beaudine) (co); *Playing with Souls* (Ince); *The Monster* (West); *He Who Laughs Last* (Nelson)

1926   *Sparrows* (*Human Sparrows*) (Beaudine) (co); *The Marriage Clause* (Weber); *The High Hand* (Maloney); *The Third Degree* (Curtiz)

1927   *The Girl from Chicago* (Enright); **The Jazz Singer** (Crosland); *Slightly Used* (Mayo); *Bitter Apples* (Hoyt); *Old San Francisco* (Crosland); *A Million Bid* (Curtiz); *The Heart of Maryland* (Bacon)

1928   *Tenderloin* (Curtiz); *Glorious Betsy* (Crosland); *The Wedding March* (von Stroheim) (co); *Noah's Ark* (Curtiz) (co); *The Last Warning* (Leni)

1929   *Broadway* (Fejos); *Shanghai Lady* (*The Girl from China*) (Robertson); *Last Performance* (*The Last Call*) (Fejos)

1930   *Captain of the Guard* (Robertson) (co); *The Cohens and Kellys in Africa* (Moore); *Outward Bound* (Milton); *The Cat Creeps* (Julian) (co); *Big Boy* (Crosland); *King of Jazz* (Anderson) (co); *The Czar of Broadway* (Craft)

1931   *The Common Law* (Stein); *A Woman of Experience* (Harry Joe Brown); *Devotion* (Milton); *The Big Gamble* (Niblo)

1932   *A Woman Commands* (Stein); *Lady with a Past* (*Reputation*) (Edward H. Griffith); *Weekends Only* (Crosland); *The First Year* (Howard); *Tess of the Storm Country* (Santell)

1933   *State Fair* (King); *The Warrior's Husband* (Walter Lang); *I Loved You Wednesday* (King); *The Worst Woman in Paris* (Bell); *As Husbands Go* (MacFadden); *The Devil's in Love* (Dieterle)

1934   *Carolina* (*The House of Connelly*) (King); *David Harum* (Cruze); *Change of Heart* (Blystone); *Charlie Chan's Courage* (Hadden); *Servants' Entrance* (Lloyd)

1935   *The County Chairman* (Blystone); *Under Pressure* (Walsh); *A Midsummer Night's Dream* (Dieterle and Reinhardt); *Captain Blood* (Curtiz)

1936   *The Walking Dead* (Curtiz); *Bullets or Ballots* (Keighley); *The Green Pastures* (Keighley and Connelly); *Ladies in Love* (Edward H. Griffith)

1938   *I Met My Love Again* (Logan and Ripley)

1939   *Back Door to Heaven* (Howard) (co); *The Under-Pup* (Wallace); *Rio* (Brahm); *Destry Rides Again* (Marshall)

Hal Mohr (left)

1940	*Where the Daltons Rode* (Marshall); *Pot o' Gold* (*The Golden Hour*) (Marshall); *International Lady* (Whelan)
1941	*Cheers for Mrs. Bishop* (Garnett)
1942	*Lady in a Jam* (La Cava); *Twin Beds* (Whelan)
1943	*Watch on the Rhine* (Shumlin) (co); *Top Man* (Lamont); *The Phantom of the Opera* (Lubin) (co); *This Is the Life* (Feist)
1944	*Ladies Courageous* (Rawlins); *San Diego, I Love You* (Le Borg); *The Climax* (Wagner); *My Gal Loves Music* (Lilley); *Enter Arsene Lupin* (Beebe); *Prices Unlimited* (Kenton)
1945	*Because of Him* (Wallace); *Shady Lady* (Waggner); *Salome, Where She Danced* (Lamont) (co); *Her Lucky Night* (Lilley)
1946	*Night in Paradise* (Lubin); *I'll Be Yours* (Seiter)
1947	*Song of Scheherazade* (Reisch); *Pirates of Monterey* (Werker); *The Lost Moment* (Gabel)
1948	*Another Part of the Forest* (Gordon); *An Act of Murder* (*Live Today for Tomorrow*; *The Case Against Calvin Cooke*) (Gordon)
1949	*Johnny Holiday* (Goldbeck)
1950	*Of Men and Music* (Reis); *The Second Woman* (*Ellen*) (Kern); *Woman on the Run* (Foster)
1951	*The Big Night* (Losey)

1952	*Rancho Notorious* (Lang); *The Four Poster* (Reis)
1953	*The Member of the Wedding* (Zinnemann); *The Wild One* (Benedek)
1956	*The Boss* (Haskin)
1957	*Baby Face Nelson* (Siegel)
1958	*The Line-Up* (Siegel); *The Gun Runners* (Siegel); *Imagination in Motion* (Lyford)
1960	*The Last Voyage* (Stone); *Underworld U.S.A.* (Fuller)
1962	*Creation of the Humanoids* (Barry)
1963	*The Man from the Diners' Club* (Tashlin)
1967	*Jack and the Beanstalk* (Kelly—for TV)
1968	*The Bamboo Saucer* (*Collision Course*) (Telford)

Publications

By MOHR: articles—

''Moving Pictures: Hal Mohr's Cinematography,'' an interview with Richard Koszarski, in *Film Comment* (New York), September-October 1974.

On MOHR: articles—

Film Comment (New York), vol. 8, no. 2, Summer 1972.
Focus on Film (London), Special Cinematography Issue, no. 13, 1973.
Obituary in *New York Times*, 12 May 1974.
Obituary in *Variety* (New York), 15 May 1974.
''A.S.C. Mourns Hal Mohr,'' in *American Cinematographer* (Hollywood), June 1974.
Maltin, Leonard, in *The Art of the Cinematographer*, New York, 1978.
Film Dope (Nottingham), March 1990.

*　　*　　*

Cinematographer Hal Mohr was an expert at serving the director by creating whatever look or visual effect that director required for his film. He was one of Hollywood's outstanding innovators with regard to photographic technique, and he is the only person ever to earn an Academy Award on a write-in vote (for 1935's *A Midsummer Night's Dream*; he also won an Oscar in 1943 for *The Phantom of the Opera*).

In an era when most film people remained employed by one studio, Mohr jumped from backlot to backlot; from the 1950s on, he worked mainly in television. A majority of the scores of films he shot during his 50-odd years as a director of photography were made during the sound era, beginning symbolically with *The Jazz Singer* in 1927. Even though the movies had learned to talk, Mohr showed how they need not stop moving. Particularly in *Broadway*, there is startling use of the moving camera: Mohr pioneered the extensive usage of boom and dolly shots, resulting in complicated, dazzling visuals that are among the most stunning examples of early Hollywood expressionism. It also was around this time that he designed a camera crane that remained in use for years. According to the *New York Evening Journal*, 10 April 1937, ''Last week it was rising up, rearing back, pirouetting and generally behaving like a cross between a drunken ballerina and a ferris wheel, garnering in wild shots of rioting in German streets after the Armistice for (Universal's) super-production of *The Road Back*.''

By the 1940s and 1950s, Mohr had become a master of creating just the right visuals to mirror a film's mood, whether that mood be eerie (in *The Phantom of the Opera*), solemn (*Watch on the Rhine*), or stark and cool (*The Wild One*). The 1930s, however, was the cinematographer's most innovative decade. In *Captain Blood*, miniatures (including 18-foot-long ships) are flawlessly combined with process shots, and there is effective integration between shots made on the backlot and on location. Even more significantly, Mohr experimented with deep-focus photography in *Bullets or Ballots* and *The Green Pastures*, predating Gregg Toland's work on *Citizen Kane*.

Whatever artistic success *A Midsummer Night's Dream* achieved—the film, to this day, has its admirers and detractors—is due as much to Mohr's creativity as the direction of Max Reinhardt and William Dieterle and the decidedly offbeat casting of James Cagney (playing Bottom), Mickey Rooney (as Puck), Joe E. Brown (as Flute), and other Warners' contract players as Shakespeare's characters. In the scenario, sprites and fairies mix in the same shots with human beings; sequences filmed in real settings are intertwined with those filmed on obviously painted sets. Mohr's cinematography perfectly mirrors this combination of reality and fantasy via his utilization of soft photography and lighting to create an effect that is shimmering—at once magical and romantic. In his pan of Reinhardt's ''lavish and fanciful rather than imaginative'' approach to the material, Graham Greene, writing in the 18 October 1935 edition of *The Spectator*, nonetheless noted that, ''in (Reinhardt's) treatment of the Athenian woodland, the silver birches, thick moss, deep mists and pools, there are sequences of great beauty. . . .'' Writing in the November 1935 *National Board of Review Magazine*, John Alfred Thomas opined that, ''as Shakespeare, the production is almost photographically accurate. . . .'' (Typically, Mohr's name cannot be found in either reviews, or in most analyses of the films to which he contributed.) In accepting his Oscar, the cinematographer observed that while working on *A Midsummer Night's Dream*, he had the opportunity to ''explore a few of the possibilities of our marvelous art-science,'' adding that ''we must constantly seek new ways of picturing old stories, or we cease to progress.''

In addition to Mohr's willingness to let his imagination roam free as he experimented with then-unheard-of techniques, his career is a testimony to the fact that filmmaking is a collaborative art form. While working on *Sparrows*, he and art director Harry Oliver united to create an impressive-looking boat-chase sequence in a swamp, utilizing miniatures that were pulled through a tray of flaxseed and dry aluminum powder. Mohr lit the setting with high lights and crosslights. This, and other effects in the film, were accomplished by what Mohr described in an interview late in his life as ''the combined efforts of a group of exquisite craftsmen.''

''I get hundreds of letters from boys wanting to know how to become studio cameramen,'' he explained, in an interview published in the 17 May 1936 *New York Herald-Tribune*. ''. . . Begin at home as an amateur camera man. Practice with your friends with your home camera. Learn all you can about trick photography, lighting effects, enlarging and finishing.''

Years before in San Francisco, this is precisely how Mohr pursued his youthful interest in cinematography. It was, of course, a time when film schools did not exist; while still in high school, Mohr exhibited the resourcefulness that was to typify his career by converting a toy movie projector into a motion-picture camera. The projector's take-up arm ran the take-up magazine, with the projector's lens becoming the picture-taking lens. Soon, Mohr began photographing local events; he developed his own negative, and struck his own prints. ''I sold some of these to our motion picture theater,'' Mohr told the *New York Herald-Tribune*, ''and they were instantly popular. This beginning finally led to Hollywood. . . .''

—Rob Edelman

MORRICONE, Ennio

Composer. **Nationality:** Italian. **Born:** Rome, 10 November 1928. **Education:** Studied with Goffredo Petrassi; Santa Cecilia Conservatory, Rome, diploma in composition, in trombone, and in orchestra direction. **Career:** Composer of symphonic and chamber works, and for theater, radio, and television; also songwriter and arranger; 1961—first film score, for *Il federale*; 1975—music for TV miniseries *Moses the Lawgiver*, and for *Marco Polo*, 1982. **Awards:** British Academy Anthony Asquith Award for Film Music, for *Days of Heaven*; British Academy Awards, for *Days of Heaven*, 1980, *Once upon a Time in America*, 1985, *The Mission*, 1987, and *The Untouchables*, 1988, *Cinema Paradiso*, 1991; Golden Globe awards, for *The Mission*, 1987, *La Leggenda del pianista sull'oceano*, 2000; Italian National Syndicate of Film Journalists Silver Ribbon Awards

Ennio Morricone

for Best Score for *Per un pugno do dollari*, 1965, *Metti una sera a cena*, 1970, *Sacco e Vanzetti*, 1972, *Once Upon a Time in America*, 1985, *The Untouchables*, 1988, Special Silver Ribbon for research for *La Leggenda del pianista sull'oceano*, 1999; Los Angeles Film Critics Association Award for *Once Upon a Time In America*, 1984; Grammy Award for Best Album of Original Background Score Written for a Motion Picture or Television for *The Untouchables*, 1988; Locarno International Film Festival, Leopard of Honour, 1989; Venice Film Festival Career Goldn Lion, 1995; David di Donatello award "David," for *La Leggenda del pianista sull'oceano*, 1999; European Film Awards Life Achievement Award, 1999. **Address:** c/o General Music, Viale Leigi 41, 00198 Rome, Italy.

Films as Composer:

1961   *Il federale* (*The Fascist*) (Salce)
1962   *Diciotteni al sole* (*Eighteen in the Sun*) (Mastrocinque); *La voglia matta* (*Crazy Desire*) (Salce); *La cuccagne* (Salce)
1963   *Il successo* (*The Success*) (Morassi and Risi); *Le monachine* (*The Little Nuns*) (Salce); *I basilischi* (*The Lizards*) (Wertmüller); *Le ore dell'amore*
1964   *Per un pugno di dollari* (*A Fistful of Dollars*) (Leone) (credited as Leo Nichols); *I malamondo* (*Malamondo*) (Cavara); *Prima della revoluzione* (*Before the Revolution*) (Bertolucci) (co)
1965   *Amanti d'oltretombo* (*Nightmare Castle*) (Caiano); *I pugni in tasca* (*Fist in His Pocket*) (Bellocchio); *Una pistola per Ringo* (*A Pistol for Ringo*) (Tessari); *El Greco* (Salce); *Il trionfo di Ringo* (Tessari); *Per qualche dollaro in più* (*For a Few Dollars More*) (Leone)

1966   *Sette pistole per i MacGregor* (*Seven Guns for the MacGregors*) (Giraldi); *Uccelacci e uccellini* (*The Hawks and the Sparrows*) (Pasolini); ***Il buono, il brutto, il cattivo*** (*The Good, the Bad, and the Ugly*) (Leone); *La battaglia di Algeri* (*The Battle of Algiers*) (Pontecorvo); *Un uomo a metà* (De Seta); *Un fiume di dollari* (*The Hills Run Red*) (Lizzani); *Svegliati e uccidi* (*Wake Up and Die*) (Lizzani); *Un dollaro a testa* (*Navajo Joe*) (Corbucci) (credited as Leo Nichols); *Sette donne per i MacGregor* (*Up the MacGregors*) (Giraldi); *Matchless* (Lattuada)
1967   *Le streghe* (*The Witches*) (Visconti and others) (co); *Il giardino delle delizie* (Agosti); *La Cina è vicina* (*China Is Near*) (Bellocchio); *La ragazza e il generale* (*The Girl and the General*) (Festa Campanile); *Ad ogni costo* (*Grand Slam*) (Montaldo); *Da uomo a uomo* (*Death Rides a Horse*) (Petroni); *O.K. Connery* (*Operation Kid Brother*) (De Martino) (co); *Arabella* (Bolognini); *La Bataille de San Sebastian* (*Guns for San Sebastian*) (Verneuil); *La resa dei conti* (*The Big Gundown*) (Sollima); *L'Harem* (Ferreri); *Faccia a faccia* (Sollima); *I crudeli* (Corbucci) (credited as Leo Nichols)
1968   *Dalle Ardenne all'inferno* (*Dirty Heroes*) (De Martino) (co); *Galileo* (Cavani); *Escalation* (Faenza); *Teorema* (*Theorum*) (Pasolini); *Diabolik* (*Danger: Diabolik*) (Bava); *Partner* (Bertolucci); *Grazia, zia* (*Come Play with Me*) (Samperi); *Ruba al prossimo tuo* (*A Fine Pair*) (Maselli); ***C'era una volta il west*** (*Once upon a Time in the West*) (Leone); *Scusi, facciamo l'amore?* (*Listen, Let's Make Love*) (Caprioli); *Un tranquillo posto di campagna* (*A Quiet Place in the Country*) (Petri); *Un bellissimo novembre* (*That Splendid November*) (Bolognini); *Il mercenario* (*The Mercenary*) (Corbucci); *Fräulein Doktor* (Lattuada); *Vergogna schifosi* (*The Dirty Angels*) (Severino); *La monaca di Monza* (*The Lady of Monza*) (E. Visconti); *Comandamenti per un gangster* (Caltabiano); *Il grande silenzio* (Corbucci); *Roma come Chicago* (*Banditi a Roma*) (De Martino) (co); *H. 2 S.* (Faenza); *L'alibi* (Lucignani, Gassman, and Celi); *Et per tetto un cielo di stelle* (Petroni); *Corri uomo corri* (Sollima)
1969   *Gli intoccabili* (*Machine Gun McCain*) (Montaldo); *Metti, une sera a cena* (Patroni Griffi); *Una breve stagione* (*Brief Season*) (Castellani); *Le Clan des Siciliens* (*The Sicilian Clan*) (Verneuil); *Un esercito di cinque uomini* (*The Five Man Army*) (Taylor); *Queimada!* (*Burn!*) (Pontecorvo); *L'uccello dalle piume di cristallo* (*The Bird with the Crystal Plumage*) (Argento); *Metello* (Bolognini); *Tepepa* (Petroni); *La stagione dei sensi* (Franciosa); *Cuore di mamma* (Samperi); *L'assoluto naturale* (Bolognini); *Mangiala* (Casaretti); *Ecce Homo—I soparavvissuti* (Gaburro); *Sai cosa faceva Stalin alle donne* (Liverani); *La donna invisibile* (Spinola); *Senza sapere niente di lei* (Comencini)
1970   *Hornets' Nest* (Karlson); *Two Mules for Sister Sara* (Siegel); *I cannibali* (Cavani); *Indagine su un cittadino al di sopra di ogni sospetto* (*Investigation of a Citizen above Suspicion*) (Petri); *La califfa* (Bevilacqua); *Gott mit uns* (Montaldo); *Maddalena* (Kawaletowicz); *La moglie più bella* (Damiani); *Città violenta* (Sollima); *Quando le donne avevano la coda* (Festa Campanile); *Uccidete il vitello grasso ed arrostitelo*

615

(Samperi); *Vamos a matar, companeros* (Corbucci); *Giocchi particolari* (Indovina)

1971　*Krasnaya palatka* (*La tenda rossa*; *The Red Tent*) (Kalatazov); *Sacco e Vanzetti* (Montaldo); *L'istruttoria è chiusa, dimentichi!* (Damiani); *Le Casse* (*The Burglars*) (Verneuil); *La classe operaia va in paradiso* (*The Working Class Goes to Heaven*; *Lulu the Tool*) (Petri); *Forza G* (Tessari); *Oceano* (Quilici); *Quattro mosche di vellato grigio* (Argento); *La tarantola dal ventro nero* (Cavara); *Veruschka—Poesia di una donna* (Rubartelli); *Addio fratello credele* (Patroni Griffi); *Incontro* (Schivazappa); *Una lucertola con la pelle di donna* (Fulci); *Tre nel mille* (Indovina) (co); *Il gatto a nove code* (Argento); *Gli occhi freddi della paura* (Castellari); *Le foto proibite de una signora per bene* (Ercoli); *Il Decameron* (*The Decameron*) (Pasolini) (co); *La corta notte della bambole di vetro* (Lado); *Lui per lei* (Rispoli)

1972　*Il diavolo nel cervello* (*Devil in the Brain*) (Sollima); *Sans mobile apparent* (*Without Apparent Motive*) (Labro); *Giù la testa* (*Duck, You Sucker!*) (Leone); *Barbe-Bleue* (*Bluebeard*) (Dmytryk); *L'Attentat* (*The French Conspiracy*) (Boisset); *Le Serpent* (*The Serpent*) (Verneuil); *Anche se volessi lavorare che faccio?* (Mogherini); *Il Maestro e Margherita* (Petrovic); *Correva l'anno di grazio 1870...* (Giannetti); *Questa specie d'amore* (Bevilacqua); *Violenza: quinto potere* (Vancini); *Quando le donne persero la coda* (Festa Campanile); *Cosa avete fatto a Solange* (Dallamano); *Les Deux Saisons de la vie* (Pavel); *Giornata nera per l'Ariete* (Bazzoni); *Mio caro assassino* (Valeri); *La banda J & S* (*Cronaca criminale del Far West*; *Far West Story*) (Corbucci); *La vita, a volta è molto dura, vero Provvidenza* (Petroni); *I bambini chiedono perchè* (Zanchin); *D'amore si muore* (Carunchio); *I raccoti di Canterbury* (*The Canterbury Tales*) (Pasolini) (co); *Chi l'ha vista morire?* (Lado); *Quando l'amore è sensualità* (De Sisti); *L'ultimo uomo di Sara* (Onorato); *Il retorno di Clint il solitario* (Martin)

1973　*Un uomo di rispettare* (*Hearts and Minds*) (Lupo); *La propietà non è più un furto* (Petri); *Rappresaglia* (*Massacre in Rome*) (Cosmatos); *Giordano Bruno* (Montaldo); *La cosa buffa* (Lado); *Libera amore mio* (Bolognini); *Il mio nome e nessuno* (Valeri); *Sepolta viva* (Lado); *Crescete e moltiplicatevi* (Petroni); *Revolver* (Sollima); *Spogliati, protesta, uccidi?* (De Sisti); *Che c'entriamo noi con la rivoluzione?* (Corbucci); *Ci risiamo, vero Provvidenza?* (De Martino); *Fiorina la vacca* (De Sisti)

1974　*Le Trio infernal* (Girod); *Allonsanfan* (P. and V. Taviani); *Le Secret* (Enrico); *Mussolini: Ultimo Atto* (Lizzani); *Fatti di gente perbene* (*La Grande Bourgeoise*; *The Murri Affair*; *Drama of the Rich*) (Bolognini); *Il sorriso del grande tentatore* (*The Devil Is a Woman*) (Damiani); *Peur sur la ville* (*Night Caller*) (Verneuil); ***Il fiore delle mille et una notta*** (*A Thousand and One Nights*) (Pasolini); *L'anticristo* (De Martino); *Il giro del monde degli innamorati di Paynet* (Perfetto) (co); *Macchie solari* (Crispino); *Space 1999* (Katzin, Austin, and Tomlin—from TV eps.); *Sesso in confessionale* (De Sisti); *La cugina* (Lado); *Spasmo* (Lenzi); *Milano odia: la polizia no puo sparare* (Lenzi)

1975　*Der Richter und sein Henker* (*The End of the Game*) (Schell); *Salo, o le 120 giornate di Sodoma* (*Salo—the 120 Days of*

Sodom) (Pasolini); *La donna della domenica* (*The Sunday Woman*) (Comencini); *Divina creatura* (Patroni Griffi); *Un genio, due compari, un pollo* (Damiani); *La faille* (*La smagliature*) (Fleischmann); *Storie di vita e malavita* (Lizzani); *Attenti al buffone* (Bevilacqua); *Leonor* (J. L. Buñuel); *Human Factor* (Dmytryk); *L'ultimo treno della notte* (Lado); *Gente di rispetto* (Zampa)

1976　*Novecento* (*1900*) (Bertolucci); *L'eredità Ferramonti* (*The Inheritance*) (Bolognini); *René la Canne* (Girod); *Per le antiche scale* (*Down the Ancient Stairs*) (Bolognini); *Labbra di lurido blu* (Petroni); *San Babila ore 20: un delitto inutile* (Lizzani); *Per amore* (Giarda); *Todo modo* (Petri)

1977　*Le désert des Tartares* (*Il deserto dei tartari*; *The Desert of the Tartars*) (Zurlini); *L'Agnese va a morire* (Montaldo); *Exorcist II: The Heretic* (Boorman); *Il prefetto di ferro* (Squitieri); *La orca* (*Orca*; *Orca—Killer Whale*) (M. Anderson); *Pedro Peramo* (Velo); *Holocaust 2000* (De Martino); *Il gatto* (Comencini); *Una vita venduta* (Florio); *Stato interessante* (Nasca); *Il mostro* (Zampa); *Autostop rosso sangue* (Festa Campanile)

1978　*Le mani sporche* (Petri); *La Cage aux Folles* (Molinaro); ***Days of Heaven*** (Malick); *Corleone* (Squitieri); *Viaggio con Anita* (*Travels with Anita*) (Monicelli); *Forza Italia!* (Faenza); *122 rue de Provence* (Gion); *Cosi comme sei* (Lattuada); "Saro tuto per te" ep. of *Dove vai in vacanza?* (Bolognini); *L'immoralità* (Pirri)

1979　*Bloodline* (Young); *Il prato* (*The Meadow*) (P. and V. Taviani); *I... comme Icare* (Verneuil); *La luna* (Bertolucci); *Ogro* (*Operation Ogre*) (Pontecorvo); *Le buone notizie* (Petri); *Un sacco bello* (Verdone); *Il ladrone* (*The Thief*) (Festa Campanile); *Il giocattolo* (Montaldo); *L'umanoide* (Lado and Lewis); *Dedicato al mare Eglo* (Ikeda); *Windows* (Willis)

1980　*La Cage aux Folles II* (Molinaro); *The Island* (Ritchie); *So Fine* (A. Bergman); *La vera storia della signora della camelie* (*The True Story of Camille*) (Festa Campanile); *Uomini e no* (Orsini); *Stark System* (Balducci); *Si salvi chi vuole* (Faenza); *Professione Figlio* (*Buzie Bianche*) (Rolla)

1981　*La tragedia di un uomo ridicolo* (*The Tragedy of a Ridiculous Man*) (Bertolucci); *Le Professionnel* (Lautner); *Bianco, rosso, e verdone* (Cerdone); *Espion, lève-toi* (Boisset); *Occhio alla penna* (Lupo); *La disubbidienza* (Lado)

1982　*The Thing* (Carpenter); *Nana* (Wolman); *Butterfly* (Cimber); *Le Ruffian* (Giovanni)

1983　*Hundra* (Cimber); *The Scarlet and the Black* (London); *La chiave* (*The Key*) (Brass); *Order of Death* (*Cop Killer*) (Faenza); *A Time to Die* (Cimber) (co); *Treasure of the Four Crowns* (Baldi)

1984　***Once upon a Time in America*** (Leone); *The Seven Magnificent Gladiators* (Mattei); *Sahara* (McLaglen)

1985　*La gabbia* (*The Trap*) (Griffi); *La Cage aux folles III* (*Elles se marient*) (Lautner); *Kommando Leopard* (*Commando Leopard*) (Dawson) (co); *Il pentito* (Squitieri); *Die Einsteiger* (Götz); *Via mala* (Toelle); *Le due vite di Mattia Pascal* (*The Two Lives of Mattia Pascal*) (Monicelli); *Die Forstenbuben*; *The Link* (De Martino); *La messe e finita*; *Il pentito* (Squitieri); *Red Sonja* (Fleischer)

1986　*Il cammorista*; *Ginger e Fred* (Fellini); *Good Morning Babylon* (P. and T. Taviani); *The Mission* (Joffé); *Pourvue que* ce soit une fille (*Let's Hope It's a Girl*) (Monicelli); *La Venexiana* (Bolognini)

1987 *Il giorno prima* (*The Day Before*; *Control*) (Montaldo); *Mosca addio* (Bolognini); *Quartière* (Agosti); *Rampage* (Friedkin); *The Untouchables* (De Palma); *Frantic* (Polanski); *Les Exploits d'un jeune Don Juan* (Mingozzi); *Intervista* (*The Interview*) (Fellini); *Gli occhiali d'oro* (Montaldo); *La sposa era bellissima* (Gábor); *Strana la vita* (Bertolucci)

1988 *A Time of Destiny* (Nava); *Cinema Paradiso* (Tornatore); *I cammelli* (Bertolucci); *Domani accadra* (Luchetti); *Drole d'endroit pour une rencontre* (*A Strange Place to Meet*) (Dupeyron) (song); *Manifesto* (Makavejev); *La soule* (Sibra); *Strange Life!*; *Young Einstein* (Roach) (song)

1989 *Gli indifferente* (*A Time of Indifference*) (Bolognini—for TV); *Casualities of War* (De Palma); *Fat Man and Little Boy* (*Shadow Makers*) (Joffé); *I promessi sposi* (*The Betrothed*) (Nocita—for TV); *¡Atame!* (*Tie Me Up! Tie Me Down!*) (Almodovar); *Tempo di uccidere* (*The Short Cut*; *Time to Kill*) (Montaldo); *Voyage of Terror: The Achille Lauro Affair* (Negrin—for TV); *The Endless Game* (Forbes—for TV); *Dimenticare Palermo* (*To Forget Palermo*; *Oublier Palerme*; *The Palermo Connection*) (Rosi); *L'appassionata* (Mingozzi); *Australia* (Andrien); *La cintura* (Gamba); *Disamistade: O Re* (Magni); *Palombella Rossa* (Moretti)

1990 *Stanno tutti bene* (*Everybody's Fine*) (Tornatore); *State of Grace* (Joanon); *Tre colonne in cronaca* (Vanzina); *Mio caro Dr. Gräsler* (*Dear Dr. Gräsler*; *The Bachelor*) (Faenza); *The Big Man* (*Crossing the Line*) (Leland); *Il principe del deserto* (*Lion in the Desert*; *The Law of the Desert*) (Tessari—for TV); *Hamlet* (Zeffirelli); *Il male oscuro* (*Obscure Evil*) (Monicelli); *Il sole anche di notte* (*The Sun Also Shines at Night*) (Taviani); *Tracce di una vita amorosa* (Del Monte); *Le voce della luna* (*Voices of the Moon*) (Fellini)

1991 *La Domenica specialmente* (*Especially on Sunday*) (Tornatore, Tognazzi, Giuseppe Bertolucci, Barilli, and Giordana); *Money* (Stern); *Deutsches Mann Geil! Die Geschichte von Ilona und Kurti* (Schwabenitzky); *Bugsy* (Levinson); *La Villa del Venerdi* (*Husbands and Lovers*) (Bolognini)

1992 *City of Joy* (Joffé); *Beyond Justice* (Tessari); *Rampage* (Friedkin)

1993 *In the Line of Fire* (Petersen)

1994 *Disclosure* (Levinson); *Love Affair* (Caron); *La Scotta* (*The Escort*) (Tognazzi); *White Dog* (Fuller); *Wolf* (Nichols); *The Long Silence* (Von Trotta)

1995 *Joseph* (Young—for TV); *Pasolini, un delitto italiano* (*Who Killed Pasolini*) (Marco Tullio Giordana); *L'Uomo delle stelle* (*The Star Maker*) (Tornatore)

1996 *Ninfa plebea* (*The Nymph*) (Wertmüller); *Marianna Ucrìa* (Faenza); *I Magi randagi* (*We Free Kings*) (Citti); *Afirma Pereira* (*According to Pereira*) (Faenza); *Nostromo* (Reid—mini for TV); *La Sindrome di Stendhal* (*Stendhal's Syndrome*) (Argento); *Moses* (Young—for TV) (title music); *Vite strozzate* (*Strangled Lives*) (Tognazzi); *La Lupa* (Lavia); *Samson and Delilah* (Roeg—for TV)

1997 *Naissance des stéréoscopages* (Marty); *In fondo al cuore* (Perelli—for TV); *David* (Markowitz—for TV); *Con rabbia e con amore* (Angeli); *La Casa bruciata* (Spano—for TV); *Cartoni animati* (Franco Citti and Sergio Citti); *U Turn* (Stone); *Lolita* (Lyne); *Solomon* (Young—for TV)

1998 *Ultimo* (Reali—for TV); *Il Fantasma dell'opera* (*The Phantom of the Opera*) (Argento); *Bulworth* (Beatty); *La Leggenda del pianista sull'oceano* (*The Legend of 1900*) (Tornatore)

1999 *Esther*

2000 *Vatel*; *Mission to Mars*; *Canone inverso* (Tognazzi); *La Tour Secrète* (for TV)

Films as Musical Director:

1965 *Centomila dollari per Ringo* (De Martino)

1966 *Quien sabe?* (*A Bullet for the General*) (Damiani)

1967 *Gentleman Jo . . . uccidi* (Finley)

1972 *Giù la testa* (*A Fistful of Dynamite*) (Leone and Santi)

1975 *Per le antiche scale* (*Down the Ancient Stairs*) (Bolognini)

Publications

By MORRICONE: articles—

Soundtrack! (Hollywood), March 1978.
Soundtrack! (Hollywood), June 1978.
Positif (Paris), April 1983.
Cinefantastique (New York), April/May 1983.
Cinema Papers (Melbourne), December 1984.
Film und Fernsehen (Potsdam), January 1990.
Soundtrack! (Mechelen), June 1990.
Interview with Gianni Bergamino and Dmitri Riccio in *Soundtrack*, 1 December 1992.

On MORRICONE: books—

Miceli, Sergio, *La Musica nel Film: Arte e Artigianato*, Florence, 1982.
Lhassa, Anne and Jean Lhassa, *Ennio Morricone*, Lausanne, 1989.
Miceli, Sergio, *Morricone, la Musica, il Cinema*, Modena, 1994.

On MORRICONE: articles—

Films in Review (New York), August/September 1970, additions in April 1972.
Image et Son (Paris), January 1974.
Image et Son (Paris), March 1974.
Ecran (Paris), September 1975.
Ciné Revue (Paris), 5 February 1976.
Film Review (London), September 1976.
Soundtrack! (Hollywood), October 1976.
Skoop (Amsterdam), March 1978.
Skoop (Amsterdam), May 1978.
International Filmusic Journal, no. 1, 1979.
Film Français (Paris), 2 February 1979.
Film Français (Paris), 16 January 1981.
Filmusic (Leeds), 1982.
Film Français (Paris), 4 May 1984.
Soundtrack! (Hollywood), December 1987.
Soundtrack! (Hollywood), June 1990.
American Film (Washington, D.C.), February 1991.

Rivista del Cinematografo, vol. 63, December 1993.

Variety (New York), 22 January 1996.

Film Score Monthly (Los Angeles), May 1996.

Film en Televisie + Video (Brussels), January 1997.

Gore, Joe, "Ennio Morricone: Spaghetti Western Maestro," in *Guitar Player*, 01 April 1997.

Briggs, Nick, review of *La Leggenda del pianista sull'oceaneo*, in *Film Review* (London), January 2000.

*　　*　　*

Ennio Morricone ranks among the most prolific and imaginative composers of film scores currently working in the field. Born and educated in Rome and initially a composer of traditional classical music, Morricone began scoring Italian motion pictures in the early 1960s. He has since worked internationally as well, with more than 175 films to his credit.

Morricone once referred to film scoring as "one art applied to another," and he effectively uses music as a sort of aural paint to create the proper blend of sound and vision. At his best, he ignores the limits of conventionality; his scores mix-and-match rock, jazz, blues, pop, folk, and classical music with innovative instrumentation and an apt gift for melody. He also makes adventurous use of percussion, brass, vocal/choral, and other sound effects—whips, gunshots, animal and bird calls, and particularly the human whistle.

Often the results are remarkable. Morricone has long and most effectively been associated with Italian director Sergio Leone, headmaster of the "spaghetti Western" school of filmmaking. Morricone's rousing and memorable work for the Leone/Clint Eastwood "Man with No Name" trilogy brought him early prominence. The scores—*A Fistful of Dollars, For a Few Dollars More,* and *The Good, the Bad, and the Ugly*—match ideally the violence, emotion, and black humor inherent in the genre.

His masterpiece, the score for *Once upon a Time in the West*, is a beautiful complement to Leone's best film. Morricone provides a powerful emotional accompaniment with his accurate, gut-level renderings of the spectacle and myth of the Old West. Also particularly evocative among his credits is the pastorale score for Terrence Malick's *Days of Heaven* (a portrait of farm-workers set in 1916 Texas), which has as its centerpiece a short theme borrowed from the nineteenth-century French romantic composer Saint-Saëns.

Occasionally the eclecticism yields less-than-unified, if still interesting, efforts (such as *My Name Is Nobody*). Morricone's inevitable weakness, naturally, is his prolificacy, which leads at times to listless scores and a certain repetition of the most facile ingredients of his distinctive style. Some of his more recent aims at the pop mainstream—*Bloodline, So Fine, Butterfly, The Thing*—miss the mark, serviceable but strictly unmemorable movie soundtracks. *Once upon a Time in America* teamed him once again with Leone in rather familiar musical territory, which won the composer his second British Academy Award.

In the late 1990s Morricone has shown no sign of reducing his musical output, continuing to turn out a prodigious quantity of scores, including *La Leggenda del pianista sull'oceano*, which has won several awards, including a Golden Globe, and *Bulworth. La Leggenda* tells the story of a man born in 1900 who never leaves the boat on which he lives, learning about the world from what people tell him. The score is central to the story: inspired by jazz and ragtime,

Morricone has been commended for his careful historical research and painstaking attention to detail.

Morricone's versatile talent has served him well. He has composed for Westerns, romances, epics, thrillers, comedies, dramas. That his best music remains listenable independent of the films for which it was written is a worthy and enduring legacy.

—Richard Sater, updated by Christopher John Stephens and Chris Routledge

MORRIS, Oswald

Cinematographer. **Nationality:** British. **Born:** Ruislip, Middlesex, England, 22 November 1915. **Education:** Attended Bishopshalt School, Hillingdon. **Military Service:** Served as bomber pilot during World War II; awarded D.F.C. and A.F.C. **Career:** Projectionist during school vacations, then unpaid assistant and clapper boy at Wembley Studios; 1935—assistant cameraman, and cameraman from 1938 at BIP and Pinewood; 1950—first film as cinematographer, *Golden Salamander*; developed innovative print color saturation with 4-strip Technicolor in 1950s. **Awards:** British Academy Award for *The Pumpkin Eater*, 1964; *The Hill*, 1965; *The Spy Who Came In from the Cold*, 1966; Academy Award for *Fiddler on the Roof*, 1971. British Society of Cinematographers Golden Camera for *Moulin Rouge*, 1953; *The Spy Who Came In from the Cold*, 1966; *The Taming of the Shrew*, 1967; *Fiddler on the Roof*, 1971.

Oswald Morris

Films as Cameraman:

1946 *Green for Danger* (Gilliat)
1947 *Captain Boycott* (Launder)
1948 *Oliver Twist* (Lean); *Blanche Fury* (Allegret)
1949 *Passionate Friends* (Lean)

Films as Cinematographer:

1950 *Golden Salamander* (Neame); *Cairo Road* (MacDonald)
1951 *Circle of Danger* (Tourneur); *The Adventurers* (*Fortune in Diamonds*) (MacDonald)
1952 *The Card* (*The Promoter*) (Neame); *Saturday Island* (*Island of Desire*) (Heisler); *So Little Time* (Bennett)
1953 *Moulin Rouge* (Huston); *South of Algiers* (*The Golden Mask*) (Lee); *Stazione Termini* (*Indiscretion of an American Wife*) (De Sica) (co)
1954 *Beat the Devil* (Huston); *Beau Brummell* (Bernhardt); *Monsieur Ripois* (*Knave of Hearts*; *Lovers, Happy Lovers*) (Clément)
1956 *The Man Who Never Was* (Neame); *Moby Dick* (Huston)
1957 *Heaven Knows, Mr. Allison* (Neame); *A Farewell to Arms* (C. Vidor) (co)
1958 *The Key* (Reed); *The Roots of Heaven* (Huston)
1959 *Look Back in Anger* (Richardson); *Our Man in Havana* (Reed)
1960 *The Entertainer* (Richardson)
1961 *The Guns of Navarone* (Lee Thompson)
1962 *Satan Never Sleeps* (*The Devil Never Sleeps*) (McCarey); **Lolita** (Kubrick); *Term of Trial* (Glenville)
1963 *Come Fly with Me* (Levin); *The Ceremony* (Harvey)
1964 *Of Human Bondage* (Hughes); *The Pumpkin Eater* (Clayton); *The Battle of the Villa Fiorita* (*Affair at the Villa Fiorita*) (Daves)
1965 *Mister Moses* (Neame); *The Hill* (Lumet)
1966 *The Spy Who Came In from the Cold* (Ritt); *Life at the Top* (Kotcheff); *Stop the World—I Want to Get Off* (Saville); *The Winter's Tale* (Dunlop)
1967 *The Taming of the Shrew* (Zeffirelli); *Great Catherine* (Flemyng)
1968 *Reflections in a Golden Eye* (Huston); *Oliver!* (Reed)
1969 *Goodbye Mr. Chips* (Ross)
1970 *Scrooge* (Neame); *Fragment of Fear* (Sarafian)
1971 *Fiddler on the Roof* (Jewison)
1972 *Lady Caroline Lamb* (Bolt); *Sleuth* (Mankiewicz)
1973 *The Mackintosh Man* (Huston); *Dracula* (Curtis) (TV, UK cinema)
1974 *The Odessa File* (Neame); *The Man with the Golden Gun* (Hamilton) (studio only)
1975 *The Man Who Would Be King* (Huston)
1976 *The Seven-Per-Cent Solution* (Ross)
1977 *Equus* (Lumet)
1978 *The Wiz* (Lumet)
1980 *Just Tell Me What You Want* (Lumet)
1981 *The Great Muppet Caper* (Henson)
1982 *The Dark Crystal* (Henson and Oz)

Publications

By MORRIS: articles—

On *Fiddler on the Roof* in *American Cinematographer* (Hollywood), December 1970.
Focus on Film (London), December 1971.
Film Heritage (Dayton, Ohio), no. 3, 1977.
Films and Filming (London), April 1977.
On *The Wiz*, in *American Cinematographer* (Hollywood), November 1978.
Millimeter (New York), November 1978.
Filmmakers Newsletter (Ward Hill, Massachusetts), December 1978.
American Cinematographer (Hollywood), May 1979.
On *The Dark Crystal* in *American Cinematographer* (Hollywood), December 1982.
American Cinematographer (Hollywood), April 1985.

On MORRIS: articles—

Hill, Derek, on *Moby Dick* in *American Cinematographer* (Hollywood), September 1966.
Screen International (London), 22 November 1975.
Films & Filming (London), April 1977.
American Cinematographer (Hollywood), November 1978; May 1979; December 1982; April 1985.
Film Dope, September 1990.
Perfect Vision (Hollywood), Spring 1994.

*   *   *

Following in that fine British tradition of being in the right place at the right time, Oswald "Ossie" Morris entered the film industry as an unpaid projectionist whilst still at school, and through good fortune and perseverance managed to secure his first paid post as clapper boy and factotum at the small Wembley Studios during the early 1930s.

His early film education included spells working with such luminaries as Michael Powell on the production line "quota quickies" which were made for a pound per foot of film. Morris's progress from camera assistant to camera operator was interrupted by the outbreak of World War II, in which he served as a bomber pilot. He returned to the business in 1946, working for Ronald Neame at Pinewood Studios as camera operator on a series of low-key, but solidly made, British films. *Green For Danger* was the first, to be followed by *Captain Boycott*, *Oliver Twist* and *Passionate Friends*—the latter two for David Lean—during which time he began to apply the lessons he had learned.

Morris's career blossomed during a golden era in British cinematography. The likes of Jack Cardiff, Freddie Young, Geoffrey Unsworth, Freddie Francis and Morris's acknowledged mentor Guy Green were variously photographing, assisting and focus pulling during this time and he finally made his debut as cinematographer on Ronald Neame's *Golden Salamander*. Unable to keep working in the top job under contract, Morris took the bold decision to go freelance and never looked back. He continued to ply his trade on small-scale British films, only two of which were shot in Technicolor, before John Huston invited him to photograph *Moulin Rouge*, the big-budget story of artist Toulouse Lautrec. Always a keen innovator, Morris was given a free rein by Huston and devised many stylish lighting effects for the film. Using fog on the set together with bold colour choices and a combination of diffused and filtered light, Morris created stunning effects.

Certainly Technicolor executives were stunned. They practically disowned the film when they saw it, but supported by his director, Morris weathered the storm and was amused to receive a congratulatory letter from the same executives when the film opened to positive reviews with particular praise for its photography. Up until that time the saturated, overripe Technicolor look was all, but Morris and Huston broke up the line, muted the colour and challenged the accepted wisdom of day.

His triumph on the film was all the more remarkable for his inexperience with Technicolor, used for only a couple of his early films and a day or two shooting second unit on John Boulting's *The Magic Box*. Following this early triumph Morris worked with John Huston on seven other pictures. But the next of them, *Beat the Devil*, was notable mainly for the in-jokes and happy reunion of several favourite Huston actors. It was not until their next association that the Huston-Morris partnership was to challenge the accepted use of Technicolor once more.

For *Moby Dick* Huston demanded a new look, and Morris together with the now cooperative Technicolor boffins worked to produce a bleak, washed out effect for the screen. The starkness of the pictures they shot perfectly complimented the steely, ethereal quality of so many of the characters; the effect was achieved by printing a negative overlaid onto another negative of the same shot. When lit by a revolving light, the effect produced a sublime outline to the characters which echoed the biblical sense of doom that pervaded Ahab's obsession with the great white whale.

Morris maintained his status as a cinematographer-for-hire when a lesser man might have settled for a staff job. His overwhelming talent seems to have been his ability to work with some of the more demanding directors of the period. Matched with his professional competence and adaptability, his solid and unostentatious work lent character and depth to a wide variety of films. He provided vivid and evocative images in an altogether different location for another Huston film, *Heaven Knows Mr. Allison*, as well as working on three occasions with Carol Reed, a director renowned for his irascible attitude towards technicians.

But no matter what the provocation, or how fearsome the reputation of those with whom he worked, Morris discharged his duties with quiet authority, proving himself to be unflashy but thoroughly dependable. As a result, he worked steadily, and when some of his peers found quality work harder to come by in the late '50s, Morris was adopted by the British new wave, led by Tony Richardson with his *Look Back in Anger*. He worked with Richardson again two years later, photographing Laurence Olivier in *The Entertainer*. He approached both films as a straightforward exercise in putting the cinematographer at the service of the story. There are few gimmicks or distractions—such elements being superfluous with actors such as Richard Burton and Olivier in any event—and Morris was certainly not weighed down by an ego that needed to boast of his talents to the world.

While he worked steadily, his films were rarely the subject of award nominations. He had to wait until *The Pumpkin Eater* for his first British Academy Award, to be followed by the searing heat and docu-drama style of *The Hill*, and the contrast offered by his next film, *The Spy Who Came in from the Cold*, which had a damp and shadowy quality that seemed thoroughly appropriate for the downbeat Cold War story that unfolded.

For a few years in the 1960s Morris was in greater demand than ever, and worked on a selection of films that seemed to sum up his whole career. The contrast of scale, theme, demands of stars, variable story quality and the continuous switch between black-and-white and colour stocks seemed not to bother him at all. In that time he rattled up credits such as *The Taming of the Shrew, Reflections in a Golden Eye* and *Oliver!* (the latter film making him the only person other than Charles Dickens to have a connection with both Carol Reed's film and David Lean's).

Fiddler on the Roof won Morris his only Oscar. His work on this film spanned all four seasons and a variety of locations, and although it was an example of the kind of unfussy approach that was his forte, there were no obvious signs that this was a Morris film. Indeed, Morris insists that he had no conscious trademark during his active career, and this clearly was one factor in his remarkable adaptability and longevity. By his own standards, the 1970s signalled a period of winding down, highlighted by a brush with Bond—completing studio shooting on *The Man with the Golden Gun*—his last professional encounter with Huston on *The Man Who Would Be King*, and the gloriously left-field *The Wiz*, which gave Morris his one and only experience of working on location in the United States. He made the most of it, lighting the New York Trade Center with thousands of multicoloured bulbs for one sequence.

Having collaborated with some of the greats on a selection of good, bad and forgettable movies made in the last forty years, his easygoing approach has served him well, the product of a unique education in the prewar British film industry, as well as the white heat of war itself. The result is a very British, very unassuming, very satisfying success story.

—Anwar Brett

MOSKVIN, Andrei

Cinematographer. **Nationality:** Russian. **Born:** Andrei Nikolaievich Moskvin in St. Petersburg, 14 February 1901. **Career:** 1922—co-founder, with Kozintsev, Trauberg, and Yutkevich, FEKS, and worked as cinematographer for these directors as well as for Eisenstein. **Awards:** Stalin Prize, 1946, 1948. **Died:** In Leningrad, 28 February 1961.

Films as Cinematographer:

1926   *Deviatoe yanvaria* (*Ninth of January*) (Viskovsky) (co); *Shinel* (*The Cloak*) (Kozintsev and Trauberg); *Katka bumazhnyi ranet* (*Katka's Reinette Apples*) (Johanson and Ermler) (co); *Chyortovo koleso* (*The Devil's Wheel*) (Kozintsev and Trauberg)

1927   *Bratichka* (*Little Brother*) (Kozintsev and Trauberg); *S.V.D.* (*Soyuz Velikogo Dela*; *The Club of the Big Deed*) (Kozintsev and Trauberg); *Turbina nr. 3* (*Turbine no. 3*) (Timoshenko) (co); *Pobediteli nochi* (*Victory of the Night*) (Timoshenko) (co); *Lektro* (*Electra*) (Timoshenko) (co); *Soikina lyubov* (*Soikin's Love*) (Timoshenko) (co); *Chuzhoy pidzhak* (*Ships*) (co)

1929   ***Novyi Vavilon*** (*The New Babylon*) (Kozintsev and Trauberg) (co)

1931   *Odna* (*Alone*) (Kozintsev and Trauberg); *Gopak* (Chakanovsky—short)
1932   *Hayl-Moskau* (Schmidgof) (co)
1935   *Yunost Maksima* (*The Youth of Maxim*) (Kozintsev and Trauberg)
1937   **Vozvrashcheniye Maksima** (*The Return of Maxim*) (Kozintsev and Trauberg)
1939   *Vyborgskaya storona* (*New Horizons*; *The Vyborg Side*) (Kozintsev and Trauberg) (co)
1943   *Aktrisa* (*The Actress*) (Trauberg)
1944   **Ivan Grozny** (*Ivan the Terrible, Part I*) (Eisenstein) (co)
1947   *Pirogov* (Kozintsev) (co)
1953   *Belinsky* (Kozintsev); *Nad Nemanom rassvet* (Fainzimmer)
1955   *Ovod* (*The Gadfly*) (Fainzimmer)
1956   *Prostiye lyudi* (*Simple People*) (Kozintsev and Traubert—produced in 1946) (co)
1957   *Don Quixote* (Kozintsev) (co); *Rasskazi o Lenine* (*Stories about Lenin*) (Yutkevich)
1958   **Ivan Grozny II: Boyarskii Zagovor** (*Ivan the Terrible, Part II: The Boyars' Plot*) (Eisenstein—produced in 1946)
1960   *Dama s sobachkoy* (*The Lady with the Dog*) (Heifitz) (co)
1963   *Hamlet* (Kozintsev) (co)

Publications

On MOSKVIN: articles—

Focus on Film, no. 13, 1973.
Iskusstvo Kino (Moscow), August 1996.

*   *   *

Andrei Moskvin was one of the most gifted of Soviet cinematographers. A few years younger than Edward Tisse, he did not have Tisse's background in newsreel photography, but he was fortunate in being able to work with the leading Soviet directors and, for the Kozintsev films, with the art director Yevgeni Enei, who was a perfect collaborator. Most of Moskvin's films were directed by Kozintsev and Trauberg, but even as early as 1927 he was a master of light and dark contrasts and highlighting in *The Club of the Big Deed*. Using Enei's fantastic sets in *The New Babylon*, his studio photography glittered to match the sardonic mood of the film, and in *Alone* he experimented with a narrow range of white tones. The Maxim trilogy (*The Youth of Maxim*, *The Return of Maxim*, and *The Vyborg Side*) made in the late 1930s is possibly the best work he did with Kozintsev and Trauberg. The careful selection of images as seen through Maxim's eyes (particularly in the first film) avoid virtuosity or artiness, but the films nevertheless take on a complete reality and mood of growing awareness and growth. But inevitably Moskvin is probably most famous for his work on Eisenstein's *Ivan the Terrible, Part I* and *Part II*. The ornate pictorial compositions of *Part I* are masterful, and the climax, the "true coronation" by the people of Ivan, brilliantly fits Eisenstein's thematic movement. *Part II*, for which Tisse himself filmed the exteriors, works boldly with a mixture of black-and-white interiors and color exterior sequences, culminating in the cathedral climax. Moskvin's last completed film was the masterpiece *The Lady with the Dog*, revealing his complete authoriy and control. He died while filming Kozintsev's *Hamlet*.

MÜLLER, Robby

Cinematographer. **Nationality:** Dutch. **Born:** Robert Müller in Curacao, Dutch West Indies, 4 April 1940; moved to Amsterdam, Holland, 1953. **Career:** 1964—assistant to cameraman Gerard Vandenberg in the Nederlandse Filmacademie, Amsterdam; moved to Germany where began collaboration with Wim Wenders. **Address:** c/o Smith Gosnell Nicholson & Associates, Pacific Palisades, CA, U.S.A.

Films as Cinematographer:

1963   *Megapolis I* (de la Parra) (+ ro); *Vogel* (*Bird*) (Sebestik)
1964   *De Lengte van een Ster* (*The Length of a Star*) (van Doorn) (co)
1966   *Eiland* (*Island*) (Terpstra) (co)
1967   *Bacher* (Tholen); *Norwegian Wood* (Meter); *Toets* (*Touch*) (Tholen) (co)
1968   *Objectief gezien* (*Objective Seen*) (van Doorn); *Don't Miss, Miss Pizz* (Kothuys); *Der Fall Lena Christ* (Geissendörfer—for TV)
1969   *She Is Like a Rainbow* (Kothuys) (co); *Jonathan* (Geissendörfer); *Alabama: 2000 Light Years* (Wenders) (co)
1970   *Frankenstein cum Cannabis* (Paape) (co); *Eine Rose für Jane* (Geissendörfer—for TV); *Pakbo* (Koch—for TV)
1971   *Het bezoek* (*The Visit*) (van de Staak); *Summer in the City* (Wenders); *Carlos* (Geissendörfer—for TV)
1972   *Can* (Przygodda) (co); *Die Scharlachrote Buchstabe* (Wenders); *Die Angst des Tormanns beim Elfmeter* (Wenders)
1973   *Die Reise nach Wien* (Reitz); *Jonathan* (Geissendörfer)
1974   *Alice in den Städten* (*Alice in the Cities*) (Wenders) (co); *Ein bisschen Liebe* (von Furstenberg); *Falsche Bewegung* (*The Wrong Move*) (Wenders)
1975   *Nathalie* (von Weitershausen); *Im Lauf der Zeit* (Wenders) (co)
1976   *Es herrscht Ruhe im Land* (Lilienthal) (co); *Die Wildente* (Geissendörfer); **Im Lauf der Zeit** (*Kings of the Road*) (Wenders)
1977   **Der amerikanische Freund** (*The American Friend*) (Wenders); *Avatar, the Return of the Wolf* (Zeillemaker); *Die linkshändige Frau* (*The Left-handed Woman*) (Handke)
1978   *Mysteries* (de Lussanet); *Die gläserne Zelle* (Geissendörfer)
1979   *Opname* (*In for Treatment*) (van Zuylen and Kok); *Saint Jack* (Bogdanovich)
1980   *Honeysuckle Rose* (*On the Road Again*) (Schatzberg)
1981   *They All Laughed* (Bogdanovich); *Die Gläserne Zelle* (*The Glass Cell*) (Geissendörfer)
1982   *Een zwoele zomeravond* (*A Sultry Summer Evening*) (Weisz and Strooker)
1983   *Les Îles* (Azimi) (co); *Un Dimanche de flics* (Vianey); *Les Tricheurs* (Schroeder) (+ ro); *Klassenfeind* (Stein)
1984   *Repo Man* (Cox); **Paris, Texas** (Wenders); *Body Rock* (Epstein); *Der Klassenfeind* (*Class Enemy*) (Stein); *Finnegan Begin Again* (Joan Micklin Silver—for TV)
1985   *The Longshot* (Bartel); *To Live and Die in L.A.* (Friedkin)
1986   *Down by Law* (Jarmusch)

1987   *Barfly* (Schroeder); *The Believers* (Schlesinger)
1988   *Il piccolo diavolo* (*The Little Devil*) (Benigni)
1989   *Coffee and Cigarettes II* (Jarmusch—short); *Mystery Train* (Jarmusch); *Aufzeichnungen zu Kleidern und Städten* (Wenders) (co)
1990   *Korczak* (Wajda)
1991   *A Notebook on Cities and Clothes* (Wenders—doc) (co); *Bis ans Ende der Welt* (*Until the End of the World*; *Jusqu'au bout du monde*) (Wenders)
1993   *Mad Dog and Glory* (McNaughton)
1995   *Dead Man* (Jarmusch); *Par-delà les nuages* (*Beyond the Clouds*) (Wenders)
1996   **Breaking the Waves** (von Trier)
1997   *The Tango Lesson* (Potter)
1998   *Shattered Image* (Ruiz)
1999   *Buena Vista Social Club* (Wenders); *Ghost Dog: The Way of the Samurai* (Jarmusch)
2000   *Dancer in the Dark*

Film as Actor:

1983   *Tricheurs* (*Youthful Sinners*) (Schroeder)
1990   *Motion and Emotion* (Joyce)
1993   *De Domeinen Ditvoorst* (*The Ditvoorst Domains*) (Hoffman)
1999   *Foot on the Moon* (Pijman)

Publications

By MÜLLER: articles—

Skrien (Amsterdam), Winter 1986–87.
Cahiers du Cinéma (Paris), no. 423, September 1989.

On MÜLLER: articles—

American Cinematographer (Hollywood), vol. 66, no. 2, February 1985.
American Film (Washington, D.C.), vol. 13, no. 3, December 1987.
Hollywood Reporter, vol. 306, no. 31, 7 March 1989.
Film Comment (New York), vol. 25, no. 5, September/October 1989.
Film Dope (Nottingham), March 1991.

*   *   *

Described by *Cinema Today*—perhaps a little fancifully—as "the greatest Dutchman with light since Vermeer," Robby Müller has worked on both sides of the Atlantic, photographing movies for directors with widely varying visions. He first sprung to prominence as Wim Wenders's camera magician, as the lensman behind such classics of the New German Cinema as *Kings of the Road*, *The American Friend*, and *Alice in the Cities*. Not all of Müller and Wenders's collaborations have had happy results: *Until the End of the World*, for instance, is an unfocused epic shot in more than a dozen countries. Nonetheless, Müller is arguably as important to the filmmaker as Nykvist was to Bergman.

By complete contrast to his "road" movies with Wenders, Müller has also shot intimate pictures, firmly rooted to place: there was his photography of *Barfly* for Barbet Schroeder, where he caught the bleary-eyed, slightly surreal Bukowski underground of late-night drinking dens, of alcoholic brawls and love affairs. Then there was his work on Jarmusch's *Down by Law*, in moody black and white, and his superb evocation of the sprawling, seething city in Friedkin's *To Live and Die in L.A.* Perhaps his most celebrated picture, again with Wenders, is *Paris, Texas*. Here, he depicts several different sides of American culture and myth: first, there is Ford's legendary West, familiar from *The Searchers*, a rugged terrain of deserts, eagles, and mountains; next, there are the antiseptic Californian suburbs, the haunt of affluent, middle-class families; and, finally, there are the grim, impersonal facades of Houston, a businessman's city whose skyscrapers, endless towers of glass and steel, are the antithesis of the great outdoors shown at the outset.

In the same year, 1984, he helped English director Alex Cox make a remarkably assured debut with the cultish *Repo Man*, which takes the same elements used elegiacally for Wenders on *Paris, Texas*—the long roads, sand, sky, cars—and recasts them in a comic vein. Müller has distinct ideas on how to light for laughs and how to set the visual tone for heavier drama. As he told the *Hollywood Reporter*, "Filming a comedy is different from (shooting) a dramatic film with documentary elements that are sometimes dark. Comedy needs another type of lighting, more light, more clarity."

Unlike Michael Ballhaus, another European cinematographer to carve out a substantial niche in 1980s Hollywood, Müller has not worked on blockbusters or overtly mainstream movies. He has tended to choose offbeat projects with innovative directors who will allow him the license to experiment: Jim Jarmusch, Joan Micklin Silver, Peter Bogdanovich, and Paul Bartel are names which spring to mind. Like one of those endlessly peripatetic characters with which Wenders fills his movies, Müller likes to travel, to change directions, to push back boundaries. Apart from America, Germany, and his native Holland, he has worked in the Far East, on Bogdanovich's underrated *Saint Jack*, and in Italy. (Wenders, of course, has dragged him all over the globe.)

Nevertheless, despite his versatility, Robby Müller is not in the top rank of cinematographers working today. He has not shot a great, stylized studio-based picture along the lines of a *Dick Tracy* (a triumph for the camera operator if not for the director) or anything of the grandeur of *1900* or *The Last Emperor*. *Paris, Texas* apart, there are few of his films that are uniquely, distinctly his, and that would have been beyond the ken of any other cinematographer. Perhaps Müller does not yet match up to the standards set by Gordon Willis or Vittorio Storaro, those two acknowledged "masters of light." Still, Müller is an endlessly resourceful lensman whose oeuvre marks a consistently fascinating clash between European and Hollywood aesthetics. In his European movies of the 1970s, particularly projects such as *The American Friend*, the Hollywood influence is manifest. By contrast, in his American pictures—particularly *Barfly* and his work with Jarmusch—he seems to strive for a looser, more fluid "European" feel. Storaro may have observed that "the emphasis in the average Hollywood film is on acting and story structure, and cinematographers are confined to recording performances." One thing is for sure, however: on whichever side of the Atlantic Müller chooses to work, he will never be confined merely to recording performance.

—Geoffrey Macnab, updated by Rob Edelman

MURAKI, Yoshiro

Art Director. **Nationality:** Japanese. **Born:** Tokyo, 1924. **Education:** Studied architecture, China University. **Family:** Married the art director Shinobu (Muraki). **Career:** 1947—joined Toho Studio as assistant art director; 1955—first film as art director, *Record of a Living Being*, first of many films directed by Kurosawa; 1970—with his wife, formed the independent art designing company Komu. **Awards:** Japanese Academy Award for *Ran*, 1985.

Films as Art Director:

1954   *Renai tokkyu* (*Love Express*) (Suzuki and Sugie) (asst)

1955   *Tenka taihei* (*The World Is Peaceful*) (Sugie—2 parts) (asst); *Ikomono no kiroku* (*Record of a Living Being*; *I Live in Fear*) (Kurosawa)

1956   *Kuroobi sangoku-shi* (*Black Belt History of Three Countries*) (Taniguchi); *Chiemi no haihiiru* (*Chiemi's High Heeled Shoes*) (Suzuki); *Aoi me* (*Blue Bud*) (Suzuki)

1957   *Kumonosu-jo* (*The Throne of Blood*) (Kurosawa); *Bibou no miyako* (*Beauty Capital*) (Matsubayashi); *Donzoko* (*The Lower Depths*) (Kurosawa)

1958   *Shachou sandai-ki* (*The Record of Three Generations of Presidents*) (Matsubayashi—2 parts); *Kakushi toride no sanakunin* (*The Hidden Fortress*) (Kurosawa)

1959   *Daigaku no oneichan* (*Young Girl at the University*) (Sugie); *Watash iwa kai ni naritai* (*I Want to Be a Shellfish*) (Hashimoto); *Aruhi watashi wa* (*One Day, I . . .*) (Okamoto); *Uwayaku shitayaku godouyaku* (*Seniors, Juniors, Colleagues*) (Honda); *Oneichan makari touru* (*Young Girl Dares to Pass*) (Sugie)

1960   *Otoko tai otoko* (*Man vs. Man*) (Taniguchi); *Warui yatsu hodo yoku nemuru* (*The Bad Sleep Well*) (Kurosawa); *Sarariiman Chushingura* (*Salaried Men's Loyal Ronin Story*) (Sugie—2 parts)

1961   *Minami no kaze to nami* (*South Wind and Waves*) (Hashimoto); *Yojimbo* (*The Bodyguard*) (Kurosawa); *Toiretto buchou* (*Toilet Section Chief*) (Kakei)

1962   *Sanjuro* (Kurosawa); *Shachou koukou-ko* (*The Story of the Company President's Overseas Travels*) (Sugie—2 parts); *Koukousei to onna kyoushi: hijou no seishun* (*High School Student and Woman Teacher: Merciless Youth*) (Onchi)

1963   *Tengoku to jigoku* (*High and Low*) (Kurosawa); *Goju man-nin no isan* (*The Legacy of the 500,000*) (Mifune); *Nippon ichi no iro-otoko* (*The Best Playboy in Japan*) (Furusawa)

1965   *Akahige* (*Red Beard*) (Kurosawa); *Tanuki no taishou* (*Badger General*) (Yamamoto); *Kemonomichi* (*The Way of the Beast*) (Sugawa)

1966   *Onna wa ikuman aritotemo* (*Although There Are Millions of Women*) (Sugie); *Jajauma narashi* (*The Taming of the Shrew*) (Sugie); *Sanbiki no tanuki* (*Three Badgers*) (Suzuki); *Tanuki no kyujitsu* (*Badger's Holiday*) (Yamamoto)

1967   *Jouiuchi* (*Rebellion*) (Kobayashi)

1968   *Toshigoro* (*The Prime of Life*) (Deme)

1969   *Dankon* (*Bullet Wound*) (Moritani)

1970   *Tora! Tora! Tora!* (Fleischer, Masuda, and Fukasaku); *Dodesukaden* (*Dodeskaden*) (Kurosawa)

1971   *Dare no tame ni aisuruka* (*For Whom Do We Love?*) (Deme)

1972   *Kaigun tokubetsu nenshouhei* (*Navy's Special Boy Sailors*) (Imai)

1973   *Ningen kakumei* (*Human Revolution*) (Masuda and Nakano); *Nippon chiubotsu* (*The Sinking of Japan*; *Tidal Wave*) (Moritani and Nakano)

1974   *Nosutoradamusu no daiyogen* (*Nostradamus's Great Prophecy*) (Masuda, Nakano, and Sakano)

1975   *Seishun no mon* (*The Gate of Youth*) (Urayama); *Tokyo-wan enjou* (*Tokyo Bay on Fire*) (Ishida and Nakano)

1976   *Suri Lanka no ai to wakare* (*Love and Separation in Sri Lanka*) (Kinoshita); *Zoku ningen kakumai* (*Human Revolution: Sequel*) (Masadu)

1977   *Seishun no mon: Jiritsu hen* (*The Gate of Youth: Independence*) (Urayama)

1978   *Seishoku no ishique* (*The Foundation of Ordination*) (Moritani)

1980   *Kagemusha* (*The Shadow Warrior*; *The Double*) (Kurosawa)

1982   *Maboroshi no mizuumi* (*Lake of Illusion*) (Hashimoto); *Kaikyou* (*Strait*) (Moritani)

1983   *Shousetsu Yoshida gakkou* (*Novel: Yoshida School*) (Moritani); *Izakaya Chouji* (*Chouki the Bar Owner*) (Kouhata)

1985   ***Ran*** (Kurosawa) (co)

1990   *Dreams* (Kurosawa) (co)

1991   *Rhapsody in August* (Kurosawa)

1999   *Ame agaru* (*After the Rain*) (Koizumi)

*   *   *

Although Yoshiro Muraki has worked on more than 60 films since the mid-1950s, he is most famous for his collaboration with Akira Kurosawa. He and his colleague and future wife Shinobu were nominally assistant art directors for Kurosawa's *Stray Dog*, but in fact were primarily responsible for the difficult job of constructing many sets under time and budget pressures.

He was promoted to art director in 1955, and his first work as art director for Kurosawa was in *Record of a Living Being*. Since that film, he has worked on all of the master director's films except *Dersu Uzala*. Kurosawa's extremely high standards challenged Muraki to create memorable production designs for each of his films. For example, the dark shining floors and audaciously simple interior sets of the castle of *The Throne of Blood* are an ideal backdrop for the intrigues of its occupants. Other memorable sets include the houses and restaurants along a road where gusts of wind swirl the dust in *Yojimbo*, the spacious hilltop mansion and the overheated hovel below in *High and Low*, and the erratic shapes of the living spaces in the slum in *Dodeskaden*.

As the scale and expense of Kurosawa's productions grew (limiting his filmmaking opportunities), Muraki's work came to symbolize the uncompromising standard of craftsmanship which Kurosawa demands from his crew. For *Kagemusha* and *Ran*, Muraki recreated the castles and battlefields of the sixteenth-century Japanese civil war period with meticulous care, choosing authentic furniture and construction materials in order to create the proper setting for the drama. His work is based on his own thorough historical research, as well as on his ingenuity in varying the scale of the sets and props to create the images which will work most effectively on film.

At Toho Studio, Muraki had worked on many other film genres, including white-collar office comedies, melodramas, youth romances, and action films. Since establishing his own design company in 1970, he has collaborated on many big-budget war films and disaster films.

—Kyoko Hirano

MURCH, Walter

Film Editor, Re-recording Engineer, Writer and Director. **Nationality:** American. **Education:** Attended Johns Hopkins University, Baltimore; graduate work at University of Southern California, Los Angeles. **Career:** 1969—first collaboration with the director Francis Ford Coppola, *The Rain People*; 1985—co-wrote and directed the film *Return to Oz*. **Awards:** British Academy (BAFTA) Film Awards for Best Film Editing and Best Sound Track, for *The Conversation*, 1974 (editing and sound); Academy Award for Best Sound, for *Apocalypse Now*, 1979; Lifetime Achievement Award, Cinema Audio Society, 1994; Academy Awards for Best Film Editing and Best Sound, American Cinema Editors Eddie Award for Best Edited Feature Film, BAFTA Film Award for Best Editing, for *The English*

Walter Murch

Patient, 1997; Maverick Tribute Award, Cinequest San Jose Film Festival, 1998.

Films as Supervising Sound Editor/Re-recording Engineer:

1969   *The Rain People* (Coppola)
1971   *THX 1138* (Lucas) (+ co-wr)
1972   ***The Godfather*** (Coppola)
1973   ***American Graffiti*** (Lucas)
1974   ***The Godfather, Part II*** (Coppola)
1979   ***Apocalypse Now*** (Coppola) (+ ed)
1981   *Dragonslayer* (M. Robbins)
1990   *Ghost* (Zucker) (+ ed); *The Godfather, Part III* (Coppola) (+ ed)
1993   *House of Cards* (Lessac) (+ ed)
1994   *Romeo Is Bleeding* (Medak) (+ ed); *Crumb* (Zweigoff)
1995   *First Knight* (Zucker) (+ ed)

Films as Editor:

1974   ***The Conversation*** (Coppola)
1977   *Julia* (Zinnemann)
1986   *Captain Eo* (Coppola)
1988   *The Unbearable Lightness of Being* (Kaufman)
1996   *The English Patient* (Minghella)
1999   *The Talented Mr. Ripley* (Minghella); *Dunbarton Bridge* (Koppelman) (consulting editor)

Film as Director and Co-Writer:

1970   *THX 1138* (co-sc only)
1985   *Return to Oz*

Publications

By MURCH: book—

In the Blink of an Eye, Sydney, 1992.

By MURCH: articles—

''Interview with Walter Murch, Sound Designer,'' in *Positif* (Paris), no. 335, January 1989.
Introduction to *Audio-Vision*, by Michel Chion, New York, 1994.
Chapter on Sound Design, in *Projections 4*, London, 1995.
''From Here to Eternity,'' in *DGA Magazine* (Los Angeles), May-June 1997.

On MURCH: articles—

Filmmakers Newsletter (Ward Hill, Massachusetts), December 1974.
Cinefax, December 1980.
Journal of the University Film and Video Association, Vol. 33, No. 4, Fall 1981.

"Sound Mixing and *Apocalypse Now*," in *Film Sound: Theory and Practice*, edited by Elisabeth Weis and John Belton, New York, 1985.
Cinefax, June 1985.
Jones, Alan, on *Return to Oz* in *Cinefantastique* (New York), July 1985.
American Film (Washington, D.C.), October 1989.
Weaver, J.M., "Auditieve auteurs," in *Skrien* (Amsterdam), February/March 1995.

*   *   *

Walter Murch calls himself a sound designer, disdaining the traditional title sound editor, and refers to his work as a sound montage, not a sound track. To some degree, these changes reflect the growing accommodation of moviemaking craft to the cultural area of art. Long associated with Francis Coppola and George Lucas, Murch is very much identified with the movement now termed retrospectively as the "Hollywood Renaissance," a period of American filmmaking that manifested, in part, a rejection of commercial approaches and a flourishing of European-derived ideas of cinema art. To term the sound track a montage, of course, is nothing new; film theorists from Eisenstein to the semioticians have recognized the complex ways in which sounds themselves may be layered and the resulting "mix" juxtaposed with the succession of images. Murch expresses this traditional view when he says: "Out of the juxtaposition of what the sound is telling you and what the picture is telling you, you (the audience) come up with a third idea which is composed of both picture and sound and resolves their superficial differences."

Yet Murch's description of his activity as sound designer does reflect a significant change within the industry, a change Murch himself has been somewhat responsible for. For even as various techniques have enabled a richer, more powerful, and layered sound track to be produced, so have films become more aural (if not less visible), with sound contributing much more than in the past to the total cinematic experience.

Murch's work on Coppola's *The Conversation* is both exemplary and instructive in this regard. The film concerns the morally dubious activities of a professional eavesdropper, a technician who is the film's self-reflexive image of its own preoccupations with the sound mix. Murch's effects are complicated here and take full advantage of the fact that sound, unlike image, can be "located" both within the story world and outside it, in the realm of narrative comment. The film's initial bravura sequence, justly celebrated, features a gradual zoom in to a crowded city park where the actions and conversation of a "target" couple are to be recorded. While the camera has no trouble providing a more or less unproblematic series of images, the sound track is filled with audio bleeps, distorting noises, gaps, and inadequate levels. The spectator is disoriented by the montage of clear image track and unclear sound, but this disorientation is soon revealed as "motivated," that is, we are seeing and hearing with the surveillers. Both image and sound are provided by diegetic narrators, and the limitations of both are reproduced by the film's narrator. The subsequent editing of the recorded conversation is depicted and eventually leads to the revelation that the eavesdropper has been used by his employers as part of a murder scheme. The sound images of this conversation (and occasionally the visual ones as well) also figure subjectively in the film, as part of the main character's consciousness and memory. Though the film has nondiegetic music (mainly a simple piano melody which plays expressively, in the traditional way, over certain diegetic sound silent sequences), it has no music director.

Murch is responsible, as sound designer, for the integration of music *and* sound. In fact, nondiegetic noise often performs the traditional function of musical phrases. As the eavesdropper examines the motel toilt which, he thinks, may reveal the traces of the murder for which he is partly responsible, we hear, louder than normal, the sound of the toilet valve on the sound track. Gradually, this diegetic sound is merged with audio bleeps reminding us of the recorded conversation, and this sound in turn is transformed into a very loud and grating nondiegetic synthesized noise (which resembles very squeaky train brakes). Though nondiegetic, this sound expresses the horror and becomes the narrational correlative of the eavesdropper's discovery: as he flushes the toilet, it spills over with blood and bandages, revealing his fears to be justified. Murch here appears to be developing further the use of "shrieking violins" in *Psycho*. He also anticipates much contemporary sound design where the distinction between music ("organized noise") and other expressive nondiegetic sounds has been problematized.

Murch's other work is similarly interesting, if less foregrounded by the dramatic elements of the films in question. In *THX 1138*, a modernist science-fiction film scripted by George Lucas and Murch (with Coppola as executive producer), Murch demonstrates how much our sense of reality depends on the myriad of sounds we constantly hear. The horrifying vision of a future world inhabited by exploited workers forced by the government to take mind-altering drugs is completed by an alternate reality of unpleasant, disorienting sounds which are constantly difficult to "read." *THX 1138* is a rare, perhaps unique production in which the sound designer is also responsible in part for the script (an interesting reversal of the more ordinary case in which the director, whose province is largely the image, is also the film's writer). Not a commercial success, the film is nonetheless a minor masterpiece of the genre because it demonstrates the centrality of sound and hearing in our relationship to the real.

Apocalypse Now offered Murch a different kind of challenge: not creating an alternate reality, but forging a hyperreality, an intersection between a dense world of aural experience and the subjectivity of those trapped within it. The most notable and typical sound image in this film is thus the aural equivalent of a fade out/fade in. As he lies in a Saigon hotel room in a drunken, drugged stupor, the film's protagonist dreams of a nightmare jungle, engulfed by flames, traversed by ghostly helicopters, their rotors beating a surreal, otherworldly "whoosh." He wakes and the whoosh "bleeds" into the whirr of the overhead fan. This is indeed an effect aptly termed a montage, and it demonstrates the incredible talent of Murch and the importance of his contributions to the art cinema of the Hollywood Renaissance.

During the last decade and a half, Murch has continued to find steady employment in a very different kind of Hollywood, one unfortunately devoted to the kinds of special effects—those that produce violent spectacle and visual fantasy—in which he has less interest. Nevertheless he has been able to work on projects outside the mainstream action film. *Return to Oz* allowed Murch to revisit a favored childhood story; the result is a rather ordinary, if quite competent, film substantially aided by his direction and screenwriting contributions. *The Godfather, Part III*, with its epic sweep and several complex sequences, challenged his sound editing and rerecording skills, as did *Ghost*, with its need for otherworldly visual and sound images; the success of both films is to be credited in part to Murch's abilities. Even Murch's artistry could not save the dismal production of *First Knight* from failure; yet it is undeniable that his effects create the proper aural ambience for an Arthurian fantasy. The neo-noirness of *Romeo Is Bleeding* unfortunately did not offer Murch a chance to recreate his stunning effects from *The Conversation*; even Murch's considerable skills as an editor were not up to the task of rescuing director Medak's confusingly told story from tedium and, frequently, inconsequence. Murch was more successful in editing *The Unbearable Lightness of Being*, based on the complex and often obscure Milan Kundera novel; here Murch is able to articulate the intimate connection between erotic and political events through judicious cutting, though he proved unable to reduce the film to a manageable commercial length (it runs almost three hours).

Murch's most notable recent project, editing the film adaptation of surrealistic Michael Ondratjie novel *The English Patient*, offered Murch even better opportunities to create meaning through the editing process, a task whose joys and discontents are experienced by his closest fictional reflex, the harried private detective and sound engineer of *The Conversation*. The novel's confusingly implausible, even absurd plot was expertly trimmed by scenarist/director Anthony Minghella, yielding a still complex story of bizarrely intertwined fates; Murch's contribution was to make sure the plot's intricately connected segments of present action and flashback made sense and did not appear to be simply disconcerting fragments. Despite the considerable challenge, Murch was extremely successful, making the most of Mighella's fine direction of a talented cast and John Seale's lushly poetic cinematography.

—R. Barton Palmer

MUREN, Dennis

Visual Effects Director. **Nationality:** American. **Born:** Glendale, California, 1 November 1946. **Education:** Pasadena City College, California, 1966–68; studied business at California State University, Los Angeles. **Family:** Married Zara Pinfold, 1981. **Career:** 1968–75—Freelance special effects expert (specializing in stop motion and miniature photography); 1975–76—camera operator for Cascade of California, Hollywood; 1976—recruited for the Industrial Light and Magic company; 1980—promoted to ILM visual effects director, pioneering work in computer animation; currently senior special effects supervisor at ILM. Television work: 1978, *Battlestar Galactica*; 1984, *Caravan of Courage* (*The Ewok Adventure*). **Awards:** Academy Awards for effects (shared) for *The Empire Strikes Back*, *E.T.*, *Return of the Jedi*, *Indiana Jones and the Temple of Doom*, *Innerspace*, *The Abyss*, *Terminator 2: Judgement Day*, *Jurassic Park*, and *Star Wars: Episode I—The Phantom Menace;* Special Academy Scientific/Technical Award for the development of a Motion Picture Figure Mover for animation photography, 1981; British Academy of Film and Television Awards (shared) for *Return of the Jedi*, *Indiana Jones and the Temple of Doom*, *Terminator 2: Judgement Day,* and *Jurassic Park*; Emmy Award for *Caravan of Courage*; Star on the Walk of Fame; Academy of Science Fiction, Horror, and Fantasy Films Saturn Award for *Star Wars: Episode I—The Phantom Menace*, 2000. **Member:** American Society of Cinematographers; Academy of Motion Picture Arts and Sciences.

Films (all special effects credits in collaboration):

1971   *Equinox* (J. Woods)
1974   *Flesh Gordon* (Ziehm, Benveniste) (miniatures; rear projection)

1977   ***Star Wars*** (Lucas) (animation sequence); ***Close Encounters of the Third Kind*** (Spielberg)
1980   ***The Empire Strikes Back*** (Kershner)
1981   *Dragonslayer* (M. Robbins) (miniatures; optics)
1982   ***E.T.*** (Spielberg) (visual sfx supervisor)
1983   ***Return of the Jedi*** (R. Marquand)
1984   *Indiana Jones and the Temple of Doom* (Spielberg)
1985   *Young Sherlock Holmes* (Levinson)
1986   *Captain Eo* (Coppola) (short)
1987   *Innerspace* (Dante); *Empire of the Sun* (Spielberg)
1988   *Willow* (R. Howard)
1989   *Ghostbusters II* (Reitman); *The Abyss* (Cameron)
1991   *Terminator 2: Judgement Day* (Cameron)
1993   *Jurassic Park* (Spielberg) (full motion dinosaurs)
1995   *Casper* (B. Silberling); *Jumanji* (J. Johnston)
1996   *Twister* (de Bont)
1997   *The Lost World: Jurassic Park* (Spielberg); *Deconstructing Harry* (Allen)
1999   ***Star Wars: Episode I—The Phantom Menace*** (Lucas)

*   *   *

From the endearingly arthritic monsters of *Equinox* to the eye-popping big-as-life dinosaurs of *Jurassic Park* and its sequels, the career of special effects artist Dennis Muren offers a virtual step-by-step guide to the evolution of cinema wizardry over the past three decades. Associated with George Lucas' groundbreaking effects house Industrial Light & Magic since its precarious beginnings in 1975, Muren's work in the ever-expanding field of computer animation has (somewhat ironically) supplanted the now outmoded stop motion techniques that attracted him to the industry in the first place. Muren is a multiple Academy Award winner from *The Empire Strikes Back* onwards. His regular collaborations with fantasy giants Lucas and Steven Spielberg illustrate all too clearly the double-edged nature of state-of-the-art effects technology: the more marvels there are available at the touch of a keyboard button, the less room there is for individual flair and imagination (not to mention restraint). The *Jurassic Park* dinosaurs may be flawless in digital execution and jaw-dropping on screen, yet they remain oddly anonymous when compared with the best work of stop motion specialists Willis O'Brien and Ray Harryhausen. Similarly, the menagerie of CGI space creatures in *Phantom Menace* seems to have strayed into the film from some ultra high-tech arcade game, existing only to be blasted into oblivion for maximum points. Muren and colleagues can guarantee a special effects roller coaster ride; what they can no longer promise is a monster to remember.

Begun when its creator was still a teenager, Muren's debut effort *Equinox* (1966–69) should be viewed charitably. Working as producer, co-director, co-photographer and co-special effects man, he enlisted the assistance of fellow animation fan Dave Allen, with a little professional help from Academy Award nominee Jim Danforth. If the amateur 16mm production did not quite do justice to the intriguing story of a missing professor (a cameo from fantasy writer Fritz Leiber), an occult bible and monsters from an infernal dimension, there was at least a show of promise, though the "professional" version released in 1971 by producer Jack E. Harris (with new footage) didn't set the world on fire. Muren's first real professional feature film work, handling some of the miniature and rear projection shots for the watered-down porno parody *Flesh Gordon*, was still on

Dennis Muren (second from left)

the very fringes of mainstream filmmaking but, combined with his work on television commercials, it got him noticed by George Lucas.

Founded to handle the unprecedented number of effects shots needed for *Star Wars* (363), Industrial Light & Magic (ILM) consisted of over 70 employees. While others worked on the revolutionary computerised motion-control scenes (which permitted the camera and model spacecraft movements to be synchronised in a preplanned sequence), Muren handled the brief scene featuring animated chess figures. Though almost a throwaway in the finished film, the miniature monsters stick in the mind, each given just enough hint of bizarre personality. Having become acquainted with Spielberg on *Close Encounters of the Third Kind*, Muren came into his own with *The Empire Strikes Back*, which made striking use of stop motion animation, most notably the Evil Empire's giant four-legged attack machines.

Promoted to visual effects supervisor on *E.T.*, Muren contributed impressive work but not the one special effect everyone remembered: *E.T.* himself (a mechanical device designed by Carlo Rambaldi). Overseeing the climactic space battle in *Return of the Jedi*, he freely admitted to both a visible error in a multispacecraft crossover shot and the occasional feeling that the end results never quite lived up to

expectations. With the unlovely *Indiana Jones and the Temple of Doom*, Muren went back to stop motion work, ingeniously adapting a standard 35mm stills camera to take shots of a model mine car and its occupants. Edited into a chase sequence, the resulting footage didn't quite work, the animation jarring with the live action. Clearly a case of room for improvement. *Young Sherlock Holmes* showcased some of ILM's first work with computer animation, bringing a stained-glass knight to impressive life. Basically the computer manipulation of digitally stored images (either scanned or computer generated), the process was further refined in *Willow*, an amiable (if violent) reworking of *Star Wars* in a sword and sorcery milieu. Alongside a two-headed, troll-chomping monster (unkindly compared by some to *Flesh Gordon*'s penisaurus), the film introduced audiences to the techno-miracle of morphing, the computerised transformation of one digitally stored image into another. Thus enchanted enchantress Patricia Hayes could be seamlessly metamorphosed into a goat, an ostrich, a tiger and finally herself. *Terminator II* gave the technique a sinister slant, with its ''liquid metal'' cyborg assassin.

With *Jurassic Park*, Muren and his collaborators finally convinced audiences that dinosaurs do indeed walk the earth. What neither he nor Spielberg could achieve was a sequence to match the Giant Gorilla-Allosaurus fight in the original *King Kong* or the caveman-dinosaur set-to devised by Harryhausen for *One Million Years BC*. Revisiting Jurassic territory for the disappointing *Lost World* sequel, Muren threw in a whole family of human-chomping Tyranosaurus Rex yet couldn't escape the law of diminishing returns (not helped by Spielberg's blatant lack of interest in the proceedings). Spectacle and shocks are fine but the effect is transitory. *Phantom Menace*, which reduces the once fresh and inventive *Star Wars* formula to a series of dull, merchandise-oriented set-pieces, lacks even the most superficial thrills. Hamstrung by poor storytelling and non-existent characterisation, ILM couldn't achieve an engaging or believable alien universe. Muren's most interesting effect of recent years is Robin Williams' permanently out-of-focus actor in *Deconstructing Harry*, a relatively small-scale piece of trickery that enhances rather than overwhelms the accompanying storyline. This aside, it remains to be seen if Muren can still impose the kind of imagination that fired *Equinox* on the vast bank of digital marvels at his disposal.

—Daniel O'Brien

MUSURACA, Nicholas

Cinematographer. **Nationality:** Italian. **Born:** 1892; sometimes billed as Nick Musuraca in the 1920s. **Career:** 1913—projectionist, editor, and assistant director, Vitagraph, New York, and from 1918 cameraman; joined Robertson-Cole, and stayed with its successor companies, FBO and RKO, until 1954; then freelance, often for TV. **Died:** In 1975.

Films as Cinematographer:

1923   *On the Banks of the Wabash* (Blackton)
1926   *Hell Bent for Heaven* (Blackton); *The Passionate Quest* (Blackton); *The Gilded Highway* (Blackton); *Bride of the Storm* (Blackton); *Shameful Behavior?* (Kelley); *His New York Wife* (Kelley)
1927   *The Sonora Kid* (De Lacey); *The Cherokee Kid* (De Lacey); *South Sea Love* (R. Ince); *Lightning Lariats* (De Lacey); *Cyclone of the Range* (De Lacey); *Splitting the Breeze* (De Lacey); *Tom's Gang* (De Lacey)
1928   *Last Lap* (Mitchell); *Orphan of the Sage* (L. King); *Rough Ridin' Red* (L. King); *Red Riders of Canada* (De Lacey); *Tropic Madness* (Vignola); *Tyrant of Red Gulch* (De Lacey); *When the Law Rides* (De Lacey); *The Avenging Rider* (Fox); *Terror* (L. King); *The Charge of the Gauchos* (Kelley); *Dog Justice* (Storm)
1929   *The Freckled Rascal* (L. King); *Gun Law* (De Lacey or Burch); *Idaho Red* (De Lacey); *The Pride of Pawnee* (De Lacey); *Side Street* (St. Clair); *The Red Sword* (Vignola); *The Trail of the Horse Thieves* (De Lacey)
1930   *The Cuckoos* (Sloane); *Inside the Line* (Pomeroy); *The Conspiracy* (Cabanne); *Half Shot at Sunset* (Sloane); *Hook, Line, and Sinker* (Cline)

1931   *Cracked Nuts* (Cline); *The Sin Ship* (Wolheim); *Three Who Loved* (Archainbaud); *Too Many Cooks* (Seiter); *Everything's Rosie* (Bruckman); *Smart Woman* (La Cava)
1932   *Come on Danger* (Hill); *Men of Chance* (Archainbaud); *Haunted Gold* (Wright)
1933   *Crossfire* (Brower); *Cheyenne Kid* (Hill); *Scarlet River* (Brower); *Son of the Border* (Nosler); *Flying Devils* (Birdwell); *Headline Shooter* (*Evidence in Camera*) (Brower); *Chance at Heaven* (Seiter)
1934   *Long Lost Father* (Shoedsack); *Sing and Like It* (Seiter); *Where Sinners Meet* (Ruben); *Murder on the Blackboard* (Archainbaud); *We're Rich Again* (Seiter); *The Richest Girl in the World* (Seiter); *By Your Leave* (Corrigan); *Romance in Manhattan* (Roberts)
1935   *Old Man Rhythm* (Ludwig); *Murder on a Honeymoon* (Corrigan); *Village Tale* (Cromwell); *To Beat the Band* (Stoloff)
1936   *Two in the Dark* (Stoloff); *Silly Billies* (Guiol); *Second Wife* (Killy); *The Farmer in the Dell* (Holmes); *The Plot Thickens* (Holmes); *Murder on a Bridle Path* (Killy and Hamilton)
1937   *Saturday's Heroes* (Killy); *We're on the Jury* (Holmes); *China Passage* (Killy); *Too Many Wives* (Holmes); *There Goes My Girl* (Holmes); *Border Cafe* (Landers); *The Big Shot* (Killy); *Flight from Glory* (Landers); *Living on Love* (Landers); *Danger Patrol* (Landers)
1938   *Quick Money* (Killy); *Crashing Hollywood* (Landers); *Blind Alibi* (Landers); *Everybody's Doing It* (Cabanne); *Night Spot* (Cabanne); *Condemned Women* (Landers); *Law of the Underworld* (Landers); *Smashing the Rackets* (Landers); *Tarnished Angel* (Goodwins)
1939   *Golden Boy* (Mamoulian); *Pacific Liner* (Landers); *Sorority House* (Farrow); *Twelve Crowded Hours* (Landers); *Five Came Back* (Farrow); *Allegheny Uprising* (*The First Rebel*) (Seiter)
1940   *A Bill of Divorcement* (Farrow); *Swiss Family Robinson* (Ludwig); *Tom Brown's School Days* (Stevenson); *The Stranger on the Third Floor* (Ingster)
1941   *Lady Scarface* (Woodruff); *Repent at Leisure* (Woodruff); *Little Man* (McLeod); *The Gay Falcon* (Reis); *Obliging Young Lady* (Wallace); *Play Girl* (Woodruff); *Hurry, Charlie, Hurry* (Roberts)
1942   **Cat People** (Tourneur); *The Navy Comes Through* (Sutherland); *Pirates of the Prairie* (Seitz); *Call Out the Marines* (Ryan and Hamilton); *The Tuttles of Tahiti* (C. Vidor)
1943   *The Ghost Ship* (Robson); *Forever and a Day* (Clair and others) (co); *The Fallen Sparrow* (Wallace); *The Seventh Victim* (Robson); *Bombardier* (Wallace); *Gangway for Tomorrow* (Auer)
1944   *Curse of the Cat People* (Wise); *Marine Raiders* (Schuster); *Bride by Mistake* (Wallace); *The Falcon in Hollywood* (Douglas); *Girl Rush* (Douglas)
1945   *Back to Bataan* (Dmytryk); *The Spiral Staircase* (Siodmak); *China Sky* (Enright)
1946   *Deadline at Dawn* (Clurman); *Bedlam* (Robson); *The Locket* (Brahm)
1947   *The Bachelor and the Bobby-Soxer* (*Bachelor Knight*) (Reis) (co); ***Out of the Past*** (*Build My Gallows High*) (Tourneur)
1948   *I Remember Mama* (Stevens); *Blood on the Moon* (Wise)
1949   *Stagecoach Kid* (Landers); *The Mysterious Desperado* (Selander)

1950   *Born to Be Bad* (Ray); *The Woman on Pier 13* (*I Married
         a Communist*) (Stevenson); *Riders from Tucson* (Selander);
         Dynamite Pass (Landers); *Where Danger Lives* (Farrow);
         The Company She Keeps (Cromwell); *Hunt the Man Down*
         (Archainbaud)
1951   *Hot Lead* (Gilmore); *Roadblock* (Daniels); *The Whip Hand*
         (Menzies)
1952   *Clash By Night* (F. Lang); *A Girl in Every Port* (Erskine);
         Trail Guide (Selander)
1953   *Split Second* (Powell); *Susan Slept Here* (Tashlin); *The Blue
         Gardenia* (F. Lang); *Devil's Canyon* (Werker); *The Hitch-
         Hiker* (Lupino)
1957   *The Story of Mankind* (Allen); *Man on the Prowl* (Napoleon)
1958   *Too Much Too Soon* (Napoleon) (co)

Publications

On MUSURACA: article—

Focus on Film, no. 13, 1973.
Turner, George, in *American Cinematographer* (Hollywood),
     March 1984.
Film Dope (Nottingham), March 1991.
Turner, G., "Wrap Shot," in *American Cinematographer* (Holly-
     wood), October 1997.

*   *   *

Nicholas Musuraca's name remains unjustly obscure among the
ranks of cinematographers from Hollywood's golden age. In his
prime years at RKO during the 1940s, Musuraca shuttled back and
forth between A- and B-films, prestige pictures, and genre potboilers.
For this reason, and because many of the motion pictures photographed by Musuraca have attained a classic or landmark status only
recently, he remains a neglected master.

Along with Gregg Toland's work on *Citizen Kane*, Musuraca's
cinematography for *The Stranger on the Third Floor* defined the
visual conventions for the *film noir* and codified the RKO look for the
1940s. Musuraca's photography begins and ends with shadows,
owing a major debt to German Expressionism, and can be seen as the
leading factor in the resurrection of the style in Hollywood in the
1940s. The dominant tone in his work is black, a stylistic bias that lent
itself to the *film noir* and the moody horror films of Val Lewton. But
even within the confines of the studio system Musuraca succeeded in
transposing his style to other genres. The western *Blood on the Moon*
and George Stevens's nostalgic family drama *I Remember Mama* are
both infused with the same shadowy visuals that Musuraca brought to
the horror film in *Cat People* and the *film noir* in *The Locket*. Through
the conventions of varying genres and the differing requirements of
numerous directors, Musuraca maintained a uniform personal aesthetic.

The whole of Musuraca's readily identifiable style can be broken
down into five consistent fragments: the use of the complete tonal
range of black and white; the low placement of lighting sources;
narrow beams of high-key light within a dark frame; a silhouetting
technique with an emphasis on lighting for contour; and a penchant
for abstraction. The first of these stylistic signatures is the use of the
full tonal range of black and white. Best exemplified by the outdoor
sequences in *Out of the Past*, Musuraca created the moving equivalent
of Ansel Adams's "Zone System" of photography in which deep
blacks, smooth grays, and sharp whites coexist within the frame. The
motion pictures which Musuraca photographed possess a richness
and variety of tone that give even the low-budget films an opulent
texture. His second rule provided a naturalistic means to achieve an
expressionistic result. The low placement of light sources—often in
the guise of table lamps, but also fireplaces and campfires—netted
a highly expressionistic look as the illuminated subject was trapped
by his or her own shadow looming on the walls and ceiling above. The
creation of claustrophobia within the frame provided visual collusion
for the onerousness of *film noir* narratives. The third Musuraca trait
called for tightly defined high-key light focused on objects, most
often faces, in the black void. The technique simultaneously directs
the eye to the primary point of interest within the frame while
emphasizing the surrounding darkness leading to a tension as the
conflicting tones attempt to dominate. Musuraca's fourth and most
readily identifiable trademark is a skimming-silhouetting technique.
Figures or faces in the foreground are lit from the side or rear,
emphasizing contour while leaving the front largely dark. The resulting highlighted contour of the silhouetted object separates it from the
background adding depth to the frame. It is this individual trait that
accounts for much of the "archetypal" *noir* look of *The Locket* and *Out
of the Past*.

A strong reliance on tonal tension featuring large areas of black led
Musuraca to the verge of abstraction in many cases. This fifth trait is
evident in a number of the films he photographed as the frame is
shattered into geometric patterns of light and shadow. In *The Seventh
Victim* a cosmetics factory at night becomes little more than a collection of rectangular shapes of varying tone. Similarly, many shots of
nocturnal San Francisco in *Out of the Past* suggest that the city is
constructed of black quadrangles and white squares of light rather
than brick and mortar. In *Cat People* threat is conveyed by the
changing density of the reflected patterns of rippling water on the
walls and ceiling surrounding an indoor pool. Musuraca formulated
a personal style in a more pronounced way than many other
cinematographers working within the studio system, a style that
dictated that any place could be threatening at any time. The shadows
with which he spoke were just as ominous in the warm kitchen of
a turn-of-the-century home as they were in a contemporary landscape
or an 18th-century insane asylum. With darkness and light as his
instruments, Musuraca charted the topography of menace with unparalleled consistency and artistry.

—Eric Schaefer

N

NEAME, Ronald

Cinematographer and director. **Nationality:** British. **Born:** London, 23 April 1911; father, Elwin Neame, director of silent films, mother Ivy Close, actress. **Education:** University College School and Hurstpierpoint College. **Family:** Married 1) Beryl Heanly 15 October 1933; one son, Christopher Elwin; 2) Dona Friedberg 12 September 1993. **Career:** Became messenger and tea boy at British International Film Studios, 1925; clapper boy and camera assistant on Hitchcock's *Blackmail*, 1929; became director of photography, 1934; became producer at Cineguild with Noel Coward, David Lean and Anthony Havelock-Allen (company made *Great Expectations* (1946), *Oliver Twist* (1947), and *The Passionate Friends* (1948); as director of photography became known for the quality of colour filming; turned to directing in 1947; teacher of direction at University of California, Los Angeles from 1992; member of Directors' Guild of America, American Film Institute, Academy of Motion Pictures, Arts and Sciences (Governor, 1977–79), British Academy of Film and Television Arts (London and Los Angeles), Savile Club (London). **Awards:**

Ronald Neame

Commander of the British Empire (CBE), 1996. **Address:** 2317 Kimridge Road, Beverley Hills, CA 90210, U.S.A.

Films as Cinematographer:

1933   *Happy* (Zelnik)
1934   *Give Her a Ring* (*Giving You the Stars*) (Woods); *Girls Will Be Boys* (Varnel)
1935   *A Star Fell From Heaven* (Merzbach); *Weekend Millionaire* (Woods); *Music Hath Charms* (Bentley, Esway, Summers and Woods); *Joy Ride* (Hughes); *Invitation to the Waltz* (Reinhardt); *Honours Easy* (Brenon); *Drake of England* (*Drake the Pirate*, *Elizabeth of England*) (Woods)
1936   *Once in a Million* (Woods); *The Improper Duchess* (Hughes); *The Crimes of Stephen Hawke* (King); *Cafe Colette* (*Danger in Paris*) (Stein)
1937   *Keep Fit* (Kimmins); *Feather Your Nest* (Beaudine); *Brief Ecstasy* (*Dangerous Secrets*) (Bréville); *Against the Tide* (Bryce)
1938   *Who Goes Next?* (Elvey); *The Ware Case* (Stevenson); *Second Thoughts* (*The Crime of Peter Frame*) (Parker); *Penny Paradise* (Reed); *It's in the Air* (*George Takes the Air*) (Kimmins); *I See Ice* (Kimmins); *The Gaunt Stranger* (*The Phantom Strikes*) (Forde)
1939   *Young Man's Fancy* (Stevenson); *Trouble Brewing* (Kimmins); *Let's Be Famous* (Forde); *The Four Just Men* (*The Secret Four*) (Forde); *Come on George* (Kimmins); *Cheer Boys Cheer* (Forde)
1940   *Saloon Bar* (Forde); *Return to Yesterday* (Stevenson); *Let George Do It* (Varnel)
1941   *Major Barbara* (Pascal, French and Lean)
1942   *One of Our Aircraft Is Missing* (Powell and Pressburger); *In Which We Serve* (Coward and Lean)
1944   *This Happy Breed* (Lean) (+ sc)
1945   *Blithe Spirit* (Lean) (+ sc)

Films as Director:

1947   *Take My Life*
1950   *The Golden Salamander* (+ co-pr, co-sc)
1952   *The Card* (*The Promoter*)
1953   *The Million Pound Note* (*Man with a Million*)
1956   *The Man Who Never Was*
1957   *The Seventh Sin*
1958   *Windom's Way*; *The Horse's Mouth* (+ pr)
1960   *Tunes of Glory*
1962   *Escape from Zahrain* (+ pr)

1963   *I Could Go on Singing*
1964   *The Chalk Garden*
1965   *Mister Moses*
1966   *A Man Could Get Killed*; *Gambit*
1968   *Prudence and the Pill*
1969   *The Prime of Miss Jean Brodie*
1970   *Scrooge*
1972   *The Poseidon Adventure*
1974   *The Odessa File* (*Die Akte Odessa, Der Fall Odessa*)
1979   *Meteor* (+ ro as British Representative)
1980   *Hopscotch*
1981   *First Monday in October*
1986   *Foreign Body*
1990   *The Magic Balloon* (+ sc)

Other Films:

1929   *Blackmail* (Hitchcock) (asst ph)
1946   *Brief Encounter* (Lean) (co-pr, co-sc); *Great Expectations*
          (Lean) (co-pr, sc)
1948   *Oliver Twist* (Lean) (pr)
1949   *The Passionate Friends* (*One Woman's Story*) (Lean) (pr)
1951   *The Magic Box* (Boulting) (pr)
1999   *Hitchcock: Shadow of a Genius* (*Dial H Hitchcock: The
          Genius Behind the Showman, Dial H for Hitchcock*)
          (Haimes—for TV) (ro as himself)

Publications

By NEAME: articles—

"Return of the Native," interview with G. Fuller, in *Stills*, no. 25,
    March 1986.
"Remembering Hitchcock," in *DGA* (Los Angeles), vol. 22, no. 2,
    May-June 1997.

On NEAME: books—

Pratley, Gerald, *The Cinema of David Lean*, South Brunswick, New
    Jersey, 1973.
Silver, Alain, and James Ursini, *David Lean and his Films*, Lon-
    don, 1974.
Low, Rachel, *Film Making in 1930s Britain*, London, 1985.

On NEAME: articles—

Bawden, J., "Ronald Neame," in *Films in Review* (New York), vol.
    38, no. 1, January 1987.
Pulleine, T., "Practically Born in a Film Studio," in *Films and
    Filming* (London), no. 391, April 1987.
"1207 Ronald Neame," in *Film Dope* (Nottingham), no. 47, Decem-
    ber 1991.
"Icons: Ronald Neame," in *Films in Review* (London), 1 May 1996.
Quinlan, David, "Ronald Neame," in *Quinlan's Directors*, Lon-
    don, 1999.

On NEAME: film—

Ronald Neame on the Director, 1985.

*   *   *

A key figure in the British film industry in the mid-twentieth century Ronald (sometimes known as Ronnie) Neame has been involved in some capacity in over some seventy feature films. Besides his work as a cinematographer, he has had success as a producer, a screenwriter, and, since 1947, as a director. Although he continued to work into the 1990s, he will best be remembered as director of the 1970 disaster movie, *The Poseidon Adventure*, and of comedies such as *The Million Pound Note* and *The Card*. As a cinematographer Neame made his most important contributions through his use of Technicolor on the David Lean films *This Happy Breed* and *Blithe Spirit*. Given that he was born in 1911, it is perhaps surprising that Neame was the second generation of his family to be involved in filmmaking. Even though his father, Elwin Neame, was a director of silent films in which his mother starred, Ronald Neame did not begin his career with any privileges. But within seven years, he did work his way up from tea boy to director of photography at British International Film Studios. It is interesting, given his father's profession, that Neame's most significant contribution before he became director of photography was as assistant to cinematographer Clyde de Vinna on Alfred Hitchcock's thriller, *Blackmail*. Hitchcock's eleventh feature was released in both silent and sound versions, placing the beginning of Neame's career at the very start of British sound film. *Blackmail* is also important from the point of view of cinematography because it was one of the earliest films to have been made using cameras mounted on wheels, anticipating modern "dollies" by several years.

It was in his collaboration with Noël Coward, David Lean, and Anthony Havelock-Allen, however, that Neame produced his best work as a cinematographer. Together they formed Cineguild, establishing David Lean as among the best British directors, and Ronald Neame as his equal in colour cinematography. Neame was one of only four cinematographers used by Lean in his fifty year career. In *This Happy Breed* and *Blithe Spirit*, for which Neame also wrote the screenplays, he set new standards in the use of the Technicolor process. Both films are noted for the warmth of their colour photography and the effectiveness with which the camera catches the quality of light.

Neame's enthusiasm for filmmaking, and for colour photography in particular, led him to producing and finally directing by the late 1940s. *Take My Life*, his directorial debut, is a strong thriller, which builds the tension through a series of small-scale set pieces, and is helped along by the photography of Guy Green, another of Lean's favoured cinematographers. Such attention to detail would seem to be a consequence of his career behind the camera, for it became a hallmark of Neame's direction. His ability to place the camera became ever more assured, and in the 1950s he was at the forefront of colour film direction.

Neame's detailed visual style has proved successful for a range of film types, from thrillers to melodramas. But it is in gentle comedies, such as *The Million Pound Note*, an adaptation of a Mark Twain story in which Gregory Peck struggles to spend the large denomination banknote of the title, that his direction seems most comfortable. At his best, he also drew excellent performances from his leading actors. Alec Guinness in the title role of *The Card* and Gene Hackman as the troubled but heroic priest in *The Poseidon Adventure* both give of their best, while Maggie Smith is impressive in the entertaining but otherwise thin adaptation, *The Prime of Miss Jean Brodie*. Neame has been nominated for Oscars as a writer, producer, director, and for special effects. Probably his best film, *Tunes of Glory*, a tense army melodrama, was nominated for a BAFTA in 1961. Although his technical accomplishments in the 1930s and 1940s undoubtedly helped when it came to directing, his films, good-looking though most of them are, lack the broad insight of a master such as Lean. Nevertheless, Neame's output has consistently scored at the box office if not with the critics.

From his beginnings running errands, to his retirement with a knighthood as a grand old man of British cinema, Ronald Neame has played a part in most aspects of the filmmaking process. With a history that spans a century of cinema, the Neame family business continues with his son, Christopher, who works as a film producer.

—Chris Routledge

NEWMAN, Alfred

Composer. **Nationality:** American. **Born:** New Haven, Connecticut, 17 March 1901. **Education:** Studied piano with Rubin Goldmark and George Wedge; also studied with Schoenberg. **Career:** Pianist in vaudeville and on Broadway; studied conducting with William Daly: conductor for *George White's Scandals of 1920* and other shows; 1930—first film as arranger and musical director, *Whoopee!*; 1940–60—head of 20th Century-Fox music department; also guest conductor for various orchestras. **Award:** Academy Awards for *Alexander's Ragtime Band*, 1938; *Tin Pan Alley*, 1940; *The Song of Bernadette*, 1943; *Mother Wore Tights*, 1947; *With a Song in My Heart*, 1952; *Call Me Madam*, 1953; *Love Is a Many-Splendored Thing*, 1955; *The King and I*, 1956; *Camelot*, 1967. **Died:** In Hollywood, California, 17 February 1970.

Films as Composer:

1931 *The Devil to Pay* (Fitzmaurice); *Reaching for the Moon* (Goulding); *Kiki* (Taylor); *Indiscreet* (McCarey); *Street Scene* (K. Vidor); *The Unholy Garden* (Fitzmaurice); *The Age for Love* (Lloyd); *Corsair* (West); *Around the World in Eighty Minutes with Douglas Fairbanks* (Fleming)

1932 *Arrowsmith* (Ford); *Cock of the Air* (Buckingham); *The Greeks Had a Word for Them* (L. Sherman); *Sky Devils* (Sutherland); *Rain* (Milestone); *Cynara* (K. Vidor); *Mr. Robinson Crusoe* (Sutherland)

1933 *Secrets* (Borzage); *I Cover the Waterfront* (Cruze); *The Bowery* (Walsh); *Blood Money* (Brown); *Advice to the Lovelorn* (Werker); *The Masquerader* (Wallace); *Gallant Lady* (La Cava); *The House of Rothschild* (Werker)

1934 *Looking for Trouble* (Wellman); *Nana* (*Lady of the Boulevards*) (Arzner); *Born to Be Bad* (L. Sherman); *The Affairs of Cellini* (La Cava); *The Last Gentleman* (Lanfield); *Bulldog Drummond Strikes Back* (Del Ruth); *The Cat's Paw* (Taylor); *Our Daily Bread* (K. Vidor); *Transatlantic Merry-Go-Round* (Stoloff); *We Live Again* (Mamoulian);

The Count of Monte Cristo (Lee); *The Mighty Barnum* (W. Lang)

1935 *Clive of India* (Boleslawsky); *The Wedding Night* (K. Vidor); *Les Miserables* (Boleslawsky); *Cardinal Richelieu* (Lee); *The Call of the Wild* (Wellman); *Barbary Coast* (Hawks); *She* (Pichel and Holden); *Splendor* (Nugent); *Metropolitan* (Boleslawsky)

1936 *These Three* (Wyler); *Dodsworth* (Wyler); *Come and Get It* (Wyler and Hawks)

1937 *Beloved Enemy* (Potter); *You Only Live Once* (F. Lang); *History Is Made at Night* (Borzage); *Woman Chases Man* (Blystone); *Slave Ship* (Garnett); *Wee Willie Winkie* (Gord); *Stella Dallas* (K. Vidor); *Dead End* (Wyler); *The Prisoner of Zenda* (Cromwell)

1938 *The Hurricane* (Ford); *The Cowboy and the Lady* (Potter); *Trade Winds* (Garnett)

1939 *Gunga Din* (Stevens); *Wuthering Heights* (Wyler); **Young Mr. Lincoln** (Ford); *Beau Geste* (Wellman); *The Rains Came* (Brown); *The Real Glory* (Hathaway); *Drums Along the Mohawk* (Ford); *The Hunchback of Notre Dame* (Dieterle); *Stanley and Livingstone* (H. King); *Vigil in the Night* (Stevens)

1940 *The Blue Bird* (W. Lang); **The Grapes of Wrath** (Ford); *Little Old New York* (H. King); *Earthbound* (Pichel); *Foreign Correspondent* (Hitchcock); *Brigham Young—Frontiersman* (Hathaway); *They Knew What They Wanted* (Kanin); *The Mark of Zorro* (Mamoulian)

1941 *Hudson's Bay* (Pichel); *Belle Starr* (Cummings); *Charley's Aunt* (*Charley's American Aunt*) (Mayo); *Man Hunt* (F. Lang); *Wild Geese Calling* (Brahm); *Ball of Fire* (Hawks); *Son of Fury* (Cromwell); *Remember the Day* (H. King); *How Green Was My Valley* (Ford)

1942 *The Battle of Midway* (Ford); *To the Shores of Tripoli* (Humberstone); *Ten Gentlemen from West Point* (Hathaway); *This above All* (Litvak); *The Pied Piper* (Pichel); *Girl Trouble* (Schuster); *The Black Swan* (H. King); *Life Begins at 8:30* (Pichel)

1943 *December 7th* (Toland and Ford); *The Moon Is Down* (Pichel); *My Friend Flicka* (Schuster); *Heaven Can Wait* (Lubitsch); *Claudia* (Goulding); *The Song of Bernadette* (H. King); *Prelude to War* (Capra) (in **Why We Fight** series)

1944 *The Purple Heart* (Milestone); *Wilson* (H. King); *Sunday Dinner for a Soldier* (Bacon); *The Fighting Lady* (doc); *The Keys of the Kingdom* (Stahl)

1945 *A Tree Grows in Brooklyn* (Kazan); *A Royal Scandal* (*Czarina*) (Preminger); *A Bell for Adano* (H. King)

1946 *Leave Her to Heaven* (Stahl); *Drangonwyck* (Mankiewicz); *The Razor's Edge* (Goulding); *13 Rue Madeleine* (Hathaway)

1947 *Captain from Castille* (H. King); *Gentleman's Agreement* (Kazan)

1948 *Call Northside 777* (Hathaway); *Sitting Pretty* (W. Lang); *The Walls of Jericho* (Stahl); *Cry of the City* (Siodmak); *Yellow Sky* (Wellman)

1949 *Come to the Stable* (Koster) (song); *Chicken Every Sunday* (Seaton); *A Letter to Three Wives* (Mankiewicz); *Mother Is a Freshman* (Bacon); *Down to the Sea in Ships* (Hathaway); *Mr. Belvedere Goes to College* (Nugent); *Pinky* (Kazan); *Prince of Foxes* (H. King); *Twelve O'Clock High* (H. King); *Thieves' Highway* (Dassin)

1950 *When Willie Comes Marching Home* (Ford); *The Big Life* (Seaton); *The Gunfighter* (H. King); *Panic in the Streets* (Kazan); *No Way Out* (Mankiewicz); ***All about Eve*** (Mankiewicz); *For Heaven's Sake* (Seaton)

1951 *The Guest* (Forest—short); *Fourteen Hours* (Hathaway); *Take Care of My Little Girl* (Negulesco); *David and Bathsheba* (H. King)

1952 *Wait till the Sun Shines, Nellie* (H. King); *What Price Glory?* (Ford); *The Snows of Kilimanjaro* (H. King) (song); *Way of a Gaucho* (Tourneur) (co, uncredited); *The Prisoner of Zenda* (Thorpe); *Night without Sleep* (Baker) (co); *The President's Lady* (Levin)

1953 *The Robe* (Koster)

1954 *Desirée* (Koster) (song); *Hell and High Water* (Fuller); *The Egyptian* (Curtiz) (co)

1955 *A Man Called Peter* (Koster); *The Seven Year Itch* (Wilder); *Love Is a Many-Splendored Thing* (H. King)

1956 *Bus Stop* (Logan) (co); *Anastasia* (Litvak)

1958 *A Certain Smile* (Negulesco); *The Bravados* (H. King) (co)

1959 *The Diary of Anne Frank* (Stevens); *The Best of Everything* (Negulesco)

1961 *The Pleasure of His Company* (Seaton); *The Counterfeit Traitor* (Seaton)

1962 *How the West Was Won* (Hathaway, Ford, and Marshall); ***The Man Who Shot Liberty Valance*** (Ford) (theme from ***Young Mr. Lincoln***)

1965 *The Greatest Story Ever Told* (Stevens)

1966 *Nevada Smith* (Hathaway)

1967 *Firecreek* (McEveety)

1970 *Airport* (Seaton)

Films as Musical Director:

1930 *Whoopee!* (Freeland)

1931 *Campus Sweetheart* (Fitzmaurice—short); ***City Lights*** (Chaplin) (orchestration); *Palmy Days* (Sutherland); *Tonight or Never* (LeRoy)

1932 *The Kid from Spain* (McCarey)

1933 *Hallelujah, I'm a Bum* (Milestone); *Broadway Thru a Keyhole* (L. Sherman); *Roman Scandals* (Tuttle)

1934 *Moulin Rouge* (Lanfield); *One Night of Love* (Schertzinger); *Kid Millions* (Del Ruth)

1935 *Folies Bergere* (*The Man from the Folies Bergere*) (Del Ruth); *The Dark Angel* (Franklin); *Broadway Melody of 1936* (Del Ruth); *The Melody Lingers On* (Burton)

1936 *Strike Me Pink* (Taurog); *One Rainy Afternoon* (Lee); *Dancing Pirate* (Corrigan); ***Modern Times*** (Chaplin) (orchestration); *Ramona* (H. King); *The Gay Desperado* (Mamoulian); *Born to Dance* (Del Ruth)

1937 *When You're in Love* (*For You Alone*) (Riskin); *52nd Street* (Young)

1938 *The Goldwyn Follies* (Marshall); *The Adventures of Marco Polo* (Mayo); *Alexander's Ragtime Band* (H. King)

1939 *The Star Maker* (Del Ruth); *Barricade* (Ratoff); *They Shall Have Music* (*Melody of Youth*) (Mayo)

1940 *Lillian Russell* (Cummings); *Maryland* (H. King); *Young People* (Dwan); *Tin Pan Alley* (W. Lang); *Broadway Melody of 1940* (Taurog); *Public Debt No. 1* (Ratoff); *The Westerner* (Wyler)

1941 *That Night in Rio* (Cummings); *The Great American Broadcast* (Mayo); *Blood and Sand* (Mamoulian); *Tobacco Road* (Ford); *A Yank in the R.A.F.* (H. King); *Weekend in Havana* (W. Lang); *Moon over Miami* (W. Lang)

1942 *Song of the Islands* (W. Lang); *Orchestra Wives* (Mayo); *Rings on Her Fingers* (Mamoulian); *Prelude to War* (Capra); *My Gal Sal* (Cummings); *Springtime in the Rockies* (Cummings); *Moontide* (Mayo); *China Girl* (Hathaway)

1943 *Coney Island* (W. Lang); *Immortal Sergeant* (Stahl); *Wintertime* (Brahm); *The Gang's All Here* (*The Girl He Left Behind*) (Berkeley)

1944 *Irish Eyes Are Smiling* (Ratoff) (co); *The Sullivans* (*The Fighting Sullivans*) (Bacon)

1945 *Billy Rose's Diamond Horseshoe* (Seaton) (co); *State Fair* (W. Lang) (co); *The Dolly Sisters* (Cummings)

1946 *Centennial Summer* (Preminger); *Three Little Girls in Blue* (Humberstone); *Margie* (H. King); *My Darling Clementine* (Ford)

1947 *Boomerang!* (Kazan); *The Shocking Miss Pilgrim* (Seaton) (co); *The Foxes of Harrow* (Stahl); *Mother Wore Tights* (W. Lang); *I Wonder Who's Kissing Her Now* (Bacon); *The Late George Apley* (Mankiewicz); *Moss Rose* (Ratoff); *Miracle on 34th Street* (Seaton)

1948 *Fury at Furnace Creek* (Humberstone); *That Lady in Ermine* (Lubitsch) (co); *That Wonderful Urge* (Sinclair); *Unfaithfully Yours* (P. Sturges); *The Iron Curtain* (Wellman); *When My Baby Smiles at Me* (W. Lang); *The Snake Pit* (Litvak)

1949 *Dancing in the Dark* (Reis); *You're My Everything* (W. Lang); *Oh, You Beautiful Doll* (Stahl); *Everybody Does It* (Goulding)

1950 *Broken Arrow* (Daves); *Whirlpool* (Preminger); *Two Flags West* (Wise); *My Blue Heaven* (Koster)

1951 *On the Riviera* (W. Lang); *Call Me Mister* (Bacon); *Half Angel* (Sale) (+ song); *House on Telegraph Hill* (Wise); *People Will Talk* (Mankiewicz)

1952 *With a Song in My Heart* (W. Lang); *Viva Zapata!* (Kazan); *O. Henry's Full House* (Hathaway and others); *Les Miserables* (Milestone); *Kangaroo* (Milestone); *Pony Soldier* (Newman); *Stars and Stripes Forever* (Koster); *Destination Gobi* (Wise)

1953 *The Desert Rats* (Wise); *Tonight We Sing* (Leisen); *Call Me Madam* (W. Lang); *The Treasure of the Golden Condor* (Daves); *How to Marry a Millionaire* (Negulesco) (co)

1954 *There's No Business Like Show Business* (W. Lang) (co)

1955 *Daddy Long Legs* (Negulesco)

1956 *Carousel* (H. King); *The King and I* (W. Lang) (co)

1957 *April Love* (Levin) (co-adaptation)

1958 *South Pacific* (Logan) (co)

1962 *Flower Drum Song* (Koster); *State Fair* (J. Ferrer)

1967 *Camelot* (Logan)

Publications

By NEWMAN: articles—

In *Film Score*, edited by Tony Thomas, South Brunswick, New Jersey, 1979.

Soundtrack! (Hollywood), December 1990.

On NEWMAN: articles—

Jacobs, Jack, in *Films in Review* (New York), August-September 1959.

(letter) *Films in Review* (New York), October 1959.

Thomas, Tony, in *Music for the Movies*, South Brunswick New Jersey, 1973.

Film (London), April 1974.

Darby, Ken, in *Film Music Notebook* (Calabasas, California), vol. 2, no. 2, 1976.

Films in Review (New York), June 1976.

Films in Review (New York), August-September 1978.

Films in Review (New York), April 1980.

Bertolina, Gian Carlo, "Alfred Newman alla Fox," in *Rivista del Cinematografo* (Rome), August-September 1980.

Dirigido por . . . (Barcelona), September and October 1982.

Lacombe, Alain, in *Hollywood*, Paris, 1983.

Films in Review (New York), August-September 1989.

Films in Review (New York), October 1990.

Palmer, Christopher, in *Composers in Hollywood*, London, 1990.

Docherty, J., "Alfred Newman," in *Film Dope*, no. 47, December 1991.

Vallerand, F., "Nostalgie," in *Sequences*, no. 156, January 1992.

Cook, P., "The sound track," in *Films in Review*, no. 43, 1992.

Giltz, M., "Scoring," in *Premiere*, no. 6, March 1993.

Neumeyer, David, "Melodrama as a Compositional Resource in Early Hollywood Sound Cinema," in *Current Musicology*, January 1995.

Handzo, Stephen, "The Golden Age of Film Music," in *Cineaste* (New York), Winter-Spring 1995.

Smith, Jack, "The Soundtrack," in *Films in Review*, vol. 48, January-February 1997.

Raynes, D., "*Wuthering Heights*: A Tribute to Alfred Newman," in *Soundtrack*, September 1997.

Berthomieu, Pierre, in *Positif* (Paris), October 1998.

*   *   *

Even allowing for the hyperbole associated with Hollywood there is little risk in claiming Alfred Newman as a titan in the art, craft, and business of supplying films with music. In addition to being an imaginative and inventive composer and possibly the best conductor in film history, he was also the head of a major music department. From 1940 to 1960 Newman was in command of music for 20th Century-Fox and assembled a stable of top arrangers, composers, and musicians. Always keenly aware of sound, he said, "In the recording of music for motion pictures it is possible to achieve total perfection of performance. Don't settle for anything less."

Newman was a pianistic prodigy. He was also the eldest of ten children in a poor family and the opportunities for his musical education were few. Friends brought about the winning of a scholarship and he was placed with Sigismond Stojowski in New York. He studied composition as well as the piano but by the age of 14 it was necessary for him to find work to help support his family. He was hired by the Strand Theatre on Broadway as a boy-wonder pianist, which led to offers in vaudeville and opportunities in the musical theatre. Feeling limited as a pianist, Newman found bigger challenges as a conductor and by the age of 17 was thus engaged. With *George White's Scandals of 1920* his career began in earnest and he was busy as a theatre conductor all through that decade.

In 1930 Irving Berlin contracted Newman as the music director for his film *Reaching for the Moon* and with that success Newman was thereafter a man of the movies. The Berlin film was made at the Goldwyn Studios and its owner asked Newman to be his music director. In 1933 Darryl F. Zanuck set up his 20th Century Films at the Goldwyn Studios and made a similar request, which Newman was able to accept, in addition to his Goldwyn duties. Once clear of his Goldwyn contract he joined Zanuck in 1940 as his music director. No film musician received more honors than Newman. Of 45 Oscar nominations, he won on nine occasions, although he readily pointed out that these wins were as a music director and involved the work of other men. The Oscar for which he was most proud was for *The Song of Bernadette*. Among the other original dramatic scores nominated: *How Green Was My Valley*, *Captain from Castile*, *All about Eve*, *David and Bathsheba*, *Anastasia*, *The Diary of Anne Frank*, and, his final film, *Airport*. In all he worked on more than 250 films, always claiming that he much preferred the gregarious job of the conductor to the loneliness of the composer. Newman wrote no music other than for film and claimed no interest in any other form of composition. Of his business he said, "The music must always be inspired by the picture of which it is a part, not by the desire of the composer to express himself. The effect of music in films is largely one of association, the important thing being to evoke the proper mood and spirit. If you can't accept these terms—stay away from films."

—Tony Thomas

NEWMAN, Thomas

Composer. **Nationality:** American. **Born:** 20 October 1955. **Family:** Married to Ann Marie. **Education:** University of Southern California where he studied with Frederick Lesemann and David Raksin; Yale where he studied with Jacob Druckman, Bruce MacCombie, and Robert Moore, with a masters in musical composition. **Career:** Played keyboard in The Innocents rock band; composed first feature score for James Foley's *Reckless*, 1984; composed music for *Amazing Stories* TV series, 1985; commissioned to create a seven-minute symphonic piece, "Reach Forth Our Hands" for the city of Cleveland bicentennial, 1996. **Awards:** Australian Film Institute Award, Best Original Music Score, for *Oscar and Lucinda*, 1998. **Agent:** Gorfaine and Schwartz Agency, 13245 Riverside Drive, Suite 450, Sherman Oaks, CA 91423–2172, U.S.A.

Films as Composer

1984   *Reckless* (Foley); *Revenge of the Nerds* (Kanew); *Grandview U.S.A.* (Kleiser); *The Seduction of Gine (Another High Roller)* (Freedman)

1985   *Real Genius* (Coolidge) *The Man With One Red Shoe* (Dragoti); *Desperately Seeking Susan* (Seidelman); *Girls Just Want to Have Fun* (Metter)

1986   *Jumpin' Jack Flash* (Marshall); *Gung Ho (Working Class Man)* (Howard)

1987   *The Lost Boys* (Schumacher); *Light of Day* (Schrade); *Less Than Zero* (Kanievska)

1988   *The Prince of Pennsylvania* (Nyswaner); *The Great Outdoors* (Deutch)

1989 *Cookie* (Seidelman)
1990 *Welcome Home, Roxy Carmichael* (Abrahams); *Naked Tango* (Schrade); *Men Don't Leave* (Brickman); *Heat Wave* (— for TV) (Hooks)
1991 *Deceived* (Harris); *Career Opportunities* (*One Wild Night*) (Gordon); *The Rapture* (Tolkin); *The Linguini Incident* (Shepard); *Fried Green Tomatoes* (*Fried Green Tomatoes at the Whistle Stop Cafe*) (Avnet)
1992 *Whispers in the Dark* (Crowe); *Scent of a Woman* (Brest/Smithee); *Those Secrets* (—for TV) (Manson); *The Player* (Altman); *Citizen Cohn* (—for TV) (Pierson)
1993 *Josh and S. A. M* (Weber); *Flesh and Bone* (Kloves)
1994 *The War* (Avnet); *Threesome* (Fleming); *The Shawshank Redemption* (Darabont); *Little Women* (Armstrong); *The Favor* (Petrie); *Corrina, Corrina* (themes) (Nelson)
1995 *Unstrung Heroes* (Keaton); *How to Make an American Quilt* (Moorhouse)
1996 *Up Close & Personal* (Dansie); *Phenomenon* (Turteltaub); *American Buffalo* (Corrente); *The People vs. Larry Flint* (Forman)
1997 *Mad City* (Costa-Gauras); *Red Corner* (Avnet); *Oscar and Lucinda* (Armstrong)
1998 *The Horse Whisperer* (Redford); *Meet Joe Black* (Brest/Smithee)
1999 *American Beauty* (Mendes); *The Three Kings* (Russell); *The Green Mile* (*Stephen King's The Green Mile*) (Darabont)
2000 *Erin Brokovich*; *My Khmer Heart*

Publications

By NEWMAN: articles—

"Thomas Newman Continues to Be Interesting and Good," an interview with Doug Adams, in *Film Score Monthly*, no. 162, Winter 1996.

On NEWMAN: articles—

"*Little Women*," review in *Entertainment Weekly*, 3 February 1995.
"*How to Make an American Quilt*," review in *National Review*, 23 October 1995.
"*The People vs. Larry Flynt*," review in *Entertainment Weekly*, 13 December 1996.
"*The People vs. Larry Flynt*," review in *The New Republic* (New York), 20 January 1997.
"*Oscar and Lucinda*," review in *Newsweek* (New York), 12 January 1998.
"Stanley Kauffman on Films: In the Midst of Life," in *The New Republic* (New York), 7 December 1998.

*   *   *

Thomas Newman was born into that outstanding cinemusical dynasty, the Newmans of Hollywood, on 20 October 1955. His father was Alfred Newman, the legendary composer, conductor, and musical director of 20th Century-Fox studios, and one of the key figures in the development and refinement of film music during the studio era.

His uncles were Lionel and Emile Newman, also both prominent composers and conductors at Fox during the same period.

Newman attended college for two years at the University of Southern California, before graduating with a Masters in Music from Yale University. After graduation Newman garnered experience in both performing and in writing for musical theater. For several years he played the keyboard in a rock band, The Innocents, and with an improvisational group, Tokyo 77. During this same period, and under the championship of musical theater legend, Stephen Sondheim, Newman made a musical theater piece, *Three Mean Fairy Tales*, produced as a workshop production by the Stuart Ostrow Foundation.

Newman reports that his indoctrination into film music was occasioned by his relationship with his uncle, Lionel Newman: "Because my uncle Lionel was head of music at Fox during my high school and college years, I went down there a lot and watched John Williams conduct some of his early Irwin Allen movies like *The Towering Inferno* and *The Poseidon Adventure*. I think because of my uncle Lionel's relationship with John Williams, one of my first gigs in Hollywood was orchestrating one of the cues from *Return of the Jedi* (1983), when Darth Vader dies at the end. John's sketch was so complete that it was more of an exercise and a bone-toss, though it was a very nice bone-toss!" The first film Newman scored on his own was *Reckless* in 1984, but the young composer's breakthrough-movie was the Madonna vehicle *Desperately Seeking Susan* in 1985. His rhythmic, ethnic flavored score was prominently featured and drew much attention.

Like many contemporary film scores Newman's works are often a fusion of orchestral and electronic techniques, such as his early scores for *The Lost Boys* and *Less Than Zero*. Newman comments that he is fascinated by both orchestral and electronic techniques. "I hate the notion that electronics are a cheesy way of doing things and that orchestra is the 'only' true approach to scoring. But you can understand those critics, because electronics allow you to make easy choices, Anyone can do it. But while synthesizers are things you hide behind sounds, they can also be put in places you'd never expect. I've always wanted these boundaries to be amorphous."

Another attention getter for Newman was his score for *The Rapture*, a controversial film about a hedonistic young woman who converts to super-Fundamentalism and, at the film's bizarre climax, literally ascends into heaven during the "end times." For this unusual and extremely specialized feature Newman fused a chamber-sized ensemble of acoustic instruments with ambient electronic sounds and colors. He continued his fusion experiments with his next film, *Men Don't Leave*, and later commented: "I learned on those scores by trial and error."

Newman's first mainstream Hollywood film was *Scent of a Woman* in 1992. The composer's experimental sound crystallized with this and ensuing major scores, and it was soon to earn him numerous awards and nominations. His critically acclaimed scores for *Little Women* and *The Shawshank Redemption* were both nominated for Academy Award in the same year, and he was also nominated for *Unstrung Heroes* in 1995.

A 1995 *Entertainment Weekly* review of the Sony Classical CD release of Newman's score for *Little Women* commented: "Pastiche-Copland often sounds tired, but Thomas Newman's glowing score to the latest version of *Little Women* proves that it can also, occasionally, be inspired. If Newman's score works so miraculously well, it may be because he seems to have peppered the Coplandisms with canny seasonings from Charles Ives, the mad genius of Danbury, Connecticut." The following year the same publication commented on the CD from *The People vs. Larry Flint* : "This elegant and austere orchestral score by Thomas Newman becomes progressively more abstract and brooding, absorbing the country, gospel, and pop songs studding the album."

However, in a *New Republic* review of *Meet Joe Black*, Stanley Kauffmann complained that "Thomas Newman's music should not pass without a protest: it's the nosiest compilation of bangs and surges in several weeks." It might also be noted that the complaints of elder critic Kauffmann were not dissimilar to certain grumblings voiced against another young genius of modern film music, Elmer Bernstein, in the early 1950s.

Contemporary film music has changed radically from the days when Newman's father, Alfred, created his legendary symphonic scores for 20th Century-Fox, and today's Hollywood composers often find themselves providing supplementary instrumental scoring for a collection of chart-hopeful pop-music chart tracks. While Thomas Newman does not possess the readily recognizable style of his father and other classic Golden Age musicians, he is an amazingly versatile musician with the uncanny gift for creating a new and utterly appropriate sound for each new film he scores. In addition to his AA nominations Newman has received five BMI Music Awards, and several Grammy and Golden Globe nominations. Newman was again nominated for an Oscar for his score for *American Beauty*, the film which won for Best Picture in 2000.

—Ross Care

NICHOLS, Dudley

Writer. Nationality: American. **Born:** Wapakoneta, Ohio, 6 April 1895. **Education:** Attended the University of Michigan, Ann Arbor. **Family:** Married Esta Vacez Gooch-Collins, 1924. **Career:** 1913—Ship's radio operator on Great Lakes; 1918–19—served in the United States Navy (devised electronic device to protect mine-sweepers); 1920–29—journalist for New York *Evening News* and New York *World*; also freelance writer; 1930—first film as writer, *Men without Women*; 1938–39—President, Screenwriters Guild; 1943—first film as director, *Government Girl*. **Awards:** Venice Festival Prize and Academy Award for *The Informer*, 1935; Writers Guild Laurel Award, 1953. **Died:** 4 January 1960.

Films as Writer:

1930 *Men without Women* (Ford); *On the Level* (Cummings); *Born Reckless* (Ford); *One Mad Kiss* (Silver); *A Devil with Women* (Cummings); *El Precio de un beso*
1931 *Seas Beneath* (Ford); *Hush Money* (Lanfield); *Not Exactly Gentlemen* (Stoloff); *Skyline* (Taylor)
1932 *This Sporting Age* (Bennison and Erickson); *Robber's Roost* (King)
1933 *Pilgrimage* (Ford); *Hot Pepper* (Blystone); *The Man Who Dared* (MacFadden)
1934 *You Can't Buy Everything* (Reisner); *Hold That Girl* (MacFadden); *Wild Gold* (Marshall); *Call It Luck* (Tinling); *Judge Priest* (Ford); *The Lost Patrol* (Ford)

1935 *Steamboat 'round the Bend* (Ford); *Mystery Woman* (Forde); ***The Informer*** (Ford); *The Arizonian* (C. Vidor); *The Crusades* (DeMille) (co); *The Three Musketeers* (Lee)
1936 *Mary of Scotland* (Ford); *The Plough and the Stars* (Ford)
1937 *The Toast of New York* (Lee); *The Hurricane* (Ford and Heisler)
1938 ***Bringing Up Baby*** (Hawks); *Carefree* (Sandrich)
1939 *Stagecoach* (Ford); *The 400 Million* (Ivens and Ferno)
1940 *The Long Voyage Home* (Ford)
1941 *Man Hunt* (F. Lang); *Swamp Water* (Renoir)
1943 *This Land Is Mine* (Renoir); *Air Force* (Hawks); *For Whom the Bell Tolls* (Wood); *Government Girl* (+ d)
1944 *It Happened Tomorrow* (Clair); *The Sign of the Cross* (DeMille) (prologue)
1945 *And Then There Were None* (Clair); *The Bells of St. Mary's* (McCarey)
1946 *Scarlet Street* (F. Lang); *Sister Kenny* (+ d)
1947 *Mourning Becomes Electra* (+ d)
1948 *The Fugitive* (Ford)
1949 *Pinky* (Kazan)
1951 *Rawhide* (Hathaway)
1952 *Return of the Texan* (Daves); *The Big Sky* (Hawks)
1954 *Prince Valiant* (Hathaway)
1956 *Run for the Sun* (R. Boulting)
1957 *The Tin Star* (A. Mann)
1959 *The Hangman* (Curtiz)
1960 *Heller in Pink Tights* (Cukor)

Publications

By NICHOLS: books—

The Informer (script) in *Modern British Drama*, edited by Harlan Thatcher, New York, 1941.
With Jean Renoir, *Stagecoach* (script) and *This Land Is Mine* (script) in *Twenty Best Film Plays*, edited by Nichols and John Gassner, New York, 1943.
Editor, with John Gassner, *The Best Film Plays of 1943–44*, New York, 1946.

By NICHOLS: articles—

Screen Guild's Magazine, March and April 1935.
"Film Writing," in *Theatre Arts* (New York), December 1942.
"The Writer and the Film," in *Theatre Arts* (New York), October 1943.
"Death of a Critic," in *Theatre Arts* (New York), April 1947.

On NICHOLS: articles—

On *The Informer* in *Novels into Film*, by George Bluestone, Baltimore, Maryland, 1957.
Cinéma (Paris), March 1960.
Avant-Scène (Paris), February 1965.
Kino Lehti (Helsinki), no. 6, 1970.
Jensen, Paul, in *Film Comment* (New York), Winter 1970–71.
Films in Review (New York), February 1971.

Lesser, Stephen O., in *American Screenwriters*, edited by Robert E. Morsberger, Lesser, and Randall Clark, Detroit, Michigan, 1984.
"Dudley Nichols," in *Film Dope*, no. 47, December 1991.
Sesonske, Alexander, "Jean Renoir in America: 1942, *This Land is Mine*," in *Persistence of Vision* (Maspeth), no. 12–13, 1996.

*   *   *

Dudley Nichols started his Hollywood career in 1930, and collaborated with John Ford on his films of the 1930s and early 1940s. While these films are somewhat dated, they are still highly valued. Nichols did other scripts, but the ones he wrote for Ford constitute the real contributions to cinema. The single possible exception would be the screwball comedy he wrote with Hagar Wilde—Howard Hawks's *Bringing Up Baby*. It is significant that the script for this comedy lacks the sentimentality that often flaws Nichols's scripts for Ford. It may be, then, that Nichols was above all a collaborator. Concerning his work with Ford, Nichols was self-deprecating. In a letter dated 24 February 1941 (in the Lilly Library collection) he wrote to the director that screenwriting "is not a creative act like directing."

Men without Women and *Born Reckless*, both made in 1930, were the first films Nichols and Ford worked on and contain some of the themes and settings that the two were to handle so successfully in the coming decade. *Born Reckless* certainly offers one important characteristic of the best of Nichols's screenplays—a brooding urban underworld of lights and shadows. In this scenario, Nichols demonstrates a careful attention to dialects and street idioms. There is also the element of maternal/filial affection between Ma Beretti and her son. *Men without Women* (also in the Lilly collection) opens with a characteristic *chiaroscuro* street-scene, carefully described in the "stage" descriptions. This scene is set in front of an American bar in Shanghai; it ends with the redemption of a traitor, like that in *The Informer*, Nichols constructs *The Informer* as a labyrinthine journey through misty streets. *Men without Women* also contains a noble self-sacrifice, as does *The Long Voyage Home*. The latter film culminates in the paternal sacrifice of an older sailor's life so a young sailor can experience what all sailors dream of, but often fail to achieve—a voyage home. By directing the several O'Neill plays towards this spiritual culmination, Nichols ably gives the material a dramatic unity not in the original.

With a characteristic expansive, exuberant humanity, Nichols poured out 146 pages of a densely packed rough-draft script for *Stagecoach* (the released dialogue-continuity is 40 sparsely covered pages). In the process of realizing the script on film, Ford had severely pared down Nichols's script. Nichols's screenplay shows a real sense of cinematic techniques; yet the masterstrokes of Ford—like the tracking shot up to Ringo's (John Wayne's) face—had to be added in the filming. All in all Nichols's script seems to have been a rich and varied grab-bag of ideas from which Ford could pick and choose.

—Rodney Farnsworth

NIHALANI, Govind

Cinematographer. **Nationality:** Indian. **Born:** Karachi (now in Pakistan) in early 1940s; lived in Udaipur, India, after the partition of India. **Education:** Attended S. J. Polytechnic, Bangalore, graduated 1962. **Career:** 1962–72—assistant cameraman to V. K. Murthy and Promod Chakravarty; also made advertising films; 1970—first film as cinematographer, Shantata, *Court Chalu Ahe*; 1974—first of several films for Shyam Benegal; 1981—directed his first film, *Akrosh*. **Award:** Indian National Film Award for *Possessed*, 1978.

Films as Cinematographer (Selected List):

1970 *Shantata, Court Chalu Ahe* (Karnad)
1974 *Ankur* (*The Seedling*) (Benegal)
1975 *Nishant* (*Night's End*) (Benegal); *Charandas Chor* (*Charandas the Thief*) (Benegal)
1976 *Manthan* (*The Churning*) (Benegal)
1977 **Bhumika** (*The Role*) (Benegal); *Kondura* (*The Boom*) (Benegal)
1978 *Junoon* (*The Obsession*) (Benegal)
1979 *Womb of Power* (doc); *A Fine Tolerance* (doc)
1980 *Hari Hondal Burgadar* (*Share Cropper*) (Benegal)
1981 *Kalyug* (*The Machine Age*) (Benegal); *Akrosh* (+ d); *Gandhi* (Attenborough)
1982 *Satyajit Ray—Film Maker* (Benegal—doc)
1983 *Vijeta* (+ d); *Ardha Satya* (+ d)
1984 *Party* (+ d)
1985 *Aaghat* (+ d)
1987 *Tamas* (*Darkness*) (+ d; sc—for TV)
1991 *Drishti* (+ d; sc—for TV)
1998 *Hazaar Chaurasi Ki Maa* (*Mother of 1084*) (+ d, pr)
1999 *Thakshak* (+ d)

Publications

By NIHALANI: article—

Film a Doba (Prague), vol. 33, no. 8, August 1987.

On NIHALANI: book—

Habibulah, Shama, *Govind Nihalani*, 1981.

On NIHALANI: articles—

Pradhan, Shalini, in *Filmfare*, 16–31 December 1983.
Masud, Iqbal, in *Cinema India International*, March 1985.
Cinema in India, vol. 4, 1993.

*   *   *

Govind Nihalani is more a master craftsman than an artist. His directorial talent is an outcome of his skill and experience as a cinematographer. Having learned all aspects of cinematography at the S. J. Polytechnic in Bangalore, and assisted V. K. Murthy for ten years thereafter, Nihalani was already a respected cameraman when he came to be associated with Shyam Benegal and Girish Karnad. His association with Shyam Benegal, however, chiselled his cinematographic sense and ability. In Benegal's films, art and commerce meet. The features that Nihalani shot for Benegal are among the best of his works. This vast experience also made him an established filmmaker in his own right. And in the excellent films that he has made so far, it is difficult to separate the able director from the ace cinematographer.

While working in texture films, Nihalani also filmed documentaries and advertisements. This trained him to extract and encapsulate the required information into a small time-frame. It was during these 12 years that Nihalani worked hard, experimented and matured as a cameraman. His vision was enriched by documentary observations and a keen sense of the theatrical. The latter probably came from Nihalani's close association with the well-known Marathi playwright Vijay Tendulkar, who scripted his *Akrosh* and *Ardha Satya*. His debut as a cinematographer was made in 1970 in a Marathi film, based on a Tendulkar play. The undercurrent of anger and violence that runs through the play also characterizes Nihalani's films, which explore the roots of violence and anger in society. *Junoon*, for example, by Benegal, set against the turbulent Sepoy Mutiny of 1857, was to Nihalani an ideal camera subject, and won him an award for best colour cinematography.

Nihalani, however, does not, like Subrata Mitra, recapture moods, the finesse of reflexes and reactions, or introspection on celluloid. Action, movement, and aggression attract him more, both as director and cinematographer. This perhaps made Richard Attenborough employ him as head of the second unit of the most ambitious film to be produced in India, *Gandhi*.

—Shohini Ghosh

NITZSCHE, Jack

Composer. **Nationality:** American. **Born:** Bernard Nitzsche in Chicago, Illinois, 1937. **Education:** Attended Howard City Elementary and High School, Michigan, 1943–55; studied at West Lake College of Music, 1956–57. **Family:** Married to the singer Buffy St. Marie. **Career:** Worked as musical copyist for Specialty Records; 1962—worked as arranger for Phil Spector; worked on Rolling Stones first American tour and on nine of their albums; arranged and produced Neil Young's first solo album and joined Neil Young's backing band Crazy Horse; 1972—composition "St. Giles Cripplegate" recorded with London Symphony Orchestra, conductor David Measham; composer of numerous film scores since 1970. **Awards:** Academy Award for "Up Where We Belong," from *An Officer and a Gentleman*, 1982.

Films as Composer:

1965	*Village of the Giants* (Gordon)
1970	*Performance* (Cammell and Roeg)
1972	*Greaser's Palace* (Downey)
1973	*The Exorcist* (Friedkin) (additional music)
1975	**One Flew over the Cuckoo's Nest** (Forman)
1977	*Heroes* (Kagan)
1978	*Blue Collar* (Schrader)
1979	*When You Comin' Back, Red Rider?* (Katselas); *Heart Beat* (Byrum); *Hardcore* (*The Hardcore Life*) (Schrader)
1980	*Cruising* (Friedkin)
1981	*Cutter's Way* (*Cutter and Bone*) (Passer)

Jack Nitzsche

1982	*An Officer and a Gentleman* (Hackford); *Personal Best* (Towne); *Cannery Row* (Ward)
1983	*Without a Trace* (Jaffe); *Breathless* (McBride)
1984	*Windy City* (Bernstein); *The Razor's Edge* (Byrum); *Starman* (Carpenter)
1985	*The Jewel of the Nile* (Teague)
1986	*The Stripper* (Gary); *9½ Weeks* (Lyne); *Stand by Me* (R. Reiner); *The Whoopee Boys* (Byrum); *Streets of Gold* (Roth)
1988	*The Seventh Sign* (Schultz)
1989	*Next of Kin* (Irvin)
1990	*Revenge* (T. Scott); *The Last of the Finest* (*Blue Heat*) (Mackenzie); *The Hot Spot* (Hopper); *Mermaids* (Benjamin)
1991	*The Indian Runner* (S. Penn)
1994	*Blue Sky* (Richardson—produced in 1990)
1995	*Crossing Guard* (S. Penn)

Publications

On NITZSCHE: articles—

Screen International, 20 June 1981.
Film Dope (London), December 1991.

* * *

Before Jack Nitzsche started on a career as one of Hollywood's more inventive and individual composers for film, he was already a veteran of the Los Angeles rock scene, cutting his teeth as an arranger for Phil Spector and having worked with a wide range of performers, from Doris Day and Frankie Laine to The Rolling Stones and Neil Young. Though some of his most characteristic scores for such films as *Performance*, *Blue Collar*, and *The Hot Spot* reflect this background in rock and roll and rhythm and blues, his work also draws on classical music, jazz, and the European avant-garde.

Nitzsche has been involved in films since the sixties. He was the musical director on *The TAMI Show* (1964), a concert film that included performances by the Rolling Stones and the Beach Boys, and he provided music for *Village of the Giants*, a low-budget teenage sci-fi spoof. His career as a film composer, however, effectively began in 1970 when he was called in to do the music for *Performance*, Donald Cammell and Nicolas Roeg's mesmerizing game of shifting identities, played out between a burnt-out rock star (Mick Jagger) and a sadistic East End gangster (James Fox). Jagger and Keith Richard were originally scheduled to do the music, but tensions surrounding the filming had caused a temporary rift in their writing partnership. Nitzsche assembled an eclectic group of musicians, including Ry Cooder, Randy Newman, Merry Clayton, Buffy St. Marie, and Stevie Winwood. The resulting score, with its echoes of Robert Johnson and Ligeti, is, by turns, sinister and exhilarating. Ghostly synthesizers, Cooder's stinging bottleneck guitar and Clayton's chanted vocals provide an eerie complement to the film's hallucinatory picture of London at the end of the sixties.

Nitzsche soon demonstrated another facet of his musical sophistication. In 1972 he recorded "St. Giles Cripplegate" an accomplished neoclassical piece performed by the London Symphony Orchestra, conducted by David Measham. Though the album was not a commercial success, Nitzsche described it as a useful calling card: "It helped me tell people that I could write for a 110 piece orchestra in a classical kind of way." Milos Forman heard the record and was impressed enough to commission Nitzsche to write the music for *One Flew over the Cuckoo's Nest*, the film based on Ken Kesey's antiauthoritarian fable set in a microcosmic mental institution. The score proved highly successful, yielding a best-selling album and an Academy Award nomination. The music is elegiac (the film's main theme), and occasionally ironic (the waltz that accompanies the ritual of medication for the hospital's inmates). Nitzsche also employed unconventional instrumentation—musical saw and crystal glass—to add a haunting dimension to the score.

Although he has been involved in a number of high-profile mainstream films—including *An Officer and a Gentleman*, its featured ballad, "Up Where We Belong," earning an Oscar for best song, and *Jewel of the Nile*—some of Nitzsche's most memorable work has been for less commercial, more personal films. Notable among these is the sound track for Paul Schrader's debut as director, *Blue Collar*. This hard-edged thriller, set among the unions on the automobile assembly lines of Detroit, is given a driving industrial rhythm-and-blues score, featuring Cooder. The film's remarkable credit sequence has a hypnotic sledgehammer beat and growled vocals from Captain Beefheart pounding over gritty stop-motion images from the factory floor. In John Byrum's *Heart Beat*, a soft-centered account of a triangular relationship between Jack Kerouac, Neal Cassady, and Carolyn Cassady, the music moves fluently between a plangent main theme, pastiche Eisenhower-era pop songs, and a memorable jazz sequence orchestrated by Shorty Rogers and featuring luminaries of the west coast jazz scene, including Art Pepper, Bud Shank, Bob Cooper, and Shelly Manne. In Ivan Passer's post-Vietnam film noir, *Cutter and Bone*, Nitzsche develops the

"glass harmonica" sound featured in *One Flew over the Cuckoo's Nest* to create a sparse, haunted theme. For Dennis Hopper's sultry thriller *The Hot Spot* he uses the inspired pairing of John Lee Hooker and Miles Davis to provide a tense blues-drenched score, Hooker vocalizing wordlessly over Davis's shimmering trumpet.

Despite working in an industry that encourages self-promotion, Jack Nitzsche has kept a low public profile. In a rare 1981 interview for *Screen International*, when discussing the difficulty he had experienced working with a particular director, he offered this downbeat assessment of his work "I don't think I could ever be like Henry Mancini or Lalo Schifrin. I can't just sit back and give them what they want." Schrader, in discussing Nitzsche's work on *Blue Collar* and *Hard Core*, offered an oblique reflection of Nitzsche's influence on film music since the seventies: "I've tried to find a music that has a life of its own, which meant going into a music that wasn't yet in the vernacular of films. For the first two I used Jack Nitzsche who had just come out of rock and roll, working with Phil Spector and the Rolling Stones, but by the time [*American*] *Gigolo* came along that sound was already in the mainstream."

—Dominic Power

NORSTEIN, Yuri

Animator. **Nationality:** Russian. **Born:** Yuri Borisovich Norstein, 1942. **Family:** Married; has children. **Career:** Joined Soyuzmultfilm, Moscow; 1968—first film as animator, *25 October, First Day*; 1971—co-directed the film *Battle under the Walls of Kerchenetz* with Ivan Ivanov-Vano.

Films as Animator:

1968	*25 October, First Day* (co)
1971	*Battle under the Walls of Kerchenetz* (with Ivan Ivanov-Vano)
1973	*The Vixen and the Hare*
1975	*The Heron and the Crane*
1976	*Hedgehog in the Mist*
1980	*The Tale of Tales*

Publications

By NORSTEIN: articles—

Banc-Titre (Paris), September 1982.
Banc-Titre (Paris), November 1984.
Positif (Paris), November 1985.
Filmkultura (Budapest), November 1986.
Film a Doba (Prague), vol. 33, no. 4, April 1987.
Iskusstvo Kino (Moscow), April 1989.
Positif (Paris), December 1989.
Cahiers du Cinéma (Paris), January 1990.
Vertigo (Paris), 6–7 1991.
Télérama (Paris), 21 July 1993.
Kino (Moscow), March 1997.

On NORSTEIN: articles—

Banc-Titre (Paris), December 1980.
Sightlines, Fall/Winter 1982–83.
Cinéma (Paris), January 1985.
Revue du Cinéma/Image et Son (Paris), January 1985.
Soviet Film (Moscow), July 1986.
Film a Doba (Prague), November 1986.
24 Images (Montreal), no. 43, Summer 1989.
Kino (Warsaw), July 1990.
Kino (Warsaw), September 1990.
Filmkultura (Budapest), July 1994.
Kino (Warsaw), June 1995.

On NORSTEIN: film—

Yuri Norstein, directed by Tarabanov, 1991.

*   *   *

Yuri Norstein, who has been working for years under the veteran Russian animator Ivan Ivanov-Vano, has emerged as one of the world's leading animators. His film, *The Tale of Tales*, was considered the most artistic production to come out of Eastern Europe in years. The success of this film, as well as others such as *Hedgehog in the Mist*, *The Vixen and the Hare*, and *The Heron and the Crane*, is due to his unique style of multidimensional figures and backgrounds that have depth, roundness, and shading, giving a visual quality to his scenes seldom seen in other films. His humor is full of human observation, contrasting emotion over a broad scale from gaiety and laughter to sadness and disappointment. The fact that these moods are happening to animals and birds with their own particular environment provides an element of magic, and once again proves that the art of animation can bridge the biological barrier between human and animal worlds.

Norstein considers animation to be a new field of art, but underestimated, its artistic plasticity and social significance not having been explored so far. According to him its principles are taken from life, avoiding a documentary approach in describing a social situation. Aristotle said, ''art, above all teachers, allows people to enjoy life.'' This principle still holds. Norstein takes his own material from an ordinary situation and develops it in his own particular way. His material consists of human emotions: joy, tears, love, and all levels of emotion within the experiences of life. Norstein, apart from being a filmmaker, is also a good painter and brilliant illustrator, which explains the high visual quality of his backgrounds and the expressions of his characters. He has a close relationship with his young children and closely considers their reactions before making a film. He thinks that only those who understand children's psychology should make a film for them. If one has sympathy with them and can play with them, one is able to look at the world through their minds and eyes.

On the question of visual quality, he thinks that animated film directors should be interested in fine arts, especially painting, since films have a dual objective: the creation of a new and original setting and a defined dramatic action within the setting. The spectator should be able to adapt to such a background and participate in the film on the terms present in the subject. Norstein recognizes that a film is composed of various elements. It contains myth, fantasy, cosmographic ideas, sound, absolute realism, and naturalism. The combined quality of these elements could be of great value, lifting animation above all other media, but so far he has not seen any film, short or long, able to make full use of such total potentialities. He holds that a feature-length film should not only tell a story but present the richness of human life, make full use of the specific properties of animation, and look for its own way of development.

—John Halas

NORTH, Alex

Composer. **Nationality:** American. **Born:** Chester, Pennsylvania, 10 December 1910. **Education:** Attended Curtis Institute; Juilliard School, New York; studied with Ernst Toch, Copland, and Revueltas. **Family:** Married Annemarie (North); two sons and one daughter. **Career:** 1933–34—enrolled at the Moscow Conservatory; 1935–40—composed for ballet; began composing for documentaries; 1951—first score for fiction film, *A Streetcar Named Desire*; also composer for TV, including the series *The Man and the City*, 1971–72, and the mini-series *Rich Man, Poor Man*, 1976, and *The Word*, 1978. **Award:** Special Academy Award, 1986. **Died:** Of cancer in California, 8 September 1991.

Films as Composer:

1937   *Heart of Spain* (doc); *People of the Cumberland* (Meyers and Hill—doc)
1945   *A Better Tomorrow* (Hackenschmeid—doc)
1951   *A Streetcar Named Desire* (Kazan); *The Thirteenth Letter* (Preminger); *Death of a Salesman* (Benedek)
1952   *Viva Zapata!* (Kazan); *Les Miserables* (Milestone); *Pony Soldier* (Newman)
1953   *The Member of the Wedding* (Zinnemann)
1954   *Go, Man, Go* (Howe); *Desirée* (Koster); *The American Road* (Stoney—doc)
1955   *The Racers (Such Men Are Dangerous)* (Hathaway); *Unchained* (Bartlett); *The Rose Tattoo* (Daniel Mann); *Man with the Gun (The Trouble Shooter)* (Wilson)
1956   *I'll Cry Tomorrow* (Daniel Mann); *The Bad Seed* (LeRoy); *The Rainmaker* (Anthony); *Four Girls in Town* (Sher); *The King and Four Queens* (Walsh)
1957   *The Bachelor Party* (Delbert Mann)
1958   *The Long Hot Summer* (Ritt); *Stage Struck* (Lumet); *Hot Spell* (Daniel Mann); *South Seas Adventure* (Thompson and others)
1959   *The Sound and the Fury* (Ritt); *The Wonderful Country* (Parrish)
1960   *Spartacus* (Kubrick)
1961   *The Children's Hour* (Wyler); *Sanctuary* (Ritt); *The Misfits* (Huston)
1962   *All Fall Down* (Frankenheimer)
1963   *Cleopatra* (Mankiewicz)
1964   *The Outrage* (Ritt)
1965   *Cheyenne Autumn* (Ford); *The Agony and the Ecstasy* (Reed)

1966   *Who's Afraid of Virginia Woolf?* (Nichols)
1967   *Africa* (doc)
1968   *The Devil's Brigade* (McLaglen); *The Shoes of the Fisherman* (Anderson)
1969   *A Dream of Kings* (Daniel Mann); *Hard Contract* (Pogostin)
1971   *Willard* (Daniel Mann)
1972   *Pocket Money* (Rosenberg)
1973   *Once Upon a Scoundrel* (Schaefer)
1974   *Shanks* (Castle); *Lost in the Stars* (Daniel Mann)
1975   *Bite the Bullet* (Brooks); *Journey into Fear* (Daniel Mann)
1976   *The Passover Plot* (Campus)
1978   *Somebody Killed Her Husband* (Johnson)
1979   *Wise Blood* (Huston)
1980   *Carny* (Kaylor)
1981   *Dragonslayer* (Robbins)
1982   *Sister, Sister* (Berry)
1984   *Under the Volcano* (Huston)
1985   *Prizzi's Honor* (Huston)
1987   **The Dead** (*The Dubliners*) (Huston); *Good Morning Vietnam* (Levinson); *John Huston and the Dubliners* (Sievernich)
1988   *The Penitent* (Osmond)
1990   *Ghost* (Zucker) (song)
1991   *Le Dernier Papillon*

Publications

By NORTH: articles—

Variety (New York), 12 October 1960.
Cinema (Los Angeles), Fall 1969.
In *Knowing the Score*, by Irwin Bazelon, New York, 1975.
Soundtrack! (Hollywood), March 1985.

On NORTH: articles—

Spolar, Betsey, and Merrilyn Hammond, in *Theatre Arts* (New York), August 1953.
Cinestudio (Madrid), June 1972.
Films in Review (New York), October 1972.
Thomas, Tony, in *Music for the Movies*, South Brunswick, New Jersey, 1973.
Ecran (Paris), September 1975.
Palmer, Christopher, in *Film Music Notebook* (Calabasas, California), vol. 3, no. 1, 1977.
Pro Musica Sana (New York), Summer 1982.
Soundtrack! (Hollywood), December 1982.
Soundtrack! (Hollywood), March 1983.
Films in Review (New York), June-July 1986.
Palmer, Christopher, in *The Composer in Hollywood*, London 1990.
Obituary in *Variety* (New York), 16 September 1991.
Obituary in *Séquences* (Haute-Ville), November 1991.
Obituary in *Soundtrack*, December 1991.
Obituary in *Sight & Sound* (London), February 1992.
Film Dope (Nottingham), July 1992.
Kendall, L., "The Re-making of Alex North's *2001*: An Interview with Robert Townson," in *Film Score Monthly* (Los Angeles), August-September 1993.

Grant, B., "The Art of Film Music: Special Emphasis on Hugo Friedhofer, Alex North, David Raskin, Leonard Rosenman," in *Choice*, January 1995.
Johnson, Victoria E., "The Art of Film Music: Special Emphasis on Hugo Friedhofer, Alex North, David Raskin, Leonard Rosenman," in *Film Quarterly* (Berkeley), Fall 1995.
Kalinak, Kathryn, "The Art of Film Music: Special Emphasis on Hugo Friedhofer, Alex North, David Raskin and Leonard Rosenman," in *Historical Journal of Film, Radio and Television*, March 1996.

*   *   *

In 1986, Alex North became the first composer to be voted an honorary Academy Award. The honor was overdue; he had never won despite 15 nominations between 1951 and 1984.

North came to films with a background in documentary and ballet music under the sponsorship of Elia Kazan. Kazan had a difficult time convincing Warner Bros.' music department to accept New Yorker North as composer for *A Streetcar Named Desire*, but Kazan persisted and the resulting score caused a reconceptualization of the role of music in films. The symphonic film score—rich, lushly orchestrated—had been a staple of the medium since the 1930s. In *Streetcar*, North wrote music that was heavily influenced by jazz and the blues yet preserved the structure of the classical film score. Cat-house blues piano and mournful trumpet wails functioned to evoke character, be it Stanley Kowalski's coarseness or Blanche DuBois's fragility. And it fit.

North's score for *Viva Zapata!* enabled him to use musical experience gained during a two-year stay in Mexico. It also gave him further opportunities to display a flair for unorthodox orchestration, but with a purpose: a sequence depicting peasants clicking stones together as a gesture of solidarity for the captured Zapata rises in volume, and as the scene progresses North adds an underlay of bongos, timbales, flutes, guitars, and plucked strings. The orchestra has added its rhythmic voice to the protest of the peasants' primitive percussion, extending in music the dramatic essence of the sequence.

Scoring against conventional expectations in Mike Nichols's volatile adaptation of *Who's Afraid of Virginia Woolf?*, North toyed with and abandoned jazz and twelve-tone approaches to the project and produced a quasi-Baroque score: a tranquil guitar theme played against muted violin chords and harp *pizzicati*. As North said: "I wanted to get to the soul of these people and suggest they were really meant for each other. Frenetic music would have tipped the scales too much in one direction. You have to let the scenes play themselves."

Although North preferred intimate and personal subjects, his mammoth scores for Kubrick's *Spartacus* and Mankiewicz's *Cleopatra* are among his most celebrated works. On both he was afforded a luxury rarely given the film composer: a year to work preparing each project, collaborating in both cases at every stage of the production with musically sensitive directors. For *Spartacus*, North attempted to "capture the feeling of pre-Christian Rome using contemporary musical techniques." To this end, he researched music of the period and unearthed unorthodox instruments such as the dulcimer and the *ondioline* in a quest for exotic tone color. Inspired by Prokofiev's score for *Alexander Nevsky*, North utilized a large brass section to evoke the barbaric quality of the times. He withheld the violins' appearance until the film's love story blossomed, at that point proving himself more than equal to the lyrical effloressence of the "traditional" film scores of the past. It is a tragedy that in their only subsequent collaboration, Kubrick decided to jettison the 40 minutes of original music North wrote for *2001: A Space Odyssey*; the director fell in love with his classical ''temporary'' track and decided to retain it.

In the 1980s, *Dragonslayer*'s gothic, stentorian strains and *Carny's* expressionist grotesquerie displayed North's flair for the fantastic and the surreal. *Under the Volcano* marked his third teaming with John Huston and was a return to the Mexican inspiration of his youth. North's mischievous streak was showcased in his witty orchestral adaptation of Italian arias that wryly comment on the black comedy of Huston's *Prizzi's Honor*.

In all, North's achievement was to realize what he saw as the function of film scoring: ''to extend the characters on screen by writing music that penetrates the soul of the individual.'' He was an innovator and experimenter who never lost sight of his considerable lyric gifts.

—Lee Tsiantis

NUGENT, Frank S.

Writer. Nationality: American. **Born:** Frank Stanley Nugent in New York City, 27 May 1908. **Education:** Attended Columbia University, New York, degree in journalism. **Family:** Married 1) Dorothy Rivers, 1939 (divorced 1952); 2) Jean Lavell, 1953; one son. **Career:** 1929–34, reporter, and film critic, 1934–40, New York *Times*; 1940—first filmwriting work, as script doctor; 1948—first film as writer, and first of several films for John Ford, *Fort Apache*; 1957–58—President, Screen Writers Guild. **Died:** 29 December 1965.

Films as Writer:

1948   *Fort Apache* (Ford); *Three Godfathers* (Ford)
1949   *Tulsa* (Heisler); *She Wore a Yellow Ribbon* (Ford)
1950   *Wagonmaster* (Ford); *Two Flags West* (Wise)
1952   *The Quiet Man* (Ford)
1953   *Angel Face* (Preminger)
1954   *The Paratrooper* (Young); *Trouble in the Glen* (Wilcox); *They Rode West* (Karlson)
1955   *Mister Roberts* (Ford and LeRoy); *The Tall Men* (Walsh)
1956   **The Searchers** (Ford)
1957   *The Rising of the Moon* (Ford)
1958   *Gunman's Walk* (Karlson); *The Last Hurrah* (Ford)
1960   *Flame over India* (Lee Thompson)
1961   *Two Rode Together* (Ford)
1963   *Donovan's Reef* (Ford)
1966   *Incident at Phantom Hill* (Bellamy)

Publications

On NUGENT: articles—

Cahiers du Cinéma (Paris), April 1966, translated in *Cahiers du Cinéma in English*, January 1967.
Film Comment (New York), Winter 1970–71.
Film Comment (New York), Summer 1972.
Film Dope, no. 48, July 1992.

*   *   *

Frank S. Nugent, who worked as a Hollywood screenwriter for nearly 20 years, started as a news reporter at the *New York Times*, and moved to the film department as an assistant, then top reviewer. In the latter capacity Nugent sang high praise for some of the biggest hits of Hollywood's waning Golden Age (*Modern Times, Stagecoach, Snow White and the Seven Dwarfs, A Star Is Born, Gone with the Wind*), as well as the growing number of imports that were to help internationalize filmmaking in the postwar years (*Grand Illusion, Pygmalion, The Lady Vanishes*).

Among the movies Nugent panned were those starring such romantic leads as Robert Taylor and Tyrone Power. Nugent's review of *The Story of Alexander Graham Bell* praised the film for *not* including Power in its cast, and resulted in a serious reduction of 20th Century-Fox's advertising in the *New York Times* for nearly a year. Then, after Nugent's effulgent re-review of that studio's *The Grapes of Wrath*, he received an offer from Darryl F. Zanuck to work there as a script doctor. (Zanuck's maneuver was privately called ''a tacit exercise of the theory that if you can't fire 'em, hire 'em,'' the *Times* obituary of Frank Nugent stated 25 years later.)

At 20th Century-Fox, Nugent worked on scores of scripts, and there was talk of his becoming a producer there. However, that didn't materialize, and he returned to journalism, writing freelance movie articles for such magazines as *Colliers, Saturday Evening Post, Good Housekeeping*, and the *New York Times Magazine*. One such assignment for the latter took Nugent to Mexico where John Ford was directing *The Fugitive*. Nugent later reported that Ford ''knocked me right off my seat by asking how I'd like to write for him. . . . He gave me a list of about 50 books to read. . . . Later he sent me down into the Old Apache country to nose around.'' Ford also asked Nugent to write complete biographies of every character in the film, from childhood to the moment he or she entered the screenplay. It was a practice that Nugent continued throughout his screenwriting career.

Eleven of the 21 scripts Nugent wrote were for Ford films, including *She Wore a Yellow Ribbon, Wagonmaster, The Quiet Man*, and *The Searchers*. The story of the Nugent-Ford association is somewhat befogged by the report, which has been published in numerous sources, that Nugent was married to John Ford's daughter, Barbara, the same year that Ford asked him to write his first script, *Fort Apache*. But the obituaries of both Barbara Ford and Frank Nugent mention two marriages each, but not to one another.

Nugent had been an ardent Ford fan since his days as the *New York Times* film critic, writing in his review of *Stagecoach* for example, that Ford had ''swept aside the years of artifice and talkie compromise and . . . made a motion picture that sings a song of camera . . . a movie of the grand old school, a genuine rib-thumper and a beautiful sight to see.'' That Nugent and Ford should eventually meet and work together seems as predestined as the meeting and collaboration of James Agee and John Huston, a few years later.

Richard Corliss, in his chapter on Nugent in *Talking Pictures*, writes that Nugent's work ''culminated in his brilliant and self-effacing script for *The Searchers*—that rare Hollywood film that can be called indisputably ineffable cinema.'' Corliss points out that *The Searchers* is the ''ultimate 'door' movie, with more than a score of shots in which doors describe or extend the psychological milieu.''

The film also helped create a new persona for the aging John Wayne, as Ethan Edwards, the outsider who thinks and feels on an essentially inner psychological terrain before he acts.

—Cecile Starr

NUYTTEN, Bruno

Cinematographer and Director. **Nationality:** French. **Born:** Melun, 28 August 1945. **Family:** A son, Barnabe, by the actress Isabelle Adjani. **Career:** 1968—first film as cinematographer; 1989—first film as director, 1984—hosted TV programme *Photographie et cinema*. **Awards:** César awards for *Tchao Pantin, 1984; Camille Claudel*, 1988.

Films as Cinematographer:

1968   *Joseph ou comment petit-on être Vosgien?* (Béraud—short)
1969   *Marie Perrault* (Dion—short)
1970   *L'Espace vital* (Leconte—short); *La Loi du coeur* (Baudry); *Une Regression exemplaire* (Béraud—short)
1971   *La Quille, bon dieu* (Zingg—short); *Alice Babar et les 40 nénuphars* (Berthomier), *La Poule* (Béraud—short); *La Mort de Janis Joplin* (Kane—short); *Les Machines de l'existence* (Dion—short)
1972   *L'Audition* (Dion—short); *Fleurs de Jones* (Berthomier—short); *Nichna* (Charlin—short); *Le Maire* (Béraud—short)
1973   *Tristan et Iseult* (Legrange—short); *L'Attente* (Legrange—short); *Ce que savait Morgan* (Béraud—short); *Music on the streets* (Combe—short); *Le Jeu des preuves* (Béraud—short)
1974   *Les Valseuses* (*Going Places*) (Blier); *La Femme du Gange* (Duras); *Le Photographe Lassine* (Marconnier—short); *Fantaisie blanche* (co, Parrain— short)
1975   *India Song* (Duras); *Souvenirs d'en France* (Téchiné); *Les Vécés étaient fermés de l'intérieur* (Leconte); *L'Assassin musicien* (Jacquot); *Mon Coeur est rouge* (Rosier)
1976   *Barocco* (Téchiné); *La Meilleure Façon de marcher* (*The Best Way to Get Along*) (Miller); *Son nom de Vénise dans Calcultta désert* (Duras)
1977   *Le Camion* (Duras); *La Nuit tous les chats vent gris* (Zingg); *L'Exercice du pouvoir* (Galland)
1978   *La Tortue sur le dos* (Béraud); *Zoo Zero* (A. Fleischer); *Les Soeurs Bronte* (Téchiné)
1979   *French Postcards* (Huyck)
1980   *Brubaker* (Rosenberg); *Un Assassin qui passe* (*A Passing Killer*) (Vianey)
1981   *Possession* (Zulawski); *Garde à vue* (Miller); *Hôtel des Amériques* (Téchiné)
1982   *L'Invitation au voyage* (Del Monte); *Retour d'Allemagne* (Berthomier)
1983   *La Vie est un roman* (*Life is a Bed of Roses*) (Resnais); *Tchao Pantin* (Berri)
1984   *Fort Saganne* (Alain Corneau); *La Pirate* (Doillon); *Les Enfants* (Duras)

1985   *Détective* (Godard)
1986   *Jean de Florette* (Berri); *Manon des sources* (*Manon of the Spring*) (Berri)

Films as Director:

1989   *Camille Claudel* (+ co-sc)
1992   *Albert Souffre* (+ sc)
2000   *Passionnément* (*Passionately*) (+ sc)

Publications

By NUYTTEN: articles—

Cinématographe, no. 23, January 1977; no. 70, September 1981; no. 88, April 1983; no. 101, June 1984.
Cahiers du Cinéma, no. 289, June 1978; nos. 371/372, May 1985; no. 501, April 1996.
Technicien du Film, no. 324, April 1984.
Première, no. 141, December 1988.
Film Quarterly (Berkeley), Summer 1996.

On NUYTTEN: articles—

Cinéma no. 212, 1976.
Télérama, no. 1570, February 1980.
Premiere, vol. 3, no. 7, March 1990.
Film Dope, no. 48, July 1992.
Mensuel du Cinéma, April 1993.
Cahiers du Cinéma (Paris), April 1996.
Film Français, no. 1665, February 1997; no. 1937, March 1993; no. 2982, March 1984; no. 2026, March 1985; no. 2131, 1 March 1987.
Literature/Film Quarterly (Salisbury), April 1998.

*   *   *

After studying cinematography under Ghislain Cloquet at the Belgian film school INSAS, Bruno Nuytten gained valuable experience as assistant to Ricardo Aronovitch and Claude Lecomte, but his most influential mentor was Cloquet who introduced him into the world of Marguerite Duras with *Jaune le soleil* (1971) and *Nathalie Granger* (1972). In the early seventies he also made short films with the rising generation of filmmakers, notably Luc Béraud (*La Poule*, 1971), and Yvan Lagrange for whom he provided the lyrical images of *Tristan et Iseult* (1973). A brief spell in publicity films conditioned him against elaborate preparation and pleonastic camera work.

From the mid-seventies Nuytten worked with successive directors whose methods and budgets varied considerably, from the spare style of Duras or Jacquot to the lavish wide-screen productions of Berri or Corneau, or the expressionist excesses of Zulwaski (*Possession*, 1981). He served established directors like Godard and Resnais, and collaborated in the experimental approaches of Alain Fleischer (*Zoo zero*, 1978) and Peter Del Monte (*L'Invitation au voyage*, 1982). In the late seventies his association with Andre Téchiné saw continued experimentation with various styles, while a period in America brought Willard Huyck's *French Postcards* (1979) and Rosenberg's disturbingly graphic exposure of prison brutality in *Brubaker* (1980).

His work for Duras represented an unusual challenge in that the director privileged sound over image, using the temporal disjunction of voice and image to explore perception and memory. After *La Femme du Gange* (1974), characterized by long fixed takes, *India Song* (1975) deploys slow tracking shots in a series of languid tableaux, but achieves striking emphasis through the juxtaposition of colourful gardens and arresting close-ups of remembered objects: a bicycle; a bouquet of fading roses; joss sticks on a piano. The spare, contemplative visual style is further extended in *Son nom de Vénise dans Calcutta désert* (1976) with long fixed takes and slow pan shots exploring abandoned rooms in half-light before focusing on memory-charged details. *Le Camion* (1977) takes the minimalism much further. Duras and Depardieu are filmed reading the script of the potential film with intercut shots of the eponymous heavy lorry crossing ugly industrial suburbs.

In complete contrast are lavish eighties super productions, particularly for Alain Corneau and Claude Berri. For Corneau's epic adventure story, *Fort Saganne* (1984) with locations in France, Tunisia and Mauritania, Nuytten overcame the problems of filming in the desert to produce superb wide-screen colour cinematography. After his brilliantly created tonality of evil in Berri's darkly atmospheric murder investigation, *Tchao Pantin* (1983) with its dimly lit streets and shadowy passageways, he then provided the director with luxuriant colour images for *Jean de Florette* and *Manon des sources* (1986). Once more overcoming difficulties of filming in harsh natural light, Nuytten used his highly mobile camera to produce stunning cinemascope images of bone-dry Provence under the August sun.

His work for Téchiné also enjoyed high production values. After the non-naturalist sets and lighting of *Souvenirs d'en France* (1975), which explores subjectivity and the march of history, came the highly referential *Barroco* (1976). Nuytten's interest in German expressionist lighting is apparent in his oneiric Amsterdam rendered in gray-blue tones through long travelling shots. In the painterly *Les Soeurs Bronte* (1978), which exploits color thematically, claustrophobic interiors are set against bare, desolate landscapes registered through slow forward travelling shots, while *Hôtel des Amériques* (1981), with its cars and rain-soaked streets is shot effectively in film noir style.

Nuytten's flexibity and wilingness to experiment was recognized by Resnais and Godard. For *La Vie est un roman* (1983) Resnais required predominantly very flat lighting except for emotionally charged moments, and to achieve this contrast, Nuytten experimented with various film emulsions. The differently textured images, some resplendent with colour, create the surreal qualities Resnais sought in his complex tripartite narrative set in a castle at different historical moments. In *Détective* (1985), Godard's constant reshaping of Sarde's script about murderous events in a hotel created problems particularly in lighting continuity, but Nuytten nevertheless achieved some telling compositions, notably the close-ups of dead white mice and pamphlets on a breakfast tray.

For Claude Miller there were contrastive undertakings. If *La Meilleure façon de marcher* (1976) required location shooting in the Auvergne as well as theatrical interiors for the costume ball, *Garde à vue* (1981), set largely in the interrogation roon of a police station required a different approach. Although presented with a storyboard, Nuytten visually ignored it as symptomatic of the overpreparation he abhorred.

In two quite different films Nuytten's use of searching close-ups is particularly marked. In Béraud's debut feature, *La Tortue sur le dos* (1978), the romanticised vision of the tortured writer is exposed in a head-on shooting style in which the protagonist seems imprisoned

within the frame, while in Doillon's intimate study of a female relationship, *La Pirate* (1984), Nuytten used frequent zooms to capture the faces of the two protagonists. Shot in black and white, the film also conveys both the dull grayness of the hotel and the translucent beauty of the North sea.

In 1988, with the encouragement of Isabelle Adjani, Nuytten made a remarkable directorial debut with *Camille Claudel*. In a handsome period production, telling the turbulent life-story of the vulnerable sculptress, Nuytten conveys with a fresh immediacy the triumphs and tribulations of artistic creation. His second film, *Albert Souffre* (1992), most notable for a strident sound track, focuses on the frenetic activities of the emotionally demanding protagonist.

In his association with directors whether established or emerging, Nuytten involved himself in every aspect of the cinematography from framing and lighting to choice of film stock. Each film, whether notable for an idiosyncratic use of zooms, close-ups, mobile camera work or expressionist lighting, represents no more than a formative stage in a continuously evolving cinematic style. Nuytten's incarnation as a director deprives other filmmakers of a talented, innovative cinematographer but opens up exciting prospects for French filmmaking in the nineties.

—R. F. Cousins

NYKVIST, Sven

Cinematographer and Director. **Nationality:** Swedish. **Born:** Moheda, 3 December 1922. **Family:** Father of the director-writer Carl-Gustav Nykvist. **Career:** Assistant cameraman from early 1940s; 1945—first film as cinematographer; 1953—first of many films for Ingmar Bergman, *The Naked Night*; 1956—co-directed first film, *Gorilla*; 1996—cinematographer for TV mini-series *Enskilda samtal*. **Awards:** Best Cinematography Academy Award and National Society of Film Critics Best Cinematography Award, for *Cries and Whispers*, 1972, Jury Specialbagge Guldbagge Award, 1973; Best Cinematography Cesar Award, for *Black Moon*, 1975; Best Cinematography Academy Award, Best Cinematography British Academy Award, Best Cinematography British Society of Cinematographers, Los Angeles Film Critics Association Best Cinematography, for *Fanny and Alexander*, 1982; Cannes Film Festival Best Artistic Contribution, for *The Sacrifice*, 1986; Best Cinematography Independent Spirit Award, for *The Unbearable Lightness of Being*, 1988; Camerimage Lifetime Achievement Award, 1993; American Society of Cinematographers Lifetime Achievement Award, 1996; Camerimage Special Award (shared with Ingmar Bergman), 1998.

Films as Cinematographer:

1941   *The Poor Millionaire* (asst)
1945   *Barnen från Frostmofjället* (*The Children of Frostmofjället*) (Husberg) (asst); *Gomorron Bill* (Falk-Winner); *Tretton stolar* (*Thirteen Chairs*) (Larsson)
1946   *Saltstänk och krutgubbar* (Bauman)
1947   *Maj på Malö* (Bauman); *Lata Lena och blåögda Per* (Wallén)
1949   *Lång-Lasse i Delsbo* (Johansson); *Hin och smålänningen* (co); *Bohus bataljon* (Cederstrand-Spjuth); *Sjösalavår* (*Spring at Sjösala*) (Wallén)

Sven Nykvist

1950   *Loffe blir polis* (Ahrle) (co)
1951   *Rågens rike* (Johansson)
1952   *Under Södra Korset* (*Under the Southern Cross*) (+ co-d, co-sc—doc); *Nar syrenerna blommar* (*When Lilacs Blossom*) (Johansson)
1953   *Barabbas* (Sjöberg) (co); *Vägen till Kolckrike* (Skoglund); **Gycklarnas afton** (*The Naked Night*; *Sawdust and Tinsel*) (Bergman) (co)
1954   *Salka Valka* (Mattsson); *Karin Mansdotter* (Sjöberg); *Storm over Tjurö* (Mattsson)
1955   *Sista ringen* (Skoglund); *Den underbara lögnen* (Road)
1956   *Gorilla* (+ co-d); *Nattbarn* (*Children of the Night*) (Hellström); *Flickan i frack* (*Girl in a Dressing Gown*) (Mattsson); *Blänande hav* (Skoglund); *Alskling på vågen* (Bauman) (co); *Ett kungligt äventyr* (Birt); *Den tappre soldaten Jönsson* (Bergström)
1957   *En drömmares vandring* (*A Dreamer's Walk*) (Lindgren); *Gäst i eget hus* (Olin); *Synnöve Solbakken* (Hellström)
1958   *Damen i svart* (*Lady in Black*) (Mattsson); *Laila—Liebe unter der Mitternachtssonne* (*Make Way for Lila*) (Husberg)
1959   *Får jag låna din fru?* (Mattsson)

1960   *Jungfrukällan* (*The Virgin Spring*) (Bergman); *Domaren* (*The Judge*) (Sjöberg); *De sista stegen* (*A Matter of Morals*) (Cromwell)
1961   *Sasom i en spegel* (*Through a Glass Darkly*) (Bergman)
1963   *Nattsvardsgästerna* (*Winter Light*; *The Communicants*) (Bergman); **Tystnaden** (*The Silence*) (Bergman)
1964   *För att inte talla om all dessa kvinnor* (*All These Women*; *Now about All These Women*) (Bergman); *Att älska* (*To Love*) (J. Donner); *Alskande par* (*Loving Couples*) (Zetterling)
1965   *Lianbron* (*The Vine Bridge*) (+ d)
1966   **Persona** (Bergman)
1968   *Vargtimmen* (*Hour of the Wolf*) (Bergman); *Skammen* (*The Shame*) (Bergman)
1969   *Riten* (*The Ritual*; *The Rite*) (Bergman); *En passion* (*The Passion of Anna*; *Passion*) (Bergman)
1970   *Erste Liebe* (*First Love*) (Schell)
1971   *Beröringen* (*The Touch*) (Bergman); *The Last Run* (Fleischer); *One Day in the Life of Ivan Denisovich* (Wrede)
1972   **Viskningar och rop** (*Cries and Whispers*) (Bergman); *Siddhartha* (Rooks)
1973   *Scener ur ett äktenskap* (*Scenes from a Marriage*) (Bergman)

1974 *The Dove* (Jarrott); *Ransom* (*The Terrorists*) (Wrede);
      Trollflöjten (*The Magic Flute*) (Bergman)
1975 *Black Moon* (Malle)
1976 *Ansikte not ansikte* (*Face to Face*) (Bergman); *Le Locataire*
      (*The Tenant*) (Polanski)
1977 *Das Schlangenei* (*The Serpent's Egg*) (Bergman)
1978 *En och en* (*One Plus One*) (+ co-d); *Pretty Baby* (Malle); *King
      of the Gypsies* (Pierson); *Herbstsonate* (*Autumn Sonata*)
      (Bergman)
1979 *Hurricane* (Troell); *Starting Over* (Pakula)
1980 *Willy and Phil* (Mazursky); *Aus dem Leben der Marionetten*
      (*From the Life of the Marionettes*) (Bergman)
1981 *The Postman Always Rings Twice* (Rafelson)
1982 **Fanny och Alexander** (*Fanny and Alexander*) (Bergman);
      Cannery Row (Ward)
1983 *Un Amour de Swann* (*Swann in Love*) (Schlondörff); *La
      Tragédie de Carmen* (*The Tragedy of Carmen*) (Brook);
      Star 80 (Fosse)
1984 *Efter Repetitioner* (*After the Rehearsal*) (Bergman)
1985 *Agnes of God* (Jewison)
1986 **Offret** (*The Sacrifice*) (Tarkovsky)
1988 *The Unbearable Lightness of Being* (Kaufman); *Another
      Woman* (W. Allen); *Katinka* (*Vid Vgen*; *Ved Vejen*)
      (von Sydow)
1989 *Crimes and Misdemeanors* (W. Allen); ''Oedipus Wrecks''
      ep. of *New York Stories* (W. Allen)
1991 *Buster's Bedroom* (Horn)
1992 *Chaplin* (Attenborough)
1993 *What's Eating Gilbert Grape* (Hallstrom); *Sleepless in Seattle*
      (N. Ephron)
1994 *With Honors* (Keshishian); *Only You* (Jewison); *Mixed Nuts*
      (N. Ephron)
1995 *Something to Talk About* (Hallström); *Kristin Lavransdotter*
      (Ullmann)
1996 *Enskilda samtal* (*Private Conversation*) (Ullmann—
      mini for TV)
1998 *Celebrity* (Allen)
1999 *Curtain Call* (Yates)

Other Films:

1977 *A Look at Liv* (Kaplan) (doc) (ro as Himself)
1992 *The Ox* (d, sc)
1992 *Visions of Light: The Art of the Cinematographer* (Glassman,
      McCarthy, Samuels) (doc) (ro as Interviewee)
1995 *Lumiere et compagnie* (*Lumiere and Company*) (various) (ro)
1997 *Liv Ullmann scener fra et liv* (Hambro) (doc) (ro as Interviewee)
2000 *Ljuset haller mig sallskap* (*Light Keeps Me Company*) (Carl-
      Gustav Nykvist) (doc) (ro as Interviewee)

Publications

By NYKVIST: articles—

''Photographing the Films of Ingmar Bergman,'' in *American Cinema-
    tographer* (Hollywood), October 1962.
''A Passion for Light,'' in *American Cinematographer* (Hollywood),
    April 1972.

Chaplin (Stockholm), no. 5, 1973.
Deutsche Kameramann (Munich), September 1974.
On *The Magic Flute* in *American Cinematographer* (Hollywood),
    August 1975.
On *Face to Face* in *Filmmakers Newsletter* (Ward Hill, Massachu-
    setts), May 1976.
Filmkritik (Munich), May 1976.
Millimeter (New York), July/August 1976.
On *Cannery Row* in *American Cinematographer* (Hollywood),
    April 1981.
Millimeter (New York), May 1981.
On Location (Hollywood), November 1983.
American Film (Washington, D.C.), March 1984.
Stills (London), June/July 1984.
Eyepiece (London), July/August 1984.
Positif (Paris), May 1986.
Positif (Paris), February 1988.
American Cinematographer (Hollywood), March 1989.
Film Comment (New York), September/October 1989.
Time Out (London), 7 April 1993.

On NYKVIST: articles—

Filmwoche, 8 July 1961.
Chaplin (Stockholm), December 1965.
Film in Sweden, no. 1, 1968.
Film World (Bombay), October/December 1968.
Focus on Film (London), Winter 1970; corrections in no. 13, 1973.
Eder, R., in *New York Times*, 7 April 1976.
Denby, D., in *New York Times*, 25 April 1976.
On *From the Life of the Marionettes* in *Film* (London), 15 Novem-
    ber 1982.
Curtin, J., in *New York Times*, 12 June 1983.
Block, Bruce A., in *American Cinematographer* (Hollywood),
    April 1984.
Cahiers du Cinéma (Paris), no. 385, June 1986.
Film Dope (Nottingham), July 1992.
Chaplin (Stockholm), vol. 34, no. 6, 1992/1993.
Filmkultura (Budapest), July 1993.
Fisher, B., ''ASC salutes Sven Nykvist,'' in *American Cinema-
    tographer* (Hollywood), February 1996.
Edmunds, M., ''A master lenser looks back,'' in *Variety* (New York),
    17–23 February 1997.
Fujiwara, Chris, ''Soulful Eye,'' in *Boston Phoenix*, 18–25 May 2000.

*   *   *

Sven Nykvist's color cinematography on the films of the director
Ingmar Bergman has won him praise, awards—and endless imitators.
Nykvist was the director of photography on all of Bergman's films
and most of his television productions from *The Virgin Spring*
through *Fanny and Alexander* and *After the Rehearsal*. So well does
Nykvist's cinematography fit Bergman's later films that it is difficult
to untangle their mutual influence on each other's work.

When he was part of Bergman's tightly knit 18-person crew,
Nykvist's responsibilities included lighting and actually working the
camera, as well as designing the cinematography for the production.
This may account for the decline in quality (from superb down to
excellent) when Nykvist works on American films, and must delegate

part of his duties among the crew. Nevertheless, there is also clearly a symbiotic matching of tastes and temperaments between himself and Bergman that Nykvist has not shared with other directors. Both Swedes are the sons of pastors, both had difficult childhoods (Nykvist's parents were African missionaries, and left him at home in Sweden for much of his childhood), and both fondly recall an early fascination with the power of film and light over the imagination.

Nykvist's pioneering with natural light sources complements Bergman's penchant for location shooting and minimalist shot compositions (''two faces and a teacup''). While Nykvist builds upon the Swedish tradition of filmmaking in his style, he has brought the national tradition of stark psychological landscape into international favor with color cinematography that achieves iconographical beauty by eschewing the distracting prettiness generally associated with color film. Initially, Nykvist was reluctant to move from black and white to color because color's tendency to prettify subjects and emphasize detail made it difficult to show something as convincingly ''ugly.'' When color became a commercial necessity, Nykvist and Bergman got off to a false start in *Now about All These Woman*, released in 1964, which made them run for cover back to black and white until they shot *Passion* in 1969. By ignoring much of the conventional wisdom about using color film, Nykvist finally managed to bring an iconographical style to *Cries and Whispers*, his fourth color film for Bergman.

Nykvist emphasizes that he strives for realism, but his use of the term is misleading. He portrays psychological truth rather than social realism, and his heavy reliance on natural light and geometrically precise shot composition gives his work the convincing quality of a dream, not a documentary. Nykvist explains that light is the key to his cinematography, and that light is a character in Bergman's films. The significance of an actor's actions often is determined by subtle differences in lighting. This fascination with light is probably linked to both men's experience of Sweden's sunless winters and unblinking summer sun. On *Cries and Whispers* the two men spent weeks simply gauging the natural light at different times of day inside the house which served as the main interior for the film. This careful preproduction work in terms of light is typical of their style.

Although each of Nykvist's films for Bergman has its own unique look, Nykvist typically favors a soft bounce lighting. Careful positioning of highlights prevents the usual flattening effect of such lighting, and gives actors a rounded, three-dimensional look which is flattering. He uses a minimum of color saturation, and sets and costumes are usually chosen in muted tones. In his Hollywood films, the demands of directors and time schedules has sometimes forced him to experiment with technical gimmicks. He steered away from them in Bergman films, however, relying instead on a dogged determination to wait until the natural light was right to shoot. One exception to this is Bergman's fantasy *The Magic Flute*, shot in a studio, in which Nykvist used a good many colored filler and key lights and a strong backlight rather than his usual bounce lighting; yet he still preferred to manipulate the light rather than use extensive lab work or distorting lenses and filters. More typical of his style is his bravura camerawork on *Scenes from a Marriage*, which included ten-minute takes with as many as 20 zooms per take, plus complex camera movements. His ability to track an actor precisely and sensitively during a long take is phenomenal, and most of *Scenes from a Marriage* was shot with only one camera, held, of course, by Nykvist. Despite his technical mastery and careful preplanning, he relies heavily on instinct and a feel for shots, and approaches his work more as an artist than a technician.

For decades, foreign cinematographers had little chance of working in American films. The easing of union regulations in the 1970s, however, allowed European directors of photography an increasing visibility in the American film industry. Since then, Nykvist has photographed a variety of American films, from *Agnes of God* to *What's Eating Gilbert Grape*. And over the years, he has worked for other filmmakers, including Louis Malle, Roman Polanski, Andrei Tarkovsky, Volker Schlöndorff, Philip Kaufman, Lasse Hallstrom, Nora Ephron, Liv Ullmann (in which he maintained his Bergman connection), and Woody Allen, and directed his own films. Particularly notable is his work with Allen on *Another Woman, Crimes and Misdemeanors, Celebrity*, and the ''Oedipus Wrecks'' episode of *New York Stories*. But Nykvist still remains synonymous with Ingmar Bergman, with their collaboration producing the cinematographer's most innovative, influential, and renowned work. In *Light Keeps Me Company*, a documentary directed by Nykvist's son, Carl-Gustav, Bergman noted, ''Sven and I saw things alike, thought things alike; our feeling for light was the same. We had the same basic moral positions about camera placement.''

—Patricia Ferrara, updated by Rob Edelman

O

O'BRIEN, Willis H.

Special Effects Technician. **Nationality:** American. **Born:** Oakland, California, 2 March 1886. **Family:** Married 1) Hazel Ruth Collette, 1917 (died 1934); two sons; 2) Darlyne Prenett, 1934. **Career:** Cartoonist for San Francisco *Daily News*; commercial sculptor (work exhibited at San Francisco World's Fair, 1913); 1914—began experimenting with special effects in short films; from mid-1920s—worked on special effects for feature films. **Died:** 8 November 1962.

Films as Director, Writer, Photographer, and Special Effects Technician (Shorts):

1914	*The Dinosaur and the Missing Link*
1916	*The Birth of a Flivver*
1917	*R.F.D. 10,000 B.C.*; *Prehistoric Poultry*; *Curious Pets of Our Ancestors*; *Mickey's Naughty Nightmares*; *Morpheus Mike*; *In the Villain's Power*; *Mickey and His Goat*; *Sam Lloyd's Famous Puzzles*; *Nippy's Nightmare*
1918	*The Ghost of Slumber Mountain*

Films as Special Effects Technician (Features):

1925	*The Lost World* (Hoyt)
1933	**King Kong** (Cooper and Schoedsack); *Son of Kong* (Schoedsack)
1935	*The Last Days of Pompeii* (Schoedsack)
1936	*The Dancing Pirate* (Corrigan)
1949	*Mighty Joe Young* (Schoedsack)
1952	*This Is Cinerama* (Thompson and others) (uncredited)
1955	*This Animal World* (Allen)
1957	*The Black Scorpion* (Ludwig)
1959	*The Giant Behemoth* (*Behemoth, the Sea Monster*) (Lourie)
1960	*The Lost World* (Allen) (uncredited)
1962	*It's a Mad, Mad, Mad, Mad World* (Kramer) (uncredited)

Film as Writer:

1956	*The Beast of Hollow Mountain* (Nassour)

Publications

By O'BRIEN: book—

The Lost World of Willis O'Brien: The Original Shooting Script of the 1925 Landmark Special Effects Dinosaur Film, edited by Roy Kinnard, Jefferson, North Carolina, 1993.

On O'BRIEN: books—

Archer, Steve, *Willis O'Brien: Special Effects Genius*, Jefferson, North Carolina, McFarland, 1993.
Jensen, Paul M., *The Men Who Made the Monsters*, New York, 1996.

On O'BRIEN: articles—

Midi-Minuit Fantastique (Paris), October 1962.
Shay, Don, ''Willis O'Brien, Creator of the Impossible,'' in *Focus on Film* (London), Autumn 1973.
Classic Film Collector (Indiana, Pennsylvania), Summer 1974.
Cinema Papers (Melbourne), July 1974.
The Saga of Special Effects, by Ron Fry and Pamela Fourzon, Englewood Cliffs, New Jersey, 1977.
Vampir (Nuremberg), March 1977.
Ecran Fantastique (Paris), no. 6, 1978.
Starburst (London), no. 28, 1980.
Cahiers du Cinéma (Paris), November 1980.
''O'Brien Issue'' of *Cinefex* (Riverside, California), January 1982.
Banc-Titre (Paris), February 1982.
Movie Maker (Hemel Hempstead, Hertfordshire), February 1985.
Film Dope, no. 48, July 1992.
Cinefantastique, vol. 24, no. 2, 1993.
Boxoffice (Chicago), June 1997.

*   *   *

While screen monsters will always be with us, it seems likely that the days of the animated monster are gone. The amount of time (and therefore money) tied up in producing a well-crafted live-action feature employing this special effects process has limited its use almost from the beginning. The career of Willis H. O'Brien, the man who pioneered the use of model animation, reflects only too well the inherent problems associated with the technique; yet he is without doubt a major figure, not only in the history of special effects but in the history of the cinema as a whole.

Any discussion of O'Brien's work must centre around *King Kong*. His major project, the film is probably still the most successful of this particular subgenre. The effects are not allowed to dominate the overall film to its detriment (as has sometimes been the case in the work of O'Brien's successor, Ray Harryhausen), but are properly integrated into the skillfully worked out ''beauty and the beast'' storyline. Most importantly, Kong is a character rather than an impersonal instrument of destruction. As many critics have pointed out, he expresses emotions (such as his affection for Ann Darrow [Fay Wray], his anger when he loses her, a childlike curiosity as he examines the bodies of creatures he has just vanquished) and motivation. O'Brien's achievement is to make us regard Kong as a living being, not just as a piece of clever effects work. *King Kong* may have been improved on technically, but never on the level of characterization.

O'Brien's career after *King Kong* was, unfortunately, very patchy. Despite the film's commercial success, it did not become any easier to launch animation projects. *Son of Kong*, while impressive in the effects area, falls flat in all other departments. Several titles, such as *War Eagle* and *Gwangi* were put into preproduction in the 1930s and 1940s but then abandoned. The films made in the 1950s suffered from low budgets. Some, such as *The Black Scorpion*, contain good special effects sequences, but O'Brien's involvement with them was to a lesser degree than his earlier work (he supervised the animation for *The Giant Behemoth* and merely provided the original story for *The Beast of Hollow Mountain*).

The one major animation project O'Brien worked on following *King Kong* was *Mighty Joe Young*, produced by the same team, Merian C. Cooper and Ernest B. Shoedsack, for RKO. Joe Young lacks Kong's grandeur but like him comes across as a character and not just a creature. In the most memorable scenes he accidentally demolishes a nightclub while drunk and, at the climax, rescues children from a burning orphanage. Unlike Kong, who ends up riddled with bullets, Joe's act of heroism earns him forgiveness (the police were sent to destroy him after the nightclub episode) and he returns home to Africa.

Aided by a team of assistants that included Marcel Delgado (who built the models for many of the films) and, later, Ray Harryhausen, O'Brien demonstrated with *King Kong* and *Mighty Joe Young* how effectively model animation can be employed in live-action films. It is certain that neither of the films could have worked so well had some other method been used (compare the original *King Kong* with the 1976 remake). Even the relatively crude models employed in *The Lost World* are infinitely preferable to the genuine reptiles used as dinosaurs in the 1960 version of the same story. Whatever the disappointments of O'Brien's career, he was responsible for some of the best-known images in cinema history.

—Daniel O'Brien

ONDŘÍČEK, Miroslav

Cinematographer. **Nationality:** Czech. **Born:** Prague, 4 November 1934. **Education:** 1957–59—attended Film Academy (FAMU), Prague. **Career:** Worked in amateur theatre, and as focus puller, grip, and laboratory technician; 1953–56—assistant at documentary film studio; 1963—photographed the first of many films for Milos Forman, *Talent Competition*; worked on films for Lindsay Anderson in England, 1967–68, and on international films after 1972. **Award:** British Academy Award for *Amadeus*, 1985.

Films as Cinematographer:

1957   *Snadný život* (Makovec) (asst); *Váhavý střelec* (Toman) (asst)
1958   *Cesta zpátky* (Krška) (asst); *Dnes naposled* (*Today for the Last Time*) (Frič); *Zde jsou lvi* (Krška) (asst)
1960   *Holubice* (Vláčil) (asst); *Kouzelný den* (Valášek) (asst)
1961   *Králíci ve vysoké trávě* (Gajer)
1962   *Deštivý den* (*Rainy Day*) (Bělka) (asst)
1963   *Až přijde kocour* (*The Cat*) (Jasný); *Konkurs* (*Talent Competition*) (Forman); *Křik* (*The Cry*) (Jireš)
1964   *Démanty noci* (*Diamonds of the Night*) (Němec)

1965   *Intimní osvětlení* (*Intimate Lighting*) (Passer) (co); ***Lásky jedné pla vovlásky*** (*Loves of a Blonde*) (Forman); "Perlicky na dne" ep. of *Podvodníci* (Němec)
1966   *Mučedníci lásky* (*Martyrs of Love*) (Němec); "The Arrivals" ep. of *The White Bus* (Anderson)
1967   *Hoří, má penenko* (*The Fireman's Ball*) (Forman); *Prag Legende* (Lahola) (TV)
1968   *Co nidky nepochopím. . .* (Roháč) (TV)
1969   *If . . .* (Anderson); *Tělo Diany* (Richard)
1970   *Slaughterhouse-Five* (Hill) (exteriors); *Taking Off* (Forman)
1972   *Homolka a tobolka* (Papousek)
1973   *O Lucky Man!* (Anderson)
1974   *Drahé tety a já* (Podskalsky); *Televize v Bublicích aneb Bublice v televizi* (Papoušek)
1975   *Dvojí svět hotelu Pacifik* (Majewski); *Hřiště* (Skalský)
1976   *Jakub* (Koval); *Konečně si rozumíme* (Papoušek); *Slovácká suita* (TV)
1977   *Antonín Dvořák: Symfonie č. 9 e moll, op. 95 "Z Nového světa"* (TV); *Příběh lásky a cti* (Vávra)
1978   *Nechci nic slyšet* (Koval)
1979   *Božská Ema* (*The Divine Emma*) (Krejčík); *Hair* (Forman)
1980   *Ragtime* (Forman); *Temné slunce* (Vávra)
1981   *The World According to Garp* (Hill)
1982   *Silkwood* (Nichols)
1983   *Amadeus* (Forman)
1984   *The River* (Rydell)
1985   *F/X* (Mandel); *Heaven Help Us* (Dinner)
1986   *Distant Harmony* (Sage)
1987   *Big Shots* (Mandel)
1988   *Hashigaon Hagadol* (*Funny Farm*) (Alter)
1989   *Valmont* (Forman)
1990   *Awakenings* (P. Marshall)
1992   *A League of Their Own* (P. Marshall)
1995   *Let It Be Me* (Bergstein)
1996   *The Preacher's Wife* (Marshall)

Publications

By ONDŘÍČEK: articles—

On *Ragtime* in *American Cinematographer* (Hollywood), May 1982.
American Cinematographer (Hollywood), February 1991.

On ONDŘÍČEK: articles—

Kino (Prague), no. 10, 1967
Wiener, D. J., on *Silkwood* in *American Cinematographer* (Hollywood), February 1984.
Lee, Nova, on *Amadeus* in *American Cinematographer* (Hollywood), April 1985.
American Cinematographer (Hollywood), vol. 73, July 1992.
Film Dope (Nottingham), June 1993.

*   *   *

The international career of Miroslav Ondříček began in the 1960s through his work with such directors of the Czechoslovak New Wave as Jan Nemec, Ivan Passer, and especially Milos Forman. As their films received prestigious awards at international festivals, Ondříček's photography was recognized as a chief factor determining the movement's style and form. His camera work in such films as *Loves of a Blonde*, *Intimate Lighting*, and *The Firemen's Ball* shows his skill in social documentary and satire. The mixture of the unobtrusive, predominantly medium shots and telling close-ups registering multitudes of momentary human reactions and feelings, created the unique style of the New Wave and demonstrated Ondříček's sensitivity to the film medium. Ondříček's talent for satire comes through especially in Forman's *The Firemen's Ball*, where his alert and often merciless camera catches the comic in the common and everyday. Without Ondříček's masterful cinematography, Forman's film would have lost much of its continuous, snowballing humor.

The success of Forman's films abroad led to Ondříček's first job outside Czechoslovakia. In 1966, although he did not know any English, Ondříček was invited by Lindsay Anderson to photograph *The White Bus*. Anderson liked his work so much that he employed him again for his two most well-known films, *If . . .* and *O Lucky Man!* Photographing each of them was a new challenge for Ondříček. In *If . . .* , following Anderson's directions, he successfully undercut a straightforward and realistic story with surrealistic portions giving the picture its ambiguous mixture of fantasy and reality, its quality of "assumed" reality. In *O Lucky Man!*, Ondříček's photography marvelously interplayed with Alan Price's songs and abruptly changed settings to portray the episodic adventures of its modern picaro.

Ondříček's high professional reputation today rests on his 30-year-long association with his compatriot, Milos Forman who, forced to remain in the West after the Soviet invasion of his homeland, established himself as one of the most successful contemporary Hollywood filmmakers. Ondříček shot all but two of Forman's films, creating photography for such hits as *Hair*, *Ragtime*, and *Amadeus*. Shooting each of these films was a completely different experience. After all, each was a creative adaptation of a different genre (musical, novel, and play, respectively), and each dealt with a radically different period of time. In *Hair* Ondříček's dynamic camera work helped give the film a coherent and fluent story line naturally highlighted by choreography and popular songs.

Ondříček's lighting and predominantly medium shots created the film's nostalgic and romanticized portrayal of the radical 1960s. *Ragtime*, for which Ondříček received an Oscar nomination, required a meticulous recreation of early 20th-century New York. Following the photographic style of the time, Ondříček depended on the natural outside light for interior sequences, avoided shots of human profiles, and positioned the camera usually at lower angles. Most of *Amadeus* was shot in historic Prague, Ondříček's home city, which was easily transformed into 18th-century Vienna. Many opera sequences were photographed in the old Tyl Theater where Mozart conducted his *Don Giovanni*.

Although the limited indoor space greatly reduced the freedom of his camera movement, all his interior scenes look dynamic and lively. Moreover, the candlelight and Chinese lanterns housing color-sprayed 250-watt bulbs gave his interior photography a realistic, warm 18th-century look. *Amadeus*, Ondříček's most lavish and challenging production so far, demonstrated the full scope of his remarkable talent. His photography gave the film its narrative flow, dynamism and splendor in the group sequences, and the intimacy of Mozart's personal life—all dramatically punctuated with the composer's enchanting music. For the first time in his career, Ondříček photographed a film that combined his love of filmmaking, music, and his hometown, Prague.

Ondříček's work with Forman gave him opportunities to work with other American directors, notably George Roy Hill and Mike Nichols. In Hill's *Slaughterhouse-Five*, a rather dull, humorless adaptation of Kurt Vonnegut's famous novel, his photography effectively conveyed the film's intricate narrative structure and its abruptly shifting time levels. A large part of that film was shot in Czechoslovakia. In Nichols's *Silkwood* Ondříček's photography subtly contrasted Karen's private and professional lives. To emphasize the characters' radioactive contamination, Ondříček used special make-up and fluorescent light for the sequences inside the plutonium plant. For scenes in Karen's house, on the other hand, he used only natural outside light from the windows.

Ondříček's photography does not exhibit any consistent stylistic or formal features. It simply demonstrates versatile technical professionalism, discipline, and artistic intuition which has always given him that rare ability to translate the director's vision into convincing visual images. After all, in an interview for *American Cinematographer* (May 1982), Ondříček plainly admitted, "Give me the right story and director, and I believe that I can find any cinematographic style that is needed."

—Tomasz Warchol

ORRY-KELLY

Costume Designer. **Nationality:** American. **Born:** John Orry Kelly in Kiama, New South Wales, 31 December 1897; emigrated to the United States, 1923. **Education:** Studied singing and art in Sydney. **Career:** Worked as mural painter in Sydney before emigrating, then worked as waiter, clerk, actor, decorative painter for shops and theater productions, and for Fox silent film titles, and costume designer for vaudeville shows at the Palace Theater, New York; 1931—moved to Hollywood, then chief designer for Warner Bros., 1932–43, 20th Century Fox, 1943–47, Universal, 1947–50, and then freelance. **Awards:** Academy Award for *An American in Paris*, 1951; *Les Girls*, 1957; *Some Like It Hot*, 1959. **Died:** Hollywood, California, 26 February 1964.

Films as Costume Designer:

1932   *The Rich Are Always with Us* (Green) (co); *So Big* (Wellman); *You Said a Mouthful* (Bacon); **I Am a Fugitive from a Chain Gang** (LeRoy); *The Crash* (Dieterle); *The Match King* (Bretherton and Keighley); *One Way Passage* (Garnett); *Week-End Marriage* (Freeland); *Winner Takes All* (Del Ruth); *Crooner* (Bacon); *Tiger Shark* (Hawks); *Two against the World* (Mayo) (co); *Cabin in the Cotton* (Curtiz); *Three on a Match* (LeRoy); *Scarlet Dawn* (Dieterle); *Lawyer Man* (Dieterle); *Employees Entrance* (Del Ruth); *Frisco Jenny* (Wellman); *Twenty Thousand Years in Sing Sing* (Curtiz); *Ladies They Talk About* (Bretherton)

1933   *Captured* (Del Ruth); *Central Airport* (Wellman); *Convention City* (Mayo); *Ex-Lady* (Florey); *Female* (Curtiz); **42nd Street** (Bacon) (co); *Hard to Handle* (LeRoy); *The House on 56th Street* (Florey) (co); *The Narrow Corner* (Green); *The Picture Snatcher* (Bacon); *Private Detective 62* (Curtiz); *The Working Man* (Adolfi); *The Mystery of the Wax Museum*

Orry-Kelly with Kay Francis

(Curtiz); *Voltaire* (Adolfi); *The Little Giant* (Del Ruth); *The Mind Reader* (Del Ruth); *The King's Vacation* (Adolfi); *Parachute Jumper* (Green); *Grand Slam* (Dieterle); *Blondie Johnson* (Enright); *Gold Diggers of 1933* (LeRoy); *Baby Face* (Green); *The Life of Jimmy Dolan* (*The Kid's Last Fight*) (Mayo); *Lilly Turner* (Wellman); *Heroes for Sale* (Wellman); *The Mayor of Hell* (Mayo); *The Silk Express* (Enright); *Mary Stevens M.D.* (Bacon); *The Kennel Murder Case* (Curtiz); *She Had to Say Yes* (Berkeley and Amy); *College Coach* (Wellman); *The World Changes* (LeRoy); *Son of a Sailor* (Bacon); *Massacre* (Crosland); *Journal of a Crime* (Keighley); *Harold Teen* (*The Dancing Foot*) (Roth)

1934 *As the Earth Turns* (Green); *British Agent* (Curtiz); *The Circus Clown* (Enright); *Dames* (Enright); *Dark Hazard* (Green); *Desirable* (Mayo); *Dr. Monica* (Keighley); *The Dragon Murder Case* (Humberstone); *Easy to Love* (Keighley); *Fashions of 1934* (Dieterle); *The Firebird* (Dieterle); *Flirtation Walk* (Borzage); *Happiness Ahead* (LeRoy); *Hi, Nellie* (LeRoy); *Housewife* (Green); *I Am a Thief* (Florey); *Kansas City Princess* (Keighley); *The Key* (Curtiz); *Madame Du Barry* (Dieterle); *The Merry*

Frinks (Green); *Merry Wives of Reno* (Humberstone); *Midnight Alibi* (Crosland); *Murder in the Clouds* (Lederman); *The Personality Kid* (Crosland); *Return of the Terror* (Bretherton); *Wonder Bar* (Bacon); *Babbitt* (Keighley); *I've Got Your Number* (Enright); *Gambling Lady* (Mayo); *Heat Lightning* (LeRoy); *Jimmy the Gent* (Curtiz); *Bedside* (Flrey); *A Modern Hero* (Pabst); *Twenty Million Sweethearts* (Enright); *Smarty* (*Hit Me Again*) (Florey); *He Was Her Man* (Bacon); *Underworld* (Del Ruth); *A Very Honorable Guy* (Bacon); *Fog over Frisco* (Dieterle); *Here Comes the Navy* (Bacon); *Registered Nurse* (Florey); *Friends of Mr. Sweeney* (Ludwig); *Side Street* (Green); *The Case of the Howling Dog* (Crosland); *A Lost Lady* (Green); *Big Hearted Herbert* (Keighley); *Gentlemen Are Born* (Green); *The St. Louis Kid* (*A Perfect Weekend*) (Enright); *I Sell Anything* (Florey); *Maybe It's Love* (McG ann); *The Secret Bride* (*Concealment*) (Dieterle); *Gold Diggers of 1935* (Berkeley)

1935 *Bordertown* (Mayo); *Broadway Gondolier* (Bacon); *Broadway Hostess* (McDonald); *Dangerous* (Green); *The Frisco Kid* (Bacon); *G-Men* (Keighley); *I Found Stella Parish*

(LeRoy); *In Caliente* (Bacon); *Living on Velvet* (Borzage); *Miss Pacific Fleet* (Enright); *Page Miss Glory* (LeRoy) (co); *The Payoff* (Florey); *Shipmates Forever* (Borzage); *Stars over Broadway* (Keighley); *Sweet Adeline* (LeRoy); *The Widow from Monte Carlo* (Collins); *The Woman in Red* (Florey); *Front Page Woman* (Curtiz); *The Goose and the Gander* (Green); *Special Agent* (Keighley); *Stranded* (Borzage); *The Petrified Forest* (Mayo); *The Case of the Curious Bride* (Curtiz); *The Florentine Dagger* (Florey); *Going Highbrow* (Florey); *The Girl from Tenth Avenue* (*Men on Her Mind*) (Green); *Bright Lights* (*Funny Face*) (Berkeley); *The Irish in Us* (Bacon); *I Live for Love* (*I Live for You*) (Berkeley); *Little Big Shot* (Curtiz); *Ceiling Zero* (Hawks); *Freshman Love* (*Rhythm on the River*) (McGann)

1936   *China Clipper* (Enright); *Colleen* (Green); *Gold Diggers of 1937* (Bacon); *The Golden Arrow* (Green); *Hearts Divided* (Borzage); *I Married a Doctor* (Mayo); *Isle of Fury* (McDonald); *Jailbreak* (Grinde); *The Law in Her Hands* (Clemens); *Murder by an Aristocrat* (McDonald); *Polo Joe* (McGann); *Satan Met a Lady* (Dieterle); *The Singing Kid* (Keighley); *Snowed Under* (Enright); *Stage Struck* (Berkeley); *Stolen Holiday* (Curtiz); *Times Square Playboy* (McGann); *The White Angel* (Dieterle); *Cain and Mabel* (Bacon); *The Walking Dead* (Curtiz); *Three Men on a Horse* (LeRoy); *Jailbreak* (*Murder in the Big House*) (Grinde); *Give Me Your Heart* (*Sweet Aloes*) (Mayo); *Here Comes Carter* (*Voice of Scandal*) (Clemens)

1937   *Another Dawn* (Dieterle); *Call It a Day* (Mayo); *First Lady* (Hogan); *The Go-Getter* (Berkeley); *Green Light* (Borzage); *Hollywood Hotel* (Berkeley); *It's Love I'm After* (Mayo); *Kid Galahad* (Curtiz); *Marked Woman* (Bacon); *That Certain Woman* (Goulding); *Ever Since Eve* (Bacon); *The King and the Chorus Girl* (*Romance Is Sacred*) (LeRoy); *The Singing Marine* (Enright); *Tovarich* (Litvak) (co)

1938   *Confession* (May); *Angels with Dirty Faces* (Curtiz); *Four Daughters* (Curtiz) (co); *Four's a Crowd* (Curtiz); *Jezebel* (Wyler); *My Bill* (Farrow); *Secrets of an Actress* (Keighley); *The Sisters* (Litvak); *Comet over Broadway* (Berkeley); *Women Are Like That* (Logan)

1939   *Dark Victory* (Goulding); *Juarez* (Dieterle); *King of the Underworld* (Seiler); *The Oklahoma Kid* (Bacon); *The Old Maid* (Goulding); *Women in the Wind* (Farrow); *The Private Lives of Elizabeth and Essex* (Curtiz); *On Your Toes* (Enright); *Wings of the Navy* (Bacon); *When Tomorrow Comes* (Stahl); *Indianapolis Speedway* (*Devil on Wheels*) (Bacon)

1940   *All This, and Heaven Too* (Litvak); *The Letter* (Wyler); *The Sea Hawk* (Curtiz); *'Til We Meet Again* (Goulding); *My Love Comes Back* (Bernhardt); *A Dispatch from Reuters* (*This Man Reuter*) (Dieterle); *No Time for Comedy* (Keighley)

1941   *The Bride Came C.O.D.* (Keighley); *The Great Lie* (Goulding); *Kings Row* (Wood); **The Little Foxes** (Wyler); **The Maltese Falcon** (Huston); *The Man Who Came to Dinner* (Keighley); *The Strawberry Blonde* (Walsh); *Affectionately Yours* (Bacon); *Million Dollar Baby* (Bernhardt); *They Died with Their Boots On* (Walsh)

1942   **Casablanca** (Curtiz); *In This Our Life* (Huston); **Now, Voyager** (Rapper); *The Hard Way* (V. Sherman); *George Washington Slept Here* (Keighley)

1943   *Old Acquaintance* (V. Sherman); *This Is the Army* (Curtiz); *Mission to Moscow* (Curtiz); *Edge of Darkness* (Milestone); *Watch on the Rhine* (Shumlin); *Princess O'Rourke* (Krasna)

1944   *Arsenic and Old Lace* (Capra); *Mr. Skeffington* (V. Sherman)

1945   *The Corn Is Green* (Rapper); *The Dolly Sisters* (Cummings); *Conflict* (Bernhardt); *London Town* (*My Heart Goes Crazy*) (Ruggles); *Temptation* (Pichel)

1946   *A Stolen Life* (Bernhardt)

1947   *The Shocking Miss Pilgrim* (Seaton); *Ivy* (Wood); *Something in the Wind* (Pichel); *Mother Wore Tights* (W. Lang) (co); *Night Song* (Cromwell); *A Woman's Vengeance* (Z. Korda)

1948   *For the Love of Mary* (de Cordova); *Larceny* (G. Sherman) (co); *One Touch of Venus* (Seiter); *Rogues' Regiment* (Florey); *Berlin Express* (Tourneur) (co)

1949   *Family Honeymoon* (Binyon); *The Lady Gambles* (Gordon); *South Sea Sinner* (*East of Java*) (Humberstone); *Undertow* (Castle); *Johnny Stool Pigeon* (Castle); *Woman in Hiding* (Gordon); *Take One False Step* (Erskine); *Once More My Darling* (Montgomery)

1950   *Deported* (Siodmak); *Under the Gun* (Tetzlaff); *Behave Yourself* (Beck); *One Way Street* (Fregonese); *Harvey* (Koster)

1951   **An American in Paris** (Minnelli) (co); *The Lady Says No!* (Ross)

1952   *Pat and Mike* (Cukor); *The Star* (Heisler)

1953   *I Confess* (Hitchcock)

1954   *She Couldn't Say No* (*Beautiful but Dangerous*) (Bacon)

1955   *Oklahoma!* (Zinnemann) (co)

1957   *Les Girls* (Cukor)

1958   *Auntie Mame* (Da Costa)

1959   *Too Much, Too Soon* (Napoleon); *The Hanging Tree* (Daves) (co); **Some Like It Hot** (Wilder)

1962   *The Chapman Report* (Cukor); *Five Finger Exercise* (Daniel Mann); *The Four Horsemen of the Apocalypse* (Minnelli) (co); *Gypsy* (LeRoy); *A Majority of One* (LeRoy); *Sweet Bird of Youth* (Brooks); *Two for the Seesaw* (Wise)

1963   *In the Cool of the Day* (Stevens) (co); *Irma La Douce* (Wilder)

1964   *Sunday in New York* (Tewksbury)

1965   *Lady L.* (Ustinov)

Publications

On ORRY-KELLY: articles—

Chierichetti, David, in *Hollywood Costume Design*, New York, 1976.
Leese, Elizabeth, in *Costume Design in the Movies*, New York, 1976.
LaVine, Robert, in *In a Glamorous Fashion*, New York, 1980.
Gibb, Bill, in *Films and Filming* (London), December 1983.

*   *   *

Orry-Kelly studied art in Australia but came to New York as an actor. Between stints as a song-and-dance man, he designed for vaudeville and Broadway productions. After arriving in Hollywood, Jack Warner promised him a job in the costume department if he could please leading ladies Kay Francis and Ruth Chatterton. It was money in the bank for Orry-Kelly.

His style differed from those of other Hollywood designers. He avoided Adrian's black-and-white contrasts in favor of a wide range of grays. His fabrics were of as high quality as Travis Banton's, but he disdained the Paramount ''shimmer.'' Nonetheless, costumes by Orry-Kelly were never dull. He cut with style and enhanced with intricate details. Tiny pleats and piping created subtle surface shadows, as did the textured embroideries, open work, crocheted lace, and trapunto. Appreciating skilled handiwork, he even included handpainted fabrics for some of his designs. As more daring decoration, he might add polka dots or punctuate with rows of buttons.

However, decoration was not his aim when working with Bette Davis. As a former actor, he understood the necessity of depicting a character's depth. Davis demanded that each role have a life of its own, with costumes playing a significant part in defining each character's image. At times, Orry-Kelly virtually resculpted her body to achieve a desired effect, and their successes included *Jezebel, Dark Victory, The Little Foxes, Now, Voyager*, and many others. One of Davis's earliest and least favorite films, *Fashions of 1934*, which stars some of Orry-Kelly's more imaginative creations, stands out as a delightful spoof of the fashion world.

Orry-Kelly's unpretentious style well served Warner Bros. He peopled its gritty gangster features with many a well-heeled moll. He'd take the kind of girl that ''a man's man'' could ''go for,'' and wrap her in wools as beautiful as chinchilla. His costumes for *The Maltese Falcon* and *Casablanca* spoke with the rich spareness of Hemingway.

But the Orry-Kelly style hardly suited everyone. The studio delegated Busby Berkeley production numbers to Milo Anderson, who also designed most of the Olivia de Havilland pictures. And when Orry-Kelly worked at Fox in the 1940s, he was never quite comfortable with those glitzy Betty Grable extravaganzas.

Freelancing in the 1950s widened Orry-Kelly's range. He put Katharine Hepburn in sportswear for *Pat and Mike*, Shirley Jones in gingham for *Oklahoma!*, Rosalind Russell in everything for *Auntie Mame*, and Marilyn Monroe in barely anything for *Some Like It Hot*. The early 1960s assigned Orry-Kelly to several adult dramas, including *Sweet Bird of Youth* and *Five Finger Exercise*.

—Edith C. Lee

O'STEEN, Sam

Editor. **Nationality:** American. **Born:** 6 March 1923. **Career:** 1956— assistant editor, became full editor in mid-1960s; 1976—directed first theatrical feature film, *Sparkle*.

Films as Editor:

1964 *Kisses for My President* (Bernhardt); *Robin and the Seven Hoods* (G. Douglas); *Youngblood Hawke* (Daves)
1965 *Marriage on the Rocks* (Donohue); *None but the Brave* (Sinatra)
1966 *Who's Afraid of Virginia Woolf?* (Nichols)
1967 ***The Graduate*** (Nichols); *Hotel* (Quine); *Cool Hand Luke* (Rosenberg)
1968 ***Rosemary's Baby*** (Polanski)
1969 *The Sterile Cukoo* (Pakula)
1970 *Catch-22* (Nichols)
1971 *Carnal Knowledge* (Nichols)

1972 *Portnoy's Complaint* (Lehman)
1973 *The Day of the Dolphin* (Nichols)
1974 ***Chinatown*** (Polanski)
1978 *Straight Time* (Grosbard)
1979 *Hurricane* (Troell)
1982 *Amityville II: The Possession* (Damiani)
1983 *Silkwood* (Nichols)
1986 *Heartburn* (Nichols)
1987 *Nadine* (Benton)
1988 *Frantic* (Polanski); *Biloxi Blues* (Nichols); *Working Girl* (Nichols)
1989 *A Dry White Season* (Palcy)
1990 *Postcards from the Edge* (Nichols)
1991 *Regarding Henry* (Nichols)
1992 *Consenting Adults* (Pakula)
1994 *Wolf* (Nichols)
1997 *Night Falls on Manhattan* (Lumet)

Films as Director:

1973 *A Brand New Life* (for TV)
1974 *I Love You, Goodbye* (for TV)
1975 *Queen of the Stardust Ballroom* (for TV)
1976 *Sparkle*; *Look What's Happened to Rosemary's Baby* (for TV); *High Risk* (for TV)
1981 *The Best Little Girl in the World* (for TV)
1985 *Kids Don't Tell* (for TV)

Publications

On O'STEEN: articles—

Film Dope (Nottingham), June 1993.
Warga, W., ''Sam O'Steen: Sparkle,'' in *Action*, November-December 1997.

*   *   *

Sam O'Steen has been at the heart of some of the most important and award-winning films of the last 30 years. O'Steen began his career in the mid-1950s as an assistant editor and rapidly rose up to a full editor in the early 1960s on such films as *Robin and the Seven Hoods* and *Youngblood Hawke*.

In 1966 O'Steen teamed up with a young director named Mike Nichols on the acclaimed *Who's Afraid of Virginia Woolf?* Known for his creative editing style, O'Steen and the director forged a relationship which has lasted the better part of three decades. O'Steen received an Academy Award nomination for *Who's Afraid of Virginia Woolf?* O'Steen and Nichols's partnership produced some of the most respected films of the late 1960s and early 1970s. Nowhere are O'Steen's skills more apparent than in Dustin Hoffman's classic debut film, *The Graduate*. O'Steen gives the audience time to study the performer's face before cutting the scene. O'Steen allows for long, personal looks at Hoffman's facial expressions to give the viewers an idea of what the character is thinking instead of the ''quick-cutting'' seen so often in modern films. In *The Graduate*

Hoffman's expressions at the party scene are as important to the character as any bit of dialogue and O'Steen does not cut the scene short.

O'Steen also worked with renowned director Roman Polanski on *Rosemary's Baby* and *Chinatown*, which garnered O'Steen's second Academy Award nomination. *Chinatown* is one of the best films of the 1970s and O'Steen's seamless editing keeps the film from slowing down. *Chinatown* is shot almost entirely in close-ups of the characters talking, yet it feels as though the action never stops. As Jack Nicholson solves the mystery, the audience solves the mystery so every scene is invaluable. Each scene is edited so that once a piece of information is revealed, it ends. One of the interesting things about *Chinatown* is information is discovered as much through Nicholson's facial expressions as it is through actual clues, so O'Steen's editing had to hold the scenes long enough for the audience to keep up with the story. Faye Dunaway's famous revelation scene near the end of *Chinatown* shows O'Steen's skill as an editor. The scene lasts long enough for Nicholson (and the audience) to comprehend the magnitude of John Huston's incestuous relationship with Dunaway without lingering into overkill.

In 1976 O'Steen took a shot at directing feature films with the unremarkable *Sparkle*, a story about the rise of a black singing group. He has also directed a number of made-for-television movies.

Sam O'Steen has been a part of many of the most memorable movies of the last 30 years. He tends to be surrounded by quality directors and performers. In addition to Hoffman and Nichols, Polanski and Nicholson, he has worked with such heavyweights as Paul Newman in *Cool Hand Luke*, Harrison Ford in *Regarding Henry*, and Meryl Streep in the 1983 film *Silkwood*, for which he received his third Academy Award nomination.

In the end, Sam O'Steen will be forever linked with old pro Mike Nichols. In 1988 they worked together with Harrison Ford and Melanie Griffith on *Working Girl*, and teamed up with an old friend from the *Carnal Knowledge* days, Jack Nicholson, for the 1994 film *Wolf*. Sam O'Steen continues to be one of the most respected film editors in the business.

—Patrick J. Sauer

PAL, George

Animator, Special Effects Designer, and Producer. **Nationality:** American. **Born:** Cegled, Hungary, 1 February 1908; became citizen of the United States. **Education:** Educated in architecture, Budapest Academy of Arts. **Family:** Married Zsoka Grandjean, 1930. **Career:** Before 1930—titler at Hunnia Films, Budapest; 1930–32—head of UFA cartoon department; 1932—opened own studio; 1933—opened Prague studio; opened Paris studio, 1934, and one in Holland, 1935; 1939—joined Paramount, U.S.A.; 1949—began producing feature films. **Awards:** Special Academy Award for the development of novel methods and techniques in the production of short subjects known as Puppetoons, 1943; Special Effects Academy Award for *Destination Moon*, 1950; *When Worlds Collide*, 1951; *War of the Worlds*, 1953; *Tom Thumb*, 1958; *The Time Machine*, 1960. **Died:** 2 May 1980.

Films as Director of Puppetoons at Paramount:

1941   *Western Daze*; *Dipsy Gypsy*; *Hoola Boola*; *The Gay Knighties*; *Rhythm in the Ranks*
1942   *Jasper and the Watermelons*; *The Sky Princess*; *Mr. Strauss Takes a Waltz*; *Tulips Shall Grow*; *The Little Broadcast*; *Jasper's Haunted House*
1943   *Jasper and the Choo-Choo*; *Bravo, Mr. Strauss*; *The 500 Hats of Bartholomew Cubbins*; *Jasper's Music Lesson*; *The Truck That Flew*; *Jasper Goes Fishing*; *Good Night, Rusty*
1944   *A Package for Jasper*; *Say Ah Jasper*; *And to Think I Saw It on Mulberry Street*; *Jasper Goes Hunting*; *Jasper's Paradise*; *2 Gun Rusty*
1945   *Hotlips Jasper*; *Jasper Tell*; *Hatful of Dreams*; *Jasper's Minstrels*; *Jasper's Booby Traps*; *Jasper's Close Shave*; *Jasper and the Beanstalk*; *My Man Jasper*
1946   *Olio for Jasper*; *Together in the Weather*; *Jasper's Derby*; *John Henry and the Inky Poo*; *Jasper in a Jam*; *Shoe Shine Jasper*
1947   *Wilbur the Lion*; *Tubby the Tuba*; *A Date with Duke*; *Rhapsody in Wood*

Films as Producer and Special Effects Designer (Features):

1949   *The Great Rupert* (Pichel)
1950   *Destination Moon* (Pichel)

George Pal

1951   *When Worlds Collide* (Maté)
1953   *War of the Worlds* (Haskin); *Houdini* (Marshall)
1954   *The Naked Jungle* (Haskin)
1955   *The Conquest of Space* (Haskin)

Films as Producer, Director, and Special Effects Designer:

1958   *Tom Thumb*
1959   *The Time Machine*
1960   *Atlantis, the Lost Continent*
1962   *The Wonderful World of the Brothers Grimm* (co-d)
1964   *The Seven Faces of Dr. Lao*

Films as Producer:

1968   *The Power* (Haskin)
1975   *Doc Savage, the Man of Bronze* (Anderson)

Publications

By PAL: articles—

Castle of Frankenstein (New York), June 1975.
Cinefantastique (Oak Park, Illinois), no. 2, 1976.
SPFX (El Paso, Texas), January 1977.
Millimeter (New York), February 1978.

On PAL: book—

Hickman, G.M., *The Films of George Pal*, South Brunswick, New Jersey, 1977.

On PAL: articles—

Sight and Sound (London), Summer 1936.
Hollywood Quarterly, July 1946.
Cinefantastique (Oak Park, Illinois), Fall 1971.
Starlog (New York), December 1977.
Starlog (New York), May 1978.
Cinefantastique (Oak Park, Illinois), Summer 1979.
RBCC (San Diego), September 1979.
Fantastic Films (Chicago), October 1979.
Starlog (New York), September 1980.
Films in Review (New York), November 1980.
Cinefex (Riverside, California), no. 25, February 1986.
Literature-Film Quarterly (Salisbury), July 1989.
Scarlet Street, no. 6, Spring 1992.
Nosferatu (San Sebastian), February 1994.
Film Dope (Nottingham), April 1994.
Minor, M., "Through Time and Space with George Pal," in *Monsterscene* (Lombard), no. 5, Summer/Fall 1995.

*   *   *

George Pal's motion picture career can be divided into two different phases. He first achieved worldwide recognition as the creator of the Puppetoons. Pal was originally an illustrator and animator, but he felt that the two-dimensional cel cartoons were too flat. He preferred the three-dimensional look of puppets, which he brought to life in his studio through the process of stop-motion animation. The "actors" in the Puppetoons were quite complex characters, being sculpted in wood and constructed with wire limbs that enabled them to be easily posed. In addition, these puppets were designed to use replacement parts, particularly the heads. By replacing heads with different expressions, the puppets could talk and indicate emotions. Central characters in the Puppetoons could have as many as 100–200 different replacement heads.

The 42 Puppetoons which Pal made for Paramount (Pal estimated that he created over 200 such short films in Europe) are not your typical "cat-chase-mouse" cartoons. Even within these short eight-minute films, Pal tried to construct a meaningful story and, perhaps, a lesson. For example, he created at least two anti-Nazi propaganda films: *Tulips Shall Grow* and *Bravo, Mr. Strauss*. Both films emphasized man's struggle for individual freedom against the oppression of

a mindless army. The theme of *John Henry and the Inky Poo* was the conflict between man and machine, proving man's will to dominate, rather than be dominated by machines. The Puppetoons remained extremely popular with the public through the 1940s, and in 1943 George Pal was awarded an Academy Award for the further "development of animation techniques." In 1948 the Puppetoons finally succumbed to skyrocketing production costs and Pal's studio at Paramount was closed. However, the end of the Puppetoons was also the beginning of George Pal's feature film career.

As a feature film producer Pal carried with him an immense enthusiasm for fantasy plus a wide knowledge of special effects techniques. (In fact, five of his features won Academy Awards for special effects.) This combination paved the way for some of the classics of the science-fiction genre, such as *Destination Moon, War of the Worlds*, and *The Time Machine*. Although these and other films can be categorized as science-fiction, Pal's films mainly emphasize the human quality of the story. Whereas most science-fiction films are dark, pessimistic visions of the future, Pal's films hold forth hope for mankind. For example, the time traveler of *The Time Machine* is searching for a world without war; Dr. Lao in *The Seven Faces of Dr. Lao* shows us that there is good in everybody; and the theme of *When Worlds Collide* is self-sacrifice amidst a struggle for survival.

Although Pal was never given the opportunity to work with a large budget (most of his films were produced for between $500,000 and $1,000,000), his enthusiasm for his work produced the best possible product for the money, and the majority of his films were great financial successes. Today many of George Pal's feature films and Puppetoons continue to be revived in both theaters and on television. However, some of his Puppetoons, particularly those featuring a little black boy named Jasper, have met with criticism for being racist. Such criticism both surprised and saddened Pal who, in his innocence, was not aware of such possible interpretations when he made the films. In fact, it is this "innocent" quality in Pal's films that gives them much of the charm that other producer/directors find difficult to express in their work.

—Linda Obalil

PAN, Hermes

Choreographer. **Nationality:** American. **Born:** Hermes Panagiotopoulos, Nashville, Tennessee, 1910. **Career:** Left school at age 12; worked in laboratories of Edison Company; then dancer in saloons and on stage (in *Topspeed*, 1929) and singer; 1933—first film as choreographer, *Flying Down to Rio*. **Awards:** Academy Award for *A Damsel in Distress*, 1937; National Film Award for achievement in cinema, 1980; Special Award from the Joffrey Ballet, 1986. **Died:** 19 September 1990, Beverly Hills, California.

Films as Choreographer:

1933   *Flying Down to Rio* (Freeland)
1934   *The Gay Divorcee* (*The Gay Divorce*) (Sandrich)

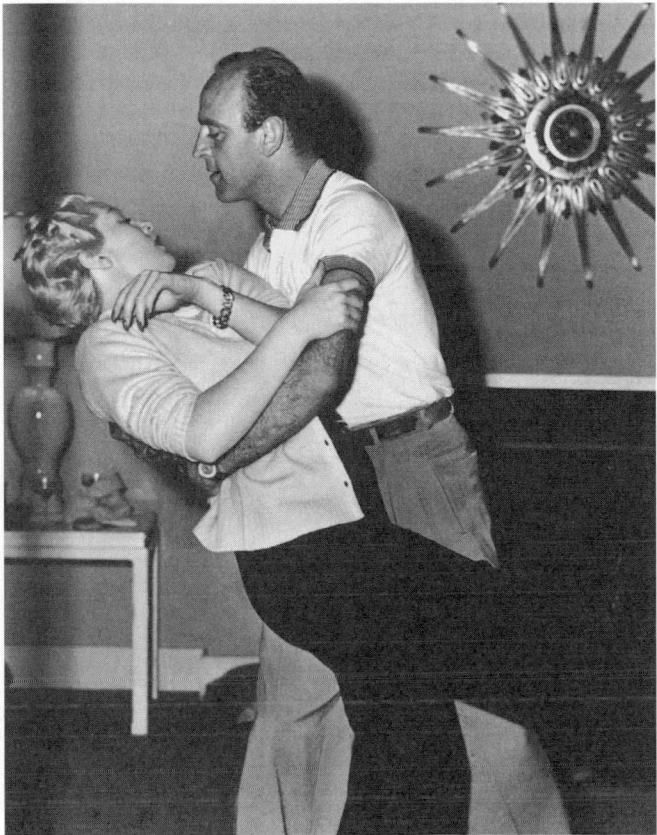

Hermes Pan with Lana Turner

1935   *Roberta* (Seiter); **Top Hat** (Sandrich); *Old Man Rhythm*
        (Ludwig); *I Dream Too Much* (Cromwell); *In Person*
        (Seiter)
1936   *Follow the Fleet* (Sandrich); *Swing Time* (Stevens)
1937   *Shall We Dance* (Sandrich); *A Damsel in Distress* (Stevens)
1938   *Carefree* (Sandrich); *Radio City Revels* (Stoloff)
1939   *The Story of Vernon and Irene Castle* (Porter)
1941   *Second Chorus* (Potter); *That Night in Rio* (Cummings);
        Moon over Miami (W. Land) (+ ro as dancer); *Sun Valley
        Serenade* (Humberstone); *Rise and Shine* (Dwan); *Week-
        end in Havana* (W. Lang)
1942   *Song of the Islands* (W. Lang); *Footlight Serenade* (Ratoff);
        My Gal Sal (Cummings) (+ ro as dancer); *Springtime in the
        Rockies* (Cummings)
1943   *Coney Island* (W. Lang); *Sweet Rosie O'Grady* (Cummings)
1944   *Pin Up Girl* (Humberstone) (+ ro as dancer); *Irish Eyes Are
        Smiling* (Ratoff)
1945   *Billy Rose's Diamond Horseshoe* (Seaton); *All-Star Musical
        Revue* (short) (co)
1946   *Blue Skies* (Heisler)
1947   *I Wonder Who's Kissing Her Now* (Bacon)
1948   *That Lady in Ermine* (Lubitsch)
1949   *The Barkleys of Broadway* (Walters)
1950   *Let's Dance* (McLeod); *Three Little Words* (Thorpe); *A Life of
        Her Own* (Cukor) (+ ro as dancer)
1951   *Texas Carnival* (Walters); *Excuse My Dust* (Rowland)
1952   *Lovely to Look At* (LeRoy)
1953   *Kiss Me Kate* (Sidney); *Sombrero* (Foster)

1954   *The Student Prince* Thorpe); *Hit the Deck* (Rowland)
1955   *Jupiter's Darling* (Sidney)
1956   *Meet Me in Las Vegas* (Rowland)
1957   *Silk Stockings* (Mamoulian); *Pal Joey* (Sidney)
1959   *Porgy and Bess* (Preminger)
1960   *Can-Can* (W. Lang)
1961   *The Pleasure of His Company* (Seaton) (co); *Flower Drum
        Song* (Koster)
1963   *Cleopatra* (Mankiewicz)
1965   *The Great Race* (Edwards)
1968   *Finian's Rainbow* (Coppola)
1970   *Darling Lili* (Edwards)
1972   *Lost Horizon* (Jarrott)

Publications

By PAN: articles—

Classic Images (Indiana, Pennsylvania), October 1982.
Cineaste (New York), vol 12, no. 4, 1983.
American Classic Screen (Shawnee Mission, Kansas), May-June 1983.
Inter/View (New York), September 1985.

On PAN: articles—

Classic Images (Indiana, Pennsylvania), January 1983.
Obituary in *Variety* (New York), 24 September 1990.
Obituary in *Dance Magazine*, January 1991.
Film Dope (Nottingham), April 1994.

*   *   *

Hermes Pan began his career as a Broadway dancer and stayed in New York for three years. During this time, he met Ginger Rogers when they danced together in the show *Top Speed*. Both dancers soon moved to Hollywood. Pan first met Fred Astaire on the set of *Flying Down to Rio* in 1933 at a time when dancing pictures hardly existed. The two men bore an uncanny physical resemblance to each other, not only facially but in their slim physiques, elegant personal style, professional modesty and professionalism. Astaire once told Pan that he was the only person who could dance the way Astaire did. They became very close friends as well as collaborators and it is reported that their artistic relationship even extended to Pan sometimes doubling as Astaire in long shots as well as taking the woman's role opposite Astaire in preliminary rehearsals. ''We thought so much alike about music and rhythms. The minute I saw him dance I said 'Oh, this is the kind of dancing I love.' He seemed to be able to do everything I felt inside and wanted to do.''

Pan became dance director on all of Astaire's films and choreographed nine of the 10 films pairing Astaire with Ginger Rogers—*Roberta, Top Hat, Follow the Fleet, The Barkleys of Broadway* are amongst the best remembered.

In the 1950s Pan choreographed a series of slick musicals transposed from stage to screen including *Kiss Me Kate* with Kathryn Grayson, Howard Keel and Ann Miller, *Flower Drum Song, Silk*

Stockings, *Pal Joey*, *The Student Prince*, *Finian's Rainbow* and *Can-Can*. The sleekest of all was *My Fair Lady*, and he also designed the non-dancing but nevertheless spectacular staging of *Cleopatra* in 1963 starring Elizabeth Taylor.

Occasionally, he would appear on screen performing his own dance steps—in *Moon over Miami*, *My Gal Sal*, and with Lana Turner and Ray Milland, in *A Life of Her Own*. He also was able to choreograph off the dance floor onto ice for Sonja Heine and in water for Esther Williams. All in all, Hermes Pan provided the routines for 55 films, and other notable dancers who appeared in his films included Juliet Prowse, Cyd Charisse, and Betty Grable.

Together with Astaire, Hermes Pan changed the face of the screen musical, dispensing with the accepted practice of frequent cutting during numbers, and creating routines so meticulously for the camera that the dances give an impression of being filmed in a continuous take. Their collaboration resulted in dance scenes of wit, mastery, elegance, and spontaneity. Pan will always be remembered as one of the great names of the Hollywood musical along with Busby Berkeley, Robert Alton and the Kelly-Donen team.

—Sylvia Paskin

PARK, Nick

Animator, Writer, and Director. **Nationality:** British. **Born:** Nicholas W. Park in Preston, Lancashire, 1958. **Education:** Took communication arts course at Sheffield Art School; studied animation at National Film and Television School, Beaconsfield, 1980–83. **Career:** Drew cartoons as a child, began experimenting with animation at age 13; 1975—early film, *Archie's Concrete Nightmare*, shown on BBC TV; started work on *A Grand Day Out* as graduation piece; 1983—joined Aardman Animation Studios, Bristol; 1989—completed *A Grand Day Out* (nominated for an Oscar). **Awards:** British Academy Award, for *A Grand Day Out*, 1989; Academy Award, for *Creature Comforts*, 1989, *The Wrong Trousers*, 1991, and *A Close Shave*, 1995; Honorary Doctor of Arts degree from Bath University, England, 1996; Commander of the Order of the British Empire, 1997. **Address:** Aardman Animation, Gas Ferry Road, Bristol BS1 6UN, England.

Films as Animator and Director:

1975 *Archie's Concrete Nightmare*
1978 *Jack and the Beanstalk*
1986 *Sledgehammer* (pop promo, animation only)
1989 *A Grand Day Out* (+ co-sc); *Creature Comforts*; *War Story* (animation only)
1991 *The Wrong Trousers* (+ sc)
1995 *A Close Shave* (+ sc)
1996 *Wallace & Gromit: The Best of Aardman Animation*; *Wallace & Gromit: The Aardman Collection 2*
2000 *Chicken Run* (+ sc)

Publications

By PARK: articles—

''A Lot Can Happen in a Second,'' interview with Kevin Macdonald, in *Projections 5: Film-makers on Film-making*, edited by John Boorman and Walter Donohue, London, 1996.
''Deux secondes par jour!,'' interview with Christine Haas, in *Première* (Paris), May 1996.
''By Gum, It's the Man behind Wallace and Gromit,'' an interview with Alison Graham, in *Radio Times* (London), 16 December 1995.

On PARK: articles—

Clarke, Jeremy, ''Gagged by Accident,'' in *What's on in London*, 19 December 1990.
Buss, Robin, ''Creatures Great and Small,'' in *Independent on Sunday* (London), 7 November 1993.
Franks, Alan, ''Fame in Slow Motion,'' in *Times* (London), 2 April 1994.
Gibson, Janine, ''A Close Shave,'' in *Televisual* (London), August 1995.
Graham, Alison, ''By Gum, It's the Man behind Wallace and Gromit,'' in *Radio Times* (London), 16 December 1995.
Westbrook, Caroline, ''Park and Pride,'' in *Empire* (London), January 1996.
Sight & Sound (London), May 1996.

Nick Park with Wallace and Gromit

Biodrowski, S., "Wallace & Gromit: 'A Close Shave'," in *Cinefantastique* (Forest Park), vol. 28, no. 1, 1996.

Klein, A., "Park: Oscar's Shorts King," in *Variety* (New York), 24/30 June 1996.

Major, W., "English Extra: Animator Nick Park," in *Box Office* (Chicago), July 1996.

* * *

If Academy Awards are any indication, Nick Park is the greatest animator in the history of the cinema. With just four films (apart from juvenilia) under his belt he has scored three Best Animated Film Awards and a nomination; the one that failed to win the Oscar picked up a BAFTA Award. Not even Disney ever had such a record. But perhaps yet more impressive than the Oscar bandwagon is the universality of his films' appeal. His ultra-English, even ultra-provincial characters, Wallace the eccentric inventor and his quick-thinking dog Gromit, have convulsed audiences in every country where they have been seen—which includes most of the world. It is a triumph for flat-voiced, faux-naïf Lancashire humor unparalleled since the heyday of George Formby.

Animated films, of course, have always crossed frontiers with an ease that live-action movies, since the advent of sound, can rarely rival, and cartoon icons from Mickey Mouse to the Simpsons have found international acceptance. What is unusual about Park's characters is the unanimous affection they inspire—an affection that clearly reflects the warmth he himself puts into his creations. Wallace's quirky inventiveness draws on memories of Park's own father, and though the increasing complexity of his films has obliged him to hand over elements of the animation to his colleagues, he admits to finding it "very, very difficult to trust anybody with Wallace and Gromit," whom he thinks of as real people.

This emotional involvement with his films also comes out in Park's scrupulous attention to detail, another key element in his success. His chosen medium, stop-frame plasticine animation, is by its nature a painstaking and labor-intensive process, where computers can be of only marginal assistance, and in Park's films no corners are cut: Wallace and Gromit are always framed and lit like live actors, and indeed perform like them. Park selects his fellow-animators as though auditioning actors: "You have to give a performance through the plasticine." Every frame of his films—especially of the two most recent Wallace and Gromit vehicles, *The Wrong Trousers* and *A Close Shave*—is packed with incidental details and jokes that repay multiple viewing. Among the reading matter favored by Gromit, a canine intellectual, are Pluto's *Republic* and—during his wrongful imprisonment—*Crime and Punishment* by Doystoyevsky.

This love of intricacy—several of Wallace's inventions show the strong influence of another celebrator of English eccentricity, the illustrator William Heath Robinson—is often combined with remarkable economy of means when it comes to characterization. Gromit has no mouth and an inexpressive blob of a nose: his emotions are vividly conveyed via his eyes, eyebrows, and ears. The villain of *The Wrong Trousers*, a sinister penguin, has no facial features at all save an immobile beak and boot-button eyes, yet he radiates malignity; by way of disguise he pulls an orange rubber glove on his head, thus (it seems) convincing everyone he is a chicken.

The very idea of choosing a penguin, that lovable buffoon of the animal kingdom, as his villain, typifies the unpredictability of Park's

offbeat humor. What he lacks—unusually among animators, notoriously a sadistic lot—is a true sense of malice. Even his darkest character yet, the *Terminator*-style robot bulldog of *A Close Shave*, is redeemed in the final reel. It is impossible to imagine Park indulging in the slash-and-burn mayhem of Tom & Jerry or the brutalities of Svankmajer, let alone subjecting Gromit to the indignities visited upon Daffy Duck by Chuck Jones in *Duck Amuck*. Right from the first work that brought him to fame, the *vox pop* animals of *Creature Comforts*, Park's films have conveyed an innate gentleness and good humor. In the long run, this may prove a limitation. But for the time being it is these same qualities that have helped gain his films the approval of Academy Award voters and worldwide audiences alike.

—Philip Kemp

PARKER, Claire

See **ALEXEIEFF, Alexander, and Claire PARKER**

PARRISH, Robert

Director, Editor, and Actor. **Nationality:** American. **Born:** Columbus, Georgia. 4 January 1916. **Family:** Brother of the actress Helen Parrish. **Career:** 1920s—began career as a child actor in such films as

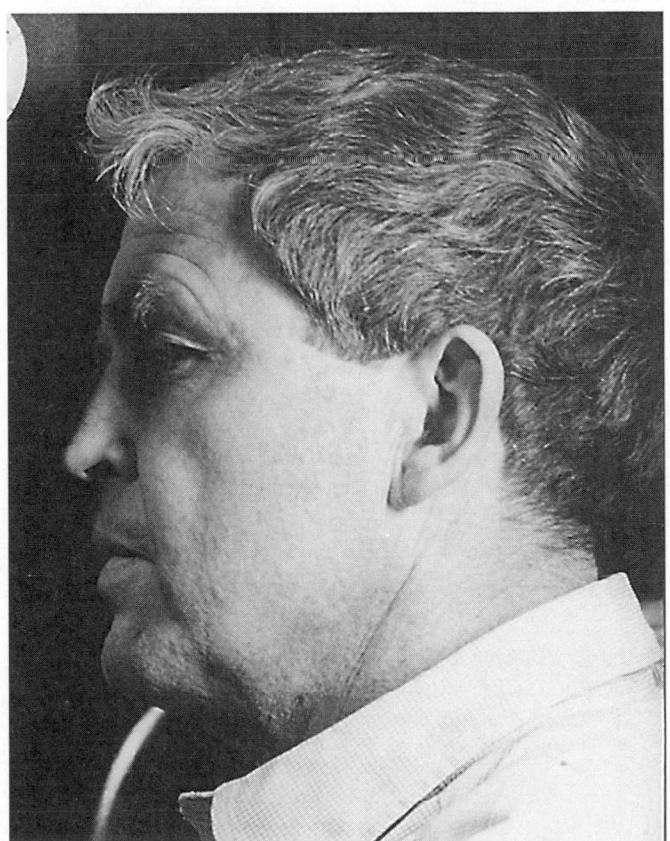

Robert Parrish

Mother Machree, *City Lights*, and *Our Gang* comedies; 1930s—became assistant editor, then sound editor; 1940s—served with John Ford as cameraman and editor on documentaries during World War II; 1947—won Academy Award for co-editing Robert Rossen's *Body and Soul*, his first feature after the war; 1948—nominated for second Academy Award for co-editing *All the King's Men*, again for Rossen; 1951—directorial debut with *Cry Danger*; 1976—published first book of memoirs, *Growing Up in Hollywood*; 1988—second memoirs book published, *Hollywood Doesn't Live Here Anymore*; 1983—last film, *Mississippi Blues*, a documentary made with Bertrand Tavernier. **Awards:** Academy Award for *Body and Soul*, 1947. **Died:** In Southampton, New York, 4 December 1995.

Films as Actor:

1928   *Mother Machree*; *Four Sons* (Ford)
1929   *The Iron Mask* (Dwan)
1930   *Men without Women* (Ford); **All Quiet on the Western Front**
            (Milestone); *Up the River* (Ford); *The Right to Love* (Wallace)
1931   **City Lights** (Chaplin)
1933   *Dr. Bull* (Ford)
1934   *Judge Priest* (Ford)
1935   *The Whole Town's Talking* (Ford); **The Informer** (Ford)
1936   *The Prisoner of Shark Island* (Ford)

Films as Sound Editor:

1939   **Young Mr. Lincoln** (Ford); *Drums along the Mohawk* (Ford)
1940   **The Grapes of Wrath** (Ford); *The Long Voyage Home* (Ford)
1941   *Tobacco Road* (Ford)

Films as Editor:

1936   *Mary of Scotland* (Ford) (asst)
1942   *The Battle of Midway* (doc, short)
1943   *December 7th* (doc, short)
1947   *Body and Soul* (Rossen) (co)
1948   *A Double Life* (Cukor); *No Minor Vices* (Milestone)
1949   **All the King's Men** (Rossen) (co); *Caught* (Ophüls)
1950   *Of Men and Music* (concert feature) (co)

Films as Director:

1951   *Cry Danger*; *The Mob*
1952   *The San Francisco Story*; *Assignment-Paris*; *My Pal Gus*
1953   *Rough Shoot* (*Shoot First*)
1954   *The Purple Plain*
1955   *Lucy Gallant*
1957   *Fire Down Below*
1958   *Saddle the Wind*
1959   *The Wonderful Country*

1963   *In the French Style* (*À la française*) (+ co-pr)
1965   *Up from the Beach*
1967   **Casino Royale** (co-d with several others); *The Bobo*
1968   *Duffy*
1969   *Doppelganger* (*Journey to the Far Side of the Sun*)
1971   *A Town Called Bastard* (*A Town Called Hell*)
1974   *The Marseille Contract* (*The Destructors*)
1983   *Pays d'Octobre* (*Mississippi Blues*) (co-d with Bertrand
            Tavernier—doc)

Publications

By PARRISH: books—

Growing Up in Hollywood, 1976.
Hollywood Doesn't Live Here Anymore, 1988.

By PARRISH: articles—

On Preston Sturges, in *Positif* (Paris), December 1977/January 1978.
On Max Ophüls, in *Positif* (Paris), July/August 1980.
On John Ford, in *American Film* (Washington, D.C.), July/August 1985.
American Film (Washington, D.C.), April 1986.
On *The Paper Chase*, in *American Film* (Washington, D.C.), March 1988.
''University of Southern California Film School,'' in *Positif* (Paris), June 1994.
''O.K. Freddie,'' in *Audience* (Simi Valley), August/September 1996.

On PARRISH: article—

Film Comment (New York), March/April 1977.
Film Dope (Nottingham), April 1994.
Obituary in *Variety* (New York), 11 December 1995.
Obituary in *Classic Images* (Muscatine), January 1996.
Obituary in *Audience* (Simi Valley), February/March 1996.

*   *   *

A lifetime spent in the film world ended when director/editor/actor Robert Parrish died in December of 1995. He was clearly a man who loved the movies. In his lifetime working with such directing greats as John Ford and Robert Rossen, he edited powerful dramas and shot and edited World War II documentaries then unequaled for authenticity.

He began his career as a child actor, working with Charlie Chaplin in *City Lights* as well as in Ford productions and *Our Gang* comedies. He continued with Ford, first as an assistant editor, then as editor and cameraman with Ford's O.S.S. department during World War II, making landmark documentaries of the U.S. war efforts.

He received his only Academy Award for co-editing duties on Rossen's *Body and Soul* and a follow-up nomination for co-editing Rossen's *All the King's Men*. Initial critical response was enthusiastic to his directorial debut, *Cry Danger*, an action drama that was generic but exciting. Throughout his career, he would receive the best critical response to other genre films, such as the military drama, *The Purple Plain*, and the Western, *Saddle the Wind*. With writer Irwin Shaw,

Parrish co-produced *In the French Style*, a lightweight drama that enthused Parrish but failed to excite critics. Leaving the United States for Europe, Parrish found most of his sixties and seventies work "second rate and getting second rater," in his own words. Neither critics nor audiences would argue with his assessment as he churned out dull thrillers, comedies, and even an Italian Western.

His final film, completed upon his return to the United States, was a documentary that touched on civil rights, *Mississippi Blues*, co-directed with an old friend, Bertrand Tavernier. The film, while considered heartfelt, was also found to be somewhat listless and received little attention. Other than his excellent editing work and early directing, Parrish may be most remembered as storyteller from his two books of Hollywood memoirs.

—Allen Grant Richards

PASTERNAK, Joe

Producer. **Nationality:** American. **Born:** Szilagy-Somlyo, Romania (now Hungary), 19 September 1901; emigrated to the United States, 1921; naturalized, 1927. **Education:** School in Szilagy-Somlyo. **Married:** (second marriage) Dorothy Darrel, 1942; three sons. **Career:** Worked as busboy and waiter in Paramount studios in early 1920s, and worked as assistant director (especially for Allan Dwan); 1928–35—manager of Universal's operations in Berlin—also producer in Berlin; 1935–40—producer for Universal in Hollywood;

Joe Pasternak

then worked for MGM after 1942. Retired in 1968. **Died:** In Los Angeles, California, 13 September 1991.

Films as Producer:

1929   *Das Schweigen im Walde* (Dieterle)

1930   *Zwei Menschen* (Waschneck); *Die Grosse Sehnsucht* (Sekely)

1932   *Die unsichtbare Front* (Eichberg); *Unter falscher Flagge* (Meyer); *Paprika* (Boese)

1933   *Skandal in Budapest* (Sekely and von Bolvary); *Früchten (Csibi, der Fratz)* (Eichberg and Neufeld)

1934   *Grüss and küss Veronika* (Boese); *Frühjahrsparade* (von Bolvary and Wratschko)

1935   *Kleine Mutter*; *Katharina, die Letzte* (Kosterlitz)

1936   *Three Smart Girls* (Koster)

1937   *100 Men and a Girl* (Koster)

1938   *Mad about Music* (Taurog); *That Certain Age* (Ludwig); *Youth Takes a Fling* (Connolly)

1939   *Three Smart Girls Grow Up* (Koster); *The Under-Pup* (Wallace); *First Love* (Koster); *Destry Rides Again* (Marshall)

1940   *It's a Date* (Seiter); *Spring Parade* (Koster); *A Little Bit of Heaven* (Marton); *Seven Sinners* (Garnett)

1941   *Nice Girl?* (Seiter); *The Flame of New Orleans* (Clair); *It Started with Eve* (Koster)

1942   *Seven Sweethearts* (Borzage)

1943   *Presenting Lily Mars* (Taurog), *Thousands Cheer* (Sidney)

1944   *Song of Russia* (Ratoff); *Two Girls and a Sailor* (Thorpe)

1945   *Music for Millions* (Koster); *Thrill of a Romance* (Thorpe); *Anchors Aweigh* (Sidney); *Her Highness and the Bellboy* (Thorpe)

1946   *Two Sisters from Boston* (Koster); *Holiday in Mexico* (Sidney); *No Leave, No Love* (Martin)

1947   *The Unfinished Dance* (Koster); *This Time for Keeps* (Thorpe)

1948   *Three Daring Daughters* (Wilcox); *Big City* (Taurog); *On an Island with You* (Thorpe); *A Date with Judy* (Thorpe); *Luxury Liner* (Whorf); *The Kissing Bandit* (Benedek)

1949   *In the Good Old Summertime* (Leonard); *That Midnight Kiss* (Taurog)

1950   *Nancy Goes to Rio* (Leonard); *The Duchess of Idaho* (Leonard); *Summer Stock* (Walters); *The Toast of New Orleans* (Taurog)

1951   *The Great Caruso* (Thorpe); *Rich, Young, and Pretty* (Taurog); *The Strip* (Kardos)

1952   *Skirts Ahoy!* (Lanfield); *The Merry Widow* (Bernhardt); *Because You're Mine* (Hall)

1953   *Small Town Girl* (Kardos); *Latin Lovers* (LeRoy); *Easy to Love* (Walters)

1954   *The Flame and the Flesh* (Brooks); *The Student Prince* (Thorpe); *Athena* (Thorpe)

1955   *Hit the Deck* (Rowland); *Love Me or Leave Me* (C. Vidor)

1956   *Meet Me in Las Vegas* (Rowland); *The Opposite Sex* (Miller)

1957   *Ten Thousand Bedrooms* (Thorpe); *This Could Be the Night* (Wise)

1958   *Party Girl* (Ray)

1959   *Ask Any Girl* (Walters)

1960   *Please Don't Eat the Daisies* (Walters); *Where the Boys Are* (Levin)

1962   *The Horizontal Lieutenant* (Thorpe); *Jumbo* (*Billy Rose's Jumbo*) (Walters) (co)
1963   *The Courtship of Eddie's Father* (Minnelli); *A Ticklish Affair* (Sidney)
1965   *Girl Happy* (Sagal)
1966   *Penelope* (Hiller) (exec); *Made in Paris* (Sagal); *Spinout* (Taurog)
1968   *The Sweet Ride* (Hart)

Film as Director:

1972   *The Casting*

Publications

By PASTERNAK: book—

Easy the Hard Way, London, 1956.

On PASTERNAK: articles—

Picturegoer (London), 23 September 1939.
Film Daily, 5 February 1953.
ABC Review, March 1963.
Bawden, James, in *Films in Review* (New York), February 1985.
Obituary in *Variety* (New York), 23 September 1991.
Obituary in *Filmvilag* (Budapest), no. 2, 1992.

*   *   *

Joe Pasternak was a Hungarian immigrant whose successful career as a motion picture producer was marked by three distinct achievements. He was responsible for developing the career of the singer actress Deanna Durbin, whose money-making films for Universal literally saved that studio from bankruptcy. He almost single-handedly revived the faltering career of ''box-office poison'' Marlene Dietrich with three films at Universal, most notably *Destry Rides Again*. And during the 1940s and 1950s, he was the second string producer, after Arthur Freed, of a series of light musical entertainments for MGM.

Pasternak arrived in the States while still in his teens and after working at Paramount as both a busboy and waiter in the studio commissary, then as a second assistant director, he joined Universal as manager of that studio's Berlin office. He produced four popular films starring Franciska Gaal: *Paprika, Skandal in Budapest, Fruchten, Frühjahrsparade* and *Katharina die Letzte*. With the rise of Nazism, Pasternak implored his studio for a post in Hollywood. Universal offered him a production job for himself and two of his fellow Hungarians, the director Henry Kosterlitz (Koster) and the writer Felix Jaochimson (Jackson). Later Pasternak imported his brother-in-law, S. Z. ''Cuddles'' Sakall, who became one of the most endearing character actors of the 1940s, and the composer Nicholas Brodsky.

Pasternak's first assignment for Universal was luckily *Three Smart Girls*, a musical built around a new singing sensation, Deanna

Durbin. Pasternak produced and Koster directed, and they struck upon a formula which would make Durbin one of Hollywood's top money-making stars—they cast her in a series of fairy-tale plots which used her keen sense of humor, her instinctive charm, and her beautiful singing voice for both popular and classical songs. Pasternak went on to produce a string of ten such successes, alternating director Koster with Norman Taurog and Norman Krasna, and literally put Universal's slumping ledgers back into the black. While at Universal, Pasternak initiated three projects for Marlene Dietrich which took her down from the pedestal created by Josef von Sternberg, capitalized upon her tempestuous personality, and overcame her ''box-office poison'' label. The films—*Destry Rides Again, Seven Sinners*, and *The Flame of New Orleans*—helped create a larger audience for her newly found flesh-and-blood image.

In 1942, Pasternak moved over to the more prestigious MGM and continued his successful formula of light-hearted musicals which frequently combined popular and classical music. At that studio. Arthur Freed rated the first-class assignments, but nonetheless Pasternak was able to produce dozens of successful musicals such as *Presenting Lily Marks, Anchors Aweigh, In the Good Old Summertime, The Great Caruso, The Merry Widow*, and *Love Me or Leave Me* using the services of MGM's wonderful stock company of stars—Judy Garland, Frank Sinatra, Kathryn Grayson, Mario Lanza, Jane Powell, and Cyd Charisse.

—Ronald Bowers

PATHÉ, Charles

Producer. **Nationality:** French. **Born:** Chevry-Cossigny, 25 December 1863. **Career:** Exhibited the Edison phonograph in France; 1984—set up phonograph business; 1896—formed the Pathé Frères company with his three brothers; 1900—moved into film production; 1902—built studio at Vincennes; 1907—controlled worldwide network of production, distribution and exhibition; 1914—business dwindled after onset of the First World War; 1929—retired. **Died:** In Los Angeles, California, 13 September 1957.

Films as Producer (Selected List):

1896   *L'Arrivée d'un train de Vincennes*
1897   *Execution capitale à Berlin; Coucher d'Yvette et Pierreuse; Le déshabillé du modèle; Le Pompier et la servante; Sainte-Antoine de Padoue*
1898   *Cambriolage sur les toits*
1899   *L'Affaire Dreyfus; Les Dernières Cartouches; La Belle et le bête; Le Muet Mélomane*
1900   *Aladin; Le Petit poucet; La Guerre du Transvaal; Mariage de raison*
1901   *Histoire d'un crime; Quo Vadis; L'Enfant prodigue; Les Sept Chateaux du diable; La Conquête de l'air; Assassinat de Mac Kinley; Tempête dans une chambre à coucher; Idylle sous un tunnel*

Charles Pathé

1902   *La Passion; Les Victimes de l'alcoolisme; La Poule merveilleuse; Catastrophe de la Martinique; Assassinat du Duc de Guise; L'Amous à tous les étages; Samson et Delila*

1903   *La Vie d'un joueur; Suite de la passion; Don Quichotte, le chat botté; Guillaume Tell; Massacre de la famille royale de Serbie; Films comiques*

1904   *Roman d'amour; La Guerre Russo-Japonais; La Règne de Louis XIV; La Grève; Peau d'âne; Christoph Colomb; Les Metamorphoses du Roi de Pique*

1905   *Les Apaches de Paris; Dix Femmes pour un mari; Première sortie; Au pays noir; Suite de la passion; Au bagne; Vendetta; L'Alcoolisme engendre la tuberculose; L'Incendiare; Les Petits Vagabonds; Toto-Gâte-Sauce; Vot'permis; Viens l'chercher; Le Voleur de bicyclette; Le Petit Poucet; La Poule aux oeufs d'or; Rêve à la lune; Potemkine*

1906   New version of *La Passion; Le Tour du monde d'un policier; Voyage autour d'un étoile; Le Billet de faveur; Le déserteur; Les Chiens contrebandiers; La Fille du sonneur; La Loi du pardon; Le Fils du biable; J'ai perdu mon lorgnon; Les Invisibles; Drame à Venise; Aladin; Un Monsieur qui suit les femmes; Boireau déménage; Le Pendu; Le Nihiliste*

1907   *Les Débuts d'un patineur; Les Apprentissages de Boireau; La Légende de Polichinelle; Faust; Monsieur et Madame veulent une bonne; Le Roman d'un malheureux*

1908   *L'Homme aux gants blancs; Les Affichés animés; Socialisme et nihilisme*

1909   *Les Miserables; Nick Carter; L'Assommois*

1910   *Re Lear* (Lo Savio)

1911   *Il Mercante di Venezia* (*The Merchant of Venice*) (Lo Savio); *Max et le quinquina*

1912   *Les Misérables*

Publications

On PATHÉ: books—

Palumbo, Mario, *L'uomo de Gallo*, 1965.
De Pathé Frères à Pathé Cinéma, Lyon, 1970.
Lefebvre, Bernard, *Les cinématographes de la Sainte Romain de Rouen 1896–1907*, Mont-Saint-Aignan, 1981.

On PATHÉ; articles—

Sight and Sound (London), Spring 1958.
Sadoul, Georges, in *Conquête du cinéma*, 1960.
Afterimage (London), vol. 3, no. 8–9, April 1981.
Avant-Scène (Paris), no. 334, November 1984.
Classic Images (Muscatine, Iowa), September 1986.
Télérama (Paris), 2 November 1992.

*   *   *

Like many of the moguls of the cinema, Charles Pathé began as a promoter of Edison's phonograph which he introduced in the early 1890s to the popular entertainment of the fairgrounds in Vincennes. He soon opened a shop selling phonographs, and also a recording studio where he made cylinders of famous theatre artists of the time. An association with Henry Joly got him interested in moving pictures and the purchase of an Edison Kinetoscope took him back to the fairgrounds. He also acquired a camera. In 1896, with the help of his brothers, he founded the firm of Pathé Frères and opened an establishment at 98 rue de Richelieu, Paris. He was convinced that "the cinema would be the theatre, the newspaper and the school of the future."

Attracting an infusion of 100,000 francs into his business through his association with an electrical manufacturer, Grivolas, in 1898 he founded the Compagnie Generale, marketing phonographs, cinematographs and precision instruments. He employed Ferdinand Zecca, who came from a theatrical family, to supervise the making of films. The great Paris Exhibition of 1900 provided a suitable showcase for the new invention and very soon, the establishment of a film studio at Joinville-le Pont became a necessity. Pathé was making 500 films a year. His company was expanding rapidly, with branches in Great Britain, Germany, Italy, Spain, Russia, the United States, and India. Pathé was now head of a great industrial empire.

His early films were plagiarisms of the successes of other people's films, as copyright did not exist at the time. But his director Zecca was making a name for himself with films such as *Histoire d'un crime* and *Les Victimes de l'alcoolisme*. The range of the Pathé output was considerable. His band of comics was to include Max Linder, the precursor of Chaplin, and others like Andre Deed, Rigadin, and Jean Durand. His Pathé color system was seen to good effect in many historical dramas and of course he launched the Pathé Journal, one of the finest newsreels to adorn the cinema screens. He was also associated with the more ambitious Film d'Art, and S.C.A.G.L., an organization of literary patrons of the cinema.

He spent some years in America from 1914, developing the Pathé Exchange there. On his return he found his empire beginning to crumble. The First World War had affected his distribution and the cost of filmmaking had increased enormously. America had taken over the programming of cinemas with its elaborate publicity and star system and super-productions like Griffith's *Birth of a Nation* and *Intolerance*. The French public had been weaned off the Pathé product.

Gradually, in the ensuing years Pathé lost many of his most valuable assets. Filmmaking in France no longer seemed to be profitable, with no chance of breaking into the American market. He shed his associations with S.C.A.G.L. and Film d'Art. He lost his Pathé Exchange in 1920. In 1926 Kodak took over his film-stock factory. Eventually Pathé ceded his organization to Bernard Natan, a one-time pornographic filmmaker but now a powerful figure on the French film scene. Under Natan, the organization retained the prestigious Pathé name, but only lasted a few years, from 1930 to 1934. Natan ended up in prison in both France and Germany.

Pathé was above all else a businessman but with a passionate interest in the cinema. His early life had been tough and the world of the film pioneer was beset by imitators and hostile competition. But he carried on the great tradition of Méliès and Lumière and placed French filmmaking in the spotlight in those early days. It might also be recalled that he introduced the Pathé Baby camera and projector to encourage home movies. He made it possible to see—even in very edited versions—great films of the past which no doubt inspired many a young cinéaste who went on to professional work in later years.

—Liam O'Leary

PAXTON, John

Writer. **Nationality:** American. **Born:** Kansas City, Missouri, 21 March 1911. **Education:** Kansas City Central High School; University of Missouri, Columbia, B.A. in journalism,1934. **Family:** Married Sarah Jane Miles, 1948. **Career:** 1935–36—worked for Theatre Guild of New York, then associate editor, *State* magazine, 1937–38, and freelance writer and publicist for Theatre Guild; 1943—writer for RKO: first film as writer, *My Pal, Wolf*, followed by a series of films directed by Edward Dmytryk. **Award:** Writers Guild Award for *Kotch*, 1971. **Died:** In Santa Monica, California, 5 January 1985.

Films as Writer:

1944   *My Pal, Wolf* (Werker)
1945   *Murder, My Sweet* (*Farewell, My Lovely*) (Dmytryk)
1946   *Cornered* (Dmytryk); *Crack-Up* (Reis)
1947   **Crossfire** (Dmytryk); *So Well Remembered* (Dmytryk)
1949   *Rope of Sand* (Dieterle)
1950   *Of Men and Mice* (Reis)
1951   *Fourteen Hours* (Hathaway)
1953   *The Wild One* (Benedek)
1955   *Prize of Gold* (Robson)

1956   *The Cobweb* (Minelli); *Interpol* (*Pickup Alley*) (Gilling)
1959   *How to Murder a Rich Uncle* (Patrick) (+ pr); *On the Beach* (Kramer)
1971   *Kotch* (Lemmon)
1973   *The Great Man's Whiskers* (Leacock)

Publications

By PAXTON: articles—

In *The Hollywood Screenwriter*, edited by Richard Corliss, New York, 1972.
Marshall, J.D., in *Blueprint in Babylon*, New York, 1978.

On PAXTON: articles—

Film Comment (New York), Winter 1970–71.
Focus on Film (London), Spring 1972.
Présence du Cinéma (Paris), June 1972.
Weaver, John D., in *UCLA Librarian* (Los Angeles), July-August 1978.
Obituary in *Variety* (New York), 16 January 1985.
Weaver, John D., in *Los Angeles Times*, 10 March 1985.
Feldman, Ellen, in *American Screenwriters*, 2nd series, edited by Randall Clark, Detroit, Michigan, 1986.

*   *   *

Perhaps the most amazing achievement in John Paxton's career as a screenwriter in Hollywood was that he remained untouched by the blacklist. The third member of the RKO team that made *Murder, My Sweet*, *Cornered*, and *Crossfire*, Paxton escaped the wrath of the witch-hunters while his colleagues, the producer Adrian Scott and the director Edward Dmytryk, were to become charter members of the "Hollywood Ten." But those three important examples of *film noir* represent Paxton's best work, particularly *Crossfire*, which attracted the special attention of the House Committee on Un-American Activities.

The initial Paxton screenplay for the Scott-Dmytryk team was an adaptation of Raymond Chandler's *Farewell, My Lovely*. Retitled *Murder, My Sweet* for the screen, it was the first incarnation of Philip Marlowe in motion pictures, and successfully transformed Dick Powell's image of boyish crooner into that of hard-boiled hero. Paxton was forced to simplify Chandler's complex narrative to fit into a 90-minute package while maintaining the spirit of the novelist's mean streets. Much of the Chandler tone was perpetuated through Marlowe's first-person narration, the device justified by the framework of a police interrogation of the detective. Rather than using the narration to advance the story, Paxton fashioned it to function as a vehicle for Chandler's similes and wisecracks as Marlowe comments on the action. Along with Chandler's own screenplay for *Double Indemnity* in the same year, Paxton's script for *Murder, My Sweet* established cynical first-person narration as a convention of the *film noir*, particularly in its detective movie form. *Cornered* solidified Powell's tough-guy image and was one of the earliest films to place the returning soldier in the role of a vengeful hunter utilizing his skill at combat to settle a personal score.

Crossfire remains one of Paxton's most accomplished screenplays and one of the best films of the 1940s. Richard Brooks's didactic Second World War novel about unbridled prejudice and the murder of a homosexual by a soldier was reshaped by Paxton into a "message picture." To meet production-code restrictions, the victim was changed from a homosexual to a Jew and the film became an attack on anti-Semitism wedged into the genre framework of a murder mystery. Yet of far more interest than the "message" aspect of the film is Paxton's updating of the novel by several years to place it squarely in the postwar milieu and his shift of the novel's emphasis on the accused murderer to the collective of demobilized soldiers in Washington, D.C. The group of soldiers works together to ferret out the real murderer within their ranks, a narrative scheme which resulted in accusations of socialism in some quarters. Politics aside, the move to a story without a clearly defined protagonist yielded a film with a diffuse point-of-view, serving to dramatize the aimlessness of the soldiers and the country after the war. Paxton was able to take the character of "The Man," a pathological liar and pimp in the novel, and, by placing him within the new context, create a disillusioned everyman. "The Man" became the spiritual center of the film, emblematic of not only the soldiers, but the country as a whole, as he searches for direction and purpose within his own conflicting stories of identity. The murder victim's monologue about the nation's desultory state and residual wartime hate was a clear summation on the atmosphere which led to the HUAC hearings.

Paxton's screenplay for *Crossfire* went beyond the problem of anti-Semitism to accent other social issues, notably the decaying family and the culture's obsession with material goods. The emphasis on the collective, national ennui and a variety of social problems made *Crossfire* a central target of the House Committee on Un-American Activities. But it is that combination of factors which, couched within a genre mold, makes the film the most concise and revealing portrait of the confused national psyche following the Second World War.

With the Scott-Dmytryk team silenced by HUAC, the assignments Paxton received became fewer and more sporadic. The success of the RKO team and Paxton's place in it was not to be repeated on the same sustained level. His last major contribution was his screenplay for *The Wild One* which in many respects operates as a continuation of the themes of a decaying society presented in *Crossfire*, but without the saving grace of cooperation within a collective. Buoyed by be-bop dialogue, *The Wild One* displayed both the motorcycle gang and the community as groups gone amok, with little hope offered for a stable society. The reply Marlon Brando gives to the question "What're you rebelling against, Johnny?"—"What've you got?"—was not only the canonizing agent that made him into the patron saint of the youth culture, but was a rallying cry of the disaffected and disillusioned for the next 20 years. Indeed, the aimless soldiers of *Crossfire* seemed to find their logical extension as the wandering band of bikers in *The Wild One*.

—Eric Schaefer

PEPLOE, Clare

Writer. **Nationality:** British. **Born:** Tanzania. **Education:** Studied French at the Sorbonne in Paris; studied Italian at Perugia University. **Family:** Married the director Bernardo Bertolucci; sister of screenwriter

Mark Peploe. **Career:** Met Michaelangelo Antonioni in the late 1960s and collaborated with him on his film of radical politics on a U.S. college campus, *Zabriskie Point;* began working with Bertolucci in mid-1970s, co-writing *La Luna* in 1979. **Agent:** Duncan Heath, International Creative Management, 8899 Beverly Boulevard, Los Angeles, CA 90048, U.S.A.

Films as Writer:

1970 *Zabriskie Point* (Antonioni) (co)
1979 *La Luna* (Bertolucci) (co)
1988 *High Season* (+d)
1995 *Rough Magic* (+d)
1998 *Besieged* (Bertolucci—for TV) (+ assoc pr)
2001 *The Triumph of Love*

Other Films:

1975 *Novecento* (*1900*) (Bertolucci) (asst d)

Publications

By PEPLOE: articles—

Interview with Jonathan Demme, in *Interview* (New York), May 1988.

On PEPLOE: articles—

Kael, Pauline, "High Season," in *The New Yorker*, 4 April 1988.
Sragow, Michael, "Bertolucci's Better Half," http://www.salon.com/ent/col/srag/1999/06/17/peploe/, May 2000.

*   *   *

In many ways, Clare Peploe had the perfect upbringing for a writer of movies. Both filmmakers and writers must have the ability to view their subjects with a certain detachment, even if the subject is themselves. Born in Africa to British parents who were both longtime ex-patriots, Peploe divided her youth among two continents and five countries. She still commutes between Italy and London, feeding an enduring longing for both the vibrant urban energy and the sensual Mediterranean sun. This life of contradictions has given Peploe an intimate knowledge of the fish-out-of-water experience that is often at the center of any dramatic production. The paradoxical search for both an individual identity and a place of belonging has become the focus of much of Peploe's own work.

Peploe's parents never owned a television, and, as a girl, she shied away from visual arts, citing her grandfather's fame in Scotland as a painter. But when she was a teenager in London, friends at Oxford introduced her to film. Her fascination with the cinema remained with her during her own multi-national college career, and when she met director Michaelangelo Antonioni in the late 1960s, she was open to the opportunity to be part of a film's production.

The spirit of rebellious questioning that characterized the times both contributed to Peploe's vision and provided her with her opportunity to develop her craft. "Getting into film wasn't so much about professional training then," she told *Salon* interviewer Michael Sragow, "Films were much more personal, and had more of a personal signature." Her collaborative work with Antonioni and, later, with her husband, Italian director Bernardo Bertolucci, helped her develop her own personal style.

Though panned by some critics for its stilted dialog and surrealistic approach, *Zabriskie Point* was a dream-like look at youthful rebellion. Co-written by an Italian and a pan-European British woman, the film necessarily embodies the outsider's view of very American cultural events. In *La Luna*, her first co-writing effort with Bertolucci, Peploe continues to explore the consciousness of the outsider, detailing the struggles of a boy to reconnect with his own heritage by finding his birth father, while floundering through drug use and a semi-incestuous relationship with his mother.

If her partnership with the famous Italian directors had resulted in weighty, even pretentious films, Peploe's own movies were much more lighthearted affairs, as if still rooted in the outsider's search for home and self. Using adventure, mystery, and even screwball comedy, Peploe shows a sure hand as a director, weaving the many complex concepts of her story into films that offer viewers a rousing good time.

Set in a tiny village on the island of Rhodes, *High Season*, released in 1988, is a comic mystery that draws upon Peploe's own ex-patriot background. A madcap romance largely overlooked by critics, it is nonetheless mightily entertaining and a successful film in terms of its own goals—to expose the contradictions inherent in both ex-patriotism, patriotism, and tourism—as well as revealing Peploe's gentle affection for the exotic lands in which she grew up.

Rough Magic, set in the jungles of Mexico in the 1950s, is a road movie and a lively blend of adventure and spirituality. A dark comedy, which some uneasy critics labeled "harsh" and "strange," the film exhibits Peploe's sharp eye for a literary work which will adapt successfully to the screen. Originally a James Hadley Chase story called "Miss Shumway Waves a Wand," *Rough Magic* tells the story of a young woman's search for a Mexican shaman and for magic, which she ultimately finds both within herself and in hilarious reality. Peploe films the story with such quirky fun that her poke at cultural imperialism passes almost unnoticed.

Peploe continues to collaborate with her husband, and she has taken both her skill at adaptation and her finely tuned sense of irony and humor back to Bertolucci. Their 1999 release, *The Besieged*, received critical accolades. Adapted from James Lesdun's *The Siege*, the film recounts the unlikely romance between a British classical musician and his African housekeeper, both living in Italy. Because she is so completely a cinematic rather than a theatrical writer, Peploe has kept her script spare, allowing facial expression and music to drive the movie as clearly as dialog. Critics have praised the gentler, more romantic Bertolucci that is evident in this film.

Peploe has a gift for finding the stories her life has given her a passion to tell, and her point of view is informed by many different cultural perspectives. This multicultural outlook, coupled with an acute sense of mischief, has enabled her to make incisive films that never lose sight of one of cinema's most important functions—to entertain.

—Tina Gianoulis

PEREIRA, Hal

Art Designer, Supervising Studio Art Director. **Nationality:** American. **Born:** Chicago, Illinois, 1905 or 1910 (sources vary). **Education:** University of Illinois. **Career:** 1933–40—worked as theatrical designer in Chicago; 1942—joined Paramount as unit art director; 1947—promoted to executive position on the staff for domestic and international companies; 1950—became supervising art director for the studio; 1968—retired from filmmaking to work as a design consultant at the architectural firm of his brother, William L. Pereira. **Award:** Academy Award, for *The Rose Tatoo*, 1955. **Died:** In Los Angeles, California, 17 December 1983.

Films as Art Designer:

1944 ***Double Indemnity***; *The Ministry of Fear*
1951 *Detective Story*
1952 *Son of a Paleface*
1953 *The War of the Worlds*
1957 *The Tin Star*

Films as Collaborating Art Designer:

1951 *Ace in the Hole*; *The Lemon Drop Kid*; *Peking Express*; *Here Comes the Groom*; *When Worlds Collide*; *Red Mountain*
1952 *My Son John*; *The Greatest Show on Earth*; *Carrie*; *Caribbean*; *The Turning Point*
1953 *Come Back*; *Little Sheba*; *Shane*; *Stalag 17*; *Houdini*; *Sangaree*; *Roman Holiday*; *Botany Bay*
1954 *Knock on Wood*; *The Naked Jungle*; *Elephant Walk*; *Jivaro*; *Rear Window*; *Sabrina*; *White Christmas*
1955 *Conquest of Space*; *Run for Cover*; *Strategic Air Command*; *The Far Horizons*; *The 7 Little Foys*; *To Catch a Thief*; *The Desperate Hours*; *The Trouble with Harry*; *The Rose Tatoo*; *Artists and Models*
1956 *The Court Jester*; *The Man Who Knew Too Much*; *The Proud and the Profane*; *That Certain Feeling*; *The Vagabond King*; *The Mountain*; *The Ten Commandments*
1957 *Three Violent People*; *Fear Strikes Out*; *Funny Face*; *Lonely Man*; *The Gunfight at the OK Corral*
1958 *Teacher's Pet*; ***Vertigo***; *Hot Spell*; *The Space Children*; *Houseboat*; *The Buccaneer*
1959 *The Five Pennies*; *That Kind of Woman*; *L'il Abner*
1960 *The Bellboy*
1961 *One-Eyed Jacks*; *The Ladies' Man*; ***Breakfast at Tiffany's***; *Pocketful of Miracles*; *The Errand Boy*
1962 *Hell is for Heroes*; *Hatari!*
1963 *Hud*; *The Nutty Professor*; *Come Blow Your Horn*; *Donovan's Reef*; *McLintock!*; *Who's Minding the Store*; *Love with the Proper Stranger*
1964 *Robinson Crusoe on Mars*; *The Patsy*; *The Disorderly Orderly*
1965 *Sylvia*; *The Family Jewels*; *Harlow*; *The Sons of Katie Elder*
1966 *Red Line 7000*; *The Night of the Grizzly*; *Nevada Smith*; *This Property is Condemned*; *Waco*; *The Swinger*
1967 *Warning Shot*; *Chuka*; *The Caper of the Golden Bulls*; *El Dorado*; *The Spirit is Willing*; *The President's Analyst*
1968 *No Way to Treat a Lady*

Publications

On PEREIRA: articles—

Obituary in *Variety* (New York), 28 December 1983.

*   *   *

Trained by a number of steady and profitable years of theatrical work, Hal Pereira began work in 1942 as a unit art designer for Paramount, the studio most noted for its sumptuous use of *mise-en-scène* to create entertaining films. Pereira rose rapidly through the ranks, becoming supervising art director in 1950 and thus responsible for art design in the studio's production as a whole, though he continued to work, usually with others, on individual projects.

Like all studio technicians of this era, Pereira was required to be flexible and work on many different kinds of films. He created interesting design effects from the Wellsian scientific apocalypse *War of the Worlds*, one of the most terrifying of the many early fifties entries in this genre, perfecting ideas he had used in an earlier coproduction, *When Worlds Collide*. Called upon to summon up appropriate images of the biblical past, Pereira helped design convincing sets for the epic story of *The Ten Commandments;* he was at least competent in other period pictures as well, notably *Botany Bay*, *The Proud and the Profane*, and *The Buccaneer*. At least two of the westerns he worked on, *Nevada Smith* and *Shane*, required well-designed interiors—uncharacteristic of the genre—and Pereira was up to the task, creating sets that allowed dramatic interior scenes equivalent to the exteriors, which benefitted much from natural scenery in each case. Pereira also did excellent work for a number of comedies, especially Jerry Lewis films such as *The Disorderly Orderly* and *The Bellboy*, which required appropriate sets for complicated interior sequences. He also worked on nearly all the Alfred Hitchcock color films of the fifties, imparting a richness and, sometimes, glamour that perfectly suited the director's interests at the time in offering exciting, adult drama with a fair amount of visual stylization.

Interestingly, though he worked for a studio that for much of its corporate life specialized in more or less elaborate forms of escapism, Pereira was obviously most at home in designing urban interiors and exteriors. It is significant that his first major project for Paramount, Billy Wilder's *Double Indemnity*, was very much a departure for the studio. One of the earliest *films noirs*, *Double Indemnity* notably transforms the ambiance of James M. Cain's gritty story of adultery and murder for profit; Raymond Chandler's screenplay firmly locates the drama in a somewhat pretentious upper middle class California milieu, perfectly expressed by Pereira's design for the Dietrichson house—with an interior that is not as rich or well-appointed as expected, the ideal setting for a debunking of bourgeois claims to respectability. His work for Wilder on this project is firmly rooted in the naturalism of both Cain's and Chandler's vision of the American character; there is no trace in the film of the more abstract kind of design, of German Expressionist origin, that is also a notable aspect of *film noir*. In his next project, however, for Fritz Lang's version of Graham Greene's *The Ministry of Fear*, Pereira designed a patently unreal wartime England, defined by threatening wastescapes and impossibly entrapping interiors, that is the precise correlative of the protagonist's paranoia and helplessness. Here Pereira cooperates successfully with Lang's stylistic interests, creating one of the most stylized and expressionistic of *film noirs*.

What most distinguishes Pereira's interior design for gritty urban dramas, however, is not stylistic versatility, the art director's competence with both realistic and more abstract conceptions. It is, instead, his ability to indicate the moral and economic values of an interior environment with a series of well-chosen effects. His design of the police station in *Detective Story* deliberately deglamorizes this agency of the law through a certain tattiness and careless disorder that suit precisely this story of moral failure and self-destructive redemption. For *Ace in the Hole* Pereira captures perfectly the dusty desperation of small-town rural American life, once again the setting for a drama of moral failure and entrapment (the set for the mine cave-in usefully epitomizes how the characters relate to but can never touch one another). Claustrophobic interior effects are also important thematically for *Rear Window*, which shares with *Ace in the Hole* a *noir* concern with dead-ends and confinement. For *The Desperate Hours* Pereira helped design not just an effective playspace for complex interior action sequences (the film was based on a stage play), but an upper middle class environment in which everything finds its tastefully designed place and from which the very possibility of evil or disorder is banished until it comes knocking on the front door. *Hud* offers a perfect re-creation of small-town southwestern ranch and town life, a setting that, with its simplicity and barrenness, nicely defines this drama of elemental character conflict and maturation. Pereira's last film, *No Way to Treat a Lady*, the story of a psychopath who, with a variety of disguises, murders a number of older women living alone, offered him a final opportunity to create a series of interior sets with just the right class and social value, here lower middle class. His designs form the perfect backdrop for Rod Steiger's scenery chewing performance as the madman, adding the right touch of realism to a story that, had it not been so grounded, could easily have deteriorated from the dramatic to the ridiculous.

Because most of his films were collaborations, and because the Hollywood film in general is an intensely collaborative effort, it is difficult to determine precisely what contributions Pereira made to a substantial body of commercially successful and, often, artistically noteworthy films. However there is no doubt that he was not only one of the top designers in the business during his twenty-five year career, but an important influence on the way Hollywood films in general developed a more substantial, more detailed, more expressive approach to art design, especially as this was influenced during the postwar period by greater demands for realism. The triumph of Pereira's contribution is probably *The Rose Tatoo*, a difficult production, based on the earthy but intellectually schematic Tennessee Williams play, in which Pereira and others at Paramount were able to design a series of interiors and exteriors that both evoked small-town life on the Gulf coast and expressed the natural law that all human beings must embrace the earthy, the physical, the sexual. Here the abstract and the actual merge, providing the perfect correlative for the art director's job, which is to surmount the paradox of designing the real.

—R. Barton Palmer

PÉRINAL, Georges

Cinematographer. **Nationality:** French. **Born:** Paris, 1897. **Career:** in French films from 1913, working on documentaries and short films; 1933—persuaded by Alexander Korda to join London Films, and later worked in the United States. **Award:** Academy Award for *The Thief of Bagdad*, 1940. **Died:** In London, 23 April 1965.

Films as Cinematographer:

1923   *Chartres* (Grémillon)
1924   *La Bière* (Grémillon)
1925   *L'Auvergne* (Grémillon); *La Justicière* (Gleize and de Marsan)
1926   *Au pays de George Sand* (Epstein)
1927   *Maldone* (Grémillon); *Six et demi onze* (Epstein); *Gratuités* (Grémillon)
1928   *Les Nouveaux Messieurs* (Feyder) (co); *La Zone* (Lacombe); *La Tour* (Clair) (co)
1929   *Ces dames aux chapeaux verts* (Berthomieu); *Gardiens de phare* (Grémillon)
1930   *David Golder* (Duvivier); *Mon ami Victor* (Berthomieu); **Le Sang d'un poète** (*The Blood of a Poet*) (Cocteau); *Sous les toits de Paris* (*Under the Roofs of Paris*) (Clair)
1931   *Dainah la metisse* (Grémillon); **A nous la liberté** (Clair); **Le Million** (Clair); *Le Parfum de la dame en nois* (L'Herbier); *Jean de la Lune* (Choux)
1932   *The Girl from Maxim's* (Z. Korda); *La Femme en homme* (Genina); *Hotel des étudiants* (Tourjansky); *Le Picador* (Jaquelux); *La Petite Chocolatière* (M. Allegret); *Pomme d'amour* (Dreville); *Quatorze juillet* (Clair)
1933   **The Private Life of Henry VIII** (Z. Korda)
1934   *Catherine the Great* (Czinner); *The Private Life of Don Juan* (Z. Korda); *Maria Chapdelaine* (*The Naked Heart*) (Duvivier)
1935   *Escape Me Never* (Czinner); *Sanders of the River* (Z. Korda); **Things to Come** (Menzies)
1936   *Rembrandt* (A. Korda)
1937   *Dark Journey* (Saville); *The Squeaker* (W. Howard); *Under the Red Robe* (Sjöström); *I, Claudius* (von Sternberg—unfinished)
1938   *The Challenge* (Rosmer); *The Drum* (*Drums*) (Z. Korda); *Prison without Bars* (Hurst)
1939   *The Four Feathers* (Z. Korda)
1940   *The Thief of Bagdad* (Berger, Powell, and Whelan); *Old Bill and Son* (Dalrymple)
1942   *The First of the Few* (L. Howard); *The Jungle Book* (Z. Korda)
1943   **The Life and Death of Colonel Blimp** (Powell and Pressburger)
1945   *Perfect Strangers* (*Vacation from Marriage*) (A. Korda)
1946   *A Man about the House* (Arliss)
1947   *An Ideal Husband* (Z. Korda); *The Life and Adventures of Nicholas Nickleby* (Cavalcanti)
1948   *The Fallen Idol* (Reed)
1949   *The Forbidden Street* (*Brittania Mews*) (Negulesco)
1950   *My Daughter Joy* (Ratoff); *That Dangerous Age* (Ratoff); *The Mudlark* (Negulesco)
1951   *I'll Never Forget You* (Baker); *No Highway* (*No Highway in the Sky*) (Koster)
1955   *L'Amant de Lady Chatterley* (*Lady Chatterley's Lover*) (M. Allégret); *The Man Who Loved Redheads* (French); *Three Cases of Murder* (O'Ferrall)
1956   *Loser Takes All* (Annakin); *Satellite in the Sky* (Dickson)
1957   *A King in New York* (Chaplin); *Saint Joan* (Preminger)
1958   *Bonjour Tristesse* (Preminger); *Tom Thumb* (Pal)
1959   *Serious Charge* (*Immoral Charge*; *A Touch of Hell*) (Young)
1960   *Once More, with Feeling!* (Donen); *Oscar Wilde* (Ratoff); *The Day They Robbed the Bank of England* (Guillermin)
1961   *The Four Horsemen of the Apocalypse* (Minnelli)

Publications

By PÉRINAL: article—

Film Weekly (London), 4 May 1934.

On PÉRINAL: articles—

Cine Technician (London), April-June 1942.
Hill, Derek, in *American Cinematographer* (Hollywood), August 1958.
Clair, René, in *Film and TV Technician* (London), May 1965.
Focus on Film (London), no. 13, 1973.

*   *   *

One of the most influential cinematographers in the history of the cinema, Georges Périnal had a career extending from his early work in the French silent cinema (*Chartres*, *L'Auvergne*, and other films), to films for Jean Cocteau (*The Blood of a Poet*), the Kordas (*The Private Life of Henry VIII*, *I, Claudius*, and his Academy Award-winning Technicolor photography on *The Thief of Bagdad*), then on to assignments for Charlie Chaplin (*A King in New York*), and Otto Preminger (*Saint Joan*). He retired in 1960 after the production of *Oscar Wilde*, and died shortly thereafter.

Périnal's work is a curiously continental hybrid of a delicately gallic lighting style modified by the various directional sensibilities he labored under. For Cocteau, he gave *The Blood of a Poet* a dreamlike, ethereal quality, shooting on silver nitrate black-and-white stock through a variety of filters and gauzes to achieve a fluid, phantasmagorical look, ideally suited to Cocteau's vision of "a realistic documentary of unreal events." Périnal received the assignment from Cocteau when the director sent out postcards to all cameramen working in Paris at that time, asking each one to come to Cocteau's flat for an interview the following morning. Périnal was the first to arrive, and Cocteau was immediately taken with him. The film proved an international triumph, and a classic of the avant-garde, still frequently revived today. During that same year, for the director René Clair, Périnal also photographed *Sous les toits de Paris*, which was a great success; and in 1931, he shot *A nous la liberté*, also for Clair, which many consider to be the director's masterpiece. All three of these early films showed an imaginative flair for combining music and image in a variety of complimentary ways, usually by closely synchronizing the movements of the actors and/or props with a quirky, effervescent score.

After this initial success, Périnal began a long association with Alexander Korda, starting with *The Private Life of Henry VIII* which starred Charles Laughton. Although this film was in every way a more conventional project than the films Périnal had previously been associated with, he nevertheless collaborated effectively on the project, giving his images a sense of light and shadow consistent with Laughton's hearty performance, and prefiguring in many ways his moody, atmospheric work on *Rembrandt*, which also starred Laughton. On *Rembrandt*, Périnal purposely designed each shot as though it were a painting by the great artist, with light shafting in through the windows of the sets in sharp contrast to the Stygian gloom of the interiors. Yet these films, and *Things to Come* (which he shot for Korda under the stylistically astute direction of art-director-turned-film-director William Cameron Menzies), show that Périnal was interested in being commercially successful as well as artistically innovative. *Things to Come* is a particular disappointment: although the film is undeniably spectacular, and uses the considerable talents of such excellent actors as Sir Cedric Hardwicke and Raymond Massey, Périnal's lighting of Menzies's gigantic sets is too often flat and perfunctory. Perhaps this was intentional, as the appropriate manner in which to light and photograph the world of the futuristic, totalitarian ''science-state'' in *Things to Come*, but Périnal's lighting here falls into the category of one strategy, perfunctorily extended and seldom modified. One could say the same of his work in *Rembrandt* and even *The Jungle Book*, which is so lushly lit and shot that its sumptuousness borders, at times, on the suffocating. Nevertheless, Périnal's work in these productions set the style for a generation of British cameramen, and he continued working in the British cinema for most of the balance of his career.

Certainly, Périnal's is an intensely romantic style, full of pronounced lighting contrasts and glossy, hard-edged key lighting. Yet one misses the airy, gentle lyricism he brought to his photography of the two Clair films and *Blood of a Poet*. Ironically, some of Périnal's best work during this ''middle period'' can be found in his work on the unfinished *I, Claudius*, directed by Josef von Sternberg. The film was abandoned after only a few days' shooting, principally because of Laughton's inability to get along with the strong-willed director or to ''come to grips'' with the role of Claudius. The few tantalizingly brief scenes that survive, which were woven into an excellent documentary by Bill Duncalf (*The Epic That Never Was*) on the making of *I, Claudius*, show that the film might have been Korda's supreme achievement. In addition to von Sternberg's direction and the performances of Laughton and Oberon, Emlyn Williams appears effectively in the incomplete footage as a debauched, languidly corrupt Caligula, and William Cameron Menzies designed the appropriately grandiose sets. Périnal's work on the film is at once seductive and sinuous; working with von Sternberg, an excellent cinematographer in his own right, Périnal blends bold, stark lighting patterns in the wide shots with gently, ''cookied'' close-ups of the protagonists, making the world of *I, Claudius* somewhat of an extension of von Sternberg's cinematographic vision in *Morocco* or *Shanghai Express*.

Perhaps Périnal's last truly realized work is his photography of *Nicholas Nickleby* in 1947, although one could make a strong case for his exquisite black-and-white photography on Graham Greene's *The Fallen Idol*, which starred Ralph Richardson, in 1948. Thereafter, Périnal's work, though not diminishing in quantity, went into a period of stasis. *The Mudlark*, *No Highway in the Sky*, and *Saint Joan* are all journeyman assignments, and Périnal apparently walked through them with little enthusiasm or interest. The same could certainly be said of his contributions to *Tom Thumb* and *Once More, with Feeling!* Yet, even in the midst of these frankly commercial productions, Périnal was capable of creditable work on Preminger's *Bonjour Tristesse*, one of the director's most affecting works, and *A King in New York*, although Chaplin's visual sense in this film is distinctly utilitarian, and gives Périnal little space to work in.

Despite, then, a certain adventurousness in Périnal's work as evidenced by his rapid assimilation into the Korda movie machine, the cinematographer emerges as a formidable commercial stylist, whose work between 1930–31 set the foundation for much of

what was to come in both classic and New Wave French cinema, through his expressive use of naturalistic techniques and a gracefully fluid moving camera. In his second phase, from 1933–46, Périnal became the architect of one of the great classical British styles of cinematography: brooding and dramatic, reveling in off-angled close-ups, and inextricably tied to the use of studio facilities. Certainly, Périnal is a major figure in the history of motion-picture cinematography, and his influence continues to be felt in both British and French studio work to the present day.

—Wheeler Winston Dixon

PIERCE, Jack P.

Makeup Artist. **Nationality:** American. **Born:** New York City, 1889. **Career:** 1910—projectionist; then theater manager, stage actor, film stuntman and actor, assistant director; 1914—cameraman for Universal; then became makeup man in late 1920s: at Universal until late 1940s; then freelance makeup work in films and on TV: worked on *Fireside Theatre* and *You Are There* series. **Died:** In 1968.

Films as Makeup Artist (selected list):

1926   *Buffalo Bill on the U.P. Trail* (Mattison); *Davy Crockett at the Fall of the Alamo* (Bradbury)
1927   *The Monkey Talks* (Walsh)
1931   **Dracula** (Browning); **Frankenstein** (Whale)
1932   *The Mummy* (Freund); **The Old Dark House** (Whale)
1933   *The Invisible Man* (Whale)
1935   **The Bride of Frankenstein** (Whale); *The Werewolf of London* (Walker); *The Raven* (Landers); *The Black Cat* (*House of Doom*) (Ulmer)
1939   *Son of Frankenstein* (Lee)
1941   *The Wolf Man* (Waggner)
1942   *The Mummy's Tomb* (Young); *The Ghost of Frankenstein* (Kenton); *Frankenstein Meets the Wolf Man* (Neill)
1943   *The Mummy's Ghost* (Le Borg); *Captive Wild Women* (Dmytryk)
1944   *The Mummy's Curse* (Goodwins); *The House of Frankenstein* (Kenton)
1945   *House of Dracula* (Kenton)
1947   *Abbott and Costello Meet Frankenstein* (Barton)
1959   *Beyond the Time Barrier* (Ulmer); *The Amazing Transparent Man* (Ulmer)
1961   *The Devil's Hand* (*Live to Love*) (Hole)
1962   *The Creation of the Humanoids* (Barry)
1963   *Beauty and the Beast* (Cahn)

Other Films:

1922   *The Man Who Waited* (Luddy) (ro)
1923   *Desert Rider* (Bradbury) (asst d)
1925   *The Speed Demon* (Bradbury) (ro)
1929   *Masquerade* (Birdwell) (ro)

Publications

By PIERCE: article—

"The Monstrous Genius of Jack Pierce," an interview with Chuck Crisafulli, in *Filmfax* (Evanston), October-November 1992.

On PIERCE: articles—

Film Comment (New York), November-December 1978.
Taylor, Al, and Sue Roy, in *Making a Monster*, New York, 1980.
American Cinematographer (Hollywood), January 1985.
Scarlet Street, no. 9, Winter 1993.

*   *   *

With the death of Lon Chaney in 1930, Universal began its search for a new "Man of a Thousand Faces." In spite of the studio's later publicity which placed the Chaney mantle on Boris Karloff's square shoulders, the rightful successor to the title was a meticulous, soft-spoken makeup man. Jack Pierce spent some 20 years at Universal creating the monsters that have populated nightmares since the early 1930s.

After a career in semi-pro baseball, Pierce drifted to Hollywood, entering production as an actor and assistant cameraman. Eventually finding his niche as a makeup artist, causing an early sensation with his ape makeup for the 1927 Fox production *The Monkey Talks*. But it was his transformation of Boris Karloff into Frankenstein's monster in 1931 that made Pierce the movies' premier conjurer of gruesome and fantastic creatures for a generation. Like Dr. Frankenstein's monster, Pierce's creature was made up of pieces—pieces of information from books on anatomy, surgery, criminology, and burial custom shaped a thing with veracity to physiological fact and constructed with the help of volatile collodion and greasepaint. The monster's pot-lid head, abnormally long arms, and distorted features not only gave it a nightmarishly plausible appearance, but also were representative of its inner suffering. The greatest achievement in Pierce's design was that it left Karloff's gaunt features free enough to express a range of emotions that gave the monster its pathos and humanity. The vulnerable quality which emanated from beneath the creature's frightening visage has made the monster, fashioned by Pierce and Karloff, the most enduring icon of Hollywood horror. The makeup was so distinctive that Universal copyrighted it, later receiving huge royalties (of which Pierce saw none) from the licensing of toys and masks.

Unlike the monsters created by today's special effects wizards, Pierce's designs focused on the human face. Pierce, like Chaney before him, possessed the innate knowledge that it is in the face where the cruelty and pain which dwell in a soul become manifest. The Frankenstein monster was only the first in a long series of horrors Pierce shaped for Universal. The same time and attention to detail that went into *Frankenstein* extended to *The Mummy*, in which Karloff was subjected to two makeups. For the role of the 3000-year-old mummy, Im-Ho-Tep, Pierce swathed the actor in beauty clay and cotton, rendering him almost immobile. And for the role of Ardeth Bey, the mummy's 20th-century incarnation, Karloff's face was desiccated into a tight expression, evoking centuries of bitterness. Edgar G. Ulmer's Bauhaus poem to necrophilia and spiritual anguish, *The Black Cat*, featured one of Pierce's subtlest and most effective makeups. The makeup man sculpted Karloff's hairline into a sharp widow's peak, cropping the hair on top into a plateau and thinning it at the sides. The angular effect transformed the actor's benign face into a permanent scowl touched with satanic glamour which blended perfectly with the geometric sets and costumes of the production. Equally effective was Pierce's contribution to the visible portion of Claude Rains in *The Invisible Man*. The ragged wrappings about the head, outcroppings of thatchy hair and socket-like goggles contrived to suggest the madness in the mind beneath the bandages. Even for those not in starring roles Pierce devised intricate treatments. Bela Lugosi's best performance, the supporting role of the shepherd Ygor in *Son of Frankenstein*, came from under heavy makeup. The shaggy hair, hooked teeth, and twisted neck submerged the actor's matinee idol looks, and permitted him a greate range of expression and depth of character than earlier roles had allowed.

Because of his heavy reliance on the face, Pierce's artistry could be constrained by the canvas on which he was forced to work. Universal's two forays into lycanthropy featured two very different Pierce designs, dictated by two very different actors. *The Wolf Man*, in which Lon Chaney, Jr. became the beast by the light of the full moon, was endowed with a more complete mythology, as well as a better script and direction. Yet Pierce's makeup for Chaney was limited by the actor's own round, jowly features and was ultimately a far less ferocious creation than the earlier monster in *The Werewolf of London*. The star, Henry Hull, refused to cooperate with Pierce's original makeup plans for the earlier werewolf movie; the heavy yak hair design eventually became Chaney's "baby" in the 1940s. For Hull, Pierce developed a lean creature, pared of excess hair, a makeup that fully exploited the severe lines and high forehead of the actor's face. The lupine viciousness of Hull's werewolf could not be equalled by the more elaborate Chaney creature.

By 1947 Universal's monsters were left with only B-budgets and plotlines buckling under the weight of their own clichés. The simple shudders created by Frankenstein's monster and the Wolfman were no match for the horrors of the Second World War and the dawning atomic age. And Pierce's painstaking process of makeup application was giving way to foam rubber and other quicker, less expensive techniques. Pierce found himself unceremoniously dumped from the studio payroll and freelancing for other studios and for television. But the monsters he created have become permanent fixtures in our national mythology.

—Eric Schaefer

PINELLI, Tullio

See **FLAIANO, Ennio, and Tullio PINELLI**

PINTER, Harold

Writer. **Nationality:** British. **Born:** Hackney, London, 10 October 1930. **Education:** Attended Hackney Downs Grammar School, London; Royal Academy of Dramatic Art, London. **Family:** Married 1) the actress Vivien Merchant, 1956 (divorced 1980), one son; 2) the writer Lady Antonia Fraser, 1980. **Career:** 1950—professional debut as actor under name David Baron; 1957—first play produced—followed by a series of plays; 1963—first film as writer, *The Servant*;

Harold Pinter

also stage director; 1973— first film as director, *Butley*; 1973—
associate director, National Theatre, London. **Awards:** New York
Film Critics Award, for *The Servant*, 1963; British Academy Award,
for *The Pumpkin Eater*, 1964, and *The Go-Between*, 1971. Commander, Order of the British Empire, 1966. **Address:** c/o ACTAC
Ltd., 16 Cadogan Lane, London S.W.1, England.

Films as Writer:

1963   ***The Servant*** (Losey) (+ ro as society man); *The Caretaker*
        (*The Guest*) (Donner)
1964   *The Pumpkin Eater* (Clayton)
1966   *The Quiller Memorandum* (Anderson)
1967   ***The Accident*** (Losey) (+ ro as Bell)
1968   *The Birthday Party* (Friedkin)
1971   *The Go-Between* (Losey)
1973   *The Homecoming* (Hall)
1976   *The Last Tycoon* (Kazan)
1981   *The French Lieutenant's Woman* (Reisz)
1983   *Betrayal* (D. Jones)
1985   *Turtle Diary* (Irvin) (+ ro as man in bookshop)
1987   *The Room* (Altman) (adapter); *The Dumb Waiter* (Altman);
        The Birthday Party (Ives—for TV) (+ ro)
1988   *Mountain Language* (+ d—for TV)
1989   *L'ami retrouvé* (*Reunion*; *Der Wiedergefundene Freund*)
        (Schatzberg); *The Heat of the Day* (Morahan—for TV)
1990   *The Handmaid's Tale* (Schlöndorff)

1991   *The Comfort of Strangers* (Schrader); *The Lover* (Kemp-Welch)
1993   *The Trial* (D. Jones)
1999   *Bez pogovora* (Jovanovic—for TV)
2000   *The Pickwick Papers*

Films as Director:

1973   *Butley*
1979   *Rear Column*
1981   *The Hothouse*

Films as Actor:

1970   *The Rise and Rise of Michael Rimmer* (Billington) (as
        Steven Hench)
1973   *The Tamarind Seed* (Edwards)
1982   *Doll's Eye* (Worth)
1996   *Breaking the Code* (Wise—for TV) (as John Smith)
1997   *Mojo* (Butterworth) (as Sam Ross)
1998   *Ritratto di Harold Pinter* (Andò) (as himself)
1999   *Mansfield Park* (Rozema) (as Sir Thomas Bertram)
2000   *Catastrophe* (for TV)

Publications

By PINTER: plays—

The Birthday Party and Other Plays, London, 1960.
The Caretaker, London, 1960.
A Slight Ache and Other Plays, London, 1961.
The Collection, London, 1962.
The Collection, and *The Lover*, 1963.
The Dwarfs and Eight Revue Sketches, New York, 1965.
The Homecoming, London, 1965.
Tea Party, London, 1965.
Tea Party and Other Plays, London, 1967.
Landscape, London, 1968.
Landscape, and *Silence*, London, 1969.
Five Screenplays (includes *The Caretaker*, *The Pumpkin Eater*,
        Accident, *The Servant*, *The Quiller Memorandum*), London, 1971;
        modified edition, omitting *The Caretaker* and including *The Go-
        Between*, London, 1971.
Old Times, London and New York, 1971.
Monologue, London, 1973.
No Man's Land, London and New York, 1975.
Plays, 4 vols., London, 1975–81; as *Complete Works*, New York,
        4 vols., 1977–81.
The Proust Screenplay: À la Recherche du Temps Perdu, New
        York, 1977.
Betrayal, London, 1978.
The Hothouse, London and New York, 1980.
Family Voices, London and New York, 1981.
Other Places, London, 1983.
One for the Road, London, 1984.
Mountain Language, London, 1988.
The Heat of the Day, London, 1989.

Moonlight, New York, 1995.
Ashes to Ashes, New York, 1997.
The Proust Screenplay: A la Recherche du Temps Perdu, New York, 1999.
The Hothouse, New York, 1999.

By PINTER: other books—

Mac (nonfiction), 1968.
Poems, London, 1968.
Poems and Prose 1949–1977, London, 1978.
I Know the Place (poetry), London, 1979.
The Screenplay of The French Lieutenant's Woman, London, 1981.
The Comfort of Strangers and Other Screenplays, London, 1990.
The Dwarfs (fiction), London, 1990.
I Know the Place, New York, 1990.
Party Time & the New World Order, New York, 1993.
One Hundred Poems by One Hundred Poets, New York, 1995.
99 Poems in Translation, New York, 1997.
Various Voices: Prose, Poetry, Politics, 1948–1998, New York, 1999.

By PINTER: articles—

Sight and Sound (London), Autumn 1966.
Positif (Paris), July/August 1985.
Film Comment (New York), May/June 1989.

On PINTER: books—

Hayman, Ronald, *Harold Pinter*, London, 1968.
Gordon, Lois, *Strategems to Uncover Nakedness: The Dramas of Harold Pinter*, Columbia, Missouri, 1969.
Taylor, John Russell, *Harold Pinter*, London, 1969.
Esslin, Martin, *The Peopled Wound: The Plays of Harold Pinter*, London, 1970, revised edition, London, 1977.
Hollis, James H., *Harold Pinter*, Carbondale, Illinois, 1970.
Sykes, Arlene, *Harold Pinter*, Brisbane, Queensland, 1970.
Burkman, Katherine H., *The Dramatic World of Harold Pinter*, Columbus, Ohio, 1971.
Ganz, Arthur, editor, *Pinter: A Collection of Critical Essays*, Englewood Cliffs, New Jersey, 1972.
Trussler, Simon, *The Plays of Harold Pinter*, London, 1973.
Quigley, Austin E., *The Pinter Problem*, Princeton, New Jersey, 1975.
Dukore, Bernard F., *Where Laughter Stops: Pinter's Tragi-Comedy*, Columbia, Missouri, 1977.
Gale, Steven H., *Butter's Going Up: A Critical Analysis of Harold Pinter's Plays*, Durham, North Carolina, 1977.
Bold, Alan, editor, *Harold Pinter: You Never Heard Such Silence*, London, 1984.
Klein, Joanne, *Making Pictures: The Pinter Screenplay*, Columbus, Ohio, 1985.
Cahn, Victor L., *Gender and Power in the Plays of Harold Pinter*, New York, 1993.
Hall, Ann. C., *A Kind of Alaska: Women in the Plays of O'Neill, Pinter, and Shepard*, Carbondale, Illinois, 1993.
Homan, Sidney, *Pinter's Odd Man Out: Staging and Filming* Old Times, Lewisburg, Pennsylvania, 1993.
Knowles, Ronald, *Understanding Harold Pinter*, Columbia, South Carolina, 1995.

Merritt, Susan H., *Pinter in Play: Critical Strategies & the Plays of Harold Pinter*, Durham, 1995.
Regal, Martin S., *Harold Pinter: A Question of Timing*, New York, 1995.
Gussow, Mel, *Conversations with Pinter*, New York, 1996.
Billington, Michael, *The Life & Work of Harold Pinter*, New York, 1997.
Peacock, D. Keith, *Harold Pinter & the New British Theatre*, Westport, 1997.
Armstrong, Raymond, *Kafka & Pinter: Shadow-Boxing: The Struggle Between Father & Son*, New York, 1999.

On PINTER: articles—

Cinema Nuovo (Turin), May/June 1967.
Cinema Nuovo (Turin), July/August 1967.
Imagen y Sonido, September 1967.
Roud, Richard, in *Sight and Sound* (London), Summer 1971.
Jones, Edward T., on *The Go-Between* in *Literature/Film Quarterly* (Salisbury, Maryland), April 1973.
National Film Theatre Booklet (London), February 1978.
Avant-Scène (Paris), Autumn 1978.
Literature/Film Quarterly (Salisbury, Maryland), vol. 10, no. 1, 1982.
Skoop (Amsterdam), vol. 22, 4 June 1986.
Literature/Film Quarterly (Salisbury, Maryland), April and July 1988.
Chase, D., ''The Pinter Principle,'' in *American Film* (Washington, D.C.), October 1990.
Films in Review (New York), vol. 43, July/August 1992.
Literature/Film Quarterly (Salisbury, Maryland), vol. 21, no. 1, 1993.
Tucker, Stephanie, ''Despair Not, Neither to Presume,'' in *Literature/Film Quarterly* (Salisbury, Maryland), vol. 24, no. 1, January 1996.
Hudgins, Christopher C., ''Lolita 1995: the Four Filmscripts,'' in *Literature/Film Quarterly* (Salisbury, Maryland), vol. 25, no. 1, January 1997.
Dodson, Mary Lynn, ''The French Lieutenant's Woman: Pinter and Reisz's Adaptation of John Fowles's Adaptation,'' in *Literature/Film Quarterly* (Salisbury, Maryland), vol. 26, no. 4, October 1998.

*   *   *

Harold Pinter began his professional career as an actor, touring the provinces with English and Irish repertory companies before achieving success as a major playwright and screenwriter. Although he has made subsequent acting appearances, generally in small roles in his own films (among them *The Servant* and *Accident*), and has acquired a strong reputation as a director of plays for the British stage, Pinter's fame owes much to his complex, nuance-charged writing for stage and screen.

In his early play *The Birthday Party*, filmed in 1968, two mysterious men terrorize a third named Stanley as he cowers in a tawdry English rooming house. The three enact a series of ritual games in an atmosphere of mounting menace, culminating in the utterly broken Stanley's removal to an unspecified destination—presumably an asylum. In post-absurdist fashion, Pinter denies his audience virtually all clarification of his characters' histories and likely futures, prompting one frustrated viewer to write: ''I would be obliged if you would kindly explain to me the meaning of your play. These are the points which I do not understand: 1. Who are the two men? 2. Where did

Stanley come from? 3. Were they all supposed to be normal? You will appreciate that without the answers to my questions, I cannot fully understand your play.'' Pinter replied: ''Dear Madam: I would be obliged if you would kindly explain to me the meaning of your letter. These are the points which I do not understand: 1. Who are you? 2. Where do you come from? 3. Are you supposed to be normal? You will understand that without the answers to my questions, I cannot fully understand your letter.'' This interchange helps to define the characteristically elusive Pinter style and attitude. Both are based on familiarity with life's perpetual uncertainty. The little dramas we observe in life, sometimes as unwilling participants, tend to occur without benefit of sequential beginning, middle, or end. People say one thing and mean another. Strangers, casual acquaintances, close family members deny us information they prefer to withhold. Bizarre events unfold without preparation. Moods change with mercurial suddenness. To live is to be continually perplexed by others.

Pinter's dramatic methods seek to reenforce such a view of life. He rejects traditional story telling structures in favor of fractured chronology and elliptical dialogue. ''The desire for verification on the part of all of us, with regard to our own experience and the experience of others, is understandable but cannot always be satisfied,'' he once wrote. ''We are also faced with the immense difficulty, if not the impossibility of verifying the past. I don't mean merely years ago, but yesterday, this morning.''

Time and memory thus serve as central Pinter subjects, functioning both technically and thematically to deny the audience the verification it instinctively desires. In *Betrayal*, for example, Pinter examines the romantic triangle that has developed among a married couple and the husband's best friend by reversing chronology and moving steadily backward in time, concluding the drama when the adulterous relationship first began, nine years before the start of the film. The backward telling of the tale radically alters the viewer's response and shifts attention from plot outcome to narrative point of view. The audience is mesmerized by its uncertainty, forced repeatedly to question who knew what about the relationship and when. Whose memory portrays events most accurately? The answer of course is no one's: ''We all interpret a common experience quite differently,'' Pinter has said. ''There's a common ground all right, but it's more like quicksand.''

Time also figures prominently in Pinter's adaptation of three difficult novels whose narrative ambiguity he reinterprets in filmic terms. In *The Go-Between* (from L. P. Hartley's novel), the past is remembered as ''a foreign country; they do things differently there.'' Here, the shifting narrative between past and present enables Pinter to emphasize the effects of cruelty so endemic to the British class system, a subject also explored in his adaptation of John Fowles's *The French Lieutenant's Woman*, a novel whose dazzling narrative pyrotechnics would appear to have rendered it undramatizable. Pinter's controversial solution rests on an alternation between Fowles's Victorian England and the enactment of that world in a film being shot in contemporary London. Actors acting in a film within the film thus become an appropriate Pinter metaphor for the invisible line between illusion and reality, with one story implicitly commenting on the other.

Pinter's characters say less than they mean as a thin veneer of civilized restraint keeps threatening to erupt into violence. In *Accident*, *Homecoming*, *Betrayal*, and other screenplays, sexual power struggles are obliquely fought in language that mocks the comedy of manners. His dialogue reads as if it were meant to be spewed, not spoken, to be articulated in tones of innuendo and menace that suggest meaning underived from the words alone. In that respect, Pinter's experience as actor and director has made a substantial if unrecognized contribution to the dynamics of his language.

Pinter also wrote the screen adaptations of novels for several films which were released in the early 1990s, including Margaret Atwood's *The Handmaid's Tale*, a feminist, Orwellian classic about a woman's ordeal under the authoritarian rule of the extreme right. He also wrote the screenplay for Ian McEwan's *The Comfort of Strangers*, the story of a young couple whose vacation in Venice evolves into a nightmare of sadomasochistic torture and murder.

Undoubtedly Pinter's greatest screenwriting challenge of the early 1990s was the offer to write the screenplay of Franz Kafka's *The Trial*. Pinter stated in 1992, that when he was first asked to adapt *The Trial*, ''I immediately said yes, since I have, more or less, been waiting for this opportunity for 45 years.'' That Pinter was greatly inspired by Kafka would seem self-evident to anyone who had studied Pinter's early works. *The Birthday Party* in particular, has often been directly compared to *The Trial* by Pinter's critics. *The Trial* is, of course, the story of Joseph K., the senior bank clerk who awakens on his 30th birthday to find himself arrested by an unknown court, for an unknown crime, from which he can never be exonerated.

The Trial was released in 1993 by Angelika Films. It was filmed in Prague and was directed by David Jones who also directed the film version of Pinter's play *Betrayal*. Overall, Pinter's adaptation is quite faithful to the novel. The novel's famous chapter ''The Cathedral'' is noticeably abridged, but this is obviously necessary due to the time constraints of the filmic form.

The colorful and beautiful backdrop created for Joseph K.'s nightmarish world is a sharp contrast to Orson Welles's 1962, futuristic black-and-white adaptation of *The Trial*. Pinter explained in an interview that the film was intended to be ''very plain without grotesqueries,'' unlike Welles's version which he described as being a ''phantasmagoria.''

The use of surreal special effects and lighting in *The Trial* would certainly have only detracted from this ultimate marriage of Kafka and Pinter. For Pinter is a dramatist and screenwriter whose gift it has been to make nightmarish worlds unfold by disrupting the ordinary, through the powers of language and silence.

—Mark W. Estrin, updated by Áine Doyle

PLANER, Franz

Cinematographer. **Nationality:** Czech. **Born:** Karlsbad (now Karlovy Vary), 29 March 1894; used the name Frank Planer in Hollywood. **Education:** Trained as photographer in Vienna. **Career:** 1910s— newsreel and still photographer, in Vienna and Paris; 1920s and 1930s—worked in German films for Emelka Company, Munich; after 1937—in Hollywood. **Died:** 10 January 1963.

Films as Cinematographer:

1912   *Der Todesritt in Riesenrad*
1920   *Der Klosterjäger* (Osten?); *Der Ochsenkrieg* (Osten)
1921   *Der Brunnen des Wahnsinns* (Ostermayr); *Die Nacht der Einbrecher* (Krafft); *Die Trommeln Asiens* (Krafft); *Die Trutze von Trutzberg* (Ostermayr)

1922　*Der Favorit der Königin* (Seitz); *Um Liebe und Thron* (Osten); *Das schwarze Gesicht* (Osten)

1924　*Die Finanzen des Grossherzogs* (*The Grand Duke's Finances*) (Murnau) (co); *Gehetzte Menschen* (Schönfelder); *Schicksal* (Basch)

1925　*Finale der Liebe* (Basch); *Der Mann seiner Frau* (Basch)

1926　*Funfuhrtee in zerin* (Morel-Molander); *Der Sohn des Hannibal* (Basch)

1927　*Die Achtzehnjährigen* (Noa); *Die Ausgestossenen* (Berger); *Einbruch* (Osten); *Das Frauenhaus von Rio* (Steinhoff); *Glanz und Elend der Kurtisanen* (Noa); *Der grosse Unbekannte* (Noa); *Die Pflicht zu schweigen* (Wilhelm); *Wie heirate ich meinen Chef* (Schall); *Alraune* (Mandrake; *Unholy Love*; *A Daughter of Destiny*) (Galeen)

1928　*Heut' spielt der Strauss* (Wiene); *Die Rothausgasse* (Oswald); *Weib in Flammen* (Reichmann); *Wolga-Wolga!* (Toujansky)

1929　*Die Flucht vor der Liebe* (Behrendt); *Frauen am Abgrund* (Jacoby); *Die Liebe der Brüder Rott* (Waschneck); *Der Narr seiner Liebe* (Tschechowa); *Stud. Chem. Helene Willfüer* (Sauer)

1930　*Die Drei von der Tankstelle* (Thiele); *Hans in allen Gassen* (Froelich); *Heute Nacht—Eventuell* (Emo); *Der Sohn der weissen Berge* (Bonnard); *Zapfenstreich am Rhein* (Speyer); *Le Chemin du paradis* (de Vaucorbeil—French version of Thiele's *Die Drei von der Tankstelle*); *La Folle Aventure* (Antoine—French version of Froelich's *Hans in allen Gassen*)

1931　*Der Herr Bürovorsteher* (Behrendt); *Der Herzog von Reichstadt* (Tourjansky); *Nie wieder Liebe* (Litvak); *Sein Scheidungsgrund* (Zeisler); *L'Aiglon* (Tourjansky); *Der Storch streikt* (Emo); *Calais-Douvre* (Boyer—French version of Litvak's *Nie weider Liebe*)

1932　*Der Prinz von Arkadien* (Hartl); *Das erste Recht des Kindes* (Wendhausen); *Die Gräfin von Monte Cristo* (Hartl); *Der schwarze Husar* (Lamprecht); *Teilnehmer antwortet nicht* (Katscher and Sorkin); *Eine Stadt steht Kopf* (Gründgens); *Le Chant du marin* (Gallone)

1933　*Der Choral von Leuthen* (Froelich); *Ihre Durchlaucht, die Verkäuferin* (Hartl); *Liebelei* (Ophüls); *Leise flehen meine Lieder* (*Unfinished Symphony*) (Forst); *Caprice de Princesse* (Clouzot—French version of Hartl's *Ihre Durchlaucht, die Verkäuferin*); *La Garrison amoureuse* (de Vaucorbeil)

1934　*Maskerade* (*Masquerade in Vienna*) (Forst); *So endete eine Liebe* (Hartl); *Les Nuits moscovites* (*Moscow Nights*) (Granowsky); *The Dictator* (*The Love Affair of a Dictator*; *Loves of a Dictator*) (Saville); *Dactylo se marie* (Pujol and May)

1935　*Casta Diva* (*The Divine Spark*) (Gallone)

1936　*Tarass Boulba* (Granowsky); *The Beloved Vagabond* (Bernhardt); *Im Sonneschein* (*Opernring*; *Thank You Madame*) (Gallone); *Premiere* (Von Bolvary); *Ave Maria* (Ophüls—short); *La Valse brillante* (Ophüls—short)

1937　*Capriolen* (Gründgens)

1938　*Holiday* (Cukor); *Girl's School* (Brahm); *Adventure in Sahara* (Lederman)

1940　*Glamour for Sale* (Lederman); *Escape to Glory* (Brahm)

1941　*The Face behind the Mask* (Florey); *Meet Boston Blackie* (Florey); *They Dare Not Love* (Whale); *Time Out for Rhythm* (Salkow); *Our Wife* (Stahl); *Sweetheart of the Campus* (Dmytryk); *Three Girls about Town* (Jason)

1942　*The Adventures of Martin Eden* (Salkow); *Harvard, Here I Come* (Landers); *The Wife Takes a Flyer* (Wallace); *Flight Lieutenant* (Salkow); *Sabotage Squad* (Landers); *The Spirit of Stanford* (Barton) (co); *Sing for Your Supper* (Barton); *Honolulu Lu* (Barton); *Canal Zone* (Landers)

1943　*The Daring Young Man* (Strayer); *Tropicana* ; *Something to Shout About* (Ratoff); *Appointment in Berlin* (Green); *My Kingdom for a Cook* (Wallace); *Destroyer* (Seiter); *The Heat's On* (Ratoff)

1944　*Once Upon a Time* (Hall); *Secret Command* (Sutherland); *Carolina Blues* (Jason); *Strange Affair* (Green)

1945　*I Love a Bandleader* (Lord); *Leave It to Blondie* (Berlin)

1946　*The Chase* (Ripley); *Snafu* (Moss); *Her Sister's Secret* (Ulmer)

1947　*The Exile* (Ophüls); ***Letter from an Unknown Woman*** (Ophüls); *One Touch of Venus* (Seiter)

1949　*Criss Cross* (Siodmak); *Once More, My Darling* (Robson); *Champion* (Robson)

1950　*711 Ocean Drive* (Newman); *Three Husbands* (Reis); *Cyrano de Bergerac* (Gordon); *Vendetta* (M. Ferrer)

1951　*Death of a Salesman* (Benedek); *The Blue Veil* (Bernhardt); *The Scarf* (*The Dungeon*) (Dupont); *Decision before Dawn* (Litvak)

1953　*Roman Holiday* (Wyler) (co); *The 5000 Fingers of Dr. T.* (Rowland); *99 River Street* (Karlson); *Bad for Each Other* (Rapper)

1954　*20,000 Leagues under the Sea* (Fleischer); *The Long Wait* (Saville); *The Caine Mutiny* (Dmytryk); *A Bullet Is Waiting* (Farrow)

1955　*Not As a Stranger* (Kramer); *The Left Hand of God* (Dmytryk)

1956　*The Mountain* (Dmytryk)

1957　*The Pride and the Passion* (Kramer)

1958　*Stage Struck* (Lumet) (co); *The Big Country* (Wyler)

1959　*The Nun's Story* (Zinnemann)

1960　*The Unforgiven* (Huston)

1961　***Breakfast at Tiffany's*** (Edwards); *King of Kings* (Ray)

1962　*The Children's Hour* (Wyler)

Publications

On PLANER: articles—

Lawton, Ralph, on *Champion* in *American Cinematographer* (Hollywood), June 1949.

American Cinematographer (Hollywood), April 1951.

Lightman, Herb A., on *Decision before Dawn* in *American Cinematographer* (Hollywood), February 1952.

Rowan, Arthur, on *The 5000 Fingers of Dr. T.* in *American Cinematographer* (Hollywood), January 1953.

On *Not As a Stranger* in *American Cinematographer* (Hollywood), July 1955.

''Shooting Black and White in Color,'' in *American Cinematographer* (Hollywood), August 1959.

Film Comment (New York), Summer 1972.

Focus on Film (London), no. 13, 1973.

*　　*　　*

Franz Planer has never achieved the critical stature of fellow European emigré cinematographers such as Karl Freund, in spite of the fact that no less a critic than Lotte Eisner placed him, along with Freund, Eugen Schüfftan, and Fritz Arno Wagner, among the greatest directors of photography in Weimar Germany. Planer's work in America is demonstrably significant and creative. Even his colleagues were unsure of what to make of the man who buried his origins under the anglicized credit title "Photographed by Frank Planer" yet whose images had a frankly expressionistic tinge redolent of his experience in Germany. Certain of Planer's projects, such as *Decision before Dawn* and *The 5000 Fingers of Dr. T*, were as genuinely experimental as anything in the commercial cinema of the postwar era, while others found such favor among industry insiders that he was nominated for five Academy Awards for cinematography. Yet even *American Cinematographer* bemusedly referred to the enigmatic Planer as "a conscientious little man" in April 1951. The answer to the mystery of Franz Planer is in fact easily solved by viewing his biography with an eye to the way he successfully fused German and American photographic traditions into a personal style.

After newsreel and still photography work, Planer became chief cameraman of the Emelka Company in Munich; it was from this base that he developed his reputation in the world of European commercial filmmaking. Yet in spite of almost constant activity, Planer worked on none of the great films of the German Expressionist canon, and this is undoubtedly a partial explanation for his critical obscurity. He *did*, however, shoot secondary works of Murnau and Galeen. Planer also shot some of the most popular films of the period, including *Die Drei von der Tankstelle*. With the coming of the Nazis to power, Planer, like others, found his German career ending.

Planer's early career in Hollywood was a strange one. Like many other European cinematographers, he was enraptured by the scale and technical sophistication of Hollywood production. It is a myth that photographers such as Planer remained glum and homesick during their stays in Hollywood, longing for European artistry in the face of American commercial concerns. Yet, it *is* true that Planer and his compatriots missed the tradition of the "Regiesitzung," or preproduction planning meeting, at which director, cinematographer, writers, designers, and even actors would debate the conceptualization of the upcoming film. Hollywood's hyperdepartmentalization defeated this slower, more democratic method, and throughout his career Planer sought other avenues for asserting preproduction input on his assignments, as well as ways of gaining greater-than-usual control over the shoot itself.

Hired by Columbia Pictures, Planer, like many of the studio's photographers, was called upon to shoot in all genres, budgets, and even structural formats. His first film in the U.S. was *Holiday*, but thereafter he spent a number of years working strictly on B-films and low-budget A-productions at Columbia. Yet even as early as *Holiday*, a Planer style is in evidence. Utilizing characteristic long or extremely long takes, Planer's camera moves easily through Stephen Goosens's glistening white settings of cavernous ballrooms and apartments with complex floorplans, becoming an intimate part of the drama. It follows crucial scenes up and down staircases, and comments on the action through exclusionary framing and staging of actors. Planer's camera, as much as Cukor's direction, is responsible for the transformation of *Holiday* from its theatrical glibness to a sophisticated comedy of class interest.

But the opportunity to do *Holiday* turned out to have been an aberration for Planer at the studio during this period, and his career reached a temporary nadir in 1945 with *Leave It to Blondie*, which restricted him to stock sets, low budgets, and series formula. Planer thus seized on his next assignment, *The Chase*, with its higher budget

and flashback structure, to create the first of his *film noir* set pieces, a pursuit through a Latin American city during carnival time. Following *The Chase*, Planer was recognized as a top-line freelance cinematographer, and helped to create some of the finest work produced by Hollywood's Germanic emigrés, working with Max Ophüls, Robert Siodmak, Edgar Ulmer, Curtis Bernhardt, and Anatole Litvak. In this period, several films stand out, but Ophüls's *Letter from an Unknown Woman* is especially rich. Planer's trademark of shooting dialogue scenes in dynamic fashion, with a moving camera often taking the place of shot-reverse shot patterning, had been in place as early as *Holiday*, and thus much of the credit for the extravagant use of these devices in the film must be assigned to Planer rather than to Ophüls, as is common in criticism about the film.

In the same period, Planer's work began to take on a poetic realist tone, influenced by the readiness of studios to permit increased location shooting. Beginning with *Criss Cross*, with its exteriors of the run-down Bunker Hill section of Los Angeles, and running through *The Nun's Story*, Planer used practical interiors and location shooting for a documentary feel, and eagerly sought out films without "superstar" actors, specifically to avoid being typed as a "glamour cinematographer." For several of his films, he also took on the task of location scouting—a further way of guaranteeing a personalized look. *Champion* and *711 Ocean Drive* were both influential arguments in their time for the aesthetics of location shooting.

This increasingly hard-edged realism, inflected with a growing use of visual irony, is an important component of Planer's work in the 1950s. However, Planer also had opportunities to reformulate an expressionist aesthetic around Hollywood conventions through his work in two fantasy films. Brought in early for the production of *The 5000 Fingers of Dr. T*, Planer brought a unique imagination to this nightmarish fantasy of a nine-year-old boy tyrannized by his piano teacher, from a scenario by Dr. Seuss. Entirely studio-shot, the film at one time utilized every soundstage on the Columbia lot for its mammoth sets. Planer devised radically new techniques, coloring his sets with light instead of paint, and utilizing experimental lighting instruments for his first film in Technicolor. His work on *20,000 Leagues under the Sea* was less spectacular but better integrated into a more standard vision of the fantasy genre. Sacrificing spectacle, using as few of the characteristically awkward Disney mattes as possible, Planer's camera focuses on the interior of the Nautilus, the story's prototype submarine. The craft appears cramped and cloistered; spiny-looking cast-iron decks and bulkheads are in view, space is clearly contiguous, and dark colors and grotesque Victorian bric-a-brac give the ship a jarring, unsettling appearance.

The Caine Mutiny fully naturalizes Planer's colorizing within a realistic genre, using light to give an explicitly ironic tint to several scenes. Planer clearly felt comfortable in new formats; from 1954 onwards, most of his work was in color, widescreen, or both. *Breakfast at Tiffany's* shows how efficiently he incorporated colorization into an ironic mode. The credit sequences of the film are shot in an unsaturated black-and-white-in-color style, while the interiors of Holly Golightly's and Paul Varjak's Manhattan apartments are done in strange, icy blues and grays, with garish red accents. These sets have an uncomfortable feel to them, accentuated by Planer's complex camera movements in closely defined and contiguous spaces. Planer also constantly interposes colored objects such as bead curtains between camera and subject in order to comment on the action, then just as suddenly removes them. Much of the action is shot from slightly too-high or too-low angles, with Holly's breakdown scene shot from a bizarre overhead perspective.

The film demonstrates that Planer's style depended as much on graphic schemes as on color, and, in fact, his style was called "black-and-white-in-color" long before such an appellation had come into general usage. Indeed, Planer returned periodically to black-and-white films, and found in the Kramer unit a suitable and hospitable home for his talents, for the company prided itself on the realism of its subjects and a lofty, high-art approach to its stories. Of his work there, *Not As a Stranger* is the clearest melding of these two aims. The film, a medical story, was shot in black and white, unusual for melodramas in this period. Kramer took realism to preposterous heights, forcing Planer to film an actual operation. This meant that standard, high wattage lamps could not be used as the heat generated would damage the tender flesh around open incisions. Planer was forced to rely on low-intensity lamps and bounced light off the reflective walls. Planer, unvanquished, used extremely fast Tri-X Pan stock to capture unusual, slow tracking movements in the operating room, making these sequences harrowing in their avoidance of traditional editing patterning in favor of suspenseful, fluid action. The rest of the film rewrites convention as well, favoring low-key lighting for the melodramatic sections, as against the glaring high-key style of the more well-known 1950s melodramas of Sirk and Minnelli.

Yet Planer's masterpiece is surely *Decision before Dawn*. Entirely location-shot, the film gave Planer his favorite ingredients in one mix: a "no-name" cast of excellent performers, months of preparation, a director (Litvak) whose visual imagination was in synch with his own, and a film with a significant moral dimension to its story line. The result is the only genuine example of an American neorealist style in the 1940s. Its photography is so striking that nearly 40 years later Francis Coppola had the film screened as an example for his cinematographer and cameramen to follow during production of *Rumblefish*.

The film was an extraordinary logistical undertaking, utilizing footage shot in 16 cities in war-ravaged Europe, including the ruins of Mannheim and Nuremberg. Completely eschewing the use of stock, process, and miniature work, Planer painstakingly supervised the pushing of the exposed footage in processing to achieve a remarkable clarity of image. "It was our aim to make a picture with all the blunt realism of a U.S. Army Signal Corps documentary," said Planer at the time, yet this claim is disingenuous, for the film has a fictional sense of irony and *trompe l'oeil* as profound as any in American film. The interiors are images of sheer devastation; no building, it seems, has been untouched by Allied bombs. Planer's camera relentlessly probes ruined castles, hospitals and inns, going up stairways, through doorways, down hallways, and into the rooms themselves, capturing a weird architecture of lavish period decor, now dilapidated, overlaid with odd trappings of military occupation. Outside, the landscape is composed of masterfully organized crowd scenes; refugees stone-facedly inhabit blasted streets, shattered bridges, and sluggish, endless truck convoys. This depiction of a society broken in spirit is a succession of set pieces, each unique in the problems confronting the cinematographer, and each a triumph for Planer.

Accounts differ, but it is likely the location-scouting trips to Europe were Planer's first visits to Germany since he had left in the mid-1930s. He had fully adopted American working methods by this time, and been fully adopted by the American industry, yet the cool detachment of the film's images suggests an artist caught between two worlds and a meditation on them both. *Decision before Dawn* is relentlessly analytical without being judgmental, nostalgic without being sentimental. It poses a moral problem through a visual lexicon, and is thus one of the great philosophical and rhetorical achievements of the American cinema.

—Kevin Jack Hagopian

PLUNKETT, Walter

Costume Designer. **Nationality:** American. **Born:** Oakland, California, 5 June 1902. **Education:** Attended the University of California, Berkeley. **Career:** Vaudeville and stock actor; designed costumes for touring vaudeville chorus; 1926–40—designer for FBO (later RKO); 1940–47—freelance designer; 1947–66—designer for MGM; also designer for Broadway shows and Metropolitan Opera productions. **Award:** Academy Award for *An American in Paris*, 1951. **Died:** 8 March 1982.

Films as Costume Designer:

1926 *Ain't Love Funny?* (Andrews); *One Minute to Play* (Wood); *Red Hot Hoofs* (Delacy); *A Regular Scout* (Kirkland)

1927 *Boy Rider* (L. King); *Clancy's Kosher Wedding* (Gillstrom); *The Gingham Girl* (Kirkland); *Her Summer Hero* (Dugan); *Legionnaires in Paris* (Gillstrom); *Lightning Lariat* (DeLacy); *The Magic Garden* (Meehan); *Shanghaied* (R. Ince); *Hard-Boiled Haggerty* (Brabin); *The Bandit's Son* (Fox)

1928 *Sinners in Love* (Melford); *Bantam Cowboy* (L. King); *Captain Careless* (Storm); *Chicago after Midnight* (R. Ince); *Circus Kid* (Seitz); *Headin' for Danger* (Bradbury); *Hey Rube!* (Seitz); *Hit of the Show* (R. Ince); *Phantom of the Range* (Dugan); *Sally of the Scandals* (Shores); *Son of the Golden West* (Forde); *Tropic Madness* (Vignola); *Wallflowers* (Meehan); *When the Law Rides* (DeLacy); *Wizard of the Saddle* (Clark); *Stolen Love* (Shores); *Stocks and Blondes* (Murphy)

1929 *The Red Sword* (Vignola); *Love in the Desert* (Melford); *Air Legion* (Glennon); *Amazing Vagabond* (Fox); *The Big Diamond Robbery* (Forde); *Come and Get It* (Fox); *Dance Hall* (M. Brown); *Delightful Rogue* (Shores); *Freckled Rascal* (L. King); *Gun Law* (DeLacy or Burch); *Half Marriage* (Cowen); *Hardboiled* (R. Ince); *The Jazz Age* (Shores); *Laughing at Death* (Fox); *The Little Savage* (L. King); *Night Parade* (St. Clair); *Outlawed* (Fogwell); *The Pride of Pawnee* (DeLacy); *Seven Keys to Baldpate* (Barker); *Street Girl* (Ruggles); *Syncopation* (Glennon); *Tanned Legs* (Neilan); *Vagabond Lover* (Neilan); *The Very Idea* (Rosson); *Voice of the Storm* (Shores); *Queen Kelly* (Von Stroheim); *The Woman I Love* (Melford)

1930 *The Case of Sergeant Grischa* (Brenon); *The Cuckoos* (Sloane); *Dixiana* (Reed); *The Fall Guy* (Pearce); *Half Shot at Sunrise* (Sloane); *Lawful Larceny* (Sherman); *Leathernecking* (Cline); *Love Comes Along* (Julian); *Midnight Mystery* (Seitz); *Second Wife* (Mack)

1931 *Cimarron* (Ruggles)

1932 *Night after Night* (Mayo); *The Conquerors* (Wellman); *The Phantom of Crestwood* (Ruben); *Secrets of the French Police* (Sutherland)

Walter Plunkett with Gene Tierney

1933   *The Past of Mary Holmes* (Thompson); *Double Harness* (Cromwell); *Morning Glory* (Sherman); *The Right to Romance* (Santell); *Ace of Aces* (Ruben); *Aggie Appleby, Maker of Men* (Sandrich); *Ann Vickers* (Cromwell) (co); *Blind Adventure* (Schoedsack); *Chance at Heaven* (Seiter); *Christopher Strong* (Arzner) (co); *Cross Fire* (Brower); *Emergency Call* (Cahn); *The Great Jasper* (Ruben); *Lucky Devils* (R. Ince); *Melody Cruise* (Sandrich); *Midshipman Jack* (Cabanne); *No Marriage Ties* (Ruben); *No Other Woman* (Ruben); *One Man's Journey* (Robertson); *Professional Sweetheart* (Seiter); *Rafter Romance* (Seiter); *Scarlet River* (Brower); *The Silver Cord* (Cromwell); *Sweepings* (Cromwell); *Tomorrow at Eight* (Enright); *Little Women* (Cukor); *Flying Down to Rio* (Freeland) (co); **King Kong** (Cooper and Schoedsack)

1934   *The Little Minister* (Wallace); *Spitfire* (Cromwell); *Finishing School* (Tuchock and Nicholls); *Sing and Like It* (Seiter); *Where Sinners Meet* (Ruben); *Stingaree* (Wellman); *The Life of Vergie Winters* (Santell); *Bachelor Bait* (Stevens); *Cockeyed Cavaliers* (Sandrich); *Strictly Dynamite* (Nugent); *The Age of Innocence* (Moeller); *The Fountain* (Cromwell);

His Greatest Gamble (Robertson); *We're Rich Again* (Seiter); *Down to Their Last Yacht* (*Hawaiian Nights*) (Sloane); *The Gay Divorcee* (*The Gay Divorce*) (Sandrich); *Anne of Green Gables* (Nicholls); *Kentucky Kernels* (Stevens); *The Silver Streak* (Atkins); *Wednesday's Child* (Robertson); *By Your Leave* (Corrigan); *Dangerous Corner* (Rosen); *Lightning Strikes Twice* (Holmes); *The Crime Doctor* (Robertson); *Gridiron Flash* (Tyron); *A Hat, a Coat, and a Glove* (Miner); *Keep 'em Rolling* (Archainbaud); *Long Lost Father* (Schoedsack); *Man of Two Worlds* (Ruben); *Meanest Gal in Town* (Mack); *Of Human Bondage* (Cromwell); *Romance in Manhattan* (Roberts); *Success at Any Price* (Ruben); *Their Big Moment* (Cruze); *This Man Is Mine* (Cromwell); *Woman in the Dark* (Rosen)

1935   *Mary of Scotland* (Ford); *Hooray for Love* (W. Lang); ***The Informer*** (Ford); *The Arizonian* (C. Vidor); *Jalna* (Cromwell); *Alice Adams* (Stevens); *Hot Tip* (McCarey and Gleason); *Freckles* (Killy and Hamilton); *His Family Tree* (C. Vidor); *The Three Musketeers* (Lee); *The Rainmakers* (Guiol); *To Beat the Band* (Stoloff); *Hi, Gaucho!* (Atkins); *The Return of Peter Grimm* (Nicholls); *Annie Oakley*

(Stevens); *Another Face* (Cabanne); *Captain Hurricane* (Robertson); *Chasing Yesterday* (Nicholls); *A Dog of Flanders* (Sloman); *Enchanted April* (Beaumont); *Grand Old Girl* (Robertson); *Murder on a Honeymoon* (Corrigan); *Seven Keys to Baldpate* (Hamilton and Killy); *Strangers All* (C. Vidor); *Sylvia Scarlett* (Cukor) (co); *Village Tale* (Cromwell)

1936   *The Plough and the Stars* (Ford); *The Soldier and the Lady* (*Michael Strogoff*) (Nicholls); *Chatterbox* (Nicholls)

1937   *Quality Street* (Stevens); *The Woman I Love* (*The Woman Between*) (Litvak); *Nothing Sacred* (Wellman) (co); *The Adventures of Tom Sawyer* (Taurog)

1939   *Allegheny Uprising* (*The First Rebel*) (Seiter); *Stagecoach* (Ford); *The Story of Vernon and Irene Castle* (Potter); **Gone with the Wind** (Fleming); *The Hunchback of Notre Dame* (Dieterle); *Abe Lincoln in Illinois* (Cromwell); *Vigil in the Night* (Stevens)

1940   *Captain Caution* (Wallace)

1941   *The Corsican Brothers* (Ratoff); *Lydia* (Duvivier) (co); *Ladies in Retirement* (C. Vidor); *Sundown* (Hathaway); *Go West, Young Lady* (Strayer); *Lady for a Night* (Jason)

1942   *To Be or Not to Be* (Lubitsch)

1943   *Commandoes Strike at Dawn* (Farrow); *In Old Oklahoma* (*The War of the Wildcats*) (Rogell); *The Heat's On* (*Tropicana*) (Ratoff); *Knickerbocker Holiday* (H. Brown)

1944   *Can't Help Singing* (Ryan); *A Song to Remember* (C. Vidor) (co)

1945   *Along Came Jones* (Heisler)

1946   *Song of Love* (C. Brown) (co); *Because of Him* (Wallace) (co)

1947   *My Brother Talks to Horses* (Zinnemann); *Duel in the Sun* (K. Vidor); *Sea of Grass* (Kazan); *Summer Holiday* (Mamoulian) (co); *Green Dolphin Street* (Saville) (co); *Fiesta* (Thorpe) (co)

1948   *The Three Musketeers* (Sidney); *The Kissing Bandit* (Benedek); *Little Women* (LeRoy)

1949   *The Secret Garden* (Wilcox); *Madame Bovary* (LeRoy) (co); *That Forsyte Woman* (*The Forsyte Sage*) (Bennett) (co); **Adam's Rib** (Cukor); *Ambush* (Wood); *Black Hand* (Thorpe); *The Outriders* (Rowland)

1950   *Stars in My Crown* (Tourneur); *Annie Get Your Gun* (Sidney) (co); *Devil's Doorway* (A. Mann); *Father of the Bride* (Minnelli) (co); *The Happy Years* (Wellman); *Summer Stock* (Walters) (co); *Toast of New Orleans* (Taurog) (co); *King Solomon's Mines* (Bennett and Marton); *The Miniver Story* (Potter) (co); *Two Weeks with Love* (Rowland) (co); *The Magnificent Yankee* (*The Man with Thirty Sons*) (J. Sturges); *Payment on Demand* (Bernhardt) (co); *Vengeance Valley* (Thorpe); *Soldiers Three* (Garnett); *Mr. Imperium* (*You Belong to My Heart*) (Hartman)

1951   *Kind Lady* (J. Sturges) (co); *Man with a Cloak* (Markle) (co); *Show Boat* (Sidney); *The Law and the Lady* (Knopf) (co); **An American in Paris** (Minnelli) (co); *Across the Wide Missouri* (Wellman); *Westward the Women* (Wellman); **Singin' in the Rain** (Kelly and Donen)

1952   *Carbine Williams* (Thorpe); *Plymouth Adventure* (C. Brown); *The Prisoner of Zenda* (Thorpe); *Million Dollar Mermaid* (*One Piece Bathing Suit*) (LeRoy) (co)

1953   *Young Bess* (Sidney); *Scandal at Scourie* (Negulesco); *Ride, Vaquero!* (Farrow); *The Actress* (Cukor); *All the Brothers Were Valiant* (Thorpe); *Kiss Me Kate* (Sidney)

1954   *Seven Brides for Seven Brothers* (Donen); *The Student Prince* (Thorpe); *Valley of the Kings* (Pirosh); *Athena* (Thorpe)

(co); *Deep in My Heart* (Donen) (co); *Jupiter's Darling* (Sidney) (co); *The Glass Slipper* (Walters) (co); *Many Rivers to Cross* (Rowland)

1955   *Moonfleet* (F. Lang); *The Scarlet Coat* (J. Sturges); *The King's Thief* (Leonard); *Diane* (Miller); *Forbidden Planet* (Wilcox) (co); *Tribute to a Bad Man* (Wise)

1956   *Lust for Life* (Minnelli); *The Wings of Eagles* (Ford); *The Fastest Gun Alive* (Rouse)

1957   *Gun Glory* (Rowland); *Raintree County* (Dmytryk); *The Brothers Karamazov* (Brooks); *Merry Andrew* (Kidd)

1958   *The Sheepman* (Marshall); *The Law and Jake Wade* (J. Sturges); *Some Came Running* (Minnelli)

1959   *Home from the Hill* (Minnelli)

1960   *Pollyanna* (Swift); *Bells Are Ringing* (Minnelli); *Cimarron* (A. Mann)

1961   *Pocketful of Miracles* (Capra) (co); *The Four Horsemen of the Apocalypse* (Minnelli) (co)

1962   *Two Weeks in Another Town* (Minnelli)

1963   *How the West Was Won* (Ford, Marshall, and Hathaway)

1965   *Marriage on the Rocks* (Donohue)

1966   *Seven Women* (Ford)

Publications

By PLUNKETT: article—

The Velvet Light Trap (Madison, Wisconsin), Spring 1978.

On PLUNKETT: articles—

Films in Review (New York), January 1973, additions in August-September 1973 and December 1974.

Chierichetti, David, in *Hollywood Costume Design*, New York, 1976.

Leese, Elizabeth, in *Costume Design in the Movies*, New York, 1976.

LaVine, W. Robert, in *In a Glamorous Fashion*, New York, 1980.

American Classic Screen (Shawnee Mission, Kansas), July-August 1982.

American Classic Screen (Shawnee Mission, Kansas), September-October 1982.

*   *   *

Walter Plunkett lacked the knack of high couture. He could not compete in the world of super-rich chic with Paris-trained Adrian or Travis Banton. Instead, Plunkett excelled in designing glorious garments of days gone by. With the fervor of a 19th-century archeologist, Plunkett worked to make his name virtually synonymous with the "period" picture.

Originally an actor, Plunkett prepared as if trained by Stanislavsky. Endowing his costumes with presence and character, even the humblest handmade, as seen in *Little Women*, was seamed with integrity. Plunkett worked especially well with Katharine Hepburn at RKO because both artists aimed for veracity in character and era. Because Plunkett's dresses were assuredly accurate even in the way in which they were made, Hepburn rehearsed in costume to achieve proper movement. She insisted on learning how to maneuver hoops and how to turn her head in stiffly starched ruffs as if such movements were natural to her in order to insure that costume and characterization became one. Plunkett also was responsible for the Fred Astaire-Ginger Rogers look. Their dance attire, integral to that ''carefree'' image, depended on Plunkett's elegant lines, as they inhibited or released areas of mobility. Astaire, of course, insisted on comfort and optimum freedom. Rogers preferred glamour and eye-catching gimmicks.

For David Selznick's *Gone with the Wind*, Plunkett chronicled the fall and rebirth of the Deep South through Scarlett O'Hara's well-researched wardrobe, which marked her passage from selfish innocence to hardened maturity. For example, the famous ''dining-room curtains'' dress, ornamented with jaunty tassels and a smart, one-shoulder cape, illustrated Scarlett's spunky calculation in the face of adversity. As one of the first technicolor movies, *Gone with the Wind* dazzled with picture-postcard color. Plunkett had already worked within the limited range of the two-color process at RKO, but now he filled the screen with sapphire, dusty rose, antique blue, claret red, and infinite shades of green. Still remembered today, the gowns of this film reflected an emerging post-Depression fashion trend. However, the Second World War aborted the cinch waist and wide, fabric-consuming skirt symbolic of prosperity and the romantic ideal of womanhood; only after the war were they resurrected in Dior's postwar ''New Look.''

Plunkett's later pictures echoed some interesting modern trends. His *American in Paris* sequence depicted the artists' ball in abstract blacks and whites, more like the flamboyant visions of Adrian than traditional Plunkett. They splashed the screen abstractly as if flung from Jackson Pollock's paint brush.

Throughout the 1950s, Plunkett continued his successful ''period'' creations. At the same time, he began to mimic the very popular culture that he and other designers had created. His mannerish garb for Judy Garland's *Summer Stock*, for example, recalls Travis Banton's collaborations with Marlene Dietrich. Plunkett's greatest homage to the silver screen however was in *Singin' in the Rain*. Exaggerated American motifs paid glorious tribute to those brash Hollywood musicals of his earlier days in the business.

—Edith C. Lee

POLGLASE, Van Nest

Art Director. **Nationality:** American. **Born:** Brooklyn, New York, 25 August 1898. **Education:** Studied architecture, Beaux Arts, New York. **Career:** Architect with Berg and Orchard, New York; 1919—followed his architectural colleague Wiard Ihnen to Famous Players-Lasky; 1927–32—worked for Paramount; 1932–42—at RKO; also worked for Columbia. **Died:** 20 December 1968.

Films as Art Director:

1925   *A Kiss in the Dark* (Tuttle); *Lovers in Quarantine* (Tuttle); *Stage Struck* (Dwan)

1928   *The Magnificent Flirt* (D'Arrast)

1929   *Untamed* (Conway)

1933   *Bed of Roses* (LaCava); *Little Women* (Cukor); *Morning Glory* (L. Sherman); *Ann Vickers* (Cromwell); *Flying Down to Rio* (Freeland); *The Past of Mary Holmes* (Thompson and Vorkapich); *Melody Cruise* (Sandrich); *Emergency Call* (Cahn); *No Marriage Ties* (Ruben); *One Man's Journey* (Robertson); *Midshipman Jack* (Cabanne); *Ace of Aces* (Ruben); *Chance at Heaven* (Seiter); *After Tonight* (Archainbaud); *Professional Sweetheart* (Seiter); *Christopher Strong* (Arzner); *Headline Shooter* (Brower); *If I Were Free* (Nugent); **King Kong** (Cooper and Schoedsack)

1934   *Romance in Manhattan* (Roberts); *Finishing School* (Tuchock and Nicholls); *Rafter Romance* (Seiter); *This Man Is Mine* (Cromwell); *Of Human Bondage* (Cromwell); *The Lost Patrol* (Ford); *Spitfire* (Cromwell); *The Gay Divorcee* (*The Gay Divorce*) (Sandrich); *The Fountain* (Cromwell); *Bachelor Bait* (Stevens); *Long Lost Father* (Schoedsack); *The Little Minister* (Wallace)

1935   *Roberta* (Seiter); *Village Tale* (Cromwell); *Jalna* (Cromwell); *The Last Days of Pompeii* (Schoedsack and Cooper); *I Dream Too Much* (Cromwell); *In Person* (Seiter); *Star of Midnight* (Roberts); *Break of Hearts* (Moeller); **The Informer** (Ford); *The Return of Peter Grimm* (Nicholls); *Sylvia Scarlett* (Cukor); *Laddie* (Stevens); *The Nitwits* (Stevens); **Top Hat** (Sandrich); *Alice Adams* (Stevens); *Annie Oakley* (Stevens); *She* (Pichel and Holden); *The Three Musketeers* (Lee); *Seven Keys to Baldpate* (Hamilton and Killy)

1936   *Winterset* (Santell); *Mary of Scotland* (Ford); *Swing Time* (Stevens); *The Plough and the Stars* (Ford); *Follow the Fleet* (Sandrich); *Mummy's Boys* (Guiol); *Muss 'em Up* (C. Vidor); *The Ex-Mrs. Bradford* (Roberts); *The Lady Consents* (Roberts); *A Woman Rebels* (Sandrich); *The Big Game* (Nicholls and Killy)

1937   *Hideaway* (Rosson); *The Big Shot* (Killy); *Fight for Your Lady* (Stoloff); *Forty Naughty Girls* (Cline); *Living on Love* (Landers); *Meet the Missus* (Santley); *Music for Madame* (Blystone); *New Faces of 1937* (Jason); *On Again—Off Again* (Cline); *Sea Devils* (Stoloff); *Shall We Dance* (Sandrich); *Stage Door* (LaCava); *Super Sleuth* (Stoloff); *The Toast of New York* (Lee); *Too Many Wives* (Holmes); *The Woman I Love* (Litvak), *Hitting a New High* (Walsh); *A Damsel in Distress* (Stevens)

1938   *Affairs of Annabel* (Stoloff); *Carefree* (Sandrich); *I'm from the City* (Holmes); *The Law West of Tombstone* (Tryon); *A Man to Remember* (Kanin); *Room Service* (Seiter); *The Saint in New York* (Holmes); *Tarnished Angel* (Goodwins); *Vivacious Lady* (Stevens); *Condemned Women* (Landers); *Having a Wonderful Time* (Santell); **Bringing Up Baby** (Hawks)

1939   *In Name Only* (Cromwell); *Love Affair* (McCarey); *The Story of Vernon and Irene Castle* (Potter); *Bachelor Mother* (Kanin); *Fifth Avenue Girl* (La Cava); *Allegheny Uprising* (Seiter); *Five Came Back* (Farrow); *The Girl from Mexico* (Goodwins); *The Great Man Votes* (Kanin); *Gunga Din* (Stevens); *Mexican Spitfire* (Goodwins); *The Hunchback of Notre Dame* (Dieterle); *Reno* (Farrow); *Panama Lady* (Hively); *That's Right—You're Wrong* (Butler)

1940   *Abe Lincoln in Illinois* (Cromwell); *Primrose Path* (La Cava); *They Knew What They Wanted* (Kanin); *Vigil in the Night* (Stevens); *Curtain Call* (Woodruff); **Dance, Girl, Dance** (Arzner); *I'm Still Alive* (Reis); *Kitty Foyle* (Wood); *Laddie* (Hively); *Let's Make Music* (Goodwins); *Lucky Partners* (Milestone); *Married and in Love* (Farrow); *Mexican Spitfire Out West* (Goodwins); *My Favorite Wife* (Kanin); *Millionaire Playboy* (Goodwins); *Millionaires in Prison*

681

(McCarey); *One Crowded Night* (Reis); *Pop Always Pays* (Goodwins); *The Stranger on the Third Floor* (Ingster); *Sued for Libel* (Goodwins); *Tom Brown's School Days* (Stevenson); *Too Many Girls* (Abbott); *Wagon Train* (Killy); *You Can't Fool Your Wife* (McCarey); *You'll Find Out* (Butler)

1941   *All That Money Can Buy* (Dieterle); *The Bandit Trail* (Killy); **Citizen Kane** (Welles); *Cyclone on Horseback* (Killy); *The Gay Falcon* (Reis); *Look Who's Laughing* (Dwan); *Mr. and Mrs. Smith* (Hitchcock); *Suspicion* (Hitchcock); *Tom, Dick, and Harry* (Kanin)

1943   *What a Woman!* (Cummings); *The Fallen Sparrow* (Wallace)

1944   *Together Again* (C. Vidor); *Kiss and Tell* (Wallace); *She Wouldn't Say Yes* (Hall)

1946   **Gilda** (C. Vidor); *The Thrill of Brazil* (Simon)

1949   *The Crooked Way* (Florey)

1950   *The Admiral Was a Lady* (Rogell); *The Fireball* (Garnett); *The Man Who Cheated Himself* (Feist); *Johnny One-Eye* (Florey); *Never Fear (The Young Lovers)* (Lupino)

1954   *Silver Lode* (Florey); *Passion* (Dwan); *Cattle Queen of Montana* (Dwan)

1955   *Escape to Burma* (Dwan); *Pearl of the South Pacific* (Dwan); *Tennessee's Partner* (Dwan)

1956   *Slightly Scarlet* (Dwan)

1957   *The River's Edge* (Dwan)

Publications

By POLGLASE: article—

"The Studio Art Director," in *How Talkies Are Made*, edited by Joe Bonica, Hollywood, 1930.

On POLGLASE: articles—

Spiegel, Ellen, in *The Velvet Light Trap* (Madison, Wisconsin), Fall 1973.
In *The Art of Hollywood*, edited by John Hambley, London, 1979.

*   *   *

Along with Cedric Gibbons at MGM, Van Nest Polglase was Hollywood's most influential supervising art director, responsible for the look of RKO's product from 1932 to 1942. Disputes linger over the precise nature and extent of Polglase's contribution to those films on which he received credit for art direction since they were most often collaborations, though it is generally conceded that he had the first and last say on all designs. However, little doubt remains that it was Polglase, with his scrupulous attention to detail, who was responsible for the eclectic look of the RKO product, a look which continued for some time after his departure. Whether it was one of the vast glossy spaces of an Astaire-Rogers musical, the moody streets of a thriller, or a stone and shingle structure for a historical drama, the RKO films under Polglase were redolent with that most sought after but elusive quality in production design—atmosphere.

Polglase practiced a perfectionism that gave his historical sets an accuracy which extended beyond the creations of other studios. The RKO-built stone and thatch Paris for *The Hunchback of Notre Dame*

exemplifies Polglase's attention to detail and his proclivity for designing sets around large open spaces, as evidenced by the cathedral's interior and the public square in front of the structure. Polglase also held a latent inclination for expressionism, a predisposition which surfaced in his foggy, angular Dublin for *The Informer*, as well as in *The Stranger on the Third Floor* and *Citizen Kane*.

Polglase's best-known and most visually exciting designs were those for RKO's series of Fred Astaire-Ginger Rogers musicals. Along with his associate Carroll Clark, Polglase supervised the creation of a series of sets that were, and continue to be, the hallmark of cosmopolitan design for the 1930s. The Big White Set, or BWS, became the centerpiece for these films, a massive space of elegant white that could accommodate both the practical concerns of the dance and the public's demand for fantasy. Over the course of the series Polglase's vision swept from the fantastic but functional to the abstract, and eventually touched down on the wholly realistic. The growing love affair between man and machine found its artistic outlet in the Art Deco movement and, in Deco, Polglase found the ideal counterpart to the choreography of Astaire and Hermes Pan and the lightweight scripts. The choices of material, including glass, chrome, and compounds like celluloid and bakelite met themes of mechanics and speed to produce generally smooth geometric forms. Polglase's use of Deco coupled with the free-flowing moves of the dance team gave the films a seamless, streamlined quality.

Beginning with *Flying Down to Rio* Polglase established the tenor of the series by employing motifs of movement and flight in the production design. Airplanes, butterflies, and even a bandstand in the form of a hot air balloon transmit the concept of motion and are reinforced by the sweeping rails and staircases that abound on the sets. Curved chromium rails, consisting of double or triple parallel lines, served Polglase with a consistent metaphor for movement through most of the film of the series. In *The Gay Divorcee* Polglase employs two variations of Deco. The first is the neo-classicism evidenced by the Greco-Roman busts, urns, and multi-square patterns. The second variation is the strictly abstract use of curvilinear form such as the walls along the esplanade, bisected by a set of dual horizontal lines which in turn are interrupted by a series of circular windows set in square frames. Refining and expanding the neo-classical Deco for *Top Hat*, Polglase removed the complexity from classical forms such as the scroll and the arch and then expanded them to a gigantic scope for the creation of the fantastic Venice set. Like the plot of the film, the set bore no resemblance to reality, and pushed the level of abstraction beyond that of the earlier movies. The same gigantism infected the Polglase-supervised sets for Xanadu in *Citizen Kane*.

In *Shall We Dance* Polglase reached the ultimate level of abstraction culminating in sets that were both outlandish and the epitome of Art Deco. For the engine room of the *S.S. Queen Anne* where Astaire performs "Slap That Bass," all relation to reality was dismissed. The vast space was turned into a sea of stylized white and chrome cylinders, mechanical fittings and pumping arms. The mechanisms were spread over a reflective bakelite floor and multiple levels were joined by sweeping gangways topped with razor-sharp silver rails.

After attaining the peak of abstraction the only direction left was realism. *Carefree* carried Astaire and Rogers through sets that were, for the first time, based largely on reality and which made use more of natural materials like wood and stone with a few Deco motives added for flair. The last film in the RKO series, *The Story of Vernon and Irene Castle*, returned the team firmly to earth with its pre-war setting and basis in biographical fact.

Polglase utilized the Deco concept of "total design" through the Astaire-Rogers series. Design motifs carried over into all phases of the production, such as the repetition of line in one of Alice Brady's dresses in *The Gay Divorcee*, which echoed a feature used throughout the film. Several of Polglase's favorite motifs return in film after film.

Increasing problems with alcoholism led to Polglase's dismissal from RKO in 1942 and to a series of freelance positions. He served as production designer for a number of notable films, including a series of eight Allan Dwan movies in the 1950s. Even though he never again had the money or the resources at his disposal that he controlled during his tenure at RKO, Polglase continued to develop worthy designs, and his influence on RKO resonated throughout the 1940s.

—Eric Schaefer

POLITO, Sol

Cinematographer. **Nationality:** American. **Born:** Palermo, Sicily, 1892; emigrated to New York at an early age. **Education:** Attended schools in New York. **Career:** Still photographer, then laboratory and camera assistant; 1917—first film as cinematographer, *Queen X*; worked for several studios, then for Warner Brothers in 1930s and 1940s. **Died:** In 1960.

Films as Cinematographer:

1914 *Rip Van Winkle* (asst)
1916 *The Sins of Society* (asst); *The World against Him* (Crane) (asst)
1917 *Queen X* (O'Brien); *Her Second Husband* (Henderson)
1918 *The Imposter* (Henderson); *Who Loved Him Best* (O'Brien); *Her Husband's Honor* (B. King); *Treason* (B. King)
1919 *What Love Forgives* (Vekroff); *The Love Defender* (Johnson); *Are You Legally Married?* (Thornby); *Bill Apperson's Boy* (Kirkwood); *Burglar by Proxy* (Dillon); *Soldiers of Fortune* (Dwan); *Should a Woman Tell?* (J. Ince)
1920 *Alias Jimmy Valentine* (Karger); *Price of Redemption* (Fitzgerald)
1921 *The Roof Tree* (Dillon); *Misleading Lady* (Irving)
1922 *Trimmed* (Pollard); *The Loaded Door* (Pollard); *Strength of the Pines* (Lewis) (co)
1923 *Mighty Lak' a Rose* (Carewe); *The Girl of the Golden West* (Carewe) (co); *The Badman* (Carewe); *Bishop of the Ozarks* (Fox)
1924 *Why Men Leave Home* (Stahl); *The Lightning Rider* (Ingraham); *Roaring Rails* (Forman); *The Siren of Seville* (Stromberg and Storm); *A Café in Cairo* (Withey); *The Flaming Forties* (Forman)
1925 *Beyond the Border* (Dunlap); *Soft Shoes* (Ingraham); *The People vs. Nancy Preston* (Forman); *The Crimson Runner* (Forman); *Silent Sanderson* (Dunlap); *The Bad Lands* (Henderson); *Paint and Powder* (Stromberg)
1926 *Driftin' Thru* (Dunlap); *The Seventh Bandit* (Dunlap); *Senor Daredevil* (Rogell); *The Frontier Trail* (Dunlap); *Satan Town* (Mortimer); *The Unknown Cavalier* (Rogell)

1927 *The Overland Trail* (Dunlap); *Somewhere in Sonora* (Rogell); *The Land beyond the Law* (H. Brown); *Lonesome Ladies* (Henabery); *Hard Boiled Haggerty* (Czabin); *Gun Gospel* (H. Brown)
1928 *The Shepherd of the Hills* (Rogell); *Burning Daylight* (Brabin); *The Hawk's Nest* (Christensen); *Heart to Heart* (Beaudine); *Show Girl* (Santell); *Burning Bridges* (Hogan); *The Border Patrol* (Hogan); *The Haunted House* (Christensen)
1929 *Scarlet Seas* (Dillon); *Seven Footprints to Satan* (Christensen); *House of Horror* (Christensen) (co); *Broadway Babies* (LeRoy); *The Man and the Moment* (Fitzmaurice); *Twin Beds* (Santell); *The Isle of Lost Ships* (Willat); *Paris* (Badger)
1930 *Girl of the Golden West* (Dillon); *Playing Around* (LeRoy); *No, No Nanette* (Badger); *Show Girl in Hollywood* (LeRoy); *Numbered Men* (LeRoy); *The Widow from Chicago* (Cline); *Madonna of the Streets* (Robertson)
1931 *Going Wild* (Seiter); *The Hot Heiress* (Badger); *Woman Hungry* (Badger) (co); *Upper Underworld* (Lee); *Big Business Girl* (Seiter); *The Bargain* (Milton); *Five Star Final* (LeRoy); *The Ruling Voice* (Lee); *Local Boy Makes Good* (LeRoy); *Suicide Fleet* (Rogell)
1932 *Union Depot* (Green); *Fireman, Save My Child* (Bacon); *It's Tough to Be Famous* (Green); *Two Seconds* (LeRoy); *Dark Horse* (Green); *Blessed Event* (Del Ruth); *Three on a Match* (LeRoy); ***I Am a Fugitive from a Chain Gang*** (LeRoy)
1933 ***42nd Street*** (Bacon); *The Picture Snatcher* (Gering); *Mind Reader* (Del Ruth); *Gold Diggers of 1933* (LeRoy)
1934 *Hi, Nellie* (LeRoy); *Dark Hazard* (Green); *Wonder Bar* (Bacon); *Dr. Monica* (Keighley); *Madame DuBarry* (Dieterle); *Flirtation Walk* (Borzage) (co)
1935 *Sweet Adeline* (LeRoy); *Go into Your Dance* (Mayo) (co); *The Woman in Red* (Florey); *The G-Men* (Keighley); *In Caliente* (Bacon) (co); *Shipmates Forever* (Borzage); *Frisco Kid* (Bacon)
1936 *The Petrified Forest* (Mayo), *Colleen* (Green) (co); *Sons o' Guns* (Bacon); *The Charge of the Light Brigade* (Curtiz) (co); *Three Men on a Horse* (LeRoy)
1937 *Ready, Willing, and Able* (Enright); *The Prince and the Pauper* (Keighley); *Varsity Show* (Keighley)
1938 *Gold Is Where You Find It* (Curtiz); ***The Adventures of Robin Hood*** (Curtiz and Keighley) (co); *Gold Diggers in Paris* (Enright) (co); *Boy Meets Girl* (Bacon); *Angels with Dirty Faces* (Curtiz); *Valley of the Giants* (Keighley) (co)
1939 *Dodge City* (Curtiz); *You Can't Get Away with Murder* (Seiler); *The Private Lives of Elizabeth and Essex* (Curtiz) (co); *Four Wives* (Curtiz); *Confessions of a Nazi Spy* (Litvak)
1940 *Virginia City* (Curtiz); *The Sea Hawk* (Curtiz); *City for Conquest* (Litvak) (co); *Sante Fe Trail* (Curtiz)
1941 *Navy Blues* (Bacon) (co); *The Sea Wolf* (Curtiz); *Sergeant York* (Hawks) (co)
1942 *Captains of the Clouds* (Curtiz) (co); *The Gay Sisters* (Rapper); ***Now, Voyager*** (Rapper)
1943 *This Is the Army* (Curtiz) (co); *Old Acquaintance* (V. Sherman)
1944 *The Adventures of Mark Twain* (Rapper); *Arsenic and Old Lace* (Capra)
1945 *The Corn Is Green* (Rapper); *Rhapsody in Blue* (Rapper) (co)
1946 *Cinderella Jones* (Berkeley); *A Stolen Life* (Bernhardt) (co); *Cloak and Dagger* (F. Lang)

1947   *The Long Night* (Litvak); *Escape Me Never* (Godfrey); *Voice of the Turtle* (Rapper)
1948   *Sorry, Wrong Number* (Litvak)
1949   *Anna Lucasta* (Rapper)

Publications

On POLITO: book—

Lazarou, George A., *Images in Low Key: Cinematographer Sol Polito A.S.C.*, Athens, 1985.

On POLITO: articles—

Film Comment (New York), Summer 1972.
Focus on Film (London), no. 13, 1973.
Reid, J.H., and G. Aachen, "*Captains of the Clouds*," in *Reid's Film Index* (Wyong, New South Wales), no. 24, 1996.

*   *   *

Like most of the technicians who created collectively, if unself-consciously, what is now known as the "classic Hollywood style," Sol Polito received little formal training in his craft, but instead learned the intricacies of cinematography on the job, first as an assistant during a three-year apprenticeship and then as head camera-man. If Polito was hardly an artist whose innovations inspired others, even as he broke with established practices, he was something much more valuable in the factory system of film production that emerged with the vertical integration of the studios in the twenties and the incredible expansion of the medium: a craftsman with a deep and abiding interest in a job well-done who was eager to create the best possible product by following industry guidelines even as he perfected their application.

The studio system in general suited Polito's temperament and work ethic; it is no accident that he thrived in the rather authoritarian setting of Warner Brothers, where studio head Jack Warner was notorious for demanding efficiency, competence, and fiscal responsibility (meaning, of course, no extra expense that did not justify itself in the finished product). As a studio technician, Polito found it necessary to work on a wide variety of projects in the different genres Warners then specialized in, most particularly what may be best described as the crime melodrama—gritty, hard-hitting pictures often based on events taken directly from yesterday's headlines. For these films, Polito and the other chief cinematographer at Warners, Tony Gaudio, devised an unglamorized look, not softened by flattering lighting effects, that made much use of the chiaroscuro contrasts between dark and light that were a heritage of German Expressionism. This style is the ancestor of the film noir cinematography that emerged to popularity in the late forties, an evolution based to some degree on technical advances (e.g., faster film stock and deep focus techniques) and a more thoroughgoing interest in realism promoted by wartime filmmaking and postwar developments abroad. Polito's work for the classic Warners crime melodrama *I Am a Fugitive from a Chain Gang*, however, bears comparison with that later style in its outstanding, expressive effects—most memorably, an overall somberness to which director Mervyn LeRoy's effective staging certainly contributed. Interestingly, though film noir evolved during

the last decade of Polito's work at Warners and the studio was itself in the forefront of this thematic and stylistic innovation (the 1941 Warners version of *The Maltese Falcon* is often regarded as the most important early noir film), Polito was not centrally involved, as other cinematographers of his generation, such as John Alton, were. Nevertheless, he ceated for Anatole Litvak's classic noir melodrama *Sorry, Wrong Number* a washed-out, hazy look that fails to define clearly much of what is in the frame, a perfect correlative for this story of moral ambivalence, failure of character, infantile preoccupations, and anomie. In this film, Polito's lighting and exposure values deprive the upscale home of the invalid main character of any sense of richness or security. How different an inflection he gives to the same tonality of grays by making the lighting scheme more glamorizing, emphasizing soft focus in close-ups of star Bette Davis, in *Now, Voyager*, the classic forties melodrama in which the world of the rich is offered as exquisitely textured, the realm for the setting of the purest romantic fantasy. Neither film makes use of the hard contrast between white and black for which Warners became famous in the thirties, and thus each exemplifies the flexibility within a dominant studio style.

Polito, however, like any studio technician, did not enjoy the luxury of working simply in one genre and perfecting his handling of nuance within overall expressive requirements. His action photography for the studio's specialist in swashbuckling epics, Michael Curtiz, is excellent in another way. *The Adventures of Robin Hood*, in particular, shows how Polito could impart a highly effective glow to a Technicolor film, a medium then rather difficult to handle well. Polito's lighting and exposure values create a depth and crispness that are entirely appropriate to the story. Working with the studio's new tank and fog machines in the similar project *The Sea Hawk*, Polito is able to inflect this tale of maritime adventure with the appropriate atmospherics, a misty, often smoky look pervades the action sequences in a story that is darker and more brooding than the moral simplicity of the children's fable of the defeat of the evil King John by Robin Hood. Polito's other black-and-white work for Curtiz is exemplary, particularly in *The Charge of the Light Brigade* where his clear images and unusual setups perfectly complement the director's fascination with exciting action.

—R. Barton Palmer

POMMER, Erich

Producer. **Nationality:** German. **Born:** Hildesheim, 20 July 1889. **Education:** Studied in Gottingen. **Military Service:** Injured during World War I. **Family:** Married Gertrude Levy, 1913; one son. **Career:** Worked in clothing factory, Berlin; 1907–14—worked for Gaumont, first in Berlin, then after 1909 in Paris, first as salesman, then becoming the company's director of operations in Central Europe; 1915—founded the production company Decla (Deutsche Eclair), which merged with Bioscop to become Decla-Bioscop; 1923—company absorbed into UFA: continued to produce films for UFA until 1933; with rise of Nazis, began long exile in Paris, 1933, Hollywood, 1934, London, where he founded Mayflower Pictures with Charles Laughton, Hollywood again, 1940; 1946–56—helped

Erich Pommer

oversee the restoration of the German film industry; 1956—returned to Hollywood. **Died:** In Hollywood, California, 8 May 1966.

Films as Producer:

1917   *Die verschleierte Dame* (Oswald); *Und Wandern sollst du ruhelos* (Oswald)

1919   *Die Pest von Florenz* (Rippert); *Die Frau mit den Orchiden* (Rippert); *Der Herr der Liebe* (Lang); ***Das Kabinett des Dr. Caligari*** (*The Cabinet of Dr. Caligari*) (Wiene); *Halbblut* (Lang)

1919–20   *Die Spinnen* (*The Spider*) (Lang—2 parts)

1920–21   *Das indische Grabmal* (*The Indian Tomb*) (May—2 parts)

1921   *Der müde Tod* (*Between Worlds*; *Destiny*) (Lang); *Schloss Vogelöd* (*Haunted Castle*) (Murnau)

1922   *Ein Glas Wasser* (Berger); *Vanina* (von Gerlach); *Luise Millerin—Kabale und Liebe* (Froelich); ***Dr. Mabuse der Spieler*** (*Dr. Mabuse the Gambler*) (Lang); *Phantom* (Murnau); *Der brennende Acker* (*Burning Soil*) (Murnau)

1923   *Der verlorene Schuh* (Berger); *Nora* (Viertel); *Der steinerne Reiter* (Wendhausen); *Austreibung—Die Macht der zweiter Frau* (Murnau); *Der Evangelimann* (Holger-Madsen); *Tatjana* (Dinesen); *Der Wetterwart* (Froelich); *Seine Frau, die Unbekannte* (Christensen)

1924   *Dekameron-Nächte* (Wilcox—German version of *Decameron Nights*); *Der Turm des schweigens* (Bertram); ***Die Nibelungen*** (Lang—2 parts); ***Der Letzte Mann*** (*The Last Laugh*) (Murnau); *Michael* (Dreyer); *Die Finanzen des Grossherzogs* (*The Grand Duke's Finances*) (Murnau)

1925   *Pietro, der Korsar* (Robison); *Wege zu Kraft und Schönheit* (Prager); *Liebe macht blind* (Mendes); *Tartüff* (*Tartuffe*) (Murnau); *Ein Walzertraum* (*The Waltz Dream*) (Berger); *Der Geiger von Florenz* (Czinner); ***Variété*** (*Variety*) (Dupont)

1926   ***Metropolis*** (Lang); *Manon Lescaut* (Robison); *Faust* (Murnau)

1927   *Hotel Imperial* (Stiller) (+ co-sc); *Barbed Wire* (Lee)

1928   *Spione* (*Spies*) (Lang); *Ungarische Rhapsodie* (*Hungarian Rhapsody*) (Schwarz); *Heimkehr* (*Homecoming*) (May)

1929   *Melodie des Herzens* (*Melody of the Heart*) (Schwarz); *Die underbare Lüge der Nina Poetrowna* (*The Wonderful Lies of Nina Petrovna*) (Schwarz); *Die Frau im Mond* (*The Woman in the Moon*) (Lang); *Asphalt* (May)

1930   *Liebeswalzer* (Thiele); *Die Drei von der Tankstelle* (Thiele); **Die blaue Engel** (*The Blue Angel*) (von Sternberg); *The Temporary Widow* (Ucicky—English version of *Hokuspokus*); *Einbrecher* (Schwarz)

1931   *Ihre Hoheit befiehlt* (Schwarz); *Voruntersuchung* (*Inquest*) (Siodmak); *Bomben auf Monte Carlo* (*Monte Carlo Madness*) (Charell); *Der Kongress tanzt* (*The Congress Dances*) (Charell); *Stürme der Leidenschaft* (*Storms of Passion*) (Siodmak)

1932   *F.P.1. antwortet nicht* (*F.P.1 Does Not Answer*) (Hartl); *Ein blonder Traum* (*A Blonde Dream*) (Martin); *Ich bei Tag und Du bei Nacht* (*Early to Bed*) (Berger); *Quick* (Siodmak); *Happy Ever After* (Martin and Stevenson)

1933   *The Only Girl* (*Heart Song*) (Hollaender); *On a volé un homme* (Ophüls); *Liliom* (Lang)

1934   *Music in the Air* (May)

1937   *Farewell Again* (*Troopship*) (Whelan); *Fire over England* (Howard)

1938   *Vessel of Wrath* (*The Beachcomber*) (+ d); *St. Martin's Lane* (*The Sidewalks of London*) (Whelan)

1939   *Jamaica Inn* (Hitchcock); *The Hunchback of Notre Dame* (Dieterle)

1940   **Dance, Girl, Dance** (Arzner); *They Knew What They Wanted* (Kanin)

1947   *Zwischen Gestern und Morgen* (Braun); *. . . und über uns der Himmel* (von Baky)

1948   *Lang ist der Weg* (Fredersdrof and Goldstein); *Morituri* (York)

1952   *Illusion in Moll* (Jugert); *Nachts auf den Strassen* (Jugert)

1954   *Ein Liebesgeschichte* (Jugert)

1955   *Kinder, Mütter, und ein General* (Benedek)

Publications

By POMMER: articles—

"Film parlant, film muet," in *La Revue des Savants* (Paris), no. 10, 1931.
Film Weekly (London), 27 February 1937.
Film Weekly (London), 10 December 1938.

On POMMER: book—

Jacobsen, Wolfgang, *Erich Pommer: ein Produzent macht Filmgeschichte*, Berlin, 1989.

On POMMER: articles—

Sight and Sound (London), April-June 1952.
Film Blätter, no. 13, 1959.
Luft, H.G., in *Films in Review* (New York), October and November 1959.
Films in Review (New York), December 1959.
Films in Review (New York), February 1960.
Films in Review (New York), May 1960.
Film Français (Paris), 20 May 1966.
Cahiers du Cinéma (Paris), July 1966.
EPD Film (Frankfurt), March 1989.

Jeune Cinéma (Paris), no. 195, June-July 1989.
EPD Film (Frankfurt), March 1989.
Film und Fernsehen (Berlin), November 1990.

*   *   *

Erich Pommer was not only Germany's greatest film producer but one of the most versatile of international showmen. His career chronicles the history of European cinema, and while a great many of the films he supervised appropriately fall into the category of motion picture entertainment, he was responsible for having shaped the artistic professionalism of the German cinema during the 1920s and 1930s and for closely supervising the creation of numerous cinematic masterpieces such as *The Cabinet of Dr. Caligari*, *The Last Laugh*, *Metropolis*, *Variety*, and *The Blue Angel*. Pommer was extremely knowledgeable about all aspects of the motion picture industry; however, his most outstanding talents were his keen sense of story values and his ability to nurture young, creative, and frequently temperamental talents like Fritz Lang, Josef von Sternberg, Emil Jannings, Carl Mayer, Marlene Dietrich, and Charles Laughton.

The debonair, charming young Pommer began his career in films in the sales department of the Berlin branch of Gaumont in 1909. After being wounded in the German army in the First World War, Pommer founded his own production company, Decla, which turned out a series of Sherlock Holmes films starring Albin Neuss. Among the new talent Pommer nurtured at Decla were Fritz Lang, who directed *Die Spinnen*, and Carl Mayer, who co-scripted *The Cabinet of Dr. Caligari*. Pommer had a shrewd sense of what the public would accept, and it was at his insistence, over the objections of the writers, that the framing story was added to *Caligari*. This device explained that the machinations of the evil hypnotist and his somnambulist were a "madman's delusions." Pommer's demand for this change resulted in this landmark Expressionistic film reaching a far wider audience. By 1921, Pommer merged his Decla company with UFA, and it was here he produced his greatest German films and helped develop that studio into Europe's finest and most efficient production center. His output is impressive, and includes a series of landmark films: *Phantom* (Murnau); *Dr. Mabuse der Spieler* (Lang), *Die Nibelungen* (Lang), *Michael* (Dreyer), *The Last Laugh* (Murnau), for which Pommer insisted upon a happy ending, *Metropolis* (Lang), *Tartuffe* (Murnau), *The Blue Angel* (von Sternberg), and *Variety* (Dupont) and *The Waltz Dream* (Berger), his two biggest commercial successes.

On 31 January 1933, the day that Hitler became chancellor of the Third Reich, Pommer resigned from UFA and joined Fox-Europa in Paris, where his first production was Max Ophüls's *On a volé un homme*. He then hired Lang to direct *Liliom*, which introduced him to a young composer named Franz Wachsman (Pommer later brought him to the U.S. as Franz Waxman). In 1934, Fox's Sidney Kent brought Pommer to America and set him up with his own production unit, where he produced *Music in the Air* starring Gloria Swanson and directed by Joe May. When Fox merged with 20th Century a year later Pommer was out of a job, so he went to England where he signed to produce two films for Alexander Korda.

Fire over England starred the young Laurence Olivier and Vivien Leigh and was directed by William K. Howard; *Troopship* starred Leslie Howard and was directed by Tim Whelan.

Pommer next formed another company called Mayflower Pictures in association with Charles Laughton and had a releasing deal through United Artists. Laughton's four films for Mayflower contain some of his most interesting work: *The Beachcomber*, *The Sidewalks of*

London, Jamaica Inn, and *The Hunchback of Notre Dame.* For *Jamaica Inn,* Pommer discovered a 16-year old lass named Maureen O'Hara and signed her to a personal 7-year contract. He used her again in *Hunchback* and after dissolving his company he sold her contract to RKO. Also for RKO, he produced *They Knew What They Wanted,* starring Laughton and directed by Garson Kanin. Poor health took its toll on Pommer's career during the early 1940s and he retired. In 1946, he returned to Germany under the auspices of the U.S. government to help restore the war-torn German film industry. He produced several films there in the 1950s, but none was of the caliber of his earlier successes.

Pommer was a stern, Teutonic disciplinarian but he knew the question every exceptional producer must ask—''What will the public accept?'' He angered many of his creative artists by insisting upon a tight production rein, yet most of his colleagues recognized his business acumen. Carl Dreyer recalled: ''For the conscientious film director, Pommer was the ideal producer. Once a decision was made on the major problems, such as script, casting, sets, etc., he would not interfere with the director's work.''

—Ronald Bowers

PONTI, Carlo

Producer. **Nationality:** French. **Born:** Magenta, Milan, Italy, 11 December 1910 (some sources say 1912); became French citizen, 1964. **Education:** Studied law: degree. **Family:** Married 1) the

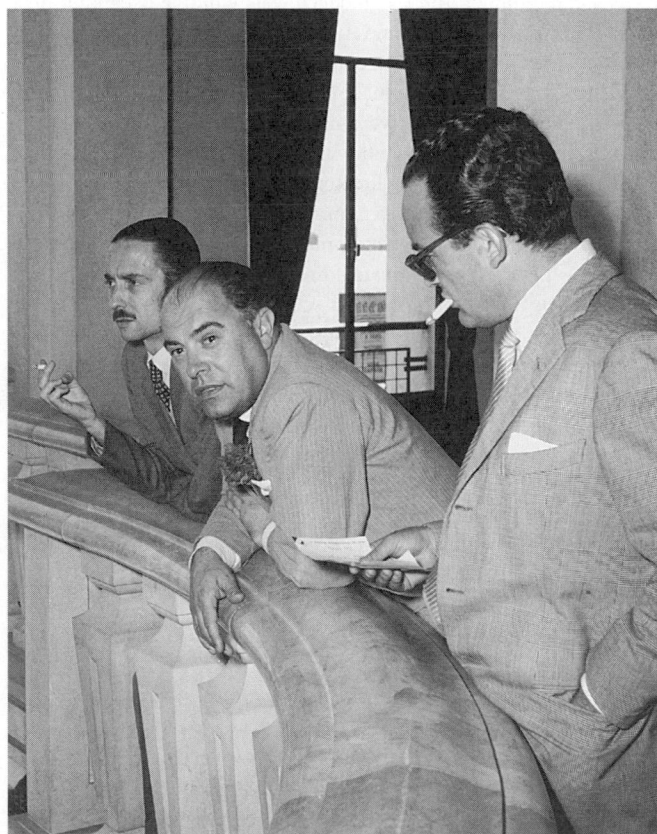

Carlo Ponti (center) with Dino De Laurentiis

actress Sophia Loren, 1957 (second marriage) (annulled, 1962), sons: Carlo Jr. and Eduardo; 2) Sophia Loren, 1966. **Career:** Producer from early 1940s; 1950–57—in partnership with Dino De Laurentiis; then international producer; 1979—complications concerning divorce/remarriage resulted in four-year jail sentence by Italian court on currency violation, but as French citizen could not be extradited; 1988—producer of TV mini-series *Mario Puzo's The Fortunate Pilgrim.*

Films as Producer:

1941 *Sissignora* (Poppioli); *Piccolo mondo antico* (*Old-Fashioned World*) (Soldati)

1942 *Giacoma l'idealista* (Lattuada)

1944 *Due lettere anonime* (Camerini)

1945 *La freccia nel fianco* (Lattuada)

1946 *Un Americano in vacanza* (*A Yank in Rome*) (Zampa); *Vivere in Pace* (*To Live in Peace*) (Zampa); *La primula bianca* (Bragaglia)

1947 *I miserabili* (Freda); *Gioventù perduta* (*Lost Youth*) (Germi)

1948 *Senza pietà* (*Without Pity*) (Lattuada)

1949 *Il mulino del Po* (*The Mill on the Po*) (Lattuada); *Fuga in Francia* (Soldati); *Campane a martello* (*Children of Change*) (Zampa); *Quel bandito sono io!* (Soldati); *L'imperatore di Capri* (Comencini)

1950 *Cuori senza fontiere* (*The White Line*) (Zampa); *Totò cerca casa* (*Toto Wants a Home*) (Steno and Monicelli); *Vita di cani* (Steno and Monicelli); *E arrivato il cavaliere* (Steno and Monicelli); *Il brigante Musolini* (Camerini)

1951 *Sensualità* (Fracassi)

1952 *Europa '51* (Rossellini); *Anna* (Lattuada)

1953 *Anni facili* (*Easy Years*) (Zampa)

1954 *Un giorno in pretura* (*A Day in Court*) (Steno) (co-exec); *Un Americano a Roma* (Steno); *La strada* (Fellini); *Ulisse* (*Ulysses*) (Camerini)

1955 *Attila flagello di dio* (*Attila the Hun*) (Francisci); *Ragazze d'oggi* (Zampa); *L'ultimo amante* (De Benedetti); *Mambo* (Rossen); *L'oro di Napoli* (*Gold of Naples*) (De Sica); *La donna del fiume* (Soldati); *La bella mugnaia* (*The Miller's Beautiful Daughter*) (Camerini)

1956 *War and Peace* (K. Vidor); *La risaia* (*Rice Girl*) (Matarazzo); *Il ferroviere* (*The Railroad Man*) (Germi); *La diciottenni* (Mattòli); *Peccato di castità* (Franciolini); *Guendalina* (Lattuada); *Le notti di Cabiria* (*Cabiria*) (Fellini)

1957 *Nata di marzo* (Pietrangeli); *Susanna tutta panna* (Steno); *Femmine tre volte* (Steno); *Marisa la civetta* (Bolognini); *Camping* (Zeffirelli)

1959 *The Black Orchid* (Ritt); *That Kind of Woman* (Lumet)

1960 *Heller in Pink Tights* (Cukor); *Lettere di una novizia* (Rita) (Lattuada); *La ciociara* (*Two Women*) (De Sica); *A Breath of Scandal* (*Olympia*) (Curtiz)

1961 *Lola* (Demy); *Une Femme est une femme* (*A Woman Is a Woman*) (Godard)

1962 *L'isola di Arturo* (*Arturo's Island*) (Damiani); *Cléo de 5 à 7* (*Cleo from 5 to 7*) (Varda) (co-exec); *L'Oeil du malin* (*The Third Lover*) (Chabrol); *Boccaccio '79* (Fellini and others); *I sequestri di Altona* (*The Condemned of Altona*) (De Sica)

1963 *Landru* (*Bluebeard*) (Chabrol); *Le Doulos* (*Doulos—the Finger Man*) (Melville); *Le Mépris* (*Contempt*) (Godard);

La noia (*The Empty Canvas*) (Damiani); *Ieri, oggi, e domani* (*Yesterday, Today, and Tomorrow*) (De Sica); *Les Carabiniers* (Godard)

1964 *Matrimonio all'italiana* (*Marriage Italian Style*) (De Sica); *La donna scimmia* (*The Ape Woman*) (Ferreri)

1965 *Operation Crossbow* (Anderson); *Casanova '70* (Monicelli); *Doctor Zhivago* (Lean); *La decima vittima* (*The Tenth Victim*) (Petri); *Lady L* (Ustinov); *Oggi, domani, e dopodomani* (De Filippo—English-language version *Kiss the Other Sheik*, additional scenes directed by Salce; section directed by Ferreri released as *The Man with the Balloons*)

1966 **Blow-Up** (Antonioni); **Ostre sledované vlaky** (*Closely Watched Trains*) (Menzel)

1967 *La ragazze e il generale* (*The Girl and the General*) (Festa Campanile); *C'era una volta* (*More than a Miracle*) (Rosi); *Smashing Time* (Davis); *Questi fantasmi* (*Ghosts—Italian Style*) (Castellani); *La Vingt-cinquième Heure* (*The 25th Hour*; *La 25e Heure*) (Verneuil); *A Countess from Hong Kong* (Chaplin)

1968 *Gli amanti* (*A Place for Lovers*) (De Sica); **O Slavnosti a hostech** (*A Report on the Party and the Guests*) (Nemec)

1969 *I girasoli* (*Sunflower*) (De Sica)

1970 *Zabriskie Point* (Antonioni)

1971 *La moglie del prete* (*The Priest's Wife*) (Risi); *La mortadella* (*Lady Liberty*) (Monicelli)

1972 *Che?* (*What?*) (Polanski); *Rappresaglia* (*Massacre in Rome*) (Cosmatos)

1973 *Bianco, rosso, e . . .* (*White Sister*) (Lattuada); *I corpi presentano tracce di violenza carnale* (*Torso*) (Martino); *Il viaggio* (*The Voyage*) (De Sica)

1974 *Le Testament* (*Jury of One*; *The Verdict*) (Cayatte); *Brief Encounter* (Bridges); *Poopsie* (*Gun Moll*) (Capitani); *Carne per Frankenstein* (*Andy Warhol's Frankenstein*) (Morrissey); *Dracula cerca sangue di vergine e . . . mori di sete!!!* (*Andy Warhol's Dracula*) (Morrissey and Dawson)

1975 *L'infermiera* (*The Nurse*; *I Will If You Will*) (Rossati); **Professione: Reporter** (*The Passenger*) (Antonioni); *Le Baby-Sitter* (*Wanted: Babysitter*) (Clément)

1976 *Brutti, sporchi, cattivi* (*Down and Dirty*) (Scola)

1977 *The Cassandra Crossing* (Cosmatos); *Una giornata particolare* (*A Special Day*) (Scola)

1989 *Running Away*; *Sabato, Domenica e Lunedi* (*Saturday, Sunday and Monday*) (Wertmüller)

1991 *Oscar* (Landis)

1998 *Liv* (Edoardo Ponti)

Publications

By PONTI: articles—

"Ponti on Producers," in *Today's Cinema*, 12 May 1970.
Film Français (Paris), 11 June 1976.

On PONTI: article—

Screen International (London), 22 November 1975.

*   *   *

Although he produced some light comedies in the early 1940s, Carlo Ponti's reputation as a producer fortuitously coincided with the rise of Italian neorealism from 1943 to 1950. He produced serious films by Germi, Lattuada, and Zampa, including *A Yank in Rome*, which established the latter as a major director. In 1950 he joined with Dino De Laurentiis to form a partnership that lasted until 1957, when both men went on to produce films independently. While partners, they produced important films by directors who would achieve international reputations—Roberto Rossellini's *Europa '51*, Federico Fellini's *La strada*, and his *Cabiria*—as well as the critically acclaimed *War and Peace* by veteran director King Vidor, and *Mambo* by Robert Rossen. Following the breakup of the partnership, Ponti became more of an international producer. American directors George Cukor, Sidney Lumet, Martin Ritt, and Michael Curtiz had films produced by Ponti during the 1960s; each film starred Sophia Loren, Ponti's wife since 1957.

Although Ponti had encouraged other Italian film actresses, among them Gina Lollobrigida, Ponti's career after 1957 was, for the most part, tied closely to Sophia Loren. She had a bit part in *Anna*, a Ponti-De Laurentiis production, and subsequently appeared regularly in Ponti productions, although her best film was Vittorio De Sica's *Two Women*, which won Loren an Oscar in an uncharacteristic performance. Loren, who by her own admission, had played in "confectionery parts" during her "English-speaking film odyssey," was induced by De Sica to play the role of the mother after Anna Magnani not only refused it, but sarcastically suggested that Loren, then aged 26, should play the mother rather than her intended role as the daughter. Loren has suggested that before the film she was a "performer," but the film made her an "actress." Unfortunately for Loren, her post-*Two Women* career under Ponti's guidance was, with the exception of *A Countess from Hong Kong* and *A Special Day*, mostly comprised of less-than-memorable Italian sex comedies and ponderous Mann epics.

Many of Ponti's films made without Loren after 1960 were Franco-Italian films which were noted for big stars, large budgets, lush settings, and romantic sentimentality, but he also produced some remarkable films by major directors: Godard's political films and Antonioni's *Blow-Up*, *Zabriskie Point*, and *The Passenger*. In addition, there were films by Agnès Varda, Claude Chabrol, De Sica, and Polanski—there were few major directors who did not work with Ponti. During this period he also produced David Lean's *Doctor Zhivago*, a popular award-winning film ideally suited to Ponti's sensibility. After 1970 Ponti produced few quality films, with the notable exception of *The Passenger*, and the careers of Ponti and Loren were in decline. His work included a film for television, Paul Morrissey's films about Andy Warhol's *Frankenstein* and *Dracula*, and some unsuccessful attempts in 1977 to produce some Brazilian films. At about the same time he and Loren came under investigation about currency transfers in Italy. Ponti left Italy but was convicted; Loren was acquitted of the charges.

In 1981 Italy dropped his arrest warrant but left some charges pending. His legal problems occupied much of his time, and between 1977 and 1988, he did not produce any films. Of the three works he produced between 1988 and 1991, only one—directed by Lina Wertmüller, herself past her filmmaking peak—is noteworthy. During his lifetime, however, he produced major films by major directors, helped bring Italian and French films international recognition, and guided the career of a prolific film performer. His career essentially has reflected the rise of neorealism and the French New Wave—in fact, he helped develop both movements. His influence as a producer of Italian films was second only to that of De Laurentiis, and his is a lasting contribution to international cinema.

—Thomas L. Erskine

POPESCU-GOPO, Ion

Animator and Director. **Nationality:** Romanian. **Born:** Bucharest, 1 May 1923. **Education:** Studied sculpture and graphic design at the Academy of Art, Bucharest. **Career:** Joined Animafilm (animation studio): first animated film, *The Naughty Duck*, 1950; 1953—first live-action film, *The Little Liar*; mid-1960s—film officer, World Health Organization, two years. **Died:** In 1990.

Films as Director (Animation):

1950	*The Naughty Duck*; *The Bee and the Dove*
1952	*Two Little Rabbits*; *The Mischievous Hedgehog*
1954	*Marinica*
1955	*Murinica's Bodkin*
1957	*A Short History*
1958	*The Seven Arts*
1960	*Homo Sapiens*
1962	*Allo! Hallo! Alo!*
1966–67	*Pill* (2 parts)
1969	*The Kiss*
1972	*The Hour Glass*
1974	*Intermezzo*
1975	*One Two Three*
1976	*Study Opus I—Man*
1977	*Infinity*
1979	*Three Apples*
1983	*Quo Vadis Homo Sapiens*
1985	*Ramasagul*; *The Sorcerer's Apprentice*

Films as Director (Live-Action):

1953	*Fetita mincinoasa* (*The Little Liar*)
1954	*O musca cu bani* (*A Fly with Money*)
1961	*S-a furat o bomba* (*A Bomb Was Stolen*)
1963	*Pasi spre lune* (*Steps to the Moon*)
1965	*De-as fi Harap Alb* (*The White Moor*)
1967	*Orasul meu* (*My City*)
1968	*Sancta Simplicitas*

Publications

By POPESCU-GOPO: book—

Filme Filme Filme, Bucharest, 1963, as *All about Film*, Bucharest, 1963.

By POPESCU-GOPU: articles—

Revista del Cinematografo (Rome), August 1964.
''Introduction au dessin animé,'' in *Bulletin de l'ASIFA*, no. 13, 1966.
Cinema International (London), no. 18, 1968.
Ecran (Paris), February 1975.
Cinema (Bucharest), April 1983.
Romanian Film, no. 2, 1987.

On POPESCU-GOPO: articles—

Image et Son (Paris), March 1958.
Deutsche Filmkunst, no. 9, 1960.
Film Rutan, no. 3, 1963.
Image et Son (Paris), November 1967.
Romanian Film (Bucharest), 1968.
Cinema (Bucharest), July 1976.
Filmowy Servis Prasowy (Warsaw), 1–15 January 1983.
Film a Doba (Prague), July 1985.

* * *

Ion Popescu-Gopo made witty animated films, all of which have a dual philosophical content. His main character, Homo Sapiens, figured in most of his films, and was a reflection of himself, almost a self-portrait. On the surface, Homo Sapiens appears to be a lost creature, an innocent party, not knowing how and why he came about. But as the plot develops he adjusts his outlook and attains the upperhand. Along the way, the oddity and the drollness of existence is emphasized. It was enterprising and quite unusual, at the time, to employ only one main character in European animation as Popescu-Gopo did for 25 years, with his Homo Sapiens character. This was at a time when such trends only existed in TV series mass-produced by the Japanese and the Hollywood type of animated cartoons. For his treatment, as well as for his simple graphic style, he became an internationally known artist whose films were regularly chosen for international festivals.

Eventually, after several live-action movies to his credit, it emerged that he was not as entirely comfortable handling live actors and human situations as he was with animated cartoons. He returned to animation but the experience gained in live-action production had enriched and expanded his skills as a filmmaker even further. *The Sorcerer's Apprentice*, using the combined technique of live action and puppet animation, shows evidence of his early experiences as a sculptor. The location is Popescu-Gopo's own studio. The live character is Popescu-Gopo himself, watched by his alter-ego, the wooden puppet. While Popescu-Gopo is away from the studio having tea, the puppet comes to life and takes over the studio activities, but without any coordination or sense of order. By the time Popescu-Gopo returns everything is chaos and the studio is ruined. The situation is handled beautifully and the film could be considered as a small masterpiece.

When asked what was his most precious wish for the future, Popescu-Gopo's reply was: ''That the Martians should see my film *Homo Sapiens*.''

—John Halas

PORTER, Cole

Composer and Lyricist. **Nationality:** American. **Born:** Peru, Indiana, 9 June 1891. **Education:** Studied piano and violin as a child; attended Worcester Academy, Massachusetts, 1905–09; Yale University, New Haven, Connecticut, 1909–13, B.A. 1913; Harvard Law School, Cambridge, Massachusetts, 1913–14, and Harvard Graduate School, 1914–15; also studied orchestration and counterpoint with d'Indy, 1920. **Family:** Married Linda Lee, 1919 (died 1954). **Career:** 1916—first Broadway show (composer and lyricist); worked with Duryea Relief Party in France during World War I; 1929—wrote songs for film *The Battle of Paris*; later musicals filmed (without Porter's participation) include *Fifty Million Frenchmen*, 1931, *The Gay Divorcee*, 1934, *Anything Goes*, 1936, *Panama Hattie*, 1942, *DuBarry Was a Lady*, 1943, *Let's Face It*, 1943, *Kiss Me Kate*, 1953, and *Can-Can*, 1959; 1936—first film score for *Born to Dance*; 1937—riding accident, resulting in amputation of leg. **Died:** Of pneumonia, in Santa Monica, California, 15 October 1964.

Films as Composer and Lyricist:

1929   *The Battle of Paris* (Florey) (songs)
1936   *Born to Dance* (Del Ruth)
1937   *Rosalie* (Van Dyke)
1940   *Broadway Melody of 1940* (Taurog)
1941   *You'll Never Get Rich* (Lanfield)
1943   *Something to Shout About* (Ratoff)

Cole Porter

1948   *The Pirate* (Minnelli)
1957   *High Society* (Walters); *Les Girls* (Cukor); *Silk Stockings* (Mamoulian)
1958   *Aladdin* (Nelson)

Publications

By PORTER: books—

Cole Porter Song Album, New York, 1935.
103 Lyrics of Cole Porter, edited by Fred Lounsberry, New York, 1954.
The Cole Porter Song Book, edited by Robert Kimball, New York, 1959.
Cole, edited by Robert Kimball, New York, 1971.
Music and Lyrics by Cole Porter, edited by Robert Kimball, New York, 1972.
The Unpublished Cole Porter, edited by Robert Kimball, New York, 1975.
The Complete Lyrics of Cole Porter, edited by Robert Kimball, New York, 1983.

On PORTER: books—

Ewen, David, *The Cole Porter Story*, New York, 1965.
Hubler, Richard G., *The Cole Porter Story*, Cleveland, Ohio, 1965.
Eells, George, *The Life That Late He Led: A Biography of Cole Porter*, New York, 1967.
Kimball, Robert, and Brendan Gill, *Cole*, New York, 1971.
Schwartz, Charles, *Cole Porter*, New York, 1977.
Citron, Stephen, *Noel and Cole: The Sophisticates*, New York, 1993.
Morella, Joe, *Genius and Lust: The Creative and Sexual Lives of Noel Coward and Cole Porter*, New York, 1995.
Cuellar, Carol, editor, *Porter on Broadway*, Miami, 1995.
Kimball, Robert, *You're Sensational: Cole Porter in the 20s, 40s & 50s*, Bloomington, 1999.
Prince, Pamela, editor, *You're the Top: A Song by Cole Porter*, New York, 1999.

On PORTER: articles—

Kimball, Robert, "The Cole Porter Collection at Yale," in *Yale University Library Gazette* (New Haven, Connecticut), July 1969.
Nolan, J. E., "Films on TV," in *Films in Review* (New York), August-September 1973.
Hemming, Roy, in *The Melody Lingers On: The Great Songwriters and Their Movie Musicals*, New York, 1986.
Custen, G. F., "Night and Day: Cole Porter, Warner Bros., and the Re-creation of a Life," in *Cineaste* (New York), vol. 19, no. 2–3, 1992.
Gill, Brendan, "Deluxe Delights," *The New Yorker*, vol. 69, 31 May 1993.
Forte, Allen, "Secrets of Melody: Line and Design in the Songs of Cole Porter," *Musical Quarterly*, vol. 77, Winter 1993.
Clark, Robert S., "You're the Top: Cole Porter in the 1930s," in *Hudson Review*, Winter 1993.
"The Secret Life of a Music Man," in *Maclean's*, 19 October 1998.
Schleifer, Ronald, "'What Is This Thing Called Love?': Cole Porter and the Rhythms of Desire," in *Criticism*, Winter 1999.

*   *   *

Urbane, witty, incisive, and, sometimes, sentimental, Cole Porter's music brought a true sophistication to the Hollywood movie musical. Versatile as well as stylish, he provided tailor-made material for a wide range of talents, from Fred Astaire to Ethel Merman to Bing Crosby.

Porter was born on a farm near the town of Peru, Indiana. Heir to a large fortune, he studied at Yale and entered Harvard Law School which he soon abandoned for music. Porter was equally talented as a composer and a lyricist, allowing him to work alone. He struggled to establish himself in the New York theater during the 1920s, finally breaking through in 1929 with his score for *Fifty Million Frenchmen*. The 1930s followed with an indefatigable series of distinctive scores and hit tunes.

His first few adaptations on film were less remarkable. His songs "They All Fall in Love" and "Here Comes the Bandwagon" were included in an early talking picture, *The Battle of Paris*; Warners' screen version of *Fifty Million Frenchmen* did not use Porter's lyrics, and his music was reduced to background instrumentals. Porter's score for *The Gay Divorce*, retitled *The Gay Divorcee*, did not fare much better; only "Night and Day" survived from the original.

It was not until Porter actually moved to Hollywood in 1935 to write a complete score for *Born to Dance* that he became significantly involved in writing for motion pictures. From then until his death in 1964, Porter continued to divide his time between New York and Los Angeles, spending four to six months each year on the west coast.

Porter began his Hollywood career in earnest at MGM, and although he worked for several important studios, MGM's lavish budgets and tasteful pictures gave Porter's music and lyrics their proper setting. Likewise, Louis B. Mayer provided Porter with a working relationship which respected the composer's talent and sensibilities.

Some of the films containing Porter's songs have faded in relative obscurity, such as *Born to Dance* or *Rosalie*, but the melodies in them ("I've Got You under My Skin" and "In the Still of the Night") continue to be as fresh and provocative as when they first appeared. And while the censorship which prevailed in Hollywood during Porter's lifetime frequently forced changes in his original lyrics, they seemed to survive the limitations, to emerge equally biting and remarkably clever.

Porter's cinematic successes and failures proved unpredictable. "Don't Fence Me In," an unpretentious cowboy song which was introduced by Roy Rogers in *Hollywood Canteen*, sold millions of copies, while the film version of *Kiss Me Kate*, Porter's longest-running broadway show, was a disappointment at the box office.

Porter's music also inspired several classic dance sequences—particularly, Fred Astaire and Ginger Rogers' "Night and Day" (*The Gay Divorcee*); Astaire and Eleanor Powell in "Begin the Beguine" (*Broadway Melody of 1940*); and Gene Kelly's *tour de force* "The Pirate Ballet" (*The Pirate*).

Throughout his life, Porter promoted entertaining stories of his heroic days in the French Foreign Legion and of his carefree life on the Riviera, which were as much fiction as fact. So, in 1945 when Warner Bros. produced a film biography of Porter's life which indulged in more than the usual literary license, Porter could hardly complain. Censorship prevented the studio from addressing his homosexuality, so it compensated by overly romanticizing his marriage to the society beauty Linda Lee. The casting of Cary Grant as Porter and the inclusion of an impressive collection of 14 of his already famous songs helped make the film a box-office success.

Originally, the producer intended to cast various celebrities performing the numbers they made famous, but, in the end, only Monty Woolley (Porter's close friend) and Mary Martin, recreating "My Heart Belongs to Daddy," were engaged to play themselves.

The composer projected two distinct images to the public—Cole Porter the glamourous, naughty *bon vivant*, and Cole Porter the diligent, prolific worker. Whatever engaged him, Porter seemed to attack it with an unquenchable zest for living. In the fall of 1937, however, his life dramatically changed when a fall from a horse crushed both legs, resulting in over thirty operations, and the eventual amputation of his right leg. Although his career was fully resumed by the end of 1938, Porter suffered intense pain the remainder of his life. Bouts of depression became so severe that he underwent electroshock therapy. Still, his music continued to express unmistakable vitality and vigor.

—Joanne L. Yeck

PREISNER, Zbigniew

Composer. **Nationality:** Polish. **Born:** Bielsko-Biala, Poland, 20 May, 1955. **Education:** Studied history and philosophy in Krakow, private music studies. **Career:** Sometimes credited as Van den Budenmayer. Composed music for *Dekalog* (*The Decalogue*), TV series, 1986–88. **Awards:** Silver Berlin Bear, for the music to *The Island on Bird Street*, Berlin International Film Festival, 1997; Best Music, for *Élisa*, César Awards, 1996; Best Music, for *Trois couleurs: Rouge*, César Awards, 1995; Best Music, for *Olivier, Olivier*, *The Secret Garden*, and *Trois couleurs: Bleu*, Los Angeles Film Critics Association Awards, 1993; Best Music, for *Damage*, Los Angeles Film Critics Association Awards, 1992; Best Music, for *Europa, Europa, Double Life of Véronique*, and *At Play in the Fields of the Lord*, Los Angeles Film Critics Association Awards, 1991; Award for outstanding achievements in the presentation of Polish Culture abroad, Minister of Foreign Affairs, Poland, 1992; Honorary member of the French Film Academy, since 1994.

Films as Composer:

1981	*Prognoza pogody* (*The Weather Forecast*) (Krauze)
1985	*Bez konca* (*No End*) (Kieslowski); *Przez dotyk* (*By Touch*) (Lazarkiewicz)
1986	*Ucieczka* (*Escape*) (Szadkowski)
1987	*Kocham Kino* (*I Love Cinema*) (Lazarkiewicz); *The Lullabye* (Sevella)
1988	*Zabic ksiedza* (*To Kill a Priest*) (Holland); *Krótki film o zabijaniu* (*A Short Film About Killing*) (Kieslowski); *Krótki film o milosci* (*A Short Film About Love*) (Kieslowski)
1989	*Ostatni dzwonek* (*The Last Schoolbell*) (Lazarkiewicz)
1990	*Hitlerjunge Salomon* (*Europa Europa*) (Holland)
1991	*La Double vie de Véronique* (*The Double Life of Veronique*) (*Podwojne zycie Weroniki*) (Kieslowski); *At Play in the Fields of the Lord* (Babenco); *Eminent Domain* (Irvin)
1992	*Olivier, Olivier* (Holland); *Zwolnieni z zycia* (*Dismissed from Life*) (Krzystek)
1993	*O Fio do Horizonte* (*The Line of the Horizon*) (Lopes); *Trois couleurs: Bleu* (*Three Colors: Blue*; *Trzy kolory: Niebieski*)

(Kieslowski); *The Secret Garden* (Holland); *Fatale* (*Damage*) (Malle)

1994　*Trois couleurs: Rouge* (*Three Colors: Red*; *Trzy kolory: Czerwony*) (Kieslowski); *Trois couleurs: Blanc* (*Three Colors: White*; *Trzy kolory: Bialy*) (Kieslowski); *Radetzky Marsch* (Corti and Roll) TV mini-series; *Mouvements du désir* (*Desire in Motion*) (Pool); *When a Man Loves a Woman* (Mandoki)

1995　*Feast of July* (Menaul); *Élisa* (Becker); *De Aegypto* (Ptaszynska) (doc); *Krzysztof Kieslowski: I'm So-So. . .* (Wierzbicki)

1996　*Bruggen* (*Bridges*)

1997　*Øen i fuglegaden* (*The Island on Bird Street*) (Kragh-Jacobsen); *FairyTale: A True Story* (Sturridge)

1998　*Dancing at Lughnasa* (O'Connor); *Corazón iluminado* (*Foolish Heart*) (Babenco); *Liv* (Ponti)

1999　*Dreaming of Joseph Lees* (Styles); *The Last September* (Warner)

2000　*Aberdeen*

Publications

On PREISNER: book—

Stok, Danusia, *Kieslowski on Kieslowski*, Boston and London, 1993.

On PREISNER: article—

Preisner, Zbigniev, in *BFI Companion to Eastern European and Russian Cinema*, London, 2000.

On PRIESNER: web sites:—

http://www.lpg.fi/preisner July 2000.
http://www.preisner.com/ July 2000.

*　　*　　*

Zbigniew Preisner is Poland's foremost film music composer and one of the leading film music figures worldwide. Largely self-taught in music, he credits as his major influences Paganini and Sibelius, along with the members of the Polish Romantic Movement in music. Preisner's style is easily recognized as he tends to employ a range of classical Baroque elements in a post-modern blend of sounds that emphasizes melody and polyphony.

Along with screenwriter Krzysztof Piesiewicz, Preisner was the closest collaborator of famous Polish director Krzysztof Kieslowski for almost a decade. The two met in 1981, at the time when Preisner was making his debut as a composer working on the Polish satire *Weather Forecast* (directed by Antony Krauze). Their meeting resulted in an extensive collaboration over the next fifteen years. Preisner wrote the scores for Kieslowski's *No End* (1984), for the acclaimed TV series *The Decalogue* (1986–1988, as well as for the film spin-offs of series number 5 and 6, the award-winning *A Short Film about Killing* and *A Short Film about Love*), for the award-winning *The Double Life of Veronique* (1991), and for the trilogy *Three Colors: Blue* (1993), *White* (1994) and *Red* (1994). Preisner also wrote the score for Krzysztof Wierzbicki's biographical documentary *Krzysztof Kieslowski: I'm So-So. . .* (1995).

Preisner is a proponent of the auteurist view of the film composer. He is known for working on the score closely with the director. He takes part in the development of the project as early as scripting and storyboarding, as well as in post-production. To him, the composer, along with the cinematographer and the screenwriter, is one of the most important collaborators of the director and has a decisive impact on the overall aesthetic of the final product. This conviction is revealed in his long lasting commitment to cultivating the tasteful and memorable musical scores of Kieslowski's films, best revealed in *The Double Life of Veronique*, a film which, even though mostly financed by France, was a major international success for the Polish school of filmmaking. For *Veronique* Preisner wrote a concerto, which he mystified and presented as the work of Dutch composer Van den Budenmayer, hence the alias he continues using occasionally. The *Three Colors* films, which won numerous international awards, brought the next major success for Kieslowski and his team of collaborators, including Preisner. Even though after the *Three Colors* trilogy Kieslowski declared an official retirement from cinema in 1995, he was planning a return. His next project was supposed to be a trilogy tentatively called *Heaven*, *Hell*, and *Purgatory*, and Preisner was to work on the musical score. These plans were abruptly interrupted by the director's death on 13 March 1996.

In the early 1990s, Kieslowski and Preisner, along with screenwriter Krzysztof Piesiewicz, had also discussed a stage project, which was supposed to be a multi-media performance, combining operatic singing and a mystery play. The intention had been to premiere the event on the Acropolis in Athens, and to eventually develop a further series of performances to be scheduled in selected locations around the world. The untimely death of Kieslowski, however, put an end to these plans as well. Nonetheless, Preisner continued working on the music he had started writing for the project, and it developed into a unique musical opus, combining singing and instrumental music. *Requiem for My Friend* (1998), the first part of which is dedicated to Kieslowski's memory, featured the singing of remarkable Polish soprano Elzbieta Towarnicka, whose voice had been a highlight of Preisner's scores in *Veronique*, *Blue*, and *Red*. The *Requiem* was recorded with the Warsaw Symphony Orchestra and Warsaw's Chamber Choir and premiered in 1998.

Besides his close collaboration with Kieslowski, Preisner also worked with Agnieszka Holland, an internationally acclaimed director of Polish background. He wrote the scores for her *To Kill a Priest*, *Europa, Europa*, *Olivier, Olivier*, and *The Secret Garden*. He maintains long-standing working relationship with Polish feminist director Magdalena Lazarkiewicz for whom he worked on *Przez dotyk* (*By Touch*) and *Ostatni dzwonek* (*The Last Schoolbell*). More and more frequently, as his fame grows, Preisner works internationally. He has written music for directors worldwide, such as French-American Louis Malle's *Fatal* (*Damage*), British Charles Sturridge's *Fairy Tale: A True Story*, and Brazilian Hector Babenco's *At Play in the Fields of the Lord* and *Corazón iluminado* (*Foolish Heart*). Preisner continues working on musical scores for international directors and in Poland.

—Dina Iordanova

PRÉVERT, Jacques

Writer. **Nationality:** French. **Born:** Jacques Henri Marie Prévert in Neuilly-sur-Seine, 4 February 1900. **Military Service:** 1920–21. **Family:** Brother of the director Pierre Prévert. Married 1) Simone

Jacques Prévert (2nd from right)

Dienne, 1925; 2) Janine Tricotet, 1947. **Career:** 1915–20—worked in Bon Marché and other stores in Paris; worked for Argus de la Presse, 1921, and for the publicity agency Damour, 1930; author of plays, verse, songs, and, from 1932, film scripts; 1936—began ten-year collaboration with the director Marcel Carné. **Died:** In Omonville-la-Petite, 11 April 1977.

Films as Writer:

1932   *L'Affaire est dans le sac* (*It's in the Bag*) (P. Prévert) (+ ro); *Ténériffe* (Y. Allégret—short)

1933   *Ciboulette* (Autant-Lara); *Comme une carpe* (Heyman—short)

1934   *L'Hotel du libre échange* (M. Allégret)

1935   *Un Oiseau rare* (Pottier)

1936   *My Partner Mr. Davis* (*The Mysterious Mr. Davis*) (Autant-Lara); *Jeunesse d'abord* (Stelli); *Jenny* (Carné); *Mantonnet* (Sti); **Le Crime de Monsieur Lange** (*The Crime of Monsieur Lange*) (Renoir)

1937   *Drôle de drame* (*Bizarre Bizarre*) (Carné)

1938   **Quai des brumes** (*Port of Shadows*) (Carné); *Ernest le rebelle* (*C'était moi*) (Christian-Jaque)

1939   **Le Jour se lève** (*Daybreak*) (Carné)

1941   *Remorques* (*Stormy Waters*) (Grémillon); *Le Soleil a toujours raison* (Billon)

1942   *Les Visiteurs du soir* (*The Devil's Envoys*) (Carné)

1943   *Lumière d'été* (Grémillon); *Adieu Leonard* (P. Prévert)

1944   *Sortiléges* (*The Bellman*) (Christian-Jaque)

1945   **Les Enfants du paradis** (*Children of Paradise*) (Carné)

1946   *Les Portes de la nuit* (*Gates of the Night*) (Carné); *Aubervilliers* (Lotar—short); *Voyage-Surprise* (P. Prévert); **Une Partie de campagne** (Renoir)

1947   *L'Arche de Noé* (Jacques)

1948   *Le Petit Soldat* (Grimault—anim)

1949   *Les Amants de Vérone* (*The Lovers of Verona*) (Cayatte)

1950   ''La Statuette'' and ''Le Violon'' eps. of *Souvenirs perdus* (Christian-Jaque)

1951   *Bim, le petit âne* (Lamorisse—short) (commentary)

1956   *Notre-Dame de Paris* (*The Hunchback of Notre Dame*) (DeLannoy)

1958   *La Faim du monde* (Grimault—anim); *Paris mange son pain* (P. Prévert—short)

1959   *Paris la belle* (P. Prévert—revised version of short produced 1928)

1960   *Les Primitifs du XIII* (Bilbeaud—short)

1961   *Les Amours célèbres* (Boisrond)

1964   *Le Petit Claus et le grand Claus* (P. Prévert)

1965   *La Maison du passeur* (P. Prévert)

1966   *A la belle étoile* (P. Prévert)

1980   *Le Roi et l'oiseau* (*The King and the Bird*) (Grimault—incorporates footage from repudiated film *La Bergère et le ramoneur*, 1952)

Publications

By PRÉVERT: poetry—

Paroles, Paris, 1945, as *Selections from Paroles*, San Francisco, 1958.
With André Verdet, *Histoires*, Paris, 1946.
C'est à Saint-Paul-de-Vence, Paris, 1949.
Spectacle, Paris, 1951.
La Pluie et le beau temps, Paris, 1955.
Lumières d'hommes, Paris, 1955.
Images, Paris, 1957.
Poèmes, edited by J.H. Douglas and D.J. Girard, 1961.
Fatras, Paris, 1965.
Blood and Feathers: Selected Poems of Jacques Prévert, translated by Harriet Zinnes, Mount Kisco, NY, Moyer Bell, 1993.

By PRÉVERT: other books—

Enfants, 1945.
Le Rendez-vous (ballet), 1945.
With André Verdet and André Virel, *Le Cheval de Troie*, Paris, 1946.
Le Petit Lion, Paris, 1947.
Contes pour enfants pas sages, Paris, 1947.
Les Visiteurs du soir (script), Paris, 1947.
Les Amants de Verone (script), Paris, 1948.
Des Bêtes, Paris, 1950.
Charmes de Londres, Paris, 1952.
Grand bal de printemps, Paris, 1952.
Lettre des îles Baladar, Paris, 1952.

L'Opéra de la lune, Paris, 1952.

Miró, Paris, 1956.

Bim, le petit âne, Paris, 1951, as *Bim, the Little Donkey*, London, 1957.

Portrait de Picasso, Paris, 1959.

Couleur de Paris, Paris, 1961, as *Paris in Colour*, London, 1962.

Diurnes, Paris, 1962.

Histoires, et d'autre histoires, Paris, 1963.

Les Chiens ont soif, Paris, 1964.

Le Jour se lève (script) in *Avant-Scène* (Paris), November 1965, translated as *Le Jour se lève*, New York, 1970.

Arbres, Paris, 1968.

Children of Paradise (script), New York, 1968, as *Les Enfants du paradis*, London, 1968.

Varengeville, Paris, 1968.

Imaginaires, Paris, 1970.

Choses et autres, Paris, 1972.

With André Pozner, *Hebdomadaires* (interviews), Paris, 1972, revised edition 1982.

Drôle de drame (script), Paris, 1974.

Arbres, 1976.

Le Quai des brumes (script) in *Avant-Scène* (Paris), 15 October 1979.

On PRÉVERT: books—

Amengual, Barthélémy, *Prévert, du cinéma*, Algiers, 1952.

Queval, Jean, *Jacques Prévert*, Paris, 1955.

Guillot, Gérard, (ed.), *Les Préverts*, Paris, 1966.

Baker, William E., *Jacques Prévert*, 1967.

Greet, Anne Hyde, *Jacques Prévert's Word Games*, 1968.

Bergens, Andrée, *Jacques Prévert*, Paris, 1969.

Fauré, Michel, *Le Groupe Octobre*, Paris, 1977.

Rachline, Michel, *Jacques Prévert*, Paris, 1981.

Blakeway, Claire, *Jacques Prévert: Popular French Theatre and Cinema*, London, 1990.

Gilson, René, *Les Mots et merveilles, Jacques Prévert*, Paris, 1990 + filmo.

Sieber, Anja, *Vom Hohn zur Angst: Die Sozialkritik Jacques Préverts in den Filmen von Marcel Carne*, Rodenbach, Avinus Verlag, 1993.

Andry, Marc, *Jacques Prévert*, Paris, Editions de Fallois, 1994 + filmo.

Gasiglia-Laster, Daniele, *Jacques Prévert: Celui qui rouge de coeur*, Paris, Seguier, 1994.

On PRÉVERT: articles—

Leenhardt, Roger, in *Fontaine* (Paris), May 1945.

Rougeuil, J., and M. Sergines, "Les Préverts," in *Ecran* (Paris), 25 September 1946.

Sight and Sound (London), Winter 1946–47.

Laroche, Pierre, Jean-Paul Le Chanois, and Georges Sadoul, in *Ciné-Club* (Paris), January 1949.

Queval, Jean, in *Mercure de France* (Paris), 1 June 1949.

Nadal, Pierre, "Carné, Prévert, et le reportage," in *Raccords* (Paris), April 1950.

Cinémonde (Paris), 7 August 1953.

Chaboud, Charles, in *Image et Son* (Paris), October-November 1956.

Brunelin, André G., in *Cinéma* (Paris), November 1959.

Bazin, André, "*Le Jour se lève*," in *Regards neufs sur le cinéma*, Paris, 1963.

Tabes, René, in *Télé-Revue* (Paris), 20 October 1963.

"Les Frères Prévert Issue" of *Image et Son* (Paris), December 1965.

Durgnat, Raymond, in *Films and Filming* (London), July 1969.

Cinéma (Paris), June 1977.

Film Comment (New York), November-December 1981.

"Prévert Issue" of *Filmkritik* (Munich), August 1983.

Brunius, Jacques, in *En marge du cinéma française*, Lausanne, 1987.

Sight and Sound (London), Summer 1988.

Journal of Popular Film and Television (Washington, D.C.), Spring 1991.

Film Quarterly (Berkeley), Summer 1991.

Cineforum, vol. 32, no. 318, 1992.

Curchod, Olivier, and others, "Partie de campagne de Jean Renoir," in *Positif* (Paris), February 1995.

Télérama (Paris), 21 February 1996.

French Review, October 1997.

* * *

For convinced auteurists, Jacques Prévert comes as something of a stumbling block. With Prévert as scriptwriter, Marcel Carné directed several supreme classics of French cinema; when the two split up, Carné sank into obscure mediocrity. *A bas* Carné, then, cold and formal craftsman helplessly limited by his material, and *vive* Prévert, true begetter of *Le Jour se lève* and *Les Enfants du paradis*? And yet—if Prévert scripted Carné's greatest successes, he also wrote *Les Portes de la nuit*, the disastrous postwar flop from which neither of their careers ever recovered. And if Carné minus Prévert looks flat and uninspired, Prévert's scripts for other directors—with one or two exceptions—rarely attained the level of his best work with Carné.

Barthélémy Amengual split Prévert the scriptwriter into three periods: there was Prévert *rosse* (a tough word to translate—"offensive" or "bloody-minded" might get near it), Prévert *noir*, and Prévert *rose*. Prévert *rosse* was the subversive, tossing surrealist firecrackers under the wheels of bourgeois ceremonial. Prévert *noir* was the poet of melancholy, the fatalist whose doomed lovers succumbed to the machinations of Destiny. And Prévert *rose* purveyed charming, sentimental fables in which oppression is overthrown by the forces of love and good-hearted innocence. The Carné films were evidently the work of Prévert *noir*—with the exception of *Drôle de drame*, seen by Amengual as the last fling of Prévert *rosse*.

Prévert's roots were deep in the interwar leftist avant-garde. He was a member of the Surrealist group—until expelled by Breton for irreverence—and of the agit-prop theatre Groupe Octobre. His Marxism, though, owed nearly as much to Groucho as to Karl. The same delight in puns and wordplay, in jokes and fantasy deployed in the cause of class warfare which fuelled his poetry, bubbles through the early films—*Drôle de drame*, far more Prévert than Carné, and *L'Affaire est dans le sac*, first of the three directed by his brother Pierre, and Prévert's own favourite of all his films.

For his only completed feature with Renoir, Prévert rechanneled his exuberance into a more controlled political stance. *Le Crime de Monsieur Lange*, witty, touching, and bright with the new-found hope of the Front Populaire, shows both Renoir and Prévert operating near the top of their form, and arouses regret that two men with so much in common worked together so little. Too much in common, perhaps. "It's wonderful, but it's left me nothing to do," commented Renoir on Prévert's script for *Une Partie de campagne*—which therefore remained the most perfect of all incomplete movies.

The necessary creative tension seems to have been more fruitfully present in the relationship between Prévert and Carné, spurring them both into producing their finest work. In *Quai des brumes*, *Le Jour se lève*, *Les Visiteurs du soir* and *Les Enfants du paradis*, the smoky, shimmering malaise and colloquial lyricism of Prévert's scripts meld with Carné's cool technique and superb handling of actors into some of the richest masterpieces of romantic cinema. Their bittersweet fatalism, distillation of the political mood of the period, has sometimes been seen as imposed on Prévert by Carné's pessimism. "Carné never really believed in happiness," Ivo Jarosy asserted; "Prévert believed in nothing else." An oversimplification, perhaps. But certainly the outcome of the Prévertian eternal triangle—a man, a woman, and Fate—tended to be less invariably doom-laden in the hands of other directors, as for example Grémillon (*Remorques, Lumière d'été*).

Even at his darkest, though, Prévert never indulged in the unrelieved, misanthropic pessimism that often distorted the work of Duvivier or Clouzot. For him the power of friendship, of art, above all of love could always transcend the forces of oppression, and even ultimately death. This Tristan-and-Isolde view of love as transfiguring, eternal, and self-justifying can slide at times perilously close to mush, as in *Visiteurs du soir*'s closing image of the entwined statues whose hearts still beat, or in Baptiste's statement (*Les Enfants du paradis*), "If all the people who live together loved each other, the earth would shine like the sun." It can also lead into some fairly questionable morality. "Everything is allowed to those who love each other"—a sentiment that Penn's Bonnie and Clyde ("They're young, they're in love, and they kill people") would have wholeheartedly applauded.

Prévert's greatest achievement as a scriptwriter lies in his transmutation of ordinary, banal speech into a lyrical street poetry, reinvesting clichés with their original emotional truth. His characters speak, not perhaps as the ordinary people of Paris ever do speak, but how they might wish to at their most eloquent. Through subtleties of rhythm, wordplay, and repetition, commonplaces acquire unsuspected resonance. Quotation is problematic, since so much depends on inflection and context, and translation tends to flatten the lines back into banality; but something of the fury of the beleaguered Gabin haranguing the crowd below his window in *Le Jour se lève* still comes through: "Mais oui, je suis un assassin! Mais les assassins, ça courent les rues! Il y en a partout! Partout! Tout le monde tue! Tout le monde tue un petit peu, seulement on tue à douceur, alors ça ne se voit pas!" [That's right, I'm a murderer! But the streets are running with murderers! They're everywhere! Everybody kills—only quietly, bit by bit, so it doesn't show!] Or, from the same film, Arletty describing Jules Berry: "C'est formidable ce qu'il cause bien, cet homme-là. Il a un façon de remuer les mains en parlant—souvent les mots, vous croiriez qu'il les sort de ses manches." [It's wonderful how he can talk, that man. He's got a way of moving his hands—you'd think he had the words hidden up his sleeves.] And immediately the image comes of Berry (whom we have just met on stage putting trained dogs through their paces) as a conjuror, or a card sharp, fluently dealing out words like marked cards off a crooked deck.

For some ten years, from 1935 to 1945, Prévert was probably the greatest single influence on French cinema. Not everyone has thought it an influence for good. Claude Mauriac referred disparagingly to "le virus Prévert," and Truffaut, in his famous *Cahiers* onslaught on the "tradition de qualité," wrote "one takes to regretting Prévert's scenarios. He believed in the Devil, thus in God. . . ." Prévert can

be—and has been—faulted for an overschematic morality, for characters neatly divided into executioners or victims, for reflex anticlericalism and a sentimental idealization of the working class, for theatricality, for the moments when the streetwise poetics of his dialogue topple into pretension or bathos. None of these charges is without substance. Yet they diminish when set against his qualities: the dramatic vigour, the richness of narrative texture, the warmth and compassion of his characterisation, the brilliance and humour of his dialogue, lyricism flowering from the disregarded rubbish-tips of everyday speech. Few screenwriters have served their actors better; to have furnished Gabin, Arletty, Barrault, and Jules Berry with their finest screen roles is a formidable achievement. If it is true, as Jacques Brunius attested, that Prévert's greatest scenarios remained unfilmed, "imprisoned in drawers," the loss is considerable.

—Philip Kemp

PREVIN, André

Composer and Music Director. **Nationality:** American. **Born:** Andreas Ludwig Prewin in Berlin, Germany, 6 April 1929; son of the musician Charles Previn; emigrated to the United States, 1939; naturalized citizen, 1943. **Education:** Studied at conservatories in Berlin and Paris; also studied with Pierre Monteux, Joseph Achron, and Castelnuovo-Tedesco; attended Beverly Hills High School. **Family:** Married 1) the singer Betsy Bennett (divorced), two daughters; 2) the singer and composer Dory Langan (i.e., Dory Previn), 1959 (divorced

André Previn

1970); 3) the actress Mia Farrow, 1970 (divorced, 1979), twin sons, three adopted children; 4) Heather Sneddon, 1982, one son (separated). **Career:** Joined MGM as arranger while still in his teens; then composer and conductor: conductor of the Houston Symphony Orchestra, 1967–69, the London Symphony Orchestra, 1968–75, the Pittsburgh Symphony Orchestra, 1976–86, the Royal Philharmonic Orchestra, London, since 1985, and the Los Angeles Philharmonic Orchestra, 1986–89. **Awards:** Academy Award, for *Gigi*, 1958, *Porgy and Bess*, 1959, *Irma La Douce*, 1963, and *My Fair Lady*, 1964.

Films as Composer:

1948   *The Sun Comes Up* (Thorpe)
1949   *Border Incident* (A. Mann); *Tension* (Berry); *Scene of the Crime* (Rowland); *Challenge to Lassie* (Thorpe)
1950   *Dial 1119* (*The Violent Hour*) (Mayer); *Kim* (Saville); *The Great Sinner* (Siodmak); *The Outriders* (Rowland)
1951   *Cause for Alarm* (Garnett)
1953   *The Girl Who Had Everything* (Thorpe)
1954   *Bad Day at Black Rock* (J. Sturges)
1955   *Kismet* (Minnelli)
1956   *Invitation to the Dance* (Kelly); *The Fastest Gun Alive* (Rouse); *The Catered Affair* (Brooks)
1957   *Hot Summer Night* (Friedkin); *House of Numbers* (Rouse); *Designing Woman* (Minnelli); *Silk Stockings* (Mamoulian)
1960   *Elmer Gantry* (Brooks); *Who Was That Lady?* (Sidney)
1961   *All in a Night's Work* (Anthony); *One, Two, Three* (Wilder)
1962   *Long Day's Journey into Night* (Lumet); *Two for the Seesaw* (Wise) (song); *The Four Horsemen of the Apocalypse* (Minnelli)
1963   *Irma La Douce* (Wilder)
1964   *Goodbye Charlie* (Minnelli); *Kiss Me Stupid* (Wilder); *Dead Ringer* (Henreid)
1965   *Inside Daisy Clover* (Mulligan)
1966   *Harper* (*The Moving Target*) (Smight) (song); *The Fortune Cookie* (Wilder); *The Swinger* (Sidney) (song)
1967   *Valley of the Dolls* (Robson) (songs)
1969   *Paint Your Wagon* (Logan) (songs)
1970   *The Music Lovers* (Russell)
1971   *Mrs. Pollifax—Spy* (Martinson)
1975   *Rollerball* (Jewison)
1980   *The Elephant Man* (Lynch)
1982   *Six Weeks* (Bill)
1990   *Romeo and Juliet* (Acosta)
1998   *Streetcar Named Desire* (Graham)

Films as Musical Director:

1946   *Undercurrent* (Minnelli) (supervisor)
1950   *Three Little Words* (Thorpe)
1953   *Small Town Girl* (Kardos); *Kiss Me Kate* (Sidney); *Give a Girl a Break* (Donen)
1955   *It's Always Fair Weather* (Donen and Kelly)
1958   *Gigi* (Minnelli)
1959   *Porgy and Bess* (Preminger)
1960   *Bells Are Ringing* (Minnelli)
1964   *My Fair Lady* (Cukor)
1967   *Thoroughly Modern Millie* (Hill) (co); *The Way West* (McLaglen)
1973   *Jesus Christ Superstar* (Jewison)

Publications

By PREVIN: books—

With Antony Hopkins, *Music Face to Face*, London, 1971.
(Editor), *Orchestra*, New York, 1979.
André Previn's Guide to Music, New York, 1983.
No Minor Chords, London, 1991.

On PREVIN: books—

Greenfield, Edward, *André Previn*, London, 1973.
Bookspan, Martin, and Ross Yockey, *André Previn: A Biography*, New York, 1981.
Ruttencutter, Helen, *Previn*, London, 1985.
Freedland, Michael, *André Previn*, London, 1991.

On PREVIN: articles—

Films and Filming (London), May 1968.
Thomas, Tony, in *Music for the Movies*, South Brunswick, New Jersey, 1973.
Ecran (Paris), September 1975.
Lacombe, Alain, in *Hollywood*, Paris, 1983.
Care, R., "Previn, Andre. No Minor Chords," in *Film Quarterly* (Berkeley), vol. 47, no. 1, 1993.

*   *   *

André Previn was born in Berlin and began piano studies at the Berlin Conservatory at the age of six. The family moved to Paris in 1938 and the next year to Los Angeles, where Previn continued his studies with the composers Joseph Achron and Mario Castelnuovo-Tedesco. At 16 Previn was hired on a part-time basis as an arranger and pianist, and two years later became a full-time employee. In 1948 he was given his first assignment as the composer of a complete, original score, *The Sun Comes Up*, followed by a stream of other films, both as a composer and the music director for musicals, and it is in the latter capacity that most of his Oscar nominations have been given. Previn won Oscars for his work arranging and conducting the scores of *Gigi* and *Porgy and Bess* and for his original music for *Irma La Douce*, and as the music director of *My Fair Lady*. He was also nominated for the song he wrote for *Two for the Seesaw* and for his music direction of *Three Little Words*, *Kiss Me Kate*, *Bells Are Ringing*, *Thoroughly Modern Millie*, and *Jesus Christ Superstar*. Of his serious film scores *Elmer Gantry* and *The Four Horsemen of the Apocalypse* are considered his finest, and of the more comedic scores *One, Two, Three* and *The Fortune Cookie* are notable.

Despite this enviable record of success in films and the popularity of his many record albums as a stylish jazz pianist, Previn put it all behind him when he accepted the position of conductor of the Houston Symphony Orchestra in 1967. The following year he was contracted as the principal conductor of the London Symphony Orchestra and held the position until 1975, establishing a solid reputation and becoming a popular figure in England with his many concerts, recordings and appearances on television. He accepted the post of conductor of the Pittsburgh Symphony Orchestra in 1976 and held it until his appointment in Los Angeles, which allowed for him to appear as a guest conductor internationally. In addition to piano and chamber works, Previn has written a symphony for strings, concertos for cello, violin and guitar, and with lyricist Tom Stoppard the choral work *Every Good Boy Deserves a Favor*. For the theater, Previn has written the scores for *Coco* (1969) and *The Good Companions* (1971). In looking back on his career in films, Previn is emphatic that it is long gone and finished, and appears to hold only one grudge. This concerns the attitude of American music critics. ''They might forgive you for having been the Boston Strangler but never for having written a movie score. You don't have this in Europe.''

—Tony Thomas

PROKOFIEV, Sergei

Composer. **Nationality:** Russian. **Born:** Sergei Sergeyevich Prokofiev in Sontsovka, Ukraine, 23 April 1891. **Education:** Studied the piano with Glière; then studied at the St. Petersburg Conservatory with Rimsky-Korsakov, Liadov, Wihtol, Tcherepnin, and Essipov until 1914. **Family:** Married Lina Llubera, 1923; two sons. **Career:**

Sergei Prokofiev

Composer as a child; important works performed in the late 1910s; 1918–27—lived in the United States and Paris; 1927—returned to the Soviet Union; composer of orchestra and stage works; 1934—first film score, for *Lieutenant Kizhe*. **Died:** In Moscow, 5 March 1953.

Films as Composer:

1934   *Poruchik Kizhe* (*Lieutenant Kizhe*) (Fainzimmer)
1938   ***Alexander Nevsky*** (Eisenstein)
1941   *Lermontov* (Gendelstein)
1942   *Kotovsky* (Fainzimmer); *Partizani v stepyakh Ukrainy* (*The Partisans in the Ukrainian Steppes*) (Savchenko)
1944   ***Ivan Grozny*** (*Ivan the Terrible, Part I*) (Eisenstein)
1958   *Ivan Grozny II: Boyarskii Zagovor* (*Ivan the Terrible, Part II: The Boyars' Plot*) (Eisenstein—produced 1946)

Publications

By PROKOFIEV: books—

Autobiography, Articles, Reminiscences, edited by Semyon Shlifshteyn, Moscow, 1965.
Prokofiev by Prokofiev: A Composer's Memoir, London, 1979.
Soviet Diary, 1927 & Other Writings, Boston, 1992.
Selected Letters of Sergei Prokofiev, edited and translated by Harlow Robinson, Boston 1998.

On PROKOFIEV: books—

Nestyev, I.V., *Prokofiev*, New York, 1946.
Hanson, L. and E., *Prokofiev*, London, 1964.
Rayment, M., *Prokofiev*, London, 1965.
Seroff, Victor, *Sergei Prokofiev*, New York, 1968.
Blok, Vladimir, (ed.), *Sergei Prokofiev: Materials, Articles, Interviews*, Moscow, 1978.
Robinson, Harlow, *Sergei Prokofiev: A Biography*, New York, 1987.
Gutman, David, *Prokofiev: The Illustrated Lives of the Great Composers*, New York, 1996.
Jaffe, Daniel, *Sergey Prokofiev*, New York, 1998.

On PROKOFIEV: articles—

Cahiers du Cinéma (Paris), May 1953.
Soviet Film (Moscow), November 1964.
Trolle, Borge, in *Kosmorama* (Copenhagen), December 1966, translated in *Cinema TV Digest*, Fall 1967.
Trolle, Borge, in *Kosmorama* (Copenhagen), February 1967, translated in *Cinema TV Digest*, Winter 1967–68.
Eisenstein, Sergei, *Soviet Film* (Moscow), April 1971.
Eisenstein (correspondence), in *Cinema Journal* (Evanston, Illinois), Fall 1973.
Gallez, Douglas W., in *Cinema Journal* (Evanston, Illinois), Spring 1978, addenda in Autumn 1978.
Studies in Comparative Communism (Los Angeles, California), Fall-Winter 1984–85.

Film Quarterly, vol. 48, Winter 1994.
New York Times, section 2, 28 May 1995.
Séquences (Haute-Ville), March-April 1996.
Journal of Musicological Research, Winter 1999.
Opera Review, vol. 64, November 1999.

*   *   *

Unlike his Soviet colleague Shostakovich, Prokofiev wrote relatively little film music—only six scores, barring a couple of unrealised projects and some filmed adaptations of his stage ballets. But those six include probably the best-known film music ever written, and two of the greatest collaborations between composer and director in the history of the cinema.

In the case of *Lieutenant Kizhe*, the popularity of the music (or rather, of the suite the composer drew from it) has far outstripped that of the film. With good reason—anybody who searches out Alexander Fainzimmer's comedy expecting to see the wit of Prokofiev's score reflected on screen will be sadly disappointed. Where the film's humour is ponderous and overemphatic, Prokofiev's contribution—''lightly serious, or seriously light,'' as he described it—satirises the czarist court with playful pastiche that hints, in its melodic flow, at the world of Tchaikovsky. In his music for the ''death scene'' he even creates the equivalent of a cinematic montage, with brief flashbacks to earlier motifs from the life of the nonexistent lieutenant.

In Eisenstein Prokofiev met a talent to match his own. The two men developed great mutual regard. Prokofiev admired Eisenstein not only as a brilliant director, but as ''a man of fine musical understanding.'' For his part, Eisenstein felt that in Prokofiev he and Eduard Tissé, his cinematographer, had ''found the third companion in our crusade for the kind of sound cinema we had been dreaming of.'' In working on *Alexander Nevsky* and *Ivan the Terrible*, the composer displayed an intuitive grasp of the cinematic process. ''I have always wondered,'' Eisenstein wrote, ''how Prokofiev, knowing only the number of seconds allotted to him and having seen the rushes two or three times at most, can have the music ready on the very next day—music which corresponds unerringly and precisely in all its caesuras and accents not only with the general rhythm of the entire episode, but with all the subtlest nuances of the montage development.''

For *Nevsky* Prokofiev rejected Eisenstein's initial suggestion of using authentic 13th-century Russian material, reasoning that this would merely seem quaint and remote to the audience. Instead, he devised a 13th-century music ''not as it really sounded at the time, but as we would imagine it sounding today.'' Since the main action of the film concerns the clash between the Teutonic Crusaders and the Russian people, Prokofiev constructs his score around vivid tonal contrasts. For the Germans, he uses complex polytonal themes, heavy, inexorable rhythms, harsh harmonies and strident instrumentation. The Russians are given clear, folk-based diatonic melodies, exultant or poignant according to mood, and transparently scored.

Recognising the limitations of the sound equipment of the period, Prokofiev turned them to advantage. He had the horns heralding the arrival of the Crusaders blown directly into the microphone; the resulting distortion, he explained, evoked the terror the sound would have aroused among the Russian populace. The score shared in the success of the film, which was widely acclaimed. Jean Mitry hailed it as ''the first masterpiece of a new art: the audio-visual art.'' Prokofiev later reworked his music into a cantata for concert performance.

On *Ivan the Terrible* composer and director worked together even more closely. Sometimes Prokofiev would provide music, in the normal way, for Eisenstein's footage; but often they reversed the order, with Eisenstein shooting material to fit passages Prokofiev had already written. Even when Prokofiev followed the standard procedure, Eisenstein noted, his music was ''incredibly plastic; it never becomes mere illustration. It shows in an amazing way the *inward* progress of events, their dynamic structure in which emotion and the sense of what is happening take definite form.''

In keeping with Eisenstein's approach, Prokofiev's music for the two parts of *Ivan* is less overtly dramatic than his score for *Nevsky*, more operatic and psychological in concept. *Nevsky*, with its straightforward heroic dualism, scarcely called for much in the way of character analysis, but in *Ivan* Prokofiev uses thematic patterns to comment on the development of character. Thus the material associated with Ivan himself gradually darkens, taking on brutal overtones from the bumptious songs of his bodyguards, the Oprichniki, as the Czar, soured by suspicion and bereavement, turns increasingly tyrannical.

The other movies on which Prokofiev worked are rarely shown outside Russia, and their music has never been available on disc. (He apparently regarded the scores as mere wartime propaganda stuff, written to order.) His reputation as a film composer rests on *Lieutenant Kizhe*, *Alexander Nevsky*, and *Ivan the Terrible*. But these three films would, by themselves, be enough to justify Eisenstein's description of him as ''the perfect composer for the screen.''

—Philip Kemp

PTUSHKO, Alexander

Animator. **Nationality:** Russian. **Born:** Alexander Lukich Ptushko in Lugansk, 6 April 1900. **Education:** Attended Plekhanov Institute of Economics. **Career:** 1920s—actor, newspaper correspondent, and painter in Don region; 1927—entered film industry, writing, directing, and animating shorts combining cartoon and trick work; 1935—*New Gulliver* claimed to be first feature-length puppet (wax figure) animated film ever made; during World War II—''combat director'' of many films, continued to make animated and trick films; 1944—became head of Animation Studios; 1946—instrumental in developing use of color, beginning with live-action *The Stone Flower* (mostly shot at Barrandov Studios, Prague); 1956—made first Soviet widescreen feature, *Ilya Muromets*; 1958—pioneer in combining animation and special effects in Soviet-Finnish coproduction *Sampo*. **Awards:** First Prize for Color Film, Cannes Festival, for *The Stone Flower*, 1946; State Prize for *The Stone Flower*, 1947; Silver Lion, Venice Festival, for *Sadko*, 1953; People's Artist of the RSFSR, 1957.

Films as Director:

1928   *Chto delat'* (*What to Do*); *Shifrovanny Document* (*Document in Cipher*)

1929   *Kniga v derevne* (*Book in the Country*); *Sluchi na stadione* (*Event in the Stadium*); *Stet priklyuchenni* (*100 Adventures*)

1930   *Kino v derevne* (*Cinema in the Country*); *Krepi oboronu*

1932   *Vlasteli byta (How Rulers Live)*; *Begstvo Puankare (The Flight [or Desertion] of Poincaré)*

1935   *Novy Gulliver (The New Gulliver)*

1937   *Skazka o rybake i rybke (Tale of the Fisherman and the Little Fish)*; *Vesyoli musikanti (The Jolly Musicians)*

1939   *Zolotoi klyuchik (The Golden Key)*

1946   *Kammeny tsvetok (The Stone Flower)*

1948   *Tri vstrechi (Three Encounters)* (co-d)

1952   *Sadko*

1956   *Ilya Myromets*

1958   *Sampo*

1961   *Alye parusa (Red Sails)*

1964   *Tale of Lost Time*

1966   *The Tale of Czar Sultan*

Publications

By PTUSHKO: article—

"Stepping Out of the Soviet," in *Films and Filming* (London), January 1960.

On PTUSHKO: articles—

Iskusstvo Kino (Moscow), July 1973.
Iluzjon, vol. 2, 1987.
Iskusstvo Kino (Moscow), March 1997.
Outré (Evanston), vol. 1, no. 7, 1997.

*   *   *

The "actors" in Alexander Ptushko's most important movies are neither flesh-and-blood professionals nor amateurs, but puppets—three-dimensional modelled figures. Ptushko expanded the art-form initiated by Wladyslaw Starewicz, who first produced stop-motion films in Russia prior to the Revolution. Starewicz's works were ingeniously animated, and it is to his credit that three-dimensional figure animation is thought of as a native Russian art. However, Ptushko added sound to the images, as well as more complex plotlines and feature-length running times.

Ptushko began his career as a cartoonist, one of the most sardonic of the 1920s. His first short sound films, also employing puppets, were only adequate, but he perfected his technique from year to year and project to project. His most famous film is his first full-length movie, *Novy Gulliver (The New Gulliver)*, based on Jonathan Swift's *Gulliver's Travels*—easily the best of all Soviet animated films, and the world's first feature starring puppets.

Unlike Dave Fleischer's 1939 animated cartoon, the scenario does not remain faithful to Swift. Instead, *The New Gulliver* is *Gulliver's Travels* with a twist. It is framed by a reading in a camp of Young Pioneers: Gulliver arrives in a Lilliput under the control of a dimwitted king and his secret police, and assists the oppressed during a workers' revolt. One human performer does appear: a boy (V. Konstantinov), who falls asleep and dreams himself into the story as Gulliver.

The New Gulliver took three years to produce, and was made before Walt Disney released his first animated feature, *Snow White and the Seven Dwarfs*. It is the first Soviet sound film to utilize extended multiplication and reproduction from models: the puppets—which are actually dolls—are not moved like marionettes but photographed motionless, in innumerable positions, a process similar to that in animation. They are modelled in clay, and there are no hidden mechanisms. Each has between two and 300 separate heads (or, if you will, masks), all interchangeable and featuring a wide array of gestures and expressions. These puppets feel and think, love and hate—in short, they become human: one contemporary reviewer predicted that they could successfully compete with Clark Gable and Joan Crawford in the Academy Awards competition. In its own modest way, *The New Gulliver* ranks with *Battleship Potemkin* in innovation. The film was Ptushko's first to be widely distributed outside the Soviet union. Portions were screened at the second film festival of Venice in 1934.

"I have striven (in my films)," Ptushko wrote, "to portray the theme I love best—mankind's dream of a better life, of happiness for people in general." This is fulfilled in *The New Gulliver*—though within a "party line" framework—as the populace liberates itself from its crazed ruler. This spirit was also carried into Ptushko's later career, when he directed live-action features adapted from Russian folk stories.

Myths and legends are Ptushko's most prevalent subject matter, whether his films feature puppets or actors. But those starring small figures cast in the likeness of the human form are regarded with special preference and affection.

—Rob Edelman

PUTTNAM, (Sir) David

Producer. **Nationality:** British. **Born:** London, 25 February 1941. **Career:** 1960s—photographer's agent in London; 1970—first film as producer, *Melody*; 1986—moved to Hollywood as production boss for Columbia; 1988—returned to England. **Awards:** Academy Award for *Chariots of Fire*, 1981; Michael Balcon Award, 1981. Knighthood, 1995. **Address:** Enigma Productions Ltd., 15 Queens Gate Place Mews, London SW7 5BG, England.

Films as Producer/Executive Producer:

1970   *S.W.A.L.K. (Melody)* (Hussein)

1972   *The Pied Piper* (Demy)

1973   *Mahler* (Russell); *Swastika* (Mora); *That'll Be the Day* (Whatham)

1974   *Brother, Can You Spare a Dime?* (Mora); *Stardust* (Apted)

1975   *James Dean, the First American Teenager* (Connolly); *Lisztomania* (Russell)

1976   *Bugsy Malone* (Parker)

1977   *The Duellists* (Scott)

1978   *Midnight Express* (Parker)

1980   *Foxes* (Lyne)

1981   *Chariots of Fire* (Hudson)

1982   *Experience Preferred But Not Essential* (Duffell—for TV); *P'tang Yang Kipperbang* (Apted—for TV); *Secrets*

1983   *Arthur's Hallowed Ground* (Young—for TV); *Local Hero* (Forsyth); *Red Monarch* (Gold); *Sharma and Beyond*

David Puttnam

(Gilbert—for TV); *Those Glory Glory Days* (Saville—for TV)
1984   *Cal* (O'Connor); *Forever Young* (Drury); *The Killing Fields* (Joffé); *Winter Flight* (Battersby)
1985   *Defence of the Realm* (Drury); *The Frog Prince* (Gilbert); *Mr. Love* (Battersby—for TV)
1986   *Knights and Emeralds* (Emes); *The Mission* (Joffé)
1990   *Memphis Belle* (Caton-Jones)
1991   *Meeting Venus* (Szabo)
1993   *Being Human* (Forsyth)
1994   *The Burning Season* (Frankenheimer—for TV); *The War of the Buttons* (Roberts)
1995   *Le Confessionnal* (*The Confessional*) (Robert Lepage)
1999   *My Life So Far* (Hudson)

Publications

By PUTTNAM: articles—

Sight and Sound (London), vol. 53, no. 2, Spring 1984.
American Film (Washington, D.C.), October 1986.
The Listener (London), vol. 120, no. 3081, 22 September 1988.
''Art and the Bottom Line,'' in *Sight and Sound* (London), Spring 1989.
Screen International (London), no. 825, 20 September 1991.
Time Out (London), 25 September 1991.
''Art and Science Must Unite behind the Screen,'' in *Times Educational Supplement* (New York), no. 4122, 30 June 1995.

On PUTTNAM: books—

Yule, Andrew, *Enigma: David Puttnam: The Story So Far*, Edinburgh, 1988.
Kipps, Charles, *Out of Focus: Power, Pride and Prejudice*, New York, 1989.
Yule, Andrew, *David Puttnam, Columbia Pictures & the Fast Fade*, New York, 1989.
Eberts, Jake, and Terry Ilott, *My Indecision is Final: The Rise and Fall of Goldcrest Films*, London, 1990.

On PUTTNAM: articles—

Walker, Alexander, in *National Heroes: British Cinema in the Seventies and Eighties*, London, 1985.
Stills (London), November 1986.
Hollywood Reporter, vol. 298, no. 50, 18 September 1987.
Films and Filming (London), no. 398, November 1987.
Cahiers du Cinéma (Paris), no. 402, December 1987.
Variety (New York), 18 and 25 May 1988.
American Cinemeditor (Hollywood), vol. 38, no. 1, Spring 1988.
Premiere (Hollywood), no. 137, August 1988.
Film Comment (New York), vol. 25, no. 1, January-February 1989.
The Listener (London), vol. 122, no. 3105, 16 March 1989.
Sight and Sound (London), vol. 58, no. 4, Autumn 1989.
Starburst (London), no. 137, January 1990.
In *Talking Films: The Best of the Guardian Lectures*, edited by Andrew Britton, London, 1991.
Film Journal, vol 94, no. 9, June 1991.
Time Out, vol. 1101, 25 September 1991.
Variety (New York), vol. 349, 25 January 1993.
New York Times, 30 August 1994.
The Nation, vol. 259, 10 October 1994.
Times Educational Suppledment, no. 4087, 28 October, 1994.
Times Educational Supplement, no. 4160, 22 March 1996.
Variety (New York), 23/29 June 1997.

*   *   *

In Vincente Minnelli's 1952 film, *The Bad and the Beautiful*, Kirk Douglas gives a bravura performance as a Hollywood tycoon who manages to be both venal and visionary, a cultured philistine: he is at once a wheeler/dealer, with the nous to shimmy all the way to the top of the greasy pole, and an ardent cinephile, whose determination to make challenging and popular films is unwavering. He will go to extraordinary lengths to help his loved ones, but will betray a lifelong friend at the drop of a hat if it is to the advantage of the movie on the lot. This great ball of contradictions may have been based on MGM's wonderboy of the 1930s, Irving Thalberg, but his foibles and qualities are precisely those which characterize Britain's most prominent producer of recent years, David Puttnam.

A former advertising executive, Puttnam broke into the film business in the early 1970s, when Goodtimes, the company he formed with ex-agent Sandy Lieberson, backed the whimsical, somewhat saccharine *Melody*, which charted a schoolboy's love affair. To add a little lustre to this gooey teen romance, Puttnam filled the film with Bee Gees songs, and cast Mark Lester, who had recently starred as *Oliver*, in the leading role. It may not have seemed a particularly auspicious way to start, but *Melody* at least proved Puttnam could get a project off the ground. It was followed by two trenchant satires on the British rock and roll myth, *That'll Be the Day* and *Stardust*. These managed to combine posturing adolescent male rebellion *à la* James Dean with a canny, ironic portrait of British provincial life in the 1960s; to reconcile "swinging sixties" glamour with an irredeemable 1970s seediness.

In the early days, Puttnam's single greatest contribution as a producer was recognizing and harnessing the pool of filmmaking talent which lay untapped in British advertising. Alan Parker, Ridley Scott, who cut his teeth on *The Duellists*, Hugh Hudson, who directed Puttnam's greatest success of all, *Chariots of Fire*, and Adrian Lyne all made more or less successful transitions from TV commercials to the big screen under Puttnam's auspices.

Puttnam proved far less adept in dealing with established cinema names. His collaboration with the French director Jacques Demy yielded a mediocre Donovan vehicle, *The Pied Piper*; his brief alliance with Ken Russell threatened to bankrupt him when *Lisztomania* rocketed over budget. Worst of all, his documentary with Marcel Ophüls, *A Memory of Justice*, a movie later lauded by the New York critics, ended in recrimination as he tried to elbow the French filmmaker off the project. Such heavy handed behaviour didn't become a producer ostensibly committed to nurturing and protecting creative talent. Puttnam's chutzpah and energy were undeniable, but his choice of material was sometimes questionable, and his facility for making enemies of anybody who stood up to or crossed him did him no favours at all.

After the 1982 success of *Chariots of Fire*—a success more closely identified with Puttnam than with the picture's director, Hugh Hudson, its stars, and even its Oscar-winning scriptwriter, Colin Welland—there was a predictable backlash against the bearded marvel: critics scoffed at Puttnam, decrying his resolutely middle-brow aesthetic vision. He in turn lambasted the critics, suggesting they bore much of the responsibility for the parlous state of the British film industry. Too many filmmakers, he suggested, were hamstrung by these critics, and ended up neglecting the needs and wants of the wider audience by making introspective, obscure films which never had a chance of success at the box office, however favourable their notices.

Still, there is no denying that Puttnam, along with Jake Eberts, the former banker who founded Goldcrest, were circumspect about the projects they backed. Generally, they plumped for tales of male heroism, rousing stories with a historical foundation and a rattling narrative to stir the emotions. They both seemed to share a patriarchal public service ethos, reminiscent of Reith's vision for the BBC, where entertainment and education went hand-in-hand: *The Killing Fields*, *Chariots of Fire*, *The Mission*, and *Memphis Belle* were all high-testosterone action adventures which came laced with a message. No gangsters or morally ambivalent figures clouded these movies, full as they were of Olympic runners, Jesuit priests, raw young American airmen and crusading journalists. Puttnam seemed to hold his nose at the prospect of sex and violence, and eviscerated his films as a consequence. Only *Midnight Express*, a project which he did not originate but which he oversaw for the American production company, Casablanca, delved into the seamier side of the human psyche.

Puttnam seems to see himself as the spiritual descendant of Sir Michael Balcon, the patrician boss at Ealing, whose studios "projected Britain and the British character." *Local Hero*, the West Highland fable he produced for director Bill Forsyth, is self-consciously in the tradition of Ealing's *Whisky Galore*, *The Maggie*, et al. However, Puttnam's only experience of running a studio was very different to Balcon's. From 1987 to 1988 he was chairman and chief executive of Columbia Pictures in Hollywood, and a major "player." It was not a happy experience. While his aims were laudable enough, his approach to being a Hollywood bigwig was arguably self-destructive. He wanted to get away from making sequels or gung-ho war pictures like *Rambo*, to rationalize studio practices and to reduce budgets. With this in mind, he himself lived modestly. As Charles Kipps observes, while his second-in-command drove a Rolls Royce, the less flamboyant Brit would turn up to work in an Audi: "It was as if the prince was brought to the palace in a gilded carriage while the king was deposited in an ox-cart."

He refused to play the game, and many respected him for it. But, to outsiders, he seemed as nepotistic as any of his predecessors. While turning down projects from such established names as Norman Jewison and Ray Stark, he gave a green light to pictures from his old British protégés: Bill Forsyth's *Housekeeping* and Ridley Scott's *Someone to Watch Over Me* were two of the earliest movies he developed at Columbia. There were also suspicions that he obliquely tried to sink the ill-fated Hoffman/Beatty extravaganza, *Ishtar*. After all, he *had* called Hoffman a "worrisome American pest" when he had been involved in the production *Agatha*, which he felt the American actor had hijacked, and he had savaged the extravagance of *Reds* when the infinitely cheaper *Chariots of Fire* beat it to the 1981 Best Picture Oscar. Furthermore, to placate Hudson, who had been aggrieved at what little credit he was given for *Chariots'* success, he suggested Hudson ought to have won the Best Director Oscar instead of Beatty.

Politicking has never been Puttnam's strongest suit, so it is little wonder his stay at Columbia was cut short. However, leaving Columbia by no means meant leaving motion pictures. Puttnam's Enigma Films, in joint venture with Warner Bros., among others, produced *Memphis Belle* and then *Meeting Venus*, featuring Glenn Close. *Meeting Venus* appropriately parallels Wagner's intentions that his opera *Tannhauser* reflect the chaos and alliances of the political factions of the day.

Controversy surrounded Puttnam's production of the HBO movie *The Burning Season*, which documents the murder of Brazilian activist Chico Mendes. Letters written by Puttnam to executives at Time Warner were discovered and published in *The Nation*. In these, Puttnam would appear to have sacrificed political, environmental, and perhaps even moral concerns in favor of liaisons with the government of Ecuador, Revlon, and Gulf Oil (who have significantly damaged the Brazilian rain forest, with dire consequences for the indigenous peoples of the region). When the film premiered in Los Angeles, representatives from two rain-forest activist groups were present to distribute leaflets in protest.

Working again with Welland in *The War of the Buttons*, Puttnam adapts the 1962 French original to the conflicts of Ireland. Using the landscape and political tension as a backdrop, he addresses the conflict experienced between children and adults, particularly when the former imitate the latter in the horrors of war. While many films have portrayed children as savage by nature, easily as corrupt as adults, Puttnam's young characters in *The War of the Buttons* affirm the innocence and purity of children.

Puttnam is a contradictory figure, difficult to warm to and easy to attack. But, whatever his detractors might say, he remains one of the few figures left with the gumption to get pictures made in Britain. At home in both the artistic and financial halls of the motion picture industry, Puttnam often emphasizes the educational potential of motion pictures. Denying that his pictures are didactically message oriented, however, Puttnam argues that his films strive for a balance between social and political issues and human relationships, providing an audience not only with entertainment but also with enlightenment. Perhaps Puttnam's passion for learning was inspired by his father's work as a journalist; indeed, journalists and the quest for knowledge and understanding feature prominently in many of his films. Puttnam insists that the British must lead the way in integrating education and media. Not only as a film producer, but as a Governor of the National Film School, a lobbyist for British film interests, and as a teacher, his contribution to British film culture in general has been immense.

—Geoffrey Macnab, updated by Carrie O'Neill

RABIER, Jean

Cinematographer. **Nationality:** French. **Born:** Paris, 21 April 1927. **Career:** Industrial artist, then camera operator and cinematographer in the 1950s, especially on short films; 1959—first of many films for Claude Chabrol, *Les Cousins.*

Films as Cinematographer:

(shorts)

1951   *L'Eveil d'un monde* (Dupont); *Okomé* (Dupont); *Voilà vous* (Dupont); *Palmes* (Dupont); *Trains sans fumée* (Cantagrel)
1952   *La Grande Case* (Dupont)
1955   *Les Araignées rouges* (Tadié and Lacoste); *Les Pucérons* (Tadié and Lacoste); *Le Carpocapse des pommes* (Tadié and Lacoste); *La Tavelure du pommier et du poirier* (Tadié and Lacoste); *Le Débroussaillage chimique* (Tadié and Lacoste); *La Tordeuse orientale* (Tadié and Lacoste); *La Banque* (Vilardebo); *Les Vers de la grappe* (Tadié and Lacoste); *La Vie du moyen age* (Vilardebo); *Le Cercle enchanté* (de Gastyne); *L'Homme, notre ami* (de Gastyne)
1956   *Israel . . . terre retrouvée* (de Gastyne); *Propre à rien* (de Gastyne)
1957   *Robinson* (de Gastyne)
1958   *Le Château du passé* (de Gastyne)
1960   *Mille villages* (Vilardebo); *Soleils* (Vilardebo)
1961   *Orchestre et diamants* (Rancy)
1962   *La Dormeuse* (Pons)
1969   *Autresville d'art* (de Gastyne)

(features)

1955   *Crève-Coeur* (Dupont)
1958   *Le Beau Serge* (*Bitter Reunion*) (Chabrol) (cam)
1959   *Les Cousins* (*The Cousins*) (Chabrol); *A double tour* (*Web of Passion*; *Leda*) (Chabrol)
1961   ***Cléo de 5 à 7*** (*Cléo from 5 to 7*) (Varda); ''L'Avarice'' ep. of *Les Sept Péchés capitaux* (*The Seven Deadly Sins*) (Chabrol); *Les Godelureaux* (Chabrol)
1962   *Ophélia* (Chabrol); ''Illibatezza'' ep. of *Rogopag* (Rossellini)
1963   *Landru* (*Bluebeard*) (Chabrol); *La Baie des anges* (*Bay of the Angels*) (Demy); *Peau de banane* (*Banana Peel*) (Marcel Ophüls)
1964   *Les Parapluies de Cherbourg* (*The Umbrellas of Cherbourg*) (Demy); ''L'Homme qui vendit la Tour Eiffel'' ep. of *Les*

Plus Belles Escroqueries du monde (*The Beautiful Swindlers*) (Chabrol); *Le Tigre aime la chair fraiche* (*The Tiger Likes Fresh Blood*) (Chabrol)
1965   *Le Bonheur* (Varda); *Les Iles enchantées* (Vilardebo); *Marie-Chantal contre le Docteur Kha* (Chabrol); ''La Muette'' ep. of *Paris vu par . . .* (*Six in Paris*) (Chabrol); *Le Tigre se parfume à la dynamite* (*An Orchid for the Tiger*) (Chabrol)
1966   *La Ligne de démarcation* (Chabrol)
1967   *Le Scandale* (*The Champagne Murders*) (Chabrol); *Un Idiot à Paris* (Korber); *La Petite Vertu* (Korber); *La Route de Corinthe* (*Who's Got the Black Box?*) (Chabrol)
1968   *Les Biches* (*The Does*) (Chabrol)
1969   ***La Femme infidèle*** (*Unfaithful Wife*) (Chabrol); *L'Homme orchestre* (Korber); *Que la bête meure* (*This Man Must Die!*) (Chabrol); ***Le Boucher*** (*The Butcher*) (Chabrol)
1970   *La Rupture* (*The Breakup*) (Chabrol)
1971   *Juste avant la nuit* (*Just Before Nightfall*) (Chabrol); *La Décade prodigieuse* (*Ten Days' Wonder*) (Chabrol)
1972   *Docteur Popaul* (Chabrol)
1973   *Les Noces rouges* (*Wedding in Blood*) (Chabrol)
1974   *Nada* (*The Nada Gang*) (Chabrol)
1975   *Les Innocents aux mains sales* (*Dirty Hands*) (Chabrol); *Une Partie de plaisir* (*Pleasure Party*) (Chabrol); *Les Magiciens* (Chabrol)
1976   *Folies bourgeoises* (*The Twist*) (Chabrol)
1977   *Alice, ou la dernière fugue* (*Alice, or the Last Escapade*) (Chabrol); *Swingmen in Europe* (Mazéas)
1978   *Les Liens de sang* (*Blood Relatives*) (Chabrol); *Violette Nozière* (*Violette*) (Chabrol)
1980   *Le Cheval d'orgueil* (Chabrol)
1982   *Les Fantômes du Chapelier* (Chabrol)
1986   *Inspector Lavardin* (Chabrol)
1987   *Le Cri du hibou* (Chabrol); *Masques* (Chabrol)
1988   *A notre regrettable epoux* (Pertitdidier); *Une Affaire de femmes* (Chabrol); *En toute innocence* (Jessua)
1990   *Dr. M* (*Club Extinction*) (Chabrol); *Jours tranquilles à Clichy* (*Quiet Days at Clichy*) (Chabrol)
1991   *Madame Bovary* (Chabrol)

Publications

By RABIER: articles—

Cinéma (Paris), December 1964.
Image et Son (Paris), November 1970.
Cinéma (Paris), January 1973.
Film Reader, January 1977.

On RABIER: articles—

Monthly Film Bulletin (London), 1965.
Focus on Film (London), no. 12, Winter 1972, additions in nos. 13 and 15, 1973.
Film Français (Paris), 29 April 1977.

*   *   *

Jean Rabier, the distinguished cinematographer of the French New Wave, has been most consistently and significantly associated with the films of Claude Chabrol. Although Rabier has worked in black-and-white, providing nicely atmospheric images in films such as *Le Beau Serge* and *Ophélia*, his most integrated work is undoubtedly in Chabrol's color films. Rabier's cinematography is distinguished at once by its incredible beauty and expressiveness, as well as by its lack of the kind of boring picture-postcard prettiness which is all too often associated with color cinematography. His first color film for Chabrol, *A double tour*, is almost deliriously colorful in its imagery.

In Rabier's best work for Chabrol, the cinematography is totally at the service of the director's theme: thus, in *La Femme infidèle*, in which Chabrol depicts the violence and passion hidden within the apparently civilized bourgeoisie, Rabier emphasizes the beautiful patina of that bourgeoisie: the sheen of crystal, the impressionistic soft-focus prettiness of flower arrangements and manicured yard, and particularly the extraordinarily photographed face of Stéphane Audran, who is turned into an exquisite bourgeois goddess.

In *Le Boucher*, Rabier's cinematography of the small-town landscape resembles nothing so much as a Cézanne painting; some of the film's final images, in which Rabier purposely drains his palette to photograph Audran's eyes as pools of light surrounded by darkness, reveal the influence of American *film noir* and never fail to move. As in *A double tour* and *Ten Days' Wonder*, an explosion of color is present also in the climax of *La Rupture*, in which Audran's gradual movement to blue and transcendence is captured visually by Rabier with the use of an increasingly longer lens, and, ultimately, a liberating rupture of laboratory-processed color which is one of the most memorable displays of virtuosity in all New Wave cinema. And yet this mastery of color expressiveness is achieved alongside a sense of improvisation and of natural light.

Finally, one must note as well the mobility of Rabier's camera, which—undoubtedly as a result of his collaboration with Chabrol and the requirements of the mise-en-scène—uses a wide variety of angles and perspectives and often constructs whole scenes around incredibly fluid and expressive camera movements. One immediately thinks of the final tracking shot of *La Femme infidèle*, or the moving camera expressing the father's grief in *Que la bête meure*, or the very impressive tracking shot of several minutes' duration in the beginning of *Le Boucher* which effortlessly reveals the layout of the town. Perhaps the signature image of Rabier and Chabrol is the expressive lateral camera movement into or away from dark trees, which, generally surrounded by beautiful color images, works to convey visually the epigraph of *La Rupture* and the theme implicit in all Chabrol's work: "What an utter darkness suddenly surrounds me!"— the darkness of the soul blotting out the color and beauty of the world.

—Charles Derry

RAKSIN, David

Composer. **Nationality:** American. **Born:** Philadelphia, Pennsylvania, 4 August 1912. **Education:** Attended the University of Pennsylvania, Philadelphia, Mus. B. 1934; also studied with Schoenberg and Isadore Freed. **Family:** Married Joanne Carol Kaiser, 1959, two sons and one daughter. **Career:** 1924—leader of his own band; composer from late 1920s: orchestra and chamber works, and works for ballet and stage; arranger, Harms music publisher, New York; 1936–43—arranger, orchestrator, and collaborator (often with Buttolph and Mockridge) on films; 1950s—composed music for Mr. Magoo cartoons; since 1958—teacher at University of California, Los Angeles.

Films as Composer:

1936   *Dancing Pirate* (Corrigan) (co)
1937   *San Quentin* (Bacon) (co); *52nd Street* (Young) (co); *Wings over Honolulu* (Potter) (co); *Marked Woman* (Bacon) (co); *Marry the Girl* (McGann) (co); *Let Them Live!* (*The Stones Cry Out*) (Young) (co); *As Good as Married* (Buzzell); *Midnight Court* (McDonald) (co); *The Kid Comes Back* (*Don't Pull Your Punches*) (Eason) (co); *She's Dangerous* (Foster and Carruth) (co); *The Mighty Treve* (Collins) (co)
1938   *Suez* (Dwan)
1939   *Hollywood Cavalcade* (Cummings) (co); *Stanley and Livingstone* (H. King) (co); *Mr. Moto's Last Warning* (Foster) (co); *Frontier Marshal* (Dwan) (co); *The Adventures of Sherlock Holmes* (*Sherlock Holmes*) (Werker) (co)
1941   *The Men in Her Life* (Ratoff) (co); *Dead Men Tell* (Lachman) (co); *Ride On, Vaquero* (Leeds) (co)
1942   *The Magnificent Dope* (W. Lang) (co); *Dr. Renault's Secret* (Lachman) (co); *Manila Calling* (Leeds) (co); *The Man Who Wouldn't Die* (Leeds) (co); *Whispering Ghosts* (Werker) (co); *Just Off Broadway* (Leeds) (co); *Thru' Different Eyes* (Loring) (co); *The Postman Didn't Ring* (Schuster) (co); *Who Is Hope Schuyler?* (Loring) (co)
1943   *City without Men* (Salkow) (co); *The Gang's All Here* (Berkeley) (co); *The Undying Monster* (*The Hammond Mystery*) (Brahm) (co)
1944   *Tampico* (Mendes); **Laura** (Preminger)
1945   *Billy Rose's Diamond Horseshoe* (Seaton); *Attack in the Pacific* (doc); *Don Juan Quilligan* (Tuttle); *Where Do We Go from Here?* (Ratoff); *Fallen Angel* (Preminger)
1946   *Smoky* (L. King); *The Shocking Miss Pilgrim* (Seaton)
1947   *The Homestretch* (Humberstone); *Forever Amber* (Preminger); *Daisy Kenyon* (Preminger); *The Secret Life of Walter Mitty* (McLeod)
1948   *Fury at Furnace Creek* (Humberstone); *Apartment for Peggy* (Seaton)
1949   *Force of Evil* (Polonsky)
1950   *Whirlpool* (Preminger); *Grounds for Marriage* (Leonard); *The Next Voice You Hear* (Wellman); *Giddyap* (cartoon); *Right Cross* (J. Sturges); *The Magnificent Yankee* (J. Sturges); *The Reformer and the Redhead* (Panama and Frank)
1951   *Kind Lady* (J. Sturges); *The Man with a Cloak* (Markle); *Across the Wide Missouri* (Wellman)

1952   *Sloppy Jalopy* (cartoon); *The Girl in White* (J. Sturges); *Pat and Mike* (Cukor); *Madeline* (cartoon); *The Bad and the Beautiful* (Minnelli); *Carrie* (Wyler); *It's a Big Country* (Weis and others); *Just for You* (Nugent)
1953   *The Unicorn in the Garden* (cartoon)
1954   *Suddenly* (Lewis); *Apache* (Aldrich)
1955   *The Big Combo* (Lewis)
1956   *Seven Wonders of the World* (Tetzlaff and others); *Jubal* (Daves); *Hilda Crane* (Dunne); *Bigger than Life* (Ray)
1957   *Man on Fire* (MacDougall); *Gaslight Ridge* (Lyon); *The Vintage* (Hayden); *Until They Sail* (Wise)
1958   *Twilight for the Gods* (Pevney); *Separate Tables* (Delbert Mann)
1959   *Al Capone* (Wilson)
1960   *Pay or Die* (Wilson)
1961   *Night Tide* (Harrington); *Too Late Blues* (Cassavetes)
1962   *Two Weeks in Another Town* (Minnelli)
1963   *The Patsy* (Lewis); *Sylvia* (Douglas); *Invitation to a Gunfighter* (Wilson)
1965   *Love Has Many Faces* (Singer)
1966   *A Big Hand for the Little Lady* (Cook); *The Redeemer* (Breen)
1968   *Will Penny* (Gries)
1970   *Glass Houses* (Singer); *The Over-the-Hill Gang Rides Again* (McGowan—for TV)
1971   *What's the Matter with Helen?* (Harrington)
1978   *The Ghost of Flight 401* (Stern—for TV)
1979   *The Suicide's Wife* (Newland—for TV)
1983   *The Day After* (Meyer—for TV)
1989   *Lady in the Corner* (Levin—for TV)

Film as Arranger:

1936   *Modern Times* (Chaplin)

Publications

By RAKSIN: articles—

''Raksin on Film Music,'' in *Journal of University Film Association* (Carbondale, Illinois), vol. 26, no. 4, 1974.
''Whatever Became of Movie Music?,'' in *Film Music Notebook* (Calabasas, California), Fall 1974.
In *Knowing the Score*, by Irwin Bazelon, New York, 1975.
Interview with Elmer Bernstein in *Film Music Notebook* (Calabasas, California), vol. 2, nos. 2 and 3, 1976.
With Charles Berg, '''Music Composed by Charlie Chaplin': Auteur or Collaborator?,'' in *Journal of University Film Association* (Carbondale, Illinois), Winter 1979.
Interview with Jeannie Pool, in *Cue Sheet* (Hollywood), vol. 10, no. 1–2, Spring 1993–1994.

On RAKSIN: articles—

Morton, Lawrence, in *Quarterly of Film, Radio, and Television* (Berkeley, California), Winter 1951.
Thomas, Anthony, in *Films in Review* (New York), January 1963.

Films in Review (New York), October 1971.
Thomas, Tony, in *Music for the Movies*, South Brunswick, New Jersey, 1973.
Film Music Notebook (Calabasas, California), Fall 1974.
Films in Review (New York), June/July 1981.
Lacombe, Alain, in *Hollywood*, Paris, 1983.
Score, no. 90, March 1994.
Soundtrack! (Hollywood), vol. 13, March 1994.
Cue Sheet (Hollywood), vol. 10, no. 3–4, 1993–94.
Cue Sheet (Hollywood), vol. 12, no. 1, January 1996.

*   *   *

Arriving in Hollywood in 1935, David Raksin was perhaps the first American film composer to set out with the idea of being one. At that time, most of the men employed in film scoring had come from the theater or the concert halls. The idea of music in films had fascinated the young Raksin, whose father conducted accompaniment to silent films in Philadelphia. Raksin Sr. also operated a music store, in which Raksin worked while attending Central High School. He studied piano and with the aid of his clarinetist father mastered that instrument. At the University of Pennsylvania, Raksin studied composition with Harl McDonald and earned his tuition playing in dance bands and the orchestra of the CBS radio station in Philadelphia. At 21 he was in New York, playing in, and arranging for, a number of dance bands, which led to a position as arranger on the staff of the music publishing house of Harms, Inc. After a year with Harms, two Hollywood orchestrators, Eddie Powell and Herbert Spencer, recommended Raksin to Alfred Newman, who needed someone to work with Charlie Chaplin on the score the comedian wanted to devise for *Modern Times*. Although he had a keen sense of the use of music in films and could invent melodies, Chaplin could neither play the piano nor write music.

The success of the score bolstered Raksin's belief that this was the area of composition in which he wanted to be active. Over the next six years, he was engaged in arranging, adapting, and writing music for a large number of features, shorts, cartoons, and documentaries. He received wide attention in 1944 with his score for *Laura*, the main theme of which would become a song standard, with lyrics by Johnny Mercer, and one of the most often recorded of all melodies. The score is regarded as a textbook example of the effective use of music in film.

Speaking with a voice very much his own, Raksin's scores tended to be more modernistic than the average and stylistically ahead of their time. He was nominated for an Oscar for *Forever Amber* and *Separate Tables*. Other of his scores highly regarded by students of film composition include *Force of Evil*, *The Bad and the Beautiful*, *Carrie*, *Too Late Blues*, *Will Penny*, and *What's the Matter with Helen?* In 1958 Raksin began his association with the University of California, Los Angeles, conducting classes in film music theory and technique. Since 1968 he has also taught urban ecology. One of the most recounted of film music anecdotes is attributable to Raksin. When Alfred Hitchcock was making *Lifeboat* at Twentieth Century-Fox in 1944, Raksin, then on staff, let it be known he would be interested in writing the score. An intermediary informed the composer, ''Mr. Hitchcock feels that since the entire action of the film takes place in a lifeboat in the middle of the ocean, where would the music come from?'' Replied Raksin, ''Ask Mr. Hitchcock to explain where the cameras come from and I'll tell him where the music comes from.''

—Tony Thomas

RALSTON, Ken

Special-Effects Supervisor and Cameraman. **Born:** c.1955. **Career:** 1971–77—Cascade Pictures, visual-effects commercial house, doing ads for the Pillsbury Doughboy and Green Giant characters, among others; 1977–81—joined George Lucas's Industrial Light & Magic as cameraman on *Star Wars*, *The Empire Strikes Back*, and *Dragonslayer*; 1982—first visual-effects supervisor on *Star Trek II: The Wrath of Khan*; 1991—in addition to visual-effects supervisor title, added second-unit director on *The Rocketeer* for first time; 1994 ''You Murderer'' episode of TV series, *Tales from the Crypt*; 1995—left ILM to become president of Sony Pictures Imageworks. **Awards:** Academy Award and British Academy Award, for *Return of the Jedi*, 1983, *Who Framed Roger Rabbit?*, 1988, *Death Becomes Her*, 1992, and *Forrest Gump*, 1994; Academy Award for *Cocoon*, 1985; British Academy Award, for *Back to the Future Part II*, 1989.

Films as Cameraman:

1977   ***Star Wars*** (Lucas)
1980   ***The Empire Strikes Back*** (Kershner)
1981   *Dragonslayer* (Robbins)

Films as Visual-Effects Supervisor:

1982   *Star Trek II: The Wrath of Khan* (Meyer)
1983   ***Return of the Jedi*** (Marquand) (co-effects supervisor)
1984   *Star Trek III: The Search for Spock* (Nimoy)
1985   *Cocoon* (Petrie); *Out of Africa* (Pollock) (train at beginning of film); *Back to the Future* (Zemeckis)
1986   *Star Trek IV: The Voyage Home* (Nimoy); *The Golden Child* (Ritchie)
1988   *Who Framed Roger Rabbit?* (Zemeckis)
1989   *Cocoon: The Return* (Petrie); *Back to the Future Part II* (Zemeckis)
1990   *Back to the Future Part III* (Zemeckis); *Akira Kurosawa's Dreams* (*Dreams*) (Kurosawa)
1991   *The Rocketeer* (Johnston) (+ 2nd-unit d)
1992   *Death Becomes Her* (Zemeckis) (+ 2nd-unit d)
1994   *Forrest Gump* (Zemeckis)
1995   *Jumanji* (Johnston); *The American President* (R. Reiner); *Sabrina* (Pollock)
1996   *Phenomenon* (Turteltaub) (special effects); *Michael* (Ephron) (senior visual effects supervisor)
1997   *Contact* (Zemeckis) (senior visual effects supervisor)

Films as Director:

2000   *Jumanji 2*

Publications

By RALSTON: article—

''Special Effects for *Star Trek II*: Mama Eel and the Nebulae,'' in *American Cinematographer* (Hollywood), October 1982.
''Astonishing Effects Slate for Future,'' an interview with Ron Magid, in *American Cinematographer* (Hollywood), December 1989.
''Gump Gallops Through Time/ILM Breaks New Digital Ground for Group,'' in *American Cinematographer* (Hollywood), October 1994.

On RALSTON: articles—

On *Cocoon*, in *American Cinematographer* (Hollywood), December 1985.
On *Roger Rabbit*, in *American Cinematographer* (Hollywood), July 1988.
On *Jumanji*, in *American Cinematographer* (Hollywood), February 1996.
On *Contact*, in *Cinefex* (Riverside), September 1997.

*   *   *

Ken Ralston is a leading member of a generation of special-effects wizards who came of age during the seventies, swept the eighties film world and, in the nineties, sit as the designated heads of mainstream Hollywood, as cinema all but gave itself over to the otherworldly visuals available through computer-enhanced imagery.

Ralston spent his childhood ''making movies in my garage, using claymation and a crummy Kodak 8mm camera.'' His obsession with filmic images led to an apprenticeship at a special-effects house, working on such ads as those featuring the Pillsbury Doughboy and the Green Giant.

After joining George Lucas's Industrial Light & Magic as a cameraman on the original *Star Wars* film, Ralston made ILM his home for the next 18 years. While effects are unquestionably a team effort, it was Ralston's drive to perfect the visual techniques that quickly found him earning the title visual-effects supervisor for the first time on *Star Trek II: The Wrath of Khan*.

Onboard for two other *Star Trek* feature-film voyages, Ralston brought an added magic that made the films visually intriguing and technically vastly superior to the series' television namesake. Audiences flocked to them and critics were more-often-than-not gentle to the films. But Ralston found the boundaries of imagery acceptable to *Star Trek*'s loyal fans confining and moved on to other challenges. While he has been instrumental in taking audiences literally and figuratively to new frontiers, Ralston and his special-effects team nearly overwhelmed the unpleasant comedy, *Death Becomes Her*, and the misguided family film, *Jumanji*.

Career highlights of Ralston's would have to include the groundbreaking smash, *Who Framed Roger Rabbit?*, which merged live action with animation in a farcical plot. Equally, the visuals on *Forrest Gump*, which at one point allowed Gump to convincingly shake hands with the late President Kennedy, satisfied the audience of this whimsical allegory of an extremely simple man in complex times, helping to make it one of the all-time box-office hits.

After years spent challenging the cinema's visual limitations with otherworldly tales, 1995 found Ralston bringing his film magic to two down-to-earth romantic fairy tales, *The American President* and the less enchanting *Sabrina*. It was the year that also found Ralston breaking away from his career home of 18 years at ILM to become president of Sony Pictures Imageworks.

—Allen Grant Richards

RANK, J. Arthur (Lord)

Producer. **Nationality:** British. **Born:** Joseph Arthur Rank in Hull, Yorkshire, 22 December 1888. **Family:** Married Laura Ellan Marshall; two daughters. **Career:** Mill apprentice; inherited father's flour milling fortune but made a loss on the business; Methodist Sunday School teacher; 1930s—formed the Religious Film Society as a means to promote his beliefs; owned Pinewood, Islington, and Denham Studios; 1941—chairman of the board, Gaumont British and Odeon cinema chains; 1945—owned 60% of the British film industry; expanded into Hollywood; 1950s—production slowed down; 1962— retired. **Award:** Peerage, 1957. **Died:** In 1972.

Films as Executive Producer:

1931   *A Night in Montmartre* (Hiscott)
1932   *Jack's the Boy* (Forde); *Love on Wheels* (Saville); *Man of Aran* (Flaherty)
1933   *Aunt Sally* (Whelan); *Channel Crossing* (Rosmer); *The Fire Raisers* (Powell); *It's a Boy* (Whelan); *Just Smith* (Walls); *The Lucky Number* (Asquith), *Red Ensign* (Powell); *Turkey Time* (Walls)
1934   *The Camels Are Coming* (Whelan); *Chu Chin Chow* (Forde); *Cup of Kindness* (Walls); *Dirty Work* (Walls); *Evensong* (Saville); *Jack Ahoy* (Forde); *Lady in Danger* (Walls); *Little Friend* (Viertel); *My Old Dutch* (Hill); *Oh Daddy!* (Cutts and Melford); *Princess Charming* (Elvey); *Road House* (Elvey); *Things Are Looking Up* (de Courville); *Wild Boy* (de Courville)
1935   *Boys Will Be Boys* (Beaudine); *Bulldog Jack* (Forde); *Car of Dreams* (Cutts and Melford); *The Clairvoyant* (Elvey); *Fighting Stock* (Walls); *Fly Away Peter* (Saunders); *Foreign Affairs* (Walls); *The Guv'nor* (Rosmel); *Heat Wave* (Elvey); *The Iron Duke* (Saville); *Me and Marlborough* (Saville); *Pot Luck* (Walls); *R.A.F.* (Betts); *Stormy Weather* (Walls); *The Turn of the Tide* (Walker)
1936   *East Meets West* (Mason); *Everybody Dance* (Reisner); *Everything Is Thunder* (Rosmer); *It's Love Again* (Saville); *King of the Damned* (Forde); *The Man Who Changed His Mind* (Stevenson); *Seven Sinners* (de Courville); *Where There's a Will* (Beaudine)
1937   *Alf's Button Afloat* (Varnel); *Non-Stop New York* (Stevenson); *O.H.M.S.* (*Born for Glory*; *You're in the Army Now*) (Walsh); *Oh, Mr. Porter!* (Varnel)

1938   *Bank Holiday* (Reed); *Convict 99* (Varnel); *Crackerjack* (de Courville); *Hey! Hey! U.S.A.* (*King Kelly of the U.S.A.*) (Varnel); *Love in Waiting* (Pierce); *Penny and the Pownall Case* (Hand); *A Piece of Cake* (Irwin)
1939   *The Arsenal Stadium Mystery* (Dickinson); *Climbing High* (Reed); *The Frozen Limits* (Varnel); *Neutral Port* (Varnel); *Band Waggon* (Varnel)
1940   *Freedom Radio* (*Voice in the Night*) (Asquith); *Gasbags* (Varnel)
1941   *Cottage to Let* (Asquith); *The Ghost Train* (Forde); *I Thank You* (Varnel); *Hi, Gang!* (Varnel)
1942   *Back Room Boy* (Mason); *The Day Will Dawn* (*The Avengers*) (French); *The Great Mr. Handel* (Walker); *In Which We Serve* (Coward and Lean); *King Arthur Was a Gentleman* (Varnel); *Secret Mission* (French); *Unpublished Story* (French)
1943   *The Demi-Paradise* (*Adventure for Two*) (Asquith); *The Flemish Farm* (Dell); *The Gentle Sex* (Howard); *It's That Man Again* (Forde); *The Life and Death of Colonel Blimp* (Powell and Pressburger); *The Man in Grey* (Arliss); *Millions Like Us* (Launder and Gilliat); *Miss London Ltd.* (Guest); *The Silver Fleet* (Sewell and Wellesley); *They Met in the Dark* (Lamac); *We Dive at Dawn* (Asquith)
1944   *Bees in Paradise* (Guest); *A Canterbury Tale* (Powell and Pressburger); *Don't Take It to Heart* (Dell); *English without Tears* (French); *Fanny By Gaslight* (*Man of Evil*) (Asquith); *Give Us the Moon* (Guest); *Love Story* (*A Lady Surrenders*) (Arliss); *Madonna of the Seven Moons* (Crabtree); *Mr. Emmanuel* (French); *Tawny Pipit* (Miles); *Time Flies* (Forde); *2,000 Women* (Launder); *The Way Ahead* (Reed)
1945   ***Brief Encounter*** (Lean); ***Henry V*** (Olivier); *I Know Where I'm Going* (Powell and Pressburger); *I'll Be Your Sweetheart* (Guest); *A Place of One's Own* (Knowles); *The Rake's Progress* (*The Notorious Gentleman*) (Gilliat); *The Seventh Veil* (Bennett); *They Knew Mr. Knight* (Walker); *They Were Sisters* (Crabtree); *Waterloo Road* (Gilliat); *The Way to the Stars* (Asquith)
1946   *Beware of Pity* (Elvey); *Caravan* (Crabtree); *Carnival* (Haynes); *Dear Murderer* (Crabtree); ***Great Expectations*** (Lean); *Green for Danger* (Gilliat); *I See a Dark Stranger* (*The Adventuress*) (Launder); *London Town* (*My Heart Goes Crazy*) (Ruggles); ***A Matter of Life and Death*** (*Stairway to Heaven*) (Powell and Pressburger); *Men of Two Worlds* (*Kissenga, Man of Africa*) (Dickinson); *The Overlanders* (Watt); *School for Secrets* (*The Secret Flight*) (Ustinov); *Theirs Is the Glory* (Hurst—doc); *The Way We Live* (Craigie—doc); *The Wicked Lady* (Arliss); *Caesar and Cleopatra* (Pascal)
1947   ***Black Narcissus*** (Powell and Pressburger); *The Brothers* (MacDonald); *Bush Christmas* (Smart); *Captain Boycott* (Launder); *The Captive Heart* (Dearden); *Easy Money* (Knowles); *End of the River* (Twist); *Fame Is the Spur* (Boulting); *Frieda* (Dearden); *Holiday Camp* (Annakin); *Hungry Hill* (Hurst); *Johnny Frenchman* (Frend); *The Magic Bow* (Knowles); *The Mark of Cain* (Hurst); *The Master of Bankdam* (Forde); *Odd Man Out* (Reed); *Root of*

J. Arthur Rank (center) with Douglas Farrar (left) and A. Galperson

All Evil (Williams); *So Well Remembered* (Dmytryk); *Take My Life* (Neame); *This Happy Breed* (Lean); *Uncle Silas* (Frank); *The Upturned Glass* (Huntington); *Vice Versa* (Ustinov); *When the Bough Breaks* (Huntington); *The Woman in the Hall* (Lee)

1948   *Against the Wind* (Crichton); *The Bad Lord Byron* (MacDonald); *Blanche Fury* (Allegret); *Blind Goddess* (French); *Broken Journey* (Annakin); *Calendar* (Crabtree); *Corridor of Mirrors* (Young); *Daybreak* (Bennett); *Diamond City* (MacDonald); *Double Pursuit*; *Dulcimer Street* (*London Belongs to Me*) (Gilliat); *Esther Waters* (Dalrymple); *Good-Time Girl* (MacDonald); *Hamlet* (Olivier); *Helter Skelter* (Thomas); *Here Come the Huggetts* (Annakin); *High Pavement* ; *It Always Rains on Sunday* (Hamer); *It's Hard to Be Good* (Dell); *Jassy* (Knowles); *The Lamp Still Burns* (Elvey); *Miranda* (Annakin); *Mr. Perrin and Mr. Traill* (Huntington); *My Brother's Keeper* (Roome); *Nicholas Nickelby* (Cavalcanti); *The October Man* (Baker); *Oliver Twist* (Lean); *Once a Jolly Swagman* (Lee); *Once upon a Dream* (Thomas); *One Night with You* (Young); *The PassionateFriends* (*One Woman's Story*) (Lean); *Portrait*

from Life (*The Girl in the Painting*) (Fisher); *Quartet* (Annakin, Crabtree, French, and Smart); ***The Red Shoes*** (Powell and Pressburger); *Saraband for Dead Lovers* (*Saraband*) (Dearden and Relph); *Scott of the Antarctic* (Frend); *The Smugglers* (*The Man Within*) (Knowles); *Snowbound* (MacDonald); *Third Time Lucky* (Parry); *Trottie True* (*The Gay Lady*) (Hurst); *Trouble in the Air* (Saunders); *The Weaker Sex* (Baker); *The White Unicorn* (Knowles); *Woman Hater* (Young)

1949   *Adam and Evalyn* (French); *All over the Town* (Twist); *The Blue Lagoon* (Launder); *A Boy, a Girl and a Bike* (Smart); *Boys in Brown* (Tully); *Cardboard Cavalier* (Forde); *The Chiltern Hundreds* (*The Amazing Mr. Beecham*) (Carstairs); *Christopher Columbus* (MacDonald); *Dear Mr. Prohack* (Freeland); *Don't Ever Leave Me* (Crabtree); *Eureka Stockade* (Watt); *Floodtide* (Wilson); *Fools Rush In* (Carstairs); *The History of Mr. Polly* (Pelissier); *The Huggetts Abroad* (Annakin); *It's Not Cricket* (Roome); *The Lost People* (Knowles); *Madeleine* (*The Strange Case of Madeleine*) (Lean); *Madness of the Heart* (Bennett); *Marry Me* (Fisher); *Morning Departure* (*Operation Disaster*)

(Baker); *The Perfect Woman* (Knowles); *Poet's Pub* (Wilson); *The Reluctant Widow* (Knowles); *The Rocking-Horse Winner* (Pelissier); *Sleeping Car to Trieste* (Carstairs); *The Spider and the Fly* (Hamer); *Sto-Press Girl* (Barry); *Traveler's Joy* (Thomas); *Vote for Huggett* (Annakin); *Warning to Wantons* (Wilson)

1950   *The Astonished Heart* (Fisher and Darnborough); *The Dark Man* (Dell); *The Golden Salamander* (Neame); *Highly Dangerous* (Baker); *Prelude to Fame* (McDonnell); *So Long at the Fair* (Fisher and Darnborough); *They Were Not Divided* (Young); *Trio* (Annakin and French)

1951   *Appointment with Venus* (*Island Rescue*) (Thomas); *The Browning Version* (Asquith); *Encore* (Jackson, Pelissier, and French); *High Treason* (Boulting); *Night without Stars* (Pelissier); *Secret People* (Dickinson)

1952   *Curtain Up* (Smart); *Hunted* (*The Stranger in Between*) (Crichton); *The Importance of Being Earnest* (Asquith); *It Started in Paradise* (Bennett); *The Long Memory* (Hamer); *Made in Heaven* (Carstairs); *Meet Me Tonight* (*Tonight at 8.30*) (Pelissier); *The Penny Princess* (Guest); *Planter's Wife* (*Outpost in Malaya*) (Annakin); *Something Money Can't Buy* (Jackson); *Top of the Form* (Carstairs); *Venetian Bird* (*The Assassin*) (Thomas)

1953   *Always a Bride* (Smart); *The Desperate Moment* (Bennett); *Genevieve* (Cornelius); *Gentlemen, the Queen* ; *John Wesley* (Walker); *The Kidnappers* (*The Little Kidnappers*) (Leacock); *Lady Godiva Rides Again* (Launder); *The Malta Story* (Hurst); *The Net* (*Project M. 7*) (Asquith); *Never Let Me Go* (Daves); *A Personal Affair* (Pelissier); *A Queen Is Crowned* (doc); *Street Corner* (*Both Sides of the Law*) (Box); *Trouble in Store* (Carstairs); *Turn the Key Softly* (Lee); *You Know What Sailors Are* (Annakin)

1954   *The Beachcomber* (Box); *Doctor in the House* (Thomas); *Fast and Loose* (Parry); *Forbidden Cargo* (French); *Mad about Men* (Thomas); *The Million Pound Note* (*Man with a Million*) (Neame); *One Good Turn* (Carstairs); *The Purple Plain* (Parrish); *The Queen's Royal Tour* (Hugham—doc); *Romeo and Juliet* (Castellani); *The Seekers* (*Land of Fury*) (Annakin); *The Teckman Mystery* (Toye); *To Paris with Love* (Hamer); *Up to His Neck* (Carstairs); *The Young Lovers* (*Chance Meeting*) (Asquith)

1955   *All for Mary* (Toye); *An Alligator Named Daisy* (Lee Thompson); *As Long as They're Happy* (Lee Thompson); *Doctor at Sea* (Thomas); *Jumping for Joy* (Carstairs); *Lost* (Green); *Man of the Moment* (Carstairs); *One Way Out* (Searle); *Passage Home* (Baker); *Simba* (Hurst); *Simon and Laura* (Box); *Who Done It?* (Relph and Dearden); *A Woman for Joe* (O'Ferrall)

1956   *The Battle of the River Plate* (*Pursuit of the Graf Spee*) (Powell and Pressburger); *Black Tent* (Hurst); *Breakaway* (Cass); *Eyewitness* (*Peril in the Night*) (Box); *The Feminine Touch* (Jackson); *House of Secrets* (*Triple Deception*) (Green); *Jacqueline* (Baker); *Long Arm* (Frend); *Reach for the Sky* (Gilbert); *The Secret Place* (Donner); *The Spanish Gardener* (Leacock); *Tiger in the Smoke* (Baker); *True as a Turtle* (*Plain Sailing*) (Toye); *Up in the World* (Carstairs)

1957   *Across the Bridge* (Annakin); *Above Us the Waves* (Thomas); *Campbell's Kingdom* (Thomas); *Checkpoint* (Thomas); *Dangerous Exile* (Hurst); *Doctor at Large* (Thomas); *Hell Drivers* (Endfield); *High Tide at Noon* (Leacock); *Ill Met* *By Moonlight* (*Night Ambush*) (Powell and Pressburger); *It Happened in Rome* (Pietrangeli); *Just My Luck* (Carstairs); *Miracle in Soho* (Amyes); *The Naked Truth* (Zampi); *The One That Got Away* (Baker); *Passionate Summer* (Brabant); *Robbery Under Arms* (Lee); *Seven Thunders* (Fregonese); *Tears for Simon* (Green); *A Town Like Alice* (*The Rape of Malaya*) (Lee); *Value for Money* (Annakin); *Windom's Way* (Neame)

1958   *Bachelor of Hearts* (Rilla); *Big Money* (Carstairs); *Carve Her Name with Pride* (*The Last Dawn*) (Gilbert); *Floods of Fear* (Crichton); *The Gypsy and the Gentleman* (Losey); *Heart of a Child* (Donner); *Innocent Sinners* (Leacock); *The Long Knife* (Tully); *Man with a Gun* (Tully); *A Night to Remember* (Baker); *Nor Moon By Night* (*Elephant Gun*) (Annakin); *Rockets Galore* (*Mad Little Island*) (Relph); *Rooney* (Pollock); *Sea of Sand* (Green); *A Tale of Two Cities* (Thomas); *Violent Playground* (Dearden); *The Wind Cannot Read* (Thomas)

1959   *The Captain's Table* (Lee); *Ferry to Hong Kong* (Gilbert); *Follow a Star* (Asher); *Heart of a Man* (Wilcox); *Hidden Homicide* (Young); *Northwest Frontier* (*Flame over India*) (Lee Thompson); *Operation Amsterdam* (McCarthy); *Sapphire* (Dearden); *Sea Fury* (Endfield); *The Square Peg* (Carstairs); *The Thirty-Nine Steps* (Thomas); *Tiger Bay* (Lee Thompson); *Too Many Crooks* (Zampi); *Upstairs and Downstairs* (Thomas); *Whirlpool* (Allen)

1960   *Bulldog Breed* (Asher); *Conspiracy of Hearts* (Thomas); *Doctor in Love* (Thomas); *League of Gentlemen* (Dearden); *Let's Get Married* (Scott); *Make Mine Mink* (Asher); *Man in the Moon* (Dearden); *The Royal Ballet* (Czinner)

1961   *Flame in the Streets* (Baker); *In the Doghouse* (Conyers); *No Love for Johnnie* (Thomas); *No, My Darling Daughter* (Thomas); *The Singer Not the Song* (Baker); *Very Important Person* (*A Coming-Out Party*) (Annakin); **Victim** (Dearden); *Whistle Down the Wind* (Forbes)

1962   *All Night Long* (Dearden); *Life for Ruth* (*Condemned to Life*) (Dearden); *On the Beat* (Asher); *A Pair of Briefs* (Thomas); *Tiara Tahiti* (Kotcheff); *Waltz of the Toreadors* (Guillermin); *The Wild and the Willing* (*Young and Willing*) (Thomas)

Publications

On RANK: books—

Wood, Alan, *Mr. Rank*, London, 1952.
Balcon, Michael, *A Lifetime in Films*, 1969.
Limbacher, James, *The Influence of J. Arthur Rank on the History of the British Film*, 1971 + filmo.
Macnab, G. C., *J. Arthur Rank and the British Film Industry*, London, 1993.

On RANK: articles—

Sight and Sound (London), October-December 1952.
Today's Cinema, no. 9865, 15 December 1970.
Obituary in *Ecran*, no. 5, May 1972.
Cinema and TV Today, 8 April 1982.
Sight and Sound (London), vol. 51, no. 4, Autumn 1982.
Economist, 1 May 1993.

Sight and Sound (London), June 1993.
Film Quarterly (Berkeley), Fall 1994.
Films in Review (New York), May-June 1996.

*   *   *

Though the Rank Organisation all but dominated British film production between the early 1940s and the late 1960s, its founder, J. Arthur Rank, born into the Yorkshire flour-milling business, was nearly 40 before his proprietorship of the *Methodist Times* led, indirectly, to film. Dissatisfied with existing films for church purposes, he sponsored his own, through producer John Corfield, and in 1933 moved into mainstream cinema, establishing British National with another idealistic millionaire, Lady Yule. Together they produced *The Turn of the Tide*, a realistic yarn of a Yorkshire fishing family. It won third prize at the Venice Film Festival, only to be shunned by British distributors. Legend long had it that this rejection sparked his determination to rescue the film business from vulgar minds. In 1937 Rank acquired the brand-new Pinewood studios and C. M. Woolf's General Film Distributors (with its familiar gong trademark), and in 1939 bought into Oscar Deutch's Odeon cinema circuit (smallest, newest, but most glamorous of the three chains dominating the market), thus becoming a ''vertically integrated combine.'' In 1940 he acquired Gaumont-British cinemas, with their 89 subsidiary companies, and by 1943 he controlled about two-thirds of the British movie business, including newsreels, laboratories, and optical technology. Though the Rank ''Empire'' was little larger than one of the Hollywood Big Five, he enjoyed the strategic advantage of sharing a duopoly (with Associated British Cinemas) over British exhibition. In 1945 his principal production companies were Two Cities (under Del Giudice), Gainsborough (under the Ostrers and Ted Black), and Independent Producers, Rank's own set-up, which offered unprecedented artistic freedom to The Archers (Powell and Pressburger), Cineguild (Lean, Neame, and Havelock-Allan), Individual (Launder and Gilliat), Wessex (Ian Dalrymple), and the notoriously extravagant Gabriel Pascl; Ealing (Balcon) was, loosely, associated. Rank's high-minded loss-makers ranged from *This Modern Age*, an English counter to Time-Life's *March of Time*, to special children's films, in order, in his words, ''to break Hollywood's grip on the child's mind.'' His drive to get good British films into the jealously guarded American mass market, often through Eagle-Lion, GFD's international complement, was spearheaded by expensive spectaculars, notably Olivier's *Henry V*, Pascal's *Caesar and Cleopatra*, and Powell and Pressburger's *A Matter of Life and Death*, while less lavish efforts, like *Brief Encounter*, and the Ealing comedies, did much to develop the American arthouse audience, disdained by Hollywood. However, Rank's high-risk internationalism, including the establishment of 200 Odeon cinemas in Canada, ran into enormous problems. His ''combine'' was an untidy aggregation of units; the deaths of Woolf and Deutsch deprived him of guiding advice from veteran showmen, and Pascal and others produced some costly and spectacular flops. During 1947-48 the Labour government's erratic misjudgments brought the Rank giant to its knees. Legislation intended to stem the postwar dollar drain goaded Hollywood to withhold new product; so Rank, having to feed over 600 cinemas, hastily expanded production. Meanwhile, the government abruptly reversed its policy, exposing this hastily run-up product to stockpiled Hollywood competition, and a new Quota Act brought to Rank an undeserved ill will from Hollywood. Only ''King Rank'' could have recouped the enormous losses; they intensified the rigorous

rationalisation, under John Davis' tough accountant's mind, driving most of Rank's prestigious filmmakers to his rival, Korda. Davis became chair on Rank's retirement, with the organisation diversified into other fields, notably, Rank-Xerox. By 1980 film production was minimal, though exhibition, distribution, and Southern Television, are still prominent.

Rank's predominance was inevitably controversial, especially given the convulsions and changes of 1946-48. His combination of a Christian sense of mission, financial acumen, and the low necklines in films like Gainsborough's *The Wicked Lady*, attracted many scathing comments from the critics, while socialists cast him as the demon semimonopolist. But the power of his ''nonconformist conscience'' was well attested, by his financial probity (and his continuing devotion to teaching home-town Sunday School classes). Alan Wood's account plausibly suggests that Rank, far from setting out to monopolise British film, felt *drawn*, by a chain of opportunities (the 1936-37 production crisis, wartime upheavals, existing corporate interlocks, and industry's aversion to Hollywood grabbing the last British bulwark, exhibition) to stabilise, save, and assert a key sector of national and moral culture. Writers often contrast Rank, the provincial, religious, puritan, businessman, with Korda the cosmopolitan, ''cavalier,'' and artwise impresario. Rank's own tastes are suggested by various Norman Walker films; the religious and moral tendencies discernible in Rank's features of the 1950s may well owe something to his sense of mission. The pros and cons and ifs and buts of industry history are interminably debatable, but history may well regard him with a warmth which will startle his detractors.

—Raymond Durgnat

RAPHAELSON, Samson

Writer. **Nationality:** American. **Born:** New York City, 30 March 1896. **Education:** Attended Lewis Institute, Chicago; University of Illinois, Urbana, B.A., 1917. **Family:** Married 1) Raina (Raphaelson), 1918 (divorced); 2) Dorothy Wegman, 1927; one son and one daughter. **Career:** 1917-18—reporter, City News Service, Chicago; 1918-20—publisher's assistant; 1920-21—teaching assistant, University of Illinois; 1921-22—police reporter, New York *Times*; 1925—first play produced, *The Jazz Singer*; 1929-30—contracts with RKO, then with Paramount; began association with Ernst Lubitsch; 1931—first film as writer, *The Smiling Lieutenant*; alternated between screenwriting and stage work until early 1950s, then retired to study photography; early 1970s—involved in the Israeli film industry as adviser; 1976-83—adjunct professor of cinema, Columbia University, New York. **Award:** Writers Guild Laurel Award, 1976. **Died:** In New York City, 16 July 1983.

Films as Writer:

1931   *The Smiling Lieutenant* (Lubitsch); *Magnificent Lie* (Viertel)
1932   *One Hour with You* (Lubitsch and Cukor); *Broken Lullaby (The Man I Killed)* (Lubitsch); **Trouble in Paradise** (Lubitsch)
1934   *The Merry Widow* (Lubitsch); *Caravan* (Charrell); *Servants' Entrance* (Lloyd); *The Queen's Affair (Runaway Queen)* (Wilcox)

1935   *Ladies Love Danger* (Humberstone); *Dressed to Thrill*
       (Lachman)
1937   *The Last of Mrs. Cheyney* (Boleslawsky); *Angel* (Lubitsch)
1940   *The Shop around the Corner* (Lubitsch)
1941   *Suspicion* (Hitchcock)
1943   *Heaven Can Wait* (Lubitsch)
1946   *The Harvey Girls* (Sidney); *Ziegfeld Follies* (Minnelli)
1947   *Green Dolphin Street* (Saville)
1948   *That Lady in Ermine* (Lubitsch and Preminger)
1953   *Main Street to Broadway* (Garnett)

Publications

By RAPHAELSON: plays—

The Jazz Singer, New York, 1925.
Young Love, New York, 1928.
The Wooden Slipper, New York, 1934.
Accent on Youth, and White Man, New York, 1935.
Skylark, New York, 1939, also novelization, 1939.
Jason, New York, 1942.
The Perfect Marriage, New York, 1945.
The Human Nature of Playwriting, New York, 1949.
Hilda Crane, New York, 1951.
Three Screen Comedies (includes *Trouble in Paradise, The Shop
      around the Corner, Heaven Can Wait*), Madison, Wisconsin, 1983.

By RAPHAELSON: articles—

Film Comment (New York), May-June 1976.
American Film (Washington, D.C.), December-January 1977.
Film Comment (New York), September-October 1979.

On RAPHAELSON: articles—

Film Comment (New York), Winter 1970–71.
Film Comment (New York), May-June 1978.
Film Comment (New York), September-October 1983.
Sabath, Barry, in *American Screenwriters, 2nd series*, edited by
      Randall Clark, Detroit, Michigan, 1986.
Cineforum (Bergamo), July-August 1993.
Simon, John, "Know-brainers," in *New York*, 15 November 1999.

*   *   *

Samson Raphaelson's great talent was in making true love seem so much more than a boy-meets-girl plot device, while at the same time cherishing the delicate patterns and structures of that device. Music and camerawork celebrate the artifice in *One Hour with You* and are elaborate in design; the revelation of an affair is given in soliloquy.

Trouble in Paradise is about the attraction of two calculating thieves in Venice. Their initial flirtation is a tricky blend of teasing, charm, and a veiled threat to betray the other to the police. Gaston declares his love for Lily, and also the fact that she stole a gentleman's wallet that was in his possession. With a flourish, he tenderly returns a diamond brooch he lifted from her. Lily, poise intact, asks him the

time. Gaston discovers his watch is missing and Lily, smiling triumphantly, hands it back to him. "It was five minutes slow, but I regulated it for you."

Amid the garbage, gondolas, and glittering evening dress, a state of romantic pandemonium revolves around Gaston's moonlit passion for his "mark," Mariette. Money means nothing to Mariette and everything to Lily, but causes Gaston, seeking more carnal conquest, reason for pause. Social conventions, male pride, and feminine curiosity add to the problem; but true love for Lily, in the end, weaves an even lovelier picture. The director Ernst Lubitsch regarded *Trouble in Paradise* as the favorite of his own films.

The Shop around the Corner is an excellent work that shows Raphaelson's strict adherence to structure and craft. In this tale set in a tidy Hungarian shop, two lonelyhearts seek love and find their ideals through letters. Personally, Klara and Kralik lock horns in petty rivalry as clerks. Kralik finds her out first and, having the upper hand, makes a shrewd game of playing the smug Klara against the woman of his dreams—who is one and the same person. Passion and conflict find expression in oblique and indirect ways throughout. The plot mechanics mesh like the gears of a music box, fittings perfect.

Raphaelson collaborated with Ernst Lubitsch in nine pictures. Their first collaboration was *The Smiling Lieutenant*. The next, *The Man I Killed*, was an artistically important tragedy about a French soldier's lone odyssey for conscience and solace in Germany during the First World War. It was Lubitsch's only sound drama.

They worked most often with a Hungarian play as a springboard and finished with something entirely different, save for the bare bones of the original plot. Raphaelson himself tended to dismiss "writing in the Lubitsch vein," as his theatrical and literary concerns were most important to him, but the two of them (and let us not exclude Ernest Vajda) inspired one another "past all sanity."

Raphaelson's *The Jazz Singer* was produced as a play in 1925. It was, he reflected, "heartfelt, corny and dramatic. It hurtled me into a lifetime dedicated to never again being so shamelessly effective." This solid star vehicle has been filmed three times to date, as was his 1934 play *Accent on Youth*. The story of a middle-aged Broadway playwright (a songwriter in the Crosby picture, a producer in the Gable picture) who is found attractive by his much younger secretary hadn't lost its spark in its numerous adaptations.

Raphaelson considered *Suspicion*, for Alfred Hitchcock, "in many ways my best screenplay." The heroine's role was tailored to the talent of Joan Fontaine, who won an Oscar. All the situations and dialogue led indirectly and cumulatively to Cary Grant trying to murder her. However, the ending insisted on by the studio made Grant innocent and the rewritten ending was unconvincing. Although meticulous from a technical point of view, *Suspicion* does not really match the best work Raphaelson did with Lubitsch.

—Rob Pinsel

RAPPENEAU, Jean-Paul

Writer and Director. **Nationality:** French. **Born:** Auxerre, 8 April 1932. **Education:** Attended Lycée Jacques-Amyot, Auxerre; Law Faculty, Paris. **Family:** Married Claude-Lise Cornély, 1971; two sons. **Career:** 1953–55—assistant director; 1955–57—production manager of short films; 1957—script writer; 1958—began directing films. **Awards:** Prix Louis Delluc for *La Vie de château*, 1966; Special Jury Prize at the Karlovy-Vary Festival, 1966. **Member:** President of ADRC (Agence pour le Dévelopment Régional du Cinéma), 1991. **Address:** 24 rue Henri Barbusse, 75005 Paris, France.

Films as Writer:

1957   *Entre la terre et le ciel* (Vilardebo—short)

1958   *Chronique provinciale* (+ d—short); *Signé Arsène Lupin* (Robert)

1960   *Zazie dans le métro* (*Zazie*) (Malle); ''Le Mariage'' ep. of *La Française et l'amour* (*Love and the Frenchwoman*) (Clair)

1962   *La Vie privée* (*A Very Private Affair*) (Malle); *Le Combat dans l'île* (Cavalier)

1964   *L'Homme de Rio* (*That Man from Rio*) (de Broca)

1965   *La Fabuleuse Aventure de Marco Polo* (*Marco the Magnificent*) (de la Patellière, Howard, and Christian-Jaque)

1966   *La Vie de château* (*A Matter of Resistance*) (+ d)

1970   *Les Mariés de l'an II* (+ d)

1975   *Le Sauvage* (+ d)

1982   *Tout feu, tout flamme* (+ d)

1990   **Cyrano de Bergerac** (+ d)

1995   *Le Hussard sur le toit* (*The Horseman on the Roof*) (+ d)

Publications

By RAPPENEAU: articles—

Cinéma (Paris), February 1965.

Art et Essai (Paris), February 1966.

La Vie de Château (script) in *Avant-Scène* (Paris), April 1966.

Cinéma (Paris), May 1966.

Show Business (Paris), 26 March 1971.

Cinéma (Paris), June 1971.

Film Français (Paris), 23 May 1978.

Unifrance Film (Paris), February 1982.

Cinématographe (Paris), February 1984.

Film Français (Paris), no. 2285, February 1990.

Studio Magazine (Paris), April 1990.

Première (Paris), no. 157, April 1990; September 1995.

Séquences (Montreal), September 1990.

Télérama (Paris), no. 2338, November 1994; no. 2384, September 1995.

Studio Magazine, no. 103, October 1995.

On RAPPENEAU: articles—

Chaplin (Stockholm), no. 2, 1970.

Cinématographe (Paris), July-August 1982.

Revue du Cinéma (Paris), no. 459, April 1990.

Empire, no. 19, January 1991; no. 80, February 1996.

Film Français (Paris), no. 2340, March; no. 2347, April; nos. 2348/9, May 1991.

Première (Paris), no. 208, July 1994.

Ciné-Bulles (Montreal), vol. 14, no. 4, Winter 1995.

Télérama (Paris), 11 January 1995.

Télérama (Paris), 23 September 1995.

Segnocinema (Vicenza), March/April 1996.

*   *   *

Jean-Paul Rappeneau entered films in a traditional way, as a second assistant to Jean Dréville on *Suspects*, as collaborator on Vilardebo's short film *Entre la terre et le ciel*, and as the director of the short *Chronique provinciale*. During the next few years he concentrated on writing, and acquired a solid reputation with scripts for *Signé Arsène Lupin*, two films by Louis Malle, *Zazie dans le métro* and *La Vie privée*, and a short film by René Clair in *La Française et l'amour*. The commercially successful *L'Homme de Rio*, directed by Philippe de Broca and starring Jean-Paul Belmondo, was followed by an international co-production, *La Fabuleuse Aventure de Marco Polo*.

These films had crystalized his own tastes and ambitions, and in 1966 he directed his first long film, *La Vie de château*, a brilliant comedy situated in Normandy on the eve of the invasion by the allies during the Second World War. This film, showing a maturity unusual in a first work, is far from being a simple or banal entertainment. Using a humorous framework, Rappeneau describes a France that is both egotistical and on the sidelines, constructing its own happiness away from the world. Using a minutely planned scenario prepared with the collaboration of Claude Sautet and Alain Cavalier (with dialogue by Daniel Boulanger), the film is revealed as the work of an elegant filmmaker who is also sensible to the playing of the actors, particularly Catherine Deneuve, Pierre Brasseur, and Philippe Noiret. His next film, *Les Mariés de l'an II*, a comedy where heroism is mixed with romance and burlesque with tragedy, is set during the French Revolution, and belongs to the genre of Christian-Jaque's *Fanfan la tulipe* and Clair's *Fêtes galantes*. Other of his films confirm his professional qualities. If the social and psychological analysis in *Tout feu, tout flamme* does not always ring true, the action is vivid, the images (shot by Pierre L'Homme) and the charm of Yves Montand and Isabelle Adjani are memorable, and the result is a successful attempt to make a commercial film of quality.

After working previously with his own original scripts, Rappeneau turned his attention to adaptation, and to works he deemed initially to be unfilmable: Edmond Rostand's *Cyrano de Bergerac* and Jean Giono's *Le Hussard sur le toit*. With Gérard Depardieu cast as the larger-than-life, swashbuckling romantic hero, *Cyrano* deservedly brought Rappeneau international attention. His version, co-adapted with Jean-Claude Carrière, retains the play's verse form and remains close to the original, with the seventeenth-century setting convincingly reproduced. The director's meticulous preparation is evident from the opening sequence in the theatre, the carefully choreographed sword fights and the impressively orchestrated battle scenes involving over 2000 extras. If Rappeneau was largely faithful to Rostand, in the case of Giono's *Le Hussard sur le toit* changes were necessary. Character motivation has been clarified and the narrative more tightly focused, but the essential story of unrequited love set against the beautiful Provence landscape remains intact. Careful attention to period detail once more characterizes the director's approach in his beautifully crafted evocation of 1830s France. Both films, along with productions such as Berri's *Jean de Florette, Manon des Sources*, or *Germinal*, are indicative of a particular trend in French filmmaking (not so far removed from post-war literary cinema) in which classic texts are transformed through film to become a new cultural phenomenon: heritage cinema.

—Karel Tabery, updated by R. F. Cousins

RATTIGAN, (Sir) Terence

Writer. **Nationality:** British. **Born:** London, 10 June 1911. **Education:** Attended Harrow School and Oxford University. **Career:** Playwright; first play, *French without Tears*, also screenplay. **Awards:** CBE, 1958; Knight Bachelor, 1971. **Died:** Of bone cancer in Bermuda, 30 November 1977.

Films as Writer:

1939   *French without Tears* (Asquith)
1942   *Quiet Wedding* (Asquith) (co); *The Day Will Dawn* (*The Avengers*) (French) (co); *Uncensored* (Asquith) (co)
1943   *English without Tears* (French) (co)
1945   *Journey Together* (Boulting) (co); *The Way to the Stars* (Asquith)
1946   *While the Sun Shines* (Asquith)
1948   *Bond Street* (Parry) (co); *The Winslow Boy* (Asquith)
1951   *The Browning Version* (Asquith)
1952   *The Sound Barrier* (*Breaking the Sound Barrier*) (Lean)
1953   *The Final Test* (Asquith)

Terence Rattigan

1954   *The Man Who Loved Redheads* (French)
1955   *The Deep Blue Sea* (Litvak)
1957   *The Prince and the Showgirl* (*The Sleeping Prince*) (Olivier)
1958   *Separate Tables* (Delbert Mann) (co)
1963   *The V.I.P.s* (*International Hotel*) (Asquith)
1964   *The Yellow Rolls-Royce* (Asquith)
1969   *Goodbye Mr. Chips* (Wood)
1973   *Bequest to the Nation* (*The Nelson Affair*) (Cellan Jones)
1976   *In Praise of Love* (Rakoff)

Publications

On RATTIGAN: books—

Darlow, Michael, and Gillian Hodson, *Terence Rattigan, the Man and His Work*, London, 1979.
Ruskino, Susan, *Terence Rattigan*, New York, 1983.
Wansell, Geoffrey, *Terence Rattigan: A Biography*, New York, 1997.

On RATTIGAN: articles—

Obituary in *Variety* (New York), 7 December 1977.
Obituary in *International Film Collector*, no. 21, March 1978.
National Film Theatre booklet (London), July 1979.
Modern Drama, September 1990.

*   *   *

Terence Rattigan's screenplays belong to the long and not altogether successful—cinematically speaking—British tradition of filming adaptations of established novels and plays. Rattigan contributed to over 20 screenplays, seven based on his own plays, but he only ever really regarded cinema as a financial safety net. He advised screenwriters "to throw off the shackles of the director" and remember that the modern cinema is "the child not only of its mother, the silent film, but also of its father, the drama."

Rattigan began his professional career in the writers' room at the old Teddington Studios, an experience he hated. His first ever screenplay was torn up in front of his eyes but he freely admitted in later years that this early experience had been invaluable in that it taught him the most ruthless economy of technique. His marvellous grasp of film craft is evident in his adaptations of his stage successes like *The Browning Version*, *French without Tears*, *Separate Tables*, *The Winslow Boy*, *The Deep Blue Sea*, and *The Man Who Loved Redheads*. His best work consists of polished dramas with a strong sense of social justice and he had a very assured touch with regard to audience involvement and emotional satisfaction. He also wrote original screenplays, notably *The V.I.P.s* and *The Yellow Rolls-Royce* where the gaiety of the jokes drowns out the deep moan of human discontent and unhappiness, but only superficially. Even in these polished comedies it is evident that Rattigan's outlook is essentially tragic. *French without Tears*, for example, is ostensibly a simple comedy centred around the romantic entanglements of a group of young Englishmen in a French crammer. However, Rattigan manages to reveal much of the underlying mood of the wealthy younger generation of the 1930s, hinting at the deeper conflicts in their political and sexual attitudes.

Rattigan contributed incalculably to Anthony Asquith's *The Way to the Stars* and *Journey Together*. *The Way to the Stars* is a classic evocation of wartime Britain which concentrates on the relationships of groups of British and American airmen. Originally commissioned to create a propaganda exercise to promote Allied understanding, Asquith and Rattigan managed to craft a film of great emotional depth and power.

The best of Rattigan's writing exemplified on the surface the cool, orderly gentlemanly code of English playwriting (rather in the style of Noël Coward with whom he is often compared both dramatically and cinematically), but the subtext was always a remorseless attack on the British fear of emotion and its relentless repression. He made moving pleas in his work for affection, kindness, and understanding as well as forgiveness. His masterpiece is *The Browning Version*, expanded by the author from his one-act play into Asquith's most satisfying film. It is a minutely observed study of a sickly schoolmaster, in which the playwright orchestrates a series of petty humiliations and minor crises which lead to a final emotional climax of great force. The film's philosophical implications go well beyond the story's naturalistic setting, and gave Michael Redgrave, as the schoolmaster, arguably the finest part in his distinguished career.

—Sylvia Paskin

REINIGER, Lotte

Animator. **Nationality:** British. **Born:** Berlin, 2 June 1899; became citizen of Great Britain. **Education:** 1916–17—attended Max Reinhardt theater school, Berlin. **Family:** Married Carl Koch, 1921 (died 1963).

Lotte Reiniger

Career: 1916—created silhouettes for intertitles of Paul Wegener's *Rübezahls Hochzeit*; 1918—introduced by Wegener to film group associated with Dr. Hans Cürlis; 1919—Cürlis's newly founded Institut für Kulturforschung, Berlin, sponsored Reiniger's first film; mid-1930s—with Koch moved to Britain, worked with G.P.O. Film Unit with Len Lye and Norman McLaren; 1936—made *The King's Breakfast*, first film in England; 1946—worked with Märchentheater of city of Berlin at Theater am Schiffbauerdamm; beginning 1950—lived and worked mainly for TV, in England; 1950s and 1960s—created sets and figures for English puppet and shadow theater Hoghart's Puppets; 1953—Primrose Productions set up, sponsored productions for American TV; 1975—began collaboration with National Film Board of Canada; 1979—*The Rose and the Ring* premiered at American Film Festival. **Awards:** Silver Dolphin, Venice Biennale, for *Gallant Little Tailor*, 1955; Filmband in Gold, West Germany, for service to German cinema, 1972; Verdienst Kreuz, West Germany, 1978. **Died:** 19 June 1981.

Films as Animator:

1919   *Das Ornament des verliebten Herzens (The Ornament of the Loving Heart)*

1920   *Amor und das standhafte Liebespaar*

1921   *Der fliegende Koffer; Der Stern von Bethlehem*

1922   *Aschenputtel; Dornröschen*

1923–26   *Die Geschichte des Prinzen Achmed (Die Abenteuer des Prinzen Achmed; Wak-Wak, ein Märchenzauber; The Adventures of Prince Achmed)*

1928   *Der scheintote Chinese* (originally part of *Die Geschichte des Prinzen Achmed*); *Doktor Dolittle und seine Tiere (The Adventures of Dr. Dolittle)* (in 3 parts: *Abenteuer: Die Reise nach Afrika; Abenteuer: Die Affenbrücke; Abenteuer: Die Affenkrankheit*)

1930   *Zehn Minuten Mozart*

1931   *Harlekin*

1932   *Sissi* (intended as interlude for premiere of operetta *Sissi* by Fritz Kreisler, Vienna 1932)

1933   *Carmen*

1934   *Das rollende Rad; Der Graf von Carabas; Das gestohlene Herz (The Stolen Heart)*

1935   *Der kleine Schornsteinfeger (The Little Chimney Sweep); Galathea; Papageno*

1936   *The King's Breakfast*

1937   *Tocher*

1939   *Dream Circus* (not completed); *L'elisir d'amore* (not released)

1944   *Die goldene Gans* (not completed)

1951   *Mary's Birthday*

1953   *Aladdin* (for U.S. TV); *The Magic Horse* (for U.S. TV); *Snow White and Rose Red* (for U.S. TV)

1954   *The Three Wishes* (for U.S. TV); *The Grasshopper and the Ant* (for U.S. TV); *The Frog Prince* (for U.S. TV); *The Gallant Little Tailor* (for U.S. TV); *The Sleeping Beauty* (for U.S. TV); *Caliph Storch* (for U.S. TV)

1955   *Hansel and Gretel* (for U.S. TV); *Thumbelina* (for U.S. TV); *Jack and the Beanstalk* (for U.S. TV)

1956   *The Star of Bethlehem* (theatrical film)

1957   *Helen la Belle* (theatrical film)

1958   *The Seraglio* (theatrical film)

1960   *The Pied Piper of Hamelin* (interlude for theatrical performance)
1961   *The Frog Prince* (interlude for theatrical performance)
1962   *Wee Sandy* (interlude for theatrical performance)
1963   *Cinderella* (interlude for theatrical performance)
1974   *The Lost Son* (interlude for theatrical performance)
1976   *Aucassin et Nicolette* (interlude for theatrical performance)
1979   *The Rose and the Ring* (interlude for theatrical performance)

Other Films:

1916   *Rübezahls Hochzeit* (Wegener) (silhouettes for intertitles);
       Die Schöne Prinzessin von China (Gliese) (set decoration,
       props, and costumes)
1918   *Apokalypse* (Gliese) (silhouettes for intertitles); *Der
       Rattenfänger von Hameln* (*The Pied Piper of Hamelin*)
       (Wegener) (silhouettes for intertitles)
1920   *Der verlorene Schatten* (Gliese) (silhouette sequence)
1923   *Die Nibelungen* (Lang) (silhouette sequence, not used)
1929–30   *Die Jagd nach dem Glück* (*Running after Luck*) (Gliese)
       (co-story + co-sc + co-sound)
1933   *Don Quichotte* (Pabst) (opening silhouette sequence)
1937   *La Marseillaise* (Renoir) (created shadow theater seen in film)

Publications

By REINIGER: books—

(Illustrator) *Das Loch im Vorhang*, Berlin, 1919.
Venus in Seide, Berlin, 1919.
Die Abenteuer des Prinzen Achmed, 32 pictures from film, with
    narration, Tubingen, 1926 (reprinted 1972; text translated into
    English by Carman Educational Associates, Pine Grove,
    Ontario, 1975).
Der böse Gutsherr und die guten Tiere, Berlin, 1930.
Wander Birds, Bristol, 1934.
Der ewige Esel, Zurich/Fribourg, 1949.
King Arthur and His Knights of the Round Table, London, 1952.
Mondscheingarten—Gedichte, Gütersloch, 1968.
Shadow Theatres and Shadow Films, London and New York, 1970.
Das gestohlene Herz, Tübingen, 1972.

By REINIGER: articles—

''Scissors Make Films,'' in *Sight and Sound* (London), Spring 1936.
''*The Adventures of Prince Achmed*,'' in *Silent Picture* (London),
    Autumn 1970.
''Lotte Reiniger et les ombres chinoises,'' interview with L. Bonneville,
    in *Séquences* (Montreal), July 1975.

On REINIGER: books—

White, Eric, *Walking Shadows*, London, 1931.
Russett, Robert, and Cecile Starr, *Experimental Animation*, New
    York, 1976.
Rondolino, Gianni, *Lotte Reiniger*, Torino, 1982 + filmo.

On REINIGER: articles—

Weaver, Randolph, ''*Prince Achmed* and Other Animated Silhou-
    ettes,'' in *Theatre Arts* (New York), June 1931.
Coté, Guy, ''Flatland Fairy Tales,'' in *Film* (London), October 1954.
''She Made First Cartoon Feature,'' in *Films and Filming* (London),
    December 1955.
''The Films of Lotte Reiniger,'' in *Film Culture* (New York),
    no. 9, 1956.
Beckerman, H., ''Animated Women,'' in *Filmmakers Newsletter*
    (Ward Hill, Massachusetts), Summer 1974.
Gelder, P., ''Lotte Reiniger at Eighty,'' in *Sight and Sound* (London),
    no. 3, 1979.
Starr, Cecile, ''Lotte Reiniger's Fabulous Film Career,'' in *Sightlines*
    (New York), Summer 1980.
Hurst, H., ''Zum Tode Lotte Reiniger,'' in *Frauen und Film* (Berlin),
    September 1981.
''Lotte Reiniger au pays des ombres,'' in *Image et Son* (Paris),
    December 1981.
Film a Doba (Prague), vol. 36, no. 1, January 1990.
Filmihullu, no. 5, 1990.
EPD Film (Frankfurt), October 1994.
Film-Dienst (Cologne), 13 September 1994.
Moritz, William, ''Some Critical Perspective on Lotte Reiniger,'' in
    Animation Journal (Orange), Fall 1996.
Elsaesser, Thomas, ''Hollywood Berlin,'' in *Sight and Sound* (Lon-
    don), November 1997.

*   *   *

Lotte Reiniger's career as an independent filmmaker is among the
longest and most singular in film history, spanning some 60 years
(1919–79) of actively creating silhouette animation films. Her *The
Adventures of Prince Achmed* is the world's first feature-length
animation film, made when she was in her mid-twenties and winning
considerable acclaim.

Silhouette animation existed before 1919, but Reiniger was its
preeminent practitioner, transforming a technically and esthetically
bland genre to a recognized art form. Since childhood she had
excelled at freehand cut-outs and shadow theaters. As a teenager at
Max Reinhardt's acting studio, she was invited by actor-director Paul
Wegener to make silhouette decorations for the credits and intertitles
of *The Pied Piper of Hamelin* (1918); she also helped animate the
film's wooden rats, when live guinea pigs proved unmanageable. The
rest of Reiniger's professional life was wholeheartedly devoted to
silhouette animation, with an occasional retreat to shadow plays or
book illustrations when money was not available for films.

Prominent among Reiniger's talents was her transcendence of the
inherent flatness and awkwardness of silhouette animation through
her dramatic *mise en scène* and her balletic movements. Her female
characters are especially lively and original, displaying wit, sensuous-
ness, and self-awareness rarely found in animated cartoons (from
whose creative ranks women animators were virtually excluded until
the 1970s). Few real-life actresses could match the expressiveness
with which Reiniger inspired the gestures of her lead-jointed figures
as she moved and filmed them fraction by fraction, frame by frame.

For over four decades, Reiniger shared her professional life with
her husband, Carl Koch, who designed her animation studio and, until

715

his death in 1963, served as her producer and camera operator. ''There was nothing about what is called film-technique that he did not know,'' Jean Renoir wrote in his autobiography. (In the late 1930s, Koch collaborated on the scripts and production of Renoir's celebrated *Grand Illusion* and *Rules of the Game*, and on *La Marseillaise* for which Reiniger created a shadow-play sequence.)

Aside from *The Adventures of Prince Achmed*, Reiniger ventured into feature filmmaking only once, in *Running after Luck*, the story of a wandering showman, part animation and part live-action, which she codirected with Rochus Gliese. It was a critical and financial failure, perhaps because of its imperfect sound system. The rest of her films were shorts, mainly one or two reels in length.

Reiniger worked outside commercial channels, with minimal support. She said she never felt discrimination because she was a woman, but she did admit resenting that great sums were spent on films of little or no imagination while so little was available for the films she wanted to make. In the 1970s she was coaxed from her retirement to make two films in Canada; she also toured much of Europe, Canada, and the United States under the auspices of the Goethe House cultural centers of the West German government, showing her films and demonstrating her cut-out animation technique.

Hans Richter, who knew Reiniger in the early Berlin years, later wrote that she ''belonged to the avant-garde as far as independent production and courage were concerned,'' but that the spirit of her work seemed Victorian. Renoir placed her even further back in time, as ''a visual expression of Mozart's music.'' It is more likely that, like the fables and myths and fairy tales on which many of her films are based, her work transcends time and fashion.

—Cecile Starr

REISCH, Walter

Writer and Director. **Nationality:** Austrian. **Born:** Vienna, 23 May 1903. **Education:** Attended the Reform-Real Gymnasium, 1913–22. **Family:** Married 1) Ina Schulthess, 1927 (divorced 1930); 2) Lisl Handl. **Career:** Extra, title-writer, and assistant to Alexander Korda at Sascha Film while still a student; 1923—camera assistant to Stefan Lorant, Berlin; then assistant cameraman for International Newsreels, Geneva; 1925–27—film writer in Vienna: first film as scenario writer, *Der Fluch*; 1927–30—writer for AAFA, Berlin, and then for UFA, Berlin, 1930–33; 1933–37—worked in Vienna to escape the Nazis; 1937—first film in Hollywood, *Men Are Not Gods*; 1938–48—contract with MGM; 1939—collaborator with Charles Brackett, at first with Billy Wilder, and after 1951 with Richard Breen; 1954–55—wrote and directed two films in Germany. **Award:** Academy Award for *Titanic*, 1953. **Died:** Of cancer, 28 March 1983.

Films as Writer:

1921 *Miss Hobbs* (*Los vom Mann*; *Die Tolle Miss*) (Kreisler) (titles)
1925 *Der Fluch* (Land); *Frauen aus der Wiener Vorstadt* (*15 Jahre schweren Kerker*) (Hanus); *Ein Walzer von Strauss* (Neufeld and Kreisler)
1926 *Küssen ist keine Sünd* (*Die letzte Einquartierung*) (Walther-Fein); *Schützenliesl* (Walther-Fein)
1927 *Der Bettelstudent* (J. and L. Fleck); *Die Dollarprinzessin und ihre sechs Freier* (Basch); *Die elf Teufel* (Z. Korda); *Faschingzauber* (Walther-Fein); *Das Heiratsnest* (Walther-Fein); *Die indiskrete Frau* (Boese); *Ein Mädel aus dem Volke* (J. and L. Fleck); *Pratermizzi* (+ co-d); *Ein rheinisches Mädchen beim rheinischen Wein* (Guter); *Seine Hoheit, der Eintänzer* (*Das entfesselte Wein*) (Leiter); *Tingel-Tangel* (Ucicky); *Trommelfeuer der Liebe* (Hartl)
1928 *Dragonerliebchen* (Walther-Fein); *Der Faschingsprinz* (Walther-Fein)
1929 *Fräulein Fähnrich* (Sauer); *Die Frau, die jeder liebt, bist du!* (Froelich); *Der Held aller Mädchenträume* (Land); *Der lustige Witwer* (Land); *Der schwarze Domino* (Janson); *Schwarzwaldmädel* (Janson); *Die Nacht gehört uns* (Froelich); *Dich hab' ich geliebt* (*Because I Loved You*) (Walther-Fein)
1930 *Donauwalzer* (Janson); *Brand in der Oper* (*Barcarole*) (Froelich); *Das Flötenkonzert von Sanssouci* (*The Flute Concert at Sans Souci*) (Ucicky); *Mach' mir die Wely zum Paradies* (Merzbach); *Das Lied ist aus* (von Bolvary); *Der Herr auf Bestellung* (von Bolvary); *Hokuspokus* (*Hocuspocus*) (Ucicky); *Wie werde ich reich und glücklich?* (Reichmann); *Ein Tango für dich* (von Bolvary); *Va banque* (Waschneck); *Zwei Herzen im 3/4 Takt* (von Bolvary)
1931 *Im Geheimdienst* (Ucicky); *Die lustigen Weiber von Wein* (von Bolvary); *Der Raub der Mona Lisa* (*The Theft of the Mona Lisa*) (von Bolvary)
1932 *Ein blonder Traum* (*The Blonde Dream*) (Martin); *Der Prinz von Arkadien* (Hartl); *F.P. 1 antwortet nicht* M.(*F.P. 1*; *F.P. 1 Does Not Answer*) (Hartl); *Die Gräfin von Monte Cristo* (Hartl)
1933 *Ich und die kaiserin* (*Heart Song*) (Holländer); *Leise flehen meine Lieder* (*Schuberts unvollendete Symphonie*; *Unfinished Symphony*) (Forst); *Saison in Kairo* (Schünzel)
1934 *Maskerade* (*Masquerade in Vienna*) (Forst)
1935 *Episode* (+ d); *Escapade* (Leonard)
1936 *Silhouettes* (+ d)
1937 *Men Are Not Gods* (+ d)
1938 *The Great Waltz* (Duvivier); *Gateway* (Werker)
1939 **Ninotchka** (Lubitsch)
1940 *My Love Came Back* (Bernhardt); *Comrade X* (K. Vidor)
1941 *That Hamilton Woman* (*Lady Hamilton*) (A. Korda); *That Uncertain Feeling* (Lubitsch)
1942 *Seven Sweethearts* (Borzage); *Somewhere I'll Find You* (Ruggles)
1943 *The Heavenly Body* (Hall)
1944 *Gaslight* (Cukor)
1946 *Song of Scheherazade* (+ d)
1948 *The Countess of Monte Cristo* (de Cordova)
1949 *The Fan* (*Lady Windermere's Fan*) (Preminger)
1951 *The Model and the Marriage Broker* (Cukor); *The Mating Season* (Leisen)
1953 *Niagara* (Hathaway); *Titanic* (Negulesco)
1954 *Die Mucke* (+ d)
1955 *Der Cornet* (+ d); *The Girl in the Red Velvet Swing* (Fleischer)

1956   *Teenage Rebel* (Goulding)
1957   *Stopover Tokyo* (Breen); *Journey to the Center of the Earth*
        (Levin); *The Remarkable Mr. Pennypacker* (Levin)

Publications

By REISCH: book—

With Charles Brackett and Billy Wilder, *Ninotchka* (script), New
    York, 1966.

On REISCH: article—

Cameron, Evan William, in *American Screenwriters, 2nd series*,
    edited by Randall Clark, Detroit, Michigan, 1986.

*   *   *

The noted Hollywood screenwriter Walter Reisch really had
a two-part career. In the first half he functioned as one of the most
important screenwriters of late silent and early sound films in
Germany. Like many others he fled the Nazi regime and eventually
made his way to Hollywood. From the late 1930s through the 1950s
Walter Reisch functioned as a ''writer's writer'' in the Golden Age of
the Hollywood studio system.

Reisch entered the Austrian film industry as an extra in 1918. But
the movie capital of Europe after the First World War was Berlin.
Once he terminated his education Reisch moved to Berlin to make his
mark in the new art form. He did everything, learning filmmaking
from all sides. He translated title cards for silent films, worked as an
assistant camera operator for features and newsreels, and helped as an
assistant director.

But just as sound was coming in, Reisch saw that the industry
would need more screenwriters and permanently moved into that
niche of motion picture production. Quickly he rose to become one of
the top writers at UFA, then Germany's largest studio and one of the
more powerful movie corporations outside Hollywood. The seizure
of power by Adolph Hitler changed everything and eventually forced
Reisch to emigrate to the United States.

Although he wrote his first Hollywood screenplay for United
Artists he made his way to MGM and settled at that studio from
1938–48. And the hits began to flow at once. *The Great Waltz*, the
fictionalized biography of Johann Strauss, earned millions. In 1939
Reisch wrote the script for *Ninotchka* with another expatriot, Billy
Wilder, and Charles Brackett. Yet another emigré, Ernst Lubitsch,
directed. Swedish-born Greta Garbo starred. The film was a major hit
and earned the writers an Academy Award nomination.

Reisch's career at MGM then settled into a routine. It was not until
Reisch moved to 20th Century-Fox that he was again united with
Charles Brackett to do more of his best work. Their collaborations did
well at the box office and stand up well on repeated showings: *The
Model and the Marriage Broker*, *The Mating Season*, *Niagara*, and
Titanic.

Reisch's career then closed with a series of mediocre films. He
retired gracefully and freelanced as uncredited ''script doctor'' and

lectured widely at universities throughout the world. He provided
many a student with tales of what it had been like to work at MGM
during the Golden Days of the studio system.

—Douglas Gomery

RENNAHAN, Ray

Cinematographer. **Nationality:** American. **Born:** Las Vegas, New
Mexico, 1 May 1896. **Career:** 1917–1943—cameraman/assistant/
director of photography for Technicolor; 1943–1950s—independent
director of photography; also served at various times as president and
secretary of the ASC (American Society of Cinematographers).
Award: Academy Award for *Gone with the Wind*, 1939. **Died:** In
Tarzana, California, 19 May 1980.

Films as Cophotographer (Technicolor):

1923   *Blood Test* (dir ph); *The Ten Commandments* (De Mille)
        (color sequences only)
1929   *Gold Diggers of Broadway* (del Ruth)
1930   *The King of Jazz* (Murray Anderson); *The Vagabond King*;
        Whoopee! (Freeland)
1932   *Doctor X* (Curtiz); *Ebb Tide*
1933   *Mystery of the Wax Museum* (Curtiz) (dir ph)
1935   **Becky Sharp** (Mamoulian) (dir ph)
1937   *Wings of the Morning* (Schuster) (dir ph)
1938   *Her Jungle Love* (Archainbaud) (dir ph)
1939   *Drums along the Mohawk* (Ford) (dir ph); **Gone with the
        Wind** (Fleming)
1940   *The Blue Bird* (Lang); *Chad Hanna* (King); *Down Argentine
        Way* (Cummings); *Maryland* (King)
1941   *Belle Starr* (Cummings); *Blood and Sand* (Mamoulian); *Loui-
        siana Purchase* (Cummings); *That Night in Rio* (Cummings)

Films as Cinematographer:

1943   *For Whom the Bell Tolls* (Wood)
1944   *Lady In The Dark* (Leisen); *Up in Arms* (Nugent)
1945   *Incendiary Blonde* (Marshall); *A Thousand and One
        Nights* (Green)
1946   *California* (Farrow); *A Duel in the Sun* (Vidor)
1947   *The Perils of Pauline* (Marshall); *Unconquered* (De Mille)
1948   *The Paleface* (McLeod); *Whispering Smith* (Fenton)
1949   *A Connecticut Yankee in King Arthur's Court* (Garnett);
        Streets of Laredo (Fenton)
1950   *The Great Missouri Raid* (Douglas)
1951   *Flaming Feather* (Enright); *Silver City* (Haskin); *Warpath*
        (Haskin)
1952   *The Denver and Rio Grande* (Haskin); *Hurricane Smith*
        (Hopper)

1953   *Arrowhead* (Marquis Warren)
1953   *Pony Express* (Hopper)
1955   *A Lawless Street* (Lewis)
1956   *Seventh Cavalry* (Lewis)
1957   *The Guns of Fort Petticoat* (Marshall); *The Halliday Brand* (Lewis)
1958   *Terror in a Texas Town* (Lewis)

Publications

On RENNAHAN: articles—

Focus on Film, no. 13, 1973.
"Ray Rennahan, ASC Honored by Star in Hollywood's 'Walk of Fame'," in *American Cinematographer* (Hollywood), January 1979.
Obituary, in *Variety* (New York), 28 May 1980.

*   *   *

As one of the premier Technicolor photographers in Hollywood, Ray Rennahan was a prominent figure in the industry's transition to color. During the experimental period of the 1920s and 1930s, Rennahan was responsible for supervising such early Technicolor endeavors as *Gold Diggers of Broadway* (1929), *The King of Jazz* (1930), and *Whoopee!* (1930). As Technicolor's rendering grew more proficient, Rennahan's reputation grew. By the early 1940s he was one of the busiest photographers in Hollywood, supervising many of the industry's great Technicolor films. Though his career during the 1950s lacked the impact of his earlier years, Rennahan's commitment to the Technicolor image remained unchanged—after over fifty years in the industry, his name, more than that of any other, has become synonymous with the art and history of color photography.

When Rennahan entered the industry in 1917 to work with Technicolor, the concept of color film was not yet a viable option. Tinting, toning and hand coloring were commonly practiced, but the actual technology of recording color was still very much in its infancy. Operating as a service firm, Technicolor had established itself to develop and promote a feasible system of recording the natural spectrum. With its own cameras and developing laboratories, it would lease its service to a particular studio and oversee the filming of an assigned project. As company photographer, Rennahan found himself working with various studios as supervisor/assistant to the studio cameraman.

The company's earliest experiments were novel but not successful. For example, in *Whoopee!*, an Eddie Cantor vehicle shot at MGM, Rennahan's photography lacks clarity, while the colors, garish and unreal, are ill defined and muddy. Though the film was reasonably successful in its initial weeks at the box office, attendance soon died down. Returns were not sufficient to warrant the high costs of the process, and the industry deemed it impractical.

In the mid-1930s Technicolor introduced the three-color system. Though the same in principle as the two-color system (it used three negatives—red, green, and blue—instead of two), it offered a wider range of spectrum and a clearer, crisper picture. The first feature to be shot with the system was *Becky Sharp* (1935), Rouben Mamoulian's rather stagy version of Thackery's *Vanity Fair*. However, as photographer Rennahan gave the picture a radiance and fidelity never before seen. One sequence, in which a ball in Brussels is interrupted by the cannon fire of Napoleon's army, brilliantly conveys the ensuing panic through a movement from the subtle greys and blues of the ballroom to the violent reds of the soldier's uniforms. In retrospect, however, the film seems a little too in awe of its own capabilities, with color at times overused, often to the point of distraction. Nevertheless, the film proved that color could entrance both audience and critics alike. When the picture was released, *The Post* declared it a dramatic indication of hitherto unrealized possibilities in the art of the motion picture.

Rennahan's work for Technicolor continued. He went to England in 1937 to shoot the country's first Technicolor film, *Wings of the Morning*. While there he proved a considerable influence on British cinematographer Jack Cardiff, with whom he worked. (Cardiff would later work on such Powell/Pressburger films as *Black Narcissus* [1946] and *The Red Shoes* [1948].) Rennahan returned to the U.S. the following year to add a colorful touch to *Her Jungle Love* (1938) and *Drums along the Mohawk* (1939). In 1939 began work on *Gone with the Wind*. Working closely with Ernest Haller the cophotographer, and production designer/codirector William Cameron Menzies, Rennahan helped create an intimacy and grandeur through the film's ground-breaking, superlative use of low-key photography. Made just four years after the advent of three-color production, the film remains the most extravagant and breathtaking example of the use of the technology. Though many talents contributed to the look of the film, Rennahan's efforts remained significant enough for him to collect his first Academy Award, shared with Haller.

Technicolor at this stage had mastered the industry. Rennahan continued, under his contract with Technicolor, to move from one studio to the next, and in 1941 he shot what is perhaps his greatest achievement. *Blood and Sand*, a remake of the Valentino silent concerning the rise and fall of a Spanish bullfighter, was directed by Mamoulian, with Tyrone Power in the starring role. Influenced by the styles of various Spanish painters, Rennahan and Mamoulian used the vivid and striking hues of Goya for the film's dramatic bullfight scenes, while the solemn hues of El Greco were employed for many of the film's quieter, more reflective moments. In short, the color not only aided the tone of the action—the bullfight scenes owe more to the actual photography than either the editing (which never fails to hide the use of a double) or the acting (Power is unsuitably timid in his role)—but also helped to articulate the theme. Rennahan's use of shadow and gloom perfectly captures the film's foreshadowing of, and preoccupation with, death.

In 1943, with the epic, somber-toned *For Whom the Bell Tolls*, Rennahan left Technicolor and began a career as an independent director of photography. His subsequent films ranged from colorful musicals (*Up in Arms* [1944]), to exotic fantasies (*A Thousand and One Nights* [1945]), and lavish westerns (*A Duel in the Sun* [1946]). Much of his later career was identified with rather formulaic westerns, and in the late 1950s he retired from the motion picture industry and worked for a period in television. His work there was associated with such shows as *Wells Fargo, Suspicion*, and *Laramie*. At various times he served as president and secretary of the American Society of Cinematographers. In 1980, after a long, productive career, he died at the age of eighty-four.

—Peter Flynn

RENOIR, Claude

Cinematographer. **Nationality:** French. **Born:** Paris, 4 December 1914. **Family:** Son of the actor Pierre Renoir, nephew of the director Jean Renoir. **Education:** Attended Lycée Lakanal, Paris. **Career:** General assistant on Jean Renoir's films in early 1930s, then assistant photographer to Christian Matras and Boris Kaufman; 1939–43—in film department of French navy; then resumed cinematography work. **Died:** In Troyes, 5 September 1993.

Films as General Assistant and Cameraman:

1932　*La Nuit du carrefour* (*Night at the Crossroads*) (J. Renoir); *Boudu sauvée des eaux* (J. Renoir)

1936　*La Vie est à nous* (*The People of France*) (J. Renoir)

1937　*Le Chanteur de minuit* (Joannon); **La Grande Illusion** (*Grand Illusion*) (J. Renoir) (+ asst d)

1938　**La Bête humaine** (*The Human Beast*) (J. Renoir) (+ asst d); *La Marseillaise* (J. Renoir); *Légions d'honneur* (Gleize); *Lumières de Paris* (Pottier); *La Piste de sud* (Billon); *Les Rois de la flotte* (Pujol)

1939　*Le Dernier Tournant* (Chenal); *L'Enfer des anges* (Christian Jaque); *Sérénade* (Boyer)

Films as Cinematographer:

1935　*Toni* (J. Renoir)

1938　*Prison sans barreaux* (Moguy) (co)

1942　*Opéra-Musette* (+ co-d)

1943　*Bonsoir mesdames, bonsoir messieurs* (Tual); *L'Aventure est au coin de la rue* (Daniel-Norman)

1945　*Le Couple idéal* (Roland); *L'Extravagante Mission* (Calef); *Jéricho* (Calef)

1946　*Les Chouans* (Calef); *La Mission sous la mer* (Calef); *Le Père tranquille* (*Mr. Orchid*) (Clément and Noël-Noël); **Une Partie de campagne** (*A Day in the Country*) (J. Renoir—produced 1936)

1947　*Monsieur Vincent* (Cloche); *La Grande Volière* (Péchet)

1948　*L'Impasse des deux anges* (Tourneur); *Docteur Laënnac* (Cloche); *Alice au pays des merveilles* (*Alice in Wonderland*) (Bunin and others) (co); *Pyrénées, terre de legends* (Lods—short) (co)

1949　*Rendezvous de juillet* (Becker); *Prélude à la gloire* (Lacombe); *Images gothiques* (Cloche—short); *Sculptures au moyen-âge* (Cloche—short)

1950　*Né de père inconnu* (Cloche); *Knock* (Lefranc); *Clara de Montargis* (Decoin)

1951　*The River* (J. Renoir); *Monsieur Fabre* (Diamant-Berger); *The Green Glove* (Maté)

1953　**Le Carrosse d'or** (*The Golden Coach*) (J. Renoir); *Puccini* (Gallone); *Maddalena* (Genina)

1954　*India favolosa* (Macchi)

1955　*Madame Butterfly* (Gallone); *Un Missionaire* (Cloche); *Le Mystère Picasso* (Clouzot)

1956　*Eléna et les hommes* (*Paris Does Strange Things*) (J. Renoir); *Crime et châtiment* (Lampin); *Les Sorcières de Salem* (Rouleau)

1957　*Une Vie* (Astruc)

1958　*Délit de fuite* (Borderie); *Les Tricheurs* (*The Cheaters*) (Carné)

1959　*La Valse du gorille* (Borderie); *Sergent X* (Borderie)

1960　*Et mourir de plaisir* (*Blood and Roses*) (Vadim); *Terrain vague* (Carné)

1961　*Les Amants de Teruel* (Rouleau); *Lafayette* (Dréville)

1962　*Symphonie pour un massacre* (Deray)

1963　*Cleopatra* (Mankiewicz) (2nd unit)

1964　*Circus World* (*The Magnificent Showman*) (Hathaway) (2nd unit); *L'Insoumis* (Cavalier)

1965　*Paris au mois d'août* (Granier-Deferre)

1966　*La Curée* (*The Game Is Over*) (Vadim); *La Grande Vadrouille* (Oury)

1968　*Barbarella* (Vadim); *Histoires extraordinaires* (*Spirits of the Dead*) (Fellini, Malle, and Vadim)

1969　*The Madwoman of Chaillot* (Forbes) (co)

1970　*The Lady in a Car with Glasses and a Gun* (Litvak); *The Adventurers* (Gilbert); *The Horsemen* (Frankenheimer)

1971　*Le Casse* (Verneuil); *Les Mariés de l'an deux* (Rappeneau)

1972　*Hellé* (Vadim); *Le Tueur* (de la Patellière); *Le Serpent* (Verneuil)

1973　*L'Impossible Objet* (*Impossible Object*) (Frankenheimer); *Paul and Michelle* (Gilbert)

1974　*La Traque* (Leroy)

1975　*Docteur Françoise Gailland* (Bertuccelli); *French Connection II* (Frankenheimer)

1976　*L'Aile, ou la cuisse* (Zidi); *Attention les enfants regardent* (Leroy); *The Spy Who Loved Me* (Gilbert)

1978　*La Zazanie* (Zidi)

1979　*La Toubib* (Granier-Deferre)

Film as Producer:

1939　**Règle du jeu** (*Rules of the Game*) (J. Renoir)

Publications

By RENOIR: articles—

Le Technicien du Film (Paris), January 1949; no. 209, November 1973.

Cahiers du Cinéma (Paris), vol. 2, no. 8, January 1952.

Ciné France Mensuel, January 1965.

Le Technicien du Film (Paris), November-December 1973.

On *The Spy Who Loved Me* in *American Cinematographer* (Hollywood), May 1977.

Cinéma Pratique, no. 160, 1979.

Cinématographe (Paris), April 1979.

On RENOIR: articles—

Monthly Film Bulletin (London), vol. 32, no. 375, April 1965.

Monthly Film Bulletin (London), no. 13, 1973.

Film Français (Paris), no. 2346, April 1991; no. 2472, September 1993.

The Guardian (London), 8 September 1993.

New York Times, 13 September 1993.
Facts on File, 16 September 1993.
Variety, 8 September 1993; 27 September 1993.
Daily Telegraph (London), 23 September 1993.
Classic Film Images (London), no. 220, October 1993.

*   *   *

In a distinguished career tragically foreshortened by failing eyesight, Claude Renoir demonstrated his versatility and technical ingenuity in over eighty films and, though principally associated with luxuriant color photography, he also achieved notable successes with monochrome. His early mentors included Jean Bachelet, Maurice Lucien, and Joseph Louis Mundwiller, although the cinematographers who most marked his development were Christian Matras and Boris Kaufman. His formative years were almost inevitably associated with the work of his pre-eminently famous uncle, Jean Renoir, and in the prewar period he gained invaluable experience of filmmaking both as his general assistant and cameraman. In the latter role he showed considerable physical courage to produce airborne shots in *La Grande Illusion* (1937), and to capture the dangerous high-speed train sequences for *La Bête humaine* (1938) when, strapped to a platform on the side of the engine, he almost lost his life as the train entered a narrower-then-expected tunnel.

In terms of his uncle's monochrome films, Renoir's sensitivity to light and composition are perhaps most in evidence in *Toni* (1935) and *Une Partie de campagne* (1946). In *Toni*, relying only on natural light for the exteriors, his deep, fluid camerawork delicately framed the protagonists in their romantic country setting, while in the dramatic switch of mood in the murder sequence, he achieved memorable tension through tightly framed close-ups. The observant, unobtrusive camera work tracing the characters through their natural setting anticipates in style a key determinant of postwar Italian neorealism. The exploitation of light is again intrinsic to the creation of the more lyrical mood of *Une Partie de campagne* which is steeped in the vibrant atmosphere of Auguste Renoir's Impressionist canvases. Of particular interest is the lyrical swing sequence, seemingly inspired by the painter's *La balançoire*, in which a mobile camera moves in harmony with the swing's oscillations, thus bringing the audience to share directly in the sensation of motion. The cinematographer's most celebrated monochrome achievement, however, came with *Monsieur Vincent* (1947) directed by Maurice Cloche, in which the unemphatic beauty of his compositions were integral to the depiction of the self-denying subject, the sixteenth-century priest, Vincent de Paul.

Renoir's first tentative excursion into color photography was at the instigation of Jean Renoir who had decided to experiment with the color format for his film *The River* (1951), filmed on location in India. Unimpressed by Hollywood's eye-catching use of color, the director sought more muted tones and these the photographer achieved with such success that previously dismissive attitudes in France towards color were changed fundamentally. Thereafter color photography could be taken seriously and in successive films during the fifties, Renoir exploited to the full the potential of polychromatic film. For Renoir's high-spirited, theatrical story *Le Carosse d'or* (1953), with its exotic Peruvian setting and magnificent costumes, he deployed color to bring a warm, carefree glamour, while in *Eleanor et les hommes* (1956), he presented Paris of the 1880s as a series of color prints, often working closely within a striking range of contrastive reds and blues. In much darker vein, in his only feature film for Alexandre Astruc, *Une Vie* (1957), he created deeply resonant images of the damp, green Normandy landscape to translate the pessimistic mood of Maupassant's tragic romance.

The sixties brought an association with the former fashion photographer Roger Vadim who now, as film director, sought to bring a visual sensuality to the cinema. Renoir readily espoused this aesthetic and in turn provided the elegantly modulated tones of *Et Mourir de plaisir* (1960) with its striking dream sequence composed in black, white and red, the suggestive color compositions of *La Curée* (1966), which includes visual references to Antonioni's color experiments in *Il Deserto rosso* (1964) and the lurid, psychedelic registers of the futuristic *Barbarella* (1968). For Oury in *La Grande Vadrouille* (1966), Renoir excelled in capturing the beauty of the Meursault locations, while his misty sequence in a Turkish bath produced images of captivating delicacy. The decade also brought work with American filmmakers, though initially only as second unit for Mankiewicz's *Cleopatra* (1963), and Hathaway's *Circus World* (1964). For Frankenheimer, using super panavison, he captured the rugged wilds of Afghanistan for *The Horseman* (1970) and after this director's scenic action film *French Connection II* (1975), Claude Renoir again showed his ability to distill the essence of exotic locations in Gilbert's *The Spy Who Loved Me* (1976), while also drawing on his accumulated experience of lighting to make the most, in dramatic terms, of the huge Pinewood set.

No account of Renoir's film career would be complete without reference to his documentary work. After *Monsieur Vincent*, he continued his association with Maurice Cloche and brought his skills as a lighting cameraman to studies of the plastic arts in *Images gothiques* (1949) and *Sculptures au moyen-âge* (1949). Renoir's most interesting achievement in this domain, however, was *Le Mystère, Picasso* (1955) for Henri Clouzot. Using specially prepared transparent "canvases," he was able to film the painter at work and thus produce a unique record of artistic creation.

Throughout his four decades as a cinematographer, Renoir adapted readily to the requirements of successive directors and was equally at home with documentaries, delicately observed romances, discreetly narrated stories of self-effacing characters or rumbustuous, all-action movies. Acknowledged by his peers as an articulate commentator on the craft of the cinematographer, he contributed articles to professional journals on color photography and technical innovation. His eye for color and composition frequently redeemed otherwise indifferent films and his intelligent contribution both to the theory and practice of cinematography was entirely worthy of the illustrious Renoir name.

—R. F. Cousins

REVILLE, Alma

Writer. **Nationality:** British. **Born:** England, 14 August 1899. **Family:** Married the director Alfred Hitchcock, 1926 (died, 1980); daughter: Patricia. **Career:** Early 1920s—editor's assistant, London Film, then Famous Players-Lasky, London; 1925—script girl on Hitchcock's *The Pleasure Garden*, then writer of many of his scripts, as well as scripts for other directors; 1939—emigrated to the United States with Hitchcock. **Died:** 6 July 1982.

Films as Cowriter for Alfred Hitchcock:

1927 *The Ring*
1929 *Juno and the Paycock*
1930 *Murder*
1931 *The Skin Game*; *Rich and Strange* (*East of Shanghai*)
1932 *Number Seventeen*
1934 *Waltzes from Vienna* (*Strauss's Great Waltz*)
1935 **The 39 Steps**
1936 *The Secret Agent*; *Sabotage* (*A Woman Alone*)
1937 *Young and Innocent* (*The Girl Was Young*)
1938 **The Lady Vanishes**
1939 *Jamaica Inn*
1941 *Suspicion*
1944 *Shadow of a Doubt*
1947 *The Paradine Case*
1950 *Stage Fright*
1953 *I Confess* (uncredited)

Other Films as Cowriter:

1928 *The Constant Nymph* (Brunel); *The First Born* (Mander)
1929 *After the Verdict* (Galeen)
1931 *The Outsider* (Lachman); *Sally in Our Alley* (Elvey)
1932 *The Water Gipsies* (Elvey); *Nine till Six* (Dean)
1934 *Forbidden Country* (Rosen)
1935 *The Passing of the Third Floor Back* (Viertel)
1945 *It's in the Bag* (Wallace)

Film as Editor:

1923 *Woman to Woman* (Cutts)

Publications

By REVILLE: articles—

Sight and Sound (London), Autumn 1976.
Wilson Library Bulletin, December 1988.

On REVILLE: articles—

Taylor, John Russell, "Alma Hitchcock," in *Take One* (Toronto), May 1976.
Obituary, in *Cinématographe*, no. 82, October 1982.

*   *   *

Alma Reville's career is difficult to assess, since during most of it she worked exclusively on the films of her husband, director Alfred Hitchcock. Her contribution to his work fluctuated during the course of their 50-year marriage. It was sometimes that of a professional screenwriter or consultant, more often that of a supportive and knowledgeable wife.

Reville entered the British film industry even earlier than her husband, whose career spanned both the silent and sound eras. From the age of 16, Reville worked as a cutter (editor), first at the London Film Company, then at Famous Players-Lasky's English branch at Islington. Hitchcock's courtship of her began at the latter studio when he invited her to work as a cutter on *Woman to Woman*, an independent production which he was assistant directing under Graham Cutts at Islington; thus from the beginning, the couple's relationship was based on a combination of personal and professional interests. She shared her first screenwriting credit with Hitchcock as cowriter of his boxing melodrama *The Ring* in 1927, while continuing to work with other directors as scriptwriter, continuity girl, and assistant director.

Ambitious and talented, Reville sought to move into the director's chair herself. But the birth of a daughter, Patricia Alma, in 1928 and the family's subsequent move to America altered her ambitions. Joan Harrison, whom Hitchcock hired as a secretary in 1935, quickly took over many of the routine production duties which had previously been Reville's responsibility, while Reville focused exclusively on preparation of her husband's scripts. Harrison eventually became involved in this capacity too, often sharing screen credit with Reville. When the Hitchcocks moved to America in 1939 so that Hitchcock could work under personal contract to David O. Selznick, Harrison went along.

The scripts Reville worked on for Hitchcock in Hollywood were *Suspicion*, a troubled project which was nearly not released; *The Paradine Case*, on which producer Selznick was more exasperating in his interference with Hitchcock than usual; *Stage Fright*; and *I Confess*, which was made on Reville's initiative, but proved to be a box office failure. Three of these films concern a man who betrays a woman. Reville was partly responsible for this pattern, which probably reflected her attitude toward her husband, whose interest in her waxed and waned; the couple's marriage was reportedly celibate after the birth of their daughter as Hitchcock's romantic fancy attached itself silently and unreciprocally to the various glamorous blondes in his films.

In the mid-1950s, at the peak of Hitchcock's confidence and power, Reville retreated firmly into the background and stayed there. He still sought and respected his wife's judgment on potential projects and relied on her keen eye for detail during the editing process. A famous story about *Psycho* has it that Reville saved its most famous sequence from being marred by a significant blemish that no one else had caught during months of editing. As the final cut was being prepared for release, Hitchcock showed it to her. She alone spotted a single blink of Janet Leigh's eye as the actress lay "dead" following the notorious shower murder scene. The gaffe was replaced with a cutaway shot, and *Psycho* went out to theaters, the sequence shocking audiences around the world and making film history.

—Patricia Ferrara, updated by John McCarty

REYNOLDS, William H.

Editor. **Nationality:** American. **Born:** Elmira, New York, 14 June 1910. **Career:** 1934—swing gang laborer, Fox; 1936–38—assistant editor to Robert Simpson; 1938–42—editor at Paramount; 1942–62—editor, 20th Century-Fox; then freelance editor. **Awards:** Academy Award, for *The Sound of Music*, 1965, and *The Sting*, 1973. **Died:** 16 July 1997, in South Pasadena, California, of cancer.

Films as Assistant Editor:

1935   *The Farmer Takes a Wife* (Fleming); *The Gay Deception* (Wyler)

1936   *Big Brown Eyes* (Walsh); *Her Master's Voice* (Santley); *Palm Springs* (Scotto); *Spendthrift* (Walsh); *John Meade's Woman* (E. Griffith)

1939   *Honeymoon in Bali* (E. Griffith)

1940   *A Night at Earl Carroll's* (Neumann); *Typhoon* (L. King)

Films as Editor:

1937   *52nd Street* (Young)

1938   *Algiers* (Cromwell)

1941   *So Ends Our Night* (Cromwell)

1942   *Moontide* (Mayo)

1947   *Carnival in Costa Rica* (Ratoff)

1948   *Give My Regards to Broadway* (Bacon); *The Street with No Name* (Keighley); *You Were Meant for Me* (Bacon)

1949   *Come to the Stable* (Koster); *Mother Is a Freshman* (Bacon)

1950   *The Big Lift* (Seaton) (co); *Halls of Montezuma* (Milestone)

1951   *The Day the Earth Stood Still* (Wise); *The Frogmen* (Bacon); *Take Care of My Little Girl* (Negulesco)

1952   *The Outcasts of Poker Flat* (Newman); *Red Skies of Montana* (Newman)

1953   *Beneath the 12-Mile Reef* (Webb); *Dangerous Crossing* (Newman); *The Kid from Left Field* (Jones)

1954   *Desiree* (Koster); *Three Coins in the Fountain* (Negulesco)

1955   *Daddy Long Legs* (Negulesco); *Good Morning, Miss Dove* (Koster); *Love Is a Many-Splendored Thing* (H. King)

1956   *Bus Stop* (Logan); *Carousel* (H. King)

1958   *In Love and War* (Dunne); *South Pacific* (Logan) (co)

1959   *Beloved Infidel* (H. King); *Blue Denim* (Dunne); *Compulsion* (Fleischer)

1960   *Wild River* (Kazan); *Fanny* (Logan)

1962   *Taras Bulba* (Lee Thompson) (co); *Tender Is the Night* (H. King)

1963   *Kings of the Sun* (Lee Thompson)

1964   *Ensign Pulver* (Logan)

1965   *The Sound of Music* (Wise)

1966   *Our Man Flint* (Daniel Mann); *The Sand Pebbles* (Wise)

1968   *Star!* (Wise)

1969   *Hello, Dolly!* (Kelly)

1970   *The Great White Hope* (Ritt)

1971   *What's the Matter with Helen?* (Harrington)

1972   ***The Godfather*** (Coppola) (co)

1973   *The Sting* (Hill); *Two People* (Wise)

1975   *The Great Waldo Pepper* (Hill); *The Master Gunfighter* (Laughlin) (co)

1976   *The Entertainer* (Wrye) (co); *The Seven-Per-Cent Solution* (Ross) (supervising ed)

1977   *The Turning Point* (Ross)

1979   *A Little Romance* (Hill)

1980   *Heaven's Gate* (Cimino)

1982   *Making Love* (Hiller); *Author! Author!* (Hiller)

1983   *Yellowbeard* (Damski)

1984   *The Lonely Guy* (Hiller) (co); *The Little Drummer Girl* (Hill)

1986   *Pirates* (Polanski) (co)

1987   *Dancers* (Ross); *Ishtar* (E. May)

1988   *A New Life* (Alda)

1989   *Rooftops* (Wise)

1990   *Taking Care of Business* (Hiller)

1992   *Newsies* (Ortega)

1993   *Gypsy* (Ardolino—for TV)

1996   *Carpool* (Hiller)

Publications

By REYNOLDS: articles—

American Cinemeditor (Los Angeles), Summer/Fall 1981.
American Cinemeditor (Los Angeles), Winter 1984/Spring 1985.

On REYNOLDS: article—

Film Comment (New York), March/April 1977.

*   *   *

William H. Reynolds is a consummate film editor who takes a straightforward approach to his craft, relying on seamless editing which never calls attention to itself. In nearly six decades as an editor he has cut some of the most popular commercial American movies, including *The Sting*, *The Godfather* (with Peter Zinner), *Algiers*, *The Sound of Music*, and *South Pacific*. Reynolds has been fortunate to work with strong directors appreciative of the editing process, such as Robert Wise, George Roy Hill, Elia Kazan, and Francis Ford Coppola.

Reynolds started at Fox in 1934 as a laborer on the swing gang, moving props around the studio. He had a chance to observe firsthand the workings of the studio system assembly line, and quickly focused on editing. He learned his trade from editor Robert Simpson, who took him along to Paramount in 1936 as his assistant. Paramount was the only studio with a policy of keeping the editor on the set, enabling the assistant editor to assemble the first cut, in addition to the usual assistant chores of logging, syncing, and maintaining the edit trims and paperwork. This was an invaluable training ground, and while at Paramount Reynolds also assisted such old-line editors as Stuart Gilmore, Eda Warren, and Alma MacCrorie.

After only two years as an assistant, Reynolds quickly became an editor when editor-turned-director Harold Young asked him to cut the musical *52nd Street* for the Walter Wanger organization. Wanger was pleased enough with young Reynolds's work to ask him to edit his important production of *Algiers*, an American remake of the French *Pépé le Moko*. Charles Boyer and Hedy Lamarr played the star-crossed lovers in the exotic romantic drama directed by John Cromwell. A scene-by-scene re-creation of the Duvivier original, *Algiers* was a commercial success and established Reynolds's reputation. His greatest challenge on the film was making Lamarr's inadequate performance work. Reynolds also cut *So Ends Our Night*, an intelligent World War II drama, for Cromwell.

In 1942 Reynolds signed as a staff editor with Twentieth Century-Fox. Studio chief Darryl F. Zanuck was himself a brilliant editor and maintained the best editorial department in Hollywood. Zanuck was extremely involved in postproduction, and Reynolds refined his editing skills under Zanuck's auspices, working with such veteran directors as Henry King, Lewis Milestone, Archie Mayo, Lloyd Bacon, and William Keighley. During his 20 years at Fox, Reynolds emerged as a top editor.

Musicals were a staple at the studio, and Reynolds was entrusted with cutting *Give My Regards to Broadway*, *Daddy Long Legs*, *Carousel*, *South Pacific*, and *The Sound of Music*, subtly blending musical sequences with the narrative. Reynolds credits Zanuck's expertise as a creative producer, and has noted that Zanuck would excise an expensive number if he felt it did not work within the context of the completed picture. Reynolds also handled the editing chores on such slick romantic dramas as *Desiree*, *Three Coins in the Fountain*, and *Love Is a Many-Splendored Thing*. Fox was the home of CinemaScope, and these titles were shot in the process. Reynolds helped bring montage to CinemaScope, since the early 'Scope films tended to play as much action as possible in a single shot, with minimal cutting.

At Fox, Reynolds was teamed with two directors with whom he did some of his best work, Robert Wise and Joshua Logan. Wise, a former editor (*Citizen Kane*), called Reynolds one of his favorite editors, and they worked together on the science-fiction classic *The Day the Earth Stood Still*, as well as *The Sound of Music*, *The Sand Pebbles*, *Star!*, and *Two People*. The Wise films reflect a great diversity of style and content, from the high-budget adventure of *The Sand Pebbles* to the intimate character study of *Two People*. *The Sound of Music* was unique in its integration of the traditional musical form with a highly dramatic story; an attempt to equal its success with *Star!*, a biography of Gertrude Lawrence, failed at the box office. *The Day the Earth Stood Still* and *The Sand Pebbles* are the best of the Wise-Reynolds collaborations, both impeccably paced and edited in an engrossing manner with an emphasis on drama and suspense.

Reynolds has also had a productive relationship with Joshua Logan on *Bus Stop*, *South Pacific* (co-edited with Robert Simpson), *Fanny*, and *Ensign Pulver*. Reynolds was present on the set for these pictures to assist the theater director Logan in his transition to screen directing. *Bus Stop* gave Marilyn Monroe one of her best vehicles; *South Pacific* was an enormously successful musical adapted from the Broadway hit; and *Ensign Pulver* a competent sequel to *Mister Roberts*. *Fanny* is an underrated work, a poignant romance that Reynolds and Logan managed to keep moving despite a 133 minute running time. In the midst of these entertainments, Reynolds edited two powerful dramas, Richard Fleischer's *Compulsion* and Elia Kazan's *Wild River*, atypical Hollywood fare.

In the 1970s and 1980s, Reynolds was very much in demand by some of the industry's top directorial talent. Most notably, his work included the blockbusters *The Godfather* and *The Sting*, and two ambitious failures, *Heaven's Gate* and *Pirates*. On *The Godfather*, he shared editing chores with Peter Zinner, alternating scenes during the film's New York production. During the postproduction period in San Francisco, director Coppola assigned Reynolds the first half of the gangster epic, and Zinner the second portion. Reynolds's work includes the lengthy wedding sequence up to and including the murder of Sollozzo in the restaurant. Reynolds has commented that his main challenge on *The Godfather* was coordinating the multitude of characterization and action in the wedding scene.

For Hill's *The Sting*, Reynolds emulated the editing stylistics of the 1930s, in keeping with the period flavor of the Paul Newman-Robert Redford con story. Reynolds's other films for Hill include *The Great Waldo Pepper*, about the daredevil barnstorming pilots of the Roaring Twenties, marked by inspired aerial sequences; the charming *A Little Romance*; and *The Little Drummer Girl*, adapted from John le Carré's best-seller about terrorism. Reynolds worked on two interesting commercial failures, Polanski's long-awaited but ultimately disappointing *Pirates*, and Michael Cimino's epic *Heaven's Gate*.

Reynolds cut the prologue (set in Oxford) and the epilogue (set in Newport) on *Heaven's Gate*, then stayed with the picture through the disastrous opening.

For more than 50 years, on about 70 movies, William Reynolds has invested his work with "invisible" editing that serves to move the narrative forward with a minimum of editing tricks. In an interview with this writer, he stated that his job is to "try to make the best possible version of what you as editor take to be the director's idea of the film." Reynolds has won two Oscars for editing (on *The Sting* and *The Sound of Music*) and earned an additional five nominations (*Fanny*, *The Sand Pebbles*, *Hello, Dolly!*, *The Godfather*, *The Turning Point*), but perhaps his greatest accolade came in 1977, when in a *Film Comment* poll of his colleagues, Reynolds was named one of the three top film editors, along with William Hornbeck and Dede Allen.

—John A. Gallagher

RISKIN, Robert

Writer. **Nationality:** American. **Born:** New York City, 30 March 1897. **Education:** Attended public schools in New York and Baltimore. **Military Service:** Served in the United States Navy during World War I. **Family:** Married the actress Fay Wray, 1942; two daughters and one son. **Career:** Left school at 13 to work in textile mill; as a youth, studio manager on short films for Victor Moore in Florida; freelance writer: plays *She Couldn't Say No*, *A Lady in Love*, *Bless You, Sister*, *The Lady Lies*, and *Many a Slip* were produced in

Robert Riskin

New York, 1926–30; 1931—first film as writer, *Men in Her Life*: contract at Columbia, often working with Frank Capra; 1941—adviser to British government on film as propaganda; then worked with the Office of War Information: created the Overseas Motion Picture Bureau, and served as its chief, 1942–45; 1945—formed Robert Riskin Productions; 1950—stroke ended his writing career. **Awards:** Academy Award for *It Happened One Night*, 1934; Writers Guild Laurel Award, 1954. **Died:** 20 September 1955.

Films as Writer:

1931   *Men in Her Life* (Beaudine); *Platinum Blonde* (Capra); *Three Wise Girls* (Beaudine)

1932   *The Big Timer* (Buzzell); *American Madness* (Capra); *Night Club Lady* (Cummings); *Virtue* (Buzzell); *Shopworn* (Grinde)

1933   *Ann Carver's Profession* (Buzzell); *Lady for a Day* (Capra); *Ex-Lady* (Florey)

1934   ***It Happened One Night*** (Capra); *Broadway Bill* (Capra)

1935   *Carnival* (W. Lang); *The Whole Town's Talking* (Ford)

1936   *Mr. Deeds Goes to Town* (Capra)

1937   *When You're in Love* (+ d); *Lost Horizon* (Capra)

1938   *You Can't Take It with You* (Capra)

1941   ***Meet John Doe*** (Capra)

1944   *The Thin Man Goes Home* (Thorpe) (+ pr)

1947   *Magic Town* (Wellman) (+ pr)

1950   *Mister 880* (Goulding)

1951   *Half Angel* (Sale); *Here Comes the Groom* (Capra)

Films as Associate Producer:

1939   *They Shall Have Music* (Mayo); *The Real Glory* (Hathaway)

Publications

By RISKIN: books—

Lady for a Day and *It Happened One Night* (scripts) in *Four-Star Scripts*, edited by Lorraine Noble, New York, 1936.
Mr. Smith Goes to Washington (script) in *Twenty Best Film Plays*, edited by John Gassner and Dudley Nichols, New York, 1943.
Six Screenplays by Robert Riskin: Platinum Bonde, American Madness, It Happened One Night, Mr. Deeds Goes to Town, Lost Horizon, Meet John, Berkeley, 1997.

On RISKIN: articles—

Film Comment (New York), Winter 1970–71.
Films and Filming (London), March 1972.
Corliss, Richard, "Capra and Riskin," in *Films and Filming* (London), November-December 1972.
Frank, Sam, in *American Screenwriters*, edited by Robert E. Morsberger, Stephen O. Lesser, and Randall Clark, Detroit, Michigan, 1984.
Hicks, Jimmie, "Frank Capra (Part 2)," in *Films in Review* (New York), January-February 1993.

"Whey You're In Love," in *Reid's Film Index* (New South Wales), no. 20, 1996.
Turner, G., in *American Cinematographer* (Hollywood), July 1997.

*   *   *

A writer of sophisticated stage plays in the late 1920s and early 1930s, Robert Riskin had over 20 screen credits in a career which lasted two-and-a-half decades. More than half of his work was with Frank Capra—a creative union which culminated in some of Riskin's best screenplays. Among these works are *American Madness*, *Lady for a Day*, *It Happened One Night*, *Mr. Deeds Goes to Town*, *Lost Horizon*, and *Meet John Doe*. Of these only *Lost Horizon* is an adaptation—and it is a solid translation of the novel that became a successful film that won popular and critical acclaim.

The collaboration of Capra and Riskin evidently became a vital force in creating a body of some of the best Capra films. While it is difficult to judge how much Riskin added to a Capra film, a close reading of the director's work indicates that his favorite writer probably influenced some of the satirical and sophisticated tone of the films—not necessarily changing Capra's overall vision, but polishing many of the aspects of his creation. Since Riskin was schooled in the sophisticated stage comedy he was well able to provide Claudette Colbert, the rich man's daughter in *It Happened One Night*, with plausible and sparkling dialogue. Working for other directors in the early 1930s, Riskin handled urbane characters in such works as *Men in Her Life*, *Night Club Lady*, and *Virtue*. Even in these minor works critics lauded the characterization and the wisecracks as they had praised his dialogue and comedy characters for the stage dramas *Bless You, Sister* and *Many a Slip*. Riskin added insight and effective dialogue for the protagonist bank president and his high-society friends in Capra's *American Madness*. The director, although also a writer, was not noted for handling this type of material in his 1920s films.

Some of the Riskin touch is evident in even his most atypical work, the adaptation of *Lost Horizon*. Two characters, played by Edward Everett Horton and Thomas Mitchell, were given comic characteristics that did not exist in the novel. In the 1940s Riskin became a producer-writer on his own and created the fifth in the series of "thin man" pictures, *The Thin Man Goes Home*, plus a film called *Magic Town*, a work that had many of the characteristics of a Capra picture. But the magic in Riskin's dialogue began to fade and he would never equal his best work of the past, when he had a marvelous symbiotic relationship with Frank Capra.

—Donald W. McCaffrey

ROACH, Hal

Producer and Director. **Nationality:** American. **Born:** Elmira, New York, 14 January 1892. **Military Service:** Made propaganda and training films during World War II: colonel. **Family:** Son: the producer Hal Roach, Jr.; daughter: Margaret. **Career:** 1910—mule-skinner and gold rusher in Alaska; 1912—arrived in Hollywood, entered films as stuntman and actor for Universal; 1914—formed Rolin Film Company: "Willie Work" series with Harold Lloyd, followed by popular "Lonesome Luke" series; then produced (and often directed and wrote) many short comedy films with Harry

Hal Roach (right) with Oliver Hardy and Stan Laurel

Pollard, Will Rogers, Charlie Chase, Edgar Kennedy, Laurel and Hardy, Our Gang, Thelma Todd and ZaSu Pitts, and others; TV producer, with his son, after World War II: company finally dissolved, 1962. **Awards:** Academy Award for *Bored of Education*, 1936; Special Academy Award, 1983. **Died:** 2 November 1992.

Films as Producer (Shorts):

1914 *Willie* (Campbell); *Willie's Haircut* (MacGregor); *Willie Goes to Sea* (Campbell)

1920 *Number Please* (Newmeyer)

1921 *Now or Never* (Newmeyer); *Among Those Present* (Newmeyer); *Never Weaken* (Newmeyer)

1922 *The Timber Queen* (Jackman—serial); *The Ropin' Fool* (Badger); *Fruits of the Faith* (Badger); *Our Gang* (McGowan); *Young Sherlocks* (McGowan and McNamara)

1923 *Her Dangerous Path* (Clements—serial); *Get Your Man* (Jeske); *The Smile Wins* (Jeske); *Boys to Board* (McNamara); *Good Riddance* (Jeske); *Jus' Passin' Through* (Parrott); *Hustlin' Hawk* (Pembroke); *Uncensored Movies* (Clements); *Two Wagons, Both Covered* (Wagner)

1924 *Short Kilts* (Jeske); *Smithy* (Jeske); *Postage Due* (Jeske); *Zeb vs. Paprika* (Cedar); *Near Dublin* (Cedar); *Brothers under the Chin* (Cedar); *The Cowboy Shiek* (Howe); *The Cake Eater* (Howe); *Big Moments from Little Pictures* (Howe); *High Brow Stuff* (Wagner); *Going to Congress* (Wagner); *Rupert of Cole Slaw* (*Rupert of Hee-Haw*) (Pembroke);

Wide Open Spaces (Jeske); *Our Congressman* (Wagner); *A Truthful Liar* (Del Ruth); *Gee Whiz Genevieve!* (Howe); *Don't Park There!* (Guiol); *Jubilo, Jr.* (McGowan)

1925 *Is Marriage the Bunk* (McCarey); *Isn't Life Terrible?* (McCarey); *Yes, Yes, Nanette* (Laurel and Hennecke); *Wandering Papas* (Laurel)

1926 *Madame Mystery* (Laurel and Wallace); *Long Live the King* (McCarey); *Thundering Fleas* (McGowan); *Along Came Auntie* (Guiol); *Crazy Like a Fox* (McCarey); *Be Your Age* (McCarey); *The Nickel Hopper* (Jones); *Should Men Walk Home?* (McCarey); *Should Tall Men Marry* (Bruckman)

1927 *Why Girls Say No* (McCarey); *Slipping Wives* (Guiol); *The Honorable Mr. Buggs* (Jackman); *Fluttering Hearts* (Parrott); *Love 'em and Weep* (Guiol); *Why Girls Love Sailors* (Guiol); *With Love and Hisses* (Guiol); *Sailors Beware* (Guiol); *Hats Off* (Yates); *Love 'em and Feed 'em* (Bruckman); *Do Detectives Think?* (Guiol); *Call of the Cuckoo* (Bruckman); *Assistant Wives* (Parrott); *Flying Elephants* (Butler); *Galloping Ghosts* (Parrott); *Putting Pants on Philip* (Bruckman); *The Lighter That Failed* (Parrott)

1928 *The Boy Friend* (Guiol); *Spook-Spoofing* (McGowan); *Rainy Days* (Mack); *The Finishing Touch* (Bruckman); *The Family Group* (Guiol); *Dumb Daddies* (Yates); *Edison, Marconi, & Co.* (Mack); *Spoofing* (McGowan); *Aching Youth* (Guiol); *From Soup to Nuts* (Kennedy); *Came the Dawn* (Heath); *Barnum and Ringling, Inc.* (McGowan); *Blow By Blow* (Parrott); *You're Darn Tootin'* (Kennedy); *Limousine Love* (Guiol); *Tell It to the Judge* (Guiol and Yates); *The Fight Pest* (Guiol); *Fair and Muddy* (Oezle); *Should Women Drive?* (Yates); *Crazy House* (McGowan); *That Night* (Heath); *School Begins* (Mack); *The Ol' Gray Hoss* (McGowan); *Early to Bed* (Flynn); *Imagine My Embarrassment* (Yates); *Is Everybody Happy?* (Yates), *Should Married Men Go Home?* (Parrott); *The Battle of the Century* (Bruckman); *The Booster* (Yates); *Do Gentlemen Snore?* (Heath); *Growing Pains* (Mack); *A Pair of Tights* (Yates); *Their Purple Moment* (Parrott); *Habeas Corpus* (Parrott)

1929 *Bacon Grabbers* (Foster); *Double Whoopee* (Foster); *Hotter Than Hot* (Foster); *Men o' War* (Foster); *Railroadin'* (McGowan); *Crazy Feet* (Doane); *Lazy Days* (McGowan); *Boxing Gloves* (Mack); *Little Mother* (McGowan); *Wiggle Your Ears* (McGowan); *Loud Soup* (Foster); *The Holy Terror* (Mack); *Dog Heaven* (Mack); *Berth Marks* (Foster); *Big Business* (Horne); *The Hoose-Gow* (Parrott); *The Big Squawk* (Doane); *Cat, Dog, & Co.* (Mack); *Bouncing Babies* (McGowan); *Shivering Shakespeare* (Mack); *The Real McCoy* (Doane); *Noisy Noises* (McGowan); *Movie Nights* (Foster); *Snappy Sneezer* (Doane); *The Perfect Day* (Parrott); *Sky Boy* (Rogers); *They Go Boom* (Parrott); *Thin Twins* (Horne); *Leaping Love* (Doane); *That's My Wife* (French); *Angora Love* (Foster); *Feed 'em and Weep* (Guiol); *The Head Guy* (Guiol); *Rainy Days* (Mack); *Skirt Shy* (Rogers); *Stepping Out* (Foster); *Unaccustomed as We Are* (Foster); *Saturday's Lesson* (McGowan)

1930 *Pups Is Pups* (McGowan); *Below Zero* (Parrott); *Blotto* (Parrott); *The King* (Horne and Rogers); *When the Wind Blows* (Horne); *The Big Kick* (Doane); *Fast Work* (Horne); *Night Owls* (Parrott); *The Brats* (Parrott); *A Tough Winter* (McGowan); *The Laurel and Hardy Murder Case* (Parrott);

The Fighting Parson (Rogers and Guiol); *The Shrimp* (Rogers); *The First Seven Years* (McGowan); *All Teed Up* (Kennedy)

1931   *Call a Cop!* (Stevens); *Shiver My Timbers* (McGowan); *High Gear* (Stevens); *Catch-as-Catch-Can* (Neilan); *Dogs Is Dogs* (McGowan); *One Good Turn* (Horne); *Come Clean* (Horne); *The Kick-Off!* (Stevens); *One of the Smiths* (Parrott); *The Panic Is On* (Parrott); *Helpmates* (Parrott); *Beau Hunks* (*Beau Chumps*) (Horne); *Big Ears* (McGowan); *Hasty Marriage* (Pratt); *Readin' and Writin'* (McGowan); *Skip the Maloo* (Parrott); *War Mamas* (Neilan); *What a Bozo* (Parrott)

1932   *Wild Babies* (Mack and French); *Free Eats* (McCarey); *Hook and Ladder* (McGowan); *The Old Bull* (Marshall); *First in War* (Doane); *Love Pains* (Horne); *The Nickel Nurser* (Doane); *Free Wheeling* (McGowan); *The Pooch* (McGowan); *Scram* (McCarey); *A Lad an 'a Lamp* (McGowan); *Spanky* (McGowan); *You're Telling Me!* (French and Mack); *The Soilers* (Marshall); *Their First Mistake* (Marshall); *Strictly Unreliable* (Marshall); *Alum and Eve* (Marshall); *Girl Grief* (Parrott); *Hot Spot* (Lord); *Show Business* (White); *Too Many Women* (Mack and French); *What Price Taxi* (Lord); *Young Ironsides* (Parrott); *The Chimp* (Parrott); *Choo-Choo* (McGowan); *County Hospital* (Parrott); *In Walked Charley* (Doane); *The Knock-out* (Mack and French); *The Music Box* (Parrott); *Red Noses* (Horne)

1933   *Sons of the Desert* (Seiter); *Busy Bodies* (French); *Wild Poses* (McGowan); *Asleep in the Feet* (Meins); *One Track Minds* (Meins); *Bedtime Worries* (McGowan); *Luncheon at Twelve* (Parrott); *Crook's Tour* (McGowan); *The Rummy* (Lord); *Thundering Taxis* (Lord); *Midsummer Mush* (Parrott); *The Cracked Ice Man* (Parrott); *Beauty and the Bus* (Meins); *Dirty Work* (French); *Sherman Said It* (Parrott); *Twin Screws* (Parrott); *Rhapsody in Brew* (Gilbert); *Mush and Milk* (McGowan); *Forgotten Babies* (McGowan); *The Kid from Borneo* (McGowan); *Maids à la Mode* (Meins); *Taxi Barons* (Meins); *Wreckety Wrecks* (Lord); *Air Fright* (Meins); *Backs to Nature* (Meins); *Fallen Arches* (Meins); *The Bargain of the Century* (Parrott); *Twice Two* (Parrott); *The Midnight Patrol* (French)

1934   *Opened By Mistake* (Parrott); *The Live Ghost* (Rogers); *The Caretaker's Daughter* (French); *For Pete's Sake* (Meins); *Going Bye-Bye!* (Rogers); *A Duke for a Day* (Parrott); *The First Round-Up* (Meins); *I'll Take Vanilla* (Parrott and Dunn); *Four Parts* (Parrott and Dunn); *Fate's Fathead* (Parrott); *Washee Ironee* (Parrott); *Next Week-End* (Dunn); *Them Thar Hills* (Rogers); *Movie Daze* (Meins); *Another Wild Idea* (Parrott and Dunn); *Apples to You!* (Jason); *Babes in the Goods* (Meins); *Bum Voyage* (Grinde); *Hi Neighbor!* (Meins); *Honky-Donkey* (Meins); *I'll Be Suing You* (Meins); *Maid in Hollywood* (Meins); *Mike Fright* (Meins); *Mrs. Barnacle Bill* (French); *Mixed Nuts* (Parrott); *Nosed Out* (Yates); *The Private Life of Oliver the Eighth* (French); *Something Simple* (Parrot and Weems); *Soup and Fish* (Meins); *Speaking of Relations* (Yates); *Three Chumps Ahead* (Meins); *You Bring the Ducks* (Yates); *You Said a Hatful!* (Parrott); *One Horse Farmers* (Meins); *Benny from Panama* (Parrott); *Music in Your Hair* (Parrott); *Roamin' Vandals* (Jason and Yates); *Done in Oil* (Meins)

1935   *Hot Money* (Horne); *The Four Star Boarder* (Parrott); *The Tin Man* (Parrott); *Twin Triplets* (Terhune); *Nurse to You* (Parrott); *Treasure Blues* (Parrott); *Shrimps for a Day* (Meins); *Anniversary Trouble* (Meins); *The Chases of Pimple Street* (Parrott); *The Fixer-Uppers* (Rogers); *The Infernal Triangle* (Douglas); *Little Papa* (Meins); *Little Sinner* (Meins); *Lucky Beginners* (Douglas); *Mama's Little Pirate* (Meins); *Manhattan Monkey Business* (Parrott and Law); *The Misses Stooge* (Parrott); *Our Gang Follies of 1936* (Meins); *Poker at Eight* (Parrott); *Public Ghost No. 1* (Parrott and Law); *Sing, Sister, Sing* (Parrott); *Slightly Static* (Terhune); *Southern Exposure* (Parrott); *Sprucin' Up* (Meins); *Teacher's Beau* (Meins); *Thicker Than Water* (Horne); *Tit for Tat* (Rogers); *Top Flat* (Terhune and Jevne); *Life Hesitates at Forty* (Parrott and Law); *Pay As You Exit* (Douglas); *Divot Diggers* (McGowan); *Vamp till Ready* (Parrott and Law); *Neighborhood House* (Parrott and Law); *The Pinch Singer* (Newmeyer); *Second Childhood* (Meins); *The Count Takes the Count* (Parrott and Law); *An All American Toothache* (Meins); *Arbor Day* (Newmeyer); *At Sea Ashore* (Terhune); *Hill Tillies* (Meins); *On the Wrong Trek* (Parrott and Law); *Pan Handlers* (Terhune); *Spooky Hooky* (Douglas); *Two Too Young* (Douglas); *Bored of Education* (Douglas)

1937   *Nobody's Baby* (Meins); *Pick a Star* (Sedgwick); *Night 'n' Gales* (Douglas); *Rushin' Ballet* (Douglas); *Roamin' Holiday* (Douglas); *Our Gang Follies of 1938* (Douglas); *Fishy Tales* (Douglas); *Framing Youth* (Douglas); *Glove Taps* (Douglas); *Mail and Female* (Newmayer); *Reunion in Rhythm* (Douglas); *Hearts Are Thumps* (Douglas); *Three Smart Boys* (Douglas)

1938   *Came the Brawn* (Douglas); *Party Fever* (Sidney); *Mein in Fright* (Sidney); *Hide and Shriek* (Douglas); *Football Romeo* (Sidney); *Practical Jokers* (Sidney); *Canned Fishing* (Douglas); *Feed 'em and Weep* (Douglas); *Three Men in a Tub* (Watt)

1939   *Dog Daze* (Sidney); *Joy Scouts* (Cahn); *Auto Antics* (Cahn); *Clown Princes* (Sidney); *Cousin Wilbur* (Sidney)

Films as Producer and Director (Shorts):

1914   *Just Nuts*; *Lonesome Luke*; *Once Every Ten Minutes*; *Spit Ball Sadie*; *Fresh from the Farm*; *Soaking the Clothes*; *Pressing His Suit*; *Terribly Stuck Up*; *A Mix-Up for Maisie*; *Some Baby*; *Giving Them Fits*; *Bughouse Bell Hops*; *Ragtime Snapshots*; *Great While It Lasted*; *Tinkering with Trouble*; *A Foozle at a Tea Party*; *Peculiar Patients' Pranks*; *Social Gangster*; *Ruses, Rhymes, Roughnecks*

1916   *Luke Leans to the Literary*; *Luke Lugs Luggage*; *Luke Lolls in Luxury*; *Luke the Candy Cut-Up*; *Luke Foils the Villain*; *Luke Pipes the Pippins*; *Skylight Sleep*; *Luke's Late Lunches*; *Luke Laughs Last*; *Luke's Fatal Flivver*; *Them Was the Happy Days*; *In Soft in a Studio*; *Lonesome Luke, Circus King*; *Lady Killers*; *Luke's Society Mix-Up*; *Luke's Washful Waiting*; *Luke Rides Roughshod*; *Luke, Crystal Gazer*; *Luke's Lost Lamb*; *Braver Than the Bravest*; *Luke Does the Midway*; *Caught in a Jam*; *Luke Joins the Navy*; *Busting the Beanery*; *Luke and the Mermaids*; *Jailed*; *Luke's Speedy Club Life*; *Luke's Preparedness Preparation*; *Luke and the*

Bang-Tails; *Luke, the Chauffeur; Luke and the Bomb Throwers; Reckless Wrestlers; Luke, Gladiator; Luke, Patient Provider; Luke's Movie Muddle; Luke's Fireworks Frizzle; Luke Locates the Loot; Luke's Shattered Sleep; Trouble Enough; Luke and the Rural Roughnecks; Luke's Double*

1917   *Lonesome Luke's Lively Life; Skinny Gets a Goat; Skinny's False Alarm; Skinny's Shipwrecked Sand-Witch; Lonesome Luke on Tin Can Alley; Lonesome Luke's Honeymoon; Lonesome Luke—Plumber; Stop! Luke! Listen!; Lonesome Luke—Messenger; Lonesome Luke—Mechanic; Lonesome Luke's Wild Women; Over the Fence; Lonesome Luke Loses Patients; Pinched Bliss; Rainbow Island; Love, Laughs, and Lather; Bashful; All Aboard; By the Sad Sea Waves; The Flirt; Lonesome Luke from London to Laramie; Birds of a Feather; Clubs Are Trump; We Never Sleep; Move On; One Quarter Inch; The Tip; Luke's Last Liberty; Luke's Busy Days; Luke's Trolley Trouble; Lonesome Luke—Lawyer; Luke Wins Ye Ladye Faire; Lonesome Luke's Lively Rifle*

1918   *The Movie Dummy; The Big Idea; The Lamb; Hello Teacher; Hit Him Again; A One Night Stand; Beat It; A Gasoline Wedding; Look Pleasant Please; Here Come the Girls; Let's Go; On the Jump; Follow the Crowd; Pipe the Whiskers; It's a Wild Life; Hey There!; His Busy Day; Kicked Out; The Non-Stop Kid; Two-Gun Gussie; The Junkman; Fireman, Save My Child; The City Slicker; Sic 'em Towser; Somewhere in Turkey; Cleopatsy; Are Crooks Dishonest?; The Furniture Movers; Bees in His Bonnet; Step Lively; An Ozark Romance; Fire the Cook; Kicking the Germ Out of Germany; Beach Nuts; That's Him; Do Husbands Deceive?; Bride and Gloom; Nipped in the Bud; Two Scrambled; The Dippy Daughter; The Great Water Peril; Swing Your Partners; No Place Like Jail; Why Pick on Me?; An Enemy of Soap; Just Rambling Along; Hear 'em Rave; Nothing But Trouble; Take a Chance; Check Your Baggage; She Loves Me Not; Wanted $5,000; Going! Going! Gone!; Ask Father; On the Fire; Look Out Below; Next Aisle Over*

1919   *Do You Love Your Wife?; Love's Young Scream; Hustling for Health; Toto's Troubles; Hoot Man; I'm on My Way; The Dutiful Dub; A Sammy in Siberia; Just Dropped In; Crack Your Heels; Ring Up the Curtain; Young Mr. Jazz; Si Senor; Before Breakfast; The Marathon; Back to the Woods; Pistols for Breakfast; Swat the Crook; Off the Trolley; Spring Fever; Billy Blazes, Esq.; Just Neighbors; At the Old Stage Door; Never Touched Me; A Jazzed Honeymoon; Count Your Change; Chop Suey & Co.; Heap Big Chief; Don't Shove; Be My Wife; The Rajah; He Leads, Others Follow; Soft Money; All at Sea; Call for Mr. Caveman; Giving the Bride Away; It's a Hard Life; From Hand to Mouth; His Only Father; Pay Your Dues; Bumping into Broadway; Captain Kidd's Kids; His Royal Slyness*

1920   *Order in the Court; How Dry I Am; Red Hot Hottentots; Why Go Home?; Slippery Slickers; The Dippy Dentist; Looking for Trouble; Tough Luck; The Floor Below; All Lit Up; Getting His Goat; Waltz Me Around; Raise the Rent; Find the Girl; Fresh Paint; Flat Broke; Cut the Cards; The Dinner Hour; Speed to Spare; Don't Weaken; Shoot on Sight; The Eastern Westerner; Haunted Spooks; Drink Hearty; Trotting Through Turkey; Merely a Maid; All*

Dressed Up; Grab the Ghost; You're Pinched; Start the Show; High and Dry; All in a Day; Any Old Port; Don't Rock the Boat; Hello Uncle; The Home Stretch; Call a Taxi; Little Miss Jazz; A Regular Pal; Go As You Please; Rock-a-bye Baby; Money to Burn; Doing Time; Fellow Citizens; Alias Aladdin; Mamma's Boy; The Sandman; When the Wind Blows; Insulting the Sultan; Queens Up; The Dear Departed; Park Your Car; Cracked Wedding Bells; A London Bobby; June Madness; Live and Learn

1921   *The Sleepy Head; Greek Meets Greek; The Morning After; Pinning It On; Burglars Bold; Open Another Bottle; Prince Pistachio; Cash Customers; A Straight Crook; Big Game; Save Your Money; I Do (co-d); Bubbling Over; Catching a Coon; Fellow Romans; Fifteen Minutes; His Best Girl; Hobgoblins; Hurry West; The Kiljoys; The Love Lesson; Make It Snappy; On Location; Paint and Powder; No Children; Oh, Promise Me; Penny-in-the-Slot; Rush Orders; Running Wild; Where's the Fire?; Own Your Home; The High Rollers; You're Next; The Bike Bug; At the Ringside; What a Whopper; No Stop-Over; Teahing the Teacher; Spot Cash; Name the Day; Stop Kidding; The Jail Bird; On Their Way; Late Lodgers; The Chink; Rough Seas; Gone to the Country; The Lucky Number; Sweet By and By; A Zero Hour; Dodge your Debts; Law and Order; Late Hours; Trolley Troubles; The Joy Rider; The Hustler; The Pickaninny; Sink or Swim; Shake 'em Up; The Corner Pocket; Try, Try Again; Lose No Time; Loose Change; Call the Witness*

1922   *Years to Come; Blow 'em Up; Stage Struck; Rich Man, Poor Man; Down and Out; Pardon Me; The Bow Wows; High Tide; Hot Off the Press; The Anvil Chorus; Jump Your Job; Stand Pat; Full o' Pep; Kill the Nerve; Days of Old; Light Showers; Do Me a Favor; The Movie; Punch the Clock; Strictly Modern; Hale and Hearty; Many Happy Returns; Some Baby; Friday the 13th; Fair Week; The Man Haters; A Bed of Roses; The Late Lamented; The Dumb-Bells; The Sleuth; The Bride-to-Be; Busy Bees; Take Next Car; The Stone Age; Touch All the Bases; The Truth Juggler; Rough on Romeo; Wet Weather; One Terrible Day; 365 Days; The Landlubber; Bone Dry; Soak the Sheik; Face the Camera; The Uppercut; The Fire Fighters; The Old Sea Dog; Out on Bail; Shiver and Shake; Shine 'em Up; Hook, Line, and Sinker; Washed Ashore; The Flivver; Blaze Away; The Golf Bug; Saturday Morning; Between Meals; Pay the Cashier; Dig Up; Paste and Paper; The Green Cat; The Only Son; The Champeen; Before the Public; Good Morning, Judge; Hired and Fired; I'll Take Vanilla; Leave It to Me; Fire the Fireman; Newly Rich; The Non-Skid Kid; A Quiet Street; The Roustabout; A Tough Winter; Watch Your Wife; A White Blacksmith*

1923   *Don't Say Die; Harvest Hands; Mr. Hyppo; Once Over; Jailed and Bailed; A Loose Tightwad; The Cobbler; Tight Shoes; The Big Show; Shoot Straight; Do Your Stuff; For Safe Keeping; A Pleasant Journey; Bowled Over; Where Am I? Sunny Spain; Speed the Swede; California or Bust; The Noon Whistle; White Wings; Giants vs. Yanks; Don't Flirt; Sold at Auction; For Art's Sake; Back Stage; Under Two Jags; The Watch Dog; Fresh Eggs; Pick and Shovel; Courtship of Miles Sandwich; Dogs of War; Collars and Cuffs; The Uncovered Wagon; Kill or Cure; Jack Frost; For*

Guests Only; *Lodge Night*; *Gas and Air*; *Oranges and Lemons*; *Post No Bills*; *The Mystery Man*; *Be Honest*; *Live Wires*; *July Days*; *Short Orders*; *Take the Air*; *The Walkout*; *Let's Build*; *A Man about Town*; *No Noise*; *Finger Prints*; *Roughest Africa*; *Stepping Out*; *No Pets*; *Frozen Hearts*; *Winner Take All*; *Stage Fright*; *Heavy Seas*; *It's a Gift*; *Derby Day*; *Save the Ship*; *Go West*; *The Soilers*; *Sunday Calm*; *Fully Insured*; *Scorching Sands*; *The Great Outdoors*; *Join the Circus*; *Mother's Joy*; *Lovey Dovey*; *It's a Boy*; *The Darkest Hour*; *One of the Family*; *At First Sight*; *Tire Troubles*; *The Big Idea*; *Bowled Over*; *The Knockout*; *Once Over*

1924　*The White Sheep* (+ sc); *The Bar Fly*; *Help One Another*; *Just a Minute*; *Big Business*; *Powder and Smoke*; *The Man Pays*; *Political Pull*; *Hard Knocks*; *Love's Detour*; *The Buccaneers*; *Love's Reward*; *Hunters Bold*; *Don't Forget*; *The Fraidy Cat*; *Seein' Things*; *Friend Husband*; *Our Little Nell*; *Hit the High Spots*; *One at a Time*; *Get Busy*; *Commencement Day*; *Publicity Pays*; *North of 50–50*; *April Fool*; *Bottle Babies*; *Position Wanted*; *Cradle Robbers*; *Up and at 'em*; *Fast Black*; *Suffering Shakespeare*; *Jeffries, Jr.*; *Why Husbands Go Mad*; *Radio Mad*; *A Ten Minute Egg*; *Seeing Nellie Home*; *It's a Bear*; *A Hard-Boiled Tenderfoot*; *Sweet Daddy*; *High Society*; *Why Men Work*; *South o' the North Pole*; *Outdoor Pajamas*; *The Sun Down Limited*; *Sittin' Pretty*; *Should Landlords Live?*; *The Lost Dog*; *Too Many Mammas*; *The Goofy Age*; *Every Man for Himself*; *Bungalow Boobs*; *The Sky Plumber*; *Hot Stuff*; *Accidental Accidents*; *Hot Heels*; *Fast Company*; *All Wet*; *Are Blond Men Bashful?*; *Deaf, Dumb, and Daffy*; *The Poor Fish*; *Meet the Missus*; *The Mysterious Mystery*; *The Royal Razz*; *Just a Good Guy*; *The Rubberneck*; *The Wages of Tin*; *The Rat's Knuckles*; *The Big Town*; *Hello Baby*; *Laugh That Off*; *The Family Entrance*; *Fighting Fluid*; *A Perfect Lady*; *Stole Goods*; *Young Oldfield*

1925　*All Wool*; *Are Husbands Human?*; *Are Parents Pickles?*; *Ask Grandma*; *Bad Boy*; *Better Movies*; *The Big Kick*; *Big Red Riding Hood*; *Black Hand Blues*; *The Bouncer*; *Boys Will Be Joys*; *The Caretaker's Daughter*; *Change the Needle*; *Chasing the Chaser*; *Circus Fever*; *Cuckoo Love*; *Daddy Goes a-Grunting*; *Dog Days*; *Excuse My Glove*; *Flaming Flappers*; *The Fox Hunt*; *Grief in Bagdad*; *Hard Boiled*; *The Haunted Honeymoon*; *His Wooden Wedding*; *Hold My Baby*; *In the Grease!*; *Innocent Husbands*; *Laughing Ladies*; *Looking for Sally*; *The Love Bug*; *Madame Sans Jane*; *Mary, Queen of Tots*; *Moonlight and Noses*; *No Father to Guide Him*; *Official Officers*; *One Wild Ride*; *Papa, Be Good!*; *Plain and Fancy Girls*; *A Punch in the Nose*; *Riders of the Kitchen Range*; *The Royal Four Flush*; *A Sailor Papa*; *Sherlock Sleuth*; *Shootin' Injuns*; *Should Husbands Be Watched?*; *Should Sailors Marry?*; *Solid Ivory*; *Somewhere in Somewhere*; *Starvation Blues*; *Sure-Mike*; *Tame Men and Wild Women*; *Tell It to a Policeman*; *There Goes the Bride*; *Thundering Landlords*; *The Uneasy Three*; *Unfriendly Enemies*; *What Price Goofy?*; *Wild Papa*; *Your Own Back Yard*

1926　*Tol'able Romeo*; *Hold Everything*; *Good Cheer*; *What's the World Coming To?*; *Charley My Boy*; *Long Pants*; *Your Husband's Past*; *Buried Treasure*; *The Hug Bug*; *Mam, Behave*; *Monkey Business*; *Dizzy Daddies*; *Wife Tamers*;

Do Your Duty; *Ukelele Sheiks*; *Baby Clothes*; *Scared Stiff*; *Mum's the Word*; *Don Key, Son of Burro*; *Say It with Babies*; *Uncle Tom's Uncle*; *He Forgot to Remember*; *Never Too Old*; *Cow's Kimono*; *Mighty Like a Moose*; *Merry Widower*; *Shivering Spooks*; *Fourth Alarm*; *Bromo and Juliet*; *Wise Guys Prefer Brunettes*; *Tell 'em Nothing*; *Get 'em Young*; *On the Front Page*; *War Feathers*; *There Ain't No Santa Claus*; *45 Minutes fromHollywood*; *Telling Whoppers*; *Many Scrappy Returns*

1927　*Bring Home the Turkey*; *Are Brunettes Safe?*; *Duck Soup*; *Ten Years Old*; *Forgotten Sweeties*; *Love My Dog*; *Jewish Prudence*; *Bigger and Better Blondes*; *Tired Business Men*; *Eve's Love Letters*; *Don't Tell Everything*; *Glorious Fourth*; *What Women Did for Me*; *Olympic Games*; *Should Husbands Come First?*; *The Way of All Pants*; *What Every Iceman Knows*; *A One-Mama Man*; *Now I'll Tell One*; *Chicken Feed*; *Fighting Fathers*; *The Smile Wins*

1929　*Dad's Day*; *Hurdy Gurdy*; *When Money Comes*; *Madame Q*; *Why Is a Plumber?*; *Thundering Toupees*

1931　*Let's Do Things*; *The Pajama Party*

1932　*On the Loose*

1933　*Arabian Tights*; *Nature in the Wrong*

1934　*The Ballad to Paducah Jail*

Films as Producer (Features):

1921　*A Sailor Made Man* (Newmeyer) (+ co-sc)

1922　*Grandma's Boy* (Newmeyer) (+ co-sc); *Dr. Jack* (Newmeyer) (+ co-sc)

1923　*Safety Last* (Newmeyer and Taylor) (+ co-sc); *Why Worry?* (Newmeyer and Taylor); *The Call of the Wild* (Jackman)

1924　*The King of Wild Horses* (Jackman) (+ sc); *Hot Water* (Taylor and Newmeyer); *The Battling Orioles* (Wilde and Guiol) (+ sc)

1925　*Black Cyclone* (Jackman) (+ sc)

1931　*Pardon Us* (Parrott)

1932　*Pack Up Your Troubles* (Marshall and McCarey)

1934　*Babes in Toyland* (Rogers and Meins)

1935　*Vagabond Lady* (Taylor); *Bonnie Scotland* (Horne)

1936　*The Bohemian Girl* (Horne and Rogers); *Kelly the Second* (Meins); *Mister Cinderella* (Sedgwick); *Our Relations* (Lachman)

1937　*Way Out West* (Horne)

1938　*Merrily We Live* (McLeod); *Swiss Miss* (Blystone); *Block-Heads* (Blystone); *There Goes My Heart* (McLeod)

1939　*Topper Takes a Trip* (McLeod); *Zenobia* (Douglas)

1940　*Of Mice and Men* (Milestone); *A Chump at Oxford* (Goulding); *Saps at Sea* (Douglas); *Captain Caution* (Wallace)

1941　*Broadway Limited* (Douglas); *Tanks a Million* (Guiol); *All American Co-Ed* (Prinz and H. Roach, Jr.); *Niagara Falls* (Douglas); *Miss Polly* (Guiol); *Fiesta* (Prinz); *Hay Foot* (Guiol); *Topper Returns* (Del Ruth)

1942　*Dudes Are Pretty People* (H. Roach, Jr.); *Brooklyn Orchid* (Neumann); *About Face* (Neumann); *Calaboose* (H. Roach, Jr.); *Fall In* (Neumann); *Flying with Music* (Archainbaud); *The McGuerins from Brooklyn* (Neumann); *Nazty Nuisance* (Tryon); *Prairie Chickens* (H. Roach, Jr.); *Taxi, Mister* (Neumann); *Yanks Ahoy* (Neumann); *The Devil with Hitler* (Douglas)

1947 *The Fabulous Joe* (Foster) (exec); *Curley* (Carr) (exec)
1948 *Here Comes Troubles* (Guiol) (exec); *Who Killed Doc Robbin*
      (Carr) (exec)
1966 *One Million Years B.C.* (Chaffey) (co)

Films as Producer and Director (Features):

1924 *Girl Shy*
1926 *The Devil Horse*
1930 *Men of the North*
1933 *Fra Diavolo* (*The Devil's Brother*) (co-d)
1936 *General Spanky*
1939 *Captain Fury*; *The Housekeeper's Daughter*
1940 *One Million B.C.* (co); *Turnabout*
1941 *Road Show*
1967 *The Crazy World of Laurel and Hardy* (compilation)

Publications

By ROACH: articles—

"The Gag's the Thing," in *Popular Mechanics* (Chicago), May 1935.
"Living with Laughter," in *Films and Filming* (London), October 1964.
The Silent Picture (London), Spring 1970.
In *Hollywood Speaks! An Oral History*, by Mike Steen, New York, 1974.
"Golden Silents," in *Time Out* (London), 20 November 1991.

On ROACH: book—

Everson, William K., *The Films of Hal Roach*, New York, 1970.

On ROACH: articles—

Sight and Sound (London), Autumn 1964.
Rosenberg, Bernard, and Harry Silverstein, in *The Real Tinsel*, New York, 1970.
"Hal Roach on Laurel & Hardy," in *Pratfall*, no. 1, 1972.
Classic Images (Indiana, Pennsylvania), July 1983.
"Hal Roach Studios," in *Pratfall*, no. 2, 1985.
Bann, R.H., "Hal Roach: A Legendary Producer's Beverly Hills Estate," in *Architectural Digest* (Los Angeles), April 1990.
Facts on File, 5 November 1992.
Obituary in *The New York Times*, 3 November 1992.
Obituary in *Variety* (New York), 9 November 1992.
Obituary in *Sight and Sound* (London), February 1993.
"Hal Roach," in *Films in Review* (New York), September-October and November-December 1993.
Hogue, P., "Charley with a Y," in *Film Comment*, March/April 1995.
"10 Years Ago," in *Forbes*, 10 February 1997.

*   *   *

Hal Roach was a producer and motion picture executive best remembered for two things. First, he helped create one of the great comedy factories of all time. In the 1920s his studio launched the careers of Laurel and Hardy, and fostered the talents of Harold Lloyd, one of the serious rivals to Charlie Chaplin, and Buster Keaton. The Roach comedy factory produced many of the best-remembered short subjects of the 1930s, including the *Our Gang* comedies which continue to grind away on television some 60 years after their creation.

By the 1920s Hal Roach had become an established producer, and his comedies had begun to rival the then "King of Comedy," Mack Sennett. Roach smoothly survived the transition to sound, but Sennett did not. Thus, by the mid-1930s it was Roach, distributing through the then dominant major studio, MGM, who could properly be labeled the "King of Comedy." The *Our Gang* series, the teaming of Laurel and Hardy, and the comedies of Charlie Chase made Roach into a powerful, respected producer of comedy shorts. But Roach did not neglect the talent behind the camera. Indeed his studio helped foster the careers of George Stevens and Leo McCarey, both of whom would move on to become major directors.

The Great Depression served as the Golden Age for the Roach comedy factory. Unfortunately the studio could not develop any stars to rival "Our Gang" and Laurel and Hardy. By 1935 the Roach studio was on the decline as the major studios squeezed them out by creating more and more double features and less and less non-animated shorts subjects. In 1938 Roach sold "Our Gang" to MGM and moved on to try independent feature filmmaking with United Artists.

Roach did as well as any producer at United Artists in the late 1930s and 1940s. It was hard to lose money during the Second World War boom era. Between 1938 and 1941 Roach tendered 14 films through United Artists, including *Topper Takes a Trip* starring Constance Bennett and Billie Burke, *Of Mice and Men* starring Lon Chaney, Jr. and Burgess Meredith, and *Saps at Sea* starring an aging Laurel and Hardy. But a military career creating training films ended what success he had with these low-budget films.

In a less well-known, but equally important contribution, Roach pushed the film industry into the television production business. For example, he set up an early series called *Screen Director's Playhouse* on which such talents as Leo McCarey, John Ford, and Tay Garnett worked. Unfortunately little came of its efforts in long-term monetary gain. Thus though *Fireside Theatre* was turned out in quickie fashion at Roach studio for NBC in the late 1940s and early 1950s, the Roaches, Senior and Junior, could not create a permanent relationship with the network. Their greatest success came with a comedy show Roach Junior did with Gale Storm called *My Little Margie* which aired from 1952 to 1955 and many more years in syndication. Hal Roach, Sr. pioneered with television but not well enough to prevent his studio from going bankrupt in 1959 and providing him with an ungraceful retirement.

—Douglas Gomery

ROBBE-GRILLET, Alain

Writer and Director. **Nationality:** French. **Born:** Brest, 18 August 1922. **Education:** Attended Lycée de Brest; lycées Buffon and St. Louis, Paris; National Institute of Agronomy, Paris, diploma 1944. **Family:** Married Catherine Rstakian, 1957. **Career:** Sent to work in German tank factory during World War II; 1945–49—engineer, National Statistical Institute, Paris; 1949–51—engineer, Institute of

Alain Robbe-Grillet

Colonial Fruits and Crops, Morocco, French Guyana, and Martinique; then full-time writer; since 1955—literary consultant, Editions de Minuit, Paris; 1961—script for first film, *L'Année dernière à Marienbad*; 1963—directed first film, *L'Immortelle*. **Awards:** Officer, Order of Merit; Chevalier, Legion of Honor. **Address:** 18, Boulevard Maillot, 92200 Neuilly-sur-Seine, France.

Films as Writer:

1961   ***L'Année dernière à Marienbad*** (*Last Year at Marienbad*) (Resnais)

1988   *Taxandria* (Servais) (co)

Films as Writer and Director:

1963   *L'Immortelle*

1966   *Trans-Europ-Express*

1968   *L'Homme qui ment* (*The Man Who Lies*)

1971   *L'Eden et après* (and TV version *N'a pris les dés*)

1974   *Les Glissements progressifs du plaisir; Le Jeu avec le feu*

1983   *La Belle Captive* (*The Beautiful Prisoner*)

1995   *Un Bruit qui rend fou* (*The Blue Villa*) (co-d with De Clercq)

Publications

By ROBBE-GRILLET: fiction—

Les Gommes, Paris, 1953, as *The Erasers*, New York, 1964.

Le Voyeur, Paris, 1955, as *The Voyeur*, New York, 1958.

La Jalousie, Paris, 1957, as *Jealousy*, New York, 1959.

Dans le labyrinthe, Paris, 1959, as *In the Labyrinth*, New York, 1960.

L'Année dernière à Marienbad, Paris, 1961, as *Last Year at Marienbad*, New York, 1962.

Instantanés, Paris, 1962, as *Snapshots*, with *Towards a New Novel*, London, 1965.

L'Immortelle, Paris, 1963, as *The Immortal One*, London, 1971.

La Maison de rendez-vous, Paris, 1965, as *La Maison de Rendez-vous*, New York, 1966, as *The House of Assignation*, London, 1970.

Projet pour une révolution à New York, Paris, 1970, as *Project for a Revolution in New York*, New York, 1972.
Glissements progressifs du plaisir, Paris, 1974.
Topologie d'une cité fantôme, Paris, 1976, as *Topology of a Phantom City*, New York, 1977.
Un Régicide, Paris, 1978.
Souvenirs du triangle d'or, 1978, as *Memories of the Golden Triangle*, London, 1984.
Djinn, Paris, 1981, as *Djinn*, New York, 1982.
A Kukkolo, 1992.
Les Derniers Jours de Corinthe, 1994.
Taxandria (screenplay), 1996.
La Belle Captive: A Novel, Berkeley, 1996.

By ROBBE-GRILLET: other books—

Pour un nouveau roman, Paris, 1963, as *Towards a New Novel*, with *Snapshots*, London, 1965, as *For a New Novel*, New York, 1966.
Rêves de jeunes filles (photographs by David Hamilton), Paris, 1971, as *Dreams of a Young Girl*, New York, 1971, as *Dreams of Young Girls*, London, 1971.
Les Demoiselles d'Hamilton (photographs by David Hamilton), Paris, 1972, as *Sisters*, New York, 1973.
With René Magritte, *La Belle Captive*, Paris, 1976.
With Irina Ionesco, *Temple aux miroirs*, Paris, 1977.
The Erotic Dream Machine: Interviews with Alain Robbe-Grillet on His Films, with Anthony G. Fragola, Carbondale, 1995.

By ROBBE-GRILLET: articles—

Cahiers du Cinéma (Paris), September 1961.
Cinéma (Paris), February 1963.
Art et Essai (Paris), no. 6, 1965.
In *Film Makers on Filmmaking*, edited by Harry M. Geduld, Bloomington, Indiana, 1967.
Cinémonde (Paris), 15 May 1970.
Cinématographe (Paris), April/May 1974.
Filmmakers Newsletter (Ward Hill, Massachusetts), July 1976.
Cinéma (Paris), July/August 1980.
Cinématographe (Paris), February 1985.
Literature/Film Quarterly (Salisbury, Maryland), April 1989.

On ROBBE-GRILLET: books—

Stoltzfus, Ben Frank, *Robbe-Grillet and the New French Novel*, Carbondale, Illinois, 1964.
Parnell, Martin, editor, *Alain Robbe-Grillet*, Nottingham, 1968.
Gardies, André, *Alain Robbe-Grillet*, Paris, 1972.
Fraizer, Dale W., editor, *Robbe-Grillet: An Annotated Bibliography of Critical Studies 1953–1972*, Metuchen, New Jersey, 1973.
Morrissette, Bruce, *The Novels of Robbe-Grillet*, Ithaca, New York, 1975.
Van Wert, William F., *The Film Career of Alain Robbe-Grillet*, London, 1977.
Nepoti, Roberto, *Alain Robbe-Grillet*, Florence, 1978.
Chateau, Dominique, *Nouveau cinema, nouvelle sémiologie*, Paris, 1979.
Gardies, André, *Approche du recit filmique: sur* L'Homme qui ment *d' Alain Robbe-Grillet*, Paris, 1980.
Armes, Roy, *The Films of Robbe-Grillet*, Amsterdam, 1981.

Fletcher, John, *Robbe-Grillet*, London, 1983.
Gardies, André, *Le Cinéma de Robbe-Grillet*, Paris, 1983.
Leki, Ilona, *Alain Robbe-Grillet*, Boston, Massachusetts, 1983.
Morrissette, Bruce, *Novel and Film*, Chicago, 1985.
Stoltzfus, Ben Frank, *Alain Robbe-Grillet: The Body of the Text*, London, 1985.
Roland, Lillian D., *Women in Robbe-Grillet: A Study in Thematics and Diegetics*, New York, 1993.
Harger-Grinling, Virginia, and Chadwick, Tony, editors, *Robbe-Grillet and the Fantastic: A Collection of Essays*, Westport, Connecticut, 1994.
Hellerstein, Marjorie H., *Inventing the Real World: The Art of Alain Robbe-Grillet*, Susquehanna, 1998.

On ROBBE-GRILLET: articles—

Huston, Penelope, in *Sight and Sound* (London), Autumn 1961.
Brunius, Jacques, in *Sight and Sound* (London), Summer 1962.
Cahiers du Cinéma (Paris), December 1962.
Doniol-Valcroze, Jacques, in *Cahiers du Cinéma* (Paris), May 1963.
Ashmore, Jerome, in *University Review* (Kansas City, Missouri), Spring 1964.
Art et Essai (Paris), February 1967.
Filmcritica (Rome), November/December 1967.
Ward, John, in *Sight and Sound* (London), Spring 1968.
Avant-Scène (Paris), June 1968.
"Robbe-Grillet Issue" of *Kinema* (London), June 1968.
Chaplin (Stockholm), no. 12, 1970.
Cinéma (Paris), September/October 1970.
Film Comment (New York), May/June 1973.
National Film Theatre Booklet (London), September/November 1973.
Films and Filming (London), January 1974.
Avant-Scène (Paris), June 1974.
Cahiers de la Cinémathèque (Paris), Christmas 1977.
Doniol-Valcroze, Jacques, in *Cahiers du Cinéma* (Paris), September 1982.
Doniol-Valcroze, Jacques, in *Cahiers du Cinéma* (Paris), April 1985.
Journal of Film and Video (Boston, Massachusetts), Fall 1990.
Creative Screenwriting (Washington), vol. 3, no. 1, Summer 1996.
Filmihullu (Helsinki), vol. 3, 1997.

* * *

Alain Robbe-Grillet had already published four novels before he came to the cinema as screenwriter of one of the most controversial and innovative films of the early 1960s, Alain Resnais's *L'Année dernière à Marienbad*. Subsequently his work as a novelist has continued alongside his filmmaking activity, often pursuing its own distinctive paths though undoubtedly influenced by the preparation for publication, as *ciné-romans*, of three of his scripts. *L'Année dernière à Marienbad* is a complex work in which the diverging contributions of its two very different authors can now be seen more clearly than in 1961, when discussion of the film tended to be based on the self-proclaimed myth of their perfect collaboration.

Robbe-Grillet's own work as a writer-director has followed paths very different from Resnais's and falls into two periods of very unequal value, with *La Belle Captive* coming as something of a coda in 1983. Between 1963 and 1968 Robbe-Grillet made the three black-and-white feature films on which his reputation as a filmmaker largely rests. *L'Immortelle*, set in Turkey and dealing with a trio of characters designated in the published screenplay as simply L, M, and N, is strikingly original in his handling of narrative. In effect it constitutes a set of variations and distortions on the themes and stylistic devices set out in its 22-shot prologue. *Trans-Europ-Express*, Robbe-Grillet's most approachable film, combines its play with reality and imagination with a humor hitherto absent from his work. Full of mirror images, disguises, distortions of reality, impossible happenings, and duplications, the film makes no pretense of having a conventional narrative. Rather the plot invents itself as it proceeds, creating and ignoring problems, inconsistencies, and downright impossibilities. Robbe-Grillet's major work as a director, *L'Homme qui ment*, carries these formal experiments through to their logical conclusion. Shot on location in Czechoslovakia and set in an old chateau amid the forests, it is the story of a man who invents his own character, past, and emotions as he goes along. But the words which create his reality are eventually turned against him and he is driven back to limbo in the forest. Though lacking a coherent plot in the conventional sense, *L'Homme qui ment* offers many of the same satisfactions as a normal narrative through its complex patterning in terms of symmetry, reversal, and inversion. By fastening on two basic aspects of the film image—its unique present tense quality and its potentiality for an inextricable mixture of reality and falsehood—Robbe-Grillet has fashioned a film which is both approachable and highly innovative.

Robbe-Grillet's color films of the early 1970s—*L'Eden et après*, *Les Glissements progressifs du plaisir*, and *Le Jeu avec le feu*—are equally novel but far less successful. On a thematic level they are undermined by a blatant and self-indulgent eroticism that never achieves the distance which would allow the obsessive subject matter to acquire an aesthetic impact. For this reason these films, which experiment with overelaborate and virtually unreadable serial structures, come to resemble all too closely the drab and dispiriting commercial exploitation movies whose stereotyped formulas Robbe-Grillet claims to be parodying.

Robbe-Grillet's status within French cinema is controversial and his situation is not helped by his own taste for both oversimplifying and mystifying his work. Many of the conventional critics and historians of French cinema ignore his work—like that of Marguerite Duras—altogether. But Robbe-Grillet's work, particularly the masterly *L'Homme qui ment*, has enormous theoretical interest and its impact on a whole generation of young French critics and theorists has been both profound and fruitful.

—Roy Armes, updated by David Levine

RÖHRIG, Walter

Art Director. **Nationality:** German. **Born:** Berlin, 13 April 1897 (some sources give 1892 and 1893). **Career:** Painter, associated with Der Sturm Expressionists in 1910s; stage designer, then film designer: 1919—first film, *Das Kabinett des Dr. Caligari*; often collaborated with Robert Herlth. **Died:** In Potsdam, 1945.

Films as Art Director/Production Designer:

1919　***Das Kabinett des Dr. Caligari*** (*The Cabinet of Dr. Caligari*) (Wiene); *Die Pest von Florenz* (Rippert)

1920　*Der Golem* (*The Golem*) (Wegener); *Irrende Seelen* (Froelich); *Masken* (Wauer); *Das Geheimnis von Bombay* (Holz); *Der Menschheit anwalt* (Rippert)

1921　*Toteninsel* (Froelich); *Der Müde Tod* (*Between Two Worlds*); *Destiny* (Lang); *Satansketten* (Lasko); *Das Spiel mit dem Feuer* (Wiene and Kroll); *Pariserinnen* (Lasko); *Die Intriguen der Madame de la Pommeraye* (Wendhausen)

1922　*Luise Millerin* (Froelich); *Fräulein Julie* (*Miss Julie*) (Basch); *Der Graf von Essex* (Felner) (+ costumes)

1923　*Der Schatz* (*The Treasure*) (Pabst)

1924　*Komödie des Herzens* (Gliese); ***Der letzte Mann*** (*The Last Laugh*) (Murnau)

1925　*Zur Chronik von Grieshaus* (*At the Grey House*) (von Gerlach); *Tartüff* (*Tartuffe*) (Murnau)

1926　*Faust* (Murnau) (+ costumes)

1927　*Luther* (Kyser)

1928　*Looping the Loop* (Robison); *Rutschbahn* (Eichberg)

1929　*Asphalt* (May); *The Informer* (Robison); *Die wunderbare Lüge der Nina Petrovna* (*The Wonderful Lie of Nina Petrovna*) (Schwarz); *Manolescu* (Tourjansky)

1930　*Der unsterbliche Lump* (Ucicky); *Hokuspokus* (*Hocuspocus*) (Ucicky); *Das Flötenkonzert von Sanssouci* (Ucicky); *Rosenmontag* (Steinhoff); *Ein Burschenlied aus Heidelberg* (Hartl); *Der Mann, der seinen Mörder sucht* (Siodmak)

1931　*Der Kongress tanzt* (*The Congress Dances*) (Charell); *Der falsche Ehemann* (Guter); *Nie wieder Liebe* (Litvak); *Im Geheimdienst* (Ucicky); *Der Kleine Seitensprung* (Schünzel); *Yorck* (Ucicky)

1932　*Die Gräfin von Monte Cristo* (Hartl); *Mensch ohne Namen* (*Man without a Name*) (Ucicky); *Der schwarze Husar* (*The Black Hussar*) (Lamprecht)

1933　*Walzerkrieg* (*Waltz Time in Vienna*) (Berger); *Fluchtlinge* (Ucicky); *Saison in Kairo* (Schünzel); *Morgenrot* (Ucicky); *Ich und die Kaiserin* (*The Only Girl*) (Hollaender)

1934　*Die Csarsasfürstin* (Jacoby); *Ich bin du* (Hoffmann); *Der junge Baron Neuhaus* (Ucicky); *Prinzessin Turandot* (Lamprecht)

1935　*Das Mädchen Johanna* (Ucicky); *Frischer Wind aus Kanada* (Kenter and Holder); *Barcarole* (Lamprecht); *Amphitryon* (Schünzel); *Königswalzer* (Maisch)

1936　*Hans im Glück* (Herlth); *Savoy-Hotel 217* (Ucicky); *Unter heissem Himmel* (Ucicky); *Verräter* (Ritter)

1937　*Urlaub und Ehrenwort* (Ritter); *Patrioten* (Ritter); *Mein Sohn, der Herr Minster* (Harlan); *Unternehman Michael* (Ritter); *Brillanten* (von Borsody)

1938　*Capriccio* (Ritter); *Pour le Mérite* (Ritter)

1939　*Die Hochzeitreise* (Ritter)

1940　*Bal paré* (Ritter); *Des Herz des Königin* (Froelich)

1941　*Heimkehr* (Ucicky); *Uber Alles in der Welt* (Ritter); *Kadetten* (Ritter)

1942　*G.P.U.* (Ritter); *Rembrandt* (Steinhoff)

1943　*Gefährlicher Frühling* (Deppe); *Liebesgeschichte* (Tourjansky); *Der kleine Grenzverkehr* (Deppe)

1945　*Via Mala* (von Baky)

Publications

On RÖHRIG: articles—

Rotha, Paul, "Plastic Design," in *Close Up* (London), September 1929.
Cinématographe (Paris), February 1982.

* * *

The German painter and, initially, stage-set designer Walter Röhrig was closely associated with the Berlin Sturm group, and so a practitioner in the so-called Expressionist movement in the fine arts. Hermann Warm, another designer in the group, claimed in reaction against naturalism that "films must be drawings brought to life," and both Warm and Röhrig, along with Walter Reimann, another Expressionist, came to the fore as film designers in the Expressionist style with the celebrated film *The Cabinet of Dr. Caligari* in 1919, directed by Robert Wiene immediately after Germany's defeat in the First World War. With the lowest of budgets, the film's three designers were instructed to create, out of stretched-canvas flats, simple backdrops, and minimal furnishing worthy of a small provincial repertory theatre, sets which would give the impression of a medieval town (fairground, civic offices, houses, both interior and exterior, roofs, bridges) all in a distorted form revealing the warped vision of the young madman who is the hero of this romantic horror film. Their success in scene after scene combined Expressionist distortion of actuality with a haunted beauty; psychological realism gives way to sets painted over with spectacular curves and whorls, rostra interset at cunning angles, doors, windows, and roofs melodramatically askew, but all combined to achieve an extraordinary pictorial effect when lit and photographed. [The artistry of *Caligari* is very fully discussed by Paul Rotha—a former student of fine art—in his book *The Film till Now*]

Both Röhrig and Warm had highly creative careers in the silent cinema, supported by the inspired visual taste of many of Germany's leading directors. Röhrig in particular worked with another partner, Robert Herlth, on four key films made by F.W. Murnau, partly in the Expressionist manner [excellently described by Lotte Eisner in her books *The Haunted Screen* and *Murnau*], but also widened to achieve greater psychological intensity and fantasy than Expressionism proper allowed within its bounds. Inevitably Expressionism and Baroque fantasy merged in film after film by Murnau and others as a result of the atmospheric needs of each individual film. The films by Murnau on which Röhrig worked along with Herlth were *The Last Laugh*, *Tartuffe* (with its beautiful and meticulously executed period settings), and *Faust*, as well as the initial drawings for Murnau's American film *The Four Devils*. Röhrig also worked for Fritz Lang, Murnau's great rival among Germany's leading directors, on *Destiny* and on Arthur von Gerlach's legendary Bohemian film *Zur Chronik von Grieshaus*.

Like Herlth, Röhrig served as art director on many merely routine but decorative German sound films before and during the period of the Third Reich, the more notable being *The Congress Dances*, *Amphitryon*, the anti-Polish Nazi film, *Heimkehr*, and *Rembrandt*, the effects of Expressionism long since gone. A fine example of Röhrig's sketch work for *Faust* can be seen in Eisner's *Murnau*, and the general atmosphere of collaboration between director, screenwriter, set designers, and the director of cinematography is admirably described by Robert Herlth for Eisner in the same book.

—Roger Manvell

ROSE, Helen

Costume Designer. **Nationality:** American. **Born:** c. 1904. **Education:** Attended Chicago Academy of Fine Arts. **Career:** Worked for Lester Costume Company and Ernie Young's costume house, Chicago; designer for Fanchon and Marco's Ice Follies, 14 years; 1942—costume designer for MGM until her retirement, 1966. **Awards:** Academy Award for *The Bad and the Beautiful*, 1952; *I'll Cry Tomorrow*, 1955. **Died:** In Palm Springs, California, 9 November 1985.

Films as Costume Designer:

1943 *Coney Island* (W. Lang) (co); *Hello Frisco, Hello* (Humberstone) (co); *Stormy Weather* (Stone)
1946 *The Harvey Girls* (Sidney) (co); *Two Sisters from Boston* (Koster) (co); *Ziegfeld Follies* (Minnelli) (co); *Till the Clouds Roll By* (Whorf) (co)
1947 *Good News* (Walters) (co); *Merton of the Movies* (Alton) (co); *The Unfinished Dance* (Koster)

Helen Rose

1948   *Act of Violence* (Zinnemann); *A Date with Judy* (Thorpe);
        Homecoming (LeRoy); *Words and Music* (Taurog) (co);
        Luxury Liner (Whorf) (co); *The Bride Goes Wild* (Taurog)

1949   **On the Town** (Kelly and Donen); *The Red Danube* (Sidney);
        The Stratton Story (Wood); *Take Me Out to the Ball Game*
        (Berkeley) (co); *East Side, West Side* (LeRoy)

1950   *A Life of Her Own* (Cukor); *Nancy Goes to Rio* (Leonard);
        Pagan Love Song (Alton); *Summer Stock* (Walters) (co);
        Three Little Words (Thorpe); *To Please a Lady* (Brown);
        The Toast of New Orleans (Taurog) (co); *The Reformer and
        the Redhead* (Panama and Frank); *Annie Get Your Gun*
        (Sidney) (co); *Father of the Bride* (Minnelli) (co); *The
        Duchess of Idaho* (Leonard); *The Big Hangover* (Minnelli);
        Grounds for Marriage (Leonard)

1951   *Father's Little Dividend* (Minnelli); *The Great Caruso* (Thorpe)
        (co); *The Light Touch* (Brooks); *Texas Carnival* (Walters);
        The Unknown Man (Thorpe); *Excuse My Dust* (Rowland)
        (co); *No Questions Asked* (Kress); *Strictly Dishonorable*
        (Panama and Frank); *The Strip* (Kardos); *Too Young to Kiss*
        (Leonard); *Callaway Went Thataway* (Frank and Panama);
        The People Against O'Hara (J. Sturges) (co); *Love Is Better
        Than Ever* (Donen)

1952   *The Girl in White* (J. Sturges) (co); *Because You're Mine*
        (Hall); *Above and Beyond* (Panama and Frank); *Glory Alley*
        (Walsh); *The Bad and the Beautiful* (Minnelli); *Invitation*
        (Bernhardt); *Holiday for Sinners* (Mayer); *The Merry Widow*
        (Bernhardt) (co); *Million Dollar Mermaid* (LeRoy) (co);
        Skirts Ahoy! (Lanfield); *The Belle of New York* (Walters)
        (co); *Washington Story* (Pirosh)

1953   *Dangerous When Wet* (Walters); *Dream Wife* (Sheldon) (co);
        Jeopardy (J. Sturges); *Latin Lovers* (LeRoy) (co); *Mogambo*
        (Ford); *Sombrero* (Foster); *The Story of Three Loves*
        (Reinhardt and Minnelli); *Torch Song* (Walters); *I Love
        Melvin* (Weis); *Small Town Girl* (Kardos); *Remains to Be
        Seen* (Weis); *Easy to Love* (Walters)

1954   *Athena* (Thorpe) (co); *Executive Suite* (Wise); *Green Fire*
        (Marton); *Her Twelve Men* (Leonard); *The Last Time I Saw
        Paris* (Brooks); *Rhapsody* (C. Vidor); *The Long, Long
        Trailer* (Minnelli); *Rogue Cop* (Rowland); *Rose Marie*
        (LeRoy) (co); *The Student Prince* (Thorpe) (co); *The Glass
        Slipper* (Walters) (co)

1955   *Bedevilled* (Leisen) (co); *Deep in My Heart* (Donen) (co); *Hit
        the Deck* (Rowland); *I'll Cry Tomorrow* (Daniel Mann);
        Interrupted Melody (Bernhardt); *It's Always Fair Weather*
        (Kelly and Donen); *Jupiter's Darling* (Sidney) (co); *Love
        Me or Leave Me* (C. Vidor); *The Rains of Ranchipur*
        (Negulesco) (co); *The Tender Trap* (Walters)

1956   *Forbidden Planet* (Wilcox) (co); *Gaby* (Beaumont); *High
        Society* (Beaudine); *Meet Me in Las Vegas* (Rowland); *The
        Opposite Sex* (Miller); *The Power and the Prize* (Koster);
        Ransom! (Segal); *The Swan* (C. Vidor); *Tea and Sympathy*
        (Minnelli); *These Wilder Years* (Rowland)

1957   *Designing Woman* (Minnelli); *Don't Go Near the Water*
        (Walters); *The Seventh Sin* (Neame); *Silk Stockings*
        (Mamoulian); *Something of Value* (Brooks); *Tip on a Dead
        Jockey* (Thorpe); *Ten Thousand Bedrooms* (Thorpe)

1958   *Cat on a Hot Tin Roof* (Brooks); *Party Girl* (Ray); *The High
        Cost of Loving* (J. Ferrer); *Saddle the Wind* (Parrish);
        The Reluctant Debutante (Minnelli) (co); *The Tunnel of
        Love* (Kelly)

1959   *Ask Any Girl* (Walters); *Count Your Blessings* (Negulesco); *It
        Started with a Kiss* (Marshall); *The Mating Game* (Marshall)

1960   *All the Fine Young Cannibals* (Anderson); *Butterfield 8*
        (Daniel Mann); *The Gazebo* (Marshall); *Never So Few* (J.
        Sturges)

1961   *Ada* (Daniel Mann); *Bachelor in Paradise* (Arnold); *Go
        Naked in the World* (MacDougall); *The Honeymoon Machine*
        (Thorpe)

1963   *The Courtship of Eddie's Father* (Minnelli)

1964   *Goodbye Charlie* (Minnelli)

1966   *Made in Paris* (Sagal), *Mister Buddwing* (Delbert Mann);
        How Sweet It Is! (Paris)

Publications

On ROSE: articles—

Chierchetti, David, in *Hollywood Costume Design*, New York, 1976.
Leese, Elizabeth, in *Costume Design in the Movies*, New York, 1976.
LaVine, W. Robert, in *In a Glamorous Fashion*, New York, 1980.
Obituary in *Variety* (New York), 13 November 1985.

*   *   *

Helen Rose was born on Chicago's south side on a yet undetermined date. (Rose came from an era when women felt compelled not to reveal their true age.) Dates vary from 1904 to 1918. Because of this, she often appears as precocious as Mozart with her list of early achievements. However, it is most likely that Rose started her career in her late teens.

She began studies at Chicago Academy of Fine Arts. While still in school she got a job at the Lester Costume Company creating ''girlie'' costumes for vaudeville and night club extravaganzas. She developed tremendous versatility turning chorus girls into, amongst other things, dancing cupcakes. She then worked at Ernie Young's costume house for three years gaining more experience and earning a highly regarded reputation as a theatrical designer. She expanded creatively and technically working for Young and at other companies, and learned the difficult art of chiffon design, a skill that she would later find useful in Hollywood. Continuing in the costume business, Rose moved to Los Angeles in 1929 to a company that supplied wardrobes for film studios. For several months she worked at 20th Century-Fox until a political upheaval in their costume department put an end to that assignment. She then became designer for the Ice Follies and stayed with them for 14 years. She was content with this work until MGM gave her a financial offer she could not refuse. The studio was still searching for a replacement for Adrian and did not feel confident that any of their current designers had taken his place. Irene was working at MGM at the time and Rose was assigned to design clothes only for the younger stars. However, while the two designers were jointly doing a film for director Joe Pasternak, he so openly preferred Rose that Irene angrily left the studio.

Pasternak was not the only one who favored Rose. Even in their private lives, stars would ask for Helen. She created wedding gowns for Liz Taylor, Ann Blyth, Jane Powell, Pier Angeli, and Debbie Reynolds. It greatly upset Edith Head when Head's good friend Grace Kelly requested a Helen Rose gown for her marriage to the Prince of

Monaco. Rose was also a favorite of Louis B. Mayer, who referred to her as "my sweetheart Rose." In general she was well-liked at the studio and dressed almost every major actress for MGM. Others who wore her costumes in addition to those mentioned above were Ava Gardner, Deborah Kerr, Cyd Charisse, Jane Powell, and Lena Horne.

Rose's designs were well structured with a strong emphasis on the silhouette. She kept her use of decoration simple and subdued. Her designs were elegant and understated, yet innovative, looking natural in spite of their theatrical nature. Like her rival at Paramount, Edith Head, Rose used designs that suited the new demands of the 1950s. They were more practical than fanciful; the sort of clothes a nice upper-middle-class suburbanite might wear. These clothes were also a goal to which less affluent members of the audience could aspire. However, Rose was not limited to the contemporary look and could equally design excellent and accurate period costuming, as in *The Swan*.

Clothing manufacturers were not blind to the fact that Rose's designs were popular with the public. Her wedding dress for *Father of the Bride* was extensively copied by New York fashion designers. Her inventive bathing suits for the Esther Williams pictures, made of light new fabrics, influenced bathing suit manufacturers such as Catalina, Jantzen, and Rose Marie Reid. In 1958 in *Cat on a Hot Tin Roof* Liz Taylor's white chiffon gown with the revealing décolletage caused a sensation. The star asked for a copy for her personal wardrobe and Rose received so many additional requests for copies that she decided to enter the wholesale garment business. Her expensive ready-to-wear was sold under franchise to exclusive department stores and speciality shops across the country. In making this move Rose may have reasoned that she could express herself more creatively and make a better living as a ready-to-wear designer. However, she might have also suspected that the time of the great studio costume designers was coming to an end.

By the time she left the studio in 1966, Rose had designed over 200 pictures and had received two Academy Awards for *The Bad and the Beautiful* and *I'll Cry Tomorrow*.

—Edith C. Lee

ROSENBLUM, Ralph

Editor. **Nationality:** American. **Born:** Brooklyn, New York, 1925. **Education:** Attended Public School 186, Brooklyn. **Family:** Married; two children. **Career:** 1942–43—worked in garment factory; 1943–46—assistant, then assistant editor, Office of War Information, New York; after the war, worked for a year for Max Rothstein's editing service, a year with the United Nations film section, and two years as editor for Obelisk Films making religious documentaries; 1948—assistant editor to Helen Van Dongen, *Louisiana Story*; 1950–51—editor of TV commercials, Tempo production company; 1951–55—TV and documentary editor, Transfilm: editor of the TV series *The Search*, 1953–55; 1955–61—founding director, with Gene Milford and Sidney Katz, MKR Films: TV work includes *Omnibus*, 1955–59, *Guy Lombardo Show*, two years; *The Patty Duke Show*, 1963–65, and *The American Sportsman*, 1966–67; 1969—edited first Woody Allen film, *Take the Money and Run*. **Awards:** British Academy Award for *Annie Hall*, 1977. **Died:** 4 September 1995.

Films as Editor:

1948 *Louisiana Story* (Flaherty) (asst)
1950 *Coney Island* (Sherry—short)
1958 *Country Music Holiday* (Ganzer)
1960 *Pretty Boy Floyd* (Leder); *Murder, Inc.* (Balaban and Rosenberg)
1961 *Mad Dog Coll* (Balaban)
1962 *Jacktown* (Martin); *Long Day's Journey into Night* (Lumet); *Two Tickets to Paris* (Garrison)
1963 *Gone Are the Days!* (Webster)
1964 *Fail Safe* (Lumet)
1965 *The Fool Killer* (Gonzalez) (supervising ed); *The Pawnbroker* (Lumet); *A Thousand Clowns* (Coe)
1966 *The Group* (Lumet); *Terror in the City* (Baron); *The Love Song of Barney Kempinski* (Praeger)
1967 *Bach to Bach* (Leaf—short); *A Great Big Thing* (Till); *The Producers* (Brooks)
1968 *The Night They Raided Minsky's* (Friedkin); *Bye Bye Braverman* (Lumet) (co)
1969 *Don't Drink the Water* (Morris); *Goodbye Columbus* (Peerce); *Take the Money and Run* (Allen) (supervising ed); *Trilogy* (Perry) (co)
1970 *Something for Everyone* (Prince)
1971 *Bananas* (Allen); *Born to Win* (Passer)
1972 *Bad Company* (Benton) (co)
1973 *Sleeper* (Allen)
1975 *Love and Death* (Allen)
1976 *Bernice Bobs Her Hair* (Silver)
1977 *Remember Those Poker Playing Monkeys* (Jacoby); **Annie Hall** (Allen)
1978 *Interiors* (Allen)
1981 *Summer Solstice* (+ d)
1983 *Stuck on You!* (Herz)

Other Films:

1972 *Turner* (d)
1977 *The President's Women* (Avildsen) (consultant)
1981 *By Design* (Jutra) (consultant)
1982 *Any Friend of Nicholas Nickleby Is a Friend of Mine* (d); *America* (Harvey) (consultant)
1983 *Marvin and Tige* (Weston) (consultant)
1986 *Amy and the Angel* (d—for TV); *Forever Lulu* (Kollek) (consultant)

Publications

By ROSENBLUM: book—

With Robert Karen, *When the Shooting Stops . . . the Cutting Begins: A Film Editor's Story*, New York, 1979.

By ROSENBLUM: articles—

American Cinematographer (Hollywood), Autumn 1972.
American Cinematographer (Hollywood), Winter 1972–73.
Millimeter (New York), March 1977.

735

On ROSENBLUM: articles—

Film Comment (New York), March-April 1977.
American Film (Washington, D.C.), December 1985.
Obituary in *The New York Times*, 8 September 1995.
Obituary in *Variety* (New York), 16 October 1995.
American Jewish History, December 1996.

*   *   *

Ralph Rosenblum did a service to editors everywhere with the 1979 publication of his memoir *When the Shooting Stops . . . the Cutting Begins*, a popular volume which gave the first insider's explanation of what really goes into film editing. Rosenblum traced the evolution of editing from Griffith through Eisenstein, and recounted the peculiar manipulations of material that resulted in such films as *The Producers, Annie Hall, Goodbye Columbus*, and *The Pawnbroker*. For years audiences have been blind to the intricacies of the cutting room, and critics only a little less so, giving credit to directors for a particularly brilliant piece of editing. In the book Rosenblum revealed that he had saved several films by creatively re-shaping the footage, such as William Friedkin's *The Night They Raided Minsky's* and Woody Allen's first major film as a director, *Take the Money and Run*. Rosenblum's revelations helped bring credit to the film editing profession, and forced scholars to reconsider editorial contributions.

Rosenblum began his career in New York during the First World War as an apprentice in the Office of War Information, working on propaganda documentaries. His experience there led him to work with documentary editors Sidney Meyers and Helen Van Dongen, and after the war he became Van Dongen's assistant on Robert Flaherty's *Louisiana Story*. Rosenblum's documentary training was invaluable, teaching him how best to turn dailies into a cohesive, unified film. He had his earliest opportunities to cut on commercials and industrials. After cutting a short-lived TV series, *The Search*, Rosenblum and Sid Katz set up their own editorial service, and were joined by veteran editor Gene Milford, for years the chief editor at Columbia Pictures. Their company, MKR films, became quite successful cutting spots, promotionals, industrials and corporate films, TV pilots, and the acclaimed TV series *Omnibus* and the popular *Guy Lombardo Show*. It was truly a wonderful training ground, and Rosenblum was frequently called upon to transform a shapeless mass of footage into a coherent whole.

He moved into features cutting three low-budget New York gangster movies, *Pretty Boy Floyd, Murder, Inc.*, and *Mad Dog Coll*, before establishing a relationship with Sidney Lumet. Their films together—*Long Day's Journey into Night, Fail Safe, The Pawnbroker, The Group*—are some of the most serious American movies of the decade. *Long Day's Journey* and *The Group* were somewhat straightforward in presentation, but *Fail Safe* and *The Pawnbroker* demonstrated Rosenblum's editorial finesse. The montage ending of *Fail Safe*, depicting the last few moments of life on earth, and the use of concentration camp flashbacks in *The Pawnbroker*, brought Rosenblum his first industry recognition.

Oddly, most of Rosenblum's subsequent editing jobs have been comedies. *A Thousand Clowns*, directed by Fred Coe and an uncredited Herb Gardner from Gardner's play, was the first of a series of pictures which called upon Rosenblum to mold difficult material into a hit movie. Lengthy and constant re-editing were required to save *A Thousand Clowns*, and a similar situation prevailed with Mel Brooks's *The Producers* and William Friedkin's *The Night They Raided Minsky's*. The difficulties of working with Brooks and Friedkin are discussed in agonizing detail in Rosenblum's book; both pictures ironically stand up as superior comedies.

Working with Rosenblum's editorial collaboration, Woody Allen came into his own with such pictures as *Take the Money and Run, Bananas, Sleeper, Love and Death*, and *Annie Hall*. Rosenblum was an integral part of Allen's filmmaking process; *Take the Money and Run* and *Annie Hall* went through major restructuring in post-production. From the early slapdash style of *Take the Money and Run* and *Bananas*, through the increasing comic sophistication of *Sleeper* and *Love and Death*, to the Oscar-winning brilliance of *Annie Hall*, the Allen-Rosenblum association is marked by a strong sense of rhythm and tempo, with a reliance on short, concise scenes. This style of editing continued with Woody Allen's Bergman-like drama *Interiors*.

—John A. Gallagher

ROSENMAN, Leonard

Composer. **Nationality:** American. **Born:** Brooklyn, New York, 7 September 1924. **Education:** Studied under Schoenberg, Sessions, and Dallapiccola. **Military Service:** Served in World War II. **Career:** Painter; then composer of chamber and choral works, and for films from the mid-1950s; taught at the University of Southern California, Los Angeles; musical director of New Muse chamber orchestra; composer for TV mini-series *Murder in Texas*, 1981, and *Celebrity*, 1984. **Awards:** Academy Award, for *Barry Lyndon*, 1975, and *Bound for Glory*, 1976.

Films as Composer:

1954 *East of Eden* (Kazan)
1955 *The Cobweb* (Minnelli); ***Rebel without a Cause*** (N. Ray)
1956 *Edge of the City* (Ritt)
1957 *The Young Stranger* (Frankenheimer); *Bombers B-52* (Douglas)
1958 *The Hidden World* (Snyder—doc); *Lafayette Escadrille* (Wellman)
1959 *Pork Chop Hill* (Milestone); *The Bramble Bush* (Petrie); *The Savage Eye* (Strick, Maddow, and Meyers)
1960 *The Crowded Sky* (Pevney); *The Plunderers* (Pevney); *The Rise and Fall of Legs Diamond* (Boetticher)
1961 *The Outsider* (Delbert Mann)
1962 *Convicts 4* (*Reprieve*) (Kaufman); *Hell Is for Heroes* (Siegel); *The Chapman Report* (Cukor)
1966 *Fantastic Voyage* (Fleischer)
1967 *A Covenant with Death* (Johnson)
1968 *Countdown* (Altman); *Hellfighters* (McLaglen)

Leonard Rosenman

1969   *This Savage Land* (McEveety—from TV segments)

1970   *A Man Called Horse* (Silverstein); *Beneath the Planet of the Apes* (Post)

1971   *The Todd Killings* (*Skipper*) (Shear)

1972   *Prophecy* (Frankenheimer)

1973   *Battle for the Planet of the Apes* (Lee Thompson)

1975   *Barry Lyndon* (Kubrick); *Race with the Devil* (Starrett); *Rooster Cogburn* (Millar)

1976   *Bound for Glory* (Ashby); *Birch Interval* (Delbert Mann); *The Return of a Man Called Horse* (Kershner)

1977   *September 30, 1955* (*9/30/55*) (Bridges); *The Car* (Silverstein); *An Enemy of the People* (Schaefer)

1978   *Lord of the Rings* (Bakshi)

1979   *Promises in the Dark* (Hellman); *Prophecy* (Frankenheimer)

1980   *City in Fear* (Smithee); *Hide in Plain Sight* (Caan); *The Jazz Singer* (Fleischer)

1982   *The Wall* (Markowitz); *Making Love* (Hiller)

1984   *The Return of Marcus Welby M.D.* (Singer—for TV); *Celebrity* (Wendkos—for TV); *Sylvia* (Firth); *Heart of the Stag* (Firth)

1986   *Star Trek IV: The Voyage Home* (Nimoy)

1990   *Where Pigeons Go to Die* (Landon—for TV); *Ambition* (Goldstein); *Robocop II* (Kershner)

1991   *Aftermath: A Test of Love* (G. Jordan—for TV)

1992   *Keeper of the City* (Roth—for TV)

1994   *The Color of Evening* (Stafford)

1995   *The Face on the Milk Carton* (Hussein—for TV); *Mrs. Munck* (Diane Ladd)

1997   *Levitation* (Goldstein)

Publications

By ROSENMAN: articles—

''Notes from a Sub-Culture,'' in *Perspectives of New Music* (Yardley, Pennsylvania), vol. 7, no. 1, 1968.

In *Knowing the Score*, by Irwin Bazelon, New York, 1975.

In *Film Score*, edited by Tony Thomas, South Brunswick, New Jersey, 1979.

In *Soundtrack!*, September 1995.
In *Soundtrack!*, December 1995.

On ROSENMAN: articles—

Thomas, Tony, in *Music for the Movies*, South Brunswick, New
    Jersey, 1973.
International Filmusic Journal, no. 2, 1980.
Palmer, Christopher, in *The Composer in Hollywood*, New York, 1990.
Indiana Theory Review, vol. 11, Spring/Fall, 1990.
Cue Sheet (Hollywood), vol. 11, no. 1, 1995.

*   *   *

Leonard Rosenman is one of a handful of film composers who
have successfully incorporated contemporary compositional techniques into conventional film scoring. Rosenman's use of Arnold
Schoenberg's 12-tone technique set a standard for the use of various
avant-garde, atonal, and serial effects. The composer has also demonstrated an ability to employ authentic period music in a number of
films dealing with historical subject matter.

Brought to the attention of director Elia Kazan by one of his piano
students, James Dean, Rosenman collaborated with the actor and
director on *East of Eden* and *Rebel without a Cause*. For the former
Rosenman opted for selective instrumentation at many points in the
score rather than the large orchestral sound common in films of the
time, and also provided an extended musical passage at the end of the
film, running several minutes in length and giving the composer an
opportunity to develop and combine themes heard throughout the film.

The use of the 12-tone technique for *The Cobweb* demonstrated
the potential for such techniques in film scoring and led to the
utilization by composers of more contemporary sounds, both in
similar psychological dramas and later in other types of films. While
Rosenman himself has continued to experiment in such sounds (as in
Fantastic Voyage), he has refused to become typed as a "modern"
composer. Rosenman has also shown an ability to adapt more
traditional musical forms to his scores, ranging from the use of an
ancient Chinese tune in *Pork Chop Hill* to the incorporation of
authentic Native American music into the score for *A Man Called
Horse*. His Academy Awards have been for arranging rather than
original compositions. Rosenman received awards for his adaptation
of Woody Guthrie songs in *Bound for Glory* and for the arrangements
of classical pieces in Kubrick's *Barry Lyndon*, although Rosenman
has expressed dissatisfaction with the final result and Kubrick's
overuse of one particular theme at the expense of many of the
composer's other variations.

The multiple facets of Rosenman's work are reflected in his
extensive score for *Lord of the Rings*, which combines richly textured
chordal structures and unusual tonalities with more lyrical passages
and a unifying march motif. In recent years Rosenman has turned to
more intimate personal dramas requiring less experimental approaches.
In addition to his film work Rosenman has remained active in
composing concert music and has worked extensively in television,
although he referred to the latter in an interview for the American
Film Institute as "the quintessential schlock medium," adding that
much of the music for the medium had a generic quality and was little
more than "wallpaper."

—Richard R. Ness

ROSHER, Charles

Cinematographer. **Nationality:** British. **Born:** England, 1885. **Fam-
ily:** Children: the actress Joan Marsh and the photographer Charles
(Chuck) Rosher, Jr. **Career:** Lived in the United States after 1908,
and in Hollywood after 1911; 1912—first film as photographer, *Early
Days Out West*; worked on several Mary Pickford films, and later for
MGM and other studios; made numerous technical innovations;
1918—founding member, American Society of Cinematographers.
Awards: Academy Award for *Sunrise*, 1927–28; *The Yearling*, 1946.
Died: In 1974.

Films as Cinematographer:

1912   *Early Days Out West* (Turner)
1914   *With General Pancho Villa in Mexico* ; *In Bermuda* (Dawley);
        The Oath of a Viking (Gordon); *The Next in Command*
        (Gordon); *The Mystery of the Poisoned Pool* (Gordon)
1915   *Gene of the Northland* (Clarke); *The Smugglers' Lass* (Clarke);
        The Mad Maid of the Forest (Clarke)
1916   *The Dumb Girl of Portici* (Smalley and Weber); *Blackbirds*
        (McGowan); *Voice in the Fog* (McGowan); *Pudd'nhead
        Wilson* (Reicher); *The Sowers* (W. De Mille); *The Blacklist*
        (W. De Mille); *Anton the Terrible* (W. De Mille); *The Plow
        Girl* (Leonard); *The Clown* (W. De Mille); *Common Ground*
        (W. De Mille)
1917   *On Record* (Leonard); *At First Sight* (Leonard); *Hashimura
        Togo* (W. De Mille); *The Primrose Ring* (Leonard); *Secret
        Game* (W. De Mille); *Mormon Main* (Leonard); *A Little
        Princess* (Neilan) (co)
1918   *Too Many Millions* (Cruze); *The Dub* (Cruze); *Till I Come
        Back to You* (C. DeMille) (co); *Widow's Might* (W. De
        Mille); *One More American* (W. De Mille); *Honor of His
        House* (W. De Mille); *How Could You, Jean?* (Taylor);
        White Man's Law (Young); *Johanna Enlists* (Taylor);
        Captain Kidd, Jr. (Taylor)
1919   *The Hoodlum* (Franklin); *Daddy Long Legs* (Neilan); *Heart o'
        the Hills* (Franklin)
1920   *Pollyanna* (Powell); *Suds* (Dillon)
1921   *The Love Light* (Marion); *Through the Back Door* (Green);
        Little Lord Fauntleroy (Green and J. Pickford); *Saint Ilario*
        (Kolker)
1922   *Smilin' Through* (Franklin); *Tess of the Storm Country*
        (Robertson)
1923   *Tiger Rose* (Franklin); *Rosita* (Lubitsch)
1924   *Dorothy Vernon of Haddon Hall* (Neilan)

Charles Rosher

1925   *Little Annie Roonie* (Beaudine) (co)

1926   *Sparrows* (Beaudine) (co)

1927   *Sunrise* (Murnau) (co); *My Best Girl* (Taylor)

1928   *Tempest* (Taylor)

1929   *Atlantic* (Dupont); *The Vagabond Queen* (von Bolvary)

1930   *La Route est belle* (Wolfe and Florey); *Two Worlds* (Dupont); *Knowing Men* (Glyn); *War Nurse* (Selwyn); *Paid* (Wood)

1931   *Dance, Fool, Dance* (Milton); *This Modern Age* (Grinde); *Laughing Sinners* (Beaumont); *Silence* (Gasnier and Marcin); *Beloved Bachelor* (Corrigan)

1932   *Two against the World* (Mayo); *What Price Hollywood?* (Cukor); *Rockabye* (Cukor)

1933   *Bed of Roses* (La Cava); *After Tonight* (Archainbaud); *Our Betters* (Cukor); *The Past of Mary Holmes* (Thompson and Vorkapich); *Silver Cord* (Cromwell)

1934   *Flaming Gold* (R. Ince); *What Every Woman Knows* (La Cava); *Outcast Lady* (Leonard); *Moulin Rouge* (Lanfield); *The Affairs of Cellini* (La Cava); *After Office Hours* (Leonard); *The Call of the Wild* (Wellman)

1935   *Broadway Melody of 1936* (Del Ruth)

1936   *Small Town Girl* (Wellman); *Little Lord Fauntleroy* (Cromwell)

1937   *Men Are Not Gods* (Reisch); *The Woman I Love* (Litvak); *The Perfect Specimen* (Curtiz); *Hollywood Hotel* (Berkeley) (co)

1938   *Hard to Get* (Enright); *White Banners* (Goulding)

1939   *Espionage Agent* (Bacon); *Hell's Kitchen* (Seiler and Dupont); *Off the Record* (Flood); *Yes, My Darling Daughter* (Keighley)

1940   *A Child Is Born* (Bacon); *My Love Came Back* (Bernhardt); *Three Cheers for the Irish* (Bacon); *Brother Rat and a Baby* (Enright)

1941   *Four Mothers* (Keighley); *Million Dollar Baby* (Bernhardt); *One Foot in Heaven* (Rapper)

1942   *Stand By for Action* (Leonard); *Mokey* (Root); *Pierre of the Plains* (Seitz)

1943   *Swing Fever* (Whelan); *Assignment in Brittany* (Conway)

1944   *Kismet* (Dieterle)

1945   *Yolanda and the Thief* (Minnelli)

1946   *The Yearling* (Brown) (co); *Ziegfeld Follies* (Minnelli) (co)

1947   *Fiesta* (Thorpe) (co); *Song of the Thin Man* (Buzzell); *Dark Delusion* (Goldbeck)

1948   *On an Island with You* (Thorpe); *Words and Music* (Taurog) (co)

1949   *Neptune's Daughter* (Buzzell); *The Red Danube* (Sidney); *East Side, West Side* (LeRoy)

1950   *Pagan Love Song* (Alton); *Annie Get Your Gun* (Sidney)
1951   *Show Boat* (Sidney)
1952   *Scaramouche* (Sidney)
1953   *The Story of Three Loves* (Reinhardt and Minnelli) (co);
        Young Bess (Sidney); *Kiss Me Kate* (Sidney)
1955   *Jupiter's Darling* (Sidney) (co)

Publications

By ROSHER: article—

American Cinematographer (Hollywood), February 1982.

On ROSHER: articles—

Sidney, George, on *Show Boat* in *American Cinematographer* (Hollywood), August 1951.
Film Comment (New York), Summer 1972.
Focus on Film (London), no. 13, 1973.
American Cinematographer (Hollywood), August 1973.
Variety (New York), 30 January 1974.
American Cinematographer (Hollywood), March 1974.
BKSTS Journal (London), April 1974.

*   *   *

Charles Rosher first worked as a photographer of portraits, then he began filming westerns. It is therefore no surprise that when in 1913 the notorious Pancho Villa signed a film contract with Mutual Film Corporation, Rosher was chosen to do the filming.

Great Hollywood directors often have one actress who seems to bring out the best in them; for Lee Garmes it was Dietrich; for William Daniels, Garbo; for Rosher, Mary Pickford. The 1921 version of *Little Lord Fauntleroy*, starring Pickford, called forth considerable inventive genius on Rosher's part to achieve some intricate moving-camera shots.

His collaboration with Karl Struss on the cinematography of *Sunrise* led to a *tour de force* in photographing people against a landscape of lights. They photograph, in the country scenes, water reflecting light and, in the city scenes, glass. *Sunrise* visually bears comparison with the great French Impressionists and Post-Impressionists, presenting a world which is realistic, and yet also inviting the viewer into the romantic world of the young lovers. This film's successful mixture of realism with romanticism is all the more miraculous when one considers that it was adapted from a novel of dismal and unrelieved naturalism. The film's superior qualities are in great part due to the cameramen. Except for Murnau's demands for a moving camera and his interest in reflected light, he allowed the cinematographers a free hand with the visuals. In order to achieve a shimmering effect, Rosher and Struss shot towards the sun. They sought twilight effects of light coming out of the doors of the village houses.

Rosher photographed the 1936 version of *Little Lord Fauntleroy*. Later in his career, he filmed musicals—*Show Boat* and *Kiss Me Kate*—in the Christmas-card technicolor that predominated then. Rosher's real talent, however, was working in black and white, during the silent era. Although many of Rosher's contributions to

cinematography were made before there were Academy Awards, he did win Oscars for *Sunrise* and *The Yearling*.

—Rodney Farnsworth

ROSSON, Hal

Cinematographer. **Nationality:** American. **Born:** Harold Rosson in New York City, 1895. **Family:** Brother of the directors Arthur Rosson and Richard Rosson; Married 1) the actress Jean Harlow, 1933 (divorced 1935); 2) Yvonne Crellin (divorced). **Career:** 1908— bit player at Vitagraph, and worked in various production capacities before becoming a camera operator in 1915, and a cinematographer in 1917; then worked mainly for MGM. **Award:** Special Academy Award, 1936. **Died:** In Florida, 6 September 1988.

Films as Cinematographer:

1915   *David Harum* (Dwan) (cam)
1917   *Panthea* (Dwan) (co)
1919   *The Cinema Murder* (Baker)
1920   *Polly of the Storm Country* (Baker)
1921   *Heliotrope* (Baker); *Buried Treasure* (Webb); *Everything for Sale* (O'Connor)
1922   *A Homespun Vamp* (O'Connor); *A Virginia Courtship* (O'Connor); *The Cradle* (Powell); *For the Defense* (Powell); *Through a Glass Window* (Campbell)
1923   *Quicksands* (Conway) (co); *Lawful Larceny* (Dwan); *Garrison's Finish* (A. Rosson); *Dark Secrets* (Fleming); *The Glimpses of the Moon* (Dwan); *Zaza* (Dwan)
1924   *Manhattan* (Burnside); *A Society Scandal* (Dwan); *Manhandled* (Dwan); *The Story without a Name* (Willat)
1925   *A Man Must Live* (Sloane); *Too Many Kisses* (Sloane); *The Little French Girl* (Brenon); *The Street of Forgotten Men* (Brenon); *Classified* (Santell)
1926   *Infatuation* (Cummings); *Up in Mabel's Room* (Hopper); *For Wives Only* (Heerman); *Say It Again* (La Cava); *Almost a Lady* (Hopper); *Man Bait* (Crisp)
1927   *Rough House Rosie* (Strayer) (co); *Jim the Conqueror* (Seitz); *Getting Gertie's Garter* (Hopper); *Evening Clothes* (Reed); *Service for Ladies* (D'Arrast); *A Gentleman of Paris* (D'Arrast); *Open Range* (Smith)
1928   *The Docks of New York* (von Sternberg); *Gentlemen Prefer Blondes* (St. Clair); *The Sawdust Paradise* (Reed); *Three Week Ends* (Badger); *The Drag Net* (von Sternberg); *Abie's Irish Rose* (Fleming)
1929   *The Far Call* (Dwan); *Trent's Last Case* (Hawks); *Frozen Justice* (Dwan); *South Sea Rose* (Dwan); *The Case of Lena Smith* (von Sternberg)
1930   *Hello Sister* (W. Lang); *This Mad World* (C. DeMille) (co); *Madame Satan* (C. DeMille); *Passion Flower* (W. De Mille)
1931   *Men Call It Love* (Selwyn); *The Prodigal* (Pollard); *The Squaw Man* (C. DeMille); *Son of India* (Feyder); *Sporting Blood* (Brabin); *The Cuban Love Song* (Van Dyke)
1932   *Red Headed Woman* (Conway); *Red Dust* (Fleming); *Tarzan, the Ape Man* (Van Dyke); *When a Feller Needs a Friend*

(Pollard); *Are You Listening?* (Beaumont); *Downstairs* (Bell); *Kongo* (Cowan)

1933 *Hold Your Man* (Wood); *Bombshell* (Fleming); *Hell Below* (Conway); *The Barbarian* (Wood); *Turn Back the Clock* (Selwyn); *Penthouse* (Van Dyke) (co)

1934 *The Cat and the Fiddle* (Howard) (co); *This Side of Heaven* (Howard); *Treasure Island* (Fleming) (co)

1935 *The Scarlet Pimpernel* (Young)

1936 *As You Like It* (Czinner); *The Ghost Goes West* (Clair); *The Man Who Could Work Miracles* (Mendes); *The Devil Is a Sissy* (Van Dyke) (co); *The Garden of Allah* (Boleslawsky) (co)

1937 *Captains Courageous* (Fleming); *They Gave Him a Gun* (Van Dyke); *The Emperor's Candlesticks* (Fitzmaurice)

1938 *Too Hot to Handle* (Conway); *A Yank at Oxford* (Conway)

1939 **Gone with the Wind** (Fleming) (co); **The Wizard of Oz** (Fleming)

1940 *Boom Town* (Conway); *I Take This Woman* (Van Dyke); *Flight Command* (Borzage); *Edison the Man* (Brown); *Dr. Kildare Goes Home* (Bucquet)

1941 *The Penalty* (Bucquet); *Men of Boys Town* (Taurog); *Washington Melodrama* (Simon); *Honky Tonk* (Conway); *Johnny Eager* (LeRoy)

1942 *Somewhere I'll Find You* (Ruggles); *Tennessee Johnson* (Dieterle)

1943 *Slightly Dangerous* (Ruggles)

1944 *Thirty Seconds over Tokyo* (LeRoy) (co); *An American Romance* (K. Vidor); *Between Two Women* (Goldbeck)

1946 *Three Wise Fools* (Buzzell); *No Leave, No Love* (Martin) (co); *My Brother Talks to Horses* (Zinnemann)

1947 *The Hucksters* (Conway); *Living in a Big Way* (La Cava); *Duel in the Sun* (K. Vidor) (co)

1948 *Command Decision* (Wood); *Homecoming* (LeRoy)

1949 **On the Town** (Kelly and Donen); *Any Number Can Play* (LeRoy), *The Stratton Story* (Wood)

1950 *To Please a Lady* (Brown); *Key to the City* (Sidney); **The Asphalt Jungle** (Huston)

1951 *The Red Badge of Courage* (Huston)

1952 *The Lone Star* (V. Sherman); *Love Is Better Than Ever* (Donen); **Singin' in the Rain** (Kelly and Donen)

1953 *The Actress* (Cukor); *I Love Melvin* (Weis); *The Story of Three Loves* (Reinhardt and Minnelli) (co); *Dangerous When Wet* (Walters)

1954 *Mambo* (Rossen); *Ulisse* (*Ulysses*) (Camerini)

1955 *Strange Lady in Town* (LeRoy); *Pete Kelly's Blues* (Webb)

1956 *The Bad Seed* (LeRoy); *Toward the Unknown* (LeRoy)

1957 *The Enemy Below* (Powell)

1958 *No Time for Sergeants* (LeRoy); *Onionhead* (Taurog)

1967 *El Dorado* (Hawks)

Publications

By ROSSON: article—

In *The Art of the Cinematographer*, by Leonard Maltin, New York, 1978.

On ROSSON: articles—

Wayne, Palma, in *Saturday Evening Post* (Philadelphia), 22 July 1933.

Lightman, Herb A., in *American Cinematographer* (Hollywood), August 1950.

Film Comment (New York), Summer 1972.

Focus on Film (London), no. 13, 1973.

American Cinematographer (Hollywood), October 1973.

Obituary in *Variety* (New York), 14 September 1988.

Obituary in *American Cinematographer* (Hollywood), November 1988.

*   *   *

Louis B. Mayer once said to the cinematographer Hal Rosson: "If it's an MGM film, it has to look like an MGM film." Rosson, one of the pioneers in motion picture photography—his career spanned the years 1915 to 1967—spent 23 of those years at Metro-Goldwyn-Mayer and is one of the photographers who helped create and maintain the "polished look" that was so integral a part of the studio's films.

Rosson was an actor with Vitagraph as early as 1908 and became a camera operator in 1915. By 1920 he was a full-fledged cinematographer at Paramount where he enjoyed close working relationships with such directors as Allan Dwan, Harry D'Arrast, Mal St. Clair, and Josef von Sternberg, working on such films as *Manhandled*, *A Gentleman of Paris*, *Gentlemen Prefer Blondes*, and *The Docks of New York*. Rosson recalled that during those days one experimented, listened, and watched to learn and develop one's craft. Technical difficulties were approached and surmounted as they occurred, with no pretensions to "art." In doing so, Rosson became one of the finest exponents of his craft.

He joined MGM in 1930 and it was there that he perfected his own skills and aided that studio in developing the glossy patina which would become an MGM trademark. One beautifully photographed film was *Red Dust*, starring Jean Harlow (whom he married). MGM loaned him to Selznick International for *The Garden of Allah* in 1936, and Rosson recalled that while he knew nothing about color film at the time, he decided "to control color, to eliminate color unless it could be used dramatically. I didn't want color to control me." For his efforts, he and cophotographer W. Howard Greene, received special Academy Award plaques. His most outstanding achievement with color was for MGM's *The Wizard of Oz*, though again he modestly described his work as simply a matter of "controlling color." He received Academy Award nominations for his MGM work on such black-and-white films as *Boom Town*, *Thirty Seconds over Tokyo*, and *The Asphalt Jungle*, and ended his MGM years with excellent color work on *Singin' in the Rain* and *The Story of Three Loves*. After 1955 he worked at various studios, and received an Oscar nomination for *The Bad Seed* at Warner Bros. His last film was Howard Hawks's *El Dorado* for Paramount. Rosson was proud of his years at MGM, and fondly recalled its *esprit de corps*: "The spirit was such that we were proud to be at MGM."

—Ronald Bowers

ROTA, Nino

Composer. **Nationality:** Italian. **Born:** Nini Rinaldi in Milan, 31 December 1911. **Education:** Attended St. Cecilia Academy, Rome, diploma, 1930; Curtis Institute, Philadelphia; also studied with Giacome Orefice and others. **Career:** Child prodigy: composer of oratorios, operas, incidental music for stage plays; 1933—first film score, for *Treno popolare*; 1937–38—taught at Liceo Musicale, Taranto; 1939—taught at Bari Conservatory, and director, 1950–78. **Awards:** British Academy Award for *The Godfather*, 1972; Academy Award for *The Godfather, Part II*, 1974. **Died:** In Rome, 10 April 1979.

Films as Composer:

1933   *Treno popolare* (Matarazzo)

1943   *Zazà* (Castellani); *Il birichino di papa* (Matarazzo)

1945   *La freccia nel fianco* (Lattuada); *Un Americano in vacanza* (*A Yank in Rome*) (Zampa)

1946   *Le miserie del Signor Travet* (Soldati); *Roma città libera* (Pagliero); *Vivere in pace* (*To Live in Peace*) (Zampa); *Mio figlio professore* (Castellani)

1947   *Daniele Cortis* (Soldati); *Come persi la guerra* (Borghesio); *Il delitto di Giovanni Episcopo* (*Flesh Will Surrender*) (Lattuada); *Albergo Luna, Camera 34* (Bragaglia)

1948   *Amanti senza amore* (Franciolini); *Arrivederci Papà* (Mastrocinque); *I pirati di Capri* (Ulmer and Scotese);

Nino Rota

Senza pietà (*Without Pity*) (Lattuada); *Fuga in Francia* (Soldati); *In nome della legge* (Germi); *Molti sogni per le strade* (Camerini); *The Glass Mountain* (Cass); *Proibito rubare* (*Guaglio*) (Comencini); *E primavera* (Castellani)

1949   *Obsession* (*The Hidden Room*) (Dmytryk); *Campane a martello* (*Children of Change*) (Zampa)

1950   *Napoli milionaria* (de Filippo); *Vita da cani* (Steno and Monicelli); *Donne e briganti* (Soldati); *E più facile che un camello* (*His Last Twelve Hours*) (Zampa)

1951   *Due mogli somo troppe* (Camerini); *Anna* (Lattuada); *Filum ena Marturano* (de Filippo); *Due soldi di speranza* (Castellani); *Era lui . . . sîà! sîà!* (Metz, Marchesi, and Girolami); *Peppino e Violetta* (Cloche); *Valley of Eagles* (Young)

1952   *Marito e moglie* (de Filippo); *The Venetian Bird* (*The Assassin*) (Thomas); *Something Money Can't Buy* (Jackson); *Le sceicco bianco* (*The White Sheik*) (Fellini); *Le meravigliose avventure di Guerrin Meschino* (Francisci); *La Regina di Saba* (Francisci); *I sette dell'orsa maggiore* (Coletti); *Totò e i re di Roma* (Steno and Monicelli)

1953   *L'Ennemi public no. 1* (*The Most Wanted Man*) (Verneuil) (co); *Gli uomini che mascalzoni* (Pellegrini); *I vitelloni* (Fellini); *Anni facili* (*Easy Years*) (Zampa); *Fanciulle di lusso* (Vorhaus); *Noi due sole* (Metz, Marchesi, and Girolami); *Scampolo '53* (Bianchi); *Star of India* (Lubin); *La mano della straniero* (*The Stranger's Hand*) (Soldati)

1954   **La strada** (Fellini); *Proibito* (Monicelli); *Mambo* (Rossen); *Musodoro* (Bennati); *Senso* (Visconti); *La grande speranza* (Coletti); *La domenica della buona gente* (Majano); *Via Padova 46* (Bianchi); *Le due orfanelle* (Gentilomo)

1955   *Il bidone* (Fellini); *Un eroe dei nostri tempi* (Monicelli); *Amici per la pelle* (*Friends for Life*) (Rossi); *La bella di Roma* (Comencini)

1956   *War and Peace* (K. Vidor); *Le notti di Cabiria* (*Cabiria. Nights of Cabiria*) (Fellini)

1957   *Le notte bianche* (*White Nights*) (Visconti); *Fortunella* (de Filippo); *Londra chiama Polo Nord* (Coletti); *El medico e lo stregone* (Monicelli); *Il momento più bello* (Emmer); *Italia piccola* (Soldati)

1958   *Barrage contre le Pacifique* (*This Angry Age*; *The Sea Wall*) (Clément); *Città di notte* (Trieste); *Un ettaro di cielo* (Casadio); *La Loi . . . c'est la loi* (*The Law Is the Law*) (Christian-Jaque); *Giovani mariti* (Bolognini); *Gli Italiani sono matti* (Coletti)

1959   *La grande guerra* (*The Great War*) (Monicelli); *Sons and Lovers* (Cardiff); *Never Take No for an Answer* (Cloche and Smart)

1960   **La dolce vita** (Fellini); *Plein soleil* (*Purple Noon*) (Clément); *Sotto dieci bandiere* (*Under Ten Flags*) (Coletti and Narizzano); *Rocco e i suoi fratelli* (*Rocco and His Brothers*) (Visconti)

1961   *The Best of Enemies* (Hamilton); *Il brigante* (Castellani); *Fantasmi a Roma* (Pietrangeli)

1962   *Boccaccio '70* (Fellini and Visconti episodes); *L'isola di Arturo* (*Arturo's Island*) (Damiani); *I sequestrati di Altona* (*The Condemned of Altona*) (De Sica); *Il mafioso* (*Mafioso*) (Lattuada) (co); *The Reluctant Saint* (Dmytryk)

1963	*Mare matto* (Castellani); **Otto e mezzo** (*81/2*) (Fellini); **Il gattopardo** (*The Leopard*) (Visconti); *Il maestro di Vigevano* (Petri)
1965	*Giulietta degli spiriti* (*Juliet of the Spirits*) (Fellini)
1966	*Spara forte, piu forte, non capisco* (*Shout Loud, Louder . . . I Don't Understand*) (de Filippo)
1967	*The Taming of the Shrew* (Zeffirelli)
1968	''Tre passi nel delirio'' ep. of *Histoires extraordinaires* (*Spirits of the Dead*) (Fellini); *Romeo and Juliet* (Zeffirelli)
1969	*Satyricon* (Fellini)
1970	*I clowns* (*The Clowns*) (Fellini); *Waterloo* (Bondarchuk)
1972	**The Godfather** (Coppola); *Roma* (Fellini)
1973	**Film d'amore e d'anarchia** (*Love and Anarchy*) (Wertmüller); *Amarcord* (Fellini); *Sunset, Sunrise* (Kurohara)
1974	*The Abdication* (Harvey); **The Godfather, Part II** (Coppola)
1976	*Caro Michele* (Monicelli); *Casanova* (Fellini); *Ragazzo di borgata* (*Slum Boy*) (Paradisi) (co)
1978	*Death on the Nile* (Guillermin)
1979	*Prova d'orchestra* (*Orchestra Rehearsal*) (Fellini); *Hurricane* (Troell)
1986	*I Soliti ignoti . . . vent'anni dopo*
1987	*Federico Fellini's Intervista* (Fellini)
1990	**The Godfather, Part III** (Coppola)

Publications

By ROTA: article—

Nuova Rivista Musicale Italiana (Rome), vol. 5, no. 1, 1971.

On ROTA: books—

De Santi, Pier Marco, *La musica di Nino Rota*, Bari, 1983.
Comuzio, Ermanno, and Paolo Vecchi, *1381/2: i film di Nino Rota*, Rome, 1986.
Latorre, José Maria, *Nino Rota: La Imagen de la música*, Barcelona, 1989.

On ROTA: articles—

Films in Review (New York), June-July 1971.
Dirigido por . . . (Barcelona), December 1973.
Film Quarterly (Berkeley, California), Winter 1974–75.
Ecran (Paris), September 1975.
Soundtrack! (Hollywood), March 1978.
Take One (Montreal), May 1979.
Bianco e Nero (Rome), July-August 1979.
Image et Son (Paris), September 1979.
Cinema Nuovo (Turin), December 1981.
Score (Lelystad, Netherlands), January 1983.
Soundtrack! (Hollywood), March and June 1987.
Mannino, F., ''Nino Rota neorealista,'' in *Revisto del Cinematografo*, no. 63, April 1993.
Vallerand, F., ''Musique 'classique','' in *Sequences*, no. 165, July/August 1993.

Dossier, in *Cahiers du Cinéma* (Paris), December 1993.
Deutsch, D.C., ''Film Music,'' in *Soundtrack!* (Hollywood), December 1996.
Simon, John, ''*Nights of Cabiria*,'' in *National Review*, 17 August 1998.

*   *   *

Nino Rota is best known for his unique 28-year-long association with Federico Fellini and his popular and prolific musical work (he composed 143 scores) for film and television.

Almost all of the music used in Fellini's films from 1951 until 1979, were written or chosen by Rota. Simple, melodious, stanzaic, and, almost always, diatonic formulation characterizes the orchestration of many of his scores for Fellini. Due to Fellini's fragmentary style, Rota's compositions became the unifying force which gave continuity to Fellini's films. For Fellini, Rota never wrote a pure accompaniment to the action nor did his music only represent a few underlying emotional or dramatic moments. His music always contributed to the classification of the structure, of the characters, of the similarities between various situations, of the bond (often not explicit) between the facts and the action. It maintained an undisputed autonomy that paralleled the role and the value of the scenic action and narration. Fellini, because of his limited knowledge of music and because of his appreciation for Rota's talent, gave the composer creative control of the musical scores. To acquire a certain rhythm and to create a certain atmosphere for a scene, Fellini often filmed to Rota's music or to the music he had chosen. The director would simply suggest a sentiment or situation to Rota and Rota would spontaneously compose something which reflected and clarified the director's intent.

Rota, a child prodigy, was classically trained in composition and piano and composed his first oratorio, *The Childhood of John the Baptist*, at age 11. Toscanini and D'Annunzio admired his work and became his patrons. He studied under Ildebrano Pizzetti and Alfredo Cassela, and at the Milan Conservatory, the Academy of Santa Cecilia in Rome, and from 1930–32, the Curtis Institute in Philadelphia. There he studied composition under Rosaria Scalero. Through her, he became familiar with the historic development of various styles and musical forms. This knowledge later enabled Rota to write for almost any period or in any style of music and contributed to his success as a composer for film. While at the Curtis Institute, he met and became friends with Aaron Copland, who inspired Rota's interest in film. He warned Rota not to assume the prejudice and the snobbish attitude that music written for film was not to be taken seriously and was simply silly enjoyment. He also became familiar with American music and musicians like Cole Porter, Irving Berlin, and George Gershwin. Rota's citation, in *Amarcord*, of the song ''Stormy Weather'' reflects American music's influence on him.

In 1931 he composed his first film score for *Treno popolare*, directed by Raffaello Matarazzo. This was the only score he wrote in the 1930s. The film was a critical failure and Rota did not want to be associated with it. He feared his career in film was finished, and decided to establish himself as a ''serious'' composer. From 1934 until 1937, he wrote mainly chamber music and his college thesis, and he taught music in a high school in Taranto. In 1939, he began teaching composition at the Bari Conservatory.

During the 1940s and 1950s he was the principal composer for Lux Films and was often forced to collaborate on ''shoddy'' films;

however, it was during this time that he began subtly combining leitmotif with symphonic structure to comment, in a melodious way, on characters and situations. He achieved fame as a composer for epoch films, and also gained recognition for his operas.

From 1951 until his death, his work with directors like Fellini, Franco Zeffirelli, Luchino Visconti, and Francis Ford Coppola brought him additional fame. Rota once said he felt it unfortunate that a film score was, usually, only a ''secondary'' element of a film, ''subservient'' to the visual images, ''a mere tool, used to recall and give credence to the images and the emotions those images try to evoke.''

Rota's critics often called him unoriginal, ''a mimic'' with a facility musically to reproduce a mood or ambience of a specific period. Many critics called him too melodious to be taken seriously. In reference to these criticisms, Rota responded: ''Originality can not necessarily be found in a new syntax or new musical grammar. Actually, originality of music is in its substance, in the message it contains, not in its exterior form; that is, it must have canons of immediacy. If something is said to be melodic, who fears that it relates to a theme or a period in history? Simple melody brings up easy relationships, revelations, and derivations. It is a silly fear and anticultural. Every idea and inspiration has precise roots. Nothing comes from nothing.''

In 1972 he was nominated for an Oscar for his score for *The Godfather*; however, someone unjustly accused him of plagiarism. He protested this accusation and the charges were dropped because the music from which the theme song had been derived was a song he had written in 1946. Then in 1974 he won an Oscar for *The Godfather, Part II*. Besides composing popular scores for film and television, he wrote four symphonies, eight operas, ballet scores, concertos, and other orchestral work.

—Suzanne Thomas

ROTUNNO, Giuseppe

Cinematographer. **Nationality:** Italian. **Born:** Rome, 19 March 1923. **Career:** 1940—still photographer; 1945—camera assistant to G. R. Aldo; 1955—became director of photography; 1962—first film with Fellini, *Boccaccio '70*. **Award:** British Academy Award for *All That Jazz*, 1980.

Films as Cinematographer:

1954   *Senso* (Visconti) (cam)
1955   *Pane, amore e . . .* (*Scandal in Sorrento*) (Risi)
1956   *The Monte Carlo Story* (*Monte Carlo*) (Taylor); *Tosca* (Gallone)
1957   *La ragazza del Palio* (*The Love Specialist*; *The Girl Who Rode in the Palio*) (Zampa); *Le notti bianchi* (*White Nights*) (Visconti)
1958   *Borgo a Mozzano* (Gandin); *Anna di Brooklyn* (*Anna of Brooklyn*) (Denham); *The Naked Maja* (Koster); *Attila, flagello di Dio* (*Attila the Hun*) (Francisci); *Fast and Sexy*
1959   *On the Beach* (Kramer)

1960   *Jovanka e le altre* (*Five Branded Women*) (Ritt); *The Angel Wore Red* (*La sposa bella*) (Johnson); *Rocco e i suoi fratelli* (*Rocco and His Brothers*) (Visconti)
1961   *I due nemici* (*The Best of Enemies*) (Hamilton); *Fantasmi a Roma* (*Ghosts in Rome*; *Phantom Lovers*) (Pietrangeli)
1962   ''Il lavoro'' (''The Job'') ep. of *Boccaccio '70* (Fellini); *Cronica familiare* (*Family Diary*) (Zurlini); *Il gattopardo* (*The Leopard*) (Visconti)
1963   *Levi, oggi, domani* (*Yesterday, Today and Tomorrow*) (De Sica); *I compagni* (*The Organizer*) (Monicelli)
1966   *La Bibbia* (*The Bible*) (Huston)
1967   *Lo straniero* (*The Stranger*) (Visconti)
1968   *Lo sbarco di Anzio* (*Battle for Anzio*; *Anzio*) (Dmytryk); *Candy* (Marquand); *Histoires extraordinaires* (*Spirits of the Dead*) (Fellini, Malle and Vadim)
1969   *I girasoli* (*Sunflower*) (De Sica); *Satyricon* (Fellini); *The Secret of Santa Vittoria* (Kramer)
1971   *Carnal Knowledge* (Nichols)
1972   *Roma* (Fellini); *L'uomo della Mancha* (*The Man of La Mancha*)
1973   *Amarcord* (Fellini); *Film d'amore e d'anarchia* (*Love and Anarchy*) (Wertmüller)
1974   *Il bestione*; *Tutto a posto e niente in ordine*
1975   *La divina creatura* (Patroni and Griffi)
1976   *Il Casanova de Federico Fellini* (*Fellini's Casanova*) (Fellini); *Stürmtruppen* (Samperi)
1977   *The End of the World in Our Usual Bed in a Night Full of Rain* (Wertmüller)
1978   *Prova d'orchestra* (*Orchestra Rehearsal*) (Fellini)
1979   *All That Jazz* (Fosse)
1980   *La citta delle donne* (*City of Women*) (Fellini); *Popeye* (Altman)
1981   *Rollover* (Pakula)
1982   *Bello mia bellezza mia*; *Five Days One Summer* (Zinnemann)
1983   *E la nave va* (*And the Ship Sails On*) (Fellini)
1984   ''Paris'' sequences of *American Dreamer* (Rosenthal); *Desiderio* (Tato); *Non ci resta che piangere* (Troisi)
1985   *The Assisi Underground* (Ramati); *Red Sonja* (Fleischer)
1986   *Hotel Colonial* (Torrini)
1987   *Julia and Julia* (del Monte)
1988   *The Adventures of Baron Münchhausen* (Gilliam); *Haunted Summer* (Passer); *Rent-a-Cop* (London)
1989   *Rebus* (Guglielmi)
1990   *Mio caro Dr. Gräsler* (*Dear Dr. Gräsler*; *Bachelor*) (Faenza)
1991   *Regarding Henry* (Nichols)
1992   *Once Upon a Crime* (Levy)
1994   *Wolf* (Nichols); *The Night and the Moment* (Tatò)
1995   *Sabrina* (Pollack)
1996   *La Sindrome di Stendhal* (*Stendhal's Syndrome*) (Argento)
1997   *Marcello Mastroianni: mi ricordo, sì, io mi ricordo* (*Marcello Mastroianni: I Remember, Yes I Remember*) (Tatò)
2000   *The White Hotel*

Publications

By ROTUNNO: articles—

In *La bottega della luce: i direttori della fotografia*, by Stefano Consiglio and Fabio Ferzetti, Milan, 1983.
Positif (Paris), no. 266, April 1983.

Cahiers du Cinéma (Paris), no. 355, January 1984.
Cinema Nuovo (Bari), May-June 1986.
Cinema Nuovo (Bari), January-February 1991.
Cinema Nuovo (Bari), November-December 1993.

On ROTUNNO: articles—

Focus on Film (London), special cinematography issue, no. 13, 1973
 + filmo.
American Cinematographer (Hollywood), vol. 69, no. 3, March 1988.
American Cinematographer (Hollywood), vol. 70, no. 3, March 1989.
Film Comment (New York), vol. 25, no. 5, September-October 1989
 + filmo.
American Cinematographer (Hollywood), vol. 75, June 1994.

* * *

From Kramer's *On The Beach* to Fellini's *Satyricon*, Visconti's *The Leopard* to Fosse's *All That Jazz*, Zurlini's *Cronica familiare* to Altman's *Popeye*, Giuseppe Rotunno, more than almost any other European lighting cameraman, has explored every corner of filmmaking. Despite his popularity with American directors, his best work has been in Italy, especially with Visconti, whose operator he was on *Senso* and who later used him on nearly all his films, including *The Leopard*, the glorious sun-struck Sicilian exteriors of which suggest that Rotunno, in slightly different circumstances, might have been one of the cinema's great photographers of vistas.

Rotunno is essentially a cameraman of colour. While Gianni di Venanzo, on films like *La notte*, *L'eclisse* and *Salvatore Giuliano*, was refining a style of matte blacks and blisteringly pale whites, Rotunno plunged into a sensual Goyaesque darkness (of which there is only a hint, sadly, in his shooting of Henry Koster's murky Goya bio-pic *The Naked Maja*). The prevailing sense in Rotunno's photography became one of rich colour, thickened and diluted with black. Before Gordon Willis won the title, he was surely cinema's reigning "Prince of Darkness," a fact which makes doubly odd Visconti's decision to use Pasqualino de Santis on *The Damned*, the most penumbral of all his films.

In Mario Monicelli's *The Organiser* and Valerio Zurlini's underrated *Cronica familiare*, Rotunno showed he could adapt his style to working-class reality, but he truly established himself as a master with Visconti's episode "The Job" for the omnibus film *Boccaccio '70*, where a wealthy wife suggests, out of boredom and perversity, that she replace, for money, her husband's latest mistress. His lighting of the voluptuous Romy Schneider as she strolls half-nude around her claustrophobic lush bedroom perfectly conveys the life of people so gorged on sensation that they've lost their ability to relish anything but gutter flavours. Obviously the style ignited Fellini's interest, since he used it (and Rotunno) on almost all his later films, including *Satyricon*, the blackest and most gross of them all.

As European cinema declined in the 1970s, Rotunno worked increasingly in the United States, though seldom on films as interesting as his lighting of them. Often working for directors with reputations as mavericks or martinets (Altman on *Popeye*, Mike Nichols on *Carnal Knowledge* and *Regarding Henry*, Alan Pakula on *Rollover*, Bob Fosse on *All That Jazz*), he has had a bumpy Hollywood career, not helped by the fact that all his films, including even the staid *Five Days One Summer* with Fred Zinnemann, have almost uniformly flopped. But from the man who photographed *The Leopard*, much may yet be expected.

—John Baxter

ROUSSELOT, Philippe

Cinematographer. **Nationality:** French. **Born:** Meurthe et Moselle, France, 4 September 1945; moved from Paris to New York. **Education:** Attended ''Vaugirard,'' Ecole Louis Lumiere Film School in Paris, 1964–66. **Family:** Married 1981; one daughter. **Career:** Early work on documentaries; worked as loader for Nestor Almedros on *Ma Nuit Chez Maud (My Night at Maud's)*, 1969; worked in commercials and still photography with Sara Moon; camera assistant on Eric Rohmer films; directorial debut, *The Serpent's Kiss*, 1996. **Awards:** Prix Jean Vigo, for *Paradiso*, 1972; Prix Special, Cannes, for *La Drolesse*, 1978; National Society of Film Critics Award (USA) for Best Cinematography, and Cesar Award (France) for Best Cinematography, for *Diva*, 1982; Cesar Award for Best Cinematography, for *Theresa*, 1987; National Society of Film Critics Award for Best Cinematography, and British Society of Cinematographers Award for Best Cinematography, for *Hope and Glory*, 1987; Academy Award for Best Cinematography, for *A River Runs Through It*, 1993; British Society of Cinematographers Award for Best Cinematography, and BAFTA (UK) Award for Best Cinematography, for *Interview With the Vampire: The Vampire Chronicles*, 1994; Cesar Award for Best Cinematography, for *La Reine Margot (Queen Margot)*, 1995. **Agent:** David Gersh, Gersh Agency, 232 N. Canon Drive, Beverly Hills, CA 90210, U.S.A.

Films as Cinematographer:

1970 *Clair de Terre* (Gilles)
1971 *Absences Repetees* (Gilles)
1972 *Paradiso* (Bricoult); *L'Affiche Rouge (The Red Poster)* (Cassenti); *Pour Clemence* (Belmont)
1973 *La Raison du Plus Fou* (Reichenbach); *Il Pleut Toujours* (Simon)
1975 *Couple Temoin* (Klein)
1977 *Diabolo Menthe (Peppermint Soda)* (Kurys); *Adam* (Benamou)
1978 *La Drolesse* (Doillon); *La Vie de Jean-Jacques Rousseau* (Goretta)
1979 *Cocktail Molotov* (Kurys)
1980 *La Provinciale (The Girl From Lorraine)* (Goretta)
1981 ***Diva*** (Beineix); *La Gueule du Loup* (Leviant); *Guy de Maupassant* (Drach)
1982 *La Lune dans le Caniveau (Moon in the Gutter)* (Beineix); *Les Voleurs de la Nuit* (Fuller)
1983 *Nemo* (Selignac)
1984 *Emerald Forest* (Boorman); *Night Magic* (Furey)
1985 *Therese* (Cavaliere)

1986 *Hope and Glory* (Boorman)
1987 *L'ours* (Annaud)
1988 *Dangerous Liasons* (Frears); *Trop belle pour toi* (Blier)
1989 *Henry and June* (Kaufman); *We're No Angels* (Jordan)
1990 *The Miracle* (Jordan); *Merci la vie* (Blier)
1991 *A River Runs Through It* (Redford)
1992 *Sommersby* (Amiel); *Flesh and Bone* (Kloves)
1993 *La Reine Margot (Quenn Margot)* (Chereau)
1994 *Interview With the Vampire: The Vampire Chronicles* (Jordan); *Mary Riley* (Frears)
1996 *The People vs. Larry Flint* (Forman)
1998 *Instinct* (Turteltaub)
1999 *Random Hearts* (Pollack)
2000 *Remember the Titans*; *The Tailor of Panama*

Films as Camera Assistant:

1969 *Ma Nuit Chez Maud (My Night at Maud's)* (Rohmer)
1970 *Le Genou de Claire (Claire's Knee)* (Rohmer)
1972 *L'Amour l'apres-midi (Chloe in the Afternoon)* (Rohmer)

Other Films:

1997 *The Serpent's Kiss* (d)

Publications

On ROUSSELOT: articles—

Hewitt, C., "Anguish and Light Balls," in *Eyepiece* (Middlesex), vol. 15, no. 4, 1994.
"Interview with the Vampire," in *American Cinematographer* (Hollywood), January 1995.
"Rousselot at 'Serpent' Helm," in *Hollywood Reporter*, 5 February 1996.
Geffner, David, "Shooting Stars: Interviews with the World's Greatest Living Cinematographers," in *MovieMaker*, no. 29, July 1998.

*   *   *

Philippe Rousselot first caught the attention of Hollywood with his work as cinematographer on the John Boorman film *Hope and Glory* in 1986, but he had been celebrated throughout Europe and in his native France for many years prior. His work on the 1982 *Diva* won the Cesar (the French equivalent of the Academy Award) for Best Cinematography and propelled his career to new levels. He received another Cesar for *Therese*, a 1985 work which chronicled the life of a fiercely faithful Carmelite nun. Rousselot's work is lyrical, passionate, and subtle in its execution. His films never suffer from apparent technique, but reveal an appreciation for the sublime qualities of light and color.

Rousselot began his career as a camera assistant on several Eric Rohmer films. The first was *Ma Nuit Chez Maud* (1969), where he worked beside esteemed cinematographer Nestor Almendros as a camera loader. This apprenticeship was apparently instrumental in

Rousselot's development. Rousselot credits this experience as a profound influence, along with his work in commercials with still photographer Sara Moon. Before this, though, there was Jean Cocteau. Rousselot was a child of eleven when he first saw the French avant-garde filmmaker's work, and he found them "so moving, emotionally, visually, and intellectually. They were complete magic to me," he told *MovieMaker* interviewer David Geffner. Other films which expanded his horizons included the works of Ingmar Bergman, Frederico Fellini, and the German Expressionists.

Rousselot embraced the masters from an early age, and he undoubtedly learned a great deal from all this study. By 1970 he was working as the Director of Photography on the French film *Clair de Terre*, and found such success that he performed in the same capacity in nearly two films per year in the first decade of his career. This prolific pace continued, with quality never suffering as Rousselot shaped important works by such directors as Phillip Kaufman (*Henry and June*), Neil Jordan (*We're No Angels*, *Interview With the Vampire*), Robert Redford, Sidney Pollack, Milos Forman, and many others.

Rousselot's work has won much praise from his peers. In 1993, he won the Academy Award for Best Cinematography for Redford's fly-fishing film *A River Runs Through It*. It was his third nomination for the award. Honor has also come from the French Cesar Awards, where he has claimed the title of Best Cinematographer three times, for Beineix' *Diva*, Cavaliere's *Therese*, and Chereau's *La Reine Margot (Queen Margot)*. Rousselot received the BAFTA, similar to the Cesar and the Academy Awards, for his work in Jordan's 1994 film *Interview With the Vampire: The Vampire Chronicles*, based on the best-selling book by Anne Rice.

Rousselot's work is highly praised in part because of his delicate lighting design. He uses such devises as Chinese lanterns to soften spectral light and shape his elegant compositions. He works to complement film content and tone with tailored illumination. This is especially evident in such films as *Therese*, where the lighting shifts to enhance the feeling of holiness within this tale of a young, remarkably passionate nun. His *Henry and June* shows a loving replication of tonal qualities seen in the still photographs of Brassai, a peripheral character in the film. One wonders where Rousselot's fine artistic sensibilities will lead him next, as he continues to work on an astonishing number of films from the most important directors of our time.

—Tammy Kinsey

ROZSA, Miklos

Composer. **Nationality:** American. **Born:** Nicholas Rozsa in Budapest, Hungary, 18 April 1907. **Education:** Studied the violin under Lajos Berkovits, and the viola and piano; attended secondary schools in Budapest; studied under Hermann Grabner and Theodor Kroyer at the Conservatory and University in Leipzig, diplomas 1929. **Career:** Composer from 1915; composer of orchestra works; 1932–35—lived in Paris, and in London, 1935–40; 1937—first film score, for *Knight without Armour*; 1940—settled in Hollywood; contracts with Paramount and MGM; 1945—Professor of Composition, University of Southern California, Los Angeles. **Awards:** Academy Awards for *Spellbound*, 1945; *A Double Life*, 1947; *Ben-Hur*, 1959; César award for *Providence*, 1977. **Died:** 27 July 1995.

Miklos Rozsa

Films as Composer:

1937 *Knight without Armour* (Feyder); *Thunder in the City* (Gering); *The Squeaker* (*Murder on Diamond Row*) (Howard)

1938 *The Divorce of Lady X* (Whelan)

1939 *The Four Feathers* (Z. Korda); *Ten Days in Paris* (*Missing Ten Days*; *Spy in the Pantry*) (Whelan); *The Spy in Black* (*U-Boat 29*) (Powell); *On the Night of the Fire* (*The Fugitive*) (Hurst)

1940 *Four Dark Hours* (*The Green Cockatoo*; *Race Gang*) (Menzies); *The Thief of Bagdad* (Powell, Berger, and Whelan)

1941 *That Hamilton Woman* (*Lady Hamilton*) (A. Korda); *Lydia* (Duvivier); *Sundown* (Hathaway)

1942 *Rudyard Kipling's Jungle Book* (*The Jungle Book*) (A. Korda); *Jacare* (*Jacare—Killer of the Amazon*) (C. Ford)

1943 *Five Graves to Cairo* (Wilder); *So Proudly We Hail* (Sandrich); *Sahara* (Z. Korda); *The Woman of the Town* (Archainbaud)

1944 *The Hour Before Dawn* (Tuttle); **Double Indemnity** (Wilder); *Dark Waters* (de Toth); *The Man in Half Moon Street* (Murphy)

1945 *A Song to Remember* (C. Vidor); *Blood on the Sun* (Lloyd); *Lady on a Train* (David); **The Lost Weekend** (Wilder); *Spellbound* (Hitchcock)

1946 *Because of Him* (Wallace); **The Killers** (Siodmak); *The Strange Love of Martha Ivers* (Milestone)

1947 *The Red House* (Daves); *Song of Scheherazade* (Reisch); *The Macomber Affair* (Z. Korda); *The Other Love* (Z. Korda);

Time Out of Mind (*Illusions*) (Siodmak); *Desert Fury* (Allen); *Brute Force* (Dassin); *A Double Life* (Cukor)

1948 *The Secret Behind the Door* (F. Lang); *A Woman's Vengeance* (*The Giaconda Smile*) (Z. Korda); *The Naked City* (Dassin); *Criss Cross* (Siodmak); *Kiss the Blood Off My Hands* (*Blood on My Hands*) (Foster)

1949 *Command Decision* (Wood); *The Bribe* (Leonard); *Madame Bovary* (Minnelli); *The Red Danube* (Sidney); **Adam's Rib** (Cukor); *East Side, West Side* (LeRoy)

1950 **The Asphalt Jungle** (Huston); *Crisis* (Brooks); *The Miniver Story* (Potter)

1951 *Quo Vadis* (LeRoy); *The Light Touch* (Brooks)

1952 *Ivanhoe* (Thorpe); *Plymouth Adventure* (Brown)

1953 *Julius Caesar* (Mankiewicz); *Young Bess* (Sidney); ''Mademoiselle'' ep. of *The Story of Three Loves* (Minnelli); *All the Brothers Were Valiant* (Thorpe); *Knights of the Round Table* (Thorpe)

1954 *Men of the Fighting Lady* (*Panther Squadron*) (Marton); *Valley of the Kings* (Pirosh); *Green Fire* (Marton); *Seagulls over Sorrento* (*Crest of the Wave*) (J. & R. Boulting)

1955 *Moonfleet* (F. Lang); *The King's Thief* (Leonard); *Diane* (Miller)

1956 *Tribute to a Badman* (Wise); *Bhowani Junction* (Cukor); *Lust for Life* (Minnelli)

1957 *Something of Value* (Brooks); *The Seventh Sin* (Neame); *Tip on a Dead Jockey* (Thorpe)

1958 *A Time to Love and a Time to Die* (Sirk)

1959 *The World, the Flesh, and the Devil* (MacDougall); *Ben-Hur* (Wyler)

1961 *King of Kings* (Ray); *El Cid* (A. Mann)

1962 *Sodom and Gomorrah* (Aldrich)

1963 *The V.I.P.s* (Asquith)

1968 *The Power* (Haskin); *The Green Berets* (Wayne and Kellogg)

1970 *The Private Life of Sherlock Holmes* (Wilder)

1973 *The Golden Voyage of Sinbad* (Hessler)

1977 *Providence* (Resnais)

1978 *The Private Files of J. Edgar Hoover* (Cohen); *Fedora* (Wilder)

1979 *The Last Embrace* (Demme); *Time after Time* (Meyer)

1980 *Eye of the Needle* (Marquand)

1981 *Dead Men Don't Wear Plaid* (Reiner)

1982 *The Atomic Cafe* (K. Rafferty, P. Rafferty, and Loader)

1987 *Dragnet* (T. Mankiewicz) (song)

1989 *Gesucht: Monika Ertl* (Baudissin)

Publications

By ROZSA: book—

Double Life (autobiography), New York, 1982.

By ROZSA: articles—

''Quo Vadis,'' in *Film/TV Music*, November-December 1951.
''Music from Historical Films,'' in *Film/TV Music*, March-April 1952.
''Julius Caesar,'' in *Film/TV Music*, September-October 1953.
Cinema TV Today (London), 20 January 1973.
Film Music Notebook (Calabasas, California), vol. 2, no. 4, 1976.
Positif (Paris), January 1977.

Films and Filming (London), May and June 1977.
Ecran (Paris), November 1978.
In *Film Score*, edited by Tony Thomas, South Brunswick, New Jersey, 1979.
National Film Theatre booklet (London), March 1980.
Première (Paris), March 1980.
Télérama (Paris), 15–21 March 1980.
Photoplay (London), June 1980.
Cinéma (Paris), June 1980.
Ecran Fantastique (Paris), no. 18, 1981.
24 Images (Longueuil, Quebec), April 1982.
Soundtrack! (Hollywood), September 1982.
New Zealand Film Music Bulletin (Invercargill), November 1982.
Soundtrack! (Hollywood), December 1982.
Cinemasessante (Rome), January-February 1983.

On ROZSA: book—

Palmer, Christopher, *Miklos Rozsa: A Sketch of His Life and Work*, London, 1974.

On ROZSA: articles—

Sternfeld, Frederick W., "The Strange Music of Martha Ivers," in *Hollywood Quarterly*, April, 1947.
Films in Review (New York), June-July 1959.
Doeckel, Ken, in *Films in Review* (New York), November 1963.
Films in Review (New York), November 1965.
Films and Filming (London), June 1970.
Palmer, Christopher, in *Performing Right* (London), May 1971.
Thomas, Tony, in *Music for the Movies*, South Brunswick, New Jersey, 1973.
Films in Review (New York), June-July 1974.
Ecran (Paris), September 1975.
Caps, John, in *Film Music Notebook* (Calabasas, California), vol. 2, no. 1, 1976.
Films in Review (New York), January 1976.
Films in Review (New York), August-September 1976.
Positif (Paris), November 1976.
Dale, S.S., in *The Strand* (London), January 1977.
Ecran Fantastique (Paris), no. 4, 1978.
Dirigido por . . . (Barcelona), February 1978.
Palmer, Christopher, in *Monthly Film Bulletin* (London), March 1978.
"Rozsa Supplement" in *Score* (Lelystad, Netherlands), April 1979.
Films in Review (New York), November 1979.
Films in Review (New York), February 1980.
Soundtrack! (Hollywood), April 1980.
Films in Review (New York), June-July 1980.
Cinéma (Paris), July-August 1980.
Positif (Paris), July-August 1981.
Filmusic (Leeds), 1982.
National Film Theatre booklet (London), June 1982.
Lacombe, Alain, in *Hollywood*, Paris, 1983.
New Zealand Film Music Bulletin (Invercargill), May 1983.
New Zealand Film Music Bulletin (Invercargill), November 1984.
New Zealand Film Music Bulletin (Invercargill), February 1985.
New Zealand Film Music Bulletin (Invercargill), May 1985.
Soundtrack! (Hollywood), June 1986.
Soundtrack! (Hollywood), July 1986.
Films in Review (New York), January-February 1990.

Palmer, Christopher, in *The Composer in Hollywood*, New York, 1990.
Cinema Nuovo (Bari), January-February 1991.
Cook, P., "The sound track," in *Films in Review*, March/April 1992.
Horton, R., "Music man," in *Film Comment*, November/December 1995.
Obituary in *The New York Times*, 29 July 1995.
Obituary in *Variety* (New York), 31 July 1995.
David, Peter, "Symphonic Cinema: Émigré Composers in Hollywood," in *New York*, 6 November 1995.
Eder, Bruce, in *Films in Review* (New York), March-April 1996.
Obituary in *Cue Sheet* (Hollywood), April 1996.
Barbour, Alan, "*Videosyncracy*," in *Films in Review*, May-June 1996.
Teachout, Terry, "I Heard it at the Movies," in *Commentary*, November 1996.

*　　*　　*

The extensive composing career of Miklos Rozsa can be divided into a number of distinct periods based on associations with particular studios or genres. Yet despite the diversity of his work Rozsa's scores have a readily identifiable style and consistency. The composer's later scores in a number of different genres have a similar structure and texture and are marked by characteristic techniques Rozsa has developed and modified throughout his career.

Rozsa's first period began with his association with the Korda brothers, for whom he scored a number of opulent period and fantasy productions. These scores are distinguished by a richness of texture and variety of instrumentation ranging from a sweeping romanticism to orchestration in the fantasy films reminiscent of Rimsky-Korsakov. In addition to an opportunity for dynamic effects and oriental stylings, the scores for films such as *The Thief of Bagdad* and *The Jungle Book* allowed Rozsa to include lyrical operatic song melodies which reappeared in variations throughout the scores. *The Jungle Book* score was founded on a series of motifs which were later presented in a concert suite with narration designed largely as a children's piece, one of the many points at which his film and concert work (referred to in his autobiography as his "double life") would converge.

The work with Korda resulted in Rozsa's migration to Hollywood, where a contract with Paramount led to an association with Billy Wilder. Rozsa's score for Wilder's *Five Graves to Cairo* served to bridge the gap between his work in films centered around exotic locales and his move into more serious psychological melodramas. Rozsa became a prominent contributor to the rising *film noir* style with his work for Wilder's *Double Indemnity* and *The Lost Weekend*, and the music was characterized by brooding and unsentimentalized themes, driving rhythms which give way abruptly to jolting chords and a use of strings as much for disturbing as for romantic effect.

The Lost Weekend also introduced the therimin to provide a wailing accompaniment for the alcoholic protagonist's delirium states and the instrument became a favorite for psychological subjects, employed by Rozsa himself for *The Red House* and in one of his best-remembered scores, for Hitchcock's *Spellbound*. Such works demonstrated that film music could be serious and contemporary while still remaining within the symphonic tradition, and further evidence was provided by Rozsa's association with the producer Mark Hellinger. The scores for *The Killers*, *The Naked City*, and *Brute Force* contain a raw urban power that perfectly complements the realistic visual emphasis of *film noir*.

The emotionalism and power evident in such works was also apparent in a series of scores that in many other respects are the opposite of Rozsa's contemporary psychological period. The composer's contract with MGM in the late 1940s led to his work in historical and religious pictures which would continue for over a decade. Rather than being regarded as a step back to the Korda period, Rozsa's scores for the MGM epics can be seen as a kind of progression into a recognizable style, combining the exoticism of the Korda scores with the strong emotional drive of the *film noir* period.

The scores also provided Rozsa with an opportunity to delve into musical antiquity, striving for realism in works like *Quo Vadis*, *Ivanhoe*, and *El Cid*. Consequently, the scores are characterized by an array of fanfares, marches, and dance pieces woven into a richly textured orchestral tapestry. Rozsa's work for these epics often included ascending choral passages combined with orchestra for strong emotional impact. Despite Rozsa's typecasting as a composer of such scores, the MGM period also provided opportunities for lighter, more contemporary subjects as well as chances for experimentation, as in the combination of romanticism and impressionism provided for *Lust for Life*.

With a greater emphasis given to popular modern styles in the 1960s, Rozsa became less active in films and turned his attention more and more to concert works. His famous Violin Concerto, commissioned by Jascha Heifetz in 1953, served as the inspiration for Billy Wilder's *The Private Life of Sherlock Holmes* and led to Rozsa's reunion with the director. For the Holmes film Rozsa rearranged and varied principal themes of the concerto as well as providing new material, and the deliberately nostalgic style of both film and score were repeated in *Fedora*, with Wilder's reflection on the passing of Hollywood's Golden Age matched by Rozsa's overtly symphonic accompaniment.

Rozsa's most recent period in film scoring was characterized not by identification with a specific studio or genre but by a distinct musical style which has been applied to a broad range of subjects. *The Power*, for example, contains a hard-driving theme played on a cimbalom which is later modified for more conventional presentation by strings, including a florid ''gypsy'' arrangement for solo violin. The dynamic percussive passages and soaring love theme are characteristic of many later scores by Rozsa, which juxtapose driving rhythms against lyrical, often waltz-like passages. Many of these works represent deliberate modifications of Rozsa's past achievements. *Time after Time* draws on the exotic orchestrations of previous fantasy works in places, while a straightforward presentation of the *film noir* style is provided for the Steve Martin comedy *Dead Men Don't Wear Plaid*. Collectively, Rozsa's last works represent not redundancy or repetition but rather a consistency which marks a distinctive personal musical approach. Despite association with a number of directors and studios and in a variety of genres Rozsa was an individual stylist in both his film and concert works and was one of a small group of composers to gain recognition and respect in both capacities.

—Richard R. Ness

RUTTENBERG, Joseph

Cinematographer. **Nationality:** American. **Born:** St. Petersburg, Russia, 4 July 1889; emigrated to Boston aged four years. **Family:** Married Rose (Ruttenberg); daughter: Virginia. **Career:** Newsboy, then reporter and news photographer, Boston; 1914—formed his own newsreel production company; 1915—joined Fox as photographer; 1917—first film as cinematographer, *A Painted Madonna*; 1935–68—worked for MGM. **Awards:** Academy Award for *The Great Waltz*, 1938; *Mrs. Miniver*, 1942; *Somebody Up There Likes Me*, 1956; *Gigi*, 1958. **Died:** In Los Angeles, California, 1 May 1983.

Films as Cinematographer:

1917 *A Painted Madonna* (Lund); *Thou Shalt Not Steal* (Seurat)
1918 *Doing Their Bit* (Buel); *The Debt of Honor* (Lund); *The Woman Who Gave* (Buel); *Women, Women*
1919 *The Fallen Idol* (Buel); *My Little Sister* (Buel)
1920 *Tiger's Club* (Giblyn); *From Now On* (Walsh); *The Shark* (Henderson)
1921 *Beyond Price* (Dawley); *Know Your Men* (Giblyn); *The Mountain Woman* (Giblyn); *A Virgin Paradise* (Dawley)
1922 *Who Are My Parents?* (Dawley); *The Town That Forgot God* (Millarde); *Over the Hill* (Millarde); *My Friend the Devil* (Millarde)
1923 *If Winter Comes* (Millarde); *Does It Pay* (Horan)
1925 *School for Wives* (Halperin); *The Fool* (Millarde)
1926 *Summer Bachelors* (Dwan)
1929 *Applause* (Mamoulian) (uncredited); *The Cocoanuts* (Florey and Santley) (uncredited); *The Battle of Paris* (*The Gay Lady*) (Florey) (uncredited)
1931 *The Struggle* (Griffith); *The Smiling Lieutenant* (Lubitsch) (uncredited)
1935 *Gigolette* (Lamont); *Frankie and Johnnie* (Auer); *People's Enemy* (Wilbur); *Man Hunt* (Clemens)
1936 *Three Godfathers* (Boleslawsky); **Fury** (F. Lang); *Piccadilly Jim* (Leonard); *Mad Holiday* (Seitz)
1937 *A Day at the Races* (Wood); *The Big Day* (Borzage)
1938 *The Great Waltz* (Duvivier); *The First Hundred Years* (Thorpe); *Everybody Sing* (Marin); *Three Comrades* (Borzage); *The Shopworn Angel* (Potter); *Spring Madness* (Simon); *Ice Follies of 1939* (Schünzel) (co)
1939 *Tell No Tales* (Fenton); *On Borrowed Time* (Bucquet); *The Women* (Cukor) (co); *Balalaika* (Schünzel)
1940 *Broadway Melody of 1940* (Taurog) (co); *Waterloo Bridge* (LeRoy); **The Philadelphia Story** (Cukor); *Comrade X* (K. Vidor)
1941 *Dr. Jekyll and Mr. Hyde* (Fleming); *Two Faced Woman* (Cukor)
1942 *Woman of the Year* (Stevens); **Mrs. Miniver** (Wyler); *Crossroads* (Conway); *Random Harvest* (LeRoy)
1944 *Gaslight* (Cukor); *Mrs. Parkington* (Garnett)
1945 *Valley of Decision* (Garnett); *Adventure* (Fleming)
1947 *Desire Me* (Cukor); *Killer McCoy* (Rowland)
1948 *Julia Misbehaves* (Conway); *B.F.'s Daughter* (Leonard)
1949 *The Bribe* (Leonard); *Side Street* (A. Mann); *That Forsyte Woman* (Bennett)
1950 *The Miniver Story* (Potter); *The Magnificent Yankee* (J. Sturges)
1951 *The Great Caruso* (Thorpe); *Cause for Alarm* (Garnett); *Kind Lady* (J. Sturges); *Too Young to Kiss* (Leonard)
1952 *Because You're Mine* (Hall); *The Prisoner of Zenda* (Thorpe); *Young Man with Ideas* (Leisen)
1953 *Julius Caesar* (Mankiewicz); *Small Town Girl* (Kardos); *Latin Lovers* (LeRoy); *The Great Diamond Robbery* (Leonard)

1954   *The Last Time I Saw Paris* (Brooks); *Her Twelve Men* (Leonard); *Brigadoon* (Minnelli)
1955   *Interrupted Melody* (Bernhardt) (co); *The Prodigal* (Thorpe); *Kismet* (Minnelli)
1956   *The Swan* (C. Vidor) (co); *Somebody Up There Likes Me* (Wise); *Invitation to the Dance* (Kelly) (co)
1957   *The Vintage* (Hayden); *Man on Fire* (MacDougall); *Until They Sail* (Wise)
1958   *Gigi* (Minnelli); *The Reluctant Debutante* (Minnelli)
1959   *Green Mansions* (M. Ferrer); *Wreck of the Mary Deare* (Anderson)
1960   *The Subterraneans* (MacDougall); *Butterfield 8* (Daniel Mann) (co)
1961   *Two Loves* (Walters); *Ada* (Daniel Mann); *Bachelor in Paradise* (Arnold)
1962   *Who's Got the Action?* (Daniel Mann)
1963   *The Hook* (Seaton); *It Happened at the World's Fair* (Taurog); *Who's Been Sleeping in My Bed?* (Daniel Mann)
1964   *A Global Affair* (Arnold)
1965   *Sylvia* (Douglas); *Harlow* (Douglas); *Love Has Many Faces* (Singer)
1966   *The Oscar* (Rouse)
1968   *Speedway* (Taurog)

Film as Cameraman:

1939   **Gone with the Wind** (Fleming)

Publications

By RUTTENBERG: articles—

"Overhead Lighting for Overall Set Illumination," in *American Cinematographer* (Hollywood), December 1952.
"Photographing Pre-Production Tests," in *American Cinematographer* (Hollywood), January 1956.
"Sound-Stage Sea Saga," in *American Cinematographer* (Hollywood), April 1960.
Positif (Paris), September 1972.
Seminar in *American Cinematographer* (Hollywood), July 1975.
Focus on Film (London), Spring 1976.
In *Dance in the Hollywood Musical*, by Jerome Delamater, Ann Arbor, Michigan, 1981.
Film History (Philadelphia), vol. 1, no. 1, 1987.
Eyman, Scott, in *Five American Cinematographers*, Metuchen, New Jersey, 1987.

On RUTTENBERG: articles—

Lawton, Ralph, "Tyro in Technicolor," in *American Cinematographer* (Hollywood), September 1949.
Gavin, Arthur, on *Gigi* in *American Cinematographer* (Hollywood), July 1958.
Film Comment (New York), Summer 1972.
Focus on Film (London), no. 13, 1973.
Revue du Cinéma (Morges, Switzerland), July-August 1983.

The Annual Obituary 1983, Chicago, 1984.
Film & History, vol. 1, no. 1, 1987.

*   *   *

"The old pro" to studio executives, actors, and film directors, Joseph Ruttenberg was a cinematographer whose technical mastery was matched by a visual artistry that enriched the films of directors more concerned with drama and acting than visual style. When he worked with directors who *did* care about lighting and composition, the films they made often were nominated for Academy Awards. Ruttenberg earned ten nominations, and won Oscars four times. In all he filmed about 110 movies between 1917 and 1968.

Born in Russia, Ruttenberg was brought to the United States as a very young boy. His first job was as a copy boy on the *Boston American* (where he was also an occasional personal messenger for William Randolph Hearst). At the *American* Ruttenberg discovered photography. First as a runner who hand delivered news film to the laboratory, then as a darkroom technician, then as a press photographer, Ruttenberg learned how to make pictures with speed and under adverse conditions. One night, for example, when he couldn't use his own flash equipment, he opened the shutter on his camera and waited for the flashes of other photographers. To photograph theatrical sets he used different colored lights to register the appropriate contrasts of color in his black-and-white images. This combination of expertise and invention won him a commission to photograph European stage sets for the Boston Opera. There, in Paris, on the eve of the First World War, he fell under the spell of the moving picture.

In America in 1914, the movies were chiefly regarded as an amusement. But in Europe they were perceived as a graphic art, as an educational tool, as an historical record, and as a dramatic medium. One of the notions current in Europe in 1914 was that film could be an archive of the images of people and events of historical importance. Ruttenberg developed a variation of this while he was in Paris. When the approach of war sent him and the other Americans of his party back to the United States, Ruttenberg returned with an ambitious proposal to assemble a visual encyclopedia on motion-picture film.

This idea, so extraordinary for an American in 1914, reveals how profoundly Ruttenberg had been affected by European concepts of the potential of film. Though he was unable to find backing for his encyclopedia in Boston, Ruttenberg chose not to return to his previous work in still photography. Instead he formed a partnership with a Yale friend—who had money and mechanical ability. They purchased a hand-cranked movie camera, built a film processing unit in a Boston loft, and for nearly six months produced a weekly newsreel for the local Loews theaters. Minimal profits and a demanding schedule led the two to eventually abandon the enterprise, but the experience was to be useful when Ruttenberg moved to New York City and employment with William Fox in 1916.

Again Ruttenberg rose through the ranks, from slate-holder and still photographer (at $18 a week) to assistant cameraman and then cinematographer (when he left Fox in 1926 he was making $175 a week). Using Pathé and Bell and Howell cameras, Ruttenberg shot at least 26 films between *A Painted Madonna* (his first as cinematographer) in 1917, and *The Struggle* for D.W. Griffith in 1931. A complete filmography for Ruttenberg remains to be assembled because in these years Ruttenberg often collaborated on films but received no on-screen credit. Rouben Mamoulian's *Applause* is one of these; Lubitsch's *The Smiling Lieutenant* is another—both were credited to George Folsey, one of Ruttenberg's closest friends. Though they worked 50/50, only Folsey got credit for legal reasons.

Lighting, camera movement, and location filming were inhibited in the first years of sound movies. There can be little doubt that Ruttenberg was wary about moving west in such circumstances. So when the Fox production company moved to Hollywood in 1926, Ruttenberg chose to remain in New York, where he soon was making screen tests with sound for MGM, RKO, and Universal. (Some of the actors he tested with the new sound systems were the Marx Brothers, Helen Hayes, Fred Astaire, Walter Huston, and Claudette Colbert.)

In the mid-1920s, Ruttenberg actually wanted to return to Europe, to work with the German directors Fritz Lang and F.W. Murnau. Ironically, though Ruttenberg finally did get to work with Lang on *Fury*, it was not until 1950 when he photographed *Side Street* for Anthony Mann that he was able to work in the conventions of a style (*film noir*) that was rooted in German Expressionism.

Though D.W. Griffith chose Ruttenberg to film *The Struggle* because he liked his camera tests made for the film, Ruttenberg also wanted to work with Griffith who was always (Ruttenberg recalled) "experimenting. He went into a foundry to [record] pretty good sound, . . . and would say 'We'll try these things'." Ruttenberg embraced challenges; when CinemaScope was introduced in the 1950s Ruttenberg enthusiastically wrote to Louis B. Mayer that "it was the best thing since sound."

In 1935 Ruttenberg finally made the move to Hollywood, briefly working at Warner Bros., and then shifting to MGM; by this time the traumatic period of the transition to sound was over, and Ruttenberg's talent as a lighting cinematographer could be used with the same freedom as in the 1920s.

Ruttenberg's camerawork was distinctive for three reasons. First, he composed the film image on two planes. The primary subject of interest, one or more actors, would appear in sharp focus, and the background would be softer, slightly out of focus. In consequence, actors would "project" out of the screen, acquiring an almost three-dimensional weight. Ruttenberg considered the "deep focus" technique used by Gregg Toland for William Wyler and Orson Welles to be a mistake, the loss of an opportunity to direct the eye of the spectator. (Nevertheless, in *Somebody Up There Likes Me*, Ruttenberg and the director Robert Wise did use deep focus for several sequences, including a wonderful allusion to the breakfast sequence of

Citizen Kane; in the film, Everett Sloane, who played Bernstein in *Kane*, is seen on the floor with Paul Newman's children in deep focus, echoing the nursery visit Kane insists Bernstein may want to make—but does not—to see Kane's children in *Citizen Kane*.)

The second reason was his lighting. While many cinematographers delegate lighting to assistants, Ruttenberg believed lighting was central to cinematography. With it he could mould and change what was in front of the camera. Often he would defy union rules to handle the lights himself. (And it was not until he moved to Hollywood that he used a light meter; his years of experience in still photography, as well as in the movies, gave him a sure sense of exposure.) Katharine Hepburn, like scores of other actresses, wanted Ruttenberg to shoot her films because his lighting flattered her (Hepburn liked shadows on her neck).

The importance of lighting in films like *Gaslight*, *Dr. Jekyll and Mr. Hyde*, and *Waterloo Bridge*, where shadows *are* atmosphere, does not need to be pointed out. Less obvious is the lighting used for a film like *A Day at the Races*. Filming the Marx Brothers, Ruttenberg often noted, was an adventure because they never did the same thing twice, especially on retakes. Multiple cameras, and an even, relatively shadowless lighting scheme was necessary if separate shots were to be cut together smoothly when the film was completed. *Three Comrades*, shot in 1938 for Frank Borzage, is one of Ruttenberg's masterpieces of lighting. The "spirituality" of Borzage's characters is given tangible substance in this film: Margaret Sullivan, at times, is almost luminous.

Ruttenberg's camerawork was also distinctive in a third way. Given the opportunity, and at times on his own initiative, he would seek to film whole sequences in a single take. As early as the 1920s, when he was working at the Astoria Studio without screen credit, Ruttenberg constructed dolly mechanisms, camera cranes, even rolling bridges so that shots of 30 or more seconds could be made. Some of his shots defy understanding: in *Gigi* he films in a room full of mirrors, but the camera and lights are not seen, and in *Brigadoon* his camera sweeps around dancers on a hilltop, hovering and flying, floating in a space that seems free of gravity.

—Robert A. Haller

SARDE, Philippe

Composer. **Nationality:** French. **Born:** Neuilly-sur-Seine, 21 June 1945. **Education:** Attended the Paris Conservatory; also studied with Noël Gallon. **Career:** 1970—first of several films for Sautet, *Les Choses de la vie*. **Award:** César awards for *Barocco* and *Le Juge et l'assassin*, 1976.

Films as Composer:

1970   *Les Choses de la vie (The Things of Life)* (Sautet); *La Liberté en croupe* (Molinaro); *Sortie de secours* (Kahane)
1971   *Max et les ferrailleurs* (Sautet); *Le Chat* (Granier-Deferre)
1972   *Le Fils* (Granier-Deferre); *Liza* (Ferreri); *Le Droit à aimer (The Right to Love)* (Le Hung)
1973   *Les Corps célestes* (Carle); *Charlie et ses deux nénettes* (Séria); *La Grande Bouffe (La Grande Abuffata; Blow-Out)* (Ferreri); *Le Train (The Train)* (Granier-Deferre)
1974   *Le Mariage à la mode* (Mardore); *La Valise* (Lautner); *Touche pas à la femme blanche* (Ferreri); *L'Horloger de Saint-Paul (The Clockmaker)* (Tavernier); *César et Rosalie* (Sautet); *Dorothea* (Fleischman); *Les Seins de glace* (Lautner); *Souvenirs d'en France* (Téchiné); *Lancelot du Lac (Lancelot of the Lake)* (Bresson); *Vincent, François, Paul ... et l'autres (Vincent, François, Paul ... and the Others)* (Sautet)
1975   *Un Divorce heureux (A Happy Divorce)* (Carlsen); *Folle à tuer* (Boisset); *Un Sac de billes* (Doillon); *Deux hommes dans la ville* (Giovanni); *La Cage* (Granier-Deferre); *Pas de problèmes* (Lautner); *Les Galettes de Pont Aven* (Séria)
1976   *Barocco* (Téchiné); *Juge Fayard dit le sheriff* (Boisset); *Le Juge et l'assassin (The Judge and the Assassin)* (Tavernier); *L'ultima donna (The Last Woman)* (Ferreri); *On aura tout vu! (The Bottom Line)* (Lautner); *La Race des ''Seigneurs'' (The ''Elite'' Group)* (Granier-Deferre); *Adieu poulet* (Granier-Deferre); *Sept morts par ordonnance* (Rouffio); *Mado* (Sautet); *Marie poupée (Marie the Doll)* (Séria); *Le Locataire (The Tenant)* (Polanski)
1977   *Le Diable, probablement (The Devil, Probably)* (Bresson); *Des enfants gâtés (Spoiled Children)* (Tavernier); *La Vie devant soi (Madame Rosa)* (Mizrahi); *Le Crabe Tambour* (Schöndörfer); *Un Taxi mauve (The Purple Taxi)* (Boisset); *Mort d'un pourri* (Lautner); *Violette et François (Violette and François)* (Rouffio)
1978   *Morte di un operatore (The Death of a Corrupt Man)* (Rosati); *Rêve de singe* (Ferreri); *Une Histoire simple* (Sautet); *Ciao maschio (Bye Bye Monkey)* (Ferreri); *La Clef sur la porte (The Key Is in the Door)* (Boisset); *Passe-Montagne (Mountain Pass)* (Stevenin); *Le Sucre (The Sugar)* (Rouffio); *Les Soeurs Brontë (The Brontë Sisters)* (Téchiné)

1979   *Tess* (Polanski); *Flic ou voyou (Cop or Hood)* (Lautner); *Le Toubib (The Medic)* (Granier-Deferre); *Chiedo asilo (My Asylum)* (Ferreri); *L'Adolescente (The Adolescent Girl)* (Moreau)
1981   *Il faut tuer Birgitt Haas (Birgitt Haas Must Be Killed)* (Heynemann); *Ghost Story* (Irvin); *Cher inconnue (I Sent a Letter to My Love)* (Mizrahi); *Beaupère* (Blier); *La Guerre du feu (The Quest for Fire)* (Annaud); *Coup de touchon (Clean Slate)* (Tavernier); *Storia di ordinaria follia (Tales of Ordinary Madness)* (Ferreri); *Choix des armes (Choice of Arms)* (Corneau)
1982   *L'Etoile du nord* (Granier-Deferre)
1983   *Garçon!* (Sautet); *My Other ''Husband''* (Lautner); *Lovesick* (Brickman); *J'ai épousé une ombre (I Married a Shadow)* (Davis)
1985   *Le Cowboy; Devil in the Flesh; Harem* (A. Joffé); *Joshua Then and Now* (Kotcheff); *L'Homme aux yeux d'argent* (Granier-Deferre); *Hors-la-loi* (Davis); *Mon beau-frere a tué ma soeur; Rendezvous; La Tentation d'Isabelle* (Doillon)
1986   *Cours privé* (Granier-Deferre); *L'Etat de grace* (Rouffio); *Every Time We Say Goodbye* (Mizrahi); *Le Lieu du crime (Scene of the Crime)* (Téchiné); *The Manhattan Project* (Brickman); *Pirates* (Polanski); *Sincerely Charlotte* (C. Huppert); *La Puritaine* (Doillon)
1987   *Comédie! (Comedy!)* (Doillon); *De guerre lasse; Les Deux Crocodiles* (Seria); *Ennemis intimes* (Amar); *Funny Boy* (Le Hemonet); *Les Innocents* (Téchiné); *L'Eté dernier à Tangier* (Arcady); *La Maison assassinée* (Lautner); *Les Mois d'avril sont meurtriers* (Heynemann); *Noyade interdite* (Granier-Deferre); *Poker* (Corsini)
1988   *La Couleur du vent* (Granier-Deferre); *La Maison de jade* (N. Trintignant); *Mangeclous* (Mizrahi); *L'Ours (The Bear)* (Annaud); *Quelques jours avec moi* (Sautet); *La Travestie* (Boisset)
1989   *Chambre à part* (Cukier); *Hiver 54, l'abbé Pierre* (Amar); *L'Invité surprise* (Lautner); *Lost Angels* (Hudson); *Music Box* (Costa-Gavras); *Reunion* (Schatzberg)
1990   *Lung Ta—les cavaliers du vent* (Ponchevil le) (co); *Le Petit Criminel* (Doillon); *La Baule les pins* (Kurys); *Faux et usage de faux* (Heynemann); *Lord of the Flies* (Hook)
1991   *La Tribu (The Tribe)* (Boisset) (+ pr); *Eve of Destruction* (Gibbins); *La Vieille qui marchait dans la mer (The Old Lady Who Walked in the Sea)* (Heynemann); *L'Amérique en otage (Iran: Days of Crisis)* (Connor); *J'embrasse pas (I Don't Kiss)* (Téchiné)
1992   *Room Service* (Lautner); *L.627* (Tavernier); *La Voix (The Voice)* (Granier-Deferre); *Max et Jérémie (Max and Jeremy)*
1993   *La Petite apocalypse (The Little Apocalypse)* (Costa-Gavras); *Le Jeune Werther (Young Werther)* (Doillon); *Ma saison*

préférée (*My Favorite Season*) (Téchiné); *Poisson lune*
(*Sunfish*) (Van Effenterre); *Taxi de nuit* (*Night Taxi*) (Leroy)

1994 *Uncovered* (McBride); *La Fille de d'Artagnan* (*Revenge of the Musketeers*) (Tavernier); *Le Fils préféré* (*The Favorite Son*) (Garcia)

1995 *Dis-moi oui* (Arcady); *Nelly & Monsieur Arnaud* (Sautet)

1996 *Les Voleurs* (*The Child of the Night*) (Téchiné); *Ponette* (Doillon); *L'Insoumise* (Trintignant—for TV)

1997 *Le Rouge et le noir* (Verhaeghe—mini for TV); *Lucie Aubrac* (Berri); *K* (Arcady); *Un frère* (*Brother*) (Verheyde); *Mad City* (Costa-Gavras); *Le Bossu* (*On Guard*) (de Broca)

1998 *Alice et Martin* (Téchiné); *Je suis vivante et je vous aime* (*I'm Alive and I Love You*) (Kahane)

2000 *Là-bas . . . mon pays* (*Return to Algiers*); *Princesses*

Publications

By SARDE: articles—

Lumière du Cinéma (Paris), April 1977.
Positif (Paris), January 1979.
Ecran (Paris), 15 December 1979.
Film Français (Paris), 16 January 1981.
Cinématographe (Paris), May 1985.
Soundtrack! (Hollywood), June 1985.
Soundtrack! (Hollywood), September 1985.
Film en Televisie + Video (Brussels), April 1994.

On SARDE: articles—

Ecran (Paris), September 1975.
Cinéma Française (Paris), no. 13, 1977.
Soundtrack! (Hollywood), vol. 3, no. 2, 1977.
Soundtrack! (Hollywood), November 1977.
Film Français (Paris), 2 February 1979.
Score (Lelystad, Netherlands), June 1980.
Soundtrack! (Hollywood), vol. 4, no. 15, September 1985.
Cue Sheet (Hollywood), vol. 11, no. 1, 1995.

* * *

Philippe Sarde describes himself as a "man of the cinema." He is he first French musician to dedicate himself exclusively to composing film music. Since beginning his career in the late 1960s, he has been linked to a whole generation of directors (Sautet, Tavernier, Granier-Deferre) and has become one of France's most prolific screen composers. In 1980, he was nominated for an Academy Award for Polanski's *Tess* and has won Césars.

Sarde has composed music of an astonishingly wide range and at an amazing rate. Some critics find his body of work devoid of an overall style or personal imprint, but that is Sarde's intent. For Sarde, the music evolves from the film, from the director's idea of the film and his directorial style. Consequently, his musical compositions are as diverse as the films he scores.

Once he decided to devote his career to film music, Sarde spent ten years on film sets. He wanted to learn how the camera is used, how a lens will affect a shot, how 35- or 70-mm film will affect close-ups. He now feels that he has the necessary training to understand the technical aspects of filming and no longer needs to be on the film set

to compose the music. He prefers to start work as early as possible in the film's production and uses the director's style and vision as a point of departure in his musical process.

Collaboration with the director is of the utmost importance in Sarde's musical process. Sarde wants to know what ideas the director has about the film. If the director wants certain musical instruments or if there is a particular sound he wants to hear, Sarde will incorporate these ideas in the music. He also wants to know how the director plans to film the movie; how he intends to use such techniques as close-ups, sequences and deep focus as each technique will call for different music. How the camera is used and techniques such as zoom, tracking, or panorama will also influence the music. Sarde says he needs to imagine the whole scene to compose music that will compliment it.

Sarde combines the director's style and vision of the movie with elements of the story. If the film is set in a particular country, Sarde will incorporate local ethnic themes into the music. Sarde compares his work to that of Ravel who never wrote an original theme but readapted folklore themes to make a completely new work. *Tess* is a good example of this. Sarde used old English ballads and readapted the themes into full-blooded orchestrations. Once when the music of *Music Box* was considered to be like the music of Goldsmith, Sarde rebutted that it was essentially folkloric. However, Sarde avoids music that comes with a built-in rhetoric and emotionalism such as the music of Bruckner or Mahler. His musical world is that of Debussy, Milhaud, Poulenc and, of course, Ravel.

Sarde is able to incorporate musical forms with visual elements. For *Fort Saganne*, he felt that the script called for a concerto and he wrote one for cello and orchestra. Musically representing the desert was a problem since the director of the movie did not want to use synthetic musical effects. Sarde solved the problem by incorporating an organ into the concerto. His use of the organ evoked images of mirages and shimmering sun. In using the concerto musical form, he was able to place the organ in between the cello and the orchestra which added a valuable element to the desert scenes.

Musical themes are incorporated in films to emphasize the emotional impact of the story. In *Ghost Story*, Sarde employed a ghost theme, terror theme, and love theme. In *The Quest for Fire*, he used a love theme, action theme, and a choral chant. For *The Tenant*, the music was atonal and he included a dirge-like song. In *Les Seins des Glace*, Sarde wanted the music to cause fear and composed music that was atonal with a strange character giving a feeling of malaise.

Sarde is the quintessential film composer. For Sarde, film music must always serve the film and he has proven himself able to incorporate classical music forms, ethnic and folkloric themes and a director's vision into music that compliments and enhances a visual story.

—Renee Ward

SARGENT, Alvin

Writer. **Nationality:** American. **Career:** Writer for television; 1966—first film as writer, *Gambit*. **Awards:** Writers Guild of America WGA Screen Award—Best Comedy Adapted from Another Medium, for *Paper Moon*, 1973; Best Screenplay Based on Material from Another Medium Academy Award, Best Screenplay British Academy Award, Writers Guild of America WGA Screen Award—Best Drama Adapted from Another Medium, for *Julia*, 1977; Best Screenplay Based on Material from Another Medium Academy Award, Writers Guild of America WGA Screen Award—Best Drama Adapted from Another Medium, for *Ordinary People*, 1980; Writers Guild of America Laurel Award for Screen Writing Achievement, 1991.

Films as Writer:

1966   *Gambit* (Neame)
1968   *The Stalking Moon* (Mulligan)
1969   *The Sterile Cuckoo* (*Pookie*) (Pakula)
1970   *I Walk the Line* (Frankenheimer)
1972   *The Effects of Gamma Rays on Man-in-the-Moon Marigolds* (Newman); *Love and Pain and the Whole Damn Thing* (Pakula)
1973   *Paper Moon* (Bogdanovich)
1977   *Bobby Deerfield* (Pollack); *Julia* (Zinnemann)
1978   *Straight Time* (Grosbard)
1979   *The Electric Horseman* (Pollack)
1980   *Ordinary People* (Redford)
1987   *Nuts* (Ritt)
1988   *Dominick and Eugene* (*Nicky and Gino*) (Young)
1990   *White Palace* (Mandoki)
1991   *What about Bob* (Oz) (co-story only); *Other People's Money* (Jewison)
1992   *Hero* (Frears) (co)
1996   *Bogus* (Jewison)
1999   *Anywhere But Here* (Wang) (co)
2001   *Unfaithful*

Other Films:

1953   *From Here to Eternity* (Zinnemann) (ro as Nair, uncredited)

Publications

On SARGENT: article—

Cinéma (Paris), July/August 1973.

*   *   *

Alvin Sargent's aesthetic is firmly rooted in the best dramatic tradition of the early years of American television, the medium in which he honed his talent prior to commencing his screenwriting career in the mid-1960s. While that aesthetic cannot be labeled radical, it most certainly is progressive, intellectual, enlightened, committed—and, finally, humanist.

Sargent's works have dealt with political and societal themes: capitalist greed in *Other People's Money*, for example, or media manipulation in *Hero* (whose story he co-wrote) and judicial-system abuse in *Straight Time*. Nonetheless, he has most consistently been concerned with the effect of contemporary society on the individual. One of Sargent's dominant interests has been the structure of, and interrelationships within, the suburban American family. This is explored most notably in *Ordinary People*, the story of a controlled,

controlling upper-class clan whose material comfort belies its members' spiritual barrenness and inability to communicate meaningfully. There is the son (Timothy Hutton), withdrawn, unhappy, and fresh from a suicide attempt after the accidental drowning of his older brother; the father (Donald Sutherland), passive, solicitous, and self-deluded; and the mother (Mary Tyler Moore), an all-American beauty who, beneath her cheerfulness, is icy-cold and unforgiving.

Nuts is the story of Claudia Faith Draper (Barbra Streisand), a woman with upper-class roots who is victimized by a less-than-ideal childhood. As a result, she has become a $100-an-hour hooker; and because she has not done what ''good white girls'' are supposed to, she is labeled by her mother, stepfather, and family lawyer as insane and irresponsible for her actions. Ultimately, her role within the scenario is that of speaker of truth in a world of everyday lies and hypocrisies.

A number of Sargent's screenplays focus on complex male characters: Dustin Hoffman's ex-con in *Straight Time*; the young intern (Ray Liotta) and his childlike twin brother (Tom Hulce) in *Dominick and Eugene*; and Timothy Hutton's teenager in *Ordinary People*. But his scripts (most of which are adaptations) more consistently feature complicated, interesting female characters of all ages and classes. Joining *Nuts* is *Julia* (based on the controversial Lillian Hellman memoir *Pentimento*), the story of a pair of women of action: Hellman (Jane Fonda), who was unconventional for her time in that she funneled her creative instincts into a career as a successful dramatist and carried on a long-term romantic relationship with Dashiell Hammett (Jason Robards); and the title character (Vanessa Redgrave), Hellman's wealthy childhood friend, who becomes a political activist in Europe and involves Hellman in a scheme to smuggle bribe money into Nazi Germany.

In *Other People's Money*, a watered-down (but still-biting) version of Jerry Sterner's play, Danny DeVito's Wall Street corporate raider is contrasted to Penelope Ann Miller's equally cagey young attorney, who sets out to outmaneuver him when he becomes determined to devour a family-owned company.

Then there is *Paper Moon*, a fairytale in which a nine-year-old (Tatum O'Neal) unites with a con man (Ryan O'Neal) in Depression-era Kansas. This character is no sweet Shirley Temple, but rather a headstrong, tough-talking, cigarette-smoking scamp who loves to mug, and is determined to be corrupted. *The Sterile Cuckoo* is the coming-of-age story of Pookie (rhymes with kookie) Adams (Liza Minnelli), a brash, insecure college student. Here is one Sargent heroine who is not strong; still, she (rather than the boy with whom she falls in love) is the focus of the scenario.

Anywhere But Here is another coming-of-age tale, with the spotlight on a child and parent: Ann August (Natalie Portman), a young teenager, and her mother Adele (Susan Sarandon), who move from Wisconsin to Beverly Hills where they struggle to adapt to a new life—and clash with each other. The young characters in *Ordinary People* and *The Sterile Cuckoo* are troubled; here, the opposite is the case. Ann is settled and happy in the Midwest, and resents being needlessly uprooted by the restless, flirty Adele. In *Anywhere But Here*, the child takes on the role of the adult, while the mother acts more like the child.

Most intriguing of all is the heroine in *White Palace*, which chronicles the romantic relationship between Max Baron (James Spader), a twentysomething advertising executive with a fine education and an upper-class, liberal-elitist background, and Nora Baker (Susan Sarandon), a fortysomething waitress with limited education and a grim family history. Even though she would not know Gloria

Steinem from Gloria Jean, Nora's integrity transforms her into a feminist heroine. She has lived in the world, and she knows what she likes and wants. She, rather than he, initiates their meeting, and their first sexual activity; even though Nora falls for Max, she will not be intimidated by his background, his income, or his family. (Here again is a scenario in which the "family" stifles the individual, who must assert him or herself and break away to ensure his or her happiness.) Max may be a regal "baron" to Nora's lowly "baker," but it is he who will have to accommodate her if their relationship is to survive.

That relationship is one of instinct versus intellect, and Sargent clearly prefers that the former prevail. Even in *Julia*, whose characters are by nature intellectual, it is the passion of the creative act that sparks the communication between Hellman and Hammett; in her political activity, Julia is a creature of emotion and zeal; and Hellman's choice to act, and risk her life, on behalf of her friend is instinctual rather than rational.

This is not to say that Sargent is anti-intellectual. Rather, he is anti-intellectual hypocrisy or pomposity. Whatever their sex or class, the best Sargent characters are those who transcend the barriers of intellectual passivity and become people who act, who take stands that transcend a mere nodding of one's head in response to injustice. The upper-class patriarch in *White Palace*, who babbles on about how the working class is exploited by Republican politics as he is served dinner by a maid, is shown to be a hypocrite; Julia, who forsakes her privileged background to take political action, and pays for this with her life, is shown to be a heroine. It is the contrasting personalities of these two characters that most acutely mirror the truth of Sargent's creative sensibilities.

—Rob Edelman

SAULNIER, Jacques

Art Director. **Nationality:** French. **Born:** Paris, 8 September 1928. **Education:** Attended the Institut des Hautes Etudes Cinématographiques, 1948–49. **Career:** 1948–58—assistant art director to the directors Jean Andre, Max Douy, and Alexandre Trauner; 1958–59—co-art director with Bernard Evein. **Awards:** César award for *Providence*, 1977; *Swann in Love*, 1984.

Films as Assistant Art Director:

1954   *Le Rouge et le noir* (Autant-Lara)
1955   *Land of the Pharaohs* (Hawks); *Marguerite de la nuit* (Autant-Lara); *Les Mauvaises Rencontres*
1956   *Eléna et les hommes* (*Paris Does Strange Things*) (Renoir); *La Traversée de Paris*; *He Who Must Die*; *Sait-on jamais*
1958   *The Vikings* (Fleischer); *En cas de malheur* (*Love Is My Profession*) (Autant-Lara)

Films as Art Director:

1957   *V. Proudech* (*Liberté surveillef*) (Vloek and Aisner)
1958   *Les Amants* (*The Lovers*) (Malle) (co)
1959   *A Double Tour* (*Web of Passion*; *Leda*) (Chabrol) (co); *Les Cousins* (Chabrol) (co); *La Sentence* (Valère) (co)

1960   *La Proie pour l'ombre* (*Shadow of Adultery*) (Astruc); *Les Jeux d'amour* (*Suzanne et les roses*; *Playing at Love*) (de Broca) (co); *Le Farceur* (*The Joker*) (de Broca); *Les Scélérats* (*Torment*) (Hossein) (co)
1961   *L'Année dernière à Marienbad* (*Last Year at Marienbad*) (Resnais); *Vu de Pont* (*View from the Bridge*) (Lumet); *La Morte-Saison des amours* (*The Season for Love*) (Kast); *L'Education sentimentale* (Astruc); *La Gamberge* (Carbonnaux); *Le Petit Garcon de l'ascenseur* (Granier-Deferre); *Germinal* (Carné)
1962   *Landru* (*Bluebeard*) (Chabrol); *Du mouron pour les petits oiseaux* (Carné)
1963   *Muriel, ou le temps d'un retour* (*Muriel*) (Resnais); *La Bonne Soupe* (*How to Make a French Dish*) (Thomas); *Les Aventures de Salavin* (Granier-Deferre); *La Confession de minuit* (Granier-Deferre)
1964   *La Fabuleuse Aventure de Marco Polo* (*Marco the Magnificent*) (de la Patellière, Howard, and Christian-Jaque); *L'Echivoier de dieu* (de la Patellière)
1965   *What's New, Pussycat?* (Donner); *La Vie de château* (*A Matter of Resistance*) (Rappeneau); *La Metamorphose des cloportes* (Granier-Deferre)
1966   *La Guerre est finie* (*The War Is Over*; *Adventures in History*) (Resnais); *Mademoiselle* (*Un, deux, trois, quatre!*) (Richardson); *Le Voleur* (Malle); *Caroline Cherie* (Aurel)
1967   *Tante Zita* (Enrico)
1968   *La Prisonnière* (Clouzot); *Ho!* (Enrico)
1969   *Le Clan des siciliens* (Verneuil); *La Horse* (Granier-Deferre)
1970   *Le Chat* (Granier-Deferre)
1971   *La Veuve Coudere* (Granier-Deferre); *Le Casse* (*The Burglars*) (Verneuil)
1972   *Le Fils* (Granier-Deferre)
1973   *Le Train* (Granier-Deferre); *Le Serpent* (*The Serpent*) (Verneuil)
1974   *Stavisky* (Resnais)
1975   *French Connection II* (Frankenheimer); *La Cage* (Granier-Deferre)
1977   *Providence* (Resnais)
1980   *Mon oncle d'Amerique* (*My American Uncle*) (Resnais)
1983   *La Vie est un roman* (*Life Is a Bed of Roses*) (Resnais)
1984   *Swann in Love* (*Un Amour de Swann*) (Schlöndörff); *Les Morfalous* (Verneuil); *L?Amour à mort* (Resnais); *Le Jumeau* (Robert)
1986   *Mélo* (Resnais)
1987   *Les Exploits d'un jeune Don Juan* (Mingozzi)
1989   *L'Autrichienne* (Granier-Deferre); *I Want to Go Home* (*Je veux rentrer à la maison*) (Resnais)
1992   *Archipelago* (Granier-Deferre); *La Voix* (*The Voice*) (Granier-Deferre)
1993   *Smoking/No Smoking* (Resnais)
1997   *On connaît la chanson* (*Same Old Song*) (Resnais)

Publications

By SAULNIER: articles—

Cinématographe (Paris), no. 88, April 1983.
Positif (Paris), no. 307, September 1986.
Positif (Paris), no. 329–330, July-August 1988.

On SAULNIER: articles—

Lumière du Cinéma (Paris), no. 1, February 1977.
Film Français (Paris), no. 1710, February 1978.
Film Français (Paris), no. 2131, 6 March 1987.
Positif (Paris), January 1994.
Filmbulletin (Winterthur), vol. 36, no. 6, 1994.
Positif (Paris), December 1995.

*　　*　　*

The museum of the Cinématheque Française in Paris displays two models in its foyer as examples of contemporary film decor. That by Bernard Evein from Jacques Demy's 1988 musical *Trois places pour le 26* is a diaphanous abstraction of wires and coloured panels, typical of a designer who is less an architect than a painter. By contrast, Jacques Saulnier's design for *Mon oncle d'Amerique*, one of many Alain Resnais films he designed, is solid as a brick, a meticulous rendering of a bourgeois French apartment of the 1970s, right down to the Dubuffet art and designer rugs.

The contrast reveals the differences in style between two men who dominated French film design in the period following the *Nouvelle Vague*. Saulnier and Evein (like Resnais) graduated from the highly theoretical Institut des Haute Etudes Cinématographiques. Saulnier however went on to the Ecole des Beaux Arts, giving his talent a formal gloss it never lost, and then entered movies as assistant to Max Douy and Alexandre Trauner. Despite the striking variation in their styles, between 1958 and 1960 Saulnier and Evein worked as a team. The château of Louis Malle's *Les Amants* and the Paris interiors of Chabrol's *Les Cousins* seem mostly Saulnier's work, but Chabrol's *A double tour*, their first film in colour, includes a Japanese-style pavilion for Antonella Lualdi that may be their first true collaboration.

The team broke up with *L'Année dernière à Marienbad*, for which Evein takes the costume credit and Saulnier that for set design. Saulnier meticulously copied 18th-century decorated plaster ceilings and mirrored interiors for the film so that the hotel in some un-named resort is perfectly integrated with the raked and barbered gardens where Resnais shot his exteriors. Some found the effect claustrophobic but without this strict formal consistency *Marienbad* is unlikely to have achieved its subsequent international success. Resnais and Saulnier had created a world which fitted only these characters and this story.

Established now as a master of authentic design, Saulnier did the New York slum sets for Sidney Lumet's European production of Arthur Miller's *View from the Bridge*, then Astruc's adaptation of *L'Education Sentimentale*. Claude Chabrol's sinister *Landru* on the other hand showed the humour that was to figure occasionally in Saulnier's work during the 1970s. In telling the story of France's mass murderer of women during the First World War, Chabrol aimed for an almost playful artificiality, interwoven with reminders (*via* newsreel footage) of the trench war taking place just over the horizon. Saulnier responded with gaudy interiors in dense purples, greens and roses (colours Evein used around the same time in *Les Parapluies de Cherbourg*, an echo of their shared history). He interspersed these with reminders of Landru's trade, notably in the laboratory-like kitchen with its bare green/white walls, big stove, and coal-scuttles brimming in anticipation of the next victim. When Chabrol wanted crowd and railway station scenes beyond the scope of the budget, Saulnier also fabricated a train from puffs of smoke and suggested a busy street with a partly curtained shop window outside which a procession of ladies' hats circulated on a conveyor belt.

This subversive contrast between formal perfection and wit runs through Saulnier's career. He continued his collaboration with Resnais on films as stylistically various as *Muriel, La Guerre est finie*, the discreet but perfectly realised art deco *Stavisky*, the studiedly artificial *Providence* with its stiff interiors and blatant use of painted backdrops, *La Vie est un roman*, which amusingly integrated comic book panels into the action, *Mon oncle d'Amerique*, and Resnais' adaptations of two plays by British writer Alan Ayckbourn, *Smoking* and *No Smoking*. At the same time, he created rowdy Edwardian interiors for Malle's *Le Voleur* and plunged into art nouveau and whorehouse baroque for the Peter O'Toole/Peter Sellers comedy *What's New Pussycat?* The film was a nightmare for Saulnier, with rival egos employing the decor as a battlefield, private apartments and houses being desperately co-opted, and sets rebuilt overnight when, for instance, a distraught Paula Prentiss rejected a bathroom design because she could not stand to look at herself; it thus became the world's only bathroom without mirrors. Even so, Saulnier's use of his favourite hot purples, reds, and yellows created an effect of opulence and Parisian playfulness which producers would struggle for the next decade to match.

Saulnier's meticulousness has created problems for directors and especially cameramen. "Saulnier frequently uses sombre colours," Leon Barsacq says, "which some cameramen have been reluctant to photograph because of lighting difficulties." Such reservations did not stop producers from hiring Saulnier to bring a reassuring realism and "Hollywood Look" to such films as *Le Clan des siciliens, Le Chat, The Burglars, The Serpent*, and *French Connection II*. In them, Barsacq has said admiringly, "his rooms, ingeniously adjusted in relation to one another, are of normal dimensions, but he always manages to give them an airiness by using openings and passages." These CinemaScope thrillers set in Antibes villas and Paris apartments, interspersed with parking garages and airport lounges, sit oddly with Saulnier's work for Resnais, though there is a consistency in their realistic effect. Like his teacher Trauner, Saulnier can make an interior created under totally theatrical constraints appear as if it has been in place for centuries.

—John Baxter

SAUNDERS, John Monk

Writer. **Nationality:** American. **Born:** Hunckley, Minnesota, 22 November 1897. **Education:** Attended the University of Minnesota, St. Paul, B.A.; Oxford University (Rhodes scholar), M.A. 1923. **Military Service:** 1914–18—served in the United States Flying Corps. **Family:** Married 1) Avis Hughes, 1922 (divorced 1927); 2) the actress Fay Wray, 1927 (divorced 1939); one daughter. **Career:** Journalist with Los Angeles *Times*, 1922, New York *Tribune*, 1923; associate editor, *American Magazine*, 1924, and regular contributor to *Cosmopolitan* and *Liberty*; 1925—first film as writer, *Too Many Kisses*. **Award:** Academy Award for *The Dawn Patrol*, 1930–31. **Died:** (Suicide) in Fort Meyers, Florida, 10 March 1940.

Films as Writer:

1925   *Too Many Kisses* (Sloane); *The Shock Punch* (Sloane)
1927   *Wings* (Wellman)
1928   *The Legion of the Condemned* (Wellman); *The Docks of New York* (von Sternberg)
1929   *She Goes to War* (H. King)
1930   *The Dawn Patrol* (Hawks)
1931   *The Finger Points* (Dillon); *The Last Flight* (Dieterle); *Dirigible* (Capra) (uncredited)
1933   *The Eagle and the Hawk* (Walker); *Ace of Aces* (Ruben)
1935   *West Point of the Air* (Rosson); *Devil Dogs of the Air* (Bacon and Keighley); *I Found Stella Parrish* (LeRoy)
1938   *The Dawn Patrol* (Goulding); *A Yank at Oxford* (Conway) (story idea); *Star of the Circus* (*Hidden Menace*) (de Courville)
1939   *The Four Feathers* (Z. Korda) (uncredited)

Publications

By SAUNDERS: books—

With George Palmer, *Brain Tests*, New York, 1925.
Wings (novelization of script), New York, 1927.
Single Lady, New York, 1930.
Nikki (play), New York, 1931.

On SAUNDERS: articles—

Slide, Anthony, in *American Screenwriters*, edited by Robert E. Morsberger, Stephen O. Lesser, and Randall Clark, Detroit, Michigan, 1984.

*   *   *

The best known of John Monk Saunders's contributions to the cinema is the original story for the first Academy Award winner for Best Picture, *Wings*. This drama of comradeship between two members of the Aviation Section of the Signal Reserve Corps during the First World War is a film which both glorifies war and also depicts its horror. It is a pacifist film which is not overtly pacifist. As *Wings* very clearly and skillfully illustrates, Saunders never—thankfully—lived up to his claim that "Action is the thing" in screenwriting. Certainly there is plenty of the latter, but *Wings* also examines the emotional relationship between two men. Both love the same woman, but, ultimately, they love each other more.

Wings is the quintessential John Monk Saunders story, based on an unpublished novel of his, and it led to the writer's creating a succession of dramas dealing with flying and the First World War, none of which had quite the same intensity as *Wings* (*The Legion of the Condemned*, *The Dawn Patrol*, *West Point of the Air*, and *Devil Dogs of the Air*).

The later lives of First World War pilots was the basis for Saunders's most highly personal film project, *The Last Flight*. It is based on a series of short stories by Saunders which appeared in

Liberty magazine, and deals with a disillusioned group of flyers failing to come to grips with their lives in postwar Paris. The central character is an eccentric and wealthy American girl, Nikki, whose favorite expression is "I'll take vanilla," and who makes ridiculous statements, such as claiming that she can walk faster in red shoes. The Nikki character is obviously based on Saunders's second wife, the actress Fay Wray, and, indeed, she starred in a short-lived stage musical based on the stories, titled *Nikki* and produced in 1931.

Aside from reflecting some of the disillusionment which Saunders must have felt with his own life, *The Last Flight* illustrates his deep affection for Wray (she starred in one of his films, *The Legion of the Condemned*, and in two films to which he made uncredited contributions, *The Four Feathers* and *Dirigible*). The break-up of the couple's marriage obviously had such a profound effect on Saunders that eventually he committed suicide.

Despite the overwhelming theme of flying in Saunders's screenplays, it should not be overlooked that he contributed the original story for Josef von Sternberg's first major film, *The Docks of New York*, and utilized knowledge of his early career as a journalist in *The Finger Points*, and of Oxford University, from which he graduated, in *A Yank at Oxford*.

—Anthony Slide

SAVINI, Tom

Makeup Artist and Makeup Effects Designer. **Nationality:** American. **Born:** Pittsburgh, Pennsylvania, 3 November 1946. **Family:** Married Nancy Hare, 1984. **Education**: Journalism major at Carnegie-Mellon University, Pittsburgh. **Career:** Actor in North Carolina; 1976—first association with the director George A. Romero who cast him in *Martin*; television work includes episodes of *Tales from the Dark Side*.

Films as Makeup Artist and/or Makeup Effects Designer Actor:

1972   *Deathdream* (*Dead of Night*) (Clark)
1973   *Deranged* (Gillen/Ormsby)
1976   *Martin* (Romero) (+ role as Arthur)
1978   *Effects* (Nelson) (+ role as Nicky); *Dawn of the Dead* (Romero) (+ role as Motorcycle Rider)
1980   *Maniac* (Lustig) (+ role as Disco Boy); *The Awakening* (Russo); *Friday the Thirteenth* (Cunningham); *The Burning* (Maylam)
1981   *Eyes of a Stranger* (Wiederhorn); *Prowler* (Zito); *Friday the Thirteenth, Part II* (Miner); *Midnight* (Russo); *Nightmare* (Scavolini)
1982   *Creepshow* (Romero) (+ role as Garbage Man #2); *Alone in the Dark* (Sholder)
1984   *Maria's Lovers* (Konchalovsky); *Friday the Thirteenth: The Final Chapter* (Zito)
1985   *Day of the Dead* (Romero); *Invasion USA* (Zito)
1986   *The Texas Chainsaw Massacre Part 2* (Hooper)
1987   *Creepshow II* (Gormick) (+ role as The Creep)
1988   *Monkey Shines* (Romero)

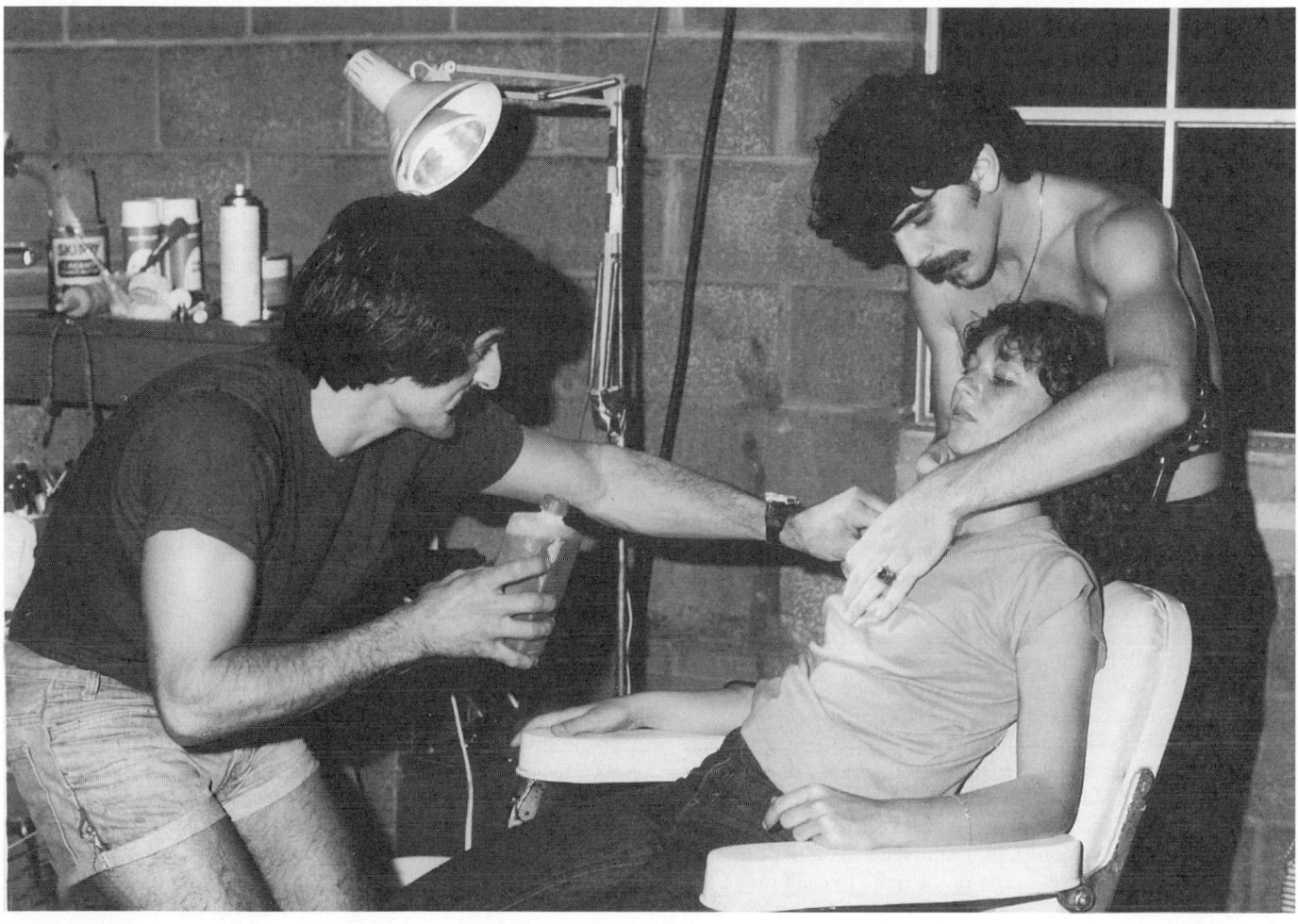

Tom Savini (left)

1989   *Red Scorpion* (Zito)
1990   *Due occhi diabolici* (*Two Evil Eyes*; *The Facts in the Case of
            M*; *Valdemar*; *The Black Cat*; *Edgar Allan Poe*) (Romero,
            Argento)
1991   *Bloodsucking Pharoahs in Pittsburgh* (Smithee/Tschetter)
1993   *Trauma* (Argento); *Heartstopper* (Russo)
1994   *Killing Zoe* (Avary); *Necronomicon* (Gans/Kaneko)
1995   *The Stitch* (Avary—for TV)
1996   *The Assassination File* (Harrison—for TV) (+ role as Chemi-
            cal Weapons Engineer)
1998   *Cutting Moments* (Buck); *Claustrophobia* (+ d, role)
1999   *Cold Hearts* (Masciantonio)

Other Films:

1981   *Knightriders* (Romero) (role as Morgan)
1990   *Night of the Living Dead* (d)
1992   *Innocent Blood* (Landis) (role as News Photographer)
1995   *The Demolitionist* (Kurtzman) (role as Roland)
1996   *From Dusk Till Dawn* (Rodriguez) (role as Sex Machine)
1997   *Eyes Are Upon You* (Goldberg) (role as Eddie Rao); *Wishmaster*
            (Kurtzman) (role as Pharmacist Helper)

Publications

By SAVINI: books—

Bizarro, New York, 1983.
*Grand Illusions: A Learn-by Example Guide to the Art and Technique
    of Special Make-up Effects from the Films of Tom Savini*, Pitts-
    burgh, 1993.

By SAVINI: articles—

Segnocinema (Vicenza), March 1982.
Écran fantastique (Paris), no. 33, April 1983.
Time Out (London), 22 September 1993.

On SAVINI: books—

McCarty, John, in *Splatter Movies: Breaking the Last Taboo of the
    Screen*, New York, 1984.
Russo, John A., *Making Movies*, New York, 1989.
Wiater, Stanley, *Dark Visions: Conversations with the Masters of the
    Horror Film*, New York, 1992.
Brown, Paul, and Nigel Burrell, *Tom Savini: The Wizard of Gore*,
    Mark V. Zeising Publisher, n.d.

On SAVINI: articles—

Film Comment (New York), vol. 17, no. 4, July-August 1981.
Starburst (London), no. 47, 1982.
Écran fantastique (Paris), no. 24, May 1982.
Cinéfantastique (New York), vol. 21, no. 3, December 1990.

*   *   *

Tom Savini, a makeup artist who specializes in special effects scenes of bodily disfigurement and mutilation, has (for better or worse) played a major role in the development of the modern horror film. It was his innovative work in prosthetics and latex, alongside that of other makeup effects designers such as Rick Baker and Rob Bottin, which at the end of the 1970s assisted at the unholy birth of what has come to be known in critical circles and the fan press as the "splatter movie." This is a form of horror film which brushes aside the Manichean struggles between Good and Evil which had characterized earlier horror films, offering instead a fascination with the impact of violence on the human body. In splatter movies, objects of violence which were usually hidden from view—most notably, the internal organs—are displayed to the film audience in graphic and unforgiving detail.

Savini worked for three years as a combat photographer in Vietnam, and it was there that he first encountered the scenes of violent death which he would later recreate on film. "[In Vietnam], I almost stepped on an arm once," he says. "A Viet Cong was shot by a buddy of mine and when he fell, a grenade he'd had primed under his armpit went off and just blew him to smithereens. I saw a lot of grisly stuff all right, and my stuff in films has been pretty grisly. If I've got anything of a reputation at all, I'm probably notorious for how *real* my stuff looks . . . well, most of the time. I would say in that respect, the realism of my stuff, the grisliness, the *anatomical* correctness of it probably does come from that experience. But I don't want to give the impression that I do this work because of my Vietnam experience. Not at all. It's all in the script. Somebody writes this stuff."

Returning to America, he pursued journalism then an acting career for a short while before following in the footsteps of his idol, the silent screen star and makeup master Lon Chaney, and moved into the area of effects makeup for the stage, then the screen. He quickly made a name for himself through his involvement with a number of major (and quite a few minor) horror films, including *Friday the 13th* and, perhaps most significantly, a series of films for director George Romero—*Martin, Dawn of the Dead, Creepshow, Day of the Dead, Monkey Shines.*

It can be argued that Savini, through his effects work, offers us a distinctly modern view of an alienated human existence. The assaulted bodies he creates are all flesh, and no spirit. They function as mere containers of organs and liquid substances, as sites upon which various makeup skills and techniques can be unleashed. Like Rick Baker and Rob Bottin, Savini has acquired a substantial cult following, most notably in the pages of *Fangoria* magazine, but also through books and videotapes detailing his work.

Savini's signature effect is the exploding head: shotgun-to-the-cranium gimmicks feature in *Maniac, The Prowler,* and *Day of the Dead.* But the importance of Romero's input to Savini's oeuvre can be gauged by comparing the uninspired decapitations and stabbings of such glumly misanthropic items as *Maniac* or *Friday the 13th* with the outrageous, transgressive "splatstick" of Romero's zombie movies—which offer a ghoul losing the top of his head to a helicopter blade like a breakfast egg, a severed head used as a bowling ball with eye-socket fingerholes, or a villain snarling "'choke on 'em'' to the zombies gobbling his entrails. Recently, his collaboration with Romero has been eclipsed by work for the Italian visionary Dario Argento, who produced *Dawn of the Dead,* directed (with Romero) the two-part *Two Evil Eyes* (for which Savini recreated Poe horrors like the naked woman bisected by a pendulum and the exhumed corpse with all its teeth plucked) and the drab decapitation-saga *Trauma* (featuring a handy noose gadget that automatically guillotines with as much resonance as an electric can-opener). His fame can be seen as part of the shift in the nature of horror to which he himself has contributed. Within this the increasing foregrounding of and fascination with special effects techniques, both in films and in horror fanzines, has made him as much a star of the genre as any actor or director. "Yes, I think the effects people *are* becoming the stars of the films," he says. "What the critics say about films like *Friday the 13th*— that they don't have much plot or characterization and are an exercise in one death after another—is absolutely true. The special effects are the stars of those movies. I can't say that [this] bothers me. But I will say that there was a magic alive in a lot of the older movies—the horror films, the swashbucklers, whatever—that we don't see today. I personally feel that it's a lot smarter to leave things to a person's imagination, let him fill things in for himself. When your mind completes something, it's much more valuable to you, I think."

Part of Savini's familiarity with audiences may also boil down to the fact that he has indeed worked as an actor—taking major supporting roles for Romero in *Martin* and *Knightriders,* enjoying himself as a monster-fighting biker dude in *Dawn of the Dead* and Robert Rodriguez's *From Dusk Till Dawn,* and playing Jack the Ripper in the made-for-video *The Ripper*—and branched into direction, with a few installments of *Tales from the Darkside* on TV and a Romero-scripted remake of Romero's seminal *Night of the Living Dead,* which surprisingly holds back on the gory make-up effects as it plays clever variations on the original film.

—Peter Hutchings, updated by Kim Newman and John McCarty

SCHAMUS, James

Producer and Writer. **Nationality:** American. **Born:** Detroit, Michigan, 7 September 1959. **Family:** Married Nancy Jean Kricorian; children: Nona Esther, Djuna Mariam. **Education:** University of California at Berkeley, A.B., 1982, M.A., 1984. **Career:** Assistant professor, Columbia University, 1991–97; associate professor, Columbia University, New York, from 1997; co-president, Good Machine, New York, from 1990. **Awards:** Brian Greenbaum award, 1994; Best Screenplay, Cannes Film Festival, for *The Ice Storm,* 1997. **Address:** Good Machine, 417 Canal Street, 4th Floor, New York, NY, 10013–1902, U.S.A.

Films as Producer:

1990   *The Golden Boat* (Ruiz)
1991   *Ambition* (Hartley); *Thank You and Good Night* (Oxenberg); *Poison* (Haynes) (exec)

1992   *Tui shou (Pushing Hands)* (Lee) (+ sc); *Warrior: The Life of Leonard Peltier* (Baer) (exec); *Swoon* (Kalin) (exec); *In the Soup* (Rockwell) (assoc); *I Was on Mars* (Levy) (line)

1993   *Hsi yen (The Wedding Banquet)* (Lee) (+ sc); *Dottie Gets Spanked* (Haynes—for TV) (coordinating)

1994   *Roy Cohn/Jack Smith* (Godmilow); *Yin shi nan nu (Eat Drink Man Woman)* (Lee) (assoc + sc); *What Happened Was. . .* (Noonan) (exec)

1995   *Sense and Sensibility* (Lee) (co-pr); *The Brothers McMullen* (Burns) (exec); *Safe* (Haynes) (exec)

1996   *She's the One* (Burns); *Walking and Talking* (Holofcener)

1997   *Arresting Gena* (Weyer) (exec); *Love God* (Grow) (exec); *The Myth of Fingerprints* (Freundlich) (exec); *Office Killer* (Sherman) (exec); *The Ice Storm* (Lee) (+ sc)

1998   *Happiness* (Solondz) (exec)

1999   *The Lifestyle* (Schisgall) (exec); *Lola and Bilidikid (Lola and Billy the Kid)* (Ataman) (exec); *Ride with the Devil* (Lee) (+ sc)

2000   *Crouching Tiger, Hidden Dragon* (Lee) (exec + sc)

Films as Writer:

2000   *X-Men* (Singer) [uncredited]

Publications

On SCHAMUS: articles—

Magnegard, C., "Hip-Mogulen," in *Chaplin* (Stockholm), vol. 34, no. 3, 1992.

Alexander, M., "Above the Line," in *Variety* (New York), vol. 354, no. 4, 28 February 1994.

*   *   *

As an associate professor of film at Columbia University, James Schamus has taught everything from film theory, to the films of Carl Theodor Dreyer, to popular genres like film noir and the Western. The diversity of his interests in the world of cinema is equally apparent in the work he has done within the industry. Although Schamus has become a leading figure in the world of independent film, he has also worked steadfastly to bring such independent film to a larger audience, often working with major studios and distributors to get small, and at times markedly experimental independents to as many screens as possible. And as both a producer and a writer, Schamus has helped to prove the commercial and popular viability of independent film.

In 1991, James Schamus began the production company Good Machine with Ted Hope, with whom he had worked with as a freelance script reader for New Line Cinema. Among the company's first productions was Ang Lee's *Tui shou (Pushing Hands)* which failed to gain U.S. distribution. But when Lee's next picture, *His yen (The Wedding Banquet)*, grossed $7.5 million in the United States and more than four times that in foreign revenues, Schamus and Hope learned the importance of the foreign market, especially in the marketing of independent film. Since then, Good Machine, Intl., has become a significant force in international sales and marketing of films, even becoming October Film's agent for foreign sales. The revenue from these sales has allowed Schamus and Good Machine to make further inroads into Hollywood filmmaking, and has given them the clout to back adventurous and sometimes controversial pictures like Todd Haynes' *Poison*, Tom Kallin's *Swoon*, and Todd Solondz's *Happiness*. As much success as earlier productions may have had, Ang Lee's 1995 film version of *Sense and Sensibility* was a watershed for Good Machine and co-producer Schamus, garnering seven Academy Awards nominations (including a win for Emma Thompson's screenplay adaptation of the Jane Austen novel) and a greater commercial viability for the production company. The door was now open for Schamus and Good Machine to produce major studio films like *The Ice Storm* and *Ride with the Devil*, which while unquestionably Hollywood films, still maintain an element of the independent spirit by which Schamus made his name.

As a writer, Schamus has collaborated extensively with Ang Lee in creating uncommonly quiet films. In an industry wherein flamboyance often seems the norm, Schamus's films demonstrate a striking understatement. His first three writing credits, which he shares with Lee, were the "Taiwanese trilogy" consisting of *Tui shou (Pushing Hands)*, *His yen (The Wedding Banquet)*, and *Yinshi nan nu (Eat Drink Man Woman)*. Each of these films explores the breakdown of communications that occurs between both generations and cultures. Consequently the scripts are spare, letting silence speak as much as any words might. Schamus continued with a variation on this theme with his next screenplay, an adaptation of Rick Moody's novel *The Ice Storm* which likewise deals with intergenerational alienation, this time in the 1970s in New Canaan, Connecticut. In this, Schamus and Lee's first American collaboration, however, the taciturn characters are replaced by characters who generally speak incessantly, but without saying much of substance. Still, Schamus skillfully uses silence. The last fifteen minutes of the film are, in fact, virtually silent, and it is only when this silence becomes paramount to the rhetoric of politics and pop psychology that the familial bonds of the movie's characters are reaffirmed.

Schamus followed up *The Ice Storm* with two more Lee directed scripts, the Civil War epic *Ride with the Devil*, based on Daniel Woodrell's novel *Woe to Live On*, and the martial arts period piece *Crouching Tiger, Hidden Dragon*. These films mark a departure for both Schamus and Lee, demonstrating an action aesthetic unhinted at in their earlier collaborations. But in *Ride with the Devil*, impressive as the action scenes may be, it is their contrast with the quieter moments of interpersonal communication, written in striking period-accurate dialect, which truly drive the emotional impact of the film. Ultimately, the mixture of tones in the picture might well be reflective of the entirety of James Schamus's work in film, which seeks to balance the world of independent film with the business of Hollywood.

—Marc Oxoby

SCHARY, Dore

Producer and Writer. **Nationality:** American. **Born:** Newark, New Jersey, 31 August 1905. **Education:** Central High School, Newark. **Family:** Married Miriam Svet, 1932; three children. **Career:**

Dore Schary

1926–32—stage director, actor, publicity director, and newspaper writer; 1933–37—film writer for Paramount, Warner Bros., and Columbia; 1938–41—writer, MGM; 1943–46—producer, David O. Selznick Productions; 1948–56—vice president in charge of production and studio operations, MGM; 1959—founded Schary Productions and Schary Television Productions. **Award:** Academy Award for script of *Boys Town*, 1938. **Died:** New York City, 7 July 1980.

Films as Writer:

1933   *Fury of the Jungle* (Neill); *Fog* (Rogell); *He Couldn't Take It* (Nigh)
1934   *The Most Precious Thing in Life* (Hillyer); *Let's Talk It Over* (Neumann); *Murder in the Clouds* (Lederman); *Young and Beautiful* (Santley)
1935   *Mississippi* (Sutherland); *The Raven* (Landers); *Chinatown Squad* (Roth); *Storm over the Andes* (Cabanne); *Red Hot Tires* (Lederman); *The Silk Hat Kid* (Humberstone); *Your Uncle Dudley* (Forde)
1936   *Timothy's Quest* (Barton); *Her Master's Voice* (Santley)
1937   *Outcast* (Florey); *Mind Your Own Business* (McLeod); *Girl from Scotland Yard* (Vignola); *Big City* (Borzage)
1938   *Boys Town* (Taurog)
1940   *Behind the News* (Santley); *Broadway Melody of 1940* (Taurog); *Young Tom Edison* (Taurog); *Edison the Man* (Brown)
1941   *Married Bachelor* (Buzzell)
1950   *It's a Big Country* (Thorpe and others)

Films as Producer (Personally Supervised):

1941   *The Penalty* (Bucquet)
1942   *Joe Smith, American* (Thorpe); *Nazi Agent* (Dassin); *Grand Central Murder* (Simon); *Northwest Rangers* (Newman); *Kid Glove Killer* (Zinnemann); *Sunday Punch* (Miller); *The War Against Mrs. Hadley* (Bucquet); *A Yank on the Burma Road* (Seitz); *Fingers at the Window* (Lederer); *The Omaha Trail* (Buzzell); *Journey for Margaret* (Van Dyke); *Eyes in the Night* (Zinnemann); *The Affairs of Martha* (Dassin); *Apache Trail* (Thorpe)
1943   *Harrigan's Kid* (Reisner); *Lassie Come Home* (Wilcox); *Pilot No. 5* (Sidney); *Bataan* (Garnett); *A Stranger in Town* (Rowland); *Lost Angel* (Rowland); *Young Ideas* (Dassin)
1944   *The Youngest Profession* (Buzzell)
1945   *I'll Be Seeing You* (Dieterle)
1946   *The Spiral Staircase* (Siodmak); *Till the End of Time* (Dmytryk)
1947   *The Bachelor and the Bobby-Soxer* (Reis); *The Farmer's Daughter* (Potter); **Crossfire** (Dmytryk)
1948   **They Live By Night** (Ray); *The Boy with the Green Hair* (Losey); *Mr. Blandings Builds His Dream House* (Potter)
1949   *Battleground* (Wellman)
1950   *Walk Softly Stranger* (Stevenson); *The Next Voice You Hear* (Wellman); *Go for Broke* (Pirosh)
1951   *Westward the Women* (Wellman)
1952   *Plymouth Adventure* (Brown); *Washington Story* (Pirosh)
1953   *Take the High Ground* (Brooks); *Dream Wife* (Sheldon)
1955   *Trial* (Robson); *Bad Day at Black Rock* (J. Sturges)
1956   *The Last Hunt* (Brooks); *The Swan* (C. Vidor); *Battle of Gettysburg* (doc) (+ sc)
1957   *Designing Woman* (Minnelli)
1959   *Lonelyhearts* (Donehue) (+ sc)
1960   *Sunrise at Campobello* (Donehue) (+ sc)
1963   *Act One* (+ d + sc)

Publications

By SCHARY: books—

With Charles Palmer, *Case History of a Movie*, New York, 1950.
Sunrise at Campobello (play), New York, 1958.
The Highest Tree (play), New York, 1961.
For Special Occasions (autobiography), New York, 1962.
With Sinclair Lewis, *Storm in the West* (script), New York, 1963.
Heyday: An Autobiography, Boston, Massachusetts, 1979.

By SCHARY: article—

American Film (Washington, D.C.), October and November 1979.

On SCHARY: book—

Schary Zimmer, Jill, *With a Cast of Thousands*, New York, 1963.

On SCHARY: articles—

Films in Review (New York), November 1950.
Lambert, Gavin, in *Sight and Sound* (London), March 1951.
Ross, Lillian, in *Picture*, New York, 1952.

Rosenberg, Bernard, and Harry Silverstein, in *The Real Tinsel*, New York, 1970.
Take One (Montreal), July 1979.
The Annual Obituary 1980, New York, 1981.
Cinématographe (Paris), May 1984.
Carty, Brad, "*Sunrise at Campobello*," in *Wilson Library Bulletin*, May 1990.
Linden, Sheri, in *Variety* (New York), 17 March 1997.

*   *   *

Dore Schary was the head of production at MGM from 1948 until 1956. As such he was ultimately responsible for such famous films as *Singin' in the Rain*, *On the Town*, *Adam's Rib*, *Father of the Bride*, *The Asphalt Jungle*, *Ivanhoe*, *The Band Wagon*, *Kiss Me Kate*, and *Seven Brides for Seven Brothers*. While this may not have been MGM's Golden Age in terms of making money, if for nothing else Schary will be remembered as the head of the studio at which Arthur Freed's wonderful musicals were created. Schary let Freed loose to work with Stanley Donen and Gene Kelly to create some of the greatest film musicals Hollywood has ever known.

But that is not to say the Schary-led MGM did not keep an eye on the box office. Indeed in the early 1950s, the beginning of his tenure, MGM seemed to do just fine. While Schary was in charge MGM produced the second biggest money maker of 1950, *Battleground*, the second biggest money maker of 1951, *Showboat*, and the second biggest box-office hit of 1952, *Quo Vadis*. Unfortunately after that the totals were not as good. Schary was fired in November 1956.

The problem was that Schary was never fully in charge and thus did not get the credit he deserved. Louis B. Mayer fought Schary's projects until he was let go in 1951. Nicholas M. Schenck, long-time boss in New York, failed to help Schary with the conversion to widescreen technology in the 1950s. Schenck retired in 1956. MGM would not adapt, and thus never was able to return to the glory days of the 1930s. Unfortunately for Schary he had to captain a ship that was sinking.

In retrospect it always seemed odd that Schary, a former screenwriter and self-professed liberal supporter of message movies, ever got as far as he did. Indeed, his initial success in Hollywood came at MGM with small films about smalltown America. He helped write *Boys Town*, starring Spencer Tracy and Mickey Rooney, and *Young Tom Edison*, with Rooney reaching the peak of his popularity.

These films earned Schary his spurs as a producer. He did some B-films for MGM, and helped David O. Selznick with *The Spiral Staircase* starring Rhonda Fleming and George Brent and *The Farmer's Daughter* starring Loretta Young. He also helped run RKO for Howard Hughes for a short time.

Once the MGM experience was over Schary returned to what he did best, the creation of certain pet projects. To many he will always be best known for *Sunrise at Campobello* in both its play and movie form. He not only produced both versions, he also wrote the play. Yet surprisingly, considering all his experience in Hollywood, Schary himself never supervised a movie of lasting importance. He will always best be remembered for his tenure at RKO and MGM when many an interesting film came from those working for him.

—Douglas Gomery

SCHENCK, Joseph and Nicholas

JOSEPH. Producer. **Nationality:** American. **Born:** Rybinsk, Russia, 25 December 1878; emigrated to the United States with his family, 1893. **Family:** Married the actress Norma Talmadge, 1916 (divorced 1934). **Career:** 1919—left Loew's to become independent producer; 1924—chairman of the board of United Artists; 1933—co-founded, with Darryl F. Zanuck, 20th Century Pictures; 1935—20th Century merged with Fox; 1941—resigned after being sentenced to a year in prison for tax offenses (served four months), then executive producer with the company. **Awards:** Special Academy Award, 1952. **Died:** 22 October 1961.

NICHOLAS. Producer. **Nationality:** American. **Born:** Rybinsk, 14 November 1881; emigrated to the United States, 1893. **Family:** Married Pansy Wilcox, three daughters. **Career:** 1919—became chief lieutenant in charge of Loew's theaters; 1924—vice president and general manager of Loew's; 1927—president of Loew's Inc. on Marcus Loew's death; 1956—resigned. **Died:** Of a stroke in Miami, Florida, 5 March 1969.

After Joseph worked his way up from being an errand boy, the brothers acquired drug stores in New York; 1908—opened amusement park, Fort George, New York; 1912—bought Palisades Amusement Park, Fort Lee, New Jersey; partnered Marcus Loew in movie theater chain (to become MGM).

Films as Producer and Executive Producer—Joseph:

1917   *Butcher Boy*; *Panthea*
1918   *The Forbidden City* (Franklin); *Salome* (Edwards)
1919   *The Way of a Woman* (Leonard)
1920   *The Right of Way* (Dillon)
1921   *The Passion Flower* (Brenon); *Lessons in Love* (Withey); *The Sign on the Door* (Brenon); *Mama's Affair* (Fleming); *Wedding Bells* (Withey); *The Wonderful Thing* (Brenon); *Woman's Place* (Fleming); *Love's Redemption* (Parker)
1922   *Polly of the Follies* (Emerson); *Smilin' Through* (Franklin); *The Primitive Lover* (Franklin); *The Eternal Flame* (Lloyd); *East Is West* (Franklin); *Cops* (Keaton)
1923   *Within the Law* (Lloyd); *Our Hospitality* (Keaton and Blystone); *Ashes of Vengeance* (Lloyd); *The Dangerous Maid* (Heerman); *Three Ages* (Keaton and Cline); *The Voice from the Minaret* (Franklin); *The Song of Love* (Franklin and Marion)
1924   *The Goldfish* (Storm); *The Only Woman* (Olcott); *Secrets* (Borzage); *Sherlock, Jr.* (Keaton); *The Navigator* (Crisp and Keaton); *Her Night of Romance* (Franklin)
1925   *The Lady* (Borzage); *Learning to Love* (Franklin); *Seven Chances* (Keaton); *Graustark* (Buchowetzki); *Her Sister from Paris* (Franklin); *Go West* (Keaton)
1926   *Kiki* (Brown); *Battling Butler* (Keaton); *The Duchess of Buffalo* (Franklin)

Nicholas Schenck (right) with Franklin Delano Roosevelt and Basil O'Connor

1927   ***The General*** (Keaton and Bruckman); *Venus of Venice* (Neilan); *Breakfast at Sunrise* (St. Clair); *Camille* (Niblo); *College* (Horne); *Sorrell and Son* (Brenon); *The Dove* (West)

1928   *Steamboat Bill, Jr.* (Reisner); *The Woman Disputed* (H. King and Taylor); *The Battle of the Sexes* (Griffith)

1929   *Lady of the Pavements* (Griffith); *Alibi* (West); *Eternal Love* (Lubitsch); *New York Nights* (Milestone)

1930   *Be Yourself!* (Freeland); *The Bad One* (Fitzmaurice); *One Romantic Night* (Stein); *The Lottery Bride* (Stein); *Puttin' on the Ritz* (Sloman); *Lummox* (Brenon); *Abraham Lincoln* (Griffith); *Du Barry—Woman of Passion* (Taylor); *The Bat Whispers* (West)

1936   *As You Like It* (Czinner) (co)

Publications

On SCHENCK (Joseph): articles—

Zierold, Norman, in *The Moguls*, New York, 1969.
Cinématographe (Paris), May 1984.

On SCHENCK (Nicholas): articles—

Giles, D., "The Ghost of Thalberg: MGM 1946–1951," in *Velvet Light Trap* (Austin), no. 18, Spring 1978.

*   *   *

No two siblings ever acquired more power in the American film industry than the brothers Schenck. One might make the case for the brothers Warner, but in their heyday Joseph Schenck functioned as the chief operating officer of Twentieth Century-Fox while his younger brother Nicholas lorded over the Loew's, Inc. empire, that had as one subsidiary, Metro-Goldwyn-Mayer, the most famous moviemaking operation in the world. The Warners may have had a mighty empire, but the Schencks ran two.

Joseph Schenck was the more famous of the two, as the mentor of noted movie stars from Buster Keaton to Marilyn Monroe. He first entered independent film production in the 1910s, from a base in the vaudeville industry. (Indeed, both Schenck brothers began as assistants to Marcus Loew.) By the early 1920s Joseph began to manage the careers and produce the films of Roscoe "Fatty" Arbuckle,

Buster Keaton, and the Talmadge sisters, one of whom he married. Since United Artists was the company through which many of these stars distributed their films, Joseph Schenck became the head of the then floundering company in the mid-1920s and therefore one of the more powerful studio heads based in Hollywood.

Joseph was known widely to the general public as spokesman and co-founder of the Academy of Motion Picture Arts and Sciences. But for pure economic power, in the 1920s, his brother, Nicholas, had much, much more economic might. Metro-Goldwyn-Mayer, with its internationally famous symbol of a roaring ''Leo the Lion,'' stood for a more famous studio than United Artists. But in a business sense MGM simply functioned as one successful unit in a larger enterprise, Loew's Inc., a fully integrated movie company, controlling not only a movie studio, but also a network for international distribution, and a highly profitable theater chain.

Nicholas Schenck ran a tight corporate empire from his office high atop the Loew's State Theater building in the heart of Times Square in New York City. Known as ''the General,'' Nicholas Schenck took over from founder Marcus Loew in the days just before the coming of sound. A trusted team of assistants, many of whom remained loyal to ''the General'' for almost 30 years, executed his every order. Louis B. Mayer, head of production at the Hollywood lot, may have been more famous to the public at large, but he did not execute any more than the most trivial decision without first checking with ''the General'' in New York.

Loew's Inc.'s longtime fiscally conservative business practices provided the company with few costly mortgages during the Great Depression, and thus Loew's Inc. never experienced any of the red ink its competitors did during that economic calamity. During the early 1930s Loew's Inc. stood at the top of the world's movie business. Indeed MGM's very method of film production reflected Schenck's conservative business philosophy. Schenck played it close to the vest. During the early 1930s the studio created only top-drawer feature films as well as distributing high-class series from the Hal Roach studio (short subjects), and the Hearst enterprises (newsreels).

One Schenck brother always sought to help the other. In the early 1930s Joseph Schenck grew tired of bickering with the founding partners of United Artists, and created his own production company Twentieth Century Pictures, with partner Darryl F. Zanuck. This he did with the financial backing of Loew's Inc. In 1935 the ailing Fox film company sought out new management, and merged with Twentieth Century Pictures to bring Joseph Schenck and Zanuck on board. To help brother Joseph take over Fox, Nicholas Schenck put up monies from Loew's and his own personal fortune.

Thereafter, as Zanuck handled the chief of production chores at the new Twentieth Century-Fox, Joseph Schenck took up the role his brother had long established at Loew's, operating as chief executive officer, always from behind the scenes, hidden from public view. Joseph Schenck coordinated production with distribution and ran Twentieth Century-Fox's chain of theaters.

The two Schencks would have remained beloved figures had they retired in the late 1940s. Instead, both hung on in the movie business until the changing economic climate of the 1950s made the methods that they had employed for nearly 30 years obsolete. With new audiences and television as a serious competitor, the Schencks lost their positions of power. Joseph never gave up and during the 1950s plunged again into independent production with Todd-AO business. Nicholas Schenck was forced to retire in 1956 after a bitter proxy battle for the very corporation many considered his brainchild. It is

unfortunate that with their ignominious endings, neither is granted the praise for helping build Hollywood into the most powerful film business in the world during the 1930s and 1940s.

—Douglas Gomery

SCHIFRIN, Lalo

Composer. **Nationality:** Argentinian. **Born:** Buenos Aires, 21 June 1932. **Education:** Attended Paris Conservatoire; studied the violin; also studied with Juan Carlos Paz and Messiaen. **Career:** Organized his own jazz group; arranger for Zavier Cugat; worked with Dizzy Gillespie in the United States; composer for films from 1964, and for TV series *The Partners*, 1971–72, *Planet of the Apes*, 1974, *Petrocelli*, 1974, *Bronk*, 1975–76, *Starsky and Hutch*, 1975–79, and *Most Wanted*, 1976–77, the theme-songs for many series (including *Mission Impossible*), and the mini-series *Princess Daisy*, 1983, *Hollywood Wives*, 1985, and *A.D.*, 1985; also composer for orchestra and jazz groups; has taught composition, University of California, Los Angeles. **Awards:** Grammy Award for Best Original Score Written for a Motion Picture or Television Show, for *Mission: Impossible*, 1966; Imagen Foundation Lifetime Achievement Award, 1999.

Lalo Schrifin

Address: 710 North Hillcrest Road, Beverly Hills, California 90210, U.S.A.

Films as Composer:

1964   *Rhino!* (Tors); *See How They Run* (Rich); *Les Félins* (*The Love Cage*; *Joy House*) (Clement)

1965   *Once a Thief* (Nelson); *The Cincinnati Kid* (Jewison); *The Liquidator* (Cardiff); *Dark Intruder* (Hart)

1966   *I Deal in Danger* (Grauman); *Blindfold* (Dunne); *Way . . . Way Out* (Douglas); *Murderers' Row* (Levin); *The Doomsday Flight* (Graham)

1967   *The Venetian Affair* (Thorpe); *Sullivan's Empire* (Hart and Carr); *Who's Minding the Mint?* (Morris); *Cool Hand Luke* (Rosenberg); *The President's Analyst* (Flicker); *How I Spent My Summer Vacation* (Hale)

1968   *The Fox* (Rydell); *Sol Madrid* (Hutton); *Where Angels Go . . . Trouble Follows!* (Neilson); *The Brotherhood* (Ritt); *Bullitt* (Yates); *Coogan's Bluff* (Siegel); *Hell in the Pacific* (Boorman); *Deadly Roulette* (Hale); *The Rise and Fall of the Third Reich* (Kauffman); *Mission Impossible versus the Mob* (Stanley)

1969   *Che!* (Fleischer); *Eye of the Cat* (Rich); *The Young Lawyers* (Hart)

1970   *Kelly's Heroes* (Hutton); *Imago* (Bosnick); *Pussycat, Pussycat, I Love You* (Amateau); *WUSA* (Rosenberg); *I Love My Wife* (Stuart); *The Mask of Sheba* (Rich); *The Aquarians* (MacDougall)

1971   *THX 1138* (Lucas); *Pretty Maids All in a Row* (Vadim); *The Beguiled* (Siegel); *Escape* (Moxey); *Earth II* (Gries)

1972   *The Neptune Factor* (*The Neptune Disaster*) (Petrie); **Dirty Harry** (Siegel); *The Wrath of God* (Nelson); *Prime Cut* (Ritchie); *Welcome Home, Johnny Bristol* (McGowan); *Joe Kidd* (J. Sturges)

1973   *Rage* (Scott); *Magnum Force* (Post); *Enter the Dragon* (Clouse); *Charley Varrick* (Siegel); *St. Ives* (Lee Thompson); *Hunter* (Horn); *Hit* (Furie); *Harry in Your Pocket* (Geller)

1974   *Night Games* (Taylor); *Golden Needles* (Clouse)

1975   *Delancey Street: The Crisis Within* (Frawley); *Starsky and Hutch* (Shear); *The Four Musketeers* (Lester); *Foster and Laurie* (Moxey); *Guilty or Innocent: The Sam Sheppard Murder Case* (Lewis); *The Master Gunfighter* (Laughlin)

1976   *Man on a Swing* (Perry); *The Eagle Has Landed* (J. Sturges); *Sky Riders* (Hickox); *Special Delivery* (Wendkos); *Voyage of the Damned* (Rosenberg); *Brenda Starr* (Stuart); *Day of the Animals* (Girdler)

1977   *Rollercoaster* (Goldstone); *Good Against Evil* (Wendkos)

1978   *Love and Bullets* (Rosenberg); *Telefon* (Siegel); *The Manitou* (Girdler); *The Return from Witch Mountain* (Hough); *The President's Mistress* (Moxey); *The Nativity* (Kowalski); *The Cat from Outer Space* (Tokar); *Nunzio* (Williams)

1979   *Escape to Athena* (Cosmatos); *The Amityville Horror* (Rosenberg); *Institute for Revenge* (Annakin); *Boulevard Nights* (Pressman); *The Concorde—Airport '79* (*Airport '80—The Concorde*) (Rich)

1980   *Loophole* (Quested); *Brubaker* (Rosenberg); *Serial* (Persky); *The Big Brawl* (Clouse); *The Nude Bomb* (Donner); *The Competition* (Oliansky)

1981   *Buddy Buddy* (Wilder); *Caveman* (Gottlieb); *When Time Ran Out* (*Earth's Final Fury*) (Goldstone); *La pelle* (*The Skin*) (Cavani); *Las viernes de la eternidad* (*The Fridays of Eternity*) (Olivera); *Chicago Story* (London)

1982   *The Seduction* (Schmoeller); *A Stranger Is Watching* (Cunningham); *Class of 1984* (Lester); *Amityville II: The Possession* (Damiani); *Victims* (Freedman); *Fast-Walking* (Harris); *Falcon's Gold* (*Robbers of the Sacred Mountain*) (Schulz)

1983   *Starflight One: The Plane That Couldn't Land* (Jameson); *The Sting II* (Kagan); *Doctor Detroit* (Pressman); *The Osterman Weekend* (Peckinpah); *Rita Hayworth, the Love Goddess* (Goldstone); *Sudden Impact* (Eastwood)

1984   *Tank* (Chomsky); *The Mean Season* (Borsos); *Spraggue* (Elikann)

1985   *Bad Medicine* (Miller); *The New Kids* (Cunningham)

1986   *Black Moon Rising* (Cokliss); *Beverly Hills Madam* (Hart—for TV); *The Ladies Club* (A. Allen)

1987   *The Fourth Protocol* (Mackenzie); *The Silence at Bethany* (Oliansky)

1988   *Berlin Blues* (Franco); *The Dead Pool* (Van Horn); *Little Sweetheart* (Simmons—for TV); *Return From the River Kwai* (McLaglen)

1989   *Return to the River Kwai* (McLaglen)

1990   *Naked Tango* (Schrader); *Face to Face* (Antonio)

1991   *FX2: The Deadly Art of Illusion* (Franklin)

1993   *The Beverly Hillbillies* (Spheeris)

1996   *Mission: Impossible* (Bay) (theme); *Manhattan Merengue!* (Vasquez-video)

1997   *Money Talks* (Ratner)

1998   *Something to Believe In* (Hough); *Tango* (Saura); *Rush Hour* (Ratner)

2000   *Mission: Impossible II* (Woo) (theme); *Jack of All Trades*

Publications

By SCHIFRIN: articles—

In *Knowing the Score* by Irwin Bazelon, New York, 1975.
Photoplay (London), February 1977.

On SCHIFRIN: articles—

Films and Filming (London), August 1968.
Thomas, Tony, in *Music for the Movies*, South Brunswick, New Jersey, 1973.
Ecran (Paris), September 1975.
Cook, Page, "The Sound Track," in *Films in Review* (US), October 1977.
Ciné Revue (Paris), 6 April 1978.
Score (Lelystad, Netherlands), September 1979.
New Zealand Film Music Bulletin (Invercargill), February 1983.
Soundtrack! (Hollywood), June 1983.
Soundtrack! (Hollywood), September 1983.

                *   *   *

Because he has bridged so successfully the worlds of traditional and film music, Lalo Schifrin is undoubtedly the most important film composer of the post-Mancini and post-*Psycho* era. During the height of the Hollywood studio period, film underscoring was heavily indebted to Romantic, basically symphonic sources, with a pronounced emphasis on melodramatic principles, that is, the music was meant to key the emotionality of the scene (and was thus more prominent in genres, like the woman's picture, where emotionality was more at issue). Though these were "unheard melodies," to borrow Claudia Gorbman's phrase, there was no doubt that the underscoring composed and orchestrated by the Franz Waxmans and Max Steiners of the period (with often a substantial debt to Tchaichovsky or Chopin) was in fact music in the obvious, accepted sense of that term. In the fifties and sixties, however, the nature of underscoring changed as its "musical" elements became increasingly assimilated to other aspects of sound design. Henry Mancini's jazz scorings are an early example of the trend, while Bernard Herrmann's shrieking violins for the shower sequence in *Psycho* problematize the separation of music—organized sound—from other types of expressive sound effects. What is interesting, of course, is that art music of the same period was moving in more or less an identical direction, away from traditional harmonic forms of organization toward aleatory and serial approaches to the design of music.

Schifrin, the son of a concertmaster, rebelled at an early age from his father's rigid tastes (no Wagner or even Debussy allowed) and went to France to study (having won a scholarship to the prestigious Paris Conservatoire), but really in order to learn more about jazz. There Schifrin played with prominent jazz musicians such as Chet Baker, but developed eclectic tastes in modern, especially popular music. Returning to Argentina, he put together a "big band" a la Count Basie and became hugely successful. At the same time, he indulged his interests for more traditional music, writing chamber music, compositions for ballet, and even symphonies. Schifrin represented Argentina in the Third International Jazz Festival, and soon after, in 1958, moved to New York at the invitation of Dizzy Gillespie, who had heard his band during a South American tour. Schifrin played with Gillespie for three years before accepting the offer of MGM Records to begin a Hollywood career. Within a short while, he had become the most prominent and productive member of a new generation of film composers.

One of the factors contributing to his success, which is witnessed in his huge number of film credits, is that Schifrin has always accepted the subsidiary role of music within the mixed, multi-track construction of the medium. This is not to say that his musical effects, almost always an eclectic mix of techniques, genres, and modes, have not been noteworthy in themselves. In *The Hellstrom Chronicles*, for example, a pseudo-scentific jeremiad that predicts how insects will take over the earth, Schifrin used a very avant-garde mix of aleatory, electronic, and serial techniques to create music that was expressive both of the film's main characters—the unstoppable hordes of ravening insects—and the film's strident, uncomfortable message. No one who has seen and listened to the film could forget the terrifying effect created by Schifrin's loud electronic sounds, synchronized piano effects, and unpredictable moments of loud percussion. But is this music or sound effects? Schifrin and sound designers such as Walter Murch, in any event, share much in common. For *Hell in the Pacific*, an arty, "psychological" war film, Schifrin designed a sequence where the Japanese soldier marooned on a Pacific Island hears loud cicadas, which then blend into "music" (two high-pitched, very loud piccolos) that segues into more traditional scoring. Similarly, for *Bullitt* Schifrin scored the famous car chase sequence by using music—a hard-driving jazz theme—which subtly fades into more traditional sound effects—screeching tires, squealing breaks. Compare the similar uses of expressive noise employed by Murch in the sequence in *The Conversation* where the snooping detective finds the bloody traces of a murder in a hotel bathroom. The two masters of modern sound design, Murch and Schifrin, even had a chance to collaborate, on George Lucas's science fiction film *THX 1138*, which has perhaps the most complex and expressive sound of any film during the seventies.

Of course, Schifrin is also expert at less subtle kinds of scoring, particularly at composing what are now known as "action themes." His action theme scoring for the TV show *Mission: Impossible* is probably one of the most recognizable on the contemporary music scene (recently recycled for the feature film remake of the series) and it is built on a very simple theme with a prominent rhythmic structure and unusual instrumentation (very prominent bongo drums, a kind of tribute to Mancini-esque fifties jazz scorings). Though more traditional symphonic underscorers still find work in Hollywood—John Williams is by far the most successful—the kind of expressive underscoring perfected by Schifrin has defined what film music has largely become in the post-studio era. If his career has declined somewhat in the nineties, his pervasive influence on the presence of sound and music in the commercial film has not.

—R. Barton Palmer

SCHLESINGER, Leon

Producer. **Nationality:** American. **Born:** Philadelphia, 1884. **Education:** Attended local schools in Philadelphia. **Career:** Worked as an usher in Philadelphia, then in the box office of a Chicago theater, and was later appointed as its cashier; also held jobs as a press agent, agent for opera libretti, manager for road and vaudeville shows, as salesman for Metro Pictures, and various positions in the import/export aspect of the film business; 1923—came to Hollywood as west coast manager for AGFA Films; 1925—founded the Pacific Title and Art Studio, a business in which he later sold his interest; 1930—entered the cartoon business at the suggestion of Jack Warner with whom he became associated; 1934–44—produced cartoons for Warner Bros. and Vitaphone; 1944—sold out to Warner Bros.; worked briefly as a producer for Columbia Pictures. **Died:** In Los Angeles, 26 December 1949.

Publications

ON SCHLESINGER: articles—

World Encyclopedia of Cartoons, New York.

* * *

Leon Schlesinger was an important member of that group of east coast promoters, businessmen, and hustlers who transformed the American film business into a well-established, respectable, and profitable industry, with the American middle-class as its paying customers. After a number of different jobs at the margins of the industry, he found himself at the beginning of the sound era working in a field—title design—which was likely to be less lucrative now that a different kind of film was beginning to be produced. Fortunately for him, Schlesinger took friend Jack Warner's advice and became involved in animation, then a relatively new field just beginning to establish its wares—first and most important the musical cartoon—as an essential item on the theatrical bill.

Schlesinger himself was a somewhat rough customer. A devotee of racetracks and an ardent gambler, he was also interested in sports, particularly deep-sea angling, at which he excelled. Though Disney had established the popularity of animation and pioneered the methods by which a successful animation studio could be run, Schlesinger was anything but an imitator of either the Disney style, with its often saccharine appeal, or management technique; he ran his studio in a loose, good-natured, and flexible style that nurtured the talents of artists who probably would not have been happy under Disney's authoritarian rule. The Looney Tunes and Merrie Melodies cartoons he produced for Warner Bros. and others were distinctly more adult in flavor than those done by Disney. The wisecracking, often sophisticated humor of Bugs Bunny and Daffy Duck, two series which began under his direction, owe much to Schlesinger's personal style and taste. Even if he was seldom involved directly in the production of cartoons, unlike Disney, who exercised a firmer hand, Schlesinger was smart to hire and nurture the careers of artists who were able to tap into the national popular taste for almost twenty years. These included Hugh Harman, Rudolph Ising, Fritz Freleng, Bob Clampett, Robert McKimson, Tex Avery, Frank Tashlin, and Chuck Jones, all of whom were greatly influential on the development of animation in America (Tashlin even went on to become a director of note in ''live'' productions). Not all his projects enjoyed the success of the Looney Tunes and Merrie Melodies series; the *Buddy's Show Boat* series for Vitaphone was less popular.

But, even though he was never quite the creative equal of Disney, who molded his productions much more in the image of his own taste and obsessions and pushed for prestige projects such as *Fantasia*, Schlesinger must be credited with having exercised an important and formative influence on screen animated comedy.

—R. Barton Palmer

SCHNEE, Charles

Writer and Producer. **Nationality:** American. **Born:** Bridgeport, Connecticut, 6 August 1916. **Education:** Attended Yale University, New Haven, Connecticut, B.A.; Yale Law School, LL.B. **Career:** Lawyer; 1943—author of play, *Apology*; 1947—first film as writer, *I Walk Alone*; 1953–57—producer and production executive; then returned to writing. **Award:** Academy Award for *The Bad and the Beautiful*, 1952. **Died:** In 1963.

Films as Writer:

1947   *I Walk Alone* (Haskin); *Cross My Heart* (Berry)
1948   **They Live by Night** (*The Twisted Road*) (Ray); **Red River** (Hawks) (co)
1949   *Scene of the Crime* (Rowland); *Easy Living* (Tourneur)
1950   *Paid in Full* (Dieterle) (co); *The Next Voice You Hear* (Wellman); *The Furies* (A. Mann); *Right Cross* (J. Sturges); *Born to Be Bad* (Ray)
1951   *Bannerline* (Weis); *Westward the Women* (Wellman)
1952   *When in Rome* (Brown) (co); *The Bad and the Beautiful* (Minnelli)
1960   *Butterfield 8* (Daniel Mann); *The Crowded Sky* (Pevney)
1962   *Two Weeks in Another Town* (Minnelli)

Films as Producer:

1953   *Torch Song* (Walters); *Jeopardy* (J. Sturges)
1955   *The Prodigal* (Thorpe); *Trial* (Robson)
1956   *Somebody up There Likes Me* (Wise)
1957   *The Wings of Eagles* (Ford); *House of Numbers* (Rouse); *Until They Sail* (Wise)

Publications

On SCHNEE: articles—

Présence du Cinéma (Paris), June 1962.
Film Comment (New York), Winter 1970–71.
Film Comment (New York), January-February 1981.

*   *   *

Charles Schnee's early death (at the age of 47) prevented him from becoming one of Hollywood's most famous names, although his abilities as screenwriter (an Oscar-winner for *The Bad and the Beautiful*) and producer (*Somebody Up There Likes Me*, *The Wings of Eagles*) had already been proved. His relatively small list of films is distinguished enough to make a thorough analysis of his work worthwhile, but since he had only just established himself as a producer when he died, it is as a screenwriter he is best remembered.

Most of Schnee's films seem to be unselfconscious updatings of old genres, presenting the values and concerns of the postwar world. However, his scripts, by his own definition, stressed character rather than genre. Although he wrote three successful westerns (*Red River*, *The Furies*, and *Westward the Women*), his work is perhaps best grouped under the general definition of ''stories about people under the stress of transition.'' This transition might be social, physical, political, economic, or emotional, as Schnee, originally trained as a lawyer, could bring his remarkable attention to detail and keen powers of observation to many different kinds of settings. For instance, Schnee's first screenplay, *I Walk Alone*, is a look at gangsters in the nightclub business. Instead of the typical rough bootleggers of the 1930s, these hoods are big businessmen, and when one of their former group (Burt Lancaster) gets out of prison, he is clearly anachronistic in the new, more polished world of crime. He must make a transition from his old ways to the new, or die. *They Live*

Charles Schnee (left) with Ray Harryhausen

by Night presents a young outlaw, in love and on the run from the law in the tradition of Fritz Lang's *You Only Live Once*, but his problem becomes more psychological than social as he falls in love and faces a transition point in his life. In *Easy Living*, one of Jacques Tourneur's lesser-known but excellent films, Victor Mature plays an aging professional football player, a man in transition between his former fame and the need to retire and take up a simpler life. *The Next Voice You Hear* is a 1950s movie in which the postatomic world contemplates the meaning of it all as God broadcasts to the little people to warn them about their new ability to destroy all of mankind. (These people are in the biggest transition of them all.)

Schnee's best work tends to be melodrama, and even his westerns reflect that tendency. Setting aside *Red River*, which was largely written by Borden Chase, the other two Schnee westerns are films in which women are central to the story: *The Furies* and *Westward the Women*. Both are superior, underrated films with strong stories and performances, well directed by Anthony Mann and William Wellman, respectively. In the former, Barbara Stanwyck struggles to take control of her life and her inheritance, attempting to wrestle it from her more backward looking father. In the latter, a motley group of women, the downtrodden and the outcast, set out on a wagon trek west

to find new homes, new lives, and new husbands. Although both films contain conventions of the western genre, and *The Furies* is also a *film noir* and *Westward the Women* a women's film, both are clearly melodramas.

Schnee's most famous screenplay is his Oscar-winner, *The Bad and the Beautiful*. Impeccably directed by Vincente Minnelli, its story is a perfectly balanced presentation on the Hollywood collaborative force. Three artists—director, writer, and star—are carefully manipulated and controlled by a producer, who orchestrates the transitional moment in each of their lives in order to further his own career. As the film begins, he is in his own crisis of transition, and each of the three stories is told in flashback, in an attempt to convince each that the manipulation had actually been to their own advantage. Like all Minnelli films, it tends to be about art and the act of creating art, and it is unquestionably Minnelli's film. However, Schnee's contribution to both this and Minnelli's companion piece, *Two Weeks in Another Town*, cannot be discounted.

Schnee's collection of screenplays taken together seem to present the postwar world—more corporate, less individualistic, less mythic, less reassuring, and with its values all in question. Thus his stories of people in various forms of transition mark him as an important postwar talent whose best contributions may well have been ahead of him at the time of his death.

—Joanne Yeck

SCHOONMAKER, Thelma

Editor. **Nationality:** American. **Born:** 3 January 1940 in North Africa. **Education:** Attended Cornell University, New York University. **Family:** Married Michael Powell (1984; died 1990). **Career:** Met Martin Scorsese while both were students at New York University; cut Scorsese's debut feature, *Who's That Knocking at My Door?*, 1969. **Awards:** Best Film Editing Academy Award, Best Editing British Academy Award, Best Edited Feature Film American Cinema Editors Eddie, for *Raging Bull*, 1980; Best Editing British Academy Award, for *GoodFellas,* 1990.

Films as Editor:

1965   *Pages From James Joyce's Finnegan's Wake*
1968   *The Virgin President* (co)
1969   *Who's That Knocking at My Door?* (Scorsese)
1970   *Street Scenes* (Scorsese) (co) *Woodstock* (Wadleigh) (chief ed) (+ asst d)
1979   *The Kids Are Alright* (1979) (special consultant)
1980   ***Raging Bull*** (Scorsese)
1983   *The King of Comedy* (Scorsese) (+ production supervisor)
1985   *After Hours* (Scorsese)
1986   *The Color of Money* (Scorsese)
1988   *The Last Temptation of Christ* (Scorsese)
1989   "Life Lessons" ep. of *New York Stories* (Scorsese)
1990   ***GoodFellas*** (Scorsese)
1991   *Cape Fear* (Scorsese)
1993   *The Age of Innocence* (Scorsese)
1995   *Casino* (Scorsese)
1996   *Grace of My Heart* (Anders)
1997   *Kundun* (Scorsese)
1999   *Bringing Out the Dead* (Scorsese)
2000   *Gangs of New York* (Scorsese)

Other Films:

1995   *A Personal Journey with Martin Scorsese Through American Movies* (Scorsese—for TV) (doc) (supervising ed)
1998   *In Search of Kundun with Martin Scorsese* (Wilson) (doc) (editorial consultant)

Publications

By SCHOONMAKER: articles—

"Scorsese's Klipp(a)," interview with J. Aghed, in *Chaplin* (Stockholm), no. 5, 1993.
"Accents and Umlauts," interview with Louise Tanner, in *Films in Review* (Denville), March-April 1995.

"Martin Scorsese," interview with Jean-Pierre Coursodon and Michael Henry, in *Positif* (Paris), March 1996.
"Why Thelma Loves Marty. . . and Michael," interview with J. Sherlock, in *Cinema Papers* (Fitzroy, Victoria, Australia), December 1996.
"Martin Scorsese," interview with Hubert Niogret and Michael Henry, in *Positif* (Paris), May 1998.

On SCHOONMAKER: articles—

Arkush, Allan, "I Want My KEM TV," in *American Film* (Washington, D.C.), December 1985.
Talty, Stephan, "Invisible Woman," in *American Film* (Washington, D.C.), vol. 16, no. 9, September-October 1991.
Pizzello, Stephen, "Thelma Schoonmaker: assembling art with Marty," in *American Cinematographer* (Hollywood), October 1993.
Lally, Kevin, "The Art of Michael Powell Finds a New Audience," in *Film Journal* (New York), April 1995.
Jousse, Thierry, Nicolas Saada, and Serge Toubiana, "Casino," in *Cahiers du Cinéma* (Paris), March 1996.
"Inside Moves," in *Sight and Sound* (London), May 1996.
Anders, Allison, "Cut to the 'Grace'," in *Premiere* (New York), October 1996.

*   *   *

An axiom of Hollywood post-production holds that the best editing maintains a seamless invisibility; that the best editors don't draw attention to their work. Thelma Schoonmaker simultaneously embodies and shatters that axiom. On one hand, she is certainly one of Hollywood's most self-effacing editors, perhaps understandably so working as Martin Scorsese's editor. Editing all his films from *Raging Bull* on, she always claims the credit goes to Scorsese since he shoots for and edits with her. On the other hand, her contributions to Scorsese's films are far from insignificant; although her editing functions within classical Hollywood parameters, it draws attention to itself as a fully realized art form and provides a compendium of what contemporary editing can accomplish. As Jeffrey Ressner says, "*Raging Bull, GoodFellas*, and *Casino* have pushed the editing craft into a postmodern, almost hallucinogenic art. They are what films can be."

Schoonmaker's "postmodern" editing synthesizes a number of different influences, approaches, and devices: Nouvelle Vague, music videos, classical continuity editing (particularly shot/reverse shot dialogue editing), long takes and intrasequence cutting, montage, freeze frames, dissolves, jump cuts, temporal ellipses, extreme close-ups, and irises. One might expect to see all these devices in a TV commercial or a music video, yet Schoonmaker's successfully employs them in narrative features. She established this "hallucinatory" battery of techniques in her first commercial narrative, *Raging Bull*, which according to Stephan Talty, "is one of the most obsessively crafted and exhaustively edited films in American cinema."

The techniques Schoonmaker initiated with *Raging Bull* won her an Oscar for best editing and she continued to use and expand them as her career progressed. Since 1980, her editing has become so innovative, complex, and continually evolving that addressing all aspects of it in a short essay is as unfair as it is impossible. Nonetheless, certain characteristics that help describe her editorial signature may be singled out.

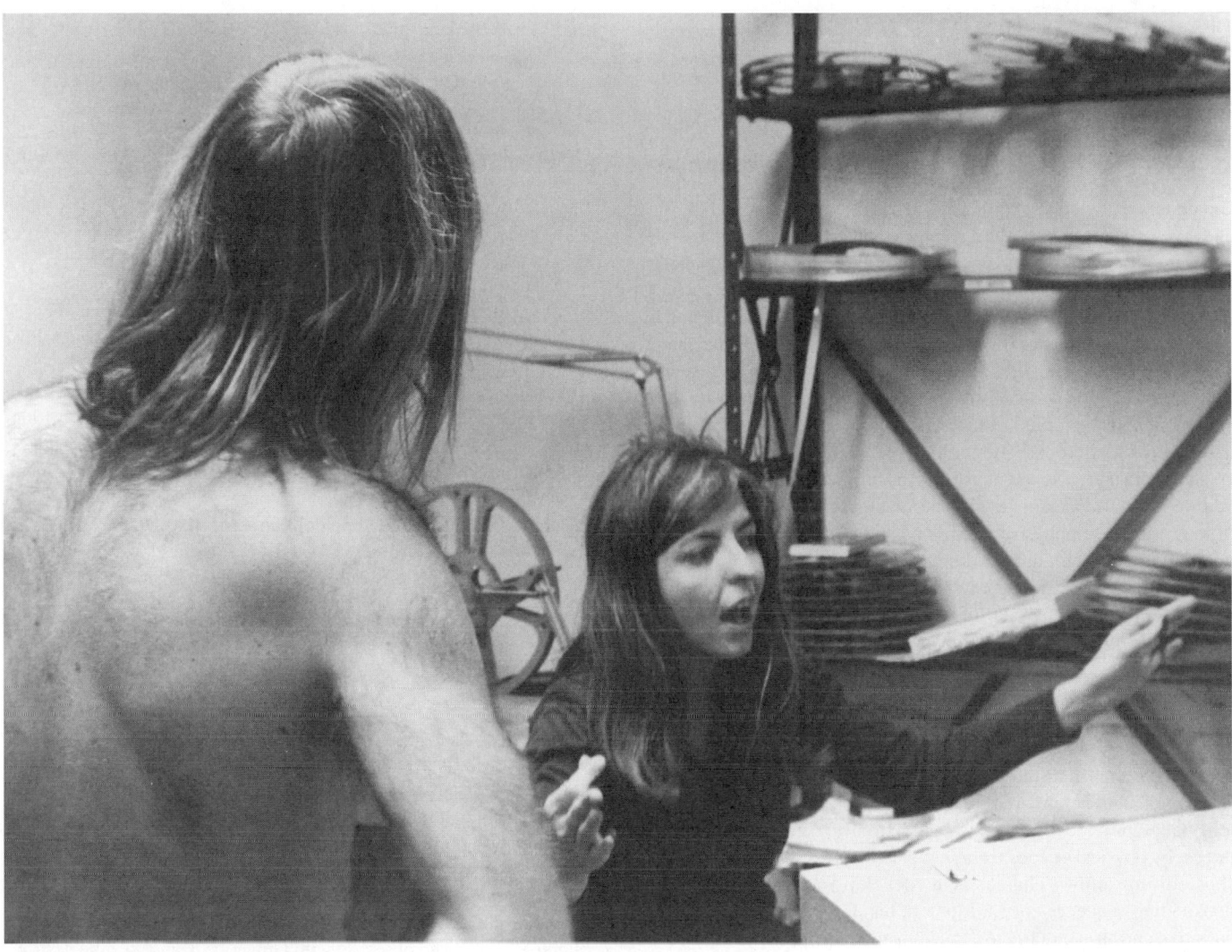

Thelma Schoonmaker

Raging Bull appears documentary-like: shot in black and white, using subtitles to specify time and place, and telling the biography of Jake La Motta. Schoonmaker contributes to this appearance by utilizing long takes and intercutting "home movies" of La Motta and his friends and family. She also employs the naturalism associated with classical Hollywood editing by structuring much of the film around traditional shot/reverse shot dialogue sequences. But any sense of realism or naturalism these techniques may suggest shrinks behind the style she gives to the rest of the film. Most obviously, the eight fight sequences allow Schoonmaker to do anything she wants. She puts each sequence together in a different way with a different tempo, but all rely on montage and sound manipulation. Extreme close-ups are cut next to long shots; low angle shots are cut next to high angle shots; normal speed shots are cut next to slow and fast motion shots; long camera takes are cut next to split-second shots of camera flashes; the boxers and audience are cut next to objects (round cards, the bell, water buckets); freeze frames are cut next to Stedicam shots; sound intensifies, drops out, becomes subjective, becomes abstract. All of this makes each fight literally "explosive," especially when compared to the slower pacing of rest of the film. Schoonmaker explains that while working on "Round 13" of the third Sugar Ray

Robinson fight, she first edited for narrative structure and then reworked the scene for movement, lighting, and effects—exactly the concerns which push her editing to the foreground.

Outside the fight sequences Schoonmaker employs subtler, but just as untraditional, editing techniques. Perhaps her most influential innovations occurred in this area: expanding the accepted boundary of the temporal ellipse and challenging the limitations of match action editing. All editors eliminate unimportant information that a viewer can infer. For example, an editor will not bother showing a character getting into a car, driving to a new location, and then getting out of the car. Typically, we would see the character get into the car, drive out of the frame, and then exit the car at the new location. The viewer understands that the car was driven between two points without needing to see it. Schoonmaker pushes this in a number of ways, but most interestingly by using this technique when we do not expect to see it. For example, while standing at a poolside soda stand, La Motta first sees Vicki. Then a cut shows us Vicki in close-up (from La Motta's point of view). When another cut returns us to La Motta he is sitting down at a table. We don't see him move from the soda stand to the table, but we know he did. Later, during La Motta's courtship of Vicki, she accompanies him to his apartment. As he closes the refrigerator door, a cut shows him sitting down at a table across the room. Again, unorthodox but fully comprehendible.

Traditional match action editing requires two things to make the cut "invisible": (1) cutting at the point of strongest action and (2) maintaining exact screen position and direction. Failure to follow these two conventions produces "bad editing" or "jump cuts." By traditional standards, Schoonmaker's editing borders on the "bad." But under contemporary editing aesthetics (heavily influenced by TV and music videos) her editing delivers an excitement impossible under the strict parameters of match action editing. Points of strongest action and exact screen position are replaced by jump cuts which produce a rhythmic pacing, an emphasis on character and dialogue (and actors' performances), and narrative intensification. In the many shot/reverse shot dialogue sequences, the street vernacular the characters speak, with its staccato tempo, perfectly complements and supports these editorial decisions and produces the edgy tension associated with Scorsese's films.

Schoonmaker also demonstrates a deft hand at intrasequence cutting. Brian Henderson defines intrasequence cutting as the linking of long takes to emphasize the rhythm and movement within a long duration shot. Each cut breaks that rhythm or movement but then replaces it with a different rhythm or movement of the next shot. Scorsese employs long takes usually with elaborate camera movements made possible by the Stedicam. In the Marcel Cerdan fight, the camera follows La Motta out of his dressing room, down a number of hallways, through the crowded arena, and into the ring as the camera (now on a crane) moves into a high angle shot. Schoonmaker uses such long takes in combination with her montage inspired editing to break and establish different editing tempos.

Immediately before or after a montage sequence, cutting together long takes provides a needed respite from a taxing emotional or intensely physical scene. Combining long takes with shot/reverse shot editing allows characters to develop more naturally. The bookending sequences of La Motta in his dressing room set up the narrative and structure of the film with an efficiency no other editing technique could accomplish.

In *The King of Comedy*, she pushed the temporal ellipse to include a spatial aspect. Straight cutting on dialogue in a typical shot/reverse shot pattern we move freely between Rupert's basement and his (fantasized) luncheon at Sardi's with Jerry Langford. Rupert's first conversation with Rita at a bar does the same thing: on a line of continuous dialogue over a shot/reverse shot cut we relocate to a restaurant. Schoonmaker and Scorsese indulge in a bit of Nouvelle Vague reflexivity here. In the long takes and intrasequence cutting which structures this scene, a patron behind Rupert gazes at the camera and mocks Rupert's gestures and facial expressions. In a film which questions the thin line between reality and fantasy, this scene in particular demonstrates the impossibility of film to ever be real.

The opening title sequence of *The King of Comedy* superimposes credits over a freeze frame of Marsha's clawing hands. Schoonmaker develops the freeze frame until it becomes one of her signature devices. She uses the freeze frame extensively in *GoodFellas*. Whenever Henry Hill's voice over makes an important point, Schoonmaker freezes the image. In *GoodFellas*, she also employs long takes (especially in the famous track back/zoom in shot at the diner), intrasequence cutting (Karen and Henry and the Copacabana and the Saturday May 11 sequence), spatial and temporal ellipses (all of the violence and the gifts of money at the wedding reception), and jump cuts (Karen at the beauty parlor and at Janet Rossi's apartment).

In *The Color of Money*, Schoonmaker uses extreme close-ups of cue chalk, billiard balls, cigarettes, and money as a visual leitmotif to stress the theme of the film. She balances long takes with montage sequences; Vincent's "Werewolves of London" pool cue performance juxtaposed to the increased speed, overhead jump cuts, and extreme close-ups for a series of pool games. She plays much cutting on moving camera against a precise visual symmetry (the left/right balance of Vincent and Eddie's grudge match). In Vincent's game with Grady, Schoonmaker employs dissolves and superimpositions to convey the various deceits and facades of the two players.

Schoonmaker also develops the dissolve until it becomes another of her signature devices. She uses the dissolve extensively in *The Age of Innocence* and *Casino*. Whereas her earlier films used the dissolve traditionally (to indicate simultaneity or a passage of time), her later films use it to disorient. In *The Age of Innocence*, the opera sequence which opens the film immediately undercuts the period setting. Dissolves link shots which traditionally would be joined in one long take or through match action. Combining this unsettling technique with jump cuts (during the pan of the theatre) and abandoned eye-line matches (an audience member looks up across the theatre, yet the next shot is down to a performer on the stage) provides a commentary on the hidden meanings of exterior actions. Schoonmaker takes advantage of the period setting to employ irises. A silent film device before editing used close-ups, an iris focused the viewer's attention on a specific part of the screen. Here Schoonmaker uses translucent irises as another visual metaphor for disguised appearances.

In *Casino*, Schoonmaker uses both devices but for different reasons. The dissolves work as point of view commentary (especially since the film is narrated in voice over). For example, as Sam explains how he eliminated professional cheaters from the Tropicana we see him determine how two men have won $140,000 in blackjack. Schoonmaker presents this to us through dissolves that link Sam to the two tables involved in the scam. When Nicky and Jennifer first meet Ginger, we see her through Nicky's eyes in a three shot dissolve which augments her approach. In *Casino*, the iris functions to suggest blindness. Sam is so obsessed with Ginger he cannot see the destruction their relationship will cause; an iris leads us to his head and then an extreme close-up of a flash bulb exploding. Both films also make extensive use of intrasequence cutting, temporal ellipses, cutting on moving camera, and montage.

These techniques also work well in the context of a suspense film. In *Cape Fear*, Schoonmaker melded her editing techniques with the action cutting demanded of a genre film. The result was a film that frightened, and exhibited an innovative twist on an old format. She used negative imagery to comment on the lack of clear difference between guilt and innocence. Her jump cutting and temporal ellipses added a new edge of terror and excitement to the final houseboat sequence (involving miniatures and special effects) as well as Sam Bowden's first sighting of Max Cady in town (three jump cuts from long shot to medium shot to close up on passing cars). Cady's seduction of Danielle on the school stage expertly demonstrates intrasequence cutting. Scorsese shot the improvised scene in one continuous, nine minute take with two cameras. Schoonmaker seamlessly melded the two takes so it looks like a typical shot/reverse shot sequence even though she is linking long takes.

The approaches mentioned above outline the unique style of Schoonmaker's editing technique. Perhaps more than any other contemporary Hollywood editor, her distinct editorial signature positions her as an auteur. Working almost exclusively with Scorsese certainly supports this claim and demonstrates not only that editing must be viewed as an art but that film can function as a collaborative act of creativity.

And indeed, as each new Scorsese project is initiated, you can be sure that he again will be working with Schoonmaker. Such was the case with *Kundun*, the undertaking of which was a special challenge for the editor. Schoonmaker has described the film as "a visual poem" and, indeed, *Kundun* is a banquet of resplendent images; it also is unlike Scorsese's other works in that it features non-professional actors and less of a concern with character and dialogue. The film consists of episodes in the life of its subject, the Dalai Lama, which are dazzlingly photographed (by Roger Deakins) and fluidly and superlatively edited.

Schoonmaker's affiliation with Scorsese even extends beyond the films he directs. One of her rare non-Scorsese projects was Allison Anders's *Grace of My Heart*; however, Scorsese was the film's executive producer.

—Greg S. Faller, updated by Rob Edelman

SCHÜFFTAN, Eugen

Cinematographer. **Nationality:** American. **Born:** in Breslau (now Wroclaw), Germany; emigrated to the United States, 1940; naturalized, 1947; used the name Eugene Shuftan in the United States. **Education:** Studied fine arts in Breslau. **Career:** Painter, sculptor, designer, and architect; worked in German films in the 1920s as a photographic effects specialist: invented the Schüfftan process (using miniature backgrounds with action foregrounds); cinematographer from 1929; 1933–40—worked in France after the rise of the Nazis; worked in the United States after 1940, and internationally in the 1950s and 1960s. **Awards:** Academy Award for *The Hustler*, 1961; Billy Bitzer Award, 1975. **Died:** 6 September 1977.

Films as Special Effects Photographer:

1924   *Die Nibelungen* (Lang—2 parts)
1925   *Ein Walzertraum* (Berger); *Variété* (*Variety*) (Dupont); *Eifersucht* (Grune)
1926   *Dagfin* (May)
1927   *Metropolis* (Lang); *Königin Luise* (*Queen Louise*) (Grune)
1929   *Narkose* (Abel)

Films as Cinematographer:

1929   *Menschen am Sonntag* (*People on Sunday*) (Siodmak and Ulmer)
1930   *Abscheid* (Siodmak); *Das gestohlene Gesicht* (Schmidt and Mayring); *Dann Schon lieber Lebertran* (Ophüls)
1931   *Gassenhauer* (Pick); *Meine Frau, die Hochstaplerin* (Gerron); *Das Ekel* (co, + co-d)
1932   *L'Atlantide* (Pabst) (co); *Zigeuner der nacht* (Schwarz)
1933   *Der Läufer von Marathon* (*The Marathon Runner*) (Dupont); *Du haut en bas* (*High and Low*) (Pabst); *Les Requins du pétrole* (Decoin); *La Voix sans visage* (Mittler); *Unsichtbare Gegner* (Katscher)

1934   *Ademai aviateur* (Tarride); *La Crise est finie* (*The Slump Is Over*) (Siodmak); *Le Scandale* (L'Herbier)
1935   *La Tendre Ennemi* (*The Tender Enemy*) (Ophüls); *The Invader* (Brunel)
1936   *Mademoiselle Docteur* (Pabst); *La Symphonie des brigands* (Feher)
1937   *Forfaiture* (L'Herbier); *Yoshiwara* (Ophüls); *Drôle de drame* (*Bizarre Bizarre*) (Carné)
1938   *Mollenard* (*Hatred*) (Siodmak); *Les Trois Valses* (Berger); *Le Drame de Shanghaï* (*The Shanghai Drama*) (Pabst) (co); **Quai des brumes** (*Port of Shadows*) (Carné)
1939   *Les Musiciens du ciel* (Lacombe)
1940   *L'Emigrante* (Joannon); *Sans lendemain* (Ophüls)
1944   *Summer Storm* (Sirk)
1947   *Carnegie Hall* (Ulmer)
1950   *Les Joyeux Pélerins* (Pasquali); *Le Traqué* (*Gunman in the Streets*) (Lewin and Tuttle)
1952   *Le Banquet des fraudeurs* (*Dans Bankett der Schmugger*) (Storck); *La P . . . respecteuse* (*The Respectable Prostitute*) (Pagliero and Brabant); *Le Chemin de Damas* (Glass); *Nina de Vanghel* (Clavel and Barry)
1953   *Le Rideau cramoisi* (*The Crimson Curtain*) (Astruc)
1954   *Une parigina a Roma* (*Begegnung in Rom*) (Kobler and Tolnay)
1955   *Marianne de ma jeunesse* (Duvivier)
1958   *La Tête contre les murs* (Franju)
1959   *The Bloody Brood* (Roffman); **Les Yeux sans visage** (*The Horror Chamber of Dr. Faustus*) (Franju)
1960   *Un Couple* (Mocky)
1961   **The Hustler** (Rossen); *Something Wild* (Garfein)
1962   *Les Vièrges* (Mocky)
1963   *Captain Sinbad* (Haskin) (co)
1964   *La Grande Frousse* (Mocky); *Lilith* (Rossen)
1965   *Trois chambres à Manhattan* (Carné)
1966   *Angeklagt nach N.218* (*The Doctor Says*) (A. Ford)

Other Films:

1943   *It Happened Tomorrow* (Clair) (technical d)
1946   *The Dark Mirror* (Siodmak) (technical supervisor)
1955   *Ulisse* (*Ulysses*) (Camerini) (special ph)
1967   *Chappaqua* (Rooks) (consultant)

Publications

On SCHÜFFTAN: articles—

Focus on Film (London), no. 13, 1973.
Brandlmeier, A., in *Film und Ton* (Munich), October 1974.
Gerely, A., in *Film und Ton* (Munich), December 1977.
Filme (Berlin), May-June 1981.
Pruemm, K., in *Archives: Institut Jean Vigo* (Perpignan), December 1997.

*   *   *

When Eugen Schüfftan was nominated for the 1961 Academy Award for *The Hustler*, *American Cinematographer* magazine was unable to provide much background in their customary profile; when

Schüfftan's name was announced as the winner on Oscar night, Howard Keel blithely accepted the award, declaring, "I don't know where he is." Clearly, Schüfftan's work on *The Hustler*, rather than an obvious accumulation of Hollywood credits or an enormous popularity within the industry, was responsible for the award. His credits, however, are extensive, both as a cameraman and an inventor.

His most acclaimed contribution to cinema technology is his invention of the Schüfftan process. Originally designed for the unrealized German production of *Gulliver's Travels*, it was first employed by Fritz Lang on *Metropolis* and subsequently by many other directors, including Alfred Hitchcock and Fred Zinnemann. This process—one of the many trick photographic effects Schüfftan pioneered at UFA—involved placing a semitransparent mirror at a 45-degree angle in front of the camera lens, reflecting the image of a scale model or actual location onto the visual field. Blending credibly with the live-action being photographed, this process allows architectural figures of all dimensions to be mapped onto the image, thus reducing the enormous costs of monumental set construction or overcoming the difficulties of shooting in certain locations. In *Metropolis* Lang effectively used this process to depict his futuristic vision; Hitchcock employed it in *Blackmail* for the climactic chase around the roof of the British Museum.

As a cameraman, Schüfftan is now best known for his work in France, particularly the atmospheric black-and-white images of doom and despair created for Marcel Carné in the 1930s—most notably *Quai des brumes*—and for Georges Franju in the 1950s—notably *Les Yeux sans visage*. For Schüfftan, an effective ambience created by lighting is the key to cinematography: he preferred to establish mood by lighting the action rather than the performer.

During the 1940s Schüfftan worked in Hollywood as a "supervisor" (a Guild title) on projects by the European implants Douglas Sirk, Edgar G. Ulmer, Robert Siodmak, and René Clair; disenchanted, he returned to Europe after three years and eight projects. Schüfftan's return to the United States ten years later was facilitated by Jack Garfein who sought him for his second feature, *Something Wild*, a New York film about a rape victim who contemplates suicide. (Garfein had difficulty convincing the New York Cinematographers Guild to allow Schüfftan—only an Honorary member—work papers.) Then during production, Garfein fortuitously introduced Schüfftan to Robert Rossen who was seeking a strong black-and-white cinematographer for *The Hustler*, his gritty tale of a New York pool player. Following the success of that film, Schüfftan remained in New York to shoot Rossen's final film, *Lilith*, before returning to Europe. He shot only a few additional projects before retiring, among them the final film for his old collaborator Marcel Carné, *Trois chambres à Manhattan*.

—Doug Tomlinson

SCHWARTZ, Stephen

Composer and lyricist. **Nationality:** American. **Born:** Stephen Michael Schwartz, New York City, 6 March 1948. **Education:** Studied piano and composition at Julliard School of Music while still in high school; Carnegie Mellon University, B.F.A. in drama, 1968. **Career:** Worked briefly as a producer for RCA Records, 1968; composer of music and lyrics for theatre, since 1969, and for film, since 1973; wrote title song

for the Broadway play *Butterflies Are Free*, 1969; first major commercial and critical success with Off Broadway musical *Godspell*, 1972; recorded albums *Stephen Michael Schwartz*, RCA, 1974, *Godspell*, Jay 1997, and *Reluctant Pilgrim*, Midder, 1997; appeared on numerous albums, from 1974. **Awards:** Academy Awards for Best Music, Original Musical or Comedy Score (with Allen Menken), and Best Music, Song ("Colors of the Wind"; with Menken), Golden Globe Award for Best Original Song-Motion Picture ("Colors of the Wind"; with Menken), and Grammy Award for Best Song Written Specifically for a Motion Picture ("Colors of the Wind"; with Menken), for *Pocahontas*, 1996; Academy Award for Best Music, Song ("When You Believe"), 1999, and ASCAP Film and Television Music Award for Most Performed Songs from Motion Pictures ("When You Believe"; with Kenneth "Babyface" Edmonds), 2000, for *The Prince of Egypt*. **Agent:** Gorfaine & Schwartz Agency, 13245 Riverside, Suite 405, Sherman Oaks, CA 91423, U.S.A.

Films as Composer/Lyricist:

1973 *Godspell* (Greene)
1981 *Pippin* (Fosse—for TV)
1982 *Working* (Marshall—for TV) (with others)
1983 *Echoes* (Seidelman) (with Gerard Bernard Cohen); *The Magic Show* (Campbell—for TV)
1995 *Pocahontas* (Gabriel and Goldberg) (lyrics with Alan Menken)
1996 *The Hunchback of Notre Dame* (Trousdale and Wise) (lyrics with Alan Menken)
1998 *The Prince of Egypt* (Chapman, Hickner, and Wells) (songs only)
2000 *Geppetto* (Moore—for TV)

Other Films:

1975 *Sweet Hostage* (Philips—for TV) (singer)

Publications

By SCHWARTZ: articles—

"Carrying the Tunes," interview in *People Weekly*, 24 July 1995.
"It's An Art: Reflections on a Life in Song," an interview with Jem Aswad, "ASCAP Film and TV Legends," http://www.ascap.com/filmtv/schwartz.html, May 2000.

On SCHWARTZ: articles—

"Songwriter Schwartz Shifts Gears," in *Billboard*, 28 June 1997.
"*Reluctant Pilgrim*" (review), in *People Weekly*, 16 February 1998.

*   *   *

The steady demise of the original American Broadway musical, combined with the rather surprising rise in mass popularity of the Broadway-*style* animated movie musical, revived the careers of a select number of Broadway composers and lyricists in the last decade of the 20th century. One of the most welcome career revivals occasioned by this animation renaissance was that of composer/ lyricist Stephen Schwartz. Born in 1948 in New York City, before the age of 25 Schwartz had composed the songs for *Godspell* and *Pippin*, two popular stage hits which also became two of the last late Broadway properties to enter the standard musical theater repertory.

Schwartz studied piano and composition at the Julliard School of Music while still in high school, and graduated from Carnegie Mellon University in Pittsburgh, Pennsylvania, with a B.F.A. in Drama. While still in college the multi-talented Schwartz did summer stock, playing the multiple roles of director, musical director, and choreographer. Upon graduation he worked as a producer for RCA Victor Records, and shortly thereafter commenced a career in Broadway theater.

Schwartz's first Broadway credit was the title song for the 1969 comedy, *Butterflies Are Free*, but his greatest success came in 1971, when he composed the songs for the Off-Broadway rock musical *Godspell*, a modern version of the story of Christ as enacted by 1960s-style hippies. The score included a popular hit, "Day by Day," and that same year Schwartz was selected to contribute the English lyrics to Leonard Bernstein's controversial concert work, "Mass," which opened at the Kennedy Center in Washington. In 1973 *Godspell* was filmed on location in New York City, but failed to gain the acclaim or commercial success it had earned on stage.

In 1972 Schwartz had his second major success (and his first on Broadway) with the big musical, *Pippin*, a contemporary and fanciful retelling of the story of the son of Charlemagne, and directed by Bob Fosse. After these two theatrical successes the young composer's career flagged, a falling off at least partially due to the confused state of live Broadway theater from the 1970s on. Schwartz composed several songs for a review showcasing magician Doug Henning, *The Magic Show*, in 1974, and the score for a 1976 musical entitled *The Baker's Wife*. Though the latter closed before reaching Broadway, its original cast album achieved cult status and led to several revivals, including one by Trevor Nunn in London in 1988. In 1986 Schwartz provided the lyrics for composer Charles Strouse's music for *Rags* which, after an unsuccessful Broadway run, went on to a number of well-received revival productions. On his long creative gap between the *Pippin* in 1972 and *Rags* in 1986, Schwartz commented in an ASCAP interview: "Basically I just burned out and stopped working. I hid out—I don't know any other way to put it."

Schwartz's last Broadway project of the 1970s was his unusual 1978 musical adaptation of Studs Terkel's book, *Working*. He both adapted and directed, but contributed only four songs to a pastiche score featuring numbers by a variety of contemporary pop and theater songwriters (including James Taylor and Dorothy Rodgers). *Working* was filmed for public television's "American Playhouse" series in 1982, and a revised version (featuring new material) eventually opened at the Signature Theater in Washington, D.C. *Pippin* was also filmed for television in 1981, directed by Fosse and starring William Katt, Martha Ray, and Chita Rivera. *The Magic Show* was filmed for TV in 1983, with Henning and Didi Conn.

Rags was Schwartz's last contribution to the increasingly risky and British (i.e., Andrew Lloyd Webber) dominated Broadway scene. With the death of lyricist Howard Ashman, Schwartz joined forces with Alan Menken and the Walt Disney Studio. The team of Menken and Ashman had of course created the popular Off-Broadway success, *The Little Shop of Horrors*, and went on to much greater fame (and fortune) with their work for the Disney animated musicals, *The Little Mermaid* and *Beauty and the Beast*. When Ashman died of AIDS in 1991, Schwartz collaborated on songs for the 1994 Disney film *Life with Mikey* with Alan Menken (though he was not credited). The films that placed Schwartz squarely back in the public eye, if only for his lyrics, were *Pocahontas* in 1995 and *The Hunchback of Notre Dame* in 1996. Both scores were nominated for Academy Awards, and Schwartz shared an Oscar with composer Menken for Best Song for "Colors of the Wind" from *Pocahontas*. Following these two career-reviving scores Schwartz was assigned to write both the music and lyrics for the big DreamWorks-SKG animated musical spectacle *Prince of Egypt* in 1998. His song, "When You Believe," earned another Oscar in 1999, and Schwartz also shared a nomination for Best Music, Original Musical or Comedy with orchestral score composer, Hans Zimmer. Schwartz returned to Disney in 2000 to compose the songs for a live action television version of Disney's classic *Pinocchio*, now entitled *Geppetto*. The revival of Schwartz's career also resulted in his first solo album, *Reluctant Pilgrim*, and in his joining forces with Disney and ASCAP to oversee their Musical Theater Workshop.

When Broadway music, like all American popular music, changed radically with the extreme cultural and social shifts of the 1960s, Schwartz was one of the few theater composers willing and able to change with it, and to make the transition with any degree of artistic and commercial success. Schwartz's transition from Broadway to animated movie musicals is certainly a welcome one. Songs like "Day by Day" (from *Godspell*) and "Corner of the World" (from *Pippin*) are among the best the late-period American musical theater has to offer, and this tradition of quality has now extended into 2000 with his Schwartz's score for *Geppetto*. Schwartz's songs have always been noted for their witty, well-crafted lyrics, and for their alternately exhilarating and moving music. Schwartz's score for *Geppetto* ranges from droll operatic parodies and operetta-like ensembles to a lyrical and potentially commercial ballad, "Since I Gave My Heart Away," this latter one of the songwriter's best tunes since "Corner of the World."

—Ross Care

ŚCIBOR-RYLSKI, Aleksander

Writer and Director. **Nationality:** Polish. **Born:** Grudziadzh, 16 March 1928. **Education:** Attended the University of Warsaw, graduated 1950. **Career:** Writer; 1951—first film script, for *Sailors*; 1963—directed first film, *Everyday*; 1972–78—director of the film group *Pryzmat*; 1977—author of TV series *Lalka*. **Died:** In Warsaw, 3 April 1983.

Films as Writer:

1951   *Matrosowcy* (*Sailors*) (Banach—short)
1952   *Wesoła II* (Wesiewicz—short)
1956   *Cień* (*The Shadow*) (Kawalerowicz)
1958   *Pigulki dla Aurelii* (*Pills for Aurelia*) (Lenartowicz); *Ostatni strzał* (*The Last Shot*) (Rybkowski)
1959   *Ocalenie* (Kluba—short)
1960   *Rok pierwszy* (*The First Years*) (Lesiewicz); *Dotknięcie nocy* (*The Touch of Night*) (Bareja)
1961   *Komedianty* (*The Comedians*) (Kaniewska)

1962   *Dom bez okien* (*House without Windows*) (Jędryka); *Czarne skrzydła* (*Black Wings*) (E. & C. Petelscy)
1963   *Ich dzień powszedni* (*Everyday*) (+ d)
1964   *Późne popołudnie* (*Late Afternoon*) (+ d)
1965   *Popioły* (*Ashes*) (Wajda); *Jutro Meksyk* (*Mexico Soon*) (+ d)
1967   *Morderca zostawia ślad* (*The Murderer Leaves Traces*) (+ d); *Wilcze echa* (*Wolf Echoes*) (+ co-d)
1969   *Sasiedzi* (*The Neighbors*) (+ d)
1970   *Południk zero* (*Meridian Zero*) (Podgórski)
1971   *Seksolatki* (Hübner); *Złote koło* (*Gold Ring*) (Wohl); *Agent Nr. 1* (Kuźmiński); *Trad* (*Leprosy*) (Trzos-Rastawiecki)
1974   *Gniazdo* (*The Nest*) (Rybkowski)
1976   *Dagny* (Sandoy); **Człowiek z marmuru** (*Man of Marble*) (Wajda)
1981   *Człowiek z żelaza* (*Man of Iron*) (Wajda)

Publications

By ŚCIBOR-RYLSKI: books—

Orczewski i jego brygada, Warsaw, 1949.
Górnicze gołębie pokoju, Warsaw, 1950.
"Pancerze" Józefa Szulca, Warsaw, 1950.
Staszek Kaluga staje do współzawodnictwa, Warsaw, 1950.
Dwanaście felietonów, Warsaw, 1951.
Węgiel, Warsaw, 1952.
Wieczór u Hanysa Dębiczka, Warsaw, 1953.
Iwan, Warsaw, 1954.
Sprawa Szymka Bielasa, Warsaw, 1954.
Cień i inne opowiadania, Warsaw, 1955.
Styczén, Warsaw, 1956.
Bliski nieznajomy, Warsaw, 1968.
Rodeo, Warsaw, 1969.
Ich dzień powszedni, Warsaw, 1972.
Człowiek z marmuru, Człowiek z żelaza, London, 1982.

By ŚCIBOR-RYLSKI: articles—

Film (Warsaw), no. 48, 1960.
Special issue of *Kino* (Munich), 1982.

On ŚCIBOR-RYLSKI: articles—

Film (Warsaw), no. 899, 1966.
Film (Warsaw), 7 September 1969.
Filmowy Serwis Prasowy (Warsaw), 1–15 April 1977.
Filmowy Serwis Prasowy (Warsaw), 1–15 August 1977.
Jeune Cinéma (Paris), July-August 1981.
Iluzjon (Warsaw), April-June 1991.
Kino (Munich), vol. 26, September 1992.

*   *   *

Aleksander Ścibor-Rylski was a fiction writer, playwright, publicist, screenwriter, and film director. His main claim to fame, however, was as a scriptwriter, to which he devoted himself from 1951 until his death. Like Jerzy Stefan Stawinsky and Tadeusz Konwicki, he was especially sensitive towards social and moral conflicts stemming from the Second World War, and from the difficulties in the founding and stabilizing of the people's government of Poland. *Pills for Aurelia*, directed by Stanislaw Lenartowicz, captured the experiences of its characters during the occupation with unusual violence and cruelty. Witold Lesiewicz's *The First Years* portrays postwar difficulties, showing with what drastic force political opinions can divide honest people.

His work in film, however, is highly diverse. He did not specialize in any theme or genre, and worked with a relatively wide circle of directors. Among his most important works are his scripts for Andrzej Wajda's films, the historical epic *Ashes* and the drama *Man of Marble*; the script for Jerzy Kawalerowicz's film *The Shadow*—three stories from the period of the occupation about a faceless man who is provocateur, traitor, and saboteur; the script for Andrzej Trzos-Rastawiecki's *Leprosy* about gangs and hooliganism; and the script for Jan Rybkowski's *The Nest*, a historical drama about the origins of the Polish state. His scripts are noted for their courageous view of events, dynamism, convincing characterizations, and logical structure.

After the "revolt of the scriptwriters" in the early 1960s, which he led together with Stawinsky, he, too, began to direct films. Except for the chamber stories *Everyday* and *Late Afternoon*, noted for the "little realism" with which he told ordinary stories of ordinary people, and his attempt at a Polish western, *Wolf Echoes*, about the struggle of a soldier with a postwar terrorist gang, his stints as a director have not been highly regarded. His main contribution to Polish cinema remains his scriptwriting.

—B. Urgošíková

SEALE, John

Cinematographer. **Nationality:** Australian. **Born:** John Clement Seale, Warwick, Queensland, Australia, 29 May 1943. **Education:** Graduated from High School, Sydney. **Family:** Married Louise lee Mutton, 23 September 1967; one son, Derin Anthony; one daughter, Brianna Lee. **Career:** Camera assistant in the film department, Australian Broadcasting Corporation, 1962–1968; freelance technician and camera operator on various films, series and commissions, 1968–1976; director of photography for various film companies, 1976; director of photography for Mirsch Agency, L.A. from 1976. **Awards:** Australian Film Institute Award, Best Achievement in Cinematography, for *Careful, He Might Hear You*, 1983; Australian Cinematographers Society Cinematographer Awards for *Goodbye Paradise*, 1983 and *Witness*, 1985; Los Angeles Film Critics Association Awards, Best Cinematography, for *The English Patient*, 1996; Chicago Film Critics Association Award, Best Cinematography, European Film Award, Best Cinematography, Golden Satellite Award, Outstanding Cinematography, British Academy Awards, American Society of Cinematographers Award, Outstanding Achievement in Cinematography in Theatrical Releases, Academy Award for Best Cinematography, for *The English Patient*, 1997; Honorary Doctorate, Griffith University, 1997. **Address:** P. O. Box 1422, Mona Vale, New South Wales, NSW 1660, Australia.

Films as Cinematographer:

1976 *Deathcheaters* (Smith)
1980 *Fatty Finn* (Murphy)
1981 *The Survivor* (Hemmings); *Doctors & Nurses* (Murphy)
1982 *Fighting Back* (Caulfield); *Ginger Meggs* (Dawson)
1983 *Goodbye Paradise* (Schultz); *Careful, He Might Hear You* (Schultz); *BMX Bandits* (Trenchard-Smith)
1984 *Silver City* (Haskin)
1985 *Top Kid* (Schultz); *Witness* (Weir); *The Empty Beach* (Thomson)
1986 *The Mosquito Coast* (Weir); *The Hitcher* (Harmon); *Children of a Lesser God* (Haines)
1987 *Stakeout* (Badham)
1988 *Rain Man* (Levinson); *Gorillas in the Mist* (Apted)
1989 *Dead Poets Society* (Weir)
1991 *The Doctor* (Haines)
1992 *Lorenzo's Oil* (Miller)
1993 *The Firm* (Pollack)
1994 *The Paper* (Howard)
1995 *Beyond Rangoon* (Boorman) (also camera operator); *The American President* (Reiner)
1996 **The English Patient** (Minghella); *Ghosts of Mississippi* (*Ghosts From the Past*) (Reiner)
1998 *City of Angels* (Silberling)
1999 *At First Sight* (Winkler); *The Talented Mr. Ripley* (Minghella)
2000 *The Perfect Storm* (Petersen)
2001 *Cold Mountain*

Other Films:

1973 *Alvin Purple* (Burstall) (camera operator)
1975 *Picnic at Hanging Rock* (Weir) (camera operator)
1976 *Mad Dog Morgan* (Mora) (camera operator); *Caddie* (Crombie) (camera operator)
1977 *The Last Wave* (Weir) (camera operator); *Break of Day* (Weir) (camera operator)
1978 *The Irishman* (Crombie) (camera operator); *Weekend of Shadows* (Jeffrey) (camera operator)
1979 *Born to Run* (Chaffey—for TV) (camera operator)
1981 *Gallipoli* (Weir) (camera operator)
1982 *The Year of Living Dangerously* (Weir) (photographer: second unit)
1990 *Till There Was You* (director)
1992 *Visions of Light* (*Visions of Light: The Art of Cinematography*) (Glassman, McCarthy, Samuels)
1997 *Underworld* (Christian) (first assistant camera: "c" camera)

Publications

On SEALE: books—

McFarlane, Bryan, *Australian Cinema 1970–1985*, London, 1987.
McFarlane, Bryan, and Geoff Mayer, *New Australian Cinema: Sources and Parallels in American and British Film*, Cambridge, England, 1992.

On SEALE: articles—

"John Seale, ACS, Lends Firm Hand to Law Thriller," in *American Cinematographer* (Los Angeles), 1 July 1993.
Colbert, Mary, "Beyond Effects/DOP John Seale," in *Cinema Papers* (North Melbourne, Australia), 1 April 1997.
Calhoun, John, "Celestial Navigation," in *Lighting Dimensions* (South Laguna, California), 1 May 1998.

*   *   *

Straight-talking Australian cinematographer John Seale has worked on many of the most influential Hollywood movies of the 1980s and 1990s, and is noted for his collaborations with director Peter Weir, whom he met while working with cinematographer Russell Boyd on *Picnic at Hanging Rock*. The greatest moment of his career so far came in 1997 when he won the Best Cinematography Oscar for *The English Patient*, but he has received awards and nominations for his work from film institutions around the world, including Oscar nominations for *Rain Man* and *Witness*. Seale is praised in particular for his realistic use of light, and his most impressive work tends to be in the photographing of large-scale landscapes and brightly lit outdoor locations.

After learning his craft as a camera operator during the 1970s Seale began working as a cinematographer in a cinematic tradition that seemed intent on exploring Australia's landscape and past. *Goodbye Paradise*, Carl Schultz's clever parody of the private eye movie genre, which comments on the migratory habits of Australia's senior citizens, is also notable for its images of Queensland, while *Careful, He Might Hear You* sets the individual's struggle for self-definition against an Australian past of struggle and adversity. In both these very different films, the landscape encroaches on the narrative, and it is perhaps because of these early projects that Seale's best work, such as *The English Patient*, and *Gorillas in the Mist*, tends to be on films that explore the relationship between people and their surroundings.

Seale moved to Hollywood with Weir to make the thriller *Witness*, and has been a regular collaborator with the director on films as diverse as *The Mosquito Coast* and *Dead Poets Society*. Although Seale remains committed to the development of Australian cinema, his output since the late 1980s has largely originated, even if it has not always been filmed, in America. *Dead Poets Society* in particular is vividly American in its attachment to Romantic individualism, and its fascination with the verdant grounds of the New England school in which the film is set. Other films, like *Rain Man*, and *The Firm* (both Tom Cruise vehicles) are resolutely Hollywood in their look and story lines.

Like many Australian filmmakers who work outside the Australian film industry, Seale seems happy to travel widely to film on location, and work in other countries. Many of his most successful films have been filmed in remote locations, such as the rain forests of South America (*The Mosquito Coast*), Burma (*Beyond Rangoon*), or Africa (*Gorillas in the Mist*). Capturing landscapes successfully on film is among the most difficult tasks for the cinematographer, yet Seale manages to convey the vastness of these settings without overwhelming the smaller scale human action on which the film narratives depend. His most recent successful collaborations with British filmmaker Anthony Minghella, *The English Patient* and *The Talented Mr Ripley*, both exploit Seale's talent for filming real places in a convincing and realistic way. In the case of *The Talented Mr*

Ripley, Seale preferred to film the tale of Tom Ripley's dark subconscious in glorious sunshine, the beauty of Italy contrasting jaggedly with the horror of the human story played out there.

Seale has so far made only one foray into directing, making his own first feature as director, *Till There Was You* in Australia. The film fits in with the themes of movies he has worked on as cinematographer; namely, the urge to define personal identity in a landscape and tradition that seems overwhelming and mysterious. Although he has travelled widely, Seale prefers to be at home, recently exploiting film's increasing digitization to do the post-production work on *The Perfect Storm* by satellite from his home in Sydney.

—Chris Routledge

SEITZ, John F.

Cinematographer. **Nationality:** American. **Born:** Chicago, Illinois, 23 June 1893. **Family:** Brother of the director George B. Seitz. Married; two children. **Career:** 1909—worked for St. Louis Motion Picture Company as laboratory technician; 1913—first film as photographer; 1916—joined Metro Pictures; many technical innovations: invented the matte shot (prephotographed backgrounds with action foregrounds), and held 18 patents on photographic inventions; 1920—first of many films for Rex Ingram; 1929–30—President, American Society of Cinematographers; 1960—retired. **Died:** In Woodland Hills, California, 27 February 1979.

Films as Cinematographer:

1913   *Ranger of Lonesome Gulf* ; *The Quagmire*
1915   *Edged Tools*
1917   *Souls in Pawn* (H. King); *Whose Wife?* (Sturgeon)
1918   *Beauty and the Rogue* (H. King); *Powers That Prey* (H. King)
1919   *The Westerners* (Sloman)
1920   *The Sagebrusher* (Sloman); *Hearts Are Trumps* (Ingram); *Shore Acres* (Ingram)
1921   *The Conquering Power* (Ingram); **The Four Horsemen of the Apocalypse** (Ingram); *Uncharted Seas* (Ruggles)
1922   *The Prisoner of Zenda* (Ingram); *Trifling Women* (Ingram); *Turn to the Right* (Ingram)
1923   *Scaramouche* (Ingram); *Where the Pavement Ends* (Ingram)
1924   *The Price of a Party* (Giblyn); *The Arab* (Ingram); *Classmates* (Robertson) (co)
1926   *The Magician* (Ingram); *Mare Nostrum* (Ingram)
1927   *The Fair Co-ed* (Wood)
1928   *Across to Singapore* (Nigh); *Adoration* (Lloyd); *Outcast* (Seiter); *The Patsy* (K. Vidor)
1929   *The Divine Lady* (Lloyd); *Careers* (Dillon); *Hard to Get* (Beaudine); *Her Private Life* (A. Korda); *A Most Immoral Lady* (Wray); *The Painted Angel* (Webb); *Saturday's Children* (La Cava); *The Squall* (A. Korda); *The Trail of '98* (Brown)
1930   *Back Pay* (Sieter); *The Bad Man* (Badger); *In the Next Room* (Cline); *Kismet* (Dillon); *Murder Will Out* (Badger); *Road to Paradise* (Beaudine); *Sweethearts and Wives* (Badger); *Misbehaving Ladies* (Beaudine)

1931   *East Lynne* (Lloyd); *Young Sinners* (Blystone); *Hush Money* (Lanfield); *Men of the Sky* (Green); *Merely Mary Ann* (H. King); *Age for Love* (Lloyd) (co); *Over the Hill* (H. King)
1932   *She Wanted a Millionaire* (Blystone); *Careless Lady* (MacKenna); *Woman in Room 13* (H. King); *Passport to Hell* (Lloyd); *Six Hours to Live* (Dieterle)
1933   *Dangerously Yours* (Tuttle); *Ladies They Talk About* (Bretherton and Keighley); *Adorable* (Keighley); *Paddy, the Next Best Thing* (Lachman); *Mr. Skitch* (Cruze)
1934   *Coming Out Party* (Blystone); *All Men Are Enemies* (Fitzmaurice); *Springtime for Henry* (Tuttle); *Marie Galante* (H. King)
1935   *Helldorado* (Cruze); *One More Spring* (H. King); *Our Little Girl* (Robertson); *Curly Top* (Cummings); *Beauty's Daughter* (Dwan) (co); *The Littlest Rebel* (Butler)
1936   *The Country Doctor* (H. King) (co); *Captain January* (Butler); *Poor Little Rich Girl* (Cummings); *Fifteen Maiden Lane* (Dwan)
1937   *Between Two Women* (G. Seitz); *Madame X* (Wood); *Navy Blue and Gold* (Wood)
1938   *Love Is a Headache* (Thorpe); *Lord Jeff* (Wood); *Young Dr. Kildare* (Bucquet); *Stablemates* (Wood); *The Crowd Roars* (Thorpe)
1939   *Huckleberry Finn* (Thorpe); *Sergeant Madden* (von Sternberg); *Six Thousand Enemies* (G. Seitz); *Thunder Afloat* (G. Seitz); *Bad Little Angel* (Thiele)
1940   *Dr. Kildare's Strange Case* (Bucquet); *A Little Bit of Heaven* (Marton); *Dr. Kildare's Crisis* (Bucquet)
1941   **Sullivan's Travels** (P. Sturges)
1942   *Fly By Night* (Siodmak); *This Gun for Hire* (Tuttle); *The Moon and Sixpence* (Lewin); *Lucky Jordon* (Tuttle)
1943   *Five Graves to Cairo* (Wilder)
1944   *The Miracle of Morgan's Creek* (P. Sturges); *Hour Before Dawn* (Tuttle); **Double Indemnity** (Wilder); *Hail the Conquering Hero* (P. Sturges); *Casanova Brown* (Wood)
1945   *The Unseen* (Allen); **The Lost Weekend** (Wilder)
1946   *The Well Groomed Bride* (Lanfield); *Home Sweet Homicide* (Bacon); *Wild Harvest* (Garnett)
1947   *The Imperfect Lady* (Allen); *Calcutta* (Farrow)
1948   *Saigon* (Fenton); *The Big Clock* (Farrow); *A Miracle Can Happen* (*On Our Merry Way*) (Fenton and K. Vidor) (co); *Beyond Glory* (Farrow); *The Night Has a Thousand Eyes* (Farrow)
1949   *The Great Gatsby* (Nugent); *Chicago Deadline* (Allen)
1950   *Captain Carey, U.S.A.* (Leisen); **Sunset Boulevard** (Wilder); *The Goldbergs* (Hart)
1951   *Dear Brat* (Seiter); *Appointment with Danger* (Allen); *When Worlds Collide* (Maté) (co)
1952   *The San Francisco Story* (Parrish); *The Savage* (Marshall); *The Iron Mistress* (Douglas)
1953   *Desert Legion* (Pevney); *Invaders from Mars* (Menzies); *Botany Bay* (Farrow)
1954   *Saskatchewan* (Walsh); *Rocket Man* (Rudolph); *Rogue Cop* (Rowland)
1955   *Many Rivers to Cross* (Rowland); *The McConnell Story* (*Tiger in the Sky*) (Douglas); *Hell on Frisco Bay* (Tuttle)
1956   *Santiago* (Douglas); *A Cry in the Night* (Tuttle)
1957   *The Big Land* (Douglas)
1958   *The Deep Six* (Maté); *The Badlanders* (Daves)

1959   *Island of Lost Women* (Tuttle); *The Man in the Net* (Curtiz)
1960   *Guns of the Timberland* (Webb)

Publications

On SEITZ: articles—

Lightman, Herb A., in *American Cinematographer* (Hollywood), September 1950.
Films in Review (New York), October 1967.
Film Comment (New York), Summer 1972.
Focus on Film (London), no. 13, 1973.
Obituary in *Variety* (New York), 7 March 1979.
Obituary in *Ecran*, 15 April 1979.
Obituary in *Cinematographe*, April 1979.

*   *   *

The development of the photographic artistry of John F. Seitz is virtually synonymous with the evolution of cinematography itself into the sophisticated form of expression it is today. At the time of his death in 1979, he held as many as 18 patents for different photographic processes and the technology to implement them. Although he was best known for the invention of the matte shot and the use of intense low-key lighting, he was instrumental in creating a distinctive visual style for a variety of landmark films spanning both the silent and sound eras.

His career began in 1909 with the St. Louis Motion Picture Company but, in 1916, he moved to Hollywood to join Metro Pictures. There, he collaborated with the director Rex Ingram in filming such classics as *The Conquering Power*, *The Four Horsemen of the Apocalypse*, *The Prisoner of Zenda*, *Where the Pavement Ends*, and *Mare Nostrum*.

It was during his collaboration with Ingram that Seitz invented the matte process. In this procedure, a mask was employed to expose just one area of the film frame in a particular pattern. When the film was subsequently rewound and used to photograph live action, a unique artistic effect was achieved. Although employed at first for relatively simple maneuvers such as shots through keyholes and binocular views, the process quickly developed the ability to produce spectacular effects by combining live action with photographic images, backgrounds, and physical objects.

He is probably best known for his work during the 1940s when he collaborated principally as a lighting cameraman with such directors as Billy Wilder and Preston Sturges. His most famous works include *Sullivan's Travels*, *The Miracle of Morgan's Creek*, and *Hail the Conquering Hero* for Sturges as well as *Double Indemnity* and *Sunset Boulevard* for Billy Wilder.

—Stephen L. Hanson

SELIG, William N.

Producer. **Nationality:** American. **Born:** William Nicholas Selig in Chicago, Illinois, 14 March 1864. **Career:** Magician, then ran a minstrel show; 1896—after duplicating the Lumière Cinematographe in workshop, developed the Selig Standard Camera and the Selig Polyscope (a projector): opened loft in Chicago, and began producing films as Selig Polyscope Company; 1909—produced *Hunting Big Game in Africa* (based on Theodore Roosevelt's lion-hunting trip to Africa), and made other ''jungle'' films; set up studio in Hollywood (the first producer to do so); also had studio in New Orleans; produced the news series *Hearst-Selig News Pictorial*, then the *Selig Tribune*; produced the first serial in the United States; introduced Tom Mix; 1918—the Polyscope Company closed; 1922—retired. **Award:** Special Academy Award, 1947. **Died:** Hollywood, 16 July 1948.

Films as Producer (selected list):

1896   *The Tramp and the Dog*
1905   *Trapped By Bloodhounds, or The Lynching at Cripple Creek*; *The Tomboys*
1906   *The Tramp and the Dog*; *The Female Highwayman*; *Who's Who*; *Lights of a Great City*
1907   *Western Justice* (Anderson); *Dolly's Papa*
1908   *The Count of Monte Cristo* (Boggs); *Dr. Jekyll and Mr. Hyde*
1909   *Hunting Big Game in Africa* (Boggs); *In the Sultan's Power* (Boggs); *On the Little Big Horn, or Custer's Last Stand* (Boggs); *Up San Juan Hill* (Boggs); *On the Border* (Boggs)
1910   *The Merry Wives of Windsor* (Boggs?); *Davy Crockett* (Boggs); *Wizard of Oz* (Turner)
1911   *Zulu-Land*; *The Two Orphans* (Turner); *Cinderella* (Campbell), *Lost in the Jungle* (Boggs)
1912   *The Coming of Columbus* (Campbell); *Kings of the Forest* (Campbell); *Sergeant Byrne of the N.W.M.P.* (Campbell)
1913   *The Three Wise Men*; *Roses of Yesterday* (Kirkland); *Alone in the Jungle* (Campbell); *Seligettes* (series of animated designs); *Seeds of Silver* (Huntley)
1914   *The Adventures of Kathlyn* (Grandon—serial); *The Spoilers* (Campbell); *The Royal Box* (Eagle); *Rosemary, That's for Remembrance* (Grandon); *Abyss* (Santschi); *Dawn* (Le Saint); *The Fifth Man* (Grandon)
1915   *Pals in Blue* (Mix); *The House of a Thousand Candles* (Heffron)
1916   *The Ne'er-Do-Well* (Campbell); *The Black Orchid* (Heffron); *The Garden of Allah* (Campbell)
1917   *A Brother's Sacrifice* (Grandon); *Brass Monkey* (Richmond)
1918   *A Hoosier Romance* (Campbell)
1921   *The Hunger of the Blood* (Watt); *The Last Chance* (Cullison); *The Mask* (Bracken); *Kazan* (Bracken); *The Fighting Stranger* (Cullison)
1922   *The Rosary* (Storm) (co)

Publications

By SELIG: article—

''Cutting Back,'' in *Photoplay* (New York), February 1920.

*   *   *

William N. Selig was an important film producer in the early days of the motion picture industry. A Chicago-born magician, he began

779

his film career in 1895 after he saw a Dallas vaudeville hall demonstration of Thomas Edison's Kinetoscope while he was running a travelling minstrel show. Returning to Chicago, he had a projector devised by dissembling and duplicating the Lumière Cinematographe. Working with a machinist, he patented the Selig Standard Camera and the Selig Polyscope, and incorporated his equipment business, a motion-picture studio and a film processing plant as the Selig Polyscope Company in 1896.

Within a few years, Selig's Chicago-based company became the largest filmmaking plant in the United States. At his studio on the city's outskirts, he produced westerns, adventure films, and melodramas utilizing both indoor and outdoor filmmaking. Among the people he trained was G. M. ("Broncho Billy") Anderson, who worked as an actor and director for Selig from 1905 to 1907 and then formed a rival company (Essanay) with Chicago businessman George Spoor.

Selig was among the first movie producers who considered Los Angeles as a versatile moviemaking location. After sending crews there for two years, he opened a permanent Los Angeles studio in 1909. The studio became particularly important for his business when, in 1909, President Theodore Roosevelt would not allow a Selig cameraman to accompany his big game expedition to Africa. So Selig bought an aging lion from a Los Angeles zoo and staged his own tropical jungle hunt with a lead character named "Teddy." When the newspaper wire services announced that Roosevelt had "bagged" a lion, Selig released his fictional film entitled *Hunting Big Game in Africa* and scored a smash hit. The film was so successful that Selig bought an entire zoo for his Los Angeles studio and began making jungle adventure films.

Selig's company often capitalized on topical newspaper headlines, deliberately blurring the distinction between documentary and fiction. Like the Edison Company, Selig sent camera crews all over the country to shoot newsworthy events and to film background locations for fiction films. He maintained full travelling companies in both Florida and Colorado, where he shot the first movie serials. *The Adventures of Kathlyn* (1914) featured the now familiar clichés of perilous, "cliffhanger" adventures befalling a spunky but sweet heroine. Colorado's treacherous rivers and sheer mountainous drops provided both a breathtaking and realistic background for the series. The series itself, however, ended when the leading actress—executing her own stunts—drowned during the shooting of a river rapids scene.

Selig also played an important role in the industry-wide consolidation that occurred with the Motion Picture Patents Company in 1909. The 1907 outcome of an Edison Company patents infringement case against American Biograph and Mutoscope validated Edison's claim for patents ownership but did not apply the claim to Biograph's film or equipment. Stymied in its efforts to control the film industry, Edison Company instead filed suit against Selig Polyscope as an alternate means to begin an industry-wide takeover. Even before Edison vs. Selig was resolved in a Chicago Circuit Court in 1908, Selig and many Chicago film exchanges (or distributors) joined with Edison in a licensing and distribution agreement that gave Edison a lion's share of the profits while the Chicago companies retained regulatory control. The power of this association and Selig's allegiance were important weapons when Edison subsequently fought George Kleine and Biograph for control of the entire industry, a battle which resulted in the monopolistic Motion Picture Patents Company (1909).

Following the outcome of a 1915 antitrust suit, the Motion Picture Patents Company dissolved, and the fortunes of Selig's company declined. By 1918, he had been forced to close both the Chicago and Los Angeles studios, and in 1922 he retired.

—Lauren Rabinovitz

SELZNICK, David O.

Producer. **Nationality:** American. **Born:** David Oliver Selznick in Pittsburgh, Pennsylvania, 10 May 1902. **Education:** Attended Columbia University, New York. **Family:** Son of the film executive Lewis J. Selznick; brother of the producer and agent Myron Selznick; married 1) Irene Mayer (divorced); son: the producer Jeffrey Selznick; 2) the actress Jennifer Jones, 1949. **Career:** Worked for his father in promotion, production, and distribution; 1923—producer of short films; 1926–27—assistant story editor and associate producer, MGM; 1927–31—associate director, Paramount; 1931–33—vice president in charge of production, RKO; 1933–36—vice president and producer, MGM; 1936—formed Selznick International. **Awards:** Irving G. Thalberg Award, 1939; Academy Awards for *Gone with the Wind*, 1939; *Rebecca*, 1940. **Died:** 22 June 1965.

Films as Producer:

1923   *Will He Conquer Dempsey?* (short); *Rudolph Valentino and His 88 American Beauties* (short)
1924   *Roulette* (Taylor)

David O. Selznick

1927   *Spoilers of the West* (Van Dyke)
1928   *Forgotten Faces* (Schertzinger); *Wyoming* (Van Dyke)
1929   *The Four Feathers* (Cooper, Schoedsack, and Mendes);
        Chinatown Nights (Wellman); *The Man I Love* (Wellman);
        The Dance of Life (Cromwell and Sutherland); *Fast Company* (Sutherland)
1930   *Street of Chance* (Cromwell); *Sarah and Son* (Arzner)
1932   *A Bill of Divorcement* (Cukor); *Symphony of Six Million* (La
        Cava); *What Price Hollywood?* (Cukor); *State's Attorney*
        (Archainbaud); *Bird of Paradise* (K. Vidor); *Westward
        Passage* (Milton); *The Lost Squadron* (Archainbaud); *Roar
        of the Dragon* (Ruggles); *The Animal Kingdom* (*The Woman
        in His House*) (Griffith); *The Conqueror* (*Pioneer Builders*)
        (Wellman); *The Age of Consent* (La Cava); *Rockabye*
        (Cukor); *The Half-Naked Truth* (La Cava)
1933   **King Kong** (Cooper and Schoedsack); *Our Betters* (Cukor);
        Topaze (D'Arrast); *The Great Jasper* (Ruben); *Dinner at
        Eight* (Cukor); *Christopher Strong* (Arzner); *Dancing Lady*
        (Leonard); *Night Flight* (Brown); *Sweepings* (Cromwell);
        The Monkey's Paw (Ruggles); *Meet the Baron* (W. Lang);
        Little Women (Cukor)
1934   *Viva Villa!* (Conway); *Manhattan Melodrama* (Van Dyke)
1935   *David Copperfield* (Cukor); *Restless* (Fleming); *Vanessa—
        Her Love Story* (Howard); *Anna Karenina* (Brown); *A Tale
        of Two Cities* (Conway)
1936   *Little Lord Fauntleroy* (Cromwell); *The Garden of Allah*
        (Boleslawsky)
1937   *A Star Is Born* (Wellman); *Nothing Sacred* (Wellman); *The
        Prisoner of Zenda* (Cromwell)
1938   *The Adventures of Tom Sawyer* (Taurog); *The Young in Heart*
        (Wallace)
1939   *Made for Each Other* (Cromwell); *Intermezzo* (Ratoff); **Gone
        with the Wind** (Fleming)
1940   *Rebecca* (Hitchcock)
1944   *Since You Went Away* (Cromwell) (+ sc); *Reward Unlimited* (short)
1945   *Spellbound* (Hitchcock)
1946   *Duel in the Sun* (K. Vidor) (+ sc)
1948   *The Paradine Case* (Hitchcock) (+ sc); *Portrait of Jennie*
        (*Jennie*) (Dieterle)
1949   **The Third Man** (Reed) (co)
1950   *Gone to Earth* (*The Wild Heart*) (Powell and Pressburger)
1953   *Stazione Termini* (*Indiscretion of an American Wife*) (De Sica)
1957   *A Farewell to Arms* (C. Vidor)

Publications

By SELZNICK: book—

Memo from David O. Selznick, edited by Rudy Behlmer, New
    York, 1972.

By SELZNICK: article—

Cinéma (Paris), December 1985.

On SELZNICK: books—

Thomas, Bob, *Selznick*, New York, 1970.
Bowers, Ronald L., *The Selznick Players*, Stamford, 1976.
Haver, Ronald, *David O. Selznick's Hollywood*, New York, 1980.
Thompson, David, *Showman: The Life of David O. Selznick*, New
    York, 1992.
Vertrees, Alan D., *Selznick's Vision: Gone with the Wind & Holly-
    wood Filmmaking*, Austin, 1997.
Leff, Leonard J., *Hitchcock & Selznick: The Rich & Strange Collabo-
    ration of Alfred Hitchcock & David O. Selznick in Hollywood*,
    Berkeley, 1999.
Rawbin, Marcella, *Yes, Mr. Selznick: Recollections of Hollywood's
    Golden Era*, Pittsburgh, 1999.

On SELZNICK: articles—

Picturegoer (London), 15, 22, and 29 July 1950.
Films and Filming (London), January 1958.
Films in Review (New York), June-July and August-September 1963.
Cahiers du Cinéma (Paris), December 1965.
Zierold, Norman, in *The Moguls*, New York, 1969.
Journal of Screen Producers Guild (Beverly Hills, California), Decem-
    ber 1972.
Haver, Ronald, in *American Film* (Washington, D.C.), Novem-
    ber 1980.
Télérama (Paris), 14–20 July, 21–27 July, 28 July-3 August, and 4–10
    August 1981.
Cinématographe (Paris), May 1984.
Cahiers du Cinéma (Paris), November 1984.
Leff, Leonard J., in *Hitchcock and Selznick*, New York, 1987.
Schatz, Thomas, in *The Genius of the System*, New York, 1988.
Journal of Film and Video (Boston, Massachusetts), vol. 41, no. 1,
    Spring 1989.
Edwards, Anne, in *Architectural Digest* (Los Angeles), April 1992.
Lyons, Donald, "David Thomson, the Movies, and the U.S.A.," in
    Film Comment (New York), January-February 1993.
Maltby, Richard, "Overlength, Over Budget," in *Sight & Sound*
    (London), May 1993.
Fyne, Robert, in *Historical Journal of Film, Radio and Television*
    (Abingdon), March 1995.
Light, Alison, "*Rebecca*," in *Sight & Sound* (London), May 1996.
Thompson, David, in *Esquire*, September 1997.
Leff, Leonard J., in *Atlantic Monthly*, December 1999.

*   *   *

David O. Selznick will always be remembered as the producer
who created the most popular feature film made during the Golden
Age of Hollywood, *Gone with the Wind*. As such Selznick has long
signified in the mind of the filmgoing public the typical movie
producer of Hollywood's greatest era. Yet Selznick was not representative at all. He worked on his own, avowedly seeking to throw off
the restrictions and confines of laboring for a studio. He labored long
and hard to be his own boss, and because of his success "working
outside the studio system" he should be remembered as one of the
Hollywood's greatest independent filmmakers. This made him a pioneer, one who showed the way to the Hollywood of the latter half of
the twentieth century when independents became the norm. *Gone*

with *The Wind* was an exception to Hollywood practice of the 1930s, not a classic example of the studio rule.

In short David O. Selznick was always struggling to be independent and thus never came to any position of power with any degree of ease.The lone exception was his first job. This came easy for him because his father, Lewis J. Selznick, was a film industry pioneer and the head of his own production company in the late 1910s when son David began to desire to enter filmmaking himself. His father's New York City-based Selznick Pictures eventually went bankrupt, but not before his son had been tutored in all phases of industry practice. As an apprentice, David edited the company magazine, and then moved up to head of newsreel and short subjects production.

In the early 1920s David O. Selznick moved to Hollywood and through his father's connections took a job as an assistant producer at MGM. From 1928 to 1936 he moved to other studios and tried various jobs, all with little success. He simply chaffed at laboring in a studio. Yet his experience from 1928 to 1936 would prove invaluable as he learned the craft of producing feature films at three different studios. At Paramount, from 1928 to 1931, he supervised a number of significant films including *The Four Feathers* and *The Man I Love*. He then moved to RKO where from 1931 to 1933 he could not have picked a worse time to try his hand at the weakest of the major studios. Yet Selznick's experience at RKO enabled him to first gain a reputation as a producer who could produce first-rate features under severe and often straining conditions. At RKO Selznick finally moved out of the shadow of this father with films that included *What Price Hollywood?*, directed by George Cukor and starring Constance Bennett, *A Bill of Divorcement*, also directed by Cukor and starring John Barrymore and Katherine Hepburn, and one of the features most associated with RKO of the 1930s, *King Kong*. But Selznick knew he was headed nowhere at RKO and so moved on to the studio headed by his then father-in-law, Louis B. Mayer. At MGM Selznick helped create *Dinner at Eight*, directed again by Cukor and starring Jean Harlow and Marie Dressler, *David Copperfield*, starring W.C. Fields, and *A Tale of Two Cities* with Ronald Colman. No one was surprised that Selznick did not last long under the glaring eye of the domineering Mayer. In 1936 Selznick left the plush confines of MGM to form his own company to distribute films through United Artists. Contrary to the myth, the hits did not come instantly. But with the blockbuster of *Gone with the Wind* Selznick was set for life.

Or was he? Sadly Selznick spent the rest of his career searching for a follow up to *Gone with the Wind*. Only *Duel in the Sun*, starring Jennifer Jones and directed by King Vidor, ever matched its box-office clout. Money became harder and harder to find and so gradually Selznick productions emerged at a slower and slower rate. During the 1950s he fashioned but two features, ending a career that seemed so promising but a decade earlier. At the end of his life he was a celebrated "has-been," living off the wealth of his wife, actress Jennifer Jones. It was a tragic close to a career which peaked at age 37 with the single most famous Hollywood film of its day.

—Douglas Gomery

SEMPRUN, Jorge

Writer. **Nationality:** Spanish. **Born:** Jorge Maura Semprun in Madrid, 10 December 1923. **Education:** Studied philosophy and literature, Sorbonne. **Career:** Joined the Spanish Communist Party, and fought

Jorge Semprun

against Franco during the Spanish Civil War, 1930s, deported from Spain to France, 1942; fought in the French Underground against the Nazis, and was imprisoned for two years in the Buchenwald concentration camp, 1942–1945; worked as a journalist for UNESCO, 1950s; began writing novels and screenplays, 1960s; expelled from the communist party, 1965; appointed Minister of Culture in post-Franco Spain, 1988. **Awards:** Edgar Allan Poe Award (shared with Costa-Gavras), Best Motion Picture for *Z*, 1969; Jerusalem Prize for Literature, 1997.

Films as Screenwriter:

1966 *Objectif 500 millions* (Schoendoerffer) (co-sc); *La Guerre est finie* (*The War Is Over*) (Resnais) (+ ro as Narrator)
1969 *Z* (Costa-Gavras)
1970 *L'Aveu* (*The Confession*) (Costa-Gavras)
1972 *L'Attentat* (*The French Conspiracy*) (Boisset) (co-sc)
1973 *Les Deux memoires* (*The Two Memories*) (+ d)
1974 *Stavisky. . .* (Resnais)
1975 *Section speciale* (*Special Section*) (Costa-Gavras) (co-sc)
1976 *Une femme a sa fenetre* (*A Woman at Her Window*) (Granier-Deferre) (co-sc, dialogue)
1978 *Les Routes du sud* (*Roads to the South*) (Losey)

1986 *Les Trottoirs de saturne* (Santiago)
1994 *L'Affaire Dreyfus* (Boisset—for TV) (co-sc)
1997 *K* (Arcady) (co-sc)

Other Films:

1966 *Je t'aime, je t'aime* (Resnais) (ro, uncredited)
1991 *Netchaiev est de retour* (*Netchaiev Is Back*) (Deray) (based on novel)

Publications

By SEMPRUN: books—

La Guerre est finie, Paris, 1966.
L'Evanouissement, Paris, 1967.
Le Grand voyage, Paris, 1969.
La Deuxieme mort de Ramon Mercader, Paris, 1969.
Le 'Stavisky' d'Alain Resnais, Paris, 1974.
Autobiografia de Federico Sanchez, Barcelona, 1977.
El desvanecimiento, Barcelona, 1979.
Quel beau dimanche, Paris, 1980.
L'Algarabie, Paris, 1981.
Montand, la vie continue, Paris, 1983.
La Montagne blanche, Paris, 1986.
Netchaiev est de retour, Paris, 1987.
Federico Sanchez se despide de ustedes, Barcelona, 1993.
L'Écriture ou la vie, Paris, 1994.
Semprun, Wiesel: se taire est impossible, Paris, 1995.
Adieu, vive clarte, Paris, 1998.
Le Retour de Carola Neher, Paris, 1998.

By SEMPRUN: articles—

"Les Deux memoires," interview with G. Braucourt, in *Ecran* (Paris), February 1974.
"Alain Resnais, Jorge Semprun et *'Stavisky'*," interview in *Ecran* (Paris), July 1974.
Interview in *Amis du Film et de la Television* (Brussels), July/August 1974.
Semprun, Jorge, and P. Kjaeruiff-Schmidt, "En form for politisk film," in *Chaplin* (Stockholm), no. 3, 1976
"The Truth Is Always Revolutionary," interview with T. Blomquist, in *Cineaste* (New York), no. 4, 1979.
Interview in *Cinema 80* (Paris), July/August 1980.

On SEMPRUN: books—

Faber, Richard, *Erinnern und Darstellen des Unausloschlichen: uber Jorge Semprun's KZ-Literatur*, Berlin, 1995.
Soto-Fernandez, Liliana, *La Autobiografia ficticia en Miguel de Unamuno, Carmen Martin Gaite y Jorge Semprun*, Madrid, 1996.
Nicoladze, Francoise, *La Deuxieme vie de Jorge Semprun: une ecriture tressee aux spirales de l'histoire*, Castelnau-le-Lez, 1997.
Cortanze, Gerard de, *Le Madrid de Jorge Semprun*, Paris, 1997.

On SEMPRUN: articles—

Gardner, Paul, "Perhaps Another '*Marienbad*?'," in *New York Times*, 2 January 1966.
Flatley, Guy, "Movies Are Passions and My Great Passion Is Politics," in *New York Times*, 11 January 1970
Grenier, Cynthia, "The '*Z*' People Make a Confession," in *New York Times*, 6 December 1970.
Davis, Melton S., "Agent Provocateur—Of Films," in *New York Times*, 21 March 1971.
Klemesrud, Judy, "Costa-Gavras: I'm Not Anti-American," in *New York Times*, 22 April 1973.
Alvarez, A., "Alain Resnais—The Man Who Makes Movies of the Mind," in *New York Times*, 10 October 1976.

*   *   *

Jorge Semprun's filmography is sparse. Since earning his first screenwriting credit in 1966, he has worked on barely over a dozen features. Most of his significant celluloid contributions came early in his career, on films directed by Costa-Gavras (*Z*, *L'Aveu*, and *Section speciale*) and Alain Resnais (*La Guerre est finie* and *Stavisky. . .*). His most characteristic films are explorations of time and memory, and evolve directly out of his life experience. They are overtly political in nature, and feature thinly veiled recollections of his early idealism and struggles, with his status as an exile and his political disillusionment often reverberating throughout.

For Semprun, film primarily is a political tool, a medium with which to express his left-of-center concerns. His screenplays often spotlight characters who are leftists, and explore the nature of their political commitment, their personal struggles, and how their views directly impact on their lives. Nonetheless, it must be stressed that Semprun is no dogmatic armchair radical, a theorist who spouts rhetoric while ignoring everyday practicality. Nor will he lambaste the excesses of right wing dictatorships while justifying those of communist governments. In his heart he is a humanist, and he would be quick to acknowledge that oppression exists on all sides of the political spectrum. He would condemn a political leader or regime that trounces on human rights, whether that government was left- or right-leaning.

While still in his teens, Semprun became a member of the Spanish Communist Party and fought against Franco in the Spanish Civil War. Eventually, he wound up in Paris as an exile—and almost a quarter-century later he scripted *La Guerre est finie*, one of his most personal works. *La Guerre est finie* is a biting portrait of a character who easily might be Semprun's alter ego: an aging, weary Spanish communist (played by Yves Montand), long exiled in Paris. He may be fiercely committed to his political beliefs, yet despite his years of resistance his efforts to foster change have been futile. Another Semprun credit, *Les Routes du sud*, directed by Joseph Losey, is an extension of *La Guerre est finie*. It also explores Franco-ruled Spain, only here the year is 1975 and the head of state has ruled for decades. Semprun's hero (also played by Montand) is another veteran political activist who has long-opposed Franco, and long been banished to France; he remains consumed by memory as he mourns lost political struggles—and, in case there be any ambiguity, Semprun even makes the character a screenwriter. His past is endlessly impacting on his present, with his fixation on yesteryear resulting in a strained relationship with his son—and then his wife, and fellow activist, is killed in a car accident while on a mission to Spain. At their core, *La Guerre est finie* and *Les Routes du sud* are ruminations on the personal price one pays for political commitment.

Semprun's scripts are elegantly written, yet terse and to the point. For example, in *Les Routes du sud*, the writer's son accuses him of living in "a paradise of memory." "You know," he tells his father, "usually paradise is for tomorrow. Yours was yesterday. A paradise of memory. The day Franco really goes . . . when the real problems begin, you'll lose interest." The writer defends himself by retorting, "You must know the past to dominate the future." His son responds with a telling question: "What do you dominate?" The writer's failures are further mirrored when the details of his wife's death are described while a celebration of Franco's 39th anniversary in power plays on a television set. Later on, a news report informs the world that Franco has passed away. "He died in bed," the writer notes. "We didn't overthrow him."

"In Spain, we have a long history of knowing how to die," is a line from *Stavisky. . . .* Set during the early 1930s, *Stavisky. . .* is the story of the real-life title character, a penny-ante con man, palm greaser, and informer whose charisma allows him to maneuver his way into the upper echelons of French politics and industry. Yet clearly, it was a morally dissolute character like Stavisky who helped to weaken France during the pre-World War II years; he is contrasted to Leon Trotsky, who at the outset is granted asylum in France and, at the finale, is deported.

Semprun's scripts, *Stavisky. . .* included, are filled with exiled characters. In addition to Trotsky, there is a Jewish-German actress who exiled herself to Paris upon Hitler's coming to power. Then there is the line that, perhaps more than any other, helps to define Semprun: "Exile is never happy!" Another significant Semprun credit is *Les Deux memoires*, which he directed as well as scripted. *Les Deux memoires* includes interviews with those who, like Semprun, were exiled from Spain; their recollections are compared to footage of the real events of the Spanish Civil War, and remarks by those on the other side of the political spectrum.

Given the period in which Semprun himself went into exile in Paris, it is not surprising that his life there was anything but placid. First he fought in the French Underground, and then was imprisoned for two years in Buchenwald. His script for *Section Speciale*—the story of a German naval officer who is assassinated by French communists, and the Vichy government's placating the Nazis by ordering the execution of six essentially harmless French prisoners—is a stinging portrait of the abuse of power and misappropriation of justice in Occupied France.

Semprun's scripts expose right-wing political corruption, and offer sharp-eyed portraits of blundering fascists/military bureaucrats. His scenario for *Z*, the film that solidified Costa-Gavras' international reputation, involves the aftermath of the assassination of a charismatic political leader who clearly is based on Greek humanist-pacifist-leftist Gregorious Lambrakis. Conversely, *L'Aveu*—which, like *Z* is a based-on-fact account—explores the excesses of communists in power. It is the story of a loyal Czech communist and government official who finds himself arrested, thrown into solitary confinement, and coerced into admitting imaginary treasonous activity. In *Les Routes du sud*, Semprun's screenwriter/alter ego has just penned a script about a communist who is a soldier in the army of the Third Reich. The night before Hitler is set to attack the USSR, the soldier deserts and warns the Russians. Not only does Stalin refuse to believe him, but has him executed as a provocateur. Indeed, Stalin is for Semprun an ever-present villain. In *Stavisky. . .* , it is casually

noted that, according to Trotsky, Stalin betrayed the Revolution—but, sadly, the Party followed Stalin. Semprun emphasizes that it was just such miscalculations that resulted in the failure of communism.

As the decades passed, Semprun became disillusioned by communism—and, in *Les Routes du sud*, the son might as well be describing Semprun when he characterizes his father as an "ex-resistance fighter . . . ex-fighter for communism . . . 20 years devoted to the cult of Stalin . . . then 20 years wondering 'why' . . . ." He continues, "Ex-fighter for the avant-garde novel . . . ex-fighter for the political film . . . And the day death was really there around the corner . . . you let [your wife] take your place." Here, as is so often the case, Semprun is being pointedly introspective and self-critical.

It is customary for a filmmaker to automatically receive credit for the content of a film; the screenwriter's contribution often is downplayed, if not altogether ignored. Granted that the sensibilities of those who directed Semprun's scripts are linked to their content; Costa-Gavras was a Greek expatriate when he made *Z*, and Losey still was an exile from the Hollywood blacklist when he directed *Les Routes du sud*. Nonetheless, both these films—and, in fact, all the films on which he worked, no matter the director—bear the unmistakable stamp of Semprun.

—Rob Edelman

SERANDREI, Mario

Editor. **Pseudonyms:** Mark Sirandrews; Mark Suran. **Nationality:** Italian. **Born:** Naples, 23 May 1907. **Career:** 1942—began editing career with Luchino Visconti's *Ossessione* (based on James M. Cain's *The Postman Always Rings Twice*); coined the term "neorealism," first used to describe *Ossessione* and later Italian films of the 1950s and 1960s. **Awards:** Received acclaim in special Italian cinema awards for *Ossessione*, *Rocco and his Brothers*, and *The Battle of Algiers*. **Died:** 17 April 1966.

Films as Editor:

1942   *Ossessione* (Visconti)
1948   *La Terra Trema* (*The Earth Trembles*) (Visconti)
1951   *Bellissima* (Visconti)
1954   *Senso* (*Wanton Contessa*) (Visconti)
1955   *Il Bidone* (*The Swindle*) (Fellini)
1957   *Le Notti Bianche* (*White Nights*) (Visconti)
1960   *La Ragazza con la Valigia* (*Girl with a Suitcase*) (Zurlini); *Rocco e i suoi fratelli* (*Rocco and His Brothers*; *Rocco et ses freres*) (Visconti)
1961   *Estate Violenta* (*Violent Summer*) (Boisroud)
1962   *Boccaccio '70* (Visconti, De Sica, and Fellini); *Salvatore Giuliano* (Visconti)
1963   *Il Gattopardo* (*The Leopard*) (Visconti)
1964   *La Donna Scimmia* (*The Ape Woman*); *Le grande Olimpiade* (*The Grand Olympics*) (doc)
1965   *La Battaglia Di Algeri* (*The Battle of Algiers*) (Pontecorvo); *Italiano Brava Gente* (*Attack*) (De Santis)
1968   "The Witch Burned Alive" ep. of *Le Streghe* (*The Witches*) (Visconti)

Publications

On SERANDREI: articles—

"Visconti's *Rocco*," in *New York Times*, 21 September 1991.
"Neorealism and Style," in *American Cinematographer* (Hollywood), May 1972.
"*Ossessione* and Neorealism," in *Film Quarterly* (Berkeley), Spring 1985.

*   *   *

When we hear the word "neorealism," we associate it with the movement in Italian cinema when film was evolving into a phase of extreme reality, in which moviemaking was attempting to replicate everyday life. This era began in 1942 with Luchino Visconti's *Ossessione*—an Italian masterwork based on James M. Cain's *The Postman Always Rings Twice*. This film marked the quintessential debut for budding film editor Mario Serandrei, who incidentally was the one who coined the term "neorealism."

Throughout the course of cinema history, the film director has been credited with being an "auteur," but essentially it is the genius of the editor in postproduction who allows the director's voice to resonate. Along these lines, it can be said that Serandrei, along with the unique formal contributions of Visconti and other directors, is one of the "fathers" of neorealism.

In the same way film theoreticians and critics were able to detect specific stylistic and thematic motifs present in a director's ouevre (such as the French writers of *Cahiers du Cinéma*), the same can be accomplished with the works of the film editor. Perhaps one of the reasons that it was Serandrei who recognized this new phase of neorealism is that he himself had his own vision of film form. Unlike the earlier films of Sergei Eisenstein (*Battleship Potemkin* and *Strike*) which practiced the rapid juxtaposition of shots known as montage Serandrei's style is quite different; essentially, it can be deduced that Serandrei—quite aware of technique—was taking an anti-montage approach with his editing.

Beginning as early as *Ossessione*, Serandrei appeared to have a critical eye for depicting reality on the screen. This film—along with Visconti's *Bellissima* and *Rocco and his Brothers*—as well as Federico Fellini's *The Swindle* became critical neorealist movies. Serandrei's meticulous editing took on new conventions as he practiced this anti-montage style. These films—which had a number of long shots and parallel camera movements—were replete with limited cuts; this preserved the continuity of the form and story lines. The benefits of these infrequent cuts allowed the directors' shots to be studied at greater lengths, and consequently the films could be viewed as true illusions of reality.

Unlike contemporary film editor Thelma Schoonmaker (Martin Scorcese's editor for such films as *Taxi Driver*, *Raging Bull*, and *Goodfellas*) who argues that continuous editing is overrated, Serandrei is more interested in bringing the concept of "real time" to the silver screen. This concept is supported by film scholar André Bazin who wrote extensively on Visconti, De Sica, and other neorealist directors of the time in *Cahiers du Cinéma*. Although these writings focused on the directors, the work of Serandrei and his contributions to neorealism certainly can not be overlooked.

After *Ossessione*, Serandrei entered the post-World War II years. His first films after the war included *La Terra Trema*—a less recognized work—along with Visconti's *Bellissima*, *Senso*, and *White Nights*. In 1960 he edited two rather prominent neorealism films—Visconti's *Rocco and his Brothers* and *Girl with a Suitcase*, directed by Valerio Zurlini; once again, Serandrei's editing reflected this postwar realism. After the war, cinema took a drastic turn internationally; many movies were commenting on society, pop culture, and politics. Serandrei worked within the norms of technical cinema to show that film was attempting to be more raw and candid in attempting to display real events in a real society.

In 1964, he edited his first documentary, *The Grand Olympics*. Within the realm of this very different style of filmmaking, Serandrei continued to practice his neorealistic techniques to create a sense of reality. Although not considered a major work in the neorealistic movement, editing this documentary allowed him to get as close to the truth of reality as possible.

By practically inventing the term "neorealism," it is apparent that Serandrei was more or less an auteur of sorts; he was able to analyze the different signatures of Visconti, Fellini and even De Sica. In 1962 Serandrei edited *Boccaccio '70*—a trilogy of stories directed by these three great directors (perhaps the film was the precursor to the American *New York Stories*). The three episodes that made up the film were De Sica's "The Raffle," Visconti's "The Job," and Fellini's "The Temptation of Dr. Antonio." Nearing the twilight of his career, this film explores Serandrei's technical wizardry. As an editor, it was essential for him to depict the neorealistic styles of Visconti and De Sica as well as the peculiar and surreal form of Fellini. In this film, it appears that Serandrei combines his editing skills in an advanced manner; he utilizes anti-montage in the Visconti and De Sica films—but is challenged to do quite the opposite with Fellini. The juxtaposition of shots in Fellini's film are entirely dream-oriented, and thus the style of editing is purposely fragmented and discontinuous: reality versus nonreality.

Serandrei seemed to retire in 1968 after he edited a short Visconti episode in *The Witches*. He is a man who made his mark in cinema history; he will always be remembered and studied as not only a talented technical artist—but as *the* man who started the entire Italian Neorealism revolution.

—David Gonthier, Jr.

SHAMROY, Leon

Cinematographer. **Nationality:** American. **Born:** New York City, 16 July 1901. **Education:** Attended Cooper Union, New York; City College of New York; Columbia University, New York. **Family:** Married the actress Mary Anderson. **Career:** Mechanical engineer: assistant to Nicholas J. Shamroy, and developed the Lawrence motor; work as laboratory technician and photographer on experimental films attracted producers' attention: 1927—first film as cinematographer; then worked at 20th Century-Fox for 30 years. **Awards:** Academy Award for *The Black Swan*, 1942; *Wilson*, 1944; *Leave Her to Heaven*, 1945; *Cleopatra*, 1963. **Died:** July 1974.

Films as Cinematographer:

1927 *Catch As Catch Can* Hutchinson); *Land of the Lawless* (Buckingham); *Hidden Aces* (Mitchell); *Pirates of the Sky* (Andrews); *Tongues of Scandal* (Clements); *The Trunk Mystery* (Crane)

1928 *Bitter Sweets* (Hutchinson); *The Last Moment* (Fejos); *Out with the Tide* (Hutchinson); *The Tell-Tale Heart* (Klein—short)

1930 *Alma de Gaucho* (Otto)

1931 *Women Men Marry* (Hutchinson)

1932 *Stowaway* (Whitman); *A Strange Adventure* (Whitman and Del Ruth)

1933 *Jennie Gerhardt* (Gering); *Her Bodyguard* (Beaudine) (co); *Three Cornered Moon* (Nugent)

1934 *Good Dame* (Gering); *Thirty Day Princess* (Gering); *Kiss and Make Up* (Thompson); *Ready for Love* (Gering); *Behold My Wife* (Leisen)

1935 *Private Worlds* (La Cava); *She Married Her Boss* (La Cava); *Accent on Youth* (Ruggles); *She Couldn't Take It* (Garnett); *Fugitive* (Howard)

1936 *Soak the Rich* (Hecht and MacArthur); *Fatal Lady* (Ludwig); *Spendthrift* (Walch); *Wedding Present* (Wallace)

1937 *You Only Live Once* (F. Lang); *Her Husband Lies* (Ludwig); *The Great Gambini* (C. Vidor); *She Asked for It* (Kenton); *Blossoms on Broadway* (Wallace)

1938 *Young in Heart* (Wallace)

1939 *Made for Each Other* (Cromwell); *The Story of Alexander Graham Bell* (Cummings); *The Adventures of Sherlock Holmes* (Werker)

1940 *Little Old New York* (H. King); *I Was an Adventuress* (Ratoff) (co); *Lillian Russell* (Cummings); *Four Sons* (Mayo); *Down Argentine Way* (Cummings) (co); *Tin Pan Alley* (W. Lang)

1941 *That Night in Rio* (Cummings) (co); *The Great American Broadcast* (Mayo) (co); *Moon over Miami* (W. Lang) (co); *A Yank in the RAF* (H. King); *Confirm or Deny* (Mayo)

1942 *Roxie Hart* (Wellman); *Ten Gentlemen from West Point* (Hathaway); *The Black Swan* (H. King)

1943 *Crash Dive* (Mayo); *Stormy Weather* (Stone); *Claudia* (Goulding)

1944 *Buffalo Bill* (Wellman); *Greenwich Village* (W. Lang) (co); *Wilson* (H. King)

1945 *A Tree Grows in Brooklyn* (Kazan); *Where Do We Go from Here?* (Ratoff); *State Fair* (W. Lang); *The Shocking Miss Pilgrim* (Seaton); *Leave Her to Heaven* (Stahl)

1947 *Forever Amber* (Preminger); *Daisy Kenyon* (Preminger)

1948 *That Lady in Ermine* (Lubitsch and Preminger)

1949 *Prince of Foxes* (H. King); *Twelve O'Clock High* (H. King)

1950 *Cheaper by the Dozen* (W. Lang); *Two Flags West* (Wise)

1951 *On the Riviera* (W. Lang); *David and Bathsheba* (H. King)

1952 *With a Song in My Heart* (W. Lang); *Wait 'till the Sun Shines, Nellie* (H. King); *Down among the Sheltering Palms* (Goulding); *The Snows of Kilimanjaro* (H. King)

1953 *Tonight We Sing* (Leisen); *Call Me Madame* (W. Lang); *The Girl Next Door* (Sale); *White Witch Doctor* (Hathaway); *The Robe* (H. King); *King of the Khyber Rifles* (H. King)

1954 *The Egyptian* (Curtiz); *There's No Business Like Show Business* (W. Lang)

1955 *Daddy Long Legs* (Negulesco); *Love Is a Many Splendored Thing* (H. King); *Good Morning Miss Dove* (Koster)

1956 *The King and I* (W. Lang); *The Best Things in Life Are Free* (Curtiz); *The Girl Can't Help It* (Tashlin)

1957 *The Desk Set* (W. Lang)

1958 *South Pacific* (Logan) (co); *The Bravados* (H. King); *Rally 'round the Flag, Boys* (McCarey)

1959 *Porgy and Bess* (Preminger); *The Blue Angel* (Dmytryk); *Beloved Infidel* (H. King)

1960 *Wake Me When It's Over* (LeRoy); *North to Alaska* (Hathaway)

1961 *Snow White and The Three Stooges* (W. Lang)

1962 *Tender Is the Night* (H. King)

1963 *Cleopatra* (Mankiewicz); *The Cardinal* (Preminger)

1964 *What a Way to Go* (Lee Thompson)

1965 *John Goldfarb, Please Come Home* (Lee Thompson); *The Agony and the Ecstasy* (Reed); *Do Not Disturb* (Levy)

1966 *The Glass Bottom Boat* (Tashlin)

1967 *Caprice* (Tashlin)

1968 *Planet of the Apes* (Schaffner); *The Secret Life of an American Wife* (Axelrod)

1969 *Skidoo* (Preminger); *Justine* (Cukor)

Publications

By SHAMROY: articles—

"Evolution of a Cameraman," in *Films in Review* (New York), April 1951.

"Filming the Big Dimension," in *American Cinematographer* (Hollywood), May 1953.

"Shooting in CinemaScope," in *Films in Review* (New York), May 1953.

Cahiers du Cinéma (Paris), September 1963.

In *Sources of Light*, edited by Charles Higham, London, 1970.

On SHAMROY: articles—

Gavin, Arthur, on *South Pacific* in *American Cinematographer* (Hollywood), May 1958.

Gavin, Arthur, on *Porgy and Bess* in *American Cinematographer* (Hollywood), August 1959.

Gavin, Arthur, on *Cleopatra* in *American Cinematographer* (Hollywood), July 1963.

Lightman, Herb A., on *The Cardinal* in *American Cinematographer* (Hollywood), June 1964.

Lightman, Herb A., on *Planet of the Apes* in *American Cinematographer* (Hollywood), April 1968.

Film Comment (London), no. 13, 1973.

Obituary in *American Cinematographer* (Hollywood), August 1974.

Luft, Herbert, in *Films in Review* (New York), January 1975.

"Wrap Shot," in *American Cinematographer* (Hollywood), May 1997.

*   *   *

Leon Shamroy's films of the 1950s demonstrate a mastery of Technicolor. He is a colorist, and he only achieved his best work with the advent of color in the cinema. If another Hollywood cameraman,

Lee Garmes, resembles Rembrandt, as many critics feel, then it can be said that Shamroy is the cinema's equivalent to Peter Paul Rubens.

Shamroy's black-and-white films still have some interest because of their strong independent strains. In the late 1920s he participated in the making of experimental films. *The Last Moment*, which he worked on with Paul Fejos, was the first silent film made without intertitles and filmed entirely with subjective, point-of-view shots. Shamroy worked for a while with Robert Flaherty, which may have developed the cameraman's realistic side. During 1930 he did extensive documentary work more for his own enjoyment than for anything else. Reality had its own intrinsic interest for Shamroy. In forwarding his desire to make the medium of film better able to render real objects in actual space, Shamroy employed lighting in such a way as to achieve high-contrast with lots of shadows.

Nevertheless, for all his realism, he drew heavily on the artifice of film. In *Private Worlds* Shamroy was among the first to employ zoom lenses. Further, his realism was not the sort that concentrated on the slightest detail, but rather more resembles the later form of realism created by the French Impressionists; he strove for a sense of the actual world captured through light, in a glance. During the 1930s Shamroy began his association with Charles MacArthur and Ben Hecht; also, at 20th Century-Fox, Shamroy's experimental spirit was allowed to blossom under the light and nourishing control of Darryl F. Zanuck.

In the 1940s Shamroy got his great chance to work in Technicolor. It was then too that he earned three Academy Awards—in 1942 for *The Black Swan*, in 1944 for *Wilson*, and in 1945 for *Leave Her to Heaven*. He continued to perfect his color techniques. He evocatively employed studio light to suggest the natural light of Africa in *The Snows of Kilimanjaro* and *The Egyptian*—two neglected pieces of cinematic virtuosity. In *Justine*, Shamroy used one major light, with two secondary bulbs, to suggest dawn light. Shamroy was very much at home in the studio.

The peculiar balance of Shamroy's cinematography between actuality and artifice becomes clearest in *South Pacific*, where Shamroy had to use color-filter effects against his will. The shots containing these expressionistic effects, forced on him by the director Joshua Logan, are poorly integrated into the impressionistic reality of the film, done for the most part on location in the South Pacific. Shamroy was a painstaking craftsman when Hollywood was offering its strange studio blend of reality and artistry. He was much more in his element when filming the studio sets of *The King and I*, and this film is a rich and shimmering feast for the eye—one of the finest among the filmed musicals.

—Rodney Farnsworth

SHANKAR, Ravi

Composer. **Nationality:** Indian. **Born:** Benares, 7 April 1920. **Education:** Attended a French Catholic school, Paris, 1930–32; studied Kathak and Kathakali styles of classical Indian dance, Calcutta. **Family:** Married Annapurna Akbar, children: one son. **Career:** Musician and dancer with Uday Shankar Company of Hindu Dancers and Musicians in Paris, early 1930s, composer and performer on the sitar from 1939; 1945—first film as composer, *Dharti Ke Lal*;

Ravi Shankar

1945–46—music director of communist party cultural group IPTA, Bombay; 1946–47—co-founder, Indian Renaissance Artists musical group; 1949—director of music, All India Radio External Services Division (with Home Service Division, 1952); 1954—beginning of international career: toured in U.S.S.R., and later tours in the United States and Europe; 1967—opened school of Indian classical music, Los Angeles; later opened school at Varanasi.

Films as Composer:

1945   *Dharti Ke Lal* (Abbas); *Neecha Nagar* (Anand)
1955   ***Pather Panchali*** (*Father Panchali*) (S. Ray)
1956   ***Aparajito*** (*The Unvanquished*) (S. Ray); *Chairy Tale*
1957   *Parash Pathar* (Ray); *En djungelsaga* (*The Flute and the Arrow*) (Sucksdorff)
1959   ***Apur Sansar*** (*The World of Apu*) (S. Ray)
1960   *Anuradha* (Mukherjee)
1961   *Kabuliwala* (Sinha); *Megh* (U. Dutt)
1962   *Godan*
1964   *Ghum Bhangaar Gaan* (U. Dutt)
1965   *Chappaqua* (Rooks)
1968   *Charly* (Nelson)
1972   *Alice's Adventures in Wonderland* (Miller)
1977   *Mira* (Gulzar)
1982   *Gandhi* (Attenborough)
1986   *Génésis* (Sen)

Publications

By SHANKAR: books—

My Music, My Life, New York, 1968.
Sri Sri Ravi Shankar: The Way of Grace, Fairfield, 1996.

By SHANKAR: article—

Montage, July 1966.

On SHANKAR: article—

Current Biography 1968, New York, 1968.

*   *   *

Although Ravi Shankar composed small pieces on the sitar (a seven-stringed Indian instrument which he has made world-famous) as background scores for some commercial Hindi films, and composed complete scores for two offbeat Hindi films in the mid-1940s, he did not come to be known as a film composer until Satyajit Ray's *Pather Panchali* made a world sensation in 1955. Shankar composed the music after seeing only a few sequences at the request of Ray, a family friend, and recorded it in one session of 11 hours.

Although Shankar is a profound practitioner of Indian classical music on many types of instruments, his style is more fluid and innovative than most great Indian sitarists, such as Ustad Bilayet Khan who composed the score of Ray's musical film *Jalsaghar*. This is evident from his soul-stirring scores for the Apu trilogy, *Gandhi*, and *Anuradha*. In *Pather Panchali*, which remains his best film score, the sequence of the improvident father's return home with a sari for the dead daughter and the mother's breakdown in tears would not have been half as moving if it were not enhanced by a little-known string instrument, *tar sanai*. Similarly, the pathos of the sequence of Gandhi's offer of a cloth to an ill-clad woman bathing in Ganges would not have been so cathartic if accompanied by a rigid classical raga on any other instrument.

Shankar never took his film scores too seriously; they were mostly concessions to friends and admirers. Nor are his scores dramatic or cinematic enough to bring home a situation or a dialogue in a lighter vein. He is too sublime to condescend to ''ridiculous'' moments in a film, one of the reasons Ray did not use him beyond the Apu trilogy. Nevertheless, the fluidity of his style and improvisations had a free play on the soundtrack of the trilogy. According to him, Indian classical music *can* convey the entire gamut of human emotions and feelings in films if it is played with an admixture of folk music, ''or each by itself.'' ''It is wrong to say that Indian classical music cannot convey emotion.'' He is himself pleased with his scores for the trilogy and for two of Utpal Dutt's films. The ''pure gold'' in Ravi Shankar which, according to Yehudi Menuhin, drew American youth to him, also shone in his film scores, because in these casual playful pieces ''there was a synthesis of the immediacy of expression, the spontaneity, truth, and integrity of action suited to the moment that is a form of honesty characteristic of both the innocent child and the great artist.''

—Bibekananda Ray

SHARAFF, Irene

Costume Designer. **Nationality:** American. **Born:** Boston, Massachusetts, 1910. **Education:** Attended the New York School of Fine and Applied Arts, Art Students League, New York, and La Grande Chaumiere, Paris. **Career:** 1928–30—assistant designer to Aline Bernstein, Civic Repertory Theatre Company; 1932—designer for Broadway plays, and for several ballet companies; 1943–45—costume designer, MGM, then freelance designer for films. **Awards:** Academy Awards for *An American in Paris*, 1951; *The King and I*, 1956; *West Side Story*, 1961; *Cleopatra*, 1963; *Who's Afraid of Virginia Woolf?*, 1966. **Died:** 16 August 1993.

Films as Costume Designer:

1943   *Girl Crazy* (Taurog); *I Dood It* (Minnelli) (co); *Madame Curie* (LeRoy) (co); *Broadway Rhythm* (Del Ruth)
1944   **Meet Me in St. Louis** (Minnelli); *Bathing Beauty* (Sidney)
1945   *Yolanda and the Thief* (Minnelli) (co)
1946   **The Best Years of Our Lives** (Wyler); *The Dark Mirror* (Siodmak); *Ziegfeld Follies* (Minnelli) (co)
1947   *The Bishop's Wife* (Koster); *The Secret Life of Walter Mitty* (McLeod); *A Song Is Born* (Hawks)
1948   *Every Girl Should Be Married* (Hartman)
1951   **An American in Paris** (Minnelli)
1953   *Call Me Madam* (W. Lang)

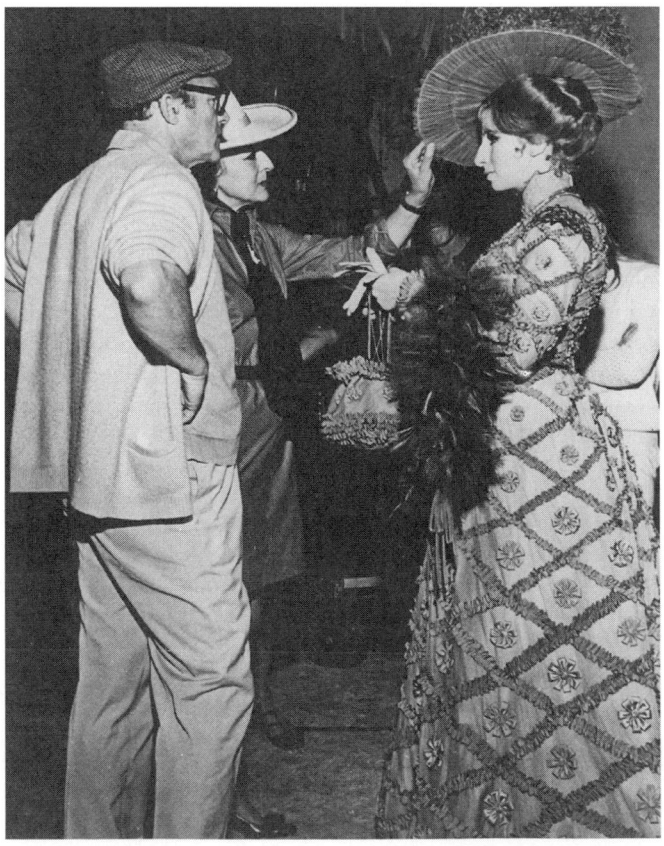

Irene Sharaff (center)

1954 *A Star Is Born* (Cukor) (co); *Brigadoon* (Minnelli)
1955 *Guys and Dolls* (Mankiewicz)
1956 *The King and I* (W. Lang)
1959 *Porgy and Bess* (Preminger)
1960 *Can-Can* (W. Lang)
1961 *Flower Drum Song* (Koster); **West Side Story** (Wise and Robbins)
1963 *Cleopatra* (Mankiewicz) (co)
1965 *The Sandpiper* (Minnelli)
1966 *Who's Afraid of Virginia Woolf?* (Nichols)
1967 *The Taming of the Shrew* (Zeffirelli) (co)
1968 *Funny Girl* (Ross)
1969 *Hello, Dolly!* (Kelly); *Justine* (Cukor)
1970 *The Great White Hope* (Ritt)
1974 *The Way We Were* (Pollack) (co)
1981 *Mommie Dearest* (Perry)

Publications

By SHARAFF: book—

Broadway and Hollywood: Costumes Designed by Irene Sharaff, New York, 1976.

By SHARAFF: article—

"Is Fashion an Art?" in *Metropolitan Museum of Art Bulletin* (New York), November 1967.
"Les costumes de *Cléopâtre*," in *Positif* (Paris), May 1977.
"*Un Américain à Paris*," in *Positif* (Paris), July-August 1996.

On SHARAFF: articles—

Theatre Arts (New York), November 1949.
Chierchetti, David, in *Hollywood Costume Design*, New York, 1976.
Leese, Elizabeth, in *Costume Design in the Movies*, New York, 1976.
LaVine, W. Robert, in *In a Glamorous Fashion*, New York, 1980.
Obituary in *The New York Times*, 17 August 1993.
Obituary in *Variety* (New York), 30 August 1993.
Dance Magazine, November 1993.
Current Biography, March 1997.

*   *   *

Making motion pictures often demands more from an artist than the duties suggested by an official title. Had "costume designer" Irene Sharaff merely sketched pretty dresses for stunning starlets, prestigious MGM studios would have slammed shut the pages of her drawing pad. But Sharaff's talent included a strong intellect, a fine eye, intuitive insights, and ingenious ability for original adaptation, and an integrating mind that united all into workable designs.

Sharaff succeeded quickly as a New York stage designer. She showed a clever use of color in her costumes for Irving Berlin's *Easter Parade*. For this stage revue, various shades of browns, tans, and other neutrals mimicked the pages of the *New York Times* rotogravure. Sharaff's designs for *Alice in Wonderland* won acclaim

as reconstructions of the original Tenniel illustrations. These successes caught the attention of MGM filmmakers who hoped to translate Sharaff's theatrical skills into bankable Hollywood ventures. Specifically, they sought a suitable designer to deal with the new technicolor process. Sharaff did not disappoint them after she joined the staff in 1942.

MGM designated Sharaff's skills to the Freed unit, which made some of the world's most memorable musicals. Almost immediately, her touch turned projects into screen gold. *Meet Me in St. Louis*, for instance, was a nostalgic valentine of lace, swiss dots, and ruffles. But the *An American in Paris* ballet sequence proved the costume designer's finest hour, as it utilized a multitude of her various talents. For this ballet, Sharaff based her visuals on a number of famous French painters. Paying homage to the Impressionists and several Post-Impressionists, she translated the colors and techniques of individual artists to set design and costume, even as she facilitated Gene Kelly's dances with garments constructed specifically for movement. Even the fabrics flowed with harmonizing rhythms.

Sharaff's career displayed considerable variety. *The King and I* sparkled with exotic ethnic dress. *Can-Can* offered an imaginative "Adam and Eve" ballet complete with guises from animal to insect. *West Side Story* glorified the uniforms of working-class New York toughs. A few years later, *The Sandpiper* peopled the beaches of Big Sur with contemporary bohemians. Sharaff often dressed Elizabeth Taylor, be it as Egyptian queen (*Cleopatra*), a brilliant but testy Renaissance jewel (*The Taming of the Shrew*), or an overweight, aging slob (*Who's Afraid of Virginia Woolf?*). Late in her career, her designs for *Mommie Dearest* amplified the lurid lustre of Hollywood glamour in the '40s and '50s.

Throughout her remarkable 50-year career, Sharaff translated her visions from stage to screen, using all the artistries of the world as inspiration. Understanding the natures of film, the stage, and ballet, she recognized their similarities and differences. Starting with this knowledge, she splashed it with just the right colors and elevated each creation to optimum advantage. Sharaff will best be remembered for taking the superficial show out of show business and replacing it with the depth of fine art.

—Edith C. Lee, updated by Denise Delorey

SHEARER, Douglas

Sound Technician. **Nationality:** Canadian. **Born:** Westmont, Quebec, 17 November 1899. **Family:** Brother of the actress Norma Shearer. Married Avice (Shearer); two sons. **Career:** 1917—worked for Northern Electric Company; 1918–20—machinist and traveling representative for an industrial power plant firm; 1920—partner in Ford automobile dealership, Montreal; 1925—worked in MGM publicity department; 1925–28—prop man at Warner Bros. and assistant cameraman at MGM; 1927–28—head of MGM Sound Department (and director of Technical Research Department, 1955–68); made many technical innovations, including devising MGM's Camera 65. **Awards:** Academy Award for *The Big House*, 1929–30; *Naughty Marietta*, 1935; *San Francisco*, 1936; *Strike Up the Band*, 1940; *Thirty Seconds over Tokyo*, 1944; *Green Dolphin Street*, 1947; *The Great Caruso*, 1951; Academy Technical Award, 1936, 1937, 1941, 1955, 1959, 1963. **Died:** In Culver City, California, 5 January 1971.

Films as Sound Technician (selected list):

1929   *The Broadway Melody* (Beaumont); *Devil-May-Care* (Franklin); *Dynamite* (DeMille); **Hallelujah** (K. Vidor); *The Trial of Mary Dugan* (Veiller); *Voice of the City* (Mack)

1930   *Anna Christie* (Brown); *The Big House* (Hill); *Call of the Flesh* (Brabin); *Let Us Be Gay* (Leonard); *Lord Byron of Broadway* (Nigh and Beaumont); *Madam Satan* (DeMille); *Min and Bill* (Hill); *The Rogue Song* (L. Barrymore); *The Sea Bat* (Ruggles); *The Unholy Three* (Conway); *Way Out West* (Niblo)

1934   **The Thin Man** (Van Dyke)

1935   *Naughty Marietta* (Van Dyke); **A Night at the Opera** (Wood)

1936   *San Francisco* (Van Dyke); *Romeo and Juliet* (Cukor)

1939   *Balalaika* (Schünzel); **Ninotchka** (Lubitsch); **The Wizard of Oz** (Fleming)

1940   *Strike Up the Band* (Berkeley); **The Philadelphia Story** (Cukor)

1944   *Thirty Seconds over Tokyo* (LeRoy)

1947   *Green Dolphin Street* (Saville)

1950   **The Asphalt Jungle** (Huston)

1951   *The Great Caruso* (Thorpe)

1952   **Singin' in the Rain** (Kelly and Donen)

Publications

By SHEARER: articles—

''The ABC of Sound,'' in *Cinema Arts*, September 1937.
In *Behind the Screen*, edited by Stephen Watts, London, 1938.
In *The Real Tinsel*, by Bernard Rosenberg and Harry Silverstein, New York, 1970.

On SHEARER: articles:—

Beatty, Jerome, in *American Magazine*, May 1937.
Film Weekly (London), 10 May 1935.

*   *   *

Douglas Shearer represented an anomaly within the film industry during the introduction of sound: whereas the embryonic sound departments of studios like Warner Bros. and RKO were initially ruled by the college-educated technicians provided by the manufacturers of their systems, Western Electric and RCA, Metro-Goldwyn-Mayer placed technical responsibility for its sound film production with Shearer, a 28-year-old Canadian high school dropout. Despite the lack of academic training, Shearer nevertheless headed both MGM's Sound Department and Technical Research Department for 41 years, winning many Oscars and holding patents ranging from studio dubbing processes to radio navigation systems for aircraft, and became perhaps one of Hollywood's most visible technicians.

In contrast to most of his counterparts at other studios, Shearer harkened back to the *bricoleur* era within the motion picture's technological evolution, when self-trained tinkerers like Francis Jenkins and Thomas Armat represented the cutting edge of technical progress. Born near Montreal in 1899, Shearer left school before graduation to pursue a number of jobs, including a relatively long stint

as a traveling representative for an industrial power plant firm which, according to Shearer, provided him with the broad background in matters mechanical and electrical that formed the technical foundation for his later pursuits in Hollywood. After visiting his sister Norma in Hollywood, Shearer decided to stay in the United States, securing various jobs at both Warner Bros. and MGM. While working in the MGM camera department in 1927, Shearer was appointed to create the studio's sound department despite his lack of specific training in the field. However, his appointment was perhaps not that unusual. Obviously, with his sister one of the studio's biggest stars and his brother-in-law being Irving Thalberg, MGM's powerful production chief, Shearer had studio contacts far beyond those of other middle echelon production employees. However, Shearer had also demonstrated prodigious technical proficiency at MGM before his assumption of sound duties, being involved in projects ranging from constructing optical printers to experimenting with early zoom lenses. Most important, perhaps, upon his arrival in Hollywood in 1925 Shearer engineered an early prompter system by which MGM publicity films shown in local theaters could be synchronized with the stars' voices broadcast over KPO radio, an audacious and early attempt at synchronized talking pictures. Also, Shearer, an attractive and athletic aviator, provided the studio with an ideal personality for publicizing the basically unglamorous technical aspect of sound film production.

During his tenure at MGM, Shearer was involved in virtually every aspect of the motion picture's technical evolution following the coming of sound; with John Arnold of the studio's Camera Department, Shearer established MGM at the forefront of studio-originated research into motion-picture technology. While disc systems were the industry standard, Shearer advocated the use of sound-on-film for production and subsequent transfer to disc, allowing far more efficient recording control and editing; later during the early days of sound, Shearer's department participated in the development of improved traveling microphones, blimped cameras, and mixing processes, and later new antiflutter mechanisms and biased push-pull recording systems. As a result, Shearer's department received early recognition, winning the first Oscar for sound recording in 1930, and consistently received Oscars throughout the years. During the remainder of his career, Shearer's accomplishments were not limited to sound. His other work included investigations of new color and projection processes, including MGM's Camera 65 widescreen process (for which he won an Oscar in 1953). Additionally, he served as a government consultant in the development of radar. By 1955, as the studio's technical research director, Shearer oversaw all aspects of the studio's technical concerns until retiring in 1968.

As the brother of one of the studio's major stars, MGM's publicity seized upon Shearer as a means of personalizing the studio's implementation of sound, promoting him as the originator of a number of technical innovations. As his patents and Oscars indicate, Shearer did possess a precocious technical mind. However, some of his technological accomplishments, like push-pull recording, undisputedly had their origins in the mammoth research laboratories of RCA and Bell Labs. Nevertheless, Shearer made a profound contribution to all aspects of motion picture technology, establishing MGM as a center of technical research while, more importantly, serving as the implementer into motion-picture practice of the technical amelioration effected by the nation's major electronic research laboratories at RCA and Bell.

—William Lafferty

SHEPARD, Sam

Writer, Director, and Actor. **Nationality:** American. **Born:** Samuel Shepard Rogers VII, Fort Sheridan, Illinois, 5 November 1943. **Education:** Attended Duarte High School, California, graduated 1960; Mount San Antonio Junior College, Walnut, California, 1960–61. **Family:** Married the actress O-Lan Johnson, 1969 (divorced), son: Jesse Mojo; children with the actress-producer Jessica Lange, daughter: Hannah Jane, and son: Samuel Walker. **Career:** Hot walker on the Santa Anita racetrack; stable hand; sheepherder and shearer; orange picker; 1962—actor with Bishop's Company Repertory Company, Burbank, California; car wrecker, Massachusetts; 1963–64—bus boy; 1964—first play produced, *Cowboys*; 1971–74—moved to England; 1974—returned to the U.S. **Awards:** Obie award, 1967, 1970, 1973, 1975, 1978 (two), 1980, 1984; Pulitzer Prize, 1979. **Agents:** Toby Cole, 234 West 44th Street, New York, NY 10036, U.S.A.

Films as Writer:

1968   *Me and My Brother* (Frank) (co-sc)
1970   *Zabriskie Point* (Antonioni) (co)
1971   *Ringaleevio*; *Oh! Calcutta!* (Levy) (co)
1978   *Renaldo and Clara* (Dylan) (co)
1984   ***Paris, Texas*** (Wenders)

Sam Shepard

1985   *Fool for Love* (Altman) (+ ro as Eddie)
1988   *Far North* (+ d)
1992   *Silent Tongue* (+ d, ro)
1994   *Curse of the Starving Class* (McClary)
1999   *Simpatico* (Warchus)

Films as Actor:

1969   *Bronco Bullfrog* (Platts-Mill) (as Jo)
1970   *Brand X*
1978   ***Days of Heaven*** (Malick) (as the Farmer)
1980   *Resurrection* (Daniel Petrie) (as Cal Carpenter)
1981   *Raggedy Man* (Fisk) (as Bailey)
1982   *Frances* (Clifford) (as Harry York)
1983   *Joe Chairkin Going On* (Gomer); *The Right Stuff* (Kaufman) (as Chuck Yeager)
1984   *Country* (Pearce) (as Gil Ivy)
1986   *Crimes of the Heart* (Beresford) (as Doc Porter)
1987   *Baby Boom* (Shyer) (as Dr. Jeff Cooper)
1989   *Steel Magnolias* (Ross) (as Spud Jones)
1991   *Defenseless* (Martin Campbell) (as George Beutel); *Voyager* (*Homo Faber*) (Schlöndorff) (as Walter Faber); *Bright Angel* (Fields) (as Jack Russell)
1992   *Thunderheart* (Apted) (as Frank Coutelle)
1993   *The Pelican Brief* (Pakula) (as Thomas Callahan)
1994   *Safe Passage* (Ackerman) (as Patrick Singer)
1995   *The Good Old Boys*
1996   *Lily Dale* (Masterson—for TV) (as Peter Davenport)
1998   *The Only Thrill* (Masterson) (as Reece McHenry)
1999   *One Kill*; *Curtain Call* (Yates) (as Will Dodge); *Purgatory* (Edel—for TV) (as Sheriff Forrest/Wild Bill Hickok); *Dash and Lilly* (as Dashiell Hammett); *Snow Falling on Cedars* (Hicks) (as Arthur Chambers)
2000   *Hamlet* (as Ghost); *One Kill* (for TV—as Major Nelson Gray); *Texas*; *The Pledge*; *All the Pretty Horses* (as Banker)
2001   *Wild Geese* (as Caleb Gare); *Just to Be Together*

Publications

By SHEPARD: plays—

Five Plays (includes *Chicago, Icarus's Mother, Fourteen Hundred Thousand, Red Cross, Melodrama Play*), Indianapolis, 1967.
La Turista, Indianapolis, 1968.
Operation Sidewinder, Indianapolis, 1970.
The Unseen Hand and Other Plays (includes *The Rock Garden, 4-H Club, Forensic and the Navigators, Cowboys #2, The Holy Ghostly, Shaved Splits, Back Bog Beast Bait*), Indianapolis, 1971.
Mad Dog Blues and Other Plays (includes *Cowboy Mouth, Cowboys #2*), New York, 1971.
The Tooth of Crime and Geography of a Horse Dreamer, New York, 1974.
Action, and The Unseen Hand, London, 1975.
Angel City and Other Plays (includes *The Rock Garden, Cowboys #2, Cowboy Mouth, Mad Dog Blues, Action, Killer's Head, Curse of the Starving Class*), New York, 1976.

Buried Child and Other Plays (includes *Suicide in B Flat*, *Seduced*), New York, 1979.

Four Two-Act Plays (includes *La Turista*, *The Tooth of Crime*, *Geography of a Horse Dreamer*, *Operation Sidewinder*), New York, 1980.

Buried Child, and Seduced, and Suicide in B Flat, London, 1980.

True West, London, 1981.

Seven Plays (includes *Buried Child*, *Curse of the Starving Class*, *The Tooth of Crime*, *La Turista*, *True West*, *Tongues*, *Savage/Love*), New York, 1981.

Chicago and Other Plays, 1982.

Fool for Love, and The Sad Lament of Pecos Bill on the Eve of Killing His Wife, San Francisco, 1983.

Fool for Love and Other Plays (includes *Angel City*, *Cowboy Mouth*, *Suicide in B Flat*, *Seduced*, *Geography of a Horse Dreamer*, *Melodrama Play*), New York, 1984.

A Lie of the Mind, New York, 1987.

States of Shock, Far North, Silent Tongue, New York, 1993.

Simpatico: A Play in Three Acts, New York, 1996.

The Unseen Hand and the Other Plays, New York, 1996.

Buried Child, New York, 1996.

Eyes for Consuela, New York, 1998.

By SHEPARD: other books—

Hawk Moon: A Book of Short Stories, Poems, and Monologues, Los Angeles, 1973.

Rolling Thunder Logbook, New York, 1977.

Motel Chronicles, San Francisco, 1982; as *Motel Chronicles and Hawk Moon*, London, 1985.

With Wim Wenders, *Paris, Texas* (screenplay), edited by Chris Sievernich, New York, 1984.

Cruising Paradise: Tales, New York, 1996.

By SHEPARD: articles—

Inter/View (New York), vol. 1, no. 3, 1969.

American Film (Washington, D.C.), vol. 10, no. 1, October 1984.

Interview (New York), vol. 18, no. 9, September 1988.

On SHEPARD: books—

Marranca, Bonnie, editor, *American Dreams: The Imagination of Sam Shepard*, New York, 1981.

Patraka, Vivian M., and Mark Siegel, *Shepard*, Boise, Idaho, 1985.

Shewey, Don, *Sam Shepard*, New York, 1985.

Oumano, Ellen, *Sam Shepard: The Life and Work of an American Dreamer*, New York, 1986.

Webster, Duncan, *Looka Yonda!: The Imaginary America of Popular Culture*, London, 1988.

Chaiken, Joseph, *Joseph Chaiken & Sam Shepard: Letters and Texts*, New York, 1989.

DeRose, David J., *Sam Shepard*, New York, 1992.

Benet, Carol, *Sam Shepard on the German Stage: Critics, Politics, Myths*, New York, 1993.

Hall, Ann C., *A Kind of Alaska: Women in the Plays of O'Neill, Pinter and Shepard*, Carbondale, Illinois, 1993.

McGhee, Jim, *True Lies: The Architecture of the Fantastic in the Plays of Sam Shepard*, New York, 1993.

Wilcox, Leonard, editor, *Rereading Shepard: Contemporary Critical Essays on the Plays of Sam Shepard*, New York, 1993.

Graham, Laura, *Sam Shepard: Theme, Image, and the Director*, New York, 1995.

McDonough, Carla J., *Staging Masculinity: Male Identity in Contemporary American Drama*, Jefferson, 1996.

Wade, Leslie A., *Sam Shepard & the American Theatre*, Westport, 1997.

Bottoms, Stephen J., *The Theatre of Sam Shepard: States of Crisis*, New York, 1998.

Callens, Johan, *Sam Shepard: Between the Margin & the Center 1 & 2*, Newark, 1998.

On SHEPARD: articles—

Film Comment (New York), vol. 19, no. 6, November/December 1983.

Lahr, John, in *Automatic Vaudeville*, New York, 1984.

Positif (Paris), no. 303, May 1986.

Image et son (Paris), no. 449, May 1989.

Literature/Film Quarterly, vol. 20, no. 2, 1992.

Special Sam Shepard and Contemporary American Drama issue, *Modern Drama*, vol. 36, no. 1, March 1993.

Modern Drama, vol. 37, no. 3, Fall 1994.

Modern Drama, vol. 37, no. 4, Winter 1994.

*   *   *

Sam Shepard has worked as a playwright, musician, director, actor, and screenwriter. As the last, Shepard gained early recognition as a co-scripter of Antonioni's *Zabriskie Point*. Earlier he wrote the little-seen *Me and My Brother*, a harsh semidocumentary treatment of mental illness and the homeless. In the 1970s he contributed to a trio of films with similarly troubled distribution histories: *Ringaleevio*, *Oh! Calcutta!*, and Bob Dylan's *Renaldo and Clara*. After this line of quirky and mainly obscure films, Shepard vaulted into prominence as a film writer in the mid-1980s with the release of *Paris, Texas*, a film which has the resonance of his best stage plays and which takes up some of their concerns. Avoiding the facile regeneration-of-the-nuclear-family plots that have traditionally meant good box office, Shepard has closely examined some of the same questions, rejecting the reassurances about the family for which mainstream Hollywood is well known (his film actor-only roles, by contrast, often fit more comfortably into the Hollywood mold, as in *The Right Stuff* and *Baby Boom*).

Paris, Texas revolves around a father and son attempting reconciliation, often a primary thematic concern of Shepard's plays. The story also offers some symptomatic dualities: both sprawling and tightly organized, both dreamy and wonderfully concrete. As such it seems a worthy companion piece to Shepard's mature stage work, which also seeks to push the conventions of contemporary drama to their limits. The film is formally organized by the wanderings of Travis (Harry Dean Stanton), which describe a rambling circuit of the American Southwest—Shepard territory for sure. Motifs of fire and water figure importantly and help pull together the enigmatic narrative. Travis is obsessed with water in the early parts of the film:

carrying a water jug, eating ice, leaving a shower running, playing with a faucet. At first this obsession seems related to his physical burning in the desert, perhaps a symptom of madness; later it is revealed that he has an emotional fire he cannot quite put out. In a more isolated instance, there is a doom-shouter whom Travis encounters on an overpass. At first the prophet's words are dissociated, free-floating, apparently nondiegetic. When Travis passes by the shouter, the abstract becomes concrete again, and the scene has a wonderful formal power. While some of the credit for this work must also go to L. M. Kit Carson, who wrote the adaptation from Shepard's story, Shepard's later film work shows increasing control on his part.

Fool for Love is his first and, so far, only film adaptation of one of his own plays. Director Robert Altman and Shepard open up the story visually and make some interesting choices, particularly in the intermingling of past and present, of thought and action. Again, figures of forbidden love and problematic fatherhood appear prominently. Eddie (Sam Shepard) and May (Kim Basinger) share a passion that they cannot quite consummate and cannot quite contain. Here, fire imagery builds and becomes literal at the climax. The Old Man (Harry Dean Stanton), an incredibly divisive father figure, is at the root of all this trouble. Rootlessness, on the other hand, is also a main concern. For instance, Eddie's journey to May, stated as one of thousands of miles contained in a relatively smaller geographic area, suggests a circuitous route, and the description of it melds with the serpentine workings of the plot. Also, Eddie and the Old Man take an apparently aimless walk, similar to wanderings in both *Paris, Texas* and *Far North*.

Shepard wrote the original screenplay for *Far North*, which was also his directorial debut. Shepard took advantage of this amount of control to film his most satisfying, and most completely personal, screenplay yet. The film examines "a notable lack of menfolk" regarding one family in particular and contemporary society in general, in a shading on the concerns central to both *Paris, Texas* and *Fool for Love*. Shepard's wordplay with Midwestern vernacular in *Far North* helps make the "personal idea of justice" speech by Bertrum (Charles Durning) and the "teaching/learning" monologue by Kate (Jessica Lange) rate with his best. Together, these speeches highlight the basically incompatible spheres of influence the sexes occupy in Shepard's world view: while men are out doing destructive things, women take the time for family, for nurturing. Men act this way out of personal concern. Women think more of group welfare. Attempts made by one group to teach the other will be ignored, or at least not learned. An organizing device in *Far North* has men and women doing similar things, first drinking and later taking a journey through the woods, to dissimilar effect in each case: violent men drift apart, and nurturing women come together. Throughout his work this pattern remains consistent. In just these three films Shepard's voice has been powerful enough to create an important countercurrent to the Hollywood mainstream.

Although Shepard has frequently directed and written for the screen, since the 1980s he has worked most often as a actor. With a cleft chin and lanky physique contributing to his rugged good looks, Shepard has habitually played leading men in films and received an Academy Award nomination in 1983 for his portrayal of astronaut Chuck Yeager in *The Right Stuff*.

—Mark Walker, updated by David Levine

SHERRIFF, R. C.

Writer. **Nationality:** British. **Born:** London, 1896. **Career:** Insurance clerk; 1928—first play, *Journey's End*, an overnight success; 1931—hired as writer by the director James Whale at Universal Studios in Hollywood; returned to Britain; 1935—returned to Hollywood, remained during World War II; returned to Britain after the war. **Died:** In London, 1975.

Films as Writer:

1930   *Journey's End* (Whale)
1932   ***The Old Dark House*** (Whale) (dialogue)
1933   *The Invisible Man* (Whale)
1934   *One More River* (*Over the River*) (Whale)
1937   *The Road Back* (Kenyon)
1938   *Three Comrades* (Borzage) (uncredited)
1939   *The Four Feathers* (Z. Korda); *Goodbye Mr. Chips* (Wood)
1941   *Lady Hamilton* (*That Hamilton Woman*) (A. Korda)
1942   *This above All* (Litvak); ***Mrs. Miniver*** (Wyler) (uncredited)
1943   *Forever and a Day* (Clair)
1947   *Odd Man Out* (Reed)
1948   *Quartet* (Crabtree)
1950   *Trio* (Annakin)
1951   *No Highway* (Koster)

R. C. Sherriff

1952   *Home at Seven* (Richardson)
1955   *Storm over the Nile* (Young); *The Dam Busters* (Anderson);
         The Night My Number Came Up (Norman)

Publications

By SHERRIFF: book—

No Leading Lady (autobiography), 1969.

On SHERRIFF: article—

Radio Times (London), vol. 259, no. 3388, 5 November 1988.

*   *   *

R. C. Sherriff's career as a writer began with the play *Journey's End*, a bleak study of life in the trenches during the First World War. Sherriff, a veteran of the war, was an insurance clerk when he wrote the play for his local amateur dramatics society. Favourable notices brought *Journey's End* to the attention of an aspiring actor, Laurence Olivier, and the director James Whale, both of whom were instrumental in arranging a West End production of the play. Despite the fact that *Journey's End* carried an antiwar message and had "no leading lady" (the title of Sherriff's autobiography), it was an enormous success and established the insurance clerk as an esteemed author virtually overnight.

When subsequent success in the West End eluded him, Sherriff joined James Whale at Universal Studios in Hollywood in 1931, where he adapted J. B. Priestley's *The Old Dark House* and H. G. Wells' *The Invisible Man*. These were very successful and are now regarded as classic horror films. Sherriff did not return to the horror genre, but found himself in demand as a writer of films concerning the First World War (*The Road Back*, *Three Comrades*) and as a faithful adaptor of British novels. In the late 1930s these adaptations had developed a patriotic flavour. *Goodbye Mr. Chips*, for example, is a nostalgic celebration of British traditions, while *The Four Feathers* wholeheartedly endorses British rule over the Empire.

Goodbye Mr. Chips set the tone for Hollywood's many tributes to Britain at war; and Sherriff, along with expatriate writers James Hilton, Arthur Wimperis and Claudine West became one of the leading writers of this genre. *Lady Hamilton*, a costume melodrama that told the story of the adulterous love affair of Lady Hamilton and Lord Nelson, was also the story of Nelson's triumph over Napoleon, and the contemporary parallels to Hitler were broadly drawn. It was one of Sherriff's few original screenplays, and was reportedly Winston Churchill's favourite film. *This above All*, an adaptation of a novel by Eric Knight, was a more typical example of Hollywood's wartime "British" melodramas. The usual British stereotypes—the haughty aristocrats and the quaint Cockneys—are portrayed as working together for the common wartime cause.

It was *Mrs. Miniver*, though, that made the most impact. The story of an "average" British housewife facing the blitz won six Oscars and was MGM's top grossing film of the 1940s. Although Sherriff did not receive a screen credit, he wrote two key scenes for *Mrs. Miniver*:

the opening scene, in which a frivolous prewar Mrs. Miniver shops for hats; and the scene in the bomb shelter that shows Mrs. Miniver reading *Alice in Wonderland* to her family during an air raid. The latter scene was almost identical to scenes in *Journey's End* and *Goodbye Mr Chips*, in which we witness the same example of the British stiff-upper-lip in action. In *Journey's End*, however, the reading scene has an ironic edge, as the men's bravery leads to their death. In the later films the irony has been removed, and the bravery of Mr. Chips and Mrs. Miniver is presented in the spirit of "Britain can take it." Patriotic propaganda was the order of the day, and the author of the "antiwar" *Journey's End* proved to be particularly adept at providing it.

In Britain after the war, Sherriff's thematic concerns continued to centre on the archetypal, understated Englishman and how he responds to war. *The Dam Busters*, for example, shows an English intellectual applying his genius to defeat the Germans; and the plot of *Home at Seven* hinges upon the aftereffects of the war on a suburban gentleman. In the late 1950s, with the "kitchen sink" in vogue in British theatre and cinema, Sherriff found his patriotic themes and middle-class characters out of date, and he retired. Despite his long career and impressive filmography, his usual epitaph states that he never quite lived up to the standard set by *Journey's End*.

—H. M. Glancy

SHERWOOD, Robert E.

Writer. **Nationality:** American. **Born:** Robert Emmett Sherwood in New Rochelle, New York, 4 April 1896. **Education:** Attended Milton Academy, Massachusetts; Harvard University, Cambridge, Massachusetts, B.A. 1918. **Military Service:** 1917–19—served in the Canadian Black Watch in France. **Family:** Married 1) Mary Brandon, 1922 (divorced 1934); one daughter; 2) Madeline Hurlock Connelly, 1935. **Career:** Journalist: drama editor, *Vanity Fair*, New York, 1919–20, film critic, 1920–24, and motion picture editor, 1924–28, *Life* magazine, and literary editor, *Scribner's Magazine*, 1928–30; 1924—first film as writer, *The Hunchback of Notre Dame*; 1926—first play produced, *The Road to Rome*; 1937–40—President, Dramatists Guild; 1938—founder, with S. N. Behrman and others, Playwrights Company; 1939–42—Special Assistant to the Secretary of War, then Director of the Overseas Branch of the Office of War Information, 1942–44, and Special Assistant to the Secretary of the Navy, 1945. **Awards:** Pulitzer Prize (for drama) for *Idiot's Delight*, 1936; *Abe Lincoln in Illinois*, 1939; *There Shall Be No Night*, 1941; (for biography) for *Roosevelt and Hopkins*, 1949; Academy Award for *The Best Years of Our Lives*, 1946. **Died:** 14 November 1955.

Films as Writer:

1924   *The Hunchback of Notre Dame* (Worsley)
1926   *The Lucky Lady* (Walsh)
1931   *The Age for Love* (Lloyd); *Around the World in Eighty Minutes with Douglas Fairbanks* (Fleming)
1932   *Cock of the Air* (Buckingham)
1933   *Roman Scandals* (Tuttle)
1935   *The Scarlet Pimpernel* (Young)

Robert E. Sherwood

1936　*The Ghost Goes West* (Clair)
1937　*Thunder in the City* (Gering)
1938　*The Adventures of Marco Polo* (Mayo); *The Divorce of Lady X* (Whelan)
1939　*Idiot's Delight* (Brown)
1940　*Abe Lincoln in Illinois* (Cromwell); *Rebecca* (Hitchcock)
1946　**The Best Years of Our Lives** (Wyler)
1947　*The Bishop's Wife* (Koster)
1953　*Man on a Tightrope* (Kazan); *Main Street to Broadway* (Garnett)

Publications

By SHERWOOD: plays—

The Road to Rome, New York, 1927.
The Queen's Husband, New York, 1928.
Waterloo Bridge, New York, 1930.
This Is New York, New York, 1931.
Reunion in Vienna, New York, 1932.
The Petrified Forest, New York, 1935.
Idiot's Delight, New York, 1936.
Tovarich, New York, 1937.
Abe Lincoln in Illinois, New York, 1939.
There Shall Be No Night, New York, 1940.
Miss Liberty, New York, 1948.
Small War on Murray Hill, New York, 1957.

By SHERWOOD: other books—

(Editor), *The Best Moving Pictures of 1922–23*, Boston, Massachusetts, 1923.
The Virtuous Knight (novel), New York, 1931, as *The Unending Crusade*, London, 1932.
The Ghost Goes West (script) in *Successful Film Writing*, by Seton Margrave, London, 1936.
The Adventures of Marco Polo (script) in *How to Write and Sell Film Stories*, by Frances Marion, New York, 1937.
With Joan Harrison, *Rebecca* (script) in *Twenty Best Film Plays*, edited by John Gassner and Dudley Nichols, New York, 1943.
Roosevelt and Hopkins, New York, 1948, as *The White House Papers of Harry L. Hopkins*, 2 vols., London 1948–49.
Robert E. Sherwood: Film Critic, Brooklyn, 1973.

By SHERWOOD: articles—

"Renaissance in Hollywood," in *American Mercury* (New York), April 1929.
Picturegoer (London), 11 August 1934.
Film Weekly (London), 2 July 1938.
"They're Film Writers, Not Juke Boxes," in *New York Times Magazine*, 2 December 1946.

On SHERWOOD: books—

Shuman, R. Baird, *Robert E. Sherwood*, New York, 1964.
Brown, John Mason, *The Worlds of Robert E. Sherwood: Mirror to His Times 1896–1939*, New York, 1965.
Brown, John Mason, *The Ordeal of a Playwright: Robert E. Sherwood and the Challenge of War*, New York, 1970.
Meserve, Walter J., *Robert E. Sherwood, Reluctant Moralist*, New York, 1970.

On SHERWOOD: articles—

Film Comment (New York), Winter 1970–71.
Hagemann, E.R., "An Extraordinary Picture: The Film Criticism of Robert E. Sherwood," in *Journal of Popular Film* (Bowling Green, Ohio), Spring 1972.
Film Comment (New York), September-October 1972.
Wolfe, Ralph Haven, in *American Screenwriters*, edited by Robert E. Morsberger, Stephen O. Lesser, and Randall Clark, Detroit, Michigan, 1984.

*　　*　　*

Robert E. Sherwood probably is best known for his plays (*Waterloo Bridge*, *The Petrified Forest*, *Idiot's Delight*, and *Abe Lincoln in Illinois*) and his book on President Franklin D. Roosevelt (*Roosevelt and Hopkins*). But it should not be forgotten that he had a long and distinguished association with the movies.

Sherwood began his association with the movies as a film critic for the humor magazine *Life*. His film criticism gave him an entree to Hollywood, and his first film work came in 1924 when he was paid the handsome sum of $2,500 to rewrite subtitles for the classic silent version of *The Hunchback of Notre Dame*.

Sherwood probably did his best screenwriting for the producer Sam Goldwyn. In 1933 Robert Sherwood and George S. Kaufman turned George Bernard Shaw's *Androcles and the Lion* into Goldwyn's *Roman Scandals*, starring Eddie Cantor. But surely Sherwood's greatest effort in the movies came with Goldwyn's award-winning *The Best Years of Our Lives*. This classic film not only pleased the critics of its day but its reputation has remained high, as it is recognized as the best of Hollywood's many looks at the American soldier's reentry into society after the Second World War. *The Best Years of Our Lives* swept the Academy Awards of its day and continues to be regularly shown in revival houses, on the late show, and now on video cassette. Much of the credit for the film's touching dialogue belongs to Sherwood. It is also reported that Sherwood tendered many of the suggestions for the final cut, along with the director Wyler and Goldwyn. *The Best Years of Our Lives* stands as a great example of Hollywood filmmaking at its peak.

Sherwood also turned Daphne du Maurier's best-selling novel *Rebecca* into an equally popular film starring Laurence Olivier and Joan Fontaine. Today *Rebecca* is remembered as Alfred Hitchcock's first Hollywood film. The writer also spent considerable time adapting his popular plays into movies. This series of adaptations reached a peak in the years immediately preceding the Second World War. *Idiot's Delight*, based on his 1936 Pulitzer Prize-winning play, was the first of his plays he adapted for the screen. Starring Norma Shearer and Clark Gable, the film was one of Hollywood's rare antiwar movies. Also adopted from a Sherwood Pulitzer Prize-winning play was *Abe Lincoln in Illinois*, in which Raymond Massey recreated an image of Lincoln which would stand paramount for a generation.

—Douglas Gomery

SHOSTAKOVICH, Dmitri

Composer. **Nationality:** Russian. **Born:** Dmitri Dimitriyevich Shostakovich in St. Petersburg, 25 September 1906. **Education:** Studied under Nikolayev, Steinberg, and Glazunov at the Leningrad Conservatory, 1919–25. **Career:** Important compositions performed in mid-1920s; 1929—first film score, for *The New Babylon*; composer of orchestra and stage works. **Died:** In Moscow, 9 August 1975.

Films as Composer:

1929 *Novyi Vavilon* (*The New Babylon*) (Kozintsev and Trauberg)
1931 *Odna* (*Alone*) (Kozintsev and Trauberg); *Zlaty gori* (*Golden Hills*) (Yutkevich)
1932 *Vstrechnyi* (*Counterplan*) (Yutkevich and Ermler)
1935 *Yunost Maxima* (*The Youth of Maxim*) (Kozintsev and Trauberg); *Podrugi* (*Girl Friends*) (Arnstam)
1937 *Vozvrashcheniye Maxima* (*The Return of Maxim*) (Kozintsev and Trauberg); *Volochayevskiye dni* (*The Days of Volotchayev*) (G. and S. Vasiliev)
1938 *Chelovek s ruzhyom* (*The Man with a Gun*) (Yutkevich)
1938–39 *Velikii grazhdanin* (*A Great Citizen*) (Ermler—2 parts)
1939 *Vyborgskaya storona* (*New Horizons*; *The Vyborg Side*) (Kozintsev and Trauberg)
1944 *Zoya* (Arnstam)
1947 *Molodaya gvardiya* (*Young Guard*) (Gerasimov); *Pirogov* (Kozintsev)
1948 *Michurin* (Dovzhenko)

1949 *Vstrecha na Elbe* (*Encounter at the Elbe*) (Alexandrov); *Padeniye Berlina* (*The Fall of Berlin*) (Chiaureli)
1952 *Nezabyvayemyi 1919-god* (*The Unforgettable Year 1919*) (Chiaureli)
1953 *Belinsky* (Kozintsev)
1954 *Das Lied der Ströme* (*Songs of the Rivers*) (Ivens)
1955 *Ovod* (*The Gadfly*) (Fainzimmer)
1956 *Prostiye lyudi* (*Simple People*) (Kozintsev and Trauberg—produced 1945); *Pervye eshelon* (*The First Echelon*) (Kalatazov)
1959 *Khovanshchina* (Stroyeva)
1960 *Pyat dney—pyat nochey* (*Five Days—Five Nights*) (Arnstam)
1962 *I sequestrati di Altona* (*The Condemned of Altona*) (De Sica)
1963 *Cheryomushki* (*Song over Moscow*) (Rappaport); *Hamlet* (Kozintsev)
1967 *Katerina Izmailova* (Shapiro) (+ sc); *Oktiabr* (*October*) (Eisenstein) (new version); *Sofiya Perovskaya* (Arnstam)
1971 **Korol Lir** (*King Lear*) (Kozintsev)

Publications

By SHOSTAKOVICH: books—

The Power of Music, New York, 1968.
Testimony: The Memoirs of Shostakovich, edited by Solomon Volkov, New York, 1979.
Dimitry Shostakovich: About Himself and His Times, edited by L. Grigoryev and Yakov Platek, Moscow, 1981.
Pisma k drugu: Dimitrii Shostakovich [Correspondence. Selections], with commentary by I. D. Glikmana, Moscow, DSCH, 1993.

On SHOSTAKOVICH: books—

Seroff, Victor, *Dimitry Shostakovich*, New York, 1943, revised edition 1970.
Rabinovich, D., *Dimitry Shostakovich, Composer*, London, 1959.
Kay, Norman, *Shostakovich*, London, 1971.
Roseberry, Eric, *Shostakovich*, London, 1981.
Hulma, Derek C., *Dimitry Shostakovich: Catalogue, Bibliography, and Discography*, Muir of Ord, Scotland, 1982.
Norris, Christopher, *Shostakovich*, London, 1982.
Martynov, Ivan I., *Dimitri Shostakovich: The Man & His Work: Music Book Index*, Temecula, 1993.
Meyer, Krzysztof, *Dimitri Chostakovitch*, Paris, Fayard, 1994.
Wilson, Elizabeth, *Shostakovich: A Life Remembered*, Princeton, NJ, University Press, 1994.
Shostakovich Studies, edited by David Fanning, New York, Cambridge University Press, 1995.

On SHOSTAKOVICH: articles—

Soviet Film (Moscow), May 1964.
Iskusstvo Kino (Moscow), July 1967.
Soviet Film (Moscow), August 1967.
Soviet Film (Moscow), September 1976.
Filmcritica (Rome), May-June 1980.
Iskusstvo Kino (Moscow), December 1981.
Cineforum, vol. 31, no. 308, 1991.
DSCH Journal, no. 1, Summer 1994.

Dmitri Shostakovich

Atlantic Monthly, vol. 275, February 1995
Commentary, vol. 99, February, 1995.
Index on Censorship, November-December 1998.
Commentary, vol. 107, June 1999.
Commentary, vol. 108, October 1999.
Mosaic (Winnipeg), December 1999.
Forbes, 20 March 2000.

*   *   *

No other major composer devoted more of his career to film music than Dmitri Shostakovich. Altogether he composed scores for 36 films, from *The New Babylon* in 1929 to *King Lear* in 1971. (He also started work on a further project, *The Envoys of Eternity*, but the film was never realised.) Movies provided an invaluable source of income for Shostakovich at those times when he fell into official disfavour, but he also had a genuine love of cinema. One of his earliest jobs was providing piano accompaniment in a movie house; he was sacked for laughing so much at a Hollywood comedy that he forgot to play.

Since he was sensitive to the specific demands of the medium, Shostakovich's film music tends to be written in a more accessible idiom than most of his orchestral or chamber works. But there was never anything careless or slipshod about it. He brought to the task unfailingly scrupulous craftsmanship, and once when asked about the subject quoted a remark of Gogol's about writing for children: ''The same as for adults, only better.'' And in his film scores, no less than in the symphonies and string quartets, can be seen every aspect of his complex and often paradoxical musical personality.

His first score, to accompany Kozintsev and Trauberg's silent *New Babylon*, is full of the parodistic, nose-thumbing humour that characterises so much of his early work. Scenes of the outbreak of the Franco-Prussian War are accompanied, not by the expected martial rhythms, but by oompah circus tunes and pratfalls from the percussion. Irreverent quotation figures strongly, with Offenbach's *Orpheus* can-can at one point interwoven with the Marseillaise. Shostakovich's approach perfectly matched the film's sardonic expressionism, but the score aroused widespread hostility and many cinemas refused to use it.

Undeterred, he followed similar principles in his first sound film, *Alone*, also for Kozintsev and Trauberg. Shostakovich established a lifelong rapport with Kozintsev, scoring all his sound films except *Don Quixote*. The two were in complete agreement on the essential function of film music: not to illustrate the action but to add an entirely new dimension, often running in counterpoint to the visuals or even undercutting them.

Shostakovich's keen dramatic sense, and his mercurial skill in juxtaposing frivolity with despair—often using one to suggest the other—served him particularly well in his film music. To say that much of it is trivial is no condemnation: he valued trivial music, granting it a legitimate role in even his most serious symphonic compositions. Few composers could have been better suited to animated films, and it is a great shame that Mikhail Tsekhanovsky's feature-length "cartoon comic-opera," *The Tale of the Priest and His Servant Balda*, was never completed (and the footage subsequently lost). Luckily, Shostakovich's exuberant score survives, so vivid that one can almost see the visuals it accompanied.

For the patriotic films of the 1940s and 1950s Shostakovich supplied more conventional material, although an undercurrent of scepticism and personal anguish, as in the 7th and 8th Symphonies, prevented him falling back on bombastic Soviet cliché. His score for *Five Days—Five Nights* creates a poignant vision of the shattered city of Dresden, with pity for war's victims (of whatever nationality) and hope for the future expressed in a passionate orchestral climax built around a theme from Beethoven's Choral Symphony.

Shostakovich's film music also gave vent to the romantic side of his character—though tempered, once again, by a pervasive sense of irony. For *The Unforgettable Year 1919* he devised a single-movement piano concerto that rivals Addinsell's Warsaw Concerto in its lush Rachmaninovian pastiche. *The Gadfly*, a period swashbuckler set in Austrian-occupied Italy, inspired one of his most tuneful and approachable scores, including a Romance that became something of a popular hit as theme music for the British TV serial *Reilly, Ace of Spies*.

The sparse textures and sombre tones of Shostakovich's late style colour his scores for Kozintsev's two powerful Shakespeare films, *Hamlet* and *King Lear*. *Hamlet* is full of obsessive, driving rhythms, punctuated by fierce outbursts of percussion, while passages of high skittering woodwind suggest mental disturbance. The music for *Lear* is even darker, with slow rumbling brass chorales reflecting the inexorable disaster overtaking king and country alike. Both scores do full justice to Kozintsev's epic conception of the plays, and bring Shostakovich's career as a film composer to an impressive conclusion.

—Philip Kemp

SIODMAK, Curt

Writer and Director. **Nationality:** American. **Born:** Kurt Siodmak in Dresden, Germany, 10 August 1902; brother of the director Robert Siodmak. **Education:** Attended the University of Zurich, Ph.D. 1927. **Family:** Married Henrietta de Perrot, 1931, one son. **Career:** Reporter, freelance writer, and railway engineer; 1929—first film as writer, *People on Sunday*; 1930—first novel published; 1934–37—writer for Gaumont-British; 1937—moved to the United States, and writer for Paramount, 1938–40, and Universal, 1940–46; 1951—first film as director, *Bride of the Gorilla*; 1952—formed production company with Ivan Tors.

Films as Writer:

1929   *Menschen am Sonntag* (*People on Sunday*) (R. Siodmak and Ulmer—doc)
1931   *Der Mann, der seinen Mörder sucht* (*Looking for His Murderer*) (R. Siodmak); *Le Bal* (Thiele)
1932   *F.P.1 antwortet nicht* (*F.P.1*; *F.P.1 Does Not Answer*; *F.P.1 Does Not Reply*) (Hartl)
1934   *La Crise est finie* (*The Slump Is Over*) (R. Siodmak); *Girls Will Be Boys* (Varnel)
1935   *Transatlantic Tunnel* (*The Tunnel*) (Elvey); *It's a Bet* (Esway)
1936   *I Give My Heart* (*The Loves of Madame Du Barry*) (Varnel)
1937   *Non-Stop New York* (Stevenson)
1938   *Her Jungle Love* (Archainbaud)
1940   *The Invisible Man Returns* (May); *Black Friday* (Lubin); *The Ape* (Nigh)
1941   *Pacific Blackout* (Murphy); *The Invisible Woman* (Sutherland); *Aloma of the South Seas* (Santell); *Midnight Angel* (Murphy)
1942   *Invisible Agent* (Marin); *London Black-Out Murders* (*Secret Motive*) (G. Sherman); *The Wolf Man* (Waggner)
1943   *Son of Dracula* (R. Siodmak); *Frankenstein Meets the Wolf Man* (Neill); *I Walked with a Zombie* (J. Tourneur); *The Purple V* (G. Sherman); *The Mantrap* (G. Sherman); *False Faces* (G. Sherman)
1944   *House of Frankenstein* (Kenton); *The Climax* (Waggner)
1945   *Shady Lady* (Waggner); *Frisco Sal* (Waggner)
1946   *The Return of Monte Cristo* (Levin)
1947   *The Beast with Five Fingers* (Florey)
1948   *Berlin Express* (J. Tourneur)
1949   *Tarzan's Magic Fountain* (Sholem); *Four Days' Leave* (*Swiss Tour*) (Lindtberg)
1953   *Riders to the Stars* (Carlson)
1955   *Creature with the Atom Brain* (Cahn)
1956   *Earth vs. Flying Saucers* (Sear)
1962   *Sherlock Holmes und das Halsband des Todes* (*Sherlock Holmes and the Deadly Necklace*) (Fisher)
1970   *Hauser's Memory* (Sagal—for TV)

Films as Writer and Director:

1951   *Bride of the Gorilla*
1953   *The Magnetic Monster*
1956   *Curucu, Beast of the Amazon*
1957   *Love Slaves of the Amazon* (+ pr)
1962   *The Devil's Messenger* (Strock) (co-d)
1967   *Liebespiele im Schnee* (*Ski Fever*)
1968   *Custer of the West*

Publications

By SIODMAK: fiction—

Schlüss in Tonfilmatelier, Berlin, 1930.
F.P.1 antwortet nicht, Berlin, 1931, as *F.P.1 Does Not Reply*, Boston, Massachusetts, 1933, as *F.P.1 Fails to Reply*, London, 1933.

Stadt hinter Nebeln, Salzburg, 1931.
Die Madonna aus der Markusstrasse, Leipzig, 1932.
Rache im Ather, Leipzig, 1932.
Bis ans Ende der Welt, Leipzig, 1933.
Die Macht im Dunkeln, Zurich, 1937.
Donovan's Brain, New York, 1943.
Whomsoever I Shall Kiss, New York, 1952.
Skyport, 1959.
For Kings Only, New York, 1961.
Hauser's Memory, New York, 1968.
The Third Ear, New York, 1971.
City in the Sky, New York, 1974.

By SIODMAK: articles—

Films and Filming (London), November 1968.
American Film (Washington, D.C.), August 1990.
Filmfax (Evanston), March-April 1996.

On SIODMAK: articles—

Kino Lehti (Helsinki), no. 4, 1972.
Cinéma (Paris), October 1978.
Ecran Fantastique (Paris), April, May, and June 1983.
Mace, Kevin, in *American Screenwriters, 2nd series*, edited by Randall Clark, Detroit, Michigan, 1986.
Segnocinema (Vicenza), January 1988.
EPD Film (Frankfurt/Main), October 1996.
Filmbulletin (Winterthur), January 1998.

*   *   *

Curt Siodmak was almost single-handedly responsible for the flowering of the second horror-film cycle. He wrote the best of Universal's 1940s horror films and influenced all the others. While by no means a great writer, Siodmak is a gifted, sometimes inspired hack, who, in the course of a prolific career, has created many striking and enduring characters and concepts. He has described himself as an idea man, and he has certainly come up with ideas on which he and others have rung variations, time and again.

One of Siodmak's first horror-film scripts was *Black Friday*, a story about a gangster's brain tissue being injected into a normal man, causing criminal tendencies in the recipient. The idea was like *The Hands of Orlac*, only more "cerebral." It probably inspired Siodmak's own *Donovan's Brain* (published two years later and filmed three times since), whose plot concerns an industrialist's disembodied brain exerting influence over the scientist who keeps it alive. Siodmak returned to the theme in *Hauser's Memory*, his later, semi-sequel to *Donovan's Brain* and his last screen credit, filmed as a television movie, in which a scientist injects himself with a colleague's brain fluid and relives the man's World War II experiences. (In between, Siodmak scripted another "head" film, *Creature with the Atom Brain*, adding a contemporary nuclear touch to his frequent subject.)

Siodmak began screenwriting as a practitioner of the *fantastic mundane*. His early science-fiction work in Germany is patterned after Fritz Lang's pedestrian *Frau im Mond* rather than Lang's more fabulous *Metropolis*; Siodmak took one futuristic or fantastic idea

(a floating air strip, a subterranean link between Europe and America, a supersonic flight across the Atlantic) and wove an ordinary melodrama around it. This approach served him well when he began writing in the United States, where for a long time audiences seemed to resist outright fantasy and wanted it couched in "reality." So Siodmak used invisibility as the gimmick in his story of a wronged man proving his innocence in *The Invisible Man Returns*. He then used invisibility in a war film (*Invisible Agent*) and a comedy (*The Invisible Woman*). Universal's subsequent Invisible Man films (*The Invisible Man's Revenge*, *Abbott and Costello Meet the Invisible Man*), though not written by Siodmak, followed the pattern he had established.

Siodmak's most effective realization of the *fantastic mundane* (and also his best picture as director) is the science-fiction film *The Magnetic Monster*, about a radioactive isotope that implodes every 11 hours, increasing in size as it does. His heroes are a couple of workmanlike, *Dragnet*-style scientists, yet—despite the nondramatic nature of his "monster" and the drab personalities of his protagonists—he manages to generate quite a bit of suspense and to make skillful use in the film's exciting climax of the laboratory sequence from a 1934 *fantastic mundane* German film, *Gold*.

Siodmak was one of numerous science-fiction film practitioners in the 1950s, but in the 1940s he was *the* horror-film practitioner. He gave new life to all of Universal's famous monsters. His story for *Son of Dracula* gave a film noir twist to the vampire legend. It was a sort of supernatural *Double Indemnity*, featuring a superbly icy femme fatale who manipulates, for her own devices, both the man and monster who love her. Despite its title, the film was about a true daughter of Dracula, and head and shoulders above the anemic *Dracula's Daughter* made nine years earlier.

Siodmak's greatest creation during this period was *The Wolf Man*, a movie that exhibits a purity and economy of structure and a unity of action, time, and place similar to Greek tragedy. The script abounds with subtle nuances: Larry Talbot comes on like a wolf to Gwenn Conliff, then becomes an actual wolf, attacking her at the picture's end; Larry's brother, John, has died in a hunting accident—perhaps at the hands of their father, Sir John, who favored John and whose wrongheaded, strained attempts to get close to his second son ultimately lead to wolf man Larry's death in another "hunting accident" at the hands of Sir John. Most of what is today considered standard werewolf lore actually originated with Siodmak in this picture and its two sequels. He invented the famous four-line verse ("Even a man who is pure in heart") and the business about silver bullets and full moons, and provided Lon Chaney, Jr., with his second-best (after Lennie) and most enduring film role.

Siodmak continued to develop the personality of the unfortunate lycanthrope in the sequel, *Frankenstein Meets the Wolf Man*, which began the practice of teaming Universal's monsters (a practice initiated because of a chance remark Siodmak jokingly made to Universal producer George Waggner). Under Roy William Neill's direction, the first half of the film is atmospheric and exciting, but the second half is less successful because of meddling by the studio. Siodmak had followed the continuity from the earlier *Ghost of Frankenstein*, which had left the monster blind, with the brain (and voice) of Ygor (Bela Lugosi). Universal cut the monster's (Lugosi's) dialogue and all references to the creature's blindness, rendering his actions incomprehensible, and destroying the effect of a moment near the end where the monster is recharged, opens his eyes, and smiles malevolently: he can *see* again.

House of Frankenstein, based on Siodmak's story "The Devil's Brood," adds Dracula to the group, and takes Larry Talbot to his romantic-tragic end: as the wolf man, he is killed by a silver bullet, shot from the hand of "one who loves enough to understand"—his Gypsy girlfriend. Once again, Universal's subsequent films in this series, *House of Dracula* and *Abbott and Costello Meet Frankenstein*, though not written by Siodmak, followed the pattern he had established.

When Siodmak turned to directing (usually his own scripts), the overall quality of his writing suffered, as the titles of those films, from *Bride of the Gorilla* to *Ski Fever*, indicate. And his direction (except for *Magnetic Monster*) was weak. But (even discounting his work on two films which some critics rate highly: *I Walked with a Zombie*—a voodoo *Jane Eyre*, one of Val Lewton's pseudo-horror follow-ups to *Cat People*—and *The Beast with Five Fingers*, a hoax horror picture—the disembodied *Hand of Orlac*), he had already left a rich genre-film legacy that makes up for a dozen films such as *Curucu, Beast of the Amazon* and *Love Slaves of the Amazon*.

—Anthony Ambrogio

SLOCOMBE, Douglas

Cinematographer. **Nationality:** British. **Born:** London, 10 February 1913. **Education:** Attended school in Paris. **Career:** Journalist and feature writer, then photo-journalist for *Life*, *Paris-Match*, and other magazines; footage used in the American documentary *Lights Out in*

Douglas Slocombe

Europe, and, after he joined Ealing Studios and was attached to the military services during World War II, in such films as *Ships with Wings*, *The Big Blockade*, *Find, Fix, and Strike*, *San Demetrio London*, and *Greek Testament*; 1945—first film as cinematographer, *Dead of Night*. **Awards:** British Academy Award for *The Servant*, 1963; *The Great Gatsby*, 1974; *Julia*, 1978.

Films as Cinematographer:

1945   **Dead of Night** (Crichton, Dearden, and Hamer)
1946   *The Captive Heart* (Dearden)
1947   *Hue and Cry* (Crichton) (co); *The Loves of Joanna Godden* (Frend); *It Always Rains on Sunday* (Hamer)
1948   *Saraband for Dead Lovers* (*Saraband*) (Dearden and Relph); *Another Shore* (Crichton)
1949   *Kind Hearts and Coronets* (Hamer); *A Run for Your Money* (Frend)
1950   *Dance Hall* (Crichton); *Cage of Gold* (Dearden)
1951   **The Lavender Hill Mob** (Crichton); *The Man in the White Suit* (Mackendrick); *His Excellency* (Hamer)
1952   *Mandy* (*The Story of Mandy*; *Crash of Silence*) (Mackendrick)
1953   *The Titfield Thunderbolt* (Crichton); *The Love Lottery* (Crichton)
1954   *Lease of Life* (Frend); *Ludwig II* (Käutner)
1955   *Touch and Go* (*The Light Touch*) (Truman)
1956   *Sailor Beware!* (Barry); *The Man in the Sky* (Crichton); *Heaven and Earth* (Brook)
1957   *The Smallest Show on Earth* (*Big Time Operators*) (Dearden); *Davy* (Relph); *Barnacle Bill* (Frend)
1958   *Tread Softly Stranger* (Parry)
1960   *Circus of Horrors* (Hayers); *The Boy Who Stole a Million* (Crichton)
1961   *The Mark* (Green); *Taste of Fear* (*Scream of Fear*) (Holt); *The Young Ones* (*Wonderful to Be Young*) (Furie)
1962   *Freud: The Secret Passion* (Huston); *The L-Shaped Room* (Forbes)
1963   **The Servant** (Losey); *The Third Secret* (Crichton)
1964   *Guns at Batasi* (Guillermin); *A High Wind in Jamaica* (Mackendrick)
1965   *Promise Her Anything* (Hiller)
1966   *The Blue Max* (Guillermin)
1967   *Dance of the Vampires* (*The Fearless Vampire Killers*) (Polanski)
1968   *Boom* (Losey); *The Lion in Winter* (Harvey)
1969   *The Italian Job* (Collinson)
1970   *The Buttercup Chain* (Miller)
1971   *The Music Lovers* (Russell); *Murphy's War* (Yates)
1972   *Travels with My Aunt* (Cukor)
1973   *Jesus Christ Superstar* (Jewison)
1974   *The Great Gatsby* (Clayton); *The Marseille Contract* (*The Destructors*) (Parrish)
1975   *Rollerball* (Jewison); *Love among the Ruins* (Cukor); *The Maids* (Miles); *Hedda* (Nunn)
1976   *The Sailor Who Fell from Grace with the Sea* (Carlino); *Nasty Habits* (Lindsay-Hogg)
1977   *Julia* (Zinnemann); **Close Encounters of the Third Kind** (Spielberg) (co)
1978   *Caravans* (Fargo)
1979   *Lost and Found* (Frank); *The Lady Vanishes* (Page); *The Corn Is Green* (Cukor)

1980 *Nijinsky* (Ross)
1981 ***Raiders of the Lost Ark*** (Spielberg)
1983 *The Pirates of Penzance* (Leach); *Never Say Never Again*
       (Kershner)
1984 *Indiana Jones and the Temple of Doom* (Spielberg)
1985 *Water* (Clement)
1986 *Lady Jane* (Nunn)
1989 *Indiana Jones and the Last Crusade* (Spielberg)

Publications

By SLOCOMBE: articles—

Sight and Sound (London), Summer 1940.
Sight and Sound (London), Summer 1965.
Image et Son (Paris), May 1969.
Film Making (London), June 1976.
On *Julia* in *American Cinematographer* (Hollywood), March 1978.
Cinématographe (Paris), July 1981.
Positif (Paris), September 1981.
American Cinematographer (Hollywood), November 1981.
On *Raiders of the Lost Ark* in *American Cinematographer* (Hollywood), May 1982.
American Cinematographer (Hollywood), June 1989.

On SLOCOMBE: articles—

Monthly Film Bulletin (London), 1965.
Focus on Film (London), no. 13, 1973.
Screen International (London), 17 January 1976.
American Cinematographer (Hollywood), May 1978.

*   *   *

Douglas Slocombe's career remains indelibly associated with his work at Ealing Studios and especially with its most radical and enduringly relevant films. It is impossible to think of *Kind Hearts and Coronets*, or *Man in the White Suit*, or *Mandy* aside from their particular look, the precision and integrity of their black-and-white cinematography, the "real blacks and pure whites" that Slocombe mentions in interview, the subtlety of their shading, all are as much part of their meaning as the performances or direction.

His career falls into three periods: Ealing, to 1959; a free-lance period dominated by work with Losey, John Huston, Mackendrick and Polanski, through the sixties and early seventies; and a final period of work with Steven Spielberg from 1977. In between were a variety of varyingly successful international productions which have left him with a certain scepticism concerning large budgets and bankable names. He works best with directors who have a very intense and personal vision.

Slocombe's early experiences as a news cameraman thrust into the action during the early years of the war in Europe with nothing more than a camera and an instinct for catching the essence of an event, have remained seminal to his mode of work, his enjoyment of cinema and his scepticism concerning received wisdom. It was Cavalcanti, Ealing's "creative catalyst," who invited him to join the studio, after his war footage had been used in several documentaries. He shot exteriors for Crichton's *For Those in Peril*, and had the briefest initiation to studio work as camera operator on *Champagne Charlie*, before starting work, without any formal training, as cinematographer. Knowing from his newsreel experience how to shoot in natural light, he now had to learn, on his feet, how to simulate that effect. Even now, he has said, called on to shoot a courtroom scene he thinks not of how such scenes are usually shot but of the very particular needs and opportunities offered by the project in hand. Ealing remains for him a memory of passionate debate and fervent exploration. With Mackendrick, Hamer and Crichton he found directors who in their different ways were similarly working "on the edge" and to an extent against the grain. It is typical that he should solve the technical problem of Alec Guinness's multiple characters in *Kind Hearts and Coronets* in the camera itself, a solution that demanded absolute preclusion (the camera was nailed to the floor and no one but Slocombe was permitted to rewind the film). Likewise, never having seen anyone shoot a night scene in the studio, he had to improvise from observation and early experience as a photographer.

With *Saraband for Dead Lovers*, his first colour film, he was determined to bring to it the same scale of contrast as he had used with black-and-white film, rather than follow the rules for shooting with Technicolour, a decision not welcomed at the time. The final effect was romantic and expressive, and despite the film's lack of success, he looks back with affection on the technical complexity of the Technicolour process (it necessitated over printing the separate colours) and relishes the fact that printing from Technicolour negatives remains pure and accurate despite the passage of time. He wrestled with the short-lived Todd-AO, much hyped at the time, and welcomed Eastmancolour's increased subtlety of tone and greater resolution. On *Cage of Gold* he began working with Chic Waterson, who remained his operator for some twenty-five years. What Slocombe lost in the physicality of handling the camera he made up in accurate awareness of detail in shot.

Both *The Servant*, a dark look at class and power in sixties Britain, and John Huston's *Freud*, offered him opportunities to continue and develop explorations in black-and-white cinematography which he had begun at Ealing. Losey required a new intricacy of camera movement and atmospheric lighting, while Huston required the creation of five very different visual styles to signal, narrative, flashback, dream, nightmare and memory. On both films Slocombe exploited negative overexposure in order to emphasise contrast. Elsewhere work for Polanski (*The Fearless Vampire Killers*) and Mackendrick (*A High Wind in Jamaica*) offered opportunities for varyingly ironic and romantic use of colour.

Nothing could be further from the claustrophobia of Losey's *The Servant* than the expansive world of the Indiana Jones films. After shooting the India footage on Spielberg's earlier *Close Encounters of the Third Kind*, Slocombe was rehired for *Raiders of the Lost Ark* and moved from films which might require some 300 setups to ones which could involve some 2,000. Working with a director who was fully conversant with both cinema aesthetics and technical detail offered opportunity for discussion and manoevre. Characteristically Slocombe looked for the simplest solutions. Two shots might be filmed as one. A different lens would obviate the need for a zoom. The key, he has said, is to look for the essential, "for what would catch the imagination," for the simplest way to tell a story, for what would most forcefully embody the drama and carry greatest impact. With all the technical sophistication at hand, that was sometimes simply the face of the actor Harrison Ford itself. Arguably the recourse to these close and medium shots underscores the adventure stories' human scale and deepens their romanticism.

Slocombe's long career has not been free from duds, but in common with the very greatest cinematographers, his best work derives its integrity and precision from its absolute faithfulness to the particular nature of the project in hand, and to the basic physical interaction of camera, light and film.

—Verina Glaessner

SMITH, Dick

Makeup Artist. **Nationality:** American. **Born:** Larchmont, New York, 26 June 1922. **Education:** Attended Yale University, New Haven, Connecticut, graduated 1943. **Military Service:** During World War II. **Career:** Worked in theater groups; 1945—joined NBC as staff artist, then founded and head of makeup department for NBC-TV until 1959, and responsible for all shows, including *The Last War*, 1946, *A Christmas Carol*, 1948, *Cyrano*, 1949; *Macbeth*, 1954, *Alice in Wonderland*, 1955, *Victoria Regina*, 1957, *The Alligator People*, 1959, *The Moon and Sixpence*, 1959, *Way Out*, *Dark Shadow*, and *The Picture of Dorian Gray*; later TV work includes *The Power and the Glory*, 1961, and *Mark Twain Tonight!*, 1967; 1962—first makeup film design, for *Requiem for a Heavyweight*. **Awards:** Academy Award and British Academy Award, for *Amadeus*, 1984.

Films as Makeup Artist and Special Effects Makeup Artist:

1962   *Requiem for a Heavyweight* (Nelson); *All the Way Home* (Segal); *It's a Mad, Mad, Mad, Mad World* (Kramer) (co)
1963   *The Cardinal* (Preminger) (co)
1964   *What a Way to Go!* (Lee Thompson) (co); *Marco the Magnificent* (de la Patellière); *The World of Henry Orient* (Hill)
1965   *Harvey Middleman, Fireman* (Pintoff)
1969   *Me, Natalie* (Coe); *Midnight Cowboy* (Schlesinger) (consultant)
1970   *House of Dark Shadows* (Curtis); *Little Big Man* (Penn) (co)
1971   *Who Is Harry Kellerman and Why Is He Saying Those Terrible Things about Me?* (Grosbard)
1972   **The Godfather** (Coppola)
1973   *The Exorcist* (Friedkin)
1974   **The Godfather, Part II** (Coppola)
1975   *The Sunshine Boys* (Ross); *The Stepford Wives* (Forbes)
1976   *Burnt Offerings* (Curtis); **Taxi Driver** (Scorsese)
1977   *Marathon Man* (Schlesinger); *The Sentinel* (Winner); *Exorcist II: The Heretic* (Boorman)
1978   *The Fury* (De Palma) (uncredited); **The Deer Hunter** (Cimino)
1980   *Altered States* (Russell)
1981   *Ghost Story* (Irvin); *Nighthawks* (Malmuth); *Dogs of War* (Irvin); *Scanners* (Cronenberg); *The Fan* (Bianchi)
1982   *Tootsie* (Pollack)
1983   *The Hunger* (Scott) (co)
1984   *Amadeus* (Forman)
1988   *Poltergeist III* (Sherman); *Everybody's All American* (Hackford)
1989   *Suito Homu* (*Sweet Home*) (Kiyoshi Kurosawa)
1990   *Tales from the Darkside: The Movie* (Harrison)

Publications

By SMITH: articles—

Filmmakers Newsletter (Ward Hill, Massachusetts), April 1974.
Cinefantastique (New York), Winter 1974.
Ecran Fantastique (Paris), nos. 21 and 22, 1981–82.
Cinefantastique (New York), February 1982.
Cinefantastique (New York), April/May 1985.
Cinefantastique (New York), July 1985.
Cinefex (Riverside), June 1995.

On SMITH: articles—

Photoplay (London), October 1978.
Film Comment (New York), November/December 1978.
Taylor, Al, and Sue Roy, *Making a Monster*, New York, 1980.
Cinefantastique (New York), Summer 1981.
Mandell, Paul R., in *American Cinematographer* (Hollywood), August 1983.
Shannon, J., "Aging Gracefully with Dick Smith," in *Cinefex* (Riverside, California), no. 33, February 1988.
Morgan, D., "Death and Aging. A Corleone Chronicle," in *Cinefex* (Riverside, California), no. 46, May 1991.
TCI, May 1993.
Crisafulli, C., "Making It Up as You Go Along: The "Way Out" World of Dick Smith," in *Filmfax* (Evanston), no. 41, October/November 1993.

*   *   *

After years of lobbying for attention, the makeup artists of Hollywood finally won recognition with the establishment of a permanent makeup Academy Award category in 1981. It is unfortunate that it took the grotesqueries of the modern horror film to garner such recognition, for much extremely creative work has been done in the makeup field throughout the history of the cinema, from the obvious brilliance of Karloff's Frankenstein and Welles's Kane to the more subtle changes that made Marilyn Monroe the most remarkable face of the 1950s.

Among the artists long overdue recognition is Dick Smith. While he shared the 1984 Oscar with Paul Le Blanc for *Amadeus*, his remarkable career began in the 1930s when he was a student doing makeup for the Yale drama group. Unquestionably the first important makeup artist of television—he was the first staff makeup artist at NBC and was director of their makeup department for 14 years—he worked on such plays as *Way Out*, *Dark Shadow*, the "live" presentation of *Victoria Regina* in which Claire Bloom aged from 28 to 80 during the hour-long presentation, and David Susskind's production of *The Picture of Dorian Gray*. His many developments and inventions during that tenure include makeup for color television and foam-latex masks flexible enough to allow for the performer's own facial expressions.

In the 1960s Smith began to work in feature films. Throughout the 1970s and 1980s he created an impressive gallery of remarkable faces: Dustin Hoffman as the 121-year-old Jack Crabbe in *Little Big Man*; Marlon Brando as the aging Mafia boss Don Corleone in *The Godfather*; Linda Blair as the levitating, venom-spitting Regan, object of aged Max von Sydow's priestly ministrations, in *The Exorcist*; Robert De Niro as the increasingly manic Travis Bickle in *Taxi Driver*; William Hurt as Eddie Jessup metamorphosed into a Neanderthal man in *Altered States*; David Bowie's transformations from 18 through 190 in *The Hunger*.

Much of Smith's work took a considerable length of time and the patience of the performer involved. For *Little Big Man* Smith made 12 appliances which, linked together, covered Hoffman's head, a process which took five hours a day to apply. Nevertheless, when necessary Smith was able to adapt to the performer's demands: when Marlon Brando preferred not to undergo extensive daily makeup preparations for *The Godfather*, Smith used his university training in dentistry, implanting a dental plumper which pushed out the skin at the jowls. Many of Smith's most ingenious effects evolved from his extensive knowledge of his materials: for the "HELP ME" which appeared like welts on Linda Blair's stomach in *The Exorcist*, Smith painted the words on her latex bodysuit with a cleaning fluid which puffed up through a chemical reaction.

His work in makeup also involved the invention of other visual effects. While abhorring excessive violence, he cleverly invented several horrifying effects for 1970s cinema, notably the realistic depiction of bullet hits: in a 1982 interview with the *Los Angeles Herald-Examiner*, Smith explained the effect achieved for Sterling Hayden's assassination in *The Godfather*: "I made a precise hole by putting a thin metal disk on Sterling Hayden's forehead to protect it; sticking a little explosive squib on the disk; running the wires back through his hair; applying an entire foam-rubber forehead over the disk, leaving an unglued pocket around the squib; injecting 'blood' into the pocket. When the squib was detonated, it blew a hole in the skin—and the 'blood' came leaking out."

While inspiring a new generation of makeup artists—among his protégés the Oscar-winner Rick Baker—Smith remained low-key, working out of his studio in Larchmont, New York. Among his other accomplishments: *Monster Makeup and Horror Makeup Kits*, mass-marketed in 1976. Having indulged in horror fantasies as a college student by terrorizing Yale students with various incarnations, he thus made available the tools of such fantasies to a new generation of would-be makeup artists.

—Doug Tomlinson

SMITH, Jack Martin

Art Director. **Nationality:** American. **Education:** Studied architecture, University of Southern California, Los Angeles. **Career:** 1938–53—sketch artist and designer, MGM; then designer, 1953–61, and supervising art director, 1961–75, 20th Century-Fox. **Awards:** Academy Award, for *Cleopatra*, 1963, *Fantastic Voyage*, 1966, and *Hello, Dolly!*, 1969.

Films as Art Director:

1939   *The Wizard of Oz* (Fleming)
1944   *Meet Me in St. Louis* (Minnelli)
1945   *Yolanda and the Thief* (Minnelli)

1946   *Holiday in Mexico* (Sidney); *Ziegfeld Follies* (Minnelli)
1948   *The Pirate* (Minnelli); *Summer Holiday* (Mamoulian); *Easter Parade* (Walters); *Words and Music* (Taurog)
1949   *Madame Bovary* (Minnelli); **On the Town** (Kelly and Donen)
1950   *Nancy Goes to Rio* (Leonard); *Summer Stock* (Walters)
1951   *Royal Wedding* (Donen); *Show Boat* (Sidney); **An American in Paris** (Minnelli) (uncredited)
1952   *The Belle of New York* (Walters); *Million Dollar Mermaid* (LeRoy)
1953   *I Love Melvin* (Weis); *Dangerous When Wet* (Walters); *Easy to Love* (Walters)
1954   *Valley of the Kings* (Pirosh)
1955   *White Feather* (Webb); *Soldier of Fortune* (Dmytryk); *Seven Cities of Gold* (Webb)
1956   *Carousel* (H. King); *The Man in the Gray Flannel Suit* (Johnson); *Bigger than Life* (N. Ray); *Bandido* (Fleischer); *Teenage Rebel* (E. Goulding)
1957   *Boy on a Dolphin* (Negulesco); *An Affair to Remember* (McCarey); *Peyton Place* (Robson)
1958   *The Barbarian and the Geisha* (Huston)
1959   *Woman Obsessed* (Hathaway); *The Best of Everything* (Negulesco)
1960   *Can-Can* (W. Lang); *North to Alaska* (Hathaway)
1961   *All Hands on Deck* (Taurog); *The Comancheros!* (Curtiz); *Marines, Let's Go!* (Walsh); *Pirates of Tortuga* (Webb); *Return to Peyton Place* (J. Ferrer); *Sanctuary* (Richardson); *The Second Time Around* (V. Sherman); *Snow White and The Three Stooges* (W. Lang); *Voyage to the Bottom of the Sea* (I. Allen); *Wild in the Country* (Dunne)
1962   *Bachelor Flat* (Tashlin); *Five Weeks in a Balloon* (I. Allen); *Hemingway's Adventures of a Young Man* (Ritt); *Mr. Hobbs Takes a Vacation* (Koster); *State Fair* (J. Ferrer); *Tender Is the Night* (H. King)
1963   *Cleopatra* (Mankiewicz); *Move Over, Darling* (Gordon); *The Stripper* (Schaffner); *Take Her, She's Mine* (Koster)
1964   *Fate Is the Hunter* (Nelson); *Goodbye Charlie* (Minnelli); *The Pleasure Seekers* (Negulesco); *Rio Concho* (Douglas); *Shock Treatment* (Sanders); *What a Way to Go!* (Lee Thompson)
1965   *The Agony and the Ecstasy* (Reed); *Dear Brigitte* (Koster); *Do Not Disturb* (Levy); *John Goldfarb, Please Come Home!* (Lee Thompson); *Morituri* (Wicki); *The Reward* (Bourguignon); *Von Ryan's Express* (Robson)
1966   *Batman* (Martinson); *Fantastic Voyage* (Fleischer); *I Deal in Danger* (Grauman); *Our Man Flint* (Daniel Mann); *Smoky* (G. Sherman); *Stagecoach* (Douglas); *Way . . . Way Out* (Douglas)
1967   *Caprice* (Tashlin); *Doctor Dolittle* (Fleischer); *A Guide for the Married Man* (Kelly); *Hombre* (Ritt); *In Like Flint* (Douglas); *Tony Rome* (Douglas); *The St. Valentine's Day Massacre* (Corman); *Valley of the Dolls* (Robson); *The Flim-Flam Man* (Kershner)
1968   *Bandolero!* (McLaglen); *The Boston Strangler* (Fleischer); *The Detective* (Douglas); *Planet of the Apes* (Schaffner); *Pretty Poison* (Black); *The Sweet Ride* (Hart); *The Secret Life of an American Wife* (Axelrod)
1969   *Butch Cassidy and the Sundance Kid* (Hill); *Che!* (Fleischer); *Hello, Dolly!* (Kelly); *Justine* (Cukor); *Daughter of the Mind* (Grauman—for TV)

1970   *Beneath the Planet of the Apes* (Post); *Beyond the Valley of the Dolls* (Meyer); *Cover Me, Babe* (Black); ***M*A*S*H*** (Altman); *Move* (Rosenberg); *Myra Breckenridge* (Sarne); *Tora! Tora! Tora!* (Fleischer, Masuda, and Fukasaku); *The Challenge* (Smithee); *Tribes* (*The Soldier Who Declared Peace*) (Sargent)
1971   *Escape from the Planet of the Apes* (Taylor); *Powderkeg* (Heyes)
1972   *Fireball Forward* (Chomsky); *The Culpepper Cattle Company* (Richards)
1973   *Ace Eli and Rodger of the Skies* (Erman); *Emperor of the North Pole* (Aldrich)
1974   *Rhinoceros* (O'Horgan)
1975   *The Reincarnation of Peter Proud* (Lee Thompson); *Bug* (Szwarc); *Strange New World* (Butler)
1976   *The Great Scout and Cathouse Thursday* (Taylor)
1977   *Pete's Dragon* (Chaffey—animation) (co)

Publications

By SMITH: articles—

Film Comment (New York), May/June, 1978.
In *Dance in the Hollywood Musical*, by Jerome Delamater, Ann Arbor, Michigan, 1981.

On SMITH: books—

Gussow, Mel, *Don't Say Yes Until I Finish Talking*, New York, 1971.
Fordin, Hugh, *The World of Entertainment: Hollywood's Greatest Musicals*, New York, 1975.
Barsacq, Leon, *Caligari's Cabinet and Other Grand Illusions*, Boston, 1976.
Delamater, Jerome, *Dance in the Hollywood Musical*, Ann Arbor, Michigan, 1981.

On SMITH: articles—

Classic Images (Muscatine), April 1994.

*   *   *

Jack Martin Smith symbolizes the master Hollywood art director. In a 40-year career he worked on the greatest of studio films, and the finest of location efforts. He probably reached his peak of public fame in the 1960s, beginning with the spectacle of *Cleopatra* and ending with the impressive work in *Tora! Tora! Tora!*. He won the Oscar (with others) for *Cleopatra* and an Academy Award nomination for *Tora! Tora! Tora!*. In between he also earned Academy Awards for *Fantastic Voyage* and *Hello, Dolly!* All these films were made for Twentieth Century-Fox during the final years of the reign of Darryl F. Zanuck. All established a style of the spectacular which Hollywood would abandon in the 1970s, and which we probably will not see again. Smith was among the best at plying the trade of the art director during an era when nonscience-fiction, noncomputer-generated images mattered.

But Smith's career had another equally significant phase. During his first 15 years in the business he labored as a member of the Freed unit on some of the greatest films ever made at MGM, including many of the famous musicals: *Meet Me in St. Louis*, *Yolanda and the Thief*, *Easter Parade*, and *An American in Paris* (the last uncredited). As such Smith and others built up the fantasy world which Arthur Freed, Gene Kelly, Vincente Minnelli, Judy Garland, and Fred Astaire set to music and dance.

Just consider the case of *Meet Me in St. Louis*. This film set a vision of St. Louis at the turn of the century which many film fans think perfectly represented that era. Surely it was a vision of American family life to which all aspired, but few actually achieved. Yet Minnelli and his skillful crew never ventured outside MGM's Culver City backlot. It was Smith, and others, who created the mythical "St. Louis" which thousands have grown to love.

In the 1950s, with the collapse of the MGM factory, Smith moved to Twentieth Century-Fox. There he became the supervisor of art directors, and participated in little actual day-to-day designing. During this period filming moved more and more on location, and *Cleopatra* was made in Italy rather than Hollywood. But still the flair of the art director was required. Smith moved easily from genre to genre. In *Fantastic Voyage* his design team created the inside of a human; for *Hello, Dolly!* he had to "best" the sets of a Broadway musical almost everyone had seen. These opportunities provided Smith with the conditions to project some of his greatest designs.

—Douglas Gomery

SOLINAS, Franco

Writer. **Nationality:** Italian. **Born:** Sardinia, 1927. **Career:** Journalist for *L'Unità*; member of Italian communist party; 1951—first film writing, for *Persiane chiuse*; 1956—published novel *Squarciò*. **Died:** 14 September 1982.

Films as Writer:

1951   *Persiane chiuse* (*Behind Closed Shutters*) (Comencini)
1952   *Gli eroi della domenica* (Camerini)
1955   *La donna più bella del mondo* (Leonard)
1956   *I difanzati della morte* (Marcellini)
1957   "Giovanna" ep. of *Die Windrose* (*The Wind Rose*) (Pontecorvo); *La grande strada azzurra* (*The Long Blue Road*) (Pontecorvo)
1960   *Kapò* (Pontecorvo); *Les Dents du diable* (*The Savage Innocents*) (Ray)
1961   *Madame Sans-Gêne* (*Madame*) (Christian-Jaque); ***Salvatore Giuliano*** (Rosi); *Vanina Vanini* (*The Betrayer*) (Rossellini)
1965   *Le soldatesse* (*The Camp Followers*) (Zurlini); *La vita violenta* (Heusch and Rondi)
1966   ***La battaglia di Algeri*** (*The Battle of Algiers*) (Pontecorvo)
1967   *Quien sabe?* (*A Bullet for the General*) (Damiani)
1968   *Il mercenario* (*The Mercenary*) (Corbucci); *La resa dei conti* (*The Big Gundown*) (Sollima)
1969   *Tepepa* (Petroni); *Queimada!* (*Burn!*) (Pontecorvo) (co)
1972   *Etat de siège* (*State of Siege*) (Costa-Gavras)
1974   *Il sospetto* (Maselli)

1977   *Mr. Klein* (Losey)
1983   *Hanna K* (Costa-Gavras)

Publications

By SOLINAS: books—

Squarciò (novel), 1956, as *Squarciò, the Fisherman*, London, 1958.
With Gillo Pontecorvo, *The Battle of Algiers* (script), New York, 1973.
With Costa-Gavras, *State of Siege* (script), New York, 1973.
La battaglia (script), Rimini, 1984.

On SOLINAS: book—

Cosulich, Callisto, *Scrivere il cinema: Franco Solinas*, Rimini, 1984 + filmo.

On SOLINAS: articles—

Michalczyk, John, "Franco Solinas: The Dialectic of Screenwriting," in *Cineaste* (New York), vol. 13, no. 2, 1984.
Bianco e Nero (Rome), April-June 1984.
Positif (Paris), July-August 1985.

*   *   *

One of the most politically committed of European screenwriters, Franco Solinas joined the French Resistance at age 16 and after the Second World War became a member of the Italian Communist Party. He also worked for its daily paper, *L'Unità*, and for *Paese Sera*.

As a screenwriter Solinas' name is inextricably linked with that of the director Gillo Pontecorvo. They first worked together when Pontecorvo directed Solinas' *Giovanna*, a characteristic story about a woman coming to political consciousness, and an episode in the Joris Ivens project *Die Windrose*, a compendium film about the political commitment of women on an international scale. In 1957 Solinas published his novel *Squarciò*, which concerned a fisherman fighting oppressive and corrupt forces in the fishing industry. He adapted this for the cinema as *La grande strada azzurra*, and Pontecorvo, who directed it, described the film as the work of his apprenticeship. His other films with Pontecorvo were *Kapò*, set in the Nazi death camps, *The Battle of Algiers*, a remarkably detailed film about the war in Algeria which distinguished itself both by its tremendous dramatic energy and its refusal to caricature the colonialist forces while nonetheless firmly taking the side of the freedom fighters, and *Queimada!*, an extremely subtle analysis of colonialism, starring Marlon Brando, which was clearly influenced by the writings of Frantz Fanon. His work with Costa-Gavras was slightly less successful; in particular *State of Siege*, though undeniably a powerful film on the emotional level, lacks the political complexities and subtleties of his work with Pontecorvo.

Solinas has always been drawn to violent confrontations at politically significant moments of history. Following the Rossellinian principle of broadly didactic filmmaking (he worked, significantly, on the script of Rossellini's *Vanina Vanini*) he has, as John Michalczyk put it in *Cineaste*, always "walked the tightrope between politicized fiction and fictionalized politics," writing not documentary scripts but extremely carefully documented ones. His films are notable for

their awareness of and adequacy to political complexity and contradiction, and their avoidance of facile analyses and solutions.

Although Solinas is probably best known for his films with Pontecorvo and Costa-Gavras, he also made a notable contribution to several interesting "spaghetti westerns." Again, his decision to work within a popular genre was a characteristically political act. As he himself explained: "movies have an accessory and not a decisive usefulness in the various events and elements that contribute to the transformation of society. It is naive to believe that you can start a revolution with a movie and even more naive to theorize about doing so. Political films are useful on the one hand if they contain a correct analysis of reality and on the other if they are made in such a way as to have that analysis reach the largest possible audience." Solinas wrote the dialogue for Damiani's *A Bullet for the General*, the story of Sollima's *The Big Gundown*, and with Giorgio Arlorio, with whom he had worked on *Queimada!*, the story of Corbucci's *A Professional Gun*. As Christopher Frayling has pointed out in his book *Spaghetti Westerns*, the central relationship between Sir William Walker and José Dolores in *Queimada!* finds various distinct echoes in these films, all of which "share a loose allegiance to Fanonism, which means that the targets they attack are at least underpinned by a coherent social and political analysis." *A Bullet for the General* even includes a critique of the politics of Kazan's *Viva Zapata!* and a possible reference to Eisenstein's *Que Viva Mexico*, as well as discussions of guerrilla tactics and the problems of the consolidation of power.

How the politically astute Solinas would have reacted to changing political circumstances will, unfortunately, never be known. He died on the eve of departing for the United States, where he was going to write a film for the director Martin Scorsese.

—Julian Petley

SOUTHERN, Terry

Writer. **Nationality:** American. **Born:** Alvarado, Texas, 1 May 1924. **Education:** 1945–48—Northwestern University, English major; 1948–52—Sorbonne, Paris. **Military Service:** 1942–44—WWII service, U.S. Army (Europe). **Career:** 1950s—wrote for expatriate publications: *New Story; Zero; Merlin; The Paris Review;* 1964 onwards—screenwriter. Television work: *Saturday Night Live* — 1981—82 season. **Died:** 30 October 1995.

Films as Writer:

1964   *Dr. Strangelove* (Kubrick) (co-sc)
1965   *The Cincinnati Kid* (Jewison) (co-sc); *The Loved One* (T. Richardson) (co-sc)
1967   *Eye of the Devil* (Lee Thompson) (co-sc, uncredited); *Casino Royale* (J. Huston, V. Guest, Parrish, McGrath, K. Hughes, Talmadge) (co-sc, uncredited)
1968   *Barbarella* (Vadim) (co-sc); *Candy* (C. Marquand) (original novel only)

1969   *Easy Rider* (D. Hopper) (co-sc); *The Magic Christian*
          (McGrath) (co-sc, from orig novel)
1970   *End of the Road* (Avakian) (co-sc)
1988   *The Telephone* (Torn) (co-sc)

Publications

By SOUTHERN: articles—

''Now dig this,'' an interview with Mike Golden, in *Creative
    Screenwriting* (Washington, D.C.), Winter 1996.

By SOUTHERN: novels—

Flash and Filigree, 1958.
The Magic Christian, 1959.
As ''Maxwell Kenton,'' with Mason Hoffenberg, *Candy*, 1964.
Red Dirt Marijuana, 1968, re-issued, 1990.
Blue Movie, 1970.
Texas Summer, 1992.

On SOUTHERN: articles—

Dassanowsky-Harris, R., ''The Southern Journey: *Candy* and *The
    Magic Christian* as Cinematic Picaresques,'' in *Studies In Popu-
    lar Culture*, no. 1, 1992.
Obituary in *Variety* (New York), 6 November 1995.
Obituary in *Time*, 13 November 1995.
Obituary in *EPD Film* (Frankfurt), December 1995.
Grand Street, Spring 1996.
Obituary in *Paris Review*, Spring 1996.
Obituary in *Sewanee Review*, Summer 1996.
New Yorker, 22 June 1998.

                    *   *   *

Terry Southern's place in the sixties counterculture pantheon rests
on decidedly slim ground when it comes to the movies, despite
working on two of the decade's most influential films. His cowriting
credit on the hit apocalyptic black comedy *Dr. Strangelove* appeared
to herald a long and lucrative sojourn in the cinema, yet of his seven
subsequent films only *Easy Rider* enjoyed anything approaching the
same impact. When the sixties ceased to swing, so did Southern's
career, his belated one-off comeback proving a barely-seen disaster.
A specialist in off-the-wall black humour, Southern could undoubtedly score points off satire's favourite targets (politics, militarism,
racism, corporate and individual greed, sexual hypocrisy, dehumanising
science) but appears to have spent any genuine ire on *Strangelove*,
obliging later work to settle for jaded leftovers.

A cult success since the late 1950s, Southern found himself
heading into the mainstream in 1963 when *Magic Christian* fans
Stanley Kubrick and Peter Sellers invited him on board for *Dr.
Strangelove*. Though working from a ''straight'' original, Peter
George's novel *Red Alert*, Kubrick found himself drawn to the
terrible absurdity of immanent nuclear annihilation, an approach

ideally suited for Southern. While most cold-war dramas now appear
wearily dated, the nightmare comedy of *Strangelove* remains compelling, if overly mannered, the idea that the world could be ended by
a middle-aged general driven insane by his impotence (which he
blames on the Russians) both amusing and awful. As with most
multiauthored scripts, Southern's exact contribution to the film is
difficult to determine. The childishly obscene/absurd character names
(Strangelove, Merkin Muffley, Buck Turgidson, Bat Guano) have
a Southern ring, as does George C. Scott's oft quoted ''I don't say we
wouldn't get our hair mussed, but I do say no more than ten to twenty
million people killed.'' Coupled with the mainstream publication of
Candy, Southern's then scandalous reworking of *Candide*, *Strangelove*
turned him into a hot film property. The MGM-affiliated outfit
Filmways was first in line, though two of the projects on offer called
for rewrites rather than original inspiration. For *The Cincinnati Kid*,
Southern did an efficient, if straightforward job of shaping up the
story of poker-hustlers assembling for the game of the decade (the
best Southern touch is the throwaway moment where sluttish femme
fatale Ann-Margaret cuts up a piece of jigsaw puzzle to make it fit
where she wants it to fit). Injecting some Strangelovian touches into
Christopher Isherwood's screenplay for *The Loved One*, Southern
fumbled the satirical ball, contributing to an ungainly, uneven charade
of ''daring'' bad taste as various whacked-out characters do their
thing in a world of funeral parlours and thwarted lust. Filmways let
Southern in on *Eye of the Devil* more or less at the start, but the weird
period tale of ritual pagan sacrifice in a noble French family proved
alien territory for a talent happier with more contemporary oddities.

Recruited for the ''adult'' comic strip movie *Barbarella*, Roger
Vadim's dubious attempt to transform then-wife Jane Fonda into the
thinking man's fantasy sex doll, Southern had the chance to develop
a *Candy*-like narrative of decadent corruption defeated by honest
sexual passion, yet the perils of scriptwriting by committee took their
toll. Cobbled together by Southern, Vadim, original creator Jean
Claude Forest and at least five others, *Barbarella* amounts to little
more than a loosely structured series of demurely kinky sexual
encounters spiced with a little campy sadism (such as the infamous
snapping dolls). Southern had some say in the casting, selecting
fashionable friend Anita Pallenberg for the role of the Black Queen
(voice courtesy of Fenella Fielding), and contributed at least one
decent line (''A lot of dramatic situations begin with screaming'')
only to find his efforts passed over in the general critical derision.
Ironically, *Candy* itself made it to the big screen in the same year, as
a coy, smug cop-out sex romp assembled with no input from either
Southern or coauthor Mason Hoffenberg (it flopped).

Following a fruitless stint working on Kubrick's screen version of
A Clockwork Orange, Southern finally got a much needed break with
the ultimate ''sleeper'' project *Easy Rider*, a vaguely antiestablish-
ment mix of sex, drugs, bikes, and rock and roll devised by Peter
Fonda and Dennis Hopper. Hired mainly to add some structure and
narrative drive to the existing outline (also to lend big-name distinction to a generally sneered on project), Southern developed the
borderline-normal character of small-town lawyer George Hanson
(a career-making role for Jack Nicholson) and came up with the title,
slang for a whore's old man. Effective satire requires a recognisable
target, however (cliched gun-toting rednecks hardly count), and *Easy
Rider* fails to deliver. Southern dropped out early on, later complain-
ing that Hopper and Fonda denied him proper credit for his work.

Having failed to get back with Kubrick, Southern agreed to a reteaming with Peter Sellers on an adaptation of his own *The Magic Christian*. Heavily reworked from the original, mostly by uncredited Pythons John Cleese and Graham Chapman, the film lacks the book's drive and aggression, with only the various star turn attractions (notably drag artist Yul Brynner) holding much curiosity value. The infamous finale, with besuited businessmen symbolically diving for cash in a vat of excrement, repulsed both the film's backers (obliging Sellers and friends to raise their own completion money) and audiences. The cult hit that launched Southern's movie career became his first credited flop. The appropriately titled *End of the Road*, directed and cowritten by fellow Paris veteran Aram Avakian, offered more substance (and better acting) but the conventionally absurd madness-is-the-only-true-sanity theme now seemed both old hat and smug. After nearly two decades in the unproduced screenplay wilderness, Southern's collaboration with Rip Torn (director) and Harry Nilsson (cowriter) on *The Telephone* proved a disastrous "comeback," its story of an out-of-work actress experiencing mental problems provoked no audience interest at all (star Whoopi Goldberg attempted to sue the producers to stop the film's release.) It is fair to say (as Southern readily confessed) that the looming shadow of *Dr. Strangelove* was just too big to escape.

—Daniel O'Brien

SPAAK, Charles

Writer. **Nationality:** Belgian. **Born:** Brussels, 25 May 1903; brother of the statesman Paul-Henri Spaak. **Family:** Married Janine (Spaak), daughters: the actresses Agnès Spaak and Catherine Spaak. **Career:** Secretary to the director Jacques Feyder; 1928—first screenplay, *La Torture par l'espérance*; 1949—directed the film *Le Mystère Barton*; 1953—author of the play *Musique pour sourds*. **Died:** In Nice, 4 February 1975.

Films as Writer:

1928 *La Torture par l'espérance* (Modot—short)
1929 *Les Nouveaux Messieurs* (Feyder)
1930 *La Petite Lise* (Grémillon); *Accusée, levez-vous!* (M. Tourneur)
1931 *Un Coup de téléphone* (Lacombe); *Dainah la métisse* (Grémillon—short); *Pan! Pan!* (Lacombe—short)
1932 *Ce conchon de Morin* (Lacombe); *Affaire classée* (Vanel—short); *Le Martyre de l'obèse* (Chenal); *Il a été perdu une mariée* (Joannon)
1933 *L'Abbé Constantin* (Paulin); *La Maison dans la dune* (Billon)
1934 *Le Grand Jeu* (Feyder); *Aux portes de Paris* (Barrois); *Le Voyage imprévu* (de Limur)
1935 *Pension Mimosas* (Feyder); *Veille d'armes* (L'Herbier); *Les Gaietés de la finance* (Forrester); *Sous la griffe* (Christian-Jaque); *Les Epoux scandaleux* (Lacombe); *La Bandera* (Duvivier); *Les Beaux Jours* (M. Allégret); **La Kermesse héroïque** (*Carnival in Flanders*) (Feyder); *La Terre qui meurt* (Vallée); *Adémaï au moyen age* (de Marguenat)

1936 *Le Secret de Polichinelle* (Berthomieu); *La Belle Equipe* (Duvivier); *Les Loups entre eux* (Mathot); *Le Mioche* (Moguy); *L'Homme du jour* (*The Man of the Hour*) (Duvivier); *La Porte du large* (L'Herbier); *Les Bas-fonds* (*The Lower Depths*) (Renoir)
1937 *Une Femme sans importance* (Choux); *Mollenard* (Siodmak); *Aloha, le chant des îles* (Mathot); *Gueule d'amour* (Grémillon); *Orage* (M. Allégret); **La Grande Illusion** (*Grand Illusion*) (Renoir)
1938 *L'Etrange Monsieur Victor* (Grémillon); *L'Entraîneuse* (Valentin); *Le Récif de corail* (Gleize); *La Fin du jour* (*The End of the Day*) (Duvivier); *Le Dernier Tournant* (Chenal)
1940 *Remorques* (Grémillon); *L'Empreinte du Dieu* (Moguy); *Untel Père et Fils* (*The Heart of a Nation*) (Duvivier)
1941 *L'Assassinat du Père Noël* (Christian-Jaque); *Péchés de jeunesse* (M. Tourneur); *Premier bal* (Christian-Jaque); *La Maison des sept jeunes filles* (Valentin)
1942 *Le Lit à colonnes* (Tual); *À la belle frégate* (Valentin); *Le Comte de Monte Cristo* (Vernay)
1943 *Carmen* (Christian-Jaque); *L'Escalier sans fin* (Lacombe); *Le Ciel est à vous* (Grémillon); *La Vie de plaisir* (Valentin)
1944 *Les Caves du Majestic* (Pottier); *Le Père Goriot* (Vernay)
1945 *Jéricho* (Calef); *Patrie* (Daquin); *La Part de l'ombre* (Delannoy)
1946 *L'Affaire du collier de la reine* (*The Queen's Necklace*) (L'Herbier); *L'Idiot* (*The Idiot*) (Lampin); *Panique* (Duvivier); *L'Homme au chapeau rond* (Billon); *Les Chouans* (Calef); *La Revanche de Roger-la-Honte* (Cayatte)
1947 *Une Belle Garce* (Daroy); *Eternel conflit* (Lampin); *Route sans issue* (Stelli)
1948 *D'homme à hommes* (*Man to Men*) (Christian-Jaque); *Le Dessous des cartes* (Cayatte); *Retour à la vie* (Cayatte, Lampin, and Dréville); *Combats sans haine* (Michel—doc)
1949 *Le Mystère Barton* (+ d); *Black Jack* (Duvivier); *Portrait d'un assassin* (Roland)
1950 *Justice est faite* (*Justice Is Done*) (Cayatte); *Albert 1er, Roi des Belges* (Gaspard-Huit—doc)
1951 *Le Banquet des fraudeurs* (Storck); *La Nuit est mon royaume* (Lacombe)
1952 *Nous sommes tous des assassins* (Cayatte); *Les Sept Péchés capitaux* (*The Seven Capital Sins*) (De Filippo); *Adorables Créatures* (*Adorable Creatures*) (Christian-Jaque)
1953 *La Pensionnaire* (Lattuada); *Jeunes Mariés* (Grangier); *Opinione pubblica* (Corgnati); *Avant le déluge* (Cayatte)
1954 *Le Grand Jeu* (*Flesh and Women*) (Siodmak); *Thérèse Raquin* (Carné); *Scuola elementare* (Lattuada)
1955 *Vestire gli ignudi* (Pagliero); *Recontre à Paris* (Lampin); *Le Dossier noir* (Cayatte)
1956 *Paris-Palace-Hôtel* (Verneuil); *Crime et châtiment* (Lampin)
1957 *Charmants garçons* (Decoin); *Quand la femme s'en mêle* (Y. Allégret)
1958 *Christine* (Gaspard-Huit); *Les Tricheurs* (*The Cheaters*) (Carné)
1959 *Normandie-Niemen* (Dréville); *Vers l'extase* (Wheeler)
1960 *Katia* (*Magnificent Sinner*) (Siodmak); "Le Divorce" ep. of *La Française et l'amour* (*Love and the Frenchwoman*) (Christian-Jaque)
1962 *Le Caporal épinglé* (Renoir); *Mathias Sandorf* (Lampin); *La Chambre ardente* (*The Burning Court*) (Duvivier); *Cartouche* (de Broca)
1963 *La Glaive et la balance* (*Two Are Guilty*) (Cayatte); *Germinal* (Y. Allégret); *Blague dans le coin* (Labro)

1965 *Un Milliard dans un billard* (Gessner)
1973 *La Main à couper* (Perier)

Publications

By SPAAK: books—

With others, *La Kermesse héroïque* (script) in *Avant-Scène* (Paris), May 1963.
With Jean Renoir, *Grande Illusion* (script), New York, 1968.

By SPAAK: articles—

Eventail (Paris), 11 January 1925–14 February 1926.
''Gaston Modot,'' in *Cinéa-Ciné pour tous*, no. 80, 1927.
''A propos du *Capitaine Fracasse* (Alberto Cavalcanti),'' in *Cinegraph*, no. 5, 1929.
''Cagliostro (Richard Oswald),'' in *Cinegraph*, no. 4, 1929.
''Jean Gabin ou *Gueule d'amour* sur un fond de taffetas,'' in *Cinémonde*, no. 476, 1937.
''Trop tard . . .,'' in *L'Écran français*, no. 8, 1945.
''Le Pain des rêves,'' in *Le Cinéma en l'an 2000*, Edition Rond-Point, 1945.
''*La Grande Illusion*,'' in *Paris-Cinéma*, no. 47, 1946.
''Mes 31 mariages'' (serialized) in *Paris-Cinéma*, nos. 4–29, 31 October 1945–23 April 1946.
''Autour d'un verdict,'' in *Paris-Cinéma*, no. 62, 1947.
''*Les Chouans*,'' in *L'Ecran français*, no. 92, 1947.
''Des scénaristes et du scénario,'' in *Syntheses*, no. 2, 1947.
''Jacques Feyder, scénariste,'' in *Ciné-Club* (Paris), no. 2, December 1948.
''*Le Mystère Barton*,'' in *L'Ecran français*, no. 216, 1949.
''Le Scénario,'' in *Le Cinéma par ceux qui le font*, Paris, 1949.
''La censure cinématographique,'' in *Le Courrier de l'Unesco*, vol. 4, no. 9, 1951.
''*Le Banquet des fraudeurs*,'' in *Notre Europe*, no. 13, 1952.
Film Culture (New York), December 1957.
''Jean . . .,'' in *Les Lettres Françaises*, 3 December 1959.
''Normandie-Niemen,'' in *Les Lettres Françaises*, 25 February 1960.
''Le Scénariste, ce métier de dupe,'' in *Cinéma univers de l'absence?*, PUF, éditions Privat, 1960.
''Le Scénariste, ce métier de dupe,'' in *Télécine* (Paris), January/February 1961.
Nouveau Cinémonde (Paris), 30 September 1969.
''Des producteurs: Nos petites auberges,'' in *Cinéma* (Paris), November 1983.

On SPAAK: books—

Spaak, Janine, *Charles Spaak, mon mari*, Paris, 1977.
Bernat, Mario, and Jacqueline Van Nypelseer, *Charles Spaak, les Années d'apprentissage (1919–27)*, 1994.

On SPAAK: articles—

Unifrance Film (Paris), August 1950.
Vincent, C., in *Cinéma* (Paris), no. 109, 1953.

Radio Cinéma Télévision (Paris), no. 173, May 1953, and no. 182, July 1953.
Film Culture, vol. 3, no. 5, December 1957.
Film Français (Paris), no. 1571, March 1975.
Technicien du Film (Paris), no. 224, March 1975.
Ecran (Paris), no. 35, April 1975.
Gauteur, Claude, and Geneviève Sellier, in *Cinéma* (Paris), November 1983.
Film Français (Paris), no. 2511, June 1994.

*   *   *

In a career that embraced both the silent era and the New Wave, Charles Spaak was a mainstay of the French cinema for some 40 years, providing more than 100 scripts for more than 40 directors. If he lacked the enviable originality of Prévert or Jeanson's brilliance for dialogue, Spaak outstripped his two contemporaries as a sure-footed, prolific writer of neatly crafted scenarios noted for clear structures and well-delineated character parts. For Spaak filmmaking was a symbiotic undertaking between scriptwriter and director and, for the partnership to work, shared moral, political, and philosophical attitudes were essential. The most fruitful exchange of creative energy came with Feyder, Renoir, Grémillon and Cayatte, though few would discount his collaborations with Duvivier, Christian-Jaque, or Carné.

Spaak's early career was fostered by his fellow Belgian, Jacques Feyder, initially as his secretary then as co-adapter of *Les Nouveaux Messieurs*. Original scenarios followed in the mid-thirties, with indications of Spaak's abiding themes and concern for tightly woven narratives. In *Le Grand Jeu*, set in a Moroccan cabaret, the themes of fate and self-destructive passion are explored through a legionnaire's obsession for a Parisian vamp, while in *Pension Mimosas*, the owner of a Nice guest house is consumed by a secret passion for her wayward godson. The same year saw the triumph of *La Kermesse héroïque* which, through a deftly constructed narrative replete with dramatic set-pieces, tells how resourceful Flemish women, abandoned by their cowardly husbands, handled to their own satisfaction, invading Spaniards.

The thirties also saw important associations begin with Duvivier and Renoir. Spaak's work with Duvivier included five original scenarios and three adaptations, namely *La Bandera*, *Panique*, and *La Chambre ardente*. If all testify to Spaak's skill in distilling workable scenarios with attractive main roles, *La Bandera* is particularly significant as the film which established Jean Gabin as the sympathetic male destroyed by a treacherous woman. The collaborative chemistry, so essential to Spaak, was occasionally lacking with Duvivier, but in their two undoubted successes the writer's abiding concern with community is evident. In *La Belle Equipe*—frequently taken to embody the collectivist ideology of the Popular Front—a group of unemployed men wins the lottery and opens a restaurant, only to find their unity of purpose threatened by another of Spaak's alluring vamps. Collective commitment is again central to *La Fin du jour* where a heterogeneous group of actors, often disputing between themselves, defend their retirement home against closure. Both films derive dramatic intensity from Spaak's typically tight focus on place and action.

Spaak's limited work with Renoir was also amongst his finest. After the contentious free rendering of Gorky's *Les Bas-Fonds* came collaboration on an original scenario: *La Grande Illusion*. Here, in an expression of the humanistic values dear to both men, fraternity and collective endeavor are tested in a World War I prison camp setting. The simple narrative allows a marvelous array of emblematic characters, all clearly differentiated through Spaak's dialogue. In the senseless world of conflict, honorable foes display their common humanity and seek to mitigate the evil in which they are haplessly embroiled.

Spaak's third major partner in the thirties and early forties was Jean Grémillon. After the melodramatic tale of self-sacrifice in *La Petite Lise*, their most notable collaborations were a psychological study of a man prepared to see his neighbor condemned for his own crime, *L'Étrange Monsieur Victor*; the uplifting account of individual endeavor in *Le Ciel est à vous* where a determined garage-owner's wife learns to fly; and two films featuring Jean Gabin: *Gueule d'amour* and *Remorques*. In the first, Gabin is the eponymous *gueule d'amour*, the handsome playboy driven to kill a flirtatious woman he cannot control, while in the second he plays a happily married tugboat captain tragically besotted with a woman he rescues. Both films extended Gabin's screen image as the attractive male ensnared by sexually dangerous women.

Spaak's postwar portfolio is largely characterized by his association with André Cayatte, but significant films with several other directors confirm the writer's admirable range. He co-wrote Calef's *Jéricho* exposing myths about French heroism during the Occupation; co-wrote Christian-Jaque's film about a fashion designer's memories in *Adorables Créatures*; worked with Carné on a free adaptation of Zola's *Thérèse Raquin;* and provided the original scenario for Storck's *Le Banquet des fraudeurs*. His association with Cayatte came to fruition in the fifties with films concerned with fundamental moral issues. *Justice est faite* explores euthanasia through the trial of a woman who kills her terminally ill lover; in *Nous sommes tous des assassins*, capital punishment is brought into question through the exposure of a criminal's social circumstances; while in *Avant le déluge* the problem of delinquency is investigated when youths kill a security guard. The cycle is completed by *Le Dossier noir*, highlighting deficiencies in the judicial system, and *Le Glaive et la balance*, where natural justice becomes an issue as a lynch mob take revenge on acquitted kidnappers.

In the course of his long career Spaak adapted numerous literary classics, though he never articulated a theory of adaptation. For Yves Allégret he scripted a scaled-down version of Zola's *Germinal*; with Carné he updated and transposed the action of *Thérèse Raquin* to 1950s Lyons and with Lampin he relocated *Crime et châtiment* to modern-day Paris, while reworkings of *L'Idiot* and *Les Bas-fonds* also espoused the tradition of artistic freedom. Common to all Spaak's adaptations is the practiced screenwriter's awareness of what is filmically viable.

Although Spaak worked closely with many different directors, his personal, morally conservative, often misogynistic, but steadfastly humanistic vision emerges from his original scenarios and the emphasis achieved in adaptation. Despite a belief in human solidarity, a pessimism permeates his scenarios with their characteristically unhappy endings. Well-intentioned individuals are overcome by forces outside their control, decent males are led astray by treacherous females. Spaak's practice led to solid, well-oiled plot mechanisms, often shaped through flashback, with richly satisfying parts differentiated through convincing, character-specific, dialogue. Though applauding the technical innovations of the New Wave, Spaak was unhappy with the cult of amoral individualism and immediacy, while as a conscientious, painstaking craftsman, the emphasis on creative spontaneity and unscripted dialogue was an anathema. His high-quality scenarios for successive generations of directors constituted

an enduring benchmark for other writers: few, however, could emulate his colossal achievement either in quality or quantity.

—R. F. Cousins

SPENCER, Dorothy

Editor. **Nationality:** American. **Born:** Covington, Kentucky, 2 February, 1909. **Career:** Hollywood film editor: first film, *Married in Hollywood*, 1929; 1945–79—worked at Twentieth Century Fox.

Films as Editor:

1929 *Married in Hollywood*; *Nix on Dames*
1934 *As Husbands Go* (McFadden); *Coming Out Party*; *She Was a Lady*
1936 *The Case against Mrs. Ames* (Seiter); *The Luckiest Girl in the World* (Buzzell)
1937 *Stand-In* (Garnett); *Vogues* (*Vogues of 1938*) (Cummings)
1938 *Blockade* (Dieterle); *Trade Winds* (Garnett)
1939 *Eternally Yours* (Garnett); *Stagecoach* (Ford); *Winter Carnival* (Riesner)
1940 *Foreign Correspondent* (Hitchcock); *The House across the Bay* (Mayo); *Slightly Honorable* (Garnett)
1941 *Sundown* (Garnett)
1942 *To Be or Not To Be* (Lubitsch)
1943 *Happy Land* (Pichel); *Heaven Can Wait* (Lubitsch)
1944 *Lifeboat* (Hitchcock); *Sweet and Low-Down* (Mayo)
1945 *A Royal Scandal* (Lubitsch); *A Tree Grows in Brooklyn* (Kazan)
1946 *Cluny Brown* (Lubitsch); *Dragonwyck* (Mankiewicz); **My Darling Clementine** (Ford)
1947 *The Ghost and Mrs. Muir* (Mankiewicz)
1948 *The Snake Pit* (Litvak); *That Lady in Ermine* (Lubitsch)
1949 *Down to the Sea in Ships* (Hathaway)
1950 *Three Came Home* (Hathaway); *Under My Skin* (Negulesco)
1951 *Fourteen Hours* (Hathaway)
1952 *Decision before Dawn* (Litvak); *Lydia Bailey* (Negulesco); *What Price Glory?* (Ford)
1953 *Man on a Tightrope* (Kazan); *Tonight We Sing* (Leisen)
1954 *Black Widow* (Johnson); *Demetrius and the Gladiators* (Daves); *Night People* (Johnson)
1955 *The Left Hand Of God* (Dmytryk); *Prince of Players* (Dunne); *The Rains of Ranchipur* (Negulesco); *Soldier of Fortune* (Dmytryk)
1956 *The Best Things in Life are Free* (Curtiz); *The Man in the Gray Flannel Suit* (Johnson)
1957 *A Hatful of Rain* (Zinnemann)
1958 *The Young Lions* (Dmytryk)
1959 *The Journey* (Litvak); *A Private's Affair* (Walsh)
1960 *From the Terrace* (Robson); *North to Alaska* (Hathaway); *Seven Thieves* (Hathaway)
1961 *Wild in the Country* (Dunne)
1963 *Cleopatra* (Mankiewicz)
1964 *Circus World* (Hathaway)
1965 *Von Ryan's Express* (Robson)
1966 *Lost Command* (Robson)

1967   *A Guide for the Married Man* (Kelly); *Valley of the Dolls*
       (Robson)
1969   *Daddy's Gone A-Hunting* (Robson)
1971   *Happy Birthday, Wanda June* (Robson)
1972   *Limbo* (*Women in Limbo*) (Robson)
1974   *Earthquake* (Robson)
1979   *The Concorde—Airport '79* (Lowell Rich)

Publications

On SPENCER: articles—

Winetrabe, Maury, "How Do You Edit an Earthquake?," *American Cinemeditor*, Fall-Winter 1974–1975.
"Silver Anniversary Eddie Awards," *American Cinemeditor*, Spring 1975.

*   *   *

Dorothy Spencer's career as film editor spanned five decades in the industry. Beginning at the dawn of talking pictures, her work continued through the glory days of the Hollywood studio system to the widescreen extravagance of the 1950s and 1960s, working under such directors as John Ford, Alfred Hitchcock, Ernst Lubitsch, Henry Hathaway and Mark Robson. Though her early days are affiliated with independent producer Walter Wanger, she involved herself exclusively with Twentieth Century-Fox from the late 1940s until her retirement in 1979. Despite a distinguished and varied career, she was nominated for an Oscar only four times, losing out on each occasion.

Beginning her career at the age of twenty, Spencer worked as cutter on many of Wanger's Thirties productions, including *The Case against Mrs. Ames* (1936) and *Winter Carnival* (1939). She also found herself working with director Tay Garnett on *Stand In* (1937), *Trade Winds* (1938) and *Eternally Yours* (1939). Her career with Wanger reached its peak with John Ford's seminal western, *Stagecoach* (1939) and Hitchcock's *Foreign Correspondent* (1940). In *Stagecoach* the editing principals of the Russian Formalists were deftly employed to convey suspense and pace. Most apparent is the chase sequence—in which the stagecoach is pursued by hostile Comanches—where the cutting is deliberately disorienting to convey the consternation of the passengers, while the crosscutting (alternating between the passengers' point of view and shots of the besetting Indians) increases the scene's tempo. The film was to earn Spencer her first Academy Award nomination.

In the early 1940s she began to work with Ernst Lubitsch, editing *To Be or Not to Be* (1942), *Heaven Can Wait* (1943), *A Royal Scandal* (1944) and *Cluny Brown* (1946). She also completed work on her second (and final) Hitchcock film, the propagandist wartime drama, *Lifeboat* (1944). Notable for its expert use of limited space (the entire film is set on a lone lifeboat in the middle of the Atlantic), the film is by and large muted. However, two scenes do stand out—the harrowing build-up to a necessary amputation and the lynching of a German U-boat commander—both of which build to their climax through a methodical use of montage. *A Tree Grows in Brooklyn* (1945), directed by Elia Kazan, marked her first film for Twentieth Century-Fox. Among her early projects for the corporation were *Dragonwyck* (1946), *The Ghost and Mrs. Muir* (1947), and John Ford's broodingly low-key western, *My Darling Clementine* (1946). Lacking significant

mood music, *Clementine* achieved its suspense—most spectacularly in the famous O.K. Corral gunfight sequence—in its editing, a tight, pared-down construction in which only the barest (and most pertinent) of information is conveyed.

In 1948, Spencer began the first of her two assignments under producer/director Anatole Litvak; the acclaimed *The Snake Pit* was followed by *Decision before Dawn* (1952), a suspenseful espionage thriller which afforded Spencer her second Oscar nomination. It was her success in the latter that gave rise to Spencer's long association with big-budget actioners, an association which would direct the rest of her career. In the same year as *Decision before Dawn*, she edited *Lydia Baily* and *What Price Glory?*, and shortly thereafter embarked upon a long list of the Fox-patented Cinemascope pictures, beginning with *Black Widow* in 1954.

Though the widescreen format brought an initial rethinking of the medium's form—traditional framing was reformulated for the wider format and the duration of scenes increased to allow audiences time to register the spectacle—such modifications were limited. By and large the editor's task remained unaltered and Spencer's work, from the mid-1950s onward, shows no apparent change in technique. She worked on a variety of pictures, from large-scale Biblical epics (*Demetrius and the Gladiators* [1954]) to Cold War anticommunist pictures (*Night People* [1954]) to war movies (*The Young Lions* [1958]). Her career in editing widescreen blockbusters reached its peak with Joseph L. Mankiewicz's labored epic *Cleopatra* (1963). Taking more than four years to produce, with countless writers and a $40 million budget, the film provided Spencer with more than 70,000 feet (120 miles) of film to reduce to the final print's 22,000 feet. A gargantuan task on every level, the film won four Academy Awards with Spencer receiving her third nomination.

Many of Spencer's later efforts were under the direction of Mark Robson. In total they worked together on seven pictures, including *Von Ryan's Express* (1965), *Valley of the Dolls* (1967) and *Earthquake* (1967). Expressing many of the concerns of the industry at the time, being big, expensive, and destructive, *Earthquake* marked the crowning achievement of Spencer's work in the 1970s. A huge success, the film managed to enthrall audiences with the scale and magnitude of its destruction, much of which depended on Spencer's competent skills as editor. In between her collaborations with Robson, Spencer worked with directors Gene Kelly on *A Guide for the Married Man* (1967), Henry Hathaway on *Circus World* (1964) and with David Lowell Rich on her final picture, *The Concord—Airport 79* (1979).

After fifty years in the industry Dorothy Spencer retired. A consummate studio craftsperson, her work traced the rise and fall of the Hollywood system. Rejecting the reactionist editing styles that emerged in the late 1960s, such as Dede Allen's work on *Bonnie and Clyde* (1967) and Sam O'Steen's on *The Graduate* (1967), she continued to employ the classical style formulated in the mid-teens. As with all editors however, her impact on the films she edited is difficult to gauge. Since the editor's role is secondary to that of the director's, and subservient to the nature and style of the film itself, a critical analysis of her own individual input is difficult to realize. Some of her best work was under such autocrats as John Ford, Alfred Hitchcock and Ernst Lubitsch, all of whom would have assumed complete responsibility for the style of the cutting employed. However, despite the lack of any auteurist evidence, her competence in the field, her success within the industry, and her devotion to her craft remain uncontested.

—Peter Flynn

SPIEGEL, Sam

Producer. **Nationality:** Austrian. **Born:** Samuel Spiegelglass in Jaroslau, (now Jaroslaw, Poland), 11 November 1903; used the name S. P. Eagle in 1940–54. **Education:** Attended schools in Poland. **Family:** Married 1) Rachel Agronovich, c. 1922 (divorced c. 1926); children: one daughter; 2) the actress Lynn Baggett, 1948 (divorced 1953); 3) Betty Benson, 1957. Also one son by Ann Pennington. **Career:** 1926–27—cotton broker and stock promoter in Europe; special adviser to Paul Bern at MGM on European plays; transferred to Universal; served five months in California jail for passing a bad cheque; 1930—deported to Poland; 1930–33—worked in Berlin producing French and German versions of Universal films; 1933–35—independent producer in Vienna; 1936—jailed in London for bad cheques; deported to France; then to Mexico; 1939—entered US illegally as S.P. Eagle; 1947—given legal residence; worked as independent producer. **Awards:** Academy Awards for *On the Waterfront*, 1954; *The Bridge on the River Kwai*, 1957; *Lawrence of Arabia*, 1962; Irving G. Thalberg Award, 1963; Michael Balcon award, 1983. **Died:** St. Martin, Antilles, 31 December 1985.

Films as Producer:

1933   *Unsichtbare Gegner* (Katscher); *Les Requins du pétrole* (Katscher and Decoin); *Mariage à responsabilité limitée* (de Limur)
1936   *The Invader* (*An Old Spanish Custom*) (Brunel) (co)

Sam Spiegel

1939   *Dernière la façade* (Lacombe and Mirande)
1942   *Tales of Manhattan* (Duvivier) (co)
1946   *The Stranger* (Welles)
1949   *We Were Strangers* (Huston)
1950   *The Prowler* (Losey)
1951   *When I Grow Up* (M. Kanin)
1952   ***The African Queen*** (Huston)
1953   *Melba* (Milestone)
1954   ***On the Waterfront*** (Kazan)
1957   *The Strange One* (*End As a Man*) (Garfein); *The Bridge on the River Kwai* (Lean)
1959   *Suddenly Last Summer* (Mankiewicz)
1962   ***Lawrence of Arabia*** (Lean) (co)
1966   *The Chase* (Penn)
1967   *The Happening* (Silverstein); *The Night of the Generals* (Litvak)
1971   *Nicholas and Alexandra* (Schaffner)
1976   *The Last Tycoon* (Kazan)
1982   *Betrayed* (Jones)

Publications

By SPIEGEL: article—

Film Index (Mosman Bay, New South Wales), no. 11, 1971.

On SPIEGEL: book—

Sinclair, Andrew, *Spiegel: The Man Behind the Pictures*, London, 1987.

On SPIEGEL: articles—

Today's Cinema, 5 March 1971.
Avant-Scène (Paris), 15 September 1977.
Jacobson, Harlan, in *Film Comment* (New York), March-April 1983.
Cinématographe (Paris), May 1984.
Obituary in *Variety* (New York), 8 January 1986.
Positif (Paris), no. 301, March 1986.
Sight and Sound (London), Autumn 1987.
Commentary, July 1988.
Cineaste (New York), October 1994.
Variety (New York), 8 January 1996.
Cineaste (New York), Spring 1996.

*   *   *

Sam Spiegel was the producer of a number of Oscar-winning films of the 1950s and 1960s including *The African Queen*, *On the Waterfront*, *The Bridge on the River Kwai*, and *Lawrence of Arabia*. Indeed he defined the image of the independent producer of his era. Prior to Spiegel, producers worked directly for one studio, following the orders of the top mogul. In the 1950s, with the collapse of the studio system, producers became independent entrepreneurs. This required a daring vision because the producer now had to rise or fall on the virtues of a single film.

Spiegel seemed to thrive in the new Hollywood of the 1950s, the very prototype of the successful packager of the color blockbuster film which was Hollywood's mainstay in the difficult years of the

1950s. Spiegel did this by developing a limited number of projects and then hiring top directors (David Lean, Orson Welles, Elia Kazan, Joseph Losey) and first-rate screenwriters (Tennessee Williams, Gore Vidal, Budd Schulberg, Lillian Hellman). United Artists, then a firm on the verge of bankruptcy, prospered by offering independent producers a chance to bring together the elements for a single film. Spiegel achieved his first success with *The African Queen* in 1952, starring Humphrey Bogart and Katharine Hepburn and directed by John Huston. From then on he became identified with big-scale productions made at sizable intervals from each other. This pattern would be adopted by all big name producers from the 1950s to the present day. In time he became to represent the Old Hollywood, the one which young turks like George Lucas and Steven Spielberg turned upside down in the 1970s.

The peak of his power came between 1957 and 1962. *The Bridge on the River Kwai*, made for $2.7 million, grossed more than $30 million and won the Academy Award for Best Picture in 1957. *Lawrence of Arabia*, starring the then-unknown Peter O'Toole, was an even bigger hit at the box office, and earned yet another Best Picture Oscar, this time in 1962. Both were directed by David Lean, making that unknown British director one of the highest paid of his profession in Hollywood. Although after *Lawrence of Arabia* Spiegel would never have another such blockbuster, he continued regularly to turn out films, including *The Chase, Nicholas and Alexandra*, and his long-cherished, but highly unsuccessful project, *The Last Tycoon*.

—Douglas Gomery

STALLICH, Jan

Cinematographer. **Nationality:** Czech. **Born:** Prague, 19 March 1907. **Career:** 1924–27—worked in A-B film laboratory; 1927—head of Kavalirka film laboratory; first film as cinematographer; also attended evening classes at graphics school, and made news and publicity films; 1949–73—taught at the national film school FAMU, Prague. **Died:** In Prague, 14 June 1973.

Films as Cinematographer:

1927   *Kašpárek kouzelníkem* (*Punch the Magician*) (Kokeisl); *Perníková chaloupka* (*Babes in the Wood*) (Kokeisl); *Provaz z oběšence* (*The Rope from the Hanged Man*) (Spelina)

1928   *Pramen lásky* (*The Source of Love*) (Kokeisl); *Stín ve svetle* (*Shadow in Light*) (Kokeisl); *U sv. Mateje* (*By St. Matthias*) (Kokeisl); *V blouzneni* (*In a Fantastic Vision*) (Kokeisl)

1929   *Horské volání SOS* (*SOS in the Mountains*) (Marten and Studecky); *Chudá holka* (*Poor Girl*); *Neviňátka* (*The Innocents*) (Innemann); *Svaty Václav* (*St. Wenceslas*) (Kollár) (co); *Z českých mlýnu* (*From the Czech Mills*) (Innemann and Seidl)

1930   *Za rodnou hroudu* (*For Native Soil*) (Kmínek) (co); *Opeřené stíny* (*Fledged Shadows*) (Marten); *Černý plamen* (*The Black Flame*) (Krnansky)

1931   *Dobrý voják švejk* (*The Good Soldier Schweik*) (Fric); *Kariera Pavla Čamrdy* (*Pavel Camrda's Career*) (Krnansky); *Obrácení Ferdyše Pištory* (*The Conversion of Ferdys*

Pistora) (Kodiček) (co); *Poslední bohém* (*The Last Bohemian*) (Innemann); *Skalní ševci* (*The Die-Hard Shoemakers*) (Lonegen); *Spejblovo filmové opojení* (*The Film Elation of Spejbl*) (Skupa); *Třetí rota* (*The Third Squad*) (Innemann)

1932   *Devčátko, neříkej ne!* (*Little Girl, Don't Say No!*) (Medeotti-Baháč); *Bouře nad Tatrami* (*Storm in Tatra*) (co); *Funebrak* (Lamac) (co); *Lelíček ve službách Sherlocka Holmese* (*Lelichek in Sherlock Holme's Service*) (Lemac); *Pepina Rejholcová* (Binovec) (co); *Právo na hřích* (*The Title for the Sin*) (Slavínský) (co); *Ružové konbiné* (*The Pink Slip*) (Marten); *Vezen no Bezdeze* (*The Prisoner on Bezdez*) (Vladimírov); *Zlaté ptáče* (*The Little Gold Bird*) (Kmínek); *Extase* (*Ecstasy*) (Machatý)

1933   *Diagnoza X* (*The X-Diagnosis*) (Marten); *Dum no předmestí* (*The Suburban House*) (Cikan) (co); *Její lékař* (*Her Doctor*) (Slavínský); *Jsem devče s čertem v tele* (*I Am a Girl with the Devil in My Body*) (Anton) (co); *Madla z cihelny* (*Madla from the Brick-Kiln*) (Slavínský); *Na sluneční strane* (*On the Sunnyside*) (Vancura) (co); *Okénko* (*Little Window*) (Slavínský); *Revisor* (*The Inspector*) (Fric); *Reka* (*The River*) (Rovenský); *Srdce za písničku* (*The Heart for a Song*) (Hašler) (co); *Strýček z Ameriky* (*Uncle from America*) (Vladimfrov); *Svítání* (*Dawn*) (Kubásek); *Štvaní lidé* (*Outcasts*) (Fehér and Sviták) (co); *Záhada modrého pokoje* (*The Mystery of the Blue Room*) (Cikán)

1934   *Pán na roztrhání* (*Very Busy Gentlemen*) (Cikán); *Z bláta do louže* (*Out of the Frying Pan into the Fire*) (Innemann); *Žena, která ví co chce* (*A Woman Who Knows What She Wants*) (Binovec) (co); *Život vojenský, život veselý* (*Military Life, Pleasant Life*) (Sviták)

1935   *A život jde dál* (*Life Continues*) (Junghans); *At žije nebožtik* (*Long Lives the Deceased*) (Fric); *Jrdina jedné noci* (*Hero for a Night*) (Fric); *Jedna z milonu* (*One in a Million*) (Slavínský); *Koho jsem včera líbal* (*Who I Kissed Yesterday*) (Svoboda) (co); *The Silent Passenger* (Denham)

1936   *Whom the Gods Love* (*Mozart*) (Dean); *Golem* (Duvivier); *The Lonely Road* (*Scotland Yard Commands*) (Dean); *Guilty Melody* (Potter)

1937   *Moonlight Sonata* (*The Charmer*) (Mendes); *The Show Goes On* (Dean); *The First and the Last* (*21 Days*; *21 Days Together*) (Dean)

1938   *Ideál Septimy* (*Septima's Ideal*) (Kubásek); *Klapzubova jedenáctka* (*Klabzuba's Eleven*) (Brom); *Pod jednou střechou* (*Safe Home*) (Krňanský); *Stříbrná oblaka* (*Silver Skies*) (Slegl); *Svet, kde se žebrá* (*The Beggar Life*) (Cikán); *Skola, základ života* (*School, the Basis of Life*) (Fric)

1939   *Dedeckem proti své vuli* (*Grandpa Involuntarily*) (Slavínský); *Men without Honour* (Newman); *Carmen fra i rossi*; *Jiný vzduch* (*Another Air*) (Fric); *Kdybych byl tátou* (*If I Was a Daddy*) (Cikán); *Osmnáctiletá* (*Eighteen-Year Old Girl*) (Cikán); *U pokladny stál* (*Standing by the Treasury*) (Lamac)

1940   *Abbandano* (Mattoli); *Caravaggio* (Alessandrini); *Captain Fracassa* (Coletti); *L'assedio dell'Alcazar* (Genina); *La figlia del corsaro verde* (Guazzoni)

1941   *Beatrice Cenci* (Brignone); *Il fiacre nr. 13*; *La maschera di Cesare Borgia* (Coletti); *Ore nove lezione di chimica* (Mattoli); *I pini di Roma*; *Ridi, pagliaccio!* (Mastrocinque)

1942   *Wiener Blut* (Forst); *I due orfanelle* (Gallone)

1943   *Frauen sind keine Engel* (Forst); *Germanin* (Kimmich)

1944   *Ein Blick zurück* (Menzel); *Glück bei Frauen* (Brauer); *Hundstage* (von Cziffra)

1945   *Wiener Mädeln* (Forst); *Vlast vítá* (*Welcome Home*) (Holman and Vavra); *Cesta ka barikádám* (*The Road to the Barricades*) (Vávra—doc); *Muži bez křídel* (*Men without Wings*) (Cáp); *Třináctý revír* (*Beat 13*) (Fric and Holman)

1947   *Jan Roháč z dubé* (*Warriors of Faith*) (Borský); *Předtucha* (*Presentiment*) (Vávra)

1948   *O ševci Matoušovi* (*Matous the Shoemaker*) (Cikán); *Zelená knížka* (*The Green Book*) (Mach)

1949   *Léto* (*Summer*) (Walló); *Revolucní rok 1848* (*The Revolutionary Year 1948*) (Krska)

1950   *Temno* (*Darkness*) (Stekly)

1951   *Císařuv pekař a pekařuc císař* (*The Emperor's Baker and the Baker's Emperor*) (Fric)

1952   *Dovolená s andelem* (*Holidays with an Angel*) (Zeman)

1953   *Tajemství krve* (*The Secret of Blood*) (Fric); *A nyní hraje dechovka* (short); *Akrobat na hrazde* (short); *Harmonikář* (short); *Jmenuji se Fifinka* (short); *Lev a krotitel* (short); *Spejbl a Hurvínek* (short—2 parts); *Tamburaši u Spejbla a Hurvínka* (short); *Vzorná výchova* (short)

1954   *Krejčovská povíkda* (*The Tailor's Story*); *Setkání v Bukurešti* (*The Meeting in Bucharest*); *Večery s Jindřichem Plachtou* (*Evenings with Jindrich Plachta*) (Duba and Zelenda—doc); *Psohlavci* (*Dog-Heads*) (Fric)

1955   *Rudá záže nad Kladnem* (*Red Glow over Kladno*) (Vlcek)

1956   *Hrátky s čertem* (*Playing with the Devil*) (Mach); *Kudy kam* (*Whence and Where To*) (Borský); *Mladé dny* (*The Young Days*); *Spartakiáda* (*Spartakiad*) (Fric—doc)

1957   *Florence 13.30* (*The Bus Terminal*) (Mach)

1958   *Páté kolo u vozu* (*Granny Takes Over*) (Zeman)

1959   *Mstitel* (*The Avenger*) (Stekly); *Slečna od vody* (*The Young Lady from the Riverside*) (Zeman)

1960   *Otomar Korbelář* (doc); *Případ Lupínek* (*The Lupinek Case*) (Vorlíček)

1961   *Tažní ptáci* (*Birds of Passage*) (Mach)

1962   *Hoffmanovy povídky* (*The Tales of Hoffman*) (Kašlík); *Rusalka* (Kaslík); *Objec na střapaté hurce* (*Discovery on the Shaggy Mountain*) (Steklý)

1964   *Starci na chmelu* (*The Hop Pickers*) (Rychman)

1966   *Lidé z maringotek* (*Life on Wheels*)

1967   *Když má svátek Dominika* (*Dominika's Name Day*); *Liebesspiele im Schnee* (*Ski Fever*) (Siodmak)

1968   *Naše bláznivá rodina* (*Our Crazy Family*)

1970   *Cosi fan tutte* (Kašlík)

1971   *Pinocchiova dobrodružstvi* (*The Adventures of Pinocchio*)

Publications

By STALLICH: book—

Kamera umeleckeho filmu, Prague, 1955.

On STALLICH: articles—

Film a Doba (Prague), no. 4, 1957.
Film a Doba (Prague), no. 8–9, 1959.

*   *   *

Jan Stallich was the youngest of the trio of famous Czech cameramen (with Heller and Vích). Like the other two, he achieved international acclaim but, unlike them, after 1945 he resumed his work for Czechoslovak cinematography to which he dedicated nearly half a century. His exceptionally fast entry into the sphere of filmmaking was made possible by his father, Julius Stallich, who belonged among the pioneers of Czech cinematography. He served his apprenticeship in the film laboratories of the studio A-B and graduated from a graphic school after attending evening classes. By 1924, he was already working in the laboratories of the Kavalirka studio which he took charge of at a later date. As a cameraman, he began with news and film advertisements. There, for the first time, he was able to apply his perfect technical knowledge which he later proved many times over raised to the level of artistic design. During the silent era, he shot 12 fairly insignificant films. More notable was his contribution to Kollár's historical epic *St. Wenceslas*.

However, in 1934 at the Venice festival, four Czech films were awarded the City of Venice Cup: *Ecstasy*, *The River*, *The Earth Sings*, and *Storm in Tatra*. Two of these, *The River* and *Ecstasy*, Stallich shot alone, and on *Storm in Tatra* he worked with V. Vích. It was his unusual camerawork in the short film *Storm in Tatra* which led Machatý to entrust him with the camera work in *Ecstasy*. Stallich succeeded like Vích in *Erotikon* to elevate the camera into becoming the leading form of expression in film. In harmony with the director's vision, he took advantage of many innovative and photographically effective (e.g., the glass bottom of a barrel) and emotionally evocative (fixing the camera on the workman's pick-axe, shooting the husband's mad driving with a hand-held camera, etc.) ideas. On several other occasions, he demonstrated his taste for functional effect and utilization of technical finesse, for example, in a postwar historical comedy set in the reign of Rudolf II, *The Emperor's Baker and the Baker's Emperor*. The success of *The River*, with its poetic mood, and, for his day, the daring *Ecstasy*, brought Stallich to the attention of such directors as Basil Dean and Carol Reed in Great Britain, Mattoli and Genina in Italy, and Willy Forst in Austria and Germany. With Forst he made his first colour film, *Wiener Mädeln*. Most outstanding is his collaboration on the films of Martin Fric. In Rovenský's *The River* he also demonstrated his poetic vision of nature as a way of expressing the action rather than just the setting for he action. In *The River*, as in *Ecstasy*, he used several innovations: for example, shooting the struggle of the young hero with a giant pike through the glass wall of the swimming pool, giving it exceptional dramatic power. Alongside the overall shots he enriched the portrayal of nature with detailed shots of various animals in movement.

After the liberation, he worked in Czechoslovakia, initially on documentary films and later on several historical dramas, including *Warriors of Faith*. He also shot a biographical film dedicated to the famous Czech haematologist J. Janský, *The Secret of Blood*. After a series of not very successful comedies, he had a further opportunity to utilize all the various styles of his highly individual craft in J. Rychman's musical *The Hop Pickers*. He combines the poetry of summer evenings with dramatic shots of dance scenes, and through resourceful placing of the camera he celebrates human labour in the hop garden. He also executed exceptionally demanding camera work in film adaptations of two operatic works: Offenbach's *The Tales of Hoffman*, shot for Laterna Magica, and *Rusalka*. The perfect knowledge of various camera techniques and styles as well as his knowledge of laboratory processes, together with many years of practical experience, brought him both a place at the forefront of his profession and a teaching role in Prague's FAMU.

—Milos Votruba

STALLING, Carl

Composer. **Nationality:** American. **Career:** 1920s—accompanist for silent films; 1928—musical director at Walt Disney's studios; 1931–36—employed by Ub Iwerks's studio; 1936–57—musical director for Warner Bros. cartoons. **Died:** 29 November 1972.

Films as Musical Director:

1928 *Steamboat Willie* (Disney)
1929 *The Merry Dwarfs* (Disney); *When the Cat's Away*
1936 *Gold Diggers of '49* (Clampett and Jones); *Porky's Poultry Plant* (Williams and White); *Toytown Hall* (McKimson and Walker); *Milk and Money* (Jones); *Porky's Moving Day* (Smith); *Boulevardier from the Bronx* (Smith); *Don't Look Now* (Clampett); *Little Beau Porky* (Tashlin); *The Village Smithy* (Avery); *Coo-Coo Nut Grove* (Freleng); *Porky of the Northwoods* (Tashlin)
1937 *He Was Her Man* (Freleng); *Porky the Wrestler* (Avery); *Pigs Is Pigs* (Freleng); *Porky's Road Race* (Tashlin); *I Only Have Eyes for You* (Avery); *Picador Porky* (Avery); *The Fella with the Fiddle* (Freleng); *She Was an Acrobat's Daughter* (Freleng); *Porky's Romance* (Tashlin); *Porky's Duck Hunt* (Avery); *Ain't We Got Fun* (Avery); *Porky and Gabby* (Iwerks); *Clean Pastures* (Freleng); *Porky's Building* (Tashlin); *Steamlined Greta Green* (Freleng); *Sweet Sioux* (Freleng); *Porky's Super Service* (Iwerks); *Uncle Tom's Bungalow* (Avery); *Egghead Rides Again* (Avery); *Porky's Badtime Story* (Clampett); *Plenty of Money and You* (Freleng); *Porky's Railroad* (Tashlin); *A Sunbonnet Blue* (Avery); *Get Rich Quick Porky* (Clampett); *Speaking of the Weather* (Tashlin); *Porky's Garden* (Avery); *Dog Daze* (Freleng); *I Wanna Be a Sailor* (Avery); *Rover's Rival* (Clampett); *The Lyin' Mouse* (Freleng); *The Case of the Stuttering Pig* (Tashlin); *Little Red Walking Hood* (Avery); *Porky's Double Trouble* (Tashlin); *The Woods Are Full of Cuckoos* (Tashlin); *Porky's Hero Agency* (Clampett); *September in the Rain* (Freleng)
1938 *Daffy Duck and Egghead* (Avery); *Porky's Poppa* (Clampett); *Porky at the Crocadero* (Tashlin); *What Price Porky* (Clampett); *Porky's Phoney Express* (Dalton and Howard); *Porky's Five and Ten* (Clampett); *Porky's Hare Hunt* (Hardaway and Dalton); *Injun Trouble* (Clampett); *Porky the Fireman* (Tashlin); *Porky's Party* (Clampett); *Porky's Spring Planting* (Tashlin); *Porky and Daffy* (Clampett); *Wholly Smoke* (Tashlin); *Porky in Wackyland* (Clampett); *Porky's Naughty Nephew* (Clampett); *Porky in Egypt* (Clampett); *The Daffy Doc* (Clampett); *Daffy Duck in Hollywood* (Avery); *Porky the Gob* (Hardaway and Dalton)
1939 *The Lone Stranger and Porky* (Clampett); *It's an Ill Wind* (Hardaway and Dalton); *Porky's Tire Trouble* (Clampett);

Porky's Movie Mystery (Clampett); *Prest-O Change-O* (Jones); *Chicken Jitters* (Clampett); *Porky and Teabiscuit* (Dalton and Hardaway); *Kristopher Kolumbus, Jr.* (Clampett); *Polar Pals* (Clampett); *Scalp Trouble* (Clampett); *Old Glory*; *Porky's Picnic* (Clampett); *Wise Quacks* (Clampett); *Hare-Um Scare-Um* (Hardaway and Dalton); *Porky's Hotel* (Clampett); *Jeepers Creepers* (Clampett); *Naughty Neighbors* (Clampett); *Pied Piper Porky* (Clampett); *Porky the Giant Killer* (Freleng); *The Film Fan* (Clampett)
1940 *Porky's Last Stand* (Clampett); *The Early Worm Gets the Bird* (Avery); *Africa Squeaks* (Clampett); *Mighty Hunters* (Jones); *Ali Baba Bound* (Clampett); *Busy Bakers* (Hardaway and Dalton); *Elmer's Candid Camera* (Jones); *Pilgrim Porky* (Clampett); *Cross Country Doctors* (Avery); *Confederate Honey* (Freleng); *Slap Happy Pappy* (Clampett); *The Bear's Tale* (Avery); *The Hardship of Miles Standish* (Freleng); *Porky's Poor Fish* (Clampett); *Sniffles Takes a Trip* (Jones); *You Ought to Be in Pictures* (Freleng); *A Gander at Mother Goose* (Avery); *The Chewin' Bruin* (Clampett); *Tom Thumb in Trouble* (Jones); *Circus Today* (Avery); *Porky's Baseball Broadcast* (Freleng); *Little Blabbermouse* (Freleng); *The Egg Collector* (Jones); *A Wild Hare* (Avery); *Ghost Wanted* (Jones); *Patient Porky* (Clampett); *Ceiling Hero* (Avery); *Malibu Beach Party* (Freleng); *Calling Dr. Porky* (Freleng); *Stage Fright* (Jones); *Prehistoric Porky* (Clampett); *Holiday Highlights* (Avery); *Good Night Elmer* (Jones); *The Sour Puss* (Clampett); *Wacky Wildlife* (Avery); *Bedtime for Sniffles* (Jones); *Porky's Hired Hand* Freleng); *Of Fox and Hounds* (Avery); *The Timid Toreador* (McCabe and Clampett); *Shop, Look and Listen* (Freleng)
1941 *Elmer's Pet Rabbit* (Jones); *Porky's Snooze Reel* (McCabe and Clampett); *The Fighting 69½th* (Freleng); *Sniffles Bells the Cat* (Jones); *The Haunted Mouse* (Avery); *The Crackpot Quail* (Avery); *The Cat's Tale* (Freleng); *Joe Glow the Firefly* (Jones); *Tortoise Beats Hare* (Avery); *Porky's Bear Facts* (Freleng); *Goofy Groceries* (Clampett); *Toy Trouble* (Jones); *Porky's Preview* (Avery); *The Trial of Mr. Wolf* (Freleng); *Porky's Ant* (Jones); *Hollywood Steps Out* (Avery); *A Coy Decoy* (Clampett); *Hiawatha's Rabbit Hunt* (Freleng); *Porky's Prize Pony* (Jones); *The Wacky Worm* (Freleng); *Meet John Doughboy* (Clampett); *The Heckling Hare* (Avery); *Inki and the Lion* (Jones); *Aviation Vacation* (Avery); *We, the Animals, Squeak* (Clampett); *Sport Chumpions* (Freleng); *The Henpecked Duck* (Clampett); *All This and Rabbit Stew* (Avery); *Notes to You* (Freleng); *The Brave Little Bat* (Jones); *The Bug Parade* (Avery); *Robinson Crusoe, Jr.* (McCabe); *Rookie Revue* (Freleng); *The Cagey Canary* (Avery); *Porky's Midnight Matinee* (Jones); *Rhapsody in Rivets* (Freleng); *Wabbit Twouble* (Clampett); *Porky's Pooch* (Clampett)
1942 *The Bird Came C.O.D.* (Jones); *Aloha Hooey* (Avery); *Who's Who in the Zoo* (McCabe); *Porky's Cafe* (Jones); *Conrad the Sailor* (Jones); *Crazy Cruise* (Avery); *The Wabbit Who Came to Supper* (Freleng); *Saps in Chaps* (Freleng); *Dog Tired* (Jones); *Daffy's Southern Exposure* (McCabe); *The Wacky Wabbit* (Clampett); *The Draft Horse* (Jones); *Nutty News* (Clampett); *Lights Fantastic* (Freleng); *Hold the Lion, Please* (Jones); *Gopher Goofy* (McCabe); *Double Chaser* (Freleng); *Wacky Blackouts* (Clampett); *Bugs Bunny Gets the Boid* (Clampett); *Foney Fables* (Freleng); *The*

Ducktators (McCabe); *Eatin' on the Cuff* (Clampett); *Fresh Hare* (Freleng); *The Impatient Patient* (McCabe); *The Dover Boys* (Jones); *The Hep Cat* (Clampett); *The Daffy Duckaroo* (McCabe); *The Hare-Brained Hypnotist* (Freleng); *A Tale of Two Kitties* (Clampett); *My Favorite Duck* (Jones); *Ding Dog Daddy* (Freleng); *Case of the Missing Hare* (Jones)

1943 *Coal Black and de Sebben Dwarfs* (Clampett); *Confusions of a Nutzy Spy* (McCabe); *Pigs in a Polka* (Freleng); *Tortoise Wins by a Hare* (Clampett); *Fifth Column Mouse* (Freleng); *To Duck or Not to Duck* (Jones); *Flop Goes the Weasel* (Jones); *Hop and Go* (McCabe); *Super Rabbit* (Jones); *The Unbearable Bear* (Jones); *The Wise Quacking Duck* (Clampett); *Greetings Bait* (Freleng); *Tokio Jokio* (McCabe); *Jack-Wabbit and the Beanstalk* (Freleng); *The Aristo-Cat* (Jones); *Yankee Doodle Daffy* (Freleng); *Wackiki Wabbit* (Jones); *Tin Pan Alley Cats* (Clampett); *Porky Pig's Feat* (Tashlin); *Scrap Happy Daffy* (Tashlin); *Hiss and Make Up* (Freleng); *A Corny Concerto* (Clampett); *Fin 'n' Catty* (Jones); *Falling Hare* (Clampett); *Inki and the Minah Bird* (Jones); *Daffy the Commando* (Freleng); *Puss 'n' Booty* (Clampett)

1944 *Little Red Riding Rabbit* (Freleng); *What's Cookin', Doc?* (Clampett); *Meatless Flyday* (Freleng); *Tom Turk an d Daffy* (Jones); *Bugs Bunny and the Three Bears* (Jones); *I Got Plenty of Mutton* (Tashlin); *The Weakly Reporter* (Jones); *Tick Tock Tuckered* (Clampett); *Bugs Bunny Nips the Nips* (Freleng); *The Swooner Crooner* (Tashlin); *Russian Rhapsody* (Clampett); *Duck Soup to Nuts* (Freleng); *Angel Puss* (Jones); *Slightly Daffy* (Freleng); *Hare Ribbin'* (Clampett); *Brother Brat* (Tashlin); *Hare Force* (Freleng); *From Hand to Mouse* (Jones); *Birdy and the Beast* (Clampett); *Buckaroo Bugs* (Clampett); *Goldilocks and the Jivin' Bears* (Freleng); *Plane Daffy* (Tashlin); *Lost and Foundling* (Jones); *Booby Hatched* (Tashlin); *The Old Grey Hare* (Clampett); *Stage Door Cartoon* (Freleng)

1945 *Odor-able Kitty* (Jones); *Herr Meets Hare* (Freleng); *Draftee Daffy* (Clampett); *The Unruly Hare* (Tashlin); *Trap Happy Porky* (Jones); *Life with Feathers* (Freleng); *Behind the Meat Ball* (Tashlin); *Hare Trigger* (Freleng); *Ain't That Ducky* (Freleng); *A Gruesome Twosome* (Clampett); *A Tale of Two Mice* (Tashlin); *Wagon Heels* (Clampett); *Hare Conditioned* (Jones); *Fresh Airedale* (Jones); *The Bashful Buzzard* (Clampett); *Peck Up Your Troubles* (Freleng); *Hare Tonic* (Jones); *Nasty Quacks* (Tashlin)

1946 *Book Revue* (Clampett); *Baseball Bugs* (Freleng); *Holiday for Shoestrings* (Freleng); *Quentin Quail* (Jones); *Baby Bottleneck* (Clampett); *Hare Remover* (Tashlin); *Daffy Doodles* (McKimson); *Hollywood Canine Canteen* (McKimson); *Hush My Mouse* (Jones); *Hair-Raising Hare* (Jones); *Kitty Kornered* (Clampett); *Hollywood Daffy* (Freleng); *Acrobatty Bunny* (McKimson); *The Great Piggy Bank Robbery* (Clampett); *Bacall to Arms* (Clampett); *Walky Talky Hawky* (McKimson); *Racketeer Rabbit* (Freleng); *Fair and Wormer* (Jones); *The Big Snooze* (Clampett); *The Mouse-merized Cat* (McKimson); *Rhapsody Rabbit* (Freleng)

1947 *The Gay Anties* (Freleng); *A Hare Grows in Manhattan* (Freleng); *Rabbit Transit* (Freleng); *Easter Yeggs* (McKimson); *Crowing Pains* (McKimson); *A Pest in the House* (Jones); *Little Orphan Airedale* (Jones); *Slick Hare*

(Freleng); *Mexican Joyride* (Davis); *Catch As Cats Can* (Davis)

1948 *Gorilla My Dreams* (McKimson); *Two Gophers from Texas* (Davis); *What Makes Daffy Duck* (Davis); *What's Brewin', Bruin?* (Jones); *Daffy Duck Slept Here* (McKimson); *A Hick, a Slick and a Chick* (Davis); *Back Alley Oproar* (Freleng); *I Taw a Putty Tat* (Freleng); *Rabbit Punch* (Jones); *Nothing But the Tooth* (Davis); *Buccaneer Bunny* (Freleng); *Bugs Bunny Rides Again* (Freleng); *The Rattled Rooster* (Davis); *The Shell Shocked Egg* (McKimson); *Haredevil Hare* (Jones); *You Were Never Duckier* (Jones); *Dough Ray Me-ow* (Davis); *Hot Cross Bunny* (McKimson); *The Pest That Came to Dinner* (Davis); *Hare Splitter* (Freleng); *Odor of the Day* (Davis); *The Foghorn Leghorn* (McKimson); *A Lad in His Lamp* (McKimson); *Daffy Dilly* (Jones); *Kit for Kat* (Freleng); *The Stupor Salesman* (Davis); *Riff Raffy Daffy* (Davis); *My Bunny Lies over the Sea* (Jones); *Scaredy Cat* (Jones)

1949 *Wise Quackers* (Freleng); *Hare Do* (Freleng); *Holiday for Drumsticks* (Davis); *The Awful Orphan* (Jones); *Porky Chops* (Davis); *Daffy Duck Hunt* (McKimson); *Rebel Rabbit* (McKimson); *Mouse Wreckers* (Jones); *High Diving Hare* (Freleng); *The Bee-devilled Bruin* (Jones); *Curtain Razor* (Freleng); *Bowery Bugs* (Davis); *Mouse Mazurka* (Freleng); *Long-Haired Hare* (Jones); *Henhouse Henry* (McKimson); *Knights Must Fall* (Freleng); *Bad Ol' Putty Tat* (Freleng); *The Greyhounded Hare* (McKim son); *The Windblown Hare* (McKimson); *Dough for the Do-Do* (Freleng); *Fast and Furry-ous* (Jones); *Each Dawn I Crow* (Freleng); *Frigid Hare* (Jones); *Swallow the Leader* (McKimson); *Bye Bye Bluebeard* (Davis); *For Scent-imental Reasons* (Jones); *Hippety Hopper* (McKimson); *Which Is Witch?* (Freleng); *Bear Feat* (Jones); *Rabbit Hood* (Jones); *A Ham in a Role* (McKimson)

1950 *Home Tweet Home* (Freleng); *Hurdy Gurdy Hare* (McKimson); *Boobs in the Woods* (McKimson); *Mutiny on the Bunny* (Freleng); *The Lion's Busy* (Freleng); *The Scarlet Pumpernickel* (Jones); *Homeless Hare* (Jones); *Strife with Father* (McKimson); *The Hypochondri-Cat* (Jones); *Big House Bunny* (Freleng); *The Leghorn Blows at Midnight* (McKimson); *His Bitter Half* (Freleng); *An Egg Scramble* (McKimson); *What's Up, Doc?* (McKimson); *All Abir-r-rd* (Freleng); *8 Ball Bunny* (Jones); *It's Hummer Time* (McKimson); *Golden Yeggs* (Freleng); *Hillbilly Hare* (McKimson); *Dog Gone South* (Jones); *The Ducksters* (Jones); *A Fractured Leghorn* (McKimson); *Bunker Hill Bunny* (Freleng); *Canary Row* (Freleng); *Stooge for a Mouse* (Freleng); *Pop 'im Pop* (McKimson); *Bushy Hare* (McKimson); *Caveman Inki* (Jones); *Dog Collared* (McKimson); *Rabbit of Seville* (Jones); *Two's a Crowd* (Jones)

1951 *Hare We Go* (McKimson); *A Fox in a Fix* (McKimson); *Canned Feud* (Freleng); *Rabbit Every Monday* (Freleng); *Putty Tat Trouble* (Freleng); *Corn Plastered* (McKimson); *Bunny Hugged* (Jones); *Scentimental Romeo* (Jones); *A Bone for a Bone* (Freleng); *Fair-haired Hare* (Freleng); *A Hound for Trouble* (Jones); *Early to Bet* (McKimson); *Rabbit Fire* (Jones); *Chow Hound* (Jones); *His Hare Raising Tale* (Freleng); *Cheese Chasers* (Jones); *Lovelorn Leghorn* (McKimson); *Tweety's S.O.S.* (Freleng); *Ballot*

Box Bunny (Freleng); *A Bear for Punishment* (Jones); *Sleepy Time Possum* (McKimson); *Drip-Along Daffy* (Jones); *Big Top Bunny* (McKimson); *Tweet, Tweet, Tweety* (Freleng); *The Prize Pest* (McKimson)

1952   *Who's Kitten Who?* (McKimson); *Operation: Rabbit* (Jones); *Feed the Kitty* (Jones); *Gift Wrapped* (Freleng); *Foxy by Proxy* (Freleng); *Thumb Fun* (McKimson); *14 Carrot Rabbit* (Freleng); *Little Beau Pepe* (Jones); *Kiddin' the Kitten* (McKimson); *Water, Water Every Hare* (Jones); *Little Red Rodent Hood* (Freleng); *Sock a Doodle Doo* (McKimson); *Beep, Beep* (Jones); *Hasty Hare* (Jones); *Ain't She Tweet* (Freleng); *The Turn-Tale Wolf* (McKimson); *Cracked Quack* (Freleng); *Oily Hare* (McKimson); *Hoppy Go Lucky* (McKimson); *Going! Going! Gosh!* (Jones); *Bird in a Guilty Cage* (Freleng); *Mouse Warming* (Jones); *Rabbit Seasoning* (Jones); *The Egg-cited Rooster* (McKimson); *Tree for Two* (Freleng); *The Super Snooper* (McKimson); *Rabbit's Kin* (McKimson); *Terrier Stricken* (Jones); *Fool Coverage* (McKimson); *Hare Lift* (Freleng)

1953   *Don't Give Up the Sheep* (Jones); *Snow Business* (Freleng); *A Mouse Divided* (Freleng); *Forward March Hare* (Jones); *Kiss Me Cat* (Jones); *Duck Amuck* (Jones); *Upswept Hare* (McKimson); *A Peck 'o' Trouble* (McKimson); *Fowl Weather* (Freleng); *Muscle Tussle* (McKimson); *Southern Fried Rabbit* (Freleng); *Ant Pasted* (Freleng); *Much Ado about Nutting* (Jones); *There Auto Be a Law* (McKimson); *Hare Trimmed* (Freleng); *Tom-Tom Tomcat* (Freleng); *Wild over You* (Jones); *Duck Dodgers in the 24 1/2th Century* (Jones); *Bully for Bugs* (Jones); *Plop Goes the Weasel* (McKimson); *Cat-Tails for Two* (McKimson); *A Street Cat Named Sylvester* (Freleng); *Zipping Along* (Jones); *Duck! Rabbit! Duck* (Jones); *Easy Peckin's* (McKimson); *Catty Cornered* (Freleng); *Of Rice and Hen* (McKimson); *Cats A-weigh* (McKimson); *Robot Rabbit* (Freleng); *Punch Trunk* (Jones)

1954   *Dog Pounded* (Freleng); *Captain Hareblower* (Freleng); *Feline Frame-Up* (Jones); *Wild Wife* (McKimson); *No Barking* (Jones); *The Cat's Bah* (Jones); *Design for Leaving* (McKimson); *Bell Hoppy* (McKimson); *No Parking Hare* (McKimson); *Doctor Jerkyl's Hide* (Freleng); *Claws for Alarm* (Jones); *Little Boy Boo* (McKimson); *Devil May Hare* (McKimson); *Muzzle Tough* (Freleng); *The Oily American* (McKimson); *Bewitched Bunny* (Jones); *Satan's Waitin'* (Freleng); *Stop, Look and Hasten!* (Jones); *Gone Batty* (McKimson); *Goo Goo Goliath* (Freleng); *From A to Z-Z-Z* (Jones); *Quack Shot* (McKimson); *Lumber Jack Rabbit* (Jones); *Sheep Ahoy* (Jones)

1955   *Beanstalk Bunny* (Jones); *All Fowled Up* (McKimson); *Sandy Claws* (Freleng); *Jumpin' Jupiter* (Jones); *Hyde and Hare* (Freleng); *Speedy Gonzales* (Freleng); *Guided Muscle* (Jones); *Pappy's Puppy* (Freleng)

1956   *The High and the Flighty* (McKimson); *The Unexpected Pest* (McKimson); *Stupor Duck* (McKimson); *Barbary Coast Bunny* (Jones); *Half-Fare Hare* (McKimson); *Raw! Raw! Rooster* (McKimson); *Slap-Hoppy Mouse* (McKimson); *Wideo Wabbit* (McKimson); *There They Go-Go-Go* (Jones)

1957   *Scrambled Aches* (Jones) (co); *Ali Baba Bunny* (Jones) (co); *Cheese It, the Cat* (McKimson) (co); *Fox Terror* (McKimson) (co); *Piker's Peak* (Freleng) (co); *Tabasco Road* (McKimson) (co); *Bugsy and Mugsy* (Freleng) (co); *Zoom and Bored* (Jones) (co); *Mouse-taken Identity* (McKimson) (co); *Gonzales' Tamales* (Freleng) (co); *Feather Bluster* (McKimson) (co); *To Itch His Own* (Jones)

Publications

By STALLING: article—

Velvet Light Trap (Madison, Wisconsin), no. 15, Fall 1975.

On STALLING: articles—

Funnyworld, no. 13, Spring 1971.
Soundtrack! (Hollywood), March 1991.
Filmfax, no. 34, August-September 1992.
Film Comment, vol. 28, September-October 1992.
Animatrix (Los Angeles), no. 7, 1993.
Film Score Monthly (Los Angeles), May 1995.

*   *   *

''I love music,'' said Warners' animator Friz Freleng. ''Music inspires my visual thinking. I time my cartoons to music . . . everything is done rhythmically.''

Musical director Carl Stalling was one of the unsung ''back-room boys'' of the Golden Age of the Hollywood cartoon from around 1930–60, working in a medium where even the directors and animators (and Stalling, especially at Warner Bros., worked with the best) have only recently begun to receive the acclaim their brilliant creations deserve.

Stalling broke into the movie business in the 1920s in time-honoured fashion accompanying silent movies and conducting theatre orchestras, principally in Kansas City. It was here that he met Walt Disney, who hired him as musical director in 1928 as the age of sound was about to dawn.

The importance of Carl Stalling's musical contribution to the success of the Mickey Mouse cartoons and other early Disney work should not be underestimated. Animation and music fused in these cartoons, the visual rhythm of movement and the punchlines of gags dancing to the beats of the soundtrack. Without music, reaction to the earliest Mickey Mouse cartoons (*Plane Crazy* and *Gallopin' Gaucho*) had been disappointing but the introduction of Stalling's music to the third cartoon, *Steamboat Willie*, transformed the situation. It was Stalling, also, who proposed the idea for the 1929 classic *Skeleton Dance* and launched the ''Silly Symphonies'' series for Disney.

A period in the early 1930s working for animator Ub Iwerks (who poached Stalling from Disney when he left to form his own studio) produced little opportunity for Stalling to shine (Iwerks' own cartoons were not outstanding) but this changed when Stalling joined Warners in 1936 after the failure of Iwerks' studio.

At Warner Bros., Stalling not only had brilliant cartoons to work on but also, thanks to the studio's ownership of several music publishers, access to a catalogue of hundreds of popular tunes. His grounding in the work of the masters of the clever tune/apt lyric brigade gave his arrangements an incredible diversity—light, graceful and witty—which complemented the on-screen action without ever distracting from it. He was helped considerably by an incredible recall which allowed him to select titles suited to the action or image, a facility which Chuck Jones referred to as "his computer." This helped Stalling in keeping up with the pace of work imposed at Warners where, as the principal person scoring for each of the cartoon "teams," he would often have to come up with an entire six-minute cartoon score every week. Along with the sound-effects of Treg Brown, Stalling's scores became an integral part of the output.

The reflex selection of music according to a title related to what was on-screen did, however, run the risk of descending into cliché. "Sometimes it worked and sometimes it didn't," said Jones, before adding that "it didn't mean anything because nobody knew the damn songs even then." This is only partly true, since even if Warner Bros. fans didn't know the titles, Stalling's method meant they came to recognize the tunes! The swingtime of "Powerhouse" became the hallmark for any mechanical activity, "California, Here I Come" accompanied trains going anywhere, and all games became jazzed up contests played out to "Freddie the Freshman."

Stalling had a particular soft spot for the catchy, energetic work of Raymond Scott (who wrote "Powerhouse," as well as such cartoony titles as "Reckless Night on Board an Ocean Liner" and "Dinner Music for a Pack of Hungry Cannibals") though he would latch onto anything with a crazy title, clearing the rights to songs such as "They Gotta Quit Kickin' My Dog Around," "Honey Bunny Boo," "Huckleberry Duck," "The Girl-Friend of the Whirling Dervish" and "Go Get the Ax."

The logic Stalling applied in his selection of music often, in fact, mirrored the remorseless extensions of logic which underlay the cartoon mayhem on screen which would take things and stretch them or put them in an oddball context. Stalling's efforts even earned the praise of the famous writer and critic James Agee for his pastiche of Lizst in the 1946 cartoon *Rhapsody Rabbit*: "A good musician must have worked on this . . . I have never seen anything done from so deep inside the ham."

If Stalling's musical eclecticism (ragtime, swing, the classics and just about any kind of popular ditty) let him down, it was only with faster jazz of the late 1940s and 1950s, when occasionally directors would bring in an outsider for a soundtrack (e.g. in *Mouse Mazurka* (1949) Friz Freleng turned to jazzman Shorty Rogers for music).

The pressure under which he had to work may have dictated his reliance on borrowing and playing with the work of others—as did the desire to pastiche everything which hung in the air on the Warners' cartoon lot—but Stalling was also a consummate musician, well able to compose his own themes or songs when the opportunity arose. Bugs' theme song, "What's Up, Doc?," was composed by Stalling in 1944 and saw the light of day to marvelous effect in the great rabbit's 1950 spoof bio-pic of the same name. Footage of this number, with Bugs doing terrible things to a deadpan Elmer, later appeared in Peter Bogdanovich's 1972 feature film *What's Up, Doc?*.

If Stalling's contribution in his 20 years at Warners' was a backdrop to the on-screen pyrotechnics it was an important one. An actor needs a platform to act upon and Stalling's music provided part of that platform. He was brilliant at adapting a staggering range of musical material to back up the cartoons' comic pace, mimicking the referential gifts of the animators with his own musical one. Chuck Jones has called Stalling "probably the most inventive musician who ever worked in animation," but perhaps he was only obeying the rarely heeded advice of producer Leon Schlesinger: "Hit 'em with the fast music."

—Norman Miller

STAREWICZ, Ladislaw

Animator and Director. **Nationality:** Polish. **Born:** Wladyslaw Starewicz in Moscow (of Polish parents), 6 August 1882 (some sources give 1892 or 1893). **Family:** Married Anna, daughters: Irene and Nina. **Education:** Studied art and entomology. **Career:** Worked as a bookkeeper before embarking on a film career; 1909—directed first film, *Nad Nyemen*. 1911—made first animated fiction film, *Beautiful Lukanida*; 1913—directed first live-action feature, *Strashnaya myest*; 1919—emigrated to France; 1928–41—worked on his first (and only) animated feature, *Le Roman de Renard*; 1939–46—made numerous publicity films. **Died:** Fontenay-sous-Bois, France, 28 February 1965.

Films as Director and Animator:

(all shorts unless otherwise noted)

1910   *Valka zukov rogachi (Battle of the Stag Beetles)* (doc, animation)
1911   *Prekrasnya Lukanida (Beautiful Lukanida); Myest kinematografichyeeskovo operator (The Cameraman's Revenge); Aviatsionnaya nyedyelya nasyekomich (The Insects' Aviation Week); Rozhdyestvo obitateli lyesa (The Insects' Christmas; The Birth of the Host of the Forest); Stryekosa i muravey (The Ant and the Grasshopper)*
1912   *Novogodnaya szutka (The Newborn Insect); Pyegaz i pyetuch (Pegasus and the Cock); Putyeshyestviye na luna (Voyage to the Moon)*
1913   *Chetirye chorta (Four Devils)*
1914   *Vsyak na Russi i tango tantzuyet (Everyone's Dancing the Tango in Russia); Pasinok Marsa (Mars's Stepson)*
1915   *Lilya Belgii (The Lily from Belgium)*
1920   *Dans les griffes de l'araignée*
1921   *Le mariage de Babylas; L'épouvantail*
1922   *Les grenouilles qui demandait un roi*
1923   *La voix du rossignol; Amour noir et amour blanc*
1924   *La petite chanteuse des rues; Les yeux du dragon*
1926   *Le rat des villes et le rat des champs*
1927   *La cigale et le fourmi; La reine des papillons*
1928   *L'horloge magique*
1930   *La petite parade*
1932   *Le lion et le moucheron; Le lion devenu vieux*
1933   *Fétiche-mascotte*
1934   *Fétiche prestidigitateur*
1935   *Fétiche se marie*
1936   *Fétiche en voyage de noces*
1937   *Fétiche chez les sirènes*
1941   *Le roman de Renard (The Tale of the Fox)* (feature; co-d and co-sc with Irene Starewicz; German version released in 1936)
1947   *Zanzabelle à Paris* (co-anim Sonika Bo)
1949   *Fleur de fougère*
1953   *Gazouilly petit oiseau* (co-anim Sonika Bo)
1954   *Gueule de bois*
1955   *Un dimanche de Gazouilly* (co-anim Sonika Bo)
1956   *Le nez au vent*
1958   *Caroussel boréal*
1965   *Comme chien et chat* (unfinished)

Live-Action Films as Director:

1909   *Nad Nyemen* (*Beyond the River Nyemen*) (doc, short); *Zhichiye vazki* (*Life of the Dragonfly*) (doc, short); *Skarabyozi* (*Beetles*) (doc, short)

1912   *Pyeresmyesznik* (ep. of serial)

1913   *Strashnaya myest* (*The Terrible Vengeance*); *Noch pyeryed rozhdyestvo* (*The Night before Christmas*); *Snyegurochka* (*Girl of the Snows*); *Ruslan i Ludmila*; *Kogda zvuchat strunnyi svedtza* (*For the Love of a Singer*) (+ ro)

1914   *Skazka pro nyemyetskovo groznovo voyakou Goguel Moguel i pro chortya Balbyeskou* (*The Great Captain Goguel Moguel and the Devil Balbeskou*) (short)

1915   *Byez zhen* (*Without a Wife*) (+ ro); *Smyatiye tsvyeti* (*Faded Flowers*); *O chem shyeptalo morye* (*The Murmuring Sea*) (doc, short); *I posledniye chorti* (*The Last of the Devils*) (short) (+ ro); *Portryet* (*The Portrait*); *Eros i Psyche* (unfinished); *Kak nyemyets obyezyanov vidumal* (*How the German Invented the Ape*) (short, part-anim); *Zhityel nyeobitayemovo ostrava* (*The Inhabitants of a Desert Island; Fawn*) (+ ro)

1916   *Nochnye priklucheniye dariyat nam naslazhdeniye* (*Nocturnal Adventure*); *Zhenschini kurorta nye boyatsa dazhe chorta* (*The Island Women Aren't Afraid of the Devil*); *Taman*; *Na Varsavkom traktye* (*On the Warsaw Highway*); *Pan Tvardovsky* (*Mr Tvardovsky*) (part-anim)

1917   *Pan Tvardovsky v Rimye* (*Mr. Tvardovsky in Rome*) (part-anim); *Malenkaya aktrisa* (*The Little Actress*); *Pyesn Taiga* (*Song of the Taiga*); *Sachka nayezdnik* (*Little Sacha, Jockey*); *Leya Lifshits*; *Eto tyebye prinadlezit* (*It's Fine for You*); *Dvye vstryechi* (*Two Meetings*); *Glupichkiye zanmimayestsya sportom* (*The Idiot Sportsman*) (short); *Tyemnaya sila* (*Dark Strength*); *K narodnoi vlasti* (*The Popular Official*)

1918   *Kaliostro*; *Yola*; *Vij*; *Sorochinskaya yamarka* (*Sorochinksy Fair*); *Maiskaya noch* (*May Night*); *Stella Maris*; *Kobila Lord Mortona* (*Lord Morton's Twin*); *Lyubov odna lyubov* (*One Love or the Other*)

Other Films:

1913   *Domik v kolomne* (Chardynin) (sc)

1920   *Aux murs du couvent* (Uralsky) (ph); *Pour une nuit d'amour* (Protazanov) (ph); *L'angoissante aventure* (Protazanov) (ph)

1934   *Crainquebille* (de Baroncelli) (puppet seq)

Publications

On STAREWICZ: books—

Gilson, Paul, *Cine-Magic*, Paris, 1951.

Pilling, Jayne, editor, *Starewicz 1882–1965*, Edinburgh, 1983.

Béatrice, L., and F. Martin, *Ladislas Starewitch: Filmographie illustrée*, Annecy, 1991.

Bendazzi, Gianalberto, *Cartoons: One Hundred Years of Cinema Animation*, London, 1994.

On STAREWICZ: articles—

Estes, Oscar G., ''The Master of Animation,'' in *Classic Film Collector* (Indiana, Pennsylvania), Winter/Spring 1966/67.

Jenkins, Alan, ''Animal Magic,'' in *Stills* (London), July/August 1983.

Pagliano, Jean-Pierre, ''Starewitch au pays des merveilles,'' in *Positif* (Paris), June 1990.

Parsons, Scott, ''The Cameraman's Revenge and Other Fantastic Tales: The Amazing Puppet Animation of Ladislaw Starewicz,'' in *Library Journal*, 15 September 1994.

Atkinson, Michael, ''The Night Countries of the Brothers Quay,'' in *Film Comment* (New York), September-October 1994.

Pummell, Simon, ''Of Rats and Men,'' in *Sight and Sound* (London), May 1995.

Skotak, R., ''Red Star Rising: the Lost Years of *Fantastika* in the Soviet Union,'' in *Outré* (Evanston), no. 6, 1996.

Pummell, Simon, ''Ladislaw Starewicz: Cut Off Their Tails with a Carving Knife,'' in *Projections 5: Film-makers on Film-making*, edited by John Boorman and Walter Donohue, London, 1996.

*   *   *

''The film you are about to see,'' announces a title at the start of Ladislaw Starewicz's *Le roman de Renard*, ''is not an animated cartoon. It is a revolution in the history of the cinema.'' The note of arrogance can be forgiven. Starewicz's film, the first-ever stop-action puppet-animation feature film, would be an impressive enough achievement had it emanated from a well-staffed studio, aided by all the modern technology of animatronics and computers. In fact it was created almost entirely (barring the actors' voices and the music score) by two people: Starewicz and his daughter Irene, who made all the puppets, costumes, and props, designed and built the sets, devised the lighting, operated the camera and executed all the millions of infinitely subtle movements and changes of expression needed to tell the story. ''Millions'' is no exaggeration: one three-minute sequence alone, during the final siege of the Fox's castle of Malpertuis by the forces of King Lion, required 273,000 different movements.

Although he was a talented cartoonist whose work appeared in newspapers, Starewicz never set out to be an animator. His first films were documentaries, stemming from his interest in landscape and natural history. Only when he tried to make a film about the mating battles of stag beetles did he stumble by chance into stop-action. The beetles proved uncooperative and one of them died, from which Starewicz realized that he could wire up the corpse and, by moving it one frame at a time, make it ''perform'' as he wanted. From this it was a short step to his first masterpiece, *The Cameraman's Revenge*, in which a comic melodrama of jealousy and adultery is played out by insects.

Insects feature strongly in Starewicz's work; their jagged, scuttling vitality clearly appealed to his spiky imagination. In *Beautiful Lukanida* beetles play out a parody of the Helen of Troy legend, and in other early films, he creates an entire world in which insects dance at weddings, ride bicycles, or celebrate Christmas. But this is never Disney-style anthropomorphism (nothing very mouselike about Mickey, after all); Starewicz's creatures, though parodying human activities, remain unnervingly insectish in their movements. What he does tend to do (as B. Ruby Rich points out in the anthology edited by Jayne Pilling) is assign specific temperaments to particular species: ''The grasshoppers are generally disagreeable: vengeful rival, foppish painter . . . , etc. The frogs are usually comic relief, fatuous and also bad-tempered.'' Even once Starewicz had moved on to featuring mammals as his main players, insects often show up in supporting roles, typically dancing or playing musical instruments.

As Rich's remarks also hint, there is little that is lovable, let alone sugary, about Starewicz's work at its best. (His late films, made after 1945, do sometimes succumb to cuteness.) Violence, of an alarmingly graphic sort, crops up a lot in his films, never softened by the pretense that mangled bodies will simply (as in *Tom & Jerry*) resuscitate unharmed in the next frame. Starewicz's world is cruel, even sadistic. Sharp things slice and sever; limbs are lopped off; creatures are eaten alive, struggling desperately. In his first French film, *Dans les griffes de l'araignée*, an empty-headed young fly, flouncing carelessly off to the big city, is seduced and gobbled up by the city-slicker spider. Two whole armies of insects attack each other without quarter in *La reine des papillons*. In *Fétiche-mascotte* toys struggle to escape from a speeding car: a white-costumed clown jumps clear, only for the wheels of another car to sever his neck. The head rolls into the gutter; the body twitches a couple of times, then lies still.

But though often bizarre and not infrequently unsettling, Starewicz's work is exhilarating in its energy, inventiveness, and sardonic humor. The influence of Gogol, some of whose stories Starewicz used for his live-action films, can be detected in much of his work; like Gogol, Starewicz often drew on folktales and fables, lending them a sardonic slant. *Le rat des villes et le rat des champs* catapults La Fontaine into the jazz age, complete with decadent scenes of rattish debauchery (sexy flapper-rats in scanty costumes) and some blatantly phallic imagery involving severed tails. *Amour noir et amour blanc* mixes its mythologies still more deliriously, with Chaplin, Tom Mix and Lillian Gish interacting with a pair of cupids (one black, one white), a dog-powered truck, a randy demon-faced camera and a moon borrowed from Méliès. The pot-bellied puppy hero of *Fétiche-mascotte* finds himself in a grotesque Bosch-like night-world populated by mobile garbage (fish-skeletons, rotting vegetables, and the like), malignant Parisian *apaches*, a balloon that plays saxophone, and a beanpole limbed devil. Such is the richness of Starewicz's imagination that his films often seem to burst at the seams with ideas, and much of the time there is far more going on in the frame than can be taken in at a single viewing.

While taking endless pains to create the illusion of realism (some of the puppets in *Renard* had as many as 150 different heads to convey changes of expression), Starewicz loved to point up the manipulation behind his work. The whole action of *Renard* is presented as a film shown, in the prologue, by a monkey projectionist (this film-within-a-film device was anticipated as early as *The Cameraman's Revenge*), and the pseudo-medieval setting is mocked by providing the combat between fox and wolf with a radio commentator. This play with illusion and reality lies at the heart of Starewicz's fantastic art; the sheer abundance of detail, nominally at the service of the story, becomes an end in itself and redirects our attention to the artifice of what we are seeing. (The contrast with the work of George Pal, the other great pioneer of stop-action, could not be more total; Pal's stick-figure minimalism and primary-colored sets scorn any attempt at realism, leaving his story line clear and uncluttered.) Gothic and romantic, primitive and ultra-sophisticated, Starewicz's work thrives on its double-edged contradictions; his vision is obsessive and intriguingly unique.

—Philip Kemp

STARK, Ray

Producer. Nationality: American. **Born:** c. 1914. **Education:** Attended Rutgers University, New Brunswick, New Jersey. **Family:** Married Frances Brice; two children. **Career:** Newsman and publicity writer; after World War II, radio writer representative, then literary agent and talent agent for Famous Players; 1957—cofounder, with Eliot Hyman, Seven Arts Productions: produced the stage musical *Funny Girl*, 1964; 1966—left the company to pursue independent film projects (including Barbra Streisand films); formed Rastar Company. **Award:** Irving G. Thalberg Award, 1979. **Address:** c/o Rastar Films, Sony Studios, Hepburn West, 10202 W. Washington, Culver City, California 90232, U.S.A.

Films as Producer:

1960   *The World of Suzie Wong* (Quine)
1964   *The Night of the Iguana* (Huston)
1967   *Oh Dad, Poor Dad, Mama's Hung You in the Closet and I'm Feelin' So Sad* (Quine)
1968   *Funny Girl* (Wyler)
1970   *The Owl and the Pussycat* (Ross)
1972   *Fat City* (Huston)
1973   *The Way We Were* (Pollack)
1975   *Funny Lady* (Ross); *The Sunshine Boys* (Ross)
1976   *Murder By Death* (Moore)
1977   *The Goodbye Girl* (Ross)
1978   *Casey's Shadow* (Ritt); *The Cheap Detective* (Moore); *California Suite* (Ross)
1979   *The Electric Horseman* (Pollack); *Chapter Two* (Moore)
1980   *Seems Like Old Times* (Sandrich); *The Hunter* (Kulik)
1982   *Annie* (Huston)
1985   *The Slugger's Wife* (Ashby)
1986   *Brighton Beach Memoirs* (Saks)
1988   *Biloxi Blues* (Nichols)
1989   *Steel Magnolias* (Ross)
1992   *Revenge* (Scott)
1993   *Barbarians at the Gate* (Jordan); *Lost in Yonkers* (Coolidge)

Publications

On STARK: articles—

Jacobson, Harlan, ''Stark Reality,'' in *Film Comment* (New York), July-August 1982.
Time Out (London), 3–9 September 1982.

*   *   *

Ray Stark should be remembered as the archetypal movie producer of the television age. This ultimate Hollywood hustler turned agent turned producer created deal after deal in the 1960s, 1970s, and 1980s that more often than not became very popular feature films. Few ever became mega-blockbusters; fewer still lost money. The studio bosses of the era loved Stark, because when he brought them a project they almost certainly had a ''sure thing.''

Stark made his reputation utilizing the talents of two very popular entertainers. First came the fabulously successful Barbra Streisand films: *Funny Girl, The Owl and the Pussycat, The Way We Were,* and *Funny Lady,* the sequel to *Funny Girl.* In their years of release these films finished second, fifth, eleventh, and tenth on *Variety*'s ranking of money earning power. Stark had long sought to produce the story of the life of noted vaudeville comic Fanny Brice, his mother-in-law. He started on Broadway fashioning *Funny Girl* into a Broadway smash. Hollywood success easily followed.

In the 1970s Stark turned to a second consistent source of making money, transforming the plays of Neil Simon into movie hits. Thus audiences came to adore *The Sunshine Boys, Murder By Death, The Goodbye Girl,* and *California Suite.* All ranked high in *Variety*'s yearly list of top money making films for their respective year of release.

But while Stark was basking in the glow of Hollywood's praise, forces were changing the industry. George Lucas and Steven Spielberg transformed the movie business of the 1970s with their films for young people, while Stark stuck with proven adult fare. Stark continued to package hits in his proven way and continued to make money, but his greatest success was behind him.

Stark then ascended into myth. He showcased his enormous wealth, estimated to be well in excess of $100 million. He hid his origins, telling all who would listen of his "rags to riches" life story. So, despite his considerable fame, we do not know when he was born; the best guess is sometime around 1914. His rise to fame as a producer we think includes brief careers as a college student, a journalist, a movie publicist, a literary agent, and a talent agent. He only lets us in on what he deems the highlights: writing "Red Ryder" scripts for radio, representing such authors as Ben Hecht and Raymond Chandler, serving as a talent agent for Marilyn Monroe, Richard Burton, and Kirk Douglas.

Some details are firm. In 1957 he did form Seven Arts Productions (with Eliot Hyman). In 1960 he did produce his first independent feature film, *The World of Suzie Wong.* In 1968 he resigned as executive vice president and head of production of Seven Arts to form Rastar, his own independent production company. In 1979 he did win Oscar's Irving G. Thalberg Award. But it is the legend that he would like us to focus on, a career that combined serious, ambitious projects with regular commercial success.

—Douglas Gomery

STAWIŃSKI, Jerzy Stefan

Writer. **Nationality:** Polish. **Born:** Zakret, 1 July 1921. **Education:** Attended law school, graduated. **Career:** Novelist; 1956—first film as writer, *Man on the Track*; 1963—first film as director, *No More Divorces*; television work includes the series *Wielka miłość Balzaka (Balzac's Great Loves).*

Films as Writer:

1956 *Czołwiek na torze (Man on the Track)* (Munk) (co)
1957 **Kanał** *(The Loved Life)* (Wajda); **Eroica** (Munk)

1958 *Dezerter (The Deserter)* (Lesiewicz); *Zamach (Answer to Violence)* (Passendorfer)
1960 *Zezowate szczęście (Bad Luck)* (Munk); *Krżacy (The Teutonic Knights)* (Ford) (co)
1961 *Historia współczesna (A Contemporary Story)* (Jakubowska)
1962 "Warszawa" ep. of *L'Amour à vingt ans (Love at Twenty)* (Wajda)
1963 *Rozwodów nie bedzie (No More Divorces)* (+ d)
1964 *Pingwin (The Penguin)* (+ d)
1965 *Przedświaeczny wieczór (Christmas Eve)* (+ co-d); *Andremo in città* (N. Risi)
1967 *Zabijaka* (Lenartowicz-for TV); *Poczmistrs* (Lenartowicz)
1968 *Adolphe* (Toublanc-Michel + Moal)
1970 *Pogon za Adamem (Chase After Adam)* (Zarzycki)
1971 *Kto wierzy w bociany (Who Believes in the Stork)* (+ co-d)
1973 *Godzina szczytu* (+ d); *Fortuna (Good Luck)* (Amiradzibi-for TV); *Wielka mloso Balzaka (Balzac's Great Love)* (Solarz—TV series) (co)
1974 *Urodziny Matyldy* (+ d)
1977 *Akcja pod Arsenalem (Action under Arsenal)* (Lomnicki)
1978 *Bilet powrotny* (E. & C. Petelscy)
1979 *Godzina W* (Morgenstern—TV)
1980 *Urodziny modego warszawiaka (Birthday of the Young Inhabitants of Warsaw)* (E. & C. Petelscy); *Ojciec królowej* (Solarz)
1981 *Do oszalalem dla niej (I Became Mad for Her Sake)*
1984 *Piec dni z zycla emeryta (Five Days from the life of a Pensioner)*
1988 *Obywatel Piszczyk (Citizen Piszczyk)* (Kotkowski) (co)
1995 *Plukownik Kwiatkowski (Colonel Kwiatkowski)* (Kutz)

Publications

By STAWIŃSKI: books—

Światło we mgle, 1952.
Herkulesy, 1953.
Katarzyna, 1955.
Godzina W. Wegrzy Kana, 1956.
Ujcieczka: Casalarga, 1958.
Sześć wcieleń Jana Piszczyka, 1959.
Ojciec królowej (play), 1961.
Pogoń za Adamem, 1963.
Wieczór przedświateczny, 1965.
Godzina szczytu, 1968.
Nie zawijajac do portou, 1970.
Pamiętnik z trzech morz i jednego oceanu, 1973.
I bedziesz miał dom . . . , 1976.
Młodego warszawiaka zapiski z urodzin, 1977.
Notatki scenarzysty (memoirs), 2 vols., 1979.

By STAWIŃSKI: articles—

Film (Warsaw), 3 August 1980.
Film (Warsaw), no. 8, 1985.
Kino (Warsaw), August 1985.
Iluzjon (Warsaw), July-December 1991.

On STAWIŃSKI: articles—

Film Polski (Warsaw), January 1964.
Image et Son (Paris), no. 223, 1968.
Kino (Warsaw), April 1974.
Filmowy Serwis Prasowy (Warsaw), 1–15 January 1978.
Filmowy Serwis Prasowy (Warsaw), 16–30 June 1981.

*   *   *

Jerzy Stefan Stawiński has three artistic professions: writer, scriptwriter, and film director. From a historical viewpoint, the most important for Polish culture is his scriptwriting, stemming from his literary works which distinctly helped to determine the appearance of "the Polish film school." He started as a writer but the content and themes of his stories and novels resonated with the movement of young new filmmakers, so in 1956 Andrzej Munk filmed *Man on the Track* from his script on the deformation of contemporary life affected by the personality cult. Later Stawiński cooperated with Munk on two other films, *Eroica* and *Bad Luck*. His short story "Kanal," about the trial of a group of freedom-fighters from the Warsaw uprising of 1944, became the basis of the script of the famous film by Andrzej Wajda.

From the beginning of his work in films, Stawiński showed himself to be a brilliant scriptwriter with a special sense for the specifics of film. His scripts have literary value, but to some extent they are left open-ended, therefore leaving space for the director's imagination. As a result he was able to work successfully with directors of completely different artistic signatures, the sober, analytical, rational and ironic Munk or the emotional Wajda. At the same time, he was able to realise through their work his own ideas and communicate his own views.

The point of departure for Stawiński's artistic work was his personal experience of war. An active soldier in the national army, he was a participant in the defeated Warsaw uprising, during which he and his comrades sought the safety of the underground sewers in the same way as the heroes of *Kanał*. Having exhausted this source to some extent, he moved temporarily on to other projects: for example, he wrote the script based on the historical novel *The Teutonic Knights* for Aleksander Ford. He enquired into themes of contemporary life, and also several times cooperated on films abroad. He was again reminded of the war towards the end of his artistic career: for example, in the films *Action under Arsenal* and *Birthday of the Young Inhabitants of Warsaw*. However, he never appeared in the films he himself directed.

In 1963 Stawiński directed his first film, the comedy *No More Divorces*. This debut, together with the debut of another writer, Aleksander Ścibor-Rylski, was preceded by the stormy and dramatic discussion which history designated the "revolt of scriptwriters." Both brought out a manifesto in which they criticised the relationship between directors and scriptwriters and expressed their dissatisfaction with the way that texts were treated. They decided as authors to direct their own scripts. It was not the most fortunate of decisions. Stawiński's direction showed a good mastery of craft but brought nothing strikingly new or original. Years later, he revised his views on scriptwriting, directing, and many other things in his two-volume memoirs.

Stawiński has written few scripts during the last fifteen years. In 1988 his script for the film *Citizen Piszczyk* was filmed. He based this tale of an unlucky person who commands both laughter and compassion on the film *Bad Luck* directed by Andrzej Munk. *Citizen Piszczyk*, directed by Andrzej Kotkowski, is less humorous than the original. Loosely filmed from Stawiński's excellent script, it depicts an aging hero unwillingly involved in a conflict with state power.

—B. Urgošíková

STEINER, Max

Composer and Arranger. **Nationality:** Austrian. **Born:** Maximilian Raoul Walter Steiner in Vienna, 10 May 1888; his father and grandfather were impressarios of operetta. **Education:** Studied at the Vienna Imperial Academy of Music, with Robert Fuchs, Herman Graedner, Felix Weingartner and briefly Gustav Mahler. **Career:** Child prodigy, as composer and conductor: his own operetta *The Pretty Greek Girl* was produced when he was 16; 1905–11—musical comedy conductor, London; then worked in Paris, Berlin, Moscow, and Johannesburg; 1914–29—worked in New York as a Broadway orchestrator, arranger and conductor; 1929–36—music director for RKO Radio Pictures; 1936–65—with Warner Bros., with loanouts to Selznick Pictures in the earlier years. **Awards:** Academy Award for *The Informer*, 1935; *Now, Voyager*, 1942; *Since You Went Away*, 1944; Venice Festival award for *The Treasure of the Sierra Madre*, 1948. **Died:** In Hollywood, 28 December 1971.

Max Steiner (right)

Films as Composer, Arranger and/or Music Director:

1929 *The Bondman* (Wilcox); *Rio Rita* (Reed)

1930 *Dixiana* (Reed); *Half Shot at Sunrise* (Sloane); *Check and Double Check* (Brown); *Beau Ideal* (Brenon); *Cimarron* (Ruggles)

1931 *Kept Husbands* (Bacon); *Cracked Nuts* (Cline); *Young Donovan's Kid* (Niblo); *Transgression* (Brenon); *Friends and Lovers* (Schertzinger) (co); *The Public Defender* (Ruben); *Traveling Husbands* (Sloane); *The Runaround* (Craft); *The Gay Diplomat* (Boleslawsky); *Way Back Home* (Seiter); *Fanny Foley Herself* (Brown); *Secret Service* (Ruben); *Consolation Marriage* (Sloane); *Are These Our Children?* (Ruggles)

1932 *Men of Chance* (Archainbaud); *Girl of the Rio* (Brenon); *Ladies of the Jury* (L. Sherman); *Young Bride* (Seiter); *The Lost Squadron* (Archainbaud); *State's Attorney* (Archainbaud); *Symphony of Six Million* (*Melody of Life*) (La Cava); *Westward Passage* (Milton); *Is My Face Red?* (Seiter); *What Price Hollywood?* (Cukor); *Roar of the Dragon* (Ruggles); *Bird of Paradise* (K. Vidor); *The Phantom of Crestwood* (Ruben); *The Most Dangerous Game* (Schoedsack and Pichel); *A Bill of Divorcement* (Cukor); *Little Orphan Annie* (Robertson); *Thirteen Women* (Archainbaud); *Renegades of the West* (Robinson); *The Conquerors* (*Pioneer Builders*) (Wellman); *The Sport Parade* (Murphy); *Rockabye* (Cukor); *The Half Naked Truth* (La Cava); *Penguin Pool Murder* (Archainbaud); *The Animal Kingdom* (*The Woman in His House*) (Griffith); *The Monkey's Paw* (Ruggles); *Lady with a Past* (*Reputation*) (Griffith); *Secrets of the French Police* (Sutherland)

1933 *No Other Woman* (Ruben); *The Cheyenne Kid* (Hill); *Lucky Devils* (R. Ince); *The Great Jaspers* (Ruben); **King Kong** (Schoedsack and Cooper); *Our Betters* (Cukor); *Topaze* (D'Arrast); *Christopher Strong* (Arzner); *Sweepings* (Cromwell); *Diplomaniacs* (Seiter); *The Silver Cord* (Cromwell); *Son of the Border* (Nosler); *Emergency Call* (Cahn); *Professional Sweetheart* (Seiter); *Flying Devils* (Birdwell); *Melody Cruise* (Sandrich); *Bed of Roses* (La Cava); *Double Harness* (Cromwell); *Headline Shooter* (Brower); *Before Dawn* (Pichel); *No Marriage Ties* (Ruben); *Morning Glory* (L. Sherman); *Blind Adventure* (Schoedsack); *One Man's Journey* (Robertson); *Rafter Romance* (Seiter); *Midshipman Jack* (Cabanne); *Ann Vickers* (Cromwell); *Ace of Aces* (Ruben); *Chance at Heaven* (Seiter); *After Tonight* (Archainbaud); *Little Women* (Cukor); *The Right to Romance* (Santell); *Aggie Appleby, Maker of Man* (Sandrich); *If I Were Free* (Nugent); *Flying Down to Rio* (Freeland); *Son of Kong* (Schoedsack) (co)

1934 *Man of Two Worlds* (Ruben); *Long Lost Father* (Schoedsack); *The Meanest Girl in Town* (Mack); *Two Alone* (Nugent); *Hips, Hips, Hooray!* (Sandrich); *The Lost Patrol* (Ford); *Keep 'em Rolling* (Archainbaud); *Spitfire* (Cromwell); *Sing and Like It* (Seiter); *Success at Any Price* (Ruben); *This Man Is Mine* (Cromwell); *The Crime Doctor* (Robertson); *Finishing School* (Tuchock and Nicholls); *Strictly Dynamite* (Nugent); *Where Sinners Meet* (Ruben); *Stingaree* (Wellman); *The Life of Vergie Winters* (Santell); *Murder on the Blackboard* (Archainbaud); *Let's Try Again* (Miner); *Of Human Bondage* (Cromwell); *We're Rich Again* (Seiter);

His Greatest Gamble (Robertson); *Hat, Coat, and Glove* (Miner); *Bachelor Bait* (Stevens); *Their Big Moment* (Cruze); *Down to Their Last Yacht* (Sloane); *The Fountain* (Cromwell); *The Age of Innocence* (Moeller); *The Richest Girl in the World* (Seiter); *The Gay Divorcee* (*The Gay Divorce*) (Sandrich); *Dangerous Corner* (Rosen); *Gridiron Flash* (Tryon); *Wednesday's Child* (Robertson); *Kentucky Kernels* (Stevens); *By Your Leave* (Corrigan); *Anne of Green Gables* (Nicholls); *The Little Minister* (Wallace); *The World Moves On* (Ford)

1935 *Romance in Manhattan* (Roberts); *Enchanted April* (Beaumont); *Roberta* (Seiter); *Laddie* (Stevens); *Star of Midnight* (Robert); **The Informer** (Ford); *Break of Hearts* (Moeller); **Becky Sharp** (Mamoulian); *She* (Pichel and Holden); *Alice Adams* (Stevens); **Top Hat** (Sandrich); *The Three Musketeers* (Lee); *I Dream Too Much* (Cromwell)

1936 *Little Lord Fauntleroy* (Cromwell); *The Charge of the Light Brigade* (Curtiz); *The Garden of Allah* (Boleslawsky); *Winterset* (Santell); *God's Country and the Woman* (Keighley), *Follow the Fleet* (Sandrich); *Two in Revolt* (Tryon); *M'Liss* (Nicholls)

1937 *Green Light* (Borzage); *Slim* (Enright); *Kid Galahad* (Curtiz) (co); *A Star Is Born* (Wellman); *The Life of Emile Zola* (Dieterle); *That Certain Woman* (Goulding); *First Lady* (Logan); *Submarine D-1* (Bacon); *Tovarich* (Litvak)

1938 *Gold Is Where You Find It* (Curtiz); *Jezebel* (Wyler); *The Adventures of Tom Sawyer* (Taurog); *Crime School* (Seiler); *White Banners* (Goulding); *The Amazing Dr. Clitterhouse* (Litvak); *Four Daughters* (Curtiz); *The Sisters* (Litvak); *Angels with Dirty Faces* (Curtiz); *The Dawn Patrol* (Goulding)

1939 *They Made Me a Criminal* (Berkeley); *Dodge City* (Curtiz); *The Oklahoma Kid* (Bacon); *Dark Victory* (Goulding); *Confessions of a Nazi Spy* (Litvak); *Each Dawn I Die* (Keighley); *Daughters Courageous* (Curtiz); *The Old Maid* (Goulding); *Dust Be My Destiny* (Seiler); *Intermezzo: A Love Story* (Ratoff); *We Are Not Alone* (Goulding); **Gone with the Wind** (Fleming)

1940 *Four Wives* (Curtiz); *Dr. Ehrlich's Magic Bullet* (Dieterle); *Virginia City* (Curtiz); *All This, and Heaven Too* (Litvak); *City for Conquest* (Litvak); *A Dispatch from Reuter's* (Dieterle); *The Letter* (Wyler); *Santa Fe Trail* (Curtiz); *The Great Lie* (Goulding); *Shining Victory* (Rapper); *The Bride Came C.O.D.* (Keighley); *Dive Bomber* (Curtiz); *Sergeant York* (Curtiz); *One Foot in Heaven* (Rapper)

1942 *They Died with Their Boots On* (Walsh); *In This Our Life* (Huston); *Captains of the Clouds* (Curtiz); *The Gay Sisters* (Rapper); *Desperate Journey* (Walsh); **Now, Voyager** (Rapper)

1943 **Casablanca** (Curtiz); *Mission to Moscow* (Curtiz); *Watch on the Rhine* (Shumlin); *This Is the Army* (Curtiz)

1944 *Passage to Marseille* (Curtiz); *The Conspirators* (Negulesco); *The Adventures of Mark Twain* (Rapper); *Since You Went Away* (Cromwell); *Arsenic and Old Lace* (Capra)

1945 *Roughly Speaking* (Curtiz); *The Corn Is Green* (Rapper); *Rhapsody in Blue* (Rapper); **Mildred Pierce** (Curtiz); *Tomorrow Is Forever* (Pichel)

1946 *San Antonio* (Butler and Walsh); *My Reputation* (Bernhardt); *Saratoga Trunk* (Wood); *One More Tomorrow* (Godfrey);

A Stolen Life (Bernhardt); ***The Big Sleep*** (Hawks); *Cloak and Dagger* (F. Lang), *Night and Day* (Curtiz)

1947   *The Man I Love* (Walsh); *The Beast with Five Fingers* (Florey); *Pursued* (Walsh); *Love and Learn* (De Cordova); *Cheyenne* (Walsh); *The Unfaithful* (V. Sherman); *Deep Valley* (Negulesco); *Life with Father* (Curtiz); *The Voice of the Turtle* (Rapper); *My Wild Irish Rose* (Butler) (co)

1948   ***The Treasure of the Sierra Madre*** (Huston); *My Girl Tisa* (Nugent); *Winter Meeting* (Windust); *The Woman in White* (Godfrey); *Silver River* (Walsh); *Key Largo* (Huston); *Johnny Belinda* (Negulesco); *Fighter Squadron* (Walsh); *The Decision of Christopher Blake* (Godfrey); *A Kiss in the Dark* (Daves)

1949   *The Adventures of Don Juan* (*The New Adventures of Don Juan*) (V. Sherman); *South of St. Louis* (Enright); *Flamingo Road* (Curtiz); *The Fountainhead* (K. Vidor); *Without Honor* (Pichel); *Beyond the Forest* (K. Vidor); ***White Heat*** (Walsh); *Mrs. Mike* (L. King); *The Lady Takes a Sailor* (Curtiz), *Oh You Beautiful Doll* (Stahl)

1950   *Caged* (Cromwell); *The Flame and the Arrow* (Tourneur); *The Glass Menagerie* (Rapper); *Rocky Mountain* (Keighley); *Sugarfoot* (*Swirl of Glory*) (Marin); *Dallas* (Heisler)

1951   *Operation Pacific* (Waggner); *Lightning Strikes Twice* (K. Vidor); *Raton Pass* (Marin); *I Was a Communist for the FBI* (Douglas); *On Moonlight Bay* (Del Ruth); *Jim Thorpe, All-American* (Curtiz); *Force of Arms* (Curtiz); *Close to My Heart* (Keighley); *Distant Drums* (Walsh); *Come Fill the Cup* (Douglas)

1952   *Room for One More* (Taurog); *The Lion and the Horse* (L. King); *Mara Maru* (Douglas); *Springfield Rifle* (De Toth); *The Miracle of Our Lady of Fatima* (Brahm); *The Iron Mistress* (Douglas)

1953   *The Jazz Singer* (Curtiz); *This Is Cinerama* (Cooper and others); *Trouble Along the Way* (Curtiz); *By the Light of the Silvery Moon* (Butler); *The Desert Song* (Humberstone); *So Big* (Wise); *The Charge at Feather River* (Douglas); *So This Is Love* (*The Grace Moore Story*) (Douglas)

1954   *The Boy from Oklahoma* (Curtiz); *The Caine Mutiny* (Dmytryk); *King Richard and the Crusaders* (Butler); *The Violent Man* (Maté)

1955   *Battle Cry* (Walsh); *The Last Command* (Lloyd); *The McConnell Story* (*Tiger in the Sky*) (Douglas); *Illegal* (Allen); *Come Next Spring* (Springsteen)

1956   *Hell on Frisco Bay* (Tuttle); *Helen of Troy* (Wise); ***The Searchers*** (Ford); *Bandido!* (Fleischer); *All Mine to Give* (*The Day They Gave Babies Away*) (Reisner); *Death of a Scoundrel* (Martin)

1957   *Band of Angels* (Walsh); *Escapade in Japan* (Lubin), *China Gate* (Fuller)

1958   *Fort Dobbs* (Douglas); *Marjorie Morningstar* (Rapper); *Darby's Raiders* (*The Young Invaders*) (Wellman)

1959   *The Hanging Tree* (Daves); *John Paul Jones* (Farrow); *The FBI Story* (LeRoy); *A Summer Place* (Daves)

1960   *Cash McCall* (Pevney); *Ice Palace* (V. Sherman); *The Dark at the Top of the Stairs* (Delbert Mann)

1961   *The Sins of Rachel Cade* (Douglas); *Parrish* (Daves); *Portrait of a Mobster* (Pevney); *Susan Slade* (Daves); *A Majority of One* (LeRoy)

1962   *Lovers Must Learn* (*Rome Adventure*) (Daves)

1963   *Spencer's Mountain* (Daves)

1964   *A Distant Trumpet* (Walsh); *FBI Code 98* (Martinson); *Youngblood Hawke* (Daves)

1965   *Those Calloways* (Tokar); *Two on a Guillotine* (Conrad)

Publications

By STEINER: articles—

''Scoring the Film,'' in *We Make the Movies*, edited by Nancy Naumberg, New York, 1937.

In *The Real Tinsel*, by Bernard Rosenberg and Harry Silverstein, New York, 1970.

In *Film Score*, edited by Tony Thomas, South Brunswick, New Jersey, 1979.

On STEINER: books—

Gorbman, Claudia, *Unheard Melodies: Narrative Film Music*, Bloomington, Indiana, 1987.

Darby, William, and Jack Du Bois, *American Film Music: Major Composers, Techniques, Trends, 1915–1990*, Jefferson, North Carolina, 1990.

Kalinak, Kathryn, *Settling the Score: Music and the Classical Hollywood Film*, Madison, Wisconsin, 1992.

On STEINER: articles—

Haun, Harry, and George Raborn, in *Films in Review* (New York), June-July 1961, corrections in August-September and October 1961.

Films in Review (New York), November 1967.

Cineforum (Bergamo), October-November 1971.

Montage (London), no. 21, 1972.

Classic Film Collector (Indiana, Pennsylvania), Spring 1972.

Ecran (Paris), March 1972.

Films in Review (New York), March 1972.

International Film Collector, August 1972.

Thomas, Tony, in *Music for the Movies*, South Brunswick, New Jersey, 1973.

Bender, Albert K., in *Film Music Notebook* (Calabasas, California), Fall 1974.

Gollner, Orville, and George E. Turner, in *The Making of King Kong*, New York, 1975.

Positif (Paris), November 1976.

Fiedel, Robert, in *American Film* (Washington, D.C.), March 1977.

Ecran Fantastique (Paris), no. 6, 1978.

Dirigido por . . . (Barcelona), nos. 66 and 67, 1979.

Filmcritica (Rome), August 1979.

24 Images (Longueuil, Quebec), May-June 1981.

Rivista del Cinematografo (Rome), December 1981.

Velvet Light Trap (Madison, Wisconsin), no. 19, 1982.

Lacombe, Alain, in *Hollywood*, Paris, 1983.

Séquences (Montreal), no. 135–6, September 1988.

Palmer, Christopher, in *The Composer in Hollywood*, New York, 1990.

Buchman, Chris, ''The Television Scene,'' in *Films in Review* (New York), July-August 1992.

Neumeyer, David, ''Melodrama as a Compositional Resource in Early Hollywood Sound Cinema,'' in *Current Musicology*, January 1995.

Handzo, Stephen, "The Golden Age of Film Music," in *Cineaste* (New York), Winter-Spring 1995.

Walsh, J.S., "The Ten Most Influential Film Composers," in *Film Score Monthly* (Los Angeles), January/February/March 1996.

Berthomieu, Pierre, in *Positif* (Paris), October 1998.

*   *   *

The jungle drums of *King Kong*, the soaring theme from *Gone With the Wind*, the brooding dramatic music for *Mildred Pierce* and *The Big Sleep*: all come from the pen of Max Steiner, one of the most influential of all Hollywood film composers. Though criticized by some for sentimentality, excessive scoring and "mickeymousing," Steiner is widely acknowledged as one of the first to use an extended original background score for a motion picture, and to work with click tracks to aid in the synchronization of music to film action. Steiner was also one of the most prolific of all film composers, famed for going with extremely little sleep while completing major projects, including the three hours and twenty minutes of music for *Gone With the Wind*. Though most of his RKO films required only opening and closing music, or arrangements of preexisting music for musicals, he began in 1932 to compose full scores, and created the music for most of Warner Brothers' biggest films from the late 1930s though the 1940s.

While films of the silent era normally had a continuous musical accompaniment (usually pastiches of classical, popular and folk tunes), early talkies normally included *no* background music at all, except for opening and closing credits, and for music that was diegetic, i.e., part of the film's story world. This absence had to do with both the lack of available technology for postdubbing and an assumption that talkie audiences would always want to see the source of the music it was hearing (a party in the next room, perhaps). But in 1932 Steiner began writing nondiegetic music to heighten the drama in selected scenes throughout such films as *Symphony of Six Million*, *Bird of Paradise*, and *The Most Dangerous Game*, and in the following year contributed importantly to the success of *King Kong*. In the latter film Steiner used no background music, after the opening credits, until the arrival at Skull Island, a quarter of the way into the picture; but then, beginning with harp and strings on the soundtrack to suggest the island in the mist, followed by skillfully blended diegetic and nondiegetic "primitive" music for the natives, Steiner's music takes us from the mundane world of the Depression and a sea voyage into the fantastic realm of Kong.

At least three prominent characteristics of Steiner's film music style have always been singled out. One is his skillful blending of original music with popular or folk tunes. Prominent examples are found in his Oscar-winning scores for *The Informer*, with its Irish melodies (establishing a musical pattern for other composers to follow in John Ford films, a tradition Steiner himself continued years later in his mixing of original and traditional Western tunes in *The Searchers*), and for *Gone With the Wind* ("Dixie" and Stephen Foster songs). For *Casablanca* Steiner worked many permutations upon the song "As Time Goes By," and made great use of "La Marseillaise" as well: e.g., when it is heard in a minor key as Captain Renault contemptuously looks down at a bottle of Vichy water.

Another common Steiner practice was his use of the Wagnerian leitmotif: not merely labelling a character or object with a musical theme, but transforming that theme to reflect changes in the drama. *Mildred Pierce* provides especially good examples. Mildred's theme, heard in the opening credits, is in a major key, but its first three notes are soon restated with tragic force in a minor key as Mildred contemplates suicide, and near the end of the film the theme is harmonized in a way to suggest resignation as Mildred tells the police the true story. Another theme, jaunty and innocent-sounding, accompanies the first shot of her daughter Veda, but is heard in quite distorted form when Veda reveals the full extent of her wickedness in the final flashback.

The third characteristic is one for which Steiner has most often been criticized: his mickeymousing, i.e., writing musical cues that very closely mirror (or ape, if one disapproves) onscreen actions. The name comes from the practice common in cartoons ever since Disney's first talkie, *Steamboat Willie*, but examples can be found much earlier in operatic music (even if such cues are pointedly ignored by modern stage directors), most notably in Richard Wagner, as in the sword-forging scene in *Siegfried*. In *The Informer*, for example, music precisely imitates a wanted poster blowing against the informer-to-be's leg, and later mimics the arc of coins tossed onto a table. In Steiner's defense, one might note that the musical emphasis most often simply accompanies visual emphasis through close-ups and other strategies; whether such emphasis should be considered redundancy or effective reinforcement may be debated.

During the 1950s Steiner's style of musicmaking began to seem old-fashioned, as the pop score (featuring a marketable title song, as in *Three Coins in the Fountain*) and the occasional jazz score (e.g, *The Man with the Golden Arm*) became more favored. Yet Steiner continued to write scores for Warner Brothers, most often romantic melodramas, until the mid-1960s, and retired reluctantly. In retrospect, his prominent place in the history of music in motion pictures seems very secure.

—Joseph Milicia

STEWART, Donald Ogden

Writer. **Nationality:** American. **Born:** Columbus, Ohio, 30 November 1894. **Education:** Attended Phillips Exeter Academy, New Hampshire; Yale University, New Haven, Connecticut, B.A. 1916. **Military Service:** Served in the United States Navy during World War I. **Family:** Married 1) Beatrice Ames, 1926 (divorced 1938); children: one daughter and one son; 2) Ella Winter, 1939. **Career:** 1919–20—clerk for AT&T, Minneapolis; then a freelance writer: first book published in 1921, regular contributor to *Vanity Fair*; 1926—first film as writer, *Brown of Harvard*; 1930—his play *Rebound* produced; 1949—investigated by the House Un-American Activities Committee, and eventually blacklisted: moved to London, and did occasional film writing. **Award:** Academy Award for *The Philadelphia Story*, 1940. **Died:** In London, 2 August 1980.

Films as Writer:

1926   *Brown of Harvard* (Conway)
1930   *Laughter* (D'Arrast)
1931   *Tarnished Lady* (Cukor)

Donald Ogden Stewart

1932   *Smilin' Through* (Franklin)
1933   *The White Sister* (Fleming); *Another Language* (E. Griffith);
        Going Hollywood (Walsh); *Dinner at Eight* (Cukor)
1934   *The Barretts of Wimpole Street* (Franklin)
1935   *No More Ladies* (E. Griffith)
1937   *The Prisoner of Zenda* (Cromwell)
1938   *Holiday* (Cukor); *Marie Antoinette* (Van Dyke)
1939   *Love Affair* (McCarey); *Night of Nights* (Milestone)
1940   **The Philadelphia Story** (Cukor); *Kitty Foyle* (Wood)
1941   *That Uncertain Feeling* (Lubitsch); *A Woman's Face* (Cukor);
        Smilin' Through (Borzage)
1942   *Tales of Manhattan* (Duvivier); *Keeper of the Flame* (Cukor)
1944   *Forever and a Day* (Clair and others)
1945   *Without Love* (Bucquet)
1947   *Life with Father* (Curtiz); *Cass Timberlane* (Sidney)
1949   *Edward, My Son* (Cukor)
1953   *Melba* (Milestone)
1954   *Europa 51* (*The Greatest Love*) (Rossellini) (English dialogue)
1955   *Escapade* (Leacock) (as Gilbert Holland)
1960   *Malaga* (*Moment of Danger*) (Benedek) (co)

Films as Actor:

1930   *Not So Dumb* (K. Vidor)
1931   *Devotion* (Milton)
1943   *Cynara* (K. Vidor)

Publications

By STEWART: books—

A Parody Outline of History, New York, 1921.
Perfect Behavior, New York, 1922.
Aunt Polly's Story of Mankind, New York, 1923.
Mr. and Mrs. Haddock Abroad, New York, 1924.
The Crazy Fool, New York, 1925.
Mr. and Mrs. Haddock in Paris, France, New York, 1926.
Father William, New York, 1929.
Rebound, New York, 1931.
(Editor), *Fighting Words*, New York, 1940.
By a Stroke of Luck! (autobiography), New York, 1975.

By STEWART: articles—

Photoplay (New York), February 1930.
''Writing for the Movies,'' in *Focus on Film* (London), Winter 1970.
Time Out (London), 24–30 May 1974.
In *Backstory: Interviews with Screenwriters of Hollywood's Golden Age*, edited by Pat McGilligan, Berkeley, California, 1986.

On STEWART: articles—

Carey, Gary, in *Film Comment* (New York), Winter 1970–71.
National Film Theatre booklet (London), April-June 1976.
Obituary in *Variety* (New York), 6 August 1980.
Obituary in *Cinematographe*, October 1980.
The Annual Obituary 1980, New York, 1981.
American Film (Washington, DC), July-August 1982. Byrge, Duane, in *American Screenwriters*, edited by Robert E. Morsberger, Stephen O. Lesser, and Randall Clark, Detroit, Michigan, 1984.
Wide Angle (Baltimore, Maryland), vol. 12, no. 3, July 1990.

*   *   *

Screenwriters who specialize in adapting for the screen the work of others are somewhat difficult to pigeonhole as creative forces. Donald Ogden Stewart, one of the most prominent of such screenwriters, is probably best described as one of the supreme play doctors of the 1930s and 1940s. For the most part, his career rests on the seven films he worked on for the director George Cukor, the best of these being *Holiday* and *The Philadelphia Story* (for which he received the Academy Award). While remaining true to playwright Philip Barry's original plays for these two films, Stewart was expert at tightening up loose ends and at knowing precisely what was cinematic about an original piece, and his satirical wit is very much evident in these two fast-moving, sparkling comedies.

Born in Columbus, Ohio, and educated at Yale, Stewart moved to New York in the early 1920s and began writing satiric novels, then very much in fashion. Philip Barry based the character of Nick Potter in *Holiday* on Stewart, and the producer Arthur Hopkins cast Stewart in the role on Broadway in 1928. The experience inspired him to write his own light comedy, *Rebound*, the main character of which was an extension of Barry's Nick Potter. After a second play, *Fine and*

Dandy, Stewart migrated to Hollywood, and although he acted in three films—*Not So Dumb*, *Devotion*, *Cynara*—his purpose in going west was to write for the movies.

His second job, *Laughter*, remains one of his best. Stewart supplied the sassy dialogue for Harry D'Arrast's script (about a chorus girl who marries a millionaire) and earned an Oscar nomination. His original story for *Tarnished Lady*, starring Tallulah Bankhead, was a flop, but initiated his seven-picture association with George Cukor. Stewart's collaboration with that director was as important to Cukor in the 1930s and 1940s as his later collaborative efforts with Ruth Gordon and Garson Kanin would be in the 1940s and 1950s. Stewart's second effort with Cukor, *Dinner at Eight*, was outstanding, and remains one of the best comedies of the era. The original granted script was by two sharp professionals—Herman J. Mankiewicz and Frances Marion—with Stewart called in to ''doctor'' the dialogue. *Holiday*, directed by Cukor from Barry's play, is definitely a Stewart script; Cukor took great pains to state that Stewart was the sole author, though studio politics added Sidney Buchman's name as co-author. *Holiday* was also Stewart's first effort to insert his political beliefs into his work. In this film he adds to Barry's play a discernible dislike for the rich. As well as these assignments for Cukor, Stewart worked on *The Barretts of Wimpole Street*, *Marie Antoinette*, and *Kitty Foyle*, then on Katharine Hepburn's favorite vehicle, *The Philadelphia Story*, again from a Barry play directed by Cukor. He worked again with Cukor on *A Woman's Face*, *Keeper of the Flame*—which he accepted because ''he felt it could be a contribution to this war against Hitler''—and *Edward, My Son* a much underrated Spencer Tracy vehicle.

Stewart's involvement with the Hollywood Anti-Nazi League resulted in MGM's demanding he ''answer questions'' before the HUAC. Stewart refused and he was blacklisted. With the help of Ruth Gordon and Garson Kanin he tried out his play *The Kidder* in Cambridge, Massachusetts, in 1951, but found no Broadway takers. The following year he moved to London with his wife, Ella Winter, the politically committed widow of Lincoln Steffens. In 1955, he wrote the script to *Escapade*, starring John Mills and Alastair Sim under the pseudonym Gilbert Holland, and in 1960 co-authored the script for *Malaga*, but he was never able to revive his screenwriting career. He published his autobiography, *By a Stroke of Luck!*, in 1975. The book carried an opening note from his friend and colleague, Katharine Hepburn, in which she described him as a ''man who is willing to pay the price of his own passionate beliefs,'' ''one of the great wits of the late 20s, 30s and 40s,'' and ''my friend.''

—Ronald Bowers

STORARO, Vittorio

Vittorio Storaro

Cinematographer. **Nationality:** Italian. **Born:** Rome, 24 June 1940. **Education:** Attended Duca D'Aosta photography school from age 11; Italian Cinemagraphic Training Center; degree, age 18; Centro Sperimentale di Cinematografia. **Career:** Apprenticed to a photographic studio; assistant to photographers Aldo Scavarda and Marco Scarpelli; made short films during the 1960s; 1969—first feature film as cinematographer, *Giovinezza, giovinezza*; first of several films for Bertolucci, *The Spider's Strategem*. **Awards:** Academy Award, for *Apocalypse Now*, 1979, *Reds*, 1981, and *The Last Emperor*, 1987; British Academy Award, for *The Sheltering Sky*, 1991; British Society of Cinematographers, Best Cinematography Award, for *The Last Emperor*, 1998. **Address:** Via Divino Amorez, 00040 Frattocchie (Rome) Italy.

Films as Cinematographer:

(shorts)

1961   *Etruscologia (Profanatori de tombe)* (Romitelli)
1965   *L'urlo* (Bazzoni)
1966   *Sortilegio* (Bazzoni); *Il laborinto* (Maestranzi); *Sirtaki* (Bazzoni)
1967   *Rapporto segreto* (Bazzoni)
1968   *Sed Lodge*
1973   *I Grandi naïf jugoslavi* (Bazzoni)
1986   *Captain Eo*

(features)

1969   *Giovinezza, giovinezza* (Rossi); *Delitto al circolo del tennis* (Rossetti); *La strategia del ragno (The Spider's Strategem)* (Bertolucci); *L'uccello dalle piume di cristallo (The Bird with the Crystal Plumage)* (Argento)
1970   *Il conformista (The Conformist)* (Bertolucci); *L'Eneide* (Rossi)

1971   *Addio fratello crudele* (Patroni Griffi); *Giornata nera per l'ariete* (Bazzoni); *Corpo d'amore* (Carpi)

1972   *Orlando furioso* (Ronconi); **Last Tango in Paris** (*L'ultimo tango a Parigi*; *Le dernier tango a Paris*) (Bertolucci); *Bleu gang . . .* (Bazzoni)

1973   *Malizia* (Samperi); *Giordano Bruno* (Montaldo); *Identikit* (Patroni Griffi)

1974   *Le orme* (Bazzoni)

1975   *Scandalo* (Samperi)

1976   *Novecento* (*1900*) (Bertolucci)

1979   *La luna* (Bertolucci); *Agatha* (Apted); **Apocalypse Now** (Coppola) (co)

1981   *Reds* (Beatty)

1982   *One from the Heart* (Coppola) (co)

1983   *Wagner* (Palmer)

1985   *Ladyhawke* (Donner)

1987   *Ishtar* (E. May); *The Last Emperor* (Bertolucci)

1988   *Tucker: The Man and His Dream* (Coppola)

1988–94   *Roma: Imago Urbis* (L. Bazzoni)

1989   "Life without Zoe" ep. of *New York Stories* (Coppola)

1990   *The Sheltering Sky* (Bertolucci); *Dick Tracy* (Beatty)

1992   *Little Buddha* (Bertolucci)

1993   *Tosca* (G. Patroni Griffi)

1994   *Flamenco* (C. Saura)

1995   *Taxi* (C. Saura)

1998   *Bulworth* (Beatty); *Tango* (C. Saura)

1999   *Mirka* (Benhadj); *Goya en Burdeos* (*Goya in Bordeaux*)

2000   *Picking Up the Pieces*; *La Traviata* (for TV); *Dune* (for TV—mini-series)

Publications

By STORARO: articles—

Chaplin (Stockholm), no. 4, 1978.

Positif (Paris), September 1979.

On *Apocalypse Now* in *American Cinematographer* (Hollywood), May 1980.

Cinema e Cinema (Bologna), July/September 1980.

On *Reds* in *American Cinematographer* (Hollywood), May 1982.

Segnocinema (Vicenza), March 1983.

Cinema Nuovo (Turin), August/October 1983.

Cinemasessanta (Rome), September/October and November/December 1983.

In *Masters of Light: Conversations with Contemporary Cinematographers*, by Dennis Schaefer and Larry Salvato, Berkeley, California, 1984.

Cineforum (Bergamo), January/February 1984.

Films (London), July 1984.

Post Script (Jacksonville, Florida), Autumn 1984 and Winter 1985.

American Cinematographer (Hollywood), March 1989.

Film Comment (New York), September/October 1989.

Griffithiana (Gemona), no. 37, December 1989.

Kino (Sofia), /9–10, 1991.

Cinema Nuovo (Bari), May-June 1991.

Kino (Warsaw), no. 28, February 1994.

Film Quarterly (Berkeley), vol. 48, no. 2, 1994/1995.

American Cinematographer (Hollywood), February 1995.

On STORARO: articles—

Filme (Berlin), no. 6, 1980.

Williams, A.L., in *American Cinematographer* (Hollywood), July 1980.

Assayas, O., in *Cahiers du Cinéma* (Paris), September 1981.

Film und TV Kameramann (Munich), June 1982.

Zambelli, M. I., in *Cineforum* (Bergamo), January/February 1984.

Delli Colli, Laura, in *Les Metiers du cinéma*, Paris, 1986.

In Camera (Hemel Hempstead, Hertfordshire), Autumn 1988.

Iskusstvo Kino (Moscow), no. 8, 1995.

Positif (Paris), March 1996.

Sight & Sound (London), May 1996.

*   *   *

Among many other things, *Apocalypse Now* by Francis Ford Coppola shows the conflict between two opposing civilizations. This battle finds expression through two visual emblems with distinctive sources of light and energy, the jungle and the spectacle. Kurtz (Marlon Brando) discovers in the jungle, and in the civilization which covers it, a primitive and vital energy, and it is this flux which fascinates him, and allows him to rediscover his own self.

In the character of Kurtz, Vittorio Storaro's art could not have found a better metaphor. His photography always tries to reach the spectator placed in the center of a conflict between antagonistic sources of energy, either natural or artificial. Storaro himself has defined his work: "Conflicts between night and day, shadows and light, white and black, technology and energy are things always recognized in me and my work." This conflict appeared already outlined in *Giovinezza, giovinezza*, his first film, through his treatment of light, as if Storaro wished to affirm the history of its use in a pictorial culture going back to the Renaissance, aligning himself in this way in the artistic tradition of Italian cinematography, along with Giuseppe Rotunno and Pasquale De Santis.

In the first phase of his work, up to *Apocalypse Now*, this conflict between opposing sources of energy appears essentially through his treatment of light, gaining true aesthetic definition after his meeting with Bernardo Bertolucci. In *The Spider's Strategem*, the first film they made together, Storaro explores all the possibilities of natural light, evoking, in the opinion of several European critics, the visual fascination of Visconti. By contrast, *The Conformist* seems to be an exercise in shadow and light, as if to transmit to the spectator the idea, central to history, of claustrophobia. In an interview in *Film Quarterly*, Storaro added: "*The Conformist* is almost a black-and-white picture in the beginning. But in the last half in Paris, you see differently. You see the light going into the shadows. It's like two sections that are united once more."

It is this same dualism and equilibrium between contraries that dominate *Last Tango in Paris*. Here Storaro attempts to reproduce winter light in Parisian exteriors, artificial light in the interiors, and mixes this with hot tones, especially the color orange, to reproduce the passion of the characters.

His photography of the Bertolucci films, which attained its most lyrical expression in *Novecento*, attracted the attention of Coppola, and *Apocalypse Now* crowns this first phase of his career. Hyperrealistic sequences such as the napalm bombardment, the *Playboy*-bunny show, and the nocturnal firing on Do Lung bridge, contrast with the natural jungle light. This contrast can be summed up perhaps in the comparison of the olive-oil lamp and the searchlight.

The second phase of Storaro's career also begins with Bertolucci, but attains its major splendor with both Bertolucci and Coppola. In *La luna* and *Reds*, Storaro claims to have established a color symbolism that had, unconsciously, emerged in *The Conformist* and *Last Tango in Paris*. In *One from the Heart*, Storaro's continued search for a system of color symbols, using opposing colors to identify his protagonists and a subtle correspondence between chromatic shades and characters' emotions, produces a beautiful contrast between the realism of action and the hyperrealism of photography. This exploration continues in *The Last Emperor*, which, arguably, ranks with *Apocalypse Now* as Storaro's greatest achievement. In recording the visuals that accompany the story of Pu Yi, the last emperor of China, Storaro evokes the many moods of a story which expands across the decades, as China evolves from feudalism to revolution. Especially memorable is the spectacle of the expansive, medieval Forbidden City (where Storaro shot on location). It also must be noted, however, that even such lesser Bertolucci works as *The Sheltering Sky* and *Little Buddha* benefit from Storaro's presence behind the camera as a true master of light.

To divide the career of Storaro into two phases is somewhat arbitrary. In fact, few cinematographers have maintained such a stylistic unity, based on a theoretical awareness and a historical consciousness of a pictorial tradition going back to Piero della Francesca and Caravaggio. Let us give Storaro himself the last word: "Since the first graffiti was scratched on the walls of caves, since the first Egyptian drawings, since Piero della Francesca, we have had ways to express emotional stories and emotional figures in a particular style. There is no question that when you make a design, shoot a picture, or photograph a movie, it is the representation of all two thousand years of history, whether you are conscious of it or not."

—M. S. Fonseca, updated by Rob Edelman

STOTHART, Herbert

Composer and Music Director. **Nationality:** American. **Born:** Milwaukee, Wisconsin, 11 September 1885. **Education:** Attended the University of Wisconsin, Madison; also studied in Europe. **Career:** Teacher; then composer and conductor on Broadway in 1920s: composer of musicals (including *Rose Marie* with Friml) and orchestral music (including *Heart Attack: A Symphonic Poem*, 1947); 1928—composer for films: became general music director at MGM. **Award:** Academy Award for *The Wizard of Oz*, 1939. **Died:** Of cancer, in Los Angeles, California, 1 February 1949.

Films as Composer or Supervisor:

1928   ***Konyets Sankta-Peterburga*** (*The End of St. Petersburg*) (Pudovkin)

1929   *Dynamite* (DeMille); *Devil-May-Care* (Franklin)

Herbert Stothart

1930   *In Gay Madrid* (Leonard); *Madam Satan* (DeMille); *The Rogue Song* (L. Barrymore); *A Lady's Morals* (Franklin); *Montana Moon* (St. Clair); *The Floradora Girl* (Beaumont); *The Call of the Flesh* (Brabin)

1931   *The Squaw Man* (DeMille); *New Moon* (Conway); *The Southerner* (*The Prodigal*) (Pollard)

1932   *The Son-Daughter* (Brown)

1933   *Night Flight* (Brown); *Rasputin and the Empress* (Boleslawsky); *Riptide* (Goulding); *Queen Christina* (Mamoulian); *The White Sister* (Fleming); *Peg o' My Heart* (Leonard); *Turn Back the Clock* (Selwyn); *The Barbarian* (Wood); *Going Hollywood* (Walsh)

1934   *The Barretts of Wimpole Street* (Franklin); *The Merry Widow* (Lubitsch); *The Painted Veil* (Boleslawsky); *Laughing Boy* (Van Dyke); *What Every Woman Knows* (La Cava); *The Spectacle Maker* (short); *Chained* (Brown); *Stamboul Quest* (Wood); *Treasure Island* (Fleming)

1935   *Naughty Marietta* (Van Dyke); *Mutiny on the Bounty* (Lloyd); *Ah, Wilderness!* (Brown); *Biography of a Bachelor Girl* (Griffith); *The Night Is Young* (Murphy); *Vanessa* (Howard); *China Seas* (Garnett); *Sequoia* (Franklin); *Anna Karenina* (Brown); *A Tale of Two Cities* (Conway); *David Copperfield* (Cukor); ***A Night at the Opera*** (Wood) (mus d)

1936   *After the Thin Man* (Van Dyke) (co); *Moonlight Murder* (Marin) (co); *The Robin Hood of El Dorado* (Wellman); *Small Town Girl* (Wellman); *The Devil Is a Sissy* (*The Devil Takes the Count*) (Van Dyke); *Wife vs. Secretary* (Brown) (co); *Romeo and Juliet* (Cukor); ***Camille*** (Cukor)

1937   *The Firefly* (Leonard); *The Good Earth* (Franklin)

1938   *The Girl of the Golden West* (Leonard); *Of Human Hearts* (Brown); *Rosalie* (Van Dyke); *Marie Antoinette* (Van Dyke)

1939   *Idiot's Delight* (Brown); *Balalaika* (Schünzel); *Broadway Serenade* (*Serenade*) (Leonard)

1940   *Pride and Prejudice* (Leonard); *Northwest Passage* (K. Vidor); *New Moon* (Leonard); *Bitter Sweet* (Van Dyke); *Susan and God* (*The Gay Mrs. Trexel*) (Cukor); *Edison the Man* (Brown)

1941   *Ziegfeld Girl* (Leonard); *Andy Hardy's Private Secretary* (Seitz); *Come Live with Me* (Brown); *Blossoms in the Dust* (LeRoy); *Men of Boys' Town* (Taurog); *The Chocolate Soldier* (Del Ruth) (co); *Smilin' Through* (Borzage); *Waterloo Bridge* (LeRoy); *They Met in Bombay* (Brown)

1942   *Rio Rita* (Simon); *The Human Comedy* (Brown); *Random Harvest* (LeRoy); **Mrs. Miniver** (Wyler); *I Married an Angel* (Van Dyke)

1943   *Tennessee Johnson* (*The Man on America's Conscience*) (Dieterle); *Madame Curie* (LeRoy); *Three Hearts for Julia* (Thorpe)

1944   *Song of Russia* (Ratoff); *The White Cliffs of Dover* (Brown); *Dragon Seed* (Conway); *A Guy Named Joe* (Fleming); *Thirty Seconds over Tokyo* (LeRoy); *Kismet* (Dieterle)

1945   *National Velvet* (Brown); **The Picture of Dorian Gray** (Lewin); *Adventure* (Fleming); *The Valley of Decision* (Garnett)

1946   *The Green Years* (Saville); *They Were Expendable* (Ford)

1947   *High Barbaree* (Conway); *If Winter Comes* (Saville)

1948   *Three Daring Daughters* (*The Birds and the Bees*) (Wilcox); *Hills of Home* (Wilcox); *Desire Me* (Cukor); *The Three Musketeers* (Sidney)

1949   *Big Jack* (Thorpe)

Other Films:

1933   *The Cat and the Fiddle* (Howard) (mus d)

1934   *Viva Villa* (Conway) (arranger)

1936   *Rose Marie* (Van Dyke) (mus d); *San Francisco* (Van Dyke) (mus d)

1937   *Maytime* (Leonard) (mus d); *Conquest* (Brown) (mus d)

1938   *Sweethearts* (Van Dyke) (mus d)

1939   **The Wizard of Oz** (Fleming) (mus d)

1941   *Cairo* (Van Dyke) (mus d)

1944   *Thousands Cheer* (Sidney) (mus d)

1945   *Son of Lassie* (Simon) (arranger)

1946   *Undercurrent* (Minnelli) (mus d); *The Yearling* (Brown) (arranger)

1947   *The Unfinished Dance* (Koster) (mus d); *Sea of Grass* (Kazan) (arranger)

Publications

By STOTHART: article—

"Film Music," in *Behind the Screen*, edited by Stephen Watts, London, 1938.

On STOTHART: articles—

Films (New York), Winter 1940.

Stothart Jr., Herbert, in *Films in Review* (New York), December 1970.

Lacombe, Alain, in *Hollywood*, Paris, 1983.

Rosar, W.H., "Herbert Stothart Tribute at U.S.C.," in *Cue Sheet* (Hollywood), January 1984.

Hemming, Roy, "Hollywood Bowl Orchestra: Hollywood Dreams," in *Stereo Review*, October 1991.

Neumeyer, David, "Melodrama as a Compositional Resource in Early Hollywood Sound Cinema," in *Current Musicology*, January 1995.

*   *   *

Herbert Stothart's place in the history of film music is clearly marked. It spanned the 20 years between 1929 and 1949, and it was a period spent entirely at MGM. It is further marked by the fact that it was Stothart who scored most of the MGM films derived from classic literature, such as *Treasure Island*, *The Barretts of Wimpole Street*, *David Copperfield*, *Anna Karenina*, *A Tale of Two Cities*, *Camille*, and *Romeo and Juliet*, in addition to the music direction of the studio's operettas. Almost all the MGM films of Jeanette MacDonald and Nelson Eddy, whether together or separately, were supervised and conducted by Stothart. It was a period in which the studio had a definite musical sound, a somewhat softer and less assertive style than the others, the orchestration often favoring the strings, and it was a sound very much devised by this composer. Stothart's first contact with music was as a choirboy, and during his school years he developed a strong interest in composing and conducting. He chose a career as a teacher, but his involvement in staging amateur theatrical productions gradually took up more of his time and interest. The success of *Manicure Shop* in Chicago, a musical he had written for the University of Wisconsin, spurred him to take up the theatre professionally and he proceeded to study composition in Europe. In 1914 Stothart was hired by producer Arthur Hammerstein as the conductor of the touring company of the Rudolf Friml musical *High Jinks*. After five years with touring companies he was brought by Hammerstein to New York and then spent all of the 1920s as a conductor of musicals on Broadway, including those written by Friml, Youmans, and Gershwin. In many instances Stothart contributed songs of his own to these productions; two of the songs in *Rose Marie*, for example ("Hard Boiled Herman" and "Why Shouldn't We?"), are his.

With the coming of sound on film in 1929, he was invited to MGM by Louis B. Mayer and from then until his death from cancer in 1949 Stothart worked constantly as an arranger, conductor, and composer on a total of 130 films. In style and substance he was very much a musician of Hollywood's Golden Years, and no retrospective of MGM in those years can overlook his contributions. Asked about his technique he said: "The composer, through experience, learns what elements generate certain moods. Anger can be generated by what I call red tones, which slightly clash in orchestrations, and so, mentally irritate. A tranquil mood can be inspired by quiet, gently flowing melody. Alarm can be created by clashing harmonies; unrest by monotonous beat of tomtoms and by effects strange in musical principle, and hence, played to unaccustomed ears. Sonorous bells and deep tones of the organ inspire reverence. These are all matters of elemental psychology. By deciding to what extent to use them, one gets the shades in between the basic classifications.''

—Tony Thomas

STRADLING, Harry

Cinematographer. **Nationality:** American. **Born:** England (some sources give Nesen, Germany, or Newark, New Jersey), 1901. **Family:** Son: the photographer Harry Stradling, Jr. **Career:** In the United States by his teens; 1921—first film as cinematographer, *Jim the Penman*; worked in France and England in the 1930s, then returned to Hollywood. **Awards:** Academy Awards for *The Picture of Dorian Gray*, 1945; *My Fair Lady*, 1964. **Died:** In February 1970.

Films as Cinematographer:

1921   *Jim the Penman* (Blackwell); *The Devil's Garden* (Blackwell); *The Great Adventure* (Blackwell)

1922   *His Wife's Husband* (Webb); *Fair Lady* (Webb); *How Women Love* (Webb); *Secrets of Paris* (Webb)

1925   *The Substitute Wife* (May); *Wandering Fires* (Campbell)

1927   *Burnt Fingers* (Campbell); *The Nest* (Nigh)

1929   *Mother's Boy* (Parker) (co); *Lucky in Love* (Webb) (co)

1930   *Le Réquisitoire* (Buchowetski—French version of *Manslaughter*)

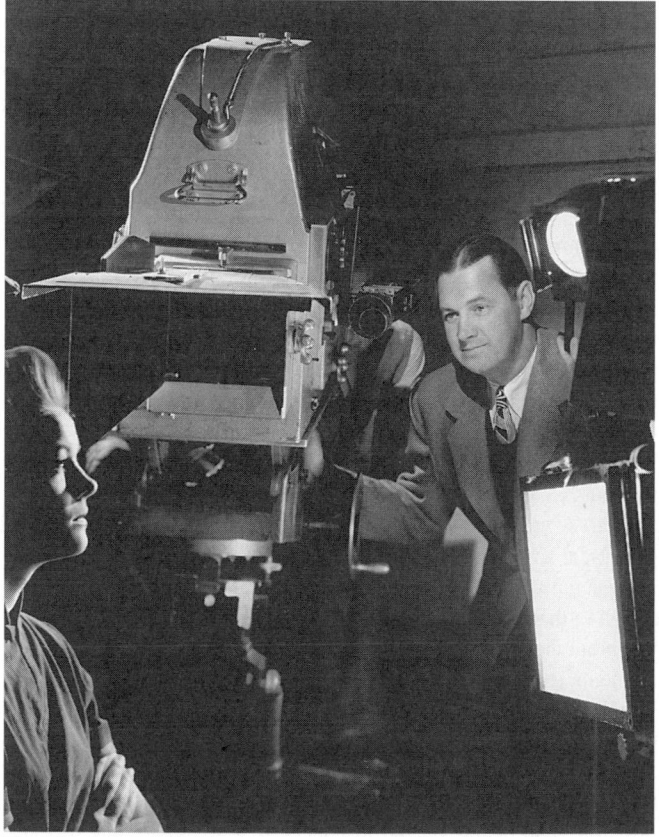

Harry Stradling

1931   *Die Männer um Lucie* (A. Korda—and French version, *Rive Gauche*); *Il est charmant* (Mercanton); *Mistigri* (Lachman)

1933   *Rund um eine Million* (Neufeld); *Le Maître des forges* (Rivers)

1934   *Le Grand Jeu* (Feyder); *Compartiment de dames seules* (Christian-Jaque); *Le Bonheur* (L'Herbier); *Jeanne* (Tourjansky); *Nous ne sommes plus des enfants* (Genina); *Jeunesse* (Lacombe); *La Dame aux camélias* (Gance); *Poliche* (Gance); *La Porteuse de pain* (Sti)

1935   *Quelle drôle de gosse!* (Joannon); *Arènes joyeuses* (Anton); **La Kermesse héro** (*Carnival in Flanders*) (Feyder); *Episode* (Reisch)

1936   *Ungekusst soll man nicht schlaten geh'n* (Emo); *Le Grand Refrain* (Mirande)

1937   *Knight without Armour* (Feyder); *Action for Slander* (Whelan)

1938   *The Divorce of Lady X* (Whelan); *The Citadel* (K. Vidor); *South Riding* (Savil le); *Pygmalion* (Asquith and Howard)

1939   *Over the Moon* (Freeland); *Jamaica Inn* (Hitchcock); *Q Planes* (*Clouds over Europe*) (Whelan); *The Lion Has Wings* (Hurst)

1940   *My Son, My Son* (C. Vidor)

1941   *They Knew What They Wanted* (Kanin); *Suspicion* (Hitchcock); *Mr. and Mrs. Smith* (Hitchcock); *The Devil and Miss Jones* (Wood); *The Men in Her Life* (Ratoff); *Mr. and Mrs. North* (Sinclair); *The Corsican Brothers* (Ratoff)

1942   *Fingers at the Window* (Lederer) (co); *Nazi Agent* (Dassin); *Her Cardboard Lover* (Cukor) (co); *Maisie Gets Her Man* (Del Ruth); *White Cargo* (Thorpe)

1943   *The Human Comedy* (Brown); *Swing Shift Maisie* (McLeod)

1944   *Song of Russia* (Ratoff); *Bathing Beauty* (Sidney)

1945   *The Picture of Dorian Gray* (Lewin); *Thrill of a Romance* (Thorpe); *Her Highness and the Bellboy* (Thorpe)

1946   *Holiday in Mexico* (Sidney); *Easy to Wed* (Buzzell); *Till the Clouds Roll By* (Whorf) (co)

1947   *Song of Love* (Brown); *Sea of Grass* (Kazan)

1948   *The Pirate* (Minnelli); *Easter Parade* (Walters); *Words and Music* (Taurog) (co)

1949   *In the Good Old Summertime* (Leonard); *The Barkleys of Broadway* (Walters); *Tension* (Berry)

1950   *The Edge of Doom* (Robson); *The Yellow Cab Man* (Donohue)

1951   *Valentino* (Allen); **A Streetcar Named Desire** (Kazan); *A Millionaire for Christy* (Marshall); *I Want You* (Robson)

1952   *My Son John* (McCarey); *Androcles and the Lion* (Erskine); *Hans Christian Andersen* (C. Vidor)

1953   *Angel Face* (Preminger); *A Lion Is in the Streets* (Walsh); *Forever Female* (Rapper)

1954   **Johnny Guitar** (Ray)

1955   *Guys and Dolls* (Mankiewicz); *Helen of Troy* (Wise)

1956   *The Eddie Duchin Story* (Sidney)

1957   *A Face in the Crowd* (Kazan); *The Pajama Game* (Abbott and Donen)

1958   *Marjorie Morningstar* (Rapper); *Auntie Mame* (Da Costa)

1959   *The Young Philadelphians* (V. Sherman); *A Summer Place* (Daves)

1960   *Who Was That Lady?* (Sidney); *The Dark at the Top of the Stairs* (Delbert Mann); *The Crowded Sky* (Pevney)

1961   *Parrish* (Daves); *On the Double* (Shavelson)

1962   *A Majority of One* (LeRoy); *Five Finger Exercise* (Daniel Mann); *Gypsy* (LeRoy)

1963   *Island of Love* (Da Costa); *Mary, Mary* (LeRoy)

1964   *My Fair Lady* (Cukor)
1965   *How to Murder Your Wife* (Quine); *Synanon* (Quine)
1966   *Moment to Moment* (LeRoy); *Walk, Don't Run* (Walters); *Penelope* (Hille); *Who's Afraid of Virginia Woolf?* (Nichols)
1968   *Funny Girl* (Wyler); *With Six You Get Eggroll* (Morris)
1969   *Hello, Dolly!* (Kelly); *The Good Guys and the Bad Guys* (Kennedy)
1970   *On a Clear Day You Can See Forever* (Minnelli); *The Owl and the Pussycat* (co)

Publications

By STRADLING: article—

On *Walk, Don't Run* in *American Cinematographer* (Hollywood), October 1957.

On STRADLING: articles—

Lightman, Herb A., in *American Cinematographer* (Hollywood), October 1951.
Lightman, Herb A., on *Parrish* in *American Cinematographer* (Hollywood), May 1961.
Lawton, Ralph, in *American Cinematographer* (Hollywood), July 1962.
Gavin, Arthur, on *My Fair Lady* in *American Cinematographer* (Hollywood), November 1964.
Film Comment (New York), Summer 1972.
Focus on Film (London), no. 13, 1973.

*   *   *

The veteran cinematographer Harry Stradling was one of the great camera talents in the history of Hollywood. He worked in every film genre and for many good and bad directors. His peers recognized his abilities and nominated him for 13 Oscars. His career represents a scope and quality matched by few cameramen.

Like many of his contemporaries who entered the American film industry during the 1920s, Stradling spent more than a decade learning his craft filming minor works. His uncle, Walter Stradling, who for many years was Mary Pickford's cameraman, got him his initial job. (His son, Harry Stradling, Jr., continues the family tradition behind the camera.) During his on-the-job training Stradling spent the 1920s on unimportant films, even working on shorts for the minor studio Pathé. At this point his career took an uncommon turn. Stradling journeyed to Europe to establish his reputation. Thus he worked on a fine 1930s French film, *Carnival in Flanders*. In this film Stradling and director Jacques Fedyer successfully captured the image of Flemish paintings, and offered up a distinctive, highly successful art film of its day.

For this effort Alexander Korda hired Stradling to photograph the fine British film *Knight without Armour*, starring Marlene Dietrich and Robert Donat. Besides the low-key impressionistic backgrounds representing Moscow, the film placed Stradling in a line of famous cameramen who boosted the career of Dietrich. This led to a series of major assignments in the United Kingdom (*Pygmalion*, *The Citadel*, and *Jamaica Inn*). From these successes Stradling was able to make his way back to Hollywood to work with Hitchcock on *Mr. and Mrs.*

Smith and *Suspicion*. He soon moved to the top rung of Hollywood cinematographers.

Possibly because of his experience in Europe, Stradling was willing to experiment. This was extremely rare in conservative Hollywood of the 1940s. A famous film for its special effects was *The Corsican Brothers*, in which Douglas Fairbanks, Jr., played twin brothers. Critics praised the scenes in which the two brothers appeared as amazingly real.

Like most ace cinematographers of his day, Stradling never stuck to one genre, but he did build up a reputation for a style which emphasized glamour and Technicolor. For example, Stradling was the man behind the camera for such MGM musicals as *Till the Clouds Roll By* and *The Barkleys of Broadway*. Later he would work on *Guys and Dolls*, *Auntie Mame*, and *Gypsy*. All these films earned him nominations for Academy Awards.

The final flare of Harry Stradling's long, distinguished career came with *Funny Girl*. Barbra Streisand thanked ''dear Harry Stradling'' in her acceptance speech for her Oscar. They later worked together on *On a Clear Day You Can See Forever* and *Hello, Dolly!*, and he died while working on yet another Streisand vehicle, *The Owl and the Pussycat*. Ironically he passed away the very day after he had been nominated for his final Academy Award, for *Hello, Dolly!*

—Douglas Gomery

STROMBERG, Hunt

Producer. **Nationality:** American. **Born:** Louisville, Kentucky, 12 July 1894. **Career:** Sports writer, St. Louis *Times*; early 1920s—publicity director for Goldwyn company in New York; 1921—personal representative for Thomas Ince, Hollywood; 1921—formed Hunt Stromberg Productions: produced first film, *The Foolish Age*; also occasional director: *A Ladies' Man*, 1922; 1925–42—producer and ''supervisor'' for MGM; 1942–51—independent producer, releasing through United Artists; then retired. **Award:** Academy Award for *The Great Ziegfeld*, 1936. **Died:** 25 August 1968.

Films as Producer:

1921   *The Foolish Age* (Seiter) (+ co-sc)
1922   *Boy Crazy* (Seiter); *A Ladies' Man* (+ d)
1923   *Breaking into Society* (+ d + sc); *Rob 'em Good* (+ d); *Snowed Under* (+ d); *Two Twins* (+ d)
1924   *The Night Hawk* (Paton); *Roaring Rails* (Forman); *The Fire Patrol* (+ d); *The Flaming Forties* (Forman); *The Siren of Seville* (+ co-d); *The Lightning Rider* (Ingraham); *A Cafe in Cairo* (Withey); *Tiger Thompson* (Eason)
1925   *Soft Shoes* (Ingraham) (+ co-sc); *Beyond the Border* (Dunlap); *The Bad Lands* (Henderson); *The Crimson Runner* (Forman); *Paint and Powder* (+ d); *The Man from Red Gulch* (Mortimer); *Off the Highway* (Forman); *Silent Sanderson* (Dunlap); *The People vs. Nancy Preston* (Forman)
1926   *The Torrent* (Bell)
1928   *Our Dancing Daughters* (Beaumont); *White Shadows in the South Seas* (Van Dyke)
1929   *Thunder* (Nigh); *The Bridge of San Luis Rey* (Brabin)

Hunt Stromberg

1930 *Our Blushing Brides* (Beaumont)
1931 *Guilty Hands* (Van Dyke)
1932 *Letty Lyndon* (Brown); *Red Dust* (Fleming); *The Wet Parade* (Fleming)
1933 *Penthouse* (Van Dyke); *The White Sister* (Fleming); *Bombshell* (*Blonde Bombshell*) (Fleming); *The Prizefighter and the Lady* (*Every Woman's Man*) (Van Dyke)
1934 ***The Thin Man*** (Van Dyke); *Treasure Island* (Fleming); *The Painted Veil* (Boleslawsky); *Hide Out* (Van Dyke); *Chained* (Brown)
1935 *Naughty Marietta* (Van Dyke); *Ah, Wilderness!* (Brown)
1936 *Rose-Marie* (Van Dyke); *Wife vs. Secretary* (Brown); *The Great Ziegfeld* (Leonard); *After the Thin Man* (Van Dyke); *Small Town Girl* (Wellman)
1937 *Maytime* (Leonard); *Night Must Fall* (Thorpe); *The Firefly* (Leonard)
1938 *Marie Antoinette* (Van Dyke); *Sweethearts* (Van Dyke)
1939 *Idiot's Delight* (Brown); ***The Women*** (Cukor); *Another Thin Man* (Van Dyke)
1940 *Northwest Passage* (K. Vidor); *Pride and Prejudice* (Leonard); *Susan and God* (*The Gay Mrs. Trexel*) (Cukor)
1941 *They Met in Bombay* (Brown); *Shadow of the Thin Man* (Van Dyke)
1942 *I Married an Angel* (Van Dyke)
1943 *Lady of Burlesque* (Wellman)
1944 *Guest in the House* (Brahm)
1946 *The Young Widow* (Marin); *The Strange Woman* (Ulmer)
1947 *Lured* (Sirk) (exec); *Dishonored Lady* (Stevenson)

1949 *Too Late for Tears* (Haskin)
1950 *Between Midnight and Dawn* (Douglas)
1951 *Mask of the Avenger* (Karlson)

Film as Story Writer:

1926 *Winning the Futurity* (Dunlap)

Publications

By STROMBERG: article—

''The Producer,'' in *Behind the Screen*, edited by Stephen Watts, London, 1938.

On STROMBERG: article—

Filme Cultura (Rio de Janeiro), November 1968.

*   *   *

Hunt Stromberg was one of a handful of supervisory producers who helped create the great MGM films of the 1930s. As a protégé of Irving Thalberg, the boy-genius executive producer at MGM until his death in 1936, Stromberg helped bring together such classics as *The Thin Man*, *Naughty Marietta*, and *Marie Antoinette*. His *The Great Ziegfeld* earned the Academy Award for Best Picture in 1936.

In the MGM system under Thalberg, a handful of supervisory producers handled the day-to-day operations of the creation of the 52 feature films. Producers developed genre specialties, usually associated with the careers of certain stars. Stromberg achieved remarkable success in the 1930s by first formulating films for Jean Harlow and Joan Crawford, and later with the Jeanette McDonald-Nelson Eddy cycle of musicals and the ''Thin Man'' series. In short over the decade of the 1930s, including the Great Depression, Stromberg was a money maker of the top rank in Hollywood.

But with Thalberg's death in September 1936, Stromberg began to chafe under a new regime dominated by Louis B. Mayer. (Many other producers also did and the studio slowly went downhill.) Flush with the success associated with the Second World War era, the greatest relative movie-going period in Hollywood history, Mayer permitted Stromberg to leave for a career as an independent producer at United Artists. Mayer refused to meet Stromberg's demands for setting up independent production through MGM, so Stromberg sacrificed guaranteed millions at MGM for the power to run his own shop.

He should have stayed at MGM. He never did as well at United Artists as he had during his salad days under Thalberg. His United Artists debut, *Lady of Burlesque*, starring Barbara Stanwyck, was a smash, but that can not be said for what followed: *The Young Widow*, *The Strange Woman*, and *Dishonored Lady*. One of the problems was budget constraint. At MGM Thalberg never permitted Stromberg to exceed certain financial limitations. At United Artists Stromberg had no such master and spent millions too much to create box-office failures which could not be written off against other successful studio efforts.

Yet Stromberg never lacked for wealth. This independent minded producer had made himself a rich man through shrewd investments outside the movies. He was an avid horseman and made millions by investing in the Santa Anita and Hollywood racetracks. Thus gradually with failure after failure at United Artists, Stromberg seemed to lose interest in the movie business. He retired, a rich man, to play the role of the Hollywood elder statesman.

—Douglas Gomery

STRUSS, Karl

Cinematographer. **Nationality:** American. **Born:** Karl Fischer Struss in New York City, 30 November 1886. **Education:** Attended night classes in photography with Clarence White, Columbia University, New York, 1908–12. **Family:** Married Ethel Wall, 1921. **Career:** 1903–14—worked in his father's bonnet-wire factory; 1914–17—studio photographer, New York; 1916—cofounder, Pictorial Photographers of America; 1917–19—served in World War I: did experiments on infrared photography; 1919–22—still photographer, then cameraman, for Cecil B. DeMille at Famous Players-Lasky, Hollywood, then worked for B.P. Schulberg, 1922–24, other companies, D.W. Griffith, 1927–30, and for Paramount after 1931; TV work includes the series *Broken Arrow*, 1950, and *My Friend Flicka*, 1957; exhibited his still photographs throughout his career. **Award:** Academy Award for *Sunrise*, 1928–29. **Died:** 16 December 1981.

Films as Cinematographer:

1920 *Something to Think About* (C. DeMille)
1921 *The Affairs of Anatol* (C. DeMille); *Fool's Paradise* (C. DeMille) (co); *The Law and the Woman* (Stanlaws)
1922 *Fools First* (Neilan) (co); *Minnie* (Neilan) (co); *Rich Men's Wives* (Gasnier); *Saturday Night* (C. DeMille) (co); *Thorns and Orange Blossoms* (Gasnier)
1923 *Daughters of the Rich* (Gasnier); *The Hero* (Gasnier); *Maytime* (Gasnier); *Mothers-in-Law* (Gasnier); *Poor Men's Wives* (Gasnier)
1924 *Idle Tongues* (Hillyer); *The Legend of Hollywood* (Hoffman); *Poisoned Paradise: The Forbidden Story of Monte Carlo* (Gasnier); *White Man* (Gasnier)
1925 *The Winding Stair* (Wray)
1926 *Ben-Hur* (Niblo) (co); *Forever After* (Weight); *Hell's 400* (Wray); *Meet the Prince* (Henabery); *Sparrows* (Beaudine) (co)
1927 *Babe Comes Home* (Wilde); *Sunrise* (Murnau) (co)
1928 *The Battle of the Sexes* (Griffith) (co); *Drums of Love* (Griffith) (co); *The Night Watch* (A. Korda)
1929 *Coquette* (Taylor); *Lady of the Pavements* (Griffith); *Taming of the Shrew* (Taylor)
1930 *Abraham Lincoln* (Griffith); *The Bad One* (Fitzmaurice); *Be Yourself* (Freeland) (co); *Danger Lights* (Seitz) (co); *Lummox* (Brenon); *One Romantic Night* (*The Swan*) (Stein)
1931 *Kiki* (Taylor); *Skippy* (Taurog); *Up Pops the Devil* (Sutherland); *Women Love Once* (Goodman); *Murder by the Clock* (Sloman); *The Road to Reno* (Wallace)

1932 ***Dr. Jekyll and Mr. Hyde*** (Mamoulian); *Two Kinds of Women* (W. De Mille); *Dancers in the Dark* (Burton); *The World and the Flesh* (Cromwell); *Forgotten Commandments* (Gasnier and Schorr); *The Man from Yesterday* (Viertel); *Guilty As Hell* (Kenton); *The Sign of the Cross* (C. DeMille); *Island of Lost Souls* (Kenton)
1933 *The Girl in 419* (*Identity Unknown*) (Hall and Somnes); *Tonight Is Ours* (Walker); *The Woman Accused* (Sloane); *The Story of Temple Drake* (Roberts); *Disgraced* (Kenton); *Torch Singer* (Hall and Somnes)
1934 *Four Frightened People* (C. DeMille); *Belle of the Nineties* (McCarey); *The Pursuit of Happiness* (Hall); *Here Is My Heart* (Tuttle)
1935 *Goin' to Town* (Hall); *Two for Tonight* (Tuttle)
1936 *Anything Goes* (Milestone); *The Preview Murder Mystery* (Florey); *Too Many Parents* (McGowan); *Rhythm of the Range* (Taurog); *Hollywood Boulevard* (Florey); *Go West, Young Man* (Hathaway); *Let's Make a Million* (McCarey)
1937 *Waikiki Wedding* (Tuttle); *Mountain Music* (Florey); *Double or Nothing* (Reed); *Thunder Trail* (Barton)
1938 *Every Day's a Holiday* (Sutherland); *Thanks for the Memory* (Archainbaud); *Sing, You Sinners* (Ruggles)
1939 *Paris Honeymoon* (Tuttle); *Zenobia* (Douglas); *Some Like It Hot* (Archainbaud); *Island of Lost Men* (Neumann); *The Star Maker* (Del Ruth)
1940 ***The Great Dictator*** (Chaplin) (co)
1941 *Caught in the Draft* (Butler); *Aloma of the South Seas* (Santell) (co)
1943 *Happy Go Lucky* (Bernhardt) (co); *Journey into Fear* (Foster); *Riding High* (Marshall) (co)
1944 *And the Angels Sing* (Marshall); *Rainbow Island* (Murphy); *For Whom the Bell Tolls* (Wood) (2nd unit)
1945 *Bring on the Girls* (Lanfield); *Tarzan and the Leopard Woman* (Neumann)
1946 *Suspense* (Tuttle); *Mister Ace* (Marin)
1947 *The Macomber Affair* (Z. Korda) (co); *Heaven Only Knows* (Rogell)
1948 *The Dude Goes West* (Neumann); *Siren of Atlantis* (Ripley and Tallas); *Tarzan's Magic Fountain* (Sholem)
1949 *Bad Boy* (Neumann)
1950 *Rocket Ship X-M* (Neumann); *It's a Small World* (Castle); *The Return of Jesse James* (Hilton); *The Texan Meets Calamity Jane* (Lamb); *Father's Wild Game* (Leeds)
1951 *Tarzan's Peril* (Haskin)
1952 *Rose of Cimarron* (Keller); *Tarzan's Savage Fury* (Endfield); *Limelight* (Chaplin); *Lady Possessed* (Spier and Kellino); *Mesa of Lost Women* (Tevos and Ormond)
1953 *Tarzan and the She Devil* (Neumann); *Il piu comico spettacolo del mondo* (Mattoli) (co); *Il Turco napoletano* (Mattoli) (co); *Cavalleria rusticana* (Gallone) (co); ''The Secret Shame'' ep. of *Face to Face* (Brahm)
1954 *Attila* (Francisci) (co); *Due notte con Cleopatra* (Mattoli) (co)
1955 *Mohawk* (Neumann)
1957 *She Devil* (Neumann); *Kronos* (Neumann); *The Deerslayer* (Neumann)
1958 *The Rawhide Trail* (Gordon); *The Fly* (Neumann); *Machete* (Neumann); *The Hot Angel* (Parker)
1959 *Here Come the Jets* (Fowler); *The Sad Horse* (Clark); *The Rebel Set* (Fowler); *The Alligator People* (Del Ruth); *Counterplot* (Neumann)

Publications

By STRUSS: book—

Pictured with the Struss Pictorial Lens (catalogue), New York, 1915.

By STRUSS: articles—

''Color Photography,'' in *American Photography*, August 1917.
''Photographic Modernism and the Cinematographer,'' in *American Cinematographer* (Hollywood), November 1934.
In *Sources of Light*, edited by Charles Higham, London, 1970.
Journal of Popular Film (Bowling Green, Ohio), vol. 4, no. 4, 1975.

On STRUSS: books—

Harvith, Susan, and John, *Karl Struss: Man with a Camera*, Ann Arbor, Michigan, 1976.
McCandless, Barbara, Yochelson, Bonnie, and Koszarski, Richard, *New York to Hollywood: The Photography of Karl Struss*, Fort Worth, TX, Amon Carter Museum, 1995.

On STRUSS: articles—

Fritz, James L., in *American Cinematographer* (Hollywood), February 1935.
Blanchard, Walter, in *American Cinematographer* (Hollywood), June 1941.
Rosenberg, Bernard, and Harry Silverstein, in *The Real Tinsel*, New York, 1970.
Film Comment (New York), Summer 1972.
American Cinematographer (Hollywood), July 1973.
American Cinematographer (Hollywood), March 1977.
Everson, William K., in *Variety* (New York), 10 September 1980.
The Annual Obituary 1981, New York, 1982.
Carcassonne, P., in *Cinématographe* (Paris), January 1982.
American Cinematographer (Hollywood), February 1982.
Eyman, Scott, in *Five American Cinematographers*, Metuchen, New Jersey, 1987.
Loke, Margarett, ''Karl Struss,'' in *ARTnews*, February 1993.
Naugrette, Jean-Pierre, and Michel Ciment, ''Cinémas, cinéma: Un jour à New York,'' in *Positif* (Paris), November 1995.

*   *   *

Karl Struss has been accurately described as ''by temperament a pictorialist, by instinct an illusionist, and by accomplishment one of the great cameramen in the floridly creative quarter-century of filmmaking that followed *The Birth of a Nation*,'' and is probably best-known as the winner (along with Charles Rosher) of the first Academy Award for cinematography, for his work on Murnau's *Sunrise*. However, his undoubted triumphs as a cinematographer in Hollywood's golden age have somewhat eclipsed his earlier achievements as a still photographer, and it was not until a few years before his death, thanks to a pioneering exhibition at the University of Michigan Museum of Art, that his photographs received any kind of critical recognition at all.

Fleeing his father's manufacturing business, Struss enrolled in art photography classes at Columbia University in 1909. These were under the direction of the renowned photographer Clarence H. White,

making him one of the youngest members of Alfred Stieglitz's Photo-Secession and a contributor to the seminal journal *Camera Work*. In 1914 he set up his own studio and began doing pictorial photography—mostly illustrations for stories—for *Vogue*, *Vanity Fair* and *Harpers Bazaar*, much of it drawn from material gathered on a long photographic vacation in Europe in 1909. He also photographed New York, and did portraits of the stars of the Metropolitan Opera Company for publicity purposes. According to the New York *Times* photography critic Gene Thornton, ''Struss was one of the great photographers of New York. Some of his Whistleresque impressions of the city at twilight rank with anything in that mode by Stieglitz and Steichen.''

It was no accident, then, that Struss started off in Hollywood as a still photographer—with Cecil B. DeMille on St. Patrick's Day, 1919. After a month or so he became a third cameraman, and was shortly thereafter put under contract. He still did the occasional portraits (of DeMille, Gloria Swanson, Bebe Daniels, and *Sunrise* star George O'Brien, for example), and there exist some fascinating studies done on the set of *Sunrise*, but his main career from then on was as a cinematographer, working with directors such as Griffith, Mamoulian, Welles, Chaplin, and stars of the calibre of Mary Pickford, Mae West, Charles Laughton, Fredric March, Cary Grant, and Bing Crosby. Amongst his best known films are *Ben-Hur* (of which he reckons to have shot around 60 percent of the finished picture, although René Guissart received the main credit for the cinematography), *Abraham Lincoln*, *Dr. Jekyll and Mr. Hyde*, *The Sign of the Cross*, *Island of Lost Souls*, *Belle of the Nineties*, *The Great Dictator* and *Limelight*.

Struss left the operation of the camera to his operator, concentrating himself on lighting, camera angles, sets and other production work. When once asked whether he considered directors a hindrance or a help, he replied ''they were usually a help. Every picture was something different; I tried not to use the same formula. It depended on the story. The way I look at it is this: the director is the captain of the ship; I'm the first lieutenant, and the rest of the crew worked directly under me. The director shouldn't care a whoop about anything else; he's got his own problems. I'm his interpreter and I have to give him what I think is good for that story.'' Of Griffith he remarked that ''the photography was independent of the direction. He never bothered you about the lighting. He was mainly concerned with the actors,'' while on *Sunrise* ''Murnau left the whole visual side of the picture to us; he concentrated entirely on the actors. Of course, he'd see what size the image was, and he was interested in the permanently moving camera . . . he was the first director I ever worked with who really knew what was going on when he started to move the camera. He not only knew when to move but how long to move.'' Is there, then, such a thing as a Struss ''look?'' Some clue may be found in the technical innovations which he developed, such as a soft-focus lens which nevertheless provided the foundation of an essentially sharp image, the Lupe reflector which became extremely popular in face lighting, the graduated red-green filter which, used in conjunction with certain makeup facilitated the smooth transformation scenes in *Dr. Jekyll and Mr. Hyde* and the healing of the lepers in *Ben-Hur*, and the graduated gauze filters which facilitated the characteristic changing lighting effects in *Sunrise*. Struss' trademarks, then, at the height of his career, are a myriad of grey tonalities avoiding grittiness or harsh contrasts, a gauzed, romantic approach to the image (witness especially *The Sign of the Cross*, which was filmed entirely through bright red gauze ''to give a feeling of a world remembered''), and, in general, all those qualities one associates with classical photography and the Hollywood studio system at their respective peaks. It is significant, for example, that what he most admired about the director Louis Gasnier was his "European sense of composition—lovely tableaux," that in the opening scene of *Dr. Jekyll and Mr. Hyde* he used an oval gauze with soft edges "to make every shot of every student look like a portrait," and that of his work on *Sunrise* he remarked that "today it's all mechanised; then we were artists."

By the time his contract with Paramount expired in the early 1940s, Struss already had his finest work behind him, although *Journey Into Fear* and *Limelight* are both notable films. However, he still continued to experiment (with 3-D, for example, and with special lenses and filters on *Rocketship X-M*), and to display his customary versatility by working in television on series such as *My Friend Flicka* and *Broken Arrow*. Never typecast, and always adaptable, he made the very best of changed circumstances and styles, though it is hard to avoid the conclusion that his was a talent that gave of its best in the conditions of traditional Hollywood in its heyday.

—Julian Petley

SULLIVAN, C. Gardner

Writer and Producer. **Nationality:** American. **Born:** Charles Gardner Sullivan in Stillwater, Minnesota, 18 September 1886. **Education:** Attended the University of Minnesota, St. Paul. **Family:** Married; four children. **Career:** 1907—journalist, St. Paul *Daily News*, and for papers in other cities during the next few years; 1912—first film based on a screenstory, *Her Polished Family*; 1914—hired by Thomas Ince: wrote films for William S. Hart; 1915–17—head of the scenario department of the recently merged New York Motion Picture Company and Triangle; 1917–19—under contract with Paramount; freelance writer, but associated with Cecil B. DeMille after 1926, and worked as script supervisor for Universal, 1930–31, and for MGM, 1931–33; 1940—retired. **Died:** 5 September 1965

Films as Writer:

1912 *Her Polished Family*; *The Altar of Death* (West); *The Army Surgeon* (F. Ford); *The Invaders* (F. Ford and T. Ince)

1913 *A Shadow of the Past* (T. Ince); *Days of '49* (T. Ince); *The Witch of Salem* (West)

1914 *The Battle of Gettysburg* (T. Ince); *One of the Discard* (+ co-d); *The Bargain* (Barker); *The Passing of Two-Gun Hicks* (Hart)

1915 *The Italian* (Barker); *Satan McAllister's Heir*; *The Last of the Line* (T. Ince); *The Roughneck* (Hart and Smith); *The Ruse* (Hart and Smith); *Pinto Ben* (Hart); *On the Night Stage* (Barker); *The Cup of Life* (West); *The Painted Soul* (Sidney); *The Iron Strain* (Barker); *The Coward* (Barker); *Matrimony* (Sidney); *The Winged Idol* (Edwards ?); *The Golden Claw* (Barker); *The Edge of the Abyss* (West ?)

1916 *The Beckoning Flame* (Edwards ?); *The Conqueror* (Barker); *The Green Swamp* (Sidney); *Honor's Altar* (West ?); *Peggy* (Giblyn); *Hell's Hinges* (Hart and Swickard); *The Moral Fabric* (West ?); *The Stepping Stone* (Barker); *The Aryan* (Hart and Smith); *Civilization's Child* (Giblyn); *The No-Good Guy* (Edwards); *The Beggar of Cawnpore* (Swickard);

Not My Sister (Giblyn); *The Market of Vain Desire* (Barker); *The Bugle Call* (Barker); *Civilization* (T. Ince and others); *The Eye of the Night* (Edwards); *The Payment* (West); *Shell '43* (Barker); *Home* (Miller ?); *The Thoroughbred* (Bartlett); *The Wolf Woman* (Willat or Edwards); *A Corner in Colleens* (Miller); *The Dawn Maker* (Hart); *Plain Jane* (Miller); *The Return of "Draw" Egan* (Hart); *The Criminal* (Barker)

1917 *The Iced Bullet* (Barker); *The Pinchhitter* (Schertzinger—reedited version, 1925); *Happiness* (Barker)

1918 *Those Who Pay* (Wells); *Love Me* (Neill); *Naughty, Naughty!* (Storm); *Selfish Yates* (Hart); *Shark Monroe* (Hart); *The Vamp* (Storm); *The Border Wireless* (Hart); *Branding Broadway* (Hart)

1919 *Happy though Married* (Niblo); *The Poppy Girl's Husband* (Hart and Hillyer); *The Haunted Bedroom* (Niblo); *Other Men's Wives* (Schertzinger); *The Virtuous Thief* (Niblo); *Wagon Tracks* (Hillyer); *Stepping Out* (Niblo); *The Market of Souls* (De Grasse); *John Petticoats* (Hillyer); *Sahara* (Rosson); *Dangerous Hours* (Niblo)

1920 *Sex* (Niblo); *The False Road* (Niblo); *Hairpins* (Niblo); *Love Madness* (Henabery)

1921 *Mother o' Mine* (Niblo); *Greater than Love* (Niblo); *Good Women* (Gasnier); *Hail the Woman* (Wray)

1922 *White Hands* (Hillyer)

1923 *Human Wreckage* (Wray); *Soul of the Beast* (Wray); *Dulcy* (S. Franklin); *Strangers of the Night* (Niblo); *The Dangerous Maid* (Heerman); *Long Live the King* (Schertzinger)

1924 *The Goldfish* (Storm); *The Marriage Cheat* (Wray); *Wandering Husbands* (Beaudine); *Dynamite Smith* (R. Ince); *The House of Wrath* (R. Ince); *The Only Woman* (Olcott); *Cheap Kisses* (R. Ince and Tate); *Idle Tongues* (Hillyer); *The Mirage* (Archainbaud)

1925 *The Monster* (West); *Playing with Souls* (R. Ince); *Wild Justice* (C. Franklin); *If Marriage Fails* (J. Ince); *Tumbleweeds* (Baggot)

1926 *Three Faces East* (Julian); *Bachelor Brides* (Howard); *Sparrows* (Beaudine)

1927 *The Bugle Call* (Sedgwick)

1928 *Sadie Thompson* (Walsh) (+ pr); *Tempest* (Taylor); *The Woman Disputed* (H. King and Taylor)

1929 *Alibi* (West); *The Locked Door* (Fitzmaurice)

1931 *The Cuban Love Song* (Van Dyke)

1932 *Huddle* (Wood); *Strange Interlude* (*Strange Interval*) (Leonard); *Skyscraper Souls* (Selwyn)

1933 *Men Must Fight* (Selwyn)

1934 *Father Brown, Detective* (Sedgwick)

1935 *Car 99* (Barton)

1936 *Three Live Ghosts* (Humberstone)

1938 *The Buccaneer* (DeMille)

1939 *Union Pacific* (DeMille)

1940 *Northwest Mounted Police* (DeMille)

1942 *Jackass Mail* (McLeod)

Films as Producer:

1926 *Corporal Kate* (Sloane); *Her Man o' War* (Urson); *Gigolo* (Howard); *The Clinging Vine* (Sloane)

1927 *The Fighting Eagle* (Crisp); *White Gold* (Howard); *Turkish Delight* (Sloane); *Vanity* (Crisp); *Yankee Clipper* (Julian)

Publications

By SULLIVAN: article—

New York *Telegraph*, 1 October 1916.

On SULLIVAN: articles—

Cahiers du Cinéma (Paris), January 1966.
Koszarski, Diane, in *American Screenwriters*, edited by Robert E. Morsberger, Stephen O. Lesser, and Randall Clark, Detroit, 1984.

*   *   *

Though the claim is probably fraudulent, it is both interesting and revealing that D. W. Griffith boasted he needed no scenario to film his three-hour epic *The Birth of a Nation*, relying instead upon handwritten notes, often penned the night before, that he kept in his pocket while the production unfolded. During the silent period, the scenario, such as it was, was often composed by the director prior to shooting; in fact, a clear division between the two roles was never made even during the later studio period as directors often collaborated, sometimes substantially with the writers on a production. If films were to be identified as having a creative source, an artist responsible for their final form, that responsibility was awarded to the director. The influential French *politique des auteurs*, often translated as the "auteur theory," suggests, in fact, more or less following industry practice and custom, that the film's "author" is its director, thereby eliding the obvious contributions of whoever composed the scenario. Though the American cinema has hardly recognized the contribution of screenwriters, creating a plan for the film (even before sound cinema required the devising of substantial dialogue) has been of crucial importance since the invention of feature-length narrative around 1903. The career of C. Gardner Sullivan, often termed the "dean of American screenwriters," usefully exemplifies that importance.

Like many who would enter this emerging profession, Sullivan developed his writing skills as a journalist, a line of work that at the time required considerable narrative talent as "stories" were an important element of journalistic fare. Writing for the *Evening Journal* in New York, Sullivan tried his hand at composing some sketches for vaudeville and soon afterward attempted to interest area film producers in scenarios. His first sale was to Edison: *Her Polished Family*, a lighthearted satire on the foibles of recent college graduates. After this success, he continued as a freelancer, selling a number of short treatments—for one-reelers—to Lubin and Edison; many of these were based on the adventure melodramas then popular and with which D. W. Griffith was making a substantial reputation. In 1913 Sullivan sold the first of several "Indian-military thrillers" to Thomas W. Ince's New York Motion Picture company. Soon Ince had made Sullivan the offer of a regular job: he was to join the California production end of the same company, the western location where Ince and others filmed this kind of story. This was an important event within the New York-based industry. Sullivan had acquired quite a reputation, and his hiring by Ince was something that the filmmaker boasted about in the trade papers. If the public were unaware of the importance of screenwriters, those within the business were not. Reluctant to leave New York, Sullivan was persuaded by a handsome

financial offer, one that attests to the importance that producers such as Ince, who were committed to the quick production of quality story films, placed on having a scenario writer who could produce shootable scripts under deadline pressure.

Ince taught Sullivan that the scripts he wanted should include not only a clear story line, but should offer short "biographies" of the characters, notes on location and set design, even suggestions for the shooting process (camera angles, framing, art design, etc.). If the scripts Sullivan produced for Ince do not follow the modern model precisely in offering numbered sequences of shots with full instructions for framing, they represented a significant advance in the scenario writer's responsibilities; Sullivan was now called upon to provide a coherent plan or recipe for each production, not just an outline of the story that would inspire the director to devise framings, locations, and narrative coherence. Sullivan drew upon his journalistic experience in writing human interest stories to devise under deadline pressure what were for the time elaborate scenarios for Ince's productions.

The change to full-feature production after 1915 did not severely test Sullivan's talents. He continued to turn out well-done scripts that Ince transformed into successful films. These were in a number of different genres, including big-budget melodrama—*Civilization's Child*—Westerns for Ince star William S. Hart—*Hell's Hinges, The Passing of Two-Gun Hicks*—and social problem melodramas—*The Moral Fabric, The Market of Vain Desire*. Sullivan had perhaps the most personal interest in this last film type. An adherent of Social Darwinism like many Progressive-era intellectuals, he had a deep, abiding concern for what he saw as social ills capable of remediation through Christian loving-kindness and benevolent government regulation; his scripts often touched on prostitution, drug addiction, adultery, and marital breakup, issues that the very straitlaced screenwriter, who was strongly religious, approached always from a moralistic and not an exploitative angle. As Ince developed a stock company of talented performers such as Hart, Charles Ray, H. B. Warner, Louise Glaum, and Dorothy Dalton, as well as a stable of skilled directors with their own peculiar talents such as Raymond West and Reginald Barker, Sullivan learned to write for his fellow Ince employees, producing what we would now term "vehicles."

After Ince's merger with Triangle, Sullivan was entrusted with a further responsibility, overseeing the scenario department, which then was responsible for both features and the numerous short subjects that filled out the weekly programs. Soon administrative duties were so onerous that Sullivan found himself writing little. In 1917, Ince left Triangle for Adolph Zukor's Paramount; Sullivan moved with him, but Ince's next shift within a rapidly altering business—to Associated Producers—did not appeal to Sullivan, and he became a freelancer once again. In the twenties, he was able to expand to Broadway plays, mostly working as an adaptor, and successfully adapted himself to the new tastes of a different era. The screenwriter who had written such religiously fervent melodramas of social reform came to produce the scenarios for titillating sex comedies such as *Wandering Husbands* and *Cheap Kisses*, which he even produced himself. Disdaining an association with the studios who now cornered the market on filmmaking, Sullivan spent most of the twenties in association with the last of the major independents, Cecil B. DeMille, for whom he concocted a number of exotic/adventure scenarios—such as *Yankee Clipper* and *Turkish Delight* as well as sexy melodramas, notably *Gigolo*. Reinventing himself once again, in a sound era that required extensive dialogue but rather static setups, he worked on one of the most prestigious "modern literature" projects of that era, an adaptation of Eugene O'Neill's *Strange Interlude*.

Like most of the technicians of the silent and early studio eras, Sullivan was only able intermittently to impose his own personality and interests on the work he did for a bewildering variety of projects. Writer of nearly 400 scenarios in about three decades, Sullivan was primarily notable for his flexibility and bottomless inspiration, the virtues of a top journalist that he made the basis for a successful career in a new medium.

—R. Barton Palmer

SURTEES, Robert L.

Cinematographer. **Nationality:** American. **Born:** Covington, Kentucky, 8 September 1906. **Family:** Married Maydell (Surtees); children: two daughters and two sons, including the photographer Bruce Surtees. **Career:** Photographer and retoucher in a portrait studio, Cincinnati; camera assistant Universal, from mid-1920s: assisted Gregg Toland, Joseph Ruttenberg, Hal Mohr, Stanley Cortez, and others for the next 15 years; 1942—first film as cinematographer, *This Precious Freedom*; then worked for MGM, and freelance. **Awards:** Academy Award for *King Solomon's Mines*, 1950; *The Bad and the Beautiful*, 1952; *Ben-Hur*, 1959. **Died:** In Carmel, California, 5 January 1985.

Robert L. Surtees

Films as Cinematographer:

1942	*This Precious Freedom* (Oboler)
1943	*Lost Angel* (Rowland)
1944	*Meet the People* (Reisner); *Music for Millions* (Koster); *Thirty Seconds over Tokyo* (LeRoy) (co); *Two Girls and a Sailor* (Thorpe)
1945	*Our Vines Have Tender Grapes* (Rowland)
1946	*No Leave, No Love* (Martin) (co); *Two Sisters from Boston* (Koster)
1947	*Unfinished Dance* (Koster)
1948	*The Big City* (Taurog); *Tenth Avenue* (Rowland); *The Kissing Bandit* (Benedek); *A Date with Judy* (Thorpe); *Act of Violence* (Zinnemann)
1949	*Big Jack* (Thorpe); *Intruder in the Dust* (Brown); *That Midnight Kiss* (Taurog)
1950	*King Solomon's Mines* (Bennett)
1951	*The Light Touch* (Brooks); *The Strip* (Kardos); *Quo Vadis* (LeRoy) (co)
1952	*The Wild North* (Marton); *The Merry Widow* (Bernhardt); *The Bad and the Beautiful* (Minnelli)
1953	*Ride Vaquero* (Farrow); *Mogambo* (Ford) (co); *Escape from Fort Bravo* (J. Sturges)
1954	*The Long, Long Trailer* (Minnelli); *Valley of the Kings* (Pirosh)
1955	*The Mark* (Robson); *Oklahoma!* (Zinnemann)
1956	*The Swan* (C. Vidor) (co); *Tribute to a Bad Man* (Wise)
1957	*Les Girls* (Cukor); *Raintree Country* (Dmytryk)
1958	*Merry Andrew* (Kidd); *The Law and Jake Wade* (J. Sturges)
1959	*Ben-Hur* (Wyler)
1960	*It Started in Naples* (Shavelson)
1961	*Cimarron* (A. Mann)
1962	*Mutiny on the Bounty* (Milestone)
1963	*PT-109* (Martinson)
1964	*Kisses for My President* (Bernhardt)
1965	*The Satan Bug* (J. Sturges); *The Hallelujah Trail* (J. Sturges); *The Collector* (Wyler) (co); *The Third Day* (Smight)
1966	*The Lost Command* (Robson)
1967	**The Graduate** (Nichols); *Dr. Dolittle* (Fleischer)
1968	*Sweet Charity* (Fosse)
1969	*The Arrangement* (Kazan)
1970	*The Liberation of L.B. Jones* (Wyler)
1971	*Summer of '42* (Mulligan); **The Last Picture Show** (Bogdanovich); *The Cowboys* (Rydell); *The Other* (Mulligan)
1972	*Lost Horizon* (Jarrott); *Oklahoma Crude* (Kramer)
1973	*The Sting* (Hill)
1975	*The Great Waldo Pepper* (Hill); *The Hindenburg* (Wise)
1976	*A Star Is Born* (Pierson)
1977	*The Turning Point* (Ross)
1978	*Same Time, Next Year* (Mulligan); *Blood Brothers* (Mulligan)

Publications

By SURTEES: articles—

On *Quo Vadis* in *American Cinematographer* (Hollywood), October 1951.

"Using the Camera Emotionally," in *Action* (Hollywood), September-October 1967.

On *The Graduate* in *Films in Review* (New York), February 1968.

On *The Last Picture Show* in *American Cinematographer* (Hollywood), January 1972.

American Cinematographer (Hollywood), April 1973.

On *The Hindenburg* in *American Cinematographer* (Hollywood), January 1976.

Action (Hollywood), January-February 1976.

On *The Turning Point* in *American Cinematographer* (Hollywood), December 1977.

On SURTEES: articles—

Lightman, Herb A., on *Oklahoma!* in *American Cinematographer* (Hollywood), April 1955.

Rowan, Arthur, "Pictorial Emphasis in Cinematography," in *American Cinematographer* (Hollywood), February 1956.

Grandi, Leo, on *Ben-Hur* in *American Cinematographer* (Hollywood), October 1959.

Scot, Darrin, on *Mutiny on the Bounty* in *American Cinematographer* (Hollywood), February 1963.

Lightman, Herb A., on *The Lost Command* in *American Cinematographer* (Hollywood), July 1966.

Lightman, Herb A., "Cinematography with a Split Personality," in *American Cinematographer* (Hollywood), February 1968.

Critisch Filmforum (The Hague), 7 August 1968.

Film Comment (New York), Summer 1972.

Focus on Film (London), no. 13, 1973.

Take One (Montreal), no. 2, 1978.

American Cinematographer (Hollywood), May 1978.

American Cinematographer (Hollywood), May 1979.

Obituary in *Variety* (New York), 16 January 1985.

Obituary in *American Cinematographer* (Hollywood), March 1985.

American Cinematographer (Hollywood), August 1986.

*   *   *

Robert L. Surtees's career as a cameraman spanned almost 50 years—from camera assistant in the late 1920s to cinematographer on his last film in 1978, from the silent era to the new Hollywood. A significant part of that career was as a cinematographer in the classic Hollywood style, that "invisible" style of filmmaking that dominated American films from the introduction of sound well into the 1960s.

Analyzing such a long career is similar to taking a survey course in the history of American cinema. As a young cameraman, Surtees was an assistant to such influential cinematographers as Gregg Toland and Joseph Ruttenberg, whose work helped set the technical standard in the industry for several decades. As a studio cinematographer for MGM for almost 20 years, Surtees photographed films in almost every popular genre, from small comedies such as *Lost Angel* to westerns such as *Escape from Fort Bravo* to blockbuster musicals like *Oklahoma!* When he began working for MGM in the early 1940s, the studio system was in its heyday and the classic Hollywood style—characterized by an even, balanced lighting, match cutting, and linear narratives—was the norm. During that era, the producers and the studio exerted creative control, not the directors. Thus, each studio developed its own "look." At MGM, this look was one of opulence, which was revealed through the use of high-key lighting. Surtees's work at MGM at this time was indicative of that studio's style. During the 1950s, when the studio system began to crumble partly from the competition of television, films became grander in scale and larger in scope. Widescreen films and spectacular Technicolor epics were popular successes, and Surtees's filmography from this decade—which includes *Quo Vadis*, *Raintree County*, and *Ben-Hur*—reflects this trend. The decade of the 1960s was one of transition in the industry when the old studio system finally gave way to the rise of independent producers and the importance of the director as the creative force. Surtees's tenure at MGM ended in 1962 and he became a freelance cinematographer working for such stalwarts as William Wyler (*The Collector*) as well as for up-and-coming directors like Mike Nichols (*The Graduate*). Surtees continued working into the 1970s, by this time for the "new Hollywood," characterized by independent producers and directors whose personal vision shaped the style of a film, sometimes in a rather self-conscious manner. It is fitting that Surtees was chosen by Peter Bogdanovich as the cinematographer for *The Last Picture Show*, for the film subtly alludes to the end of the old Hollywood studio system—a system that Surtees saw rise and fall. It is a tribute to Surtees's talent and adaptability that he could succeed from one era through he next.

Searching for one type of film or a particular style that Surtees specialized in is difficult. However, after analyzing his filmography and studying reviews of his films, it can be said that Surtees was adept at lush Technicolor cinematography, particularly that found in such big-budget A-films as *King Solomon's Mines* (for which he won an Oscar), *Quo Vadis*, *Mogambo*, *Oklahoma!*, *Raintree County*, *Ben-Hur* (for which he won his third Oscar), *Mutiny on the Bounty*, and *Dr. Dolittle*. So influential was his work on *King Solomon's Mines*, for example, that the excess footage was used in other jungle films, most notably *Watusi*. Analyses or critiques of these films do not fail to mention the excellent or beautiful cinematography. As one critic so eloquently stated, "Each frame of celluloid is like a painting."

—Susan Doll

ŠVANKMAJER, Jan

Animator and Director. **Nationality:** Czech. **Born:** Prague, 4 September 1934. **Education:** Attended the Arts and Crafts School, Prague, 1950–54; Theatre Faculty of the Academy of Music and Dramatic Art (DAMU), Prague, 1954–58. **Family:** Married Eva Kostelec. **Career:** Graphic artist and painter; 1958–64—worked in puppet theatre, in Liberec, and then formed his own Theatre of Masks in Prague; also associated with Laterna Magica and Black Theatre; 1964—first film as director, *The Last Trick*; member of surrealist group in Prague; 1974—began experimentation with "touch objects." **Award:** Golden Bear award, Berlin Film Festival, for *Mozenosti dialogu*, 1982; Karlovy-Vary Festival, Special Jury Prize, for *Lekce Faust*, 1994.

Films as Writer and Director:

1964   *Poslední trik pana Schwarzwalldea a pana Edgara* (*The Last Trick of Mr. Schwarzwald and Mr. Edgar*) (+ prod design)

1965   *J.S. Bach: Fantasia G-Moll* (*J.S. Bach: Fantasy in G Minor*) (short) (+ prod design); *Spiel mit Steinen* (*A Game with Stones*) (short) (+ prod design)

1966   *Rakvickárna* (*Punch and Judy*) (short) (+ prod design); *Et cetera* (short) (+ prod design)
1967   *Historia naturae* (short) (+ prod design)
1968   *Zahrada* (*The Garden*) (short); *Byt* (*The Flat*) (short); *Picnick mit Weismann* (*Picnic with Weisman*) (short) (+ prod design)
1969   *Tichy tyden v domee* (*A Quiet Week in a House*) (short) (+ prod design)
1970   *Kostnice* (*The Ossuary*) (short) (+ prod design); *Don Sajn* (*Don Juan*) (+ prod design)
1971   *Jabberwocky* (short) (+ prod design)
1972   *Leonarduv deník* (*Leonardo's Diary*) (short)
1973–79   *Otrantsky zámek* (*The Castle of Otranto*) (short) (+ prod design)
1980   *Zanik domu Usheru* (*The Fall of the House of Usher*) (short) (+ prod design)
1982   *Mozenosti dialogu* (*Dimensions of Dialogue*) (short) (+ prod design); *Do pivnice* (*Down to the Cellar*) (short)
1983   *Kyvadlo, jáma, a nadeeje* (*The Pit, the Pendulum, and Hope*) (+ prod design)
1987   *Alice*
1988   *Muzné Hry* (*Virile Games*) (short) (+ prod design); *Another Kind of Love* (short) (+ prod design); *Autoportrét* (*Self-Portraits*) (short)
1989   *Zamilované maso* (*Meat in Love*) (short); *Tma-svetlo-tma* (*Darkness-Light-Darkness*) (short) (+ prod design); *Flora* (short) (+ prod design)
1990   *Konec stalinismu v Cechách* (*The Death of Stalinism in Bohemia*) (short) (+ prod design)
1992   *Jídlo* (*Food*) (short) (+ prod design)
1994   *Lekce Faust* (+ prod design)
1996   *Spikelenci slasti*
2000   *Otesánek* (+ prod design)

Other Films:

1958   *Faust* (Radok) (puppeteer)
1966   *Ceíslice* (*Ciphers*) (Procházka) (art d)
1977   *Adéla jeste nevecerela* (*Adela Hasn't Had Her Supper Yet*) (Lipsky) (co-art d; animator)
1979   *Hodinárova svatební cesta korálovym moren* (Svoboda)
1980   *Blazni vodníci a podvodníci* (*Fools, Water Sprites, and Imposters*) (Svoboda)
1981   *Tajemstvi hradu v Karpatech* (*The Mysterious Castle in the Carpathians*) (Lipsky) (co-art d; animator); *Monstrum z galaxie Arkana* (*Monsters from the Arcane Galaxy*) (Vukotic) (designer of monster)
1984   *Barrandovské nocturno aneb Jak film tancil a zpíval* (*Barrandov Nocturne, or How Films Dance and Sing*) (Sís) (animator) (short)
1985   *Skalpel, prosím* (*Scalpel, Please*) (Svoboda) (co-art d)

Publications

By ŠVANKMAJER: books—

Hmat a imaginace, Prague, 1995.
Editor, *Otevreená hra* (surrealist anthology), Prague, n.d.
Opak zrcadla (surrealist anthology), Prague, n.d.

Transmutace smyslu [*Transmutation of the Senses*], Prague, n.d.
Dark Alchymie, London, n.d.

By ŠVANKMAJER: articles—

Film a Doba (Prague), no. 5, 1982.
Positif (Paris), November 1985.
Dryje, F., "Jan Švankmajer. Rozhovor. Tri filmy Jana Švankmajera," an article and interview by F. Dryje, *Film a Doba* (CZ), Spring 1991.
"A Faust Buck," an interview with Geoff Andrew, *Time Out* (UK), September 7, 1994.
Švankmajer, Jan, "Coming Attractions," in *Time Out* (UK), February 12, 1997.

On ŠVANKMAJER: articles—

Film a Doba (Prague), no. 10, 1966.
Poseová, Katereina, in *Film a Doba* (Prague), no. 7, 1968.
Film a Doba (Prague), no. 9, 1969.
Horeejseí, Jan, in *Magazín Kina* (Prague), 1969–70.
Effenberger, Vratislav, in *Film a Doba* (Prague), no. 3, 1972.
Banc-Titre (Paris), no. 1–2, 1978.
Sauvaget, Daniel, in *Image et Son* (Paris), June 1978.
Positif (Paris), November 1979.
Svab, Ludvik, in *Film a Doba* (Prague), no. 10, 1984.
Zvoníceek, Petr, in *Film a Divadlo* (Bratislava), no. 19, 1984.
O'Pray, Mike, "In the Capital of Magic," in *Monthly Film Bulletin* (London), July 1986 + filmo.
Special Švankmajer Section, in *Afterimage*, no. 13, Autumn 1987.
Cahiers du Cinéma (Paris), no. 424, October 1989.
Donald, James, in *Fantasy and the Cinema*, London, 1989.
O'Pray, Michael, in *Het Ludicatief Principe: Jan Švankmajer*, Antwerpe Film Stichting, n.d..
Film a doba (Prague), no. 3, 1994 + filmo.
Lidové noviny (Prague), 30 September 1994.
O'Pray, Michael, "Between Slapstick and Horror," in *Sight and Sound* (UK), September 1994.

*   *   *

Ever since Jan Švankmajer's 12-minute short, *Mozenosti dialogu* (*Dimensions of Dialogue*), won a Golden Bear at the Berlin Film Festival in 1982 which resulted in his "discovery" by the West, this director of enigmatic animated films has become one of the world's best known contemporary Czechoslovakian artists, rivaled in renown only by Milos Forman, Milan Kundera, and Václav Havel. As a whole, his work draws from a distinctive matrix of influences and qualities, precariously synthesized as if by a magical dialectic, balancing indigenous Czechoslovakian surrealism on the one hand, with international literary sources on the other (Lewis Carroll and Edgar Allan Poe in particular). His films play off highly personal imagery and concerns against veiled political and social critique, juxtaposing violence and tenderness, humour and pathos. He and his team of collaborators (including his wife, Eva Švankmajerova), are recognized as some of the most technically accomplished animators, especially of object animation, in the business. His belated fame, after 20 years of filmmaking in relative obscurity, has had a twofold influence: inspiring a generation of independent animators working both in the commercial market and the more rarefied field of the festival circuit, while also helping to build a greater audience for a medium seen, hitherto, primarily as one only suitable for children.

Ironically, while his films are often characterized by others as "adult" animation, Švankmajer himself insists that, "I'm interested, in the first instance, in a dialogue with my own childhood. *Childhood is my alter ego.... Animation can bring the imagery of childhood back to life and give it back its credibility. The animation of objects upholds the truth of our childhood.*" (Italics his.) Thus, all of Švankmajer's works, even the most abstract, like *Johann Sebastian Bach: Fantasia G-Moll* (1965) and *Spiel mit Steinen* (1965), function in part as an act of reparation for the lost or repressed animistic beliefs of childhood. Many of his films feature children—*Do pivnice* (1983), *Alice* (1988)—exploring a menacing landscape of animated *objets trouvés*, responding alternately with fear, bravery, and retributive aggression to an incomprehensible and threatening world. One of his finest early works, *Jabberwocky* (1971), evokes children all the more strongly by their virtual absence, as a nursery comes to life and performs a sinister cabaret, starring dolls born from the stuffing of a larger doll, a dancing penknife that kills itself, and a sailor suit which acts as host to their performances. The spanking which opens this film is characteristic of the sadism and cruelty which pervades his work, and is especially notable in his other adaptation of Lewis Carroll, *Alice*, his only feature film to date. There the heroine is tempted by jars of marmalade that contain hidden drawing pins and threatened by a scissors-wielding rabbit. Like Freud, whom he greatly admires, Švankmajer is interested in exploring the obscure sexuality of childhood, the polymorphous perversity which has not yet learned to separate the animate from the ianimate as a source of pleasure, which discovers sensual delight in the materiality of objects, no matter how decrepit and tawdry. His representation of the body as a plastic site of decay and transformation, pleasure and pain, often recalls Buñuel, Borowczyk, and Fellini as well as Breton, Duchamps, and the Surrealists and Dadaist movements.

Despite the international breadth of his influences, Švankmajer's "militant surrealism" and that of the Czech Surrealist Group of which he is a long-standing member, grew as much out of the history of Prague itself—once a centre for the study of Alchemy and the Cabala in the court of Rudolf II—and from the highly decorative and stylized Mannerist style of the 16th century whose best known artist, Arcimboldo, is "quoted" in the composite heads of *Dimensions of Dialogue*. Czech-language marionette and puppet theatres have a long and lively history in Prague, and it was at the Black Theatre and Magic Lantern of Prague that Švankmajer served his apprenticeship and was first introduced to filmmaking. However, Švankmajer does not merely *use* puppetry in several films, for example *The Last Trick* (1964), *Punch and Judy* (1966), and *Don Juan* (1970), as much as he defamiliarizes it, exploring and exploding its narratives and recurrent tropes of violence.

Švankmajer's Mannerist mannerisms have been aped by many aspirant animators and his figures duplicated for beer commercials and pop videos, but one of the most important aspects of his work, his oblique political commentary, has proved less transferable. Like many artists living under politically repressive states, Švankmajer has had to mask his critique in ambiguous symbols, such as the menacing and senseless regime of the flat in *The Flat* (1968), the tea party in *Alice*, or the intercut shots of daily life in *Leonardo's Diary* (1973). The latter film so angered the authorities, Švankmajer was forbidden from doing any filmmaking for eight years. The self-confessed "work of agit-prop," *The Death of Stalinism in Bohemia* (1990), made after the fall of Communism, formed a kind of animated

revenge on his past oppressors, and seemed to mark a departure for his work into a new transparency of meaning, disparaged by some critics. Yet, its final images, which fade to black before it is revealed what has been "born" from the erstwhile "free" Czechoslovak state, begs more questions than the film cares to answer, a strategy reminiscent of Švankmajer's quizzical *oeuvre* as a whole.

—Leslie Felperin Sharman

SWERLING, Jo

Writer. **Nationality:** American. **Born:** Joseph Swerling in Bardichov, Russia, 8 April 1897; emigrated with his family to the United States. **Family:** Married; two children, including son: the television producer Jo Swerling, Jr. **Career:** 1916—journalist: reporter, editorial writer, columnist, and comic-strip author for Chicago *Herald and Examiner*; Chicago correspondent for *Variety*; also a playwright and short-story writer: produced plays include *One of Us*, 1918, *One Helluva Night*, 1924, *The New Yorkers*, 1927, *Kibitzer*, with Edward G. Robinson, 1929, and *Guys and Dolls*, 1950; 1930—first film as writer, *Ladies of Leisure*: contract with Columbia, and association with Frank Capra; 1964—retired from film writing. **Died:** October 1964.

Films as Writer:

1930   *Ladies of Leisure* (Capra); *Melody Lane* (based on his unpublished play "The Understander"); *Sisters* (Flood); *Rain or Shine* (Capra); *Hell's Island* (Sloman)

1931   *The Last Parade* (Kenton); *Dirigible* (Capra); *Ten Cents a Dance* (L. Barrymore); *The Miracle Woman* (Capra); *Platinum Blonde* (Capra)

1932   *Forbidden* (Capra); *Behind the Mask* (Dillon); *War Correspondent* (Sloane); *Washington Merry-Go-Round* (Cruze)

1933   *Below the Sea* (Rogell); *Man's Castle* (Borzage)

1934   *No Greater Glory* (Borzage); *The Defense Rests* (Hillyer); *Lady by Choice* (Burton)

1935   *The Whole Town's Talking* (Ford); *Love Me Forever* (Schertzinger)

1936   *The Music Goes 'round* (Schertzinger); *Pennies from Heaven* (McLeod)

1937   *Double Wedding* (Thorpe)

1938   *I Am the Law* (Hall); *Doctor Rhythm* (Tuttle)

1939   *Made for Each Other* (Cromwell); *The Real Glory* (Hathaway); ***Gone with the Wind*** (Fleming)

1940   *The Westerner* (Wyler)

1941   *Blood and Sand* (Mamoulian); *New York Town* (C. Vidor); *Confirm or Deny* (Mayo)

1942   *Pride of the Yankees* (Wood)

1943   *Crash Dive* (Mayo); *A Lady Takes a Chance* (Seiter)

1944   *Lifeboat* (Hitchcock)

1945   *Leave Her to Heaven* (Stahl)

1946   ***It's a Wonderful Life*** (Capra)

1953   *Thunder in the East* (C. Vidor)

1956   *The Lord Don't Play Favorites* (co-written with Hal Stanley for NBC's *Producers' Showcase*)

1961   *King of the Roaring Twenties* (*The Big Bankroll*) (J. Newman)

Publications

By SWERLING: books—

Typo Tales and Verses, Chicago, 1915.
Kibitzer (play), New York, 1929.

On SWERLING: articles—

Film Comment (New York), Winter 1970–71.
Slater, Thomas, in *American Screenwriters, 2nd series*, edited by Randall Clark, Detroit, 1986.

*   *   *

The conversion to sound in the late twenties meant that the American film industry needed to hire a different kind of screenwriter, one used to creating effective dialogue rather than simply outlining a workable scenario and devising title materials. Hollywood found such writers in the top ranks of journalists and successful playwrights. Swerling is perhaps the only of these to have achieved outstanding success in both fields. After selling papers as a youngster, he moved up to join the staff of the *Chicago Herald and Examiner*, where he excelled in a number of roles, most memorably as the author of the popular comic strip "Gallagher and Shean," then a well-known vaudeville act. The Marx brothers admired his writing, and Swerling was subsequently invited to write a musical comedy for them that, unfortunately, was not successful. Convinced, however, that his future lay in playwriting, Swerling returned to his hometown New York and wrote four comedy dramas, most with a New York Jewish flavor, that were produced with some success; the most notable of these is perhaps *Kibitzer*, in which Swerling persuaded Edward G. Robinson to star.

The opportunity to make what was then a huge amount of money writing for the sound pictures proved impossible to resist despite a thriving Broadway career, and Swerling moved to the west coast where he spent six years under contract to Columbia, collaborating most importantly with Frank Capra, whose optimistic vision of the American common man and distrust for the wealthy establishment Swerling very much shared. After establishing himself in Hollywood, Swerling made a comfortable living freelancing until his retirement in 1964. Like Capra, in the early thirties Swerling had little interest in probing the limits of public taste with titillating or erotic drama, then much in vogue. Swerling's characters, in contrast, display that Horatio Algerism that is very much associated with Capra, a kind of optimistic faith in the national institutions and down-home decency that is often derided as "Capra-Corn." His early films often feature women who have made early, but not disastrous, mistakes in their lives; by the end of the final reel of *The Defense Rests* and *Ladies of Leisure*, the heroine has faced up to her error, made the best of the strong virtues she inherently possesses, and embarked upon a life devoted to decency and respectability.

An important reason for Swerling's success with such films is that his vision of American life was very much in harmony with what conservative moral forces in the country, particularly the Catholic Legion of Decency, were demanding that the studios provide. The adoption of the Production Code in 1934 institutionalized the Victorian version of moral uplift that Swerling saw as the essence of the American experience: a rejection of modern temptation (especially of the big-city variety) in favor of time-tested traditional values. If Swerling's heroes are eager to achieve material success in a world that seems inhospitable to such aims (an accurate reflection of Depression era sentiments), they are never served well by political (read "communist" or "socialist") solutions, always in the end holding fast to republican ideals of self-reliance and community service. The main characters are often petite bourgeoisie, such as the owners of a small circus in a Capra collaboration, *Rain or Shine*, whose livelihood is threatened by an employee strike; or the struggling young couple in *Made for Each Other*, whose love for each other is nearly destroyed by dire economic straits. The threat to happiness, however, may just as easily come from above as from below. In another Capra film, the heroine in *Ladies of Leisure* finally recognizes that her successful efforts at self-advancement have made her a kind of prostitute; she then forswears material comfort for a life of romantic bliss with a poor but honest "Mr. Right"; in *Platinum Blonde*, also for Capra, Swerling explores the gender difficulties faced by a gritty newspaper reporter who marries a wealthy woman, and therefore abandons the traditional American-male role of breadwinner.

The limitations and glories of Swerling's vision of American life can be seen in his two most famous scripts, for *Pride of the Yankees*, co-written with Herman J. Mankiewicz, the life story of the most sentimentalized American hero of the early forties, Lou Gehrig; and *It's a Wonderful Life*, a project that whose 11th-hour script difficulties Swerling was called upon to solve by a desperate Capra. *Pride of the Yankees* is vintage Swerling, an emotionally affecting paean of praise of the most cherished elements of the national character: hard work, selflessness, devotion to family, patient acceptance of adversity, and endurance. Like his main character, Swerling possessed incredible stamina; seemingly supplied with endless inspiration, he carved out a secure living in a business where a writer was only as good as his or her last picture. The darker aspects of Gehrig's experience, especially the inevitable rivalry with teammate Babe Ruth, whose showmanship and flashiness garnered him more notoriety and a higher salary, are elided in Swerling's treatment; the screenplay never even hints at the contrast between the free-living Ruth and his conservative teammate, at their achievement of very different kinds of fame. In other words, Gehrig is provided with no alternative way of life, a source of temptation that is avoided only through moral diligence and innate strength of character. The film, lacking a central struggle, fails to be interestingly dramatic, though it is a tribute to Swerling's ability to keep the narrative flowing that *Pride of the Yankees* is never boring. It is typical of Swerling that the script's most interesting moments are provided by expertly evoked sentiment, especially in the closing sequences where Gehrig tries to hide the disease that is soon to kill him from his wife, who already knows but is desperate to maintain the illusion in which his pride and considerateness are so invested.

In contrast, *It's a Wonderful Life* is structured around the most basic of life's struggles, against a despair born of hostile and unrewarding circumstance that can rob even the strongest and most virtuous of the will to live. Completely beyond the experience of Swerling's Lou Gehrig is the urge for self-annihilation to which George Bailey is reduced by the apparent victory of pure chance and malevolence over his self-sacrificing efforts to serve others. At the film's center is the heavenly effort, directed by one of the Hollywood screen's most charming angels, to convince George that he must go on living. This psychological task is not achieved by holding out an alternative vision of the life George might subsequently lead, but by a kind of moral subtraction, the reduction of George to an identity-less being who must experience the horror of the world as it would have been had he never lived, a nightmare vision of what would have happened had George not been there to prevent it. Like Swerling's protagonists in *The Defense Rests* and *The Miracle Woman*, George undergoes a moral rehabilitation that is essentially self-generated, the product not of changed circumstances, but of a transformed sensibility. The film ends in classic Horatio Alger fashion, with George's moral virtue rewarded by benefaction, in this case the generous gifts of money that allow George to avoid going to jail for bank fraud. This touch seems pure Swerling.

What Capra undoubtedly was responsible for, in contrast, was the presentation of the hero in extremis (shades of the filibuster in *Mr. Smith Goes to Washington*, on which Swerling did not collaborate); for Capra, the fight for virtue is always barely won, the product of an immense suffering that wins the day (e.g., the moral collapse of the crooked senator in *Mr. Smith* who cannot stand the agony of watching his youthful protégé endure the unendurable). For Swerling, however, the victory of virtue is always, already assured by the protagonist's moral righteousness, a quality that will ensure that he or she does the right thing once the proper kind of self-recognition has been achieved. Even more so than Capra's patriotic populism, such a belief in the innate invincibility of good people made Swerling the ideal voice for a Hollywood dedicated from 1934 until the mid-sixties to the making of films where good inevitably triumphs over evil, where virtue is always more attractive than vice, where the simple faith of simple people is to be preferred to the dangerous sophistication, the idle self-indulgence of the rich. As Hollywood turned to different forms of entertainment in the fifties and sixties, Swerling became much less in demand. In *Thunder in the East*, Swerling demonstrates the enduring power of the old entertainment formula; in this effective recycling of *Casablanca*, an immoral gunrunner operating in the Far East is persuaded to support the cause of democracy and freedom by a beautiful blind woman. Less successful was *King of the Roaring Twenties*, a screen biography of gangster Arnold Rothstein, most famous for fixing the 1919 World Series; Swerling's heart was obviously not in this late noir portrayal of decadence and the criminal demimonde, which forms a kind of reverse image to *Pride of the Yankees*. In 1964 Swerling retired from a quite different Hollywood than the one he contributed so much to in the thirties and forties.

—R. Barton Palmer

SYLBERT, Richard

Art Director. **Nationality:** American. **Born:** Brooklyn, New York, 1928; twin brother of the designer Paul Sylbert. **Education:** Attended Tyler School of Art, Philadelphia. **Career:** 1951–53—TV art director (including the series *Inner Sanctum*); film designer from mid-1950s; 1975–78—head of production, Paramount. **Awards:** Academy Award, for *Who's Afraid of Virginia Woolf?*, 1966; Academy Award, Best Art Direction and Set Direction, for *Dick Tracy*, 1991; British Academy Award, Best Production Design, for *Dick Tracy*, 1991; Lifetime Achievement Award, Society of Motion Picture and Television Art Directors, 2000.

Films as Art Director/Production Designer:

1956   *Crowded Paradise* (Pressburger); *Baby Doll* (Kazan)
1957   *A Face in the Crowd* (Kazan); *Edge of the City* (Ritt)

1958   *Wind Across the Everglades* (Ray)
1960   *The Fugitive Kind* (Lumet); *Murder, Inc.* (Balaban and Rosenberg)
1961   *Mad Dog Coll* (Balaban); *Splendor in the Grass* (Kazan); *The Young Doctors* (Karlson)
1962   *Walk on the Wild Side* (Dmytryk); *The Manchurian Candidate* (Frankenheimer); *The Connection* (Clarke); *Long Day's Journey into Night* (Lumet)
1963   *All the Way Home* (Segal)
1964   *Lilith* (Rossen)
1965   *How to Murder Your Wife* (Quine); *The Pawnbroker* (Lumet); *What's New, Pussycat?* (Donner)
1966   *Who's Afraid of Virginia Woolf?* (Nichols); *Grand Prix* (Frankenheimer)
1967   **The Graduate** (Nichols)
1968   **Rosemary's Baby** (Polanski)
1969   *The April Fools* (Rosenberg); *The Illustrated Man* (Smight)
1970   *Catch-22* (Nichols)
1971   *Carnal Knowledge* (Nichols)
1972   *Fat City* (Huston); *The Heartbreak Kid* (May)
1973   *The Day of the Dolphin* (Nichols)
1974   **Chinatown** (Polanski)
1975   *The Fortune* (Nichols); *Shampoo* (Ashby); *Last Hours Before Morning* (Hardy)
1979   *Players* (Harvey)
1981   *Reds* (Beatty)
1982   *Partners* (Burrows); *Frances* (Clifford)
1983   *Breathless* (McBride)
1984   *The Cotton Club* (Coppola)
1986   *Under the Cherry Moon* (Prince)
1988   *Shoot to Kill* (*Deadly Pursuit*) (Spottiswoode); *Tequila Sunrise* (Towne)
1990   *The Bonfire of the Vanities* (De Palma); *Dick Tracy* (Beatty)
1991   *Mobsters* (Karbelnikoff)
1992   *Ruby Cairo* (*Deception*) (Clifford)
1993   *Carlito's Way* (De Palma)
1996   *Mulholland Falls* (Tamahori) (+ ro as Coroner)
1997   *Blood and Wine* (Rafelson); *My Best Friend's Wedding* (Hogan); *Red Corner* (Avnet)
2000   *In the Boom Boom Room*
2001   *Unconditional Love*; *Uprising*

Publications

By SYLBERT: articles—

Film Heritage (Dayton, Ohio), Fall 1975.
Film Comment (New York), January/February 1982.
Stills (London), May 1985.
American Film (Washington, D.C.), December 1985.
American Film (Washington, D.C.), December 1989.

On SYLBERT: article:

Premiere, vol. 7, December 1993.

*   *   *

Though the importance of Richard Sylbert's contribution to art direction in the American cinema is undeniable, it is legitimate to ask if the abandonment of the great studios, continuing in Hollywood during the 1960s and 1970s, limited the complete expression of his talent. Nevertheless, Sylbert is one of the principal links, if not *the* principal, in the history of the classic art department, maintaining a tradition of design which has undergone a considerable renewal since the 1980s.

In his twenties, Sylbert worked with William Cameron Menzies, perhaps the major American film designer, claiming: "Menzies taught me about getting hold of the whole thing, about making the connections and keeping control of it and making rules." If Sylbert, through Menzies, is heir to the idea of "structural rules," to Elia Kazan, Sylbert owes the notion of the independence of the creative process. Sylbert says: "Kazan taught me a wonderful thing. Here was this man who was one of the greatest directors we ever had. I would sometimes go up to him and say, 'Gadge, what do you think we ought to do here?' And he would look at me and say, 'What would you do if I were dead?' I treat all directors as if they're dead."

A fidelity to these two influences allowed Sylbert to bring to the design of his films an individual vision, stressing the scripts' most central ideas. He has said, for instance, that the design for *Chinatown* follows the basic orientation of the film: it can be summed up, in his opinion, as "Find the girl." Sylbert uses color, space, and architecture to effect a "visual rewriting" of the script. In general, a color emerges as the deepest unifying factor of his design: in *Chinatown* a rediscovery of *film noir* leads to a utilization of "open" colors which tend toward luminous and hot whites; in *Reds* neutral browns dominate, contrasting only with the sequence of lively colors worn by Louise Bryant; in *The Cotton Club*, in which Sylbert is again involved in "reinventing a genre," a profusion of brilliants and reflections dominate the look of the film, reinforcing the illusion of spectacle and the mythology of gangsters.

Some of Sylbert's sets are both realistic and full of atmosphere, like the second floor of the house in *Baby Doll*, his first film with Kazan, and Martha's house in *Who's Afraid of Virginia Woolf?*, one of the five films he made for Mike Nichols. Both examples show the same line of unity: the sets carry a large psychological freight, with few decorative details (a studied disarrangement) and a confining space. The empty walls of *Carnal Knowledge* ("it's really about memory," the designer says) and the claustrophobic apartment of *Rosemary's Baby* also show this psychological vision of space.

The art of Richard Sylbert is a long search for the correspondences between the psychology of the characters and the appearances of his sets. A Sylbert design possesses a liberty and an abstraction that approaches those of music. As he himself has said: "There's no question, if you look at *Reds*, it's a romantic symphony. You look at a picture like *Chinatown*, and it's a concerto for instant brass. The idea in *Cotton Club* is that there's no classical type structure. Jazz is not written down. *Cotton Club* is a syncopated movie."

—M. S. Fonesca

TAKEMITSU, Toru

Composer. **Nationality:** Japanese. **Born:** Tokyo, 8 October 1930; grew up in Manchuria. **Education:** Studied with Kasuji Kiyose. **Career:** Member of the avant-garde group Jikken Kobo; entered films as assistant to Fumio Hayasaka; 1955—first film score, for *Ginrin*; has composed orchestra works; 1975—taught at Yale University, New Haven, Connecticut. **Awards:** Japanese Academy Award and Los Angeles Film Critics Award, for *Ran*, 1985. **Died:** 16 February 1996.

Films as Composer:

1955 *Ginrin* (*Silver Circle*) (Matsumoto) (co); *Kinegraphy* (Ohtsuji)

1956 *Kurutta kajitsu* (*Crazed Fruit*) (Nakahira); *Shu to midori* (*Red and Green*) (Nakamura); *Tsuyu no atosaki* (*Toward the Rainy Season*) (Nakamura)

1957 *Doshaburi* (*Hard Rain*) (Nakamura); *Kaoyaku* (*The Boss*) (Nakamura)

1959 *Haru o matsu hitobito* (*Those Who Wait for Spring*) (Nakamura); *Kiyen ryoko* (*Dangerous Voyage*) (Nakamura); *Asu e no seiso* (*Tomorrow's Costume*) (Nakamura); *Itazura* (*The Joke*) (Nakamura)

1960 *José Torres* (Teshigahara—short); *Kawaita mizuumi* (*Youth in Fury*) (Shinoda)

1961 *Mozu* (Shibuya); *Furyo shonen* (*Bad Boys*) (Hani); *Hanjo* (Nakamura); *Mitasareta seikatsu* (*A Full Life*) (Hani)

1962 *Karami-ai* (*Heritage*) (Kobayashi); *Otoshiana* (*Pitfall*) (Teshigahara); *Namida o shishi no tategami no* (*Tears in the Lion's Mane*) (Shinoda); *Seppuku* (*Harakiri*) (Kobayashi); "Japan" ep. of *L'Amour à vingt ans* (*Love at Twenty*) (Ishihara); *Ratai* (*The Body*) (Narusawa)

1963 *Kawaita hana* (*Pale Flower*) (Shinoda); *Subarashii akujo* (*Wonderful Bad Woman*) (Onchi); *Miren* (*Regrets*) (Chiba); *Taiheiyo hitoribotchi* (*My Enemy, the Sea*; *Alone on the Pacific*) (Ichikawa) (co); *Shiro to kuro* (*Pressure of Guilt*) (Horikawa); *Koto* (*Twin Sisters of Kyoto*) (Nakamura); *Sunna no onna* (*Woman in the Dunes*) (Teshigahara); *Kanojo to kare* (*She and He*) (Hani)

1964 *Nijuissa no chichi* (*A Father at 21*) (Nakamura); "Ako" ep. of *La Fleur de l'age* (*The Adolescents*) (Teshigahara); *Ansatsu* (*Assassination*) (Shinoda); *Nihon dashutsu* (*Escape from Japan*) (Yoshida); *Te o tsunagu ko-ra* (*Children Hand in Hand*) (Hani); *Jidosha doroba* (*Car Thief*) (Wada); *Kaidan* (*Kwaidan*) (Kobayashi); *Shiroi asa* (*White Morning*) (Teshigahara—short); *Jotai* (*The Call of Flesh*) (Onchi); *Le Mystère Koumiko* (*The Koumiko Mystery*) (Marker)

1965 *Utsukushisa to kanashimi to* (*With Beauty and Sorrow*) (Shinoda); *Saigo no shinpan* (*The Last Judgment*) (Horikawa); *Ibun Sarutobi sasuke* (*Samurai Spy*) (Shinoda); *Kemonomichi* (*Beast Alley*) (Sugawa); *José Torres, Part II* (Teshigahara—doc); *Yotsuya kaidan* (*Illusion of Blood*) (Toyoda); *Buwana Toshi no uta* (*Bwana Toshi*) (Hani)

1966 *Shokei no shima* (*Punishment Island*) (Shinoda); *Monokurohmu no gaka: Yves Kline* (*Monochrome Painter Yves Kline*) (Noda); *Ki no kawa* (*Ki River*) (Nakamura); *Tanin no kao* (*The Face of Another*) (Teshigahara); *Akogare* (*Once a Rainy Day*) (Onchi)

1967 *Akanegumo* (*Clouds at Sunset*) (Shinoda); *Joi-Uchi* (*Rebellion*) (Kobayashi); *Izol no odoriko* (Onchi); *Midaregumo* (*Two in the Shadow*) (Naruse)

1968 *Meguriai* (*The Meeting*) (Onchi); *Moetikuta chizu* (*The Man without a Map*) (Teshigahara); *Nihon no seishun* (*Japanese Youth*) (Kobayashi); *Kyo* (*Kyoto*) (Ichikawa); *Hatsukoi jigokuhen* (*Nanami: Inferno of First Love*) (Hani)

1969 *Dankon* (*Bullet Wound*) (Moritani); *Shinju ten no amijima* (*Double Suicide*) (Shinoda)

1970 *Taiyo no karyudo* (*Hunter of the Sun*) (Onchi); *Dodesukaden* (*Dodeskaden*) (Kurosawa); *Yomigaeru daichi* (*The Rebirth of the Soil*) (Nakamura); *Tokyo senso sengo hiwa* (*He Died after the War*) (Oshima); *Inochi bonifuro* (*Inn of Evil*) (Kobayashi)

1971 *Gishiki* (*The Ceremony*) (Oshima); *Chinmoko* (*Silence*) (Shinoda)

1972 *Natsu no imoto* (*Dear Summer Sister*) (Oshima); *Wonder World* (Funakoshi); *Summer Soldiers* (Teshigahara); *Seigenki* (*Time without Memory*) (Narushima)

1973 *Kaseki no mori* (*The Petrified Forest*) (Shinoda)

1974 *Himiko* (Shinoda); *Shiawase* (*Happiness*) (Onchi)

1975 *Sakura no mori no mankai no shita* (*Under the Cherry Blossoms*) (Shinoda); *Kaseki* (*Fossils*) (Kobayashi)

1976 *Nihontou: Miyairi Kouhei no waza* (*Japanese Swords: The Work of Kouhei Miyairi*) (Yamauchi)

1977 *Sabita honoo* (*Rusty Flame*) (Sadanaga); *Hanare goze Orin* (*The Ballad of Orin*) (Shinoda)

1978 *Ai no borei* (*Empire of Passion*) (Oshima); *Moeru aki* (*Burning Autumn*; *Glowing Autumn*) (Kobayashi)

1979 *Le Musée du Louvre* (*The Louvre Museum*) (Uruta); *Kataku* (*This World*) (Kawamoto)

1980 *Tenpyou no iraka* (*Slates of the Tenpyo Period*) (Kumai)

1982 *Yogen* (*Prophecy*) (Hani)

1983 *Tokyo saiban* (*The Tokyo Trial*) (Kobayashi—doc)

1984 *Himatsuri* (*Fire Festival*) (Yanagimachi)

1985 *Antonio Gaudi* (Teshigahara); **Ran** (Kurosawa); *Shokutaku no nai ie* (*Family without a Dinner Table*) (Kobayashi); *Yari no Gonza* (*Gonza the Spearman*) (Shinoda)

1990 *Kuroi Ame* (*Black Rain*) (Imamura)

1991 *Rikyu* (Teshigahara)

1993 *Rising Sun* (Kaufman)

1994 *Music for the Movies: Toru Takemitsu* (Zwerin—doc) (+ ro as interviewee)

Publications

By TAKEMITSU: book—

Confronting Silence: Selected Writings, Berkeley, California, 1995.

By TAKEMITSU: article—

Cinejap (Paris), September 1978.

On TAKEMITSU: book—

Ohtake, Norike, *Creative Sources for the Music of Toru Takemitsu*, Hertfordshire, England, 1993.

On TAKEMITSU: articles—

Chaplin (Stockholm), April-May 1965.
Focus on Film (London), March-April 1970.
Ecran (Paris), September 1975.
Revue du Cinéma (Paris), September 1985.
Obituary in *Cue Sheet* (Hollywood), January 1996.
Obituary in *Variety* (New York), 26 February 1996.

*   *   *

Toru Takemitsu was not only one of the greatest contemporary Japanese composers and theoreticians of experimental music, but he was also a cinema fanatic who wrote music for more than 80 films. His film career began in the mid-1950s after he studied with the master composer Fumio Hayasaka. His first feature film was Kou Nakahira's *Crazed Fruit*, a popular film about sensational bourgeois youth, which also attracted critical attention for its refreshing sensibility.

After working on a number of films by Noboru Nakamura, a successful Shochiku Studio melodrama director, Takemitsu began to work for the most ambitious young directors of his generation such as Masahiro Shinoda, Susumu Hani, Hiroshi Teshigahara, Nagisa Oshima, and Yoshishige Yoshida, as well as master directors including Masaki Kobayashi, Kon Ichikawa and Akira Kurosawa.

Takemitsu's modern and unconventional style has greatly advanced Japanese film music. He responded to the highly experimental and stylized visual images created by Shinoda, Hani, Teshigahara, Oshima, and Yoshida with equally bold, often dissonant and avant-garde sounds. His scores compel the audience to perceive a film as a montage of visual and auditory images.

Takemitsu experimented with Japanese traditional instruments and musical concepts, as evidenced in Kobayashi's *Kwaidan* and Kurosawa's *Ran*. His use of silence and his sense of taste and timing were particularly effective in conveying suspense.

—Kyoko Hirano

TARADASH, Daniel

Writer. **Nationality:** American. **Born:** Louisville, Kentucky, 29 January 1913. **Education:** Attended Harvard University, Cambridge, Massachusetts, B.A. 1933; Harvard Law School, LL.B. 1936. **Military Service:** 1941–46—served in the United States Army in the infantry (captain), and as a writer in the Signal Corps: scripts for the *Fighting Men* series. **Family:** Married Madeleine Forbes, 1944; three children. **Career:** 1939—first film as writer, *Golden Boy*: contract with Columbia; 1977–79—President, Writers Guild of America, West, 1970–73—President, Motion Picture Academy. **Awards:** Academy Award and Writers Guild Award for *From Here to Eternity*, 1953; Writers Guild Valentine Davies Award, 1970; Morgan Cox Award, 1988; Edmund H. North Award, 1991. **Address:** 9140 Hazen Drive, Beverly Hills, California 90210, U.S.A.

Films as Writer:

1939   *Golden Boy* (Mamoulian); *For Love or Money* (Rogell)
1940   *A Little Bit of Heaven* (Marton)
1948   *The Noose Hangs High* (Barton)
1949   *Knock on Any Door* (Ray)
1952   *Rancho Notorious* (F. Lang); *Don't Bother to Knock* (Baker)
1953   **From Here to Eternity** (Zinnemann)
1954   *Desiree* (Koster)
1955   *Picnic* (Logan)
1956   *Storm Center* (+ d)
1958   *Bell, Book, and Candle* (Quine)
1965   *Saboteur: Code Name Morituri* (*Morituri*) (Wicki)
1966   *Hawaii* (Hill)
1969   *Castle Keep* (Pollack)
1971   *Doctors' Wives* (Schaeffer)
1977   *The Other Side of Midnight* (Jarrott)
1980   *Bogie* (V. Sherman—for TV)

Publications

By TARADASH: articles—

"Into Another World," in *Films and Filming* (London), no. 8, 1959.
In *Blueprint in Babylon*, by J. D. Marshall, Los Angeles, 1978.
American Film (Washington, D.C.), May 1979.
Literature/Film Quarterly (Salisbury, Maryland), vol. 29, no. 1, January 1991.

On TARADASH: articles—

Présence du Cinéma (Paris), June 1962.
Kino Lehti (Helsinki), no. 7, 1972.
Boyer, Jay, in *American Screenwriters, 2nd series*, edited by Randall Clark, Detroit, Michigan, 1986.
American Film (Washington, D.C), August 1990.
Literature/Film Quarterly (Salisbury), vol. 19, no. 1, January 1991.
The Journal: Writers Guild of America, West, (Los Angeles), April 1996.

*   *   *

Daniel Taradash's career more often suggests the lawyer he was intended to become before he started writing, than the high-priced screenwriting technician he later became. Yet the law was the ambition of his father rather than of Taradash himself, and after graduating Taradash bargained a year in New York out of him before taking up the bar. Rouben Mamoulian, looking for someone to rewrite

Clifford Odets' *Golden Boy*, picked Taradash and Lewis Maltzer out of the same playwriting course, and Taradash found himself at Columbia. After war service, he went back to become one of the few screenwriters to endure and tame the autocratic Harry Cohn.

Knock on Any Door for Bogart under Nicholas Ray's quirky direction helped build Taradash's reputation for soothing tempers and getting on with the unruly—he same skills that would make him sought after for countless committees of the Academy of Motion Picture Arts and Sciences and the Writers' Guild. He tried his skills with Broadway producer Jed Harris, but though his play *Red Gloves* ran more than 100 performances, Taradash could never endure the tyrannical producer ("I *loathed* Jed Harris. He was a terrible sadist"), and fled back to Hollywood and the equally feared Fritz Lang. However *Rancho Notorious*, a high baroque Western with Dietrich's Altar Keene queering it in tight trousers over the outlaw hideout Chuckaluck until she succumbs to the improbable charms of a young Arthur Kennedy, became a backdoor success. Also Langian in tone, *Don't Bother to Knock*, the high-point of British director Roy Ward Baker's brief Hollywood career, with Marilyn Monroe as a homicidal babysitter, won Taradash praise.

Taradash's triumph was turning *From Here to Eternity* into an acceptable screenplay. Having paid $85,000 for James Jones's erotic and profane novel of Pearl Harbour, Cohn was convinced he'd wasted his money. When Taradash asked if he could work on the adaptation at home, Cohn snapped, "With this book, you can write it in a whorehouse." But Taradash managed to find a censor-proof story in the bestseller without doing too much violence to its text. After seeing the film, which won the scriptwriter an Oscar, Jones told the producer, "Please tell Dan Taradash how much I liked it."

Thereafter, Taradash mostly occupied himself condensing fat bestsellers and "opening up" hit Broadway plays. He admitted wintry Manhattan light and air into John van Druten's witchcraft comedy *Bell, Book and Candle*, toned down the rural eroticism of William Inge's *Picnic* (as well as inserting the picnic which didn't appear in the original) and, in *Desirée*, reduced Annemarie Selinko's epic of Napoleon's love life to managable proportions for Marlon Brando. Noël Coward had planned to direct. Instead journeyman Henry Koster took over, and Brando, piqued that he was not the centre of the story, sulked his way through his lines.

In 1956, Taradash belatedly pinned his liberal heart to his sleeve when he made a failed stab at direction with *Storm Center*, a moral fable about a smalltown librarian defying local book-bumers and having the library torched for her trouble. The script had been kicking around for years. Mary Pickford had intended to star after decades of nonactivity, but dropped out. So did Irene Dunne, and Bette Davis took the part. Four years after *High Noon*, the lesson was no longer topical, and even those critics inclined to give Taradash the benefit of the doubt on the basis of his work with Lang and Ray were unimpressed. He spent 1960 and 1961 trying to adapt James Michener's sprawling *Hawaii*. His solution was to make not one film of the book but two, and sell tickets by the pair, but director Fred Zinnemann could never find funds for such a giant project. The script passed to Dalton Trumbo, the direction to George Roy Hill, and *Hawaii*, as one film, flopped.

Taradash's later credits were mostly European. Brando persuaded him to write *The Saboteur: Codename Morituri*, a rambling story of a World War II German blockade runner being chased all over the ocean by the allies with Brando as an undercover anti-Nazi on board. Bernhard Wicki's direction snuffed out what quality Brando's rewrites and improvisations left in the script. *Castle Keep*, a fable of Americans who stumble into the medieval atmosphere of a remote French castle, was a cheap small picture inflated to an $8 million dud when Burt Lancaster became involved.

Taradash did repair work on Edward Dmytryk's western *Alvarez Kelly*. He was fired from Sidney Sheldon's *The Other Side of Midnight*, though his signature remains on a script which one French critic praised as "*delirant*," perhaps out of loyalty to a film that tried, without success, to launch Marie-France Pisier as an international star. Taradash's great disappointment is that he failed to see his adaptation of *Andersonville* produced. Mackinlay Kantor's novel of the Civil War prison camp where 15,000 troops died seemed to offer the combination of epic scope and liberal politics which brought out the best in him, but no Hollywood studio would touch it. He remains a screenwriter never given his due by the film factory system he supported so vigorously.

—John Baxter

TAVOULARIS, Dean

Art Director. **Nationality:** American. **Born:** Lowell, Massachusetts, 1932. **Education:** Studied architecture at Otis Art Institute, Los Angeles. **Career:** Worked in animation department, then in live production, Walt Disney studios, before becoming art director. **Awards:** Academy Award, for *The Godfather, Part II*, 1974; British Academy Award, for *Tucker: The Man and His Dream*, 1988. **Address:** c/o Academy of Motion Picture Arts and Sciences, 8949 Wilshire Boulevard, Beverly Hills, CA 90211, U.S.A.

Film as Assistant Art Director:

1965   *Ship of Fools* (Kramer); *Inside Daisy Clover* (Mulligan)

Films as Art Director/Production Designer:

1967   ***Bonnie and Clyde*** (Penn)
1968   *Candy* (Marquand); *Petulia* (Lester)
1970   *Zabriskie Point* (Antonioni); *Little Big Man* (Penn)
1972   ***The Godfather*** (Coppola)
1974   *The Conversation* (Coppola); ***The Godfather, Part II*** (Coppola)
1975   *Farewell, My Lovely* (Richards)
1978   ***Apocalypse Now*** (Coppola); *The Brink's Job* (Friedkin)
1982   *One from the Heart* (Coppola); *The Escape Artist* (Deschanel); *Hammett* (Wenders)
1983   *The Outsiders* (Coppola); *Rumble Fish* (Coppola); *Testament* (Littman)
1986   *Peggy Sue Got Married* (Coppola)
1987   *Gardens of Stone* (Coppola); *Heat* (Richards); *Un Homme amoreux (A Man in Love)* (Kurys)
1988   *Tucker: The Man and His Dream* (Coppola)
1989   "Life without Zoe" ep. of *New York Stories* (Scorsese, Coppola and Allen)
1990   *The Godfather, Part III* (Coppola)
1992   *Final Analysis* (Joanou)
1993   *Rising Sun* (Kaufman)
1994   *I Love Trouble* (Shyer)

Dean Tavoularis (left)

1996   *Jack* (Coppola)
1998   *Bulworth* (Beatty); *The Parent Trap* (N. Meyers)
1999   *The Ninth Gate* (Polanski)
2001   *Angel Eyes*

Publications

By TAVOULARIS: article—

Positif (Paris), September 1979.
Cine, vol. 2, no. 23, March 1980.
Cineaste (New York), vol. 23, no. 4, July 1998.

*   *   *

Since the mid-1960s, the production designs of Dean Tavoularis have been particularly noteworthy of his brilliant handling of twentieth-century period settings. Tavoularis trained as an architect at the Otis Art Institute and later worked as an animator for the Disney Studios before beginning his career as an art director and, ultimately, production designer.

His most notable work has appeared in films directed by Coppola and Antonioni. In addition, Tavoularis has developed a particular working relationship with the art director Angelo Graham. Tavoularis defines the production designer as the person who "should be involved in all visual aspects of the film," as opposed to the art director, who is primarily involved in the technical aspects of settings. Graham and Tavoularis worked together throughout the 1970s on films including *The Godfather, Part II*; *Farewell, My Lovely*; and *Apocalypse Now*.

Among his early work, Tavoularis was assistant set designer on *Inside Daisy Clover*, which makes conspicuous use of abstract set designs reflecting a nostalgia for the artifice of early 1930s Hollywood musicals. These sets recall the work of designers such as Van Nest Polglase and Anton Grot, but their style is more minimal, revealing an affinity with their own time. Likewise, as art director on *Bonnie and Clyde*, Tavoularis conceived an image of the Depression era so heavily glamorized as to sacrifice all but the barest traces of historical accuracy. This romantic image was conveyed through costumes, settings, and the highly artificial rosy and golden coloring used throughout the film. Nevertheless, his sets contain something of the spirit of the age they depict, and, although the film has not worn particularly well, the look of *Bonnie and Clyde* exerted a strong and lasting influence on fashion in both dress and décor.

Set in the contemporary American west, Antonioni's *Zabriskie Point* contrasted harsh reality with nostalgic escapism—the heroine drives a 20-year-old Buick—both of which were finely represented by the exactness of details of setting, properties, and costume, all under the supervision of Tavoularis. His background in animation may have lent authenticity to the "explosion" sequence towards the end of the film in which the contents of a well-appointed modern American residence are blasted into the atmosphere in slow motion. This minute examination of domestic consumerism encapsulates the attitudes of the film towards bourgeois materialism in a time of political unrest.

Tavoularis's work moved from the somewhat naive historicism of *Bonnie and Clyde* to the more archaeologically accurate portrayal of twentieth-century styles in Coppola's *The Godfather* (both parts) in which the panoramic history of the Corleone family is set against insightful and precise backgrounds relating not only to the particular historical moment but also to the changing moods and the ethnic qualities of the narrative. *Farewell, My Lovely* continued the archaeo-logical approach even more ambitiously as Tavoularis designed the revival, in color, of a classic 1940s film noir. His masterful handling of a subdued color range and his sophisticated use of the telling detail support Tavoularis's position at the top of his profession.

—Gregory Votolato

TERRY, Paul

Animator and Producer. **Nationality:** American. **Born:** Paul Houlton Terry in San Mateo, California, 19 February 1887. **Career:** News photographer, then syndicated cartoonist for Hearst newspaper chain; 1915—joined Bray Studios as animator; 1919—formed own studio, and produced cartoon series *Aesop's Film Fables*; 1930—founded Terrytoons: collaborated with Frank Moser until 1936; after 1936, individual directors were assigned to the films; cartoon series include Farmer Al Falfa, Peg Leg Pete, Puddy the Pup, Kiko the Kangaroo, Gandy Goose, Dinky Duck, Mighty Mouse, Heckle and Jeckle, Little Roquefort, and Casper the Ghost; 1955—sold studio and films to CBS, and retired. **Died:** In New York City, October 1971.

Films as Animator and Producer with Frank Moser:

1930   *Caviar*; *Pretzels*; *Spanish Onions*; *Indian Pudding*; *Roman Punch*; *Hot Turkey*; *Hawaiian Pineapple*; *Swiss Cheese*; *Codfish Balls*; *Hungarian Goulash*; *Bully Beef*; *Kangaroo Steak*; *Monkey Meat*; *Chop Suey*; *French Fried*; *Dutch Treat*; *Irish Stew*; *Fried Chicken*; *Jumping Beans*; *Scotch Highball*; *Salt Water Taffy*; *Golf Nuts*; *Pigskin Capers*

1931   *Popcorn*; *Club Sandwich*; *Razzberries*; *Go West, Big Boy*; *Quack Quack*; *The Explorers*; *Clowning*; *Sing Sing Prison*; *The Fireman's Bride*; *The Sultan's Cat*; *A Day to Live*; *2000 B.C.*; *Blues*; *By the Sea*; *Her First Egg*; *Jazz Mad*; *Canadian Capers*; *Jesse and James*; *The Champ*; *Around the World*; *Jingle Bells*; *The Black Spider*; *China*; *The Lorelei*; *Summertime*; *Aladdin's Lamp*

1932   *The Villain's Curse*; *Noah's Outing*; *The Spider Talks*; *Peg Leg Pete*; *Play Ball*; *Ye Olde Songs*; *Bullero*; *Radio Girl*; *Woodland*; *Romance*; *Bluebeard's Brother*; *Farmer Al-falfa's Bedtime Story*; *The Mad King*; *Cocky Cockroach*; *Spring Is Here*; *Farmer Alfalfa's Ape Girl*; *Sherman Was*

Right; *Burlesque*; *Southern Rhythm*; *Farmer Alfalfa's Birth-day Party*; *College Spirit*; *Hook and Ladder Number One*; *The Forty Thieves*; *Toyland*; *Hollywood Diet*; *Ireland or Bust*

1933   *Jealous Lover*; *Robin Hood*; *Hansel and Gretel*; *Tale of a Shirt*; *Down on the Levee*; *Who Killed Cock Robin?*; *Oh Susanna*; *Romeo and Juliet*; *Pirate Ship*; *Tropical Fish*; *Cinderella*; *King Zilch*; *The Banker's Daughter*; *The Oil Can Mystery*; *Fanny in the Lion's Den*; *Hypnotic Eyes*; *Grand Uproar*; *Pick-Necking*; *Fanny's Wedding Day*; *A Gypsy Fiddler*; *Beanstalk Jack*; *The Village Blacksmith*; *Robinson Crusoe*; *Little Boy Blue*; *In Venice*; *The Sunny South*

1934   *Holland Days*; *The Three Bears*; *Rip Van Winkle*; *The Last Straw*; *The Owl and the Pussycat*; *A Mad House*; *Joe's Lunch Wagon*; *Just a Clown*; *The King's Daughter*; *The Lion's Friend*; *Pandora*; *Slow but Sure*; *See the World*; *My Lady's Garden*; *Irish Sweepstakes*; *Busted Blossoms*; *Mice in Council*; *Why Mules Leave Home*; *Jail Birds*; *The Black Sheep*; *The Magic Fish*; *Hot Sands*; *Tom, Tom the Piper's Son*; *Jack's Shack*; *South Pole or Bust*; *The Dog Show*

1935   *The First Snow*; *What a Night*; *The Bullfight*; *Fireman Save My Child*; *The Moth and the Spider*; *Old Dog Tray*; *Flying Oil*; *Peg Leg Pete the Pirate*; *A Modern Red Riding Hood*; *Five Puplets*; *Opera Night*; *King Looney XIV*; *Moan and Groans*; *Amateur Night*; *The Foxy-Fox*; *Chain Letters*; *Birdland*; *Circus Days*; *Hey Diddle Diddle*; *Foiled Again*; *Football*; *A June Bride*; *Aladdin's Lamp*; *Southern Horse-pitality*; *Ye Olde Toy Shop*; *The Mayflower*

1936   *The Feud*; *The 19th Hole Club*; *The Alpine Yodeler*; *Barnyard Amateurs*; *Off to China*; *The Western Trail*; *A Wolf in Cheap Clothing*; *Rolling Stones*; *The Runt*; *The Busy Bee*; *The Sailor's Home*; *A Tough Egg*; *Puddy the Pup and the Gypsies*; *Farmer Alfalfa's Prize Package*

Other Films as Animator and Producer:

1916   *Cat-astrophe*; *Wolfhound*

1921   *The Country Mouse and the City Mouse*; *The Fox and the Grapes*; *The Frog That Wanted a King*

1922   *The Spendthrift*; *The Eternal Triangle*; *The Model Diary*

1923   *Cat's Whiskers*

1927   *Carnival Week*

1936   *The Hot Spell* (Davis and Gordon); *Kiko and the Honey Bears* (Davis and Gordon); *The Health Farm* (Davis and Gordon); *A Bully Frog* (Davis and Gordon); *Kiko Foils a Fox* (Davis and Gordon); *Sunken Treasure* (Davis and Gordon); *A Battle Royal* (Davis and Gordon); *Robin Hood in an Arrow Escape* (Davis and Gordon); *Farmer Alfalfa's Twentieth Anniversary* (Davis and Gordon); *Cats in the Bag* (Davis and Gordon); *Slanked Again* (Davis and Gordon)

1937   *Salty McQuire* (Davis and Gordon); *The Tin Can Tourist* (Davis and Gordon); *The Book Shop* (Davis and Gordon); *The Big Game Hunt* (Davis and Gordon); *Red Hot Music* (Davis and Gordon); *Flying South* (Davis and Gordon); *The Hay Ride* (Davis and Gordon); *Bug Carnival* (Davis and Gordon); *School Birds* (Davis and Gordon); *Puddy's Coro-nation* (Davis and Gordon); *Ozzie Ostrich Comes to Town* (Davis and Gordon); *Play Ball* (Davis); *The Mechanical*

Cow (Zander); *Pink Elephants* (Gordon); *The Homeless Pup* (Gordon); *The Paper Hangers* (Davis); *Trailer Life*; *The Villain Still Pursued Her*; *Kiko's Cleaning Day* (Gordon); *A Close Shave* (Davis); *The Dancing Bear*; *The Saw Mill Mystery* (Rasinski); *The Dog and the Bone* (Gordon); *The Timid Rabbit* (Davis); *The Billy Goat Whiskers* (Foster); *The Barnyard Boss* (Rasinski)

1938 *The Lion Hunt* (Davis); *Bugs Beetle and His Orchestra* (Foster); *His Off Day* (Rasinski); *Just Ask Jupiter* (Davis); *Gandy the Goose* (Foster); *Happy and Lucky* (Rasinski); *A Mountain Romance* (Davis); *Robinson Crusoe's Broadcast* (Foster); *Maid in China* (Rasinski); *The Big Top* (Davis); *Devil of the Deep* (Foster); *Here's to Good Old Jail* (Donnelly); *The Last Indian* (Rasinski); *Milk for Baby* (Davis); *Mrs. O'Leary's Cow* (Donnelly); *Eliza Runs Again* (Rasinski); *Chris Columbo* (Donnelly); *String Bean Jack* (Foster); *Goose Flies High* (Foster); *Wolf's Side of the Story* (Rasinski); *The Glass Slipper* (Davis); *The Newcomer* (Davis); *The Stranger Rides Again* (Davis); *Housewife Herman* (Donnelly); *Village Blacksmith* (Davis); *Doomsday* (Rasinski); *The Frame-Up* (Rasinski)

1939 *The Owl and the Pussy Cat* (Donnelly); *One Gun Gary in Nick of Time* (Donnelly); *The Three Bears* (Davis); *Frozen Feet* (Rasinski); *G-Man Jitters* (Donnelly); *The Nutty Network* (Davis); *The Cuckoo Bird* (Davis); *Barnyard Eggcitement* (Rasinski); *Nick's Coffee Pot* (Rasinski); *The Prize Guest* (Davis); *A Bully Romance* (Donnelly); *Africa Squawks* (Rasinski); *Barnyard Baseball* (Davis); *Old Fire Horse* (Donnelly); *Two Headed Giant* (Rasinski); *The Golden West* (Davis); *Sheep in the Meadow* (Davis); *Hook, Line, and Sinker* (Donnelly); *The Orphan Duck* (Rasinski); *The Watchdog* (Donnelly); *One Mouse in a Million* (Rasinski); *A Wicky-Wacky Romance* (Davis); *The Hitchhiker* (Donnelly); *The Ice Pond* (Davis); *The First Robin* (Rasinski)

1940 *A Dog in a Mansion* (Donnelly); *Edgar Runs Again* (Davis); *Harvest Time* (Rasinski); *The Hare and the Hounds* (Donnelly); *All's Well That Ends Well* (Davis); *Much Ado about Nothing* (Rasinski); *It Must Be Love* (Rasinski); *Just a Little Bull* (Donnelly); *Wot's All th' Shootin, Fer* (White); *Swiss Ski Yodelers* (Donnelly); *Catnip Capers* (Davis); *Professor Offkeyski* (Rasinski); *Rover's Rescue* (White); *Rupert the Runt* (Davis); *Love in a Cottage* (White); *Billy Mouse's Akwakade* (Donnelly); *Club Life in Stone Age* (Davis); *The Lucky Duck* (Rasinski); *Touchdown Demons* (White); *How Wet Was My Ocean* (Donnelly); *Happy Haunting Grounds*; *Landing of the Pilgrims* (Rasinski); *The Magic Pencil* (White); *Plane Goofy* (Donnelly); *Snowman* (Davis); *Temperamental Lion* (Rasinski); *The Mouse of Tomorrow* (Donnelly)

1941 *What a Little Sneeze Will Do* (Donnelly); *Hairless Hector* (White); *Mississippi Swing* (Rasinski); *Fishing Made Easy* (Donnelly); *The Home Guard* (Davis); *When Knights Were Bold* (White); *The Baby Seal* (Rasinski); *Uncle Joey* (Davis); *The Dog's Dream* (Donnelly); *The Magic Shell* (Davis); *What Happens at Night* (Rasinski); *Horse Fly Opera* (Donnelly); *Good Old Irish Tunes* (Rasinski); *Bringing Home the Bacon* (Davis); *Twelve O'Clock and All Ain't Well* (Donnelly); *The Old Oaken Bucket* (Rasinski); *The Ice Carnival* (Donnelly); *The One Man Navy* (Davis); *Uncle Joey Comes to Town* (Davis); *Welcome Little Stranger*

(Rasinski); *The Frozen North* (Rasinski); *Slap Happy Hunters* (Donnelly); *Back to the Soil* (Donnelly); *The Bird Tower* (Davis); *A Yarn about Yarn* (Rasinski); *Flying Fever* (Davis)

1942 *The Torrid Toreador* (Donnelly); *Happy Circus Days* (Rasinski); *Funny Bunny Business* (Donnelly); *Cat Meets Mouse* (Davis); *Eat Me, Kitty, Eight to the Bar* (Davis); *Sham Battle Shenanigans* (Rasinski); *Oh Gentle Spring* (Rasinski); *Lights Out* (Donnelly); *Tricky Business* (Donnelly); *Neck and Neck* (Davis); *The Stork's Mistake* (Donnelly); *All about Dogs* (Rasinski); *Willful Willie* (Rasinski); *The Outpost* (Davis); *Tire Trouble* (Donnelly); *All Out for "V"* (Davis); *Life with Fido* (Rasinski); *The Big Build-Up* (Davis); *School Daze*; *Night Life in the Army* (Davis); *Doing Their Bit*; *Ickle Meets Pickle* (Rasinski); *Frankenstein's Cat* (Davis); *Barnyard WAAC* (Donnelly); *Somewhere in the Pacific* (Davis)

1943 *Scrap for Victory* (Rasinski); *He Dood It Again* (Donnelly); *Barnyard Blackout* (Davis); *Shipyard Symphony* (Donnelly); *Patriotic Pooches* (Rasinski); *The Last Round-Up* (Davis); *Pandora's Box* (Rasinski); *Mopping Up* (Donnelly); *Keep 'em Growing* (Davis); *Super Mouse Rides Again* (*Mighty Mouse Rides Again*) (Davis); *Camouflage* (Donnelly); *Somewhere in Egypt* (Davis); *Down with Cats* (Rasinski); *Aladdin's Lamp* (Donnelly); *Lion and the Mouse* (Davis); *Yokel Duck Makes Good* (Donnelly); *The Hopeful Donkey* (Davis)

1944 *The Butcher of Seville* (Donnelly); *The Helicopter* (Donnelly); *Wreck of the Hesperus* (Davis); *A Day in June* (Donnelly); *The Champion of Justice* (Davis); *The Frog and the Princess* (Donnelly); *Mighty Mouse Meets Jekyll and Hyde Cat* (Davis); *My Boy Johnny* (Donnelly); *Eliza on the Ice* (Rasinski); *Wolf! Wolf!* (Davis); *The Green Line* (Donnelly); *Carmen's Veranda* (Davis); *The Cat Came Back* (Rasinski); *The Two Barbers* (Donnelly); *The Ghost Town* (Davis); *Sultan's Birthday* (Tytle); *A Wolf's Tale* (Rasinski); *At the Circus* (Donnelly); *Gandy's Dream Girl* (Davis); *Dear Old Switzerland* (Donnell y)

1945 *Mighty Mouse and the Pirates* (Rasinski); *Port of Missing Mice* (Donnelly); *Ants in Your Pantry* (Davis); *Raiding the Raiders* (Rasinski); *Post War Inventions* (Rasinski); *Fisherman's Luck* (Donnelly); *Mighty Mouse and the Kilkenny Cats* (Davis); *Mother Goose Nightmare* (Rasinski); *Smokey Joe* (Rasinski); *The Silver Streak* (Donnelly); *Aesop's Fable: The Mosquito* (Davis); *Mighty Mouse and the Wolf* (Donnelly); *Gypsy Life* (Rasinski); *The Fox and the Duck* (Davis); *Swooming the Swooners* (Rasinski); *The Watch Dog* (Donnelly); *Who's Who in the Jungle* (Donnelly); *Mighty Mouse Meets Bad Bill Bunion* (Davis); *The Exterminator* (Donnelly); *Mighty Mouse in Krakatoa* (Rasinski)

1946 *The Talking Magpies* (Davis); *Svengali's Cat* (Donnelly); *The Fortune Hunters* (Rasinski); *The Wicked Wolf* (Davis); *My Old Kentucky Home* (Donnelly); *It's All in the Stars* (Rasinski); *Throwing the Bull* (Rasinski); *The Golden Hen* (Davis); *Dinky Finds a Home* (Donnelly); *The Johnstown Flood* (Rasinski); *Peace-Time Football* (Davis); *The Trojan Horse* (Davis); *The Tortoise Wins Again* (Rasinski); *Winning the West* (Donnelly); *The Electronic Mouse Trap* (Davis); *The Jail Break* (Donnelly); *The Snow Man* (Rasinski); *The Housing Problem* (Davis); *The Crackpot*

King (Donnelly); *The Uninvited Pests* (Rasinski); *The Hepcat* (Davis); *Beanstalk Jack* (Donnelly)

1947   *Crying Wolf* (Rasinski); *McDougal's Rest Farm* (Davis); *Deadend Cats* (Donnelly); *Happy Go Lucky* (Rasinski); *Mexican Baseball* (Davis); *Aladdin's Lamp* (Donnelly); *Cat Trouble* (Rasinski); *The Sky Is Falling* (Davis); *The Intruders* (Donnelly); *Mighty Mouse Meets Deadeye Dick* (Rasinski); *Flying South* (Davis); *Date for Dinner* (Donnelly); *Fishing by the Sea* (Rasinski); *The First Snow* (Davis); *One Note Tony* (Rasinski); *Super Salesman* (Donnelly); *A Fight to the Finish* (Rasinski); *The Wolf's Pardon* (Donnelly); *Hitch Hikers* (Rasinski); *Swiss Cheeze Family Robinson* (Davis); *Lazy Little Beaver* (Donnelly)

1948   *Felix the Fox* (Davis); *Taming the Cat* (Rasinski); *Mighty Mouse and the Magician* (Donnelly); *Gandy Goose and the Chipper Chipmunk* (Davis); *Hounding the Hares* (Donnelly); *The Feuding Hillbillies* (Rasinski); *Mystery in the Moonlight* (Donnelly); *Seeing Ghosts* (Davis); *Sleepless Night* (Rasinski); *The Witch's Cat* (Davis); *Magpie Madness* (Donnelly); *Love's Labor Won* (Davis); *The Hard Boiled Egg* (Rasinski); *The Mysterious Stranger* (Donnelly); *Triple Trouble* (Donnelly); *Out Again, in Again* (Rasinski); *Free Enterprise* (Davis); *Magic Slipper* (Davis); *Gooney Golfers* (Rasinski)

1949   *The Wooden Indian* (Rasinski); *Power of Thought* (Donnelly); *Racket Buster* (Davis); *Dingbat Land*; *Lion Hunt* (Donnelly); *Stowaways* (Rasinski); *Cold Romance* (Davis); *The Kitten Sitter* (Donnelly); *Happy Landing*; *The Catnip Gang* (Donnelly); *Hula Hula Land* (Davis); *The Lyin' Lion* (Rasinski); *Mrs. Jones' Rest Farm* (Donnelly); *The Covered Pushcart* (Davis); *A Truckload of Trouble* (Rasinski); *Perils of Pearl Pureheart* (Donnelly); *Dancing Shoes* (Davis); *Flying Cups and Saucers* (Rasinski); *Paint Pot Symphony* (Rasinski); *Stop, Look, and Listen* (Donnelly)

1950   *Comic Book Land* (Davis); *Fox Hunt* (Rasinski); *Better Late Than Never* (Donnelly); *Anti-Cats* (Davis); *Aesop's Fable*; *Foiling the Fox* (Rasinski); *The Beauty Shop* (Donnelly); *Merry Chase* (Davis); *Dream Walking* (Rasinski); *Law and Order* (Donnelly); *The Red Headed Monkey* (Davis); *All This and Rabbit Stew* (Rasinski); *The Dog Show* (Donnelly); *King Tut's Tomb* (Davis); *Cat Happy* (Rasinski); *If Cats Could Sing* (Donnelly); *Mouse and Garden* (Davis); *Beauty on the Beach* (Rasinski); *Wide Open Spaces* (Donnelly); *Sour Grapes* (Davis); *Mother Goose's Birthday Party* (Rasinski)

1951   *Rival Romeos* (Donnelly); *Squirrel Crazy* (Davis); *Three Is a Crowd* (Rasinski); *Woodman Spare That Tree* (Donnelly); *Stage Struck* (Davis); *Sunny Italy* (Rasinski); *Songs of Erin* (Rasinski); *Bulldozing the Bull* (Donnelly); *Spring Fever* (Davis); *Goons from the Moon* (Rasinski); *Musical Madness* (Donnelly); *The Elephant Mouse* (Davis); *The Rain Makers* (Rasinski); *Injun Trouble* (Donnelly); *Seasick Sailors* (Davis); *Tall Timber Tale* (Rasinski); *Aesop's Fable: Golden Egg Goosie* (Donnelly); *A Swiss Miss* (Davis); *Steeple Jacks* (Rasinski); *Little Problems* (Donnelly); *Pastry Panic* (Davis); *The Helpful Genie* (Rasinski); *'Sno Fun* (Donnelly); *A Cat's Tale* (Davis); *Beaver Trouble* (Rasinski); *The Haunted Cat* (Donnelly)

1952   *Papa's Little Helpers* (Davis); *Movie Madness* (Rasinski); *Mechanical Bird* (Donnelly); *Seaside Adventure* (Davis);

City Slicker (Davis); *Prehistoric Perils* (Rasinski); *Papa's Day of Rest* (Davis); *Flat Foot Fledgling* (Davis); *Time Gallops On* (Davis); *Off to the Opera* (Rasinski); *The Happy Cobblers* (Davis); *Hypnotized* (Davis); *Hansel and Gretel* (Rasinski); *Flipper Frolics* (Rasinski); *Little Anglers* (Rasinski); *Foolish Duckling* (Davis); *House Busters* (Rasinski); *Mysterious Cowboy* (Davis); *Happy Valley* (Donnelly); *Good Mouse Keeping* (Davis); *Nice Doggy* (Donnelly); *Happy Holland* (Donnelly); *Moose on the Loose* (Davis); *Sink or Swim* (Rasinski); *Flop Secret* (Donnelly); *Picnic with Papa* (Davis)

1953   *Soapy Opera* (Rasinski); *Thrifty Cubs* (Davis); *Hair Cut-Ups* (Donnelly); *Wise Quacks* (Davis); *Mouse Meets Bird* (Rasinski); *Snappy Snap Shots* (Donnelly); *Hero for a Day* (Davis); *Pill Peddlars* (Rasinski); *Featherweight Champ* (Donnelly); *Playful Puss* (Davis); *Plumber's Helpers* (Rasinski); *Hot Rods* (Donnelly); *Ten Pin Terrors* (Rasinski); *The Orphan Egg* (Donnelly); *Friday the 13th* (Davis); *When Mousehood Was in Flower* (Rasinski); *Open House* (Donnelly); *Bargain Daze* (Davis); *Sparky the Firefly* (Rasinski); *Mouse Menace* (Donnelly); *The Reluctant Pup* (Davis); *How to Keep Cool* (Rasinski); *Log Rollers* (Davis); *Growing Pains* (Donnelly)

1954   *Spare the Rod* (Rasinski); *Runaway Mouse* (Davis); *How to Relax* (Rasinski); *Blind Date* (Donnelly); *Nonsense Newsreel* (Davis); *Helpless Hippo* (Rasinski); *Pet Problems* (Donnelly); *Prescription for Percy* (Davis); *Satisfied Customers* (Rasinski); *Tall Tale Teller* (Rasinski); *Arctic Rivals* (Davis); *Howling Success* (Rasinski); *Pride of the Yard* (Donnelly); *Cat's Revenge* (Davis); *Reformed Wolf* (Rasinski); *Blue Plate Symphony* (Rasinski)

1955   *Barnyard Actor* (Rasinski); *A Yokohama Yankee* (Rasinski); *Duck Fever* (Rasinski); *The First Flying Fish* (Rasinski); *No Sleep for Percy* (Rasinski); *An Igloo for Two* (Rasinski); *Good Deed Daily* (Rasinski); *Bird Symphony* (Rasinski); *Phoney News Flashes* (Rasinski); *Foxed by a Fox* (Rasinski); *Last Mouse of Hamlin* (Rasinski); *Little Red Hen* (Rasinski)

Publications

On TERRY: articles—

The Cartoonist, August 1967.
Classic Film/Video Images (Muscatine, Iowa), July 1979.
Maltin, Leonard, in *Of Mice and Magic*, New York, 1980.
Griffithiana (Gemona), no. 28, December 1986.
Times Literary Supplement, 16 August 1996.

*   *   *

Paul Terry was the Kmart producer of theatrical cartoons. He was strictly a businessman and cartoons were his business. His goal was to make cartoons as inexpensively as possible. Because his cartoons were simplistic, they were produced faster, allowing Terrytoons to have more cartoons showing in the theaters. Terrytoons were cheap and uninspired. Terry ruled his kingdom with an iron hand, with ultimate control over all stories and characters. He preferred to make one-shot cartoons instead of using continuing characters like Disney and others. Outstanding creative talents were stifled at the studio, and animators of high caliber went on to greener creative pastures. Regardless of this, some memorable cartoon characters were eventually created by the Terrytoon Studios.

In 1940 Isidore Klein proposed a parody of the popular Superman series by having a fly with similar superhuman powers. Terry rejected this idea only to come back a few weeks later and propose a mouse with these superhuman powers. Thus Mighty Mouse (originally known as Super Mouse) was born in *The Mouse of Tomorrow* and Terrytoons had created its first superstar. *The Mouse of Tomorrow* told the story of a mouse who escapes from terrorizing cats. He hides out in a supermarket where he washes in Super Soap, eats Super Soup, Super Celery, and Super Cheese, and turns into Super Mouse. Then he returns to save the rest of micedom and throttle the cats. Several films were produced with the Super Mouse character until a conflict of interest developed between the cartoon and a Super Mouse comic book. So Terry changed the mouse's name to Mighty Mouse. To enhance the one-dimensional character of Mighty Mouse musical spoofs of opera were used with Mighty Mouse singing his dialogue. All of the successful formulas were used to death by Terry but the longevity of the series indicates its popularity.

In the meantime Terry had created another successful series, Heckle and Jeckle. Terry's idea was to use the look-a-like concept in a new cartoon. This was an innovative idea, never used before. Heckle and Jeckle were mischievous magpies who talked with accents, one British, the other New York, and the two were never distinguishable from one another. Heckle and Jeckle was a very self-reflexive cartoon, and the magpies often referred to their animated status. *The Power of Thought* was an entire cartoon focusing on animation of the characters. As with all of Terry's cartoons, the formula was used repeatedly. But the characters of Heckle and Jeckle were so strong that they survived repetition better than the rest.

With the success of Heckle and Jeckle and Mighty Mouse, Terry began to change his attitude about continuing characters. The studio began creating other continuing characters, some meeting with success, others failing after one or two episodes. In 1952 Terrytoons was the first studio to sell its cartoons to television. In 1955 he sold out completely to CBS, thus ending his involvement in the production of Terrytoons. Terrytoons were always simple, pleasant, and non-violent (with the possible exception of Heckle and Jeckle). They worked very well on television because although limited in the quality of animation they were considerably better than average. Terrytoons owes a great debt to television and the endurance that these cartoons have found in the medium.

—Maryann Oshana

THALBERG, Irving G.

Producer. **Nationality:** American. **Born:** Irving Grant Thalberg in Brooklyn, New York, 30 May 1899. **Family:** Married the actress Norma Shearer, 1927. **Career:** Secretary; 1918—worked as Carl Laemmle's assistant in New York office of Universal, and sent to Hollywood as troubleshooter; 1923—Vice president and head of production for Louis B. Mayer: with merger into MGM, became vice president and supervisor of production: over the next decade helped make MGM the leading film studio; mid-1930s—ill health reduced

Irving Thalberg with Gloria Swanson

his control; 1937—Motion Picture Academy instituted the Irving G. Thalberg Memorial Award. **Awards:** Academy Awards for *Grand Hotel*, 1931–32; *Mutiny on the Bounty*, 1935. **Died:** Of pneumonia in Hollywood, 14 September 1936.

Films as Producer:

1921   *Foolish Wives* (von Stroheim)
1923   *Merry-Go-Round* (Julian); *The Hunchback of Notre Dame* (Worsley)
1924   *He Who Gets Slapped* (Sjöström)
1925   *The Merry Widow* (von Stroheim); **The Big Parade** (K. Vidor); *The Great Divide* (Barker)
1926   *Ben-Hur* (Niblo)
1927   *Flesh and the Devil* (Brown)
1928   **The Crowd** (K. Vidor)
1929   **Hallelujah** (K. Vidor)
1930   *Anna Christie* (Brown); *The Big House* (Hill)
1931   *Private Lives* (Franklin); *Grand Hotel* (Goulding)
1932   *Freaks* (Browning); *Strange Interlude* (Leonard)
1933   *The Merry Widow* (Lubitsch); *The Barretts of Wimpole Street* (Franklin)
1935   *Mutiny on the Bounty* (Lloyd); *China Seas* (Garnett); **A Night at the Opera** (Wood); *Biography of a Bachelor Girl* (R. Griffith)
1936   *Romeo and Juliet* (Cukor)
1937   **Camille** (Cukor); *The Good Earth* (Franklin)

Publications

By THALBERG: articles—

Film Weekly (London), 14 July 1933.
"The Modern Photoplay," in *Journal of the Producers Guild of America* (Beverly Hills, California), June 1971.

On THALBERG: books—

Thomas, Bob, *Thalberg: Life and Legend*, New York, 1969.
Marx, Samuel, *Mayer and Thalberg: The Make-Believe Saints*, London, 1976.
Flamini, Roland, *Thalberg: The Last Tycoon and the World of M-G-M*, New York, 1994.

On THALBERG: articles—

Sight and Sound (London), Summer 1976.
Télérama (Paris), 15–21 March 1980.
Cinématographe (Paris), May 1984.
Films in Review (New York), June-July 1987.
Sight & Sound (London), no. 4, 1989.
Architectural Digest (Los Angeles), April 1990.
Sight & Sound (London), November 1994.
Film History (London), vol. 7, no. 4, Winter 1995.

*   *   *

Irving Thalberg was the head of film production at MGM during that studio's glory years of the late 1920s and early 1930s. While Louis B. Mayer ran the studio, it was Thalberg who by and large saw to it that the required feature films were regularly turned out. In his day Thalberg was hailed as boy-wonder, a genius. His years at the studio were certainly its best in terms of making money. And after his death in 1936 (at age 37) MGM slid, albeit gradually at first, down and downhill.

Despite severe health problems from birth and the lack of any significant industry connections, Thalberg took power at a remarkably early age. It was Carl Laemmle, the founder of Universal Pictures, who served as Thalberg's patron. In 1918 the nineteen year old Thalberg so impressed Laemmle that he hired him as his private secretary. A year later Laemmle appointed Thalberg studio manager at Universal City. Laemmle remained in charge in New York while his young protege supervised what was Hollywood's biggest back lot.

At Universal Thalberg quickly showed why the elder Laemmle had placed him in charge. Despite a slight build he was ruthless in terms of cutting costs. Unafraid he took on the once mighty. For example, he battled with director Erich von Stroheim on a daily basis during the making of *Foolish Wives;* during von Stroheim's next Universal project, *Merry-Go- Round*, Thalberg fired him.

Thalberg left Universal in 1923, wooed by yet another patron, Louis B. Mayer of the then forming Metro-Goldwyn-Mayer. Thalberg worked under Mayer, supervising all the great and profitable films which came out of MGM film factory from 1924 through 1936. Notably Thalberg built up a loyal staff of associate producers including Hunt Stromberg and Albert Lewin. Yet only the slick films produced near the end of his career does any one now associate with Thalberg himself: *The Barretts of Wimpole Street*, starring Thalberg's wife Norma Shearer, *The Merry Widow*, starring Maurice Chevalier and Jeanette McDonald, *Mutiny on the Bounty*, starring Clark Gable and Charles Laughton, *The Good Earth*, starring Louise Rainer, and *Camille*, starring Greta Garbo in what may have been her finest role.

In the end the long term impact of Irving Thalberg is difficult to appraise. Since he is the subject of F. Scott Fitzgerald's novel *The Last Tycoon*, Thalberg is surely the most famous movie mogul of Hollywood's Golden Age, and because of his early death one of the most nostalgically remembered. He surely ranked in the Hollywood elite as best seen in his creation of the Academy of Motion Picture Arts and Science, and its celebrated Oscars. (Thalberg provided the name for the award given to "creative producers whose body of work reflects a consistently high quality of motion picture production.")

But as the head of production for MGM for a dozen years he reported to studio chief, Louis B. Mayer, and to corporate head, Nicholas M. Schenck. Mayer and Schenck protected Thalberg and enabled him to "simply produce." Thalberg did his best work mentoring fabled stars, line producers, mediocre directors, and talented writers. Perhaps he is so fondly remembered because he alone seemed to take talent seriously, and thus represented the lone sensitive, mannered head of production in a Hollywood filled with ruthless, cut throat executives.

—Douglas Gomery

THEODORAKIS, Mikis

Composer. **Nationality:** Greek. **Born:** Chios Island, 29 July 1925. **Education:** Attended the Conservatory of Patras; Athens Conservatory; studied with Messiaen in Paris. **Family:** Married Myrto Altinoglou, 1953, children: one son and one daughter. **Career:** Arrested as a student, and deported during the Greek civil war, 1947–52; lived in Europe during most of the 1950s: first film as composer, *Barefoot Battalion*, 1953; 1961—returned to Greece, and elected to Parliament, 1963, but imprisoned by the military junta, 1967–70, and again in exile; 1974—returned to Greece again, and served as member of Parliament, 1981–85; composer of works for the theater, as well as songs and orchestral works. **Awards:** British Academy Award, for Z, 1969. **Address:** 111 rue Notre-Dame-des-Champs, 75006 Paris France.

Films as Composer:

1953 *Barefoot Battalion* (Tallas); *Eva* (Plyta)
1957 *Ill Met by Moonlight* (*Night Ambush*) (Powell and Pressburger)
1959 *Luna de miel* (*Honeymoon*) (Powell)
1960 *Faces in the Dark* (Eady)
1961 *The Shadow of the Cat* (Gilling)
1962 *Manolis* (Crosfield); *Electra* (Cacoyannis); *Phaedra* (Dassin); *Le Couteau dans la plaie* (*Five Miles to Midnight*) (Litvak); *Les Amants de Teruel* (*The Lovers of Teruel*) (Rouleau) (co)
1964 *Bloko* (*The Blockade*) (Kyrou)
1965 *Une Balle au coeur* (Pollet); *Zorba the Greek* (Cacoyannis)
1967 *The Day the Fish Came Out* (Cacoyannis)
1968 *Falak* (Kovacs)
1969 *Z* (Costa-Gavras)

1971 *État de Siège* (*State of Siege*) (Costa-Gavras); *The Trojan Women* (Cacoyannis)
1973 *Sutiejka* (Delic); *Serpico* (Lumet)
1974 *Partizani* (*Hell River*) (Jankovic); *The Story of Jacob and Joseph* (Cacoyannis)
1975 *Der Geheimnistrager* (Gottlieb)
1976 *Actas de Merusia* (Litvin); *Iphigenia* (Cacoyannis)
1979 *Asymvivastos* (*Easy Road*) (Thomopoulos); *Hell River Bad Company* (Paulou); *Kostas*
1980 *O Anthropos me to garyfallo*; *Nela* (Fischer)
1981 *Belladonna* (Rex); *The Savage Hunt* (Scavolini) (song)
1983 *Mod att leva* (Romare)
1986 *Les Clowns de dieu* (Schmidt)
1989 *Sis* (*The Mist*) (Livaneli)
1998 *Barluschke*
2000 *Fovou tous Ellines . . .* (*Beware of Greeks Bearing Arms*; *Beware of Greeks Bearing Guns*)

Publications

By THEODORAKIS: books—

Gia ten Hellenike mousike (on Greek music), Athens, 1961.
Journal de résistance, Paris, 1971, as *Journal of Resistance*, New York, 1973.
To chreos, 2 vols., Athens, 1971.
Amesa politika proviemata, London, 1972.
Culture et dimensions politiques, Paris, 1972.
Mousike gia tis mazes (on Greek music), Athens, 1972.
Les Fiancés de Pénélope: Conversations avec Denis Bourgeois, Paris, 1975.

On THEODORAKIS: books—

Holst, Gail, *Theodorakis: Myth and Politics in Modern Greek Music*, Amsterdam, 1980.
Phlessas, Giannes, *Hodoiporiko me to Mike Theodorake*, Aigokeros, 1994.

On THEODORAKIS: articles—

Focus on Film (London), Spring 1974, additions in Spring 1977.
Ecran (Paris), September 1975.
Film Score Monthly (Los Angeles), November 1993.
Soundtrack! (Hollywood), vol. 13, March 1994.

*   *   *

Although he has become recognized as much for his political involvements as for his compositions, Mikis Theodorakis has had a significant role in the development of contemporary Greek music, not only for films but in other fields as well. His film work, especially for Michael Cacoyannis and Constantin Costa-Gavras, has gained him an international reputation. Theodorakis's music combines folk-oriented pieces and traditional instrumentation with contemporary musical approaches emphasizing rhythmic dancelike pieces, and

consequently he has been most often associated with films concerning contemporary ethnic subjects.

Deported in the early 1950s because of his political convictions, Theodorakis moved to Paris where he began composing concert works as well as scores for ballet, theater, and films (primarily in England). He returned to Greece in 1961 and began his association with Cacoyannis, providing an appropriate mixture of modern musical styles and traditional Greek instrumentation to the director's updating of Greek tragedies. The score for *Electra* shows a tendency toward jazz and rock influences, while the music for *Zorba the Greek*, one of the composer's most famous scores, contains rhythmic dance pieces that capture of the spirit of the title character's more philosophical nature. *The Day the Fish Came Out* further demonstrates the composer's familiarity with rock and more experimental musical approaches which nevertheless reflect in their orchestration a nationalistic tradition.

Following his imprisonment in 1967 both his assignments and the music itself became more politically oriented. While the composer maintained his association with Cacoyannis on the film version of *The Trojan Women* and later, following Theodorakis's return to Greece, on *Iphigenia*, he also began collaborating with Costa-Gavras. Much of the score for *Z* was written while the composer was in exile and compiled from previously written material, and lends a decided specificity to the unidentified locale of the film. This, coupled with the awareness of the composer's own political activities, makes the musical messages as significant as those inherent in the script.

While *Z* made Theodorakis a logical choice for further politically oriented films, the distinct Greek inflections in his scores have not always been appropriate to the subject matter. The score for *Serpico* contains restrained passages recalling the quieter moments of *Zorba*, combined with jazzlike themes to provide a contemporary urban sound. The music tries to capture some of the main character's Italian background but much of it still maintains an atmosphere reflecting the composer's own traditions. The score for Costa-Gavras's *State of Siege* aims for an authentic folk flavor performed by South American musicians, and is particularly effective in its driving percussive passages. While such scores show only marginal ability to break away from his instant identification with a "Greek sound," Theodorakis's body of work for films as a whole serves as a reflection of that country's rich heritage, from its traditional styles to its contemporary musical development.

—Richard R. Ness

THOMSON, Virgil

Composer. **Nationality:** American. **Born:** Virgil Garnett Thomson in Kansas City, Missouri, 25 November 1896. **Education:** Attended Central High School, Junior College, Kansas City, and Harvard University, Cambridge, Massachusetts. **Career:** Childhood prodigy; music critic, *Vanity Fair*; 1928—moved to Paris, studied under Nadia Boulanger; 1933—wrote opera with the writer Gertrude Stein, *Four Saints in Three Acts*; 1936—first music for film, *The Plow That Broke the Plains*; 1940—returned to US; music critic for New York *Herald Tribune*. **Award:** Pulitzer Prize for *Louisiana Story*, 1948. **Died:** In New York, 30 September 1989.

Virgil Thomson

Films as Composer:

1936   *The Plow That Broke the Plains* (Lorentz)
1937   **The River** (Lorentz); **The Spanish Earth** (Ivens)
1945   *Tuesday in November* (Houseman)
1948   **Louisiana Story** (Flaherty)
1957   *The Goddess* (Cromwell)
1958   *Power among Men* (Hackenschmied)
1964   *Voyage to America* (Jackson—short)

Publications

By THOMSON: books—

The State of Music, New York, 1939.
The Musical Scene, New York, 1945.
The Art of Judging Music, New York, 1948.
Music Right and Left, New York, 1951.
Everbest Ever: Virgil Thomson's Correspondence with Bay Area Friends, Lanham, 1996.

On THOMSON: book—

Hoover, Kathleen, and John Cage, *Virgil Thomson: His Life and Music*, New York, 1959.
Kirkpatrick, John, *20th Century American Masters: Ives, Thomson, Sessions & Cowell*, New York, 1997.

Tommasini, Anthony, *Virgil Thomson: Composer on the Aisle*, New York, 1998.
Watson, Steven, *Prepare for Saints: Gertrude Stein, Virgil Thomson, and the Mainstreaming of American Modernism*, New York, 1999.

On THOMSON: articles—

Films and Filming (London), vol. 8, no. 3, December 1961.
New Zealand Film Music Bulletin (Invercargill), no. 36, November 1981.
Obituary in *Variety* (New York), 11 October 1989.
New Zealand Film Music Bulletin (Invercargill), no. 69, February 1990.
Wide Angle (Baltimore), no. 1, 1995.
Advocate, 8 July 1997.
Commentary, July 1997.
Music & Letters, February 1998.
Opera Quarterly, Spring 1999.

*   *   *

Virgil Thomson's reputation as a composer of film music is out of all proportion to his output. He wrote scores for only eight movies, six of them documentaries. Yet these scores—and two of them in particular—exerted a lasting influence on the development of 20th-century American music, not only for films but in the concert hall as well.

Born in Missouri, Thomson studied during the 1920s with Nadia Boulanger in Paris, revelling in the musical and artistic ferment of the era. Invited in 1936 to provide a score for Pare Lorentz's documentary, *The Plow That Broke the Plains*, he responded with music that treated indigenous American folk themes with a wit, litheness and affectionate irony learnt from Satie and the composers of Les Six, creating an engaging blend of naivety and sophistication.

Lorentz's film, commissioned by the US Department of Agriculture, dealt with the Dustbowl disaster of the American Midwest, when thousands were driven off the land by economic and ecological breakdown. Working closely with Lorentz—and virtually for nothing, since the director had long since overspent his minuscule budget—Thomson wove further strands of association around the film's evocative images. For the arrival of cattle on the high plains, banjo and guitar pick out the plangent melancholy of cowboy songs like ''Streets of Laredo,'' while scenes of rampant financial speculation are treated to a raunchy, sardonic blues, vibrant with saxophones, that recalls the Weill of *Dreigroschenoper*.

Thomson's score for *The Plow* reached wider audiences through the orchestral suite he drew from it, and so did the music for his second collaboration with Lorentz. Backed, like its predecessor, by Roosevelt's New Deal Administration, *The River* sketched a brooding, elegiac account of the Mississippi valley, culminating in a celebration of Roosevelt's pet scheme, the Tennessee Valley Authority. Once again Thomson's score set off the images—and Lorentz's incantatory script—with a piquant mix of original material and indigenous melodies: hymn-tunes, spirituals and popular songs, including (for scenes of booming industrial expansion) an uproarious handling of ''Hot Time in the Old Town Tonight.''

To Aaron Copland, Thomson's score for *The River* provided ''a lesson in how to treat Americana.'' Its influence can be heard in

Copland's own ballet scores—*Rodeo, Billy the Kid, Appalachian Spring*—as well as in the work of associated composers such as Roy Harris and Walter Piston. But in the specific field of film music Thomson's two scores for Lorentz established an alternative mode to the lush Germanic romanticism then prevalent in Hollywood movies. Not only through Copland's own film scores (and via Copland, those of his followers such as Bernard Herrmann and Alex North) but for American film music in general Thomson set out options of concision and spareness, of a clean, sharply-etched idiom rather than an overall impressionistic haze.

"The movie," Thomson once wrote, "is a true musical form, as truly a musical form as the opera, though without the opera's inseparable marriage of music to words." Nowhere was his theory better demonstrated than in his score for Flaherty's *Louisiana Story*. The film, financed by Standard Oil, showed the coming of oil prospectors to the swamp wilderness of the bayous, seen through the eyes of a native Cajun boy. Drawing this time on an anthology of Cajun folk song, Thomson clothed the haunting melodic lines in a rich variety of instrumental texture, combining them as before with original passages of his own. Though employing complex formal devices—a twelve-tone chorale, a passacaglia, a chromatic double fugue—the music never seems academic, nor loses the simplicity and rhythmic freedom appropriate to its basic material and to Flaherty's lyrical images.

Thomson's score for *Louisiana Story* won him a Pulitzer Prize, the first Pulitzer award ever granted to a film score. Once again he adapted the music for concert use, deriving from it two separate orchestral suites and a ballet, *The Bayou*.

The only feature film Thomson scored was *The Goddess*, the rise to fame of a Monroesque Hollywood star directed by John Cromwell from a script by Paddy Chayefsky. Less distinctive than his documentary work, the music suggests that Thomson felt hampered by composing for fiction film, with its limited scope for elongated lines and symphonic development. Even so, *The Goddess* allowed him to exercise his talent for spot-on pastiche. At various points in the film (which covers the years 1928–58) a radio is turned on and jazz emerges, each time perfectly in period in its style and instrumentation. Yet all of it is Thomson's original work—further evidence of his exact and appreciative ear for indigenous American music of every kind.

—Philip Kemp

TIOMKIN, Dimitri

Composer. **Nationality:** American. **Born:** St. Petersburg, Russia, 10 May 1899; emigrated to the United States, 1925; naturalized citizen, 1937. **Education:** Attended St. Petersburg Conservatory and St. Petersburg University; studied with Glazunov and Blumenthal in St. Petersburg and with Petri, Zadora, and Busoni in Berlin. **Family:** Married 1) the ballerina and choreographer Albertina Rasch, 1925 (died 1967); 2) Olivia Cynthia Patch, 1972. **Career:** Composer and pianist in Berlin and Paris during the 1920s (played European premier of Gershwin's Concerto, 1928); 1929–68—lived in Hollywood; music director, Signal Corps films during World War II; 1968—settled in London. **Awards:** Academy Award, for *High Noon* and the song "High Noon," 1951, *The High and the Mighty*, 1954, and *The*

Old Man and the Sea, 1958. Chevalier, Legion of Honor. **Died:** London, 12 November 1979.

Films as Composer:

1929   *Devil May Care* (Franklin) (co)
1930   *Our Blushing Brides* (Beaumont); *The Rogue Song* (L. Barrymore) (co); *Lord Byron of Broadway* (Nigh and Beaumont) (co)
1931   *Resurrection* (Carewe)
1933   *Broadway to Hollywood* (Mack) (co); *Alice in Wonderland* (McLeod)
1934   *Roast-Beef and Movies* (Bearwitz—short)
1935   *Naughty Marietta* (Van Dyke) (co); *The Casino Murder Case* (Marin); *I Live My Life* (Van Dyke); *Mad Love* (*The Hands of Orlac*) (Freund)
1936   *Mr. Deeds Goes to Town* (Capra)
1937   *Lost Horizon* (Capra); *The Road Back* (Whale)
1938   *Spawn of the North* (Hathaway); *The Great Waltz* (Duvivier); *You Can't Take It with You* (Capra)
1939   *Only Angels Have Wings* (Hawks); **Mr. Smith Goes to Washington** (Capra)
1940   *Lucky Partners* (Milestone); *The Westerner* (Wyler)
1941   *Meet John Doe* (Capra); *Forced Landing* (Wiles); *The Corsican Brothers* (Ratoff); *Scattergood Meets Broadway* (*Blonde Menace*) (Cabanne); *Flying Blind* (McDonald)
1942   *A Gentleman after Dark* (Marin); *Twin Beds* (Whelan); *The Moon and Sixpence* (Lewin); *Shadow of a Doubt* (Hitchcock)
1942–45   **Why We Fight** series (Capra and Litvak)
1943   *Unknown Guest* (Neumann)
1944   *The Imposter* (Duvivier); *The Bridge of San Luis Rey* (Lee); *Ladies Courageous* (Rawlins); *When Strangers Marry* (*Betrayed*) (Castle); *The Battle of San Pietro* (Huston); *Forever Yours* (Nigh)
1945   *Dillinger* (Nosseck); *China's Little Devils* (Bell); *Pardon My Past* (Fenton)
1946   *Whistle Stop* (Moguy); *Black Beauty* (Nosseck); *Angel on My Shoulder* (Mayo); *The Dark Mirror* (Siodmak); *Duel in the Sun* (K. Vidor); **It's a Wonderful Life** (Capra)
1947   *The Long Night* (Litvak)
1948   *Tarzan and the Mermaids* (Florey); *The Dude Goes West* (Neumann); *So This Is New York* (Fleischer); **Red River** (Hawks); *Portrait of Jennie* (Dieterle)
1949   *Canadian Pacific* (Marin); *Champion* (Robson); *Home of the Brave* (Robson); *Red Light* (Del Ruth)
1950   *Dakota Lil* (Selander); *Guilty Bystander* (Lerner); *Champagne for Caesar* (Whorf); *D.O.A.* (Maté); *The Men* (Zinnemann); *Mr. Universe* (Lerner); *Cyrano de Bergerac* (Gordon)
1951   *The Thing* (*The Thing from Another World*) (Nyby); **Strangers on a Train** (Hitchcock); *Peking Express* (Dieterle); *The Well* (Popkin and Rouse); *Drums in the Deep South* (Menzies); *Bugles in the Afternoon* (Rowland); **High Noon** (Zinnemann)
1952   *Mutiny* (Dmytryk); *My Six Convicts* (Fregonese); *Lady in the Iron Mask* (Murphy); *The Happy Time* (Fleischer); *The Big Sky* (Hawks); *The Four Poster* (Reis); *The Steel Trap* (Stone); *Angel Face* (Preminger); *I Confess* (Hitchcock);

Return to Paradise (Robson); *Jeopardy* (J. Sturges); *Blowing Wild* (Fregonese)
1953   *Take the High Ground* (Brooks); *Cease Fire!* (Crump); *Dial M for Murder* (Hitchcock)
1954   *His Majesty O'Keefe* (Haskin); *The Command* (Butler); *The High and the Mighty* (Wellman); *A Bullet Is Waiting* (Farrow); *The Adventures of Hajji Baba* (Weis); *Strange Lady in Town* (LeRoy)
1955   *Land of the Pharoahs* (Hawks); *The Court-Martial of Billy Mitchell* (Preminger)
1956   **Giant** (Stevens); *Friendly Persuasion* (Wyler); *Tension at Table Rock* (Warren)
1957   *Gunfight at the O.K. Corral* (J. Sturges); *Night Passage* (Nielson); *Search for Paradise* (O. Lang); *The Young Land* (Tetzlaff); *Wild Is the Wind* (Cukor)
1958   *The Old Man and the Sea* (J. Sturges)
1959   **Rio Bravo** (Hawks); *Last Train from Gun Hill* (J. Sturges)
1960   *The Unforgiven* (Huston); *The Alamo* (Wayne); *The Sundowners* (Zinnemann)
1961   *The Guns of Navarone* (Lee Thompson); *Town without Pity* (Reinhardt); *Without Each Other* (Swimmer)
1963   *55 Days at Peking* (N. Ray)
1964   *The Fall of the Roman Empire* (A. Mann); *Circus World* (Hathaway)
1965   *36 Hours* (Seaton)
1967   *The War Wagon* (Kennedy)
1968   *Great Catherine* (Flemyng); *Tchaikovsky* (+ d, exec pr)

Film as Co-Producer:

1969   *Mackenna's Gold* (Lee Thompson)

Publications

By TIOMKIN: book—

With P. Buranelli, *Please Don't Hate Me* (autobiography), New York, 1959.

By TIOMKIN: articles—

"Composing for Films," in *Films in Review* (New York), November 1951.
Etude (Philadelphia), February 1953.
Music Journal (New York), April 1955.
"Writing Symphonically for the Screen," in *Music Journal* (New York), January 1959.
"The Music of Hollywood," in *Music Journal* (New York), November/December 1962.
Cinema (Los Angeles), July 1966.
In *Film Score*, edited by Tony Thomas, South Brunswick, New Jersey, 1979.

On TIOMKIN: books—

Elley, Derek, *Dmitri Tiomkin: The Man and His Music*, London, 1986.
McIntosh, *High Noon—Friendly Persuasion & More Classic Themes by Dimitri Tiomkin*, Miami, 1993.

On TIOMKIN: articles—

Performing Right (London), May 1970.
"Tiomkin's Tchaikovsky," in *Musical Opinion* (Luton, Bedfordshire), 1971.
"The Music of Dimitri Tiomkin," in *Film* (London), Winter 1971.
Film (London), Spring 1972.
Thomas, Tony, in *Music for the Movies*, South Brunswick, New Jersey, 1973.
Ecran Fantastique (Paris), no. 6, 1978.
Film Music Notebook (Calabasas, California), vol. 4, no. 2, 1978.
Cinéma (Paris), January 1980.
Cinema 2002 (Madrid), January 1980.
Rivista del Cinematografo (Rome), May 1980.
Fistful of Soundtracks (London), October 1980.
Fistful of Soundtracks (London), November 1981.
Lacombe, Alain, in *Hollywood*, Paris, 1983.
National Film Theatre Booklet (London), February 1986.
Sight and Sound (London), Spring 1986.
Soundtrack! (Hollywood), March 1986.
Palmer, Christopher, in *The Composer in Hollywood*, London, 1990.
Cue Sheet (Hollywood), no. 3/4, 1993/1994.
Brown, Royal S., in *Cineaste* (New York), Winter-Spring 1995.
Soundtrack! (Hollywood), March 1996.
Film Score Monthly (Los Angeles), June 1996.
Films in Review (New York), January-February 1997.

*   *   *

On receiving an Academy Award in 1955 for *The High and the Mighty*, Dimitri Tiomkin began his acceptance speech by saying "I would like to thank Beethoven, Brahms, Wagner, Strauss, Rimsky-Korsakov." That the audience greeted this as a joke and roared with laughter accordingly is not surprising, for Tiomkin, his pronounced Russian accent untouched by years in America, enjoyed a reputation as a flamboyant, larger-than-life character. Nor is it surprising that Tiomkin should protest that he was, in fact, deadly serious, for though he was the consummate Hollywood professional, his roots, like so many Hollywood composers of his generation, belonged in the European classical tradition.

Tiomkin was trained in Tsarist Russia, studying under Alexander Glazunov at the St. Petersburg Conservatory. He had his first brush with the movies at this time, working in a cinema playing the piano to accompany silent films. After the revolution he studied under Busoni in Berlin. Subsequently he moved between Paris (where he gave the first European concert performance of Gershwin's *Concerto in F*) and America, where he eventually settled. The first film for which he was solely responsible for the music was Norman Z. McLeod's *Alice in Wonderland*, but his first major break came when Frank Capra asked him to compose the music for *Lost Horizon*, the film based on James Hilton's Utopian fantasy about the lost kingdom of Shangri-La. Tiomkin's lush, oriental pastiche, with its clustered woodwinds and angelic choirs, was enormously successful at the time, but opinion has been divided as to its merits. Irving Bazelon, in his book *Knowing the Score*, notes that though the film is set in Tibet "not one note of Tibetan music appears on the soundtrack," while William H. Rosar, in an essay analyzing Tiomkin's work for the film argues that the score "contributed much to the film's faraway mood and enchantment." Capra expressed no reservations: "Tiomkin's music not only captured the mood, it damn near captured the film." Tiomkin became

857

Capra's favored composer, and worked with him on *Mr. Smith Goes to Washington*, *Meet John Doe*, *You Can't Take It With You*, and *It's a Wonderful Life*, as well as more than 20 wartime documentaries, supervised by Capra and directed by Capra, John Huston, Anatole Litvak, and Joris Ivens.

In his four decades as a composer for Hollywood, Tiomkin covered the entire spectrum of film music, from film noir to comedy, from Western to melodrama. He freely incorporated elements from the romantic European tradition and from American folk music. While something of a musical conservative (''For mass appeal, melody is the important thing. . . . To hell with musical intellectuals. Who cares about them?''), he could be adventurous when adapting to the requirements of the film. He showed a surprising affinity for the Western, scoring films by Howard Hawks, John Sturges, King Vidor's *Duel in the Sun*, William Wyler's *Friendly Persuasion*, and winning two Oscars for Fred Zinnemann's *High Noon*. When asked how a Russian could write for a Western, Tiomkin's characteristic response was ''Did our producer on *Red River* know how to lasso a steer?'' *High Noon* perhaps shows Tiomkin at his most effective—a simple score featuring harmonica—building tension through repetition. The ballad, with lyrics by Ned Washington, which runs through the film, comments on the story, as if the events taking place on the screen have already passed into oral history. The song became a hit in its own right, which, in turn, helped boost the film commercially. Tiomkin continued to develop the ballad form in subsequent films, using it even more ambitiously in John Sturges's *Gunfight at the O.K. Corral*. He also provided the score for *Rio Bravo*, Howard Hawks's answer to the implied pacifism of *High Noon*. The featured ballad, sung during the film by Rick Nelson, is an echo of Tiomkin's earlier score for Hawks's *Red River*.

Tiomkin was philosophical about the loss of his earlier aspirations as a concert composer. He immersed himself in the new art of creating music for the cinema, apparently at ease with the imposed commercial criteria. In his genial autobiography *Please Don't Hate Me*, Tiomkin offers this sober assessment of his talent, ''I could never have been a Beethoven, Chopin, or Wagner . . . had I devoted myself to composition in the concert field I think I might have been as good as Rachmaninov . . . I've gone over to the technology of motion pictures, music for the masses, music for the machine in an age of machines.''

Tiomkin's long and prolific career, embracing myriad musical styles for a wide variety of films, defies easy assessment. He could create rousing Western scores for films such as *Red River* and *The Big Sky*, or bring out simple touches of Americana, as in *Friendly Persuasion*. He provided effective scores for Alfred Hitchcock, notably with a series of sinister variations on the ''Merry Widow Waltz'' for *Shadow of a Doubt*. He could also lapse into moments of vulgarity—his powerful score for Rudolph Maté's doom-laden film noir, *D.O.A.*, is marred by the bizarre intrusion of the sliding woodwind wolf whistle that marks the appearance of a pretty woman. His relations with directors were not always trouble-free; Fred Zinnemann was upset by what he considered an intrusive, inappropriate score for *The Men*, the story of crippled World War II veterans, and Howard Hawks apparently dropped Tiomkin from *Hatari!* because he refused to use authentic African instruments.

In addition to the two Oscars (for score and song) for *High Noon*, Tiomkin received Academy Awards for *The High and the Mighty* and *The Old Man and the Sea*. In his autobiography he offered this unsentimental description of his work for the movies: ''I followed the changes in progressive jazz. When calypso came along I wrote in the

West Indian vein. I could write rock and roll if necessary. In Hollywood vernacular, I could write commercial.''

—Dominic Power

TISSE, Edward

Cinematographer. **Nationality:** Russian. **Born:** Edward Kazimirovich Tisse in Lithuania, 13 April 1897. **Career:** Newsreel cameraman; 1918—photographer on the ''agit-trains'' during the Russian Revolution (footage used by both Esther Shub and Dziga Vertov); photographed the first Soviet film, *Signal*; worked with Sergei Eisenstein during his entire career, and accompanied him to Western Europe and the United States, photographed documentary or chronicle films *Warm Company*, *Kino-Pravda no. 21* (*Cine-Truth about Lenin*), *The Kremlin Past and Present*, *Face the Village*, *From Ore to Rail*, *Poisonous Gases*, and Roman Karman's film on the Kara-Kum expedition. **Died:** In Moscow 18 November 1961.

Films as Cinematographer:

1918   *Signal* (Arkatov) (co)
1921   *Serp i molet* (*Sickel and Hammer*) (Gardin); *Golod . . . golod . . . golod* (*Hunger . . . Hunger . . . Hunger*) (Pudovkin and Gardin)

Edward Tisse

1924   *Starets Vasili Gryaznov* (*Elder Vasili Gryaznov*) (Sabinsky)
1925   *The Gold Reserve* (Gardin); **Stachka** (*Strike*) (Eisenstein) (co); **Bronenosets Potemkin** (*Battleship Potemkin*) (Eisenstein)
1926   *Medvezhya svadba* (*The Bear's Wedding*) (Gardin and Eggert) (co)
1928   **Oktiabr** (*October; Ten Days That Shook the World*) (Eisenstein)
1929   *Staroie i novoie* (*Old and New; The General Line*) (Eisenstein)
1930   *Romance sentimentale* (Eisenstein and Alexandrov); *Frauennot-Frauenglück*(+ d)
1931   *Que Viva Mexico!* (Eisenstein—unfinished; various films edited from this footage include *Thunder over Mexico, Death Day, Eisenstein in Mexico, Time in the Sun*, and others)
1935   *Aerogard* (*Air City; Frontier*) (Dovzhenko) (co)
1938   **Alexander Nevsky** (Eisenstein)
1939   *The Ferghana Canal* (Eisenstein)
1944   **Ivan Grozny** (*Ivan the Terrible, Part I*) (Eisenstein) (co)
1946   *In the Mountains of Yugoslavia* (Room)
1949   *Vsetrecha na Elba* (*Meeting on the Elbe*) (Alexandrov)
1952   *Kompozitor Glinka* (*Glinka; Man of Music*) (Alexandrov)
1956   *The Immortal Garrison* (+ co-d)
1958   *Ivan Grozny II: Boyarskii Zagover* (*Ivan the Terrible, Part II: The Boyars' Plot*) (Eisenstein—produced 1946) (co)

Publications

By TISSE: articles—

On *Old and New* in *Sovietsky Ekran* (Moscow), 11 December 1926.
Iskusstvo Kino (Moscow), no. 2, 1929.
Sovietsky Ekran (Moscow), 25 January 1929.
Cinema Nuovo (Turin), October 1956.
Film und Fernsehen (Berlin), no. 3, 1980.

On TISSE: articles—

Films in Review (New York), January 1954.
Iskusstvo Kino (Moscow), no. 12, 1961.
Focus on Film (London), no. 13, 1973.
Film und Fernsehen (Berlin), no. 1, 1978.
American Cinematographer (Hollywood), July 1991.
Iskusstvo Kino (Moscow), August 1996.

*   *   *

Edward Tisse is best known for his work with director Sergei Eisenstein. Tisse was, however, among the pioneers of the Soviet cinema, working with such people as Vertov and Pudovkin before his long, successful partnership with Eisenstein began. His early career as a newsreel cameraman on World War and Russian Civil War fronts earned him a reputation as both a skilled and fearless technician. He participated in newsreel and feature film projects which would later be viewed as the beginnings of a new Russian cinema.

Tisse headed the film crew of the first "agit-train," a train staffed and equipped to produce printed materials, plays, and films specifically for the moral support of the Red Army troops. In addition, he photographed what is sometimes referred to as the first "Soviet"

feature film—director Alexander Arkatov's *Signal*. The film was the first feature produced by the Moscow branch of the Cinema Committee, the first Soviet Russia film organization. Tisse's demonstrated skill with both newsreel footage and features, his bold personality, and his enthusiasm for experimentation led to a collaboration which spanned almost a quarter of a century. In 1923, Tisse was selected to photograph Eisenstein's first film, *Strike*.

The realization of *Strike* was due to a great extent to Tisse. He not only possessed the technical knowledge which Eisenstein lacked at the time, but also understood and agreed with the director's "montage of attractions." The partnership continued to develop with the shooting of Eisenstein's second feature, *Battleship Potemkin*. The two artists complemented each other. Tisse was inspired to further experimentation with the technology at his disposal to make Eisenstein's artistic vision a filmic reality. For the Odessa Steps sequence, Tisse set up a camera trolley the length of the steps, creating one of the first dolly shots in Russian film history. The origins of what would become conventions of documentary film technique are also visible in scenes like the one shot in an actual ship's engine room.

Tisse continued to work with Eisenstein on *Old and New* (*The General Line*) and *October*. Eisenstein's detailed planning of each film coupled with the fact that director and cameraman understood each other so well made it possible for Tisse to shoot scenes with the eventual juxtaposition of images in mind. This facilitated editing of every montage sequence but was particularly beneficial in the production of *October*, with its numerous and complex intellectual montage sequences.

During the early 1930s Tisse left Russia to travel with Eisenstein through Europe, America, and Mexico. The official reason for the trip was the study of sound film techniques in other countries. In addition to this pursuit, other projects were undertaken. Much time was devoted to researching and filming Eisenstein's never completed *Que Viva Mexico!* Also during this period, Tisse directed a feature-length film on abortion while in Switzerland.

Upon returning to Russia, Tisse resumed his experimentation with tone and emotional tension begun in earlier films. He had previously used shades of light and darkness and different degrees of soft focus to create emotional tension. He perfected these techniques during Eisenstein's sound film period. Tisse's mastery of tonal composition is best demonstrated in *Alexander Nevsky*. In one exemplary sequence the choice of lenses and the use of a special filter transformed the atmosphere of a hot July day into the "Battle on the Ice." In this particular scene Tisse also slowed down the hand-cranked camera to control the rhythm and the tension of the battle. He utilized similar methods in photographing the exterior scenes for both parts of *Ivan the Terrible*, Eisenstein's final films.

—Marie Saeli

TODA, Jusho

Art Director. **Nationality:** Japanese. **Born:** Tokyo, 1928. **Education:** Studied painting and sculpture at Junior High School of Aoyama Gakuin University; studied industrial design in the army. **Military Service:** Served in the Japanese army during World War II. **Career:** 1945–46—engineer for Hokkaido University; then a painter and sculptor, and architect and industrial designer; 1953—assistant art director: worked with Hiroshi Mizutani and Kisaku Ito; 1962—first film as art director, *The Entanglement*; 1966—first of several films for Nagisa Oshima. **Died:** 1 February 1987.

Films as Art Director:

1962   *Karami-ai* (*The Entanglement*) (Kobayashi); *Sanga ari* (*There Are Mountains and Rivers*) (Matsuyami); *Seppuku* (*Harakiri*) (Kobayashi)

1963   *Kawaita hana* (*Pale Flower*) (Shinoda)

1964   *Kaidan* (*Kwaidan*) (Kobayashi)

1966   *Shokei no shima* (*Punishment Island*) (Shinoda); *Hakuchu no torima* (*Violence at Noon*) (Oshima)

1967   *Akanegumo* (*Clouds at Sunset*) (Shinoda); *Nippon shunka-ko* (*A Treatise on Japanese Rowdy Songs*) (Oshima); *Murishinju: Nippon no natsu* (*Japanese Summer: Double Suicide*) (Oshima)

1968   **Koshikei** (*Death By Hanging*) (Oshima); *Kaettekita yopparai* (*Three Resurrected Drunkards*) (Oshima)

1969   *Shinjuku dorobo nikki* (*Diary of a Shinjuku Thief*) (Oshima); **Shonen** (*Boy*) (Oshima)

1970   *Buraikan* (*The Scandalous Adventures of Buraikan*) (Shinoda); *Tokyo senso sengo hiwa* (*The Man Who Left His Will on Film*) (Oshima)

1971   *Gishiki* (*The Ceremony*) (Oshima)

1972   *Nasu no imoto* (*Summer Sister*) (Oshima)

1974   *Ranru no hata* (*Ragged Flag*) (Yoshimura)

1976   *Ai no corrida* (*In the Realm of the Senses*) (Oshima)

1978   *Ai no borei* (*Empire of Passion*) (Oshima)

1983   *Senjo no merii kurisumasu* (*Merry Christmas, Mr. Lawrence*) (Oshima)

1985   *Shokutaku no nai ie* (*The Family without a Dinner Table*) (Kobayashi)

Publications

On TODA: article—

Obituary in *Revue du Cinéma* (Paris), no. 427, May 1987.

*   *   *

Jusho Toda was one of the most imaginative production designers in Japan. He was first acclaimed for the ambitious set design of Masaki Kobayashi's *Seppuku*, for which he created appropriately striking black-and-white backgrounds to highlight the powerful story of a struggle between samurai. The Daliesque images he created for Kobayashi's *Kwaidan*, such as a pair of eyes in an orange-yellow sky and a palace floating over the smoke on colorful waters, were particularly noted for the audacious quality they gave to this anthology of ghost stories.

Nagisa Oshima invited the eccentric art director to join his filmmaking group, and their collaboration has continued for two decades, from *Violence at Noon* to *Merry Christmas, Mr. Lawrence*. Challenged by the budgetary limitations of Oshima's independent productions, Toda created ingenious settings for the spontaneous and radical ideas of this ideologically conscious director. Parts of the sets in *Death By Hanging* were made out of newspapers; similarly, many sets in other Oshima films use abstract plastic shapes to emphasize

theatricality. The altars he often used in both interior and exterior scenes were similar to those of the Shinto religion, and gave a ritualistic quality. One of the most idiosyncratic of the images he created for Oshima is the Japanese national flag whose "Rising Sun" in the center is painted in black, a symbol of the dark side of authority.

The sets Toda designed for Oshima's *In the Realm of the Senses*, *Empire of Passion*, and *Merry Christmas, Mr. Lawrence*, are comparatively realistic but nonetheless help create the powerful atmosphere of passionate love, violence, and abstract eroticism.

Toda was also responsible for the simple yet striking black-and-white interior settings for the gambling scenes of Masahiro Shinoda's *Pale Flower*, as well as for the elaborate color schemes of the director's *The Scandalous Adventures of Buraikan*. Toda was also acclaimed for the solemn interiors he created for Kobayashi's serious family drama, *The Family without a Dinner Table*.

—Kyoko Hirano

TOLAND, Gregg

Cinematographer. **Nationality:** American. **Born:** Charleston, Illinois, 29 May 1904. **Military Service:** 1941–45—photographer and camera designer for Navy Photographic Unit and Office of Strategic Services. **Family:** Married the actress Virginia Thorpe, 1945. **Career:** Messenger boy, then camera assistant to Al St. John at William Fox Studio; later, assistant to Arthur Edeson; 1926—began

Gregg Toland

long-term association with Goldwyn Studio; 1929—first film as co-cinematographer (with George Barnes), *This Is Heaven*; he and Barnes designed "blimp" to replace the immobile sound-proof camera booth. **Awards:** Academy Awards for *Wuthering Heights*, 1939; *December 7th* (documentary), 1943. **Died:** Of heart attack in West Hollywood, 28 September 1948.

Films as Co-Cinematographer with George Barnes:

1929   *This Is Heaven* (Santell); *Bulldog Drummond* (Jones); *Condemned* (Ruggles); *The Trespasser* (Goulding)

1930   *Whoopee!* (Freeland) (co); *Raffles* (D'Arrast); *One Heavenly Night* (Fitzmaurice)

Films as Cinematographer:

1931   *The Devil to Pay* (Fitzmaurice); *The Unholy Garden* (Fitzmaurice); *Indiscreet* (McCarey) (co); *Tonight or Never* (LeRoy); *Palmy Days* (Sutherland)

1932   *Playgirl* (Enright); *Man Wanted* (Dieterle); *The Tenderfoot* (Enright); *The Washington Masquerade* (Brabin); *The Kid from Spain* (McCarey)

1933   *The Nuisance* (Conway); *Tugboat Annie* (LeRoy); *The Masquerader* (Wallace); *Roman Scandals* (Tuttle)

1934   *Jazz River* (Seitz); *Forsaking All Others* (Van Dyke) (co); *Nana* (Arzner); *We Live Again* (Mamoulian)

1935   *The Wedding Night* (Vidor); *Public Hero No. 1* (Ruben); *Les Miserables* (Boleslawsky); *Mad Love* (Freund) (co); *The Dark Angel* (Franklin); *Splendor* (Nugent)

1936   *Strike Me Pink* (Taurog) (co); *These Three* (Wyler); *Come and Get It* (Hawks and Wyler) (co); *The Road to Glory* (Hawks); *Beloved Enemy* (Potter)

1937   *History Is Made at Night* (Borzage); *Woman Chases Man* (Blystone); *Dead End* (Wyler)

1938   *The Goldwyn Follies* (Marshall); *Kidnapped* (Werker); *The Cowboy and the Lady* (Potter)

1939   *Wuthering Heights* (Wyler); *They Shall Have Music* (Mayo); *Intermezzo: A Love Story* (Ratoff)

1940   *Raffles* (Wood); ***The Grapes of Wrath*** (Ford); *The Westerner* (Wyler); *The Long Voyage Home* (Ford)

1941   ***Citizen Kane*** (Welles); ***The Little Foxes*** (Wyler); *Ball of Fire* (Hawks)

1943   *December 7th* (+ co-d); *The Outlaw* (Hughes)

1946   *The Kid from Brooklyn* (McLeod); *Song of the South* (Foster and Jackson); ***The Best Years of Our Lives*** (Wyler)

1947   *The Bishop's Wife* (Koster); *A Song Is Born* (Hawks)

1948   *Enchantment* (Reis)

Publications

By TOLAND: articles—

On *Citizen Kane* in *American Cinematographer* (Hollywood), February 1941.

On *Citizen Kane* in *Popular Photoplay* (New York), June 1941.

"Motion Picture Cameraman," in *Theatre Arts* (New York), September 1941.

Revue du Cinéma (Paris), January 1947.

Screenwriter (London), December 1947.

With G. Turner, "Xanadu in Review: *Citizen Kane* Turns 50," in *American Cinematographer* (Hollywood), August 1991.

On TOLAND: articles—

Blaisdell, G., "*Citizen Kane*'s New Technique," in *Movie-Makers*, March 1941, reprinted in *Classic Film Collector* (Muscatine, Iowa), Winter 1977.

Alekan, Henri, in *Ecran* (Paris), 30 November 1948.

Slocombe, Douglas, and William Wyler, in *Sequence* (London), Summer 1949, also letter in Autumn 1949.

Film (New York), September 1953.

Mitchell, G., in *Films in Review* (New York), December 1956.

Filmmaker's Newsletter (Ward Hill, Massachusetts), May 1971.

Film Comment (New York), Summer 1972.

Focus on Film (London), no. 13, 1973.

Chaplin (Stockholm), vol. 15, no. 2, 1973.

Filme (Berlin), no. 6, 1980.

Film Psychology Review (Salem, New York), Summer-Fall 1980.

Carringer, R.L., on Toland and Welles in *Critical Inquiry* (Chicago), no. 4, 1982.

Turner, George, in *American Cinematographer* (Hollywood), November 1982, corrections in letter, January 1983.

Allen, R., in *Framework* (Norwich, Norfolk), Summer 1983.

Skinner, James M., "*December 7*: Filmic Myth Masquerading as Historical Fact," in *Journal of Military History*, October 1991.

Turner, George, "*Sharp Practice: The Innovators 1940–1950*," in *Sight and Sound* (London), July 1999.

*   *   *

Gregg Toland was one of the greatest cinematographers of the Hollywood studio era—if not *the* greatest. Much more than a competent technician, Toland was a visual stylist and an innovator. He often supervised the set construction on his films, and he always worked closely with his directors to plan lighting and camerawork that would go beyond the technical requirements of filmmaking to create the proper mood for a scene.

Toland's most productive association with a director was his six-film collaboration with William Wyler. It was on the Wyler films of the late 1930s that the cinematographer began experimenting with the composition-in-depth and deep-focus photography for which he is best known. Composition-in-depth is the arrangement of characters and action on several planes within the frame at once. The different planes need not all be in focus simultaneously for composition-in-depth to be effective; if, however, foreground, middleground, and background are all in sharp focus at the same time, this effect is called deep-focus photography.

Wyler liked to use long takes, long shots, and composition-in-depth: he preferred to create dramatic tension by spreading his actors out across the frame and on different planes within the frame, rather than by cutting back and forth between them. In *The Little Foxes*, for example, the death of Horace involves a very lengthy shot and two planes of action. In the shot the focus stays on Regina, who sits motionless in the foreground, while the paralyzed Horace struggles and then dies of a heart attack—out of focus—on the stairs in the background.

Toland experimented with composition-in-depth and deep focus on other films—John Ford's *The Long Voyage Home*, for example—and then perfected the deep-focus technique on Orson Welles's masterpiece, *Citizen Kane*. Toland's use of high-intensity arc lamps and the newly available light sensitive Eastman Super XX film stock allowed him to close down the aperture of his 24mm lens to f8 or less; the combination of the wide-angle lens and narrow aperture gave Toland sharp focus on objects from five to 50 feet or more away from the camera.

Welles and Toland used deep focus extensively in *Citizen Kane*—sometimes as a functional alternative to shot-reaction shot editing, and sometimes expressively, to create a mood or a visual metaphor. In one shot early in the film, Charlie Kane's mother and a banker, in the foreground, sign an agreement that will allow young Charlie to be taken away from his parents and later inherit a fortune; Charlie's father, uncertain about the agreement, paces back and forth in the middleground; Charlie, seen through a window, plays unsuspectingly in the snow in the background. Thus, one of the film's themes—Kane's alienation from the others—is established visually in this early scene.

After *Citizen Kane*—his crowning achievement—Toland continued his fine work on films such as Wyler's *The Best Years of Our Lives*, until his distinguished career was cut short by his premature death in 1948.

—Clyde Kelly Dunagan

TOLL, John

Cinematographer. **Nationality:** American. **Born:** Cleveland, Ohio. **Education:** Attended school in Ohio before moving to Los Angeles at the age of 19 to attend college. **Family:** Married Lois Burwell (a makeup artist). **Career:** Production assistant, Wolper Productions, 1970s; served as an assistant on feature films before working as assistant camera operator for cinematographers John Alonzo, Jordan Cronenweth, Allen Daviau, Conrad Hall, and Robbie Greenberg; television credits include cinematography for *A China Odyssey: Steven Spielberg's "Empire of the Sun"* (CBS, 1987), *The Young Riders* (ABC, 1989), and *Good Night, Sweet Wife: A Murder in Boston* (CBS, 1990); shot hundreds of television commercials since 1988. **Awards:** Academy Award, Best Cinematography, for *Legends of the Fall*, 1994; Camerimage Golden Frog (Poland), for *Legends of the Fall*, 1995; Academy Award, Best Cinematography, American Society of Cinematographers (ASC) Award, Outstanding Achievement in Cinematography in Theatrical Releases, both 1995, and British Academy Award, Best Cinematography, 1996, for *Braveheart*; New York Film Critics Circle Award, National Society of Film Critics Award, Best Cinematography, both 1998, ASC Award, Outstanding Achievement in Cinematography in Theatrical Releases,

Berlin International Film Festival Honorable Mention for Outstanding Camerawork, Chicago Film Critics Association Award, Best Cinematography, and Golden Satellite Award, Best Motion Picture Cinematography, all 1999, all for *The Thin Red Line*. **Agent:** Judy Marks Agency, 119 N. Larchmont Boulevard, Los Angeles, CA 90004–3704, U.S.A.

Films as Cinematographer:

1971 *The Young Graduates* (Anderson)
1972 *The Hoax* (Anderson)
1987 *A China Odyssey: Steven Spielberg's "Empire of the Sun"* (for TV) (doc)
1989 *The Kid*, pilot for *The Young Riders* series (for TV)
1990 *Good Night, Sweet Wife: A Murder in Boston* (Freedman—for TV)
1992 *Wind* (Ballard)
1994 *Legends of the Fall* (Zwick)
1995 *Braveheart* (Gibson)
1996 *Jack* (Coppola)
1997 *The Rainmaker* (Coppola)
1998 *The Thin Red Line* (Malick)
1999 *Simpatico* (Warchus)
2000 *Almost Famous* (Crowe)
2001 *Captain Corelli's Mandolin*

Other Films:

1979 *Tom Horn* (Wiard) (camera operator); *Norma Rae* (Ritt) (camera operator)
1980 *The Boy Who Drank Too Much* (Freedman—for TV) (camera operator)
1981 *Zorro, the Gay Blade* (Medak) (camera operator)
1983 *Scarface* (De Palma) (camera operator)
1984 *The Falcon and the Snowman* (Schlesinger) (camera operator)
1986 *Peggy Sue Got Married* (Coppola) (camera operator); *Black Widow* (Rafelson) (camera operator)
1988 *Tequila Sunrise* (Towne) (ph: second unit); *The Milagro Beanfield War* (Redford) (camera operator)
1989 *Blaze* (Shelton) (ph: second unit); *Always* (Spielberg) (additonal ph: Montana unit)

Publications

By TOLL: articles—

"Cinematographer John Toll," interview with David Morgan, in *Wide Angle/Closeup*, http://members.aol.com/morgands1/closeup/text/toll.htm, June 1991.
"Filmmakers' Forum: ASC Members Riposte *Variety* Article," in *American Cinematographer* (Hollywood), August 1996.
"John Toll, ASC Details His Experiences on *The Thin Red Line*," interview with Stephen Pizzello, in *American Cinematographer* (Hollywood), February 1999.

On TOLL: articles—

Heuring, David, "Cinematographers Honor Their Own," in *American Cinematographer* (Hollywood), May 1990.
Daily Variety (Hollywood), 17 February 1995.
Pizzello, Stephen, "*Legends of the Fall* Exploits Scenic Locale," in *American Cinematographer* (Hollywood), March 1995.
Probst, Chris, "Cinematic Transcendence: The ASC and the Academy of Motion Picture Arts and Sciences Honor 1995's Standout Feature-film Cinematographers," in *American Cinematographer* (Hollywood), June 1996.
Thompson, Andrew O., "Production Slate: ASC and Digital Domain Explore New Frontiers," in *American Cinematographer* (Hollywood), August 1996.
Shoot, May 15, 1998.
American Cinematographer (Hollywood), February 1999.

*   *   *

In a 1991 interview on the Newport, Rhode Island, location of Carroll Ballard's *Wind*, John Toll divulged that he did not have an individual style. After almost ten years of working his way up through the ranks from assistant camera operator to camera operator—under the tutelage of such distinguished cinematographers as John Alonzo and Jordan Cronenweth—he had landed his first job as director of photography on this theatrical feature. Within a decade, the fledgling cinematographer who proclaimed "I don't really have a visual definition of myself" would develop a signature look.

Toll belongs to the school that believes the cinematographer's art is one of illusion. He prefers an unobtrusive, uncluttered style in which the hand of the director of photography is almost invisible. The Ohio native favors images captured in natural light—or at least those that appear that way. He had little choice while shooting the America's Cup sailing adventure *Wind* on a twelve-meter boat in the open seas. The cramped quarters and difficult circumstances forced him to work with existing daylight conditions. Although Edward Zwick's *Legends of the Fall* (1994) offered plenty of wide-open space on location in western Canada, the shoot was plagued by rainstorms and floods, requiring Toll to make constant technical adjustments. Matching shots posed a particular difficulty, as cloud cover alternated with brilliant sunlight. Despite these challenges, Toll remained committed to his naturalistic aesthetic of making "the lighting feel natural, and not manipulated." His striking widescreen cinematography captured breathtaking vistas in the "big sky" tradition of classic Westerns and earned him an Oscar for Best Cinematography in 1994.

Toll's experience with shifting, unpredictable weather patterns and his flexibility in dealing with change proved invaluable on his next project, Mel Gibson's *Braveheart* (1995). Shot in Ireland and Scotland, where the climate seemingly cycled through four seasons in a single day, the historical epic was a difficult shoot. He achieved a "very rough, raw, stark, dark and graphic—almost primitive" feel suitable for the uncivilized Middle Ages in which the story of Scottish freedom fighter William Wallace takes place. Similar to *Legends of the Fall*, the subject matter called for realism and a degree of visual stylization to elevate the heroic protagonist to mythic stature. In both films, Toll linked characters to the surroundings that shaped them in wide shots of bold composition. The imagery recalls John Ford's Western films, especially those set in Monument Valley, and David Lean's *Lawrence of Arabia*—influences that Toll has cited. His backlighting gave the characters a romantic quality, adding golden highlights to the long tresses of the adventuresome Tristan (Brad Pitt) in *Legends of the Fall* and the valiant Wallace (Mel Gibson) in *Braveheart*. Although executed with existing light sources, the stylized photography marked a new direction in the cinematographer's work.

The strength of Toll's action-sequence photography lies in his ability to plunge the spectator into the midst of a scene. Using handheld cameras aboard the racing yachts in *Wind*, he simulated the visceral experience of being ravaged by the forces of nature. Shots of sea water splashing against the camera lens make viewers feel as though they are being hit in the face by a wave. Handheld cameras were also used to shoot the sweeping battle sequences of *Braveheart*. "We wanted to create a sense of immediacy and make the audience feel as if they were participants, that they were witnessing the battle from close range," Toll was quoted by Chris Probst in *American Cinematographer*. He used longer focal-length lenses to fill the frame with close-ups of the combatants. The unsteady images and moving camera created visual chaos, capturing the confusion of the fighting. Toll's creative and logistical accomplishments earned him a second Best Cinematography Oscar for *Braveheart* in 1995, making him the first cinematographer in almost fifty years to win back-to-back Academy Awards.

Collaborating with Terrence Malick on *The Thin Red Line* in 1998, Toll elevated his artistry to a new level. The screen became his canvas, and he transformed images into poetry. Based on James Jones's 1962 novel about the 1942–43 battle for Guadalcanal, *The Thin Red Line* unfolds like an impressionist mood piece. Instead of using traditional master shots and coverage, Toll's camera drifts from soldier to soldier, following the emotional thread of each scene as the scared men question why they are there and ponder the meaning of life. The spontaneous camera work and high contrast images mimic the unpredictability of combat and contribute to the feeling that things are out of control. The wide-screen format situates the Americans within the Pacific paradise, an environment violated and scarred by the war. Nature becomes the most powerful character. Shots of vegetation and wildlife—grasslands undulating in the wind, a leaf riddled with bullet-like holes, a crocodile easing into shimmering water, a cluster of bats—are intercut with the drama. Putting the viewer into the action, Toll's moving camera stalks American soldiers through waist-high grass as they try to overtake a Japanese hilltop bunker. When red blood splatters a blade of grass, the effect is jolting. Not only has life been lost, but nature has been defiled. Toll's stunning, lyrical work earned him a third Academy Award nomination for Best Cinematography in 1999, although the Oscar went to Janusz Kaminski for another war film, *Saving Private Ryan*. John Toll has teamed with visual directors ranging from Carroll Ballard to Francis Coppola to Terrence Malick. He became their eyes and turned their visions into photographic reality. Even when shots were technically difficult to achieve, he favored a naturalistic approach of working within existing set conditions. In less than a decade, Toll evolved from a craftsman of no distinguishable style to an internationally acclaimed cinematographer with a style all his own.

—Susan Tavernetti

TOWNE, Robert

Writer. **Nationality:** American. **Born:** Los Angeles, 23 November 1935. **Education:** Attended Pomona State College, California; studied acting with Jeff Corey. **Family:** Two daughters. **Military Service:** U.S. Army. **Career:** Sold real estate and worked as a commercial fisherman; 1960—first film as writer, *The Last Woman on Earth*; then worked as script doctor and for TV; 1970–71—negotiator between San Pedro tuna fishermen and environmentalists. **Awards:** Academy Award and Writers Guild Award, for *Chinatown*, 1974; British Academy Award, for *Chinatown* and *The Last Detail*, 1974; Writers Guild Award, for *Shampoo*, 1975. **Agent:** Contemporary Artists Agency, 9830 Wilshire Boulevard, Beverly Hills, CA 90212, U.S.A.

Films as Writer:

1960   *The Last Woman on Earth* (Corman) (+ ro)
1965   *The Tomb of Ligeia* (Corman)
1967   ***Bonnie and Clyde*** (Penn) (consultant)
1968   *Villa Rides* (Kulik) (co)
1973   *The Last Detail* (Ashby)
1974   ***Chinatown*** (Polanski)
1975   *Shampoo* (Ashby) (co); *The Yakuza* (Pollack) (co)
1982   *Personal Best* (+ d)
1984   *Greystoke: The Legend of Tarzan, Lord of the Apes* (Hudson) (credited as P. H. Vazak)
1988   *Tequila Sunrise* (+ d)
1990   *Days of Thunder* (T. Scott); *The Two Jakes* (Nicholson) (from original characters)
1993   *The Firm* (co) (Pollack)
1994   *Love Affair* (co) (Caron)
1996   *Mission: Impossible* (co) (De Palma)
1998   *Without Limits* (+ d); *Armageddon* (Bay) (additional writing [uncredited])
1999   *Mission: Impossible II* (Woo)

Film as Producer:

1987   *The Bedroom Window* (Hanson) (exec pr)

Film as Actor:

1987   *The Pick-Up Artist* (Toback) (as Stan)

Publications

By TOWNE: articles—

American Film (Washington, D.C.), December 1976.
In *The Craft of the Screenwriter* by John Brady, New York, 1981.

Time Out (London), 1–7 July 1983.
Towne, Robert, "On Moving Pictures," in *Scenario* (US), vol 1, no.1, Winter, 1995.
"I Wanna Make it Like Real Life," interview with Hadani Ditmars, in *Sight and Sound* (London), vol.9, no. 2, February 1999.

On TOWNE: articles—

Sragow, Michael, "Ghost Writers Unraveling the Enigma of Movie Authorship," in *Film Comment* (New York), March-April 1983.
Bellman, Joel, in *American Screenwriters, 2nd series*, edited by Randall Clark, Detroit, 1986.
Sight and Sound (London), Autumn 1986.
American Film (Washington, D.C.), January/February 1989.
Film Comment (New York), November/December 1990.
Engel, Joel, in *Screenwriters on Screenwriting*, New York, 1995.

*   *   *

The main characters in Robert Towne's technically impeccable scripts are outsiders flirting with coming in from the cold. Jack Nicholson's J. J. Gittes in *Chinatown*; Warren Beatty's George in *Shampoo*; Mariel Hemingway's Chris, the novice athlete, and Patrice Donnelly's Tory, the veteran, in *Personal Best*; the two petty officers, Otis Young's Mulhall and Jack Nicholson's unruly Buddusky, and their childlike prisoner, Meadows (Randy Quaid), in *The Last Detail*; Christopher Lambert's Tarzan in *Greystoke*; Robert Mitchum's American hero and his Japanese cohort (Ken Takakura) in *The Yakuza*—these are characters living on the fringe. Towne's misfit protagonists are caught at society's margins, and his screenplays find them at the moment when they confront the mainstream. The overarching sadness at the end of Towne's scripts has to do with their remaining on the outside, having realized that is where they belong. As with Tarzan in *Greystoke*, their inability to be integrated into the system only underscores their dignity and the hollowness of society. All the characters above, as well as Bonnie and Clyde, Vito Corleone in his twilight days in *The Godfather*, and Michael Corleone contemplating vengeance, are all figures as alien to "civilization" as Tarzan.

One of the major changes Towne made in adapting Darryl Ponicsan's novel *The Last Detail* for the screen concerned stripping away Buddusky's eccentricities, eliminating his closet intellectualism and his beautiful wife. Shaped in the mold of a typical Towne protagonist, Buddusky could not get off Towne's existential hook: he could not, as the book's character could, retreat into ideas, nor take any comfort from the fact that waiting at the end of this detail was a pretty wife. And Towne's decision to alter the ending so that Buddusky does not die makes him a lonely survivor rather than a martyr. Like J. J. Gittes, he ends up wrapped in solitude. Towne's heroes are characters for whom neat dramatic resolutions do not exist. Tarzan remains a "wild man." George, the notorious ladies' man, is the odd man out at the conclusion of *Shampoo*. Tory, who got Chris a place on the track team and gave her support, love, and consolation, is left far behind at the end of *Personal Best*.

Towne gained fame in Hollywood as a consummate "script doctor," a writer who could fix ailing scripts of films already in production. Among his most noted house calls is an on-the-set revision of *Bonnie and Clyde*. But his most famous doctoring is the patio scene he wrote for *The Godfather*. The scene, between the retired Don Vito Corleone (Marlon Brando) and his son Michael (Al

Robert Towne (right) with Mel Gibson

Pacino), who has taken over the family business, is a key one in the film. Technically, it was a difficult scene to write (there was no comparable scene in the book) because it had to do two things at once. As an exposition scene, it had to provide the audience with crucial information about an upcoming betrayal and attempt on Michael's life. Moreover, director Francis Ford Coppola wanted a scene where, as he put it, father and son "say they love each other." Towne's solution was brilliant. He placed the scene's hard information—who the Corleones' enemies were, how and when they would try to assassinate Michael—at the beginning and end. In between he wrote a tender encounter between father and son, as touching as it was universal. It subtly showed the transfer of power and hinted at the Don's senility and Michael's self-doubt. More importantly, it gave Don Corleone the opportunity to speak about his failed dreams. As powerful as he is, Don Corleone is a father who like many fathers has regrets about how his children's lives turned out. "There wasn't enough time, Michael," Don Corleone says, thinking of things that will never be and expressing feelings any parent could sympathize with, "there just wasn't enough time."

In Robert Towne's screenwriting career, *The Godfather*'s patio scene is one in a series of telling, bittersweet moments. Towne's is

a dark, uncaring world, but one of the things that makes his vision so penetrating is that it is so complete. In the Towne universe, life may be mostly hopeless, but not completely so. The scenes that stand out in relief amidst the bleakness are those in which a glimmer of hope shines through, where one character shows another some warmth and kindness. In *The Last Detail* it is the glance exchanged by Buddusky and Mulhall when they almost let Meadows escape. In *Personal Best* it is Chris's encouragement of Tory at the climactic Olympic trials. In *Chinatown* it is Mrs. Mulwray's attempt to get her sister-daughter out of the clutches of her father and Gittes's fumbling attempts to help. In *Shampoo* it is Jack Warden's puffed-up character of Lester forgiving, accepting, and proposing to his mistress (Julie Christie). And it is George's awkward but moving explanation of his philandering to Jill (Goldie Hawn) when he says, "I go into an elevator or walk down the street and see a pretty girl, and that's it: It makes my day. I can't help it. I feel like I'm gonna live forever. Maybe it means I don't love them, and maybe it means I don't love you, but nobody's gonna tell me I don't *like* them very much." In *Greystoke* it is Tarzan's grandfather (Ralph Richardson) embracing his long-lost heir.

Towne's outsiders are not allowed in, but, ultimately, they never really wanted in—they adhere to a code society will not honor. That the outsider-insider gulf cannot be bridged, that person-to-person goodness is so rare, is not the result of evil in Towne's screenplays; it is the very root of evil. But along the way his characters do encounter some goodness, and the fact that it is present at all is considerable consolation. Towne's characters exist to bear witness to the ongoing—but all too fleeting—presence of goodness.

—Charles Ramírez Berg

TRAUNER, Alexandre

Art Director. **Nationality:** French. **Born:** Sandor Trauner in Budapest, Hungary, 3 August 1906; emigrated to France, 1929; naturalized, 1944. **Education:** Studied painting, School of Fine Arts, Budapest, 1925–29. **Career:** Assistant art director to Lazare Meerson, in early 1930s, then art director in France, Hollywood, and elsewhere; also stage designer; 1936—founder member, Cinémathéque Française. **Awards:** Academy Award for *The Apartment*, 1960; César awards for *Mr. Klein*, 1977; *Don Giovanni*, 1979; *Subway*, 1985. **Died:** 6 December 1993 at Omonville-La-Petite.

Films as Assistant Art Director:

1930   *Sous les toits de Paris* (*Under the Roofs of Paris*) (Clair); *David Golder* (Duvivier)
1931   *Jean de la Lune* (Choux); *A nous la liberté* (Clair)
1932   *L'Affaire est dans le sac* (*It's in the Bag*) (P. Prévert); *Quatorze juillet* (Clair); *Danton* (Roubaud)
1933   *Ciboulette* (Autant-Lara); *Amok* (Ozep); *Faut réparer Sophie* (Ryder)

Films as Art Director/Production Designer:

1934   *L'Hôtel du libre-échange* (M. Allégret) (co); *Sans famille* (M. Allégret) (co)
1935   **La Kermesse heroïque** (*Carnival in Flanders*) (Feyder) (co)
1937   *Gribouille* (M. Allégret); *La Dame de Malacca* (M. Allégret) (co); *Drôle de drame* (*Bizarre Bizarre*) (Carné); *Mollenard* (Siodmak)
1938   **Quai des Brumes** (*Port of Shadows*) (Carné); *Entrée des artistes* (*The Curtain Rises*) (M. Allégret) (co); *Hôtel du Nord* (Carné)
1939   **Le Jour se lève** (*Daybreak*) (Carné)
1940   *Soyez les bienvenus* (de Baroncelli)
1941   *Remorques* (*Stormy Weather*) (Grémillon); *Le Soleil a toujours raison* (Billon) (co)
1942   *Les Visiteurs du soir* (*The Devil's Envoys*) (Carné) (co)
1943   *Lumière d'été* (Grémillon) (co)
1945   **Les Enfants du paradis** (*Children of Paradise*) (Carné) (co); *Les Malheurs de Sophie* (Audry)
1946   *Les Portes de la nuit* (*Gates of the Night*) (Carné); *Rêves d'amour* (Stengel) (co); *Voyage surprise* (P. Prévert) (co)
1947   *La Fleur de l'âge* (Carné—unfinished)
1949   *La Marie du port* (Carné) (co)
1950   *Manèges* (*The Cheat*) (Y. Allégret); *Les Miracles n'ont lieu qu'une fois* (Y. Allégret)

1951   *Juliette, ou la clé des songes* (Carné); *The Green Glove* (Maté)
1952   *Othello* (Welles); *Les Sept Péchés capitaux* (*The Seven Deadly Sins*) (Y. Allégret); *La Jeune Folle* (Y. Allégret)
1953   *Un Acte d'amour* (*Act of Love*) (Litvak)
1954   *Land of the Pharoahs* (Hawks)
1955   **Du Rififi chez les hommes** (*Rififi*) (Dassin) (co); *L'Amant de Lady Chatterley* (*Lady Chatterley's Lover*) (M. Allégret)
1956   *The Happy Road* (Kelly); *En effeuillant la Marguerite* (*Mam'zelle Striptease*) (M. Allégret)
1957   *Love in the Afternoon* (Wilder)
1958   *Witness for the Prosecution* (Wilder); *The Nun's Story* (Zinnemann)
1959   *Le Secret du Chevalier d'eon* (Audry)
1960   *Once More with Feeling* (Donen); **The Apartment** (Wilder)
1961   *Romanoff and Juliet* (Ustinov); *Paris Blues* (Ritt); *Aimez-vous Brahms* (*Goodbye Again*) (Litvak); *One, Two, Three* (Wilder)
1962   *Le Couteau dans la plaie* (*Five Miles to Midnight*) (Litvak)
1963   *Irma La Douce* (Wilder); *Behold a Pale Horse* (Zinnemann)
1964   *Kiss Me, Stupid* (Wilder)
1966   *How to Steal a Million* (Wyler)
1967   *The Night of the Generals* (Litvak); *La Puce à l'oreille* (*A Flea in Her Ear*) (Charon)
1968   *Uptight* (Dassin)
1970   *The Private Life of Sherlock Holmes* (Wilder); *Les Mariés de l'an II* (Rappeneau)
1971   *La Promesse de l'aube* (*Promise at Dawn*) (Dassin)
1972   *L'Impossible Objet* (*The Impossible Object*) (Frankenheimer); *Grandeur nature* (Berlanga)
1975   *The Man Who Would Be King* (Huston)
1976   *La Première Fois* (Berri)
1977   *Mr. Klein* (Losey); *Les Routes du sud* (Losey)
1978   *Fedora* (Wilder)
1979   *Don Giovanni* (Losey); *The Fiendish Plot of Dr. Fu Manchu* (Haggard)
1981   *Coup de torchon* (*Clean Slate*) (Tavernier)
1982   *The Trout* (Losey)
1983   *Tchao Pantin* (Berri)
1984   *Vive les femmes!* (Confortes)
1985   *Harem* (A. Joffé); *Subway* (Bresson)
1986   *Round Midnight* (*Autour de minuit*) (Tavernier)
1987   *Le Moustachu* (Chaussois)
1988   *La Nuit bengali* (Klotz)
1989   *Comédie d'amour* (Gobbi); *Réunion* (Schatzberg) (+ ro)

Publications

By TRAUNER: articles—

Image et Son (Paris), December 1965.
Positif (Paris), October and November 1979, additions in January 1980.
Film Comment (New York), January-February 1982.
Cinématographe (Paris), March 1982.
Film Français (Paris), 13 August 1984.
Télérama (Paris), 17–23 November 1984.
Revue du Cinéma/Image et Son (Paris), December 1984.
Cinéma (Paris), September-October 1985.
Cinéma (Paris), no. 453, January 1989.

On TRAUNER: books—

Alexandre Trauner: Cinquante ans de cinéma, Paris 1986.
Alexandre Trauner: Décors de cinéma, Paris 1988.

On TRAUNER: articles—

Calibano, "Scenografia di Trauner," in Libro e Moschetto (Milan), no. 24, 1943.
Unifrance (Paris), November 1951.
Gray, Martin, "Design for Living," in Films and Filming (London), January 1957.
Monthly Film Bulletin (London), November 1967.
Film Français (Paris), 18 February 1977.
Cinéma Français (Paris), April 1980.
Film Français (Paris), 30 October 1981.
Film Français (Paris), 2 March 1984.
National Film Theatre booklet (London), October-November 1984.
Cinéma (Paris), 25 September 1985.
Télérama, no. 1894, April 1986.
Cinéma (Paris), 7 May 1986.
Film Français, no. 2077, February 1986 and no. 2087, May 1986.
Sight and Sound (London), Autumn 1986.
Filmkultura (Budapest), March 1987.
Film en televisie (Brussels), no. 368, January 1988.
Première, no. 140, November 1988.
Avant-Scène (Paris), no. 374, October 1988.
Positif, no. 352, June 1990.
Film Français, no. 2848, December 1993.
Obituary, in Variety, 20 December 1993.
Studio Magazine, no. 82, April 1994.
Classic Images, no. 226, April 1994.

*   *   *

Alexandre Trauner's vast career is mentioned and analyzed in all books about production design, but he remained modest and disliked to talk about his skills. "I work in the shadow of the authors, and it's just as well," he said. "A designer is a manipulator, he makes believe . . . and makes audiences believe. And as a magician, he should not reveal too much of his tricks!"

What kind of tricks has Trauner used, for instance, to build houses, towns, atmospheres that have become for millions of people throughout the world, the houses, the towns, the atmospheres of Paris, London, or the Pharaohs' Egypt? Even those who do not precisely remember the docks in Quai des Brumes or the boulevard in Children of Paradise imagine them just as Trauner has designed them.

"What makes my job most interesting," said Trauner, "is that there are no two identical films, even though producers would like to repeat indefinitely the same success. Every time I start working on a movie, I try to forget all that I have experienced."

He claimed that invention is the one and only acceptable rule. That is trick number one. Another of his tricks might be called friendship. The best of his work was done with people who were his friends: poet and screenwriter Jacques Prévert; directors Billy Wilder, Orson Welles, Joseph Losey, composer Maurice Jaubert, designers Ray and Charles Eames, actors Jean Gabin, Yves Montand, Jack Lemmon, and others.

"Shooting a film is collective work," said Trauner, and something he enjoyed. "Each member of the team contributes, everything is important, but what's decisive for me is to have an adventure in common!"

Trauner's sets are immediately recognizable. During the Second World War, when France was occupied and he worked undercover, everyone in the profession felt his touch and knew that he had designed Grémillon's Lumière d'été and Carné's Les Visiteurs du soir, for his style is unmistakable. The basic trick was simplicity. He banished the picturesque and loathes the decorative. "It's useless," he said, "to fill the screen with superfluous things. Come to think about it, what a designer refrains from doing is almost more important than what he actually does. He's like a sculptor who eliminates material from the marble block. He cannot show everything; he chooses the significant elements, the unexpected ones, and these must look true, they must sound right."

That was how Trauner achieved the sturdiest, the most meaningful and imaginative of sets. He created the Paris that many people have in their minds, but he believed that movies become interesting when they do not stick to reality. Showing reality was not enough: the picture must be new and surprising. Only then does it become real. "It's a question of point of view, just as painting is a question of vision, and from Far Eastern to European painting, there are many different visions!" said Trauner.

Painting, since his beginnings at the Fine Arts School of Budapest, remained essential for him. He was the best known of production designers, the most ignored of painters. Only his close friends, Prévert or Picasso, knew about it, as he was always too modest or careless to do or let do anything about it; his set designs turn out to be fascinating pieces of painting. They were made with paint and a brush, just as the sets were made of plaster, wood, and sunlight. They were made by a person whose trick, all said and done, was to have no tricks—only an incisive eye, a keen understanding of people and places, and talent, as they say.

With Trauner's death in 1993, the cinema lost one of its truly international art directors. In a career spanning five decades, he served leading directors in Europe and America, winning an Oscar and three Césars for his production designs. He saw his role as helping "the mise en scène so that the spectator has an immediate grasp of the characters' psychology," and with over eighty films to his credit, there is ample evidence of his wide-ranging achievement. Comparing himself more readily to a painter than to an architect, he acknowledged the influence of Cubism and Impressionism, though it was Lazare Meerson who shaped his initial predilection for non-naturalistic designs. If in France his early career was synonymous with those of Carné and Grémillon, he was equally at home in later years with Tavernier or the hi-tech world of Besson. Outside France, his associations with Wilder and Losey were particularly creative, whether designing the huge, Kafkaesque office for The Apartment or exploiting the natural locations of Palladio to exquisite effect in Don Giovanni. From the monumental to the intimate, from fantasy 15th-century castles to 19th-century French boulevards or the London of Sherlock Holmes, from seedy hotels and working class tenements in France to exotic locations in West Africa or India, Trauner excelled in creating the necessary framework for the director's narrative to unfold. In 1986 his achievements were marked in Paris by retrospectives of his films at the Cinémathèque and of his set designs at the Ecole des Beaux Arts.

—André Pozner, updated by R. F. Cousins

TRNKA, Jiří

Animator. **Nationality:** Czech. **Born:** Pilsen, 24 February 1912. **Education:** Attended Arts and Crafts School (UMPRUM), Prague, 1928–35. **Family:** Married Ružena Trnková. **Career:** 1923—began making puppets; 1926—shop assistant, designer in modern puppet theater of Josef Skupa; 1928–35—while student at UMPRUM, newspaper cartoonist; 1936—founded puppet theater "Dřevěné divadlo" (Wooden Theatre); late 1930s—graphic artist, painter, and book illustrator; 1937—Wooden Theatre fails; 1941–44—scenic artist at National Theatre; 1945—began working in animation at invitation of members of studio that becomes "Bratři v triku" Studio; 1946—began making puppet films. **Awards:** National Artist; Order of Labor. **Died:** In Prague, 30 December 1969.

Films as Animator, Writer, and Art Director:

1945   *Zasadil dědek řepu* (*Grandpa Planted a Beet*) (cartoon)
1946   *Zvířátka a Petrovští* (*The Animals and the Brigands*) (cartoon); *Dárek* (*The Gift*) (cartoon); *Pérák a SS* (*The Springer and SS-Men*) (cartoon)
1947   "Masopust" (Carnival), "Jaro" (Spring), "Legenda o svatém Prokopu" (Legend of St. Prokop), "Pout" (Fair), "Posvícení" (Feast), "Betlém" (Bethlehem) eps. of *Spaliček* (*The Czech Year*) (puppet film)
1948   *Císařuv slavík* (*The Emperor's Nightingale*) (puppet film)
1949   *Román s basou* (*Novel with a Contrabass*) (puppet film); *Arie prérie* (*The Song of the Prairie*) (puppet film)
1950   *Certuv mlýn* (*The Devil's Mill*) (puppet film); *Bajaja* (*Bayaya*) (puppet film); *Veselý cirkus* (*The Merry Circus*) (puppet film) (+ paper-cut animation)
1951   *O zlaté rybce* (*The Golden Fish*) (cartoon)
1953   **Staré pověsti cěské** (*Old Czech Legends*) (puppet film); *Jak stařeček měnil až vyměnil* (*How Grandpa Changed Till Nothing Was Left*) (cartoon)
1954   *Dva mrazíci* (*Two Frosts*) (puppet film); *Kutásek a Kutilka, jak ráno vstávali* (*Kutásek and Kutilka*) (puppet film)
1955   "Z Hatvanu do Haliče" (From Putim to Putim), "Svejkovy nehody ve vlaku" (Schweik's Difficulties on the Train), and "Svejkova budějovická anabase" (Schweik and Cognac) eps. of *Osudy dobrého vojáka Svejka* (*The Good Soldier Schweik*) (puppet film); *Cirkus Hurvínek* (*Hurvínek's Circus*) (puppet film)
1958   *Proč UNESCO?* (*Why UNESCO?*) (cartoon)
1959   *Sen noci svatojánské* (*A Midsummer Night's Dream*) (puppet film)
1961   *Vášeň* (*Passion*) (puppet film)

1962   *Kybernetická babička* (*Cybernetic Granny*) (puppet film)
1964   *Archanděl Gabriel a paní Husa* (*Archangel Gabriel and Mistress Goose*) (puppet film)
1965   *Maxplatte, Maxplatten* (puppet film); *Ruka* (*The Hand*) (puppet film)

Other Films:

1947   *Capkovy povídky* (*Tales By Capek*) (Frič) (art d); *Liska a džbán* (*The Fox and the Jug*) (Látal) (art d + co-sc)
1951   *Perníková chaloupka* (*Gingerbread Hut*) (Pojar, puppet film) (art d); *Císařuv pekař—Pekařuv císař* (*The Emperor's Baker and the Baker's Emperor*) (Fric) (art d)
1953   *O skleničkú víc* (*One Glass Too Much*) (Pojar, puppet film) (art d)
1954   *Byl jednou jeden král* (*Once Upon a Time There Was a King*) (Bořivoj Zeman) (art d); *Jan Hus* (Vávra) (art d)
1955   *Spejbl na stopě* (*Spejbl on the Trail*) (Pojar, puppet film) (art d); *Jan Zizka* (*A Hussite Warrior*) (Vávra) (co-costume des)
1957   *Proti všem* (*Against All*) (Vávra) (co-costume des); *Paraplíčko* (*The Brolly*) (Pojar, puppet film) (des "magic grandpa" puppet)
1959   *Bombomanie* (*Bombomania*) (Pojar, puppet film) (art d)
1960   *Pulnoční příhoda* (*The Midnight Event*) (Pojar, puppet film) (art d)
1966   *Blaho lásky* (*The Bliss of Love*) (Brdečka, cartoon) (art d)

Publications

By TRNKA: articles—

"The Puppet Film as an Art," interview with Jaroslav Brož, in *Film Culture* (New York), no. 5–6, 1955.
"An Interview with the Puppet-Film Director, Jiří Trnka," with Jaroslav Brož, in *Film* (London), January-February 1956.
"20 let Cs.filmu—vypovídá Jiří Trnka," interview with Jaroslav Brož, in *Film a Doba* (Prague), no. 6, 1965.

On TRNKA: books—

Benešová, Marie, *Od Spalíčku ke Snu noci svatojánské*, Prague, 1961.
Boček, Jaroslav, *Jiří Trnka, Artist and Puppet Master*, Prague, 1963.
Hoffmeister, Adolf, *Cas se nevrací!*, Prague, 1965.
Benešová, Marie, *Jiří Trnka*, brochure, Prague, 1970.
Trnková, Ružena, and Helena Chvojková, *Muj syn*, Prague, 1972.

On TRNKA: articles—

Metzl, E., "Four European Illustrators," in *American Artist*, December 1955.
Orna, Bernard, "Trnka's Little Men," in *Films and Filming* (London), November 1956.
Polt, Harriet, "The Czechoslovak Animated Film," in *Film Quarterly* (Berkeley, California), Spring 1964.
Bocek, Jaroslav, "Trnkovské postskriptum," in *Film a Doba* (Prague), no. 3, 1966.
"Trnkaland," in *Newsweek* (New York), March 1966.
Obituary in the *New York Times*, 31 December 1969.

Fiala, Miloš, "O Jiřím Trnkovi se Stanislavem Látalem a Břetislavem Pojarem," in *Film a Doba* (Prague), no. 4, 1970.

Fiala, Miloš, "O Jiřím Trnkovi s Václavem Trojanem a Jiřím Brdečkou," in *Film a Doba* (Prague), no. 5, 1970.

Obituary in *Newsweek* (New York), 12 January 1970.

Film a Doba (Prague), February 1987.

CinémAction (Conde-sur-Noireau), no. 51, April 1989.

Film a Doba (Prague), April 1990.

Nosferatu (San Sebastian), February 1992.

Meils, Cathy, in *Variety* (New York), 9 June 1997.

* * *

A puppeteer at heart, a skilled painter and renowned illustrator, Jiří Trnka was 33 years old in 1945 when associates at the animated film studio (later the "Bratři v triku" Studio) asked him to collaborate with them.

In only one year he created four animated films in rapid succession, making a strong impact on the development of the genre. With their naive charm and an artistic conception based on unfettered drawing and a new method of film narration that was well received by the international moviegoing public, these works demonstrated huge innovations in animation, and broke the monopoly in this area of art previously enjoyed by Walt Disney. However, Trnka did not find animated films artistically satisfying, and after leaving the studio he went off to a small atelier to attempt a film with puppets. He immediately produced a magnificent work, *Spaliček (The Czech Year)*, in which he depicted the Czech year from spring through winter in the customs, rituals, work, holidays, and legends of country life. *Spaliček* is a key work which portrays the Czech attitudes towards life, work, love, faith, and death. It anticipates a number of motifs from his later work, motifs which Trnka would develop at various places in various genres and which resonate throughout his *oeuvre*.

Along the pathway of the puppet film Trnka would create his own world, but he would also show that the expressive possibilities of the puppet film are boundless. He depicts ancient times in legends and myths, visions of the future, and the worlds of fairy tales and of modern times. He switches genres from comedy through parody, satire, and pantomime to drama and parable. He translates into cinematic form the works of Andersen [*Císařuv slavík (The Emperor's Nightingale)*], Chekhov [*Román s basou (Novel with a Contrabass)*], Němcová [*Bajaja (Bayaya)*], Hašek [*Osudy dobrého vojáka Svejkova (The Good Soldier Schweik)*], Shakespeare [*Sen noci svatojánské (A Midsummer Night's Dream)*], and Boccaccio [*Archandĕl Gabriel a paní Husa (Archangel Gabriel and Mistress Goose)*]. He recognizes the encroachment of technology into human life as one of the greatest threats to mankind [*Císařuv slavik (The Emperor's Nightingale)*] and returns to this theme again in the film *Vášerí (Passion)* and in the science-fiction film *Kybernetická babička (Cybernetic Granny)*. In his last work, the philosophical study *Ruka (The Hand)*, Trnka creates a timeless parable about man and the detrimental effects of power.

Until the end of his life, however, he continued to devote himself to illustrating, woodcarving, sculpture, and painting, in order, as he put it, "to capture a story, but in a single phrase." He was awarded the Andersen Prize *in memoriam* for his illustration work.

Trnka was an extraordinarily talented and hard-working individual. He painted and wrote and was a woodcutter, a sculptor, and an illustrator. In all his films he was not only a writer and graphic artist but also an editor, a designer and builder of puppets, and a designer of puppet costumes. Often misunderstood and attacked by the critics, he never bent to any pressures.

The work he produced was well-rounded, full of human warmth, tenderness, wisdom, humor, and grace. He succeeded in bringing the puppet film out of the periphery and into mature prominence. He brought the masterworks of literature into the purview of the puppet film and expressed philosophical ideas and emotions with such urgency that his films have become not only a landmark but also a yardstick for puppet films yet to be made.

Truly a unique genius of Czech culture in the second half of the twentieth century, Trnka demonstrated by his work that the animated film can convey all the conditions of the human spirit.

—Vladimír Opěla

TROTTI, Lamar

Writer and Producer. **Nationality:** American. **Born:** Lamar Jefferson Trotti in Atlanta, Georgia, 18 October 1900. **Education:** Attended the University of Georgia, Athens, degree in journalism 1921; studied writing at Columbia University, New York. **Family:** Married; three children. **Career:** 1922–25—city editor, Atlanta *Georgian*; 1925–32—publicist and editor of trade magazine for Motion Picture Association of America, first in New York, then in Hollywood; 1932–52—contract writer at Fox, later at 20th Century-Fox: first film as writer, *The Man Who Dared*, 1933; frequent collaborator with Dudley Nichols; writer-producer after 1942. **Awards:** Academy Award for *Wilson*, 1944; Writers Guild Award for *Yellow Sky*; Writers Guild Founders Award, 1970. **Died:** Of heart attack, 28 August 1952.

Films as Writer:

1933 *The Man Who Dared* (MacFadden)
1934 *You Can't Buy Everything* (Reisner); *Hold That Girl* (MacFadden); *Wild Gold* (Marshall); *Call It Luck* (Tinling); *Judge Priest* (Ford); *Bachelor of Arts* (L. King)
1935 *Steamboat 'round the Bend* (Ford); *Life Begins at 40* (Marshall); *This Is the Life* (Neilan)
1936 *The Country Beyond* (Forde); *The First Baby* (Seiler); *Ramona* (H. King); *Pepper* (Tinling); *Career Woman* (Seiler); *Can This Be Dixie?* (Marshall)
1937 *Slave Ship* (Garnett); *This Is My Affair* (*His Affair*) (Seiter); *Wife, Doctor, and Nurse* (W. Lang)
1938 *In Old Chicago* (H. King); *The Baroness and the Butler* (W. Lang); *Alexander's Ragtime Band* (H. King); *Kentucky* (Butler); *Gateway* (Werker)
1939 *The Story of Alexander Graham Bell* (*The Modern Miracle*) (Cummings); **Young Mr. Lincoln** (Ford); *Drums along the Mohawk* (Ford)
1940 *Brigham Young—Frontiersman* (Hathaway); *Hudson's Bay* (Pichel)
1941 *Belle Starr* (Cummings)
1942 *To the Shores of Tripoli* (Humberstone); *Tales of Manhattan* (Duvivier)
1943 *Guadalcanal Diary* (Seiler)
1944 *Wilson* (H. King)
1946 *The Razor's Edge* (Goulding)

1952   ''The Cop and the Anthem'' ep. of *O. Henry's Full House*
          (Koster)
1954   *There's No Business Like Show Business* (W. Lang) (story)

Films as Writer and Producer:

1942   *Thunderbirds* (Wellman)
1943   *The Immortal Sergeant* (Stahl); *The Ox-Bow Incident* (*Strange
          Incident*) (Wellman)
1945   *A Bell for Adano* (H. King) (co)
1947   *Captain from Castile* (H. King); *Mother Wore Tights* (W. Lang)
1948   *The Walls of Jericho* (Stahlo); *When My Baby Smiles at Me*
          (W. Lang); *Yellow Sky* (Wellman)
1949   *You're My Everything* (W. Lang) (co-sc)
1950   *Cheaper by the Dozen* (W. Lang); *My Blue Heaven* (Koster)
          (co-sc); *American Guerilla in the Philippines* (*I Shall
          Return*) (F. Lang); *I'd Climb the Highest Mountain* (H. King)
1952   *With a Song in My Heart* (W. Lang); *Stars and Stripes
          Forever* (*Marching Along*) (Koster)

Film as Producer:

1946   *Colonel Effingham's Raid* (*Man of the Hour*) (Pichel)

Publications

By TROTTI: screenplays—

Wilson and *The Ox-Bow Incident* in *Best Film Plays 1943–1944*,
    edited by John Gassner and Dudley Nichols, New York, 1945.

On TROTTI: articles—

Tereba Smith, Maynard, in *Films in Review* (New York), August-
    September 1958.
Tereba Smith, Maynard, in *American Screenwriters, 2nd series*,
    edited by Randall Clark, Detroit, Michigan, 1986.

                              *   *   *

With the exception of one screenplay for MGM in 1934, *You
Can't Buy Everything*, Lamar Trotti worked exclusively for 20th
Century-Fox from 1933 until his death in 1952. This identification
with a single studio (and its stable of stars and craftsmen), coupled
with his growing power within that company, gives Trotti's work an
uncommon consistency. His 50-odd films cover a variety of styles
and genres: westerns (*The Ox-Bow Incident, Yellow Sky*), musicals
(*Mother Wore Tights, My Blue Heaven*), war films (*Guadalcanal
Diary, American Guerilla in the Philippines*), and biographies (*Stars
and Stripes Forever, The Story of Alexander Graham Bell, Young Mr.
Lincoln* and *Wilson*). Directors as diverse as Ford, Wellman, King,
and Koster brought his words to the screen. But Trotti's body of work
is bound together by his amiable, low-key style, his historian's eye
and ear, his casual gravity.

The typical Trotti screenplay is imbued with an earnest feeling for
the American past and is characterized by an easy pace, nearly
plotless structure, and a concentration on human values as opposed to
spectacle or melodrama. ''Americana'' is what Trotti did best. Films
as diverse as *Young Mr. Lincoln* and *Cheaper By the Dozen* share
a graceful—yet never sugar-coated—view of the American landscape, an appreciation of rustic character, a respect for the principles
and attitudes of earlier, ''simpler'' times.

Trotti was born in Georgia at the turn of the century; both the land
and the era of his origins were to influence his work enormously. *I'd
Climb the Highest Mountain* and *Colonel Effingham's Raid* are set in
Georgia; many others of his films take place in the South; only
a handful are set in the present. That Trotti's father allegedly fought in
the American Civil War might help to explain Trotti's lifelong
obsession with that conflict (though, certainly, such an obsession is
not rare in the South). The shadow of that war falls across much of
Trotti's work: *Judge Priest* celebrates the camaraderie of a group of
aging Confederate veterans; *Young Mr. Lincoln* is imbued with
a prescience of the upcoming conflict and of Lincoln's fateful role in
it; *The Ox-Bow Incident, Yellow Sky*, and *Belle Starr* take place in the
period after the war when disillusion and despair have turned its
soldiers into ruthless martinets or cynical outlaws.

Trotti's insistent return to the theme of the American Civil War
and to more general ''Southern'' stories is no coincidence; it speaks
of a deliberation and interest that transcends the simple typecasting
which was (and is) so rampant in Hollywood. Trotti subtly bent the
demands and conventions of the popular film to his own ends.

There is a strong streak of sentiment in Trotti's films which can
sometimes impede appreciation of his enormous skill and integrity as
a screenwriter by ''modern'' viewers. But true warmth and honest
sentiment are as rare in the cinema as deep thought or original ideas.
A writer can sometimes fake having brains; he can never fake having
a heart.

Henry Fonda once called Trotti ''one of the very few people in the
film industry for whom I have any respect.'' The sincere and
unpretentious character which inspired such a comment translated
itself with uncommon purity into Trotti's screenplays. His work,
when taken as a whole, makes up something very much like an
autobiography.

                                                    —Frank Thompson

TRUMBO, Dalton

Writer. **Pseudonyms:** Robert Rich, Arnold Schulman, Sally
Stubblefield, and Les Crutchfield. **Nationality:** American. **Born:**
Montrose, Colorado, 9 December 1905. **Education:** Attended the
University of Colorado, Boulder, 1924–25; University of California,
Los Angeles, 1925–27; University of Southern California, Los Angeles, 1927–29. **Family:** Married Cleo Beth Fincher, 1939; children:
two daughters and one son. **Career:** 1930–34—newspaper reporter;
1934—script reader, Warner Bros.; 1935—first novel published;
1936—first film as writer, *Love Begins at Twenty*; then writer for
Warner Bros., RKO, and MGM; 1945—founder and editor, *The
Screenwriter*; 1947—investigation by the House Un-American Activities Committee: cited for contempt of congress, 1949, and served 10-
month prison sentence; blacklisted; then wrote under pseudonyms;

1960—resumed writing under his own name; 1971—directed his own script, *Johnny Got His Gun*. **Awards:** Academy Award for *The Brave One*, 1956 (awarded in 1975 because of the blacklisting); Writers Guild Laurel Award, 1969. **Died:** 10 September 1976.

Films as Writer:

1936   *Love Begins at Twenty* (McDonald); *Tugboat Princess* (Selman); *Road Gang* (L. King)

1937   *Devil's Playground* (Kenton); *That Man's Here Again* (L. King)

1938   *A Man to Remember* (Kanin); *Fugitive for a Night* (Goodwins)

1939   *Sorority House* (Farrow); *Career* (Jason); *The Flying Irishman* (Jason); *Five Came Back* (Farrow); *The Kid from Kokomo* (Seiler)

1940   *Heaven with a Barbed Wire Fence* (Cortez); *A Bill of Divorcement* (Farrow); *Curtain Call* (Woodruff); *Half a Sinner* (Christie); *The Lone Wolf Strikes* (Salkow); *We Who Are Young* (Bucquet); *Kitty Foyle* (Wood)

1941   *Accent on Love* (McCarey); *You Belong to Me* (Ruggles)

1942   *The Remarkable Andrew* (Heisler)

1943   *Tender Comrade* (Dmytryk); *A Guy Named Joe* (Fleming)

1944   *Thirty Seconds over Tokyo* (LeRoy)

1945   *Our Vines Have Tender Grapes* (Rowland)

1946   *Jealousy* (Machaty)

1949   **Gun Crazy** (Lewis) (credited to Millard Kaufman); *The Beautiful Blonde from Bashful Bend* (P. Sturges) (credited to Earl Felton)

1951   *He Ran All the Way* (Berry) (credited to Hugh Butler); *The Prowler* (Losey) (credited to Hugh Butler); *The Brave Bulls* (Rossen) (credited to John Bright)

1953   *Roman Holiday* (Wyler) (credited to Ian Hunter)

1954   *Carnival Story* (Neumann) (uncredited)

1956   *The Brave One* (Rapper) (story, as Robert Rich); *The Boss* (Haskin) (credited to Ben Perry)

1957   *Wild Is the Wind* (Cukor) (as Arnold Schulman); *The Green-Eyed Blonde* (Girard) (as Sally Stubblefield); *The Abominable Snowman* (Guest) (credited to Nigel Kneale)

1958   *Cowboy* (Daves) (credited to Edmund North)

1959   *Last Train from Gun Hill* (J. Sturges) (as Les Crutchfield)

1960   *Exodus* (Preminger); *Spartacus* (Kubrick)

1961   *Town without Pity* (Reinhardt) (uncredited); *The Last Sunset* (Aldrich)

1962   *Lonely Are the Brave* (Miller)

1965   *The Sandpiper* (Minnelli)

1966   *Hawaii* (Hill)

1968   *The Fixer* (Frankenheimer)

1971   *Johnny Got His Gun* (+ d); *The Horsemen* (Frankenheimer)

1972   *F.T.A.* (*Foxtrot Tango Alpha*; *Free the Army*; *Fuck the Army*) (Parker) (co)

1973   *Papillon* (Schaffner) (+ ro); *Executive Action* (Miller)

1978   *Ishi, the Last of His Tribe* (Miller)

Publications

By TRUMBO: fiction—

Eclipse, London, 1935.
Washington Jitters, New York, 1936.

Johnny Got His Gun, Philadelphia, 1939.
The Remarkable Andrew, Philadelphia, 1941.
Night of the Aurochs, edited by Robert Kirsch, New York, 1979.

By TRUMBO: other books—

Harry Bridges (nonfiction), New York, 1941.
An Appeal to the People (nonfiction), Los Angeles, 1942.
Thirty Seconds over Tokyo (script) in *Best Film Plays, 1945*, edited by John Gassner and Dudley Nichols, New York, 1946.
The Time of the Toad (nonfiction), Hollywood, 1948.
The Biggest Thief in Town (play), New York, 1949.
The Devil in the Book (nonfiction), Los Angeles, 1956.
Additional Dialogue: Letters of Dalton Trumbo, edited by Helen Manfull, New York, 1970.
The Time of the Toad and Two Related Pamphlets, New York, 1972.

By TRUMBO: articles—

"Stepchild of the Muses," in *North American Review*, December 1933.
"Blacklist Equals Black Market," in *Nation* (New York), 4 May 1957.
Positif (Paris), no. 64–65, 1965.
Cinema Canada, January-February 1969.
Cinema Canada, September-October 1969.
Jeune Cinéma (Paris), May 1971.
Cinéma (Paris), July-August 1971.
"The Blacklist Was a Time of Evil," in *Film Culture* (New York), Fall-Winter 1971.
Ecran (Paris), April 1972.
In *Blueprint in Babylon*, by J. D. Marshall, Los Angeles, 1978.
"Who Killed Spartacus?" with D. Cooper, and Gary Crowdus, in *Cineaste* (New York), vol. 18, no. 3, 1991.

On TRUMBO: book—

Cook, Bruce, *Dalton Trumbo*, New York, 1977.

On TRUMBO: articles—

Présence du Cinéma (Paris), June 1962.
Hanson, Curtis Lee, "Dalton Trumbo—Writer, Director, Producer Relationships," in *Cinema* (Beverly Hills, California), July-August 1965.
Zinnemon, Jerry, in *Esquire* (New York), March 1971.
Madsen, Axel, in *Sight and Sound* (London), Summer 1971.
In *The Hollywood Screenwriters*, edited by Richard Corliss, New York, 1972.
Rivista del Cinematografo (Rome), August-September 1975.
American Film (Washington, DC), October 1975.
Cinemateca Revista (Montevideo), July 1981, additions in August 1981.
Moore, James, in *American Screenwriters*, edited by Robert E. Morsberger, Stephen O. Lesser, and Randall Clark, Detroit, Michigan, 1984.
Dick, Bernard F., in *Radical Innocence: A Critical Study of the Hollywood Ten*, Lexington, Kentucky, 1989.
Smith, J. P., "A Good Business Proposition," in *Velvet Light Trap* (Madison, Wisconsin), no. 23, Spring 1989.
Cineaste (New York), vol. 43, no. 3, 1991.
Rectangle, no. 38–39, Spring 1992.

Time, vol. 141, 24 May 1993.
Advocate, 14 December 1993.
McGilligan, Patrick, "John Berry: Man of Principle," in *Film Comment* (New York), May-June 1995.
Cineaste (New York), Spring 1996.
Variety (New York), 9 September 1996.
Nation, 5 April 1999.

*   *   *

Dalton Trumbo's life is perhaps more exciting than any of the films he wrote. He was a successful screenwriter in the 1940s, one of the highest paid in Hollywood. He has been compared to Wilde and Shaw in his capacity as a witty man of letters. He wrote magnificent letters (collected in *Additional Dialogue*) as well as one of the most stirring antiwar novels ever written, *Johnny Got His Gun*, a story written from the point of view of a quadriplegic. Then, as the House Un-American Activities Committee searched for Communists in Hollywood, he joined the ranks of the infamous Hollywood Ten.

Trumbo was forced into exile but this did not stop the spunky writer from working under a multitude of pseudonyms. He won Hollywood's highest honors while using the names of others. Finally, after 13 years in limbo and a change in the climate of the country, Trumbo returned a hero. The world finally acknowledged his previously uncredited pictures and he served as a director for the film version of his controversial masterpiece, *Johnny Got His Gun*.

Unfortunately for the history of cinema, Trumbo's life was more gripping than any of his film creations. His achievements include *Spartacus*, *Exodus*, *The Sandpiper*, and *Hawaii*. These films deal with important issues but are painted in such broad, melodramatic tones that they trivialize the very points they try to make. They are Hollywood "message" films, reflecting the conventions of a genre more than serious social reality. That is not to say that they cannot have moving moments. In *Spartacus*, when his men are asked to turn in their leader (Kirk Douglas), and Tony Curtis, and one by one each of the others, declares "I am Spartacus," it is a very poignant moment (in spite of Curtis's inappropriate Brooklyn accent which was hardly Trumbo's fault). Then there is the memorable scene in *Lonely Are the Brave* when Kirk Douglas, as the last cowboy, gets run over by a truck. Dalton's films are capable of great drama and poetic ironies. They can make great entertainment. However, these films never really make the significant social impact on the filmgoer that Trumbo would have liked. He had intended "to use art as a weapon for the future of mankind, rather than as an adornment for the vanity of aesthetes and poseurs." The book *Johnny Got His Gun* is capable of changing an opinion for life. The Trumbo films, however, only make great trivia questions for film buffs.

Trumbo's movies lacked sophistication. They hit you over the head with a sledgehammer. They tended to be preachy and "more liberal than thou." On the other hand. Trumbo's superpatriot war films, created shortly after he wrote *Johnny Got His Gun*, are even more astounding. In *A Guy Named Joe*, a highly chauvinistic screenplay written to propagandize the Second World War, he has his good-guy hero die and then return to earth to help teach other guys named Joe the art of better bombing.

The film critic Richard Corliss suggests several reasons for the disparity between Trumbo's literary efforts and his film works. It could have been the fault of the film industry, with Trumbo trying to conform in order to sneak through the important ideas he wanted to get across. It could have been Trumbo's attempt to reach as large an audience as possible by relying on the tried and true Hollywood dramatic conventions. In any case, the legend of Trumbo's life is a far more important statement to be remembered than any of his films, and no doubt will be.

—Edith C. Lee

TRUMBULL, Douglas

Special Effects Technician. **Nationality:** American. **Born:** Los Angeles, California, 8 April 1942. **Education:** Studied architecture at El Camino College, Torrance, California. **Career:** Mid-1960s—educational and technical filmmaker for Graphic Films, Los Angeles; 1974—founded Future General Corporation: developed Showscan process.

Films as Special Effects Technician:

1964   *To the Moon and Beyond* (+ d—short)
1968   *Candy* (Marquand) (co); ***2001: A Space Odyssey*** (Kubrick) (co)
1971   *The Andromeda Strain* (Wise) (co)
1973   *The Borrowers* (Miller)
1977   ***Close Encounters of the Third Kind*** (Spielberg)
1979   *Star Trek: The Motion Picture* (Meyer)
1982   ***Blade Runner*** (R. Scott)

Douglas Trumbull

Films as Director:

1971   *Silent Running*
1983   *Brainstorm* (+ pr)
1984   *New Magic* (+ pr)
1989   *Leonardo's Dream*
1990   *To Dream of Roses*
1991   *Back to the Future—;The Ride*
1993   *In Search of the Obelisk* (+ pr)

Publications

By TRUMBULL: articles—

"The Slit-Scan Process," in *American Cinematographer* (Hollywood), October 1969.
With Jon Bloom and David Graham, on *The Andromeda Strain*, in *American Cinematographer* (Hollywood), May 1971.
Action (Los Angeles), May/June 1972.
Filmmakers Newsletter (Ward Hill, Massachusetts), December 1977.
American Cinematographer (Hollywood), January 1978.
Cinefantastique (New York), Spring 1978.
Take One (Montreal), May 1978.
Films Illustrated (London), June 1978.
Cinefantastique (New York), Autumn 1978.
Ecran Fantastique (Paris), no. 18, 1981.
Cahiers du Cinéma (Paris), April 1982.
Film Comment (New York), September/October 1983.
Cinefantastique (New York), December 1983/January 1984.
Cahiers du Cinéma (Paris), February 1984.
Ecran Fantastique (Paris), February 1984.
Starburst (London), February 1984.
Sight and Sound (London), Spring 1985.
American Cinematographer (Hollywood), August 1993.
American Cinematographer (Hollywood), vol. 75, August 1994.

On TRUMBULL: articles—

Show (New York), 23 July 1970.
American Film (Washington, D.C.), January 1978.
American Cinematographer (Hollywood), February 1979.
Cahiers du Cinéma (Paris), November 1980.
Image et Son/Ecran (Paris), September 1981.
Ecran Fantastique (Paris), no. 26, 1982.
Duncan, Pamela, in *Cinefex* (Riverside, California), April 1982.
Revue du Cinéma/Image et Son (Paris), February 1984.
American Film (Washington, D.C.), May 1984.
American Cinematographer (Hollywood), vol. 73, August 1992.
American Cinematographer (Hollywood), vol. 74, August 1993.
Sight & Sound (London), May 1995.

*   *   *

From the late 1960s through the mid-1980s, Douglas Trumbull symbolized the new Hollywood special-effects wizards. He showed that blockbusters could be built around more than a good story and a top cast of stars. Inventor/cameraman/special-effects masters such

as himself could make such films as *2001: A Space Odyssey*, *The Andromeda Strain*, *Close Encounters of a Third Kind*, *Star Trek: The Motion Picture*, and *Blade Runner* big hits. A cult of film fans began to worship his creative efforts which turned a motion picture into a complete new world. Directors Steven Spielberg, Stanley Kubrick, and Ridley Scott skillfully took advantage of Trumbull's considerable talents to create a handful of the most important science-fiction films in Hollywood history. And for a time even official Hollywood recognized him with Oscar nominations.

Yet however successful he was Douglas Trumbull possessed a strong independent spirit and chaffed working for others. As a consequence it was not surprising that in the early 1980s he turned to his own projects, wanting to present his world view on his own films. But total control proved harder than he had anticipated. For example, he tried his hand at the film *Brainstorm* which had been begun by others. In the process of filming, Natalie Wood, the film's star, died in a controversial boating accident; Trumbull took over a film no one else wanted and tried, through his technological magic, to turn it into a blockbuster. He failed. The released film lost millions of dollars.

New Magic and *Leonardo's Dream* did not do any better. Trumbull then tried to pioneer new cinema technology and unveiled Showscan. Shot at 60 frames per second (versus 24 frames per second for traditional 35mm film), Trumbull sought to bombard the viewer with 150 percent more visual information. By using a larger screen, set closer to the audience, plus a powerful, state-of-the-art stereo sound system, plus 70mm film stock, Trumbull wanted to make the ticket buyer unaware she or he was even watching a motion picture.

Trumbull's dream never passed the experimental stage. He and his backers were unable to persuade the public to want this "super realism." Ironically, during the very period Trumbull sought to develop Showscan, film fans were turning more and more to the inferior images found on home video. Trumbull gave up and turned his considerable talents to making rides for theme parks, most notably the "Back to the Future" attraction at the Universal Studios theme park.

—Douglas Gomery

TSUBURAYA, Eiji

Special Effects Technician. **Nationality:** Japanese. **Born:** Fukushima, 7 July 1901. **Education:** Attended Sugugama-Chori Elementary School; Kanda Electronic School. **Military Service:** 1921–23—served in correspondence corps of Japanese army. **Family:** Married Masano Araki, 1930; children: three sons. **Career:** 1919–21—assistant cinematographer for Kokkatsu Studios; 1923–25—cameraman for Ogasaware Productions; 1925–35—cameraman and occasional special effects man for Shochiku-Shimogamo Studio, Nikkatsu-Taihei Studios, Taihei-Hasei Studio, and J.O. Studios; 1936—began concentrating on special effects; 1939—joined Toho Studios and established the Special Effects Section; 1945—retired from Toho; 1949—established the Tsuburaya Laboratory for technical studies; 1950—returned to Toho; 1954—created first monster, Godzilla; began association with Inoshiro Honda; 1963—established his own Special Effects Laboratory; created exhibits for the Mitsubishi Pavilion for the World Expo; 1964—established Tsuburaya Productions for television; created *Ultra Q* and *Ultraman* series; 1969—directed the construction and development of the *Holi-Mirror* for the Mitsubishi Pavilion for the World Expo. **Died:** 25 January 1970.

Films as Cameraman (selected list):

1924 *Enmeiin no semushiotoko (Hunchback of Enmeiin)*

1925 *Kurutta l peiji* (Kinugasa) (asst)

1927 *Chigo no kenpo (Sword of the Child)* (Otsuka); *Rangun* (Otsuka); *Komori-zoshi* (Yamazaki); *Gekla no kyoba* (Kinugasa); *Tenpo hiken roku*

1928 *Fununjo shi*; *Ashibi*; *Shirai gonpachi*; *Ose no hangoro*; *Kaito Sayamaro(Savamaro the Great Thief)*; *Oedo no saigon*; *Rozeki mono*

1929 *Meiran (Brightness and Darkness)*; *Chimatsuri (Carnival of Blood)*; *Yoma Kidan (Tales of Monsters)*

1930 *Nogitsune sanji* ; *Shiobara tasuke* ; *Chohichiro matsudaira* (+ special effects)

1931 *Benikmori (Red Bat)*

1932 *Kwaidan yanagi zoshi*

1934 *Tenka no igagoe*

1935 *Kaguyahimi*

Films as Special Effects Technician (selected list):

1936 *Koutareki*; *Atarshiki tsuchi (New Earth)* (Frank and Itami)

1938 *Ah! Nango shosa* (+ d + ph)

1940 *Kodo nipon* (doc); *Kaigun bakugekitai (Navy Bombers)* (doc); *Moyuru ozora (Burning Sky)* (doc); *Songoku* (2 parts)

1941 *Hachyyuhachinenme no taiyo*; *Syanhai no tsuki*

1942 *Shiroi hekiga*; *Nankai no hanatabe*; *Suikoden*; *Hawaii marei oki haisen (Battle of Hawaii)* (Yamamoto)

1943 *Guraida* (+ ph—doc); *Aken senso* (+ ph); *Hyoraku yume monogatari* (+ ph); *Hikoki wa naze tobuka* (+ ph—doc); *Kessen no osorae* (+ ph); *Syonen hyoryuki* (+ ph)

1944 *Ano hata oute*; *Kato hayabusa sento tai*; *Ikari no umi*; *Raigeki tai shutsudo*

1950 *Sasaki kojiro*

1953 *Anatahan (Saga of Anatahan)* (von Sternberg); *Taiheizo no washi (Eagle of the Pacific)*

1954 *Saraba rabauru*; *Tomei ningen (The Invisible Man)* (Oda); **Gojira** *(Godzilla)* (Honda)

1955 *Gojira no gyakushu (Revenge of Godzilla*; *Gigantis the Fire Monster)* (Oda); *Jujin Kuki-Otoko (The Abominable Snowman)* (Honda)

1956 *Hakufujin no yoren (Mysterious Love of Mrs. White)* (Toyeda); *Sorano Daikaijyu Rodan (Rodan)* (Honda)

1957 *Chikyu boeigun (The Mysterious)* (Honda)

1958 *Daikaiju Baran (Varan the Unbelievable)* (Baerwitz); *Bijo to ekitai ningen (The H-Man)* (Honda)

1959 *Songoku*; *Sensuikan T-57*; *Kofuku sezu*; *Nippon tanjo (The Three Treasures)* (Inagaki); *Uchu daisensu (Battle in Outer Space)* (Honda)

1960 *Taiheiyo no arashi (I Bombed Pearl Harbor*; *The Storm of the Pacific)* (Matsubayashi); *Denso ningen (Secret of the Telegian)* (Fukuda); *Gasu ningen daiichigo (The Human Vapor)* (Honda)

1961 *Osaka-jo monogatari (Daredevil in the Castle)* (Inagaki); *Mosura (Mothra)* (Honda); *Gen to Fudo-myoh (The Youth and His Amulet)* (Inagaki); *Sekai dai senso (The Last War)* (Matsubayashi)

1962 *King Kong tai Gojira (King Kong vs. Godzilla)* (Honda); *Yosei Goraith (Yosei Gorasu*; *Gorath)* (Honda)

1963 *Taiheiyo no tsubasi*; *Chintao yosai bakugeki merrei (Siege of Fort Bismark)* (Furusawa); *Mantango (Mantango—Fungus of Terror)* (Honda); *Dartozoku*

1964 *Kaitei gunkan (Atragon)* (Honda); *Gojira tai Mosura (Godzilla vs. The Thing)* (Honda); *Daitozoku (Samurai Pirate*; *The Lost World of Sinbad)* (Taniguchi); *Uchu daikaiju Dogora (Dogora—The Space Monster)* (Honda); *Dai tatsumaki (Whirlwind)* (Inagaki)

1965 *Kisuka*; *Daiboken*; *Sandai kaiju chikyu saidai no kessen (Ghidrah, the Three-Headed Monster*; *The Biggest Fight on Earth*; *The Greatest Battle on Earth)* (Honda); *None but the Brave* (Sinatra); *Taiheiyo Kiseki no sakusen Kisuka (Retreat from Kiska)* (Maruyama)

1966 *Furankenshutain tai Barogon (Frankenstein Conquers the World*; *Frankenstein vs. the Giant Devilfish)* (Honda); *Dai kusen (Zero Fighter)* (Moritani); *Nankai no daiketto (Ebirah—Terror of the Deep)* (Fukuda); *Furankenshutain no kaiju—Sanda tai Gailah (Sanda tai Gailha*; *The War of the Gargantuas)* (Honda); *Kaiju daisenso (Monster Zero*; *Invasion of the Astro-Monsters*; *Battle of the Astros*; *Invasion of the Astros)* (Honda)

1967 *Kingu Kongu no gyakushu (King Kong Escapes)* (Honda); *Ultraman* (Hajime); *Gojira no musuko (Son of Godzilla)* (Fukuda)

1968 *Yamamoto Isoroku (Admiral Yamamoto)* (Maruyama); *Kaiju soshingeki (Destroy All Monsters)* (Honda)

1969 *Ido Zero daisakusen (Latitude Zero)* (Honda); *Nihonkai daikaisen (Battle of the Japan Sea)* (Maruyama)

Publications

On TSUBURAYA: book—

Tsuburaya, Hajime, editor, *The Films of Eiji Tsuburaya*, Tokyo, 1973.

On TSUBURAYA: articles—

Harrington, C., ''Japan's Master of Monsters,'' in *American Cinematographer* (Hollywood), August 1960.

Famous Monsters of Filmland, September 1964.

Image et Son (Paris), April 1970.

''The Films of Eiji Tsuburaya,'' in *Little Shoppe of Horrors* (Waterloo, Iowa), February 1974.

*   *   *

The 1950s are known in science-fiction circles as the decade of classic atomic-bomb monster movies. Fantasy films of this era explored what might happen to nature and mankind when the unknown power of nuclear devices was unleashed. Typically an explosion caused rapid mutation and accelerated growth resulting in gigantic creatures. Although films with building-size insects (*Them!*, *The Black Scorpion*, *The Deadly Mantis*) and human abnormalities (*The Amazing Colossal Man*, *The Incredible Shrinking Man*, *Attack of the 50-Foot Woman*) ranked high in number, the most popular subgenre was prehistoric or ''prehistoric-like'' creatures, usually reptiles. No one capitalized on this fascination with enormous reptilian monsters better than Eiji Tsuburaya. Starting with *Godzilla* in 1954, he created a menagerie of over 50 creatures for film and television.

His best-known beings, Godzilla (reportedly the nickname of a tough looking fellow who worked on the Toho lot), Mothra, Rodan, Ghidrah, and Ultraman, always conducted battles in Tokyo, levelling the city to ruins. To facilitate the numerous battles and speed production, Toho built a standing miniature set of Tokyo upon which Tsuburaya wrought his wholesale destruction. The popularity of Godzilla and his companions resulted in many sequels which cast them against one another. Eventually they changed into folk heroes and teamed together to protect the citizenry from the latest monster threatening Tokyo.

Tsuburaya not only constructed and photographed these creatures, but also dreamt them up, wrote stories around them, and occasionally functioned as producer to bring them to the screen. His giants were not animated models like those used by Willis O'Brien or Ray Harryhausen, but either actors in costume or mechanized miniatures. Compared to their work, Tsuburaya's effects were less convincing and, many felt, laughable. But given the studio system in Japan and its need for quantity of film product, Tsuburaya's economical methods (multiple cameras simultaneously filming long shots and close-ups) allowed for reasonable effects. Perhaps the best that can be said about his monster pictures is that they achieve an impression of scale and solidity, created by the detailed miniatures his crews built and high speed filming. Frequently shot at 240 frames-per-second, the monster would move normally when projected at the standard speed of 24 frames-per-second.

While his specialty was weird creatures, Tsuburaya was also responsible for all the miniature and special effects work needed by any Toho film in production. His water effects and sea battles easily bettered his monster work in execution if not popularity, from his first major assignment, *Battle of Hawaii*, to his last, *Battle of the Japan Sea*. One of his most curious collaborations was with Josef von Sternberg in 1953 on *Saga of Anatahan*, a film which explored the relationships among a group of men shipwrecked on an island with one woman. *Anatahan* required no ostensible special effects, but took production design to a realm of experimental surrealism never again attempted.

Tsuburaya's legacy continues as old monsters make comebacks (*Godzilla 1985*) and new ones appear on Japanese children's television and in films. A recent creature that might have made Tsuburaya smile because of its humorous implausibility is Gamera—an eighty-ton, jet-propelled, prehistoric turtle. Today, Tsuburaya's simple techniques fail to compete with the sophisticated technology now available in the field of special effects, but during the 1950s and 1960s they offered an inexpensive way to visualize the fantastic and entertain millions.

—Greg S. Faller

UNSWORTH, Geoffrey

Cinematographer. **Nationality:** British. **Born:** London, 1914. **Career:** 1932—camera assistant, then camera operator from 1937; 1942—made the documentary *Teeth of Steel*, followed by others in the mid-1940s, then feature films and international productions; collaborated on several technical innovations, including a special front-projection technique. **Awards:** British Academy Award for *Becket*, 1964; *2001: A Space Odyssey*, 1968; *Cabaret* and *Alice's Adventures in Wonderland*, 1972; *A Bridge Too Far*, 1977; *Tess*, 1981; Academy Award for *Cabaret*, 1972; *Tess*, 1980. Officer, Order of the British Empire. **Died:** In Brittany, France, 29 October 1978.

Films as Cameraman:

1937 *The Drum* (*Drums*) (Z. Korda)
1939 *The Four Feathers* (Z. Korda)
1940 *The Thief of Bagdad* (Berger, Powell, and Whelan)
1942 *The Great Mr. Handel* (Walker); *Teeth of Steel* (doc); *Gardens of England* (doc); *World Gardens* (doc)
1943 **The Life and Death of Colonel Blimp** (*Colonel Blimp*) (Powell and Pressburger); *The People's Land* (doc); *Power on the Land* (doc)
1944 *Men of Science* (doc)
1945 *Make Fruitful the Land* (doc)
1946 **A Matter of Life and Death** (*Stairway to Heaven*) (Powell and Pressburger); *Meet the Navy* (doc)

Films as Cinematographer:

1947 *Jassy* (Knowles); *Paris on the Seine* (doc); *The Man Within* (*The Smugglers*) (Knowles)
1948 *Blanche Fury* (M. Allégret) (co)
1949 *The Blue Lagoon* (Launder); *Fools Rush In* (Carstairs); *Scott of the Antarctic* (Frend); *The Spider and the Fly* (Hamer)
1950 *Trio* (French); *The Clouded Yellow* (Thomas); *Double Confession* (Annakin)
1952 *The Planter's Wife* (*Outpost in Malaya*) (Annakin); *Made in Heaven* (Carstairs); *The Story of Robin Hood and His Merrie Men* (Annakin); *Penny Princess* (Guest)
1953 *The Sword and the Rose* (Annakin); *Turn the Key Softly* (Lee); *The Million Pound Note* (*Man with a Million*) (Neame)
1954 *The Purple Plain* (Parrish); *The Seekers* (*Land of Fury*) (Annakin)
1955 *Simba* (Hurst); *Value for Money* (Annakin)
1956 *A Town Like Alice* (*The Rape of Malaya*) (Lee); *Jacqueline* (Baker)
1957 *Eric Winstone's Coach* (short); *Hell Drivers* (Endfield); *Dangerous Exile* (Hurst)
1958 *A Night to Remember* (Baker); *Bachelor of Hearts* (Rilla)
1959 *North West Frontier* (*Flame over India*) (Lee Thompson); *Whirlpool* (Allen)
1960 *The World of Suzie Wong* (Quine)
1961 *On the Double* (Shavelson); *Don't Bother to Knock* (*Why Bother to Knock*) (Frankel); *The Lion of Sparta* (*The Three Hundred Spartans*) (Maté)
1962 *The Main Attraction* (Petrie); *The Playboy of the Western World* (Hurst)
1963 *An Evening with the Royal Ballet* (Havelock-Allan and Asquith); *Tamahine* (Leacock)
1964 *Becket* (Glenville)
1965 *Genghis Khan* (Levin); *Pop Gear* (*Go Go Mania*) (Goode); *You Must Be Joking!* (Winner)
1966 *Othello* (Burge)
1967 *Oh Dad, Poor Dad, Mamma's Hung You in the Closet and I'm Feelin' So Sad* (Quine)
1968 *Half a Sixpence* (Sidney); *The Bliss of Mrs. Blossom* (McGrath); **2001: A Space Odyssey** (Kubrick); *The Dance of Death* (Giles)
1969 *The Assassination Bureau* (Dearden)
1970 *Cromwell* (Hughes); *Goodbye, Gemini* (Gibson); *The Magic Christian* (McGrath); *The Three Sisters* (Olivier)
1971 *Unman, Wittering, and Zigo* (MacKenzie)
1972 **Cabaret** (Fosse); *Alice's Adventures in Wonderland* (Sterling)
1973 *Baxter* (Jeffries); *Love and Pain and the Whole Darn Thing* (Pakula); *Zardoz* (Boorman)
1974 *The Internecine Project* (Hughes); *The Abdication* (Harvey); *Murder on the Orient Express* (Lumet)
1975 *The Return of the Pink Panther* (Edwards); *Royal Flash* (Lester); *Lucky Lady* (Donen)
1976 *A Matter of Time* (Minnelli)
1977 *A Bridge Too Far* (Attenborough)
1978 *Superman* (Donner)
1979 *Tess* (Polanski) (co)
1981 *Superman II* (Lester) (co)

Publications

By UNSWORTH: articles—

"The Director of Photography," in *Films and Filming* (London), April 1957.
Cinema TV Today (London), 15 December 1973.
On *The Return of the Pink Panther*, in *American Cinematographer* (Hollywood), April 1975.
On *A Bridge Too Far*, in *American Cinematographer* (Hollywood), April 1977.

On UNSWORTH: articles—

Focus on Film (London), October 1971, corrections in December 1971, July 1972, and no. 13, 1973.
Castell, D., on *Murder on the Orient Express* in *Films Illustrated* (London), December 1974.
Screen International (London), 18 October 1975.
Film and TV Technician (London), December 1978.
MacDonald, Peter, on *Superman* in *American Cinematographer* (Hollywood), January 1979.
Cinématographe (Paris), July-August 1979.
American Cinematographer (Hollywood), May 1981.

*   *   *

When Geoffrey Unsworth died in 1978, the film industry lost one of its best-loved and most accomplished cinematographers. Although his work was renowned for its lush qualities, it was his versatility and craftsmanship, rather than any distinctive personal style, which elevated him to the top ranks of his profession. Unsworth was an artistic chameleon, capable of adapting to a wide range of directors, genres, and environmental conditions, and of evoking radically different cinematic moods. Ambitious, expensively budgeted costume dramas such as *Cromwell*, and intimate, modestly financed films such as *The Three Sisters*, might pose different technical and aesthetic challenges, but variations in scale had no bearing on the amount of professionalism and enthusiasm which Unsworth invested. He enjoyed making period films such as *Becket* because they provided him with opportunities to use cinematography's basic grammar to establish ambience and verisimilitude. Yet he was equally adept at creating visual moods appropriate to films set in our own time, such as *The Return of the Pink Panther*. Although he learned his craft in the artificial and malleable context of studio production, he proved capable of superior work in the intractable and unpredictable conditions of location filmmaking, as *A Bridge Too Far* amply demonstrated.

Unsworth's career began in 1932 when he joined Gaumont British as a camera apprentice. In time he was promoted to camera operator, and, after moving to Technicolor, worked with such luminaries as Georges Périnal on *The Drum*, *The Four Feathers*, and *The Thief of Bagdad*, and Jack Cardiff on *Colonel Blimp* and *A Matter of Life and Death* (*Stairway to Heaven*). He joined the Rank Organization in 1946, and remained there as a director of photography for 13 years, working frequently with the directors Ken Annakin and Roy Baker. His reputation established, Unsworth turned freelance in 1959, and soon became a highly sought-after director both in his native England and in America.

His best work was realized in the 1960s and 1970s. The frosty magnificence of *2001: A Space Odyssey*, the elegance of *Murder on the Orient Express*, the chimerical aura of *Zardoz*, the ethereal and comic-book elements of *Superman*, and grandeur of *Becket* and *Cromwell*, and the softened representation of war in *A Bridge Too Far*, all owe a great deal to Unsworth's work. His finest accomplishment, however, was undoubtedly *Cabaret*. The grotesquerie of the Kit Kat Klub, and the decaying fabric of pre-Second World War Germany are impeccably rendered by Unsworth's expressionistic camerawork. The effort to draw the cinema audience into the mood of the nightclub by aligning its visual perspective with that of the clientele is highly successful. One of the most interesting aspects of Unsworth's work on *Cabaret* is that it proved he had no lack of imagination when it came to translating theatre into cinema. Not too many years earlier, he had been castigated by the critics for excessive deference to theatrical conventions in his photography of plays performed by Britain's National Theatre (*Othello*, *The Three Sisters*, and *The Dance of Death*). *Cabaret*, however, with its fluid camera movements, varied angles, and stunning lighting effects, was one of the most successful attempts ever to adapt a theatrical work for the film medium.

Cabaret earned Unsworth his first Academy Award. His second was for *Tess*, a movie which failed to satisfy Hardy purists but whose visual poetry seemed to strike a chord among cinema audiences. Unsworth died during the making of *Tess*; principal photography was completed by Ghislain Cloquet, who shared the Oscar.

Unsworth enjoyed a harmonious and unusually long partnership with his camera assistant and operator Peter MacDonald. Their association spanned two decades and about 30 features. MacDonald describes Unsworth as an ''impressionist,'' and has said that he was an intuitive, as opposed to a technical, cameraman who preferred to be guided by his instincts rather than by elaborate advance planning in the selection of lighting, angles, and composition. He was not renowned as an innovator, but he was always willing to experiment. If called upon to execute a particularly difficult shot, he would respond by searching for a solution rather than by dismissing the idea as technically impossible. Indeed, as director of photography on *2001: A Space Odyssey*, he was a key member of the team which applied advanced technology towards the realization of the director Stanley Kubrick's highly complex vision of the future. Unsworth's cinematography, coupled with Douglas Trumbull's pioneering special effects, helped to create the film's documentary feel as well as its exceptional visual clarity.

Unsworth was committed to the principle that the cameraman's input should be unobtrusive. He believed that cinematography should not call attention to itself but support directorial intent and the flow of the action. Yet, even though he believed that his contribution should be imperceptible, there is little doubt that his craftsmanship and artistry have left an indelible impression on modern cinema.

—Fiona Valentine

URUSEVSKY, Sergei

Cinematographer. **Nationality:** Russian. **Born:** 1908. **Education:** Institute of Fine Arts, Moscow. **Military Service:** Front-line cameraman, World War II. **Career:** Worked as a graphic designer and photographer in the 1930s; cinematographer, Mosfilm Studios, after World War II; directed two films toward the end of his life. **Awards:** Special Award, Cannes Film Festival, for *Sorok pervyj*, 1957; Golden Palm, Cannes Film Festival, for *Letyat zhuravli*, 1958; Archival Award, National Society of American Film Critics, for *I am Cuba* (1965), 1995. **Died:** In Moscow, 1974.

Films as Cinematographer:

1945   *Poyedinok* (*Duel*) (Legoshin)
1947   *Selskaya uchitelnitsa* (*The Village Teacher*) (Donskoy)
1949   *Alitet ukhodit v gory* (*Alitet Leaves for the Hills*) (Donskoy)
1952   *Vozvrashcheniye Vasiliya Bortnikova* (*The Return of Vasili Bortnikov*) (Pudovkin)

1955   *Urok zhizni* (*Lesson of Life*) (Raizman)
1955   *Pervyi eshelon* (*The First Echelon*) (Kalatozov)
1956   *Sorok pervyi* (*The Forty-first*) (Chukhrai)
1957   *Letyat zhuravli* (*Cranes Are Flying*) (Kalatozov)
1959   *Neotpravlennoye pismo* (*The Letter Never Sent*) (Kalatozov)
1963   *Kavalier zolotoi zvezdy* (*Cavalier of the Golden Star*) (Raizman)
1964   *Ya Kuba* (**Soy Cuba**; *I Am Cuba*) (Kalatozov)

Films as Director:

1969   *Proshschaj, Gjulsary!* (*The Ambler's Race*)
1971   *Poy pesnyu, poet!* (*Sing Your Song, Poet*)

Publications

By URUSEVSKY: articles—

"About the Form," in *Izkusstvo kino* (Moscow), no. 2, 1966.

On URUSEVSKY: articles—

Barnet, Enrique Pineda, "The Slogan is Friendship," in *Soviet Screen*, No. 15, 1964.
Harvey, Dennis, "Soy Cuba/Ja Cuba," in *Variety*, 17 May 1993.
Guthmann, Edward, "Soviet Bird's-Eye View of Cuba: Sweeping, Swooping Propaganda Piece," in *San Francisco Chronicle*, 14 April 1995.
Rosenberg, Scott, "1964 film *I Am Cuba* Mixes Art and Propoganda," in *San Francisco Examiner*, 14 April 1995.
Turner, George, "The Astonishing Images of *I Am Cuba*," in *American Cinematographer* (Hollywood), July 1995.
Ebert, Roger, "I am Cuba," in *Chicago Sun-Times*, 8 December 1995.
West, Dennis, "*I Am Cuba*," in *Cineaste* (New York), vol. 22, no. 2, Spring 1996.

*   *   *

Sergei Urusevsky will be remembered as one of the most innovative and resourceful figures in the history of cinematography, a proponent of a filmmaking in which a subjective camera narrates the film. He advocated a camera technique that would edit the film with its own movement and make montage obsolete. Urusevsky was influenced by the other main figure of Soviet cinematography, Eisenstein's cameraman Eduard Tisse. While celebrated internationally, at home he was often blamed for his obsession with form.

Urusevsky studied under graphic artist Vladimir Favorsky and other Russian constructivists in Moscow. In the 1930s he worked as a graphic designer and photographer. He was a Picasso admirer, and was particularly proud that he visited with Picasso once and received some ceramic pieces from the painter. During the war he was mobilized and worked as a combat cameraman. He became a DP only later, and worked with directors Mark Donskoy and Yuli Raizman, as well as on the last picture of veteran Vsevolod Pudovkin. Little of Urusevsky's formalist philosophy is to be seen in his earlier work. His best-known film from that period is Grigoriy Chukhrai's *Sorok pervyi* (1956), a conventionally shot studio-set adaptation of a popular short story by Boris Lavrenyev, recounting a doomed love affair unraveling in the background of Russia's civil war.

Urusevsky's interest in cinematic form found its adequate expression only after he began working with director Mikhail Kalatozov. Their first collaboration was the war-time romance drama *Pervyi eshelon* (1955), but it was not until the triumph of *Letyat zhuravli* (1957) that Urusevsky's innovative approach to film narration was recognized. Besides receiving the top award at Cannes, the film marked a decisive turn in Soviet war cinema: for a first time the experience of war was discussed through the utterly personal anxieties of the protagonists. Hand-held camera shots were used as often as technology allowed. There was even a scene where the protagonist, Veronica, runs away in a moment of trauma, surrounded by a shaky background of trees and buildings, reflecting her state of mind. For this subjective shot Urusevsky is said to have asked actress Tatiana Samoilova to hold the camera herself while running.

Kalatozov and Urusevsky then collaborated on *Neotpravlennoye pismo* (*The Letter Never Sent*, 1959), a romantic story of geologists facing a hostile nature. Elements of the cinematography of this film are believed to have influenced some scenes in Francis Ford Coppola's *Apocalypse Now*. Urusevsky's masterpiece remains his last picture as cinematographer, *Ya Kuba* (*I Am Cuba*, 1965). It was an important and lavishly financed joing project of the Soviet Union and newly socialist Cuba, meant to further the iconography and mythology of the revolutionary aesthetic, and to become the cinematic cornerstone of the "Cuban craze" that characterized the Soviet Union in the mid-1960s.

The film runs close to three hours and consists of four unrelated stories, recounting the fates of ordinary Cubans involved in situations of class confrontation that in the end lead them all into revolution. Otherwise an ordinary propaganda feature, *I Am Cuba* is outstanding for its extraordinary cinematography and design influenced by the work of Cuban painter Jose Portocarrero. Urusevsky chose to make the film in lush black and white, as he believed that the powerful emotional impact of contrasting shadows was crucial in cinema. For *I Am Cuba*, he used special infrared stock to achieve a fairy effect of the white island and palms on the dark background of sea and sky. Most of the film was shot with a 9.8 lens that slightly distorts the proportions and gives the images a dizzy, engulfing feel.

The shots in *I Am Cuba* are long and elaborately composed; many consist of a single take that runs over two minutes. In order to secure the changes in angles and the twists in the point of view the camera had not only been hand-held most of the time, but at times had to be handled by two operators. The nearly three-minute-long complex single-take opening scene on the hotel roof had to be shot 17 times; it involves vertical and horizontal movement of the camera operator, a combination of panoramic shots and extreme close ups, as well as the coordination of more than 100 extras.

The innovative cinematography of *I Am Cuba* was also influenced by the presence of young and inventive camera operator Aleksander Calzatti on the set. Calzatti, who eventually emigrated to Israel and the United States, had spent long hours discussing the film with Urusevsky and Kalatozov. He had seen Hitchcock's *Psycho*, and described to them its opening shot where the camera moves from a panoramic view of the city to a close-up of the window behind which the action of the film begins to unravel. Urusevsky was impressed by this description, and planned some of the long takes in *I Am Cuba* around the concept of combination of far and near. In the famous funeral scene, in one unbroken take the camera moves over a street overlooking a funeral procession, then enters a room through a window, travels over the heads of the workers in a third floor cigar factory, then goes out of the window again and continues wandering over the top of the procession. The shot was made possible with a system of cranes and an elaborate cable system.

Upon its release, *I Am Cuba* was accused of formalism. In an extensive discussion organized by *Iskusstvo Kino* in 1965 various filmmakers and critics shared their admiration for its experimentation with cinematic form, but noted that excessive attention to form had led to neglected character development and psychological complexity of the protagonists. The overtly aesthetic approach was considered inappropriate since it had subjected content to form. The filmmakers were accused of misleading viewers into enjoying the beauty of the images instead of sympathizing with the sorrows of the disinherited protagonists. It seemed that the cameraman had taken over directing, and was rather preoccupied with demonstrating the means of expression he had at his disposal while forgetting the goal these means were supposed to serve.

Urusevsky defended himself: "There cannot be art beyond form," he insisted, alluding to Eisenstein. "It has never interested me, as cameraman, to just register what is going on in front of the camera." On the contrary, Urusevsky claimed that his goal had always been to "make the image very active."

I Am Cuba was rediscovered at the Telluride Film Festival in 1992, and screened to a standing ovation at the 1993 San Francisco International Film Festival. It was then restored, released in the United States as a presentation of Martin Scorsese and Francis Coppola, and enjoyed enthusiastic reviews and acclaim in the arthouse circuit.

Toward the end of his life, Urusevsky turned to directing. In 1969 he adapted for the screen the popular short novel by Kirghiz writer Chingiz Aitmatov *Farewell, Gulsary!*, and in 1971 he worked on a film based on the works of Russian poet Sergei Yesenin, who committed suicide in 1925. After Urusevsky's death, an exhibition of his paintings was organized in Moscow.

—Dina Iordanova

V

VACHON, Christine

Producer. **Nationality:** American. **Born:** New York, 1962. **Education:** Attended Brown University. **Career:** Worked odd film jobs to learn the trade while also working as a freelance copy editor; co-founded Apparatus Productions, 1987, to produce expiremental work; co-founder, with Pamela Koffler, of production company Killer Films, 1996. **Awards:** Frameline Award for Outstanding Achievement in Lesbian and Gay Media, 1994; Muse Award for Outstanding Vision and Achievement, New York Women in Film and Television, 1996; Producer Award, Gotham Awards, 1999. **Address:** Killer Films, 380 Lafayette Street, Suite 302, New York, NY 10003, U.S.A.

Films as Producer:

1989   *He Was Once* (Hestand)
1990   *Oreos with Attitude* (Carty)

Christine Vachon

1991   *Poison* (Haynes) (+ first asst d)
1992   *Swoon* (Kalin)
1993   *Dottie Gets Spanked* (Haynes—for TV)
1994   *Postcards from America* (McLean); *Go Fish* (Troche) (exec)
1995   *Stonewall* (Finch); *Kids* (Clark) (co-pr); *Safe* (Haynes)
1996   *Plain Pleasures* (Kalin); *I Shot Andy Warhol* (Harron)
1997   *Office Killer* (Sherman); *Kiss Me Guido* (Vitale)
1998   *I'm Losing You* (Wagner); *Velvet Goldmine* (Haynes); *Happiness* (Solondz)
1999   *Wild Flowers* (Painter) (exec); *Boys Don't Cry* (Peirce)
2000   *The Fluffer* (Glatzer and Westmoreland) (exec); *Women in Film* (Wagner); *Crime and Punishment in Suburbia* (Schmidt)

Other Films:

1987   *Magic Sticks* (Keglevic) (third asst d); *My Demon Lover* (Loventhal) (prod co-ord)
1990   *The Laserman* (Wang) (second unit asst d)

Publications:

By VACHON: book—

With David Edelstein, *Shooting to Kill: How an Independent Producer Blasts through the Barriers to Make Movies that Matter*, New York, 1998.

On VACHON: articles—

Huisman, Mark J., "Screen Gem," in *The Advocate* (New York), no. 724–5, 21 January 1997.
Grey, Ian, "Urban Independent," in *Sex, Stupidity, and Greed: Inside the American Movie Industry*, New York, 1997.
Premiere (Boulder), October 1998.
Wallace, Amy, "Where Others Fear to Tread, She Steps In," in *Los Angeles Times*, 28 January 2000.

*   *   *

Independent producer Christine Vachon has been described as fearless, relentless, radical, and determined. Director Todd Haynes said of the woman who raised the bar in independent filmmaking, "She is the kind of producer who will lay down in front of a train" to get a film made. She is a risk-taker who has bucked the establishment by bringing subjects to the screen that were once considered untouchable. Dubbed the "Godmother of Independent Films," Vachon makes intelligent art pictures that have become commercially as well as critically successful.

Vachon began making movies in 1987 when she formed a production company with fellow Brown University alumni Todd Haynes. As Vachon later noted, "Our mandate was to make movies by young filmmakers just starting out." Their first effort was Haynes' *Superstar: The Karen Carpenter Story*, starring a Barbie Doll as the anorexic Karen. The Sundance Film Festival fan favorite was blocked from release when the Carpenter family filed suit against the project. Even unreleased, the film became a cult hit and brought Haynes and Vachon the clout to finance their next project, *Poison.* Inspired by the writings of Jean Genet, *Poison* skillfully interweaves three stories to create what Leonard Maltin called a "jarring, disturbing film about what it means to be different, to be alienated from the mainstream." A difficult film, *Poison* found its audience in a gay community so unrecognized and underserved by mainstream filmmakers that it flocked to see the film because it contained some gay content.

Vachon next produced *Swoon* (1992), Tom Kalin's surrealistic vision of the Leopold-Loeb murders. Unlike previous film interpretations of the famous 1920s thrill killing of a young Chicago boy, *Swoon* did not shy away from the homosexuality of the two murderers. Shot in black and white, with what Roger Ebert called "the look of modern men's fashion photography," *Swoon* was immediately touted as the epitome of the new queer cinema, even as it was roundly criticized for depicting homosexuals as murderers. Vachon, however, was quick to note that, for her, filmmaking was about telling stories, not presenting a unified front of gay identity. And in her other gay-themed films, Vachon has presented gay life from a wide range of angles and experiences.

In Rose Troche's *Go Fish* (1994), Vachon brought a witty and innovative lesbian love story to the screen—this one played by a largely non-professional cast. And Todd Haynes' *Velvet Goldmine* used a Citizen Kane flashback approach to chronicle London's glam rock era, a time in which sexual experimentation with androgyny and bisexuality stemmed from a spirit of rebellion, optimism, and hero worship.

Though she was dubbed "the Queen of Queer Cinema," Vachon detested the appellation and certainly never limited herself to producing gay-themed films. Larry Clark's *Kids* (1995) took on the uncomfortable subject of HIV-infected teenagers in a world of streetwise kids whose hellish lives revolve around sexual conquest and drugs. That same year Vachon reteamed with Todd Haynes to make *Safe,* a film about a woman who is allergic to her environment. As Roger Ebert noted, "The movie starts out dealing with one problem (environmental poisoning) and ends up attacking another (a blissed-out cult that charges big dollars from suffering people, who pay to hear the leader blame them for their troubles)." But it moves to another level when it suggests that, in fact, Moore's character may be responsible for much of her own illness. In a directorial style characterized by Ebert as "sneaky and insidious," Haynes never blames anyone, leaving the audience to work through its own discomfort.

The film that catapulted Vachon to popular acclaim was the gay-themed *Boys Don't Cry,* director Kimberly Pierce's docudrama about the Brandon Teena story. A film lauded by many critics as one of the best of the year, *Boys Don't Cry* avoided cliché by letting superb actors, led by Academy Award and Golden Globe winner Hilary Swank and Academy Award nominee Chloe Sevigny, and pure, forceful filmmaking tell a powerful and distressing true story of sexual identity and confusion in Middle America.

Although the groundbreaking film brought Vachon widespread recognition and praise, she has made it clear that she has no intention of abandoning her independent filmmaking ethos. But one can only look forward to the inevitable merging of the mainstream money and attention bound to come Vachon's way with her relentless belief in the puissant voice and vision of the independent filmmaker.

—Victoria Price

VAJDA, Ernest

Writer. **Nationality:** Hungarian. **Born:** Ernö Vajda in Romaron, 27 May 1887. **Education:** Attended the College of the Benedictine Monks, Paps, Hungary, degree in electrochemistry 1904; Peter Pazmany University, Budapest, Ph.D. 1908. **Career:** secretary to Thalia Theatre Company: first play produced, 1909; editor of *A Het,* and founder-editor of *Kepes Ujsag;* editorial writer, *Hirlap;* several other plays produced in Hungary and New York: later plays include *The Crown Prince,* 1923, *Grounds for Divorce,* 1924, *The Littlest Angel,* 1924, *Bottom of the Pile,* 1951, and *Royal Suite,* 1954; 1925–31—contract writer with Paramount: first film as writer *The Crown of Lies,* 1926; 1929—first of several films for Ernst Lubitsch; 1931–38—worked for MGM, often collaborating with Claudine West; 1942—retired from screenwriting. **Died:** In Woodland Hills, California, 3 April 1954.

Films as Writer:

1926 *The Crown of Lies* (Buchowetzki); *The Cat's Pajamas* (Wellman); *You Never Know Women* (Wellman)
1927 *Service for Ladies* (D'Arrast); *Serenade* (D'Arrast)
1928 *A Night of Mystery* (Mendes); *His Tiger Lady* (Henley); *Loves of an Actress* (Lee); *Manhattan Cowboy* (McGowan); *His Private Life* (Tuttle); *Manhattan Cocktail* (Arzner)
1929 *Innocents of Paris* (Wallace); *The Love Parade* (Lubitsch); *Marquis Preferred* (Tuttle)
1930 *Such Men Are Dangerous* (Hawks and Burke); *Monte Carlo* (Lubitsch)
1931 *The Smiling Lieutenant* (Lubitsch); *Tonight or Never* (LeRoy); *Son of India* (Feyder); *The Guardsman* (Franklin)
1932 *Smilin' Through* (Franklin); *Payment Deferred* (Mendes); *Service for Ladies* (*Reserved for Ladies*) (A. Korda); *Broken Lullaby* (*The Man I Killed*) (Lubitsch)
1933 *Reunion in Vienna* (Franklin)
1934 *The Barretts of Wimpole Street* (Franklin); *The Merry Widow* (Lubitsch)
1936 *A Woman Rebels* (Sandrich)
1937 *Personal Property* (Van Dyke); *The Great Garrick* (Whale)
1938 *Marie Antoinette* (Van Dyke); *Dramatic School* (Sinclair)
1940 *He Stayed for Breakfast* (Hell)
1941 *They Dare Not Love* (Whale)

Publications

By VAJDA: plays—

Rozmarin Neni [Aunt Rose Marie], Budapest, 1909.
Mister Bobby, Budapest, 1912.
A váratlan vendég [The Unexpected Guest], Budapest, 1915.

Szerelem Vására, Budapest, 1920.
Délibáb, Budapest, 1922, as *Fata Morgana*, New York, 1924.
The Harem, New York, 1924.

By VAJDA: book—

The Monkey Man and the Man Monkey (fiction), Budapest, 1916.

On VAJDA: article—

Kupferberg, Audrey, in *American Screenwriters, 2nd series*, edited by Randall Clark, Detroit, Michigan, 1986.

*   *   *

Ernest Vajda was one of the hundreds of talented Europeans lured to Hollywood during the 1920s. Vajda had constructed a major career as a playwright in Budapest prior to his coming to America. Although writing popular plays offered a first-rate career, Hollywood dangled its lures in front of many Europeans who were caught up in an era of high inflation and political chaos.

Vajda's career in Hollywood can be divided into two distinct periods. In the first, Vajda made his way through the complicated transition to talkies. At Paramount he became associated with witty comedies starring Adolph Menjou. Although these have not made their way into the pantheon of American movie classics of the late silent era, they did make money for what was then Hollywood's most powerful movie company. *Service for Ladies* may have been the best of these, in part because it was directed by a first-rate talent, Harry D'Arrast.

There is no question that Vajda's career peaked at Paramount once he commenced his association with the noted director and fellow emigré Ernst Lubitsch. The Berlin-born Lubitsch and Vajda could exchange their ideas for comedies from the continent in German and English. And some of Hollywood's best early sound films came about as a result. Their initial collaboration, *The Love Parade*, is now considered a classic of the early sound era. Jeanette MacDonald and Maurice Chevalier represented a new style of comedy actor for movie-goers, and box-office results indicated fans throughout the world loved their films. Before he left for MGM Vajda collaborated with Lubitsch on three more films. None were as good as *The Love Parade*, but all stood among the better products of that early era of talkies: *Monte Carlo*, *The Smiling Lieutenant*, and *The Man I Killed*.

At this point Ernest Vajda moved to MGM where he remained until 1938. As might be expected, during his first three years there the studio tried to use him to create Lubitsch-like comedies. The results were acceptable at the box office, but will be remembered by few today. Only when Lubitsch was lured to MGM to direct *The Merry Widow*, again with MacDonald and Chevalier, did a fine movie result.

In the mid-1930s the genre of the European light musical comedy faded, replaced by other forms of comedy. With it Vajda's career also came to a close. MGM dropped him in 1939, and after a few efforts elsewhere, he retired. Vajda helped write many a great film, but only in a genre which lasted from the late 1920s through the mid-1930s.

—Douglas Gomery

VAN DONGEN, Helen

Editor. **Nationality:** Dutch. **Born:** Amsterdam, 5 January 1909. **Family:** Married Kenneth Durant, 1950. **Career:** 1928—assisted Joris Ivens on *The Bridge*, and later works; 1930—studied soundtrack recording and editing, Tobis Klangfilm Studios, and also studied at UFA, Berlin; 1934—assistant and observer at Joinville Studios, Paris, studied at the Academy of Cinematography, Moscow, under Eisenstein, Pudovkin, and Vertov, 1934–36, and observer in Hollywood studios, 1936; late 1930s—worked as producer on education films; abortive job as editor on film project of Nelson Rockefeller, the co-ordinator of Inter-American Affairs, during World War II; another abortive project as deputy commissioner for the Netherlands East Indies (Ivens was to serve as Commissioner); 1950—retired upon marriage.

Films as Editor:

1928 *De brug* (*The Bridge*) (Ivens) (asst)
1929 *Regen* (*Rain*) (Ivens) (asst); *Wy brouwen* (*We Are Building*) (Ivens) (asst)
1931 *Philips-Radio* (*Industrial Symphony*) (Ivens); *Zuiderzee Dike* (doc); *Nieuwe polders* (doc); *Creosoot* (*Creosote*) (Ivens) (asst)
1933 *Zuyderzee* (Ivens)
1934 **Nieuwe Gronden** (*New Earth*) (Ivens); *Misère au Borinage* (*Borinage*) (Ivens)
1935 *Borza* (*The Struggle*) (von Wagenheim)
1936 *Spain in Flames* (+ pr)
1937 **The Spanish Earth** (Ivens)
1938 *You Can Draw* (+ d, ph)
1939 *The 400 Million* (*China's 400 Million*) (Ivens); *Pete Roleum and His Cousins* (Losey)
1940 *Power and the Land* (Ivens)
1942 **The Land** (Flaherty); *Russians at War* (compilation)
1943 *Netherlands America* (+ d); *Peoples of Indonesia* (+ d)
1945 *News Review No. 2* (compilation)
1946 *Gift of Green* (+ co-d—16 mm)
1948 **Louisiana Story** (Flaherty) (+ co-pr)
1950 *Of Human Rights* (+ d)

Publications

By VAN DONGEN: books—

Joris Ivens, Berlin, 1963.
The Adirondack Guide-Book and Related Essays, Blue Mountain Lake, New York, 1971.

By VAN DONGEN: articles—

"350,000 Feet of Film," in *The Cinema 1951*, edited by Roger Manvell, London, 1951.
"Imaginative Documentary," in *The Technique of Film Editing*, by Karel Reisz, London, 1958.

"Notes on *Louisiana Story*," "Robert Flaherty," and "Tonschnitt bei *Louisiana Story*," in *Robert Flaherty*, edited by Wolfgang Klaue, Berlin, 1964.

"Robert J. Flaherty 1884–1951," in *Film Quarterly* (New York), Summer 1965.

Film Quarterly (New York), Winter 1976–77.

On VAN DONGEN: articles—

Films and Filming (London), December 1961.
Ivens, Joris, in *The Camera and I*, New York, 1969.
Skoop (Amsterdam), November 1978.

* * *

There is a famous story recounted by *Time* magazine's Richard Corliss in a 1980 essay on Robert Flaherty. Helen Van Dongen, working as the editor of the filmmaker's *The Land*, showed him a sequence she had cut together and he fervently disapproved. A few days later she screened the same sequence for him and he said "Now you've got it." Van Dongen proved ably up to the task of working with Flaherty, transmuting the director's seemingly random and chaotic footage into, as Corliss writes, "a brilliant 'as told to' autobiography. If [Flaherty's] spirit informed their project, then [Van Dongen's] will gave its final form."

In the truest spirit of the title, Van Dongen was an editor whose techniques, honed by early work with Joris Ivens, extended beyond mere physical assemblage and continuity supervision to thoughtful documentary theory and to complex and creative sound work. In Flaherty's *Louisiana Story*, in which she served as editor and as associate producer, she worked closely with composer Virgil Thompson in creating specific themes for characters and sequences, and manipulated the sound track by disassembling sounds and then reconfiguring them: a scene on a bridge at night may contain up to 20 separate sounds (some of which were not endemic to the location) or a human scream could be a fusing of a dozen voices. Her exhaustive analysis of the film can be found in *The Technique of Film Editing* and is a fascinating look not only at how sequences were structured and sound was used, but also the reasons why—both the pragmatic and the dramatic.

Though her two World War II compilation documentaries, *Russians at War* and *News Review No. 2* were well received, having been compared favorably with the *World at War* series by Frank Capra, her two films with Flaherty have proven her most enduring works. Her extensive diaries of the production histories of *The Land* and *Louisiana Story* provide a telling memoir of working on location and in the editing room with the often opaque and stubborn Flaherty (he referred to her as his "Dutch mule"), while also revealing a uniquely productive and successful collaboration. Though certainly a tempestuous relationship, it was never overtly adversarial; in fact when Van Dongen had to trick Flaherty into providing the narration for *The Land* because no narrator could capture his intonations (she earlier had corralled Ernest Hemingway into reciting his own written words on Ivens's *The Spanish Earth*), he was by all accounts incensed, but later conceded Van Dongen was right because it benefited the film. While their goals were the same, Van Dongen admitted her greatest challenge was in having to continually interpret and reinterpret Flaherty's admittedly elusive vision (which often led to gross continuity gaps and over- and undershooting) and then shape it into a cohesive and viewable motion picture. When she first began to work

with Flaherty, she said she was "completely baffled by his method" and wrote to Ivens for help in understanding. Ivens's reply was equally cryptic: "Observe, look and listen and you'll find what he wants." Only when she was able to view the footage through Flaherty's realm of understanding, she said, and then decipher Flaherty's reaction while watching footage could she gauge the direction—and ultimately, the success—of the film. She wrote, "Had I myself gone to direct Flaherty's story, it would have looked quite different. But working with already filmed material, filmed under the influence of Flaherty . . . essentially my editing would have resulted in approximately the same story and form. This would have been inevitable because, to use the random material to full value, the editor has to discover not only the inherent qualities of each shot but also must know the how's and why's, the director's reasoning behind each shot, or must know that no one else but Flaherty would have shot such a scene." Her ability to read the director in this way no doubt made her the best editor for Flaherty, but more importantly, made Flaherty's films better.

Though both *The Land* and *Louisiana Story* are prime examples of Flaherty's filmmaking sensibility, much of the beauty and emotional gravity of the films is owed to Van Dongen's delicately focused sound and film editing. They move beyond what film history regards as documentary (and perhaps to a degree beyond what fiction can do as well), and into something ultimately more lyrical. In an interview with Ben Achtenberg, Van Dongen herself resisted the label of documentary: "To me Flaherty is *not* a documentarian; he makes it all up. He does use the documentary style and background but, except for *The Land*, they are all, to a degree, stories. . . . They are part of our history of filmmaking, but I do hesitate to call them documentaries. They are Flaherty-films, and worthwhile enjoying."

—Jon Lupo

VANGELIS

Composer. **Nationality:** Greek. **Born:** Evangelos O. Papathanassiou in Valez, 1944. **Career:** Composer and performer with European techno-rock bands Formynx and Aphrodite's Child (with Demis Roussos), then solo career; recordings since 1968, often with the singer Jon Anderson; also composer for TV commercials and other TV music. **Awards:** Academy Award for *Chariots of Fire*, 1981.

Films as Composer:

1970   *Sex Power* (Chapier)
1973   *Amour* (Chapier); *L'Apocalypse des animaux* (Rossif)
1974   *Entends-tu les chiens aboyer?* (Reichenbach)
1975   *Le Fête sauvage* (Rossif)
1981   *Chariots of Fire* (Hudson)
1982   *Missing* (Costa Gavras); **Blade Runner** (Scott)
1984   *Sauvage et beau* (Rossif); *The Bounty* (Donaldson)
1987   *Nosferatu a venezia*; *Someone to Watch Over Me* (Scott) (song)
1988   *Francesco* (*Franziskus*) (Cavani); *Le Diner des bustes* (Matouk)
1989   *Russicum* (Squitieri) (song)
1992   *1492: The Conquest of Paradise* (Scott); *Bitter Moon*; *Starwatcher*
1996   *Cavafy* (Smaragdis)

Vangelis

Publications

On VANGELIS: articles—

Atkinson, Terry, "Scoring with synthesizers," in *American Film* (Washington, D.C.), September 1982.
Score (Lelystad, Netherlands), no. 89, December 1993.

*   *   *

Vangelis' forte has been composing music for films in which characters seek to transcend their limitations in achieving some great goal or quest. Indeed, Vangelis became well-known for his musical score for *Chariots of Fire*, where he enveloped scenes of Olympic victory with that particularly exalting music of triumph he creates with such perfection. It was certainly a feat to weld music consisting in great part of synthesized or mechanically processed sounds to essentially realistic visuals. It is certainly true that many of the film's more impressive shots have been transformed by slow motion; yet the completely fantastic visuals of horror or futuristic films have been the traditional forum for what is generally considered to be experimental music. Vangelis' music, however, is not just synthetic. The composer prides himself on using echo chamber and other effects to blur the distinction between synthesized sounds and traditional instruments, as well as choir. Indeed, Vangelis' mixed-media arrangement of the Anglican hymn "Jerusalem" perfectly matches the patriarchal vision of this rather reactionary film glorifying God and Empire, and it is a phrase from this hymn that provides the film its title.

Beginning the 1982, Vangelis had the chance of providing music for two directors whose talents equaled his—first for Peter Weir. A portion from Vangelis' suite for synthesizer *Opera Sauvage* somewhat upstages Maurice Jarre's reticent score for Peter Weir's *The Year of Living Dangerously*. Vangelis' music underscores the exhilarating curfew ride of Guy (Mel Gibson) and Jill (Sigourney Weaver)—their moment of living very dangerously and of driving to their first night of love. The same is true of the scene where Jill makes the decision to tell Guy top secret information to save his life—a trust he betrays. In 1982, the composer wrote the full score for the first of two very interesting works by Ridley Scott whose misty lights and velvety darks find perfect counterparts in Vangelis' nuanced, but wide-ranging harmonies and timbres.

Vangelis accompanies the titles of Scott's *Blade Runner* with percussive sounds played under a tentative statement of the film's main theme. The opening establishing shot showing Los Angeles, in 2019, is accompanied by the percussive sounds which seem to be real explosions of burn-off from huge refinery towers, while the main theme is given a full statement with simulated brass and strings. Vangelis enjoys this playing with diegetic sounds (sounds that fit something in the plot) and extra-diegetic music (mere accompaniment): are we hearing explosions that sound like percussive instruments or the opposite? It may very well be the ambiguity of this synthesized music that makes it fit so well with both the high-tech bleeps of the futuristic world and the mysterious twists of the plot. And yet, again, Vangelis demonstrates his readiness to move beyond electronically fabricated sound to that of traditional instruments at precisely those moments when meaning and expression demand it. The love theme—a melancholy jazz melody—for the love scenes or quieter moments is done with real instruments, piano and saxophone, as if to emphasize the fact that we finally are witnessing something human, something transcendent of the fact that one of the couple is an android. Here again, Vangelis plays with diegetic/extra diegetic music by having the two (played by Harrison Ford and Sean Young) each pick out fragments of the melody on a piano. The final credit music is a magnificent toccata with a driving bass. His ability to find just the right synthetic sounds to underscore psychological intensity and depth is apparent, not only in *Blade Runner*, but in the dark quest of Costa Gavas' *Missing* and in the cross-cutting between the two desperate bands of a fragmented ship's crew in the finale of Roger Donaldson's fine effort *The Bounty*. However impressive each one of the efforts prior to 1992, not one of them prepares one for the full power of Vangelis' music for Scott's *1492: The Conquest of Paradise*. Indeed, this score seems to combine all the excellent qualities of the earlier efforts. He has composed a score to be compared, in its imaginative richness and inventive transformations, with scores by Sergei Prokofiev or Aaron Copland. This originality is not lessened, but rather greatly increased by Vangelis' having undertaken to evoke the music of Juan dal Encina and other composers of the court of Ferdinand and Isabella. Since he is dealing with a period piece set in the Renaissance and since that was a period where choral forms dominated, the prevalence he gives to sections for chorus and the artistry he lavishes on them is absolutely on the mark. In general, he uses chorus in combination with traditional instruments. When there is need, Vangelis appeals again to that side of his talent that created the euphoric, exultant texture of *Chariots of Fire*: for the departure of the ships of Columbus on their first voyage; for the royal celebration in church upon his return; for the hoisting of the giant church bell for the first settlement in the New World. And when hurricanes, white-colonial greed, Native-American uprisings, and enemies in Spain ruin Columbus' Utopian vision, Vangelis draws on his deeper, richer, darker tone poetics.

—Rodney Farnsworth

VAN HEUSEN, James

Songwriter. **Nationality:** American. **Born:** Edward Chester Babcock in Syracuse, New York, 26 January 1913. **Education:** Attened Syracuse University. **Family:** Married Mrs. William Perlberg. **Career**: 1928—radio announcer for WSYR; 1933—composed songs for Cotton Club revue; 1933–38—staff pianist at various Tin Pan Alley music publishers, including Santly Brothers and Remick's; 1939—composer for Broadway musical *Swingin' on a Dream*, songwriter for popular bands; 1940–74—songwriter for films. **Awards**: Academy Award, for "Swinging on a Star," from *Going My Way*, 1944, "All the Way," from *The Joker Is Wild*, 1957, "High Hopes," from *A Hole in the Head*, 1959, and "Call Me Irresponsible," from *Papa's Delicate Condition*, 1963; Emmy Award, for "Love And Marriage," "Our Town," and other songs from *Our Town*, 1955. **Died**: February 1990.

Films as Songwriter:

1940	*Love Thy Neighbor* (Sandrich)
1941	*The Road to Zanzibar* (Schertzinger); *Playmates* (Butler)
1942	*My Favorite Spy* (Garnett); *The Road to Morocco* (Butler)
1943	*Dixie* (A. Sutherland)
1944	*Lady in the Dark* (Leisen); *Take It Big* (McDonald); *And the Angels Sing* (Binyon); *Going My Way* (McCarey); *The Road to Utopia* (Walker); *The Belle of the Yukon* (Seiter)
1945	*Duffy's Tavern* (Walker); *The Bells of Saint Mary's* (McCarey); *The Great John L.* (Tuttle)
1946	*Cross My Heart* (Berry); *My Heart Goes Crazy* (Ruggles)
1947	*Welcome Stranger* (Nugent); *Variety Girl* (Marshall); *Magic Town* (Wellman); *The Road to Rio* (McLeod)
1948	*The Emporer Waltz* (Wilder); *Mystery in Mexico* (Wise)
1949	*A Connecticut Yankee in King Arthur's Court* (Garnett); *Top O' the Morning* (Miller)
1950	*Riding High* (Capra); *Mr. Music* (Haydn)
1953	*The Road to Bali* (Walker); *Little Boy Lost* (Seaton)
1954	*Young at Heart* (Douglas)
1955	*The Tender Trap* (Walters); *Not as a Stranger* (Kramer); *Our Town* (Bettis for—TV)
1956	*Anything Goes* (Lewis); *Pardners* (Taurog)
1957	*The Joker Is Wild* (C. Vidor)
1958	*Some Came Running* (Minnelli); *Indiscreet* (Donen); *Paris Holiday* (Oswald)
1959	*Hole in the Head* (Capra); *They Came to Cordura* (Rossen); *Say One for Me* (Tashlin); *Career* (Anthony); *This Earth Is Mine* (H. King); *Night of the Quarter Moon* (Haas); *Holiday for Lovers* (Levin)
1960	*High Time* (Edwards); *Wake Me When It's Over* (LeRoy for—TV); *Who Was That Lady?* (Sidney); *The World of Suzie Wong* (Quine); *Let's Make Love* (Cukor); *Ocean's Eleven* (Milestone)
1961	*A Pocketful of Miracles* (Capra)
1962	*Boys Night Out* (Gordon); *The Road to Hong Kong* (Panama)
1963	*Papa's Delicate Condition* (Marshall); *Come Blow Your Horn* (Yorkin); *Under the Yum Yum Tree* (Swift); *Four for Texas* (Aldrich); *My Six Loves* (Champion); *Johnny Cool* (Asher); *Come Fly with Me* (Levin)
1964	*Robin and the Seven Hoods* (Douglas); *Where Love Has Gone* (Dmytryk); *The Pleasure Seekers* (Negulesco); *Honeymoon Hotel* (Levin)
1965	*The Second Best Secret Agent in the Whole Wide World* (Shonteff)
1967	*Thoroughly Modern Millie* (Hill)
1968	*Star!* (Wise)

1969   *The Great Bank Robbery* (Averback)
1974   *Journey Back to Oz* (H. Sutherland—animation)

Publications

On VAN HEUSEN: articles—

Ewen, David, in *Great Men of American Popular Song*, New Jersey, 1970.
Cahn, Sammy, in *I Should Care*, New York, 1974.
White, Mark, in *You Must Remember This*, New York, 1985.
Hemming, Roy, in *The Melody Lingers On*, New York, 1986.
Obituary in *New York Times*, 8 February 1990.
Obituary in *Variety* (New York), 21 February 1990.
Obituary in *Classic Images* (Muscatine), March 1990.
Obituary in *Current Biography*, April 1990.
Lichtman, Irv, in *Billboard*, 30 January 1993.

*   *   *

Well-respected by his peers and popular with the ladies, James Van Heusen was as multifaceted as the music he wrote. Privately a role model for Frank Sinatra, among others, he was both loud and sublime, qualities which would manifest themselves in his most popular works.

Before being summoned by Hollywood, Van Heusen was a fledgling composer who used his photographic musical memory to transcribe songs for a radio orchestra long before any sheet music was available. His special talent allowed him to dissect hit songs and understand them. In his ten-year career through radio, nightclubs, and Tin Pan Alley, he peppered the Hit Parade with his own stylish hits until "Imagination" caught the ear of Hollywood and he was called upon to compose songs for the Jack Benny vehicle *Love Thy Neighbor*.

It was Van Heusen's next assignment which would cement his position in Hollywood by giving him an important mouthpiece for his music. Beginning with *The Road to Zanzibar*, Van Heusen would compose songs for about 20 Bing Crosby movies. Songs from Crosby and Hope's *Road* pictures, such as "Road to Morocco," "Moonlight Becomes You," and "Personality" became national favorites. Crosby's easygoing, relaxed style was amiably buoyed by Van Heusen's smooth compositions, and this is nowhere more apparent than in *Going My Way*. Van Heusen and lyricist Johnny Burke were instructed to write the Ten Commandments as a rhythm song. They came up with "Swing on a Star," an enduring and charming number which is still a favorite for children.

After his longtime lyricist Burke fell ill, Van Heusen fell into a partnership with Sammy Cahn, the lyricist behind the popular song "Bei Mir Bist Du Schoen" and the Oscar-winning "Three Coins in the Fountain." Together, they formed a powerhouse of a songwriting team, with Cahn's goofy lyrics playing well with Van Heusen's sweeping compositions. They became Hollywood's "Kings of the Title Songs" and also the unofficial official songwriters for Van Heusen's old friend, Frank Sinatra, who was reemerging in his career. This three-way partnership would literally redefine all their careers and create a body of work for which all three men are primarily identified.

Van Heusen's work for Crosby could never project the good-time, playboy image that he had personally, but with Sinatra as his new musical face, that attitude took precedence. Their first collaboration as a threesome was the title track to the film *The Tender Trap*, a hard-hitting and vibrant number with lyrics espousing the evils of marriage and music representing the beauties of bachelorhood. They followed this up with songs for a television production of Thornton Wilder's *Our Town*, featuring "Love and Marriage," the antithesis to "Tender Trap" in which Cahn's optimistic and naive lyrics are bounced around by Van Heusen's melodramatic circus waltz, which seems to illustrate the ups and downs of marriage that Cahn's lyrics overlook.

Van Heusen also had a strength for using his ballads, which are considered overlooked and deserving of the same praise as Jerome Kern's, to reveal the other side of a rather coarse character. In *Papa's Delicate Condition*, "Call Me Irresponsible" creates some sympathetic pathos for an alcoholic, played by Jackie Gleason, and is generally considered to be the only good thing about the movie. In the superb *The Joker Is Wild*, Frank Sinatra plays an unlikable singer who has his throat cut. The song "All the Way" was specifically written by Van Heusen, note by note, for the character to have some difficulty singing it once his throat is cut. Cahn's double-entendre lyrics glide over Van Heusen's sentimental and sweeping music to create a remarkable soliloquy for a snake.

Van Heusen's lesser work was of a playful nature. If there was not an "All the Way" for every picture, there was at least a "Career," an easygoing lament from the film of the same name, sung by Dean Martin. Highlights of Van Heusen's secondary work include "Young at Heart," from the movie of the same name, a sentimental and sweet number; "High Hopes" from *A Hole in the Head*, a playful children's song; "Ain't that a Kick in the Head," from *Ocean's 11*, a rollicking tour de force performed by Dean Martin; "My Kind of Town" from *Robin and the Seven Hoods*, an equally rollicking paean to Chicago which has become one of Sinatra's most beloved standards; and "Come Fly with Me," sung by Frankie Avalon for the film of the same name, has also become a beloved Sinatra standard, a testament to the lifestyle that singer and songwriter both held as their preferred one.

As the sixties wore on, musicals fell out of the vogue, as did songs in Van Heusen's style. While there were attempts at musicals, such as *Thoroughly Modern Millie*, they often fell flat, and Cahn and Van Heusen were left to write title songs for such films as *The Second Best Secret Agent in the Whole Wide World*. Twenty-five years later the world turned around and Van Heusen compositions have been given a new life. "Love and Marriage" was used as the theme to the popular television sitcom *Married . . . With Children*, though now Sinatra's version sounds even more sarcastic and doom-saying than ever before. "Young at Heart," as performed by Sinatra, was featured in the 1994 film *It Could Happen to You*. The revived popularity of crooners such as Dean Martin and Frank Sinatra has meant that songs such as "Ain't that a Kick in the Head" and "Come Fly with Me" have been reissued on CDs now being marketed to college-age music lovers. Van Heusen's music has come full circle.

—John E. Mitchell

VAN RUNKLE, Theodora

Costume Designer. **Born:** c. 1940. **Education:** Attended Chouinard Art Institute, Los Angeles, California. **Career:** Commercial artist; then sketch artist on *Hawaii*; 1967—first film as costume designer, *Bonnie and Clyde*.

Films as Costume Designer:

1966   *Hawaii* (Hill) (sketch artist)
1967   **Bonnie and Clyde** (Penn)
1968   *Bullitt* (Yates); *The Thomas Crown Affair* (Jewison) (co); *I Love You, Alice B. Toklas!* (Averback); *Amanti* (*A Place for Lovers*) (De Sica) (co)
1969   *The Reivers* (Rydell); *The Arrangement* (Kazan)
1970   *Myra Breckenridge* (Sarne)
1971   *Johnny Got His Gun* (Trumbo)
1973   *Kid Blue* (Frawley)
1974   *Mame* (Saks); **The Godfather, Part II** (Coppola)
1978   *Heaven Can Wait* (Beatty and Henry) (co); *New York, New York* (Scorsese)
1979   *The Jerk* (C. Reiner)
1981   *S.O.B.* (Edwards); *Heartbeeps* (Arkush) (co)
1982   *The Best Little Whorehouse in Texas* (Higgins)
1984   *Rhinestone* (Clark)
1986   *Native Son* (Freedman); *Peggy Sue Got Married* (Coppola)
1988   *Everybody's All-American* (Hackford); *Wildfire* (Z. King)
1989   *Troop Beverly Hills* (Kanew)
1990   *Stella* (Erman)
1991   *The Butcher's Wife* (Hughes)
1992   *Leap of Faith* (Pearce)
1995   *Kiss of Death* (Schroeder); *White Dwarf* (Markle—for TV)
1997   *The Last Don* (Clifford—mini for TV)
1998   *I'm Losing You* (Wagner)
1999   *Goodbye Lover* (Joffé); *The Championship Season* (Paul Sorvino—for TV)

Publications

By VAN RUNKLE: article—

Cinema (Beverly Hills, California), no. 35, 1976.

On VAN RUNKLE: article—

American Film, vol. 16, no. 9, September-October 1991.

*   *   *

In 1967 miniskirts maintained their hold on the world of women's fashions. With the release of *Bonnie and Clyde*, however, hemlines began to fall as fashion magazines featured the midi-look Theodora Van Runkle revived for that film. And while women were wearing midi-skirts with silk blouses, men began sporting wide lapeled, double-breasted suits.

Prior to *Bonnie and Clyde*, Van Runkle had worked as an ad illustrator before making her film debut as a sketch artist for Dorothy Jeakins on *Hawaii*. When Jeakins had to turn down *Bonnie and Clyde* due to a prior commitment, she recommended Van Runkle: it was a golden opportunity for the young designer with an admitted passion for 1930s clothing design. With her debut as a designer, Van Runkle was thrust into the spotlight: an Oscar nomination (she lost to John Truscott for *Camelot*), a Golden Tiberius from the Italian design industry, and numerous offers for more film work.

Bonnie and Clyde catapulted not only Van Runkle to fame, but Faye Dunaway as well; over the next few years, the star used Van Runkle to design her clothes both offscreen and on, establishing her fashion image as one based on soft silks which both reveal and disguise. In discussing her approach to dressing Dunaway for *The Thomas Crown Affair*, Van Runkle noted her use of accessories to counterpoint the outfit: Dunaway's passion is signified by her clothing, her control by her jewelry.

While Van Runkle has done a wide variety of period pieces, from the sock-hop styles of the 1950s in *Peggy Sue Got Married* to the hippie atrocities of *I Love You, Alice B. Toklas!*, she claims her favorite period is that from the beginning of World War I to the end of World War II. With *Mame* Van Runkle re-created a fashion obsession with hats that prompted the Millinery Institute of America to award her their Golden Crown, while with *New York, New York*, she redefined Liza Minnelli's fashion image by dressing her in tailored outfits. With *The Godfather, Part II* Van Runkle was able to cover much of the period between the wars, outfitting the mob in an exquisite array of tailored suits.

That tailored look remains one of her two favorites, the other being what she calls her "romantic" style: sensual satins, furs, lace, and velvet. With *The Best Little Whorehouse in Texas*, she was allowed to indulge that latter penchant to great effect, director Colin Higgins agreeing with her that costumes are an effective shorthand to character. In that film Dolly Parton was never more appropriately, nor more lavishly attired: one costume, dubbed "Miss Mona Aflame with Passion," cost $7,000.

—Doug Tomlinson

VEILLER, Anthony

Writer and Producer. **Nationality:** American. **Born:** New York City, 23 June 1903. **Education:** Attended Antioch College, Ohio; Union College, New York. **Family:** Son of the writer and director Bayard Veiller. Married; two children and one step-child. **Career:** 1925–30—reporter, publicist, and theater manager; 1932—first film as writer, *Breach of Promise*; then writer for RKO and other studios; 1942–45—writer for the *Why We Fight* series for the Office of War Information; 1949–52—worked mainly as producer. **Award:** Academy Award for *Stage Door*, 1937. **Died:** Of cancer, 27 June 1965.

Films as Writer:

1932   *Breach of Promise* (Stein)
1934   *The Notorious Sophie Lang* (Murphy)
1935   *Jalna* (Cromwell); *Break of Hearts* (Moeller); *Star of Midnight* (Roberts); *Seven Keys to Baldpate* (Hamilton and Killy)
1936   *The Lady Consents* (Roberts); *A Woman Rebels* (Sandrich); *The Ex-Mrs. Bradford* (Roberts); *Winterset* (Santell)
1937   *The Soldier and the Lady* (*Michael Strogoff*) (Nichols); *Stage Door* (La Cava); *The Woman I Love* (Litvak)
1938   *Radio City Revels* (Stoloff)
1939   *Let Us Live* (Brahm); *Disputed Passage* (Borzage); *Barricade* (Ratoff)
1942   *Her Cardboard Lover* (Cukor); **Prelude to War** (**Why We Fight** series) (Capra—doc)
1943   *Assignment in Brittany* (Conway); **The Nazis Strike** (**Why We Fight** series) (Capra and Litvak—doc) (+ co-narration);

Divide and Conquer (**Why We Fight** series) (Capra and Litvak—doc); *The Battle of Britain* (**Why We Fight** series) (+ d + co-narration—doc)

1944 *The Battle of Russia* (**Why We Fight** series) (Litvak—doc) (+ co-narration); *The Battle of China* (**Why We Fight** series) (Litvak and Capra—doc) (+ co-narration); *Tunisian Victory* (Capra—doc)

1945 *Adventure* (Fleming); *War Comes to America* (**Why We Fight** series) (Litvak—doc) (+ co-narration)

1946 *The Killers* (Siodmak); *The Stranger* (Welles)

1948 *State of the Union* (Capra)

1953 *Moulin Rouge* (Huston)

1955 *That Lady* (Young)

1956 *Safari* (Young)

1957 *Monkey on My Back* (de Toth)

1959 *Timbuktu* (Tourneur); *Solomon and Sheba* (K. Vidor)

1963 *The List of Adrian Messenger* (Huston)

1964 *The Night of the Iguana* (Huston)

Films as Producer:

1940 *Victory* (Cromwell)

1949 *Colorado Territory* (Walsh); *Backfire* (Sherman)

1950 *Chain Lightning* (Heisler); *Along the Great Divide* (Walsh)

1951 *Dallas* (Heisler); *Force of Arms* (Curtiz)

1952 *Red Planet Mars* (Horner) (+ co-sc)

Publications

On VEILLER: book—

Bohn, Theodore Thomas, *An Historical and Descriptive Analysis of the "Why We Fight" Series*, New York, 1977.

On VEILLER: article—

Slater, Thomas, in *American Screenwriters, 2nd series*, edited by Randall Clark, Detroit, Michigan, 1986.

*   *   *

The screenwriting career of Anthony Veiller reached its peak near the end of his career. Indeed, his final two screenplays, both for the director John Huston, probably represent his best known and best crafted: *The List of Adrian Messenger* and *The Night of the Iguana*. But Veiller did have a long and fruitful career prior to these two successes, one which spanned the Golden Age of the Hollywood studio system.

Unlike many of his generation, Veiller was born into the movie business. His father, Bayard, was a modestly successful director and screenwriter in the silent era. Once his father settled in Hollywood in the early 1930s, he brought his son in on several projects for Paramount and MGM. Having completed his brief apprenticeship, the son moved to Poverty Row with RKO, writing two or three screenplays per year. Few would care to remember the titles, save two which starred Katharine Hepburn in the early part of her career, *Break of Hearts* and *A Woman Rebels*.

During the Second World War, Veiller joined Frank Capra's documentary unit and he worked on several of the *Why We Fight* series. This work must have helped Veiller deal with the Hollywood studio system, for after the war he had the first of his two successful creative periods. *The Stranger* is now considered one of Orson Welles's minor classics. *The Killers*, a *film noir* starring Burt Lancaster and Ava Gardner, was directed by Robert Siodmak and earned Veiller an Academy Award nomination. In 1948 Veiller turned to work with his buddy from the *Why We Fight* series, Frank Capra. *State of the Union* was not Capra's best, but it did well enough at the box office. Veiller then worked as a producer, and returned to writing only in 1952, but his films of the 1950s lack the power or impact of the three efforts which came after the Second World War. It took an alliance during the 1960s with John Huston to revitalize Veiller's writing career. It was a shame that he died in 1965, for Huston and he had just begun *The Man Who Would Be King*.

—Douglas Gomery

VETCHINSKY, Alex

Art Director. **Nationality:** British. **Career:** 1930s—draughtsman at Gainsborough Studios; set designer at Gainsborough and Gaumont British until 1970s; 1977—retired from films. **Died:** In 1980.

Films as Art Director/Production Designer:

1931 *Michael and Mary* (Saville); *Sunshine Susie* (Saville); *Faithful Heart* (Saville)

1932 *Love on Wheels* (Saville); *Jack's the Boy* (Forde)

1933 *The Lucky Number* (Asquith); *It's a Boy* (Whelan); *Falling for You* (Stevenson and Hulbert); *Friday the Thirteenth* (Saville) (co); *Aunt Sally* (Whelan)

1935 *The Phantom Light* (Powell); *Stormy Weather* (Walls); *Boys Will Be Boys* (Beaudine); *Foreign Affairs* (Walls)

1936 *Jack of All Trades* (Stevenson and Hulbert); *Tudor Rose* (Stevenson); *The Man Who Changed His Mind* (Stevenson); *Where There's a Will* (Beaudine); *Everybody Dance* (Reisner); *All In* (Varnel); *Windbag the Sailor* (Beaudine) (co)

1937 *Good Morning, Boys* (Varnel); *OK for Sound* (Varnel); *Said O'Reilly to McNab* (Beaudine); *Dr. Syn* (Neill); *Oh Mr. Porter!* (Varnel); *Bank Holiday* (Reed)

1938 *The Lady Vanishes* (Hitchcock) (co); *Owd Bob* (Stevenson); *Old Homes of the River* (Vernal); *Hey, Hey, USA* (Varnel); *Convict 99* (Varnel); *Alf's Button Afloat* (Varnel)

1939 *A Girl Must Live* (Reed)

1940 *Night Train to Munich* (Reed)

1941 *The Young Mr. Pitt* (Reed); *Charley's Aunt* (Forde); *The Ghost Train* (Forde); *Kipps* (Reed); *Cottage to Let* (Asquith); *I Thank You* (Varnel)

1942 *Uncensored* (Asquith); *The Flemish Farm* (Dell)

1943 *The Lamp Still Burns* (Elvey); *Tawny Pipit* (Miles and Saunders)

1944 *Don't Take It to Heart* (Dell); *Waterloo Road* (Gilliat)

1946 *Beware of Pity* (Elvey)

1947 *Hungry Hill* (Hurst); *The October Man* (Baker)

1948   *The Mark of Cain* (Hurst); *Escape* (Mankiewicz)

1949   *Give Us This Day* (Dmytryk)

1950   *Morning Departure* (Baker); *Highly Dangerous* (Baker)

1951   *High Treason* (Boulting); *Hunted* (Crichton)

1952   *Something Money Can't Buy* (Jackson); *The Long Memory* (Hamer); *Single-Handed* (Boulting)

1953   *Trouble in Store* (Carstairs); *Hell below Zero* (Robson); *The Black Knight* (Garnett)

1954   *The Colditz Story* (Hamilton); *Up to His Neck* (Carstairs)

1955   *Value for Money* (Annakin); *Passage Home* (Baker)

1956   *House of Secrets* (Green); *Ill Met by Moonlight* (Powell); *A Town Like Alice* (Lee)

1957   *Robbery under Arms* (Lee)

1958   *A Night to Remember* (Baker); *Carry on Sergeant* (G. Thomas)

1959   *Carry on Nurse* (G. Thomas); *Operation Amsterdam* (McCarthy); *Carry on Teacher* (G. Thomas); *North West Frontier* (Lee Thompson)

1960   *Conspiracy of Hearts* (R. Thomas)

1961   **Victim** (Dearden); *The Singer Not the Song* (Baker)

1962   *Life for Ruth* (Dearden); *Tiara Tahiti* (Kotcheff)

1963   *Doctor in Distress* (R. Thomas)

1964   *Carry on Spying* (G. Thomas)

1965   *The Amorous Adventures of Moll Flanders* (Young)

1966   *Deadlier Than the Male* (R. Thomas); *Rotten to the Core* (Boulting)

1967   *The Long Duel* (Annakin)

1968   *Carry On up the Khyber* (G. Thomas)

1969   *David Copperfield* (Mann)

1970   *Jane Eyre* (Mann)

1972   *Kidnapped* (Mann)

1974   *Gold* (Hunt)

Publications

On VETCHINSKY: articles—

Screen International (London), no. 233, 22 March 1980.
Film and Television Technician, May 1980.

*   *   *

Alfred Hitchcock's return to Britain in 1971 to direct *Frenzy* was marked by a banquet at Pinewood studios. Seated next to the director was his set designer from *The Lady Vanishes* (as "a reminder of old times," publicists claimed). To Alex Vetchinsky the honour must have seemed ambiguous. Even though his employer Michael Balcon produced most of Hitchcock's films of the 1930s, he had assigned Vetchinsky to none of them. While the more flamboyant Alfred Junge worked with innovators like Hitchcock and Michael Powell, Vetchinsky remained at Balcon's low-budget Gainsborough studios, mostly ignored.

Balcon launched Gainsborough Films in 1924 on the cramped Famous Players lot in inner London's Islington. Driven to keep up a supply of comedies, musicals and crime stories, many of them (under a deal with UFA's Erich Pommer) copied from German or French originals but aimed at the American market, he recruited a directorial team which, while it included Victor Saville and Carol

Reed, more often fell back on such minor talents as Marcel Varnel and failing American pros like William Beaudine who had learned to work quickly and cheaply in Depression Hollywood. It was a cheerless *milieu*. "Mickey Balcon had a Programme," commented Michael Powell, "and when as a filmmaker you have a Programme, you have lost your soul."

Vetchinsky joined Gainsborough at the age of 23 and within a year was designing sets. He did little else for the next two decades. A vital cog in the Balcon "Programme," he provided at the rate of three or four a year the country mansions, Swiss finishing schools, Riviera casinos, London Art Deco nightclubs, trans-Atlantic liners and innumerable trains and stations demanded by the standard Gainsborough films. These were often comedy musicals (*Sunshine Susie*, *Love on Wheels*, *Falling for You*, *Jack of All Trades*) or farces featuring the ex-vaudeville Crazy Gang and Will Hay, for whose most popular films, *Good Morning, Boys* and *Oh Mr. Porter!*, Vetchinsky provided the minimal sets.

The Lady Vanishes had already been started by American director Roy William Neill but cancelled after problems during Yugoslav location shooting. Needing to direct a film, to complete a two-picture contract, Hitchcock took over not only the script but also the available Gainsborough talent including Vetchinsky, who could by then have provided designs for the film's trains, stations and snowbound Ruritanian hotel from stock. Nobody, least of all Vetchinsky, seems to have imagined the film would become the most successful of Hitchcock's British career. Having designed the period smuggling melodrama *Dr. Syn* before *The Lady Vanishes*, Vetchinsky (who shared the art direction credit with Maurice Carter and Albert Jullion) moved on immediately afterwards to two Will Hays films, two Crazy Gang films, and *Owd Bob*, the lachrymose tale of a Scots shepherd and his dog.

All the same, Vetchinsky's 1930s work does show ability and imagination. His sets for *Tudor Rose*, Robert Stevenson's 1936 version of the life of Lady Jane Grey, were widely applauded, though his true style, more modern and naturalistic, is apparent in the shadowy lighthouse interiors of Michael Powell's *The Phantom Light*. Powell made research expeditions to the Eddystone Light but Vetchinsky amplified reality with the cluttered, almost claustrophobic interiors of which he had become a master.

As his reputation increased Vetchinsky created authentically seedy seaside settings for Carol Reed's *Bank Holiday* and an expressionistic attic dormitory for the apprentices in the same director's *Kipps*, with a ceiling of slanting planes and bizarre angles that is among his finest work. For the next three decades he worked mainly on the big-budget films produced in Britain by American studios, especially 20th Century-Fox, for whom he designed Reed's Napoleonic *The Young Mr. Pitt*. After the Second World War, however, he seldom collaborated with directors of Reed's calibre.

North West Frontier and the *Titanic* story *A Night to Remember* were Edwardian dramas which submerged his talent for realism in the fussy period detail that signified in Hollywood's eyes "a British Film."

The Vetchinsky signature is more apparent in *The October Man*, a contemporary thriller with John Mills set mostly in a London suburban boarding house surrounded by a fog-shrouded park skillfully hinted at but never actually seen. Ironically Vetchinsky's one film of this time with a major artist was Michael Powell's *Ill Met By Moonlight* which takes place almost totally on Cretan hillsides. After *Carry on Nurse* in 1959, a farce which must have recalled the bad old

Gainsborough days, his reputation revived with the 1974 thriller *Gold*. Set largely in the depths of a South African gold mine which, for the climax, is also flooded, *Gold* offered the sort of challenge to which someone trained in the hard school of Gainsborough could respond perfectly.

—John Baxter

VIERNY, Sacha

Cinematographer. **Nationality:** French. **Born:** Bois-le-Roi, 10 August 1919. **Education:** Attended IDHEC, 1946. **Career:** 1948—assistant director to André Berthomieu and Louis Daquin; also photographer on several documentaries in the 1950s; 1959—first film as cinematographer, *Le Bel-âge*; first of several films for Resnais, *Hiroshima, mon amour*. **Awards:** Catalonian International Film Festival Award, Best Cinematography, for *The Cook, the Thief, His Wife and Her Lover,* 1989; Catalonian International Film Festival Award, Best Cinematography, for *The Baby of Macon,* 1993; Catalonian International Film Festival Award, Best Cinematography, Art Film Festival Award, Best Cinematography, for *The Pillow Book,* 1996.

Films as Cinematographer (Features):

1959   *Le Bel-âge* (Kast); **Hiroshima, mon amour** (Resnais); *Natercia* (Kast)
1961   **L'Année dernière à Marienbad** (*Last Year at Marienbad*) (Resnais); *La Morte Saison des amours* (Kast)
1962   *Climats* (Lorenzi)
1963   *Muriel, ou le temps d'un retour* (Resnais)
1964   *Aimez-vous les femmes?* (Léon)
1966   **Belle de jour** (Buñuel); *The Dance of the Heron* (Rademaker); *La Guerre est finie* (*The War Is Over*) (Resnais); *La Musica* (Duras and Seban); *De Dans van de Reiger*
1967   *Caroline chérie* (de la Patellière)
1968   *Le Tatoué* (de la Patellière)
1969   *La main* (Glaeser)
1970   *Bof!* (Faraldo); *La Nuit des Bulgares* (Mitrani); *L'Anatomie d'un livreur*
1972   *Les Granges brûlées* (Chapot); *Le Moine* (Kyroui)
1973   *La Sainte Famille* (Marchou)
1974   *Stavisky* (Resnais)
1975   *Je suis Pierre Rivière* (Lipinska)
1976   *Le Diable dans la boîte* (Lary)
1977   *Baxter, Vera Baxter* (Duras); *La Vocation suspendue* (*Suspended Vocation*) (Ruiz); *Eclipse sur un ancien chemin vers Compostelle* (Férié)
1978   *Les Aventures de Holly and Wood* (Pansard-Besson); *Le Fils puni* (Collin); *L'Hypothèse du tableau volé* (*The Hypothesis of the Stolen Painting*) (Ruiz); *La Bravade legendaire*
1979   *Le Chemin perdu* (Moraz)
1980   *Mon oncle d'Amerique* (*My American Uncle*) (Resnais)
1981   *Beau-Père* (Blier)
1982   *Letter from Siberia* (Marker); *Les Trois Couronnes du matelot* (*The Sailor's Three Crowns*) (Ruiz)
1984   *L'Avenir d'Emilie* (*The Future of Emily*) (Sanders-Brahms); *L'Amour à mort* (*Love unto Death*) (Resnais); *Clash* (Delpard); *La Femme publique* (Zulawski); *Flugel und Fellein*
1986   *A Zed and Two Noughts* (Greenaway)
1987   *The Belly of an Architect* (Greenaway)
1988   *Drowning By Numbers* (Greenaway)
1989   *The Cook, the Thief, His Wife and Her Lover* (Greenaway)
1991   *Prospero's Books* (Greenaway); *M Is for Man, Music, Mozart* (Greenaway—for TV)
1992   *Rosa* (Greenaway)
1993   *The Baby of Macon* (Greenaway)
1996   *The Pillow Book* (Greenaway)
1998   *Dormez, je le veux* (Jouannet)
1999   *8 1/2 Women* (Greenaway)

Publications

By VIERNY: articles—

Cinéma (Paris), July-August 1980.
Cinématographe (Paris), July 1981.
Cahiers du Cinéma (Paris), March 1983.
Positif (Paris), April 1986.

On VIERNY: articles—

Cinéma (Paris), no. 91, 1964.
Focus on Film (London), no. 13, 1973.
Film Français (Paris), 22 April 1977.
Film Français (Paris), 1 March 1985.

*   *   *

France in the 1960s became the cradle of innovative cinematography as faster film stocks, lighter cameras, and a directorial community unafraid to bend or occasionally discard forever the old rules, leveled the Hollywood formalism that ruled post-war film. Among the great French lighting cameraman of that generation, Sacha Vierny has cut his own path. Never in sympathy with the shoot-and-see guerilla tactics of Raoul Coutard, unwilling to follow Jean Rabier into his world of gaudy primaries, more adventurous than the formal Henri Decaë, Vierny has worked so closely with directors, notably Alain Resnais and Peter Greenaway, that he is less a technician than their collaborator, replicating famous pre-war relationships between cameraman and director such as that of Boris Kaufmann and Jean Vigo.

Born in 1919, Vierny was in the 1946 class at the Institut des Haute Etudes Cinématographiques. In the 1950s, with French cinema closed to new talent, Vierny, Resnais, and their colleagues made documentaries under the government grant scheme. Vierny first worked for Resnais in 1956 as assistant to Ghislain Cloquet on the concentration camp documentary *Nuit et brouillard*. The following year he lit Resnais's last short, *Le Chant du styrene*, a sponsored film about plastics manufacture turned on its head by Vierny's dazzling visuals and a Raymond Queneau commentary written in alexandrines.

Vierny shot Chris Marker's *Lettre de Siberie*, then Pierre Kast's *La Bel-âge*, his first feature. Resnais had meanwhile found funding to film Marguerite Duras's script of *Hiroshima, mon amour*, of which Vierny shot the French sections (the Japanese component is by Mishio Takahashi). Vierny's style is already apparent in this film, with its painterly taste for darkness and texture, wide ranges of contrast between scenes, and considerable courage in working with low light sources. At first viewing, the film seemed to many critics disorganised, lacking formal photographic style, even carelessly underlit. Only later did its unifying intelligence become clear.

The film won the Palme d'Or at Cannes in 1959, establishing Resnais's career along with that of Vierny and Duras and launching the *Nouvelle Vague*. Vierny went on to shoot *L'Année dernière à Marienbad* in 1961. The photography was no less chancy than on *Hiroshima*, but Vierny is philosophical about its technical drawbacks. ''The fact that there are diffused images, that we sometimes shot on sound stock, that we are not really satisfied, that we think it's a little hasty, a little botched; is that important?'' Resnais had showed the cameraman old newspapers and silent films as examples of the effects he was aiming at. ''That the whites flared and the blacks were limpid,'' said Vierny. ''That's what Resnais asked of me.''

For the next two decades, Vierny shot every Resnais film except *Je t'aime je t'aime* and *Providence*, establishing a rapport that Resnais found invaluable. Vierny is so quick, Resnais has commented, that simply the way the director looks through his viewfinder tells Vierny and his operator Philippe Brun which lens and framing he has chosen. Vierny also lit *Belle de jour* for Buñuel, *Baxter, Vera Baxter* for Marguerite Duras, and a variety of low-budget films, including *The Hypothesis of the Stolen Painting* and others for Paris-based Chilean Raul Ruiz, which suggest his continuing interest in maverick filmmaking. Many of these, especially the Ruiz productions with their discontinuous narratives and use of colour effects and filters, have been sporadically brilliant, but they lack the intensity of Vierny's best work. He did not enter into another long-term relationship with any director until his films with Peter Greenaway.

Fascinated with painting and anxious to instill some of the same values into his films as he finds in artists like Vermeer, Greenaway is a challenging collaborator for any lighting cameraman, particularly one like Vierny who shares his taste for saturated colours and low light. Their work together on films like *Drowning By Numbers* and *The Cook, the Thief, His Wife and Her Lover*, most of which are shot at night and involve intricate tracking shots through semidarkness, is rich and distinctive. At the same time, Vierny adapted with relative ease to the baroque extravagance of Greenaway's *Prospero's Books*, a flamboyant adaptation of Shakespeare's *The Tempest*, which employed the new technology of digital manipulation to render the cinema image as a page of illuminated manuscript in constant and inventive change. Indeed, throughout the 1990s Vierny more than ably served as Greenaway's house cinematographer. (His lone non-Greenaway credit from 1986's *A Zed and Two Noughts* through the end of the century is Irene Jouannet's *Dormez, je le veux*.) His images in *The Baby of Macon* and *The Pillow Book* are especially resplendent; viewing the latter (the story of a young Japanese woman who develops an appetite for having her body painted) is equal to watching a moving canvas.

Vierny, however, rejects photographic richness for its own sake. ''My satisfaction is that the photography is not remarked on too much for itself,'' he has said. To underline his preference for atmosphere over formal perfection Vierny boasts that he uses neither viewfinder nor light meter. The light meter, he says, is ''an instrument that measures essentially the *quantities* of light, and that doesn't correspond to the feelings I have about my work. What is the use of measuring? The meter will only verify that it's right.'' Such confidence would be arrogant in any lighting cameraman who had not proved, as Vierny has, his absolute mastery of the art.

—John Baxter, updated by Rob Edelman

VINTON, Will

Animator. **Nationality:** American. **Born:** 1947 (some sources say 1948); McMinville, Oregon. **Career:** 1974—first film, *Closed Mondays*, using clay-animation; the Will Vinton Studios has also done commercials and special effects projects for live-action films. **Awards:** Academy Award for *Closed Mondays*, 1974.

Films as Animator:

1974	*Closed Mondays*
1976	*Mountain Music*; *Martin the Cobbler*
1978	*Rip Van Winkle*; *Claymation* (doc)
1979	*Legacy*; *The Little Prince*
1980	*Dinosaur*; *A Christmas Gift*
1981	*The Diary*
1982	*The Creation*; *The Great Cognito*
1985	*Return to Oz* (Murch) (special effects)
1986	*The Adventures of Mark Twain*
1987	*Festival of Claymation*; *Claymation Christmas Celebration*
1988	*Meet the Raisins: The Story of the California Raisins* (Bruce)
1990	*Raisins Sold Out!*
1991	*Claymation Comedy of Horrors Show* (Bruce) (exec pr)
1999	*The PJs* (Gustafson—series for TV) (+ exec pr)

Publications

By VINTON: articles—

Banc-Titre (Paris), June 1980.
American Cinematographer (Hollywood), November 1985.

On VINTON: articles—

Cinefantastique (New York), Winter 1980.
Funnyworld, Spring 1983.
Banc-Titre (Paris), September 1983.
American Cinematographer (Hollywood), May 1985.
CinémAction (Conde-sur-Noireau), no. 51, April 1989.
Cinefantastique (New York), vol. 27, no. 7, 1996.

*   *   *

Traditionally, the earliest successful use of the medium of clay for animation-cinematography is credited to the American Eliot Noyes whose 1964 work *Clay* constitutes a rough sketch for the type of animation which Will Vinton was to make famous just a decade later with his award-winning short *Closed Mondays*. A contrast of the two films provides excellent insight into Vinton's styles and structures.

Whereas Noyes's *Clay* is best classified as "experimental animation," being the total production of Noyes himself and consisting of a series of rough-hewn representational clay shapes (animals and abstract geometric forms) which metamorphose one-to-another without regard to any narrative or "story," Vinton's production—though likely influenced by Noyes's experiments—is far more open to popular appreciation. *Closed Mondays* is at once more collaborative than *Clay* and more realistic, more highly representational in its sculpting of the various elements which mark its mobile mise-en-scènes. For while *Closed Mondays* echoes *Clay* in its employ of elaborate metamorphoses, its traditional narrative also emphasizes the classical continuity which became the hallmark of Disney's realistic cel-animation. Within *Closed Mondays*'s narrative regard for cinematic scenes (with retained axis-lines, matched action, and clear presentation of diegetic time) are clay constructions which depict human beings, buildings, furniture, and the like in a manner that is charming in its realism. When a bust of the physicist Einstein appears, for example, it is doubtless Einstein, complete with old sweater, mustache, and long unkempt hair. Comparably, Vinton's movements are realistic—with the exception of the intrinsically surreal metamorphoses.

The story of *Closed Mondays* depicts a drunk who wanders into a museum to enjoy a solitary, sarcastic appreciation of various paintings and sculptures. The drunk's walk, gestures, movements, and speech rest upon an aesthetic of extraordinary verisimilitude. Only his seemingly hallucinatory regards of paintings which "come to life," or sculptures which transform from shape-to-shape by means of clay's wonderful plastic resource for metamorphic meltings and reformations, stand in contradistinction to this same highly representational base.

Closed Mondays was Vinton's first film, and proved so successful (winning an Academy Award) that it came to launch a unique company of clay animators who work under Vinton's direction. They produced: *Mountain Music* which depicts rock musicians in conflict with natural environments and which culminates in a metamorphic cataclysm; *Rip Van Winkle*, based upon the original Washington Irving story; *The Creation*, a revision of the biblical Genesis; and *The Great Cognito*. An excellent insight into Vinton's small company and realistic clay construction during this period is provided by the 17-minute documentary *Claymation*, produced at the Will Vinton Studios.

Through this "early period," Vinton's work tended toward short subjects (including some television public service announcements), but he began to enter the realm of features with his award-winning (special effects) work on Disney's *Return to Oz*. This same transition led to the 1986 release of Vinton's first feature, *The Adventures of Mark Twain*, designed—as is all of Vinton's work—for both children and adult audiences. Using the actor James Whitmore's voice for the character of Twain, the 90-minute feature retells both Twain's life and a number of Twain's classic tales, such as "The Celebrated Jumping Frog of Calaveras County."

Finally, Vinton has realized equal success with popular television commercials as well as music videos. All these productions—from Twain through the commercials and Fogerty's "Vanz Kant Danz"—are marked by Vinton's careful realism-cum-magical metamorphoses.

—Edward S. Small

von BRANDENSTEIN, Patrizia

Production Designer. **Nationality:** American. **Born:** In Arizona. **Family:** Married the production designer Stuart Wurtzel. **Career:** Late 1960s-early 1970s—worked on stage productions for the American Conservatory Theater in San Francisco; assistant to production designer Stuart Wurtzel; 1975–77—served as art director on *Hester Street*; painted scenery for PBS; worked as costume designer on *Saturday Night Fever*; 1979—first major production-design work on *Breaking Away*. **Awards:** Academy Award for *Amadeus*, 1984.

Films as Costume Designer:

1977   *Between the Lines* (J. Silver); *Saturday Night Fever* (Badham)
1982   *A Little Sex* (Paltrow)

Films as Production Designer:

1978   *Girlfriends* (Weill)
1979   *Breaking Away* (Yates)
1980   *Tell Me a Riddle* (L. Grant)
1981   *Heartland* (Pearce)
1983   *Silkwood* (Nichols); *Touched* (Flynn)
1984   *Amadeus* (Forman); *Beat Street* (Lathan)
1985   *A Chorus Line* (Attenborough)
1986   *The Money Pit* (Benjamin); *No Mercy* (Pearce)
1987   *The Untouchables* (De Palma)
1988   *Betrayed* (Costa-Gavras); *Working Girl* (Nichols)
1990   *The Lemon Sisters* (Chopra); *Postcards from the Edge* (Nichols); *State of Grace* (Joanou)
1991   *Billy Bathgate* (Benton)
1992   *Leap of Faith* (Pearce); *Sneakers* (Robinson)
1993   *Six Degrees of Separation* (Schepisi)
1995   *Just Cause* (Glimcher); *The Quick and the Dead* (Raimi)
1996   *The People vs. Larry Flint* (Forman)
1998   *Mercury Rising* (Becker); *A Simple Plan* (S. Raimi)
1999   *Witness Protection* (Pearce—for TV); *Man on the Moon* (Forman)
2000   *Shaft*

Other Films:

1972   *The Candidate* (Ritchie) (set designer)
1975   *Hester Street* (J. Silver) (art d)
1981   *Ragtime* (Forman) (art d)

Publications

On VON BRANDENSTEIN: articles—

New York, 14 January 1985.
Film Comment (New York), March/April 1986.

American Film (New York), August 1990.
Premiere (New York), Special Issue, 1993.

*   *   *

Patrizia von Brandenstein made history in 1985 by becoming the first woman ever to win an Oscar for production design, for Milos Forman's ornate, pictorial *Amadeus*. But even if she had never won an Oscar, or never worked on *Amadeus*, her versatility alone would rank her at the top of her profession. Her credits show an astonishing range of subjects, styles, and periods: what does the low-budget, break-dancing musical *Beat Street* have in common with the expensive plutonium-plant melodrama *Silkwood*, besides von Brandenstein? Believing that a production designer can become as typecast as actors and actresses, and despite receiving Academy recognition only for her big-budgeted period pieces (*Ragtime*, *Amadeus*, and *The Untouchables*), von Brandenstein makes a concerted effort to avoid repeating herself or latching onto familiar subjects. This openness to challenge and diversity complicates any analysis of von Brandenstein's designing "style," for she has worked in so many genres her achievements resist categorization. Although not every film she worked on was a success—critically or financially—the enthusiasm she brings to such disparate pictures as *A Chorus Line* and *The Quick and the Dead* is always visible: these films, however flawed, catch the eye.

Von Brandenstein won some instant notoriety in 1977 as costume designer on *Saturday Night Fever*: the white disco-dance outfit she created for John Travolta appeared on the cover of *Newsweek*, sparking a fad. But it was her association with Stuart Wurtzel, her production design mentor (and future husband) that established ties with director Milos Forman. As Wurtzel's assistant on *Hair*, von Brandenstein worked well with Forman, and later served as art director on *Ragtime*, supervising construction of a nickelodeon and a lush rooftop garden that captured the film's nostalgic tone: they are relics of a bygone era, still glowing and functional, as if dropped from a time capsule. Her ability to establish historical verisimilitude dominates *Ragtime* and later films such as *Amadeus*, *The Untouchables*, and *Billy Bathgate*, where the visual design is so vivid and evocative the story and characters seem less interesting. For example, von Brandenstein and Forman scouted castles and palaces in Czechoslovakia to select appropriate sets for *Amadeus*, and even gained access to Prague's Tyl Theatre, where Mozart conducted the premiere of *Don Giovanni* in 1787. With all this rich architecture as background scenery, the dynamics of Peter Shaffer's stage play are somewhat stifled; the viewer is too busy gawking at the sets to concentrate on the vicious envy of F. Murray Abraham's mediocre composer. Less problematic are *The Untouchables* and *The Quick and the Dead*, period films by flamboyant directors uninterested in the psychological dimensions of their characters: here, von Brandenstein's bold re-creation of 1920s Chicago, and her hilarious rendering of a rotting, ramshackle western town match the films' comic-book plots and directorial flourishes.

Some of her best work, however, is not pure re-creation. Films with contemporary settings can challenge von Brandenstein even more than period pieces. She believes that for every picture, a production designer's main goal is to orchestrate visual material to establish the director's idea of the story's characters and central ideas, whatever the setting. Two films directed by Mike Nichols show her labors: In *Silkwood*, she conveys Karen Silkwood's paranoia and feelings of entrapment by designing her home in the same featureless, pale-green

hue as the plutonium plant where she works; only Drew, Karen's free-wheeling lover, brings life to the place with his American flags and bright-red hot rod. In *Postcards from the Edge*, von Brandenstein plays illusion/reality games meant to represent the Hollywood heroine's disorientation: a tree-lined background proves to be a set painting when a stagehand walks right through it; a building shifts behind Dennis Quaid as Meryl Streep drives away, but it is the building that is on wheels; and, most famously, Streep hangs off a ledge over moving traffic, an illusion broken when Streep lifts her hands and does not fall—both the ledge and the traffic are fake. The viewer reads these images subconsciously, hardly aware that von Brandenstein is building emotion with colors and giant props. The sets are an outgrowth of the characters' personalities and conflicts, as in *The Money Pit*, where a crumbling mansion is a comic metaphor for a crumbling marriage.

Von Brandenstein also enjoys tricking an audience with realistic sets that, in terms of the plot and the characters, become absurd and unsettling. The first half of Costa-Gavras's race-hate picture *Betrayed* depicts an underground network of para-military bigots as deceptively simple country boys fond of beer, horses, and barbecues, an extended conceit tailored to the subjective view of outsiders like ourselves. (As soon as the country boys are exposed as out-and-out racists, though, the picture loses tension and belabors the obvious Klan rallies and right-wing militia training exercises.) The eclectic *Six Degrees of Separation* extends the visual trickery to knock down social barriers: vastly different New York environments (penthouse, hovel, bookstore, police station) are inhabited by the same characters at various points, making everyone look slightly out of place. A dirt-poor young actress, for instance, barges into a high-priced apartment complex to meet a rich art dealer, who has to come downstairs to a grubby little boiler room—it is a double clash of cultures. The production design in *Six Degrees* achieves total authenticity, unlike the broad, expressionist *Silkwood*; but it is the authenticity of the locations that parodies the characters in their bizarre explorations. The art dealer would not be laughable if the boiler room did not look real.

A film designed by von Brandenstein is guaranteed to be visually interesting, and von Brandenstein herself continues to expand her territory. *The Quick and the Dead* is her first Western after 20 years of movie work, and her memorable, dilapidated designs for that film prove both her virtuosity and her readiness to take a risk.

—Ken Provencher

von DASSANOWSKY, Elfi

Nationality: Austrian/American. **Born:** Elfriede Maria Elisabeth Charlotte von Dassanowsky in Vienna, Austria, 2 February 1924; became citizen of the United States, 1962; now holds dual citizenship. **Education:** A child prodigy in piano, she was the youngest female student to be admitted to Vienna's Hochschule für Musik und darstellende Kunst (Academy of Music and Performing Arts); studied piano with German concert pianist Emil von Sauer, voice with Paula Mark-Neusser, and acting with Eduard Volters. **Family:** Married L. Harris de Czonkas, 1953 (divorced); children: two sons (one deceased), one daughter. **Career:** Piano coach for actor Curd Jürgens and director Karl Hartl, 1942; offered star contract by UFA Studios Berlin, 1944; opera debut as Susanna in Mozart's *The Marriage of Figaro*, St. Pölten, Austria, 1946; co-founded Belvedere Film Studios, Vienna, 1946; guest appearances in opera and operetta, as concert singer, pianist, and actress in Austria and West Germany; broadcast announcer for Allied Forces Broadcasting and BBC, Vienna; creator and performer of musical recitals for Allied High Command, Vienna, 1947–49; administrator and casting director, Phoebus International Films, Hamburg, 1951–53; master classes in piano and voice in Europe and United States; Hollywood vocal coach and businesswoman, from 1962; reestablished Belvedere Film Productions, Los Angeles/Vienna, 1999. **Awards:** Order of Merit in Gold, Austria, 1991; Gold Medal of the City of Vienna, 1996; 2 February 1996 named Elfi von Dassanowsky Day by California Senate; honored by city of Los Angeles, 1996; UNESCO Mozart Medal, 1997; Austrian Film Archive Lifetime Achievement Medal, 1998; honorary title of professor granted by Austrian President, 1998; Women's International Center Living Legacy Award, 2000. **Address:** c/o Belvedere Film Prod., 13052 Moorpark Street, Suite 203, Studio City, CA 91604, U.S.A.

Films as Producer:

1946 *Symphonie in Salzburg* (Diglas)
1947 *Kunstschätze des Klosterneuburger Stiftes* (Hanus); *Die Glucksmühle* (*The Mill of Good Fortune*) (Hanus) (+ ro); *Wer küßt wen?* (*Glück mußt Du haben auf dieser Welt*) (Friese)
1948 *Der Leberfleck (The Freckle)* (Carl) (+ ro)
1949 *Dr. Rosin* (de Glahs); ***Märchen vom Glück*** (*Traum vom Glück*; *Kiss Me Casanova*) (de Glahs)

Other Films:

1942 *Wen die Götter lieben (Mozart)* (Hartl) (mus asst)
1943 *Frauen sind keine Engel* (Forst) (mus asst)
1948 *The Mozart Story* (Hartl) (mus asst)
1952 *Walzer von Strauss (Waltz by Strauss)* (Silbermann) (ro as narrator)
1998 *Porträt von Elfi von Dassanowsky* (Wessely—for TV) (ro)

Publications

By von DASSANOWSKY: articles—

"Besides, ich bin Österreicherin," interview with Gertraud Steiner, in *Wiener Zeitung*, 2 August 1996.
"A Life of Devotion to Austrian Culture," interview with Birgit Schwarz, in *Austrian Information*, vol. 3, 1996.
"Die Diva und der Professor," interview with Inge Dalma, in *Rot-Weiss-Rot*, no. 3, 1996.
"Austria's Shining Light," interview with Carol Bidwell, in *Los Angeles Daily News*, 6 October 1997.
Interview with Hyde Flippo, in *The German-Hollywood Connection*, http://www.german-way.com/cinema/dass.html, 1998.

"An Hour with 'World-Citizen' Elfi von Dassanowsky," interview with Hedda Egerer, in *Noblesse*, no. 18, 1998
"Nazi Offer Spurned, Star Rises," interview with Patricia Ward Biedermann, in *Los Angeles Times*, 29 February 1999.
"Märchen vom Glück am Bauernmarkt—Erinnerungen an die Belvedere-Filme," in *Wiener Zeitung*, 10 September 1999.

On von DASSANOWSKY: articles—

Ulrich, Rudolf, *Österreicher in Hollywood*, Vienna, 1993.
Whitesell, Heidi, "Woman in the Arts," in *German Life*, April/May 1996.
Hoffmann, Robert, "Ahead of Her Time," in *Austria Kultur*, no. 4, 1997.
Dassanowsky, Robert, "Male Sites/Female Visions: Four Female Austrian Film Pioneers," in *Modern Austrian Literature*, vol. 32, no. 1, 1999.
Ulrich, Rudolf, "Zum 75. Geburtstag einer Wiener Filmpionierin," in *Blimp Film Magazine*, no. 41, 1999.

* * *

Gertraud Steiner suggests in her 1996 interview with Elfi von Dassanowsky that she has been a multi-talent—film producer, opera singer, pianist, theater actress, cultural diplomat—not only because she could be but also because she had to be. Reinvention and innovation was the only road to creative power for the women of her generation. Von Dassanowsky has also maintained that it was precisely the lack of men and the sociocultural rupture in postwar Central Europe that allowed her to slip into a leadership role in film at age 23—as Austria's second major female producer/studio head and as one of the handful in international cinema history to that time. Her background and her career show a distinct maverick spirit and a creative prowess that often ran counter to expectations and showed a strong sociopolitical conscience. Despite her classical beauty and dramatic voice which Nazi, Soviet, and Hollywood interests all attempted and failed to utilize, von Dassanowsky preferred to remain behind the camera and create on her own terms.

A musical prodigy in piano, von Dassanowsky entered Vienna's famed Academy of Music at age fifteen in 1939, one year after the annexation of Austria by Nazi Germany. Her accomplishments allowed her to teach as a student and in 1942 she was hired by director Karl Hartl to instruct rising star Curd Jürgens in piano so he could perform on camera in the Mozart-biopic, *Wen die Götter lieben*. Although Jürgens ultimately switched instruments for the role, von Dassanowsky continued to coach him for his next film and she would again be his vocal trainer in Hollywood during the 1960s. Von Dassanowsky refused to join any Nazi youth or arts organizations and subsequently her early operatic and piano careers were halted for two years of intense labor service. In 1944 UFA Studios in Berlin offered her a film contract, hoping to create another glamorous musical star along the lines of Zarah Leander, who had fallen into political disfavor. Despite prompting from the Propaganda Ministry, von Dassanowsky rejected the offer but escaped repercussions because of the collapse of the Reich.

With the Allied occupation of Austria, von Dassanowsky launched her opera career, performed a wide range of roles in the theater, had a stint at radio broadcasting, and directed and performed in musical entertainment at the behest of the Allied High Command. She turned down a Soviet offer of ''stardom'' and narrowly escaped a kidnapping attempt by Stalin's forces. Her desire to help rebuild Austrian cinema—which was hampered by Soviet control of the major studios— led her to join August Diglas and silent-film director Emmerich Hanus in founding Belvedere Film in Vienna in 1946. Not simply one of the many production companies that sprang up in Austria and West Germany in the era, Belvedere was conceived as a traditional studio, which despite its early limited space and lack of material support, discovered and cultivated technical and performance talent. Although the studio made only seven films, it was instrumental, as John Walker puts it in *Halliwell's Who's Who in Movies (13th Ed.)*, in ''kick starting'' postwar German-language film.

As producer responsible for creative decisions, von Dassanowsky attempted a re-vision of the *Heimatfilm* and the Viennese musical genres that had been tainted by Nazism. The early films, in which she also made appearances, were popular and but escaped critical attention. The last two productions, however, transcend the norms of the period. *Dr. Rosin*, the story of a gifted Viennese physician who is lost to the opium trade during the First World War, manages to evoke a half-dozen exotic locales in its back-lot production and predicts the on-location sweep of a David Lean epic. *Märchen vom Glück*, the most ambitious of the studio's productions, gave first roles to future European cinema and television stars Nadja Tiller, Gunther Philipp, and Evelyn Künneke, and fostered the comebacks of film icons O.W. Fischer and Maria Holst. The film, a satirical romance/musical set in a fictional country, echoes *Duck Soup* and American screwball comedy, but its iconoclastic political and gender-role subtext was provocative, and the kaleidoscopic style points towards the all-star Anglo-American satire extravaganzas of the mid-1960s.

Von Dassanowsky claims that both *Dr. Rosin* and *Märchen vom Glück* were actually directed by her co-producers, Emmerich Hanus and August Diglas, under the pseudonym Arthur de Glahs. During this period, von Dassanowsky also convinced young theater star Oskar Werner of his future in film, but before she could find him a suitable project, her former employer, Karl Hartl, cast him in *Der Engel mit der Posaune (Angel with a Trumpet)*, which made Werner an international star. Although von Dassanowsky was responsible for the creative growth of the studio and encouraged experimentation, her warnings against over-expenditure went unheeded and ultimately *Märchen vom Glück's* star salaries and escalating budget ended Belvedere's run. She joined a fledgling German film company in Hamburg in 1951, where she worked as an administrator, casting director, and finally star—of the company's only documentary feature, now lost. She also brought together various contacts in the Allied Command in Vienna that helped pave the way for the international co-productions in German-language cinema.

By 1955, von Dassanowsky had settled in New York, and by 1962, she had reached Hollywood. Unfortunately, she could not find the leadership opportunities there that she had in Austria and West Germany in the 1940s and 1950s. Producer/director Otto Preminger, one of the interwar Austrian cinema exiles, encouraged her to go the starlet route. Frustrated by the sexism of the times, she instead returned to her musical talents as a vocal coach to film actors, and later became a businesswoman and promoter of Austrian-American cultural exchange. Her pioneering career attained international recognition in the 1990s, during which time became a writer and re-established Belvedere Films as a production company.

—Robert von Dassanowsky

896

VON HARBOU, Thea

Writer. **Nationality:** German. **Born:** Tauperlitz, 27 December 1888. **Family:** Married 1) the actor Rudolf Klein-Rogge (divorced); 2) the director Fritz Lang, 1924 (divorced 1934). **Career:** actress in Dusseldorf, 1906, Weimar, 1908–10, Chemnitz, 1911–12, and Aachen, 1913–14; novelist; 1920—first film script, *Die heilige Simplizie*; also wrote several scripts with Lang; joined Nazi party in the 1930s, and appointed official scriptwriter; directed two films in the 1930s. **Died:** In Berlin, 1 July 1954.

Films as Writer:

1920   *Die heilige Simplizie* (May); *Das wandernde Bild* (*Wandernder Held*) (Lang)

1921   *Die Frauen von Gnadenstein* (Dinesen); *Kämpfende Herzen* (Lang); *Das indische Grabmal* (*The Indian Tomb*) (May); *Der müde Tod* (*Between Two Worlds; Beyond the Wall*) (Lang); *Der Leidensweg der Inge Krafft* (May)

1922   *Der brennende Acker* (*Burning Soil*) (Murnau); **Dr. Mabuse, der Spieler** (*Dr. Mabuse, the Gambler*) (Lang); *Phantom* (Murnau)

1923   *Die Austreibung* (*Driven from Home*) (Murnau); *Die Prinzessin Suwarin* (Guter)

1924   *Die Finanzen des Grossherzogs* (*The Grand Duke's Finances*) (Murnau); *Michael* (Dreyer); **Die Nibelungen** (Lang—2 parts)

1925   *Zur Chronik von Grieshuus* (*At the Grey House*) (von Gerlach)

1927   **Metropolis** (Lang)

1928   *Spione* (*Spies*) (Lang)

1929   *Die Frau im Mond* (*By Rocket to the Moon; The Woman in the Moon*) (Lang)

1931   *M* (Lang)

1932   *Das erste Recht des Kindes* (*Aus dem Tagebuch einer Frauenärzin*) (Wendhausen)

1933   **Das Testament des Dr. Mabuse** (*The Testament of Dr. Mabuse*) (Lang); *Der Läufer von Marathon* (Dupont)

1934   *Hanneles Himmelfahrt* (+ d); *Prinzessin Tourandot* (Lamprecht); *Was bin ich ohne Dich?* (Rabenalt)

1935   *Der alte und der junge König* (Steinhoff); *Ein idealer Gatte* (Selpin); *Ich war Jack Mortimer* (Froelich); *Der Mann mit der Pranke* (van der Noss)

1936   *Eine Frau ohne Bedeutung* (*A Woman of No Importance*) (Steinhoff); *Eskapade* (*Seine offizielle Frau*) (Waschneck); *Die unmögliche Frau* (Meyer)

1937   *Der Herrscher* (*The Ruler*) (Harlan); *Versprich mir nichts!* (Liebeneiner); *Mutterlied* (Gallone); *Der zerbrochene Krug* (*The Broken Jug*) (Ucicky)

1938   *Jugend* (*Youth*) (Harlan); *Verwehte Spuren* (Harlan); *Die Frau am Scheidewege* (von Baky)

1939   *Hurra! Ich bin Papa!* (Hoffmann)

1940   *Lauter Liebe* (Rühmann); *Wie konntest du, Veronika?* (Habich)

1941   *Annelie* (*Die Geschichte eines Lebens*) (von Baky); *Am Abend auf der Heide* (von Alten)

1942   *Mit den Augen einer Frau* (Külb)

1943   *Die Gattin* (Jacoby); *Gefährten meines Sommers* (Buch)
1944   *Eine Frau für drei Tage* (Kirchhoff)
1948   *Fahrt ins Glück* (Engel—produced 1945); *Via Mala* (*Die Strasse des Bösen*) (von Baky—produced 1944)
1950   *Es kommt ein Tag* (Jugert); *Erzieherin gesucht* (Erfurth—produced 1944)
1951   *Dr. Holl* (Hansen)
1953   *Dein Herz ist meine Heimat* (Häussler)

Film as Director:

1934   *Elisabeth und der Narr*

Publications

By VON HARBOU: fiction—

Die nach uns kommen, Stuttgart, 1910.
Von Engeln und Teufelchen, Stuttgart, 1913.
Der Krieg and Die Frauen, Stuttgart, 1913.
Die Masken des Todes, Stuttgart, 1915.
Der unsterbliche Acker, Stuttgart, 1915.
Aus Abend und Morgen ein neuer Tag, Heilbronn, 1916.
Gold in Feuer, Stuttgart, 1916.
Das Mondscheinprinzesschen, Stuttgart, 1916.
Der belagerte Tempel, Berlin, 1917.
Das indische Grabmal, Berlin, 1917.
Adrian Drost und sein Land, Berlin, 1918.
Sonderbare Heilige, Berlin, 1919.
Das Haus ohne Tür und Fenster, Berlin, 1920.
Legenden, Berlin, 1920.
Das Nibelungenbuch, Munich, 1923.
Mann zwischen Frauen, Leipzig, 1927.
Metropolis, Berlin, 1926, translated as *Metropolis*, London, 1927.
Frau im Mond, Berlin, 1928, as *The Girl in the Moon*, London, 1930.
Die Insel der Unsterblichen, Berlin, 1928.
Spione, Berlin, 1928, as *The Spy*, London, 1928.
Rocket to the Moon, New York, 1930.
Du bist unmöglich Jo, Berlin, 1931.
Aufblühender Lotos, Berlin, 1941.
Gartenstrasse 64, Berlin, 1952.

By VON HARBOU: other books—

Deutsche Frauen, Leipzig, 1914.
Die junge Wacht am Rhein, Stuttgart, 1915.
Die deutsche Frau im Weltkrieg, Leipzig, 1916.
Die unheilige Dreifaltigkeit, Heilbronn, 1920.
Liebesbriefe aus St. Florin, Leipzig, 1935.
Das Dieb von Bagdad, Holzminden, 1949.
With Fritz Lang, *M* (script), edited by Gero Gandert and Ulrich Gregor, Hamburg, 1963, translated as *M*, New York, 1968.
With Fritz Lang, *Metropolis* (script) in *Avant-Scène* (Paris), 1 December 1977.

On VON HARBOU: book—

Keiner, Reinhold, *Thea Von Harbou und der deutsche Film bis 1933*, Hildesheim, 1984.

On VON HARBOU: articles—

Mein Film (Vienna), 29 August 1952.
Filmblätter, 8 January 1954.
Chaplin (Stockholm), December 1968.
Nenno, Nancy P., ''Kinomythen: 1920–1945, Die Filmentwurfe der Thea von Harbou,'' in *German Quarterly*, Summer 1996.

*   *   *

Thea Von Harbou worked as Fritz Lang's principal scenarist from 1924 to 1932, when she split with Lang on political matters, and enthusiastically joined the Nazi Party. If we are to believe Fritz Lang's later statements, made in the 1960s in America, it was Von Harbou who turned Lang in to Joseph Goebbels, the head of the Reich Propaganda Ministry.

Von Harbou's work as a scenarist for Lang includes her scripts for *Metropolis*, *By Rocket to the Moon*, *Dr. Mabuse, the Gambler*, and *Spies*. She also worked with Murnau, Dreyer and Joe May. After writing the screenplay of Lang's most anti-Nazi film, *The Testament of Dr. Mabuse* (in which Hitler's words are put in the mouth of Dr. Mabuse, a criminal madman), Von Harbou made a fatal decision, deciding for the nihilistic vision of the Nazis over the humanistic if sometimes brooding realism of the best of Lang's works. She worked continually up to her death on screen fare of decreasing distinction, ending her career with the screenplay for the mediocre film *Dein Herz ist meine Heimat*.

In all of Von Harbou's screenplays, one can easily detect the strident notes of propaganda. Her work with Lang is the most restrained and fleshed-out of her long career, but, Lang later claimed that Von Harbou was, at her best, merely a journeyman screenwriter who lacked the ability to get inside the motivations of her characters. Because Von Harbou supported a regime which took a dim view of individualism or artistry without state direction, it is to be expected that her work under the Hitler regime, such as the screenplay for *Jugend*, a study of the Hitler Youth Movement, would fail as both propaganda and cinematic art.

Between 1945 and 1951 Von Harbou was prevented from working in the German cinema by order of the Nuremburg Tribunal, but clearly her major work, for better or worse, was long behind her. She also directed two films under the Nazis, *Elisabeth und der Narr* and *Hanneles Himmelfahrt*. Neither was a commercial or critical success. The same must be said of her work as a screenwriter between 1933 and 1945. That her resultant efforts were quickly forgotten by both the public and the critics seems an inescapable by-product of Von Harbou's ardent espousal of the Nazi cause. For the researcher, prints of Von Harbou's work during the Second World War are available for screening at the National Archive in Washington, D.C. Although Von Harbou was undoubtedly one of the key figures in the Expressionist movement of the 1920s, her work from 1937 to 1945, founded as it inevitably was on a doctrine of racial hatred, simply has no place in a thoughtful or caring society.

—Wheeler Winston Dixon

VORKAPICH, Slavko

Special Effects Technician and Director. **Nationality:** Yugoslav. **Born:** Slavko Vorkapic in Dobrna, 17 March 1895. **Education:** Belgrade, Budapest, and Paris. **Military Service:** Served in a student regiment during World War I. **Career:** 1920—settled in the United States; 1922—first film work as actor in Rex Ingram films; 1927—codirector of *The Life and Death of a Hollywood Extra*; then worked in providing montage sequences for RKO and, from 1933 to 1939, for MGM; 1949–51—head of film department, University of Southern California, Los Angeles; lectured in Europe in the 1950s, and artistic adviser, Avala Film Studios, Belgrade, and teacher, Belgrade Academy of Art; 1959–60—editor of TV series *John Gunther's High Road*. **Died:** Of diabetes in Mijas, Spain, 20 October 1976.

Films as Director of Montage Sequences:

1930   *Safety in Numbers* (Schertzinger)
1931   *Girls about Town* (Cukor); *I Take This Woman* (co)
1932   *The Conquerors* (*The Pioneer Builders*) (Wellman); *What Price Hollywood?* (Cukor)
1933   *No Other Woman* (Ruben); *Christopher Strong* (Arzner); *Turn Back the Clock* (Selwyn); *Dancing Lady* (Leonard); *The Past of Mary Holmes* (co)
1934   *Viva Villa!* (Conway); *Manhattan Melodrama* (Van Dyke); *Crime without Passion* (Hecht and MacArthur); *The President Vanishes* (*Strange Conspiracy*) (Wellman)
1935   *David Copperfield* (Cukor)
1936   *Romeo and Juliet* (Cukor)
1937   *The Good Earth* (Franklin); *Maytime* (Leonard); *The Firefly* (Leonard); *The Broadway Melody of 1938* (Del Ruth); *The Last Gangster* (Ludwig)
1938   *Test Pilot* (Fleming); *Yellow Jack* (Seitz); *Three Comrades* (Borzage); *The Shopworn Angel* (Potter); *Marie Antoinette* (Van Dyke); *Port of Seven Seas* (Whale); *Sweethearts* (Van Dyke); *Of Human Hearts* (Brown); *The Girl of the Golden West* (Leonard)
1939   *Idiot's Delight* (Brown); **Mr. Smith Goes to Washington** (Capra); *Air Waves* (short)
1940   *The Howards of Virginia* (*The Tree of Liberty*) (Lloyd)
1941   *Meet John Doe* (Capra)
1942   *Moscow Strikes Back* (Varlamov and Kopalin) (ed. of US version of *Razgrom nemetzkikhy voisk pod Moskvoi*)
1945   *A Song to Remember* (C. Vidor)

Films as Director (shorts):

1942   *Private Smith of the U.S.A.*; *Conquer by the Clock*; *Moods of the Sea* (co)
1943   *Lieutenant Smith*; *Sailors All*
1944   *Mail Call*
1945   *New Americans*; *T.V.A.*
1946   *Fingal's Cave*
1947   *Forest Murmurs*

Films as Actor:

1922   *The Prisoner of Zenda* (Ingram); *Trifling Woman* (*Black Orchid*) (Ingram)
1923   *Scaramouche* (Ingram)

Other Films:

1927   *The Life and Death of a Hollywood Extra* (*The Life and Death of 9413—A Hollywood Extra*) (co-d + co-sc, ph, ed)
1948   *Joan of Arc* (Fleming—full-length) (assoc d)
1955   *Hanka* (d+ co-sc, ed—full-length)
1961   *The Mask* (*The Eyes of Hell*) (Roffman—full-length) (co-sc)

Publications

By VORKAPICH: articles—

''Cinematics,'' in *Cinematographic Annual 1930*, Hollywood, 1930.
''Towards True Cinema,'' in *Film Culture* (New York), April 1959.
Film Culture (New York), Fall 1965.
Making Film in New York (New York), June 1970.
''A Fresh Look at the Dynamics of Film-Making,'' in *American Cinematographer* (Hollywood), February 1972.
American Cinematographer (Hollywood), July 1973.
''*The Life and Death of a Hollywood Extra*,'' (script) in *Framework* (Norwich), Summer 1983.

On VORKAPICH: books—

Goodman, Ezra, *The Fifty-Year Decline and Fall of Hollywood*, New York, 1961.
Whittemore, Don and Cecchettini, Philip Alan, *Passport to Hollywood: Film Immigrants Anthology*, New York, 1976.

On VORKAPICH: articles—

American Cinemeditor (Los Angeles), Spring 1972.
Farber, Stephen, in *Film Comment* (New York), September 1972.
Films in Review (New York), June-July 1975.
Petric, Vlada, in *American Film* (Washington, D.C.), March 1978.Brown, Geoff, ''Vorkapich around Vorkapich,'' in *Monthly Film Bulletin* (London), September 1981.
Ekran (Ljubljana), vol. 7, nos. 3–4, 1982.
Zecevic, B., and Richard Allen, ''Archaeology of Film Theory 7: Slavko Vorkapich—a Hollywood Extra,'' in *Framework*, no. 21, Summer 1983.
Dakovic, N., ''Recent Books from Yugoslavia (Serbia and Montenegro),'' in *Historical Journal of Film, Radio and Television* (Abingdon), no. 2, 1995.

*   *   *

To today's audiences, brought up on high-speed editing and slick narrative elisions, the pace of classic 1930s Hollywood cinema can sometimes seem ponderous. Events are too explained, too paced-out—except when, about mid-way through certain films, the action abruptly slips into a montage sequence like a sedately-flowing stream suddenly diving into a narrow canyon. Adagio turns to presto: whole pages of dull exposition are eliminated as, in a cascade of images often lasting less than a minute, months or years hurtle past, thousands of miles are traversed by road or rail, the fortunes of the hero (or of whole empires) rise or fall. The inventor and master of this telescoping technique was Slavko Vorkapich, cinema's first-ever montage editor.

After studying to be a painter, Vorkapich began his film career acting in minor roles (and working on dissolves) for Rex Ingram, whose rhapsodic imagery may have influenced the young extra. But the chief influences on the work that brought him to fame, the experimental short *The Life and Death of 9413, a Hollywood Extra*, were those of German expressionism and the Russian school of montage. Reputedly made on a kitchen table for $96, in collaboration with Robert Florey and Gregg Toland, this was the first experimental film to gain wide distribution in the USA and Vorkapich, who had edited it as well as codirecting, found himself in demand in Hollywood as a master of the latest in editing techniques.

Hired by Paramount, and later by RKO and MGM, to construct what were initially called "transition sequences" in feature films, Vorkapich rapidly developed a technique of his own that owed little to the classic theories of the Soviet filmmakers. Where Eisenstein set out to create a dialectic through contrasted images, and Pudovkin's "linkages" aimed at guiding the thoughts and emotions of the viewer, Vorkapich's "symphonies of visual movement," as he called them, were chiefly designed to advance the story as rapidly and vividly as possible. These sequences, with their headlong, seemingly unstoppable pace, were especially well suited to depicting cataclysms both natural and man-made: the collapse of Wall Street in *The Conquerors*, the outbreak of the Mexican Revolution in *Viva Villa!*, the ravages of famine in *The Good Earth*, and of the plague in *Romeo and Juliet*. When working with filmmakers of an adventurous frame of mind, Vorkapich seized the opportunity to introduce expressionist elements into his work, and some of his most imaginative effects occur in the montages he devised, working closely with cinematographer Lee Garmes, for Hecht and MacArthur's *Crime without Passion*. The opening credits show three winged Furies darting through the canyons of New York to seize at random upon their victims; when crooked lawyer Claude Rains shoots the dancer who is blackmailing him, the Furies emerge from a drop of her blood as it falls in slow-motion and wheel vengefully out into the night, feasting their eyes on the violence of the city.

Much of the time, though, Vorkapich's work found itself incongruously spliced into films with which, in terms of style and mood, it had little or nothing in common. His montages feature in four of the Nelson Eddy-Jeanette MacDonald musicals, stranded amid the apple blossom and whipped cream of MGM's cloying prettiness. As Geoff Brown noted (in *Monthly Film Bulletin* of Sept. 1981), Vorkapich's "attempts to slice through this cinematic wedding cake are honourable but doomed." He would have fitted in far better with the pacy, staccato rhythms of Warner Bros.—but Warners, oddly enough, is one of the few major studios where he seems never to have worked.

As fashions in filmmaking changed towards the end of the 1930s, Vorkapich's style of montage came to seem outmoded and was decreasingly in demand. During the war he directed propaganda shorts for Frederick Ullman, Jr.'s *This is America* series, and afterwards returned only once more to Hollywood, dispatching Cornel Wilde's Chopin on a triumphal pan-European tour in *A Song to*

Remember. Thereafter he withdrew into academia, taking up a teaching post at the University of Southern California. In the 1950s, he returned for a while to his native Yugoslavia, where he taught at the Belgrade Academy, acted as artistic adviser at the Avala Film Studios and directed his sole feature film, *Hanka*. Towards the end of his life, Vorkapich gave a series of public lectures expounding his theory of film as an autonomous visual language. They attracted large and prestigious audiences, not least for Vorkapich's iconoclastic readiness to lambaste some of the most revered names of cinema (Eisenstein, Ford, Bergman) for what he saw as technical incompetence. For a while, he was considered one of the great film theoreticians, though since his death his reputation has faded. But his influence remains strong on mainstream Hollywood editing and narrative techniques, both directly via his montage-editor successors like Peter Ballbusch and Don Siegel, and more widely on editors and cinematographers in general. To a large extent, those same slick, well-oiled narrative conventions that today's audiences take so much for granted can be traced back to Vorkapich's trailblazing work.

—Philip Kemp

VUKOTIĆ, Dušan

Animator. **Nationality:** Yugoslav. **Born:** Bileca, 1927. **Education:** Studied architecture in Zagreb. **Career:** Cartoonist for *Kerempuh* magazine; 1950—first animated film, *A Big Rally*; 1951–52—worked at Duga Film until its collapse; formed animation company with several colleagues that became Zagreb Film, 1956. **Awards:** Academy Award for *Ersatz*, 1961. **Died:** 8 July 1998, in Zagreb, Croatia, of natural causes.

Films as Animator:

1950   *A Big Rally* (co)
1951   *How Kico Was Born*
1952   *The Enchanted Castle in Dudinci*
1956   *The Playful Robot* (*The Disobedient Robot*); *The Magic Catalogue*
1957   *Cowboy Jimmie*; *Carobni zvuci* (*The Magic Sounds*)
1958   *Abracadabra*; *Osvetnic* (*Revenger*); *Veliki strah* (*The Great Fear*); *Koncert za masinsku pusku* (*Concerto for Sub-Machine Gun*)
1959   *Krava na mjescu* (*The Cow on the Moon*); *My Tail's My Ticket*; *All the Drawings of the Town*
1960   *Piccolo*; *1001 Drawings*
1961   *Ersatz*; *The Lion Tamer*; *A Doll*
1962   *Play*
1963   *Astromutts*
1964   *A Visit from Space*; *Put oko svijeta* (*Trip around the World*) (Jovanovic) (animation sequences)
1966   *Sedmi kontinent* (*The Seventh Continent*) (+ co-sc)
1967   *Man and His World*; *Time*
1968   *A Stain on the Conscience*; *Opera Cordis*; *Gorilla's Dance*
1969   *OTC*
1970   *Ars Gratia Artis*
1971   *Flight 54321*; *Maternity Hospital*
1974   *Gubecziana*

1975   *Grasshopper*
1977   *Operation Stadium*
1979   *Amy Goes to Buy Some Bread*
1981   *Monstrum z galaxie Arkana* (*Monsters from the Arcane Galaxy; Visitors form the Galaxy*)
1983   *Gavrilovic II*
1984   *Zagreb Title*
1993   *Dobro dosli na planet Zemlju*

Publications

By VUKOTI,: articles—

Filmska Kultura, no. 27, 1962.
Film und Fernsehen (Berlin), no. 11, 1978.
Film a Doba (Prague), no. 12, 1981.

On VUKOTI,: articles—

Jugoslavia Film, March 1964.
Durand, P., in *Cinéma* (Paris), no. 98, 1965.
Film (London), no. 60, 1970.
Ekran (Yugoslavia), vol. 14, no. 5–6, 1977.
Ekran (Yugoslavia), vol. 18, no. 6–7, 1981.
Filmowy Serwis Prasowy (Warsaw), vol. 29, no. 6, 16–31 March 1983.

*   *   *

Dušan Vukotić is an important animator and co-founder of the widely acclaimed Zagreb Film Studio. Known throughout the world as the ''Zagreb School,'' the Yugoslavian animation company achieved fame in the 1960s for its political satire expressed through visual experimentation. Vukotić played a significant role in establishing the structure and aesthetic direction of the Zagreb Studio styles.

Vukotić began his animation career shortly after World War II when he collaborated with other artists on an animated cartoon commemorating Yugoslavia's break from the Soviet bloc, *A Big Rally*. The artists involved in this project had all met working on the satirical magazine *Kerempuh*, a popular publication which employed young writers and artists (Vukotić himself had been trained as an architect). Using old American cartoons as a guide, the group was so successful in their first effort that they were able to start an animation studio, Duga Film.

The Duga Film studio employed a staff of approximately 100 young artists in four animation units modeled after the Walt Disney studio as well as the Disney aesthetic. Between 1951 and 1952, Vukotić worked at Duga and developed a highly individualistic style of animation. Within the company, he led a rival movement away from anthropomorphic imitation, naturalistic movement, and costly full-animation processes. When, in 1952, Duga closed the studio because it was not economically efficient, Vukotić and others (including Nikola Kostelac, Zlatko Bourek, Aleksandar Marks, and Boris Kolar) left to form an animation company for advertising films.

The success of the new company relied upon the importance of reduced animation. Requiring far fewer animation cels—or drawn frames—for each cartoon, reduced animation was less expensive, quicker, and aesthetically more radical than the full-animation technique of drawing or painting every individual frame in order to achieve the illusion of smooth, naturalistic movement. Influenced by Jiří Trnka's films for their nationalist character as well as by the United Productions of America cartoons that employed streamlined graphics and reduced animation, Vukotić developed a style dependent on minimalized, abstract graphics and upbeat tempos. Freed from anthropomorphic limitations and realistic imitation, the films that Vukotić directed had both a contemporary look and topical subject matter.

Between 1955 and 1958, the new animation company took shape both legally and aesthetically as the Zagreb Film Studio. In 1956 Vukotić directed the studio's first attempt at story animation (*The Playful Robot*), and in 1958 the company received important international recognition at the Oberhausen, Cannes, and Venice festivals. Vukotić continued the practice that he learned at *Kerempuh* of employing young writers, architects, sculptors, and painters so that the films assumed important influences from the graphic arts and maintained a vanguard aesthetic quality.

Vukotić's own oeuvre is highly eclectic. His earliest Zagreb cartoons were highly successful satires of American movie genres: *Cowboy Jimmie*, *The Great Fear*, and *Concerto for Sub-Machine Gun*. *Piccolo*, which Vukotić directed, designed, and animated himself, was among the first in a wave of Zagreb cartoons that reflected Vukotić's strongly held belief in auteurism and individual style. In the late 1960s Vukotić experimented with live-action combined with animation in such films as *Ars Gratia Artis*, a satire on contemporary art and on general relationships between an individual and the masses. In addition to winning many international animation awards, Vukotić was the first artist to receive an Academy Award for a cartoon produced outside the United States, *Ersatz*.

—Lauren Rabinovitz

WAGNER, Fritz Arno

Cinematographer. **Nationality:** German. **Born:** Schmiedefeld am Rennsteig, 5 December 1891 (other sources give 1889 and 1894). **Education:** Studied commercial subjects at the University of Leipzig; attended Academy of Fine Arts, Paris. **Career:** 1911—clerk for Pathé, Paris; newsreel cameraman during the 1910s; 1919—joined Decla-Bioscop, Berlin: first film as cinematographer, *Der Galeerensträfling*; after World War II, worked at DEFA, Babelsburg. **Died:** In automobile accident, 18 August 1958.

Films as Cinematographer:

1919   *Der Galeerensträfling* (co)
1920   *Arme Violetta* (*The Red Peacock*) (Stein); *Die Geshchlossene Kette* (Stein); *Das Martyrium* (Stein); *Das Skelett des Herrn Markutius* (Janson)
1921   *Der müde Tod* (*Between Two Worlds*) (Lang) (co); *Schloss Vogelöd* (*The Haunted Castle*) (Murnau) (co); *Nachtbesuch in der Northernbank* (Grune); *Pariserinnen* (Lasko); *Das Spiel mit dem Feuer* (Wiene and Kroll)
1922   *Der brennende Acker* (*Burning Soil*) (Murnau) (co); *Nosferatu* (*Nosferatu the Vampire*) (Murnau) (co); *Schatten* (*Warning Shadows*) (Robison); *Bardame* (Guter); *Der Graf von Essex* (Felner); *Das hohe Lied der Liebe* (Schall); *Lebenshunger* (Guter); *Der Ruf des Schicksals* (Guter)
1923   *Der Grossindustrielle* (Kaufman); *Die Magyarenfürstin* (Funck); *Zwischen Abends und Morgens* (Robison)
1924   *Der Sprung ins Leben* (Guter)
1925   *Zur Chronik von Grieshuus* (*At the Grey House*) (von Gerlach) (co); *Das Fräul ein vom Amt* (Schwarz); *Pietro der Korsar* (*Peter the Pirate*) (Robison)
1926   *Die drei Kuckucksuhren* (Mendes); *Liebeshandel* (Speyer); *Vater werden ist nicht schwer . . .* (Schönfelder)
1927   *Am Rande der Welt* (Grune); *Eine DuBarry von Heute* (*A Modern DuBarry*) (Z. Korda); *Der Liebe der Jeanne Ney* (*The Love of Jeanne Ney*) (Pabst) (co)
1928   *Das letzte Fort* (Bernhardt); *Marquis d'Eon, der Spion der Pompadour* (Grune); *Waterloo* (Grune); *Spione* (*Spies*) (Lang)
1929   *Napoleon à Sainte-Hélène* (Pick); *Wenn du einmal dein Herz verschenkst* (Guter)
1930   *Brand in der Oper* (Froelich); *Dolly macht Karriere* (Litvak); *Die Jagd nach dem Glück* (*Running after Luck*) (Gliese and Koch); *Skandal um Eva* (*Scandalous Eva*) (Pabst); *Westfront 1918* (*Comrades of 1918*) (Pabst) (co)

1931   *M* (*Mörder unter uns*) (Lang); *Ronny* (Schünzel); *Kameradschaft* (*Comradeship*) (Pabst) (co); *Die Dreigroschenoper* (*The Threepenny Opera*; *The Beggar's Opera*) (Pabst)
1932   *Es wird schon wieder besser* (Gerron); *Das Lied einer Nacht* (Litvak); *Das schöne Abenteuer* (Schünzel)
1933   *Das Testament des Dr. Mabuse* (*The Testament of Dr. Mabuse*) (Lang) (co); *Flüchtlinge* (Ucicky); *Die Nacht der grossen Liebe* (von Bolvary); *Das Schloss im Süden* (von Bolvary); *Spione am Werk* (Lamprecht)
1934   *Liebe, Tod, und Teufel* (Hilpert and Steinbicker); *Ein Mann will nach deutschland* (Wegener); *Prinzessin Turandot* (Lamprecht); *Spiel mit dem Feuer* (Robert)
1935   *Amphitryon* (Schünzel); *Schwarze Rosen* (Martin)
1936   *Savoy-Hotel 217* (Ucicky); *Unter heissem Himmel* (Ucicky)
1937   *Der Mann, der Sherlock Holmes war* (Hartl); *Tango notturno* (Kirchhoff); *Der zerbrochene Krug* (Ucicky)
1938   *Das Mädchen mit dem guten Ruf* (Schweikart); *Schatten über St. Pauli* (Kirchhoff)
1939   *Ein hoffnungloser Fall* (Engel); *Der Vierte kommt nicht* (Kimmlich); *Robert Koch, der Bekämpfer des Todes* (Steinhoff)
1940   *Aus erster Ehe* (Verhoeven); *Feinde* (Tourjansky); *Friedrich Schiller* (Maisch); *Der Fuchs von Glenarvon* (Kimmich)
1941   *Ohm Krüger* (Steinhoff); *Was geschah in dieser Nacht* (Lingen)
1942   *Die Entlassung* (Liebeneiner); *Der Fall Rainer* (Verhoeven)
1943   *Altes Herz wird wieder Jung* (Engel); *Ein glucklicher Mensch* (Verhoeven); *Herr Sanders lebt gefährlich* (Stemmle); *Lache Bajazzo* (Hainisch); *Ich werde dich auf Händen tragen* (Hoffmann)
1945   *Das kleine Hofkonzert* (Verhoeven); *Meine Herren Söhne* (Stemmle)
1949   *Die Brücke* (*The Bridge*) (Pohl); *Mädchen hinter gittern* (Braun)
1950   *Frauenarzt Dr. Prätorius* (Goetz and Gillmann)
1952   *1 April 2000* (Liebeneiner)
1954   *Heideschulmeister Uwe Karsten* (Deppe)
1955   *Hotel Adlon* (von Baky)
1956   *Hochzeit auf Immenhof* (von Collande)
1957   *Ferien auf Immenhof* (Leitner)
1958   *Das Czardas-König* (Philipp)

Publications

By WAGNER: articles—

Film Art (London), Summer 1934.
''I Believe in the Sound Film,'' in *Film Art* (London), vol. 3, no. 8, 1936.

On WAGNER: articles—

Kosmorama (Copenhagen), no. 39, 1958.
Focus on Film (London), no. 13, 1973.
Filme (Berlin), May-June 1981.

*   *   *

Fritz Arno Wagner is responsible for photographing some of the most iconographic images in German cinema from 1919 to 1933: Max Schreck's Nosferatu looming over a ship's hold, talons extended; Peter Lorre's child murderer in *M*, cowering in a storeroom; Rudolf Forster's Mackie Messer in *Die Dreigroschenoper*, surrounded by prostitutes and observed by a *fin-de-siècle* statue of a negress. Except for Karl Freund, no other cameraman of the period achieved Wagner's level of versatility and technical expertise. His collaborations with G.W. Pabst, Fritz Lang and F.W. Murnau are a virtual catalog of the expressive potential of the cinematographer's art, from Expressionist *Stimmung* to documentary realism. *Stimmung* is the operative word Lotte Eisner coined to describe the mood or atmosphere evoked by many films of the German silent era—brooding and introspective in tone, illuminated by pools or shafts of light, the total effect reflecting the characters' states of mind. Wagner's most extreme contribution to this genre was Robison's *Warning Shadows*, in which a conjuror releases the repressed unconscious desires of the protagonists, who act out their fantasies in silhouette, shadow, or double exposure.

Ironically, the most obtrusive of Wagner's photographic contributions to Murnau's celebrated *Nosferatu* are what have made portions of the film date badly: undercranking the camera provides an absurd effect when Nosferatu is loading his coffins, and the use of negative film in the woods seems more perplexing than eerie or spectral. Undeniably more effective are the moments in which Wagner evokes Nosferatu's presence through naturalistic means, as in the sweepingly atmospheric natural vistas during the monster's voyage to Bremen by raft and ship. There is no denying the quasi-Expressionist treatment of the film's early sequences (the visit to Nosferatu's castle, with its alternating light and dark arches) and its climax (the vampire's shadow advancing up the wall of the stairwell). Yet it is surprising how little noted it is that *Nosferatu* is as much a film of daytime and nature (and its perversion) as it is of darkness.

Despite his reputation as a cinematographer of *Stimmung*, it could be argued that the naturalistic or documentary aspect of Wagner's work is more interesting when viewed today. In Pabst's *The Love of Jeanne Ney*, Wagner photographed Paris as if the camera was discovering it for the first time, tracking through the city, reveling in the details of train stations and busy streets. Yet, in the same film, Pabst could call on Wagner to diffuse the image with the facility of a portrait photographer when the hero and heroine enter a church. Lang's *M* permitted Wagner a synthesis of styles: on one hand, an objective study of police procedure, the camera sniffing out clues along with the protagonists; on the other hand, a shadowy emanation of the murderer's state of mind as he is progressively cornered like a rat, in one shot circumscribed in both the camera frame and a garden trellis.

Pabst's ''Social Trilogy''—*Westfront 1918*, *Kameradschaft*, and *Die Dreigroschenoper*—represent the pinnacles of Wagner's art. His major achievement in these films is the expressive use of camera movement, so often difficult to facilitate during the early sound period. Wagner was lucky to work with collaborators who were equal to the formidable technical challenges Pabst posed in each film. The set designer Ernö Metzner worked closely with Wagner in devising apparatus to mask the movement of the camera in Pabst's astonishing evocation of a mining disaster, *Kameradschaft*. The horror of fire and collapsing shafts in the claustrophobic confines of the mine were recreated with painstaking verisimilitude. Wagner's camera seems to be everywhere, tracking in front of a fleeing worker or receding from a trio searching for survivors, the retreat gradually revealing more and more of Metzner's artfully designed chaos. Similarly, Wagner's camera evokes the horror of war in *Westfront 1918*, tracking alongside soldiers as they make their way from crater to crater. Ironically, Pabst's controversial adaptation of *Die Dreigroschenoper* marked a return for Wagner to the techniques of *Stimmung*, André Andrejew's stylized studio sets photographed in a manner recalling the gloomy visions of the 1920s. Camera movement seems less organic to this film, Pabst here more concerned with character than spectacle.

Wagner continued to work in Germany, producing competent, craftsmanlike work throughout the Second World War and up to his death in an automobile accident in 1958, but with the export or suppression of talent after 1933, opportunities became infrequent for the kind of visual experimentation that made his early work so innovative.

—Lee Tsiantis

WAKHÉVITCH, Georges

Art Director. **Nationality:** French. **Born:** Odessa, Russia, 18 August 1907; emigrated with his parents to France, 1921. **Education:** Attended Lycée Buffon, Paris; studied painting with Edwin Scott and stage design with Pavel Tchelitchew; attended the School of Decorative Arts, Paris. **Family:** Married Marie Pück, 1947; one son and one daughter from earlier marriage. **Career:** Entered films as assistant to Lazare Meerson in late 1920s: first film as art director, *Baroud*, 1931; designer of stage productions for Barrault and Petit, of plays in England, and operas at La Scala; 1940—cofounder of Centre Artistique et Technique des Jeunes du Cinéma, predecessor of IDHEC. Member, Legion of Honor. **Died:** Of heart attack, in Paris, 11 February 1984.

Films as Art Director:

1930   *Tarakanova* (Bernard) (asst)
1931   *Baroud* (*Love in Morocco*) (Ingram); *Le Chanteur inconnu* (Tourjansky)
1932   *Les Bleus de l'amour* (de Marguenat) (co); *Plaisirs de Paris* (Gréville); *La Tête d'un homme* (Duvivier)
1933   *Ce cochon de Morin* (Lacombe); *Don Quichotte* (Pabst) (co); *L'Homme à l'Hispano* (Epstein); *L'Agonie des aigles* (Richebe) (co); *Quelqu'un a tué* (Forrester) (co); *Le Voyage de Mr. Perrichon* (Tarride) (co)
1934   *Madame Bovary* (Renoir) (co); *Les Filles de la concierge* (J. Tourneur) (co); *Un Tour de cochon* (Tzipine) (co)
1935   *La Kermesse héroïque* (*Carnival in Flanders*) (Feyder) (co)
1936   *Nitchevo* (de Baroncelli) (co); *A nous deux, Madame la vie* (Mirande and Guissart)

1937 *Feu!* (de Baroncelli); *Nostalgie* (Tourjansky) (co); *Le Temps des cerises* (Le Chanois); *Le Chanteur de minuit* (Joannon); **La Grande Illusion** (*Grand Illusion*) (Renoir) (asst)

1938 *La Marseillaise* (Renoir) (co); *Prison sans barreaux* (*Prison without Bars*) (Moguy); *La Maison du Maltais* (Chenal); *La Belle Etoile* (de Baroncelli) (co); *Gibraltar* (Ozep)

1939 *Conflits* (Moguy); *Louise* (Gance); *Le Dernier Tournant* (Chenal); *Pièges* (*Personal Column*) (Siodmak); *Sérénade* (Boyer)

1940 *Faut ce qu'il faut* (*Monsieur Bibi*) (Pujol) (co)

1941 *Le Club des soupirants* (Gleize); *Le Soleil a toujours raison* (Billon) (co); *Mélodie pour toi* (Rozier) (co)

1942 *Les Visiteurs du soir* (*The Devil's Envoys*) (Carné) (co)

1943 *La Vie de Bohème* (L'Herbier); *L'Eternel Retour* (*The Eternal Return*) (Delannoy); *Le Mort ne reçoit plus* (Tarride); *Béatrice devant le désir* (de Marguenat); *La Boite aux rêves* (Choux and Y. Allégret)

1944 *Mademoiselle X* (Billon)

1945 *Vingt-quatre heures de perm'* (Cloche—produced 1940); *L'Invité de la lle* (Cloche)

1946 *Sérénade aux nuages* (Cayatte); *Les Démons de l'aube* (Y. Allégret); *L'Homme au chapeau rond* (Billon); *Martin Roumagnac* (Lacombe); *La Danse de mort* (Cravenne) (co); *Miroir* (Lamy) (co)

1947 *Ruy Blas* (Billon); *L'Aigle à deux têtes* (*The Eagle with Two Heads*) (Cocteau)

1948 *Dédée d'Anvers* (*Dédée*) (Y. Allégret); *Now Barrabas* (*Now Barrabas Was a Robber . . .*) (Parry)

1949 *Miquette et sa mère* (*Miquette*) (Clouzot)

1950 *L'Aiguille rouge* (Reinert)

1951 *Barbe-Bleue* (*Bluebeard*) (Christian-Jaque); *Les Sept Péchés capitaux* (*The Seven Deadly Sins*) (Rim); *The Medium* (Menotti)

1952 *Nez de cuir* (Y. Allégret)

1953 *The Beggar's Opera* (Brook); *Mam'zelle Nitouche* (Y. Allégret); *Innocents in Paris* (Parry); *Le Chair et le diable* (Josipovici)

1954 *Ali Baba et les 40 voleurs* (*Ali Baba*) (Jacques Becker)

1955 *Don Juan* (Berry)

1956 *Si le roi savait ça* (Canaille)

1957 *Escapade* (Habib); *Tamango* (Barry); *Clara et les méchants* (André); *Me and the Colonel* (Glenville)

1958 *Paris Holiday* (Oswald); *La Femme et le pantin* (Duvivier); *Jeux dangereux* (Chenal) (co)

1959 *Marie Octobre* (*Secret Meeting*) (Duvivier); *L'Ambitieuse* (Y. Allégret)

1960 *Les Collants noirs* (*Black Tights*) (Young)

1961 *King of Kings* (Ray); *Les Amours Célèbres* (Boisrond)

1962 *Le Crime ne paie pas* (*Crime Does Not Pay*) (Oury)

1963 *Shéhérazade* (Gaspard-Huit); *Peau de banane* (*Banana Peel*) (Marcel Ophüls); *Le Journal d'une femme de chambre* (*Diary of a Chambermaid*) (Buñuel)

1964 *Echappement libre* (*Backfire*) (Jean Becker); *Par un beau matin d'été* (Deray)

1965 *Les Fêtes galantes* (Clair); *Monnaie de singe* (Jean Becker)

1966 *Tendre voyou* (*Tender Scoundrel*) (Jean Becker)

1967 *Toutes folles du lui* (Carbonnaux); *Oscar* (Molinaro); *Carmen* (von Karajan)

1968 *Mayerling* (Young)

1970 *King Lear* (Brook); *I pagliacci* (von Karajan)

1971 *La Folie des grandeurs* (Oury)

1978 *Meetings with Remarkable Men* (Brook)

1983 *La Tragédie de Carmen* (*The Tragedy of Carmen*) (Brook)

Films as Designer:

1932 *Les Trois Mousquetaires* (Diamant-Berger)

1955 *Marianne de ma jeunesse* (Duvivier)

Publications

By WAKHÉVITCH: book—

L'Envers des décors, Paris, 1977

By WAKHÉVITCH: articles—

Cinématographe (Paris), March 1982.
Positif (Paris), May 1982.
On Cocteau in *Cinéma* (Paris), March 1983

On WAKHÉVITCH: book—

Georges Wakhévitch: Décors et costumes 1930–1980, Marseilles, 1980.

On WAKHÉVITCH: articles—

Film Français (Paris), 4 February 1977.
Obituary in *Variety* (New York), 22 February 1984.
Obituary in *Cinématographe*, no. 98, March 1984.
Obituary in *The Annual Obituary 1984*, Chicago, 1985.

*   *   *

Before he entered films in the late 1920s, Georges Wakhévitch studied painting and the decorative arts, a training he put to good use as he designed costumes and sets for many stage, opera, and ballet productions, as well as important films. He would be as comfortable with gritty realism as with the fanciful, period studies for which he is best known. Combining design with solid constructions, he would design realistic sets creating illusions of reality that few others could accomplish. The 60 films he worked on are the mark of his refined personality and his taste for the baroque. His most characteristic films are *Les Visiteurs du soir, L'Eternal Retour, Ruy Blas, L'Aigle à deux têtes*, and *Dédée d'Anvers*.

Wakhévitch started his career as the assistant of Lazare Meerson and Serge Pimenoff, participating in such films as *Le Chanter Inconnu* (1931), *L'Homme à l'Hispano* (1933), and *Ce Cochon de Morin* (1933). His real debut, however, was *Madame Bovary* in 1934.

He also worked with Jean Renoir on *La Grande Illusion* and *La Marseillaise*. Renoir's *La Grande Illusion* was filmed in a documentary style and called for a look as realistic as possible. Wakhévitch was able to achieve perfect illusions of reality in this story of World War I prisoners caught in the dry rot of inaction. The *film noir, Dédée d'Anvers*, is another example of Wakhévitch's use of realism. The tawdry streets and café ribaldry of the Antwerp waterfront establish the film's melancholy mood.

In contrast to these films are the French historical superproductions and period fantasies with which Wakhévitch is most associated. He applied his taste for the theatrical to make memorable contributions to such films as Pierre Chenal's *La Maison du Maltais*, Marcel L'Herbier's *La Vie de Bohème*, Abel Gance's *Louise*, and Marcel Carne's *Les Visiteurs du soir*. *Les Visiteurs du soir* was set in the Middle Ages, and for this film, Wakhévitch, much to the horror of some critics, designed a new, white medieval castle. *Louise* was a film adaptation of the French opera set in springtime Paris.

Wakhévitch was often solicited by foreign directors. He designed *The Beggar's Opera* and *King Lear* for Peter Brook, *Mayerling* for Terence Young, and *King of Kings* for Nicholas Ray. *Mayerling*, a 19th-century period piece set in Austria, called for the colorful dresses, furniture, and settings for which Wakhévitch is known. *The Beggar's Opera* is another marriage between film and opera. In this film, Wakhévitch used impressive backgrounds and a restrained use of color. It included scenes of high and low life in London: Newgate Prison's sordidness; gay and boisterous mobs in the streets; and flashing dance scenes in a tavern, sumptuous surroundings where the rich gambled. In short, it provided a kaleidoscope of colorful views of London. In Peter Brook's *King Lear*, Wakhévitch used black-and-white film, which Brook thought would add to the overall theme of the story. To compliment the gray tones of the sand dunes and the stormy Danish seas, the interiors were shot with deep shadows that wrap the images in darkness.

Wakhévitch was active in films until the 1980s, finishing his career with two more Peter Brooks films, *Meetings with Remarkable Men* and *La Tragédie de Carmen*.

—Renee Ward

WALAS, Chris

Special Effects and Creature Makeup Artist. Nationality: American. **Born:** Chicago. **Education:** William Paterson College, New Jersey; Los Angeles City College. **Career:** 1978—began with Roger Corman productions doing makeup and effects on such low-budget films as *Piranha* and *Humanoids from the Deep*; 1981—graduated to first-class productions with *Raiders of the Lost Ark*; 1984—first major credit on a major studio film with *Gremlins*; 1989—directorial debut with *The Fly II*; TV work: directed two episodes of *Tales from the Crypt* series. **Awards:** Academy Award, Best Makeup, for *The Fly*, 1986.

Films as Makeup/Creature-Effects Artist:

1978 *Piranha* (Dante); *Screamers* (*The Island of the Fish Men*; *L'isola degli uomini Pesci*) (Martino and Miller)
1980 *Humanoids from the Deep* (Peeters); *Galaxina* (Sachs); *Dragonslayer* (Robbins)
1981 *Scanners* (Cronenberg); ***Raiders of the Lost Ark*** (Spielberg); *Caveman* (Gottlieb)
1983 ***Return of the Jedi*** (Marquand)
1984 *Gremlins* (Dante); *Romancing the Stone* (Zemeckis)
1985 *Enemy Mine* (Petersen)
1986 *The Fly* (Cronenberg)
1987 *House II: The Second Story* (Wiley)
1988 *The Kiss* (Densham); *Child's Play* (Holland)

1990 *Arachnophobia* (F. Marshall); *Look Who's Talking Too* (Heckerling)
1991 *Naked Lunch* (Cronenberg)
1995 Jade (Friedkin); *Virtuosity* (Leonard)

Films as Director:

1989 *The Fly II*
1992 *The Vagrant*

Publications

On WALAS: book—

Brouwer, Alexandra, and Thomas Lee Wright, *Working in Hollywood: 64 Film Professionals Talk about Moviemaking*, New York, 1990.

On WALAS: articles—

Gentry, R., *Millimeter*, September 1984.
Salza, G., *Segno*, January 1986.

* * *

Chris Walas's work as special effects and makeup artist saw him move into feature filmmaking at a time when the visuals became both more innovative and more graphic, often even grisly. He has said that when he started his attitude was to "think of something nobody's ever thought of before" and then do it.

Even as he did this, he attempted to take an organic approach, to make the makeup and effects logical to the situation. For instance, on his Academy Award-winning work on David Cronenberg's *The Fly*, he sought to figure out just why the creature, played by actor Jeff Goldblum, would evolve physically in a certain manner—then try to create it with the makeup. The result in that case, while hardly for the weak of heart, clearly won over its audience and the award committee.

Beginning his creature work at a Halloween mask-making company in California in the late 1970s, Walas was able to work on the feature films that came to the company for makeup assistance. When he went out on his own, he found himself in the employ of ultra-low-budget icon Roger Corman, creating fish, severed limbs, and cuts.

Walas made his leap to major productions with *Raiders of the Lost Ark*. But he did not feel he had reached his potential until *Gremlins* blossomed from an independent film to a studio work during preproduction, making him responsible for an endless array of good and evil puppet creatures.

By the time it came time to make the sequel to *The Fly*, Walas was eager to branch out into direction. Unfortunately, the result—*The Fly II*—was poorly received by both critics and audiences. Critics often cited the makeup as seeming to take precedence over the story. Walas's second stab at directing, *The Vagrant*, was a troubled production from the start, seeing a seemingly endless turnover in crew during shooting then barely receiving a release. The critics again savaged it and again pointed out that the special effects seemed much stronger than the story line.

At this juncture in his career, Walas has won accolades for the makeup effects he has created, bringing the whole art to a new level.

Nevertheless, he has stated a determination to find work as a film director, a role at which he has not yet found equal success.

—Allen Grant Richards

WALD, Jerry

Producer and Writer. **Nationality:** American. **Born:** Jerome Irving Wald in Brooklyn, New York, 16 September 1911. **Education:** Studied journalism at New York University, 1929–31. **Family:** Married Eleanor Rudolph, 1935 (divorced 1936). **Career:** 1929–31—radio columnist, New York *Graphic*; 1933–50—produced shorts, then script writer, and from 1941 producer, Warner Bros.; 1950—formed production company with Norman Krasna; 1952–56—Vice-President in Charge of Production, Columbia; 1956—formed Jerry Wald Productions, releasing through 20th Century-Fox. **Award:** Irving G. Thalberg Award, 1948. **Died:** In Hollywood, California, 13 July 1962.

Films as Writer:

1934 *Twenty Million Sweethearts* (Enright); *Gift of Gab* (Freund)
1935 *Sweet Music* (Green); *Maybe It's Love* (McGann); *Living on Velvet* (Borzage); *In Caliente* (Bacon); *Broadway Gondolier* (Bacon); *I Live for Love* (Berkeley); *Little Big Shot* (Curtiz); *Stars over Broadway* (Keighley)

Jerry Wald

1936 *Sons o' Guns* (Bacon); *Sing Me a Love Song* (Enright)
1937 *Ready, Willing, and Able* (Enright); *Varsity Show* (Keighley); *Hollywood Hotel* (Berkeley)
1938 *Gold Diggers in Paris* (Enright); *Garden of the Moon* (Berkeley); *Brother Rat* (Keighley); *Hard to Get* (Enright); *Going Places* (Enright)
1939 *The Kid from Kokomo* (Seiler); *Naughty but Nice* (Enright); *On Your Toes* (Enright); *The Roaring Twenties* (Walsh)
1940 *Brother Rat and a Baby* (Enright); *Three Cheers for the Irish* (Bacon); *Flight Angels* (Seiler); *Torrid Zone* (Keighley); *They Drive by Night* (Walsh)
1941 *Million Dollar Baby* (Bernhardt); *Out of the Fog* (Litvak); *Manpower* (Walsh)
1943 *Air Force* (Hawks) (co)
1944 *Shine On, Harvest Moon* (Butler) (co)

Films as Producer:

1941 *Navy Blues* (Bacon) (+ co-sc); *The Man Who Came to Dinner* (Keighley)
1942 *All through the Night* (V. Sherman); *Larceny, Inc.* (Bacon); *Juke Girl* (Bernhardt); *Across the Pacific* (Huston); *Desperate Journey* (Walsh); *George Washington Slept Here* (Keighley)
1943 *The Hard Way* (V. Sherman) (+ co-sc); *Action in the North Atlantic* (Bacon) (+ co-sc); *Background to Danger* (Walsh)
1944 *Destination Tokyo* (Daves) (+ co-sc); *In Our Time* (V. Sherman) (+ co-sc); *The Very Thought of You* (Daves) (+ co-sc)
1945 *Objective, Burma!* (Walsh) (+ co-sc); *Pride of the Marines* (Daves); **Mildred Pierce** (Curtiz)
1946 *Humoresque* (Negulesco)
1947 *Possessed* (Bernhardt); *The Unfaithful* (V. Sherman) (+ co-sc); *Dark Passage* (Daves)
1948 *To the Victor* (Daves) (+ co-sc); *Key Largo* (Huston); *Johnny Belinda* (Negulesco)
1949 *One Sunday Afternoon* (Walsh); *The Adventures of Don Juan* (*The New Adventures of Don Juan*) (V. Sherman); *John Loves Mary* (Butler); *Flamingo Road* (Curtiz); *Task Force* (Daves) (+ co-sc); *Always Leave Them Laughing* (Del Ruth); *The Inspector General* (Koster)
1950 *Young Man with a Horn* (Curtiz); *Perfect Strangers* (Windust); *The Damned Don't Cry* (V. Sherman) (+ co-sc); *Caged* (Cromwell) (+ co-sc); *The Breaking Point* (Curtiz); *The Glass Menagerie* (Rapper)
1951 *Storm Warning* (Heisler) (+ co-sc); *Behave Yourself* (Beck); *The Blue Veil* (Bernhardt)
1952 *Clash by Night* (F. Lang); *The Lusty Men* (Ray)
1954 *Miss Sadie Thompson* (Bernhardt)
1955 *The Queen Bee* (MacDougall)
1956 *The Eddie Duchin Story* (Sidney)
1957 *An Affair to Remember* (McCarey); *No Down Payment* (Ritt); *Peyton Place* (Robson); *Kiss Them for Me* (Donen)
1958 *The Long Hot Summer* (Ritt); *In Love and War* (Dunne); *Mardi Gras* (Goulding); *The Sound and the Fury* (Ritt); *The Best of Everything* (Negulesco); *Hound-Dog Man* (Siegel); *Beloved Infidel* (H. King)
1960 *The Story on Page One* (Odets); *Sons and Lovers* (Cardiff); *Let's Make Love* (Cukor)

1961　*Return to Peyton Place* (J. Ferrer); *Wild in the Country* (Dunne); *Hemingway's Adventures of a Young Man* (Ritt)
1962　*Mr. Hobbs Takes a Vacation* (Koster)
1963　*The Stripper* (Schaffner)

Films as Executive Producer:

1953　*From Here to Eternity* (Zinnemann); ***The Big Heat*** (F. Lang); *Gun Fury* (Walsh)
1954　*Bad for Each Other* (Rapper); *It Should Happen to You* (Cukor); *Pushover* (Quine); *The Caine Mutiny* (Dmytryk); *Human Desire* (F. Lang); *Phffft!* (Robson); *They Rode West* (Karlson)
1955　*The Violent Men* (Maté); *Three for the Show* (Potter); *Cell 2455, Death Row* (Sears); *Tight Spot* (Karlson); *Five against the House* (Karlson); *The Long Gray Line* (Ford); *My Sister Eileen* (Quine)
1956　*The Last Frontier* (A. Mann); *Picnic* (Logan); *The Harder They Fall* (Robson); *Jubal* (Daves); *The Solid Gold Cadillac* (Quine); *You Can't Run Away from It* (Powell)

Publications

By WALD: book—

Editor, with Richard Macaulay, *The Best Pictures 1939–1940*, New York, 1940.

By WALD: article—

Films and Filming (London), September 1958.

On WALD: articles—

Goodman, Ezra, "How to be a Hollywood Producer," in *Harper's* (New York), May 1948.
Nolan, Jack Edmund, in *Films in Review* (New York), August-September 1961, corrections in October 1961.
Matteson, A., in *Chaplin* (Stockholm), vol. 14, no. 2, 1972.

*　　*　　*

Jerry Wald's ambition, his often unbridled creative drive, and his desire to make every picture in town—all at once—characterized this highly energetic writer-producer from his arrival in Hollywood in 1933 until his untimely death in 1962.

Born in Brooklyn, Wald began his writing career at the age of 19 by creating a radio column for the New York *Graphic* while studying journalism at New York University. He quickly advanced and soon persuaded Warner Bros. to produce a series of short subjects featuring radio stars called "Rambling 'round Radio Row." But it was a biographical article he ghostwrote for the crooner Russ Columbo that gave Wald his break in motion pictures. Warners bought the story, and signed Wald to collaborate on *Twenty Million Sweethearts*, featuring their rising musical star Dick Powell. Between 1934 and 1941, Wald worked in some capacity on some 30 pictures and was

credited with several original stories. His most frequent cowriters were Julius Epstein (who later gained fame collaborating with his brother Philip) and the ex-magazine writer Richard Maccauly. During these early years, Wald's films were primarily formula musicals (*In Caliente, Ready, Willing, and Able, Hollywood Hotel*) and lightweight comedies (*Sons o' Guns, Hard to Get, Brother Rat*).

Despite Wald's status as a writer, he desperately wanted to function as a producer. Even in the mid-1930s he was acting as an "idea" man—generating original story ideas or suggesting plot blendings or remakes—and depended on dedicated writers like Epstein or Maccauly to develop and execute the concepts. Towards the end of the decade, Wald's pictures incorporated more dramatic material. Associations with the writer-producer Mark Hellinger led to credits on *The Roaring Twenties, Torrid Zone, They Drive By Night*, and *Manpower*, and steered Wald in the direction which would characterize many of his productions of the 1940s: Realism. Hellinger also provided Wald with his step up to associate producer on *Navy Blues* when in the middle of the picture Hellinger fell out with Jack Warner, left the studio, and Wald took over, finishing the production.

Once promoted to associate producer, Wald established himself with gritty dramas like *The Hard Way* and a series of popular war pictures, *Across the Pacific, Action in the North Atlantic, Destination Tokyo*, and *Objective, Burma!*. He was personally responsible for resurrecting Joan Crawford's career after her dismissal from MGM by casting her in her Academy Award-winning role in *Mildred Pierce*; he sustained her comeback with a series of starring roles in *Humoresque, Possessed, Flamingo Road*, and *The Damned Don't Cry*. He believed there was "no such thing as a washed-up star, only washed-up stories," and proved it not only with Crawford but with Jane Wyman (*Johnny Belinda*), Claire Trevor (*Key Largo*), and Lana Turner (*Peyton Place*).

In contrast to a methodical, detail-oriented producer like David Selznick, Wald's industrious, enterprising nature drove him to move quickly from one project to the next. Typically, he would initiate an idea, find the appropriate writer, director, and cast, switch to another project (or two) and then only become seriously involved again to promote the finished project. He was a voracious reader and never gave up his New York connections for fresh stories and new writers. He kept massive files with picture ideas and notebooks jammed with partially developed future projects, most of which he knew would never be realized. He ended his astonishingly prolific and long association with Warner Bros. in 1950, having produced an impressive list of critical and box office successes. In eight years, he had produced 30 more pictures, 12 of them based on his own stories, and prepared at least ten additional properties which were eventually turned over to other producers on the lot. He considered his pinnacle at Warners to be *Johnny Belinda*, a story of a deaf-mute girl which Jack Warner believed was too obscure to have box-office appeal. The film, however, not only won an Academy Award for Best Actress for Jane Wyman but also earned Wald the prestigious Irving G. Thalberg Award.

At RKO Wald ran an independent production company with his partner, the writer Norman Krasna, under studio-head Howard Hughes. After only two years, he moved again to become Harry Cohn's vice president in charge of production at Columbia Pictures. He enjoyed another profitable tenure, this time at 20th Century-Fox where he formed Jerry Wald Productions, and produced another string of hits, beginning in 1957 with the blockbuster *Peyton Place*. Unlike his films at Warners, his Fox productions were lavish, often in CinemaScope and/or Technicolor. They covered everything from serious social topics (*No Down Payment*) to glossy biographies (*Beloved Infidel*) to escapistic romance (*An Affair to Remember*).

Although Hollywood legend has it that Jerry Wald provided the model for Budd Schulberg's famous character Sammy Glick in *What Makes Sammy Run?*, Wald's body of work clearly indicates that he was more than just an ambitious showman who capitalized on the talents of others. A more accurate evaluation of the producer's contribution is perhaps the sentiment attributed to Darryl F. Zanuck, ''If it were possible, I'd have ten Jerry Walds working at the studio!''

—Joanne L. Yeck

WALKER, Joseph B.

Cinematographer. **Nationality:** American. **Born:** Denver, Colorado, 22 August 1892. **Career:** Worked as wireless telephone engineer and inventor; then film cameraman in middle 1910s; aerial cinematographer, and photographer of Red Cross documentaries during World War I; 1920—first feature film as cinematographer, *Back to God's Country*; 1925–52—photographer for Columbia; involved in technical aspects of photography: invented the Double Exposure System, c. 1917, several zoom lenses (the earliest in 1929), Duomar Lens for motion picture cameras, 1931 (and for television cameras in the 1940s), the Variable Diffusion Device, 1931, and the Facial Make-Up Meter, 1941, as well as lightweight camera blimps and optical diffusion techniques. **Award:** Gordon Sawyer Award, 1980. **Died:** In Las Vegas, Nevada, 1 August 1985.

Joseph Walker (left) with Rosalind Russell and Alexander Hall

Films as Cinematographer:

1920 *Back to God's Country* (Shipman)

1921 *The Girl from God's Country* (Shipman and van Tuyle)

1923 *Danger* (Elfelt); *The Grub Stake* (van Tuyle); *Richard the Lion Hearted* (Withey)

1924 *The Girl on the Stairs* (Worthington); *The Wise Virgin* (Ingraham); *No More Women* (Ingraham); *What Shall I Do?* (Woods); *Chalk Marks* (Adolfi)

1925 *Let Women Alone* (Powell); *Clash of the Wolves* (Smith); *My Neighbor's Wife* (Geldert); *Fighting Courage* (Elfelt); *The Pleasure Buyers* (Withey); *The North Star* (Powell)

1926 *The Dixie Flyer* (Hunt); *Flying Fury* (Hogan); *Tentacles of the North* (Chaudet)

1927 *Tarzan and the Golden Lion* (McGowan); *The Outlaw Dog* (McGowan); *The Baited Trap* (Paton); *Temporary Sheriff* (Hatton); *Great Mail Robbery* (Seitz); *Fire and Steel* (Bracken) (co); *Isle of Forgotten Women* (Seitz); *The Warning* (Seitz); *Death Valley* (Powell); *Shanghaied* (R. Ince); *The Flying U Ranch* (de Lacy); *College Hero* (W. Lang); *Aflame in the Sky* (McGowan); *The Tigress* (Seitz); *Stage Kisses* (Kelly)

1928 *That Certain Thing* (Capra); *Modern Mothers* (Rosen); *After the Storm* (Seitz); *Virgin Lips* (Clifton); *Ransom* (Seitz); *Lady Raffles* (Neill); *Say It with Sables* (Capra); *Beware of Blondes* (Seitz); *Submarine* (Capra); *Court Martial* (Seitz); *Street of Illusion* (Kenton); *Driftwood* (Cabanne); *Nothing to Wear* (Kenton); *Restless Youth* (Cabanne); *Side Show* (Kenton)

1929 *Object Alimony* (Dunlap); *Eternal Woman* (McCarthy); *Trial Marriage* (Kenton); *The Quitter* (Henabery); *Flight* (Capra); *Song of Love* (Kenton)

1930 *Murder on the Roof* (Seitz); *Dirigible* (Capra); *Broadway Hoofers* (Archainbaud); *Ladies of Leisure* (Capra); *Around the Corner* (Glennon); *Midnight Mystery* (Seitz); *Rain or Shine* (Capra); *Ladies Must Play* (Cannon)

1931 *Subway Express* (Newmeyer); *The Miracle Woman* (Capra); *Fifty Fathoms Deep* (Neill); *Platinum Blonde* (Capra)

1932 *Forbidden* (Capra); *Shopworn* (Grinde); *By Whose Hand?* (Stoloff); *American Madness* (Capra); *Virtue* (Buzzell)

1933 *The Bitter Tea of General Yen* (Capra); *Air Hostess* (Rogell); *Below the Sea* (Rogell); *Lady for a Day* (Capra)

1934 ***It Happened One Night*** (Capra); *The Lady Is Willing* (Miller); *One Night of Love* (Schertzinger); *Broadway Bill* (Capra)

1935 *The Best Man Wins* (Kenton); *Let's Live Tonight* (Schertzinger); *Eight Bells* (Neill); *Love Me Forever* (Schertzinger); *The Girl Friend* (Buzzell); *A Feather in Her Hat* (Santell)

1936 *The Music Goes Around* (Schertzinger); *Mr. Deeds Goes to Town* (Capra); *Theodora Goes Wild* (Boleslawsky)

1937 *When You're in Love* (Riskin); *Lost Horizon* (Capra); *There Goes My Girl* (Holmes); *It Happened in Hollywood* (Lachman); *The Awful Truth* (McCarey)

1938 *The Joy of Living* (Garnett); *Start Cheering* (Rogell); *There's That Woman Again* (Hall); *You Can't Take It with You* (Capra)

1939 *Only Angels Have Wings* (Hawks); ***Mr. Smith Goes to Washington*** (Capra)

1940 ***His Girl Friday*** (Hawks); *Too Many Husbands* (*My Two Husbands*) (Ruggles); *He Stayed for Breakfast* (Hall); *Arizona* (Ruggles) (co)

1941 *This Thing Called Love* (Hall); *Penny Serenade* (Stevens); *Here Comes Mr. Jordan* (Hall); *You Belong to Me* (Ruggles); *Bedtime Story* (Hall)

1942 *They All Kissed the Bride* (Hall); *Tales of Manhattan* (Duvivier); *My Sister Eileen* (Hall)

1943 *A Night to Remember* (Wallace); *What's Buzzin Cousin?* (Barton); *First Comes Courage* (Arzner); *What a Woman* (Cummings)

1944 *The Impatient Years* (Cummings); *Mr. Winkle Goes to War* (Green); *Together Again* (C. Vidor)

1945 *Roughly Speaking* (Curtiz); *She Wouldn't Say Yes* (Hall)

1946 *Tars and Spars* (Green); *The Jolson Story* (Green); ***It's a Wonderful Life*** (Capra)

1947 *The Guilt of Janet Ames* (Levin); *The Velvet Touch* (Gage)

1948 *The Mating of Millie* (Levin); *The Dark Past* (Maté)

1949 *Mr. Soft Touch* (Levin); *Tell It to the Judge* (Foster)

1950 *Harriet Craig* (V. Sherman); *A Woman of Distinction* (Buzzell); *No Sad Songs for Me* (Maté); *Born Yesterday* (Cukor); *Never a Dull Moment* (Marshall)

1951 *The Mob* (Parrish)

1952 *The Marrying Kind* (Cukor); *Affair in Trinidad* (V. Sherman)

Publications

By WALKER: articles—

"Danger in God's Country," in *American Cinematographer* (Hollywood), May 1985.

By WALKER: book—

With Juanita Walker, *The Light on Her Face*, Hollywood, 1984.

On WALKER: articles—

Film Comment (New York), Winter 1970–71.
Dusing, Lysa, in *American Cinematographer* (Hollywood), July 1981.
American Cinematographer (Hollywood), March 1982.
Obituary in *Variety* (New York), 7 August 1985.
Obituary in *American Cinematographer* (Hollywood), October 1985.

*   *   *

Joseph B. Walker's career could have flourished in any of a number of directions. His pioneering work in the development of the wireless transmitter with Dr. Lee DeForest gave him a head start in the new world of radio broadcasting. His lifelong fascination with the workings of motion-picture cameras led him to put his name to an impressive list of inventions: the first zoom lens patent, a comparator exposure meter, a panoramic television camera, and many others. But it was as cinematographer on some 160 feature films that Walker made his mark.

After some years of freelancing as a newsreel photographer Walker shot his first feature, *Back to God's Country*, in 1919 on

a formidable location near the Arctic Circle. For the next seven years he worked steadily at a variety of minor studios, occasionally with good directors like W.S. Van Dyke, Francis Ford, and George B. Seitz. More often Walker photographed low-budget programmers. His huge collection of camera lenses (and his intimate knowledge of their possibilities) made him invaluable to the directors of these quickies. Walker could, by changing lenses, shoot a close, medium, or long shot without moving the camera, thus saving precious time in shooting westerns like *Fighting Courage* or serials like *Officer 444*.

In 1927 Walker photographed *The Warning*, directed by Seitz, his first film at Columbia. Walker was to remain almost exclusively with this studio until his retirement in 1952. At the time, Columbia was the least of the majors; Walker, through his long association with Frank Capra, would help to change that.

Walker found Capra a most congenial collaborator, a director who could at once keep a tight rein on his artistic vision while allowing Walker remarkable experimental leeway. Though Walker was a master at composition and elaborate camera movement, his most memorable images come from his brilliant mastery of lighting: Barbara Stanwyck and David Manners by the fireside in *The Miracle Woman*; the delicate mists of the moonlit haystack scene in *It Happened One Night*; the shimmering, Baroque visions of *The Bitter Tea of General Yen*; the stunning torchlight funeral in *Lost Horizon*.

Though Walker's best work was with Capra, the cinematographer also had occasion to work with directors as diverse as Hawks (*Only Angels Have Wings*, *His Girl Friday*), Garnett (*The Joy of Living*), McCarey (*The Awful Truth*) and Schertzinger (*Love Me Forever*, *Let's Live Tonight*), George Stevens (*Penny Serenade*) and Alexander Hall (*Here Comes Mr. Jordan*). It's difficult, in fact, to come up with many first-rate Columbia films of the era on which Walker did not work.

In his amiable and informative autobiography, *The Light On Her Face*, Walker quotes Columbia head Harry Cohn: "Y'know, there's one thing that's always made me curious about you. Practically *every* money-making picture we've had at Columbia, you've worked on it. How do you account for that? And don't tell me it's the photography! Photography doesn't sell pictures!" Maybe not. But those silvery images stay in the mind long after the movies' plots have faded from memory. The elegance of Walker's cinematography even survives the indignities of being shrunk down and contrasted out for television, though the delicacy of his lighting suffers on video. Walker, like many another of his gifted peers who worked predominantly in black-and-white, seem sadly relegated to a medium for which their work was not designed and which does not have the sensitivity properly to display the beautiful and precious images it chews up as so much fodder. But should the viewer have the willingness and the opportunity to return to Walker's films as they were originally intended—on 35 mm film—he or she will find that there were few more gifted practitioners of the art of cinematography.

—Frank Thompson

WALLIS, Hal B.

Producer. **Nationality:** American. **Born:** Harold Brent Wallis in Chicago, Illinois, 14 September 1899. **Family:** Married 1) the actress Louise Fazenda, 1927 (divorced); son: the producer Hal B. Wallis, Jr.;

Hal B. Wallis (right) with Dean Martin and Lizabeth Scott

2) the actress Martha Hyer. **Career:** Left school at 14, and worked as office boy and salesman for electric heating company; 1922—manager of Garrick film theatre, Los Angeles; 1923—joined Warner Bros. as assistant to head of publicity, then became head of publicity; 1928—made studio manager; 1928–31—production executive 1933–42—executive producer in charge of production; 1942—formed Hal Wallis Productions, releasing through Paramount and, after 1969, through Universal. **Awards:** Irving G. Thalberg Award, 1938, 1943; Academy Award for *Casablanca*, 1943. **Died:** In Rancho Mirage, California, 5 October 1986.

Films as Producer:

1930   *The Dawn Patrol* (Hawks); *Sally* (Dillon); *Little Caesar* (LeRoy)
1931   *Five Star Final* (LeRoy)
1932   **I Am a Fugitive from a Chain Gang** (LeRoy)
1933   *Mystery of the Wax Museum* (Curtiz); *The World Changes* (LeRoy); *Gold Diggers of 1933* (LeRoy); *Footlight Parade* (Bacon); **42nd Street** (Bacon)

1934   *Flirtation Walk* (Borzage)
1935   ''*G*'' *Men* (Keighley); *Sweet Adeline* (LeRoy); *A Midsummer Night's Dream* (Reinhardt and Dieterle); *Captain Blood* (Curtiz)
1936   *The Story of Louis Pasteur* (Dieterle); *Anthony Adverse* (LeRoy); *Green Pastures* (Connelly and Keighley); *Green Light* (Borzage); *The Charge of the Light Brigade* (Curtiz); *Stolen Holiday* (Curtiz); *God's Country and the Woman* (Keighley)
1937   *Marked Woman* (Bacon); *Kid Galahad* (Curtiz); *The Life of Emile Zola* (Dieterle); *First Lady* (Logan); *That Certain Feeling* (Goulding); *Back in Circulation* (Enright); *It's Love I'm After* (Mayo); *Confession* (May); *Call It a Day* (Mayo); *The Go Getter* (Berkeley); *The Prince and the Pauper* (Keighley); *Slim* (Enright); *Marry the Girl* (McGann); *The Perfect Specimen* (Curtiz); *Tovarich* (Litvak) (co); *Hollywood Hotel* (Berkeley)
1938   *A Slight Case of Murder* (Bacon); *Jezebel* (Wyler) (co); **The Adventures of Robin Hood** (Curtiz and Keighley); *Boy Meets Girl* (Bacon); *Four Daughters* (Curtiz); *The Sisters* (Litvak); *Brother Rat* (Keighley); *Swing Your Baby* (Enright);

Love, Honor, and Behave (Logan); *Gold Is Where You Find It* (Curtiz); *White Banners* (Goulding); *Gold Diggers in Paris* (Enright); *Cowboy from Brooklyn* (Bacon); *Hard to Get* (Enright); *Dawn Patrol* (Goulding); *Going Places* (Enright)

1939 *Dark Victory* (Goulding); *Juarez* (Dieterle) (co); *The Old Maid* (Goulding) (co); *The Roaring Twenties* (Walsh) (co); *Daughters Courageous* (Curtiz); *The Private Lives of Elizabeth and Essex* (Curtiz) (co); *They Made Me a Criminal* (Berkeley); *Wings of the Navy* (Bacon); *The Kid from Kokomo* (Seiler) (co); *Yes, My Darling Daughter* (Keighley); *We Are Not Alone* (Goulding); *A Child Is Born* (Bacon)

1940 *Dr. Ehrlich's Magic Bullet* (Dieterle); *Brother Orchid* (Bacon) (co); *Torrid Zone* (Keighley); *They Drive By Night* (Walsh) (co); *The Sea Hawk* (Curtiz); *A Dispatch from Reuters* (Dieterle); *The Letter* (Wyler) (co); *Four Wives* (Curtiz); *The Fighting 69th* (Keighley); *Brother Rat and a Baby* (Enright) (co); *Invisible Stripes* (Bacon); *Three Cheers for the Irish* (Bacon); *Virginia City* (Curtiz); *It All Came True* (Seiler) (co); *'Til We Meet Again* (Goulding); *Saturday's Children* (V. Sherman); *All This, and Heaven Too* (Litvak) (co); *My Love Came Back* (Bernhardt); *No Time for Comedy* (Keighley); *City for Conquest* (Litvak); *Knute Rockne—All American* (Bacon); *Santa Fe Trail* (Curtiz)

1941 **High Sierra** (Walsh) (co); *The Sea Wolf* (Curtiz); *The Great Lie* (Goulding) (co); *Sergeant York* (Hawks); **The Maltese Falcon** (Huston) (co); *Out of the Fog* (Litvak); *Footsteps in the Dark* (Bacon); *The Wagons Roll at Night* (Enright); *Affectionately Yours* (Bacon); *Shining Victory* (Rapper); *Million Dollar Baby* (Bernhardt); *Underground* (V. Sherman); *The Bride Came C.O.D.* (Keighley); *Manpower* (Walsh) (co); *Navy Blues* (Bacon) (co); *Dive Bomber* (Curtiz); *One Foot in Heaven* (Rapper) (co); *The Strawberry Blonde* (Walsh); *They Died with Their Boots On* (Walsh)

1942 *The Man Who Came to Dinner* (Keighley) (co); *Kings Row* (Wood); *Yankee Doodle Dandy* (Curtiz); **Now, Voyager** (Rapper); *Captains of the Clouds* (Curtiz); *Brother Orchid* (Bacon); *The Male Animal* (Nugent); *Larceny, Inc.* (Bacon); *Juke Girl* (Bernhardt); *In This Our Life* (Huston); *Desperate Journey* (Walsh)

1943 **Casablanca** (Curtiz); *Air Force* (Hawks); *Watch on the Rhine* (Shumlin); *Princess O'Rourke* (Krasna); *This Is the Army* (Curtiz)

1944 *Passage to Marseilles* (Curtiz)

1945 *Love Letters* (Dieterle); *The Affairs of Susan* (Seiter); *You Came Along* (Farrow); *Saratoga Trunk* (Wood)

1946 *The Strange Love of Martha Ivers* (Milestone); *The Searching Wind* (Dieterle); *The Perfect Marriage* (Allen)

1947 *I Walk Alone* (Haskin); *Desert Fury* (Allen)

1948 *So Evil My Love* (Allen); *Sorry, Wrong Number* (Litvak); *The Accused* (Dieterle)

1949 *Rope of Sand* (Dieterle); *My Friend Irma* (G. Marshall); *File on Thelma Jordan* (Siodmak)

1950 *Paid in Full* (Dieterle); *The Furies* (A. Mann); *Dark City* (Dieterle); *My Friend Irma Goes West* (Walker)

1951 *September Affair* (Dieterle); *That's My Boy* (Walker); *Peking Express* (Dieterle); *Red Mountain* (Dieterle); *Sailor Beware* (Walker); *The Stooge* (Taurog)

1952 *Come Back Little Sheba* (D. Mann); *Jumping Jacks* (Taurog); *Scared Stiff* (Marshall)

1953 *Cease Fire!* (Crump); *Money from Home* (Marshall)

1954 *About Mrs. Leslie* (D. Mann); *Three Ring Circus* (Pevney)

1955 *The Rose Tattoo* (D. Mann)

1956 *Artists and Models* (Tashlin); *The Rainmaker* (Anthony); *Hollywood or Bust* (Tashlin)

1957 *Gunfight at the O.K. Corral* (J. Sturges); *Loving You* (Kanter); *The Sad Sack* (Marshall); *Wild Is the Wind* (Cukor)

1958 *King Creole* (Curtiz); *Hot Spell* (Daniel Mann)

1959 *Last Train from Gun Hill* (J. Sturges); *Career* (Anthony); *Don't Give Up the Ship* (Taurog)

1960 *G.I. Blues* (Taurog)

1961 *All in a Night's Work* (Anthony); *Blue Hawaii* (Taurog); *Summer and Smoke* (Glenville)

1962 *A Girl Named Tamiko* (J. Sturges); *Girls! Girls! Girls!* (Taurog)

1963 *Wives and Lovers* (Rich); *Fun in Acapulco* (Thorpe)

1964 *Becket* (Glenville); *Roustabout* (Rich)

1965 *The Sons of Katie Elder* (Hathaway); *Boeing Boeing* (Rich)

1966 *Paradise—Hawaiian Style* (Moore)

1967 *Easy Come, Easy Go* (Rich); *Barefoot in the Park* (Saks)

1968 *5 Card Stud* (Hathaway)

1969 *True Grit* (Hathaway); *Anne of the Thousand Days* (Jarrott)

1970 *Norwood* (Haley)

1971 *Red Sky at Morning* (Goldstone)

1972 *Shoot Out* (Hathaway); *Mary, Queen of Scots* (Jarrott); *Follow Me* (*The Public Eye*) (Reed)

1973 *A Bequest to the Nation* (*The Nelson Affair*) (Jones); *The Don Is Dead* (Fleis cher)

1975 *Rooster Cogburn* (Millar)

Publications

By WALLIS: articles—

Today's Cinema, 18 August 1969.
Films and Filming (London), December 1969.
Cinéma (Paris), November 1970.
Stills (London), May-June 1983.

On WALLIS: book—

Mancia, Adrienne, editor, *Hal Wallis, Film Producer*, New York, 1970.

On WALLIS: articles—

Kine Weekly (London), 20 September 1969.
"Wallis Issue" of *Dialogue on Film* (Beverly Hills, California), March 1975.
Cinématographe (Paris), May 1984.
Obituary in *Variety* (New York), 15 October 1986.
Obituary in *Films and Filming* (London), December 1986.

Obituary in *Sight and Sound* (London), Winter 1986–87.

Film Comment (New York), July-August 1989.

Corliss, Richard, "14-Karat Oomph," in *Film Comment* (New York), July-August 1989.

Woodcock, J.M., "The Name Dropper," in *American Cinemeditor* (Encino), no. 1, 1990.

Edwards, Anne, "Hal Wallis: The Producer's Valley Farm," in *Architectural Digest* (Los Angeles), April 1992.

Dolven, F., "Hal B. Wallis: The golden-arm producer," in *Classic Images*, no. 220, October 1993.

* * *

Hal B. Wallis was one of the most important movie producers from the Golden Age of Hollywood filmmaking of the 1930s and 1940s. On one classic Warner Bros. movie after another Hal B. Wallis' name is listed under the title: Warner's studio boss, Jack L. Warner, was the brother in charge of the west coast studio, but surely his right-hand man, Hal Wallis, did most of the day to day work producing.

In the 1930s Wallis produced many of the classic genre films. *Little Caesar*, *'G' Men*, and *The Roaring Twenties* defined the gangster form. There were few more honored films of the decade than *I Am a Fugitive from the Chain Gang*, *Anthony Adverse*, and *Jezebel*. *Gold Diggers of 1933*, *Footlight Parade*, *42nd Street*, and *Gold Diggers in Paris* swung with music and dance. Captain *Blood*, *The Charge of the Light Brigade*, and *The Adventures of Robin Hood* defined what an adventure film should be.

Although film scholars have traditionally associated Wallis with his classic Warner period of the 1930s, he reached his creative peak at the studio in the early 1940s. Wallis produced a remarkable string of classic films: *Sergeant York*, *The Maltese Falcon*, *High Sierra*, *The Bride Came C.O.D.*, *The Strawberry Blond*, *Now, Voyager*, *Yankee Doodle Dandy*, and *Casablanca*. But Wallis' career was hardly over when he left Warner Bros. in 1944. He would remain a key force in the Hollywood film industry until 1975, when he produced his final film, *Rooster Cogburn*, starring John Wayne in a sequel to yet another Wallis hit, the 1969 *True Grit*. In 1944 Wallis sought greater independence as a producer. Understandably he chaffed under the yoke provided by Jack L. Warner. He weighed several offers and went with Paramount. At Paramount Wallis' career fell into four phases. In the first he continued producing genre films, in this case thrillers in the late 1940s and westerns during the early 1950s. But his career changed dramatically in 1956 with the release of *Artists and Models*, setting in motion a string of Jerry Lewis and Dean Martin comedies. A third phase began in 1958 when Wallis began producing the predictable, but high-grossing films starring Elvis Presley. Few find these Elvis formula movies complex or sophisticated cinema, but they made money, lots of money. Indeed *Blue Hawaii* finished as the eleventh highest grossing film of all of 1962 according to *Variety*'s figures.

Wallis' final period of filmmaking followed Elvis and lasted from 1964 to 1975. He is probably best remembered for making two very different types of films in this period. The first were westerns starring John Wayne including the aforementioned *True Grit* and *Rooster Cogburn*, as well as *The Sons of Katie Elder*. Far different were the tales of royalty, costume dramas which Wallis called in his autobiography his "royal histories." These included the very successful *Becket*, *Anne of a Thousand Days*, and *Mary, Queen of Scots*. Wallis was a consummate producer, taking project after project that both interested him and seemed destined to make a great deal of money. He

skillfully flowed with the times, and in the process helped several major eras of Hollywood history. In nearly a half century he produced, coproduced, and/or supervised more than 400 films. Few individuals have been as successful as Hollywood producers; few have made a greater stamp in defining how Hollywood operated as a business.

—Douglas Gomery

WALTON, William

Composer. **Nationality:** British. **Born:** William Turner Walton in Oldham, Lancashire, 29 March 1902. **Education:** Attended Cathedral Choir School, Christ Church College, Oxford, sent down; lived with the Sitwell family for fifteen years. **Family:** Married Susana Gil Passo, 1946. **Career:** 1923—composed *Facade*, to poems by Edith Sitwell, other works include *The Viola Concerto*, 1929, *Belshazzar's Feast* oratorio, 1931, coronation marches for King George VI and Queen Elizabeth II; 1935—composed first symphony; first film score, *Escape Me Never*. **Died:** On the island of Ischia, 8 March 1983.

Films as Composer/Musical Director:

1935   *Escape Me Never* (Czinner)
1936   *As You Like It* (Czinner)

William Walton

1941   *Major Barbara* (Pascal)
1942   *The First of the Few* (Howard); *The Foreman Went to France* (Frend); *Next of Kin* (Dickinson); *Went the Day Well?* (Cavalcanti)
1944   **Henry V** (Olivier)
1948   *Hamlet* (Olivier)
1955   *Richard III* (Olivier)
1969   ''Battle in the Air'' sequence of *Battle of Britain* (Hamilton)
1970   *Three Sisters* (Olivier)

Publications

On WALTON: books—

Craggs, Stewart R., *William Walton*, Oxford, 1977.
Walton, Susana, *William Walton: Behind the Facade*, Oxford, 1988.
Kennedy, Michael, *Portrait of Walton*, New York, 1998.
Craggs, Stewart R., editor, *William Walton: Music & Literature*, 1999.

On WALTON: articles—

National Film Theatre booklet (London), July 1982.
Obituary in *Variety* (New York), 16 March 1983.
Séquences (Montreal), no. 112, April 1983.
New Statesman, 25 March 1988.
Score (Lelystad, Netherlands), no. 75, June 1990 + filmo.
Segnocinema (Vicenza), May-June 1995.
Cineforum (Bergamo), October 1996.
American Heritage, October 1998.
Choice, January 2000.

*   *   *

William Walton was born in Oldham, Lancashire. His father was a choir-master and singing teacher and his mother had a fine contralto voice. By the age of 12 he was already composing music of his own and attended Christ Church Cathedral School in Oxford. He quickly made his name as a composer during the glittering 1920s and was friend and confidante of Siegfried Sassoon, Constant Lambert, George Gershwin, Sir Thomas Beecham and Diaghilev. All in all he composed the music to 14 films beginning in 1935 with a score for *Escape Me Never*, but he did not capture attention for his film work until the 1942 film *The First of the Few* with its famous ''Prelude and Fugue for Spitfire.'' What marked him out for special attention and acclaim were the scores he wrote for three of Laurence Olivier's films, the most illustrious of which was for *Henry V*. It has been highly praised by music critics both as film music and as a concert suite in its own right. When the film was released in 1944, many music critics published detailed reviews of the score and extracts of it were presented at the Promenade concerts in 1945. Olivier's enchanting and spectacular historical pageant version of Shakespeare's patriotic epic is as memorable for Walton's sumptuous and rousing music as it is for its magnificent acting, directing, photography, sets and costumes, and most especially for the stirring music for the French cavalry charge at Agincourt.

Walton's second collaboration with Olivier on a Shakespeare adaptation—*Hamlet*—was once again completely interlocked with the director's perception of it. The mime within a mime scene has the soundtrack devoted to Walton's music. The third film with Olivier,

Richard III, was remembered by Walton as ''the fruit of mutual confidence and esteem.'' His final collaboration with Olivier came in 1970 when he wrote the score for *Three Sisters* where the music has a distinctly mellow, autumnal and muted feel to it in keeping with the tragic dimensions of the play. The year before, Walton had written the music for the film *Battle of Britain* but the score was not considered commercial enough and in the end only a small part of the original score was used—the ''Battle in the Air'' sequence—and for many years United Artists refused to release the original score for performance in spite of anguished letters from Walton's fans.

Walton is one of this century's most celebrated British composers— he said of his contribution to cinema; ''The value to a film of its musical score rests chiefly in the creation of mood, atmosphere, and the sense of period.'' No other British composer has given greater value to the films he worked on.

—Sylvia Paskin

WANGER, Walter

Producer. **Nationality:** American. **Born:** Walter Feuchtwanger in San Francisco, California, 11 July 1894 (some sources give 16 October). **Education:** Attended Dartmouth College, Hanover, New Hampshire. **Military Service:** Served in Army Intelligence during World War I, and on President Wilson's staff at Paris Peace Conference. **Family:** Married the actress Joan Bennett (second marriage),

Walter Wanger

1940 (divorced 1965). **Career:** Theatrical producer in New York in 1910s; opened cinema in Brighton, and worked in England as theatre manager after war; returned to the United States; general manager, Paramount, then vice president of Columbia, and producer, MGM; 1939–44—president, Motion Picture Academy; 1945—formed Diana Productions with Fritz Lang and his wife Joan Bennett; 1951—served jail sentence for shooting Bennett's agent; 1950–56—producer, Allied Artists. **Awards:** Special Academy Awards, 1945 and 1948. **Died:** In New York City, 18 November 1968.

Films as Producer:

1929   *The Cocoanuts* (Santley and Florey); *Applause* (Mamoulian) (co)

1932   *The Bitter Tea of General Yen* (Capra); *Washington Merry-Go-Round* (Cruze)

1933   *Another Language* (Griffith) (production associate); *Going Hollywood* (Walsh); *Queen Christina* (Mamoulian); *Gabriel over the White House* (La Cava)

1934   *The President Vanishes* (Wellman); *Stamboul Quest* (Wood)

1935   *Private Worlds* (La Cava); *Mary Burns, Fugitive* (Howard); *Shanghai* (Flood); *Every Night at Eight* (Walsh); *Smart Girl* (Scotto)

1936   *Big Brown Eyes* (Walsh); *Spendthrift* (Walsh); *The Moon's Our Home* (Seiter); *Fatal Lady* (Ludwig); *The Case Against Mrs. Ames* (Seiter); *Palm Springs* (Scotto); *Her Master's Voice* (Santley); *Sabotage* (Hitchcock); *The Trail of the Lonesome Pine* (Hathaway)

1937   *You Only Live Once* (F. Lang); *Stand-In* (Garnett); *52nd Street* (Young); *Vogues of 1938* (*Walter Wanger's Vogues of 1938*) (Cummings)

1938   *I Met My Love Again* (Ripley and Logan); *Blockade* (Dieterle); *Algiers* (Cromwell); *Trade Winds* (Garnett)

1939   *Winter Carnival* (Reisner); *Stagecoach* (Ford) (exec); *Eternally Yours* (Garnett)

1940   *The Long Voyage Home* (Ford); *Slightly Honorable* (Garnett); *The House Across the Bay* (Mayo); *Foreign Correspondent* (Hitchcock)

1941   *Sundown* (Hathaway)

1942   *Eagle Squadron* (Lubin); *Arabian Nights* (Rawlins)

1943   *We've Never Been Licked* (Rawlins); *Gung Ho!* (Enright)

1944   *Ladies Courageous* (Rawlins)

1945   *Salome, Where She Danced* (Lamont); *Scarlet Street* (F. Lang) (exec)

1946   *Canyon Passage* (Tourneur); *A Night in Paradise* (Lubin)

1947   *The Lost Moment* (Gabel); *Smash-Up: The Story of a Woman* (*A Woman Destroyed*) (Heisler)

1948   *The Secret beyond the Door* (F. Lang); *Joan of Arc* (Fleming); *Tap Roots* (Marshall)

1949   *Tulsa* (Heisler); *The Reckless Moment* (Ophüls); *Reign of Terror* (*The Black Book*) (A. Mann)

1952   *Aladdin and His Lamp* (Landers); *Battle Zone* (Selander); *Lady in the Iron Mask* (Murphy) (co)

1953   *Kansas Pacific* (Nazarro); *Fort Vengeance* (Selander)

1954   *Riot in Cell Block 11* (Siegel); *The Adventures of Hajii Baba* (Weis)

1956   *Invasion of the Body Snatchers* (Siegel); *Navy Wife* (Bernds)

1958   *I Want to Live!* (Wise)

1963   *Cleopatra* (Mankiewicz) (replaced by Zanuck)

Publications

By WANGER: book—

With Joe Hyams, *My Life with "Cleopatra,"* New York, 1963.

On WANGER: book—

Bernstein, Matthew, *Walter Wanger: Hollywood Independent*, Minneapolis, 2000.

On WANGER: articles—

Films and Filming (London), December 1960.

Brownlow, Kevin, in *Film* (London), no. 39, 1964.

Rosenberg, Bernard, and Harry Silverstein, in *The Real Tinsel*, New York, 1970.

Cinématographe (Paris), May 1984.

Velvet Light Trap (Madison, Wisconsin), no. 22, 1986.

Velvet Light Trap (Madison, Wisconsin), no. 28, Fall 1991.

Doherty, Thomas, "Walter Wanger: Hollywood Independent," in *Film Quarterly* (Berkeley), Summer 1996.

*   *   *

Leaving aside the headline-grabbing incidents that blighted the last decade of his career, Walter Wanger stands as the epitome of the inspirational Hollywood producer, committed to artistry as much as profit, provocation as much as pleasure. Renowned and respected for his hands-off approach, entrusting his collaborators with creative freedom, contributing his ideas as suggestions rather than dictates, Wanger enjoyed fruitful partnerships with the likes of Fritz Lang, John Ford, Alfred Hitchcock and Don Siegel. Working in a wide variety of genres and styles, the biggest constant in his career is an enduring concern with the blind, dehumanising force of legal/social retribution and the way a decent person can be hounded to the grave by one minor indiscretion or unlucky break. Cannily trading off his "serious" efforts (*Scarlet Street*) with pure box-office hokum (*Salome Where She Danced*), Wanger's instincts were skewed only by a tendency towards literary awe (placing troubled talents F. Scott Fitzgerald and Dorothy Parker under contract despite a demonstrable lack of screenwriting ability). It says something about his ability that Wanger's avowed dislike of being second best in anything comes across not as typical front-office arrogance but a simple statement of fact.

Employed by most of the big studios at one time or another, Wanger first came to prominence at Paramount, facilitating the Marx Brothers' big screen debut in *The Cocoanuts* and director Rouben Mamoulian's striking first film, the location-shot vaudeville star-loses-love-of-daughter melodrama *Applause*. A two-film stint at Columbia included Frank Capra's still enticing miscegenation fantasy *The Bitter Tea of General Yen*. Pausing at MGM long enough to endorse Franklin Roosevelt's New Deal (in *Gabriel over the White House*) and produce the definitive Greta Garbo vehicle, Mamoulian's *Queen Christina*, Wanger settled at Paramount in the mid-1930s, becoming acquainted with wife-to-be Joan Bennett (costar of the medical drama *Private Worlds*). The same year he brought out his first miscarriage-of-justice melodrama, *Mary Burns, Fugitive*, with Sylvia Sidney as the former gangster's moll undone by circumstance and prejudice. Having teamed Sidney with Henry Fonda on the technicolour hillbilly drama *Trail of the Lonesome Pine*, Wanger reunited the stars, regular writer Graham Baker and regular cameraman Leon Shamroy for the independently produced *You Only Live Once*. Under Fritz Lang's unflinching eye, the story of a petty crook framed for murder took on a tragic dimension, the gripping victimised-love-on-the-run plot undermined only by the sentimental Hays Office friendly conclusion. Confident on home ground, Wanger's ambitions fell flat the following year with *Blockade*, a bland, laughably apolitical Spanish Civil War adventure which managed to mention neither Franco nor the Fascists as simple farmer Henry Fonda turns fighter in defense of his land.

Running with a winning streak at the end of the decade, notably the John Ford-John Wayne-Dudley Nichols team-ups *Stagecoach* and *The Long Voyage Home* (the former relocating its producer's usual outsider-prejudice theme to the Old West), Wanger found more effective antifascist propaganda in Hitchcock's *Foreign Correspondent*, which even Joseph Goebbels had to admire. Signing on with Universal shortly after, he alternated further fighting-spirit efforts (*Sundown, Gung Ho!*) with escapism (*Arabian Nights*). The end of hostilities brought *Scarlet Street*, a moody noir reuniting Lang, Bennett, Edward G. Robinson, and Dan Duryea from the previous year's hit *The Woman in the Window*, a lighter non-Wanger thriller. Remarkable at the time for showing a murderer go officially unpunished (downtrodden clerk Robinson kills deceitful prostitute mistress Bennett; sleazy pimp Duryea goes to the chair), the film suggests that state sanctioned execution is preferable to the inner torments suffered by the now vagrant Robinson at the conclusion (in a turnaround on the usual Wanger take, no one will believe that the pathetic man is guilty).

Over the next few years, Wanger lost form, the special "moral stature" Academy Award handed out for the notorious dud *Joan of Arc* fooling no-one. The trash melodrama *The Reckless Moment*, a Columbia-backed vehicle for Bennett and James Mason, won a few European admirers, largely thanks to Max Ophüls' ultra stylish handling. There were fewer takers for the dreary Bennett-Lang psycho-melodrama *The Secret beyond the Door*. Already associating with downmarket outfits such as Eagle Lion, Wanger's industry standing took a rapid downward turn in 1952 when he shot Joan Bennett's agent-turned-lover in the groin. Serving his four month jail sentence in a relatively easy-going honour camp, Wanger nevertheless emerged with a burning desire to expose the corruption and injustices of the penal system and also to relaunch his career. Teaming up with poverty row exploitation specialists Allied Artists (formerly Monogram), Wanger was fortunate to be joined on *Riot in Cell Block 11* by director Don Siegel, an expert in alienated, violent outsiders (here inside), and ferocious leading man Neville Brand. *Riot* hit home and Wanger reunited with Siegel for *Invasion of the Body Snatchers*, an unsurpassed nightmare fantasy on the loss of individuality. Back in demand, Wanger made a shaky return to the capital punishment debate with the based-on-fact *I Want to Live!*, an awkward (if award winning) vehicle for frequent collaborator Susan Hayward. In the same year he started work on a modestly budgeted historical tale, *Cleopatra*, a Fox-backed project for minor contract star Joan Collins. The rest is dismal history: five years worth of cast changes, director changes (Mamoulian making way for Joseph Mankiewicz), location changes, mounting costs, general chaos and financial disaster, all centred arond chronically unhealthy million-dollar-star Elizabeth Taylor. Fired by Darryl Zanuck towards the end of production, Wanger and assorted Fox personnel attempted to sue each other into the ground. For a man who once remarked that nothing was as cheap

as a hit, no matter how much it cost, this career finale marked a particularly sad end.

—Daniel O'Brien

WARM, Hermann

Art Director. **Nationality:** German. **Born:** Berlin, 5 May 1889. **Education:** Studied design at Kunstgewerbeschule, Berlin, c. 1905–07; trained in stage design at the Szenograph, Berlin, c. 1908–09, and the Schauspielhaus, Dusseldorf, c. 1910–11. **Career:** Painter, associated with Der Sturm Expressionists, Berlin; 1912—entered German films as set designer for Vitaskop, then for Union, Decla, Decla-Bioskop, and Greenbaum; also freelance architect and set designer in Hungary, France, and England, 1924–33, and in Switzerland, 1941–44; worked in Germany, 1947–60. **Died:** In Berlin, 1976.

Films as Art Director:

1913   *Der Shylock von Krakau* (Wilhelm); *Menschen und Masken* (Piel); *Der letzte Tag* (Mack); *Wo ist Coletti?* (Mack); *Der König* (Mack); *Die blaue Maus* (Mack); *Der Andere* (Mack)

1914   *Die Geschichte der stillen Mühle* (Oswald); *Pauline* (Etiévant); *Der Hund von Baskerville* (Oswald—2 parts); *Der Spion* (Schmidt-Häsler); *Die beiden Rivalen* (Etiévant); *Die Millionen-Mine* (Piel)

1919   *Totentanz* (Rippert); *Der Volontär* (Neuss); *Die Pest von Florenz* (Rippert) (co); *Der Tunnel* (Meinert and Wauer); *Die Spinnen, Part 1: Der goldene See* (*The Spiders, Part 1: The Golden Lake*) (F. Lang)

1920   *Die Spinnen, Part 2: Das Brillantenschiff* (*The Spiders, Part 2: The Diamond Ship*) (F. Lang); **Das Kabinett des Dr. Caligari** (*The Cabinet of Dr. Caligari*) (Wiene); *Die Toteninsel* (Froelich) (co); *Masken* (Wauer); *Das Blut der Ahnen* (Gerhardt); *Das Haupt des Juarez* (Guter); *Der Richter von Zalamea* (Berger); *Kämpfende Herzen* (*Der Vier um die Frau*; *Four around a Woman*) (F. Lang) (co)

1921   *Der müde Tod: Ein Deutsches Volkslied im Sechs Versen* (*The Weary Death*; *Between Two Worlds*; *Beyond the Wall*; *Destiny*) (F. Lang) (co); *Der ewige Fluch* (Wendhausen); *Die fliegenden Briganten* (Felmy); *Die Jagd nach dem Tode* (Gerhardt); *Schloss Vogelöd* (*Haunted Castle*) (Murnau); *Zirkus des Lebens* (Guter)

1922   *Phantom* (Murnau) (co)

1923   *Das Spiel der Königin* (*Ein Glas Wasser*) (Berger) (co); *Der Kaufmann von Venedig* (Flener); *Quarantine* (Mack)

1924   *Gräfin Donelli* (*Countess Donelli*) (Pabst); *Rosenmontag* (*Eine Offizierstragödie*; *Rose Monday*) (Meinert) (co); *Königsliebchen* (Schall) (co)

1925   *Mädels von heute* (*Liebesgeschichten*) (Friesler); *Die rote Maus* (Meinert); *Soll man heiraten?* (*Intermezzo einer Ehe in sieben Tagen*) (Noa)

1926   *Das süsse Mädel* (Noa) (co); *Der Student von Prag* (*The Student of Prague*; *The Man Who Cheated Life*) (Galeen); *Fräulein Josette, meine Frau* (*Mademoiselle Josette, ma femme*) (Ravel); *Die Frau ohne Namen* (Jacoby) (co); *Die*

Flucht in die Nacht (Pelermi); *Die Frauen von Folies Bergères* (Obal); *Die Insel der verbotenen Küsse* (Jacoby) (co); *Liebe (Die Herzogin von Langeais)* (Czinner) (co); *Parkettsessel 47 (Le Fauteuil 47)* (Ravel)

1927 *Die Liebe der Jeanne Ney (The Love of Jeanne Ney)* (Pabst) (co); *Die Jagd nach der Braut* (Jacoby) (co); *Colonialskandal (Liebe im Rausch)* (Jacoby); *Millionenraub im Rivieraexpress* (Delmont)

1928 *La Passion de Jeanne d'Arc (The Passion of Joan of Arc)* (Dreyer); *Eine Nacht in London (A Night in London)* (Pick); *Priscillas fahrt ins Glück* (Asquith)

1929 *Die weissen Rosen von Ravensberg* (Meinert); *Masken* (Meinert); *Fundvogel* (Hoffmann-Harnisch); *Das Erlebnis einer Nacht* (Brignone); *Freiheit in Fesseln* (Weolff); *Vertauschte Gesichter* (Randolf)

1930 *Dreyfus* (Oswald); *Es kommt alle Tage vor . . .* (Natge)

1931 *Der Mann, der den Mord beging (Nächte am Bosporus; The Man Who Murdered)* (Bernhardt); *Der Herr Finanz-direktor* (Friedmann-Frederich)

1932 **Vampyr** *(The Dream of Allan Gray)* (Dreyer); *Friederike* (Friedmann-Frederich); *Gehetzte Menschen* (Feher)

1933 *Hochzeit am Wolfgangsee* (Behrendt); *Wenn am Sonntagabend die Dorfmusik spielt* (Schündler)

1934 *Peer Gynt* (Wendhausen); *Wenn ich König wär!* (Hübler-Kahla); *Musik im Blut* (Waschneck); *Peter, Paul, und Nanette* (Engels); *Pappi* (Rabenalt); *Zigeunerblut (Ungarmädel)* (Klein)

1935 *Der Student von Prag (The Student of Prague)* (Robison); *Mazurka* (Forst); *Ich liebe alle Frauen* (Lamac); *Krach im Interhaus* (Harlan)

1936 *Ein Hochzeitstraum* (Engel); *Mädchenjahre einer Königin* (Engel); *Die Nacht mit dem Kaiser* (Engel)

1937 *Gefährliches Spiel* (Engel); *Ein Volksfeind* (Steinhoff); *Die Warschauer Zitadelle* (Buch)

1938 *Jugend* (Harlan); *Verwehte Spuren* (Harlan)

1939 *Das unsterbliche Herz* (Harlan)

1940 *Die Geierwally* (Steinhoff)

1943 *Le Corbeau (The Raven)* (Clouzot)

1947 *Wozzeck* (Klaren) (co)

1948 *Morituri* (York) (co); *Vors uns liegt das Leben (Die Fünf von Titan)* (Ritau) (co)

1949 *Tragödie einer Leidenschaft* (Meisel) (co)

1950 *Königskinder* (Käutner); *Sehnsucht des Herzens* (Martin) (co)

1951 *Das ewige Spiel* (Cap) (co)

1952 *Herz der Welt* (Braun) (co); *Cuba Cabana* (Buch) (co)

1953 *Die Privatesekretärin (Private Secretary)* (Martin) (co); *Hokuspokus* (Hoffmann) (co)

1954 *Der Raub des Sabinerinnen* (Hoffmann) (co)

1955 *Verrat an Deutschland* (Harlan) (co); *Hamusse Hanussen* (Fischer) (co); *Königswalzer* (Tourjansky) (co)

1956 *Dany, bitte schreiben sie!* (von Borsody) (co)

1959 *Helden (Arms and the Man)* (Wirth) (co); *Die Nackte und der Satan (The Head)* (Trivas) (co); *Die Wahrheit über Rosemarie (Love Now, Pay Later)* (Jugert)

1960 *Die Botschafterin* (Braun)

Film as Actor:

1960 *Männer sind zum Lieben da* (Schmidt)

Publications

By WARM: articles—

"Meine Arbeit," in *Filmkunst* (Vienna), no. 43, 1965.
Film (Hanover), July 1965.
Kosmorama (Copenhagen), October 1965.

On WARM: articles—

Kosmorama (Copenhagen), no. 90, 1969.
Schöpferische Filmarchitektur, by Walter Kaul, Berlin, 1971.
Cinématographe (Paris), February 1982.
Kosmorama (Copenhagen), Summer 1993.

*   *   *

Trained as a stage designer and a painter by avocation, Hermann Warm was perfectly suited to become a leading figure in a Weimar cinema that would be dominated in part by a merging of the artistic and cinematic, a freeing of films from various forms of recapturing the real from naive realism to impressionism. Such filmmaking was to challenge the truism that the essence of the new medium was the photographic process, which, for many at the time, seemed to be defined by a mechanical reproduction of what exists.

Warm was already engaged on a substantial project, Fritz Lang's *The Spiders*—to become an important film of this newly emerging film style—when he was offered to chance to work on what would be the defining text of the movement: *The Cabinet of Dr. Caligari.* Authors Carl Mayer and Hans Janowitz had originally thought that Alfred Kubin, a designer much interested in chiaroscuro effects, should do the art work, but producer Erich Pommer thought otherwise. It is not certain whether it was actually Pommer or Rudolf Meinert, whose involvement in the project is disputed, who actually hired Warm to design the sets, but the decision was crucial to the eventual look of the film. Instead of a Goyaesque horror landscape of light and shadow, probably the treatment Kubin would have advocated, *Caligari* became an experiment in eccentricity, with its sets made out of painted canvas, an artificial look that was duplicated in nonnaturalistic makeup and stage props (for the most part). The distorted world of *Caligari*, which turns out to be not "real" but a madman's vision of the truth, is not created by any special photographic effects (compare the use of anamorphic lenses in Abel Gance's *La Folie du Docteur Tube* to evoke insanity) but entirely by set design.

The principle of Warm's conception is the Expressionist notion of *Ballung*, that crystallization of the inner reality of objects, concepts, and people through an artistic expression that cuts through and discards a false exterior. Warm's sets for the film correspondingly evoke the twists and turnings of a small German medieval town, but in a patently unrealistic fashion (e.g., streets cut across one another at impossible angles and paths are impossibly steep). The roofs that Cesare the somnambulist crosses during his nighttime depredations rise at unlikely angles to one another, yet still afford him passage so that he can reach his victims. In other words, the world of *Caligari* remains "real" in the sense that it is not offered as an alternative one to what actually exists. On the contrary, Warm's design is meant to evoke the essence of German social life, offering a penetrating critique of semiofficial authority (the psychiatrist) that is softened by the addition of a framing story. As a practicing artist with a deep commitment to the political and intellectual program of Expressionism, Warm was the ideal technician to do the art design for the film, which bears out Warm's famous manifesto that ''the cinema image must become an engraving.''

One of a number of art designers with similar training and commitments (e.g, Walter Röhrig, Otto Hunte, and Robert Herlth), Warm proved able to create many different kinds of effects, as indeed his more standard work for less extraordinary commercial projects during the war had shown. For Fritz Lang's *Destiny*, for example, he created sumptuous period stylizations that provide appropriate backdrop in the Venetian and Arabian sequences. The emphasis on elaborate decoration that is simultaneously accurate and expressive recalls the similar staging effects of Max Reinhardt's Deutsches Theater productions (Reinhardt rejected the scrupulous naturalism of the previous generation for more startling visual effects, to be achieved mainly by innovative lighting and costuming). For Heinrick Galeen's *The Student of Prague*, Warm appropriately reconstructed an authentic nineteenth-century ambience, whose only distortions can be traced to the romantic sensibilities of the story.

More in line with the abstractive *Ballung* of *Caligari* is Warm's design for Dreyer's *The Passion of Joan of Arc*, which involved the re-creation of much of a medieval town. Working with Jean Hugo, Warm abstracted from medieval paintings a certain fundamental medievality that he made the basis of an architecture that is somewhat unrealistic with its smooth, neutral walls. Unfortunately for Warm, director Dreyer decided to shoot this film largely in close-up so that set design figures as only a scarcely seen backdrop to what is essentially a drama played out in facial expressions and camerawork.

Though he would enjoy a long and productive career in the film business, the end of the Weimar cinema in the early 1930s meant that Warm would subsequently work on projects that depended less on the genius and artistic inventiveness of the art designer.

—R. Barton Palmer

WARNER, Jack L.

Producer. **Nationality:** American. **Born:** Jack Leonard Warner in London, Ontario, 2 August 1892. **Education:** Attended schools in Ohio. **Family:** Married 1) Irma (Warner) (divorced 1935); 2) Ann Boyar; one son and one daughter. **Career:** Worked in brother Harry's shoe repair store in Baltimore; 1905—sang illustrated song slides in nickelodeons; with brothers opened Le Bijou nickelodeon in Pittsburgh; 1906—formed the Duquesne Amusement Supply Company; opened production studios in St. Louis and Santa Paula, California; 1917—*My Four Years in Germany* established Jack as a major producer; 1918—took sole charge of Warner Bros. Hollywood operation; controlled the studio until 1967, then independent producer. **Awards:** Academy Awards for *The Life of Emile Zola*, 1937; *Casablanca*, 1943, and *My Fair Lady*, 1964; Irving Thalberg Award, 1958; US Medal of Merit; Order of British Empire. **Died:** Of heart disease in Los Angeles, California, 9 September 1978.

Films as Producer/Executive Producer (Selected List):

1917   *My Four Years in Germany*
1922   *Dangerous Adventure* (+ co d with Sam Warner)

Jack Warner

1926   *Don Juan* (Crosland)
1927   ***The Jazz Singer*** (Crosland)
1928   *The Lights of New York* (Foy); *The Singing Fool* (Bacon)
1929   *Disraeli* (Green)
1930   ***Little Caesar*** (LeRoy)
1931   ***The Public Enemy*** (Wellman); *The Secret Six* (Hill)
1932   *I Am a Fugitive from a Chain Gang* (LeRoy)
1933   ***42nd Street*** (Bacon); *Gold Diggers of 1933* (LeRoy); *Footlight Parade* (Bacon); *Wild Boys of the Road* (*Dangerous Days*) (Wellman)
1935   *Captain Blood* (Curtiz); *Gold Diggers of 1935* (Berkeley)
1936   *The Story of Louis Pasteur* (Dieterle); *Anthony Adverse* (LeRoy)
1937   *They Won't Forget* (LeRoy); *The Life of Emile Zola* (Dieterle); *Gold Diggers of 1937* (Bacon)
1938   *The Amazing Dr. Clitterhouse* (Litvak); *Gold Diggers in Paris* (*The Gay Imposters*) (Enright)
1939   *Confessions of a Nazi Spy* (Litvak)
1941   *The Bride Came C.O.D.* (Keighley)
1943   *Action in the North Atlantic* (Bacon); *Air Force* (Hawks); ***Casablanca*** (Curtiz); *Mission to Moscow* (Curtiz); *Watch on the Rhine* (Shumlin); *Destination Tokyo* (Daves)
1944   *Journey to Marseilles* (Curtiz); *Objective Burma* (Walsh)
1945   *Christmas in Connecticut* (*Indiscretion*) (Godfrey)
1946   *Night and Day* (Curtiz)
1947   *Life with Father* (Curtiz)
1948   ***Treasure of the Sierra Madre*** (Huston); *Johnny Belinda* (Negulesco)
1949   *Montana* (Enright)

1951	*A Streetcar Named Desire* (Kazan)	
1953	*House of Wax* (De Toth)	
1955	*East of Eden* (Kazan); *Rebel without a Cause* (Ray)	
1956	*Moby Dick* (Huston); *Giant* (Stevens)	
1957	*The Prince and the Showgirl* (Olivier); *Chase a Crooked Shadow* (Anderson)	
1958	*Auntie Mame* (da Costa)	
1959	*The Nun's Story* (Zinnemann)	
1960	*The Sundowners* (Zinnemann)	
1962	*PT-109* (Martinson)	
1964	*My Fair Lady* (Cukor)	
1965	*The Great Race* (Edwards)	
1966	*Who's Afraid of Virginia Woolf?* (Nichols)	
1967	*Camelot* (Logan); *Bonnie and Clyde* (Penn)	
1972	*1776* (Hunt); *Dirty Little Billy* (Dragoti)	

Publications

By WARNER: book—

My First Hundred Years in Hollywood, New York, 1964.

On WARNER: books—

The Colonel: An Affectionate Remembrance of Jack L. Warner, Los Angeles, 1980.
Freedland, Michael, *The Warner Bros.*, London, 1983.
Thomas, Bob, *Clown Prince of Hollywood*, New York, 1990.

On WARNER: articles—

Obituary in *Hollywood Reporter*, vol. 253, no. 12, 11 September 1978.
Gabler, Neal, in *An Empire of Their Own: How the Jews Invented Hollywood*, New York, 1988.
Film Comment (New York), vol. 25, no. 4, July-August 1989.
"Freedom Fighter," in *Economist*, 14 October 1989.
Lockwood, Charles, "Jack L. Warner: The Beverly Hills Estate of the Archetypal Hollywood Mogul," in *Architectural Digest*, April 1992.
Bart, Peter, "Recalling Jack's Warning," in *Variety* (New York), 4 April 1994.
Stein, Jean, "West of Eden: The Rise and Fall of Jack L. Warner's Paradise," in *New Yorker*, 23 February 1998.

*   *   *

During the Golden Age of Hollywood Warner Bros. (never Brothers unless referring to the four men themselves) represented the only true family run studio operation. Eldest brother Harry functioned as company president, making all key decisions from the New York office. Next youngest brother Abe supervised distribution, also from New York City. "Baby" Jack headed the studio filmmaking operation in California, churning out hundreds of feature films, animated short subjects, and newsreels. (Their brother Sam, who pioneered the coming of sound, died in 1927.)

Like most newcomers to the movie business, the brothers Warner began as nickelodeon operators, in this case in western Pennsylvania and eastern Ohio. They struggled on the margins of the industry until the early 1920s; in 1922, on the verge of expansion, the Warner company was but one hundredth of the size of industry leader, Famous Players-Lasky. Harry Warner and his brothers realized they needed to grow or face extinction. So they gambled and copied the strategies that were working so well for Adolph Zukor and Famous Players-Lasky by producing expensive feature films, setting up world-wide distribution, and buying theaters, all backed by the Wall Street banking house of Goldman Sachs.

During this initial phase of corporate growth, Sam Warner learned of AT&T's inventions for recording and reproducing sounds electronically. He and Harry Warner devised a means by which to use sound to make their company grow. Warner Bros. would not rock the boat, rather, the company would make recordings of popular vaudeville acts, and offer them as novelties to exhibitors along with Warner Bros. feature length (silent) films. Jack Warner helped supervise these early forays into "talking pictures." Abe Warner's sales pitch stressed that these so-called "vaudeville" sound shorts could substitute for the then omnipresent stage shows offered by picture palaces around the country. Thus, the very first "talkers" were conceived as short recordings of the acts of top musical, comic, and variety talent then touring the United States.

This strategy worked. In August, 1926 Warners premiered the *Vitaphone* with a package of shorts accompanying Jack Warner's latest silent film spectacular, *Don Juan*, with music on a sound track replacing the usual live orchestra for the feature film. As Warner Bros. developed more "packages of sound movies" (a silent feature film with orchestral music on disc plus "vaudeville" short), the brothers Warner quickly realized the movie-going public preferred recordings of popular musical acts to opera stars. Logically and systematically, Warner Bros. inserted "vaudeville" numbers into its features, the first being Al Jolson as *The Jazz Singer*, premiering in October 1927. (Jack Warner would make his greatest contribution as a line producer in these pioneering days.) The three brothers Warner knew they had made it into Hollywood's pantheon based on the overwhelming response to a *Jazz Singer* sequel, *The Singing Fool*, also starring Al Jolson, released in September 1928.

The Singing Fool established box-office records that lasted a decade and took *Gone with the Wind* to shatter. By the early 1930s Jack Warner had ceased working on individual projects and settled into running thriving sets of studios (in Hollywood and Burbank, California) and hiring and firing talented filmmakers, scriptwriters, and other filmmaking personnel. Because of his distance from actual productions, historians debate Jack Warner's day-to-day impact, but he surely set the direction for studio production.

The 1930s and 1940s proved a heyday for Warners. We now properly celebrate the studio for its social expose films (*I Was a Fugitive on the Chain Gang* and *Wild Boys of the Road*), innovative gangster films (*Public Enemy* and *The Secret Six*), and backstage musicals (*The Gold Diggers of 1933* and *Footlight Parade*). Jack Warner took proper credit for the 1937 Academy Award winner, *The Life of Emile Zola*. But he also never produced regular profits until World War II brought the film industry out of the Great Depression. From a box-office point of view Warner's films of the early 1930s only helped the company lose more than $30 million. Steady profits only commenced in the 1940s with the release of such popular fare as the Bette Davis and James Cagney comedy *The Bride Came C.O.D.*; the romantic *Christmas in Connecticut*, starring Barbara Stanwyck and Dennis Morgan; a film biography of Cole Porter *Night and Day*, starring Cary Grant and Alexis Smith; the Broadway hit *Life With Father*, starring Irene Dunne and William Powell; and Jane Wyman's

Oscar winning performance in *Johnny Belinda*. By the late 1940s there was no one in Hollywood with more power than Jack Warner.

The brothers' dynasty began to fall apart with the coming of television. Although the company pioneered in TV production (with such early hits as *77 Sunset Strip* and *Maverick*) corporate profits began to fall. Harry and Abe Warner had made their fortunes and sold their stakes in the company in the mid-1950s. Jack Warner would stay on to run Warner Bros. for another decade, but worked for other corporate owners. He could not simply appeal to his older brothers and thus never again possessed the power he had from the late 1920s through the early 1950s. He became just another independent filmmaker, occasionally turning out hits such as *My Fair Lady* and *The Great Race*. These would prove the swan song for the final remaining member of one of Hollywood's most important families.

—Douglas Gomery

WASSERMAN, Lew

Film, Recording, and Talent Agency Executive. **Nationality:** American. **Born:** Cleveland, Ohio, 1913. **Career:** 1936–38—national director, advertising and publicity, Music Corporation of America; 1939—vice president, Music Corporation of America; 1940—vice president in charge of motion picture division; 1973–1996—chairman, chief executive officer, director, member, executive committee, Music Corporation of America; also chairman of the board, chief executive officer, director, subsidiary corporations; 1996—director, Seagrams

Lew Wasserman

Corp. **Award:** Jean Hersholt Humanitarian Award, Academy of Motion Picture Arts and Sciences, 1973. **Member:** Chairman Emeritus, Association of Motion Picture and TV producers; president, Hollywood Canteen Foundation.

Publications

By WASSERMAN: article—

"Lew Wasserman Compares: TV Fans Only View, Moviegoers Partake," in *Boxoffice*, 10 December 1973.

On WASSERMAN: articles—

Sansweet, Stephen J., "Movie Industry Hurt by Writers' Strike," in *The Wall Street Journal*, 17 June 1981.
Fabrikant, G., "A Movie Giant's Unfinished Script," in *The New York Times*, 20 October 1984.
Egan, Jack, "A Hollywood Thriller: MCA vs. the Sharks," in *U.S. News and World Report*, 7 September 1987.
Cieply, Michael, "Wasserman—An Astute Giant Remains Behind the Myth," in *Los Angeles Times*, 20 February 1988.
Bart, Peter, "Still Standing Tall," in *Variety*, 15 March 1993.
Harris, Kathryn, and John Lippman, "The Clock is Ticking," in *Los Angeles Times*, 20 October 1994.
Fabrikant, Geraldine, "At the Crossroads," in *The New York Times*, 13 October 1994.
Sterngold, James, "A Marriage Not Made in Heaven," in *The New York Times*, 7 April 1995.
Tobenkin, David, "Seagram Buy Could Shake up MCA TV," in *Broadcasting and Cable*, 10 April 1995.
Rose, Frank, "Twilight of the Last Mogul," in *Los Angeles Times*, 21 May 1995.
Weinrab, Bernard, "For MCA and Hollywood, a Generational Shift," in *The New York Times*, 12 July 1995.
Farhi, Paul, "The Man who Remade Hollywood," in *The Washington Post*, 23 July 1995.
Brown, David, "Exit Lew," in *The New Yorker*, 31 July 1995.
Peterkin, Chris, "More Than the Man Behind the Deal," in *Variety*, 28 August 1995.
Laksi, Beth, "Showman of the Century," in *Variety*, 28 August 1995.

*   *   *

Although Lew Wasserman might legitimately be considered the last great Hollywood mogul, he does not fit the stereotype. In an industry built on hyperbole and showmanship, his style is characterized by discipline and restraint. Yet, he reigns as the entertainment industry's deal maker supreme.

During a 59 year career with the talent agency MCA, he reshaped the entertainment business by shifting the focus of programming from motion pictures to television and from producers to onscreen talent. Indeed, Wasserman virtually invented most of what has now come to be standard business practice for the film and television industries.

Wasserman began his show business career at the very bottom as an usher in a Cleveland theater in 1933. This job was quickly followed by a stint as a promoter for a small-time nightclub called the Mayfair Casino. During the latter job, he was spotted by Jules Stein, a Chicago eye doctor turned band booker who hired him in 1936 for his fledgling talent agency, Music Corporation of America (MCA).

In 1938, the agency packed him off to Los Angeles to operate a branch office for motion picture talent. Within ten years, he had assembled a roster of talent headed by such stars as Betty Grable, Bette Davis, Billy Wilder, Gene Kelly, Alfred Hitchcock, Joan Crawford, Jimmy Stewart, and Ronald Reagan, and had ascended to the agency presidency. Through it all, Wasserman managed to keep a low profile and asked that his staff do the same. ''I've always felt,'' he said, ''that, in the agency business, publicity is for the client. Our responsibility is to do our job.''

With all of this talent on hand and competition for radio and film jobs heating up, Wasserman converted MCA into a programming entity by inventing the concept of ''packaging.'' Instead of merely booking talent on existing radio shows, for example, the agency head put his staff to work creating programs and projects which would feature predominately MCA talent. This strategy would eventually be transferred to motion pictures and ultimately to the newer medium of television where it would become standard practice by the 1960s.

Television presented Wasserman with a unique problem when it began to take hold in the late 1940s and early 1950s. As the major studios lost their monopolies on production, exhibition and exploitation of talent in the years following World War II, they unanimously turned their backs on the newer medium reasoning that it would be suicidal to allow their major stars to appear on television since if American audiences could see them for free in their living rooms, no one would go to the movies.

When MCA moved to fill the void with its own television production entity, Revue Productions, it was barred from using two members of the Screen Actors Guild (SAG) on live TV broadcasts. However, Wasserman found a loophole. With the sponsorship of Coca-Cola, he began to produce series shot totally on film and was thus able to negotiate a waiver from SAG allowing him to employ ''big screen'' names such as Alfred Hitchcock as long as the shows were shot entirely on film. By the end of the 1960s almost all shows were either produced on film or videotape, and MCA and the William Morris Agency controlled 80 percent of the talent appearing on TV.

Yet, the MCA head viewed ''talent'' as a diminishing asset. Although he had negotiated the first million-dollar contract in 1946 tying Ronald Reagan to Warner Bros. for seven years and followed it with another precedent a decade later by creating the first ''percentage'' profit sharing package for Jimmy Stewart for starring in Universal's *Winchester 73*, he realized that his bargaining power would cease if the actor walked out the door and went with another agency. ''What I did wasn't such a big deal,'' he emphasized. ''Ronald Coleman got a percentage of his pictures in the 1920s.''

Yet, Wasserman's gamble in trading Stewart's $250,000 salary for a percentage of the film's net gross which ultimately amounted to several million dollars for the actor, actually put the ''onscreen talent'' in the position of virtually dictating which projects could be made by the studios. ''Wasserman and Stein built the first real powerhouse agency,'' attested Samuel Goldwyn, Jr., chairman of the Samuel Goldwyn Co., in 1995. ''They really created the concept of stars producing pictures long before ICM and Creative Artists Agency came along.''

But, Wasserman, pragmatist that he was, knew that his agency had to acquire other firmer, more tangible assets that investors could count on. Accordingly, in 1958, he obtained Paramount Picture's pre-1948 film library for the then unheard of sum of $10 million. (By contrast, Ted Turner paid almost $1.5 billion for the MGM library

three decades later.) Although Paramount executives crowed that the sale generated more revenues than would several years of actually making and exhibiting films, MCA had the last laugh by obtaining more than $30 million from TV stations for broadcast rights to the films within the first month.

Four years later, Wasserman took an even larger gamble by purchasing Universal Studios and its parent company Decca Records. It was his intention to transform his new company into Hollywood's first vertically integrated entertainment corporation which would ultimately grow to encompass film, television, music production, theatrical exhibition, home entertainment and theme parks. However, the MCA chief's initial steps were viewed as a potential monopoly by the Justice Department which stepped in and forced MCA to divest itself of its talent business. At the height of his most ambitious reach, his fear of diminishing assets had seemingly come true.

Yet, the merged company with its sizable assets weathered the crisis and the regulatory setback, if anything, actually forced Wasserman to become even more creative in his deal making. He went from an apolitical stance at the opening of the 1960s to active political involvement in the ensuing decades courting Presidents Lyndon Johnson and Jimmy Carter (both of whom offered him cabinet positions) and eventually reteamed with his old client Ronald Reagan.

By 1973, when Jules Stein retired naming Wasserman his successor as MCA chairman, the company was valued at $160 million. Twelve years later, the younger man had turned it into an empire with a net worth $3.6 million including 420 acres in Los Angeles; two hotels; office buildings; an open-air amphitheater; the Universal Studio Tour (the third ranked tourist attraction in the U.S.); and half interest in the Cineplex Odeon theater chain. Much of this was aided by the relaxed attitude of the Reagan Justice Department toward antitrust issues.

The secret of Wasserman's success during this period was that although MCA continued to expand and diversify, it never strayed from its core business which was entertainment. However, within those basic boundaries, experimentation was conducted at an extremely high level. For example, the company pioneered longform television movies during the 1980s which allowed Universal to keep a full slate of producers, directors and writers at work around the clock while spreading the company's overhead over a full 365 days instead of the usual less than 200 for its competitors. Also, at least one third of these long-form movies wound up becoming weekly series, including such major hits as *The Rockford Files* and *Columbo* among their number. Wasserman thus achieved the best of all worlds—low overhead and a launching pad for high revenue continuing programming with incredible long-term syndication potential.

During the 1980s MCA became one of the largest suppliers of longform programming to the T.V. networks with such hits as *Kojak*, *Columbo*, *Miami Vice*, and *Murder She Wrote*. At the same time, the motion picture division of Universal, long known for relatively low-brow entertainment began to ride the crest of such acclaimed films as the Academy Award-winning *The Deer Hunter* and *Out of Africa*. But, it was another Wasserman gamble made in 1975 that really produced dividends in the ensuing decades. He agreed to finance a film version of the best-selling novel *Jaws* as a vehicle for his protege Steven Spielberg, who would go on to give Universal three of the biggest money winners of all time, including the box office champ *E.T—The Extra-Terrestrial*. In 1990, Wasserman pulled his biggest deal of all, selling MCA to the giant Japanese electronics firm Matsushita. In addition to keeping his chairmanship at an annual salary of $3 million, he exchanged his common shares of stock for preferred shares carrying a value of $327 million. But, the free wheeling dealer was finally reigned in by the financial conservatism of his new partners, and MCA began to decline until it was again sold in 1995 to Seagram's Distillers, which effectively ended Wasserman's involvement in the day-to-day operations of the company.

His only regret, he said at the end, was that the possibilities of the industry that he pioneered "seem endless. I just wish I could be around to see all the changes to come." However, if show business's past is any indicator, its future will still bear the Wasserman imprint.

—Steve Hanson

WATKIN, David

Cinematographer. **Nationality:** British. **Born:** Margate, England, 23 March 1925. **Career:** Messenger boy with a documentary film unit, then cameraman; 1965—first film as cinematographer, *The Knack— and How to Get It,* first of several films for Richard Lester; supervised development of "Wendy Light"; 1977—cinematographer for TV mini-series *Jesus of Nazareth.* **Awards:** Academy Awards, and British Academy Award, for *Out of Africa,* 1985.

Films as Cinematographer:

1965   *The Knack—and How to Get It* (Lester); *Help!* (Lester)
1967   ***Marat/Sade*** (Brook); *How I Won the War* (Lester)
1968   *The Charge of the Light Brigade* (Richardson)
1969   *The Bed-Sitting Room* (Lester)
1970   *Catch-22* (Nichols)
1971   *The Devils* (Russell); *The Boy Friend* (Russell)
1973   *The Homecoming* (Hall); *A Delicate Balance* (Richardson)
1974   *The Three Musketeers* (Lester)
1975   *The Four Musketeers* (Lester); *Mahogony* (Gordy)
1976   *To the Devil a Daughter* (Sykes); *Robin and Marian* (Lester)
1977   *Joseph Andrews* (Richardson)
1979   *Hanover Street* (Hyams)
1981   *Endless Love* (Zeffirelli); *Chariots of Fire* (Hudson)
1983   *Yentl* (Streisand)
1984   *The Hotel New Hampshire* (Richardson)
1985   *Return to Oz* (Murch); *Out of Africa* (Pollack); *White Nights* (Hackford)
1986   *Journey to the Center of the Earth* (Lemorande); *Sky Bandits* (Perisic)
1987   *Moonstruck* (Jewison)
1988   *The Good Mother* (Nimoy); *Last Rites* (Bellisario); *Masquerade* (Swaim)
1990   *Hamlet* (Zeffirelli); *The Cabinet of Dr. Ramirez* (Sellars); *Memphis Belle* (Caton-Jones)
1991   *The Object of Beauty* (Lindsay-Hogg)
1992   *Hallo Mister God, This Is Anna* (Fairfax); *Used People* (Kidron)
1993   *This Boy's Life* (Caton-Jones); *Bopha!* (Freeman)
1994   *Milk Money* (Benjamin)

1996   *Jane Eyre* (Zeffirelli); *Bogus* (Jewison)
1997   *Night Falls on Manhattan* (Lumet); *Obsession* (Sehr); *Critical Care* (Lumet)
1999   *Gloria* (Lumet); *Tea with Mussolini* (Zeffirelli)

Publications

By WATKIN: articles—

American Cinematographer (Hollywood), May 1985.
Eyepiece (Middlesex, Great Britain), vol. 13, no. 5, 1992.

On WATKIN: articles—

Screen International (London), 27 September 1975.
Chase, Donald, in *American Cinematographer* (Hollywood), March 1984.
American Cinematographer (Hollywood), February and April 1986.
McCarthy, T., in *Film Comment* (New York), vol. 25, September/ October 1989.

*   *   *

David Watkin stands out as a maverick even in a field renowned for individualism. One of Britain's most gifted cinematographers, Watkin has always spurned the conventional in the pursuit of his art. His love of experimentation, whether in lighting, composition, or use of film stock, has earned him a reputation as a true innovator. His originality has been brought to bear on such diverse subjects as the Beatles, Jesus of Nazareth, the Four Musketeers, Robin Hood, and the inhabitants of Oz. Watkin's work has displayed a variety of texture, ranging from the crisp, high-contrast photography of *The Knack* to the muted visual narrative of *Yentl.*

Although Watkin believes in matching his style to directorial intent, he favors naturalism. Working with director Caton-Jones, he photographed *This Boy's Life,* the cinematic adaptation of Tobias Wolf's memoir, a disturbing childhood portrait of boredom and violence. Watkin's naturalistic cinematography in *This Boy's Life* has been praised as among the most remarkable features of the film. Concrete, Washington, is rendered as visually dreary as its name suggests. In the film, images of the mundane, of the brutal in Concrete, are juxtaposed with the state's more majestic landscapes— the resulting photographic contrast reinforcing the central character's sense of entrapment in a dull world and an abusive situation.

Few cinematographers are better at using light to echo the experiences of real life. Yet despite the breadth and quality of his achievements, Watkin has not earned the recognition enjoyed by many of his contemporaries. It was only when he earned the 1985 Academy Award for *Out of Africa* that Watkin stepped out of the shadows and shared the spotlight with the top names in cinematography.

Watkin's early career was spent in documentaries. Starting out as a messenger boy, he worked his way up through the industry, making his debut as a cameraman on *Holiday* in 1955. He switched to features in 1965. At that time, a crop of young directors was struggling to help the British film industry break free from the constraints of studio production and was developing a fresh, more natural visual language.

Cameramen such as Watkin, with backgrounds in the more adventurous fields of commercials and documentaries, were eagerly sought out by these directors. Watkin was chosen by American-born director Richard Lester to film *The Knack*, a witty statement on the changing moral climate of 1960s London. Watkin's giddy camerawork intensified the film's mood of spontaneity, and his sharp, monochromic photography underscored its thematic emphasis on opposing viewpoints. Watkin and Lester have since worked together on more than a half-dozen films—the director's eclecticism in subject matter having been equally matched by the cinematographer's stylistic diversity. Their collaboration includes *Help!*, a vividly colored Beatles romp; *How I Won the War*, an antiwar movie in which alternating use of colored, monochromic, and tinted footage functions as a Brechtian alienating device; and *The Three Musketeers* and *The Four Musketeers*, for which Watkin harnessed the dazzling light of the Spanish locations to create exceptionally rich tableaux.

Watkin is nothing if not unconventional. When filming *Out of Africa*, he reversed traditional applications of film stock, using fast film for night and interior shots (situations in which slow film would normally be used) and slow film for exterior shots. The intention was to give the film a soft quality, appropriate to its lush, romantic mood. For *The Charge of the Light Brigade*, Watkin used Ross Express lenses, equipment which had long since passed out of favor with most cinematographers because of its unpredictable effects, but which Watkin drenched certain scenes in a single, dramatic color—in one case a lurid red, in another an electric blue. Stark coloration of this kind is typically shunned by filmmakers because of its highly stylized effects, but for Watkin it was a way of signposting the film's shifting emotional currents. Although Watkin is now very much part of mainstream cinema, in his early career he was associated with directors who were themselves considered unconventional—Ken Russell, Peter Brook, Tony Richardson, and Lester.

Watkin's ingenuity is best exemplified by the ''Wendy Light,'' a lighting unit whose development he supervised. The ''Wendy Light'' consists of some 200 bulbs and is mounted on a crane at heights of up to 150 feet. It functions as a single, powerful light source capable of producing natural effects in both exterior and interior conditions. The unit creates the type of shadows and degree of smoothness found in the real world.

Watkin brings a painterly quality to his work. Like the Dutch artist Vermeer, he often illuminates his subjects with light passing through windows. *Yentl*, *The Hotel New Hampshire*, *White Nights*, and *The Four Musketeers* all contain striking examples of his use of this technique. His work is full of arresting images—a decaying apple in *Robin and Marian*, a huddle of athletes running across the sand in *Chariots of Fire*, an eviscerated serviceman in *Catch-22*, and the majestic Kenyan plains in *Out of Africa*. Yet while there are certain Watkin trademarks, it is incorrect to describe him as having a fixed style. He has always varied his techniques to fit narrative logic and to facilitate the director's aims. One needs only compare *Marat/Sade*'s dizzy camera movements and unpredictable changes of focus (designed to simulate the feel of live theater) with the stately images of *Out of Africa* to appreciate the range of his professional vocabulary. Although his opinions on certain matters are unshakable—the superiority of Zeiss lenses over all their competitors, for example—after nearly 30 years in features, Watkin is still striving to attempt something new.

—Fiona Valentine, updated by Carrie O'Neill

WAXMAN, Franz

Composer. **Nationality:** Polish. **Born:** Franz Wachsmann in Königshütte, Germany (now Chorzow, Poland), 24 December 1906. **Education:** Studied at the Dresden Music Academy and the Berlin Conservatory. **Career:** Piano player in cafes, and with the Weintraub Syncopaters group; 1930—arranged and conducted Hollaender's score for *Der blaue Engel*; 1933—original score for Lang's *Liliom*; 1934–35—lived in Paris; 1935–36—worked for Paramount, then for MGM, 1936–43, Warner Bros., 1943–48, then freelance; 1947—founding director, Los Angeles Musical Festival; conducted widely in the US and Europe. **Awards:** Academy Awards for *Sunset Boulevard*, 1950 and *A Place in the Sun*, 1951. **Died:** In Los Angeles, California, 24 February 1967.

Films as Composer:

1930 *Das Kabinett des Dr. Larifari* (Wohlmuth) (co)
1932 *La Petite de Montparnasse* (Schwarz)
1933 *Ich und die Kaiserin* (Hollaender) (co)
1934 *Liliom* (F. Lang); *Gruss und kuss Veronika* (Boese); *The Only Girl* (*Heart Song*) (Hollaender)
1935 **The Bride of Frankenstein** (Whale); *Diamond Jim* (Sutherland); *The Affair of Susan* (Neumann); *His Night Out* (Nigh); *Three Kids and a Queen* (Ludwig); *East of Java*

Franz Waxman

(Melford); *Remember Last Night?* (Whale); *The Great Impersonation* (Crosland); *Magnificent Obsession* (Stahl)

1936   *The Invisible Ray* (Hillyer); *Next Time We Love* (Griffith); *Don't Get Personal* (Nigh); *Love Before Breakfast* (W. Lang); *Sutter's Gold* (Cruze); *Absolute Quiet* (Seitz); *Trouble for Two* (*The Suicide Club*) (Roberts); **Fury** (F. Lang); *The Devil Doll* (Browning); *His Brother's Wife* (Browning); *Love on the Run* (Van Dyke)

1937   *Personal Property* (Van Dyke); *A Day at the Races* (Wood); *Captains Courageous* (Fleming); *The Emperor's Candlesticks* (Fitzmaurice); *The Bride Wore Red* (Arzner); *Man-Proof* (Thorpe)

1938   *Arsene Lupin Returns* (Fitzmaurice); *Test Pilot* (Fleming); *Port of Seven Seas* (Whale); *Three Comrades* (Borzage); *Too Hot to Handle* (Conway); *The Shining Hour*; (Borzage); *The Young in Heart* (Wallace); *Dramatic School* (Sinclair); *A Christmas Carol* (Marin)

1939   *At the Circus* (Buzzell); *Honolulu* (Buzzell); *The Adventures of Huckleberry Finn* (Thorpe) (co); *On Borrowed Time* (Bucquet); *Lady of the Tropics* (Conway)

1940   *Strange Cargo* (Borzage); *Florian* (Marin); *Rebecca* (Hitchcock); *Sporting Blood* (Simon); *Boom Town* (Conway); *Escape* (*When the Door Opened*) (LeRoy); *Flight Command* (Borzage); **The Philadelphia Story** (Cukor)

1941   *The Bad Man* (*Two Gun Cupid*) (Thorpe); *Kathleen* (Bucquet); *Dr. Jekyll and Mr. Hyde* (Fleming); *Unfinished Business* (La Cava); *The Feminine Touch* (Van Dyke); *Honky Tonk* (Conway); *Suspicion* (Hitchcock); *Design for Scandal* (Taurog)

1942   *Seven Sweethearts* (Borzage); *Woman of the Year* (Stevens); *Her Cardboard Lover* (Cukor); *Journey for Margaret* (Van Dyke); *Reunion in France* (Dassin)

1943   *Air Force* (Hawks); *Edge of Darkness* (Milestone); *Old Acquaintance* (V. Sherman)

1944   *Destination Tokyo* (Daves); *In Our Time* (V. Sherman); *Mr. Skeffington* (V. Sherman); *The Very Thought of You* (Daves)

1945   *Objective, Burma!* (Walsh); *To Have and Have Not* (Hawks); *Hotel Berlin* (Godfrey); *God Is My Co-Pilot* (Florey); *The Horn Blows at Midnight* (Walsh); *Pride of the Marines* (Daves); *Confidential Agent* (Shumlin)

1946   *Her Kind of Man* (De Cordova)

1947   *Nora Prentiss* (V. Sherman); *The Two Mrs. Carrolls* (Godfrey); *Possessed* (Bernhardt); *Cry Wolf* (Godfrey); *Dark Passage* (Daves); *The Unsuspected* (Curtiz); *That Hagen Girl* (Godfred); *The Paradine Case* (Hitchcock)

1948   *Sorry, Wrong Number* (Litvak); *No Minor Vices* (Milestone)

1949   *Whiplash* (Seiler); *Rope of Sand* (Dieterle); *Alias Nick Beal* (*The Contact Man*) (Farrow); *Night unto Night* (Siegel); *Task Force* (Daves)

1950   *Johnny Holiday* (Goldbeck); *Night and the City* (Dassin); *The Furies* (A. Mann); **Sunset Boulevard** (Wilder); *Dark City* (Dieterle)

1951   *Only the Valiant* (Douglas); *He Ran All the Way* (Berry); **A Place in the Sun** (Stevens); *Anne of the Indies* (Tourneur); *The Blue Veil* (Bernhardt); *Red Mountain* (Dieterle); *Decision Before Dawn* (Litvak)

1952   *Phone Call from a Stranger* (Negulesco); *My Cousin Rachel* (Koster); *Lure of the Wilderness* (Negulesco)

1953   *Come Back, Little Sheba* (Daniel Mann); *I, the Jury* (Essex); *Man on a Tightrope* (Kazan); *Stalag 17* (Wilder); *A Lion Is in the Streets* (Walsh); *Botany Bay* (Farrow)

1954   *Prince Valiant* (Hathaway); *Elephant Walk* (Dieterle); *Demetrius and the Gladiators* (Daves); **Rear Window** (Hitchcock); *This Is My Love* (Heisler); *Miracle in the Rain* (Maté)

1955   *The Silver Chalice* (Saville); *Untamed* (H. King); *Mister Roberts* (Ford and LeRoy); *The Virgin Queen* (Koster); *The Indian Fighter* (De Toth)

1956   *Crime in the Streets* (Siegel); *Back from Eternity* (Farrow)

1957   *The Spirit of St. Louis* (Wilder); *Peyton Place* (Robson); *Sayonara* (Logan)

1958   *Run Silent, Run Deep* (Wise); *Home Before Dark* (LeRoy)

1959   *Count Your Blessings* (Negulesco); *The Nun's Story* (Zinnemann); *Career* (Anthony); *Beloved Infidel* (H. King)

1960   *The Story of Ruth* (Koster); *Cimarron* (A. Mann); *Sunrise at Campobello* (Donohue)

1961   *Return to Peyton Place* (J. Ferrer); *My Geisha* (Cardiff); *King of the Roaring Twenties—The Story of Arnold Rothstein* (Newman)

1962   *Hemingway's Adventures of a Young Man* (Ritt); *Taras Bulba* (Lee Thompson)

1966   *Lost Command* (Robson)

1967   *The Longest Hundred Miles* (Weis)

Films as Musical Director:

1930   **Der blaue Engel** (von Sternberg)

1934   *Music in the Air* (May)

1939   *The Ice Follies of 1939* (Conway) (co)

1940   *I Love You Again* (Van Dyke)

1942   *I Married a Witch* (Clair)

1945   *Roughly Speaking* (Curtiz); *San Antonio* (Butler and Walsh)

1947   *Humoresque* (Negulesco)

1957   *Love in the Afternoon* (Wilder)

1958   *Dino* (Carr)

Publications

By WAXMAN: articles—

Hollywood Quarterly, Winter 1950.
In *Film Score*, edited by Tony Thomas, South Brunswick, New Jersey, 1979.
Soundtrack! (Hollywood), vol. 6, no. 21, March 1987.

On WAXMAN: articles—

Films in Review (New York), August-September 1968.
Thomas, Tony, in *Music for the Movies*, South Brunswick, New Jersey, 1973.
International Film Collector, May 1973.
Frankenstein, Alfred, in *Film Music Notebook* (Calabasas, California), Spring 1975.

Positif (Paris), November 1976.

Ecran Fantastique (Paris), no. 6, 1978.

Rivista del Cinematografo (Rome), April 1982.

Lacombe, Alain, in *Hollywood*, Paris, 1983.

Soundtrack! (Hollywood), vol. 5, no. 19, September 1986.

Palmer, Christopher, in *The Composer in Hollywood*, New York, 1990.

Waxman, John, in *Films in Review* (New York), September-October 1991.

Larson, R.D., "Franz Waxman (1907–1967): Two Unrecorded Scores from 1936: 'Fury' and 'Devil Doll'," *Film Score Monthly* (Los Angeles), no. 39, November 1993.

Handzo, Stephen, "The Golden Age of Film Music," in *Cineaste* (New York), Winter-Spring 1995.

Smith, Jack, "The Soundtrack," in *Films in Review* (New York), September-October 1996.

*   *   *

Part of the ironic benefit bestowed on the American film industry by the Nazi regime, Franz Waxman was the most prominent of the German musicians who advanced the craft of film scoring in Hollywood. Aside from his distinguished work in films, Waxman was a fine conductor, and invested much of his time in creating and guiding the Los Angeles Music Festival, which began in 1947 and lasted until his death 20 years later. He won Oscars for *Sunset Boulevard* and *A Place in the Sun*, and he was the only composer to set the style for a whole genre; his first dramatic score in Hollywood, *The Bride of Frankenstein* (1935), written for Universal, was subsequently used, either in pieces or in imitation, for dozens of horror movies made by that studio in the following decade.

Waxman began piano studies at six but was not encouraged by his businessman father to pursue music as a career. At the age of 16 he began work as a bank teller in his hometown of Königshütte, but within a year he made the decision to enroll in the Dresden Music Academy. In 1923 Waxman went to Berlin to study composition and conducting at the conservatory and supported himself by playing the piano in night clubs and cafes. He was hired by the Weintraub Syncopaters, then a popular jazz band, and began making arrangements in addition to playing the piano. He was befriended by the composer Frederick Hollaender (also an emigré to Hollywood during the Nazi period), who persuaded the producer Erich Pommer at UFA to engage Waxman as an arranger in 1930.

One of his first assignments was arranging Hollaender's songs for *The Blue Angel*, the success of which assured Waxman continuous work. In 1933 Fritz Lang gave him his first job writing an original dramatic score, *Liliom*, filmed in Paris. Because of the adverse political climate in Berlin, Waxman decided to stay there, but after only one assignment he was called to Hollywood by Pommer, who was filming Jerome Kern's *Music in the Air*, to be the music director. It resulted in a two-year contract from Universal, followed by terms with MGM and Warners. In addition to his two Oscars, Waxman was nominated for *The Young in Heart*, *Dr. Jekyll and Mr. Hyde*, *Objective, Burma!*, *Humoresque*, *The Silver Chalice*, *The Nun's Story*, and *Taras Bulba*. Very much a serious composer, he felt deeply about the value of film as an outlet for contemporary composers and resented the disregard of most American music critics toward the medium. "There are still too many who look down their noses at

anything written for films. This is a very silly attitude, and it does not exist in Europe, where critics have not condemned composers because they write for the screen."

—Tony Thomas

THE WESTMORE FAMILY

Makeup artists. **George:** Born in Newport, Isle of Wight, England, 27 June 1879. **Mont:** Born Montague George Westmore in Newport, Isle of Wight, 22 July 1902. **Perc:** Born Percival Harry Westmore in Canterbury, Kent, 1904 (twin of Ern). **Ern:** Born Ernest Henry Westmore in Canterbury, Kent, 1904 (twin of Perc). **Wally:** Born Walter James Westmore in Canterbury, Kent, 1906. **Bud:** Born Hamilton Adolph Westmore in Los Angeles, California, 1918. **Frank:** Born in Maywood, California, 13 April 1923. **Education:** George and his four oldest sons left school as youths to begin work as wigmakers or hairdressers; Bud and Frank attended various military and other schools; Frank graduated from Hollywood High School, 1938. **Military Service:** George: served in the British Army during Boer War. Frank: 1943–45—served in US Coast Guard: makeup artist for Coast Guard touring show *Tars and Spars*. **Family:** George: married 1) Ada Savage, 1901; 19 children, including the six sons listed above, a daughter Dorothy, and others who died young; 2) Anita Salazar, 1925; daughter: Patricia. Mont: married 1) Edith McCarrier (divorced); sons: Mont, Jr., Marvin, and Michael; 2) Cora Williams; 3) remarried Edith McCarrier, 1934. Perc: married 1) Virginia Thomas, 1924 (divorced 1936); daughters: Norma and Virginia; 2) the actress Gloria Dickson, 1938 (divorced 1940); 3) Julietta Novis, 1941; 4) Margaret Donovan, 1942; 5) Ola Carroll, 1951. Ern: married 1) Venida Snyder, 1922 (divorced 1929); daughter: Muriel; 2) Ethelyne Claire, 1930; daughter: Lynn; 3) Peggy Kent, 1940 (divorced 1940); 4) Betty Harron, 1941. Wally: married Edwina Shelton; son: James; daughter: Ann. Bud: married 1) the actress Martha Raye, 1937 (divorced 1937); 2) the actress Rosemary Lane, 1941 (divorced 1954); daughter: Bridget; 3) Jeanne Shores, 1955; sons: Robert, Timothy, and Charles; daughter: Melinda. Frank: married 1) Fran Shore, 1950 (divorced 1951); 2) Johnnie Fay Rector, 1955 (divorced 1955); 3) Gloria Christian, 1968. **Career:** George: 1901—opened hair dressing salon, Newport, then worked in Canterbury, Kent, until after 1906, in Montreal, Toronto, and Quebec, Canada, and Pittsburgh, San Antonio, New Orleans, Buffalo, St. Louis, and Washington, D.C.; 1913—added makeup to his repertory, Cleveland; began teaching Perc and Ern the art of wigmaking when they were nine; 1917—worked at Maison Cesare, Los Angeles, then for Selig Studio (opening the first film studio makeup department), Triangle, and other studios: responsible for Mary Pickford's curls in the late 1910s. Mont: worked in lumberyard, then as busboy at Famous Players-Lasky studio; valet, then makeup artist for Rudolph Valentino (created the clean Latin look); and freelance artist for Gloria Swanson, Clara Bow, and Sonia Henie; worked for Selznick International Studios in late 1930s. Perc: worked at Maison Cesare from age 16, then worked on individual actors' hair and makeup; 1923–50—established and headed makeup department at First National (later

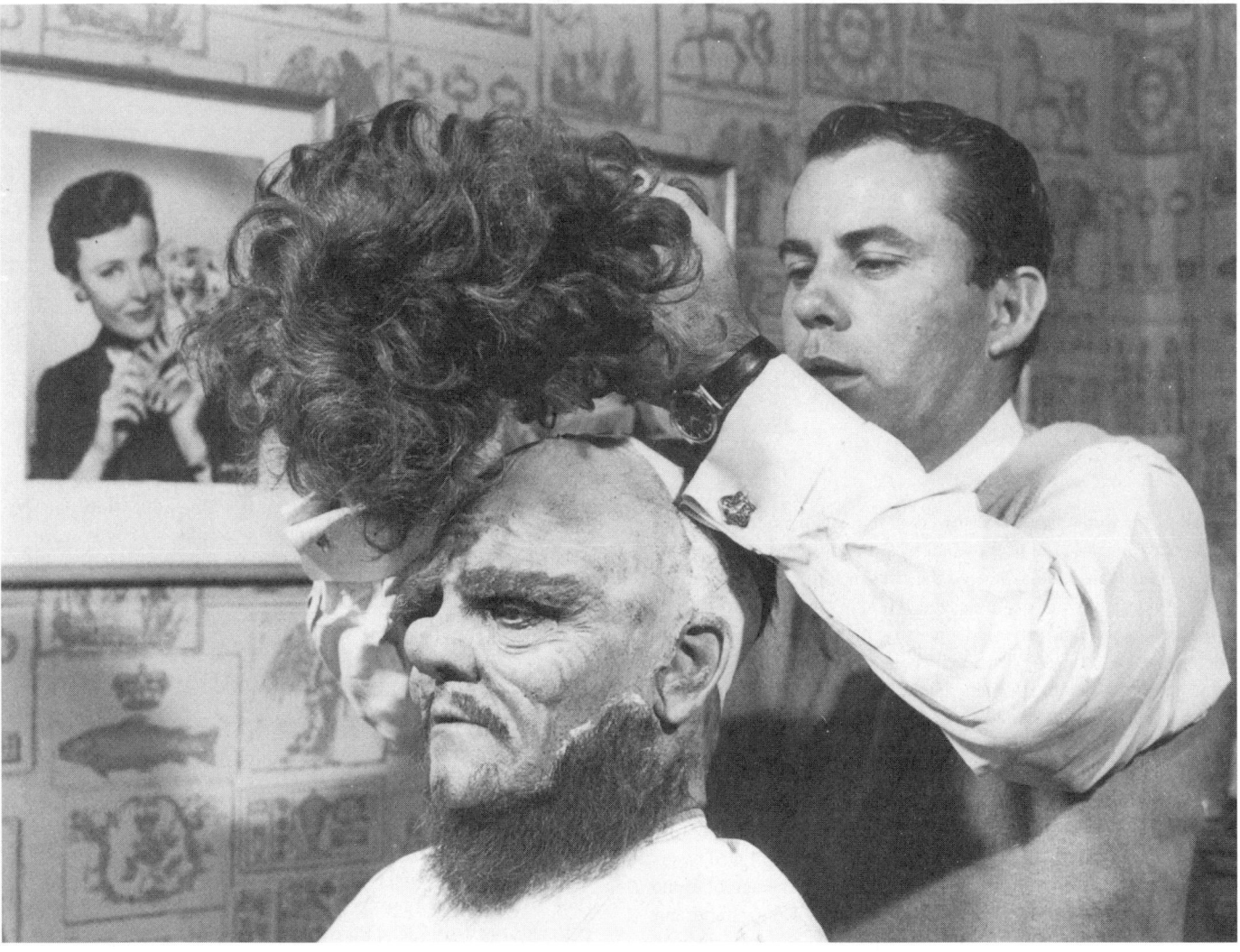

Bud Westmore

Warner Bros.); 1950s—regular guest on Art Linkletter's *House Party* show (radio and TV), and special makeup artist on *Queen for a Day* for 11 years; then worked at Universal for two years, and again at Warner Bros.: did the TV series *The Munsters* and *The Bill Cosby Show*. Ern: 1924–28—worked at Warner Bros., then at RKO, 1929–31, 20th Century-Fox, 1935–39, then freelance; 1950s—did *Hollywood Glamour Show* on TV; cosmetic salesman in New York. Wally: worked as mechanic, then at Brunton studio and Warner Bros.; 1926–69—head of makeup department, Paramount. 1935–65—Mont, Perc, Ern, and Wally set up House of Westmore beauty salon, run in later years mainly by Perc (Ern sold his share, 1939). Bud: apprentice to Perc at Warner Bros. at age 15, then worked at 20th Century-Fox and as head of makeup department at Eagle-Lion Studio; 1946–70—head of makeup department, Universal. Frank: worked at House of Westmore from age 15, then apprentice at Paramount, 1942; worked at Paramount after the war, then freelance, including the TV series *Bonanza*, *It Takes a Thief*, *The Jimmy Stewart Show*, *Planet of the Apes*, and *Kung Fu*. **Award:** Ern: Special Academy Award for *Cimarron*, 1930. **Died:** George died (suicide) 12 July 1931; Mont died of a heart attack in Hollywood, April 1940; Ern died of a heart attack in New York City, 1 February 1968; Perc died of a heart attack in Hollywood, 30 September 1970; Wally died 3 July 1973; Frank died 14 May 1985.

Films as Hairdresser or Makeup Artist (selected list):

George:

1922   *Smilin' Through* (Franklin)
1924   *Secrets* (Borzage)

Mont:

1922   *Blood and Sand* (Niblo)
1923   *Monsieur Beaucaire* (Olcott)
1924   *A Sainted Devil* (Henabery)
1925   *Cobra* (Henabery); *The Eagle* (Brown)
1926   *Son of the Sheik* (Fitzmaurice); *The King of Kings* (DeMille)
1929   *Mexicali Rose* (Kenton)
1932   *Scarface* (Hawks)

1934   *The House of Rothschild* (Werker)
1935   *Mutiny on the Bounty* (Lloyd)
1939   *Intermezzo* (Ratoff); ***Gone with the Wind*** (Fleming)
1940   *Rebecca* (Hitchcock)

Perc:

1925   *Stella Dallas* (H. King); *The Lost World* (Hoyt)
1934   *Bordertown* (Mayo)
1935   *Captain Blood* (Curtiz); *A Midsummer Night's Dream* (Reinhardt and Dieterle)
1936   *Cain and Mabel* (Bacon); *The Story of Louis Pasteur* (Dieterle); *The Walking Dead* (Curtiz)
1937   *The Life of Emile Zola* (Dieterle); *Dead End* (Wyler)
1939   *The Private Lives of Elizabeth and Essex* (Curtiz); *The Return of Dr. X* (V. Sherman); *Juarez* (Dieterle); *The Hunchback of Notre Dame* (Dieterle)
1941   *Kings Row* (Wood)
1942   ***Casablanca*** (Curtiz)
1951   *The Blue Veil* (Bernhardt)
1956   *The Catered Affair* (Brooks)
1966   *Munster, Go Home!* (Bellamy)
1969   *The Arrangement* (Kazan)
1970   *There Was a Crooked Man . . .* (Mankiewicz)

Ern:

1926   *The Sea Beast* (Webb)
1930   *Cimarron* (Ruggles)
1931   *Way Back Home* (*Old Greatheart*) (Seiter)
1932   *A Bill of Divorcement* (Cukor)
1937   *Lost Horizon* (Capra)

Wally:

1931   ***Dr. Jekyll and Mr. Hyde*** (Mamoulian); *Island of Lost Souls* (Kenton)
1933   *Alice in Wonderland* (McLeod)
1936   *The General Died at Dawn* (Mielstone)
1938   *Spawn of the North* (Hathaway); *Professor Beware* (Nugent)
1942   *The Great Man's Lady* (Wellman)
1961   ***Breakfast at Tiffany's*** (Edwards); *One-Eyed Jacks* (Brando)
1962   ***The Man Who Shot Liberty Valance*** (Ford)
1963   *Hud* (Ritt)
1964   *The Carpetbaggers* (Dmytryk); *Lady in a Cage* (Grauman); *Robinson Crusoe on Mars* (Haskin)
1965   *Harlow* (Douglas)
1966   *The Oscar* (Rouse); *This Property Is Condemned* (Pollack)
1967   *Barefoot in the Park* (Saks)
1968   *The Odd Couple* (Saks); *Will Penny* (Gries)
1970   *The Molly Maguires* (Ritt); *There Was a Crooked Man . . .* (Mankiewicz)

Bud:

1948   *Mr. Peabody and the Mermaid* (Pichel)
1954   *The Creature from the Black Lagoon* (Arnold)
1955   *Tarantula* (Arnold); *This Island Earth* (Newman)
1956   *Creature Walks among Us* (Sherwood); *The Mole People* (Vogel)

1957   *Deadly Mantis* (Juran); *Land Unknown* (Vogel); *Man of a Thousand Faces* (Pevney)
1961   *Flower Drum Song* (Koster); *Lover Come Back* (Delbert Mann)
1962   *Lonely Are the Brave* (Miller); *That Touch of Mink* (Delbert Mann); *To Kill a Mockingbird* (Mulligan)
1963   *The List of Adrian Messenger* (Huston); *Captain Newman, M.D.* (Miller)
1965   *I Saw What You Did* (Castle); *The War Lord* (Schaffner)
1966   *Madame X* (Rich); *The Plainsman* (Rich)
1967   *Thoroughly Modern Millie* (Hill); *The War Wagon* (Kennedy)
1968   *Madigan* (Siegel)
1969   *Death of a Gunfighter* (Smithee); *Sweet Charity* (Rosse); *Tell Them Willie Boy Is Here* (Polonsky)
1970   *Airport* (Seaton); *The Forbin Project* (Sargent)
1973   *Soylent Green* (Fleischer)

Frank:

1942   *Beyond the Blue Horizon* (Santell)
1946   *Tars and Spars* (Green)
1947   *Unconquered* (DeMille)
1948   *Let's Live a Little* (Wallace)
1950   *Storm Warning* (Heisler)
1952   *Rancho Notorious* (F. Lang)
1953   *All I Desire* (Sirk)
1954   *Abbott and Costello Meet Dr. Jekyll and Mr. Hyde* (Lamont)
1956   *The Mountain* (Dmytryk); *The Ten Commandments* (DeMille)
1957   *The Joker is Wild* (C. Vidor); *The Buster Keaton Story* (Sheldon)
1958   *Hot Spell* (Daniel Mann); *Houseboat* (Shavelson); *The Matchmaker* (Anthony); *The Buccaneer* (Quinn)
1960   *The Rat Race* (Mulligan)
1962   *My Geisha* (Cardiff); *Two for the Seesaw* (Wise)
1963   *Irma La Douce* (Wilder)
1964   *What a Way to Go!* (Lee Thompson)
1965   *The Flight of the Phoenix* (Aldrich)
1970   *Two Mules for Sister Sara* (Siegel)
1971   *Fool's Paradise* (McLaglen); *The Beguiled* (Siegel)
1972   *Kung Fu* (Thorpe)
1974   *The Towering Inferno* (Guillermin and Allen); *Mr. Ricco* (Bogart)
1975   *Farewell, My Lovely* (Richards)

Publications

By WESTMORE family: book—

Westmore, Frank, and Muriel Davidson, *The Westmores of Hollywood*, Philadelphia, 1976.

By WESTMORE family: articles—

Westmore, Perc, "Make-Up and Coiffure," in *Movie Merry-Go-Round*, edited by John Paddy Carstairs, London, 1937.
Westmore, Perc, in *Hollywood Speaks! An Oral History*, by Mike Steen, New York, 1974.
Westmore, Frank, in *Photoplay* (London), January 1977.
Westmore, Frank, in *American Cinematographer* (Hollywood), July 1984.

On WESTMORE family: articles—

Elkins, M., "The Westmores: Sculpting the Faces of the World," in *American Cinematographer* (Hollywood), July 1984.

Laimans, S., "In Laimans' Terms: George Westmore, Movie Makeup Magic," in *Classic Images*, no. 203, May 1992.

Essman, S., "Behind the Masks," in *Cinefex* (Riverside), December 1996.

* * *

A family of makeup artists all working in Hollywood would deserve a place in film history on this basis alone. However, while the six sons of George Westmore (himself best known for restyling Rudolph Valentino's hair) may not have all achieved the same degree of prominence, their careers offer more than mere curiosity value. Employed at different studios, most of their work was of the kind that does not attract attention to itself. The best known of the brothers, Bud and Wally, gained their fame through work in the horror/fantasy field where the makeup artist has the most scope for the creation of spectacular effects.

Bud Westmore had the best opportunities to make a name for himself, in that from the mid-1940s until 1970 he was head of makeup at Universal Studios (he took over from Jack Pierce, the man responsible for Boris Karloff's monster makeup in *Frankenstein* [1931]). The studio's move from horror to science-fiction brought about the need for bizarre new creations. Of these, the monster in *The Creature from the Black Lagoon*, co-created with Jack Kevan, is Bud Westmore's most famous work. Though obviously a man (Ricou Browning) in a rubber suit, the design is striking, and some of the eerie underwater scenes are well enough staged to make audiences suspend their disbelief. Less well known, but almost as impressive, is the Metaluna Mutant from *This Island Earth*, with bulging eyes, visible brains and pincers. Perhaps the most ambitious assignment on which he worked was one outside the fantasy genre, the 1957 bio-pic of Lon Chaney, *Man of a Thousand Faces*. If ultimately he failed to recreate the latter's makeup designs for James Cagney, it is no reflection on his skill. No one but Chaney would be willing to endure the extremely painful devices he employed to distort his face for the required grotesque effect.

The lurid designs created by Bud Westmore for 1950s science-fiction sagas work well within the context of the overall films. Wally Westmore's work in fantasy films, while exhibiting talent, does on occasion go over the top. His makeup for the 1932 version of *Dr. Jekyll and Mr. Hyde*, which helped Fredric March win an Oscar, is hopelessly overdone, making the embodiment of the doctor's perverse desires look like a comical ape-man. The ugly "manimals" in *Island of Lost Souls* are far more effective.

Perc Westmore seems by and large to have pursued a more mainstream career in the makeup field. His most notable departure into the outlandish was Charles Laughton's makeup in the 1939 remake of *The Hunchback of Notre Dame*. Aided by George Bau, Westmore created an image of extreme ugliness (to the extent of having one of Quasimodo's eyes lower than the other) which, in conjunction with Laughton's acting, is at the same time very touching.

It may seem unfair to acclaim work that by its very nature must draw audience attention to itself while more subtle effects go unappreciated. There might be a case for arguing that *The Creature from the Black Lagoon* required no more skill than Frank Westmore's transformation of Shirley Maclaine into a Japanese girl for *My*

Geisha. Had none of the brothers ever ventured into the realms of the monstrous or bizarre, however, it is unlikely that they would be so well remembered, whatever their talent. Not even membership in a Hollywood family dynasty can compare with bringing to life an archetypal screen monster.

—Daniel O'Brien

WEXLER, Haskell

Cinematographer and Director. **Nationality:** American. **Born:** Chicago, Illinois, 6 February 1926. **Education:** Attended the University of Chicago. **Career:** Merchant seaman for four years; amateur filmmaker since his teens; made educational and industrial films for ten years; 1960—first feature film as cinematographer, *The Savage Eye*; 1969—directed first feature film, *Medium Cool*; mid-1970s—formed Wexler Hall Inc., with Conrad Hall, to make commercials. **Awards:** Academy Awards, for *Who's Afraid of Virginia Woolf?*, 1966, and *Bound for Glory*, 1976.

Films as Cinematographer:

1955 *The Living City* (+ d—short); *Picnic* (Logan) (2nd unit)
1959 *Five Bold Women* (Lopez-Portillo)
1960 *The Savage Eye* (Maddow, Meyers, and Strick); *Studs Lonigan* (Lerner)
1961 *The Hoodlum Priest* (Kershner); *Angel Baby* (Wendkos) (co); *Jangadero* (Guggenheim)
1962 *T for Tumbleweed* (short)
1963 *A Face in the Rain* (Kershner); *America, America* (Kazan)
1964 *The Best Man* (Schaffner)
1965 *The Loved One* (Richardson) (+ co-pr); *The Bus* (+ d, pr, sc)
1966 *Who's Afraid of Virginia Woolf?* (Nichols)
1967 *In the Heat of the Night* (Jewison)
1968 *The Thomas Crown Affair* (Jewison)
1969 *Medium Cool* (+ d, co-pr, sc)
1970 *Interviews with My Lai Veterans* (Strick—short) (co); *Gimme Shelter* (D. & A. Maysles) (co)
1971 *Brazil: A Report on Torture* (+ co-d, co-pr); *Interview with President Allende* (+ co-d, co-pr)
1972 *Trial of the Catonsville Nine* (Davidson)
1973 *American Graffiti* (Lucas) (consultant)
1974 *Introduction to the Enemy* (+ co-d, co-pr, co-sc)
1975 ***One Flew over the Cuckoo's Nest*** (Forman) (co)
1976 *Underground* (+ co-d, co-pr, co-sc); *Bound for Glory* (Ashby)
1978 *Coming Home* (Ashby); ***Days of Heaven*** (Malick)
1980 *No Nukes* (Schlossberg, Goldberg, and Potenza)
1981 *Second Hand Hearts* (Ashby)
1982 *Lookin' to Get Out* (Ashby); *The Kid from Nowhere* (Bridges) (special ph); *Richard Pryor Live on the Sunset Strip* (Layton)
1983 *The Man Who Loved Women* (Edwards); *Bus II* (co-d only)
1985 *Latino* (+ d)
1987 *Matewan* (Sayles)
1988 *Colors* (Hopper)
1989 *Three Fugitives* (Veber); *Blaze* (Shelton)

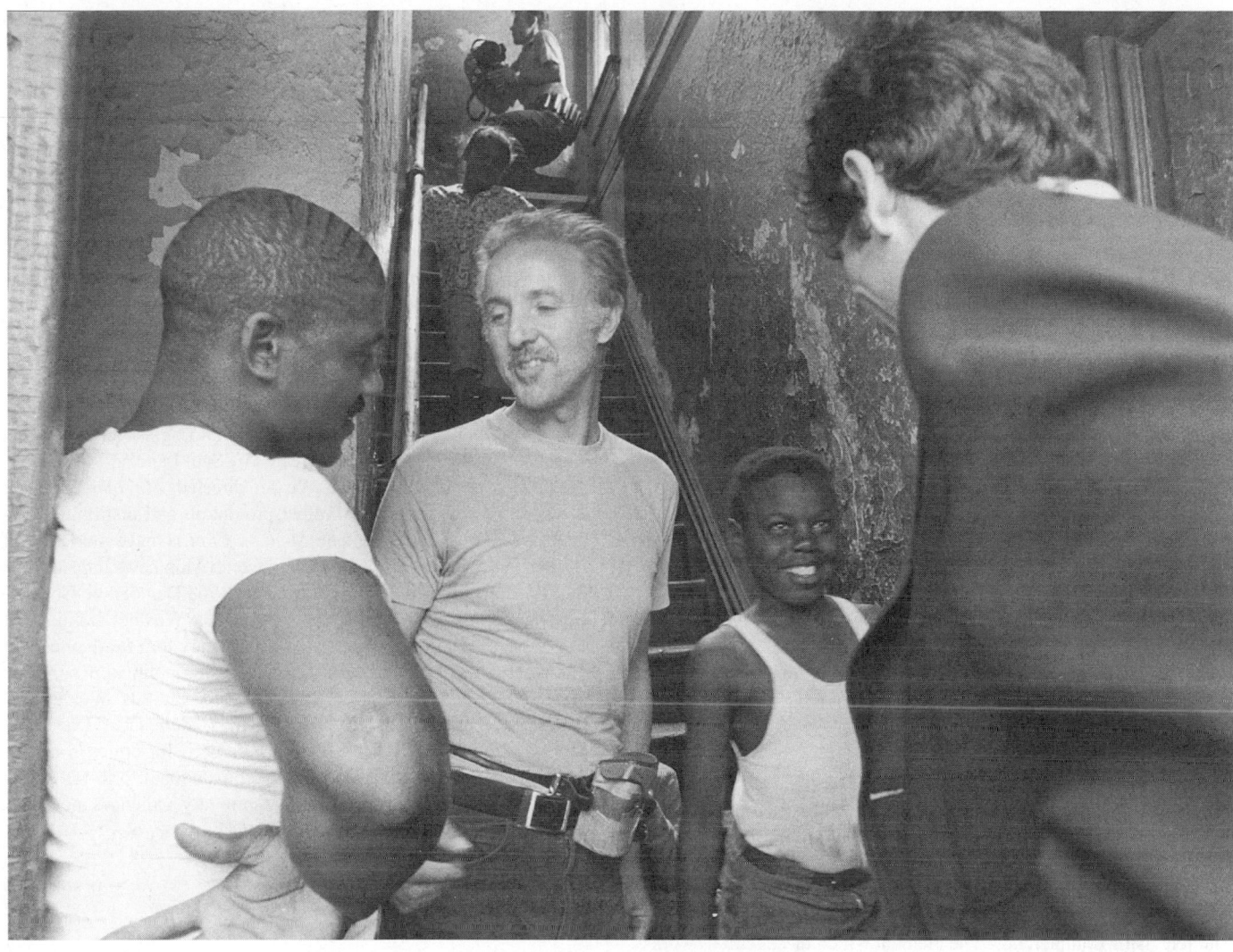

Haskell Wexler (center)

1990	*Other People's Money* (Jewison); *The Babe* (Hiller); *Through the Wire* (Rosenblum—for TV); *To the Moon, Alice* (Nelson—short)
1991	*Other People's Money* (Jewison)
1992	*The Babe* (Hiller)
1994	*The Secret of Roan Inish* (Sayles); *Canadian Bacon* (Moore)
1996	*Mulholland Falls* (Tamahari); *The Bishop, the Warrior and Rebellion in Chiapas* (Landau—doc-in-progress) (co-pr); *The Rich Man's Wife* (A. H. Jones)
1999	*Limbo* (Sayles); *Bus Rider's Union*

Publications

By WEXLER: articeles—

Action (Hollywood), May/June 1967.
Film Quarterly (Berkeley, California), Spring 1968.
Cinéma (Paris), May 1970.
Kosmorama (Copenhagen), September 1970.

Take One (Montreal), no. 3, 1972.
Sight and Sound (London), Winter 1975.
"How to Convert a 16mm Zoom Lens into a 35mm Zoom Lens," in *American Cinematographer* (Hollywood), January 1975.
Film Français (Paris), 23 April 1976.
On *Bound for Glory* in *American Cinematographer* (Hollywood), July 1976.
Seminar in *American Cinematographer* (Hollywood), June and July 1977.
Filmmakers Newsletter (Ward Hill, Massachusetts), March 1978.
Cinématographe (Paris), March 1979.
On *One Flew over the Cuckoo's Nest* in *American Film* (Washington, D.C.), September 1979.
Filme (Berlin), no. 6, 1980.
In *Masters of Light: Conversations with Contemporary Cinematographers*, by Dennis Schaefer and Larry Salvato, Berkeley, California, 1984.
Jeune Cinéma (Paris), July/August 1985.
On TV commercials in *On Location* (Hollywood), October 1985.
Stills (London), November 1985.
Cinéaste (New York), vol. 14, no. 3, 1986.

American Film (Washington, D.C.), October 1988.
American Cinematographer (Hollywood), February 1990.

On WEXLER: articles—

Lightman, Herb A., on *Who's Afraid of Virginia Woolf?* in *American Cinematographer* (Hollywood), August 1966.
Lightman, Herb A., on *The Thomas Crown Affair* in *American Cinematographer* (Hollywood), October 1968.
Film Quarterly (Berkeley, California), Winter 1969.
Chaplin (Stockholm), no. 3, 1970.
Jones, R. B., in *Take One* (Montreal), March/April 1970.
Film Comment (New York), Summer 1972.
Focus on Film (London), no. 13, 1973.
Film a Doba (Prague), March 1973.
Hess, J., in *Jump Cut* (Chicago), August/September 1975.
Cook, B., ''Commercials: Another Form of Filmmaking,'' in *American Film* (Washington, D.C.), October 1977.
Take One (Montreal), no. 2, 1978.
Goodwin, M., on Wexler and Kovacs in *Moving Image* (San Francisco), March/April 1982.
Film Comment (New York), March/April 1984.
American Cinematographer (Hollywood), November 1991.
American Cinematographer (Hollywood), February 1993.
Entertainment Weekly (New York), 5 May 1995.
American Cinematographer (Hollywood), June 1996.
American Cinematographer (Hollywood), January 1997.

*   *   *

Haskell Wexler has worked alternately and successfully inside and outside the commercial film industry throughout his career. He has a reputation as a radical documentary filmmaker, yet he is also an Academy Award-winning Hollywood cameraman. Wexler's cinematography credits include documentaries, Hollywood features, and television commercials. The element which these various works share is Wexler's camera technique. He consciously brings his experience in documentary film to every project in which he is involved.

During the 1950s Wexler learned his craft working in the American *cinéma vérité* style of documentary film. His first feature was uncredited work on Irvin Kershner's *Stakeout on Dope Street*. Kershner also came from a documentary background. The two experimented, mixing *cinéma vérité* and fiction narrative conventions. The film was shot on location rather than in a studio, and hand-held cameras were used. Wexler continued to incorporate the visual techniques of documentary film into features, including two more with Kershner in subsequent years. The harsh, realistic style of such films as *The Savage Eye*, *America, America*, and *The Loved One* is characteristic of his early work in features.

Realism is still emphasized in Wexler's later cinematic style, although the documentary elements vary in degree from film to film. He uses nonfiction film techniques creatively to heighten the tension and mood of a narrative film. In *Who's Afraid of Virginia Woolf?*, a work about intensely personal emotions, Wexler effectively uses a hand-held camera more forcefully to project the tension in some scenes. His camera work gives a gritty reality to the dust storms and shanty towns in *Bound for Glory*. The documentary-style interview scenes with Vietnam veterans in *Coming Home* remind viewers that the fictional drama represents actual issues. The realistic portrayal of the violence-ridden streets of East Los Angeles in *Colors* is too powerful for some viewers and even some critics.

Wexler's documentary experience is also evident in films that have a more traditional cinematic look. In *Other People's Money*, Wexler captures the visual reality and personality of a small New England town and its resident wire and cable company. Both are so stable and old-fashioned that the company becomes too static to deal with a Wall Street takeover. In *The Babe*, he visually conveys a behind-the-scenes look at baseball's dark, seedy side.

While Wexler has worked in feature films since the 1950s, he has never stopped making documentaries. The subject matter of these films has often been politically controversial—the Vietnam War, torture practices of governments, nuclear power. Because of their theater circulation, *Interviews with My Lai Veterans* and *No Nukes* are probably the best-known documentaries that Wexler has photographed. His most recent project to date is *The Bishop, the Warrior and Rebellion in Chiapas*, a documentary-in-progress on the current Zapatista rebellion in Mexico, directed by Saul Landau.

The two feature films that Wexler directed, *Medium Cool* and *Latino*, received extremely limited promotion and distribution because of their political content. *Medium Cool* is an examination of responsibility and accountability in the television news industry and in government set, in Chicago during the 1968 Democratic Convention. The film's form complements its themes. Wexler uses many of the conventions of reportage-style documentary film for this feature. His more recent work *Latino* presents a strong political position on American foreign policy in Nicaragua in the mid-80s. Wexler uses a more conventional narrative form than in *Medium Cool*. Documentary technique is used, as in previous features, for effect in certain scenes. Wexler decided to use a more conventional form for *Latino* because he felt it would appeal to contemporary audiences more than a documentary format.

—Marie Saeli

WHEELER, Lyle

Art Director. **Nationality:** American. **Born:** Woburn, Massachusetts, 2 February 1905. **Education:** Attended the University of Southern California School of Architecture, Los Angeles. **Career:** Magazine illustrator and industrial designer; then art director for David O. Selznick in late 1930s, and MGM, early 1940s; 1944–47—supervising art director, and 1940–60, head of the art department, 20th Century-Fox; then freelance art director. **Awards:** Academy Awards for *Gone with the Wind*, 1939, *Anna and the King of Siam*, 1946, *The Robe*, 1953, *The King and I*, 1956, and *The Diary of Anne Frank*, 1959. **Died:** In Los Angeles, California, 10 January 1990.

Films as Art Director:

1936   *The Garden of Allah* (Boleslawsky)
1937   *A Star Is Born* (Wellman); *The Prisoner of Zenda* (Cromwell)
1938   *Nothing Sacred* (Wellman); *The Young in Heart* (Wallace); *The Adventures of Tom Sawyer* (Taurog)
1939   **Gone with the Wind** (Fleming); *Made for Each Other* (Cromwell); *Intermezzo* (Ratoff)
1940   *Rebecca* (Hitchcock)

1941   *That Hamilton Woman* (*Lady Hamilton*) (A. Korda)

1942   *Keeper of the Flame* (Cukor); *The Jungle Book* (*Rudyard Kipling's Jungle Book*) (Z. Korda); *Cairo* (Van Dyke)

1943   *Bataan* (Garnett)

1944   ***Laura*** (Preminger); *Dragon Seed* (Conway and Bucquet); *Thirty Seconds over Tokyo* (LeRoy); *Winged Victory* (Cukor); *Wing and a Prayer* (Hathaway)

1945   *Hangover Square* (Brahm); *Leave Her to Heaven* (Stahl); *A Tree Grows in Brooklyn* (Kazan); *The Dolly Sisters* (Cummings) (co); *The House on 92nd Street* (Hathaway); *Fallen Angel* (Preminger)

1946   *Anna and the King of Siam* (Cromwell); *Cluny Brown* (Lubitsch); ***My Darling Clementine*** (Ford); *Centennial Summer* (Preminger); *Wake Up and Dream* (Bacon); *Dragonwyck* (Mankiewicz)

1947   *Daisy Kenyon* (Preminger); *Forever Amber* (Preminger); *The Foxes of Harrow* (Stahl); *Gentlemen's Agreement* (Kazan); *Kiss of Death* (Hathaway); *Nightmare Alley* (Goulding)

1948   *Call Northside 777* (Hathaway); *The Art Director* (doc); *That Lady in Ermine* (Lubitsch); *Unfaithfully Yours* (P. Sturges); *The Iron Curtain* (Wellman); *Cry of the City* (Siodmak); *Give My Regards to Broadway* (Bacon); *The Snake Pit* (Litvak); *Street with No Name* (Keighly)

1949   *Thieves' Highway* (Dassin); *Whirlpool* (Preminger); *Pinky* (Kazan); *Chicken Every Sunday* (Seaton); *Twelve O'Clock High* (H. King); *Mother Is a Freshman* (Bacon); *Slattery's Hurricane* (De Toth); *I Was a Male War Bride* (Hawks); *House of Strangers* (Mankiewicz); *The Fan* (Preminger); *A Letter to Three Wives* (Mankiewicz); *Dancing in the Dark* (Reis); *Down to the Sea in Ships* (Hathaway)

1950   *Panic in the Streets* (Kazan); *Cheaper by the Dozen* (W. Lang); ***All about Eve*** (Mankiewicz); *Broken Arrow* (Daves); *American Guerilla in the Philippines* (F. Lang); *Two Flags West* (Wise); *When Willie Comes Marching Home* (Ford); *No Way Out* (Mankiewicz); *Where the Sidewalk Ends* (Preminger)

1951   *Fourteen Hours* (Hathaway); *Bird of Paradise* (Daves); *The House on Telegraph Hill* (Wise); *David and Bathsheba* (H. King); *Halls of Montezuma* (Milestone); *Fixed Bayonets* (Fuller); *Rawhide!* (Hathaway); *The Guy Who Came Back* (Newman); *Golden Girl* (Bacon); *The Frogmen* (Bacon); *The Day the Earth Stood Still* (Wise); *Call Me Mister* (Bacon); *Anne of the Indies* (Tourneur); *People Will Talk* (Mankiewicz); *Love Nest* (Newman); *The Thirteenth Letter* (Preminger); *You're in the Navy Now* (Hathaway); *The Desert Fox* (Hathaway)

1952   *Deadline—U.S.A.* (Brooks); *My Cousin Rachel* (Koster); *Viva Zapata!* (Kazan); *The President's Lady* (Levin); *The Snows of Kilimanjaro* (H. King); *Five Fingers* (Mankiewicz); *Monkey Business* (Hawks); *Return of the Texan* (Daves); *The Model and the Marriage Broker* (Cukor); *Red Skies of Montana* (Newman); *Diplomatic Courier* (Hathaway); *My Pal Gus* (Parrish); *Pony Soldier* (Newman); *Something for the Birds* (Wise); *Way of a Gaucho* (Tourneur)

1953   *The Robe* (Koster); *Call Me Madam* (W. Lang); *Titanic!* (Negulesco); *Gentlemen Prefer Blondes* (Hawks); *The Farmer Takes a Wife* (Levin); *Man in the Attic* (Fregonese);

Treasure of the Golden Condor (Daves); *Dangerous Crossing* (Newman); *How to Marry a Millionaire* (Negulesco); *Pickup on South Street* (Fuller); *White Witch Doctor* (Hathaway); *The I Don't Care Girl* (Bacon); *Niagara* (Hathaway); *King of the Khyber Rifles* (H. King)

1954   *River of No Return* (Preminger); *Three Coins in the Fountain* (Negulesco); *Garden of Evil* (Hathaway); *The Egyptian* (Curtiz); *Desirée* (Koster); *Hell and High Water* (Fuller); *The Siege at Red River* (Maté); *Demetrius and the Gladiators* (Daves); *There's No Business Like Show Business* (W. Lang)

1955   *Love Is a Many-Splendored Thing* (H. King); *The Racers* (Hathaway); *The Girl in the Red Velvet Swing* (Fleischer); *Daddy Long Legs* (Negulesco); *The Seven Year Itch* (Wilder); *Violent Saturday* (Fleischer); *House of Bamboo* (Fuller); *The Tall Men* (Walsh); *The Left Hand of God* (Dmytryk)

1956   *Bus Stop* (Logan); *Teenage Rebel* (Goulding); *The King and I* (W. Lang); *The Bottom of the Bottle* (Hathaway); *Carousel* (H. King); *The Lieutenant Wore Skirts* (Tashlin); *The Man in the Gray Flannel Suit* (Johnson); *The Revolt of Mamie Stover* (Walsh); *Bigger Than Life* (Ray); *The Lazy Wagon* (Daves); *The Girl Can't Help It* (Tashlin); *Between Heaven and Hell* (Fleischer)

1957   *The Sun Also Rises* (H. King); *A Hatful of Rain* (Zinnemann); *Peyton Place* (Robson); *Will Success Spoil Rock Hunter?* (Tashlin); *An Affair to Remember* (McCarey); *Stopover Tokyo* (Breen); *The Three Faces of Eve* (Johnson); *Kiss Them for Me* (Donen); *No Down Payment* (Ritt)

1958   *South Pacific* (Logan); *A Certain Smile* (Negulesco); *The Young Lions* (Dmytryk); *From Hell to Texas* (Hathaway); *Ten North Frederick* (Dunne); *The Bravados* (H. King); *The Long Hot Summer* (Ritt); *The Hunters* (D. Powell); *The Barbarian and the Geisha* (Huston); *These Thousand Hills* (Fleischer); *The Fiend Who Walked the West* (Douglas); *Rally 'round the Flag, Boys!* (McCarey)

1959   *Compulsion* (Fleischer); *Blue Denim* (Dunne); *Journey to the Center of the Earth* (Levin); *A Farewell to Arms* (C. Vidor); *The Diary of Anne Frank* (Stevens); *The Sound and the Fury* (Ritt); *Woman Obsessed* (Hathaway); *Say One for Me* (Tashlin); *Hound Dog Man* (Siegel); *The Man Who Understood Women* (Johnson); *The Story on Page One* (Odets)

1960   *From the Terrace* (Robson); *Wild River* (Kazan); *Wake Me When It's Over* (LeRoy); *Seven Thieves* (Preminger); *Can-Can* (W. Lang)

1962   *Advise and Consent* (Preminger)

1963   *The Cardinal* (Preminger)

1964   *The Best Man* (Schaffner)

1965   *In Harm's Way* (Preminger)

1967   *The Big Mouth* (Lewis)

1968   *The Swimmer* (Perry); *Where Angels Go . . . Trouble Follows!* (Neilson)

1969   *Marooned* (J. Sturges)

1970   *Tell Me That You Love Me, Junie Moon* (Preminger)

1971   *The Love Machine* (Haley); *Doctors' Wives* (Schaefer)

1972   *Bless the Beasts and Children* (Kramer); *Stand Up and Be Counted* (Cooper)

1975   *Posse* (K. Douglas)

929

Publications

By WHEELER: article—

Film Comment (New York), May-June 1978.

On WHEELER: article—

Obituary in *New York Times*, 13 January 1990.
Obituary in *Variety* (New York), 17 January 1990.
Obituary in *Classic Images* (Muscatine), March 1990.

*   *   *

Lyle Wheeler began his career in art direction on a high note, precociously winning an Academy Award for *Gone with the Wind*. His role was to execute the sets which were painstakingly sketched by William Cameron Menzies, the production designer. Wheeler's talent for creating historically accurate sets is not only evident in this epic but is also seen in his later films, such as *That Hamilton Woman* (with Vincent Korda), about the lives of Lord Nelson and Lady Hamilton, and *The Robe*.

Wheeler's black-and-white films are characterized by a sharp, clean look. In the contemporary psychological thrillers *Rebecca* and *Laura*, the sharp shadows cast on and around the characters became more overbearing during tense moments. Though Wheeler's black-and-white films are much admired, he regretted that some of them could not have been made in color. The Academy Award-winning *Anna and the King of Siam* was made in black-and-white because of a painters' strike. To compensate for the lack of color, Wheeler built the sets of plaster treated to appear in varying values. The result is a monochrome film so vivid that it almost convinces the audience that it was shot in color.

Wheeler's color films are as beautiful as his black-and-white. He was able to design the *Anna and the King* story in bold, stunning colors when he worked on the musical version, *The King and I*. Wheeler even made the unusual decision to shoot one of the *noir* films, *Leave Her to Heaven*, in color. Instead of the dark, rain-soaked streets typical of that genre, this tale of deception is set effectively against bright country lawns and sunny skies.

From 1944 to 1960, Wheeler was supervising art director at 20th Century-Fox. As such, he oversaw the visual aspects of each film from its inception, as he worked with the writer, scouted locations with the art director assigned to each film, and approved all sketches.

During his career as an art director, Wheeler was in on the ground floor of many advances in film technology. He experimented with Technicolor as early as 1936 when he worked on *The Garden of Allah* with producer David O. Selznick. He led 20th Century-Fox through the transition from black-and-white to color production and from the standard shot-size to CinemaScope.

—Lois Miklas

WHITLOCK, Albert

Special Effects Technician. **Nationality:** British. **Born:** London, England, 1915. **Family:** Married; two sons. **Career:** 1930s—worked at a variety of jobs in British film industry; then painted backdrops

Albert Whitlock

and designed titles until 1954; 1954–61—worked at Disney studios, Hollywood; 1961–63—freelance designer; 1963— designer for Universal; TV work includes special effects for the miniseries *A.D.*, 1985. **Awards:** Academy Award for *Earthquake*, 1974; Special Achievement Award, 1975. **Died:** 17 October 1982.

Films as Special Effects Technician:

1955   *The Man Who Knew Too Much* (Hitchcock)
1961   *Greyfriars Bobby* (Chaffey)
1963   *Captain Newman, M.D.* (Miller)
1964   *I'd Rather Be Rich* (Smight); *Island of the Blue Dolphins* (Clark)
1965   *Mirage* (Dmytryk); *Shenandoah* (McLaglen); *Ship of Fools* (Kramer); *That Funny Feeling* (Thorpe); *The War Lord* (Schaffner)
1966   *Beau Geste* (Heyes); *Blindfold* (Dunne); *Munster, Go Home!* (Bellamy); *The Rare Breed* (McLaglen)
1967   *The King's Pirate* (Weis); *The Reluctant Astronaut* (Montagne); *Rough Night in Jericho* (Laven); *Tobruk* (Hiller); *Thoroughly Modern Millie* (Hill); *The War Wagon* (Kennedy)
1968   *The Ballad of Josie* (McLaglen); *Counterpoint* (Nelson); *Hellfighters* (McLaglen); *In Enemy Country* (Keller); *P.J.* (Guillermin); *The Shakiest Gun in the West* (Rafkin)
1969   *The Learning Tree* (Parks); *Topaz* (Hitchcock)
1970   *Catch-22* (Nichols); *The Forbin Project* (Sargent); *Skullduggery* (Douglas and Wilson)
1971   *Diamonds Are Forever* (Hamilton) (co)

1972   *Short Walk to Daylight* (Shear)
1973   *The Sting* (Hill)
1974   *The Questor Tapes* (Colla); *Killdozer* (London); *Earthquake*
        (Robson)
1975   *Day of the Locust* (Schlesinger); *The Hindenburg* (Wise); *The
        Man Who Would Be King* (Huston)
1976   *Bound for Glory* (Ashby)
1977   *The Car* (Silverstein); *MacArthur* (Sargent); *High Anxiety*
        (Brooks); *Airport '77* (Jameson); *Exorcist II: The Heretic*
        (Boorman)
1979   *Dracula* (Badham); *The Prisoner of Zenda* (Quine); *The
        Wiz* (Lumet)
1980   *Cheech and Chong's Next Movie* (*High Encounters of the
        Ultimate Kind*) (Chong); *The Blues Brothers* (Landis)
1981   *Ghost Story* (Irvin); *Heartbeeps* (Arkush); *History of the
        World, Part I* (Brooks)
1982   *Missing* (Costa Gavras); *The Thing* (Carpenter); *Cat People*
        (Schrader); *The Best Little Whorehouse in Texas* (Higgins)
1983   *Psycho II* (Franklin)
1984   *The Lonely Guy* (Hiller); *Dune* (Lynch); *Greystoke: The
        Legend of Tarzan* (Hudson)
1985   *Red Sonja* (Fleischer)

Other Films:

1963   *The Birds* (Hitchcock) (design)
1964   *Marnie* (Hitchcock) (design)
1966   *Torn Curtain* (Hitchcock) (design)
1985   *Clue* (Lynn) (consultant)

Publications

By WHITLOCK: articles—

Filmmakers Newsletter (Ward Hill, Massachusetts), October 1974.
Cinefantastique (New York), February 1982.
Cahiers du Cinéma (Paris), June 1982.

On WHITLOCK: articles—

Fry, Ron, and Pamela Fourson, in *The Saga of Special Effects*,
    Englewood Cliffs, New Jersey, 1977.
National Film Theatre booklet (London), October-December 1982.
Starburst (London), no. 56, 1983.
American Cinematographer (Hollywood), January 1986.
Variety (New York), 1 November 1999.

*   *   *

As one of Hollywood's leading special effects artists, Albert
Whitlock was in the unusual position of being most successful when
he was least recognized. He was a master of matte painting, and often
his work is on the screen for only a few seconds. Through his art, he
was able to create for the screen images that are impossible to achieve
realistically, whether they be from periods of the past, such as 1930s
Chicago (*The Sting*) or Los Angeles (*Day of the Locust*), or disasters,
such as two for which his illusions won Academy Awards, *Earthquake* and *The Hindenburg*.

The space and science-fiction films of the late 1970s and 1980s
focused attention on special effects artists in Hollywood. Generally,
these effects were obvious ones, involving other planets, prehistoric
times, fantastic robots, or organic creatures. These kind of effects did
not interest Whitlock, whose idea of a great effect was one that the
public does not recognize as one. Whitlock's art furthers the illusion
that what is seen on the screen is ''real'' and causes the thrill that often
accompanies such illusionism. Whitlock was an artist of the natural
world, creating images of things that cannot be filmed realistically
because of their violent nature, such as an earthquake or a dust-storm
(*Bound for Glory*), or because of their cost to build, such as an entire
castle (*Dracula* and *The Prisoner of Zenda*) or a mountaintop city
(*The Man Who Would Be King*).

Whitlock's art made movies cheaper to produce. His was a world
of matte paintings, models, and filming at different speeds. In his
emphasis on illusionism, Whitlock can be seen as part of an artistic
tradition going back to the Italian Renaissance and the invention of
perspective to make two-dimensional pictures appear to be windows
on the world. In his painting style, however, he considered himself
closer to Impressionism, than to academic painting because he was
more interested in the study of phenomena and the effects of light than
in objects themselves.

In the late 1950s, Whitlock was influenced by working under Peter
Ellenshaw, an effects supervisor for Disney studios. He was associated with Universal from 1963 and worked with a number of art
directors, including Robert Boyle (*The Birds*). Though his work may
go unrecognized because it is so convincing, Whitlock's artistry with
special effects is important in understanding three concepts: the
collaboration necessary in movie-making, the need to use effects for
budgetary reasons, and the fact that film is a two-dimensional
illusionistic medium.

—Floyd W. Martin

WILCOX, Herbert

Producer and Director. **Nationality:** British. **Born:** Cork, Ireland
(some sources say Norwood, South London), 19 April 1892 (some
sources say 1890). **Education:** Attended school in Brighton, England. **Military Service:** Royal Flying Corps, during World War I:
pilot. **Family:** Married 1) Maude Bower, three daughters, one son;
2) Anna Neagle, 1943. **Career:** Worked as journalist until 1914;
1919—entered film rental business with Astra Films; 1920—founded
Graham Wilcox Productions with director Graham Cutts; 1922—
produced first feature film, *The Wonderful Story;* 1929—set up
British and Dominion Productions; 1932—first film with Anna
Neagle, *Goodnight Vienna*; 1937—chairman and managing director,
Imperator Film Productions; 1938—signed distribution agreement
with RKO; 1940–42—directed for RKO in Hollywood before returning to Britain; 1945—signed distribution agreement with 20th Century-Fox; 1964—declared bankrupt. **Died:** In London, 15 May 1977.

Films as Producer:

1922   *The Wonderful Story* (Cutts); *Flames of Passion* (Cutts)
1923   *Paddy-the-Next-Best-Thing* (Cutts); *Chu Chin Chow* (+ d)

Herbert Wilcox

1924   *Southern Love* (+ d); *Decameron Nights* (+ d)
1925   *The Only Way* (+ d)
1926   *Nell Gwyn* (+ d, sc); *London* (*Limehouse*) (+ d, sc)
1927   *Tiptoes* (+ d, sc); *Madame Pompadour* (+ d); *Mumsie* (+ d); *The Luck of the Navy* (Paul) (co-pr)
1928   *Dawn* (+ d); *The Bondman* (+ d);
1929   *The Woman in White* (+ d); *Splinters* (Raymond)
1930   *Rookery Nook* (Walls); *The Loves of Robert Burns* (+ d); *Wolves* (*Wanted Men*) (de Courville); *Canaries Sometimes Sing* (Walls); *Plunder* (Walls); *Tons of Money* (Walls)
1931   *Chance of a Night-Time* (co-d, Lynn); *Carnival* (+ d); *Almost a Divorce* (Varney); *The Speckled Band* (Raymond); *Up for the Cup* (Raymond); *Mischief* (Raymond)
1932   *Thark* (Walls); *The Flag Lieutenant* (Edwards); *Say It with Music* (Raymond); *The Love Contract* (Selpin); *The Blue Danube* (+ d); *Goodnight Vienna* (*Magic Night*); *Mayor's Nest* (Rogers); *Money Means Nothing* (Templeman); *Leap Year* (Walls)
1933   *Yes Mr. Brown* (+ d); *The King's Cup* (+ d); *Bitter Sweet* (+ d); *Sorrell and Son* (Raymond); *The Little Damozel* (+ d); *Just My Luck* (Raymond); *Up for the Derby* (Rogers); *The Blarney Stone* (Walls); *Night of the Garter* (Raymond); *Summer Lightning* (Rogers); *Up to the Neck* (Raymond); *That's a Good Girl* (Buchanan); *Trouble* (Rogers)
1934   *The Queen's Affair* (+ d); *Nell Gwyn* (+ d); *The King of Paris* (Raymond); *It's a Cop* (Raymond); *Girls Please!* (Raymond)
1935   *Brewster's Millions* (Freeland); *Escape Me Never* (Czinner); *Peg of Old Drury* (+ d); *Where's George?* (*The Hope of His Side*) (Raymond and Young); *Come out of the Pantry* (Raymond)
1936   *Limelight* (+ d); *The Three Maxims* (+ d); *This'll Make You Whistle* (+ d); *Fame* (Hiscott); *Millions* (Hiscott)
1937   *The Gang Show* (Goulding); *The Frog* (Raymond); *The Rat* (Goulding); *Sunset in Vienna* (*Suicide Legion*) (Walker); *London Melody* (*Girl in the Street*) (+ d); *Our Fighting Navy* (*Torpedoed*) (+ d); *Victoria the Great* (+ d); *Splinters in the Air* (Goulding)
1938   *Blondes for Danger* (Raymond); *Sixty Glorious Years* (+ d); *Return of the Frog* (Elvey)
1939   *Nurse Edith Cavell* (+ d)
1940   *Irene* (+ d); *No, No Nanette* (+ d)
1941   *Sunny* (+ d)
1942   *They Flew Alone* (*Wings and the Woman*) (+ d); *Queen Victoria* (reedited amalgamation of *Victoria the Great* and *Sixty Glorious Years*) (+ d)
1943   *Forever and a Day* (co-pr,+ co-d); *The Yellow Canary* (+ d)
1945   *I Live in Grosvenor Square* (*A Yank in London*) (+ d)
1946   *Piccadilly Incident* (+ d)
1947   *The Courtneys of Curzon Street* (*Kathy's Love Affair*) (+ d)
1948   *Spring in Park Lane* (+ d); *Elizabeth of Ladymead* (+ d)
1949   *Maytime in Mayfair* (+ d)
1950   *Odette* (+ d); *Into the Blue* (co-pr, + d)
1951   *The Lady with the Lamp* (+ d)
1952   *Derby Day* (+ d)
1953   *Trent's Last Case* (+ d); *The Beggar's Opera* (Brook) (co-pr); *Laughing Anne* (+ d)
1954   *Trouble in the Glen* (+ d); *Lilacs in the Spring* (*Let's Make Up*) (+ d)
1955   *King's Rhapsody* (+ d)
1956   *My Teenage Daughter* (+ d)
1957   *Yangtse Incident* (*Battle Hell*) (Anderson)
1958   *The Man Who Wouldn't Talk* (+ d)
1959   *The Lady Is a Square* (+ d); *The Navy Lark* (Parry)

Films as Director Only:

1957   *These Dangerous Years* (*Dangerous Youth*)
1958   *Wonderful Things*
1959   *The Heart of a Man*

Publications

By WILCOX: book—

25,000 Sunsets: The Autobiography of Herbert Wilcox, London, 1967.

On WILCOX: books—

Neagle, Anna, *It's Been Fun*, London, 1949.
Low, Rachael, *The History of the British Film 1918–1929*, London, 1971.
Neagle, Anna, *There's Always Tomorrow*, London, 1974.
Armes, Roy, *A Critical History of the British Cinema*, London, 1978.
Low, Rachael, *The History of the British Film 1929–1939: Film Making in 1930s Britain*, London, 1985.

On WILCOX: articles—

Obituary in *New York Times*, 16 May 1977.
Obituary in *Vareity* (New York), 18 May 1977.
Passek, Jean-Loup, ''Herbert Wilcox,'' in *Cinéma* (Paris), August/September 1977.
Stimpson, Mansel, ''When His Taste Was Our Taste,'' in *What's On in London*, 11 April 1990.
Bagh, Peter von, ''Kuninkaankuvia,'' in *Filmihullu* (Helsinki), no. 1, 1998.

*　　*　　*

The function of the film producer is so imprecise that most producers are perhaps best defined in terms of some other role. Of the three leading British producers between the wars, Michael Balcon was a studio boss; Alexander Korda was a mogul; and Herbert Wilcox was, above all, a showman.

Like most showmen, Wilcox regarded truth as a flexible commodity, and many of the claims he made for himself in his floridly entitled autobiography, *25,000 Sunsets*, need to be treated with care. (Even his romantic Irish origins now seem doubtful; more recent research suggests he may have been born, not in County Cork as he gave out, but more prosaically in the south London suburb of Norwood.) But what is not disputed is that Wilcox was a key figure, along with Balcon, in establishing the British cinema on a reasonably sound financial basis during the crucial period of the twenties when it seemed in danger of going under to the Hollywood invaders.

Even before Balcon, Wilcox devised the survival strategy of importing American stars and German technical know-how to boost his films' appeal and production values. Each of his productions was exploited to the hilt. ''His plans,'' Rachael Low noted (in her 1920s volume), ''were always on a grand scale. Each film was a major property, not a little commodity.'' When sound arrived, Wilcox lost no time in setting up his own British and Dominion Studios at Elstree, fully equipped with Western Electric Sound. The early thirties were his most prolific period as a producer. Gathering around him a stable of solid, journeyman directors, he oversaw a steady string of decently crafted movies, often featuring established theatrical stars like Jack Buchanan and Tom Walls, most of which did well at the box office.

If anything, he was too prolific. His partner, Richard Norton (quoted by Low in her thirties volume), described him as ''the quickest man to start making pictures you ever saw; if you took your eyes off him for a moment two or three more would be on the way, and of course . . . you used up all your working capital.'' After a financial crisis or two Wilcox was gradually persuaded to cut back and concentrate on a few big pictures each year—many of them, by this stage, starring Anna Neagle. He always had a flair for rooting out acting talent—Clive Brook and Madeleine Carroll were among those he brought to the screen—but it was his discovery of Neagle, and subsequent long partnership with her (both professional and personal) that shaped the rest of his filmmaking career.

Neagle was to star in almost all the films for which Wilcox is now best remembered. Before the war there were the grand historical pageants, with Neagle impersonating Nell Gwyn, Peg Woffington and, most famously, Queen Victoria. After the war came the string of escapist light comedies set in a high-society never-neverland—*Spring in Park Lane*, *Maytime in Mayfair* and the like. Neither cycle much impressed the critics—''Both the director and the star seem to labour under the impression that they are producing something

important,'' noted Graham Greene of *Sixty Glorious Years*—but for a while at least the public responded with enthusiasm.

In many ways Wilcox, though a far less pompous and more likable figure, had a good deal in common with Cecil B. DeMille. Both men prided themselves on having their fingers on (or, as Joe Mankiewicz suggested in DeMille's case, up) the pulse of the public; both succeeded for much of their careers in operating as a virtually autonomous force within the industry. Both, quite early on, hit on a fairly simple audience-pleasing formula and stuck with it; and both, having started out as innovators known for making daring and even mildly scandalous films, saw public taste evolve past them while they stood still, so that they became outdated, almost ludicrous figures. The main difference, of course, is that DeMille, the shrewder operator of the two, ended up outdated but rich, while Wilcox wound up outdated and broke, unable to adapt and blaming audiences for rejecting his offerings. ''The public wants horror and sadism,'' he complained after his bankruptcy in 1964. ''I make pleasant films about pleasant people.''

''Pleasant''—in that revealing word may lie the reason why Wilcox now seems, when set beside Balcon, Korda, or Del Giudice, a marginal figure in the history of British cinema. Both as producer and director he set out to please his audiences, and very often succeeded. But the idea that he might try to challenge them, to overturn or subvert their assumptions—in short, that the cinema should aim to be anything beyond a medium of entertainment—never seems to have occurred to him. (Or if it did, he promptly dismissed the idea.) Herbert Wilcox's success as a filmmaker was his ability, during the greater part of his career, to gauge just what the public wanted and give it to them. But in the long run, that was also his failure.

—Philip Kemp

WILLIAMS, John

Composer. **Nationality:** American. **Born:** John Towner Williams, Long Island, New York, 8 February 1932; credited as Johnny Williams during early career. **Education:** Attended University of California, Los Angeles; Juilliard School, New York; studied with Castelnuovo-Tedesco and others. **Military Service:** U.S. Air Force, 1951–54. **Career:** Composer and conductor; 1960–62—music for TV series *Checkmate*; 1980–93—conductor, Boston Pops Orchestra. **Awards:** Academy Awards, for *Fiddler on the Roof*, 1971, *Jaws*, 1975, *Star Wars*, 1977, *E.T.—The Extra-Terrestrial*, 1982, and *Schindler's List*, 1993; British Academy Award, for *Jaws* and *The Towering Inferno*, 1975, *Star Wars*, 1977, *The Empire Strikes Back*, 1980, *E.T.—The Extra-Terrestrial*, 1982, *Empire of the Sun*, 1987, and *Schindler's List*, 1993.

Films as Composer:

1960	*I Passed for White* (Wilcox); *Because They're Young* (Wendkos)
1961	*The Secret Ways* (Karlson)
1962	*Bachelor Flat* (Tashlin)
1963	*Stark Fear* (Hockman) (co); *Gidget Goes to Rome* (Wendkos); *Diamond Head* (Green)
1964	*The Killers* (Siegel)

John Williams

1965   *None but the Brave* (Sinatra); *John Goldfarb, Please Come Home!* (Lee Thompson)
1966   *Penelope* (Hiller); *How to Steal a Million* (Wyler); *Not with My Wife, You Don't!* (Panama); *The Rare Breed* (McLaglen); *The Plainsman* (Rich)
1967   *A Guide for the Married Man* (Kelly); *Fitzwilly* (Delbert Mann); *Valley of the Dolls* (Robson)
1968   *Storia di una donna* (*Story of a Woman*) (Bercovici); *Sergeant Ryker* (Kulik)
1969   *The Reivers* (Rydell)
1970   *Jane Eyre* (Delbert Mann—for TV); *Daddy's Gone a-Hunting* (Robson)
1971   *The Cowboys* (Rydell)
1972   *The Screaming Woman* (Smight); *Images* (Altman); *The Poseidon Adventure* (Neame); *Pete 'n' Tillie* (Ritt)
1973   *The Long Goodbye* (Altman); *The Man Who Loved Cat Dancing* (Sarafian); *Cinderella Liberty* (Rydell); *The Paper Chase* (Bridges)
1974   *Sugarland Express* (Spielberg); *Conrack* (Ritt)
1975   *The Towering Inferno* (Guillermin); *Earthquake* (Robson); ***Jaws*** (Spielberg); *The Eiger Sanction* (Eastwood)
1976   *Family Plot* (Hitchcock); *The Missouri Breaks* (Penn); ***Black Sunday*** (Frankenheimer); *Midway* (*The Battle of Midway*) (Smight)
1977   ***Star Wars*** (Lucas); ***Close Encounters of the Third Kind*** (Spielberg)
1978   *Jaws II* (Szwarc); *Superman* (Donner); *The End* (Reynolds); *The Fury* (De Palma); ***The Deer Hunter*** (Cimino)

1979   *Dracula* (Badham)
1980   *1941* (Spielberg); ***The Empire Strikes Back*** (Kershner)
1981   ***Raiders of the Lost Ark*** (Spielberg); *Heartbeeps* (Arkush)
1982   *Yes, Giorgio* (Schaffner); *Monsignor* (Perry); ***E.T.—The Extra-Terrestrial*** (Spielberg)
1983   ***Return of the Jedi*** (Marquand)
1984   *The River* (Rydell); *Indiana Jones and the Temple of Doom* (Spielberg)
1986   *SpaceCamp* (Winer)
1987   *The Witches of Eastwick* (Miller); *Empire of the Sun* (Spielberg); *Jaws: The Revenge* (Sargent); *Superman IV: The Quest for Peace* (Nimoy)
1988   *The Accidental Tourist* (Kasdan)
1989   *Born on the Fourth of July* (Stone); *Always* (Spielberg); *Indiana Jones and the Last Crusade* (Spielberg)
1990   *Home Alone* (Columbus); *Presumed Innocent* (Pakula); *Stanley and Iris* (Ritt)
1991   ***JFK*** (Stone); *Hook* (Spielberg)
1992   *Far and Away* (R. Howard); *Home Alone 2: Lost in New York* (Columbus)
1993   *Jurassic Park* (Spielberg); ***Schindler's List*** (Spielberg)
1995   *Sabrina* (Pollack); *Nixon* (Stone)
1996   *Sleepers* (Levinson)
1997   *Rosewood* (Singleton); *The Lost World: Jurassic Park* (Spielberg); *Seven Years in Tibet* (Annaud); *Amistad* (Spielberg)
1998   *Saving Private Ryan* (Spielberg); *Stepmom* (Columbus)
1999   *Star Wars: Episode I—The Phantom Menace* (Lucas); *Angela's Ashes* (Parker)
2000   *The Patriot* (Emmerich)

Other Films:

1959   *Gidget* (Wendkos) (arranger)
1970   *Goodbye, Mr. Chips* (Ross) (mus d)
1971   *Fiddler on the Roof* (Jewison) (mus d)
1973   *Tom Sawyer* (Taylor) (mus d)

Publications

By WILLIAMS: articles—

In *Knowing the Score*, by Irwin Bazelon, New York, 1975.
Films and Filming (London), July and August 1978.
Radio Times (London), 17–23 May 1980.
Soundtrack! (Hollywood), March 1982.
Cue Sheet (Hollywood), vol. 8, no. 1, March 1991.
Soundtrack! (Hollywood), September 1993.
Film Score Monthly (Los Angeles), December 1995.
Soundtrack! (Hollywood), March 1996.

On WILLIAMS: articles—

Films Illustrated (London), May 1972.
Focus on Film (London), Summer 1972.

Ecran (Paris), September 1975.

Caps, John, in *Film Music Notebook* (Calabasas, California), vol. 2, no. 3, 1976.

Soundtrack! (Hollywood), October 1978.

Cook, Page, in *Films in Review* (New York), October 1979.

Filmcritica (Rome), April 1983.

Soundtrack! (Hollywood), June 1985.

Soundtrack! (Hollywood), September 1985.

Segnocinema (Vicenza), vol. 8, no. 33, May 1988.

Film Score Monthly (Los Angeles), January/February/March 1996.

Variety (New York), 22/28 January 1996.

Segnocinema (Vicenza), vol. 8, no. 33, May 1988.

Positif (Paris), no. 452, October 1998.

* * *

The success of John Williams as a film composer can easily be understood by the mere listing of his number of awarded Oscars and Oscar nominations. His first Oscar was as the music director of *Fiddler on the Roof*; the others are for original compositions: *Jaws*, *Star Wars*, *E.T.*, and *Schindler's List*. Also nominated were *Valley of the Dolls*, *The Reivers*, *The Poseidon Adventure*, *Cinderella Liberty*, *The Towering Inferno*, *Close Encounters of the Third Kind*, *Superman*, *The Empire Strikes Back*, *Raiders of the Lost Ark*, *Return of the Jedi*, *Indiana Jones and the Temple of Doom*, and *The River*.

Williams began his musical education at the University of California, Los Angeles, studying composition with Mario Castelnuovo Tedesco. Following military service, he studied piano with Rosina Lhevinne at the Juilliard School of Music in New York, with the object—like many successful film score composers before him—of pursuing a musical career on the concert stage not the sound stage. In Williams' case, he wanted to be a concert pianist. As Williams was also adept at jazz piano, he was able to find work and support himself doing recording sessions. This experience enabled him to gain employment as a studio pianist when he returned to Los Angeles in the early 1950s. By the mid-1950s, he had drifted into arranging then scoring title themes (many with a jazz motif) and background music under the name Johnny Williams for countless television programs during what is now known as The Golden Age of Television. His TV work at this time included just about every major and minor hit series. Among them: *Alcoa Presents*, *General Electric Theater*, *Kraft Music Hall*, *Playhouse 90*, *Tales of Wells Fargo*, *Bachelor Father*, *Wagon Train*, *M Squad*, *Checkmate*, *The Virginian*, *Gilligan's Island*, *Lost in Space*, *The Time Tunnel*, and *Land of the Giants*. Some of his TV show themes—notably those for *M Squad* and *Checkmate*—won huge popularity with the public.

With no prior interest in being a film composer, Williams claims, "I stumbled [from TV] into films." He scored his first feature film, the low budget exploitation vehicle *I Passed for White*, in 1960 and kept busy all through the 1960s jumping from TV to film work, honing his skills as a scorer of, primarily, light comedies (*Gidget Goes to Rome*, *John Godfarb, Please Come Home!*, *Penelope*, *How to Steal a Million*, *Not With My Wife, You Don't!*, *A Guide to the Married Man*, *Fitzwilly*)—with an occasional western (*The Rare Breed*), war film (*None But the Brave* for star and first-time director Frank Sinatra), and thriller (*The Secret Ways*, *The Killers*) intervening.

The success of his music for the Steve McQueen film *The Reivers*, generally regarded as a fine example of musical Americana, brought him into focus as a mainline composer; with the music for the telefilm

Jane Eyre, then the big screen western *The Cowboys*, and blockbuster *Jaws*, Williams became a much in demand, versatile new master of the form. His score for *Jaws* contributed so much to that film's scariness, said its director, Steven Spielberg, that he insisted on using Williams as composer for all his films ever since—forming one of the most mutually-supportive and identifiable (but longer-lasting) director-composer partnerships since Alfred Hitchcock and Bernard Herrmann split up.

The tremendous success of George Lucas' *Star Wars* and its sequels, in addition to other romantic adventure films of similarly epic scope, has tended to typecast Williams and draw attention away from the more subtle and often more interesting work he has done on less high-profile films, such as *Family Plot*, Hitchcock's last movie, and Robert Altman's send-up of the private eye genre, *The Long Goodbye*, for which Williams contributed the delightfully satiric score with its many and varied refrains of the standard *Hooray for Hollywood*.

Williams's success in the movie business has, however, not deterred him from pursuing his concert hall ambitions. Indeed, his success in the one field (largely because of his contributions to the films of box office kings Spielberg and Lucas) no doubt gave him the financial independence, confidence—and clout—to pursue the other. Among his concert works are two symphonies, a flute concerto, and a violin concerto, none of which bear much stylistic comparison with his film scores. In 1980 his career took on another dimension when he was appointed Arthur Fiedler's successor as the conductor of the Boston Pops Orchestra, a job that required only his summer months and left him free for guest conducting with other orchestras as well as continuing work in films. He left the Pops in the early nineties to devote his full energies to motion picture scoring, where he has further demonstrated his versatility on such diverse projects as the dinosaur-thrillers *Jurassic Park* and *The Lost World: Jurassic Park*, and the historical dramas *Schindler's List* and *Amistad* (all four films made by Spielberg as a demonstration, perhaps, of his own versatility); Oliver Stone's controversial speculation-cum-historical docudramas *JFK* and *Nixon*; and the World War II epic *Saving Private Ryan* (again for Spielberg). After an almost two decade hiatus since the last *Star Wars* adventure (*Return of the Jedi*), the *Star Wars* franchise geared up again in 1999 with *The Phantom Menace*—the maiden voyage of a new trilogy of *Star Wars* films from producer-director George Lucas. Williams again provided the rousing score, which he will undoubtedly do for the next two episodes in the trilogy as well.

—Tony Thomas, updated by John McCarty

WILLIAMS, Richard

Animator. **Nationality:** Canadian. **Born:** Montreal, 19 March 1933; emigrated to the United Kingdom, 1955. **Career:** Worked for Disney and United Productions of America (UPA) in early 1950s; 1955—moved to England: first animated film, *The Little Island*, 1958; his own studio produced animated films, commercials, and special effects and titles for live-action films; 1992—forced to close studio. **Awards:** Academy Award, for *A Christmas Carol*, 1971; Special Achievement Award and Visual Effects Academy Award, and two British Academy Awards, for *Who Framed Roger Rabbit?*, 1988.

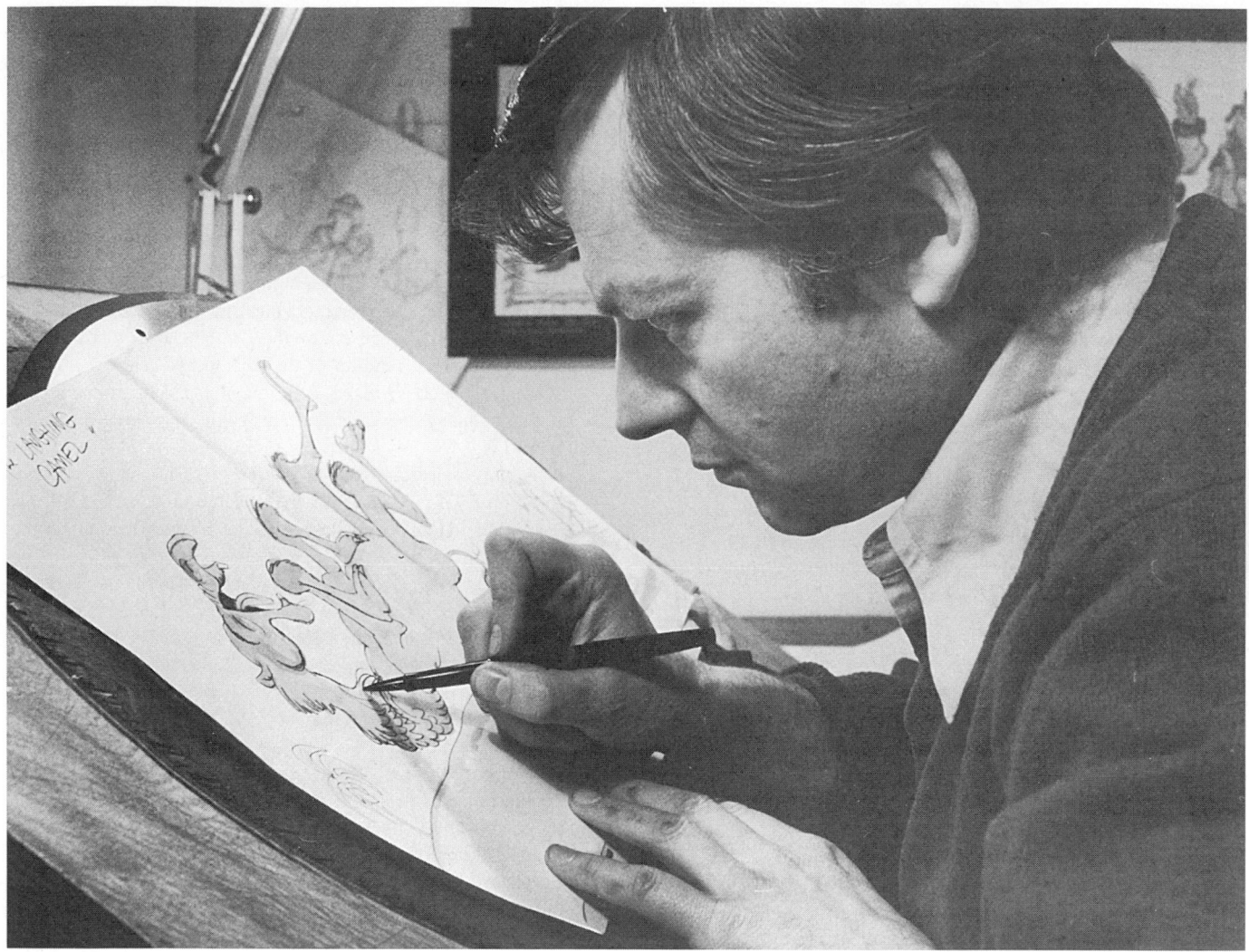

Richard Williams

Films as Animator:

1958   *The Little Island*; *The Story of the Motorcar Engine*
1961   *A Lecture on Man*
1962   *Love Me, Love Me, Love Me*
1964   *Circus Drawings*
1965   *Diary of a Madman* (not completed); *The Dermis Probe*;
        What's New Pussycat? (Donner) (animated sequences)
1966   *Pubs and Beaches*; *The Liquidator* (Cardiff) (animated se-
        quences); *The Spy with a Cold Nose* (Petrie) (animated
        sequences); *A Funny Thing Happened on the Way to the
        Forum* (Lester) (animated sequences)
1967   ***Casino Royale*** (Huston and others) (animated sequences); *I
        Vor Pittfalks* (not completed); *The Sailor and the Devil*
1968   *Prudence and the Pill* (Cook) (animated sequences); *The
        Charge of the Light Brigade* (Richardson) (animated
        sequences)
1969   *Don't Drink the Water* (Morris) (animated sequences)
1971   *A Christmas Carol*
1977   *Raggedy Ann and Andy*
1982   *Ziggy's Gift*

1988   *Who Framed Roger Rabbit?* (Zemeckis) (+ ro as voice
        of Droopy)
1995   *Arabian Knight* (*The Thief and the Cobbler*) (+ sc)

Publications

By WILLIAMS: articles—

"Animation and *The Little Island*," in *Sight and Sound* (London),
    Autumn 1958.
Contrast, Spring 1963.
Cinéma (Paris), January 1970.
Screen International (London), 18 June 1977.
Funnyworld, Fall 1978.
Funnyworld, Summer 1979.
Films and Filming (London), April 1982.
Screen International (London), 11–18 December 1982.
Television Weekly, 25 May 1984.
Starburst (London), September 1985.

Films and Filming (London), August 1988.
The Listener (London), 20 October 1988.

On WILLIAMS: articles—

Sight and Sound (London), Spring 1963.
Films and Filming (London), October 1963.
Roudévitch, Michel, in *Cinéma* (Paris), no. 98, 1965.
Cinema TV Today (London), 9 December 1972.
Filmmakers Newsletter (Ward Hill, Massachusetts), May 1973.
Monthly Film Bulletin (London), October 1973, additions in September 1974.
Movie Maker (London), December 1975.
Stills (London), May/June 1983.
National Film Theatre Booklet (London), April 1985.
Film Comment (New York), July/August 1988.
Times (London), 1 September 1989.
Films in Review (New York), November-December 1995.
Duncan, Celia, in *Screen International* (London), 22 March 1996.
Animato! (Springfield), no. 35, Summer 1996.

*   *   *

By general informed consensus, Richard Williams is probably the finest animator alive—in Chuck Jones's words, "the only 'genius' genius to come along in animation in years." His style—fluid, dynamic, assured, painstakingly detailed—consciously harks back to the golden age of full animation, when the Disney studio was at its creative peak: the years of *Fantasia*, *Pinocchio*, and *Dumbo*. Williams himself, though heartily sick of being dubbed "the new Disney," readily acknowledges his indebtedness. "Nobody has ever surpassed Disney. . . . He did everything. We have to go back and study him." No other contemporary animator is more constantly aware of the tradition he inherits—though it may be that this awareness has served to inhibit as much as to inspire him.

"An animator," Williams has said, "should be able to draw like Degas." He has never been shy of invoking the highest possible standards, both for himself and for those who work with him: not only Disney, Jones, and Max Fleischer, but the weightiest names in the whole field of human art. "I don't think in terms of animation. . . . My standards come from music, painting, and literature. . . . I'm in the same business as Goya and Rembrandt. I may be rotten at it with nothing of the same quality and talent, but that's my business." Not surprisingly, his view of the cheap, limited-animation material prevalent on television is dismissive. "It's like the three-chord trick in music. It's quick, easy, and you don't need any real training to do it. . . . But don't call it animation."

Williams's first film gained him immediate and worldwide renown. *The Little Island*, which took three years to make (and is said to be the longest film ever drawn and animated single-handedly), is a half-hour philosophical allegory; Roger Manvell called it "at once absurd and violent, madly serious and wildly funny." Three small, pear-shaped people land on a desert island. They personify, respectively, Goodness, Beauty, and Truth. Goodness and Beauty, dangerous monomaniacs, soon clash, piling increasingly grandiose structures on their rival concepts, until they metamorphose into ferocious monsters whose vast collision shudders the globe. Truth, meanwhile, bemused and conscientious, keeps score on a blackboard which takes on the shape of a nuclear bomb. The film uses no words; the most complex abstract ideas are brilliantly conveyed in purely visual terms. *The Little Island* picked up a stack of awards, and Williams—who founded his London studio on its success—was hailed as an animator of infinite promise.

More than 30 years on, that promise still awaits fulfillment. The films that Williams has completed on his own account—*Love Me, Love Me, Love Me*; *The Dermis Probe*; *The Sailor and the Devil*—though accomplished, are relatively banal in content, lacking the dazzling originality, the sense of ideas in full spate, that fueled *The Little Island*. They suggest a major talent coasting at half-throttle. *A Christmas Carol*, commissioned by ABC TV, displayed impressive technique, for which it well deserved its Oscar, although Williams's imagination was constrained by fidelity to the Dickens text. His only feature-length film to date, *Raggedy Ann and Andy*, was also an American commission, and one which he thoroughly regretted accepting. "The lesson I learned was the Golden Rule: 'Whoever has the gold makes the rules.'"

Much of his finest work, from a technical standpoint, has been seen in commercials, and in title sequences for live-action features. Far from regarding advertising as a demeaning chore, to be undertaken with disdain, Williams always welcomed the chance to extend his team's range, comparing commercials to calisthenics: "You try new things, you get all this extra technique." His studio, turning out over 100 ads a year in a staggering variety of styles, was reckoned probably the best, and certainly the most versatile, commercial animation house in the world. Several of Williams's commercials became classics, while his titles often outclassed the films they adorned. In Tony Richardson's *The Charge of the Light Brigade*, his superb linking passages, based on Victorian political cartoons, were widely admired; the rest of the film flopped. "It's a pity," Pauline Kael remarked acidly, "that Richardson didn't leave the Charge itself to Williams."

Yet after all the years of limbering up, all the flexing of creative muscle and development of technique, the Big Event is still to come. From time to time tantalizing fragments—storyboards, sketches, even sections of film—have surfaced: *I Vor Pittfalks*, the rise of a demagogue; *Circus Drawings*, based on sketches Williams made in Spain; a treatment of Gogol's *Diary of a Madman*; all, to date, unfinished.

And for more than 25 years there was the great Asian epic, "banana-skin Ali Baba or slapstick 1,001 Nights," that grew out of illustrations for a book about the legendary wise fool, Mullah Nasrudin. Started in 1967, the project changed titles a dozen times (though *The Thief and the Cobbler* was the longest-running favorite) and was repeatedly announced as "nearing completion." Williams promised that when it eventually appeared, it would "change the face of animation."

For a while, it seemed the arrival of this long-awaited magnum opus might be speeded by the success of *Who Framed Roger Rabbit?*, which integrated live-action and animation at an unprecedented level of technical complexity. It was Steven Spielberg, producing the film in tandem with Disney's Touchstone Studios, who persuaded Williams to provide *Rabbit*'s animated element. Technically dazzling and packed with in-jokes for animation buffs, the film triumphed at the box office and gained Williams a Special Achievement Oscar—the first animator to win one since Disney himself.

This international acclaim, Williams hoped, would help him raise funding; he could pull out of commercial work and concentrate on finishing *The Thief*. But potential investors feared that the release of

Disney's *Aladdin* might spoil the market, and in 1992, Williams's studio, overwhelmed by debts, laid off all its staff and ceased operations. Taken out of his hands by a Los Angeles completion bond company, his film was radically altered against his wishes and finally released (as *Arabian Knight*) in 1995. It flopped dismally at the U.S. box office.

Williams has plans to return to production with two animated features ''based on ancient stories.'' But for the time being, doubts must still remain whether Richard Williams is not so much ?the new Disney? as the Orson Welles of animation—a prodigious talent foundering amid a mass of incomplete projects.

—Philip Kemp

WILLINGHAM, Calder

Writer. **Nationality:** American. **Born:** Atlanta, Georgia, 23 December 1922. **Education:** Attended The Citadel and The University of Virginia. **Family:** Married 1) Helen Rothenberg (divorced), son Paul; 2) Jane Marie Bennett, five children. **Career:** First novel, *End as a Man*, was a popular success. Published nine others. 1957—brought to Hollywood to write screenplay for film version of *End as a Man*.; worked in Hollywood until 1974, when he retired to write fiction full time; 1978—wrote with Del Reisman the teleplay *Thou Shalt Not Commit Adultery*. **Died:** Of lung cancer, in Laconia, New Hampshire, 19 February 1995.

Films as Writer:

1957	*The Strange One* (Garfein)
1957	*Paths of Glory* (Kubrick) (co with Jim Thompson and Kubrick)
1958	*The Vikings* (R. Fleischer)
1961	*One-Eyed Jacks* (Marlon Brando) (co with Guy Trosper)
1967	*The Graduate* (Nichols) (co with Buck Henry)
1970	*Little Big Man* (Penn)
1974	*Thieves Like Us* (Altman)
1978	*Thou Shalt Not Commit Adultery* (co with Del Reisman—TV)

Publications

By WILLINGHAM: books—

End as a Man, New York, 1947
Geraldine Bradshaw, New York, 1950
The Gates of Hell, New York, 1951
Reach to the Stars, New York, 1951
Natural Child, New York, 1952
To Eat a Peach, New York, 1955
Eternal Fire, New York, 1963
Providence Island, New York, 1969
Rambling Rose, New York, 1972
The Big Nickel, New York, 1975
The Building of Venus Four, New York, 1977

On WILLINGHAM: articles—

Millichap, Joseph, in *Dictionary of Literary Biography*, edited by Randall Clark, Robert E. Morsberger, and Stephen O. Lessner, vol. 44, Detroit, 1986.
Obituary in *Facts on File*, 23 February 1995.
Obituary in *Variety* (New York), 27 February 1995.
Obituary in *Classic Images* (Muscatine), April 1995.
Obituary in *Psychotronic Video* (Narrowsburg), no. 20, 1995.
Loggia, Cynthia, ''*Graduate* Scribes Work Together After Decades,'' in *Variety* (New York), 24 January 2000.

*   *   *

Calder Willingham's first novel, *End as a Man*, proved a success with critics and readers alike, who appreciated the novelist's finely detailed study of military school life (based on Willingham's own years at The Citadel) and his exploration of male codes of conduct. A sudden shift of representational modes, to an expressionistic black humor, probably doomed his next book to a disappointing reception. Four novels published in quick succession likewise failed to make the favorable impression of Willingham's initial effort, and with a growing family to support he was happy to be hired by Columbia to adapt *End as a Man* for the screen; the story was retitled *The Strange One* for a marketing campaign that emphasized the bizarrely charismatic but cruel behavior of the main character, played with Method angst and power by Ben Gazzara. With its strong support of institutional convention and traditional pieties, the film was conservative in a late fifties, Cold War sense, offering no challenge to the military status quo despite the focus on an exceptional loner who tellingly probes the weaknesses of ''the system'' from the inside and reveals the limitations of following the rules. The film bears interesting comparison to *From Here to Eternity* (Fred Zinnemann, 1953), which treats, with quite different conclusions, a similar encounter between an exceptional individual and the military system that cannot accommodate his individuality.

The Strange One proved Willingham's ability to write tight and effective screenplays, a rare ability in novelists, who often find the restrictions of the form overwhelming. What Willingham's first effort showed in particular was a flair for staging in brief dramatic scenes what the novelist needed quite different narrative techniques to express. Willingham, in essence, showed how he could create bold and arresting character with an economy of effort, an important skill in adapting novels, the film versions of which must always be summaries in some sense. Though he despised film work and never took it seriously, Willingham stayed in Hollywood in order to support his growing family. His work for *The Strange One* had caught the eye of Stanley Kubrick, then a young director working on the margins of the industry, who engaged Willingham to, first, attempt an adaptation of Stefan Zweig's story ''The Burning Secret,'' a project that was never realized. Instead, Willingham soon set to work, along with pulp writer Jim Thompson and director Stanley Kubrick, on adapting Humphrey Cobb's novel about the French army mutiny of 1917,

Paths of Glory. The resulting film is an interesting and effective mixture of authorial interests. *Paths of Glory* exemplifies Kubrick's fascination with the interaction between men and environment, Jim Thompson's obsession with elemental differences in character and ethics, and Willingham's concern with the struggle against, but ultimately necessary accommodation to a flawed institution. In particular, Willingham's influence on the film's literate, highly dramatic script—unusual for what is in essence an ''action'' picture—is most clearly seen in the character of Colonel Dax, a man of conscience who protests against suicidally stupid orders and venal, self-serving general officers, but who willingly shares the undeserve and brutal fate of the men under his command, finding some consolation in the basic human quality—a desire for comradeship and love—that binds them. With its art house black and white photography, self-conscious stylization, and political tendentiousness (the film was banned from the screen in France), *Paths of Glory* was a prestige project that offered Willingham a suitable opportunity for his considerable talents, despite his reluctance about film work in general.

Willingham's ability to create complex, interesting character was tested more severely in his next project, which was to write a screenplay from Dale Wasserman's ''treatment'' of Edison Marshall's *The Viking*. The film that eventually emerged as *The Vikings* was not intended for art house exhibition or to please a literate film audience; it was instead a big-budget, star-studded, action-packed, wide-screen, full-color epic in the proven fifties mold of historical recreations. And yet Willingham, though unable to reproduce the novel's interesting complexities of setting and custom, does a more than credible job of re-imagining it in terms of brotherly ties and loyalty to a shared code of masculine conduct; what distinguished the finished film from other costume spectaculars of the period, including Kubrick's *Spartacus* (1960), is the deep sense of character that effectively motivates the action set pieces.

In *The Vikings*, the hero and his antagonist are bound together by the very brotherhood (kept secret from them until the plot's climactic moment) that lends them the impulsiveness and self-assertion that makes them mortal enemies. Willingham's screenplay for *One-Eyed Jacks*, based on Charles Neider's novel *The Authentic Death of Hendry James*, re-structures that familial conflict in Oedipal terms. Handsome young Rio (Marlon Brando) robs banks with the aptly named Dad (Karl Malden) until the older man, saving his own skin, leaves Rio behind to be captured by the Mexican police. Escaping from jail, Rio seeks revenge on the now-respectable Dad, who has married and become a sheriff, by seducing his former friend's stepdaughter and subjecting him to public shame. Dad replies in kind, publicly whipping Rio after a trumped up charge and then mutilating his gun hand. Forswearing further vengeance because of his genuine love for Dad's stepdaughter, Rio is forced to confront Dad in a final shootout and kills him. The film emphasizes Brando's compelling Method performance as the betrayed young man who finds a better way to live, but the ethical dilemma and the way it works to discover the goodness in Rio and moral emptiness in Dad was Willingham's substantial contribution. Like Colonel Dax, Rio discovers in authentic human connections a reason to live in a world otherwise characterized by the immoral and ruthless pursuit of self-interest.

Much the same can be said of Willingham's script for *The Graduate*, his most masterful and acclaimed screenwriting effort. Paired perfectly with Buck Henry, whose penchant for black humor

and arresting character matched his own, Willingham here vastly improves on Charles Webb's weakly structured novel. Benjamin Braddock (Dustin Hoffman), confused about what direction to take now that he has graduated from college, lets himself be seduced by a sexual predatory older woman, who only takes an interest in his body. Where Rio has to break his self-destructive attachment to a vicious father figure, Benjamin must abandon his infantilizing connection with a substitute mother; in both instances, the protagonists discover a conventional Hollywood adulthood in the arms of a faithful, loving woman. Henry and Willingham deepen the significance of this *bildungsroman* with an acerbic look at contemporary American society, whose adult establishment is populated by plastics salesman out to make a killing, horny housewives, pathetically indulgent parents, and mindlessly materialistic adolescents. The film's antiestablishmentarianism perfectly caught the mood of the late sixties (though the more obvious social and political issues of that period rate nary a mention).

More *engagé* was Willingham's next project, the adaptation of Thomas Berger's anti-western, *Little Big Man*, also starring Hoffman, who effectively recycles the naive righteousness of Benjamin Braddock. His Jack Crabb is a picaresque figure whom Willingham, following Berger closely, utilizes as a narrative *entrée* into various aspects of Western life, whose conventional meanings are debunked as the white settlers are shown to be venal and stupid, while the Indians the helplessly innocent victims of an overpowering social change. Usually presented as a tragic hero, Willingham's George Custer is a bloodthirsty savage, demented by his hatred of the Indians and his own delusions of grandeur. The story was episodic even in its original form, and Willingham's *Little Big Man* appears too much the summary of a larger, more coherent work. Yet the film works largely because of the writer's skillful imagining of dramatic encounters and the virtuoso performance of Hoffman, who portrays effectively nearly eighty years in Jack Crabb's life.

Little Big Man represents a thematic departure for Willingham, whose characters previously had chosen to live within the flawed structures of a society they cannot improve. Perhaps this change was due to alterations within the industry as a whole, where angry youth pictures became the rage after the success of *Easy Rider* (Dennis Hopper, 1969), a maturation story that took its rebellious heroes to a very different political and personal destination than Benjamin Braddock discovers at the end of *The Graduate*. But it may be that Willingham himself had begun to take a more jaundiced view of the American establishment. That this is the case is certainly suggested by his next and final Hollywood project, an adaptation of Edward Anderson's forties novel *Thieves Like Us*, a social realist examination of class structure and criminality in American life, previously filmed by Nicholas Ray in 1949 as *They Live by Night*. Anderson's novel examines what happens to an essentially moral if underprivileged country boy named Bowie who finds himself convicted of a murder that was likely simple self-defense. Escaping from jail, he forms a criminal gang of the similarly dispossessed, only to fall in love with a good woman, Keechie. Willingham's version not surprisingly emphasizes the ethical dilemma that Bowie finds himself in: yearning for a better life with Keechie, Bowie cannot escape from his life of crime to working class respectability because of his loyalty to his criminal comrades. Unlike Benjamin Braddock, Bowie cannot break cleanly with the criminal past because it holds real value for him, an authenticity that proper society had denied him.

Though he always deprecated his film work, seeing it simply as a way of paying the bills, Willingham must be counted one of the postwar era's most successful screenwriters. Because he was talented and reliable, he more readily made a name and reputation for himself in screenwriting. Working steadily and profitably during the late sixties and early seventies, that period of American commercial film art usually termed the "Hollywood Renaissance," Willingham gave important literary value to the films of several noted directors. Ironically he was denied the same kind of success from novel readers and reviewers. The American cinema was impoverished by his decision in 1974 to resume a novel writing career full time, but, in any event, the turn of the American cinema away from character-driven drama to various forms of sexual and violent spectacle would have likely left him underemployed in Reaganite Hollywood.

—R. Barton Palmer

WILLIS, Gordon

Cinematographer. **Nationality:** American. **Born:** New York City, 1931. **Education:** Attended Manhasset High School, New York. **Military Service:** Served in the U.S. Air Force as a photographer in the early 1950s. **Family:** Married; three children. **Career:** After Air Force, assistant cameraman and photographer on documentaries and commercials; 1969—first film as cinematographer, *End of the Road*; 1977—first of several films for Woody Allen, *Annie Hall*.

Films as Cinematographer:

1969   *End of the Road* (Avakian)
1970   *Loving* (Kershner); *The Landlord* (Ashby); *The People Next Door* (Greene)
1971   *Little Murders* (Arkin); *Klute* (Pakula)
1972   *The Godfather* (Coppola); *Bad Company* (Benton); *Up the Sandbox* (Kershner)
1973   *The Paper Chase* (Bridges)
1974   *The Parallax View* (Pakula); *The Godfather, Part II* (Coppola)
1975   *The Drowning Pool* (Rosenberg)
1976   *All the President's Men* (Pakula)
1977   *Annie Hall* (Allen); *September 30, 1955 (9/30/55)* (Bridges)
1978   *Interiors* (Allen); *Comes a Horseman* (Pakula)
1979   *Manhattan* (Allen)
1980   *Stardust Memories* (Allen); *Windows* (+ d)
1981   *Pennies from Heaven* (Ross)
1982   *A Midsummer Night's Sex Comedy* (Allen)
1983   *Zelig* (Allen)
1984   *Broadway Danny Rose* (Allen)
1985   *The Purple Rose of Cairo* (Allen); *Perfect* (Bridges); *The Money Pit* (Benjamin)
1987   *The Pick-Up Artist* (Toback)
1988   *Bright Lights, Big City* (Bridges)
1990   *The Godfather, Part III* (Coppola); *Presumed Innocent* (Pakula)
1993   *Malice* (H. Becker)
1997   *The Devil's Own* (Pakula)

Publications

By WILLIS: articles—

On *The Godfather* in *American Cinematographer* (Hollywood), June 1971.
American Cinematographer (Hollywood), September and October 1978.
Seminar in *Cinema Canada* (Montreal), September 1983.
Masters of Light: Conversations with Contemporary Cinematographers, by Dennis Schaefer and Larry Salvato, Berkeley, California, 1984.
American Cinematographer (Hollywood), April 1984.
American Cinematographer (Hollywood), August 1994.

On WILLIS: articles—

Take One (Montreal), no. 2, 1978.
Stevenson, J., in *New Yorker*, 16 October 1978.
Filme (Berlin), no. 6, 1980.
Goodhill, D., on *Manhattan* in *American Cinematographer* (Hollywood), November 1982.
Films and Filming (London), December 1982.
Maslin, Janet, in *New York Times*, 1 August 1983.
Film Comment (New York), March/April 1984.
McDonough, Tom, in *American Film* (Washington, D.C.), April 1986.
American Film (Washington, D.C.), May 1986.
Variety (New York), 24/30 October 1994.

*   *   *

At a time in film history when cinematographers are receiving an unprecedented amount of attention and credit for their contributions to the art of filmmaking, Gordon Willis has emerged as one of the screen's most gifted and creative cameramen. Working closely with his directors, Willis manages in film after film to create a visual style that is uniquely suited to the story's thematic intentions. His work on such widely varied films as *The Godfather*, *Annie Hall*, *All the President's Men*, and *Zelig* has helped establish him as a cinematographer able to translate a director's vision into a physical reality while still planting his own particular stamp on a film's visual style.

The son of a Hollywood makeup man, Willis initially considered a career as an actor before an early interest in photography and the theater led him into behind-the-scenes jobs involving scenery and stage lighting. After a brief stint working on documentaries and television commercials, Willis began his career as a cinematographer on feature films with *End of the Road*, and was soon earning critical acclaim for his work on such films as *Klute*, *All the President's Men* and the first two *Godfather* films. In each of these pictures, the photography takes its cue from the mood of the story.

Klute, a hard-edged psychological thriller, has a chilly, dark, claustrophobic style, while *All the President's Men* shifts between the bright fluorescent lights of the Washington *Post* newsroom to the shadowy settings of Woodward and Bernstein's meetings with the informant known as "Deep Throat." The *Godfather* films make use of muted colors, richly photographed and darkly lit, to evoke the secretive, somber atmosphere of the criminal underworld. *The Godfather, Part II* contrasts this style with the sunny scenes of Vito Corleone's childhood in Sicily and the golden and sepia tones of his days as a young immigrant in New York City. Both of the *Godfather* films received Best Picture Oscars (as did *Annie Hall* in 1977) and *All the President's Men* was a Best Picture nominee, yet Willis himself was not nominated for a cinematography Oscar until *Zelig* in 1983. It is an oversight that has been a source of great controversy, with Willis's admirers maintaining that his resolutely east coast-based career has led the Hollywood establishment to snub him as an outsider.

Annie Hall began Willis's long and mutually profitable collaboration with Woody Allen, who has utilized the cinematographer's talents on eight films so far. *Annie Hall* contrasts the warm, glowing scenes of Annie and Alvy's New York romance with the slightly overexposed glare of the film's California scenes, while *Manhattan* is a richly textured black-and-white paean to the beauty and diversity of the city itself. In *Interiors* and *Stardust Memories*, Willis creates echoes of Ingmar Bergman and Federico Fellini, using stark whites in the former to convey the emotional sterility of the troubled Bergmanesque family that is the focus of the film, and a harsh, almost surrealistic black and white in the latter, which many critics have labeled Allen's *8?* The hazy golds and browns of *A Midsummer Night's Sex Comedy* capture the bucolic quality of the film's witty merry-go-round of romances, while the wisecracking show-business fairy tale of *Broadway Danny Rose* is enhanced by Willis's gritty blacks and whites. *The Purple Rose of Cairo*'s Depression-era setting is conveyed in the film's subdued, washed-out tones, a look which also comments on the bleak reality of the heroine's life. The pair's most remarkable collaborative achievement, however, is *Zelig*, Allen's fictional mock-documentary. Imitating the style and tone of early newsreels, Allen and Willis "aged" their own film stock by scratching and marking its surface, matching their footage seamlessly with actual newsreels from the 1920s and 1930s. In several astonishing shots, Willis superimposes Allen's character, Leonard Zelig, onto the older footage, creating the impression that Zelig is actually a part of the newsreels and is conversing with well-known historical figures.

Willis has directed a film of his own, *Windows*, which drew mixed notices, but his true talents lie in his ability to translate a director's concepts into precise and compelling visual terms. He has stated that his job is to "make movies *with* directors . . . ultimately it's their idea that I'm executing." In Willis's case, however, the execution is often one of the most creative aspects of the film itself.

In 1993, the critically acclaimed film *Visions of Light* examined 26 leading directors of photography, one of whom was Gordon Willis.

—Janet Lorenz, updated by David Levine

WILSON, Michael

Writer. **Nationality:** American. **Born:** McAlester, Oklahoma, 1 July 1914. **Education:** Attended the University of California, Berkeley, graduated 1936; studied in France 1937–38. **Military Service:** Served in

Michael Wilson

the Marine Corps during World War II: Lieutenant. **Family:** Married Zelma (Wilson); two daughters. **Career:** teacher and writer; 1941—first film as writer, *The Men in Her Life*; 1951—refused to answer questions before the House Un-American Activities Committee, and blacklisted: for several later film projects he used a pseudonym or received no credit; 1954–64—lived in France. **Awards:** Writers Guild Award and Academy Award for *A Place in the Sun*, 1951; *The Bridge on the River Kwai* (awarded to Pierre Boulle because of the blacklisting), 1957. **Died:** Of a heart attack, in California, 9 April 1978.

Films as Writer:

1941   *The Men in Her Life* (Ratoff)
1943   *Border Patrol* (Selander); *Colt Comrades* (Selander); *Bar 20* (Selander)
1944   *Forty Thieves* (Selander)
1951   **A Place in the Sun** (Stevens)
1952   *Five Fingers* (Mankiewicz)
1954   **Salt of the Earth** (Biberman)
1956   *Friendly Persuasion* (Wyler) (uncredited)
1957   *The Bridge on the River Kwai* (Lean) (uncredited)
1958   *La tempesta* (*Tempest*) (Lattuada)
1960   *Jovanka e l'altri* (*Five Branded Women*) (Ritt)
1962   **Lawrence of Arabia** (Lean) (co)
1965   *The Sandpiper* (Minnelli)
1968   *Planet of the Apes* (Schaffner)
1969   *Che!* (Fleischer)

Publications

By WILSON: book—

Salt of the Earth (script) in *Salt of the Earth: The Story of a Film*, by Herbert J. Biberman, Boston, Massachusetts, 1965.

By WILSON: articles—

Positif (Paris), no. 64–65, 1965.
In *The Hollywood Screenwriter*, edited by Richard Corliss, New York, 1972.

On WILSON: articles—

Présence du Cinéma (Paris), June 1962.
Film Comment (New York), Winter 1970–71.
Ecran (Paris), October 1976.
Tuchman, Michael, in *Take One* (Montreal), September 1978.
Hodson, M., "Who Wrote *Lawrence of Arabia*? Sam Spiegel and David Lean's Denial of Credit to a Blacklisted Screenwriter," in *Cineaste* (New York), vol. 20, no. 4, 1994.
Crowdus, Gary, and Michael Wilson, and Robert Bolt, "The Writer's Guild of America vs. the Blacklist: *Lawrence of Arabia*: Elements and Facets of the Theme: Apologia," in *Cineaste* (New York), vol. 21, no. 4 1995.
New York Times, Section D, 14 September 1995.
New York Times, Section A, 16 September 1995.

*   *   *

After being identified by the House Committee on Un-American Activities as "a Communist, past or present," Michael Wilson was denied work by the same industry which had given him an Oscar for *A Place in the Sun*, the screen adaptation he wrote with Harry Carr of Theodore Dreiser's *An American Tragedy*, and his films after the time of his "blacklisting" seem to reflect this. They are much less charitable toward human nature than his earlier work, often about sudden, drastic changes in one's fate. But they are also about more than that.

Wilson is at his best when he is exploring the dynamics of the group, and it is surely here that his greatest contribution as a writer is to be found. His chief weakness is his dialogue. The best one can say about a conversation written by Wilson is that it is passable movie dialogue. Never does it ring to the ear like a conversation between two individuals. But then neither does Wilson really offer us individuals. Rather, his characters take their definition from a larger body of people, alternately trying to accommodate that group, lead it, understand it, rebel against it, or find their place within it.

This is true of films as otherwise diverse as *Salt of the Earth*, *The Bridge on the River Kwai*, *Lawrence of Arabia*, *Planet of the Apes*, and *Che!*. In each case the group is depicted as a delicate balance of conflicting interests. Perhaps influenced by what he learned from McCarthyism, the group, in Wilson's scripts, is always corruptible, and always in danger of being weakened from within.

Wilson made a point of his penchant for working alone, even when the screen credits would suggest that he was worked with a partner,

"In every case save one (*The Sandpiper*)," he has said, "there was no collaboration. I either preceded or followed another writer." That's true, but it is also misleading, for it was his willingness to collaborate that made him attractive to so many directors.

It is no accident that Wilson's name has become identified with "big money" projects, productions involving extraordinarily large casts, extensive location work, or unusually costly support functions, for he was known as a writer who worked closely with directors. At once able and willing to adjust continuity, plot, and characterization without compromising the integrity of the story, he enjoyed the reputation of a seasoned professional who understands—perhaps only too well—the possibilities and limitations which movie making can provide.

—Jay Boyer

WINKLER, Irwin

Producer. **Nationality:** American. **Born:** New York City, 28 May 1931. Attended Columbia University Business School, graduated 1955. **Career:** Mailboy at William Morris Agency; secretary; projectionist; formed management agency with Robert Chartoff; 1966—produced first film in partnership with Chartoff, *Double Trouble*; 1985—independent producer. **Award:** Academy Award for *Rocky*, 1976.

Films as Producer with Robert Chartoff:

1966 *Double Trouble* (Taurog)
1967 *Point Blank* (Boorman)
1968 *Blue* (Narizzano); *The Split* (Flemyng)
1969 *Leo the Last* (Boorman); *They Shoot Horses, Don't They?* (Pollack); *The Strawberry Statement* (Hagmann)
1971 *Believe in Me* (Hagmann); *The Gang That Couldn't Shoot Straight* (Goldstone)
1972 *The Mechanic* (*Killer of Killers*) (Winner); *The New Centurions* (*Precinct 45: Los Angeles Police*) (Fleischer); *Thumb Tripping* (Masters); *Up the Sandbox* (Kershner)
1973 *Busting* (Hyams)
1974 *The Gambler* (Reisz); *Spies*
1975 *Breakout* (Gries); *Peeper* (Hyams)
1976 *Nickelodeon* (Bogdanovich); *Rocky* (Avildsen)
1977 *New York, New York* (Scorsese); *Valentino* (Russell)
1978 *Comes a Horseman* (Pakula); *Uncle Joe Shannon*
1979 *Rocky II* (Stallone)
1980 ***Raging Bull*** (Scorsese)
1981 *True Confessions* (Grosbard)
1982 *Author! Author!* (Hiller); *Rocky III* (Stallone)
1983 *The Right Stuff* (Kaufman)
1985 *Revolution* (Hudson)

Other Films as Producer:

1985 *Rocky IV* (Stallone)
1986 *Round Midnight* (*Autour de minuit*) (Tavernier)

Irwin Winkler

1988   *Betrayed* (Costa-Gavras)
1989   *Music Box* (Costa-Gavras)
1990   *Rocky V* (Avildsen) (co); *GoodFellas* (Scorsese)
1991   *Guilty by Suspicion* (+ d + sc); *Night and the City* (+ d)
1992   *Basic Instinct* (Verhoeven) (orig pr)
1995   *The Net* (+ d)
1999   *At First Sight* (+ d)
2000   *The Shipping News*

Publications

By WINKLER: book—

Guilty by Suspicion (screenplay), Warner Bros., 1991.

By WINKLER: articles—

Positif (Paris), no. 307, September 1986.
American Film (Washington, D.C.), vol. 15, no. 1, October 1989.
Films in Review (New York), December 1989.

Time Out (London), no. 1092, 24 July 1991.
Time Out (London), no. 1311, 4 October 1995.
Fade In (Beverly Hills), vol. 2, no. 3, 1996.

On WINKLER: articles—

American Film (Washington, D.C.), vol. 2, no. 3, December-January 1976–7.
Stills (London), no. 20, June-July 1985.
Positif (Paris), no. 307, September 1986.
American Premiere, May/June 1991.
Segnocinema, no. 61, May/June 1993.
DGA (Los Angeles), September-October 1996.

*   *   *

The career of producer Irwin Winkler is so involved with that of his long-time partner Robert Chartoff—in 1983 screenwriter William Goldman described them as ''best friends forever, and partners for damn near as long''—that though the business relationship ended in the 1980s, it is still difficult to consider them separately.

943

Chartoff and Winkler left New York for California in the early 1960s. They shared with fellow east coast emigrés Mike Nichols, Sidney Lumet, and Arthur Penn a taste for liberal themes, but in attempting to turn this preoccupation into profitable films the producers singularly failed. Two edgily intellectual thrillers with English directors, John Boorman's *Point Blank* and Gordon Flemyng's *The Split*, puzzled the American audience, as did Boorman's eccentric *Leo the Last*, while Stuart Hagmann's *Believe in Me* and *The Strawberry Statement*, the former an anti-drug story, the latter one of many miserable attempts of the time to transmute student revolt into salable cinema, also foundered. However, Sidney Pollack's version of Horace McCoy's *They Shoot Horses, Don't They?* with Jane Fonda and Gig Young did briefly gain Chartoff and Winkler the critical respect they craved.

From 1970 the team affiliated with United Artists, supplying films of medium budget and low risk to this studio without production facilities. *The Gang That Couldn't Shoot Straight* and *The New Centurions*, crime stories from best-selling books by Jimmy Breslin and Joseph Wambaugh, were modest successes as were *Busting* and *Peeper*, better-than-average comedy thrillers by Peter Hyams. Even Michael Winner and Charles Bronson were coaxed to lift their game with an everyday tale of assassinating folk, *The Mechanic*. Less successful was *The Gambler*, by Karel Reisz after Dostoyevsky, though the team did at least freshen their social conscience credentials with *Up the Sandbox*, a Barbra Streisand vehicle about the trials of a young New York mother.

In 1976, against UA's advice, Chartoff and Winkler championed a $1 million boxing picture starring and written by a minor actor, Sylvester Stallone. To the surprise of even its producers *Rocky* earned more than $100 million worldwide and an Academy Award for Best Picture. In addition, since the partners had attached themselves to the project, the production company could make no sequels without their involvement. *Rocky*s *I* to *IV* made Chartoff and Winkler rich and powerful. They relocated to luxury offices and enjoyed fees from UA labeled by one insider as "astronomical." Success also made them in the words of then-UA vice-president Steven Bach "proud and difficult to argue with. Sooner or later Rocky Balboa's boxing glove . . . would settle any argument. In their minds at least."

The team's budgets rose with prosperity but not their success rate. *Nickelodeon*, Peter Bogdanovich's tribute to the silent cinema, flopped, as did Ken Russell's *Valentino*. More intent on critical success than ever, they funded a stark 1940s western by Alan Pakula, *Comes a Horseman*, and bought *The Right Stuff*, Tom Wolfe's sprawling "fraction" best-seller about the Apollo astronauts.

Having financed Martin Scorsese's ill-fated musical *New York, New York* the partners now also took on his most controversial project, a violent biography of the boxer Jake LaMotta, *Raging Bull*. Winkler is generally credited with negotiating the deal between UA, Scorsese, and Robert De Niro, a feat which, according to Steven Bach, involved an uncredited rewrite of the script by director and star. Chartoff and Winkler then shepherded *Raging Bull* to production and saw it become one of the most highly regarded Hollywood films of all time.

Raging Bull was the team's greatest achievement, and its last. When William Goldman delivered the screenplay for *The Right Stuff*, for which UA had paid the largest fee in its history, and which portrayed the astronauts as symbols of a braver, better America, he learned that director Phil Kaufman now preferred to emphasise the character of test pilot Chuck Yaeger, conceived by Goldman and Wolfe as the loser in the race for space. Goldman has claimed since that Chartoff sided with Kaufman in the resulting dispute and Winkler with the writer. Finally Goldman resigned, his screenplay was shelved and Kaufman wrote his own. Chartoff and Winkler subsequently dissolved their partnership—over, Goldman implies, this disagreement.

As an independent, Winkler has produced Costa-Gavras's anti-Fascist *Music Box*. He also made his debut as director in 1991 with *Guilty by Suspicion*. Robert De Niro played a 1950s filmmaker hounded for communist sympathies. Blacklist veterans were cast in minor roles and Winkler used the sets from the covertly anti-McCarthy *High Noon* for the cheap western De Niro is forced to direct. Most critics found the film heavy-handed, and writer/director Abraham Polonsky further soured the reaction by claiming it cribbed elements from his life.

Neither of Winkler's subsequent outings as director convinces one that he's capable of better. His 1992 remake of Jules Dassin's *Night and the City*, with de Niro in Richard Widmark's old role as a desperate hustler trying to set up a wrestling match (altered by Winkler to boxing), and running foul of harder men in the process, was long on decor but short on impact. In *The Net*, Sandra Bullock is wasted as the computer nerd who stumbles on a secret in her job as free-lance programmer, and is harried by unseen enemies who cancel her credit cards, invalidate her driver's licence, sell her house, and all but erase her identity, replacing it with that of a dope-dealing prostitute. A potentially apt film which might have commented incisively on the growing power of those who process electronic information is invalidated by the writers' and director's resort to all the clichés of 1960s girl-on-the-run movies. Winkler learned the lessons of paranoia taught by the McCarthy era, but has so far proved incapable of extending his knowledge beyond simple didacticism. Liberal and intellectual legitimacy seem as far from his grasp now as when he produced *The Strawberry Statement*.

—John Baxter

WINSTON, Stan

Makeup and special effects artist. **Nationality:** American. **Born:** Virginia, c. 1946. **Career:** 1969—Walt Disney Studios makeup department; 1971–1977—freelance televsion and motion picture makeup and prosthetic effects artist; 1978—Stan Winston Studio; 1993—Digital Domain. **Awards:** Academy Award, *Aliens*, 1986 (effects); Academy Award, *Terminator 2: Judgement Day*, 1991 (effects, makeup); *Jurassic Park*, 1993 (effects); Emmy Award, *Gargoyles*, 1972 (makeup); *The Autobiography of Miss Jane Pittman*, 1974 (makeup).

Films as Director:

1988   *Pumpkinhead*
1991   *Adventures of a Gnome Named Gnorm*
1996   *T2 3-D: Battle Across Time*
1997   *Ghosts*

Films as Makeup and Special Effects Artist:

1972   *Gargoyles* (television)
1974   *Masquerade* (television); *The Autiobiograhy of Miss Jane Pittman* (television)
1975   *The Man in the Glass Booth*
1976   *Pinocchio* (television); *W. C. Fields and Me*
1977   *An Evening with Diana Ross* (television); *Roots* (television)
1978   *The Wiz*
1980   *The Exterminator*
1981   *Dead and Buried*; *Heartbeeps*; *The Hand*
1982   *The Thing*; *Parasite*
1983   *Something Wicked This Way Comes*
1984   *The Terminator*; *Starman*
1985   *The Vindicator*
1986   *Aliens*; *Invaders from Mars*
1987   *Monster Squad*; *Predator*
1988   *Alien Nation*
1989   *Leviathan*
1990   *Edward Scissorhands*; *Predator 2*
1991   *Terminator 2: Judgement Day*
1992   *Batman Returns*
1993   *Jurassic Park*
1994   *Interview with the Vampire*
1995   *Tank Girl*; *Congo*
1996   *The Island of Dr. Moreau*
1999   *Instinct*; *Lake Placid*; *Inspector Gadget*; *End of Days*; *Galaxy Quest*

Publications

On WINSTON: articles—

Hogan, D. J., "How Makeup Expert Stan Winston Solved an Unusual Effects Problem on *The Entity*," in *Cinefantastique*, no. 5, 1983.

Salza, G. "Bio-filmografia dei nuovi tecnici di effetti special," in *Segnocinema*, January 1986.

Genild, P., "Effektive Marsmonstre," in *Levende Billeder*, 1 June 1987.

Vincenzi, L., "A New Direction," in *Millimeter*, September 1987.

Magid, R., "A Planetful of Aliens," in *Cinefex*, November 1988.

Pollack, Andrew, "Computer Images are Staking Out Star Roles in Movies," in *The New York Times*, 24 July 1991.

Duncan, J., "A Once and Future War," in *Cinefex*, August 1991.

Stephens, C., "Master of Animatronics & Makeup," in *On Production*, no. 5, 1992.

Moerk, Christian, "*Jurassic* Looks Like an f/x Classic; Tech Industry Expects Pic to Revolutionize Field," in *Variety*, 7 September 1992.

McGowan, Chris, "IBM, Movie Veterans Enter Digital Technology Domain," in *Billboard*, 3 April 1993.

Biodrowski, S., "Stan Winston," in *Cinefantastique*, no. 2, 1993.

Duncan, J., "The Beauty in the Beasts," in *Cinefex*, August 1993.

Magid, R., "Effects Team Brings Dinosaurs Back from Extinction," in *American Cinematographer*, June 1993.

Impoco, Jim, "Big Blue Goes Hollywood," in *U.S. News and World Report*, 19 September 1994.

Johnson, Ross, "Winston Gratification," in *The Hollywood Reporter*, 16 June 1995.

Diorio, Carl, "Mighty Morphin," in *The Hollywood Reporter*, 16 June 1995.

Duncan, Jody, "Moreau's Menagerie," in *Cinefex* (Riverside), December 1996.

Duncan, Jody, "On the Shoulders of Giants," in *Cinefex* (Riverside), June 1997.

*   *   *

Stan Winston, has, at various points in his career, been typecast as a makeup artist, a special effects whiz, a computer animator, and a puppeteer. Yet, while all of these terms are accurate, they do little to either define the man or his unique art. He is perhaps most accurately described as a storyteller and a creator of characters. In fact, his resume includes creating memorable persona in some of the biggest grossing films in the world including *Aliens*, *Terminator 2*, *Batman Returns*, and *Jurassic Park*. He has even directed two creature-based films, *Pumpkinhead* and *Adventures of a Gnome Named Gnorm*. As a result of an early fascination with the acting profession, focused in particular on those roles that involved bizarre characters such as werewolves or Jekyll and Hyde transformations, Winston discovered that it could be more fulfilling to go beyond human actors playing parts and to actually create artificial characters that could act. As a result, he now bases his creations, whether puppets, computer images or prosthetic makeup effects, within the context of the performances being given by live actors in a well-told story. Audiences, he believes, do not walk out of a movie theater remembering makeup or creature effects. They will remember them only if they are a realistic part of a ground-breaking story or paired with an actor's powerful performance.

He points to 1986's *Aliens* as a case in point. Although, he constructed 15 warrior aliens for the film, it was his full scale 14-foot tall Queen Alien who came to life and slugged it out with the film's star Sigourney Weaver "live on the set" and helped her to achieve an Academy Award nominated performance. Although the Queen rig was operated by a two man crew assisted by a cable rig and a team of cable controllers, in Winston's view, his technicians were actors giving a performance in creating the alien character who would take part on an equal basis with any other performer in the film. In the finished film, the Queen emerges as an actual character. According to Winston, she comes across as elegant in her form, feminine but nasty—definitely a woman you do not want to mess with.

What makes Winston unique in a profession that thrives on labeling its practitioners and forcing them into pigeonholes is that he is constantly reinventing himself and his craft. Early in his career, he carved out a reputation as a makeup artist who specialized primarily in realistic facial prosthetics. However, building on his childhood experiences with puppetry, he graduated to the more specialized field of makeup effects and was soon designing characters with animated faces that were controlled and operated externally. He then extended the external animation to the entire creature, pioneering the new art form of animatronics and robotic design which was to reach its high point through his collaborations with director James Cameron on *Terminator 2* and Steven Spielberg on *Jurassic Park*. At the Stan Winston Studio which he founded in 1978, Winston's staff routinely works with images of virtually every creature existing in nature including man. The characteristics of these creatures are then excerpted and incorporated in designs of beings that have no existence outside of the imagination. Yet, the reality of these new creatures is heightened by the fact that they reflect expressions, gestures, and movements that build on the audiences' own memories and experiences. Regardless of how exotic the creature is, whether alien or Terminator, something about it is strangely familiar to the viewer. The bottom line, Winston emphasizes, is to do what has never been done before—to take the writer's wildest ideas and somehow turn them into cinematic reality—on a daily basis.

Winston's art was expanded in 1993 when he teamed with Industrial Light and Magic designer Scott Ross and director James Cameron to form Digital Domain, a firm focusing on digital and other "high tech" special effects for motion pictures. D.D.'s first project was the fall 1994 release *Interview with the Vampire* which Winston considered to be a major turning point in his career.

Although he had started out successfully as a makeup artist, he had become typecast as a "creature maker" as a result of the phenomenal success of *Jurassic Park*. He had to literally do some fast talking to get the job. "I realized that there were still things that I wanted to try with subtle nuances of makeup but nobody would give me the chance because I was the guy who does dinosaurs," he stated in 1995. "That job was very important to me."

Winston's reason for selecting *Vampire* was his profound interest in creating characters. Director Neil Jordan's film called for a more subtle, elegant, almost spiritual type of effect than did a film dealing with 20-ton dinosaurs. The merger of makeup and small scale mechanical effects with the computer's potential for creating and cloning realistic images extended Winston's range in a remarkable way. Winston's studio took care of the prosthetics, makeup and the mechanical effects—one of which was a crawling robotic Tom Cruise in Lestat's near death scene—while Digital Domain provided computer-generated imagery, miniatures and digital compositing.

From an artistic point of view, the blending of puppetry with computer animation, usually results in the computer getting the credit. For example, out of 16 minutes of dinosaur footage in *Jurassic Park*, 60 percent was actually Winston's full-size creatures and not electronic images. Similarly, in *Interview With the Vampire*, the prosthetic and mechanical touches were seamlessly interwoven with the computer-generated effects. Yet, most viewers credited the work to Industrial Light and Magic's computers in the former and to Digital Domain in the latter, because the effects were simply too realistic to be puppets.

However, Winston sees this as vindication of his approach to creature building. He views the computer and other technological innovations as simply new tools to help with the creation of characters in order to create an undetectable blend between what is alive and what's on computer. In Winston's view, if he has done his job correctly, the mechanical characters and the computer-generated images are no less real than the human actors appearing in the finished product. The bottom line is that all three have to be able to act and to make the viewer believe in them. "If you look at a film that I have contributed to," he says, "and my work is apparent, I have failed. But, if it is instead identifiable as a Tim Burton, a James Cameron, or Steven Spielberg film, that's a pat on the back to me."

—Steve Hanson

YODA, Yoshikata

Writer. **Nationality:** Japanese. **Born:** Kyoto City, 1909. **Education:** Attended Kyoto Second Commercial High School. **Career:** 1927–29—worked for Sumitomo Bank, Kyoto: left after being arrested for political activities; 1930—joined Nikkatsu's Kyoto Studio to study screenwriting: first film as writer, *A Port without a Sea*, 1931; 1936—first of many films for Kenji Mizoguchi: wrote for him until 1955; taught screenwriting, Osaka Art College. **Awards:** Several Japanese film prizes.

Films as Writer:

1931   *Umi no nai minato* (*A Port without a Sea*) (Murata); *Shiroi ane* (*White Elder Sister*) (Murata—2 parts)

1932   *Kyouba to nyoubou* (*Horse-Race and Wife*) (Tokunaga); *Youki no seidayo* (*It's Because of Good Weather*) (Takechisa); *Tokaku omna to iu mono wa* (*Women Tend to . . .*) (Kurata); *Minato no jojoushi* (*Lyric of a Port*) (Saegusa)

1933   *Haha yo ko yo* (*Mother and Child*) (Taguchi); *Seishun no koro* (*Time of Youth*) (Kurata); *Bokura no otouto* (*Our Younger Brother*) (Kumagai and Sunohara)

1934   *Judo senshu no koi* (*Love of a Judo Player*) (Chiba); *Yume no naka no ojousan* (*Young Lady in a Dream*) (Ohtani); *Gurentai no uta* (*Gangster's Song*) (Taguchi)

1936   ***Naniwa ereji*** (*Osaka Elegy*) (Mizoguchi); *Gion no shimai* (*Sisters of the Gion*) (Mizoguchi); *Adauchi hizakurige* (*Walking Trip of Revenge*) (Mori)

1937   *Otsuru junreika* (*Otsuru's Pilgrim Song*) (Oshimoto); *Samurai ondo* (*Samurai Song*) (Kimura); *Aienkyo* (*The Straits of Love and Hate*) (Mizoguchi)

1938   *Ishin no uta* (*The Song of Restoration*) (Inuzuka); *Tenryu shibuki* (*Splash of Tenryu*) (Iwata); *Aa furusato* (*Ah, My Home Town*) (Mizoguchi); *Aija no musume* (*Daughter of Asia*) (Tanaka and Numamani); *Ninjutsu Sekigahara Sarutobi Sasuke* (*Ninja Sasuke Sarutobi of Sekigahara*) (Mori); *Akatsuki no hatakaze* (*Flag Wind of Dawn*) (Hoshi)

1939   *Kyouenroku* (*Record of Manhood and Eros*) (Tanaka and Suyama); *Oise mairi* (*Pilgrimage to Ise*) (Mori); *Bunbuku chagama* (*Badger's Tea Pot*) (Mokudou); ***Zangiku monogatari*** (*The Story of the Last Chrysanthemums*) (Mizoguchi); *Tsukiyo garasu* (*Crow on a Moonlit Night*) (Inoue—2 parts); *Umi o yuku bushi* (*The Warrior Who Crosses the Sea*) (Inoue); *Ukiyo kouji* (*Alley of the World*) (Makino)

1940   *Hataoka junsa* (*Policeman Hataoka*) (Ushihara); *Naniwa onna* (*Osaka Woman*) (Mizoguchi); *Harekodose* (*Formal Kimono*) (Ushihara)

1941   *Geidou ichidai otoko* (*The Life of an Actor*) (Mizoguchi); *Meoto daiko* (*A Couple's Drum*) (Mori); *Musume tabigeinen* (*Troubador Girl*) (Mokudou); *Iga Kottou gunryu* (*Iga Kottou Military Style*) (Nishina)

1941–42   *Genroku chushingura* (*The Loyal 47 Ronin*) (Mizoguchi—2 parts)

1942   *Ninin sugata* (*Two Together*) (Ohba)

1943   *Kikuchi senbonyari* (*Kikuchi's Thousand Spears*) (Ikeda and Shirai)

1944   *Takadanobaba* (Matsuda—2 parts); *Kodachi o tsukau onna* (*A Woman Using a Small Sword*) (Marune)

1945   *Hanamuko Taiheiki* (*Bridegroom's Taiheiki*) (Marune); *Sennichimae fukin* (*Around Sennichimae*) (Makino)

1946   *Tobira o hiraku onna* (*Woman Opening a Door*) (Kimura); *Utamaro o meguru gonin no onna* (*Utamaro and His Five Women*) (Mizoguchi)

1947   *Tenka no goikenban o Ikensuru otoko* (*The Adviser of the World's Adviser*) (Kimura); *Moderu to wakatono* (*The Model and the Young Lord*) (Takeno); *Joyu Sumako no koi* (*The Love of Sumako the Actress*) (Mizoguchi)

1948   *Yamaneko rei jou* (*Miss Wildcat*) (Mori); *Yogoreta hanazono* (*Spoiled Garden*) (Kosaka); *Yoru no onnatachi* (*Women of the Night*) (Mizoguchi); *Gonin no mokugekisha* (*Five Witnesses*) (Matsuda), *Busou keikantai* (*Armed Police Force*) (Ohsone)

1949   *Waga koi wa moenu* (*My Love Burns*) (Mizoguchi); *Watashi no na wa joufu* (*My Name Is Mistress*) (Mori)

1949–50   *Hebihme douchuh* (*The Travels of Princess Snake*) (Kimura and Marune—2 parts)

1950   *Haruka narishi haha no kuni* (*Mother's Country Is Far*) (Ito); *Aru fujinkai no kokuhaku* (*Confessions of Gynecologist*) (Mori); *Sengoku dawara* (*Rice Packages*) (Makino); *Fukkatsu* (*Resurrection*) (Nobuchi); *Minami no bara* (*Roses of the South*) (Mori); *Yuki Fujin ezu* (*A Picture of Madame Yuki*) (Mizoguchi); *Shimau-boshi* (*Sister Stars*) (Nobuchi)

1951   *Oboro kago* (*Sedan Chair in the Mist*) (Ito); *Otsuya goroshi* (*Murder of Otsuya*) (Makino); *Shunen* (*Spring Grudge*) (Kosugi); *Oyu-sama* (*Miss Oyu*) (Mizoguchi); *Musashino Fujin* (*Lady Musashino*) (Mizoguchi); *Aizen-bashi* (*Bridge of Love*) (Nobuchi); *Oh-Edo gonon otoko* (*Five Men of Great Edo*) (Ito)

1952   ***Saikaku ichidai onna*** (*The Life of Oharu*) (Mizoguchi); *Taki no shiraito* (*Water Magician; The White Thread of the Waterfall*) (Nobuchi); *Koikaze gojusan-tsugi* (*53 Stations of the Wind of Love*) (Nakagawa)

1953   *Kettou gofun-mar* (*Five Minutes to the Duel*) (Adachi); ***Ugetsu monogatari*** (*Ugetsu; Tales of a Pale and Mysterious Moon after the Rain*) (Mizoguchi); *Gion bayashi* (*Gion Festival Music*) (Mizoguchi)

1954   *Sansho dayu* (*Sansho the Bailiff*) (Mizoguchi); *Chushingura*
        (47 Loyal Ronin) (Ohsone); *Uwawa no onna* (*The Woman*
        of the Rumor) (Mizoguchi); *Chikamatsu monogatari* (*A*
        Story from Chikamatsu) (Mizoguchi)

1955   *Toujin Okichi* (*The Foreigner's Okichi*) (Wakasugi); *Yoidore*
        bayashi (*Drunken Music*) (Takiuchi); *Maiko sanjushi* (*The*
        Three Musketeers of the Apprentice Geishas) (Amano);
        Tojuro no koi (*The Love of Tojuro*) (Mori); *Yokihi* (*The*
        Princess Yang Kwei-Fei) (Mizoguchi); *Shin Heike*
        monogatari (*New Tale of the Taira Clan*) (Mizoguchi)

1956   *Tanuki* (*Badger*) (Hagiyama); *Zangiku monogatari* (*The Story*
        of the Last Chrysanthemums) (Shima); *Chichiko-daka* (*Fa-*
        ther-Son Falcons) (Matsuda); *Ninjutsu senshuken jiai* (*Ti-*
        tle Match of Magic) (Yasuda); *Gion no shimai* (*Sisters of*
        Gion) (Nomura); *Kiri no oto* (*Sound of Fog*) (Shimizu);
        Haha shirayuki (*Mother's White Snow*) (Yasuda)

1957   *Abarenbou kaido* (*Wild Main Line*) (Uchida); *Osaka monogatari*
        (*An Osaka Story*) (Yoshimura); *Adauchi Suzenjinobaba*
        (*Revenge of Suzenjinobaba*) (Makino); *Ibo koudai* (*Step-*
        Brothers) (Ieki)

1959   *Niguruma no uta* (*The Song of the Cart*) (Yamamoto); *Aijou*
        dudou (*Immobile Love*) (Saeki); *Chiyoda-jo enjo* (*Chiyoda*
        Castle on Fire) (Yasuda); *Todoke haha no uta* (*Reach,*
        Mother's Song) (Fukuda); *Kakureta ninkimono* (*Secret*
        Popular Character) (Sakai)

1960   *Abarenbou taishou* (*Wild Boss*) (Kimura); *Hana no Yoshiwara*
        hyakunin-giri (*One Hundred Killings of Flowery Yoshiwara*)
        (Uchida); *Buki naki tatakai* (*Battle without Weapons*)
        (Yamamoto)

1961   *Harekodose* (*Formal Kimono*) (Yasuda); *Kodachi o tsukau*
        onna (*A Woman Using a Small Sword*) (Ikehiro); *Shin*
        akumyo (*New Bad Names*) (Mori and Tanaka—2 parts);
        Akumyo (*Bad Names*) (Tanaka—2 parts)

1962   *Fukeizu* (*Women's Origin*) (Misumi); *Aru Osaka no onna*
        (*Ayako*) (Sugawa); *Koi ya koinasuna koi* (*Love, Not Loving*
        Love) (Uchida)

1963   *Daisan no akumyo* (*The Third Bad Name*) (Tanaka); *Bushidou*
        zankku monogatari (*Cruel Story of the Samurai Code*)
        (Imai); *Akumyo hatoba* (*The Port of Bad Names*) (Mori);
        Akumyo ichiba (*The Market of Bad Names*) (Mori); *Jokei*
        kazoku (*Family of Women*) (Misumi)

1965   *Chouchou Yuji no meoto zenzai* (*The Nice Couple, Chouchou*
        and Yuni) (Makino); *Akumyo niwaka* (*Suddenly Bad Names*)
        (Tanaka); *Akumyo muteki* (*Invincible Bad Names*) (Tanaka)

1966   *Akumyo zakura* (*Bad Names' Cherry Blossoms*) (Tanaka)

1967   *Akumyo ichidai* (*Lives of Bad Names*) (Yasuda); *Namida-*
        Gawa (*The River of Tears*) (Misumi)

1968   *Akumyo juhachi-ban* (*Bad Names' Best Trick*) (Mori); *Botab*
        dourou (*Peony Lantern*) (Yamamoto)

1969   *Nemuri Kyoshiro no manji-giri* (*Kyoshiro Nemuri's Swasti-*
        ka-Slash) (Ikehiro)

1974   *Akumyo nawabari arashi* (*Bad Names' Breaking of Territo-*
        ries) (Masumura)

1978   *Ogin sama* (*Miss Ogin*) (Kumai)

1979   *Tenpyo no iraka* (*Slates of the Tenpyo Period*) (Kumai)

1989   *Sen no rikyu* (*Death of a Teamaster*) (Kumai)

Publications

On YODA: articles—

Martin, Marcel, "Recontre avec Yoshikata Yoda," in *Image et Son*,
    October 1982.

*   *   *

The screenwriter Yoshikata Yoda is best known for his long-time association with the director Kenji Mizoguchi. Their collaboration began with *Osaka Elegy* and lasted for two decades, until the director's death. This 1936 film made history with its effective use of the Osaka dialect. Critics hailed this device as the force behind "Mizoguchi realism" which flourished in the new medium of talking films. It is fundamental to the harshly authentic portrayal of the strong-willed heroine who tries to exploit men using her youth and beauty, but in the end is herself exploited, betrayed, and rejected by her family and her lovers alike. Mizoguchi told the writer Yoda to adapt the plot from a short story in a magazine, and then demanded that he rewrite the script more than 20 times, so that it would best express the character's tenacious scheming to survive. Thoroughly trained by this difficult task, Yoda emerged as one of the most promising young screenplay writers, and became indispensable to the work of the master director.

Yoda's next screenplay for Mizoguchi was *Sisters of the Gion*, which emphasizes the contrasts between two sisters who are lower-class geisha. One is traditional, the other modern, but both end up betrayed by men and enslaved by what they must do to earn money. The director, who always insisted those involved in his projects do first-hand research on their subjects, demanded that the writer become fully acquainted with the world of the geisha. Yoda carried out this task by sitting in the kitchen of a geisha house in his native Kyoto, taking notes on everything. He conveyed his experiences through the story and characterizations of this film, which was another great success due to its realistic unsentimentality and avoidance of an easy solution to the heroines' problems.

Mizoguchi and Yoda are most highly acclaimed for their portrayals of lower-class women in feudal and capitalist societies. Their men are usually weak and cannot be depended on either materially or psychologically. Therefore, it is the heroines who are forced not only to be financially independent but also to help their selfish and foolishly ambitious men. Often forced into prostitution to do so, they are exploited by men and by the social system, but retain both their inner strength and their gentleness despite all. Mizoguchi and Yoda tried to expose the injustices of the system, with mercy for none except for the women themselves. The director and writer conveyed this almost Buddhist image of gracious women with profound reverence, in characters such as Otoku in *The Story of the Last Chrysanthemums* and Miyaki in *Ugetsu*.

Yoda continued to work prolifically after Mizoguchi's death, producing a number of excellent screenplays for other directors. His deep sympathy for those exploited by society has been well expressed in the films of leftist directors such as Satsuo Yamamoto, Tadashi Imai, and Miyoji Teki. His talent for writing high-quality entertainment-oriented scripts is evident in the 12 scripts he has written for the enormously popular *Bad Name* action-comedy series featuring Shintaro

Katsu of *Zatoichi* fame. Yoda has also written many period films, historical epics, and adaptations of literary works.

—Kyoko Hirano

YOUNG, Freddie

Cinematographer. **Nationality:** British. **Born:** Frederick A. Young in England, 9 October 1902. **Military Service:** British Army's Kinetographic Unit during World War II. **Career:** Entered films at age 15, and worked in various capacities before becoming cinematographer in late 1920s; worked on international productions from the 1950s; 1962—first collaboration with David Lean, *Lawrence of Arabia*. **Awards:** Academy Award, for *Lawrence of Arabia*, 1962, *Doctor Zhivago*, 1965, and *Ryan's Daughter*, 1970; International Award, American Society of Cinematographers, 1993. Officer, Order of the British Empire, 1970. **Died:** 1 December 1998, in London, England, of natural causes.

Films as Cinematographer:

1926 *The Flag Lieutenant* (Edwards) (co)
1930 *The W Plan* (Saville) (co)
1931 *The Speckled Band* (Raymond)
1932 *The Little Damozel* (Wilcox); *The Blue Danube* (Wilcox)
1933 *Bitter Sweet* (Wilcox)
1934 *Nell Gwynn* (Wilcox); *The Queen's Affair* (Wilcox)
1935 *The Runaway Queen* (Wilcox); *Peg of Old Drury* (Wilcox)
1936 *When Knights Were Bold* (Raymond)
1937 *Victoria the Great* (Wilcox) (co); *The Rat* (Raymond)
1938 *Sixty Glorious Years* (*Queen of Destiny*) (Wilcox)
1939 *Nurse Edith Cavell* (Wilcox); *Goodbye, Mr. Chips* (Wood)
1940 *Contraband* (Powell); *Busman's Holiday* (*Haunted Honeymoon*) (Woods)
1941 *49th Parallel* (*The Invaders*) (Powell)
1942 *The Young Mr. Pitt* (Reed)
1946 *Caesar and Cleopatra* (Pascal) (co); *Bedelia* (Comfort)
1947 *So Well Remembered* (Dmytryk)
1948 *The Winslow Boy* (Asquith); *Escape* (Mankiewicz)
1949 *Edward, My Son* (Cukor); *The Conspirator* (Saville)
1950 *Treasure Island* (Haskin)
1952 *Time Bomb* (Tetzlaff); *Ivanhoe* (Thorpe)
1953 *Mogambo* (Ford) (co)
1954 *Knights of the Round Table* (Thorpe)
1956 *Lust for Life* (Minnelli) (co); *Bhowani Junction* (Cukor); *Invitation to the Dance* (Kelly)
1957 *The Barretts of Wimpole Street* (Franklin); *Island in the Sun* (Rossen); *Gideon of Scotland Yard* (*Gideon's Day*) (Ford)
1958 *The Inn of the Sixth Happiness* (Robson); *Indiscreet* (Donen)
1959 *Solomon and Sheba* (K. Vidor); *The Wreck of the Mary Deare* (Anderson)
1960 *Macbeth* (Schaefer)
1961 *The Greengage Summer* (Gilbert)
1962 **Lawrence of Arabia** (Lean)
1964 *The Seventh Dawn* (Gilbert)
1965 *Lord Jim* (R. Brooks); *Rotten to the Core* (J. Boulting); *Doctor Zhivago* (Lean)
1967 *The Deadly Affair* (Lumet); *You Only Live Twice* (Gilbert)
1968 *Elfrida and the Pig* (+ d)
1969 *Battle of Britain* (Hamilton); *Sinful Davey* (Huston)
1970 *Ryan's Daughter* (Lean)
1972 *Nicholas and Alexandra* (Schaffner)
1974 *Luther* (Green); *The Tamarind Seed* (Edwards); *Great Expectations* (Hardy)
1975 *Permission to Kill* (Frankel)
1976 *The Blue Bird* (Cukor) (co)
1977 *The Man in the Iron Mask* (Newell)
1978 *Stevie* (Enders)
1979 *Bloodline* (T. Young)
1980 *Rough Cut* (Siegel)
1981 *Richard's Things* (Harvey)
1983 *Invitation to the Wedding* (J. Brooks); *Sword of the Valiant: The Legend of Gawain and the Green Knight* (Weeks) (co)
1985 *Invitation to the Wedding* (J. Brooks)

Film as Director:

1985 *Arthur's Hallowed Ground*

Publications

By YOUNG: book—

With P. Petzold, *The Work of the Motion Picture Cameraman*, New York, 1972.

By YOUNG: articles—

"A Method of Pre-Exposing Color Negative for Subtle Effect," in *American Cinematographer* (Hollywood), August 1966.
Films Illustrated (London), June 1973.
On *The Tamarind Seed* in *American Cinematographer* (Hollywood), July 1974.
On *The Blue Bird* in *American Cinematographer* (Hollywood), December 1975.
Screen International (London), 13 March 1976.
Screen International (London), 21–28 May 1983.

On YOUNG: articles—

Hill, Derek, on *Indiscreet* in *American Cinematographer* (Hollywood), April 1958.
American Cinematographer (Hollywood), July 1968.
Skoop (Amsterdam), March 1969.
Lightman, Herb A., on *Ryan's Daughter* in *American Cinematographer* (Hollywood), August 1969.
American Cinematographer (Hollywood), June 1971.
Cinema TV Today (London), 25 March 1972.
Films Illustrated (London), May 1972.
Cinema TV Today (London), 1 July 1972.

Freddie Young

Focus on Film (London), no. 13, 1973.

Films in Review (New York), February 1973.

Crowdus, Gary, "Just Make It Marvelous, Freddie," *Cineaste* (New York), Vol. xxi, No. 3, 1995.

Obituary in *Variety* (New York), 7 December 1998.

*   *   *

Freddie Young stands as one of contemporary cinema's most creative cinematographers. As such he represents an era of filmmaking in which production has truly taken on an international flavor, for Young has achieved fame and fortune and *not* moved to Hollywood. One of Britain's most noted cinematographers, once Young took over as David Lean's cameraman he began regularly to earn Oscars. In a remarkably short time in the 1960s, he won three, for *Lawrence of Arabia*, *Doctor Zhivago*, and *Ryan's Daughter*.

Like many great cinematographers, Young spent decades learning his craft before he received any awards. (He was 60 before he won his first Oscar.) His career began in Great Britain in the old glass-topped Gaumont Studios in Lime Grove, London. At first he did a bit of everything from taking stills, developing and printing exposed movie film, editing shorts and features, and operating the camera under the direction of an experienced cinematographer. Young's first credit as cinematographer came in 1926.

During the 1930s he toiled as a cinematographer. He was under contract to British impresario Herbert Wilcox and photographed several of Anna Neagle's films. But during the 1930s the British film industry suffered from the impact of Hollywood. Young adapted and thus worked for several Hollywood films shot in Britain, including *Goodbye, Mr. Chips*. At the outbreak of World War II, Young was actually in Hollywood, about to begin a career in the movie capital of the world. He immediately returned to the United Kingdom to serve as chief cameraman for the British Army's Kinematographic Unit. After the war, Young worked on many of MGM's British-based productions, with such directors as George Cukor, Gene Kelly, and Richard Thorpe. Young earned his first Oscar nomination for one of these productions, *Ivanhoe* in 1953. During this period, he also worked on two second-rate John Ford films. Yet the experience impressed him: "John Ford struck me as something special." Ford was willing to try effects conventional Hollywood directors would avoid, though few would rank *Mogambo* and *Gideon's Day* among his best works.

Then came the break: Young's association with David Lean. The remarkably successful *Lawrence of Arabia* came first. Personally Young liked *Doctor Zhivago* the best of his three Oscar winners because it gave him the greatest chance to try a variety of techniques.

—Douglas Gomery

YOUNG, Victor

Composer and Arranger. **Nationality:** American. **Born:** Chicago, Illinois, 8 August 1900. **Education:** Studied the violin from age 6; studied in Warsaw with Roman Statlovsky and others. **Career:** 1917—violinist with Warsaw Philharmonic; interned, first by Russians, then by Germans, during World War I; from 1920—worked in New York as violinist, concert director, and composer of songs and musicals, and for radio; music director for Decca records; 1935—joined Paramount. **Award:** Academy Award, for *Around the World in Eighty Days*, 1956. **Died:** In Palm Springs, California, 10 November 1956.

Films as Arranger and Musical Director:

1936   *Anything Goes* (*Tops Is the Limit*) (Milestone); *Klondike Annie* (Walsh); *Frankie and Johnnie* (Auer); *Fatal Lady* (Ludwig) (co); *Rhythm on the Range* (Taurog); *Three Cheers for Love* (McCarey); *Big Broadcast of 1937* (Leisen); *Hideaway Girl* (Archainbaud); *College Holiday* (Tuttle)
1937   *Waikiki Wedding* (Tuttle); *Make Way for Tomorrow* (McCarey); *Turn Off the Moon* (Seiler); *Mountain Music* (Florey); *Artists and Models* (Walsh); *Double or Nothing* (Reed); *Walter Wanger's Vogues of 1938* (Cummings)

Films as Composer:

1937   *Champagne Waltz* (Sutherland) (co); *Maid of Salem* (Lloyd); *Swing High, Swing Low* (Leisen) (co); *Ebb Tide* (Hogan); *Wells Fargo* (Lloyd)
1939   *Man of Conquest* (Nicholls); *Heritage of the Desert* (Selander); *Golden Boy* (Mamoulian); *Range War* (Selander); *Our Neighbors, the Carters* (Murphy); *The Night of Nights* (Milestone); *The Llano Kid* (Venturini); *Gulliver's Travels* (Fleischer); *The Light That Failed* (Wellman)
1940   *Raffles* (Wood); *The Way of All Flesh* (L. King); *Dark Command* (Walsh); *Buck Benny Rides Again* (Sandrich); *Three Faces West* (Borhaus); *Untamed* (Archainbaud); *I Want a Divorce* (Murphy); *Moon over Burma* (L. King); *Arise My Love* (Leisen); *Three Men from Texas* (Selander); *North West Mounted Police* (DeMille); *Arizona* (Ruggles); *The Mad Doctor* (*A Date with Destiny*) (Whelan)
1941   *Virginia* (Griffith); *I Wanted Wings* (Leisen); *Reaching for the Sun* (Wellman); *Caught in the Draft* (Butler); *Aloma of the South Seas* (Santell); *Hold Back the Dawn* (Leisen); *Skylark* (Sandrich)
1942   *The Remarkable Andrew* (Heisler); *Reap the Wild Wind* (DeMille); *The Great Man's Lady* (Wellman); *Beyond the Blue Horizon* (Santell); *Take a Letter, Darling* (Leisen);

The Forest Rangers (Marshall); *Flying Tigers* (Miller); *Mrs. Wiggs of the Cabbage Patch* (Murphy); *The Glass Key* (Heisler); *Young and Willing* (Griffith); *The Palm Beach Story* (P. Sturges); *The Crystal Ball* (Nugent); *Silver Queen* (Bacon)
1943   *The Outlaw* (Hughes and Hawks—produced 1941); *Salute for Three* (Murphy); *Buckskin Frontier* (Selander); *Riding High* (*Holiday Inn*) (Marshall); *China* (Farrow); *For Whom the Bell Tolls* (Wood); *Hostages* (Tuttle); *True to Life* (Marshall); *No Time for Love* (Leisen)
1944   *The Uninvited* (Allen); *The Story of Dr. Wassell* (DeMille); *The Great Moment* (P. Sturges); *Frenchman's Creek* (Leisen); *Ministry of Fear* (F. Lang); *Practically Yours* (Leisen); *And Now Tomorrow* (Pichel)
1945   *Kitty* (Leisen); *A Medal for Benny* (Pichel); *You Came Along* (Farrow); *The Great John L.* (*A Man Called Sullivan*) (Tuttle); *Love Letters* (Dieterle); *Hold That Blonde!* (Marshall)
1946   *The Blue Dahlia* (Marshall); *The Searching Wind* (Dieterle); *Our Hearts Were Growing Up* (Russell); *To Each His Own* (Leisen); *Two Years before the Mast* (Farrow)
1947   *Suddenly It's Spring* (Leisen); *California* (Farrow); *The Imperfect Lady* (*Mrs. Loring's Secret*) (Allen); *Calcutta* (Farrow); *The Trouble with Women* (Lanfield) (co); *I Walk Alone* (Haskin); *Unconquered* (DeMille); *Golden Earrings* (Leisen)
1948   *State of the Union* (Capra); *The Big Clock* (Farrow); *The Emperor Waltz* (Wilder); *Dream Girl* (Leisen); *So Evil My Love* (Allen) (co); *Miss Tatlock's Millions* (Haydn); *The Night Has a Thousand Eyes* (Farrow); *The Paleface* (McLeod)
1949   *The Accused* (Dieterle); *Streets of Laredo* (Fenton); *A Connecticut Yankee in King Arthur's Court* (Garnett); *Samson and Delilah* (DeMille); *Sands of Iwo Jima* (Dwan); *Song of Surrender* (Leisen); *Chicago Deadline* (Allen); *Deadly Is the Female* (**Gun Crazy**) (Lewis); *Our Very Own* (Miller); *My Foolish Heart* (Robson)
1950   *Thelma Jordan* (*The File on Thelma Jordan*) (Siodmak); *The Fireball* (Garnett); *Paid in Full* (Dieterle); *Bright Leaf* (Curtiz); *Rio Grande* (Ford)
1951   *September Affair* (Dieterle); *Belle Le Grand* (Dwan); *Payment on Demand* (Bernhardt); *The Lemon Drop Kid* (Lanfield); *The Bullfighter and the Lady* (Boetticher); *Honeychile* (Springsteen); *Appointment with Danger* (*United States Mail*) (Allen); *A Millionaire for Christy* (Marshall); *My Favorite Spy* (McLeod); *The Wild Blue Yonder* (*Thunder across the Pacific; Bombs over Japan*) (Dwan)
1952   *The Quiet Man* (Ford); *Anything Can Happen* (Seaton); *Something to Live For* (Stevens); *Scaramouche* (Sidney); *The Greatest Show on Earth* (DeMille); *One Minute to Zero* (Garnett); *The Star* (Heisler); *Thunderbirds* (Auer); *Blackbeard the Pirate* (Walsh)
1953   *The Stars Are Singing* (Taurog); *Fair Wind to Java* (Kane); *A Perilous Journey* (Springsteen); *The Sun Shines Bright* (Ford); **Shane** (Stevens); *Flight Nurse* (Dwan); *Little Boy Lost* (Seaton); *Forever Female* (Rapper)
1954   *Jubilee Trail* (Kane); **Johnny Guitar** (Ray); *Three Coins in the Fountain* (Negulesco); *Trouble in the Glen* (Wilcox); *About Mrs. Leslie* (Daniel Mann); *Drum Beat* (Daves); *The Country Girl* (Seaton); *Timberjack* (Kane)

951

1955   *Strategic Air Command* (A. Mann); *Son of Sinbad* (Tetzlaff);
        A Man Alone (Milland); *The Left Hand of God* (Dmytryk);
        The Tall Men (Walsh); *The Conqueror* (Powell)
1956   *The Maverick Queen* (Kane); *The Proud and the Profane*
        (Seaton); *Around the World in Eighty Days* (Anderson)
1957   *The Brave One* (Rapper); *The Buster Keaton Story* (Sheldon);
        Run of the Arrow (Fuller); *Omar Khayyam* (Dieterle);
        Istanbul (Pevney); *China Gate* (Fuller) (completed by Max
        Steiner)

Films as Musical Director:

1938   *Army Girl* (Nicholls); *Thrill of a Lifetime* (Archainbaud);
        Breaking the Ice (Cline); *The Gladiator* (Sedgwick); *Peck's
        Bad Boy with the Circus* (Cline); *Flirting with Fate*
        (McDonald)
1939   *Fisherman's Wharf* (Vorhaus); *Man about Town* (Sandrich);
        Way Down South (Vorhaus); *Escape to Paradise* (Kenton)
1940   *Road to Singapore* (Schertzinger); *Those Were the Days*
        (Reed); *Rhythm on the River* (Schertzinger); *Dancing on
        a Dime* (Santley); *Love thy Neighbor* (Sandrich)
1941   *Las Vegas Nights* (Murphy); *Road to Zanzibar* (Schertzinger);
        Kiss the Boys Goodbye (Schertzinger); *Glamour Boy*
        (Murphy)
1942   *Sweater Girl* (Clemens); *True to the Army* (Rogell); *The
        Fleet's In* (Schertzinger) (co); *Priorities on Parade* (Rogell);
        Road to Morocco (Butler)
1944   *And the Angels Sing* (Marshall and Binyon)
1945   *Out of This World* (Walker); *Masquerade in Mexico* (Leisen)
1950   *High* (Capra)
1952   *The Story of Will Rogers* (Curtiz)
1954   *Knock on Wood* (Panama)
1956   *The Vagabond King* (Curtiz)

Publications

By YOUNG: article—

Music Journal (New York), September 1956.

On YOUNG: articles—

Thomas, Tony, in *Music for the Movies*, South Brunswick, New
    Jersey, 1973.
Bertolina, Gian Carlo, in *Rivista del Cinematografo* (Rome), Janu-
    ary 1981.
Lacombe, Alain, in *Hollywood*, Paris, 1983.
DeMary, T., "*Shane:* A Tribute to Victor Young," in *Film Score
    Monthly* (Los Angeles), November 1996.
Deutsch, D.C., "*Shane:* A Tribute to Victor Young," in *Soundtrack!*
    (Hollywood), December 1996.

"*Shane*: A Tribute to Victor Young," in *Score* (Lelystad), Decem-
    ber 1996.
Bennett, R., "Sometimes They Do Make Them Like They Used To,"
    in *Home Theater*, no. 11, 1997.

*   *   *

It was said of Victor Young that he needed only to sit at the piano
for the melodies to fall out of his sleeves. Certainly his productivity
was incredible. He arrived in Hollywood in 1936 and by the time he
died 20 years later he had either arranged or composed, and conducted
or supervised the music for more than 300 films. That, however, was
only part of his musical life; at the same time he also wrote and
conducted music for many of the top radio programs of the time,
while also working as a recording artist for Decca Records. No film
composer of the period made more recordings, or had more hit songs
drawn from his scores: "Love Letters," "Stella by Starlight," "My
Foolish Heart," "Golden Earrings," "When I Fall in Love," and
"Around the World in Eighty Days," among others.

Young began playing the violin at the age of six. Four years later
the family returned to Poland and the boy was enrolled in the Imperial
Conservatory of Warsaw, after which he was engaged as a soloist
with various orchestras. Returning to America in 1920, he accepted
the position of concertmaster with the Central Park Theater in
Chicago, the anchor theatre in the Balaban and Katz chain of movie
theaters. By the mid-1920s Young was a music director for the chain
and writing accompaniments to silent films. In 1931 he signed with
Brunswick Records and over the next four years became the best-
known music director in radio and a leading conductor in the record
business.

Paramount offered him a contract in 1935 and the majority of his
scores through his film years were for that studio. Most of Young's
early assignments were for light entertainments but his score for the
epic *Wells Fargo* caused producers to regard him more seriously.
Cecil B. DeMille was so taken with his score for *North West Mounted
Police* that he would consider no other composer thereafter. Young
was preparing to score *The Ten Commandments* at the time of his
death, after which Elmer Bernstein was hired to write a "Young-
like" score. A man of extraordinary facility, Young wrote with
apparent ease, albeit in a conventional form, and of his vast number of
scores the one for which he seemed to have the most regard was *For
Whom the Bell Tolls*. That and nine others were nominated for Oscars
but he did not live to receive his one Academy Award. Young died in
1956; the following March he was awarded a posthumous Oscar for
Around the World in Eighty Days.

Young could never explain why he became a film composer, it
was simply something that happened to him. He said, "Why, indeed,
would any trained musician let himself in for a career that calls for the
exactitude of an Einstein, the diplomacy of Churchill, and the
patience of a martyr. Yet I can think of no other medium that offers
this challenge and excitement, provided that your interest in the
universe is unflagging and your knowledge of musical forms is
gargantuan."

—Tony Thomas

Z

ZANUCK, Darryl F.

Producer and writer. **Nationality:** American. **Born:** Darryl Francis Zanuck in Wahoo, Nebraska, 5 September 1902; credited as Gregory Rogers, Melville Crossman, and Mark Canfield as writer in 1920s. **Education:** Page Military Academy; Manual Training High School; also studied under private tutors. **Military Service:** Joined Nebraska National Guard at age 15: served in France during World War I. **Family:** Married Virginia Fox, 1924; children: Darrylin, Susan Marie, and the producer Richard Darryl. **Career:** Worked as laborer, drugstore clerk, and writer; 1923–33—worked as writer, then studio manager, 1928, executive, 1929, and in charge of production, 1931, Warner Bros.; 1933—cofounder, with Joseph Schenck, 20th Century Pictures: merged with Fox, 1934, and remained President in charge of productions until 1956; then independent producer: 1962–69—returned to 20th Century-Fox as President, and Chairman and Chief Executive, 1969–71. **Awards:** Irving G. Thalberg Award, 1937, 1944, 1950; Academy Awards for *How Green Was My Valley*, 1941; *Gentleman's Agreement*, 1947; *All about Eve*, 1950. Decorated, Legion of Honor. **Died:** 22 December 1979.

Films as Writer:

1924   *Find Your Man* (St. Clair); *Lighthouse By the Sea* (St. Clair)
1925   *On Thin Ice* (St. Clair); *The Limited Mail* (Hill); *Red Hot Tires* (Kenton); *Hogan's Alley* (Del Ruth)
1926   *The Little Irish Girl* (Del Ruth); *The Social Highwayman* (Beaudine); *Footloose Widows* (Del Ruth); *Across the Pacific* (Del Ruth); *The Better 'ole* (Reisner); *Oh! What a Nurse!* (Reisner)
1927   *Tracked by the Police* (Enright); *The Missing Link* (Reisner); *Irish Hearts* (Haskin); *Old San Francisco* (Crosland); *The First Auto* (Del Ruth); *The Black Diamond Express* (Bretherton); *State Street Sadie* (Mayo); *The Desired Woman* (Curtiz)
1928   *Tenderloin* (Curtiz); *The Midnight Taxi* (Adolfi); *My Man* (Mayo)
1929   *Noah's Ark* (Curtiz); *Say It with Songs* (Bacon); *Madonna of Avenue A* (Curtiz)
1930   *The Life of the Party* (Del Ruth)
1933   *Baby Face* (Green) (co)
1935   *"G" Men* (Keighley) (co)
1942   *Thunderbirds* (Wellman) (co)
1943   *China Girl* (Hathaway) (co)

Films as Producer:

1927   **The Jazz Singer** (Crosland)
1929   *Disraeli* (Green)
1930   *The Office Wife* (Bacon) (+ co-sc); *The Doorway to Hell* (Mayo)
1931   **Little Caesar** (LeRoy) (+co-sc); *Illicit* (Mayo); **The Public Enemy** (Wellman); *Smart Money* (Green); *Five Start Final* (LeRoy)
1932   *The Crowd Roars* (Hawks); *The Mouthpiece* (Flood and Nugent) (+ co-sc); *The Dark Horse* (Green) (+ co-sc); **I am a Fugitive from a Chain Gang** (LeRoy) (+co-sc)
1933   **42nd Street** (Bacon); *The Bowery* (Walsh) (+ sc); *Broadway Thru' a Keyhole* (L. Sherman) (+ co-sc); *Blood Money* (Brown) (+ co-sc); *Advice to the Lovelorn* (Werker)
1934   *Gallant Lady* (LaCava) (+ co-sc); *Moulin Rouge* (Lanfield); *The House of Rothschild* (Werker); *Looking for Trouble* (Wellman); *Born to Be Bad* (L. Sherman) (+ co-sc); *Bulldog Drummond Strikes Back* (Del Ruth); *The Affairs of Cellini* (La Cava); *The Last Gentleman* (Lanfield) (+ co-sc); *The Mighty Barnum* (W. Lang) (+ co-sc)
1935   *Clive of India* (Boleslawsky); *Folies Bergere* (Del Ruth); *Cardinal Richelieu* (Lee); *Les Miserables* (Boleslawsky);

Darryl F. Zanuck

Call of the Wild (Wellman); *Metropolitan* (Boleslawsky); *Thanks a Million* (Del Ruth); *The Man Who Broke the Bank at Monte Carlo* (Roberts); *Show Them No Mercy* (Marshall)

1936 *King of Burlesque* (Lanfield); *The Prisoner of Shark Island* (Ford); *Professional Soldier* (Garnett); *It Had to Happen* (Del Ruth); *The Country Doctor* (H. King); *A Message to Garcia* (Marshall); *Captain January* (Butler); *Under Two Flags* (Lloyd); *Half Angel* (Lanfield); *White Fang* (Butler); *Sins of Man* (Brower and Ratoff); *The Road to Glory* (Hawks); *Sing Baby, Sing* (Lanfield); *Lloyds of London* (H. King); *Pigskin Parade* (Butler)

1938 *In Old Chicago* (H. King); *Happy Landing* (Del Ruth); *Kidnapped* (Werker) (+ co-sc); *Little Miss Broadway* (Cummings) (+ co-sc); *I'll Give a Million* (W. Lang); *Alexander's Ragtime Band* (H. King) (+ co-sc); *Josette* (Dwan); *Three Blind Mice* (Seiter); *Hold That Co-Ed* (Marshall); *Suez* (Dwan); *Submarine Patrol* (Ford); *Straight, Place and Show* (Butler); *Just Around the Corner* (Cummings); *Thanks for Everything* (Seiter); *Kentucky* (Butler

1939 *Jesse James* (H. King); *Tail Spin* (Del Ruth); *The Little Princess* (W. Lang); *The Story of Alexander Graham Bell* (Cummings) (+ co-sc); *Young Mr. Lincoln* (Ford); *Susannah of the Mounties* (Seiter); *The Gorilla* (Dwan); *Second Fiddle* (Lanfield); *Wife, Husband, and Friend* (Ratoff); *Stanley and Livingstone* (H. King); *Hotel for Women* (Ratoff); *Hollywood Cavalcade* (Cummings) (+ co-sc); *Drums along the Mohawk* (Ford); *Daytime Wife* (Ratoff); *The Return of the Cisco Kid* (Leeds); *Rose of Washington Square* (Ratoff); *The Rains Came* (Brown)

1940 *Swanee River* (Lanfield); *The Blue Bird* (W. Lang); *Little Old New York* (H. King); *The Grapes of Wrath* (Ford); *Chad Hanna* (H. King); *Johnny Apollo* (Hathaway); *He Married His Wife* (Del Ruth); *Star Dust* (W. Lang); *I Was an Adventuress* (Ratoff); *Lillian Russell* (Cummings); *Four Sons* (Mayo); *Maryland* (H. King); *The Man I Married* (Pichel); *Public Debt No. 1* (Ratoff) (+ co-sc); *The Return of Frank James* (F. Lang); *Brigham Young—Frontiersman* (Hathaway); *Down Argentine Way* (Cummings) (+co-sc); *The Great Profile* (W. Lang)

1941 *Tobacco Road* (Ford); *Blood and Sand* (Mamoulian); *A Yank in the R.A.F.* (H. King); *How Green Was My Valley* (Ford)

1942 *Son of Fury* (Cromwell); *To the Shores of Tripoli* (Humberstone); *This above All* (Litvak); *The Pied Piper* (Pichel)

1943 *At the Front* (doc)

1944 *Lifeboat* (Hitchcock) (co); *The Song of Bernadette* (H. King); *The Purple Heart* (Milestone); *Wilson* (H. King); *Laura* (Preminger); *Winged Victory* (Cukor)

1946 *Dragonwyck* (Mankiewicz); *The Razor's Edge* (Goulding); *My Darling Clementine* (Ford)

1947 *Gentleman's Agreement* (Kazan)

1949 *Pinky* (Kazan)

1950 *Twelve O'Clock High* (H. King)

1951 *David and Bathsheba* (H. King); *People Will Talk* (Mankiewicz)

1952 *Viva Zapata!* (Kazan); *The Snows of Kilimanjaro* (H. King)

1954 *The Egyptian* (Curtiz); *The Man in the Gray Flannel Suit* (Johnson)

1957 *Island in the Sun* (Rossen); *The Sun Also Rises* (H. King)

1958 *The Roots of Heaven* (Huston)

1960 *Crack in the Mirror* (Fleischer)

1961 *The Big Gamble* (Fleischer)

1962 *The Longest Day* (Annakin, Marton, and Wicki)

1963 *Cleopatra* (Mankiewicz) (replaced Wanger)

1965 *Those Magnificent Men in Their Flying Machines* (Annakin)

1970 *Hello and Goodbye* (Negulesco) (+ sc, as Canfield)

Films as Executive Producer:

1943 *Coney Island* (W. Lang)

1945 *A Tree Grows in Brooklyn* (Kazan); *The House on 92nd Street* (Hathaway); *Diamond Horseshoe* (Seaton)

1947 *13 Rue Madeleine* (Hathaway); *Boomerang* (Kazan); *Miracle on 34th Street* (Seaton); *Kiss of Death* (Hathaway); *Mother Wore Tights* (W. Lang)

1948 *The Snake Pit* (Litvak); *Unfaithfully Yours* (P. Sturges); *Call Northside 777* (Hathaway); *Sitting Pretty* (W. Lang); *When My Baby Smiles at Me* (W. Lang)

1949 *A Letter to Three Wives* (Mankiewicz); *Yellow Sky* (Wellman)

1950 *The Gunfighter* (H. King); *No Way Out* (Mankiewicz); *All about Eve* (Mankiewicz); *Mister 880* (Goulding)

1952 *Five Fingers* (Mankiewicz); *The Robe* (Koster)

1970 *Tora! Tora! Tora!* (Fleischer)

Publications

By ZANUCK: articles—

''Hollywood v. Communism,'' in *Films and Filming* (London), June 1961.

''A Blank Cheque for the Real Thing,'' in *Films and Filming* (London), November 1962.

''The Future of the Film Industry,'' with David Levin in *Today's Cinema*, 8 October 1969.

Film Francais (Paris), October 1970.

On ZANUCK: books—

Guild, Leo, *Zanuck, Hollywood's Last Tycoon*, Los Angeles, 1970.

Gussow, Mel, *Don't Say Yes Until I Finish Talking: A Biography of Darryl F. Zanuck*, New York, 1971.

Mosley, Leonard, *Zanuck: The Rise and Fall of Hollywood's Last Tycoon*, Boston, Massachusetts, 1984.

Silverman, Stephen M., *The Fox That Got Away*, Secaucus, New Jersey, 1988.

Solomon, Aubrey, *Twentieth Century-Fox: A Corporate and Financial History*, London, 1988.

Harris, Marlys J., *The Zanucks of Hollywood*, London, 1990.

Behlmer, Rudy, editor, *Memo From Darryl F. Zanuck*, New York, 1993.

On ZANUCK: articles—

Films and Filming (London), January 1959.

Zierold, Norman, in *The Moguls*, New York, 1969.

Bielecki, Stanley, in *Films and Filming* (London), August 1969.

Canham, Kingsley, in *Screen* (London), January-February 1970.

Quarterly Review of Film Studies (Pleasantville, New York), Winter 1978.

Cinématographe (Paris), May 1984.

Films (New York), July 1984.

Télérama (Paris), 16–22 March 1985.

Positif (Paris), April 1985.

Wiseman, J.B., ''Darryl F. Zanuck and the failure of *One World*,'' in *Historical Journal of Film, Radio and Television* (Abingdon, Oxfordshire), vol. 7, no. 3, 1987.

Films in Review (New York), February 1989.

Film Comment (New York), July-August 1989.

Library Journal, 1 November 1993.

Europe, May 1994.

Film Quarterly (Berkeley), Fall 1994.

Historical Journal of Film, Radio and Television (Abingdon), October 1994.

''De Luxe Tour,'' in *Reid's Film Index* (Wyong), no. 17, 1995.

Dossier, in *Cahiers du Cinéma* (Paris), December 1997.

* * *

Darryl F. Zanuck ranks as one of the most famous, long-lived of Hollywood's movie moguls, earning the Thalberg Award a record three times. He is properly celebrated for helping revive and create Twentieth Century-Fox, and functioned as its chief of production from the mid-1930s until the mid-1950s, and then again, after a stint as an independent producer, through much of the 1960s. With the exception of the years during the Second World War, when he served as a lieutenant colonel in charge of a documentary filmmaking unit, no studio executive's power exceeded Zanuck's.

Zanuck took a rare and strange route to Hollywood power. He began as a writer, and during the confusion caused by the coming of sound at his then employer Warner Bros. found himself in charge of production—at age 27! But Zanuck quickly chaffed under the scrutiny of brother Jack L. Warner who had all final decision power, and in a celebrated huff left and fashioned his own company—with partner Joseph M. Schenck. Two years later Schenck and Zanuck merged their Twentieth Century Pictures into a near bankrupt Fox Film company.

Zanuck took over as production chief at the ailing Fox studio during the summer of 1935. He inherited only two important stars (Shirley Temple and Janet Gaynor) while bringing along three from Twentieth Century Pictures (Frederic March, Ronald Colman, and Loretta Young). Zanuck then developed an extraordinary set of stars who pulled the new Twentieth Century-Fox from the depths of the industry to it apex.

The first of these new talents was skater Sonja Henie whose first film, *One in a Million* (1936), proved to be an unexpected smash hit. Henie remained a major star until she left Fox in 1943. Alice Faye and Tyrone Power came next. For *In Old Chicago* (1938), they teamed the pair who would bring in millions into Fox's coffers. But it was Betty Grable, filmed in Technicolor, which made Twentieth Century-Fox a true power house studio operation, a Hollywood colossus second to none. Too long unappreciated these Zanuck-produced Grable spectacles should rank among the most popular films of the Golden Age of Hollywood, in particular *Coney Island, Diamond Horseshoe*, and *Mother Wore Tights*. After serving his country in the Second World War, Zanuck moved Twentieth Century-Fox in a far different direction that the Technicolor fluff of Betty Grable and company. Based on his war experience, he authorized a series of films dealing with important social themes, from racism in America to the cruelty of mental hospitals. And they made money, all of them, including the much celebrated and honored *Gentlemen's Agreement*, *Pinky*, and *The Snake Pit*. But like many of the moguls from the Golden Age of the 1930s and 1940s, Zanuck had little success in dealing with television. It was new corporate boss at Fox, Spyros Skouras, not Zanuck, who moved the studio into CinemaScope as the corporate technological savior. In 1956 Zanuck left Fox after two decades, and entered independent production. *The Sun Also Rises*, *The Roots of Heaven*, and *Crack in the Mirror* made him little money. He did not hit the jackpot until 1962 with his *The Longest Day*. The early 1960s nearly proved the unmaking of the Fox studio, and so the board of directors kicked out Skouras and his management team, and brought back Zanuck. Zanuck his son, Richard (age 28), in charge of day-to-day production and together the Zanucks did well for a time, principally on the strength of a single mega-hit, *The Sound of Music*. But Hollywood was changing and based on excess spending and declining attendance, the board that hired Zanuck, kicked him out. An era had ended at one of Hollywood's major studios.

—Douglas Gomery

ZANUCK, Richard D.

Producer, Production Executive. **Nationality:** American. **Born:** Los Angeles, 13 December 1934, the son of studio executive Darryl F. Zanuck. **Family:** Married 1) Lili Gentle (divorced), daughters Virginia and Janet; 2) Linda Harrison (divorced), sons Harrison and Dean; 3) producer/director Lili Fini. **Education:** Stanford University. **Career:** Worked in the story department of 20th Century Fox, his father's studio, while a college student; 1956—became vice president in charge of U.S. operations of Darryl F. Zanuck Productions, his father's newly formed independent production company; 1962—when Darryl regained control of 20th Century Fox, was appointed vice president in charge of production; briefly became company president, but was removed after a proxy fight, 1971–72—served as senior executive vice president; 1972—formed his own production company in partnership with David Brown with release though Universal; produced with Brown two of the biggest grossing films of the seventies, *The Sting* (1973) and *Jaws* (1975). **Awards:** Academy Awards for *The Sting*, 1974 and *Driving Miss Daisy*, 1990. **Address:** 202 North Canon Drive, Beverly Hills, California 90210, U.S.A.

Films as Producer:

1959   *Compulsion*

1961   *Sanctuary*

1962   *The Chapman Report*

With David Brown:

1973   *SSSSSSS*; *Willie Dynamite*

1974   *The Sugarland Express*; *The Black Windmill*; *The Girl from Petrovka*

1975   *The Eiger Sanction*; **Jaws**

1977   *MacArthur*

1978   *Jaws 2*

1980   *The Island*

Richard D. Zanuck (right) with Steven Spielberg

1981   *Neighbors*
1982   *The Verdict*
1985   *Cocoon* (with L. F. Zanuck)
1985   *Target*
1988   *Cocoon: The Return* (with L. F. Zanuck)
1989   *Driving Miss Daisy* (with L. F. Zanuck)
1991   *Rush* (with L. F. Zanuck)
1993   *Rich in Love* (with L. F. Zanuck)
1994   *Clean Slate*
1995   *Wild Bill*
1996   *Mulholland Falls*
1998   *Deep Impact* (Leder)
1999   *True Crime* (Eastwood)
2000   *Rules of Engagement* (Friedkin)

Films as Assistant to the Producer:

1956   *The Sun Also Rises*
1957   *Island in the Sun*
1962   *The Longest Day*

Films as Executive Producer:

1973   *The Sting*
1987   *Barrington* (for TV)
1996   *Chain Reaction*

Publications

 By ZANUCK: articles—

Films & Filming, April 1983.
Stills, October 1985.
American Film, July 1990.

 On ZANUCK: articles—

American Film, October 1975.
Films in Review (New York), March 1990.

*   *   *

Perhaps because the producer's contribution to the film that actually screens is difficult to measure, Richard D. Zanuck's contributions to filmmaking in the last twenty years, like those of his collaborators David Brown and Lili F. Zanuck, have gone largely unrecognized by the movie going public. Zanuck may take some consolation in the fact that the film industry has seen fit to reward him for his efforts (but this may be due somewhat to the peculiarity of the Academy Award system in deciding upon a ''best picture,'' for which the award goes to the producers, who may or may not have contributed to a quality effort).

If the producer is as invisible to the public as the director once was (but is no more), that does not mean that his influence on filmmaking is negligible, confined only to a kind of glorified accountancy and financial deal making. Zanuck was brought up in the film business, where his father Darryl was first a studio executive and then later an independent producer, a man who very forcefully put his mark on the films made under his auspices. Zanuck, in fact, worked as assistant producer on the project—*The Longest Day*, an epic tribute to the Normandy invasion—that most obviously belonged to his father. Darryl Zanuck fought for the film's length, its expensive production values, its cast of many notable stars, and its vignettish realism, in stark contrast to the usual Hollywood procedure for making war films. Just as his career is modeled in other ways on that of his father, so Zanuck's choice of film projects, and the way in which these were produced, had not a little to do with his own vision of what a good entertainment film should be, a vision that is discernible often in the final product despite the contributions of others, most notably the directors in each case and his coproducers, often David Brown and Lili F. Zanuck, strong personalities in their own right.

Like his father, Zanuck worked successfully for a time within the confines of the Hollywood system. It was a very volatile industry in the late 1960s and early 1970s, one faced by continual financial crisis, rapid changes in public taste, and uncertain conditions of exhibition. Zanuck was employed first by Darryl F. Zanuck Productions when a college student, but then, when his father once again took a position inside the studio system, he followed him there: initially as vice president in charge of production (in effect, his father's right hand man) and later, while Darryl Zanuck became in a bitter proxy fight for control, as president. When Darryl Zanuck lost the struggle for control, Zanuck stayed on briefly as senior executive vice president, but, like his father before him, yearned for more control of production and founded his own company in partnership with David Brown in 1972.

The early 1970s were a time of great marketing uncertainty for the industry, which had lost much of its original audience base, but had as potential customers a huge population of the young who already had an enthusiasm for movie going. Zanuck and Brown began operations by producing a number of more or less alternative youth films that attempted to cater to this taste. Some of these were very forgettable (*Willie Dynamite*), others more successful, most notably *Sugarland Express*, where Zanuck and Brown worked closely with a new director—Steven Spielberg—on a modern remake of *Bonnie and Clyde*. What Zanuck had in common with his director was a desire to emphasize the sympathetic character of the protagonists—a desperate young mother and a kidnapped policeman—and thus impart a very strong melodramatic quality to a narrative that was handled during this period quite differently by other directors (compare Altman's *Thieves Like Us* and Hopper's *Easy Rider*). These same elements—an adventure narrative energized by interesting character relationships—were recycled by Spielberg and Zanuck/Brown in one of the most

successful films of that period, *Jaws*, a monster hit that helped re-establish filmgoing as an essential American pastime. The various remakes of that film have failed to match the original's riveting approach to storytelling, but *Jaws 2*, done by Zanuck/Brown but without Spielberg, shows the same interest in character relationships. Perhaps attempting to recycle his father's success with a World War II subject, Zanuck/Brown produced *MacArthur*, a biography of the noted general; the film was a *Patton* wannabe, but simply lacked the strengths of Coppola's script and George C. Scott's performance for that earlier film. However, once again we can glimpse Zanuck's interest in compelling character, in dramatic conflicts and interests that motivate the audience's fascination with well-orchestrated spectacle. Of more purely dramatic interest is one of Zanuck/Brown's most notable other films, *The Verdict*, notable for providing Paul Newman with one of his best opportunities for character portrayal.

Much the same may be said about the extremely popular productions *Cocoon* and *Driving Miss Daisy* that Zanuck worked on with director/producer wife Lili. Here melodrama of a sentimental but not saccharine kind (one particularly associated with aging Americans) predominates over spectacle, proving that, sometimes at least, an industry trend can be resisted. In general, however, the kinds of films that Zanuck has been interested in making are no longer as popular as they once were, a fact that may account for his gradual marginalization within the industry during the 1990s. *Mulholland Falls* is a disastrously disjointed attempt to recapture the magic of *The Sting*; the 1990s were no longer an era interested in the subtle dramatics of male relationships, the magic that made not only *The Sting* but also *Jaws* a success with audiences. In this case, Zanuck lacked not only the dynamic casting of Robert Redford and Paul Newman, he also did not base his film around a good, solid script, a fundamental mistake he would probably never have made earlier in his career. *True Crime*, in contrast, is what Zanuck's father might have termed a solid programmer; this Clint Eastwood vehicle is an expertly produced and slick entertainment vehicle. Much the same could be said for *Deep Impact*, which is far and away the best entry in the recently revived disaster film genre, far superior to either *Independence Day* or *Armageddon*. Working once again with David Brown, Zanuck made the most of the well-constructed screenplay by Michael Tolkin and Bruce Joel Rubin, assembling a stellar international cast (shades of *The Longest Day*) that includes Robert Duvall, Morgan Freeman, and Vanessa Redgrave, and ably supervising a very complicated production. Here is good solid Hollywood entertainment, with tragedy and melodramatic triumph enough for an audience of all ages, that is unencumbered by profound thoughts of any kind. *Deep Impact* is precisely the kind of film that many years ago Darryl Zanuck taught his son to make, and fortunately for him it still can claim a profitable niche in today's international market.

—R. Barton Palmer

ZAVATTINI, Cesare

Writer. **Nationality:** Italian. **Born:** Luzzura, 20 September 1902. **Education:** Studied in Parma. **Married:** Olga Berni. **Career:** Journalist in Parma, then in Milan, then a fiction writer; 1935—first film script, *Darò un milione*; 1941—first of several films for Vittorio De Sica, *Teresa Venerdi*. **Died:** In Rome, 13 October 1989.

Cesare Zavattini

Films as Writer:

1935   *Darò un milione* (Camerini)

1936   *La danza delle lancette* (Baffico)

1938   *I'll Give a Million* (W. Lang)

1939   *Bionda sottochiave* (Mastrocinque)

1940   *Una famiglia impossibile* (Bragaglia); *Senza cielo* (Guarini); *Capitan Fracassa* (Coletti); *San Giovanni Decollato* (Palermi)

1941   *É caduta una donna* (Guarini); *Teresa Venerdi* (De Sica); *La scuola del timidi* (Bragaglia)

1942   *C'é sempre un ma!* (Zampa); *Don Cesare di Bazan* (Freda); *Quattro passi fra le nuvole* (*Four Steps in the Clouds*) (Blasetti); *I setti peccati* (Kish); *Quarta pagina* (Manzari and Gambino)

1943   *Gian Burrasca* (Tofano); *Silenzio: si gira!* (Campogalliani); *L'ippocampo* (Rosmino); *I nostri sogni* (Cottafavi); *Il birichino di Papà* (Matarazzo)

1944   *Romanzo a passo di danzo* (Capelli); *I bambini ci guardano* (De Sica)

1945   *La freccia nel fianco* (Lattuada); *Canto ma sottovoce* (Brignone); *Il mondo vuole cosi* (Bianchi)

1946   *Il testimone* (Germi); *Il marito povero* (Amato); *Un giorno nella vita* (Blasetti); *L'angeloc il diavolo* (Camerini); ***Sciuscià*** (*Shoeshine*) (De Sica); *La porta del cielo* (De Sica)

1947   *Sperduti nel buio* (Mastrocinque); *Caccia tragica* (*The Tragic Pursuit*) (De Santis); *Lo sconosciuto di San Marino* (Waszynski, Cottafavi and De Sica); *La grande aurora* (Scotese and Waszynski)

1948   *Roma città libera* (Pagliero); ***Ladri di biciclette*** (*The Bicycle Thief*) (De Sica); *Guerra alle guerra* (Marcellini and Simonelli)

1949   *Fabiola* (Blasetti); *Au-delà des grilles* (*The Walls of Malapaga*) (Clément); *Miracolo a loreto* (Moccheggiani—short); *La sposa non può attendere* (Franciolini)

1950   *Vent'anni* (Bianchi); *La roccia incantata* (Morelli); *Domenica d'agosto* (Emmer); *Il cielo è rosso* (*The Sky Is Red*) (Gora); *Prima communione* (Blasetti); *E primavera* (*It's Forever Springtime*) (Castellani); *É più facile che un cammello*; ***Miracolo a Milano*** (*Miracle in Milan*) (De Sica)

1951   *Bellissima* (Visconti); *Mamma Mia, che impressione!* (Savarese and De Sica)

1952   *Roma ore 11* (*Rome, Eleven O'Clock*) (De Santis); *Il cappotto* (*The Overcoat*) (Lattuada); **Umberto D** (De Sica); *Buongiorno elefante!* (*Hello Elephant!*) (Franciolini); *Cinque poveri in automobile* (*The Lucky Five*) (Mattoli)

1953   *Lettere di condamnati a morte della resistenza italiana* (Fornari—short); *La voce de silenzio* (Pabst); *Amore in città* (Antonioni and others); *Siamo donne* (Rossellini and others); *Un marito per Anna Zaccheo* (De Santis); *Donne proibite* (Amato); *La passeggiata* (Rascel); *Piovuto dal cielo* (De Mitri); *Stazione Termini* (*Indiscretion of an American Wife*) (De Sica)

1954   *San Miniato, Iuglio 1944* (Orsini and P. & V. Taviani—short); *L'oro di Napoli* (*The Gold of Naples*) (De Sica); *Ali Baba et les 40 voleurs* (Becker)

1955   *Il segno di Venere* (Risi)

1956   *Il tetto* (*The Roof*) (De Sica); *La cavallina storna* (Morelli); *Suor Letizia* (*The Awakening*) Camerini); *Era di venerdi 17* (Soldati)

1957   *La donna del giorno* (*The Doll That Took the Town*) (Maselli); *Amore e chiacchiere* (Blasetti); *Uomini e lupi* (De Santis)

1959   *Nel blu dipinto di blu* (Tellini)

1960   *Il rossetto* (*Lipstick*) (Damiani); *Rat* (Bulajic); *La ciociara* (*Two Women*) (De Sica); *La lunga calza verde* Gavioli); *Chi legge?* (*Viaggio lungo il Tirreno*) (Soldati); *Arriba el campesino* (Gallo—short)

1961   *Un quarto d'Italia* (Tosi); *El joven rebelde* (Espinosa); *Il sicario* (Damiani); *Il giudizio universale* (*The Last Judgment*) (De Sica); *Le Italiane e l'amore* (Mazzetti and others); *L'oro di Roma* (Lizzani)

1962   *I sequestrati di Altona* (*The Condemned of Altona*) (De Sica); "*La Riffa*" ep. of *Boccaccio '70* (De Sica); *L'isola di Arturo* (*Arthur's Island*) (Damiani)

1963   *Cinegiornale della pace* (+co-d—short); *Il boom* (De Sica); *I misteri di Roma* (Bizzari and others); *Ieri, oggi, domani* (De Sica)

1964   "*Cocaina di comenica*" ep. of *Controssesso* (Rossi)

1965   *Con il cuore fermo, Sicilia* (Mingozzi—short); *Ein Arbeitstag* (Nelli)

1966   *Andremo in città* (Risi); *Caccia alla volpe* (*After the Fox*) (De Sica); *Un mondo nuovo* (*A Young World*) (De Sica)

1967   "*La strega bruciata viva*" and "*Una sera come le altre*" eps. of *Le streghe* (*The Witches*) (Visconti and De Sica); *Sette volte donna* (*Woman Times Seven*) (De Sica)

1968   "*La gelosia*" ep. of *Capriccio all' italiana* (Bolognini); *I sette fratelli Cervi* (Puccini); *Amanti* (*A Place for Lovers*) (De Sica); *Parliamo tanto di me* (Carpi)

1970   *I girasoli* (*Sunflower*) (DeSica); "*Il leone*" ep. of *Le coppie* (De Sica)

1972   *Cesare Zavattini e il "Campo di grano dei corvi" di Van Gogh* (Emmer—short); *Lo chiameremo Andrea* (De Sica)

1973   *Una breve vacanza* (*A Brief Vacation*) (De Sica)

1977   *Un cuore semplice* (Ferrara)

1978   *The Children of Sanchez* (Bartlett); *Ligabue* (Nocita)

1982   *La veritá* (+ d); *La "follia" de Zavattini* (Giannarelli)

1983   *Césare Zavattini: I milione, I milione di idee* (Gambetti and Di Laura—for TV)

Publications

By ZAVATTINI: books—

Parliamo tanto di me, Milan, 1931.
I poveri sono matti, Milan, 1937.
Io sono il diavolo, Milan, 1942.
Totò il buono, Milan, 1943.
With De Sica, *Umberto D* (script), Milan, 1953.
Ipocrita 1943, Milan, 1955.
Un paese, Turin, 1955.
Il tetto (script), edited by Michele Gandin, Bologna, 1956.
Come nasce un soggetto cinematografico, Milan, 1959.
With De Sica, *Il giudizio universale* (script), Rome, 1961.
"*Lariffa*" ep. of *Boccaccio '70* (script), edited by Carlo Di Carlo and Gaio Fratini, Bologna, 1961.
I misteri di Roma, edited by F. Bolzoni, Bologna, 1963.
Fiume Po, Turin, 1966.
Straparole, Milan, 1967.
With others, *Bicycle Thieves* (script), London, 1968, as *The Bicycle Thief*, New York, 1968.
Saturno contro la terra, Milan, 1968.
Non libro più disco, Milan, 1970.
Le grandi firme del fumetto italiano, Milan, 1971.
Stricarm' in d' na parola, Milan, 1973.
Romanzi, diari, poésie, edited by Renato Barilli, Milan, 1974.
Le voglie litterarie, Bologna, 1974.
Opere, Milan, 1974.
Ligabue, Milan, 1974.
Otto canzonette sporche, Rome, 1975.
Un paesevent' anni dopo, Turin, 1976.
Prime mostra antologica, Aula magna delle scuole medie . . . 1976, edited by Franco Solmi, Bologna, 1976.
Al macero 1927–1940, edited by Gustavo Marchesi and Giovanni Negri, Turin, 1976.
La notte che ho dato uno schiaffo a Mussolini, Milan, 1976.
Basta coi soggetti, edited by Roberto Mazzoni, Milan, 1979.
Diario cinematografico, edited by Valentina Fortichiari, Milan, 1979.
With Paolo Monti, *Foto d'archivio: Italia tra '800 e '900*, Milan, 1979.
Neorealismo ecc., edited by Mino Argentieri, Milan, 1979.
Zavattini parla di Zavattini, edited by Silvana Cirillo, Cosenza, 1980.
Cesare Zavattini Milanese, Milan, 1982.
La Verità (script), edited by Maurizio Grande, Milan, 1983.
Gli altri, edited by Pier Luigi Raffaelli, Milan, 1986.
Zavattini Mago e tecnico, edited by Giacomo Gambetti, Rome, 1986.
Zavattini cinema, edited by Tullio Masini and Paolo Vecchi, Bologna, 1988.
Zavattini pittura, edited by Renato Barilli, Bologna, 1988.
Una, cento, mille lettere, edited by Silvano Cirillo, Milan, 1988.
Ciao Zavattini, edited by Aldo Bernardino and Jean Gili, Paris, 1990.

By ZAVATTINI: articles—

Sight and Sound (London), October-December 1953.
Cahiers du Cinéma (Paris), December 1953.
Cahiers du Cinéma (Paris), August 1959.
Filmselezione (Bologna), December 1961.
Filmkritik (Munich), no. 2, 1962.
Bianco e Nero (Rome), June 1963.
Jeune Cinéma (Paris), February 1970.

Ecran (Paris), June-July 1975.
Image et Son (Paris), May 1977.
Cinemasessante (Rome), March-April 1979.
Rivista del Cinematografo (Rome), August 1981.
Soviet Film (Moscow), no. 11, 1983.
Cahiers de la Cinémathèque (Paris), Summer 1984.
Cinema Nuovo (Bari), January-February 1987.
Cinema Nuovo (Bari), November-December 1989.
Cinema Nuovo (Bari), January-February 1990.
Cinema Nuovo (Bari), March-April 1990.

On ZAVATTINI: books—

Angioletti, Lina, *Invito all lettura di Cesare Zavattini*, Milan, 1978.
Bernardino, Aldo, and Jean A. Gili, *Cesare Zavattini*, Paris, 1990.

On ZAVATTINI: articles—

Hawkins, Robert F., in *Films in Review* (New York), May 1951.
Cahiers du Cinéma (Paris), December 1951.
Image et Son (Paris), April 1952.
Films and Filming (London), November 1954.
Sight and Sound (London), Summer 1964.
Jeune Cinéma (Paris), June-July 1965.
Cinema Nuovo (Turin), November-December 1974.
"Zavattini Section" of *Cinema e Cinema* (Bologna), July-September 1979.
Aristarco, Guido, in *Cinema Nuovo* (Turin), June 1980.
"Zavattini Issue" of *Bianco e Nero* (Rome), April-June 1983.
Cine Cubano (Havana), no. 108, 1984.
Codelli, Lorenzo, and Antonella Cristofaro, *in Cahiers de la Cinémathèque* (Paris), Summer 1984.
Cinema Nuovo (Bari), November-December 1988.
Filmcritica (Montepulciano), April 1989.
Obituary in *Cinema Nuovo* (Bari), no. 320–321, July-October 1989.
Obituary in *Variety* (New York), 18 October 1989.
Obituary in *New Republic*, 27 November 1989.
EPD Film (Frankfurt), vol. 7, no. 1, January 1990.
Cine Cubano (Havana), no. 129, 1990.
Cinéma (Paris), no. 473, January 1991.
Cinema Nuovo (Bari), no. 330, March-April 1991.
Cinema Nuovo (Bari), January-February 1992.
Cinema Nuovo (Bari), November-December 1992.
Cinémaction (Courbevoie), January 1994.
Jeune Cinéma (Paris), Summer 1994.
Positif (Paris), October 1998.

*   *   *

Cesare Zavattini's contribution to the development of cinema can easily be compared with that of Griffith and Eisenstein. Within two decades of the invention of sound for celluloid film, Zavattini brought about a revolution in the scripting of feature films in Italy and ushered in the neorealist movement through his collaboration with Rossellini, De Sica, and Fellini. The movement sought to bring film closer to daily life and influenced many filmmakers in the major filmmaking

cities of Europe and the U.S.A., and even as far away as India and Japan. His script for De Sica's *The Bicycle Thief*, for example, influenced India's Satyajit Ray to make *Pather Panchali* in 1955. His influence and neorealist credo persisted into the 1970s, although the *cinéma vérité* which he tried rather unsuccessfully, in *Amore in città* and *I misteri di Roma*, had little following in Europe or elsewhere.

The greatness of Zavattini lay in freeing cinema from Hollywood conventions and capitalist elitism. In his enthusiasm, he also understandably overstated his aims. Beginning with the narrative tradition of Italian cinema, he came to discard "story" altogether, as it was to him "simply a technique of superimposing dead formulas over living social facts." He used the Irish novelist James Joyce's "stream of consciousness" as a technique to recapture on celluloid the Heraclitean flux of life. "Life is not what is invented in stories; life is another matter. To understand it involves a minute and patient search." He also favored doing away with professional actors, because "to want one person to play another implies a calculated plot." He would even do away with technical paraphernalia which tended to distance reality.

His other feverish crusade was against capitalistic elitism in cinema. "The cinema's capitalist structure has a tremendous influence over its true function." Neorealist films, he thought, had, *ipso facto*, to depict poverty, because "it is one of the most vital realities of our time and I challenge anyone to prove the contrary. . . . The theme of poverty, of rich and poor, is something one can dedicate one's life to." This social concern in cinema abided throughout his restless career in Italian new wave cinema of more than four decades of script-writing and collaboration.

—Bibekananda Ray

ZEMAN, Karel

Animator. **Nationality:** Czech. **Born:** Ostroměř, 3 November 1910. **Career:** 1930–36—worked in France as poster designer, window dresser, artist with various advertising agencies; 1943—animator in Bata Film Studio at Zlín (now Gottwaldov); assistant director to Hermína Týlová; 1945—director, organizer of 2nd production group for puppet films at Gottwaldov Film Studio; 1955—*A Journey into Primeval Times* established international reputation. **Awards:** National Artist, 1970; Order of the Republic, 1980. **Died:** In Gottwaldov, 5 April 1989.

Films as Animator, Writer and Art Director:

1946   *Vánočni* (*The Christmas Dream*) (co-d + sc only; comb. puppet and feature film); *Podkova pro štěstí* (*A Hoseshoe for Luck*) (Puppet film); *Křeček* (*The Hamster*) (Puppet film)

1947   *Pan prokouk úřaduje* (*Mr. Prokouk in the Office*) (puppet film); *Pan Prokouk v pokušeni* (*Mr. Prokouk in Temptation*) (puppet film); *Brigady* (*Mr. Prokouk Leaves for Volunteer Work*) (puppet film)

1948   *Pan Prokouk filmuje* (*Mr. Prokouk Is Filming*) (puppet film); *Pan Prokouk vynálezcem* (*Mr. Prokouk, the Inventor*) (puppet film)

Karel Zeman

1949   *Inspirace (Inspiration)* (puppet film)
1950   *Král Làvra (King Lavra)* (puppet film)
1952   *Poklad Ptačího ostrova (The Treasure of Bird Island)* (puppet film)
1955   *Cesta do pravěku (A Journey into Prehistory; A Journey into Primeval Times)* ("trick-film"); *Pan Prokouk, přítel zvířátek (Mr. Prokouk, the Animal Lover)* (puppet film)
1958   *Vynález zkàzy (An Invention for Destruction)* ("trick-film")
1961   ***Baron Prášil** (Baron Münchhausen)* ("trick-film")
1964   *Bláznova Kronika (A Jester's Tale)* (puppet film)
1966   *Ukradená vzducholod (The Stolen Airship)* ("trick-film")
1970   *Na Kometě (On the Comet)* ("trick-film")
1974   *Pohádky tisíce a jedné noci (A Thousand and One Nights)* (paper cut animation)
1977   *Carodějuv učen (Krabat)* (paper cut animation)
1980   *Pohádka o Honzikovi a Mařence (The Tale of John and Mary)* (paper cut animation)

Other Films:

1955   *Strakonický dudák (The Piper of Strakonice)* (co-special effects); *Cerný démant (The Black Diamond)* (sc + art d)
1957   *Pan Prokouk detektivem (Mr. Prokouk, the Detective)* (sc)
1958   *Pan Prokouk abrobat (Mr. Prokouk, the Acrobat)* (sc + art d)
1972   *Pan Prokouk hodinářem (Mr. Prokouk, the Watchmaker)* (sc + art d)

Publications

By ZEMAN: articles—

"Comment j'ai tourné *Une Invention diabolique*," in *Image et Son* (Paris), November 1959.
Midi-Minuit Fantastique (Paris), December-January 1966–67.

On ZEMAN: books—

Benešová, Marie, *Karel Zeman*, Prague, 1968.
Karel Zeman (in French), Ceskoslovensky Filmexport, Prague, 1968.
Hořejši, J., *Karel Zeman*, Prague, 1970.
Asenin, Sergei, *Fantastičeskij kinomir Karela Zemana*, Moscow, 1979.

On ZEMAN: articles—

Martin, Marcel, "Karel Zeman, ou, L'Impossible n'est pas tchèque," in *Cinéma* (Paris), no. 34, 1959.
Delahaye, Michel, "Aventures fantastiques," in *Cinéma* (Paris), no. 38, 1959.
Thirard, P.-L., "Le Diabolique Karel Zeman," in *Les Lettres françaises* (Paris), 15 January 1959.
Libuse, Konradova, "Putting on a Style," in *Films and Filming* (London), June 1961.
Philippe, P., "Le Baron de Crac rencontre le mage Zeman," in *Les Lettres françaises* (Paris), 26 April 1962.
Polt, Harriet, "The Czechoslovak Animated Film," in *Film Quarterly* (Berkeley, California), Spring 1964.
Benesová, Marie, "Karel Zeman ce nouveau Méliès," in *Jeune Cinéma* (Paris), December-January 1964–65.
Hrbas, J., "Karel Zeman—Puvab chlapecké romantiky," in 3 parts, in *Film a Doba* (Prague), January, February, and March 1974.
Kliment, J., "Odpovědnost umělcova—odpovědnost k umělci," in *Film a Doba* (Prague), October 1974.
Boček, Jaroslav, "Zlínští po osvobozeni," in *Panorama* (Prague), no. 3, 1978.
Benešová, M., "Zápas o tvar," in *Film a Doba* (Prague), December 1980.
Film a Doba (Prague), November 1985.
CinémAction (Conde-sur-Noireau), no. 51, April 1989.
Obituary in *EPD Film* (Frankfurt), vol. 6, no. 5, May 1989.
Film a Doba (Prague), July 1989.
Film a Doba (Prague), August 1989.
Monsterscene (Lombard), Summer/Fall 1995.

*   *   *

After 1945 Karel Zeman, Hermína Týlová's assistant, began independent work with a piece promoting recycling, *Podkova Pro štěsti (A Horseshoe for Luck)*. Everyone in the studio was surprised at the positive response. The main animated character in the film, Mr. Prokouk, a sort of indifferent citizen with petty bourgeois traits, enjoyed tremendous popularity. Thus there emerged over the course of two years a series of five cartoons that responded to the needs of the time: nimble, tendentious grotesques with rapid-fire gags and Mr. Prokouk in the leading role. Zeman conceived the theme and wrote the script, and worked as graphic artist, animator, and director. In complete contrast to these cartoons, he then hastily produced a remarkable piece, a cinematic poem devoted to the work of Czech glass-makers in which he brought to life the fragile beauty of figures of blown glass. *Inspirace (Inspiration)* possesses the beauty of a perfect work of art and is one of the pinnacles of his career. Here, Zeman demonstrated great technical resourcefulness and an ability to experiment. The folk tale *Poklad Ptačího ostrova (The Treasure of Bird Island)*, an evening-long animated film with a combination of flat and three-dimensional figures and an artistic form inspired by Persian miniatures, was intended for children. Also made for children was his next film, *Cesta do pravěku (A Journey into Primeval Times)*. This is the story of four boys sailing against the current of time and encountering on their journey the natural world of past geological eras. The film's creative form gives it a special place: it is a popular science film, a scientific fantasy film, and combines animation, special effects, and live-action. Here again, Zeman showed his abilities as an experimenter.

While in *Cesta do pravěku* Zeman attempted to reconstruct a world that once existed, in his work *Vynález zkázy (An Invention for Destruction)*, based on Jules Verne's novel *Face au drapeau*, he created a new world inspired by the illustrations that accompanied the first editions of Verne's novels. With considerable grace, Zeman attained in this film the magic of the old Verne stories, "that enchantment from naiveté, poetry, and geniality of Verne's novels that anticipated technical discoveries at the end of the century" (M. Benešová). In a perfect form he joined the techniques of the cartoon, animated, and live-action film and created a film in which actor, cartoon figure, structure, and scenery are a part of the graphic style. With this work Zeman revived and refined the forgotten Méliès mode of filmmaking and created his own style—that of the graphic special-effects film. Encouraged by the film's worldwide success, Zeman made another in the same style. This time he chose Bürger's novel *Baron Prášil (Baron Münchhausen)*. Here, too, the graphic design is based on the original illustrations for the novel. Unlike its predecessor, however, this film was devoted more to the acting, while the graphic aspect was enriched through the emotive use of color. In subsequent films of this tendency the live-action component began to predominate.

In the 1970s he returned to the animated film and experimented with three-dimensional technique. He filmed folk tales for children. Along with Jiří Trnka and Hermína Týlová, Karel Zeman was the co-creator of the Czech animated film. The outstanding features of his talent were technical ingenuity and an experimental searching, which led him to the graphic special-effects film. His supreme work *Vynález zkázy (An Invention for Destruction)* was a unique landmark of world cinematography, which revived and refined the forgotten Méliès tradition.

—Vladimír Opěla

ZIMMER, Hans

Composer. **Nationality:** German. **Born:** Hans Florian Zimmer in Frankfurt, Germany, 12 September 1957; moved to London, 1971. **Education:** Attended high school in London; no formal music education. **Family:** Married to Suzanne Zimmer; two children. **Career:** Composed advertising jingles, 1973–75; wrote songs for rock bands The Buggles, Tangerine Dream, and Ultravox; rock musician and composer, 1970s and 1980s; first film soundtrack, 1982; worked

Hans Zimmer

as assistant to and established Lillie Yard Studio with Stanley Myers, 1982; first solo film score, 1988; scored several television series, including *Millenium*, 1992, *Space Rangers*, 1993, *The Critic*, 1994, and *High Incident*, 1996; established Media Ventures, 1992; head of the music department at DreamWorks SKG, 1997. **Awards:** Academy Award for Best Music, Original Score, Grammy Award for Best Instrumental Arrangement with Accompanying Vocals, and Golden Globe for Best Original Score-Motion Picture, for *The Lion King*, 1994; Tony Award for Best Original Score for Broadway, for *The Lion King*, 1995; Grammy Award for Best Instrumental Composition Written for a Motion Picture or for Television, for *Crimson Tide*, 1996; BMI Award for lifetime achievement, 1996; Glaubber Award for Best Original Score-Comedy or Musical (Brazil), for *As Good As It Gets*, 1998; Golden Satellite Award for Best Motion Picture Score, for *The Thin Red Line*, 1999. **Agent:** Gorfaine-Schwartz Agency, 3301 Barham Blvd., Suite 301, Los Angeles, CA 90068, U.S.A.

Films as Composer:

1982   *Moonlighting* (Skolimowski) (with Stanley Myers)
1984   *Histoire d'O: Chapitre 2 (Story of O, Part II)* (Rochat) (with Myers); *Success Is the Best Revenge* (Skolimowski) (with Myers)

1985 *Insignificance* (Roeg) (with Myers); *Wild Horses* (Lowry— for TV) (with Myers)

1986 *Separate Vacations* (Anderson) (with Myers)

1987 *Comeback* (Ambrose—for TV); *Terminal Exposure* (Mastorakis); *The Wind* (Mastorakis)

1988 *A World Apart* (Menges); *Twister* (Almereyda); *Burning Secret* (Birkin); *The Fruit Machine* (*Wonderland*) (Saville); *Nature of the Beast* (with Myers); *Paperhouse* (Rose); *Rain Man* (Levinson) (+ musical score); *Spies Inc.* (Thomas); *Taffin* (Megahy)

1989 *Black Rain* (Scott); *Dark Obsession* (*Diamond Skulls*) (Broomfield); *Driving Miss Daisy* (Beresford); *Prisoners of Rio* (*Wiezien Rio*) (Majewski); *First Born* (miniseries—for TV)

1990 *Bird on a Wire* (Badham); *Chicago Joe and the Showgirl* (Rose); *Days of Thunder* (Scott); *Fools of Fortune* (O'Connor); *Green Card* (Weir); *Pacific Heights* (Schlesinger); *To the Moon, Alice* (Nelson—for TV) (as Hans Florian Zimmer); *Nightmare at Noon* (Mastorakis)

1991 *Regarding Henry* (Nichols); *Backdraft* (Howard); *K2* (European version) (Roddam); *Thelma & Louise* (Scott)

1992 *A League of Their Own* (Marshall); *Power of One* (Avildsen); *Radio Flyer* (Donner); *Where Sleeping Dogs Lie* (Finch); *Toys* (Levinson)

1993 *Calendar Girl* (Whitesell); *Point of No Return* (Badham); *Cool Runnings* (Turteltaub); *True Romance* (Scott); *The House of the Spirits* (August); *Younger and Younger* (Adlon)

1994 *Renaissance Man* (Marshall); *I'll Do Anything* (Brooks); *Drop Zone* (Badham); *The Lion King* (Allers and Minkoff); *Africa: The Serengeti* (Casey)

1995 *Beyond Rangoon* (Boorman); *Crimson Tide* (Scott); *Nine Months* (Columbus); *Something to Talk About* (Hallstrom); *Two Deaths* (Roeg); *The Preacher's Wife* (Marshall)

1996 *The Whole Wide World* (Ireland); *The Fan* (Scott); *Broken Arrow* (Woo); *The Rock* (Bay) (+ score arranger); *Muppet Treasure Island* (Henson)

1997 *The Peacemaker* (Leder); *Scream 2* (Craven); *Fräulein Smillas Gespür für Schnee* (*Smilla's Sense of Snow*) (August); *As Good As It Gets* (Brooks) (+ music arranger and song producer [uncredited])

1998 *The Last Days* (Moll); *The Prince of Egypt* (Chapman, Hickman, others) (+ lyricist); *The Thin Red Line* (Malick)

1999 *El Candidato* (for TV); *Chill Factor* (Johnson)

2000 *The Road to El Dorado* (Bergeron, Finn, others); *Gladiator* (Scott); *Mission Impossible 2* (Woo)

2001 *Hannibal*; *Pearl Harbor*

Other Films:

1982 *Eureka* (Roeg) (additional composer)

1985 *My Beautiful Laundrette* (Frears) (music producer)

1987 *The Last Emperor* (Bertolucci) (score producer)

1991 *White Fang* (Kleiser) (additional music)

1993 *Sniper* (Llosa) (additional music)

1994 *Monkey Trouble* (Amurri) (additional music)

1996 *White Squall* (Scott) (music producer)

1997 *The Borrowers* (Hewitt) (score producer); *Fame L.A.* (Green, Miller, others—for TV) (score producer); *Face/Off* (Woo) (score producer)

1998 *Endurance* (Greenspan and Woodhead) (music producer); *With Friends Like These. . .* (music producer); *Antz* (Darnell, Gutterman, others) (executive music producer)

Publications

On ZIMMER: books—

Karlin, Fred, *Listening to Movies: The Film Lover's Guide to Film Music*, New York, 1994.

Marill, Alvin H., *Keeping Score: Film and Television Music, 1988–1997*, Landham, Maryland, 1998.

On ZIMMER: articles—

Marans, Michael, ''Hans Zimmer,'' in *Keyboard*. vol. 15, no. 6, June 1989.

Widders-Ellis, ''A World View: Under the Gun with *Days of Thunder*,'' in *Keyboard*, vol. 16, June 1990.

Kimble, Christopher, ''Cameos: Composer Hans Zimmer,'' in *Premiere*, vol. 4, no. 9, May 1991.

Reece, D. Menken, ''Zimmer Honored at BMI Film, TV Awards,'' in *Billboard*, 8 June 1996.

Burlingame, Jon, ''They Shoot, He Scores,'' in *Los Angeles Times*, 15 December 1998.

Essay in Craggs, Stewart A., *Soundtracks: An International Dictionary of Composers for Film*, Aldershot, England, and Brookfield, Vermont, 1998.

Black, Edwin, ''Interview with Hans Zimmer,'' in *Film Score Monthly: The Online Magazine of motion Picture and Television Music Appreciation*, http://www.filmscoremonthly.com/features/zimmer.asp, March 2000.

''Hans Zimmer Biography,'' http://www.mediaventures.com/htmls/zimmer_bs.html, March 2000.

''Hans Zimmer,'' http://www.german-way.com/cinema/zimmer.html, June 2000.

''The Hans Zimmer Worship Page,'' http://www.lionking.org/~zimmer, June 2000.

* * *

Hans Zimmer is a pioneer in computer technology, digital synthesizers, and electronic keyboards. His successful integration of digital electronics with traditional orchestral music can be heard in over 65 popular, successful, and critically acclaimed films and television shows. Despite his lack of formal training, Zimmer currently ranks among the highest paid and most fiercely sought-after Hollywood composers. His scores range from quiet and sentimental to loud and pulse-raising. In *Film Score Monthly*, Zimmer described himself as a ''loose cannon—all over the place. I can do action movies and romantic comedies. And I'm a good collaborator—which means I'm cantankerous and opinionated. I compose from a point of view. Point of view is the most important thing to have, and it doesn't necessarily have to be the director's point of view.'' Zimmer's versatile sampling style and emotional attunement to the film themes contribute to his ongoing success and market appeal. His mixing of genres extends to his music education, which he describes as growing up with classical music, but reaching adolescence in rock and roll.

Zimmer has been playing piano since the age of three. By the time he was six, he knew he wanted to be a composer. His family moved all over Europe until he was 14, when they settled in London. He began his musical career in London during his late teens, composing advertising jingles. In the 1970s, he stepped onto the rock music scene and reached success with the hit song, "Video Killed the Radio Star" (1979); he also made an album entitled *The Age of Plastic* for the band The Buggles and promoted the use of computers live on stage with the groups Tangerine Dream and Ultravox before turning to film scores.

He ventured into film soundtracks in the 1980s with electronic effects for Jerzy Skolimowski's *Moonlighting* (1982). With the film composer Stanley Myers (best known for *The Deerhunter*), Zimmer began to fuse two musical forms, electronic and classical. Together they created Lillie Yard Studio in London to advance digital music technology. Collaborating with Myers, Zimmer created scores for *Success Is The Best Revenge* (1984) and Nicholas Roeg's *Insignificance* (1985). In the mid-1980s, Zimmer produced the score for Stephen Frear's quirky art-house film, *My Beautiful Laundrette* (1985). He worked with David Byrne and Ryiuichi Sakamoto to produce the music for Bertolucci's *The Last Emperor* (1987). He also composed the music for the Faye Dunaway and Klaus Maria Brandauer feature, *Burning Secret* (1988). Zimmer clearly was influenced by his apprenticeship with Myers; he has founded his own company, Media Ventures, in the early 1990s to assist fledgling talent in the film music industry.

Zimmer went solo with his haunting tribal anthems for an epic, groundbreaking film about the historic struggle in South Africa, *A World Apart* (1988). His music quickly caught Hollywood's attention: within the next year, he received Oscar nominations for the scores of *Rain Man* (1988) and *Driving Miss Daisy* (1989). Zimmer credits his break into Hollywood to Barry Levinson: "When you are European wanting to break into the Hollywood film business you don't stand a chance. But Barry Levinson gave me a shot in *Rain Man*, and that was very gracious and courageous."

The African-inspired rhythms of Disney's blockbuster, *The Lion King* (1994), for which he was music supervisor, song arranger, and producer, earned Zimmer his only Academy Award to date. It took him took about three and a half weeks to compose the music. *The Lion King* also won the Golden Globe, Chicago Film Critics Award, two Grammys, American Music Award for Best Album of the Year, and a Tony nomination for Best Original Score for *The Lion King on Broadway*. He received a Grammy for his *Crimson Tide* (1995) soundtrack, which features a majestic symphonic score and a large choir, as well as powerful 3-D sound effects that enhance the on-screen action and suspense. In the early 1990s, Zimmer also worked on compelling and invigorating music/scores for *Bird on a Wire*, John Schlesinger's suspenseful *Pacific Heights*, and *Days of Thunder*, starring Tom Cruise. His synthesizing can be heard in the background of *Regarding Henry* and Peter Weir's *Green Card*. Zimmer's dreamy, evocative, and emotional music enhances Ridley Scott's *Thelma and Louise* (1991) and Richard Donner's poignant *Radio Flyer* (1992). Penny Marshall's *A League of Their Own*, a film about the first female baseball league, starring Geena Davis, Tom Hanks, and Madonna also features a score by Zimmer. Zimmer has also ventured into the light and emotional, penning the infectious score for Barry Levingson's *Toys* (1992) starring Robin Williams, and *Muppet Treasure Island* (1996).

Zimmer has also placed his mark on films outside of Hollywood. Zimmer composed the score for his second South African film, *The Power of One*, directed by John Avildsen in 1992. He has worked with director Percy Adlon on *Younger and Younger* (1993), and with Billie August on *Smilla's Sense of Snow* (1997).

Zimmer was been frequently recognized for his scores, earning Oscar nominations for *The Preacher's Wife* (1996) and *As Good As It Gets* (1997). For the latter he lost out to the soundtrack for the blockbuster adventure *Titanic*. Zimmer was twice nominated in 1999 for Best Score Oscars for Terrence Malick's phenomenal *The Thin Red Line* (1998) and Disney's animated telling of the Ten Commandments, *The Prince of Egypt* (1998), for which he also received a Golden Globe nomination. The elegiac, lyrical music in *Thin Red Line* combines simple American hymns, indigenous music from the Solomon Islands, orchestral compositions with rich bass and cello lines, and a complete absence of the usual militaristic flourishes of brass, marching rhythms, and fanfares to create a tone poem that works magic with Malick's somber portrayal of the losses and anguish of war.

In 1997 Zimmer became head of the music department at DreamWorks SKG. Of the music he has composed, Zimmer claims to be proudest of *A World Apart*, *Driving Miss Daisy* and *Crimson Tide*.

—Jill Gillespie

ZSIGMOND, Vilmos

Cinematographer. **Nationality:** Hungarian. **Born:** Szeged, 16 June 1930; credited as William Zsigmond on early films. **Education:** Attended Budapest Film School, graduated 1956. **Career:** 1956—escaped to Austria during Hungarian Revolution with the cinematographer Laszlo Kovacs, then to the United States, 1957; worked as still photographer, laboratory technician, and camera assistant; 1963—first film as cinematographer; TV work includes *The Protectors* series, 1969–70, and the mini-series *Flesh and Blood*, 1979. **Awards:** Academy Award, for *Close Encounters of the Third Kind*, 1977; British Academy Award, for *The Deer Hunter*, 1978.

Films as Cinematographer:

1957 *Hungarn in Flammen* (*Revolt in Hungary*) (Erdelyi—doc) (co)
1963 *The Sadist* (*Profile of Terror*) (James Landis); *Living between Two Worlds* (Johnson)
1964 *What's up Front* (Wehling); *The Time Travelers* (Melchior); *The Incredibly Strange Creatures Who Stopped Living and Became Crazy Mixed-Up Zombies!!?* (Steckler) (co)
1965 *Rat Fink* (*My Soul Runs Naked*) (James Landis); *The Nasty Rabbit* (*Spies A-Go-Go*) (James Landis); *Deadwood '76* (James Landis); *Tales of a Salesman* (Russell); *A Hot Summer Game* (Bruner); *Psycho A-Go-Go!* (Adamson—revised version, *The Fiend with the Electronic Brain*)
1966 *Road to Nashville* (Zens)
1967 *Mondo Mod* (Perry—doc) (co)

Vilmos Zsigmond

1968   *The Name of the Game Is Kill!* (*The Female Trap*) (Hellstrom);
        Jennie, Wife/Child (James Landis and Cohen)
1969   *The Monitors* (Shea); *Hot Rod Action* (McCabe); *Five Bloody
        Graves* (*Gun Riders*) (Adamson); *Futz!* (O'Horgan); *The
        Picasso Summer* (Bourguignon)
1970   *Horror of the Blood Monsters* (*Vampire Men of the Lost
        Planet*) (Adamson) (co)
1971   *Red Sky at Morning* (Goldstone); *The Ski Bum* (Clark);
        McCabe and Mrs. Miller (Altman); *The Hired Hand* (Fonda)
1972   *Images* (Altman); ***Deliverance*** (Boorman)
1973   *The Long Goodbye* (Altman); *Scarecrow* (Schatzberg); *Cin-
        derella Liberty* (Rydell)
1974   *The Sugarland Express* (Spielberg); *The Girl from Petrovka*
        (Miller)
1976   *Sweet Revenge* (Schatzberg); *Obsession* (De Palma)
1977   ***Close Encounters of the Third Kind*** (Spielberg) (co)
1978   *The Last Waltz* (Scorsese) (co); *The Rose* (Rydell); ***The Deer
        Hunter*** (Cimino)
1979   *Winter Kills* (Richert)
1980   *Heaven's Gate* (Cimino)
1981   *Blow Out* (De Palma)

1982   *Jinxed* (Siegel); *The Border* (Richardson) (co)
1983   *Table for Five* (Lieberman)
1984   *The River* (Rydell); *No Small Affair* (Schatzberg)
1985   *Real Genius* (Coolidge)
1987   *The Witches of Eastwick* (Miller)
1988   *Journey to Spirit Island* (L. Pal)
1989   *Fat Man and Little Boy* (Joffé)
1990   *The Two Jakes* (Nicholson); *The Bonfire of the Vanities*
        (De Palma)
1993   *Sliver* (Noyce)
1994   *Maverick* (R. Donner); *Intersection* (Rydell)
1995   *The Crossing Guard* (S. Penn); *Assassins* (R. Donner)
1996   *The Ghost and the Darkness* (Hopkins)
1998   *Illegal Music* (Zidel); *Playing by Heart* (Carroll)
1999   *The Argument* (Cammell)

Films as Director:

1992   *The Long Shadow*

Publications

By ZSIGMOND: articles—

American Cinematographer (Hollywood), June 1974.
Dialogue on Film (Beverly Hills, California), July 1974.
Dialogue on Film (Beverly Hills, California), October 1974.
Film Heritage (Dayton, Ohio), Spring 1977.
American Cinematographer (Hollywood), January 1978.
On *The Deer Hunter* in *American Cinematographer* (Hollywood), October 1978.
American Film (Washington, D.C.), June 1979.
On *Heaven's Gate* in *American Cinematographer* (Hollywood), November 1980.
On *Heaven's Gate* in *Millimeter* (New York), January 1981.
Films and Filming (London), September 1982.
In *Masters of Light: Conversations with Contemporary Cinematographers*, by Dennis Schaefer and Larry Salvato, Berkeley, California, 1984.
American Cinematographer (Hollywood), June 1987.
Filmkultura (Budapest), vol. 25, no. 6, 1989.
American Cinematographer (Hollywood), November 1989.
American Cinematographer (Hollywood), April 1990.
American Cinematographer (Hollywood), November 1990.
American Film (Washington, D.C.), November 1990.
American Cinematographer (Hollywood), November 1991.

On ZSIGMOND: articles—

Lightman, Herb A., on *Deliverance* in *American Cinematographer* (Hollywood), August 1971.
Focus on Film (London), Autumn 1972, corrections in no. 13, 1973.
Lipnick, Edward, on *The Long Goodbye* in *American Cinematographer* (Hollywood), March 1973.
Gosnold, H. G., in *American Cinematographer* (Hollywood), March 1977.
Take One (Montreal), no. 2, 1978.
American Cinematographer (Hollywood), May 1978.
Carcassonne, P., and J. Fieschi, in *Cinématographe* (Paris), March 1979.
American Cinematographer (Hollywood), May 1979.
Lyman, D., in *Filmmakers Monthly* (Ward Hill, Massachusetts), June 1979.
Vallely, J., in *Rolling Stone* (New York), 21 February 1980.
Films and Filming (London), May 1980.
McCarthy, T., in *Film Comment* (New York), March/April 1984.
Patterson, Richard, in *American Cinematographer* (Hollywood), November 1984.
Betro, A., ''Reaching Out to Europe,'' in *American Cinematographer* (Hollywood), June 1992.
Lueker, Rob, ''At the Master's Feet,'' in *American Cinematographer* (Hollywood), February 1996.
Williams, D. E., ''Night of the Hunters,'' in *American Cinematographer* (Hollywood), November 1996.

*　　*　　*

Arriving in the United States in 1956 after escaping from Hungary with fellow cameraman and sometime collaborator Laszlo Kovacs, Vilmos Zsigmond toiled in the low-budget exploitation field throughout the 1960s, and then emerged as a major director of photography in the 1970s and 1980s, working with the directors Steven Spielberg, Brian De Palma, Martin Scorsese, Michael Cimino, Jerry Schatzberg, John Boorman, Mark Rydell and, most often, Robert Altman. Like Kovacs, Zsigmond established himself with a few intriguing lower-case credits, making his debut—credited as William Zsigmond—as a cinematographer on *The Sadist*, a high-energy black-and-white psycho picture based on the incident that inspired *Badlands*. Zsigmond went on to work with the incredibly strange Ray Dennis Steckler on *The Incredibly Strange Creatures Who Stopped Living and Became Crazy Mixed-Up Zombies!!?* which has moments so awful they could pass for surreal. After such oddities as the documentary *Mondo Mod*, the psychotic desert picture *The Name of the Game Is Kill!*, the improvisational science-fiction comedy *The Monitors*, and the off-Broadway adaption *Futz!*, Zsigmond fell in with Al Adamson—a poverty-stricken auteur who made Ray Dennis Steckler look talented—for *Five Bloody Graves* and *Horror of the Blood Monsters*, the former a horror Western narrated by Death, the latter a patchwork of tinted Filipino science-fiction footage with John Carradine explaining the plot.

Something about the deserts of *The Sadist*, *The Name of the Game Is Kill!*, and *Five Bloody Graves* must have registered, for Zsigmond's breakthrough from the blood monsters and psycho-a-go-go girls came with a series of Western or Western-flavored movies in 1970, commencing with James Goldstone's coming-of-age drama set in New Mexico during World War II, *Red Sky at Morning* and taking in Peter Fonda's rugged, ragged ''acid Western'' *The Hired Hand*. The most important of these films was Altman's *McCabe and Mrs. Miller*, in which Zsigmond captured the magic of the muddy small town and caught Altman's stranded characters in the uncharacteristic snowy wastes of the film's western Canada setting. For Altman, Zsigmond then tackled the seductive but hollow post-Chandler Los Angeles of *The Long Goodbye*, which also includes a side-trip to a lushly corrupt Mexico; the pristine Scots autumn backdrop to Susannah York's nervous breakdown in *Images*; and the teeming canvas of the over-populated but glowing *A Wedding*. Meanwhile, he also established relationships with Steven Spielberg, transferring from the Altmanesque road movieness of *The Sugarland Express* to the Oscar-winning lightshow of *Close Encounters of the Third Kind*; Jerry Schatzberg, also on the road in *Scarecrow* and homing in for the miscalculated *Sweet Revenge* and *No Small Affair*; Mark Rydell, from the grubby *Cinderella Liberty* through the showbiz sleaze of *The Rose* to the nouveau Western of *The River*; Brian De Palma, at his iciest and most intriguingly Hitchcock-cum-Antonioniesque in *Obsession* and *Blow Out* (prompting Zsigmond to far more whirling effects than Spielberg's aliens did); and Michael Cimino, stepping from the un-Altmanesque ethnic marriages and rat-trap horrors of *The Deer Hunter* to the expansive western crowds and massacres of *Heaven's Gate*. That a career could encompass *Five Bloody Graves* and *Heaven's Gate* is bizarre enough, but even stranger is the continuity between the cheap disaster and the super-produced disaster, both of which are marked by Zsigmond's daring look. Daring, because it can sometimes seem pretty—pretty enough to win an Oscar—but more often gets accused of being muddy, fuzzy, foggy, and indistinct, even ugly. It could be argued, however, that Zsigmond's contribution to the Western and the western-set road movie—including, besides the films cited above, Tony Richardson's draggy *The Border* and John Boorman's backwoods *Deliverance*—was crucial to the evolution, even the death, of the form in the 1970s and 1980s, imposing a countercultural hairiness on the straight-arrow Americanism of the genre. Certainly, as a Hungarian, Zsigmond has been involved in a succession of almost archetypal American movies—the Eastern European heritage touched on only in *The Deer Hunter* and *The Girl from Petrovka*—that have taken him into the most prized American genre forms—horror, Western, private eye, family weepie (*Table for Five*), rock 'n' roll concert (*The Last Waltz*)—and even, in *Winter Kills*, near the White House. He has a sometimes-exercised gift for fantasy that dates back to the *Incredibly Strange Creatures* days and is undaunted by the special effects of *Close Encounters* or *The Witches of Eastwick*. He has been somewhat in eclipse in the late 1980s and 1990s, but he is well-enough established as a proficient craftsman as well as an unimpeachable artist, to still land the plum assignments. His penchant for being attached to famous disasters persists with *The Bonfire o the Vanities*, for which De Palma steered Zsigmond through a memorably redundant tour-de-force opening shot. He has turned out a few entirely anonymous but slick jobs (*Sliver*, *Maverick*, and *Assassins*) between ambitious oddments (*Fat Man and Little Boy* and *The Crossing Guard*). In the late 1990s, Zsigmond continued to turn in creditable efforts. The pleasant clarity of his images and lighting in *Playing by Heart* provide a warm and reassuring setting for the light melodrama and comedy of this updated woman's picture. *The Ghost and the Darkness* called for a substantially different approach. This true story of man-eating African lions demanded just the combination of *National Geographic* photographic painting and expressionistic stylization that Zsigmond employs. As in an unfortunately large number of the projects he has worked on in his career, his cinematography is the most successfully conceived and executed element in an otherwise very ordinary and forgettable production.

—Kim Newman, updated by R. Barton Palmer

Adolph Zukor

ZUKOR, Adolph

Producer. **Nationality:** Hungarian-American. **Born:** Risce, Hungary, 7 January 1873, emigrated to the United States, 1889. **Family:** Married Lottie Kaufman. **Career:** Furrier in Chicago; 1903—opened a string of penny arcades with partner Marcus Loew; 1905—treasurer of extensive Loew's theatre chain; 1912—distributor of European productions; formed own production and distribution company, Famous Players; 1916—joined with the Jesse Lasky Feature Play Company; president; the company renamed Paramount; 1936—replaced by Barney Balaban; remained as chairman of the board until his death. **Award:** Special Academy Award, 1948. **Died:** In Los Angeles, California, 10 June 1976.

Films as Producer/Executive Producer:

1912 *Queen Elizabeth* (Desfontaines); *The Count of Monte Cristo* (Porter)

1913 *A Good Little Devil* (Porter); *The Man from Mexico*; *Charlie Fadden*; *The Prisoner of Zenda* (Porter)

1914 *The Squaw Man* (DeMille)

1915 *Peer Gynt* (Apfel); *Zaza* (Ford); *The Cheat* (DeMille); *Carmen* (DeMille); *Madame Butterfly* (Olcott)

1916 *Miss George Washington* (Dawley); *Oliver Twist* (Twist)

1917 *Seventeen*; *Great Expectations* (Vignola); *Tom Sawyer* (Taylor); *A Modern Musketeer* (Dwan); *The Bluebird* (Tourneur); *Barbary Sheep* (Tourneur)

1918 *The Doll's House* (Tourneur); *Uncle Tom's Cabin* (Dawley); *Battling Jane* (Clifton); *Old Wives for New* (DeMille); *The Greatest Thing in Life* (Griffith); *Come on In*

1919 *My Cousin* (José); *String Beans* (Schertzinger); *Pettigrew's Girl* (Melford); *The Knickerbocker Buckaroo* (Parker); *Valley of the Giants* (Cruze); *The Miracle Man* (Tucker); *23 1/2 Hours Leave* (King); *The Admirable Crichton (Male and Female)* (DeMille); *The Misleading Widow* (Robertson)

1920 *Remodelling Her Husband*; *Dr. Jekyll and Mr. Hyde* (Robertson); *Humoresque* (Borzage); *Deception (Anna Boleyn)* (Lubitsch); *Miss Lulu Bett* (W. De Mille); *Broadway Jones Der Silberkoenig (The Silver King)*

1921 *The Gilded Lily* (Leonard); *The Great Moment* (Wood); *The Affairs of Anatol* (DeMille); *Fool's Paradise* (DeMille)

1922 *The Old Homestead* (Cruze); *The Sheik* (Melford); *Three Live Ghosts* (Fitzmaurice); *The Young Rajah* (Rosen); *Manslaughter* (DeMille); *Belladonna*

1923 *The Covered Wagon* (Cruze); *Why Worry?* (Taylor); *Safety Last* (Taylor)

1924 *Forbidden Paradise* (Lubitsch); *Peter Pan* (Brenon); *Monsieur Beaucaire* (Olcott); *Girl Shy* (Newmeyer); *Manhandled* (Dwan); *Wanderer of the Wasteland* (Willat); *Grass* (Schoedsack); *The Ten Commandments* (DeMille); *Hot Water* (Newmeyer and Taylor); *A Sainted Devil* (Henabery)

1925 *Madame Sans-Gêne* (Perret); *The Freshman* (Newmeyer); *Cobra* (Henabery)

1926 *Beau Geste* (Brenon); *The Kid Brother* (Wilde); *Aloma of the South Seas*

1927   *For Heaven's Sake* (Taylor); *Underworld* (von Sternberg)
1928   *The Last Command* (von Sternberg); *The Vanishing Race* (Seitz); *Gentlemen Prefer Blondes* (St. Clair); *Speedy* (Wilde); *Way of All Flesh* (Fleming); *Chang* (Cooper); *Gentlemen of the Press* (Webb); *Beau Sabreur* (Waters); *The Patriot* (Lubitsch)
1929   *College Days* (Wood); *The Wedding March* (von Stroheim); *Innocents of Paris* (Wallace); *Wings* (Wellman); *The Cocoanuts* (Florey and Santley); *The Mysterious Dr. Fu Manchu* (Lee); *Legion of the Condemned* (Wellman)
1930   *Welcome Danger* (Bruckman); *Love Parade* (Lubitsch); *The Mighty* (Cromwell); *The Four Feathers* (Mendes); *The Vagabond King* (Berger); *The Virginian* (Fleming); *The Big Pond* (Henley); *Monte Carlo* (Lubitsch); *Morocco* (von Sternberg); *Playboy of Paris* (Berger)
1931   *The Royal Family of Broadway* (*Theatre Royal*) (Cukor); *Sarah and Son* (Arzner); *Feet First* (Bruckman); *The Texan* (Cromwell); *Dishonoured* (von Sternberg); *Fighting Caravans* (Brower and Burton); *City Streets* (Mamoulian); *Skippy* (Taurog); *Tarnished Lady* (Cukor); *Paramount on Parade* (Arzner, Brower, Goulding, Heerman, Knopf, Lee, Lubitsch, Mendes, Schertzinger, Sutherland, and Tuttle); *Anybody's Woman* (Arzner); *The Smiling Lieutenant* (Lubitsch); *Grumpy* (Cukor and Gardner)
1932   *Huckleberry Finn* (Taurog); *Secrets of a Secretary* (Abbott); *Tomorrow and Tomorrow* (Wallace); *Service for Ladies* (*Reserved for Ladies*) (A. Korda); *Once a Lady* (McClintic); *I Take This Woman* (Gering and Vorkapitch); *Ladies of the Big House* (Gering); **Dr. Jekyll and Mr. Hyde** (Mamoulian); *Ladies' Man* (Mendes); *Devil and the Deep* (Gering); *Shanghai Express* (von Sternberg); *The Miracle Man* (McLeod); *Merrily We Go to Hell* (Arzner); *Dancers in the Dark* (Burton); *The Strange Case of Clara Dean* (Gasnier and Marcin);
1933   *One Hour with You* (Cukor and Lubitsch); *Forgotten Commandments* (Gasnier and Schoor); *Sinners in the Sun* (Hall); *The Man from Yesterday* (Viertel); *Blonde Venus* (von Sternberg); *Horse Feathers* (McLeod); *The Night of June 13* (Roberts); *Love Me Tonight* (Mamoulian); *Trouble in Paradise* (Lubitsch); *Night after Night* (Mayo); *If I Had a Million* (Lubitsch, Taurog, Roberts, McLeod, Cruze, Seiter and Humberstone); *Madame Butterfly* (Gering); *Tonight Is Ours* (Walker); **She Done Him Wrong** (Sherman); *No Man of Her Own* (Ruggles); *The Sign of the Cross* (DeMille); *A Farewell to Arms* (Vidor); *Jennie Gerhardt* (Gering); *Alice in Wonderland* (McLeod)
1934   *Song of Songs* (Mamoulian); *This Day and Age* (DeMille); *One Sunday Afternoon* (Roberts); *The Way to Love* (Taurog); *Three Cornered Moon* (Nugent); *I'm No Angel* (Ruggles); *Tillie and Gus* (Martin); *White Woman* (Walker); **Duck Soup** (McCarey); *Design for Living* (Lubitsch); *Six of a Kind* (McCarey); *Four Frightened People* (DeMille); *Search for Beauty* (Kenton); *Bolero* (Ruggles); *The Scarlet Empress* (von Sternberg); *Death Takes a Holiday* (Leisen); *Murder at the Vanities* (Leisen); *Cleopatra* (DeMille)
1935   *Belle of the Nineties* (McCarey); *Mrs. Wiggs of the Cabbage Patch* (Taurog); *The Old-Fashioned Way* (Beaudine); *Crime without Passion* (Hecht and MacArthur); *Now and Forever* (Hathaway); *Limehouse Blues* (*East End Chant*) (Hall); *It's a Gift* (McLeod); *The Pursuit of Happiness* (Hall); *Behold*

My Wife (Leisen); *Father Brown—Detective* (Hamer); *Here Is My Heart* (Tuttle); *The Lives of a Bengal Lancer* (Hathaway); *The Gilded Lily* (Ruggles); *The Milky Way* (McCarey); *Wings in the Dark* (Flood); *Rumba* (Gering); *Ruggles of Red Gap* (McCarey); *Mississippi* (Sutherland); *Four Hours to Kill* (Leisen); *The Devil Is a Woman* (von Sternberg); *The Scoundrel* (Hecht and MacArthur); *Goin' to Town* (Hall)

Publications

By ZUKOR: book—

The Public Is Never Wrong, 1953.

On ZUKOR: books—

Edmonds, I.D., and Raiko Mimura, *Paramount Pictures and the People Who Made Them*, New York, 1980.
Eames, John Douglas, *The Paramount Story*, London, 1985.

On ZUKOR: articles—

Motion Picture Herald, vol. 193, no. 1, 3 October 1953.
French, Philip, in *The Movie Moguls*, London, 1969.
Sight and Sound (London), vol. 42, no. 1, Winter 1972–73.
Obituary in *Hollywood Reporter*, vol. 241, no. 44, 11 June 1976.
Films in Review (New York), vol. 38, no. 10, October 1987.
Dyer MacCann, Richard, in *The First Tycoons*, London, 1987.
Gabler, Neal, in *An Empire of Their Own: How the Jews Invented Hollywood*, New York, 1988.
Luft, H. G., "Hommage à Adolph Zukor," in *Filmkunst*, no. 128, 1990.
Stephens, C., "The Legacy of Adolph Zukor," in *Variety's On Production* (Los Angeles), no. 3, 1996.

*   *   *

By 1920 Hollywood had risen to define the cinema in the United States as well as throughout the world. Stars like Charlie Chaplin and Mary Pickford were among the most famous people of their era. The American cinema dominated world filmmaking and distribution as no other popular cultural force had ever done. And no executive was more responsible for the creation of Hollywood than Adolph Zukor.

Hollywood commenced with the failure of the Motion Picture Patents Company Trust. A number of independent production companies rose to challenge the Trust, but quickly Adolph Zukor and his company, "Famous Players in Famous Plays," led the way by transforming basic business practices.

He differentiated his company's products. Gone were the days when film was sold by the foot; for Zukor each "photoplay" became a unique product, heavily advertised by emphasizing popular stories and then developing movie stars to act in them. Zukor had his studio develop a system by which to regularly and efficiently manufacture feature-length films. Soon this method became known as the Hollywood system of production.

This transformation began in 1912 when Zukor and his partners began to produce feature films including *The Count of Monte Cristo* starring James O'Neill, father of the famous playwright, *The Prisoner of Zenda* starring James Hackett, *Queen Elizabeth* starring Sarah

Bernhardt, and *Tess of the D'Urbervilles* starring Minnie Maddern Fiske. These early stars were drawn from the stage, but soon Zukor realized that he would have to create his own stars. He reached the ultimate early on with Mary Pickford, a Canadian-born vaudeville performer. We can best see "Little Mary's" rise to fame through her salary ascendancy: $1000 a week in 1914, $2000 per week in 1915, $10,000 per week in 1916; and a million dollars a year in 1917. Zukor willingly anted up such fabulous amounts because he knew the vast audiences Pickford drew at the box office.

It was Adolph Zukor and his Famous Players' Company which taught the world how to fully exploit the features of Pickford, Douglas Fairbanks, Gloria Swanson, Pauline Frederick, Blanche Sweet, and Norma and Constance Talmadge. He accomplished this through merger and acquisitions. In 1916 alone Zukor took over 12 smaller producers and formed Famous Players-Lasky Corporation. Partner Jesse Lasky became his studio boss. By 1921 Zukor had turned Famous Players-Lasky into the largest film production company in the world.

Zukor learned how to squeeze theater owners because he alone could deliver the biggest stars in Hollywood. Zukor's principle means of exploitation became "block booking." That is if a theater owner wanted to show the films of Pickford, he or she had to take motion pictures with less well known, up-and-coming Famous Players-Lasky stars. In turn, Famous Players-Lasky used these guaranteed bookings to test and develop new stars.

Soon enough theater owners caught on, and formed their own "booking cooperatives." In turn Zukor reacted, and in 1919 began to purchase theaters. He could not finance such a large set of takeovers simply with cash on hand and so became the first movie company to approach Wall Street bankers. Famous Players-Lasky borrowed $10 million through Wall Street's Kuhn, Loeb and became the first motion picture company listed on the New York Stock Exchange. Zukor, who had come to the United States penniless 30 years earlier, had hit the big time.

Nothing stopped him. By the mid-point of 1921 he owned 300 theaters. Four years later, he merged his theaters with Balaban & Katz, the most important and innovative theater chain in the United States, and renamed the enterprise Paramount, which up to then had been the name of his distribution arm. By 1931 Paramount's Publix theater circuit had become the largest in the world, double the size of its nearest competitor. Paramount Pictures produced many of the most popular films of the silent film era, from *The Covered Wagon* to *The Ten Commandments*, from *Beau Geste* to *Wings*. Zukor innovated a third major change in movie industry practice. It was not enough that the Hollywood companies simply control all the movie stars and studios. Their long-run economic security depended on the construction and maintenance of networks for national and international distribution. Once a feature film was made, the majority of its cost had been accumulated. It then cost relatively little to market it throughout the world. If somehow the producer could expand the territory to include greater and greater portions of the planet, the additional revenues overwhelmed any extra costs.

In 1914 Zukor began his assault on national distribution. W. W. Hodkinson had merged eleven regional distributors to create the Paramount distribution network. But Hodkinson had no steady supply of feature films, and thus sold out to Zukor. Quickly Zukor took over other national distributors and soon had a strangle hold on the marketplace for film distribution throughout the United States. Zukor then turned his attentions to world distribution. The First World War had curtailed distribution powers of rival European movie makers, and into that gap stepped Zukor. By the end of hostilities, he had Paramount distributing Famous Players-Lasky films around the world. During the 1920s, prior to the coming of sound, only the Soviet Union, with a Marxist government, Germany with its rise of nationalism and then fascism, and Japan, with a strong nationalist economy and film industry of its own, were able to keep Zukor and his films at bay.

It took something outside Zukor's control to do him in — the Great Depression. Business declined, theaters were sold, and Paramount teetered on the brink of bankruptcy. By 1936 Barney Balaban had replaced Zukor atop the Paramount chain of command, but for 40 more years Zukor offered the company he had created his wise counsel. He was still regularly going into the office until only a few years before his death at age 103.

—Douglas Gomery

PICTURE ACKNOWLEDGMENTS

The editors wish to thank the copyright holders of the photographs included in this volume and the permissions managers of many book and magazine publishing companies for assisting us in securing reproduction rights. We are also grateful to the staffs of the Detroit Public Library, the Library of Congress, the University of Detroit Mercy Library, Wayne State University Purdy/Kresge Library Complex, and the University of Michigan Libraries for making their resources available to us. Every effort has been made to trace copyright, but if omissions have been made, please bring them to the attention of the editors. The following is a list of the copyright holders who have granted us permission to reproduce material in the *International Dictionary of Films and Filmmakers* as well as from where said resources were received:

Dede Allen. Dede Allen.

AP/Wide World Photos. Rick Baker; Barney Balaban; Lucien Ballard; Walter Bernstein; Mel Blanc; Margaret Booth; Charles Brackett; Albert R. Broccoli; Bill Conti; Sir Noel Coward; Louis De Rochemont; Jim Henson; David Alam Mamet; Alan Menken; Nick Park; Harold Pinter; Andre Previn; Sir Terence Rattigan; Ravi Shankar; Robert Emmet Sherwood; Vangelis.

Archive Photos, Inc. Hoagy Carmichael; Danny Elfman, photograph by Scott Harrison; Jerry Goldsmith, photograph by Nosta Alexander; Samuel Goldwyn; Arthur Honegger/Limot; Maurice Jarre, photograph by Frank Edwards; Sherry Lansing; Val Lewton; Anita Loos/American Stock; Henry Mancini; Louis B. Mayer; Ismail Merchant, photograph by Frank Capri; Ennio Morricone, photograph by Jean-marie De Craene/Reuters; Cole Porter; Sergei Prokofiev; Alain Robbe-Grillet; Sam Shepard; Max Steiner; Sir William Turner Walton; Franz Waxman; John Williams, photograph by David Strick.

Jerry Bauer. Marguerite Duras.

CORBIS. Ken Adam; Malcolm Arnold; Burt Bacharach/UPI; Michael Ballhaus; Travis Banton; Richard Rodney Bennett/Hulton-Deutsch Collection; Lajos Biro; Enos Edward Canutt; Jean-Claude Carriere; Ernest Dickerson, photograph by Jim Spellman; Hanns Eisler; Julius and Philip Epstein; Leon Gaumont; William Goldman; Frances Goodrich and Albert Hackett; Dave Grusin; Tony Havelock-Allan; Sidney Coe Howard; Chuck Jones; Janusz Kaminski; Marcus Loew/Bettmann; Herman Mankiewicz; Winsor McCay/Bettmann-UPI; Johnny Mercer; Jerry Wald.

Film Music Associates. Angelo Badalamenti, photograph by L. Wong. Copyright © 1990 Capital Cities/ABC, Inc.

All remaining images were provided courtesy of the Kobal Collection.

NOTES ON ADVISERS AND CONTRIBUTORS

ALWYN, Richard. Essayist. Freelance writer. English-language assistant, University of Paris III, 1983–85. Contributor to many British film journals. **Essays:** de Beauregard; Douy; Jeanson; Kosma.

AMBROGIO, Anthony. Essayist. Formerly film and composition instructor, Wayne State University, Detroit. Contributor to *Film Criticism* and *Pukka Afflatus.* **Essay:** Siodmak.

ARMES, Roy. Essayist. Professor of film at Middlesex University, London. Author of *French Cinema Since 1946,* 1966, 1970; *The Cinema of Alain Resnais,* 1968; *French Film,* 1970; *Patterns of Realism,* 1972, 1983; *Film and Reality,* 1974; *The Ambiguous Image,* 1976; *A Critical History of British Cinema,* 1978; *The Films of Alain Robbe-Grillet,* 1981; *French Cinema,* 1985; *Third World Filmmaking and the West,* 1987; *On Video,* 1988; *Studies in Arab and African Film* (with Lizbeth Malkmus), 1991; *Action and Image,* 1994; bilingual *Dictionary of North African Film Makers,* 1996. **Essay:** Robbe-Grillet.

ATTERBERRY, Giselle. Essayist. Instructor, Parkland College, Champaign, Illinois, since 1986. Contributor, *New Art Examiner.* **Essay:** Leven.

BARTONI, Doreen. Essayist. Artist-in-residence, Columbia College, Chicago, 1986–87. **Essays:** Hecht; Loos.

BASINGER, Jeanine. Adviser and essayist. Corwin-Fuller Professor of Film, Wesleyan University, Middletown, Connecticut. Trustee, American Film Institute, National Center for Film and Video Preservation. Member of advisory board, Foundation for Independent Video and Film. Author of *Working with Kazan,* 1973; *Shirley Temple,* 1975; *Gene Kelly,* 1976; *Lana Turner,* 1977; *Anthony Mann: A Critical Analysis,* 1979; *The World War II Combat Film: Anatomy of a Genre,* 1986; *The ''It's a Wonderful Life'' Book,* 1986; *A Woman's View: How Hollywood Spoke to Women, 1930–60,* 1993; *American Cinema: 100 Years of Filmmaking,* 1994; and numerous articles. **Essays:** Chase; Harrison; Hornbeck; Levien; Mirisch.

BAXTER, John. Essayist. Novelist, screenwriter, TV producer, and film historian. Visiting lecturer, Hollins College, Virginia, 1974–75; broadcaster with BBC Radio and Television, 1976–91. Author of *Hollywood in the Thirties,* 1968; *The Australian Cinema,* 1970; *Science Fiction in the Cinema,* 1970; *The Gangster Film,* 1970; *The Cinema of Josef von Sternberg,* 1971; *The Cinema of John Ford,* 1971; *Hollywood in the Sixties,* 1972; *Sixty Years of Hollywood,* 1973; *An Appalling Talent: Ken Russell,* 1973; *Stunt,* 1974; *The Hollywood Exiles,* 1976; *King Vidor,* 1976; with Brian Norris, *The Video Handbook,* 1982; and *Filmstruck,* 1989. **Essays:** Bumstead; Cristaldi; Evein; Raymond and Robert Hakim; Harlan; Kräly; Krasna; Rotunno; Saulnier; Taradash; Vetchinsky; Vierny; Winkler.

BERG, Charles Ramírez. Essayist. Instructor in film, University of Texas, Austin. **Essays:** Alcoriza; Almendros; Goldman; Towne.

BERGAN, Ronald. Adviser. Regular contributor, *The Guardian* (London); consultant and writer for several TV documentaries; lectured on literature, theatre, and film during ten years in France; author of numerous books on the cinema, including biographies of the Coen Brothers, Sergei Eisenstein, Jean Renoir, Anthony Perkins, and Dustin Hoffman, as well as *The United Artists Story* and *The Great Theatres of London.*

BJORNSSON, Nina. Essayist. **Essay:** Duras.

BOWERS, Ronald. Essayist. Financial editor, E. F. Hutton and Company, since 1982. Editor, *Films in Review,* 1979–81. Author of *The MGM Stock Company,* with James Robert Parish, 1973; and *The Selznick Players,* 1976. **Essays:** C. Brackett; Coward; Howe; Lasky; MacGowan; Mankiewicz; Pasternak; Pommer; Rosson; Stewart.

BOYER, Jay. Essayist. Freelance writer. **Essay:** Wilson.

BRETT, Anwar. Essayist. Freelance writer. **Essays:** Menken; Morris.

BRITO, Rui Santana. Adviser. Film historian, Cinemateca Portuguesa, Lisbon.

BROPHY, Stephen. Essayist. Writer on international, independent, and classic films for publications in the Boston area. **Essays:** Amidei; Di Venanzo; Dutta.

BROUSSARD, Rick. Essayist. Freelance writer, Atlanta, Georgia. Contributor to *Atlanta Magazine, Southline, Open City,* and other journals. **Essay:** MacArthur.

CAMPER, Fred. Essayist. Independent filmmaker, writer and lecturer on film, since 1965. Has taught at various American colleges and universities. **Essay:** Breer.

CARE, Ross. Essayist. Composer/arranger for the films *Otto Messmer and Felix the Cat, The Wizard's Son, General Sutter* (orch. only); and other film and theater scores; author of film music column, ''The Record Rack,'' for *Scarlet Street* magazine, since 1993; contributor to the Library of Congress ''Performing Arts'' book series (1986, 2001), the *St. James Encyclopedia of Popular Culture, Film Quarterly, Sight and Sound, Quarterly Journal of the Library of Congress, Millimeter,* and other periodicals. **Essays:** Addinsell; Bennett; Loew; Mandel; Newman; Schwartz.

CHATTEN, Richard. Essayist. Film historian. **Essay:** Metty.

COLE, Lewis. Adviser. Professor of screenwriting, Columbia University, co-founder Mediterranean Film Institute, chair of Film Division, Columbia University, 1996–2000. Television critic, *Nation Magazine,* 1994–97. Author of *A Loose Game,* 1978; *Dream Team,* 1982; *Never Too Young to Die,* 1990; and *This Side of Glory,* 1996. Also author of numerous screenplays and articles.

COUSINS, R. F. Essayist. Senior lecturer in French studies, University of Birmingham, England. Author of *Zola's Thérèse Raquin,* 1991; and contributor to *University Vision, Literature/Film Quarterly, Francophonie,* and *Excavatio.* Formerly executive member of British Universities Film and Video Council. Forthcoming books include, *Zola and the Cinema* and *Introduction to French Film Studies.* **Essays:** Alekan; Aurenche and Bost; Coutard; D'Eaubonne; Decaë; Fradetal; Jaubert; Meerson; Mnouchkine; Nuytten; Rappeneau; Renoir; Spaak; Trauner.

CROWDUS, Gary. Adviser. Founder and editor-in-chief, *Cineaste* magazine; editor of *A Political Companion to American Film.*

DASSANOWSKY, Robert von. Adviser and essayist. Associate professor of languages and cultures, director of film studies, and head of German studies, University of Colorado, Colorado Springs; vice president, Austrian American Film Association; actor, television writer and independent film producer; author of *Phantom*

977

Empires: The Novels of Alexander Lernet-Holenia, 1996; and *Cinema: From Vienna to Hollywood and Back* (forthcoming); contributing editor, ''Austria's Hollywood/Hollywood's Austria,'' special issue of *Filmkunst,* 1997; contributing editor, *Gale Encyclopedia of Multicultural America,* 2000. **Essay:** von Dassanowsky.

DAVIAU, Gertraud Steiner. Essayist. Lecturer at the Universities of Vienna and Klagenfurt, Austria; visiting scholar, University of California, Riverside, and University of California, Los Angeles; civil servant, Austrian Federal Chancellery/ Federal Press Service, Austria; working on a research project and screenplay for the documentary *Austria's Hollywood—Hollywood's Austria*; author of *Die Heimat-Macher. Kino in Österreich 1946–1966,* 1987; *Filmbook Austria,* 2nd edition, 1997, and *Traumfabrik Rosenhügel (The Dream Factory of Rosenhügel),* 1997. **Essay:** Kolowrat-Krakowsky.

DELAMATER, Jerome. Essayist. Associate professor and Film Track coordinator, Department of Communication Arts, Hofstra University, Hempstead, New York. Formerly director of Motion Picture Studies, Wright State University, Dayton, Ohio. Author of *Dance in the Hollywood Musical,* 1981. **Essay:** Cole.

DELOREY, Denise. Essayist. Writer and educator. Taught history of narrative film at Massachusetts Institute of Technology, 1989, 1991, and American literature at Emerson College, 1994–95. Author of ''Parsing the Female Sentence: The Paradox of Containment in Virginia Woolf's Narratives,'' in *Ambiguous Discourse: Feminist Narratology and British Women Writers,* North Carolina University Press, forthcoming, summer 1996. **Essays:** Fraker; Hall; Lantz; Sharaff.

DERRY, Charles. Essayist. Head of Motion Picture Studies, Wright State University, Dayton, Ohio. Author of *Dark Dreams: A Psychological History of the Modern Horror Film,* 1978; *The Film Book Bibliography 1940–1975* (coauthor), 1980; and *The Suspense Thriller: Films in the Shadow of Alfred Hitchcock,* 1988. **Essays:** Allen; Hunter; Rabier.

DIXON, Wheeler Winston. Essayist. Director, Film Studies Program, University of Nebraska at Lincoln. Filmmaker. Author of *The ''B'' Directors: A Biographical Dictionary,* 1985; *The Cinematic Vision of F. Scott Fitzgerald,* 1986; *Terence Fisher: The Critical Reception,* 1991; and *The Early Film Criticism of François Truffaut,* 1992. Contributor to *Films in Review, Velvet Light Trap, Literature/Film Quarterly,* and *Post Script.* **Essays:** Auric; Bernard; Crosby; Delerue; Francis; Iwerks; Périnal; Von Harbou.

DIXTER, Robert. Essayist. Degree in film and communications, McGill University. Masters candidate, Emerson College. **Essay:** Lundgren.

DOLL, Susan. Essayist. Instructor in film at Oakton Community College and at the School of the Art Institute of Chicago. Author of *Marilyn: Her Life and Legend,* 1990; and *The Films of Elvis Presley,* 1991. **Essays:** Edlund; Fraker; V. Miller; Surtees.

DOYLE, Aine. Essayist. Freelance writer. Candidate in the John W. Draper Master's Program in Liberal Studies at New York University. **Essay:** Pinter.

DUNAGAN, Clyde Kelly. Essayist. Instructor in mathematics, University of Wisconsin Center, Sheboygan, 1983–84. Since 1984,

Instructor in mathematics, film, and television, Louisiana School for Math, Science and the Arts, Natchitoches. **Essays:** Goldwyn; Toland.

DURGNAT, Raymond. Essayist. Visiting professor of film, University of East London. Author of numerous publications on film, including *Durgnat on Film,* 1975; *King Vidor—American,* 1988. **Essays:** Braunberger; de Grunwald; Heckroth; Rank.

EDELMAN, Rob. Essayist. Author of *Great Baseball Films,* 1994; and *Baseball on the Web,* 1998. Co-author of *Angela Lansbury: A Life on Stage and Screen,* 1996; *The John Travolta Scrapbook,* 1997; and *Meet the Mertzes,* 1999. Contributing editor of *Leonard Maltin's Movie & Video Guide; Leonard Maltin's Movie Encyclopedia;* and *Leonard Maltin's Family Film Guide.* Director of programming of Home Film Festival. Contributor to *The Political Companion to American Film; Women Filmmakers & Their Films; Total Baseball; The Total Baseball Catalog; International Film Guide;* and *The Whole Film Sourcebook.* Film critic/commentator, WAMC (Northeast) Public Radio. Lecturer, University at Albany. Former film critic/columnist, New Haven Register and Gazette Newspapers. Former adjunct instructor, The School of Visual Arts, Iona College, Sacred Heart University. **Essays:** Almendros; Ballhaus; Bass; E. Bernstein; N. Brown; Burel; Carrière; Conti; Disney; Hunter; Jarrico; Jhabvala; Q. Jones; Lansing; Loquasto; Mancini; Menges; Miyagawa; Mohr; Müller; Nykvist, Ptushko; Sargent; Schoonmaker; Semprun; Storaro; Vierny.

ERSKINE, Thomas L. Essayist. Professor of English, Salisbury State University, Maryland. Founder, *Literature/Film Quarterly.* Formerly chairman, film division of the Modern Language Association. **Essays:** Bitzer; Krasker; Lassally; Ponti.

ESTRIN, Mark W. Essayist. Professor of English and director of film studies, Rhode Island College, Providence, since 1966. Editor of *Critical Essays on Lillian Hellman,* 1986, 1989; and *Conversations with Eugene O'Neill,* 1990. Author of *Lillian Hellman: Plays, Films, Memoirs,* 1980. Contributor to *Literature/Film Quarterly, Modern Drama,* and *Journal of Narrative Technique.* **Essays:** Comden and Green; Kanin; Pinter.

FALLER, Greg S. Essayist. Professor, Department of Electronic Media & Film, Towson University, Towson, Maryland, since 1986; Assistant/associate editor of *The International Dictionary of Films & Filmmakers,* first edition, vols. 3, 4, and 5, and *Journal of Film & Video,* 1985–87; adviser, *The International Dictionary of Films & Filmmakers,* second and third editions. **Essays:** D. Allen; Baker; Carré; Edouart; Guillemot; Herlth; Jenkins; Magnusson; Schoonmaker; Tsuburaya.

FARNSWORTH, Rodney. Essayist. Associate professor of comparative studies, Indiana University-Purdue University, Fort Wayne. Has published in numerous international scholarly publications including, most recently, *Literature/Film Quarterly.* **Essays:** Cooper; Cortez; Daniels; Garmes; Jarre; A. Miller; Nichols; Rosher; Shamroy; Vangelis.

FELLEMAN, Susan. Adviser and essayist. Assistant professor of cinema studies, Southern Illinois University, Carbondale; author of *Botticelli in Hollywood: The Films of Albert Lewin,* 1997; and many articles on art and film. **Essay:** Justin.

FERRARA, Patricia. Essayist. Member of the faculty, Georgia State University, Atlanta; contributor to *New Orleans Review.* **Essays:** Fischer; Nykvist; Reville.

FLYNN, Peter. Essayist. Freelance writer. **Essays:** Edens; Kahn; Rennahan; Spencer.

FONSECA, M. S. Essayist. Researcher, Programming Department, Cinemateca Portuguesa, Lisbon, since 1981. Film critic for *Expresso* newspaper, Lisbon. Author or coauthor of *Cinema Americano anos 60/70,* 1981; *Panorama do Cinema Dinamarqués,* 1983; *Helma Sanders,* 1984; *Michelangelo Antonioni,* 1985; and *Cinema Novo Portugués,* 1985. **Essays:** Branco; de Almeida; Edeson; Storaro; Sylbert.

FOREMAN, Alexa L. Essayist. Account executive, Video Duplications, Atlanta, since 1986. Theatre manager, American Film Institute, 1978–80. Author of *Women in Motion,* 1983. **Essays:** L. Brackett; Johnson; Macpherson.

GALLAGHER, John A. Essayist. Writer, filmmaker, and lecturer. Member of National Board of Review of Motion Pictures, since 1982. Writer-director, *Beach House,* 1982; *Long Walk to Forever,* 1983; *One Life Is Not Enough,* 1985; *Hell Soldier,* 1986; producer, *Biograph Days, Biograph Nights,* and *The Directors* series; screenwriter, *Time Capsule,* 1986. Author of *Tay Garnett,* 1986. **Essays:** Barnes; Buchman; Canutt; Clothier; De Laurentiis; Gaudio; Glennon; Jennings; Laszlo; S. Miller; Reynolds; Rosenblum.

GARCIA-MYERS, Sandra. Essayist. Associate director, Cinema-Television Library and Archives of the Performing Arts, 1996—; humanities/social science librarian, Southern Oregon State College, 1992–95. **Essays:** Loquasto; Marshall.

GENSCH, Heidi. Essayist. Freelance film critic. **Essay:** Golan and Globus.

GHOSH, Shohini. Essayist. Producer-director of educational films and teaching assistant, Mass Communication Research Centre, Jamia Milia Islamia, New Delhi. **Essays:** Biswas; Nihalani.

GIANOULIS, Tina. Essayist. Freelance writer; contributor to *St. James Encyclopedia of Popular Culture,* 1999; *Gay and Lesbian Literature,* 1997; www.mystories.com (daytime drama website), 1997–98; *Common Lives, Lesbian Lives, Sinister Wisdom,* and others. **Essay:** Peploe.

GILLESPIE, Jill. Essayist. Doctoral candidate, Department of German Studies, Cornell University. **Essays:** Elfman; Zimmer.

GLAESSNER, Verina. Essayist. Film critic, London. Contributor to *The Economist, Monthly Film Bulletin, Sight and Sound, Focus on Film,* and *The Guardian.* **Essays:** Cecchi d'Amico; Delli Colli; Fisher; Slocombe.

GLANCY, H. M. Essayist. Freelance writer and lecturer. **Essay:** Sherriff.

GOMERY, Douglas. Adviser and essayist. Professor of media history, University of Maryland; author of ten books including *Media in America,* 1998; and *Shared Pleasures: A History of Movie Presentation in the United States,* 1992. **Essays:** Alonzo; Ballard; Berman; Blanke; Booth; Cahn; Deutsch; Fields; Fox; Haller; Carl Laemmle, Sr. and Carl Laemmle, Jr.; Lang; Levine; Maté; L. Mayer; McCord;

Reisch; Roach; Schary; Joseph and Nicholas Schenck; Selznick; Sherwood; J. Smith; Spiegel; Stark; Stradling; Stromberg; Thalberg; Trumbull; Vajda, Veiller; Wallis; Warner; F. Young; Zanuck; Zukor.

GONTHIER, David, Jr. Essayist. **Essay:** Serandrei.

GOSTANIAN, Martin A. Essayist. Freelance writer and advertising professional. Historian and collector of vintage TV/radio programs and commercials. Head of consulting firm specializing in research, film, and audiovisual recordings on the history of broadcasting and advertising. Former champion on the quiz show *Jeopardy!* **Essay:** Hanna and Barbera.

GUSTAINIS, Justin. Essayist. Professor of communication at Plattsburgh State University, Plattsburgh, New York. **Essays:** Goldman; Goldsmith; Legrand.

HAGAN, John. Essayist. Producer and host, Arts Forum, WNYC, 1978–79. Collaborator on *Voices of Film Experience,* and contributor to *Film before Griffith, Cinema 1900 1906, Millennium Film Journal, Thousand Eyes, Cinefantastique, October,* and *Les Cahiers de la Cinémathèque.* **Essay:** Maddow.

HAGOPIAN, Kevin Jack. Essayist. Freelance writer. Contributor to *Velvet Light Trap,* and *Film Criticism.* **Essays:** Krasner; Planer.

HALAS, John. Essayist. See entry on Halas and Batchelor. **Essays:** Bozzetto; Dinov; Driessen; Grimault; Havelock-Allan; Ivanov-Vano; V. Korda; Norstein; Popescu-Gopo.

HALLER, Robert A. Essayist. Assistant director for development, Staten Island Institute of Arts and Sciences; secretary-treasurer, National Alliance of Media Arts Centers. Executive director, Pittsburgh Film-Makers Inc., 1973–80, and Anthology Film Archives, 1980–84. Editor of *Field of Vision* magazine and *Brakhage Scrapbook: Collected Writings 1964–1980,* 1982. Author of *Kenneth Anger,* 1986. **Essays:** Foreman; Ruttenberg.

HANSON, Patricia King. Essayist. Executive editor, American Film Institute, Los Angeles, since 1983. Film critic, Screen International, since 1986. Associate editor, Salem Press, 1978–83. Editor of *American Film Institute Catalog of Feature Films 1911–20 and 1931–40.* Coeditor of *Film Review Index,* vols. I and II, 1986–87, and of *Source Book for the Performing Arts,* 1988. **Essays:** Cronjager; Mandell.

HANSON, Stephen L. Essayist. Director, Cinema-Television Library and Archives of Performing Arts, University of Southern California, Los Angeles, since 1990. Humanities biographer, University of Southern California, Los Angeles, 1969–90. Coauthor with Patricia King Hanson, *Lights, Camera, Action, A History of the Movies in the Twentieth Century,* 1991; coauthor with Anthony Slide and Patricia King Hanson, *Sourcebook for the Performing Arts,* 1988; coauthor with Patricia King Hanson, *Film Review Index 1950–1985,* 1987; coauthor with Patricia King Hanson, *Film Review Index, 1882–1949,* 1986. Film reviewer, *Screen International,* 1987–90. Feature writer for *Stills,* 1983–86. Associate editor with Patricia King Hanson, *Magill's Survey of Cinema, Series I,* 1979; *Magill's Bibliography of Literary Criticism,* 1979; and *Magill's Survey of Cinema, Silent Films,* 1981. **Essays:** La Shelle; Seitz; Wasserman; Winston.

HELDRETH, Leonard G. Essayist. Professor of English, Northern Michigan University, Marquette, since 1970. Head of film and TV,

International Association for the Fantastic in the Arts, 1985–87. Film reviewer, WNMU-FM. **Essay:** Harryhausen.

HESS, Mary. Essayist. Film reviewer, *Magill's Cinema Annual* and *6Degrees* magazine; Ph.D. student, American History, Michigan State University; lecturer, State University of New York, Geneseo; teaches courses on film and history; frequent contributor, *Rochester Magazine*. **Essays:** Biziou; Dawson.

HIRANO, Kyoko. Essayist. Film program coordinator, Japan Society, New York, since 1986. Editor, *Cinéma Gras,* Tokyo, 1977–79. Contributor to *Cineaste,* and *Theater Craft* magazines. **Essays:** Hayasaka; Miyagawa; Muraki; Takemitsu; Toda; Yoda.

HUTCHINGS, Peter. Essayist. Lecturer in film studies in the Department of Historical and Critical Studies at Newcastle Polytechnic. **Essays:** Alcott; Savini.

IORDANOVA, Dina. Essayist. Contributing editor, BFI's Companion to Eastern European and Russian Cinema; works in the field of Balkan cinema and transnational film. **Essays:** Mindadze; Preisner; Urusevskii.

JOHNSON, Mark. Essayist. Freelance writer. BGS, University of Kansas, 1989. MA, University of Texas at Austin, 1993. Author of *The Swedish Sexpot Stereotype Anita Ekberg and the American Fifties,* 1993. Associate editor of the *Velvet Light Trap,* 1989–91. **Essays:** J. Allen; Dykstra.

JOHNSTON, Nancy Jane. Essayist. Taught at Baker University, Baldwin, Kansas, 1984–86. Author of *James Agee: An Annotated Bibliography of Primary and Secondary Sources 1925–1985,* 1987. **Essays:** Freund; Kidd.

KARNEY, Robyn. Adviser. London-based freelance writer, critic, and editor specializing in film subjects; editor-in-chief of *The Chronicle of the Cinema,* 1995, 1998; co-author, *The Faber Foreign Film Guide,* 1993; author of *A Star Danced: The Life of Audrey Hepburn,* 1995; *A Singular Man: Burt Lancaster,* 1998; and numerous other publications.

KEMP, Philip. Adviser and essayist. London-based freelance reviewer and film historian; contributor to *Sight and Sound, Variety,* and *Film Comment;* author of *Lethal Innocence: The Cinema of Alexander Mackendrick,* 1991; and of a forthcoming biography of Michael Balcon. **Essays:** Alton; Balcon; Bass; Carreras; Carrière; T. Clarke; Daring; Fischinger; Godfrey; Henson; Honegger; Ibert; A. Korda; Lehman; Mamet; Merchant; Milhaud; Park; Prévert; Prokofiev; Shostakovich; Starewicz; Thomson; Vorkapich; Wilcox; R. Williams.

KINSEY, Tammy. Essayist. Assistant professor of film, University of Toledo, Ohio, since 1997; made her first film at the age of eight; M.F.A. in Filmmaking, Virginia Commonwealth University, 1996. **Essays:** Kaminski; Rousselot.

LAFFERTY, William. Essayist. Associate professor of theatre arts, Wright State University, Dayton, Ohio, since 1981. **Essays:** de Rochemont; Shearer.

LARSEN, Susan K. Adviser. Assistant professor of Russian literature, University of California, San Diego; author of *Reading and Writing Girlhood in Late Imperial Russia* (forthcoming) and many articles on Russian film and popular culture; former chair of the

Working Group on Cinema and Television in Eastern Europe and the Former Soviet Union.

LEE, Edith C. Essayist. Staff member, Synthesis Concepts, Chicago. Editor, META Magazine. Worked in video division, Columbia Pictures, 1981–82. **Essays:** Adam; Adrian; Ames; Andrejew; Banton; Day; Dillon; Donati; Dreier; Gibbons; Horner; LeMaire; Orry-Kelly; Plunkett; Rose; Sharaff; Trumbo.

LEV, Peter. Essayist. Assistant professor of mass communication, Towson State University, Baltimore, since 1983. Taught at University of Texas, Austin, 1980–82. Author of *Claude Lelouch, Film Director,* 1983. **Essays:** Gégauff; Lai.

LEVINE, David. Essayist. Freelance writer. **Essays:** Robbe-Grillet; Shepard; Willis.

LIMBACHER, James. Essayist. Film historian and audio-visual librarian, Dearborn, Michigan Department of Libraries, 1955–83; national president, American Federation of Film Societies, 1962–65, and Educational Film Library Association, 1966–70. Host of the television series *Shadows on the Wall, The Screening Room,* and *Talking Pictures.* Author of *Four Aspects of the Film,* 1968; *Film Music: From Violins to Video,* 1974; *Haven't I Seen You Somewhere Before?,* 1979; *Sexuality in World Cinema,* 1983; *Keeping Score,* 1991; and *Feature Films on 8mm, 16mm and Video,* 7 editions. **Essay:** Dunn.

LORENZ, Janet. Essayist. Associate editor and film critic, *Z Channel Magazine,* since 1984. Assistant supervisor, University of Southern California Cinema Research Library, Los Angeles, 1979–82; film critic, SelecTV Magazine, 1980–84. **Essays:** Dunne; Freed; Jhabvala; Willis.

LUPO, Jon. Essayist. Freelance writer. Film editor and critic, *Massachusetts Daily Collegian,* 1991–96. Editor and publisher, *Cinefile* cinema journal, 1995—. **Essay:** Van Dongen.

MacCANN, Richard Dyer. Essayist. Professor of film, University of Iowa, Iowa City, from 1970 (emeritus professor since 1986). Editor, *Cinema Journal,* 1967–76. Author of *Hollywood in Transition,* 1962; *The People's Films: A Political History of U.S. Government Motion Pictures,* 1973; *The First Tycoons,* 1987; and *The First Film Makers,* 1989. Editor of *Film and Society,* 1964; *Film: A Montage of Theories,* 1966; *The New Film Index,* 1975; and *Cinema Examined,* 1982. **Essays:** Cohn; Houseman.

MACNAB, Geoffrey. Essayist. Freelance writer, London. Author of *J. Arthur Rank and the British Film Industry,* 1993. **Essays:** Ballhaus; Puttnam.

MANVELL, Roger. Essayist. Formerly professor of film, Boston University. Director, British Film Academy, London, 1947–59, and a governor and head of the Department of Film History, London Film School, until 1974; Bingham Professor of the Humanities, University of Louisville, 1973. Editor, *Penguin Film Review,* 1946–49, and the Pelican annual *The Cinema,* 1950–52; associate editor, *New Humanist,* 1968–75; member of the board of directors, *Rationalist Press,* London, from 1966; editor-in chief, *International Encyclopedia of Film,* 1972. Vice-chairman, National Panel of Film Festivals, British Council, London, 1976–78. Author of *Film,* 1944; *The Animated Film,* 1954; *The Film and the Public,* 1955; *On the Air,* 1955; *The Technique of Film Music,* 1957, 1976; *The Technique of Film*

Animation, with John Halas, 1959; *The Living Screen,* 1961; *Design in Motion,* with John Halas, 1962; *What Is a Film?,* 1965; *New Cinema in Europe,* 1966; *This Age of Communication,* 1967; *New Cinema in the U.S.A.,* 1968; *New Cinema in Britain,* 1969; *Art in Movement,* 1970; *The German Cinema,* with Heinrich Fraenkel, 1971; *Shakespeare and the Film,* 1971; *Films and the Second World War,* 1975; *Love Goddesses of the Movies,* 1975; *Theatre and Film,* 1979; *Art and Animation: Halas and Batchelor 1940–1980,* 1980; *Ingmar Bergman,* 1980; and *Images of Madness: The Portrayal of Insanity in the Feature Film,* with Michael Fleming, 1985; also author of novels, biographies of theatrical personalities and of personalities of the Third Reich. Died 1987. **Essays:** Arnold; Biro; Galeen; Halas and Batchelor; Mathieson; Mathis; C. Mayer; Röhrig.

MARTIN, Floyd W. Essayist. Professor of art history, University of Arkansas, Little Rock, since 1982. **Essays:** Beaton; K. Brown; Gherardi; Grot; Menzies; Whitlock.

McCAFFREY, Donald W. Essayist. Emeritus professor of English, University of North Dakota. Author of *Four Great Comedians: Chaplin, Lloyd, Keaton, and Langdon,* 1968; *The Golden Age of Sound Comedy: Comic Films and Comedians of the Thirties,* 1973; *Three Classic Silent Screen Comedies of Harold Lloyd,* 1976; and *Assault on Society: Satirical Literature to Film,* 1992. Editor of *Focus on Chaplin,* 1971. **Essays:** Goodrich and Hackett; Riskin.

McCARTY, John. Essayist. Supervising writer and co-director of *The Fearmakers: Screen Masters of Suspense and Terror,* a video documentary series based on his 1994 book of the same name; author of numerous books on film, including *Splatter Movies: Breaking the Last Taboo of the Screen,* 1984; *The Modern Horror Film: 50 Contemporary Classics,* 1990; *John McCarty's Official Splatter Movie Guide, Vols. 1 and 2,* 1989, 1992; and *Hollywood Gangland,* 1993. **Essays:** Adam; Alonzo; Biroc; Donaggio; Francis; Goldman; Goldsmith; C. Jones; Mainwaring; Reville; Savini; J. Williams.

McCLUSKEY, Audrey T. Adviser. Director of the Black Film Center/Archive and associate professor of Afro-American Studies, Indiana University-Bloomington; specializes in education, gender, and cultural studies; co-editor, with Elaine M. Smith, *Mary McLeod Bethune: Building a Better World,* 2000.

MERHAUT, Vacláv. Essayist. Film historian and member of staff, Film Archives of Czechoslovakia, Prague. Author of *Actors and Actresses of the Italian Cinema.* **Essay:** Bosustow.

MIKLAS, Lois. Essayist. Intern, 1982–83, and assistant to program coordinator, 1983–84, Children's Museum, Indianapolis; also participant-interpreter, Conner Prairie Pioneer Settlement, Noblesville, Indiana. **Essay:** Wheeler.

MILICIA, Joseph. Essayist. Professor of English, University of Wisconsin, Sheboygan; writes about film and literature for such periodicals as *Multicultural Review* and *The New York Review of Science Fiction.* **Essays:** Badalamenti; Burwell; Dickerson; Flaiano and Pinelli; Herrmann; Steiner.

MILLER, Norman. Essayist. Journalist and author, London. Author of *Toontown: Cartoons, Comedy and Creativity,* and contributor to a variety of periodicals. **Essay:** Stalling.

MITCHELL, John E. Humor writer/comic book writer, and publisher. Author of *Very Vicky* comic books 1993–95; *That Skinny*

Bastard: Frank Sinatra, 1995; *Calling All Hillbillies* comic books, 1995; *Very Vicky Junior Hepcat Funbook,* 1996. **Essays:** Irene; Van Heusen.

MONTY, Ib. Adviser. Director of Det Danske Filmmuseum, Copenhagen, since 1960. Literary and film critic for the newspaper *Morgenavisen Jyllands-Posten,* 1958–94. Editor in chief of the film periodical *Kosmorama,* 1960–67; member, Danish Film Council, 1965–69. Adviser for the journal *Film History.* Member of the editorial board of *Journal of Film Preservation.* Author of *Leonardo da Vinci,* 1953; editor, with Morten Piil, *Se-det er film I-iii* (anthology of articles on film), 1964–66, and TV-broadcasts on films and filmmakers, 1972.

MORRIS, Gary. Adviser. Editor and publisher, *Bright Lights* film journal, formerly print, now online as *brightlightsfilm.com.* Author of *Roger Corman,* 1985. Regular film critic for *Bay Area Reporter* and *San Francisco Weekly* and author of numerous articles for various American and Italian newspapers, magazines, film festival catalogs, and online journals.

MORRISON, James. Essayist. Lecturer in the English Department, North Carolina State University, Raleigh. Contributor to *New Orleans Review, Centennial Review,* and *Film Criticism.* **Essay:** Burks.

MRAZ, John. Essayist. Researcher, Center for the Study of Contemporary History, University of Puebla, Mexico, since 1984. Distinguished visiting professor, Mexican American Studies, San Diego State University, 1991. Visiting professor, Art and Latin American Studies, University of Connecticut, 1990. Visiting professor of history, University of California, Santa Cruz, 1988. Coordinator of graphic history, Center for the Historical Study of the Mexican Labor Movement. 1981–83. Contributor to *Jump Cut.* **Essays:** Figueroa; Herrera.

NASTA, Dominique. Essayist. Assistant professor, Department of Film Studies, Université Libre de Bruxelles, Belgium, since 1990. Author of *Mooning in Film: Relevant Structures in Soundtrack and Narrative;* and of articles on film music, melodrama, Michelangelo Antonioni, André Delvaux, Andrei Tarkovsky, and Jaco Van Dormael. Editor of Jacques Ledoux issue of *Revue Beige du Cinéma,* 1995. **Essays:** Age and Scarpelli; Cloquet.

NESS, Richard R. Essayist. Freelance writer. **Essays:** Donaggio; Goldsmith; Q. Jones; Legrand; Rosenman; Rozsa; Theodorakis.

NEWMAN, Kim. Essayist. Freelance writer and broadcaster. Author of *Nightmare Movies,* 1988; and *Wild West Movies,* 1990. Contributor to *Sight and Sound, Empire, New Musical Express,* and other periodicals. Also a fiction writer. **Essays:** Berlin; Blanc; Cardiff; Golan and Globus; Kovacs; Savini; Zsigmond.

NISSEN, Dan. Adviser. Deputy curator, 1988–1998, head of Department Archive & Cinematheque, since 1998, Danish Film Institute. Teacher of film and literature, 1978–88; film critic for the daily newspaper *Information,* since 1976; editor of the film periodical *Kosmorama,* since 1988; contributor to several books and dictionaries on film.

NORDEN, Martin F. Essayist. Professor of communication, University of Massachusetts-Amherst; author of *The Cinema of Isolation: A History of Physical Disability in the Movies,* 1994; and *John Barrymore: A Bio-Bibliography,* 1995. **Essay:** W. Bernstein.

OBALIL, Linda. Essayist. Assistant, Special Effects Unit, Dreamscape, Bruce Cohn Curtis Productions/Bella Productions, since 1983. **Essays:** Avery; Cohl; C. Jones; Pal.

O'BRIEN, Daniel. Essayist. Contributor to *The Hutchison Encyclopedia* and *Dark Side* magazine; publications include *Robert Altman: Hollywood Survivor,* 1995; *Clint Eastwood: Film Maker,* 1996; and *The Frank Sinatra Film Guide,* 1998. **Essays:** Biddle; Challis; Muren; O'Brien; Southern; Wanger; The Westmore Family.

O'LEARY, Liam. Essayist. Formerly film viewer, Radio Telefis Eireann, Dublin; director, Liam O'Leary Film Archives, Dublin. Producer, Abbey Theatre, Dublin, 1944; director of the Film History Cycle at the National Film Theatre, London, and acquisitions officer, National Film Archive, London, 1953–66. Cofounder, 1936, and honorary secretary, 1936–44, Irish Film Society. Director of the films *Our Country,* 1948; *Mr. Careless,* 1950; and *Portrait of Dublin,* 1951. Author of *Invitation to the Film,* 1945; *The Silent Cinema,* 1965; and *Rex Ingram, Master of the Silent Cinema,* 1980. Died 1992. **Essays:** Aldo; Gaumont; Golovnya; Heller; Hunte; Jaenzon; Lassally; Metzner; Pathé.

O'NEILL, Carrie. Essayist. Freelance writer and editor. Assistant, Danieleweski Professional Writers/Actors/Directors Workshops, 1982–83; graduate instructor, Department of Theatre, Speech, and Cinema, Brigham Young University, 1986–88; tutorial instructor, Department of Theatre Studies, University of New South Wales, 1988–89; dramaturg, Australia's National Institute for Dramatic Art, 1989–90; assistant professor of English composition and literature, Arkansas State University, 1990–95; assistant to creative director, Righel, Inc., 1995–96. Author of "The Translation to Stage and Screen of an Original Script," *Forbidden Colors,* and "Analysis of the Processes Involved in Workshopping a Text for Two Unique Media"; "The Australian Male as Myth: A Survey of the Subject of Masculinity in the Contemporary Drama of Australia." Productions include, *Games Played Darkly,* 1989; *Forbidden Colors,* 1988; *Confederate Air Force,* 1987; and *Half in Love with Easeful Death,* 1983. **Essays:** Enei; Puttnam; Watkin.

OPĚLA, Vladimír. Essayist. Film historian, Czechoslovakian Film Archives, Prague. **Essays:** Brdečka; Trnka; Zeman.

OSCHERWITZ, Dayna. Essayist. Doctoral candidate in French and Francophone studies, University of Texas at Austin; specializes in twentieth-century French and Francophone literature and French cinema; author of articles on Calixthe Beyala, Gisèle Pineau, and Patrick Chamoiseau; writing a dissertation entitled "*Re*presenting the Nation: Literature, Cinema and the Struggle for National Identity in Late Twentieth-Century France." **Essay:** Lhomme.

OSHANA, Maryann. Essayist. Film historian, Northwestern University, Evanston, Illinois. Author of *Women of Color: A Filmography of Minority and Third World Women,* 1985. **Essays:** Lantz; Terry.

OXOBY, Marc. Essayist. Ph.D. candidate, University of Nevada, Reno; contributor of essays on film to *Film and History* and the *St. James Encyclopedia of Popular Culture,* 1999. **Essay:** Schamus.

PALMER, R. Barton. Essayist. Calhoun Lemon Professor of Literature and Director of the South Carolina Film Institute, Clemson University; books include *Hollywood's Dark Cinema, Perspectives on Film Noir,* and *Joseph Mankiewicz: A Bibliographical and Critical Study.* **Essays:** Balaban; Barker; Broccoli; Eszterhas; Hamlisch; Mercer; Merchant; Murch; Pereira; Polito; Schifrin; Schlesinger; Sullivan; Swerling; Warm; Willingham; R. Zanuck; Zsigmond.

PASKIN, Sylvia. Essayist. Teacher in media studies, BRIT School of Performing Arts and Technology, London. Contributor to various film journals and books, including *The New Television in Europe,* 1993. **Essays:** Carmichael; Pan; Rattigan; Walton.

PETEN, Soon-Mi. Doctoral candidate in film studies, Université Libre de Bruxelles, Belgium. Thesis focuses on a comparative study of the mythic component in American and European cinema. Member of the editorial board of the *Revue Beige du Cinéma;* contributor to issues on filmmaker Jaco Van Dormael and film archivist Jacques Ledoux. **Essay:** Guerra.

PETLEY, Julian. Adviser and essayist. Lecturer in communications, Brunel University. Contributor to *Index on Censorship, Vertigo, New Statesman* and *Society.* **Essays:** Guerra; Hall; Haskin; Hoffmann; Menges; Solinas; Struss.

PILLING, Jayne. Adviser. Animation festival director, British Film Institute.

PINSEL, Rob. Essayist. Author of *Rating the Movie Stars,* 1983; researcher on *The Best, Worst, and Most Unusual Musicals,* 1982; *The Filmgoer's Companion,* 1982–84; and *Who Was Who on Screen,* 3rd ed., 1983. **Essays:** Bruckman; Hoffenstein; Raphaelson.

POLAN, Dana. Adviser. Professor of critical studies, School of Cinema-TV, University of Southern California. Author of *Pulp Fiction* (BFI Modern Classics); *In a Lonely Place* (BFI Film Classics); two other books, and numerous essays on film and cultural studies; former president of the Society for Cinema Studies.

POWER, Dominic. Essayist. Core tutor, National Film and Television School, since 1989. Lecturer on film history, Kingston University (School of Three Dimensional Design), since 1996. Adviser to the Film Panel of the Eastern Arts Board, since 1994. Writer for stage, radio, and television. Recent work includes *Tales of the Undead,* stage play, produced in Bristol and London; 1990, *Measure for Measure* (with Andrew Hilton) stage play, from Shakespeare, produced Bristol, 1992. Film history consultant and writer, *Buffalo Bill,* BBC Timewatch documentary, broadcast, 1993; *Riddley Walker,* radio adaptation of Russell Hoban's novel, commissioned by the BBC, 1996. **Essays:** Bacharach; Nitzsche; Tiomkin.

POZNER, André. Essayist. Writer and journalist, Chécy, France. **Essay:** Trauner.

PRICE, Victoria. Essayist. Writer for A&E's *Biography* series; author of *Vincent Price: A Daughter's Biography,* 1999; currently working on a biography of actress Dorothy McGuire for the University Press of Mississippi; completing her doctorate in American Studies at the University of New Mexico. **Essays:** Grusin; Vachon.

PRICHARD, Susan Perez. Essayist. Freelance writer. Author of *Film Costume: An Annotated Bibliography,* 1981. **Essay:** Jeakins.

PROVENCHER, Ken. Essayist. Graduate Student. B.A. Psychology and English, UMass Lowell, 1994; M.A. English, UMass Boston, 1996. Arts and entertainment staff writer and editor, *The Lowell Connector,* 1991–94. **Essays:** Burtt; Edlund; von Brandenstein.

RABINOVITZ, Lauren. Essayist. Associate professor of American studies and communications, University of Iowa, Iowa City, since 1986. Author of *Points of Resistance: Women, Power and Politics in the New York Avant Garde Cinema 1943–1971*, 1991. Coauthor of *The Rebecca Project* (with Greg Easley), 1995; coeditor of *Seeing through the Media: The Persian Gulf War* (with Susan Jeffords). **Essays:** Max and Dave Fleischer; McCay; Selig; Vukotic.

RAY, Bibekananda. Adviser and essayist. Far Eastern correspondent of All India Radio, based in Singapore, 1996—. All India Radio News Services division, Calcutta and New Delhi, 1970–96. Indian Ministry of Defence: Editor in chief, *Sainik Samachar* (Pictorial Weekly of India's Armed Forces), public relations officer, 1977–79, and deputy director of public relations, 1981–83. Contributor to *Sight and Sound,* London. Forthcoming writings include, centenary history of Indian cinema to be published by the government of India. **Essays:** Burman; Chandragupta; Mitra; Shankar; Zavattini.

RICHARDS, Allen Grant. Essayist. Freelance writer. **Essays:** Lanci; Littleton; Parrish; Ralston; Walas.

ROBSON, Arthur G. Essayist. Professor and chairman, Department of Classics, and professor of comparative literature, Beloit College, Wisconsin, since 1966. Editor of *Latin: Our Living Heritage, Book III*, 1964; author of *Euripides' 'Electra': An Interpretive Commentary*; and author, with Rodney Farnsworth, of *Alexandre Alexeieff and Claire Parker: The Artistry of Animation.* **Essay:** Alexeieff and Parker.

ROUTLEDGE, Chris. Essayist. Freelance writer and lecturer in literature and film; published essays on detective fiction, popular culture, and poetics; co-editor of *Mystery in Children's Literature* (2001). **Essays:** Adam; Bryan; Bumstead; Hall; Hambling; Kästner; Kovacs; Kureishi; Lathrop; Marshall; McAlpine; Menken; Morricone; Neame; Scale.

SAELI, Marie. Essayist. Instructor in English and the humanities, Triton College, River Grove, Illinois, since 1983. **Essays:** Tisse; Wexler.

SATER, Richard. Essayist. Freelance writer and film critic. **Essay:** Morricone.

SAUER, Patrick J. Essayist. Graduate writing program, Emerson College. Past member, Jesuit Volunteer Corps. Associate editor, *The Daily Record,* Coatesville, until 1995. Writer, director, and performer in the Boston-based comedy troupe "Not in the Face." **Essays:** Goosson; O'Steen.

SCHAEFER, Eric. Essayist. Film critic. **Essays:** D'Agostino; Guffey; Musuraca; Paxton; Pierce; Polglase.

SCHUTH, H. Wayne. Essayist. Professor of drama and communications, University of New Orleans. Author of *Mike Nichols,* 1978. Member of the board of trustees of the University Film and Video Foundation. **Essay:** Henry.

SHARMAN, Leslie Felperin. Essayist. Doctoral candidate in animation, University of Kent at Canterbury. Freelance writer; and lecturer, Goldsmiths College, University of London. Contributor to *Screen* and *Sight and Sound.* **Essays:** Bray; Lenica; McLaren; Messmer; Svankmajer.

SILET, Charles L. P. Essayist. Professor of English, Iowa State University, Ames. Author of *Lindsay Anderson: A Guide to References and Resources,* 1979; and coeditor of *The Pretend Indians:*

Images of American Indians in the Movies, 1980. Contributor to *Quarterly Review of Film, Film Heritage, Journal of Popular Film Criticism,* and *Magill's Cinema Annual.* **Essays:** Furthman; Hayes; Koch; Lardner; Lederer.

SLIDE, Anthony. Essayist. Freelance writer. Associate film archivist, American Film Institute, 1972–75; resident film historian, Academy of Motion Picture Arts and Sciences, 1975–80. Author of *Early American Cinema,* 1970; *The Griffith Actresses,* 1973; *The Films of D. W. Griffith,* with Edward Wagenknecht, 1975; *The Idols of Silence,* 1976; *The Big V: A History of the Vitagraph Company,* 1976; *Early Women Directors,* 1977; *Aspects of American Film History Prior to 1920,* 1978; *Films on Film History,* 1979; *The Kindergarten of the Movies: A History of the Fine Arts Company,* 1980; *Fifty Great American Silent Films 1912–1920,* with Edward Wagenknecht, 1980; *The Vaudevillians,* 1981; *A Collector's Guide to Movie Memorabilia,* 1983; *Fifty Classic British Films 1932–1982,* 1985; *The American Film Industry: A Historical Dictionary,* 1986; and *The International Film Industry: A Historical Dictionary,* 1989. Editor of *Selected Film Criticism 1896–1950,* 7 volumes, and the Scarecrow Press Filmmakers series. **Essays:** Buckland; C. Clarke; Dean; Ince; Lye; Saunders.

SMALL, Edward S. Essayist. Associate professor of communication, and chairman of the Interdisciplinary Program in Film Studies, University of Missouri, Columbia, since 1983. **Essays:** Kuri; Vinton.

STARR, Cecile. Essayist. Freelance writer, lecturer, and filmmaker. Film reviewer, *Saturday Review,* 1949–59. Author of *Discovering the Movies,* 1972. Coeditor of *Experimental Animation,* 1976. **Essays:** Kaufman; Marion; Nugent; Reiniger.

STEPHENS, Christopher John. Essayist. Freelance writer and educator. AmeriCorps/VISTA worker, 1994–95. Contributor to *Shaping the Short Essay,* 1991. **Essay:** Morricone.

STREIBLE, Dan. Essayist. Author of film notes for University of North Carolina film series and Cinema Texas. **Essay:** Messter.

TABERY, Karel. Essayist. Film researcher, archivist, and historian, France, Czech Republic. Historian/archivist, Czechoslovakian Film Archives, Prague, 1974–82; Centre National de la Cinématographie, Paris, 1991–92; and National Film Archive, Prague, 1993–96. **Essays:** Alekan; Colpi; Rappeneau.

TAVERNETTI, Susan. Essayist. Instructor of film, De Anza College, Cupertino, California; film reviewer and writer, *Palo Alto Weekly,* since 1988; co-author, with Margo Kasdan, of *The Critical Eye: An Introduction to Looking at Movies,* 1998; author of "Native Americans in a Revisionist Western: *Little Big Man*" in *Hollywood's Indian: The Portrayal of the Native American in Film,* 1997. **Essays:** Boyd; Toll.

TELOTTE, J. P. Essayist. Associate professor of English, Georgia Institute of Technology, Atlanta, since 1979. Coeditor, *Post Script.* Author of *Dreams of Darkness: Fantasy and the Films of Val Lewton,* 1985; *Voices in the Dark: The Narrative Patterns of Film Noir,* 1989; and *The Cult of Film Experience: Beyond All Reason,* 1991. **Essay:** Lewton.

THOMAS, Suzanne. Essayist. Researcher and translator, Emerson College, Boston, since 1986. Has worked as assistant and production manager for N.A. Productions, Jaguar TV Production, and Cineteam Realizzazioni, 1982–85. **Essay:** Rota.

THOMAS, Tony. Essayist. Freelance writer. Announcer and writer-producer for Canadian radio in 1940s and 1950s. Author of numerous books, including *The Films of Errol Flynn,* 1969; *Ustinov in Focus,* 1971; *The Films of Kirk Douglas,* 1972; *The Films of Marlon Brando,* 1973; *The Busby Berkeley Book,* 1973; *Music for the Movies,* 1973; *Cads and Cavaliers: The Gentlemen Adventurers of the Movies,* 1973; *The Films of Gene Kelly,* 1974; *Harry Warren and the Hollywood Musical,* 1975; *The Films of Ronald Reagan,* 1980; *The Films of Olivia De Havilland,* 1983; *That's Dancing,* 1984; *The Cinema of the Sea,* 1988; *The West That Never Was,* 1989; and *Errol Flynn: The Spy Who Never Was,* 1990. Editor of *Film Score: The View from the Podium,* 1979. **Essays:** Alwyn; Bernstein; Duning; Friedhofer; Green; Kaper; Korngold; Mancini; Newman; Previn; Raksin; Stothart; Waxman; J. Williams; V. Young.

THOMPSON, Frank. Essayist. Author of *William A. Wellman,* 1983. Editor, *Between Action and Cut: Five American Directors,* 1985. **Essays:** August; Biroc; Hoch; Trotti; Walker.

TOMASULO, Frank P. Adviser. Professor of film, Georgia State University; editor, *Journal of Film and Video,* 1992–97, and *Cinema Journal,* 1998–2003; author of over 50 scholarly articles and 100 conference papers.

TOMLINSON, Doug. Essayist. Assistant professor of film studies, Montclair State College, New Jersey. Principal researcher, *Voices of Film Experience,* edited by Jay Leyda, 1977, and editor of *Actors on Acting for the Screen,* 1989. **Essays:** Lourié; Schüfftan; D. Smith; Van Runkle.

TSIANTIS, Lee. Essayist. Former lecturer in film, now publicist for 20th Century-Fox, Atlanta, Georgia. **Essays:** North; Wagner.

URGOŠÍKOVÁ, B. Adviser and essayist. Film historian, Czechoslovakian Film Archives, Prague. Author (in Czech) of *Famous Era of the Swedish Film,* 1970; *SF—From Meliès to Tarkovsky,* 1974;

Remakes, 1981; and *Science Fiction Films,* 1983. **Essays:** Ścibor-Rylski; Stawiński.

VALENTINE, Fiona. Essayist. Member of faculty, School of Speech, Northwestern University, Evanston, Illinois. **Essays:** Barry; Head; Unsworth; Watkin.

VASUDEVAN, Ravi. Essayist. Fellow, Nehru Centre for Contemporary Studies, New Delhi. Formerly film critic of *The Sunday Observer,* Delhi. **Essay:** Abbas.

VOTOLATO, Gregory. Essayist. Senior lecturer of art and design, Buckinghamshire College, England, since 1980. **Essays:** Barsacq; Basevi; Junge; Tavoularis.

VOTRUBA, Miloš. Essayist. Chairman of the Czechoslovakian Film Club (active in the Czech film club movement since 1956). **Essay:** Stallich.

WALKER, Mark. Essayist. Teacher and freelance writer, Maryland. Author of *Writing for Television,* 1988; and *Vietnam Veteran Films,* 1992. **Essay:** Shepard.

WARCHOL, Tomasz. Essayist. Assistant professor of English, Georgia Southern College, since 1984. Senior assistant in English, Gdansk University, 1977–81. Contributor to *Sight and Sound* and *Ball State University Forum.* **Essay:** Ondříček.

WARD, Renee. Essayist. Freelance writer. **Essays:** Boyle; Ellenshaw; Louis; Matras; Sarde; Wakhévitch.

WEBB, Graham. Essayist. Freelance writer, artist, and researcher. Animator on *Yellow Submarine* film, 1967. Coeditor, *The Great Movie Cartoon Parade,* 1975; and *The Great Cartoon Stars: A Who's Who,* 1979. **Essays:** Clampett; Dunning; Hubley; McKimson.

YECK, Joanne L. Essayist. Lecturer on humanities and film, Art Center College of Design, Pasadena, California, since 1983. **Essays:** Diamond; Julius and Philip Epstein; Howard; Porter; Schnee; Wald.

NATIONALITY INDEX

American

Adrian
Dede Allen
Jay Presson Allen
John A. Alonzo
Preston Ames
Joseph H. August
Tex Avery
Joseph Barbera
Burt Bacharach
Angelo Badalamenti
Rick Baker
Barney Balaban
Lucien Ballard
Travis Banton
George S. Barnes
Ronald Bass
Saul Bass
Irving Berlin
Pandro S. Berman
Elmer Bernstein
Walter Bernstein
Joseph Biroc
Billy Bitzer
Mel Blanc
Margaret Booth
Robert Boyle
Charles Brackett
Leigh Brackett
J. R. Bray
Robert Breer
Albert R. Broccoli
Karl Brown
Nacio Herb Brown
Clyde Bruckman
Sidney Buchman
Wilfred Buckland
Henry Bumstead
Ben Burtt
Carter Burwell
Sammy Cahn
Yakima Canutt
Hoagy Carmichael
Borden Chase
Bob Clampett
Charles G. Clarke
William H. Clothier
Harry Cohn
Jack Cole
Betty Comden
Bill Conti
Merian C. Cooper
Stanley Cortez
Edward Cronjager
Floyd Crosby
Mason Daring
Richard Day
Louis De Rochemont
Adolph Deutsch
I. A. L. Diamond

Ernest Dickerson
Walt Disney
George Duning
Linwood Dunn
Philip Dunne
John Dykstra
Roger Edens
Arthur Edeson
Richard Edlund
Farciot Edouart
Danny Elfman
Julius Epstein
Philip Epstein
Joe Eszterhas
Verna Fields
Dave Fleischer
Max Fleischer
Carl Foreman
William Fox
William A. Fraker
Arthur Freed
Hugo Friedhofer
Jules Furthman
Lee Garmes
Cedric Gibbons
Arnold Gillespie
Bert Glennon
William Goldman
Jerry Goldsmith
Samuel Goldwyn
Frances Goodrich
Stephen Goosson
Adolph Green
Dave Grusin
Burnett Guffey
Albert Hackett
Conrad Hall
Ernest Haller
Marvin Hamlisch
William Hanna
Russell Harlan
Ray Harryhausen
Byron Haskin
John Michael Hayes
Edith Head
Ben Hecht
Buck Henry
Jim Henson
Bernard Herrmann
Winton C. Hoch
Samuel Hoffenstein
William Hornbeck
Harry Horner
John Houseman
Sidney Howard
James Wong Howe
John Hubley
Ross Hunter
Thomas H. Ince
Irene

Ub Iwerks
Paul Jarrico
Dorothy Jeakins
George Jenkins
Talbot Jennings
Ruth Prawer Jhabvala
Nunnally Johnson
Chuck Jones
Quincy Jones
George Justin
Garson Kanin
Michael Kidd
Howard W. Koch
Erich Wolfgang Korngold
Norman Krasna
Milton Krasner
Joseph La Shelle
Carl Laemmle, Jr.
Carl Laemmle, Sr.
Charles B. Lang
Sherry Lansing
Walter Lantz
Ring Lardner, Jr.
Jesse L. Lasky
Philip H. Lathrop
Charles Lederer
Charles Lemaire
Boris Leven
Sonya Levien
Joseph E. Levine
Val Lewton
Carol Littleton
Marcus Loew
Anita Loos
Santo Loquasto
Charles MacArthur
Kenneth MacGowan
Jeanie MacPherson
Ben Maddow
Daniel Mainwaring
David Mamet
Henry Mancini
Johnny Mandel
Daniel Mandell
Herman Mankiewicz
Frances Marion
Frank Marshall
June Mathis
Louis B. Mayer
Winsor McCay
Ted McCord
Robert McKimson
William Cameron Menzies
Johnny Mercer
Otto Messmer
Russell Metty
Arthur C. Miller
Seton I. Miller
Virgil Miller
Walter Mirisch

Hal Mohr
Walter Murch
Dennis Muren
Alfred Newman
Thomas Newman
Dudley Nichols
Jack Nitzsche
Alex North
Frank S. Nugent
Willis H. O'Brien
Sam O'Steen
Orry-Kelly
George Pal
Hermes Pan
Claire Parker
Robert Parrish
Joe Pasternak
John Paxton
Hal Pereira
Jack P. Pierce
Walter Plunkett
Van Nest Polglase
Sol Polito
Cole Porter
André Previn
David Raksin
Samson Raphaelson
Ray Rennahan
William H. Reynolds
Robert Riskin
Hal Roach
Helen Rose
Ralph Rosenblum
Leonard Rosenman
Hal Rosson
Miklos Rozsa
Joseph Ruttenberg
John Monk Saunders
Tom Savini
James Schamus
Dore Schary
Joseph Schenck
Nicholas Schenck
Leon Schlesinger
Charles Schnee
Thelma Schoonmaker
Stephen Schwartz
John F. Seitz
William N. Selig
David O. Selznick
Leon Shamroy
Irene Sharaff
Sam Shepard
Robert E. Sherwood
Curt Siodmak
Dick Smith
Jack Martin Smith
Terry Southern
Dorothy Spencer
Carl Stalling

Ray Stark
Donald Ogden Stewart
Herbert Stothart
Harry Stradling
Hunt Stromberg
Karl Struss
C. Gardner Sullivan
Robert L. Surtees
Jo Swerling
Richard Sylbert
Daniel Taradash
Dean Tavoularis
Paul Terry
Irving G. Thalberg
Virgil Thomson
Dimitri Tiomkin
Gregg Toland
John Toll
Robert Towne
Lamar Trotti
Dalton Trumbo
Douglas Trumbull
Christine Vachon
James Van Heusen
Anthony Veiller
Will Vinton
Patrizia von Brandenstein
Chris Walas
Jerry Wald
Joseph B. Walker
Hal B. Wallis
Walter Wanger
Jack L. Warner
Lew Wasserman
Haskell Wexler
Lyle Wheeler
John Williams
Calder Willingham
Gordon Willis
Michael Wilson
Irwin Winkler
Stan Winston
Victor Young
Darryl F. Zanuck
Richard D. Zanuck

Argentinian
Lalo Schifrin

Australian
Russell Boyd
Robert Krasker
Donald McAlpine
John Seale

Austrian
Alexander Kolowrat-Krakowsky
Carl Mayer
Walter Reisch
Sam Spiegel
Max Steiner

Belgian
Ghislain Cloquet
Charles Spaak

British
Ken Adam
Richard Addinsell
John Alcott
William Alwyn
Malcolm Arnold
Michael Balcon
William George Barker
John Barry
James Basevi
Joy Batchelor
Cecil Beaton
Richard Rodney Bennett
James Bernard
Adrian Biddle
Peter Biziou
John Bryan
Jack Cardiff
James Carreras
Christopher Challis
T. E. B. Clarke
Noël Coward
Beatrice Dawson
Basil Dean
Carmen Dillon
Peter Ellenshaw
Gerry Fisher
Freddie Francis
Bob Godfrey
John Halas
Gerry Hambling
Joan Harrison
Anthony Havelock-Allan
Otto Heller
Alexander Korda
Vincent Korda
Hanif Kureishi
Muir Mathieson
Chris Menges
Oswald Morris
Ronald Neame
Nick Park
Clare Peploe
Harold Pinter
David Puttnam
J. Arthur Rank
Terence Rattigan
Lotte Reiniger
Alma Reville
Charles Rosher
R. C. Sherriff
Douglas Slocombe
Geoffrey Unsworth
Alex Vetchinsky
William Walton
David Watkin
Albert Whitlock

Herbert Wilcox
Freddie Young

Bulgarian
Todor Dinov

Canadian
Stephen Bosustow
George Dunning
Douglas Shearer
Richard Williams

Cuban
Jorge Herrera

Czech
Jiří Brdečka
Miroslav Ondříček
Franz Planer
Jan Stallich
Jan Švankmajer
Jiří Trnka
Karel Zeman

Dutch
Paul Driessen
Robby Müllcr
Helen Van Dongen

Egyptian
Raymond Hakim
Robert Hakim

French
Henri Alekan
Jean Aurenche
Georges Auric
Pierre Bost
Pierre Braunberger
Léonce-Henry Burel
Ben Carré
Jean-Claude Carrière
Emile Cohl
Raoul Coutard
Georges De Beauregard
Henri Decaë
Jean D'Eaubonne
Marguerite Duras
Bernard Evein
Marcel Fradetal
Léon Gaumont
Paul Gégauff
Paul Grimault
Agnès Guillemot
Jacques Ibert
Maurice Jarre
Maurice Jaubert
Henri Jeanson
Joseph Kosma
Francis Lai
Michel Legrand
Jan Lenica
Pierre Lhomme
Jean Louis

Christian Matras
Darius Milhaud
Bruno Nuytten
Charles Pathé
Georges Périnal
Carlo Ponti
Jacques Prévert
Jean Rabier
Jean-Paul Rappeneau
Claude Renoir
Alain Robbe-Grillet
Philippe Sarde
Jacques Saulnier
Alexandre Trauner
Sacha Vierny
Georges Wakhévitch

German
Michael Ballhaus
Henry Blanke
Curt Courant
Hans Dreier
Hanns Eisler
Oskar Fischinger
Karl Freund
Hein Heckroth
Robert Herlth
Carl Hoffmann
Otto Hunte
Alfred Junge
Erich Kästner
Hanns Kräly
Walter Lassally
Oskar Messter
Erich Pommer
Walter Rohrig
Thea von Harbou
Fritz Arno Wagner
Hermann Warm
Hans Zimmer

Greek
Mikis Theodorakis
Vangelis

Hungarian
John Alton
Joy Batchelor
Lajos Biro
Yevgeni Enei
John Halas
Ernest Laszlo
Rudolph Maté
Ernö Metzner
Ernest Vajda
Vilmos Zsigmond

Indian
K. A. Abbas
Anil Biswas
S. D. Burman

Bansi Chandragupta
Dulal Dutta
Ismail Merchant
Subrata Mitra
Govind Nihalani
Ravi Shankar

Israeli
Yoram Globus
Menahem Golan

Italian
Age
G. R. Aldo
Sergio Amidei
Bruno Bozzetto
Suso Cecchi D'Amico
Franco Cristaldi
Dino De Laurentiis
Tonino Delli Colli
Gianni Di Venanzo
Pino Donaggio
Danilo Donati
Ennio Flaiano
Tony Gaudio
Piero Gherardi
Tonino Guerra
Giuseppe Lanci
Ennio Morricone
Nicholas Musuraca
Tullio Pinelli
Nino Rota
Giuseppe Rotunno
Scarpelli
Mario Serandrei
Franco Solinas
Vittorio Storaro
Cesare Zavattini

Japanese
Fumio Hayasaka
Yoji Kuri
Kazuo Miyagawa
Yoshiro Muraki
Toru Takemitsu
Jusho Toda
Eiji Tsuburaya
Yoshikata Yoda

Mexican
Luis Alcoriza
Gabriel Figueroa

New Zealander
Len Lye

Polish
Janusz Kaminski
Bronislau Kaper
Boris Kaufman
Aleksander Ścibor-Rylski
Ladislaw Starewicz
Jerzy Stefan Stawiński
Franz Waxman

FILM TITLE INDEX

The following list of titles cites all films included in the *Writers and Production Artists* volume of this series, including cross-references for alternative or English-language titles. The name(s) in parentheses following the title and date refer the reader to the appropriate entry or entries where full information is given. Titles appearing in bold are covered in the *Films* volume.

$, 1971 (Jones) NOTE: Name is "$"
1 April 2000, 1952 (Wagner)
1 x 1 der Ehe, 1949 (Herlth)
2 Drops of Water. *See* Do Boond Pani, 1972
2 Gun Rusty, 1944 (Pal)
3 Dumb Clucks, 1937 (Bruckman)
3-Ring Wing-Ding, 1968 (Blanc)
3:10 to Yuma, 1957 (Cohn; Duning; Louis)
4 Carrot Rabbit, 1952 (Blanc)
4 for Texas, 1963 (Cahn)
5 Branded Women, 1960 (Jarrico)
5 Card Stud, 1968 (Jarre; Wallis)
7 Little Foys, 1955 (Pereira)
7 Women, 1965 (Bernstein)
8 Ball Bunny, 1950 (Blanc; Stalling)
8 Seconds, 1994 (Conti)
8 1/2, 1963 (Flaiano and Pinelli)
8 1/2. *See* **Otto e mezzo**, 1963
8 1/2 Women, 1999 (Vierny)
9½ Weeks, 1986 (Nitzsche)
9/30/55. *See* September 30, 1955, 1977
10, 1979 (Mancini)
10 Seconds to Hell, 1959 (Adam)
10th Avenue Angel, 1947 (Irene)
10th Victim. *See* Decima vittima, 1965
10:30 P.M. Summer, 1966 (Duras)
12 Angry Men, 1957 (Justin)
12 to the Moon. *See* Twelve to the Moon, 1960
13 Rue Madeline, 1946 (Basevi; de Rochemont; Newman; Zanuck)
13th Warrior, 1999 (Goldsmith)
14 Carrot Rabbit, 1952 (Stalling)
15 from Rome. *See* I mostri, 1963
15 Jahre schweren Kerker. *See* Frauen aus der Wiener Vorstadt, 1925
19th Hole Club, 1936 (Terry)
21 Days, 1937 (Hornbeck; Korda)
21 Days. *See* First and the Last, 1937
21 Days Together. *See* 21 Days, 1937
21 Days Together. *See* First and the Last, 1937
$21.00 a Day Once a Month, 1941 (Lantz)
22 Misfortunes. *See* Dvadzatdva neshchastia, 1930
23 Paces to Baker Street, 1956 (Krasner)
23 1/2 Hours Leave, 1919 (Zukor)
23 1/2 Hours Leave, 1937 (Carré)
24 Hours, 1931 (Haller)
24 Hours in an Underground Market. *See* Chikagai 24-jikan, 1947
24 Hours of a Woman's Life, 1952 (Francis)
25 October, First Day, 1968 (Norstein)
25e Heure. *See* Vingt-cinquième Heure, 1967
25th Hour. *See* Vingt-cinquième Heure, 1967
27 Down, 1973 (Chandragupta)
36 Chowringhee Lane, 1981 (Chandragupta)
36 Hours, 1954 (Carreras)
36 Hours, 1964 (Lathrop; Tiomkin)
36 Hours to Kill, 1936 (Miller)
39 Steps, 1935 (Balcon; Reville)
40 Carats, 1973 (Legrand)
40-Horse Hawkins, 1924 (Miller)
42nd Street, 1933 (Orry-Kelly; Polito; Wallis; Warner; Zanuck)
45 Minutes from Hollywood, 1926 (Roach)
47 Loyal Ronin. *See* Chushingura, 1954

47 morto che parla, 1950 (Age and Scarpelli)
48 heures d'amour, 1968 (de Beauregard)
48-Hour Prison Break. *See* Shutsugoku yonjuhachi jikan, 1969
48 Hours. *See* Went the Day Well?, 1942
49th Parallel, 1941 (Mathieson; Young)
52 Pick-Up, 1986 (Golan and Globus)
52nd Street, 1937 (Newman; Raksin; Reynolds; Wanger)
53 Stations of the Wind of Love. *See* Koikaze gojusan-tsugi, 1952
55 Days at Peking, 1963 (Fisher; Tiomkin)
58-59, 1959 (Almendros)
65, 66, och jag, 1936 (Fischer)
66, 1966 (Breer)
69, 1968 (Breer)
70, 1970 (Breer)
77, 1977 (Breer)
80 Steps to Jonah, 1969 (La Shelle)
99 and 44/100% Dead, 1974 (Mancini)
99 River Street, 1953 (Planer)
100 Adventures. *See* Stet priklyuchenni, 1929
100 Men and a Girl, 1937 (Pasternak)
100 Rifles, 1968 (Goldsmith)
101 Dalmatians, 1996 (Biddle)
102 Dalmatians, 2000 (Biddle)
113, 1935 (Clothier)
122 rue de Provence, 1978 (Morricone)
300 Din Ke Baad, 1938 (Biswas)
317e Section, 1964 (Coutard; de Beauregard)
365 Days, 1922 (Roach)
400 Blows. *See* **Quatre Cents Coups**, 1959
491, 1964 (Fischer; Lundgren)
500 Hats of Bartholomew Cubbins, 1943 (Pal)
633 Squadron, 1964 (Koch)
711 Ocean Drive, 1950 (Planer)
$1,000 a Touchdown, 1939 (Head)
1001 Arabian Nights, 1959 (Bosustow)
1001 Drawings, 1960 (Vukotić)
1066 and All That, 1994 (Godfrey)
1492: The Conquest of Paradise, 1992 (Biddle; Vangelis)
1776, 1972 (Jenkins; Warner)
1776, or Hessian Renegades, 1909 (Bitzer)
1789, 1973 (Mnouchkine)
1814, 1910 (Gaumont)
1880, 1963 (Braunberger)
1900. *See* **Novecento**, 1976
1941, 1979 (Fraker; Williams)
1984, 1955 (Arnold)
1999, 1998 (Henry)
2000 B.C., 1931 (Terry)
2,000 Women, 1944 (Bryan; Rank)
2001: A Space Odyssey, 1968 (Alcott; Trumbull; Unsworth)
2010, 1984 (Edlund)
3,000 Mile Chase, 1977 (Bernstein)
5000 Fingers of Dr. T. , 1953 (Planer)
20,000 Leagues under the Sea, 1954 (Disney; Ellenshaw; Iwerks; Planer)
20,000 Years in Sing Sing, 1932 (Grot; Haskin)
70,000 Witnesses, 1932 (Krasner)
20 Million Miles to Earth, 1957 (Harryhausen)
400 Million, 1939 (Eisler; Nichols; van Dongen)

A, 1964 (Delerue; Lenica)
A 111-es, 1919 (Korda)
A becsapott újságíró, 1914 (Korda)
À bientôt j'espère, 1968 (Lhomme)
A bout de souffle, 1960 (Coutard; de Beauregard)
A Caixa, 1994 (Branco)
A Carta, 1999 (Branco)
A Casa, 1997 (Branco)
A cavallo della tigre, 1961 (Age and Scarpelli)
A cheval, 1950 (Decaë)
A Cruz de Ferro, 1968 (de Almeida)
A csikós, 1917 (Korda)
A divina comedia, 1991 (Branco)
A estrangeira, 1983 (Branco; de Almeida)
A été perdu une mariée, 1932 (Burel; Meerson; Spaak)
A fleur de peau, 1962 (Kosma)
A fleur d'eau, 1970 (Braunberger)
A Flor do Mar, 1986 (de Almeida)
A gólyakalifa, 1917 (Korda)
A-Haunting We Will Go, 1942 (Day)
A-Haunting We Will Go, 1966 (McKimson)
A-Hunting We Will Go, 1932 (Fleischer)
A-Hunting We Won't Go, 1943 (Fleischer)
A. I., 2001 (Kaminski)
A Ilha dos Amores, 1982 (de Almeida)
A ketlekü asszony, 1917 (Korda)
A ketszívü férfi, 1916 (Korda)
A kis lord, 1918 (Korda)
A la belle étoile, 1966 (Prévert)
À la belle frégate, 1942 (Spaak)
À la française. See In the French Style, 1963
A la mémoire du rock, 1962 (Braunberger)
A l'aube du troisième jour, 1963 (Kosma)
A Lei da Terra—Alentejo 76, 1976 (de Almeida)
A l'Heure ou les grandes fauves vont boire, 1993 (Mnouchkine)
A media luz los tres, 1957 (Alcoriza)
A nagymama, 1916 (Korda)
A nevtö Szaszkia, 1916 (Korda)
A notre regrettable epoux, 1988 (Rabier)
A nous deux, 1979 (Lai)
A nous deux, Madame la vie, 1936 (Wakhévitch)
À nous la liberté, 1931 (Auric; Meerson; Périnal; Trauner)
A nous quatre, Cardinal, 1973 (Douy)
A nyní hraje dechovka, 1953 (Stallich)
A Paris . . . un jeudi, 1954 (Kosma)
A peleskei notárius, 1917 (Korda)
A propos de Jivago, 1962 (Alexeieff and Parker)
A propos de Nice, 1930 (Kaufman)
A proposito Lucky Luciano, 1973 (Cristaldi)
A riporterkirály, 1917 (Korda)
A rosa de areia, 1989 (de Almeida)
A Sagrada Família, 1972 (de Almeida)
A Sombra dos Abutres, 1998 (de Almeida)
A Tempestade da Terra, 1998 (de Almeida)
A testör, 1918 (Korda)
A tiszti kardbojt, 1915 (Korda)
A tous les vents, 1945 (Decaë)
A tout casser, 1953 (Colpi; Decaë)
à Valparaiso, 1963 (Delerue)
A Votre santé!, 1950 (Fradetal)
A život jde dál, 1935 (Heller; Stallich)
Aa furusato, 1938 (Yoda)
Aaamour , 1978 (Brdečka)
Aaghat, 1985 (Nihalani)
Aakash, 1953 (Biswas)
Aaraam, 1951 (Biswas)

Aarohan, 1982 (Chandragupta)
Aaron Slick from Punkin Crick, 1952 (Bumstead; Head; Lang)
Aasman Mahal, 1965 (Abbas)
Aasraa, 1941 (Biswas)
Aath Din, 1946 (Burman)
Ab Mitternacht, 1938 (Hoffmann)
Abandonadas, 1944 (Figueroa)
Abandoned, 1949 (Boyle; Daniels)
Abarenbou kaido, 1957 (Yoda)
Abarenbou taishou, 1960 (Yoda)
Abbandano, 1940 (Stallich)
Abbé Constantin, 1933 (Burel; Spaak)
Abbott and Costello Go to Mars, 1953 (Boyle)
Abbott and Costello in Hollywood, 1945 (Irene)
Abbott and Costello Meet Captain Kidd, 1952 (Cortez)
Abbott and Costello Meet Dr. Jekyll and Mr. Hyde, 1954
    (Westmore Family)
Abbott and Costello Meet Frankenstein, 1947 (Pierce)
A.B.C., 1958 (Lassally)
A.B.C.A., 1943 (Alwyn)
Abdication, 1974 (Rota; Unsworth)
Abduction of Saint Anne, 1975 (Duning)
Abductors, 1957 (La Shelle)
Abdul the Damned, 1935 (Eisler)
Abdulla the Great, 1954 (Auric; Garmes)
Abdullah's Harem. See Abdulla the Great, 1954
Abe Lincoln in Illinois, 1940 (Howe; Plunkett; Polglase; Sherwood)
Abeilles, 1956 (Braunberger)
Abeille et les hommes, 1960 (Braunberger)
Abel Gance, the Charm of Dynamite, 1968 (Menges)
Abenteurer, 1921 (Courant)
Abenteuer: Die Affenbrücke. See Doktor Dolittle und seine Tiere, 1928
Abenteuer: Die Reise nach Afrika. See Doktor Dolittle und seine
    Tiere, 1928
Abenteuer des Prinzen Achmed. See Geschichte des Prinzen
    Achmed, 1923-26
Abenteuer des Till Ulenspiegel, 1956 (Matras)
Abenteuer eines Zehnmarkscheinen, 1927 (Freund)
Aberdeen, 2000 (Preisner)
Abhijan, 1962 (Chandragupta; Dutta)
Abhilasha, 1938 (Biswas)
Abhiman, 1957 (Biswas)
Abhiman, 1973 (Burman)
Abie's Irish Rose, 1929 (Banton; Furthman; Mankiewicz; Rosson)
Abito nero da sposa, 1943 (Flaiano and Pinelli)
Abominable Homme des douanes, 1963 (Delerue)
Abominable Snow Rabbit, 1961 (Blanc; Jones)
Abominable Snowman, 1957 (Carreras; Trumbo)
Abominable Snowman. See Jujin Kuki-Otoko, 1955
About Face, 1942 (Roach)
About Face, 1951 (Glennon)
About Last Night. . . , 1986 (Mamet)
About Mrs. Leslie, 1954 (Head; Laszlo; Wallis; Young)
Above and Beyond, 1952 (Friedhofer; Rose)
Above Suspicion, 1943 (Irene; Kaper; Mayer)
Above the Abyss. See Nad propastí, 1921
Above Us the Waves, 1957 (Rank)
Abracadabra, 1958 (Vukotić)
Abraham Lincoln, 1924 (Marion)
Abraham Lincoln, 1930 (Menzies; Schenck; Struss)
Abraham Valley. See Vale Abraão, 1993
Abscheid, 1930 (Schüfftan)
Abseits vom Blück, 1916 (Freund)
Abseits vom Glück, 1914 (Messter)
Absence, 1993 (Branco)
Absence of Malice, 1981 (Grusin)

Absences Repetees, 1971 (Rousselot)
Absent-Minded Professor, 1961 (Disney; Ellenshaw)
Absent-Minded Waiter, 1977 (Hamlisch; Henry)
Absolute Beginners, 1986 (Hambling)
Absolute Power, 1997 (Bumstead; Goldman)
Absolute Quiet, 1936 (Waxman)
Abus de confiance, 1937 (Burel)
Abyss, 1914 (Selig)
Abyss, 1989 (Muren)
Academician Ivan Pavlov, 1949 (Enei)
Academy Awards Film, 1951 (Clarke)
Accadde al penitenziario, 1955 (Delli Colli)
Accattone, 1961 (Delli Colli)
Accent on Love, 1941 (Clarke; Day; Trumbo)
Accent on Youth, 1935 (Shamroy)
Accident, 1961 (Kosma)
Accident, 1967 (Dillon; Fisher; Pinter)
Accident. *See* Uberfall, 1928
Accidental Accidents, 1924 (Roach)
Accidental Tourist, 1988 (Littleton; Williams)
Accordéon et ses vedettes, 1946 (Decaë)
According to Pereira. *See* Afirma Pereira, 1996
Accordion Joe, 1930 (Fleischer)
Accordion Song , 1974 (Brdečka)
Accused, 1948 (Dreier; Head; Krasner; Wallis; Young)
Accused, 1988 (Lansing)
Accusée, levez-vous!, 1930 (Douy; Spaak)
Accusing Finger, 1936 (Head)
Ace. *See* Great Santini, 1979
Ace Eli and Rodger of the Skies, 1973 (Goldsmith; Smith)
Ace in the Hole, 1951 (Edouart; Friedhofer; Lang; Pereira)
Ace of Aces, 1933 (Cooper; Plunkett; Polglase; Saunders; Steiner)
Ace of Spades, 1931 (Fleischer)
Aces High, 1976 (Fisher)
Achanak, 1973 (Abbas)
Aching Youth, 1928 (Roach)
Acht Mädels im Boot, 1932 (Junge)
Achtung banditi!, 1951 (Di Venanzo)
Achtung Harry! Augen auf!, 1926 (Galeen)
Achtung! Liebe-Lebensgefahr!, 1929 (Metzner)
Achtzehnjährigen, 1927 (Planer)
Ack, du är some en ros, 1967 (Fischer)
Acqua, 1960 (Almendros)
Acquaintances of the Street. *See* Známosti z ulice, 1929
Acquittal, 1923 (Furthman)
Acrobatic Toys. *See* Freres Boutdebois, 1908
Acrobatty Bunny, 1946 (Blanc; McKimson; Stalling)
Across the Atlantic, 1928 (Blanke)
Across the Bridge, 1957 (Rank)
Across the Great Divide, 1977 (Badalamenti)
Across the Heart, 1986 (Branco)
Across the Pacific, 1926 (Haskin; Zanuck)
Across the Pacific, 1942 (Deutsch; Edeson; Haskin; Wald)
Across the Pacific, 1957 (Bernard)
Across the Plains, 1912 (Ince)
Across the Plains. *See* War on the Plains, 1912
Across the Wide Missouri, 1951 (Basevi; Jennings; Plunkett; Raksin)
Across to Singapore, 1928 (Gibbons; Mayer; Seitz)
Act of Love, 1953 (Hornbeck)
Act of Love. *See* Acte d'amour, 1953
Act of Murder, 1948 (Boyle; Mohr)
Act of Violence, 1948 (Kaper; Rose; Surtees)
Act One, 1963 (Schary)
Actas de Merusia, 1976 (Theodorakis)
Acte d'amour, 1953 (Trauner)
Action for Slander, 1937 (Korda; Stradling)

Action in the North Atlantic, 1943 (Deutsch; Gaudio; Haskin; McCord; Wald; Warner)
Action Man. *See* Soleil des voyous, 1967
Action under Arsenal. *See* Akcja pod Arsenalem, 1977
Actor, 1978 (Kidd)
Actors and Sin, 1952 (Garmes; Hecht)
Actress, 1928 (Daniels; Day; Gibbons; Mayer)
Actress, 1953 (Gibbons; Kaper; Plunkett; Rosson)
Actress. *See* Aktrisa, 1943
Actress. *See* Joyu, 1947
Actualités burlesques, 1948 (Braunberger)
Actualités: ça c'est des nouvelles!, 1949 (Braunberger)
A.D., 1985 (Houseman)
Ad ogni costo, 1967 (Morricone)
Ada, 1961 (Kaper; Rose; Ruttenberg)
Adam, 1977 (Rousselot)
Adam 2. *See* Adam II, 1969
Adam and Eva, 1923 (Gaudio)
Adam and Evalyn, 1949 (Rank)
Adam and Evil, 1927 (Day; Gibbons)
Adam at 6 A.M., 1970 (Grusin)
Adam Had Four Sons, 1941 (Cohn)
Adam II, 1969 (Lenica)
Adam's Rib, 1923 (Buckland; Gillespie; Macpherson)
Adam's Rib, 1949 (Gibbons; Kanin; Mayer; Plunkett; Rozsa)
Adamo e Eva, 1950 (de Laurentiis)
Adamson i Sverige, 1966 (Fischer)
Adauchi hizakurige, 1936 (Yoda)
Adauchi Suzenjinobaba, 1957 (Yoda)
Addams Family, 1991 (Allen)
Addams Family Values, 1993 (Adam)
Adding Machine, 1968 (Hambling; Lassally)
Addio, amore!, 1944 (Amidei)
Addio fratello crudele, 1971 (Morricone; Storaro)
Address Unknown, 1944 (Maté; Menzies)
Adela Hasn't Had Her Supper Yet. *See* Adéla jeste nevecerela, 1977
Adéla jeste nevecerela, 1977 (švankmajer)
Adelita, 1938 (Figueroa)
Adémaï au moyen age, 1935 (Spaak)
Ademai aviateur, 1934 (Schüfftan)
Adieu . . . Léonard!, 1943 (Douy)
Adieu Leonard, 1943 (Kosma; Prévert)
Adieu Philippine, 1960 (de Beauregard)
Adieu poulet, 1975 (Mnouchkine; Sarde)
Adios. *See* Lash, 1930
Adiós, Mariquita linda, 1944 (Figueroa)
Adjunkt Vrba, 1929 (Heller)
Adjutant seiner Hoheit, 1933 (Heller)
Admirable Crichton, 1919 (Zukor)
Admirable Crichton, 1957 (Addinsell)
Admiral Nakhimov. *See* Amiral Nakhimov, 1946
Admiral Was a Lady, 1950 (Cortez; Polglase)
Admiral Yamamoto. *See* Yamamoto Isoroku, 1968
Admission Free, 1932 (Fleischer)
Adolescent Girl. *See* Adolescente, 1979
Adolescente, 1979 (Sarde)
Adolescents. *See* Fleur de l'age, ou les adolescents, 1964
Adolf & Marlene, 1976 (Ballhaus)
Adolphe, 1968 (Stawiński)
Adolphe, ou l'age tendre, 1968 (Evein)
Adorabili e bugiarde, 1957 (Delli Colli)
Adorable, 1933 (Seitz)
Adorable Creatures. *See* Adorables créatures, 1952
Adorables créatures, 1952 (Matras; Spaak)
Adoration, 1928 (Biro; Seitz)
Adressatin verstorben, 1911 (Messter)

Africana. *See* Ruckkehr, 1990

After a Lifetime, 1971 (Menges)

After Dark, My Sweet, 1990 (Jarre)

After Hours, 1985 (Ballhaus; Schoonmaker)

After Many Years, 1908 (Bitzer)

After Midnight, 1927 (Day; Gibbons)

After Office Hours, 1935 (Adrian; Mankiewicz; Rosher)

After the Ball, 1929 (Fleischer)

After the Ball, 1932 (Balcon; Junge)

After the Ball, 1957 (Mathieson)

After the Dance, 1935 (August)

After the Fox, 1966 (Bacharach)

After the Fox. *See* Caccia alla volpe, 1966

After the Rain. *See* Ame agaru, 1999

After the Rehearsal. *See* Efter Repetitioner, 1984

After the Storm, 1928 (Walker)

After the Thin Man, 1936 (Brown; Freed; Goodrich and Hackett; Mayer;
    Stothart; Stromberg)

After the Verdict, 1929 (Galeen; Reville)

After Tomorrow, 1932 (Howe; Levien)

After Tonight, 1933 (Cooper; Polglase; Rosher; Steiner)

Aftermath: A Test of Love, 1991 (Rosenman)

Against All. *See* Proti všem, 1957

Against All Flags, 1952 (Metty)

Against All Odds, 1984 (Mainwaring)

Against the Tide, 1937 (Neame)

Against the Wind, 1948 (Balcon; Clarke; Rank)

Agakuk. *See* Shadow of the Wolf, 1993

Agantuk, 1991 (Dutta)

Agatha, 1979 (Mandel; Storaro)

Agatha. *See* Agatha et les lectures illimitées, 1981

Agatha Christie's Ordeal by Innocence, 1984 (Donaggio; Golan
    and Globus)

Agatha et les lectures illimitées, 1981 (Duras)

Agaton and Fina. *See* Agaton och Fina, 1912

Agaton och Fina, 1912 (Jaenzon)

Age des artères, 1959 (Delerue)

Age d'or, 1930 (Braunberger)

Age for Love, 1931 (Newman; Seitz; Sherwood)

Age ingrat, 1964 (Delerue)

Age of Consent, 1932 (Berman; Selznick)

Age of Indiscretion, 1935 (Haller)

Age of Infidelity. *See* Muerte de un ciclista, 1955

Age of Innocence, 1934 (Berman; Plunkett; Steiner)

Age of Innocence, 1993 (Ballhaus; Bass; Bernstein; Schoonmaker)

Age tendre, 1974 (Guillemot)

Agence matrimoniale, 1951 (Douy; Kosma)

Agent de poche, 1909 (Cohl)

Agent et le violoniste. *See* Violoniste, 1908

Agent Nr. 1, 1971 (ścibor-Rylski)

Aggie Appleby, Maker of Men, 1933 (Plunkett; Steiner)

Aggressor, 1911 (Ince)

Agnes of God, 1985 (Adam; Delerue; Nykvist)

Agnese va a morire, 1976 (Age and Scarpelli; Morricone)

Agonie de Byzance, 1913 (Gaumont)

Agonie des aigles, 1933 (Wakhévitch)

Agony and the Ecstasy, 1965 (Dunne; Goldsmith; North;
    Shamroy; Smith)

Agosta, 1986 (Branco; de Almeida)

Agression, 1974 (Braunberger)

Ague di Primavera, 1989 (Mnouchkine)

Ah, My Home Town. *See* Aa furusato, 1938

Ah! Nango shosa, 1938 (Tsuburaya)

Ah Sweet Mouse-Story of Life, 1965 (Jones)

Ah, Wilderness!, 1935 (Goodrich and Hackett; Mayer; Stothart;
    Stromberg)

Ahava Ilemeth, 1982 (Golan and Globus)

Ahí viene Martín Corona, 1952 (Figueroa)

Ahijado de la muerte, 1946 (Alcoriza)

Ai no borei, 1978 (Takemitsu; Toda)

Ai no corrida, 1976 (Toda)

Ai no sanga, 1950 (Miyagawa)

Ai yo hoshi to tomoni, 1947 (Hayasaka)

Aienkyo, 1937 (Yoda)

Aigle à deux têtes, 1947 (Auric; Matras; Mnouchkine; Wakhévitch)

Aiglon, 1931 (Burel; Planer)

Aiguille rouge, 1950 (Wakhévitch)

Aija no musume, 1938 (Yoda)

Aijou dudou, 1959 (Yoda)

Aile, ou la cuisse, 1976 (Renoir)

Ailes du désir. *See* **Himmel über Berlin**, 1987

Aime le bruit, 1912-14 (Cohl)

Aimez-vous Brahms?, 1961 (Auric; Trauner)

Aimez-vous les femmes?, 1964 (Evein; Vierny)

Ainé des Ferchaux, 1963 (Decaë; Delerue)

Ain't Love Funny?, 1926 (Plunkett)

Ain't Misbehavin', 1955 (Cahn)

Ain't She Sweet, 1933 (Fleischer)

Ain't She Tweet, 1952 (Blanc; Stalling)

Ain't That Ducky, 1945 (Blanc; Stalling)

Ain't We Got Fun, 1937 (Avery; Stalling)

Air, 1972 (Driessen)

Air Circus, 1928 (Carré; Miller)

Air City. *See* Aerogard, 1935

Air Express, 1937 (Lantz)

Air Force, 1943 (Haskin; Howe; Nichols; Wald; Wallis;
    Warner; Waxman)

Air Force One, 1997 (Ballhaus; Edlund; Goldsmith)

Air Fright, 1933 (Roach)

Air Hostess, 1933 (Walker)

Air Legion, 1929 (Glennon; Plunkett)

Air Mail, 1932 (Laemmle)

Air Outpost, 1937 (Alwyn)

Air pur, 1939 (Douy; Lourié)

Air Waves, 1939 (Vorkapich)

Airborne, 1973 (Jarre)

Airheads, 1994 (Burwell)

Airmail, 1932 (Freund)

Airplane!, 1980 (Bernstein)

Airplane II: The Sequel, 1982 (Bernstein; Biroc)

Airport, 1970 (Ames; Dunn; Head; Hunter; Laszlo; Newman;
    Westmore Family)

Airport '75, 1974 (Head; Lathrop)

Airport '77, 1977 (Head; Lathrop; Whitlock)

Airport '79. *See* Concorde: Airport '79, 1979

Airport '80: The Concorde. *See* Concorde: Airport '79, 1979

Aizen-bashi, 1951 (Yoda)

Akadou Suzunosuke, 1958 (Miyagawa)

Akahige, 1965 (Muraki)

Akai shuriken, 1965 (Miyagawa)

Akanegumo, 1967 (Takemitsu; Toda)

Akasen chitai, 1956 (Miyagawa)

Akash Kusum, 1965 (Mitra)

Akatsuki no dasso, 1950 (Hayasaka)

Akatsuki no hatakaze, 1938 (Yoda)

Akcja pod Arsenalem, 1977 (Stawiński)

Aken senso, 1943 (Tsuburaya)

Akira Kurosawa's Dreams, 1990 (Ralston)

Akogare, 1966 (Takemitsu)

Akrobat na hrazde, 1953 (Stallich)

Akrosh, 1981 (Nihalani)

Akte Odessa,. *See* Odessa File, 1974

Aktenskapsbrydån, 1913 (Jaenzon)
Aktenskapsleken, 1935 (Jaenzon)
Aktrisa, 1943 (Moskvin)
Akuma no kanpai, 1947 (Miyagawa)
Akuma-to, 1980 (Miyagawa)
Akumyo, 1961 (Miyagawa; Yoda)
Akumyo hatoba, 1963 (Yoda)
Akumyo ichiba, 1963 (Yoda)
Akumyo ichidai, 1967 (Yoda)
Akumyo juhachi-ban, 1968 (Yoda)
Akumyo muteki, 1965 (Miyagawa; Yoda)
Akumyo nawabari arashi, 1974 (Miyagawa; Yoda)
Akumyo niwaka, 1965 (Miyagawa; Yoda)
Akumyo zakura, 1966 (Miyagawa; Yoda)
Al Capone, 1959 (Ballard; Raksin)
Al di là del bene a del male, 1980 (Donaggio)
Al di là delle nuvole, 1995 (Guerra)
Al Treleor Muscle Exercises, 1905 (Bitzer)
Alabama: 2000 Light Years, 1969 (Müller)
Aladdin, 1953 (Reiniger)
Aladdin, 1958 (Porter)
Aladdin, 1992 (Menken)
Aladdin and His Lamp, 1952 (Wanger)
Aladdin and His Wonderful Lamp, 1939 (Fleischer)
Aladdin and the Wonderful Lamp, 1934 (Iwerks)
Aladdin's Lamp, 1931 (Terry)
Aladdin's Lamp, 1935 (Terry)
Aladdin's Lamp, 1943 (Terry)
Aladdin's Lamp, 1947 (Terry)
Aladin, 1900 (Pathé)
Aladin, 1906 (Pathé)
Alamo, 1960 (Clothier; Tiomkin)
Alan Smithee Film: Burn Hollywood Burn, 1997 (Eszterhas)
Alarm Clock Andy, 1919 (Ince)
Alarmstufe V, 1941 (Hoffmann)
Alaska Seas, 1954 (Head; Mainwaring)
Alaska Sweepstakes, 1936 (Lantz)
Alaskan, 1924 (Howe)
Albergo Luna, Camera 34, 1947 (Rota)
Alberobello, "Au pays des trulli'', 1957 (Braunberger)
Albert, R.N., 1953 (Arnold)
Albert 1er, Roi des Belges, 1950 (Spaak)
Albert Souffre, 1992 (Nuytten)
Albigeois, 1964 (Braunberger)
Alby's Delight. See Over the Brooklyn Bridge, 1984
Alchimie, 1966 (Delerue)
Alcoolisme engendre la tuberculose, 1905 (Pathé)
Alerte au sud, 1953 (Kosma)
Alerte en Méditerranée, 1938 (Mnouchkine)
Alex and the Gypsy, 1976 (Mancini)
Alex in Wonderland, 1970 (Kovacs)
Alex the Great, 1928 (Miller)
Alexander den Store, 1917 (Jaenzon)
Alexander Nevsky, 1938 (Prokofiev; Tisse)
Alexander the Great, 1955 (Andrejew; Krasker)
Alexander the Great. See Alexander den Store, 1917
Alexander's Ragtime Band, 1931 (Fleischer)
Alexander's Ragtime Band, 1938 (Berlin; Leven; Newman;
    Trotti; Zanuck)
Alexandra, 1914 (Messter)
Alf, Bill, and Fred, 1964 (Godfrey)
Alf's Button Afloat, 1938 (Rank; Vetchinsky)
Alfie, 1965 (Heller)
Alfredo, Alfredo, 1973 (Flaiano and Pinelli)
Algiers, 1938 (Howe; Irene; Reynolds; Wanger)
Ali Baba, 1936 (Iwerks)

Ali Baba. See Ali Baba et les 40 voleurs, 1954
Ali Baba Bound, 1940 (Blanc; Clampett; Stalling)
Ali Baba Bunny, 1957 (Blanc; Jones; Stalling)
Ali Baba et les 40 voleurs, 1954 (Wakhévitch; Zavattini)
Ali Baba Goes to Town, 1937 (Canutt)
Alias Aladdin, 1920 (Roach)
Alias Bulldog Drummond. See Bulldog Jack, 1935
Alias Jesse James, 1959 (Head)
Alias Jimmy Valentine, 1915 (Carré)
Alias Jimmy Valentine, 1920 (Polito)
Alias Jimmy Valentine, 1929 (Gibbons; Mayer)
Alias Mary Flynn, 1925 (Berman)
Alias Nick Beal, 1949 (Dreier; Waxman)
Alias Texas Pete Owens. See Sell 'em Cowboy, 1924
Alias the Deacon, 1940 (Cortez)
Alias the Doctor, 1932 (Grot)
Alibaba, 1940 (Biswas)
Alibi, 1929 (Menzies; Schenck; Sullivan)
Alibi, 1937 (Auric; Fradetal; Lourié)
Alibi, 1939 (Auric)
Alibi, 1942 (Heller)
Alibi, 1968 (Morricone)
Alice, 1987 (švankmajer)
Alice, 1990 (Loquasto)
Alice Adams, 1923 (Barnes)
Alice Adams, 1935 (Berman; Plunkett; Polglase; Steiner)
Alice and the Dog Catcher, 1924 (Disney)
Alice and the Three Bears, 1924 (Disney)
Alice at the Carnival, 1927 (Disney)
Alice at the Rodeo. See Alice's Rodeo, 1927
Alice au pays des merveilles, 1948 (Renoir)
Alice Babar et les 40 nénuphars, 1971 (Nuytten)
Alice Cans the Cannibals, 1924 (Disney)
Alice Charms the Fish, 1926 (Disney)
Alice Chops the Suey, 1925 (Disney)
Alice Cuts the Ice, 1926 (Disney)
Alice et Martin, 1998 (Sarde)
Alice Foils the Pirates, 1927 (Disney)
Alice Gets in Dutch, 1924 (Disney)
Alice Gets Stung, 1925 (Disney)
Alice Helps the Romance, 1926 (Disney)
Alice Hunting in Africa, 1924 (Disney)
Alice in den Städten, 1974 (Müller)
Alice in the Alps, 1927 (Disney)
Alice in the Big League, 1927 (Disney)
Alice in the Cities. See Alice in den Städten, 1974
Alice in the Jungle, 1925 (Disney)
Alice in the Klondike, 1927 (Disney)
Alice in the Wooly West, 1926 (Disney)
Alice in Wonderland, 1933 (Edouart; Glennon; Menzies; Tiomkin;
    Westmore Family; Zukor)
Alice in Wonderland, 1951 (Disney)
Alice in Wonderland. See Alice au pays des merveilles, 1948
Alice Loses Out, 1925 (Disney)
Alice on the Farm, 1925 (Disney)
Alice, or the Last Escapade. See Alice, ou la dernière fugue, 1977
Alice, ou la dernière fugue, 1977 (Rabier)
Alice Picks the Champ, 1925 (Disney)
Alice Plays Cupid, 1925 (Disney)
Alice Rattled by Rats, 1925 (Disney)
Alice Solves the Puzzle, 1925 (Disney)
Alice Stage Struck, 1925 (Disney)
Alice the Beach Nut, 1927 (Disney)
Alice the Collegiate, 1927 (Disney)
Alice the Fire Fighter, 1926 (Disney)
Alice the Golf Bag, 1927 (Disney)

998

Alice the Jail Bird, 1925 (Disney)
Alice the Peacemaker, 1924 (Disney)
Alice the Piper, 1924 (Disney)
Alice the Toreador, 1924 (Disney)
Alice the Whaler, 1927 (Disney)
Alice Wins the Derby, 1925 (Disney)
Alice's Adventures in Wonderland, 1972 (Barry; Shankar; Unsworth)
Alice's Auto Race, 1927 (Disney)
Alice's Balloon Race, 1925 (Disney)
Alice's Brown Derby, 1926 (Disney)
Alice's Channel Swim, 1927 (Disney)
Alice's Circus Daze, 1927 (Disney)
Alice's Day at Sea, 1924 (Disney)
Alice's Egg Plant, 1925 (Disney)
Alice's Fishy Story, 1924 (Disney)
Alice's Knaughty Knight, 1927 (Disney)
Alice's Little Parade, 1925 (Disney)
Alice's Medicine Show, 1927 (Disney)
Alice's Monkey Business, 1926 (Disney)
Alice's Mysterious Mystery, 1925 (Disney)
Alice's Ornery Orphan, 1925 (Disney)
Alice's Picnic, 1927 (Disney)
Alice's Restaurant, 1970 (Allen)
Alice's Rodeo, 1927 (Disney)
Alice's Spanish Guitar, 1926 (Disney)
Alice's Spooky Adventure, 1924 (Disney)
Alice's Three Bad Eggs, 1927 (Disney)
Alice's Tin Pony, 1925 (Disney)
Alice's Wild West Show, 1924 (Disney)
Alice's Wonderland, 1923 (Disney)
Alien, 1915 (Ince)
Alien, 1979 (Biddle; Burtt; Goldsmith)
Alien 3, 1992 (Edlund)
Alien from L.A., 1988 (Golan and Globus)
Alien Nation, 1988 (Winston)
Alien: Resurrection, 1997 (Goldsmith)
Aliens, 1986 (Biddle; Winston)
Aliki, 1962 (Maté)
Aliki in the Navy. See Aliki sto naftiko, 1960
Aliki, My Love. See Aliki, 1962
Aliki sto naftiko, 1960 (Lassally)
Alina, 1950 (Delli Colli)
Alitet Leaves for the Hills. See Alitet ukhodit v gory, 1949
Alitet ukhodit v gory, 1949 (Urusevsky)
Alive, 1993 (Marshall)
All Abir-r-rd, 1950 (Blanc; Stalling)
All Aboard, 1917 (Roach)
All about Dogs, 1942 (Terry)
All about Eve, 1950 (Head; Krasner; Lemaire; Newman; Wheeler; Zanuck)
All American Chump, 1936 (Clarke)
All American Co-Ed, 1941 (Roach)
All American Toothache, 1935 (Roach)
All Ashore, 1952 (Duning)
All at Sea, 1919 (Roach)
All at Sea, 1929 (Gibbons)
All at Sea. See Barnacle Bill, 1957
All Dressed Up, 1920 (Roach)
All Fall Down, 1962 (Ames; Houseman; Jeakins; North)
All Fired Up. See Tout feu, tout flamme, 1981
All for a Woman. See Danton, 1921
All for Mary, 1955 (Rank)
All Fowled Up, 1955 (Blanc; McKimson; Stalling)
All Hands, 1940 (Balcon)
All Hands on Deck, 1961 (Smith)
All I Desire, 1953 (Hunter; Westmore Family)

All In, 1936 (Balcon; Vetchinsky)
All in a Day, 1920 (Roach)
All in a Night's Work, 1961 (Head; La Shelle; Previn; Wallis)
All Lit Up, 1920 (Roach)
All Lit Up, 1959 (Halas and Batchelor)
All Man, 1916 (Marion)
All Men Are Enemies, 1934 (Hoffenstein; Seitz)
All Mine to Give, 1956 (Steiner)
All My Sons, 1948 (Lathrop; Metty)
All Night Long, 1961 (Jarrico; Rank)
All Night Long, 1981 (Lathrop)
All of Me, 1934 (Banton; Buchman)
All One Night. See Love Begins at Twenty, 1936
All Out for "V", 1942 (Terry)
All over the Town, 1949 (Rank)
All Quiet on the Western Front, 1930 (Edeson; Freund; Gaudio; Laemmle; Parrish)
All Square. See Gang War, 1928
All-Star Musical Revue, 1945 (Pan)
All Teed Up, 1930 (Roach)
All That Heaven Allows, 1955 (Hunter; Metty)
All that I Have, 1951 (Biroc)
All That Jazz, 1979 (Rotunno)
All That Money Can Buy, 1941 (August; Herrmann; Polglase)
All the Brothers Were Valiant, 1953 (Berman; Plunkett; Rozsa)
All the Drawings of the Town, 1959 (Vukotić)
All the Fine Young Cannibals, 1960 (Berman; Daniels; Rose)
All the King's Horses, 1935 (Banton)
All the King's Men, 1949 (Cohn; Guffey; Parrish)
All the Marbles, 1981 (Biroc)
All the President's Men, 1976 (Goldman; Jenkins; Willis)
All the Pretty Horses, 2000 (Shepard)
All the Right Noises, 1969 (Fisher)
All the Way Home, 1963 (Kaufman; Smith; Sylbert)
All the World to Nothing, 1918 (Furthman)
All the Young Men, 1960 (Duning)
All These Women. See För att inte tala om alla dessa kvinnor, 1964
All This, and Heaven Too, 1940 (Friedhofer; Haller; Haskin; Orry-Kelly; Steiner; Wallis)
All This and Rabbit Stew, 1941 (Avery; Blanc; Stalling)
All This and Rabbit Stew, 1950 (Terry)
All Through the Night, 1942 (Deutsch; Mercer; Wald)
All Wet, 1924 (Roach)
All Wet, 1927 (Disney)
All Women Do It. See Così fan tutte, 1992
All Women Have Secrets, 1939 (Head)
All Wool, 1925 (Roach)
All's Fair at the Fair, 1938 (Fleischer)
All's Well, 1941 (Fleischer)
All's Well That Ends Well, 1940 (Terry)
Allá en el rancho grande, 1936 (Figueroa)
Allá en el trópico, 1940 (Figueroa)
Allan Quatermain and the Lost City of Gold, 1987 (Golan and Globus; Goldsmith)
Allegheny Uprising, 1939 (Musuraca; Plunkett; Polglase)
Allegretto, 1936 (Fischinger)
Allegro non troppo, 1976 (Bozzetto)
Allegro squadrone, 1954 (Cecchi D'amico)
Alles für Geld, 1923 (Kräly)
Alley in Paradise. See Ulička v Ráji, 1936
Alley of the World. See Ukiyo kouji, 1939
Alliance, 1970 (Carrière)
Alligator Named Daisy, 1955 (Rank)
Alligator People, 1959 (Struss)
Allo! Hallo! Alo!, 1962 (Popescu-Gopo)
Allonsanfan, 1974 (Morricone)

Ame de clown, 1933 (D'Eaubonne)
Amère victoire, 1957 (D'Eaubonne)
America, 1924 (Bitzer)
America, 1982 (Rosenblum)
America 3000, 1986 (Golan and Globus)
America, America, 1963 (Allen; Wexler)
Américain, 1969 (Mnouchkine)
Américain se détend, 1957 (Braunberger)
American Aristocracy, 1916 (Loos)
American Beauty, 1999 (Hall; Newman)
American Buffalo, 1996 (Mamet; Newman)
American Christmas Carol, 1979 (Baker)
American Dream, 1966 (Mandel)
American Dream, 1977 (Lundgren)
American Dreamer, 1971 (Kovacs)
American Dreamer, 1984 (Rotunno)
American Empire, 1942 (Harlan)
American Friend. *See* **Amerikanische Freund**, 1977
American Graffiti, 1973 (Fields; Murch; Wexler)
American Guerilla in the Philippines, 1950 (Lemaire; Trotti; Wheeler)
American Hot Wax, 1977 (Fraker)
American in Paris, 1951 (Alton; Ames; Edens; Freed; Gibbons; Green; Orry-Kelly; Plunkett; Sharaff; Smith)
American Madness, 1932 (Cohn; Riskin; Walker)
American March, 1941 (Fischinger)
American Ninja II, 1987 (Golan and Globus)
American President, 1995 (Ralston; Seale)
American Road, 1954 (North)
American Romance, 1944 (Irene; Rosson)
American Soldier in Love and War, 1903 (Bitzer)
American Success. *See* American Success Company, 1979
American Success Company, 1979 (Jarre)
American Tail, 1986 (Marshall)
American Tail: Fievel Goes West, 1991 (Marshall)
American Tragedy, 1931 (Banton; Dreier; Garmes; Hoffenstein)
American Werewolf in London, 1981 (Baker; Bernstein)
Americanization of Emily, 1964 (Challis; Lathrop; Mandel; Mercer)
Americano a Roma, 1954 (Ponti)
Americano, 1917 (Loos)
Americano in vacanza, 1946 (Ponti; Rota)
Amerikanische Freund, 1977 (Müller)
Amérique en otage, 1991 (Sarde)
Amérique insolite, 1958 (Braunberger)
Amérique insolite, 1960 (Legrand)
Amérique Lunaire, 1962 (Braunberger)
Amérique vue par un français. *See* Amérique insolite, 1960
Ames d'orient, 1919 (Gaumont)
Ami Fritz, 1933 (D'Eaubonne)
Ami retrouvé, 1989 (Mnouchkine; Pinter)
Ami viendra ce soir, 1945 (Honegger)
Amiche, 1955 (Cecchi D'amico; Di Venanzo)
Amici miei, 1975 (Flaiano and Pinelli)
Amici miei III, 1984 (Flaiano and Pinelli)
Amici miei atto II, 1983 (Flaiano and Pinelli)
Amici per la pelle, 1955 (Rota)
Amico del giaguaro, 1958 (Delli Colli)
Amico magico: il maestro Nino Rota, 1999 (Cecchi D'amico)
Amigos, 1972 (Delli Colli)
Amiral Nakhimov, 1946 (Golovnya)
Amistad, 1997 (Kaminski; Williams)
Amitiés particulières, 1964 (Aurenche and Bost; Matras)
Amityville II: The Possession, 1982 (O'Steen; Schifrin)
Amityville Horror, 1979 (Schifrin)
Amok, 1934 (Courant; Meerson; Trauner)
Among the Living, 1941 (Head)
Among the Missing, 1934 (August)

Among Those Present, 1921 (Roach)
Amoozin' But Confoozin', 1944 (Fleischer)
Amor, amor, amor, 1965 (Figueroa)
Amor de perdicao, 1981 (Branco)
Amor tiene cara de mujer, 1973 (Figueroa)
Amor und das standhafte Liebespaar, 1920 (Reiniger)
Amore, 1948 (Flaiano and Pinelli)
Amore a Roma, 1960 (Flaiano and Pinelli)
Amore amaro, 1974 (Cecchi D'amico)
Amore canta, 1941 (de Laurentiis)
Amore e chiacchiere, 1957 (Zavattini)
Amore e ginnastica, 1973 (Cecchi D'amico)
Amore e rabbia, 1969 (Guillemot)
Amore in città, 1953 (Di Venanzo; Flaiano and Pinelli; Zavattini)
Amore in quattro dimensioni, 1963 (Delli Colli)
Amore pericolosi, 1964 (Delli Colli)
Amore, piombo, e furore, 1978 (Donaggio)
Amores de une viuda, 1948 (Alcoriza)
Amori di Manon Lescaut, 1954 (Flaiano and Pinelli)
Amori di mezzo secolo, 1953 (Delli Colli)
Amorous Adventures of Moll Flanders, 1965 (Vetchinsky)
Amorous General. *See* Waltz of the Toreadors, 1962
Amorous Prawn, 1962 (Barry)
Amour, 1973 (Vangelis)
Amour à la chaîne, 1964 (Delerue)
Amour à mort, 1984 (Mnouchkine; Vierny)
Amour à vingt ans, 1962 (Coutard; Delerue; Stawiński; Takemitsu)
Amour autour de la maison, 1946 (Kosma)
Amour avec des si . . . , 1963 (Braunberger)
Amour chante, 1930 (Braunberger)
Amour de pluie, 1974 (Lai)
Amour de poche, 1957 (Cloquet)
Amour de Swann, 1983 (Carrière; Nykvist; Saulnier)
Amour d'un métier, 1950 (Colpi)
Amour en cage, 1934 (Heller)
Amour en fuite, 1979 (Almendros; Delerue)
Amour est le plus fort. *See* Viaggio in Italia, 1953
Amour et discipline, 1931 (D'Eaubonne)
Amour et la veine, 1932 (D'Eaubonne)
Amour existe, 1961 (Braunberger; Delerue)
Amour fou, 1968 (de Beauregard)
Amour l'après-midi, 1972 (Almendros; Rousselot)
Amour noir et amour blanc, 1923 (Starewicz)
Amoureux du France, 1963 (Legrand)
Amoureux sont seuls au monde, 1948 (Jeanson)
Amours célèbres, 1961 (Jarre; Prévert; Wakhévitch)
Amours finissent à l'aube, 1953 (Alekan)
Amous à tous les étages, 1902 (Pathé)
Amphitryon, 1935 (Herlth; Röhrig; Wagner)
Amsterdam Affair, 1968 (Fisher)
Amuletten, 1911 (Magnusson)
Amy and the Angel, 1986 (Rosenblum)
Amy Goes to Buy Some Bread, 1979 (Vukotić)
Ana, 1981 (Branco)
Ana, 1982 (de Almeida)
Anarchists Doom, (undated) (Barker)
Anastasia, 1956 (Andrejew; Newman)
Anastasia nio fratello, 1973 (Amidei)
Anatahan, 1953 (Tsuburaya)
Anatolian Smile. *See* America, America, 1964
Anatomie d'un livreur, 1970 (Vierny)
Anatomy of a Murder, 1959 (Bass; Leven)
Anatomy of Love. *See* Tempi nostri, 1953
Anche se volessi lavorare che faccio?, 1972 (Morricone)
Anchors Aweigh, 1945 (Cahn; Hanna and Barbera; Irene; Mayer; Pasternak)

Ancient Law. *See* Alte Gesetz, 1923
Ancient Mariner, 1925 (August)
And Baby Makes Three, 1949 (Duning; Guffey)
And Hope to Die. *See* Course du lièvre à travers les champs, 1972
And Justice for All, 1979 (Grusin)
And Life Goes On. *See* A Život jde dál, 1935
And Now for Something Completely Different, 1971 (Godfrey)
And Now My Love. *See* Toure une vie, 1974
And Now Tomorrow, 1944 (Dreier; Head; Young)
And Suddenly It's Murder. *See* Crimen, 1960
And the Angels Sing, 1944 (Dreier; Head; Struss; Young; van Heusen)
And the Band Played On, 1993 (Burwell)
And the Earth Shall Give Back Life, 1953 (Kaufman)
And the Green Grass Grew All Around, 1931 (Fleischer)
And the Ship Sails On. *See* E la nave va, 1983
And the Wild, Wild Women. *See* Nella città l'inferno, 1958
And Then There Were None, 1945 (Nichols)
And to Think I Saw It on Mulberry Street, 1944 (Pal)
Andelský kabát, 1948 (Brdečka)
Andere, 1913 (Warm)
Andere, 1924 (Hoffmann)
Andere Ich, 1918 (Kolowrat-Krakowsky)
Anderson Tapes, 1971 (Jones; Justin)
André Masson et les quatre éléments, 1958 (Delerue)
Andreas Hofer, 1909 (Messter)
Andreas Schlüter, 1942 (Herlth)
Andremo in città, 1966 (Delli Colli; Stawiński; Zavattini)
Androcles and the Lion, 1952 (D'Agostino; Dunn; Horner; Stradling)
Andromeda Strain, 1971 (Dykstra; Leven; Trumbull)
Andy Clyde Gets Spring Chicken, 1939 (Bruckman)
Andy Hardy's Blonde Trouble, 1944 (Irene)
Andy Hardy's Private Secretary, 1941 (Stothart)
Andy Plays Hookey, 1946 (Bruckman)
Andy Warhol's Dracula. *See* Dracula cerca sangue di vergine e . . . mori di sete!!!, 1974
Andy Warhol's Frankenstein. *See* Carne per Frankenstein, 1974
Ane de Bruidan, 1932 (Douy)
Angarey, 1954 (Burman)
Ange gardien, 1933 (Meerson)
Ange que j'ai vendu, 1938 (Barsacq)
Angeklagt nach N.218, 1966 (Schüfftan)
Angel, 1937 (Banton; Dreier; Lang; Raphaelson)
Angel, 1982 (Menges)
Angel and Sinner. *See* Boule de suif, 1945
Angel and the Badman, 1946 (Canutt)
Angel Baby, 1961 (Wexler)
ángel exterminador, 1962 (Alcoriza; Figueroa)
Angel Eyes, 2001 (Tavoularis)
Angel Face, 1952 (D'Agostino; Nugent; Stradling; Tiomkin)
Angel Heart, 1987 (Hambling)
Angel Levine, 1970 (Jenkins)
Angel of Broadway, 1927 (Adrian; Miller)
Angel on Earth. *See* Engel auf Erden, 1959
Angel on My Shoulder, 1946 (Tiomkin)
Angel Puss, 1944 (Blanc; Jones; Stalling)
Angel Street. *See* Gaslight, 1939
Angel with the Trumpet, 1949 (Korda; Krasker)
Angel Wore Red, 1960 (Johnson; Kaper; Rotunno)
Angel's Coat. *See* Andelský kabát, 1948
Angela, 1973 (Delerue)
Angela, 1984 (Mancini)
Angela's Ashes, 1999 (Hambling; Williams)
Angèle, 1934 (Honegger)
Angeles de Puebla, 1966 (Figueroa)
Angelica, 1939 (Ibert)
Angelina. *See* Onorevole Angelina, 1947

Angelo bianco, 1955 (Delli Colli)
Angeloc il diavolo, 1946 (Zavattini)
Angels One Five, 1952 (Challis; Francis)
Angels Over Broadway, 1940 (Cohn; Garmes; Hecht)
Angels Wash Their Faces, 1939 (Deutsch)
Angels with Dirty Faces, 1938 (Friedhofer; Orry-Kelly; Polito; Steiner)
Angélus, 1899 (Gaumont)
Angie, 1994 (Goldsmith)
Angoissante aventure, 1920 (Starewicz)
Angoisse, 1913 (Gaumont)
Angola, 1984 (Branco)
Angora Love, 1929 (Roach)
Angry Barbara. *See* Bařbora rádí, 1935
Angry Hills, 1959 (Adam; Bennett)
Angry Red Planet, 1960 (Cortez)
Angry Silence, 1960 (Arnold)
Angst, 1954 (Amidei)
Angst des Tormanns beim Elfmeter, 1972 (Müller)
Angulimaal, 1960 (Biswas)
Anhonee, 1951 (Abbas)
Ani Ohev Otach Rosa, 1971 (Golan and Globus)
Aniceko, vrate se!, 1926 (Heller)
Anichti epistoli, 1968 (Lassally)
Anicka, Come Back!. *See* Aniceko, vrate se!, 1926
Anillo de compromiso, 1951 (Alcoriza)
Anima persa, 1977 (Delli Colli; Lai)
Animal Crackers, 1930 (Green)
Animal Farm, 1954 (Halas and Batchelor; de Rochemont)
Animal Kingdom, 1932 (Irene; Mandell; Selznick; Steiner)
Animal Vegetable Mineral, 1955 (Halas and Batchelor)
Animal World, 1955 (Harryhausen)
Animals, 1973 (Halas and Batchelor)
Animals and the Brigands. *See* Zvířátka a Petrovští, 1946
Animas Trujano, el hombre importante, 1961 (Figueroa)
Animated Matches. *See* Allumettes animées, 1908
Animaux, 1963 (Jarre)
Anita in Paradise. *See* Anita v Ráji, 1934
Anita v Ráji, 1934 (Heller)
Anjuta, the Dancer. *See* Balettprimadonnan, 1916
Ankur, 1974 (Nihalani)
Ann Carver's Profession, 1933 (Riskin)
Ann Vickers, 1933 (Berman; Cooper; Plunkett; Polglase; Steiner)
Anna, 1951 (de Laurentiis; Ponti; Rota)
Anna and the King of Siam, 1946 (Day; Herrmann; Jennings; Miller; Wheeler)
Anna Boleyn, 1920 (Messter)
Anna Christie, 1923 (Ince)
Anna Christie, 1930 (Adrian; Daniels; Day; Gibbons; Marion; Mayer; Shearer; Thalberg)
Anna di Brooklyn, 1958 (Rotunno)
Anna Karenina, 1927 (Gibbons)
Anna Karenina, 1935 (Adrian; Daniels; Gibbons; Levien; Mayer; Selznick; Stothart)
Anna Karenina, 1948 (Alekan; Andrejew; Beaton; Korda)
Anna Karenina. *See* Love, 1927
Anna Lucasta, 1949 (Cahn; Polito)
Anna Lucasta, 1958 (Ballard; Bernstein)
Anna of Brooklyn. *See* Anna di Brooklyn, 1958
Anna Oz, 1996 (Lhomme)
Annabel Takes a Tour, 1938 (Metty)
Annabelle's Affairs, 1931 (Clarke)
Annaluise and Anton. *See* Pünktchen und Anton, 1999
Annapolis, 1928 (Miller)
Annapolis Salute, 1937 (Metty)
Annapolis Story, 1955 (Mainwaring; Mirisch)
Anne Boleyn, 1920 (Kräly)

Après le vent des sables, 1974 (Lassally)
April Fool, 1924 (Roach)
April Fools, 1969 (Bacharach; Hamlisch; Sylbert)
April in Paris, 1952 (Cahn)
April Love, 1957 (Lemaire; Newman)
Aprile, 1998 (Lanci)
Apur Sansar, 1959 (Chandragupta; Dutta; Mitra; Shankar)
Aqua Duck, 1963 (Blanc; McKimson)
Aquarians, 1970 (Schifrin)
Aquí está Heraclio Bernal, 1957 (Figueroa)
Arab, 1915 (Buckland)
Arab, 1924 (Mayer; Seitz)
Arabella, 1924 (Metzner)
Arabella, 1967 (Morricone)
Arabesque, 1966 (Challis; Mancini)
Arabia, 1922 (Fox)
Arabian Bazaar. *See* World Window, 1937-40
Arabian Knight, 1995 (Williams)
Arabian Love, 1922 (August; Fox; Furthman)
Arabian Nights, 1942 (Krasner; Wanger)
Arabian Tights, 1933 (Roach)
Arachnophobia, 1990 (Marshall; Walas)
Aradhana, 1969 (Burman)
Araignées rouges, 1955 (Rabier)
Aranyer Din Ratri, 1970 (Chandragupta; Dutta)
Arbeitstag, 1965 (Zavattini)
Arbor Day, 1936 (Krasner; Roach)
Arbre de Noel, 1969 (Alekan)
Arcadian Maid, 1910 (Bitzer)
Arcano incantatore, 1996 (Donaggio)
Arch of Triumph, 1948 (Alekan; Head; Menzies; Metty)
Archandĕl Gabriel a paní Husa, 1964 (Trnka)
Archangel Gabriel and Mistress Goose. *See* Archandĕl Gabriel a paní Husa, 1964
Arche, 1919 (Freund)
Arche de Noé, 1946 (Kosma; Prévert)
Arche de Noé, 1967 (Grimault)
Archie's Concrete Nightmare, 1975 (Park)
Archipelago, 1992 (Saulnier)
Architects of England, 1941 (Alwyn)
Architecture de lumière, 1953 (Colpi)
Architecture et chauffage d'aujourd'hui, 1960 (Delerue)
Arctic Rivals, 1954 (Terry)
Ardha Satya, 1983 (Nihalani)
Arditi civili, 1940 (Amidei)
Are Blond Men Bashful?, 1924 (Roach)
Are Brunettes Safe?, 1927 (Roach)
Are Crooks Dishonest?, 1918 (Roach)
Are Husbands Human?, 1925 (Roach)
Are Husbands Necessary?, 1942 (Head; Lang)
Are Parents People?, 1925 (Glennon)
Are Parents Pickles?, 1925 (Roach)
Are These Our Children?, 1931 (Steiner)
Are You a Failure?, 1923 (Lang)
Are You Legally Married?, 1919 (Polito)
Are You Listening?, 1932 (Rosson)
Are You There?, 1930 (Goosson)
Arènes joyeuses, 1935 (Stradling)
Argent, 1928 (Meerson)
Argent, 1936 (Matras)
Argent de poche, 1976 (Jaubert)
Argentine Nights, 1940 (Cahn)
Argument, 1999 (Zsigmond)
Aria, 1987 (Henry)
Ariane, 1931 (Mayer)
Arie prérie, 1949 (Brdečka; Trnka)

Arise, My Love, 1940 (Brackett; Dreier; Head; Irene; Lang; Young)
Aristo, 1934 (D'Eaubonne)
Aristo-Cat, 1943 (Blanc; Jones; Stalling)
Aristotle. *See* Jak se moudrý Aristoteles stal jeste moudřejšim, 1970
Arizona, 1940 (Cohn; Walker; Young)
Arizona Cyclone, 1928 (Laemmle)
Arizona Express, 1924 (Fox)
Arizona Kid, 1930 (Fox)
Arizona Mahoney, 1937 (Head)
Arizona Romeo, 1925 (Fox)
Arizona Wildcat, 1927 (Fox)
Arizonian, 1935 (Nichols; Plunkett)
Arjun Pandit, 1976 (Burman)
Arkansas Judge, 1941 (Lardner)
Arkansas Traveler, 1938 (Dreier; Head)
Arlésienne, 1922 (Burel)
Arlington Road, 1999 (Badalamenti)
Armageddon, 1998 (Kaminski; Towne)
Arman, 1953 (Burman)
Armand and Michaela Denis, 1955 (Balcon)
Armata Brancaleone, 1966 (Age and Scarpelli; Gherardi)
Armavir, 1991 (Mindadze)
Arme Eva. *See* Frau Eva, 1915
Arme Violetta, 1920 (Kräly; Wagner)
Armed Police Force. *See* Busou keikantai, 1948
Armée d'Agenor, 1909 (Cohl)
Armée des ombres, 1969 (Lhomme)
Armistice, 1929 (Balcon)
Armoire, 1969 (Braunberger)
Armored Attack. *See* North Star, 1943
Armored Car, 1937 (Cortez)
Armored Command, 1961 (Haller; Haskin)
Arms and the Man. *See* Helden, 1959
Arms and the Woman, 1916 (Grot; Miller)
Army Girl, 1938 (Young)
Army In the Shadows. *See* Armée des ombres, 1969
Army of Darkness, 1993 (Elfman)
Army Surgeon, 1912 (Sullivan)
Army Surgeon, 1942 (Metty)
Arnelo Affair, 1947 (Irene)
Arnold, 1973 (Duning)
Aroma of the South Seas, 1931 (Balcon)
Around Is Around, 1950-51 (McClaren)
Around Sennichimae. *See* Sennichimae fukin, 1945
Around the Corner, 1930 (Glennon; Walker)
Around the World in 80 Days, 1956 (Menzies)
Around the World in Eighty Days, 1956 (Adam; Bass; Coward; Young)
Around the World in Eighty Minutes with Douglas Fairbanks, 1931 (Newman; Sherwood)
Around the World with Fanny Hill. *See* Jorden runt med Fanny Hill, 1974
Around the World, 1931 (Terry)
Around the World, 1943 (Metty)
Arousers. *See* Sweet Kill, 1972
Arrangement, 1969 (Surtees; Westmore Family; van Runkle)
Arrest Bulldog Drummond, 1939 (Dreier; Head)
Arresting Gena, 1997 (Schamus)
Arretez les tambours, 1960 (Delerue)
Arriba el campesino, 1960 (Zavattini)
Arrival from the Dark. *See* Příchozí z temnot, 1921
Arrivano i miei, 1983 (Cristaldi)
Arrivano i nostri, 1951 (Age and Scarpelli)
Arrivano i Titani, 1961 (Cristaldi; Mnouchkine)
Arrivederci Papà, 1948 (Rota)
Arrivée du Président de la République au pesage, 1895-97 (Gaumont)
Arrivée d'un train de Vincennes, 1896 (Pathé)
Arrivistes, 1959 (Barsacq)

Arrivistes. *See* Trübe Wasser, 1959

Arroseur arrosé, 1907 (Gaumont)

Arrowhead, 1953 (Head; Rennahan)

Arrowsmith, 1931 (Day; Goldwyn; Howard; Newman)

Arruza, 1968 (Ballard)

Ars Gratia Artis, 1970 (Vukotić)

Arsenal Stadium Mystery, 1939 (Rank)

Arsene Lupin, 1931 (Adrian)

Arsène Lupin, détective, 1936 (Fradetal)

Arsene Lupin Returns, 1938 (Gibbons; Waxman)

Arsenic and Old Lace, 1944 (Burks; Epstein; Friedhofer; Haskin; Mandell; Orry-Kelly; Polito; Steiner)

Art de la turlutte, 1969 (Braunberger)

Art Director, 1948 (Wheeler)

Art for Art's Sake, 1960 (Halas and Batchelor)

Art Haut-Rhénan, 1951 (Braunberger)

Art Lovers, 1960 (Halas and Batchelor)

Art of Love, 1965 (Hunter; Metty)

Art pour l'art, 1965 (Godfrey)

Arte e realtà, 1950 (Delli Colli)

Artful Kate, 1911 (Gaudio; Ince)

Arthur, 1981 (Bacharach)

Arthur 2: On the Rocks, 1988 (Bacharach)

Arthur's Hallowed Ground, 1983 (Puttnam)

Arthur's Hallowed Ground, 1985 (Young)

Arthur's Island. *See* Isola di Arturo, 1962

Article 99, 1992 (Elfman)

Artifices, 1963 (Braunberger)

Artist's Dream, 1910 (Bray)

Artists and Models, 1937 (Banton; Dreier; Head; Young)

Artists and Models, 1955 (Edouart; Head; Pereira; Wallis)

Artists and Models Abroad, 1938 (Dreier; Head)

Arturo's Island. *See* Isola di Arturo, 1962

Aru fujinkai no kokuhaku, 1950 (Yoda)

Aru koroshiya, 1967 (Miyagawa)

Aru koroshiya no kagi, 1967 (Miyagawa)

Aru Osaka no onna, 1962 (Yoda)

Aruba, Bonaire, Curazao. *See* A.B.C., 1958

Aruhi watashi wa, 1959 (Muraki)

Aryan, 1916 (August; Sullivan)

Arzoo, 1950 (Biswas)

As armas e o Povo, 1975 (de Almeida)

As Bodas de Deus, 1999 (Branco)

As Dark as the Night, 1959 (Lassally)

As Good As It Gets, 1997 (Zimmer)

As Good As Married, 1937 (Krasna; Raksin)

As Husbands Go, 1934 (Friedhofer; Lasky; Levien; Mohr; Spencer)

As in a Looking-Glass, 1911 (Bitzer)

As It Is in Life, 1910 (Bitzer)

As Long as They're Happy, 1955 (Rank)

As Long as We Live. *See* Inochi aru kagiri, 1947

As Man Made Her, 1917 (Marion)

As negro, 1944 (Figueroa)

As Old as the Hills, 1950 (Halas and Batchelor)

As Summer Dies, 1989 (Legrand)

As Summers Die. *See* As Summer Dies, 1989

As the Bells Rang Out, 1910 (Bitzer)

As the Devil Commands, 1932 (August)

As the Earth Turns, 1934 (Haskin; Orry-Kelly)

As You Desire Me, 1932 (Adrian; Daniels; Mayer)

As You Like It, 1936 (Cardiff; Meerson; Rosson; Schenck; Walton)

As Young As We Are, 1958 (Bumstead)

As Young as You Are, 1958 (Head)

As Young as You Feel, 1952 (Lemaire)

Asani Sanket, 1973 (Dutta)

Ascending Scale. *See* Aarohan, 1982

Ascension du Mont-Blanc, 1900 (Gaumont)

Aschenputtel, 1922 (Reiniger)

Asesino se embarca, 1966 (Figueroa)

Asfar, 1950 (Burman)

Ash Wednesday, 1973 (Head; Jarre)

Ashes, 1930 (Balcon)

Ashes. *See* Popioły, 1965

Ashes of Vengeance, 1923 (Gaudio; Schenck)

Ashibi, 1928 (Tsuburaya)

Ask Any Girl, 1959 (Pasternak; Rose)

Ask Father, 1918 (Roach)

Ask Grandma, 1925 (Roach)

Asleep in the Feet, 1933 (Roach)

Aspern, 1981 (Branco; de Almeida)

Asphalt, 1929 (Herlth; Pommer; Röhrig)

Asphalt Jungle, 1950 (Gibbons; Maddow; Mayer; Rosson; Rozsa; Shearer)

Ass and the Stick, 1974 (Halas and Batchelor)

Assassin(s), 1997 (Burwell)

Assassin. *See* Venetian Bird, 1952

Assassin a peur la nuit, 1942 (Auric)

Assassin habite au 21, 1942 (Andrejew)

Assassin musicien, 1975 (Nuytten)

Assassin qui passe, 1980 (Nuytten)

Assassinat de la rue du Temple, 1904 (Gaumont)

Assassinat de Mac Kinley, 1901 (Pathé)

Assassinat du courrier de Lyon, 1904 (Gaumont)

Assassinat du Duc de Guise, 1902 (Pathé)

Assassinat du Père Noël, 1941 (Spaak)

Assassination, 1986 (Golan and Globus)

Assassination, 1987 (Golan and Globus)

Assassination. *See* Ansatsu, 1964

Assassination at Sarajevo. *See* Sarajevsky Atentat, 1975

Assassination Bureau, 1969 (Unsworth)

Assassination File, 1996 (Savini)

Assassino, 1961 (Cristaldi; Guerra)

Assassins, 1995 (Zsigmond; de Laurentiis)

Assault and Matrimony, 1987 (Mandel)

Assault and Peppered, 1965 (Blanc; McKimson)

Assault on a Queen, 1966 (Daniels; Head)

Assedio dell'Alcazar, 1940 (Stallich)

Assignment: Paris, 1952 (Guffey; Duning; Parrish)

Assignment in Brittany, 1943 (Irene; Rosher; Veiller)

Assignment Skybolt, 1966 (Lassally)

Assisi Underground, 1985 (Rotunno)

Assistant Wives, 1927 (Roach)

Associate. *See* Associé, 1979

Association de malfaiteurs, 1986 (Lai)

Associations de bienfaiteurs, 1994 (Carrière)

Associé, 1979 (Carrière)

Assoluto naturale, 1969 (Morricone)

Assommois, 1909 (Pathé)

Astonished Heart, 1949 (Coward; Rank)

Astroduck, 1966 (Blanc; McKimson)

Astromutts, 1963 (Vukotić)

Asu e no seiso, 1959 (Takemitsu)

Asunaro monogatari, 1955 (Hayasaka)

Asunto privado, 1996 (de Almeida)

Asymvivastos, 1979 (Theodorakis)

At a Quarter of Two, 1911 (Gaudio)

At Bay, 1915 (Miller)

At Breakneck Speed, 1900 (Bitzer)

At Dawn We Die. *See* Tomorrow We Live, 1942

At First Sight, 1917 (Rosher)

At First Sight, 1923 (Roach)

At First Sight, 1999 (Seale; Winkler)

Auto-portrait, 1963 (Braunberger)
Auto Races, Ormonde, Fla., 1905 (Bitzer)
Autobahn, 1979 (Halas and Batchelor)
Autobiography of a Princess, 1975 (Jhabvala; Lassally; Merchant)
Autobiography of Miss Jane Pittman, 1974 (Baker; Winston)
Autogram, 1984 (Ballhaus)
Autogrimpeurs, 1962 (Delerue)
Automania 2000, 1963 (Halas and Batchelor)
Automate, 1908 (Cohl)
Automatic Monkey. See Beaux-Arts de Jocko, 1909
Automation, 1959 (Alexeieff and Parker)
Automation Blues, 1960 (Halas and Batchelor)
Automobile Ride, 1921 (Fleischer)
Autoportrét, 1988 (švankmajer)
Autostop rosso sangue, 1977 (Morricone)
Autour de minuit. See Round Midnight, 1986
Autre, 1970 (Braunberger)
Autre Femme, 1964 (Delerue)
Autre homme, une autre chance, 1977 (Cortez; Lai; Mnouchkine)
Autresville d'art, 1969 (Rabier)
Autrichienne, 1989 (Saulnier)
Autumn Crocus, 1934 (Dean)
Autumn Leaves, 1956 (Lang; Louis)
Autumn Sonata. See Herbstsonate, 1978
Auvergne, 1925 (Périnal)
Aux confins d'une ville, 1952 (Fradetal)
Aux frontières de l'homme, 1954 (Cloquet)
Aux lions les chrétiens, 1911 (Carré; Gaumont)
Aux murs du couvent, 1920 (Starewicz)
Aux portes de Paris, 1934 (Spaak)
Aux yeux du souvenir, 1948 (Auric; Jeanson)
Ava & Gabriel, 1990 (Dickerson)
Avalanche, 1919 (Miller)
Avalanche, 1928 (Mankiewicz)
Avalanche, 1950 (Cloquet)
Avalanche. See Lawine, 1923
Avalanche Express, 1979 (Dykstra)
Avalanche Patrol, 1947 (Arnold)
Avant le déluge, 1953 (Spaak)
Avant-veille du grand soir, 1969 (Braunberger)
Avanti!, 1972 (Diamond)
Avatar, the Return of the Wolf, 1977 (Müller)
Avatar botanique de Mlle. Flora, 1964 (Braunberger; Coutard)
Ave Caesar!, 1919 (Korda)
Ave Maria, 1936 (Planer)
Avec André Gide, 1952 (Braunberger)
Avec les gens de voyage, 1953 (Decaë)
Avec les peaux des autres, 1966 (D'Eaubonne)
Avec les pilotes de porte-avions, 1953 (Delerue)
Avenger. See Mstitel, 1959
Avengers. See Day Will Dawn, 1942
Avenging Conscience, 1914 (Bitzer; Brown)
Avenging Force, 1986 (Golan and Globus)
Avenging Rider, 1928 (Musuraca)
Avenging Trail, 1917 (Gaudio)
Avenir d'Emilie, 1984 (Vierny)
Avenir devoile par les lignes des pieds, 1917 (Cohl)
Aventure à Paris, 1936 (Lourié)
Aventure, c'est l'aventure, 1972 (Lai; Mnouchkine)
Aventure est au coin de la rue, 1943 (Renoir)
Aventures d'Arsène Lupin, 1957 (Cloquet)
Aventures de Clementine, 1916 (Cohl)
Aventures de Holly and Wood, 1978 (Vierny)
Aventures de Rabbi Jacob, 1973 (Decaë)
Aventures de Robert Macaire, 1925 (Meerson)
Aventures de Salavin, 1963 (Saulnier)

Aventures de Till l'Espiègle, 1956 (Auric; Barsacq; Mnouchkine)
Aventures des Pieds-Nickelés, 1948 (Braunberger)
Aventures du roi Pausole, 1933 (Amidei; Jeanson; Maté)
Aventures d'un bout de papier, 1911 (Cohl)
Aventures en Laponie, 1960 (Braunberger)
Aventyret, 1936 (Fischer; Jaenzon)
Aveu, 1970 (Coutard; Evein; Semprun)
Aveugle, 1907 (Gaumont)
Aveux les plus doux, 1971 (Coutard; Delerue)
Aviation Vacation, 1941 (Avery; Blanc; Stalling)
Aviatsionnaya nyedyelya nasyekomich, 1911 (Starewicz)
Avventura, 1959 (Guerra)
Avventure di Pinocchio, 1971 (Gherardi)
Awaara. See **Awara**, 1952
Awakened Conscience. See Probuzené svedomí, 1919
Awakening, 1909 (Bitzer)
Awakening, 1928 (Barnes; Berlin; Goldwyn; Marion; Menzies)
Awakening, 1980 (Savini)
Awakening. See Suor Letizia, 1956
Awakenings, 1990 (Ondříček)
Awara, 1952 (Abbas)
Away All Boats, 1956 (Daniels)
Awful Orphan, 1949 (Blanc; Jones; Stalling)
Awful Spook, 1921 (Bray)
Awful Truth, 1937 (Cohn; Goosson; Walker)
Axe and the Lamp, 1963 (Halas and Batchelor)
Axe Me Another, 1934 (Fleischer)
Ayako. See Aru Osaka no onna, 1962
Az aranyember, 1918 (Korda)
Az egymillió fontos bankó, 1916 (Korda)
Až přijde kocour, 1963 (Brdečka; Ondříček)
Azais, 1930 (D'Eaubonne)
Aztecas, 1976 (Figueroa)

B.F.'s Daughter, 1948 (Irene; Kaper; Ruttenberg)
Baag ki Jyoti, 1953 (Biswas)
Baaji, 1951 (Burman)
Baat Ek Raat Ki, 1962 (Burman)
Baba-Ali, 1952 (Colpi)
Babbitt, 1934 (Orry-Kelly)
Babe, 1975 (Ames; Goldsmith)
Babe, 1992 (Bernstein; Wexler)
Babe Comes Home, 1927 (Struss)
Babes in Arms, 1939 (Brown; Edens; Freed)
Babes in the Goods, 1934 (Roach)
Babes in the Wood. See Perníková chaloupka, 1927
Babes in Toyland, 1934 (Roach)
Babes in Toyland, 1961 (Disney)
Babes on Broadway, 1941 (Edens; Freed; Mayer)
Babette Goes to War. See Babette s'en va-t-en guerre, 1959
Babette s'en va-t-en guerre, 1959 (Mnouchkine)
Babla, 1953 (Burman)
Baby, 1932 (Heller)
Baby, 1985 (Alcott)
Baby and the Stork, 1911 (Bitzer)
Baby Be Good, 1935 (Fleischer)
Baby Blue Marine, 1976 (Kovacs)
Baby Boogie, 1955 (Bosustow)
Baby Boom, 1987 (Conti; Fraker; Shepard)
Baby Bottleneck, 1946 (Blanc; Stalling)
Baby Buggy Bunny, 1954 (Blanc; Jones)
Baby Butch, 1954 (Hanna and Barbera)
Baby Clothes, 1926 (Roach)
Baby Cyclone, 1928 (Gibbons)
Baby Doll, 1956 (Kaufman; Sylbert)
Baby Face, 1933 (Grot; Orry-Kelly; Zanuck)

Baby Face Harrington, 1935 (Johnson)
Baby Face Nelson, 1957 (Mainwaring; Mohr)
Baby It's You, 1983 (Ballhaus)
Baby Love. See Roman Zair, 1983
Baby Mine, 1917 (Edeson)
Baby Mine, 1928 (Gibbons)
Baby of Macon, 1993 (Vierny)
Baby Puss, 1943 (Hanna and Barbera)
Baby Seal, 1941 (Terry)
Baby—Secret of the Lost Legend, 1984 (Goldsmith)
Baby-Sitter, 1975 (Lai; Ponti)
Baby Story, 1978 (Bozzetto)
Baby the Rain Must Fall, 1964 (Bernstein; Laszlo)
Baby Wants a Bottle-ship, 1942 (Fleischer)
Babylon, 1980 (Menges)
Baby's Shoe, 1909 (Bitzer)
Baby's Day Out, 1994 (Baker)
Babysitter, 1980 (Houseman)
Bacall to Arms, 1946 (Blanc; Clampett; Stalling)
Baccara, 1936 (Lourié)
Bach Millionnaire, 1933 (Jeanson)
Bach to Bach, 1967 (Rosenblum)
Bachelor. See Mio caro Dr. Gräsler, 1990
Bachelor and the Bobby-Soxer, 1947 (Musuraca; Schary)
Bachelor Bait, 1934 (Plunkett; Polglase; Steiner)
Bachelor Brides, 1926 (Sullivan)
Bachelor Daddy, 1941 (Krasner)
Bachelor Father, 1931 (Adrian)
Bachelor Flat, 1962 (Smith; Williams)
Bachelor in Paradise, 1961 (Mancini; Rose; Ruttenberg)
Bachelor Knight. See Bachelor and the Bobby-Soxer, 1947
Bachelor Mother, 1939 (Irene; Kanin; Krasna; Polglase)
Bachelor of Arts, 1934 (Trotti)
Bachelor of Hearts, 1958 (Rank; Unsworth)
Bachelor Party, 1957 (La Shelle; North)
Bachelor's Folly. See Calender, 1931
Bacher, 1967 (Müller)
Back Alley Oproar, 1948 (Blanc; Stalling)
Back at the Front, 1952 (Boyle)
Back Door to Heaven, 1939 (Head; Mohr)
Back from Eternity, 1956 (D'Agostino; Waxman)
Back from the Dead, 1957 (Haller)
Back Home From the Dead. See Bury Me Dead, 1947
Back in Circulation, 1937 (Miller; Wallis)
Back of the Man, 1917 (Ince)
Back Pay, 1922 (Marion)
Back Pay, 1930 (Seitz)
Back Roads, 1981 (Alonzo; Mancini)
Back Room Boy, 1942 (Rank)
Back Stage, 1923 (Roach)
Back Street, 1932 (Freund; Laemmle)
Back Street, 1941 (Daniels)
Back Street, 1961 (Cortez; Hunter; Louis; Lourié)
Back to Bataan, 1945 (D'Agostino; Musuraca)
Back to God's Country, 1920 (Walker)
Back to God's Country, 1927 (Laemmle)
Back To School, 1986 (Elfman)
Back to the Future, 1985 (Marshall; Ralston)
Back to the Future Part II, 1989 (Marshall; Ralston)
Back to the Future Part III, 1990 (Marshall; Ralston)
Back to the Future . . . The Ride, 1991 (Trumbull)
Back to the Soil, 1911 (Gaudio)
Back to the Soil, 1941 (Terry)
Back to the Woods, 1919 (Roach)
Backdraft, 1991 (Zimmer)
Backfire, 1950 (Grot; Veiller)

Backfire. See Echappement libre, 1964
Background to Danger, 1943 (Gaudio; Wald)
Backlash, 1956 (Chase)
Backs to Nature, 1933 (Roach)
Backstairs. See Hintertreppe, 1921
Backstreet Dreams, 1990 (Conti)
Backstreet Strays. See Backstreet Dreams, 1990
Backstreets of Paris. See MacAdam, 1946
Backtrack, 1969 (Chase)
Backwoods Bunny, 1959 (Blanc; McKimson)
Bacon Grabbers, 1929 (Roach)
Bad and the Beautiful, 1952 (Gibbons; Houseman; Raksin; Rose; Schnee; Surtees)
Bad Bascomb, 1946 (Irene)
Bad Blonde. See Flanagan Boy, 1953
Bad Boy, 1925 (Roach)
Bad Boy, 1935 (Glennon)
Bad Boy, 1949 (Struss)
Bad Boys, 1983 (Conti)
Bad Boys. See Furyo shonen, 1961
Bad Company, 1931 (Miller)
Bad Company, 1972 (Rosenblum; Willis)
Bad Company, 1995 (Burwell)
Bad Day at Black Rock, 1955 (Gibbons; Previn; Schary)
Bad Day at Cat Rock, 1965 (Jones)
Bad for Each Other, 1953 (Planer; Wald)
Bad Girls, 1994 (Goldsmith)
Bad Jim, 1989 (Golan and Globus)
Bad Lands, 1925 (Polito; Stromberg)
Bad Little Angel, 1939 (Seitz)
Bad Lord Byron, 1948 (Rank)
Bad Luck. See Zezowate szczęście, 1960
Bad Luck Blackie, 1949 (Avery)
Bad Man of Deadwood, 1941 (Canutt)
Bad Man, 1930 (Seitz)
Bad Man, 1941 (Waxman)
Bad Medicine, 1985 (Schifrin)
Bad Men of Tombstone, 1948 (Harlan)
Bad Men's Money, 1929 (Canutt)
Bad Names. See Akumyo, 1961
Bad Names' Best Trick. See Akumyo juhachi-ban, 1968
Bad Names' Breaking of Territories. See Akumyo nawabari arashi, 1974
Bad Names' Cherry Blossoms. See Akumyo zakura, 1966
Bad News Bears, 1976 (Alonzo)
Bad Ol' Putty Tat, 1949 (Blanc; Stalling)
Bad One, 1930 (Berlin; Menzies; Schenck; Struss)
Bad Seed, 1956 (North; Rosson)
Bad Sister, 1931 (Freund; Laemmle)
Bad Sleep Well. See Warui yatsu hodo yoku nemuru, 1960
Badge or the Cross. See Sarge, 1971
Badger. See Tanuki, 1956
Badger General. See Tanuki no taishou, 1965
Badgers Green, 1948 (Arnold)
Badger's Holiday. See Tanuki no kyujitsu, 1966
Badger's Tea Pot. See Bunbuku chagama, 1939
Badi Bahu, 1951 (Biswas)
Badlanders, 1958 (Seitz)
Badlanders, 1991 (Golan and Globus)
Badlands of Dakota, 1941 (Cortez)
Badman, 1923 (Polito)
Badman's Territory, 1946 (D'Agostino)
Baeus, 1987 (Bozzetto)
Bag and Baggage, 1923 (Mohr)
Bagarres, 1948 (Kosma)
Bagdad, 1949 (Metty)
Bagpipes, 1960 (Halas and Batchelor)

Bahama Passage, 1941 (Dreier; Head)
Bahar, 1951 (Burman)
Bahen, 1941 (Biswas)
Baie des anges, 1963 (Evein; Legrand; Rabier)
Baignades dans le torrent, 1901 (Gaumont)
Baignoire, 1912-14 (Cohl)
Bain d'X, 1956 (Alexeieff and Parker)
Baiser. See Ronde, 1974
Baisers, 1963 (Coutard; de Beauregard)
Baises volés, 1968 (Guillemot)
Baited Trap, 1927 (Walker)
Baja Oklahoma, 1988 (Ballhaus)
Bajaja, 1950 (Trnka)
Bajo el cielo de México, 1937 (Figueroa)
Baku wa Toukichiroh, 1955 (Miyagawa)
Bakuro ichidai, 1951 (Hayasaka)
Bal, 1931 (Siodmak)
Bal. See Ballando ballando, 1983
Bal Cupidon, 1948 (Mnouchkine)
Bal du Comte d'Orgel, 1970 (Matras)
Bal paré, 1940 (Röhrig)
Bala, 1976 (Dutta)
Bala peridida, 1959 (Alcoriza)
Balaclava, 1930 (Balcon)
Balada da Praia dos Cães, 1986 (de Almeida)
Balalaika, 1939 (Adrian; Freund; Gibbons; Kahn; Ruttenberg; Shearer; Stothart)
Balance, 1982 (Mnouchkine)
Balao, 1913 (Gaumont)
Balatum, 1938 (Alexeieff and Parker)
Balayeur, 1961 (Delerue)
Balcony, 1963 (Fields; Maddow)
Balettprimadonnan, 1916 (Jaenzon; Magnusson)
Baleydier, 1931 (Braunberger)
Balia, 1999 (Lanci, Giuseppe ("beppe"))
Ball, 1931 (Meerson)
Ball. See Ballando ballando, 1983
Ball of Fire, 1941 (Brackett; Goldwyn; Head; Mandell; Newman; Toland)
Ball Player and the Bandit, 1912 (Ince)
Ballad of Cable Hogue, 1970 (Ballard; Goldsmith)
Ballad of Josie, 1967 (Krasner; Whitlock)
Ballad of Orin. See Hanare goze Orin, 1977
Ballad of the Sad Café, 1991 (Lassally; Merchant)
Ballad to Paducah Jail, 1934 (Roach)
Ballade parisienne, 1954 (Braunberger)
Ballade sur les fils, 1957 (Braunberger)
Ballando ballando, 1983 (Age and Scarpelli)
Balle au coeur, 1965 (Theodorakis)
Ballet. See Étoile, 1988
Ballet adagio, 1972 (McClaren)
Ballet Girl. See Ballettens born, 1954
Ballet-Oop, 1954 (Bosustow)
Ballettens born, 1954 (Fischer)
Balloonland, 1935 (Iwerks)
Balloons, 1923 (Fleischer)
Ballot Box Bunny, 1951 (Blanc; Stalling)
Ballroom Tragedy, 1905 (Bitzer)
Balthasar. See Au hasard Balthazar, 1966
Baltimore Bullet, 1980 (Mandel)
Balún Canán, 1976 (Figueroa)
Balzac's Great Love. See Wielka mloso Balzaka, 1973
Bambi, 1942 (Disney; Hubley)
Bambole, 1965 (Flaiano and Pinelli; Gherardi)
Bamboo Doll of Echizen. See Echizen take ningyo, 1963
Bamboo Prison, 1954 (Guffey)
Bamboo Saucer, 1968 (Mohr)

Banana Peel. See Peau de banane, 1963
Bananas, 1971 (Hamlisch; Rosenblum)
Banco de prince, 1950 (Burel)
Band Master, 1931 (Lantz)
Band of Angels, 1957 (Ballard; Steiner)
Band of Outsiders. See Bande à part, 1964
Band Waggon, 1939 (Rank)
Band Wagon, 1953 (Ames; Comden and Green; Deutsch; Edens; Freed; Gibbons; Kidd)
Banda degli onesti, 1956 (Age and Scarpelli; de Laurentiis)
Banda J & S, 1972 (Morricone)
Bande à part, 1964 (Coutard; Guillemot; Legrand)
Bandera, 1935 (Spaak)
Bandida, 1962 (Figueroa)
Bandido, 1956 (Laszlo; Smith; Steiner)
Bandini, 1963 (Burman)
Bandit and the Preacher , 1914 (August)
Bandit General. See Del odio nació el amor, 1949
Bandit of Sherwood Forest, 1946 (Friedhofer; Gaudio; Goosson)
Bandit of Zhobe, 1959 (Broccoli)
Bandit Trail, 1941 (Polglase)
Banditi a Milano, 1968 (de Laurentiis)
Banditi a Roma. See Roma come Chicago, 1968
Bandito, 1946 (de Laurentiis)
Bandits. See Attention Bandits, 1987
Bandit's Son, 1927 (Plunkett)
Bandolero!, 1968 (Cahn; Clothier; Goldsmith; Smith)
Bang!, 1986 (Breer)
Bang, 1967 (Godfrey)
Banished Orin. See Hanare goze Orin, 1977
Banjo on My Knee, 1936 (Johnson)
Bank Detective. See Bank Dick, 1940
Bank Dick, 1940 (Krasner)
Bank Holiday, 1938 (Rank; Vetchinsky)
Banker's Daughter, 1927 (Disney)
Banker's Daughter, 1933 (Terry)
Banker's Daughters, 1910 (Bitzer)
Banner of Youth. See Sztandar młodych, 1958
Bannerline, 1951 (Schnee)
Banning, 1967 (Bumstead; Jones)
Banque, 1955 (Rabier)
Banque Nemo, 1934 (Meerson)
Banquet des fraudeurs, 1952 (Schüfftan; Spaak)
Bantam Cowboy, 1928 (Plunkett)
Banty Raids, 1963 (Blanc; McKimson)
Banzai, 1913 (Ince)
Baptême, 1988 (Lhomme)
Bar 20, 1943 (Wilson)
Bar 20 Justice, 1938 (Head)
Bar de la fourche, 1972 (de Beauregard)
Bar Fly, 1924 (Roach)
Bar L Ranch, 1930 (Canutt)
Bar Twenty, 1943 (Harlan)
Bara en kypare, 1960 (Lundgren)
Barabba, 1961 (de Laurentiis)
Barabbas, 1953 (Nykvist)
Barabbas. See Barabba, 1961
Barbara Frietchie, 1924 (Ince)
Barbarella, 1968 (Jarre; Renoir; Southern; de Laurentiis)
Barbarian, 1933 (Adrian; Brown; Freed; Loos; Mayer; Rosson; Stothart)
Barbarian and the Geisha, 1958 (Clarke; Friedhofer; Lemaire; Smith; Wheeler)
Barbarian, Ingomar, 1908 (Bitzer)
Barbarians, 1987 (Donaggio; Golan and Globus)
Barbarians. See Revak, lo schiavo di Cartagine, 1960
Barbarians at the Gate, 1993 (Stark)

Barbary Coast, 1935 (Day; Goldwyn; Hecht; Newman)
Barbary Coast Bunny, 1956 (Blanc; Jones; Stalling)
Barbary Sheep, 1917 (Carré; Zukor)
Barbe-Bleue, 1935 (Jaubert)
Barbe-Bleue, 1951 (Jeanson; Matras; Wakhévitch)
Barbe-Bleue, 1972 (Legrand; Morricone)
Barbed Wire, 1927 (Banton; Furthman; Glennon; Pommer)
Barbeque Brawl, 1956 (Hanna and Barbera)
Barberousse, 1917 (Burel; Gaumont)
Bařbora rádí, 1935 (Heller)
Barcarole, 1935 (Herlth; Röhrig)
Barcarole. See Brand in der Oper, 1930
Bardame, 1922 (Wagner)
Bardelys the Magnificent, 1926 (Basevi; Daniels; Day; Gibbons; Mayer)
Bare Essence, 1982 (Ames)
Barefaced Flatfoot, 1951 (Bosustow; Hubley)
Barefoot Battalion, 1953 (Theodorakis)
Barefoot Boy, 1924 (Cohn)
Barefoot Boy, 1938 (Brown)
Barefoot Contessa, 1954 (Cardiff; Hornbeck)
Barefoot in the Park, 1967 (Edouart; Head; La Shelle; Mercer; Wallis; Westmore Family)
Barefoot Mailman, 1951 (Duning)
Barfly, 1987 (Golan and Globus; Müller)
Bargain, 1914 (Sullivan)
Bargain, 1931 (Polito)
Bargain Daze, 1953 (Terry)
Bargain of the Century, 1933 (Roach)
Barker, 1928 (Garmes; Grot; Mankiewicz)
Barking-Donkey Sonichi. See Shiriboe Sonichi, 1969
Barkleys of Broadway, 1949 (Comden and Green; Freed; Irene; Mayer; Pan; Stradling)
Barluschke, 1998 (Theodorakis)
Barn Dance, 1929 (Disney; Iwerks)
Barna från Blåsjöfjället, 1980 (Lundgren)
Barnaby—Father Dear Father, 1962 (Halas and Batchelor)
Barnaby—Overdue Dues Blues, 1962 (Halas and Batchelor)
Barnacle Bill, 1930 (Fleischer)
Barnacle Bill, 1941 (Gibbons; Kaper)
Barnacle Bill, 1957 (Clarke; Slocombe)
Barnen från Frostmofjället, 1945 (Nykvist)
Barnet, 1912 (Jaenzon; Magnusson)
Barnstormers, 1905 (Bitzer)
Barnum and Ringling, Inc., 1928 (Roach)
Barnyard Actor, 1955 (Terry)
Barnyard Amateurs, 1936 (Terry)
Barnyard Baseball, 1939 (Terry)
Barnyard Battle, 1929 (Disney; Iwerks)
Barnyard Blackout, 1943 (Terry)
Barnyard Boss, 1937 (Terry)
Barnyard Brat, 1939 (Fleischer)
Barnyard Concert, 1930 (Disney)
Barnyard Eggcitement, 1939 (Terry)
Barnyard Five, 1936 (Lantz)
Barnyard WAAC, 1942 (Terry)
Barocco, 1976 (Nuytten; Sarde)
Baron de Crac. See Monsieur de Crac, 1910
Baron Munchhausen, 1943 (Kästner)
Baron Münchhausen. See Baron Prášil, 1961
Baron of Arizona, 1950 (Howe)
Baron Prášil, 1961 (Brdečka; Zeman)
Baroness and the Butler, 1938 (La Shelle; Miller; Trotti)
Baroon, 1976 (Burman)
Baroud, 1931 (Burel; Wakhévitch)
Barrage contre le Pacifique, 1958 (Rota; de Laurentiis)
Barrage du Chatelot, 1950 (Fradetal)

Barrage du Châtelot, 1953 (Colpi)
Barrandov Nocturne, or How Films Dance and Sing. See Barrandovské nocturno aneb Jak film tancil a zpíval, 1984
Barrandovské nocturno aneb Jak film tancil a zpíval, 1984 (švankmajer)
Barretts of Wimpole Street, 1934 (Adrian; Booth; Daniels; Gibbons; Mayer; Stewart; Stothart; Thalberg; Vajda)
Barretts of Wimpole Street, 1957 (Junge; Kaper; Young)
Barricade, 1939 (Freund; Newman; Veiller)
Barrier, 1926 (Mayer)
Barrier, 1937 (Barnes; Head)
Barrington, 1987 (Zanuck)
Barry Lyndon, 1975 (Adam; Alcott; Rosenman)
Barry MacKenzie Holds His Own , 1974 (McAlpine)
Bartered Bride. See Prodaná nevesta, 1933
Bartholomew versus the Wheel, 1964 (Blanc; McKimson)
Barton Fink, 1991 (Burwell)
Baruch. See Alte Gesetz, 1923
Baruffe Chiozzotte. See Paese senza pace, 1943
Baruten Bukvar, 1977 (Dinov)
Bas-fonds, 1936 (Lourié; Spaak)
Basant, 1943 (Biswas)
Baseball Bugs, 1946 (Blanc; Stalling)
Bashful, 1917 (Roach)
Bashful Buzzard, 1945 (Blanc; Clampett; Stalling)
Basic Instinct, 1992 (Eszterhas; Goldsmith; Winkler)
Basketball Fix, 1951 (Cortez; Leven)
Basta che non si sappia in giro, 1976 (Age and Scarpelli)
Bat, 1926 (Edeson; Menzies)
Bat, 1959 (Biroc)
Bat Whispers, 1930 (Schenck)
Bataan, 1943 (Gibbons; Gillespie; Kaper; Mayer; Schary; Wheeler)
Bataille d'Austerlitz, 1909 (Cohl)
Bataille de boules de neige, 1901 (Gaumont)
Bataille de San Sebastian, 1967 (Morricone)
Bataille d'oreillers, 1907 (Gaumont)
Bataille du rail, 1945 (Alekan)
Batavernas trohetsed, 1957 (Fischer)
Batavians' Oath of Fidelity. See Batavernas trohetsed, 1957
Bateau sur l'herbe, 1971 (Evein)
Bathing Beauty, 1944 (Green; Irene; Mayer; Sharaff; Stradling)
Bathroom, 1970 (Kuri)
Bâtisseurs, 1938 (Honegger)
Batman, 1966 (Smith)
Batman, 1989 (Elfman)
Batman & Robin, 1997 (Baker; Dykstra)
Batman Forever, 1995 (Baker; Dykstra)
Batman Returns, 1992 (Elfman; Winston)
Baton Bunny, 1959 (Blanc; Jones)
Bats in the Belfry, 1960 (Lantz)
Battaglia di Algeri, 1965 (Morricone; Serandrei; Solinas)
Battement de coeur, 1939 (Barsacq)
*batteries not included, 1987 (Marshall)
Battle at Apache Pass, 1952 (Hunter)
Battle at Elderbush Gulch, 1914 (Bitzer)
Battle Circus, 1953 (Alton; Basevi; Berman)
Battle Cry, 1955 (Steiner)
Battle Dust. See Senjin, 1935
Battle for Anzio. See Sbarco di Anzio, 1968
Battle for the Planet of the Apes, 1973 (Rosenman)
Battle Ground, 1949 (Gibbons)
Battle Hell. See Yangtse Incident, 1957
Battle Hymn, 1957 (Hunter; Metty)
Battle in Outer Space. See Uchu daisensu, 1959
Battle of Algiers. See Battaglia di Algeri, 1965
Battle of Austerlitz. See Bataille d'Austerlitz, 1909
Battle of Britain, 1943 (Hornbeck; Veiller)

Battle of Britain, 1969 (Arnold; Walton; Young)
Battle of China, 1944 (Hornbeck; Veiller)
Battle of Gettysburg, 1913 (Ince; Sullivan)
Battle of Gettysburg, 1955 (Deutsch; Schary)
Battle of Hawaii. *See* Hawaii marei oki haisen, 1942
Battle of Midway, 1942 (Newman; Parrish)
Battle of Midway. *See* Midway, 1976
Battle of Neretva. *See* Bitka na Neretvi, 1968
Battle of New Orleans, 1960 (Godfrey)
Battle of Paris, 1929 (Porter; Ruttenberg)
Battle of Russia, 1944 (Hornbeck; Veiller)
Battle of San Pietro, 1944 (Tiomkin)
Battle of the Astros. *See* Kaiju daisenso, 1966
Battle of the Bulge, 1965 (Lourié)
Battle of the Century, 1928 (Bruckman; Roach)
Battle of the Japan Sea. *See* Nihonkai daikaisen, 1969
Battle of the Red Men, 1912 (Ince)
Battle of the River Plate, 1956 (Challis; Heckroth; Rank)
Battle of the Sexes, 1914 (Bitzer)
Battle of the Sexes, 1928 (Bitzer; Schenck; Struss)
Battle of the Sexes, 1959 (Francis)
Battle of the Stag Beetles. *See* Valka zukov rogachi, 1910
Battle of the V1, 1958 (Adam)
Battle of the Villa Fiorita, 1965 (Dillon; Morris)
Battle Royal, 1936 (Lantz; Terry)
Battle Stations, 1944 (Kanin)
Battle Stations, 1955 (Guffey)
Battle under the Walls of Kerchenetz, 1971 (Ivanov-Vano; Norstein)
Battle without Weapons. *See* Buki naki tatakai, 1960
Battle Zone, 1952 (Wanger)
Battle, 1911 (Bitzer)
Battle, 1923 (Fleischer)
Battleground, 1949 (Schary)
Battles of Chief Pontiac, 1952 (Bernstein)
Battleship Potemkin. *See* **Bronenosets Potemkin**, 1925
Battleship Potemkin Survivor, 1968 (Lassally)
Battlestar: Galactica, 1978 (Dykstra)
Battletruck, 1981 (Menges)
Battling Buckaroos, 1933 (Canutt)
Battling Butler, 1926 (Schenck)
Battling Jane, 1918 (Zukor)
Battling Orioles, 1924 (Roach)
Battling with Buffalo Bill, 1931 (Canutt)
Batty Baseball, 1944 (Avery)
Baule les pins, 1990 (Sarde)
Baxter, 1973 (Unsworth)
Baxter, Vera Baxter, 1977 (Duras; Vierny)
Bay of the Angels. *See* Baie des anges, 1963
Bayaya. *See* Bajaja, 1950
Be Honest, 1923 (Roach)
Be Human, 1936 (Fleischer)
Be Kind to Aminals, 1935 (Fleischer)
Be My Wife, 1919 (Roach)
Be Up to Date, 1938 (Fleischer)
Be Your Age, 1926 (Roach)
Be Yourself!, 1930 (Menzies; Schenck; Struss)
Beach, 2000 (Badalamenti)
Beachcomber. *See* Vessel of Wrath, 1938
Beach Blanket Bingo, 1965 (Crosby)
Beach Combers, 1936 (Lantz)
Beach Nuts, 1918 (Roach)
Beachcomber, 1939 (Head)
Beachcomber, 1954 (Rank)
Beaches, 1988 (Delerue)
Beaks to the Grindstone, 1985 (Godfrey)
Beanstalk Bunny, 1955 (Blanc; Jones; Stalling)

Beanstalk Jack, 1933 (Terry)
Beanstalk Jack, 1946 (Terry)
Bear, 1984 (Conti)
Bear, 1989 (Henson)
Bear. *See* Ours, 1988
Bear Feat, 1949 (Blanc; Jones; Stalling)
Bear for Punishment, 1951 (Blanc; Jones; Stalling)
Bear Hug, 1964 (Hanna and Barbera)
Bear Knuckles, 1964 (Hanna and Barbera)
Bear that Wasn't, 1967 (Jones)
Bear Up!, 1963 (Hanna and Barbera)
Bearly Able, 1962 (Hanna and Barbera)
Bear's Tale, 1940 (Avery; Blanc; Stalling)
Bear's Wedding. *See* Medvezhya svadba, 1926
Beast Alley. *See* Kemonomichi, 1965
Beast at Bay, 1912 (Bitzer)
Beast from 20,000 Fathoms, 1953 (Boyle; Harryhausen; Lourié)
Beast of Hollow Mountain, 1956 (O'Brien)
Beast with Five Fingers, 1947 (Friedhofer; Siodmak; Steiner)
Beastmaster, 1982 (Alcott)
Beat, 1988 (Burwell)
Beat 13. *See* Třináctý revír, 1945
Beat Girl, 1960 (Barry; Lassally)
Beat It, 1918 (Roach)
Beat Me Daddy, Eight to the Bar!, 1940 (Krasner)
Beat Street, 1984 (Von Brandenstein)
Beat the Devil, 1953 (Francis; Morris)
Beata Loro, 1975 (Cristaldi)
Beating the Game, 1921 (Gibbons)
Beatrice Cenci, 1926 (Amidei)
Beatrice Cenci, 1941 (Stallich)
Béatrice devant le désir, 1943 (Wakhévitch)
Beau and Arrows, 1932 (Lantz)
Beau Beste, 1933 (Lantz)
Beau Broadway, 1928 (Gibbons)
Beau Brummell, 1954 (Addinsell; Francis; Junge; Morris)
Beau Chumps. *See* Beau Hunks, 1931
Beau fixe, 1953 (Legrand)
Beau Geste, 1926 (Zukor)
Beau Geste, 1939 (Dreier; Head; Newman)
Beau Geste, 1966 (Bumstead; Whitlock)
Beau Hunks, 1931 (Roach)
Beau Ideal, 1930 (Steiner)
Beau James, 1957 (Cahn; Head)
Beau Revel, 1921 (Ince)
Beau Sabreur, 1928 (Banton; Zukor)
Beau Serge, 1958 (Rabier)
Beau Voyage, 1947 (Matras)
Beau-Père, 1981 (Sarde; Vierny)
Beaubourg, 1977 (Almendros)
Beauté de l'effort, 1953 (Decaë)
Beauté du diable, 1949 (Barsacq; Di Venanzo)
Beauties of the Night. *See* Belles de nuit, 1952
Beautiful Banff and Lake Louise, 1935 (Hoch)
Beautiful Blonde from Bashful Bend, 1949 (Trumbo)
Beautiful Budapest, 1938 (Hoch)
Beautiful but Dangerous. *See* She Couldn't Say No, 1954
Beautiful but Deadly. *See* Don Is Dead, 1973
Beautiful But Poor. *See* Belle ma povere, 1957
Beautiful Cheat, 1945 (Banton)
Beautiful Gambler, 1921 (Barnes)
Beautiful Katya. *See* Krasavice Ka a, 1919
Beautiful Lukanida. *See* Prekrasnya Lukanida, 1911
Beautiful Margaret. *See* Tout Petit Faust, 1910
Beautiful Nuisance. *See* On peut le dire sans se fâcher!, 1978
Beautiful Prisoner. *See* Belle Captive, 1983

Beautiful Rebel. *See* Janice Meredith, 1924
Beautiful Stranger, 1954 (Arnold)
Beautiful Swindlers. *See* Plus Belles Escroqueries du monde, 1964
Beauty, 1994 (Elfman)
Beauty. *See* Beauty for Sale, 1933
Beauty and the Beast, 1962 (Friedhofer; Pierce)
Beauty and the Beast, 1987 (Baker; Golan and Globus)
Beauty and the Beast, 1991 (Menken)
Beauty and the Beast. *See* **Belle et la bête**, 1946
Beauty and the Bus, 1933 (Roach)
Beauty and the Devil. *See* Beauté du diable, 1949
Beauty and the Rogue, 1918 (Seitz)
Beauty Capital. *See* Bibou no miyako, 1957
Beauty for Sale, 1933 (Adrian; Howe)
Beauty for the Asking, 1939 (Jarrico)
Beauty on the Beach, 1950 (Terry)
Beauty Shop, 1950 (Terry)
Beauty Shoppe, 1936 (Lantz)
Beauty Treatment, 1960 (Halas and Batchelor)
Beauty's Daughter, 1935 (Maté; Seitz)
Beaux Arts mysterieux, 1910 (Cohl)
Beaux Jours, 1935 (D'Eaubonne; Meerson; Spaak)
Beaux-Arts de Jocko, 1909 (Cohl)
Beaver Trouble, 1951 (Terry)
Bébé de l'escadron, 1935 (Douy; Lourié)
Bebo's Girl. *See* Ragazza di Bube, 1963
Because I Loved You. *See* Dich hab' ich geliebt, 1929
Because of Him, 1946 (Mohr; Plunkett; Rozsa)
Because of You, 1952 (Metty)
Because They're Young, 1960 (Williams)
Because You're Mine, 1952 (Cahn; Green; Pasternak; Rose; Ruttenberg)
Becket, 1964 (Bryan; Mathieson; Unsworth; Wallis)
Beckoning Flame, 1916 (Sullivan)
Becky, 1927 (Gibbons)
Becky Sharp, 1935 (Cooper; MacGowan; Rennahan; Steiner)
Becoming Colette, 1992 (Mnouchkine)
Bed. *See* Secrets d'alcove, 1954
Bed and Board. *See* Domicile conjugal, 1970
Bed of Roses, 1922 (Roach)
Bed of Roses, 1933 (Cooper; Polglase; Rosher; Steiner)
Bed-Sitting Room, 1969 (Watkin)
Bedazzled, 2000 (Edlund)
Bedelia, 1930 (Fleischer)
Bedelia, 1946 (Young)
Bedevilled, 1955 (Alwyn; Junge; Rose)
Bedevilled Rabbit, 1957 (Blanc; McKimson)
Bedknobs and Broomsticks, 1971 (Ellenshaw)
Bedlam, 1946 (D'Agostino; Lewton; Musuraca)
Bedroom Window, 1987 (Towne)
Bedside, 1934 (Orry-Kelly)
Bedtime, 1923 (Fleischer)
Bedtime for Bonzo, 1951 (Fleischer)
Bedtime for Sniffles, 1940 (Blanc; Jones; Stalling)
Bedtime Story, 1933 (Johnson; Lang)
Bedtime Story, 1941 (Irene; Walker)
Bedtime Worries, 1933 (Roach)
Bee and the Dove, 1950 (Popescu-Gopo)
Bee-Devilled Bruin, 1949 (Blanc; Joncs; Stalling)
Beef for and After, 1962 (Hanna and Barbera)
Beekeeper. *See* O Melissokomos, 1986
Beep, Beep, 1952 (Blanc; Jones; Stalling)
Beep Prepared, 1961 (Blanc; Jones)
Beer, 1985 (Conti)
Bees in His Bonnet, 1918 (Roach)
Bees in Paradise, 1944 (Rank)
Beetles. *See* Skarabyozi, 1909

Before Breakfast, 1919 (Roach)
Before Dawn, 1933 (Steiner)
Before I Hang, 1940 (Brown)
Before Matriculation. *See* Před maturitou, 1932
Before Midnight, 1925 (Furthman)
Before the Monsoon, 1979 (Menges)
Before the Public, 1922 (Roach)
Before the Revolution. *See* Prima della revoluzione, 1964
Befriete Hände, 1939 (Hoffmann)
Beg, Borrow, or Steal, 1937 (Daniels)
Begegnung in Rom. *See* Parigina a Roma, 1954
Beggar Life. *See* Svet, kde se žebrá, 1938
Beggar of Cawnpore, 1916 (Sullivan)
Beggar on Horseback, 1925 (Brown)
Beggar's Opera, 1953 (Wakhévitch; Wilcox)
Beggar's Opera. *See* **Dreigroschenoper**, 1931
Beggar's Uproar, 1960 (Halas and Batchelor)
Beginning of the End, 1947 (Gillespie; Irene)
Begone Dull Care, 1949 (McClaren)
Begstvo Puankare, 1932 (Ptushko)
Beguiled, 1971 (Schifrin; Westmore Family)
Behave Yourself, 1951 (Howe; Krasna; Orry-Kelly; Wald)
Behemoth, the Sea Monster. *See* Giant Behemoth, 1959
Behind Closed Doors. *See* S vyloučenim veřejnosti, 1933
Behind Closed Shutters. *See* Persiane chiuse, 1951
Behind That Curtain, 1929 (Fox; Levien)
Behind the Door, 1919 (Ince)
Behind the Door. *See* Man with Nine Lives, 1940
Behind the Door. *See* Oltre la porta, 1982
Behind the Headlines, 1937 (Metty)
Behind the Make-Up, 1930 (Lang; Miller)
Behind the Mask, 1932 (Swerling)
Behind the Mask, 1958 (Krasker)
Behind the Meat Ball, 1945 (Blanc; Stalling)
Behind the News, 1940 (Schary)
Behind the Rising Sun, 1943 (Metty)
Behind the Stockade, 1911 (Ince)
Behold a Pale Horse, 1964 (Jarre; Trauner)
Behold My Wife, 1935 (Shamroy; Zukor)
Behold We Live. *See* If I Were Free, 1932
Beichte des Feldkuraten, 1927 (Kolowrat-Krakowsky)
Beiden Gatten der Frau Ruth, 1919 (Galeen)
Beiden Rivalen, 1914 (Warm)
Being Human, 1993 (Puttnam)
Being John Malkovich, 1999 (Burwell)
Being There, 1979 (Mandel)
Bekenntnisse des Hochstaplers Felix Krull, 1957 (Herlth)
Bel Age, 1959 (Cloquet; Delerue)
Bel Ami, 1954 (Eisler)
Bel Indifférent, 1957 (Evein; Fradetal; Jarre)
Bel-âge, 1959 (Vierny)
Bel-Ami, 1954 (Barsacq)
Believe in Me, 1971 (Winkler)
Believe It or Else, 1939 (Avery)
Believers, 1987 (Müller)
Belinsky, 1953 (Moskvin; Shostakovich)
Bell for Adano, 1945 (La Shelle; Newman; Trotti)
Bell Hoppy, 1954 (Blanc; McKimson; Stalling)
Bell of Austi, 1914 (Ince)
Bell ouvrage, 1943 (Alekan)
Bell, Book and Candle, 1958 (Duning; Howe; Louis; Taradash)
Bella di Lodi, 1962 (Delli Colli)
Bella di Roma, 1955 (Rota)
Bella Donna, 1923 (Miller)
Bella mugnaia, 1955 (Ponti; de Laurentiis)
Belladonna, 1922 (Zukor)

Belladonna, 1981 (Theodorakis)

Bellamy Trial, 1929 (Gibbons; Miller)

Bellboy, 1960 (Bumstead; Head; Pereira)

Belle, 1973 (Cloquet)

Belle Américaine, 1961 (Cloquet)

Belle au bois dormant, 1935 (Alexeieff and Parker)

Belle Aventure, 1942 (Auric; Burel)

Belle Captive, 1983 (Alekan; Robbe-Grillet)

Belle de Cadix, 1953 (Barsacq)

Belle de jour, 1967 (Carrière; Hakim; Vierny)

Belle Emmerdeuse. *See* On peut le dire sans se fâcher!, 1978

Belle Equipe, 1936 (Spaak)

Belle et la bête, 1946 (Alekan; Auric)

Bclle ct lc bête, 1899 (Pathé)

Belle et l'empereur, 1959 (Matras)

Belle Etoile, 1938 (Wakhévitch)

Belle Fille comme moi, 1972 (Delerue)

Belle Garce, 1947 (Spaak)

Belle Histoire, 1991 (Lai)

Belle Journée, 1954 (Cloquet)

Belle Journée, 1972 (Colpi)

Belle Le Grand, 1951 (Young)

Belle ma povere, 1957 (Delli Colli)

Belle Marinière, 1932 (Maté)

Belle Marinière, 1963 (Cloquet)

Belle of New York, 1952 (Freed; Deutsch; Mercer; Rose; Smith)

Belle of the Nineties, 1934 (Banton; Dreier; Struss; Zukor)

Belle of the Yukon, 1944 (Fields; van Heusen)

Belle of Yorktown, 1913 (Ince)

Belle que voilà, 1949 (Douy; Kosma)

Dellc Starr, 1941 (Banton; Day; MacGowan; Newman; Rennahan; Trotti)

Belle Starr, 1980 (Alonzo)

Belles de nuit, 1952 (Barsacq)

Belles of St. Clement's, 1936 (Havelock-Allan)

Belles of St. Trinian's, 1954 (Arnold; Korda)

Belles on Their Toes, 1952 (Carmichael; Jeakins; Lemaire)

Bellissima, 1951 (Cecchi D'amico; Serandrei; Zavattini)

Bellissimo novembre, 1968 (Morricone)

Bellman. *See* Sortiléges, 1944

Bello mia bellezza mia, 1982 (Rotunno)

Bells, 1982 (Houseman)

Bells. *See* Murder by Phone, 1981

Bells Are Ringing, 1960 (Ames; Comden and Green; Freed; Krasner; Plunkett; Previn)

Bells Go Down, 1943 (Balcon)

Bells of St. Mary's, 1945 (Barnes; D'Agostino; Head; Nichols; van Heusen)

Belly of an Architect, 1987 (Vierny)

Beloved, 1998 (Littleton)

Beloved. *See* Del odio nació el amor, 1949

Beloved Adventuress, 1917 (Marion)

Beloved Bachelor, 1931 (Rosher)

Beloved Brat, 1938 (Barnes)

Beloved Enemy, 1936 (Day; Goldwyn; Newman; Toland)

Beloved Infidel, 1959 (Reynolds; Shamroy; Wald; Waxman)

Beloved Rogue, 1927 (August; Menzies)

Beloved Vagabond, 1936 (Andrejew; Milhaud; Planer)

Below the Chinese Restaurant. *See* Sotto il ristorante Cinese, 1987

Below the Sea, 1933 (Swerling; Walker)

Below Zero, 1930 (Roach)

Ben, 1972 (Metty)

Ben-Hur, 1925 (Gibbons; Gillespie; Goldwyn; Mathis; Mayer; Struss; Thalberg)

Ben-Hur, 1959 (Adam; Canutt; Gillespie; Rozsa; Surtees)

Benazir, 1964 (Burman)

Bend of the River, 1952 (Chase)

Beneath the 12-Mile Reef, 1953 (Cronjager; Herrmann; Jeakins; Lemaire; Reynolds)

Beneath the Planet of the Apes, 1970 (Krasner; Rosenman; Smith)

Bengal Brigade, 1954 (Miller)

Bengal Lancers, 1984 (Lassally)

Bengazi, 1955 (Biroc)

Benikmori, 1931 (Tsuburaya)

Benjamin ou les mémoires d'un puceau, 1968 (Cloquet)

Benny & Joon, 1993 (Littleton)

Benny from Panama, 1934 (Roach)

Benny Goodman Story, 1955 (Daniels; Mancini)

Benten Boy. *See* Benten kozou, 1958

Benten kozou, 1958 (Miyagawa)

Beqasoor, 1950 (Biswas)

Bequest to the Nation, 1973 (Fisher; Legrand; Rattigan; Wallis)

Berg-Ejvind och hans hustru, 1918 (Jaenzon; Magnusson)

Bergère et le ramoneur, 1952 (Kosma)

Bergère et le ramoneur. *See* Roi et l'oiseau, 1980

Bergkatze, 1921 (Kräly)

Berkeley Square, 1933 (Lasky; Levien)

Berlin Affair, 1970 (Lai)

Berlin Affair, 1985 (Donaggio; Golan and Globus)

Berlin Blues, 1988 (Schifrin)

Berlin Correspondent, 1942 (Day; Miller)

Berlin—Die Symphonie einer Grossstadt, 1927 (Freund; Mayer)

Berlin Express, 1948 (Ballard; D'Agostino; Orry-Kelly; Siodmak)

Berlin-Jérusalem, 1989 (Alekan)

Berlin—Symphony of a Big City. *See* **Berlin—Die Symphonie einer Grossstadt**, 1927

Berlin—Symphony of a Great City. *See* **Berlin—Die Symphonie einer Grossstadt**, 1927

Bermuda Mystery, 1944 (Basevi; La Shelle)

Bernadette, 1988 (Lai)

Bernard-l'hermite, 1931 (Jaubert)

Bernardine, 1957 (Lemaire; Mercer)

Bernice Bobs Her Hair, 1976 (Rosenblum)

Beröringen, 1971 (Fischer; Lundgren; Nykvist)

Berre, cité du pétrole, 1953 (Delerue)

Berth Mark, 1926 (Fleischer)

Berth Marks, 1929 (Roach)

Bertha, the Sewing Machine Girl, 1926 (Fox)

Bertoldo, Bertoldino e Cacasenno, 1984 (Cecchi D'amico)

Bertrand, coeur de lion, 1950 (Braunberger; Decaë)

Beside a Moonlit Stream, 1938 (Fleischer)

Besieged, 1998 (Peploe)

Bespoke Overcoat, 1955 (Auric)

Best Foot Forward, 1943 (Freed; Irene)

Best Friends, 1982 (Legrand)

Best Little Girl in the World, 1981 (O'Steen)

Best Little Whorehouse in Texas, 1982 (Fraker; Whitlock; van Runkle)

Best Man, 1964 (Jeakins; Wexler; Wheeler)

Best Man Wins, 1935 (Walker)

Best Mouse Loses, 1920 (Bray)

Best of Cinerama, 1956 (Cooper)

Best of Enemies. *See* I due nemici, 1961

Best of Everything, 1959 (Cahn; Newman; Smith; Wald)

Best of the Badmen, 1951 (Cronjager)

Best People, 1925 (Howe)

Best Playboy in Japan. *See* Nippon ichi no iro-otoko, 1963

Best Things in Life Are Free, 1956 (Lemaire; Shamroy; Spencer)

Best Way to Get Along. *See* Meilleure Façon de marcher, 1976

Best Years of Our Lives, 1946 (Carmichael; Friedhofer; Goldwyn; Jenkins; Koch; Mandell; Sharaff; Sherwood; Toland)

Bestaire d'amour, 1963 (Braunberger; Carrière)

Bestia negra, 1939 (Figueroa)

Bestiaire d'amour, 1965 (Delerue)

Bestioles Artistes, 1911 (Cohl)
Bestione, 1974 (Rotunno)
Besuch, 1963 (Barsacq)
Bête a l'affût, 1959 (Jarre; Matras)
Bête errante, 1931 (Douy)
Bête humaine, 1938 (Courant; Douy; Hakim; Kosma; Lourié; Renoir)
Bethsabée, 1947 (Kosma)
Bethune: The Making of a Hero, 1990 (Coutard)
Betragen ungenuend, 1933 (Heller)
Betrayal, 1929 (Dreier; Kräly)
Betrayal, 1983 (Pinter)
Betrayal from the East, 1945 (Metty)
Betrayed, 1954 (Junge)
Betrayed, 1982 (Spiegel)
Betrayed, 1988 (Conti; Eszterhas; Von Brandenstein; Winkler)
Betrayed. *See* When Strangers Marry, 1944
Betrayed by a Handprint, 1908 (Bitzer)
Betrayer. *See* Vanina Vanini, 1961
Betrothed. *See* I promessi sposi, 1989
Betsy, 1978 (Barry; Bernstein; Jeakins)
Bettelstudent, 1927 (Reisch)
Better Late Than Never, 1950 (Terry)
Better Late than Never, 1983 (Fisher; Mancini)
Better Movies, 1925 (Roach)
Better 'ole, 1926 (Carré; Zanuck)
Better Tomorrow, 1945 (Kaufman; North)
Better Way, 1909 (Bitzer)
Better Way, 1911 (Gaudio)
Better Wife, 1919 (Edeson)
Betty Boop, 1931 (Fleischer)
Betty Boop, 1933 (Fleischer)
Betty Boop, 1935 (Fleischer)
Betty Boop and Grampy, 1935 (Fleischer)
Betty Boop and Little Jimmy, 1936 (Fleischer)
Betty Boop and the Little King, 1936 (Fleischer)
Betty Boop for President, 1932 (Fleischer)
Betty Boop Limited, 1932 (Fleischer)
Betty Boop M.D., 1932 (Fleischer)
Betty Boop with Henry the Funniest Living American, 1935 (Fleischer)
Betty Boop's Bamboo Isle, 1932 (Fleischer)
Betty Boop's Big Boss, 1933 (Fleischer)
Betty Boop's Birthday Party, 1933 (Fleischer)
Betty Boop's Bizzy Bee, 1932 (Fleischer)
Betty Boop's Crazy Inventions, 1933 (Fleischer)
Betty Boop's Hallowe'en Party, 1933 (Fleischer)
Betty Boop's Ker-choo, 1933 (Fleischer)
Betty Boop's Life Guard, 1934 (Fleischer)
Betty Boop's Little Pal, 1934 (Fleischer)
Betty Boop's May Party, 1933 (Fleischer)
Betty Boop's Museum, 1932 (Fleischer)
Betty Boop's Penthouse, 1933 (Fleischer)
Betty Boop's Prize Show, 1934 (Fleischer)
Betty Boop's Rise to Fame, 1934 (Fleischer)
Betty Boop's Ups and Downs, 1932 (Fleischer)
Betty Co-ed, 1931 (Fleischer)
Betty in Blunderland, 1934 (Fleischer)
Betty in Search of a Thrill, 1915 (Marion)
Between Heaven and Hell, 1956 (Friedhofer; Lemaire; Wheeler)
Between Meals, 1922 (Roach)
Between Men, 1915 (August)
Between Midnight and Dawn, 1950 (Duning; Stromberg)
Between the Dances, 1905 (Bitzer)
Between the Darkness and the Dawn, 1985 (Lathrop)
Between the Lines, 1977 (Von Brandenstein)
Between Two Women, 1937 (Adrian; Seitz)
Between Two Women, 1944 (Irene; Rosson)

Between Two Worlds, 1944 (Friedhofer; Korngold)
Between Two Worlds. *See* Müde Tod, 1921
Between Wars, 1974 (Boyd)
Between Worlds. *See* Müde Tod, 1921
Beverley of Graustark, 1926 (Day)
Beverly Hillbillies, 1993 (Schifrin)
Beverly Hills Cop III, 1994 (Harryhausen)
Beverly Hills Madam, 1986 (Schifrin)
Beverly of Graustark, 1926 (Gibbons)
Bewaqoof, 1960 (Burman)
Beware My Lovely, 1952 (D'Agostino; Horner)
Beware of a Holy Whore. *See* Warnung vor einer Heiligen Nutte, 1971
Beware of Barnacle Bill, 1935 (Fleischer)
Beware of Blondes, 1928 (Walker)
Beware of Children. *See* No Kidding, 1960
Beware of Greeks Bearing Arms. *See* Fovou tous Ellines . . . , 2000
Beware of Greeks Bearing Guns. *See* Fovou tous Ellines . . . , 2000
Beware of Pity, 1946 (Beaton; Rank; Vetchinsky)
Beware of Widows, 1927 (Laemmle)
Bewitched, 1945 (Kaper)
Bewitched Bunny, 1954 (Blanc; Jones; Stalling)
Bewitched Matches, 1913-14 (Cohl)
Beyond All Limits. *See* Flor de mayo, 1957
Beyond Evil. *See* Al di là del bene a del male, 1980
Beyond Glory, 1948 (Dreier; Head; Seitz)
Beyond Justice, 1992 (Morricone)
Beyond London, 1928 (Berman)
Beyond Price, 1921 (Fox; Ruttenberg)
Beyond Rangoon, 1995 (Seale; Zimmer)
Beyond the Blue Horizon, 1942 (Dreier; Head; Westmore Family; Young)
Beyond the Border, 1925 (Polito; Stromberg)
Beyond the Clouds. *See* Par-delà les nuages, 1995
Beyond the Forest, 1949 (Blanke; Burks; Head; Steiner)
Beyond the Mountains. *See* Más allá de las montañas, 1967
Beyond the Poseidon Adventure, 1979 (Ames)
Beyond the Reef, 1981 (Lai)
Beyond the River. *See* Bottom of the Bottle, 1956
Beyond the River Nyemen. *See* Nad Nyemen, 1909
Beyond the Rockies, 1932 (McCord)
Beyond the Time Barrier, 1959 (Pierce)
Beyond the Tropopause, 1968 (Menges)
Beyond the Valley of the Dolls, 1970 (Smith)
Beyond the Wall. *See* Müde Tod, 1921
Beyond This Place, 1959 (Adam; Cardiff)
Beyond Tomorrow, 1940 (Garmes)
Beyond Victory, 1931 (Mandell)
Bez konca, 1985 (Preisner)
Bez pogovora, 1999 (Pinter)
Bezdetná, 1935 (Heller)
Bhookh, 1947 (Biswas)
Bhowani Junction, 1956 (Berman; Levien; Rozsa; Young)
Bhumika, 1977 (Nihalani)
Bianco, rosso, e . . . , 1971 (Guerra; Ponti)
Bianco, rosso, e verdone, 1981 (Morricone)
Bibbia, 1966 (Dunn; de Laurentiis; Rotunno)
Bible. *See* Bibbia, 1966
Bible . . . in the Beginning. *See* Bibbia, 1965
Bible Stories, 1980 (Halas and Batchelor)
Bibou no miyako, 1957 (Muraki)
Biches, 1968 (Gégauff; Rabier)
Bicycle Thief. *See* **Ladri di biciclette**, 1948
Bicyclette bleue, 2000 (Legrand)
Bidone, 1955 (Flaiano and Pinelli; Rota; Serandrei)
Bidrohi, 1935 (Burman)
Bien amada, 1951 (Figueroa)
Bienamados, 1965 (Figueroa)

Bienvenuto Cellini, 1910 (Gaumont)

Bière, 1924 (Périnal)

Biffen and the Banana. *See* Biffen och bananen, 1951

Biffen och bananen, 1951 (Fischer)

Big, 1988 (Bass; Hamlisch; Loquasto)

Big Adventure, 1921 (Miller)

Big Bang, 1990 (Bozzetto)

Big Bankroll. *See* King of the Roaring Twenties, 1961

Big Beat, 1957 (Mancini)

Big Blockade, 1942 (Addinsell; Balcon)

Big Blue. *See* Grand Bleu, 1988

Big Boodle, 1956 (Garmes)

Big Boy, 1930 (Mohr)

Big Brain, 1933 (Edeson)

Big Brawl, 1980 (Schifrin)

Big Broadcast of 1932, 1932 (Head)

Big Broadcast of 1936, 1935 (Head)

Big Broadcast of 1937, 1936 (Banton; Dreier; Fischinger; Head; Young)

Big Broadcast of 1938, 1938 (Dreier; Head)

Big Brown Eyes, 1936 (Reynolds; Wanger)

Big Build-Up, 1942 (Terry)

Big Business, 1924 (Roach)

Big Business, 1929 (Roach)

Big Business Girl, 1931 (Polito)

Big Calibre, 1935 (Alton)

Big Carnival, 1951 (Head)

Big Carnival. *See* Ace in the Hole, 1951

Big Chief Ko-Ko, 1925 (Fleischer)

Big Chief Ugh-Amugh-Ugh, 1938 (Fleischer)

Big Chill, 1983 (Littleton)

Big Circus, 1959 (Hoch)

Big City, 1928 (Day; Gibbons)

Big City, 1937 (Gibbons; Krasna; Schary)

Big City, 1948 (Ames; Pasternak; Surtees)

Big City. *See* Mahanagar, 1963

Big City Blues, 1932 (Grot; Kahn)

Big Clock, 1948 (Dreier; Head; Seitz; Young)

Big Combo, 1955 (Alton; Raksin)

Big Country, 1958 (Bass; Planer)

Big Crash. *See* Stora Skrällen, 1943

Big Cube, 1969 (Figueroa)

Big Dan, 1923 (August; Fox)

Big Day, 1937 (Ruttenberg)

Big Deal at Dodge City. *See* A Big Hand for the Little Lady, 1966

Big Deal on Madonna Street. *See* I soliti ignoti, 1958

Big Deal on Madonna Street. . .20 Years Later. *See* I soliti ignoti vent'anni dopo, 1986

Big Decision. *See* Basketball Fix, 1951

Big Diamond Robbery, 1929 (Plunkett)

Big Ears, 1931 (Roach)

Big Fisherman, 1959 (Garmes)

Big Fix, 1947 (Miller)

Big Fix, 1978 (Conti; Head)

Big Frame. *See* Lost Hours, 1952

Big Gamble, 1931 (Mohr)

Big Gamble, 1961 (D'Eaubonne; Jarre; Zanuck)

Big Game, 1921 (Roach)

Big Game, 1936 (Berman; Polglase)

Big Game Haunt, 1968 (Blanc)

Big Game Hunt, 1937 (Terry)

Big Gundown. *See* Resa dei conti, 1966

Big Hand for the Little Lady, 1966 (Garmes; Mercer; Raksin)

Big Hangover, 1950 (Deutsch; Krasna; Rose)

Big Heart. *See* Miracle on 34th Street, 1947

Big Hearted Herbert, 1934 (Orry-Kelly)

Big Heat, 1953 (Cohn; Lang; Louis; Wald)

Big Heel-watha, 1944 (Avery)

Big House, 1930 (Gibbons; Marion; Mayer; Shearer; Thalberg)

Big House Bunny, 1950 (Blanc; Stalling)

Big Hug. *See* Stora famnen, 1939

Big Idea, 1918 (Mohr; Roach)

Big Idea, 1923 (Roach)

Big Jack, 1949 (Stothart; Surtees)

Big Jake, 1971 (Bernstein; Clothier)

Big Jim Garrity, 1916 (Miller)

Big Kick, 1925 (Roach)

Big Kick, 1930 (Roach)

Big Killing, 1928 (Mankiewicz)

Big Knife, 1955 (Bass; Laszlo)

Big Land, 1957 (Seitz)

Big Lebowski, 1998 (Burwell)

Big Life, 1950 (Newman)

Big Lift, 1950 (Clarke; Reynolds)

Big Man, 1990 (Morricone)

Big Moments from Little Pictures, 1924 (Roach)

Big Money, 1958 (Rank)

Big Mouse-Take, 1965 (Hanna and Barbera)

Big Mouth, 1967 (Wheeler)

Big News, 1929 (Miller)

Big Night, 1951 (Lardner; Mohr)

Big Noise, 1928 (Hecht)

Big Operator, 1959 (Ames)

Big Pal, 1925 (Furthman)

Big Parade, 1925 (Basevi; Gibbons; Mayer; Thalberg)

Big Parade, 1952 (Godfrey)

Big Party, 1930 (Fox)

Big Pond, 1930 (Green; Zukor)

Big Punch, 1921 (Fox; Furthman)

Big Race, 1937 (Lantz)

Big Race, 1960 (Halas and Batchelor)

Big Race. *See* Texan, 1930

Big Rally, 1950 (Vukotić)

Big Red. *See* Miracle of the White Stallions, 1962

Big Red Riding Hood, 1925 (Roach)

Big Risk. *See* Classe tous risques, 1960

Big Shot, 1932 (Miller)

Big Shot, 1937 (Musuraca; Polglase)

Big Shot, 1942 (Deutsch)

Big Shots, 1987 (Eszterhas; Ondříček)

Big Show, 1923 (Roach)

Big Show, 1936 (Canutt)

Big Show, 1961 (Heller)

Big Sky, 1952 (D'Agostino; Harlan; Jeakins; Nichols; Tiomkin)

Big Sleep, 1946 (Brackett; Furthman; Steiner)

Big Snooze, 1946 (Blanc; Clampett; Stalling)

Big Squawk, 1929 (Roach)

Big Stampede, 1932 (McCord)

Big Steal, 1949 (Mainwaring)

Big Stickup at Brink's. *See* Brink's Job, 1978

Big Street, 1942 (Metty)

Big Time, 1929 (Fox)

Big Time Operators. *See* Smallest Show on Earth, 1957

Big Timer, 1932 (Riskin)

Big Top, 1938 (Terry)

Big Top Bunny, 1951 (McKimson; Stalling)

Big Top Pee-wee, 1988 (Edlund; Elfman)

Big Town, 1924 (Roach)

Big Town, 1947 (Mainwaring)

Big Town after Dark, 1947 (Mainwaring)

Big Town Scandal, 1948 (Mainwaring)

Big Trail, 1930 (Edeson; Friedhofer)

Big Trees, 1951 (Glennon)

Black Bag, 1922 (Miller)
Black Bart, 1948 (Friedhofer)
Black Beauty, 1946 (Tiomkin)
Black Beauty, 1971 (Menges)
Black Belt History of Three Countries. *See* Kuroobi sangoku-shi, 1956
Black Bird, 1926 (Gibbons; Gillespie; Mayer)
Black Bird, 1975 (Booth; Horner; Lathrop)
Black Book. *See* Reign of Terror , 1949
Black Caesar, 1973 (Baker)
Black Camel, 1931 (Carré)
Black Cat, 1935 (Pierce)
Black Cat, 1941 (Cortez)
Black Cat. *See* Due occhi diabolici, 1990
Black Cat. *See* Gatto nero, 1981
Black Cauldron, 1985 (Bernstein)
Black Coin, 1936 (Canutt)
Black Cyclone, 1925 (Roach)
Black Diamond. *See* Cerný démant, 1955
Black Diamond Express, 1927 (Zanuck)
Black Doll, 1938 (Cortez)
Black Eyes and Blues, 1941 (Bruckman)
Black Flame. *See* Černý plamen, 1930
Black Flowers for the Bride. *See* Something for Everyone, 1970
Black Friday, 1940 (Siodmak)
Black Fury, 1935 (Haskin)
Black Ghost, 1932 (Canutt)
Black Glove. *See* Face the Music, 1954
Black Hand Blues, 1925 (Roach)
Black Hand, 1906 (Bitzer)
Black Hand, 1949 (Plunkett)
Black Hole, 1979 (Barry; Ellenshaw)
Black Horse Canyon, 1954 (Mainwaring)
Black Hussar. *See* Schwarze Husar, 1932
Black Jack, 1927 (Fox)
Black Jack, 1949 (Spaak)
Black Jack, 1950 (Kosma)
Black Jack, 1979 (Menges)
Black Knight, 1954 (Broccoli; Vetchinsky)
Black Legion, 1936 (Barnes)
Black Magic, 1929 (Fox)
Black Magic, 1949 (Annenkov; D'Eaubonne)
Black Marble, 1979 (Jarre)
Black Masks. *See* De svarta maskerna, 1912
Black Moon Rising, 1986 (Schifrin)
Black Moon, 1934 (August)
Black Moon, 1975 (Nykvist)
Black Narcissus, 1947 (Cardiff; Ellenshaw; Heckroth; Junge; Rank)
Black Noon, 1971 (Duning)
Black on White, 1954 (Alwyn)
Black Orchid, 1916 (Selig)
Black Orchid, 1958 (Burks; Head; Ponti)
Black Orchid. *See* Trifling Woman, 1922
Black Oxen, 1923 (Kräly)
Black Palm Trees. *See* Svarta palmkronor, 1968
Black Paradise, 1926 (Fox)
Black Patch, 1957 (Goldsmith)
Black Rain. *See* Kuroi Ame, 1989
Black Rainbow, 1987 (Fisher)
Black Room, 1935 (Goosson)
Black Rose, 1950 (Addinsell; Cardiff; Jennings; Mathieson)
Black Sail. *See* Chornyi parus, 1929
Black Scorpion, 1957 (O'Brien)
Black Sheep, 1912 (Bitzer)
Black Sheep, 1934 (Terry)
Black Sheep, 1935 (Miller)
Black Sheep of Whitehall, 1941 (Balcon)

Black Shield of Falworth, 1954 (Maté)
Black Spider, 1931 (Terry)
Black Stallion Returns, 1983 (Delerue)
Black Sunday, 1977 (Alonzo; Lehman; Williams)
Black Swan, 1942 (Basevi; Day; Hecht; Miller; Newman; Shamroy)
Black Tent, 1956 (Alwyn; Rank)
Black Tights. *See* Collants noirs, 1960
Black Tuesday, 1954 (Cortez)
Black Tulip. *See* Tulipe noire, 1963
Black Viper, 1908 (Bitzer)
Black Watch, 1929 (August; Fox)
Black Whip, 1956 (Biroc)
Black Widow, 1951 (Carreras)
Black Widow, 1954 (Clarke; Johnson; Lemaire; Spencer)
Black Widow, 1986 (Bass; Hall; Mamet)
Black Windmill, 1974 (Zanuck)
Black Wings. *See* Czarne skrzydła, 1962
Black Zoo, 1963 (Crosby)
Blackbeard the Pirate, 1952 (Young)
Blackbeard's Ghost, 1968 (Ellenshaw)
Blackbirds, 1916 (Rosher)
Blackboard Jungle, 1955 (Berman; Gibbons; Harlan)
Blackboard Revue, 1940 (Iwerks)
Blackguard, 1925 (Balcon)
Blacklist, 1916 (Rosher)
Blackmail, 1929 (Neame)
Blackout. *See* Contraband, 1940
Blackout. *See* Murder By Proxy, 1955
Blade Runner, 1982 (Trumbull; Vangelis)
Blague dans le coin, 1963 (Spaak)
Blaho lásky, 1965 (Brdečka; Trnka)
Blåjackor, 1945 (Fischer)
Blänande hav, 1956 (Nykvist)
Blanc comme neige, 1947 (Cloquet)
Blanc de chine, 1988 (Coutard)
Blanc et le noir, 1932 (Braunberger)
Blanche comme neige, 1908 (Cohl)
Blanche Fury, 1947 (Bryan; Havelock-Allan; Morris; Rank; Unsworth)
Blanchisserie américaine, 1915 (Cohl)
Blarney, 1926 (Gibbons; Mayer)
Blarney Stone, 1933 (Wilcox)
Blaue Engel, 1930 (Hunte; Pommer; Waxman)
Blaue Laterne, 1918 (Messter)
Blaue Maus, 1913 (Warm)
Blaze, 1989 (Wexler)
Blaze Away, 1922 (Roach)
Blaze of Glory, 2000 (Eszterhas)
Blaze of Noon, 1947 (Deutsch; Dreier; Head)
Blazes, 1961 (Breer)
Blazing Days, 1927 (Laemmle)
Blazing Guns, 1934 (Canutt)
Blazing Saddles, 1974 (Biroc)
Blazni vodníci a podvodníci, 1980 (švankmajer)
Bláznova Kronika, 1964 (Zeman)
Blé en herbe, 1953 (Aurenche and Bost; Douy)
Blechtrommel, 1979 (Carrière; Jarre)
Bless the Beasts and Children, 1972 (Wheeler)
Blessed Event, 1932 (Polito)
Bleu gang . . . , 1972 (Storaro)
Bleu perdu, 1972 (Driessen)
Bleus de l'amour, 1932 (Wakhévitch)
Blick zurück, 1944 (Stallich)
Blighty, 1927 (Balcon)
Blind Adventure, 1933 (Plunkett; Steiner)
Blind Alibi, 1938 (Musuraca)
Blind Alley, 1939 (Ballard)

Blind Date, 1954 (Terry)
Blind Date, 1959 (Bennett; Challis)
Blind Date, 1987 (Mancini)
Blind Desire. *See* Part de l'ombre, 1945
Blind Goddess, 1926 (Banton)
Blind Goddess, 1948 (Rank)
Blind Husbands, 1919 (Daniels; Day)
Blind Love, 1979 (Legrand)
Blind Man's Bluff. *See* A Caixa, 1994
Blind Princess and the Poet, 1911 (Bitzer)
Blind Terror, 1971 (Bernstein; Fisher)
Blinde, 1911 (Messter)
Blinded by the Light, 1980 (Alonzo)
Blindfold, 1928 (Fox)
Blindfold, 1966 (Bumstead; Dunne; Schifrin; Whitlock)
Blinkity Blank, 1954-55 (McClaren)
Blinky, 1923 (Miller)
Bliss of Love. *See* Blaho lásky, 1966
Bliss of Mrs. Blossom, 1968 (Godfrey; Unsworth)
Blithe Spirit, 1945 (Addinsell; Coward; Havelock-Allan; Neame)
Blitz Wolf, 1942 (Avery)
Blitzzug der Liebe, 1925 (Hoffmann)
Blixt och dunder, 1938 (Fischer)
Blob, 1958 (Bacharach)
Block-Heads, 1938 (Roach)
Blockade, 1938 (Basevi; Irene; Maté; Spencer; Wanger)
Blockade. *See* Bloko, 1964
Blodets röst, 1913 (Jaenzon)
Bloko, 1964 (Theodorakis)
Blonde Bombshell. *See* Bombshell, 1933
Blonde Crazy, 1931 (Haller)
Blonde Dream. *See* Blonder Traum, 1932
Blonde Fever, 1944 (Irene)
Blonde from Brooklyn, 1945 (Guffey)
Blonde Inspiration, 1941 (Kaper)
Blonde Menace. *See* Scattergood Meets Broadway, 1941
Blonde Saint, 1926 (Gaudio)
Blonde Trouble, 1937 (Head)
Blonde Venus, 1932 (Banton; Furthman; Glennon; Zukor)
Blonder Traum, 1932 (Pommer; Reisch)
Blondes for Danger, 1938 (Wilcox)
Blondie Goes to College, 1942 (Bruckman; Cahn)
Blondie Johnson, 1933 (Gaudio; Orry-Kelly)
Blondie of the Follies, 1932 (Barnes; Freed; Loos; Marion)
Blondie's Blessed Event, 1942 (Cahn)
Blood Alley, 1955 (Clothier)
Blood and Roses. *See* Et mourir de plaisir, 1960
Blood and Sand, 1922 (Mathis; Westmore Family)
Blood and Sand, 1941 (Banton; Day; Newman; Rennahan; Swerling; Zanuck)
Blood and Steel, 1959 (Crosby)
Blood and Wine, 1997 (Sylbert)
Blood from the Mummy's Tomb, 1971 (Carreras)
Blood In. . .Blood Out. *See* Bound By Honor, 1993
Blood Kin, 1969 (Howe; Jones)
Blood Money, 1933 (D'Agostino; Newman; Zanuck)
Blood Oath, 1989 (Boyd)
Blood of a Poet. *See* **Sang d'un poète**, 1930
Blood of Dracula's Castle, 1967 (Kovacs)
Blood of Hussain, 1977 (Lassally)
Blood on My Hands. *See* Kiss the Blood Off My Hands, 1948
Blood on the Moon, 1948 (D'Agostino; Musuraca)
Blood on the Sun, 1945 (Rozsa)
Blood Orange, 1954 (Carreras)
Blood Oranges, 1997 (Badalamenti)
Blood Relatives. *See* Liens de sang, 1978

Blood Ship, 1927 (Cohn)
Blood Simple, 1984 (Burwell)
Blood Sisters. *See* Sister, 1972
Blood Test, 1923 (Rennahan)
Blood Will Tell, 1912 (Ince)
Blood Will Tell, 1927 (Fox)
Bloodbrothers, 1978 (Bernstein; Surtees)
Bloodhounds of Broadway, 1952 (Cronjager; Lemaire)
Bloodline, 1979 (Morricone; Young)
Bloodsport, 1988 (Golan and Globus)
Bloodsucking Pharoahs in Pittsburgh, 1991 (Savini)
Bloody Brood, 1959 (Schüfftan)
Bloody Kids, 1979 (Menges)
Bloody Mama, 1970 (Alonzo)
Bloomfield, 1969 (Heller)
Blossoms in the Dust, 1941 (Adrian; Freund; Gibbons; Loos; Mayer; Stothart)
Blossoms on Broadway, 1937 (Head; Shamroy)
Blot on the Scutcheon, 1911 (Bitzer)
Blotto, 1930 (Roach)
Blow By Blow, 1928 (Roach)
Blow 'em Up, 1922 (Roach)
Blow Me Down, 1933 (Fleischer)
Blow Out, 1981 (Donaggio; Zsigmond)
Blow Out, 1936 (Avery)
Blow-Out. *See* Grande Bouffe, 1973
Blowing Wild, 1952 (Tiomkin)
Blowup, 1966 (Guerra; Ponti)
Blue, 1968 (Cortez; Winkler)
Blue and the Gold. *See* Annapolis Story, 1955
Blue Angel, 1959 (Friedhofer; Shamroy)
Blue Angel. *See* **Blaue Engel**, 1930
Blue Bird, 1918 (Carré)
Blue Bird, 1940 (Day; Miller; Newman; Rennahan; Zanuck)
Blue Bird, 1976 (Young)
Blue Blazes Rawden, 1918 (August)
Blue Bud. *See* Aoi me, 1956
Blue Cat Blues, 1956 (Hanna and Barbera)
Blue Collar, 1978 (Nitzsche)
Blue Dahlia, 1946 (Dreier; Head; Houseman; Young)
Blue Danube, 1928 (Adrian; Grot; Miller)
Blue Danube, 1932 (Wilcox; Young)
Blue Denim, 1959 (Brackett; Dunne; Herrmann; Reynolds; Wheeler)
Blue Eagle, 1926 (Fox)
Blue Gardenia, 1953 (Musuraca)
Blue Grass Romance, 1913 (Ince)
Blue Hawaii, 1961 (Edouart; Head; Lang; Wallis)
Blue Heat. *See* Last of the Finest, 1990
Blue Jeans. *See* Blue Denim, 1959
Blue Knight, 1975 (Mancini)
Blue Lagoon, 1949 (Rank; Unsworth)
Blue Lagoon, 1979 (Almendros)
Blue Lamp, 1950 (Balcon; Clarke)
Blue Max, 1966 (Goldsmith; Slocombe)
Blue Monday, 1938 (Hanna and Barbera)
Blue Monday, 1988 (Breer)
Blue Murder at St. Trinian's, 1958 (Arnold)
Blue Peter, 1958 (Lassally)
Blue Planet, 1990 (Burtt)
Blue Plate Symphony, 1954 (Terry)
Blue Skies, 1929 (Fox)
Blue Skies, 1946 (Berlin; Head; Lang; Pan)
Blue Skies Again, 1983 (McAlpine)
Blue Sky, 1994 (Nitzsche)
Blue Steel, 1934 (Canutt)
Blue Thunder, 1983 (Alonzo)

Blue Veil, 1951 (Hakim; Krasna; Planer; Wald; Waxman; Westmore Family)
Blue Velvet, 1986 (Badalamenti; de Laurentiis)
Blue Villa. *See* Bruit qui rend fou, 1995
Blue, White, and Perfect, 1941 (Chase)
Bluebeard. *See* Barbe-Bleue, 1951
Bluebeard. *See* Barbe-Bleue, 1972
Bluebeard. *See* Landru, 1962
Bluebeard's Brother, 1932 (Terry)
Bluebeard's Castle. *See* Herzog Blaubart's Burg, 1964
Bluebeard's Eighth Wife, 1938 (Banton; Brackett; Dreier)
Bluebeard's Seven Wives, 1925 (Haller)
Bluebird, 1917 (Zukor)
Bluebird, 1976 (Head)
Bluejackets. *See* Blåjackor, 1945
Blueprint for Murder, 1953 (Lemaire)
Blues, 1931 (Terry)
Blues Brothers, 1980 (Whitlock)
Blues in the Night, 1941 (Blanke; Haller; Mercer)
Bluets dans la tête, 1969 (Almendros)
Bluff, 1916 (Gaumont)
Blume in Love, 1973 (Conti)
Blunder Below, 1942 (Fleischer)
Blusen König, 1917 (Kräly)
Blushing Bride, 1921 (Fox; Furthman)
Blut der Ahnen, 1920 (Warm)
Bly jednou jeden Král, 1955 (Brdečka)
BMX Bandits, 1983 (Seale)
Boats under Oars, 1901 (Bitzer)
Bob and Carol and Ted and Alice, 1969 (Bacharach; Jones; Lang)
Bob and the Pirates, 1960 (Haller)
Bob Hampton of Placer, 1921 (Carré)
Bob le flambeur, 1956 (Decaë)
Bob, Son of Battle. *See* Thunder in the Valley, 1947
Bobbed Hair, 1924 (Haskin)
Bobby, 1973 (Abbas)
Bobby Deerfield, 1977 (Decaë; Grusin; Sargent)
Bobby the Coward, 1911 (Bitzer)
Bobby's Kodak, 1908 (Bitzer)
Bobo, 1967 (Cahn; Lai; Parrish)
Boccaccio '70, 1962 (Cecchi D'amico; Flaiano and Pinelli; Gherardi; Rota; Rotunno; Ponti; Serandrei; Zavattini)
Bodily Harm. *See* Operation, 1990
Body. *See* Ratai, 1962
Body and Soul, 1927 (Gibbons; Gillespie)
Body and Soul, 1931 (Furthman; Grot)
Body and Soul, 1947 (Friedhofer; Howe; Parrish)
Body and Soul, 1981 (Golan and Globus)
Body Bags, 1993 (Baker)
Body Double, 1984 (Donaggio)
Body Heat, 1981 (Barry; Littleton)
Body of Evidence, 1993 (de Laurentiis)
Body of My Enemy. *See* Corps de mon ennemi, 1976
Body Rock, 1984 (Müller)
Body Snatcher, 1945 (D'Agostino; Lewton)
Bodyguard, 1944 (Hanna and Barbera)
Bodyguard. *See* Yojimbo, 1961
Boeing Boeing, 1965 (Ballard; Head; Wallis)
Bof!, 1970 (Vierny)
Bogie, 1980 (Taradash)
Bogus, 1996 (Adam; Sargent; Watkin)
Bohème, 1923 (Dreier; Kräly)
Boheme, 1926 (Carré; Gibbons; Gillespie; Mayer)
Bohemian Girl, 1936 (Roach)
Bohus bataljon, 1949 (Lundgren; Nykvist)
Boilesk, 1933 (Fleischer)

Boireau déménage, 1906 (Pathé)
Bois des amants, 1960 (Douy)
Bois et cuivres, 1958 (Decaë)
Boite aux rêves, 1943 (Wakhévitch)
Boite diabolique, 1911 (Cohl)
Bokura no otouto, 1933 (Yoda)
Bold Adventure. *See* Aventures de Till l'Espiègle, 1957
Bold Caballero, 1937 (Canutt)
Bold Cavalier. *See* Bold Caballero, 1937
Bold King Cole, 1936 (Messmer)
Bolero, 1934 (Banton; Zukor)
Bolero, 1984 (Bernstein; Golan and Globus)
Bolero. *See* Uns et les autres, 1981
Bolero de Raquel, 1956 (Figueroa)
Bolly, 1968 (Halas and Batchelor)
Bolwieser, 1978 (Ballhaus)
Bom Povo Português, 1980 (de Almeida)
Boman på utstallningen, 1923 (Magnusson)
Bomb Mania. *See* Bombománie, 1959
Bomb Was Stolen. *See* S-a furat o bomba, 1961
Bomba and the African Treasure. *See* African Treasure, 1962
Bomba and the Elephant Stampede. *See* Elephant Stampede, 1951
Bomba and the Hidden City. *See* Hidden City, 1950
Bomba and the Jungle Girl, 1962 (Mirisch)
Bomba and the Lion Hunters. *See* Lion Hunters, 1962
Bomba on Panther Island, 1950 (Mirisch)
Bomba the Jungle Boy, 1949 (Mirisch)
Bombai Ka Babu, 1960 (Burman)
Bombardier, 1943 (Dunn; Musuraca)
Bombay Clipper, 1941 (Cortez)
Bombay Talkie, 1970 (Jhabvala; Merchant; Mitra)
Bombe par hasard, 1969 (Grimault)
Bomben auf Monte Carlo, 1931 (Pommer)
Bombero atómico, 1952 (Figueroa)
Bombers B-52, 1957 (Clothier; Rosenman)
Bomber's Moon, 1943 (Ballard; Basevi)
Bombomania. *See* Bombománie, 1959
Bombománie, 1959 (Brdečka; Trnka)
Bombs over Japan. *See* Wild Blue Yonder, 1951
Bombshell, 1933 (Adrian; Booth; Furthman; Mayer; Rosson; Stromberg)
Bombsight Stolen. *See* Cottage to Let, 1941
Bon Appetit, Mama. *See* Ed and His Dead Mother, 1993
Bon Dieu sans confession, 1953 (Douy)
Bon et les méchants, 1976 (Lai)
Bon Voyage, 1962 (Disney)
Bonanza Bunny, 1959 (Blanc; McKimson)
Bonaventure. *See* Thunder on the Hill, 1951
Bonchi, 1960 (Miyagawa)
Bond between Us, 1953 (Metty)
Bond Street, 1948 (Heller; Rattigan; de Grunwald)
Bondage, 1933 (Friedhofer)
Bondman, 1929 (Steiner; Wilcox)
Bone Dry, 1922 (Roach)
Bone for a Bone, 1951 (Blanc; Stalling)
Bone, Sweet Bone, 1948 (Blanc)
Bones, 2000 (Dickerson)
Bones. *See* Ossos, 1997
Bonfire of the Vanities, 1990 (Grusin; Sylbert; Zsigmond)
Bonheur, 1934 (Stradling)
Bonheur, 1935 (Douy)
Bonheur, 1965 (Rabier)
Bonheur est pour demain, 1962 (Delerue)
Bonjour sourire, 1955 (Burel)
Bonjour Tristesse, 1958 (Auric; Bass; Périnal)
Bonjour, Monsieur La Bruyère, 1958 (Braunberger)
Bonne à tout faire. *See* Difficulté d'être infidèle, 1963

Bonne Absinthe, 1899 (Gaumont)

Bonne Année, 1973 (Lai)

Bonne Aventure, 1932 (Fradetal)

Bonne Soupe, 1963 (Saulnier)

Bonnes à tuer, 1954 (D'Eaubonne)

Bonnes Causes, 1963 (Jeanson)

Bonnes Femmes, 1960 (Decaë; Gégauff; Hakim)

Bonnie and Clyde, 1967 (Allen; Guffey; Tavoularis; Towne; Warner; van Runkle)

Bonnie Prince Charlie, 1948 (Korda; Krasker)

Bonnie Scotland, 1935 (Roach)

Bons baisers de Dinard, 1949 (Decaë)

Bonsoir mesdames, bonsoir messieurs, 1943 (Renoir)

Bonsoir Paris, bonjour l'amour, 1956 (D'Eaubonne)

Bonsoirs, 1910 (Cohl)

Bonsoirs russes, 1910 (Cohl)

Boo, Boo, Theme Song, 1933 (Fleischer)

Boob, 1926 (Daniels; Gibbons)

Boobs in the Woods, 1950 (Blanc; McKimson; Stalling)

Booby Hatched, 1944 (Blanc; Stalling)

Booby Traps, 1943 (Clampett)

Boogie Doodle, 1939-41 (McClaren)

Boogie Woogie Bugle Boy of Company B, 1941 (Lantz)

Book, 1926 (Carré)

Book Bargain, 1937-39 (McClaren)

Book in the Country. See Kniga v derevne, 1929

Book Revue, 1946 (Blanc; Clampett; Stalling)

Book Shop, 1937 (Terry)

Booloo, 1938 (Head)

Boom!, 1968 (Barry; Coward; Slocombe)

Boom, 1963 (Zavattini; de Laurentiis)

Boom, 1999 (Age and Scarpelli)

Boom. See Kondura, 1977

Boom Town, 1940 (Adrian; Canutt; Gibbons; Gillespie; Mayer; Rosson; Waxman)

Boomerang!, 1947 (Basevi; Day; Lemaire; Newman; de Rochemont; Zanuck)

Boomerang, 1913 (Ince)

Boop-Oop-a-Doop, 1932 (Fleischer)

Booster, 1928 (Roach)

Boots Malone, 1951 (Bernstein; Guffey)

Bopha!, 1993 (Watkin)

Bordello of Blood, 1996 (Elfman)

Border, 1982 (Zsigmond)

Border Cafe, 1937 (Musuraca)

Border Cavalier, 1927 (Laemmle)

Border Feud. See Gränsfolken, 1913

Border Film, 1990 (Branco)

Border Flight, 1936 (Dreier; Head)

Border G-Man, 1938 (August)

Border Incident, 1949 (Alton; Koch; Previn)

Border Line, 1999 (Bass)

Border Patrol, 1928 (Polito)

Border Patrol, 1943 (Harlan; Wilson)

Border Vigilantes, 1941 (Harlan; Head)

Border Weave, 1942 (Alwyn; Cardiff)

Border Wireless, 1918 (August; Sullivan)

Borderland, 1937 (Head)

Borderline, 1949 (Cahn)

Borderlines. See Caretakers, 1963

Bordertown, 1935 (Gaudio; Orry-Kelly; Westmore Family)

Bored of Education, 1935 (Roach)

Borghese piccolo piccolo, 1977 (Amidei)

Borgo a Mozzano, 1958 (Rotunno)

Borinage. See Misère au Borinage, 1934

Born for Glory. See Brown on Revolution, 1935

Born for Glory. See O.H.M.S., 1937

Born Free, 1966 (Barry; Foreman)

Born on the Fourth of July, 1989 (Mancini; Williams)

Born Reckless, 1930 (Fox; Nichols)

Born Reckless, 1959 (Biroc)

Born to Be Bad, 1934 (Day; Newman; Zanuck)

Born to Be Bad, 1950 (Musuraca; Schnee)

Born to Dance, 1936 (Adrian; Edens; Mayer; Newman; Porter)

Born to Kill. See Cockfighter, 1974

Born to Peck, 1952 (Lantz)

Born to Run, 1979 (Seale)

Born to Sing. See Almost Angels, 1962

Born to the West, 1937 (Head)

Born to Win, 1971 (Rosenblum)

Born Yesterday, 1950 (Cohn; Horner; Louis; Walker)

Born Yesterday, 1993 (Kanin)

Borrowers, 1973 (Allen; Trumbull)

Borrowers, 1997 (Zimmer)

Borsalino, 1970 (Carrière)

Borza, 1935 (van Dongen)

Bosambo. See Sanders of the River, 1935

Bosphore, 1963 (Delerue)

Boss, 1915 (Carré)

Boss, 1956 (Haskin; Mohr; Trumbo)

Boss. See Kaoyaku, 1957

Boss of Camp Four, 1922 (Fox)

Boss Said No. See Blondie Goes to College, 1942

Boss' Wife, 1986 (Conti)

Bossu, 1934 (Lourié)

Bossu, 1944 (Annenkov; Auric; Matras)

Bossu, 1997 (Sarde)

Boston Blackie, 1923 (Fox)

Boston Quackie, 1957 (Blanc; McKimson)

Boston Strangler, 1968 (Day; Smith)

Bostonians, 1984 (Jhabvala; Lassally; Merchant)

Botab dourou, 1968 (Yoda)

Botany Bay, 1953 (Pereira; Seitz; Waxman)

Both Sides of the Law. See Street Corner, 1953

Botschafterin, 1960 (Warm)

Botta di vita, 1988 (Age and Scarpelli)

Botta e risposta, 1951 (de Laurentiis)

Botte di Natale, 1994 (Donaggio)

Bottle Babies, 1924 (Roach)

Bottom Line. See On aura tout vu!, 1976

Bottom of the Bottle, 1956 (Garmes; Lemaire; Wheeler)

Bottoms Up, 1934 (Kahn; Miller)

Boucher, 1969 (Rabier)

Boucher, la star, et l'orpheline, 1974 (Cloquet)

Boudoir Diplomat, 1930 (Freund; Laemmle)

Boudu sauvée des eaux, 1932 (Renoir)

Bouevard du Rhum, 1971 (Douy)

Bought and Paid For, 1916 (Edeson; Marion)

Boulder Wham, 1965 (Blanc)

Boule de suif, 1945 (Barsacq; Jeanson; Matras)

Boulevard Nights, 1979 (Schifrin)

Boulevardier from the Bronx, 1936 (Stalling)

Bouncer, 1925 (Roach)

Bouncing Babies, 1929 (Roach)

Bound and Gagged, 1919 (Grot)

Bound By Honor, 1993 (Conti)

Bound for Glory, 1976 (Rosenman; Wexler; Whitlock)

Bound on the Wheel, 1915 (Furthman)

Bounty, 1984 (Vangelis; de Laurentiis)

Bouquets de fleurs, 1913 (Gaumont)

Bourdelle, 1950 (Honegger)

Bourdelle, sculpteur monumental, 1962 (Coutard)

Bouře nad Tatrami, 1932 (Stallich)
Bourgeois Gentilhomme, 1958 (Alekan)
Bourse. *See* Valise diplomatique, 1909
Boutique de l'Orfèvre. *See* Jeweller's Shop, 1987
Bouvard et Pecuchet, 1991 (Carrière)
Bow Bells, 1954 (Lassally)
Bow Wows, 1922 (Roach)
Bowery, 1933 (Day; Newman; Zanuck)
Bowery Bimboes, 1930 (Lantz)
Bowery Bugs, 1949 (Blanc; Stalling)
Bowled Over, 1923 (Roach)
Bowling Alley-Cat, 1942 (Hanna and Barbera)
Bowling Bimboes, 1930 (Lantz)
Boxe de la France, 1943 (Honegger)
Boxer, 1997 (Hambling; Menges)
Boxing Gloves, 1929 (Roach)
Boxing Kangaroo, 1920 (Fleischer)
Boy. *See* **Shonen**, 1969
Boy, a Girl and a Bike, 1949 (Rank)
Boy Crazy, 1922 (Stromberg)
Boy Detective, 1908 (Bitzer)
Boy Friend, 1926 (Gibbons)
Boy Friend, 1928 (Roach)
Boy Friend, 1971 (Watkin)
Boy from Oklahoma, 1954 (Steiner; Burks)
Boy in Blue. *See* Knabe in Blau, 1919
Boy in the Barrel, 1903 (Bitzer)
Boy in the Tree. *See* Pojken i trädet, 1961
Boy Meets Girl, 1938 (Edeson; Polito; Wallis)
Boy on a Dolphin, 1957 (Friedhofer; Krasner; Smith)
Boy Rider, 1927 (Plunkett)
Boy Slaves, 1939 (Berman)
Boy Ten Feet Tall. *See* Sammy Going South, 1963
Boy Trouble, 1939 (Head)
Boy Who Could Fly, 1986 (Edlund)
Boy Who Stole a Million, 1960 (Slocombe)
Boy Who Turned Yellow, 1972 (Challis)
Boy with Green Hair, 1948 (Barnes; D'Agostino; Schary)
Boyhood Daze, 1957 (Blanc; Jones)
Boys Don't Cry, 1999 (Vachon)
Boys from Brazil, 1978 (Decaë; Goldsmith)
Boys in Brown, 1949 (Rank)
Boys' Night Out, 1962 (Cahn; van Heusen)
Boys on the Side, 1994 (Adam)
Boys' Ranch, 1946 (Irene)
Boys to Board, 1923 (Roach)
Boys Town, 1938 (Mayer; Schary)
Boys Will Be Boys, 1935 (Balcon; Rank; Vetchinsky)
Boys Will Be Joys, 1925 (Roach)
Božská Ema, 1979 (Ondříček)
Bracos de Sologne, 1933 (Aurenche and Bost)
Braddock: Missing in Action III, 1988 (Golan and Globus)
Brahim, 1956 (Cloquet)
Brahma Diamond, 1909 (Bitzer)
Brain. *See* Vengeance, 1962
Brain Snatcher. *See* Man Who Changed His Mind, 1936
Brains Repaired. *See* Retapeur de Cervelles, 1911
Brainstorm, 1965 (Duning)
Brainstorm, 1983 (Trumbull)
Bram Stoker's Dracula, 1992 (Ballhaus)
Bramble Bush, 1960 (Ballard; Rosenman)
Brancaleone alle crociate, 1970 (Age and Scarpelli)
Branches of the Tree. *See* Shakha Proshakha, 1990
Brand in der Oper, 1930 (Reisch; Wagner)
Brand New Life, 1973 (O'Steen)
Brand X, 1970 (Shepard)

Branded, 1950 (Dreier; Head; Lang; Maté)
Branded a Bandit, 1924 (Canutt)
Branded Sombrero, 1928 (Fox)
Branded Woman, 1920 (Loos)
Brandherd. *See* Verlogene Moral, 1921
Branding Broadway, 1918 (August; Sullivan)
Brandos Costumes, 1974 (de Almeida)
Branle-bas de combat, 1936 (Ibert)
Brannigan, 1975 (Fisher)
Brannigar, 1935 (Jaenzon)
Branningar, eller Stulen lycka, 1912 (Jaenzon; Magnusson)
Braque, 1950 (Cloquet)
Brasher Doubloon, 1947 (Basevi)
Brass Bottle, 1964 (Bumstead)
Brass Bowl, 1924 (Fox)
Brass Buttons, 1919 (Furthman)
Brass Commandments, 1923 (Fox)
Brass Knuckles, 1927 (Blanke)
Brass Monkey, 1917 (Selig)
Brass Monkey. *See* Lucky Mascot, 1948
Brat, 1919 (Mathis)
Brat, 1931 (August; Levien)
Bratichka, 1927 (Enei; Moskvin)
Brats, 1930 (Roach)
Bravade legendaire, 1978 (Vierny)
Bravados, 1958 (Friedhofer; Lemaire; Newman; Shamroy; Wheeler)
Brave and the Beautiful. *See* Magnificent Matador, 1955
Brave Bulls, 1951 (Crosby; Howe; Trumbo)
Brave Hare, 1955 (Ivanov-Vano)
Brave Little Bat, 1941 (Blanc; Jones; Stalling)
Brave One, 1956 (Cardiff; Trumbo; Young)
Brave Tin Soldier, 1934 (Iwerks)
Braver Than the Bravest, 1916 (Roach)
Braves Gens, 1912 (Gaumont)
Braves Petits Soldats de plomb, 1915 (Cohl)
Bravissimo!, 1955 (Age and Scarpelli)
Bravo Alpha, 1957 (Jarre)
Bravo for Billy, 1979 (Halas and Batchelor)
Bravo, Mr. Strauss, 1943 (Pal)
Brazil: A Report on Torture, 1971 (Wexler)
Breach of Promise, 1932 (Miller; Veiller)
Bread, 1924 (Mayer)
Bread Cast upon the Water, 1913 (Ince)
Break in the Circle, 1955 (Carreras)
Break of Day, 1977 (Boyd; Seale)
Break of Hearts, 1935 (Berman; Biroc; Polglase; Steiner; Veiller)
Break the News, 1937 (Meerson)
Break to Freedom. *See* Albert, R.N., 1953
Breakaway, 1956 (Rank)
Breakdance 2: Electric Boogaloo, 1984 (Golan and Globus)
Breakdown, 1997 (de Laurentiis)
Breaker Morant , 1980 (McAlpine)
Breakers, or Stolen Happiness. *See* Branningar, eller Stulen lycka, 1912
Breakfast at Sunrise, 1927 (Schenck)
Breakfast at Tiffany's, 1961 (Edouart; Head; Mancini; Mercer; Pereira; Planer; Westmore Family)
Breakfast Club, 1985 (Allen)
Breakfast in Hollywood, 1945 (Metty)
Breakfast of Champions, 1999 (Henry)
Breakheart Pass, 1975 (Ballard; Canutt; Goldsmith)
Breaking Away, 1979 (Von Brandenstein)
Breaking into Society, 1923 (Stromberg)
Breaking Point, 1924 (Howe)
Breaking Point, 1950 (McCord; Wald)
Breaking the Code, 1996 (Pinter)
Breaking the Ice, 1938 (Young)

Broadway Melody of 1936, 1935 (Adrian; Brown; Edens; Freed; Mayer; Newman; Rosher)
Broadway Melody of 1938, 1937 (Adrian; Brown; Daniels; Edens; Freed; Gibbons; Mayer; Vorkapich)
Broadway Melody of 1940, 1940 (Adrian; Mayer; Newman; Porter; Ruttenberg; Schary)
Broadway Melody, 1929 (Brown; Freed; Gibbons; Mayer; Shearer)
Broadway Musketeers, 1938 (Deutsch)
Broadway Nights, 1927 (Haller)
Broadway or Bust, 1924 (Miller)
Broadway Peacock, 1922 (Fox)
Broadway Rhythm, 1944 (Green; Irene; Kahn; Mayer; Sharaff)
Broadway Serenade, 1939 (Adrian; Kahn; Kaufman; Kräly; Lederer; Renoir; Stothart; Wakhévitch)
Broadway Thru a Keyhole, 1933 (Newman; Zanuck)
Broadway to Hollywood, 1933 (Daniels; Tiomkin)
Broceliande, 1969 (Jarre)
Bröderna, 1913 (Jaenzon)
Bröderna Lejonhjärta, 1977 (Lundgren)
Broken Arrow, 1950 (Friedhofer; Newman; Wheeler)
Broken Arrow, 1996 (Zimmer)
Broken Blossoms, 1919 (Bitzer; Brown)
Broken Blossoms, 1936 (Courant)
Broken Butterfly, 1919 (Carré)
Broken Chains, 1922 (Haskin)
Broken Cross, 1911 (Bitzer)
Broken Doll, 1910 (Bitzer)
Broken Hearts of Hollywood, 1926 (Miller)
Broken Journey, 1948 (Rank)
Broken Journey. See Uttoran, 1994
Broken Jug. See Zerbrochene Krug, 1937
Broken Lance, 1954 (Lemaire)
Broken Land, 1961 (Crosby)
Broken Leghorn, 1959 (Blanc; McKimson)
Broken Locket, 1909 (Bitzer)
Broken Lullaby, 1932 (Raphaelson; Vajda)
Broken Lullaby. See Man I Killed, 1932
Broken Ways, 1913 (Bitzer)
Bröllopet på Ulfåsa, 1911 (Jaenzon)
Brollopet pa Ulfasa, 1909 (Magnusson)
Bröllopsresan, 1935 (Jaenzon)
Brolly. See Paraplíčko, 1957
Bromo and Juliet, 1926 (Roach)
Broncho Buster, 1927 (Laemmle)
Broncho Twister, 1927 (Fox)
Bronco Billy, 1980 (Lourié)
Bronco Bullfrog, 1969 (Shepard)
Bronco Buster, 1935 (Lantz)
Bronco Buster, 1952 (Boyle)
Bronenosets Potemkin, 1925 (Tisse)
Brontë Sisters. See Soeurs Brontë, 1978
Bronze Bell, 1921 (Barnes)
Brooklyn Orchid, 1942 (Roach)
Broomstick Bunny, 1956 (Blanc)
Brother. See Frére, 1997
Brother Brat, 1944 (Blanc; Stalling)
Brother, Can You Spare a Dime?, 1974 (Puttnam)
Brother from Another Planet, 1984 (Daring; Dickerson)
Brother John, 1950 (Fleischer)
Brother John, 1970 (Jones)
Brother Orchid, 1940 (Burks; Gaudio; Haskin; Wallis)
Brother Rat, 1938 (Haller; Wald; Wallis)
Brother Rat and a Baby, 1940 (Rosher; Wald; Wallis)
Brother Sun, Sister Moon. See Fratello sole, sorella luna, 1972
Brotherhood, 1968 (Kaufman; Schifrin)
Brotherhood of Man, 1946 (Bosustow; Hubley; Lardner)

Brotherhood of the Bell, 1970 (Goldsmith)
Brotherhood of the Yakuza. See Yakuza, 1975
Brotherly Love, 1928 (Gibbons)
Brotherly Love, 1936 (Fleischer)
Brothers, 1912 (Bitzer)
Brothers, 1947 (Rank)
Brothers. See Bröderna, 1913
Brother's Atonement, 1914 (Barker)
Brothers Carry Mouse Off, 1965 (Jones)
Brothers Karamazov, 1958 (Alton; Berman; Epstein; Kaper; Plunkett)
Brothers McMullen, 1995 (Schamus)
Brothers Rico, 1957 (Boyle; Duning; Guffey; Louis)
Brother's Sacrifice, 1917 (Selig)
Brothers under the Chin, 1924 (Roach)
Brothers Wod. See Freres Boutdebois, 1908
Brouillard sur la ville. See Gaz mortels, 1916
Brown of Harvard, 1926 (Gibbons; Gillespie; Mayer; Stewart)
Brown on Revolution, 1935 (Junge)
Browning Version, 1951 (Dillon; Rank; Rattigan)
Brubaker, 1980 (Nuytten; Schifrin)
Brücke, 1949 (Wagner)
Bruggen, 1996 (Preisner)
Bruit qui rend fou, 1995 (Robbe-Grillet)
Bruna indiavolata, 1951 (Age and Scarpelli)
Brunnen des Wahnsinns, 1921 (Planer)
Bruno aspetta in macchina, 1996 (Cecchi D'amico)
Bruno is Waiting on the Car. See Bruno aspetta in macchina, 1996
Brutality, 1912 (Bitzer)
Brute, 1987 (Guillemot)
Brute. See Bruto, 1953
Brute Force, 1947 (Daniels; Rozsa)
Bruto, 1953 (Alcoriza)
Brutti, sporchi, cattivi, 1976 (Ponti)
Bubbles of Song, 1951 (Fleischer)
Bubbles, 1922 (Fleischer)
Bubbling Over, 1921 (Roach)
Buccaneer, 1938 (Dreier; Head; MacPherson; Sullivan)
Buccaneer, 1958 (Bernstein; Head; Pereira; Westmore Family)
Buccaneer Bunny, 1948 (Blanc; Stalling)
Buccaneers, 1924 (Roach)
Buccaneer's Girl, 1950 (Boyle; Metty)
Buch des Lasters, 1917 (Hoffmann)
Buchanan Rides Alone, 1958 (Ballard; Boyle)
Bûche, 1999 (Legrand)
Büchse der Pandora, 1928 (Andrejew)
Buck Benny Rides Again, 1940 (Dreier; Head; Lang; Young)
Buck Privates, 1928 (Laemmle)
Buck Privates, 1941 (Krasner)
Buckaroo Bugs, 1944 (Blanc; Clampett; Stalling)
Buckaroo Kid, 1926 (Laemmle)
Bucking the Barrier, 1923 (Fox)
Bucking the Line, 1921 (Fox)
Bucking the Truth, 1926 (Laemmle)
Bucklige und die Tänzerin, 1920 (Freund; Mayer)
Buckskin Frontier, 1943 (Harlan; Young)
Buddenbrooks, 1959 (Herlth)
Buddy, 1997 (Bernstein)
Buddy Buddy, 1981 (Diamond; Schifrin)
Buena Vista Social Club, 1999 (Müller)
Buffalo Bill, 1944 (Basevi; Shamroy)
Buffalo Bill and the Indians, 1976 (de Laurentiis)
Buffalo Bill on the U.P. Trail, 1926 (Pierce)
Buffy the Vampire Slayer, 1992 (Burwell; Elfman)
Bug, 1975 (Smith)
Bug Carnival, 1937 (Terry)
Bug Parade, 1941 (Avery; Blanc; Stalling)

Bug Vaudeville, 1921 (McCay)
Bugambilia, 1944 (Figueroa)
Bugged by a Bee, 1969 (Blanc; McKimson)
Bughouse Bell Hops, 1914 (Roach)
Bugle Call, 1916 (Sullivan)
Bugle Call, 1927 (Gibbons; Sullivan)
Bugles in the Afternoon, 1952 (Mainwaring; Tiomkin)
Bugs and Thugs, 1954 (Blanc)
Bugs Beetle and His Orchestra, 1938 (Terry)
Bugs Bonnets, 1956 (Blanc; Jones)
Bugs Bunny and the Three Bears, 1944 (Blanc; Jones; Stalling)
Bugs Bunny Gets the Boid, 1942 (Blanc; Clampett; Stalling)
Bugs Bunny Nips the Nips, 1944 (Blanc; Stalling)
Bugs Bunny Rides Again, 1948 (Blanc; Stalling)
Bugs Bunny—Superstar, 1975 (Clampett)
Bugs Bunny's Third Movie, 1982 (Jones)
Bugs n' Daffy Show, 1996 (Jones)
Bugsy, 1991 (Morricone)
Bugsy and Mugsy, 1957 (Blanc; Stalling)
Bugsy Malone, 1976 (Biziou; Hambling; Puttnam)
Build and Marry. See Koffer des Herrn O.F., 1931
Build My Gallows High. See **Out of the Past**, 1947
Buisson ardent, 1955 (Alexeieff and Parker)
Buki naki tatakai, 1960 (Yoda)
Bull Dog, 1937 (Biswas)
Bull Rushes, 1931 (Balcon)
Bulldog Breed, 1960 (Hambling; Rank)
Bulldog Drummond , 1929 (Barnes; Goldwyn; Howard; Menzies; Toland)
Bulldog Drummond Comes Back, 1937 (Dreier; Head)
Bulldog Drummond Escapes, 1937 (Head)
Bulldog Drummond in Africa, 1938 (Dreier; Head)
Bulldog Drummond Strikes Back, 1934 (Day; Johnson; Newman; Zanuck)
Bulldog Drummond's Bride, 1939 (Dreier; Head)
Bulldog Drummond's Peril, 1938 (Dreier; Head)
Bulldog Drummond's Revenge, 1937 (Head)
Bulldog Drummond's Secret Police, 1939 (Head)
Bulldog Jack, 1935 (Balcon; Junge; Rank)
Bulldozing the Bull, 1938 (Fleischer)
Bulldozing the Bull, 1951 (Terry)
Bullero, 1932 (Terry)
Bullet for a Badman, 1964 (Biroc; Bumstead)
Bullet for Joey, 1955 (Mainwaring)
Bullet for the General. See Quien sabe?, 1966
Bullet Is Waiting, 1954 (Planer; Tiomkin)
Bullet Scars, 1942 (McCord)
Bullet Wound. See Dankon, 1969
Bulletproof, 1996 (Bernstein; Dickerson)
Bullets for O'Hara, 1941 (McCord)
Bullets or Ballots, 1936 (Miller; Mohr)
Bullets over Broadway, 1994 (Loquasto)
Bullfight, 1935 (Terry)
Bullfight. See Course de tauraux, 1951
Bullfighter and the Lady, 1951 (Young)
Bullitt, 1968 (Fraker; Schifrin; van Runkle)
Bulloney, 1933 (Iwerks)
Bullseye!, 1990 (Golan and Globus)
Bully, 1932 (Iwerks)
Bully Beef, 1930 (Terry)
Bully for Bugs, 1953 (Blanc; Jones; Stalling)
Bully Frog, 1936 (Terry)
Bully Romance, 1939 (Terry)
Bulworth, 1998 (Morricone; Storaro; Tavoularis)
Bum Bandit, 1931 (Fleischer)
Bum Voyage, 1934 (Roach)
Bummelstudenten, 1917 (Freund)

Bumping into Broadway, 1919 (Roach)
Bunbuku chagama, 1939 (Yoda)
Bunch of Flowers, 1914 (Loos)
Bundle of Joy, 1956 (Krasna)
Bungalow Boobs, 1924 (Roach)
Bungle Uncle, 1962 (Hanna and Barbera)
Bungled Bungalow, 1949 (Bosustow)
Bunker Hill Bunny, 1950 (Blanc; Stalling)
Bunnies Abundant, 1962 (Hanna and Barbera)
Bunny and Claude, 1968 (Blanc; McKimson)
Bunny Hugged, 1951 (Blanc; Jones; Stalling)
Bunny Lake Is Missing, 1965 (Bass; Coward; Fisher)
Bunny-mooning, 1937 (Fleischer)
Buon appetito, 1956 (Delli Colli)
Buone notizie, 1979 (Morricone)
Buongiorno, elefante!, 1952 (Cecchi D'amico; Zavattini)
Buono, il brutto, il cattivo, 1966 (Age and Scarpelli; Delli Colli; Morricone)
Buraikan, 1970 (Toda)
Burbs, 1989 (Goldsmith)
Bureau des mariages, 1962 (Delerue)
Bureau of Missing Persons, 1933 (Blanke)
Burglar, 1928 (Hornbeck)
Burglar, 1987 (Fraker)
Burglar by Proxy, 1919 (Polito)
Burglar Catcher, 1960 (Halas and Batchelor)
Burglars. See Casse, 1971
Burglars Bold, 1921 (Roach)
Burglar's Dilemma, 1912 (Bitzer)
Burglar's Mistake, 1909 (Bitzer)
Buried Treasure, 1921 (Rosson)
Buried Treasure, 1926 (Roach)
Burke & Wills, 1986 (Boyd)
Burlesque, 1925 (Balcon)
Burlesque, 1932 (Terry)
Burn!. See Queimada!, 1969
Burn, Witch, Burn. See Night of the Eagle, 1961
Burn-'em-Up Barnes, 1934 (Canutt)
Burning, 1980 (Savini)
Burning Autumn. See Moeru aki, 1978
Burning Beds. See Brennende Betten, 1988
Burning Bridges, 1928 (Polito)
Burning Court. See Chambre ardente, 1962
Burning Daylight, 1928 (Polito)
Burning Heart. See Brennende Herz, 1929
Burning Hills, 1956 (McCord)
Burning Sands, 1922 (Clarke; Glennon; Howe)
Burning Season, 1994 (Puttnam)
Burning Secret, 1988 (Zimmer)
Burning Soil. See Brennende Acker, 1922
Burning Words, 1923 (Laemmle)
Burnt Fingers, 1927 (Stradling)
Burnt Offerings, 1976 (Lourié; Smith)
Burro, 1989 (Guerra)
Burschenlied aus Heidelberg, 1930 (Herlth; Hoffmann; Röhrig)
Bury Me Dead, 1947 (Alton)
Bus, 1964 (Fields)
Bus, 1965 (Wexler)
Bus II, 1983 (Wexler)
Bus Rider's Union, 1999 (Wexler)
Bus Riley's Back in Town, 1965 (Louis; Metty)
Bus Stop, 1956 (Krasner; Lemaire; Newman; Reynolds; Wheeler)
Bus Terminal. See Florence 13.30, 1957
Bush Christmas, 1947 (Rank)
Busher, 1919 (Ince)
Bushidou zankku monogatari, 1963 (Yoda)

Bushwackers, 1952 (Biroc)
Bushwhacked, 1995 (Conti)
Bushy Hare, 1950 (Blanc; McKimson; Stalling)
Business as Usual, 1987 (Golan and Globus)
Business Must Not Interfere, 1912-14 (Cohl)
Busker, 1976 (Menges)
Busman's Holiday, 1940 (Young)
Busman's Honeymoon, 1940 (Junge)
Busou keikantai, 1948 (Yoda)
Busted Blossoms, 1934 (Terry)
Buster, 1923 (Fox)
Buster, 1988 (Jarre)
Buster Keaton Story, 1957 (Head; Westmore Family; Young)
Buster's Bedroom, 1991 (Nykvist)
Busting the Beanery, 1916 (Roach)
Busting, 1973 (Winkler)
Busy Bakers, 1940 (Blanc; Stalling)
Busy Barber, 1932 (Lantz)
Busy Bee, 1936 (Terry)
Busy Bees, 1922 (Roach)
Busy Bodies, 1933 (Roach)
Busy Body, 1967 (Green)
Busy Buddies, 1956 (Hanna and Barbera)
But I Don't Want to Get Married!, 1967 (Duning)
But Not for Me, 1959 (Burks; Hayes; Head)
But the Flesh Is Weak, 1932 (Adrian)
Butch and Sundance: The Early Days, 1979 (Goldman; Kovacs)
Butch Cassidy and the Sundance Kid, 1969 (Bacharach; Goldman; Hall;
 Head; Smith)
Butcher. See Boucher, 1969
Butcher Boy, 1917 (Schenck)
Butcher Boy, 1932 (Lantz)
Butcher Boy, 1997 (Biddle)
Butcher of Seville, 1944 (Terry)
Butcher's Wife, 1991 (van Runkle)
Butley, 1974 (Dillon; Fisher; Pinter)
Buttercup Chain, 1970 (Bennett; Slocombe)
Butterfield 8, 1960 (Berman; Hayes; Kaper; Rose; Ruttenberg; Schnee)
Butterflies Are Free, 1972 (Lang)
Butterflies in the Rain, 1926 (Laemmle)
Butterfly, 1924 (Laemmle)
Butterfly, 1982 (Morricone)
Butterfly Ball, 1974 (Halas and Batchelor)
Butterfly on the Wheel, 1915 (Carré)
Button My Back, 1929 (Hornbeck)
Buttons, 1927 (Gibbons; Gillespie)
Buwana Toshi no uta, 1965 (Takemitsu)
Buy Me That Town, 1941 (Dreier; Head)
Buzie Bianche. See Professione Figlio, 1980
Buzzy Boop, 1938 (Fleischer)
Buzzy Boop at the Concert, 1938 (Fleischer)
Bwana Devil, 1952 (Biroc; Clampett)
Bwana Magoo, 1959 (Bosustow)
Bwana Toshi. See Buwana Toshi no uta, 1965
By Candlelight, 1933 (Kräly; Laemmle)
By Design, 1981 (Rosenblum)
By Love Possessed, 1961 (Bernstein; Cahn; Metty; Mirisch)
By Rocket to the Moon. See Frau im Mond, 1929
By St. Matthias. See U sv. Mateje, 1928
By Super Strategy. See Restitution, 1918
By the Beautiful Sea, 1931 (Fleischer)
By the Light of the Silvery Moon, 1926 (Fleischer)
By the Light of the Silvery Moon, 1931 (Fleischer)
By the Light of the Silvery Moon, 1953 (Steiner)
By the Sad Sea Waves, 1917 (Roach)
By the Sea, 1931 (Terry)

By the Sword, 1991 (Conti)
By Touch. See Przez dotyk, 1985
By Whose Hand?, 1932 (Walker)
By Word of Mouse, 1954 (Blanc)
By Your Leave, 1934 (Berman; Musuraca; Plunkett; Steiner)
Bye Bye Birdie, 1963 (Biroc; Green)
Bye Bye Bluebeard, 1949 (Blanc; Stalling)
Bye Bye Braverman, 1968 (Kaufman; Rosenblum)
Bye Bye Monkey. See Ciao maschio, 1978
Byez zhen, 1915 (Starewicz)
Byl jednou jeden král, 1954 (Trnka)
Był sobie raz . . . , 1957 (Lenica)
Byt, 1968 (švankmajer)

C.H.O.M.P.S., 1979 (Hanna and Barbera)
Cabaret, 1972 (Allen; Unsworth)
Cabin in the Cotton, 1932 (Orry-Kelly)
Cabin in the Sky, 1943 (Edens; Freed; Gibbons; Irene; Mayer)
Cabina, 1973 (Bozzetto)
Cabinet of Dr. Caligari. See **Kabinett des Dr. Caligari**, 1920
Cabinet of Dr. Ramirez, 1990 (Watkin)
Cabiria. See Notti di Cabiria, 1956
Cabiria. Nights of Cabiria. See Notti di Cabiria, 1956
Cable Car Murder, 1971 (Goldsmith)
Cable Laying, 1940 (Balcon)
Cabo Blanco, 1979 (Goldsmith)
Caccia alla volpe, 1966 (Bryan; Zavattini)
Caccia tragica, 1947 (Zavattini)
Cactus Cure, 1925 (Canutt)
Cactus Flower, 1969 (Diamond; Jones; Lang)
Cactus Kid, 1930 (Disney)
Cadaveri eccellenti, 1976 (Guerra)
Caddic, 1976 (Seale)
Caddies, 1960 (Halas and Batchelor)
Caddy, 1953 (Head)
Caddyshack, 1980 (Mandel)
Cadeau, 1982 (Legrand)
Cadence, 1990 (Delerue)
Cadet Girl, 1941 (Clarke)
Cadet Rousselle, 1946 (Dunning)
Cadres fleuris, 1910 (Cohl)
Caduta degli dei, 1969 (Jarre)
Caesar and Cleopatra, 1946 (Auric; Bryan; Cardiff; Heckroth; Krasker;
 Mathieson; Rank; Young)
Café Colón, 1958 (Figueroa)
Cafe Colette, 1936 (Neame)
Café de Paris, 1938 (Matras)
Café Electric, 1927 (Kolowrat-Krakowsky)
Café Express, 1980 (Cristaldi)
Café in Cairo, 1924 (Polito; Stromberg)
Cafe in the Main Street. See Kavárna na hlavní třide, 1954
Cafe Metropole, 1937 (Johnson)
Café Society, 1939 (Dreier; Head)
Café Waiter's Dream. See Songe d'un garçon de café, 1910
Cage, 1975 (Sarde; Saulnier)
Cage aux Folles, 1978 (Morricone)
Cage aux Folles II, 1980 (Morricone)
Cage aux folles III, 1985 (Morricone)
Cage of Doom. See Terror from the Year 5000, 1958
Cage of Gold, 1950 (Auric; Balcon; Slocombe)
Caged, 1950 (Steiner; Wald)
Cagey Canary, 1941 (Avery; Blanc; Clampett; Stalling)
Cagliostro, 1928 (Meerson)
Cagliostro. See Black Magic, 1947
Cagna, 1972 (Carrière; Flaiano and Pinelli)
Cahill. See Cahill, United States Marshal, 1973

Cahill, United States Marshal, 1973 (Bernstein; Biroc)
Caids, 1972 (Douy)
Cain and Mabel, 1936 (Barnes; Orry-Kelly; Westmore Family)
Caine Mutiny, 1954 (Cohn; Planer; Steiner; Wald)
Cairo, 1942 (Stothart; Wheeler)
Cairo Road, 1950 (Morris)
Cake Eater, 1924 (Roach)
Cake-Walk de la pendule, 1904 (Gaumont)
Cal, 1984 (Puttnam)
Calaboose, 1942 (Roach)
Calabuch, 1956 (Flaiano and Pinelli)
Calais-Douvre, 1931 (Planer)
Calamitous Elopement, 1908 (Bitzer)
Calcutta, 1947 (Dreier; Head; Miller; Seitz; Young)
Calendar, 1948 (Rank)
Calendar Girl, 1993 (Zimmer)
Calender, 1931 (Balcon)
Calico Vampire, 1916 (Loos)
Califfa, 1970 (Morricone)
California, 1946 (Dreier; Head; Miller; Rennahan; Young)
California Dolls. See All the Marbles, 1981
California in '49 , 1924 (Canutt)
California or Bust, 1923 (Roach)
California Romance, 1922 (August; Fox; Furthman)
California Straight Ahead, 1925 (Mandell)
California Suite, 1978 (Booth; Stark)
Caligula, 1976 (Donati)
Caliph Storch, 1954 (Reiniger)
Call, 1909 (Bitzer)
Call a Cop!, 1931 (Roach)
Call a Taxi, 1920 (Roach)
Call for Mr. Caveman, 1919 (Roach)
Call from Space, 1988 (Cardiff)
Call Girl. See Models, Inc., 1952
Call Harry Crown. See 99 and 44/100% Dead, 1974
Call Her Savage, 1932 (Garmes)
Call It a Day, 1937 (Blanke; Haller; Orry-Kelly; Wallis)
Call It Luck, 1934 (Nichols; Trotti)
Call Me Bwana, 1963 (Broccoli)
Call Me Madam, 1953 (Berlin; Newman; Sharaff; Wheeler)
Call Me Madame, 1953 (Shamroy)
Call Me Mister, 1951 (Lemaire; Newman; Wheeler)
Call Northside 777, 1948 (Lemaire; Newman; Wheeler; Zanuck)
Call of Flesh. See Jotai, 1964
Call of the Canyon, 1923 (Howe)
Call of the Cuckoo, 1927 (Bruckman; Roach)
Call of the Flesh, 1930 (Gibbons; Shearer; Stothart)
Call of the Heart, 1927 (Laemmle)
Call of the Mate, 1924 (Furthman)
Call of the North, 1914 (Buckland)
Call of the Song, 1911 (Gaudio)
Call of the Wild, 1923 (Roach)
Call of the Wild, 1935 (Day; Newman; Rosher; Zanuck)
Call Out the Marines, 1942 (Musuraca)
Call the Witness, 1921 (Roach)
Call to Arms, 1910 (Bitzer)
Callahans and the Murphys, 1927 (Gibbons; Marion)
Callaway Went Thataway, 1951 (Rose)
Calle Mayor, 1956 (Kosma; de Beauregard)
Calligraphie japonaise, 1961 (Braunberger)
Calling All Husbands, 1940 (McCord)
Calling Bulldog Drummond, 1951 (Junge)
Calling Dr. Death, 1943 (Miller)
Calling Dr. Magoo, 1956 (Bosustow)
Calling Dr. Porky, 1940 (Blanc; Stalling)
Calling of Dan Matthews, 1935 (Brown)

Calling Wild Bill Hickok, 1943 (Canutt)
Callisto, 1943 (Honegger)
Calmos, 1975 (Delerue)
Calveras, 1969 (Grimault)
Calvert's Folly. See Calvert's Valley, 1922
Calvert's Valley, 1922 (Fox; Furthman)
Cambio de sexo, 1976 (Almendros)
Cambriolage sur les toits, 1898 (Pathé)
Came the Brawn, 1938 (Roach)
Came the Dawn, 1928 (Roach)
Caméléone, 1996 (Branco)
Camelia, 1953 (Figueroa)
Camelot, 1967 (Newman; Warner)
Camels Are Coming, 1934 (Balcon; Rank)
Cameo Kirby, 1923 (Fox)
Camera d'albergo, 1981 (Age and Scarpelli)
Camera Makes Woopee, 1934-35 (McClaren)
Cameraman, 1928 (Bruckman; Mayer)
Cameraman's Revenge. See Myest kinematografichyeeskovo
    operator, 1911
Cameramen at War, 1944 (Lye)
Cameriera bella presenza offresi, 1951 (Flaiano and Pinelli)
Cameriere, 1959 (Delli Colli)
Camicie rosse, 1950 (Gherardi)
Camilla, 1954 (Cristaldi; Flaiano and Pinelli)
Camille, 1915 (Carré; Marion)
Camille, 1921 (Mathis)
Camille, 1927 (Menzies; Schenck)
Camille, 1937 (Adrian; Booth; Daniels; Freund; Gibbons; Marion; Mayer;
    Stothart; Thalberg)
Camille Claudel, 1988 (Lhomme; Nuytten)
Camille without Camelias. See Signora senza camelie, 1953
Caminito de Gloria, 1939 (Alton)
Camion, 1977 (Duras; Nuytten)
Cammino della speranza, 1950 (Flaiano and Pinelli)
Cammorista, 1986 (Morricone)
Camorra. See Complicato intrigo di Bonne vicoli e delitti, 1985
Camouflage, 1943 (Terry)
Camouflage Kiss, 1918 (Furthman)
Camp Followers. See Soldatesse, 1965
Camp of Mischli-Mischloch. See Nachtlager von Mischli-Michloch, 1917
Camp on Blood Island, 1958 (Carreras)
Campagne de France 1814-(?), 1916 (Cohl)
Campane a martello, 1949 (Gherardi; Ponti; Rota)
Campbell Soups, 1912 (Cohl)
Campbell's Kingdom, 1957 (Rank)
Campcment 13, 1938 (Alekan)
Camping, 1957 (Ponti)
Campus Confessions, 1938 (Dreier; Head)
Campus Sweetheart, 1931 (Newman)
Can, 1972 (Müller)
Can Heironymus Merkin Ever Forget Mercy Humppe and Find True
    Happiness?, 1969 (Heller)
Can Horses Sing?, 1971 (Lassally)
Can This Be Dixie?, 1936 (Glennon; Trotti)
Can You Take It?, 1934 (Fleischer)
Can-Can, 1960 (Daniels; Lederer; Pan; Sharaff; Smith; Wheeler)
Canada Is My Piano, 1967 (Dunning)
Canadian Bacon, 1994 (Bernstein; Wexler)
Canadian Capers, 1931 (Terry)
Canadian Pacific, 1949 (Tiomkin)
Canadian Pacific Railroad Shots, 1899 (Bitzer)
Canadians, 1961 (Mathieson)
Canal Zone, 1942 (Planer)
Cananea, 1976 (Figueroa)
Canard aux cérises, 1951 (Kosma)

Canaries Sometimes Sing, 1930 (Wilcox)
Canary Murder Case, 1929 (Banton; Mankiewicz)
Canary Row, 1950 (Blanc; Stalling)
Canasta de cuentos mexicanos, 1956 (Figueroa)
Canasta uruguaya, 1951 (Alcoriza)
Cancel My Reservation, 1972 (Metty)
Canción del alma, 1938 (Figueroa)
Canción del milagro, 1940 (Figueroa)
Candid Candidate, 1937 (Fleischer)
Candidate, 1972 (Von Brandenstein)
Candidate for a Killing. See Sudario a la medida, 1969
Candidato, 1999 (Zimmer)
Candlelight in Algeria, 1943 (Heller)
Candlemaker, 1956 (Halas and Batchelor)
Candy, 1968 (Grusin; Henry; Rotunno; Southern; Tavoularis; Trumbull)
Candy House, 1934 (Lantz)
Candy Lamb, 1935 (Lantz)
Canicule, 1983 (Lai)
Canned Feud, 1951 (Blanc; Stalling)
Canned Fishing, 1938 (Roach)
Cannery Row, 1982 (Nitzsche; Nykvist)
Cannery Woe, 1961 (Blanc; McKimson)
Cannon for Cordoba, 1970 (Bernstein)
Canon, 1964 (McClaren)
Canon City, 1948 (Alton)
Canone inverso, 2000 (Morricone)
Can't Help Singing, 1944 (Plunkett)
Cantaclaro, 1945 (Figueroa)
Cantata de Chile, 1975 (Herrera)
Canterbury Tale, 1944 (Junge; Rank)
Canterbury Tales. See I racconti di Canterbury, 1971
Canto ma sottovoce, 1945 (Zavattini)
Cantoria d'Angeli, 1949 (Di Venanzo)
Canyon Hawks, 1930 (Canutt)
Canyon of Adventure, 1928 (McCord)
Canyon of Light, 1926 (Fox)
Canyon Passage, 1946 (Banton; Carmichael; Cronjager; Wanger)
Canzoni, canzoni, canzoni, 1953 (Flaiano and Pinelli)
Cap de l'Espérance, 1951 (Kosma; Mnouchkine)
Cape Fear, 1962 (Boyle; Herrmann)
Cape Fear, 1991 (Bass; Bernstein; Bumstead; Francis; Herrmann; Marshall; Schoonmaker)
Cape Forlorn, 1930 (Junge)
Caper of the Golden Bulls, 1966 (Head; Levine; Pereira)
Capitaine Corsaire. See Mollenard, 1937
Capitaine Cyrano, 1995 (Carrière)
Capitaine Fracasse, 1942 (Honegger)
Capital Story, 1945 (Kaufman)
Capitan Fantasma, 1953 (Age and Scarpelli)
Capitan Fracassa, 1940 (Stallich; Zavattini)
Capkovy povídky, 1947 (Trnka)
Caporal épinglé, 1962 (Kosma; Spaak)
Cappello da prete, 1944 (Amidei)
Cappotto, 1952 (Zavattini)
Cappotto di Astrakan, 1979 (Cristaldi; Mnouchkine)
Caprelles et pantopodes, 1930 (Jaubert)
Capriccio, 1938 (Röhrig)
Capriccio all'italiana, 1968 (Age and Scarpelli; Delli Colli; Zavattini)
Capriccio Espagnol. See Spanish Fiesta, 1941
Caprice, 1967 (Shamroy; Smith)
Caprice de Noël, 1963 (McClaren)
Caprice de Princesse, 1933 (Planer)
Caprices, 1941 (Andrejew)
Caprices de Maria, 1969 (Delerue)
Caprices of Kitty, 1915 (Marion)
Capricorn One, 1977 (Goldsmith)

Capriolen, 1937 (Planer)
Captain America, 1992 (Golan and Globus)
Captain Blood, 1935 (Friedhofer; Grot; Haller; Korngold; Mohr; Wallis; Warner; Westmore Family)
Captain Blood, Fugitive. See Captain Pirate, 1952
Captain Boycott, 1947 (Alwyn; Morris; Rank)
Captain Cap, 1963 (Braunberger)
Captain Careless, 1928 (Miller; Plunkett)
Captain Carey, U.S.A., 1950 (Dreier; Friedhofer; Seitz)
Captain Caution, 1940 (Plunkett; Roach)
Captain China, 1949 (Alton)
Captain Clegg, 1962 (Carreras)
Captain Courtesy, 1915 (Marion)
Captain Cowboy, 1929 (Canutt)
Captain Eo, 1986 (Baker; Murch; Muren; Storaro)
Captain from Castile, 1947 (Basevi; Clarke; Day; Lemaire; Newman; Trotti)
Captain Fury, 1939 (Canutt; Roach)
Captain Hareblower, 1954 (Blanc; Stalling)
Captain Hurricane, 1935 (Plunkett)
Captain Is a Lady, 1940 (Kaper)
Captain January, 1936 (Seitz; Zanuck)
Captain Kidd, 1926 (Bray)
Captain Kidd, Jr., 1919 (Marion; Rosher)
Captain Kidd's Kids, 1919 (Roach)
Captain Kleinschmidt's Adventures in the Far North. See Adventures in the Far North, 1923
Captain Lash, 1929 (Fox)
Captain Lightfoot, 1955 (Hunter)
Captain Newman, M.D., 1963 (Metty; Westmore Family; Whitlock)
Captain of Koepenick. See I Was a Criminal, 1945
Captain of the Guard, 1930 (Laemmle; Mohr)
Captain Pirate, 1952 (Duning)
Captain Salvation, 1927 (Daniels; Gibbons)
Captain Sinbad, 1963 (Haskin; Schüfftan)
Captains Courageous, 1937 (Gibbons; Gillespie; Kahn; Mayer; Rosson; Waxman)
Captains Courageous, 1977 (Lathrop)
Captain's Kid, 1936 (Haller)
Captains of the Clouds, 1942 (Haskin; Hoch; Mercer; Polito; Steiner; Wallis)
Captains Outrageous, 1952 (Bosustow)
Captain's Paradise, 1953 (Arnold; Korda)
Captain's Table, 1959 (Challis; Rank)
Captian Hates the Sea, 1934 (August)
Captive, 1915 (Buckland; MacPherson)
Captive, 2000 (Branco)
Captive City, 1952 (Garmes)
Captive God, 1916 (August)
Captive Heart, 1946 (Balcon; Rank; Slocombe)
Captive in the Land, 1990 (Conti)
Captive Wild Women, 1943 (Pierce)
Capture, 1950 (Cronjager)
Captured, 1933 (Orry-Kelly)
Car, 1977 (Rosenman; Whitlock)Car, 1977 (Rosenman; Whitlock)
Car 99, 1935 (Head; Sullivan)
Car of Dreams, 1935 (Balcon; Junge; Rank)
Car of Tomorrow, 1951 (Avery)
Car Thief. See Jidosha doroba, 1964
Car-Tune Portrait, 1937 (Fleischer)
Carabina 30-30, 1958 (Figueroa)
Carabiniere a cavallo, 1961 (Di Venanzo; Gherardi)
Carabiniers, 1963 (Coutard; Guillemot; Ponti; de Beauregard)
Caravaggio, 1940 (Stallich)
Caravan, 1934 (Kahn; Raphaelson)
Caravan, 1945 (Bryan; Rank)

Caravane au Jardin d'Acclimatation, 1895-97 (Gaumont)
Caravane de la lumière, 1947 (Fradetal)
Caravans, 1978 (Slocombe)
Carbine Williams, 1952 (Plunkett)
Carbon Arc Projection, 1947 (Hoch)
Carbon Copy, 1981 (Conti)
Card, 1952 (Alwyn; Bryan; Morris; Neame)
Card Game. See Poker, 1920
Cardboard Cavalier, 1949 (Dillon; Rank)
Cardboard Lover, 1928 (Gibbons)
Cardinal, 1963 (Bass; Shamroy; Smith; Wheeler)
Cardinal Richelieu, 1935 (Day; Johnson; Newman; Zanuck)
Cardinal's Conspiracy, 1909 (Bitzer; Ince)
Career, 1939 (Trumbo)
Career, 1959 (Cahn; Head; La Shelle; Wallis; Waxman; van Heusen)
Career: Medical Technologists, 1954 (Bernstein)
Career Opportunities, 1991 (McAlpine; Newman)
Career Woman, 1936 (Trotti)
Careers, 1929 (Seitz)
Carefree, 1938 (Berlin; Berman; Nichols; Pan; Polglase)
Careful, He Might Hear You, 1983 (Seale)
Careful, Soft Shoulders, 1942 (Clarke; Day)
Careless Lady, 1932 (Friedhofer; Seitz)
Caretaker, 1963 (Pinter)
Caretakers, 1963 (Ballard; Bernstein)
Caretaker's Daughter, 1925 (Roach)
Caretaker's Daughter, 1934 (Roach)
Cargamento prohibibo, 1965 (Figueroa)
Cargo of Innocents. See Stand by for Action, 1943
Cargo to Capetown, 1950 (Duning)
Cari fottutissimi amici, 1993 (Cecchi D'amico)
Caribbean, 1952 (Head; Pereira)
Carillons sans joie, 1962 (Auric; Cloquet)
Cariñoso, 1958 (Alcoriza)
Carlito's Way, 1993 (Sylbert)
Carlos, 1971 (Müller)
Carmen, 1915 (Buckland; MacPherson; Zukor)
Carmen, 1918 (Kräly)
Carmen, 1926 (Meerson)
Carmen, 1933 (Reiniger)
Carmen, 1943 (Spaak; Jeanson)
Carmen, 1967 (Wakhévitch)
Carmen, 1984 (Guerra)
Carmen fra i rossi, 1939 (Stallich)
Carmen Jones, 1954 (Bass)
Carmen von St. Pauli, 1928 (Junge)
Carmen's Veranda, 1944 (Terry)
Carnal Knowledge, 1971 (Levine; O'Steen; Rotunno; Sylbert)
Carnaval à la Nouvelle Orléans, 1957 (Braunberger)
Carnaval à Nice, 1913 (Gaumont)
Carne de presidio, 1951 (Alcoriza)
Carne per Frankenstein, 1974 (Ponti)
Carnegie Hall, 1947 (Schüfftan)
Carnet de bal, 1937 (Jaubert; Jeanson)
Carnets du Major Thompson, 1957 (Matras)
Carnevale di Venezia, 1927 (Amidei)
Carniere, 1997 (Donaggio)
Carnival, 1931 (Wilcox)
Carnival, 1935 (Riskin)
Carnival, 1946 (Dillon; Rank)
Carnival Boat, 1932 (McCord)
Carnival Capers, 1932 (Lantz)
Carnival Girl, 1926 (Garmes)
Carnival in Costa Rica, 1947 (Hoffenstein; Reynolds)
Carnival in Flanders. See Kermesse héroïque, 1935
Carnival in the Clothes Cupboard, 1940 (Halas and Batchelor)

Carnival of Thieves. See Caper of the Golden Bulls, 1966
Carnival on Costa Rica, 1947 (Basevi)
Carnival Rock, 1957 (Crosby)
Carnival Story, 1954 (Haller; Trumbo)
Carnival Week, 1927 (Terry)
Carny, 1980 (North)
Caro Diaro, 1994 (Lanci, Giuseppe ("beppe"))
Caro Michele, 1976 (Cecchi D'amico; Delli Colli; Guerra; Rota)
Caro Papà, 1979 (Delli Colli)
Carobni zvuci, 1957 (Vukotić)
Carodějuv učen, 1977 (Zeman)
Carola, 1975 (Lourié)
Carolina, 1934 (Mohr)
Carolina Blues, 1944 (Cahn; Duning; Planer)
Carolina Rediviva, 1920 (Magnusson)
Caroline au pays natal, 1951 (Decaë)
Caroline chérie, 1950 (Auric)
Caroline chérie, 1967 (Saulnier; Vierny)
Caroline du Sud, 1952 (Decaë)
Carousel, 1956 (Clarke; Newman; Reynolds; Smith; Wheeler)
Caroussel boréal, 1958 (Starewicz)
Carpetbaggers, 1964 (Bernstein; ;Edouart; Hayes; Head; Levine;Westmore Family)
Carpocapse des pommes, 1955 (Rabier)
Carpool, 1996 (Reynolds)
Carrara, 1950 (Di Venanzo)
Carré de valets, 1947 (Jeanson)
Carrefour, 1938 (Burel; D'Eaubonne)
Carrefour des passion, 1948 (Kosma)
Carrefour du crime, 1947 (Burel)
Carrie, 1952 (Head; Pereira; Raksin)
Carrie, 1977 (Donaggio)
Carried Away by the Current. See Proudy, 1922
Carro armata dell'otto settembre, 1960 (Guerra)
Carrosse d'or, 1953 (Renoir)
Carry on Constable, 1960 (Dillon)
Carry on Cruising, 1962 (Dillon)
Carry on Milkmaids, 1974 (Halas and Batchelor)
Carry on Nurse, 1959 (Vetchinsky)
Carry on Sergeant, 1958 (Vetchinsky)
Carry on Spying, 1964 (Vetchinsky)
Carry on Teacher, 1959 (Vetchinsky)
Carry On up the Khyber, 1968 (Vetchinsky)
Carrying the Mail, 1934 (Canutt)
Carson City Raiders, 1948 (Canutt)
Carte américaine, 1912-14 (Cohl)
Carter Case. See Mr. District Attorney in the Carter Case, 1942
Cartes sur table, 1965 (Carrière; D'Eaubonne)
Cartoni animati, 1997 (Morricone)
Cartoon Factory, 1925 (Fleischer)
Cartoonland, 1921 (Fleischer)
Cartouche, 1934 (Fradetal)
Cartouche, 1962 (Delerue; Matras; Mnouchkine; Spaak)
Carve Her Name with Pride, 1958 (Alwyn; Rank)
Carved in Ivory, 1974 (Lassally)
Caryl Chessman Story. See Kill Me If You Can, 1977
Cas du Docteur Laurent, 1956 (Alekan; Kosma)
Casa bruciata, 1997 (Morricone)
Casa colorado, 1947 (Figueroa)
Casa de cristal, 1967 (Alcoriza)
Casa de Lava, 1994 (Branco)
Casa del ogro, 1938 (Figueroa)
Casa del pelicano, 1977 (Figueroa)
Casa del rencor, 1941 (Figueroa)
Casa Ricordi, 1954 (Age and Scarpelli)

Casablanca, 1942 (Edeson; Epstein; Friedhofer; Koch; Orry-Kelly; Steiner; Wallis; Warner; Westmore Family)
Casanova, 1927 (Burel)
Casanova, 1976 (Donati; Rota; de Laurentiis)
Casanova '70, 1965 (Age and Scarpelli; Cecchi D'amico; Guerra; Levine; Ponti)
Casanova Brown, 1944 (Fields; Johnson; Seitz)
Casanova Cat, 1951 (Hanna and Barbera)
Casanova de Federico Fellini, 1976 (Rotunno)
Casanova's Return. *See* Retour de Casanova, 1992
Case Against Calvin Cooke. *See* Act of Murder, 1948
Case Against Mrs. Ames, 1936 (Spencer; Wanger)
Case for Life, 1996 (Mirisch)
Case for PC 49, 1951 (Carreras)
Case of Jonathan Drew. *See* Lodger: A Story of the London Fog, 1926
Case of Lena Smith, 1929 (Banton; Dreier; Furthman; Rosson)
Case of Marcel Duchamp, 1983 (Lassally)
Case of Sergeant Grischa, 1930 (Plunkett)
Case of the Black Parrot, 1941 (McCord)
Case of the Curious Bride, 1935 (Grot; Laszlo; Orry-Kelly)
Case of the Howling Dog, 1934 (Orry-Kelly)
Case of the Lost Sheep, 1935 (Lantz)
Case of the Lucky Legs, 1935 (Gaudio)
Case of the Missing Blonde. *See* Lady in the Morgue, 1938
Case of the Missing Hare, 1942 (Blanc; Jones; Stalling)
Case of the Stuttering Pig, 1937 (Blanc; Stalling)
Case of the Velvet Claw, 1936 (Blanke)
Casey at the Bat, 1927 (Furthman)
Casey's Shadow, 1978 (Alonzo; Stark)
Cash, 1933 (Korda)
Cash and Carry, 1937 (Bruckman)
Cash Customers, 1921 (Roach)
Cash McCall, 1960 (Blanke; Steiner)
Cash on Demand, 1963 (Carreras)
Cash Parrish's Pal, 1915 (August)
Casino, 1995 (Bass; Schoonmaker)
Casino de Paree. *See* Go into Your Dance, 1935
Casino Murder Case, 1935 (Clarke; Tiomkin)
Casino Royale, 1967 (Bacharach; Fisher; Parrish; Southern; Williams)
Caso Mattei, 1972 (Cristaldi; Guerra)
Caso moro, 1986 (Donaggio)
Casper, 1995 (Muren)
Casque d'or, 1952 (D'Eaubonne; Hakim)
Cass Timberlane, 1947 (Irene; Levien; Mayer; Stewart)
Cassandra Crossing, 1976 (Goldsmith; Ponti)
Casse, 1971 (Morricone; Renoir; Saulnier)
Casse Pieds, 1948 (Burel)
Cassidy of Bar 20, 1938 (Head)
Cassis Colank, 1958-59 (Breer)
Cast a Giant Shadow, 1965 (Bernstein)
Cast a Long Shadow, 1959 (Mirisch)
Casta Diva, 1935 (Planer)
Casta diva, 1955 (Age and Scarpelli)
Castle. *See* Project X, 1968
Castle in the Desert, 1942 (Miller)
Castle Keep, 1969 (Decaë; Douy; Legrand; Taradash)
Castle of Otranto. *See* Otrantsky zámek, 1973-79
Castle on the Hudson, 1940 (Deutsch; Edeson; Haskin; Miller)
Casualities of War, 1989 (Morricone)
Cat, 1921 (Laemmle)
Cat. *See* Až přijde kocour, 1963
Cat. *See* Chatte, 1958
Cat Above and the Mouse Below, 1964 (Jones)
Cat and Duplicat, 1967 (Jones)
Cat and Mouse. *See* Chat et la souris, 1975
Cat and the Canary, 1927 (Laemmle)

Cat and the Canary, 1939 (Dreier; Head; Lang)
Cat and the Fiddle, 1934 (Adrian; Clarke; Rosson; Stothart)
Cat and the Mermouse, 1949 (Hanna and Barbera)
Cat Came Back, 1944 (Terry)
Cat Concerto, 1947 (Hanna and Barbera)
Cat Creeps, 1930 (Laemmle; Mohr)
Cat Feud, 1958 (Blanc; Jones)
Cat Fishin', 1947 (Hanna and Barbera)
Cat from Outer Space, 1978 (Ames; Schifrin)
Cat Happy, 1950 (Terry)
Cat Meets Mouse, 1942 (Terry)
Cat Napping, 1951 (Hanna and Barbera)
Cat Nipped, 1932 (Lantz)
Cat on a Hot Tin Roof, 1958 (Daniels; Rose)
Cat People, 1942 (D'Agostino; Dunn; Lewton; Musuraca)
Cat People, 1982 (Whitlock)
Cat That Hated People, 1948 (Avery)
Cat Trouble, 1947 (Terry)
Cat Women of the Moon, 1953 (Bernstein)
Cat, Dog, & Co., 1929 (Roach)
Cat-astrophe, 1916 (Terry)
Cat-Tails for Two, 1953 (Blanc; McKimson; Stalling)
Catacombs, 1988 (Donaggio)
Catapult and the Kite. *See* Prak a drank, 1960
Catastrophe, 2000 (Pinter)
Catastrophe de la Martinique, 1902 (Pathé)
Catch As Catch Can , 1927 (Shamroy)
Catch as Catch Can. *See* Scatenato, 1967
Catch As Cats Can, 1947 (Blanc; Stalling)
Catch Him! *See* Chytte ho!, 1924
Catch Me a Spy, 1971 (Braunberger; Challis; Dillon)
Catch Meow, 1961 (Hanna and Barbera)
Catch My Smoke, 1922 (Fox)
Catch My Soul, 1973 (Hall)
Catch-22, 1970 (Henry; O'Steen; Sylbert; Watkin; Whitlock)
Catch-as-Catch-Can, 1931 (Roach)
Catching a Coon, 1921 (Roach)
Catered Affair, 1956 (Alton; Previn; Westmore Family)
Cathédrale, 1947 (Braunberger)
Catherine the Great, 1934 (Biro; Korda; Krasker; Mathieson; Périnal)
Catherine, il suffit d'un amour, 1969 (Douy)
Catholics, 1973 (Fisher)
Catnip Capers, 1940 (Terry)
Catnip Gang, 1949 (Terry)
Cats, 1956 (Breer)
Cats A-Weigh!, 1953 (Blanc; McKimson; Stalling)
Cats and Bruises, 1965 (Blanc)
Cats and Dogs, 1932 (Lantz)
Cat's Bah, 1954 (Blanc; Jones; Stalling)
Cat's Cradle, 1974 (Driessen)
Cat's Eye, 1985 (Cardiff; de Laurentiis)
Cats in the Bag, 1936 (Terry)
Cat's Me-Ouch, 1965 (Jones)
Cat's Meow, 1956 (Avery)
Cat's Nine Lives, 1927 (Lantz)
Cat's Pajamas, 1926 (Banton; Vajda)
Cat's Paw, 1934 (Newman)
Cat's Paw, 1959 (Blanc)
Cat's Revenge, 1954 (Terry)
Cat's Tale, 1941 (Blanc; Stalling)
Cat's Tale, 1951 (Terry)
Cat's Whiskers, 1923 (Terry)
Cat's Whiskers, 1926 (Lantz)
Cattiva, 1992 (Age and Scarpelli)
Cattle Call, 1999 (Golan and Globus)
Cattle Queen of Montana, 1954 (Alton; Polglase)

Chair, 1963 (Kuri)
Chair, 1967 (Dunning)
Chair de l'orchidée, 1974 (Carrière; Lhomme)
Chair de poule, 1963 (Burel; Delerue; Hakim)
Chair et le diable, 1953 (Auric; Wakhévitch)
Chairman, 1969 (Maddow)
Chairman. *See* Most Dangerous Man in the World, 1969
Chairy Tale, 1956 (McLaren; Shankar)
Chaleur du foyer, 1955 (Auric)
Chalis Baba Ek Chor, 1954 (Burman)
Chalk Garden, 1964 (Arnold; Dillon; Hayes; Hunter; Neame)
Chalk Marks, 1924 (Walker)
Challenge, 1922 (Fleischer)
Challenge, 1938 (Korda; Krasker; Périnal)
Challenge, 1970 (Smith)
Challenge, 1982 (Goldsmith)
Challenge. *See* Sfida, 1958
Challenge for Robin Hood, 1967 (Carreras)
Challenge to Lassie, 1949 (Previn)
Chalti Ka Naam Gaddi, 1958 (Burman)
Chamade, 1968 (Lhomme; Mnouchkine)
Chamber, 1996 (Burwell; Goldman)
Chamberlain. *See* Kammarjunkaren, 1914
Chambre, 1964 (Cloquet)
Chambre 34, 1945 (Braunberger)
Chambre à part, 1989 (Sarde)
Chambre ardente, 1962 (Auric; Spaak)
Chambre de bonne, 1970 (Braunberger)
Chambre en ville, 1982 (Evein)
Chambre verte, 1978 (Almendros; Jaubert)
Champ, 1931 (Marion; Mayer; Terry)
Champ, 1979 (Grusin)
Champ du possible, 1962 (Delerue)
Champagne amer, 1986 (Lhomme)
Champagne Charlie, 1944 (Balcon; Clarke)
Champagne for Caesar, 1950 (Tiomkin)
Champagne Murders. *See* Scandale, 1967
Champagne Waltz, 1937 (Banton; Young)
Champeen, 1922 (Roach)
Champion, 1949 (Foreman; Planer; Tiomkin)
Champion du jeu à la mode, 1910 (Cohl)
Champion of Justice, 1944 (Terry)
Champions juniors, 1950 (Fradetal; Kosma)
Champions: A Love Story, 1979 (Alonzo)
Championship Season, 1999 (van Runkle)
Champs-Elysées, 1928 (Kaufman)
Chance, 1994 (Donaggio)
Chance. *See* Being There, 1979
Chance at Heaven, 1933 (Cooper; Musuraca; Plunkett; Polglase; Steiner)
Chance Deception, 1912 (Bitzer)
Chance et l'amour, 1964 (de Beauregard)
Chance Meeting. *See* Blind Date, 1959
Chance Meeting. *See* Young Lovers, 1954
Chance of a Night-Time, 1931 (Wilcox)
Chances, 1931 (Haller)
Chances Are, 1989 (Fraker; Jarre)
Chandu the Magician, 1932 (Howe; Menzies)
Chang, 1927 (Cooper; Zukor)
Change Meeting. *See* Blind Date, 1959
Change of Habit, 1969 (Metty)
Change of Heart, 1909 (Bitzer)
Change of Heart, 1934 (Friedhofer; Hoffenstein; Levien; Mohr)
Change of Heart. *See* Two and Two Make Six, 1962
Change of Seasons, 1980 (Lathrop)
Change the Needle, 1925 (Roach)
Changing Husbands, 1924 (Glennon)

Channel Crossing, 1933 (Junge; Rank)
Chans, 1962 (Lundgren)
Chanson de gestes, 1966 (Braunberger)
Chanson de rue, 1945 (Decaë)
Chanson du pavé, 1951 (Colpi)
Chansons de Paris, 1934 (Barsacq)
Chant de l'amour, 1935 (D'Eaubonne)
Chant du marin, 1932 (Planer)
Chant du Styrène, 1958 (Braunberger; Delerue)
Chanteur de minuit, 1937 (Matras; Renoir; Wakhévitch)
Chanteur inconnu, 1931 (Courant; Wakhévitch)
Chanteur inconnu, 1946 (Barsacq)
Chanteurs des cours, 1899 (Gaumont)
Chantons sous l'occupation, 1976 (Colpi)
Chants populaires, 1944 (Dunning)
Chants retrouvés, 1948 (Colpi)
Chaos. *See* **Kaos**, 1984
Chapeau de paille d'Italie, 1927 (Meerson)
Chapeaux des belles dames, 1909 (Cohl)
Chaplin, 1992 (Barry; Goldman; Nykvist)
Chapman Report, 1962 (Orry-Kelly; Rosenman; Zanuck)
Chappaqua, 1966 (Schüfftan; Shankar)
Chapter Two, 1979 (Booth; Hamlisch; Stark)
Char Ankhen, 1944 (Biswas)
Char dil Char rahen, 1959 (Biswas)
Charade, 1953 (Biroc)
Charade, 1963 (D'Eaubonne; Lang; Mancini; Mercer)
Charandas Chor, 1975 (Nihalani)
Charandas the Thief. *See* Charandas Chor, 1975
Charcutier de Machonville, 1946 (Decaë; Fradetal)
Charette fantôme, 1939 (Ibert)
Charge at Feather River, 1953 (Steiner)
Charge Is Murder. *See* Twilight of Honor, 1963
Charge of the Gauchos, 1928 (Musuraca)
Charge of the Light Brigade, 1936 (Canutt; Friedhofer; Polito; Steiner; Wallis)
Charge of the Light Brigade, 1968 (Watkin; Williams)
Chariot de Thespis, 1941 (Alekan)
Chariots of Fire, 1981 (Puttnam; Vangelis; Watkin)
Chariots of Fur, 1994 (Jones)
Charlemagne, 1933 (Douy)
Charleston, 1979 (Bernstein)
Charleston. *See* Sur un air de Charleston, 1927
Charley in "Your Very Good Health'', 1946-47 (Halas and Batchelor)
Charley in the New Mines, 1946-47 (Halas and Batchelor)
Charley in the New Schools, 1946-47 (Halas and Batchelor)
Charley in the New Towns, 1946-47 (Halas and Batchelor)
Charley Junior's Schooldays, 1946-47 (Halas and Batchelor)
Charley My Boy, 1926 (Roach)
Charley Varrick, 1973 (Schifrin)
Charley's American Aunt. *See* Charley's Aunt, 1941
Charley's Aunt, 1941 (Banton; Day; Newman; Vetchinsky)
Charley's March of Time, 1946-47 (Halas and Batchelor)
Charlie & Louise—Das Doppelte Lottchen, 1993 (Kästner)
Charlie Chan at the Olympics, 1937 (Miller)
Charlie Chan at the Wax Museum, 1940 (Day; Miller)
Charlie Chan at Treasure Island, 1939 (Day; Miller)
Charlie Chan in Honolulu, 1938 (Clarke; Day)
Charlie Chan in Panama, 1940 (Day; Miller)
Charlie Chan in Reno, 1939 (Miller)
Charlie Chan in Rio, 1941 (Day)
Charlie Chan in the City of Darkness, 1939 (Miller)
Charlie Chan's Chance, 1931 (August)
Charlie Chan's Courage, 1934 (Miller; Mohr)
Charlie Chan's Murder Cruise, 1940 (Miller)
Charlie Chan's Secret, 1936 (Maté)

Charlie et ses deux nénettes, 1973 (Sarde)
Charlie Fadden, 1913 (Zukor)
Charlotte et son Jules, 1958 (Braunberger)
Charlotte Löwenskjöld, 1930 (Jaenzon)
Charlotte's Web, 1972 (Hanna and Barbera)
Charly, 1968 (Shankar)
Charmants garçons, 1957 (Legrand; Spaak)
Charme discret de la bourgeoisie, 1972 (Carrière)
Charmer, 1925 (Howe)
Charmer. *See* Moonlight Sonata, 1937
Charmeuse de serpents, 1895-97 (Gaumont)
Charming Sinners, 1929 (Banton)
Charting the Seas, 1948 (Arnold)
Chartres, 1923 (Périnal)
Chartreuse de Parme, 1948 (Annenkov; D'Eaubonne)
Charulata, 1964 (Chandragupta; Dutta; Mitra)
Chase, 1946 (Planer)
Chase, 1966 (Barry; Day; La Shelle; Spiegel)
Chase a Crooked Shadow, 1957 (Warner)
Chase After Adam. *See* Pogon za Adamem, 1970
Chaser on the Rocks, 1965 (Blanc)
Chases of Pimple Street, 1935 (Roach)
Chasing Danger, 1939 (Miller)
Chasing Rainbows, 1930 (Gibbons)
Chasing the Chaser, 1925 (Roach)
Chasing the Limited, 1915 (Furthman)
Chasing the Moon, 1922 (Fox)
Chasing Through Europe, 1929 (Fox)
Chasing Yesterday, 1935 (Plunkett)
Chasse au lion à l'arc, 1965 (Braunberger)
Chassé-croisé, 1931 (Fradetal)
Chasseur, 1970 (Braunberger)
Chasseur de chez Maxim's, 1927 (Meerson)
Chaste Suzanne, 1937 (D'Eaubonne)
Chat, 1970 (Saulnier)
Chat, 1971 (Sarde)
Chat et la souris, 1975 (Lai)
Château de verre, 1950 (Aurenche and Bost; Barsacq)
Château du passé, 1958 (Decaë; Rabier)
Chateaux stop . . . sur la Loire, 1962 (Delerue)
Chatelaine du Liban, 1933 (Matras)
Chatte, 1958 (Kosma)
Chatte sort ses griffes, 1959 (Kosma)
Chatterbox, 1936 (Plunkett)
Chaudronnier, 1948 (Fradetal)
Chauncy Explains, 1905 (Bitzer)
Chausette surprise, 1978 (Carrière)
Chaussures matrimoniales, 1909 (Cohl)
Chauve-souris, 1931 (Heller)
Che!, 1969 (Schifrin; Smith; Wilson)
Che?, 1972 (Ponti)
Che c'entriamo noi con la rivoluzione?, 1973 (Morricone)
Che gioia vivere, 1961 (Aurenche and Bost; Decaë)
Cheap Detective, 1978 (Alonzo; Booth; Houseman; Stark)
Cheap Kisses, 1924 (Sullivan)
Cheaper by the Dozen, 1950 (Lemaire; Shamroy; Trotti; Wheeler)
Cheaper to Marry, 1925 (Gibbons; Mayer)
Cheat, 1915 (Buckland; Zukor)
Cheat, 1923 (Miller)
Cheat. *See* Manèges, 1950
Cheated Hearts, 1921 (Laemmle; Miller)
Cheated Love, 1921 (Glennon; Levien)
Cheater Reformed, 1921 (Fox; Furthman)
Cheaters. *See* Tricheurs, 1958
Cheating Cheaters, 1919 (Edeson)
Cheating Cheaters, 1927 (Laemmle)

Check and Double Check, 1930 (Steiner)
Check to Song, 1951 (Halas and Batchelor)
Check Your Baggage, 1918 (Roach)
Checking Out, 1989 (Burwell; Eszterhas)
Checkmate, 1935 (Havelock-Allan)
Checkpoint, 1956 (Dillon; Rank)
Cheech and Chong's Next Movie, 1980 (Whitlock)
Cheer Boys Cheer, 1939 (Balcon; Neame)
Cheer Up and Smile, 1930 (Fox)
Cheerful Fraud, 1927 (Laemmle)
Cheers for Mrs. Bishop, 1941 (Mohr)
Cheers of the Crowd, 1935 (Krasner)
Cheese Chasers, 1951 (Blanc; Jones; Stalling)
Cheese It—the Cat!, 1957 (Blanc; McKimson; Stalling)
Chef-Lieu de Canton, 1910 (Gaumont)
Chefs de demain, 1944 (Alekan)
Chefs d'oeuvres de Bébé, 1910 (Cohl)
Chelovek iz restorana, 1929 (Golovnya)
Chelovek s ruzhyom, 1938 (Shostakovich)
Chemical Ko-Ko, 1929 (Fleischer)
Chemin de Damas, 1952 (Schüfftan)
Chemin de la terre, 1962 (Delerue)
Chemin de Rio, 1936 (Jeanson)
Chemin des écoliers, 1959 (Aurenche and Bost; Barsacq; Matras)
Chemin du bonheur, 1933 (Kaufman)
Chemin du paradis, 1930 (Planer)
Chemin perdu, 1979 (Vierny)
Cher inconnue, 1981 (Sarde)
Cher vieux Paris!, 1950 (Decaë)
Cherchez la femme, 1921 (Kolowrat-Krakowsky)
Chère inconnue, 1980 (Cloquet; Evein)
Chère Louise, 1972 (Delerue; Mnouchkine)
Chères vieilles choses, 1957 (Colpi; Delerue)
Chéri Bibi, 1954 (Auric)
Cherokee Kid, 1927 (Musuraca)
Cherokee Strip, 1940 (Harlan; Head)
Cheryomushki, 1963 (Shostakovich)
Chess Fever. *See* Shakmatnaya goryachka, 1925
Chess Players. *See* Shatranj Ke Khilari, 1977
Chess-nuts, 1932 (Fleischer)
Chetirye chorta, 1913 (Starewicz)
Chetniks!, 1943 (Day; Friedhofer)
Chetniks—the Fighting Guerillas. *See* Chetniks!, 1943
Cheval d'orgueil, 1980 (Rabier; de Beauregard)
Chevaliers de la table ronde, 1990 (Braunberger)
Chevaux d'acier. *See* Moissons d'aujourd'hui, 1949
Chevaux de Vaugirard, 1961 (Delerue)
Chevaux du Vercors, 1942 (Alekan)
Chèvre d'or, 1942 (Aurenche and Bost)
Chèvre, 1961 (Fradetal)
Chewin' Bruin, 1940 (Blanc; Clampett; Stalling)
Cheyenne, 1947 (Friedhofer; Steiner)
Cheyenne Autumn, 1964 (Clothier; Day; North)
Cheyenne Cyclone, 1932 (Canutt)
Cheyenne Kid, 1933 (Musuraca; Steiner)
Cheyenne Social Club, 1970 (Clothier)
Chhoti Chhoti Baten, 1965 (Biswas)
Chhupa Rustam, 1973 (Burman)
Chi legge?, 1960 (Zavattini)
Chi l'ha vista morire?, 1972 (Morricone)
Chiameremo Andrea, 1972 (Zavattini)
Chiave, 1983 (Morricone)
Chicago, 1927 (Adrian)
Chicago after Midnight, 1928 (Plunkett)
Chicago Deadline, 1949 (Seitz; Young)
Chicago Joe and the Showgirl, 1990 (Zimmer)

Chicago Kid, 1945 (Brown)

Chicago Masquerade. *See* Little Eygpt, 1951

Chicago Story, 1981 (Schifrin)

Chicago Streets, 1975 (Menges)

Chicago, Chicago. *See* Gaily, Gaily, 1969

Chichiko-daka, 1956 (Yoda)

Chicken à la King, 1919 (Garmes)

Chicken à la King, 1928 (Fox)

Chicken à la King, 1937 (Fleischer)

Chicken Every Sunday, 1948 (Epstein; Lemaire; Newman; Wheeler)

Chicken Feed, 1927 (Roach)

Chicken Fraca-See, 1962 (Hanna and Barbera)

Chicken Jitters, 1939 (Blanc; Clampett; Stalling)

Chicken Reel, 1934 (Lantz)

Chicken Run, 2000 (Park)

Chicken Thief, 1921 (Bray)

Chicken-Hearted Wolf, 1963 (Hanna and Barbera)

Chicken-Wagon Family, 1939 (Cronjager)

Chiedo asilo, 1979 (Sarde)

Chief Crazy Horse, 1955 (Boyle)

Chief's Daughter, 1911 (Bitzer)

Chiemi no haihiiru, 1956 (Muraki)

Chiemi's High Heeled Shoes. *See* Chiemi no haihiiru, 1956

Chien andalou, 1929 (Braunberger)

Chien dans un jeu de quilles, 1962 (Gégauff)

Chien de pique, 1960 (Legrand)

Chien fou, 1966 (Guillemot)

Chien Mélomane, 1973 (Grimault)

Chienne, 1931 (Braunberger)

Chiens contrebandiers, 1906 (Pathé)

Chiens perdus sans collier, 1955 (Aurenche and Bost)

Chiffonniers d'Emmaüs, 1954 (Kosma)

Chigo no kenpo , 1927 (Tsuburaya)

Chiisana tobosha, 1967 (Miyagawa)

Chikagai 24-jikan, 1947 (Hayasaka)

Chikamatsu monogatari, 1954 (Hayasaka; Miyagawa; Yoda)

Chikyu boeigun, 1957 (Tsuburaya)

Child. *See* Barnet, 1912

Child in the House, 1956 (Adam; Heller)

Child Is Born, 1939 (Rosher; Wallis)

Child Is Waiting, 1962 (La Shelle)

Child of the Ghetto, 1910 (Bitzer)

Child of the Night. *See* Voleurs, 1996

Child Psykolojiky, 1941 (Fleischer)

Child Sock-Cology, 1961 (Hanna and Barbera)

Child Thou Gavest Me, 1921 (Mayer)

Child under a Leaf, 1974 (Lai)

Child Went Forth, 1941 (Eisler)

Childhood's Vow, 1900 (Bitzer)

Childless. *See* Bezdetná, 1935

Children. *See* Enfants, 1985

Children and Cars, 1971 (Halas and Batchelor)

Children Feeding Ducklings, 1899 (Bitzer)

Children Hand in Hand. *See* Te o tsunagu kora, 1963

Children in the Crossfire, 1984 (Lassally)

Children in the Surf, 1904 (Bitzer)

Children Making Cartoons, 1973 (Halas and Batchelor)

Children of a Lesser God, 1986 (Seale)

Children of Change. *See* Campane a martello, 1949

Children of Divorce, 1927 (Banton)

Children of Frostmofjället. *See* Barnen från Frostmofjället, 1945

Children of Paradise. *See* **Enfants du paradis**, 1945

Children of Pleasure, 1930 (Gibbons)

Children of Sanchez, 1978 (Figueroa; Zavattini)

Children of the Earth. *See* Dharti Ke Lal, 1947

Children of the Night, 1921 (Fox)

Children of the Night. *See* Nattbarn, 1956

Children of the Revolution. *See* Kinder der Revolution, 1923

Children of the Street. *See* Gatans barn, 1914

Children of the Sun, 1960 (Hubley)

Children Remember the Holocaust, 1995 (Burwell)

Children Upstairs, 1955 (Lassally)

Children's Corner, 1956 (Lassally)

Children's Friend, 1909 (Bitzer)

Children's Hour, 1961 (Hayes; Jeakins; North; Planer)

Child's Faith, 1910 (Bitzer)

Child's Impulse, 1910 (Bitzer)

Child's Play, 1988 (Walas)

Child's Remorse, 1912 (Bitzer)

Child's Strategem, 1910 (Bitzer)

Chile con Carmen, 1930 (Lantz)

Chile, Land of Charm, 1937 (Hoch)

Chili Corn Corny, 1965 (Blanc; McKimson)

Chili Weather, 1963 (Blanc)

Chill Factor, 1999 (Zimmer)

Chilly Willy in the Legend of Rockabye Point, 1955 (Avery)

Chiltern Hundreds, 1949 (Rank)

Chimatsuri , 1929 (Tsuburaya)

Chimmie Fadden, 1915 (Buckland)

Chimmie Fadden Out West, 1915 (Buckland; MacPherson)

Chimp, 1932 (Roach)

Chimp and Zee, 1968 (Blanc)

China, 1931 (Lantz; Terry)

China, 1943 (Dreier; Head; Young)

China 9, Liberty 37. *See* Amore, piombo, e furore, 1978

China Bound, 1929 (Gibbons)

China Clipper, 1936 (Edeson; Orry-Kelly)

China Doll, 1958 (Clothier)

China Fights, 1942 (Eisler)

China Gate, 1957 (Biroc; Steiner; Young)

China Girl, 1942 (Basevi; Day; Friedhofer; Garmes; Hecht; Newman; Zanuck)

China Is Near. *See* Cina è vicina, 1967

China Jones, 1959 (Blanc; McKimson)

China Moon, 1994 (Littleton)

China Passage, 1937 (Musuraca)

China Seas, 1935 (Adrian; Brown; Freed; Furthman; Gibbons; Mayer; Stothart; Thalberg)

China Sky, 1945 (Musuraca)

China Strikes Back, 1937 (Maddow)

China Syndrome, 1979 (Edlund; Jenkins)

Chinaman, 1920 (Fleischer)

Chinaman's Chance, 1933 (Iwerks)

China's 400 Million. *See* 400 Million, 1939

China's Little Devils, 1945 (Tiomkin)

Chinasisches Roulette, 1976 (Ballhaus)

Chinatown, 1974 (Alonzo; Goldsmith; Justin; O'Steen; Sylbert; Towne)

Chinatown My Chinatown, 1929 (Fleischer)

Chinatown Nights, 1929 (Selznick)

Chinatown Squad, 1935 (Schary)

Chinese Box, 1997 (Carrière)

Chinese Coffee, 2000 (Bernstein)

Chinese Honeymoon, 1920 (Bray)

Chinese Parrot, 1927 (Laemmle)

Chinese Room, 1966 (Figueroa)

Chinese Roulette. *See* Chinasisches Roulette, 1976

Chink, 1921 (Roach)

Chinmoko, 1971 (Takemitsu)

Chinmoku, 1971 (Miyagawa)

Chinoise, 1967 (Coutard; Guillemot)

Chintao yosai bakugeki merrei, 1963 (Tsuburaya)

Chips Are Down. *See* Jeux sont faits, 1947

Chiriakhana, 1967 (Dutta)
Chirurgien distrait, 1909 (Cohl)
Chisum, 1970 (Clothier)
Chittor Vijay, 1947 (Burman)
Chitty Chitty Bang Bang, 1968 (Adam; Broccoli; Challis)
Chiuzoi pidzak, 1927 (Enei)
Chivato, 1961 (Haller)
Chiyoda Castle on Fire. See Chiyoda-jo enjo, 1959
Chiyoda-jo enjo, 1959 (Yoda)
Chloe in the Afternoon. See Amour l'après-midi, 1972
Chocolate Soldier, 1941 (Freund; Gibbons; Kahn; Kaper; Mayer; Stothart)
Chohichiro matsudaira, 1930 (Tsuburaya)
Choice of Arms. See Choix des armes, 1981
Choices of the Heart, 1983 (Houseman)
Choirboys, 1977 (Biroc)
Choix d'assassins , 1966 (de Beauregard)
Choix des armes, 1981 (Sarde)
Cholly Polly, 1942 (Fleischer)
Choo-Choo, 1932 (Roach)
Choo Choo Swing, 1948 (Fleischer)
Choose Your Partner. See Two Girls on Broadway, 1940
Choose Your Weppins, 1935 (Fleischer)
Choosing a Husband, 1909 (Bitzer)
Chop Suey, 1930 (Terry)
Chop Suey & Co., 1919 (Roach)
Chopin, 1958 (Cloquet)
Choral von Leuthen, 1933 (Planer)
Chornyi parus, 1929 (Enei)
Chorus Line, 1985 (Hamlisch; Von Brandenstein)
Chosen, 1982 (Bernstein)
Choses de la vie, 1970 (Sarde)
Chotard et Cie, 1933 (Douy)
Chouans!, 1988 (Delerue)
Chouans, 1946 (Kosma; Renoir; Spaak)
Chouchou Yuji no meoto zenzai, 1965 (Yoda)
Chouki the Bar Owner. See Izakaya Chouji, 1983
Chow Hound, 1951 (Blanc; Jones; Stalling)
Chris Columbo, 1938 (Terry)
Chris Columbus, Jr., 1934 (Lantz)
Christ Stopped at Eboli. See **Cristo si è fermato a Eboli**, 1979
Christa Hartungen, 1917 (Freund)
Christina, 1929 (Fox)
Christine, 1958 (Auric; D'Eaubonne; Matras; Spaak)
Christine of the Big Tops, 1926 (Levien)
Christmas Burglars, 1908 (Bitzer)
Christmas Carol, 1938 (Waxman)
Christmas Carol, 1971 (Jones; Williams)
Christmas Carol. See Scrooge, 1951
Christmas Comes But Once a Year, 1936 (Fleischer)
Christmas Crackers. See Caprice de Noël, 1963
Christmas Dream. See Vánočni, 1946
Christmas Eve. See Przedświaeczny wieczór, 1965
Christmas Feast, 1974 (Halas and Batchelor)
Christmas Gift, 1980 (Vinton)
Christmas Holiday, 1944 (Berlin; Mankiewicz)
Christmas in Connecticut, 1945 (Head; Warner)
Christmas in July, 1940 (Dreier; Head)
Christmas Tree. See Arbre de Noel, 1969
Christmas Visitor, 1958 (Halas and Batchelor)
Christmas without Snow, 1980 (Houseman)
Christoph Colomb, 1904 (Pathé)
Christopher Bean, 1933 (Daniels)
Christopher Columbus, 1949 (Mathieson; Rank)
Christopher Crumpet, 1953 (Bosustow)
Christopher Crumpet's Playmate, 1955 (Bosustow)

Christopher Strong, 1933 (Berman; Glennon; Plunkett; Polglase; Selznick; Steiner; Vorkapich)
Chronicle of a Death Foretold. See Cronaca di una morte annunciata, 1987
Chronique d'un été, 1960 (Coutard)
Chronique provinciale, 1958 (Jarre; Rappeneau)
Chto delat', 1928 (Ptushko)
Chu Chin Chow, 1923 (Wilcox)
Chu Chin Chow, 1934 (Balcon; Metzner; Rank)
Chu Chu and the Philly Flash, 1981 (Jarre)
Chudá holka, 1929 (Stallich)
Chuka, 1967 (Head; Pereira)
Chump at Oxford, 1940 (Roach)
Chump Champ, 1950 (Avery)
Chupke Chupke, 1975 (Burman)
Churning. See Manthan, 1976
Chushingura, 1954 (Yoda)
Chutes de pierres, danger du mort, 1958-59 (Breer)
Chuzhoy pidzhak, 1927 (Moskvin)
Chyortovo koleso, 1926 (Enei; Moskvin)
Chytte ho!, 1924 (Heller)
Ci risiamo, vero Provvidenza?, 1973 (Morricone)
Ciao maschio, 1978 (Sarde)
Ciboulette, 1933 (Courant; Meerson; Prévert; Trauner)
Cid, 1961 (Canutt; Fields; Krasker; Rozsa)
Ciel est à vous, 1943 (Douy; Spaak)
Ciel est par-dessus le toit, 1956 (Cloquet)
Cielito lindo, 1936 (Figueroa)
Cielo Cade, 2000 (Cecchi D'amico)
Cielo è rosso, 1950 (Zavattini)
Cielo sulla palude, 1948 (Aldo; Cecchi D'amico)
Cień, 1956 (ścibor-Rylski)
Cigale et la fourmi, 1953 (Kosma)
Cigale et le fourmi, 1927 (Starewicz)
Cigarettes Bastos, 1938 (Alexeieff and Parker)
Ciklámen, 1916 (Korda)
Cimarron, 1931 (Clothier; Cronjager; Dunn; Plunkett; Steiner; Westmore Family)
Cimarron, 1960 (Gillespie; Plunkett; Surtees; Waxman)
Cin Cin. See A Fine Romance, 1992
Cina è vicina, 1967 (Delli Colli; Morricone)
Cincinnati Kid, 1965 (Lardner; Lathrop; Schifrin; Southern)
Cinco Dias, Cinco Noites, 1996 (Branco)
Cinderella, 1911 (Selig)
Cinderella, 1922 (Disney)
Cinderella, 1925 (Lantz)
Cinderella, 1933 (Terry)
Cinderella, 1937 (Kaufman)
Cinderella, 1949 (Iwerks)
Cinderella, 1950 (Disney)
Cinderella, 1963 (Reiniger)
Cinderfella, 1960 (Bumstead; Head)
Cinderella Jones, 1946 (Cahn; Polito)
Cinderella Liberty, 1973 (Williams; Zsigmond)
Cinderella Meets Fella, 1938 (Avery)
Cinderella of the Hills, 1921 (Fox)
Cine è vicina, 1967 (Cristaldi)
Cinegiornale della pace, 1963 (Zavattini)
Cinéma cinéma, 1969 (Braunberger)
Cinema d'altri tempi, 1950 (Gherardi)
Cinema d'altri tempi, 1953 (Age and Scarpelli)
Cinema in the Country. See Kino v derevne, 1930
Cinema Murder, 1919 (Marion; Rosson)
Cinema Paradiso. See Nuovo cinema paradiso, 1988
Cinerama Holiday, 1955 (de Rochemont)
Cinq cents balles, 1961 (Braunberger)

Cinq gars pour Singapour, 1967 (Amidei)
Cinq Gentlemen maudits, 1931 (Ibert; Meerson)
Cinq jours en juin, 1989 (Legrand)
Cinque poveri in automobile, 1952 (Zavattini)
Cintura, 1989 (Morricone)
Cintura di castità, 1949 (Flaiano and Pinelli)
Cintura di castità, 1968 (Donati)
Ciociara, 1960 (Levine; Ponti; Zavattini)
Ciphers. *See* Ceíslice, 1966
Circe the Enchantress, 1924 (Gibbons)
Circle, 1925 (Basevi; Gibbons)
Circle, 1976 (Houseman)
Circle. *See* Vicious Circle, 1957
Circle of Danger, 1951 (Harrison; Morris)
Circle of Death, 1935 (Canutt)
Circle of Deceit. *See* Fälschung, 1981
Circle of Love. *See* **Ronde**, 1964
Circo, 1943 (Figueroa)
Circus, 1920 (Fleischer)
Circus, 1932 (Iwerks)
Circus Ace, 1927 (Fox)
Circus Clown, 1934 (Orry-Kelly)
Circus Comes to Town. *See* Under the Big Top, 1938
Circus Cowboy, 1924 (Fox)
Circus Days, 1935 (Terry)
Circus Drawings, 1964 (Williams)
Circus Fever, 1925 (Roach)
Circus Friends, 1956 (Heller)
Circus Kid, 1928 (Plunkett)
Circus of Horrors, 1960 (Mathieson; Slocombe)
Circus of Love. *See* Carnival Story, 1954
Circus of Sin. *See* Salto mortale, 1931
Circus Queen Murder, 1933 (August)
Circus Rookies, 1928 (Day; Gibbons)
Circus Shadow. *See* Shadow, 1937
Circus Star, 1960 (Halas and Batchelor)
Circus Today, 1940 (Avery; Blanc; Stalling)
Circus World, 1964 (Fisher; Hecht; Renoir; Spencer; Tiomkin)
Cirkus Hurvínek, 1955 (Trnka)
Císařuv pekař, pekařuv císař, 1951 (Stallich; Trnka)
Císařuv slavík, 1948 (Brdečka; Trnka)
Cita de amor, 1956 (Figueroa)
Citadel, 1938 (Junge; Mayer; Meerson; Stradling)
Citadelle du silence, 1937 (Andrejew; Honegger; Milhaud)
Cité d'argent, 1955 (Delerue)
Cité de la joie. *See* City of Joy, 1992
Cité des enfants perdus, 1995 (Badalamenti)
Cités du ciel, 1959 (Fradetal)
Citizen Cohn, 1992 (Newman)
Citizen Kane, 1941 (Dunn; Herrmann; Mankiewicz; Polglase; Toland)
Citizen of Tomorrow, 1942 (Alwyn)
Citizen Piszczyk. *See* Obywatel Piszczyk, 1988
Citizens Band. *See* Handle with Care, 1977
Citta delle donne, 1980 (Rotunno)
Città di notte, 1958 (Rota)
Città dolente, 1948 (Delli Colli)
Città si difende, 1951 (Flaiano and Pinelli)
Città violenta, 1970 (Morricone)
City, 1914 (Ince)
City, 1926 (Fox)
City for Conquest, 1940 (Friedhofer; Haskin; Howe; Polito; Steiner; Wallis)
City Girl, 1930 (Carré; Fox)
City Gone Wild, 1927 (Furthman; Glennon; Mankiewicz)
City Government. *See* A City Speaks, 1947
City Hall, 1996 (Goldsmith)

City in Fear, 1980 (Rosenman)
City Is Dark. *See* Crime Wave, 1954
City Lights, 1931 (Newman; Parrish)
City of Angels, 1998 (Seale)
City of Bad Men, 1953 (Clarke; Jeakins; Lemaire)
City of Chance, 1939 (Day)
City of Darkness, 1915 (August; Ince)
City of Darkness, 1939 (Day)
City of Dim Faces, 1918 (Marion)
City of Fear, 1958 (Ballard; Goldsmith)
City of Hope, 1991 (Daring)
City of Joy, 1992 (Biziou; Hambling; Morricone)
City of Lost Children. *See* Cité des enfants perdus, 1995
City of Masks, 1920 (Brown)
City of Pirates. *See* Ville des pirates, 1983
City of Play, 1929 (Balcon)
City of Women. *See* Citta delle donne, 1980
City Park, 1934 (Brown)
City Slicker, 1918 (Roach)
City Slicker, 1952 (Terry)
City Slickers II: The Legend of Curly's Gold, 1994 (Biddle)
City Speaks, 1947 (Alwyn)
City Streets, 1931 (Garmes; Zukor)
City That Never Sleeps, 1924 (Brown)
City Vamp, 1915 (Marion)
City without Men, 1943 (Raksin)
Citydreams. *See* Dear Mr. Wonderful, 1982
Civil Action, 1998 (Elfman; Hall)
Civilian, 1912 (Ince)
Civilization, 1916 (Ince; Sullivan)
Civilization's Child, 1916 (August; Sullivan)
Claim Jumper, 1913 (Ince)
Clair de lune, 1932 (Fradetal)
Clair de lune espagnol, 1909 (Cohl)
Clair de Terre, 1970 (Rousselot)
Claire's Knee. *See* Genou de Claire, 1970
Clairvoyant, 1935 (Balcon; Junge; Rank)
Clan des Siciliens, 1969 (Decaë; Morricone; Saulnier)
Clancy's Kosher Wedding, 1927 (Plunkett)
Clap Your Hands, 1948 (Fleischer)
Clara and Her Mysterious Toys, 1913-14 (Cohl)
Clara Cleans Her Teeth, 1926 (Disney)
Clara de Montargis, 1950 (Renoir)
Clara et les méchants, 1957 (Wakhévitch)
Clara's Heart, 1988 (Francis; Grusin)
Clarence, 1937 (Head)
Clarissa, 1998 (Carrière)
Clash, 1984 (Vierny)
Clash by Night, 1952 (D'Agostino; Krasna; Musuraca; Wald)
Clash of the Titans, 1981 (Harryhausen)
Clash of the Wolves, 1925 (Walker)
Class, 1983 (Bernstein)
Class Action, 1991 (Hall)
Class Enemy. *See* Klassenfeind, 1984
Class of 1984, 1982 (Schifrin)
Class of '61, 1992 (Kaminski)
Class Reunion, 1982 (Lathrop)
Classe de lettres, 1953 (Cloquet)
Classe de mathématiques, 1953 (Cloquet)
Classe d'histoire, 1953 (Cloquet)
Classe operaia va in paradiso, 1971 (Morricone)
Classe tous risques, 1960 (Cloquet; Delerue)
Classified, 1925 (Mathis; Rosson)
Classmates, 1908 (Bitzer)
Classmates, 1914 (Gaudio)
Classmates, 1924 (Seitz)

Coeur de Paris, 1931 (Fradetal)
Coeur des pierres, 1967 (Colpi)
Coeur fantôme, 1996 (Branco)
Coeur gros comme ça, 1961 (Braunberger)
Coffee and Cigarettes II, 1989 (Müller)
Coffre-fort, 1908 (Cohl)
Cohen and Tate, 1989 (Conti)
Cohens and Kellys in Africa, 1930 (Mohr)
Cohens and Kellys in Paris, 1928 (Laemmle)
Cohens and Kellys in Scotland, 1930 (Laemmle)
Col. Heezaliar's Ancestors, 1924 (Lantz)
Col. Heezaliar's Forbidden Fruit, 1924 (Lantz)
Col. Heezaliar's Knighthood, 1924 (Lantz)
Col. Heezaliar's Vacation, 1924 (Lantz)
Cold Around the Heart, 1997 (Daring)
Cold Deck, 1917 (August)
Cold Feet, 1930 (Lantz)
Cold Hearts, 1999 (Savini)
Cold Land. See Terra Fria, 1990
Cold Mountain, 2001 (Seale)
Cold Romance, 1949 (Terry)
Cold Turkey, 1929 (Lantz)
Cold Wind in August, 1961 (Crosby)
Colditz Story, 1954 (Vetchinsky)
Cole Younger, Gunfighter, 1958 (Mainwaring)
Colère des dieux, 1946 (Annenkov; Burel)
Collants noirs, 1960 (Alekan; Wakhévitch)
Collars and Cuffs, 1923 (Roach)
Collectionneuse, 1967 (Almendros; de Beauregard)
Collections privées, 1979 (Braunberger)
Collector, 1965 (Jarre; Krasker; Surtees)
Colleen, 1927 (Fox)
Colleen, 1936 (Haskin; Orry-Kelly; Polito)
College, 1927 (Schenck)
College, 1931 (Lantz)
College Coach, 1933 (Freed; Mercer; Orry-Kelly)
College Days, 1929 (Zukor)
College Hero, 1927 (Walker)
College Holiday, 1936 (Head; Young)
College Love, 1929 (Laemmle)
College Scandal, 1935 (Brackett)
College Spirit, 1932 (Terry)
College Swing, 1938 (Carmichael; Dreier; Head)
College Widow, 1927 (Blanke)
Collegiate, 1936 (Head)
Collision Course. See Bamboo Saucer, 1968
Colloids, 1969 (Godfrey)
Colombo Plan, 1967 (Halas and Batchelor)
Colonel Blimp. See Life and Death of Colonel Blimp, 1943
Colonel Chabert, 1994 (Mnouchkine)
Colonel Effingham's Raid, 1945 (Cronjager; Trotti)
Colonel Heezaliar, 1923 (Bray)
Colonel Heezaliar and the Bandits, 1916 (Bray)
Colonel Heezaliar and the Torpedo, 1915 (Bray)
Colonel Heezaliar and the Zeppelin, 1915 (Bray)
Colonel Heezaliar At the Bat, 1915 (Bray)
Colonel Heezaliar At the Front, 1915 (Bray)
Colonel Heezaliar at the Vaudeville Show, 1916 (Bray)
Colonel Heezaliar Captures Villa, 1916 (Bray)
Colonel Heezaliar Foils the Enemy, 1915 (Bray)
Colonel Heezaliar Gets Married, 1916 (Bray)
Colonel Heezaliar in Africa, 1914 (Bray)
Colonel Heezaliar in Mexico, 1914 (Bray)
Colonel Heezaliar in the Haunted Castle, 1915 (Bray)
Colonel Heezaliar in the Trenches, 1915 (Bray)
Colonel Heezaliar in the Wilderness, 1914 (Bray)

Colonel Heezaliar Invents a New Kind of Shell, 1915 (Bray)
Colonel Heezaliar on Strike, 1916 (Bray)
Colonel Heezaliar on the Jump, 1917 (Bray)
Colonel Heezaliar Plays Hamlet, 1916 (Bray)
Colonel Heezaliar Runs the Blockade, 1915 (Bray)
Colonel Heezaliar Signs the Pledge, 1915 (Bray)
Colonel Heezaliar, Detective, 1917 (Bray)
Colonel Heezaliar, Dog Fancier, 1915 (Bray)
Colonel Heezaliar, Explorer, 1914 (Bray)
Colonel Heezaliar, Farmer, 1914 (Bray)
Colonel Heezaliar, Naturalist, 1914 (Bray)
Colonel Heezaliar, Nature Faker, 1924 (Bray)
Colonel Heezaliar, Shipwrecked, 1914 (Bray)
Colonel Heezaliar, Skypilot, 1924 (Bray)
Colonel Heezaliar, Spy Dodger, 1917 (Bray)
Colonel Heezaliar, Temperance Advocate, 1917 (Bray)
Colonel Heezaliar, War Aviator, 1915 (Bray)
Colonel Heezaliar, War Dog, 1915 (Bray)
Colonel Heezaliar—Ghost Breaker, 1915 (Bray)
Colonel Heezaliar's African Hunt, 1914 (Bray)
Colonel Heezaliar's Ancestors, 1924 (Bray)
Colonel Heezaliar's Bachelor Quarters, 1916 (Bray)
Colonel Heezaliar's Horseplay, 1924 (Bray)
Colonel Heezaliar's Knighthood, 1924 (Bray)
Colonel Heezaliar's Mysterious Case, 1923 (Bray)
Colonel Kwiatkowski. See Plukownik Kwiatkowski, 1995
Colonel's Ward, 1912 (Ince)
Colonialskandal, 1927 (Warm)
Color Box, 1935 (Lye)
Color Cry, 1953 (Lye)
Color of Evening, 1994 (Rosenman)
Color of Money, 1986 (Ballhaus; Schoonmaker)
Color Purple, 1985 (Jones; Marshall)
Colorado, 1921 (Laemmle; Miller)
Colorado Jim. See Colorado Pluck, 1921
Colorado Pluck, 1921 (Furthman)
Colorado Territory, 1949 (Veiller)
Colorful Bombay, 1937 (Hoch)
Colorful Islands—Madagascar and Seychelles, 1936 (Hoch)
Colors, 1988 (Wexler)
Colossus of New York, 1958 (Edouart; Lourié)
Colossus: The Forbin Project, 1970 (Head)
Colour Box. See A Color Box, 1935
Colour Cocktail, 1934-35 (McClaren)
Colour Flight , 1938 (Lye)
Colour in Clay, 1942 (Cardiff)
Colpe rovente, 1969 (Flaiano and Pinelli)
Colpo di sole, 1968 (Amidei)
Colt Comrades, 1943 (Harlan; Wilson)
Columbo: Prescription Murder. See Prescription: Murder, 1968
Coma, 1977 (Goldsmith)
Comancheros!, 1961 (Smith)
Comancheros, 1961 (Bernstein; Clothier)
Comandamenti per un gangster, 1968 (Morricone)
Comata, The Sioux, 1909 (Bitzer)
Combat dans l'île, 1961 (Evein; Lhomme)
Combats sans haine, 1948 (Spaak)
Come Across, 1929 (Laemmle)
Come and Get It, 1929 (Miller; Plunkett)
Come and Get It, 1936 (Day; Furthman; Goldwyn; Maté;
    Newman; Toland)
Come Back, 1953 (Pereira)
Come Back Charleston Blue, 1972 (Jones)
Come Back, Little Sheba, 1952 (Bumstead; Head; Howe; Waxman)
Come Back to Me. See Doll Face, 1946
Come Blow Your Horn, 1963 (Cahn; Daniels; Head; Pereira; van Heusen)

Condemned Man Escapes. *See* **Condamné à mort s'est échappé**, 1956
Condemned of Altona. *See* I sequestrati di Altona, 1962
Condemned to Life. *See* Life for Ruth, 1962
Condemned Women, 1938 (Musuraca; Polglase)
Condition of Man, 1971 (Halas and Batchelor)
Condor, 1970 (Jarre)
Condorman, 1981 (Mancini)
Conduisez-moi madame, 1932 (Meerson)
Coney Island, 1943 (Day; Newman; Pan; Rose; Zanuck)
Coney Island, 1950 (Rosenblum)
Coney Island Police Patrol Chicken Thief, 1904 (Bitzer)
Confederate Honey, 1940 (Blanc; Stalling)
Confession, 1937 (Blanke; Epstein; Grot; Orry-Kelly; Wallis)
Confession. *See* Aveu, 1970
Confession de minuit, 1963 (Saulnier)
Confession of a Military Priest. *See* Beichte des Feldkuraten, 1927
Confessional. *See* Confessionnal, 1995
Confessionnal, 1995 (Puttnam)
Confessions of a Co-ed, 1931 (Garmes)
Confessions of a Nazi Spy, 1939 (Polito; Steiner; Warner)
Confessions of a Nutzy Spy, 1943 (Blanc)
Confessions of a Queen, 1925 (Basevi; Gibbons; Mayer)
Confessions of an Opium Eater, 1962 (Biroc; Lourié)
Confessions of Felix Krull. *See* Bekenntnisse des Hochstaplers Felix Krull, 1957
Confessions of Gynecologist. *See* Aru fujinkai no kokuhaku, 1950
Confidence, 1909 (Bitzer)
Confidence, 1922 (Laemmle)
Confidence, 1933 (Lantz)
Confidence Girl, 1952 (Clothier)
Confidences d'un piano, 1957 (Decaë)
Confidential Agent, 1945 (Howe; Waxman)
Confidentially Yours. *See* Vivement dimanche!, 1982
Confirm or Deny, 1941 (Banton; Shamroy; Swerling)
Conflagration. *See* Enjo, 1958
Conflict, 1921 (Laemmle)
Conflict, 1945 (Orry-Kelly)
Conflicts of Life. *See* Livets konflikter, 1913
Conflit, 1938 (Fradetal)
Conflits, 1939 (Wakhévitch)
Conformist. *See* **Conformista**, 1970
Conformista, 1970 (Delerue; Storaro)
Confusions of a Nutzy Spy, 1943 (Stalling)
Congiura dei dieci. *See* Spadaccino di Siena, 1961
Congo, 1995 (Goldsmith; Marshall; Winston)
Congo Crossing, 1956 (Boyle; Mancini; Metty)
Congress Dances. *See* Kongress tanzt, 1931
Connecticut Yankee at King Arthur's Court, 1921 (Fox)
Connecticut Yankee in King Arthur's Court, 1949 (Dreier; Rennahan; Young; van Heusen)
Connection, 1962 (Sylbert)
Conquer by the Clock, 1942 (Vorkapich)
Conquering Christ. *See* Restitution, 1918
Conquering Power, 1921 (Mathis; Seitz)
Conquering the Women, 1922 (Barnes)
Conqueror, 1916 (Sullivan)
Conqueror, 1932 (Selznick)
Conqueror, 1956 (D'Agostino; La Shelle; Young)
Conquerors, 1932 (Clothier; Cronjager; Plunkett; Steiner; Vorkapich)
Conquest, 1937 (Adrian; Freund; Gibbons; Hoffenstein; Stothart)
Conquest of Space, 1955 (Haskin; Head; Pal; Pereira)
Conquest of the Air, 1940 (Garmes; Korda; Menzies)
Conquête de l'air, 1901 (Pathé)
Conquête des Gaules, 1922 (Burel)
Conquête du ciel. *See* Vom Blitz zum Fernsehbild, 1937
Conrack, 1974 (Alonzo; Williams)

Conrad in Search of His Youth, 1920 (Buckland)
Conrad the Sailor, 1942 (Blanc; Jones; Stalling)
Conscience, 1910 (Bitzer)
Conscientious Adolf. *See* Samvetsömma Adolf, 1936
Conseil de famille, 1986 (Delerue)
Consenting Adults, 1992 (O'Steen)
Consolation Marriage, 1931 (Steiner)
Conspiracy, 1930 (Musuraca)
Conspiracy of Hearts, 1960 (Rank; Vetchinsky)
Conspiracy Theory, 1997 (Burwell)
Conspirator, 1949 (Junge; Young)
Conspirators, 1944 (Edeson; Grot; Steiner)
Constable, 1940 (Fleischer)
Constance, 1957 (Alexeieff and Parker)
Contact, 1973 (Halas and Batchelor)
Contact, 1997 (Ralston)
Constant Husband, 1954 (Alwyn; Korda)
Constant Nymph, 1928 (Balcon; Dean; Reville)
Constant Nymph, 1934 (Balcon; Dean)
Constant Nymph, 1943 (Blanke; Friedhofer; Gaudio; Korngold)
Constant Woman, 1933 (Edeson)
Construcciones rurales, 1960 (Almendros)
Conte di Brechard, 1938 (Amidei)
Conte Max, 1991 (Age and Scarpelli)
Contemporary Story. *See* Historia współczesna, 1961
Contempt. *See* **Mépris**, 1963
Contes à dormir debout, 1954 (Cloquet)
Contessa azzurra, 1960 (Cecchi D'amico)
Contest, 1923 (Fleischer)
Continental Express. *See* Silent Battle, 1939
Continuar a Viver, 1976 (de Almeida)
Continuous Observation, 1955 (Lassally)
Contraband, 1940 (Addinsell; Junge; Mathieson; Young)
Contract on Cherry Street, 1977 (Goldsmith)
Contrebasse, 1962 (Delerue)
Control. *See* Giorno prima, 1987
Controsesso, 1964 (Guerra; Zavattini)
Controverse de Valladolid, 1992 (Carrière)
Convent. *See* O Convento, 1995
Convention City, 1933 (Blanke; Orry-Kelly)
Conversa Acabada, 1982 (Branco; de Almeida)
Conversation, 1974 (Murch; Tavoularis)
Conversation Piece. *See* Gruppo di famiglia in un interno, 1974
Conversion of Ferdys Pistora. *See* Obrácení Ferdyše Pištory, 1931
Conversion of Frosty Blake, 1915 (August)
Convert/The Roughneck , 1915 (August)
Converts, 1910 (Bitzer)
Convict 99, 1938 (Rank; Vetchinsky)
Convict 993, 1918 (Miller)
Convict Stage, 1965 (Mainwaring)
Convicted, 1950 (Duning; Guffey)
Conviction, 1994 (Lanci, Giuseppe ("beppe"))
Convicts Four, 1962 (Biroc; Rosenman)
Convict's Sacrifice, 1909 (Bitzer)
Convoy, 1927 (Haller)
Convoy, 1940 (Balcon)
Coo-Coo Nut Grove, 1936 (Stalling)
Coocoo Murder Case, 1931 (Iwerks)
Coogan's Bluff, 1968 (Schifrin)
Cook, the Thief, His Wife and Her Lover, 1989 (Vierny)
Cookie, 1989 (Newman)
Cool As Ice, 1991 (Kaminski)
Cool Cat, 1967 (Blanc)
Cool Hand Luke, 1967 (Hall; O'Steen; Schifrin)
Cool Ones, 1967 (Cahn; Crosby)
Cool Runnings, 1993 (Zimmer)

Country Mouse and the City Mouse, 1921 (Terry)
Country Music Holiday, 1958 (Bacharach; Rosenblum)
Country School, 1931 (Lantz)
Country Schoolmaster, 1906 (Bitzer)
Country Store, 1937 (Lantz)
Country Town, 1944 (Alwyn)
Countrywomen, 1942 (Alwyn)
County Chairman, 1935 (Mohr)
County Fair, 1950 (Mirisch)
County Hospital, 1932 (Roach)
Coup de bambou, 1962 (Matras)
Coup de berger, 1956 (Braunberger)
Coup de Jarnac, 1909 (Cohl)
Coup de roulis, 1931 (D'Eaubonne)
Coup de téléphone, 1931 (Lourié; Meerson; Spaak)
Coup de torchon, 1981 (Aurenche and Bost; Sarde; Trauner)
Coup du parapluie, 1980 (Decaë)
Coup pur pour rien, 1970 (Braunberger)
Coupable, 1936 (Barsacq; Ibert)
Coupe d'Or. See Golden Mary, 2000
Couple, 1960 (Schüfftan)
Couple idéal, 1945 (Renoir)
Couple Temoin, 1975 (Rousselot)
Couples and Robbers, 1981 (Menges)
Couple's Drum. See Meoto daiko, 1941
Courage of Black Beauty, 1957 (Leven)
Courage of Lassie, 1946 (Irene; Kaper)
Courageous Dr. Christian, 1940 (Alton; Lardner)
Courageous Mr. Penn. See Penn of Pennsylvania, 1941
Coureurs de brousse, 1956 (Decaë)
Courier of Lyons. See Affaire du courrier de Lyon, 1937
Couronnes, 1909 (Cohl)
Courrier Sud, 1936 (Barsacq; Ibert)
Cours d'une vie, 1966 (Delerue)
Cours privé, 1986 (Sarde)
Course à l'échalotte, 1975 (Decaë)
Course aux potirons, 1907 (Carré)
Course de taureaux, 1951 (Braunberger; Decaë)
Course des belles mères, 1907 (Gaumont)
Course du lièvre à travers les champs, 1972 (Lai)
Courses d'obstacles, 1957 (Delerue)
Court Jester, 1956 (Cahn; Head; Pereira)
Court Martial, 1928 (Walker)
Court-Martial of Billy Mitchell, 1955 (Tiomkin)
Courtesans of Bombay, 1982 (Jhabvala; Merchant)
Courtin' Wildcats, 1929 (Laemmle)
Courtneys of Curzon Street, 1947 (Wilcox)
Courtship of Eddie's Father, 1963 (Krasner; Pasternak; Rose)
Courtship of Miles Sandwich, 1923 (Roach)
Courtship of O San, 1914 (Ince)
Cousin Bobby, 1992 (Dickerson)
Cousin cousine, 1975 (Guillemot)
Cousin de Callao, 1962 (Delerue)
Cousin Wilbur, 1939 (Roach)
Cousins, 1959 (Decaë; Evein; Gégauff; Rabier; Saulnier)
Cousins, 1989 (Badalamenti)
Couteau dans la plaie, 1962 (Alekan; Theodorakis; Trauner)
Couturière de Linevile, 1931 (Maté)
Covenant with Death, 1967 (Burks; Rosenman)
Cover Girl, 1944 (Banton; Cohn; Cole; Guffey; Maté)
Cover Me, Babe, 1970 (Smith)
Cover-Up, 1949 (Laszlo)
Covered Pushcart, 1949 (Terry)
Covered Wagon, 1923 (Brown; Lasky; Zukor)
Cow and I. See Vache et le prisonnier, 1959
Cow on the Moon. See Krava na mjescu, 1959

Cow-boys français, 1953 (Decaë)
Coward, 1915 (August; Ince; Sullivan)
Coward and the Saint. See Kapurush-o-Mahapurush, 1965
Cowboy, 1958 (Bass; Duning; Trumbo)
Cowboy, 1985 (Sarde)
Cowboy and the Blonde, 1941 (Clarke; Day)
Cowboy and the Countess, 1926 (Fox)
Cowboy and the Lady, 1938 (Basevi; Day; Goldwyn; Levien; Newman; Toland)
Cowboy from Brooklyn, 1938 (Deutsch; Edeson; Mercer; Wallis)
Cowboy Jimmie, 1957 (Vukotić)
Cowboy Kid, 1928 (Fox; Miller)
Cowboy Quarterback, 1939 (McCord)
Cowboy Shiek, 1924 (Roach)
Cowboys, 1971 (Surtees; Williams)
Cowboys from Texas, 1939 (Canutt)
Cow's Husband, 1931 (Fleischer)
Cow's Kimono, 1926 (Roach)
Coy Decoy, 1941 (Blanc; Clampett; Stalling)
Crabe-Tambour, 1977 (Coutard; de Beauregard; Sarde)
Crack in the Mirror, 1960 (D'Eaubonne; Jarre; Zanuck)
Crack in the World, 1965 (Lourié)
Crack o' Dawn, 1925 (Garmes)
Crack-Up, 1946 (Paxton)
Crack Your Heels, 1919 (Roach)
Cracked Ice Man, 1933 (Roach)
Cracked Nuts, 1931 (Musuraca; Steiner)
Cracked Quack, 1952 (Blanc; Stalling)
Cracked Wedding Bells, 1920 (Roach)
Crackerjack, 1938 (Rank)
Crackers, 1984 (Kovacs)
Crackpot King, 1946 (Terry)
Crackpot Quail, 1941 (Avery; Blanc; Stalling)
Cracks, 1968 (Delerue)
Cradle, 1922 (Rosson)
Cradle of Courage, 1920 (August)
Cradle Robbers, 1924 (Roach)
Cradle Snatchers, 1927 (Fox)
Cradle Song, 1933 (Head; Lang)
Craig's Wife, 1936 (Ballard)
Crainquebille, 1934 (Starewicz)
Cranes Are Flying. See Letyat zhuravli, 1957
Crash, 1928 (McCord)
Crash, 1932 (Haller; Orry-Kelly)
Crash Dive, 1943 (Day; Shamroy; Swerling)
Crash Donovan, 1936 (Krasner)
Crash of Silence. See Mandy, 1952
Crashing Hollywood, 1938 (Musuraca)
Crashout, 1955 (Metty)
Crawlspace, 1972 (Goldsmith)
Crawlspace, 1986 (Donaggio)
Crayono, 1907 (Bitzer)
Craze, 1973 (Francis)
Crazed Fruit. See Kurutta kajitsu, 1956
Crazy Cruise, 1941 (Avery)
Crazy Cruise, 1942 (Blanc; Clampett; Stalling)
Crazy Desire. See Voglia matta, 1962
Crazy Feet, 1929 (Roach)
Crazy House, 1928 (Roach)
Crazy House, 1940 (Lantz)
Crazy House, 1943 (Cahn)
Crazy Like a Fox, 1926 (Roach)
Crazy Mixed-Up Pup, 1954 (Avery)
Crazy That Way, 1930 (Fox)
Crazy to Marry, 1921 (Brown)
Crazy Town, 1932 (Fleischer)

Crazy World of Laurel and Hardy, 1967 (Roach)
Crazy World, 1968 (Kuri)
Crazylegs, 1953 (Miller)
Creation, 1982 (Vinton)
Creation of the Humanoids, 1962 (Mohr; Pierce)
Creation of Woman, 1960 (Merchant)
Creature Comforts, 1989 (Park)
Creature from the Black Lagoon, 1954 (Mancini; Westmore Family)
Creature Walks among Us, 1956 (Mancini; Westmore Family)
Creature with the Atom Brain, 1955 (Siodmak)
Creatures the World Forgot, 1971 (Carreras)
Creeping Flesh, 1972 (Francis)
Creeping Unknown. *See* Quatermass Experiment, 1955
Creeping Unknown. *See* Shock, 1972
Creepshow, 1982 (Savini)
Creepshow II, 1987 (Savini)
Creepy Time Pal, 1960 (Hanna and Barbera)
Crème Simon, 1937 (Alexeieff and Parker)
Creo en Dios, 1941 (Figueroa)
Creosoot, 1931 (van Dongen)
Creosote. *See* Creosoot, 1931
Crescendo, 1970 (Carreras)
Crescete e moltiplicatevi, 1973 (Morricone)
Crest of the Wave. *See* Seagulls over Sorrento, 1954
Crésus, 1960 (Kosma)
Crève-Coeur, 1955 (Decaë; Rabier)
Cri du cormoran le soir, au-dessus des jonques, 1970 (D'Eaubonne)
Cri du hibou, 1987 (Rabier)
Cricket in Times Square, 1971 (Jones)
Cricket on the Hearth, 1909 (Bitzer)
Cricket on the Hearth, 1914 (Gaudio)
Cries and Whispers. *See* **Viskningar och rop**, 1972
Crime and Punishment. *See* Raskolnikoff, 1923
Crime and Punishment, 1935 (Ballard; Cohn; Goosson)
Crime and Punishment in Suburbia, 2000 (Vachon)
Crime and Punishment, U.S.A., 1959 (Crosby)
Crime by Night, 1944 (Mainwaring)
Crime de Monsieur Lange, 1936 (Grimault; ; Kosma Prévert)
Crime Doctor, 1934 (Plunkett; Steiner)
Crime Doctor's Manhunt, 1946 (Brackett)
Crime Does Not Pay. *See* Crime ne paie pas, 1962
Crime du bouif, 1951 (Braunberger)
Crime et châtiment, 1935 (Honegger; Lourié)
Crime et châtiment, 1956 (Renoir; Spaak)
Crime in the Streets, 1956 (Waxman)
Crime ne paie pas, 1962 (Aurenche and Bost; Delerue; Jeanson; Matras; Wakhévitch)
Crime Nobody Saw, 1937 (Head)
Crime of Dr. Hallett, 1938 (Krasner)
Crime of Monsieur Lange. *See* **Crime de Monsieur Lange**, 1936
Crime of Passion, 1956 (La Shelle)
Crime of Peter Frame. *See* Second Thoughts, 1938
Crime of the Century, 1933 (Banton; Head)
Crime School, 1938 (Friedhofer; Steiner)
Crime Wave, 1954 (Glennon)
Crime without Passion, 1934 (Garmes; Hecht; MacArthur; Vorkapich; Zukor)
Crimen, 1960 (Di Venanzo; Gherardi; de Laurentiis)
Crimes and Misdemeanors, 1989 (Loquasto; Nykvist)
Crime's End. *See* My Son Is Guilty, 1939
Crimes of Stephen Hawke, 1936 (Neame)
Crimes of the Heart, 1986 (Adam; Delerue; Shepard; de Laurentiis)
Criminal, 1916 (Sullivan)
Criminal, 1960 (Krasker)
Criminal at Large. *See* Frightened Lady, 1932
Criminal Code, 1931 (Cohn; Howe; Miller)

Criminal Hypnotist, 1908 (Bitzer)
Criminal Law, 1988 (Goldsmith)
Criminals. *See* Once upon a Crime, 1992
Crimson Blade. *See* Scarlet Blade, 1963
Crimson Curtain. *See* Rideau cramoisi, 1953
Crimson Dove, 1917 (Marion)
Crimson Dynasty. *See* Koenigsmark, 1936
Crimson Kimono, 1959 (Boyle)
Crimson Notebook. *See* Piros bugyelláris, 1917
Crimson Pirate, 1952 (Adam; Alwyn; Heller; Mathieson)
Crimson Runner, 1925 (Polito; Stromberg)
Crimson Tide, 1995 (Zimmer)
Crise est finie, 1934 (Schüfftan; Siodmak)
Crisis, 1912 (Ince)
Crisis, 1950 (Ames; Freed; Mayer; Rozsa)
Criss Cross, 1949 (Leven; Planer; Rozsa)
CrissCross, 1992 (Menges)
Cristo si è fermato a Eboli, 1979 (Cristaldi; Guerra)
Cristoforo Colombo, 1980 (Flaiano and Pinelli)
Critic, 1906 (Bitzer)
Critical Care, 1997 (Baker; Watkin)
Critical Decision. *See* Executive Decision, 1996
Critic's Choice, 1963 (Duning; Head; Lang)
Crockett Doodle-Do, 1960 (Blanc; McKimson)
"Crocodile" Dundee, 1986 (Boyd)
"Crocodile" Dundee II, 1988 (Boyd)
Croisières sidérales, 1942 (Aurenche and Bost)
Croissance de Paris, 1954 (Braunberger)
Croix de bois, 1931 (Douy)
Croix des vivants, 1960 (Barsacq)
Cromwell, 1970 (Unsworth)
Cronaca criminale del Far West. *See* Banda J & S, 1972
Cronaca di una morte annunciata, 1987 (Guerra; Mnouchkine)
Cronache di poveri amanti, 1954 (Amidei; Di Venanzo)
Cronica familiare, 1962 (Rotunno)
Cronoca nera, 1946 (Amidei)
Crook. *See* Voyou, 1970
Crook Who Cried Wolf, 1963 (Hanna and Barbera)
Crooked Billet, 1930 (Balcon)
Crooked Hearts, 1972 (Biroc)
Crooked Road, 1911 (Bitzer)
Crooked Way, 1949 (Alton; Polglase)
Crooks in Clover. *See* Penthouse, 1933
Crook's Tour, 1933 (Roach)
Crooner, 1932 (Orry-Kelly)
Crop Chasers, 1939 (Iwerks)
Croquemitaine et Rosalie, 1916 (Cohl)
Cross by the Brook. *See* Kríž u potoka, 1921
Cross Country Detours, 1940 (Avery)
Cross Country Doctors, 1940 (Blanc; Stalling)
Cross Creek, 1983 (Alonzo)
Cross Currents, 1935 (Havelock-Allan)
Cross Fire, 1933 (Plunkett)
Cross My Heart, 1937 (Havelock-Allan)
Cross My Heart, 1946 (Lang; Head; Schnee; van Heusen)
Cross of Iron, 1978 (Epstein)
Cross of Lorraine, 1943 (Freund; Gibbons; Kaper; Lardner)
Cross of the Living. *See* Croix des vivants, 1960
Crossed Swords. *See* Maestro di Don Giovanni, 1954
Crossed Swords. *See* Prince and the Pauper, 1978
Crossed Wires, 1923 (Laemmle)
Crossfire, 1933 (Musuraca)
Crossfire, 1947 (D'Agostino; Paxton; Schary)
Crossing Guard, 1995 (Nitzsche; Zsigmond)
Crossing the Line. *See* Big Man, 1990
Crossroads, 1942 (Kaper; Ruttenberg)

Crossroads of New York, 1922 (Hornbeck)
Crosswinds, 1951 (Head)
Crouching Tiger, Hidden Dragon, 2000 (Schamus)
Croulants se portent bien, 1961 (Auric)
Crow on a Moonlit Night. *See* Tsukiyo garasu, 1939
Crowd Roars, 1932 (Miller; Zanuck)
Crowd Roars, 1938 (Mayer; Seitz)
Crowd, 1928 (Gibbons; Gillespie; Mayer; Thalberg)
Crowded Paradise, 1956 (Kaufman; Sylbert)
Crowded Sky, 1960 (Rosenman; Schnee; Stradling)
Crowded Snores, 1932 (Lantz)
Crowing Pains, 1947 (Blanc; McKimson; Stalling)
Crown of Lies, 1926 (Glennon; Vajda)
Crown of the Year, 1943 (Alwyn)
Crow's Feat, 1962 (Blanc)
Crow's Fete, 1965 (Hanna and Barbera)
Crucial Test, 1916 (Marion)
Crucified Lovers. *See* Chikamatsu monogatari, 1954
Cruel Story of the Samurai Code. *See* Bushidou zankku monogatari, 1963
Cruel Tower, 1956 (Haller)
Cruise, 1967 (Hubley)
Cruise Cat, 1952 (Hanna and Barbera)
Cruising, 1980 (Nitzsche)
Crumb, 1994 (Murch)
Crumbs for the Poor. *See* Ulička v Ráji, 1936
Crusader, 1922 (Fox)
Crusades, 1935 (Banton; Brackett; Dreier; Head; MacPherson; Nichols)
Cry. *See* Křik, 1963
Cry Baby Killer, 1958 (Crosby)
Cry Danger, 1951 (Biroc; Day; Parrish)
Cry for Happy, 1961 (Duning; Guffey)
Cry for Help, 1912 (Bitzer)
Cry Havoc, 1943 (Freund; Goosson; Irene)
Cry in the Dark, 1988 (Golan and Globus)
Cry in the Night, 1956 (Seitz)
Cry of Battle, 1963 (Fields)
Cry of the City, 1948 (Lemaire; Newman; Wheeler)
Cry of the Weak, 1919 (Miller)
Cry of the World, 1933 (de Rochemont)
Cry Tough, 1959 (Lathrop)
Cry Wolf, 1947 (Blanke; Burks; Head; Waxman)
Cry Wolf, 1980 (Krasker)
Cry, the Beloved Country, 1951 (Korda; Krasker)
Cry, the Beloved Country, 1995 (Barry)
Crying Wolf, 1947 (Terry)
Crystal Ball, 1943 (Dreier; Head; Young)
Crystal Book. *See* Livre de cristal, 1994
Csardasfürstin, 1934 (Herlth; Röhrig)
Cuando el amor rie. *See* Ladron de amor, 1930
Cuando levanta la niebla, 1952 (Figueroa)
Cuando viajan las estrellas, 1942 (Figueroa)
Cuatro Juanes, 1964 (Figueroa)
Cub, 1917 (Carré)
Cuba Cabana, 1952 (Warm)
¡Cuba Si!, 1961 (Braunberger; Grimault)
Cuban Love Song, 1931 (Booth; Rosson; Sullivan)
Cubisme. *See* Statues d'épouvante, 1953
Cucaracha, 1934 (Cooper; MacGowan)
Cucaracha, 1958 (Figueroa)
Cuccagne, 1962 (Morricone)
Cuckoo Bird, 1939 (Terry)
Cuckoo Clock, 1950 (Avery)
Cuckoo in the Nest, 1933 (Junge)
Cuckoo Love, 1925 (Roach)
Cuckoos, 1930 (Musuraca; Plunkett)
Cueball Cat, 1950 (Hanna and Barbera)

Cuerpo de mujer, 1949 (Alcoriza; Figueroa)
Cugina, 1974 (Morricone)
Cuivres à la voix d'or, 1958 (Decaë)
Cul-de-sac, 1964 (Lenica)
Culpepper Cattle Company, 1972 (Goldsmith; Smith)
Cult of the Cobra, 1955 (Metty)
Cultured Ape, 1960 (Halas and Batchelor)
Cuore di mamma, 1969 (Morricone)
Cuore, 1984 (Cecchi D'amico)
Cuore semplice, 1977 (Zavattini)
Cuori nella tormenta, 1941 (Amidei)
Cuori nella tormenta, 1984 (Age and Scarpelli)
Cuori senza fontiere, 1950 (Ponti)
Cup of Kindness, 1934 (Balcon; Junge; Rank)
Cup of Life, 1915 (Sullivan)
Cupid's Fireman, 1923 (August; Fox)
Curare et curarisants de synthèse, 1950 (Cloquet)
Cure, 1924 (Fleischer)
Cure, 1995 (Grusin)
Cure for Love, 1949 (Alwyn; Korda)
Cure for Suffragettes, 1913 (Loos)
Curée, 1966 (Renoir)
Curious Pets of Our Ancestors, 1917 (O'Brien)
Curious Puppy, 1939 (Jones)
Curley, 1947 (Roach)
Curly Sue, 1991 (Delerue)
Curly Top, 1935 (Friedhofer; Seitz)
Curlytop, 1924 (Fox)
Curse IV: The Ultimate Sacrifice, 1993 (Donaggio)
Curse of Frankenstein, 1957 (Bernard; Carreras)
Curse of Humanity, 1914 (Ince)
Curse of the Cat People, 1944 (D'Agostino; Lewton; Musuraca)
Curse of the Demon. *See* Night of the Demon, 1957
Curse of the Mummy's Tomb, 1964 (Carreras; Heller)
Curse of the Pink Panther, 1983 (Mancini)
Curse of the Starving Class, 1994 (Shepard)
Curse of the Werewolf, 1960 (Carreras)
Curtain Call, 1940 (Metty; Polglase; Trumbo)
Curtain Call, 1999 (Henry; Nykvist; Shepard)
Curtain Call at Cactus Creek, 1949 (Metty)
Curtain Falls, 1934 (Brown)
Curtain Pole, 1908 (Bitzer)
Curtain Razor, 1949 (Blanc; Stalling)
Curtain Rises. *See* Entrée des artistes, 1938
Curtain Up, 1952 (Arnold; Rank)
Curucu, Beast of the Amazon, 1956 (Siodmak)
Custard Cup, 1923 (Fox)
Custer of the West, 1967 (D'Eaubonne; Lourié; Siodmak)
Custer's Last Raid, 1912 (Ince)
Custer's Last Stand. *See* Bob Hampton of Placer, 1921
Customers Wanted, 1939 (Fleischer)
Cut the Cards, 1920 (Roach)
Cutter and Bone. *See* Cutter's Way, 1981
Cutter's Way, 1981 (Nitzsche)
Cutting Moments, 1998 (Savini)
Cybèle, ou les dimanches de Ville d'Avray, 1962 (Decaë; Evein; Jarre)
Cybernetic Granny. *See* Kybernetická babička, 1962
Cyborg, 1988 (Golan and Globus)
Cyclamen. *See* Ciklámen, 1916
Cyclone, 1946 (Canutt)
Cyclone of the Range, 1927 (Musuraca)
Cyclone of the Saddle, 1935 (Canutt)
Cyclone on Horseback, 1941 (Polglase)
Cynara, 1932 (Day; Goldwyn; Marion; Newman)
Cynara, 1943 (Stewart)
Cynthia, 1947 (Irene; Kaper; Mayer)

Cyrano de Bergerac, 1900 (Gaumont)
Cyrano de Bergerac, 1950 (Foreman; Planer; Tiomkin)
Cyrano de Bergerac, 1990 (Carrière)
Cyrano de Bergerac, 1990 (Lhomme)
Cyrano de Bergerac, 1990 (Rappeneau)
Cyril Stapleton and the Show Band, 1955 (Carreras)
Cytherea, 1924 (Carré; Goldwyn; Marion; Miller)
Czar Durandai, 1934 (Ivanov-Vano)
Czar of Broadway, 1930 (Laemmle; Mohr)
Czardas-König, 1958 (Wagner)
Czardasfürsten, 1927 (Courant)
Czardasfürstin, 1934 (Hoffmann)
Czarina. See A Royal Scandal, 1945
Czarne skrzydła, 1962 (ścibor-Rylski)
Czech Year. See Spalíček, 1947
Czechoslovakia on Parade, 1938 (Hoch)
Człowiek z żelaza, 1981 (ścibor-Rylski)
Człowiek z marmuru, 1976 (ścibor-Rylski)
Czołwiek na torze, 1956 (Stawiński)

D' Fightin' Ones, 1961 (Blanc)
D-Day, the Sixth of June, 1956 (Brackett; Garmes; Lemaire)
D.A.R.Y.L., 1985 (Hamlisch)
D.C. Follies, 1988 (Golan and Globus)
D.F., 1978 (Figueroa)
D.O.A, 1950 (Laszlo; Maté; Tiomkin)
Da, 1988 (Bernstein)Da hält die Welt den Aten an, 1927 (Junge)
Da uomo a uomo, 1967 (Morricone)
Dachshund and the Sausage. See Artist's Dream, 1910
Dactylo, 1931 (Heller)
Dactylo se marie, 1934 (Douy; Planer)
Dad, 1989 (Marshall)
Daddy Goes a-Grunting, 1925 (Roach)
Daddy Long Legs, 1919 (Rosher)
Daddy Long Legs, 1931 (Friedhofer; Levien)
Daddy Long Legs, 1955 (Lemaire; Mercer; Newman; Reynolds; Shamroy; Wheeler)
Daddy's Gone A-Hunting, 1925 (Gibbons; Mayer)
Daddy's Gone A-Hunting, 1969 (Laszlo; Spencer; Williams)
Dad's Day, 1929 (Roach)
Daffy Dilly, 1948 (Blanc; Jones; Stalling)
Daffy Doc, 1938 (Blanc; Clampett; Stalling)
Daffy Doodles, 1946 (Blanc; McKimson; Stalling)
Daffy Duck and Egghead, 1938 (Avery; Blanc; Stalling)
Daffy Duck and the Dinosaur, 1939 (Blanc; Jones)
Daffy Duck Hunt, 1949 (Blanc; McKimson; Stalling)
Daffy Duck in Hollywood, 1938 (Avery; Blanc; Stalling)
Daffy Duck Slept Here, 1948 (Blanc; McKimson; Stalling)
Daffy Duckaroo, 1942 (Blanc; Stalling)
Daffy Duck's Movie: Fantastic Island, 1983 (Jones)
Daffy Duck's Quackbusters, 1988 (Blanc; Jones)
Daffy Rents, 1966 (Blanc; McKimson)
Daffy the Commando, 1943 (Blanc; Stalling)
Daffy's Diner, 1967 (Blanc; McKimson)
Daffy's Inn Trouble, 1961 (Blanc; McKimson)
Daffy's Romance, 1938 (Avery)
Daffy's Southern Exposure, 1942 (Blanc; Stalling)
Dagfin, 1926 (Schüfftan)
Dagger. See Dolken, 1915
Dagny, 1976 (Ścibor-Rylski)
Dagobert, 1983 (Age and Scarpelli)
Dai kusen, 1966 (Tsuburaya)
Dai tatsumaki, 1964 (Tsuburaya)
Daiboken, 1965 (Tsuburaya)
Daigaku no oneichan, 1959 (Muraki)
Daikaiju Baran, 1958 (Tsuburaya)

Dainah la métisse, 1931 (Périnal; Spaak)
Daisan no akumyo, 1963 (Miyagawa; Yoda)
Daisy, 1965 (Dinov)
Daisy Bell, 1925 (Fleischer)
Daisy Bell, 1929 (Fleischer)
Daisy Kenyon, 1947 (Lemaire; Raksin; Shamroy; Wheeler)
Daisy Miller, 1974 (Fields; Marshall)
Daitozoku, 1964 (Tsuburaya)
Dakota, 1945 (Canutt; Foreman)
Dakota Incident, 1956 (Haller)
Dakota Lil, 1950 (Leven; Tiomkin)
Dallas, 1950 (Haller; Steiner; Veiller)
Dalle Ardenne all'inferno, 1968 (Morricone)
Dam Busters, 1955 (Sherriff)
Dam the Delta, 1958 (Halas and Batchelor)
Dama s sobachkoy, 1960 (Moskvin)
Damage. See Fatale, 1992
Dame à la longue vue, 1963 (Braunberger)
Dame aux camélias, 1934 (Stradling)
Dame aux camélias, 1952 (Barsacq)
Dame de chez Maxim's, 1933 (Jeanson)
Dame de Chez Maxim's, 1950 (D'Eaubonne)
Dame de Malacca, 1937 (Trauner)
Dame, der Teufel, und die Probiermamsell, 1917 (Messter)
Dame d'onze heures, 1947 (Kosma)
Dame mit den schwarzen Handschuhen, 1919 (Kolowrat-Krakowsky)
Dame mit den Sonnenblumen, 1920 (Kolowrat-Krakowsky)
Dame mit der Maske, 1928 (Galeen)
Damen i svart, 1958 (Nykvist)
Dames, 1934 (Barnes; Orry-Kelly)
Dames Ahoy!, 1930 (Laemmle)
Dames du Bois de Boulogne, 1945 (Douy)
Damien—Omen II, 1978 (Goldsmith)
Damn Citizen, 1958 (Mancini)
Damn the Defiant!. See H.M.S. Defiant, 1962
Damnation Alley, 1977 (Ames; Goldsmith)
Damned, 1961 (Bernard; Carreras)
Damned, 1963 (Carreras)
Damned. See Caduta degli dei, 1969
Damned. See Maudits, 1947
Damned Don't Cry, 1950 (McCord; Wald)
Damned in Venice. See Nero Veneziamo, 1978
Dämon der Frauen. See Rasputin, 1932
Dämon des Himalaya, 1935 (Honegger)
Damon the Mower, 1972 (Dunning)
Dämonische Liebe, 1950 (Herlth)
D'amore si muore, 1972 (Morricone)
Damsel in Distress, 1937 (August; Berman; Pan; Polglase)
Dan, 1965 (Lassally)
Dan the Dandy, 1911 (Bitzer)
Dance Contest, 1934 (Fleischer)
Dance, Fool, Dance, 1931 (Rosher)
Dance, Girl, Dance, 1940 (Metty; Polglase; Pommer)
Dance Hall, 1929 (Plunkett)
Dance Hall, 1941 (Day; Slocombe)
Dance Macabre, 1992 (Golan and Globus)
Dance Madness, 1926 (Basevi; Daniels; Gibbons)
Dance Music, 1927 (Haller)
Dance of Death, 1968 (Unsworth)
Dance of Life, 1929 (Banton; Selznick)
Dance of Shiva, 1998 (Cardiff)
Dance of the Heron, 1966 (Slocombe; Vierny)
Dance Team, 1931 (Howe)
Dancer. See Maihime, 1989
Dancer in the Dark, 2000 (Müller)
Dancer of Paris, 1926 (Haller)

Dancers, 1925 (Fox)
Dancers, 1930 (Friedhofer)
Dancers, 1987 (Donaggio; Golan and Globus; Reynolds)
Dancers in the Dark, 1932 (Mankiewicz; Struss; Zukor)
Dances with Wolves, 1990 (Barry)
Dancing, 1991 (Bozzetto)
Dancing at Lughnasa, 1998 (Preisner)
Dancing Bear, 1937 (Terry)
Dancing Cow, 1999 (Alonzo)
Dancing Fool, 1932 (Fleischer)
Dancing Foot. See Harold Teen, 1933
Dancing Girl of Butte, 1909 (Bitzer)
Dancing in the Dark, 1949 (Lemaire; Newman; Wheeler)
Dancing Lady, 1933 (Adrian; Booth; Mayer; Selznick; Vorkapich)
Dancing Masters, 1943 (Basevi)
Dancing Mothers, 1926 (Banton)
Dancing on a Dime, 1940 (Head; Lang; Young)
Dancing on the Moon, 1935 (Fleischer)
Dancing Pirate, 1936 (Cooper; Newman; O'Brien; Raksin)
Dancing Shoes, 1949 (Terry)
Dancing with Crime, 1947 (Lassally)
Dandelion Dead, 1994 (Fisher)
Dandy in Aspic, 1968 (Challis; Dillon; Jones)
Dandy Lion, 1940 (Fleischer)
Danger, 1923 (Walker)
Danger Ahead, 1921 (Laemmle)
Danger: Diabolik. See Diabolik, 1968
Danger Grows Wild, 1966 (Alekan; Auric)
Danger in Paris. See Cafe Colette, 1936
Danger Lights, 1930 (Dunn; Struss)
Danger List, 1957 (Carreras)
Danger, Love at Work, 1937 (Miller)
Danger on the Air, 1938 (Cortez)
Danger Patrol, 1937 (Musuraca)
Danger Signal, 1945 (Deutsch; Howe)
Dangerous, 1935 (Haller; Orry-Kelly)
Dangerous Adventure, 1922 (Warner)
Dangerous Age, 1922 (Mayer)
Dangerous Age. See Beloved Brat, 1938
Dangerous Business, 1921 (Loos)
Dangerous Comment, 1940 (Balcon)
Dangerous Corner, 1934 (Plunkett; Steiner)
Dangerous Crossing, 1953 (La Shelle; Lemaire; Reynolds; Wheeler)
Dangerous Dan McFoo, 1939 (Avery)
Dangerous Days. See Wild Boys of the Road, 1933
Dangerous Exile, 1957 (Auric; Rank; Unsworth)
Dangerous Game, 1922 (Laemmle)
Dangerous Game, 1940 (Cortez)
Dangerous Game. See Gefährliches Spiel, 1919
Dangerous Hours, 1919 (Barnes; Sullivan)
Dangerous Liasons, 1988 (Rousselot)
Dangerous Maid, 1923 (Schenck; Sullivan)
Dangerous Minds, 1995 (Bass)
Dangerous Mists. See U-Boat Prisoner, 1944
Dangerous Moment, 1921 (Glennon; Laemmle)
Dangerous Moonlight, 1941 (Addinsell; Beaton; Bryan; Krasker; Mathieson)
Dangerous Moves. See Diagonale du fou, 1983
Dangerous Partners, 1945 (Freund; Irene)
Dangerous Passage, 1944 (Mainwaring)
Dangerous Secrets. See Brief Ecstasy, 1937
Dangerous to Know, 1938 (Head)
Dangerous Voyage. See Kiyen ryoko, 1959
Dangerous When Wet, 1953 (Hanna and Barbera; Mercer; Rose; Rosson; Smith)
Dangerous Woman, 1929 (Dreier)

Dangerous Woman, 1993 (Burwell)
Dangerous Youth. See These Dangerous Years, 1957
Dangerously Close, 1986 (Golan and Globus)
Dangerously Yours, 1933 (Friedhofer; Seitz)
Dangers de l'alcoolisme, 1899 (Gaumont)
Dangers of the Canadian Mounted, 1948 (Canutt)
Daniel and the Devil. See All that Money Can Buy, 1941
Daniele Cortis, 1946 (Gherardi; Rota)
Dankon, 1969 (Muraki; Takemitsu)
Dann Schon lieber Lebertran, 1930 (Kästner; Schüfftan)
Dans Arles où sont les Alyscamps, 1966 (Braunberger)
Dans Bankett der Schmugger. See Banquet des fraudeurs, 1952
Dans la poussière du soleil, 1970 (Lai)
Dans la réserve africaine, 1961 (Braunberger)
Dans la Vallée d'Ossau, 1912 (Cohl)
Dans la vie, 1911 (Gaumont)
Dans la vie tout s'arrange, 1950 (Kosma)
Dans la ville blanche, 1983 (Branco; de Almeida)
Dans les griffes de l'araignée, 1920 (Starewicz)
Dans les rues, 1933 (Andrejew; Eisler; Maté)
Dans un miroir, 1985 (de Almeida)
Danse de mort, 1946 (Wakhévitch)
Danseuse de 14 ans, 1989 (Alekan)
Danseuse nue, 1952 (Evein)
Danseuse orchidé, 1927 (Burel)
Danseuse rouge, 1937 (Alekan; Auric)
Dante n'avait rien vu, 1962 (Braunberger)
Dante's Inferno, 1924 (August; Fox)
Dante's Inferno, 1935 (Canutt; Carré; Friedhofer; Maté)
Danton, 1921 (Dreier)
Danton, 1932 (Burel; Trauner)
Danton, 1982 (Carrière)
Dany, bitte schreiben sie!, 1956 (Warm)
Danza del fuoco, 1942 (Flaiano and Pinelli)
Danza delle lancette, 1936 (Zavattini)
Daphne and the Pirate, 1916 (Brown)
Darby O'Gill and the Little People, 1959 (Disney; Hoch)
Darby's Raiders, 1958 (Steiner)
Darby's Rangers, 1957 (Clothier)
Dare no tame ni aisuruka, 1971 (Muraki)
Dare-Devil Droopy, 1951 (Avery)
Daredevil Drivers, 1938 (McCord)
Daredevil in the Castle. See Osaka-jo monogatari, 1961
Daredevils of the Red Circle, 1939 (Canutt)
Daredevil's Reward, 1928 (Fox)
Dárek, 1946 (Brdečka; Trnka)
Daring Days, 1925 (Laemmle)
Daring Young Man, 1943 (Planer)
Dark Angel, 1925 (Barnes; Goldwyn; Marion; Menzies)
Dark Angel, 1935 (Day; Goldwyn; Newman; Toland)
Dark at the Top of the Stairs, 1960 (Steiner; Stradling)
Dark Avengers, 1955 (Mirisch)
Dark City, 1950 (Dreier; Head; Wallis; Waxman)
Dark Command, 1940 (Canutt; Young)
Dark Corner, 1946 (Basevi)
Dark Crystal, 1982 (Burtt; Henson; Morris)
Dark Delusion, 1947 (Irene; Rosher)
Dark Eyes. See Oci ciornie, 1987
Dark Hazard, 1934 (Orry-Kelly; Polito)
Dark Horse, 1932 (Polito; Zanuck)
Dark Intruder, 1965 (Schifrin)
Dark Journey, 1937 (Addinsell; Biro; Hornbeck; Korda; Périnal)
Dark Light, 1951 (Carreras)
Dark Man, 1950 (Rank)
Dark Mirror, 1946 (Irene; Johnson; Krasner; Schüfftan; Sharaff; Tiomkin)
Dark Obsession, 1989 (Zimmer)

Dark of the Sun. *See* Mercenaries, 1967
Dark Page. *See* Scandal Sheet, 1951
Dark Passage, 1947 (Wald; Waxman)
Dark Past, 1948 (Duning; Maté; Walker)
Dark Road, 1917 (Ince)
Dark Secrets, 1923 (Rosson)
Dark Silence, 1916 (Carré)
Dark Streets, 1929 (Haller)
Dark Strength. *See* Tyemnaya sila, 1917
Dark Tower, 1943 (Heller)
Dark Tower, 1987 (Francis)
Dark Victory, 1939 (Friedhofer; Haller; Orry-Kelly; Steiner; Wallis)
Dark Waters, 1944 (Harrison; Rozsa)
Dark Wave, 1956 (Clarke)
Darkening Trail, 1915 (August)
Darkest Hour, 1923 (Roach)
Darkest Russia, 1917 (Marion)
Darkman, 1990 (Elfman)
Darkman II: The Return of Durant, 1994 (Elfman)
Darkman III: Die Darkman Die, 1996 (Elfman)
Darkness. *See* Tamas, 1987
Darkness. *See* Temno, 1950
Darkness and Daylight, 1923 (August)
Darkness-Light-Darkness. *See* Tma-svetlo-tma, 1989
Darling Dolly Gray, 1926 (Fleischer)
Darling, How Could You?, 1951 (Head)
Darling Lili, 1970 (Dunn; Harlan; Mancini; Mercer; Pan)
Darling of the Rich, 1922 (Goodrich and Hackett)
Darò un milione, 1935 (Zavattini)
Dartozoku, 1963 (Tsuburaya)
Darwin Was Right, 1924 (Fox)
Dash and Lilly, 1999 (Shepard)
Date, 1971 (Cortez)
Date for Dinner, 1947 (Terry)
Date to Skate, 1938 (Fleischer)
Date with an Angel, 1987 (Edlund)
Date with Destiny. *See* Mad Doctor, 1940
Date with Dizzy, 1957 (Hubley)
Date with Duke, 1947 (Pal)
Date with Judy, 1948 (Pasternak; Rose; Surtees)
Daughter of Asia. *See* Aija no musume, 1938
Daughter of Deceit. *See* Hija del angaño, 1951
Daughter of Destiny. *See* Alraune, 1927
Daughter of Luxury. *See* Five and Ten, 1931
Daughter of Shanghai, 1937 (Head)
Daughter of the Dragon, 1931 (Buchman)
Daughter of the Law, 1921 (Glennon)
Daughter of the Mind, 1969 (Smith)
Daughter of the Mountains. *See* Högfjällets dotter, 1914
Daughter of the Poor, 1916 (Loos)
Daughters Courageous, 1939 (Blanke; Epstein; Howe; Steiner; Wallis)
Daughters of Destiny. *See* Destinées, 1952
Daughters of Destiny. *See* Destini di donne, 1952
Daughters of the Night, 1924 (Fox)
Daughters of the Rich, 1923 (Struss)
Dauphine Java, 1960 (Alexeieff and Parker)
Davdas, 1955 (Burman)
David, 1977 (Driessen)
David, 1997 (Morricone)
David and Bathsheba, 1951 (Cole; Dunne; Lemaire; Newman; Shamroy; Wheeler; Zanuck)
David Copperfield, 1935 (Gibbons; Mayer; Selznick; Stothart; Vorkapich)
David Copperfield, 1969 (Anold; Vetchinsky)
David Golder, 1930 (Meerson; Périnal; Trauner)
David Harum, 1915 (Rosson)
David Harum, 1934 (Mohr)

David Niven, 1973 (Alcott)
Davy, 1957 (Slocombe)
Davy Crockett, 1910 (Selig)
Davy Crockett and the River Pirates, 1955 (Disney; Glennon)
Davy Crockett at the Fall of the Alamo, 1926 (Pierce)
Davy Crockett, King of the Wild Frontier, 1954 (Ellenshaw)
Davy Jones' Locker, 1934 (Iwerks)
Dawn, 1914 (Selig)
Dawn, 1928 (Wilcox)
Dawn. *See* Svítání, 1933
Dawn!, 1979 (Boyd)Dawning, 1988 (Biddle)
Dawn Maker, 1916 (Sullivan)
Dawn of a Tomorrow, 1924 (Clarke)
Dawn of the Dead, 1978 (Savini)
Dawn Patrol, 1930 (Haller; Miller; Saunders; Wallis)
Dawn Patrol, 1938 (Friedhofer; Gaudio; Miller; Saunders; Steiner; Wallis)
Dawn Rider, 1935 (Canutt)
Dawn Trail, 1930 (McCord)
Day After, 1983 (Raksin)
Day and Night. *See* Jour et la nuit, 1997
Day and the Hour. *See* Jour et l'heure, 1962
Day at the Races, 1937 (Edens; Gibbons; Kahn; Kaper; Mayer; Ruttenberg; Waxman)
Day at the Zoo, 1939 (Avery)
Day Before. *See* Giorno prima, 1987
Day for Night. *See* Nuit américaine, 1973
Day in Court. *See* Giorno in pretura, 1954
Day in June, 1944 (Terry)
Day in the Country. *See* **Partie de campagne**, 1946
Day Nurse, 1932 (Lantz)
Day Nursing. *See* Children's Corner, 1956
Day of Despair. *See* O Dia do Desespero, 1992
Day of Fury, 1956 (Boyle)
Day of Grace, 1957 (Carreras)
Day of the Animals, 1976 (Schifrin)
Day of the Dead, 1985 (Savini)
Day of the Dolphin, 1973 (Delerue; Fraker; Henry; Levine; O'Steen; Sylbert)
Day of the Jackal, 1973 (Delerue)
Day of the Locust, 1975 (Barry; Hall; Whitlock)
Day of the Outlaw, 1959 (Harlan)
Day One, 1989 (Daring)
Day Shall Dawn, 1944 (Lundgren)
Day Shall Dawn. *See* Jago hua savera, 1958
Day That Shook the World. *See* Sarajevsky Atentat, 1975
Day the Earth Stood Still, 1951 (Herrmann; Lemaire; Reynolds; Wheeler)
Day the Fish Came Out, 1967 (Lassally; Theodorakis)
Day the Hot Line Got Hot. *See* Rouble a Deux Faces, 1968
Day They Gave Babies Away. *See* All Mine to Give, 1956
Day They Robbed the Bank of England, 1960 (Périnal)
Day-Time Wife, 1939 (Day)
Day to Live, 1931 (Terry)
Day Will Dawn, 1942 (Addinsell; Rank; Rattigan)
Day with the Boys, 1969 (Kovacs)
Daybreak, 1948 (Rank)
Daybreak. *See* **Jour se lève**, 1939
Daybreak in Udi, 1949 (Alwyn)
Days and Nights in the Forest. *See* **Aranyer Din Ratri**, 1970
Days in the Trees. *See* Des journées entières dans les arbres, 1976
Days of '49, 1913 (Ince; Sullivan)
Days of '49, 1924 (Canutt)
Days of Glory, 1944 (Dunn; Gaudio)
Days of Heaven, 1978 (Almendros; Morricone; Shepard; Wexler)
Days of Old, 1922 (Roach)
Days of Thunder, 1990 (Mancini; Towne; Zimmer)
Days of Volotchayev. *See* Volochayevskiye dni, 1937

Days of Wine and Roses, 1962 (Lathrop; Mancini; Mercer)
Daytime Wife, 1939 (Zanuck)
Dcery Eviny, 1928 (Heller)
De abajo, 1940 (Figueroa)
De Aegypto, 1995 (Preisner)
De-as fi Harap Alb, 1965 (Popescu-Gopo)
De Babord à Tribord, 1926 (Matras)
De bouche à oreille, 1957 (Decaë)
De brug, 1928 (van Dongen)
De Dans van de Reiger, 1966 (Vierny)
De Domeinen Ditvoorst, 1993 (Müller)
De grens, 1984 (Branco)
De guerre lasse, 1987 (Aurenche and Bost; Sarde)
De la Canebière, 1938 (D'Eaubonne)
De la ferraille a l'acier victorieux, 1940 (Auric)
De l'amour, 1964 (Braunberger; Guillemot)
De landsflyktiga, 1921 (Magnusson)
De l'autre côté de l'eau, 1951 (Cortez)
De Lengte van een Ster, 1964 (Müller)
De Mayerling à Sarajevo, 1940 (Courant; D'Eaubonne; Heller)
De sista stegen, 1960 (Nykvist)
De svarta maskerna, 1912 (Jaenzon; Magnusson)
Deacon's Whiskers, 1915 (Loos)
Dead, 1987 (Jeakins; North)
Dead and Buried, 1981 (Winston)
Dead Bang, 1986 (Fisher)
Dead-Bang, 1988 (Adam)
Dead Center, 1994 (Golan and Globus)
Dead End, 1937 (Basevi; Day; Goldwyn; Mandell; Newman; Toland;
    Westmore Family)
Dead Image. See Dead Ringer, 1964
Dead Live. See Mrtví žijí, 1922
Dead Man, 1995 (Müller)
Dead Man's Return. See Manželé paní Mileny, 1921
Dead Men Don't Wear Plaid, 1982 (Head; Rosza)
Dead Men Tell, 1941 (Clarke; Raksin)
Dead Men Tell No Tales, 1920 (Haller)
Dead of Night, 1945 (Auric; Balcon; Clarke; Slocombe)
Dead of Night. See Deathdream, 1972
Dead Pays, 1912 (Ince)
Dead Poets Society, 1989 (Jarre; Seale)
Dead Pool, 1988 (Schifrin)
Dead Presidents, 1995 (Elfman)
Dead Reckoning, 1947 (Cohn; Goosson; Louis)
Dead Ringer, 1964 (Haller; Previn)
Dead Zone, 1983 (de Laurentiis)
Deadend Cats, 1947 (Terry)
Deadfall, 1968 (Barry)
Deadlier Than the Male, 1966 (Vetchinsky)
Deadline, 1930 (Haskin)
Deadline at Dawn, 1946 (Eisler; Musuraca)
Deadline, U.S.A., 1952 (Krasner; Lemaire; Wheeler)
Deadlock, 1966 (Halas and Batchelor)
Deadly Affair, 1967 (Jones; Young)
Deadly Bees, 1966 (Francis)
Deadly Companions, 1961 (Clothier)
Deadly Dream, 1971 (Grusin)
Deadly Friend, 1986 (Lathrop)
Deadly Game. See Third Party Risk, 1955
Deadly Glass of Beer, 1917 (Loos)
Deadly Honeymoon, 1972 (Bernstein)
Deadly Illusion, 1987 (Justin)
Deadly Is the Female. See **Gun Crazy**, 1949
Deadly Mantis, 1957 (Westmore Family)
Deadly Pursuit. See Shoot to Kill, 1988
Deadly Roulette, 1968 (Schifrin)

Deadly Run. See Mortelle randonnée, 1983
Deadly Trap. See Maison sous les arbres, 1971
Deadwood '76, 1965 (Zsigmond)
Deadwood Coach, 1924 (Fox)
Deadwood Dick, 1940 (Canutt)
Deadwood Sleeper, 1905 (Bitzer)
Deaf, Dumb, and Daffy, 1924 (Roach)
Deaf-Mutes Ball, 1907 (Bitzer)
Deaf Smith and Johnny Ears. See Amigos, 1972
Dear Brat, 1951 (Ames; Head; Krasna; Seitz)
Dear Brigitte, 1965 (Ballard; Duning; Smith)
Dear! Deer!, 1942 (Metty)
Dear Departed, 1920 (Roach)
Dear Detective. See Tendre Poulet, 1977
Dear Diary. See Caro Diaro, 1994
Dear Dr. Gräsler. See Mio caro Dr. Gräsler, 1990
Dear Father. See Caro Papà, 1979
Dear Heart, 1964 (Harlan; Mancini)
Dear Inspector. See Tendre poulet, 1977
Dear Margery Boobs, 1977 (Godfrey)
Dear Mr. Prohack, 1949 (Rank)
Dear Mr. Wonderful, 1982 (Ballhaus)
Dear Murderer, 1947 (Mathieson; Rank)
Dear Octopus, 1943 (Bryan)
Dear Old Switzerland, 1944 (Terry)
Dear Ruth, 1947 (Dreier; Head; Krasna; Laszlo; Mercer)
Dear Summer Sister. See Natsu no imoto, 1972
Dear Wife, 1949 (Dreier; Krasna)
Dearie, 1927 (Blanke)
Death and the Maiden, 1994 (Delli Colli)
Death Becomes Her, 1992 (Ralston)
Death By Hanging. See **Koshikei**, 1968
Death Cliff. See Shi no dangai, 1951
Death Day, 1931 (Tisse)
Death Disk, 1909 (Bitzer)
Death in California, 1985 (Biroc)
Death in Small Doses, 1995 (Fraker)
Death in the Garden. See Mort en ce jardin, 1956
Death in the Vatican. See Morte in Vaticano, 1982
Death of a Champion, 1939 (Head)
Death of a Corrupt Man. See Morte di un operatore, 1978
Death of a Cyclist. See Muerte de un ciclista, 1955
Death of a Gunfighter, 1969 (Westmore Family)
Death of a Salesman, 1951 (Cohn; North; Planer)
Death of a Salesman, 1985 (Ballhaus)
Death of a Scoundrel, 1956 (Howe; Steiner)
Death of a Teamaster. See Sen no rikyu, 1989
Death of an Angel, 1952 (Carreras)
Death of Her Innocence. See Our Time, 1974
Death of Stalinism in Bohemia. See Konec stalinismu v Cechách, 1990
Death on the Diamond, 1934 (Krasner)
Death on the Nile, 1978 (Cardiff; Rota)
Death Race 2000, 1975 (Baker)
Death Ray. See Luch smerti, 1925
Death Rides a Horse. See Da uomo a uomo, 1967
Death Squad, 1974 (Grusin)
Death Takes a Holiday, 1934 (Banton; Lang; Zukor)
Death Takes a Holiday, 1971 (Lourié)
Death Valley, 1927 (Walker)
Death Wish, 1974 (de Laurentiis)
Death Wish 4: The Crackdown, 1987 (Golan and Globus)
Deathcheaters, 1976 (Seale)
Deathdream, 1972 (Savini)
Death's Marathon, 1913 (Bitzer)
Deathtrap, 1982 (Allen; Mandel)
Deathwatch, 1966 (Fields)

Débroussaillage chimique, 1955 (Rabier)
Debt of Honor, 1918 (Ruttenberg)
Début du siècle, 1968 (Braunberger)
Debut of Thomas Cat, 1920 (Bray)
Débuts d'un patineur, 1907 (Pathé)
Décade prodigieuse, 1971 (Gégauff; Rabier)
Decameron, 1971 (Donati; Morricone)
Decameron Nights, 1924 (Pommer; Wilcox)
Deceived, 1991 (Newman)
Deceived Slumming Party, 1908 (Bitzer)
Deceiver, 1914 (Loos)
Deceiver, 1920 (Mohr)
Deceivers, 1988 (Adam; Lassally; Merchant)
December 7th, 1943 (Newman; Parrish; Toland)
Deception, 1909 (Bitzer)
Deception, 1920 (Zukor)
Deception, 1946 (Blanke; Grot; Haller; Korngold)
Deception, 1993 (Barry)
Deception. See Anna Boleyn, 1920
Deception. See Ruby Cairo, 1992
Déchaînés, 1950 (Colpi)
Décharge, 1970 (Cloquet; Legrand)
Decima vittima, 1965 (Di Venanzo; Flaiano and Pinelli; Guerra; Levine; Ponti)
Decision at Sundown, 1957 (Guffey)
Decision Before Dawn, 1951 (Planer; Spencer; Waxman)
Decision of Christopher Blake, 1948 (Freund; Steiner)
Déclassée, 1925 (Gaudio)
Deconstructing Harry, 1997 (Loquasto; Muren)
Decoy. See Lockfågeln, 1971
Decree of Destiny, 1910 (Bitzer)
Dedeckem proti své vuli, 1939 (Stallich)
Dédée d'Anvers, 1948 (Wakhévitch)
Dedicato al mare Eglo, 1979 (Morricone)
Deduce, You Say, 1956 (Blanc; Jones)
Deep, 1977 (Barry; Challis; Justin)
Deep Blue Sea, 1955 (Arnold; Korda; Rattigan)
Deep End of the Ocean, 1999 (Bernstein)
Deep Impact, 1998 (Zanuck)
Deep in My Heart, 1954 (Deutsch; Edens; Friedhofer; Plunkett; Rose)
Deep Purple, 1915 (Carré Edeson)
Deep Purple, 1920 (Menzies)
Deep Rising, 1998 (Goldsmith)
Deep Six, 1958 (Maté; Seitz)
Deep Valley, 1947 (Blanke; McCord; Steiner)
Deep Waters, 1948 (La Shelle; Lemaire)
Deer Hunter, 1978 (Smith; Williams; Zsigmond)
Deer Stalking with Camera, 1905 (Bitzer)
Deerslayer, 1957 (Struss)
Deewanjee, 1976 (Burman)
Def by Temptation, 1990 (Dickerson)
Defector. See Espion, 1967
Defence of the Realm, 1985 (Puttnam)
Defend My Love. See Difendo il mio amore, 1956
Defenders, 1959 (Justin)
Defending Your Life, 1991 (Henry)
Defense of Madrid, 1936-37 (McClaren)
Defense of the Carpathians. See Verteidigung der Karpaten, 1916
Defense Rests, 1934 (August; Swerling)
Defenseless, 1991 (Shepard)
Défenseur, 1930 (D'Eaubonne)
Défilé d'artillerie à la revue du 14 juillet 1896, 1895-97 (Gaumont)
Défilé de vaches laitières, 1901 (Gaumont)
Defizit, 1917 (Hoffmann)
Dégourdis de la onzième, 1936 (Aurenche and Bost)
Dein Herz ist meine Heimat, 1953 (Von Harbou)

Dein Schicksal, 1928 (Fischinger; Metzner)
Déjà vu, 1984 (Donaggio; Golan and Globus)
Déjeuner de soleil, 1937 (Auric; D'Eaubonne)
Déjeuner des oiseaux au Kursaal de Vienne, 1895-97 (Gaumont)
Déjeuner sur l'herbe, 1959 (Kosma)
Dekameron-Nächte, 1924 (Pommer)
Del mismo barro, 1930 (Furthman)
Del odio nació el amor, 1949 (Figueroa)
Delancey Street: The Crisis Within, 1975 (Schifrin)
Delhi. See World Window, 1937-40
Delicate Balance, 1973 (Watkin)
Delicate Delinquent, 1957 (Head)
Delicious, 1931 (Levien)
Delightful Rogue, 1929 (Plunkett)
Delightfully Dangerous, 1945 (Krasner)
Délit de fuite, 1958 (Renoir)
Delitto al circolo del tennis, 1969 (Storaro)
Delitto di Giovanni Episcopo, 1947 (Cecchi D'Amico; Rota)
Deliverance, 1972 (Zsigmond)
Delores Claiborne, 1988 (Elfman)
Delphi Bureau, 1972 (Lourié)
Delphica, 1962 (Braunberger)
Delphine, 1968 (Gégauff)
Delta de sel, 1967 (Braunberger)
Delta Force, 1986 (Golan and Globus)
Delta Force 1: The Lost Patrol, 1999 (Golan and Globus)
Delta Force 2, 1990 (Golan and Globus)
Dem Frieden entgegen, 1917 (Kolowrat-Krakowsky)
Démanty noci, 1964 (Ondříček)
Demetrius and the Gladiators, 1954 (Dunne; Krasner; Lemaire; Spencer; Waxman; Wheeler)
Demi-Bride, 1927 (Gibbons; Gillespie)
Demi-Paradise, 1943 (Dillon; Rank; de Grunwald)
Demoiselle et le violoncelliste, 1965 (Grimault)
Demoiselle et son revenant, 1951 (Burel)
Demoiselles de Rochefort, 1967 (Cloquet; Evein; Legrand)
Demoiselles ont eu 25 Ans, 1993 (Legrand)
Demolitionist, 1995 (Savini)
Demon, 1925 (Laemmle)
Démons de l'aube, 1946 (Honegger; Wakhévitch)
Demons of the Mind, 1972 (Carreras)
Den Åttonde dagen, 1979 (Lundgren)
Den Hårda leken, 1956 (Fischer; Lundgren)
Den levande mumien, 1916 (Magnusson)
Den ljusnande frantis, 1940 (Jaenzon)
Den pervyi, 1958 (Enei)
Den tappre soldaten Jönsson, 1956 (Nykvist)
Den tryanniske fästmannen, 1912 (Magnusson)
Den underbara lögnen, 1955 (Nykvist)
Denial, 1925 (Gibbons; Mayer)
Dennis the Menace, 1993 (Goldsmith)
Dénonciation, 1961 (Braunberger; Delerue)
Denso ningen, 1960 (Tsuburaya)
Dents du diable, 1960 (Mathieson; Solinas)
Denture Adventure, 1960 (Halas and Batchelor)
Denver and Rio Grande, 1952 (Head; Rennahan)
Denver Dude, 1927 (Laemmle)
Département 66, 1963 (Braunberger)
Departure of Train from Station, 1905 (Bitzer)
Deported, 1950 (Daniels; Orry-Kelly)
Deputy Droopy, 1955 (Avery)
Deranged, 1973 (Savini)
Derby Day, 1923 (Roach)
Derby Day, 1952 (Wilcox)
Dermis Probe, 1965 (Williams)
Dernier atout, 1942 (Aurenche and Bost; Douy)

Dernier des six, 1942 (Andrejew)
Dernier Eté à Tanger, 1987 (Mnouchkine)
Dernier homme, 1968 (Lhomme)
Dernier Métro, 1980 (Almendros; Delerue)
Dernier Milliardaire, 1934 (Jaubert; Maté)
Dernier Papillon, 1991 (North)
Dernier refuge, 1946 (Burel)
Dernier Refuge, 1965 (Braunberger; Delerue)
Dernier sou, 1946 (Andrejew)
Dernier tango a Paris. *See* **Last Tango in Paris**, 1972
Dernier tiercé, 1964 (Burel)
Dernier Tournant, 1939 (Matras; Renoir; Spaak; Wakhévitch)
Dernière la façade, 1939 (Spiegel)
Dernière Valse, 1936 (Burel)
Dernières Cartouches, 1899 (Pathé)
Dernières Vacances, 1947 (Barsacq)
Derniers Jours de Pompéi, 1948 (Aldo)
Déroute, 1957 (Colpi)
Derrière la fenêtre, 1966 (Delerue)
Des enfants gâtés, 1977 (Sarde)
Des gens sans importance, 1955 (Kosma)
Des gouts et des couleurs, 1960 (Delerue)
Des Herz des Königin, 1940 (Röhrig)
Des hommes . . . une doctrine, 1960 (Delerue)
Des journées entières dans les arbres, 1976 (Almendros; Duras)
Des Pfarrers Töchterlein , 1912 (Messter)
Des pissenlits par la racine, 1964 (Delerue)
Des rails sous les palmiers, 1951 (Colpi)
Des ruines et des hommes, 1958 (Delerue)
Déscente aux enfers, 1986 (Delerue)
Description d'un combat, 1960 (Cloquet)
Desdemona, 1908 (Messter)
Desert Blossoms, 1921 (Fox)
Desert Command, 1933 (Canutt)
Désert des Tartares, 1977 (Morricone)
Desert Dust, 1927 (Laemmle)
Desert Flower, 1925 (Mathis; McCord)
Desert Fox, 1951 (Johnson; Wheeler)
Desert Fury, 1947 (Cronjager; Head; Lang; Rozsa; Wallis)
Desert Gold, 1914 (Ince)
Desert Gold, 1936 (Dreier)
Desert Greed, 1926 (Canutt)
Desert Hawk, 1924 (Canutt)
Desert Hawk, 1950 (Metty)
Desert Legion, 1953 (Seitz)
Desert Man, 1917 (August)
Desert Man, 1934 (Canutt)
Desert Nights, 1929 (Gibbons; Howe)
Desert of the Tartars. *See* Désert des Tartares, 1977
Desert Outlaw, 1924 (Fox)
Desert Patrol. *See* Sea of Sand, 1958
Desert Rats, 1953 (Lemaire; Newman)
Desert Rider, 1923 (Pierce)
Desert Rose. *See* A rosa de areia, 1989
Desert Shield. *See* Finest Hour, 1992
Desert Song, 1943 (Glennon)
Desert Song, 1953 (Burks; Steiner)
Desert Valley, 1926 (Fox)
Desert Vengeance, 1931 (McCord)
Desert Victory, 1943 (Alwyn)
Desert Wooing, 1918 (Barnes)
Deserter, 1912 (Ince)
Deserter, 1916 (August; Ince)
Deserter, 1971 (de Laurentiis)
Déserteur, 1906 (Pathé)
Déserteur, 1939 (Honegger)

Deserto dei tartari. *See* Désert des Tartares, 1977
Deserto rosso, 1964 (Guerra)
Desert's Price, 1925 (Fox)
Desert's Sting, 1914 (Macpherson)
Déshabillé du modèle, 1897 (Pathé)
Desiderio, 1984 (Rotunno)
Desideria, la vita interiore, 1980 (Donaggio)
Design for Leaving, 1954 (Blanc; McKimson; Stalling)
Design for Living, 1933 (Banton; Dreier; Hecht; Zukor)
Design for Scandal, 1941 (Daniels; Waxman)
Designing Woman, 1941 (Cole)
Designing Woman, 1957 (Alton; Ames; Previn; Rose; Schary)
Designs On Jerry, 1955 (Hanna and Barbera)
Désir mène les hommes, 1957 (Decaë)
Desirable, 1934 (Haller; Orry-Kelly)
Desire, 1923 (Barnes)
Desire, 1936 (Banton; Dreier; Hoffenstein; Lang)
Desire. *See* Yukubo, 1953
Desire in Motion. *See* Mouvements du désir, 1994
Desire in the Dust, 1960 (Ballard)
Desire Me, 1947 (Irene; Ruttenberg; Stothart))
Desire, the Interior Life. *See* Desideria, la vita interiore, 1980
Desire under the Elms, 1958 (Bernstein)
Desired Woman, 1927 (Blanke; Zanuck)
Desirée, 1954 (Krasner; Lemaire; Newman; North; Reynolds; Taradash; Wheeler)
Desk Set, 1957 (Lemaire; Shamroy)
Despair, 1978 (Ballhaus)
Desperado, 1954 (Mainwaring)
Desperate Hours, 1955 (Garmes; Head; Pereira)
Desperate Hours, 1990 (de Laurentiis)
Desperate Journey, 1942 (Friedhofer; Glennon; Steiner; Wald; Wallis)
Desperate Lives, 1982 (Biroc)
Desperate Measures, 1998 (Edlund)
Desperate Moment, 1953 (Rank)
Desperate Ones. *See* Más allá de las montañas, 1967
Desperate Trails, 1921 (Laemmle)
Desperately Seeking Susan, 1985 (Loquasto; Newman)
Dessin de perspective. *See* Perspective, 1949
Dessous des cartes, 1947 (Korda; Spaak)
Destin s'amuse, 1946 (Mnouchkine)
Destination Gobi, 1952 (Clarke; Lemaire; Newman)
Destination Magoo, 1954 (Bosustow)
Destination Meatball, 1951 (Lantz)
Destination Moon, 1950 (Pal)
Destination Murder, 1950 (Leven)
Destination Tokyo, 1944 (Glennon; Wald; Warner; Waxman)
Destinées, 1952 (Aurenche and Bost; D'Eaubonne; Jeanson; Matras)
Destini di donne, 1952 (Amidei; Flaiano and Pinelli)
Destins de Manoel, 1984 (Branco; de Almeida)
Destiny, 1921 (Röhrig)
Destiny. *See* Müde Tod, 1921
Destiny in Space, 1994 (Burtt)
Deštivý den, 1962 (Ondříček)
Destroy All Monsters. *See* Kaiju soshingeki, 1968
Destroy She Said. *See* Détruire, dit-elle, 1969
Destroyer, 1943 (Chase; Planer)
Destruction of Sakura Jim. *See* Wrath of the Gods, 1914
Destructors. *See* Marseille Contract, 1974
Destry Rides Again, 1939 (Mohr; Pasternak)
Det är min musik, 1942 (Fischer)
Det gröna halsbandet, 1912 (Magnusson)
Det omrigade huset, 1922 (Magnusson)
Det röda tornet, 1914 (Jaenzon; Magnusson)
Det sjunde inseglet, 1956 (Fischer; Lundgren)
Det svänger på slottet, 1959 (Fischer)

Detective, 1930 (Lantz)
Detective, 1968 (Biroc; Goldsmith; Smith)
Détective, 1985 (Nuytten)Detective Story, 1951 (Garmes; Head; Pereira)
Detective. *See* Father Brown, 1954
Detenuto in attesa di giudizio, 1971 (Amidei)
Detgröna halsbandet, 1912 (Jaenzon)
Detour to Marriage. *See* Umweg zur Ehe, 1919
Detouring America, 1939 (Avery)
Détruire, dit-elle, 1969 (Colpi; Duras)
Deuce of Spades, 1922 (Buckland)
Deuces Wild, 2001 (Alonzo)
Deus, Pátria, Autoridade, 1975 (de Almeida)
Deutscher Frühling, 1979 (Ballhaus)
Deutsches Mann Geil! Die Geschichte von Ilona und Kurti, 1991
    (Morricone)
Deutschland im Herbst, 1978 (Ballhaus)
Deux Anglaises et le continent, 1971 (Almendros; Delerue; Donaggio)
Deux bobines et un fil, 1955 (Cloquet)
Deux Canards, 1933 (Douy)
Deux Couverts, 1934 (Fradetal)
Deux Crocodiles, 1987 (Sarde)
Deux hommes dans la ville, 1975 (Sarde)
Deux memoires, 1973 (Semprun)
Deux Orphelines, 1933 (Douy; Ibert)
Deux ou trois choses que je sais d'elle, 1967 (Coutard)
Deux "Monsieurs" de Madame, 1933 (Burel)
Deux Saisons de la vie, 1972 (Morricone)
Deux sous de violettes, 1951 (Barsacq)
Deux Timides, 1928 (Meerson)
Deux Timides, 1942 (Alekan)
Deuxième Ciel, 1969 (Braunberger)
Devčata, nedejte se!, 1937 (Heller)
Devčátko, neříkej ne!, 1932 (Stallich)
Development History of the Southern Sea: Tribes of the Ocean. *See*
    Mampou hattenshi: Umi no gouzoku, 1942
Devi, 1960 (Chandragupta; Dutta; Mitra)
Deviatoe yanvaria, 1926 (Moskvin)
Devil, 1908 (Bitzer)
Devil and Daniel Webster. *See* All That Money Can Buy, 1941
Devil and Max Devlin, 1981 (Hamlisch)
Devil and Miss Jones, 1941 (Krasna; Menzies; Stradling)
Devil and the Deep, 1932 (Lang; Zukor)
Devil and the Ten Commandments. *See* Diable et les dix
    commandements, 1962
Devil at Four O'Clock, 1961 (Biroc; Duning)
Devil by the Tail. *See* Diable par la queue, 1968
Devil Dancer, 1927 (Barnes; Goldwyn)
Devil Dogs of the Air, 1935 (Edeson; Saunders)
Devil Doll, 1936 (Gibons; Waxman)
Devil Girl from Mars, 1954 (Korda)
Devil Horse, 1926 (Canutt; Roach)
Devil Horse, 1932 (Canutt)
Devil in a Blue Dress, 1995 (Bernstein)
Devil in Silk. *See* Teufel in Seide, 1955
Devil in the Brain. *See* Diavolo nel cervello, 1972
Devil in the Flesh. *See* **Diable au corps**, 1947
Devil in the Flesh. *See* Diavolo in Corpo, 1986
Devil Is a Sissy, 1936 (Brown; Freed; Rosson; Stothart)
Devil Is a Woman, 1935 (Ballard; Banton; Dreier; Zukor)
Devil Is a Woman. *See* Sorriso del grande tentatore, 1974
Devil-May-Care, 1929 (Adrian; Day; Gibbons; Kräly; Shearer; Stothart;
    Tiomkin)
Devil May Hare, 1954 (Blanc; McKimson; Stalling)
Devil Never Sleeps. *See* Satan Never Sleeps, 1962
Devil of the Deep, 1938 (Terry)
Devil on Wheels. *See* Indianapolis Speedway, 1939

Devil Pays Off, 1941 (Alton)
Devil, Probably. *See* Diable, probablement, 1977
Devil Rides Out, 1968 (Bernard; Carreras)
Devil-Ship Pirates, 1963 (Carreras)
Devil Stone, 1917 (Buckland; Macpherson)
Devil Takes the Count . *See* Devil Is a Sissy, 1936
Devil to Pay, 1930 (Barnes; Day; Goldwyn; Newman; Toland)
Devil with Hitler, 1942 (Roach)
Devil with Women, 1930 (Fox; Friedhofer; Nichols)
Devils, 1971 (Watkin)
Devil's Advocate, 1997 (Baker)
Devil's Bait, 1959 (Alwyn)
Devil's Bride. *See* Devil Rides Out, 1968
Devil's Brigade, 1968 (Clothier; North)
Devil's Brother. *See* Fra Diavolo, 1933
Devil's Canyon, 1953 (D'Agostino; Musuraca)
Devil's Daughter. *See* Setta, 1992
Devil's Disciple, 1959 (Bennett; Fisher)
Devil's Doorway, 1950 (Alton; Canutt; Mayer; Plunkett)
Devil's Double, 1916 (August)
Devil's Envoy. *See* Visiteurs du soir, 1942
Devil's Eye. *See* Djävulens öga, 1960
Devil's Feud Cake, 1963 (Blanc)
Devil's Garden, 1921 (Stradling)
Devil's Garden. *See* Coplan sauve sa peau, 1967
Devil's Hairpin, 1957 (Head)
Devil's Hand, 1961 (Pierce)
Devil's in Love, 1933 (Mohr)
Devil's Instrument. *See* Djävulens instrument, 1967
Devil's Island. *See* Akuma-to, 1980
Devil's Lottery, 1932 (Friedhofer)
Devil's Messenger, 1962 (Siodmak)
Devil's Mill. *See* Certuv mlýn, 1950
Devil's Own, 1997 (Willis)
Devil's Own. *See* Witches, 1966
Devil's Partner, 1958 (Cronjager)
Devil's Party, 1938 (Krasner)
Devil's Pass, 1957 (Adam)
Devil's Passkey, 1919 (Daniels; Day)
Devil's Playground, 1937 (Ballard; Trumbo)
Devil's Playground. *See* Lady Who Dared, 1931
Devil's Temple. *See* Ono no sumu yakata, 1969
Devil's Toast. *See* Akuma no kanpai, 1947
Devil's Toy, 1916 (Edeson)
Devils Wanton, 1949 (Lundgren)
Devil's Wheel. *See* Chyortovo koleso, 1926
Devoir de Zouzou, 1955 (Kosma)
Devotion, 1913 (Ince)
Devotion, 1931 (Mandell; Mohr; Stewart)
Devotion, 1946 (Friedoer; Haller; Korngold)
Devushka s dalekoi reki, 1928 (Enei)
Dezerter, 1958 (Stawiński)
Dezertér, 1965 (Brdečka)
Dezertir, 1933 (Golovnya)
Dharam Ki Devi, 1935 (Biswas)
Dharti Ke Lal, 1947 (Abbas; Shankar)
D'homme à hommes, 1948 (Kosma; Matras; Spaak)
Día con el diablo, 1945 (Figueroa)
Dia de vida, 1950 (Figueroa)
Diable au corps, 1947 (Aurenche and Bost; Douy)
Diable dans la boîte, 1977 (Carrière; Vierny)
Diable et les dix commandements, 1962 (Jeanson)
Diable par la queue, 1968 (Delerue)
Diable, probablement, 1977 (Sarde)
Diable souffle, 1947 (Alekan)
Diabolical Dr. Z. *See* Miss Muerte, 1966

Diabolically Yours. *See* Diaboliquement vôtre, 1967

Diabolik, 1968 (Gherardi; Morricone; de Laurentiis)

Diabolique, 1996 (Littleton)

Diaboliquement vôtre, 1967 (Barsacq; Decaë; Gégauff)

Diaboliques, 1954 (Barsacq)

Diabolo Menthe (Peppermint Soda), 1977 (Rousselot)

Diagnostic C.I.V., 1960 (Delerue)

Diagnoza X, 1933 (Stallich)

Diagonale du fou, 1983 (Coutard; Guillemot)

Dial 1119, 1950 (Previn)

Dial H for Hitchcock. *See* Hitchcock: Shadow of a Genius, 1999

Dial M for Murder, 1953 (Burks; Tiomkin)

Dialectique, 1966 (Guillemot)

Diamant, 1969 (Grimault)

Diamond City, 1948 (Rank)

Diamond Frontier, 1940 (Krasner)

Diamond Head, 1963 (Williams)

Diamond Horseshoe, 1945 (Zanuck)

Diamond Jim, 1935 (Mandell; Waxman)

Diamond Queen, 1953 (Cortez; Lourié)

Diamond Skulls. *See* Dark Obsession, 1989

Diamond Star, 1910 (Bitzer)

Diamonds, 1975 (Golan and Globus)

Diamonds Are Forever, 1971 (Barry; Broccoli; Whitlock)

Diamonds of the Night. *See* Démanty noci, 1964

Diane, 1929 (Andrejew)

Diane, 1955 (Plunkett; Rozsa)

Diary, 1981 (Vinton)

Diary for Timothy, 1945 (Mathieson)

Diary of a Chambermaid, 1946 (Lourié)

Diary of a Chambermaid. *See* Journal d'une femme de chambre, 1963

Diary of a Country Priest. *See* **Journal d'un curé de campagne**, 1950

Diary of a Lost Girl. *See* Tagebuch einer Verlorenen, 1929

Diary of a Madman, 1965 (Williams)

Diary of a Seducer. *See* Journal de séducteur, 1996

Diary of a Shinjuku Thief. *See* Shinjuku dorobo nikki, 1969

Diary of Anne Frank, 1959 (Cardiff; Goodrich and Hackett; Lemaire; Newman; Wheeler)

Diary of Anne Frank, 1980 (Goodrich and Hackett)

Días de otoño, 1962 (Figueroa)

Dias del agua, 1971 (Herrera)

Diavolo, 1963 (de Laurentiis)

Diavolo in Corpo, 1986 (Lanci, Giuseppe; Sarde)

Diavolo nel cervello, 1972 (Cecchi D'Amico; Morricone)

Dich hab' ich geliebt, 1929 (Reisch)

Diciotteni al sole, 1962 (Morricone)

Diciottenni, 1956 (Ponti)

Dick Barton at Bay, 1950 (Carreras)

Dick Barton—Special Agent, 1948 (Carreras)

Dick Barton Strikes Back, 1949 (Adam; Carreras)

Dick Tracy, 1990 (Elfman; Storaro; Sylbert)

Dick Tracy Meets Gruesome, 1947 (D'Agostino)

Dick Tracy Returns, 1938 (Canutt)

Dick Turpin, 1925 (Fox)

Dick Turpin—Highwayman, 1956 (Carreras)

Dick Whittington's Cat, 1936 (Iwerks)

Dictator, 1922 (Brown)

Dictator, 1934 (Andrejew; Planer)

Dictionnaire des pin-up girls, 1951 (Braunberger)

Did You Ever See a Dream Walking?, 1943 (Balcon)

Die! Die! My Darling!. *See* Fanatic, 1964

Die-Hard Shoemakers. *See* Skalní ševci, 1931

Die—oder Keine, 1932 (Courant)

Diebstahl, 1917 (Kolowrat-Krakowsky)

Dieu a besoin des hommes, 1950 (Aurenche and Bost)

Dieu a choisi Paris, 1969 (Milhaud)

Dieu que les femmes sont amoureuses, 1994 (Lhomme)

Difendo il mio amore, 1956 (Cecchi D'Amico; Di Venanzo)

Different Story, 1978 (Lathrop)

Difficult Years. *See* Anni difficili, 1948

Difficulté d'être infidèle, 1963 (Braunberger; Coutard)

Dig Up, 1922 (Roach)

Diga sul Pacifico. *See* Barrage contre le Pacifique, 1958

Digging for Victory, 1942 (Halas and Batchelor)

Digging to China, 1998 (Bernstein)

Diggstown, 1992 (Fisher)

Dil Ki Rani, 1947 (Burman)

Dilemma, 1982 (Halas and Batchelor)

Dillinger, 1945 (Tiomkin)

Dimanche à Pekin, 1956 (Delerue)

Dimanche de flics, 1983 (Müller)

Dimanche de Gazouilly, 1955 (Starewicz)

Dime to Retire, 1955 (Blanc)

Dime with a Halo, 1963 (Lathrop)

Dimensions of Dialogue. *See* Mozenosti dialogu, 1982

Dimenticare Palermo, 1989 (Guerra; Morricone)

Dimmi che fai tutto per mei, 1976 (Cecchi D'Amico)

Dimples, 1936 (Glennon; Johnson)

Din stund pa jorden, 1972 (Fischer)

Dina e Django, 1981 (de Almeida)

Dinah, 1933 (Fleischer)

Diner des bustes, 1988 (Vangelis)

Ding Dog Daddy, 1942 (Blanc; Stalling)

Ding Dong Doggie, 1937 (Fleischer)

Dingbat Land, 1949 (Terry)

Dingo, 1991 (Legrand)

Dinky, 1935 (Edeson)

Dinky Doodle and the Little Orphan, 1926 (Lantz)

Dinky Doodle in Egypt, 1926 (Lantz)

Dinky Doodle in Lost and Found, 1926 (Lantz)

Dinky Doodle in the Arctic, 1926 (Lantz)

Dinky Doodle in the Army, 1926 (Lantz)

Dinky Doodle in the Circus, 1925 (Lantz)

Dinky Doodle in the Restaurant, 1925 (Lantz)

Dinky Doodle in the Wild West, 1926 (Lantz)

Dinky Doodle in Uncle Tom's Cabin, 1926 (Lantz)

Dinky Doodle's Bed Time Story, 1926 (Lantz)

Dinky Finds a Home, 1946 (Terry)

Dinner at Eight, 1933 (Adrian; Daniels; Gibbons; Mankiewicz; Marion; Mayer; Selznick; Stewart)

Dinner Date, 1960 (Halas and Batchelor)

Dinner Hour, 1920 (Roach)

Dino, 1958 (Waxman)

Dinosaur, 1980 (Vinton)

Dinosaur and the Missing Link, 1914 (O'Brien)

Dinosaurs, 1989 (Adam)

Dinosaurus!, 1960 (Cortez)

Dinty, 1921 (Carré)

Dionysos, 1984 (Braunberger)

Diplomaniacs, 1932 (Cronjager; Steiner)

Diplomatic Courier, 1952 (Ballard; Wheeler)

Dippy Daughter, 1918 (Roach)

Dippy Dentist, 1920 (Roach)

Dipsy Gypsy, 1941 (Pal)

Directed by John Ford, 1971 (Kovacs)

Direction d'acteurs par Jean Renoir, 1966 (Braunberger)

Dirigible, 1931 (Cohn; Saunders; Swerling; Walker)

Dirty Angels. *See* Vergogna schifosi, 1968

Dirty Dozen, 1967 (Johnson)

Dirty Fingers. *See* Smutsiga fingrar, 1973

Dirty Hands. *See* Innocents aux mains sales, 1975

Dirty Harry, 1972 (Schifrin)

Dr. Bethune. *See* Bethune: The Making of a Hero, 1990

Dr. Broadway, 1942 (Dreier)

Dr. Bull, 1933 (Parrish)

Dr. Christian Meets the Women, 1940 (Alton)

Dr. Cyclops, 1940 (Dreier; Edouart; Head; Hoch)

Doctor Detroit, 1983 (Schifrin)

Dr. Devil and Mr. Hare, 1964 (Blanc; McKimson)

Dr. Dippy's Sanitarium, 1906 (Bitzer)

Doctor Dolittle, 1967 (Smith; Surtees)

Dr. Dolittle, 1998 (Boyd)

Dr. Ehrlich's Magic Bullet, 1940 (Friedhofer; Steiner; Wallis)

Dr. Gillespie's Criminal Case, 1943 (Irene)

Dr. Holl, 1951 (Herlth; Von Harbou)

Doctor in Distress, 1963 (Vetchinsky)

Doctor in Love, 1960 (Rank)

Doctor in the House, 1954 (Dillon; Rank)

Dr. Jack, 1922 (Roach)

Dr. Jekyll and Mr. Hyde, 1908 (Selig)

Dr. Jekyll and Mr. Hyde, 1920 (Zukor)

Dr. Jekyll and Mr. Hyde, 1931 (Banton; Dreier; Hoffenstein; Mayer; Struss; Westmore Family; Zukor)

Dr. Jekyll and Mr. Hyde, 1941 (Adrian; Mayer; Ruttenberg; Waxman)

Dr. Jekyll and Mr. Mouse, 1947 (Hanna and Barbera)

Dr. Jekyll and Sister Hyde, 1971 (Carreras)

Doctor Jerkyll's Hide, 1954 (Blanc; Stalling)

Dr. Kildare Goes Home, 1940 (Rosson)

Dr. Kildare's Crisis, 1940 (Seitz)

Dr. Kildare's Strange Case, 1940 (Seitz)

Dr. Kildare's Victory, 1941 (Daniels)

Dr. Kildare's Wedding Day, 1941 (Kaper)

Dr. Kotnis Ki Amar Kahani, 1946 (Abbas)

Dr. M, 1990 (Rabier)

Dr. Mabuse, der Spieler, 1922 (Hoffmann; Hunte; Pommer; Von Harbou)

Doctor Maniac. *See* Man Who Changed His Mind, 1936

Dr. Monica, 1934 (Blanke; Grot; Orry-Kelly; Polito)

Dr. Morelle—the Case of the Missing Heiress, 1949 (Carreras)

Dr. No, 1962 (Adam; Barry; Broccoli)

Doctor Oswald, 1935 (Lantz)

Dr. Paul Joseph Goebbels. *See* Enemy of Women, 1944

Dr. Renault's Secret, 1942 (Day; Miller; Raksin)

Doctor Rhythm, 1938 (Crosby; Head; Lang; Swerling)

Dr. Rosin, 1949 (Von Dassanowsky)

Doctor Says. *See* Angeklagt nach N.218, 1966

Dr. Skinum, 1907 (Bitzer)

Dr. Socrates, 1935 (Gaudio; Grot)

Dr. Strangelove: Or How I Learned to Stop Worrying and Love the Bomb, 1964 (Adam; Southern)

Dr. Syn, 1937 (Vetchinsky)

Dr. Terror's House of Horrors, 1965 (Francis)

Dr. Vidya, 1962 (Burman)

Doctor Who, 1963 (Bennett)

Doctor X, 1932 (Grot; Rennahan)

Doctor Zhivago, 1965 (Jarre; Ponti; Young)

Doctors & Nurses, 1981 (Seale)

Doctors at War, 1943 (Goodrich and Hackett)

Doctor's Diary, 1937 (D'agostino; Head)

Doctor's Dilemma, 1958 (Beaton; Kosma; Krasker; de Grunwald)

Doctor's Trouble, 1912 (Ince)

Doctors' Wives, 1931 (Edeson)

Doctors' Wives, 1970 (Bernstein; Lang; Taradash; Wheeler)

Document in Cipher. *See* Shifrovanny Document, 1928

Dodesukaden, 1970 (Muraki; Takemitsu)

Dodge City, 1939 (Canutt; Friedhofer; Haskin; Polito; Steiner)

Dodge your Debts, 1921 (Roach)

Dodshoppet farn circkuskupolen, 1912 (Magnusson)

Dodskyssen, 1917 (Jaenzon)

Dodsworth, 1936 (Day; Goldwyn; Howard; Mandell; Maté; Newman)

Does. *See* Biches, 1968

Does It Pay?, 1923 (Fox; Ruttenberg)

Dog and the Bone, 1937 (Terry)

Dog Collared, 1950 (Blanc; McKimson; Stalling)

Dog Day Afternoon, 1975 (Allen)

Dog Days, 1925 (Roach)

Dog Days. *See* Rötmånad, 1970

Dog Daze, 1937 (Stalling)

Dog Daze, 1939 (Roach)

Dog Done Dog Catcher, 1955 (Halas and Batchelor)

Dog Gone It, 1927 (Lantz)

Dog Gone Modern, 1938 (Jones)

Dog Gone South, 1950 (Blanc; Jones; Stalling)

Dog-Heads. *See* Psohlavci, 1954

Dog Heaven, 1929 (Roach)

Dog House, 1952 (Hanna and Barbera)

Dog in a Mansion, 1940 (Terry)

Dog Justice, 1928 (Musuraca)

Dog of Flanders, 1935 (Plunkett)

Dog of Flanders, 1959 (Heller)

Dog Pound, 1960 (Halas and Batchelor)

Dog Pounded, 1954 (Blanc; Stalling)

Dog Show, 1934 (Terry)

Dog Show, 1950 (Terry)

Dog Snatcher, 1952 (Bosustow)

Dog Tales, 1958 (Blanc; McKimson)

Dog Tired, 1942 (Blanc; Jones; Stalling)

Dog Trouble, 1942 (Hanna and Barbera)

Dogfight, 1991 (Daring)

Doggone Cats, 1947 (Blanc)

Doggone People, 1960 (Blanc; McKimson)

Doggone Tired, 1949 (Avery)

Doggy Bag, 1999 (Legrand)

Dogora—The Space Monster. *See* Uchu daikaiju Dogora, 1964

Dogpound Shuffle, 1974 (Fisher)

Dog's Dream, 1941 (Terry)

Dogs Is Dogs, 1931 (Roach)

Dogs of War, 1923 (Roach)

Dogs of War, 1981 (Cardiff; Smith)

Dogsday. *See* Canicule, 1983

Dohyou matsuri, 1944 (Miyagawa)

Doigts de lumière, 1947 (Fradetal)

Doin' Time on Planet Earth, 1988 (Golan and Globus)

Doing Imposikible Stunts, 1940 (Fleischer)

Doing Their Bit, 1918 (Ruttenberg)

Doing Their Bit, 1942 (Terry)

Doing Time, 1920 (Roach)

Dokoku, 1952 (Hayasaka)

Doktor Dolittle und seine Tiere, 1928 (Reiniger)

Dolce cinema, 1999 (Cecchi D'Amico)

Dolce vita, 1960 (Flaiano and Pinelli; Gherardi; Rota)

Dolken, 1915 (Jaenzon)

Doll, 1961 (Vukotić)

Doll. *See* Puppe, 1919

Doll Face, 1945 (La Shelle; Leven)

Doll That Took the Town. *See* Donna del giorno, 1957

Dollar-a-Year Man, 1921 (Brown)

Dollar Dance, 1943 (McClaren)

Dollar Mark, 1914 (Carré; Edeson)

Dollaro a testa, 1966 (Morricone)

Dollarprinzessin und ihre sechs Freier, 1927 (Reisch)

Dollmaker, 1984 (Jenkins)

Dolls. *See* Bambole, 1964

Doll's Eye, 1982 (Pinter)

Doll's House, 1918 (Carré; Zukor)
Doll's House, 1973 (Barry; Fisher; Head; Legrand)
Dolly macht Karriere, 1930 (Wagner)
Dolly Put the Kettle On, 1947 (Halas and Batchelor)
Dolly Sisters, 1945 (Newman; Orry-Kelly; Wheeler)
Dolly's Papa, 1907 (Selig)
Dom, 1958 (Lenica)
Dom bez okien, 1962 (Ścibor-Rylski)
Dom v sugribakh, 1928 (Enei)
Domani accadra, 1988 (Morricone)
Domani e un altro giorno, 1951 (Aldo)
Domani si balla, 1982 (Cristaldi)
Domaren, 1960 (Nykvist)
Domenica d'agosto, 1950 (Amidei; Zavattini)
Domenica della buona gente, 1954 (Rota)
Domenica d'estate, 1962 (Amidei)
Domenica specialmente, 1991 (Guerra; Morricone)
Domestic Relations, 1922 (Glennon)
Domicile conjugal, 1970 (Almendros; Guillemot)
Domik v kolomne, 1913 (Starewicz)
Dominatore dei sette mari, 1960 (Maté)
Domingo à Tarde, 1965 (de Almeida)
Domingo salvaje, 1966 (Figueroa)
Dominick and Eugene, 1988 (Sargent)
Dominika's Name Day. See Když má svátek Dominika, 1967
Domino, 1942 (Aurenche and Bost)
Domino Killings. See Domino Principle, 1976
Domino Principle, 1976 (Laszlo)
Don Bosco, 1935 (Amidei)
Don Cesar de Bazan, 1957 (Enei)
Don Cesare di Bazan, 1942 (Amidei; Zavattini)
Don Giovanni, 1979 (Fisher; Trauner)
Don Is Dead, 1973 (Ames; Goldsmith; Head; Wallis)
Don Juan, 1922 (Metzner)
Don Juan, 1926 (Carré; Haskin; Warner)
Don Juan, 1955 (Wakhévitch)
Don Juan. See Don Sajn, 1970
Don Juan 1973, ou si Don Juan était une femme, 1973 (Decaë)
Don Juan Quilligan, 1945 (Raksin)
Don Juans letztes Abenteuer, 1918 (Kolowrat-Krakowsky)
Don Key, Son of Burro, 1926 (Roach)
Don Q, Son of Zorro, 1925 (Grot)
Don Quichotte, 1909 (Cohl)
Don Quichotte, 1933 (Andrejew; Ibert; Reiniger; Wakhévitch)
Don Quichotte, le chat botté, 1903 (Pathé)
Don Quickshot of the Rio Grande, 1923 (Laemmle)
Don Quixote, 1934 (Iwerks)
Don Quixote, 1957 (Enei; Moskvin)
Don Quixote. See Don Quichotte, 1909
Don Quixote. See Don Quichotte, 1933
Don Sajn, 1970 (Švankmajer)
Doña Juana, 1927 (Freund)
Donatella, 1956 (Delli Colli)
Donauwalzer, 1930 (Reisch)
Doncella de piedra, 1955 (Figueroa)
Done in Oil, 1934 (Roach)
Dong Kingman, 1955 (Howe)
Donkey Skin. See Peau d'âne, 1971
Donna del fiume, 1955 (Flaiano and Pinelli; Ponti; de Laurentiis)
Donna del giorno, 1957 (Zavattini)
Donna della domenica, 1975 (Age and Scarpelli; Morricone)
Donna della montagne, 1943 (de Laurentiis)
Donna è una cosa meravigliosa, 1964 (Di Venanzo; Guerra)
Donna invisible, 1969 (Morricone)
Donna più bella del mondo, 1955 (Solinas)
Donna Scimmia, 1964 (Ponti; Serandrei)

Donne e briganti, 1950 (Rota)
Donne e soldati, 1954 (Di Venanzo)
Donne proibite, 1953 (Zavattini)
Donne-moi la main, 1958 (Jarre)
Donovan Affair, 1929 (Cohn)
Donovan's Brain, 1953 (Biroc; Leven)
Donovan's Kid. See Young Donovan's Kid, 1931
Donovan's Reef, 1963 (Clothier; Edouart; Head; Nugent; Pereira)
Don's Party , 1976 (McAlpine)
Don't Axe Me, 1958 (Blanc; McKimson)
Don't Bet on Love, 1933 (Laemmle)
Don't Bother to Knock, 1952 (Ballard; Lemaire; Taradash)
Don't Bother to Knock, 1961 (Unsworth)
Don't Change Your Husband, 1918 (Buckland; MacPherson)
Don't Cry, It's Only Thunder , 1982 (Jarre; McAlpine)
Don't Drink the Water, 1969 (Rosenblum; Williams)
Don't Ever Leave Me, 1949 (Rank)
Don't Ever Marry, 1921 (Carré)
Don't Flirt, 1923 (Roach)
Don't Forget, 1924 (Roach)
Don't Forget That You're Going to Die. See N'oublie pas que tu vas mourir, 1995
Don't Get Gay with Your Manicure, 1903 (Bitzer)
Don't Get Jealous, 1929 (Hornbeck)
Don't Get Personal, 1922 (Laemmle)
Don't Get Personal, 1936 (Waxman)
Don't Give In, Girls!. See Devčata, nedejte se!, 1937
Don't Give Up. See Tappa inte sugen, 1947
Don't Give Up the Sheep, 1953 (Blanc; Jones; Stalling)
Don't Give Up the Ship, 1959 (Head; Wallis)
Don't Go Near the Water, 1957 (Cahn; Kaper; Rose)
Don't Just Stand There, 1967 (Krasner)
Don't Look Now, 1936 (Avery; Stalling)
Don't Look Now, 1973 (Donaggio)
Don't Make Grandfather Angry. See Nezlobte dedečka, 1934
Don't Make Waves, 1967 (Lathrop)
Don't Marry, 1928 (August; Fox)
Don't Miss, Miss Pizz, 1968 (Müller)
Don't Panic Chaps!, 1959 (Carreras)
Don't Park There!, 1924 (Roach)
Don't Pull Your Punches. See Kid Comes Back, 1937
Don't Push, I'll Charge When I'm Ready, 1977 (Bumstead)
Don't Raise the Bridge, Lower the River, 1967 (Heller)
Don't Rock the Boat, 1920 (Roach)
Don't Say Die, 1923 (Roach)
Don't Shoot, 1922 (Laemmle; Miller)
Don't Shove, 1919 (Roach)
Don't Take It to Heart, 1944 (Rank; Vetchinsky)
Don't Tell Everything, 1927 (Roach)
Don't Tell the Wife, 1927 (Blanke)
Don't Tempt the Devil. See Bonnes Causes, 1963
Don't Trust Your Husband, 1948 (Cronjager)
Don't Weaken, 1920 (Roach)
Donzoko, 1957 (Muraki)
Doolins of Oklahoma, 1949 (Canutt; Duning)
Doomed Caravan, 1941 (Harlan; Head)
Doomed Cargo. See Seven Sinners, 1936
Doomsday, 1928 (Banton)
Doomsday, 1938 (Terry)
Doomsday Flight, 1966 (Schifrin)
Doomsday Gun, 1994 (Bernstein)
Door, 1968 (Blanc)
Door in the Wall, 1956 (Bernard)
Doorway to Hell, 1930 (Zanuck)
Doppelganger, 1969 (Parrish)
Doppelt Lottchen. See Charlie & Louise—Das Doppelte Lottchen, 1993

Doppelte Lottchen, 1950 (Herlth; Kästner)
Dorado, 1921 (Gaumont)
Dorado, 1963 (Golan and Globus)
Dorado, 1967 (Brackett; Edouart; Pereira; Rosson)
Dorado, 1985 (Bozzetto)
Dorf unter Himmel, 1953 (Herlth)
Dormeuse, 1962 (Rabier)
Dormez, je le veux, 1998 (Vierny)
Dornröschen, 1922 (Reiniger)
Dorothea, 1974 (Sarde)
Dorothea Angermann, 1958 (Herlth)
Dorothea Tanning, ou le regard ébloui, 1960 (Delerue)
Dorotheas Rache, 1974 (Carrière)
Dorothy Vernon of Haddon Hall, 1924 (Grot; Rosher)
Dorothys Bekenntnis, 1921 (Kolowrat-Krakowsky)
Dorothy's Confession. See Dorothys Bekenntnis, 1921
Dos tipos de cuidado, 1952 (Figueroa)
Doshaburi, 1957 (Takemitsu)
Dossier noir, 1955 (Spaak)
Dot and the Line, 1965 (Jones)
Dotknięcie nocy, 1960 (ścibor-Rylski)
Dots, 1939-41 (McClaren)
Dottie Gets Spanked, 1993 (Schamus; Vachon)
Double. See Kagemusha, 1980
Double Blind. See No Sex Last Night, 1996
Double Chaser, 1942 (Blanc; Stalling)
Double Confession, 1950 (Unsworth)
Double crime sur la ligne Maginot, 1937 (Fradetal)
Double Cross Roads, 1930 (August; Fox)
Double Crossed. See Cash Parrish's Pal, 1915
Double Dealing, 1923 (Laemmle)
Double Deception. See Magiciennes, 1960
Double Dynamite, 1951 (Cahn)
Double Harness, 1933 (Cooper; Macgowan; Plunkett; Steiner)
Double Indemnity, 1944 (Dreier; Head; Pereira; Rozsa; Seitz)
Double Jeopardy, 1970 (Grusin)
Double Life, 1944 (Horner)
Double Life, 1947 (Kanin; Krasner; Rozsa)
Double Life, 1948 (Banton; Parrish)
Double Life of Veronique. See Double vie de Véronique, 1991
Double or Mutton, 1955 (Blanc; Jones)
Double or Nothing, 1937 (Head; Lederer; Struss; Young)
Double Pursuit, 1948 (Rank)
Double Reward, 1912 (Ince)
Double Suicide. See Shinju ten no amijima, 1969
Double Suicide of Sonezaki. See Sonezaki shinjuh, 1981
Double tour, 1959 (Evein; Gégauff; Hakim; Rabier; Saulnier)
Double Trouble, 1915 (Loos)
Double Trouble, 1966 (Winkler)
Double Up, 1943 (Metty)
Double vie de Véronique, 1991 (Preisner)
Double Wedding, 1937 (Adrian; Daniels; Swerling)
Double Whoopee, 1929 (Roach)
Douce, 1943 (Aurenche and Bost)
Douceur du village, 1963 (Braunberger)
Dough for the Do-Do, 1949 (B;anc; Stalling)
Dough Ray Me-ow, 1948 (Blanc; Stalling)
Doughboys, 1930 (Gibbons)
Doughgirls, 1944 (Deutsch; Haller)
Doulos, 1963 (Ponti; de Beauregard)
Douze heures de bonheur, 1952 (Evein)
Douze heures d'horloge, 1959 (Alekan)
Douze Travaux d'Hercule, 1910 (Cohl)
Dove, 1927 (Menzies; Schenck)
Dove, 1974 (Barry; Nykvist)
Dov'è la libertà?, 1953 (Delli Colli; de Laurentiis; Flaiano and Pinelli)

Dove siete' Io sono qui, 1993 (Donaggio)
Dove vai in vacanza?, 1978 (Morricone)
Dover Boys, 1942 (Blanc; Jones; Stalling)
Dover Road. See Little Adventuress, 1927
Dover Road. See Where Sinners Meet, 1934
Dovolená s andelem, 1952 (Stallich)
Down a Long Way, 1954 (Halas and Batchelor)
Down among the Sheltering Palms, 1952 (Lemaire; Shamroy)
Down among the Sugar Cane, 1932 (Fleischer)
Down and Dirty. See Brutti, sporchi, cattivi, 1976
Down and Out, 1922 (Roach)
Down and Out in Beverly Hills , 1986 (McAlpine)
Down Argentine Way, 1940 (Banton; Day; Rennahan; Shamroy; Zanuck)
Down by Law, 1986 (Müller)
Down by the Old Mill Stream, 1933 (Fleischer)
Down on the Levee, 1933 (Terry)
Down the Ancient Stairs. See Per le antiche scale, 1975
Down the River, 1951 (Fleischer)
Down the Stretch, 1926 (Laemmle)
Down to Earth, 1917 (Loos)
Down to Earth, 1947 (Cohn; Cole; Duning; Goosson; Louis; Maté)
Down to Earth. See Casa de Lava, 1994
Down to the Cellar. See Do pivnice, 1982
Down to the Sea in Ships, 1949 (Lemaire; Newman; Spencer; Wheeler)
Down to Their Last Yacht, 1934 (Cronjager; Dunn; Plunkett; Steiner)
Down Twisted, 1987 (Golan and Globus)
Down with Cats, 1943 (Terry)
Downbeat Bear, 1956 (Hanna and Barbera)
Downey Girl. See Dunungen, 1919
Downhearted Duckling, 1954 (Hanna and Barbera)
Downhill, 1927 (Balcon)
Downhill Racer, 1969 (Head)
Downstairs, 1932 (Rosson)
Downy Girl. See Dunungen, 1941
Dracula, 1931 (Freund; Laemmle; Pierce)
Dracula, 1958 (Bernard; Carreras)
Dracula, 1973 (Morris)
Dracula, 1979 (Mirisch; Whitlock; Williams)
Dracula A.D. 1972, 1972 (Carreras)
Dracula cerca sangue di vergine e . . . mori di sete!!!, 1974 (Ponti)
Dracula Has Risen from the Grave, 1968 (Bernard; Carreras; Francis)
Dracula—Prince of Darkness, 1965 (Bernard; Carreras)
Dracula's Daughter, 1936 (D'Agostino)
Draft Horse, 1942 (Blanc; Jones; Stalling)
Draftee Daffy, 1945 (Blanc; Clampett; Stalling)
Drag, 1929 (Haller)
Drag-a-long Droopy, 1953 (Avery)
Drag Net, 1928 (Mankiewicz; Rosson)
Dragées au poivre, 1963 (Decaë)
Drageurs, 1959 (Jarre)
Dragnet, 1928 (Dreier; Furthman)
Dragnet, 1987 (Boyle; Rozsa)
Dragon de Komodo, 1958 (Delerue)
Dragon Murder Case, 1934 (Blanke; Gaudio; Orry-Kelly)
Dragon Seed, 1944 (Berman; Stothart; Wheeler)
Dragonerliebchen, 1928 (Reisch)
Dragon's Gold, 1953 (Cortez)
Dragonslayer, 1981 (Murch; Muren; North; Ralston; Walas)
Dragonwyck, 1946 (Miller; Newman; Spencer; Wheeler; Zanuck)
Dragoon Wells Massacre, 1957 (Clothier)
Dragueurs, 1959 (Douy)
Drahé tety a já, 1974 (Ondříček)
Drahoušek Klementýna, 1959 (Brdečka)
Drake of England, 1935 (Neame)
Drama of Jealousy and Other Things. See Dramma della gelosia, tutti i particolari in cronaca, 1970

Duchesse de Langeais, 1994 (Carrière)
Duck Amuck, 1953 (Blanc; Jones; Stalling)
Duck Doctor, 1952 (Hanna and Barbera)
Duck Dodgers in the 241/2th Century, 1953 (Blanc; Jones; Stalling)
Duck Fever, 1955 (Terry)
Duck Hunt, 1937 (Lantz)
Duck! Rabbit! Duck, 1953 (Blanc; Jones; Stalling)Duck Soup to Nuts, 1944 (Blanc; Stalling)
Duck Soup, 1927 (Roach)
Duck Soup, 1933 (Dreier; Head; Mankiewicz; Zukor)
Duck, You Sucker!. *See* Giù la testa, 1972
Ducking the Devil, 1957 (Blanc; McKimson)
Ducksters, 1950 (Blanc; Jones; Stalling)
Ducktators, 1942 (Blanc; Stalling)
Duckweed Story. *See* Ukigusa, 1959
Dude and the Burglar, 1903 (Bitzer)
Dude Goes West, 1948 (Struss; Tiomkin)
Dudes Are Pretty People, 1942 (Roach)
Due lettere anonime, 1944 (Ponti)
Due mogli sono troppe, 1951 (Cecchi D'Amico; Rota)
Due notte con Cleopatra, 1954 (Struss)
Due occhi diabolici, 1990 (Savini)
Due orfanelle, 1954 (Rota)
Due soldi di speranza, 1951 (Rota)
Due vite di Mattia Pascal, 1985 (Cecchi D'Amico; Morricone)
Ducl, 1939 (Matras)
Duel. *See* Poyedinok, 1945
Duel in the Sun, 1946 (Basevi; Garmes; Menzies; Plunkett; Rennahan; Rosson; Selznick; Tiomkin)
Duel Personality, 1966 (Jones)
Duellists, 1977 (Biddle; Puttnam)
Duelo en las montañas, 1949 (Figueroa)
Dueña y señora, 1948 (Figueroa)
Duet for One, 1986 (Golan and Globus)
Duffy, 1968 (Heller; Parrish)
Duffy of San Quentin, 1954 (Alton)
Duffy's Tavern, 1945 (Dreier; Head; van Heusen)
Duke for a Day, 1934 (Roach)
Duke Steps Out, 1929 (Gibbons)
Duke Wore Jeans, 1958 (Heller)
Duke's Plan, 1909 (Bitzer)
Dukhiyari, 1937 (Biswas)
Dulcimer Street, 1948 (Rank)
Dulcy, 1923 (Loos; Sullivan)
Dulcy, 1940 (Kaper)
Dum no předmestí, 1933 (Stallich)
Dumb-Bells, 1922 (Roach)
Dumb Cluck, 1937 (Lantz)
Dumb Daddies, 1928 (Roach)
Dumb Dicks, 1986 (Golan and Globus)
Dumb Girl of Portici, 1916 (Rosher)
Dumb-Hounded, 1942 (Avery)
Dumb Patrol, 1964 (Blanc)
Dumb Waiter, 1928 (Hornbeck)
Dumb Waiter, 1987 (Pinter)
Dumbconscious Mind, 1942 (Fleischer; Hubley)
Dumbo, 1941 (Disney)
Dummkopf, 1920 (Mayer)
Dummy, 1929 (Mankiewicz)
Dummy Owner, 1938 (Metty)
Dunbarton Bridge, 1999 (Murch)
Dune, 1984 (de Laurentiis; Francis; Whitlock)
Dune, 2000 (Storaro)
Dungeon. *See* Scarf, 1951
Dunkirk, 1958 (Arnold)
Dunoyer de Segonzac, 1965 (Braunberger)

Dunungen, 1920 (Jaenzon; Magnusson)
Dunungen, 1941 (Fischer)
Duped Journalist. *See* A becsapott újságíró, 1914
Duplizität der Ereignisse, 1919 (Dreier)
Dupont-Barbès, 1951 (Kosma)
Durand of the Badlands, 1925 (Fox)
Durango, 1999 (Bernstein)
Durch Verrat zum Sieg, 1914 (Kolowrat-Krakowsky)
During the Roundup, 1913 (Bitzer)
Dusk to Dawn, 1922 (Barnes)
Dust Be My Destiny, 1939 (Haskin; Howe; Steiner)
Dustbin Parade, 1941 (Halas and Batchelor)
Dusty and Sweets McGee, 1970 (Fraker)
Dusty Ermine, 1937 (Courant)
Dutch Treat, 1930 (Terry)
Dutch Treat, 1987 (Golan and Globus)
Dutchman, 1966 (Barry)
Dutiful Dub, 1919 (Roach)
Duty and the Beast, 1943 (Fleischer)
Duvod k rozvodu, 1937 (Heller)
Duxorcist, 1988 (Blanc)
Dva mrazíci, 1954 (Trnka)
Dvadzatdva neshchastia, 1930 (Enei)
Dvojí svět hotelu Pacifik, 1975 (Ondříček)
Dvye vstryechi, 1917 (Starewicz)
Dweller in the Desert. *See* Burning Sands, 1922
Dying for a Smoke, 1966 (Halas and Batchelor)
Dynamite, 1929 (Adrian; Gibbons; Macpherson; Mayer; Shearer; Stothart)
Dynamite, 1938 (Biswas)
Dynamite Allen, 1921 (Fox)
Dynamite Pass, 1950 (Musuraca)
Dynamite Smith, 1924 (Sullivan)
Dynasty: The Reunion, 1991 (Conti)

E arrivato il cavaliere, 1950 (Ponti)
É caduta una donna, 1941 (Zavattini)
E la nave va, 1983 (Cristaldi; Guerra; Rotunno)
É più facile che un cammello, 1950 (Cecchi D'Amico; Rota; Zavattini)
E primavera, 1950 (Cecchi D'Amico; Rota; Zavattini)
E.T., 1982 (Burtt; Littleton; Muren; Williams)
E1 pequino proscrito. *See* Littlest Outlaw, 1954
E1 Terrible Toreador, 1929 (Disney)
Each Dawn I Crow, 1949 (Blanc; Stalling)
Each Dawn I Die, 1939 (Edeson; Steiner)
Each for All, 1946 (Alwyn)
Eadie Was a Lady, 1945 (Guffey)
Eager Beaver, 1946 (Blanc; Jones)
Eagle, 1925 (Adrian; Barnes; Kräly; Menzies; Westmore Family)
Eagle and the Hawk, 1933 (Banton; Miller; Saunders)
Eagle and the Hawk, 1950 (Howe; Mainwaring)
Eagle Has Landed, 1976 (Schifrin)
Eagle of the Pacific. *See* Taiheizo no washi, 1953
Eagle Squadron, 1942 (Cooper; Cortez; Wanger)
Eagle with Two Heads. *See* Aigle à deux têtes, 1947
Eames Lounge Chair, 1956 (Bernstein)
Earl Carroll Sketchbook, 1946 (Cahn)
Early Bird, 1965 (Hambling)
Early Bird Dood it, 1942 (Avery)
Early Days of Communication, 1958 (Halas and Batchelor)
Early Days Out West, 1912 (Rosher)
Early to Bed, 1928 (Roach)
Early to Bed. *See* Ich bei Tag und Du bei Nacht, 1932
Early to Bet, 1951 (Blanc; McKimson; Stalling)
Early to Wed, 1926 (Fox)
Early Worm Gets the Bird, 1940 (Avery; Blanc; Stalling)
Earrings of Madame de . . . . *See* **Madame de . . .**, 1953

Ehe der Maria Braun, 1979 (Ballhaus)
Ei des Fürsten Ulrich. *See* Spitzen, 1926
Eifersucht, 1925 (Schüfftan)
Eiger Sanction, 1975 (Williams; Zanuck)
Eight-Ball Bunny, 1950 (Jones)
Eight Bells, 1935 (Walker)
Eight Men Out, 1988 (Daring)
Eighteen in the Sun. *See* Diciotteni al sole, 1962
Eighteen-Year Old Girl. *See* Osmnáctiletá, 1939
Eiland, 1966 (Müller)
Einbrecher, 1930 (Pommer)
Einbrecher im Frack,, 1919 (Kolowrat-Krakowsky)
Einbruch, 1927 (Planer)
Eindringling, 1911 (Messter)
Einsteiger, 1985 (Morricone)
Einstein Revealed, 1996 (Daring)
Einstein Theory of Relativity, 1923 (Fleischer)
Eisenstein in Mexico, 1931 (Tisse)
Ek Hi Raasta, 1939 (Biswas)
Ek Ke Baad Ek, 1960 (Burman)
Ek Naujawan, 1951 (Burman)
Ekel, 1931 (Schüfftan)
El, 1952 (Alcoriza; Figueroa)
Elbowing, 1980 (Driessen)
Eld ombord, 1923 (Jaenzon; Magnusson)
Elder Vasili Gryaznov. *See* Starets Vasili Gryaznov, 1924
Eleanor and Franklin, 1977 (Barry)
Elective Affinities. *See* Affinita elettive, 1996
Electra Glide in Blue, 1973 (Hall)
Electra, 1961 (Lassally; Theodorakis)
Electra. *See* Lektro, 1927
Electric Horseman, 1979 (Grusin; Sargent; Stark)
Electronic Mouse Trap, 1946 (Terry)
Electron's Tale, 1970 (Godfrey)
Eléna et les hommes, 1956 (Kosma; Renoir; Saulnier)
Elephant Boy, 1937 (Hornbeck; Korda)
Elephant God. *See* Joi Baba Felunath, 1978
Elephant Gun. *See* Nor Moon By Night, 1958
Elephant Man, 1980 (Francis; Previn)
Elephant Mouse, 1951 (Terry)
Elephant Never Forgets, 1935 (Fleischer)
Elephant Stampede, 1951 (Mirisch)
Elephant Walk, 1954 (Head; Pereira; Waxman)
Elephantastic, 1964 (Hanna and Barbera)
Elephantrio, 1986 (Driessen)
Elet, hal l, szerelem, 1929 (Kosma)
Elevator, 1971 (Breer)
Eleventh Commandment. *See* Jedenácté preikazání, 1935
Eleventh Hour, 1923 (Fox)
Eleventh Hour Reformation, 1914 (Ince)
Elèves-maîtres, 1958 (Braunberger)
Elf Teufel, 1927 (Reisch)
Elfrida and the Pig, 1968 (Young)
Eliette, ou instants de la vie d'une femme, 1971 (Braunberger)
Élisa, 1995 (Preisner)
Elisabeth und der Narr, 1934 (Von Harbou)
Elisir d'amore, 1939 (Reiniger)
"Elite" Group. *See* Race des "Seigneurs", 1976
Eliza on the Ice, 1944 (Terry)
Eliza Runs Again, 1938 (Terry)
Elizabeth of England. *See* Drake of England, 1935
Elizabeth of Ladymead, 1948 (Wilcox)
Eliza's Horoscope, 1971 (Lourié)
Elle boit pas, elle fume pas, elle drague pas, mais . . . elle cause!, 1970 (D'Eaubonne)
Elle court, elle court, la banlieu, 1973 (Braunberger)

Ellery Queen, 1975 (Bernstein)
Elles étaient douze femmes, 1940 (Andrejew)
Elles se marient. *See* Cage aux folles III, 1985
Elmer Gantry, 1960 (Alton; Jeakins; Previn)
Elmer the Great Dane, 1935 (Lantz)
Elmer's Candid Camera, 1940 (Blanc; Jones; Stalling)
Elmer's Pet Rabbit, 1941 (Blanc; Stalling)
Elope If You Must, 1922 (Fox)
Elopement, 1907 (Bitzer)
Elopement, 1951 (La Shelle; Lemaire)
Eloping with Auntie, 1909 (Bitzer)
Elusive Corporal. *See* Caporal epinglé, 1962
Elusive Pimpernel, 1950 (Challis; Francis; Heckroth)
Elvira, Mistress of the Dark, 1988 (Edlund)
Elvis—That's the Way It Is, 1970 (Ballard)
Embajador, 1949 (Figueroa)
Embarrassing Moments, 1930 (Laemmle)
Embarrassing Moments, 1934 (Mandell)
Embassy, 1972 (Coutard)
Embezzler, 1914 (Ince)
Emerald Forest, 1984 (Rousselot)
Emergency Call, 1933 (Mandell; Plunkett; Polglase; Steiner)
Emergency Squad, 1940 (Dreier; Head)
Emergency Wedding, 1950 (Guffey)
Emigrante, 1939 (Alekan; Aurenche and Bost; Mnouchkine; Schüfftan)
Emigrants, 1971 (Lundgren)
Emil and the Detectives, 1935 (Kästner)
Emil and the Detectives, 1964 (Disney)
Emil und die Detektive, 1954 (Kästner)
Emilie Högqvist, 1939 (Fischer; Jacnzon)
Emily. *See* Americanization of Emily, 1964
Eminent Domain, 1991 (Preisner)
Emma, 1932 (Adrian; Marion)
Emmanuelle, 1974 (Lai)
Emmanuelle II: L'Anti-vierge, 1975 (Lai)
Emmerdeur, 1973 (Coutard; Mnouchkine)
Emperor Jones, 1933 (Haller)
Emperor Joseph II. *See* Kaiser Joseph II, 1912
Emperor of the North, 1973 (Biroc)
Emperor of the North Pole, 1973 (Smith)
Emperor Waltz, 1948 (Barnes; Brackett; Dreier; Edouart; Head; van Heusen; Young)
Emperor's Baker and the Baker's Emperor. *See* Císařuv pekař a pekařuc císař, 1951
Emperor's Candlesticks, 1937 (Gibbons; Rosson; Waxman)
Emperor's New Clothes, 1953 (Bosustow)
Emperor's New Clothes, 1987 (Golan and Globus)
Emperor's Nightingale. *See* Císařuv slavík, 1948
Empire de la nuit, 1962 (Legrand)
Empire of Passion. *See* Ai no borei, 1978
Empire of the Sun, 1987 (Marshall; Muren; Williams)
Empire Strikes Back, 1980 (Brackett; Burtt; Edlund; Menges; Muren; Ralston; Williams)
Emploi du temps, 1967 (Braunberger)
Employees Entrance, 1932 (Orry-Kelly)
Empreinte de Dieu, 1940 (Heller; Spaak)
Empty Beach, 1985 (Seale)
Empty Canvas. *See* Noia, 1963
Empty Hearts, 1924 (Haller)
Empty Socks, 1927 (Disney)
En attendant l'auto, 1970 (Braunberger)
En cas de malheur, 1958 (Aurenche and Bost; Douy; Saulnier)
En Crète sans les dieux, 1934 (Jaubert)
En djungelsaga, 1957 (Shankar)
En drömmares vandring, 1957 (Nykvist)
En effeuillant la Marguerite, 1956 (Trauner)

Entfesselte Wein. *See* Seine Hoheit, der Eintänzer, 1927
Enticement, 1925 (Ince)
Entity, 1983 (Bernstein)
Entlassung, 1942 (Wagner)
Entr'acte, 1924 (Auric; Braunberger)
Entrainement du toréro, 1968 (Braunberger)
Entraîneuse, 1938 (Spaak)
Entrapment, 1999 (Bass)
Entre la terre et le ciel, 1957 (Delerue; Rappeneau)
Entre onze heures et minuit, 1949 (Jeanson)
Entrée des artistes, 1938 (Auric; Jeanson; Matras; Trauner)
Entrega immediata, 1963 (Figueroa)
Entres angen, ur Dollarprinsessan, 1910 (Magnusson)
Envers du paradis, 1953 (Burel)
Eperon d'or, 1930 (Matras)
Episode, 1935 (Reisch; Stradling)
Epouse infernale, 1963 (Braunberger)
Epouvantail, 1921 (Starewicz)
Epouvantail, 1943 (Aurenche and Bost; Grimault)
Epoux scandaleux, 1935 (Spaak)
Equilibre, 1952 (Ibert)
Equinox, 1971 (Muren)
Equipage, 1927 (Burel)
Equipage, 1935 (Honegger; Jaubert)
Equivoque 1900, 1966 (Braunberger)
Equus, 1977 (Bennett; Canutt; Morris)
Er muß sie haben, 1917 (Kolowrat-Krakowsky)
Er oder ich. *See* Sein grösster Bluff, 1927
Er rächt seine Schwiegermutter, 1917 (Kolowrat-Krakowsky)
Er und seine Schwester, 1931 (Heller)
Era di venerdì 17, 1956 (Zavattini)
Era lui . . . sîa! sîa!, 1951 (Rota)
Eradicating Auntie, 1909 (Bitzer)
Erbe der Van Diemen, 1921 (Hoffmann)
Erdgeist, 1923 (Mayer)
Eredità Ferramonti, 1976 (Morricone)
Eric, 1975 (Grusin)
Eric Winstone Band Show, 1955 (Carreras)
Eric Winstone's Coach, 1957 (Unsworth)
Eric Winstone's Stagecoach, 1956 (Carreras)
Erin Brokovich, 2000 (Newman)
Erlebnis einer Nacht, 1929 (Warm)
Ernest Green Story, 1993 (Daring)
Ernest Hemingway's Adventures of a Young Man, 1962 (Garmes)
Ernest le rebelle, 1938 (Prévert)
Ernst Fuchs, 1976 (Lassally)
Eroe borghese, 1995 (Donaggio)
Eroe dei nostri tempi, 1955 (Cristaldi; Rota)
Eroe sono io, 1951 (Age and Scarpelli)
Eroi della domenica, 1952 (Solinas)
Eroica, 1957 (Stawiński)
Eroica, 1960 (Lassally)
Eros i Psyche, 1915 (Starewicz)
Erotikon, 1920 (Magnusson)
Erotissimo, 1968 (Braunberger)
Errand Boy, 1961 (Head; Pereira)
Erreur tragique, 1913 (Gaumont)
Ersatz, 1961 (Vukotić)
Erste Kuss, 1928 (Heller)
Erste Liebe, 1970 (Nykvist)
Erste Polka, 1978 (Ballhaus)
Erste Recht des Kindes, 1932 (Planer; Von Harbou)
Erzehog Otto und das Wäschermadel, 1930 (Heller)
Erzieherin gesucht, 1950 (Von Harbou)
Es herrscht Ruhe im Land, 1976 (Müller)
Es kommt alle Tage vor . . . , 1930 (Warm)

Es kommt ein Tag, 1950 (Von Harbou)
Es wird schon wieder besser, 1932 (Kaper; Wagner)
Escalation, 1968 (Morricone)
Escale, 1959 (Delerue)
Escale à Paris, 1951 (Decaë)
Escalier C, 1985 (Guillemot)
Escalier sans fin, 1943 (Matras; Spaak)
Escándalo, 1934 (Figueroa)
Escapade, 1935 (Kahn; Kaper; Mankiewicz; Reisch)
Escapade, 1955 (Stewart)
Escapade, 1957 (Wakhévitch)
Escapade in Japan, 1957 (Steiner)
Escape, 1914 (Bitzer)
Escape, 1926 (Laemmle)
Escape, 1930 (Dean)
Escape, 1939 (Cronjager; Day)
Escape, 1940 (Adrian; Mayer; Waxman)
Escape, 1948 (Alwyn; Dunne; Lemaire; Vetchinsky; Young)
Escape, 1971 (Schifrin)
Escape. *See* Ucieczka, 1986
Escape Artist, 1982 (Delerue; Tavoularis)
Escape at Dawn. *See* Akatsuki no dasso, 1950
Escape from Fort Bravo, 1953 (Surtees)
Escape from Japan. *See* Nihon dashutsu, 1964
Escape from L.A., 1996 (Baker)
Escape from the Planet of the Apes, 1971 (Biroc; Goldsmith; Smith)
Escape from Zahrain, 1962 (Head; Neame)
Escape in the Desert, 1945 (Burks; Deutsch)
Escape Me Never, 1935 (Périnal; Walton; Wilcox)
Escape Me Never, 1947 (Blanke; Friedhofer; Korngold; Polito)
Escape to Athena, 1979 (Schifrin)
Escape to Burma, 1955 (Alton; Jennings; Polglase)
Escape to Danger, 1943 (Alwyn)
Escape to Glory, 1940 (Irene; Planer)
Escape to Paradise, 1939 (Young)
Escape to the Sun, 1972 (Golan and Globus)
Escape to Victory. *See* Victory, 1981
Escape to Witch Mountain, 1975 (Mandel)
Escapulario, 1966 (Figueroa)
Esclave, 1953 (Auric)
Esclave blanche, 1938 (Alekan; Andrejew; Jaubert)
Escondida, 1955 (Figueroa)
Escort. *See* Mauvaise passe, 1999
Escort. *See* Scotta, 1994
Escort West, 1958 (Clothier)
Escuela de rateros, 1956 (Alcoriza)
Escuela para solteras, 1964 (Figueroa)
Escuela rural, 1960 (Almendros)
Esercito di cinque uomini, 1969 (Morricone)
Eskapade, 1936 (Von Harbou)
Eskimo, 1933 (Gillespie; Mayer)
Eskimo Limon, 1977 (Golan and Globus)
Eskimo Ohgen, 1985 (Golan and Globus)
Esmérelda, 1905 (Gaumont)
Espace vital, 1970 (Nuytten)
Especially on Sunday. *See* Domenica specialmente, 1991
Espectro de la novia, 1943 (Figueroa)
Esperanza, 1972 (Alcoriza)
Esperienza del cubismo, 1949 (Delli Colli)
Espion, 1967 (Coutard)
Espion, lève-toi, 1981 (Morricone)
Espionage, 1963 (Justin)
Espionage Agent, 1939 (Deutsch; Rosher)
Espions, 1955 (Auric; Matras)
Espoir, 1939 (Milhaud)
Espoir au village, 1950 (Cloquet)

Esqueleto de la señora Morales, 1959 (Alcoriza)
Esso, 1954 (Alexeieff and Parker)
Est-ce bien raisonnable, 1980 (Decaë)
Est charmant, 1931 (Stradling)
Est minuit, Docteur Schweitzer, 1952 (Cloquet)
Estafa de amor, 1954 (Figueroa)
Estate violenta, 1959 (Cecchi D'Amico; Serandrei)
Esther, 1910 (Gaumont)
Esther, 1962 (Eisler)
Esther, 1986 (Alekan)
Esther, 1999 (Morricone)
Esther Waters, 1948 (Rank)
Et cetera, 1966 (švankmajer)
Et mourir de plaisir, 1960 (Renoir)
Et per tetto un cielo di stelle, 1968 (Morricone)
Et quand vient le soir, 1969 (Braunberger)
Et Satan conduit le bal, 1962 (Coutard)
Et si nous buvions un coup, 1908 (Cohl)
Était une chaise. See A Chairy Tale, 1957
Était une fois, 1933 (Douy)
Etat de grace, 1986 (Sarde)
État de Siège, 1971 (Solinas; Theodorakis)
État sauvage, 1978 (Lhomme)
Etc., 1975 (Breer)
Eté dernier à Tangier, 1987 (Sarde)
Eté indien, 1957 (Braunberger)
Eté meurtrier, 1983 (Delerue)
Eternal City, 1923 (Goldwyn; Miller)
Eternal Fire. See World Window, 1937-40
Eternal Flame, 1922 (Gaudio; Goosson; Schenck)
Eternal Love, 1929 (Kräly; Schenck)
Eternal Mother, 1911 (Bitzer)
Eternal Return. See Eternel Retour, 1943
Eternal Sea, 1955 (Bernstein)
Eternal Struggle, 1923 (Mayer)
Eternal Triangle, 1922 (Terry)
Eternal Woman, 1929 (Walker)
Eternally Yours, 1939 (Banton; Irene; Spencer; Wanger)
Eternel conflit, 1947 (Barsacq; Matras; Spaak)
Eternel Retour, 1943 (Annenkov; Auric; Wakhévitch)
Eternity, 1990 (Legrand)
Eternity and a Day. See Mia aiwniothta kai mia mera, 1999
Etes-vous fiancée à un marin grec ou à un pilote de ligne?, 1970
    (Braunberger; Coutard)
Etes-vous jalouse?, 1937 (Kaufman)
Eto tyebye prinadlezit, 1917 (Starewicz)
Etoile, 1988 (de Almeida)
Etoile au soleil, 1942 (Aurenche and Bost)
Etoile de mer, 1959 (Delerue)
Etoile de mer, 1967 (Braunberger)
Etoile du nord, 1982 (Aurenche and Bost; Sarde)
Etoile du sud, 1968 (Coutard)
Etoile sans lumière, 1945 (D'Eaubonne)
Etoiles de Midi, 1959 (Jarre)Étrange aventure de Lemmy Caution. See
    Alphaville, 1965
Etrange Désir de Monsieur Bard, 1953 (Burel)
Etrange destin, 1945 (Burel)
Etrange Monsieur Victor, 1938 (Spaak)
Etrangère, 1930 (Burel; Meerson)
Etruscologia, 1961 (Storaro)
Ett glass vin, 1960 (Fischer)
Ett hemligt giftermäl, 1912 (Magnusson)
Ett kungligt äventyr, 1956 (Nykvist)
Ettaro di cielo, 1958 (Cristaldi; Di Venanzo; Flaiano and Pinelli;
    Guerra; Rota)
Ettore Scola. See Famiglia, 1987

Etudiants, 1960 (Delerue)
Euberfall in Feindesland, 1915 (Messter)
Eugene, the Jeep, 1940 (Fleischer)
Eugenia Grandet, 1946 (Gherardi)
Eugenie Grandet, 1993 (Carrière)
Eureka, 1982 (Zimmer)
Eureka Stockade, 1949 (Balcon; Rank)
Europa '51, 1952 (de Laurentiis; Ponti; Stewart)
Europa Europa. See Hitlerjunge Salomon, 1990
Europe, 1958 (Delerue)
Europe continentale avant 1900, 1969 (Braunberger)
Europe méridionale au temps des rois, 1969 (Braunberger)
Europeans, 1979 (Jhabvala; Merchant)
Eva, 1913 (Messter)
Eva, 1953 (Theodorakis)
Eva, 1962 (Hakim; Legrand)
Evadée, 1929 (Burel)
Evadés, 1954 (Kosma)
Evangelimann, 1923 (Pommer)
Evangeline, 1929 (Goosson)
Evas Töchter, 1928 (Heller)
Evasions de Bob Walter, 1916 (Cohl)
Eve, 1962 (Di Venanzo)
Eve Knew Her Apples, 1945 (Guffey)
Eve of Destruction, 1991 (Sarde)
Eve of St. Mark, 1944 (Basevi; La Shelle)
Eve sans trêve, 1963 (Braunberger)
Eveil d'un monde, 1951 (Rabier)
Eveillé du Pont de l'Alma, 1985 (Branco)
Evelyn Prentice, 1934 (Clarke)
Even Break, 1917 (August)
Even Cowgirls Get the Blues, 1993 (Henry)
Evènement le plus important depuis que l'homme a marché sur la lune,
    1973 (Evein; Legrand)
Evening Clothes, 1927 (Rosson)
Evening for Sale, 1932 (Banton)
Evening Glory of Heaven. See Ama no yugao, 1948
Evening with Diana Ross, 1977 (Winston)
Evening with the Royal Ballet, 1963 (Challis; Havelock-Allan; Unsworth)
Evenings with Jindrich Plachta. See Večery s Jindřichem Plachtou, 1954
Evensong, 1934 (Balcon; Junge; Rank)
Event Horizon, 1997 (Biddle)
Event in the Stadium. See Sluchi na stadione, 1929
Eventail animé, 1909 (Cohl)
Ever-Changing Motor Car, 1962 (Dunning)
Ever in My Heart, 1933 (Grot)
Ever Since Eve, 1921 (Fox)
Ever Since Eve, 1934 (Miller)
Ever Since Eve, 1937 (Barnes; Orry-Kelly)
Evergreen, 1934 (Balcon; Junge)
Everlasting Whisper, 1925 (Fox)
Every Day Except Christmas, 1957 (Lassally)
Every Day's a Holiday, 1938 (Carmichael; Struss)
Every Five Minutes, 1950 (Lassally)
Every Girl Should Be Married, 1948 (Sharaff)
Every Little Crook and Nanny, 1972 (Lathrop)
Every Man for Himself, 1924 (Roach)
Every Man's Wife, 1925 (Fox)
Every Minute Counts. See Count the Hours, 1953
Every Night at Eight, 1935 (Wanger)
Every Other Weekend. See Week-End sur deux, 1990
Every Saturday Night, 1936 (August)
Every Time We Say Goodbye, 1986 (Lanci, Giuseppe ("beppe"); Sarde)
Every Woman's Man. See Prizefighter and the Lady, 1933
Everybody Dance, 1936 (Balcon; Rank; Vetchinsky)
Everybody Does It, 1949 (Johnson; La Shelle; Lemaire; Newman)

Everybody Go Home!. *See* Tutti a casa, 1960

Everybody Sing, 1938 (Edens; Kahn; Kaper; Ruttenberg)

Everybody Sings, 1937 (Lantz)

Everybody Works but Father, 1905 (Bitzer)

Everybody's All American, 1988 (Smith; van Runkle)

Everybody's Cheering. *See* Take Me Out to the Ballgame, 1948

Everybody's Doing It, 1938 (Musuraca)

Everybody's Fine. *See* Stanno tutti bene, 1990

Everyday. *See* Ich dzień powszedni, 1963

Everyman's Woman. *See* Jedermanns Weib, 1924

Everyone Says I Love You, 1996 (Loquasto)

Everyone's Dancing the Tango in Russia. *See* Vsyak na Russi i tango tantzuyet, 1914

Everything for Sale, 1921 (Howe; Rosson)

Everything Happens at Night, 1939 (Cronjager; Day)

Everything I Have Is Yours, 1953 (Mercer)

Everything Is Thunder, 1936 (Balcon; Junge; Rank)

Everything's on Ice, 1939 (Metty)

Everything's Rosie, 1931 (Bruckman; Musuraca)

Eve's Daughters. *See* Dcery Eviny, 1928

Eves futures, 1963 (Delerue)

Eve's Leaves, 1926 (Miller)

Eve's Love Letters, 1927 (Roach)

Evidence in Camera. *See* Headline Shooter, 1933

Evidence of Blood, 1998 (Daring)

Evil Dead 3. *See* Army of Darkness, 1993

Evil Eden. *See* Mort en ce jardin, 1956

Evil Mind. *See* Clairvoyant, 1935

Evil of Frankenstein, 1964 (Carreras; Francis)

Evil Under the Sun, 1981 (Challis)

Evils of Chinatown. *See* Confessions of an Opium Eater, 1962

Evita, 1996 (Hambling)

Evita Peron, 1981 (Mandel)

Evitez le désordre, 1949 (Decaë)

Evolution, 1925 (Fleischer)

Ewige Fluch, 1921 (Warm)

Ewige Nacht, 1914 (Freund; Kräly)

Ewige Spiel, 1951 (Warm)

Ex-Bad Boy, 1931 (Loos)

Ex-Lady, 1933 (Gaudio; Orry-Kelly; Riskin)

Ex-Mrs. Bradford, 1936 (Polglase; Veiller)

Exalted Flapper, 1929 (Clarke; Fox)

Examen de minuit, 1998 (Branco)

Examination Day at School, 1910 (Bitzer)

Excellensen, 1944 (Lundgren)

Excess Baggage, 1928 (Day; Gibbons; Marion)

Exchange of Wives, 1925 (Gibbons)

Excitement, 1924 (Laemmle)

Exciters, 1923 (Levien)

Exclusive, 1937 (Head)

Exclusive Story, 1935 (Gillespie)

Excuse Me, 1925 (Gibbons; Mayer)

Excuse My Dust, 1951 (Pan; Rose)

Excuse My Glove, 1925 (Roach)

Exécution à quatre voix. *See* Wunkanal Hinrichtung fur vier Stimmen, 1984

Exécution, 1960 (Cloquet)

Execution capitale à Berlin, 1897 (Pathé)

Executive Action, 1973 (Trumbo)

Executive Decision, 1996 (Goldsmith)

Executive Suite, 1954 (Gibbons; Houseman; Lehman; Rose)

Exemple Etretat, 1962 (Braunberger; Delerue)

Exercice du pouvoir, 1977 (Nuytten)

Exile, 1917 (Carré)

Exile, 1947 (Planer)

Exiles. *See* De landsflyktiga, 1921

Exit Smiling, 1926 (Gibbons)

Exodus, 1960 (Bass; Day; Trumbo)

Exorcist, 1973 (Baker; Nitzsche; Smith)

Exorcist II: The Heretic, 1977 (Fisher; Fraker; Morricone; Smith; Whitlock)

Exorcist III, 1988 (Fisher)

Expedition. *See* Abhijan, 1962

Experience, 1921 (Miller)

Experience Preferred But Not Essential, 1982 (Puttnam)

Experiment in Terror, 1962 (Lathrop; Mancini)

Experiment Perilous, 1944 (Dunn; Gaudio)

Experimental Animation: Peanut Vendor, 1933 (Lye)

Experts, 1989 (Hamlisch)

Expert's Opinion, 1935 (Havelock-Allan)

Expiation, 1909 (Bitzer)

Exploits de Farfadet, 1916 (Cohl)

Exploits de feu-follet, 1912 (Cohl)

Exploits d'un jeune Don Juan, 1987 (Carrière; Mnouchkine; Morricone; Saulnier)

Explorers, 1986 (Goldsmith)

Explosion, 1971 (Coutard)

Explosive Generation, 1961 (Crosby)

Explosive Mr Magoo, 1958 (Bosustow)

Exposed, 1938 (Cortez)

Exposed, 1983 (Decaë; Delerue)

Exposition 1900, 1967 (Braunberger)

Exposition de Caricatures. *See* Unforeseen Metamorphosis, 1913-14

Exposition Française à Moscou, 1962 (Delerue)

Express Sedan. *See* Sutobi kago, 1952

Exquisite Sinner, 1926 (Gibbons)

Extase, 1932 (Stallich)

Exterminating Angel. *See* Angel exterminador, 1962

Exterminator, 1945 (Terry)

Exterminator, 1980 (Winston)

Exterminator 1, 1984 (Golan and Globus)

Extra Girl, 1923 (Hornbeck)

Extraconiugale, 1964 (Delli Colli)

Extraordinaires Exercices de la famille Coeur-de-Bois, 1912 (Cohl)

Extraordinary Adventures of Baron Muenchhausen. *See* Baron Munchhausen,, 1943

Extraordinary Seaman, 1968 (Jarre)

Extravagante Mission, 1945 (Renoir)

Extreme Measures, 1996 (Elfman)

Extreme Prejudice, 1987 (Goldsmith)

Eye for an Eye, 1918 (Mathis)

Eye for an Eye, 1966 (Ballard)

Eye for an Eye. *See* Oeil pour oeil, 1956

Eye of the Cat, 1969 (Head; Metty; Schifrin)

Eye of the Devil, 1967 (Southern)

Eye of the Needle, 1980 (Rozsa)

Eye of the Night, 1916 (Sullivan)

Eye on Emily, 1964 (Kanin)

Eye Witness. *See* Your Witness, 1950

Eyes Are Upon You, 1997 (Savini)

Eyes in the Night, 1942 (Schary)

Eyes of a Stranger, 1981 (Savini)

Eyes of Asia. *See* Os Olhos da Ásia, 1996

Eyes of Hell. *See* Mask, 1961

Eyes of Laura Mars, 1978 (Justin)

Eyes of the Forest, 1923 (Fox)

Eyes of the Mummy. *See* Augen der Mummie Mâ, 1918

Eyes of Youth, 1919 (Edeson)

Eyes, the Mouth. *See* Occhi, la bocca, 1982

Eyewash, 1959 (Breer)

Eyewitness, 1956 (Rank)

Eygalières, commune de France, 1957 (Braunberger)

Fascist. *See* Federale, 1961
Fashion, 1960 (Kuri)
Fashion Follies of 1934. *See* Fashions of 1934, 1934
Fashions for Men. *See* Fine Clothes, 1925
Fashions for Women, 1927 (Furthman; Mankiewicz)
Fashions in Love, 1929 (Cronjager)
Fashions of 1934, 1934 (Blanke; Orry-Kelly)
Fassbinder Produces Film No. 8, 1970 (Ballhaus)
Fast and Furious, 1927 (Laemmle)
Fast and Furry-ous, 1949 (Blanc; Jones; Stalling)
Fast and Loose, 1930 (Banton)
Fast and Loose, 1954 (Rank)
Fast and Sexy, 1958 (Rotunno)
Fast and the Furious, 1954 (Crosby)
Fast Black, 1924 (Roach)
Fast Buck Duck, 1963 (Blanc; McKimson)
Fast Companions, 1932 (Edeson)
Fast Company, 1924 (Roach)
Fast Company, 1929 (Cronjager; Selznick)
Fast Forward, 1985 (Jones)
Fast Mail, 1922 (Fox)
Fast-Walking, 1982 (Schifrin)
Fast Work, 1930 (Roach)
Fast Worker, 1924 (Laemmle)
Fast Workers, 1933 (Brown)
Fastest Gun Alive, 1956 (Plunkett; Previn)
Fastest with the Mostest, 1960 (Blanc; Jones)
Fat City, 1972 (Booth; Hall; Hamlisch; Jeakins; Stark; Sylbert)
Fat Man and Little Boy, 1989 (Morricone; Zsigmond)
Fatal Attraction, 1987 (Jarre; Lansing)
Fatal Dress Suit, 1914 (Loos)
Fatal Finger Prints, 1915 (Loos)
Fatal Glass of Beer, 1933 (Bruckman)
Fatal Hour, 1937 (Havelock-Allan)
Fatal Lady, 1936 (Shamroy; Wanger; Young)
Fatale, 1992 (
Fatale, 1993 (Biziou; Preisner)
Fatalità, 1947 (Amidei)
Fate, 1912 (Bitzer)
Fate, 1966 (Cecchi D'Amico; Gherardi; Guerra)
Fate, 1992 (Legrand)
Fate Is the Hunter, 1964 (Goldsmith; Krasner; Smith)
Fate's Fathead, 1934 (Roach)
Fate's Interception, 1912 (Bitzer)
Fate's Turning, 1910 (Bitzer)
Father at 21. *See* Nijuissa no chichi, 1964
Father Brown, 1954 (Auric; Mathieson)
Father Brown, Detective, 1934 (Head; Sullivan; Zukor)
Father Buys a Ladder, 1907 (Gaumont)
Father Gets in the Game, 1908 (Bitzer)
Father Goose, 1964 (Bumstead; Fraker; Lang)
Father Is a Bachelor, 1950 (Guffey)
Father Is a Prince, 1940 (McCord)
Father of Hell Town, 1985 (Biroc)
Father of the Bride, 1950 (Alton; Berman; Deutsch; Goodrich and Hackett; Mayer; Plunkett; Rose)
Father of the Bride Part II, 1995 (Fraker)
Father Panchali. *See* **Pather Panchali**, 1955
Father-Son Falcons. *See* Chichiko-daka, 1956
Father Vojtech. *See* Páter Vojtech, 1929
Fatherland—Singing the Blues in Red, 1986 (Menges)
Fathers and Sons. *See* Padri e figli . . . , 1957
Father's Little Dividend, 1951 (Alton; Berman; Goodrich and Hackett; Rose)
Father's Son, 1930 (Miller)
Father's Wild Game, 1950 (Struss)

Fattened for the Market, 1901 (Bitzer)
Fatti di gente perbene, 1974 (Morricone)
Fatty Finn, 1980 (Seale)
Faubourg St. Martin, 1985 (Branco)
Faun, 1917 (Korda)
Fause Alerte, 1940 (Lourié)
Fausse Maitresse, 1942 (Andrejew)
Faust, 1907 (Pathé)
Faust, 1926 (Annenkov; Herlth; Hoffmann; Pommer; Röhrig)
Faust, 1958 (švankmajer)
Faust des Riesen, 1917 (Messter)
Faustine et le bel été, 1971 (Cloquet)
Faustrecht der Freiheit, 1975 (Ballhaus)
Faut ce qu'il faut, 1940 (Wakhévitch)
Faut-il les marier?, 1932 (Heller)
Faut pas prendre les enfants du Bon Dieu pour des canards sauvages, 1968 (D'Eaubonne)
Faut-pas rire au bonheur, 1994 (Coutard)
Faut réparer Sophie, 1933 (Trauner)
Faut tuer Birgitt Haas, 1981 (Sarde)
Faute de l'Abbé Mouret, 1970 (Fradetal)
Faute des autres, 1953 (Guillemot)
Faute d'orthographie, 1919 (Gaumont)
Fauteuil 47. *See* Parkettsessel 47, 1926
Faux et usage de faux, 1990 (Sarde)
Faux Magistrat, 1914 (Gaumont)
Faux monnayeurs. *See* Farinet, oder das falsche Geld, 1939
Favor, 1994 (Newman)
Favorit der Königin, 1922 (Planer)
Favorite Son, 1913 (Ince)
Favorite Son. *See* Fils préféré, 1994
Fawn. *See* Zhityel nyeobitayemovo ostrava, 1915
Fazil, 1928 (Fox; Miller)
FBI Code 98, 1964 (Steiner)
FBI Story, 1959 (Biroc; Steiner)
Fe, esperanza y caridad, 1979 (Alcoriza)
Fear, 1989 (Mancini)
Fear, 1996 (Burwell)
Fear. *See* Angst, 1954
Fear in the Night, 1972 (Carreras)
Fear No Evil, 1991 (Ballhaus)
Fear No More, 1961 (Haller)
Fear o' God. *See* Mountain Eagle, 1926
Fear on Trial, 1975 (Houseman)
Fear Strikes Out, 1957 (Bernstein; Head; Pereira)
Fearless Fagan, 1952 (Lederer)
Fearless Little Soldier. *See* Fanfan la Tulipe, 1952
Fearless Rider, 1928 (Laemmle)
Fearless, 1993 (Jarre)
Fearless Vampire Killers, or Pardon Me, But Your Teeth Are in My Neck, 1967 (Godfrey)
Feast at Zhirmunka. *See* Pir v Girmunka, 1941
Feast of July, 1995 (Merchant; Preisner)
Feast of Life, 1916 (Marion)
Feather & Father Gang. *See* Never Con a Killer, 1977
Feather Bluster, 1958 (Blanc; McKimson; Stalling)
Feather Dusted, 1955 (Blanc; McKimson)
Feather Finger, 1966 (Blanc; McKimson)
Feather in Her Hat, 1935 (Walker)
Feather in His Hare, 1946 (Blanc; Jones)
Feather Your Nest, 1937 (Dean; Neame)
Featherweight Champ, 1953 (Terry)
Febbre di vivere, 1953 (Cecchi D'Amico)
Federal Bullets, 1937 (Brown)
Federal Operator 99, 1945 (Canutt)
Federale, 1961 (Morricone)

Federico Fellini's Intervista, 1987 (Rota)
Fedora, 1978 (Diamond; Fisher; Rozsa; Trauner)
Fedora. *See* Fehér éjszakák, 1916
Fée aux choux. *See* Sage-femme de première classe, 1902
Fee Fie Foes, 1961 (Hanna and Barbera)
Feed 'em and Weep, 1929 (Roach)
Feed the Kitty, 1952 (Blanc; Jones; Stalling)
Feeder de l'est. *See* Chaleur du foyer, 1955
Feedin' the Kiddie, 1957 (Hanna and Barbera)
Feenhände , 1912 (Messter)
Feet First, 1930 (Bruckman; Zukor)
Fehér éjszakák, 1916 (Korda)
Fehér Rosza, 1919 (Korda)
Feinde, 1940 (Wagner)
Feldgraue Krone, 1917 (Kolowrat-Krakowsky)
Félicie Nanteuil, 1942 (Ibert)
Felicità perduta, 1946 (Delli Colli)
Feline Follies, 1919 (Messmer)
Feline Frame-Up, 1954 (Blanc; Jones; Stalling)
Félins, 1964 (Decaë; Schifrin)
Felix All at Sea, 1922 (Messmer)
Felix All Balled Up, 1924 (Messmer)
Felix All Puzzled, 1925 (Messmer)
Felix at the Fair, 1922 (Messmer)
Felix Baffled By Banjos, 1924 (Messmer)
Felix Brings Home the Bacon, 1924 (Messmer)
Felix Calms His Conscience, 1923 (Messmer)
Felix Crosses the Crooks, 1924 (Messmer)
Felix Dopes It Out, 1924 (Messmer)
Felix Fans the Flames, 1926 (Messmer)
Felix Fills a Shortage, 1923 (Messmer)
Felix Finds a Way, 1922 (Messmer)
Felix Finds Out, 1924 (Messmer)
Felix Finishes First, 1924 (Messmer)
Felix Follows the Swallows, 1925 (Messmer)
Felix, Friend in Need, 1924 (Messmer)
Felix Gets Broadcasted, 1923 (Messmer)
Felix Gets It Wrong, 1916 (Messmer)
Felix Gets Left, 1922 (Messmer)
Felix Gets Revenge, 1922 (Messmer)
Felix Gets the Can, 1924 (Messmer)
Felix Goes A-Hunting, 1923 (Messmer)
Felix Goes Hungry, 1924 (Messmer)
Felix Goes West, 1924 (Messmer)
Felix Hits the Hipps, 1924 (Messmer)
Felix in Fairyland, 1923 (Messmer)
Felix in Hollywood, 1923 (Messmer)
Felix in Love, 1922 (Messmer)
Felix in Love, 1930 (Messmer)
Felix in the Bone Age, 1922 (Messmer)
Felix in the Swim, 1922 (Messmer)
Felix Laughs Last, 1923 (Messmer)
Felix Lends a Hand, 1922 (Messmer)
Felix Loses Out, 1924 (Messmer)
Felix Makes Good, 1922 (Messmer)
Felix Minds the Kid, 1922 (Messmer)
Felix on the Job, 1916 (Messmer)
Felix on the Trail, 1922 (Messmer)
Felix Out of Luck, 1924 (Messmer)
Felix Punches the Pole, 1924 (Messmer)
Felix Puts It Over, 1924 (Messmer)
Felix Rests in Peace, 1925 (Messmer)
Felix Revolts, 1923 (Messmer)
Felix Saves the Day, 1922 (Messmer)
Felix Scoots through Scotland, 1926 (Messmer)
Felix Strikes It Rich, 1923 (Messmer)

Felix the Cat and the Goose That Laid the Golden Egg, 1936 (Messmer)
Felix the Cat as Romeeow, 1927 (Messmer)
Felix the Cat Behind in Front, 1927 (Messmer)
Felix the Cat Braves the Briny, 1926 (Messmer)
Felix the Cat Busts a Bubble, 1926 (Messmer)
Felix the Cat Busts into Business, 1925 (Messmer)
Felix the Cat Collars the Button, 1926 (Messmer)
Felix the Cat Dines and Pines, 1927 (Messmer)
Felix the Cat Ducks His Duty, 1927 (Messmer)
Felix the Cat Flirts with Fate, 1926 (Messmer)
Felix the Cat Hits the Deck, 1927 (Messmer)
Felix the Cat Hunts the Hunter, 1926 (Messmer)
Felix the Cat in A Tale of Two Kitties, 1926 (Messmer)
Felix the Cat in April Maze, 1930 (Messmer)
Felix the Cat in Arabiantics, 1928 (Messmer)
Felix the Cat in Art for Hearts Sake, 1927 (Messmer)
Felix the Cat in Astronomeows, 1928 (Messmer)
Felix the Cat in At the Rainbows End, 1925 (Messmer)
Felix the Cat in Barn Yarns, 1927 (Messmer)
Felix the Cat in Blunderland, 1926 (Messmer)
Felix the Cat in Comicalamitics, 1928 (Messmer)
Felix the Cat in Daze and Knights, 1927 (Messmer)
Felix the Cat in Dough-Nutty, 1927 (Messmer)
Felix the Cat in Draggin' the Dragon, 1928 (Messmer)
Felix the Cat in Eats Are West, 1925 (Messmer)
Felix the Cat in Eskimotive, 1928 (Messmer)
Felix the Cat in Eye Jinks, 1927 (Messmer)
Felix the Cat in False Vases, 1930 (Messmer)
Felix the Cat in Film Flam Films, 1927 (Messmer)
Felix the Cat in Forty Winks, 1930 (Messmer)
Felix the Cat in Futuritzy, 1928 (Messmer)
Felix the Cat in Germ Mania, 1927 (Messmer)
Felix the Cat in Gym Gems, 1926 (Messmer)
Felix the Cat in Icy Eyes, 1927 (Messmer)
Felix the Cat in In and Out-Laws, 1928 (Messmer)
Felix the Cat in Japanicky, 1928 (Messmer)
Felix the Cat in Jungle Bungles, 1928 (Messmer)
Felix the Cat in Land O'Fancy, 1926 (Messmer)
Felix the Cat in No Fuelin', 1927 (Messmer)
Felix the Cat in Oceanantics, 1930 (Messmer)
Felix the Cat in Ohm Sweet Ohm, 1928 (Messmer)
Felix the Cat in Outdoor Indore, 1928 (Messmer)
Felix the Cat in Pedigreedy, 1927 (Messmer)
Felix the Cat in Polly-tics, 1928 (Messmer)
Felix the Cat in "Loco" Motive, 1927 (Messmer)
Felix the Cat in Reverse English, 1926 (Messmer)
Felix the Cat in Sax Appeal, 1927 (Messmer)
Felix the Cat in School Daze, 1926 (Messmer)
Felix the Cat in Scrambled Eggs, 1926 (Messmer)
Felix the Cat in Skulls and Sculls, 1930 (Messmer)
Felix the Cat in Stars and Stripes, 1927 (Messmer)
Felix the Cat in Sure-Locked Homes, 1928 (Messmer)
Felix the Cat in Tee-Time, 1930 (Messmer)
Felix the Cat in the Cold, 1925 (Messmer)
Felix the Cat in the Last Life, 1928 (Messmer)
Felix the Cat in The Non-Stop Fright, 1927 (Messmer)
Felix the Cat in the Oily Bird, 1928 (Messmer)
Felix the Cat in the Smoke Scream, 1928 (Messmer)
Felix the Cat in the Travel-Hog, 1927 (Messmer)
Felix the Cat in Two Lips Time, 1926 (Messmer)
Felix the Cat in Uncle Tom's Crabbin', 1927 (Messmer)
Felix the Cat in Whys and Otherwhys, 1927 (Messmer)
Felix the Cat in Wise Guise, 1927 (Messmer)
Felix the Cat in Zoo Logic, 1926 (Messmer)
Felix the Cat, Jack of All Trades, 1927 (Messmer)
Felix the Cat Kept Walking, 1925 (Messmer)

Felix the Cat Laughs It Off, 1926 (Messmer)
Felix the Cat Misses His Swiss, 1926 (Messmer)
Felix the Cat Misses the Cue, 1926 (Messmer)
Felix the Cat on the Farm, 1925 (Messmer)
Felix the Cat on the Job, 1925 (Messmer)
Felix the Cat Rings the Ringer, 1926 (Messmer)
Felix the Cat Seeks Solitude, 1926 (Messmer)
Felix the Cat Sees 'Em in Season, 1927 (Messmer)
Felix the Cat Shatters the Sheik, 1926 (Messmer)
Felix the Cat Spots the Spooks, 1926 (Messmer)
Felix the Cat Switches Witches, 1927 (Messmer)
Felix the Cat Tries the Trades, 1925 (Messmer)
Felix the Cat Trips Through Toyland, 1925 (Messmer)
Felix the Cat Trumps the Ace, 1926 (Messmer)
Felix the Cat Uses His Head, 1926 (Messmer)
Felix the Cat Weathers the Weather, 1926 (Messmer)
Felix the Cat Woos Whoopee, 1930 (Messmer)
Felix the Fox, 1948 (Terry)
Felix the Ghost Breaker, 1923 (Messmer)
Felix the Globe Trotter, 1923 (Messmer)
Felix the Goat Getter, 1923 (Messmer)
Felix Tries for Treasure, 1923 (Messmer)
Felix Tries to Rest, 1924 (Messmer)
Felix Trifles with Time, 1925 (Messmer)
Felix Turns the Tide, 1922 (Messmer)
Felix Wakes Up, 1922 (Messmer)
Felix Wins and Loses, 1925 (Messmer)
Felix Wins Out, 1923 (Messmer)
Fella with the Fiddle, 1937 (Stalling)
Fellini's Casanova. See Casanova de Federico Fellini, 1976
Fellow Americans, 1942 (Kanin)
Fellow Citizens, 1920 (Roach)
Fellow Romans, 1921 (Roach)
Female, 1933 (Blanke; Orry-Kelly)
Female. See Femme et le pantin, 1958
Female Animal, 1957 (Metty)
Female Highwayman, 1906 (Selig)
Female of the Species, 1912 (Bitzer)
Female on the Beach, 1955 (Lang)
Female Trap. See Name of the Game Is Kill!, 1968
Females Is Fickle, 1940 (Fleischer)
Feminine Touch, 1941 (Adrian; Waxman)
Feminine Touch, 1956 (Balcon; Rank)
Femme a sa fenetre, 1976 (Semprun)
Femme au volant, 1933 (Maté)
Femme aux bottes rouges, 1974 (Carrière)
Femme d'à côté, 1981 (Delerue)
Femmc dans la nuit, 1941 (Alekan; Kosma)
Femme de Jean, 1973 (Delerue)
Femme de mes amours. See Frullo del passero, 1988
Femme disparait, 1942 (D'Eaubonne)
Femme douce, 1969 (Cloquet)
Femme du Ganges, 1974 (Duras; Nuytten)
Femme d'une nuit, 1930 (Burel)
Femme écarlate, 1968 (Gégauff)
Femme en blanc se révolte. See Nouveau Journal d'une femme en
    blanc, 1966
Femme en homme, 1932 (Meerson; Périnal)
Femme est une femme, 1961 (Coutard; Evein; Guillemot; Legrand; Ponti;
    de Beauregard)
Femme et la fauve, 1955 (Auric)
Femme et le pantin, 1958 (Aurenche and Bost; Wakhévitch)
Femme explosive, 1996 (Carrière)
Femme fardeé, 1990 (Coutard)
Femme-Fleur, 1965 (Lenica)
Femme idéale, 1933 (D'Eaubonne)

Femme inconnue, 1923 (Burel)
Femme infidèle, 1969 (Rabier)
Femme invisible, 1933 (Meerson)
Femme mariée, 1964 (Coutard; Guillemot)
Femme noire, femme nue, 1969 (Colpi)
Femme nue, 1932 (Burel; Meerson)
Femme publique, 1984 (Vierny)
Femme sans importance, 1937 (Spaak)
Femme spectacle, 1964 (Braunberger)
Femmes au soleil, 1973 (Almendros)
Femmes de personne, 1984 (Delerue)
Femmine tre volte, 1957 (Delli Colli; Ponti)
Fencing Master, 1907 (Bitzer)
Ferghana Canal, 1939 (Tisse)
Ferien auf Immenhof, 1957 (Wagner)
Ferme aux loups, 1943 (Andrejew)
Ferme des sept péchés, 1949 (Kosma)
Ferme du pendu, 1945 (Douy)
Ferroviere, 1956 (Ponti)
Ferry to Hong Kong, 1959 (Heller; Mathieson; Rank)
Fès, 1950 (Auric)
Fesche Erzherzog, 1927 (Courant)
Fessée, 1937 (Fradetal)
Festin de Balthazar, 1910 (Carré)
Festival, 1952 (Lassally)
Festival, 1996 (Donaggio)
Festival acrobatique, 1951 (Kosma)
Festival of Claymation, 1987 (Vinton)
Festival of Nyan-nyan-myan. See Nyan-nyan-myan-hoi, 1940
Fête à Henriette, 1952 (Auric; D'Eaubonne; Jeanson)
Fête des mères, 1969 (Braunberger)
Fête des morts, 1969 (Braunberger)
Fête sauvage, 1975 (Vangelis)
Fêtes galantes, 1965 (Matras; Wakhévitch)
Fétiche chez les sirènes, 1937 (Starewicz)
Fétiche en voyage de noces, 1936 (Starewicz)
Fétiche prestidigitateur, 1934 (Starewicz)
Fétiche se marie, 1935 (Starewicz)
Fétiche-mascotte, 1933 (Starewicz)
Fetita mincinoasa, 1953 (Popescu-Gopo)
Feu!, 1937 (Ibert; Wakhévitch)
Feu. See Forêt calcinée, 1971
Feu follet, 1963 (Cloquet; Evein)
Feu Mathias Pascal, 1925 (Burel; Meerson)
Feu Nicolas, 1943 (Douy)
Feu sacré, 1942 (Burel)
Feud, 1936 (Terry)
Feud and the Turkey, 1908 (Bitzer)
Feud in the Kentucky Hills, 1912 (Bitzer)
Feud of the West, 1936 (McCord)
Feud There Was, 1938 (Avery)
Feud with a Dude, 1968 (Blanc)
Feuding Hillbillies, 1948 (Terry)
Feuer, 1914 (Freund; Kräly)
Feuerprobe, 1913 (Kolowrat-Krakowsky)
Feux de la chandeleur, 1972 (Legrand)
Fever Pitch, 1985 (Fraker)
Fcw of Us, 1996 (Branco)
Fiacre nr. 13 , 1941 (Stallich)
Fiaker Nr. 13, 1926 (Kolowrat-Krakowsky)
Fiancailles de Flambeau, 1916 (Cohl)
Fiancée du diable, 1915 (Gaumont)
Fiasco in Milan. See Audace colpo dei soliti ignoti, 1959
Fiddle-de-dee, 1947 (McClaren)
Fiddler on the Roof, 1971 (Boyle; Morris; Williams)
Fiddlers Three, 1944 (Balcon)

Fiddlesticks, 1931 (Iwerks)
Fiddling Around. *See* Just Mickey, 1930
Fiddling Buckaroo, 1933 (McCord)
Fidelio, 1956 (Eisler)
Fidélité, 2000 (Branco)
Field, 1990 (Bernstein)
Field and Scream, 1955 (Avery)
Field of Honor, 1986 (Golan and Globus)
Fiend Who Walked the West, 1958 (Lemaire; Wheeler)
Fiend with the Electronic Brain. *See* Psycho A-Go-Go!, 1965
Fiendish Plot of Dr. Fu Manchu, 1979 (Trauner)
Fierce Creatures, 1997 (Biddle; Goldman; Goldsmith)
Fiery Introduction, 1915 (Furthman)
Fiesco, 1921 (Hoffmann; Metzner)
Fiesko, 1913 (Hoffmann)
Fiesta, 1941 (Roach)
Fiesta, 1947 (Green; Irene; Mayer; Plunkett; Rosher)
Fiesta Fiasco, 1967 (Blanc)
Fiesta Story, 1977 (Alcott)
Fièvre monte à El Pao, 1959 (Alcoriza; Figueroa)
Fifteen Maiden Lane, 1936 (Seitz)
Fifteen Minutes, 1921 (Roach)
Fifth Avenue, 1916 (Miller)
Fifth Avenue Girl, 1939 (Polglase)
Fifth Avenue Models, 1925 (Laemmle)
Fifth Column Mouse, 1943 (Blanc; Stalling)
Fifth Man, 1914 (Selig)
Fifth Monkey, 1990 (Golan and Globus)
Fifty Fathoms Deep, 1931 (Walker)
Fifty Roads to Town, 1937 (August)
Fifty-Fifty Girl, 1928 (Banton)
Fig Leaves, 1926 (Adrian; August; Fox; Menzies)
Fight for Freedom, 1908 (Bitzer)
Fight for Life, 1940 (Crosby)
Fight for Your Lady, 1937 (Polglase)
Fight Pest, 1928 (Roach)
Fight to the Finish, 1947 (Terry)
Fighter, 1952 (Howe)
Fighter Squadron, 1948 (Miller; Steiner)
Fightin' Pals, 1940 (Fleischer)
Fighting 69th, 1940 (Deutsch; Friedhofer; Gaudio; Haskin; Wallis)
Fighting 691/2th, 1941 (Blanc; Stalling)
Fighting American, 1924 (Laemmle)
Fighting Back, 1982 (Seale)
Fighting Blood, 1923 (Garmes)
Fighting Breed. *See* Jackaroo of Coolabong, 1920
Fighting Buckaroo, 1926 (Fox)
Fighting Caravans, 1931 (Garmes; Zukor)
Fighting Courage, 1925 (Walker)
Fighting Coward, 1924 (Brown)
Fighting Eagle, 1927 (Adrian; Miller; Sullivan)
Fighting Fathers, 1927 (Roach)
Fighting Film Albums , 1941 (Golovnya)
Fighting Fluid, 1924 (Roach)
Fighting Guardsman, 1945 (Goosson; Guffey)
Fighting Heart, 1925 (August; Fox)
Fighting Kentuckian, 1949 (Garmes)
Fighting Lady, 1944 (Newman; de Rochemont)
Fighting Legion, 1930 (Laemmle; McCord)
Fighting Marine, 1935 (Canutt)
Fighting Marshall. *See* Cherokee Strip, 1940
Fighting O'Flynn, 1948 (Edeson)
Fighting Parson, 1930 (Barker; Roach)
Fighting Peacemaker, 1926 (Laemmle)
Fighting Pimpernel. *See* Elusive Pimpernel, 1950
Fighting Prince of Donegal, 1966 (Disney; Ellenshaw)

Fighting Seabees, 1944 (Chase)
Fighting Shepherdess, 1920 (Gaudio)
Fighting Stallion, 1926 (Canutt)
Fighting Stock, 1935 (Balcon; Rank)
Fighting Stranger, 1921 (Selig)
Fighting Streak, 1922 (Fox)
Fighting Sullivans. *See* Sullivans, 1944
Fighting Test, 1931 (Canutt)
Fighting Texans, 1933 (Canutt)
Fighting Three, 1927 (Laemmle)
Fighting Through, 1934 (Canutt)
Fighting with Kit Carson, 1933 (Canutt)
Fights of Nations, 1907 (Bitzer)
Figlia del capitano, 1947 (Flaiano and Pinelli; de Laurentiis)
Figlia del corsaro verde, 1940 (Stallich)
Figlio del corsaro rosso, 1942 (Amidei)
Figurehead, 1981 (Halas and Batchelor)
Figures de cire et tetes de bois, 1916 (Cohl)
Figures Don't Lie, 1927 (Mankiewicz)
Figures in a Landscape, 1970 (Alekan; Bennett)
File on Thelma Jordan, 1949 (Barnes; Dreier; Head; Wallis; Young)
Fille à la dérive, 1964 (Guillemot)
Fille de d'Artagnan, 1994 (Sarde)
Fille de Jephté, 1910 (Gaumont)
Fille de la mer morte, 1966 (Golan and Globus)
Fille de l'eau, 1925 (Braunberger)
Fille du cantonnier, 1909 (Gaumont)
Fille du régiment, 1933 (Heller)
Fille du sonneur, 1906 (Pathé)
Fille et des fusils, 1964 (Braunberger)
Fille nommée Madeleine, 1953 (Aurenche and Bost)
Fille pour l'été, 1959 (Delerue)
Filles de la concierge, 1934 (Wakhévitch)
Filles du Rhône, 1938 (Burel; Jaubert)
Filling the Gap, 1941 (Halas and Batchelor)
Film, 1965 (Kaufman)
Film d'amore e d'anarchia, 1973 (Rota; Rotunno)
Film Elation of Spejbl. *See* Spejblovo filmové opojení, 1931
Film Fan, 1939 (Blanc; Clampett; Stalling)
Film ohne Titel, 1947 (Herlth)
Film without Title. *See* Film ohne Titel, 1947
Filmprimadonna, 1913 (Freund; Kräly)
Films comiques, 1903 (Pathé)
Filosofská historie, 1937 (Heller)
Fils, 1972 (Sarde; Saulnier)
Fils d'Amérique, 1932 (Courant)
Fils de l'eau, 1951 (Braunberger)
Fils du biable, 1906 (Pathé)
Fils préféré, 1994 (Guillemot; Sarde)
Fils puni, 1978 (Vierny)
Filum ena Marturano, 1951 (Rota)
Fim de estação, 1981 (Branco)
Fin de Don Juan, 1911 (Gaumont)
Fin des Pyrénées, 1971 (Braunberger)
Fin du jour, 1938 (Jaubert; Matras; Spaak)
Fin du monde, 1930 (Honegger; Meerson)
Fin 'n' Catty, 1943 (Blanc; Jones; Stalling)
Final Analysis, 1992 (Tavoularis)
Final Reckoning, 1914 (Ince)
Final Settlement, 1910 (Bitzer)
Final Test, 1953 (Rattigan)
Finale der Liebe, 1925 (Planer)
Finally, Sunday!. *See* Vivement dimanche!, 1982
Finalmente sì, 1943 (Delli Colli)
Finanzen des Grossherzogs, 1924 (Freund; Planer; Pommer; Von Harbou)
Find the Girl, 1920 (Roach)

Fishing, 1921 (Fleischer)
Fishing by the Sea, 1947 (Terry)
Fishing Made Easy, 1941 (Terry)
Fishing Village. *See* Fiskebyn, 1919
Fishy Tales, 1937 (Roach)
Fiskarvals från Bohuslän, 1909 (Magnusson)
Fiskebyn, 1919 (Magnusson)
Fiskelivets favor , 1908 (Jaenzon)
Fist Fight, 1964 (Breer)
Fist in His Pocket. *See* **I pugni in tasca**, 1965
Fistful of Dollars. *See* Per un pugno di dollari, 1964
Fistful of Dynamite. *See* Giù la testa, 1972
Fistic Mystic, 1968 (Blanc; McKimson)
Fit to Be Tied, 1952 (Hanna and Barbera)
Fitting Gift, 1925 (Bray)
Fitzwilly, 1967 (Biroc; Boyle; Mirisch; Williams)
Fiume di dollari, 1966 (Morricone)
Five, 1970 (Halas and Batchelor)
Five against the House, 1955 (Cohn; Duning; Wald)
Five and Dime, 1933 (Lantz)
Five and Ten, 1931 (Adrian; Barnes; Booth)
Five Bloody Graves, 1969 (Zsigmond)
Five Bold Women, 1959 (Wexler)
Five Branded Women. *See* Giovanna e le altre, 1960
Five Came Back, 1939 (Musuraca; Polglase; Trumbo)
Five Day Lover. *See* Amant de cinq jours, 1961
Five Days, 1954 (Carreras)
Five Days—Five Nights. *See* Pyat dney—pyat nochey, 1960
Five Days from Home, 1978 (Conti)
Five Days from the life of a Pensioner. *See* Piec dni z zycla
    emeryta, 1984
Five Days in June. *See* Cinq jours en juin, 1989
Five Days One Summer, 1982 (Bernstein; Rotunno)
Five Easy Pieces, 1970 (Kovacs)
Five Finger Exercise, 1962 (Goodrich and Hackett; Orry-Kelly; Stradling)
Five Fingers, 1952 (Herrmann, Lemaire; Wheeler; Wilson; Zanuck)
Five for Four, 1942 (McClaren)
Five Golden Hours, 1961 (Challis)
Five Graves to Cairo, 1943 (Biro; Brackett; Dreier; Head; Rozsa; Seitz)
Five Guns West, 1954 (Crosby)
Five Man Army. *See* Esercito di cinque uomini, 1969
Five Men of Great Edo. *See* Oh-Edo gonon otoko, 1951
Five Miles to Midnight. *See* Couteau dans la plaie, 1962
Five Million Years to Earth. *See* Quartermass and the Pit, 1967
Five Minutes to the Duel. *See* Kettou gofun-mar, 1953
Five Pennies, 1959 (Head; Pereira)
Five Pound Man, 1937 (Dillon)
Five Puplets, 1935 (Terry)
Five Star Final, 1931 (Polito; Wallis; Zanuck)
Five Weeks in a Balloon, 1962 (Hoch; Smith)
Five Witnesses. *See* Gonin no mokugekisha, 1948
Fixed Bayonets!, 1951 (Ballard; Lemaire; Wheeler)
Fixer, 1968 (Jarre; Jeakins; Trumbo)
Fixer-Uppers, 1935 (Roach)
Flag, 1987 (Mnouchkine)
Flag Lieutenant, 1926 (Young)
Flag Lieutenant, 1932 (Wilcox)
Flag nazii, 1929 (Enei)
Flag Wind of Dawn. *See* Akatsuki no hatakaze, 1938
Flags of Nations. *See* Flag nazii, 1929
Flamands Roses de Camargue, 1969 (Braunberger)
Flambeau au pays des surprises, 1916 (Cohl)
Flambeau aux lignes. *See* Flambeau au pays des surprises, 1916
Flambeau, chien perdu. *See* Journée de Flambeau, 1916
Flame and the Arrow, 1950 (Haller; Steiner)
Flame and the Flesh, 1954 (Challis; Junge; Pasternak)

Flame dans mon coeur, 1990 (Branco; de Almeida)
Flame in My Heart. *See* Flame dans mon coeur, 1990
Flame in the Ashes, 1913 (Ince)
Flame in the Streets, 1961 (Challis; Rank)
Flame of Araby, 1951 (Hunter; Metty)
Flame of Life, 1923 (Laemmle; Miller)
Flame of New Orleans, 1941 (Krasna; Maté; Pasternak)
Flame of the Barbary Coast, 1945 (Canutt; Chase)
Flame of the Yukon, 1926 (La Shelle)
Flame over India, 1960 (Nugent)
Flame Within, 1935 (Howe)
Flamenco, 1994 (Storaro)
Flames, 1932 (Brown)
Flames of Desire, 1924 (Fox)
Flames of Life. *See* Plameny života, 1920
Flames of Passion, 1922 (Wilcox)
Flaming Barriers, 1924 (Clarke)
Flaming Feather, 1951 (Rennahan)
Flaming Flappers, 1925 (Roach)
Flaming Forest, 1926 (Gibbons)
Flaming Forties, 1924 (Marion; Polito; Stromberg)
Flaming Frontier, 1926 (Miller)
Flaming Gold, 1934 (Rosher)
Flaming Hour, 1922 (Laemmle)
Flaming Sky. *See* Moyuru oozora, 1940
Flaming Star, 1960 (Clarke; Johnson)
Flamingo Road, 1949 (McCord; Steiner, Wald)
Flamme, 1923 (Kräly)
Flamme, 1936 (D'Eaubonne)
Flanagan Boy, 1953 (Carreras)
Flap, 1970 (Hamlisch)
Flapper, 1920 (Marion)
Flash, 1990 (Elfman; Fraker)
Flash Gordon, 1979 (de Laurentiis; Donati)
Flash of Light, 1910 (Bitzer)
Flashdance, 1983 (Eszterhas)
Flat. *See* Byt, 1968
Flat Broke, 1920 (Roach)
Flat Foot Fledgling, 1952 (Terry)
Flat Top, 1962 (Mirisch)
Flathatting, 1945 (Bosustow; Hubley)
Flea Circus, 1954 (Avery)
Flea in Her Ear, 1968 (Cahn; Kaper; Lang)
Flea in Her Ear. *See* Puce à l'oreille, 1967
Fledermaus, 1931 (Heller)
Fledermaus, 1946 (Herlth)
Fledged Shadows. *See* Opeřené stíny, 1930
Fleet Air Arm, 1943 (Balcon)
Fleet's In, 1928 (Banton)
Fleet's In, 1942 (Head; Mercer; Young)
Fleets of Stren'th, 1942 (Fleischer)
Fleetwing, 1928 (Fox)
Flemish Farm, 1942 (Rank; Vetchinsky)
Flesh, 1932 (Edeson)
Flesh and Blood, 1951 (Heller; Korda; de Grunwald)
Flesh and Blood, 1997 (Bernard; Harryhausen)
Flesh and Bone, 1993 (Newman; Rousselot)
Flesh and Fantasy, 1943 (Boyle; Cortez; Head; Hoffenstein)
Flesh and the Devil, 1926 (Daniels; Gibbons; Mayer; Thalberg)
Flesh and Women. *See* Grand Jeu, 1954
Flesh Gordon, 1974 (Muren)
Flesh of the Orchid. *See* Chair de l'orchidée, 1974
Flesh Will Surrender. *See* Delitto di Giovanni Episcopo, 1947
Fletch, 1985 (Leven)
Fleur de fougère, 1949 (Starewicz)
Fleur de l'âge, 1947 (Trauner)

Fleur de l'age, 1964 (Braunberger; Takemitsu)
Fleur des ruines, 1916 (Burel; Gaumont)
Fleur d'oseille, 1967 (D'Eaubonne)
Fleurs de Jones, 1972 (Nuytten)
Fleuve invisible, 1960 (Delerue)
Fleuve: Le Tarn, 1951 (Fradetal)
Flic ou voyou, 1978 (Decaë; Sarde)
Flickan i fönstret mittemot, 1942 (Fischer)
Flickan i frack, 1956 (Nykvist)
Flickan och djävulen, 1944 (Lundgren)
Fliegende Klassenzimmer, 1954 (Herlth; Kästner)
Fliegende Klassenzimmer, 1973 (Kästner)
Fliegende Koffer, 1921 (Reiniger)
Fliegenden Briganten, 1921 (Warm)
Flies, 1923 (Fleischer)
Flies. See Mouchy, 1950
Flies Ain't Human, 1941 (Fleischer)
Flight, 1929 (Cohn; Walker)
Flight 54321, 1971 (Vukotić)
Flight Angels, 1940 (Haskin; Wald)
Flight Command, 1940 (Gillespie; Rosson; Waxman)
Flight for Freedom, 1943 (Garmes)
Flight from Ashiya, 1962 (Guffey; Lourié)
Flight from Folly, 1944 (Heller)
Flight from Glory, 1937 (Musuraca)
Flight in the Night. See Flucht in die Nacht, 1926
Flight into France. See Fuga in Francia, 1948
Flight Lieutenant, 1942 (Cohn; Planer)
Flight Nurse, 1953 (Young)
Flight of Ludlows Aerodrome, 1905 (Bitzer)
Flight of the Phoenix, 1965 (Biroc; Westmore Family)
Flight of the White Stallions. See Miracle of the White Stallions, 1962
Flight [or Desertion] of Poincaré. See Begstvo Puankare, 1932
Flight to Fame, 1938 (Ballard)
Flight to Mars, 1951 (Mirisch)
Flim-Flam Man, 1967 (Goldsmith; Jeakins; Lang; Smith)
Flintstones, 1994 (Hanna and Barbera)
Flipper Frolics, 1952 (Terry)
Flip's Circus, 1918-21 (McCay)
Flirt, 1917 (Roach)
Flirt, 1922 (Laemmle)
Flirtation Walk, 1934 (Barnes; Orry-Kelly; Polito; Wallis)
Flirting with Fate, 1938 (Young)
Flirting with Love, 1924 (McCord)
Flirty Birdy, 1945 (Hanna and Barbera)
Flivver, 1922 (Roach)
Floating Weeds. See Ukigusa, 1959
Flood Tide, 1958 (Mancini)
Floods of Fear, 1958 (Challis; Rank)
Floodtide, 1949 (Rank)
Floor Below, 1920 (Roach)
Flop Goes the Weasel, 1943 (Blanc; Jones; Stalling)
Flop Secret, 1952 (Terry)
Flor de caña, 1948 (Alcoriza)
Flor de mayo, 1957 (Figueroa)
Flor Silvestre, 1943 (Figueroa)
Flora, 1989 (švankmajer)
Floradora Girl, 1930 (Adrian; Gibbons; Stothart)
Floraison, 1913 (Burel)
Floral Studies. See Cadres fleuris, 1910
Florence 13.30, 1957 (Stallich)
Florence est folle, 1944 (Jeanson)
Florentine Dagger, 1935 (Grot; Hecht; Orry-Kelly)
Florentiner Hut, 1939 (Hoffmann)
Florentinische Nächte, 1920 (Dreier)
Florian, 1940 (Freund; Waxman)

Flötenkonzert von Sanssouci, 1930 (Herlth; Hoffmann; Reisch; Röhrig)
Flottans överman, 1958 (Lundgren)
Flow Diagram, 1966 (Halas and Batchelor)
Flower, 1967 (Kuri)
Flower Blooms. See Hana hiraku, 1948
Flower Drum Song, 1961 (Hunter; Metty; Newman; Pan; Sharaff; Westmore Family)
Flower in the Desert, 1915 (Ince)
Flower of Night, 1925 (Glennon)
Flowers from the Sumava. See Kvet ze Šumavy, 1927
Flowing Gold, 1940 (Deutsch)
Flubber, 1997 (Elfman)
Fluch, 1925 (Reisch)
Flucht in die Nacht, 1926 (Courant; Warm)
Flucht vor der Liebe, 1929 (Planer)
Flüchtlinge, 1933 (Herlth; Röhrig; Wagner
Fluchtversuch, 1976 (Lassally)
Fluffer, 2000 (Vachon)
Flug in den Tod, 1921 (Hoffmann)
Flugel und Felleln, 1984 (Vierny)
Flurina, 1970 (Halas and Batchelor)
Flurry in Art, 1914 (Loos)
Flûte à six schtroumpfs, 1976 (Legrand)
Flute and the Arrow. See En djungelsaga, 1957
Flute Concert at Sans Souci. See Flötenkonzert von Sanssouci, 1930
Flute magique, 1946 (Grimault)
Fluttering Hearts, 1927 (Roach)
Fly, 1958 (Lemaire; Struss)
Fly, 1986 (Walas)
Fly II, 1989 (Walas)
Fly about the House, 1949 (Halas and Batchelor)
Fly Away Peter, 1935 (Rank)
Fly By Night, 1942 (Seitz)
Fly in the Ointment, 1943 (Fleischer)
Fly on the Wall, 1978 (Menges)
Fly with Money. See O musca cu bani, 1954
Flying Blind, 1941 (Head; Tiomkin)
Flying Cat, 1952 (Hanna and Barbera)
Flying Children. See Enfants volants, 1991
Flying Circus, 1968 (Blanc)
Flying Classroom. See Fliegende Klassenzimmer, 1954
Flying Cups and Saucers, 1949 (Terry)
Flying Devils, 1933 (Musuraca; Steiner)
Flying Doctor, 1936 (Balcon)
Flying Down to Rio, 1933 (Cooper; Dunn; Irene; Kahn; Pan; Plunkett; Polglase; Steiner)
Flying Elephants, 1927 (Roach)
Flying Fever, 1941 (Terry)
Flying Fists, 1931 (Iwerks)
Flying Fleet, 1929 (Gibbons)
Flying Fool, 1929 (Miller)
Flying Fury, 1926 (Walker)
Flying High, 1932 (Adrian)
Flying Horseman, 1926 (August; Fox)
Flying House, 1921 (McCay)
Flying Irishman, 1939 (Berman; Trumbo)
Flying Man, 1962 (Dunning)
Flying Missile, 1950 (Duning)
Flying Oil, 1935 (Terry)
Flying Sorceress, 1956 (Hanna and Barbera)
Flying South, 1937 (Terry)
Flying South, 1947 (Terry)
Flying Tigers, 1942 (Young)
Flying Torpedo, 1916 (Brown)
Flying U Ranch, 1927 (Walker)
Flying with Music, 1942 (Roach)

FM, 1978 (Alonzo)
Focal Point. *See* Point de mire, 1977
Fog, 1933 (Schary)
Fog, 1979 (Houseman)
Fog over Frisco, 1934 ((Blanke; Gaudio; Orry-Kelly)
Foghorn Leghorn, 1948 (Blanc; McKimson; Stalling)
Foiled Again, 1935 (Terry)
Foiling the Fox, 1950 (Terry)
Foire aux cancres, 1963 (Grimault)
Foire aux chimères, 1946 (D'Eaubonne)
Folie des grandeurs, 1971 (Decaë; Wakhévitch)
Folie du Docteur Tube, 1915 (Burel; Gaumont)
Folies bourgeoises, 1976 (Rabier)
Folies d'elodie, 1981 (Gégauff)
Folies douces, 1978 (Guillemot)
Folle à tuer, 1975 (Sarde)
Folle Aventure, 1930 (Planer)
"follia" de Zavattini, 1982 (Zavattini)
Follow a Star, 1959 (Rank)
Follow Me, 1972 (Barry; Challis; Wallis)
Follow Me, Boys!, 1966 (Disney)
Follow That Car, 1964 (Halas and Batchelor)
Follow That Dream, 1962 (Lederer)
Follow the Boys, 1944 (Cahn)
Follow the Crowd, 1918 (Roach)
Follow the Fleet, 1936 (Berlin; Berman; Pan; Polglase; Steiner)
Follow the Leader, 1930 (Green; Head)
Follow the Sun, 1951 (Lemaire)
Follow Thru', 1930 (Banton)
Folly of Vanity, 1924 (August; Fox)
Folly to Be Wise, 1952 (Korda)
Fonderies Martin, 1938 (Alexeieff and Parker)
Foney Fables, 1942 (Blanc; Stalling)
Foo Foo's New Hat, 1960 (Halas and Batchelor)
Foo Foo's Sleepless Night, 1960 (Halas and Batchelor)
Food. *See* Jídlo, 1992
Food of the Gods, 1976 (Baker)
Fool, 1925 (Fox; Ruttenberg)
Fool Coverage, 1952 (Blanc; McKimson; Stalling)
Fool for Love, 1985 (Shepard)
Fool Killer, 1965 (Jeakins; Rosenblum)
Fool There Was, 1915 (Fox)
Fool There Was, 1922 (Fox)
Foolin' Around, 1979 (Lathrop)
Foolish Age, 1921 (Stromberg)
Foolish Duckling, 1952 (Terry)
Foolish Heart. *See* Corazón iluminado, 1998
Foolish Husbands, 1929 (Hornbeck)
Foolish Wives, 1921 (Daniels; Day; Laemmle; Mandell; Thalberg)
Fools First, 1922 (Struss)
Fools for Scandal, 1938 (Banton; Deutsch; Grot)
Fool's Gold. *See* Krakguldet, 1969
Fools Highway, 1924 (Laemmle)
Fools of Fate, 1909 (Bitzer)
Fools of Fortune, 1990 (Zimmer)
Fool's Paradise, 1921 (Struss; Zukor)
Fool's Paradise, 1971 (Westmore Family)
Fool's Revenge, 1909 (Bitzer)
Fools Rush In, 1949 (Rank; Unsworth)
Fools, Water Sprites, and Imposters. *See* Blazni vodníci a podvodníci, 1980
Foot and Mouth, 1955 (Lassally)
Foot on the Moon, 1999 (Müller)
Football, 1935 (Terry)
Football, 1962 (Decaë)
Football Coach. *See* College Coach, 1933

Football Fever, 1937 (Lantz)
Football Freaks, 1971 (Halas and Batchelor)
Football Romeo, 1938 (Roach)
Football Toucher Downer, 1937 (Fleischer)
Footfalls, 1921 (Fox)
Footlight Glamor. *See* Upstream, 1926
Footlight Parade, 1933 (Barnes; Grot; Wallis; Warner)
Footlight Ranger, 1923 (Fox)
Footlight Serenade, 1942 (Day; Garmes; Pan)
Footlights and Fools, 1929 (Grot)
Footloose Heiress, 1937 (Edeson)
Footloose Widows, 1926 (Zanuck)
Footsteps in the Dark, 1941 (Haller; Wallis)
Footsteps in the Fog, 1955 (Challis)
Footsteps in the Night. *See* A Honeymoon Adventure, 1931
Foozle at a Tea Party, 1914 (Roach)
For a Few Dollars More. *See* Per qualche dollaro in più, 1965
For a Woman. *See* Um ein Weib, 1917
For Alimony Only, 1926 (Adrian; Miller)
For Art's Sake, 1923 (Roach)
För att inte tala om alla dessa kvinnor, 1964 (Lundgren; Nykvist)
For Beauty's Sake, 1940 (Clarke; Day)
For Better, for Worse, 1919 (Buckland; Howe; Macpherson)
For Better for Worse, 1959 (Halas and Batchelor)
For Better or Worser, 1935 (Fleischer)
For Big Stakes, 1922 (Fox)
For Ever Mozart, 1996 (Branco)
For Freedom of Cuba, 1912 (Ince)
For Friendship. *See* För vänskaps skull, 1963
For Fun—for Play. *See* Kaleidoskop: Valeska Gert, 1979
For Guests Only, 1923 (Roach)
For Heaven's Sake, 1926 (Bruckman; Zukor)
For Heaven's Sake, 1950 (Lemaire; Newman)
För hennes skull, 1930 (Jaenzon)
For Her Brother's Sake, 1911 (Gaudio; Ince)
For Her Brother's Sake, 1914 (Ince)
For Her Father's Sins, 1913 (Loos)
For Her Sake. *See* För hennes skull, 1930
For His Son, 1911 (Bitzer)
For Keeps, 1988 (Conti)
For Love of Ivy, 1968 (Jones)
For Love of Money, 1963 (Louis)
For Love or Money, 1939 (Cortez; Taradash)
For Love or Money. *See* Cash, 1933
For Love or Money. *See* Crossroads of New York, 1922
For Me and My Gal, 1942 (Daniels; Freed)
For Native Soil. *See* Za rodnou hroudu, 1930
For Pete's Sake, 1934 (Roach)
For Pete's Sake, 1974 (Kovacs)
For Safe Keeping, 1923 (Roach)
For Sale, 1924 (McCord)
For Scent-imental Reasons, 1949 (Blanc; Jones; Stalling)
For the Boys, 1991 (Grusin)
For the Defense, 1922 (Rosson)
For the Defense, 1930 (Banton; Lang)
For the First Time. *See* Serenade einer grossen Liebe, 1958
For the Fredom of the People. *See* Za svobodu národa, 1920
For the Honor of the 7th, 1912 (Ince)
For the Love 'o Pete, 1926 (Lantz)
For the Love of a Singer. *See* Kogda zvuchat strunnyi svedtza, 1913
For the Love of Mary, 1948 (Boyle; Daniels; Orry-Kelly)
For the Love of Mike, 1927 (Haller)
For the Queen's Honor, 1911 (Gaudio)
For the Soul of Rafael, 1920 (Carré; Edeson)
For Those in Peril, 1944 (Balcon; Clarke)
För vänskaps skull, 1963 (Fischer; Lundgren)

For Whom Do We Love?. *See* Dare no tame ni aisuruka, 1971

For Whom the Bell Tolls, 1943 (Canutt; Dreier; Head; Menzies; Nichols; Rennahan; Struss; Young)

For Wives Only, 1926 (Rosson)

For You Alone. *See* When You're in Love, 1937

For You I Die, 1947 (Clothier)

For Your Daughter's Sake. *See* Common Sin, 1920

For Your Eyes Only, 1981 (Broccoli; Conti)

Forbid Them Not, 1961 (Fraker)

Forbidden, 1932 (Cohn; Swerling; Walker)

Forbidden, 1953 (Daniels; Maté)

Forbidden Adventure, 1931 (Lang)

Forbidden Cargo, 1954 (Rank)

Forbidden City, 1918 (Schenck)

Forbidden Country, 1934 (Reville)

Forbidden Dance, 1990 (Golan and Globus)

Forbidden Fruit, 1921 (Macpherson)

Forbidden Games. *See* **Jeux interdits**, 1951

Forbidden Heaven, 1935 (Krasner)

Forbidden Hours, 1928 (Day; Gibbons)

Forbidden Paradise, 1924 (Dreier; Kräly; Zukor)

Forbidden Planet, 1956 (Gibbons; Gillespie; Plunkett; Rose)

Forbidden Range, 1923 (Canutt)

Forbidden Street, 1948 (Lardner; Périnal)

Forbidden Thing, 1920 (Gaudio)

Forbidden Way. *See* Cytherea, 1924

Forbidden Woman, 1920 (Edeson)

Forbidden Woman, 1927 (Adrian; Buckland)

Forbidden Zone, 1980 (Elfman)

Forbin Project, 1970 (Westmore Family; Whitlock)

Force 10 from Navarone, 1978 (Foreman)

Force de l'argent, 1913 (Gaumont)

Force de l'enfant, 1908 (Cohl)

Force of Arms, 1951 (McCord; Steiner; Veiller)

Force of Evil, 1949 (Barnes; Day; Raksin)

Force Ten from Navarone, 1978 (Challis)

Forced Landing, 1941 (Alton; Head; Tiomkin)

Foreign Affair, 1948 (Brackett; Dreier; Head; Lang)

Foreign Affairs, 1935 (Balcon; Rank; Vetchinsky)

Foreign Body, 1986 (Neame)

Foreign Correspondent, 1940 (Guffey; Harrison; Maté; Menzies; Newman; Spencer; Wanger)

Foreign Devils, 1927 (Gibbons)

Foreigner's Okichi. *See* Toujin Okichi, 1955

Foreman Went to France, 1942 (Balcon; Walton)

Forest Murmurs, 1947 (Vorkapich)

Forest Rangers, 1942 (Dreier; Lang; Young)

Forester's Song. *See* Do lesíčka na čekanou, 1966

Forêt calcinée, 1971 (Braunberger)

Forever, 1921 (Miller)

Forever After, 1926 (Struss)

Forever Amber, 1947 (Dunne; Lardner; Lemaire; Raksin; Shamroy; Wheeler)

Forever and a Day, 1943 (Garmes; Metty; Musuraca; Sherriff; Stewart; Wilcox)

Forever Darling, 1956 (Cahn)

Forever England, 1935 (Balcon)

Forever Female, 1953 (Epstein; Head; Stradling; Young)

Forever in Love. *See* Pride of the Marines, 1945

Forever Lulu, 1986 (Rosenblum)

Forever Mine, 1999 (Badalamenti)

Forever My Love, 1962 (Bacharach)

Forever Young, 1984 (Puttnam)

Forever Young, 1992 (Boyd; Goldsmith)

Forever Yours, 1944 (Tiomkin)

Forever Yours. *See* Forget-Me-Not, 1936

Forever, Darling, 1955 (Kaper)

Forfaiture, 1937 (Braunberger; Schüfftan)

Forgery. *See* Southside 1-1000, 1950

Forget-Me-Not, 1917 (Marion)

Forget-Me-Not, 1936 (Hornbeck; Korda; Krasker)

Forgotten Babies, 1933 (Roach)

Forgotten Commandments, 1932 (Struss; Zukor)

Forgotten Faces, 1928 (Selznick)

Forgotten Man, 1971 (Grusin)

Forgotten Patriots. *See* Zapadlí vlastenci, 1932

Forgotten Sweeties, 1927 (Roach)

Forgotten Village, 1941 (Eisler)

Forgotten Woman, 1939 (Cortez)

Forlorn River, 1937 (Head)

Form Phases I, 1952 (Breer)

Form Phases II, 1953 (Breer)

Form Phases III, 1953 (Breer)

Form Phases IV, 1954 (Breer)

Formal Kimono. *See* Harekodose, 1940

Formation, 1952 (Godfrey)

Formula, 1980 (Conti)

Forrest Gump, 1994 (Ralston)

Forsaking All Others, 1922 (Laemmle)

Forsaking All Others, 1934 (Adrian; Toland)

Förseglade läppar, 1927 (Jaenzon)

Forstenbuben, 1985 (Morricone)

Försterchristel, 1926 (Andrejew)

Försterchristl, 1952 (Herlth)

Forsyte Saga. *See* That Forsyte Woman, 1949

Fort Apache, 1948 (Basevi; Clothier; Cooper; Nugent)

Fort Apache, the Bronx, 1980 (Alcott)

Fort Defiance, 1951 (Cortez)

Fort Dobbs, 1958 (Clothier; Steiner)

Fort-Dolorès, 1938 (Kaufman)

Fort Massacre, 1958 (Mirisch)

Fort Osage, 1951 (Mirisch)

Fort Saganne, 1984 (Nuytten)

Fort Vengeance, 1953 (Wanger)

Fort Yuma, 1955 (Koch)

Fortuna, 1973 (Stawiński)

Fortuna di essere donna, 1955 (Cecchi D'Amico; Flaiano and Pinelli)

Fortune, 1975 (Alonzo; Sylbert)

Fortune Cookie, 1966 (Diamond; La Shelle; Mandell; Previn)

Fortune Hunters, 1946 (Terry)

Fortune in Diamonds. *See* Adventurers, 1951

Fortune Is a Woman, 1956 (Alwyn)

Fortune Teller, 1923 (Fleischer)

Fortunella, 1957 (de Laurentiis; Flaiano and Pinelli; Rota)

Fortune's Fool. *See* Alles für Geld, 1923

Fortunes of War, 1914 (Ince)

Forty Carats, 1973 (Lang; Louis)

Forty-first. *See* Sorok pervyi, 1956

Forty Guns, 1957 (Biroc; Lemaire)

Forty Naughty Girls, 1937 (Metty; Polglase)

Forty Thieves, 1932 (Terry)

Forty Thieves, 1944 (Harlan; Wilson)

Forty Years. *See* Vertig Jaren, 1938

Forward a Century, 1951 (Lassally)

Forward March Hare, 1953 (Blanc; Jones; Stalling)

Forza G, 1971 (Morricone)

Forza Italia!, 1978 (Morricone)

Fossils. *See* Kaseki, 1975

Foster and Laurie, 1975 (Schifrin)

Foto proibite de una signora per bene, 1971 (Morricone)

Fou de la falaise, 1916 (Burel)

Fougères bleues, 1975 (de Beauregard)

Foul Ball Player, 1940 (Fleischer)

Foundation of Ordination. *See* Seishoku no ishique, 1978

Foundling, 1916 (Marion)

Fountain, 1934 (Berman; Hoffenstein; Plunkett; Polglase; Steiner)

Fountainhead, 1949 (Blanke; Burks; Steiner)

Four around a Woman. *See* Kämpfende Herzen, 1920

Four Bags Full. *See* Traversée de Paris, 1956

Four Dark Hours, 1940 (Rozsa)

Four Dark Hours. *See* Green Cockatoo, 1937

Four Daughters, 1938 (Blanke; Epstein; Friedhofer; Haller; Orry-Kelly;
    Steiner; Wallis)

Four Days in November, 1964 (Bernstein)

Four Days Leave, 1948 (Lardner)

Four Days' Leave, 1949 (Siodmak)

Four Days' Wonder, 1936 (Cortez)

Four Devils, 1929 (Fox; Mayer)

Four Devils. *See* Chetirye chorta, 1913

Four Faces of India. *See* Chaar Dil Chaar Rahen, 1959

Four Faces West, 1948 (Harlan)

Four Feathers, 1929 (Banton; Cooper; Selznick; Zukor)

Four Feathers, 1939 (Biro; Hornbeck; Korda; Krasker; Périnal; Rozsa;
    Saunders; Sherriff; Unsworth)

Four-Footed Ranger, 1927 (Laemmle)

Four for Texas, 1963 (Biroc; Guffey; Laszlo; van Heusen)

Four Friends, 1981 (Cloquet)

Four Frightened People, 1934 (Struss; Zukor)

Four Girls in Town, 1956 (North)

Four Guns to the Border, 1954 (Mancini; Metty)

Four Hearts, Four Roads. *See* Chaar Dil Chaar Rahen, 1959

Four Horsemen of the Apocalypse, 1921 (Mathis; Mohr; Seitz)

Four Horsemen of the Apocalypse, 1962 (Gillespie; Krasner; Orry-Kelly;
    Périnal; Plunkett; Previn)

Four Hours to Kill, 1935 (Head; Krasna; Zukor)

Four in the Morning, 1965 (Barry)

Four Jacks and a Jill, 1941 (Metty)

Four Jills in a Jeep, 1944 (Basevi; Friedhofer)

Four Just Men, 1939 (Balcon; Neame)

Four Little Tailors. *See* Qautre Petits Tailleurs, 1910

Four Love Stories. *See* Yottsu no koi no monogatari, 1947

Four Men and a Prayer, 1938 (Levien; Macgowan)

Four Mothers, 1940 (Blanke; Rosher)

Four Musicians of Bremen, 1922 (Disney)

Four Musketeers, 1975 (Schifrin; Watkin)

Four Nights of a Dreamer. *See* Quatre nuits d'un rêveur, 1971

Four Parts, 1934 (Roach)

Four Poster, 1952 (Bosustow; Hubley; Mohr; Tiomkin)

Four Rooms, 1995 (Jones)

Four Sided Triangle, 1952 (Arnold; Carreras))

Four Sons, 1928 (Clarke; Fox; Parrish)

Four Sons, 1940 (Day; Shamroy; Zanuck)

Four Star Boarder, 1935 (Roach)

Four Steps in the Clouds. *See* Quattro passi fra le nuvole, 1942

Four Walls, 1928 (Gibbons; Howe)

Four Weddings and a Funeral, 1994 (Bennett)

Four Wheels and No Brake, 1955 (Bosustow)

Four Wives, 1939 (Blanke; Epstein; Polito; Steiner; Wallis)

Fourflusher, 1927 (Laemmle)

Four's a Crowd, 1938 (Deutsch; Haller; Orry-Kelly)

Fourteen Hours, 1951 (Lemaire; Newman; Paxton; Spencer; Wheeler)

Fourteenth Man, 1920 (Brown)

Fourth Alarm, 1926 (Roach)

Fourth Commandment, 1927 (Laemmle)

Fourth Estate, 1940 (Mayer)

Fourth Protocol, 1987 (Schifrin)

Fourth War, 1987 (Fisher)

Fourth War, 1990 (Conti)

Fourvière, 1948 (Colpi)

Fous de Bassan, 1987 (Mnouchkine)

Fovou tous Ellines . . . , 2000 (Theodorakis)

Fowl Ball, 1930 (Lantz)

Fowl Play, 1937 (Fleischer)

Fowl Play, 1973 (McKimson)

Fowl Weather, 1953 (Blanc; Stalling)

Fox, 1967 (Fraker; Koch; Schifrin)

Fox and his Friends. *See* Faustrecht der Freiheit, 1975

Fox and the Duck, 1945 (Terry)

Fox and the Grapes, 1921 (Terry)

Fox and the Jug. *See* Liska a džbán, 1947

Fox and the Rabbit, 1935 (Lantz)

Fox Chase, 1928 (Disney)

Fox Chase, 1952 (Lye)

Fox Hunt, 1906 (Bitzer)

Fox Hunt, 1925 (Roach)

Fox Hunt, 1936 (Korda)

Fox Hunt, 1950 (Terry)

Fox Hunt. *See* Okhota na lis, 1980

Fox Hunting the Roman Compagna. *See* World Window, 1937-40

Fox in a Fix, 1951 (Blanc; Mckimson; Stalling)

Fox Movietone Follies of 1929, 1929 (Fox)

Fox Movietone Follies of 1930, 1930 (Fox; Goosson)

Fox Pop, 1942 (Blanc; Jones)

Fox Terror, 1957 (Blanc; McKimson; Stalling)

Foxed by a Fox, 1955 (Terry)

Foxes, 1980 (Puttnam)

Foxes of Harrow, 1947 (La Shelle; Lemaire; Newman; Wheeler)

Foxfire, 1955 (Daniels)

Foxfire, 1987 (Mandel)

Foxtrot Tango Alpha. *See* F.T.A., 1972

Foxy by Proxy, 1952 (Blanc; Stalling)

Foxy Duckling, 1947 (Blanc)

Foxy-Fox, 1935 (Terry)

Foxy Hunter, 1937 (Fleischer)

Foxy Pup, 1937 (Iwerks)

Fra Diavolo , 1906 (Messter)

Fra Diavolo, 1922 (Metzner)

Fra Diavolo, 1930 (Metzner)

Fra Diavolo, 1933 (Macpherson; Roach)

Fractured Leghorn, 1950 (Blanc; McKimson; Stalling)

Fragment of an Empire. *See* Oblomok imperii, 1929

Fragment of Fear, 1970 (Morris)

Fragments of Isabella, 1989 (Lassally)

Fraidy Cat, 1924 (Roach)

Fraidy Cat, 1942 (Hanna and Barbera)

Frame-Up, 1917 (Furthman)

Frame-Up, 1938 (Terry)

Framed, 1939 (Guffey)

Framed, 1947 (Goosson; Guffey; Maddow)

Framed Cat, 1950 (Hanna and Barbera)

Framing Father, 1942 (Metty)

Framing Youth, 1937 (Roach)

Främmande hamn, 1948 (Lundgren)

Française et l'amour, 1960 (Delerue; Kosma; Rappeneau; Spaak)

France, nouvelle patrie, 1948 (Kosma)

France S.A., 1973 (Carrière)

Frances, 1982 (Barry; Kovacs; Shepard; Sylbert)

Francesco, 1989 (Donati; Lanci, Giuseppe ("beppe"); Vangelis)

Francis, 1949 (Fleischer)

Francisca, 1981 (Branco)

Franciscain de Bourges, 1967 (Aurenche and Bost; Douy)

Franck Aroma, 1937 (Alexeieff and Parker)

François le rhinocéros, 1953 (Kosma)

François Villon, 1945 (Auric; Douy)

Fugitive Kind, 1959 (Justin; Kaufman; Sylbert)
Fugitive Lady. *See* Strada, 1949
Fugitive Lovers, 1934 (Gillespie; Goodrich and Hackett)
Fugitive Road, 1934 (McCord)
Fugitives, 1929 (Fox)
Fugueuses, 1995 (de Almeida)
Fuite en Avant, 1983 (Colpi)
Fuji, 1974 (Breer)
Fuji sancho, 1948 (Hayasaka)
Fukeizu, 1962 (Yoda)
Fukkatsu, 1950 (Yoda)
Full House. *See* O. Henry's Full House, 1952
Full Life. *See* Mitasareta seikatsu, 1961
Full Moon in Paris. *See* Nuits de pleine lune, 1984
Full o' Pep, 1922 (Roach)
Full of Life, 1956 (Cohn; Duning)
Full Rich Life. *See* Cynthia, 1947
Full Treatment, 1961 (Carreras)
Fulla Bluff Man, 1940 (Fleischer)
Fuller Brush Man, 1948 (Goosson)
Fully Insured, 1923 (Roach)
Fumées, 1951 (Alexeieff and Parker)
Fumo di Londra, 1966 (Amidei)
Fun and Fancy Free, 1947 (Disney; Iwerks)
Fun from the Press, 1923 (Fleischer)
Fun House, 1936 (Lantz)
Fun in Acapulco, 1963 (Head; Wallis)
Fun on the Joy Line, 1905 (Bitzer)
Functions and Relations, 1968 (Halas and Batchelor)
Fundvogel, 1929 (Warm)
Funebrák, 1932 (Heller; Stallich)
Funeral in Berlin, 1966 (Adam; Heller)
Fünf von Titan. *See* Vors uns liegt das Leben, 1948
Funfuhrtee in zerin, 1926 (Planer)
Funhouse, 1981 (Baker)
Funny Boy, 1987 (Sarde)
Funny Bunny Business, 1942 (Terry)
Funny Face, 1933 (Iwerks)
Funny Face, 1957 (Deutsch; Edens; Head; Pereira)
Funny Face. *See* Bright Lights, 1935
Funny Farm, 1988 (Bernstein; Bumstead)
Funny Farm. *See* Hashigaon Hagadol, 1988
Funny Girl, 1968 (Sharaff; Stark; Stradling)
Funny Lady, 1975 (Allen; Howe; Jenkins; Stark)
Funny Thing Happened on the Way to the Forum, 1966 (Williams)
Funnyface. *See* Bright Lights, 1935
Funtoosh, 1956 (Burman)
Fununjo shi, 1928 (Tsuburaya)
Furankenshutain no kaiju—Sanda tai Gailah, 1966 (Tsuburaya)
Furankenshutain tai Barogon, 1966 (Tsuburaya)
Furia, 1999 (Fisher)
Furies, 1950 (Bumstead; Dreier; Head; Schnee; Wallis; Waxman)
Furniture Movers, 1918 (Roach)
Fürstin Woronzoff, 1920 (Dreier)
Further up the Creek, 1958 (Carreras)
Fury at Furnace Creek, 1948 (Newman; Raksin)
Fury at Showdown, 1956 (La Shelle)
Fury of the Jungle, 1933 (Schary)
Fury Unleashed. *See* Hot Rod Gang, 1958
Fury, 1936 (Gibbons; Krasna; Mayer; Ruttenberg; Waxman)
Fury, 1978 (Baker; Smith; Williams)
Furyo shonen, 1961 (Takemitsu)
Fuss and Feathers, 1918 (Barnes)
Futore e donna, 1984 (Delli Colli)
Future Is a Woman. *See* Futore e donna, 1984
Future of Emily. *See* Avenir d'Emilie, 1984

Future's in the Air, 1936 (Alwyn)
Futuresport, 1998 (Dickerson)
Futz!, 1969 (Zsigmond)
Fuzz, 1972 (Grusin; Jeakins)
Fuzzy Pink Nightgown, 1957 (La Shelle)
FX2: The Deadly Art of Illusion, 1991 (Schifrin)

"G" Men, 1935 (Wallis; Zanuck)
G-Man Jitters, 1939 (Terry)
G-Man's Wife. *See* Public Enemy's Wife, 1936
G-Men, 1935 (Miller; Orry-Kelly; Polito)
G-Men Never Forget, 1947 (Canutt)
G.I. Blues, 1960 (Head; Wallis)
G.P.U., 1942 (Röhrig)
G.S.O., 1958 (Kosma)
Gabbia, 1985 (Morricone)
Gabby Goes Fishing, 1941 (Fleischer)
Gable and Lombard, 1976 (Head; Legrand)
Gabriel over the White House, 1933 (Adrian; Glennon; Mayer; Wanger)
Gabrielle, 1954 (Fischer)
Gaby, 1956 (Goodrich and Hackett; Lederer; Rose)
Gaby—A True Story, 1987 (Jarre)
Gadfly. *See* Ovod, 1955
Gagnant, 1935 (Fradetal)
Gaietés de la finance, 1935 (Spaak)
Gaietés de l'escadron, 1932 (Douy)
Gaiety George, 1945 (Heller)
Gaiety Girl, 1924 (Laemmle)
Gaiety Girls. *See* Paradise for Two, 1937
Gaily, Gaily, 1969 (Boyle; Mancini)
Gaines Roussel, 1939 (Alexeieff and Parker)
Gaité Parisienne. *See* Gay Parisian, 1941
Gaités de l'exposition, 1938 (Kaufman)
Gajre, 1948 (Biswas)
Gal Who Took the West, 1949 (Boyle; Daniels)
Galathea, 1935 (Reiniger)
Galaxina, 1980 (Walas)
Galaxy Quest, 1999 (Winston)
Galeerensträfling, 1919 (Wagner)
Galettes de Pont Aven, 1975 (Sarde)
Galia, 1966 (D'Eaubonne)
Galileo, 1968 (Flaiano and Pinelli; Morricone)
Gallant Blade, 1948 (Duning; Goosson; Guffey)
Gallant Journey, 1946 (Goosson; Guffey)
Gallant Lady, 1933 (Day; Newman; Zanuck)
Gallant Little Tailor, 1954 (Reiniger)
Gallina clueca, 1941 (Figueroa)
Gallina Vogelbirdie. *See* Spatne namalovaná slepice, 1963
Gallipoli, 1981 (Boyd; Seale)
Gallo de oro, 1964 (Figueroa)
Gallo en corral ajeno, 1952 (Figueroa)
Gallopin' Gals, 1940 (Hanna and Barbera)
Gallopin' Gaucho, 1928 (Disney; Iwerks)
Galloping Fury, 1927 (Laemmle)
Galloping Ghost, 1931 (Canutt)
Galloping Ghosts, 1927 (Roach)
Galveston Hurricane Shots, 1900 (Bitzer)
Gamberge, 1961 (Saulnier)
Gambit, 1966 (Jarre; Louis; Neame; Sargent)
Gamble. *See* Partita, 1988
Gambler, 1971 (Burman)
Gambler, 1974 (Winkler)
Gambler and the Lady, 1952 (Carreras)
Gambler Wore a Gun, 1960 (Crosby; Hall)
Gamblers' Story of Saruga: Broken Iron Fire. *See* Suruga yuhkyou-den: Yabure takka, 1964

Gambling Lady, 1934 (Barnes; Blanke; Grot; Orry-Kelly)
Gambling Ship, 1933 (Head; Lang)
Game Bag. *See* Carniere, 1997
Game Called Scruggs. *See* Scruggs, 1965
Game for Six Lovers. *See* Eau à la bouche, 1959
Game Is Over. *See* Curée, 1966
Game of Death, 1945 (Dunn)
Game of Death, 1978 (Barry)
Game of Love. *See* Blé en herbe, 1953
Game with Stones. *See* Spiel mit Steinen, 1965
Gamekeeper, 1980 (Menges)
Games, 1967 (Fraker)
Games, 1970 (Lai)
Gamine. *See* Uličnice, 1936
Ganashatru, 1989 (Dutta)
Gander at Mother Goose, 1940 (Avery; Blanc; Stalling)
Gandhi, 1981 (Nihalani; Shankar)
Gandy Goose and the Chipper Chipmunk, 1948 (Terry)
Gandy the Goose, 1938 (Terry)
Gandy's Dream Girl, 1944 (Terry)
Gang, 1976 (Carrière)
Gang-Busters, 1955 (Clothier)
Gang des otages, 1972 (Coutard; Legrand)
Gang in die Nacht, 1921 (Mayer)
Gang Show, 1937 (Wilcox)
Gang That Couldn't Shoot Straight, 1971 (Grusin; Winkler)
Gang War, 1928 (Glennon; Miller)
Ganga Sagar, 1979 (Chandragupta)
Gang's All Here, 1943 (Basevi; Cronjager; Friedhofer; Newman; Raksin)
Gangs of Chicago, 1940 (Brown)
Gangs of New York, 2000 (Ballhaus; Schoonmaker)
Gangster, 1964 (Alcoriza)
Gangsters and the Girl, 1914 (Ince)
Gangster's Boy, 1938 (Brown)
Gangsters du Chateau d'If, 1938 (D'Eaubonne)
Gangsters of New York, 1914 (Loos)
Gangster's Song. *See* Gurentai no uta, 1934
Gangway, 1937 (Junge)
Gangway for Tomorrow, 1943 (Musuraca)
Gaou utaggasen, 1939 (Miyagawa)
Garbo Talks, 1984 (Comden and Green)
Garce, 1984 (Coutard)
Garçon!, 1983 (Sarde)
Garçon sauvage, 1951 (Jeanson)
Garçonnière, 1960 (Guerra)
Garde à vue, 1981 (Delerue; Mnouchkine; Nuytten)
Garde-chasse, 1951 (Decaë)
Garden. *See* Zahrada, 1968Garden Gopher, 1950 (Avery)
Garden Murder Case, 1936 (Clarke)
Garden of Allah, 1916 (Selig)
Garden of Allah, 1927 (Garmes; Mayer)
Garden of Allah, 1936 (Miller; Rosson; Selznick; Steiner; Wheeler)
Garden of Eden, 1928 (Kräly; Menzies)
Garden of Eden, 1954 (Kaufman)
Garden of Evil, 1954 (Brackett; Herrmann; Krasner; Lemaire; Wheeler)
Garden of the Finzi-Contini. *See* Giardino dei Finzi-Contini, 1970
Garden of the Moon, 1938 (Mercer; Wald)
Garden of Weeds, 1924 (Brown)
Gardener, 1960 (Halas and Batchelor)
Gardener. *See* Trädgårdsmästaren, 1912
Gardens of England, 1942 (Unsworth)
Gardens of Stone, 1987 (Bass; Tavoularis)
Gardens of the Moon, 1938 (Gaudio)
Gardeoffizier. *See* Leibgardist, 1925
Gardien de la nuit, 1985 (Branco)
Gardiens de phare, 1929 (Périnal)

Gareeb, 1942 (Biswas)
Gargousse, 1938 (Jeanson)
Gargoyles, 1972 (Winston)
Garibaldi—the General, 1986 (Cristaldi)
Garment Jungle, 1957 (Biroc; Louis)
Garrison amoureuse, 1933 (Planer)
Garrison's Finish, 1923 (Rosson)
Gas and Air, 1923 (Roach)
Gasbags, 1940 (Rank)
Gaslight Ridge, 1957 (Raksin)
Gaslight, 1940 (Addinsell; Junge)
Gaslight, 1944 (Gibbons; Irene; Kaper; Reisch; Ruttenberg)
Gasoline Engagement, 1911 (Gaudio)
Gasoline Gus, 1921 (Brown)
Gasoline Wedding, 1918 (Roach)
Gaspard a un rendez-vous, 1963 (Braunberger)
Gaspard et Robinson, 1990 (Legrand)
Gaspard fait du cheval, 1963 (Braunberger)
Gaspard se marie, 1964 (Braunberger)
Gasparone, 1955 (Eisler)
Gassenhauer, 1931 (Schüfftan)
Gassi, 1960 (Delerue)
Gäst i eget hus, 1957 (Nykvist)
Gasu ningen daiichigo, 1960 (Tsuburaya)
Gatan, 1949 (Lundgren)
Gatans barn, 1914 (Magnusson)
Gate of Youth. *See* Seishun no mon, 1975
Gate of Youth: Independence. *See* Seishun no mon: Jiritsu hen, 1977
Gates of Paris. *See* Porte de Lilas, 1957
Gates of Power, 1948 (Arnold)
Gates of the Night. *See* Portes de la nuit, 1946
Gateway, 1938 (Cronjager; Reisch; Trotti)
Gateway of the Moon, 1928 (Fox)
Gateway to the Catskills, 1906 (Bitzer)
Gathering, 1977 (Barry)
Gathering of Eagles, 1963 (Bumstead; Goldsmith; Harlan; Irene)
Gator, 1976 (Fraker)
Gattin, 1943 (Von Harbou)
Gatto, 1977 (Morricone)
Gatto a nove code, 1971 (Morricone)
Gatto nero, 1981 (Donaggio)
Gattopardo, 1962 (Cecchi D'Amico; Rota; Rotunno; Serandrei)
Gaucho, 1928 (Gaudio)
Gauchos of Eldorado, 1941 (Canutt)
Gauguin, 1950 (Braunberger)
Gauguin the Savage, 1980 (Lassally)
Gauloises bleues, 1968 (Guillemot; Mnouchkine)
Gaunt Stranger, 1938 (Balcon; Neame)
Gavilan pollero, 1950 (Figueroa)
Gavrilovic II, 1983 (Vukotić)
Gay Anties, 1947 (Blanc; Stalling)
Gay Caballero, 1940 (Cronjager; Day)
Gay Deceiver, 1926 (Booth; Gaudio; Gibbons)
Gay Deception, 1935 (Lasky; Reynolds)
Gay Defender, 1927 (Cronjager; Mankiewicz)
Gay Desperado, 1936 (Day; Lasky; Newman)
Gay Diplomat, 1931 (Berman; Steiner)
Gay Divorcee, 1934 (Berman; Biroc; Hoffenstein; Pan; Plunkett; Polglase; Steiner)
Gay Falcon, 1941 (Musuraca; Polglase)
Gay Imposters. *See* Gold Diggers in Paris, 1938
Gay Knighties, 1941 (Pal)
Gay Lady. *See* Battle of Paris, 1929
Gay Lady. *See* Trottie True, 1948
Gay Mrs. Trexel. *See* Susan and God, 1940
Gay Old Bird, 1927 (Miller)

Gay Parisian, 1941 (Friedhofer; Haller)
Gay Purr-ee, 1962 (Jones)
Gay Retreat, 1927 (Fox)
Gay Senorita, 1945 (Guffey)
Gay Sisters, 1942 (Blanke; Head; Polito; Steiner)
Gaz, 1939 (Alexeieff and Parker)
Gaz de Lacq, 1960 (Guillemot)
Gaz mortels, 1916 (Burel; Gaumont)
Gazebo, 1960 (Rose)
Gazouilly petit oiseau, 1953 (Starewicz)
Gebissen wird nur Nachts—Happening der Vampire, 1971 (Francis)
Gee, If Me Mudder Could See Me, 1905 (Bitzer)
Gee Whiz Genevieve!, 1924 (Roach)
Gee Whiz-z-z, 1956 (Blanc; Jones)
Geese and Ducks' Singing Contest. See Gaou utaggasen, 1939
Gefährliche Alter, 1911 (Messter)
Gefährlicher Frühling, 1943 (Röhrig)
Gefährliches Spiel, 1919 (Kolowrat-Krakowsky)
Gefährliches Spiel, 1937 (Warm)
Gefährten meines Sommers, 1943 (Von Harbou)
Gefangene Seele, 1917 (Freund)
Gefangene Seelen, 1912 (Messter)
Geheimnis der alten Mamsell, 1925 (Andrejew)
Geheimnis von Bombay, 1920 (Herlth; Röhrig)
Geheimnisse des Orients, 1928 (Courant)
Geheimnisse einer Seele, 1926 (Metzner)
Geheimnistrager, 1975 (Theodorakis)
Geheimnisvolle Spiegel, 1928 (Hoffmann)
Gehetzte Menschen, 1924 (Messter; Planer)
Gehetzte Menschen, 1932 (Warm)
Geidou ichidai otoko, 1941 (Yoda)
Geierwally, 1940 (Warm)
Geiger von Florenz, 1925 (Pommer)
Geisha, 1914 (Ince)
Geisha Boy, 1958 (Head)
Gekla no kyoba, 1927 (Tsuburaya)
Gelbe Haus des King-Fu, 1930 (Douy)
Gelbe Schein, 1918 (Kräly)
Gèle en enfer, 1990 (Coutard)
Geliebte Feindin, 1954 (Herlth)
Geliebte Roswolskys, 1921 (Galeen)
Geliebter Lügner, 1949 (Herlth)
Gelosia, 1943 (Amidei)
Gelöste Ketten, 1916 (Freund)
Gems, 1930 (Balcon)
Gemütlich beim Kaffee, 1898 (Messter)
Gen to Fudo-myoh, 1961 (Tsuburaya)
Gendarme desconocido, 1941 (Figueroa)
Gene of the Northland, 1915 (Rosher)
Généalogies d'un crime, 1997 (Branco)
General, 1926 (Bruckman; Schenck)
General Crack, 1929 (Gaudio)
General Della Rovere. See Generale Della Rovere, 1959
General Died at Dawn, 1936 (Dreier; Westmore Family)
General Idi Amin Dada, 1974 (Almendros)
General Line. See Staroie i novoie, 1929
General Nuisance, 1941 (Bruckman)
General Spanky, 1936 (Roach)
Generale Della Rovere, 1959 (Amidei)
General's Daughter, 1999 (Burwell; Goldman)
Generation, 1969 (Grusin)
Génération du désert, 1958 (Jarre)
Génération spontanée, 1909 (Cohl)
Génésis, 1986 (Shankar)
Genevieve, 1953 (Challis; Rank)
Genghis Khan, 1965 (Mathieson; Unsworth)

Genio, due compari, un pollo, 1975 (Morricone)
Genou de Claire, 1970 (Almendros; Rousselot)
Genroku chushingura, 1941-42 (Yoda)
Gens du voyage, 1938 (D'Eaubonne)
Gens normaux n'ont rien d'exceptionnel, 1993 (Branco)
Gente da Praia da Vieira, 1975 (de Almeida)
Gente di rispetto, 1975 (Morricone)
Gente en la playa, 1961 (Almendros)
Gentle Corsican, 1956 (Lassally)
Gentle Sergeant. See Three Stripes in the Sun, 1955
Gentle Sex, 1943 (Dillon; Krasker; Rank)
Gentle Touch. See Feminine Touch, 1956
Gentleman after Dark, 1942 (Krasner; Tiomkin)
Gentleman at Heart, 1942 (Clarke)
Gentleman Daku, 1937 (Biswas)
Gentleman d'Epsom, 1963 (Legrand)
Gentleman from America, 1923 (Miller)
Gentleman from Blue Gulch. See Conversion of Frosty Blake, 1915
Gentleman from Mississippi, 1914 (Edeson)
Gentleman in Paradise. See Kedlubnový kavalír v ráji, 1928
Gentleman in Room 6, 1951 (Kaufman)
Gentleman Jo . . . uccidi, 1967 (Morricone)
Gentleman of Paris, 1927 (Mankiewicz; Rosson)
Gentleman or Thief, 1913 (Loos)
Gentleman Tramp, 1973 (Almendros)
Gentleman's Agreement, 1935 (Havelock-Allan)
Gentleman's Agreement, 1947 (Lemaire; Miller; Newman; Wheeler; Zanuck)
Gentlemen Are Born, 1934 (Orry-Kelly)
Gentlemen Marry Brunettes, 1955 (Cole; Loos)
Gentlemen of the Press, 1928 (Zukor)
Gentlemen Prefer Blondes, 1928 (Loos; Mankiewicz; Rosson; Zukor)
Gentlemen Prefer Blondes, 1953 (Carmichael; Cole; Lederer; Lemaire; Loos; Wheeler)
Gentlemen, the Queen, 1953 (Rank)
Genuine: Die Tragödie eines seltsamen Hauses, 1920 (Mayer)
Geordie, 1955 (Alwyn)
George Bernard Shaw, 1957 (Lassally)
George Raft Story, 1961 (Mainwaring)
George Takes the Air. See It's in the Air, 1938
George Wallace: Settin' the Woods on Fire, 2000 (Daring)
George Washington Slept Here, 1942 (Deutsch; Haller; Orry-Kelly; Wald)
George White's 1935 Scandals, 1935 (Friedhofer)
George White's Scandals, 1934 (Friedhofer; Garmes; Lemaire)
Georgia's Friends. See Four Friends, 1981
Georgie and the Dragon, 1951 (Bosustow; Hubley)
Geppetto, 2000 (Schwartz)
Gerald McBoing Boing, 1951 (Bosustow)
Gerald McBoing Boing on the Planet Moo, 1956 (Bosustow)
Gerald McBoing Boing's Symphony, 1953 (Bosustow)
German Calling, 1942 (Lye)
German Manpower, 1943 (Kanin)
Germania, anno zero, 1947 (Amidei)
Germanin, 1943 (Stallich)
Germany in Autumn. See **Deutschland im Herbst**, 1978
Germany, Year Zero. See Germania, anno zero, 1947
Germinal, 1961 (Saulnier)
Germinal, 1963 (Spaak)
Geronimo, 1939 (Dreier; Head)
Geronimo, 1962 (Friedhofer)
Gertie on Tour, 1918-21 (McCay)
Gertie the Dinosaur, 1914 (McCay)
Gervaise, 1955 (Aurenche and Bost; Auric)
Geschichte der stillen Mühle, 1914 (Warm)
Geschichte des Prinzen Achmed, 1928 (Reiniger)
Geschichte eines Lebens. See Annelie, 1941

Geschiendene Frau, 1953 (Herlth)
Geschlecht derer von Ringwall, 1918 (Freund)
Geschwader Fledermaus, 1958 (Eisler)
Gestärtes Rendez-vous, 1897 (Messter)
Gestes de France, 1963 (Braunberger)
Gestohlene Gesicht, 1930 (Schüfftan)
Gestohlene Herz, 1934 (Reiniger)
Gestos e Fragmentos, 1982 (de Almeida)
Gesucht: Monika Ertl, 1989 (Rozsa)
Get Busy, 1924 (Roach)
Get 'em Young, 1926 (Roach)
Get Out Your Handkerchiefs. See Preparez vos mouchoirs, 1977
Get Rich Quick Porky, 1937 (Blanc; Clampett; Stalling)
Get to Know Your Rabbit, 1972 (Alonzo)
Get Your Man, 1923 (Roach)
Getaway, 1972 (Ballard; Jones)
Getting Even, 1909 (Bitzer)
Getting Gertie's Garter, 1927 (Rosson)
Getting Gertie's Garter, 1945 (Friedhofer)
Getting His Goat, 1920 (Roach)
Getting Mary Married, 1919 (Loos)
Getting of Wisdom, 1977 (McAlpine)
Getting Out, 1994 (Daring)
Getting Straight, 1970 (Kovacs)
Gewissenswurm, 1917 (Kolowrat-Krakowsky)
Gewisser Judas, 1958 (Herlth)
Gewonnene Prozeß, 1917 (Kolowrat-Krakowsky)
Gharbar, 1963 (Merchant)
Gharc Bahire, 1982 (Dutta)
Ghidrah, the Three-Headed Monster. See Sandai kaiju chikyu saidai no kessen, 1965
Ghosks in the Bunk, 1939 (Fleischer)
Ghost, 1990 (Edlund; Jarre; Murch; North)
Ghost and Mrs. Muir, 1947 (Day; Dunne; Herrmann; Lang; Lemaire; Spencer)
Ghost and the Darkness, 1996 (Goldman; Goldsmith; Zsigmond)
Ghost Breaker, 1914 (Buckland; Macpherson)
Ghost Breakers, 1940 (Dreier; Head; Lang)
Ghost Dad, 1990 (Bumstead; Mancini)
Ghost Dog: The Way of the Samurai, 1999 (Müller)
Ghost Goes West, 1935 (Cardiff; Hornbeck; Korda; Mathieson; Rosson; Sherwood)
Ghost Goes Wild, 1947 (Alton)
Ghost of Flight 401, 1978 (Raksin)
Ghost of Frankenstein, 1942 (Krasner; Pierce)
Ghost of Slumber Mountain, 1918 (O'Brien)
Ghost of St. Michael's, 1941 (Balcon)
Ghost Ship, 1943 (D'Agostino; Lewton; Musuraca)
Ghost Story, 1981 (Cardiff; Houseman; Sarde; Smith; Whitlock)
Ghost Town, 1944 (Terry)
Ghost Town, 1955 (Biroc)
Ghost Town Gold, 1936 (Canutt)
Ghost Train, 1931 (Balcon; Biro)
Ghost Train, 1941 (Rank; Vetchinsky)
Ghost Train. See Yuhrei ressha, 1949
Ghost Valley Raiders, 1940 (Canutt)
Ghost Wanted, 1940 (Blanc; Jones; Stalling)
Ghostbusters, 1984 (Bernstein; Edlund; Kovacs)
Ghostbusters II, 1989 (Elfman; Muren)
Ghosts, 1997 (Winston)
Ghosts From the Past. See Ghosts of Mississippi, 1996
Ghosts in Rome. See Fantasmi a Roma, 1961
Ghosts—Italian Style. See Questi fantasmi, 1967
Ghosts of Mississippi, 1996 (Seale)
Ghoul, 1933 (Balcon; Junge)
Ghoul, 1975 (Francis)

Ghum Bhangaar Gaan, 1964 (Shankar)
Giacoma l'idealista, 1942 (Ponti)
Giaconda Smile. See A Woman's Vengeance, 1948
Giallo automatico, 1980 (Bozzetto)
Gian Burrasca, 1943 (Zavattini)
Giant, 1956 (Hornbeck; Leven; Tiomkin; Warner)
Giant Behemoth, 1958 (Lourié; O'Brien)
Giant Killer, 1924 (Lantz)
Giants vs. Yanks, 1923 (Roach)
Giardino dei Finzi-Contini, 1970 (Conti; Flaiano and Pinelli)
Giardino delle delizie, 1967 (Morricone)
Gibbsville: The Turning Point of Jim Malloy. See Turning Point of Jim Malloy, 1975
Gibier de potence, 1951 (Aurenche and Bost)
Gibraltar, 1938 (Fradetal; Wakhévitch)
Gibson Goddess, 1909 (Bitzer)
Giddy Yap, 1949 (Bosustow)
Giddy-yapping, 1944 (Fleischer)
Giddyap, 1950 (Raksin)
Gideon of Scotland Yard, 1957 (Adam; Young)
Gideon's Day, 1958 (Clarke)
Gideon's Trumpet, 1980 (Houseman)
Gidget, 1959 (Duning; Guffey; Williams)
Gidget Gets Married, 1972 (Biroc)
Gidget Goes Hawaiian, 1961 (Duning)
Gidget Goes to Rome, 1963 (Williams)
Gifle, 1974 (Delerue)
Gift. See Cadeau, 1982
Gift. See Dárck, 1946
Gift for Love, 1964 (Heller)
Gift of Gab, 1934 (Freund; Wald)
Gift of Green, 1946 (van Dongen)
Gift of Love, 1958 (Brackett; Krasner; Lemaire)
Gift Wrapped, 1952 (Blanc; Stalling)
Giftasvuxnar döttrar, 1933 (Jaenzon)
Gigantis the Fire Monster. See Gojira no gyakushu, 1955
Gigi, 1958 (Ames; Beaton; Freed; Previn; Ruttenberg)
Gigolette, 1935 (Ruttenberg)
Gigolo, 1926 (Adrian; Sullivan)
Gigot, 1962 (Cahn)
Gilbert and Sullivan. See Story of Gilbert and Sullivan, 1953
Gilda, 1946 (Cohn; Cole; Friedhofer; Goosson; Louis; Maté; Polglase)
Gilded Cage, 1916 (Edeson; Marion)
Gilded Highway, 1926 (Musuraca)
Gilded Lily, 1921 (Haller; Zukor)
Gilded Lily, 1935 (Banton; Zukor)
Gimme, 1923 (Gibbons)
Gimme Shelter, 1970 (Wexler)
Gina. See Mort en ce jardin, 1956
Ginger, 1935 (Glennon)
Ginger Bread Boy, 1934 (Lantz)
Ginger e Fred, 1986 (Delli Colli; Donati; Flaiano and Pinelli; Guerra; Mnouchkine; Morricone)
Ginger Meggs, 1982 (Seale)
Gingerbread Hut. See Perníková chaloupka, 1951
Gingham Girl, 1927 (Plunkett)
Gink at the Sink, 1952 (Bruckman)
Ginpei the Outlaw. See Muhoumono Ginpei, 1938
Ginrin, 1955 (Takemitsu)
Ginsberg the Great, 1927 (Blanke; Haskin)
Giocattolo, 1979 (Morricone)
Giocchi particolari, 1970 (Morricone)
Giochi particolari, 1970 (Guerra)
Gioco pericoloso, 1942 (Amidei)
Gion bayashi, 1953 (Miyagawa; Yoda)
Gion Festival Music. See Gion bayashi, 1953

Gion no shimai, 1936 (Yoda)
Giono Prima, 1987 (Mnouchkine)
Giordano Bruno, 1973 (Morricone; Storaro)
Giornata nera per l'Ariete, 1972 (Morricone; Storaro))
Giornata particolare, 1977 (Ponti)
Giorno da leone, 1961 (Cristaldi)
Giorno della civetta, 1968 (Delli Colli)
Giorno in pretura, 1954 (Ponti; de Laurentiis)
Giorno nella vita, 1946 (Zavattini)
Giorno per giorno disperatamente, 1961 (Cristaldi)
Giorno prima, 1987 (Morricone)
Giovani mariti, 1958 (Rota)
Giovanna e le altre, 1960 (de Laurentiis)
Giovanni Falcone, 1993 (Donaggio)
Gioventù alla sbarra, 1951 (Delli Colli)
Gioventù perduta, 1947 (Ponti)
Giovinezza, giovinezza, 1969 (Storaro)
Girl, a Guy and a Gob, 1941 (Metty)
Girl and Her Trust, 1912 (Bitzer)
Girl and the Gambler, 1939 (Metty)
Girl and the General. See Ragazza e il generale, 1967
Girl Can't Help It, 1956 (Kanin; Lemaire; Shamroy; Wheeler)
Girl Crazy, 1932 (Mankiewicz)
Girl Crazy, 1943 (Daniels; Freed; Irene; Mayer; Sharaff)
Girl Friend, 1935 (Walker)
Girl Friends. See Podrugi, 1935
Girl from Avenue A, 1940 (Barnes; Day)
Girl from Chicago, 1927 (Mohr)
Girl from China. See Shanghai Lady, 1929
Girl from God's Country, 1921 (Walker)
Girl from Havana, 1940 (Brown)
Girl from Jones Beach, 1949 (Diamond)
Girl from Manhattan, 1948 (Laszlo)
Girl from Maxim's, 1932 (Korda; Périnal)
Girl from Mexico, 1939 (Polglase)
Girl from Missouri, 1934 (Adrian; Gillespie; Loos)
Girl from Petrovka, 1974 (Mancini; Zanuck; Zsigmond)
Girl from Scotland Yard, 1937 (Head; Schary)
Girl from Tenth Avenue, 1935 ((Blanke; Orry-Kelly)
Girl from the Distant River. See Devushka s dalekoi reki, 1928
Girl Game. See Copacabana Palace, 1962
Girl Grief, 1932 (Roach)
Girl Happy, 1965 (Lathrop; Pasternak)
Girl He Left Behind, 1956 (McCord)
Girl in 313, 1940 (Cronjager; Day)
Girl in 419, 1933 (Furthman; Struss)
Girl in a Dressing Gown. See Flickan i frack, 1956
Girl in Black. See To koritsi me ta mavra, 1955
Girl in Every Port, 1928 (Miller)
Girl in Every Port, 1952 (Musuraca)
Girl in Lover's Lane, 1959 (Cronjager)
Girl in Overalls. See Swing Shift Maisie, 1943
Girl in Room 17. See Vice Squad, 1953
Girl in the Glass Cage, 1929 (Haller)
Girl in the Moon. See Frau im Mond, 1929
Girl in the Painting. See Portrait from Life, 1948
Girl in the Red Velvet Swing, 1955 (Brackett; Krasner; Lemaire; Reisch; Wheeler)
Girl in the Shack, 1914 (Loos)
Girl in the Show, 1929 (Day; Gibbons)
Girl in the Street. See London Melody, 1937
Girl in the Taxi. See Chaste Suzanne, 1937
Girl in the Window Opposite. See Flickan i fönstret mittemot, 1942
Girl in White, 1952 (Raksin; Rose)
Girl Loves Boy, 1937 (Brown)
Girl Most Likely, 1957 (Jarrico)

Girl Must Live, 1939 (Vetchinsky)
Girl Named Sooner, 1975 (Goldsmith)
Girl Named Tamiko, 1962 (Bernstein; Head; Lang; Wallis)
Girl Next Door, 1953 (Lemaire; Shamroy)
Girl of the Golden West, 1914 (Buckland; Macpherson)
Girl of the Golden West, 1923 (Polito)
Girl of the Golden West, 1938 (Adrian; Canutt; Gibbons; Kahn; Stothart; Vorkapich)
Girl of the Limberlost, 1945 (Guffey)
Girl of the Ozarks, 1936 (Dreier)
Girl of the Port, 1930 (Glennon)
Girl of the Rio, 1932 (Steiner)
Girl of the Snows. See Snyegurochka, 1913
Girl of Yesterday, 1915 (Marion)
Girl on a Motorcycle, 1968 (Cardiff; D'Eaubonne)
Girl on the Boat, 1962 (Bryan)
Girl on the Canal. See Painted Boats, 1945
Girl on the Front Page, 1936 (Krasner)
Girl on the Stairs, 1924 (Walker)
Girl on the Subway, 1939 (Furthman)
Girl Rush, 1944 (Musuraca)
Girl Rush, 1955 (Daniels; Head; Hornbeck)
Girl Said No, 1930 (Gibbons; MacArthur)
Girl Shy, 1924 (Roach; Zukor)
Girl-Shy Cowboy, 1928 (Miller)
Girl Swappers. See Two and Two Make Six, 1962
Girl Trouble, 1942 (Cronjager; Day; Newman)
Girl Was Young, 1937 (Harrison)
Girl Who Had Everything, 1953 (Previn)
Girl Who Rode in the Palio. See Ragazza del Palio, 1957
Girl Who Stayed Home, 1919 (Bitzer)
Girl with a Suitcase. See Ragazza con la Valigia, 1960
Girl with Ideas, 1937 (Krasner)
Girl with the Devil in Her. See Jsem devče s čertem v tele, 1933
Girl without a Room, 1933 (Banton)
Girlfriends, 1978 (Von Brandenstein)
Girlfriends. See Amiche, 1955
Girls, 1957 (Cole; Deutsch; Orry-Kelly; Porter; Surtees)
Girls about Town, 1931 (Banton; Haller; Vorkapich)
Girls and a Daddy, 1908 (Bitzer)
Girls Can Play, 1937 (Ballard; Goosson)
Girls Demand Excitement, 1931 (Clarke)
Girl's Folly, 1916 (Carré; Marion)
Girls! Girls! Girls!, 1962 (Head; Wallis)
Girls Gone Wild, 1929 (Edeson)
Girls Growing Up, 1967 (Halas and Batchelor)
Girls He Left Behind. See Gang's All Here, 1943
Girls in the Night, 1953 (Boyle)
Girls Just Want to Have Fun, 1985 (Newman)
Girls Marked Danger. See Tratta delle bianche, 1952
Girls Night Out, 1997 (Burwell)
Girls of the Big House, 1945 (Alton)
Girls on the Loose, 1958 (Lathrop)
Girls Please!, 1934 (Wilcox)
Girls' School, 1938 (Goosson; Planer)
Girls' School, 1949 (Biswas)
Girl's Strategem, 1913 (Bitzer)
Girls Will Be Boys, 1934 (Neame; Siodmak)
Giro del monde degli innamorati di Paynet, 1974 (Morricone)
Giselle, 1970 (Alekan)
Gishiki, 1971 (Takemitsu; Toda)
Gitana tenias que ser, 1953 (Alcoriza)
Gitans d'Espagne, 1945 (Braunberger)
Gitta entdeckt ihr Herz, 1932 (Courant)
Giù la testa, 1972 (Morricone)
Giudizia universale, 1961 (de Laurentiis; Zavattini))

Giulietta degli spiriti, 1965 (Di Venanzo; Flaiano and Pinelli;
  Gherardi; Rota)
Giungla, 1942 (Amidei)
Give a Girl a Break, 1954 (Goodrich and Hackett; Previn)
Give and Take. *See* Singing in the Corn, 1946
Give and Take, 1956 (Hanna and Barbera)
Give Her a Ring, 1934 (Neame)
Give Her the Moon. *See* Caprices de Maria, 1969
Give Me a Sailor, 1938 (Dreier; Head)
Give Me Your Heart, 1936 (Orry-Kelly)
Give My Regards, 1948 (Lemaire)
Give My Regards to Broadway, 1948 (Hoffenstein; Reynolds; Wheeler)
Give Us the Moon, 1944 (Rank)
Give Us This Day, 1949 (Vetchinsky)
Give Us This Day. *See* Ingeborg Holm, 1913
Give Us This Night, 1936 (Dreier; Korngold)
Giving the Bride Away, 1919 (Roach)
Giving Them Fits, 1914 (Roach)
Giving You the Stars. *See* Give Her a Ring, 1934
Glaciers, 1942 (Decaë)
Glad Rag Doll, 1929 (Haskin)
Glad Rags, 1923 (Bruckman)
Gladiator, 1938 (D'Agostino; Young)
Gladiator, 2000 (Zimmer)
Glaive et la balance, 1963 (Jeanson; Spaak)
Glamour, 1934 (Laemmle)
Glamour Boy, 1941 (Dreier; Head; Young)
Glamour for Sale, 1940 (Planer)
Glanz und Elend der Kurtisanen, 1927 (Planer)
Glas Wasser, 1922 (Pommer)
Glasberget, 1953 (Lundgren)
Gläserne Zelle, 1978 (Müller)
Glass Bottom Boat, 1966 (Shamroy)
Glass Cage, 1955 (Carreras)
Glass Cell. *See* Gläserne Zelle, 1981
Glass Houses, 1970 (Raksin)
Glass Key, 1935 (Head)
Glass Key, 1942 (Dreier; Head; Young)
Glass Menagerie, 1950 (Burks; Steiner; Wald)
Glass Menagerie, 1973 (Barry)
Glass Menagerie, 1987 (Ballhaus; Mancini)
Glass Mountain, 1948 (Rota)
Glass of Wine. *See* Ett glass vin, 1960
Glass Slipper, 1938 (Terry)
Glass Slipper, 1954 (Kaper; Plunkett; Rose)
Glass Tomb. *See* Glass Cage, 1955
Glass Wall, 1953 (Biroc)
Gleam O'Dawn, 1922 (Furthman)
Glengarry Glen Ross, 1992 (Mamet)
Glenn Miller Story, 1954 (Daniels; Mancini)
Glimpse of Austria, 1938 (Hoch)
Glimpses of Java and Ceylon, 1937 (Hoch)
Glimpses of New Brunswick, 1938 (Hoch)
Glimpses of Peru, 1937 (Hoch)
Glimpses of the Moon, 1923 (Rosson)
Glimpses of the U.S.A., 1959 (Bernstein)
Glimpses of West Bengal, 1978 (Chandragupta)
Glinka. *See* Kompozitor Glinka, 1952
Glissements progressifs du plaisir, 1974 (Robbe-Grillet)
Global Affair, 1964 (Ames; Lederer; Ruttenberg)
Gloria, 1980 (Conti; Henry)
Gloria, 1999 (Watkin)
Glorifying the American Girl, 1929 (Berlin)
Glorious Betsy, 1928 (Mohr)
Glorious Campaign. *See* Spanilá jízda, 1963
Glorious Fourth, 1927 (Roach)

Glorious Musketeers, 1973 (Halas and Batchelor)
Glory, 1989 (Francis)
Glory Alley, 1952 (Daniels; Rose)
Glory Guys, 1965 (Howe)
Glove Birds, 1942 (Bruckman)
Glove Taps, 1937 (Roach)
Glow Worm, 1930 (Fleischer)
Glowing Autumn. *See* Moeru aki, 1978
Glück bei Frauen, 1944 (Stallich)
Glück mußt Du haben auf dieser Welt. *See* Wer küßt wen?, 1947
Glücklicher Mensch, 1943 (Wagner)
Glücksmühle, 1947 (Von Dassanowsky)
Glupichkiye zanmimayestsya sportom, 1917 (Starewicz)
Gniazdo, 1974 (ścibor-Rylski)
Gnome-Mobile, 1967 (Disney; Ellenshaw)
Go and Get It, 1920 (Carré)
Go As You Please, 1920 (Roach)
Go Away Stowaway, 1967 (Blanc)
Go-Between, 1971 (Dillon; Fisher; Legrand; Pinter)
Gô chez les oiseaux, 1939 (Grimault)
Go Fish, 1994 (Vachon)
Go Fly a Kit, 1957 (Blanc; Jones)
Go for Broke, 1950 (Schary)
Go-Getter, 1937 (Edeson; Orry-Kelly; Wallis)
Go Go Amigo, 1965 (Blanc; McKimson)
Go Go Mania. *See* Pop Gear, 1965
Go into Your Dance, 1935 (Gaudio; Polito)
Go, Man, Go, 1954 (Howe; North)
Go Naked in the World, 1961 (Deutsch; Krasner; Rose)
Go See Mother . . . Father Is Working. *See* Va voir Maman . . . Papa
  travaille, 1977
Go to Blazes, 1942 (Balcon)
Go to Nowhere, 1966 (Ivanov-Vano)
Go West, 1923 (Roach)
Go West, 1925 (Mayer; Schenck)
Go West, 1940 (Edens; Kahn; Kaper)
Go West, Big Boy, 1931 (Terry)
Go West, Young Lady, 1941 (Cahn; Plunkett)
Go West, Young Man, 1936 (Banton; Dreier; Struss)
Goal Rush, 1932 (Iwerks)
Goat, 1918 (Marion)
Goat Getter, 1925 (Garmes)
Gobbo, 1960 (Gherardi; de Laurentiis)
GoBots: Battle of The Rock Lords, 1986 (Hanna and Barbera)
God Is My Co-Pilot, 1945 (Burks; Waxman)
God Needs Men. *See* Dieu a besoin des hommes, 1950
God Within, 1912 (Bitzer)
Goda vänner, trogna grannar, 1938 (Fischer)
Godan, 1962 (Shankar)
Goddess of Sagebrush Gulch, 1912 (Bitzer)
Goddess, 1957 (Justin; Thomson)
Goddess. *See* Devi, 1960
Godelureaux, 1961 (Gégauff; Rabier)
Godfather, 1972 (Murch; Reynolds; Rota; Smith; Tavoularis; Willis)
Godfather, Part II, 1974 (Murch; Rota; Smith; Tavoularis; Willis;
  van Runkle)
Godfather, Part III, 1990 (Murch; Rota; Tavoularis; Willis)
Godless Girl, 1928 (Adrian; Grot; Macpherson))
Gods and Monsters, 1998 (Burwell)
God's Country and the Woman, 1936 (Friedhofer; Gaudio;
  Steiner; Wallis)
God's Little Acre, 1958 (Bernstein; Haller; Maddow)
God's Punishment. *See* Gottesgeissel, 1920
God's Tomorrow. *See* Restitution, 1918
Godspell, 1973 (Schwartz)
Godzilla. *See* **Gojira**, 1954

Godzilla vs. The Thing. *See* Gojira tai Mosura, 1964
Godzina szczytu, 1973 (Stawiński)
Godzina W, 1979 (Stawiński)
Goin' South, 1977 (Almendros)
Goin' to Town, 1935 (Banton; Dreier; Struss; Zukor)
Going and Coming Back. *See* Partir, revenir, 1985
Going Ape!, 1981 (Bernstein)
Going Bananas, 1987 (Donaggio; Golan and Globus)
Going Bye-Bye!, 1934 (Roach)
Going Crooked, 1926 (Clarke)
Going! Going! Gone!, 1918 (Roach)
Going! Going! Gosh!, 1952 (Blanc; Jones; Stalling)
Going Highbrow, 1935 (Edeson; Orry-Kelly)
Going Hollywood, 1933 (Adrian; Brown; Freed; Marion; Stewart;
    Stothart; Wanger)
Going My Way, 1944 (Dreier; Head; van Heusen)
Going Places, 1938 (Mercer; Wald; Wallis)
Going Places. *See* Valseuses, 1974
Going Steady. *See* Yotz 'im Kavua, 1979
Going to Blazes, 1933 (Lantz)
Going to Congress, 1924 (Roach)
Going Wild, 1931 (Polito)
Gojira, 1954 (Tsuburaya)
Gojira no gyakushu, 1955 (Tsuburaya)
Gojira no musuko, 1967 (Tsuburaya)
Gojira tai Mosura, 1964 (Tsuburaya)
Goju man-nin no isan, 1963 (Muraki)
Gokuraku hanayome-juku, 1936 (Miyagawa)
Gold, 1913 (Bitzer)
Gold, 1974 (Bernstein; Vetchinsky)
Gold and Glitter, 1912 (Bitzer)
Gold and the Glory. *See* Coolangatta Gold, 1984
Gold Diggers in Paris, 1938 (Barnes; Mercer; Polito; Wald;
    Wallis; Warner)
Gold Diggers of 1933, 1933 (Grot; Orry-Kelly; Polito; Wallis; Warner)
Gold Diggers of 1935, 1935 (Barnes; Cortez; Grot; Orry-Kelly; Warner)
Gold Diggers of 1937, 1937 (Edeson; Orry-Kelly; Warner)
Gold Diggers of '49, 1936 (Avery; Stalling)
Gold Diggers of Broadway, 1929 (Rennahan)
Gold in New Frisco, 1939 (Hoffmann)
Gold Is Not All, 1910 (Bitzer)
Gold Is Where You Find It, 1938 (Friedhofer; Polito; Steiner; Wallis)
Gold of Naples. *See* Oro di Napoli, 1955
Gold of the Seven Saints, 1961 (Biroc; Brackett)
Gold Reserve, 1925 (Tisse)
Gold Ring. *See* Złote koło, 1971
Gold Seekers, 1910 (Bitzer)
Goldbergs, 1950 (Bumstead; Seitz)
Golden Arrow, 1936 (Edeson; Grot; Orry-Kelly)
Golden Arrow. *See* Three Men and a Girl, 1952
Golden Bed, 1925 (Head; Macpherson)
Golden Boat, 1990 (Schamus)
Golden Bowl, 2000 (Jhabvala)
Golden Boy, 1939 (Cohn; Freund; Musuraca; Taradash; Young)
Golden Butterfly. *See* Goldene Schmetterling, 1926
Golden Cage, 1975 (Boyd)
Golden Calf, 1930 (Friedhofer)
Golden Chance, 1916 (Buckland; Macpherson))
Golden Child, 1986 (Ralston)
Golden Claw, 1915 (Ince; Sullivan)
Golden Coach. *See* **Carrosse d'or**, 1953
Golden Cocoon, 1925 (Haskin)
Golden Days, 1914 (Brown)
Golden Earrings, 1947 (Dreier; Young)
Golden Fish. *See* O zlaté rybce, 1951
Golden Fortress. *See* Sonar Kella, 1974

Golden Gate Murders, 1979 (Foreman)
Golden Girl, 1951 (Clarke; Lemaire; Wheeler)
Golden Gloves, 1940 (Dreier; Head)
Golden Goose, 1914 (Ince)
Golden Harvest, 1933 (Krasner)
Golden Hen, 1946 (Terry)
Golden Hills. *See* Zlaty gori, 1931
Golden Horde, 1951 (Metty)
Golden Hour. *See* Pot o' Gold, 1940
Golden Key. *See* Zolotoi klyuchik, 1939
Golden Mary, 2000 (Merchant)
Golden Needles, 1974 (Schifrin)
Golden Princess, 1925 (Lang)
Golden Rendezvous, 1977 (Francis)
Golden Rule Kate, 1917 (August)
Golden Salamander, 1950 (Alwyn; Bryan; Francis; Morris; Neame; Rank)
Golden Shield. *See* Goldene Wehr, 1917
Golden Supper, 1910 (Bitzer)
Golden Touch, 1935 (Disney)
Golden Trail, 1920 (Mohr)
Golden Trail. *See* Riders of the Whistling Skull, 1937
Golden Voyage of Sinbad, 1973 (Harryhausen; Rozsa)
Golden West, 1939 (Terry)
Golden Yeggs, 1950 (Blanc; Stalling)
Goldene Abgrund, 1927 (Andrejew)
Goldene Gans, 1944 (Reiniger)
Goldene Krone, 1920 (Messter)
Goldene Schmetterling, 1926 (Kolowrat-Krakowsky)
Goldene Wehr, 1917 (Kolowrat-Krakowsky)
Goldengirl, 1979 (Conti)
Goldfinger, 1964 (Adam; Barry; Broccoli)
Goldfish, 1924 (Carré; Schenck; Sullivan)
Goldie Gets Along, 1933 (Irene)
Goldie Locks and the Three Bears, 1922 (Disney)
Goldielocks and the Three Bears, 1934 (Lantz)
Goldilocks and the Jivin' Bears, 1944 (Blanc; Stalling)
Goldimouse and the Three Cats, 1960 (Blanc)
Goldsmith's Shop. *See* Jeweller's Shop, 1987
Goldwyn Follies, 1938 (Day; Goldwyn; Hecht; Newman; Toland)
Golem, 1914 (Galeen)
Golem, 1936 (Andrejew; Stallich)
Golem, wie er in die Welt kam, 1920 (Freund; Galeen; Röhrig)
Golem—Le Jardin pétrifié, 1993 (Alekan)
Golem—L'Esprit de l'exil, 1992 (Alekan)
Golf Bug, 1922 (Roach)
Golf Nuts, 1930 (Terry)
Golfa, 1957 (Figueroa)
Golfers, 1937 (Lantz)
Golgotha, 1935 (Ibert)
Goliath and the Vampire. *See* Maciste contre il vampiro, 1961
Goliath Awaits, 1981 (Duning)
Golod . . . golod . . . golod, 1921 (Tisse)
Golowin geht durch die Stadt, 1940 (Hoffmann)
Gommes, 1968 (Delerue)
Gomorron Bill, 1945 (Nykvist)
Gondole delle chimera, 1936 (Burel)
Gone Are the Days!, 1963 (Kaufman; Rosenblum)
Gone Batty, 1954 (Blanc; McKimson; Stalling)
Gone to Earth, 1950 (Challis; Francis; Heckroth; Korda; Selznick)
Gone to Ground, 1977 (Boyd)
Gone to the Country, 1921 (Roach)
Gone with the Wind, 1939 (Canutt; Deutsch; Friedhofer; Garmes;
    Haller; Hecht; Howard; Mayer; Menzies; Plunkett; Rennahan; Rosson;
    Ruttenberg; Selznick; Steiner; Swerling; Westmore Family; Wheeler)
Gonin no mokugekisha, 1948 (Yoda)
Gonza the Spearman. *See* Yari no Gonza, 1985

Gonzales' Tamales, 1957 (Blanc; Stalling)
Goo Goo Goliath, 1954 (Blanc; Stalling)
Good Against Evil, 1977 (Schifrin)
Good and Naughty, 1926 (Glennon)
Good and the Bad. See Bon et les méchants, 1976
Good Bad Girl. See Inez from Hollywood, 1924
Good-Bad Wife, 1921 (Goodrich and Hackett)
Good-by Girls!, 1923 (August)
Good-bye-Bill, 1918 (Loos)
Good-Bye Kiss, 1928 (Hornbeck)
Good-bye, My Lady, 1955 (Clothier)
Good-bye My Lady Love, 1925 (Fleischer)
Good Cheer, 1926 (Roach)
Good Companions, 1933 (Balcon; Friedhofer; Junge; Mercer)
Good Dame, 1934 (Shamroy)
Good Deed Daily, 1955 (Terry)
Good Die Young, 1954 (Auric)
Good Earth, 1937 (Freund; Gibbons; Gillespie; Jennings; Mayer; Stothart; Thalberg; Vorkapich)
Good Egg, 1939 (Jones)
Good Fairy, 1935 (Laemmle; Mandell)
Good Fellows, 1943 (Dreier; Head)
Good Fight: The Abraham Lincoln Brigade in the Spanish Civil War, 1984 (Houseman)
Good Friends and Faithful Neighbors. See Goda vänner, trogna grannar, 1938
Good Girls Go to Paris, 1939 (Cohn)
Good Guys and the Bad Guys, 1969 (Stradling)
Good Little Devil, 1913 (Zukor)
Good Luck. See Fortuna, 1973
Good Morning Babilonia, 1986 (Guerra; Lanci, Giuseppe ("beppe"); Morricone)
Good Morning, Boys, 1937 (Vetchinsky)
Good Morning, Judge, 1922 (Roach)
Good Morning, Judge, 1943 (Boyle)
Good Morning, Miss Dove, 1955 (Reynolds, Shamroy)
Good Morning Vietnam, 1987 (North)
Good Mother, 1988 (Bernstein; Watkin)
Good Mouse Keeping, 1952 (Terry)
Good Neighbor Sam, 1964 (Guffey)
Good News, 1930 (Brown; Freed; Gibbons; Marion; Mayer)
Good News, 1947 (Comden and Green; Edens; Freed; Mayer; Rose)
Good Night Elmer, 1940 (Blanc; Jones; Stalling)
Good Night, Rusty, 1943 (Pal)
Good Noose, 1962 (Blanc; McKimson)
Good Old Boys, 1995 (Shepard)
Good Old Irish Tunes, 1941 (Terry)
Good Riddance, 1923 (Roach)
Good Sam, 1948 (Barnes)
Good Scout, 1934 (Iwerks)
Good Soldier Schweik. See Dobrý voják švejk, 1931
Good Soldier Schweik. See Osudy dobrého vojáka Svejkova, 1955
Good Soldier Svejk. See Dobry voják Švejk, 1926
Good Son, 1993 (Bernstein)
Good Sport, 1931 (Clarke)
Good Tramp Bernasek. See Dobrý tramp Bernasek, 1933
Good Will Hunting, 1997 (Elfman)
Good Will o Men*, 1955 (Hanna and Barbera)
Good Women, 1921 (Edeson; Sullivan)
Good, the Bad, and the Ugly. See **Buono, il brutto, il cattivo**, 1966
Good-Time Girl, 1948 (Rank)
Goodbye Again, 1933 (Barnes)
Goodbye Again. See Aimez-vous Brahms?, 1961
Goodbye Charlie, 1964 (Day; Krasner; Previn; Rose; Smith)
Goodbye Columbus, 1969 (Rosenblum)
Goodbye, Gemini, 1970 (Unsworth)

Goodbye Girl, 1977 (Booth; Grusin; Stark)
Goodbye Lover, 1999 (Barry; van Runkle)
Goodbye, Mr. Chips, 1939 (Addinsell; Junge; Mayer; Sherriff; Young)
Goodbye, Mr. Chips, 1969 (Adam; Morris; Rattigan; Williams)
Goodbye Mr. Moth, 1942 (Lantz)
Goodbye, My Fancy, 1951 (Blanke; McCord)
Goodbye Paradise, 1983 (Seale)
GoodFellas, 1990 (Ballhaus; Bass; Schoonmaker; Winkler)
Goodnight Vienna, 1932 (Wilcox)
Goodwill to All Dogs, 1960 (Halas and Batchelor)
Goof on the Roof, 1953 (Bruckman)
Goofy Age, 1924 (Roach)
Goofy Gophers, 1946 (Blanc; Clampett)
Goofy Groceries, 1941 (Blanc; Clampett; Stalling)
Goofy Movie, 1995 (Burwell)
Gooney Golfers, 1948 (Terry)
Goonies, 1985 (Grusin; Marshall)
Goonland, 1938 (Fleischer)
Goons from the Moon, 1951 (Terry)
Goopy Gyne Bagha Byne, 1969 (Dutta)
Goose and the Gander, 1935 (Orry-Kelly)
Goose Flies High, 1938 (Terry)
Goose Goes South*, 1941 (Hanna and Barbera)
Goose Hangs High, 1925 (Brown)
Goose Steps Out, 1942 (Balcon)
Gopak, 1931 (Moskvin)
Gopher Broke, 1958 (Blanc; McKimson)
Gopher Goofy, 1942 (Blanc; Stalling)
Gopher Trouble, 1936 (Lantz)
Gor, 1987 (Golan and Globus)
Göranssons pojke, 1941 (Jaenzon)
Gorath. See Yosei Goraith, 1962
Gorbenhurst, 2000 (Bennett)
Gordon's War, 1973 (Badalamenti)
Gore Vidal's Lincoln, 1988 (Houseman)
Gorgeous Hussy, 1936 (Adrian; Gibbons)
Gorgo, 1961 (Lourié)
Gorgon, 1964 (Bernard; Carreras)
Gorilla, 1927 (Edeson)
Gorilla, 1939 (Cronjager; Day; Zanuck)
Gorilla, 1956 (Nykvist)
Gorilla Hunt, 1939 (Iwerks)
Gorilla My Dreams, 1948 (Blanc; McKimson; Stalling)
Gorilla's Dance, 1968 (Vukotić)
Gorillas in the Mist, 1988 (Baker; Jarre; Seale)
Gospel According to St. Matthew. See **Vangelo secondo Matteo**, 1964
Gossipers, 1905 (Bitzer)
Gösta Berlings saga, 1923 (Jaenzon; Magnusson)
Gotcha!, 1985 (Conti)
Gott mit uns, 1970 (Morricone)
Gottesgeissel, 1920 (Kolowrat-Krakowsky)
Goualeuse, 1938 (Kosma)
Goubbiah, 1955 (Kosma)
Goumbé des jeunes noceurs, 1965 (Braunberger)
Government Girl, 1943 (Nichols)
Governor's Daughters. See Landshövdingens döttrar, 1916
Gow, the Head Hunter, 1928 (Cooper)
Goya en Burdeos, 1999 (Storaro)
Goya in Bordeaux. See Goya en Burdeos, 1999
Goyoukiba: Kamisori Hanzo jigokuzeme, 1973 (Miyagawa)
Grab the Ghost, 1920 (Roach)
Grace Moore Story. See So This Is Love, 1953
Grace of My Heart, 1996 (Bacharach; Schoonmaker)
Gracie Allen Murder Case, 1939 (Dreier; Head; Lang)
Gracious Living. See Vie de château, 1965

Great Caruso, 1951 (Green; Levien; Pasternak; Rose; Ruttenberg; Shearer)
Great Catherine, 1968 (Bryan; Morris; Tiomkin)
Great Cheese Robbery, 1920 (Bray)
Great Citizen. *See* Velikii grazhdanin, 1938-39
Great Cognito, 1982 (Vinton)
Great Commandment, 1939 (Banton)
Great Day, 1945 (Alwyn)
Great Day in Harlem, 1994 (Mandel)
Great Day in the Morning, 1956 (D'Agostino)
Great Deception, 1926 (Haller)
Great Diamond Robbery, 1953 (Ruttenberg)
Great Dictator, 1940 (Struss)
Great Divide, 1925 (Gibbons; Mayer; Thalberg)
Great Divide, 1929 (Garmes)
Great Escape, 1962 (Bernstein; Mirisch)
Great Event, 1979 (Mancini)
Great Expectations, 1917 (Zukor)
Great Expectations, 1946 (Bryan; Havelock-Allan; Neame; Rank; Young)
Great Expectations, 1975 (Jarre; Young)
Great Fear. *See* Veliki strah, 1958
Great Flirtation, 1934 (Banton; Krasner)
Great Gabbo, 1930 (Hecht)
Great Gambini, 1937 (D'Agostino; Head; Shamroy)
Great Garrick, 1937 (Deutsch; Grot; Haller; Vajda)
Great Gatsby, 1949 (Dreier; Head; Seitz)
Great Gatsby, 1974 (Slocombe)
Great Georgia Bank Hoax. *See* Shenanigans, 1977
Great Gilbert and Sullivan. *See* Story of Gilbert and Sullivan, 1953
Great God Gold, 1935 (Krasner)
Great Guns, 1927 (Disney)
Great Guns, 1941 (Day)
Great Guy, 1936 (Carré)
Great Heep, 1986 (Burtt)
Great Impersonation, 1935 (Krasner; Waxman)
Great Imposter, 1961 (Bumstead; Burks; Mancini)
Great Jasper, 1933 (Macgowan; Plunkett; Selznick; Steiner)
Great Jewel Mystery, 1905 (Bitzer)
Great Jewel Robbery, 1950 (Chase)
Great John L., 1945 (Young; van Heusen)
Great Lie, 1941 (Blanke; Gaudio; Orry-Kelly; Steiner; Wallis)
Great Locomotive Chase, 1956 (Disney; Ellenshaw)
Great Love, 1918 (Bitzer; Brown)
Great Love, 1927 (Mayer)
Great Lover, 1949 (Dreier; Head; Lang)
Great Madcap. *See* Gran calavera, 1949
Great Mail Robbery, 1927 (Walker)
Great Man Hunt. *See* State Secret, 1950
Great Man Votes, 1939 (Kanin; Metty; Polglase)
Great Manhunt. *See* Doolins of Oklahoma, 1949
Great Manhunt. *See* State Secret, 1950
Great Man's Lady, 1942 (Dreier; Head; Westmore Family; Young)
Great Man's Whiskers, 1973 (Paxton)
Great McGinty, 1940 (Dreier; Head)
Great Missouri Raid, 1950 (Rennahan)
Great Moment, 1921 (Zukor)
Great Moment, 1944 (Dreier; Head; Young)
Great Mouse Detective, 1986 (Mancini)
Great Mr. Handel, 1942 (Cardiff; Rank; Unsworth)
Great Mr. Nobody, 1941 (Deutsch)
Great Muppet Caper, 1981 (Henson; Morris)
Great Northfield, Minnesota Raid, 1972 (Grusin)
Great O'Malley, 1936 (Friedhofer; Haller)
Great Outdoors, 1923 (Roach)
Great Outdoors. *See* Prince of Pennsylvania, 1988

Great People of the Bible and How They Lived, 1995 (Elfman)
Great Piggy Bank Robbery, 1946 (Blanc; Clampett; Stalling)
Great Profile, 1940 (Day; Zanuck)
Great Race, 1965 (Dunn; Harlan; Head; Mancini; Mercer; Pan; Warner)
Great Redeemer, 1920 (Furthman)
Great Rupert, 1949 (Pal)
Great Sacrifice, 1912 (Ince)
Great Santini, 1979 (Bernstein)
Great Schnozzle. *See* Palooka, 1934
Great Scout and Cathouse Thursday, 1976 (Smith)
Great Secret, 1917 (Mayer)
Great Singer, 1949 (Gibbons)
Great Sinner, 1949 (Irene; Kaper; Previn)
Great St. Trinian's Train Robbery, 1966 (Arnold)
Great Swordsmen of Japan. *See* Nippon kengo-den, 1945
Great Train Robbery, 1941 (Canutt)
Great Train Robbery. *See* First Great Train Robbery, 1978
Great Victor Herbert, 1939 (Dreier; Head)
Great Waldo Pepper, 1975 (Bumstead; Goldman; Head; Mancini; Reynolds; Surtees)
Great Waltz, 1938 (Gibbons; Hoffenstein; Reisch; Ruttenberg; Tiomkin)
Great War, 1996 (Daring)
Great War. *See* Grande guerra, 1959
Great Water Peril, 1918 (Roach)
Great While It Lasted, 1914 (Roach)
Great White Hope, 1970 (Guffey; Reynolds; Sharaff)
Great Who Dood It, 1952 (Lantz)
Great Ziegfeld, 1936 (Adrian; Edens; Freund; Gibbons; Mayer; Stromberg)
Greater Glory, 1926 (Mathis)
Greater Love Hath No Man, (undated) (Barker)
Greater Than a Crown, 1925 (August)
Greater than Love, 1921 (Sullivan)
Greatest, 1977 (Lardner)
Greatest Battle on Earth. *See* Sandai kaiju chikyu saidai no kessen, 1965
Greatest Love. *See* Europa 51, 1954
Greatest Question, 1919 (Bitzer)
Greatest Show on Earth, 1952 (Barnes; Head; Jeakins; Pereira; Young)
Greatest Story Ever Told, 1965 (Day; Friedhofer; Gillespie; Newman)
Greatest Thing in Life, 1918 (Bitzer; Zukor)
Greco, 1965 (Donati; Morricone)
Greed of Gold. *See* Desert Greed, 1926
Greed, 1924 (Daniels; Day; Gibbons; Goldwyn; Mathis; Mayer)
Greedy for Tweety, 1957 (Blanc)
Greedy Humpty Dumpty, 1936 (Fleischer)
Greek Meets Greek, 1921 (Roach)
Greeks, 1965 (Lassally)
Greeks Had a Word for Them, 1932 (Barnes; Day; Goldwyn; Howard; Newman)
Green and Pleasant Land, 1955 (Lassally)
Green Berets, 1968 (Hoch; Rozsa)
Green Book. *See* Zelená knížka, 1948
Green Card, 1990 (Zimmer)
Green Carnation. *See* Trials of Oscar Wilde, 1960
Green Cat, 1922 (Roach)
Green Cockatoo, 1937 (Menzies)
Green Cockatoo. *See* Four Dark Hours, 1940
Green Dolphin Street, 1947 (Gillespie; Irene; Kaper; Mayer; Plunkett; Raphaelson; Shearer)
Green Earth. *See* Midori no daichi, 1942
Green-Eyed Blonde, 1957 (Trumbo)
Green-Eyed Woman. *See* Take a Letter, Darling, 1942
Green Fire, 1954 (Gillespie; Rose; Rozsa)
Green for Danger, 1946 (Alwyn; Mathieson; Morris; Rank)
Green Ghost. *See* Spectre vert, 1929
Green Girdle, 1941 (Cardiff)

Green Glove, 1951 (Cloquet; Kosma; Maté; Renoir; Trauner)
Green Grass of Wyoming, 1948 (Clarke; Lemaire)
Green Hell, 1940 (Freund; Marion)
Green Light, 1936 (Blanke; Friedhofer; Haskin; Orry-Kelly; Steiner;
　　Orry-Kelly; Steiner Wallis)
Green Line, 1944 (Terry)
Green Mansions, 1959 (Ames; Jeakins; Kaper; Ruttenberg)
Green Manuela. See Grüne Manuela, 1923
Green Mare. See Jument verte, 1959
Green Mile, 1999 (Newman)
Green Necklace. See Det gröna halsbandet, 1912
Green Pastures, 1936 (Blanke; Friedhofer; Korngold; Mohr; Wallis)
Green Queen. See Reine verte, 1964
Green Room. See Chambre verte, 1978
Green Scarf, 1954 (Korda)
Green Shadow, 1913 (Ince)
Green Swamp, 1916 (Sullivan)
Green Years, 1946 (Gibbons; Gillespie; Irene; Levien; Stothart)
Greengage Summer, 1961 (Addinsell; Koch; Young)
Greenhorn, 1913 (Ince)
Greenwich Village, 1944 (Basevi; Brown; Comden and Green; Shamroy)
Greetings Bait, 1943 (Blanc; Stalling)
Grehut na Malitsa, 1986 (Dinov)
Gremlins, 1984 (Goldsmith; Jones; Marshall; Walas)
Gremlins 2: The New Batch, 1990 (Baker; Goldsmith; Jones; Marshall)
Grenoble. See Treize jours en France, 1968
Grenouilles qui demandait un roi, 1922 (Starewicz)
Grève, 1904 (Pathé)
Grey Sentinel, 1913 (Ince)
Greyfriars Bobby , 1961 (Disney; Whitlock)
Greyhounded Hare, 1949 (Blanc; McKimson; Stalling)
Greystoke: The Legend of Tarzan, Lord of the Apes, 1984 (Alcott; Baker;
　　Towne; Whitlock)
Gribiche, 1925 (Meerson)
Gribouille, 1937 (Auric; Trauner)
Gricheux, 1909 (Cohl)
Gridiron Flash, 1934 (Berman; Plunkett; Steiner)
Grido, 1957 (Di Venanzo)
Grief in Bagdad, 1925 (Roach)
Grifters, 1990 (Bernstein)
Grim Game, 1919 (Buckland)
Grim Pastures, or the Fight for Fodder, 1944 (Dunning)
Gringuita en Mexico, 1951 (Alcoriza)
Grip of Fear. See Experiment in Terror, 1962
Grips, Grunts, and Groans, 1937 (Bruckman)
Grisbi. See Touchez pas au Grisbi, 1954
Grissom Gang, 1971 (Biroc)
Grit, 1915 (August)
Grizzly Golfer, 1951 (Bosustow; Hubley)
Gromaire, 1970 (Braunberger)
Gros Coup, 1964 (Delerue; Gégauff)
Gross Paris, 1973 (de Beauregard)
Gross-stadtkavaliere. See Kleine aus der Kongektion, 1925
Gross und Klein, 1980 (Ballhaus)
Grosse Attraktion, 1931 (Kaper)
Große Ekstase, 1975 (Lhomme)
Grosse Sehnsucht, 1930 (Pasternak)
Grosse Sünderin, 1913 (Messter)
Grosse Tête, 1962 (Guillemot; Legrand)
Grosse Unbekannte, 1927 (Planer)
Grosse und die kleine Welt, 1921 (Dreier)
Grosse Zapfenstreich, 1952 (Herlth)
Grossindustrielle, 1923 (Wagner)
Grossreinemachen, 1935 (Heller)
Grotesque Chicken. See Spatne namalovaná slepice, 1963
Grounds for Divorce, 1925 (Banton)

Grounds for Marriage, 1950 (Alton; Kaper; Raksin; Rose)
Group, 1966 (Buchman; Kaufman; Rosenblum)
Growing Pains, 1928 (Roach)
Growing Pains, 1953 (Terry)
Growing Up. See Asunaro monogatari, 1955
Grub Stake, 1923 (Walker)
Gruesome Twosome, 1945 (Blanc; Clampett; Stalling)
Grumbler. See Nörgler, 1917
Grumpy, 1931 (Zukor)
Grumpy Old Men, 1993 (Henry)
Grüne Manuela, 1923 (Junge)
Gruppo di famiglia in un interno, 1974 (Cecchi D'Amico)
Grüss and küss Veronika, 1934 (Pasternak; Waxman)
Guadalcanal Diary, 1943 (Basevi; Clarke; Trotti)
Guaglio. See Prohibito rubare, 1949
Guantes de Oro, 1959 (Alcoriza)
Guardian, 1990 (Alonzo)
Guardians of the Wild, 1928 (Miller)
Guardie e ladri, 1951 (Flaiano and Pinelli; de Laurentiis)
Guardsman, 1931 (Adrian; Mayer; Vajda)
Guardsman. See A testör, 1918
Gubecziana, 1974 (Vukotić)
Gubijinso, 1941 (Hayasaka)
Guendalina, 1956 (Ponti; de Laurentiis)
Guêpes, 1961 (Braunberger; Delerue)
Guerilla, 1908 (Bitzer)
Guérisseur, 1953 (Aurenche and Bost)
Guernica, 1949 (Braunberger)
Guerra alle guerra, 1948 (Zavattini)
Guerre dans le Haut Pays, 1998 (Carrière)
Guerre du feu, 1981 (Sarde)
Guerre du Transvaal, 1900 (Pathé)
Guerre est finie, 1966 (Saulnier; Semprun; Vierny)
Guerre Russo-Japonais, 1904 (Pathé)
Guess Who's Coming to Dinner, 1966 (Louis)
Guest, 1951 (Newman)
Guest. See Caretaker, 1963
Guest in the House, 1944 (Garmes; Stromberg)
Gueule d'amour, 1937 (Spaak)
Gueule de bois, 1954 (Starewicz)
Gueule du Loup, 1981 (Rousselot)
Gueule ouverte, 1974 (Almendros)
Guide, 1965 (Burman)
Guide for the Married Man, 1967 (Smith; Spencer; Williams)
Guided Muscle, 1955 (Blanc; Jones; Stalling)
Guignolo, 1979 (Decaë)
Guillaume Apollinaire, 1955 (Kosma)
Guillaume Tell, 1903 (Pathé)
Guilt of Janet Ames, 1947 (Duning; Goosson; Walker)
Guilty As Hell, 1932 (Struss)
Guilty by Suspicion, 1991 (Ballhaus; Winkler)
Guilty Bystander, 1950 (Harlan; Tiomkin)
Guilty Conscience. See Gewissenswurm, 1917
Guilty Generation, 1931 (Haskin)
Guilty Hands, 1931 (Stromberg)
Guilty Melody, 1936 (Stallich)
Guilty of Treason, 1950 (Friedhofer)
Guilty or Innocent: The Sam Sheppard Murder Case, 1975 (Schifrin)
Guinguette, 1958 (Jeanson)
Gulf Stream, 1939 (Alexeieff and Parker; Milhaud)
Gullible Canary, 1942 (Fleischer)
Gulliver's Travels, 1939 (Young)
Gulliver's Travels, 1976 (Legrand)
Gulls and Buoys, 1972 (Breer)
Gumshoe, 1971 (Menges)
Gumshoe Magoo, 1958 (Bosustow)

Gun before Butter, 1972 (Lassally)
Gun Crazy, 1949 (Harlan; Trumbo)
Gun Fury, 1953 (Wald)
Gun Glory, 1957 (Plunkett)
Gun Gospel, 1927 (Polito)
Gun Justice, 1934 (McCord)
Gun Law, 1929 (Musuraca; Plunkett)
Gun Law, 1938 (August)
Gun Moll. *See* Poopsie, 1974
Gun Riders. *See* Five Bloody Graves, 1969
Gun Runners, 1958 (Mainwaring; Mohr)
Gun the Man Down, 1956 (Clothier)
Gunfight at Comanche Creek, 1963 (Biroc)
Gunfight at Dodge City, 1958 (Mirisch)
Gunfight at the O.K. Corral, 1957 (Head; Lang; Pereira; Tiomkin; Wallis)
Gunfighter, 1917 (August)
Gunfighter, 1950 (Johnson; Lemaire; Miller; Newman; Zanuck)
Gunfighters of Casa Grande. *See* Pistoleros de Casa Grande, 1965
Gung Ho!, 1943 (Krasner; Wanger)
Gung Ho, 1986 (Newman)
Gunga Din, 1939 (August; Berman; Clothier; Dunn; Hecht; MacArthur; Newman; Polglase)
Gunman in the Streets. *See* Traqué, 1950
Gunman's Walk, 1958 (Duning; Nugent)
Gunmen, 1994 (Goldsmith)
Gunn, 1967 (Lathrop; Mancini)
Gunnar Hedes saga, 1922 (Jaenzon; Magnusson)
Gunpoint, 1966 (Bumstead)
Guns at Batasi, 1964 (Fisher; Slocombe)
Guns for San Sebastian. *See* Bataille de San Sebastian, 1967
Guns of Darkness, 1962 (Fisher; Krasker)
Guns of Fort Petticoat, 1957 (Rennahan)
Guns of Navarone, 1961 (Foreman; Halas and Batchelor; Morris; Tiomkin)
Guns of the Magnificent Seven, 1968 (Bernstein)
Guns of the Pecos, 1937 (McCord)
Guns of the Timberland, 1960 (Seitz)
Gunsight Ridge, 1957 (Jennings; Laszlo)
Gunsmoke, 1953 (Boyle)
Gunsmoke Ranch, 1937 (Canutt)
Günstling von Schönbrunn, 1929 (Junge)
Guraida, 1943 (Tsuburaya)
Gurentai no uta, 1934 (Yoda)
Guru, 1968 (Jhabvala; Merchant; Mitra)
Gus Edwards' Song Revue, 1929 (Day)
Gustav Adolfs Page, 1960 (Herlth)
Guv'nor, 1935 (Balcon; Junge; Rank)
Guy, a Gal, and a Pal, 1945 (Hunter)
Guy Could Change, 1946 (Alton)
Guy de Maupassant, 1981 (Rousselot)
Guy Named Joe, 1943 (Freund; Gibbons; Irene; Mayer; Stothart; Trumbo)
Guy Who Came Back, 1951 (La Shelle; Lemaire; Wheeler)
Guyrkoviscarna, 1920 (Magnusson)
Guys and Dolls, 1955 (Goldwyn; Kidd; Mandell; Sharaff; Stradling)
Gycklarnas afton, 1953 (Fischer; Nykvist)
Gypsy, 1962 (Orry-Kelly; Reynolds; Stradling)
Gypsy and the Gentleman, 1958 (Rank)
Gypsy Blood. *See* Carmen, 1918
Gypsy Fiddler, 1933 (Terry)
Gypsy Girl. *See* Sky, West, and Crooked, 1966
Gypsy Life, 1945 (Terry)
Gypsy Love. *See* Zigeunerliebe, 1922
Gypsy Moths, 1969 (Bernstein; Lathrop)

H. 2 S., 1968 (Morricone)
H. M. Pulham, Esq., 1941 (Gibbons; Kaper)

H.M.S. Defiant, 1962 (Mathieson)
H-Man. *See* Bijo to ekitai ningen, 1958
Ha! Ha! Ha!, 1934 (Fleischer)
Habeas Corpus, 1928 (Roach)
Habit Rabbit, 1963 (Hanna and Barbera)
Habit Troubles, 1964 (Hanna and Barbera)
Habit vert, 1937 (D'Eaubonne)
Hachyyuhachinenme no taiyo, 1941 (Tsuburaya)
Hagbard and Signe/The Red Mantle, 1967 (Lundgren)
Haha no chizu, 1942 (Hayasaka)
Haha shirayuki, 1956 (Yoda)
Haha yo ko yo, 1933 (Yoda)
Hail the Conquering Hero, 1944 (Dreier; Head; Seitz)
Hail the Woman, 1921 (Ince; Sullivan)
Haim Soutine, 1959 (Delerue)
Haine; La Dixième Symphonie, 1918 (Gaumont)
Hair, 1979 (Ondříček)
Hair Cut-Ups, 1953 (Terry)
Hair Raising Hare, 1945 (Blanc; Jones; Stalling)
Hair Trigger Baxter, 1926 (Haller)
Hairless Hector, 1941 (Terry)
Hairpins, 1920 (Barnes; Sullivan)
Hairy Hercules, 1960 (Halas and Batchelor)
Hakai, 1962 (Miyagawa)
Hakuchi, 1951 (Hayasaka)
Hakuchu no torima, 1966 (Toda)
Hakufujin no yoren, 1956 (Tsuburaya)
Halbblut, 1919 (Hoffmann; Pommer)
Hale and Hearty, 1922 (Roach)
Half a Sinner, 1940 (Trumbo)
Half a Sixpence, 1968 (Unsworth)
Half Angel, 1935 (Macgowan)
Half Angel, 1936 (Glennon; Zanuck)
Half Angel, 1951 (Krasner; Newman; Riskin)
Half-Breed, 1916 (Loos)
Half Breed, 1922 (Clarke)
Half Caste. *See* Halbblut, 1919
Half Marriage, 1929 (Plunkett)
Half Naked Truth, 1932 (Glennon; Steiner; Berman; Selznick)
Half Shot at Sunrise, 1930 (Plunkett; Steiner)
Half Shot at Sunset, 1930 (Musuraca)
Half Shot Shooters, 1936 (Bruckman)
Half-Fare Hare, 1956 (Blanc; McKimson; Stalling)
Half-Pint Pygmy, 1948 (Avery)
Half-Way to Heaven, 1929 (Lang)
Halfbreed. *See* Halvblod, 1913
Halfway House, 1944 (Balcon; Clarke)
Hall on Devil's Island, 1957 (Haller)
Hallalujah I'm a Bum!, 1933 (Day; Hecht; Newman)
Hallelujah I'm a Tramp. *See* Hallalujah I'm a Bum!, 1933
Hallelujah Trail, 1965 (Bernstein; Head; Surtees)
Hallelujah, 1929 (Berlin; Gibbons; Mayer; Shearer; Thalberg)
Halles, 1929 (Kaufman)
Halliday Brand, 1957 (Rennahan)
Hallo Everybody, 1933 (Milhaud)
Hallo Mister God, This Is Anna, 1992 (Watkin)
Hallroom Boys, 1906 (Bitzer)
Halls of Anger, 1970 (Grusin; Guffey; Mirisch)
Halls of Montezuma, 1950 (Lemaire; Reynolds; Hoch; Wheeler)
Halvblod, 1913 (Magnusson)
Ham and Eggs, 1933 (Lantz)
Ham and Eggs at the Front, 1926 (Clarke)
Ham Dard, 1953 (Biswas)
Ham in a Role, 1949 (Blanc; McKimson; Stalling)
Hamari Baat, 1943 (Biswas)
Hamateur Night, 1938 (Avery)

Hame Khelne Do, 1962 (Biswas)
Hamilton in the Musical Festival, 1961 (Halas and Batchelor)
Hamilton the Musical Elephant, 1961 (Halas and Batchelor)
Hamlet, 1920 (Courant)
Hamlet, 1948 (Dillon; Mathieson; Rank; Walton)
Hamlet, 1963 (Enei; Moskvin; Shostakovich)
Hamlet, 1969 (Fisher)
Hamlet, 1990 (Morricone; Watkin)
Hamlet, 2000 (Burwell; Shepard)
Hammarforsens brus, 1948 (Lundgren)
Hammersmith Is Out, 1972 (Head)
Hammett, 1982 (Barry; Biroc; Lathrop; Tavoularis)
Hammond Mystery. *See* Undying Monster, 1942
Hamnstad, 1948 (Fischer)
Hampelmann, 1930 (Courant)
Hams That Couldn't Be Cured, 1942 (Lantz)
Hamster. *See* Křeček, 1946
Hamusse Hanussen, 1955 (Warm)
Hana hiraku, 1948 (Hayasaka)
Hana no Yoshiwara hyakunin-giri, 1960 (Yoda)
Hanamuko Taiheiki, 1945 (Yoda)
Hanare goze Orin, 1977 (Miyagawa; Takemitsu)
Hand. *See* Ruka, 1965
Hand, 1981 (Winston)
Hand of Death, 1961 (Crosby)
Hand of Peril, 1916 (Carré)
Hand Painted Abstraction, 1934-35 (McClaren)
Handful of Love. *See* En Handfull kärlek, 1974
Handle with Care, 1977 (Conti)
Handling Ships, 1944-45 (Halas and Batchelor)
Handmaid's Tale, 1990 (Pinter)
Hands across the Table, 1935 (Krasna)
Hands, Knees, and Bumps-a-Daisy, 1969 (Dunning)
Hands of Orlac. *See* Mad Love, 1935
Hands of the Ripper, 1971 (Carreras)
Hands over the City. *See* Mani sulla cittá, 1963
Handsome Boy Trying to Rule the World. *See* Tenka o nerau
    bishounen, 1955
Handsome Priest. *See* Prete bello, 1989
Handy Andy, 1934 (Miller)
Hanging Tree, 1959 (McCord; Orry-Kelly; Steiner)
Hangman, 1959 (Bumstead; Head; Nichols)
Hangman's Knot, 1952 (Canutt)
Hangmen Also Die!, 1943 (Eisler; Howe)
Hangover Square, 1945 (Herrmann; La Shelle; Wheeler)
Hanjo, 1961 (Takemitsu)
Hanka, 1955 (Vorkapich)
Hanna K, 1983 (Solinas)
Hannah Lee. *See* Outlaw Territory, 1953
Hanna's War, 1988 (Golan and Globus)
Hanneles Himmelfahrt, 1934 (Von Harbou)
Hannibal, 2001 (Zimmer)
Hannibal Brooks, 1969 (Lai)
Hanoi Hilton, 1987 (Golan and Globus)
Hanover Street, 1979 (Barry; Watkin)
Hanran, 1954 (Hayasaka)
Hans Brinker, or the Silver Skates, 1959 (Fischer)
Hans bröllopsnatt, 1915 (Magnusson)
Hans Christian Andersen, 1952 (Day; Goldwyn; Mandell; Stradling)
Hans engelska fru, 1926 (Jaenzon)
Hans Hartung, 1971 (Braunberger)
Hans, hon, och pengarna, 1936 (Fischer)
Hans hustrus förflutna, 1915 (Jaenzon)
Hans im Glück, 1936 (Herlth; Röhrig)
Hans in allen Gassen, 1930 (Planer)
Hans le marin, 1948 (D'Eaubonne; Kosma)

Hans nåds testamente, 1919 (Magnusson)
Hansel and Gretel, 1933 (Terry)
Hansel and Gretel, 1952 (Terry)
Hansel and Gretel, 1955 (Reiniger)
Hansel and Gretel, 1987 (Golan and Globus)
Hantise, 1912 (Gaumont)
Hanussen, 1955 (Herlth)
Happening, 1966 (Day; Lathrop; Spiegel)
Happening in Calcutta, 1980 (Chandragupta)
Happiest Days of Your Life, 1950 (Korda)
Happiest Millionaire, 1967 (Ellenshaw)
Happiness, 1917 (Ince; Sullivan)
Happiness. *See* Shiawase, 1974
Happiness, 1998 (Schamus; Vachon)
Happiness Ahead, 1934 (Gaudio; Orry-Kelly)
Happiness Is No Joke. *See* Faut-pas rire au bonheur, 1994
Happy, 1933 (Neame)
Happy and Lucky, 1938 (Terry)
Happy Anniversary, 1959 (Garmes; Justin)
Happy Birthday, 1979 (Bozzetto)
Happy Birthday Switzerland, 1991 (Godfrey)
Happy Birthday Wanda June, 1971 (Leven; Spencer)
Happy Circus Days, 1942 (Terry)
Happy Cobblers, 1952 (Terry)
Happy Days, 1929 (Friedhofer)
Happy Days, 1936 (Iwerks)
Happy Divorce. *See* Divorce heureux, 1975
Happy Ending, 1969 (Hall; Legrand)
Happy Ever After, 1932 (Pommer)
Happy Face Murders, 1999 (Bernstein)
Happy Families, 1939 (Balcon)
Happy Family. *See* Merry Frinks, 1934
Happy Go Ducky, 1958 (Hanna and Barbera)
Happy Go Loopy, 1961 (Hanna and Barbera)
Happy Go Lucky, 1943 (Dreier; Head; Struss)
Happy Go Lucky, 1947 (Terry)
Happy Haunting Grounds, 1940 (Terry)
Happy Holland, 1952 (Terry)
Happy Hooldini and Lampoons, 1920 (Bray)
Happy Hooligan Earns His Dinner, 1903 (Bitzer)
Happy Land, 1943 (Basevi; La Shelle; Macgowan; Spencer)
Happy Landing, 1938 (Zanuck)
Happy Landing, 1949 (Terry)
Happy Lion. *See* Stastny lev, 1959
Happy Lovers. *See* Monsieur Ripois, 1954
Happy Mother's Day . . . Love George, 1973 (Lassally)
Happy New Year. *See* Bonne Année, 1973
Happy New Year, 1987 (Conti)
Happy Road, 1956 (Trauner)
Happy Though Married, 1919 (Barnes; Sullivan)
Happy Time, 1952 (Tiomkin)
Happy Valley, 1952 (Terry)
Happy Years, 1950 (Plunkett)
Happy You and Merry Me, 1936 (Fleischer)
Happy-Go-Nutty, 1944 (Avery)
Hara-Kiri, 1919 (Hoffmann)
Harakiri. *See* Seppuku, 1962
Harbor Scenes, 1935 (Maddow)
Hard, 1988 (Edlund)
Hard Boiled, 1925 (Roach)
Hard Boiled Egg, 1948 (Terry)
Hard Boiled Haggerty, 1927 (Polito; Plunkett)
Hard-Boiled Tenderfoot, 1924 (Roach)
Hard Contract, 1969 (North)
Hard Knocks, 1924 (Roach)
Hard Rain. *See* Doshaburi, 1957

Hard Times, 1975 (Lathrop)
Hard to Be a God, 1989 (Carrière; Delerue)
Hard to Get, 1929 (Seitz)
Hard to Get, 1938 (Grot; Mercer; Rosher; Wald; Wallis)
Hard to Handle, 1933 (Orry-Kelly)
Hard to Handle. *See* Paid to Dance, 1937
Hard Wash, 1896 (Bitzer)
Hard Way, 1943 (Howe; Wald; Orry-Kelly)
Hard Way, 1979 (Decaë)
Hard Way, 1991 (McAlpine)
Harda viljor, 1923 (Magnusson)
Hardboiled, 1929 (Plunkett)
Hardcore, 1979 (Nitzsche)
Hardcore Life. *See* Hardcore, 1979
Harder They Fall, 1956 (Cohn; Friedhofer; Guffey; Wald)
Hardhat and Legs, 1980 (Kanin)
Hardship of Miles Standish, 1940 (Blanc; Stalling)
Hare and the Hounds, 1940 (Terry)
Hare-Brained Hypnotist, 1942 (Blanc; Stalling)
Hare-breadth Hurry, 1963 (Blanc; Jones)
Hare Brush, 1955 (Blanc)
Hare Conditioned, 1945 (Blanc; Jones; Stalling)
Hare Do, 1949 (Blanc; Stalling)
Hare Force, 1944 (Blanc; Stalling)
Hare Grows in Manhattan, 1947 (Blanc; Stalling)
Hare-less Wolf, 1958 (Blanc)
Hare Lift, 1952 (Blanc; Stalling)
Hare Mail, 1931 (Lantz)
Hare Remover, 1946 (Blanc; Stalling)
Hare Ribbin', 1944 (Blanc; Clampett; Stalling)
Hare Splitter, 1948 (Blanc; Stalling)
Hare Tonic, 1945 (Blanc; Jones; Stalling)
Hare Trigger, 1945 (Blanc; Stalling)
Hare Trimmed, 1953 (Blanc; Stalling)
Hare-Um Scare-Um, 1939 (Blanc; Stalling)
Hare-way to the Stars, 1958 (Blanc; Jones)
Hare We Go, 1951 (Blanc; Stalling)
Hare-abian Nights, 1959 (Blanc)
Haredevil Hare, 1948 (Blanc; Jones; Stalling)
Harekodose, 1940 (Yoda)
Harekodose, 1961 (Yoda)
Harem, 1967 (Morricone)
Harem, 1985 (Sarde; Trauner)
Harem Scarem, 1927 (Disney)
Harems Devoid of Magic. *See* Harémy kouzla zbavené, 1922
Harémy kouzla zbavené, 1922 (Heller)
Hari Hondal Burgadar, 1980 (Nihalani)
Harlekin, 1931 (Reiniger)
Harlem, 1942 (Amidei)
Harlem Wednesday, 1958 (Hubley)
Harlow, 1965 (Hayes; Head; Levine; Pereira; Ruttenberg; Westmore Family)
Harmonikář, 1953 (Stallich)
Harmony at Home, 1930 (Miller)
Harold and Maude, 1971 (Alonzo)
Harold Robbins' The Pirate. *See* Pirate, 1978
Harold Teen, 1928 (Haller)
Harold Teen, 1933 (Orry-Kelly)
Harp in Hock, 1927 (Levien)
Harp of Tara, 1914 (Ince)
Harper, 1966 (Goldman; Hall; Mandel; Previn)
Harried and Hurried, 1965 (Blanc)
Harriet and the Piper, 1920 (Mayer)
Harriet Craig, 1950 (Duning; Walker)
Harrigan's Kid, 1943 (Chase; Schary)
Harrison and Barrison. *See* Harrison es Barrison, 1917

Harrison es Barrison, 1917 (Korda)
Harry & Son, 1984 (Allen; Bumstead; Mancini)
Harry and the Hendersons, 1987 (Baker)
Harry and Tonto, 1974 (Conti)
Harry and Walter Go to New York, 1976 (Horner; Kovacs)
Harry in Your Pocket, 1973 (Schifrin)
Harry Lauder Songs, 1931 (Balcon)
Haru no tawamure, 1949 (Hayasaka)
Haru o matsu hitobito, 1959 (Takemitsu)
Haruka narishi haha no kuni, 1950 (Yoda)
Harun al Raschid, 1924 (Kolowrat-Krakowsky)
Harvard, Here I Come, 1941 (Brown; Planer)
Harvest Hands, 1923 (Roach)
Harvest of Sin, 1913 (Ince)
Harvest Shall Come, 1942 (Alwyn)
Harvest Time, 1940 (Terry)
Harvey, 1950 (Daniels; Orry-Kelly)
Harvey Girls, 1945 (Edens; Freed; Irene; Mayer; Mercer; Raphaelson; Rose)
Harvey Middleman, Fireman, 1965 (Smith)
Has Anybody Here Seen Kelly?, 1926 (Fleischer)
Hasard et la violence, 1973 (Evein)
Hash Shop, 1930 (Lantz)
Hasher's Delirium. *See* Songe d'un garçon de café, 1910
Hashigaon Hagadol, 1986 (Golan and Globus)
Hashigaon Hagadol, 1988 (Ondříček)
Hashimura Togo, 1917 (Rosher)
Hasty Hare, 1952 (Blanc; Jones; Stalling)
Hasty Marriage, 1931 (Roach)
Hat, 1964 (Hubley)
Hat Check Honey, 1944 (Krasner)
Hat, Coat, and Glove, 1934 (Macgowan; Plunkett; Steiner)
Hataoka junsa, 1940 (Yoda)
Hatari!, 1960 (Brackett; Harlan; Head; Mancini; Mercer; Pereira)
Hatch up Your Troubles, 1949 (Hanna and Barbera)
Hatchet Man, 1932 (Grot)
Hate, 1922 (Mathis)
Hatful of Dreams, 1945 (Pal)
Hatful of Rain, 1957 (Herrmann; Lemaire; Spencer; Wheeler)
Hatred. *See* Mollenard, 1938
Hats Off, 1927 (Roach)
Hatsukoi jigokuhen, 1968 (Takemitsu)
Haunted Bedroom, 1919 (Barnes; Sullivan)
Haunted Castle. *See* Schloss Vogelöd, 1921
Haunted Cat, 1951 (Terry)
Haunted Gold, 1932 (Musuraca)
Haunted Honeymoon, 1925 (Roach)
Haunted Honeymoon. *See* Busman's Holiday, 1940
Haunted Honeymoon. *See* Busman's Honeymoon, 1940
Haunted House, 1928 (Biro; Polito)
Haunted House, 1929 (Disney; Iwerks)
Haunted Mouse, 1941 (Avery; Blanc; Stalling)
Haunted Mouse, 1965 (Jones)
Haunted Pajamas, 1917 (Gaudio)
Haunted Palace, 1963 (Crosby)
Haunted Spooks, 1920 (Roach)
Haunted Summer, 1988 (Golan and Globus; Rotunno)
Haunting, 1999 (Goldsmith)
Haunting We Will Go, 1966 (Blanc)
Haunts of the Very Rich, 1972 (Lourié)
Haupt des Juarez, 1920 (Warm)
Hauptmann von Köpenick, 1907 (Freund)
Haus ohne Lachen, 1923 (Galeen)
Haus zum Mond, 1920 (Hoffmann)
Hauser's Memory, 1970 (Siodmak)
Haut sur ces montagnes, 1945 (McClaren)

Havana, 1990 (Grusin)
Havana Widows, 1933 (Barnes)
Have a Heart, 1934 (Howe)
Havets son, 1949 (Lundgren)
Havinck, 1987 (Lanci, Giuseppe ("beppe"))
Having a Wonderful Time, 1938 (Berman; Polglase)
Havre sac, 1963 (Braunberger)
Hawaii, 1966 (Bernstein; Dunn; Harlan; Jeakins; Mirisch; Taradash; Trumbo; van Runkle)
Hawaii marei oki haisen, 1942 (Tsuburaya)
Hawaiian Aye Aye, 1964 (Blanc)
Hawaiian Birds, 1936 (Fleischer)
Hawaiian Nights, 1939 (Cortez)
Hawaiian Nights. See Down to Their Last Yacht, 1934
Hawaiian Pineapple, 1930 (Terry)
Hawaiians, 1970 (Ballard; Lathrop; Mancini; Mirisch)
Hawk. See Ride Him Cowboy, 1932
Hawkins on Murder, 1973 (Goldsmith)
Hawks and the Sparrows. See Uccelacci e uccellini, 1966
Hawk's Nest, 1928 (Polito)
Hay Foot, 1941 (Roach)
Hay Ride, 1937 (Terry)
Hay un niño en su futuro, 1952 (Figueroa)
Hayl-Moskau, 1932 (Moskvin)
Hazaar Chaurasi Ki Maa, 1998 (Nihalani)
Hazard, 1948 (Dreier)
Hazard's People, 1976 (Houseman)
He and His Sister. See On a jeho sestra, 1931
He Can't Make It Stick, 1943 (Fleischer; Hubley)
He Comes Up Smiling, 1918 (August; Marion)
He Couldn't Take It, 1933 (Schary)
He Died after the War. See Tokyo senso sengo hiwa, 1970
He Doesn't Care to Be Photographed, 1912-14 (Cohl)
He Dood It Again, 1943 (Terry)
He Forgot to Remember, 1926 (Roach)
He Found a Star, 1941 (Junge)
He Hired the Boss, 1943 (Day)
He Knew Women, 1930 (Cronjager)
He Leads, Others Follow, 1919 (Roach)
He Learned about Women, 1932 (Banton; Head; Lang)
He Likes Things Upside-Down, 1912-14 (Cohl)
He Loves to Be Amused, 1912-14 (Cohl)
He Loves to Watch the Flight of Time, 1912-14 (Cohl)
He Married His Wife, 1940 (Day; Zanuck)
He Must Have Her. See Er muß sie haben, 1917
He Poses for His Portrait, 1912-14 (Cohl)
He Ran All the Way, 1951 (Horner; Howe; Trumbo; Waxman)
He Revenges His Mother-in-Law. See Er rächt seine Schwiegermutter, 1917
He Ruins His Family Reputation, 1912-14 (Cohl)
He, She, or It. See Poupée, 1962
He Slept Well, 1912-14 (Cohl)
He Stayed for Breakfast, 1940 (Cohn; Vajda; Walker)
He Walked by Night, 1948 (Alton)
He Wants What He Wants When He Wants It, 1912-14 (Cohl)
He Was Her Man, 1934 (Barnes; Grot; Orry-Kelly)
He Was Her Man, 1937 (Stalling)
He Was Not Ill, Only Unhappy, 1912-14 (Cohl)
He Was Once, 1989 (Vachon)
He Who Gets Slapped, 1924 (Gibbons; Mayer; Thalberg)
He Who Laughs Last, 1925 (Mohr)
He Who Must Die, 1956 (Saulnier)
He Who Must Die. See Celui qui doit mourir, 1957
He, She, and the Money. See Hans, hon, och pengarna, 1936
Head. See Nackte und der Satan, 1959
Head Guy, 1929 (Roach)

Head Over Heels, 1937 (Balcon; Junge)
Headdresses of Different Periods. See Histoire de chapeaux, 1910
Headin' for Danger, 1928 (Miller; Plunkett)
Headless Horseman, 1934 (Iwerks)
Headline Shooter, 1933 (D'Agostino; Musuraca; Polglase; Steiner)
Heads Up, 1930 (Green)
Health Farm, 1936 (Terry)
Heap Big Chief, 1919 (Roach)
Hear 'em Rave, 1918 (Roach)
Hear Me Good, 1957 (Head)
Heart and Soul, 1988 (Jones)
Heart Beat, 1979 (Kovacs; Nitzsche)
Heart Beats of Long Ago, 1910 (Bitzer)
Heart for a Song. See Srdce za písničku, 1933
Heart Is a Lonely Hunter, 1968 (Grusin; Howe)
Heart Line, 1921 (Barnes)
Heart o' the Hills, 1919 (Rosher)
Heart of a Child, 1958 (Rank)
Heart of a Man, 1959 (Rank; Wilcox)
Heart of a Nation. See Untel Père et Fils, 1940
Heart of a Siren, 1925 (Lemaire)
Heart of a Texan, 1922 (Canutt)
Heart of Arizona, 1938 (Harlan; Head)
Heart of Maryland, 1927 (Mohr)
Heart of Nora Flynn, 1916 (Buckland; Macpherson)
Heart of Spain, 1937 (Maddow; North)
Heart of the Matter, 1953 (Korda)
Heart of the North, 1938 (Deutsch)
Heart of the Rockies, 1938 (Canutt)
Heart of the Stag, 1984 (Rosenman)
Heart Song. See Ich und die kaiserin, 1933
Heart Song. See Only Girl, 1933
Heart Thief, 1927 (Levien)
Heart to Heart, 1928 (Polito)
Heartaches, 1981 (Hambling)
Heartbeat, 1968 (Hakim)
Heartbeat. See Chamade, 1968
Heartbeeps, 1981 (Whitlock; Williams; Winston; van Runkle)
Heartbreak, 1931 (August; Friedhofer; Grot)
Heartbreak Hotel, 1988 (Delerue)
Heartbreak Kid, 1972 (Sylbert; Cahn)
Heartbreakers, 1984 (Ballhaus)
Heartburn, 1986 (Almendros; O'Steen)
Hearth Fires. See Feux de la chandeleur, 1972
Heartland, 1981 (Von Brandenstein)
Hearts Afire. See Hearts in Exile, 1915
Hearts Aflame, 1923 (Mayer)
Hearts and Minds. See Uomo da rispettare, 1972
Hearts Are Thumps, 1937 (Roach)
Hearts Are Trumps, 1920 (Mathis; Seitz)
Hearts Divided, 1936 (Korngold; Orry-Kelly)
Hearts in Bondage, 1936 (Brown)
Hearts in Exile, 1915 (Carré; Edeson)
Hearts of Fire, 1987 (Barry; Eszterhas)
Hearts of Lieutenants. See Löjtnantshjärtan, 1941
Hearts of the World, 1918 (Bitzer; Coward)
Heartstopper, 1993 (Savini)
Heat, 1987 (Goldman; Tavoularis)
Heat and Dust, 1982 (Lassally; Jhabvala; Merchant)
Heat Lightning, 1934 (Orry-Kelly)
Heat of the Day, 1989 (Pinter)
Heat Wave, 1935 (Rank)
Heat Wave, 1990 (Newman)
Heat Wave. See House across the Lake, 1954
Heathcliff: The Movie, 1986 (Blanc)
Heat's On, 1943 (Cahn; Planer; Plunkett)

Heave Away My Johnny, 1948 (Halas and Batchelor)
Heave Ho!. *See* Hej rup!, 1934
Heaven, 1987 (Mancini)
Heaven and Earth, 1956 (Slocombe)
Heaven and Hell of Bohemia. *See* Plameny života, 1920
Heaven Avenges, 1912 (Bitzer)
Heaven Can Wait, 1943 (Basevi; Cronjager; Newman; Raphaelson; Spencer)
Heaven Can Wait, 1978 (Fraker; Grusin; Henry; van Runkle)
Heaven Fell That Night. *See* Bijoutiers du clair de lune, 1958
Heaven Help Us, 1985 (Ondříček)
Heaven Knows, Mr. Allison, 1956 (Auric; Morris)
Heaven on Earth, 1927 (Gibbons; Gillespie)
Heaven Only Knows, 1947 (Struss)
Heaven over the Marshes. *See* Cielo sulla palude, 1948
Heaven Scent, 1956 (Blanc; Jones)
Heaven with a Barbed Wire Fence, 1939 (Cronjager; Trumbo)
Heaven with a Gun, 1969 (Mandel)
Heavenly Body, 1943 (Gillespie; Irene; Kaper; Mayer; Reisch)
Heavenly Puss, 1949 (Hanna and Barbera)
Heavens Above, 1963 (Bennett)
Heaven's Gate, 1980 (Reynolds; Zsigmond)
Heavy Metal, 1981 (Bernstein)
Heavy Petting, 1988 (Mancini)
Heavy Seas, 1923 (Roach)
Hebihime douchuh, 1949-50 (Miyagawa; Yoda)
Heckling Hare, 1941 (Avery; Blanc; Stalling)
Hedda, 1975 (Slocombe)
Hedgehog in the Mist, 1976 (Norstein)
Heer, 1956 (Biswas)
Heerak Rajar Deshe, 1979 (Dutta)
Heideschulmeister Uwe Karsten, 1954 (Wagner)
Heidi, 1937 (Miller)
Heidi's Song, 1982 (Cahn; Hanna and Barbera)
Heilige Simplizie, 1920 (Von Harbou)
Heilige und ihr Narr, 1928 (Andrejew)
Heiligen Wassern, 1960 (Heller)
Heimkehr, 1928 (Pommer)
Heimkehr, 1941 (Röhrig)
Heinrich der Vierte, 1926 (Courant)
Heir Conditioned, 1955 (Blanc)
Heir to Genghis Khan. *See* **Potomok Chingis-khan**, 1928
Heiratsnest, 1927 (Reisch)
Heiress, 1949 (Head; Hornbeck; Horner)
Heisse Ernte, 1956 (Herlth)
Heisses Blut, 1911 (Freund)
Heist. *See* $, 1971
Hej rup!, 1934 (Heller)
Hélène, 1936 (Burel)
Held aller Mädchenträume, 1929 (Reisch)
Helden, 1959 (Warm)
Helen la Belle, 1957 (Reiniger)
Helen Morgan Story, 1957 (McCord)
Helen of Troy, 1955 (Adam; Steiner; Stradling)
Helen, Queen of the Nautch Girls, 1973 (Merchant)
Helen's Babies, 1924 (Daniels)
Helicopter, 1944 (Terry)
Heliotrope, 1921 (Rosson)
Hell and High Water, 1954 (Lemaire; Newman; Wheeler)
Hell below Zero, 1953 (Broccoli; Vetchinsky)
Hell Below, 1933 (Rosson)
Hell Bent for Glory. *See* Lafayette Escadrille, 1957
Hell-Bent for Election, 1944 (Hubley)
Hell Bent for Heaven, 1926 (Musuraca)
Hell Bound for Alaska , 1915 (August)
Hell Canyon Outlaws, 1957 (Crosby)

Hell Drivers, 1957 (Rank; Unsworth)
Hell-Fire Austin, 1932 (McCord)
Hell in Korea. *See* A Hill in Korea, 1956
Hell in the Heavens, 1934 (Glennon)
Hell in the Pacific, 1968 (Hall; Schifrin)
Hell Is a City, 1960 (Carreras)
Hell Is for Heroes, 1962 (Blanke; Pereira; Rosenman)
Hell on Frisco Bay, 1955 (Seitz; Steiner)
Hell River. *See* Partizani, 1974
Hell River Bad Company, 1979 (Theodorakis)
Hell Unlimited, 1936-37 (McClaren)
Hell with Heroes, 1968 (Jones)
Hellbound, 1993 (Golan and Globus)
Helldorado, 1935 (Lasky; Seitz)
Hellé, 1972 (Gégauff; Renoir)
Heller in Pink Tights, 1960 (Bernstein; Head; Nichols; Ponti)
Heller Wahn. *See* Friends and Husbands, 1982
Hellfighters, 1968 (Clothier; Head; Rosenman; Whitlock)
Hellfire, 1949 (Canutt)
Hellhound of the Plains, 1926 (Canutt)
Hellions, 1961 (Adam)
Hello and Goodbye, 1970 (Zanuck)
Hello Baby, 1924 (Roach)
Hello Beautiful. *See* Powers Girl, 1943
Hello Charlie, 1959 (Hecht)
Hello, Dolly!, 1969 (Edens; Kidd; Lehman; Reynolds; Sharaff; Smith; Stradling)
Hello Elephant!. *See* Buongiorno elefante!, 1952
Hello, Everybody, 1933 (Head)
Hello, Frisco, Hello, 1943 (Basevi; Clarke; Leven; Rose)
Hello-Goodbye, 1970 (Decaë; Lai)
Hello, How Am I?, 1939 (Fleischer)
Hello London, 1958 (Heller)
Hello Sister, 1930 (Rosson)
Hello, Sister!, 1933 (Howe)
Hello Teacher, 1918 (Roach)
Hello Uncle, 1920 (Roach)
Hell's 400, 1926 (Struss)
Hell's Angels, 1930 (Gaudio)
Hell's Angels on Wheels, 1967 (Kovacs)
Hell's Bells, 1929 (Iwerks)
Hell's Blood Devils, 1968 (Kovacs)
Hell's Boss. *See* Meido no kaoyaku, 1957
Hell's Fire, 1934 (Iwerks)
Hell's Five Hours, 1958 (Haller)
Hell's Heels, 1930 (Lantz)
Hell's Highway, 1932 (Cronjager)
Hell's Hinges, 1916 (August; Sullivan)
Hell's Horizon, 1955 (Crosby)
Hell's Island, 1930 (Swerling)
Hell's Island, 1955 (Head)
Hell's Kitchen, 1939 (Rosher)
Hell's Worm. *See* Jigoku no mushi, 1938
Help!, 1965 (Watkin)
Help?, 1995 (Bozzetto)
Help One Another, 1924 (Roach)
Helpful Genie, 1951 (Terry)
Helpless Hippo, 1954 (Terry)
Helpmates, 1931 (Roach)
Helter Skelter, 1948 (Rank)
Hemingway's Adventures of a Young Man, 1961 (Smith; Waxman; Wald)
Hen Fruit, 1930 (Lantz)
Hen Hop, 1942 (McClaren)
Henhouse Henry, 1949 (Blanc; Stalling)
Henpecked Duck, 1941 (Blanc; Clampett; Stalling)

Henpecked Hoboes, 1946 (Avery)
Henpecked Husband, 1905 (Bitzer)
Henri Matisse, ou le talent du bonheur, 1961 (Kosma)
Henry, 1955 (Lassally)
Henry IV, 1985 (Guerra)
Henry IV. *See* Enrico IV, 1984
Henry Moore at the Tate Gallery, 1970 (Lassally)
Henry Moore, 1951 (Alwyn)
Henry V, 1944 (Dillon; Krasker; Mathieson; Rank; Walton)
Henry VIII, 1911 (Barker)
Henry 9 'til 5, 1970 (Godfrey)
Henry Aldrich, Boy Scout, 1944 (Dreier)
Henry Aldrich, Editor, 1942 (Dreier; Head)
Henry Aldrich for President, 1941 (Dreier; Head)
Henry Aldrich Gets Glamour, 1943 (Dreier; Head)
Henry Aldrich Haunts a House, 1943 (Dreier; Head)
Henry Aldrich Plays Cupid, 1944 (Dreier)
Henry Aldrich Swings It, 1943 (Dreier)
Henry Aldrich's Little Secret, 1944 (Dreier; Head)
Henry and June, 1989 (Allen; Rousselot)
Henry Cotton: This Game of Golf, 1974 (Lassally)
Henry's Cat, 1982 (Godfrey)
Hep Cat, 1942 (Blanc; Clampett; Stalling)
Hepcat, 1946 (Terry)
Her Accidental Husband, 1923 (Cohn)
Her Alibi, 1989 (Bumstead; Delerue; Francis)
Her Awakening, 1911 (Bitzer)
Her Bodyguard, 1933 (Shamroy)
Her Brother. *See* Ototo, 1960
Her Cardboard Lover, 1942 (Mayer; Stradling; Veiller; Waxman)
Her Dangerous Path, 1923 (Roach)
Her Darkest Hour, 1911 (Gaudio; Ince)
Her Dilemma. *See* Confessions of a Co-ed, 1931
Her Doctor. *See* Její lékař, 1933
Her Father's Pride, 1910 (Bitzer)
Her Favourite Husband, 1950 (Gherardi)
Her First Adventure, 1908 (Bitzer)
Her First Biscuit, 1909 (Bitzer)
Her First Egg, 1931 (Terry)
Her Highness and the Bellboy, 1945 (Mercer; Pasternak; Stradling)
Her Highness' Young Washerwoman. *See* Pradlenka Jeho Jasnosti, 1930
Her Husband Lies, 1937 (D'Agostino; Head; Shamroy)
Her Husband's Affairs, 1947 (Duning; Goosson; Hakim; Hecht; Lederer)
Her Husband's Friend, 1920 (Barnes)
Her Husband's Honor, 1918 (Polito)
Her Jungle Love, 1938 (Head; Rennahan; Siodmak)
Her Kind of Man, 1946 (Waxman)
Her Kingdom of Desire, 1922 (Mayer)
Her Kingdom of Dreams, 1920 (Gaudio)
Her Legacy, 1913 (Ince)
Her Lucky Night, 1945 (Bruckman; Mohr)
Her Mad Bargain, 1921 (Mayer)
Her Man o' War, 1926 (Sullivan)
Her Master's Voice, 1936 (Reynolds; Schary; Wanger)
Her Mother's Oath, 1913 (Bitzer)
Her Night of Promise, 1924 (Kräly)
Her Night of Romance, 1924 (Schenck)
Her Panelled Door. *See* Woman with No Name, 1950
Her Polished Family, 1912 (Sullivan)
Her Private Life, 1929 (Grot; Korda; Seitz)
Her Reputation. *See* Broadway Bad, 1933
Her Sacrifice, 1911 (Bitzer)
Her Second Husband, 1917 (Polito)
Her Sister, 1925 (Adrian)
Her Sister from Paris, 1925 (Edeson; Menzies; Schenck)
Her Sister's Secret, 1946 (Planer)

Her Summer Hero, 1927 (Plunkett)
Her Terrible Ordeal, 1909 (Bitzer)
Her Twelve Men, 1953 (Houseman; Kaper; Rose; Ruttenberg)
Héroïsme de Paddy, 1915 (Gaumont)
Herb Alpert and the Tijuana Brass Double Feature, 1966 (Hubley)
Herbier. *See* Citadelle du silence, 1937
Herbstsonate, 1978 (Nykvist)
Hercules, 1983 (Donaggio; Golan and Globus)
Hercules, 1997 (Menken)
Hercules and the Big Stick. *See* Douze Travaux d'Hercule, 1910
Here, 1960 (Hanna and Barbera)
Here and There, 1961 (Kuri)
Here Come the Girls, 1918 (Roach)
Here Come the Girls, 1953 (Head)
Here Come the Huggetts, 1948 (Rank)
Here Come the Jets, 1959 (Struss)
Here Come the Waves, 1944 (Head; Mercer)
Here Comes Carter, 1936 (Orry-Kelly)
Here Comes Cookie, 1935 (Head)
Here Comes Mr. Jordan, 1941 (Buchman; Cohn; Head; Miller; Walker)
Here Comes Santa Claus. *See* J'ai rencontré le Père Noel, 1984
Here Comes the Groom, 1951 (Barnes; Carmichael; Head; Mercer; Pereira; Riskin)
Here Comes the Navy, 1934 (Edeson; Orry-Kelly)
Here Comes the Waves, 1944 (Dreier; Lang)
Here Comes Troubles, 1948 (Roach)
Here I Am a Stranger, 1939 (Miller)
Here I Come. *See* Harvard, Here I Come, 1941
Here Is a Man. *See* All that Money Can Buy, 1941
Here Is My Heart, 1934 (Banton; Struss; Zukor)
Here Is Tomorrow, 1941 (Maddow)
Here Today, Gone Tamale, 1959 (Blanc)
Here We Go, 1951 (McKimson)
Heredity, 1912 (Bitzer)
Here's to Good Old Jail, 1938 (Terry)
Here's to Romance, 1935 (Friedhofer; Lasky; Levien)
Heritage, 1953 (Hubley)
Heritage. *See* Karami-ai, 1962
Heritage of Eve, 1913 (August)
Heritage of the Desert, 1939 (Harlan; Head; Young)
Héritier des Mondésir, 1939 (Aurenche and Bost)
Hermanos del hierro, 1961 (Figueroa)
Hero, 1923 (Struss)
Hero, 1992 (Sargent)
Hero. *See* Nayak, 1966
Hero. *See* Bloomfield, 1969
Hero and the Terror, 1988 (Golan and Globus)
Hero for a Day, 1953 (Terry)
Hero for a Night. *See* Jrdina jedné noci, 1935
Hero of Liao Yang, 1904 (Bitzer)
Hero of Little Italy, 1913 (Bitzer)
Hero of Our Time, 1985 (Burwell)
Hérodiade, 1910 (Gaumont)
Héroe desconocido, 1981 (Figueroa)
Heroes, 1977 (Nitzsche)
Heroes for Sale, 1933 (Orry-Kelly)
Heroes of Telemark, 1965 (Arnold)
Heroes of the Hills, 1938 (Canutt)
Héroes sont fatigués, 1955 (Alekan)
Héroines du mal, 1978 (Braunberger)
Heroïsme de Paddy, 1916 (Burel)
Heroismus einer Französin, 1913 (Messter)
Heron and the Crane, 1975 (Norstein)
Héros de la Marne, 1938 (Ibert)
Héros de l'air, 1962 (Delerue)
Hero's Island, 1962 (McCord)

Herr Arnes pengar, 1919 (Jaenzon)
Herr Arnes pengar, 1919 (Magnusson)
Herr auf Bestellung, 1930 (Reisch)
Herr Bürovorsteher, 1931 (Planer)
Herr der Bestien, 1921 (Hoffmann)
Herr der Liebe, 1919 (Hoffmann; Pommer)
Herr Finanz-direktor, 1931 (Warm)
Herr Meets Hare, 1945 (Blanc; Stalling)
Herr Puntila und sein Knecht Matti, 1955 (Eisler)
Herr Sanders lebt gefährlich, 1943 (Wagner)
Herr und Hund, 1963 (Herlth)
Herren der Meere, 1922 (Kolowrat-Krakowsky; Korda)
Herrin der Welt, 1920 (Hunte)
Herrin von Atlantis. See Atlantide, 1932
Herring Murder Case, 1931 (Fleischer)
Herring Murder Mystery, 1944 (Fleischer)
Herrn Zabladies seltsamer Traum, 1917 (Kolowrat-Krakowsky)
Herrscher, 1937 (Herlth; Von Harbou)
Hers to Hold, 1942 (Adrian)
Herz der Welt, 1952 (Herlth; Warm)
Herz vom Hochland, 1920 (Hoffmann)
Herzensphotograph, 1928 (Andrejew)
Herzog Blaubart's Burg, 1964 (Heckroth)
Herzog Ferrantes Ende, 1922 (Freund)
Herzog von Reichstadt, 1931 (Planer)
Herzogin von Langeais. See Liebe, 1926
Hester Street, 1975 (Von Brandenstein)
Het bezoek, 1971 (Müller)
Heterosexual. See Juliette de Sade, 1969
Heureux anniversaire, 1961 (Carrière)
Heureux qui comme Ulysse, 1970 (Colpi; Delerue)
Heut' kommt's drauf an, 1933 (Kaper)
Heut' spielt der Strauss, 1928 (Planer)
Heut tanzt Mariett, 1928 (Andrejew)
Heute heiratet mein Mann, 1956 (Herlth)
Heute Nacht—Eventuell, 1930 (Planer)
Hexer, 1932 (Heller)
Hey Cinderella, 1968 (Henson)
Hey Diddle Diddle, 1935 (Terry)
Hey! Hey! U.S.A., 1938 (Rank; Vetchinsky)
Hey Rube!, 1928 (Plunkett)
Hey There!, 1918 (Roach)
Hey There, It's Yogi Bear, 1964 (Hanna and Barbera)
Hi Diddle Diddle, 1942 (Adrian)
Hi Neighbor!, 1934 (Roach)
Hi, Gang!, 1941 (Rank)
Hi, Gaucho!, 1935 (Plunkett)
Hi-Lo Country, 1998 (Burwell)
Hi, Nellie, 1934 (Orry-Kelly; Polito)
Hiawatha, 1962 (Mirisch)
Hiawatha's Rabbit Hunt, 1941 (Blanc; Stalling)
Hibernatus, 1969 (Delerue)
Hic-Cup Pup, 1954 (Hanna and Barbera)
Hick, a Slick and a Chick, 1948 (Blanc; Stalling)
Hick Chick, 1946 (Avery)
Hicksville Epicure, 1913 (Loos)
Hickville's Finest, 1914 (Loos)
Hidden Aces, 1927 (Shamroy)
Hidden Children, 1917 (Gaudio)
Hidden City, 1950 (Mirisch)
Hidden Eye, 1945 (Irene)
Hidden Fortress. See Kakushi toride no sanakunin, 1958
Hidden Gold, 1940 (Harlan; Head)
Hidden Homicide, 1959 (Rank)
Hidden in America, 1996 (Daring)
Hidden in the Fog. See I dimma dold, 1952

Hidden Menace. See Star of the Circus, 1938
Hidden River. See Río escondido, 1947
Hidden Room. See Obsession, 1948
Hidden Scar, 1916 (Marion)
Hidden Spring, 1917 (Gaudio)
Hidden Trail, 1912 (Ince)
Hidden Valley Outlaws, 1944 (Canutt)
Hidden World, 1958 (Rosenman)
Hide and Seek, 1932 (Fleischer)
Hide and Shriek, 1938 (Roach)
Hide in Plain Sight, 1980 (Rosenman)
Hide-Out, 1933 (Freed)
Hide Out, 1934 (Brown; Goodrich and Hackett; Stromberg)
Hideaway Girl, 1936 (Head; Polglase; Young)
Hideout. See Small Voice, 1948
Hier et aujourd'hui. See Paris d'hier et d'aujourd'hui, 1956
High, 1950 (Young)
High and Dry, 1920 (Roach)
High and Handsome, 1925 (Haller)
High and Low. See Du haut en bas, 1933
High and Low. See Tengoku to jigoku, 1963
High and the Flighty, 1956 (Blanc; McKimson; Stalling)
High and the Mighty, 1954 (Clothier; Tiomkin)
High Anxiety, 1977 (Whitlock)
High Barbaree, 1947 (Irene; Stothart)
High Brow Stuff, 1924 (Roach)
High Command, 1937 (Heller)
High Commissioner. See Nobody Runs Forever, 1968
High Cost of Loving, 1958 (Rose)
High Diving Hare, 1949 (Blanc; Stalling)
High Encounters of the Ultimate Kind. See Cheech and Chong's Next Movie, 1980
High Fidelity, 2000 (Burwell)
High Frequency, 1988 (Donaggio)
High Fury. See White Cradle Inn, 1947
High Gear Jeffrey, 1921 (Furthman)
High Gear, 1931 (Roach)
High Hand, 1926 (Mohr)
High Infidelity. See Alta infedeltà, 1964
High Noon, 1951 (Crosby; Foreman; Tiomkin)
High Note, 1960 (Blanc; Jones)
High on the Range , 1985 (Canutt)
High Pavement , 1948 (Rank)
High Plains Drifter, 1972 (Bumstead)
High Rise Donkey, 1979 (Clarke)
High Risk, 1976 (O'Steen)
High Road. See Lady of Scandal, 1930
High Road to China, 1983 (Barry)
High Rollers, 1921 (Roach)
High School Hero, 1927 (Miller)
High School Student and Woman Teacher: Merciless Youth. See Koukousei to onna kyoushi: hijou no seishun, 1962
High Season, 1987 (Menges; Peploe)
High Sierra, 1941 (Deutsch; Gaudio; Haskin; Wallis)
High Society, 1924 (Roach)
High Society, 1956 (Gibbons; Green; Rose; Porter)
High Speed, 1953 (Lassally)
High Tension. See Sånt händer inte här, 1950
High Tide, 1922 (Roach)
High Tide, 1987 (Boyd)
High Tide at Noon, 1957 (Rank)
High Time, 1960 (Brackett; Cahn; Kanin; Mancini; van Heusen)
High Treason, 1951 (Rank; Vetchinsky)
High Velocity, 1976 (Goldsmith)
High Vermilion. See Silver City, 1951
High Wall, 1947 (Kaper; Mayer)

High, Wide, and Handsome, 1937 (Banton; Dreier)
High Wind in Jamaica, 1964 (Slocombe)
High Window. *See* Brasher Doubloon, 1947
Highbrow Love, 1913 (Loos)
Highlander, 1985 (Fisher)
Highly Dangerous, 1950 (Addinsell; Rank; Vetchinsky)
Highway Patrol, 1938 (Ballard)
Highway Pickup. *See* Chair de poule, 1963
Highway Runnery, 1965 (Blanc)
Highway West, 1941 (Burks; McCord)
Hija del angaño, 1951 (Alcoriza)
Hijazo de mi vidaza, 1971 (Figueroa)
Hijo de papá, 1934 (Alton)
Hijos de Satanas, 1971 (Figueroa)
Hikoki wa naze tobuka, 1943 (Tsuburaya)
Hilda Crane, 1956 (Dunne; Lemaire; Raksin)
Hilda Warren und der Tod, 1917 (Courant; Hoffmann)
Hill, 1965 (Morris)
Hill in Korea, 1956 (Francis)
Hill Tillies, 1935 (Roach)
Hillbilly Hare, 1950 (Blanc; McKimson; Stalling)
Hillbilly, 1935 (Lantz)
Hillcrest Mystery, 1918 (Miller)
Hills of Home, 1948 (Stothart)
Hills of Old Wyomin', 1936 (Head; Fleischer)
Hills Run Red. *See* Fiume di dollari, 1966
Hilly Billy, 1951 (Fleischer)
Himatsuri, 1984 (Takemitsu)
Himiko, 1974 (Takemitsu)
Himmel och pannkaka, 1959 (Lundgren)
Himmel über Berlin, 1987 (Alekan)
Hin och smålänningen, 1949 (Lundgren; Nykvist)
Hindenburg, 1975 (Jeakins; Surtees; Whitlock)
Hindle Wakes, 1931 (Balcon)
Hindoo Dagger, 1908 (Bitzer)
Hinotori, 1977 (Legrand)
Hinter Kostermann, 1952 (Herlth)
Hintertreppe, 1921 (Junge; Mayer)
Hip, Hip—Hurry!, 1958 (Blanc; Jones)
Hippety Hopper, 1949 (Blanc; Stalling)
Hippocampe, 1934 (Milhaud)
Hippydrome Tiger, 1968 (Blanc)
Hips, Hips, Hooray!, 1934 (Steiner)
Hired and Fired, 1922 (Roach)
Hired Hand, 1971 (Zsigmond)
Hired Wife, 1940 (Krasner)
Hirondelle et la mésange, 1921 (Burel)
Hirondelle et la mésange, 1983 (Colpi)
Hiroshima mon amour, 1959 (Colpi; Delerue; Duras; Vierny)
Hirt von Maria Schnee, 1919 (Hoffmann)
Hiryuh no ken, 1937 (Miyagawa)
His Affair. *See* This Is My Affair, 1937
His Awful Vengeance, 1914 (Loos)
His Best Girl, 1921 (Roach)
His Better Self, 1912 (Ince)
His Bitter Half, 1950 (Blanc; Stalling)
His Brother's Wife, 1936 (Waxman)
His Busy Day, 1918 (Roach)
His Butler's Sister, 1943 (Adrian; Hoffenstein)
His Captive Woman, 1929 (Garmes)
His Country. *See* A Ship Comes In, 1928
His Daughter, 1911 (Bitzer)
His Day of Rest, 1908 (Bitzer)
His Dog, 1927 (Adrian; Brown)
His Double Life, 1933 (Edeson)
His Dress Shirt, 1911 (Gaudio)

His Duty, 1909 (Bitzer)
His English Wife. *See* Hans engelska fru, 1926
His Excellency, 1951 (Slocombe)
His Family Tree, 1935 (Plunkett)
His First Command, 1929 (Miller)
His First Flame, 1927 (Hornbeck)
His Girl Friday, 1939 (Cohn; Hecht; Lederer; Walker)
His Glorious Night, 1929 (Daniels; Gibbons; Mayer)
His Greatest Gamble, 1934 (Buchman; Plunkett; Steiner)
His Hare Raising Tale, 1951 (Blanc; Stalling)
His Highness' Adjutant. *See* Pobočník jeho výsosti, 1933
His Hoodoo, 1913 (Loos)
His Hour, 1924 (Gibbons; Mayer)
His Hour of Manhood, 1914 (August; Ince)
His House in Order, 1920 (Miller)
His Last Adventure. *See* Battling Buckaroos, 1933
His Last Burglary, 1910 (Bitzer)
His Last Legs, 1920 (Bray)
His Last Twelve Hours. *See* E più facile che un camello, 1950
His Last Twelve Hours. *See* Mondo le condanna, 1952
His Lesson, 1912 (Bitzer)
His Lordship, 1936 (Balcon; Junge)
His Lost Love, 1909 (Bitzer)
His Majesty, Bunker Bean, 1925 (Haskin)
His Majesty O'Keefe, 1953 (Chase; Haskin; Heller; Tiomkin)
His Mother's Scarf, 1911 (Bitzer)
His Mother's Son, 1913 (Bitzer)
His Mouse Friday, 1951 (Hanna and Barbera)
His Move, 1905 (Bitzer)
His Nemesis, 1912 (Ince)
His New Lid, 1910 (Ince)
His New Stenographer, 1928 (Hornbeck)
His New York Wife, 1926 (Musuraca)
His Night Out, 1935 (Mandell; Waxman)
His Off Day, 1938 (Terry)
His Only Father, 1919 (Roach)
His Other Woman. *See* Desk Set, 1957
His Picture in the Papers, 1916 (Loos)
His Private Life, 1928 (Vajda)
His Royal Slyness, 1919 (Roach)
His Secretary, 1925 (Day; Gibbons)
His Sense of Duty, 1912 (Ince)
His Sister from Paris, 1925 (Kräly)
His Sister-in-Law, 1910 (Bitzer)
His Squaw, 1912 (Ince)
His Supreme Moment, 1925 (Goldwyn; Marion; Miller)
His Tiger Lady, 1928 (Banton; Mankiewicz; Vajda)
His Trust Fulfilled, 1910 (Bitzer)
His Trust, 1910 (Bitzer)
His Unlucky Night, 1928 (Hornbeck)
His Ward's Love, 1909 (Bitzer)
His Wedding Night. *See* Hans bröllopsnatt, 1915
His Wife's Husband, 1922 (Stradling)
His Wife's Past. *See* Hans hustrus förflutna, 1915
His Wife's Visitor, 1909 (Bitzer)
His Wooden Wedding, 1925 (Roach)
Hiss and Make Up, 1943 (Blanc; Stalling)
Histérico, 1952 (Figueroa)
Histoire comique. *See* Félicie Nanteuil, 1942
Histoire d'Adèle H., 1971 (Jaubert)
Histoire d'Adèle H., 1975 (Almendros)
Histoire de chapeaux, 1910 (Cohl)
Histoire de pin-up girls, 1950 (Braunberger)
Histoire d'eau, 1958 (Braunberger)
Histoire d'O: Chapitre 2, 1984 (Zimmer)
Histoire d'un crime, 1901 (Pathé Gaumont)

Histoire d'un petit garçon devenu grand, 1963 (Braunberger)
Histoire simple, 1978 (Sarde)
Histoire très bonne et très joyeuse de Colinot Trousse-Chemise, 1973
    (Cloquet)
Histoires extraordinaires, 1968 (Delli Colli; Renoir; Rota; Rotunno)
Historia de un amor, 1955 (Figueroa)
Historia de un gran amor, 1942 (Figueroa)
Historia naturae, 1967 (švankmajer)
Historia współczesna, 1961 (Stawiński)
Histórias Selvagems, 1978 (de Almeida)
Historical Fan. See Eventail animé, 1909
Historie blechatého psa, 1958 (Brdečka)
Historien om en moder, 1979 (Gégauff)
History and Romance of Transportation, 1939 (Maddow)
History Is Made at Night, 1937 (Basevi; Newman; Toland)
History of Adventure, 1964 (Bass)
History of Inventions, 1960 (Halas and Batchelor)
History of Mr. Polly, 1948 (Rank; Alwyn)
History of the Cinema, 1957 (Halas and Batchelor)
History of the World, Part I, 1981 (Whitlock)
Hit, 1973 (Schifrin)
Hit and Run, 1924 (Miller)
Hit Him Again, 1918 (Roach)
Hit Me Again. See Smarty, 1934
Hit of the Show, 1928 (Kahn; Plunkett)
Hit Parade of 1947, 1947 (Alton)
Hit the Deck, 1930 (Clothier)
Hit the Deck, 1954 (Levien; Pan; Pasternak; Rose)
Hit the Hay, 1946 (Hunter)
Hit the High Spots, 1924 (Roach)
Hit the Saddle, 1937 (Canutt)
Hit-the-Trail Holliday, 1918 (Loos)
Hitch-Hiker, 1953 (D'Agostino; Mainwaring; Musuraca)
Hitch Hikers, 1947 (Terry)
Hitch in Time, 1978 (Clarke)
Hitchcock: Shadow of a Genius, 1999 (Neame)
Hitcher, 1986 (Seale)
Hitchhiker, 1939 (Terry)
Hitchhiking Vietnam: Letters From the Trail, 1997 (Daring)
Hitler, 1962 (Biroc)
Hitler . . . connais pas, 1963 (Delerue)
Hitler—Dead or Alive, 1942 (Brown)
Hitler Gang, 1944 (Dreier; Goodrich and Hackett; Head; Laszlo)
Hitler Lives!, 1945 (Burks)
Hitlerjunge Salomon, 1990 (Preisner)
Hitler's Children, 1943 (Metty)
Hits of the Nineties, 1948 (Fleischer)
Hitting a New High, 1937 (Lasky; Polglase)
Hiver 54, l'abbé Pierre, 1989 (Sarde)
Hjärtats triumpf, 1929 (Jaenzon)
HMS Defiant, 1962 (Challis)
Ho!, 1968 (Saulnier)
Ho fatto splash, 1980 (Cristaldi)
Hoa-Binh, 1969 (Coutard)
Hobbs in a Hurry, 1918 (Furthman)
Hobby Horse Laffs, 1942 (Blanc)
Hobgoblins, 1921 (Roach)
Hobo Bobo, 1947 (Blanc; McKimson)
Hobson's Choice, 1953 (Arnold; Korda)
Hochstaplerin, 1926 (Maté)
Hochzeit am Wolfgangsee, 1933 (Warm)
Hochzeit auf Immenhof, 1956 (Wagner)
Hochzeit in Ekzentrik Klub, 1917 (Hoffmann)
Hochzeitglocken, 1953 (Herlth)
Hochzeitreise, 1939 (Röhrig)
Hochzeitsreise zu Dritt, 1932 (Kaper)

Hochzeitstraum, 1936 (Warm)
Hocus Pocus Powwow, 1968 (Blanc)
Hocus pocus. See Hokuspokus, 1930
Hodinárova svatební cesta korálovym moren, 1979 (švankmajer)
Hoffa, 1992 (Mamet)
Hoffmanovy povídky, 1962 (Stallich)
Hoffnungloser Fall, 1939 (Wagner)
Hogan's Alley, 1925 (Zanuck)
Högfjällets dotter, 1914 (Jaenzon; Magnusson)
Hogre andamal, 1921 (Magnusson)
Högsta vinsten, 1915 (Jaenzon)
Hohe Lied der Liebe, 1922 (Wagner)
Hohelied der Kraft, 1930 (Fischinger)
Hokuspokus, 1930 (Herlth; Hoffmann; Pommer; Reisch; Röhrig)
Hokuspokus, 1953 (Warm)
Holcroft Covenant, 1984 (Fisher)
Hold 'em Yale, 1928 (Grot; Miller)
Hold 'em Yale, 1935 (Head; Krasner)
Hold 'em, Navy, 1937 (Dreier; Head)
Hold Back the Dawn, 1941 (Brackett; Dreier; Head; Laszlo; Young)
Hold Everything, 1926 (Roach)
Hold It, 1938 (Fleischer)
Hold Me Tight, 1933 (Miller)
Hold My Baby, 1925 (Roach)
Hold That Blonde!, 1945 (Dreier; Head; Young)
Hold That Co-Ed, 1938 (Zanuck)
Hold That Girl, 1934 (Nichols; Trotti)
Hold the Lion, Please, 1941 (Blanc; Jones; Stalling)
Hold the Wire, 1936 (Fleischer)
Hold Your Man, 1933 (Adrian; Brown; Freed; Loos; Mayer; Rosson)
Hold-up, 1985 (Mnouchkine)
Holdup of Rocky Mt. Express, 1906 (Bitzer)
Hole, 1962 (Hubley)
Hole Idea, 1955 (Blanc)
Hole Ideal Dime to Retire, 1955 (McKimson)
Hole in the Head, 1959 (Cahn; Daniels; Head; Hornbeck; van Heusen)
Holiday, 1930 (Mandell)
Holiday, 1938 (Buchman; Cohn; Goosson; Planer; Stewart)
Holiday Affair, 1949 (Krasner)
Holiday Camp, 1947 (Rank)
Holiday for Drumsticks, 1949 (Blanc; Stalling)
Holiday for Henriette. See Fête à Henriette, 1952
Holiday for Lovers, 1959 (Cahn; Clarke; van Heusen)
Holiday for Shoestrings, 1946 (Blanc; Stalling)
Holiday for Sinners, 1952 (Houseman)
Holiday Highlights, 1940 (Avery; Blanc; Stalling)
Holiday in Mexico, 1946 (Brown; Hanna and Barbera; Irene; Pasternak;
    Smith; Stradling)
Holiday in Spain. See Scent of Mystery, 1960
Holiday Inn, 1942 (Berlin; Dreier; Head)
Holiday Inn. See Riding High, 1943
Holiday's End, 1937 (Havelock-Allan)
Holidays with an Angel. See Dovolená s andelem, 1952
Holland Days, 1934 (Terry)
Holland Submarine Torpedo Boat, 1904 (Bitzer)
Höllenspuk in 6 Akten. See Kurfurstendamm, 1920
Hollow Man, 2000 (Goldsmith)
Hollow Triumph, 1948 (Alton)
Holly and the Ivy, 1952 (Arnold; Korda; de Grunwald)
Hollyrock-a-Bye Baby, 1993 (Hanna and Barbera)
Hollywood Boulevard, 1936 (Dreier; Head; Struss)
Hollywood Canine Canteen, 1946 (Blanc; McKimson; Stalling)
Hollywood Canteen, 1944 (Glennon)
Hollywood Cavalcade, 1939 (Day; Raksin; Zanuck)
Hollywood Daffy, 1946 (Blanc; Stalling)
Hollywood Diet, 1932 (Terry)

Hollywood Hotel, 1937 (Barnes; Mercer; Orry-Kelly; Rosher; Wald; Wallis)
Hollywood Knights, 1980 (Fraker)
Hollywood Matador, 1942 (Lantz)
Hollywood on Trial, 1976 (Bernstein)
Hollywood or Bust, 1956 (Bumstead; Head; Wallis)
Hollywood Party, 1933 (Brown; Freed; Howe; Kahn)
Hollywood Revue of 1929, 1929 (Brown; Day; Freed; Gibbons; Mayer)
Hollywood Speaks, 1932 (Krasna)
Hollywood Steps Out, 1941 (Avery; Blanc; Stalling)
Hollywood Sunset. See Good Morning Babilonia, 1986
Hollywood Ten, 1950 (Jarrico; Lardner)
Holocaust 2000, 1977 (Morricone)
Holubice, 1960 (Ondříček)
Holy Man, 1998 (Biddle)
Holy Matrimony, 1943 (Ballard; Basevi; Johnson)
Holy Smoke, 1999 (Badalamenti)
Holy Terror, 1929 (Roach)
Homage to Jean Tinguely's Homage to New York, 1960 (Breer)
Hombre, 1966 (Howe; Smith)
Hombre de Alazan, 1958 (Alcoriza)
Hombre de papel, 1963 (Figueroa)
Hombre neustra de cada dia, 1959 (Alcoriza)
Hombres armados. See Men with Guns, 1997
Home, 1916 (Ince; Sullivan)
Home Again, 1958 (Kaufman)
Home Alone, 1990 (Williams)
Home Alone 2: Lost in New York, 1992 (Menken; Williams)
Home Alone 3, 1997 (Bumstead)
Home and School, 1946 (Alwyn)
Home and the World. See Ghare Bahire, 1982
Home at Seven, 1948 (de Grunwald)
Home at Seven, 1951 (Arnold; Korda; Sherriff)
Home Before Dark, 1958 (Biroc; Cahn; Waxman)
Home Folks, 1912 (Bitzer)
Home from the Hill, 1959 (Ames; Kaper; Krasner; Plunkett)
Home Guard, 1941 (Terry)
Home in Indiana, 1944 (Basevi; Cronjager; Friedhofer)
Home Movies, 1979 (Donaggio)
Home of the Brave, 1949 (Foreman; Tiomkin)
Home on the Rails, 1982 (Driessen)
Home on the Range, 1938 (Ballard)
Home Stretch, 1920 (Roach)
Home Stretch, 1947 (Lemaire)
Home, Sweet Home, 1914 (Bitzer)
Home Sweet Homicide, 1946 (Basevi; Leven; Seitz)
Home Talent, 1921 (Hornbeck)
Home Tweet Home, 1950 (Blanc; Stalling)
Homebreaker, 1919 (Ince)
Homecoming. See Heimkehr, 1928
Homecoming, 1947 (Kaper; Mayer; Rose; Rosson)
Homecoming, 1971 (Goldsmith)
Homecoming, 1973 (Pinter; Watkin)
Homeless Hare, 1949 (Blanc; Jones; Stalling)
Homeless Pup, 1937 (Terry)
Homespun Vamp, 1922 (Rosson)
Homesteader Droopy, 1954 (Avery)
Homestretch, 1947 (Basevi; Raksin)
Homeward Bound, 1923 (Haller)
Homicidal, 1961 (Friedhofer; Guffey)
Homicide, 1991 (Mamet)
Homicide Bureau, 1939 (Goosson)
Homme, 1946 (Braunberger; Kosma)
Homme à l'Hispano, 1933 (Wakhévitch)
Homme à l'oeillet blanc, 1953 (Cloquet)
Homme à l'oreille cassée, 1935 (Burel)

Homme à la barbiche, 1932 (Fradetal)
Homme à la Buick, 1967 (Legrand)
Homme à la mer, 1948 (Decaë)
Homme aimanté, 1907 (Gaumont)
Homme amoureux, 1987 (Delerue; Tavoularis)
Homme au chapeau rond, 1946 (Spaak; Wakhévitch)
Homme au crâne rasé, 1966 (Cloquet)
Homme aux clés d'or, 1956 (D'Eaubonne)
Homme aux gants blancs, 1908 (Pathé)
Homme aux yeux d'argent, 1985 (Sarde)
Homme de compagnie, 1916 (Gaumont)
Homme de joie, 1950 (Mnouchkine)
Homme de ma vie, 1951 (Jeanson)
Homme de nulle part, 1936 (Ibert)
Homme de Rio, 1963 (Delerue; Mnouchkine; Rappeneau)
Homme du jour, 1936 (Spaak)
Homme du large, 1920 (Gaumont)
Homme du Niger, 1939 (Burel)
Homme en colère, 1978 (Mnouchkine)
Homme en marche, 1952 (Fradetal)
Homme en or, 1934 (Burel)
Homme est mort, 1972 (Carrière)
Homme est mort, 1973 (Legrand)
Homme et la bête, 1953 (Decaë)
Homme et une femme, 1966 (Lai)
Homme et une femme: vingt ans déjà, 1986 (Lai)
Homme libre, 1973 (Lai)
Homme mystérieux. See Obsession, 1934
Homme, notre ami, 1955 (Rabier)
Homme orchestre, 1969 (Rabier)
Homme qui a perdu son ombre, 1991 (Branco)
Homme qui aimait les femmes, 1977 (Almendros; Jaubert)
Homme qui assassina, 1930 (Courant)
Homme qui joue avec le feu, 1942 (Aurenche and Bost)
Homme qui me plaît, 1969 (Lai; Mnouchkine)
Homme qui ment, 1968 (Robbe-Grillet)
Homme qui ne sais pas dire non, 1932 (Courant)
Homme sans coeur, 1936 (Kaufman)
Homme sans nom, 1937 (D'Eaubonne)
Homme sans visage, 1919 (Gaumont)
Hommes, 1972 (Lai)
Hommes d'aujourd'hui, 1952 (Fradetal)
Hommes de la baleine, 1958 (Colpi)
Hommes de la Wahgi, 1963 (Braunberger; Guillemot)
Hommes des oasis, 1950 (Cloquet)
Hommes du pétrole, 1961 (Delerue)
Hommes du Sepik, 1965 (Braunberger)
Hommes et bêtes, 1946 (Decaë)
Hommes, femmes, mode d'emploi, 1996 (Lai)
Hommes nouveaux, 1936 (Fradetal; Lourié)
Hommes sans nom, 1937 (Kaufman)
Hommes veulent vivre, 1961 (Kosma)
Homo eroticus, 1971 (Delli Colli)
Homo Faber, 1991 (Lhomme)
Homo Faber. See Voyager, 1991
Homo Sapiens, 1960 (Popescu-Gopo)
Homo Technologicus, 1981 (Bozzetto)
Homolka a tobolka, 1972 (Ondříček)
Homunculus, 1916 (Hoffmann)
Hon den enda, 1926 (Jaenzon)
Hondo, 1953 (Burks; Friedhofer)
Honest Love and True, 1938 (Fleischer)
Honey, 1930 (Mankiewicz)
Honey-mousers, 1956 (Blanc; McKimson)
Honey Pot, 1967 (Di Venanzo)
Honeychile, 1951 (Young)

Hot Dog, 1928 (Disney)
Hot Dog, 1930 (Fleischer)
Hot Feet, 1931 (Lantz)
Hot for Hollywood, 1930 (Lantz)
Hot for Paris, 1929 (Carré)
Hot Heels, 1924 (Roach)
Hot Heir, 1931 (Balcon)
Hot Heiress, 1931 (Polito)
Hot Lead, 1951 (Musuraca)
Hot Money, 1935 (Edeson; Roach)
Hot Off the Press, 1922 (Roach)
Hot Pepper, 1933 (Clarke; Nichols)
Hot Resort, 1984 (Golan and Globus)
Hot Rock, 1972 (Goldman; Jones)
Hot Rod Action, 1969 (Zsigmond)
Hot Rod and Reel, 1959 (Blanc; Jones)
Hot Rod Gang, 1958 (Crosby)
Hot Rods, 1953 (Terry)
Hot Sands, 1934 (Terry)
Hot Saturday, 1932 (Head)
Hot Spell, 1936 (Terry)
Hot Spell, 1958 (Head; North; Pereira; Wallis; Westmore Family)
Hot Spot, 1932 (Roach)
Hot Spot, 1941 (Cronjager)
Hot Spot, 1990 (Nitzsche)
Hot Stuff, 1924 (Roach)
Hot Summer Game, 1965 (Zsigmond)
Hot Summer Night, 1957 (Previn)
Hot Time in the Old Town Tonight, 1930 (Fleischer)
Hot Tip, 1935 (Plunkett)
Hot to Trot, 1988 (Elfman)
Hot Tomorrows, 1977 (Elfman)
Hot Turkey, 1930 (Terry)
Hot Water, 1924 (Roach; Zukor)
Hotel, 1967 (Head; Lang; O'Steen)
Hotel Adlon, 1955 (Wagner)
Hotel Berlin, 1945 (Waxman)
Hotel Colonial, 1986 (Donaggio; Rotunno)
Hôtel des Amériques, 1981 (Nuytten)
Hôtel des étudiants, 1932 (Périnal)
Hôtel des Invalides, 1951 (Fradetal; Jarre)
Hôtel du libre échange, 1934 (Grimault; Meerson; Prévert; Trauner)
Hôtel du Nord, 1938 (Aurenche and Bost; Jaubert; Jeanson; Trauner)
Hôtel du silence, 1908 (Cohl)
Hotel for Women, 1939 (Zanuck)
Hotel Geheimnisse, 1928 (Metzner)
Hotel Haywire, 1937 (Head)
Hotel Imperial, 1926 (Furthman; Glennon)
Hotel Imperial, 1927 (Pommer)
Hotel Imperial, 1939 (Biro; Head)
Hotel New Hampshire, 1984 (Watkin)
Hotel Paradiso, 1966 (Carrière; Decaë)
Hotel Room, 1993 (Badalamenti)
Hothouse, 1981 (Pinter)
Hothouse, 1988 (Allen)
Hotlips Jasper, 1945 (Pal)
Hotsy Footsy, 1952 (Bosustow)
Hotter Than Hot, 1929 (Roach)
Houat, 1963 (Fradetal)
Houdini, 1953 (Head; Laszlo; Pal; Pereira)
Hound Dog Man, 1959 (Clarke; Wheeler; Wald)
Hound for Trouble, 1951 (Blanc; Jones; Stalling)
Hound Hunters, 1947 (Avery)
Hound of the Baskervilles, 1939 (Day)
Hound of the Baskervilles, 1959 (Bernard; Carreras)
Hounded. See Johnny Allegro, 1949

Hounding the Hares, 1948 (Terry)
Hounds of Zaroff. See Most Dangerous Game, 1932
Hour before the Dawn, 1944 (Head; Rozsa; Seitz)
Hour Glass, 1972 (Popescu-Gopo)
Hour of 13, 1952 (Junge)
Hour of Glory. See Small Back Room, 1949
Hour of the Gun, 1967 (Ballard; Goldsmith)
Hour of the Wolf. See Vargtimmen, 1968
Hours before the Dawn, 1944 (Dreier)
Hours Between. See 24 Hours, 1931
House. See Dom, 1958
House. See A Casa, 1997
House II: The Second Story, 1987 (Walas)
House Across the Bay, 1940 (Irene; Spencer; Wanger)
House across the Lake, 1954 (Carreras)
House, after Five Years of Living, 1955 (Bernstein)
House Broken, 1936 (Havelock-Allan)
House Builder-Upper, 1938 (Fleischer)
House Busters, 1952 (Terry)
House by the River, 1949 (Cronjager; Leven)
House Calls, 1978 (Bumstead; Epstein; Mancini)
House Cleaning Blues, 1937 (Fleischer)
House Hunting Mice, 1947 (Blanc; Jones)
House in the Snow-Drifts. See Dom v sugribakh, 1928
House in the Square, 1951 (Alwyn)
House Is Not a Home, 1964 (Bacharach; Head)
House No. 44, 1955 (Burman)
House of 1,000 Women. See 2,000 Women, 1944
House of a Thousand Candles, 1915 (Selig)
House of Bamboo, 1955 (Lemaire; Wheeler)
House of Blackmail, 1953 (Lassally)
House of Bondage, 1913 (Ince)
House of Cards, 1969 (Head; Lai; Louis)
House of Cards, 1993 (Murch)
House of Connelly. See Carolina, 1934
House of Dark Shadows, 1970 (Smith)
House of Darkness, 1913 (Bitzer)
House of Doom. See Black Cat, 1935
House of Dracula, 1945 (Pierce)
House of Evil. See House on Sorority Row, 1982
House of Fate. See Muss 'em Up, 1936
House of Fear, 1939 (Krasner)
House of Fear, 1944 (Lourié Miller)
House of Frankenstein, 1944 (Pierce; Siodmak)
House of Fright. See Two Faces of Dr. Jekyll, 1960
House of Games, 1987 (Mamet)
House of Horror, 1929 (Haller; Polito)
House of Magic, 1937 (Lantz)
House of Numbers, 1957 (Previn; Schnee)
House of Pleasure. See Plaisir, 1952
House of Ricordi. See Casa Ricordi, 1954
House of Rothschild, 1933 (Day; Johnson; Newman; Westmore Family; Zanuck)
House of Secrets, 1956 (Rank; Vetchinsky)
House of Silence, 1962 (Bernstein)
House of Strangers, 1949 (Krasner; Lemaire; Wheeler)
House of the Long Shadows, 1982 (Golan and Globus)
House of the Seven Gables, 1940 (Krasner)
House of the Spirits, 1993 (Zimmer)
House of Tomorrow, 1949 (Avery)
House of Usher. See Fall of the House of Usher, 1960
House of Wax, 1953 (Glennon; Warner)
House of Wrath, 1924 (Sullivan)
House on 56th Street, 1933 (Haller; Orry-Kelly)
House on 92nd Street, 1945 (Wheeler; Zanuck; de Rochemont)
House on Carroll Street, 1988 (Ballhaus; Bernstein; Delerue)

House on Chelouche Street, 1973 (Golan and Globus)
House on Sorority Row, 1982 (Goldsmith)
House on Telegraph Hill, 1951 (Ballard; Lemaire; Newman; Wheeler)
House That Dinky Built, 1925 (Lantz)
House with the Closed Shutters, 1910 (Bitzer)
House without Laughter. *See* Haus ohne Lachen, 1918
House without Windows. *See* Dom bez okien, 1962
Houseboat, 1958 (Duning; Edouart; Head; Pereira; Westmore Family)
Householder, 1963 (Jhabvala; Mitra)
Householder. *See* Gharbar, 1963
Housekeeper's Daughter, 1939 (Irene; Roach)
HouseSitter, 1992 (Alonzo)
Housewife, 1934 (Orry-Kelly)
Housewife Herman, 1938 (Terry)
Housing Problem, 1946 (Terry)
Houston Texas, 1956 (Braunberger)
How a Man Loves. *See* Woman He Loved, 1922
How a Mosquito Operates, 1912 (McCay)
How Cocl Became Asta Pilsen. *See* Wie aus Cocl Asta Pilsen
    wurde, 1913
How Could You, Jean?, 1918 (Marion; Rosher)
How Do I Love Thee?, 1970 (Metty)
How Dry I Am, 1920 (Roach)
How Ducks Are Fattened, 1899 (Bitzer)
How Grandpa Changed Till Nothing Was Left. *See* Jak staříček měnil až
    vyměnil, 1953
How Green Was My Valley, 1941 (Banton; Day; Dunne; La Shelle;
    Miller; Newman; Zanuck)
How I Became Krazy, 1921 (Bray)
How I Spent My Summer Vacation, 1967 (Schifrin)
How I Won the War, 1967 (Watkin)
How Kico Was Born, 1951 (Vukotić)
How Man Learned to Fly. *See* Jak se člověk naucil létat, 1958
How Mike Got the Soap in His Eyes, 1903 (Bitzer)
How Not to Lose Your Head While Shotfiring, 1973 (Dunning)
How Not to Succeed in Business, 1975 (Halas and Batchelor)
How Now Boing Boing, 1954 (Bosustow)
How Rulers Live. *See* Vlasteli byta, 1932
How She Triumphed, 1911 (Bitzer)
How Stella Got Her Groove Back, 1998 (Bass)
How Sweet It Is!, 1966 (Ballard; Rose)
How the Day Was Saved, 1913 (Loos)
How the German Invented the Ape. *See* Kak nyemyets obyezyanov
    vidumal, 1915
How the Grinch Stole Christmas, 1970 (Jones)
How the Grinch Stole Christmas, 2000 (Baker)
How the West Was Won, 1962 (Cahn; Canutt; Daniels; Krasner; La
    Shelle; Lang; Newman; Gillespie; Mercer; Plunkett)
How to Be a Hostess, 1959 (Halas and Batchelor)
How to Be Very, Very Popular, 1955 (Cahn; Johnson; Krasner; Lemaire)
How to Commit Marriage, 1969 (Lang)
How to Destroy the Reputation of the Greatest Secret Agent. *See*
    Magnifique, 1973
How to Fill a Wild Bikini. *See* How to Stuff a Wild Bikini, 1965
How to Fire a Lewis Gun, 1918 (Fleischer)
How to Fire a Stokes Mortar, 1918 (Fleischer)
How to Furnish a Flat. *See* Jak zařídit byt, 1960
How to Have Love Flame on the Spot, even for the Deceased. *See* Tu
    Ten Kámen, 1923
How to Keep a Husband, 1914 (Loos)
How to Keep Cool, 1953 (Terry)
How to Keep Slim. *See* Jak na to, 1963
How to Make a French Dish. *See* Bonne Soupe, 1963
How to Make an American Quilt, 1995 (Kaminski; Newman)
How to Marry a Millionaire, 1953 (Johnson; Lemaire; Newman; Wheeler)
How to Murder a Rich Uncle, 1957 (Broccoli, Paxton)

How to Murder Your Wife, 1965 (Stradling; Sylbert)
How to Read an Army Map, 1918 (Fleischer)
How to Relax, 1954 (Terry)
How to Save a Marriage and Ruin Your Life, 1967 (Garmes; Legrand)
How to Steal a Diamond in Four Uneasy Lessons. *See* Hot Rock, 1972
How to Steal a Million, 1966 (Lang; Trauner; Williams)
How to Stuff a Wild Bikini, 1965 (Crosby)
How to Succeed in Business without Really Trying, 1966 (Boyle; Guffey)
How Wet Was My Ocean, 1940 (Terry)
How Women Love, 1922 (Stradling)
Howard the Duck, 1986 (Barry; Blanc)
Howards End, 1992 (Jhabvala; Merchant)
Howards of Virginia, 1940 (Buchman; Glennon; Vorkapich)
Howling, 1980 (Baker; Donaggio)
Howling in the Woods, 1971 (Grusin)
Howling Success, 1954 (Terry)
Hrabenka z Podskalí, 1926 (Heller)
Hrátky s čertem, 1956 (Stallich)
Hřích, 1929 (Heller)
Hřiště, 1975 (Ondříček)
Hsi yen, 1993 (Schamus)
Hubby's Latest Alibi , 1928 (Hornbeck)
Hubby's Week End Trip, 1928 (Hornbeck)
Huckleberry Finn, 1932 (Zukor)
Huckleberry Finn, 1939 (Seitz)
Huckleberry Finn, 1974 (Kovacs)
Hucksters, 1947 (Irene; Mayer; Rosson)
Hud, 1962 (Bernstein; Howe; Edouart; Head; Pereira; Westmore Family)
Huddle, 1932 (Adrian; Sullivan)
Hudson's Bay, 1940 (Banton; Barnes; Day; Trotti; Macgowan; Newman)
Hudsucker Proxy, 1994 (Burwell)
Hue and Cry, 1946 (Clarke; Auric; Balcon; Slocombe)
Huellas del pasado, 1950 (Alcoriza)
Hug Bug, 1926 (Roach)
Huggetts Abroad, 1949 (Rank)
Huguenot, 1909 (Carré; Gaumont)
Huilor, 1938 (Alexeieff and Parker; Auric)
Huis clos, 1954 (Kosma)
Huit hommes dans un château, 1942 (Aurenche and Bost; Honegger)
Huitième Jour, 1960 (Fradetal; Kosma)
Hula Hula Land, 1949 (Terry)
Hulda's Lovers, 1908 (Bitzer)
Hullabaloo over Georgie and Bonnie's Pictures, 1978 (Jhabvala; Lassally;
    Merchant)
Hum Tum aur Woh, 1938 (Biswas)
Human Beast. *See* **Bête humaine**, 1938
Human Comedy, 1942 (Stothart; Gibbons; Irene; Stradling)
Human Desire, 1919 (Mayer)
Human Desire, 1954 (Guffey; Wald)
Human Factor, 1975 (Morricone)
Human Fish, 1933 (Bruckman)
Human Growth, 1947 (Hubley)
Human Revolution. *See* Ningen kakumei, 1973
Human Revolution: Sequel. *See* Zoku ningen kakumai, 1976
Human Sparrows. *See* Sparrows, 1926
Human Tornado, 1925 (Canutt)
Human Vapor. *See* Gasu ningen daiichigo, 1960
Human Wreckage, 1923 (Ince; Sullivan)
Human Zoo, 1961 (Kuri)
Humanoids from the Deep, 1980 (Walas)
Humoresque, 1920 (Marion; Zukor)
Humoresque, 1946 (Adrian; Haller; Wald; Waxman)
Humour noir, 1964 (Aurenche and Bost; Douy)
Humpty Dumpty, 1935 (Iwerks)
Hunchback, 1914 (Loos)
Hunchback and the Dancer. *See* Bucklige und die Tänzerin, 1920

Hunchback of Notre Dame, 1923 (Goosson; Thalberg; Sherwood)
Hunchback of Notre Dame, 1939 (August; Berman; Dunn; Levien; Newman; Plunkett; Polglase; Pommer; Westmore Family)
Hunchback of Notre Dame, 1956 (Hakim; Prévert)
Hunchback of Notre Dame, 1996 (Menken; Schwartz)
Hunchback of Notre Dame. See Notre-Dame de Paris, 1956
Hunchback of Rome. See Gobbo, 1960
Hund von Baskerville, 1914 (Freund; Warm)
Hundra, 1983 (Morricone)
Hundred Pound Window, 1943 (Heller)
Hundred Thousand Children, 1955 (Lassally)
Hundstage, 1944 (Stallich)
Hungarian Goulash, 1930 (Terry)
Hungarian Rhapsody. See Ungarische Rhapsodie, 1913
Hungarian Rhapsody. See Ungarische Rhapsodie, 1928
Hungarn in Flammen, 1957 (Kovacs; Zsigmond)
Hunger, 1983 (Smith)
Hunger . . . Hunger . . . Hunger. See Gold . . . gold . . . golod, 1921
Hunger of the Blood, 1921 (Selig)
Hungry Dog, 1960 (Halas and Batchelor)
Hungry Heart, 1917 (Marion)
Hungry Hill, 1947 (Rank; Vetchinsky)
Hungry Hoboes, 1928 (Disney)
Hunky and Spunky, 1938 (Fleischer)
Hunt the Man Down, 1950 (Musuraca)
Hunted Men, 1938 (Dreier; Head)
Hunted Woman, 1925 (August)
Hunted, 1951 (Rank; Vetchinsky)
Hunter of the Sun. See Taiyo no karyudo, 1970
Hunter, 1931 (Lantz)
Hunter, 1973 (Schifrin)
Hunter, 1980 (Legrand; Stark)
Hunters, 1958 (Clarke; Lemaire; Wheeler)
Hunters Bold, 1924 (Roach)
Hunting Big Game in Africa, 1909 (Selig)
Hunting of the Hawk, 1917 (Miller)
Hunting We Will Go, 1960 (Halas and Batchelor)
Hurdy Gurdy, 1929 (Lantz; Roach)
Hurdy Gurdy Hare, 1948 (McKimson; Blanc; Stalling)
Hurra! Ich bin Papa!, 1939 (Von Harbou)
Hurrah! Ich lebe!, 1928 (Courant)
Hurricane Express, 1932 (Canutt)
Hurricane Horseman, 1931 (Canutt)
Hurricane Kid, 1925 (Miller)
Hurricane Smith, 1952 (Head; Rennahan)
Hurricane, 1937 (Basevi; Day; Glennon; Goldwyn; Nichols; Newman)
Hurricane, 1979 (Donati; Nykvist; O'Steen; Rota; de Laurentiis)
Hurricane's Pal, 1922 (Haskin)
Hurry, Charlie, Hurry, 1941 (Musuraca)
Hurry Doctor, 1931 (Fleischer)
Hurry Sundown, 1966 (Krasner)
Hurry Up, Or I'll Be Thirty, 1973 (Levine)
Hurry West, 1921 (Roach)
Hurvínek's Circus. See Cirkus Hurvínek, 1955
Husbands and Lovers, 1924 (Booth; Gaudio)
Husbands and Lovers. See Villa del Venerdi, 1991
Husbands and Wives, 1992 (Loquasto)
Husbands Beware, 1955 (Bruckman)
Hush, 1920 (Edeson)
Hush . . . Hush, Sweet Charlotte, 1964 (Biroc)
Hush Money, 1931 (Nichols; Seitz)
Hush My Mouse, 1945 (Jones; Blanc; Stalling)
Hushed Hour, 1919 (Edeson)
Hussard sur le toit, 1994 (Carrière; Rappeneau)
Hussards, 1955 (Auric)
Hussite Warrior. See Jan Zižka, 1955

Hustle, 1975 (Biroc)
Hustler, 1921 (Roach)
Hustler, 1961 (Allen; Horner; Schüfftan)
Hustlin' Hawk, 1923 (Roach)
Hustling for Health, 1919 (Roach)
Hyas, 1930 (Jaubert)
Hyde and Go Tweet, 1960 (Blanc)
Hyde and Hare, 1955 (Blanc; Stalling)
Hyena's Laugh, 1927 (Lantz)
Hyoraku yume monogatari, 1943 (Tsuburaya)
Hypnotic Eyes, 1933 (Terry)
Hypnotist, 1922 (Fleischer)
Hypnotist, 1960 (Halas and Batchelor)
Hypnotist. See London After Midnight, 1927
Hypnotist's Revenge, 1907 (Bitzer)
Hypnotized, 1932 (Hornbeck)
Hypnotized, 1952 (Terry)
Hyp-nut-tist, 1935 (Fleischer)
Hypo-Chondri-Cat, 1950 (Jones; Blanc; Stalling)
Hypocrites, 1914 (Marion)
Hypothèse du tableau volé, 1978 (Vierny)
Hypothesis of the Stolen Painting. See Hypothèse du tableau volé, 1978
Hysteria, 1964 (Carreras; Francis)
Hysterical High Spots in American History, 1941 (Lantz)

I Accuse!, 1957 (Alwyn)
I . . . comme Icare, 1979 (Morricone)
I Ain't Got Nobody, 1932 (Fleischer)
I Am a Camera, 1955 (Arnold; Korda; Mathieson)
I Am a Fugitive from a Chain Gang, 1932 (Orry-Kelly; Polito; Wallis; Warner; Zanuck)
I Am a Girl with the Devil in My Body. See Jsem devče s čertem v tele, 1933
I Am a Thief, 1934 (Blanke; Orry-Kelly)
I Am Cuba. See Ya Kuba, 1964
I Am Suzanne, 1933 (Garmes; Lasky)
I Am the Law, 1938 (Goosson; Jarrico; Swerling)
I Am Tokichiro. See Baku wa Toukichiroh, 1955
I and My Lovers. See Galia, 1966
I bambini chiedono perchè, 1972 (Morricone)
I bambini ci guardano, 1944 (Zavattini)
I basilischi, 1963 (Di Venanzo; Morricone)
I Became a Criminal. See They Made Me a Fugitive, 1947
I Became Mad for Her Sake. See Do oszalalem dla niej, 1981
I Bombed Pearl Harbor. See Taiheiyo no arashi, 1960
I cadetti di Guascogna, 1950 (Age and Scarpelli)
I cammelli, 1988 (Morricone)
I Can Get It for You Wholesale, 1950 (Lemaire; Krasner)
I Can Hardly Wait, 1942 (Bruckman)
I cannibali, 1970 (Morricone)
I Cannot Say That Person's Name. See Sono hito no na wa ienai, 1951
I Can't Escape from You, 1936 (Fleischer)
I, Claudius, 1937 (Korda; Krasker; Périnal)
I clowns, 1970 (Donati; Rota)
I compagni, 1963 (Age and Scarpelli; Cristaldi; Rotunno)
I complessi, 1965 (Age and Scarpelli)
I Confess, 1952 (Burks; Tiomkin; Orry-Kelly; Reville)
I corpi presentano tracce di violenza carnale, 1973 (Ponti)
I Could Go On Singing, 1963 (Head; Neame)
I Cover the Waterfront, 1933 (D'Agostino; Newman)
I crudeli, 1967 (Morricone)
I Deal in Danger, 1966 (Schifrin; Smith)
I delfini, 1960 (Cristaldi; Di Venanzo; Mnouchkine)
I Did It, Mama, 1909 (Bitzer)
I Died a Thousand Times, 1955 (McCord)
I difanzati della morte, 1956 (Solinas)

I dimma dold, 1952 (Fischer)
I Do, 1921 (Roach)
I Don't Care Girl, 1953 (Cole; Wheeler)
I Don't Kiss. See J'embrasse pas, 1991
I Don't Want to Make History, 1936 (Fleischer)
I Dood It, 1943 (Sharaff)
I Dream Too Much, 1935 (Berman; Pan; Polglase; Steiner)
I Dreamed of Africa, 2000 (Jarre)
I Due Castelli, 1963 (Bozzetto)
I due nemici, 1961 (Age and Scarpelli; Cecchi D'amico; Rotunno; de Laurentiis)
I due orfanelle, 1942 (Stallich)
I due orfanelli, 1947 (Age and Scarpelli)
I Eats My Spinach, 1933 (Fleischer)
I Feel Like a Feather in the Breeze, 1936 (Fleischer)
I figli chiedono perche, 1972 (Cecchi D'amico)
I Found Stella Parish, 1935 (Orry-Kelly; Saunders)
I giorni contati, 1962 (Guerra)
I girasoli, 1969 (Levine; Ponti; Rotunno; Guerra; Mancini; Zavattini)
I Give My Heart, 1936 (Siodmak)
I Give My Love, 1934 (Freund)
I Gopher You, 1954 (Blanc)
I Got Plenty of Mutton, 1944 (Blanc; Stalling)
I grandi condottieri, 1965 (Guerra)
I Grandi naíf jugoslavi, 1973 (Storaro)
I Hate Love. See J'ai horreur de l'amour, 1997
I Heard, 1933 (Fleischer)
I Know Where I'm Going!, 1945 (Junge; Rank)
I Like Babies and Infinks, 1937 (Fleischer)
I Like Mountain Music, 1933 (Fleischer)
I Like Your Nerve, 1931 (Haller)
I Live for Love, 1935 (Barnes; Epstein; Orry-Kelly; Wald)
I Live for You. See I Live for Love, 1935
I Live in Fear. See Ikomono no kiroku, 1955
I Live in Grosvenor Square, 1945 (Heller; Wilcox)
I Live My Life, 1935 (Adrian; Tiomkin)
I livets var, eller Forsta alskarinnan, 1912 (Jaenzon; Magnusson)
I Liza kai i alli, 1961 (Lassally)
I Love a Bandleader, 1945 (Planer)
I Love a Lassie, 1925 (Fleischer)
I Love a Mystery, 1945 (Guffey)
I Love a Soldier, 1944 (Head; Lang)
I Love Cinema. See Kocham Kino, 1987
I Love Melvin, 1953 (Rose; Rosson; Smith)
I Love My Wife, 1970 (Schifrin)
I Love N.Y., 1988 (Conti)
I Love That Man, 1933 (Krasner)
I Love to Singa, 1936 (Avery)
I Love Trouble, 1947 (Duning; Goosson; Tavoularis)
I Love You Again, 1940 (Lederer; Mayer; Waxman)
I Love You, Alice B. Toklas!, 1968 (Bernstein; Lathrop; van Runkle)
I Love You, Goodbye, 1974 (O'Steen)
I Love You, Rosa. See Ani Ohev Otach Rosa, 1971
I Love, You Love. See Io amo, tu ami, 1961
I Loved a Woman, 1933 (Blanke)
I Loved You Wednesday, 1933 (Menzies; Mohr)
I Magi randagi, 1996 (Donati; Morricone)
I magliari, 1959 (Cecchi D'amico; Cristaldi; Di Venanzo)
I malamondo, 1964 (Morricone)
I Married a Communist. See Woman on Pier 13, 1950
I Married a Doctor, 1936 (Haskin; Orry-Kelly)
I Married a Monster from Outer Space, 1958 (Bumstead; Head)
I Married a Shadow. See J'ai épousé une ombre, 1983
I Married a Spy. See Secret Lives, 1937
I Married a Witch, 1942 (Dreier; Head; Waxman)
I Married a Woman, 1956 (D'Agostino)

I Married a Woman, 1958 (Ballard)
I Married an Angel, 1942 (Loos; Mayer; Stothart; Stromberg)
I Married Too Young. See Married Too Young, 1961
I Married You for Fun. See Ti ho sposato per allegria, 1967
I Met Him in Paris, 1937 (Banton; Dreier)
I Met My Love Again, 1938 (Mohr; Wanger)
I miserabili, 1947 (Ponti)
I misteri di Roma, 1963 (Zavattini)
I mostri, 1963 (Age and Scarpelli)
I Need a Woman. See Adamson i Sverige, 1966
I Never Changes My Altitude, 1937 (Fleischer)
I nostri figli. See I vinti, 1952
I nostri mariti, 1966 (Age and Scarpelli)
I nostri sogni, 1943 (Zavattini)
I notti bianchi, 1957 (Cristaldi)
I nuovi mostri, 1977 (Age and Scarpelli; Delli Colli)
I Only Arsked, 1959 (Carreras)
I Only Have Eyes for You, 1937 (Avery; Stalling)
I Only Want You to Love Me. See Ich will doch nur, das Ihr mich liebt, 1976
I Ought to Be in Pictures, 1981 (Hamlisch)
I pagliacci, 1970 (Wakhévitch)
I Passed for White, 1960 (Williams)
I picari, 1987 (Cecchi D'amico)
I Piccoli maestri, 1998 (Lanci, Giuseppe ("beppe"))
I pini di Roma; Ridi, pagliaccio!, 1941 (Stallich)
I pirati di Capri, 1948 (Rota)
I posledniye chorti, 1915 (Starewicz)
I promessi sposi, 1989 (Morricone)
I Promise to Pay, 1937 (Ballard)
I protagonisti, 1967 (Flaiano and Pinelli)
I pugni in tasca, 1965 (Morricone)
I racconti di Canterbury, 1972 (Delli Colli; Donati; Morricone)
I Remember Mama, 1948 (D'Agostino; Musuraca)
I Saw What You Did, 1965 (Biroc; Westmore Family)
I See a Dark Stranger, 1946 (Alwyn; Rank)
I See Ice, 1938 (Dean; Neame)
I Sell Anything, 1934 (Orry-Kelly)
I Sent a Letter to My Love. See Chère inconnue, 1981
I sequestrati di Altona, 1962 (Rota; Shostakovich; Zavattini; Ponti)
I sette dell'orsa maggiore, 1952 (Rota)
I sette fratelli Cervi, 1968 (Zavattini)
I setti peccati, 1942 (Zavattini)
I Shall Return. See American Guerilla in the Philippines, 1950
I Shot Andy Warhol, 1996 (Vachon)
I-ski Love-ski You-ski, 1936 (Fleischer)
I sogni del Signor Rossi, 1977 (Bozzetto)
I soliti ignoti, 1958 (Age and Scarpelli; Cecchi D'amico; Cristaldi; Di Venanzo; Gherardi)
I soliti ignoti vent'anni dopo, 1986 (Age and Scarpelli; Cecchi D'amico; Rota)
I Stand Condemned. See Moscow Nights, 1935
I Stole a Million, 1939 (Krasner)
I Surrender Dear, 1931 (Hornbeck)
I Take This Woman, 1931 (Vorkapich; Zukor)
I Take This Woman, 1940 (Kaper; MacArthur; Rosson)
I Taw a Putty Tat, 1948 (Blanc; Stalling)
I Thank a Fool, 1962 (de Grunwald)
I Thank You, 1941 (Rank; Vetchinsky)
I, the Jury, 1953 (Alton; Waxman)
I, the Jury, 1982 (Conti)
I tre corsari, 1951 (Delli Colli; de Laurentiis)
I vinti, 1952 (Cecchi D'amico)
I vitelloni, 1953 (Flaiano and Pinelli; Rota)
I vo. See Fluchtversuch, 1976
I Vor Pittfalks, 1967 (Williams)

I Wake Up Screaming. *See* Hot Spot, 1941

I Walk Alone, 1947 (Dreier; Haskin; Head; Schnee; Wallis; Young)

I Walk the Line, 1970 (Sargent)

I Walked with a Zombie, 1943 (D'Agostino; Lewton; Siodmak)

I Wanna Be a Life Guard, 1936 (Fleischer)

I Wanna Be a Sailor, 1937 (Avery; Stalling)

I Wanna Mink, 1960 (Halas and Batchelor)

I Want a Divorce, 1940 (Dreier; Head; Young)

I Want Her Dead. *See* W, 1974

I Want My Dinner, 1903 (Bitzer)

I Want to Be a Shellfish. *See* Watash iwa kai ni naritai, 1959

I Want to Go Home, 1989 (Comden and Green; Saulnier)

I Want to Live!, 1958 (Hornbeck; Wanger; Mandel)

I Want You, 1951 (Day; Mandell; Stradling; Goldwyn)

I Wanted Wings, 1941 (Dreier; Edouart; Head; Young)

I Was a Communist for the FBI, 1951 (Steiner)

I Was a Criminal, 1945 (Alton)

I Was a Fireman. *See* **Fires Were Started**, 1943

I Was a Male War Bride, 1949 (Lederer; Wheeler)

I Was a Prisoner on Devil's Island, 1941 (Brown)

I Was a Spy, 1933 (Balcon; Junge)

I Was a Teenage Thumb, 1963 (Jones)

I Was a Teenage Werewolf, 1957 (La Shelle)

I Was an Adventuress, 1940 (Cronjager; Day; Johnson; Shamroy; Zanuck)

I Was Framed, 1942 (McCord)

I Was on Mars, 1992 (Schamus)

I Will, I Will . . . for Now, 1975 (Alonzo; Cahn)

I Will If You Will. *See* Infermiera, 1975

I Wished on the Moon, 1935 (Fleischer)

I Wonder Who's Kissing Her Now, 1931 (Fleischer)

I Wonder Who's Kissing Her Now, 1947 (Day; Lemaire; Leven; Newman; Pan)

I Wouldn't Be in Your Shoes, 1948 (Mirisch)

I Yabba-Dabba Do!, 1993 (Hanna and Barbera)

I Yam Love Sick, 1938 (Fleischer)

I Yam What I Yam, 1933 (Fleischer)

I.N.R.I., 1923 (Metzner)

Ibaragi Ukon, 1939 (Miyagawa)

IBM at the Fair, 1965 (Bernstein)

IBM Mathematics Peep Show, 1961 (Bernstein)

IBM Puppet Show, 1965 (Bernstein)

Ibo koudai, 1957 (Yoda)

Ibun Sarutobi sasuke, 1965 (Takemitsu)

Ice. *See* Is, 1970

Ice-Capades Revue, 1942 (Alton)

Ice-Capades. *See* Ice-Capades Revue, 1942

Ice Carnival, 1941 (Terry)

Ice Castles, 1978 (Hamlisch)

Ice Follies of 1939, 1938 (Ruttenberg; Adrian; Brown; Freed; Waxman)

Ice Man's Luck, 1929 (Lantz)

Ice Palace, 1960 (Biroc; Blanke; Steiner)

Ice Pond, 1939 (Terry)

Ice Station Zebra, 1968 (Legrand)

Ice Storm, 1997 (Schamus)

Icebound, 1924 (Buckland)

Iced Bullet, 1917 (Sullivan)

Iceland, 1942 (Day; Miller)

Iceman Cometh, 1973 (Jeakins)

Iceman Ducketh, 1964 (Blanc)

Ich bei Tag und Du bei Nacht, 1932 (Pommer)

Ich bin du, 1934 (Röhrig)

Ich bin Sebastian Ott, 1939 (Hoffmann)

Ich dzień powszedni, 1963 (ścibor-Rylski)

Ich lebe für dich, 1929 (Junge)

Ich liebe alle Frauen, 1935 (Warm)

Ich liebe dich, 1926 (Courant)

Ich puti razoshchlis, 1932 (Enei)

Ich und die Kaiserin, 1933 (Herlth; Reisch; Röhrig; Waxman)

Ich war Jack Mortimer, 1935 (Von Harbou)

Ich werde dich auf Händen tragen, 1943 (Wagner)

Ich will dich liebe lehren, 1933 (Courant)

Ich will doch nur, das Ihr mich liebt, 1976 (Ballhaus)

Ichabod and Mr. Toad, 1949 (Disney; Glennon; Iwerks)

Ici et maintenant, 1968 (Alekan)

Ickle Meets Pickle, 1942 (Terry)

ICOGRADA Congress, 1966 (Halas and Batchelor)

Iconoclast, 1910 (Bitzer)

Iconoclast, 1913 (Ince)

I'd Climb the Highest Mountain, 1931 (Fleischer)

I'd Climb the Highest Mountain, 1950 (Trotti; Cronjager; Lemaire)

I'd Love to Take Orders from You, 1936 (Avery)

I'd Rather Be Rich, 1964 (Hunter; Krasna; Metty; Whitlock)

I'd Rather Have Cold Liver Oil. *See* Dann schon lieber Lebertran, 1931

Idaho Red, 1929 (Musuraca)

Ideal Husband, 1947 (Korda; Périnal; Beaton; Biro)

Ideál Septimy, 1938 (Stallich)

Ideal Teacher. *See* Kantor Idéal, 1932

Idealer Gatte, 1935 (Von Harbou)

Idée, 1934 (Honegger)

Idée fixe, 1962 (Braunberger)

Identificazione di una donna, 1982 (Guerra)

Identikit, 1973 (Storaro)

Identité judicaire, 1951 (Jeanson)

Identity Unknown. *See* Girl in 419, 1933

Idiot. *See* Dummkopf, 1920

Idiot, 1945 (Matras; Barsacq; Spaak)

Idiot. *See* Idiot, 1945

Idiot. *See* Hakuchi, 1951

Idiot à Paris, 1967 (Rabier)

Idiot Sportsman. *See* Glupichkiye zanmimayestsya sportom, 1917

Idiot's Delight, 1939 (Adrian; Daniels; Sherwood; Stothart; Stromberg; Vorkapich)

Idle Rich, 1921 (Mathis)

Idle Rich, 1929 (Day; Gibbons)

Idle Tongues, 1924 (Struss; Sullivan)

Ido Zero daisakusen, 1969 (Tsuburaya)

Idol, 1966 (Levine)

Idol Dancer, 1920 (Bitzer)

Idol on Parade, 1959 (Broccoli)

Idols in the Dust. *See* Saturday's Heroes, 1951

Idols of Clay, 1920 (Miller)

Idylle sous un tunnel, 1901 (Pathé)

Ieri, oggi, domani, 1963 (Zavattini; Ponti)

If . . . , 1968 (Menges; Ondříček)

If a Man Answers, 1962 (Hunter; Louis; Metty)

If Cats Could Sing, 1950 (Terry)

If I Had a Million, 1932 (Buchman; Miller; Zukor)

If I Was a Daddy. *See* Kdybych byl tátou, 1939

If I Were Free, 1932 (Cronjager; Macgowan; Polglase; Steiner)

If I Were King, 1938 (Dreier)

If I'm Lucky, 1946 (Basevi)

If Marriage Fails, 1925 (Sullivan)

If This Be Sin. *See* That Dangerous Age, 1949

If Winter Comes, 1923 (Ruttenberg)

If Winter Comes, 1947 (Berman; Irene; Stothart)

If You Feel Like Singing. *See* Summer Stock, 1950

If You Had a Wife Like This, 1907 (Bitzer)

If You Still Have a Mother. *See* Wenn du noch eine Mutter hast, 1924

Iga Kottou gunryu, 1941 (Yoda)

Iga Kottou Military Style. *See* Iga Kottou gunryu, 1941

Igloo for Two, 1955 (Terry)

Ihre Durchlaucht, die Verkäuferin , 1933 (Planer)
Ihre Hoheit befiehlt, 1931 (Pommer)
Ihre Majestät die Liebe, 1931 (Andrejew)
I'Ile de sein, 1958 (Delerue)
Ikari no umi, 1944 (Tsuburaya)
Ikiru, 1952 (Hayasaka)
Ikiteiru gazo, 1948 (Hayasaka)
Ikomono no kiroku, 1955 (Hayasaka; Muraki)
Ikonostast, 1969 (Dinov)
Il Abner, 1959 (Pereira)
Île au trésor, 1985 (Branco; de Almeida)
Ile de Pâques, 1935 (Jaubert)
Ile d'Ouessant. *See* Enez Eussa, 1961
Ile Maurice, 1960 (Braunberger)
Ile mystérieuse, 1973 (Colpi)
Iles enchantées, 1965 (Rabier)
Îles, 1983 (Müller)
Ilhas Encantadas, 1965 (de Almeida)
I'll Be Glad When You're Dead, You Rascal, 1932 (Fleischer)
I'll Be Seeing You, 1944 (Gaudio; Head; Schary)
I'll Be Suing You, 1934 (Roach)
I'll Be Your Sweetheart, 1945 (Rank)
I'll Be Yours, 1946 (Mohr; Banton)
I'll Cry Tomorrow, 1955 (Mercer; Rose; Gibbons; North)
I'll Defend You My Love. *See* Difendo il mio amore, 1956
I'll Do Anything, 1994 (Ballhaus; Zimmer)
I'll Get By, 1950 (Clarke; Lemaire)
I'll Get Him Yet, 1919 (Garmes)
I'll Get You for This, 1950 (Heller)
I'll Give a Million, 1938 (Macgowan; Zanuck; Zavattini)
I'll Love You Always, 1935 (August; Buchman)
Ill Met By Moonlight, 1956 (Challis; Vetchinsky; Rank; Theodorakis)
I'll Never Crow Again, 1941 (Fleischer)
I'll Never Forget What's 'is Name, 1967 (Heller; Lai)
I'll Never Forget You, 1951 (Périnal)
I'll Never Forget You. *See* House in the Square, 1951
I'll Never Heil Again, 1941 (Bruckman)
I'll See You in My Dreams, 1951 (McCord)
I'll Take Romance, 1937 (Cohn, Goosson)
I'll Take Vanilla, 1922 (Roach)
I'll Take Vanilla, 1934 (Roach)
I'll Tell the World, 1934 (Mandell)
I'll Wait for You, 1941 (Kaper)
Illegal, 1955 (Steiner)
Illegal Divorce. *See* Second Hand Wife, 1932
Illegal Entry, 1949 (Daniels)
Illegal Music, 1998 (Zsigmond)
Illegal Traffic, 1938 (Dreier; Head)
Illicit, 1931 (Zanuck)
Illuminations, 1963 (Braunberger)
Illusion, 1947 (Braunberger)
Illusion in Moll, 1952 (Pommer)
Illusion of Blood. *See* Yotsuya kaidan, 1965
Illusioniste renversant, 1903 (Gaumont)
Illusions. *See* Time Out of Mind, 1947
Illustrated Man, 1968 (Goldsmith; Lathrop)
Illustrious Corpses. *See* Cadaveri eccellenti, 1976
Ils étaient tous des volontaires, 1954 (Milhaud)
Ils sont foux, ces sorciers!, 1978 (Decaë)
Ils sont grands ces petits, 1979 (Carrière)
Ils vont tous bien. *See* Stanno tutti bene, 1990
Ilusión viaja en tranvia, 1953 (Alcoriza)
Ilya Mourometz, 1960 (Fields)
Ilya Myromets, 1956 (Ptushko)
I'm Afraid to Come Home in the Dark, 1930 (Fleischer)
I'm Alive and I Love You. *See* Je suis vivante et je vous aime, 1998

I'm Almost Not Crazy: John Cassavetes—the Man and His Work, 1984 (Golan and Globus)
I'm Cold, 1955 (Avery)
Im Exil der ertrunkenen Tiger, 1988 (Alekan)
I'm Forever Blowing Bubbles, 1930 (Fleischer)
I'm from Missouri, 1939 (Head)
I'm from the City, 1938 (Polglase)
Im Geheimdienst, 1931 (Reisch; Röhrig; Herlth)
I'm in the Army Now, 1936 (Fleischer)
I'm Just Wild about Jerry, 1965 (Jones)
Im Lauf der Zeit, 1976 (Müller)
I'm Losing You, 1998 (Henry; van Runkle)
Im Luxuszug, 1927 (Andrejew)
I'm No Angel, 1933 (Dreier; Head; Zukor)
I'm Not Feeling Myself Tonight, 1975 (Godfrey)
I'm on My Way, 1919 (Roach)
Im Sonneschein, 1936 (Planer)
I'm Still Alive, 1940 (Polglase)
Im weissen Rössl, 1952 (Herlth)
Image, 1925 (Burel)
Image by Images I (endless loop):, 1954 (Breer)
Image by Image II, 1955 (Breer)
Image by Image III, 1955 (Breer)
Image by Images IV, 1956 (Breer)
Images, 1972 (Williams; Zsigmond)
Images de Sologne, 1959 (Delerue)
Images des mondes perdus, 1959 (Delerue)
Images d'hier et d'aujourd'hui, 1960 (Decaë)
Images gothiques, 1949 (Renoir)
Images pour Baudelaire, 1958 (Delerue)
Imagination, 1943 (Fleischer)
Imagination, 1969 (Kuri)
Imagination in Motion, 1958 (Mohr)
Imagine My Embarrassment, 1928 (Roach)
Imago, 1970 (Schifrin)
Imi Hageneralit, 1979 (Golan and Globus)
Imitation of Life, 1934 (Laemmle)
Imitation of Life, 1959 (Hunter; Louis; Metty)
Immaculate Road, 1960 (Maté)
Immobile Love. *See* Aijou dudou, 1959
Immoral Charge. *See* Serious Charge, 1959
Immoral Moment. *See* Dénonciation, 1961
Immorale, 1967 (Flaiano and Pinelli)
Immoralità, 1978 (Morricone)
Immortal Battalion. *See* Way Ahead, 1944
Immortal Garrison, 1956 (Tisse)
Immortal Land, 1958 (Bernard)
Immortal Sergeant, 1943 (Day; Miller; Newman; Trotti)
Immortal Story of Dr. Kotnis. *See* Dr. Kotnis Ki Amar Kahani, 1946
Immortelle, 1962 (Delerue)
Immortelle, 1963 (Robbe-Grillet)
Impaciencia del corazon, 1958 (Figueroa)
Impact, 1948 (Laszlo)
Impalement, 1910 (Bitzer)
Impasse des Deux Anges, 1948 (D'Eaubonne; Renoir)
Impasse d'un matin, 1964 (Delerue)
Impassive Footman, 1932 (Dean)
Impatient Maiden, 1932 (Edeson)
Impatient Patient, 1942 (Blanc; Clampett; Stalling)
Impatient Years, 1944 (Walker)
Imperatore di Capri, 1949 (Ponti)
Imperfect Lady, 1947 (Dreier; Seitz; Young)
Imperfect Wife, 1947 (Head)
Importance of Being Earnest, 1952 (Dillon; Rank)
Important c'est d'aimer, 1974 (Delerue)
Impossible. *See* Anhonee, 1951

Impossible Convicts, 1905 (Bitzer)
Impossible Object, 1973 (Legrand)
Impossible Object. See Impossible Objet, 1972
Impossible Object. See Impossible Objet, 1973
Impossible Objet, 1972 (Trauner)
Impossible Objet, 1973 (Renoir)
Impossible Years, 1968 (Ames; Daniels)
Imposter, 1914 (August)
Imposter, 1918 (Polito)
Imposter, 1944 (Lourié; Tiomkin)
Impractical Joker, 1937 (Fleischer)
Impressions de New York, 1955 (Braunberger)
Impromptu, 1991 (Mnouchkine)
Improper Conduct. See Mauvaise conduite, 1984
Improper Duchess, 1936 (Neame)
Impures, 1954 (Alekan)
Imus, 1973 (Kuri)
In a Fantastic Vision. See V blouzneni, 1928
In a Hempen Bag, 1909 (Bitzer)
In a Lonely Place, 1950 (Guffey; Cohn; Louis)
In a Monastery Garden, 1929 (Balcon)
In & Out, 1997 (Adam)
In Again, Out Again, 1917 (Loos; Edeson)
In Anfang war das Wort, 1928 (Metzner)
In Bermuda, 1914 (Rosher)
In Caliente, 1935 (Barnes; Epstein; Orry-Kelly; Polito; Wald)
In Cold Blood, 1967 (Boyle; Hall; Jones)
In Country, 1989 (Boyd)
In Custody, 1993 (Merchant)
In einer Fremden Stadt, 1963 (Herlth)
In Enemy Country, 1968 (Head; Whitlock)
In fondo al cuore, 1997 (Morricone)
In for Treatment. See Opname, 1979
In Gay Madrid, 1930 (Adrian; Day; Gibbons; Stothart)
In Geheimdienst, 1931 (Hoffmann)
In Harm's Way, 1965 (Bass; Edouart; Goldsmith; Lathrop; Wheeler)
In His Steps, 1936 (Brown)
In Hollywood with Potash and Perlmutter, 1924 (Carré; Goldwyn; Marion; Miller)
In letzter Stunde, 1919 (Kolowrat-Krakowsky)
In Life's Cycle, 1910 (Bitzer)
In Like Flint, 1967 (Daniels; Goldsmith; Smith)
In Line of Duty, 1931 (Glennon)
In Little Italy, 1909 (Bitzer)
In Love and War, 1958 (Canutt; Dunne; Friedhofer; Lemaire; Reynolds; Wald)
In My Merry Oldsmobile, 1931 (Fleischer)
In Name Only, 1939 (Banton; Berman; Polglase)
In nome del popolo italiano, 1971 (Age and Scarpelli)
In nome della legge, 1948 (Rota; Flaiano and Pinelli)
In Old Arizona, 1929 (Edeson)
In Old California, 1910 (Bitzer)
In Old Chicago, 1937 (Canutt)
In Old Chicago, 1938 (Levien; Macgowan; Trotti; Zanuck)
In Old Colorado, 1941 (Harlan; Head)
In Old Kentucky, 1909 (Bitzer)
In Old Kentucky, 1919 (Mayer; Carré; Gaudio)
In Old Kentucky, 1927 (Booth; Gibbons)
In Old Madrid, 1911 (Gaudio; Ince)
In Old Mexico, 1938 (Harlan; Head)
In Old Oklahoma, 1943 (Canutt; Plunkett)
In Our Time, 1944 (Koch; Wald; Waxman)
In Person, 1935 (Berman; Cronjager; Pan; Polglase)
In Praise of Love, 1976 (Rattigan)
In Prehistoric Days, 1914 (Bitzer)
In Search of a Sinner, 1920 (Loos)

In Search of Gregory, 1969 (Guerra; Heller)
In Search of Kundun with Martin Scorsese, 1998 (Schoonmaker)
In Search of Opportunity, 1967 (Menges)
In Search of the Castaways, 1961 (Alwyn; Disney; Ellenshaw)
In Search of the Obelisk, 1993 (Trumbull)
In Society, 1944 (Lourié)
In Soft in a Studio, 1916 (Roach)
In Spite of Danger, 1935 (Cohn)
In the Aisles of the Wild, 1912 (Bitzer)
In the Beginning, 1975 (Lassally)
In the Boom Boom Room, 2000 (Sylbert)
In the Border States, 1910 (Bitzer)
In the Cellar, 1960 (Halas and Batchelor)
In the Cool of the Day, 1963 (Houseman; Orry-Kelly)
In the Cool of the Night, 1962 (Adam)
In the Days of '49, 1911 (Bitzer)
In the Doghouse, 1961 (Rank)
In the French Style, 1962 (Kosma; Parrish)
In the Gloaming, 1997 (Grusin)
In the Good Old Summer Time, 1930 (Fleischer)
In the Good Old Summertime, 1926 (Fleischer)
In the Good Old Summertime, 1949 (Goodrich and Hackett; Irene; Pasternak; Stradling)
In the Grazing Country, 1901 (Bitzer)
In the Grease!, 1925 (Roach)
In the Hands of London Crooks, (undated) (Barker)
In the Haunts of Rip Van Winkle, 1906 (Bitzer)
In the Heart of the Catskills, 1906 (Bitzer)
In the Heat of the Night, 1967 (Jones; Mirisch; Wexler)
In the Jungle, 1960 (Halas and Batchelor)
In the Line of Fire, 1993 (Morricone)
In the Matter of Karen Ann Quinlan, 1977 (Conti)
In the Meantime, Darling, 1944 (Basevi)
In the Mountains of Yugoslavia, 1946 (Tisse)
In the N.Y. Subway, 1903 (Bitzer)
In the Name of the Father, 1993 (Biziou; Hambling)
In the Name of the Father. See Nel nome del padre, 1971
In the Name of the Italian People. See In nome del popolo italiano, 1971
In the Name of the Law. See In nome della legge, 1949
In the Next Room, 1930 (Seitz)
In the Nick, 1959 (Adam; Broccoli)
In the Palace of the King, 1923 (Mathis)
In the Ranks, 1913 (Ince)
In the Realm of the Senses. See Ai no corrida, 1976
In the Season of Buds, 1910 (Bitzer)
In the Shade of the Old Apple Sauce, 1931 (Fleischer)
In the Shade of the Old Apple Tree, 1930 (Fleischer)
In the Shadow of the Vultures. See A Sombra dos Abutres, 1998
In the Shadow of the Wind. See Fous de Bassan, 1987
In the Soup, 1992 (Schamus)
In the Spring of Life, or His First Love. See I livets vår, eller Forsta alskarinnan, 1912
In the Sultan's Garden, 1911 (Gaudio; Ince)
In the Sultan's Power, 1909 (Selig)
In the Sweet Pie and Pie, 1941 (Bruckman)
In the Villain's Power, 1917 (O'brien)
In the Watches of the Night, 1909 (Bitzer)
In the White City. See Dans la ville blanche, 1983
In the Window Recess, 1909 (Bitzer)
In This House of Brede, 1975 (Dillon)
In This Our Life, 1942 (Burks; Friedhofer; Haller; Haskin; Koch; Orry-Kelly; Steiner; Wallis)
In Time of Pestilence, 1951 (Halas and Batchelor)
In Time with Industry. See Trade Tattoo, 1937
In Venice, 1933 (Terry)
In Walked Charley, 1932 (Roach)

Invisible Power, 1921 (Gibbons)
Invisible Ray, 1936 (D'Agostino; Waxman)
Invisible Stripes, 1939 (Haller; Haskin; Wallis)
Invisible Woman, 1941 (Siodmak)
Invisibles, 1906 (Pathé)
Invitata, 1969 (Guerra)
Invitation, 1951 (Kaper)
Invitation à la chasse, 1974 (Gégauff)
Invitation au voyage, 1982 (Nuytten)
Invitation to a Gunfighter, 1963 (Raksin; Alonzo)
Invitation to Happiness, 1939 (Dreier; Head)
Invitation to the Dance, 1954 (Ibert; Junge)
Invitation to the Dance, 1956 (Freed; Hanna and Barbera; Previn;
    Ruttenberg; Young)
Invitation to the Waltz, 1935 (Neame)
Invitation to the Wedding, 1983 (Hambling; Young)
Invité de la lle, 1945 (Wakhévitch)
Invité surprise, 1989 (Sarde)
Io amo, tu ami, 1961 (de Laurentiis)
Io e papa, 1987 (Conti)
Io sono il Capataz!, 1950 (Delli Colli)
Io, io, io . . . e gli altri, 1965 (Age and Scarpelli; Cecchi D'amico;
    Flaiano and Pinelli)
Iolanda la figlia del corsaro nero, 1951 (Gherardi)
Iola's Promise, 1912 (Bitzer)
Ipcress File, 1965 (Adam; Barry; Heller)
Iphigenia, 1976 (Theodorakis)
Ippocampo, 1943 (Zavattini)
IQ, 1994 (Goldsmith)
I'm Losing You, 1998 (Vachon)
Iran: Days of Crisis. See Amérique en otage, 1991
Ireland or Bust, 1932 (Terry)
Irene, 1926 (Mathis; McCord)
Irene, 1940 (Metty; Wilcox)
Irezumi, 1966 (Miyagawa)
Irish Eyes Are Smiling, 1944 (Newman; Pan)
Irish Hearts, 1927 (Haskin; Miller; Zanuck)
Irish in Us, 1935 (Barnes; Orry-Kelly)
Irish Stew, 1930 (Terry)
Irish Sweepstakes, 1934 (Terry)
Irishman, 1978 (Seale)
Irma La Douce, 1963 (Diamond; La Shelle; Mandell; Orry-Kelly; Previn;
    Trauner; Westmore Family)
Iron Angel. See Engel aus Eisen, 1981
Iron-Carrier. See Järnbäraren, 1911
Iron Curtain, 1948 (Clarke; Lemaire; Newman; Wheeler)
Iron Duke, 1934 (Courant; Junge; Balcon; Rank)
Iron Heart, 1917 (Grot; Miller)
Iron Maiden, 1963 (Dillon)
Iron Man, 1951 (Boyle; Chase)
Iron Mask, 1929 (Carré; Menzies; Parrish)
Iron Master, 1913 (August)
Iron Mistress, 1952 (Blanke; Seitz; Steiner)
Iron Petticoat, 1956 (Dillon; Hecht)
Iron Rider, 1920 (Furthman)
Iron Road. See Buckskin Frontier, 1943
Iron Strain, 1915 (August; Ince; Sullivan)
Iron Trail, 1921 (Haller)
Iron Will, 1994 (Hayes)
Ironside, 1967 (Jones)
Irreconcilible Differences, 1984 (Fraker)
Irrende Seelen, 1920 (Herlth; Röhrig)
Irresistible Lover, 1927 (Laemmle)
Irrfahrt ins Glück, 1914 (Hoffmann)
Is, 1970 (Fischer)
Is Everybody Happy?, 1928 (Roach)

Is Marriage the Bunk, 1925 (Roach)
Is Matrimony a Failure?, 1922 (Brown)
Is My Face Red, 1932 (Krasner; Steiner)
Is My Palm Read, 1933 (Fleischer)
Is Paris Burning?. See Paris brûle-t-il?, 1966
Is There a Doctor in the Mouse, 1964 (Jones)
Is There Sex after Death, 1971 (Henry)
Is This a Record?, 1973 (Godfrey)
Isabelle, 1951 (Kosma)
Isabelle devant le désir, 1974 (Decaë)
Isadora, 1967 (Hakim)
Isadora, 1968 (Jarre)
Ishi, the Last of His Tribe, 1978 (Jarre; Trumbo)
Ishin no uta, 1938 (Yoda)
Ishq par Zor Nahin, 1970 (Burman)
Ishtar, 1987 (Grusin; Reynolds; Storaro)
Isla de mujeres, 1952 (Alcoriza)
Isla para dos, 1958 (Figueroa)
Island. See Eiland, 1966
Island, 1980 (Decaë; Morricone; Zanuck)
Island at the Top of the World, 1973 (Ellenshaw; Jarre)
Island in the Sky, 1938 (Cronjager)
Island in the Sky, 1953 (Basevi; Clothier; Friedhofer)
Island in the Sun, 1957 (Arnold; Young; Zanuck)
Island of Desire. See Saturday Island, 1951
Island of Dr. Moreau, 1977 (Fisher)
Island of Dr. Moreau, 1996 (Fraker; Winston)
Island of Lost Men, 1939 (Head; Struss)
Island of Lost Souls, 1931 (Westmore Family; Struss)
Island of Lost Women, 1959 (Seitz)
Island of Love, 1963 (Duning; Stradling)
Island of the Blue Dolphins, 1964 (Whitlock)
Island of the Fish Men. See Screamers, 1978
Island on Bird Street. See Øen i fuglegaden, 1997
Island Rescue. See Appointment with Venus, 1951
Island Women Aren't Afraid of the Devil. See Zhenschini kurorta nye
    boyatsa dazhe chorta, 1916
Islanders, 1939 (Milhaud)
Islands in the Stream, 1976 (Goldsmith)
Islas Marias, 1950 (Figueroa)
Isle of Conquest, 1919 (Loos)
Isle of Forgotten Women, 1927 (Walker)
Isle of Fury, 1936 (Orry-Kelly)
Isle of Lost Ships, 1929 (Polito)
Isle of Pingo Pongo, 1938 (Avery)
Isle of the Dead, 1945 (D'Agostino; Lewton)
Isn't It Romantic?, 1948 (Dreier; Head)
Isn't Life Terrible?, 1925 (Roach)
Isn't She Great, 2000 (Bacharach)
Isola degli uomini Pesci. See Screamers, 1978
Isola di Arturo, 1962 (Ponti; Rota; Zavattini)
Isola di Montecristo, 1948 (Delli Colli)
Israel, 1959 (Bernstein)
Israel . . . terre retrouvée, 1956 (Decaë; Rabier)
Istanbul, 1956 (Daniels)
Istanbul, 1957 (Miller; Young)
Istruttoria è chiusa, dimentichi!, 1971 (Morricone)
It, 1927 (Banton)
It All Came True, 1940 (Haller; Haskin; Wallis)
It Always Rains on Sunday, 1947 (Auric; Balcon; Slocombe; Rank)
It Came from beneath the Sea, 1955 (Harryhausen)
It Came from Outer Space, 1953 (Boyle)
It Could Happen to You, 1994 (Burwell)
It Furthers One to Have Somewhere to Go, 1971 (Halas and Batchelor)
It Had to Be You, 1947 (Goosson; Maté)
It Had to Happen, 1936 (Zanuck)

It Happened at the World's Fair, 1963 (Ames; Ruttenberg)

It Happened in Athens, 1961 (Courant)

It Happened in Brooklyn, 1946 (Cahn; Green)

It Happened in Flatbush, 1942 (Clarke; Day)

It Happened in Hollywood, 1937 (Walker)

It Happened in New York, 1935 (Miller)

It Happened in Rome, 1957 (Rank)

It Happened in the Park. *See* Villa Borghese, 1953

It Happened One Christmas, 1975 (Hall)

It Happened One Night, 1934 (Cohn; Goosson; Riskin; Walker)

It Happened to Jane, 1959 (Duning)

It Happened Tomorrow, 1943 (Schüfftan; Metzner; Nichols)

It Happens Every Spring, 1949 (Lemaire)

It Happens Every Thursday, 1953 (Metty)

It Is Hard to Please Him, But It Is Worth It, 1912-14 (Cohl)

It Is My Music. *See* Det är min musik, 1942

It Lives Again, 1978 (Baker; Herrmann)

It Must Be Love, 1940 (Terry)

It Ought to Be a Crime, 1931 (Johnson)

It Pays to Advertise, 1931 (Banton)

It Rains On Our Love, 1946 (Lundgren)

It Should Happen to You, 1953 (Cohn; Kanin; Lang; Louis; Wald)

It Shouldn't Happen to a Dog, 1946 (Basevi)

It Started in Naples, 1960 (Cecchi D'amico; Head; Surtees)

It Started in Paradise, 1952 (Arnold; Cardiff; Rank)

It Started with a Kiss, 1959 (Lederer; Rose)

It Started with Eve, 1941 (Kräly; Krasna; Pasternak; Maté)

It Takes Two, 1988 (Burwell)

Italia 61, 1961 (Lenica)

Italia piccola, 1957 (Rota)

Italian, 1915 (Ince; Sullivan)

Italian Barber, 1910 (Bitzer)

Italian Blood, 1911 (Bitzer)

Italian Job, 1969 (Coward; Jones; Slocombe)

Italian Straw Hat. *See* **Chapeau de paille d'Italie**, 1927

Italiane e l'amore, 1961 (Zavattini)

Italiani sono matti, 1958 (Rota)

Italiano Brava Gente, 1965 (Serandrei)

Italy 61. *See* Italia 61, 1961

Itazura, 1959 (Takemitsu)

Itch in Time, 1943 (Blanc; Clampett)

Itinéraire d'un enfant gaté, 1988 (Lai)

It's a 2' 6" above the Ground World, 1972 (Godfrey)

It's a Bear, 1924 (Roach)

It's a Bet, 1935 (Siodmak)

It's a Big Country, 1950 (Schary; Alton; Raksin)

It's a Boy, 1923 (Roach)

It's a Boy, 1933 (Balcon; Rank; Vetchinsky)

It's a Cop, 1934 (Wilcox)

It's a Date, 1940 (Krasna; Pasternak)

It's a Dog's Life, 1955 (Hayes)

It's a Funny, Funny World, 1978 (Golan and Globus)

It's a Gift, 1923 (Roach)

It's a Gift, 1934 (Dreier; Zukor)

It's a Good Day, 1969 (Fields)

It's a Grand Old Nag, 1947 (Clampett)

It's a Great Feeling, 1949 (Cahn; Diamond)

It's a Great Life, 1929 (Gibbons)

It's a Hap-hap-happy Day, 1941 (Fleischer)

It's a Hard Life, 1919 (Roach)

It's a Mad, Mad, Mad, Mad World, 1962 (O'brien; Smith; Dunn; Edouart; Laszlo)

It's a Small World, 1935 (La Shelle; Miller)

It's a Small World, 1950 (Struss)

It's a Wild Life, 1918 (Roach)

It's a Wise Child, 1931 (Booth)

It's a Wonderful Life, 1946 (Goodrich and Hackett; Hornbeck; Swerling; Tiomkin; Walker; Biroc)

It's a Wonderful World, 1939 (Adrian; Hecht; Mankiewicz)

It's Alive, 1973 (Herrmann; Baker)

It's Alive III: Island of the Alive, 1987 (Baker; Herrmann)

It's All in the Stars, 1946 (Terry)

It's All Yours, 1936 (Cohn; Goosson)

It's Always Fair Weather, 1955 (Comden and Green; Freed; Kidd; Previn; Rose)

It's Always Now, 1965 (Allen)

It's an Ill Wind, 1939 (Blanc; Stalling)

It's Because of Good Weather. *See* Youki no seidayo, 1932

It's Big Country, 1951 (Kaper)

It's Easy to Remember, 1935 (Fleischer)

It's Fine for You. *See* Eto tyebye prinadlezit, 1917

It's Forever Springtime. *See* E primavera, 1950

It's Good to Be Alive, 1974 (Legrand)

It's Great to Be Alive, 1933 (Friedhofer)

It's Hard to Be Good, 1948 (Rank)

It's Hummer Time, 1950 (Blanc; McKimson; Stalling)

It's in the Air, 1938 (Dean; Neame)

It's in the Bag, 1944 (Metty; Reville)

It's in the Bag. *See* Affaire est dans le sac, 1932

It's Love Again, 1936 (Balcon; Junge; Rank)

It's Love I'm After, 1937 (Orry-Kelly; Wallis)

It's Magic. *See* Romance on the High Seas, 1948

It's My Turn, 1980 (Allen)

It's Nice to Have a Mouse around the House, 1965 (Blanc)

It's No Laughing Matter, 1914 (Marion)

It's Not Cricket, 1949 (Rank)

It's Only Money, 1962 (Head)

It's Pink But Is It Mink?, 1975 (McKimson)

It's That Man Again, 1943 (Rank)

It's the Cat's, 1926 (Fleischer)

It's the Natural Thing to Do, 1939 (Fleischer)

It's Tough to Be Famous, 1932 (Polito)

Ittouryu shinan, 1936 (Miyagawa)

Ivan Grozny, 1944 (Moskvin; Prokofiev; Tisse)

Ivan Grozny II: Boyarskii Zagovor, 1958 (Moskvin; Tisse; Prokofiev)

Ivan, il figlio del diavolo bianco, 1953 (Age and Scarpelli)

Ivan the Terrible, Part I. *See* **Ivan Grozny**, 1944

Ivan the Terrible, Part II: The Boyars' Plot. *See* Ivan Grozny II: Boyarskii Zagover, 1958

Ivanhoe, 1951 (Junge; Berman; Canutt; Rozsa; Young)

I've Always Loved You, 1946 (Chase; Gaudio)

I've Got Rings on My Fingers, 1929 (Fleischer)

I've Got Your Number, 1934 (Orry-Kelly)

Ivory Hunter. *See* Where No Vultures Fly, 1951

Ivory Snuff Box, 1915 (Carré)

Ivy, 1947 (Menzies; Metty; Orry-Kelly)

Izakaya Chouji, 1983 (Muraki)

Izol no odoriko, 1967 (Takemitsu)

Izzy Able the Detective, 1921 (Bray)

Izzy and His Rival. *See* Billy's Rival, 1914

J-3, 1946 (Aurenche and Bost)

J.S. Bach: Fantasia G-Moll, 1965 (švankmajer)

J.S. Bach: Fantasy in G Minor. *See* J.S. Bach: Fantasia G-Moll, 1965

Jaal, 1952 (Burman)

Jabberwocky, 1971 (švankmajer)

Jacare, 1942 (Rozsa)

Jacare—Killer of the Amazon. *See* Jacare, 1942

J'accuse, 1919 (Burel; Gaumont)

Jack, 1996 (Tavoularis)

Jack Ahoy!, 1934 (Balcon; Junge; Rank)

Jack and the Beanstalk, 1922 (Disney)

Jack and the Beanstalk, 1931 (Fleischer; Iwerks)
Jack and the Beanstalk, 1955 (Reiniger)
Jack and the Beanstalk, 1967 (Cahn; Mohr)
Jack and the Beanstalk, 1978 (Park)
Jack Frost, 1923 (Roach)
Jack Frost, 1934 (Iwerks)
Jack Frost, 1998 (Kovacs)
Jack London, 1943 (Garmes)
Jack Mortimer, 1962 (Herlth)
Jack of All Trades, 1936 (Balcon; Vetchinsky)
Jack of All Trades, 2000 (Schifrin)
Jack Spurlock, Prodigal, 1918 (Edeson)
Jack-Wabbit and the Beanstalk, 1943 (Blanc; Stalling)
Jackal, 1997 (Burwell)
Jackaroo of Coolabong, 1920 (Glennon)
Jackass Mail, 1942 (Sullivan)
Jackie Robinson Story, 1950 (Laszlo)
Jacko the Artist. *See* Beaux-Arts de Jocko, 1909
Jackpot, 1950 (La Shelle; Lemaire)
Jackpot, 1975 (Alekan)
Jack's Shack, 1934 (Terry)
Jack's the Boy, 1932 (Balcon; Rank; Vetchinsky)
Jacktown, 1962 (Rosenblum)
Jacob's Ladder. *See* Jacobs stege, 1942
Jacob's Ladder, 1990 (Jarre)
Jacobs stege, 1942 (Fischer)
Jaconde, 1957 (Colpi)
Jacqueline, 1956 (Rank; Unsworth)
Jacques Copeau, 1963 (Grimault)
Jade, 1995 (Eszterhas; Walas)
Jagd nach dem Glück, 1929-30 (Reiniger; Wagner)
Jagd nach dem Tode, 1921 (Warm)
Jagd nach der Braut, 1927 (Warm)
Jagged Edge, 1985 (Barry; Eszterhas)
Jagirdar, 1937 (Biswas)
Jago hua savera, 1958 (Lassally)
J'ai épousé une ombre, 1983 (Sarde)
J'ai horreur de l'amour, 1997 (Branco)
J'ai perdu mon lorgnon, 1906 (Pathé)
J'ai recontré le Père Noel, 1984 (Lai)
J'ai tout donnée, 1971 (Braunberger)
J'ai tué Raspoutine, 1967 (Barsacq)
Jail Bird, 1921 (Roach)
Jail Birds, 1932 (Iwerks)
Jail Birds, 1934 (Terry)
Jail Break, 1946 (Terry)
Jailbreak, 1936 (Orry-Kelly)
Jailed and Bailed, 1923 (Roach)
Jailed, 1916 (Roach)
Jailhouse Rock, 1957 (Berman)
Jajauma narashi, 1966 (Muraki)
Jak na to, 1963 (Brdečka)
Jak se člověk naucil létat, 1958 (Brdečka)
Jak se moudrý Aristoteles stal jeste moudřejšim, 1970 (Brdečka)
Jak stařeček měnil až vyměnil, 1953 (Trnka)
Jak zařídit byt, 1960 (Brdečka)
Jakub, 1976 (Ondříček)
Jalisco nunca pierde, 1937 (Figueroa)
Jalna, 1935 (Cronjager; Macgowan; Plunkett; Polglase; Veiller)
Jalousie 1976, 1976 (Legrand)
Jalsaghar, 1958 (Chandragupta; Dutta; Mitra)
Jalti Nishani, 1957 (Biswas)
Jam Session, 1944 (Cahn)
Jamaica Inn, 1939 (Harrison; Pommer; Reville; Stradling)
Jamaica Run, 1953 (Head)
Jamais plus toujours, 1975 (Delerue)

Jambul, 1952 (Enei)
James Dean, the First American Teenager, 1975 (Puttnam)
Jamestown Baloos, 1957 (Breer)
Jamestown Exposition, 1907 (Bitzer)
Jamie, 1944 (Cahn)
Jammin' the Blues, 1944 (Burks; Cole)
Jan Hus, 1954 (Trnka)
Jan Roháč z dubé, 1947 (Stallich)
Jan Zižka, 1955 (Trnka)
Jana Aranya, 1975 (Dutta)
Jane Austen in Manhattan, 1980 (Jhabvala; Merchant)
Jane Eyre, 1943 (Herrmann; Barnes; Basevi; Macgowan)
Jane Eyre, 1970 (Vetchinsky; Williams)
Jane Eyre, 1996 (Watkin)
Jangadero, 1961 (Wexler)
Janice Meredith, 1924 (Barnes)
January Man, 1988 (Hamlisch)
Janus-Faced, 1920 (Hoffmann)
Janus-Faced. *See* Januskopf, 1920
Januskopf, 1920 (Freund; Hoffmann)
Japanese Fantasy. *See* Japon de fantaisie, 1909
Japanese Nightingale, 1918 (Furthman; Miller)
Japanese Magic. *See* Japon de fantaisie, 1909
Japanese Summer: Double Suicide. *See* Muri-shinju: Nippon no natsu, 1967
Japanese Swords: The Work of Kouhei Miyairi. *See* Nihontou: Miyairi Kouhei no waza, 1976
Japanese Youth. *See* Nihon no seishun, 1968
Japon de fantaisie, 1909 (Cohl)
Jaquar, 1967 (Braunberger)
Jardin des supplices, 1976 (Carrière)
Jardins de Paris, 1961 (Fradetal)
Jarnac's Treacherous Blow. *See* Coup de Jarnac, 1909
Järnbäraren, 1911 (Jaenzon; Magnusson)
Jason and the Argonauts, 1963 (Harryhausen; Herrmann)
Jasper and the Beanstalk, 1945 (Pal)
Jasper and the Choo-Choo, 1943 (Pal)
Jasper and the Watermelons, 1942 (Pal)
Jasper Goes Fishing, 1943 (Pal)
Jasper Goes Hunting, 1944 (Pal)
Jasper in a Jam, 1946 (Pal)
Jasper Tell, 1945 (Pal)
Jasper's Booby Traps, 1945 (Pal)
Jasper's Close Shave, 1945 (Pal)
Jasper's Derby, 1946 (Pal)
Jasper's Haunted House, 1942 (Pal)
Jasper's Minstrels, 1945 (Pal)
Jasper's Music Lesson, 1943 (Pal)
Jasper's Paradise, 1944 (Pal)
Jassy, 1947 (Unsworth; Rank)
Jaune le soleil, 1971 (Duras)
Java Head, 1923 (Glennon)
Java Head, 1934 (Dean)
Jawani, 1942 (Biswas)
Jaws, 1975 (Fields; Williams; Zanuck)
Jaws 2, 1978 (Zanuck; Williams)
Jaws of Hell. *See* Balaclava, 1930
Jaws: The Revenge, 1987 (Williams)
Jayhawkers, 1959 (Head)
Jaywalker, 1956 (Bosustow)
Jazz Age, 1929 (Plunkett)
Jazz Boat, 1960 (Broccoli)
Jazz Fool, 1929 (Disney; Iwerks)
Jazz Mad, 1931 (Terry)
Jazz River, 1934 (Toland)
Jazz Singer, 1927 (Berlin; Carré; Kahn; Mohr; Warner; Zanuck)

Jim the Penman, 1921 (Stradling)
Jim Thorpe, All-American, 1951 (Steiner; Haller)
Jimmy the Gent, 1934 (Orry-Kelly)
Jinanbou garasu, 1955 (Miyagawa)
Jindra, Countess Ostrovin. See Jindra, hrabenka Ostrovínová, 1933
Jindra, hrabenka Ostrovínová, 1933 (Heller)
Jinete fantasma, 1967 (Figueroa)
Jingle Bells, 1927 (Lantz)
Jingle Bells, 1931 (Terry)
Jinsei gekijo, 1952 (Hayasaka)
Jinxed, 1982 (Zsigmond)
Jiný vzduch , 1939 (Stallich)
Jitterbugs, 1943 (Basevi)
Jivaro, 1954 (Head; Pereira)
Jízdní hlídka, 1936 (Heller)
Jmenuji se Fifinka, 1953 (Stallich)
Jo, 1971 (Decaë)
Joan of Arc, 1947 (Hoch; Day; Friedhofer; Jeakins; Vorkapich; Wanger)
Joan of Paris, 1942 (Metty)
Joan the Woman, 1916 (Buckland; Macpherson)
Joanna, 1968 (Lassally)
Joaquin Murieta, 1969 (Goldsmith)
Jobard a tué sa belle-mere, 1911 (Cohl)
Jobard amoureux timide, 1911 (Cohl)
Jobard change de bonne, 1911 (Cohl)
Jobard chauffeur. See Jobard fiance par interim, 1911
Jobard est demande en mariage, 1911 (Cohl)
Jobard fiance par interim, 1911 (Cohl)
Jobard garçon de recettes, 1911 (Cohl)
Jobard ne peut pas rire, 1911 (Cohl)
Jobard ne peut pas voir les femmes travailler, 1911 (Cohl)
Jobard portefaix par amour, 1911 (Cohl)
Jocelyn, 1951 (Braunberger)
Joconde, 1957 (Delerue)
Jodai no chokoku, 1950 (Hayasaka)
Joe Chairkin Going On, 1983 (Shepard)
Joe Glow the Firefly, 1941 (Blanc; Jones; Stalling)
Joe Kidd, 1972 (Bumstead; Schifrin)
Joe Smith, American, 1942 (Schary)
Joe Valachi—i segreti di Cosa Nostra, 1972 (de Laurentiis)
Joe Versus the Volcano, 1990 (Marshall; Delerue)
Joe's Apartment, 1996 (Burwell)
Joe's Bed-Stuy Barbershop: We Cut Heads, 1982 (Dickerson)
Joe's Lunch Wagon, 1934 (Terry)
Johan Ulfstjerna, 1923 (Magnusson)
Johan Ulfstjerna, 1936 (Fischer; Jaenzon)
Johan, 1920 (Magnusson)
Johann Mouse, 1953 (Hanna and Barbera)
Johanna Enlists, 1918 (Marion; Rosher)
Johannes Goth, 1920 (Mayer)
Johannestraum, 1919 (Hoffmann)
John and Mary, 1969 (Jones)
John Gilpin, 1951 (Halas and Batchelor)
John Goldfarb, Please Come Home!, 1965 (Smith; Williams; Head; Shamroy)
John Henry and the Inky Poo, 1946 (Pal)
John Huston and the Dubliners, 1987 (North)
John Loves Mary, 1949 (Burks; Krasna; Wald)
John Meade's Woman, 1936 (Reynolds; D'Agostino; Head; Mankiewicz)
John Paul Jones, 1959 (Adam; Steiner)
John Petticoats, 1919 (August; Sullivan)
John Wesley, 1953 (Rank)
Johnny Allegro, 1949 (Biroc; Duning; Louis)
Johnny Angel, 1945 (Carmichael)
Johnny Apollo, 1940 (Day; Dunne; Zanuck; Miller)
Johnny Banco, 1968 (D'Eaubonne)

Johnny Belinda, 1948 (McCord; Steiner; Wald; Warner)
Johnny Comes Flying Home, 1946 (Basevi)
Johnny Cool, 1963 (Cahn; van Heusen)
Johnny Dark, 1954 (Boyle)
Johnny Doughboy, 1942 (Alton; Cahn)
Johnny Eager, 1941 (Kaper; Rosson; Mayer)
Johnny Frenchman, 1945 (Balcon; Clarke; Rank)
Johnny Got His Gun, 1971 (Trumbo; van Runkle)
Johnny Guitar, 1954 (Maddow; Stradling; Young)
Johnny Holiday, 1949 (Mohr; Carmichael; Waxman)
Johnny in the Clouds. See Way to the Stars, 1945
Johnny Nobody, 1961 (Broccoli)
Johnny O'Clock, 1947 (Duning; Goosson; Guffey; Louis; Cohn)
Johnny One-Eye, 1950 (Polglase)
Johnny Smith and Poker-Huntas, 1938 (Avery)
Johnny Stecchino, 1991 (Lanci, Giuseppe ("beppe"))
Johnny Stool Pigeon, 1949 (Orry-Kelly)
Johnny Tiger, 1965 (Mercer; Green)
Johnny Toothpick. See Johnny Stecchino, 1991
Johnny Tremain, 1957 (Disney; Ellenshaw; Iwerks)
Johnstown Flood, 1946 (Terry)
Joi Baba Felunath, 1978 (Dutta)
Join the Circus, 1923 (Roach)
Join the Marines, 1937 (Brown)
Joi-Uchi, 1967 (Takemitsu)
Joke. See Itazura, 1959
Jokei kazoku, 1963 (Miyagawa; Yoda)
Jokei, 1960 (Miyagawa)
Joker. See Farceur, 1960
Joker Is Wild, 1957 (Cahn; Head; Westmore Family; van Heusen)
Jolanda la figlia del corsaro nero, 1951 (Delli Colli; de Laurentiis)
Jolanta—den gäckande suggan, 1945 (Jaenzon)
Jolanta—the Elusive Sow. See Jolanta—den gäckande suggan, 1945
Joli Mai, 1963 (Legrand; Lhomme)
Jolly Bad Fellow, 1964 (Barry)
Jolly Green, 1970 (Coutard)
Jolly Little Elves, 1934 (Lantz)
Jolly Musicians. See Vesyoli musikanti, 1937
Jolly Whirl. See Singeries humaines, 1910
Jolson Sings Again, 1949 (Buchman; Cohn; Duning; Louis)
Jolson Story, 1946 (Berlin; Cohn; Cole; Goosson; Louis; Walker)
Jolt for General Germ, 1931 (Fleischer)
Jonathan, 1969 (Müller)
Jonathan, 1973 (Müller)
Jonathan Livingston Seagull, 1973 (Leven)
Jones and His New Neighbors, 1909 (Bitzer)
Jones and the Lady Book Agent, 1909 (Bitzer)
Jones Have Amateur Theatricals, 1909 (Bitzer)
Jonny Quest vs. the Cyber Insects, 1995 (Hanna and Barbera)
Jonque, 1964 (Guillemot)
Jorden runt med Fanny Hill, 1974 (Lundgren)
José Torres, 1960 (Takemitsu)
José Torres, Part II, 1965 (Takemitsu)
Josef Kajetán Tyl, 1925 (Heller)
Joseph, 1995 (Morricone)
Joseph Andrews, 1977 (Watkin)
Joseph Balsamo, 1971 (Douy)
Joseph ou comment petit-on être Vosgien?, 1968 (Nuytten)
Josephine Baker Story, 1992 (Delerue)
Josette, 1938 (Zanuck)
Josh and S. A. M, 1993 (Newman)
Joshua Then and Now, 1985 (Sarde)
Jotai, 1964 (Takemitsu)
Joue avec Dodo, 1912-14 (Cohl)
Jouet, 1976 (Evein)
Jouets animés, 1912 (Cohl)

Joueur, 1958 (Aurenche and Bost; Douy)
Jougasaki no ame, 1950 (Miyagawa)
Jougasaki's Rain. *See* Jougasaki no ame, 1950
Jouiuchi, 1967 (Muraki)
Joujoux savants. *See* Jouets animés, 1912
Jour et la nuit, 1997 (Jarre)
Jour et l'heure, 1962 (Decaë; Evein)
Jour se lève, 1939 (Courant; Hakim; Jaubert; Prévert; Trauner)
Journal animé, 1908 (Cohl)
Journal de la résistance, 1945 (Coward)
Journal de séducteur, 1996 (Branco)
Journal d'un curé de campagne, 1950 (Burel)
Journal d'un fou, 1963 (Delerue)
Journal d'un scélérat, 1950 (Gégauff)
Journal d'une femme de chambre, 1963 (Carrière; Wakhévitch)
Journal d'une femme en blanc, 1965 (Aurenche and Bost; Douy)
Journal masculin, 1948 (Braunberger)
Journal of a Crime, 1933 (Orry-Kelly; Blanke; Haller)
Journal of Resistance, 1944 (Balcon)
Journal tombe à cinq heures, 1942 (Honegger)
Journalist, 1979 (McAlpine)
Journalist's Tale, 1985 (Godfrey)
Journée de Flambeau, 1916 (Cohl)
Journey, 1959 (Auric; Cardiff; Spencer; Fisher)
Journey Back to Oz, 1971 (Cahn)
Journey Back to Oz, 1974 (van Heusen)
Journey for Margaret, 1942 (Schary; Waxman)
Journey into Fear, 1943 (Struss)
Journey into Fear, 1975 (North)
Journey into Medicine, 1946 (Kaufman)
Journey into Prehistory. *See* Cesta do pravěku, 1955
Journey into Primeval Times. *See* Cesta do pravěku, 1955
Journey into the Night. *See* Gang in die Nacht, 1921
Journey of Love. *See* Viaggio d'amore, 1991
Journey Through Rosebud, 1972 (Mandel)
Journey to Italy. *See* Viaggio in Italia, 1953
Journey to Marseilles, 1944 (Warner)
Journey to Spirit Island, 1988 (Zsigmond)
Journey to the Center of the Earth, 1959 (Reisch; Brackett; Cahn; Herrmann; Wheeler)
Journey to the Center of the Earth, 1986 (Golan and Globus; Watkin)
Journey to the Far Side of the Sun. *See* Doppelganger, 1969
Journey to the Pacific, 1968 (Fields)
Journey Together, 1945 (Rattigan)
Journey's End, 1930 (Balcon; Sherriff)
Jours tranquilles à Clichy, 1990 (Rabier)
Jovanka e l'altri, 1960 (Wilson)
Jovanka e le altre, 1960 (Rotunno)
Joven. *See* Young Ones, 1960
Joven rebelde, 1961 (Zavattini)
Jovenes, 1960 (Alcoriza)
Joy House. *See* Félins, 1964
Joy in the Morning, 1964 (Herrmann)
Joy Luck Club, 1993 (Bass)
Joy of Living, 1938 (Walker)
Joy of Love. *See* Blaho lásky, 1965
Joy Ride, 1935 (Neame)
Joy Rider, 1921 (Roach)
Joy Scouts, 1939 (Roach)
Joyeaux Microbes, 1909 (Cohl)
Joyeux Fantômes. *See* Fantasma a Roma, 1960
Joyeux Pélerins, 1950 (Schüfftan)
Joyu Sumako no koi, 1947 (Yoda)
Joyu, 1947 (Hayasaka)
Jrdina jedné noci, 1935 (Stallich)
Jsem devče s čertem v tele, 1933 (Heller; Stallich)

Jsouc na rece mlynár jeden, 1971 (Brdečka)
Juana Gallo, 1960 (Figueroa)
Juarez, 1938 (Blanke)
Juarez, 1939 (Friedhofer; Gaudio; Grot; Korngold; Orry-Kelly; Wallis; Westmore Family)
Jubal, 1956 (Cohn; Raksin; Wald)
Jubilee Trail, 1954 (Young)
Jubilee Widow, 1935 (Havelock-Allan)
Jubilo, Jr., 1924 (Roach)
Jud Süss, 1940 (Hunte)
Judas Money. *See* Judaspengar, 1915
Judaspengar, 1915 (Jaenzon)
Judex, 1916 (Gaumont)
Judex, 1963 (Fradetal; Jarre)
Judge. *See* Domaren, 1960
Judge Alton B. Parker, 1904 (Bitzer)
Judge and the Assassin. *See* Juge et l'assassin, 1976
Judge Dredd, 1995 (Biddle)
Judge for a Day, 1935 (Fleischer)
Judge Priest, 1934 (Nichols; Parrish; Trotti)
Judgment at Nuremberg, 1961 (Laszlo; Louis)
Judith, 1966 (Hayes)
Judith et Holopherne, 1909 (Gaumont)
Judith of Bethulia, 1914 (Bitzer)
Judith Therpauve, 1978 (Lhomme)
Judith Trachtenberg , 1920 (Galeen)
Judo School Expulsion Letter. *See* Koudoukan hamonjou, 1968
Judo senshu no koi, 1934 (Yoda)
Juego peligroso, 1966 (Alcoriza)
Jugador de ajedrez, 1980 (Figueroa)
Jugando con la muerte, 1982 (Donaggio)
Juge et l'assassin, 1975 (Aurenche and Bost; Sarde)
Juge Fayard dit lè sheriff, 1976 (Sarde)
Jugement de Dieu, 1949 (Kosma)
Jugement de minuit, 1932 (Jeanson)
Jugement dernier, 1945 (Jeanson)
Jugend, 1938 (Von Harbou; Warm)
Jugendrausch, 1927 (Hoffmann)
Juggernaut, 1974 (Fisher)
Jugnu, 1973 (Burman)
Juice, 1992 (Dickerson)
Juif polonais, 1931 (D'Eaubonne)
Jujin Kuki-Otoko, 1955 (Tsuburaya)
Juke Girl, 1942 (Deutsch; Glennon; Wald; Wallis)
Jules and Jim. *See* **Jules et Jim**, 1961
Jules et Jim, 1961 (Coutard; Delerue)
Julia, 1977 (Delerue; Dillon; Murch; Sargent; Slocombe)
Julia and Julia, 1987 (Jarre; Rotunno)
Julia Misbehaves, 1948 (Deutsch; Irene; Ruttenberg)
Julianwale, 1953 (Biswas)
Julie de Carneilhan, 1949 (Mnouchkine)
Julie Pot de Colle, 1977 (Carrière; Delerue)
Juliet of the Spirits. *See* Giulietta degli spirit, 1965
Julietta, 1953 (Alekan; Braunberger; D'Eaubonne)
Juliette de Sade, 1969 (Conti)
Juliette ou la clé des songes, 1951 (Alekan; Kosma; Trauner)
Julius Caesar, 1953 (Gibbons; Houseman; Rozsa; Ruttenberg)
July Days, 1923 (Roach)
Jumanji, 1995 (Muren; Ralston)
Jumanji 2, 2000 (Ralston)
Jumbo, 1962 (Ames; Daniels; Edens; Gillespie; Pasternak)
Jumeau, 1984 (Saulnier)
Jument verte, 1959 (Aurenche and Bost; Douy)
Jump Your Job, 1922 (Roach)
Jumpin' Jack Flash, 1986 (Boyle; Newman)
Jumpin' Jupiter, 1955 (Blanc; Jones; Stalling)

Jumping Beans, 1922 (Fleischer)
Jumping Beans, 1930 (Terry)
Jumping for Joy, 1955 (Rank)
Jumping Jacks, 1952 (Bumstead; Head; Wallis)
Junak Markos, 1953 (Dinov)
June Bride, 1935 (Terry)
June Bride, 1948 (Blanke; Grot; Head; McCord)
June Madness, 1920 (Roach)
June Night. See Juninatt, 1965
Junge Baron Neuhaus, 1934 (Herlth; Röhrig)
Junge Medardus, 1923 (Kolowrat-Krakowsky)
Junges Mädchen—ein junger Mann, 1935 (Heller)
Jungfrukällan, 1960 (Nykvist; Lundgren)
Jungle. See World Window, 1937-40
Jungle Book, 1942 (Cooper; Garmes; Hornbeck; Korda; Périnal; Wheeler)
Jungle Book. See Rudyard Kipling's Jungle Book, 1942
Jungle Book, 1967 (Disney)
Jungle Cat, 1959 (Iwerks)
Jungle Fever, 1991 (Dickerson)
Jungle Girl, 1941 (Canutt)
Jungle Jingles, 1929 (Lantz)
Jungle Jitters, 1934 (Iwerks)
Jungle Jumble, 1932 (Lantz)
Jungle Princess, 1936 (Head)
Jungle Rhythm, 1929 (Disney; Iwerks)
Jungle Trail of the Son of the Tarzan. See Son of Tarzan, 1921
Jungle Warfare, 1943 (Halas and Batchelor)
Juninatt, 1965 (Fischer)
Junior Bonner, 1972 (Ballard)
Junior Miss, 1945 (Clarke)
Junkman, 1918 (Roach)
Juno and the Paycock, 1929 (Reville)
Junoon, 1978 (Nihalani)
Jupiter. See Douze heures de bonheur, 1952
Jupiter's Darling, 1954 (Gibbons; Plunkett; Pan; Rose; Rosher)
Jurassic Park, 1993 (Muren; Williams; Winston)
Jury of One. See Testament, 1974
Jury's Secret, 1938 (Krasner)
Jus' Passin' Through, 1923 (Roach)
Jusqu'à la nuit, 1983 (Branco; de Almeida)
Jusqu'au bout du monde, 1962 (Delerue)
Jusqu'au bout du monde. See Bis ans Ende der Welt, 1991
Jusqu'au dernier, 1956 (D'Eaubonne)
Jusques au feu exclusivement, 1971 (Fradetal)
Just a Clown, 1934 (Terry)
Just a Gigolo, 1932 (Fleischer)
Just a Good Guy, 1924 (Roach)
Just a Little Bull, 1940 (Terry)
Just a Minute, 1924 (Roach)
Just a Wolf at Heart, 1963 (Hanna and Barbera)
Just Another Blonde, 1926 (Edeson)
Just around the Corner, 1921 (Marion)
Just around the Corner, 1938 (Leven; Zanuck)
Just Ask Jupiter, 1938 (Terry)
Just Before Nightfall. See Juste avant la nuit, 1971
Just Cause, 1995 (Von Brandenstein)
Just Dropped In, 1919 (Roach)
Just Ducky, 1953 (Hanna and Barbera)
Just for a Song, 1930 (Balcon)
Just for You, 1952 (Barnes; Friedhofer; Head; Raksin)
Just for You, 1956 (Carreras)
Just Gold, 1913 (Bitzer)
Just Imagine, 1930 (Friedhofer; Goosson)
Just Like a Woman, 1912 (Bitzer)
Just Like a Woman, 1966 (Godfrey)
Just Mickey, 1930 (Disney)

Just My Luck, 1933 (Wilcox)
Just My Luck, 1957 (Rank)
Just Neighbors, 1919 (Roach)
Just Nuts, 1914 (Roach)
Just Off Broadway, 1942 (Day; Raksin)
Just Once More. See Chans, 1962
Just One More Chance, 1932 (Fleischer)
Just Out of Reach, 1979 (Boyd)
Just Plane Beep, 1965 (Blanc)
Just Rambling Along, 1918 (Roach)
Just Smith, 1933 (Balcon; Junge; Rank)
Just Spooks, 1925 (Lantz)
Just Tell Me What You Want, 1980 (Allen; Morris)
Just This Once, 1951 (Basevi)
Just to Be Together, 2001 (Shepard)
Juste avant la nuit, 1971 (Rabier)
Justice est faite, 1950 (Spaak)
Justice Is Done. See Justice est faite, 1950
Justice of Society. See Samhallets dom, 1912
Justicière, 1925 (Périnal)
Justin de Marseille, 1935 (Ibert; Meerson)
Justine, 1969 (Berman; Goldsmith; Shamroy; Sharaff; Smith)
Jutro Meksyk, 1965 (ścibor-Rylski)
Juve contre Fantômas, 1913 (Gaumont)
Juvenile Court, 1938 (Cohn; Goosson)
Jwar Bhata, 1944 (Biswas)
Jyoti, 1969 (Burman)

K2, 1991 (Zimmer)
K, 1997 (Fischer; Sarde; Semprun)
K narodnoi vlasti, 1917 (Starewicz)
K und K Feldermarschall. See Falsche Feldmarschall, 1930
Kaagaz Ke Phool, 1959 (Burman)
Kabinett des Dr. Caligari, 1919 (Hunte; Pommer; Röhrig; Mayer; Warm)
Kabinett des Dr. Larifari, 1930 (Heller; Waxman)
Kabuliwala, 1961 (Shankar)
Kadetten, 1941 (Röhrig)
Kaettekita yopparai, 1968 (Toda)
Kagemusha, 1980 (Miyagawa; Muraki)
Kagi, 1959 (Miyagawa)
Kaguyahimi , 1935 (Tsuburaya)
Kaidan, 1964 (Takemitsu; Toda)
Kaigun bakugekitai, 1940 (Hayasaka; Tsuburaya)
Kaigun tokubetsu nenshouhei, 1972 (Muraki)
Kaiju daisenso, 1966 (Tsuburaya)
Kaiju soshingeki, 1968 (Tsuburaya)
Kaikyou, 1982 (Muraki)
Kaise Kahoon, 1964 (Burman)
Kaiser Joseph II, 1912 (Kolowrat-Krakowsky)
Kaitei gunkan, 1964 (Tsuburaya)
Kaito Sayamaro, 1928 (Tsuburaya)
Kak nyemyets obyezyanov vidumal, 1915 (Starewicz)
Kakedashi jidai, 1947 (Hayasaka)
Kakureta ninkimono, 1959 (Yoda)
Kakushi toride no sanakunin, 1958 (Muraki)
Kakute kamikaze wa fuku, 1944 (Miyagawa)
Kala Bazar, 1960 (Burman)
Kala Pani, 1958 (Burman)
Kaleidoscope , 1935 (Lye)
Kaleidoscope, 1966 (Challis)
Kaleidoscope, 1990 (Mandel)
Kaleidoskop: Valeska Gert, 1979 (Ballhaus)
Kalifornia, 1993 (Burwell)
Kaliostro, 1918 (Starewicz)
Kalyug, 1981 (Nihalani)

Kama Sutra Rides Again, 1971 (Godfrey)
Kamal, 1949 (Burman)
Kameradschaft, 1931 (Metzner; Wagner)
Kamilla og tyven II, 1989 (Lassally)
Kammarjunkaren, 1914 (Jaenzon)
Kammeny tsvetok, 1946 (Ptushko)
Kampf des Donald Westhof, 1927 (Courant)
Kampf um Karthago. *See* Salammbo, 1924
Kämpfende Herzen, 1920 (Warm; Von Harbou)
Kampfgegen Berlin, 1925 (Junge)
Kanał, 1957 (Stawiński)
Kanchanganga, 1962 (Mitra; Dutta)
Kangaroo, 1952 (Clarke; Newman)
Kangaroo Courting, 1954 (Bosustow)
Kangaroo Kid, 1950 (Harlan)
Kangaroo Steak, 1930 (Terry)
Kanojo to kare, 1963 (Takemitsu)
Kansan, 1943 (Harlan)
Kansas, 1988 (Donaggio)
Kansas City Kitty, 1944 (Guffey)
Kansas City Princess, 1934 (Barnes; Orry-Kelly)
Kansas Cyclone, 1941 (Canutt)
Kansas Pacific, 1953 (Wanger)
Kansas Terrors, 1939 (Canutt)
Kantor Idéal, 1932 (Heller)
Kaos, 1984 (Guerra; Lanci, Giuseppe ("beppe"))
Kaoyaku, 1957 (Takemitsu)
Kaplan von San Lorenzo, 1952 (Herlth)
Kapò, 1960 (Cristaldi; Gherardi; Solinas)
Kapurush-o-Mahapurush, 1965 (Chandragupta; Dutta)
Karami-ai, 1962 (Takemitsu; Toda)
Karate Kid, 1984 (Conti)
Karate Kid, Part II, 1986 (Conti)
Karate Kid III, 1989 (Conti)
Karel Hynek Mácha, 1937 (Heller)
Kariera Pavla Čamrdy, 1931 (Stallich)
Karin, Daughter of Ingmar. *See* Karin Ingmarsdotter, 1920
Karin Ingmarsdotter, 1920 (Magnusson)
Karin Mansdotter, 1954 (Nykvist)
Kärlek och journalistik, 1916 (Jaenzon; Magnusson))
Kärlek och kassabrist, 1932 (Jaenzon)
Kärlek starkare än hat, 1914 (Jaenzon)
Kärlekens decimaler, 1960 (Lundgren)
Karneval und Liebe, 1934 (Heller)
Karnival Kid, 1929 (Disney; Iwerks)
Karol Lear, 1971 (Enei)
Károly Bakák, 1918 (Korda)
Karusellen, 1923 (Jaenzon; Magnusson)
Kaseki no mori, 1973 (Takemitsu)
Kaseki, 1975 (Takemitsu)
Káslání a kýchani, 1950 (Brdečka)
Kašpárek kouzelníkem, 1927 (Stallich)
Kataku, 1979 (Takemitsu)
Katerina Izmailova, 1967 (Enei; Shostakovich)
Katharina die Grosse, 1920 (Freund)
Katharina, die Letzte, 1935 (Pasternak)
Kathleen, 1941 (Edens; Waxman)
Kathy's Love Affair. *See* Courtneys of Curzon Street, 1947
Katia, 1960 (Spaak)
Katie Did It, 1950 (Metty)
Katina. *See* Iceland, 1942
Katinka, 1988 (Nykvist)
Katja, 1960 (D'Eaubonne)
Katka bumazhnyi ranet, 1926 (Enei; Moskvin)
Katka's Reinette Apple. *See* Katka bumazhnyi ranet, 1926
Kato hayabusa sento tai, 1944 (Tsuburaya)

Katrina, 1943 (Jaenzon)
Kats Is Kats, 1920 (Bray)
Katya, 1960 (Kosma)
Kaufmann von Venedig, 1923 (Maté; Warm)
Kavalier zolotoi zvezdy, 1963 (Urusevsky)
Kavárna na hlavní třide, 1954 (Brdečka)
Kaviarprinzessin, 1929 (Heller)
Kawaita hana, 1963 (Takemitsu; Toda)
Kawaita mizuumi, 1960 (Takemitsu)
Kazablan, 1973 (Golan and Globus)
Kazan, 1921 (Selig)
Kdybych byl tátou, 1939 (Stallich)
Když má svátek Dominika, 1967 (Stallich)
Kean, 1956 (Cecchi D'amico; Cristaldi; Di Venanzo)
Kedlubnový kavalír v ráji, 1928 (Heller)
Keep 'em Growing, 1943 (Terry)
Keep 'em Rolling, 1934 (Plunkett; Steiner)
Keep Fit, 1937 (Neame)
Keep in Style, 1934 (Fleischer)
Keep Smilin', 1925 (Garmes; Bruckman)
Keep Smiling, 1938 (Cronjager)
Keep Your Mouth Shut, 1944 (Dunning; McClaren)
Keep Your Powder Dry, 1945 (Irene)
Keeper of the City, 1992 (Rosenman)
Keeper of the Flame, 1942 (Adrian; Daniels; Mayer; Stewart;
    Wheeler; Kaper)
Keeper of the Lions, 1937 (Lantz)
Keepers. *See* Tête contre les murs, 1958
Keeping Company, 1940 (Freund; Mankiewicz)
Keeping the Faith, 2000 (Bernstein)
Keeps Rainin' All the Time, 1934 (Fleischer)
Kein Engel ist so rein, 1950 (Herlth)
Kelly the Second, 1936 (Roach)
Kelly's Heroes, 1970 (Figueroa; Schifrin)
Kemonomichi, 1965 (Muraki; Takemitsu)
Kempy. *See* Wise Girls, 1929
Kennel Murder Case, 1933 (Orry-Kelly)
Kenny Rogers as the Gambler, 1980 (Biroc)
Keno Bates, Liar, 1915 (August)
Kenran taru satsujin, 1951 (Miyagawa)
Kentuckian, 1908 (Bitzer)
Kentuckian, 1955 (Herrmann; Laszlo)
Kentucky, 1938 (Trotti; Zanuck)
Kentucky Bells, 1931 (Lantz)
Kentucky Colonel, 1920 (Glennon)
Kentucky Feud, 1905 (Bitzer)
Kentucky Kernels, 1934 (Cronjager; Plunkett; Steiner)
Kentucky Moonshine, 1938 (Macgowan)
Kept Husbands, 1931 (Steiner)
Kermesse fantastique, 1951 (Auric)
Kermesse héroïque, 1935 (Meerson; Spaak; Wakhévitch)
Kermesse héro, 1935 (Stradling; Trauner)
Kernels of Corn, 1947 (Fleischer)
Kes, 1969 (Menges)
Kesa and Moritou. *See* Kesa to Moritou, 1939
Kesa to Moritou, 1939 (Miyagawa)
Kessen no osorae, 1943 (Tsuburaya)
Kettou gofun-mar, 1953 (Yoda)
Kevin Saves the World, 1995 (Godfrey)
Key, 1934 (Haller; Orry-Kelly)
Key, 1958 (Arnold; Foreman; Morris)
Key, 1976 (Godfrey)
Key. *See* Chiave, 1983
Key Exchange, 1985 (Daring)
Key Is in the Door. *See* Clef sur la porte, 1978
Key Largo, 1948 (Burks; Freund; Steiner; Wald)

King of Gamblers, 1937 (Dreier; Head)
King of Hearts. *See* Roi de coeur, 1966
King of Jazz, 1930 (Laemmle; MacArthur; Mohr; Rennahan)
King of Kings, 1927 (Westmore Family; Carré; Grot; Macpherson)
King of Kings, 1961 (Krasner; Planer; Rozsa; Wakhévitch)
King of Marvin Gardens, 1972 (Kovacs)
King of Paris, 1934 (Wilcox)
King of Reporters. *See* A riporterkirály, 1917
King of Soho. *See* Street of Sin, 1928
King of the Arena, 1933 (McCord)
King of the Cannibal Islands, 1908 (Bitzer)
King of the Cowboys, 1943 (Canutt)
King of the Damned, 1936 (Balcon; Rank)
King of the Gypsies, 1978 (Nykvist; de Laurentiis)
King of the Jungle, 1933 (Haller)
King of the Khyber Rifles, 1953 (Herrmann; Shamroy; Wheeler; Lemaire)
King of the Khyber Rifles. *See* Black Watch, 1929
King of the Mardi Gras, 1935 (Fleischer)
King of the Pecos, 1936 (Canutt)
King of the Ritz, 1933 (Balcon)
King of the Roaring Twenties, 1961 (Swerling; Waxman)
King of the Texas Rangers, 1941 (Canutt)
King of the Underworld, 1939 (Orry-Kelly)
King of Wild Horses, 1924 (Roach)
King on Main Street, 1925 (Howe)
King Rat, 1965 (Barry; Guffey)
King Richard and the Crusaders, 1954 (Blanke; Steiner)
King Size Canary, 1947 (Avery)
King Solomon of Broadway, 1935 (D'Agostino; Mandell)
King Solomon's Mines, 1937 (Balcon; Junge)
King Solomon's Mines, 1950 (Mayer; Plunkett; Surtees)
King Solomon's Mines, 1985 (Golan and Globus; Goldsmith)
King Steps Out, 1936 (Ballard; Buchman; Cohn; Goosson)
King Struck Dumb. *See* Rey Pasmado, 1992
King Tut's Tomb, 1950 (Terry)
King Ubu. *See* Ubu Roi, 1976
King Zilch, 1933 (Terry)
Kingdom of Diamonds. *See* Heerak Rajar Deshe, 1979
Kings and Queens, 1956 (Heller)
King's Breakfast, 1936 (Reiniger)
King's Cup, 1933 (Wilcox)
King's Daughter, 1934 (Terry)
Kings Go Forth, 1958 (Bernstein; Cahn)
King's Messenger, 1908 (Bitzer)
Kings of the Forest, 1912 (Selig)
Kings of the Road. *See* **Im Lauf der Zeit**, 1976
Kings of the Sun, 1963 (Bernstein; Reynolds)
King's Pirate, 1967 (Whitlock)
King's Rhapsody, 1955 (Wilcox)
Kings Row, 1941 (Burks; Menzies; Orry-Kelly; Westmore Family; Friedhofer; Howe; Korngold; Wallis)
King's Thief, 1955 (Plunkett; Rozsa)
King's Vacation, 1933 (Grot; Orry-Kelly)
Kingu Kongu no gyakushu, 1967 (Tsuburaya)
Kinjite, 1988 (Golan and Globus)
Kino v derevne, 1930 (Ptushko)
Kipps, 1941 (Beaton; Vetchinsky)
Kirare Yosaburou, 1960 (Miyagawa)
Kiri no oto, 1956 (Yoda)
Kirpichiki, 1925 (Golovnya)
Kismat, 1943 (Biswas)
Kismet, 1920 (Gaudio)
Kismet, 1930 (Seitz)
Kismet, 1944 (Cole; Gibbons; Irene; Rosher; Stothart)
Kismet, 1955 (Ames; Cole; Freed; Gibbons; Lederer; Previn; Ruttenberg)
Kiss, 1921 (Glennon)

Kiss, 1928 (Mayer)
Kiss, 1929 (Daniels; Day; Gibbons; Kräly)
Kiss, 1969 (Popescu-Gopo)
Kiss, 1988 (Walas)
Kiss and Make Up, 1934 (Banton; Dreier; Shamroy)
Kiss and Tell, 1944 (Polglase; Goosson; Louis)
Kiss before Dying, 1956 (Ballard)
Kiss before the Mirror, 1933 (Freund)
Kiss in the Dark, 1925 (Polglase)
Kiss in the Dark, 1948 (Burks; Steiner)
Kiss Me Again, 1925 (Kräly)
Kiss Me Again, 1931 (Garmes)
Kiss Me Casanova. *See* **Märchen vom Glück**, 1949
Kiss Me Cat, 1952 (Jones; Blanc; Stalling)
Kiss Me Deadly, 1955 (Laszlo)
Kiss Me Guido, 1997 (Vachon)
Kiss Me Kate, 1953 (Pan; Plunkett; Previn; Rosher)
Kiss Me Stupid, 1964 (Blanc; Previn; Diamond; La Shelle; Mandell; Trauner)
Kiss My Butterfly. *See* I Love You, Alice B. Toklas!, 1968
Kiss of Death, 1947 (Hecht; Lederer; Lemaire; Wheeler; Zanuck)
Kiss of Death, 1995 (van Runkle)
Kiss of Death. *See* Dodskyssen, 1917
Kiss of Evil. *See* Kiss of the Vampire, 1963
Kiss of Fire, 1955 (Boyle)
Kiss of the Vampire, 1963 (Bernard; Carreras)
Kiss the Blood Off My Hands, 1948 (Bernstein; Maddow; Metty; Rozsa)
Kiss the Boys Goodbye, 1941 (Head; Young)
Kiss the Girls and Make Them Die. *See* Se tutte le donne del mondo . . . , 1966
Kiss the Other Sheik. *See* Oggi, domani, e dopodomani, 1965
Kiss Them for Me, 1957 (Epstein; Krasner; Lemaire; Wald; Wheeler)
Kissenga, Man of Africa. *See* Men of Two Worlds, 1946
Kisses and Kurses, 1930 (Lantz)
Kisses for Breakfast, 1941 (Deutsch; Edeson)
Kisses for My President, 1964 (Kaper; O'Steen; Surtees)
Kisses, 1922 (Mathis)
Kissing Bandit, 1948 (Brown; Pasternak; Plunkett; Surtees)
Kit for Kat, 1948 (Blanc; Stalling)
Kita no sannin, 1945 (Hayasaka)
Kitchen Think, 1974 (Halas and Batchelor)
Kitchen Toto, 1987 (Golan and Globus)
Kitchen, 1961 (Hambling)
Kitten Sitter, 1949 (Terry)
Kitten with a Whip, 1964 (Biroc)
Kitty, 1945 (Dreier; Young)
Kitty Foiled, 1948 (Hanna and Barbera)
Kitty Foyle, 1940 (Polglase; Stewart; Trumbo)
Kitty from Kansas City, 1931 (Fleischer)
Kitty Kornered, 1946 (Blanc; Clampett; Stalling)
Kiyen ryoko, 1959 (Takemitsu)
Klabzuba's Eleven. *See* Klapzubova jedenáctka, 1938
Klapzubova jedenáctka, 1938 (Stallich)
Klart till drabbning, 1937 (Fischer; Jaenzon)
Klassenfeind, 1983 (Müller)
Klassenfeind, 1984 (Müller)
Kleider machen Leute, 1940 (Herlth)
Klein Dorrit, 1934 (Heller)
Kleine aus der Kongektion, 1925 (Junge)
Kleine Fernsehspiel, 1975 (Lenica)
Kleine Godard, 1978 (Ballhaus)
Kleine Grenzverkehr, 1943 (Kästner; Röhrig)
Kleine Hofkonzert, 1945 (Wagner)
Kleine Mutter, 1935 (Pasternak)
Kleine Schornsteinfeger, 1935 (Reiniger)
Kleine Seitensprung, 1931 (Herlth; Röhrig)

Kleine vom Variété, 1926 (Courant)
Klondike Annie, 1936 (Dreier; Young)
Klosterjäger, 1920 (Planer)
Klostret it sendomir, 1920 (Magnusson)
Klute, 1971 (Jenkins; Willis)
Knabe in Blau, 1919 (Hoffmann)
Knack, and How to Get It, 1965 (Barry)
Knave of Hearts. *See* Monsieur Ripois, 1954
Knickerbocker Buckaroo, 1919 (Zukor)
Knickerbocker Holiday, 1943 (Plunkett; Cahn)
Kniga v derevne, 1929 (Ptushko)
Knight in London, 1928 (Freund)
Knight-Mare Hare, 1955 (Jones)
Knight of the Road, 1911 (Bitzer)
Knight without Armour, 1937 (Biro; Cardiff; Hornbeck; Korda; Marion;
    Meerson; Rozsa; Stradling)
Knightriders, 1981 (Savini)
Knights and Emeralds, 1986 (Puttnam)
Knights for a Day, 1936 (Lantz)
Knights Must Fall, 1949 (Blanc; Stalling)
Knights of the Range, 1940 (Harlan; Head)
Knights of the Round Table, 1953 (Berman; Jennings; Junge;
    Rozsa; Young)
Knightwatch, 1988 (Alonzo)
Knighty Night Bugs, 1958 (Blanc)
Knock, 1950 (Renoir)
Knock, Knock, 1940 (Lantz)
Knock on Any Door, 1949 (Cohn; Guffey; Louis; Taradash)
Knock on the Window, the Door Is in a Jamb, 1920 (Bray)
Knock on Wood, 1953 (Kidd; Bumstead; Head; Pereira; Young)
Knock Out, 1935 (Heller)
Knockout, 1923 (Roach)
Knockout, 1932 (Roach)
Knockout, 1941 (McCord)
Knockout Reilly, 1927 (Cronjager)
Know Your Ally: Britain, 1943 (Hornbeck)
Know Your Europeans, 1994 (Godfrey)
Know Your Men, 1921 (Ruttenberg)
Knowing Men, 1930 (Rosher)
Knute Rockne—All American, 1940 (Haskin; Wallis; Gaudio)
Kobila Lord Mortona, 1918 (Starewicz)
Kocham Kino, 1987 (Preisner)
Kodachi o tsukau onna, 1944 (Miyagawa; Yoda)
Kodachi o tsukau onna, 1961 (Yoda)
Kodo nipon, 1940 (Tsuburaya)
Koenigsmark, 1936 (Ibert)
Koffer des Herrn O.F., 1931 (Kästner)
Kofuku sezu, 1959 (Tsuburaya)
Kogda zvuchat strunnyi svedtza, 1913 (Starewicz)
Koharu kyogen, 1942 (Hayasaka)
Koharu's Performance. *See* Koharu kyogen, 1942
Kohlhiessels Töchter, 1920 (Kräly)
Koho jsem včera líbal, 1935 (Stallich)
Koi ya koinasuna koi, 1962 (Yoda)
Koikaze gojusan-tsugi, 1952 (Yoda)
Koisuru tsuma, 1947 (Hayasaka)
Kokila, 1937 (Biswas)
Koko, 1977 (Almendros)
Ko-Ko at the Circus, 1926 (Fleischer)
Ko-Ko Back Tracks, 1927 (Fleischer)
Ko-Ko Baffles the Bulls, 1926 (Fleischer)
Ko-Ko Beats Time, 1929 (Fleischer)
Ko-Ko Celebrates the Fourth, 1925 (Fleischer)
Ko-Ko Chops Suey, 1927 (Fleischer)
Ko-Ko Cleans Up, 1928 (Fleischer)
Ko-Ko Eats, 1925 (Fleischer)

Ko-Ko Explores, 1927 (Fleischer)
Ko-Ko Gets Egg-cited, 1926 (Fleischer)
Ko-Ko Goes Over, 1928 (Fleischer)
Ko-Ko Heaves-Ho, 1928 (Fleischer)
Ko-Ko Hops Off, 1927 (Fleischer)
Ko-Ko Hot After It, 1926 (Fleischer)
Ko-Ko in 1999, 1924 (Fleischer)
Ko-Ko in the Rough, 1928 (Fleischer)
Ko-Ko in Toyland, 1925 (Fleischer)
Ko-Ko Kicks, 1927 (Fleischer)
Ko-Ko Kidnapped, 1926 (Fleischer)
Ko-Ko Lamps Aladdin, 1928 (Fleischer)
Ko-Ko Makes 'em Laugh, 1927 (Fleischer)
Ko-Ko Needles the Boss, 1927 (Fleischer)
Ko-Ko Nuts, 1925 (Fleischer)
Ko-Ko on the Run, 1925 (Fleischer)
Ko-Ko on the Track, 1928 (Fleischer)
Ko-Ko Packs 'em, 1925 (Fleischer)
Ko-Ko Plays Pool, 1927 (Fleischer)
Ko-Ko Sees Spooks, 1925 (Fleischer)
Ko-Ko Smokes, 1928 (Fleischer)
Ko-Ko Squeals, 1928 (Fleischer)
Ko-Ko Steps Out, 1926 (Fleischer)
Ko-Ko the Barber, 1925 (Fleischer)
Ko-Ko the Convict, 1926 (Fleischer)
Ko-Ko the Hot Shot, 1924 (Fleischer)
Ko-Ko the Kid, 1927 (Fleischer)
Ko-Ko the Knight, 1927 (Fleischer)
Ko-Ko the Kop, 1927 (Fleischer)
Ko-Ko Trains Animals, 1925 (Fleischer)
Ko-Ko's Act, 1928 (Fleischer)
Ko-Ko's Bawth, 1928 (Fleischer)
Ko-Ko's Big Pull, 1928 (Fleischer)
Ko-Ko's Big Sale, 1929 (Fleischer)
Ko-Ko's Catch, 1928 (Fleischer)
Ko-Ko's Chase, 1928 (Fleischer)
Ko-Ko's Conquest, 1929 (Fleischer)
Ko-Ko's Courtship, 1928 (Fleischer)
Ko-Ko's Crib, 1929 (Fleischer)
Ko-Ko's Dog-Gone, 1928 (Fleischer)
Ko-Ko's Earth Control, 1928 (Fleischer)
Ko-Ko's Field Daze, 1928 (Fleischer)
Ko-Ko's Focus, 1929 (Fleischer)
Koko's Germ Jam, 1928 (Fleischer)
Ko-Ko's Harem-Scarem, 1929 (Fleischer)
Ko-Ko's Haunted House, 1928 (Fleischer)
Ko-Ko's Hot Dog, 1928 (Fleischer)
Ko-Ko's Hot Ink, 1929 (Fleischer)
Ko-Ko's Hypnotism, 1929 (Fleischer)
Ko-Ko's Kane, 1927 (Fleischer)
Ko-Ko's Kink, 1928 (Fleischer)
Ko-Ko's Klock, 1927 (Fleischer)
Ko-Ko's Knock-down, 1929 (Fleischer)
Ko-Ko's Kozy Korner, 1928 (Fleischer)
Ko-Ko's Magic, 1928 (Fleischer)
Ko-Ko's Parade, 1928 (Fleischer)
Ko-Ko's Paradise, 1926 (Fleischer)
Ko-Ko's Quest, 1927 (Fleischer)
Ko-Ko's Reward, 1929 (Fleischer)
Ko-Ko's Saxaphonies, 1929 (Fleischer)
Ko-Ko's Signals, 1929 (Fleischer)
Ko-Ko's Tattoo, 1928 (Fleischer)
Ko-Ko's Thanksgiving, 1925 (Fleischer)
Ko-Ko's War Dogs, 1928 (Fleischer)
Kolingens galoscher, 1912 (Jaenzon; Magnusson)
Koloraturen, 1932 (Fischinger)

Laban Petterqvist tränär för Olympiska spelen, 1912 (Jaenzon)
Labbra di lurido blu, 1976 (Morricone)
Labirynt, 1962 (Lenica)
Labor Goes to School, 1951 (Cloquet)
Laboratoire de l'angoisse, 1971 (Braunberger)
Laborinto, 1966 (Storaro)
Laboureur, 1901 (Gaumont)
Labyrinth, 1967 (Lassally)
Labyrinth, 1986 (Henson)
Labyrinth. See Labirynt, 1962
Lac aux dames, 1934 (Auric; Meerson)
Lache Bajazzo, 1943 (Wagner)
Lachende Grauen, 1920 (Herlth)
Lachende Grille, 1926 (Andrejew)
Lacombe Lucien, 1973 (Cristaldi; Delli Colli)
Lacy and the Mississippi Queen, 1978 (Lourié)
Lad—A Dog, 1961 (Glennon)
Lad an 'a Lamp, 1932 (Roach)
Lad in His Lamp, 1948 (Blanc; Mckimson; Stalling)
Ladali, 1949 (Biswas)
Ladder, 1964 (Dunning)
Laddie, 1935 (Berman; Biroc; Polglase; Steiner)
Laddie, 1940 (Polglase)
Laddroga Maldita. See Opio, 1949
Ladenprinz, 1928 (Andrejew)
Ladies Club, 1986 (Schifrin)
Ladies Courageous, 1944 (Mohr; Tiomkin; Wanger)
Ladies in Love, 1936 (Mohr)
Ladies in Retirement, 1941 (Barnes; Plunkett)
Ladies Love Brutes, 1930 (Mankiewicz)
Ladies Love Danger, 1935 (Raphaelson)
Ladies' Man, 1922 (Stromberg)
Ladies' Man, 1931 (Banton; Mankiewicz; Zukor)
Ladies' Man, 1947 (Cahn; Dreier)
Ladies' Man, 1961 (Head; Pereira)
Ladies Must Eat, 1929 (Hornbeck)
Ladies Must Live, 1940 (Cahn; McCord)
Ladies Must Love, 1933 (Gaudio)
Ladies Must Play, 1930 (Walker)
Ladies of Leisure, 1930 (Cohn; Swerling; Walker)
Ladies of the Big House, 1932 (Zukor)
Ladies of the Chorus, 1948 (Louis)
Ladies of the Jury, 1932 (Steiner)
Ladies of Washington, 1944 (Basevi; Clarke)
Ladies Should Listen, 1934 (Dreier; Head)
Ladies They Talk About, 1933 (Orry-Kelly; Seitz)
Ladri di biciclette, 1948 (Amidei; Cecchi D'amico; Zavattini)
Ladro di Bagdad, 1960 (Delli Colli)
Ladron de amor, 1930 (Furthman)
Ladrone, 1979 (Morricone)
Lady, 1925 (Gaudio; Marion; Menzies; Schenck)
Lady and the Bandit, 1951 (Duning)
Lady and the Doctor. See Lady and the Monster, 1944
Lady and the Monster, 1944 (Alton)
Lady and the Mouse, 1913 (Bitzer; Loos)
Lady and the Tramp, 1955 (Disney; Iwerks)
Lady Be Careful, 1936 (Dreier; Head)
Lady Be Gay. See Laugh It Off, 1939
Lady Be Good, 1941 (Adrian; Edens; Freed; Mayer)
Lady Bodyguard, 1943 (Dreier; Head)
Lady by Choice, 1934 (Cohn; Swerling)
Lady Caroline Lamb, 1972 (Bennett; Cristaldi; Dillon; Morris)
Lady Chatterley's Lover. See Amant de Lady Chatterley, 1955
Lady Consents, 1936 (Polglase; Veiller)
Lady Craved Excitement, 1950 (Carreras)
Lady Dances. See Merry Widow, 1934

Lady Eve, 1941 (Head)
Lady Fights Back, 1937 (Krasner)
Lady for a Day, 1933 (Cohn; Goosson; Riskin; Walker)
Lady for a Night, 1941 (Plunkett)
Lady from Cheyenne, 1941 (Krasner)
Lady from Shanghai, 1948 (Cohn; Goosson; Louis)
Lady Gambles, 1949 (Metty; Orry-Kelly)
Lady Godiva, 1920 (Dreier)
Lady Godiva, 1955 (Boyle)
Lady Godiva Rides Again, 1951 (Alwyn; Korda; Rank)
Lady Hamilton. See That Hamilton Woman, 1941
Lady Hamilton, 1921 (Dreier; Hoffmann)
Lady Hamilton, 1941 (Maté; Sherriff)
Lady Has Plans, 1942 (Head; Lang)
Lady Helen's Escapade, 1909 (Bitzer)
Lady in a Cage, 1964 (Garmes; Head; Westmore Family)
Lady in a Car with Glasses and a Gun, 1970 (Renoir)
Lady in a Jam, 1942 (Mohr)
Lady in Black, 1913 (Loos)
Lady in Black. See Damen i svart, 1958
Lady in Cement, 1968 (Biroc)
Lady in Danger, 1934 (Balcon; Junge; Rank)
Lady in Love, 1930 (Adrian)
Lady in Question, 1940 (Cohn)
Lady in the Car with Glasses and a Gun, 1970 (Legrand)
Lady in the Corner, 1989 (Raksin)
Lady in the Dark, 1944 (Dreier; Goodrich and Hackett; Head; Renahan, van Heusen)
Lady in the Fog, 1952 (Carreras)
Lady in the Iron Mask, 1952 (Laszlo; Tiomkin; Wanger)
Lady in the Lake, 1947 (Ames; Gibbons; Irene; Mayer)
Lady in the Morgue, 1938 (Cortez)
Lady Is a Square, 1959 (Wilcox)
Lady Is Willing, 1934 (Walker)
Lady Is Willing, 1942 (Irene)
Lady Jane, 1986 (Slocombe)
Lady Killer, 1933 (Blanke; Gaudio)
Lady Killer of Rome. See Assassino, 1961
Lady Killers, 1916 (Roach)
Lady L, 1965 (Alekan; D'Eaubonne; Orry-Kelly; Ponti)
Lady Liberty. See Mortadella, 1971
Lady Luck, 1946 (D'Agostino)
Lady Marions sommarflirt, 1913 (Jaenzon; Magnusson)
Lady Marion's Summer Flirt. See Lady Marions sommarflirt, 1913
Lady Marion's Summer Flirtation. See Lady Marions sommarflirt, 1913
Lady Musashino. See Musashino Fujin, 1951
Lady of Burlesque, 1943 (Cahn; Head; Stromberg)
Lady of Chance, 1928 (Adrian; Booth; Daniels; Gibbons; Mayer)
Lady of Monza. See Monaca di Monza, 1969
Lady of Mystery. See A Close Call for Boston Blackie, 1946
Lady of Quality, 1923 (Mandell)
Lady of Scandal, 1930 (Adrian; Booth; Gibbons; Kräly; Miller)
Lady of the Lake, 1931 (Balcon)
Lady of the Night, 1925 (Gibbons)
Lady of the Pavements, 1929 (Berlin; Bitzer; Menzies; Schenck; Struss)
Lady of the Tropics, 1939 (Hecht; Waxman)
Lady on a Train, 1945 (Rozsa)
Lady Oscar, 1978 (Evein; Legrand)
Lady Paname, 1951 (Annenkov; D'Eaubonne; Jeanson)
Lady Pays Off, 1951 (Boyle; Daniels)
Lady Possessed, 1952 (Struss)
Lady Raffles, 1928 (Walker)
Lady Robinhood, 1925 (Berman)
Lady Rose's Daughter, 1920 (Miller)
Lady Says No!, 1951 (Howe; Orry-Kelly)
Lady Scarface, 1941 (Musuraca)

Lady Sen. *See* Sen-hime, 1954
Lady Sings the Blues, 1972 (Alonzo; Legrand)
Lady Surrenders, 1930 (Laemmle)
Lady Surrenders. *See* Love Story, 1944
Lady Takes a Chance, 1943 (Swerling)
Lady Takes a Sailor, 1949 (McCord; Steiner)
Lady to Love, 1930 (Gibbons; Howard; Kräly)
Lady Vanishes, 1938 (Reville; Vetchinsky)
Lady Vanishes, 1979 (Slocombe)
Lady Who Dared, 1931 (Gaudio)
Lady Windermere's Fan. *See* Fan, 1949
Lady with a Past, 1932 (Mohr; Steiner)
Lady with a Ribbon. *See* Ribon o musubu fujin, 1939
Lady with Red Hair, 1940 (Edeson)
Lady with the Black Gloves. *See* Dame mit den schwarzen
　　Handschuhen, 1919
Lady with the Dog. *See* Dama s sobachkoy, 1960
Lady with the Lamp, 1951 (Wilcox)
Lady with the Sunflowers. *See* Dame mit den Sonnenblumen, 1920
Ladyhawke, 1985 (Storaro)
Ladykillers, 1955 (Balcon; Heller)
Lady's from Kentucky, 1939 (Head)
Lady's Morals, 1930 (Adrian; Barnes; Booth; Freed; Gibbons; Kräly;
　　Mayer; Stothart)
Lady's Profession, 1933 (Banton)
Lafayette, 1961 (Renoir)
Lafayette Escadrille, 1958 (Clothier; Rosenman)
Laila—Liebe unter der Mitternachtssonne, 1958 (Nykvist)
Laisse aller, c'est une valse, 1970 (D'Eaubonne)
Laissez tirer les tireurs, 1964 (Delerue)
Lajawab, 1950 (Biswas)
Lajwanti, 1958 (Burman)
Lake of Illusion. *See* Maboroshi no mizuumi, 1982
Lake Placid, 1999 (Winston)
Lake Placid Serenade, 1944 (Alton)
Lakeboat, 2000 (Mamet)
Lal Kunwar, 1952 (Burman)
Lamb, 1918 (Roach)
Lambertville Story , 1949 (Kaufman)
Lambeth Walk, 1939 (Havelock-Allan)
Lamiel, 1967 (de Beauregard)
Lamjata, 1974 (Dinov)
L'Amour à l'américaine, 1931 (Braunberger)
L'Amour à mort, 1984 (Saulnier)
Lamp Post Favorites, 1948 (Fleischer)
Lamp Still Burns, 1943 (Krasker; Rank; Vetchinsky)
Lampe qui file, 1909 (Cohl)
Lancashire Luck, 1937 (Havelock-Allan)
Lancelot du Lac, 1974 (Sarde)
Lancelot of the Lake. *See* Lancelot du Lac, 1974
Lancer Spy, 1937 (Dunne)
Land before Time, 1988 (Marshall)
Land beyond the Law, 1927 (Polito)
Land of Dead Things, 1913 (Ince)
Land of Enchantment: Southwest U.S.A.. *See* Southwest, 1945
Land of Fury. *See* Seekers, 1954
Land of Jazz, 1920 (Furthman)
Land of Liberty, 1939 (MacPherson)
Land of Promise, 1945 (Alwyn)
Land of the Dead. *See* Trésor des Îles Chiennes, 1990
Land of the Incas, 1937 (Hoch)
Land of the Lawless, 1927 (Shamroy)
Land of the Midnight Fun, 1939 (Avery)
Land of the Pharaohs, 1955 (Harlan; Saulnier)
Land of the Pharoahs, 1955 (Garmes; Tiomkin; Trauner)
Land Unknown, 1957 (Westmore Family)

Land, 1941 (Crosby; van Dongen)
Landing of the Pilgrims, 1940 (Terry)
Landloper, 1918 (Gaudio)
Landlord, 1970 (Boyle; Willis)
Landlubber, 1922 (Roach)
Landru, 1962 (de Beauregard; Ponti; Rabier; Saulnier)
Landscape, 1974 (Lenica)
Landscape in the Mist. *See* Topio stin omichli, 1988
Landschaft im Nebel. *See* Topio stin omichli, 1988
Landshövdingens döttrar, 1916 (Jaenzon)
Landstrasse und Gross-stadt, 1921 (Hoffmann)
Lane Frost Story. *See* 8 Seconds, 1994
Lang ist der Weg, 1948 (Pommer)
Lång-Lasse i Delsbo, 1949 (Lundgren; Nykvist)
Language All My Own, 1935 (Fleischer)
Lansky, 1999 (Alonzo; Mamet)
Lantern. *See* Lucerna, 1925
Lapland, 1957 (Iwerks)
Lärarinna på vift, 1941 (Fischer)
Larceny, 1942 (Deutsch)
Larceny, 1947 (Orry-Kelly)
Larceny, Inc., 1942 (Gaudio; Wald; Wallis)
Larceny Lane. *See* Blonde Crazy, 1931
Lars Hård, 1948 (Lundgren)
Las Vegas Story, 1952 (Carmichael; Jarrico)
Laserman, 1990 (Dickerson; Vachon)
Lash, 1930 (Haller)
Lásky jedné pla vovlásky, 1965 (Ondříček)
Lásky Kaňenky Strnadové, 1926 (Heller)
Lass. *See* Trny a kveti, 1921
Lass from the Stormy Croft. *See* Tösen från stormyrtorpet, 1918
Lassie Come Home, 1943 (Gibbons; Mayer; Schary)
Last Act, 1916 (August)
Last Action Hero, 1993 (Goldman)
Last Alarm, 1900 (Bitzer)
Last American Virgin, 1982 (Golan and Globus)
Last Angry Man, 1959 (Duning; Howe; Louis)
Last Bohemian. *See* Poslední bohém, 1931
Last Call. *See* Last Performance, 1929
Last Chance, 1921 (Selig)
Last Command, 1928 (Biro; Clothier; Dreier; Glennon;
　　Mankiewicz; Zukor)
Last Command, 1955 (Steiner)
Last Convertible, 1979 (Houseman)
Last Curtain, 1937 (Havelock-Allan)
Last Dawn. *See* Carve Her Name with Pride, 1958
Last Days of Dolwyn, 1948 (Heller; Korda)
Last Days of Marilyn Monroe, 1985 (Bernstein)
Last Days of Pompeii, 1935 (Cooper; Dunn; O'Brien; Polglase)
Last Days of Pompeii. *See* Derniers Jours de Pompéi, 1948
Last Days, 1998 (Zimmer)
Last Deal, 1909 (Bitzer)
Last Detail, 1973 (Mandel; Towne)
Last Dive. *See* O Último Mergulho, 1992
Last Don, 1997 (van Runkle)
Last Drink of Whiskey, 1914 (Loos)
Last Drop of Water, 1911 (Bitzer)
Last Embrace, 1979 (Rozsa)
Last Emperor, 1987 (Storaro; Zimmer)
Last Express, 1938 (Cortez)
Last Flight, 1931 (Saunders)
Last Flight of Noah's Ark, 1980 (Jarre)
Last Frontier, 1932 (Canutt)
Last Frontier, 1956 (Wald)
Last Gangster, 1937 (Adrian; Daniels; Vorkapich)
Last Gangster. *See* Roger Touhy, Gangster, 1944

Lawless Nineties, 1936 (Canutt)

Lawless Range, 1935 (Canutt)

Lawless Rider, 1954 (Canutt)

Lawless Street, 1955 (Rennahan)

Lawrence of Arabia, 1962 (Jarre; Spiegel; Wilson; Young)

Lawyer Man, 1932 (Grot; Orry-Kelly)

Lazy Bones, 1925 (Marion)

Lazy Bones. *See* Hallelujah, I'm a Bum, 1933

Lazy Days, 1929 (Roach)

Lazy Little Beaver, 1947 (Terry)

Lazy River, 1968 (Dunning)

Lazy Wagon, 1956 (Wheeler)

Lazybones, 1934 (Fleischer)

Lea Lyon. *See* Lyon Lea, 1915

Leadbelly, 1976 (Boyle)

League of Gentlemen, 1960 (Rank)

League of Nations, 1924 (Fleischer)

League of Their Own, 1992 (Ondříček; Zimmer)

Lean on Me, 1989 (Conti)

Leap Frog Railway, 1905 (Bitzer)

Leap into the Void. *See* Salto nel Vuoto, 1980

Leap of Faith, 1992 (Von Brandenstein; van Runkle)

Leap Year, 1932 (Wilcox)

Leaping Love, 1929 (Roach)

Learn Polikeness, 1938 (Fleischer)

Learning to Love, 1925 (Loos; Schenck)

Learning Tree, 1969 (Guffey; Whitlock)

Lease of Life, 1954 (Balcon; Slocombe)

Leather and Nylon. *See* Soleil des voyous, 1967

Leather Burners, 1942 (Harlan)

Leather Saint, 1956 (Bumstead; Head)

Leather Stocking, 1909 (Bitzer)

Leatherface: Texas Chainsaw Massacre III, 1990 (Elfman)

Leathernecking, 1930 (Plunkett)

Leathernecks Have Landed, 1936 (Miller)

Leatherpushers, 1940 (Cortez)

Leave 'em Laughing, 1928 (Bruckman)

Leave Her to Heaven, 1945 (Newman; Shamroy; Swerling; Wheeler)

Leave It to Blondie, 1945 (Planer)

Leave It to John, 1936 (Iwerks)

Leave It to Lester, 1930 (Green)

Leave It to Me, 1920 (Furthman)

Leave It to Me, 1922 (Roach)

Leave Well Enough Alone, 1939 (Fleischer)

Leben unserer Präsidenten, 1951 (Eisler)

Leben Wilhelm Piecks. *See* Leben unserer Präsidenten, 1951

Lebenshunger, 1922 (Wagner)

Lebenskünstler, 1925 (Junge)

Leberfleck (The Freckle), 1948 (Von Dassanowsky)

Lecon de boxe comique, 1907 (Gaumont)

Leçon de musique, 1971 (Braunberger)

Lecteur distrait, 1907 (Gaumont)

Lecture on Man, 1961 (Williams)

Leda. *See* A double tour, 1959

Leda. *See* Plein soleil, 1959

Left Hand of God, 1955 (Lemaire; Planer; Spencer; Wheeler; Young)

Left-handed Woman. *See* Linkshändige Frau, 1977

Left Hander, 1964 (Ivanov-Vano)

Left Right and Center, 1961 (Hambling)

Legacy, 1979 (Littleton; Vinton)

Legacy of the 500,000. *See* Goju man-nin no isan, 1963

Legacy of the Hollywood Blacklist, 1987 (Jarrico)

Legal Eagles, 1986 (Bernstein; Edlund; Kovacs)

Legend, 1985 (Goldsmith)

Legend, 1995 (Goldsmith)

Legend of 1900. *See* Leggenda del pianista sull'oceano, 1998

Legend of a Cruel Giant, 1968 (Ivanov-Vano)

Legend of Bagger Vance, 2000 (Ballhaus)

Legend of Billie Jean, 1985 (Bernstein)

Legend of Frenchie King. *See* Pétroleuses, 1971

Legend of Hollywood, 1924 (Struss)

Legend of Jimmy Blue Eyes, 1964 (Alonzo)

Legend of Lobo, 1962 (Disney)

Legend of Lylah Clare, 1968 (Biroc)

Legend of the Boy and the Eagle, 1967 (Fields)

Legend of the Lone Ranger, 1981 (Barry; Fraker; Kovacs)

Legend of the Lost, 1957 (Cardiff; Hecht)

Legend of the Seven Golden Vampires, 1974 (Bernard)

Legend of the Werewolf, 1975 (Francis)

Légende de Polichinelle, 1907 (Pathé)

Légende des phares, 1909 (Gaumont)

Leggenda del pianista sull'oceano, 1998 (Morricone)

Leggenda di Faust, 1948 (Annenkov; Herlth)

Leghorn Blows at Midnight, 1950 (Blanc; McKimson; Stalling)

Leghorn Swoggled, 1951 (Blanc; McKimson)

Legion of the Condemned, 1928 (Saunders; Zukor)

Légion sauté sur Kolwezi, 1979 (Coutard; de Beauregard)

Legionnaires in Paris, 1927 (Plunkett)

Légions d'honneur, 1938 (D'Eaubonne; Matras; Renoir)

Leibgardist, 1925 (Metzner)

Leidensweg der Inge Krafft, 1921 (Von Harbou)

Leise flehen meine Lieder, 1933 (Planer; Reisch)

Lek på regnbågen, 1957 (Fischer)

Lekce Faust, 1994 (švankmajer)

Lektro, 1927 (Moskvin)

Lelakek Tatut, 1992 (Golan and Globus)

Lelíček ve službách Sherlocka Holmese, 1932 (Stallich)

Lelichek in Sherlock Holme's Service. *See* Lelíček ve službách Sherlocka Holmese, 1932

Lemmy pour les dames, 1962 (Kosma)

Lemon Drop Kid, 1951 (Head; Pereira; Young)

Lemon Popsicle. *See* Eskimo Limon, 1977

Lemon Popsicle IV. *See* Sapiches, 1982

Lemon Popsicle V. *See* Roman Zair, 1983

Lemon Popsicle VI. *See* Eskimo Ohgen, 1985

Lemon Sisters, 1990 (Von Brandenstein)

Lemonade Joe. *See* Limonádový Joe, 1964

Lena and the Geese, 1912 (Bitzer)

Lend Me Your Name, 1918 (Gaudio)

Length of a Star. *See* De Lengte van een Ster, 1964

Leo the Last, 1969 (Winkler)

Léon Morin, prêtre, 1963 (Decaë)

Leonard Part 6, 1987 (Bernstein; Edlund; Hambling)

Leonardo da Vinci, 1952 (Kaufman)

Leonardo da Vinci, 1985 (Halas and Batchelor)

Leonardo's Diary. *See* Leonarduv deník, 1972

Leonardo's Dream, 1989 (Trumbull)

Leonarduv deník, 1972 (švankmajer)

Léonce, 1913 (Gaumont)

Leonor, 1975 (Carrière; Morricone)

Leopard. *See* **Gattopardo**, 1963

Leopard Man, 1943 (D'Agostino; Lewton)

Léopold le bienaimé, 1933 (Douy)

Lepke, 1974 (Golan and Globus)

Leprosy. *See* Trad, 1971

Lermontov, 1941 (Prokofiev)

Less than Kin, 1918 (Buckland)

Less Than Zero, 1987 (Newman)

Lesser Evil, 1912 (Bitzer)

Lesson in Love. *See* En lektion i kärlek, 1954

Lesson in Mechanics, 1914 (Loos)

Lesson of Life. *See* Urok zhizni, 1955
Lessons for Wives. *See* French Dressing, 1927
Lessons in Love, 1921 (Schenck)
Let 'er Buck, 1925 (Miller)
Let 'Er Go Gallagher, 1928 (Adrian; Goosson)
Let Freedom Ring, 1939 (Hecht; Kahn)
Let George Do It, 1940 (Balcon; Neame)
Let It Be Me, 1995 (Ondříček)
Let It Bleed, 1971 (Halas and Batchelor)
Let It Ride, 1989 (Allen)
Let Joy Reign Supreme. *See* Que la fête commence, 1975
Let Me Call You Sweetheart, 1932 (Fleischer)
Let My People Go, 1961 (Lassally)
Let No Man Write My Epitaph, 1960 (Duning; Guffey)
Let Them Live!, 1937 (Raksin)
Let Us Be Gay, 1930 (Adrian; Gibbons; Marion; Mayer; Shearer)
Let Us Live, 1939 (Ballard; Veiller)
Let Women Alone, 1925 (Walker)
Léto, 1949 (Stallich)
Let's All Sing Like the Birdies Sing, 1934 (Fleischer)
Let's Be Famous, 1939 (Balcon; Neame)
Let's Build, 1923 (Roach)
Let's Celebrake, 1938 (Fleischer)
Let's Dance, 1950 (Barnes; Dreier; Head; Pan)
Let's Do Things, 1931 (Roach)
Let's Eat, 1932 (Lantz)
Let's Face It, 1943 (Cahn; Head)
Let's Get a Divorce, 1918 (Loos)
Let's Get Married, 1926 (Cronjager)
Let's Get Married, 1960 (Adam; Broccoli; Rank)
Let's Get Movin', 1936 (Fleischer)
Let's Go, 1918 (Roach)
Let's Go Hunting in the Woods. *See* Do lesíčka na čekanou, 1966
Let's Go Latin, 1947 (Fleischer)
Let's Go Native, 1930 (Banton)
Let's Go to the Movies, 1948 (Foreman)
Let's Hope It's a Girl. *See* Speriamo che sia femmina, 1986
Let's Live a Little, 1948 (Laszlo; Westmore Family)
Let's Live Tonight, 1935 (Walker)
Let's Make a Million, 1937 (Struss; Head)
Let's Make It Legal, 1951 (Ballard; Diamond; Lemaire)
Let's Make Love, 1960 (Cahn; Cole; Jeakins; Krasna; Wald; van Heusen)
Let's Make Music, 1940 (Mercer; Polglase)
Let's Make Up. *See* Lilacs in the Spring, 1954
Let's Sing a College Song, 1947 (Fleischer)
Let's Sing a Love Song, 1948 (Fleischer)
Let's Sing a Western Song, 1947 (Fleischer)
Let's Sing Again, 1936 (Carré; Kahn)
Let's Talk It Over, 1934 (Schary)
Let's Try Again, 1934 (Steiner)
Let's You and Him Fight, 1934 (Fleischer)
Letter, 1940 (Friedhofer; Gaudio; Koch; Orry-Kelly; Steiner; Wallis)
Letter. *See* A Carta, 1999
Letter for Evie, 1946 (Freund)
Letter from a Dead Woman. *See* Brief einer Toten, 1917
Letter from an Unknown Woman, 1948 (Banton; Houseman; Koch; Planer)
Letter from Siberia, 1982 (Vierny)
Letter M. *See* Slóvce M, 1964
Letter Never Sent. *See* Neotpravlennoye pismo, 1959
Letter to My Killer, 1995 (Daring)
Letter to Three Wives, 1949 (Lemaire; Miller; Newman; Wheeler; Zanuck)
Letter to Three Wives, 1985 (Mandel)
Lettere di condannati a morte della resistenza italiana, 1953 (Zavattini)
Lettere di una novizia, 1960 (Ponti)

Letters from a Killer, 1998 (Alonzo)
Letti selvaggi, 1978 (Guerra)
Letto. *See* Secrets d'alcove, 1954
Lettre de Sibérie, 1957 (Delerue)
Lettre pour vous, 1955 (Braunberger)
Lettres d'amour, 1942 (Aurenche and Bost)
Letty Lyndon, 1932 (Stromberg)
Letyat zhuravli, 1957 (Urusevsky)
Letzte Einquartierung. *See* Küssen ist keine Sünd, 1926
Letzte Erbe von Lassa, 1918 (Kolowrat-Krakowsky)
Letzte Fort, 1928 (Wagner)
Letzte Kompagnie, 1930 (Andrejew)
Letzte Mann, 1924 (Freund; Herlth; Mayer; Pommer; Röhrig)
Letzte Mann, 1955 (Herlth)
Letzte Sommer, 1954 (Herlth)
Letzte Sommer-Wenn Du nicht willst, 1998 (Cecchi D'amico)
Letzte Tag, 1913 (Warm)
Letzte Zeuge, 1919 (Dreier)
Letzten Menschen, 1919 (Freund)
Letzten werden die Ersten sein, 1957 (Herlth)
Leur dernière nuit, 1953 (Barsacq)
Lev a krotitel, 1953 (Stallich)
Levi, oggi, domani, 1963 (Rotunno)
Leviathan, 1989 (Goldsmith; Winston)
Levitation, 1997 (Rosenman)
Levy et Cie, 1930 (Douy)
Leya Lifshits, 1917 (Starewicz)
Leyenda de Balthasar el Castrado, 1995 (de Almeida)
Lianbron, 1965 (Nykvist)
Lianna, 1983 (Daring)
Liar Liar, 1997 (Boyd)
Libel, 1959 (Krasker; de Grunwald)
Libeled Lady, 1935 (Mayer)
Libera amore mio, 1973 (Morricone)
Libération de Paris, 1944 (Aurenche and Bost)
Liberation of L.B. Jones, 1970 (Bernstein; Surtees)
Liberté, 1937 (Honegger)
Liberté en croupe, 1970 (Coutard; Sarde)
Liberté surveillef. *See* V. Proudech, 1957
Libre de ne pas l'être, 1969 (Braunberger)
Licence to Kill, 1989 (Broccoli)
Licensed to Kill, 1965 (Cahn; Van Heusen)
Licht und der Mensch, 1955 (Auric)
Licht und Finsternis, 1917 (Kolowrat-Krakowsky)
Lichtkonzert Nr 1. *See* Komposition in Blau, 1935
Lichtkonzert Nr 2, 1935 (Fischinger)
Lickety Splat, 1961 (Blanc; Jones)
Licking the Raspberry. *See* Lelakek Tatut, 1992
Lidé z maringotek, 1966 (Stallich)
Lidé za kamerou, 1961 (Brdečka)
Lie. *See* No Man of Her Own, 1950
Lie of Nina Petrovna. *See* Mensonge de Nina Petrowna, 1937
Liebe, 1926 (Warm)
Liebe der Brüder Rott, 1929 (Andrejew; Planer)
Liebe der Jeanne Ney, 1927 (Hunte; Wagner; Warm)
Liebe im Rausch. *See* Colonialskandal, 1927
Liebe in Deutschland, 1983 (Legrand)
Liebe macht blind, 1925 (Pommer)
Liebe und Telephon. *See* Fräulein vom Amt, 1925
Liebe, Tod, und Teufel, 1934 (Wagner)
Liebelei, 1933 (Planer)
Liebesbrief der Königin, 1916 (Messter)
Liebesbriefe der Baronin von S. , 1924 (Galeen)
Liebesfeuer, 1925 (Courant)
Liebesgeschichte, 1943 (Röhrig)
Liebesgeschichte, 1954 (Pommer)

Liebesgeschichten. *See* Mädels von heute, 1925

Liebesglück einer Blinden, 1909 (Messter)

Liebeshandel, 1926 (Junge; Wagner)

Liebeskommando, 1931 (Andrejew)

Liebespiele im Schnee, 1967 (Siodmak)

Liebesspiel, 1931 (Fischinger)

Liebesspiele im Schnee, 1967 (Stallich)

Liebeswalzer, 1930 (Pommer)

Liebling der Frauen, 1911 (Freund)

Liebling der Frauen, 1921 (Hoffmann)

Liebschaftenden des Hektor Dalmore, 1921 (Dreier)

Lied der Mutter, 1918 (Hoffmann)

Lied der Ströme, 1954 (Shostakovich)

Lied einer Nacht, 1932 (Wagner)

Lied für Dich, 1933 (Kaper)

Lied ist aus, 1930 (Reisch)

Lied vom Leben, 1930 (Eisler)

Lied von der Glocke, 1907 (Freund)

Liens de sang, 1978 (Rabier)

Lieu du crime, 1986 (Sarde)

Lieut. Danny, U.S.A., 1916 (Ince)

Lieutenant Kizhe. *See* Poruchik Kizhe, 1934

Lieutenant Smith, 1943 (Vorkapich)

Lieutenant Wore Skirts, 1956 (Lemaire; Wheeler)

Lieutenant's Last Fight, 1912 (Ince)

Life, 1999 (Baker)

Life and Adventures of Nicholas Nickleby. *See* Nicholas Nickleby, 1947

Life and Death of 9413—A Hollywood Extra. *See* Life and Death of a Hollywood Extra, 1927

Life and Death of a Hollywood Extra, 1927 (Vorkapich)

Life and Death of Colonel Blimp, 1943 (Cardiff; Junge; Périnal; Rank; Unsworth)

Life and Times of Judge Roy Bean, 1972 (Head; Jarre)

Life at the Top, 1965 (Addinsell; Morris)

Life Begins Again, 1942 (Alwyn)

Life Begins at 40, 1935 (Trotti)

Life Begins at Eight-Thirty, 1942 (Cronjager; Day; Johnson; Leven; Newman)

Life Begins with Love, 1937 (Ballard)

Life Continues. *See* A život jde dál, 1935

Life for Ruth, 1962 (Alwyn; Heller; Rank; Vetchinsky)

Life Hesitates at Forty, 1935 (Roach)

Life in the Balance, 1954 (Horner)

Life in the Citadel. *See* Zhizn v tsitadel, 1947

Life in the Country. *See* Livet på landet, 1924

Life in the Theater, 1979 (Mamet)

Life in the Theater, 1993 (Francis; Mamet)

Life Insurance Training Film, 1975 (Halas and Batchelor)

Life Is a Bed of Roses. *See* Vie est un roman, 1983

Life is Beautiful. *See* Vita è bella, 1997

Life Line, 1919 (Carré)

Life, Love, Death. *See* Vie, l'amour, la mort, 1969

Life of a Horse Dealer. *See* Bakuro ichidai, 1951

Life of an Actor. *See* Geidou ichidai otoko, 1941

Life of Brian, 1979 (Biziou)

Life of Emile Zola, 1937 (Blanke; Friedhofer; Gaudio; Grot; Steiner; Wallis; Warner; Westmore Family)

Life of Her Own, 1950 (Kaper; Mayer; Pan; Rose)

Life of Jimmy Dolan, 1933 (Edeson; Orry-Kelly)

Life of Oharu. *See* **Saikaku ichidai onna**, 1952

Life of Reckless Matsu. *See* Muhoumatsu no issho, 1943

Life of Riley, 1949 (Daniels)

Life of the Dragonfly. *See* Zhichiye vazki, 1909

Life of the Party, 1920 (Brown)

Life of the Party, 1930 (Zanuck)

Life of Vergie Winters, 1934 (Berman; Plunkett; Steiner)

Life on the Mississippi, 1980 (Lassally)

Life on Wheels. *See* Lidé z maringotek, 1966

Life Size. *See* Grandeur nature, 1973

Life with Father, 1947 (Steiner; Stewart; Warner)

Life with Feathers, 1945 (Blanc; Stalling)

Life with Fido, 1942 (Terry)

Life with Henry, 1941 (Head)

Life With Loopy, 1960 (Hanna and Barbera)

Life with Mikey, 1993 (Menken)

Life with the Lyons, 1954 (Carreras)

Life with Tom, 1953 (Hanna and Barbera)

Lifeboat, 1944 (Basevi; Friedhofer; MacGowan; Spencer; Swerling; Zanuck)

Lifeforce, 1985 (Dykstra; Golan and Globus; Mancini)

Lifestyle, 1999 (Schamus)

Lifetime. *See* Toure une vie, 1974

Lifting the Lid, 1905 (Bitzer)

Liga de las muchachas, 1949 (Alcoriza)

Ligabue, 1978 (Zavattini)

Lighea, 1983 (Cecchi D'amico)

Light and Darkness. *See* Licht und Finsternis, 1917

Light at Heart. *See* Life Begins at Eight-Thirty, 1942

Light at the Edge of the World. *See* Luz del fin del mundo, 1971

Light in Nature, 1960 (Hoch)

Light in the Dark, 1922 (Carré)

Light in the Forest, 1958 (Disney; Ellenshaw)

Light in the Piazza, 1962 (Epstein; Freed; Heller)

Light Keeps Me Company. *See* Ljuset haller mig sallskap, 2000

Light of Day, 1987 (Newman)

Light of Heart. *See* Life Begins at Eight-Thirty, 1942

Light of the World, 1989 (Halas and Batchelor)

Light of Western Stars, 1930 (Lang)

Light of Western Stars, 1940 (Harlan; Head)

Light Showers, 1922 (Roach)

Light, Strong and Beautiful, 1971 (Bernstein)

Light That Came, 1909 (Bitzer)

Light That Failed, 1923 (Clarke)

Light That Failed, 1939 (Canutt; Dreier; Head; Young)

Light Touch, 1951 (Berman; Rose; Rozsa; Surtees)

Light Touch. *See* Touch and Go, 1955

Light Woman, 1928 (Balcon)

Lighter Than Hare, 1960 (Blanc)

Lighter That Failed, 1927 (Roach)

Lighthouse, 1906 (Bitzer)

Lighthouse by the Sea, 1924 (Garmes; Zanuck)

Lighthouse Keeper, 1911 (Gaudio)

Lighthouse Mouse, 1955 (Blanc; McKimson)

Lighting Bryce, 1919 (Canutt; Glennon)

Lightnin', 1925 (August; Marion)

Lightnin', 1930 (Levien)

Lightning Conductor, 1938 (Havelock-Allan)

Lightning Conductor, 1962 (Dinov)

Lightning Lariat, 1927 (Plunkett)

Lightning Lariats, 1927 (Musuraca)

Lightning Rider, 1924 (Polito; Stromberg)

Lightning Strikes Twice, 1934 (Cronjager; Plunkett)

Lightning Strikes Twice, 1951 (Blanke; Steiner)

Lightning—The White Stallion, 1986 (Golan and Globus)

Lightning Warrior, 1931 (Canutt)

Light's Diamond Jubilee, 1954 (Hecht)

Lights Fantastic, 1942 (Blanc; Stalling)

Lights of a Great City, 1906 (Selig)

Lights of London, (undated) (Barker)

Lights of New York, 1928 (Warner)

Lights of Old Broadway, 1925 (Carré)

Lights Out, 1942 (Terry)

Little Eygpt, 1951 (Metty)

Little Foxes, 1941 (Goldwyn; Goosson; Horner; Mandell; Orry-Kelly; Toland)

Little French Girl, 1925 (Banton; Rosson)

Little Friend, 1934 (Balcon; Junge; Rank)

Little Giant, 1933 (Orry-Kelly)

Little Giant, 1946 (Jarrico)

Little Giants, 1994 (Kaminski)

Little Girl in Blue Velvet. *See* Petite Fille en velour bleu, 1978

Little Girl Lost, 1988 (Lathrop)

Little Girl, Don't Say No!. *See* Devčátko, neříkej ne!, 1932

Little Gold Bird. *See* Zlaté ptáče, 1932

Little Guardian Angel, 1956 (Dinov)

Little Humpbacked Horse, 1947 (Ivanov-Vano)

Little Irish Girl, 1926 (Zanuck)

Little Island, 1958 (Williams)

Little Island, 1969 (Kuri)

Little Johnny Jet, 1953 (Avery)

Little Journey, 1927 (Gibbons)

Little Kidnappers. *See* Kidnappers, 1953

Little Lambkin, 1940 (Fleischer)

Little Lamby, 1937 (Fleischer)

Little Liar, 1916 (Loos)

Little Liar. *See* Fetita mincinoasa, 1953

Little Lion Hunter, 1939 (Jones)

Little Lord. *See* A kis lord, 1918

Little Lord Fauntleroy, 1921 (Goosson; Rosher)

Little Lord Fauntleroy, 1936 (Miller; Rosher; Selznick; Steiner)

Little Malcolm, 1974 (Alcott)

Little Man, 1941 (Musuraca)

Little Man, What Now?, 1934 (Laemmle)

Little Mermaid, 1989 (Menken)

Little Minister, 1934 (Berman; Plunkett; Polglase; Steiner)

Little Miss Broadway, 1938 (Miller; Zanuck)

Little Miss Jazz, 1920 (Roach)

Little Miss Marker, 1934 (Head)

Little Miss Marker, 1980 (Bernstein; Lathrop; Mancini)

Little Miss Muffet. *See* Mother Goose Presents Humpty Dumpty, 1946

Little Miss Nobody, 1936 (Glennon)

Little Mister Jim, 1946 (Irene)

Little Mother, 1929 (Roach)

Little Murders, 1971 (Willis)

Little Murmurs, 1966 (Kuri)

Little Nellie Kelly, 1940 (Freed; Mayer)

Little Nell's Tobacco, 1910 (Ince)

Little Nelly Kelly, 1940 (Edens)

Little Nemo, 1909 (McCay)

Little Nikita, 1988 (Hamlisch; Kovacs)

Little Nobody, 1935 (Fleischer)

Little Nuns. *See* Monachine, 1963

Little Old New York, 1940 (Day; Newman; Shamroy; Zanuck)

Little Orphan, 1949 (Hanna and Barbera)

Little Orphan, 1957 (Hanna and Barbera)

Little Orphan Airedale, 1947 (Blanc; Jones; Stalling)

Little Orphan Annie, 1932 (Steiner)

Little Orphan Annie, 1938 (Head)

Little Orphan Willie, 1931 (Iwerks)

Little Papa, 1935 (Roach)

Little Phantasy, 1946 (Mclaren)

Little Prince, 1974 (Barry; Challis)

Little Prince, 1979 (Vinton)

Little Princess, 1917 (Marion; Rosher)

Little Princess, 1939 (Day; Miller; Zanuck)

Little Problems, 1951 (Terry)

Little Quacker, 1950 (Hanna and Barbera)

Little Red Hen, 1934 (Iwerks)

Little Red Hen, 1955 (Terry)

Little Red Riding Hood, 1922 (Disney)

Little Red Riding Hood, 1925 (Lantz)

Little Red Riding Rabbit, 1944 (Blanc; Stalling)

Little Red Rodent Hood, 1952 (Blanc; Stalling)

Little Red Walking Hood, 1937 (Avery; Stalling)

Little Romance, 1979 (Bumstead; Delerue; Reynolds)

Little Runaway, 1952 (Hanna and Barbera)

Little Runaway. *See* Chiisana tobosha, 1967

Little Rural Riding Hood, 1949 (Avery)

Little Sacha, Jockey. *See* Sachka nayezdnik, 1917

Little Savage, 1929 (Miller; Plunkett)

Little Savage, 1959 (Haskin)

Little School Mouse, 1954 (Hanna and Barbera)

Little Sex, 1982 (Delerue; Von Brandenstein)

Little Sheba, 1953 (Pereira)

Little Shepherd of Kingdom Come, 1928 (Garmes)

Little Shepherd of Kingdom Come, 1960 (Crosby)

Little Shop of Horrors, 1986 (Menken)

Little Sinner, 1935 (Roach)

Little Soap and Water, 1935 (Fleischer)

Little Stranger, 1936 (Fleischer)

Little Swee' Pea, 1936 (Fleischer)

Little Sweetheart, 1988 (Schifrin)

Little Teacher, 1909 (Bitzer)

Little Teachers. *See* I Piccoli maestri, 1998

Little Tease, 1913 (Bitzer)

Little Theatre of Jean Renoir. *See* Petit Théâtre de Jean Renoir, 1970

Little Tinker, 1947 (Avery)

Little Tinker. *See* Dráteníček, 1920

Little Tokyo, U.S.A., 1942 (Day)

Little Turncoat, 1913 (Ince)

Little Vegas, 1990 (Daring)

Little Window. *See* Okénko, 1933

Little Women, 1933 (Cooper; MacGowan; Plunkett; Polglase; Selznick; Steiner)

Little Women, 1948 (Plunkett)

Little Women, 1949 (Deutsch; Gibbons; Jenkins; Mayer)

Little Women, 1994 (Newman)

Little-Big-Cosmos. *See* Mikromakrokosmos, 1960

Littlest Outlaw, 1954 (Disney)

Littlest Rebel, 1935 (Seitz)

Liv, 1998 (Ponti; Preisner)

Liv Ullmann scener fra et liv, 1997 (Nykvist)

Live a Little, Love a Little, 1968 (Ames)

Live and Learn, 1920 (Roach)

Live and Let Die, 1973 (Baker; Broccoli)

Live and Let Live. *See* Spy for a Day, 1940

Live Fast, Die Young, 1958 (Lathrop)

Live for Life. *See* Vivre pour vivre, 1967

Live Ghost, 1934 (Roach)

Live, Love, and Learn, 1937 (Brackett)

Live Now, Pay Later, 1962 (Fisher)

Live to Love. *See* Devil's Hand, 1961

Live Today for Tomorrow. *See* Act of Murder, 1948

Live Wires, 1923 (Roach)

Lives of a Bengal Lancer, 1935 (Banton; Dreier; Edouart; Head; Lang; Zukor)

Lives of Bad Names. *See* Akumyo ichidai, 1967

Lives of Jenny Dolan, 1975 (Ames; Hunter)

Livet i Finnskogarna, 1947 (Lundgren)

Livet på landet, 1924 (Jaenzon)

Livets konflikter, 1913 (Jaenzon)

Living. *See* **Ikiru**, 1952

Living between Two Worlds, 1963 (Zsigmond)

Living Blackboard. *See* Cauche-mar du Fantoche, 1908

Living City, 1955 (Wexler)
Living Corpse. *See* Zhivoi trup, 1928
Living Daylights, 1987 (Barry; Broccoli)
Living Dead Man. *See* **Feu Mathias Pascal**, 1925
Living Desert, 1953 (Iwerks)
Living Free, 1971 (Foreman)
Living in a Big Way, 1947 (Berman; Irene; Rosson)
Living It Up, 1954 (Head)
Living Mummy. *See* Den levande mumien, 1916
Living on Love, 1937 (Musuraca; Polglase)
Living on Velvet, 1935 (Epstein; Orry-Kelly; Wald)
Living Portrait. *See* Ikiteiru gazo, 1948
Livre de cristal, 1994 (Branco)
Liza. *See* Cagna, 1972
Liza and Her Double. *See* I Liza kai i alli, 1961
Lizards. *See* I basilischi, 1963
Lizzie, 1957 (Bacharach)
Ljuset från Lund, 1955 (Lundgren)
Ljuset haller mig sallskap, 2000 (Nykvist)
Llano Kid, 1939 (Harlan; Head; Young)
Llanto de la tortuga, 1974 (Figueroa)
Llevame en tus brazos, 1953 (Figueroa)
Lloyds of London, 1936 (Glennon; MacGowan; Zanuck)
LMNO, 1978 (Breer)
Loaded Door, 1922 (Polito)
Loan Shark, 1952 (Biroc)
Local Boy Makes Good, 1931 (Polito)
Local Hero, 1983 (Menges; Puttnam)
Locataire, 1976 (Nykvist; Sarde)
Locataires d'à côté, 1909 (Cohl)
Lock Up, 1989 (Conti)
Lock Your Doors. *See* Ape Man, 1943
Locked Door, 1929 (Menzies; Sullivan)
Locket, 1946 (D'Agostino; Musuraca)
Lockfågeln, 1971 (Lundgren)
Loco Boy Makes Good, 1941 (Bruckman)
Locus, 1963 (Kuri)
Locusts, 1997 (Burwell)
Lodge Night, 1923 (Roach)
Lodger, 1944 (Ballard; Dasevi; Friedhofer)
Lodger: A Story of the London Fog, 1926 (Balcon)
Lodging for the Night, 1912 (Bitzer)
Loffe blir polis, 1950 (Nykvist)
Log Rollers, 1953 (Terry)
Logan's Run, 1976 (Goldsmith; Laszlo)
Lohengrin, 1907 (Messter)
Loi . . . c'est la loi, 1958 (Age and Scarpelli; Cristaldi; Di Venanzo; Mnouchkine; Rota)
Loi du coeur, 1970 (Nuytten)
Loi du nord, 1942 (D'Eaubonne)
Loi du pardon, 1906 (Pathé)
Loi du printemps, 1942 (Matras)
Loin de Manhattan, 1980 (Branco)
Loin du Viêt-nam, 1967 (Cloquet)
Löjen och tårar, 1913 (Jaenzon; Magnusson)
Löjtnantshjärtan, 1941 (Jaenzon)
Lola and Bilidikid, 1999 (Schamus)
Lola and Billy the Kid. *See* Lola and Bilidikid, 1999
Lola Montès, 1955 (Annenkov; Auric; D'Eaubonne; Matras)
Lola Triana, 1936 (Clothier)
Lola, 1961 (Coutard; Evein; Legrand; Ponti; de Beauregard)
Lola. *See* **Lola Montès**, 1955
Lola. *See* Twinky, 1969
Lolita, 1962 (Morris)
Lolita, 1997 (Morricone)
Lolly Madonna War. *See* Lolly-Madonna XXX, 1973

Lolly-Madonna XXX, 1973 (Lathrop)
Lomelin, 1965 (Braunberger)
London, 1926 (Wilcox)
London after Midnight, 1927 (Gibbons; Gillespie; Mayer)
London Belongs to Me. *See* Dulcimer Street, 1948
London Black-Out Murders, 1942 (Siodmak)
London Bobby, 1920 (Roach)
London by Night, 1913 (Barker)
London Kills Me, 1991 (Kureishi)
London Melody, 1937 (Wilcox)
London Town, 1946 (Orry-Kelly; Rank)
London University, 1961 (Lassally)
Londra chiama Polo Nord, 1957 (Rota)
Lone Hand, 1922 (Miller)
Lone Ranger, 1938 (Canutt)
Lone Ranger Rides Again, 1939 (Canutt)
Lone Rider, 1930 (McCord)
Lone Star, 1951 (Chase; Rosson)
Lone Star, 1996 (Daring)
Lone Star Ranger, 1930 (Miller)
Lone Star Ranger, 1942 (Day)
Lone Stranger and Porky, 1939 (Blanc; Clampett; Stalling)
Lone Wolf in Paris, 1938 (Ballard)
Lone Wolf Strikes, 1940 (Trumbo)
Lone World Sail, 1960 (Halas and Batchelor)
Lonedale Operator, 1911 (Bitzer)
Loneliness of the Long Distance Runner, 1962 (Lassally)
Loneliness of the Long Distance Singer. *See* Solitude du chanteur de fond, 1974
Lonely Are the Brave, 1962 (Goldsmith; Lathrop; Trumbo; Westmore Family)
Lonely Guy, 1984 (Goldsmith; Reynolds; Whitlock)
Lonely Man, 1957 (Head; Pereira)
Lonely Passion of Judith Hearne, 1987 (Delerue)
Lonely Road, 1936 (Dean; Stallich)
Lonely Trail, 1936 (Canutt)
Lonely Villa, 1909 (Bitzer)
Lonely Wife. *See* **Charulata**, 1964
Lonelyhearts, 1959 (Alton; Schary)
Lonesome, 1928 (Laemmle)
Lonesome Junction, 1908 (Bitzer)
Lonesome Ladies, 1927 (Polito)
Lonesome Lenny, 1946 (Avery)
Lonesome Luke, 1914 (Roach)
Lonesome Luke from London to Laramie, 1917 (Roach)
Lonesome Luke Loses Patients, 1917 (Roach)
Lonesome Luke on Tin Can Alley, 1917 (Roach)
Lonesome Luke, Circus King, 1916 (Roach)
Lonesome Luke—Lawyer, 1917 (Roach)
Lonesome Luke—Mechanic, 1917 (Roach)
Lonesome Luke—Messenger, 1917 (Roach)
Lonesome Luke—Plumber, 1917 (Roach)
Lonesome Luke's Honeymoon, 1917 (Roach)
Lonesome Luke's Lively Life, 1917 (Roach)
Lonesome Luke's Lively Rifle, 1917 (Roach)
Lonesome Luke's Wild Women, 1917 (Roach)
Lonesome Mouse, 1943 (Hanna and Barbera)
Lonesome Trail, 1930 (Canutt)
Long Absence. *See* Aussi Longue Absence, 1961
Long Arm, 1956 (Balcon; Rank)
Long Blue Road. *See* Grande strada azzurra, 1957
Long Chance, 1922 (Daniels)
Long Dark Hall, 1951 (Johnson)
Long Day's Journey into Night, 1962 (Justin; Kaufman; Previn; Rosenblum; Sylbert)
Long des trottoirs, 1956 (D'Eaubonne; Kosma)

Long Duel, 1967 (Vetchinsky)
Long Goodbye, 1973 (Brackett; Mercer; Williams; Zsigmond)
Long Gray Line, 1954 (Duning)
Long Gray Line, 1955 (Cohn; Wald)
Long Hot Summer, 1958 (Cahn; La Shelle; Lemaire; North; Wald; Wheeler)
Long John Silver, 1954 (Haskin)
Long Knife, 1958 (Rank)
Long Live the King, 1923 (Sullivan)
Long Live the King, 1926 (Roach)
Long Lives the Deceased. *See* At žije nebožtik, 1935
Long Lost Father, 1934 (MacGowan; Musuraca; Plunkett; Polglase; Steiner)
Long Memory, 1952 (Alwyn; Rank; Vetchinsky)
Long Night, 1947 (D'Agostino; Hakim; Lourié; Polito; Tiomkin)
Long Pants, 1926 (Roach)
Long Portage, 1913 (Ince)
Long Road, 1911 (Bitzer)
Long Rope, 1961 (Alonzo)
Long Shadow, 1992 (Zsigmond)
Long Ships, 1963 (Adam; Cardiff; Challis)
Long Silence, 1994 (Morricone)
Long Voyage Home, 1940 (Basevi; Cooper; Nichols; Parrish; Toland; Wanger)
Long Wait, 1954 (Leven; Planer)
Long, Long Trailer, 1954 (Berman; Deutsch; Goodrich and Hackett; Rose; Surtees)
Long-Haired Hare, 1949 (Blanc; Jones; Stalling)
Longe da Vista, 1998 (Branco)
Longe Daqui, 1994 (Branco)
Longest Day, 1962 (Barsacq; Jarre; Korda; Zanuck)
Longest Hundred Miles, 1967 (Waxman)
Longest Yard, 1974 (Biroc)
Longshot, 1985 (Müller)
Longue Nuit, 1965 (Braunberger)
Look at Liv, 1977 (Nykvist)
Look Back in Anger, 1959 (Morris)
Look Out! *See* Pozor!, 1959
Look Out Below, 1918 (Roach)
Look Pleasant Please, 1918 (Roach)
Look Up and Laugh , 1935 (Dean)
Look What's Happened to Rosemary's Baby, 1976 (O'Steen)
Look Who's Laughing, 1941 (Polglase)
Look Who's Talking Too, 1990 (Walas)
Look Your Best, 1923 (Gibbons)
Lookin' to Get Out, 1982 (Mandel; Wexler)
Looking at the Bright Side, 1932 (Dean)
Looking for His Murderer. *See* Mann, der seinen Mörder sucht, 1931
Looking for Love, 1964 (Cahn; Krasner)
Looking for Mr. Goodbar, 1977 (Fraker)
Looking for Sally, 1925 (Roach)
Looking for Trouble, 1920 (Roach)
Looking for Trouble, 1934 (Day; Newman; Zanuck)
Looking Forward, 1933 (Adrian)
Looks and Smiles, 1981 (Menges)
Loophole, 1980 (Schifrin)
Looping, 1981 (Ballhaus)
Looping the Loop, 1928 (Herlth; Hoffmann; Röhrig)
Loops, 1939-41 (McClaren)
Loopy's Hare-Do, 1961 (Hanna and Barbera)
Loose Change, 1921 (Roach)
Loose Ends, 1930 (Cardiff)
Loose Tightwad, 1923 (Roach)
Lord Babs, 1932 (Balcon)
Lord Byron of Broadway, 1930 (Brown; Freed; Gibbons; Shearer; Tiomkin)

Lord Chumley, 1915 (Loos)
Lord Don't Play Favorites, 1956 (Swerling)
Lord Jeff, 1938 (Gibbons; Seitz)
Lord Jim, 1965 (Kaper; Mathieson; Young)
Lord Morton's Twin. *See* Kobila Lord Mortona, 1918
Lord of the Flies, 1990 (Allen; Sarde)
Lord of the Rings, 1978 (Rosenman)
Lorelei, 1931 (Terry)
Lorenzaccio, 1977 (Jarre)
Lorenzo's Oil, 1992 (Baker; Seale)
Lorna Doone, 1922 (Ince)
Lorna Doone, 1935 (Dean)
Lorna Doone, 1951 (Duning)
Lorraine of the Lions, 1925 (Miller)
Lose No Time, 1921 (Roach)
Loser Takes All, 1956 (Périnal)
Loss of Innocence. *See* Greengage Summer, 1961
Lost, 1955 (Rank)
Lost and Found, 1979 (Slocombe)
Lost and Foundling, 1944 (Blanc; Jones; Stalling)
Lost and Foundry, 1937 (Fleischer)
Lost Angel, 1943 (Irene; Schary; Surtees)
Lost Angels, 1989 (Sarde)
Lost Boundaries, 1949 (de Rochemont)
Lost Boys, 1987 (Newman)
Lost Canyon, 1942 (Harlan)
Lost Child, 1904 (Bitzer)
Lost Child. *See* Munna, 1954
Lost Command, 1966 (Spencer; Surtees; Waxman)
Lost Continent, 1968 (Carreras)
Lost Dog, 1924 (Roach)
Lost Empire, 1929 (Cooper)
Lost Highway, 1997 (Badalamenti)
Lost Horizon, 1937 (Cohn; Goosson; Riskin; Tiomkin; Walker; Westmore Family)
Lost Horizon, 1972 (Ames; Bacharach; Hunter; Louis; Pan; Surtees)
Lost Hours, 1952 (Korda)
Lost House, 1915 (Loos)
Lost in Alaska, 1952 (Boyle)
Lost in America, 1985 (Jones)
Lost in the Jungle, 1911 (Selig)
Lost in the Stars, 1974 (North)
Lost in Yonkers, 1993 (Bernstein; Stark)
Lost Jungle, 1934 (Canutt)
Lost Lady, 1934 (Orry-Kelly)
Lost Man, 1969 (Head; Jones)
Lost Moment, 1947 (Banton; Mohr; Wanger)
Lost Outpost, 1935 (Brackett)
Lost Patrol, 1934 (Cooper; Nichols; Polglase; Steiner)
Lost People, 1949 (Rank)
Lost Sentry. *See* Ztracená varta, 1956
Lost Son, 1974 (Reiniger)
Lost Son, 1999 (Menges)
Lost Soul. *See* Anima persa, 1976
Lost Souls, 2000 (Kaminski)
Lost Squadron, 1932 (Clothier; Cronjager; Mankiewicz; Selznick; Steiner)
Lost Volcano, 1950 (Mirisch)
Lost Weekend, 1945 (Brackett; Dreier; Edouart; Head; Rozsa; Seitz)
Lost World of Sinbad. *See* Daitozoku, 1964
Lost World, 1925 (Edeson; O'Brien; Westmore Family)
Lost World, 1960 (Hoch; O'Brien)
Lost World: Jurassic Park, 1997 (Kaminski; Muren; Williams)
Lost Youth. *See* Gioventù perduta, 1947
Lotte nell'ombra, 1939 (Amidei)
Lottery Bride, 1930 (Menzies; Schenck)
Lottery Lover, 1935 (Glennon)

Loud Soup, 1929 (Roach)
Louis Lecoin, 1966 (Delerue)
Louis Lumière. *See* Lumière et l'invention du cinématographe, 1953
Louisa, 1950 (Boyle)
Louise, 1939 (Courant; Wakhévitch)
Louise. *See* Chère Louise, 1972
Louise de Lavallière, 1921 (Freund)
Louisiana Hayride, 1944 (Hunter)
Louisiana Purchase, 1941 (Berlin; Dreier; Rennahan)
Louisiana Story, 1948 (Rosenblum; Thomson; van Dongen)
Loup et l'agneau, 1953 (Kosma)
Loupezeníci na Chlumu, 1927 (Heller)
Loups chassent la nuit, 1951 (Kosma)
Loups entre eux, 1936 (Spaak)
Lourdes, 1965 (Braunberger)
Louve solitaire, 1967 (Lai)
Louves, 1957 (Kosma)
Louvre Come Back to Me, 1962 (Blanc; Jones)
Louvre Museum. *See* Musée du Louvre, 1979
Lovable Cheat, 1949 (Leven)
Love, 1963 (Kuri)
Love, 1980 (Kuri)
Love, 1927 (Adrian; Daniels; Gibbons; Marion; Mayer)
Love à la carte. *See* Adua e le compagne, 1960
Love Affair, 1932 (Cohn)
Love Affair, 1939 (Berman; Maté; Polglase; Stewart)
Love Affair, 1994 (Hall; Morricone; Towne)
Love Affair in Toyland. *See* Drame chez les fantoches, 1908
Love Affair of a Dictator. *See* Dictator, 1934
Love among the Millionaires, 1930 (Mankiewicz)
Love among the Ruins, 1975 (Barry; Dillon; Slocombe)
Love and Anarchy. *See* **Film d'amore e d'anarchia**, 1973
Love and Bullets, 1978 (Schifrin)
Love and Death, 1975 (Cloquet; Rosenblum)
Love and Deficit. *See* Kärlek och kassabrist, 1932
Love and Fear. *See* Paure e Amore, 1988
Love and Hisses, 1937 (MacGowan)
Love and Larceny. *See* Mattatore, 1960
Love and Learn, 1928 (Mankiewicz)
Love and Learn, 1947 (Diamond; Steiner)
Love and Marriage, 1970 (Godfrey)
Love and Morocco. *See* Baroud, 1931
Love and Pain and the Whole Damn Thing, 1972 (Sargent; Unsworth)
Love and Separation in Sri Lanka. *See* Suri Lanka no ai to wakare, 1976
Love and the Devil, 1929 (Garmes; Korda)
Love and the Frenchwoman. *See* Française et l'amour, 1960
Love and the Journalist. *See* Kärlek och journalistik, 1916
Love and the Zeppelin. *See* Vzuchold a láska, 1947
Love As Disorder , 1963 (Maddow)
Love at 20. *See* Amour à vingts ans, 1962
Love at First Flight, 1928 (Hornbeck)
Love at Sea, 1936 (Havelock-Allan)
Love at Twenty. *See* Amour à vingt ans, 1962
Love Ban. *See* It's a 2' 6" above the Ground World, 1972
Love before Breakfast, 1936 (Banton; D'Agostino; Waxman)
Love Begins at Twenty, 1936 (Barnes; Trumbo)
Love Birds, 1934 (Mandell)
Love Brand, 1923 (Laemmle)
Love Bug, 1925 (Roach)
Love Bug, 1969 (Ellenshaw)
Love Cage. *See* Félins, 1964
Love Comes Along, 1930 (Plunkett)
Love Comes to Magoo, 1958 (Bosustow)
Love Contract, 1932 (Wilcox)
Love Crazy, 1941 (Berman; Gibbons; Lederer)
Love Defender, 1919 (Polito)

Love Doctor, 1929 (Cronjager; Mankiewicz)
Love 'em and Leave 'em, 1926 (Banton; Bruckman; Roach)
Love 'em and Weep, 1927 (Roach)
Love Expert, 1920 (Loos)
Love Express. *See* Renai tokkyu, 1954
Love Field, 1992 (Goldsmith)
Love Finds a Way, 1908 (Bitzer)
Love Finds Andy Hardy, 1938 (Edens)
Love Flower, 1920 (Bitzer)
Love from a Stranger, 1937 (Marion)
Love from a Stranger, 1947 (Gaudio)
Love Gambler, 1922 (August; Furthman)
Love God, 1997 (Schamus)
Love Has Many Faces, 1965 (Head; Raksin; Ruttenberg)
Love, Honor and Goodbye, 1945 (Alton)
Love, Honor, and Behave, 1938 (Barnes; Wallis)
Love, Honor, and Oh Baby!, 1933 (Krasna)
Love, Honor, and Oh, Baby!, 1940 (Cortez)
Love Hurts, 1992 (Bacharach)
Love in a Bungalow, 1937 (Krasner)
Love in a Cottage, 1940 (Terry)
Love in a Goldfish Bowl, 1961 (Bacharach; Head)
Love in an Apartment Hotel, 1912 (Bitzer)
Love in Germany. *See* Liebe in Deutschland, 1983
Love in Goa, 1983 (Abbas)
Love in Las Vegas. *See* Viva Las Vegas, 1964
Love in Morocco. *See* Baroud, 1931
Love in Rome. *See* Amore a Roma, 1960
Love in the Afternoon, 1957 (Diamond; Mercer; Trauner; Waxman)
Love in the City. *See* Amore in città, 1953
Love in the Desert, 1929 (Plunkett)
Love in the Hills, 1911 (Bitzer)
Love in the Rough, 1930 (Gibbons)
Love in the Suburbs, 1900 (Bitzer)
Love in Waiting, 1938 (Rank)
Love Is a Ball, 1962 (D'Eaubonne; Legrand)
Love Is a Funny Thing. *See* Homme qui me plaît, 1969
Love Is a Headache, 1938 (Adrian; Seitz)
Love Is a Many-Splendored Thing, 1955 (Lemaire; Newman; Reynolds; Shamroy; Wheeler)
Love Is Better Than Ever, 1952 (Rose; Rosson)
Love Is Everything, 1920 (Haller)
Love Is My Profession. *See* En cas de malheur, 1958
Love, Laughs, and Lather, 1917 (Roach)
Love Laughs at Andy Hardy, 1946 (Irene)
Love Lesson, 1921 (Roach)
Love Letters of a Star, 1936 (Krasner)
Love Letters, 1945 (Dreier; Garmes; Head; Wallis; Young)
Love, Life, and Laughter, 1934 (Dean)
Love Light, 1921 (Goosson; Marion; Rosher)
Love, Life, Death. *See* Vie, l'amour, la mort, 1968
Love, Live with the Stars. *See* Ai yo hoshi to tomoni, 1947
Love Lottery, 1953 (Slocombe)
Love Machine, 1971 (Lang; Wheeler)
Love Madness, 1920 (Sullivan)
Love Mart, 1927 (Garmes)
Love Match. *See* Partie de plaisir, 1975
Love Me, 1918 (Sullivan)
Love Me and the World Is Mine, 1928 (Mandell)
Love Me Forever, 1935 (Buchman; Cohn; Kahn; Swerling; Walker)
Love Me or Leave Me, 1955 (Cahn; Gibbons; Pasternak; Rose)
Love Me Tonight, 1932 (Dreier; Head; Hoffenstein; Zukor)
Love Me, Love Me, Love Me, 1962 (Williams)
Love Me, Love My Mouse, 1966 (Jones)
Love Microbe, 1907 (Bitzer)
Love My Dog, 1927 (Roach)

Love Nest, 1951 (Diamond; Lemaire; Wheeler)
Love Now, Pay Later. *See* Wahrheit über Rosemarie, 1959
Love, Not Loving Love. *See* Koi ya koinasuna koi, 1962
Love of a Judo Player. *See* Judo senshu no koi, 1934
Love of a Patriot. *See* Barbara Frietchie, 1924
Love of Jeanne Ney. *See* Liebe der Jeanne Ney, 1927
Love of Sumako the Actress. *See* Joyu Sumako no koi, 1947
Love of the Blind Girl. *See* Liebesglück einer Blinden, 1909
Love of Tojuro. *See* Tojuro no koi, 1955
Love on a Bet, 1936 (Epstein)
Love on the Dole, 1941 (Addinsell)
Love on the Riviera. *See* Racconti d'estate, 1958
Love on the Run, 1936 (Adrian; Waxman)
Love on the Run, 1985 (Lathrop)
Love on the Run. *See* Amour en fuite, 1979
Love on the Spot, 1932 (Dean)
Love on the Wing, 1937-39 (McClaren)
Love on Toast, 1937 (Head)
Love on Wheels, 1932 (Balcon; Rank; Vetchinsky)
Love Pains, 1932 (Roach)
Love Parade, 1929 (Banton; Dreier; Vajda; Zukor)
Love Piker, 1923 (Barnes; Marion)
Love Required. *See* Nagrodzone uczucie, 1957
Love Root. *See* Mandragola, 1965
Love Slaves of the Amazon, 1957 (Siodmak)
Love Song of Barney Kempinski, 1966 (Rosenblum)
Love Specialist. *See* Ragazza del Palio, 1957
Love Storm. *See* Cape Forlorn, 1930
Love Story, 1944 (Bryan; Rank)
Love Story, 1970 (Lai)
Love Streams, 1984 (Golan and Globus)
Love Stronger Than Hatred. *See* Kärlek starkare än hat, 1914
Love That Pup, 1949 (Hanna and Barbera)
Love That Pup, 1957 (Hanna and Barbera)
Love Thy Neighbor, 1934 (Fleischer)
Love Thy Neighbor, 1940 (Dreier; Head; van Heusen; Young)
Love Thy Neighbor, 1984 (Delerue)
Love Time, 1934 (Miller)
Love Toy, 1926 (Levien)
Love under Fire, 1937 (Johnson)
Love unto Death. *See* Amour à mort, 1984
Love vs. Duty, 1914 (Ince)
Love with the Proper Stranger, 1963 (Bernstein; Head; Krasner; Mercer; Pereira)
Love You to Death. *See* Deadly Illusion, 1987
Lovebound, 1923 (Furthman)
Loved Life. *See* **Kanał**, 1957
Loved One, 1965 (Southern; Wexler)
Lovelorn Leghorn, 1951 (Blanc; McKimson; Stalling)
Lovelorn, 1927 (Gibbons)
Lovely to Look At, 1952 (Adrian; Berman; Gibbons; Pan)
Lovely to Look At. *See* Thin Ice, 1937
Lovemaker. *See* Calle Mayor, 1956
Lover. *See* Amant, 1991
Lover Come Back, 1961 (Irene; Westmore Family)
Lovers?, 1927 (Booth; Gibbons)
Lovers. *See* Amants, 1958
Lovers. *See* Monsieur Ripois, 1954
Lovers Courageous, 1932 (Adrian; Booth; Daniels)
Lovers, Happy Lovers. *See* Monsieur Ripois, 1954
Lovers in Quarantine, 1925 (Polglase)
Lovers Must Learn, 1962 (Steiner)
Lovers' Net. *See* Amants du Tage, 1955
Lovers of Teruel. *See* Amants de Teruel, 1962
Lovers of Verona. *See* Amants de Vérone, 1949
Lover's Return. *See* Revenant, 1946

Love's A-Poppin', 1953 (Bruckman)
Love's Blindness, 1926 (Basevi; Gibbons)
Love's Crucible. *See* Vem dömer, 1922
Love's Detour, 1924 (Roach)
Love's Labor Won, 1948 (Terry)
Loves of a Blonde. *See* **Lásky jedné pla vovlásky**, 1965
Loves of a Dictator. *See* Dictator, 1934
Loves of an Actress, 1928 (Vajda)
Loves of an Old Criminal. *See* Kilenky starého kriminálníka, 1927
Loves of Carmen, 1948 (Goosson; Louis)
Loves of Colette. *See* Vie en rose, 1948
Loves of Edgar Allan Poe, 1942 (Day; Hoffenstein)
Loves of Isadora. *See* Isadora, 1968
Loves of Joanna Godden, 1947 (Balcon; Slocombe)
Loves of Kacenky Strnadova. *See* Lásky Kaňenky Strnadové, 1926
Loves of Madame Du Barry. *See* I Give My Heart, 1936
Loves of Omar Khayyam. *See* Omar Khayyam, 1957
Loves of Pharoah. *See* Weib des Pharao, 1922
Loves of Robert Burns, 1930 (Wilcox)
Loves of Zero, 1928 (Menzies)
Love's Redemption, 1921 (Schenck)
Love's Reward, 1924 (Roach)
Love's Sacrifice, 1914 (Ince)
Love's Young Scream, 1919 (Roach)
Lovesick, 1937 (Lantz)
Lovesick, 1983 (Fisher; Sarde)
Lovey Dovey, 1923 (Roach)
Lovey Mary, 1926 (Gibbons; Gillespie)
Lovin' the Ladies, 1930 (Cronjager)
Loving, 1970 (Lansing; Willis)
Loving Couples, 1980 (Lathrop)
Loving Couples. *See* Alskande par, 1964
Loving in the Rain. *See* Amour de pluie, 1974
Loving Memory, 1970 (Menges)
Loving You, 1957 (Head; Lang; Wallis)
Low Finance, 1960 (Halas and Batchelor)
Low-Rank Soldiers. *See* Zouhei monogatari, 1963
Lower Depths . *See* Bas-fonds, 1936
Lower Depths. *See* Donzoko, 1957
Lower the Boom, 1950 (Fleischer)
Loyal 47 Ronin. *See* Genroku chushingura, 1941-42
Loyalties, 1933 (Dean)
Lt. Robin Crusoe U.S.N., 1966 (Ellenshaw)
Lt. Robin Crusoe, U.S.N., 1966 (Disney)
Lucas, 1986 (Grusin)
Lucerna, 1925 (Heller)
Lucertola con la pelle di donna, 1971 (Morricone)
Luch smerti, 1925 (Golovnya)
Luci del varietà, 1950 (Flaiano and Pinelli)
Lucía, 1968 (Herrera)
Lucie Aubrac, 1997 (Sarde)
Luck of Ginger Coffey, 1964 (Horner)
Luck of the Irish, 1948 (Dunne; La Shelle; Lemaire)
Luck of the Navy, 1927 (Wilcox)
Luckiest Girl in the World, 1936 (Spencer)
Lucky Beginners, 1935 (Roach)
Lucky Days, 1935 (Havelock-Allan)
Lucky Devils, 1933 (Cooper; Plunkett; Steiner)
Lucky Duck, 1940 (Terry)
Lucky Ducky, 1948 (Avery)
Lucky Five. *See* Cinque poveri in automobile, 1952
Lucky in Love, 1929 (Stradling)
Lucky Jim, 1909 (Bitzer)
Lucky Jo, 1964 (Delerue)
Lucky Jordan, 1942 (Deutsch; Dreier; Head; Seitz)
Lucky Lady, 1926 (Sherwood)

Lucky Lady, 1975 (Unsworth)
Lucky Larkin, 1930 (McCord)
Lucky Luciano, 1973 (Guerra)
Lucky Mascot, 1948 (Adam)
Lucky Me, 1954 (Blanke)
Lucky Nick Cain. See I'll Get You for This, 1950
Lucky Number, 1921 (Roach)
Lucky Number, 1933 (Balcon; Rank; Vetchinsky)
Lucky Number, 1961 (Biswas)
Lucky Partners, 1940 (Irene; Polglase; Tiomkin)
Lucky Star, 1928 (Levien)
Lucky Stiff, 1949 (Laszlo)
Lucky Street, 1960 (Halas and Batchelor)
Lucky Texan, 1934 (Canutt)
Lucky to Be a Woman. See Fortuna di essere donna, 1955
Lucrèce, 1943 (Matras)
Lucrèce Borgia, 1935 (Kaufman)
Lucrèce Borgia, 1953 (Matras; Mnouchkine)
Lucrezia Borgia, 1922 (Freund)
Lucrezia Borgia. See Lucrèce Borgia, 1953
Lucy Gallant, 1955 (Bumstead; Head; Parrish)
Ludlow's Aeroplane, 1905 (Bitzer)
Ludwig, 1973 (Cecchi D'amico)
Ludwig II—Glanz und Eland eines Königs, 1954 (Heckroth; Slocomb)
Lui per lei, 1971 (Morricone)
Luise Millerin   Kabale und Liebe, 1922 (Herlth; Pommer; Röhrig)
Luke and the Bang-Tails, 1916 (Roach)
Luke and the Bomb Throwers, 1916 (Roach)
Luke and the Mermaids, 1916 (Roach)
Luke and the Rural Roughnecks, 1916 (Roach)
Luke, Crystal Gazer, 1916 (Roach)
Luke Does the Midway, 1916 (Roach)
Luke Foils the Villain, 1916 (Roach)
Luke, Gladiator, 1916 (Roach)
Luke Joins the Navy, 1916 (Roach)
Luke Laughs Last, 1916 (Roach)
Luke Leans to the Literary, 1916 (Roach)
Luke Locates the Loot, 1916 (Roach)
Luke Lolls in Luxury, 1916 (Roach)
Luke Lugs Luggage, 1916 (Roach)
Luke, Patient Provider, 1916 (Roach)
Luke Pipes the Pippins, 1916 (Roach)
Luke Rides Roughshod, 1916 (Roach)
Luke the Candy Cut-Up, 1916 (Roach)
Luke, the Chauffeur, 1916 (Roach)
Luke Wins Ye Ladye Faire, 1917 (Roach)
Luke's Busy Days, 1917 (Roach)
Luke's Double, 1916 (Roach)
Luke's Fatal Flivver, 1916 (Roach)
Luke's Fireworks Frizzle, 1916 (Roach)
Luke's Last Liberty, 1917 (Roach)
Luke's Late Lunches, 1916 (Roach)
Luke's Lost Lamb, 1916 (Roach)
Luke's Movie Muddle, 1916 (Roach)
Luke's Preparedness Preparation, 1916 (Roach)
Luke's Shattered Sleep, 1916 (Roach)
Luke's Society Mix-Up, 1916 (Roach)
Luke's Speedy Club Life, 1916 (Roach)
Luke's Trolley Trouble, 1917 (Roach)
Luke's Washful Waiting, 1916 (Roach)
Lullaby. See Sin of Madelon Claudet, 1931
Lullaby Bushu's Kite. See Komoriuta Bushu-dako, 1935
Lullabye, 1987 (Preisner)
Lulu Belle, 1948 (Laszlo; MacArthur)
Lulu the Tool. See Classe operaia va in paradiso, 1971
Lumber Camp, 1937 (Lantz)

Lumber Chumps, 1933 (Lantz)
Lumber Jack-Rabbit, 1954 (Blanc; Jones; Stalling)
Lumber Jerks, 1955 (Blanc)
Lumberjack, 1944 (Harlan)
Lumière, 1967 (Braunberger)
Lumiere and Company. See Lumiere et compagnie, 1995
Lumière d'été, 1943 (Barsacq; Douy; Prévert; Trauner)
Lumière du lac, 1988 (Guillemot)
Lumière et compagnie, 1995 (Merchant)
Lumiere et compagnie, 1995 (Nykvist)
Lumière et l'invention du cinématographe, 1953 (Cloquet; Kosma)
Lumières de Paris, 1938 (Andrejew; Courant; Jaubert; Renoir)
Lummox, 1930 (Menzies; Schenck; Struss)
Luna de miel, 1959 (Theodorakis)
Luna, 1979 (Morricone; Peploe; Storaro)
Lunch Hound, 1927 (Lantz)
Luncheon at Twelve, 1933 (Roach)
Lune dans le Caniveau (Moon in the Gutter), 1982 (Rousselot)
Lune dans son tablier, 1909 (Cohl)
Lunettes féeriques, 1909 (Cohl)
Lung Ta—les cavaliers du vent, 1990 (Sarde)
Lunga calza verde, 1960 (Zavattini)
Lunga manica, 1947 (Delli Colli)
Lupa, 1953 (de Laurentiis)
Lupa, 1996 (Morricone)
Lupič nešika. See Chytte ho!, 1924
Lupinek Case. See Pripad Lupínek, 1960
Lupo, 1970 (Golan and Globus)
Lupo della Sila, 1949 (de Laurentiis)
Lure of the Gown, 1909 (Bitzer)
Lure of the Sila. See Lupo della Sila, 1949
Lure of the Wilderness, 1952 (Cronjager; Jeakins; Lemaire; Waxman)
Lured, 1947 (Daniels; Stromberg)
Luring Lips, 1921 (Miller)
Lust for a Vampire, 1971 (Carreras)
Lust for Gold, 1949 (Duning)
Lust for Life, 1956 (Ames; Gibbons; Harlan; Houseman; Plunkett; Rozsa; Young)
Lustgården, 1961 (Fischer)
Lustige Witwer, 1929 (Reisch)
Lustigen Weiber, 1934 (Hoffmann)
Lustigen Weiber von Wein, 1931 (Andrejew; Reisch)
Lusty Men, 1952 (D'Agostino; Garmes; Krasna; Wald)
Luther, 1927 (Herlth; Röhrig)
Luther, 1974 (Young)
Lutte contre le gaspillage, 1951 (Decaë)
Luv, 1967 (Laszlo)
Luxury Girls. See Fanciulle di lusso, 1952
Luxury Liner, 1948 (Mayer; Pasternak; Rose)
Luz del fin del mundo, 1971 (Decaë)
Lyautey, bâtisseur d'empire, 1947 (Ibert)
Lycée sur la colline, 1952 (Fradetal)
Lydia, 1941 (Garmes; Hecht; Hoffenstein; Hornbeck; Korda; Plunkett; Rozsa)
Lydia Bailey, 1952 (Dunne; Friedhofer; Lemaire; Spencer)
Lyin' Lion, 1949 (Terry)
Lyin' Mouse, 1937 (Stalling)
Lyin' Tamer, 1925 (Lantz)
Lying Lips, 1921 (Ince)
Lyon Lea, 1915 (Korda)
Lyons in Paris, 1955 (Carreras)
Lyric of a Port. See Minato no jojoushi, 1932
Lyubov odna lyubov, 1918 (Starewicz)

M, 1931 (Von Harbou; Wagner)
M, 1951 (Cohn; Hubley; Laszlo)

M Is for Man, Music, Mozart, 1991 (Vierny)
Ma and Pa Kettle at Home, 1954 (Boyle)
Ma and Pa Kettle on Vacation, 1953 (Boyle)
Ma come fanno a farli cosi' belli?, 1980 (Bozzetto)
Ma cousine de Varsovie. See Meine Cousine aus Warschau, 1931
Ma famille et mon toit. See Ciel est par-dessus le toit, 1956
Ma femme est une panthère, 1960 (Matras)
Ma Jeannette et mes copains, 1954 (Kosma)
Ma mère l'eau. See Mammy Water, 1955
Ma nuit chez Maud, 1969 (Almendros; Braunberger; Rousselot)
Ma pomme, 1950 (Alekan; D'Eaubonne)
Ma saison préférée, 1993 (Sarde)
Ma tante d'Honfleur, 1931 (Fradetal)
M*A*S*H, 1970 (Lardner; Mandel; Smith)
Maan, 1954 (Biswas)
Maboroshi no mizuumi, 1982 (Muraki)
Macabre. See Macabro, 1980
Macabro, 1980 (Delli Colli)
Macadam, 1946 (D'Eaubonne)
Macão, 1952 (D'Agostino)
Macao, l'enfer du jeu. See Enfer du jeu, 1939
Macaro, 1959 (Figueroa)
Macaroni. See Maccheroni, 1985
MacArthur, 1977 (Goldsmith; Whitlock; Zanuck)
MacArthur's Children. See Setouchi shounen yakyu-dan, 1984
Macbeth, 1908 (Ince)
Macbeth, 1916 (Loos)
Macbeth, 1948 (Ibert)
Macbeth, 1954 (Addinsell)
Macbeth, 1960 (Mathieson; Young)
Maccheroni, 1985 (Age and Scarpelli)
Macchie solari, 1974 (Morricone)
Macchina ammazzacattivi, 1948 (Amidei)
MacDonald's Farm, 1951 (Fleischer)
Mach' mir die Wely zum Paradies, 1930 (Reisch)
Machete, 1958 (Struss)
Machine à parler d'amour, 1961 (Braunberger; Fradetal)
Machine Age. See Kalyug, 1981
Machine Gun Kelly, 1958 (Crosby)
Machine Gun McCain. See Intoccabili, 1969
Machines de l'existence, 1971 (Nuytten)
Macho Callahan, 1970 (Fisher)
Macht der Finsternis, 1923 (Andrejew)
Maciste all'inferno, 1926 (Amidei)
Maciste contre il vampiro, 1961 (de Laurentiis)
Maciste nella gabbia dei Leoni, 1926 (Amidei)
Mack the Knife, 1988 (Golan and Globus)
Mackenna's Gold, 1969 (Foreman; Jones; Tiomkin)
Mackintosh Man, 1973 (Jarre; Morris)
Maclovia, 1948 (Figueroa)
Macomber Affair, 1947 (Francis; Metzner; Rozsa; Struss)
Mad about Men, 1954 (Rank)
Mad about Music, 1938 (Pasternak)
Mad As a Mars Hare, 1963 (Blanc)
Mad Bridegroom. See Vzteklý ženich, 1919
Mad City, 1997 (Newman; Sarde)
Mad Doctor, 1941 (Head; Young)
Mad Dog and Glory, 1993 (Bernstein; Müller)
Mad Dog Coll, 1961 (Rosenblum; Sylbert)
Mad Dog Coll, 1991 (Golan and Globus)
Mad Dog Morgan, 1976 (Seale)
Mad Emperor. See Patriote, 1938
Mad Game, 1933 (Miller)
Mad Genius, 1931 (Grot)
Mad Ghoul, 1943 (Kräly; Krasner)
Mad Hatter, 1935 (Havelock-Allan)

Mad Holiday, 1936 (Ruttenberg)
Mad Hour, 1928 (Haller)
Mad House, 1934 (Terry)
Mad King, 1932 (Terry)
Mad Little Island. See Rockets Galore, 1958
Mad Love, 1935 (Freund; Gibbons; Tiomkin; Toland)
Mad Lover, 1944 (Alton)
Mad Magician, 1954 (Glennon)
Mad Maid of the Forest, 1915 (Rosher)
Mad Man's Money. See Bad Men's Money, 1929
Mad Max: Beyond Thunderdome, 1985 (Jarre)
Mad Miss Manton, 1938 (Berman; Epstein)
Mad Parade, 1931 (Banton)
Mad Room, 1969 (Grusin)
Madagascar, 1954 (Delerue)
Madam Kitty. See Salon Kitty, 1977
Madam Satan, 1930 (Adrian; Gibbons; MacPherson; Mayer; Shearer; Stothart)
Madam wünscht keine Kinder, 1926 (Freund)
Madam X, 1965 (Metty)
Madame. See Madame Sans-Gêne, 1961
Madame Bovary, 1933 (Lourié; Milhaud; Wakhévitch)
Madame Bovary, 1949 (Berman; Gibbons; Plunkett; Rozsa; Smith)
Madame Bovary, 1991 (Rabier)
Madame Butterfly, 1915 (Zukor)
Madame Butterfly, 1933 (Zukor)
Madame Butterfly, 1955 (Renoir)
Madame Claude 2, 1981 (Lai)
Madame Curie, 1943 (Gibbons; Irene; Mayer; Sharaff; Stothart)
Madame de . . ., 1953 (Annenkov; D'Eaubonne; Matras)
Madame de Thèbes, 1915 (Jaenzon; Magnusson)
Madame Du Barry, 1917 (Hunte; Kräly)
Madame du Barry, 1954 (Jeanson; Matras; Mnouchkine)
Madame DuBarry, 1934 (Blanke; Orry-Kelly; Polito)
Madame et le mort, 1942 (Aurenche and Bost)
Madame Milena's Husbands. See Manželé paní Mileny, 1921
Madame Mystery, 1926 (Roach)
Madame Nicotine , 1908 (Gaudio)
Madame Pimpernel. See Paris Underground, 1945
Madame Pompadour, 1927 (Marion; Wilcox)
Madame Q, 1929 (Roach)
Madame Rex, 1911 (Bitzer)
Madame Rosa. See Vie devant soi, 1977
Madame Sans Jane, 1925 (Roach)
Madame Sans-Gêne, 1925 (Zukor)
Madame Sans-Gêne, 1941 (Aurenche and Bost)
Madame Sans-Gêne, 1961 (D'Eaubonne; Jeanson; Solinas)
Madame Satan, 1930 (Day; Rosson)
Madame Sousatska, 1988 (Jhabvala)
Madame Spy, 1934 (Freund)
Madame Wants No Children. See Madam wünscht keine Kinder, 1926
Madame wünscht keine Kinder, 1933 (Kaper)
Madame X, 1929 (Gibbons)
Madame X, 1937 (Gibbons; Seitz)
Madame X, 1966 (Hunter; Louis; Westmore Family)
Madamigella di Maupin, 1965 (Gherardi)
Madcap Magoo, 1955 (Bosustow)
Mädchen aus der Ackerstrasse, 1920 (Courant)
Mädchen hinter gittern, 1949 (Wagner)
Mädchen Johanna, 1935 (Herlth; Röhrig)
Mädchen mit dem guten Ruf, 1938 (Wagner)
Mädchen von Fanö, 1940 (Hoffmann)
Mädchenjahre einer Königin, 1936 (Warm)
Maddalena, 1960 (Lassally)
Maddalena, 1970 (Morricone)
Maddalena. See Fille nommée Madeleine, 1953

Made for Each Other, 1939 (Banton; Friedhofer; Menzies; Selznick; Shamroy; Swerling; Wheeler)
Made for Love, 1926 (Miller)
Made in Britain, 1982 (Menges)
Made in Heaven, 1921 (Gibbons)
Made in Heaven, 1952 (Rank; Unsworth)
Made In Paris, 1965 (Jones; Krasner)
Made in Paris, 1966 (Ames; Pasternak; Rose)
Made in Sweden, 1968 (Fischer)
Made in U.S.A., 1966 (Coutard; Guillemot; de Beauregard)
Made on Broadway, 1933 (Adrian)
Mädel aus dem Volke, 1927 (Reisch)
Mädel aus U.S.A., 1930 (Heller)
Mädel mit der Peitsche, 1929 (Heller)
Mädel vom Ballett, 1918 (Kräly)
Mädel vom Piccadilly, 1921 (Courant)
Mädel von Nebenan, 1917 (Hoffmann)
Madeleine, 1950 (Alwyn; Bryan; Rank)
Madeline, 1952 (Bosustow; Raksin)
Madeline, 1998 (Legrand)
Madelon, 1955 (Mnouchkine)
Mädels von heute, 1925 (Warm)
Mademoiselle, 1966 (Saulnier)
Mademoiselle de la Ferté, 1948 (Cloquet)
Mademoiselle de la seiglière, 1921 (Burel)
Mademoiselle Docteur, 1936 (Alekan; Annenkov; Heller; Honegger; Schüfftan)
Mademoiselle Fifi, 1944 (D'Agostino; Lewton)
Mademoiselle France. See Reunion in France, 1942
Mademoiselle Josette ma femme, 1933 (D'Eaubonne)
Mademoiselle Josette, ma femme. See Fräulein Josette, meine Frau, 1926
Mademoiselle ma mère, 1937 (Burel)
Mademoiselle Modiste, 1926 (Barnes)
Mademoiselle X, 1944 (Matras; Wakhévitch)
Madh Bhare Nain, 1955 (Burman)
Madhatter. See Breakfast in Hollywood, 1945
Madigan, 1968 (Head; Metty; Westmore Family)
Madison Avenue, 1961 (Clarke)
Madla from the Brick-Kiln. See Madla z cihelny, 1933
Madla z cihelny, 1933 (Stallich)
Madly, 1970 (Lai)
Madmen of Mandoras, 1962 (Cortez)
Madness of King George, 1994 (Adam)
Madness of the Heart, 1949 (Rank)
Madness of Youth, 1923 (August)
Mado, 1976 (Sarde)
Madone des sleepings, 1955 (Burel)
Madonna of Avenue A, 1929 (Haskin; Zanuck)
Madonna of the Seven Moons, 1944 (Rank)
Madonna of the Streets, 1930 (Polito)
Madonna's Secret, 1946 (Alton)
Madregilda, 1993 (Branco)
Madreselva, 1938 (Alton)
Madwoman of Chaillot, 1969 (Guffey; Renoir)
Maelstrom, 1913 (Ince)
Maestro, 1964 (Halas and Batchelor)
Maestro, 1989 (de Almeida)
Maestro. See Maestro, 1989
Maestro di Don Giovanni, 1954 (Cardiff)
Maestro di Vigevano, 1963 (Age and Scarpelli; Rota)
Maestro e Margherita, 1972 (Morricone)
Mafioso, 1962 (Age and Scarpelli; Rota; de Laurentiis)
Mafu Cage, 1978 (Littleton)
Magd, 1911 (Messter)
Maggot, 1973 (Dunning)
Mágia, 1917 (Korda)

Magic, 1978 (Goldman; Goldsmith; Levine)
Magic. See Mágia, 1917
Magic Balloon, 1990 (Cardiff; Neame)
Magic Book, 1960 (Halas and Batchelor)
Magic Bow, 1947 (Rank)
Magic Box, 1951 (Alwyn; Bryan; Cardiff; Mathieson; Neame)
Magic Canvas, 1948 (Halas and Batchelor)
Magic Carpet, 1925 (Lantz)
Magic Cartoons. See Génération spontanée, 1909
Magic Catalogue, 1956 (Vukotić)
Magic Christian, 1969 (Southern; Unsworth)
Magic Eggs. See Omelette fantastique, 1909
Magic Fan. See Eventail animé, 1909
Magic Fire, 1955 (Haller; Herlth; Korngold)
Magic Fish, 1934 (Terry)
Magic Flame, 1927 (Barnes; Goldwyn; Mathis)
Magic Fluke, 1949 (Bosustow; Hubley)
Magic Flute. See Trollflöjten, 1974
Magic Garden, 1927 (Plunkett)
Magic Garden of Stanley Sweetheart, 1970 (Goldsmith)
Magic Hoop. See Cerceau magique, 1908
Magic Horse, 1953 (Reiniger)
Magic Lamp, 1924 (Lantz)
Magic Night. See Goodnight Vienna, 1932
Magic on Broadway, 1937 (Fleischer)
Magic Pencil, 1940 (Terry)
Magic Shell, 1941 (Terry)
Magic Show, 1983 (Schwartz)
Magic Slipper, 1948 (Terry)
Magic Sounds. See Carobni zvuci, 1957
Magic Statue. See Mazou, 1938
Magic Sticks, 1987 (Vachon)
Magic Strength, 1944 (Fleischer)
Magic Town, 1947 (Biroc; Hornbeck; Riskin; van Heusen)
Magical Maestro, 1951 (Avery)
Magical World of Chuck Jones, 1992 (Elfman)
Magician, 1926 (Mayer; Seitz)
Magician, 1960 (Halas and Batchelor)
Magician. See Ansiktet, 1958
Magician of Lublin. See Magier, 1979
Magiciennes, 1960 (D'Eaubonne; Matras)
Magiciens, 1975 (Gégauff; Rabier)
Magie du diamant, 1958 (Kosma)
Magier, 1979 (Golan and Globus; Jarre)
Mágnás Miska, 1916 (Korda)
Magnet, 1950 (Alwyn; Balcon; Clarke)
Magnetic Monster, 1953 (Siodmak)
Magnificent Ambersons, 1942 (Cortez; D'Agostino; Herrmann)
Magnificent Doll, 1946 (Banton)
Magnificent Dope, 1942 (Day; Raksin)
Magnificent Flirt, 1928 (Mankiewicz; Polglase)
Magnificent Fraud, 1939 (Head)
Magnificent Lie, 1931 (Raphaelson)
Magnificent Life, 1931 (Lang)
Magnificent Matador, 1955 (Ballard)
Magnificent Obsession, 1935 (Waxman)
Magnificent Obsession, 1954 (Hunter; Metty)
Magnificent Rogue, 1946 (Alton)
Magnificent Seven, 1960 (Alonzo; Bernstein; Lang; Mirisch)
Magnificent Seven Deadly Sins, 1971 (Godfrey)
Magnificent Seven Ride!, 1972 (Bernstein)
Magnificent Showman. See Circus World, 1964
Magnificent Sinner. See Katia, 1960
Magnificent Two, 1967 (Hambling)
Magnificent Yankee, 1950 (Plunkett; Raksin; Ruttenberg)
Magnifique, 1973 (Mnouchkine)

Magnum Force, 1973 (Schifrin)
Magoichi Saga. *See* Shirikurae Magoichi, 1969
Magoo Beats the Heat, 1956 (Bosustow)
Magoo Breaks Par, 1957 (Bosustow)
Magoo Goes Overboard, 1957 (Bosustow)
Magoo Goes Skiing, 1954 (Bosustow)
Magoo Goes West, 1956 (Bosustow)
Magoo Makes News, 1955 (Bosustow)
Magoo Saves the Bank, 1957 (Bosustow)
Magoo Slept Here, 1953 (Bosustow)
Magoo's Caine Mutiny, 1956 (Bosustow)
Magoo's Check-Up, 1955 (Bosustow)
Magoo's Cruise, 1958 (Bosustow)
Magoo's Express, 1955 (Bosustow)
Magoo's Glorious Fourth, 1957 (Bosustow)
Magoo's Homecoming, 1959 (Bosustow)
Magoo's Lodge Brother, 1959 (Bosustow)
Magoo's Masquerade, 1957 (Bosustow)
Magoo's Masterpiece, 1953 (Bosustow)
Magoo's Moose Hunt, 1957 (Bosustow)
Magoo's Private War, 1957 (Bosustow)
Magoo's Problem Child, 1956 (Bosustow)
Magoo's Puddle Jumper, 1956 (Bosustow)
Magoo's Three Point Landing, 1958 (Bosustow)
Magoo's Young Manhood, 1958 (Bosustow)
Magot de Joséfa, 1964 (Aurenche and Bost; Douy)
Magpie Madness, 1948 (Terry)
Magyarenfürstin, 1923 (Wagner)
Maha Geet, 1937 (Biswas)
Mahabharata, 1989 (Carrière)
Mahanagar, 1963 (Chandragupta; Dutta; Mitra)
Maharadžovo potešení. *See* Harémy kouzla zbavené, 1922
Maharajah's Pleasures. *See* Harémy kouzla zbavené, 1922
Mahatma and the Mad Boy, 1974 (Merchant)
Mahatma Kabir Munna, 1954 (Biswas)
Mahler, 1973 (Puttnam)
Mahlia la métisse, 1942 (Matras)
Mahogony, 1975 (Watkin)
Maître des forges, 1933 (Stradling)
Maid for Murder. *See* She'll Have to Go, 1962
Maid in China, 1938 (Terry)
Maid in Hollywood, 1934 (Roach)
Maid of Salem, 1937 (Banton; Young)
Maid or Man, 1911 (Gaudio; Ince)
Maid to Order, 1987 (Delerue)
Maids, 1975 (Slocombe)
Maids à la Mode, 1933 (Roach)
Maigret a Pigalle, 1967 (Amidei)
Maigret dirige l'enquête, 1955 (Kosma)
Maihime, 1989 (Miyagawa)
Maiko sanjushi, 1955 (Yoda)
Mail and Female, 1937 (Roach)
Mail Call, 1944 (Vorkapich)
Mail Early, 1941 (McClaren)
Mail Early for Christmas, 1959 (McClaren)
Main, 1969 (Vierny)
Main à couper, 1973 (Spaak)
Main Attraction, 1962 (Unsworth)
Main chaude, 1959 (Jarre)
Main du diable, 1942 (Andrejew)
Main Event, 1927 (Adrian)
Main mystérieuse, 1916 (Cohl)
Main Street of Paris, 1939 (Cardiff)
Main Street to Broadway, 1953 (Howe; Raphaelson; Sherwood)
Maine-Océan, 1984 (Branco; de Almeida)
Mains négatives, 1978/79 (Duras)

Maire, 1972 (Nuytten)
Mais où sont les nègres d'antan?, 1962 (Delerue)
Maisie, 1939 (Gibbons)
Maisie Gets Her Man, 1942 (Stradling)
Maisie Goes to Reno, 1944 (Irene)
Maiskaya noch, 1918 (Starewicz)
Maison assassinée, 1987 (Sarde)
Maison dans la dune, 1934 (Matras; Spaak)
Maison de jade, 1988 (Sarde)
Maison des Bories, 1969 (Cloquet)
Maison des sept jeunes filles, 1941 (Douy; Spaak)
Maison du Fantoche, 1916 (Cohl)
Maison du Maltais, 1938 (Courant; Ibert; Wakhévitch)
Maison du passeur, 1965 (Prévert)
Maison sous les arbres, 1971 (Buchman)
Maisons de la misère, 1937 (Jaubert)
Maître Bolbec et son mari, 1934 (D'Eaubonne)
Maîtres fous, 1955 (Braunberger)
Maîtresse, 1975 (Almendros)
Maj på Malö, 1947 (Nykvist)
Major and the Minor, 1942 (Brackett; Dreier; Head; Laszlo)
Major Barbara, 1941 (Beaton; Korda; Mayer; Neame; Walton)
Majorca, 1913 (Gaumont)
Majordôme, 1965 (Jeanson)
Majority of One, 1962 (Orry-Kelly; Steiner; Stradling)
Make Believe Ballroom, 1949 (Mercer)
Make Fruitful the Land, 1945 (Unsworth)
Make Haste to Live, 1954 (Bernstein)
Make It Snappy, 1921 (Roach)
Make Mine Mink, 1960 (Dillon; Rank)
Make Mine Music, 1946 (Disney; Iwerks)
Make Way for Lila. *See* Laila—Liebe unter der Mitternachtssonne, 1958
Make Way for Tomorrow, 1937 (Dreier; Head; Young)
Make Your Own Bed, 1944 (Burks)
Making Friends, 1936 (Fleischer)
Making Good, 1932 (Lantz)
Making It Move, 1977 (Halas and Batchelor)
Making Love, 1982 (Reynolds; Rosenman)
Making Music Together, 1973 (Halas and Batchelor)
Making of a Man, 1911 (Bitzer)
Making of Seven Brides for Seven Brothers, 1997 (Kidd)
Making Stars, 1935 (Fleischer)
Makioka Sisters. *See* Sasame-yuki, 1950
Mal, 1999 (de Almeida)
Mal des autres, 1959 (Delerue)
Mala hembre, 1950 (Alcoriza)
Malachi's Cove. *See* Seaweed Children, 1973
Malaga, 1954 (Challis; Korda)
Malaga, 1960 (Stewart)
Malamondo. *See* I malamondo, 1964
Mälarpirater, 1923 (Magnusson)
Malaya, 1949 (Head; Irene; Kaper)
Malcolm X, 1992 (Dickerson)
Maldone, 1927 (Honegger; Matras; Périnal)
Male and Female, 1919 (Buckland; Howe; MacPherson)
Male Animal, 1942 (Edeson; Epstein; Wallis)
Male Companion. *See* Monsieur de compagnie, 1964
Male Man, 1931 (Fleischer)
Male oscuro, 1990 (Cecchi D'amico; Morricone)
Male Pattern Baldness, 1998 (Eszterhas)
Maleducazione in Montagna, 1993 (Bozzetto)
Malenkaya aktrisa, 1917 (Starewicz)
Malevil, 1980 (Douy)
Malheurs de Sophie, 1945 (Trauner)
Malibu Beach Party, 1940 (Blanc; Stalling)
Malice, 1993 (Goldsmith; Willis)

Malice in Slumberland, 1942 (Fleischer)
Malice in Wonderland, 1985 (Lathrop)
Malizia, 1973 (Storaro)
Malkat Hakita, 1986 (Golan and Globus)
Malombra, 1942 (de Laurentiis)
Malou, 1983 (Ballhaus)
Malpertuis, 1972 (Delerue; Fisher)
Malquerida, 1949 (Figueroa)
Malrif, aigle royal, 1960 (Jarre)
Malta Story, 1953 (Alwyn; Krasker; Rank)
Maltese Bippy, 1969 (Daniels)
Maltese Falcon, 1941 (Blanke; Deutsch; Edeson; Orry-Kelly; Wallis)
Mam' zelle Souris series, 1958 (Delerue)
Mam, Behave, 1926 (Roach)
Mama Loves Papa, 1933 (Johnson)
Mama Steps Out, 1937 (Loos)
Mamaia, 1966 (Braunberger)
Maman et la putain, 1973 (Lhomme)
Mama's Affair, 1921 (Loos; Schenck)
Mama's Little Pirate, 1935 (Roach)
Mambo Kings, 1991 (Ballhaus)
Mambo, 1954 (Andrejew; de Laurentiis; Ponti; Rosson; Rota)
Mame, 1974 (Boyle; Lathrop; van Runkle)
Mamma Mia, che impressione!, 1951 (Zavattini)
Mamma Roma, 1962 (Delli Colli)
Mammamc, 1986 (de Almeida)
Mamma's Boy, 1920 (Roach)
Mammy, 1930 (Berlin)
Mammy Water, 1955 (Braunberger)
Mampou hattenshi: Umi no gouzoku, 1942 (Miyagawa)
Mamsell Josabeth, 1963 (Fischer)
Mam'zelle Nitouche, 1931 (Braunberger; Heller)
Mam'zelle Nitouche, 1954 (Aurenche and Bost; D'Eaubonne; Wakhévitch)
Mam'zelle Spahi, 1934 (Douy)
Mam'zelle Striptease. See En effeuillant la Marguerite, 1956
Man, 1910 (Bitzer)
Man, 1972 (Goldsmith)
Man, a Woman, and a Bank, 1979 (Conti)
Man about the House, 1946 (Korda; Périnal)
Man about Town, 1923 (Roach)
Man about Town, 1932 (Howe)
Man about Town, 1939 (Dreier; Head; Young)
Man Afraid, 1957 (Mancini; Metty)
Man Alone, 1955 (Young)
Man and a Woman. See Homme et une femme, 1966
Man and a Woman: 20 Years Later. See Homme et une femme: vingt ans déjà, 1986
Man and Boy, 1971 (Jones)
Man and His Dog Out for Air, 1957 (Breer)
Man and His Mate. See One Million B.C., 1940
Man and His Tools, 1962 (Hubley)
Man and His World, 1967 (Vukotić)
Man and Maid, 1925 (Gibbons)
Man and the Moment, 1929 (Grot; Polito)
Man and the Snake, 1972 (Fisher)
Man and the Woman, 1908 (Bitzer)
Man at Large, 1941 (Day; Miller)
Man Bait, 1926 (Rosson)
Man Bait. See Last Page, 1952
Man behind the Gun, 1952 (Glennon)
Man Between, 1953 (Andrejew; Korda)
Man Called Adam, 1966 (Levine)
Man Called Dagger, 1967 (Kovacs)
Man Called Flintstone, 1966 (Hanna and Barbera)
Man Called Gannon, 1969 (Bumstead; Chase; Grusin)

Man Called Horse, 1970 (Rosenman)
Man Called Peter, 1955 (Newman)
Man Called Sarge, 1989 (Golan and Globus)
Man Called Sullivan. See Great John L., 1945
Man Could Get Killed, 1966 (Clarke; Neame)
Man Crazy, 1953 (Crosby)
Man die zijn Haar kort liet knippen. See Homme au crâne rasé, 1966
Man Eater of Kumaon, 1948 (Haskin)
Man for All Seasons, 1966 (Delerue)
Man from Bitteridge, 1955 (Metty)
Man from C.O.T.T.O.N.. See Gone Are the Days!, 1963
Man from Colorado, 1948 (Chase; Duning; Goosson; Maddow)
Man from Del Rio, 1956 (Cortez; Horner)
Man from Down Under, 1943 (Irene)
Man from Galveston, 1963 (Glennon)
Man from Hell, 1934 (Canutt)
Man from Home, 1914 (Buckland)
Man from Home, 1922 (Miller)
Man From Hong Kong, 1975 (Boyd)
Man from Independence, 1974 (Bernstein)
Man from Kangaroo, 1920 (Glennon)
Man from Laramie, 1955 (Cohn; Duning; Lang)
Man from Mexico, 1913 (Zukor)
Man from Monterey, 1933 (McCord)
Man from Montreal, 1939 (Krasner)
Man from Red Gulch, 1925 (Stromberg)
Man from Rio. See Homme de Rio, 1964
Man from the Alamo, 1953 (Metty)
Man from the Diners' Club, 1963 (Mohr)
Man from the Folies Bergere. See Folies Bergere, 1935
Man from the Restaurant. See Chelovek iz restorana, 1929
Man from Toronto, 1933 (Balcon)
Man from Utah, 1934 (Canutt)
Man from Yesterday, 1932 (Banton; Struss; Zukor)
Man Haters, 1922 (Roach)
Man Hunt, 1935 (Ruttenberg)
Man Hunt, 1941 (Banton; Day; MacGowan; Miller; Newman; Nichols)
Man I Killed. See Broken Lullaby, 1932
Man I Love, 1929 (Banton; Mankiewicz; Selznick)
Man I Love, 1947 (Friedhofer; Steiner)
Man I Married, 1940 (Day; Zanuck)
Man in Black, 1950 (Carreras)
Man in Grey, 1943 (Rank)
Man in Half Moon Street, 1944 (Dreier; Head; Rozsa)
Man in Hiding. See Mantrap, 1952
Man in Love. See Homme amoureux, 1987
Man in Possession, 1931 (Mayer)
Man in Silence, 1959 (Halas and Batchelor)
Man in the Attic, 1953 (Lemaire; Wheeler)
Man in the Box, 1908 (Bitzer)
Man in the Dark, 1953 (Crosby)
Man in the Glass Booth, 1975 (Winston)
Man in the Gray Flannel Suit, 1956 (Clarke; Herrmann; Johnson; Lemaire; Smith; Spencer; Wheeler; Zanuck)
Man in the Iron Mask, 1977 (Young)
Man in the Middle, 1964 (Barry)
Man in the Mirror, 1936 (Courant)
Man in the Moon, 1960 (Rank)
Man in the Moon, 1991 (Francis)
Man in the Moon. See Clair de lune espagnol, 1909
Man in the Net, 1959 (Mirisch; Seitz)
Man in the Saddle, 1951 (Duning)
Man in the Sky, 1956 (Slocombe)
Man in the Trunk, 1942 (Day)
Man in the Vault, 1956 (Clothier)
Man in the White Suit, 1951 (Balcon; Slocombe)

Man in the Wilderness, 1971 (Fisher)
Man Inside, 1958 (Bennett; Broccoli)
Man Is Dead. *See* Homme est mort, 1973
Man Is Ten Feet Tall. *See* Edge of the City, 1957
Man Must Live, 1925 (Rosson)
Man Next Door, 1965 (Kuri)
Man of a Thousand Faces, 1957 (Westmore Family)
Man of Affairs. *See* His Lordship, 1936
Man of Aran, 1934 (Balcon; Rank)
Man of Bronze. *See* Jim Thorpe—All American, 1951
Man of Conquest, 1939 (August; Canutt; Head; Young)
Man of Evil. *See* Fanny by Gaslight, 1944
Man of Honor, 1919 (Gaudio)
Man of Iron. *See* Człowiek z żelaza, 1981
Man of La Mancha. *See* Uomo della Mancha, 1972
Man of Marble. *See* **Człowiek z marmuru**, 1976
Man of Music. *See* Kompozitor Glinka, 1952
Man of the Hour, 1914 (Carré)
Man of the Hour. *See* Colonel Effingham's Raid, 1945
Man of the Hour. *See* Homme du jour, 1936
Man of the Moment, 1955 (Rank)
Man of the People, 1937 (Clarke)
Man of the West, 1958 (Haller; Mirisch)
Man of the World, 1931 (Mankiewicz)
Man of Two Worlds, 1934 (Plunkett; Steiner)
Man on a String, 1960 (Duning; de Rochemont)
Man on a Swing, 1976 (Schifrin)
Man on a Tightrope, 1953 (Lemaire; Sherwood; Spencer; Waxman)
Man on America's Conscience. *See* Tennessee Johnson, 1943
Man on Fire, 1957 (Raksin; Ruttenberg)
Man on Fire, 1985 (Fisher)
Man on the Beach, 1956 (Carreras)
Man on the Box, 1914 (Buckland)
Man on the Eiffel Tower, 1949 (Cortez)
Man on the Flying Trapeze, 1934 (Fleischer)
Man on the Flying Trapeze, 1935 (Bruckman; Head)
Man on the Flying Trapeze, 1954 (Bosustow)
Man on the Moon, 1999 (Von Brandenstein)
Man on the Prowl, 1957 (Musuraca)
Man on the Track. *See* Człowiek na torze, 1956
Man Pays, 1924 (Roach)
Man Power, 1927 (Cronjager)
Man, Pride and Vengeance. *See* Uomo, l'orgoglio, la vendetta, 1967
Man steigt nach, 1927 (Metzner)
Man Taking Off His Gloves. *See* Tebukuro o nugasu otoko, 1946
Man There Was. *See* Terje vigen, 1917
Man They Could Not Arrest, 1931 (Balcon)
Man They Could Not Hang, 1939 (Brown)
Man Thou Gavest Me. *See* Eternal Struggle, 1923
Man to Men. *See* D'homme à hommes, 1948
Man to Remember, 1938 (Kanin; Polglase; Trumbo)
Man to Respect. *See* Uomo da rispettare, 1972
Man Trouble, 1930 (August)
Man under Cover, 1922 (Miller)
Man Under Water. *See* Clovek pod vodou, 1961
Man Upstairs, 1992 (Lassally)
Man vs. Man. *See* Otoko tai otoko, 1960
Man Wanted, 1932 (Toland)
Man Who Broke the Bank at Monte Carlo, 1935 (Johnson; Zanuck)
Man Who Came Back, 1930 (Edeson; Friedhofer)
Man Who Came Back. *See* Swamp Water, 1941
Man Who Came to Dinner, 1942 (Epstein; Gaudio; Orry-Kelly; Wald; Wallis)
Man Who Changed His Mind, 1936 (Balcon; Rank; Vetchinsky)
Man Who Cheated Himself, 1950 (Harlan; Polglase)
Man Who Cheated Life. *See* Student von Prag, 1926

Man Who Could Cheat Death, 1959 (Bennett; Carreras)
Man Who Could Work Miracles, 1936 (Biro; Hornbeck; Korda; Krasker; Rosson)
Man Who Dared, 1920 (Furthman)
Man Who Dared, 1933 (Miller; Nichols; Trotti)
Man Who Fell to Earth, 1976 (Henry)
Man Who Had His Hair Cut Short. *See* Homme au crâne rasé, 1966
Man Who Had Power Over Women, 1970 (Mandel)
Man Who Knew Too Much, 1934 (Balcon; Courant; Junge)
Man Who Knew Too Much, 1956 (Bumstead; Burks; Hayes; Head; Herrmann; Pereira; Whitlock)
Man Who Left His Will on Film. *See* Tokyo senso sengo hiwa, 1970
Man Who Lies. *See* Homme qui ment, 1968
Man Who Lived Again. *See* Man Who Changed His Mind, 1936
Man Who Lost His Shadow. *See* Homme qui a perdu son ombre, 1991
Man Who Loved Cat Dancing, 1973 (Williams)
Man Who Loved Redheads, 1955 (Korda; Périnal; Rattigan)
Man Who Loved Women, 1983 (Mancini; Wexler)
Man Who Loved Women. *See* Homme qui aimait les femmes, 1977
Man Who Murdered. *See* Mann, der den Mord beging, 1931
Man Who Never Was, 1956 (Korda; Mathieson; Morris; Neame)
Man Who Reclaimed His Head, 1934 (D'Agostino)
Man Who Shot Liberty Valance, 1962 (Clothier; Head; Newman; Westmore Family)
Man Who Understood Women, 1959 (Johnson; Krasner; Wheeler)
Man Who Waited, 1922 (Pierce)
Man Who Watched Trains Go By, 1952 (Heller)
Man Who Went Out, 1913 (August)
Man Who Won, 1923 (August)
Man Who Would Be King, 1975 (Head; Jarre; Morris; Trauner; Whitlock)
Man Who Wouldn't Die, 1942 (Day; Raksin)
Man Who Wouldn't Talk, 1940 (Day; Miller)
Man Who Wouldn't Talk, 1958 (Wilcox)
Man with a Cloak, 1951 (Plunkett; Raksin)
Man with a Dog, 1958 (Carreras)
Man with a Gun, 1958 (Rank)
Man with a Gun. *See* Chelovek s ruzhyom, 1938
Man with a Million. *See* Million Pound Note, 1953
Man with Bogart's Face, 1980 (Duning)
Man with Nine Lives, 1940 (Brown)
Man With One Red Shoe, 1985 (Newman)
Man with the Balloons. *See* Oggi, domani, e dopodomani, 1965
Man with the Golden Arm, 1955 (Bass; Bernstein)
Man with the Golden Arm, 1974 (Broccoli)
Man with the Golden Gun, 1974 (Barry; Morris)
Man with the Golden Touch. *See* Az aranyember, 1918
Man with the Gun, 1955 (Garmes; North)
Man with the Mask. *See* Mann mit der Maske, 1917
Man with the Scar. *See* Scar Hanan, 1925
Man with the X-Ray Eyes. *See* X, 1963
Man with Thirty Sons. *See* Magnificent Yankee, 1950
Man with Two Faces, 1934 (Gaudio)
Man with Two Hearts. *See* A ketszívü férfi, 1916
Man Within. *See* Smugglers, 1947
Man without a Face, 1993 (McAlpine)
Man without a Heart. *See* Muž bez srdce, 1923
Man without a Map. *See* Moetikuta chizu, 1968
Man without a Name. *See* Mensch ohne Namen, 1932
Man without a Star, 1955 (Chase; Metty)
Man, Woman, and Child, 1983 (Delerue)
Man, Woman, and Dog, 1964 (Kuri)
Man, Woman, and Marriage, 1921 (Carré)
Man, Woman, and Sin, 1927 (Gibbons)
Man, Woman, and Wife, 1929 (Mandell)
Man-Made Woman, 1928 (Goosson)

Man-Proof, 1937 (Freund; Waxman)
Manche et la belle, 1957 (D'Eaubonne; Matras)
Manchurian Candidate, 1962 (Koch; Sylbert)
Mandalay, 1934 (Gaudio; Grot)
Mandarin, bandit gentilhomme, 1962 (Douy)
Mandarino per Teo, 1960 (Di Venanzo)
Mandingo, 1975 (Jarre; Leven; de Laurentiis)
Mandragola, 1965 (Delli Colli; Donati)
Mandrake. See Alraune, 1927
Mandy, 1952 (Alwyn; Slocombe)
Manèges, 1950 (Trauner)
Mangeclous, 1988 (Sarde)
Mangiala, 1969 (Morricone)
Manhandled, 1924 (Rosson; Zukor)
Manhandled, 1949 (Head; Laszlo)
Manhattan, 1924 (Rosson)
Manhattan, 1979 (Willis)
Manhattan Cocktail, 1928 (Vajda)
Manhattan Cowboy, 1928 (Vajda)
Manhattan Heartbeat, 1940 (Day; Miller)
Manhattan Madness, 1916 (Loos)
Manhattan Madness. See Adventure in Manhattan, 1936
Manhattan Melodrama, 1934 (Howe; Mayer; Selznick; Vorkapich)
Manhattan Memories, 1947 (Fleischer)
Manhattan Merengue!, 1996 (Schifrin)
Manhattan Monkey Business, 1935 (Roach)
Manhattan Moon, 1935 (D'Agostino)
Manhattan Murder Mystery, 1993 (Loquasto)
Manhattan Project, 1986 (Sarde)
Manhunt. See From Hell to Texas, 1958
Manhunt of Mystery Island, 1945 (Canutt)
Mani sporche, 1978 (Morricone)
Mani sulla cittá, 1963 (Di Venanzo)
Maniac Cook, 1908 (Bitzer)
Maniac, 1963 (Carreras)
Maniac, 1980 (Savini)
Manifesto, 1988 (Golan and Globus; Morricone)
Manila Calling, 1942 (Day; Raksin)
Manitou, 1978 (Schifrin)
Manjudhar, 1947 (Biswas)
Manly Man, 1911 (Gaudio; Ince)
Mann, der den Mord beging, 1931 (Warm)
Mann, der den mord Being, 1931 (Courant)
Mann, der seinen Mörder sucht, 1930 (Herlth; Röhrig)
Mann, der seinen Mörder sucht, 1931 (Siodmak)
Mann, der Sherlock Holmes war, 1937 (Wagner)
Mann im Spiegel, 1916 (Freund; Messter)
Mann mit den sieben Masken, 1918 (Messter)
Mann mit der Maske, 1917 (Kolowrat-Krakowsky)
Mann mit der Pranke, 1935 (Von Harbou)
Mann mit Grundsaltzen?, 1943 (Herlth)
Mann seiner Frau, 1925 (Planer)
Mann um Mitternacht, 1924 (Junge)
Mann will nach deutschland, 1934 (Wagner)
Mannekängen, 1913 (Jaenzon)
Mannequin, 1926 (Brown)
Mannequin, 1938 (Adrian; Mayer)
Mannequins, 1933 (D'Eaubonne)
Männer sind zum Lieben da, 1960 (Warm)
Männer um Lucie, 1931 (Stradling)
Människor möts och ljuv musik uppstår i hjärtat, 1967 (Lundgren)
Mano della straniero, 1953 (Rota)
Manolescu, 1929 (Herlth; Hoffmann; Röhrig)
Manolescus Memoiren, 1920 (Dreier)
Manolis, 1962 (Theodorakis)
Manon, 1948 (Douy)

Manon des sources, 1986 (Nuytten)
Manon Lescaut, 1926 (Pommer)
Manon of the Spring. See Manon des sources, 1986
Manpower, 1941 (Deutsch; Haller; Haskin; Wald; Wallis)
Manque de mémoire, 1929 (Maté)
Mans, 1971 (Legrand)
Man's Best Friend, 1941 (Lantz)
Man's Castle, 1933 (August; Cohn; Swerling)
Man's Favorite Sport?, 1964 (Harlan; Mancini; Mercer)
Man's Genesis, 1912 (Bitzer)
Man's Lust for Gold, 1912 (Bitzer)
Man's Man, 1929 (Day; Gibbons)
Mansfield Park, 1999 (Pinter)
Manslaughter, 1922 (Gillespie; MacPherson; Zukor)
Manslaughter, 1930 (Stradling)
Mantango, 1963 (Tsuburaya)
Mantango—Fungus of Terror. See Mantango, 1963
Manthan, 1976 (Nihalani)
Mantle of Charity, 1918 (Furthman)
Mantonnet, 1936 (Prévert)
Mantrap, 1926 (Head; Howe)
Mantrap, 1943 (Siodmak)
Mantrap, 1952 (Carreras)
Mantrap, 1961 (Head)
Manuela, 1957 (Alwyn; Heller)
Manuela, 1966 (Herrera)
Many a Pickle, 1937-39 (McClaren)
Many Happy Returns, 1922 (Roach)
Many Happy Returns, 1934 (Head)
Many Rivers to Cross, 1955 (Plunkett; Seitz)
Many Scrappy Returns, 1926 (Roach)
Many Tanks, 1942 (Fleischer)
Manželé paní Mileny, 1921 (Heller)
Manzil, 1960 (Burman)
Mao le veut, 1965 (Lassally)
Map of the Human Heart, 1992 (Mnouchkine)
Map of the World, 1999 (Marshall)
Mar, 2000 (Branco)
Mar y tú, 1951 (Figueroa)
Mara Maru, 1952 (Burks; Steiner)
Maracaibo, 1958 (Head)
Marat/Sade, 1967 (Watkin)
Marathon, 1919 (Roach)
Marathon Man, 1976 (Goldman; Hall; Justin; Smith)
Marathon Runner. See Läufer von Marathon, 1933
Marcel, ta mère t'appelle, 1962 (Grimault)
Marcello Mastroianni: I Remember, Yes I Remember. See Marcello Mastroianni: mi ricordo, sì, io mi ricordo, 1997
Marcello Mastroianni: mi ricordo, sì, io mi ricordo, 1997 (Rotunno)
Marcello's Secret. See Tajna Marchello, 1997
March of Time, 1940 (Lye)
March of Time, 1933-43 (de Rochemont)
March of Time, 1944-51 (Lye)
March or Die, 1977 (Alcott; Jarre)
Marchand d'amour, 1935 (Jeanson)
Marchand de notes, 1943 (Aurenche and Bost; Grimault)
Marché á la volaille, 1901 (Gaumont)
Marche de la faim, 1935 (Kosma)
Marche des machines, 1928 (Kaufman)
Marche française, 1956 (Delerue)
Marche ou crève, 1959 (Delerue)
Märchen vom Glück, 1949 (Von Dassanowsky)
Marching Along. See Stars and Stripes Forever, 1952
Marcia su Roma, 1962 (Age and Scarpelli)
Marciando nel buio, 1995 (Donaggio)
Marco Polo, 1983 (Cristaldi)

Marry the Boss's Daughter, 1941 (Clarke)
Marry the Girl, 1937 (Raksin; Wallis)
Marrying Kind, 1952 (Cohn; Friedhofer; Horner; Kanin; Louis; Walker)
Mars, 1930 (Lantz)
Mars Attacks!, 1996 (Elfman)
Marseillaise, 1912 (Cohl)
Marseillaise, 1938 (Barsacq; Kosma; Reiniger; Renoir; Wakhévitch)
Marseille Contract, 1974 (Parrish; Slocombe)
Marseille, premier port de France, 1945 (Decaë)
Marshmallow Moon. *See* Aaron Slick from Punkin Crick, 1951
Mars's Stepson. *See* Pasinok Marsa, 1914
Martha, 1923 (Disney)
Martha, 1974 (Ballhaus)
Marthe Richard au service de la France, 1937 (Honegger)
Martian Through Georgia, 1962 (Blanc; Jones)
Martin, 1976 (Savini)
Martin Luther, 1953 (de Rochemont)
Martin Roumagnac, 1946 (Wakhévitch)
Martin Soldat, 1966 (Braunberger)
Martin the Cobbler, 1976 (Vinton)
Marty, 1954 (La Shelle)
Martyr of His Heart. *See* Märtyrer seines Herzens, 1918
Martyre de l'obèse, 1932 (Spaak)
Märtyrer seines Herzens, 1918 (Kolowrat-Krakowsky)
Martyrium, 1920 (Wagner)
Martyrs of Love. *See* Mučedníci lásky, 1966
Marvin and Tige, 1983 (Rosenblum)
Marx Brothers Go West. *See* Go West, 1940
Marx for Beginners, 1978 (Godfrey)
Mary Ann. *See* Az aranyember, 1918
Mary Burns, Fugitive, 1935 (Wanger)
Mary Jane's Pa, 1935 (Haller)
Mary Lou, 1928 (Andrejew)
Mary, Mary, 1963 (Stradling)
Mary of Scotland, 1936 (August; Berman; Nichols; Parrish; Plunkett; Polglase)
Mary of the Mines, 1912 (Ince)
Mary of the Movies, 1923 (Cohn)
Mary Poppins, 1964 (Disney; Ellenshaw)
Mary Queen of Scots, 1971 (Challis)
Mary Regan, 1919 (Mayer)
Mary Riley, 1994 (Rousselot)
Mary Stevens M.D., 1933 (Orry-Kelly)
Mary, Queen of Scots, 1972 (Barry; Wallis)
Mary, Queen of Tots, 1925 (Roach)
Maryland, 1940 (Barnes; Day; Newman; Rennahan; Zanuck)
Mary's Birthday, 1951 (Reiniger)
Mary's Little Lamb, 1935 (Iwerks)
Más allá de las montañas, 1967 (Matras)
Más allá del amor, 1945 (Figueroa)
Mascara, 1987 (Golan and Globus)
Máscaras, 1976 (de Almeida)
Maschera, 1988 (de Almeida)
Maschera di Cesare Borgia, 1941 (Stallich)
Masculin-féminin, 1966 (Guillemot; Lai)
Masculine-Feminine. *See* Masculin-féminin, 1966
Mashal, 1950 (Burman)
Mask, 1921 (Selig)
Mask. *See* Maschera, 1988
Mask, 1941 (Jarrico)
Mask, 1961 (Vorkapich)
Mask, 1985 (Kovacs)
Mask of Comedy. *See* Gay Deceiver, 1926
Mask of Dimitrios, 1944 (Blanke; Deutsch; Edeson)
Mask of Dust, 1954 (Carreras)
Mask of Fu Manchu, 1932 (Adrian; Gaudio)

Mask of Sheba, 1970 (Schifrin)
Mask of the Avenger, 1951 (Stromberg)
Mask-a-Raid, 1931 (Fleischer)
Masked Bride, 1925 (Carré; Gibbons; Mayer)
Masked Rider, 1916 (Gaudio)
Masked Woman, 1926 (Mathis)
Masken, 1920 (Röhrig; Warm)
Masken, 1929 (Warm)
Maskenfest der Liebe, 1918 (Messter)
Maskerade, 1934 (Planer; Reisch)
Masks of the Devil, 1928 (Adrian; Gibbons; Marion)
Masquerade in Mexico, 1945 (Dreier; Head; Young)
Masquerade in Vienna. *See* Maskerade, 1934
Masquerade, 1924 (Fleischer)
Masquerade, 1929 (Clarke; Pierce)
Masquerade, 1964 (Goldman; Heller)
Masquerade, 1974 (Winston)
Masquerade, 1988 (Barry; Watkin)
Masquerader, 1922 (Buckland)
Masquerader, 1933 (Day; Goldwyn; Newman; Toland)
Masqueraders, 1906 (Bitzer)
Masques, 1952 (Alexeieff and Parker)
Masques, 1987 (Rabier)
Mass Appeal, 1984 (Conti)
Mass Mouse Meeting, 1943 (Fleischer)
Massacre, 1912 (Bitzer)
Massacre, 1934 (Barnes; Orry-Kelly)
Massacre de la famille royale de Serbie, 1903 (Pathé)
Massacre in Rome. *See* Rappresaglia, 1973
Massacre of Sante Fe Trail, 1912 (Ince)
Master. *See* Det röda tornet, 1914
Master and the Man, 1911 (Gaudio)
Master Gunfighter, 1975 (Reynolds; Schifrin)
Master Hand, 1917 (Edeson)
Master of Ballantrae, 1953 (Adam; Alwyn; Cardiff)
Master of Bankdam, 1947 (Rank)
Master of Men, 1933 (August)
Master of the Islands. *See* Hawaiians, 1970
Master of Woman. *See* Eternal Struggle, 1923
Master Race, 1944 (Metty)
Master Samuel. *See* Mästerman, 1920
Master Touch. *See* Uomo da rispettare, 1972
Mästerjuven, 1915 (Jaenzon)
Mästerman, 1920 (Jaenzon; Magnusson)
Masters of the Sea. *See* Herren der Meere, 1922
Masters of the Universe, 1987 (Conti; Edlund; Golan and Globus)
Mat, 1926 (Golovnya)
Mata Hari, 1927 (Junge)
Mata Hari, 1931 (Daniels; Mayer)
Mata Hari, 1984 (Golan and Globus)
Mata-Hari, Agent H-21, 1964 (Delerue)
Matador Magoo, 1957 (Bosustow)
Match. *See* Partita, 1988
Match Breaker, 1921 (Mandell)
Match de catch, 1961 (Braunberger)
Match King, 1932 (Grot; Orry-Kelly)
Matchless, 1966 (Morricone)
Matchmaker, 1958 (Deutsch; Hayes; Head; Lang; Westmore Family)
Matchmaking Mamma, 1929 (Hornbeck)
Maten al león, 1975 (Figueroa)
Mater dolorosa, 1917 (Burel; Gaumont)
Matériaux nouveaux, demeures nouvelles, 1956 (Colpi)
Maternale, 1978 (Lanci, Giuseppe ("beppe"))
Maternelle, 1933 (Fradetal)
Maternité, 1934 (Ibert; Matras)
Maternity Hospital, 1971 (Vukotić)

Matewan, 1987 (Daring; Wexler)
Mathias Sandorf, 1962 (Spaak)
Matilda, 1978 (Leven)
Matinee, 1993 (Goldsmith)
Matinee Idol, 1928 (Cohn)
Matinee Idol, 1955 (Halas and Batchelor)
Matinee Ladies, 1927 (Blanke; Buchman; Haskin)
Mating Call, 1928 (Mankiewicz)
Mating Game, 1959 (Rose)
Mating of Millie, 1948 (Goosson; Walker)
Mating Season, 1951 (Brackett; Lang; Reisch)
Matous the Shoemaker. *See* O ševci Matoušovi, 1948
Matrices, 1966 (Halas and Batchelor)
Matrimaniac, 1916 (Loos)
Matrimonio all'italiana, 1964 (Guerra; Levine; Ponti)
Matrimony, 1915 (Ince; Sullivan)
Matrosowcy, 1951 (ścibor-Rylski)
Mattatore, 1960 (Age and Scarpelli)
Mattei Affair. *See* Caso Mattei, 1972
Matter of Dignity. *See* To teleftaio psemma, 1957
Matter of Innocence. *See* Pretty Polly, 1967
Matter of Life and Death, 1946 (Cardiff; Ellenshaw; Heckroth; Junge; Rank; Unsworth)
Matter of Morals. *See* De sista stegen, 1960
Matter of Resistance. *See* Vie de château, 1965
Matter of Time, 1976 (Unsworth)
Matto Grosso, 1932 (Crosby)
Maudits, 1947 (Alekan; Jeanson)
Maulkorb, 1937 (Herlth)
Maurice, 1987 (Lhomme; Merchant)
Mauvaise conduite, 1984 (Almendros)
Mauvaise passe, 1999 (Kureishi)
Mauvaise soupe, 1899 (Gaumont)
Mauvaises Rencontres, 1955 (Douy; Saulnier)
Maverick, 1994 (Goldman; Zsigmond)
Maverick Queen, 1956 (Young)
Max and Jeremy. *See* Max et Jérémie, 1992
Max and Moritz, 1978 (Halas and Batchelor)
Max et Jérémie, 1992 (Sarde)
Max et le quinquina, 1911 (Pathé)
Max et les ferrailleurs, 1971 (Sarde)
Max mon amour, 1986 (Baker; Carrière; Coutard)
Max, der Vielgeprüfte, 1920 (Dreier)
Max, My Love. *See* Max mon amour, 1986
Maxie, 1985 (Delerue)
Maxime, 1958 (Jeanson; Matras)
Maximum Overdrive, 1986 (de Laurentiis)
Maxplatte, Maxplatten, 1965 (Trnka)
May Fools. *See* Milou en mai, 1990
May Night. *See* Maiskaya noch, 1918
Maya, 1949 (Auric; Barsacq)
Maya Darpan, 1972 (Chandragupta)
Maybe It's Love, 1935 (Edeson; Orry-Kelly; Wald)
Maybe This Time, 1980 (Boyd)
Mayerling, 1936 (Andrejew; Annenkov; Honegger; Jaubert)
Mayerling, 1968 (Alekan; Lai; Wakhévitch)
Mayerling to Sarajevo. *See* De Mayerling à Sarajevo, 1940
Mayflower, 1935 (Terry)
Mayor of Hell, 1933 (Orry-Kelly)
Mayor's Nest, 1932 (Wilcox)
Maytime, 1923 (Struss)
Maytime, 1937 (Adrian; Mayer; Stothart; Stromberg; Vorkapich)
Maytime in Mayfair, 1949 (Wilcox)
Maze, 1953 (Menzies; Mirisch)
Mazel tov ou le mariage, 1968 (Cloquet)
Mazou, 1938 (Miyagawa)

Mazurka, 1935 (Warm)
McCabe and Mrs. Miller, 1971 (Zsigmond)
McCloud: Who Killed Miss U.S.A.?, 1970 (Bumstead)
McConnell Story, 1955 (Blanke; Seitz; Steiner)
McDougal's Rest Farm, 1947 (Terry)
McFadden's Flats, 1927 (Edeson)
McGuerins from Brooklyn, 1942 (Roach)
McLintock!, 1963 (Clothier; Pereira)
McQ, 1974 (Bernstein)
Me and Marlborough, 1935 (Balcon; Junge; Rank)
Me and My Brother, 1968 (Shepard)
Me and My Gal, 1932 (Miller)
Me and My Gal, 1942 (Mayer)
Me and the Colonel, 1958 (Cloquet; Duning; Guffey; Head; Wakhévitch)
Me faire ça à moi, 1961 (Legrand)
Me gustan valentones, 1958 (Alcoriza)
Me, Gangster, 1928 (Edeson)
Me, Natalie, 1969 (Jenkins; Mancini; Smith)
Meadow. *See* Prato, 1979
Meal Ticket, 1914 (Loos)
Mean Machine. *See* Longest Yard, 1974
Mean Season, 1984 (Schifrin)
Meanest Gal in Town, 1934 (Plunkett)
Meanest Girl in Town, 1934 (Steiner)
Meanest Man in the World, 1943 (Day)
Measure of Man, 1969 (Halas and Batchelor)
Meat in Love. *See* Zamilované maso, 1989
Meatballs, 1979 (Bernstein)
Meatless Flyday, 1944 (Blanc; Stalling)
Mecánica nacional, 1971 (Alcoriza)
Mechanic, 1972 (Winkler)
Mechanical Bird, 1952 (Terry)
Mechanical Cow, 1927 (Disney)
Mechanical Cow, 1937 (Terry)
Mechanical Flea, 1964 (Ivanov-Vano)
Mechanical Handy Man, 1937 (Lantz)
Mechanical Man, 1932 (Lantz)
Mechanics of the Brain. *See* Mekhanikha golovnovo mozga, 1926
Medal for Benny, 1945 (Dreier; Head; Young)
Medal for the General, 1944 (Alwyn)
Medals. *See* Seven Days Leave, 1930
Medea, 1969 (Donati)
Medianoche, 1949 (Figueroa)
Medic. *See* Toubib, 1979
Medicine Ball Caravan, 1970 (Braunberger)
Medicine Bottle, 1909 (Bitzer)
Medicine Man , 1992 (McAlpine)
Medicine Man, 1992 (Goldsmith)
Medico della Mutua, 1968 (Amidei)
Medico e lo stregone, 1957 (Age and Scarpelli; Gherardi; Rota)
Méditerréenne, 1969 (Braunberger)
Medium, 1951 (Wakhévitch)
Medium Cool, 1969 (Fields; Wexler)
Medvezhya svadba, 1926 (Tisse)
Meer ruft, 1933 (Metzner)
Meet Boston Blackie, 1941 (Planer)
Meet Dr. Christian, 1940 (Lardner)
Meet Joe Black, 1998 (Newman)
Meet John Doe, 1941 (Barnes; Goosson; Mandell; Riskin; Tiomkin; Vorkapich)
Meet John Doughboy, 1941 (Blanc; Clampett; Stalling)
Meet Me after the Show, 1951 (Cole; Lemaire)
Meet Me in Las Vegas, 1956 (Cahn; Pan; Pasternak; Rose)
Meet Me in St. Louis, 1944 (Edens; Freed; Gibbons; Irene; Mayer; Sharaff; Smith)
Meet Me on Broadway, 1946 (Goosson; Guffey)

Meet Me Tonight, 1952 (Coward; Dillon; Havelock-Allan; Rank)
Meet Mother Magoo, 1956 (Bosustow)
Meet Mr. Joad, 1942 (Balcon)
Meet Simon Cherry, 1950 (Carreras)
Meet the Baron, 1933 (Krasna; Mankiewicz; Selznick)
Meet the Missus, 1924 (Roach)
Meet the Missus, 1937 (Polglase)
Meet the Navy, 1946 (Unsworth)
Meet the People, 1944 (Irene; Surtees)
Meet the Prince, 1926 (Struss)
Meet the Raisins: The Story of the California Raisins, 1988 (Vinton)
Meet the Wildcat, 1940 (Cortez)
Meet Whiplash Willie. See Fortune Cookie, 1966
Meeting. See Meguriai, 1968
Meeting Again. See Sakai, 1953
Meeting in Bucharest. See Setkání v Bukurešti, 1954
Meeting on the Elbe. See Vsetrecha na Elba, 1949
Meeting Venus, 1991 (Puttnam)
Meetings with Remarkable Men, 1978 (Wakhévitch)
Méfaits d'un tête de veau, 1899 (Gaumont)
Megapolis I, 1963 (Müller)
Megh, 1961 (Shankar)
Meguriai, 1968 (Takemitsu)
Mehmaan, 1953 (Biswas)
Meido no kaoyaku, 1957 (Miyagawa)
Meilleur de la ville, 1984 (Branco)
Meilleure Façon de marcher, 1976 (Nuytten)
Meilleure Part, 1955 (Alekan)
Mein Herz ist eine jazzband, 1928 (Andrejew)
Mein in Fright, 1938 (Roach)
Mein Sohn, der Herr Minster, 1937 (Röhrig)
Meine Cousine aus Warschau, 1931 (Courant)
Meine Frau, die Filmschauspielerin, 1919 (Kräly)
Meine Frau, die Hochstaplerin, 1931 (Schüfftan)
Meine Herren Söhne, 1945 (Wagner)
Meineid, 1929 (Andrejew)
Meiran, 1929 (Tsuburaya)
Meissner Porzellan, 1907 (Messter)
Mekhanikha golovnovo mozga, 1926 (Golovnya)
Melba, 1953 (Andrejew; Spiegel; Stewart)
Mellah de Marrakech, 1948 (Decaë)
Mélo, 1986 (Saulnier)
Melodie der Liebe, 1932 (Kaper)
Melodie des Herzens, 1929 (Pommer)
Mélodie pour toi, 1941 (Wakhévitch)
Melody. See S.W.A.L.K., 1970
Melody Cruise, 1933 (Cooper; Glennon; Plunkett; Polglase; Steiner)
Melody for Three, 1941 (Alton)
Melody Lane, 1929 (Mandell; Swerling)
Melody Lingers On, 1935 (Dunne; Newman)
Melody of Life. See Symphony of Six Million, 1932
Melody of the Heart. See Melodie des Herzens, 1929
Melody of Youth. See They Shall Have Music, 1939
Melody Ranch, 1940 (August)
Melody Time, 1948 (Disney; Hoch; Iwerks)
Melusine, 1944 (Herlth)
Melvin and Howard, 1980 (Legrand)
Member of the Wedding, 1953 (Cohn; Mohr; North)
Memed My Hawk, 1984 (Francis)
Mémoires d'un jeune con, 1996 (Guillemot)
Memoirs of a Geisha, 2001 (Kaminski)
Memoirs of a Survivor, 1981 (Lassally)
Memoirs of an Invisible Man, 1992 (Fraker; Goldman)
Memories from the Boston Club. See Minnen fran Bostonklubben, 1909
Memories of Europe, 1941 (Hoch)
Memories of Me, 1988 (Delerue)

Memory Expert. See Man on the Flying Trapeze, 1935
Memory Lane, 1926 (Booth; Gibbons)
Memory Song Book, 1952 (Fleischer)
Memphis Belle, 1944 (Clothier)
Memphis Belle, 1990 (Puttnam; Watkin)
Men, 1950 (Foreman; Tiomkin)
Men and Wolves. See Uomini e lupi, 1956
Men Are Like That, 1930 (Mankiewicz)
Men Are Not Gods, 1936 (Hornbeck; Korda; Krasker; Reisch; Rosher)
Men Behind Bars. See Duffy of San Quentin, 1954
Men Call It Love, 1931 (Rosson)
Men Don't Leave, 1990 (Newman)
Men in Black, 1997 (Baker; Elfman)
Men in Her Life, 1931 (Riskin)
Men in Her Life, 1941 (Lemaire; Miller; Raksin; Stradling; Wilson)
Men in War, 1957 (Bernstein; Haller; Maddow)
Men in White, 1934 (Adrian; Gibbons)
Men Must Fight, 1933 (Adrian; Sullivan)
Men o' War, 1929 (Roach)
Men of Boys Town, 1941 (Rosson; Stothart)
Men of Chance, 1932 (Berman; Musuraca; Steiner)
Men of Destiny. See Men of Texas, 1942
Men of Science, 1944 (Unsworth)
Men of Sherwood Forest, 1954 (Carreras)
Men of Texas, 1942 (Krasner)
Men of the Dragon, 1974 (Bernstein)
Men of the Fighting Lady, 1954 (Rozsa)
Men of the North, 1930 (Gibbons; Mayer; Roach)
Men of the Sea. See Midshipman Easy, 1935
Men of the Sky, 1931 (Seitz)
Men of the Timberland, 1941 (Jarrico)
Men of Tomorrow, 1932 (Korda)
Men of Two Worlds, 1946 (Rank)
Men on Call, 1930 (Clarke; Friedhofer)
Men on Her Mind. See Girl from Tenth Avenue, 1935
Men with Guns, 1997 (Daring)
Men with Wings, 1938 (Head)
Men without Honour, 1939 (Stallich)
Men without Law, 1930 (McCord)
Men without Names, 1935 (Head)
Men without Wings. See Muži bez křídel, 1945
Men without Women, 1930 (August; Nichols; Parrish)
Men, Women: A User's Manual. See Hommes, femmes, mode d'emploi, 1996
Menace, 1934 (Banton)
Menace in the Night. See Face in the Night, 1958
Menaces, 1939 (Braunberger; Heller)
Mended Lute, 1909 (Bitzer)
Mender of the Nets, 1912 (Bitzer)
Mendiants, 1986 (Branco; de Almeida)
Men's Favorite Sport?, 1964 (Head)
Mensch gegen Mensch, 1924 (Junge)
Mensch ohne Namen, 1932 (Herlth; Hoffmann; Röhrig)
Menschen am Sonntag, 1929 (Schüfftan; Siodmak)
Menschen und Masken, 1913 (Warm)
Menschheit anwalt, 1920 (Röhrig)
Mensonge de Nina Petrowna, 1937 (Annenkov; Courant; Jeanson)
Menuisier, 1962 (Braunberger)
Meoto daiko, 1941 (Yoda)
Mephisto Waltz, 1971 (Goldsmith; Maddow)
Mépris, 1963 (Coutard; Delerue; Guillemot; Levine; Ponti; de Beauregard)
Mer Caribe, 1955 (Decaë)
Mer et les jours, 1958 (Colpi; Delerue)
Meraviglie di Aladino, 1961 (Delli Colli)
Meravigliose avventure di Guerrin Meschino, 1952 (Rota)

Mercante di Venezia, 1911 (Pathé)

Mercenaries, 1967 (Cardiff)

Mercenario, 1968 (Morricone; Solinas)

Mercenary. *See* Mercenario, 1968

Merchant of Venice. *See* Mercante di Venezia, 1911

Merci la vie, 1990 (Rousselot)

Mercury Rising, 1998 (Barry; Von Brandenstein)

Merely a Maid, 1920 (Roach)

Merely Mary Ann, 1931 (Furthman; Seitz)

Meri Soorat, 1963 (Burman)

Meridian Zero. *See* Południk zero, 1970

Meridian—Kiss of the Beast, 1990 (Donaggio)

Merle, 1958 (McClaren)

Merlin the Magic Mouse, 1967 (Blanc)

Mermaids, 1990 (Nitzsche)

Mermoz, 1943 (Honegger)

Merrie Melodies: Starring Bugs Bunny and Friends, 1990 (Jones)

Merrill's Marauders, 1962 (Clothier)

Merrily We Go to Hell, 1932 (Zukor)

Merrily We Live, 1938 (Irene; Roach)

Merrily We Sing, 1946 (Fleischer)

Merry Andrew, 1957 (Plunkett)

Merry Andrew, 1958 (Diamond; Kidd; Mercer; Surtees)

Merry Chase, 1950 (Terry)

Merry Christmas, Mr. Lawrence. *See* Senjo no merii kurisumasu, 1983

Merry Circus. *See* Veselý cirkus, 1950

Merry Dog, 1933 (Lantz)

Merry Dwarfs, 1929 (Disney; Stalling)

Merry Frinks, 1934 (Edeson; Orry-Kelly)

Merry Mannequins, 1937 (Iwerks)

Merry Microbes. *See* Joyeaux Microbes, 1909

Merry Minstrel Magoo, 1959 (Bosustow)

Merry Old Soul, 1933 (Lantz)

Merry Widow, 1925 (Daniels; Day; Gibbons; Mayer; Thalberg)

Merry Widow, 1934 (Adrian; Gibbons; Kahn; Loos; Mayer; Raphaelson; Stothart; Thalberg; Vajda)

Merry Widow, 1952 (Cole; Levien; Pasternak; Rose; Surtees)

Merry Widower, 1926 (Roach)

Merry Wives of Gotham. *See* Lights of Old Broadway, 1925

Merry Wives of Reno, 1934 (Haller; Orry-Kelly)

Merry Wives of Windsor, 1910 (Selig)

Merry-Go-Round, 1923 (Daniels; Day; Thalberg)

Merton of the Movies, 1924 (Brown)

Merton of the Movies, 1947 (Irene; Mayer; Rose)

Merveilleuse Journée, 1981 (Evein)

Merveilleuse Visite, 1974 (Evein)

Mes petites amoureuses, 1974 (Almendros)

Mesa of Lost Women, 1952 (Struss)

Mésaventure d'un charbonnier, 1899 (Gaumont)

Mesék az írógépröl, 1916 (Korda)

Meshi, 1951 (Hayasaka)

Meskal le contrabandier, 1909 (Gaumont)

Mesmerized, 1986 (Delerue)

Message, 1909 (Bitzer)

Message in the Bottle, 1911 (Gaudio; Ince)

Message of the Violin, 1910 (Bitzer)

Message to Garcia, 1936 (Maté; Zanuck)

Message to Gracias, 1963 (Blanc; McKimson)

Messager, 1937 (Auric; Lourié)

Messager de la lumière, 1938 (Grimault)

Messe e finita, 1985 (Morricone)

Messenger of Death, 1988 (Golan and Globus; Jarrico)

Messieurs Ludovic, 1946 (Kosma)

Metamorfeus, 1969 (Brdečka)

Metamorphose des cloportes, 1965 (Saulnier)

Metamorphoses comiques, 1912 (Cohl)

Metamorphoses du Roi de Pique, 1904 (Pathé)

Metamorphosis. *See* Fantasmagorie, 1908

Metello, 1969 (Cecchi D'amico; Morricone)

Meteor, 1979 (Neame)

Meteor Man, 1993 (Alonzo)

Meteoro vima tou Pelargou. *See* To meteoro vima to Pelargou, 1991

Métier de fous, 1948 (Burel)

Metropolis, 1927 (Freund; Hunte; Pommer; Schüfftan; Von Harbou)

Metropolitan, 1935 (Day; Maté; Newman; Zanuck)

Metti, une sera a cena, 1969 (Delli Colli; Morricone)

Meurtres, 1950 (Jeanson)

Meurtrier, 1963 (Aurenche and Bost; Douy)

Meus Amigos, 1974 (de Almeida)

Mexicali Rose, 1929 (Westmore Family)

Mexicali Shmoes, 1959 (Blanc)

Mexican. *See* Hurricane Horseman, 1931

Mexican Affair. *See* Flor de mayo, 1957

Mexican Baseball, 1947 (Terry)

Mexican Boarders, 1962 (Blanc)

Mexican Cat Dance, 1963 (Blanc)

Mexican Joyride, 1947 (Blanc; Stalling)

Mexican Mousepiece, 1966 (Blanc; McKimson)

Mexican Spitfire, 1939 (Polglase)

Mexican Spitfire Out West, 1940 (Polglase)

Mexican Spitfire Sees a Ghost, 1942 (Metty)

Mexican Sweetheart, 1909 (Bitzer)

Mexican Tragedy, 1912 (Ince)

Mexico, 1930 (Lantz)

México 2000, 1981 (Figueroa)

México mágico, 1980 (Figueroa)

Mexico Soon. *See* Jutro Meksyk, 1965

MGM Studio Tour, 1925 (Daniels)

Mi candidato, 1938 (Figueroa)

Mi negra o su negra. *See* Bestia negra, 1939

Mi viuda alegre, 1941 (Figueroa)

Mia aiwniothta kai mia mera, 1999 (Guerra)

Miarka, la fille à l'ourse, 1937 (Honegger)

Mice Follies, 1954 (Hanna and Barbera)

Mice Follies, 1960 (Blanc; McKimson)

Mice in Council, 1934 (Terry)

Mice Will Play, 1938 (Avery)

Michael and Mary, 1931 (Balcon; Biro; Vetchinsky)

Michael, 1924 (Freund; Maté; Pommer; Von Harbou)

Michael, 1996 (Ralston)

Michael Collins, 1996 (Menges)

Michael O'Halloran, 1937 (Brown)

Michael Shayne, Private Detective, 1940 (Day)

Michel Strogoff, 1925 (Burel)

Michel Strogoff, 1956 (Barsacq)

Michel's Mixed Up Bird, 1978 (Legrand)

Michigan Kid, 1946 (Miller)

Michurin, 1948 (Shostakovich)

Mickey and His Goat, 1917 (O'brien)

Mickey One, 1965 (Cloquet; Jenkins)

Mickey's Choo-Choo, 1929 (Disney; Iwerks)

Mickey's Follies, 1929 (Iwerks)

Mickey's Naughty Nightmares, 1917 (O'brien)

Micki and Maude, 1985 (Legrand)

Mid Channel, 1920 (Edeson)

Midaregumo, 1967 (Takemitsu)

Midas Run, 1969 (Bernstein)

Middies Shortening Sail, 1901 (Bitzer)

Middle of the Night, 1959 (Justin)

Middleman. *See* Jana Aranya, 1975

Midnight, 1939 (Brackett; Head; Irene; Lang)

Midnight, 1981 (Savini)Midnight Alibi, 1934 (Orry-Kelly)

Midnight Adventure, 1909 (Bitzer)
Midnight Angel, 1941 (Siodmak)
Midnight Club, 1933 (Banton)
Midnight Court, 1937 (Raksin)
Midnight Cowboy, 1969 (Barry; Smith)
Midnight Cupid, 1910 (Bitzer)
Midnight Daddies, 1930 (Hornbeck)
Midnight Event. *See* Pulnoční příhoda, 1960
Midnight Exam. *See* Examen de minuit, 1998
Midnight Express, 1978 (Hambling; Puttnam)
Midnight Frolics, 1938 (Iwerks)
Midnight in the Garden of Good and Evil, 1997 (Bumstead)
Midnight Intruder, 1938 (Krasner)
Midnight Lace, 1960 (Hunter; Irene; Metty)
Midnight Madness, 1928 (Adrian; Goosson)
Midnight Madonna, 1937 (Head)
Midnight Man, 1974 (Grusin)
Midnight Mary, 1933 (Adrian; Loos)
Midnight Melody. *See* Murder in the Music Hall, 1946
Midnight Molly, 1925 (Berman)
Midnight Mystery, 1930 (Plunkett; Walker)
Midnight Parasites, 1972 (Kuri)
Midnight Patrol, 1918 (Ince)
Midnight Patrol, 1933 (Roach)
Midnight Romance, 1919 (Mayer)
Midnight Run, 1988 (Elfman)
Midnight Snack, 1941 (Hanna and Barbera)
Midnight Sting. *See* Diggstown, 1992
Midnight Story, 1957 (Metty)
Midnight Taxi, 1928 (Zanuck)
Midori no daichi, 1942 (Hayasaka)
Midshipman, 1932 (Balcon; Junge)
Midshipman Easy, 1935 (Dean)
Midshipman Jack, 1933 (D'Agostino; Plunkett; Polglase; Steiner)
Midsummer Mush, 1933 (Roach)
Midsummer Music, 1960 (Lassally)
Midsummer Nightmare, 1957 (Halas and Batchelor)
Midsummer Night's Dream, 1935 (Blanke; Grot; Haskin; Korngold; Mohr; Wallis; Westmore Family)
Midsummer Night's Dream. *See* Sen noci svatojánské, 1959
Midsummer Night's Dream. *See* Sommernachstraum, 1924
Midsummer Night's Sex Comedy, 1982 (Loquasto; Willis)
Midway, 1976 (Mirisch; Williams)
Miel se fue de la luna, 1951 (Alcoriza)
Mientras México duerme, 1938 (Figueroa)
Mighty, 1930 (Mankiewicz; Zukor)
Mighty Aphrodite, 1995 (Loquasto)
Mighty Barnum, 1934 (Day; Newman; Zanuck)
Mighty Hunters, 1940 (Blanc; Jones; Stalling)
Mighty Joe Young, 1949 (Basevi; Cooper; Dunn; Harryhausen; O'brien)
Mighty Joe Young, 1998 (Baker; Harryhausen)
Mighty Lak' a Rose, 1923 (Polito)
Mighty Like a Moose, 1926 (Roach)
Mighty McGurk, 1946 (Irene)
Mighty Mouse and the Kilkenny Cats, 1945 (Terry)
Mighty Mouse and the Magician, 1948 (Terry)
Mighty Mouse and the Pirates, 1945 (Terry)
Mighty Mouse and the Wolf, 1945 (Terry)
Mighty Mouse in Krakatoa, 1945 (Terry)
Mighty Mouse Meets Bad Bill Bunion, 1945 (Terry)
Mighty Mouse Meets Deadeye Dick, 1947 (Terry)
Mighty Mouse Meets Jekyll and Hyde Cat, 1944 (Terry)
Mighty Mouse Rides Again. *See* Super Mouse Rides Again, 1943
Mighty Navy, 1941 (Fleischer)
Mighty Penny, 1942 (Balcon)
Mighty Treve, 1937 (Raksin)

Mikado, 1907 (Gaumont)
Mikado, 1939 (Dillon)
Mikado, 1967 (Fisher; Havelock-Allan)
Mike Fright, 1934 (Roach)
Mike's Murder, 1984 (Allen; Barry)
Mikey and Nicky, 1976 (Ballard)
Mikosch rückt ein, 1928 (Metzner)
Mikromakrokosmos, 1960 (Brdečka)
Mil e Uma, 1994 (Branco)
Milagro Beanfield War, 1988 (Allen; Grusin)
Milan, 1946 (Biswas)
Milano Miliardaria, 1951 (Delli Colli)
Milano odia: la polizia no puo sparare, 1974 (Morricone)
Milano Zero, 1983 (Bozzetto)
Mildred Pierce, 1945 (Friedhofer; Grot; Haller; Steiner; Wald)
Mile de Jules Ladoumègue, 1932 (Kaufman)
Milestones of the Movies, 1966 (Clarke)
Mili, 1975 (Burman)
Military Academy, 1940 (Brown)
Military Judas, 1913 (Ince)
Military Life, Pleasant Life. *See* Život vojenský, život veselý, 1934
Milk and Money, 1936 (Avery; Stalling)
Milk for Baby, 1938 (Terry)
Milk Money, 1994 (Marshall; Watkin)
Milkman, 1932 (Iwerks)
Milkman, 1950 (Boyle)
Milky Waif, 1946 (Hanna and Barbera)
Milky Way, 1935 (Head; Zukor)
Milky Way. *See* Voie Lactée, 1969
Mill of Good Fortune. *See* Glücksmühle, 1947
Mill on the Po. *See* Mulino del Po, 1949
Mille-et-Deuxième Nuit, 1933 (Maté)
Mille et un millions. *See* Toute la ville accuse, 1955
Mille villages, 1960 (Rabier)
Miller's Beautiful Daughter. *See* Bella mugnaia, 1955
Miller's Beautiful Wife. *See* Bella mugnaia, 1955
Miller's Crossing, 1990 (Burwell)
Milliard dans un billard, 1965 (Spaak)
Millie, 1931 (Haller)
Million, 1931 (Meerson; Périnal)
Million Bid, 1927 (Blanke; Mohr)
Million Dollar Baby, 1941 (Orry-Kelly; Rosher; Wald; Wallis)
Million Dollar Bride, 1914 (Loos)
Million Dollar Cat, 1944 (Hanna and Barbera)
Million Dollar Legs, 1932 (Mankiewicz)
Million Dollar Legs, 1939 (Head)
Million Dollar Mermaid, 1952 (Deutsch; Plunkett; Rose; Smith)
Million Dollar Mystery, 1987 (Cardiff)
Million Dollar Trio. *See* Trio: Rubenstein, Heifetz, and Piatigorsky, 1952
Million-Hare, 1963 (Blanc; McKimson)
Million Pound Note, 1953 (Alwyn; Bryan; Neame; Rank; Unsworth)
Million Pound Note. *See* Az egymillió fontos bankó, 1916
Millionaire Droopy, 1956 (Avery)
Millionaire for Christie, 1951 (Leven; Mandell; Stradling; Young)
Millionaire Playboy, 1940 (Polglase)
Millionaire Uncle. *See* Millionenonkel, 1913
Millionaires, 1926 (Haskin)
Millionaires in Prison, 1940 (Polglase)
Millionairess, 1960 (Fisher)
Millionär für 3 Tage, 1963 (Herlth)
Millionen-Mine, 1914 (Warm)
Millionenonkel, 1913 (Kolowrat-Krakowsky)
Millionenraub im Rivieraexpress, 1927 (Warm)
Millions, 1936 (Wilcox)
Millions Like Us, 1943 (Bryan; Rank)
Millones de Chaflan, 1938 (Figueroa)

Mills of the Gods, 1909 (Bitzer)
Milou en mai, 1990 (Carrière)
Min and Bill, 1930 (Gibbons; Marion; Mayer; Shearer)
Min kära är en ros, 1963 (Fischer)
Mina drömmars stad, 1976 (Lundgren)
Minami no bara, 1950 (Yoda)
Minami no kaze to nami, 1961 (Muraki)
Minato no jojoushi, 1932 (Yoda)
Mind Benders, 1963 (Auric; Mathieson)
Mind of Mr. Reeder, 1939 (Junge)
Mind Reader, 1933 (Orry-Kelly; Polito)
Mind Your Own Business, 1937 (Head; Schary)
Minding the Baby, 1931 (Fleischer)
Mine Own Executioner, 1947 (Francis; Korda)
Mine with the Iron Door, 1936 (Carré)
Miner Affair, 1945 (Bruckman)
Miner's Daughter, 1949 (Bosustow)
Mini Quark, 1988 (Bozzetto)
Minin i Pozharsky, 1939 (Golovnya)
Ministry of Fear, 1944 (Dreier; Head; Miller; Pereira; Young)
Miniver Story, 1950 (Junge; Mathieson; Mayer; Plunkett; Rozsa;
    Ruttenberg)
Minnen fran Bostonklubben, 1909 (Magnusson)
Minnie, 1922 (Marion; Struss)
Minnie the Moocher, 1932 (Fleischer)
Minotaur, 1961 (Mainwaring)
Minshu no teki, 1946 (Hayasaka)
Minstrel Mania, 1949 (Fleischer)
Minstrel's Song. See Slóvce M, 1964
Minute de verité, 1952 (Jeanson)
Mio caro assassino, 1972 (Morricone)
Mio caro Dr. Gräsler, 1990 (Morricone; Rotunno)
Mio Dio, come sono caduta in basso!, 1974 (Delli Colli)
Mio figlio Nerone, 1956 (Cristaldi)
Mio figlio professore, 1946 (Cecchi D'amico; Rota)
Mio nome e nessuno, 1973 (Morricone)
Mio West, 1999 (Donaggio)
Mioche, 1936 (Spaak)
Miquette et sa mère, 1933 (Fradetal)
Miquette et sa mère, 1949 (Wakhévitch)
Mira, 1971 (Delerue)
Mira, 1977 (Shankar)
Mira ka Chitra, 1960 (Biswas)
Miracle, 1954 (Breer)
Miracle, 1959 (Bernstein; Blanke; Haller)
Miracle, 1990 (Rousselot)
Miracle. See Miraklet, 1913
Miracle Can Happen, 1947 (Biroc; Cronjager; Laszlo; Seitz)
Miracle des roses, 1908 (Cohl)
Miracle in Milan. See **Miracolo a Milano**, 1950
Miracle in Soho, 1957 (Challis; Dillon; Rank)
Miracle in the Rain, 1956 (Hecht; Maté; Metty; Waxman)
Miracle Man, 1919 (Zukor)
Miracle Man, 1932 (Laszlo; Zukor)
Miracle of Fatima. See Miracle of Our Lady of Fatima, 1952
Miracle of Morgan's Creek, 1944 (Dreier; Head; Seitz)
Miracle of Our Lady of Fatima, 1952 (Burks; Steiner)
Miracle of the Bells, 1948 (Cahn; Hecht; Lasky)
Miracle of the White Stallions, 1962 (Disney)
Miracle on 34th Street, 1947 (Clarke; Day; Lemaire; Newman; Zanuck)
Miracle Woman, 1931 (Cohn; Swerling; Walker)
Miracle Worker, 1962 (Jenkins)·
Miracles, 1984 (Alcott)
Miracles n'ont lieu qu'une fois, 1950 (Trauner)
Miracolo a loreto, 1949 (Zavattini)

Miracolo a Milano, 1950 (Aldo; Cecchi D'Amico; Di Venanzo; Korda;
    Zavattini)
Miraculous Doctor. See Za opunu smrti, 1923
Mirage, 1924 (Sullivan)
Mirage, 1965 (Jones; Louis; Whitlock)
Mirage in the North. See Severnoe siianie, 1926
Mirages, 1937 (Burel)
Mirages de Paris, 1932 (Andrejew; Douy; Jaubert)
Miraklet, 1913 (Jaenzon; Magnusson)
Miranda, 1948 (Rank)
Miren, 1963 (Takemitsu)
Mirka, 1999 (Storaro)
Miroir, 1946 (Wakhévitch)
Mirror, 1911 (Gaudio)
Mirror Crack'd, 1980 (Challis)
Mirror Has Two Faces, 1996 (Hamlisch)
Misadventures of Merlin Jones, 1963 (Disney)
Misanthrope, 1966 (Braunberger)
Misappropriated Turkey, 1912 (Bitzer)
Misbehaving Ladies, 1930 (Seitz)
Mischief, 1931 (Wilcox)
Mischievous Hedgehog, 1952 (Popescu-Gopo)
Mise à sac, 1967 (Lhomme; Mnouchkine)
Miser, 1913 (August)
Misérables, 1912 (Pathé)
Misérables, 1934 (Douy; Honegger; Jaubert; Newman; Toland; Zanuck
Misérables, 1952 (Jeakins; La Shelle; Lemaire; Newman; North)
Misérables, 1995 (Lai; Legrand)
Misère au Borinage, 1934 (van Dongen)
Miserie del Signor Travet, 1946 (Flaiano and Pinelli; de Laurentiis; Rota)
Miser's Heart, 1911 (Bitzer)
Misery, 1990 (Goldman)
Misfits, 1961 (Metty; North)
Misguided Tour, 1960 (Halas and Batchelor)
Mishka against Yudenich. See Mishki protiv Youdenitsa, 1925
Mishki protiv Youdenitsa, 1925 (Enei)
Miska the Magnate. See Mágnás Miska, 1916
Misleading Lady, 1921 (Polito)
Misleading Widow, 1919 (Marion; Zukor)
Miss and Mrs. Sweden, 1969 (Fischer)
Miss Bracegirdle Does Her Duty, 1936 (Korda)
Miss Congeniality, 2000 (Kovacs)
Miss Evers' Boys, 1997 (Bernstein)
Miss Fix-It. See Keep Smiling, 1938
Miss George Washington, 1916 (Zukor)
Miss Glory, 1936 (Avery)
Miss Grant Takes Richmond, 1949 (Louis)
Miss Hobbs, 1921 (Reisch)
Miss India, 1957 (Burman)
Miss Josabeth. See Mamsell Josabeth, 1963
Miss Julie. See Fräulein Julie, 1922
Miss London Ltd., 1943 (Rank)
Miss Lonelyheart. See Lonelyhearts, 1959
Miss Lulu Bett, 1920 (Zukor)
Miss Mrs.. See Fräulein Frau, 1923
Miss Muerte, 1966 (Carrière)
Miss Ogin. See Ogin sama, 1978
Miss Oyu. See Oyu-sama, 1951
Miss Pacific Fleet, 1935 (Orry-Kelly)
Miss Petticoats, 1916 (Edeson)
Miss Polly, 1941 (Roach)
Miss Robin Crusoe, 1953 (Bernstein; Miller)
Miss Sadie Thompson, 1953 (Cohn; Duning; Louis; Wald)
Miss Susie Slagle's, 1945 (Dreier; Head; Houseman; Lang)
Miss Tatlock's Millions, 1948 (Brackett; Dreier; Head; Lang; Young)
Miss Uyo. See Oyu-sama, 1951

Miss Wildcat. *See* Yamaneko rei jou, 1948
Misses Stooge, 1935 (Roach)
Missile from Hell. *See* Battle of the V1, 1958
Missing, 1982 (Vangelis; Whitlock)
Missing, Believed Married, 1937 (Havelock-Allan)
Missing Evidence, 1939 (Krasner)
Missing Guest, 1938 (Krasner)
Missing in Action, 1984 (Golan and Globus)
Missing Link, 1927 (Zanuck)
Missing Link, 1989 (Baker)
Missing Mouse, 1953 (Hanna and Barbera)
Missing Ten Days. *See* Ten Days in Paris, 1939
Mission, 1986 (Menges; Morricone; Puttnam)
Mission: Impossible, 1966 (Alton)
Mission: Impossible, 1996 (Elfman; Schifrin; Towne)
Mission: Impossible 2, 2000 (Schifrin; Towne; Zimmer)
Mission Impossible versus the Mob, 1968 (Schifrin)
Mission sous la mer, 1946 (Renoir)
Mission to Mars, 2000 (Morricone)
Mission to Moscow, 1943 (Glennon; Haskin; Koch; Orry-Kelly;
   Steiner; Warner)
Missionaire, 1955 (Renoir)
Missione d'amore, 1992 (Donaggio)
Mississippi, 1935 (Dreier; Head; Lang; Schary; Zukor)
Mississippi Blues. *See* Pays d'Octobre, 1983
Mississippi Burning, 1988 (Biziou; Hambling)
Mississippi Gambler, 1929 (Brown)
Mississippi Gambler, 1952 (Maté; Miller)
Mississippi Hare, 1949 (Blanc; Jones)
Mississippi Mermaid. *See* Sirène du Mississippi, 1969
Mississippi Swing, 1941 (Terry)
Missouri Breaks, 1976 (Allen; Williams)
Missouri Traveler, 1957 (Hoch; Mercer)
Mist. *See* Sis, 1989
Mistake, 1913 (Bitzer; Loos)
Mister 44, 1916 (Gaudio)
Mr. 420. *See* Shree 420, 1955
Mr. 880, 1950 (La Shelle; Lemaire; Riskin; Zanuck)
Mister Ace, 1946 (Struss)
Mr. and Mrs. Bridge, 1990 (Jhabvala; Merchant)
Mr. and Mrs. North, 1941 (Stradling)
Mr. and Mrs. Smith, 1941 (D'Agostino; Krasna; Polglase; Stradling)
Mr. Ashton Was Indiscreet. *See* Senator Was Indiscreet, 1947
Mr. Baseball, 1992 (Goldsmith)
Mr. Belvedere Goes to College, 1949 (Lemaire; Newman)
Mr. Belvedere Rings the Bell, 1951 (La Shelle; Lang; Lemaire)
Mr. Billion, 1977 (Grusin)
Mr. Blandings Builds His Dream House, 1948 (Howe; Schary)
Mister Buddwing, 1966 (Rose)
Mr. Bug Goes to Town, 1942 (Carmichael)
Mr. Butt-In, 1906 (Bitzer)
Mr. Casanova, 1954 (Head)
Mr. Chump, 1938 (Edeson)
Mister Cinderella, 1936 (Krasner; Roach)
Mr. Cory, 1957 (Metty)
Mr. Deeds Goes to Town, 1936 (Cohn; Deutsch; Goosson; Riskin;
   Tiomkin; Walker)
Mr. Denning Drives North, 1951 (Korda)
Mr. District Attorney, 1941 (Brown)
Mr. District Attorney, 1946 (Goosson; Louis; Glennon)
Mr. District Attorney in the Carter Case, 1942 (Alton)
Mr. Dodd Takes the Air, 1937 (Deutsch; Edeson)
Mr. Doodle Kicks Off, 1938 (Metty)
Mr. Emmanuel, 1944 (Heller; Rank)
Mr. Fixit, 1918 (Edeson)
Mister Flow, 1936 (Jeanson)

Mister Freedom, 1969 (Lhomme)
Mr. Gallagher and Mr. Shean, 1931 (Fleischer)
Mr. Head. *See* Monsieur Tête, 1959
Mr. Hobbs Takes a Vacation, 1962 (Johnson; Mancini; Mercer;
   Smith; Wald)
Mister Hobo. *See* Guv'nor, 1935
Mr. Horn, 1979 (Goldman)
Mr. Hughes, 2000 (Donaggio)
Mr. Hulot's Holiday. *See* **Vacances de M. Hulot**, 1953
Mr. Hurry-Up, 1906 (Bitzer)
Mr. Hyppo, 1923 (Roach)
Mr. Imperium, 1950 (Kaper; Plunkett)
Mister Johnson, 1990 (Delerue)
Mr. Jones at the Ball, 1908 (Bitzer; Macpherson)
Mr. Jones, 1993 (Jarre)
Mr. Klein, 1977 (Fisher; Solinas; Trauner)
Mr. Know-How in Hot Water, 1962 (Dunning)
Mr. Lemon of Orange, 1931 (August)
Mr. Love, 1985 (Puttnam)
Mr. Lucky, 1943 (Barnes; Menzies)
Mr. Magoo, 1949 (Hubley)
Mr. Majestyk, 1974 (Mirisch)
Mister Moses, 1965 (Barry; Morris; Neame)
Mr. Moto Takes a Chance, 1938 (Miller)
Mr. Moto Takes a Vacation, 1939 (Clarke)
Mr. Moto's Last Warning, 1939 (Miller; Raksin)
Mr. Music, 1950 (Barnes; Dreier; Head; van Heusen)
Mr. Orchid. *See* Père tranquille, 1946
Mr. Peabody and the Mermaid, 1948 (Johnson; Leven; Mercer; Metty;
   Westmore Family)
Mr. Perrin and Mr. Traill, 1948 (Rank)
Mr. Prokouk in Temptation. *See* Pan Prokouk v pokušeni, 1947
Mr. Prokouk in the Office. *See* Pan prokouk úřaduje, 1947
Mr. Prokouk Is Filming. *See* Pan Prokouk filmuje, 1948
Mr. Prokouk Leaves for Volunteer Work. *See* Brigady, 1947
Mr. Prokouk, the Acrobat. *See* Pan Prokouk abrobat, 1958
Mr. Prokouk, the Animal Lover. *See* Pan Prokouk, přítel zvířátek, 1955
Mr. Prokouk, the Detective. *See* Pan Prokouk detektivem, 1957
Mr. Prokouk, the Inventor. *See* Pan Prokouk vynálezcem, 1948
Mr. Prokouk, the Watchmaker. *See* Pan Prokouk hodinářem, 1972
Mister Quilp, 1974 (Bernstein; Challis)
Mr. Ricco, 1974 (Westmore Family)
Mister Roberts, 1955 (Hoch; Nugent; Waxman)
Mr. Robinson Crusoe, 1932 (Newman)
Mr. Sardonicus, 1961 (Guffey)
Mr. Saturday Night, 1992 (Bass)
Mr. Scoutmaster, 1953 (La Shelle; Lemaire)
Mr. Skeffington, 1944 (Epstein; Orry-Kelly; Waxman)
Mr. Skitch, 1933 (Levien; Seitz)
Mr. Smith Carries On, 1937 (Havelock-Allan)
Mr. Smith Goes to Washington, 1939 (Buchman; Cohn; Tiomkin;
   Vorkapich; Walker)
Mr. Soft Touch, 1949 (Walker)
Mr. Strauss Takes a Waltz, 1942 (Pal)
Mr. Sycamore, 1975 (Jarre)
Mister Tao, 1988 (Bozzetto)
Mr Tvardovsky. *See* Pan Tvardovsky, 1916
Mr. Tvardovsky in Rome. *See* Pan Tvardovsky v Rimye, 1917
Mr. Universe, 1950 (Tiomkin)
Mr. Winkle Goes to War, 1944 (Walker)
Mr. Wu, 1927 (Day; Gibbons; Mayer)
Mistero di Oberwald, 1979 (Guerra)
Mistigri, 1931 (Stradling)
Mistral, 1965 (Lhomme)
Mistress. *See* Maîtresse, 1975
Mrs. Barnacle Bill, 1934 (Roach)

Mrs. Delafield Wants to Marry, 1985 (Lassally)
Mrs. Doubtfire, 1993 (Jones; McAlpine)
Mrs. Jones' Burglar, 1909 (Bitzer)
Mrs. Jones Entertains, 1908 (Bitzer; Macpherson)
Mrs. Jones Has a Card Party, 1908 (Bitzer)
Mrs. Jones' Lover, 1909 (Bitzer)
Mrs. Jones' Rest Farm, 1949 (Terry)
Mrs. Loring's Secret. See Imperfect Lady, 1947
Mrs. Mike, 1949 (Biroc; Steiner)
Mrs. Miniver, 1942 (Gibbons; Gillespie; Mayer; Ruttenberg; Sherriff; Stothart)
Mrs. Munck, 1995 (Rosenman)
Mrs. O'Leary's Cow, 1938 (Terry)
Mrs. O'Malley and Mr. Malone, 1950 (Deutsch)
Mrs. Parkington, 1944 (Irene; Kaper; Mayer; Ruttenberg)
Mrs. Pollifax—Spy, 1970 (Biroc; Previn)
Mrs. Skeffington, 1944 (Haller)
Mrs. Smithers' Boarding School, 1907 (Bitzer)
Mrs. Soffel, 1984 (Boyd)
Mrs. Tutti Frutti, 1921 (Kolowrat-Krakowsky)
Mrs. Uschyck, 1973 (Jarre)
Mrs. Wallace Reid. See Linda, 1928
Mrs. Wiggs of the Cabbage Patch, 1934 (Lang; Zukor)
Mrs. Wiggs of the Cabbage Patch, 1942 (Dreier; Head; Young)
Misty, 1961 (Garmes)
Misunderstood Boy, 1913 (Bitzer)
Mit den Augen einer Frau, 1942 (Von Harbou)
Mitasareta seikatsu, 1961 (Takemitsu)
Mitsuyu-sen, 1954 (Hayasaka)
Mitt folk är icke ditt, 1944 (Lundgren)
Mitt Me Tonight, 1941 (Bruckman)
Mivtza Kahir, 1966 (Golan and Globus)
Mix-Up for Maisie, 1914 (Roach)
Mixed Babies, 1908 (Bitzer)
Mixed Master, 1956 (Blanc; McKimson)
Mixed Nuts, 1934 (Roach)
Mixed Nuts, 1994 (Nykvist)
Mixed Values, 1915 (Loos)
Miya Bibi Raji, 1960 (Burman)
Miyamoto Musashi, 1940 (Miyagawa)
Mladé dny, 1956 (Stallich)
M'Liss, 1918 (Marion)
M'Liss, 1936 (Steiner)
Mlle. Irene the Great, 1931 (Johnson)
Mo' Better Blues, 1990 (Dickerson)
Moa Moa, 1984 (Bozzetto)
Moan and Groans, 1935 (Terry)
Mob, 1951 (Duning; Parrish; Walker)
Mobilier fidèle, 1910 (Cohl)
Mobilizing Mass. State Troops, 1905 (Bitzer)
Mobsters, 1991 (Sylbert)
Moby Dick, 1956 (Francis; Morris; Warner)
Moby Duck, 1965 (Blanc; McKimson)
Moc osudu, 1968 (Brdečka)
Mockery, 1927 (Gibbons; Mayer)
Mod att leva, 1983 (Theodorakis)
Mode rêvée, 1939 (Auric)
Model. See Mannekängen, 1913
Model and the Marriage Broker, 1951 (Brackett; Krasner; Lemaire; Reisch; Wheeler)
Model and the Young Lord. See Moderu to wakatono, 1947
Model Courtship, 1903 (Bitzer)
Model Diary, 1922 (Terry)
Model Muddle, 1955 (Halas and Batchelor)
Modelage express, 1903 (Gaumont)
Modeling, 1923 (Fleischer)

Model's Ma, 1907 (Bitzer)
Models, Inc., 1952 (Cortez)
Moderato Cantabile, 1960 (Duras)
Modern DuBarry. See DuBarry von Heute, 1927
Modern Guide to Health, 1946 (Halas and Batchelor)
Modern Hero, 1934 (Orry-Kelly)
Modern Hero. See Knute Rockne—All American, 1940
Modern Miracle. See Story of Alexander Graham Bell, 1939
Modern Mothers, 1928 (Walker)
Modern Musketeer, 1917 (Zukor)
Modern Prodigal, 1910 (Bitzer)
Modern Red Riding Hood, 1935 (Terry)
Modern Times, 1936 (Newman; Raksin)
Modern Vampires, 1998 (Elfman)
Moderne Ecole, 1909 (Cohl)
Moderní Magdalena, 1921 (Heller)
Moderu to wakatono, 1947 (Yoda)
Modesty Blaise, 1966 (Fisher)
Modification, 1969 (Lai)
Modigliani of Montparnasse. See Montparnasse 19, 1958
Moeru aki, 1978 (Takemitsu)
Moetikuta chizu, 1968 (Takemitsu)
Mogambo, 1953 (Junge; Rose; Surtees; Young)
Moglie americana, 1965 (Flaiano and Pinelli)
Moglie del prete, 1971 (Ponti)
Moglie più bella, 1970 (Morricone)
Mohammad, Messenger of God, 1976 (Jarre)
Mohawk, 1955 (Struss)
Mohawk's Way, 1910 (Bitzer)
Moi, un noir, 1958 (Braunberger)
Moine, 1972 (Carrière; Douy; Vierny)
Mois d'avril sont meurtriers, 1987 (Sarde)
Moisson sera belle, 1954 (Fradetal)
Moissons d'aujourd'hui, 1949 (Cloquet)
Moissons de l'espoir, 1969 (Braunberger)
Mojo, 1997 (Pinter)
Mokey, 1942 (Rosher)
Mole People, 1956 (Westmore Family)
Mollenard, 1937 (Milhaud; Spaak; Trauner; Alekan; Schüfftan)
Mollo tutto, 1995 (Donaggio)
Molly and Lawless John, 1972 (Mandel)
Molly and Me, 1945 (Clarke)
Molly Maguires, 1969 (Howe; Bernstein; Jeakins; Mancini; Westmore Family)
Molly O', 1921 (Goodrich and Hackett; Hornbeck)
Molodaya gvardiya, 1947 (Shostakovich)
Molti sogni per le strade, 1948 (Rota; de Laurentiis)
Mom and Dad Save the World, 1992 (Goldsmith)
Moment by Moment, 1978 (Horner; Lathrop)
Moment of Danger. See Malaga, 1960
Moment of Truth. See Minute de verité, 1952
Moment of Truth. See Momento della verità, 1965
Moment to Moment, 1966 (Mancini; Mercer; Stradling)
Momento della verità, 1965 (Di Venanzo)
Momento più bello, 1957 (Amidei; Rota)
Momentos de la vida de Martí. See Rosa blanca, 1953
Momma Don't Allow, 1956 (Lassally)
Mommie Dearest, 1981 (Mancini; Sharaff)
Mommy Loves Puppy, 1940 (Fleischer)
Mon ami Pierre, 1951 (Kosma)
Mon ami Sainfoin, 1949 (Mnouchkine)
Mon ami Victor, 1930 (Périnal)
Mon Amour est près de toi, 1943 (Andrejew)
Mon amour, mon amour, 1967 (Lai)
Mon beau-frere a tué ma soeur, 1985 (Sarde)
Mon cas, 1986 (Branco)

Mon Coeur est rouge, 1975 (Nuytten)
Mon curé chez les pauvres, 1956 (Burel)
Mon gosse de Père, 1952 (Burel)
Mon homme, 1996 (Lhomme)
Mon Journal. See Journal animé, 1908
Mon oncle d'Amerique, 1980 (Saulnier; Vierny)
Mon oncle, 1958 (Grimault)
Mon premier amour, 1978 (Legrand)
Mon royaume pour un cheval, 1978 (Jarre)
Mona, l'étoile sans nom, 1966 (Colpi; Delerue)
Monaca di Monza, 1962 (Delli Colli)
Monaca di Monza, 1968 (Morricone; Donati)
Monaca di Monza, 1987 (Donaggio)
Monachine, 1963 (Morricone)
Monasterio de los buitres, 1972 (Figueroa)
Monastery of Sendomir. See Klostret it sendomir, 1920
Monday Morning in a Coney Island Police Court, 1908 (Bitzer)
Monde des marais, 1963 (Braunberger; Delerue)
Monde en raccourci, 1958 (Grimault)
Monde est un grand chien, 1996 (Legrand)
Monde nouveau, 1965 (Douy)
Monde perdu, 1954 (Milhaud)
Monde tremblera, 1939 (Barsacq)
Monde troublant, 1953 (Decaë)
Mondo di notte, 1959 (Delli Colli)
Mondo le condanna, 1952 (Cecchi D'amico; Flaiano and Pinelli)
Mondo Mod, 1967 (Kovacs; Zsigmond)
Mondo nuovo, 1966 (Zavattini)
Mondo vuole cosi, 1945 (Zavattini)
Monella, 1999 (Donaggio)
Money, 1914 (Mohr)
Money, 1991 (Morricone)
Money Corral, 1919 (August)
Money Dance. See Zenin no odori, 1964
Money from Home, 1953 (Wallis; Head)
Money Man, 1908 (Bitzer)
Money Means Nothing, 1932 (Wilcox)
Money Money Money. See Aventure c'est l'aventure, 1972
Money Movers, 1979 (McAlpine)
Money Pit, 1985 (Willis; Marshall; Von Brandenstein)
Money Talks, 1926 (Daniels; Gibbons)
Money Talks, 1997 (Schifrin)
Money to Burn, 1920 (Roach)
Money Trap, 1966 (Bernstein)
Money, Women and Guns, 1958 (Lathrop)
Monga, 1977 (Kuri)
Monica Vogelsang, 1919 (Kräly)
Monika. See Sommaren med Monika, 1953
Monique à Vichy, 1969 (Braunberger)
Monitors, 1969 (Zsigmond)
Monje loco, 1940 (Figueroa)
Monk. See Moine, 1972
Monkey Business, 1926 (Roach)
Monkey Business, 1931 (Mankiewicz)
Monkey Business, 1952 (Diamond; Hecht; Krasner; Lederer; Lemaire; Wheeler)
Monkey into Man, 1938 (Alwyn)
Monkey Meat, 1930 (Terry)
Monkey on My Back, 1957 (Veiller)
Monkey Shines, 1988 (Savini)
Monkey Talks, 1927 (Pierce)
Monkey Trouble, 1994 (Zimmer)
Monkey Wretches, 1935 (Lantz)
Monkey's Paw, 1932 (Steiner; Selznick)
Monkey's Uncle, 1964 (Disney)
Monkeys, Go Home!, 1966 (Disney; Ellenshaw)

Monnaie de 1.000F, 1908 (Cohl)
Monnaie de lapin, 1899 (Gaumont)
Monnaie de singe, 1965 (Legrand; Wakhévitch)
Monochrome Painter Yves Kline. See Monokurohmu no gaka: Yves Kline, 1966
Monokurohmu no gaka: Yves Kline, 1966 (Takemitsu)
Monsieur Albert, 1932 (Maté)
Monsieur Albert, 1975 (Cloquet; Mnouchkine)
Monsieur Badin, 1946 (Braunberger)
Monsieur Badin, 1977 (Guillemot)
Monsieur Beaucaire, 1923 (Westmore Family; Braunberger; Zukor)
Monsieur Beaucaire, 1946 (Dreier; Head)
Monsieur Bibi. See Faut ce qu'il faut, 1940
Monsieur Bretonneau, 1939 (Courant)
Monsieur Clown chez les Lilliputiens, 1909 (Cohl)
Monsieur Cordon, 1933 (Aurenche and Bost)
Monsieur de compagnie, 1964 (Coutard; Delerue)
Monsieur de Crac, 1910 (Cohl)
Monsieur de minuit, 1931 (Maté; Meerson)
Monsieur de Pourceaugnas, 1984 (Douy)
Monsieur et la souris, 1942 (Auric)
Monsieur et Madame Curie, 1953 (Fradetal)
Monsieur et Madame veulent une bonne, 1907 (Pathé)
Monsieur Fabre, 1951 (Renoir)
Monsieur La Bruyère, 1956 (Colpi)
Monsieur Le Maréchal, 1931 (Heller)
Monsieur qui suit les femmes, 1906 (Pathé)
Monsieur Ripois, 1954 (Francis; Morris)
Monsieur Stop, 1910 (Cohl)
Monsieur Tête, 1959 (Colpi; Lenica)
Monsieur Verdoux, 1947 (Courant)
Monsieur Vincent, 1947 (Renoir)
Monsignor, 1982 (Williams)
Monsoon, 1952 (Haller; Jenkins)
Monster, 1925 (Mayer; Mohr; Sullivan)
Monster. See Mostro, 1994
Monster and the Girl, 1941 (Head)
Monster and Tiger Man, 1944 (Alton)
Monster from the Ocean Floor, 1954 (Crosby)
Monster of Highgate Pond, 1961 (Halas and Batchelor)
Monster of Piedras Blancas, 1958 (Lathrop)
Monster on the Campus, 1958 (Metty)
Monster Squad, 1987 (Edlund; Winston)
Monster Zero. See Kaiju daisenso, 1966
Monsters. See I nuovi mostri, 1977
Monsters from the Arcane Galaxy. See Monstrum z galaxie Arkana, 1981
Monsters in the Night. See Navy versus the Night Monsters, 1965
Monstrum z galaxie Arkana, 1981 (Vukotić; švankmajer)
Monstruo de la sombra, 1954 (Figueroa)
Montagne aux météores, 1958 (Braunberger)
Montagne vivante, 1964 (Delerue)
Montana, 1930 (Daniels)
Montana, 1949 (Freund; Warner; Chase)
Montana Moon, 1930 (Adrian; Brown; Freed; Gibbons; Stothart)
Monte Carlo, 1926 (Daniels; Gibbons)
Monte Carlo, 1930 (Banton; Dreier; Vajda; Zukor)
Monte Carlo. See Monte Carlo Story, 1956
Monte Carlo Madness. See Bomben auf Monte Carlo, 1931
Monte Carlo Nights, 1934 (Canutt)
Monte Carlo Story, 1956 (Rotunno)
Monte-charge, 1962 (Delerue)
Monte Walsh, 1970 (Barry; Fraker)
Montmartre, 1950 (Cardiff)
Montmartre. See Flamme, 1923
Montmartre Nocturne, 1951 (Cardiff)
Montparnasse 19, 1957 (D'Eaubonne; Annenkov; Jeanson; Matras)

Montreur d'ombres, 1959 (Delerue)
Monty Python's Life of Brian. See Life of Brian, 1979
Moochin' through Georgia, 1939 (Bruckman)
Moods of the Sea, 1942 (Vorkapich)
Moon and Sixpence, 1942 (Seitz; Tiomkin)
Moon for Your Love. See Lune dans son tablier, 1909
Moon Is Blue, 1953 (Laszlo)
Moon Is Down, 1943 (Basevi; Johnson; Miller; Newman)
Moon of Israel. See Sodom and Gomorrha, 1922
Moon over Burma, 1940 (Head; Young)
Moon over Las Vegas, 1944 (Bruckman)
Moon over Miami, 1941 (Banton; Cole; Day; Newman; Pan; Shamroy)
Moon over Parador, 1988 (Jarre; McAlpine)
Moon Pilot, 1961 (Disney)
Moon Rock, 1970 (Dunning)
Moon-Spinners, 1964 (Disney)
Moon-Struck Matador. See Clair de lune espagnol, 1909
Moon Zero Two, 1969 (Carreras)
Moonbird, 1959 (Hubley)
Moonfleet, 1955 (Houseman; Plunkett; Rozsa)
Moonflower of Heaven. See Ten no yugao, 1948
Moonlight and Melody. See Moonlight and Pretzels, 1933
Moonlight and Noses, 1925 (Roach)
Moonlight and Pretzels, 1933 (Freund)
Moonlight Follies, 1921 (Glennon)
Moonlight in Hawaii, 1941 (Cortez)
Moonlight Masquerade, 1942 (Alton)
Moonlight Murder, 1936 (Clarke; Stothart)
Moonlight Sonata, 1937 (Stallich)
Moonlighter, 1953 (Glennon)
Moonlighting, 1982 (Zimmer)
Moonraker, 1979 (Adam; Barry; Broccoli; Douy)
Moon's Our Home, 1936 (Wanger)
Moonshiners, 1904 (Bitzer)
Moonstruck, 1960 (Halas and Batchelor)
Moonstruck, 1987 (Watkin)
Moontide, 1942 (Basevi; Clarke; Day; Newman; Reynolds)
Moose Hunt in Canada, 1905 (Bitzer)
Moose on the Loose, 1952 (Terry)
Mopping Up, 1943 (Terry)
Mor och dotter, 1912 (Jaenzon; Magnusson)
Moral Fabric, 1916 (Ince; Sullivan)
Moran of the Lady Letty, 1922 (Glennon)
Moran of the Marines, 1928 (Cronjager)
Morbidone, 1965 (Di Venanzo)
Mörder sind unter uns, 1946 (Hunte)
Mörder unter uns. See **M**, 1931
Morderca zostawia ślad, 1967 (ścibor-Rylski)
More, 1969 (Almendros; Gégauff)
More Pep, 1936 (Fleischer)
More than a Miracle. See C'era una volta, 1967
More the Merrier, 1943 (Cohn)
More to Be Pitied Than Scorned, 1924 (Cohn)
More Trouble, 1918 (Furthman)
Morfalous, 1984 (Saulnier)
Morgan le Pirate, 1909 (Gaumont)
Morgan il pirata, 1961 (Delli Colli)
Morgan the Pirate. See Morgan il pirata, 1961
Morgane la Sirène, 1927 (Burel)
Morgen werde ich verhaftet, 1939 (Herlth)
Morgenrot, 1933 (Herlth; Hoffmann; Röhrig)
Morgensterne, 1977 (Lassally)
Morituri, 1948 (Pommer; Taradash; Warm)
Morituri, 1965 (Fraker; Goldsmith; Hall; Smith)
Mormon Main, 1917 (Rosher)
Morning After, 1921 (Roach)

Morning After, 1986 (Allen)
Morning Departure, 1949 (Alwyn; Rank; Vetchinsky)
Morning Glory, 1933 (Berman; Cooper; Glennon; Plunkett; Polglase; Steiner)
Morning Judge, 1926 (Fleischer)
Morning, Noon, and Night Club, 1937 (Fleischer)
Morning, Noon, and Night, 1933 (Fleischer)
Morocco, 1930 (Ballard; Banton; Dreier; Furthman; Garmes; Zukor)
Morpheus Mike, 1917 (O'brien)
Morse Code Melody, 1963 (Godfrey)
Mort, 1909 (Gaumont)
Mort de Belle, 1960 (Delerue)
Mort de Janis Joplin, 1971 (Nuytten)
Mort de Mozart, 1909 (Carré)
Mort du cygne, 1937 (Burel)
Mort d'un pourri, 1977 (Decaë; Sarde)
Mort en ce jardin, 1956 (Alcoriza)
Mort ne reçoit plus, 1943 (Wakhévitch)
Mort ne tue jamais personne, 1971 (Braunberger)
Mort qui tue, 1913 (Gaumont)
Mort, où est ta victoire?, 1963 (Jarre)
Mortadella, 1971 (Cecchi D'amico; Lardner; Ponti)
Mortal Storm, 1940 (Adrian; Daniels; Kaper)
Morte di un operatore, 1978 (Sarde)
Morte di una ragazza perbene, 1999 (Donaggio)
Morte in Vaticano, 1982 (Donaggio)
Morte Saison des amours, 1961 (Vierny; Delerue; Saulnier)
Mortelle randonnée, 1983 (Lhomme)
Morts en vitrine, 1957 (Colpi; Delerue)
Mosaic, 1965 (McClaren)
Mosaic Law, 1913 (Ince)
Mosaïque. See Mosaic, 1965
Mosca addio, 1987 (Morricone)
Moscow Nights, 1935 (Hornbeck; Korda)
Moscow Nights. See Nuits moscovites, 1934
Moscow on the Hudson, 1984 (McAlpine)
Moscow Strikes Back, 1942 (Vorkapich)
Moses, 1996 (Morricone)
Mosquito, 1922 (Fleischer)
Mosquito Coast, 1986 (Jarre; Seale)
Moss Rose, 1947 (Day; Furthman; Lemaire; Newman)
Most Dangerous Game, 1932 (Cooper; Dunn; Steiner)
Most Dangerous Man in the World, 1969 (Goldsmith)
Most Immoral Lady, 1929 (Seitz)
Most Important Thing: Love. See Important c'est d'aimer, 1974
Most Precious Thing in Life, 1934 (Schary)
Most Wanted Man. See Ennemi public no. 1, 1953
Most Wonderful Moment. See Momento più bello, 1957
Mostro, 1977 (Morricone)
Mostro, 1994 (Donati)
Mosura, 1961 (Tsuburaya)
Möten i skymningen, 1957 (Fischer)
Moth and the Spider, 1935 (Terry)
Mother, 1913 (Loos; Carré)
Mother. See **Mat**, 1926
Mother and Child. See Haha yo ko yo, 1933
Mother and Daughter. See Mor och dotter, 1912
Mother and the Whore. See Maman et la putain, 1973
Mother Carey's Chickens, 1938 (Berman)
Mother Didn't Tell Me, 1950 (La Shelle; Lemaire)
Mother Goose Land, 1925 (Fleischer)
Mother Goose Land, 1933 (Fleischer)
Mother Goose Nightmare, 1945 (Terry)
Mother Goose on the Loose, 1942 (Lantz)
Mother Goose Presents Humpty Dumpty, 1946 (Harryhausen)
Mother Goose's Birthday Party, 1950 (Terry)

Mother Hulda, 1915 (Ince)
Mother-in-Law Is Coming. *See* Svärmor kommer, 1930
Mother Is a Freshman, 1949 (Newman; Reynolds; Wheeler)
Mother, Jugs, and Speed, 1976 (Jones)
Mother Machree, 1928 (Parrish)
Mother, Mother, 1989 (Mancini)
Mother, Mother, Mother, Pin a Rose on Me, 1924 (Fleischer)
Mother o' Mine, 1921 (Sullivan)
Mother of 1084. *See* Hazaar Chaurasi Ki Maa, 1998
Mother of Mine. *See* Gribiche, 1925
Mother Pin a Rose on Me, 1929 (Fleischer)
Mother Was a Rooster, 1962 (Blanc; McKimson)
Mother Wore Tights, 1947 (Day; Lemaire; Newman; Orry-Kelly;
    Trotti; Zanuck)
Mothering Heart, 1913 (Bitzer)
Mothers and Fathers, 1967 (Halas and Batchelor)
Mother's Boy, 1929 (Stradling)
Mother's Boy. *See* Percy, 1925
Mother's Country Is Far. *See* Haruka narishi haha no kuni, 1950
Mothers-in-Law, 1923 (Struss)
Mother's Joy, 1923 (Roach)
Mother's Map. *See* Haha no chizu, 1942
Mother's White Snow. *See* Haha shirayuki, 1956
Mothra. *See* Mosura, 1961
Motion and Emotion, 1990 (Müller)
Motion Painting No 1, 1947 (Fischinger)
Motion Painting No 2, 1960 (Fischinger)
Motion Pictures, 1956 (Breer)
Motocyclette. *See* Girl on a Motorcycle, 1968
Motor Boat Mamas, 1928 (Hornbeck)
Motor Mat, 1915 (Messmer)
Motoring Mamas, 1929 (Hornbeck)
Motorkavaljerer, 1951 (Lundgren)
Mots pour le dire, 1983 (Cecchi D'amico)
Mots pour le dire, 1983 (Fisher)
Mouchette, 1967 (Cloquet)
Mouchy, 1950 (Brdečka)
Mouettes, 1916 (Burel)
Moulai Hafid et Alphonse XIII, 1912 (Cohl)
Moulin Rouge, 1928 (Junge)
Moulin Rouge, 1934 (Day; Johnson; Newman; Rosher; Zanuck)
Moulin Rouge, 1953 (Morris; Veiller; Francis; Auric)
Mountain, 1956 (Edouart; Head; Pereira; Planer; Westmore Family)
Mountain and River of Love. *See* Ai no sanga, 1950
Mountain Eagle, 1926 (Balcon)
Mountain Justice, 1915 (Furthman)
Mountain Justice, 1930 (McCord)
Mountain Justice, 1936 (Haller)
Mountain Language, 1988 (Pinter)
Mountain Music, 1937 (Dreier; Head; Lederer; Struss; Young)
Mountain Music, 1976 (Vinton)
Mountain Pass. *See* Passe-Montagne, 1978
Mountain Romance, 1938 (Terry)
Mountain Woman, 1921 (Ruttenberg)
Mountaineer's Honor, 1909 (Bitzer)
Mounties Are Coming. *See* Vigilantes Are Coming, 1936
Mourir à Madrid, 1962 (Grimault; Jarre)
Mourning Becomes Electra, 1947 (Barnes; D'Agostino; Nichols)
Mouse and Garden, 1950 (Terry)
Mouse and Garden, 1960 (Blanc)
Mouse and the Lion, 1913 (Grot)
Mouse Cleaning, 1948 (Hanna and Barbera)
Mouse Comes to Dinner, 1945 (Hanna and Barbera)
Mouse Divided, 1953 (Blanc; Stalling)
Mouse for Sale, 1955 (Hanna and Barbera)
Mouse in Manhattan, 1945 (Hanna and Barbera)

Mouse in the House, 1947 (Hanna and Barbera)
Mouse Mazurka, 1949 (Blanc; Stalling)
Mouse Meets Bird, 1953 (Terry)
Mouse Menace, 1946 (Blanc)
Mouse Menace, 1953 (Terry)
Mouse-merized Cat, 1946 (Blanc; Stalling; McKimson)
Mouse of Tomorrow, 1940 (Terry)
Mouse on 57th Street, 1961 (Blanc; Jones)
Mouse-placed Kitten, 1959 (McKimson; Blanc)
Mouse-taken Identity, 1957 (Blanc; McKimson; Stalling)
Mouse That Jack Built, 1959 (Blanc; McKimson)
Mouse That Roared, 1959 (Foreman)
Mouse Trouble, 1944 (Hanna and Barbera)
Mouse Warming, 1952 (Blanc; Stalling; Jones)
Mouse Wreckers, 1948 (Jones; Blanc; Stalling)
Moussaillon, 1943 (Aurenche and Bost)
Moustachu, 1987 (Trauner)
Moutarde me monte au nez, 1974 (Decaë)
Mouthpiece, 1932 (Zanuck)
Mouton enragé, 1908 (Cohl)
Moutons de Praxos. *See* A l'aube du troisième jour, 1963
Mouvement image par image, 1976-78 (McClaren)
Mouvements du désir, 1994 (Preisner)
Move, 1970 (Berman; Daniels; Hamlisch; Smith)
Move On, 1917 (Roach)
Move Over, Darling, 1963 (Smith)
Movie, 1922 (Roach)
Movie Crazy , 1932 (Bruckman)
Movie Daze, 1934 (Roach)
Movie Dummy, 1918 (Roach)
Movie Mad, 1931 (Iwerks)
Movie Madness, 1952 (Terry)
Movie Movie, 1978 (Kidd)
Movie Murderer, 1970 (Bumstead)
Movie Nights, 1929 (Roach)
Movie Stunt Pilot, 1954 (La Shelle)
Moving Spirit, 1951 (Halas and Batchelor)
Moving Target. *See* Harper, 1966
Moviola: This Year's Blonde, 1980 (Bernstein)
Moyuru oozora, 1940 (Hayasaka; Tsuburaya)
Mozart Story, 1948 (Von Dassanowsky)
Mozart. *See* Whom the Gods Love, 1936
Mozenosti dialogu, 1982 (švankmajer)
Mozu, 1961 (Takemitsu)
Mrtví žijí, 1922 (Heller)
M'sieur la Caille, 1955 (Kosma)
Mstitel, 1959 (Stallich)
Mučedníci lásky, 1966 (Ondříček)
Much Ado about Mousing, 1964 (Jones)
Much Ado about Nothing, 1940 (Terry)
Much Ado about Nutting, 1953 (Blanc; Jones; Stalling)
Muchacha, 1960 (Figueroa)
Mucho Locos, 1966 (Blanc; McKimson)
Mucho Mouse, 1957 (Hanna and Barbera)
Mucke, 1954 (Reisch)
Müde Tod, 1921 (Herlth; Pommer; Röhrig; Von Harbou; Wagner; Warm)
Mudlark, 1950 (Alwyn; Johnson; Périnal)
Muerte de un ciclista, 1955 (de Beauregard)
Muet Mélomane, 1899 (Pathé)
Muggsy's First Sweetheart, 1910 (Bitzer)
Mühle von Sanssouci, 1926 (Andrejew)
Muhoumatsu no issho, 1943 (Miyagawa)
Muhoumono Ginpei, 1938 (Miyagawa)
Mujer en condominio, 1956 (Figueroa)
Mujer sin cabeza, 1944 (Figueroa)
Mujer X, 1954 (Figueroa)

Mujeres mandan, 1937 (Figueroa)
Mulan, 1998 (Goldsmith)
Mule's Disposition, 1926 (Lantz)
Mulholland Drive, 2000 (Badalamenti)
Mulholland Falls, 1996 (Grusin; Sylbert; Wexler; Zanuck)
Mulino del Po, 1949 (Flaiano and Pinelli; Ponti)
Multiplicity, 1996 (Edlund; Kovacs)
Mumford, 1999 (Littleton)
Mummy, 1932 (Freund; Pierce)
Mummy, 1933 (Laemmle)
Mummy, 1959 (Carreras)
Mummy, 1999 (Biddle; Goldsmith)
Mummy Lives, 1993 (Golan and Globus)
Mummy Returns, 2001 (Biddle)
Mummy's Boys, 1936 (Polglase)
Mummy's Curse, 1944 (Pierce)
Mummy's Ghost, 1943 (Pierce)
Mummy's Shroud , 1967 (Carreras)
Mummy's Tomb, 1942 (Pierce)
Mum's the Word, 1926 (Roach)
Mumsie, 1927 (Wilcox)
Mumsy, Nanny, Sonny, and Girly, 1969 (Francis)
München-Berlin Wanderung, 1927 (Fischinger)
Münchener Bilderbogen, 1924-26 (Fischinger)
Münchhausen, 1943 (Kästner)
Munimji, 1955 (Burman)
Munna, 1954 (Abbas)
Munster, Go Home!, 1966 (Westmore Family; Whitlock)
Muppet Movie, 1979 (Henson)
Muppet Treasure Island, 1996 (Zimmer)
Muppets Take Manhattan, 1984 (Henson)
Mur de l'Atlantique, 1970 (de Beauregard)
Mura di Malapaga, 1949 (Cecchi D'amico)
Muratti greift ein, 1934 (Fischinger)
Muratti Marches On. See Muratti greift ein, 1934
Murder, 1930 (Reville)
Murder among Friends, 1941 (Clarke)
Murder at Harvard. See Mystery Street, 1950
Murder at the Vanities, 1934 (Zukor)
Murder by an Aristocrat, 1936 (Orry-Kelly)
Murder by Contract, 1958 (Ballard)
Murder by Death, 1976 (Booth; Grusin; Stark)
Murder by Phone, 1981 (Barry)
Murder By Phone. See Bells, 1982
Murder By Proxy, 1955 (Carreras)
Murder By Rope, 1936 (Havelock-Allan)
Murder by the Clock, 1931 (Struss)
Murder Elite, 1985 (Bernard)
Murder Goes to College, 1937 (Head)
Murder He Says, 1945 (Head; Dreier)
Murder in Bergen. See Let George Do It, 1940
Murder in Mississippi, 1990 (Daring)
Murder in the Air, 1940 (McCord)
Murder in the Big House. See Jailbreak, 1936
Murder in the Big House, 1942 (McCord)
Murder in the Blue Room, 1944 (Diamond)
Murder in the Clouds, 1934 (Orry-Kelly; Schary)
Murder in the Fleet, 1935 (Krasner)
Murder in the Music Hall, 1946 (Alton)
Murder in Thornton Square. See Gaslight, 1944
Murder Inc. See Enforcer, 1951
Murder, Inc., 1960 (Rosenblum; Sylbert)
Murder My Sweet, 1944 (D'Agostino; Paxton)
Murder of Otsuya. See Otsuya goroshi, 1951
Murder on a Bridle Path, 1936 (Musuraca)
Murder on a Honeymoon, 1935 (MacGowan; Musuraca; Plunkett)

Murder on Diamond Row. See Squeaker, 1937
Murder on Monday. See Home at Seven, 1948
Murder on the Blackboard, 1934 (MacGowan; Musuraca; Steiner)
Murder on the Orient Express, 1974 (Bennett; Unsworth)
Murder on the Roof, 1930 (Walker)
Murder over New York, 1940 (Day; Miller)
Murder Party. See Night of the Party, 1934
Murder Will Out, 1930 (Seitz)
Murder with Pictures, 1936 (Head)
Murder without Tears, 1953 (Miller)
Murderer. See Aru koroshiya, 1967
Murderer Dmitri Karamazov. See Brothers Karamazov, 1958
Murderer Leaves Traces. See Morderca zostawia ślad, 1967
Murderers Among Us: The Simon Wiesenthal Story, 1989 (Conti)
Murderers' Row, 1966 (Schifrin)
Murders in the Rue Morgue, 1932 (Freund; Laemmle)
Murders in the Zoo, 1933 (Haller)
Muri-shinju: Nippon no natsu, 1967 (Toda)
Muriel, 1963 (Braunberger; Delerue)
Muriel. See Muriel, ou le temps d'un retour, 1963
Muriel, ou le temps d'un retour, 1963 (Saulnier; Vierny)
Murmur of the Heart. See **Souffle au coeur**, 1971
Murmuring Sea. See O chem shyeptalo morye, 1915
Muro de silencio, 1972 (Alcoriza)
Murphy's Law, 1986 (Golan and Globus)
Murphy's Romance, 1985 (Fraker; Justin)
Murphy's War, 1971 (Barry; Slocombe)
Murri Affair. See Fatti di gente perbene, 1974
Musashino Fujin, 1951 (Hayasaka; Yoda)
Muscle Beach Tom, 1956 (Hanna and Barbera)
Muscle Tussle, 1953 (Blanc; McKimson; Stalling)
Musée des grotesques, 1911 (Cohl)
Musée du Louvre, 1979 (Takemitsu)
Musée Grévin, 1958 (Fradetal)
Museum Mystery, 1937 (Havelock-Allan)
Mush and Milk, 1933 (Roach)
Mushukunin Mikoshin no Joukichi, 1972 (Miyagawa)
Music Academy, 1964 (Halas and Batchelor)
Music Box, 1932 (Mayer; Roach)
Music Box, 1989 (Sarde; Winkler; Eszterhas)
Music for Madam, 1937 (August)
Music for Madame, 1937 (Kahn; Lasky; Polglase)
Music for Millions, 1944 (Irene; Surtees; Pasternak)
Music for the Movies: Bernard Herrmann, 1992 (Bernstein)
Music for the Movies: Toru Takemitsu, 1994 (Takemitsu)
Music Goes 'Round, 1936 (Walker; Buchman; Swerling)
Music Hath Charms, 1935 (Neame; Lantz)
Music in Darkness. See Musik i mörker, 1948
Music in Manhattan, 1944 (Metty)
Music in the Air, 1934 (Pommer; Waxman)
Music in Your Hair, 1934 (Roach)
Music Lesson, 1932 (Iwerks)
Music Lovers, 1970 (Previn; Slocombe)
Music Man, 1938 (Halas and Batchelor)
Music Man, 1962 (Burks; Jeakins)
Music Master, 1908 (Bitzer)
Music Mice-Tro, 1967 (Blanc)
Music of the Heart, 1999 (Daring)
Music on the streets, 1973 (Nuytten)
Music Room. See Jalsaghar, 1958
Musica, 1966 (Duras; Vierny)
Musical Madness, 1951 (Terry)
Musical Memories, 1935 (Fleischer)
Musical Mews, 1919 (Messmer)
Musical Mountaineers, 1939 (Fleischer)
Musical Poster No.1, 1940 (Lye)

Musiciens de la mine, 1950 (Cloquet)

Musiciens du ciel, 1939 (Alekan; Andrejew; Honegger; Schüfftan)

Musicomanie, 1910 (Cohl)

Musik bei Nacht, 1953 (Herlth)

Musik i mörker, 1948 (Lundgren)

Musik im Blut, 1934 (Warm)

Musketeers of Pig Alley, 1912 (Bitzer)

Musodoro, 1954 (Rota)

Muss 'em Up, 1936 (August; Berman; Polglase)

Mussolini: Ultimo Atto, 1974 (Morricone)

Musume tabigeinen, 1941 (Yoda)

Mutants, 1998 (de Almeida)

Mutations, 1974 (Cardiff)

Mutinés de l'Elseneur, 1936 (Honegger; Matras)

Mutiny, 1951 (Laszlo; Tiomkin)

Mutiny Ain't Nice, 1938 (Fleischer)

Mutiny on the Bounty, 1934 (Mayer; Booth; Clarke; Edeson; Furthman; Gibbons; Gillespie; Jennings; Kaper; Stothart; Thalberg; Westmore Family)

Mutiny on the Bounty, 1962 (Gillespie; Hall; Kaper; Lederer; Surtees)

Mutiny on the Bunny, 1950 (Blanc; Stalling)

Mutiny on the Buses, 1972 (Carreras)

Mutoscope Shorts, 1897 (Bitzer)

Mutt in a Rut, 1959 (Blanc; Mckimson)

Mutter Courage und ihre Kinder, 1955 (Douy)

Mütter Küsters fahrt zum Himmel, 1977 (Ballhaus)

Mütter Küsters Goes to Heaven. See Mütter Küsters fahrt zum Himmel, 1977

Mütter, verzaget nicht!, 1911 (Messter)

Mutterlied, 1937 (Von Harbou)

Muž bez srdce, 1923 (Heller)

Muži bez křídel, 1945 (Stallich)

Muzné Hry, 1988 (švankmajer)

Muzzle Tough, 1954 (Blanc; Stalling)

My American Uncle. See Mon oncle d'Amerique, 1980

My Artistical Temperature, 1937 (Fleischer)

My Asylum. See Chiedo asilo, 1979

My Baby, 1912 (Bitzer)

My Baby Just Cares for Me, 1931 (Fleischer)

My Beautiful Laundrette, 1985 (Kureishi; Zimmer)

My Best Friend's Wedding, 1997 (Bass; Kovacs; Lai; Sylbert)

My Best Girl, 1927 (Rosher)

My Bill, 1938 (Orry-Kelly)

My Blood Runs Cold, 1965 (Duning)

My Blue Heaven, 1950 (Lemaire; Newman; Trotti)

My Bodyguard, 1980 (Grusin; Houseman)

My Bonnie, 1925 (Fleischer)

My Boy Johnny, 1944 (Terry)

My Brilliant Career , 1979 (McAlpine)

My Brother Down There. See Running Target, 1956

My Brother Talks to Horses, 1946 (Irene; Rosson; Plunkett)

My Brother's Keeper, 1948 (Rank)

My Bunny Lies over the Sea, 1948 (Blanc; Jones; Stalling)

My City. See Orasul meu, 1967

My Cousin, 1919 (Zukor)

My Cousin Rachel, 1952 (Jeakins; Johnson; La Shelle; Lemaire; Waxman; Wheeler)

My Darling Clementine, 1946 (Basevi; Newman; Spencer; Wheeler; Zanuck)

My Darling Clementine. See Drahoušek Klementýna, 1959

My Daughter Joy, 1950 (Korda; Périnal)

My Dear Miss Aldrich, 1937 (Mankiewicz)

My Dear Secretary, 1948 (Biroc)

My Demon Lover, 1987 (Vachon)

My Dream Is Yours, 1949 (Haller)

My Enemy, the Sea. See Taiheiyo hitoribotchi, 1963

My Fair Lady, 1964 (Previn; Stradling; Warner; Beaton)

My Father's House, 1947 (Crosby)

My Favorite Blonde, 1942 (Dreier; Head)

My Favorite Brunette, 1947 (Dreier; Head)

My Favorite Duck, 1942 (Blanc; Jones; Stalling)

My Favorite Martian, 1999 (Elfman)

My Favorite Season. See Ma saison préférée, 1993

My Favorite Spy, 1942 (van Heusen)

My Favorite Spy, 1951 (Head; Mercer; Young)

My Favorite Wife, 1940 (Kanin; Maté; Polglase)

My Favorite Year, 1982 (Comden and Green)

My Feelin's Is Hurt, 1940 (Fleischer)

My Foolish Heart, 1949 (Day; Epstein; Garmes; Goldwyn; Head; Mandell; Young)

My Four Years in Germany, 1917 (Warner; Cohn)

My Friend Flicka, 1943 (Day; Newman)

My Friend from India, 1927 (Adrian)

My Friend Irma, 1949 (Bumstead; Dreier; Head; Wallis)

My Friend Irma Goes West, 1950 (Bumstead; Dreier; Garmes; Head; Wallis)

My Friend the Devil, 1922 (Ruttenberg)

My Friend the Monkey, 1939 (Fleischer)

My Friends. See Amici miei, 1975

My Gal Loves Music, 1944 (Mohr)

My Gal Sal, 1930 (Fleischer)

My Gal Sal, 1942 (Day; Miller; Newman; Pan)

My Geisha, 1961 (Cardiff; Krasna; Waxman; Head; Westmore Family)

My Girl Tisa, 1948 (Haller; Steiner)

My Gun Is Quick, 1957 (Leven)

My Heart Belongs to Daddy, 1942 (Dreier; Head)

My Heart Goes Crazy, 1946 (van Heusen)

My Heart Goes Crazy. See London Town, 1946

My Hero, 1912 (Bitzer)

My Khmer Heart, 2000 (Newman)

My Kingdom for a Cook, 1943 (Planer)

My Lady's Garden, 1934 (Terry)

My Lady's Garter, 1920 (Carré)

My Learned Friend, 1943 (Balcon)

My Left Foot, 1989 (Bernstein)

My Life, 1993 (Barry)

My Life So Far, 1999 (Puttnam)

My Life to Live. See Vivre sa vie, 1962

My Life with Caroline, 1941 (Miller)

My Lips Betray, 1933 (Friedhofer; Garmes; Kräly)

My Little Duckaroo, 1954 (Blanc; Jones)

My Little Girl, 1986 (Lhomme; Merchant)

My Little Sister, 1919 (Ruttenberg)

My Love Burns. See Waga koi wa moenu, 1949

My Love Came Back, 1940 (Reisch; Rosher; Wallis; Orry-Kelly)

My Love Is beyond the Mountain. See Waga ai wa yama no kanata ni, 1948

My Love Is Like a Rose. See Min kära är en ros, 1963

My Man, 1928 (Zanuck)

My Man. See Mon homme, 1996

My Man Adam , 1985 (McAlpine)

My Man and I, 1952 (Basevi)

My Man Godfrey, 1936 (Banton)

My Man Godfrey, 1957 (Daniels; Hunter)

My Man Jasper, 1945 (Pal)

My Mother the General. See Imi Hageneralit, 1979

My Name Is Bertolt Brecht—Exile in U.S.A., 1988 (Lardner)

My Name Is Julia Ross, 1945 (Guffey)

My Name Is Mistress. See Watashi no na wa joufu, 1949

My Neighbor's Wife, 1925 (Walker)

My New Partner. See Ripoux, 1984

My New Partner II. See Ripoux contre Ripoux, 1990

My Night at Maud's. *See* Ma nuit chez Maud, 1969
My Official Wife, 1926 (Blanke; Carré)
My Old China, 1931 (Balcon)
My Old Dutch, 1934 (Balcon; Rank)
My Old Kentucky Home, 1926 (Fleischer)
My Old Kentucky Home, 1946 (Terry)
My Other "Husband," 1983 (Sarde)
My Own True Love, 1948 (Bumstead; Dreier; Head; Lang; Lewton)
My Pal Gus, 1952 (Lemaire; Parrish; Wheeler)
My Pal Paul, 1930 (Lantz)
My Pal, Wolf, 1944 (Paxton)
My Partner Mr. Davis, 1936 (Prévert)
My Pony Boy, 1929 (Fleischer)
My Pop, My Pop, 1940 (Fleischer)
My Reputation, 1946 (Blanke; Grot; Head; Howe; Steiner)
My Science Project, 1985 (Baker)
My Sin, 1931 (Green)
My Sister Eileen, 1942 (Cohn; Walker)
My Sister Eileen, 1955 (Duning; Wald)
My Sister My Love. *See* Syskonbädd 1782, 1966
My Sister, My Love. *See* Mafu Cage, 1978
My Sister's Keeper, 1986 (Barry)
My Six Convicts, 1952 (Tiomkin)
My Six Loves, 1963 (Cahn; Head; van Heusen)
My Son Alone. *See* American Empire, 1942
My Son Is Guilty, 1939 (Brown)
My Son John, 1952 (Head; Pereira; Stradling)
My Son, My Son, 1940 (Stradling)
My Son the Fanatic, 1998 (Kureishi)
My Son, the Hero. *See* Arrivano i Titani, 1962
My Song for You, 1934 (Junge)
My Soul Runs Naked. *See* Rat Fink, 1965
My Stepmother Is an Alien, 1988 (Dykstra)
My Tail's My Ticket, 1959 (Vukotić)
My Teenage Daughter, 1956 (Wilcox)
My Twelve Fathers. *See* Tucet mých tatínku, 1959
My Two Husbands. *See* Too Many Husbands, 1940
My Weakness, 1933 (Miller)
My West. *See* Mio West, 1999
My Wife's Best Friend, 1952 (Lemaire)
My Wife's Gone to the Country, 1931 (Fleischer)
My Wild Irish Rose, 1947 (Burks; Edeson; Steiner)
Myest kinematografichyeeskovo operator, 1911 (Starewicz)
Myra Breckenridge, 1970 (Smith; van Runkle; Head)
Mystère Barton, 1948 (Burel; Spaak)
Mystère de la chambre jaune, 1930 (Burel; Meerson)
Mystère de la chambre jaune, 1948 (Douy)
Mystère de l'atelier 15, 1957 (Delerue; Cloquet)
Mystère du Palace Hôtel, 1953 (D'Eaubonne)
Mystère du Quai Conti, 1950 (Delerue)
Mystère Koumiko, 1964 (Takemitsu)
Mystère Picasso, 1955 (Renoir; Auric; Colpi)
Mystères de l'ombre , 1915 (Gaumont)
Mystères de Paris, 1935 (Auric)
Mystères de Paris, 1943 (Barsacq; Burel)
Mysteries, 1978 (Müller)
Mysterious. *See* Chikyu boeigun, 1957
Mysterious Castle in the Carpathians. *See* Tajemstvi hradu v Karpatech, 1981
Mysterious Cowboy, 1952 (Terry)
Mysterious Crossing, 1936 (Krasner)
Mysterious Desperado, 1949 (Musuraca)
Mysterious Dr. Fu Manchu, 1929 (Zukor)
Mysterious Encounter. *See* Arcano incantatore, 1996
Mysterious Island, 1929 (Basevi; Gibbons; Mayer)
Mysterious Island, 1961 (Harryhausen; Herrmann)

Mysterious Island. *See* Ile mystérieuse, 1973
Mysterious Jug, 1937 (Lantz)
Mysterious Lady, 1928 (Booth; Daniels; Gibbons; Mayer)
Mysterious Love of Mrs. White. *See* Hakufujin no yoren, 1956
Mysterious Mose, 1930 (Fleischer)
Mysterious Mr. Davis. *See* My Partner Mr. Davis, 1936
Mysterious Mystery, 1924 (Roach)
Mysterious Pilot, 1937 (Canutt)
Mysterious Rider, 1938 (Harlan; Head)
Mysterious Stranger, 1948 (Terry)
Mysterious Stranger, 1981 (Lassally)
Mystery, Alaska, 1999 (Burwell)
Mystery at Fire Island, 1982 (Lassally)
Mystery in Mexico, 1948 (van Heusen)
Mystery in the Moonlight, 1948 (Terry)
Mystery Lake, 1953 (Crosby)
Mystery Man, 1923 (Roach)
Mystery Man, 1944 (Harlan)
Mystery Mountain, 1934 (Canutt)
Mystery of Edwin Drood, 1935 (D'Agostino)
Mystery of Mr. X, 1934 (Adrian)
Mystery of Picasso. *See* Mystère Picasso, 1956
Mystery of the Blue Room. *See* Záhada modrého pokoje, 1933
Mystery of the Jewel Casket, 1905 (Bitzer)
Mystery of the Leaping Fish, 1916 (Brown)
Mystery of the Night. *See* Stíny, 1921
Mystery of the Poisoned Pool, 1914 (Rosher)
Mystery of the Wax Museum, 1933 (Blanke; Grot; Orry-Kelly; Rennahan; Wallis)
Mystery Ranch, 1932 (August; Friedhofer)
Mystery Sea Raider, 1940 (Dreier; Head)
Mystery Squadron, 1933 (Canutt)
Mystery Street, 1950 (Alton; Mayer)
Mystery Submarine, 1950 (Boyle)
Mystery Train, 1989 (Müller)
Mystery Woman, 1935 (Nichols)
Mystic, 1925 (Gibbons)
Mystic Pink, 1976 (McKimson)
Mystical Love-Making. *See* Drame chez les fantoches, 1908
Myth of Fingerprints, 1997 (Schamus)

N or NW, 1938 (Lye)
N.E.L. Offshore News, 1975 (Arnold)
N.I. ni-c'est fini, 1908 (Cohl)
N.Y. City Fire Dept., 1903 (Bitzer)
Na Kometě, 1970 (Zeman)
N'a pris les dés. *See* Eden et après, 1971
Na sluneční strane, 1933 (Stallich)
Na ty louce zeleny, 1936 (Heller)
Na Varsavkom traktye, 1916 (Starewicz)
Naaz, 1954 (Biswas)
Nach uns die Sintflut, 1996 (Donaggio)
Nacht der Einbrecher, 1921 (Planer)
Nacht der grossen Liebe, 1933 (Wagner)
Nacht des Grauens, 1912 (Messter)
Nacht gehört uns, 1929 (Reisch)
Nacht im Grandhotel, 1931 (Metzner)
Nacht in London, 1928 (Warm)
Nacht mit dem Kaiser, 1936 (Warm)
Nachtbesuch in der Northernbank, 1921 (Wagner)
Nächte am Bosporus. *See* Mann, der den Mord beging, 1931
Nächte von Port Said, 1931 (Junge)
Nachtfalter, 1911 (Freund)
Nachtgestalten, 1921 (Hoffmann)
Nachtgestvalten, 1920 (Dreier)
Nachtlager von Mischli-Michloch, 1917 (Kolowrat-Krakowsky)

Nachts auf den Strassen, 1952 (Pommer)
Nachtsonne. *See* Sole anche di notte, 1990
Nackte und der Satan, 1959 (Warm)
Nad Nemanom rassvet, 1953 (Moskvin)
Nad Nyemen, 1909 (Starewicz)
Nad propastí, 1921 (Heller)
Nada, 1974 (Rabier)
Nada Gang. *See* Nada, 1974
Nadie escuchaba, 1988 (Almendros)
Nadine, 1987 (Almendros; O'Steen)
Nagana, 1954 (Auric)
Nagrodzone uczucie, 1957 (Lenica)
Nai Roshani, 1941 (Biswas)
Nails, 1992 (Conti)
Nain, 1912 (Gaumont)
Naissance de l'amour, 1993 (Coutard)
Naissance des stéréoscopages, 1997 (Morricone)
Naissance du plutonium, 1960 (Delerue)
Naked Alibi, 1954 (Hunter; Metty)
Naked and the Dead, 1958 (Herrmann; La Shelle)
Naked Ape, 1973 (Alonzo)
Naked Cage, 1986 (Golan and Globus)
Naked City, 1948 (Daniels; Rozsa)
Naked Edge, 1961 (Alwyn; Dillon; Mathieson)
Naked Eye, 1957 (Bernstein)
Naked Face, 1984 (Golan and Globus)
Naked Gun, 1988 (Houseman)
Naked Heart. *See* Maria Chapdelaine, 1934
Naked in New York, 1994 (Badalamenti)
Naked Jungle, 1954 (Haskin; Head; Laszlo; Maddow; Pal; Pereira)
Naked Kiss, 1964 (Cortez; Lourié)
Naked Lunch, 1991 (Walas)
Naked Maja, 1959 (Jennings; Rotunno)
Naked Night. *See* **Gycklarnas afton**, 1953
Naked Paradise, 1957 (Crosby)
Naked Runner, 1967 (Heller)
Naked Spur, 1953 (Kaper)
Naked Street, 1955 (Crosby)
Naked Tango, 1990 (Newman; Schifrin)
Naked Truth, 1957 (Rank)
Naked under Leather. *See* Girl on a Motorcycle, 1968
Name, Age, Occupation, 1942 (Clothier; Crosby)
Name der Rose, 1986 (Mnouchkine)
Name of the Game Is Kill!, 1968 (Zsigmond)
Name of the Rose, 1986 (Cristaldi; Delli Colli)
Name the Day, 1921 (Roach)
Namenlos, 1923 (Kolowrat-Krakowsky)
Namida-Gawa, 1967 (Yoda)
Namida o shishi no tategami no, 1962 (Takemitsu)
Nan Paterson's Trial, 1905 (Bitzer)
Nana, 1926 (Braunberger)
Nana, 1934 (Banton; Day; Goldwyn; Newman; Toland)
Nana, 1954 (Jeanson; Matras)
Nana, 1982 (Golan and Globus; Morricone)
Nanami: Inferno of First Love. *See* Hatsukoi jigokuhen, 1968
Nancy Drew—Reporter, 1939 (Edeson)
Nancy Goes to Rio, 1950 (Pasternak; Rose; Smith)
Nancy Steele Is Missing, 1937 (Cronjager; Johnson)
Naniwa ereji, 1936 (Yoda)
Naniwa onna, 1940 (Yoda)
Nankai no daiketto, 1966 (Tsuburaya)
Nankai no hanatabe, 1942 (Hayasaka; Tsuburaya)
Nanny, 1965 (Bennett; Carreras)
Nanny. *See* Balia, 1999
Nao Do Egarah, 1957 (Burman)
Nao ou a vã gloria de mandar, 1990 (Branco)

Napoleon à Sainte-Hélène, 1929 (Wagner)
Napoleon Bunny-Part, 1956 (Blanc)
Napoleon Crossing the Alps , 1903 (Gaudio)
Napoleon und die kleine Wäscherin, 1920 (Dreier)
Napoléon, 1927 (Burel; Honegger; Lourié)
Napoléon, 1954 (Cloquet; Lourié)
Napoleon, 1995 (Conti)
Napoleon-Gaz, 1925 (Enei)
Napoletani a Milano, 1953 (Age and Scarpelli)
Napoli milionaria, 1950 (Gherardi; Rota; de Laurentiis)
När jag var Prins Utav Arkadien , 1909 (Magnusson)
När kärleken dödar, 1913 (Jaenzon; Magnusson)
När kärleken kom till byn, 1950 (Lundgren)
När konstnärer älska, 1914 (Jaenzon)
När larmklockan ljuder, 1913 (Jaenzon)
När syrenerna blommar, 1952 (Lundgren; Nykvist)
Narcissus, 1981-83 (McClaren)
Narcissus/Echo, 1971 (Braunberger)
Nark. *See* Balance, 1982
Narkose, 1929 (Schüfftan)
Narr seiner Liebe, 1929 (Andrejew; Planer)
Narrow Corner, 1933 (Gaudio; Orry-Kelly)
Narrow Escape, 1913 (Loos)
Narrow Path, 1918 (Miller)
Narrow Road, 1912 (Bitzer)
Narrow Trail, 1918 (August; Ince)
Naše bláznivá rodina, 1968 (Stallich)
Naše Karkulka, 1960 (Brdečka)
Nashörner, 1963 (Lenica)
Nasty Habits, 1976 (Slocombe)
Nasty Quacks, 1945 (Blanc; Stalling)
Nasty Rabbit, 1965 (Kovacs; Zsigmond)
Nasu no imoto, 1972 (Toda)
Nata di marzo, 1958 (Age and Scarpelli; Ponti)
Natercia, 1959 (Vierny)
Nathalie, 1975 (Müller)
Nathalie Granger, 1972 (Cloquet; Duras)
National Barn Dance, 1944 (Dreier; Head)
National Lampoon's Animal House, 1978 (Bernstein)
National Lampoon's Christmas Vacation, 1989 (Badalamenti)
National Lampoon's Class Reunion. *See* Class Reunion, 1982
National Velvet, 1945 (Berman; Irene; Mayer; Stothart)
Native Land, 1942 (Maddow)
Native Son, 1986 (van Runkle)
Nativity, 1978 (Schifrin)
Natsu no imoto, 1972 (Takemitsu)
Natt i hamn, 1943 (Fischer)
Nattbarn, 1956 (Nykvist)
Nattmarschen i Sankt Eriks Gränd, 1909 (Magnusson)
Nattsvardsgästerna, 1963 (Lundgren; Nykvist)
Natural Wonders of the West, 1938 (Hoch)
Naturalisée, 1962 (Delerue)
Nature in the Wrong, 1933 (Roach)
Nature morte, 1966 (Guillemot)
Nature morte, 1970 (Lenica)
Nature of the Beast, 1988 (Zimmer)
Nature's Workshop, 1933 (Lantz)
Naufrageurs, 1958 (Cloquet)
Naughty Baby, 1928 (Haller)
Naughty Blue Knickers. *See* Folies d'elodie, 1981
Naughty Boy, 1962 (Burman)
Naughty but Mice, 1939 (Jones)
Naughty but Nice, 1939 (Mercer; Wald)
Naughty Duck, 1950 (Popescu-Gopo)
Naughty Marietta, 1935 (Adrian; Daniels; Gibbons; Goodrich and Hackett; Kahn; Mayer; Shearer; Stothart; Stromberg; Tiomkin)

Naughty, Naughty!, 1918 (Barnes; Sullivan)
Naughty Neighbors, 1939 (Blanc; Clampett; Stalling)
Naulahka, 1918 (Grot; Menzies; Miller)
Navajo, 1952 (Miller)
Navajo Joe. *See* Dollaro a testa, 1966
Naval Bomber Fleet. *See* Kaigun bakugekitai, 1940
Navigation marchande, 1953 (Decaë)
Navigator, 1924 (Bruckman; Mayer; Schenck)
Navire Night, 1978 (Duras)
Navrat mrtvého. *See* Manželé paní Mileny, 1921
Navy, 1930 (Lantz)
Navy Blue and Gold, 1937 (Gibbons; Seitz)
Navy Blues, 1929 (Gibbons)
Navy Blues, 1941 (Gaudio; Howe; Mercer; Polito; Wald; Wallis)
Navy Comes Through, 1942 (Dunn; Musuraca)
Navy Lark, 1959 (Wilcox)
Navy Seals, 1990 (Alonzo)
Navy versus the Night Monsters, 1965 (Cortez)
Navy Wife, 1935 (Levien)
Navy Wife, 1956 (Wanger)
Navy's Special Boy Sailors. *See* Kaigun tokubetsu nenshouhei, 1972
Naxalites, 1981 (Abbas)
Naya Sansaar, 1943 (Abbas)
Naya Zamana, 1971 (Burman)
Nayak, 1966 (Chandragupta; Dutta; Mitra)
Nayya, 1947 (Biswas)
Nazarin, 1958 (Figueroa)
Nazi Agent, 1942 (Schary; Stradling)
Nazis Strike, 1943 (Hornbeck; Veiller)
Nazty Nuisance, 1942 (Roach)
Ne compromettez pas vos loisirs, 1949 (Decaë)
Né de père inconnu, 1950 (Renoir)
Ne le criez pas sur les toits, 1941 (Burel)
Ne réveillez pas un flic qui dort, 1988 (Coutard)
Néa, 1976 (Evein)
Neanderthal Man, 1953 (Cortez)
Neapolitan Mouse, 1954 (Hanna and Barbera)
Near Dublin, 1924 (Roach)
Near to Earth, 1913 (Bitzer)
Nearly a Burglar's Bride, 1914 (Loos)
Nearly a Lady, 1915 (Marion)
Nearly Married, 1917 (Edeson)
'Neath the Arizona Skies, 1934 (Canutt)
Necessary Roughness, 1991 (Conti)
Nechci nic slyšet, 1978 (Ondříček)
Neck and Neck, 1942 (Terry)
Neck 'n Neck, 1927 (Disney)
Necklace, 1909 (Bitzer)
Necromancy, 1972 (Hoch)
Necronomicon, 1994 (Savini)
Ned Kelly, 1970 (Fisher)
Neecha Nagar, 1945 (Shankar)
Ne'er-Do-Well, 1916 (Selig)
Ne'er-Do-Well, 1923 (Haller)
Neglected Wives, 1920 (Haller)
Negra consentida, 1948 (Alcoriza)
Nègre blanc, 1925 (Meerson)
Neiges, 1954 (Cloquet)
Neighborhood House, 1935 (Roach)
Neighbors, 1907 (Bitzer)
Neighbors, 1952 (McClaren)
Neighbors, 1981 (Conti; Zanuck)
Neighbors. *See* Sasiedzi, 1969
Neither in Nor Out. *See* Se ki, se be, 1919
Nel blu dipinto di blu, 1959 (Di Venanzo; Zavattini)
Nel Centro del Mirino, 1983 (Bozzetto)

Nel nome del padre, 1971 (Cristaldi)
Nela, 1980 (Theodorakis)
Nell Gwyn, 1926 (Wilcox)
Nell Gwyn, 1934 (Wilcox; Young))
Nella città l'inferno, 1958 (Cecchi D'amico)
Nell's Eugenic Wedding, 1914 (Loos)
Nell's Yells, 1939 (Iwerks)
Nelly & Monsieur Arnaud, 1995 (Sarde)
Nelly's Folly, 1961 (Blanc; Jones)
Nelson Affair, 1973 (Dillon)
Nelson Touch. *See* Corvette K-225, 1943
Nemico di mia moglie, 1959 (Di Venanzo)
Nemo, 1983 (Rousselot)
Nemuri Kyoshiro no manji-giri, 1969 (Yoda)
Neotpravlennoye pismo, 1959 (Urusevsky)
Nephew of Paris, 1934 (Garmes)
Neptune Disaster. *See* Neptune Factor, 1972
Neptune Factor, 1972 (Schifrin)
Neptune Nonsense, 1936 (Messmer)
Neptune's Daughter, 1949 (Blanc; Hanna and Barbera; Irene; Mayer; Rosher)
Nero Veneziamo, 1978 (Donaggio)
Nerone e Messalina, 1949 (Delli Colli)
Nero's Mistress. *See* Mio figlio Nerone, 1956
Nervous Shakedown, 1947 (Bruckman)
Nessa no byakuran, 1951 (Hayasaka)
Nest. *See* Gniazdo, 1974
Nest, 1927 (Stradling)
Net, 1953 (Rank)
Net, 1995 (Winkler)
Netchaiev est de retour, 1991 (Semprun)
Netherlands America, 1943 (van Dongen)
Neue Leben, 1918 (Kolowrat-Krakowsky)
Neuf à trois, ou la journée d'une vedette, 1957 (Decaë)
Neuf étages tout acier, 1960 (Delerue; Kosma)
Neutral Port, 1939 (Rank)
Nevada Smith, 1966 (Ballard; Hayes; Head; Levine; Newman; Pereira)
Never a Dull Moment, 1950 (Banton; Walker)
Never a Dull Moment, 1968 (Ellenshaw)
Never Con a Killer, 1977 (Lathrop)
Never Fear, 1950 (Polglase)
Never Forget, 1991 (Mancini)
Never Give an Inch. *See* Sometimes a Great Notion, 1971
Never Kick a Woman, 1936 (Fleischer)
Never Let Go, 1960 (Barry; Challis)
Never Let Me Go, 1953 (Junge; Krasker; Rank)
Never Look Back, 1952 (Carreras)
Never Love a Stranger, 1957 (Garmes)
Never Say Die, 1939 (Dreier; Head)
Never Say Goodbye, 1946 (Diamond; Edeson; Grot)
Never Say Goodbye, 1956 (Boyle)
Never Say Never Again, 1983 (Legrand; Slocombe)
Never Should Have Told You, 1937 (Fleischer)
Never So Few, 1959 (Daniels; Friedhofer; Rose)
Never Sock a Baby, 1939 (Fleischer)
Never Steal Anything Small, 1959 (Lederer)
Never Take Candy from a Stranger. *See* Never Take Sweets from a Stranger, 1960
Never Take No for an Answer, 1952 (Havelock-Allan; Heller)
Never Take No for an Answer, 1959 (Rota)
Never Take Sweets from a Stranger, 1960 (Carreras; Francis)
Never Talk to Strangers, 1995 (Donaggio)
Never Too Late, 1965 (Lathrop)
Never Too Old, 1926 (Roach)
Never Touched Me, 1919 (Roach)
Never Wave at a WAC, 1952 (Bernstein; Daniels)

Never Weaken, 1921 (Roach)
Neviditelní neprátelé, 1950 (Brdečka)
Neviňátka, 1929 (Stallich)
New Adventures of Don Juan. *See* Adventures of Don Juan, 1949
New Adventures of Get-Rich-Quick Wallingford, 1931 (MacArthur)
New Americans, 1945 (Vorkapich)
New Aunt, 1929 (Hornbeck)
New Babylon. *See* **Novyi Vavilon**, 1929
New Bad Names. *See* Shin akumyo, 1961
New Britain, 1940 (Alwyn)
New Car, 1931 (Iwerks)
New Centurions, 1972 (Jones; Leven; Winkler)
New Commandment, 1925 (Haller)
New Cowboy, 1911 (Ince)
New Deal Show, 1937 (Fleischer)
New Delhi Times, 1986 (Mitra)
New Dress, 1911 (Bitzer)
New Earth. *See* Atarshiki tsuchi, 1936
New Earth. *See* **Nieuwe gronden**, 1933
New England Idyll, 1914 (Ince)
New Eve. *See* Nouvelle Ève, 1999
New Faces of 1937, 1937 (Epstein; Polglase)
New Faces, 1953 (Ballard; Horner)
New Gentlemen. *See* Nouveaux Messieurs, 1928
New Gulliver. *See* Novy Gulliver, 1935
New Horizons. *See* **Vyborgskaya storona**, 1939
New Interns, 1964 (Ballard)
New Janko the Musician. *See* Nowy Janko muzykant, 1960
New Kid on the Block, 1999 (Bass)
New Kids, 1985 (Schifrin)
New Kind of Love, 1963 (Head)
New Land, 1973 (Lundgren)
New Life, 1988 (Reynolds)
New Life. *See* Neue Leben, 1918
New Magic, 1984 (Trumbull)
New Moon, 1931 (Adrian; Booth; Mayer; Stothart)
New Moon, 1940 (Adrian; Daniels; Stothart)
New Tale of Genji: Shuzuka and Yoshitsune. *See* Shin Heike monogatari: Shizuka to Yoshitsune, 1956
New Tales of the Taira Clan. *See* Shin Heike monogatari, 1955
New Trick, 1909 (Bitzer)
New Version of La Passion, 1906 (Pathé)
New Vision: The Life and Work of Botticelli, 1984 (Halas and Batchelor)
New Wine, 1941 (Korda)
New Wives' Conference. *See* Niizuma kaigi, 1949
New World. *See* Naya Sansaar, 1943
New Worlds for Old, 1936 (Alwyn)
New Year's Eve. *See* Sylvester: Tragödie einer Nacht, 1923
New Year's Evil, 1981 (Golan and Globus)
New York, 1916 (Miller)
New York ballade, 1955 (Braunberger)
New York Hat, 1912 (Bitzer; Loos)
New York Lightboard, 1961 (McClaren)
New York, New York, 1977 (Kovacs; Leven; van Runkle; Winkler)
New York Nights, 1929 (Furthman; Menzies; Schenck)
New York Stories, 1989 (Almendros; Loquasto; Nykvist; Schoonmaker; Storaro; Tavoularis)
New York Town, 1941 (Dreier; Head; Swerling)
Newborn Insect. *See* Novogodnaya szutka, 1912
Newcomer, 1938 (Terry)
Newly Rich, 1922 (Roach)
Newly Rich. *See* Forbidden Adventure, 1931
Newlyweds, 1910 (Bitzer)
Newman Laugh-O-Grams, 1920 (Disney)
News for the Navy, 1937-39 (McClaren)
News Review No. 2, 1945 (van Dongen)

Newsboys Home, 1938 (Krasner)
Newsies, 1992 (Menken; Reynolds)
Newspaper Train, 1941 (Lye)
Nex de cuir, 1951 (Auric)
Next Aisle Over, 1918 (Roach)
Next Door Neighbors. *See* Locataires d'à côté, 1909
Next in Command, 1914 (Rosher)
Next Karate Kid, 1994 (Conti; Kovacs)
Next of Kin, 1942 (Balcon; Walton)
Next of Kin, 1989 (Nitzsche)
Next Stop, Greenwich Village, 1976 (Conti)
Next Time I Marry, 1938 (Kanin; Metty)
Next Time We Love, 1936 (Waxman)
Next to No Time!, 1958 (Auric; Francis)
Next Voice You Hear, 1950 (Mayer; Raksin; Schary; Schnee)
Next Week-End, 1934 (Roach)
Nez, 1963 (Alexeieff and Parker)
Nez au vent, 1956 (Starewicz)
Nez de cuir, 1952 (Wakhévitch)
Nezabyvayemyi 1919-god, 1952 (Shostakovich)
Nezlobte dedečka, 1934 (Heller)
Ni pobres ni ricos, 1952 (Figueroa)
Ni sangre ni arena, 1941 (Figueroa)
Niagara, 1953 (Brackett; Jeakins; Lemaire; Reisch; Wheeler)
Niagara Falls, 1941 (Roach)
Niagara: Miracles, Myths and Magic, 1986 (Conti)
Nibelungen, 1924 (Hoffmann; Hunte; Pommer; Reiniger; Schüfftan; Von Harbou)
Nice Couple, Chouchou and Yuni. *See* Chouchou Yuji no meoto zenzai, 1965
Nice Doggy, 1952 (Terry)
Nice Girl?, 1941 (Pasternak)
Nice Little Bank That Should Be Robbed, 1958 (Lemaire)
Nichna, 1972 (Nuytten)
Nicholas and Alexandra, 1971 (Bennett; Korda; Spiege; Young)
Nicholas Nickelby, 1948 (Balcon; Rank)
Nick Carter, 1909 (Gaumont; Pathé)
Nickel Hopper, 1926 (Roach)
Nickel Nurser, 1932 (Roach)
Nickel Ride, 1974 (Grusin)
Nickelodeon, 1976 (Kovacs; Marshall; Winkler)
Nick's Coffee Pot, 1939 (Terry)
Nicky and Gino. *See* Dominick and Eugene, 1988
Nicky et Kitty, 1959 (Coutard)
Nido de viudas, 1977 (Lai)
Nie wieder Liebe, 1931 (Herlth; Planer; Röhrig)
Niemansland, 1931 (Eisler)
Niente rose per OSS 177, 1968 (Delli Colli)
Nieuwe Gronden, 1934 (Eisler; van Dongen)
Nieuwe polders, 1931 (van Dongen)
Night, 1930 (Disney)
Night. *See* **Notte**, 1960
Night after Night, 1932 (Banton; Haller; Plunkett)
Night after Night, 1933 (Zukor)
Night Ambush. *See* Ill Met By Moonlight, 1957
Night and Day, 1946 (Burks; Steiner; Warner)
Night and Day. *See* Jack's the Boy, 1932
Night and Fog. *See* **Nuit et brouillard**, 1955
Night and the City, 1950 (Lassally; Waxman)
Night and the City, 1991 (Winkler)
Night and the Moment, 1994 (Carrière; Rotunno)
Night at Earl Carroll's, 1940 (Dreier; Head; Reynolds)
Night at the Crossroads. *See* Nuit du carrefour, 1932
Night at the Opera, 1935 (Brown; Carré; Freed; Gibbons; Kaper; Mayer; Shearer; Stothart; Thalberg)
Night Beat, 1947 (Francis; Korda)

1157

Night before Christmas, 1941 (Hanna and Barbera)
Night before Christmas. *See* Botte di Natale, 1994
Night before Christmas. *See* Noch pyeryed rozhdyestvo, 1913
Night Boat to Dublin, 1945 (Heller)
Night Butterflies. *See* Yoru no cho, 1957
Night Caller. *See* Peur sur la ville, 1974
Night Club Lady, 1932 (Riskin)
Night Club Scandal, 1937 (Dreier; Head)
Night Creatures. *See* Captain Clegg, 1962
Night Crossing, 1982 (Goldsmith)
Night Digger, 1970 (Herrmann)
Night Editor, 1946 (Guffey)
Night Falls on Manhattan, 1997 (O'Steen; Watkin)
Night Flight, 1933 (Mayer; Selznick; Stothart)
Night Games, 1974 (Schifrin)
Night Games, 1989 (Donaggio)
Night Has a Thousand Eyes, 1948 (Dreier; Head; Seitz; Young)
Night Hawk, 1924 (Stromberg)
Night in Cairo. *See* Barbarian, 1933
Night in Havana. *See* Big Boodle, 1956
Night in London. *See* Nacht in London, 1928
Night in Montmartre, 1931 (Balcon; Rank)
Night in New Orleans, 1942 (Dreier)
Night in Paradise, 1946 (Banton; Mohr; Wanger)
Night in the Harbor. *See* Natt i hamn, 1943
Night in the Life of Jimmy Reardon, 1988 (Conti)
Night into Morning, 1951 (Basevi)
Night Invader, 1942 (Heller)
Night Is Ending. *See* Paris after Dark, 1943
Night Is My Future. *See* Musik i mörker, 1948
Night Is Young, 1935 (Howe; Stothart)
Night Life in the Army, 1942 (Terry)
Night Life of the Bugs, 1936 (Lantz)
Night Life of the Gods, 1935 (Laemmle)
Night Magic, 1984 (Rousselot)
Night Moves, 1975 (Allen; Jenkins)
Night Must Fall, 1937 (Mayer; Stromberg)
Night Must Fall, 1964 (Fisher; Francis)
Night My Number Came Up, 1955 (Arnold; Balcon; Sherriff)
Night 'n' Gales, 1937 (Roach)
Night of January 16th, 1941 (Dreier; Head)
Night of June 13, 1933 (Zukor)
Night of Love, 1927 (Barnes; Goldwyn)
Night of Mystery, 1928 (Mankiewicz; Vajda)
Night of Mystery, 1937 (Head)
Night of Nights, 1939 (Dreier; Head; Stewart; Young)
Night of San Lorenzo. *See* Notte di San Lorenzo, 1981
Night of Terror, 1908 (Bitzer)
Night of the Demon, 1957 (Adam; Cohn)
Night of the Eagle, 1961 (Alwyn)
Night of the Garter, 1933 (Wilcox)
Night of the Generals, 1967 (Decaë; Jarre; Spiegel; Trauner)
Night of the Grizzly, 1966 (Pereira)
Night of the Hunter, 1955 (Cortez)
Night of the Iguana, 1964 (Figueroa; Jeakins; Stark; Veiller)
Night of the Living Dead, 1990 (Golan and Globus; Savini)
Night of the Living Duck, 1988 (Blanc)
Night of the Party, 1906 (Bitzer)
Night of the Party, 1934 (Junge)
Night of the Quarter Moon, 1959 (Cahn; van Heusen)
Night on Bald Mountain. *See* **Nuit sur le Mont Chauve**, 1933
Night Owls, 1930 (Roach)
Night Parade, 1929 (Plunkett)
Night Passage, 1957 (Chase; Daniels; Tiomkin)
Night Patrol, 1926 (Lang)
Night People, 1954 (Clarke; Johnson; Lemaire; Spencer)

Night Plane from Chungking, 1943 (Head)
Night Ride, 1937 (Havelock-Allan)
Night Riders, 1939 (Canutt)
Night River. *See* Yoru no kawa, 1956
Night Runner, 1957 (Boyle)
Night Shift, 1942 (Kanin)
Night Shift, 1982 (Bacharach)
Night Song, 1947 (Ballard; Carmichael; D'Agostino; Orry-Kelly)
Night Spot, 1938 (Musuraca)
Night Stripes, 1944 (Kanin)
Night Sun. *See* Sole anche di notte, 1990
Night Taxi. *See* Taxi de nuit, 1993
Night They Invented Striptease. *See* Night They Raided Minsky's, 1968
Night They Raided Minsky's, 1968 (Justin; Rosenblum)
Night Tide, 1961 (Raksin)
Night to Remember, 1943 (Walker)
Night to Remember, 1958 (Alwyn; Rank; Unsworth; Vetchinsky)
Night Train to Munich, 1940 (Vetchinsky)
Night unto Night, 1949 (Waxman)
Night Visitor, 1970 (Lundgren; Mancini)
Night Waitress, 1936 (Metty)
Night Watch, 1928 (Biro; Korda; Struss)
Night Watch, 1941 (Alwyn)
Night Watchman, 1938 (Jones)
Night Watchman's Mistake, 1929 (Hornbeck)
Night without Sleep, 1952 (Ballard; Lemaire; Newman)
Night without Stars, 1951 (Alwyn; Rank)
Night Women. *See* Femme spectacle, 1964
Night Work, 1939 (Head)
Nightbreed, 1990 (Elfman)
Nightfall, 1956 (Duning; Guffey)
Nighthawks, 1981 (Smith)
Nightmare, 1942 (Barnes)
Nightmare, 1956 (Biroc)
Nightmare, 1963 (Francis; Carreras)
Nightmare, 1981 (Savini)
Nightmare. *See* Voices, 1973
Nightmare Alley, 1947 (Furthman; Garmes; Lemaire; Wheeler)
Nightmare at Noon, 1990 (Zimmer)
Nightmare Before Christmas, 1993 (Elfman)
Nightmare Castle. *See* Amanti d'oltretombo, 1965
Nightmare in the Sun, 1963 (Cortez)
Nightmare on Elm Street 3: Dream Warriors, 1987 (Badalamenti)
Night's End. *See* Nishant, 1975
Nights of Cabiria. *See* Notti di Cabiria, 1956
Nightsun. *See* Sole anche di notte, 1990
Nightwing, 1979 (Mancini)
Niguruma no uta, 1959 (Yoda)
Nihiliste, 1906 (Pathé)
Nihon dashutsu, 1964 (Takemitsu)
Nihon no seishun, 1968 (Takemitsu)
Nihonkai daikaisen, 1969 (Tsuburaya)
Nihontou: Miyairi Kouhei no waza, 1976 (Takemitsu)
Niizuma kaigi, 1949 (Miyagawa)
Niji o idaku shojo, 1948 (Hayasaka)
Nijinsky, 1980 (Slocombe)
Nijuissa no chichi, 1964 (Takemitsu)
Nikki, Wild Dog of the North, 1961 (Disney)
Nilo di pietra, 1956 (Delli Colli)
Nina, 1958 (D'Eaubonne)
Nina B Affair. *See* Affaire Nina B, 1962
Nina de Vanghel, 1952 (Schüfftan)
Nine 1/2 Weeks, 1986 (Biziou)
Nine Days a Queen. *See* Tudor Rose, 1936
Nine Hours to Live. *See* Nine Hours to Rama, 1963
Nine Hours to Rama, 1963 (Arnold; Bass)

Nine Lives Are Not Enough, 1941 (McCord)
Nine Men, 1943 (Balcon)
Nine Months, 1995 (McAlpine; Zimmer)
Nine till Six, 1932 (Dean; Reville)
Ninfa plebea, 1996 (Morricone)
Ningen kakumei, 1973 (Muraki)
Ninguém Duas Vezes, 1984 (de Almeida; Branco)
Ninin sugata, 1942 (Yoda)
Ninja III: The Domination, 1984 (Golan and Globus)
Ninja Sasuke Sarutobi of Sekigahara. *See* Ninjutsu Sekigahara Sarutobi
  Sasuke, 1938
Ninjutsu Sekigahara Sarutobi Sasuke, 1938 (Yoda)
Ninjutsu senshuken jiai, 1956 (Yoda)
Niño y la niebla, 1953 (Figueroa)
Ninotchka, 1939 (Adrian; Brackett; Daniels; Gibbons; Mayer; Reisch;
  Shearer)
Ninth Configuration, 1980 (Fisher)
Ninth Gate, 1999 (Tavoularis)
Ninth of January. *See* Deviatoe yanvaria, 1926
Nipped in the Bud, 1918 (Roach)
Nippon chiubotsu, 1973 (Muraki)
Nippon ichi no iro-otoko, 1963 (Muraki)
Nippon kengo-den, 1945 (Hayasaka)
Nippon shunka-ko, 1967 (Toda)
Nippon tanjo, 1959 (Tsuburaya)
Nippy's Nightmare, 1917 (O'brien)
Nirala Hindustan, 1938 (Biswas)
Nishant, 1975 (Nihalani)
Nishijin no shimai, 1952 (Miyagawa)
Nit-Witty Kitty, 1951 (Hanna and Barbera)
Nitchevo, 1936 (Honegger; Wakhévitch)
Nitwits, 1935 (Cronjager; Polglase)
Nix on Dames, 1929 (Clarke; Spencer)
Nix on Hypnotricks, 1941 (Fleischer)
Nixon, 1995 (Williams)
No. 111. *See* A 111-es, 1919
No Barking, 1954 (Blanc; Jones; Stalling)
No Biz Like Shoe Biz, 1960 (Hanna and Barbera)
No Children, 1921 (Roach)
No Dia dos Meus Anos, 1992 (Branco)
No Down Payment, 1957 (La Shelle; Lemaire; Wald; Wheeler)
No End. *See* Bez konca, 1985
No Exit. *See* Huis clos, 1954
No Eyes Today, 1929 (Fleischer)
No Father to Guide Him, 1925 (Roach)
No-Good Guy, 1916 (Sullivan)
No Greater Glory, 1934 (August; Swerling)
No Hands on the Clock, 1941 (Mainwaring)
No Highway, 1951 (Périnal; Sherriff)
No Kidding, 1960 (Dillon)
No Leave, No Love, 1946 (Ames; Irene; Pasternak; Rosson; Surtees)
No Limit, 1935 (Dean)
No Love for Johnnie, 1961 (Arnold; Rank)
No Man of Her Own, 1932 (Banton; Zukor)
No Man of Her Own, 1950 (Bumstead; Dreier; Friedhofer; Head)
No Man's Land, 1987 (Mancini)
No Man's Land. *See* Niemansland, 1931
No Marriage Ties, 1933 (Cronjager; Plunkett; Polglase; Steiner)
No Mercy, 1986 (Von Brandenstein)
No Minor Vices, 1948 (Barnes; Parrish; Waxman)
No More Divorces. *See* Rozwodów nie bedzie, 1963
No More Ladies, 1935 (Adrian; Mayer; Stewart)
No More Orchids, 1932 (August)
No More Women, 1924 (Walker)
No, My Darling Daughter, 1961 (Rank)
No! No! A Thousand Times No!, 1935 (Fleischer)

No, No, Nanette, 1930 (Grot; Polito)
No, No, Nanette, 1940 (Metty; Wilcox)
No Noise, 1923 (Roach)
No Nukes, 1980 (Wexler)
No One Man, 1932 (Buchman; Lang)
No, or the Vain Glory of Command. *See* Nao ou a vã gloria de mandar,
1990No Other One, 1936 (Fleischer)
No Other Woman, 1933 (Cronjager; Plunkett; Steiner; Vorkapich)
No Parking Hare, 1954 (Blanc; McKimson; Stalling)
No Pets, 1923 (Roach)
No Place Like Jail, 1918 (Roach)
No Place to Go, 1939 (Edeson)
No Place to Hide, 1959 (Menges)
No Questions Asked, 1951 (Rose)
No Resting Place, 1951 (Alwyn)
No Sad Songs for Me, 1950 (Duning; Koch; Maté; Walker)
No Sex Last Night, 1996 (Branco)
No Sleep for Percy, 1955 (Terry)
No Sleep till Dawn. *See* Bombers B-52, 1957
No Small Affair, 1984 (Justin; Zsigmond)
No Stop-Over, 1921 (Roach)
No Time for Comedy, 1940 (Epstein; Haller; Orry-Kelly; Wallis)
No Time for Love, 1943 (Dreier; Head; Irene; Lang; Young)
No Time for Pity. *See* Time without Pity, 1957
No Time for Sergeants, 1958 (Rosson)
No Time to Marry, 1938 (Jarrico)
No Trumpets, No Drums. *See* Trackers, 1971
No Way Out, 1950 (Krasner; Lemaire; Newman; Wheeler; Zanuck)
No Way Out, 1987 (Alcott; Jarre)
No Way to Treat a Lady, 1968 (Goldman; Jenkins; Pereira)
Noah's Ark, 1928 (Grot; Mohr; Zanuck)
Noah's Ark, 1977 (Halas and Batchelor)
Noah's Lark, 1929 (Fleischer)
Noah's Outing, 1932 (Terry)
Nob Hill, 1945 (Cronjager)
Nobody Home, 1919 (Garmes)
Nobody Listened. *See* Nadie escuchaba, 1988
Nobody Lives Forever, 1946 (Deutsch; Edeson)
Nobody Runs Forever, 1968 (Delerue)
Nobody's Baby, 1937 (Roach)
Nobody's Bridge, 1923 (Miller)
Nobody's Fool, 1921 (Glennon)
Nobody's Widow, 1927 (Miller)
Nobody's Women. *See* Femmes de personne, 1984
Noceau Lac Saint-Fargeau, 1905 (Gaumont)
Noces du sable, 1948 (Auric)
Noces rouges, 1973 (Rabier)
Noces vénetiennes. *See* Prima notte, 1958
Noch pyeryed rozhdyestvo, 1913 (Starewicz)
Noche de los mayas, 1939 (Figueroa)
Nochnye priklucheniye dariyat nam naslazhdeniye, 1916 (Starewicz)
Nocturnal Adventure. *See* Nochnye priklucheniye dariyat nam
  naslazhdeniye, 1916
Nocturne, 1919 (Gaumont)
Nocturne, 1946 (Boyle; Harrison)
Nocturne, 1954 (Alexeieff and Parker)
Nocturno de amor, 1948 (Alcoriza)
Nogitsune sanji , 1930 (Tsuburaya)
Noi donne siamo fatte cosi, 1971 (Age and Scarpelli)
Noi due sole, 1953 (Rota)
Noia, 1963 (Guerra; Levine; Ponti)
Noire et Caline, 1947 (Alekan)
Noise Annoys Ko-Ko, 1929 (Fleischer)
Noises Off, 1992 (Marshall)
Noisy Noises, 1929 (Roach)
Nomads, 1986 (Conti)

Nommé la Rocca, 1961 (Cloquet)

Non ci resta che piangere, 1984 (Rotunno)

Non coupable, 1947 (Mnouchkine)

Non, ou la vaine gloire de commande. *See* Nao ou a vã gloria de mandar, 1990

Non-Skid Kid, 1922 (Roach)

Non-Stop Kid, 1918 (Roach)

Non-Stop New York, 1937 (Rank; Siodmak)

Non uccidere. *See* Tu ne tueras point, 1961

None but the Brave, 1965 (Daniels; O'Steen; Tsuburaya; Williams)

None but the Lonely Heart, 1944 (Barnes; D'Agostino; Eisler)

None Shall Escape, 1944 (Garmes)

Nonna Sabella, 1957 (Delli Colli)

Nonsense Newsreel, 1954 (Terry)

Noon Whistle, 1923 (Roach)

Noose, 1948 (Heller)

Noose Hangs High, 1948 (Taradash)

Nor the Moon by Night, 1958 (Bernard; Rank)

Nora, 1923 (Pommer)

Nora inu, 1949 (Hayasaka)

Nora Prentiss, 1947 (Grot; Howe; Waxman)

Nord, 1991 (Guillemot)

Nordlandrose, 1914 (Messter)

Nörgler, 1917 (Kolowrat-Krakowsky)

Norma Rae, 1979 (Alonzo)

Normal People Are Nothing Exceptional. *See* Gens normaux n'ont rien d'exceptionnel, 1993

Norman Normal, 1968 (Blanc)

Normandie-Niemen, 1959 (Spaak)

North. *See* Nord, 1991

North by Northwest, 1959 (Bass; Boyle; Burks; Gillespie; Herrmann; Lehman)

North of 50-50, 1924 (Roach)

North of Hudson Bay, 1923 (Furthman)

North of the Rio Grande, 1937 (Harlan; Head)

North of the Yukon. *See* North of Hudson Bay, 1923

North or North West. *See* N or NW, 1938

North Star, 1925 (Walker)

North Star, 1943 (Goldwyn; Howe; Mandell; Menzies)

North to Alaska, 1960 (Shamroy; Smith; Spencer)

North West Frontier, 1959 (Unsworth; Vetchinsky)

North West Mounted Police, 1940 (Dreier; Macpherson; Young)

North Woods, 1931 (Lantz)

Northern Harbour. *See* Severní přístav, 1954

Northern Star. *See* Etoile du nord, 1982

Northwest Frontier, 1959 (Rank)

Northwest Hounded Police, 1946 (Avery)

Northwest Mounted Police, 1940 (Head; Sullivan)

Northwest Outpost, 1947 (Canutt)

Northwest Passage, 1940 (Jennings; Mayer; Stothart; Stromberg)

Northwest Rangers, 1942 (Schary)

Norvège, 1951 (Colpi)

Norwegian Wood, 1967 (Müller)

Norwood, 1970 (Wallis)

Nos bons étudiants, 1904 (Gaumont)

Nose. *See* Nez, 1963

Nosed Out, 1934 (Roach)

Nose's Story, 1911 (Gaudio)

Nosferatu, 1922 (Wagner)

Nosferatu a venezia, 1987 (Vangelis)

Nostalghia, 1983 (Guerra; Lanci, Giuseppe ("beppe"))

Nostalgi. *See* Nostalghia, 1983

Nostalgie, 1937 (Annenkov; Wakhévitch)

Nostradamus's Great Prophecy. *See* Nosutoradamusu no daiyogen, 1974

Nostromo, 1996 (Donati; Morricone)

Nosutoradamusu no daiyogen, 1974 (Muraki)

Not a Drum Was Heard, 1924 (August)

Not as a Stranger, 1955 (Planer; van Heusen)

Not Exactly Gentlemen, 1931 (Nichols)

Not in Nottingham, 1963 (Hanna and Barbera)

Not My Sister, 1916 (Sullivan)

Not Now, 1936 (Fleischer)

Not on My Account, 1943 (Metty)

Not on Your Life. *See* **Verdugo**, 1963

Not One Shall Die, 1957 (Guffey)

Not Quite Decent, 1929 (Clarke)

Not So Dumb, 1930 (Adrian; Gibbons; Stewart)

Not So Long Ago, 1925 (Howe)

Not So Quiet, 1930 (Lantz)

Not Wanted, 1949 (Jarrico)

Not with My Wife, You Don't!, 1966 (Bass; Head; Lang; Mercer; Williams)

Not without My Daughter, 1991 (Goldsmith)

Notary. *See* A peleskei notárius, 1917

Notebook on Cities and Clothes, 1991 (Müller)

Notes on the Popular Arts, 1978 (Bass)

Notes to You, 1941 (Blanc; Stalling)

Nothern Pursuit, 1943 (Deutsch)

Nothing but Pleasure, 1939 (Bruckman)

Nothing but the Tooth, 1948 (Blanc; Stalling)

Nothing but the Truth, 1929 (Cronjager)

Nothing but the Truth, 1941 (Dreier; Head; Lang)

Nothing but Trouble, 1918 (Roach)

Nothing but Trouble, 1944 (Irene)

Nothing in Common, 1986 (Alonzo)

Nothing Sacred, 1938 (Banton; Hecht; Plunkett; Selznick; Wheeler)

Nothing to Wear, 1928 (Walker)

Notorious, 1946 (D'Agostino; Head; Hecht)

Notorious Affair, 1930 (Grot; Haller)

Notorious Fanny Hill, 1965 (Kovacs)

Notorious Gentleman. *See* Rake's Progress, 1945

Notorious Lady, 1927 (Gaudio)

Notorious Landlady, 1962 (Duning)

Notorious Lone Wolf, 1946 (Guffey)

Notorious Sophie Lang, 1934 (Head; Veiller)

Notre Dame, cathédrale de Paris, 1957 (Delerue; Fradetal)

Notre Dame de Paris, 1956 (Aurenche and Bost; Auric; Prévert)

Notre Dame of Paris. *See* Hunchback of Notre Dame, 1956

Notre histoire, 1984 (Evein)

Notre mariage, 1984 (Branco; de Almeida)

Notre Nazi. *See* Unser Nazi, 1984

Notte, 1960 (Di Venanzo; Flaiano and Pinelli; Guerra)

Notte bianche, 1957 (Rota)

Notte delle beffe, 1940 (Amidei)

Notte delle nozze. *See* Tradita, 1954

Notte di San Lorenzo, 1981 (Guerra)

Notte di tempestà, 1945 (Gherardi)

Notte porta consiglio. *See* Roma città libera, 1946

Notti bianche, 1957 (Cecchi D'amico)

Notti Bianche, 1957 (Serandrei)

Notti bianchi, 1957 (Rotunno)

Notti di Cabiria, 1956 (Flaiano and Pinelli; Gherardi; Ponti; Rota; de Laurentiis)

N'oublie pas que tu vas mourir, 1995 (Guillemot)

Nous les gosses, 1941 (Douy)

Nous les jeunes. *See* Altitude 3.200, 1938

Nous ne sommes plus des enfants, 1934 (Stradling)

Nous n'irons plus au bois, 1963 (Carrière)

Nous sommes tous des assassins, 1952 (Spaak)

Nouveau Journal d'une femme en blanc, 1966 (Aurenche and Bost; Douy)

Nouveaux Messieurs, 1928 (Meerson; Périnal; Spaak)

Objective, Burma!, 1945 (Howe; Wald; Warner; Waxman)
Objective Seen. *See* Objectief gezien, 1968
Obliging Young Lady, 1941 (Musuraca)
Oblivion, 1994 (Donaggio)
Oblivion 2: Backlash, 1996 (Donaggio)
Oblomok imperii, 1929 (Enei)
Oboro kago, 1951 (Yoda)
Obrácení Ferdyše Pištory, 1931 (Stallich)
Obscure Evil. *See* Male oscuro, 1990
Obsession. *See* Junoon, 1978
Obsession, 1934 (Jaubert)
Obsession, 1948 (Adam; Rota)
Obsession, 1975 (Herrmann; Zsigmond)
Obsession, 1997 (Watkin)
Obusku, z pytle ven!, 1956 (Brdečka)
Obywatel Piszczyk, 1988 (Stawiński)
Ocalenie, 1959 (Ścibor-Rylski)
Occhi freddi della paura, 1971 (Morricone)
Occhi, la bocca, 1982 (Lanci, Giuseppe ("beppe"))
Occhiali d'oro, 1987 (Morricone)
Occhio alla penna, 1981 (Morricone)
Occhio selvaggio, 1967 (Guerra)
Occupe-toi d'Amélie, 1949 (Aurenche and Bost; Douy)
Ocean Breakers. *See* Brannigar, 1935
Ocean Hop, 1927 (Disney)
Oceano, 1971 (Morricone)
Ocean's Eleven, 1960 (Bass; Cahn; Daniels; Lederer; van Heusen)
Ochiyo-gasa, 1935 (Miyagawa)
Ochiyo toshigoro, 1937 (Miyagawa)
Ochiyo's Umbrella. *See* Ochiyo-gasa, 1935
Ochsenkrieg, 1920 (Planer)
Oci ciornie, 1987 (Cecchi D'amico; Lai)
OCIL 1958, 1958 (Delerue)
Octaman, 1970 (Baker)
October. *See* **Oktiabr**, 1928
October. *See* Oktiabr, 1967
October Man, 1947 (Alwyn; Rank;Vetchinsky)
Octopussy, 1983 (Barry; Broccoli)
Odd Angry Shot, 1979 (McAlpine)
Odd Couple, 1968 (Cahn; Westmore Family)
Odd Man Out, 1947 (Alwyn; Krasker; Mathieson; Rank; Sherriff)
Odd Obsession. *See* Kagi, 1959
Odds against Tomorrow, 1959 (Allen)
Ode to Billy Joe, 1976 (Legrand)
Ödemarksprästen, 1946 (Lundgren)
Odessa File, 1974 (Morris; Neame)
Odette, 1950 (Wilcox)
Odeur des fauves, 1971 (Lai)
Odna, 1931 (Enei; Moskvin; Shostakovich)
Odongo, 1956 (Alwyn; Broccoli)
Odor of the Day, 1948 (Blanc; Stalling)
Odor-able Kitty, 1945 (Blanc; Jones; Stalling)
Odplata, 1920 (Heller)
Odyssée du Capitaine Steve. *See* Walk into Paradise, 1955
Odysseus' Heimkehr, 1918 (Messter)
Odyssey of Life, 1996 (Daring)
Oedipus Rex. *See* Edipo re, 1967
Oedipus the King, 1967 (Lassally)
Oedo no saigon, 1928 (Tsuburaya)
Oeil au beurre noir, 1987 (Mnouchkine)
Oeil-du-Lynx, détective, 1936 (Kaufman)
Oeil du maître, 1957 (Braunberger)
Oeil du malin, 1962 (Ponti; de Beauregard)
Oeil pour oeil, 1956 (Aurenche and Bost; Matras)
Øen i fuglegaden, 1997 (Preisner)
Oeufs brouillés, 1975 (Carrière)

Oeuvre scientifique de Pasteur, 1946 (Fradetal)
Of Feline Bondage, 1965 (Jones)
Of Flesh and Blood. *See* Grands Chemins, 1963
Of Fox and Hounds, 1940 (Avery; Blanc; Stalling)
Of Human Bondage, 1934 (Berman; Plunkett; Polglase; Steiner)
Of Human Bondage, 1946 (Blanke; Friedhofer; Korngold)
Of Human Bondage, 1964 (Morris)
Of Human Hearts, 1938 (Stothart; Vorkapich)
Of Human Rights, 1950 (van Dongen)
Of Men and Demons, 1970 (Hubley; Jones)
Of Men and Mice, 1950 (Paxton)
Of Men and Music, 1950 (Crosby; Mohr; Parrish)
Of Mice and Men, 1940 (Roach)
Of Rice and Hen, 1953 (Blanc; McKimson; Stalling)
Of Stars and Men, 1961 (Hubley)
Of Thee I Sting, 1946 (Blanc)
Off Beat, 1986 (Allen)
Off Limits, 1953 (Head)
Off the Highway, 1925 (Stromberg)
Off the Record, 1939 (Deutsch; Rosher)
Off the Trolley, 1919 (Roach)
Off to China, 1936 (Terry)
Off to the Opera, 1952 (Terry)
Offence, 1972 (Fisher)
Office Boy, 1932 (Iwerks)
Office Girl. *See* Sunshine Susie, 1931
Office Killer, 1997 (Schamus; Vachon)
Office Wife, 1930 (Zanuck)
Officer and a Gentleman, 1982 (Nitzsche)
Officer O'Brien, 1930 (Miller)
Officer Pooch, 1940 (Hanna and Barbera)
Officer's Swordknot. *See* A tiszti kardbojt, 1915
Official Officers, 1925 (Roach)
Offizierstragödie. *See* Rosenmontag, 1924
Offret, 1986 (Colpi; Nykvist)
Oficio más antiguo, 1968 (Alcoriza)
Often an Orphan, 1949 (Blanc; Jones)
Oggi, dommani, e dopodomani, 1964 (Di Venanzo; Ponti))
Ogin sama, 1978 (Yoda)
Ogre. *See* Roi des aulnes, 1995
Ogro, 1979 (Cristaldi; Morricone)
Oh Amelia!. *See* Occupe-toi d'Amélie, 1949
Oh! Calcutta!, 1971 (Shepard)
Oh Dad, Poor Dad, Mama's Hung You in the Closet and I'm Feelin' So Sad, 1967 (Stark; Unsworth)
Oh Daddy!, 1934 (Balcon; Rank)
Oh, Doctor, 1937 (Krasner)
Oh-Edo gonon otoko, 1951 (Yoda)
Oh, for a Man!, 1930 (Clarke; Goosson)
Oh Gentle Spring, 1942 (Terry)
Oh God, Women Are So Loving. *See* Dieu que les femmes sont amoureuses, 1994
Oh! How I Hate to Get Up in the Morning, 1932 (Fleischer)
Oh, Johnny, How You Can Love!, 1940 (Krasner)
Oh, Mabel!, 1924 (Fleischer)
Oh Men! Oh Women!, 1957 (Clarke; Friedhofer; Johnson; Lemaire)
Oh Mr. Porter!, 1937 (Rank; Vetchinsky)
Oh, Promise Me, 1921 (Roach)
Oh Rosalinda!, 1955 (Challis; Heckroth)
Oh Susanna, 1933 (Terry)
Oh, Teacher, 1927 (Disney)
Oh, Uncle!, 1909 (Bitzer)
Oh, What a Knight, 1928 (Disney)
Oh What a Knight, 1982 (Driessen)
Oh! What a Nurse!, 1926 (Zanuck)
Oh, Yeah!, 1929 (Miller)

Oh, You Are Like a Rose. *See* Ack, du är some en ros, 1967
Oh, You Beautiful Doll, 1949 (Lemaire; Newman; Steiner)
Oh You Beautiful Doll, 1926 (Fleischer)
Oh, You Women!, 1919 (Loos)
Ohm Krüger, 1941 (Wagner)
Oil and Water, 1912 (Bitzer)
Oil Can Mystery, 1933 (Terry)
Oil for the Lamps of China, 1935 (Gaudio)
Oil Hell of Killing Women. *See* Onna goroshi abura jigoku, 1949
Oil's Well, 1929 (Lantz)
Oily American, 1954 (Blanc; McKimson; Stalling)
Oily Hare, 1952 (Blanc; McKimson; Stalling)
Oise mairi, 1939 (Yoda)
Oiseau de paradis, 1962 (Jarre)
Oiseau rare, 1935 (Prévert)
Oiseau s'en vole, 1960 (Alekan)
Oiseaux d'Afrique, 1961 (Braunberger)
Oiseaux vont mourir au Perou, 1968 (Matras)
Ojciec królowej, 1980 (Stawiński)
Ojojoj eller sången om den eldröda hummern, 1965 (Fischer)
OK for Sound, 1937 (Vetchinsky)
Okay, America, 1932 (Miller)
Okénko, 1933 (Stallich)
Okhota na lis, 1980 (Mindadze)
Oklahoma!, 1955 (Crosby; Deutsch; Levien; Orry-Kelly; Surtees)
Oklahoma Badlands, 1948 (Canutt)
Oklahoma Crude, 1972 (Mancini; Surtees)
Oklahoma Kid, 1939 (Deutsch; Friedhofer; Howe; Orry-Kelly; Steiner)
Oklahoma Renegades, 1940 (Canutt)
Oklahoman, 1957 (Mirisch)
Okomé, 1951 (Rabier)
Oktiabr, 1928 (Tisse)
Oktiabr, 1967 (Shostakovich)
Ol' Gray Hoss, 1928 (Roach)
Ol' Swimmin' 'ole, 1928 (Disney)
Ola och Julia, 1967 (Fischer)
Olaf, an Atom, 1913 (Bitzer)
Olaf Laughs Last, 1942 (Bruckman)
Old Acquaintance, 1943 (Blanke; Orry-Kelly; Polito; Waxman)
Old Actor, 1912 (Bitzer)
Old and New. *See* Staroie i novoie, 1929
Old Barn, 1929 (Hornbeck)
Old Bill and Son, 1940 (Korda; Périnal)
Old Black Joe, 1926 (Fleischer)
Old Blackout Joe, 1940 (Hubley)
Old Bookkeeper, 1911 (Bitzer)
Old Box, 1975 (Driessen)
Old Boyfriends, 1978 (Fraker; Henry; Houseman)
Old Bull, 1932 (Roach)
Old Confectioner's Mistake, 1911 (Bitzer)
Old Curiosity Shop, 1994 (Daring)
Old Curiosity Shop. *See* Mister Quilp, 1975
Old Czech Legends. *See* **Staré pověsti cěské**, 1953
Old Dark House, 1932 (Edeson; Laemmle; Pierce; Sherriff)
Old Dark House, 1966 (Carreras)
Old Dog Tray, 1935 (Terry)
Old Enough, 1984 (Ballhaus)
Old-Fashioned Way, 1935 (Zukor)
Old-Fashioned World. *See* Piccolo mondo antico, 1941
Old Fire Horse, 1939 (Terry)
Old Folks at Home, 1924 (Fleischer)
Old Glory, 1939 (Blanc; Jones; Stalling)
Old Greatheart. *See* Way Back Home, 1931
Old Grey Hare, 1944 (Blanc; Clampett; Stalling)
Old Homes of the River, 1938 (Vetchinsky)
Old Homestead, 1922 (Brown; Zukor)

Old Isaacs, the Pawnbroker, 1908 (Bitzer)
Old Lady 31, 1920 (Mathis)
Old Lady Who Walked in the Sea. *See* Vieille qui marchait dans la mer, 1991
Old Maid, 1939 (Blanke; Friedhofer; Gaudio; Orry-Kelly; Steiner; Wallis)
Old Maid. *See* Vieille Fille, 1972
Old Mammy's Secret Code, 1913 (Ince)
Old Man and the Sea, 1958 (Crosby; Howe; Tiomkin)
Old Man Bezouska. *See* Pantáta Bezoušek, 1927
Old Man of the Mountain, 1933 (Fleischer)
Old Man Rhythm, 1935 (Mercer; Musuraca; Pan)
Old Mother Hubbard, 1935 (Iwerks)
Old Mother Hubbard. *See* Mother Goose Presents Humpty Dumpty, 1946
Old Oaken Bucket, 1941 (Terry)
Old Rockin' Chair Tom, 1948 (Hanna and Barbera)
Old San Francisco, 1927 (Carré; Mohr; Zanuck)
Old Sea Dog, 1922 (Roach)
Old Sin. *See* Starý hřích, 1930
Old Spanish Custom. *See* Invader, 1936
Old Wives for New, 1918 (Buckland; Macpherson; Zukor)
Old Wives' Tales, 1946 (Halas and Batchelor)
Old Woman Ghost. *See* Yoba, 1976
Old Yeller, 1957 (Canutt; Disney)
Oldest Profession in the World. *See* Plus vieux métier du monde, 1967
Oleanna, 1994 (Mamet)
Olimpiada en Mexico, 1968 (Lassally)
Olio for Jasper, 1946 (Pal)
Olive Oyl and Water Don't Mix, 1942 (Fleischer)
Olive Trees of Justice. *See* Oliviers de la justice, 1962
Oliver!, 1968 (Green; Morris)
Oliver Twist, 1916 (Zukor)
Oliver Twist, 1922 (Goosson)
Oliver Twist, 1948 (Bryan; Havelock-Allan; Mathieson; Morris; Neame; Rank)
Oliver's Story, 1978 (Lai)
Olive's Boithday Presink, 1941 (Fleischer)
Olive's Sweepstake Ticket, 1941 (Fleischer)
Olivia, 1950 (D'Eaubonne; Matras)
Olivier, Olivier, 1992 (Preisner)
Oliviers de la justice, 1962 (Jarre)
Olly Olly Oxen Free, 1978 (Head)
Oltre la porta, 1982 (Donaggio)
Olvidados, 1950 (Alcoriza; Figueroa)
Olympia, 1930 (Daniels; Gibbons)
Olympia, 1938 (Herlth)
Olympia. *See* A Breath of Scandal, 1960
Olympic Games, 1927 (Roach)
Olympic Glory, 1999 (Marshall)
Olympics in Mexico. *See* Olimpiada en Mexico, 1968
Omagatsuji no ketto, 1951 (Miyagawa)
Omagatsuji's Duel. *See* Omagatsuji no ketto, 1951
Omaha Trail, 1942 (Schary)
O'Malley of the Mounted, 1921 (August)
Omar Khayyam, 1957 (Laszlo; Young)
Omar the Tentmaker, 1922 (Buckland)
Ombra, 1954 (Delli Colli)
Ombre et la nuit, 1977 (Alekan)
Ombre et lumière, 1950 (Kosma)
Omega Man, 1971 (Metty)
Omelette fantastique, 1909 (Cohl)
Omen, 1976 (Goldsmith)
Omicron, 1963 (Cristaldi)
On a Clear Day You Can See Forever, 1970 (Beaton; Stradling)
On a jeho sestra, 1931 (Heller)
On a Sunday Afternoon, 1930 (Fleischer)
On a très peu d'amis, 1998 (Branco)

On a volé la cuisse de Jupiter, 1979 (Mnouchkine)
On a volé la mer, 1962 (Delerue)
On a volé un homme, 1933 (Kaper; Pommer)
On Again—Off Again, 1937 (Polglase)
On an Island with You, 1948 (Brown; Irene; Mayer; Pasternak; Rosher)
On Approval, 1943 (Alwyn)
On aura tout vu!, 1976 (Sarde)
On Borrowed Time, 1939 (Ruttenberg; Waxman)
On connaît la chanson, 1997 (Saulnier)
On Dangerous Ground, 1916 (Marion)
On Dangerous Ground, 1951 (Herrmann; Houseman)
On Golden Pond, 1981 (Grusin; Jeakins)
On Guard. See Bossu, 1997
On Her Majesty's Secret Service, 1969 (Barry; Broccoli)
On ira lui porter des oranges, 1970 (Braunberger)
On Land, at Sea, and in the Air, 1980 (Driessen)
On Light. See O svetle, 1953
On Location, 1921 (Roach)
On Moonlight Bay, 1951 (Haller; Steiner)
On My Birthday. See No Dia dos Meus Anos, 1992
On My Way to the Crusades, I Met a Girl Who . . . . See Cintura di castità, 1968
On n'a pas besoin d'argent, 1933 (Burel)
On n'arrête pas le printemps, 1971 (Braunberger)
On ne badine pas avec l'amour, 1952 (Evein)
On ne roule pas Antoinette, 1936 (Kaufman)
On Our Merry Way. See A Miracle Can Happen, 1947
On peut le dire sans se fâcher!, 1978 (Legrand)
On Promised Land, 1994 (Daring)
On purge Bébé, 1931 (Braunberger)
On Record, 1917 (Rosher)
On Secret Service, 1912 (Ince)
On Such a Night, 1937 (Head)
On the Air, 1992 (Badalamenti)
On the Avenue, 1937 (Berlin)
On the Banks of the Wabash, 1923 (Musuraca)
On the Beach, 1959 (Paxton; Rotunno)
On the Beat, 1962 (Rank)
On the Border, 1909 (Selig)
On the Buses, 1971 (Carreras)
On the Comet. See Na Kometě, 1970
On the Double, 1961 (Head; Stradling; Unsworth)
On the Fiddle, 1961 (Arnold)
On the Fire, 1918 (Roach)
On the Firing Line, 1912 (Ince)
On the Front Page, 1926 (Roach)
On the Green Meadow. See Na ty louce zeleny, 1936
On the Jump, 1918 (Roach)
On the Level, 1930 (Nichols)
On the Little Big Horn, or Custer's Last Stand, 1909 (Selig)
On the Loose, 1932 (Roach)
On the Loose, 1951 (Lederer)
On the Night of the Fire, 1939 (Rozsa)
On the Night Stage, 1915 (August; Ince; Sullivan)
On the Reef, 1909 (Bitzer)
On the Riviera, 1951 (Cole; Lemaire; Newman; Shamroy)
On the Road Again. See Honeysuckle Rose, 1980
On the Sunnyside. See Na sluneční strane, 1933
On the Threshold of Space, 1956 (Lemaire)
On the Town, 1949 (Comden and Green; Edens; Freed; Gibbons; Mayer; Rose; Rosson; Smith)
On the Warsaw Highway. See Na Varsavkom traktye, 1916
On the Waterfront, 1954 (Cohn; Day; Justin; Kaufman; Spiegel)
On the Wrong Trek, 1935 (Roach)
On Their Own, 1940 (Miller)
On Their Way, 1921 (Roach)

On Thin Ice, 1924 (Haskin; (Zanuck)
On Trial, 1928 (Haskin)
On with the Dance, 1920 (Miller)
On with the New, 1938 (Fleischer)
On with the Show, 1929 (Gaudio)
On Your Back, 1930 (August)
On Your Toes, 1939 (Howe; Orry-Kelly; Wald)
On ze Boulevard, 1927 (Daniels; Gibbons)
Once a Jolly Swagman, 1948 (Rank)
Once a Lady, 1931 (Banton; Hoffenstein; Lang; Zukor)
Once a Rainy Day. See Akogare, 1966
Once a Thief, 1935 (Havelock-Allan)
Once a Thief, 1950 (Clothier; Leven)
Once a Thief, 1965 (Burks; Schifrin)
Once Every Ten Minutes, 1914 (Roach)
Once in a Blue Moon, 1935 (Garmes; Hecht; MacArthur)
Once in a Lifetime, 1932 (Laemmle)
Once in a Million, 1936 (Neame)
Once Is Not Enough, 1975 (Alonzo; Epstein; Mancini)
Once More, My Darling, 1949 (Harrison; Orry-Kelly; Planer)
Once More, with Feeling!, 1960 (Périnal; Trauner)
Once Over, 1923 (Roach)
Once upon a Crime, 1992 (de Laurentiis; Rotunno)
Once upon a Dream, 1948 (Rank)
Once upon a Honeymoon, 1942 (Barnes)
Once upon a Scoundrel, 1973 (Figueroa; North)
Once upon a Time, 1944 (Planer)
Once upon a Time, 1957 (Ivanov-Vano)
Once upon a Time . . . . See Był sobie raz . . . , 1957
Once upon a Time in the West. See C'era una volta il west, 1968
Once upon a Time . . . Is Now, 1977 (Fisher)
Once upon a Time There Was a King. See Byl jednou jeden král, 1954
Ondomane, 1961 (Delerue)
One 4 All. See Pour toutes, 2000
One Against Seven. See Counter-Attack, 1945
One among Many. See Een blandt mange, 1961
One Arabian Night. See Sumurun, 1920
One at a Time, 1924 (Roach)
One Born Every Minute. See Flim-Flam Man, 1967
One Busy Hour, 1909 (Bitzer)
One, But a Lion. See En, men ett lejon, 1940
One Cab's Family, 1952 (Avery)
One Can Say It without Getting Angry. See On peut le dire sans se fâcher!, 1978
One Clear Call, 1922 (Mayer)
One Crowded Night, 1940 (Polglase)
One Day, I . . . . See Aruhi watashi wa, 1959
One Day in the Life of Ivan Denisovich, 1971 (Nykvist)
One Deadly Summer. See Eté meurtrier, 1983
One Desire, 1954 (Hunter)
One Droopy Knight, 1957 (Hanna and Barbera)
One Exciting Night, 1944 (Heller)
One Exciting Week, 1946 (Alton)
One-Eyed Jacks, 1961 (Edouart; Friedhofer; Lang; Pereira; Westmore Family; Willingham)
One False Move, 1991 (Kaminski)
One Flew over the Cuckoo's Nest, 1975 (Fraker; Nitzsche; Wexler)
One Foot in Heaven, 1941 (Friedhofer; Rosher; Steiner; Wallis)
One Froggy Evening, 1955 (Blanc; Jones)
One from the Heart, 1982 (Storaro; Tavoularis)
One Glass Too Much. See O skleničkú víc, 1953
One Glorious Day, 1922 (Brown)
One Good Turn, 1931 (Roach)
One Good Turn, 1954 (Dillon; Rank)
One Great Vision, 1953 (Lassally)
One Gun Gary in Nick of Time, 1939 (Terry)

One Ham's Family, 1943 (Avery)
One Heavenly Night, 1930 (Barnes; Brown; Goldwyn; Howard; Toland)
One Horse Farmers, 1934 (Roach)
One Hour with You, 1932 (Dreier; Raphaelson; Zukor)
One Hundred and One Dalmations, 1960 (Disney; Iwerks)
One Hundred Killings of Flowery Yoshiwara. See Hana no Yoshiwara hyakunin-giri, 1960
One Hundred Men and a Girl, 1937 (Kräly)
One Hundred Years of the Telephone, 1977 (Bass)
One in a Million, 1934 (Brown)
One in a Million, 1936 (Cronjager)
One in a Million. See Jedna z milonu, 1935
One Is a Lonely Number, 1972 (Legrand)
One Is Business, the Other Crime, 1912 (Bitzer)
One Kill, 2000 (Shepard)
One Little Indian, 1973 (Goldsmith)
One Love or the Other. See Lyubov odna lyubov, 1918
One Mad Kiss, 1930 (Nichols)
One-Mama Man, 1927 (Roach)
One Man and His Bank, 1965 (Barry)
One Man Band, 1965 (Godfrey)
One Man Navy, 1941 (Terry)
One Man's Journey, 1933 (Berman; D'Agostino; Plunkett; Polglase; Steiner)
One Man's Story, 1948 (Alwyn)
One Man's Way, 1963 (Laszlo)
One Meat Brawl, 1947 (Blanc; McKimson)
One Million B.C., 1940 (Canutt; Roach)
One Million Years B.C., 1966 (Carreras; Harryhausen; Roach)
One Minute to Play, 1926 (Clarke; Plunkett)
One Minute to Zero, 1952 (Young)
One More American, 1918 (Rosher)
One More Chance, 1931 (Hornbeck)
One More Chance, 1983 (Golan and Globus)
One More River, 1934 (Laemmle; Sherriff)
One More Spring, 1935 (Seitz)
One More Tomorrow, 1946 (Blanke; Glennon; Grot; Steiner)
One Mouse in a Million, 1939 (Terry)
One Night and Then—, 1909 (Bitzer)
One Night at Susie's, 1930 (Haller)
One Night in Lisbon, 1941 (Dreier; Glennon; Head)
One Night of Love, 1934 (Cohn; Goosson; Kahn; Newman; Walker)
One Night Stand, 1918 (Roach)
One Night Stand, 1997 (Eszterhas)
One Night with You, 1948 (Rank)
One Note Tony, 1947 (Terry)
One of Our Aircraft Is Missing, 1942 (Krasker; Neame)
One of the Best, 1927 (Balcon)
One of the Discard, 1914 (Ince; Sullivan)
One of the Family, 1923 (Roach)
One of the Smiths, 1931 (Roach)
One Parisian "Knight". See Open All Night, 1924
One Piece Bathing Suit. See Million Dollar Mermaid, 1952
One Plus One, 1968 (Guillemot)
One Plus One. See En och en, 1978
One Quarter Inch, 1917 (Roach)
One Rainy Afternoon, 1936 (Day; Lasky; Newman)
One Romantic Night, 1930 (Menzies; Schenck; Struss)
One She Loved, 1912 (Bitzer)
One Sunday Afternoon, 1933 (Dreier; Zukor)
One Sunday Afternoon, 1948 (Grot; Wald)
One Terrible Day, 1922 (Roach)
One That Got Away, 1957 (Rank)
One Thousand Dollars a Touchdown, 1939 (Dreier)
One Thousand Nights on a Bed of Stones, 1959 (Abbas)
One Touch of Venus, 1947 (Orry-Kelly; Planer)

One Track Minds, 1933 (Roach)
One, Two, Three, 1961 (Diamond; Mandell; Mirisch; Previn; Trauner)
One Two Three, 1975 (Popescu-Gopo)
One Way Out, 1955 (Rank)
One Way Passage, 1931 (Grot; Orry-Kelly)
One Way Pendulum, 1965 (Bennett)
One Way Street, 1925 (Edeson)
One Way Street, 1950 (Orry-Kelly)
One Way to Love, 1946 (Goosson; Louis)
One Wild Night. See Career Opportunities, 1991
One Wild Ride, 1925 (Roach)
One Woman's Story. See Passionate Friends, 1949
Oneichan makari touru, 1959 (Muraki)
Onion Pacific, 1940 (Fleischer)
Onionhead, 1958 (Rosson)
Oniromane, 1969 (Braunberger)
Onkel Cocl am Gänsehäufel, 1912 (Kolowrat-Krakowsky)
Onkel Cocls Klassenlos, 1914 (Kolowrat-Krakowsky)
Only a Shop Girl, 1922 (Cohn)
Only a Waiter. See Bara en kypare, 1960
Only Angels Have Wings, 1939 (Cohn; Furthman; Tiomkin; Walker)
Only Game in Town, 1970 (Decaë; Jarre)
Only Girl, 1933 (Pommer; Waxman)
Only Son, 1922 (Roach)
Only the Brave, 1930 (Head)
Only the French Can. See French Can-Can, 1955
Only the Lonely, 1991 (Jarre)
Only the Valiant, 1951 (Waxman)
Only Thing, 1925 (Day; Gibbons)
Only Thrill, 1998 (Shepard)
Only Two Can Play, 1962 (Bennett; Mathieson)
Only Way, 1925 (Wilcox)
Only Woman, 1924 (Gaudio; Schenck; Sullivan)
Only Yesterday, 1933 (Laemmle)
Only You, 1994 (Nykvist)
Onna goroshi abura jigoku, 1949 (Miyagawa)
Onna to kauzoku, 1959 (Miyagawa)
Onna wa ikuman aritotemo, 1966 (Muraki)
Ono no sumu yakata, 1969 (Miyagawa)
Onorevole Angelina, 1947 (Cecchi D'amico)
Onshuh junreiuta, 1936 (Miyagawa)
Oompahs, 1952 (Bosustow)
Open All Night, 1924 (Glennon)
Open Another Bottle, 1921 (Roach)
Open City. See **Roma città aperta**, 1945
Open Gate, 1909 (Bitzer)
Open House, 1953 (Terry)
Open Letter. See Anichti epistoli, 1968
Open Range, 1927 (Canutt; Rosson)
Open Season, 1996 (Hamlisch)
Open Switch. See Whispering Smith, 1926
Open Window, 1951 (Auric)
Open Windows, 1960 (Freund)
Opened by Mistake, 1934 (Roach)
Opened by Mistake, 1940 (Dreier; Head)
Opened Shutters, 1921 (Barnes)
Opening Speech, 1960 (McClaren)
Opera, 1973 (Bozzetto)
Opera Cordis, 1968 (Vukotić)
Opéra de quatres pesos, 1970 (Braunberger)
Opéra-Mouffe, 1958 (Delerue)
Opéra-Musette, 1942 (Auric; Renoir)
Opera Night, 1935 (Terry)
Operation, 1990 (Conti)
Operation Amsterdam, 1959 (Rank; Vetchinsky)
Operation Bottleneck, 1960 (Crosby)

Operation Crossbow, 1965 (Ponti)
Operation Daybreak, 1975 (Decaë)
Operation Disaster. *See* Morning Departure, 1949
Operation Dumbo Drop, 1995 (Boyd)
Operation Eichmann, 1961 (Biroc)
Operation Heartbeat. *See* U.M.C., 1969
Operation Kid Brother. *See* O.K. Connery, 1967
Operation Mad Ball, 1957 (Boyle; Duning)
Opération Magali, 1952 (Kosma)
Operation of the K-13 Gunsight, 1944 (Hubley)
Operation Ogre. *See* Ogro, 1979
Operation Pacific, 1951 (Glennon; Steiner)
Operation Petticoat, 1959 (Harlan)
Operation: Rabbit, 1952 (Blanc; Jones; Stalling)
Operation Secret, 1952 (Blanke; McCord)
Operation Snafu. *See* On the Fiddle, 1961
Operation Stadium, 1977 (Vukotić)
Operation Thunderbolt, 1977 (Golan and Globus)
Operation Undercover. *See* Report to the Commissioner, 1974
Operation Universe, 1959 (Carreras)
Operation X. *See* My Daughter Joy, 1950
Operator 13, 1933 (Adrian; Gillespie)
Operazione Paradiso. *See* Se tutte le donne del mondo . . . , 1966
Opeřené stíny, 1930 (Stallich)
Opernball, 1939 (Herlth)
Opernring. *See* Im Sonneschein, 1936
Ophélia, 1963 (Gégauff; Rabier)
Opiate '67. *See* I mostri, 1963
Opinione pubblica, 1953 (Spaak)
Opio, 1949 (Figueroa)
Opium Den. *See* Opiumhalan, 1911
Opium Trail, 1964 (Menges)
Opium Warlords, 1974 (Menges)
Opiumhalan, 1911 (Jaenzon)
Opname, 1979 (Müller)
Oppio per oppio, 1972 (Bozzetto)
Opposite of Sex, 1998 (Daring)
Opposite Sex, 1956 (Cahn; Pasternak; Rose)
Opry House, 1929 (Disney; Iwerks)
Opta empfangt, 1936 (Alexeieff and Parker)
Optical Poem, 1937 (Fischinger)
Or dans la montagne. *See* Farinet, oder das falsche Geld, 1939
Or dans la rue, 1934 (Andrejew)
Or des mers, 1933 (Matras)
Or du Cristobal, 1939 (Lourié)
Or et le plomb, 1965 (Legrand)
Orage, 1938 (Auric; Spaak)
Oranges and Lemons, 1923 (Roach)
Oranges de Jaffa, 1938 (Alexeieff and Parker; Auric)
Orasul meu, 1967 (Popescu-Gopo)
Orca, 1977 (Morricone; de Laurentiis)
Orca. *See* Orca, 1977
Orchestra Rehearsal. *See* Prova d'orchestra, 1978
Orchestra Wives, 1942 (Ballard; Day; Newman)
Orchestre et diamants, 1961 (Rabier)
Orchid for the Tiger. *See* Tigre se parfume à la dynamite, 1965
Orchids to You, 1935 (Friedhofer)
Ordeal at Dry Red. *See* Terror at Black Falls, 1959
Order in the Court, 1920 (Roach)
Order of Death, 1983 (Morricone)
Orders Is Orders, 1933 (Balcon; Junge)
Orders to Kill, 1958 (Havelock-Allan)
Ordinary Hero. *See* Eroe borghese, 1995
Ordinary People, 1980 (Hamlisch; Sargent)
Ordini sono ordini, 1972 (Guerra)
Ordonnance, 1907 (Gaumont)

Ore dell'amore, 1963 (Morricone)
Ore nove lezione di chimica, 1941 (Stallich)
Ore nude, 1964 (Guerra)
Oregon Trail, 1936 (Canutt)
Oreos with Attitude, 1990 (Vachon)
Organ Grinder's Swing, 1937 (Fleischer)
Organization, 1971 (Biroc; Mirisch)
Organizer. *See* I compagni, 1963
Orgelstäbe, 1922-27 (Fischinger)
Orgueilleux, 1953 (Aurenche and Bost)
Orient Express, 1934 (Friedhofer)
Oriental Dream. *See* Kismet, 1944
Origin of Princess Moon. *See* Tsukihime keizu, 1958
Original Sin, 1997 (Eszterhas)
Orlando furioso, 1972 (Storaro)
Orme, 1974 (Storaro)
Ornament des verliebten Herzens, 1919 (Reiniger)
Ornament of the Loving Heart. *See* Ornament des verliebten
    Herzens, 1919
Oro di Napoli, 1955 (de Laurentiis; Ponti; Zavattini)
Oro di Roma, 1961 (Zavattini)
Orphan Duck, 1939 (Terry)
Orphan Egg, 1953 (Terry)
Orphan of the Sage, 1928 (Musuraca)
Orphan of the War, 1913 (Ince)
Orphans, 1987 (Jenkins; McAlpine)
Orphée, 1950 (Auric; D'Eaubonne)
Orpheus in the Underworld. *See* Urfeus i underjorden, 1910
Os Mutantes, 1998 (de Almeida)
Os Olhos da Ásia, 1996 (Branco)
Osa, 1985 (Daring)
Osaka Elegy. *See* **Naniwa ereji**, 1936
Osaka-jo monogatari, 1961 (Tsuburaya)
Osaka monogatari, 1957 (Yoda)
Osaka Story. *See* Osaka monogatari, 1957
Osaka Woman. *See* Naniwa onna, 1940
Oscar and Lucinda, 1997 (Boyd; Newman)
Oscar per due, 1998 (Lanci, Giuseppe ("beppe"))
Oscar per il Signor Rossi, 1960 (Bozzetto)
Oscar Wilde, 1960 (Périnal)
Oscar, 1966 (Cahn; Delerue; Head; Levine; Ruttenberg; Wakhévitch;
    Westmore Family)
Oscar, 1991 (Bernstein; Ponti)
Ose no hangoro, 1928 (Tsuburaya)
O'Shaughnessy's Boy, 1935 (Howe)
Oslerizing Papa, 1905 (Bitzer)
Osmnáctiletá, 1939 (Stallich)
Osmosis, 1948 (Kaufman)
Osram, 1957 (Alexeieff and Parker)
OSS 117 n'est pas mort, 1956 (D'Eaubonne)
Ossessione, 1942 (Serandrei)
Ossos, 1997 (Branco)
Ossuary. *See* Kostnice, 1970
Ostanovilsya poyezd, 1982 (Mindadze)
Ostatni dzwonek, 1989 (Preisner)
Ostatni strzał, 1958 (ścibor-Rylski)
Ostende, reine de plages, 1931 (Jaubert)
Osterman Weekend, 1983 (Schifrin)
'Ostler Joe, 1908 (Bitzer)
Ostre sledované vlaky, 1966 (Ponti)
Ostrich Feathers, 1937 (Lantz)
Osudy dobrého vojáka Svejkova, 1955 (Trnka)
Osvetnic, 1958 (Vukotić)
Otages, 1939 (Milhaud)
OTC, 1969 (Vukotić)
Otello, 1986 (Golan and Globus)

Otesánek, 2000 (švankmajer)
Othello, 1952 (Aldo; Trauner)
Othello, 1966 (Havelock-Allan; Unsworth)
Other, 1972 (Goldsmith; Surtees)
Other Love, 1947 (Head; Rozsa)
Other Men's Wives, 1919 (Sullivan)
Other People's Money, 1991 (Sargent; Wexler)
Other Self. See Andere Ich, 1918
Other Side of Midnight, 1977 (Legrand; Taradash)
Other Tomorrow, 1930 (Garmes)
Other Woman, 1921 (Gaudio)
Otley, 1969 (Dillon Foreman)
Otoko o sabaku onna, 1948 (Miyagawa)
Otoko tai otoko, 1960 (Muraki)
Otomar Korbelář, 1960 (Stallich)
Otoshiana, 1962 (Takemitsu)
Ototo, 1960 (Miyagawa)
Otrantsky zámek, 1973-79 (švankmajer)
Otrávené svetlo, 1921 (Heller)
Otro Cristobal, 1963 (Alekan)
Otsuru junreika, 1937 (Yoda)
Otsuru's Pilgrim Song. See Otsuru junreika, 1937
Otsuya goroshi, 1951 (Yoda)
Otto e mezzo, 1963 (Di Venanzo; Gherardi; Levine; Rota)
Oublie-moi Mandoline, 1975 (Delerue)
Oublier Palerme. See Dimenticare Palermo, 1989
Oubliette, 1912 (Gaumont)
Ouch!, 1967 (Godfrey)
Oued, la ville aux mille coupoles, 1947 (Fradetal)
Ouija Board, 1920 (Fleischer)
Our Better Selves, 1919 (Miller)
Our Betters, 1933 (Rosher; Selznick; Steiner)
Our Blushing Brides, 1930 (Adrian; Gibbons; Stromberg; Tiomkin)
Our Congressman, 1924 (Roach)
Our Country, 1944 (Alwyn)
Our Crazy Family. See Naše bláznivá rodina, 1968
Our Daily Bread, 1934 (Newman)
Our Daily Bread. See Unser täglich Brot, 1949
Our Dancing Daughters, 1928 (Barnes; Day; Gibbons; Mayer; Stromberg)
Our Fighting Navy, 1937 (Wilcox)
Our Gang, 1922 (Roach)
Our Gang Follies of 1936, 1935 (Roach)
Our Gang Follies of 1938, 1937 (Roach)
Our Hearts Were Growing Up, 1946 (Dreier; Head; Young)
Our Hearts Were Young and Gay, 1944 (Dreier; Head)
Our Hospitality, 1923 (Bruckman; Schenck)
Our Last Spring. See Eroica, 1960
Our Leading Citizen, 1939 (Head)
Our Little Girl, 1935 (Seitz)
Our Little Nell, 1924 (Roach)
Our Little Red Riding Hood. See Naše Karkulka, 1960
Our Man Flint, 1966 (Goldsmith; Reynolds; Smith)
Our Man in Havana, 1959 (Coward; Morris)
Our Miss Brooks, 1956 (La Shelle)
Our Modern Maidens, 1929 (Adrian; Gibbons; Mayer)
Our Mother's House, 1967 (Delerue)
Our Neighbors, the Carters, 1939 (Barnes; Dreier; Head; Young)
Our Relations, 1936 (Maté; Roach)
Our Russian Front, 1941 (Eisler)
Our Story. See Notre histoire, 1984
Our Time, 1974 (Legrand)
Our Town, 1940 (Glennon; Horner; Menzies)
Our Town, 1955 (van Heusen)
Our Very Own, 1950 (Day; Garmes; Goldwyn; Young)
Our Vines Have Tender Grapes, 1945 (Irene; Kaper; Surtees; Trumbo)
Our Wife, 1941 (Cohn; Planer)

Our Younger Brother. See Bokura no otouto, 1933
Ours, 1988 (Rousselot; Sarde)
Ousititi de Toto, 1913-14 (Cohl)
Out Again, in Again, 1948 (Terry)
Out All Night, 1933 (Laemmle)
Out and Out Rout, 1966 (Blanc)
Out of Africa, 1985 (Barry; Ralston; Watkin)
Out of Luck, 1923 (Miller)
Out of the Box, 1942 (Cardiff)
Out of the Clouds, 1955 (Addinsell)
Out of the Darkness. See Teenage Caveman, 1958
Out of the Fog, 1919 (Mathis)
Out of the Fog, 1941 (Blanke; Howe; Wald; Wallis)
Out of the Frying Pan into the Fire. See Z bláta do louže, 1934
Out of the Inkwell, 1915 (Fleischer)
Out of the Past, 1947 (D'Agostino; Mainwaring; Musuraca)
Out of the Ruins, 1928 (Haller)
Out of This World, 1945 (Dreier; Head; Mercer; Young)
Out-of-Towners, 1969 (Jones)
Out-of-Towners, 1999 (Adam)
Out on Bail, 1922 (Roach)
Out West, 1947 (Bruckman)
Out with the Tide, 1928 (Shamroy)
Outbreak, 1995 (Ballhaus)
Outcast, 1928 (Seitz)
Outcast, 1937 (Head; Maté; Schary)
Outcast. See Hakai, 1962
Outcast among Outcasts, 1912 (Bitzer)
Outcast Lady, 1934 (Adrian; Rosher)
Outcast of the Islands, 1951 (Francis; Korda)
Outcasts of Poker Flat, 1952 (Friedhofer; Jeakins; La Shelle; Lemaire; Reynolds)
Outcasts. See Štvaní lidé, 1933
Outcry. See Grido, 1957
Outdoor Pajamas, 1924 (Roach)
Outfoxed, 1949 (Avery)
Outlaw, 1908 (Bitzer)
Outlaw, 1943 (Furthman; Toland; Young)
Outlaw and His Wife. See Berg-Ejvind och hans hustru, 1918
Outlaw Dog, 1927 (Walker)
Outlaw Joukichi of Mikoshin. See Mushukunin Mikoshin no Joukichi, 1972
Outlaw Rule, 1934 (Canutt)
Outlaw Territory, 1953 (Garmes)
Outlawed, 1929 (Plunkett)
Outlaws of the Desert, 1941 (Harlan)
Outline Breaker, 1927 (Canutt)
Outpost, 1942 (Terry)
Outpost in Malaya. See Planter's Wife, 1952
Outrage, 1950 (Horner)
Outrage, 1964 (Howe; North)
Outrage!, 1986 (Biroc)
Outriders, 1949 (Ames; Plunkett; Previn)
Outside Man. See Homme est mort, 1972
Outsider, 1931 (Reville)
Outsider, 1961 (La Shelle; Rosenman)
Outsider. See Marginal, 1983
Outsiders, 1983 (Tavoularis)
Outward Bound, 1930 (Grot; Mohr)
Over 21, 1945 (Buchman; Cohn; Goosson; Louis)
Over My Dead Body. See Once upon a Crime, 1992
Over Silent Paths, 1910 (Bitzer)
Over the Andes, 1944 (Hoch)
Over the Brooklyn Bridge, 1984 (Donaggio; Golan and Globus)
Over the Fence, 1917 (Roach)
Over the Hill, 1922 (Ruttenberg)

Over the Hill, 1931 (Furthman; Seitz)
Over the Hills to the Poorhouse, 1908 (Bitzer)
Over the Moon, 1937 (Biro; Hornbeck; Korda)
Over the Moon, 1939 (Stradling)
Over the River. *See* One More River, 1934
Over the Top, 1986 (Golan and Globus)
Over-the-Hill Gang, 1969 (Friedhofer)
Over-the-Hill Gang Rides Again, 1970 (Raksin)
Overboard, 1987 (Alonzo)
Overcoat. *See* Cappotto, 1952
Overland Stage Raiders, 1938 (Canutt)
Overland Trail, 1927 (Polito)
Overlanders, 1946 (Balcon; Rank)
Overnight. *See* That Night in London, 1932
Ovod, 1955 (Enei; Moskvin; Shostakovich)
Owd Bob, 1938 (Vetchinsky)
Owen Marshall, Counselor at Law, 1971 (Bernstein)
Owl and the Pussy Cat, 1939 (Terry)
Owl and the Pussycat, 1934 (Terry)
Owl and the Pussycat, 1952 (Halas and Batchelor)
Owl and the Pussycat, 1970 (Adam; Booth; Henry; Justin; Stark; Stradling)
Own Your Home, 1921 (Roach)
Ox, 1992 (Nykvist)
Ox-Bow Incident, 1943 (Basevi; Day; Miller; Trotti)
Oxalá, 1979 (Branco)
Oxo Parade, 1948 (Halas and Batchelor)
Oyster Princess. *See* Austerprinzessin, 1919
Oyu-sama, 1951 (Hayasaka; Miyagawa; Yoda)
Ozark Romance, 1918 (Roach)
Ozzie of the Circus, 1929 (Lantz)
Ozzie of the Mounted, 1928 (Disney)
Ozzie Ostrich Comes to Town, 1937 (Terry)

P . . . respecteuse, 1951 (Aurenche and Bost; Auric; Schüfftan)
P. C. Josser, 1931 (Balcon)
P. J., 1968 (Louis; Whitlock)
På en bänk i en park, 1960 (Lundgren)
På livets ödesvägar, 1913 (Jaenzon)
Pa Says, 1913 (Loos)
Pace That Kills, 1928 (Laszlo)
Pace That Thrills, 1925 (McCord)
Pacemaker, 1925 (Garmes)
Pacha, 1967 (D'Eaubonne)
Pacific Blackout, 1941 (Dreier; Siodmak)
Pacific Destiny, 1956 (Bernard)
Pacific Heights, 1990 (Zimmer)
Pacific Liner, 1939 (Musuraca)
Pacific Northwest, 1942 (Maddow)
Pack Up Your Troubles, 1926 (Fleischer)
Pack Up Your Troubles, 1932 (Roach)
Pack Up Your Troubles, 1939 (Day)
Package for Jasper, 1944 (Pal)
Packaging Story, 1964 (Bass)
Pad . . . and How to Use It, 1966 (Hunter)
Paddy O'Day, 1935 (Miller)
Paddy O'Hara, 1917 (Ince)
Paddy-the-Next-Best-Thing, 1923 (Wilcox)
Paddy, the Next Best Thing, 1933 (Seitz)
Padeniye Berlina, 1949 (Shostakovich)
Padlocked, 1926 (Howe)
Padre de más de cuatro, 1938 (Figueroa)
Padri e figli, 1956 (Age and Scarpelli; Gherardi)
Paese senza pace, 1943 (Delli Colli)
Pagaille, 1991 (Age and Scarpelli)
Pagan, 1929 (Freed; Gibbons; La Shelle)

Pagan Love Song, 1950 (Brown; Deutsch; Freed; Rose; Rosher)
Page Miss Glory, 1935 (Orry-Kelly)
Page Mystery, 1917 (Edeson)
Pages d'histoire numbers 1 and 2, 1916 (Cohl)
Pages From James Joyce's Finnegan's Wake, 1965 (Schoonmaker)
Pagliacci, 1936 (Eisler)
Pahli Nazar, 1945 (Biswas)
Paid, 1930 (Gibbons; MacArthur; Mayer; Rosher)
Paid in Full, 1950 (Dreier; Head; Schnee; Wallis; Young)
Paid to Dance, 1937 (Goosson)
Paid to Kill. *See* Five Days, 1954
Paid to Love, 1927 (Miller)
Pain et le vin, 1964 (Cloquet)
Pain in the Neck. *See* Emmerdeur, 1973
Paint and Powder, 1921 (Roach)
Paint and Powder, 1925 (Polito; Stromberg)
Paint Pot Symphony, 1949 (Terry)
Paint Your Wagon, 1969 (Fraker; Previn)
Painted Angel, 1929 (Seitz)
Painted Boats, 1945 (Balcon)
Painted Desert, 1931 (La Shelle)
Painted Lady, 1912 (Bitzer)
Painted Madonna, 1917 (Ruttenberg)
Painted Soul, 1915 (Ince; Sullivan)
Painted Stallion, 1937 (Canutt)
Painted Veil, 1934 (Adrian; Daniels; Gibbons; Mayer; Stothart; Stromberg)
Painted Woman, 1932 (Friedhofer)
Pair of Briefs, 1962 (Rank)
Pair of Tights, 1928 (Roach)
Paisà, 1946 (Amidei)
Paisa hi paisa, 1956 (Biswas)
Paisan. *See* **Paisà**, 1946
Pajama Game, 1957 (Stradling)
Pajama Girl, 1903 (Bitzer)
Pajama Party, 1931 (Roach)
Pajama Party, 1964 (Crosby)
Pakbo, 1970 (Müller)
Pakt mit dem Tod, 1993 (Donaggio)
Pal Joey, 1957 (Cahn; Cohn; Duning; Louis; Pan)
Palace, 1985 (Legrand)
Palais-Royale, 1951 (Braunberger)
Palanquin des larmes, 1988 (Aurenche and Bost; Jarre)
Palavra e Utopia, 2000 (Branco)
Pale Flower. *See* Kawaita hana, 1963
Pale-Face, 1933 (Iwerks)
Paleface, 1948 (Dreier; Rennahan; Young)
Palermo Connection. *See* Dimenticare Palermo, 1989
Palermo Milano solo andata, 1995 (Donaggio)
Palimpest, 1919 (Heller)
Palissades, 1962 (Delerue)
Palm Beach Girl, 1926 (Banton; Garmes)
Palm Beach Story, 1942 (Dreier; Head; Irene; Young)
Palm Court Orchestra, 1964 (Halas and Batchelor)
Palm Springs, 1936 (Reynolds; Wanger)
Palmes, 1951 (Rabier)
Palmes de M. Schutz, 1997 (Lhomme)
Palmy Days, 1931 (Day; Goldwyn; Newman; Toland)
Paloma, 1930 (Fleischer)
Palombella rossa, 1989 (Lanci, Giuseppe ("beppe"); Morricone)
Palooka, 1934 (D'Agostino; Edeson)
Pals and Gals, 1953 (Bruckman)
Pals First, 1918 (Gaudio)
Pals in Blue, 1915 (Selig)
Pals of the Prairie, 1929 (Miller)
Pals of the Saddle, 1938 (Canutt)

Parfum de la dame en noir, 1949 (Douy)
Parfum de la dame en soie, 1931 (Meerson; Périnal)
Parigi è sempre Parigi, 1951 (Alekan; Amidei; Flaiano and
    Pinelli; Kosma)
Parigina a Roma, 1954 (Schüfftan)
Paris, 1926 (Gibbons; Mayer)
Paris, 1929 (Polito)
Paris, 1936 (Ibert)
Paris, 1951 (Cardiff)
Paris 1900, 1946 (Braunberger)
Paris after Dark, 1943 (Basevi; Friedhofer)
Paris at Midnight, 1926 (Marion)
Paris au jour d'hiver, 1965 (Braunberger)
Paris au mois d'août, 1965 (Evein; Jeanson; Renoir)
Paris au temps des cerises: La Commune, 1967 (Delerue)
Paris Blues, 1961 (Bernstein; Matras; Trauner)
Paris brûle-t-il?, 1966 (Aurenche and Bost; Jarre)
Paris by Night, 1988 (Delerue)
Paris Calling, 1941 (Krasner)
Paris des mannequins, 1962 (Braunberger)
Paris des photographes, 1962 (Braunberger)
Paris d'hier et d'aujourd'hui, 1956 (Braunberger)
Paris Does Strange Things. See Eléna et les hommes, 1956
Paris Express. See Man Who Watched Trains Go By, 1952
Paris Frills. See Falbalas, 1945
Paris Holiday, 1958 (Cahn; Wakhévitch; van Heusen)
Paris Honeymoon, 1939 (Head; Struss)
Paris in Spring, 1935 (Hoffenstein)
Paris in the Month of August. See Paris au mois d'août, 1965
Paris in the Spring, 1935 (Dreier)
Paris Interlude, 1934 (Krasner)
Paris la belle, 1959 (Colpi; Prévert)
Paris la nuit, 1904 (Gaumont)
Paris mange son pain, 1958 (Grimault; Prévert)
Paris-Mediterranée, 1931 (Douy)
Paris, mes amours, 1935 (Fradetal)
Paris-New York, 1940 (Andrejew)
Paris on Parade, 1938 (Cardiff)
Paris on the Seine, 1947 (Unsworth)
Paris-Palace-Hôtel, 1956 (D'Eaubonne; Spaak)
Paris qui ne dort pas, 1955 (Braunberger)
Paris Restaurants, 1971 (Lassally)
Paris Seen By . . . . See Paris vu Par . . . , 1964
Paris, Texas, 1984 (Müller; Shepard)
Paris Underground, 1945 (Garmes)
Paris vu Par . . . , 1964 (Almendros; Rabier)
Paris Waltz. See Valse de Paris, 1950
Paris When It Sizzles, 1963 (Coward; D'Eaubonne; Lang)
Pariserinnen, 1921 (Herlth; Röhrig; Wagner)
Parisian Nights, 1924 (Haller)
Parisienne, 1957 (Mnouchkine)
Parisiennes, 1961 (Alekan)
Parisiskor, 1928 (Jaenzon)
Park Your Car, 1920 (Roach)
Parkettsessel 47, 1926 (Warm)
Parking, 1985 (Legrand)
Parking Space, 1933 (Lantz)
Parliamo tanto di me, 1968 (Zavattini)
Parnell, 1937 (Adrian; Freund; Mayer)
Parole est du fleuve, 1961 (Delerue)
Parole Fixer, 1940 (Barnes; Head)
Parole Girl, 1933 (Krasna)
Paroles et musique, 1984 (Legrand)
Parrish, 1961 (Steiner; Stradling)
Parson of Panamint, 1941 (Harlan; Head)
Parson's Widow. See Prästänkan, 1920

Part de l'ombre, 1945 (Auric; Spaak)
Part Time Pal, 1947 (Hanna and Barbera)
Parted Curtains, 1920 (Glennon)
Particles in Space, 1961-66 (Lye)
Partie de campagne, 1946 (Braunberger; Kosma; Prévert; Renoir)
Partie de plaisir, 1975 (Gégauff; Rabier)
Partir, 1931 (Douy)
Partir, revenir, 1985 (Legrand)
Partisans in the Ukrainian Steppes. See Partizani v stepyakh
    Ukrainy, 1942
Partita, 1988 (Donaggio)
Partizani, 1974 (Theodorakis)
Partizani v stepyakh Ukrainy, 1942 (Prokofiev)
Partner, 1968 (Morricone)
Partners, 1982 (Delerue; Sylbert)
Partners Again, 1926 (Edeson; Goldwyn; Marion)
Partners in Crime, 1937 (Dreier; Head)
Partners of the Plains, 1937 (Harlan; Head)
Partners Three, 1919 (Barnes)
Party, 1968 (Ballard; Mancini)
Party, 1984 (Nihalani)
Party, 1996 (Branco)Party Crashers, 1958 (Head)
Party. See Pete's Haunted House, 1926
Party Fever, 1938 (Roach)
Party Girl, 1958 (Cahn; Pasternak; Rose)
Party's Over, 1965 (Barry)
Pas de caviar pour Tante Olga, 1965 (Cloquet)
Pas de deux, 1967 (McClaren)
Pas de pitié pour les caves, 1955 (Kosma)
Pas de problèmes, 1975 (Sarde)
Pas de souris dans le bizness, 1954 (Kosma)
Pas de week-end pour notre amour, 1949 (D'Eaubonne)
Pas folle la guêpe, 1972 (Legrand; Matras)
Pas question le samedi, 1964 (Annenkov)
Pas suspendu de la cicogne. See To meteoro vima to Pelargou, 1991
Pasi spre lune, 1963 (Popescu-Gopo)
Pasinok Marsa, 1914 (Starewicz)
Pasolini, un delitto italiano, 1995 (Morricone)
Pasqualino Settebellezza, 1975 (Delli Colli)
Pass the Ammo, 1988 (Burwell)
Passage Home, 1955 (Rank; Vetchinsky)
Passage to India, 1984 (Jarre)
Passage to Marseilles, 1944 (Howe; Steiner; Wallis)
Passagem ou a Meio Caminho, 1980 (de Almeida)
Passager de la pluie, 1969 (Lai)
Passagers de la Grande Ourse, 1939 (Grimault)
Passante. See Passante du Sans-Souci, 1981
Passante du Sans-Souci, 1981 (Delerue)
Passatore, 1947 (Flaiano and Pinelli; de Laurentiis)
Passe du diable, 1957 (Coutard; de Beauregard)
Passe-Montagne, 1978 (Sarde)
Passeggiata, 1953 (Zavattini)
Passenger. See **Professione: Reporter**, 1975
Passeurs d'hommes, 1937 (Honegger)
Passing Killer. See Assassin qui passe, 1980
Passing of the Third Floor Back, 1935 (Balcon; Courant; Reville)
Passing of Two-Gun Hicks, 1914 (August; Sullivan)
Passing Stranger, 1954 (Lassally)
Passion, 1902 (Pathé)
Passion, 1904 (Gaumont)
Passion, 1954 (Alton; Polglase)
Passion, 1982 (Coutard)
Passion. See En passion, 1969
Passion. See Madame Du Barry, 1919
Passion. See Vášeň, 1961
Passion de Jeanne d'Arc, 1928 (Maté; Warm)

Pédiluve, 1901 (Gaumont)
Pedro Páramo, 1966 (Figueroa)
Pedro Peramo, 1977 (Morricone)
Pee Wee's Big Adventure, 1985 (Elfman)
Peeper, 1975 (Winkler)
Peeping Penguins, 1937 (Fleischer)
Peeping Tom, 1959 (Heller)
Peer Gynt, 1915 (Zukor)
Peer Gynt, 1934 (Hoffmann; Warm)
Peg Leg Pete, 1932 (Terry)
Peg Leg Pete the Pirate, 1935 (Terry)
Peg o' My Heart, 1922 (Barnes)
Peg o' My Heart, 1933 (Adrian; Barnes; Booth; Brown; Freed; Marion; Stothart)
Peg of Old Drury, 1935 (Wilcox; Young)
Pegasus and the Cock. *See* Pyegaz i pyetuch, 1912
Peggy, 1916 (Ince; Sullivan)
Peggy, 1950 (Metty)
Peggy, Peg and Polly, 1950 (Fleischer)
Peggy Sue Got Married, 1986 (Barry; Tavoularis; van Runkle)
Peintre neo-impressioniste, 1910 (Cohl)
Peintres françaises d'aujourd'hui—Edouard Pignon, 1963 (Milhaud)
Peking Express, 1951 (Furthman; Head; Lang; Pereira; Tiomkin; Wallis)
Pelican Brief, 1993 (Shepard)
Pelican's Bill, 1926 (Lantz)
Pelle, 1981 (Schifrin)
Pelliccia di visone, 1956 (Age and Scarpelli; Amidei)
Penalty, 1941 (Rosson; Schary)
Pendu, 1906 (Pathé)
Penelope, 1966 (Ames; Head; Pasternak; Stradling; Williams)
Penelope, folle de son corps, 1974 (Fradetal)
Penguin. *See* Pingwin, 1964
Penguin Parade, 1938 (Avery)
Penguin Pool Murder, 1932 (Macgowan; Steiner)
Penitent, 1988 (North)
Penitentiary, 1938 (Ballard; Miller)
Penn of Pennsylvania, 1941 (Alwyn)
Pennies from Heaven, 1936 (Goosson; Swerling)
Pennies from Heaven, 1981 (Adam; Hamlisch; Willis)
Pennington's Choice, 1915 (Loos)
Penny and the Pownall Case, 1938 (Rank)
Penny Gold, 1973 (Cardiff)
Penny-in-the-Slot, 1921 (Roach)
Penny Paradise, 1938 (Dean; Neame)
Penny Princess, 1952 (Rank; Unsworth)
Penny Serenade, 1941 (Walker)
Pensez à ceux qui sont en-dessous!, 1949 (Decaë)
Pension Mimosas, 1935 (Meerson; Spaak)
Pensionnaire, 1953 (Spaak)
Penthouse, 1933 (Adrian; Goodrich and Hackett; Rosson; Stromberg)
Penthouse Mouse, 1963 (Jones)
Pentito, 1985 (Morricone)
Peony Lantern. *See* Botab dourou, 1968
People against O'Hara, 1951 (Alton; Basevi; Rose)
People Are Bunny, 1959 (Blanc; McKimson)
People behind the Camera. *See* Lidé za kamerou, 1961
People Meet and Sweet Music Fills the Air. *See* Människor möts och ljuv musik uppstår i hjärtat, 1967
People Next Door, 1970 (Willis)
People of France. *See* Vie est à nous, 1936
People of Småland. *See* Smålänningar, 1935
People of the Cumberland, 1937 (Maddow; North)
People on Sunday. *See* Menschen am Sonntag, 1929
People, People, People, 1975 (Hubley)
People vs. Larry Flint, 1996 (Newman; Rousselot; Von Brandenstein)
People vs. Nancy Preston, 1925 (Polito; Stromberg)

People Will Talk, 1935 (Head)
People Will Talk, 1951 (Krasner; Lemaire; Newman; Wheeler; Zanuck)
People's Enemy, 1935 (Ruttenberg)
People's Land, 1943 (Unsworth)
Peoples of Indonesia, 1943 (van Dongen)
Pepe, 1960 (Green; Head; Levien)
Pépé le Moko, 1937 (Hakim; Jeanson)
Pepina Rejholcová, 1932 (Stallich)
Pepper, 1936 (Trotti)
Peppino e Violetta, 1951 (Rota)
Per amore, 1976 (Morricone)
Per le antiche scale, 1976 (Flaiano and Pinelli; Morricone)
Per qualche dollaro in più, 1965 (Morricone)
Per un pugno di dollari, 1964 (Morricone)
Pérák a SS, 1946 (Brdečka; Trnka)
Perceval le Gaullois, 1978 (Almendros)
Percy, 1925 (Ince)
Perdido per cem, 1972 (Branco)
Père Goriot, 1944 (Spaak)
Père Lampion, 1934 (Kaufman)
Père Lebonnard, 1939 (Ibert)
Père Noel a les yeux bleus, 1964 (Almendros)
Père Serge, 1945 (Annenkov; Ibert)
Père tranquille, 1946 (Renoir)
Perfect, 1985 (Willis)
Perfect Alibi. *See* Birds of Prey, 1930
Perfect Crime, 1921 (Buckland)
Perfect Crime, 1928 (Glennon; Howe)
Perfect Day, 1929 (Roach)
Perfect Furlough, 1958 (Lathrop)
Perfect Gentleman, 1927 (Bruckman)
Perfect Gentleman, 1935 (Clarke; Kaper)
Perfect Kiss, 1985 (Alekan)
Perfect Lady, 1924 (Roach)
Perfect Marriage, 1946 (Head; Metty; Wallis)
Perfect Murder, 1988 (Lassally; Merchant)
Perfect Snob, 1941 (Clarke)
Perfect Specimen, 1937 (Haskin; Rosher; Wallis)
Perfect Storm, 2000 (Seale)
Perfect Strangers, 1945 (Korda; Périnal)
Perfect Strangers, 1950 (Hecht; Wald)
Perfect Understanding, 1933 (Courant)
Perfect Weekend. *See* St. Louis Kid, 1934
Perfect Woman, 1920 (Loos)
Perfect Woman, 1949 (Rank)
Perfect World, 1993 (Bumstead)
Perfectionist, 1986 (Boyd)
Perfidy of Mary, 1913 (Bitzer)
Performance, 1970 (Nitzsche)
Peril in the Night. *See* Eyewitness, 1956
Perilous Holiday, 1946 (Goosson)
Perilous Journey, 1953 (Young)
Perils of Pauline, 1914 (Miller)
Perils of Pauline, 1947 (Dreier; Head; Rennahan)
Perils of Pearl Pureheart, 1949 (Terry)
Perils of the Darkest Jungle. *See* Tiger Woman, 1944
Périscope, 1915 (Gaumont)
Perla, 1945 (Figueroa)
Permanent Record, 1988 (Mancini)
Permanent Wave, 1929 (Lantz)
Permission to Kill, 1975 (Bennett; Young)
Perníková chaloupka, 1927 (Stallich)
Perníková chaloupka, 1951 (Trnka)
Perpetual Motion, 1920 (Fleischer)
Perpetual Motion, 1975 (Dinov)
Perri, 1957 (Iwerks)

Pharao's Revenge. *See* Rache des Pharao, 1925
Phare, 1967 (Braunberger)
Phase IV, 1973 (Bass)
Phèdre, 1968 (Barsacq)
Phenix City Story, 1955 (Mainwaring)
Phénomènes électriques, 1937 (Grimault)
Phenomenon, 1996 (Newman; Ralston)
Phffft!, 1954 (Cohn; Lang; Louis; Wald)
Philadelphia Story, 1940 (Adrian; Gibbons; Mayer; Ruttenberg; Shearer; Stewart; Waxman)
Philemon, 1976 (Lourié)
Philips-Radio, 1931 (van Dongen)
Philosopher's Stone. *See* Parash Pathar, 1957
Philosophical Story. *See* Filosofská historie, 1937
Phone Call from a Stranger, 1952 (Johnson; Krasner; Waxman)
Phoney News Flashes, 1955 (Terry)
Phony Express, 1932 (Iwerks)
Photo-souvenir, 1960 (Braunberger)
Photo souvenir, 1978 (Carrière)
Photographe Lassine, 1974 (Nuytten)
Photographer, 1948 (Maddow)
Physical Culture Girls, 1903 (Bitzer)
Physical Evidence, 1988 (Alonzo; Mancini)
Piano Encores, 1954 (La Shelle)
Piano Lesson. *See* Pianolektionen, 1966
Piano, mon ami, 1957 (Decaë)
Piano panier, 1989 (Branco)
Pianolektionen, 1966 (Fischer)
Pianos mécanicos, 1965 (Delerue)
Picador, 1932 (Périnal)
Picador Porky, 1937 (Avery; Blanc; Stalling)
Picasso, 1955 (Amidei)
Picasso, romancero du picador, 1960 (Delerue)
Picasso Summer, 1969 (Zsigmond)
Picasso Summer, 1972 (Legrand)
Piccadilly, 1928 (Junge)
Piccadilly Incident, 1946 (Wilcox)
Piccadilly Jim, 1936 (Hoffenstein; Ruttenberg)
Piccola posta, 1955 (Delli Colli)
Piccolo, 1960 (Vukotić)
Piccolo diavolo, 1988 (Müller)
Piccolo mondo antico, 1941 (Ponti)
Pick a Star, 1937 (Roach)
Pick and Shovel, 1923 (Roach)
Pick-me-up est un sportsman, 1912-14 (Cohl)
Pick Me Up, ur Flickorna Jackson, 1910 (Magnusson)
Pick-Necking, 1933 (Terry)
Pick-Up Artist, 1987 (Delerue; Towne; Willis)
Pickaninny, 1921 (Roach)
Picking Up the Pieces, 1985 (Lathrop)
Picking Up the Pieces, 2000 (Storaro)
Pickle, 1993 (Legrand)
Pickpocket, 1959 (Burel)
Pickup Alley, 1957 (Bennett; Broccoli)
Pickup on South Street, 1953 (Lemaire; Wheeler)
Pickwick Papers, 2000 (Pinter)
Picnic at Hanging Rock, 1975 (Boyd; Seale)
Picnic on the Grass. *See* Déjeuner sur l'herbe, 1959
Picnic with Papa, 1952 (Terry)
Picnic with Weisman. *See* Picnick mit Weismann, 1968
Picnic, 1955 (Cohn; Duning; Howe; Louis; Taradash; Wald; Wexler)
Picnick mit Weismann, 1968 (švankmajer)
Picnics Are Fun and Dino's Serenade, 1959 (Bosustow)
Picpus, 1942 (Andrejew)
Pictura: An Adventure in Art, 1951 (Haller)

Picture of Dorian Gray, 1945 (Berman; Gibbons; Irene; Mayer; Stothart; Stradling)
Picture of Madame Yuki. *See* Yuki Fujin ezu, 1950
Picture Perfect, 1997 (Burwell)
Picture Snatcher, 1933 (Orry-Kelly; Polito)
Pictureland, 1911 (Gaudio)
Pictures at an Exhibition. *See* Tableaux d'une exposition, 1972
Picturesque South Africa, 1936 (Hoch)
Picturesque West, 1899 (Bitzer)
Pidgin Island, 1917 (Gaudio)
Piec dni z zycla emeryta, 1984 (Stawiński)
Piece of Cake, 1938 (Rank)
Piece of Pleasure. *See* Partie de plaisir, 1975
Pieces of Dreams, 1970 (Legrand)
Pied Piper, 1924 (Lantz)
Pied Piper, 1942 (Cronjager; Johnson; Newman; Zanuck)
Pied Piper, 1972 (Puttnam)
Pied Piper Malone, 1924 (Haller)
Pied Piper of Guadalupe, 1961 (Blanc)
Pied Piper of Hamelin, 1960 (Reiniger)
Pied Piper of Hamelin. *See* Rattenfänger von Hamelin, 1918
Pied Piper Porky, 1939 (Blanc; Clampett; Stalling)
Piège, 1958 (Cloquet)
Pièges, 1939 (Fradetal; Wakhévitch)
Pier 13, 1940 (Day; Miller)
Pier 13. *See* Me and My Gal, 1942
Pierre Boulez, 1965 (Braunberger)
Pierre dans la bouche, 1982 (Alekan)
Pierre et Jean, 1943 (Andrejew)
Pierre of the Plains, 1942 (Rosher)
Pierres oubliées, 1952 (Grimault)
Pierrette I. *See* Münchener Bilderbogen, 1924-26
Pierrot le fou, 1965 (Coutard; de Beauregard)
Pieta per chi cade, 1953 (Flaiano and Pinelli)
Pietro der Korsar, 1925 (Pommer; Wagner)
Pietro Micca, 1938 (Amidei)
Pigeon That Took Rome, 1962 (Head)
Pig's Curly Tail, 1926 (Lantz)
Pigs in a Polka, 1943 (Blanc; Stalling)
Pigs Is Pigs, 1937 (Stalling)
Pigskin Capers, 1930 (Terry)
Pigskin Champions, 1937 (Clarke)
Pigskin Parade, 1936 (Miller; Zanuck)
Pigsty. *See* Porcile, 1969
Pigulki dla Aurelii, 1958 (ścibor-Rylski)
Piker's Peak, 1957 (Blanc; Stalling)
Pilgrim Porky, 1940 (Blanc; Clampett; Stalling)
Pilgrimage, 1933 (Nichols)
Pilgrimage, 1972 (Delli Colli)
Pilgrimage Song of Grace and Grudge. *See* Onshuh junreiuta, 1936
Pilgrimage to Ise. *See* Oise mairi, 1939
Pilgrimage to Kevlar. *See* Vallfarten till Kevlar, 1921
Pilgrims of the Nights, 1921 (Gaudio)
Pill, 1966-67 (Popescu-Gopo)
Pill Peddlars, 1953 (Terry)
Pillaged. *See* Mise à sac, 1967
Pillola, 1983 (Bozzetto)
Pillow Book, 1996 (Vierny)
Pillow Talk, 1959 (Hunter; Louis)
Pills for Aurelia. *See* Pigulki dla Aurelii, 1958
Pilot, 1980 (Lassally)
Pilot No. 5, 1943 (Schary)
Pimpernel Smith, 1941 (de Grunwald)
Pin Feathers, 1933 (Lantz)
Pin-Up Girl, 1944 (Basevi; Pan)
Pince à ongles, 1968 (Carrière)

Pinch Hitter, 1917 (Ince)
Pinch Singer, 1935 (Roach)
Pinched Bliss, 1917 (Roach)
Pinchhitter, 1917 (Sullivan)
Pincushion Man. See Balloonland, 1935
Pinehurst, 1905 (Bitzer)
Pingwin, 1964 (Stawiński)
Pink and Blue Blues, 1952 (Bosustow)
Pink Davinci, 1975 (McKimson)
Pink Elephants, 1937 (Terry)
Pink Floyd The Wall, 1982 (Biziou; Hambling)
Pink Gods, 1922 (Levien)
Pink Jungle, 1968 (Head; Metty)
Pink Pajamas, 1929 (Hornbeck)
Pink Panther, 1964 (Lathrop; Mancini; Mercer; Mirisch)
Pink Panther Strikes Again, 1976 (Mancini)
Pink Pro, 1976 (McKimson)
Pink Slip. See Ružové konbiné, 1932
Pink String and Sealing Wax, 1945 (Balcon)
Pinky, 1949 (Dunne; Lemaire; Newman; Nichols; Wheeler; Zanuck)
Pinning It On, 1921 (Roach)
Pinocchio, 1940 (Blanc; Disney; Hubley)
Pinocchio, 1972 (Cecchi D'amico)
Pinocchio, 1976 (Winston)
Pinocchiova dobrodružstvi, 1971 (Stallich)
Pinto Ben, 1914 (August; Sullivan)
Pioneer Builders. See Conqueror, 1932
Pioneers of the West, 1940 (Canutt)
Piovuto dal cielo, 1953 (Zavattini)
Pip eye, Pup-eye, Poop-eye and Peep-eye, 1942 (Fleischer)
Pipe Dream, 1905 (Bitzer)
Pipe the Whiskers, 1918 (Roach)
Piper of Strakonice. See Strakonický dudák, 1955
Piping Hot, 1959 (Halas and Batchelor)
Pippa Passes, 1909 (Bitzer)
Pippin, 1981 (Schwartz)
Pir v Girmunka, 1941 (Golovnya)
Piranha, 1978 (Donaggio; Walas)
Pirate, 1948 (Edens; Freed; Gibbons; Goodrich and Hackett; Mayer; Porter; Smith; Stradling)
Pirate, 1978 (Conti)
Pirate, 1984 (Nuytten)
Pirate Gold, 1912 (Bitzer)
Pirate Gold, 1920 (Grot)
Pirate Ship, 1933 (Terry)
Pirates, 1986 (Reynolds; Sarde)
Pirates du Rhône, 1933 (Aurenche and Bost)
Pirate's Gold, 1908 (Bitzer)
Pirates of Blood River, 1961 (Carreras)
Pirates of Monterey, 1947 (Mohr)
Pirates of Penzance, 1983 (Slocombe)
Pirates of the Prairie, 1942 (Musuraca)
Pirates of the Sky, 1927 (Shamroy)
Pirates of Tortuga, 1961 (Smith)
Pirates on Horseback, 1941 (Harlan; Head)
Pirates on Lake Mälar. See Mälarpirater, 1923
Pirogov, 1947 (Enei; Moskvin; Shostakovich)
Piros bugyelláris, 1917 (Korda)
Piscine, 1969 (Carrière; Legrand; Levine)
Piscinia, 1976 (Bozzetto)
Píseň života, 1925 (Heller)
Piso Piselli, 1982 (Lanci, Giuseppe ("beppe"))
Piste du sud, 1938 (Matras; Renoir)
Pistol for Ringo. See Pistola per Ringo, 1965
Pistola per Ringo, 1965 (Morricone)
Pistoleros de Casa Grande, 1965 (Chase)

Pistols for Breakfast, 1919 (Roach)
Pit, 1914 (Carré)
Pit and the Pendulum, 1961 (Crosby)
Pit, the Pendulum, and Hope. See Kyvadlo, jáma, a nadeeje, 1983
Pitchin' in the Kitchen, 1942 (Bruckman)
Pitfall, 1913 (Ince)
Pitfall. See Otoshiana, 1962
Più bella serata della mia vita, 1972 (Amidei)
Piu comico spettacolo del mondo, 1953 (Struss)
Pizza Triangle. See Dramma della gelosia, tutti i particolari in cronaca, 1970
Pizza Tweety Pie, 1958 (Blanc)
Pizzicato Pussycat, 1955 (Blanc)
PJs, 1999 (Vinton)
Place for Gold, 1960 (Bernard)
Place for Lovers. See Amanti, 1968
A Place in the Sun, 1951 (Dreier; Head; Hornbeck; Waxman; Wilson)
Place of One's Own, 1945 (Rank)
Place to Live, 1941 (Maddow)Placer de matar, 1988 (de Almeida)
Places in the Heart, 1984 (Almendros; Littleton)
Placier est tenance, 1910 (Cohl)
Plague of the Zombies, 1966 (Bernard; Carreras)
Plain and Fancy Girls, 1925 (Roach)
Plain Jane, 1916 (Ince; Sullivan)
Plain Man's Guide to Advertising, 1962 (Godfrey)
Plain Pleasures, 1996 (Vachon)
Plain Sailing. See True as a Turtle, 1956
Plain Song, 1910 (Bitzer)
Plainsman, 1936 (Dreier; Macpherson)
Plainsman, 1966 (Westmore Family; Williams)
Plaisir, 1952 (Annenkov; D'Eaubonne; Matras)
Plaisir d'amour, 1968 (Braunberger)
Plaisir de plaire, 1960 (Delerue)
Plaisirs de Paris, 1932 (Wakhévitch)
Plaisirs de Paris, 1952 (D'Eaubonne)
Plameny života, 1920 (Heller)
Plane Crazy, 1929 (Disney; Iwerks)
Plane Daffy, 1944 (Blanc; Stalling)
Plane Dippy, 1936 (Avery)
Plane Gooty, 1940 (Terry)
Planet of the Apes, 1968 (Goldsmith; Shamroy; Smith; Wilson)
Planned Crops, 1943 (Lye)
Planter's Wife, 1908 (Bitzer)
Planter's Wife, 1952 (Rank; Unsworth)
Planton du colonel, 1907 (Gaumont)
Plastered in Paris, 1928 (Clarke)
Plastic Dome of Norma Jean, 1970 (Legrand)
Plastic Nightmare. See Shattered, 1991
Plastic Surgery in Wartime, 1941 (Cardiff)
Platinum Blonde, 1931 (Cohn; Riskin; Swerling; Walker)
Platinum High School, 1959 (Metty)
Platoon, 1986 (Delerue)
Play, 1962 (Vukotić)
Play Ball, 1932 (Iwerks; Terry)
Play Ball, 1937 (Terry)
Play Dirty, 1968 (Legrand)
Play for a Passenger. See Pyesa dlya passazhira, 1995
Play Girl, 1941 (Musuraca)
Play Safe, 1936 (Fleischer)
Playboy Adventure, 1936 (Havelock-Allan)
Playboy of Paris, 1930 (Zukor)
Playboy of the Western World, 1962 (Unsworth)
Player, 1992 (Henry; Newman)
Players. See Club, 1980
Players, 1979 (Goldsmith; Sylbert)
Players, 1983 (Halas and Batchelor)

Playful Pest, 1943 (Fleischer)
Playful Polar Bears, 1938 (Fleischer)
Playful Pup, 1937 (Lantz)
Playful Puss, 1953 (Terry)
Playful Robot, 1956 (Vukotić)
Playgirl, 1932 (Toland)
Playgirl and the War Minister. *See* Amorous Prawn, 1962
Playing Around, 1930 (Grot; Polito)
Playing at Love. *See* Jeux d'amour, 1960
Playing by Heart, 1998 (Barry; Zsigmond)
Playing on the Rainbow. *See* Lek på regnbågen, 1957
Playing the Game, 1918 (Ince)
Playing with Death. *See* Jugando con la muerte, 1982
Playing with Souls, 1925 (Ince; Mohr; Sullivan)
Playing with the Devil. *See* Hrátky s čertem, 1956
Playmates, 1941 (van Heusen)
Playmates, 1972 (Biroc)
Play's the Thing, 1914 (Ince)
Playthings of Destiny, 1921 (Mayer)
Plaza Suite, 1970 (Jarre)
Pleasant Journey, 1923 (Roach)
Pleasantville, 1976 (Lassally)
Please Believe Me, 1949 (Irene; Lewton)
Please Don't Eat the Daisies, 1960 (Pasternak)
Please Go 'way and Let Me Sleep, 1931 (Fleischer)
Please Keep Me in Your Dreams, 1937 (Fleischer)
Please Turn Over, 1960 (Dillon)
Pleased to Meet Cha, 1935 (Fleischer)
Pleased to Mitt You, 1940 (Bruckman)
Pleasure Buyers, 1925 (Walker)
Pleasure Garden, 1926 (Balcon)
Pleasure Garden, 1952 (Lassally)
Pleasure Garden, 1961 (Lundgren)
Pleasure Island, 1953 (Head)
Pleasure Mad, 1923 (Mayer)
Pleasure of His Company, 1961 (Burks; Cahn; Edouart; Head;
    Newman; Pan)
Pleasure of Killing. *See* Placer de matar, 1988
Pleasure Party. *See* Partie de plaisir, 1975
Pleasure Seekers, 1964 (Cahn; Smith; van Heusen)
Pledge, 2000 (Menges; Shepard)
Plein aux as, 1933 (Fradetal)
Plein soleil, 1959 (Decaë; Gégauff; Hakim; Rota)
Pleins feux sur l'assassin, 1960 (Fradetal; Jarre)
Pleins feux sur Stanislas, 1965 (Delerue)
Plenty Below Zero, 1943 (Fleischer)
Plenty of Money and You, 1937 (Stalling)
Pleut Toujours, 1973 (Rousselot)
Plop Goes the Weasel, 1953 (Blanc; McKimson; Stalling)
Plot Thickens, 1936 (Musuraca)
Plough and the Stars, 1936 (August; Nichols; Plunkett; Polglase)
Plow Boy, 1929 (Disney; Iwerks)
Plow Girl, 1916 (Rosher)
Plow That Broke the Plains, 1936 (Thomson)
Plukownik Kwiatkowski, 1995 (Stawiński)
Plumber, 1933 (Lantz)
Plumber's Helpers, 1953 (Terry)
Plumbing Is a Pipe, 1938 (Fleischer)
Plumbum, or Dangerous Game. *See* Plyumbum, ili opasnaya igra, 1986
Plunder, 1930 (Wilcox)
Plunder of the Sun, 1953 (Friedhofer)
Plunder Road, 1957 (Haller)
Plunderers, 1960 (Rosenman)
Plus Beaux Jours, 1957 (Decaë)
Plus Belles Escroqueries du monde, 1963 (Coutard; Cristaldi; Delli Colli;
    Gégauff; Guillemot; Rabier)

Plus qu'on ne peut donner, 1963 (Braunberger)
Plus Vieux Métier du monde, 1967 (Aurenche and Bost; Douy; Evein;
    Flaiano and Pinelli; Guillemot; Legrand; Lhomme)
Plymouth Adventure, 1952 (Daniels; Gillespie; Plunkett; Rozsa; Schary)
Plyumbum, ili opasnaya igra, 1986 (Mindadze)
Poacher's Daughter, 1960 (Hambling)
Pobeda, 1938 (Golovnya)
Pobediteli nochi, 1927 (Moskvin)
Pobočník jeho výsosti, 1933 (Heller)
Pobre Pérez, 1937 (Alton)
Pobres van al cielo, 1951 (Figueroa)
Pocahontas, 1995 (Menken; Schwartz)
Pocket Money, 1972 (Kovacs; North)
Pocket Policeman. *See* Agent de poche, 1909
Pocketful of Miracles, 1961 (Cahn; Head; Pereira; Plunkett; van Heusen)
Poczmistrs, 1967 (Stawiński)
Pod jednou střechou, 1938 (Stallich)
Podkova pro štěstí, 1946 (Zeman)
Podrugi, 1935 (Shostakovich)
Podvodníci, 1965 (Ondříček)
Podwojne zycie Weroniki. *See* Double vie de Véronique, 1991
Poet and Peasant, 1989 (Lantz)
Poet's Pub, 1949 (Rank)
Pogo Special Birthday Special, 1971 (Jones)
Pogon za Adamem, 1970 (Stawiński)
Pohádka o Honzikovi a Mařence, 1980 (Zeman)
Pohádky tisíce a jedné noci, 1974 (Zeman)
Poignard malais, 1930 (Douy)
Poil de carotte, 1932 (Jaubert)
Point Blank, 1967 (Lathrop; Mandel; Winkler)
Point de mire, 1977 (Decaë; Delerue)
Point of No Return, 1993 (Zimmer)
Point of Terror, 1971 (Fields)
Pointe de fuite, 1983 (Branco; de Almeida)
Pointe-Courte, 1954 (Delerue)
Poison, 1911 (Gaumont)
Poison, 1991 (Schamus; Vachon)
Poisoned Light. *See* Otrávené svetlo, 1921
Poisoned Paradise: The Forbidden Story of Monte Carlo, 1924 (Struss)
Poisson lune, 1993 (Sarde)
Pojken i trädet, 1961 (Fischer)
Poker, 1920 (Fleischer)
Poker, 1951 (Lundgren)
Poker, 1987 (Sarde)
Poker at Eight, 1935 (Roach)
Poklad Ptačího ostrova, 1952 (Zeman)
Polar Pals, 1939 (Blanc; Clampett; Stalling)
Polar Pests, 1958 (Avery)
Polenblut, 1934 (Heller)
Policarpo, ufficiale di scrittura, 1959 (Age and Scarpelli)
Police Fang: Razor Hanzo's Torture in Hell. *See* Goyoukiba: Kamisori
    Hanzo jigokuzeme, 1973
Police mondaine, 1937 (D'Eaubonne)
Police Python 357, 1975 (Delerue)
Police Story, 1973 (Goldsmith)
Policeman Hataoka. *See* Hataoka junsa, 1940
Poliche, 1934 (Meerson; Stradling)
Polish Blood. *See* Polská krev, 1934
Political Pull, 1924 (Roach)
Political Theatre. *See* Soushi gekijou, 1946
Politician's Love Story, 1909 (Bitzer)
Polka-Dot Puss, 1949 (Hanna and Barbera)
Polly of the Circus, 1932 (Adrian; Barnes)
Polly of the Follies, 1922 (Loos; Schenck)
Polly of the Storm Country, 1920 (Rosson)
Polly Wants a Doctor, 1943 (Fleischer)

Polly with a Past, 1920 (Mathis)
Pollyanna, 1920 (Marion; Rosher)
Pollyanna, 1960 (Disney; Ellenshaw; Harlan; Iwerks; Plunkett)
Polo Games, Brooklyn, 1900 (Bitzer)
Polo Joe, 1936 (Orry-Kelly)
Polská krev, 1934 (Heller)
Poltergeist, 1982 (Edlund; Goldsmith; Marshall)
Poltergeist II, 1986 (Edlund; Goldsmith)
Poltergeist III, 1988 (Smith)
Południk zero, 1970 (ścibor-Rylski)
Polygamous Polonius, 1958 (Godfrey)
Polygamous Polonius Revisited, 1985 (Godfrey)
Pomme d'amour, 1932 (Périnal)
Pompier et la servante, 1897 (Pathé)
Pompon rouge, 1951 (Braunberger)
Pomsta, 1968 (Brdečka)
Ponette, 1996 (Sarde)
Pont de Tancarville, 1959 (Delerue)
Pontcarral, colonel d'empire, 1942 (Annenkov; Matras)
Ponti e porte de Roma, 1949 (Di Venanzo)
Pony Express, 1925 (Brown)
Pony Express, 1953 (Head; Rennahan)
Pony Soldier, 1952 (Newman; North; Wheeler)
Pooch, 1932 (Roach)
Pooja, 1940 (Biswas)
Pookie. See Sterile Cuckoo, 1969
Pool of London, 1951 (Balcon)
Poopdeck Pappy, 1940 (Fleischer)
Poopsie, 1974 (Ponti)
Poor but Beautiful. See Poveri ma belli, 1956
Poor Cinderella, 1934 (Fleischer)
Poor Cow, 1967 (Menges)
Poor Fish, 1924 (Roach)
Poor Girl. See Chudá holka, 1929
Poor Little Chap He Was Only Dreaming, 1912-14 (Cohl)
Poor Little Rich Girl, 1917 (Carré; Marion)
Poor Little Rich Girl, 1936 (Seitz)
Poor Men's Wives, 1923 (Struss)
Poor Millionaire, 1941 (Nykvist)
Poor Millionaires. See Poveri milionari, 1958
Poor Old Fido, 1903 (Bitzer)
Poor Papa, 1928 (Disney)
Pop, 1970 (Kuri)
Pop Always Pays, 1940 (Polglase)
Pop and Mom in Wild Oysters, 1941 (Fleischer)
Pop Gear, 1965 (Unsworth)
Pop 'im Pop, 1950 (Blanc; McKimson; Stalling)
Popcorn, 1931 (Terry)
Popcorn Story, 1949 (Bosustow)
Pope Joan, 1972 (Jarre)
Pope of Greenwich Village, 1984 (Grusin)
Popeye, 1980 (Rotunno)
Popeye Meets Rip Van Winkle, 1941 (Fleischer)
Popeye Meets William Tell, 1940 (Fleischer)
Popeye the Sailor, 1935 (Fleischer)
Popeye the Sailor Meets Ali Baba's Forty Thieves, 1937 (Fleischer)
Popeye the Sailor Meets Sinbad the Sailor, 1936 (Fleischer)
Popielusko, 1988 (Delerue)
Popioły, 1965 (ścibor-Rylski)
Popo divorzieremo, 1940 (Amidei)
Poppy, 1917 (Banton)
Poppy, 1936 (Dreier; Head)
Poppy. See Gubijinso, 1941
Poppy Girl's Husband, 1919 (August; Sullivan)
Poppy Is Also a Flower. See Danger Grows Wild, 1966
Popular Melodies, 1933 (Fleischer)

Popular Official. See K narodnoi vlasti, 1917
Popular Sin, 1926 (Banton; Garmes)
Porcelaines tendres, 1909 (Cohl)
Porcile, 1969 (Delli Colli; Donati)
Porgy and Bess, 1959 (Goldwyn; Mandell; Pan; Previn; Shamroy; Sharaff)
Pork Chop Fooey, 1965 (Hanna and Barbera)
Pork Chop Hill, 1959 (Rosenman)
Porky and Daffy, 1938 (Blanc; Clampett; Stalling)
Porky and Gabby, 1937 (Blanc; Iwerks; Stalling)
Porky and Teabiscuit, 1939 (Blanc; Stalling)
Porky at the Crocadero, 1938 (Blanc; Stalling)
Porky Chops, 1949 (Blanc; Stalling)
Porky in Egypt, 1938 (Blanc; Clampett; Stalling)
Porky in Wackyland, 1938 (Blanc; Clampett; Stalling)
Porky of the Northwoods, 1936 (Stalling)
Porky Pig in Hollywood, 1986 (Blanc; Jones)
Porky Pig's Feat, 1943 (Blanc; Stalling)
Porky the Fireman, 1938 (Blanc; Stalling)
Porky the Giant Killer, 1939 (Blanc; Stalling)
Porky the Gob, 1938 (Blanc; Stalling)
Porky the Rain Maker, 1936 (Avery)
Porky the Wrestler, 1937 (Avery; Blanc; Stalling)
Porky's Ant, 1941 (Blanc; Jones; Stalling)
Porky's Badtime Story, 1937 (Blanc; Stalling)
Porky's Baseball Broadcast, 1940 (Blanc; Stalling)
Porky's Bear Facts, 1941 (Blanc; Stalling)
Porky's Bedtime Story, 1937 (Clampett)
Porky's Building, 1937 (Blanc; Stalling)
Porky's Cafe, 1942 (Blanc; Jones; Stalling)
Porky's Double Trouble, 1937 (Blanc; Stalling)
Porky's Duck Hunt, 1937 (Avery; Blanc; Stalling)
Porky's Five and Ten, 1938 (Blanc; Clampett; Stalling)
Porky's Garden, 1937 (Avery; Blanc; Stalling)
Porky's Hare Hunt, 1938 (Blanc; Stalling)
Porky's Hero Agency, 1937 (Blanc; Clampett; Stalling)
Porky's Hired Hand , 1940 (Blanc; Stalling)
Porky's Hotel, 1939 (Blanc; Clampett; Stalling)
Porky's Last Stand, 1940 (Blanc; Clampett; Stalling)
Porky's Midnight Matinee, 1941 (Blanc; Jones; Stalling)
Porky's Movie Mystery, 1939 (Blanc; Clampett; Stalling)
Porky's Moving Day, 1936 (Stalling)
Porky's Naughty Nephew, 1938 (Blanc; Clampett; Stalling)
Porky's Party, 1938 (Blanc; Clampett; Stalling)
Porky's Pastry Pirates, 1942 (Blanc)
Porky's Phoney Express, 1938 (Blanc; Stalling)
Porky's Picnic, 1939 (Blanc; Clampett)
Porky's Pooch, 1941 (Blanc; Clampett; Stalling)
Porky's Poor Fish, 1940 (Blanc; Clampett; Stalling)
Porky's Poppa, 1938 (Blanc; Clampett; Stalling)
Porky's Poultry Plant, 1936 (Stalling)
Porky's Preview, 1941 (Avery; Blanc; Stalling)
Porky's Prize Pony, 1941 (Blanc; Jones; Stalling)
Porky's Railroad, 1937 (Blanc; Stalling)
Porky's Road Race, 1937 (Blanc; Stalling)
Porky's Romance, 1937 (Blanc; Stalling)
Porky's Snooze Reel, 1941 (Blanc; Clampett; Stalling)
Porky's Spring Planting, 1938 (Blanc; Stalling)
Porky's Super Service, 1937 (Blanc; Iwerks; Stalling)
Porky's Tire Trouble, 1939 (Blanc; Clampett; Stalling)
Port Afrique, 1956 (Arnold; Maté)
Port Arthur, 1936 (Heller)
Port du désir, 1954 (Alekan; Kosma)
Port of Bad Names. See Akumyo hatoba, 1963
Port of Call. See Hamnstad, 1948
Port of Missing Girls, 1938 (Brown)

Port of Missing Mice, 1945 (Terry)
Port of Seven Seas, 1938 (Vorkapich; Waxman)
Port of Shadows. *See* Quai des brumes, 1938
Port without a Sea. *See* Umi no nai minato, 1931
Porta del cielo, 1946 (Zavattini)
Porte de Lilas, 1957 (Barsacq)
Porte du large, 1936 (Spaak)
Portes claquent, 1960 (Legrand)
Portes de la nuit, 1946 (Kosma; Prévert; Trauner)
Porteuse de pain, 1934 (Lourié; Stradling)
Porteuse de pain, 1963 (Decaë)
Portnoy's Complaint, 1972 (Boyle; Lathrop; Legrand; Lehman; O'Steen)
Porto Santo, 1997 (Branco; Guerra)
Portrait. *See* Portryet, 1915
Portrait de la France, 1957 (Delerue)
Portrait d'un assassin, 1949 (Spaak)
Portrait from Life, 1948 (Rank)
Portrait in Black, 1960 (Hunter; Metty)
Portrait of a Dead Girl. *See* McCloud: Who Killed Miss U.S.A.?, 1970
Portrait of a Mobster, 1961 (Steiner)
Portrait of a Sinner. *See* Rough and the Smooth, 1959
Portrait of a Stripper, 1979 (Alonzo)
Portrait of a Woman, Nude. *See* Nudo di donna, 1981
Portrait of an Album, 1985 (Jones)
Portrait of Jennie, 1948 (August; Herrmann; Selznick; Tiomkin)
Porträt von Elfi von Dassanowsky, 1998 (Von Dassanowsky)
Portryet, 1915 (Starewicz)
Ports of Industrial Scandinavia: Sweden's East Coast, 1949 (Fischer)
Poruchik Kizhe, 1934 (Prokofiev)
Poseidon Adventure, 1972 (Neame; Williams)
Position Firing, 1944 (Hubley)
Position Wanted, 1924 (Roach)
Positively True Adventures of the Alleged Texas Cheerleader-Murdering Mom, 1992 (Fisher)
Poslední bohém, 1931 (Stallich)
Poslední polibek, 1922 (Heller)
Poslední trik pana Schwarzwalldea a pana Edgara, 1964 (švankmajer)
Posse, 1975 (Jarre; Wheeler)
Posse Cat, 1954 (Hanna and Barbera)
Possédés, 1955 (Cloquet)
Possédés, 1987 (Carrière)
Possessed, 1931 (Mayer)
Possessed, 1947 (Burks; Grot; Wald; Waxman)
Possessed. *See* Possédés, 1987
Possession, 1981 (Nuytten)
Possession de l'enfant, 1909 (Gaumont)
Possession of Joel Delaney, 1970 (Justin)
Post No Bills, 1923 (Roach)
Post War Inventions, 1945 (Terry)
Postage Due, 1924 (Roach)
Postcards from America, 1994 (Vachon)
Postcards from the Edge, 1990 (Ballhaus; O'Steen; Von Brandenstein)
Postino, 1994 (Age and Scarpelli)
Postman. *See* Postino, 1994
Postman Always Rings Twice, 1946 (Gibbons; Irene; Mayer)
Postman Always Rings Twice, 1981 (Jeakins; Jenkins; Mamet; Nykvist)
Postman Didn't Ring, 1942 (Day; Raksin)
Postmaster's Daughter. *See* Nostalgic, 1937
Pot-Bouille, 1957 (Barsacq; Hakim; Jeanson)
Pot Luck, 1935 (Balcon; Rank)
Pot o' Gold, 1940 (Mohr)
Potash and Perlmutter, 1923 (Goldwyn; Marion)
Potemkine, 1905 (Pathé)
Potent Lotion, 1955 (Halas and Batchelor)
Potomok Chingis-khan, 1928 (Golovnya)
Pouce!, 1971 (Cloquet)

Poudre d'escampette, 1971 (Legrand; Mnouchkine)
Poughkeepsie Regatta, 1906 (Bitzer)
Poule, 1971 (Nuytten)
Poule aux oeufs d'or, 1905 (Pathé)
Poule merveilleuse, 1902 (Pathé)
Poule mouillée qui se sèche, 1912 (Cohl)
Poulet, 1963 (Cloquet)
Poulette grise, 1947 (McClaren)
Poulot n'est pas sage, 1912 (Cohl)
Poupée, 1962 (Coutard; Kosma)
Pour Clemence, 1972 (Rousselot)
Pour le maillot jaune, 1939 (Burel)
Pour le Mérite, 1938 (Röhrig)
Pour l'Espagne, 1963 (Jarre)
Pour rire!, 1997 (Branco)
Pour toutes, 2000 (Lai)
Pour un sou d'amour, 1931 (D'Eaubonne)
Pour une nuit d'amour, 1920 (Starewicz)
Pourquoi viens-tu si tard?, 1959 (Matras)
Pourvue que ce soit une fille, 1986 (Morricone)
Pousse des plantes, 1913 (Burel)
Poveri ma belli, 1956 (Delli Colli)
Poveri milionari, 1958 (Delli Colli)
Povorot, 1978 (Mindadze)
POW—the Escape, 1986 (Golan and Globus)
Powaqqatsi, 1988 (Golan and Globus)
Powder, 1995 (Goldsmith)
Powder and Smoke, 1924 (Roach)
Powder River, 1953 (Cronjager; Lemaire; Mainwaring)
Powderkeg, 1971 (Smith)
Power, 1967 (Haskin; Pal; Rozsa)
Power, 1980 (Jenkins)
Power. *See* Jew Süss, 1934
Power among Men, 1958 (Thomson)
Power and Glory. *See* Power and the Glory, 1933
Power and Lovers. *See* Chance, 1994
Power and the Glory, 1933 (Howe; Lasky)
Power and the Land, 1940 (Crosby; van Dongen)
Power and the Prize, 1956 (Kaper; Rose)
Power Dive, 1941 (Alton; Head)
Power for Defense, 1942 (Crosby)
Power of Destiny. *See* Moc osudu, 1968
Power of One, 1992 (Zimmer)
Power of the Camera, 1913 (Loos)
Power of the Press, 1928 (Cohn; Levien)
Power of Thought, 1949 (Terry)
Power on thc Land, 1943 (Unsworth)
Power Signal Lineman, 1953 (Lassally)
Power to Fly, 1953 (Halas and Batchelor)
Powers Girl, 1943 (Adrian; Cortez)
Powers of Ten, 1968 (Bernstein)
Powers That Prey, 1918 (Seitz)
Poy pesnyu, poet!, 1971 (Urusevsky)
Poyedinok, 1945 (Urusevsky)
Późne popołudnie, 1964 (ścibor-Rylski)
Pozor!, 1959 (Brdečka)
Pozzo dei miracoli, 1941 (Amidei)
Practical Jokers, 1938 (Roach)
Practically Yours, 1944 (Dreier; Krasna; Lang; Young)
Practice Makes Perfect. *See* Cavaleur, 1978
Pradlenka Jeho Jasnosti, 1930 (Heller)
Prag Legende, 1967 (Ondříček)
Prague Nights. *See* Pražské noci, 1968
Prairie Chickens, 1942 (Roach)
Prairie Pioneers, 1941 (Brown; Canutt)
Prairie Schooners, 1940 (Canutt)

Prairie Thunder, 1937 (Canutt)
Prak a drank, 1960 (Brdečka)
Pramen lásky, 1928 (Stallich)
Prancer, 1989 (Jarre)
Präsident Barrada, 1920 (Courant)
Prästänkan, 1920 (Magnusson)
Prästen, 1914 (Jaenzon; Magnusson)
Prater Girl. *See* Pratermizzi, 1926
Pratermizzi, 1926 (Kolowrat-Krakowsky; Reisch)
Pratidwandi, 1970 (Dutta)
Pratima, 1936 (Biswas)
Prato, 1979 (Morricone)
Právo na hřích, 1932 (Stallich)
Prayer for the Dying, 1987 (Conti)
Pražské noci, 1968 (Brdečka)
Pre-hysterical Hare, 1958 (Blanc; McKimson)
Preacher's Wife, 1996 (Ondříček; Zimmer)
Précieuses ridicules, 1900 (Gaumont)
Precinct 45: Los Angeles Police. *See* New Centurions, 1972
Precio de un beso, 1930 (Nichols)
Před maturitou, 1932 (Heller)
Predator, 1987 (McAlpine; Winston)
Predator 2, 1990 (Winston)
Prédiction, 1994 (Mnouchkine)
Předtucha, 1947 (Stallich)
Preface to a Life, 1950 (Kaufman)
Prefetto di ferro, 1977 (Morricone)
Prefontaine, 1997 (Daring)
Prehistoric Perils, 1952 (Terry)
Prehistoric Porky, 1940 (Blanc; Clampett; Stalling)
Prehistoric Poultry, 1917 (O'brien)
Prehistoric Women. *See* Slave Girls, 1968
Preis fürs Überleben, 1980 (Lassally)
Prekrasnya Lukanida, 1911 (Starewicz)
Prélude à la gloire, 1949 (Renoir)
Prélude à l'Asie, 1960 (Braunberger)
Prélude pour orchestre, voix, et caméra, 1959 (Delerue)
Prelude to Fame, 1950 (Rank)
Prelude to War, 1942 (Friedhofer; Hornbeck; Newman; Veiller)
Prem Bandhan, 1936 (Biswas)
Prem Murti. *See* Pratima, 1936
Prem Nagar, 1974 (Burman)
Prem Pujari, 1970 (Burman)
Premature Burial, 1962 (Crosby)
Premier bal, 1941 (Spaak)
Premier Jour de Vacances de Poulot, 1912 (Cohl)
Premier Pas, 1950 (Decaë)
Premier prix du conservatoire, 1942 (Decaë)
Premiere, 1936 (Planer)
Première croisière, 1955 (Delerue)
Première Fois, 1976 (Trauner)
Première Nuit, 1958 (Colpi; Delerue)
Première sortie, 1905 (Pathé)
Prenez des gants, 1960 (Delerue)
Prénom Carmen, 1983 (Coutard)
Préparez vos mouchoirs, 1978 (Delerue; Mnouchkine)
Presagio, 1973 (Alcoriza; Figueroa)
Prescription for Percy, 1954 (Terry)
Prescription for Romance, 1937 (Krasner)
Prescription: Murder, 1968 (Grusin)
Présence d'Albert Camus, 1962 (Jarre)
Present with a Future, 1943 (Haller)
Presentiment. *See* Předtucha, 1947
Presenting Lily Mars, 1943 (Edens; Pasternak)
Président, 1960 (Jarre)
President McKinley's Inauguration, 1897 (Bitzer)

President T. R. Roosevelt, July 4th, 1903 (Bitzer)
President Vanishes, 1934 (Vorkapich; Wanger)
Presidente del Borgorosso Football Club, 1970 (Amidei)
President's Analyst, 1967 (Fraker; Pereira; Schifrin)
President's Lady, 1952 (Lemaire; Newman; Wheeler)
President's Mistress, 1978 (Schifrin)
President's Women, 1977 (Rosenblum)
Presidio, 1988 (Mancini)
Press for Time, 1966 (Hambling)
Pressing His Suit, 1914 (Roach)
Pressure of Guilt. *See* Shiro to kuro, 1963
Pressure Point, 1962 (Hall; Haller)
Prest-O Change-O, 1939 (Blanc; Jones; Stalling)
Presumed Innocent, 1990 (Jenkins; Williams; Willis)
Prêt-à-Porter. *See* Ready to Wear, 1994
Prete bello, 1989 (Lanci, Giuseppe ("beppe"))
Prete, fai un miracolo, 1974 (Cecchi D'amico)
Pretender, 1947 (Alton)
Prêtres interdits, 1973 (de Beauregard)
Pretty Baby, 1950 (Furthman)
Pretty Baby, 1978 (Nykvist)
Pretty Boy Floyd, 1960 (Rosenblum)
Pretty Girl, 1950 (Duning)
Pretty Maids All in a Row, 1971 (Schifrin)
Pretty Poison, 1968 (Mandel; Smith)
Pretty Polly, 1967 (Legrand)
Pretzels, 1930 (Terry)
Preview Murder Mystery, 1936 (Dreier; Struss)
Příběh lásky a cti, 1977 (Ondříček)
Příběh jednoho dne, 1926 (Heller)
Price of a Party, 1924 (Seitz)
Price of Pride, 1917 (Edeson)
Price of Redemption, 1920 (Polito)
Price of Survival. *See* Preis fürs Überleben, 1980
Price of Wisdom, 1935 (Havelock-Allan)
Prices Unlimited, 1944 (Mohr)
Příchozí z temnot, 1921 (Heller)
Pride and Prejudice, 1940 (Adrian; Freund; Gibbons; Mayer; Stothart; Stromberg)
Pride and the Passion, 1957 (Bass; Planer)
Pride of Bluegrass, 1939 (McCord)
Pride of Pawnee, 1929 (Musuraca; Plunkett)
Pride of St. Louis, 1952 (Lemaire; Mankiewicz)
Pride of the Clan, 1917 (Carré)
Pride of the Marines, 1945 (Burks; Wald; Waxman)
Pride of the Plains, 1943 (Canutt)
Pride of the South, 1913 (Ince)
Pride of the West, 1938 (Harlan; Head)
Pride of the Yankees, 1942 (Goldwyn; Mandell; Mankiewicz; Maté; Menzies; Swerling)
Pride of the Yard, 1954 (Terry)
Priest. *See* Prästen, 1914
Priest's Wife. *See* Moglie del prete, 1971
Prigioniero di Santa Cruz, 1941 (Amidei)
Prima communione, 1950 (Zavattini)
Prima del tramonto, 1999 (Donaggio)
Prima della revoluzione, 1964 (Morricone)
Prima notte, 1958 (Di Venanzo)
Primal Call, 1911 (Bitzer)
Primary Colors, 1998 (Ballhaus)
Primavera del papa, 1949 (Di Venanzo)
Prime Cut, 1972 (Schifrin)
Prime of Life. *See* Toshigoro, 1968
Prime of Miss Jean Brodie, 1969 (Allen; Neame)
Prime of Ochiyo's Life. *See* Ochiyo toshigoro, 1937
Primera carga al machete, 1969 (Herrera)

Puddy the Pup and the Gypsies, 1936 (Terry)
Puddy's Coronation, 1937 (Terry)
Pudgy and the Lost Kitten, 1938 (Fleischer)
Pudgy and the Watchman, 1938 (Fleischer)
Pudgy Picks a Fight, 1937 (Fleischer)
Pudgy Takes a Bow-wow, 1937 (Fleischer)
Pueblerina, 1948 (Figueroa)
Pueblo, canto y esperanza, 1954 (Figueroa)
Pueblo Legend, 1912 (Bitzer)
Pueblo Terror, 1931 (Canutt)
Puerta, 1968 (Alcoriza; Figueroa)
Puerta cerrada, 1939 (Alton)
Puits aux trois vérités, 1960 (Jarre; Jeanson)
Pulcherie et ses meubles, 1916 (Cohl)
Pulnoční příhoda, 1960 (Trnka)
Pumpkin Eater, 1964 (Delerue; Morris; Pinter)
Pumpkin Race. See Course aux potirons, 1907
Pumpkinhead, 1988 (Winston)
Punch and Judy. See Rakvickárna, 1966
Punch the Clock, 1922 (Roach)
Punch the Magician. See Kašpárek kouzelníkem, 1927
Punch Trunk, 1953 (Blanc; Joens; Stalling)
Punch in the Nose, 1925 (Roach)
Punchy Deleon, 1949 (Bosustow; Hubley)
Punctured Life. See Vie crevée, 1992
Punctured Prince, 1923 (Bruckman)
Punishment, 1912 (Bitzer)
Punishment Island. See Shokei no shima, 1966
Punition, 1964 (Braunberger)
Pünktchen und Anton, 1953 (Kästner)
Puño del amo, 1958 (Figueroa)
Pup on a Picnic, 1955 (Hanna and Barbera)
Puppe, 1919 (Kräly)
Puppenmacher von Kiang-Ning, 1923 (Mayer)
Puppet Show, 1936 (Lantz)
Puppetoon Movie, 1986 (Harryhausen)
Puppet's Nightmare. See Cauche-mar du Fantoche, 1908
Puppies for Sale, 1997 (Bernstein)
Puppy Express, 1927 (Lantz)
Puppy Love, 1919 (Howe)
Puppy Love, 1932 (Iwerks)
Puppy Tale, 1954 (Hanna and Barbera)
Pups Is Pups, 1930 (Roach)
Pura Formalita, 1993 (Mnouchkine)
Pure Beauté, 1954 (Alexeieff and Parker)
Pure Hell of St. Trinian's, 1960 (Arnold)
Pure Luck, 1991 (Elfman)
Purgation, 1910 (Bitzer)
Purgatory, 1999 (Shepard)
Puritain, 1937 (Courant)
Puritaine, 1986 (Sarde)
Purlie Victorious. See Gone Are the Days!, 1963
Purple Heart, 1944 (Basevi; Miller; Newman; Zanuck)
Purple Hills, 1961 (Crosby)
Purple Noon. See Plein Soleil, 1959
Purple Plain, 1954 (Bryan; Parrish; Rank; Unsworth)
Purple Rose of Cairo, 1985 (Willis)
Purple Taxi. See Taxi mauve, 1977
Purple V, 1943 (Siodmak)
Pursued, 1947 (Howe; Steiner)
Pursuit, 1935 (Clarke)
Pursuit, 1972 (Goldsmith)
Pursuit of D. B. Cooper, 1981 (Ames)
Pursuit of Happiness, 1934 (Head; Struss; Zukor)
Pursuit of Happiness, 1971 (Grusin; Jenkins)
Pursuit of the Graf Spee. See Battle of the River Plate, 1956

Push-Button Kitty, 1952 (Hanna and Barbera)
Pushing Hands. See Tui shou, 1992
Pushover, 1954 (Wald)
Puss Gets the Boot, 1940 (Hanna and Barbera)
Puss in Boots, 1922 (Disney)
Puss in Boots, 1934 (Iwerks)
Puss in Boots, 1988 (Golan and Globus)
Puss 'n' Booty, 1943 (Blanc; Stalling)
Puss 'n' Toots, 1942 (Hanna and Barbera)
Pussy Cat!, 1954 (Hanna and Barbera)
Pussycat, Pussycat, I Love You, 1970 (Delli Colli; Schifrin)
Put oko svijeta, 1964 (Vukotić)
Put on Your Old Gray Bonnet, 1929 (Fleischer)
Puttin' on the Act, 1940 (Fleischer)
Puttin' on the Dog, 1944 (Hanna and Barbera)
Puttin' on the Ritz, 1930 (Berlin; Menzies; Schenck)
Putting Pants on Philip, 1927 (Bruckman; Roach)
Putty Tat Trouble, 1951 (Blanc; Stalling)
Putyeshyestviye na luna, 1912 (Starewicz)
Puzzle, 1923 (Fleischer)
Pyar, 1950 (Burman)
Pyasaa, 1957 (Burman)
Pyat dney—pyat nochey, 1960 (Shostakovich)
Pyegaz i pyetuch, 1912 (Starewicz)
Pyeresmyesznik, 1912 (Starewicz)
Pyesa dlya passazhira, 1995 (Mindadze)
Pyesn Taiga, 1917 (Starewicz)
Pygmalion, 1938 (Bryan; Honegger; Mayer; Stradling)
Pyhrric Victory. See Manželé paní Mileny, 1921
Pyramide humaine, 1961 (Braunberger)
Pyramides bleues, 1988 (Lai)
Pyrates, 1991 (Kaminski)
Pyrénées, terre de legends, 1948 (Renoir)
Pyrrhovo vítezství. See Manželé paní Mileny, 1921
Pythoness, 1951 (Halas and Batchelor)

Q Planes, 1937 (Mathieson)
Q Planes, 1939 (Hornbeck; Korda; Stradling)
Quack Quack, 1931 (Terry)
Quack Shot, 1954 (Blanc; McKimson; Stalling)
Quacker Tracker, 1967 (Blanc)
Quackodile Tears, 1962 (Blanc)
Quadrate, 1934 (Fischinger)
Quagmire , 1913 (Seitz)
Quai des brumes, 1938 (Alekan; Jaubert; Prévert; Schüfftan; Trauner)
Quai des illusions, 1956 (Kosma)
Quai des Orfèvres, 1947 (Douy)
Quail Hunt, 1935 (Lantz)
Quail Shooting, 1905 (Bitzer)
Quakeress, 1913 (Ince)
Quality Street, 1927 (Gibbons; Kräly)
Quality Street, 1937 (Berman; Plunkett)
Quand la femme s'en mêle, 1957 (D'Eaubonne; Spaak)
Quand la vie était belle, 1935 (Lourié)
Quand midi sonne par la France, 1960 (Kosma)
Quand minuit sonnera, 1936 (Kaufman)
Quand passent les faisans, 1965 (Legrand)
Quand sonnera midi, 1957 (Burel)
Quand tu liras cette lettre, 1953 (Alekan)
Quando l'amore è sensualità, 1972 (Morricone)
Quando le donne avevano la coda, 1970 (Morricone)
Quando le donne persero la coda, 1972 (Morricone)
Quando tramonta il sole, 1955 (Di Venanzo)
Quaranta gradi all'ombra del lenzuolo, 1975 (Guerra)
Quarantième rugissante, 1981 (Douy)
Quarantine, 1923 (Warm)

Quarantined, 1967 (Duning)
Quare Fellow, 1962 (Havelock-Allan)
Quark Economia, 1986 (Bozzetto)
Quark, 1981-83 (Bozzetto)
Quark, 1987 (Bozzetto)
Quarta pagina, 1942 (Zavattini)
Quarterback, 1926 (Cronjager)
Quarterback, 1940 (Head)
Quartet, 1948 (Rank; Sherriff)
Quartet, 1971 (Halas and Batchelor)
Quartet, 1981 (Jhabvala; Lhomme; Merchant)
Quartière, 1987 (Morricone)
Quarto d'Italia, 1961 (Zavattini)
Quatermass II, 1957 (Bernard; Carreras)
Quatermass and the Pit, 1967 (Carreras)
Quatermass Experiment, 1955 (Bernard; Carreras)
Quatorze juillet, 1932 (Jaubert; Meerson; Périnal; Trauner)
Quatorze juillet, 1961 (Braunberger)
Quatre Cents Coups, 1959 (Decaë; Evein)
Quatre Charlots mousequetaires, 1973 (Douy)
Quatre Mouches de velours gris, 1972 (Lenica)
Quatre nuits d'un rêveur, 1971 (Lhomme)
Quatre Petits Tailleurs, 1910 (Cohl)
Quatre Temps, 1956 (Alexeieff and Parker)
Quatre Vérités, 1962 (Barsacq; Cecchi D'amico)
Quattro mosche di vellato grigio, 1971 (Morricone)
Quattro passi fra le nuvole, 1942 (Zavattini)
Que fait-on ce dimanche, 1977 (de Almeida)
Que Farei Eu Com Esta Espada, 1975 (de Almeida)
Que importa es vivir, 1989 (Alcoriza)
Que la bête meure, 1969 (Gégauff; Rabier)
Que la fête commence, 1975 (Aurenche and Bost)
¡Que viene mi marido!, 1940 (Figueroa)
Que Viva Mexico!, 1931 (Tisse)
Queen Bee, 1955 (Duning; Lang; Louis; Wald)
Queen Christina, 1933 (Adrian; Daniels; Gibbons; Mayer;
   Stothart; Wanger)
Queen Cotton, 1941 (Alwyn; Cardiff)
Queen Elizabeth, 1912 (Zukor)
Queen for a Day, 1951 (Friedhofer; Miller)
Queen High, 1930 (Green)
Queen Is Crowned, 1953 (Rank)
Queen Kelly, 1929 (Plunkett)
Queen Louise. See Königin Luise, 1927
Queen of Destiny. See Sixty Glorious Years, 1938
Queen of Hearts, 1934 (Iwerks)
Queen of Hearts, 1936 (Dean)
Queen of Hearts. See Mother Goose Presents Humpty Dumpty, 1946
Queen of Outer Space, 1958 (Hecht)
Queen of Spades, 1948 (Adam; Auric; Heller; de Grunwald)
Queen of the Mob, 1940 (Dreier; Head)
Queen of the Moulin Rouge, 1922 (Carré)
Queen of the Road, 1971 (Golan and Globus)
Queen of the Stardust Ballroom, 1975 (O'Steen)
Queen Victoria, 1942 (Wilcox)
Queen X, 1917 (Polito)
Queens. See Fate, 1966
Queen's Affair, 1934 (Raphaelson; Wilcox; Young)
Queen's Necklace. See Affaire du collier de la reine, 1946
Queen's Royal Tour, 1954 (Rank)
Queens Up, 1920 (Roach)
Queimada!, 1969 (Gherardi; Morricone; Solinas)
Quel bandito sono io!, 1949 (Ponti)
Quelle drôle de blanchisserie, 1912 (Cohl)
Quelle drôle de gosse!, 1935 (Stradling)
Quelle joie de vivre. See Che gioia vivere, 1961

Quelque part, quelqu'un, 1972 (Delerue)
Quelques jours avec moi, 1988 (Sarde)
Quelqu'un a tué, 1933 (Wakhévitch)
Quentin Durward, 1955 (Berman; Challis; Kaper)
Quentin Quail, 1946 (Blanc; Jones; Stalling)
Queridísimos Verdugos, 1971 (de Almeida)
Quest, 1983 (Bass)
Quest for Fire. See Guerre du feu, 1981
Qu'est-ce qui fait courir David?, 1982 (Legrand)
Questa specie d'amore, 1972 (Morricone)
Questi fantasmi, 1967 (Delli Colli; Ponti)
Question, 1967 (Halas and Batchelor)
Question d'assurance, 1959 (Delerue)
Questor Tapes, 1974 (Whitlock)
Qui?, 1970 (Gégauff)
Qui comincia l'avventura, 1976 (Cristaldi)
Qui êtes vous, Polly Magoo, 1965 (Evein; Legrand)
Quick, 1932 (Pommer)
Quick and the Dead, 1995 (Von Brandenstein)
Quick, Before It Melts, 1964 (Ames; Harlan)
Quick Millions, 1931 (August)
Quick Millions, 1939 (Day)
Quick Money, 1938 (Musuraca)
Quicksand, 1950 (Leven)
Quicksands, 1923 (Rosson)
Quien sabe?, 1966 (Morricone; Solinas)
Quiet American, 1957 (Hornbeck; Krasker)
Quiet Days at Clichy. See Jours tranquilles à Clichy, 1990
Quiet Man, 1952 (Cooper; Hoch; Nugent; Young)
Quiet Place in the Country. See Tranquillo posto di campagna, 1968
Quiet Please!, 1945 (Hanna and Barbera)
Quiet, Please, Murder, 1942 (Day)
Quiet! Pleeze, 1941 (Fleischer)
Quiet Squad, 1967 (McKimson)
Quiet Street, 1922 (Roach)
Quiet Wedding, 1941 (Dillon; Rattigan)
Quiet Week in a House. See Tichy tyden v domee, 1969
Quille, 1961 (Guillemot)
Quille, bon dieu, 1971 (Nuytten)
Quiller Memorandum, 1966 (Barry; Pinter)
Quincannon, Frontier Scout, 1956 (Biroc; Cahn)
Quirinale, 1947 (Delli Colli)
Quits, 1915 (Furthman)
Quitter, 1929 (Walker)
Quo Vadis, 1901 (Pathé)
Quo Vadis?, 1924 (Courant)
Quo Vadis?, 1951 (Ellenshaw; Gibbons; Gillespie; Levien; Rozsa;
   Surtees)
Quo Vadis Homo Sapiens, 1983 (Popescu-Gopo)

R.A.F., 1935 (Rank)
R.F.D. 10,000 B.C., 1917 (O'brien)
R-I, ein Formspiel von Oskar Fischinger, 1927 (Fischinger)
Rabbit Every Monday, 1951 (Blanc; Stalling)
Rabbit Fire, 1951 (Blanc; Jones; Stalling)
Rabbit Hood, 1949 (Blanc; Jones; Stalling)
Rabbit of Seville, 1950 (Blanc; Jones; Stalling)
Rabbit Punch, 1948 (Blanc; Jones; Stalling)
Rabbit Rampage, 1955 (Blanc; Jones)
Rabbit Romeo, 1957 (Blanc; McKimson)
Rabbit, Run, 1970 (Lathrop)
Rabbit Seasoning, 1952 (Blanc; Jones; Stalling)
Rabbit Stew and Rabbits Too, 1969 (Blanc; McKimson)
Rabbit Test, 1978 (Ballard)
Rabbit Transit, 1947 (Blanc; Stalling)
Rabbit's Feat, 1960 (Blanc; Jones)

Rabbit's Kin, 1952 (Blanc; McKimson; Stalling)
Rabbitson Crusoe, 1956 (Blanc)
Rabindranath Tagore, 1961 (Chandragupta; Dutta)
Racconti d'estate, 1958 (Amidei; Flaiano and Pinelli)
Racconti romani, 1956 (Age and Scarpelli; Amidei)
Raccourci. See Tempo di uccidere, 1989
Race des "Seigneurs'', 1976 (Sarde)
Race for Life. See Mask of Dust, 1954
Race for Life. See Si tous les gars du monde, 1956
Race Gang. See Four Dark Hours, 1940
Race Gang. See Green Cockatoo, 1937
Race Riot, 1929 (Lantz)
Race with the Devil, 1975 (Rosenman)
Racers, 1955 (Bass; North; Wheeler)
Rache des Pharao, 1925 (Kolowrat-Krakowsky)
Rache ist mein , 1912 (Messter)
Rachel and the Stranger, 1948 (D'Agostino; Head)
Rachel, Rachel, 1968 (Allen)
Racing Luck. See Red Hot Tires, 1935
Racing Romeo, 1926 (Clarke)
Racing the Chutes at Dreamland, 1904 (Bitzer)
Racing with the Moon, 1984 (Grusin; Lansing)
Rack, 1916 (Carré)
Rack, 1956 (Deutsch)
Racket, 1928 (Gaudio)
Racket Buster, 1949 (Terry)
Racket Busters, 1938 (Deutsch; Edeson; Friedhofer)
Racketeer Rabbit, 1946 (Blanc; Stalling)
Racketeers in Exile, 1937 (Ballard)
Radetzky Marsch, 1994 (Preisner)
Radha Krishna, 1954 (Burman)
Radical Lawyer, 1973 (Menges)
Radio City Revels, 1938 (Pan; Veiller)
Radio Days, 1987 (Loquasto)
Radio Dynamics, 1942 (Fischinger)
Radio Flyer, 1992 (Kovacs; Zimmer)
Radio Girl, 1932 (Terry)
Radio Mad, 1924 (Roach)
Radio Rhythm, 1931 (Lantz)
Radio Riot, 1930 (Fleischer)
Raffles, 1930 (Barnes; Goldwyn; Howard; Menzies; Toland)
Raffles, 1940 (Banton; Basevi; Goldwyn; Howard; Toland; Young)
Raffles sur la ville, 1957 (Legrand)
Rafter Romance, 1933 (Macgowan; Plunkett; Polglase; Steiner)
Ragasse di Piazza di Spagna, 1952 (Amidei)
Ragazza con la Valigia, 1960 (Serandrei)
Ragazza del Palio, 1957 (Rotunno)
Ragazza di Bube, 1963 (Gherardi)
Ragazza e il generale, 1967 (Morricone)
Ragazza in vetrina, 1960 (Flaiano and Pinelli)
Ragazze da marito, 1952 (Age and Scarpelli)
Ragazze de San Frediano, 1954 (Di Venanzo)
Ragazze di Piazza di Spagna, 1997 (Donaggio)
Ragazze d'oggi, 1955 (Ponti)
Ragazze e il generale, 1967 (Ponti)
Ragazzi di Bube, 1963 (Cristaldi; Di Venanzo)
Ragazzo di borgata, 1976 (Rota)
Ragazzo, una ragazza, 1983 (Age and Scarpelli)
Rage, 1973 (Schifrin)
Rage, 1991 (Golan and Globus)
Rage in Harlem, 1991 (Bernstein)
Rage in Heaven, 1941 (Kaper)
Rågens rike, 1951 (Nykvist)
Ragged Flag. See Ranru no hata, 1974
Ragged Heiress, 1922 (Furthman)
Raggedy Ann and Andy, 1941 (Fleischer)

Raggedy Ann and Andy, 1977 (Williams)
Raggedy Man, 1981 (Goldsmith; Shepard)
Raggedy Rug, 1964 (Hanna and Barbera)
Raging Bull, 1980 (Schoonmaker; Winkler)
Raging Tide, 1951 (Metty)
Ragtime, 1981 (de Laurentiis; Ondříček; Von Brandenstein)
Ragtime Bear, 1949 (Bosustow; Hubley)
Ragtime Romeo, 1931 (Iwerks)
Ragtime Snapshots, 1914 (Roach)
Rahi, 1953 (Abbas; Biswas)
Raid, 1954 (Ballard)
Raid on France, 1942 (Balcon)
Raider. See Western Approaches, 1944
Raider of the Golden Gulch, 1932 (Canutt)
Raiders of the Lost Ark, 1981 (Burtt; Edlund; Marshall; Slocombe; Walas; Williams)
Raiding the Raiders, 1945 (Terry)
Raigeki tai shutsudo, 1944 (Tsuburaya)
Rail Rider, 1916 (Carré)
Railroad Man. See Ferroviere, 1956
Railroadin', 1929 (Roach)
Rain, 1932 (Day; Newman)
Rain, 1940 (Eisler)
Rain. See Regen, 1929
Rain Killer, 1990 (Kaminski)
Rain Makers, 1951 (Terry)
Rain Man, 1988 (Bass; Seale; Zimmer)
Rain of Paris, 1980 (Dinov)
Rain or Shine, 1930 (Cohn; Swerling; Walker)
Rain People, 1969 (Murch)
Rainbow, 1995 (Francis)
Rainbow Dance , 1936 (Lye)
Rainbow Island, 1917 (Roach)
Rainbow Island, 1944 (Dreier; Head; Struss)
Rainbow Jacket, 1954 (Alwyn; Clarke; Heller)
Rainmaker, 1956 (Head; Lang; North; Wallis)
Rainmaker, 1997 (Bernstein)
Rainmakers, 1935 (McCord; Plunkett)
Rains Came, 1939 (Dunne; Glennon; Miller; Newman; Zanuck)
Rains of Ranchipur, 1955 (Friedhofer; Krasner; Lemaire; Rose; Spencer)
Raintree County, 1957 (Green; Plunkett; Surtees)
Rainy Day. See Deštivý den, 1962
Rainy Days, 1928 (Roach)
Raise the Rent, 1920 (Roach)
Raise the Titanic!, 1980 (Barry)
Raising a Riot, 1955 (Challis; Korda)
Raising Arizona, 1987 (Burwell)
Raising Cain, 1992 (Donaggio)
Raising the Wind, 1961 (Dillon)
Raisins Sold Out!, 1990 (Vinton)
Raison du Plus Fou, 1973 (Rousselot)
Ráj a peklo bohemy. See Plameny života, 1920
Rajah, 1919 (Roach)
Rajgi, 1937 (Burman)
Raju aur Gangaram, 1964 (Biswas)
Rake's Progress, 1945 (Alwyn; Mathieson; Rank)
Rakvickárna, 1966 (švankmajer)
Rally 'round the Flag, Boys!, 1958 (Lemaire; Shamroy; Wheeler)
Ramasagul, 1985 (Popescu-Gopo)
Ramblin' Kid, 1923 (Miller)
Rambling Rose, 1991 (Bernstein)
Rambo: First Blood, Part II, 1985 (Cardiff; Goldsmith)
Rambo III, 1988 (Goldsmith)
Ramiet and Julio, 1915 (Bray)
Ramona, 1910 (Bitzer)
Ramona, 1928 (D'Agostino)

Ramona, 1936 (Newman; Trotti)
Ramoneur malgré lui, 1912 (Cohl)
Rampage, 1962 (Bernstein)
Rampage, 1987 (Morricone)
Rampage, 1992 (Morricone)
Ramparts We Watch, 1940 (de Rochemont)
Ramrod, 1947 (Deutsch; Harlan; Head)
Ramuntcho, 1938 (Douy; Lourié)
Ramuntcho, 1958 (Coutard; de Beauregard)
Ran, 1985 (Muraki; Takemitsu)
Ranchero's Revenge, 1913 (Bitzer)
Rancho Deluxe, 1975 (Fraker; Loquasto)
Rancho Notorious, 1952 (Friedhofer; Mohr; Taradash; Westmore Family)
Rancid Ransom, 1962 (Hanna and Barbera)
Randolph Family. *See* Dear Octopus, 1943
Random Harvest, 1942 (Mayer; Ruttenberg; Stothart)
Random Hearts, 1999 (Grusin; Rousselot)
Randy Rides Alone, 1934 (Canutt)
Randy Strikes Oil. *See* Fighting Texans, 1933
Range Defenders, 1937 (Canutt)
Range War, 1939 (Harlan; Head; Young)
Ranger and the Lady, 1940 (Canutt)
Ranger of Lonesome Gulf , 1913 (Seitz)
Rangers of Fortune, 1940 (Dreier; Head)
Rangun, 1927 (Tsuburaya)
Ranru no hata, 1974 (Toda)
Ransom, 1928 (Walker)
Ransom!, 1956 (Rose)
Ransom, 1974 (Goldsmith; Nykvist)
Rapa-Nui, 1928 (Andrejew)
Rapaces diurnes et nocturnes, 1913 (Burel)
Rape of Malaya. *See* A Town Like Alice, 1956
Rápido de las 9.15, 1941 (Figueroa)
Rappin', 1985 (Golan and Globus)
Rapporto segreto, 1967 (Storaro)
Rappresaglia, 1973 (Morricone; Ponti)
Rapt, 1934 (Honegger)
Rapture, 1965 (Delerue; Flaiano and Pinelli)
Rapture, 1991 (Newman)
Rapunzel, 1897 (Messter)
Rapunzel. *See* Story of Hansel and Gretel, 1951
Rare Breed, 1965 (Clothier)
Rare Breed, 1966 (Whitlock; Williams)
Rascals, 1938 (Cronjager)
Rascel Fifi, 1957 (Cristaldi; Di Venanzo)
Rascel Marine, 1959 (Cristaldi; Di Venanzo)
Rashomon, 1950 (Hayasaka; Miyagawa)
Raskens, 1976 (Fischer)
Raskolnikoff, 1923 (Andrejew)
Rasputin. *See* Tragédie impériale, 1938
Rasputin and the Empress, 1932 (Adrian; Courant; Daniels; MacArthur; Mayer; Stothart)
Rasputin—The Mad Monk, 1966 (Carreras)
Rasskazi o Lenine, 1957 (Moskvin)
Rasslin' Round, 1934 (Iwerks)
Rastus' Rabid Rabbit Hunt, 1915 (Bray)
Rat, 1925 (Balcon)
Rat, 1937 (Wilcox; Young)
Rat, 1960 (Zavattini)
Rat der Götter, 1950 (Eisler)
Rat des villes et le rat des champs, 1926 (Starewicz)
Rat Destruction, 1942 (Alwyn)
Rat Fink, 1965 (Zsigmond)
Rat Race, 1960 (Bernstein; Burks; Head; Kanin; Westmore Family)
Ratai, 1962 (Takemitsu)
Ratataa, 1956 (Lundgren)

Ratataplan, 1979 (Cristaldi)
Ratboy, 1986 (Baker)
Raton Pass, 1951 (Steiner)
Rat's Knuckes, 1924 (Roach)
Rätsel der Sphinx, 1921 (Dreier)
Ratten, 1921 (Freund)
Rattenfänger von Hameln, 1918 (Reiniger)
Rattled Rooster, 1948 (Blanc; Stalling)
Raub der Mona Lisa, 1931 (Andrejew; Reisch)
Raub des Sabinerinnen, 1954 (Warm)
Rausch, 1919 (Freund; Kräly)
Raven, 1935 (D'Agostino; Pierce; Schary)
Raven, 1942 (Fleischer)
Raven, 1963 (Crosby)
Raven. *See* Corbeau, 1943
Ravin sans fond, 1917 (Gaumont)
Ravissante Idiote, 1964 (Legrand)
Raw Deal, 1948 (Alton)
Raw! Raw! Rooster, 1956 (Blanc; McKimson; Stalling)
Rawhide!, 1950 (Krasner; Lemaire; Nichols; Wheeler)
Rawhide Trail, 1958 (Struss)
Rawhide Years, 1956 (Maté)
Ray's Male Heterosexual Dance Hall, 1987 (Lathrop)
Razgrom nemetzkikhy voisk pod Moskvoi, 1942 (Vorkapich)
Razor's Edge, 1946 (Day; Lemaire; Miller; Newman; Trotti; Zanuck)
Razor's Edge, 1984 (Nitzsche)
Razumov. *See* Sous les yeux d'occident, 1936
Razzberries, 1931 (Terry)
Reflection of Fear, 1971 (Fraker; Kovacs)
Regular Girl, 1919 (Marion)
Regular Pal, 1920 (Roach)
Regular Scout, 1926 (Plunkett)
Relic of Old Japan, 1914 (Ince)
Report on the Party and the Guests. *See* **O Slavnosti a hostech**, 1968
Rich Man's Son. *See* Pappas pojke, 1937
Rich Revenge, 1910 (Bitzer)
River Runs Through It, 1991 (Bernstein; Rousselot)
River Speaks, 1957 (Lassally)
Road in India. *See* World Window, 1937-40
Romance in Happy Valley, 1919 (Bitzer)
Romance of the Redwoods, 1917 (Buckland; Macpherson)
Romany Tragedy, 1911 (Bitzer)
Room in Town. *See* Chambre en ville, 1982
Room with a View, 1985 (Jhabvala; Merchant)
Rose for Everyone. *See* Rosa per tutti, 1967
Royal Scandal, 1945 (Biro; Miller; Newman; Spencer)
Rude Hostess, 1909 (Bitzer)
Run for Your Money, 1949 (Balcon; Slocombe)
Run on Gold. *See* Midas Run, 1969
Rural Elopement, 1908 (Bitzer)

S vyloučenim veřejnosti, 1933 (Heller)
S-a furat o bomba, 1961 (Popescu-Gopo)
S. Carlino, 1950 (Di Venanzo)
SAS à San Salvador, 1982 (Coutard)
SAS—Terminate with Extreme Prejudice. *See* SAS à San Salvador, 1982
S.E.A.L.S.. *See* Finest Hour, 1992
S.O.B., 1981 (Mancini; van Runkle)
S.O.S. Coastguard, 1937 (Canutt)
S.O.S. Concorde. *See* Concorde: Airport '79, 1979
S.O.S. Foch, 1931 (Ibert)
SOS in the Mountains. *See* Horské volání SOS, 1929
S.O.S. Mediterranean. *See* Alerte en Méditerranée, 1938
S.O.S. Noronha, 1956 (Decaë)
S.O.S. Pacific, 1959 (Auric)
S.O.S., 1940 (Alwyn)

Sallah. *See* Sallah Shabati, 1964
Sally, 1925 (Mathis; McCord)
Sally, 1930 (Wallis)
Sally and Saint Anne, 1952 (Maté)
Sally in Our Alley, 1931 (Dean; Reville)
Sally, Irene, and Mary, 1925 (Gibbons; Mayer)
Sally of the Scandals, 1928 (Plunkett)
Sally Swing, 1938 (Fleischer)
Sally's Irish Rogue. *See* Poacher's Daughter, 1960
Sally's Shoulders, 1928 (Miller)
Salmon Fishing, Quebec, 1905 (Bitzer)
Salo, o le 120 giornate di Sodoma, 1975 (Delli Colli; Donati; Morricone)
Salo—The 120 Days of Sodom. *See* Salo o le 120 giornate di Sodoma, 1975
Salome, 1902 (Messter)
Salome, 1918 (Schenck)
Salome, 1922 (Metzner)
Salome, 1953 (Duning; Hoch; Lang; Louis)
Salome, 1986 (Golan and Globus)
Salome of the Tenements, 1925 (Levien)
Salome, Where She Danced, 1945 (Mohr; Wanger)
Salomy Jane, 1914 (Mohr)
Salomy Jane, 1923 (Clarke)
Salon Dora Green, 1933 (Galeen)
Salon Kitty, 1977 (Adam)
Salón México, 1949 (Figueroa)
Salonique, nid d'espions. *See* Mademoiselle Docteur, 1937
Saloon Bar, 1940 (Balcon; Neame)
Salsa, 1988 (Golan and Globus)
Salsa, 2000 (Carrière)
Salt of the Earth, 1954 (Jarrico; Wilson)
Salt Water Daffy, 1941 (Lantz)
Salt Water Tabby, 1947 (Hanna and Barbera)
Salt Water Taffy, 1930 (Terry)
Salto mortale, 1931 (Junge)
Salto nel Vuoto, 1980 (Lanci, Giuseppe ("beppe"))
Saltstänk och krutgubbar, 1946 (Nykvist)
Salty McQuire, 1937 (Terry)
Salty O'Rourke, 1945 (Dreier; Head)
Saludos Amigos, 1942 (Disney)
Salut la puce, 1982 (Lai)
Salutary Lesson, 1910 (Bitzer)
Salute, 1929 (August)
Salute for Three, 1943 (Dreier; Head; Young)
Salute to France, 1944 (Kanin)
Salute to Romance. *See* Annapolis Salute, 1937
Salvador, 1986 (Delerue)
Salvation Army Lass, 1908 (Bitzer)
Salvation Nell, 1921 (D'Agostino; Haller)
Salvatore Giuliano, 1961 (Cecchi D'amico; Cristaldi; Di Venanzo; Serandrei; Solinas)
Salzburger Geschichten, 1957 (Kästner)
Sam Lloyd's Famous Puzzles, 1917 (O'brien)
Same Old Song. *See* On connaît la chanson, 1997
Same Old Story, 1982 (Driessen)
Same Time Next Year, 1978 (Bumstead; Hamlisch; Mirisch; Surtees)
Samhallets dom, 1912 (Jaenzon; Magnusson)
Sami der Seefahrer, 1916 (Kolowrat-Krakowsky)
Sami the Seafarer. *See* Sami der Seefahrer, 1916
Sammy and Rosie Get Laid, 1987 (Kureishi)
Sammy Going South, 1963 (Balcon)
Sammy in Siberia, 1919 (Roach)
Sammy Stops the World, 1978 (Loquasto)
Samourai, 1967 (Decaë)
Sampo, 1958 (Ptushko)
Samson and Delilah, 1949 (Barnes; Dreier; Head; Jeakins; Young)

Samson and Delilah, 1984 (Jarre)
Samson and Delilah, 1996 (Morricone)
Samson et Delila, 1902 (Pathé)
Samson und Delila, 1922 (Korda)
Samurai, 1965 (Kuri)
Samurai ondo, 1937 (Yoda)
Samurai Pirate. *See* Daitozoku, 1964
Samurai Song. *See* Samurai ondo, 1937
Samurai Spy. *See* Ibun Sarutobi sasuke, 1965
Samvetsömma Adolf, 1936 (Fischer; Jaenzon)
San Antonio, 1945 (Glennon; Steiner; Waxman)
San Antonio Rose, 1941 (Cortez)
San Babila ore 20: un delitto inutile, 1976 (Morricone)
San Demetrio London, 1944 (Balcon)
San Diego, I Love You, 1944 (Mohr)
San Francesco, 1966 (Flaiano and Pinelli)
San Francisco, 1906 (Bitzer)
San Francisco, 1936 (Adrian; Brown; Canutt; Edens; Freed; Gibbons; Gillespie; Kahn; Kaper; Loos; Mayer; Shearer; Stothart)
San Francisco Story, 1952 (Friedhofer; Jenkins; Parrish; Seitz)
San Giovanni Decollato, 1940 (Zavattini)
San Miniato, Iuglio 1944, 1954 (Zavattini)
San Quentin, 1937 (Raksin)
Sanbiki no tanuki, 1966 (Muraki)
Sancta Simplicitas, 1968 (Popescu-Gopo)
Sanctuary, 1961 (North; Smith; Zanuck)
Sand, 1920 (August)
Sand, 1949 (Clarke)
Sand, 1971 (Ballhaus)
Sand Pebbles, 1966 (Goldsmith; Leven; Reynolds)
Sanda tai Gailha. *See* Furankenshutain no kaiju—Sanda tai Gailah, 1966
Sandai kaiju chikyu saidai no kessen, 1965 (Tsuburaya)
Sanders of the River, 1935 (Biro; Hornbeck; Korda; Périnal)
Sandman, 1920 (Roach)
Sandpiper, 1965 (Krasner; Mandel; Sharaff; Trumbo; Wilson)
Sandra. *See* Vaghe stelle dell'orsa, 1965
Sands of Dee, 1912 (Bitzer)
Sands of Iwo Jima, 1949 (Young)
Sands of the Kalahari, 1965 (Levine)
Sandwich, 1984 (Bozzetto)
Sandy Claws, 1955 (Blanc; Stalling)
Sandy Is a Lady, 1940 (Krasner)
Sanford Meisner: The American Theatre's Best Kept Secret, 1984 (Mamet)
Sang des bêtes, 1948 (Fradetal; Kosma)
Sang d'un poète, 1930 (Auric; D'Eaubonne; Périnal)
Sanga ari, 1962 (Toda)
Sangaree, 1953 (Head; Pereira)
Sången om den eldröda blomman, 1918 (Jaenzon; Magnusson)
Sången om den eldröda blomman, 1934 (Jaenzon)
Sanjuro, 1962 (Muraki)
Sans famille, 1934 (Braunberger; Jaubert; Trauner)
Sans laisser d'adresse, 1950 (Douy; Kosma)
Sans lendemain, 1940 (Alekan; Douy; Lourié; Schüfftan)
Sans mobile apparent, 1972 (Morricone)
Sansho dayu, 1954 (Hayasaka; Miyagawa; Yoda)
Sansho the Bailiff. *See* **Sansho dayu**, 1954
Sanskar, 1958 (Biswas)
Sånt händer inte här, 1950 (Fischer)
Santa Clause, 1994 (Baker)
Santa Claus: The Movie, 1985 (Mancini)
Santa Fe Marshall, 1940 (Harlan; Head)
Santa Fe Scouts, 1943 (Canutt)
Santa Fe Stampede, 1938 (Canutt)
Santa Fe Trail, 1930 (Head)
Santa Fe Trail, 1940 (Friedhofer; Haskin; Polito; Steiner; Wallis)

Santé à l'étable, 1957 (Braunberger)
Santiago, 1956 (Seitz)
Santostefano, 1997 (Lanci, Giuseppe ("beppe"))
Sap from Syracuse, 1930 (Green)
Sapatos Pretos, 1998 (Branco)
Sapho, 1934 (Douy; Jaubert)
Sapho, 1970 (D'Eaubonne)
Sapho 63, 1963 (Alcoriza)
Sapiches, 1982 (Golan and Globus)
Sapphire, 1959 (Dillon; Rank)
Saps at Sea, 1940 (Roach)
Saps in Chaps, 1942 (Blanc; Stalling)
Sara lär sig folkvett, 1937 (Fischer; Jaenzon)
Sara Learns Manners. See Sara lär sig folkvett, 1937
Saraba rabauru, 1954 (Tsuburaya)
Saraband. See Saraband for Dead Lovers, 1948
Saraband for Dead Lovers, 1948 (Balcon; Rank; Slocombe)
Sarafina!, 1992 (Mnouchkine)
Sarah and Son, 1930 (Lang; Selznick; Zukor)
Sarajevsky Atentat, 1975 (Jarrico)
Sarariiman Chushingura, 1960 (Muraki)
Saratoga, 1937 (Gibbons; Loos)
Saratoga Trunk, 1945 (Haller; Wallis; Steiner)
Sarge, 1971 (Grusin)
Sarre, pleins feux, 1951 (Alekan; Colpi)
Sasaki kojiro, 1950 (Tsuburaya)
Sasame-yuki, 1950 (Hayasaka)
Sasiedzi, 1969 (ścibor-Rylski)
Saskatchewan, 1954 (Seitz)
Såsom i en spegel, 1961 (Lundgren)
Sasom i en spegel, 1961 (Nykvist)
Satan Bug, 1965 (Goldsmith; Surtees)
Satan McAllister's Heir, 1915 (Sullivan)
Satan Met a Lady, 1936 (Blanke; Edeson; Orry-Kelly)
Satan Never Sleeps, 1962 (Bennett; Cardiff; Morris)
Satan Town, 1926 (Polito)
Satan's Brew. See Satansbraten, 1976
Satan's Waitin', 1954 (Blanc; Stalling)
Satanas, 1920 (Freund)
Satansbraten, 1976 (Ballhaus)
Satansketten, 1921 (Herlth; Röhrig)
Satellite in the Sky, 1956 (Périnal)
Satisfied Customers, 1954 (Terry)
Saturday Afternoon, 1926 (Hornbeck)
Saturday Evening Puss, 1950 (Hanna and Barbera)
Saturday Island, 1951 (Alwyn; Morris)
Saturday Men, 1962 (Menges)
Saturday Morning, 1922 (Roach)
Saturday Night, 1922 (Macpherson; Struss)
Saturday Night. See Cerná sobota, 1960
Saturday Night and Sunday Morning, 1960 (Francis)
Saturday Night Fever, 1977 (Von Brandenstein)
Saturday Night Kid, 1929 (Head)
Saturday, Sunday and Monday. See Sabato, Domenica e Lunedi, 1989
Saturday's Children, 1929 (Seitz)
Saturday's Children, 1940 (Blanke; Deutsch; Epstein; Howe; Wallis)
Saturday's Hero, 1951 (Bernstein; Garmes)
Saturday's Heroes, 1937 (Musuraca)
Saturday's Heroes, 1951 (Buchman)
Saturday's Lesson, 1929 (Roach)
Saturn 3, 1980 (Bernstein)
Satyajit Ray—Film Maker, 1982 (Nihalani)
Satyricon, 1969 (Donati; Rota; Rotunno)
Saucy Sausages, 1929 (Lantz)
Sauerbruch—Das war mein Leben, 1954 (Herlth)
Saul and David. See Saul e David, 1964

Saul e David, 1964 (Guerra)
Sautela Bhai, 1962 (Biswas)
Sauvage, 1975 (Douy; Legrand; Lhomme; Rappeneau)
Sauvage et beau, 1984 (Vangelis)
Savage, 1952 (Head; Seitz)
Savage. See Sauvage, 1975
Savage Eye, 1960 (Fields; Maddow; Rosenman; Wexler)
Savage Hunt, 1981 (Theodorakis)
Savage Innocents. See Dents du diable, 1960
Savage Sam, 1963 (Disney)
Savage Seven, 1968 (Kovacs)
Savage State. See État sauvage, 1978
Savage Triangle. See Garçon sauvage, 1951
Savage Woman, 1918 (Edeson)
Savages, 1972 (Lassally; Merchant)
Save the Ship, 1923 (Roach)
Save the Tiger, 1973 (Hamlisch)
Save Your Money, 1921 (Roach)
Save Your Shillings and Smile, 1943 (Balcon)
Saved from Himself, 1911 (Bitzer)
Saving Grace, 1914 (Loos)
Saving Grace, 1943 (Balcon)
Saving Presence, 1914 (Loos)
Saving Private Ryan, 1998 (Kaminski; Williams)
Savitri, 1961 (Biswas)
Savoy-Hotel 217, 1936 (Herlth; Röhrig; Wagner)
Saw Mill Mystery, 1937 (Terry)
Sawdust and Tinsel. See **Gycklarnas afton**, 1953
Sawdust Paradise, 1928 (Rosson)
Sawdust Trail, 1924 (Miller)
Saxon Charm, 1948 (Krasner)
Saxophon-Susi, 1927 (Heller)
Say Ah Jasper, 1944 (Pal)
Say Anything . . . , 1989 (Kovacs)
Say It Again, 1926 (Cronjager; Rosson)
Say It in French, 1938 (Head)
Say It with Babies, 1926 (Roach)
Say It with Music. See Säg det i toner, 1929
Say It with Music, 1932 (Wilcox)
Say It with Sables, 1928 (Cohn; Walker)
Say It with Songs, 1929 (Garmes; Zanuck)
Say One for Me, 1959 (Cahn; Lemaire; Wheeler; van Heusen)
Sayonara, 1957 (Berlin; Waxman)
Sazaa, 1951 (Burman)
Sbandati, 1955 (Di Venanzo)
Sbarco di Anzio, 1968 (Rotunno; de Laurentiis)
Scalawag, 1973 (Cardiff)
Scalp Treatment, 1952 (Lantz)
Scalp Trouble, 1939 (Blanc; Clampett; Stalling)
Scalpel, Please. See Skalpel, prosím, 1985
Scalphunters, 1967 (Bernstein)
Scamp, 1957 (Francis)
Scampolo '53, 1953 (Rota)
Scampolo, ein Kind der Strasse, 1933 (Courant)
Scandal. See Skandalen, 1912
Scandal. See Shubun, 1950
Scandal at Scourie, 1953 (Plunkett)
Scandal for Sale, 1932 (Freund)
Scandal in Paris, 1946 (Eisler)
Scandal in Sorrento. See Pane, amore e . . . , 1955
Scandal Sheet, 1938 (Head)
Scandal Sheet, 1951 (Duning; Guffey; Louis)
Scandale, 1934 (Matras; Schüfftan)
Scandale, 1948 (Jeanson)
Scandale, 1967 (Gégauff; Rabier)
Scandalo, 1975 (Storaro)

Scandalous Adventures of Buraikan. *See* Buraikan, 1970
Scandalous Eva. *See* Skandal um Eva, 1930
Scandalous, 1984 (Cardiff; Grusin)
Scandals, 1935 (Lemaire)
Scanners, 1981 (Smith; Walas)
Scapegoat, 1959 (Balcon; Halas and Batchelor; Kaper)
Scapolo, 1955 (Di Venanzo)
Scar. *See* Hollow Triumph, 1948
Scar Hanan, 1925 (Canutt)
Scarab Murder Case, 1936 (Havelock-Allan)
Scaramouche, 1923 (Seitz; Vorkapich)
Scaramouche, 1952 (Gibbons; Rosher; Young)
Scarecrow, 1973 (Zsigmond)
Scared Crows, 1939 (Fleischer)
Scared Stiff, 1926 (Roach)
Scared Stiff, 1945 (Mainwaring)
Scared Stiff, 1953 (Head; Laszlo; Wallis)
Scaredy Cat, 1948 (Blanc; Jones; Stalling)
Scarf, 1951 (Planer)
Scarface, 1932 (Garmes; Hecht; Miller; Westmore Family)
Scarface, 1983 (Alonzo)
Scarlet and the Black, 1983 (Morricone)
Scarlet Angel, 1952 (Metty)
Scarlet Blade, 1963 (Carreras)
Scarlet Buccaneer. *See* Swashbuckler, 1976
Scarlet Car, 1923 (Miller)
Scarlet Coat, 1955 (Plunkett)
Scarlet Dawn, 1932 (Grot; Haller; Orry-Kelly)
Scarlet Days, 1919 (Bitzer)
Scarlet Empress, 1934 (Banton; Dreier; Glennon; Zukor)
Scarlet Hour, 1956 (Head)
Scarlet Letter, 1926 (Gibbons; Marion; Mayer)
Scarlet Pimpernel, 1935 (Biro; Hornbeck; Korda; Mathieson; Meerson; Rosson; Sherwood)
Scarlet Pumpernickel, 1950 (Blanc; Jones; Stalling)
Scarlet River, 1933 (Canutt; Musuraca; Plunkett)
Scarlet Seas, 1929 (Polito)
Scarlet Street, 1945 (Banton; Krasner; Nichols; Wanger)
Scarlet Woman. *See* Femme écarlate, 1968
Scarlett Letter, 1995 (Barry)
Scarlett O'Hara War, 1980 (Kanin)
Scars of Dracula, 1970 (Bernard; Carreras)
Scat Cats*, 1956 (Hanna and Barbera)
Scatenato, 1967 (Guerra)
Scattergood Meets Broadway, 1941 (Tiomkin)
Sceicco bianco, 1952 (Flaiano and Pinelli; Rota)
Scélérats, 1960 (Evein; Saulnier)
Scemo di guerra, 1985 (Age and Scarpelli)
Scene of the Crime, 1949 (Irene; Previn; Schnee)
Scene of the Crime. *See* Lieu du crime, 1986
Scener ur ett äktenskap, 1973 (Nykvist)
Scènes de ménage, 1954 (D'Eaubonne)
Scenes from a Marriage. *See* Scener ur ett äktenskap, 1973
Scent of a Woman, 1992 (Newman)
Scent of Mystery, 1960 (Cardiff; Korda)
Scent of the Matterhorn, 1961 (Blanc; Jones)
Scent-imental Over You, 1947 (Blanc)
Scent-imental Romeo, 1951 (Blanc; Jones; Stalling)
Scenti-Mental over You, 1946 (Jones)
Scharlachrote Buchstabe, 1972 (Müller)
Schatten, 1922 (Wagner)
Schatten der Unterwelt, 1931 (Galeen)
Schatten des Meeres, 1912 (Messter)
Schatten über St. Pauli, 1938 (Wagner)
Schatz, 1923 (Herlth; Röhrig)
Scheherazade. *See* Shéhérazade, 1963

Scheintote Chinese, 1928 (Reiniger)
Scherben, 1921 (Mayer)
Scherzo, 1932 (Cortez)
Scherzo, 1939-41 (McClaren)
Scherzo, 1983 (Age and Scarpelli)
Schicksal, 1924 (Planer)
Schicksal am Lenkrad, 1953 (Eisler)
Schindler's List, 1993 (Kaminski; Williams)
Schirm mit dem Schwan, 1915 (Messter)
Schlagende Wetter, 1923 (Metzner)
Schlangenei, 1977 (Nykvist; de Laurentiis)
Schlock, 1971 (Baker)
Schloss im Süden, 1933 (Wagner)
Schloss Vogelöd, 1921 (Herlth; Mayer; Pommer; Wagner; Warm)
Schlüssakkord, 1960 (Auric)
Schöne Abenteuer, 1932 (Wagner)
Schöne Abenteuer, 1959 (Herlth)
Schöne Prinzessin von China, 1916 (Reiniger)
School Begins, 1928 (Roach)
School Birds, 1937 (Terry)
School Days, 1932 (Fleischer; Iwerks)
School Daze, 1942 (Terry)
School Daze, 1988 (Dickerson)
School for Secrets, 1946 (Dillon; Rank)
School for Stars, 1935 (Havelock-Allan)
School for Wives, 1925 (Ruttenberg)
School, the Basis of Life. *See* Skola, základ života, 1938
School Ties, 1992 (Francis; Jarre; Lansing)
Schoolmistress on the Spree. *See* Lärarinna på vift, 1941
Schoolteacher and the Waif, 1912 (Bitzer)
Schreckensnacht in der Menagerie, 1921 (Hoffmann)
Schubert. *See* Sinfonia d'amore, 1954
Schuberts unvollendete Symphonie. *See* Leise flehen meine Lieder, 1933
Schuhpalast Pinkus, 1916 (Kräly)
Schuldig, 1913 (Messter)
Schuldig, 1928 (Courant)
Schützenliesl, 1926 (Reisch)
Schwarze Domino, 1929 (Reisch)
Schwarze Gesicht, 1922 (Planer)
Schwarze Husar, 1932 (Herlth; Planer; Röhrig)
Schwarze Rosen, 1935 (Wagner)
Schwarzwaldmädel, 1929 (Reisch)
Schwedische Nachtigall, 1941 (Herlth)
Schweigen im Walde, 1929 (Pasternak)
Schweikart. *See* Fräulein von Barnhelm, 1940
Schwere Opfer, 1911 (Messter)
Schwindende Herz, 1917 (Kolowrat-Krakowsky)
Schwur des Peter Hertatz, 1921 (Freund)
Science, 1911 (Gaudio)
Scirocco, 1987 (Donaggio)
Sciuscià, 1946 (Amidei; Zavattini)
Sconosciuto di San Marino, 1947 (Zavattini)
Scooper Dooper, 1947 (Bruckman)
Scorchers, 1991 (Burwell)
Scorching Sands, 1923 (Roach)
Scorpio, 1972 (Mirisch)
Scorpio Letters, 1967 (Grusin)
Scotch Highball, 1930 (Terry)
Scotland Yard, 1930 (Friedhofer)
Scotland Yard, 1941 (Miller)
Scotland Yard Commands. *See* Lonely Road, 1936
Scotland Yard Inspector. *See* Lady in the Fog, 1952
Scott of the Antarctic, 1948 (Balcon; Cardiff; Rank; Unsworth)
Scotta, 1994 (Morricone)
Scottish Mazurka, 1943 (Cardiff)
Scoundrel, 1935 (Coward; Garmes; Hecht; MacArthur; Zukor)

Scoundrel in White. *See* Docteur Popaul, 1972
Scout, 1994 (Conti; Kovacs)
Scoutmaster Magoo, 1958 (Bosustow)
Scram, 1932 (Roach)
Scrambled Aches, 1957 (Blanc; Jones; Stalling)
Scrap for Victory, 1943 (Terry)
Scrap Happy Daffy, 1943 (Blanc; Stalling)
Scrapper, 1922 (Miller)
Scrappily Married, 1940 (Metty)
Scream 2, 1997 (Elfman; Zimmer)
Scream of Fear. *See* Taste of Fear, 1961
Screamers, 1978 (Walas)
Screaming Mimi, 1958 (Guffey)
Screaming Skull, 1958 (Crosby)
Screaming Woman, 1972 (Head; Williams)
Screen Song, 1932 (Fleischer)
Screwball Football, 1939 (Avery)
Screwdriver, 1941 (Lantz)
Screw's Adventures. *See* Sroublkova dobrodružství, 1962
Screwy Squirrel, 1944 (Avery)
Screwy Truant, 1945 (Avery)
Scrooge, 1951 (Addinsell)
Scrooge, 1970 (Morris; Neame)
Scrooged, 1988 (Elfman; Houseman)
Scrub Me Mama with a Boogie Beat, 1941 (Lantz)
Scruggs, 1965 (Coutard)
Scudda Hoo! Scudda Hay!, 1948 (Lemaire)
Sculptor's Landscape, 1957 (Lassally)
Sculptor's Nightmare, 1908 (Bitzer)
Sculptures au moyen-âge, 1949 (Renoir)
Scuola del timidi, 1941 (Zavattini)
Scuola di Severino, 1949 (Di Venanzo)
Scuola elementare, 1954 (Spaak)
Scusi, facciamo l'amore?, 1968 (Morricone)
Scusi, lei e favorevole o contrario?, 1966 (Amidei)
Se ki, se be, 1919 (Korda)
Se la paso la mano, 1952 (Alcoriza)
Se tutte le donne del mondo . . . , 1966 (de Laurentiis; Gherardi)
Sea, 1954 (Halas and Batchelor)
Sea. *See* Mar, 2000
Sea Bat, 1930 (Gibbons; Shearer)
Sea Beast, 1926 (Haskin; Westmore Family)
Sea Chase, 1955 (Clothier)
Sea Devils, 1937 (August; Polglase)
Sea Devils, 1953 (Addinsell; Chase)
Sea Fever. *See* En rade, 1927
Sea Fury, 1959 (Rank)
Sea Hawk, 1924 (Goosson)
Sea Hawk, 1940 (Blanke; Friedhofer; Grot; Haskin; Koch; Korngold; Miller; Orry-Kelly; Polito; Wallis)
Sea Hornet, 1951 (Glennon)
Sea Horses, 1926 (Howe)
Sea of Grass, 1947 (Berman; Mayer; Plunkett; Stothart; Stradling)
Sea of Sand, 1958 (Mathieson; Rank)
Sea Shall Not Have Them, 1954 (Arnold; Mathieson)
Sea Theme, 1949 (Hall)
Sea Urchin, 1926 (Balcon)
Sea Wall. *See* Barrage contre le Pacifique, 1958
Sea Wolf, 1941 (Blanke; Friedhofer; Grot; Haskin; Korngold; Polito; Wallis)
Seagull, 1968 (Fisher)
Seagulls over Sorrento, 1954 (Junge; Rozsa)
Seal of Silence, 1913 (Ince)
Sealed Lips. *See* Förseglade läppar, 1927
Sealed Lips. *See* After Tonight, 1933
Sealed Lips, 1941 (Cortez)

Sealed Room, 1909 (Bitzer)
Sealed Verdict, 1948 (Dreier; Friedhofer; Head)
Seance on a Wet Afternoon, 1964 (Barry)
Search, 1948 (Jarrico; Mayer)
Search for Beauty, 1934 (Banton; Zukor)
Search for Bridey Murphy, 1956 (Head)
Search for Danger, 1949 (Leven)
Search for Paradise, 1957 (Tiomkin)
Search for Signs of Intelligent Life in the Universe, 1991 (Littleton)
Search for the Evil One, 1967 (Fields)
Searchers, 1956 (Basevi; Cooper; Hoch; Nugent; Steiner)
Searching Eye, 1964 (Bass)
Searching for Bobby Fischer, 1993 (Hall)
Searching Wind, 1946 (Dreier; Garmes; Wallis; Young)
Seas Beneath, 1931 (August; Nichols)
Seashore Baby, 1904 (Bitzer)
Seasick Sailors, 1951 (Terry)
Seaside Adventure, 1952 (Terry)
Season for Love. *See* Morte-Saison des amours, 1961
Seasons, 1963 (Ivanov-Vano)
Season's Beatings. *See* Bûche, 1999
Season's Greetinks, 1933 (Fleischer)
Seasons of the Heart, 1994 (Hamlisch)
Seaweed Children, 1973 (Lassally)
Sebastian, 1967 (Fisher; Goldsmith)
Sechs Wochen unter den Apachen. *See* Achtung Harry! Augen auf!, 1926
Second Best, 1994 (Menges)
Second Best Secret Agent in the Whole Wide World. *See* Licensed to Kill, 1965
Second Chance, 1953 (D'Agostino; Maté)
Second Chance. *See* Si c'était à refaire, 1976
Second Childhood, 1935 (Roach)
Second Chorus, 1941 (Leven; Mercer; Pan)
Second Daughter, 1991 (Merchant)
Second Fiddle, 1939 (Berlin; Glennon; Zanuck)
Second Hand Hearts, 1981 (Wexler)
Second Hand Wife, 1932 (Clarke; Friedhofer)
Second Son Crow. *See* Jinanbou garasu, 1955
Second Thoughts, 1938 (Neame)
Second Thoughts, 1983 (Mancini)
Second Time Around, 1961 (Mancini; Smith)
Second Wife, 1930 (Glennon; Plunkett)
Second Wife, 1936 (Musuraca)
Second Woman, 1951 (Leven; Mohr)
Seconde Vérité, 1966 (Douy)
Seconds, 1966 (Alonzo; Bass; Goldsmith; Howe)
Secret, 1974 (Morricone)
Secret Agent, 1936 (Balcon; Reville)
Secret Behind the Door, 1948 (Cortez; Rozsa)
Secret beyond the Door, 1948 (Banton; Wanger)
Secret Bride, 1934 (Blanke; Grot; Orry-Kelly)
Secret Ceremony, 1968 (Bennett; Fisher)
Secret Command, 1944 (Planer)
Secret de Delhia, 1929 (Burel)
Secret de Polichinelle, 1936 (Spaak)
Secret de Soeur Angèle, 1955 (D'Eaubonne)
Secret du chevalier d'eon, 1960 (Alekan; Trauner)
Secret Flight. *See* School for Secrets, 1946
Secret Four. *See* Four Just Men, 1939
Secret Game, 1917 (Rosher)
Secret Garden, 1949 (Gillespie; Kaper; Plunkett)
Secret Garden, 1993 (Preisner)
Secret Heart, 1946 (Irene; Kaper)
Secret Interlude. *See* Storm View from Pompey's Head, 1955
Secret Invasion, 1964 (Friedhofer)
Secret Land, 1948 (Kaper)

Secret Life of an American Wife, 1968 (Shamroy; Smith)
Secret Life of Walter Mitty, 1947 (Garmes; Goldwyn; Jenkins; Raksin; Sharaff)
Secret Lives, 1937 (Heller)
Secret Lives of Plants, 1978 (Cloquet)
Secret Marriage. See Ett hemligt giftermäl, 1912
Secret Meeting. See Marie Octobre, 1959
Secret Mission, 1942 (Rank)
Secret Motive. See London Black-Out Murders, 1942
Secret Obsession. See Champagne amer, 1986
Secret of Blood. See Tajemství krve, 1953
Secret of Blood Island, 1965 (Bernard; Carreras)
Secret of Convict Lake, 1951 (Lemaire)
Secret of Madame Blanche, 1933 (Adrian; Goodrich and Hackett)
Secret of Roan Inish, 1994 (Daring; Wexler)
Secret of Santa Vittoria, 1969 (Maddow; Rotunno)
Secret of the Ice Cave, 1989 (Golan and Globus)
Secret of the Incas, 1954 (Head)
Secret of the Telegian. See Denso ningen, 1960
Secret of the Wastelands, 1941 (Harlan; Head)
Secret of Treasure Island, 1938 (Canutt)
Secret of Yolanda. See Ahava Ilemeth, 1982
Secret People, 1951 (Rank)
Secret Place, 1957 (Bryan; Rank)
Secret Places, 1985 (Legrand)
Secret Popular Character. See Kakureta ninkimono, 1959
Secret Service, 1931 (Cronjager; Steiner)
Secret Service of the Air, 1939 (McCord)
Secret Seven. See Invincibili sette, 1964
"The Secret Sharer" and "The Bride Comes to Yellow Sky" cps. of Face to Face, 1952 (Friedhofer)
Secret Six, 1931 (Marion; Mayer; Warner)
Secret Stranger. See Rough Ridin' Rangers, 1935
Secret Voice, 1936 (Havelock-Allan)
Secret War of Harry Frigg, 1968 (Bumstead; Head; Metty)
Secret Ways, 1961 (Williams)
Secrets d'alcove, 1953 (Amidei; Burel; Matras)
Secrets of a Secretary, 1931 (Green; Zukor)
Secrets of a Soul. See Geheimnisse einer Seele, 1926
Secrets of an Actress, 1938 (Epstein; Gaudio; Orry-Kelly)
Secrets of Life, 1956 (Iwerks)
Secrets of Paris, 1922 (Stradling)
Secrets of the French Police, 1932 (Plunkett; Steiner)
Secrets of the Underground, 1943 (Mainwaring)
Secrets, 1924 (Gaudio; Marion; Schenck; Westmore Family)
Secrets, 1933 (Adrian; Day; Marion; Newman)
Secrets, 1942 (Honegger; Matras)
Secrets, 1982 (Puttnam)
Secte de Marrakech. See Brigade mondaine, 1979
Section speciale, 1975 (Douy; Semprun)
Sécurité et hygiène du travail dans la fabrication du sucre et de l'alcool, 1952 (Fradetal)
Sed Lodge, 1968 (Storaro)
Sedan Chair in the Mist. See Oboro kago, 1951
Sedmi kontinent, 1966 (Vukotić)
Sedotta e abbandonata, 1964 (Cristaldi)
Seduced and Abandoned. See Sedotta e abbandonata, 1964
Seduction, 1982 (Schifrin)
Seduction of Gine, 1984 (Newman)
Seduction of Joe Tynan, 1979 (Conti)
Seduttore, 1955 (Cristaldi)
See American Thirst, 1930 (Miller)
See Here, Private Hargrove, 1944 (Goosson; Irene)
See How They Run, 1964 (Schifrin)
See How They Won, 1935 (Iwerks)
See No Evil. See Blind Terror, 1971

See the World, 1934 (Terry)
See Ya Later Gladiator, 1968 (Blanc)
See You in Hell, Darling. See American Dream, 1966
See You in the Morning, 1989 (Jenkins; McAlpine)
Seedling. See Ankur, 1974
Seeds of Silver, 1913 (Selig)
Seein' Things, 1924 (Roach)
Seeing Ghosts, 1948 (Terry)
Seeing Nellie Home, 1924 (Roach)
Seekers, 1954 (Alwyn; Rank; Unsworth)
Seelenverkäufer, 1919 (Dreier)
Seelische Konstruktionen, 1927 (Fischinger)
Seema , 1957 (Chandragupta)
Seemabaddha, 1971 (Dutta)
Seems Like Old Times, 1980 (Booth; Hamlisch; Stark)
Seger i mörker, 1954 (Fischer)
Segno di Venere, 1955 (Flaiano and Pinelli; Zavattini)
Segreto di stato, 1995 (Donaggio)
Sehnsucht, 1920 (Hoffmann)
Sehnsucht des Herzens, 1950 (Warm)
Sehnsucht jeder Frau, 1930 (Kräly)
Seigenki, 1972 (Takemitsu)
Seigneurs des mers du sud, 1968 (Braunberger)
Sein grösster Bluff, 1927 (Galeen)
Sein ist das Gericht, 1922 (Metzner)
Sein Scheidungsgrund, 1931 (Planer)
Seine Beichte, 1919 (Dreier)
Seine et ses marchands, 1953 (Braunberger)
Seine Frau, die Unbekannte, 1923 (Pommer)
Seine Hoheit, der Eintänzer, 1927 (Reisch)
Seine Majestat das Bettelkind, 1920 (Korda)
Seine offizielle Frau. See Eskapade, 1936
Seins de glace, 1974 (Sarde)
Seishoku no ishique, 1978 (Muraki)
Seishun no koro, 1933 (Yoda)
Scishun no mon, 1975 (Muraki)
Seishun no mon: Jiritsu hen, 1977 (Muraki)
Sekai dai senso, 1961 (Tsuburaya)
Sekretär der Königin, 1916 (Messter)
Seksolatki, 1971 (scibor-Rylski)
Sel de la terre, 1950 (Fradetal)
Selena, 1997 (Grusin)
Self-Portraits. See Autoportrét, 1988
Self Service, 1974 (Bozzetto)
Selfish Yates, 1918 (August; Sullivan)
Seligettes, 1913 (Selig)
Selima, 1934 (Burman)
Sell 'em Cowboy, 1924 (Canutt)
Selling of America. See Beer, 1985
Selskaya uchitelnitsa, 1947 (Urusevsky)
Semaine en France, 1963 (Guillemot)
Semi-Tough, 1977 (Bernstein; Lardner)
Seminole, 1953 (Metty)
Sen-hime, 1954 (Hayasaka)
Sen no rikyu, 1989 (Yoda)
Sen noci svatojánské, 1959 (Brdečka; Trnka)
Senator Was Indiscreet, 1947 (Johnson; Leven; MacArthur)
Senba-zuru, 1953 (Miyagawa)
Send Me No Flowers, 1964 (Bacharach; Epstein; Louis)
Sengoku dawara, 1950 (Yoda)
Senilita, 1961 (Flaiano and Pinelli)
Seniors, Juniors, Colleagues. See Uwayaku shitayaku godouyaku, 1959
Senjin, 1935 (Miyagawa)
Senjo no merii kurisumasu, 1983 (Toda)
Senka the African, 1927 (Ivanov-Vano)
Sennichimae fukin, 1945 (Yoda)

Senor Americano, 1929 (McCord)
Senor Daredevil, 1926 (Polito)
Señor de Osanto, 1972 (Figueroa)
Señor Droopy, 1949 (Avery)
Señor fotografo, 1952 (Figueroa)
Senorella and the Glass Huarache, 1964 (Blanc)
Sensations, 1977 (Godfrey)
Sense and Sensibility, 1995 (Schamus)
Sense of Freedom, 1981 (Menges)
Sensitive, Passionate Man, 1977 (Conti)
Senso, 1954 (Aldo; Cecchi D'amico; Krasker; Rota; Rotunno; Serandrei)
Sensualità, 1951 (Gherardi; Ponti; de Laurentiis)
Sensuikan T-57, 1959 (Tsuburaya)
Sentence, 1959 (Decaë; Evein; Saulnier)
Sentimental Journey, 1946 (Hoffenstein)
Sentinel, 1977 (Smith)
Sentinel Asleep, 1911 (Gaudio)
Sentinelle endormie, 1965 (Auric)
Senza buccia, 1979 (Donaggio)
Senza cielo, 1940 (Zavattini)
Senza famiglia nullatenenti, cercano affetto . . . , 1972 (Age and Scarpelli)
Senza pietà, 1948 (Flaiano and Pinelli; Gherardi; Ponti; Rota)
Senza sapere niente di lei, 1969 (Cecchi D'amico; Morricone)
Separate Beds. See Wheeler Dealers, 1963
Separate Tables, 1958 (Head; Horner; Lang; Raksin; Rattigan)
Separate Vacations, 1986 (Zimmer)
Sepolta viva, 1973 (Morricone)
Seppuku, 1962 (Takemitsu; Toda)
Sept Chateaux du diable, 1901 (Pathé)
Sept fois femme. See Woman Times Seven, 1967
Sept morts par ordonnance, 1976 (Sarde)
Sept Pechés capitaux, 1910 (Gaumont)
Sept Péchés capitaux, 1952 (Aurenche and Bost; Spaak; Trauner; Wakhévitch)
Sept Péchés capitaux, 1962 (Decaë; Douy; Evein; Legrand; Rabier)
September, 1987 (Loquasto)
September 30, 1955, 1977 (Rosenman; Willis)
September Affair, 1950 (Dreier; Head; Lang; Wallis; Young)
September in the Rain, 1937 (Stalling)
September Storm, 1960 (Haskin; Leven)
Septième Porte, 1946 (Aurenche and Bost; Auric)
Septima's Ideal. See Ideál Septimy, 1938
Septs Péchés capitaux, 1952 (Douy)
Séquestrée, 1908 (Cohl)
Sequoia, 1935 (Stothart)
Serafino, 1968 (Flaiano and Pinelli)
Seraglio, 1958 (Reiniger)
Serenade, 1921 (Menzies)
Serenade, 1927 (Vajda)
Serenade. See Broadway Serenade, 1939
Serenade, 1956 (Blanke; Cahn)
Sérénade aux nuages, 1946 (Wakhévitch)
Serenade einer grossen Liebe, 1958 (Maté)
Serenal*, 1959 (McClaren)
Serene Siam, 1937 (Hoch)
Serge Panine, 1922 (Kolowrat-Krakowsky)
Sergeant Byrne of the N.W.M.P., 1912 (Selig)
Sergeant Deadhead, 1965 (Crosby)
Sergeant Madden, 1939 (Seitz)
Sergeant Murphy, 1938 (McCord)
Sergeant Rutledge, 1960 (Glennon)
Sergeant Ryker, 1968 (Williams)
Sergeant York, 1941 (Edeson; Friedhofer; Koch; Lasky; Polito; Steiner; Wallis)
Sergeant's Boy, 1912 (Ince)
Sergeants Three, 1962 (Hoch)

Sergent X . . . , 1959 (Auric; Renoir)
Serial, 1980 (Schifrin)
Série des bouts de Zari, 1913 (Gaumont)
Sérieux comme le plaisir, 1974 (Carrière)
Serious Charge, 1959 (Périnal)
Serious Sixteen, 1910 (Bitzer)
Serp i molet, 1921 (Tisse)
Serpent, 1972 (Morricone; Renoir; Saulnier)
Serpent's Egg. See Schlangenei, 1977
Serpent's Kiss, 1997 (Rousselot)
Serpico, 1973 (Allen; Theodorakis; de Laurentiis)
Serpico: The Deadly Game, 1976 (Bernstein)
Servant, 1963 (Hambling; Pinter; Slocombe)
Servant. See Sluga, 1988
Servants' Entrance, 1934 (Friedhofer; Mohr; Raphaelson)
Service for Ladies, 1927 (Rosson; Vajda)
Service for Ladies, 1932 (Biro; Junge; Korda; Vajda; Zukor)
Service with a Smile, 1937 (Fleischer)
Ses Ancêtres, 1915 (Cohl)
Sesso in confessionale, 1974 (Morricone)
Set-Up, 1949 (D'Agostino; Krasner)
Sete Balas para Selma, 1967 (de Almeida)
Setkání v Bukurešti, 1954 (Stallich)
Setouchi shounen yakyu-dan, 1984 (Miyagawa)
Setta, 1992 (Donaggio)
Sette chili in sette giorni, 1986 (Donaggio)
Sette donne per i MacGregor, 1966 (Morricone)
Sette pistole per i MacGregor, 1966 (Morricone)
Sette volte donna, 1967 (Zavattini)
Seul Amour, 1943 (Honegger; Matras)
Sève de la terre, 1955 (Alexeieff and Parker)
Seven Ages of Man , 1906 (Ince)
Seven Arts, 1958 (Popescu-Gopo)
Seven Beauties. See Pasqualino Settebellezza, 1975
Seven Brides for Seven Brothers, 1954 (Deutsch; Gillespie; Goodrich and Hackett; Kidd; Mercer; Plunkett)
Seven Brothers Meet Dracula. See Legend of the Seven Golden Vampires, 1974
Seven Capital Sins. See Sept Péchés capitaux, 1952
Seven Capital Sins. See Sept Péchés capitaux, 1962
Seven Chances, 1925 (Bruckman; Mayer; Schenck)
Seven Cities of Gold, 1955 (Ballard; Friedhofer; Lemaire; Smith)
Seven Days Ashore, 1944 (Metty)
Seven Days in May, 1963 (Goldsmith; Houseman)
Seven Days Leave, 1930 (Lang)
Seven Days to Noon, 1950 (Bernard; Korda)
Seven Deadly Sins. See Sept Péchés capitaux, 1952
Seven Deadly Sins. See Sept Péchés capitaux, 1962
Seven Faces, 1929 (August; Friedhofer)
Seven Faces of Dr. Lao , 1964 (Pal)
Seven Footprints to Satan, 1929 (Polito)
Seven Guns for the MacGregors. See Sette pistole per i MacGregor, 1966
Seven Hills of Rome, 1957 (Delli Colli)
Seven Indians. See Saat Hindustani, 1970
Seven Keys to Baldpate, 1929 (Cronjager; Plunkett)
Seven Keys to Baldpate, 1935 (Plunkett; Polglase; Veiller)
Seven Little Foys, 1955 (Head)
Seven Magnificent Gladiators, 1984 (Golan and Globus; Morricone)
Seven Men from Now, 1956 (Clothier)
Seven Minutes, 1989 (Delerue)
Seven Nights in Japan, 1976 (Decaë)
Seven Pearls, 1917 (Grot)
Seven-Per-Cent Solution, 1976 (Adam; Morris; Reynolds)
Seven Samurai. See **Shichinin no samurai**, 1954
Seven Seas to Calais. See Dominatore dei sette mari, 1960
Seven Sinners, 1936 (Balcon; Metzner; Rank)

Seven Sinners, 1940 (Irene; Maté; Pasternak)
Seven Sweethearts, 1942 (Pasternak; Reisch; Waxman)
Seven Thieves, 1960 (Spencer; Wheeler)
Seven Thunders, 1957 (Rank)
Seven Till Five, 1934-35 (McClaren)
Seven Women from Hell, 1961 (Crosby)
Seven Women, 1965 (La Shelle; Plunkett)
Seven Wonders of the World, 1956 (Raksin)
Seven Year Itch, 1955 (Bass; Cahn; Krasner; Lemaire; Newman; Wheeler)
Seven Years in Tibet, 1997 (Williams)
Seventeen, 1917 (Zukor)
Seventeen, 1940 (Dreier; Head)
Seventh Bandit, 1926 (Polito)
Seventh Cavalry, 1956 (Rennahan)
Seventh Continent. See Sedmi kontinent, 1966
Seventh Cross, 1944 (Berman; Freund; Gibbons; Irene; Mayer)
Seventh Dawn, 1964 (Young)
Seventh Day, 1909 (Bitzer)
Seventh Man, 1943 (Lewton)
Seventh Seal. See Det sjunde inseglet, 1957
Seventh Sign, 1988 (Nitzsche)
Seventh Sin, 1957 (Neame; Rose; Rozsa)
Seventh Veil, 1945 (Mathieson; Rank)
Seventh Victim, 1943 (D'Agostino; Musuraca)
Seventh Voyage of Sinbad, 1958 (Harryhausen; Herrmann)
Severní přístav, 1954 (Brdečka)
Severnoe siianie, 1926 (Enei)
Sevres Porcelain. See Porcelaines tendres, 1909
Sex, 1920 (Barnes; Sullivan)
Sex and the Married Woman, 1977 (Head)
Sex and the Single Girl, 1964 (Head; Lang)
Sex Hygiene, 1941 (Barnes)
Sex, Love and Marriage. See Love and Marriage, 1970
Sex O'Clock U.S.A., 1976 (Braunberger)
Sex Power, 1970 (Vangelis)
Sex Shop, 1973 (Lhomme)
Sex Symbol, 1974 (Lai; Mancini)
Sextette, 1978 (Head)
Sexual Perversity in Chicago. See About Last Night. . . , 1986
Sfida, 1958 (Cecchi D'amico; Cristaldi; Di Venanzo)
Sguardo di Ulisse. See To vlemma tou odyssea, 1995
SH-H-H-H, 1955 (Avery)
Shabnam, 1949 (Burman)
Shachou koukou-ko, 1962 (Muraki)
Shachou sandai-ki, 1958 (Muraki)
Shack Out on 101, 1955 (Crosby)
Shadow, 1937 (Ballard; Goosson)
Shadow. See Cień, 1956
Shadow, 1994 (Goldsmith)
Shadow Box, 1981 (Mancini)
Shadow in Light. See Stín ve svetle, 1928
Shadow in the Sky, 1951 (Kaper; Maddow)
Shadow Makers. See Fat Man and Little Boy, 1989
Shadow of a Doubt, 1943 (Adrian; Boyle; Reville; Tiomkin)
Shadow of a Woman, 1946 (Deutsch; Glennon)
Shadow of Adultery. See Proie pour l'ombre, 1960
Shadow of Darkness. See Yami no Kageboushi, 1938
Shadow of Doubt, 1935 (Clarke)
Shadow of Lightning Ridge, 1920 (Glennon)
Shadow of the Cat, 1961 (Theodorakis)
Shadow of the Eagle, 1932 (Canutt)
Shadow of the Eagle, 1950 (Havelock-Allan)
Shadow of the Law, 1930 (Lang)
Shadow of the Past, 1913 (Ince; Sullivan)
Shadow of the Thin Man, 1941 (Daniels; Stromberg)

Shadow of the Wolf, 1993 (Jarre)
Shadow on the Wall, 1949 (Irene)
Shadow on the Window, 1957 (Duning)
Shadow Ranch, 1930 (McCord)
Shadow Warrior. See Kagemusha, 1980
Shadows and Fog, 1992 (Loquasto)
Shadows of Fear. See Thérèse Raquin, 1928
Shadows on the Sage, 1942 (Canutt)
Shadows. See Stíny, 1921
Shadows, 1923 (Fleischer)
Shady Lady, 1945 (Mohr; Siodmak)
Shaft, 2000 (Von Brandenstein)
Shaggy Dog, 1959 (Disney)
Shahen Shah, 1953 (Burman)
Shake 'em Up, 1921 (Roach)
Shake Hands with the Devil, 1959 (Alwyn)
Shakespeare Wallah, 1965 (Jhabvala; Merchant; Mitra)
Shakespearian Spinach, 1940 (Fleischer)
Shakha Proshakha, 1990 (Dutta)
Shakiest Gun in the West, 1968 (Whitlock)
Shakmatnaya goryachka, 1925 (Golovnya)
Shalako, 1968 (Mathieson)
Shall We Dance, 1937 (Berman; Pan; Polglase)
Sham Battle Shenanigans, 1942 (Terry)
Shame. See Skammen, 1968
Shameful Behavior?, 1926 (Musuraca)
Shampoo, 1975 (Justin; Kovacs; Sylbert, Towne)
Shamrock and Roll, 1969 (Blanc; McKimson)
Shamus, 1972 (Goldsmith)
Shane, 1953 (Head; Hornbeck; Pereira; Young)
Shanghai, 1935 (Wanger)
Shanghai Bound, 1927 (Cronjager)
Shanghai Drama. See Drame de Shanghaï, 1938
Shanghai Express, 1932 (Banton; Dreier; Furthman; Garmes; Zukor)
Shanghai Gesture, 1941 (Furthman; Leven)
Shanghai Lady, 1929 (Mohr)
Shanghai Madness, 1933 (Garmes)
Shanghai Story, 1954 (Miller)
Shanghaied, 1927 (Plunkett; Walker)
Shanks, 1974 (Biroc; Leven; North)
Shantata, Court Chalu Ahe, 1970 (Nihalani)
Share Cropper. See Hari Hondal Burgadar, 1980
Shark, 1920 (Ruttenberg)
Shark Monroe, 1918 (August; Sullivan)
Shark Reef. See She-Gods of Shark Reef, 1957
Shark River, 1953 (Cortez)
Sharkey's Machine, 1982 (Fraker)
Sharkfighters, 1956 (Garmes; Mandell)
Sharma and Beyond, 1983 (Puttnam)
Sharmeelee, 1971 (Burman)
Sharp Shooters, 1928 (Clarke)
Sharpshooter, 1913 (Ince)
Shatranj Ke Khilari, 1977 (Chandragupta; Dutta)
Shattered. See Scherben, 1921
Shattered, 1991 (Kovacs)
Shattered Idols, 1921 (Gaudio)
Shattered Image, 1998 (Müller)
Shawshank Redemption, 1994 (Newman)
She, 1935 (Cooper; Dunn; Newman; Polglase; Steiner)
She, 1965 (Bernard; Carreras)
She and He. See Blaho lásky, 1965
She and He. See Kanojo to kare, 1963
She Asked for It, 1937 (Head; Shamroy)
She Couldn't Say No, 1941 (McCord)
She Couldn't Say No, 1954 (Orry-Kelly)
She Couldn't Take It, 1935 (Cohn; Goosson; Shamroy)

She Devil, 1957 (Struss)
She-Devil, 1989 (Loquasto)
She Done Him Wrong, 1933 (Head; Lang; Zukor)
She Done Him Wrong. *See* Villain Still Pursued Her, 1940
She Fell Fainting in His Arms, 1903 (Bitzer)
She Gets Her Man, 1935 (D'Agostino)
She Gets Her Man, 1945 (Bruckman)
She-Gods of Shark Reef, 1957 (Crosby)
She Goes to War, 1929 (D'Agostino; Gaudio; Saunders)
She Had to Say Yes, 1933 (Orry-Kelly)
She Is Like a Rainbow, 1969 (Müller)
She Lives to Ride, 1994 (Daring)
She Loves Me Not, 1918 (Roach)
She Loves Me Not, 1934 (Lang)
She Made Her Bed, 1934 (Krasner)
She Married an Artist, 1937 (Buchman; Goosson)
She Married Her Boss, 1935 (Buchman; Cohn; Goosson; Shamroy)
She Played with Fire. *See* Fortune Is a Woman, 1956
She Reminds Me of You, 1934 (Fleischer)
She Wanted a Millionaire, 1932 (Levien; Seitz)
She Was a Lady, 1934 (Glennon; Spencer)
She Was an Acrobat's Daughter, 1937 (Stalling)
She Went to the Races, 1945 (Irene)
She-Wolf. *See* Lupa, 1953
She Wore a Yellow Ribbon, 1949 (Basevi; Cooper; Hoch; Nugent)
She Wouldn't Say Yes, 1945 (Banton; Goosson; Polglase; Walker)
She Wronged Him Right, 1934 (Fleischer)
Sheep Ahoy, 1954 (Blanc; Jones; Stalling)
Sheep in the Deep, 1962 (Blanc; Jones)
Sheep in the Meadow, 1939 (Terry)
Sheep Stealers Anonymous, 1963 (Hanna and Barbera)
Sheepish Wolf, 1942 (Blanc)
Sheepman, 1958 (Plunkett)
Shéhérazade, 1963 (Matras; Wakhévitch)
Sheik, 1922 (Zukor)
Sheila Levine Is Dead and Living in New York, 1975 (Legrand)
Shell '43, 1916 (Sullivan)
She'll Have to Go, 1962 (Hambling)
Shell Shocked Egg, 1948 (Blanc; McKimson; Stalling)
Sheltering Sky, 1990 (Storaro)
Shenandoah, 1965 (Clothier; Whitlock)
Shenanigans, 1977 (Lassally)
Shepherd of the Hills, 1928 (Polito)
Shepherd of the Hills, 1941 (Dreier; Head; Lang)
Sher Ka Panja, 1936 (Biswas)
Sheriff of Cimarron, 1945 (Canutt)
Sheriff of Fractured Jaw, 1958 (Heller)
Sheriff's Adopted Child, 1912 (Ince)
Sheriff's Baby, 1913 (Bitzer)
Sherlock Holmes, 1932 (Barnes; Friedhofer)
Sherlock Holmes. *See* Adventures of Sherlock Holmes, 1939
Sherlock Holmes and the Deadly Necklace. *See* Sherlock Holmes und das Halsband des Todes, 1962
Sherlock Holmes in New York, 1976 (Bennett)
Sherlock Holmes und das Halsband des Todes, 1962 (Siodmak)
Sherlock, Jr., 1924 (Bruckman; Mayer; Schenck)
Sherlock Pink, 1976 (McKimson)
Sherlock Sleuth, 1925 (Roach)
Sherman Said It, 1933 (Roach)
Sherman Was Right, 1932 (Terry)
Sherriff's Son, 1919 (Ince)
She's Back on Broadway, 1953 (Blanke)
She's Dangerous, 1937 (Krasner; Raksin)
She's Gotta Have It, 1986 (Dickerson)
She's No Lady, 1937 (Head)
She's the One, 1996 (Schamus)

She's the Only One. *See* Hon den enda, 1926
She's Working Her Way Through College, 1952 (Cahn)
Shi no dangai, 1951 (Hayasaka)
Shiawase, 1974 (Takemitsu)
Shichinin no samurai, 1954 (Hayasaka)
Shido monogatari, 1941 (Hayasaka)
Shifrovanny Document, 1928 (Ptushko)
Shikari, 1945 (Burman)
Shikko yuyo, 1950 (Hayasaka)
Shimau-boshi, 1950 (Yoda)
Shin akumýo, 1961 (Yoda)
Shin Heike monogatari, 1955 (Hayasaka; Miyagawa; Yoda)
Shine 'em Up, 1922 (Roach)
Shine On Harvest Moon, 1932 (Fleischer)
Shine On, Harvest Moon, 1944 (Edeson; Wald)
Shinel, 1926 (Enei; Moskvin)
Shining, 1980 (Alcott)
Shining Hour, 1938 (Adrian; Waxman)
Shining Victory, 1941 (Howe; Koch; Steiner; Wallis)
Shinju ten no amijima, 1969 (Takemitsu)
Shinjuku dorobo nikki, 1969 (Toda)
Shinrei Jakouneko, 1940 (Miyagawa)
Shiobara tasuke , 1930 (Tsuburaya)
Ship Comes In, 1928 (Adrian; Grot; Levien)
Ship from Shanghai, 1930 (Gibbons)
Ship o' the Doom, 1954 (Haskin)
Ship of Fools, 1965 (Edouart; Laszlo; Louis; Tavoularis; Whitlock)
Ship That Died of Shame, 1955 (Alwyn)
Shipmates Forever, 1935 (Orry-Kelly; Polito)
Shipping News, 2001 (Bass; Winkler)
Ships. *See* Chuzhoy pidzhak, 1927
Ships with Wings, 1941 (Balcon)
Shipwrecked, 1931 (Lantz)
Shipyard Symphony, 1943 (Terry)
Shirai gonpachi, 1928 (Tsuburaya)
Shirasagi, 1941 (Hayasaka)
Shiriboe Sonichi, 1969 (Miyagawa)
Shirikurae Magoichi, 1969 (Miyagawa)
Shirley Valentine, 1989 (Hamlisch)
Shiro to kuro, 1963 (Takemitsu)
Shiroi ane, 1931 (Yoda)
Shiroi asa, 1964 (Takemitsu)
Shiroi hekiga, 1942 (Tsuburaya)
Shishkabugs, 1962 (Blanc)
Shiver and Shake, 1922 (Roach)
Shiver Me Timbers!, 1934 (Fleischer)
Shiver My Timbers, 1931 (Roach)
Shivering Shakespeare, 1929 (Roach)
Shivering Spooks, 1926 (Roach)
Shock, 1946 (Leven)
Shock, 1972 (Carreras)
Shock Corridor, 1963 (Cortez; Lourié)
Shock Punch, 1925 (Saunders)
Shock Treatment, 1964 (Smith)
Shocking Incident, 1903 (Bitzer)
Shocking Miss Pilgrim, 1947 (Basevi; Leven; Newman; Orry-Kelly; Raksin; Shamroy)
Shockproof, 1949 (Duning; Louis)
Shoe Shine Jasper, 1946 (Pal)
Shoein' Hosses, 1934 (Fleischer)
Shoemaker and the Hatter, 1949 (Halas and Batchelor)
Shoes, 1916 (Clarke)
Shoes of the Fisherman, 1968 (North)
Shoeshine. *See* **Sciuscià**, 1946
Shokei no shima, 1966 (Takemitsu; Toda)
Shokutaku no nai ie, 1985 (Takemitsu; Toda)

Skidoo, 1969 (Shamroy)
Skin. *See* Pelle, 1981
Skin Deep, 1989 (Kidd)
Skin Game, 1931 (Reville)
Skinny Gets a Goat, 1917 (Roach)
Skinny's False Alarm, 1917 (Roach)
Skinny's Shipwrecked Sand-Witch, 1917 (Roach)
Skip the Maloo, 1931 (Roach)
Skipper. *See* Todd Killings, 1971
Skipper of the Osprey, 1933 (Dean)
Skipper Surprised His Wife, 1950 (Kaper)
Skippy, 1931 (Struss; Zukor)
Skirmish on the Home Front, 1944 (Brackett)
Skirt Chaser. *See* Cavaleur, 1978
Skirt Shy, 1929 (Roach)
Skirts Ahoy!, 1952 (Pasternak; Rose)
Sklavenkönigin, 1924 (Kolowrat-Krakowsky)
Skola, základ života, 1938 (Stallich)
Skottet, 1914 (Jaenzon)
Skull, 1965 (Francis)
Skullduggery, 1970 (Head; Whitlock)
Sky Bandits, 1986 (Watkin)
Sky Boy, 1929 (Roach)
Sky Devils, 1932 (Gaudio; Newman)
Sky Is Falling, 1947 (Terry)
Sky Is Red. *See* Cielo è rosso, 1950
Sky Larks, 1934 (Lantz)
Sky over Berlin. *See* **Himmel über Berlin**, 1987
Sky Pilot, 1924 (Lantz)
Sky Plumber, 1924 (Roach)
Sky Princess, 1942 (Pal)
Sky Riders, 1976 (Schifrin)
Sky Scraping, 1930 (Fleischer)
Sky Scrappers, 1928 (Disney)
Sky, West, and Crooked, 1966 (Arnold; Dillon)
Sky Will Fall. *See* Cielo Cade, 2000
Sky's No Limit, 1984 (Jarre)
Sky's the Limit, 1937 (Garmes)
Sky's the Limit, 1943 (Mercer; Metty)
Skylark, 1941 (Dreier; Head; Irene; Lang; Young)
Skylight Sleep, 1916 (Roach)
Skyline, 1931 (Friedhofer; Nichols)
Skyrider, 1976 (Halas and Batchelor)
Skyscraper, 1928 (Adrian; Goosson)
Skyscraper Caper, 1968 (Blanc)
Skyscraper Souls, 1932 (Daniels; Sullivan)
Skywayman, 1920 (Furthman)
Sladká Josefínka, 1927 (Heller)
Slander the Woman, 1923 (Haskin)
Slanked Again, 1936 (Terry)
Slap. *See* Gifle, 1974
Slap Happy Hunters, 1941 (Terry)
Slap Happy Lion, 1947 (Avery)
Slap Happy Pappy, 1940 (Blanc; Clampett; Stalling)
Slap Shot, 1977 (Allen; Bernstein)
Slap-Hoppy Mouse, 1956 (Blanc; McKimson; Stalling)
Slapstick of Another Kind, 1984 (Legrand)
Slashed Yosaburo. *See* Kirare Yosaburou, 1960
Slates of the Tenpyo Period. *See* Tenpyo no iraka, 1979
Slattery's Hurricane, 1949 (Clarke; Wheeler)
Slaughterhouse-Five, 1972 (Allen; Bumstead; Ondříček)
Sláva, 1960 (Brdečka)
Slave, 1909 (Bitzer)
Slave Girls, 1968 (Carreras)
Slave of Dreams, 1995 (de Laurentiis)
Slave of Fashion, 1925 (Gibbons)

Slave Queen. *See* Sklavenkönigin, 1924
Slave Ship, 1937 (Johnson; Miller; Newman; Trotti)
Slave's Devotion, 1913 (Ince)
Slaves of New York, 1989 (Comden and Green; Merchant)
Slavka, Don't Give In!. *See* Slávko, nedej se!, 1938
Slávko, nedej se!, 1938 (Heller)
Slay It with Flowers, 1943 (Fleischer)
Slečna od vody, 1959 (Stallich)
Sledgehammer, 1986 (Park)
Sleeper, 1973 (Rosenblum)
Sleepers, 1996 (Ballhaus; Williams)
Sleeping Beauty, 1954 (Reiniger)
Sleeping Beauty, 1958 (Disney; Iwerks)
Sleeping Beauty, 1960 (Halas and Batchelor)
Sleeping Beauty, 1987 (Golan and Globus)
Sleeping Car, 1933 (Balcon; Junge)
Sleeping Car to Trieste, 1949 (Rank)
Sleeping Prince. *See* Prince and the Showgirl, 1957
Sleeping Tiger, 1954 (Arnold)
Sleeping Tiger, 1955 (Foreman)
Sleeping with the Enemy, 1991 (Bass; Goldsmith)
Sleepless in Seattle, 1993 (Nykvist)
Sleepless Night, 1948 (Terry)
Sleepy Head, 1921 (Roach)
Sleepy Hollow, 1999 (Elfman; Hall)
Sleepy Time Down South, 1932 (Fleischer)
Sleepy Time Possum, 1951 (Blanc; McKimson; Stalling)
Sleepy-Time Tom, 1951 (Hanna and Barbera)
Sleigh Bells, 1928 (Disney)
Slender Thread, 1965 (Head; Jones)
Sleuth, 1922 (Roach)
Sleuth, 1972 (Adam; Morris)
Slick Chick, 1962 (Blanc; McKimson)
Slick Hare, 1947 (Blanc; Stalling)
Slicked-Up Pup, 1951 (Hanna and Barbera)
Slide, Kelly, Slide, 1927 (Gibbons)
Slides, 1919 (Fleischer)
Slight Case of Murder, 1938 (Wallis)
Slightly Daffy, 1944 (Blanc; Clampett; Stalling)
Slightly Dangerous, 1943 (Berman; Irene; Kaper; Lederer; Rosson)
Slightly French, 1949 (Duning)
Slightly Honorable, 1940 (Banton; Spencer; Wanger)
Slightly Pregnant Man. *See* Evènement le plus important depuis que
    l'homme a marché sur la lune, 1973
Slightly Scarlet, 1930 (Banton)
Slightly Scarlet, 1956 (Alton; Polglase)
Slightly Static, 1935 (Roach)
Slightly Used, 1927 (Mohr)
Slim, 1937 (Steiner; Wallis)
Slingshot 67/8, 1951 (Lantz)
Slippery McGee, 1923 (Clarke)
Slippery Slickers, 1920 (Roach)
Slippery Slippers, 1962 (Hanna and Barbera)
Slipping Wives, 1927 (Roach)
Slipstream, 1989 (Bernstein)
Slither, 1973 (Kovacs)
Sliver, 1993 (Eszterhas; Kovacs; Zsigmond)
Slocum Disaster, 1904 (Bitzer)
Sloppy Jalopy, 1952 (Bosustow; Hubley; Raksin)
Slovácká suita, 1976 (Ondříček)
Slóvce M, 1964 (Brdečka)
Slovo dlia zashchity, 1976 (Mindadze)
Slow but Sure, 1934 (Terry)
Slow Dancing in the Big City, 1978 (Conti)
Sluchi na stadione, 1929 (Ptushko)
Sluga, 1988 (Mindadze)

Slugger's Wife, 1985 (Booth; Jones; Stark)
Slum Boy. *See* Ragazzo di borgata, 1976
Slumberland Express, 1936 (Lantz)
Slump Is Over. *See* Crise est finie, 1934
Slut, 1966 (Fischer)
Smagliature. *See* Faille, 1975
Smålänningar, 1935 (Fischer; Jaenzon)
Small Back Room, 1948 (Challis; Francis; Heckroth; Korda)
Small Czechoslovak Icon. *See* Československý ježíšek, 1918
Small Fry, 1939 (Fleischer)
Small Soldiers, 1998 (Goldsmith)
Small Talk, 1993 (Godfrey)
Small Time Crooks, 2000 (Loquasto)
Small Timers. *See* Ringards, 1978
Small Town Deb, 1941 (Miller)
Small Town Girl, 1936 (Gibbons; Gillespie; Goodrich and Hackett; Rosher; Stothart; Stromberg)
Small Town Girl, 1953 (Pasternak; Previn; Rose; Ruttenberg)
Small Town Idol, 1921 (Hornbeck)
Small Voice, 1948 (Havelock-Allan)
Smallest Show on Earth, 1957 (Alwyn; Slocombe)
Smart Girl, 1935 (Wanger)
Smart Girls Don't Talk, 1948 (Burks; McCord)
Smart Money, 1931 (Zanuck)
Smart Set, 1928 (Gibbons)
Smart Woman, 1931 (Musuraca)
Smart Woman, 1948 (Adrian; Cortez)
Smarty, 1934 (Barnes; Orry-Kelly)
Smarty Cat, 1955 (Hanna and Barbera)
Smash en direct, 1962 (Auric)
Smash Up, 1947 (Banton; Cortez)
Smash-Up on Interstate 5, 1976 (Conti)
Smash-Up: The Story of a Woman, 1947 (Wanger)
Smashing the Crime Syndicate. *See* Hell's Blood Devils, 1968
Smashing the Rackets, 1938 (Musuraca)
Smashing Through. *See* Cheyenne Cyclone, 1932
Smashing Time, 1967 (Ponti)
S'matter, Pete?, 1927 (Lantz)
Smic, Smac, Smoc, 1971 (Lai)
Smile, 1974 (Hall; Kidd)
Smile of the Child, 1911 (Bitzer)
Smile Wins, 1927 (Roach)
Smiles, 1929 (Fleischer)
Smiles of a Summer Night. *See* **Sommarnattens leende**, 1955
Smiley, 1956 (Alwyn; Korda)
Smilin' Through, 1922 (Rosher; Schenck; Westmore Family)
Smilin' Through, 1932 (Adrian; Garmes; Mayer; Stewart; Vajda)
Smilin' Through, 1941 (Adrian; Mayer; Stewart; Stothart)
Smilin' Thru, 1932 (Booth)
Smiling Irish Eyes, 1929 (Grot)
Smiling Lieutenant, 1931 (Deutsch; Dreier; Green; Raphaelson; Ruttenberg; Vajda; Zukor)
Smilla's Sense of Snow. *See* Fräulein Smillas Gespür für Schnee, 1997
Smith, Our Friend, 1946 (Lassally)
Smith's Army Life, 1928 (Hornbeck)
Smith's Boby's Birthday, 1928 (Hornbeck)
Smith's Farm Days, 1928 (Hornbeck)
Smith's Holiday, 1928 (Hornbeck)
Smith's Restaurant, 1928 (Hornbeck)
Smithsonian Institution, 1965 (Bernstein)
Smithy, 1924 (Roach)
Smitten Kitten, 1952 (Hanna and Barbera)
Smoked Husband, 1908 (Bitzer)
Smokey, 1946 (Clarke)
Smokey Joe, 1945 (Terry)
Smoking Guns, 1934 (McCord)

Smoking Lamp. *See* Lampe qui file, 1909
Smoking/No Smoking, 1993 (Saulnier)
Smoky, 1946 (Raksin)
Smoky, 1966 (Smith)
Smooth as Satin, 1925 (Berman)
Smugglers. *See* På livets ödesvägar, 1913
Smugglers. *See* Man Within, 1947
Smugglers, 1948 (Rank)
Smugglers' Lass, 1915 (Rosher)
Smuggling Ship. *See* Mitsuyu-sen, 1954
Smultronstället, 1957 (Fischer)
Smurfs and the Magic Flute. *See* Flûte à six schtroumpfs, 1976
Smutsiga fingrar, 1973 (Lundgren)
Smyatiye tsvyeti, 1915 (Starewicz)
Snadný život, 1957 (Brdečka; Ondříček)
Snafu, 1945 (Goosson; Planer)
Snaiper, 1932 (Enei)
Snake Pit, 1948 (Lemaire; Newman; Spencer; Wheeler; Zanuck)
Snakes and Ladders, 1960 (Halas and Batchelor)
Snap and the Beanstalk, 1960 (Halas and Batchelor)
Snap Goes East, 1960 (Halas and Batchelor)
Snappy Salesman, 1930 (Lantz)
Snappy Snap Shots, 1953 (Terry)
Snappy Sneezer, 1929 (Roach)
Sneak, Snoop and Snitch, 1940 (Fleischer)
Sneak, Snoop and Snitch in Triple Trouble, 1941 (Fleischer)
Sneakers, 1992 (Von Brandenstein)
Sneezing Weasel, 1937 (Avery)
Sniffles and the Bookworm, 1939 (Jones)
Sniffles Bells the Cat, 1941 (Blanc; Jones; Stalling)
Sniffles Takes a Trip, 1940 (Blanc; Jones; Stalling)
Sniper, 1952 (Guffey)
Sniper, 1993 (Zimmer)
'Sno Fun, 1951 (Terry)
Snob, 1924 (Gibbons; Mayer)
Snobs!, 1961 (Kosma)
Snoopy Loopy, 1960 (Hanna and Barbera)
Snorkel, 1958 (Carreras)
Snow Bride, 1923 (Levien)
Snow Business, 1953 (Blanc; Stalling)
Snow Creature, 1954 (Crosby)
Snow Excuse, 1966 (Blanc; McKimson)
Snow Falling on Cedars, 1999 (Bass; Marshall; Shepard)
Snow Maiden, 1952 (Ivanov-Vano)
Snow Man, 1946 (Terry)
Snow Time for Comedy, 1941 (Blanc; Jones)
Snow White, 1933 (Fleischer)
Snow White, 1987 (Golan and Globus)
Snow White and Rose Red, 1953 (Reiniger)
Snow White and the Seven Dwarfs, 1937 (Disney)
Snow White and The Three Stooges, 1961 (Shamroy; Smith)
Snowbody Loves Me, 1964 (Jones)
Snowbound, 1948 (Rank)
Snowed Under, 1923 (Stromberg)
Snowed Under, 1936 (Orry-Kelly)
Snowfire, 1958 (Fields)
Snowman, 1908 (Bitzer)
Snowman, 1940 (Terry)
Snowman's Land, 1939 (Jones)
Snows of Kilimanjaro, 1952 (Herrmann; Lemaire; Newman; Shamroy; Wheeler; Zanuck)
Snowtime, 1938 (Iwerks)
Snowy Heron. *See* Shirasagi, 1941
Snubbed by a Snob, 1940 (Fleischer)
Snyegurochka, 1913 (Starewicz)
So Big, 1924 (McCord)

So Big, 1932 (Orry-Kelly)
So Big, 1953 (Blanke; Steiner)
So Dark the Night, 1946 (Friedhofer; Guffey)
So Dear to My Heart, 1947 (Hoch; Disney)
So Does an Automobile, 1939 (Fleischer)
So endete eine Liebe, 1934 (Planer)
So Ends Our Night, 1941 (Daniels; Jennings; Menzies; Reynolds)
So Evil My Love, 1948 (Alwyn; Head; Wallis; Young)
So Fine, 1980 (Loquasto; Morricone)
So Little Time, 1952 (Morris)
So Long at the Fair, 1950 (Rank)
So Long Copper. *See* Adieu Poulet, 1975
So Long, Mr. Chumps, 1941 (Bruckman)
So Much for So Little, 1949 (Jones)
So Near Yet So Far, 1912 (Bitzer)
So Nobody Knows Hadimrsku. *See* To neznáte Hadimršku, 1931
So Proudly We Hail, 1943 (Dreier; Edouart; Lang; Rozsa)
So Red the Rose, 1935 (Banton; Dreier)
So This is Africa, 1933 (Krasna)
So This Is College, 1929 (Gibbons)
So This Is Harris!, 1933 (Glennon)
So This Is Hollywood. *See* In Hollywood with Potash and
   Perlmutter, 1924
So This Is London, 1930 (Clarke; Levien)
So This Is Love, 1928 (Cohn)
So This Is Love, 1953 (Blanke; Burks; Steiner)
So This Is Marriage, 1924 (Gibbons)
So This Is New York, 1948 (Foreman; Tiomkin)
So This Is Paris, 1926 (Kräly)
So This Is Paris, 1954 (Lourié)
So Well Remembered, 1947 (Eisler; Paxton; Rank; Young)
So's Your Uncle, 1943 (Bruckman; Krasner)
Soak the Rich, 1936 (Hecht; MacArthur; Shamroy)
Soak the Sheik, 1922 (Roach)
Soaking the Clothes, 1914 (Roach)
Soapy Opera, 1953 (Terry)
Social Celebrity, 1926 (Garmes)
Social Exile. *See* Déclassée, 1925
Social Gangster, 1914 (Roach)
Social Highwayman, 1916 (Marion)
Social Highwayman, 1926 (Zanuck)
Social Leper, 1917 (Edeson; Marion)
Social Register, 1934 (Loos)
Social Secretary, 1916 (Loos)
Socialisme et nihilisme, 1908 (Pathé)
Society, 1955 (Burman)
Society Ballooning, 1906 (Bitzer)
Society Exile, 1919 (Menzies; Miller)
Society Girl, 1932 (Barnes)
Society Lawyer, 1939 (Goodrich and Hackett)
Society Scandal, 1924 (Rosson)
Sock a Bye Baby, 1934 (Fleischer)
Sock-a-bye Baby, 1942 (Bruckman)
Sock a Doodle Doo, 1952 (Blanc; McKimson; Stalling)
Soda Squirt, 1933 (Iwerks)
Sodom and Gomorrah. *See* Sodoma e Gomorra, 1962
Sodom and Gomorrha, 1922 (Kolowrat-Krakowsky)
Sodoma e Gomorra, 1962 (Adam; Rozsa)
Soeurs Brontë, 1978 (Nuytten; Sarde)
Sofia, 1948 (Clothier)
Sofiya Perovskaya, 1967 (Shostakovich)
Soft Ball Game, 1936 (Lantz)
Soft Cushions, 1927 (Carré)
Soft Living, 1928 (August)
Soft Money, 1919 (Roach)
Soft Shoes, 1925 (Polito; Stromberg)

Soft Skin. *See* Peau douce, 1964
Sohn der Hagar, 1927 (Freund)
Sohn der weissen Berge, 1930 (Planer)
Sohn des Hannibal, 1926 (Planer)
Soho Incident, 1956 (Adam)
Soif de l'or, 1993 (Delli Colli)
Soif des bêtes, 1960 (Braunberger)
Soikina lyubov, 1927 (Moskvin)
Soikin's Love. *See* Soikina lyubov, 1927
Soilers, 1923 (Roach)
Soilers, 1932 (Roach)
Soir à Tibériade, 1966 (Kosma)
Soir de fête, 1956 (Braunberger)
Soir de notre vie, 1963 (Delerue)
Soir de rafle, 1931 (Burel)
Soir sur la plage, 1961 (Burel)
Soir, un train, 1968 (Cloquet)
Sol Madrid, 1968 (Schifrin)
Solang' es hübsche Mädchen gibt, 1955 (Herlth)
Solar Crisis, 1990 (Edlund; Jarre)
Solar Film, 1980 (Bass)
Solarbabies, 1986 (Edlund; Jarre)
Sold at Auction, 1923 (Roach)
Soldat Bom, 1948 (Fischer)
Soldatesse, 1965 (Delli Colli; Solinas)
Soldato ignoto, 1995 (Donaggio)
Soldats d'eau douce, 1950 (Cloquet)
Soldier and the Lady, 1937 (August; Berman; Plunkett; Veiller)
Soldier in the Rain, 1963 (Goldman; Lathrop; Mancini)
Soldier Man, 1926 (Hornbeck)
Soldier of Fortune, 1955 (Duning; Friedhofer; Lemaire; Smith; Spencer)
Soldier—Sailor, 1944 (Alwyn)
Soldier Who Declared Peace. *See* Tribes, 1970
Soldier's Daughter Never Cries, 1998 (Jhabvala; Merchant)
Soldier's Duties. *See* Krigsmans erinran, 1947
Soldiers of Fortune, 1919 (Polito)
Soldiers of the King, 1933 (Balcon)
Soldier's Story, 1984 (Boyd)
Soldiers Three, 1951 (Berman; Deutsch; Plunkett)
Sole anche di notte, 1990 (Lanci, Giuseppe; Guerra; Morricone)
Sole di notte. *See* Sole anche di notte, 1990
Soledad. *See* Rebozo de Soledad, 1952
Soledad. *See* Fruits amers, 1966
Soleil, 1966 (Braunberger)
Soleil a toujours raison, 1941 (Kosma; Prévert; Trauner; Wakhévitch)
Soleil dans l'oeil, 1961 (Jarre)
Soleil de pierre, 1967 (Braunberger)
Soleil des voyous, 1967 (Lai)
Soleil éteint, 1961 (Braunberger)
Soleil noir, 1966 (Barsacq)
Soleil rouge, 1971 (Alekan; Jarre)
Soleils, 1960 (Rabier)
Solid Gold Cadillac, 1956 (Cohn; Lang; Louis; Wald)
Solid Ivory, 1925 (Roach)
Solid Serenade, 1946 (Hanna and Barbera)
Solid Tin Coyote, 1966 (Blanc)
Solitaire Man, 1933 (Adrian)
Solitude du chanteur de fond, 1974 (Lhomme)
Soll man heiraten?, 1925 (Warm)
Solo, 1969 (Menges)
Solomon, 1997 (Morricone)
Solomon & Sheba, 1995 (de Laurentiis)
Solomon and Sheba, 1959 (Day; Veiller; Young)
Soltero. *See* Scapolo, 1955
Solutions françaises, 1945 (Jaubert)
Solva Saal, 1958 (Burman)

Solving the Puzzle. *See* Champion du jeu à la mode, 1910
Sombra verde, 1954 (Alcoriza)
Sombrero, 1953 (Pan; Rose)
Some Baby, 1914 (Roach)
Some Baby, 1922 (Roach)
Some Bull's Daughter, 1914 (Loos)
Some Came Running, 1958 (Bernstein; Cahn; Daniels; Plunkett; van Heusen)
Some Kind of Nut, 1969 (Guffey; Kanin; Mandel; Mirisch)
Some Liar, 1919 (Furthman)
Some Like It Hot, 1939 (Dreier; Head; Hecht; Struss)
Some Like It Hot, 1959 (Cole; Deutsch; Diamond; Hecht; Lang; Mirisch; Orry-Kelly)
Some Like It Not. *See* I'm Cold, 1955
Some Sort of Cage, 1964 (Bernstein)
Somebody Killed Her Husband, 1978 (North)
Somebody Loves Me, 1952 (Barnes; Head)
Somebody Stole My Gal, 1931 (Fleischer)
Somebody Up There Likes Me, 1956 (Cahn; Gibbons; Kaper; Lehman; Ruttenberg; Schnee)
Someone at the Door, 1950 (Carreras)
Someone Behind the Door, 1971 (Lhomme)
Someone to Watch Over Me, 1987 (Vangelis)
Something Always Happens, 1928 (Mankiewicz)
Something Big, 1971 (Hamlisch)
Something for Everyone, 1970 (Lassally; Rosenblum)
Something for the Birds, 1952 (Diamond; La Shelle; Wheeler)
Something in the Wind, 1947 (Green; Krasner; Orry-Kelly)
Something Money Can't Buy, 1952 (Rank; Rota; Vetchinsky)
Something of Value, 1957 (Berman; Harlan; Rose; Rozsa)
Something or the Birds, 1952 (Lemaire)
Something Short of Paradise, 1979 (Lassally)
Something Simple, 1934 (Roach)
Something to Believe In, 1998 (Schifrin)
Something to Live For, 1952 (Barnes; Head; Hornbeck; Young)
Something to Shout About, 1943 (Planer; Porter)
Something to Talk About, 1995 (Nykvist; Zimmer)
Something to Think About, 1920 (Macpherson; Struss)
Something Wicked This Way Comes, 1983 (Winston)
Something Wild, 1961 (Bass; Day; Justin; Schüfftan)
Something's Got to Give, 1962 (Bernstein)
Sometimes a Great Notion, 1971 (Head; Mancini)
Sometimes They Come Back, 1991 (de Laurentiis)
Somewhere I'll Find You, 1942 (Berman; Kaper; Reisch; Rosson)
Somewhere in Dream Land, 1936 (Fleischer)
Somewhere in Egypt, 1943 (Terry)
Somewhere in France. *See* Foreman Went to France, 1942
Somewhere in Somewhere, 1925 (Roach)
Somewhere in Sonora, 1927 (Polito)
Somewhere in Sonora, 1933 (McCord)
Somewhere in the City. *See* Backfire, 1948
Somewhere in the Night, 1946 (Basevi)
Somewhere in the Pacific, 1942 (Terry)
Somewhere in Time, 1980 (Barry)
Somewhere in Turkey, 1918 (Roach)
Sommaren med Monika, 1953 (Fischer; Lundgren)
Sommarlek, 1951 (Fischer)
Sommarnattens leende, 1955 (Fischer; Lundgren)
Sommarnöje sökes, 1957 (Lundgren)
Sommergäste, 1976 (Ballhaus)
Sommernachstraum, 1924 (Metzner)
Sommersby, 1993 (Carrière; Elfman; Rousselot)
Son altesse l'amour, 1931 (Courant)
Son autre amour, 1935 (Burel)
Son Copain. *See* Inconnue de Montréal, 1950
Son-Daughter, 1932 (Adrian; Booth; Stothart)

Son et Lumière, 1961 (Delerue)
Son nom de Vénise dans Calcultta désert, 1976 (Duras; Nuytten)
Son of a Paleface, 1952 (Pereira)
Son of a Sailor, 1933 (Grot; Orry-Kelly)
Son of Dracula, 1943 (Siodmak)
Son of Dracula, 1974 (Francis)
Son of Fate. *See* Mästerjuven, 1915
Son of Flubber, 1962 (Disney; Ellenshaw)
Son of Frankenstein, 1939 (Pierce)
Son of Fury, 1942 (Basevi; Day; Dunne; Newman; Zanuck)
Son of Godzilla. *See* Gojira no musuko, 1967
Son of India, 1931 (Rosson; Vajda)
Son of Kong, 1933 (O'brien; Steiner)
Son of Lassie, 1945 (Irene; Mayer; Stothart)
Son of Paleface, 1952 (Head)
Son of Sinbad, 1955 (Young)
Son of Tarzan, 1921 (Clarke)
Son of the Border, 1933 (Musuraca; Steiner)
Son of the Gods, 1930 (Haller)
Son of the Golden West, 1928 (Plunkett)
Son of the Mountains. *See* Syn hor, 1925
Son of the Pink Panther, 1993 (Mancini)
Son of the Sea. *See* Havets son, 1949
Son of the Sheik, 1926 (Barnes; Marion; Menzies; Westmore Family)
Son oncle de Normandie, 1938 (Auric)
Sonar Kella, 1974 (Dutta)
Sone, 1897? (Messter)
Sonezaki shinjuh, 1981 (Miyagawa)
Song a Day, 1936 (Fleischer)
Song and Dance Man, 1926 (Howe)
Song for Prince Charlie, 1958 (Lassally)
Song Is Born, 1947 (Friedhofer; Goldwyn; Jenkins; Mandell; Sharaff; Toland)
Song o' My Heart, 1930 (Levien)
Song of Bernadette, 1943 (Basevi; La Shelle; Miller; Newman; Zanuck)
Song of Gold. *See* Zpev zlata, 1920
Song of Heroes. *See* Pesn o geroyazh, 1932
Song of Kentucky, 1929 (Clarke)
Song of Life, 1922 (Mayer)
Song of Life. *See* Píseň života, 1925
Song of Life. *See* Lied vom Leben, 1930
Song of Love, 1923 (Gaudio; Marion; Chenck)
Song of Love, 1929 (Walker)
Song of Love, 1947 (Gibbons; Irene; Kaper; Mayer; Plunkett; Stradling)
Song of Mexico, 1945 (Alton)
Song of Restoration. *See* Ishin no uta, 1938
Song of Russia, 1944 (Irene; Jarrico; Pasternak; Stothart; Stradling)
Song of Scheherazade, 1947 (Lourié; Mohr; Reisch; Rozsa)
Song of Songs, 1933 (Banton; Dreier; Hoffenstein; Zukor)
Song of Surrender, 1949 (Bumstead; Dreier; Head; Young)
Song of Texas, 1943 (Canutt)
Song of the Birds, 1935 (Fleischer)
Song of the Caballero, 1930 (McCord)
Song of the Cart. *See* Niguruma no uta, 1959
Song of the Flame, 1930 (Garmes; Grot)
Song of the Islands, 1942 (Day; Newman; Pan)
Song of the Prairie. *See* Arie prérie, 1949
Song of the Road, 1937 (Bryan)
Song of the Scarlet Flower. *See* Sången om den eldröda blomman, 1918
Song of the Scarlet Flower. *See* Sången om den eldröda blomman, 1934
Song of the Scarlet Flower, 1956 (Lundgren)
Song of the Shirt, 1908 (Bitzer)
Song of the South, 1946 (Disney; Iwerks; Toland)
Song of the Taiga. *See* Pyesn Taiga, 1917
Song of the Thin Man, 1947 (Irene; Rosher)
Song of the West. *See* Let Freedom Ring, 1939

Song of the Wildwood Flute, 1910 (Bitzer)
Song of Victory, 1942 (Fleischer)
Song over Moscow. *See* Cheryomushki, 1963
Song Shop, 1929 (Day)
Song Shopping, 1933 (Fleischer)
Song to Remember, 1944 (Banton; Buchman; Cahn; Cohn; Gaudio;
    Plunkett; Rozsa; Vorkapich)
Song without End, 1960 (Howe)
Songe d'un garçon de café, 1910 (Cohl)
Songoku, 1940 (Tsuburaya)
Songoku, 1959 (Tsuburaya)
Songs of Erin, 1951 (Terry)
Songs of Romance, 1949 (Fleischer)
Songs of the Rivers. *See* Lied der Ströme, 1954
Songs of the Seasons, 1948 (Fleischer)
Songs That Live, 1952 (Fleischer)
Sonnou sonjuku, 1939 (Miyagawa)
Sonny, 1922 (Marion)
Sono hito no na wa ienai, 1951 (Hayasaka)
Sonora Kid, 1927 (Musuraca)
Sonotas, 1959 (Figueroa)
Sonoyo no bouken, 1948 (Miyagawa)
Sonrisa de la Virgen, 1957 (Figueroa)
Sons and Lovers, 1960 (Cardiff; Clarke; Francis; Rota; Wald)
Sons o' Guns, 1936 (Epstein; Polito; Wald)
Sons of Adventure, 1948 (Cahn; Canutt)
Sons of Ingmar. *See* Ingmarsönerna, 1919
Sons of Katie Elder, 1965 (Ballard; Bernstein; Head; Jennings;
    Pereira; Wallis)
Sons of the Desert, 1933 (Roach)
Sons of the Legion, 1938 (Dreier; Head)
Sons of the Saddle, 1930 (McCord)
Son's Return, 1909 (Bitzer)
Sophie Lang Goes West, 1937 (Head)
Sophie's Choice, 1982 (Almendros; Hamlisch; Jenkins)
Sorano Daikaijyu Rodan, 1956 (Tsuburaya)
Sorcerer's Apprentice, 1955 (Challis; Francis; Heckroth)
Sorcerer's Apprentice, 1985 (Popescu-Gopo)
Sorcières de Salem, 1956 (Delerue; Eisler; Renoir)
Sorochinsky Fair. *See* Sorochinskaya yamarka, 1918
Sorochinskaya yamarka, 1918 (Starewicz)
Sorok pervyi, 1956 (Urusevsky)
Sorority House, 1939 (Musuraca; Trumbo)
Sorrell and Son, 1927 (Howe; Menzies; Schenck)
Sorrell and Son, 1933 (Wilcox)
Sorriso del grande tentatore, 1974 (Morricone)
Sorrowful Example, 1911 (Bitzer)
Sorrowful Jones, 1949 (Dreier)
Sorrowful Shore, 1913 (Bitzer)
Sorrows of the Unfaithful, 1910 (Bitzer)
Sorrows of Young Love. *See* Werther, 1927
Sorry, Wrong Number, 1948 (Dreier; Head; Polito; Wallis; Waxman)
Sortie de secours, 1970 (Sarde)
Sortie des usines Panhard et Levessor, 1895-97 (Gaumont)
Sortie d'un vapeur du port du Havre, 1901 (Gaumont)
Sortiléges, 1944 (Prévert)
Sortilegio, 1966 (Storaro)
Sospetto, 1974 (Solinas)
Sottaceti, 1971 (Bozzetto)
Sotto dieci bandiere, 1960 (Gherardi; Rota)
Sotto il ristorante Cinese, 1987 (Bozzetto)
Sotto il sole di Roma, 1948 (Amidei)
Sotto il vestito niente, 1985 (Donaggio)
Souffle au coeur, 1971 (Cristaldi)
Soul Kill. *See* A Lady's Morals, 1930
Soul Kiss. *See* A Lady's Morals, 1930

Soul Mates, 1925 (Basevi; Gibbons)
Soul of a Monster, 1944 (Guffey)
Soul of the Beast, 1923 (Sullivan)
Soule, 1988 (Morricone)
Soulier de satin, 1985 (Branco)
Souls Adrift, 1917 (Edeson)
Souls at Sea, 1937 (Dreier; Head; Lang)
Souls in Pawn, 1917 (Furthman; Seitz)
Sound and the Fury, 1959 (Cahn; Clarke; North; Wald; Wheeler)
Sound Barrier, 1952 (Arnold; Korda; Rattigan)
Sound of Fog. *See* Kiri no oto, 1956
Sound of Fury, 1950 (Friedhofer)
Sound of Music, 1965 (Jeakins; Lehman; Leven; McCord; Reynolds)
Sound Sleeper, 1909 (Bitzer)
Sound Off, 1952 (Duning)
Sounder, 1972 (Alonzo)
Soup and Fish, 1934 (Roach)
Soup for One, 1982 (Mandel)
Soup Song, 1931 (Iwerks)
Soupçons, 1956 (Kosma)
Soupirant, 1962 (Carrière)
Sour Grapes, 1950 (Terry)
Sour Puss, 1940 (Blanc; Clampett; Stalling)
Source of Love. *See* Pramen lásky, 1928
Sourire, 1958 (Delerue)
Sourire aux lèvres. *See* Bonjour sourire, 1955
Souris blanches, 1911 (Gaumont)
Souris d'hôtel, 1928 (Meerson)
Sous la griffe, 1935 (Spaak)
Sous la terre, 1931 (Matras)
Sous les palmes de Marrakech, 1948 (Decaë)
Sous les toits de Paris, 1930 (Meerson; Périnal; Trauner)
Sous les yeux d'occident, 1936 (Auric; Lourié)
Soushi gekijou, 1946 (Miyagawa)
South o' the North Pole, 1924 (Roach)
South of Algiers, 1953 (Morris)
South of Dixie, 1944 (Bruckman)
South of Santa Fe, 1932 (Glennon)
South of St. Louis, 1949 (Freund; Steiner)
South of Tahiti, 1943 (Boyle)
South Pacific, 1958 (Jeakins; Newman; Reynolds; Shamroy; Wheeler)
South Pole or Bust, 1934 (Terry)
South Riding, 1938 (Addinsell; Korda; Meerson; Stradling)
South Sea Bubble, 1928 (Balcon)
South Sea Love, 1927 (Musuraca)
South Sea Rose, 1928 (Levien; Rosson)
South Sea Sinner, 1949 (Orry-Kelly)
South Sea Woman, 1953 (McCord)
South Seas Adventure, 1958 (North)
South Seas Bouquet. *See* Nankai no hanatabe, 1942
South Wind and Waves. *See* Minami no kaze to nami, 1961
Southbound Duckling, 1955 (Hanna and Barbera)
Southern Cinderella, 1913 (Ince)
Southern Exposure, 1935 (Roach)
Southern Fried Rabbit, 1953 (Blanc; Stalling)
Southern Horse-pitality, 1935 (Terry)
Southern Love, 1924 (Wilcox)
Southern Rhythm, 1932 (Terry)
Southern Star. *See* Éoile du sud, 1968
Southerner, 1931 (Booth; Stothart)
Southerner, 1945 (Hakim; Lourié)
Southside 1-1000, 1950 (Harlan)
Southwest, 1945 (Kaufman)
Southwest Passage, 1954 (Mainwaring)
Souvenir. *See* Aux yeux du souvenir, 1948
Souvenir d'Italie, 1957 (Age and Scarpelli)

Spinnen, Part 2: Das Brillantenschiff, 1920 (Freund; Pommer; Warm)
Spinout, 1966 (Pasternak)
Spion, 1914 (Warm)
Spione, 1928 (Pommer; Von Harbou; Wagner)
Spione am Werk, 1933 (Wagner)
Spiral Road, 1962 (Bumstead; Goldsmith; Harlan)
Spiral Staircase, 1945 (D'Agostino; Musuraca; Schary)
Spirale, 1987 (Legrand)
Spiralen, 1926 (Fischinger)
Spirit Awakened, 1912 (Bitzer)
Spirit is Willing, 1967 (Pereira)
Spirit of '76, 1905 (Bitzer)
Spirit of Notre Dame, 1931 (Laemmle)
Spirit of St. Louis, 1957 (Burks; Lederer; Waxman)
Spirit of Stanford, 1942 (Planer)
Spirit of the People . See Abe Lincoln in Illinois, 1940
Spirits of the Dead. See Histoires extraordinaires, 1968
Spiritual Constructions. See Seelische Konstruktionen, 1927
Spiritualist, 1948 (Alton)
Spiskroksvalsen, 1909 (Magnusson)
Spit Ball Sadie, 1914 (Roach)
Spite Flight, 1933 (Iwerks)
Spite Marriage, 1929 (Gibbons)
Spitfire, 1934 (Berman; Cooper; Cronjager; Plunkett; Polglase; Steiner)
Spitfire. See First of the Few, 1942
Spitting Image. See Als tween druppels water, 1963
Spitzen, 1926 (Junge)
Splash of Tenryu. See Tenryu shibuki, 1938
Splendor, 1935 (Day; Goldwyn; Newman; Toland)
Splendor in the Grass, 1961 (Kaufman; Sylbert)
Splinters, 1929 (Wilcox)
Splinters in the Air, 1937 (Wilcox)
Split, 1968 (Guffey; Jones; Winkler)
Split Image, 1982 (Conti)
Split Second, 1953 (Musuraca)
Split Second to an Epitaph, 1968 (Jones)
Splitting the Breeze, 1927 (Musuraca)
Spogliati, protesta, uccidi?, 1973 (Morricone)
Spoiled Children. See Des enfants gâtés, 1977
Spoiled Garden. See Yogoreta hanazono, 1948
Spoilers, 1914 (Brown; Selig)
Spoilers, 1942 (Krasner)
Spoilers, 1955 (Hunter)
Spoilers of the West, 1927 (Selznick)
Spöke på semester, 1951 (Lundgren)
Spoofing, 1928 (Roach)
Spook Louder, 1942 (Bruckman)
Spook Speaks, 1940 (Bruckman)
Spook-Spoofing, 1928 (Roach)
Spooks Run Wild, 1941 (Foreman)
Spooks, 1930 (Lantz)
Spooks, 1932 (Iwerks)
Spooky Hooky, 1935 (Roach)
Sport Chumpions, 1941 (Blanc; Stalling)
Sport de la voile, 1946 (Decaë)
Sport del Signor Rossi, 1975 (Bozzetto)
Sport of Kings, 1931 (Balcon)
Sport Parade, 1932 (Steiner)
Sporting, 1982 (Bozzetto)
Sporting Blood, 1931 (Rosson)
Sporting Blood, 1940 (Waxman)
Sporting Chance, 1919 (Furthman)
Sporting Goods, 1928 (Cronjager)
Sporting Life, 1918 (Carré)
Sporting Venus, 1925 (Gibbons)
Sportive Puppet. See Soyons doncs sportifs, 1909

Sports, 1973 (Halas and Batchelor)
Sports Pages, 1999 (Marshall)
Sposa bella. See Angel Wore Red, 1960
Sposa era bellissima, 1987 (Morricone)
Sposa non può attendere, 1949 (Zavattini)
Spot. See Dogpound Shuffle, 1974
Spot Cash, 1921 (Roach)
Spot of Bother, 1938 (Havelock-Allan)
Spotlight, 1927 (Mankiewicz)
Spotlight Serenade, 1948 (Fleischer)
Spotting a Cow, 1983 (Driessen)
Spraggue, 1984 (Schifrin)
Sprengbagger 1010, 1929 (Andrejew)
Spring and Saganaki, 1958 (Bosustow)
Spring and Winter, 1951 (Halas and Batchelor)
Spring at Sjösala. See Sjösalavår, 1949
Spring Call. See Vesyonnij prizyv, 1976
Spring Caprice. See Haru no tawamure, 1949
Spring Fever, 1919 (Roach)
Spring Fever, 1927 (Gibbons)
Spring Fever, 1951 (Terry)
Spring Grudge. See Shunen, 1951
Spring in Park Lane, 1948 (Wilcox)
Spring in the Park, 1934 (Lantz)
Spring Is Here, 1930 (Garmes)
Spring Is Here, 1932 (Terry)
Spring Madness, 1938 (Ruttenberg)
Spring on the Farm, 1942 (Alwyn)
Spring Parade, 1940 (Kahn; Pasternak)
Spring Reunion, 1956 (Mercer)
Spring Song, 1960 (Halas and Batchelor)
Spring Tonic, 1935 (Bruckman; Hecht)
Springer and the SS-Men. See Pérák a SS, 1946
Springfield Rifle, 1952 (Steiner)
Springtime, 1929 (Iwerks)
Springtime for Henry, 1934 (Lasky; Seitz)
Springtime for Thomas, 1946 (Hanna and Barbera)
Springtime in the Rockage, 1940 (Fleischer)
Springtime in the Rockies, 1942 (Day; Newman; Pan)
Springtime Serenade, 1935 (Lantz)
Sprucin' Up, 1935 (Roach)
Sprung ins Leben, 1924 (Wagner)
Spy for a Day, 1940 (de Grunwald)
Spy Hard, 1996 (Conti)
Spy in Black, 1939 (Hornbeck; Korda; Rozsa)
Spy in the Pantry. See Ten Days in Paris, 1939
Spy of Napoleon, 1936 (Courant)
Spy Smasher, 1942 (Canutt)
Spy Swatter, 1967 (Blanc)
Spy Train, 1960 (Halas and Batchelor)
Spy Who Came In from the Cold, 1966 (Morris)
Spy Who Loved Me, 1977 (Adam; Broccoli; Hamlisch; Renoir)
Spy with a Cold Nose, 1966 (Levine; Williams)
Spylarks. See Intelligence Men, 1965
Spys, 1974 (Fisher; Goldsmith)
Squadron Leader X, 1942 (Alwyn)
Squadron of Honor, 1937 (Ballard)
Squall, 1929 (Korda; Seitz)
Square Deal, 1915 (August)
Square Deal, 1917 (Edeson; Marion)
Square Deal Man, 1917 (August)
Square Deal Sanderson, 1919 (August)
Square Deceiver, 1917 (Gaudio)
Square Peg. See Denial, 1925
Square Peg, 1959 (Rank)
Square Ring, 1953 (Heller)

Squaw Man, 1914 (Buckland; Zukor)
Squaw Man, 1918 (Buckland)
Squaw Man, 1931 (Adrian; Mayer; Rosson; Stothart)
Squaw's Love, 1911 (Bitzer)
Squawkin' Hawk, 1942 (Blanc; Jones)
Squeak in the Deep, 1966 (Blanc; Mckimson)
Squeaker, 1937 (Korda; Krasker; Périnal; Rozsa)
Squillo, 1996 (Donaggio)
Squire's Son, 1914 (Ince)
Squirm, 1976 (Baker)
Squirrel Crazy, 1951 (Terry)
Srdce za písničku, 1933 (Stallich)
Sroublkova dobrodružství, 1962 (Brdečka)
St. Elmo, 1923 (August; Furthman)
St. Elmo Murray. See St. Elmo, 1923
St. Francis of Assisi. See Francesco, 1989
St. Helena and Its Man of Destiny, 1936 (Hoch)
St. Ives, 1976 (Ballard; Houseman; Schifrin)
St. Louis Blues, 1939 (Dreier; Head)
St. Louis Blues, 1958 (Head)
St. Louis Exposition, 1902 (Bitzer)
St. Louis Kid, 1934 (Orry-Kelly)
St. Martin's Lane, 1938 (Pommer)
St. Valentine's Day Massacre, 1967 (Krasner; Smith)
St. Wenceslas. See Svaty Václav, 1929
Stablemates, 1938 (Seitz)
Stachka, 1925 (Tisse)
Stackars miljonärer, 1936 (Kästner)
Stacked Cards, 1926 (Haller)
Stadt in Sicht, 1923 (Galeen)
Stadt steht Kopf, 1932 (Planer)
Staffan Stolle Story. See Ratataa, 1956
Stage Door, 1937 (Berman; Polglase; Veiller)
Stage Door Canteen, 1943 (Blanc; Green; Horner; Stalling)
Stage Door Magoo, 1955 (Bosustow)
Stage Fright, 1923 (Roach)
Stage Fright, 1938 (Metty)
Stage Fright, 1940 (Blanc; Stalling)
Stage Fright, 1950 (Reville)
Stage Hoax, 1952 (Lantz)
Stage Kisses, 1927 (Walker)
Stage Mother, 1933 (Adrian; Brown; Freed)
Stage Struck, 1922 (Roach)
Stage Struck, 1925 (Polglase)
Stage Struck, 1936 (Haskin; Orry-Kelly)
Stage Struck, 1951 (Terry)
Stage Struck, 1958 (North; Planer)
Stage Stunt, 1929 (Lantz)
Stagecoach, 1939 (Canutt; Cooper; Glennon; Nichols; Plunkett; Spencer; Wanger)
Stagecoach, 1966 (Clothier; Goldsmith; Smith)
Stagecoach Kid, 1949 (Musuraca)
Stagecoach War, 1940 (Harlan; Head)
Stagione all'inferno, 1971 (Jarre)
Stagione dei sensi, 1969 (Morricone)
Stain on the Conscience, 1968 (Vukotić)
Staircase, 1969 (Challis)
Stairs, 1953 (Maddow)
Stairway to Heaven. See **A Matter of Life and Death**, 1946
Stake-Out. See Police Story, 1973
Stakeout, 1987 (Seale)
Stalag 17, 1953 (Head; Laszlo; Pereira; Waxman)
Stalin, 1992 (Jarrico)
Staline, 1984 (Mnouchkine)
Stalking Moon, 1968 (Jeakins; Lang; Sargent)
Stallion Road, 1947 (Edeson)

Stamboul Quest, 1934 (Howe; Mankiewicz; Stothart; Wanger)
Stamp Fantasia, 1961 (Kuri)
Stampede; Second Sight, 1911 (Gaudio)
Stampen, 1955 (Fischer)
Stand and Deliver, 1928 (Adrian; Grot)
Stand by for Action, 1943 (Mankiewicz; Mayer; Rosher)
Stand by Me, 1986 (Nitzsche)
Stand der Dinge, 1982 (Alekan; Branco)
Stand-In, 1937 (Clarke; Spencer; Wanger)
Stand Pat, 1922 (Roach)
Stand Up and Be Counted, 1972 (Wheeler)
Standing by the Treasury. See U pokladny stál, 1939
Standing Room Only, 1944 (Dreier; Head; Lang)
Stanley and Iris, 1990 (McAlpine; Williams)
Stanley and Livingstone, 1939 (Barnes; Dunne; Macgowan; Newman; Raksin; Zanuck)
Stanley: Every Home Should Have One, 1983 (Boyd)
Stanno tutti bene, 1990 (Guerra; Morricone)
Stanza dello scirocco, 1998 (Cecchi D'amico)
Star, 1952 (Laszlo; Orry-Kelly; Young)
Star, 1953 (Leven)
Star!, 1968 (Cahn; Kidd; Laszlo; Leven; Reynolds; van Heusen)
Star 80, 1983 (Nykvist)
Star Crash, 1979 (Barry)
Star Dust, 1940 (Day; Macgowan; Zanuck)
Star Fell From Heaven, 1935 (Neame)
Star in the Night, 1945 (Burks)
Star Is Bored, 1956 (Blanc)
Star Is Born, 1937 (Selznick; Steiner; Wheeler)
Star Is Born, 1954 (Edens; Louis; Sharaff)
Star Is Born, 1976 (Surtees)
Star Is Shorn, 1939 (Ballard)
Star Maker, 1939 (Head; Newman; Struss)
Star Maker. See Uomo delle stelle, 1995
Star of Bethlehem, 1956 (Reiniger)
Star of Damaskus. See Stern von Damaskus, 1920
Star of India, 1953 (Adam; Rota)
Star of Midnight, 1935 (Berman; Polglase; Steiner; Veiller)
Star of the Circus, 1938 (Saunders)
Star Packer, 1934 (Canutt)
Star Rock. See Apple, 1980
Star Spangled Rhythm, 1942 (Dreier; Head; Mercer)
Star Struck, 1994 (Justin)
Star Trek II: The Wrath of Khan, 1982 (Ralston)
Star Trek III: The Search for Spock, 1984 (Ralston)
Star Trek IV: The Voyage Home, 1986 (Ralston; Rosenman)
Star Trek V: The Final Frontier, 1989 (Goldsmith)
Star Trek: First Contact, 1996 (Goldsmith)
Star Trek: Generations, 1994 (Alonzo)
Star Trek: Insurrection, 1998 (Goldsmith)
Star Trek: The Motion Picture, 1979 (Dykstra; Goldsmith; Trumbull)
Star Trek: The Next Generation—All Good Things, 1994 (Goldsmith)
Star Trek: Voyager—Caretaker, 1995 (Goldsmith)
Star Wars, 1977 (Baker; Burtt; Dykstra; Edlund; Muren; Ralston; Williams)
Star Wars: Episode I—The Phantom Menace, 1999 (Burtt; Muren; Williams)
Starci na chmelu, 1964 (Stallich)
Stardust, 1974 (Puttnam)
Stardust Memories, 1980 (Loquasto; Willis)
Staré pověsti čéské, 1953 (Brdečka; Trnka)
Starets Vasili Gryaznov, 1924 (Tisse)
Starflight One: The Plane That Couldn't Land, 1983 (Schifrin)
Stark, 1985 (Conti)
Stark II. See Stark: Mirror-Image, 1986
Stark Fear, 1963 (Williams)

Stark Love, 1927 (Brown)
Stark: Mirror-Image, 1986 (Conti)
Stark System, 1980 (Morricone)
Starlift, 1951 (McCord)
Starman, 1984 (Baker; Nitzsche; Winston)
Staroie i novoie, 1929 (Tisse)
Stars and Stripes, 1939-41 (McClaren)
Stars and Stripes Forever, 1952 (Clarke; Jeakins; Lemaire;
     Newman; Trotti)
Stars Are Singing, 1953 (Bumstead; Head; Young)
Stars Fell on Henrietta, 1994 (Bumstead)
Stars in My Crown, 1950 (Deutsch; Plunkett)
Stars over Broadway, 1935 (Barnes; Epstein; Orry-Kelly; Wald)
Starsky and Hutch, 1975 (Schifrin)
Starstruck, 1982 (Boyd)
Start Cheering, 1937 (Green; Walker)
Start in Life, 1943 (Alwyn)
Start the Show, 1920 (Roach)
Starting Over, 1979 (Hamlisch; Jenkins; Nykvist)
Starvation Blues, 1925 (Roach)
Starwatcher, 1992 (Vangelis)
Starý hřích, 1930 (Heller)
Stastny lev, 1959 (Brdečka)
State and Main, 2000 (Mamet)
State Fair, 1933 (Levien; Mohr)
State Fair, 1945 (Levien; Newman; Shamroy)
State Fair, 1962 (Brackett; Newman; Smith)
State of Grace, 1990 (Morricone; Von Brandenstein)
State of Siege. See Etat de siège, 1972
State of the Union, 1948 (Hornbeck; Irene; Mayer; Veiller; Young)
State of Things. See Stand der Dinge, 1982
State Secret, 1950 (Alwyn; Korda; Krasker)
State Secret. See Segreto di stato, 1995
State Street Sadie, 1927 (Zanuck)
State's Attorney, 1932 (Selznick; Steiner)
Station mondaine, 1951 (Braunberger)
Stationmaster's Wife. See Bolwieser, 1978
Stato interessante, 1977 (Morricone)
Statues d'épouvante, 1953 (Cloquet)
Statues meurent aussi, 1953 (Cloquet; Colpi)
Stavisky, 1974 (Mnouchkine; Saulnier; Semprun; Vierny)
Stay Tuned, 1992 (Jones)
Staying Alive, 1983 (Boyle; Mandel)
Stazione Termini, 1953 (Aldo; Cahn; Morris; Selznick; Zavattini)
Steady Company, 1915 (Furthman)
Steagle, 1970 (Guffey)
Steak trop cuit, 1960 (Guillemot)
Steal Wool, 1957 (Blanc; Jones)
Stealin' Ain't Honest, 1940 (Fleischer)
Steam Locomotive C-57. See Kikansha C-57, 1940
Steamboat Bill, Jr., 1928 (Schenck)
Steamboat 'round the Bend, 1935 (Nichols; Trotti)
Steamboat Willie, 1928 (Disney; Iwerks; Stalling)
Steaming, 1985 (Challis)
Steamlined Greta Green, 1937 (Stalling)
Steel, 1944 (Cardiff)
Steel Bayonet, 1957 (Carreras)
Steel Glory, Stunt Seven. See Fantastic Seven, 1979
Steel Goes to War, 1941 (Alwyn)
Steel Lady, 1953 (Crosby)
Steel Magnolias, 1989 (Alonzo; Delerue; Shepard; Stark)
Steel Town, 1952 (Hunter)
Steel Trap, 1952 (Laszlo; Tiomkin)
Steel Workers, 1937 (Lantz)
Steelyard Blues, 1972 (Kovacs)
Steeple Jacks, 1951 (Terry)

Stein Song, 1930 (Fleischer)
Steinerne Reiter, 1923 (Hoffmann; Pommer)
Stella, 1950 (Lemaire)
Stella, 1990 (van Runkle)
Stella Dallas, 1925 (Edeson; Goldwyn; Marion; Westmore Family)
Stella Dallas, 1937 (Day; Goldwyn; Maté; Newman)
Stella Maris, 1918 (Buckland; Marion; Starewicz)
Stelle emigranti, 1983 (Lanci, Giuseppe ("beppe"))
Sten Stensson Stéen fran Eslöv på nya äventyr, 1930 (Jaenzon)
Sten Stensson Stéen from Eslöv on New Adventures. See Sten Stensson
     Stéen fran Eslöv på nya äventyr, 1930
Stendhal's Syndrome. See Sindrome di Stendhal, 1996
Step-Brothers. See Ibo koudai, 1957
Step Down to Terror, 1958 (Metty)
Step Lively, 1918 (Roach)
Step Lively, 1944 (Cahn)
Step on It, 1931 (Fleischer)
Step Out of Line, 1971 (Goldsmith)
Step to Darkness. See Krok do tmy, 1938
Stepford Wives, 1974 (Goldman; Smith)
Stéphane et la garde chasse, 1966 (Braunberger)
Stephen King's The Green Mile. See Green Mile, 1999
Stepmom, 1998 (Bass; McAlpine; Williams)
Steppa, 1963 (Donati; Flaiano and Pinelli)
Steppe. See Steppa, 1963
Stepping Out, 1919 (Barnes; Sullivan)
Stepping Out, 1923 (Roach)
Stepping Out, 1929 (Roach)
Stepping Stone, 1916 (Sullivan)
Steps of Age, 1951 (Maddow)
Steps to the Moon. See Pasi spre lune, 1963
Stereo Film, 1952 (Fischinger)
Sterile Cuckoo, 1969 (Krasner; O'Steen; Sargent)
Stern von Bethlehem, 1921 (Reiniger)
Stern von Damaskus, 1920 (Kolowrat-Krakowsky)
Stet priklyuchenni, 1929 (Ptushko)
Stevedores, 1937 (Lantz)
Steven Donoghue, 1926 (Balcon)
Stevie, 1978 (Young)
Stick, Start Beating!. See Obusku, z pytle ven!, 1956
Stick to Your Guns, 1941 (Harlan)
Stier von Olivera, 1921 (Messter; Metzncr)
Stiletto, 1969 (Levine)
Still Life. See Stilleben, 1969
Still of the Night, 1982 (Almendros)
Stilleben, 1969 (Lenica)
Stimme, 1920 (Dreier)
Stimulantia, 1967 (Fischer; Lundgren)
Stín ve svetle, 1928 (Stallich)
Sting, 1973 (Bumstead; Hamlisch; Head; Reynolds; Surtees;
     Whitlock; Zanuck)
Sting II, 1983 (Schifrin)
Stingaree, 1915 (Glennon)
Stingaree, 1934 (Berman; Cooper; Kahn; Plunkett; Steiner)
Stíny, 1921 (Heller)
Stitch, 1995 (Savini)
Stitch in Time, 1963 (Hambling)
Sto-Press Girl, 1949 (Rank)
Stock-Cars. See A tout casser, 1953
Stockholm, Pride of Sweden, 1937 (Hoch)
Stocks and Blondes, 1928 (Berman; Plunkett)
Stole Goods, 1924 (Roach)
Stolen Affections. See Révoltée, 1947
Stolen Airship. See Ukradená vzducholod, 1966
Stolen Babies, 1993 (Daring)
Stolen Bride, 1927 (Korda)

Streets of Gold, 1986 (Nitzsche)
Streets of Laredo, 1949 (Dreier; Rennahan; Young)
Streghe, 1967 (Age and Scarpelli; de Laurentiis; Morricone; Serandrei; Zavattini)
Strejken, 1914 (Jaenzon; Magnusson)
Strength of the Pines, 1922 (Polito)
Stříbrná oblaka, 1938 (Stallich)
Strictly Confidential. *See* Broadway Bill, 1934
Strictly Dishonorable, 1931 (Freund)
Strictly Dishonorable, 1951 (Rose)
Strictly Dynamite, 1934 (Cronjager; Plunkett; Steiner)
Strictly for Pleasure. *See* Perfect Furlough, 1958
Strictly Modern, 1922 (Roach)
Strictly Personal, 1933 (Head; Krasner)
Strictly Unconventional, 1930 (Booth; Daniels; Gibbons)
Strictly Unreliable, 1932 (Roach)
Strife with Father, 1950 (Blanc; McKimson; Stalling)
Strike. *See* Strejken, 1915
Strike. *See* **Stachka**, 1925
Strike!. *See* Red Ensign, 1934
Strike Me Pink, 1936 (Day; Goldwyn; Newman; Toland)
Strike Up the Band, 1930 (Fleischer)
Strike Up the Band, 1940 (Edens; Freed; Mayer; Shearer)
String Bean Jack, 1938 (Terry)
String Beans, 1918 (Ince; Zukor)
String of Pearls, 1911 (Bitzer)
Strip, 1951 (Pasternak; Rose; Surtees)
Strip-Tease, 1957 (Lenica)
Stripes, 1981 (Bernstein)
Stripes and Stars, 1929 (Lantz)
Stripper, 1963 (Goldsmith; Smith; Wald)
Stripper, 1986 (Nitzsche)
Striptease, 1977 (Bozzetto)
Stromboli. *See* **Stromboli, terra di Dio**, 1949
Stromboli, terra di Dio, 1949 (Amidei)
Strong Boy, 1929 (August)
Strong to the Finich, 1934 (Fleischer)
Stronger Sex, 1931 (Balcon)
Stronger than Death, 1920 (Carré)
Stronger than Desire, 1939 (Daniels)
Stronger than Fear. *See* Edge of Doom, 1950
Strongest, 1920 (Fox)
Strongheart, 1914 (Gaudio)
Stronghold, 1952 (Cortez)
Study in Scarlet, 1933 (Edeson)
Struggle, 1931 (Loos; Ruttenberg)
Struggle. *See* Borza, 1935
Struggling Hearts. *See* Vergödö szívek, 1916
Strýček z Ameriky, 1933 (Stallich)
Stryekosa i muravey, 1911 (Starewicz)
Stuart Little, 1999 (Dykstra)
Stuck on You!, 1983 (Rosenblum)
Stud, 1978 (Cahn)
Stud. Chem. Helene Willfüer, 1929 (Planer)
Student of Prague. *See* Student von Prag, 1926
Student of Prague. *See* Student von Prag, 1935
Student Prince, 1954 (Levien; Pan; Pasternak; Plunkett; Rose)
Student Prince in Old Heidelberg, 1927 (Day; Dreier; Gibbons; Kräly; Mayer)
Student Tour, 1933 (Brown; Dunne; Freed)
Student von Prag, 1913 (Galeen)
Student von Prag, 1926 (Galeen; Warm)
Student von Prag, 1935 (Warm)
Studie Nr 5, 1929 (Fischinger)
Studie Nr 6, 1930 (Fischinger)
Studie Nr 7, 1930 (Fischinger)

Studie Nr 8, 1930 (Fischinger)
Studie Nr 9, 1930 (Fischinger)
Studie Nr 10, 1930 (Fischinger)
Studie Nr 11, 1931 (Fischinger)
Studie Nr 12, 1931 (Fischinger)
Studie Nr 13, 1931 (Fischinger)
Studie Nr 14, 1932 (Fischinger)
Studie Nr 15, 1932 (Fischinger)
Studie Nr 16, 1932 (Fischinger)
Studie Nr 17, 1933 (Fischinger)
Studie Nr 18, 1933 (Fischinger)
Studien 1-4, 1922-25 (Fischinger)
Studs Lonigan, 1960 (Fields; Goldsmith; Wexler)
Study Opus I—Man, 1976 (Popescu-Gopo)
Stuff Heroes Are Made Of, 1911 (Bitzer)
Stunden vor dem Morgengrauen, 1997 (Donaggio)
Stupid Cupid, 1944 (Blanc)
Stupor Duck, 1956 (Blanc; McKimson; Stalling)
Stupor Salesman, 1948 (Blanc; Stalling)
Stürme der Leidenschaft, 1931 (Pommer)
Stürmtruppen, 1976 (Rotunno)
Štvaní lidé, 1933 (Stallich)
Su or Letizia, 1956 (Di Venanzo)
Su última aventura, 1946 (Figueroa)
Subarashii akujo, 1963 (Takemitsu)
Subject Was Roses, 1968 (Jenkins)
Submarine, 1910 (Gaudio)
Submarine, 1928 (Cohn; Walker)
Submarine Command, 1951 (Ames; Head)
Submarine Control, 1949 (Halas and Batchelor)
Submarine D-1, 1937 (Deutsch; Edeson; Haskin; Steiner)
Submarine Patrol, 1938 (Miller; Zanuck)
Submarine Zone. *See* Escape to Glory, 1941
Subpoena Server, 1906 (Bitzer)
Substance of Fire, 1996 (Comden and Green)
Substitute Wife, 1925 (Stradling)
Subterraneans, 1960 (Freed; Ruttenberg)
Suburban House. *See* Dum no předmestí, 1933
Subway, 1985 (Trauner)
Subway Express, 1931 (Walker)
Subway Sadie, 1926 (Edeson)
Success. *See* Successo, 1963
Success. *See* American Success Company, 1979
Success at Any Price, 1934 (Cooper; Plunkett; Steiner)
Success Is the Best Revenge, 1984 (Zimmer)
Successo, 1963 (Morricone)
Such a Gorgeous Kid Like Me. *See* Belle Fille comme moi, 1972
Such a Little Queen, 1921 (Haller)
Such Good Friends, 1971 (Bass)
Such Men Are Dangerous, 1930 (Goosson; Vajda)
Such Men Are Dangerous. *See* Racers, 1955
Sucre, 1978 (Sarde)
Sudario a la medida, 1969 (Conti)
Sudden Fear, 1952 (Bernstein; Lang; Leven)
Sudden Impact, 1983 (Schifrin)
Sudden Money, 1939 (Head)
Suddenly, 1954 (Clarke; Raksin)
Suddenly. *See* Achanak, 1973
Suddenly Bad Names. *See* Akumyo niwaka, 1965
Suddenly It's Spring, 1947 (Dreier; Young)
Suddenly Last Summer, 1959 (Arnold; Fisher; Hornbeck; Louis; Spiegel)
Suddenly, Love, 1978 (Hunter)
Suds, 1920 (Rosher)
Sued for Libel, 1940 (Polglase)
Suenos de oro, 1956 (Figueroa)
Suez, 1938 (Clarke; Dunne; Raksin; Zanuck)

Sufferin' Cats!, 1943 (Hanna and Barbera)
Suffering of Susan, 1914 (Loos)
Suffering Shakespeare, 1924 (Roach)
Suffit d'une fois, 1946 (Matras)
Sugar. *See* Sucre, 1978
Sugar and Spice Series, 1930 (Balcon)
Sugar and Spies, 1966 (Blanc; McKimson)
Sugarfoot, 1950 (Cahn; Steiner)
Sugarland Express, 1974 (Fields; Williams; Zanuck; Zsigmond)
Sugihara: Conspiracy of Goodness, 2000 (Conti)
Suicídate, mi amor, 1960 (Alcoriza)
Suicide Battalion, 1958 (Crosby)
Suicide Club, 1909 (Bitzer)
Suicide Club. *See* Trouble for Two, 1936
Suicide Fleet, 1931 (Polito)
Suicide Legion. *See* Sunset in Vienna, 1937
Suicide Pact, 1913 (Loos)
Suicide Squadron. *See* Dangerous Moonlight, 1941
Suicide's Wife, 1979 (Raksin)
Suikoden, 1942 (Tsuburaya)
Suite de la passion, 1903 (Pathé)
Suite de la passion, 1905 (Pathé)
Suite en si mineur, 1969 (Braunberger)
Suited to a T., 1931 (Fleischer)
Suito Homu, 1989 (Smith)
Suitor. *See* Soupirant, 1962
Suivez l'oeuf, 1963 (Braunberger)
Sullivans, 1944 (Basevi; Newman)
Sullivan's Empire, 1967 (Schifrin)
Sullivan's Travels, 1941 (Dreier; Edouart; Head; Seitz)
Sultans, 1965 (Delli Colli)
Sultan's Birthday, 1944 (Terry)
Sultan's Cat, 1931 (Terry)
Sultan's Daughter, 1944 (Alton)
Sultry Summer Evening. *See* Een zwoele zomeravond, 1982
Summer. *See* Léto, 1949
Summer and Smoke, 1961 (Bernstein; Head; Lang; Wallis)
Summer, Autumn, 1930 (Iwerks)
Summer Bachelors, 1926 (Ruttenberg)
Summer Girl, 1916 (Marion)
Summer Guests. *See* Sommergäste, 1976
Summer Heat, 1987 (Delerue)
Summer Holiday, 1948 (Freed; Goodrich and Hackett; Irene; Mayer; Plunkett; Smith)
Summer's Idyll, 1910 (Bitzer)
Summer in the City, 1971 (Müller)
Summer Interlude. *See* Sommarlek, 1951
Summer Lightning, 1933 (Wilcox)
Summer Lightning. *See* Scudda Hoo! Scudda Hay!, 1948
Summer Love, 1958 (Mancini)
Summer Madness, 1955 (Korda)
Summer Magic, 1963 (Disney; Ellenshaw)
Summer of '42, 1971 (Legrand; Surtees)
Summer of Secrets, 1976 (Boyd)
Summer on the Farm, 1943 (Alwyn)
Summer Place, 1959 (Steiner; Stradling)
Summer School, 1987 (Elfman)
Summer Sister. *See* Nasu no imoto, 1972
Summer Soldiers, 1972 (Takemitsu)
Summer Solstice, 1981 (Rosenblum)
Summer Stock, 1950 (Green; Mayer; Pasternak; Plunkett; Rose; Smith)
Summer Storm, 1944 (Schüfftan)
Summer Story, 1988 (Delerue)
Summer Strolls. *See* Promenades d'été, 1992
Summer Tale. *See* En sommarsaga, 1912
Summer Tales. *See* Racconti d'estate, 1958

Summer Wishes, Winter Dreams, 1973 (Mandel)
Summer with Monika. *See* Sommaren med Monika, 1953
Summertime, 1931 (Terry)
Summertime, 1935 (Iwerks)
Summertime. *See* Summer Madness, 1955
Summit of Mount Fuji. *See* Fuji sancho, 1948
Sumo Festival. *See* Dohyou matsuri, 1944
Sumurun, 1920 (Kräly; Metzner)
Sun Also Rises, 1957 (Friedhofer; Lemaire; Wheeler; Zanuck)
Sun Also Shines at Night. *See* Sole anche di notte, 1990
Sun Comes Up, 1948 (Irene; Previn)
Sun Down Limited, 1924 (Roach)
Sun Shines Bright, 1953 (Cooper; Young)
Sun Valley Serenade, 1941 (Banton; Cronjager; Day; Pan)
Sunbeam, 1911 (Bitzer)
Sunbonnet Blue, 1937 (Avery; Stalling)
Sunchaser, 1996 (Jarre)
Sunday by the Sea, 1953 (Lassally)
Sunday Calm, 1923 (Roach)
Sunday Dinner for a Soldier, 1944 (Newman)
Sunday in August. *See* Domenica d'agosto, 1950
Sunday in New York, 1963 (Krasna; Orry-Kelly)
Sunday Lovers, 1981 (Age and Scarpelli; Delli Colli)
Sunday Punch, 1942 (Schary)
Sunday Woman. *See* Donna della domenica, 1975
Sundays and Cybèle. *See* Cybèle, ou les dimanches de Ville d'Avray, 1962
Sünde der Engel, 1999 (Donaggio)
Sündelbabel, 1925 (Junge)
Sundered Ties, 1912 (Ince)
Sündig und Süss, 1929 (Heller)
Sundown, 1924 (Marion)
Sundown, 1941 (Irene; Lang; Plunkett; Rozsa; Spencer; Wanger)
Sundown Trail, 1931 (McCord)
Sundowners, 1949 (Hoch)
Sundowners, 1960 (Fisher; Tiomkin; Warner)
Sunfish. *See* Poisson lune, 1993
Sunflower. *See* I girasoli, 1969
Sunk By the Census, 1940 (Metty)
Sunken Treasure, 1936 (Terry)
Sunken World. *See* Versunkene Welt, 1922
Sunna no onna, 1963 (Takemitsu)
Sunny, 1930 (Haller)
Sunny, 1941 (Metty; Wilcox)
Sunny Italy, 1951 (Terry)
Sunny Side of the Street, 1951 (Duning)
Sunny Side Up, 1929 (Friedhofer)
Sunny South, 1931 (Lantz)
Sunny South, 1933 (Terry)
Sunrise, 1927 (Mayer; Rosher; Struss)
Sunrise at Campobello, 1960 (Harlan; Schary; Waxman)
Sunset, 1988 (Mancini)
Sunset Boulevard, 1950 (Brackett; Dreier; Edouart; Head; Seitz; Waxman)
Sunset in El Dorado, 1945 (Canutt)
Sunset in Vienna, 1937 (Wilcox)
Sunset, Sunrise, 1973 (Rota)
Sunset Trail, 1939 (Harlan; Head; Metty)
Sunshine, 1999 (Jarre)
Sunshine Boys, 1975 (Booth; Smith; Stark)
Sunshine Christmas, 1977 (Head)
Sunshine Molly, 1915 (Marion)
Sunshine Sue, 1910 (Bitzer)
Sunshine Susie, 1931 (Balcon; Vetchinsky)
Sunshine through the Dark, 1911 (Bitzer)
Suor Letizia, 1956 (Zavattini)

Super Mouse Rides Again, 1943 (Terry)
Super-Pacific, 1948 (Colpi)
Super Rabbit, 1943 (Blanc; Jones; Stalling)
Super Salesman, 1947 (Terry)
Super Sleuth, 1937 (August; Polglase)
Super Snooper, 1952 (Blanc; McKimson; Stalling)
Supergirl, 1984 (Goldsmith)
Superior Duck, 1996 (Jones)
Superman, 1941 (Fleischer)
Superman, 1978 (Unsworth; Williams)
Superman II, 1981 (Unsworth)
Superman IV: The Quest for Peace, 1987 (Golan and Globus; Williams)
Superman in Billion Dollar Limited, 1942 (Fleischer)
Superman in Electric Earthquake, 1942 (Fleischer)
Superman in Terror on the Midway, 1942 (Fleischer)
Superman in The Arctic Giant, 1942 (Fleischer)
Superman in The Bulleteers, 1942 (Fleischer)
Superman in The Magnetic Telescope, 1942 (Fleischer)
Superman in The Mechanical Monsters, 1941 (Fleischer)
Superman in Volcano, 1942 (Fleischer)
Superman ki Wapasi, 1960 (Biswas)
Supernatural, 1932 (Banton)
Supertestimone, 1971 (Guerra)
Supertrain, 1979 (Lourié)
Suppose They Gave a War and Nobody Came, 1969 (Guffey)
Suppressed Duck, 1965 (Blanc; McKimson)
Sur la route de Salina, 1969 (D'Eaubonne)
Sur le pont d'Avignon, 1956 (Fradetal; Jarre)
Sur un air de Charleston, 1927 (Braunberger)
Surboum. See Déchaînés, 1950
Sure Fire, 1921 (Miller)
Sure-Mike, 1925 (Roach)
Sure Way to Peace. See Sichere Weg zum Frieden, 1917
Suri Lanka no ai to wakare, 1976 (Muraki)
Surmenés, 1957 (Braunberger; Delerue)
Surprise, 1923 (Fleischer)
Surprise-boogie, 1956 (Braunberger)
Surprise Package, 1960 (Challis; Coward)
Surprise Sock. See Chausette surprise, 1978
Surrender, 1931 (Grot; Howe; Levien)
Surrender, 1987 (Golan and Globus)
Surrounded House. See Det omrigade huset, 1922
Suruga yuhkyou-den: Yabure takka, 1964 (Miyagawa)
Surveillez votre tenue, 1949 (Decaë)
Surviving Picasso, 1996 (Jhabvala; Merchant)
Surviving the Game, 1994 (Dickerson)
Survivor, 1981 (Seale)
Susan and God, 1940 (Loos; Stothart; Stromberg)
Susan Lenox, Her Fall and Rise, 1931 (Adrian; Booth; Daniels; Gibbons; Mayer)
Susan Slade, 1961 (Alonzo; Ballard; Steiner)
Susan Slept Here, 1953 (D'Agostino; Musuraca)
Susanna, 1922 (Hornbeck)
Susanna tutta panna, 1957 (Delli Colli; Ponti)
Susannah of the Mounties, 1939 (Macgowan; Miller; Zanuck)
Suspended Step of the Stork. See To meteoro vima to Pelargou, 1991
Suspended Vocation. See Vocation suspendue, 1977
Suspense, 1946 (Struss)
Suspense au 2e Bureau, 1959 (D'Eaubonne)
Suspicion, 1941 (Harrison; Polglase; Raphaelson; Reville; Stradling; Waxman)
Süsse Mädel, 1926 (Warm)
Sussurro nel buio, 1976 (Donaggio)
Sutiejka, 1973 (Theodorakis)
Sutobi kago, 1952 (Miyagawa)
Sutter's Gold, 1936 (Waxman)

Suvorov, 1941 (Golovnya)
Suwanee River, 1925 (Fleischer)
Suzaku Gate. See Suzaku-mon, 1957
Suzaku-mon, 1957 (Miyagawa)
Suzanne et les roses. See Jeux d'amour, 1960
Suzanne et ses brigands, 1948 (Burel)
Suzanne Simonin, la religieuse de Denis Diderot, 1966 (de Beauregard)
Sváb, 1947 (Brdečka)
Svärmor kommer, 1930 (Jaenzon)
Svarta palmkronor, 1968 (Fischer)
Svatý Václav, 1930 (Heller; Stallich)
Svegliati e uccidi, 1966 (Morricone)
Svejk at the Front. See Švejk na fronte, 1926
Švejk na fronte, 1926 (Heller)
Svengali, 1931 (Grot)
Svengali, 1954 (Alwyn)
Svengali, 1983 (Barry)
Svengali's Cat, 1946 (Terry)
Svenska bilder, 1964 (Lundgren)
Svet, kde se žebrá, 1938 (Stallich)
Svet patří nám, 1937 (Heller)
Svítání, 1933 (Stallich)
Swallow the Leader, 1949 (Blanc; McKimson; Stalling)
Swamp Fire, 1946 (Mainwaring)
Swamp Water, 1941 (Day; Nichols)
Swan, 1925 (Banton)
Swan. See One Romantic Night, 1930
Swan, 1956 (Gibbons; Kaper; Rose; Ruttenberg; Schary; Surtees)
Swanee River, 1939 (Day; Dunne; Glennon; Macgowan; Zanuck)
Swann, 1996 (Bennett)
Swann in Love. See Amour de Swann, 1983
Swarm, 1978 (Goldsmith)
Swash Buckled, 1962 (Hanna and Barbera)
Swashbuckler, 1976 (Lathrop)
Swastika, 1973 (Puttnam)
Swat the Crook, 1919 (Roach)
Swat the Fly, 1935 (Fleischer)
Sweater Girl, 1942 (Dreier; Young)
Swedish Mistress, 1962 (Lundgren)
Swee' Pea. See Piso Piselli, 1982
Sweepings, 1933 (Cronjager; Plunkett; Selznick; Steiner)
Sweepstakes Winner, 1939 (Edeson)
Sweet Adeline, 1926 (Fleischer)
Sweet Adeline, 1935 (Orry-Kelly; Polito; Wallis)
Sweet Aloes. See Give Me Your Heart, 1936
Sweet and Low-Down, 1944 (Ballard; Spencer)
Sweet and Lowdown, 1999 (Loquasto)
Sweet and Twenty, 1909 (Bitzer)
Sweet Bird of Youth, 1962 (Berman; Krasner; Orry-Kelly)
Sweet By and By, 1921 (Roach)
Sweet Charity, 1969 (Head; Surtees; Westmore Family)
Sweet Cookie, 1921 (Garmes)
Sweet Daddies, 1926 (Edeson)
Sweet Daddy, 1924 (Roach)
Sweet Home. See Suito Homu, 1989
Sweet Hostage, 1975 (Schwartz)
Sweet Hunters, 1969 (Evein)
Sweet Jenny Lee, 1932 (Fleischer)
Sweet Kill, 1972 (Crosby)
Sweet Little Josefina. See Sladká Josefínka, 1927
Sweet Memories of Yesterday, 1911 (Gaudio; Ince)
Sweet Movie, 1974 (Lhomme)
Sweet Music, 1935 (Gaudio; Wald)
Sweet November, 1968 (Legrand)
Sweet Revenge, 1909 (Bitzer)
Sweet Revenge, 1976 (Zsigmond)

Sweet Ride, 1968 (Day; Pasternak; Smith)
Sweet Rosie O'Grady, 1943 (Basevi; Pan)
Sweet Sioux, 1937 (Stalling)
Sweet Smell of Success, 1957 (Bernstein; Howe; Lehman)
Sweet Sounds, 1976 (Merchant)
Sweet Talker, 1989 (Boyd)
Sweetheart of Sigma Chi, 1946 (Cahn; Hunter)
Sweetheart of the Campus, 1941 (Planer)
Sweethearts, 1938 (Adrian; Mayer; Stothart; Stromberg; Vorkapich)
Sweethearts and Wives, 1930 (Seitz)
Sweets for the Sweet, 1903 (Bitzer)
Swell Guy, 1946 (Gaudio)
Swept from the Sea, 1997 (Barry)
Swim or Sink, 1932 (Fleischer)
Swim Princess, 1928 (Hornbeck)
Swimmer, 1968 (Hamlisch; Wheeler)
Swimming Class, 1904 (Bitzer)
Swimming Pool. *See* Piscine, 1969
Swimming to Cambodia, 1987 (Littleton)
Swindle. *See* Bidone, 1955
Swing Cleaning, 1941 (Fleischer)
Swing Ding Amigo, 1966 (Blanc; McKimson)
Swing Fever, 1943 (Brown; Goosson; Rosher)
Swing Frolic, 1942 (Krasner)
Swing High, 1930 (Mandell)
Swing High, Swing Low, 1937 (Banton; Dreier; Young)
Swing It, 1936 (Cronjager)
Swing Kids, 1993 (Marshall)
Swing School, 1938 (Fleischer)
Swing Shift Cinderella, 1945 (Avery)
Swing Shift Maisie, 1943 (Irene; Stradling)
Swing Time, 1936 (Berman; Pan; Polglase)
Swing Vote, 1999 (Bass)
Swing, You Sinner, 1930 (Fleischer)
Swing Your Baby, 1938 (Wallis)
Swing Your Lady, 1937 (Deutsch; Edeson; Friedhofer)
Swing Your Partners, 1918 (Roach)
Swinger, 1966 (Biroc; Head; Pereira; Previn)
Swingin' Maiden. *See* Iron Maiden, 1963
Swinging at the Castle. *See* Det svänger på slottet, 1959
Swinging the Lambeth Walk , 1939 (Lye)
Swingmen in Europe, 1977 (Rabier)
Swingtime Johnny, 1943 (Bruckman)
Swirl of Glory. *See* Sugarfoot, 1950
Swiss Army Knife with Rats and Pigeons, 1981 (Breer)
Swiss Cheese, 1930 (Terry)
Swiss Cheeze Family Robinson, 1947 (Terry)
Swiss Family Robinson, 1940 (Dunn; Musuraca)
Swiss Family Robinson, 1960 (Alwyn; Disney; Ellenshaw)
Swiss Miss, 1938 (Roach)
Swiss Miss, 1951 (Terry)
Swiss Ski Yodelers, 1940 (Terry)
Swiss Tour. *See* Four Days' Leave, 1949
Switch, 1991 (Mancini)
Switched at Birth, 1991 (Hamlisch)
Switching Channels, 1988 (Hecht; Legrand)
Swooming the Swooners, 1945 (Terry)
Swoon, 1992 (Schamus; Vachon)
Swooner Crooner, 1944 (Blanc; Stalling)
Sword and Hearts, 1911 (Bitzer)
Sword and the Dragon, 1960 (Fields)
Sword and the Rose, 1953 (Dillon; Disney; Ellenshaw; Unsworth)
Sword in the Stone, 1963 (Disney)
Sword of Flying Dragon. *See* Hiryuh no ken, 1937
Sword of Sherwood Forest, 1960 (Carreras)

Sword of the Valiant: The Legend of Gawain and the Green Knight, 1983 (Golan and Globus; Young)
Sword of Vengeance, 1954 (Haskin)
Swords of Blood. *See* Cartouche, 1961
Swordsman, 1947 (Friedhofer; Goosson)
Swordsman of Siena. *See* Spadaccino di Siena, 1961
Syanhai no tsuki, 1941 (Tsuburaya)
Sylvester: Tragödie einer Nacht, 1923 (Mayer)
Sylvia of the Secret Service, 1917 (Grot; Miller)
Sylvia Scarlett, 1935 (August; Berman; Plunkett; Polglase)
Sylvia, 1965 (Head; Pereira; Raksin; Ruttenberg)
Sylvia, 1984 (Rosenman)
Sylvie and the Ghost. *See* Sylvie et la fantôme, 1944
Sylvie and the Phantom. *See* Sylvie et la fantôme, 1944
Sylvie et la fantôme, 1944 (Aurenche and Bost)
Sympathy for the Devil. *See* One Plus One, 1968
Sympathy Sal, 1915 (Loos)
Symphonie des brigands, 1936 (Schüfftan)
Symphonie du travail, 1943 (Alekan)
Symphonie eines Lebens, 1942 (Hoffmann)
Symphonie in Salzburg, 1946 (Von Dassanowsky)
Symphonie New York, 1956 (Braunberger)
Symphonie Nr. 3 in Es-dur, Opus 55 "Eroica" von Ludwig von Beethoven, 1967 (Colpi)
Symphonie Nr. 7 von Ludwig von Beethoven, 1966 (Colpi)
Symphonie Nr. 9 von Franz Schubert, 1966 (Colpi)
Symphonie pastorale, 1942 (Andrejew)
Symphonie pastorale, 1946 (Annenkov; Aurenche and Bost; Auric)
Symphonie pour un massacre, 1962 (Barsacq; Renoir)
Symphony for a Massacre. *See* Symphonie pour un massacre, 1963
Symphony in Slang, 1951 (Avery)
Symphony in Two Flats, 1930 (Balcon)
Symphony of Six Million, 1932 (Berman; Selznick; Steiner)
Symphony Orchestra, 1964 (Halas and Batchelor)
Syn hor, 1925 (Heller)
Synanon, 1965 (Stradling)
Synchromy, 1971 (McClaren)
Syncopated Sioux, 1940 (Lantz)
Syncopation, 1929 (Plunkett)
Synd, 1928 (Jaenzon)
Synnöve Solbakken, 1957 (Nykvist)
Syonen hyoryuki, 1943 (Tsuburaya)
Syskonbädd 1782, 1966 (Lundgren)
Sztandar młodych, 1958 (Lenica)

T for Tumbleweed, 1962 (Wexler)
T-Men, 1947 (Alton)
THX 1138, 1970 (Murch; Schifrin)
T.V.A., 1945 (Vorkapich)
TZ, 1979 (Breer)
T2 3-D: Battle Across Time, 1996 (Winston)
Ta-Ra-Ra-Boom-Der-A, 1926 (Fleischer)
Tabasco Road, 1957 (Stalling)
Tabi yakusha, 1940 (Hayasaka)
Table for Five, 1983 (Zsigmond)
Table tournante, 1989 (Grimault)
Tableaux d'une exposition, 1972 (Alexeieff and Parker)
Tableaux futuristes et incohérents, 1916 (Cohl)
Tabu, 1931 (Crosby)
Tac, tac, 1980 (Alcoriza)
Taffin, 1988 (Zimmer)
Tag, der nie zu Ende geht, 1959 (Herlth)
Tagebuch des Dr. Hart, 1916 (Hoffmann)
Tagebuch einer Verlorenen, 1929 (Metzner)
Tahiti Nights, 1944 (Guffey)
Tai-Pan, 1986 (Cardiff; de Laurentiis; Jarre)

Taiga, 1958 (Herlth)
Taiheiyo hitoribotchi, 1963 (Takemitsu)
Taiheiyo Kiseki no sakusen Kisuka, 1965 (Tsuburaya)
Taiheiyo no arashi, 1960 (Tsuburaya)
Taiheiyo no tsubasi, 1963 (Tsuburaya)
Taiheizo no washi, 1953 (Tsuburaya)
Tail of the Monkey, 1926 (Lantz)
Tail Spin, 1939 (Freund; Zanuck)
Tailor Made Man, 1922 (Irene)
Tailor of Panama, 2000 (Rousselot)
Tailor's Maid. See Padri e figli, 1956
Tailor's Story. See Krejčovská povíkda, 1954
Tainted Money. See Show Them No Mercy, 1935
Taiyo no karyudo, 1970 (Takemitsu)
Tajemstvi hradu v Karpatech, 1981 (Brdečka; švankmajer)
Tajemství krve, 1953 (Stallich)
Tajna Marchello, 1997 (Guerra)
Takadanobaba, 1944 (Yoda)
Take a Chance, 1918 (Roach)
Take a Chance, 1933 (Lemaire)
Take a Giant Step, 1959 (Epstein)
Take a Hard Ride, 1975 (Goldsmith)
Take a Letter, Darling, 1942 (Dreier; Irene; Young)
Take a Trip, 1926 (Fleischer)
Take Care of My Little Girl, 1951 (Epstein; Lemaire; Newman;
    Reynolds)
Take Her, She's Mine, 1963 (Ballard; Goldsmith; Johnson; Smith)
Take It Big, 1944 (van Heusen)
Take It or Leave It, 1944 (La Shelle)
Take Me Out to the Ball Game, 1948 (Comden and Green; Deutsch;
    Edens; Freed; Mayer; Rose)
Take Me to Town, 1953 (Hunter; Metty)
Take My Life, 1947 (Alwyn; Bryan; Havelock-Allan; Neame; Rank)
Take My Tip, 1937 (Metzner)
Take Next Car, 1922 (Roach)
Take One False Step, 1949 (Orry-Kelly)
Take the Air, 1923 (Roach)
Take the High Ground, 1953 (Alton; Schary; Tiomkin)
Take the Money and Run, 1969 (Hamlisch; Rosenblum)
Taki no shiraito, 1952 (Miyagawa; Yoda)
Taking Care of Business, 1990 (Reynolds)
Taking of Luke McVane. See Fugitive, 1914
Taking Off, 1970 (Carrière; Henry; Ondříček)
Taking the Blame, 1935 (Fleischer)
Taková láska, 1959 (Brdečka)
Tal des Lebens, 1913 (Messter)
Tal Farlow, 1980 (Lye)
Talash, 1969 (Burman)
Tale of a Dead Princess, 1953 (Ivanov-Vano)
Tale of a Shirt, 1933 (Terry)
Tale of a Wolf, 1960 (Hanna and Barbera)
Tale of Czar Sultan, 1966 (Ptushko)
Tale of John and Mary. See Pohádka o Honzikovi a Mařence, 1980
Tale of Lost Time, 1964 (Ptushko)
Tale of Sweeney Todd, 1998 (Bennett)
Tale of Tales, 1980 (Norstein)
Tale of the Fisherman and the Little Fish. See Skazka o rybake i
    rybke, 1937
Tale of the Fox. See Roman de Renard, 1941
Tale of the Magician, 1964 (Halas and Batchelor)
Tale of the Wilderness, 1911 (Bitzer)
Tale of Two Cities, 1935 (Gibbons; Mayer; Selznick; Stothart)
Tale of Two Cities, 1958 (Addinsell; Clarke; Dillon; Rank)
Tale of Two Kitties, 1942 (Blanc; Clampett; Stalling)
Tale of Two Mice, 1945 (Blanc; Stalling) <Talent Competition. See
    Konkurs, 1963

Talented Mr. Ripley, 1999 (Murch; Seale)
Tales By Capek. See Capkovy povídky, 1947
Tales from the Crypt, 1972 (Francis)
Tales from the Crypt, 1989 (Francis)
Tales From the Crypt: Demon Knight, 1995 (Dickerson)
Tales from the Darkside: The Movie, 1990 (Smith)
Tales of a Pale and Mysterious Moon after the Rain. See **Ugetsu
    monogatari**, 1953
Tales of a Salesman, 1965 (Zsigmond)
Tales of Hoffman, 1951 (Francis; Challis; Heckroth; Korda)
Tales of Hoffman. See Hoffmanovy povídky, 1962
Tales of Manhattan, 1942 (Day; Hecht; Hoffenstein; Leven; Spiegel;
    Stewart; Trotti; Walker)
Tales of Ordinary Madness. See Storie di ordinaria follia, 1981
Tales of Terror, 1962 (Crosby)
Tales of the Typewriter. See Mesék az írógépről, 1916
Tales that Witness Madness, 1973 (Francis)
Talisman. See Amuletten, 1911
Talk About a Stranger, 1952 (Alton)
Talk about Work, 1971 (Menges)
Talk of Angels, 1998 (Hambling)
Talk of the Town, 1942 (Buchman; Cohn; Irene)
Talker, 1925 (Edeson)
Talking Magpies, 1946 (Terry)
Talking through My Heart, 1936 (Fleischer)
Tall, Dark and Gruesome, 1948 (Bruckman)
Tall Guy, 1990 (Biddle)
Tall Men, 1955 (Lemaire; Nugent; Wheeler; Young)
Tall Story, 1960 (Epstein)
Tall Stranger, 1957 (Mirisch)
Tall Tale, 1994 (Kaminski)
Tall Tale Teller, 1954 (Terry)
Tall Tales, 1940 (Maddow)
Tall Target, 1951 (Gibbons; Mainwaring)
Tall Texan, 1953 (Biroc)
Tall Timber, 1928 (Disney)
Tall Timber Tale, 1951 (Terry)
Tall Trouble. See Hell Canyon Outlaws, 1957
Tamahine, 1963 (Arnold; Bryan; Unsworth)
Taman, 1916 (Starewicz)
Tamango, 1957 (Douy; Kosma; Wakhévitch)
Tamara la complaisante, 1937 (Auric)
Tamarind Seed, 1973 (Pinter; Barry; Young)
Tamas, 1987 (Nihalani)
Tamburaši u Spejbla a Hurvínka, 1953 (Stallich)
Tame Men and Wild Women, 1925 (Roach)
T'amerò sempre, 1943 (Amidei)
Taming a Husband, 1910 (Bitzer)
Taming of Dorothy. See Her Favourite Husband, 1950
Taming of the Shrew, 1908 (Bitzer)
Taming of the Shrew, 1929 (Menzies; Struss)
Taming of the Shrew, 1966 (Cecchi D'amico; Donati; Morris; Rota;
    Sharaff)
Taming of the Shrew. See Jajauma narashi, 1966
Taming of the Snood, 1940 (Bruckman)
Taming the Cat, 1948 (Terry)
Tammy. See Tammy and the Bachelor, 1957
Tammy and the Bachelor, 1957 (Hunter)
Tammy and the Doctor, 1963 (Hunter; Metty)
Tammy Tell Me True, 1961 (Hunter)
Tampico, 1944 (Basevi; Clarke; Raksin)
Tampon du capiston, 1950 (Braunberger)
Tang, 1970 (Douy)
Tangier, 1946 (Banton)
Tangled Fates, 1916 (Marion)
Tangled Travels, 1944 (Fleischer)

Tanglewood, Music School and Music Festival. *See* Tanglewood Story, 1950

Tanglewood Story, 1950 (Kaufman)

Tango, 1998 (Schifrin; Storaro)

Tango für dich, 1930 (Reisch)

Tango Lesson, 1997 (Müller)

Tango notturno, 1937 (Wagner)

Tanin no kao, 1966 (Takemitsu)

Tank, 1984 (Schifrin)

Tank Force, 1958 (Broccoli)

Tank Girl, 1995 (Winston)

Tanks a Million, 1941 (Roach)

Tanned Legs, 1929 (Plunkett)

Tant Grun, Tant Brun, och Tant Gredelin, 1945 (Fischer)

Tant que je vivrai, 1945 (Matras; Mnouchkine)

Tant qu'il est temps: le cancer, 1960 (Braunberger)

Tant qu'il y aura des femmes, 1955 (Burel)

Tant qu'on a la santé. *See* Nous n'irons plus au bois, 1963

Tantalizing Fly, 1919 (Fleischer)

Tante Zita, 1967 (Saulnier)

Tanuki, 1956 (Yoda)

Tanuki no kyujitsu, 1966 (Muraki)

Tanuki no taishou, 1965 (Muraki)

Tanya's Island, 1980 (Baker)

Tanzende Wien, 1927 (Andrejew)

Tänzer Meiner Frau, 1925 (Korda)

Tap Roots, 1947 (Hoch; Wanger)

Tapis volant, 1960 (Jarre)

Tapisserie au XXe siècle, 1955 (Kosma)

Tappa inte sugen, 1947 (Fischer)

Taps, 1981 (Jarre)

Tapum!, la storia delle armi, 1958 (Bozzetto)

Tarahumara, 1965 (Alcoriza)

Tarakanova, 1930 (D'Eaubonne; Wakhévitch)

Tarakanova, 1937 (Courant)

Tarakanowa, 1937 (Andrejew)

Tarakanowa, 1938 (Annenkov; Jeanson)

Taran, 1951 (Biswas)

Tarantel, 1920 (Messter)

Tarantola dal ventro nero, 1971 (Morricone)

Tarantula, 1912 (Macpherson)

Tarantula, 1955 (Mancini; Westmore Family)

Taras Bulba, 1962 (Reynolds; Waxman)

Tarass Boulba, 1935 (Andrejew; Planer)

Tarde Demais, 2000 (Branco)

Tare, 1911 (Gaumont)

Target, 1985 (Zanuck)

Target, 1995 (Dutta)

Target Eagle. *See* Jugando con la muerte, 1982

Target for Scandal. *See* Washington Story, 1952

Targets, 1967 (Fields; Kovacs)

Tarnish, 1924 (Carré; Goldwyn; Marion; Miller)

Tarnished Angel, 1938 (Musuraca; Polglase)

Tarnished Lady, 1931 (Banton; Stewart; Zukor)

Tars and Spars, 1946 (Cahn; Goosson; Walker; Westmore Family)

Tartarin de tarascon, 1934 (Douy; Milhaud)

Tartelette, 1968 (Grimault)

Tartu. *See* Sabotage Agent, 1943

Tartüff, 1925 (Freund; Herlth; Mayer; Pommer; Röhrig)

Tartuffe. *See* Tartüff, 1925

Tarzan and His Mate, 1934 (Clarke; Gibbons; Gillespie; Mayer)

Tarzan and the Golden Lion, 1927 (Walker)

Tarzan and the Jungle Queen, 1951 (Haskin; Struss)

Tarzan and the Leopard Woman, 1945 (Struss)

Tarzan and the Mermaids, 1947 (Figueroa; Tiomkin)

Tarzan and the She Devil, 1953 (Struss)

Tarzan and the Slave Girl, 1950 (Harlan; Horner)

Tarzan Escapes, 1935 (Brown; Mayer)

Tarzan the Ape Man, 1928 (Gillespie)

Tarzan the Ape Man, 1931 (Mayer)

Tarzan, the Ape Man, 1932 (Rosson)

Tarzan Triumphs, 1943 (Horner)

Tarzan versus I.B.M.. *See* **Alphaville**, 1965

Tarzan's Desert Mystery, 1943 (Harlan)

Tarzan's Greatest Adventure, 1959 (Fisher)

Tarzan's Magic Fountain, 1948 (Siodmak; Struss)

Tarzan's New York Adventure, 1942 (Mayer)

Tarzan's Peril. *See* Tarzan and the Jungle Queen, 1951

Tarzan's Savage Fury, 1952 (Struss)

Task Force, 1949 (Burks; Wald; Waxman)

Tassinaro, 1983 (Age and Scarpelli)

Taste for Women. *See* Aimez-vous des femmes, 1964

Taste of Catnip, 1966 (Blanc; Mckimson)

Taste of Fear, 1961 (Carreras; Slocombe)

Taste of Honey, 1961 (Lassally)

Taste the Blood of Dracula, 1970 (Bernard; Carreras)

Tatjana, 1923 (Messter; Pommer)

Tatoué, 1968 (Vierny)

Tattoo. *See* Irezumi, 1966

Tattoo, 1981 (Donaggio; Levine)

Taugenichts, 1922 (Herlth)

Tavelure du pommier et du poirier, 1955 (Rabier)

Taverne du poisson couronné, 1947 (Jeanson)

Tawny Pipit, 1943 (Rank; Vetchinsky)

Taxandria, 1988 (Robbe-Grillet)

Taxi, 1953 (Krasner; Lemaire)

Taxi, 1995 (Storaro)

Taxi 13, 1928 (Berman)

Taxi Barons, 1933 (Roach)

Taxi Beauties, 1928 (Hornbeck)

Taxi Dancer, 1927 (Mayer)

Taxi de nuit, 1993 (Sarde)

Taxi di notte, 1950 (Aldo)

Taxi Dolls, 1929 (Hornbeck)

Taxi Driver, 1927 (Gibbons)

Taxi Driver, 1954 (Burman)

Taxi Driver, 1976 (Herrmann; Smith)

Taxi for Two, 1928 (Balcon; Hornbeck)

Taxi mauve, 1977 (Delli Colli; Sarde)

Taxi, Mister, 1942 (Roach)

Taxi Scandal, 1928 (Hornbeck)

Taxi Spooks, 1929 (Hornbeck)

Taxidi sta kithira, 1985 (Guerra)

Taza, Son of Cochise, 1953 (Hunter)

Tažní ptáci, 1961 (Stallich)

Tchaikovsky, 1968 (Tiomkin)

Tchaikovsky and Rachimanova. *See* V tylu u belych, 1925

Tchao Pantin, 1983 (Nuytten; Trauner)

Tchin-Tchin. *See* A Fine Romance, 1992

Te o tsunagu ko-ra, 1964 (Takemitsu)

Te o tsunaqu kora, 1948 (Miyagawa)

Te quiero, 1978 (Figueroa)

Tea and Sympathy, 1956 (Alton; Berman; Deutsch; Rose)

Tea for Three, 1927 (Day; Gibbons)

Tea for Two, 1945 (Hanna and Barbera)

Tea with Mussolini, 1999 (Watkin)

Teacher's Beau, 1935 (Roach)

Teacher's Pest, 1931 (Fleischer; Lantz)

Teacher's Pet, 1958 (Head; Pereira)

Teaching Dad to Like Her, 1911 (Bitzer)

Teaching of the Ittou Style. *See* Ittouryu shinan, 1936

Teaching the Teacher, 1921 (Roach)

Teahouse of the August Moon, 1956 (Alton)
Team. *See* Venedig—die Insel der Glückseligen am Rande am des Untergangs, 1978
Team of Four. *See* Viererzug, 1917
Teamwork, 1977 (Dunning)
Tear Me but Satiate Me with Your Kisses. *See* Straziami ma di baci saziami, 1968
Tear on the Page, 1915 (Loos)
Tears for Simon, 1957 (Rank)
Tears in the Lion's Mane. *See* Namida o shishi no tategami no, 1962
Tears of an Onion, 1938 (Fleischer)
Tease for Two, 1965 (Blanc; McKimson)
Teaser, 1925 (Barnes)
Tebukuro o nugasu otoko, 1946 (Miyagawa)
Technocracked, 1933 (Iwerks)
Techo de la ballena, 1982 (Alekan)
Teckman Mystery, 1954 (Korda; Rank)
Teen Deviyan, 1965 (Burman)
Teen Kanya, 1961 (Chandragupta; Dutta)
Teen Wolf, 1985 (Baker)
Teenage Bonnie and Klepto Clyde, 1993 (Golan and Globus)
Teenage Caveman, 1958 (Crosby)
Teenage Mutant Ninja Turtles, 1990 (Henson)
Teenage Rebel, 1956 (Brackett; Lemaire; Reisch; Smith; Wheeler)
Teeth of Steel, 1942 (Unsworth)
Teilnehmer antwortet nicht, 1932 (Junge; Planer)
Teiva, enfant des îles, 1960 (Kosma)
Tejedor de milagros, 1961 (Figueroa)
Telecoutre sans fil, 1910 (Cohl)
Telefilm, 1928 (Fleischer)
Telefon, 1978 (Schifrin)
Telegraph Trail, 1933 (Canutt; McCord)
Telephone, 1988 (Southern)
Telephone Girl, 1924 (Garmes)
Telephone Girl and the Lady, 1912 (Bitzer; Loos)
Television Fan. *See* Zavada není na vašem přijímaci, 1961
Television Spy, 1939 (Head)
Televize v Bublicích aneb Bublice v televizi, 1974 (Ondříček)
Tell 'em Nothing, 1926 (Roach)
Tell It to a Policeman, 1925 (Roach)
Tell It to the Judge, 1928 (Roach)
Tell It to the Judge, 1949 (Walker)
Tell It to the Marines, 1926 (Gibbons; Gillespie)
Tell Me a Riddle, 1980 (Von Brandenstein)
Tell Me that You Love Me, Junie Moon, 1969 (Cortez; Kaufman; Wheeler)
Tell No Tales, 1939 (Ruttenberg)
Tell-Tale Heart, 1928 (Shamroy)
Tell-Tale Heart, 1953 (Bosustow)
Tell-Tale Heart, 1971 (Bernstein)
Tell Them Willie Boy Is Here, 1969 (Bumstead; Grusin; Hall; Head; Westmore Family)
Telling Lies in America, 1997 (Eszterhas)
Telling the World, 1928 (Booth; Daniels; Gibbons)
Telling Whoppers, 1926 (Roach)
Tělo Diany, 1969 (Ondříček)
Temip nostri, 1953 (Flaiano and Pinelli)
Temné slunce, 1980 (Ondříček)
Temno, 1950 (Stallich)
Temoin, 1979 (Amidei)
Témoin dans la ville, 1957 (Decaë)
T'empêches tout le monde de dormir, 1981 (Mnouchkine)
Temperamental Lion, 1940 (Terry)
Temperamental Wife, 1919 (Loos)
Tempest, 1928 (Menzies; Rosher; Sullivan)
Tempest. *See* Tempesta, 1958

Tempest, 1982 (McAlpine)
Tempesta, 1958 (Wilson; de Laurentiis)
Tempête dans une chambre à coucher, 1901 (Pathé)
Tempête sur l'Asie, 1938 (Fradetal)
Tempi nostri, 1953 (Cecchi D'amico)
Temple of Dusk, 1918 (Marion)
Temple of Venus, 1923 (August)
Temple Tower, 1930 (Clarke)
Tempo di uccidere, 1989 (Age and Scarpelli; Morricone)
Tempo di villeggiatura, 1956 (Age and Scarpelli)
Temporale Rosy, 1979 (Age and Scarpelli)
Temporary Sheriff, 1927 (Walker)
Temporary Truce, 1912 (Bitzer)
Temporary Widow, 1930 (Pommer)
Temps des cérises, 1937 (Kosma; Wakhévitch)
Temps détruit: lettres d'une guerre 1939-40, 1985 (Jaubert)
Temps du ghetto, 1961 (Braunberger; Fradetal; Jarre)
Temps morts, 1964 (Grimault)
Temps redonné, 1967 (Delerue)
Temps retrouvé, 1999 (Branco)
Temptation, 1915 (Buckland; Macpherson)
Temptation, 1923 (Cohn)
Temptation, 1934 (Balcon)
Temptation, 1945 (Ballard; Orry-Kelly)
Temptation Harbour, 1947 (Heller)
Temptress, 1926 (Basevi; Daniels; Gaudio; Gibbons; Mayer)
Ten Bridges, 1957 (Lassally)
Ten-Cent Adventure, 1915 (Loos)
Ten Cents a Dance, 1931 (Haller; Swerling)
Ten Commandments, 1923 (Glennon; Macpherson; Rennahan; Zukor)
Ten Commandments, 1956 (Bernstein; Head; Jeakins; Pereira; Westmore Family)
Ten Days in Paris, 1939 (Rozsa)
Ten Days That Shook the World. *See* **Oktiabr**, 1928
Ten Days' Wonder. *See* Décade prodigieuse, 1972
Ten Dollar Raise, 1921 (Gaudio)
Ten for Survival, 1979 (Halas and Batchelor)
Ten Gentlemen from West Point, 1942 (Day; Newman; Shamroy)
Ten Girls Ago, 1962 (Garmes)
Ten Laps to Go, 1936 (Canutt)
Ten Minute Egg, 1924 (Roach)
Ten no yugao, 1948 (Hayasaka)
Ten North Frederick, 1958 (Brackett; Dunne; Lemaire; Wheeler)
Ten Pin Terrors, 1953 (Terry)
Ten Seconds to Hell, 1958 (Carreras; Laszlo)
Ten Thousand Bedrooms, 1957 (Cahn; Pasternak; Rose)
Ten to Midnight, 1983 (Golan and Globus)
Ten Who Dared, 1960 (Disney; Iwerks)
Ten Years Old, 1927 (Roach)
Tenant. *See* Locataire, 1976
Tenda rossa. *See* Krasnaya palatka, 1971
Tender Comrade, 1943 (D'Agostino; Head; Metty; Trumbo)
Tender Enemy. *See* Tendre Ennemi, 1935
Tender Game, 1958 (Hubley)
Tender Hearts, 1909 (Bitzer)
Tender Is the Night, 1962 (Herrmann; Reynolds; Shamroy; Smith)
Tender Is the Night, 1985 (Bennett)
Tender Mercies, 1983 (Boyd)
Tender Scoundrel. *See* Tendre voyou, 1966
Tender Trap, 1955 (Cahn; Epstein; Rose; van Heusen)
Tenderfoot, 1932 (Toland)
Tenderfoot. *See* Bushwhacked, 1995
Tenderfoot Days. *See* Kakedashi jidai, 1947
Tenderhearted Boy, 1912 (Bitzer)
Tenderloin, 1928 (Mohr; Zanuck)
Tenderloin Tragedy, 1907 (Bitzer)

Tendre Ennemi, 1935 (Schüfftan)
Tendre Poulet, 1977 (Delerue; Mnouchkine)
Tendre voyou, 1966 (Legrand; Wakhévitch)
Ténériffe, 1932 (Prévert)
Tengoku to jigoku, 1963 (Muraki)
Tenka no goikenban o Ikensuru otoko, 1947 (Yoda)
Tenka no igagoe , 1934 (Tsuburaya)
Tenka o nerau bishounen, 1955 (Miyagawa)
Tenka taihei, 1955 (Muraki)
Tennessee Johnson, 1942 (Rosson; Stothart)
Tennessee's Partner, 1955 (Alton; Polglase)
Tennis Chumps, 1949 (Hanna and Barbera)
Tennis Club, 1982 (Bozzetto)
Tenpo hiken roku , 1927 (Tsuburaya)
Tenpyo no iraka, 1979 (Takemitsu; Yoda)
Tenryu shibuki, 1938 (Yoda)
Tension, 1949 (Previn; Stradling)
Tension at Table Rock, 1956 (Biroc; Tiomkin)
Tentacles of the North, 1926 (Walker)
Tentation d'Isabelle, 1985 (Sarde)
Tenth Avenue, 1948 (Surtees)
Tenth Victim. See Decima vittima, 1965
Teorema, 1968 (Morricone)
Tepepa, 1969 (Morricone; Solinas)
Tequila Sunrise, 1988 (Grusin; Hall; Sylbert; Towne)
Tercera palabra, 1955 (Alcoriza)
Tere Ghar Ke Saamne, 1963 (Burman)
Tere Mere Sapne, 1971 (Burman)
Teresa la ladra, 1973 (Age and Scarpelli)
Teresa Venerdi, 1941 (Zavattini)
Teri Ankhen, 1963 (Burman)
Terje vigen, 1917 (Jaenzon; Magnusson)
Term of Trial, 1962 (Morris)
Terminal Exposure, 1987 (Zimmer)
Terminator, 1984 (Winston)
Terminator 2: Judgement Day, 1991 (Muren; Winston)
Terra Fria, 1990 (de Almeida)
Terra Incognito, 1949 (Arnold)
Terra straniera, 1953 (Di Venanzo)
Terra trema, 1947 (Aldo; Di Venanzo; Serandrei)
Terrain vague, 1960 (Legrand; Renoir)
Terrazza, 1980 (Age and Scarpelli)
Terre d'amour, 1935 (Jaubert)
Terre d'insectes, 1957 (Braunberger)
Terre d'oiseaux, 1957 (Braunberger)
Terre qui meurt, 1935 (Spaak)
Terre sous-marine, 1958 (Braunberger)
Terreur en Oklahoma, 1950 (Douy)
Terrible Bout de papier, 1915 (Cohl)
Terrible Discovery, 1911 (Bitzer)
Terrible Ted, 1907 (Bitzer)
Terrible Toreador, 1929 (Iwerks)
Terrible Troubadour, 1933 (Lantz)
Terrible Vengeance. See Strashnaya myest, 1913
Terribly Stuck Up, 1914 (Roach)
Terribly Talented, 1948 (Kaufman)
Terrier Stricken, 1952 (Blanc; Jones; Stalling)
Territoire, 1981 (Alekan; Branco; de Almeida)
Territory. See Territoire, 1981
Terror, 1928 (Musuraca)
Terror Abroad, 1933 (Banton)
Terror and Black Lace. See Terrór y encajes negros, 1986
Terror at Black Falls, 1962 (Alonzo; Crosby)
Terror Faces Magoo, 1959 (Bosustow)
Terror from the Year 5000, 1958 (Allen)
Terror in a Texas Town, 1958 (Rennahan)

Terror in the City, 1966 (Rosenblum)
Terror in the Wax Museum, 1973 (Duning)
Terror of Manhattan, 1991 (Golan and Globus)
Terror of the Tongs, 1960 (Bernard; Carreras)
Terror on a Train. See Time Bomb, 1952
Terror Street. See 36 Hours, 1954
Terror Train, 1980 (Alcott)
Terror Within II, 1990 (Kaminski)
Terrór y encajes negros, 1986 (Alcoriza)
Terrore sulla città, 1956 (Di Venanzo; Flaiano and Pinelli)
Terrorists. See Ransom, 1974
Terry Fox Story, 1983 (Conti)
Terza liceo, 1954 (Amidei)
Terza luna, 1997 (Donaggio)
Tesoro di Damasco, 1999 (Donaggio)
Tess, 1979 (Cloquet; Sarde; Unsworth)
Tess of the D'Urbervilles, 1927 (Mayer)
Tess of the Storm Country, 1922 (Grot; Rosher)
Tess of the Storm Country, 1932 (Levien; Mohr)
Tess of the Storm Country, 1960 (Howe)
Test, 1909 (Bitzer)
Test by Fire. See Feuerprobe, 1913
Test of Friendship, 1908 (Bitzer)
Test Pilot, 1938 (Gillespie; Mayer; Vorkapich; Waxman)
Testament, 1974 (Ponti)
Testament, 1983 (Tavoularis)
Testament des Dr. Mabuse, 1933 (Hunte; Von Harbou; Wagner)
Testament d'Orphée, 1960 (Auric)
Testament du Docteur Cordelier, 1959 (Kosma)
Testament of Dr. Mabuse. See **Testament des Dr. Mabuse**, 1933
Testament of Orpheus. See Testament d'Orphée, 1960
Testimone, 1946 (Zavattini)
Testimonies. See Vittnesbörd om henne, 1962
Testing Block, 1920 (August)
Tête, 1973 (Grimault)
Tête contre les murs, 1958 (Jarre; Schüfftan)
Tête d'un homme, 1932 (Wakhévitch)
Tetto, 1956 (Zavattini)
Teufel führt Regie. See Dämonische Liebe, 1950
Teufel in Seide, 1955 (Herlth)
Teufel und die Madonna, 1919 (Dreier)
Teutonic Knights. See Krżacy, 1960
Tevye and His Seven Daughters. See Diamonds, 1975
Tex, 1982 (Donaggio)
Texan, 1920 (Furthman)
Texan, 1930 (Canutt; Zukor)
Texan, 1994 (Mamet)
Texan Meets Calamity Jane, 1950 (Struss)
Texans, 1938 (Edouart; Head)
Texan's Honor , 1929 (Canutt)
Texas, 2000 (Shepard)
Texas Across the River, 1966 (Cahn; Metty)
Texas Carnival, 1951 (Pan; Rose)
Texas Chainsaw Massacre II, 1986 (Elfman; Golan and Globus; Savini)
Texas in 1999, 1931 (Fleischer)
Texas Kelly at Bay, 1913 (Ince)
Texas Masquerade, 1943 (Harlan)
Texas Rangers, 1936 (Cronjager; Dreier; Head)
Texas Rangers Ride Again, 1940 (Head)
Texas Stampede, 1939 (Ballard)
Texas to Tokyo. See We've Never Been Licked, 1943
Texas Tom, 1950 (Hanna and Barbera)
Texas Tornado, 1928 (Berman)
Texas Tornado, 1934 (Canutt)
Texas Trail, 1937 (Harlan; Head)
Thakshak, 1999 (Nihalani)

Thank Heaven for Small Favors. *See* Dr"le de paroissien, 1963
Thank You, 1925 (Marion)
Thank You and Good Night, 1991 (Schamus)
Thank You Madame. *See* Im Sonneschein, 1936
Thank You, Mr. Moto, 1937 (Miller)
Thank Your Lucky Stars, 1943 (Edeson; Grot)
Thanks a Million, 1935 (Johnson; Kahn; Zanuck)
Thanks for Everything, 1938 (Zanuck)
Thanks for the Memory, 1938 (Dreier; Fleischer; Head; Struss)
Thark, 1932 (Wilcox)
That Cat. *See* Až přijde kocour, 1963
That Certain Age, 1938 (Pasternak)
That Certain Feeling, 1937 (Wallis)
That Certain Feeling, 1956 (Bumstead; Diamond; Head; Pereira)
That Certain Thing, 1928 (Cohn; Walker)
That Certain Woman, 1937 (Haller; Orry-Kelly; Steiner)
That Championship Season, 1982 (Conti; Golan and Globus)
That Chink in Golden Gulch, 1910 (Bitzer)
That Cold Day in the Park, 1969 (Kovacs; Mandel)
That Dangerous Age, 1949 (Korda)
That Dangerous Age, 1950 (Périnal)
That Darn Cat, 1965 (Disney)
That Forsyte Woman, 1949 (Kaper; Plunkett; Ruttenberg)
That Funny Feeling, 1965 (Whitlock)
That Girl from Paris, 1936 (Berman)
That Hagen Girl, 1947 (Freund; Waxman)
That Hamilton Woman, 1941 (Guffey; Hornbeck; Korda; Reisch; Rozsa; Wheeler)
That Kind of Girl. *See* Models, Inc., 1952
That Kind of Woman, 1959 (Bernstein; Head; Kaufman; Pereira; Ponti)
That Lady, 1955 (Junge; Krasker; Veiller)
That Lady in Ermine, 1948 (Lemaire; Newman; Pan; Raphaelson; Shamroy; Spencer; Wheeler)
That Little Big Fellow, 1927 (Fleischer)
That Man from Rio. *See* Homme de Rio, 1964
That Man Mr. Jones. *See* Fuller Brush Man, 1948
That Man's Here Again, 1937 (Trumbo)
That Midnight Kiss, 1949 (Ames; Mayer; Pasternak; Surtees)
That Night, 1928 (Roach)
That Night Adventure. *See* Sonoyo no bouken, 1948
That Night in London, 1932 (Korda)
That Night in Rio, 1941 (Banton; Day; Newman; Pan; Rennahan; Shamroy)
That Noise, 1961 (Godfrey)
That Obscure Object of Desire. *See* Cet obscur objet de désir, 1977
That Old Gang of Mine, 1931 (Fleischer)
That Other Woman, 1942 (Day)
That Riviera Touch, 1966 (Hambling; Heller)
That Splendid November. *See* Bellissimo novembre, 1968
That Touch of Mink, 1962 (Duning; Lourié; Metty; Westmore Family)
That Uncertain Feeling, 1941 (Barnes; Irene; Reisch; Stewart)
That Way with Women, 1947 (McCord)
That Wonderful Urge, 1948 (Clarke; Lemaire; Newman)
That'll Be the Day, 1973 (Puttnam)
That's a Good Girl, 1933 (Wilcox)
That's Dancing!, 1985 (Mancini)
That's Entertainment!, 1974 (Laszlo; Mancini; Metty)
That's Entertainment, Part II, 1976 (Bass)
That's Him, 1918 (Roach)
That's Life!, 1986 (Mancini)
That's My Boy, 1932 (August; Krasna)
That's My Boy, 1951 (Garmes; Head; Wallis)
That's My Man, 1947 (Canutt; Gaudio)
That's My Mommy, 1955 (Hanna and Barbera)
That's My Pup, 1953 (Hanna and Barbera)
That's My Wife, 1929 (Roach)

That's Right, You're Wrong, 1939 (Duning; Metty; Polglase)
That's Warner Bros!, 1995 (Jones)
Thau le pêcheur, 1957 (Coutard)
Thaumetopoea, 1960 (Guillemot)
Théâtre National Populaire, 1956 (Fradetal; Jarre)
Theatre of Life. *See* Jinsei gekijo, 1952
Theatre Royal. *See* Royal Family of Broadway, 1931
Theft. *See* Diebstahl, 1917
Theft of the Mona Lisa. *See* Raub der Mona Lisa, 1931
Their Big Moment, 1934 (Plunkett; Steiner)
Their Bridal Night. *See* Jejich svatební noc, 1922
Their First Mistake, 1932 (Roach)
Their First Misunderstanding, 1911 (Gaudio; Ince)
Their Own Desire, 1929 (Adrian; Daniels; Day; Gibbons; Marion)
Their Purple Moment, 1928 (Roach)
Their Secret Affair. *See* Top Secret Affair, 1957
Theirs Is the Glory, 1946 (Rank)
Thelma & Louise, 1991 (Biddle; Zimmer)
Thelma Jordan. *See* File on Thelma Jordan, 1949
Them!, 1954 (Kaper)
Them Thar Hills, 1934 (Roach)
Them Was the Happy Days, 1916 (Roach)
Them Were the Happy Days, 1917 (Messmer)
Then I'll Come Back to You, 1916 (Marion)
Theodora Goes Wild, 1936 (Buchman; Cohn; Goosson; Walker)
Théodore et Cie, 1933 (Douy)
Theorum. *See* Teorema, 1968
There Ain't No Justice, 1939 (Balcon)
There Ain't No Santa Claus, 1926 (Roach)
There Are Mountains and Rivers. *See* Banga ari, 1962
There Auto Be a Law, 1953 (Blanc; McKimson; Stalling)
There Goes My Baby, 1993 (Fraker)
There Goes My Girl, 1937 (August; Musuraca; Walker)
There Goes My Heart, 1938 (Irene; Roach)
There Goes the Bride, 1925 (Roach)
There Goes the Bride, 1932 (Balcon)
There Goes the Groom, 1937 (Krasner)
There They Go-Go-Go, 1956 (Blanc; Jones; Stalling)
There Was a Crooked Man, 1960 (Bryan)
There Was a Crooked Man . . . , 1970 (Westmore Family)
There Was a Miller on the River. *See* Jsouc na rece mlynár jeden, 1971
There Was Once a King. *See* Bly jednou jeden Král, 1955
There Were Days . . . and Moons. *See* Y a des jours . . . et des lunes, 1990
There You Are!, 1926 (Gibbons; Gillespie)
There's a Future in It, 1944 (Alwyn)
There's Always a Woman, 1938 (Cohn; Goosson)
There's Always Tomorrow, 1955 (Hunter; Metty)
There's Magic in Music, 1941 (Dreier; Head)
There's No Business Like Show Business, 1954 (Berlin; Cole; Lemaire; Newman; Shamroy; Trotti; Wheeler)
There's Something about a Soldier, 1934 (Fleischer)
There's Something about a Soldier, 1943 (Fleischer)
There's That Woman Again, 1938 (Cohn; Epstein; Walker)
Therese, 1916 (Jaenzon; Magnusson)
Thérèse. *See* **Thérèse Desqueyroux**, 1962
Thérèse, 1986 (Evein; Rousselot)
Thérèse and Isabelle, 1968 (Auric)
Thérèse Desqueyroux, 1962 (Jarre; Matras)
Thérèse Martin, 1938 (Ibert)
Thérèse Raquin, 1928 (Andrejew)
Thérèse Raquin, 1953 (Hakim; Spaak)
These Are the Damned. *See* Damned, 1963
These Children Are Safe, 1939 (Alwyn)
These Dangerous Years, 1957 (Wilcox)
These Kids Are Grown-Ups. *See* Ils sont grands ces petits, 1979

These Thousand Hills, 1958 (Clarke; Lemaire; Wheeler)
These Three, 1936 (Day; Goldwyn; Mandell; Newman; Toland)
These Wilder Years, 1956 (Ames; Rose)
They All Died Laughing. *See* A Jolly Bad Fellow, 1964
They All Kissed the Bride, 1942 (Cohn; Irene; Walker)
They All Laughed, 1981 (Müller)
They Asked for It, 1939 (Cortez)
They Call Me MISTER Tibbs!, 1970 (Jones; Mirisch)
They Came from beyond Space, 1967 (Francis)
They Came to a City, 1944 (Balcon)
They Came to Blow Up America, 1943 (Basevi; Friedhofer)
They Came to Cordura, 1959 (Cahn; Guffey; Louis; van Heusen)
They Dare Not Love, 1941 (Planer; Vajda)
They Died with Their Boots On, 1941 (Canutt; Glennon; Orry-Kelly;
    Steiner; Wallis)
They Done Him Right, 1933 (Lantz)
They Drive by Night, 1940 (Burks; Deutsch; Edeson; Haskin;
    Wald; Wallis)
They Flew Alone, 1942 (Alwyn; Wilcox)
They Gave Him a Gun, 1937 (Rosson)
They Go Boom, 1929 (Roach)
They Got Me Covered, 1943 (Goldwyn; Head; Mandell; Maté Mercer)
They Had to See Paris, 1928 (Levien)
They Knew Mr. Knight, 1945 (Rank)
They Knew What They Wanted, 1940 (Kanin; Newman; Polglase;
    Pommer; Stradling)
They Learned about Women, 1930 (Gibbons)
They Live by Night, 1948 (D'Agostino; Houseman; Schary; Schnee)
They Made Me a Criminal, 1939 (Grot; Howe; Steiner; Wallis)
They Made Me a Fugitive, 1947 (Heller)
They Made Me a Killer, 1945 (Mainwaring)
They Met in Bombay, 1941 (Adrian; Daniels; Loos; Stothart; Stromberg)
They Met in the Dark, 1943 (Heller; Rank)
They Might Be Giants, 1971 (Barry)
They Passed This Way. *See* Four Faces West, 1948
They Rode West, 1954 (Nugent; Wald)
They Shall Have Music, 1939 (Goldwyn; Newman; Riskin; Toland)
They Shoot Horses, Don't They?, 1969 (Green; Horner; Lathrop;
    Winkler)
They Wanted to Marry, 1937 (Metty)
They Were Expendable, 1945 (August; Mayer; Stothart)
They Were Not Divided, 1950 (Rank)
They Were Sisters, 1945 (Rank)
They Won't Believe Me, 1947 (Boyle; Harrison)
They Won't Forget, 1937 (Deutsch; Edeson; Warner)
They Would Elope, 1909 (Bitzer)
They've Kidnapped Anne Benedict. *See* Abduction of Saint Anne, 1975
Thicker Than Water, 1935 (Roach)
Thief. *See* Ladrone, 1979
Thief and the Cobbler. *See* Arabian Knight, 1995
Thief and the Girl, 1911 (Bitzer)
Thief in Paradise, 1925 (Goldwyn; Grot; Marion; Miller)
Thief in the Dark, 1928 (Edeson)
Thief in Tuxedo. *See* Einbrecher im Frack,, 1919
Thief of Bagdad, 1924 (Edeson; Grot; Menzies)
Thief of Bagdad, 1940 (Biro; Ellenshaw; Hornbeck; Korda; Krasker;
    Menzies; Mathieson Périnal; Rozsa; Unsworth)
Thief of Bagdad. *See* Ladro di Bagdad, 1960
Thief of Paris. *See* Voleur, 1967
Thief Who Came to Dinner, 1973 (Lathrop; Mancini)
Thieves' Highway, 1949 (Lemaire; Newman; Wheeler)
Thieves Like Us, 1974 (Willingham)
Thin Ice, 1937 (Cronjager)
Thin Ice, 1960 (Halas and Batchelor)
Thin Man, 1934 (Gibbons; Goodrich and Hackett; Howe; Mayer;
    Shearer; Stromberg)

Thin Man Goes Home, 1944 (Freund; Irene; Riskin)
Thin Red Line, 1964 (Arnold)
Thin Red Line, 1998 (Zimmer)
Thin Twins, 1929 (Roach)
Thing, 1951 (D'Agostino; Dunn; Harlan; Lederer; Tiomkin)
Thing, 1982 (Morricone; Whitlock; Winston)
Thing from Another World. *See* Thing, 1951
Thing That Couldn't Die, 1958 (Metty)
Thing with Two Heads, 1972 (Baker)
Things Are Looking Up, 1934 (Balcon; Rank)
Things Change, 1988 (Mamet)
Things Happen at Night, 1948 (Lassally)
Things of Life. *See* Choses de la vie, 1970
Things to Come, 1935 (Biro; Bryan; Hornbeck; Korda; Krasker;
    Mathieson; Menzies Périnal)
Think, 1964 (Bernstein)
Third Bad Name. *See* Daisan no Akumyo, 1963
Third Bell. *See* Treti zvoneni, 1938
Third Day, 1965 (Surtees)
Third Degree, 1926 (Blanke; Mohr)
Third Key. *See* Long Arm, 1956
Third Lover. *See* Oeil du malin, 1962
Third Man, 1949 (Korda; Krasker; Selznick)
Third Man on the Mountain, 1959 (Alwyn; Disney)
Third Party Risk, 1955 (Carreras)
Third Secret, 1963 (Slocombe)
Third Squad. *See* Třetí rota, 1931
Third Time Lucky, 1931 (Balcon)
Third Time Lucky, 1948 (Adam; Rank)
Third Voice, 1959 (Haller; Mandel)
Thirst. *See* Desert Nights, 1929
Thirst. *See* Törst, 1949
Thirst for Gold. *See* Soif de l'or, 1993
Thirteen Chairs. *See* Tretton stolar, 1945
Thirteen Ghosts, 1960 (Biroc)
Thirteen Hours by Air, 1936 (Head)
Thirteen Steps to Death. *See* Why Must I Die?, 1960
Thirteen Trunks of Mr. O.F., The Trunks of Mr. O.F.. *See* Koffer des
    Herrn O.F.; 1931
Thirteen West Street, 1962 (Duning)
Thirteen Women, 1932 (Steiner)
Thirteenth Chair, 1929 (Adrian; Day; Gibbons)
Thirteenth Chair, 1937 (Clarke)
Thirteenth Floor, 1999 (Ballhaus)
Thirteenth Letter, 1951 (Koch; La Shelle; Lemaire; North; Wheeler)
Thirty Day Princess, 1934 (Shamroy)
Thirty Days, 1922 (Brown)
Thirty-Nine Steps, 1959 (Rank)
Thirty Seconds over Tokyo, 1944 (Gibbons; Gillespie; Irene; Mayer;
    Rosson; Shearer; Stothart; Surtees; Trumbo; Wheeler)
Thirty-Six Hours, 1964 (Head)
This above All, 1942 (Day; Miller; Newman; Sherriff; Zanuck)
This Angry Age. *See* Barrage contre le Pacifique, 1958
This Animal World, 1955 (O'brien)
This Boy's Life, 1993 (Burwell; Watkin)
This Could Be the Night, 1957 (Cahn; Harlan; Pasternak)
This Day and Age, 1933 (Dreier; Zukor)
This Earth Is Mine, 1959 (Cahn; Friedhofer; Metty; van Heusen)
This Gun for Hire, 1942 (Dreier; Head; Seitz)
This Happy Breed, 1944 (Coward; Havelock-Allan; Neame)
This Happy Breed, 1947 (Rank)
This Happy Feeling, 1958 (Hunter)
This Hero Stuff, 1919 (Furthman)
This House of Vanity. *See* Vanity's Price, 1924
This Is a Life?, 1955 (Blanc)
This is America, Charlie Brown, 1988 (Grusin)

Three Girls from Rome. *See* Ragasse di Piazza di Spagna, 1952
Three Godfathers, 1936 (Ruttenberg)
Three Godfathers, 1948 (Basevi; Cooper; Hoch; Nugent)
Three Guys Named Mike, 1950 (Kaper)
Three Hearts for Julia, 1942 (Irene; Stothart)
Three Hundred Spartans. *See* Lion of Sparta, 1961
Three Husbands, 1950 (Planer)
Three in a Closet, 1920 (Bruckman)
Three Installations, 1952 (Lassally)
Three into Two Won't Go, 1968 (Lai; Lassally)
Three Is a Crowd, 1951 (Terry)
Three Keys, 1924 (Haller)
Three Kids and a Queen, 1935 (D'Agostino; Waxman)
Three Kings, 1999 (Burwell; Newman)
Three Lazy Mice, 1935 (Lantz)
Three Little Beers, 1936 (Bruckman)
Three Little Bops, 1957 (Blanc)
Three Little Girls in Blue, 1946 (Newman)
Three Little Pirates, 1946 (Bruckman)
Three Little Pups, 1953 (Avery)
Three Little Sew and Sews, 1938 (Ballard)
Three Little Words, 1950 (Mayer; Pan; Previn; Rose)
Three Live Ghosts, 1922 (Miller; Zukor)
Three Live Ghosts, 1929 (Menzies)
Three Live Ghosts, 1936 (Howe; Sullivan)
Three Lives and Only One Death. *See* Trois vies et une seule mort, 1996
Three Lives of Thomasina, 1963 (Disney; Iwerks)
Three Loves Has Nancy, 1938 (Adrian; Daniels; Krasna)
Three Magic Feathers. *See* Tři čarovná péra, 1970
Three Married Men, 1936 (Cronjager)
Three Maxims, 1936 (Wilcox)
Three Men and a Baby, 1987 (Hamlisch)
Three Men and a Girl, 1949 (Adam; Heller)
Three Men and a Girl, 1952 (de Grunwald)
Three Men from Texas, 1940 (Harlan; Head; Young)
Three Men in a Boat, 1933 (Dean)
Three Men in a Tub, 1938 (Roach)
Three Men in White, 1944 (Irene)
Three Men Missing. *See* Ztracenci, 1957
Three Men of the North. *See* Kita no sannin, 1945
Three Men on a Horse, 1936 (Orry-Kelly; Polito)
Three Miles Out, 1924 (Loos)
Three Minus Me. *See* Tres menos eu, 1988
Three Mountaineers, 1960 (Halas and Batchelor)
Three Musketeers, 1921 (Edeson; Menzies)
Three Musketeers, 1933 (Canutt)
Three Musketeers, 1935 (Nichols; Plunkett; Polglase; Steiner)
Three Musketeers, 1938 (Ivanov-Vano)
Three Musketeers, 1948 (Berman; Gibbons; Plunkett; Stothart)
Three Musketeers, 1974 (Legrand; Watkin)
Three Musketeers of the Apprentice Geishas. *See* Maiko sanjushi, 1955
Three Naval Rascals. *See* Sharp Shooters, 1928
Three Nights of Love. *See* Tre notti d'amore, 1964
Three on a Match, 1932 (Orry-Kelly; Polito)
Three Outcasts, 1929 (Canutt)
Three Palm Trees. *See* Três Palmeiras, 1994
Three Passions, 1929 (Burel)
Three Resurrected Drunkards. *See* Kaettekita yopparai, 1968
Three Ring Circus, 1954 (Head; Wallis)
Three Russian Girls, 1943 (Lourié)
Three Sailors and a Girl, 1953 (Cahn)
Three Sappy People, 1939 (Bruckman)
Three Sinners. *See* Meurtres, 1950
Three Sisters, 1910 (Bitzer)
Three Sisters, 1970 (Unsworth; Walton)
Three Sisters. *See* Paure e Amore, 1988

Three Smart Boys, 1937 (Roach)
Three Smart Girls, 1936 (Kahn; Kaper; Pasternak)
Three Smart Girls Grow Up, 1939 (Pasternak)
Three Smart Saps, 1942 (Bruckman)
Three Sons, 1939 (Metty)
Three Steps Away from Me. *See* Tři kroky od tela, 1934
Three Stops to Murder. *See* Blood Orange, 1954
Three Strangers, 1946 (Deutsch; Edeson; Koch)
Three Stripes in the Sun, 1955 (Duning; Guffey)
Three Themes. *See* Trois Themes, 1980
Three Treasures. *See* Nippon tanjo, 1959
Three Violent People, 1956 (Head; Maté Pereira)
Three Weekends, 1928 (Mankiewicz; Rosson)
Three Weeks, 1924 (Gibbons)
Three Who Loved, 1931 (Musuraca)
Three Wise Fools, 1923 (Mathis)
Three Wise Fools, 1946 (Irene; Kaper; Rosson)
Three Wise Girls, 1931 (Riskin)
Three Wise Men, 1913 (Selig)
Three Wishes, 1954 (Reiniger)
Three Women, 1924 (Blanke; Kräly)
Three Word Brand, 1921 (August)
Three Worlds of Gulliver, 1960 (Harryhausen; Herrmann)
Three Young Texans, 1953 (Lemaire)
Threepenny Opera. *See* **Dreigroschenoper**, 1931
Threepenny Opera. *See* Dreigroschenoper, 1962
Threepenny Opera, 1988 (Golan and Globus)
Threesome, 1994 (Newman)
Thrifty Cubs, 1953 (Terry)
Thrill Chaser, 1923 (Miller)
Thrill of a Lifetime, 1937 (Dreier; Head; Young)
Thrill of a Romance, 1945 (Cahn; Irene; Pasternak; Stradling)
Thrill of Brazil, 1946 (Cole; Goosson; Louis; Polglase)
Thrill of It All, 1963 (Boyle; Hunter; Louis; Metty)
Thriller, 1983 (Baker; Bernstein)
Thrills and Chills, 1938 (Fleischer)
Throne of Blood. *See* Kumonosu-jo, 1957
Through a Glass Darkly. *See* Såsom i en spegel, 1961
Through a Glass Window, 1922 (Rosson)
Through Austin Glen, 1906 (Bitzer)
Through Darkened Vales, 1911 (Bitzer)
Through Different Eyes, 1942 (Day)
Through the Back Door, 1921 (Rosher)
Through the Breakers, 1909 (Bitzer)
Through the Dark, 1924 (Marion)
Through the Storm. *See* Prairie Schooners, 1940
Through the Wire, 1990 (Wexler)
Through Treason to Victory. *See* Durch Verrat zum Sieg, 1914
Throwing the Bull, 1946 (Terry)
Thru Different Eyes, 1942 (Clarke; Raksin)
Thugs with Dirty Mugs, 1939 (Avery)
Thumb Fun, 1952 (Blanc; McKimson; Stalling)
Thumb Tripping, 1972 (Winkler)
Thumbelina, 1955 (Reiniger)
Thumbs Up, 1943 (Cahn)
Thunder across the Pacific. *See* Wild Blue Yonder, 1951
Thunder, 1929 (Mayer; Stromberg)
Thunder Afloat, 1939 (Seitz)
Thunder Alley, 1984 (Golan and Globus)
Thunder and Lightning. *See* Blixt och dunder, 1938
Thunder Bay, 1953 (Daniels; Hayes)
Thunder Below, 1932 (Buchman; Lang)
Thunder Birds, 1942 (Basevi; Day)
Thunder in the City, 1937 (Rozsa; Sherwood)
Thunder in the Dust. *See* Sundowners, 1949
Thunder in the East, 1953 (Friedhofer; Garmes; Head; Swerling)

Thunder in the Night, 1935 (Glennon)
Thunder in the Sun, 1959 (Cortez; Lemaire; Leven)
Thunder in the Valley, 1947 (Basevi; Clarke; Lemaire)
Thunder on the Hill, 1951 (Daniels)
Thunder over Mexico, 1931 (Tisse)
Thunder over the Plains, 1952 (Glennon)
Thunder Trail, 1937 (Head; Struss)
Thunderball, 1965 (Adam; Barry; Douy)
Thunderbirds, 1942 (Trotti; Zanuck)
Thunderbirds, 1952 (Young)
Thunderbolt, 1929 (Dreier; Furthman; Mankiewicz)
Thunderhead, Son of Flicka, 1945 (Clarke)
Thunderheart, 1992 (Shepard)
Thundering Fleas, 1926 (Roach)
Thundering Landlords, 1925 (Roach)
Thundering Taxis, 1933 (Roach)
Thundering Toupees, 1929 (Roach)
Thundering West, 1939 (Ballard)
Thursday's Children, 1953 (Lassally)
Thursday's Game, 1974 (Biroc)
Thus the Divine Wind Arrives. See Kakute kamikaze wa fuku, 1944
Thy Name Is Woman, 1924 (Carré; Mayer)
Ti ho sempre amato, 1953 (Delli Colli)
Ti ho sposato per allegria, 1967 (Age and Scarpelli)
Ti presento un'amica, 1988 (Cecchi D'amico)
Tiara Tahiti, 1962 (Heller; Rank; Vetchinsky)
Tiburoneros, 1962 (Alcoriza)
Tichy tyden v domee, 1969 (švankmajer)
Tick Tock Tuckered, 1944 (Blanc; Clampett; Stalling)
Ticket of Leave, 1936 (Havelock-Allan)
Ticket to Tomahawk, 1950 (Lemaire)
Ticklish Affair, 1963 (Gillespie; Krasner; Pasternak)
Tidal Wave. See Nippon chiubotsu, 1973
Tide of Empire, 1929 (Gibbons)
Tie Me Up! Tie Me Down!. See ¡Atame!, 1989
Ticf in Böhmerwald , 1908 (Messter)
Tierra del Fuego se apaga, 1955 (Figueroa)
Tierra del fuego, 1999 (Guerra)
Tiger, 1930 (Hoffmann)
Tiger and the Flame. See Jhansi ri-rani, 1952
Tiger and the Pussycat. See Tigre, 1967
Tiger Bay, 1959 (Rank)
Tiger in the Sky. See McConnell Story, 1955
Tiger in the Smoke, 1956 (Arnold; Rank)
Tiger Likes Fresh Blood. See Tigre aime la chair fraiche, 1964
Tiger Love, 1924 (Clarke)
Tiger Makes Out, 1967 (Justin)
Tiger Man, 1918 (August)
Tiger Man. See Monster and Tiger Man, 1944
Tiger Rose, 1923 (Rosher)
Tiger Rose, 1929 (Gaudio)
Tiger Shark, 1932 (Gaudio; Orry-Kelly)
Tiger Thompson, 1924 (Stromberg)
Tiger Walks, 1964 (Disney)
Tiger Woman, 1944 (Canutt)
Tiger's Club, 1920 (Ruttenberg)
Tigerin, 1921 (Hoffmann)
Tight Little Island. See Whiskey Galore!, 1949
Tight Shoes, 1923 (Roach)
Tight Spot, 1955 (Duning; Guffey; Wald)
Tigre, 1967 (Age and Scarpelli)
Tigre aime la chair fraiche, 1964 (Rabier)
Tigre se parfume à la dynamite, 1965 (Rabier)
Tigress, 1927 (Walker)
Tijera de oro, 1958 (Alcoriza)
'Til We Meet Again, 1940 (Orry-Kelly; Wallis)

Till glädje, 1950 (Fischer)
Till I Come Back to You, 1918 (Buckland; Rosher)
Till Osterland, 1925 (Jaenzon; Magnusson)
Till the Clouds Roll By, 1946 (Freed; Irene; Mayer; Rose; Stradling)
Till the End of Time, 1946 (D'Agostino; Schary)
Till There Was You, 1990 (Seale)
Till We Meet Again, 1936 (Head)
'Till We Meet Again, 1940 (Gaudio; Haskin)
Till We Meet Again, 1944 (Dreier; Head)
Tillie and Gus, 1934 (Zukor)
Tillie the Toiler, 1927 (Daniels; Day; Gibbons)
Tillie Wakes Up, 1917 (Marion)
Timber Queen, 1922 (Roach)
Timberjack, 1954 (Carmichael; Mercer; Young)
Timbuktu, 1959 (Veiller)
Time, 1967 (Vukotić)
Time after Time, 1979 (Rozsa)
Time Bandits, 1981 (Biziou)
Time Bomb, 1952 (Junge; Young)
Time Flies, 1944 (Bryan; Rank)
Time for Caring. See Generation, 1969
Time for Dying, 1969 (Ballard)
Time for Love, 1935 (Fleischer)
Time for Loving, 1971 (Legrand)
Time Gallops On, 1952 (Terry)
Time in the Sun, 1931 (Tisse)
Time Machine, 1959 (Pal)
Time of Destiny, 1988 (Bumstead; Morricone)
Time of Indifference. See Indifferenti, 1964
Time of the Dancer. See Vremya tantsora, 1998
Time of Your Life, 1948 (Howe)
Time of Youth. See Seishun no koro, 1933
Time on My Hands, 1932 (Fleischer)
Time Out for Love. See Grandes Personnes, 1960
Time Out for Murder, 1938 (Miller)
Time Out for Rhythm, 1941 (Cahn; Planer)
Time Out of Mind, 1947 (Rozsa)
Time Regained. See Temps retrouvé, 1999
Time, the Place and the Girl, 1946 (Edeson)
Time to Die, 1983 (Morricone)
Time to Kill, 1942 (Clarke; Day)
Time to Kill. See Tempo di uccidere, 1989
Time to Love and a Time to Die, 1958 (Metty; Rozsa)
Time Travelers, 1964 (Kovacs; Zsigmond)
Time Travelers, 1976 (Lourié)
Time without Memory. See Seigenki, 1972
Time without Pity, 1957 (Francis)
Timely Interception, 1913 (Bitzer)
Timepiece, 1965 (Henson)
Times Gone By. See Altri tempi, 1952
Times Square Playboy, 1936 (Orry-Kelly)
Timid Rabbit, 1937 (Terry)
Timid Tabby, 1957 (Hanna and Barbera)
Timid Toreador, 1940 (Blanc; Clampett; Stalling)
Timothy's Quest, 1936 (Schary)
Tin Can Tourist, 1937 (Terry)
Tin Cup, 1996 (Boyd)
Tin Drum. See Blechtrommel, 1979
Tin Hats, 1926 (Gibbons)
Tin Man, 1935 (Roach)
Tin-minh, 1919 (Gaumont)
Tin Pan Alley, 1940 (Banton; Day; Macgowan; Newman; Shamroy)
Tin Pan Alley Cats, 1943 (Blanc; Clampett; Stalling)
Tin Star, 1957 (Bernstein; Hcad; Nichols; Pereira)
Tindous, 1955 (Kosma)
Tingel Tangel, 1927 (Kolowrat-Krakowsky; Reisch)

Tinkering with Trouble, 1914 (Roach)

Tip, 1917 (Roach)

Tip on a Dead Jockey, 1957 (Lederer; Rose; Rozsa)

Tip-Off Girls, 1938 (Head)

Tipat Mazal, 1992 (Golan and Globus)

Tiptoes, 1927 (Wilcox)

Tire au flanc, 1928 (Braunberger)

Tire-au-flanc 62, 1961 (Coutard)

Tire Trouble, 1942 (Terry)

Tire Troubles, 1923 (Roach)

Tired and Feathered, 1965 (Blanc)

Tired Business Men, 1927 (Roach)

Tireman Spare My Tires, 1942 (Bruckman)

Tirez sur le pianiste, 1960 (Braunberger; Coutard; Delerue)

Tirol in Waffen, 1914 (Messter)

'Tis an Ill Wind, 1909 (Bitzer)

Tit for Tat, 1935 (Roach)

Titanic, 1953 (Brackett; Jeakins; Lemaire; Reisch; Wheeler)

Titans. See Arrivano i Titani, 1961

Titfield Thunderbolt, 1951 (Auric; Clarke; Slocombe)

Title for the Sin. See Právo na hřích, 1932

Title Match of Magic. See Ninjutsu senshuken jiai, 1956

Tito's Guitar, 1942 (Fleischer)

Tlayucan, 1961 (Alcoriza)

Tma-svetlo-tma, 1989 (švankmajer)

To Be a Crook. See Fille et des fusils, 1964

To Be or Not To Be, 1942 (Irene; Korda; Maté; Plunkett; Spencer)

To Be Seven in Belfast, 1975 (Menges)

To Beat the Band, 1935 (Mercer; Musuraca; Plunkett)

To Bed or Not to Bed. See Diavolo, 1963

To Beep or Not to Beep, 1963 (Blanc)

To Catch a Thief, 1955 (Burks; Hayes; Head; Pereira)

To Die For, 1995 (Elfman; Henry)

To Die in Madrid. See Mourir à Madrid, 1962

To Die Standing, 1990 (Kaminski)

To Dream of Roses, 1990 (Trumbull)

To Duck or Not to Duck, 1943 (Blanc; Jones; Stalling)

To Each His Own, 1946 (Brackett; Dreier; Head; Young)

To Find a Man, 1970 (Booth)

To Forget Palermo. See Dimenticare Palermo, 1989

To Hare Is Human, 1956 (Blanc; Jones)

To Have and Have Not, 1944 (Carmichael; Furthman; Mercer; Waxman)

To Have and to Hold, 1922 (Miller)

To Have and to Hold, 1951 (Carreras)

To Hell with Heroes, 1968 (Louis)

To Hell with the Kaiser, 1918 (Mathis)

To Itch His Own, 1958 (Blanc; Jones; Stalling)

To Joy. See Till glädje, 1950

To Kill a Clown, 1971 (Lassally)

To Kill a Mockingbird, 1962 (Bernstein; Bumstead; Harlan; Westmore Family)

To Kill a Priest. See Zabic ksiedza, 1988

To koritsi me ta mavra, 1955 (Lassally)

To Live and Die in L.A., 1985 (Müller)

To Live in Peace. See Vivere in pace, 1946

To Love. See Att älska, 1964

To Mary—with Love, 1936 (Macgowan)

To meteoro vima to Pelargou, 1991 (Boyle; Guerra)

To neznáte Hadimršku, 1931 (Heller)

To Our Children's Children, 1969 (Halas and Batchelor)

To Paris with Love, 1954 (Rank)

To Please a Lady, 1950 (Basevi; Kaper; Mayer; Rose; Rosson)

To Save Her Soul, 1909 (Bitzer)

To teleftaio psemma, 1957 (Lassally)

To the Devil a Daughter, 1976 (Watkin)

To the Ends of the Earth, 1948 (Buchman; Duning; Goosson; Guffey)

To the Last Man, 1923 (Howe)

To the Moon, Alice, 1990 (Wexler; Zimmer)

To the Moon and Beyond, 1964 (Trumbull)

To the Orient. See Till Osterland, 1926

To the Rescue, 1932 (Lantz)

To the Shores of Tripoli, 1942 (Cronjager; Newman; Trotti; Zanuck)

To the Victor, 1948 (Burks; Wald)

To vlemma tou odyssea, 1995 (Guerra)

To Your Health, 1956 (Halas and Batchelor)

Toast of New Orleans, 1950 (Cahn; Green; Mayer; Pasternak; Plunkett; Rose)

Toast of New York, 1937 (Nichols; Polglase)

Toast of Song, 1952 (Fleischer)

Toast of the Legion. See Kiss Me Again, 1931

Tobacco Road, 1941 (Banton; Basevi; Day; Johnson; La Shelle; Miller; Newman; Parrish; Zanuck)

Tobasco Road, 1957 (Blanc)

Tobe Hooper's Night Terrors, 1993 (Golan and Globus)

Tobira o hiraku onna, 1946 (Miyagawa; Yoda)

Tobisuke boken ryoko, 1949 (Hayasaka)

Tobisuke's Adventures. See Tobisuke boken ryoko, 1949

Toboggan, 1934 (Burel)

Tobruk, 1967 (Bumstead; Harlan; Kaper; Whitlock)

Toby Tyler, or Ten Weeks with a Circus, 1959 (Disney; Iwerks)

Toccata for Toy Trains, 1957 (Bernstein)

Tocher, 1937 (Reiniger)

Today, 1930 (D'Agostino; Howe; Miller)

Today and Tomorrow, 1945 (Alwyn)

Today for the Last Time. See Dnes naposled, 1958

Today Mexico, Tomorrow . . . the World, 1970 (Godfrey)

Todd Killings, 1971 (Rosenman)

Todesritt in Riesenrad , 1912 (Planer)

Todo modo, 1976 (Morricone)

Todoke haha no uta, 1959 (Yoda)

Toets, 1967 (Müller)

Tog Dogs, 1960 (Halas and Batchelor)

Together, 1956 (Lassally)

Together Again, 1944 (Cohn; Goosson; Louis; Polglase; Walker)

Together Brothers, 1974 (Lathrop)

Together in the Weather, 1946 (Pal)

Toilet Section Chief. See Toiretto buchou, 1961

Toiretto buchou, 1961 (Muraki)

Tojuro no koi, 1955 (Yoda)

Tokaku omna to iu mono wa, 1932 (Yoda)

Tokio Jokio, 1943 (Blanc; Stalling)

Tokojiro of Katsukake. See Kutsukake Tokojiro, 1961

Tokyo Bay on Fire. See Tokyo-wan enjou, 1975

Tokyo Blackout. See Shuto Shoshitsu, 1987

Tokyo Joe, 1949 (Louis)

Tokyo Olympiad. See **Tokyo Orimpikku**, 1965

Tokyo Orimpikku, 1965 (Miyagawa)

Tokyo Rose, 1946 (Mainwaring)

Tokyo saiban, 1983 (Takemitsu)

Tokyo senso sengo hiwa, 1970 (Takemitsu; Toda)

Tokyo Trial. See Tokyo saiban, 1983

Tokyo-wan enjou, 1975 (Muraki)

Tol'able Romeo, 1926 (Roach)

Told in the Hills, 1919 (Howe)

Tolgo il disturbo, 1992 (Lai)

Toll Bridge Troubles, 1942 (Fleischer)

Toll Gate, 1920 (August)

Tolle Miss. See Miss Hobbs, 1921

Toller Einfall, 1932 (Kaper)

Tom And Chérie, 1955 (Hanna and Barbera)

Tom and Jerry in the Hollywood Bowl, 1950 (Hanna and Barbera)

Tom and Jerry: The Movie, 1992 (Hanna and Barbera; Mancini)

Tom Brown's School Days, 1940 (Biroc; Musuraca; Polglase)
Tom Brown's Schooldays, 1951 (Addinsell)
Tom Horn, 1980 (Alonzo)
Tom Jones, 1963 (Lassally)
Tom Sawyer, 1917 (Zukor)
Tom Sawyer, 1930 (Lang)
Tom Sawyer, 1973 (Williams)
Tom Sawyer, Detective, 1938 (Head)
Tom Thumb, 1936 (Iwerks)
Tom Thumb, 1958 (Pal; Périnal)
Tom Thumb in Trouble, 1940 (Blanc; Jones; Stalling)
Tom Turk and Daffy, 1944 (Blanc; Jones; Stalling)
Tom, Dick, and Harry, 1941 (Jarrico; Kanin; Polglase)
Tom, Tom the Piper's Son, 1934 (Terry)
Tom-Tom Tomcat, 1953 (Blanc; Stalling)
Tom's Gang, 1927 (Musuraca)
Tom's Photo Finish, 1957 (Hanna and Barbera)
Tomate, 1960 (Almendros)
Tomb of Ligeia, 1965 (Towne)
Tomboy and the Champ, 1960 (Clothier)
Tomboys, 1905 (Selig)
Tombstone, 1993 (Fraker)
Tombstone, the Town Too Tough to Die, 1942 (Harlan)
Tomei ningen, 1954 (Tsuburaya)
Tommy Tucker's Tooth, 1923 (Disney)
Tomorrow and Tomorrow, 1932 (Lang; Zukor)
Tomorrow at Eight, 1933 (Plunkett)
Tomorrow at Midnight. See For Love or Money, 1939
Tomorrow Is Another Day, 1951 (Blanke; Burks)
Tomorrow Is Forever, 1945 (Louis; Steiner)
Tomorrow the World, 1944 (Lardner)
Tomorrow We Live, 1941 (de Grunwald; Heller)
Tomorrow's Costume. See Asu e no seiso, 1959
Tomorrow's Love, 1925 (Glennon)
Tomuraishi tachi, 1968 (Miyagawa)
Ton ombre est la mienne, 1962 (Jarre)
Tongues of Scandal, 1927 (Laszlo; Shamroy)
Toni, 1935 (Renoir)
Tonight and Every Night, 1945 (Cahn; Cohn; Cole; Goosson; Louis; Maté)
Tonight at 8.30. See Meet Me Tonight, 1952
Tonight at Twelve, 1929 (Mandell)
Tonight Is Ours, 1933 (Struss; Zukor)
Tonight or Never, 1931 (Goldwyn; Newman; Toland; Vajda)
Tonight We Raid Calais, 1943 (Ballard; Day)
Tonight We Sing, 1953 (Lemaire; Newman; Shamroy; Spencer)
Tonio Kroger, 1964 (Flaiano and Pinelli)
Tonka, 1958 (Disney)
Tonnelier, 1899 (Gaumont)
Tons of Money, 1930 (Wilcox)
Tony Rome, 1967 (Biroc; Smith)
Too Ardent Lover, 1903 (Bitzer)
Too Bad She's Bad. See Peccato che sia una canaglia, 1954
Too Beautiful for You. See Trop belle pour toi, 1989
Too Busy to Work, 1932 (Clarke)
Too Busy to Work, 1939 (Cronjager)
Too Far to Go, 1978 (Lassally)
Too Hop to Handle, 1956 (Blanc; McKimson)
Too Hot to Handle, 1938 (Rosson; Waxman)
Too Late Blues, 1961 (Head; Raksin)
Too Late for Tears, 1949 (Haskin; Stromberg)
Too Late the Hero, 1969 (Biroc)
Too Many Blondes, 1941 (Krasner)
Too Many Chefs. See Who Is Killing the Great Chefs of Europe?, 1978
Too Many Cooks, 1931 (Musuraca)
Too Many Crooks, 1959 (Rank)

Too Many Girls, 1940 (Polglase)
Too Many Highballs, 1933 (Bruckman)
Too Many Husbands, 1940 (Cohn; Walker)
Too Many Kisses, 1925 (Rosson; Saunders)
Too Many Mammas, 1924 (Roach)
Too Many Millions, 1918 (Rosher)
Too Many Parents, 1936 (Head; Struss)
Too Many Suspects. See Ellery Queen, 1975
Too Many Wives, 1937 (Musuraca; Polglase)
Too Many Women, 1932 (Roach)
Too Much, 1987 (Golan and Globus)
Too Much, Too Soon, 1958 (Blanke; Musuraca; Orry-Kelly)
Too Young for Love, 1959 (Head)
Too Young to Kiss, 1951 (Goodrich and Hackett; Green; Kaper; Rose; Ruttenberg)
Toot! Toot!, 1926 (Fleischer)
Tootsie, 1982 (Grusin; Smith)
Top Flat, 1935 (Roach)
Top Hat, 1935 (Berlin; Berman; Pan; Polglase; Steiner)
Top Kid, 1985 (Seale)
Top Man, 1943 (Mohr)
Top o' the Morning, 1949 (Bumstead; Dreier; van Heusen)
Top of New York, 1922 (Levien)
Top of the Form, 1952 (Rank)
Top of the Hill, 1980 (Duning)
Top of the World, 1924 (Clarke)
Top of the World, 1955 (Clothier)
Top Secret!, 1984 (Challis; Jarre)
Top Secret Affair, 1957 (Cortez; Lemaire)
Top Speed, 1930 (Grot)
Topaz, 1969 (Bumstead; Head; Jarre; Whitlock)
Topaze, 1933 (Macgowan; Selznick; Steiner)
Topeka Terror, 1945 (Canutt)
Topio stin omichli, 1988 (Guerra)
Topkapi, 1964 (Alekan; Douy)
Topper Returns, 1941 (Roach)
Topper Takes a Trip, 1939 (Friedhofer; Irene; Roach)
Tops, 1969 (Bernstein)
Tops Is the Limit. See Anything Goes, 1936
Tops With Pops, 1957 (Hanna and Barbera)
Tora! Tora! Tora!, 1970 (Day; Goldsmith; Muraki; Smith; Zanuck)
Torch. See Del odio nació el amor, 1949
Torch Singer, 1933 (Banton; Struss)
Torch Song, 1953 (Ames; Deutsch; Hayes; Rose; Schnee)
Torchy Blane in Panama, 1938 (Gaudio)
Tordeuse orientale, 1955 (Rabier)
Torgus. See Verlogene Moral, 1921
Torment. See Scélérats, 1960
Tormenta, 1955 (Mainwaring)
Tormented, 1960 (Laszlo)
Torn Curtain, 1966 (Head; Heckroth; Whitlock)
Toro negro, 1959 (Alcoriza)
Toros, 1967 (Braunberger)
Torpedo Raiders. See Forever England, 1935
Torpedo Run, 1958 (Gillespie)
Torpedoed. See Our Fighting Navy, 1937
Torrent, 1920 (Glennon)
Torrent, 1926 (Daniels; Gibbons; Mayer; Stromberg)
Torrents of Spring. See Ague di Primavera, 1989
Torrid Toreador, 1942 (Terry)
Torrid Zone, 1940 (Deutsch; Haskin; Howe; Wald; Wallis)
Torso. See I corpi presentano tracce di violenza carnale, 1973
Törst, 1949 (Fischer)
Torticola contra Frankensberg, 1952 (Kosma)
Tortilla Flaps, 1958 (Blanc; McKimson)
Tortilla Flat, 1942 (Freund)

Trackers, 1971 (Mandel)
Trad, 1971 (ścibor-Rylski)
Trade Tattoo, 1937 (Lye)
Trade Winds, 1938 (Irene; Newman; Spencer; Wanger)
Trader Horn, 1930 (Mayer)
Tradewinds, 1938 (Maté)
Trädgårdsmästaren, 1912 (Jaenzon; Magnusson)
Trading Places, 1983 (Bernstein)
Tradita, 1954 (Delli Colli)
Tradition de minuit, 1939 (Aurenche and Bost)
Traffic, 1998 (Branco)
Tragedia di un uomo ridicolo, 1981 (Morricone)
Tragédie de Carmen, 1983 (Carrière; Nykvist; Wakhévitch)
Tragédie impériale, 1938 (Lourié; Milhaud)
Tragedy of a Ridiculous Man. See Tragedia di un uomo ridicolo, 1981
Tragedy of Carmen. See Tragédie de Carmen, 1983
Tragic Love, 1908 (Bitzer)
Tragic Pursuit. See Caccia tragica, 1947
Tragic Ship. See Eld ombord, 1923
Tragödie einer Leidenschaft, 1949 (Warm)
Tragödie eines Verlorenen, 1927 (Junge)
Tragödie eines verschollenen Fürstensohnes. See Versunkene Welt, 1922
Tragodie im Haus Habsburg, 1924 (Korda)
Trail Beyond, 1934 (Canutt)
Trail Drive, 1934 (McCord)
Trail Guide, 1952 (Musuraca)
Trail of '98, 1929 (Mayer; Seitz)
Trail of the Books, 1911 (Bitzer)
Trail of the Horse Thieves, 1929 (Musuraca)
Trail of the Lonesome Pine, 1916 (Buckland; Macpherson)
Trail of the Lonesome Pine, 1923 (Howe)
Trail of the Lonesome Pine, 1926 (Fleischer)
Trail of the Lonesome Pine, 1936 (Canutt; Dreier; Friedhofer; Wanger)
Trail of the Pink Panther, 1982 (Mancini)
Trail of the Vigilantes, 1940 (Krasner)
Trailblazer Magoo, 1956 (Bosustow)
Trailer, 1959 (Breer)
Trailer Life, 1937 (Terry)
Trailer Thrills, 1937 (Lantz)
Trailin' West, 1936 (McCord)
Train, 1964 (Bernstein; Jarre; Mnouchkine)
Train, 1973 (Sarde; Saulnier)
Train d'enfer, 1984 (Legrand)
Train des suicides, 1931 (Fradetal)
Train of Events, 1948 (Balcon; Clarke)
Train on Jacob's Ladder, Mt. Washington, 1899 (Bitzer)
Train pour Venise, 1938 (D'Eaubonne)
Train Robbers, 1973 (Clothier)
Train Stopped. See Ostanovilsya poyezd, 1982
Train Trouble, 1940 (Halas and Batchelor)
Training Pigeons, 1936 (Fleischer)
Trains sans fumée, 1951 (Rabier)
Traitor, 1914 (Marion)
Traitor's Gate, 1964 (Francis)
Tramp and the Dog, 1896 (Selig)
Tramp and the Dog, 1906 (Selig)
Tramp, the Boys are Marching, 1926 (Fleischer)
Tramping Tramps, 1930 (Lantz)
Tranches de vie, 1985 (Mnouchkine)
Tranquillo posto di campagna, 1968 (Guerra; Morricone)
Trans-Europ-Express, 1966 (Robbe-Grillet)
Transatlantic, 1931 (Friedhofer; Howe)
Transatlantic Merry-Go-Round, 1934 (Newman)
Transatlantic Tunnel. See Tunnel, 1935
Transatlantique, 1997 (Branco)
Transatlantisches, 1926 (Amidei)

Transfigurations, 1909 (Cohl)
Transformation of Mike, 1911 (Bitzer)
Transgression, 1931 (Steiner)
Transports urbains, 1948 (Braunberger)
Transylvania 6-5000, 1963 (Blanc)
Trap, 1922 (Miller)
Trap, 1959 (Head)
Trap, 1966 (Krasker)
Trap. See Gabbia, 1985
Trap for Santa Claus, 1909 (Bitzer)
Trap Happy, 1946 (Hanna and Barbera)
Trap Happy Porky, 1945 (Blanc; Jones; Stalling)
Trapeze, 1956 (Arnold; Krasker)
Trapp Family. See Trapp-Familie, 1956
Trapp-Familie, 1956 (Herlth)
Trapp-Familie in Amerika, 1958 (Herlth)
Trapped, 1923 (Fleischer)
Trapped By Bloodhounds, or The Lynching at Cripple Creek, 1905 (Selig)
Traqué, 1950 (Schüfftan)
Traque, 1974 (Renoir)
Trás-os-Montes, 1976 (de Almeida)
Tratta delle bianche, 1952 (de Laurentiis)
Traum vom Glück. See **Märchen vom Glück**, 1949
Trauma, 1992 (Donaggio; Savini)
Träumende Munde, 1932 (Jaubert; Mayer)
Traveaux du tunnel sous l'Escaut, 1932 (Kaufman)
Traveler's Joy, 1949 (Rank)
Travelin' On, 1922 (August)
Traveling Actors. See Tabi yakusha, 1940
Traveling Executioner, 1970 (Goldsmith; Lathrop)
Traveling Husbands, 1931 (Steiner)
Traveling Saleslady, 1935 (Barnes; Grot)
Traveling Salesman, 1921 (Brown)
Travels of Princess Snake. See Hebihime douchuh, 1949-50
Travels of Teddy, 1915 (Messmer)
Travels with Anita. See Viaggio con Anita, 1978
Travels with My Aunt, 1972 (Allen; Slocombe)
Traversata nera, 1939 (Amidei)
Traversée de Paris, 1956 (Aurenche and Bost; Douy; Saulnier)
Travestie, 1988 (Sarde)
Travestis du diable, 1963 (Jarre)
Traviata, 2000 (Storaro)
Traviata '53, 1953 (Flaiano and Pinelli)
Tre colonne in cronaca, 1990 (Morricone)
Tre fratelli, 1981 (Guerra)
Tre nel mille, 1970 (Guerra; Morricone)
Tre notti d'amore, 1964 (Gherardi)
Tre storie proibite, 1952 (Aldo)
Tread Softly Stranger, 1958 (Slocombe)
Treason, 1918 (Polito)
Treasure. See Schatz, 1923
Treasure Blues, 1935 (Roach)
Treasure Hunt, 1952 (de Grunwald)
Treasure Hunt, 1960 (Halas and Batchelor)
Treasure Island, 1920 (Carré; Furthman)
Treasure Island, 1934 (Mayer; Rosson; Stothart; Stromberg)
Treasure Island, 1950 (Disney; Ellenshaw; Haskin; Young)
Treasure Island. See Ile au trésor, 1985
Treasure of Bird Island. See Poklad Ptačího ostrova, 1952
Treasure of Ice Cake Island, 1960 (Halas and Batchelor)
Treasure of Kalifa. See Steel Lady, 1953
Treasure of Lost Canyon, 1951 (Metty)
Treasure of the Aztecs, 1965 (Jarrico)
Treasure of the Four Crowns, 1983 (Morricone)

Trompette anti-neurasthenique, 1915 (Cohl)
Trône de France, 1937 (Alexeieff and Parker)
Troop Beverly Hills, 1989 (Boyle; Hamlisch; van Runkle)
Troopship . *See* Farewell Again, 1937
Trop belle pour toi, 1988 (Lai; Rousselot)
Tropic Holiday, 1938 (Head)
Tropic Madness, 1928 (Musuraca; Plunkett)
Tropic Zone, 1953 (Head)
Tropical Fish, 1933 (Terry)
Tropicana. *See* Heat's On, 1943
Troppo tardi t'ho conosciuta, 1939 (de Laurentiis)
Trottie True, 1948 (Rank)
Trotting Through Turkey, 1920 (Roach)
Trottoirs de saturne, 1986 (Semprun)
Trou, 1959 (Cloquet)
Troubador Girl. *See* Musume tabigeinen, 1941
Trouble, 1933 (Wilcox)
Trouble Along the Way, 1953 (Steiner)
Trouble Bound, 1992 (Kaminski)
Trouble Brewing, 1939 (Neame)
Trouble Bruin, 1964 (Hanna and Barbera)
Trouble Enough, 1916 (Roach)
Trouble for Two, 1936 (Clarke; Waxman)
Trouble in Panama. *See* Torchy Blane in Panama, 1938
Trouble in Paradise, 1932 (Banton; Dreier; Raphaelson; Zukor)
Trouble in Store, 1953 (Rank; Vetchinsky)
Trouble in Texas, 1937 (Canutt)
Trouble in the Air, 1948 (Rank)
Trouble in the Glen, 1954 (Nugent; Wilcox; Young)
Trouble Indemnity, 1949 (Bosustow; Hubley)
Trouble Shooter. *See* Man with the Gun, 1955
Trouble Shooters: Trapped Beneath the Earth, 1993 (Mirisch)
Trouble with Angels, 1966 (Goldsmith)
Trouble with Harry, 1955 (Burks; Hayes; Head; Herrmann; Pereira)
Trouble with Women, 1947 (Dreier; Head; Young)
Troublemaker, 1964 (Henry)
Troublemakers. *See* Once upon a Crime, 1992
Troublesome Satchel, 1909 (Bitzer)
Trout, 1982 (Alekan; Trauner)
Trout Fishing, Rangeley Lakes, 1905 (Bitzer)
Truants, 1907 (Bitzer)
Trübe Wasser, 1959 (Eisler)
Truc au Brésilien, 1932 (D'Eaubonne)
Truce. *See* Tregua, 1996
Truce Hurts, 1948 (Hanna and Barbera)
Truck Busters, 1943 (Haskin)
Truck That Flew, 1943 (Pal)
Truckload of Trouble, 1949 (Terry)
True as a Turtle, 1956 (Rank)
True Confession, 1937 (Head; Dreier)
True Confessions, 1981 (Delerue; Winkler)
True Crime, 1999 (Bumstead; Zanuck)
True Glory, 1945 (Alwyn; Kanin)
True Grit, 1969 (Ballard; Bernstein; Jeakins; Wallis)
True-Heart Susie, 1919 (Bitzer)
True Romance, 1993 (Zimmer)
True Story of Camille. *See* Vera storia della signora della camelie, 1980
True Story of Lynn Stuart, 1958 (Guffey)
True to Life, 1943 (Carmichael; Dreier; Head; Lang; Mercer; Young)
True to the Army, 1942 (Young)
True to the Navy, 1930 (Mankiewicz)
Truman at Potsdam, 1976 (Houseman)
Truman Show, 1998 (Biziou)
Trumpet Call . *See* Rough Riders, 1927
Trumpet Island, 1920 (Haller)
Trunk Mystery, 1927 (Shamroy)

Trunk to Cairo. *See* Mivtza Kahir, 1966
Trust, 1911 (Gaumont)
Truth about Women, 1957 (Beaton; Heller)
Truth about Youth, 1930 (Miller)
Truth Juggler, 1922 (Roach)
Truthful Liar, 1924 (Roach)
Truthful Tulliver, 1917 (August)
Trutze von Trutzberg, 1921 (Planer)
Truxton King, 1923 (August)
Truxtonia. *See* Truxton King, 1923
Try and Get It, 1924 (Furthman)
Try, Try Again, 1921 (Roach)
Trying to Get Married, 1909 (Bitzer)
Trzy kolory: Bialy. *See* Trois couleurs: Blanc, 1994
Trzy kolory: Czerwony. *See* Trois couleurs: Rouge, 1994
Trzy kolory: Niebieski. *See* Trois couleurs: Bleu, 1993
Tschetan, der Indianerjunge, 1973 (Ballhaus)
Tsukihime keizu, 1958 (Miyagawa)
Tsukiyo garasu, 1939 (Yoda)
Tsuma to onna kisha, 1950 (Hayasaka)
Tsuyu no atosaki, 1956 (Takemitsu)
Tu enfanteras sans douleur, 1956 (Delerue)
Tu es danse et vertige, 1967 (Coutard)
Tu ne tueras point, 1961 (Aurenche and Bost; Douy)
Tu ridi, 1998 (Lanci, Giuseppe ("beppe"))
Tu seras vedette, 1942 (Alekan)
Tu, solo tu, 1949 (Alcoriza)
Tu Ten Kámen, 1923 (Heller)
Tubby the Tuba, 1947 (Pal)
Tucet mých tatínku, 1959 (Brdečka)
Tucker: The Man and His Dream, 1988 (Storaro; Tavoularis)
Tudor Rose, 1936 (Balcon; Vetchinsky)
Tuesday in November, 1945 (Hubley; Koch; Thomson)
Tuesdays with Morrie, 1999 (Littleton)
Tueur, 1972 (Renoir)
Tugboat Annie, 1933 (Mayer; Toland)
Tugboat Annie Sails Again, 1940 (Deutsch; Edeson)
Tugboat Granny, 1956 (Blanc)
Tugboat Princess, 1936 (Trumbo)
Tui shou, 1992 (Schamus)
Tulák. *See* Aniceko, vrate se!, 1926
Tulilem, 1992 (Bozzetto)
Tulipe noire, 1963 (Decaë)
Tulips Shall Grow, 1942 (Pal)
Tulsa, 1949 (Hoch; Nugent; Wanger)
Tumbleweed, 1953 (Hunter; Metty)
Tumbleweeds, 1925 (August; Sullivan)
Tummy Trouble, 1990 (Marshall)
Tune in Tomorrow. *See* Aunt Julia and the Scriptwriter, 1990
Tune Up and Sing, 1934 (Fleischer)
Tunes of Glory, 1960 (Arnold; Neame)
Tunisian Victory, 1943 (Alwyn; Hornbeck; Veiller)
Tunnel, 1919 (Warm)
Tunnel, 1933 (Hoffmann)
Tunnel, 1935 (Balcon; Metzner; Siodmak)
Tunnel of Love, 1958 (Rose)
Turbina nr. 3, 1927 (Moskvin)
Turbine no. 3. *See* Turbina nr. 3, 1927
Turco napoletano, 1953 (Struss)
Turkey Dinner, 1936 (Lantz)
Turkey Hunt, Pinehurst, 1905 (Bitzer)
Turkey Time, 1933 (Balcon; Junge; Rank)
Turkish Delight, 1927 (Sullivan)
Turm des schweigens, 1924 (Pommer)
Turmoil, 1924 (Mandell)

Turn Back the Clock, 1933 (Adrian; Gillespie; Hecht; Rosson; Stothart; Vorkapich)
Turn of the Tide, 1935 (Rank)
Turn Off the Moon, 1937 (Dreier; Head; Young)
Turn-Tale Wolf, 1952 (Blanc; McKimson; Stalling)
Turn the Key Softly, 1953 (Rank; Unsworth)
Turn to the Right, 1922 (Mathis; Seitz)
Turnabout, 1940 (Roach)
Turned Out Nice Again, 1941 (Balcon)
Turner, 1972 (Rosenblum)
Turning Point, 1952 (Head; Pereira)
Turning Point, 1977 (Reynolds; Surtees)
Turning Point. See Povorot, 1978
Turning Point of Jim Malloy, 1975 (Mandel)
Turtle Beach, 1991 (Boyd)
Turtle Diary, 1985 (Pinter)
Tusalava, 1929 (Lye)
Tutankhamen. See Tu Ten Kámen, 1923
Tutti a casa, 1960 (Age and Scarpelli; de Laurentiis)
Tuttles of Tahiti, 1942 (Musuraca)
Tutto a posto e niente in ordine, 1974 (Rotunno)
Tutyu and Totyo. See Tutyu és Totyo, 1915
Tutyu és Totyo, 1915 (Korda)
Tuxedo Warrior, 1982 (Lassally)
TV of Tomorrow, 1953 (Avery)
Två konungar, 1924 (Jaenzon)
Tva man om en änka, 1933 (Jaenzon)
Två människor, 1945 (Fischer)
Två Svenska emigranters aventyr i Amerika, 1912 (Jaenzon; Magnusson)
Tvár, 1973 (Brdečka)
Twa Corbies, 1951 (Halas and Batchelor)
'Twas Ever Thus, 1915 (Marion)
Tweet and Lovely, 1959 (Blanc)
Tweet and Sour, 1956 (Blanc)
Tweet Dreams, 1959 (Blanc)
Tweet, Tweet, Tweety, 1951 (Blanc; Stalling)
Tweet Zoo, 1957 (Blanc)
Tweetie Pie, 1947 (Blanc)
Tweety and the Beanstalk, 1957 (Blanc)
Tweety's Circus, 1955 (Blanc)
Tweety's S.O.S., 1951 (Blanc; Stalling)
Twelve Angry Men, 1956 (Kaufman)
Twelve Crowded Hours, 1939 (Musuraca)
Twelve Hours to Kill, 1960 (Crosby)
Twelve Miles Out, 1926 (Gibbons; Mayer)
Twelve O'Clock and All Ain't Well, 1941 (Terry)
Twelve O'Clock High, 1949 (Newman; Shamroy; Wheeler; Zanuck)
Twelve Tasks of Asterix, 1973 (Halas and Batchelor)
Twelve to the Moon, 1960 (Alton)
Twentieth Century, 1934 (August; Cohn; Hecht; MacArthur)
Twenty-Four Hours of a Woman's Life, 1952 (Challis)
Twenty Horses, 1932 (Johnson)
Twenty Legs under the Sea, 1931 (Fleischer)
Twenty Million Sweethearts, 1934 (Orry-Kelly; Wald)
Twenty-Nine, 1968 (Godfrey)
Twenty Thousand Years in Sing Sing, 1932 (Orry-Kelly)
Twenty Three Paces to Baker Street, 1956 (Lemaire)
Twice Blessed, 1945 (Irene)
Twice 'round the Daffodils, 1962 (Dillon)
Twice Two, 1933 (Roach)
Twice Upon a Time, 1953 (Challis; Francis; Kästner; Korda)
Twilight. See Belle Aventure, 1942
Twilight, 1998 (Bernstein; Littleton)
Twilight for the Gods, 1958 (Raksin)
Twilight Meeting. See Möten i skymningen, 1957
Twilight of Honor, 1963 (Green; Lathrop)

Twilight on the Prairie, 1944 (Bruckman)
Twilight on the Rio Grande, 1947 (Canutt)
Twilight on the Trail, 1937 (Fleischer)
Twilight on the Trail, 1941 (Harlan)
Twilight Women. See Women of Twilight, 1952
Twilight Zone—The Movie, 1983 (Goldsmith; Marshall)
Twilight's Last Gleaming, 1977 (Goldsmith)
Twin Beds, 1929 (Polito)
Twin Beds, 1942 (Irene; Mohr; Tiomkin)
Twin Flames. See Tripas Coração, 1992
Twin Peaks, 1990 (Badalamenti)
Twin Peaks: Fire Walk with Me, 1992 (Badalamenti)
Twin Screws, 1933 (Roach)
Twin Sisters of Kyoto. See Koto, 1963
Twin Triplets, 1935 (Roach)
Twinkle, Twinkle, Killer Kane. See Ninth Configuration, 1980
Twinkletoes Gets the Bird, 1941 (Fleischer)
Twinkletoes in Hat Stuff, 1941 (Fleischer)
Twinkletoes—Where He Goes Nobody Knows, 1941 (Fleischer)
Twinky, 1969 (Lassally)
Twins, 1988 (Delerue)
Twins of Evil, 1971 (Carreras)
Twins of Suffering Creek, 1920 (Furthman)
Twisker Pitcher, 1937 (Fleischer)
Twist. See Folies bourgeoises, 1976
Twist of Fate. See Beautiful Stranger, 1954
Twisted Nerve, 1968 (Herrmann)
Twisted Road. See **They Live by Night**, 1948
Twisted Trail, 1910 (Bitzer)
Twister, 1988 (Zimmer)
Twister, 1996 (Muren)
Two against the World, 1932 (Orry-Kelly; Rosher)
Two-Alarm Fire, 1934 (Fleischer)
Two Alone, 1934 (Steiner)
Two and Two Make Six, 1962 (Francis)
Two April Fools, 1954 (Bruckman)
Two Arabian Knights, 1927 (August; Gaudio; Menzies)
Two Are Guilty. See Glaive et la balance, 1963
Two Bagatelles, 1952 (McClaren)
Two Barbers, 1944 (Terry)
Two Baroque Churches in Germany, 1959 (Bernstein)
Two Bits, 1995 (Burwell)
Two Bottle Babies, 1904 (Bitzer)
Two Brothers, 1910 (Bitzer)
Two Crows from Tacos, 1956 (Blanc)
Two Daughters. See Teen Kanya, 1961
Two Daghters of Eve, 1912 (Bitzer)
Two Deaths, 1995 (Zimmer)
Two Dollar Bettor, 1951 (Leven)
Two Down and One to Go!, 1945 (Hornbeck)
Two English Girls. See Deux anglaises et le continent, 1971
Two Evil Eyes. See Due occhi diabolici, 1990
Two Faced Woman, 1941 (Mayer; Ruttenberg)
Two Faces of Dr. Jekyll, 1960 (Carreras)
Two-Faced Wolf, 1961 (Hanna and Barbera)
Two-Faced Woman, 1941 (Adrian; Kaper)
Two-Fisted Justice, 1932 (Canutt)
Two-Fisted Sheriff, 1925 (Canutt)
Two Flags West, 1950 (Lemaire; Newman; Nugent; Shamroy; Wheeler)
Two Flaming Youths, 1928 (Mankiewicz)
Two Flats West, 1950 (Friedhofer)
Two for the Road, 1966 (Challis; Mancini)
Two for the Seesaw, 1962 (Leven; McCord; Mirisch; Orry-Kelly; Previn; Westmore Family)
Two for the Zoo, 1941 (Fleischer)
Two for Tonight, 1935 (Head; Struss)

Two Frosts. *See* Dva mrazíci, 1954

Two Girls and a Sailor, 1944 (Irene; Pasternak; Surtees)

Two Girls on Broadway, 1940 (Brown; Freed)

Two Girls Wanted, 1927 (Miller)

Two Gophers from Texas, 1948 (Blanc; Stalling)

Two Grilled Fish, 1968 (Kuri)

Two Gun Cupid. *See* Bad Man, 1941

Two-Gun Gussie, 1918 (Roach)

Two Gun Hicks. *See* Passing of Two Gun Hicks, 1914

Two Guys from Milwaukee, 1946 (Diamond; Edeson)

Two Guys from Texas, 1948 (Cahn; Diamond; Edeson)

Two Headed Giant, 1939 (Terry)

Two in Revolt, 1936 (Steiner)

Two in the Dark, 1936 (Musuraca)

Two in the Shadow. *See* Midaregumo, 1967

Two Jakes, 1990 (Towne; Zsigmond)

Two Kinds of Women, 1932 (Head; Struss)

Two Kings. *See* Två konungar, 1924

Two Latins from Manhattan, 1941 (Cahn)

Two Lazy Crows, 1936 (Iwerks)

Two Little Bears, 1961 (Crosby)

Two Little Indians, 1953 (Hanna and Barbera)

Two Little Lambs, 1935 (Lantz)

Two Little Rabbits, 1952 (Popescu-Gopo)

Two Little Waifs, 1910 (Bitzer)

Two Lives of Mattia Pascal. *See* Due vite di Mattia Pascal, 1985

Two Living, One Dead, 1961 (Fischer)

Two Lovers, 1928 (Barnes; Goldwyn)

Two Loves, 1961 (Kaper; Maddow; Ruttenberg)

Two Meetings. *See* Dvye vstryechi, 1917

Two Memories, 1909 (Bitzer)

Two Memories. *See* Deux memoires, 1973

Two Men and a Girl. *See* Honeymoon, 1947

Two Men and a Widow. *See* Tva man om en änka, 1933

Two Men of the Desert, 1913 (Bitzer)

Two Mouseketeers, 1952 (Hanna and Barbera)

Two Mrs. Carrolls, 1947 (Burks; Grot; Head; Waxman)

Two Mules for Sister Sara, 1970 (Figueroa; Morricone; Westmore Family)

Two of a Kind, 1951 (Duning; Guffey)

Two of a Kind, 1983 (Conti)

Two of Us. *See* Jack of All Trades, 1936

Two of Us. *See* Vieil Homme et l'enfant, 1966

Two Off the Cuff, 1968 (Godfrey)

Two on a Doorstep, 1936 (Havelock-Allan)

Two on a Guillotine, 1965 (Steiner)

Two Orphans, 1911 (Selig)

Two Outlaws, 1928 (Miller)

Two Paths, 1910 (Bitzer)

Two People. *See* Två människor, 1945

Two People, 1973 (Decaë; Reynolds)

Two Rode Together, 1961 (Nugent; Duning)

Two Scents Worth, 1955 (Blanc; Jones)

Two Scrambled, 1918 (Roach)

Two Seconds, 1932 (Grot; Polito)

Two Sides, 1911 (Bitzer)

Two Sisters from Boston, 1946 (Pasternak; Rose; Surtees)

Two Smart People, 1946 (Freund; Irene)

Two Solitudes, 1978 (Jarre)

Two Texas Knights. *See* Two Guys from Texas, 1948

Two Thousand Women. *See* 2,000 Women, 1944

Two Tickets to Broadway, 1951 (Cahn; Cronjager)

Two Tickets to London, 1943 (Krasner)

Two Tickets to Paris, 1962 (Rosenblum)

Two Times Lotte. *See* Doppelte Lottchen, 1950

Two Together. *See* Ninin sugata, 1942

Two Too Young, 1935 (Roach)

Two Topers, 1905 (Bitzer)

Two Twins, 1923 (Stromberg)

Two Wagons, Both Covered, 1923 (Roach)

Two Weeks, 1920 (Loos)

Two Weeks in Another Town, 1962 (Houseman; Krasner; Plunkett; Raksin; Schnee)

Two Weeks with Love, 1950 (Ames; Mayer; Plunkett)

Two Women. *See* Ciociara, 1960

Two Women and a Man, 1909 (Bitzer)

Two Worlds. *See* Zwei Welten, 1919

Two Worlds, 1930 (Junge; Rosher)

Two Yanks in Trinidad, 1942 (Cahn)

Two Years Before the Mast, 1946 (Dreier; Laszlo; Miller; Young)

Two's a Crowd, 1950 (Blanc; Jones; Stalling)

Twonky, 1953 (Biroc)

Tyaag, 1977 (Burman)

Tycoon, 1947 (Chase; D'Agostino)

Tyemnaya sila, 1917 (Starewicz)

Type comme moi ne devrait jamais mourir, 1976 (Guillemot)

Typhon sur Nagasaki, 1956 (Alekan)

Typhoon, 1914 (Ince)

Typhoon, 1940 (Dreier; Head; Reynolds)

Tyrannical Fiancee. *See* Den tryanniske fästmannen, 1912

Tyrant of Red Gulch, 1928 (Musuraca)

Tystnaden, 1963 (Lundgren; Nykvist)

U-Boat 29. *See* Spy in Black, 1939

U-Boat Prisoner, 1944 (Guffey)

U pokladny stál, 1939 (Stallich)

U sv. Mateje, 1928 (Stallich)

U Turn, 1997 (Morricone)

U.M.C., 1969 (La Shelle)

U.S. Marshals, 1998 (Goldsmith)

U.S. Naval Militia, 1900 (Bitzer)

U.S.S. Maine, Havana Harbor, 1898 (Bitzer)

Uber Alles in der Welt, 1941 (Röhrig)

Uberfall, 1928 (Metzner)

Uberflüssige Menschen, 1926 (Andrejew)

Ubu and the Great Gidouille. *See* Ubu et la Grande Gidouille, 1979

Ubu et la Grande Gidouille, 1979 (Lenica)

Ubu Roi, 1976 (Lenica)

Uccellacci e uccellini, 1966 (Delli Colli; Donati; Morricone)

Uccello dalle piume di cristallo, 1969 (Morricone; Storaro)

Uccidete il vitello grasso ed arrostitelo, 1970 (Morricone)

Uchu daikaiju Dogora, 1964 (Tsuburaya)

Uchu daisensu, 1959 (Tsuburaya)

Ucieczka, 1986 (Preisner)

Udienza, 1971 (Cristaldi)

Ugetsu. *See* **Ugetsu monogatari**, 1953

Ugetsu monogatari, 1953 (Hayasaka; Miyagawa; Yoda)

Ugly Dachshund, 1966 (Disney)

Ugly Dino, 1940 (Fleischer)

Ugly Duckling, 1959 (Carreras)

Ukelele Sheiks, 1926 (Roach)

Ukigusa, 1959 (Miyagawa)

Ukiyo kouji, 1939 (Yoda)

Ukradená vzducholod, 1966 (Zeman)

Ulička v Ráji, 1936 (Heller)

Uličnice, 1936 (Heller)

Ulisse, 1954 (Hecht; de Laurentiis; Ponti; Rosson; Schüfftan)

Ulla, min Ulla, 1930 (Jaenzon)

Ulla, My Ulla. *See* Ulla, min Ulla, 1930

Ultima donna, 1976 (Sarde)

Ultimate Solution of Grace Quigley, 1983 (Golan and Globus)

Ultimatum, 1938 (Fradetal)

Up Goes Maisie, 1945 (Irene)
Up in Arms, 1944 (Day; Goldwyn; Mandell; Rennahan)
Up in Central Park, 1948 (Green; Krasner)
Up in Daisy's Penthouse, 1952 (Bruckman)
Up in Mabel's Room, 1926 (Rosson)
Up in the Clouds. *See* Akash Kusum, 1965
Up in the World, 1956 (Rank)
Up Pops the Devil, 1931 (Banton; Struss)
Up San Juan Hill, 1909 (Selig)
Up She Goes. *See* Up Goes Maisie, 1945
Up the Down Staircase, 1967 (Jenkins; Justin)
Up the Junction, 1968 (Havelock-Allan)
Up the MacGregors. *See* Sette donne per i MacGregor, 1966
Up the River, 1930 (August; Parrish)
Up the Sandbox, 1972 (Horner; Willis; Winkler)
Up to His Ears. *See* Tribulations d'un chinois en Chine, 1965
Up to His Neck, 1954 (Rank; Vetchinsky)
Up to Mars, 1930 (Fleischer)
Up to the Neck, 1933 (Wilcox)
Up Your Anchor. *See* Eskimo Ohgen, 1985
Up Your Teddy Bear, 1970 (Jones)
Upfront, 1951 (Metty)
Upholding the Law, 1917 (August)
Upkeep, 1973 (Hubley)
Upland Rider, 1928 (McCord)
Upper Underworld, 1931 (Polito)
Upper World, 1934 (Hecht)
Uppercut, 1922 (Roach)
Upperworld, 1934 (Gaudio; Grot)
Upright and Wrong, 1947 (Dunning)
Uprising. *See* Aufstand, 1980
Uprising, 2001 (Sylbert)
Upstage, 1926 (Gaudio; Gibbons; Gillespie; Mayer)
Upstairs and Downstairs, 1959 (Rank)
Upstanding Sitter, 1948 (Blanc; McKimson)
Upstream, 1926 (Clarke)
Upswept Hare, 1953 (Blanc; McKimson; Stalling)
Uptight, 1968 (Hubley; Kaufman; Trauner)
Upturned Glass, 1947 (Rank)
Uranium Conspiracy, 1977 (Golan and Globus)
Urbanissimo, 1966 (Hubley)
Urfeus i underjorden, 1910 (Magnusson)
Urgence, 1985 (Lhomme)
Urgh! A Music War, 1981 (Elfman)
Uriel Acosta, 1920 (Hoffmann)
Urlaub und Ehrenwort, 1937 (Röhrig)
Urlo, 1965 (Storaro)
Urodziny Matyldy, 1974 (Stawiński)
Urodziny modego warszawiaka, 1980 (Stawiński)
Urok zhizni, 1955 (Urusevsky)
Us Paar, 1974 (Burman)
Us Two. *See* A nous deux, 1979
Used People, 1992 (Watkin)
Users, 1978 (Jarre)
Usurer, 1910 (Bitzer)
Ut Mine Stromtid, 1920 (Dreier)
Utamaro and His Five Women. *See* Utamaro o meguru gonin no onna, 1946
Utamaro o meguru gonin no onna, 1946 (Yoda)
Utrpení mladé lásky. *See* Werther, 1927
Utsukushisa to kanashimi to, 1965 (Takemitsu)
Uttoran, 1994 (Dutta)
Uwasa no onna, 1954 (Miyagawa)
Uwawa no onna. *See* Uwasa no onna, 1954
Uwayaku shitayaku godouyaku, 1959 (Muraki)

V blouzneni, 1928 (Stallich)
V for Victory, 1941 (McClarenlaren)
V. Proudech, 1957 (Saulnier)
V tylu u belych, 1925 (Enei)
Va banque, 1930 (Reisch)
Va voir Maman . . . Papa travaille, 1977 (Delerue)
Vášeň, 1961 (Trnka)
Vacances au paradis, 1959 (Delerue)
Vacances blanches, 1951 (Decaë)
Vacances de M. Hulot, 1953 (Grimault)
Vacances en enfer, 1961 (Fradetal)
Vacances portugaises, 1962 (Coutard; Delerue)
Vacanze del Signor Rossi, 1977 (Bozzetto)
Vacation, 1924 (Fleischer)
Vacation from Love, 1938 (Adrian)
Vacation from Marriage. *See* Perfect Strangers, 1945
Vache et le prisonnier, 1959 (Jeanson)
Vacuum Cleaner, 1964 (Halas and Batchelor)
Vad veta val männen?, 1933 (Jaenzon)
Vagabond. *See* Aniceko, vrate se!, 1926
Vagabond. *See* **Awara**, 1952
Vagabond Club, 1929 (Miller)
Vagabond King, 1930 (Banton; Dreier; Mankiewicz; Rennahan; Zukor)
Vagabond King, 1956 (Bumstead; Burks; Pereira; Young)
Vagabond Lady, 1935 (Roach)
Vagabond Lover, 1929 (Plunkett)
Vagabond Queen, 1929 (Rosher)
Vagabond Trail, 1924 (August)
Vagabond's Galoshes. *See* Kolingens galoscher, 1912
Vagabonde, 1931 (Fradetal)
Vägen till Kolckrike, 1953 (Nykvist)
Vaghe stelle dell'orsa, 1965 (Cecchi D'amico; Cristaldi)
Vagrant, 1992 (Walas)
Váhavý střelec, 1957 (Ondříček)
Vaisseau sur la colline, 1960 (Delerue)
Valachi Papers. *See* Joe Valachi—i segreti di Cosa Nostra, 1972
Våld, 1955 (Lundgren)
Valdemar. *See* Due occhi diabolici, 1990
Vale Abraão, 1993 (Branco)
Valencia, 1926 (Gibbons; Gillespie; Mayer)
Valentino, 1951 (Banton; Mandell; Stradling)
Valentino, 1977 (Winkler)
Valerie, 1957 (Laszlo)
Valet's Wife, 1908 (Bitzer)
Valfångare, 1939 (Fischer; Jaenzon)
Valiant, 1929 (Carré)
Valiant Is the Word for Carrie, 1936 (Banton)
Valiant Tailor, 1934 (Iwerks)
Valise, 1974 (Sarde)
Valise diplomatique, 1909 (Cohl)
Valka zukov rogachi, 1910 (Starewicz)
Vallée, 1972 (Almendros; Gégauff)
Valley. *See* Vallée, 1972
Valley of Decision, 1945 (Gillespie; Irene; Levien; Mayer; Ruttenberg; Stothart)
Valley of Eagles, 1951 (Rota)
Valley of Esopus, 1906 (Bitzer)
Valley of Gwangi, 1969 (Harryhausen)
Valley of the Dolls, 1967 (Daniels; Day; Previn; Smith; Spencer; Williams)
Valley of the Giants, 1919 (Zukor)
Valley of the Giants, 1927 (McCord)
Valley of the Giants, 1938 (Deutsch; Friedhofer; Miller; Polito)
Valley of the Kings, 1954 (Plunkett; Rozsa; Smith; Surtees)
Valley of Tomorrow, 1920 (Furthman)
Valley Town, 1940 (Maddow)

Vallfarten till Kevlar, 1921 (Magnusson)
Valmont, 1989 (Carrière; Ondříček)
Valse brillante, 1936 (Planer)
Valse brillante, 1949 (Annenkov; Burel)
Valse de Paris, 1950 (Matras)
Valse du gorille, 1959 (Renoir)
Valseuses, 1974 (Nuytten)
Value for Money, 1955 (Rank; Unsworth; Vetchinsky)
¡Vámonos con Pancho Villa!, 1936 (Figueroa)
Vamos a matar, companeros, 1970 (Morricone)
Vamp, 1918 (Barnes; Ince; Sullivan)
Vamp till Ready, 1935 (Roach)
Vampire. See Vampyren, 1912
Vampire Circus, 1972 (Carreras)
Vampire de Düsseldorf, 1964 (de Beauregard)
Vampire Happening. See Gebissen wird nur Nachts—Happening der
    Vampire, 1971
Vampire Lovers, 1970 (Carreras)
Vampire Men of the Lost Planet. See Horror of the Blood Monsters, 1970
Vampire's Ghost, 1945 (Brackett)
Vampires, 1915-16 (Gaumont)
Vampyr, 1932 (Fradetal; Maté; Warm)
Vampyren, 1912 (Jaenzon; Magnusson)
Van Gogh, 1948 (Braunberger)
Vanderbilt Cup Auto Race, 1904 (Bitzer)
Vanessa: Her Love Story, 1935 (Selznick; Stothart)
Vangelo '70. See Amore e rabbia, 1969
Vangelo secondo Matteo, 1964 (Delli Colli; Donati)
Vanille fraise, 1989 (Cristaldi)
Vanille Française, 1989 (Mnouchkine)
Vanina, 1922 (Mayer; Pommer)
Vanina Vanini, 1961 (Solinas)
Vanish, 1978 (Kuri)
Vanishing, 1993 (Goldsmith)
Vanishing Duck, 1958 (Hanna and Barbera)
Vanishing Legion, 1931 (Canutt)
Vanishing Point, 1971 (Alonzo)
Vanishing Prairie, 1954 (Iwerks)
Vanishing Race, 1928 (Zukor)
Vanishing West, 1928 (Canutt)
Vanity, 1927 (Adrian; Grot; Miller; Sullivan)
Vanity Street, 1932 (August)
Vanity's Price, 1924 (Mohr)
Vánočni, 1946 (Zeman)
Vanquished, 1953 (Head)
Väntande vatten, 1965 (Fischer)
Vantour de la Sierra, 1909 (Gaumont)
Vanya on 42nd Street, 1994 (Mamet)
Vaquero's Vow, 1908 (Bitzer)
Varan the Unbelievable. See Daikaiju Baran, 1958
Vargtimmen, 1968 (Nykvist)
Variété, 1925 (Freund; Pommer; Schüfftan)
Variétés, 1971 (Matras)
Variety. See **Variété**, 1925
Variety Girl, 1947 (Dreier; Head; van Heusen)
Variety Lights. See Luci del varietà, 1950
Variety Show, 1937 (Barnes)
Varmlanningarne, 1909 (Magnusson)
Varsity Show, 1937 (Mercer; Polito; Wald)
Vatan, 1938 (Biswas)
Vatel, 2000 (Morricone)
Vater werden ist nicht schwer . . . , 1926 (Wagner)
Vaudeville, 1924 (Fleischer)
Vdavky Nanynky Kulichovy, 1925 (Heller)
Veau, 1908 (Cohl)
Veau gras, 1939 (Kaufman)

Vecchie amicizie, 1956 (Delli Colli)
Večery s Jindřichem Plachtou, 1954 (Stallich)
Vécés étaient fermés de l'intérieur, 1975 (Nuytten)
Ved Vejen. See Katinka, 1988
Vedovo allegro, 1949 (Age and Scarpelli)
Veena, 1948 (Biswas)
Vegas Nights, 1941 (Head; Young)
Vegas Vacation, 1997 (Fraker)
Vegetarian's Dream, 1913-14 (Cohl)
Veilchenfresser, 1926 (Andrejew)
Veiled Woman, 1929 (Clarke)
Veille d'armes, 1935 (Spaak)
Vel' d'hiv', 1960 (Jarre)
Velia, 1980 (Cecchi D'amico)
Veliki strah, 1958 (Vukotić)
Velikii grazhdanin, 1938-39 (Shostakovich)
Velké dobrodružství, 1952 (Brdečka)
Velvet Fingers, 1920 (Grot)
Velvet Goldmine, 1998 (Burwell; Vachon)
Velvet Paw, 1916 (Carré)
Velvet Touch, 1948 (Banton; Walker)
Vem dömer?, 1922 (Jaenzon; Magnusson)
Vem Skot?, 1916 (Magnusson)
Vendemiaire, 1918 (Gaumont)
Vendetta, 1905 (Pathé)
Vendetta, 1950 (Planer)
Vendetta en Camargue, 1950 (Kosma)
Venedig—die Insel der Glückseligen am Rande am des Untergangs, 1978
    (Ballhaus)
Venere imperiale, 1963 (Aurenche and Bost)
Venetian Affair, 1967 (Krasner; Schifrin)
Venetian Bird, 1952 (Rank; Rota)
Venetian Woman. See Venexiana, 1986
Venexiana, 1986 (Lanci; Morricone)
Venezia, carnevale, un amore, 1981 (Donaggio)
Venezia, la luna, e tu, 1958 (Delli Colli)
Venezianische Nacht, 1914 (Freund)
Venganza de Heraclio Bernal, 1957 (Figueroa)
Vengeance, 1930 (Cohn)
Vengeance, 1962 (Francis)
Vengeance. See Pomsta, 1968
Vengeance de Riri, 1908 (Cohl)
Vengeance des esprits, 1911 (Cohl)
Vengeance du serpent à plumes, 1984 (Decaë)
Vengeance d'une orpheline russe, 1965 (Braunberger)
Vengeance Is Mine, 1917 (Miller)
Vengeance of Fate, 1912 (Ince)
Vengeance of She, 1968 (Carreras)
Vengeance Valley, 1950 (Plunkett)
Venice. See Venedig—die Insel der Glückseligen am Rande am des
    Untergangs, 1978
Venice, the Moon, and You. See Venezia, la luna, e tu, 1958
Venir du Havre, 1962 (Braunberger)
Vent se lève, 1958 (Aurenche and Bost)
Vent souffle où il veut. See **Condamné à mort s'est échappé**, 1956
Vent'anni, 1950 (Zavattini)
Vento del sud, 1959 (Cristaldi; Di Venanzo)
Ventriloquist Cat, 1950 (Avery)
Vénus, 1928 (Burel)
Vénus aveugle, 1941 (Alekan; Burel)
Venus Makes Trouble, 1937 (Ballard)
Venus of Venice, 1927 (Barnes; Schenck)
Vera Cruz, 1954 (Cahn; Chase; Friedhofer; Laszlo)
Vera storia della signora della camelie, 1980 (Morricone)
Verboten!, 1959 (Biroc)
Verbotene Weg, 1920 (Galeen)

Verdict, 1946 (Burks; Haller)
Verdict, 1982 (Mamet; Mandel; Zanuck)
Verdict. *See* Testament, 1974
Verdugo, 1963 (Delli Colli; Flaiano and Pinelli)
Verdugo de Sevilla, 1942 (Figueroa)
Veredas, 1977 (de Almeida)
Vergine moderna, 1954 (Flaiano and Pinelli)
Vergödö szívek, 1916 (Korda)
Vergogna schifosi, 1968 (Morricone)
Veritá, 1982 (Zavattini)
Vérité sur Bébé Donge, 1951 (Burel)
Verkannt, 1910 (Messter)
Verliebte Hotel, 1933 (Heller)
Verlogene Moral, 1921 (Freund; Mayer)
Verlorene Schatten, 1920 (Freund; Reiniger)
Verlorene Schuh, 1923 (Pommer)
Verrat an Deutschland, 1955 (Warm)
Verräter, 1936 (Röhrig)
Vers de la grappe, 1955 (Rabier)
Vers l'extase, 1959 (Matras; Spaak)
Versailles, 1969 (Alekan)
Versailles et ses fantômes, 1948 (Braunberger)
Verschleierte Dame, 1917 (Pommer)
Verschwöhrung zu Genua. *See* Fiesco, 1921
Verschwörung zu Genua. *See* Fiesco, 1921
Verschwundene Miniatur, 1989 (Kästner)
Verspieltes Leben, 1949 (Herlth)
Versprich mir nichts!, 1937 (Von Harbou)
Versunkene Welt, 1922 (Kolowrat-Krakowsky; Korda)
Vertauschte Braut, 1925 (Junge)
Vertauschte Braut, 1934 (Heller)
Vertauschte Gesichter, 1929 (Warm)
Verteidigung der Karpaten, 1916 (Kolowrat-Krakowsky)
Vertig Jaren, 1938 (Heller)
Vertiges, 1985 (Branco; de Almeida)
Vertigo, 1958 (Bass; Bumstead; Burks; Edouart; Head; Herrmann; Mathieson; Pereira)
Veruschka—Poesia di una donna, 1971 (Morricone)
Verwehte Spuren, 1938 (Von Harbou; Warm)
Verwehte Spuren. *See* Auf gefährlichen Spuren, 1924
Very Big Withdrawal. *See* A Man, a Woman, and a Bank, 1979
Very Busy Gentlemen. *See* Pán na roztrhání, 1934
Very Confidential, 1927 (August)
Very Handy Man. *See* Liolà, 1964
Very Honorable Guy, 1934 (Orry-Kelly)
Very Idea, 1929 (Plunkett)
Very Important Person, 1961 (Rank)
Very Merry Cricket, 1971 (Jones)
Very Private Affair. *See* Vie privée, 1962
Very Thought of You, 1944 (Glennon; Wald; Waxman)
Very Young Lady, 1941 (Cronjager; Day)
Veselý cirkus, 1950 (Trnka)
Vesire gli ignudi, 1953 (Flaiano and Pinelli)
Vessel of Wrath, 1938 (Addinsell; Pommer)
Vestire gli ignudi, 1955 (Spaak)
Vesuvius Express, 1953 (Clarke)
Vesyoli musikanti, 1937 (Ptushko)
Vesyonnij prizyv, 1976 (Mindadze)
Vêtements Sigrand, 1938 (Alexeieff and Parker)
Veuve Coudere, 1971 (Saulnier)
Veuve en or, 1969 (D'Eaubonne)
Vézélay, 1969 (Milhaud)
Vezen no Bezdeze, 1932 (Stallich)
Vi behöver varann, 1944 (Lundgren)
Vi går landsvagen, 1937 (Jaenzon)
Vi tre debutera, 1953 (Fischer)

Via Mala, 1945 (Hoffmann; Röhrig; Von Harbou)
Via mala, 1985 (Morricone)
Via Padova 46, 1954 (Rota)
Via Pony Express, 1933 (Canutt)
Viagem ao Princípio do Mundo, 1997 (Branco)
Viaggio, 1973 (Ponti)
Viaggio con Anita, 1978 (Delli Colli; Flaiano and Pinelli; Morricone)
Viaggio d'amore, 1991 (Guerra)
Viaggio di Capitan Fracassa, 1990 (Age and Scarpelli)
Viaggio in Italia, 1953 (Mnouchkine)
Viaggio lungo il Tirreno. *See* Chi legge?, 1960
Vibes, 1988 (Edlund; Littleton)
Vice and Virtue. *See* Vice et la vertu, 1963
Vice et la vertu, 1963 (Gégauff)
Vice Raid, 1959 (Cortez)
Vice Squad, 1931 (Lang)
Vice Squad, 1953 (Biroc)
Vice Squad, 1982 (Alcott)
Vice Versa, 1948 (Dillon; Rank)
Vicious Circle, 1957 (Heller)
Vicki, 1953 (Horner; Krasner)
Victim, 1961 (Heller; Rank; Vetchinsky)
Victim, 1972 (Bumstead)
Victim of Jealousy, 1910 (Bitzer)
Victimas del pecado, 1950 (Figueroa)
Victimes de l'alcoolisme, 1902 (Pathé)
Victims, 1982 (Schifrin)
Victoire en chantant, 1976 (Douy)
Victor/Victoria, 1982 (Mancini)
Victoria the Great, 1937 (Wilcox; Young)
Victorious through Serbia. *See* Siegreich durch Serbien, 1914
Victors, 1963 (Bass; Challis; Foreman)
Victory, 1919 (Carré; Furthman)
Victory, 1940 (Dreier; Head; Veiller)
Victory, 1981 (Conti; Fisher)
Victory. *See* Pobeda, 1938
Victory in Court. *See* Gewonnene Prozeß, 1917
Victory in the Dark. *See* Seger i mörker, 1954
Victory of the Night. *See* Pobediteli nochi, 1927
Victory through Air Power, 1943 (Disney)
Victuailles de Gretchen se revoltent, 1916 (Cohl)
Vid Vgen. *See* Katinka, 1988
Vida cambia, 1976 (Figueroa)
Vida no vale nada, 1954 (Alcoriza)
Vidas, 1983 (Branco; de Almeida)
Videodrome, 1983 (Baker)
Vidya, 1948 (Burman)
Vie, 1957 (Renoir)
Vie chantée, 1950 (Burel)
Vie commence demain, 1950 (Milhaud)
Vie continue, 1982 (Delerue)
Vie continue. *See* Vie devant soi, 1977
Vie crevée, 1992 (Coutard)
Vie dans l'herbe, 1957 (Braunberger)
Vie de Bohème, 1916 (Carré; Marion)
Vie de Bohème, 1943 (Wakhévitch)
Vie de château, 1965 (Legrand; Lhomme; Rappeneau; Saulnier)
Vie de Jean-Jacques Rousseau, 1978 (Rousselot)
Vie de Jésus, 1951 (Braunberger)
Vie de plaisir, 1943 (Spaak)
Vie des oiseaux en Mauritanie, 1963 (Braunberger)
Vie des termites, 1958 (Braunberger)
Vie devant soi, 1977 (Almendros; Evein; Sarde)
Vie drôle, 1914 (Gaumont)
Vie du Christ, 1898 (Gaumont)
Vie du Christ, 1906 (Gaumont)

Vie du moyen age, 1955 (Rabier)
Vie d'un fleuve: La Seine, 1932 (Jaubert; Kaufman)
Vie d'un homme, 1938 (Auric)
Vie d'un joueur, 1903 (Pathé)
Vie en rose, 1948 (Jeanson)
Vie est à nous, 1936 (Eisler; Renoir)
Vie est un roman, 1983 (Mnouchkine; Nuytten; Saulnier)
Vie parisienne, 1935 (Jaubert)
Vie privée, 1962 (Decaë; Evein; Rappeneau)
Vie, l'amour, la mort, 1969 (Lai; Mnouchkine)
Vieil Homme et l'enfant, 1966 (Delerue)
Vieille fille, 1971 (Legrand; Lhomme)
Vieille qui marchait dans la mer, 1991 (Sarde)
Vieilles Femmes de l'hospice, 1917 (Gaumont)
Vienna at War. See Wien im Krieg, 1916
Viens l'chercher, 1905 (Pathé)
Vier um die Frau. See Kämpfende Herzen, 1920
Viererzug, 1917 (Kolowrat-Krakowsky)
Vièrges, 1962 (Schüfftan)
Viernes de la eternidad, 1981 (Schifrin)
Vierte kommt nicht, 1939 (Wagner)
View from Pompey's Head, 1955 (Dunne; Lemaire)
View from the Bridge. See Vu de Pont, 1961
View to a Kill, 1985 (Barry; Broccoli)
Vigil, 1914 (Ince)
Vigil in the Night, 1940 (Newman; Plunkett; Polglase)
Vigilante's Return, 1947 (Miller)
Vigilantes Are Coming, 1936 (Canutt)
Vignes du seigneur, 1932 (D'Eaubonne)
Vij, 1918 (Starewicz)
Vijaya, 1942 (Biswas)
Vijeta, 1983 (Nihalani)
Viking Queen, 1967 (Carreras)
Vikings, 1958 (Cardiff; Saulnier; Willingham)
Viktoria, 1934 (Hoffmann)
Villa Borghese, 1953 (Amidei; Flaiano and Pinelli)
Villa del venerdi, 1992 (Lanci; Morricone)
Villa Rides, 1968 (Jarre; Towne)
Village Barber, 1931 (Iwerks)
Village Blacksmith, 1933 (Terry)
Village Cut-Up, 1906 (Bitzer)
Village dans Paris: Montmartre, 1940 (Jaubert)
Village du milieu des brumes, 1961 (Decaë)
Village in India. See World Window, 1937-40
Village magique, 1954 (Kosma)
Village of the Giants, 1965 (Edouart; Nitzsche)
Village perdu, 1947 (Honegger)
Village School of Emperor Supporters. See Sonnou sonjuku, 1939
Village Smithy, 1936 (Avery; Stalling)
Village Smitty, 1931 (Iwerks)
Village Specialist, 1932 (Iwerks)
Village Squire, 1935 (Havelock-Allan)
Village Tale, 1935 (Musuraca; Plunkett; Polglase)
Village Teacher. See Selskaya uchitelnitsa, 1947
Villain, 1971 (Challis)
Villain Still Pursued Her, 1937 (Terry)
Villain Still Pursued Her, 1940 (Ballard)
Villain's Curse, 1932 (Terry)
Ville Bidon, 1975 (Cloquet)
Ville des pirates, 1983 (Branco; de Almeida)
Vim, Vigor and Vitaliky, 1936 (Fleischer)
Vincent, François, Paul . . . and the Others. See Vincent, François, Paul . . . et l'autres, 1974
Vincent, François, Paul . . . et l'autres, 1974 (Sarde)
Vindicator, 1985 (Winston)
Vine Bridge. See Lianbron, 1965

Vingarne, 1916 (Jaenzon; Magnusson)
Vingt-cinquième heure, 1967 (Delerue; Ponti)
Vingt-quatre heures de perm', 1940 (Heller; Wakhévitch)
Vingt-quatre heures en trente minutes, 1928 (Kaufman)
Vintage, 1957 (Raksin; Ruttenberg)
Violence at Noon. See Hakuchu no torima, 1966
Violent Four. See Banditi a Milano, 1968
Violent Hour. See Dial 1119, 1950
Violent Is the Word for Curly, 1938 (Ballard)
Violent Journey, 1966 (Jeakins)
Violent Men, 1955 (Guffey; Maté; Steiner; Wald)
Violent Playground, 1958 (Rank)
Violent Saturday, 1955 (Clarke; Friedhofer; Lemaire; Wheeler)
Violent Summer. See Estate violenta, 1959
Violenza segreta, 1962 (Gherardi)
Violenza: quinto potere, 1972 (Morricone)
Violette. See Violette Nozière, 1978
Violette and François. See Violette et François, 1977
Violette et François, 1977 (Sarde)
Violette Nozière, 1978 (Rabier)
Violettes impériales, 1952 (Barsacq; Matras)
Violin Maker of Cremona, 1909 (Bitzer)
Violon de Crémone, 1968 (Delerue)
Violon et agent. See Violoniste, 1908
Violoniste, 1908 (Cohl)
Violons d'Ingres, 1940 (Jaubert)
Violons parfois, 1977 (Guillemot)
Vip mio fratello superuomo, 1968 (Bozzetto)
V.I.P.s, 1963 (Booth; de Grunwald; Fisher; Rattigan; Rozsa)
Vipères, 1911 (Gaumont)
Virgen de medianoche, 1942 (Figueroa)
Virgen que forjó una patria, 1942 (Figueroa)
Virgin Island, 1958 (Francis; Lardner)
Virgin Lips, 1928 (Walker)
Virgin Paradise, 1921 (Ruttenberg)
Virgin President, 1968 (Schoonmaker)
Virgin Queen, 1955 (Brackett; Clarke; Lemaire; Waxman)
Virgin Soldiers, 1970 (Foreman)
Virgin Spring. See Jungfrukällan, 1960
Virgin Who Embraces a Rainbow. See Niji o idaku shojo, 1948
Virginia, 1941 (Dreier; Edouart; Glennon; Head; Young)
Virginia City, 1940 (Canutt; Friedhofer; Haskin; Koch; Polito; Steiner; Wallis)
Virginia Courtship, 1922 (Rosson)
Virginia Judge, 1935 (Krasner)
Virginian, 1914 (Buckland)
Virginian, 1923 (Lang)
Virginian, 1929 (Head; Zukor)
Virginian, 1946 (Dreier; Edouart; Goodrich and Hackett; Head)
Virginie, 1962 (Braunberger; Matras)
Virile Games. See Muzné Hry, 1988
Virtue, 1932 (Riskin; Walker)
Virtuous Vamp, 1919 (Loos)
Virtuosity, 1995 (Walas)
Virtuous Thief, 1919 (Barnes; Sullivan)
Virtuous Wives, 1919 (Mayer)
Visa to Canton, 1961 (Carreras)
Visage mysterieux d'Océanie, 1970 (Braunberger)
Visages de France, 1936 (Honegger)
Visages de Paris, 1955 (Braunberger)
Visages d'enfants, 1923 (Burel)
Visconti. See Senso, 1954
Visible Manifestations, 1961 (Dunning)
Vision of Eight, 1973 (Allen)
Visione del Sabba, 1988 (Lanci)
Visions of Eight, 1973 (Lassally; Mancini)

Vous n'avez rien contre la jeunesse, 1958 (Guillemot)
Vous ne l'emporterez pas au paradis, 1974 (Mnouchkine)
Vous pigez?, 1955 (Burel)
Voyage. *See* Viaggio, 1973
Voyage à la Côte d'Azur, 1913 (Gaumont)
Voyage au Congo, 1926 (Braunberger)
Voyage autour d'un étoile, 1906 (Pathé)
Voyage d'Abdallah, 1953 (Jarre)
Voyage de Mr. Perrichon, 1933 (Wakhévitch)
Voyage de noces. *See* Jalousie 1976, 1976
Voyage du Capitaine Fracasse. *See* Viaggio di Capitan Fracassa, 1990
Voyage en Amérique, 1951 (Alekan)
Voyage en Boscavie, 1958 (Guillemot)
Voyage en Camardie, 1971 (Braunberger)
Voyage imprévu, 1934 (Spaak)
Voyage of Captain Fracasse. *See* Viaggio di Capitan Fracassa, 1990
Voyage of Terror: The Achille Lauro Affair, 1989 (Morricone)
Voyage of the Damned, 1976 (Schifrin)
Voyage surprise, 1946 (Kosma; Prévert; Trauner)
Voyage to America, 1964 (Houseman; Thomson)
Voyage to Next, 1974 (Hubley)
Voyage to the Beginning of the World. *See* Viagem ao Princípio do Mundo, 1997
Voyage to the Bottom of the Sea, 1961 (Hoch; Smith)
Voyage to the Moon. *See* Putyeshyestviyc na luna, 1912
Voyager, 1991 (Shepard)
Voyager. *See* Homo Faber, 1991
Voyageur sans bagages, 1943 (Matras)
Voyou, 1970 (Lai; Mnouchkine)
Vozvrashcheniye Maksima, 1937 (Enei; Moskvin)
Vozvrashcheniye Maxima, 1937 (Shostakovich)
Vozvrashcheniye Vasiliya Bortnikova, 1952 (Urusevsky)
Vrai Visage de Thérèse de Lisieux, 1961 (Grimault)
Vremya tantsora, 1998 (Mindadze)
Vstrecha na Elbe, 1949 (Shostakovich; Tisse)
Vstrechnyi, 1932 (Shostakovich)
Vsyak na Russi i tango tantzuyet, 1914 (Starewicz)
Vu du pont, 1962 (Aurenche and Bost; Saulnier)
Vulcan Entertains. *See* Hell's Fire, 1934
Vyborg Side. *See* **Vyborgskaya Storona**, 1939
Vyborgskaya Storona, 1939 (Enei; Moskvin; Shostakovich)
Vynález zkásy, 1958 (Brdečka; Zeman)
Vzorná výchova, 1953 (Stallich)
Vzteklý ženich, 1919 (Heller)
Vzucholod a láska, 1947 (Brdečka)

W, 1974 (Mandel)
W Plan, 1930 (Young)
Wabash Avenue, 1950 (Lederer; Lemaire)
Wabbit Twouble, 1941 (Blanc; Clampett; Stalling)
Wabbit Who Came to Supper, 1942 (Blanc; Stalling)
Wachsexperimente, 1921-26 (Fischinger)
Wachsfigurenkabinett, 1924 (Galeen; Junge)
Wackiest Ship in the Navy, 1960 (Duning)
Wackiki Wabbit, 1943 (Blanc; Jones; Stalling)
Wacky Blackout, 1942 (Blanc; Clampett; Stalling)
Wacky Wabbit, 1942 (Blanc; Clampett; Stalling)
Wacky Wildlife, 1940 (Avery; Blanc; Stalling)
Wacky Worm, 1941 (Blanc; Jones; Stalling)
Waco, 1966 (Head; Pereira)
Wag the Dog, 1997 (Mamet)
Waga ai wa yama no kanata ni, 1948 (Hayasaka)
Waga koi wa moenu, 1949 (Yoda)
Wages of Fear. *See* **Salaire de la peur**, 1953
Wages of Sin, 1903 (Bitzer)
Wages of Tin, 1924 (Roach)

Waggily Tale, 1958 (Blanc)
Wagner, 1983 (Storaro)
Wagon Heels, 1945 (Blanc; Clampett; Stalling)
Wagon Master, 1929 (McCord)
Wagon Tracks, 1919 (August; Ince; Sullivan)
Wagon Train, 1940 (Polglase)
Wagonmaster, 1950 (Basevi; Cooper; Glennon; Nugent)
Wagons Roll at Night, 1941 (Haskin; Wallis)
Wags to Riches, 1949 (Avery)
Wags to Riches, 1955 (Avery)
Wahnsinn, 1919 (Hoffmann)
Wahrheit über Rosemarie, 1959 (Warm)
Waikiki Wedding, 1937 (Head; Struss; Young)
Wail. *See* Dokoku, 1952
Wait Till the Sun Shines, Nellie, 1932 (Fleischer)
Wait till the Sun Shines, Nellie, 1952 (Lemaire; Newman; Shamroy)
Wait until Dark, 1967 (Jenkins; Lang; Mancini)
Wait Until Spring, Bandini, 1989 (Badalamenti)
Waiter No. 5, 1910 (Bitzer)
Waiting to Exhale, 1995 (Bass)
Waiting Water. *See* Väntande vatten, 1965
Waiting Women. *See* Kvinnors väntan, 1952
Wak-Wak, ein Märchenzauber. *See* Geschichte des Prinzen Achmed, 1923-26
Wakai sensei, 1941 (Hayasaka)
Wake Island, 1942 (Dreier; Head)
Wake Me When It's Over, 1960 (Cahn; Shamroy; Wheeler; van Heusen)
Wake Up and Die. *See* Svegliati e uccidi, 1966
Wake Up and Dream, 1934 (Mandell)
Wake Up and Dream, 1946 (Wheeler)
Wake Up and Live, 1937 (Cronjager; Macgowan)
Wakefield Express, 1952 (Lassally)
Waking Up the Town, 1925 (Edeson)
Wales—Green Mountain, Black Mountain, 1942 (Alwyn)
Walk, Don't Run, 1966 (Jones; Stradling)
Walk East on Beacon, 1952 (de Rochemont)
Walk in the Clouds, 1995 (Jarre)
Walk in the Forest, 1975 (Friedhofer)
Walk in the Shadow. *See* Life for Ruth, 1962
Walk in the Spring Rain, 1969 (Bernstein; Lang)
Walk in the Sun, 1945 (Harlan)
Walk into Hell, 1957 (Auric)
Walk into Paradise, 1955 (Auric; Guillemot)
Walk Like a Dragon, 1960 (Mainwaring)
Walk on the Moon, 1999 (Daring)
Walk on the Wild Side, 1962 (Bass; Bernstein; Lemaire; Sylbert)
Walk Softly Stranger, 1950 (Schary)
Walk Tall, 1960 (Crosby)
Walk with Love and Death, 1969 (Delerue)
Walkabout, 1971 (Barry)
Walking along the Main Road. *See* Vi går landsvagen, 1937
Walking and Talking, 1996 (Schamus)
Walking Back, 1928 (Adrian; Grot)
Walking Dead, 1936 (Mohr; Orry-Kelly; Westmore Family)
Walking down Broadway . *See* Hello, Sister!, 1933
Walking down Broadway, 1938 (Miller)
Walking Hills, 1950 (Louis)
Walking Trip of Revenge. *See* Adauchi hizakurige, 1936
Walkout, 1923 (Roach)
Walky Talky Hawky, 1946 (Blanc; McKimson; Stalling)
Wall, 1982 (Rosenman)
Wall. *See* Pink Floyd The Wall, 1982
Wall of Noise, 1963 (Ballard)
Wall of Tyrany, 1988 (Golan and Globus)
Wallace & Gromit: The Aardman Collection 2, 1996 (Park)
Wallace & Gromit: The Best of Aardman Animation, 1996 (Park)

Wallflower, 1948 (Freund)
Wallflowers, 1928 (Plunkett)
Walls Came Tumbling Down, 1946 (Goosson)
Walls of Jericho, 1948 (Lemaire; Miller; Newman; Trotti)
Walls of Malapaga. *See* Au-delà des grilles, 1949
Walls of Malapaga. *See* Mura di Malapaga, 1949
Walter, 1982 (Menges)
Walter and June, 1983 (Menges)
Walter Wanger's Vogues of 1938, 1937 (Young)
Walter Wanger's Vogues of 1938. *See* Vogues of 1938, 1937
Walternacht, 1917 (Kräly)
Waltz Dream. *See* Walzertraum, 1925
Waltz Me Around, 1920 (Roach)
Waltz of the Toreadors, 1962 (Addinsell; Mathieson; Rank)
Waltz Time, 1933 (Junge)
Waltz Time in Vienna. *See* Walzerkrieg, 1933
Waltz War. *See* Walzerkrieg, 1933
Waltzes from Vienna, 1933 (Junge; Reville)
Walzer von Strauss, 1925 (Reisch)
Walzer von Strauss (Waltz by Strauss), 1952 (Von Dassanowsky)
Walzerkrieg, 1933 (Herlth; Hoffmann; Röhrig)
Walzertraum, 1925 (Pommer; Schüfftan)
Wanda, la peccatrice, 1952 (Flaiano and Pinelli)
Wanderer, 1913 (Bitzer)
Wanderer, 1925 (Head)
Wanderer, 1926 (Menzies)
Wanderer of the Wasteland, 1924 (Zukor)
Wanderers of the Desert. *See* World Window, 1937-40
Wandering Fires, 1925 (Stradling)
Wandering Husbands, 1924 (Sullivan)
Wandering Papas, 1925 (Roach)
Wanderlust. *See* Mary Jane's Pa, 1935
Wandernde Bild, 1920 (Von Harbou)
Wandernde Licht, 1916 (Messter)
Wandernder Held. *See* Wandernde Bild, 1920
Waning Sex, 1926 (Gibbons; Mayer)
Wanted, a Child, 1909 (Bitzer)
Wanted: Babysitter. *See* Baby-Sitter, 1975
Wanted $5,000, 1918 (Roach)
Wanted Men. *See* Wolves, 1930
Wanters, 1923 (Mayer)
Wanton Contessa. *See* Senso, 1954
Wanton Countess. *See* Senso, 1954
War, 1994 (Newman)
War Against Mrs. Hadley, 1942 (Freund; Schary)
War and Peace, 1956 (Cardiff; Gherardi; Ponti; Rota; de Laurentiis)
War and Pieces, 1964 (Blanc)
War Arrow, 1953 (Daniels; Hayes)
War Between Men and Women, 1972 (Hamlisch)
War between the Tates, 1977 (Barry)
War Comes to America, 1945 (Hornbeck; Veiller)
War Correspondent, 1932 (Swerling)
War Feathers, 1926 (Roach)
War Game, 1962 (Menges)
War Hunt, 1962 (McCord)
War in the Highlands. *See* Guerre dans le Haut Pays, 1998
War Is Over. *See* Guerre est finie, 1966
War Lord, 1965 (Bumstead; Westmore Family; Whitlock)
War Lover, 1962 (Addinsell; Koch; Mathieson)
War Mamas, 1931 (Roach)
War Nurse, 1930 (Gibbons; Rosher)
War of the Buttons, 1994 (Puttnam)
War of the Gargantuas. *See* Furankenshutain no kaiju—Sanda tai Gailah, 1966
War of the Roses, 1989 (Bass)
War of the Satellites, 1958 (Crosby)

War of the Wildcats. *See* In Old Oklahoma, 1943
War of the Worlds, 1953 (Barnes; Haskin; Head; Pal; Pereira)
War on the Plains, 1912 (Ince)
War Story, 1989 (Park)
War Wagon, 1967 (Clothier; Tiomkin; Westmore Family; Whitlock)
Wardrobe, 1958 (Dunning)
Ware Case, 1938 (Balcon; Neame)
WarGames, 1983 (Burtt; Fraker)
Waris, 1954 (Biswas)
Warlock, 1959 (Lemaire)
Warlock, 1989 (Goldsmith)
Warlord, 1965 (Metty)
Warm Corner, 1930 (Balcon)
Warming Up, 1928 (Cronjager)
Warning, 1927 (Walker)
Warning Shadows. *See* **Schatten**, 1922
Warning Shot, 1967 (Biroc; Edouart; Goldsmith; Head; Pereira)
Warning to Wantons, 1949 (Rank)
Warnung vor einer Heiligen Nutte, 1971 (Ballhaus)
Warpath, 1951 (Haskin; Rennahan)
Warrens of Virginia, 1915 (Buckland)
Warrior Who Crosses the Sea. *See* Umi o yuku bushi, 1939
Warrior: The Life of Leonard Peltier, 1992 (Schamus)
Warrior's Husband, 1933 (Levien; Mohr)
Warriors, 1979 (Marshall)
Warriors. *See* Dark Avengers, 1955
Warriors of Faith. *See* Jan Roháč z dubé, 1947
Warschauer Zitadelle, 1937 (Warm)
Warui yatsu hodo yoku nemuru, 1960 (Muraki)
Was bin ich ohne Dich?, 1934 (Von Harbou)
Was die Liebe vermag, 1917 (Kolowrat-Krakowsky)
Was geschah in dieser Nacht, 1941 (Wagner)
Was He a Coward?, 1911 (Bitzer)
Was Justice Served?, 1909 (Bitzer)
Washed Ashore, 1922 (Roach)
Washee Ironee, 1934 (Roach)
Washington Masquerade, 1932 (Adrian; Toland)
Washington Melodrama, 1941 (Rosson)
Washington Merry-Go-Round, 1932 (Swerling; Wanger)
Washington Story, 1952 (Alton; Rose; Schary)
Wastrel. *See* Relitto, 1961
Watash iwa kai ni naritai, 1959 (Muraki)
Watashi no na wa joufu, 1949 (Yoda)
Watch Dog, 1923 (Roach)
Watch Dog, 1945 (Terry)
Watch Him Step, 1922 (Mohr)
Watch it Sailor!, 1961 (Carreras)
Watch on the Rhine, 1943 (Friedhofer; Mohr; Orry-Kelly; Steiner; Wallis; Warner)
Watch the Birdie, 1954 (Godfrey)
Watch Your Stern, 1960 (Dillon)
Watch Your Wife, 1922 (Roach)
Watchdog, 1939 (Terry)
Watchers II, 1990 (Kaminski)
Watchtower over Tomorrow, 1945 (Hecht)
Water, 1985 (Slocombe)
Water Duel, 1900 (Bitzer)
Water Engine, 1992 (Mamet)
Water for Firefighting, 1948 (Halas and Batchelor)
Water Gipsies, 1932 (Dean; Reville)
Water Hole, 1928 (Mankiewicz)
Water Magician, or The White Thread of the Waterfall. *See* Taki no shiraito, 1952
Water, Water Every Hare, 1952 (Blanc; Jones; Stalling)
Waterfront, 1928 (Garmes)
Waterfront, 1950 (Mathieson)

Waterfront Women. *See* Waterfront, 1950
Waterhole #3, 1967 (Burks; Grusin)
Waterland, 1992 (Burwell)
Waterloo, 1928 (Wagner)
Waterloo, 1970 (Louis; Rota; de Laurentiis)
Waterloo Bridge, 1931 (Edeson; Laemmle)
Waterloo Bridge, 1940 (Adrian; Gillespie; Mayer; Ruttenberg; Stothart)
Waterloo Road, 1944 (Rank; Vetchinsky)
Wax Works, 1934 (Lantz)
Waxworks. *See* Wachsfigurenkabinett, 1924
Way Ahead, 1944 (Alwyn; Mathieson; Rank)
Way Back Home, 1931 (Berman; Steiner; Westmore Family)
Way Back When a Nag Was Only a Horse, 1940 (Fleischer)
Way Back When a Night Club Was a Stick, 1940 (Fleischer)
Way Back When a Razzberry Was a Fruit, 1940 (Fleischer)
Way Back When a Triangle Had Its Points, 1940 (Fleischer)
Way Back When Women Had Their Weigh, 1940 (Fleischer)
Way Down East, 1920 (Bitzer)
Way Down East, 1935 (Friedhofer)
Way Down South, 1939 (Young)
Way Down Yonder in the Corn, 1943 (Fleischer)
Way for a Sailor, 1930 (Gibbons; MacArthur; Mayer)
Way of a Gaucho, 1952 (Dunne; Lemaire; Newman; Wheeler)
Way of a Girl, 1925 (Gibbons)
Way of a Woman, 1919 (Schenck)
Way of All Flesh, 1927 (Biro; Furthman; Zukor)
Way of All Flesh, 1940 (Biro; Furthman; Head; Young)
Way of All Pants, 1927 (Roach)
Way of Man, 1909 (Bitzer)
Way of the Beast. *See* Kemonomichi, 1965
Way of the Strong, 1926 (Cohn)
Way of the World, 1910 (Bitzer)
Way Out West, 1930 (Gibbons; Shearer)
Way Out West, 1937 (Berlin; Roach)
Way to Love, 1933 (Lang; Zukor)
Way to the Gold, 1957 (Lemaire)
Way to the Heights. *See* Cesty k výšinam, 1921
Way to the Stars, 1945 (Dillon; Rank; Rattigan; de Grunwald)
Way . . . Way Out, 1966 (Clothier; Schifrin; Smith)
Way We Live, 1946 (Rank)
Way We Were, 1973 (Booth; Hamlisch; Sharaff; Stark)
Way West, 1967 (Clothier; Kaper; Maddow; Previn)
Wayne's World 2, 1993 (Burwell)
Ways of Love. *See* Amore, 1948
Wayward Bus, 1957 (Brackett; Clarke; Lemaire)
Wayward, 1932 (Green; Head)
Wayward Life. *See* Provinciale, 1952
W. C. Fields and Me, 1976 (Head; Mancini; Winston)
We Aim to Please, 1934 (Fleischer)
We All Loved Each Other So Much. *See* C'eravamo tanto amati, 1974
We Americans, 1928 (Laemmle)
We and the Others. *See* Wir und die andern, 1917
We Are Building. *See* Wy brouwen, 1929
We Are Not Alone, 1939 (Blanke; Gaudio; Haskin; Steiner; Wallis)
We Are the Lambeth Boys, 1958 (Lassally)
We Are the Marines, 1942 (de Rochemont)
We Can't Have Everything, 1918 (Buckland)
We Did It, 1936 (Fleischer)
We Dive at Dawn, 1943 (Rank)
We Free Kings. *See* I Magi randagi, 1996
We Go Fast, 1941 (Day)
We Have Come for Your Daughters. *See* Medicine Ball Caravan, 1970
We Have Our Moments, 1937 (Krasner)
We Joined the Navy, 1962 (Heller)
We Live Again, 1934 (Day; Goldwyn; Jennings; Newman; Toland)
We Live in Two Worlds, 1937 (Jaubert)

We Moderns, 1925 (Mathis; McCord)
We Never Sleep, 1917 (Roach)
We, the Animals, Squeak, 1941 (Blanc; Clampett; Stalling)
We the Women. *See* Siamo donne, 1953
We Three. *See* Compromised, 1931
We Three Debutantes. *See* Vi tre debutera, 1953
We Were Dancing, 1942 (Kaper)
We Were Strangers, 1949 (Louis; Metty; Spiegel)
We Who Are Young, 1940 (Freund; Kaper; Trumbo)
We Who Are Young, 1952 (Lassally)
Weaker Sex, 1948 (Rank)
Weakly Reporter, 1944 (Blanc; Jones; Stalling)
Wear Willies, 1929 (Lantz)
Wearing of the Grin, 1951 (Blanc; Jones)
Weary Death. *See* Müde Tod: Ein Deutsches Volkslied im Sechs Versen, 1921
Weary River, 1929 (Haller)
Weasel Stop, 1956 (Blanc; McKimson)
Weasel While You Work, 1958 (Blanc; McKimson)
Weather Forecast. *See* Prognoza pogody, 1981
Web. *See* Après le vent des sables, 1974
Web of Desire, 1917 (Marion)
Web of Evidence. *See* Beyond This Place, 1959
Web of Passion. *See* A Double Tour, 1959
Web of Passion. *See* Plein soleil, 1959
Weber, 1927 (Andrejew)
Wedding, 1905 (Bitzer)
Wedding at Ulfåsa. *See* Bröllopet på Ulfåsa, 1911
Wedding Banquet. *See* Hsi yen, 1993
Wedding Bells, 1921 (Schenck)
Wedding Bells. *See* Royal Wedding, 1950
Wedding Belts, 1940 (Fleischer)
Wedding Breakfast. *See* Catered Affair, 1956
Wedding Gown, 1913 (Loos)
Wedding in Blood. *See* Noces rouges, 1973
Wedding in the Eccentric Club. *See* Hochzeit in Ekzentrik Klub, 1917
Wedding March, 1928 (Day; Mohr; Zukor)
Wedding Night, 1935 (Goldwyn; Newman; Toland)
Wedding Present, 1936 (Dreier; Head; Shamroy)
Wedding Rehearsal, 1933 (Biro; Korda)
Wedding Rings, 1929 (Haller)
Wedlock Deadlock, 1947 (Bruckman)
Wednesday's Child, 1934 (Berman; Macgowan; Plunkett; Steiner)
Wednesday's Luck, 1936 (Havelock-Allan)
Wee Geordie. *See* Geordie, 1955
Wee Sandy, 1962 (Reiniger)
Wee Willie Winkie, 1937 (Miller; Newman)
Weeds, 1987 (Badalamenti)
Week-end, 1967 (Gégauff)
Week-end à Zuydcoote, 1964 (Decaë; Hakim; Jarre)
Week-End at the Waldorf, 1945 (Green; Irene)
Week-end in Havana, 1941 (Day; Newman; Pan)
Week-End Marriage, 1932 (Orry-Kelly)
Week-end Pass, 1944 (Bruckman)
Week-End sur deux, 1990 (Guillemot)
Week-end total, 1965 (Braunberger)
Weekend, 1967 (Coutard; Guillemot)
Weekend. *See* **Week-end**, 1967
Weekend at Dunkirk. *See* Weekend à Zuydcoote, 1964
Weekend for Three, 1941 (Metty)
Weekend Millionaire, 1935 (Neame)
Weekend of Shadows, 1978 (Seale)
Weekend with Father, 1951 (Boyle)
Weekend with Lulu, 1961 (Carreras)
Weekends Only, 1932 (Mohr)
Weg, der qur Verdammnis führt, 1918 (Hoffmann)

Weg zum Nachbarn, 1966 (Lenica)
Wege des Schreckens, 1921 (Kolowrat-Krakowsky)
Wege zu Kraft und Schönheit, 1925 (Pommer)
Wehe, wenn die lossgelassen, 1926 (Courant)
Wehe, wenn er losgelassen, 1932 (Heller)
Weib des Pharao, 1922 (Kräly; Metzner)
Weib in Flammen, 1928 (Planer)
Weighing the Baby, 1903 (Bitzer)
Weight for Me, 1955 (Halas and Batchelor)
Weight of Water. *See* Mummy Returns, 2001
Weird Woman, 1944 (Miller)
Weisse Abenteuer, 1951 (Herlth)
Weisse Dämon, 1932 (Hoffmann)
Weisse Hölle von Piz Palü, 1929 (Metzner)
Weisse Rosen, 1914 (Kräly)
Weisse Teufal, 1930 (Courant)
Weissen Rosen von Ravensberg, 1929 (Warm)
Welcome Burglar, 1908 (Bitzer)
Welcome Danger, 1929 (Bruckman; Zukor)
Welcome Home. *See* Snafu, 1945
Welcome Home. *See* Vlast vítá, 1945
Welcome Home, 1925 (Brown)
Welcome Home, 1935 (Miller)
Welcome Home, 1989 (Mancini)
Welcome Home, Johnny Bristol, 1972 (Schifrin)
Welcome Home, Roxy Carmichael, 1990 (Newman)
Welcome Intruder, 1913 (Bitzer)
Welcome Little Stranger, 1941 (Terry)
Welcome Stranger, 1947 (Dreier; Head; van Heusen)
Welcome to Britain, 1943 (Alwyn)
Well, 1951 (Laszlo; Tiomkin)
Well-Groomed Bride, 1946 (Dreier; Head; Seitz)
Well Well Well. *See* Ojojoj eller sången om den eldröda hummern, 1965
Well Worn Daffy, 1965 (Blanc; McKimson)
Wells Fargo, 1937 (Dreier; Head; Young)
Welt will belogen sein, 1926 (Courant)
Wen die Götter lieben (Mozart), 1942 (Von Dassanowsky)
Wenn am Sonntagabend die Dorfmusik spielt, 1933 (Warm)
Wenn die Liebe auf den Hund kommt, 1917 (Kolowrat-Krakowsky)
Wenn die Sonne weider scheint, 1943 (Herlth)
Wenn du einmal dein Herz verschenkst, 1929 (Wagner)
Wenn du noch eine Mutter hast, 1924 (Kolowrat-Krakowsky)
Wenn ich König wär!, 1934 (Warm)
Went the Day Well?, 1942 (Balcon; Walton)
Wer Kennet Jonny R?, 1966 (Jarrico)
Wer küßt wen?, 1947 (Von Dassanowsky)
Wer nimmt die Liebe ernst?, 1931 (Courant)
We're All Gamblers, 1927 (Glennon)
We're Back! A Dinosaur's Story, 1993 (Marshall)
We're in the Army Now. *See* Pack Up Your Troubles, 1939
We're No Angels, 1989 (Mamet; Rousselot)
We're Not Dressing, 1934 (Dreier; Lang)
We're Not Married, 1952 (Johnson; Lemaire)
We're on the Jury, 1937 (Musuraca)
We're Rich Again, 1934 (Musuraca; Plunkett; Steiner)
Werewolf of London, 1935 (D'Agostino; Pierce)
Werther, 1927 (Heller)
Werther, 1938 (Douy; Lourié)
Wesoła II, 1952 (ścibor-Rylski)
West 11, 1963 (Heller)
West and Soda, 1965 (Bozzetto)
West of the Divide, 1934 (Canutt)
West of the Pecos, 1935 (Metty)
West of the Pesos, 1960 (Blanc; McKimson)
West of Zanzibar, 1928 (Day; Gibbons)
West Point of the Air, 1935 (Saunders)

West Point Story, 1950 (Cahn)
West Point Widow, 1941 (Dreier; Head; Kräly)
West Side Story, 1961 (Bass; Dunn; Green; Lehman; Leven; Mirsch; Sharaff)
Westbound, 1959 (Blanke)
Western Approaches, 1944 (Cardiff)
Western Daze, 1941 (Pal)
Western Isles, 1941 (Alwyn; Cardiff)
Western Justice, 1907 (Selig)
Western Story. *See* Gal Who Took the West, 1949
Western Trail, 1936 (Terry)
Western Union, 1941 (Banton; Canutt; Cronjager; Day)
Westerner, 1940 (Basevi; Goldwyn; Mandell; Newman; Swerling; Tiomkin; Toland)
Westerners, 1919 (Seitz)
Westfront 1918, 1930 (Metzner; Wagner)
Westinghouse A.B.C., 1965 (Bernstein)
Westward Bound, 1930 (Canutt)
Westward Ho, 1935 (Canutt)
Westward Ho the Wagons!, 1956 (Disney; Iwerks)
Westward Passage, 1932 (Selznick; Steiner)
Westward the Women, 1951 (Plunkett; Schary; Schnee)
Wet Hare, 1962 (Blanc; McKimson)
Wet Knight, 1932 (Lantz)
Wet Nurse. *See* Balia, 1999
Wet Parade, 1932 (Adrian; Barnes; Mayer; Stromberg)
Wet Weather, 1922 (Roach)
Wetterwart, 1923 (Pommer)
We've Come a Long Way, 1952 (Halas and Batchelor)
We've Never Been Licked, 1943 (Krasner; Wanger)
Whale for the Killing, 1980 (Lourié)
Whalers. *See* Valfångare, 1939
Wham-Bam-Slam!, 1955 (Bruckman)
Wharf Angel, 1934 (Hoffenstein; Menzies)
Wharf Rat, 1916 (Loos)
Wharves and Strays, 1935 (Korda)
What?, 1971 (Breer)
What?. *See* Che?, 1972
What a Bozo, 1931 (Roach)
What a Crazy World, 1963 (Heller)
What a Funeral. *See* Funebrák, 1932
What a Hog!, 1992 (Godfrey)
What a Life, 1932 (Iwerks)
What a Life, 1939 (Head)
What a Lion!, 1938 (Hanna and Barbera)
What a Little Sneeze Will Do, 1941 (Terry)
What a Night!, 1928 (Cronjager; Mankiewicz)
What a Night, 1935 (Terry)
What a Way to Go!, 1964 (Comden and Green; Head; Shamroy; Smith; Westmore Family)
What a Whopper, 1921 (Roach)
What a Widow!, 1930 (Barnes)
What a Woman!, 1943 (Banton; Polglase; Walker)
What about Bob?, 1991 (Ballhaus; Sargent)
What Are Best Friends For?, 1973 (Lourié)
What Did You Do in the War, Daddy?, 1966 (Dunn; Lathrop; Mancini)
What Do Men Know?. *See* Vad veta val männen?, 1933
What Dreams May Come, 1998 (Bass)
What Drink Did, 1909 (Bitzer)
What Ever Happened to Uncle Fred?, 1967 (Godfrey)
What Every Iceman Knows, 1927 (Roach)
What Every Woman Knows, 1934 (Adrian; Rosher; Stothart)
What Every Woman Learns, 1919 (Barnes)
What Fools Men Are, 1922 (Carré)
What Happened Was. . . , 1994 (Schamus)
What Happens at Night, 1941 (Terry)

What I Didn't Say to the Prince, 1975 (Brdečka)
What Is a Computer, 1967 (Halas and Batchelor)
What Kind of Fool Am I?, 1961 (Godfrey)
What Love Can Do. See Was die Liebe vermag, 1917
What Love Forgives, 1919 (Polito)
What Makes Daffy Duck, 1948 (Blanc; Stalling)
What Makes David Run?. See Qu'est-ce qui fait courir David?, 1982
What Next Corporal Hargrove?, 1945 (Irene)
What No Spinach?, 1936 (Fleischer)
What Planet Are You From?, 2000 (Ballhaus; Burwell)
What Price Beauty, 1924 (Adrian)
What Price Beauty, 1925 (Menzies)
What Price Fleadom, 1948 (Avery)
What Price Glory?, 1952 (Lemaire; Newman; Spencer)
What Price Goofy?, 1925 (Roach)
What Price Hollywood?, 1932 (Berman; Rosher; Selznick; Steiner; Vorkapich)
What Price Melody?. See Lord Byron of Broadway, 1930
What Price Porky, 1938 (Blanc; Clampett; Stalling)
What Price Taxi, 1932 (Roach)
What Price Vengeance, 1937 (Cohn)
What Shall I Do?, 1924 (Walker)
What Shall We Do with Our Old?, 1910 (Bitzer)
What the Butler Saw, 1950 (Carreras)
What the Daisy Said, 1910 (Bitzer)
What to Do. See Chto delat', 1928
What Women Did for Me, 1927 (Roach)
What's Brewin', Bruin?, 1948 (Blanc; Jones; Stalling)
What's Buzzin Cousin?, 1943 (Walker)
What's Buzzin', Buzzard?, 1943 (Avery)
What's Cookin', Doc?, 1944 (Blanc; Clampett Stalling)
What's Cooking?, 1947 (Halas and Batchelor)
What's Eating Gilbert Grape, 1993 (Nykvist)
What's Good for the Goose, 1969 (Golan and Globus)
What's His Name, 1914 (Buckland)
What's Important Is to Live. See Que importa es vivir, 1989
What's in a Number, 1948 (Lassally)
What's My Lion?, 1961 (Blanc; McKimson)
What's New, Pussycat?, 1965 (Bacharach; Saulnier; Sylbert; Williams)
What's Opera, Doc?, 1957 (Blanc; Jones)
What's So Bad about Feeling Good?, 1968 (Bumstead; Head)
What's the Matter with Helen?, 1971 (Ballard; Lourié; Raksin; Reynolds)
What's the World Coming To?, 1926 (Roach)
What's Up, Doc?, 1950 (Blanc; McKimson; Stalling)
What's Up, Doc?, 1972 (Fields; Henry; Kovacs)
What's up Front, 1964 (Zsigmond)
What's Your Hurry?, 1909 (Bitzer)
Whatcha Watchin', 1963 (Hanna and Barbera)
Whatever Happened to Aunt Alice?, 1969 (Biroc)
Whatever Happened to Baby Jane?, 1962 (Haller)
Wheel of Chance, 1928 (Haller)
Wheel of Life, 1929 (Cronjager)
Wheeler Dealers, 1963 (Lang)
Wheels of Destiny, 1934 (McCord)
When a Feller Needs a Friend, 1932 (Rosson)
When a Ma Loves, 1910 (Bitzer)
When a Man Loves, 1926 (Carré; Haskin)
When a Man Loves a Woman, 1994 (Bass; Preisner)
When A Man Rides Alone, 1918 (Furthman)
When a Man Sees Red, 1934 (McCord)
When a Woman Guides, 1914 (Loos)
When Artists Love. See När konstnärer älska, 1914
When Boys Leave Home. See Downhill, 1927
When Dinosaurs Ruled the Earth, 1970 (Carreras)
When Do We Eat?, 1918 (Barnes; Ince)
When He Wants a Dog He Wants a Dog, 1912-14 (Cohl)

When I Grow Up, 1951 (Laszlo; Spiegel)
When in Rome, 1952 (Daniels; Schnee)
When Kings Were the Law, 1912 (Bitzer)
When Knights Were Bold, 1908 (Bitzer)
When Knights Were Bold, 1936 (Young)
When Knights Were Bold, 1941 (Terry)
When Ladies Meet, 1933 (Adrian; Mayer)
When Ladies Meet, 1941 (Adrian; Kaper; Loos)
When Lee Surrenders, 1912 (Ince)
When Lilacs Blossom. See Nar syrenerna blommar, 1952
When Love Fades. See Wenn die Liebe auf den Hund kommt, 1917
When Love Kills. See När kärleken dödar, 1913
When Magoo Flew, 1955 (Bosustow)
When Money Comes, 1929 (Roach)
When Mousehood Was in Flower, 1953 (Terry)
When My Baby Smiles at Me, 1948 (Lemaire; Newman; Trotti; Zanuck)
When My Ship Comes In, 1934 (Fleischer)
When Saturday Comes, 1995 (Fisher)
When Strangers Marry, 1944 (Tiomkin)
When the Alarm Bell Rings. See När larmklockan ljuder, 1913
When the Bough Breaks, 1947 (Rank)
When the Cat's Away, 1929 (Disney; Iwerks; Stalling)
When the Desert Calls, 1922 (Carré)
When the Door Opened. See Escape, 1940
When the Girls Meet the Boys. See Girl Crazy, 1943
When the Jungle Cats Go to Drink. See A l'Heure ou les grandes fauves vont boire, 1993
When the Law Rides, 1928 (Musuraca; Plunkett)
When the Pie Was Opened, 1941 (Lye)
When the Red Red Robin Comes Bob Bob Bobbin' Along, 1932 (Fleischer)
When the Road Parts, 1915 (Loos)
When the Time Comes, 1987 (Lansing)
When the Wind Blows, 1920 (Roach)
When the Wind Blows, 1930 (Roach)
When Time Ran Out, 1981 (Foreman; Schifrin)
When Tomorrow Comes, 1939 (Orry-Kelly)
When Willie Comes Marching Home, 1950 (Lemaire; Newman; Wheeler)
When Worlds Collide, 1951 (Edouart; Head; Maté; Pal; Pereira; Seitz)
When You Comin' Back, Red Rider?, 1979 (Nitzsche)
When You're in Love, 1937 (Cohn; Goosson; Newman; Riskin; Walker)
When Yuba Plays the Rumba on the Tuba, 1933 (Fleischer)
When's Your Birthday, 1936 (Clampett)
Whence and Where To. See Kudy kam, 1956
Where Am I? Sunny Spain, 1923 (Roach)
Where Angels Go . . . Trouble Follows!, 1968 (Schifrin; Wheeler)
Where Are You? I'm Here. See Dove siete' Io sono qui, 1993
Where Danger Lives, 1950 (Musuraca)
Where Do We Go from Here?, 1945 (Raksin; Shamroy)
Where Eagles Dare, 1969 (Canutt)
Where East Is East, 1929 (Gibbons)
Where It's At, 1969 (Guffey; Kanin)
Where Love Has Gone, 1964 (Cahn; Hayes; Head; Levine; van Heusen)
Where No Vultures Fly, 1951 (Balcon)
Where Pigeons Go to Die, 1990 (Rosenman)
Where Sinners Meet, 1934 (Biroc; Musuraca; Plunkett; Steiner)
Where Sleeping Dogs Lie, 1992 (Zimmer)
Where the Boys Are, 1960 (Ames; Pasternak)
Where the Breakers Roar, 1908 (Bitzer)
Where the Daltons Rode, 1940 (Mohr)
Where the Heart Is, 2000 (Daring)
Where the Pavement Ends, 1923 (Seitz)
Where the River Bends. See Bend of the River, 1952
Where the Sidewalk Ends, 1950 (Hecht; La Shelle; Lemaire; Wheeler)
Where the West Begins, 1919 (Furthman)
Where the Worst Begins, 1925 (Haskin)

Where There's a Will, 1936 (Balcon; Rank; Vetchinsky)
Where There's Life, 1947 (Dreier; Head; Lang)
Where Were You When the Lights Went Out?, 1968 (Grusin)
Where's Charley, 1952 (Kidd)
Where's George?, 1935 (Wilcox)
Where's Jack, 1968 (Bernstein)
Where's the Fire?, 1921 (Roach)
Which Is Witch?, 1949 (Blanc; Stalling)
Which Is Witch?, 1955 (Halas and Batchelor)
Which Side Are You On?, 1985 (Menges)
Which Way Is Up?, 1977 (Alonzo)
Whiffs, 1975 (Cahn)
While the Cat's Away, 1911 (Gaudio)
While the City Sleeps, 1928 (Day; Gibbons)
While the City Sleeps, 1956 (Fields; Laszlo)
While the Patient Slept, 1935 (Edeson)
While the Sun Shines, 1946 (Rattigan)
Whip, 1917 (Carré)
Whip Hand, 1951 (Menzies; Musuraca)
Whip Woman, 1928 (Haller)
Whiplash, 1949 (Waxman)
Whipped. See Underworld Story, 1950
Whipsaw, 1935 (Howe; Mayer)
Whirlpool, 1949 (Hecht; Lemaire; Miller; Newman; Raksin; Wheeler)
Whirlpool, 1959 (Rank; Unsworth)
Whirlwind. See Dai tatsumaki, 1964
Whiskey Galore!, 1949 (Balcon)
Whisperers, 1967 (Barry)
Whispering Chorus, 1918 (Buckland; Macpherson)
Whispering Devils, 1920 (Gaudio)
Whispering Ghosts, 1942 (Ballard; Day; Raksin)
Whispering Smith, 1926 (Clarke; La Shelle)
Whispering Smith, 1948 (Deutsch; Dreier; Head; Rennahan)
Whispering Smith Hits London, 1952 (Carreras)
Whispering Smith vs. Scotland Yard. See Whispering Smith Hits London, 1952
Whispers in the Dark, 1937 (Fleischer)
Whispers in the Dark, 1992 (Newman)
Whistle, 1921 (August)
Whistle, 2000 (Mamet)
Whistle at Eaton Falls, 1951 (de Rochemont)
Whistle Down the Wind, 1961 (Alcott; Arnold; Rank)
Whistle Stop, 1946 (Metty; Tiomkin)
Whistling in Brooklyn, 1943 (Irene)
Whistling in the Dark, 1941 (Kaper)
White Angel, 1936 (Blanke; Gaudio; Grot; Orry-Kelly)
White Banners, 1938 (Blanke; Rosher; Steiner; Wallis)
White Blacksmith, 1922 (Roach)
White Buffalo, 1977 (Barry; de Laurentiis)
White Bus, 1966 (Ondříček)
White Cargo, 1942 (Kaper; Mayer; Stradling)
White Christmas, 1954 (Berlin; Head; Krasna; Pereira)
White Circle, 1920 (Furthman)
White Cliffs of Dover, 1944 (Gillespie; Irene; Mayer; Stothart)
White Cockatoo, 1935 (Blanke; Gaudio)
White Cradle Inn, 1947 (Dillon)
White Dawn, 1974 (Mancini)
White Dog, 1994 (Morricone)
White Dwarf, 1995 (van Runkle)
White Eagle, 1941 (Canutt)
White Elder Sister. See Shiroi ane, 1931
White Face, 1932 (Balcon)
White Fang, 1936 (Friedhofer; Miller; Zanuck)
White Fang, 1991 (Zimmer)
White Feather, 1955 (Ballard; Friedhofer; Smith)
White Flood, 1940 (Eisler; Maddow)

White Gold, 1927 (Grot; Sullivan)
White Hands, 1922 (Sullivan)
White Heat, 1949 (Steiner)
White Heather, 1919 (Carré)
White Hell of Piz Palü. See Weisse Hölle von Piz Palü, 1929
White Hotel, 2000 (Adam; Rotunno)
White House Years, 1977 (Barry)
White Legion, 1936 (Brown)
White Line. See Cuori senza fontiere, 1950
White Man, 1924 (Struss)
White Man's Law, 1918 (Rosher)
White Men Can't Jump, 1992 (Boyd)
White Moor. See De-as fi Harap Alb, 1965
White Morning. See Shiroi asa, 1964
White Nights, 1985 (Watkin)
White Nights. See Fehér éjszakák, 1916
White Nights. See I notti bianchi, 1957
White Nights. See Notte bianche, 1957
White Oak, 1921 (August)
White Orchid of the Heating Desert. See Nessa no byakuran, 1951
White Outlaw, 1929 (Laszlo)
White Palace, 1990 (Littleton; Sargent)
White Parade, 1934 (La Shelle; Lasky; Levien; Miller)
White Paradise. See Bílý Ráj, 1924
White Rider. See White Thunder, 1925
White Rose, 1923 (Bitzer)
White Rose. See Fehér Rosza, 1919
White Rose of the Wilds, 1911 (Bitzer)
White Savage. See South of Tahiti, 1943
White Scourge. See Bílá nemoc, 1937
White Shadow, 1924 (Balcon)
White Shadows. See White Shadow, 1924
White Shadows in the South Seas, 1928 (Mayer; Stromberg)
White Sheep, 1924 (Roach)
White Sheik. See Sceicco bianco, 1952
White Sister, 1933 (Adrian; Booth; Daniels; Stewart; Stothart; Stromberg)
White Sister. See Bianco, rosso, e . . . , 1972
White Slave Catchers, 1914 (Loos)
White Squall, 1996 (Hambling; Zimmer)
White Thread of the Waterfall. See Taki no shiraito, 1952
White Thunder, 1925 (Canutt)
White Tower, 1950 (Jarrico)
White Unicorn, 1948 (Rank)
White Water Summer, 1987 (Alcott)
White Wilderness, 1958 (Iwerks)
White Wings, 1923 (Roach)
White Witch Doctor, 1953 (Herrmann; Jeakins; Lemaire; Shamroy; Wheeler)
White Woman, 1933 (Dreier; Head; Hoffenstein; Zukor)
Whity, 1971 (Ballhaus)
Who Are My Parents?, 1922 (Ruttenberg)
Who Believes in the Stork. See Kto wierzy w bociany, 1971
Who Done It?, 1956 (Clarke; Heller; Rank)
Who Framed Roger Rabbit?, 1988 (Blanc; Jones; Marshall; Ralston; Williams)
Who Goes Next?, 1938 (Dillon; Neame)
Who Goes There!, 1952 (Korda; Mathieson)
Who Has Seen the Wind?, 1965 (Head)
Who I Kissed Yesterday. See Koho jsem včera líbal, 1935
Who Is Harry Kellerman and Why Is He Saying Those Terrible Things about Me?, 1971 (Horner; Smith)
Who Is Hope Schuyler?, 1942 (Miller; Raksin)
Who Is Killing the Great Chefs of Europe?, 1978 (Alcott; Mancini)
Who Killed Cock Robin?, 1933 (Terry)
Who Killed Doc Robbin, 1948 (Roach)
Who Killed Doc Robin?, 1931 (Balcon)

Who Killed Gail Preston?, 1938 (Goosson)
Who Killed Johnny Ringo. *See* Wer Kennet Jonny R?, 1966
Who Killed Pasolini. *See* Pasolini, un delitto italiano, 1995
Who Killed Who?, 1943 (Avery)
Who Loved Him Best, 1918 (Polito)
Who Scent You?, 1960 (Blanc; Jones)
Who Was That Lady?, 1960 (Cahn; Krasna; Louis; Previn; Stradling;
    van Heusen)
Who Will Marry Me?, 1919 (Levien)
Who's Afraid of Virginia Woolf?, 1966 (Lehman; North; O'Ssteen;
    Sharaff; Stradling; Sylbert; Warner; Wexler)
Who's Been Sleeping in My Bed?, 1963 (Bacharach; Duning; Head;
    Ruttenberg)
Who's Got the Action?, 1962 (Duning; Head; Ruttenberg)
Who's Got the Black Box?. *See* Route de Corinthe, 1967
Who's Kitten Who?, 1952 (Blanc; McKimson; Stalling)
Who's Minding the Mint?, 1967 (Biroc; Schifrin)
Who's Minding the Store?, 1963 (Head; Pereira)
Who's That Knocking at My Door?, 1969 (Schoonmaker)
Who's Who, 1906 (Selig)
Who's Who in the Jungle, 1945 (Terry)
Who's Who in the Zoo, 1942 (Blanc; Stalling)
Whoa, Be Gone!, 1958 (Blanc; Jones)
Whole Town's Talking, 1926 (Loos)
Whole Town's Talking, 1935 (August; Cohn; Parrish; Riskin; Swerling)
Whole Truth, 1958 (Hambling)
Whole Wide World, 1996 (Zimmer)
Wholly Moses!, 1980 (Houseman)
Wholly Smoke, 1938 (Blanc; Stalling)
Whom the Gods Destroy, 1934 (Buchman)
Whom the Gods Love, 1936 (Andrejew; Dean; Stallich)
Whoopee!, 1930 (Brown; Day; Garmes; Goldwyn; Goodrich and Hackett;
    Kahn; Newman; Rennahan; Toland)
Whoopee Boys, 1986 (Nitzsche)
Whoops! I'm a Cowboy, 1937 (Fleischer)
Whoops! I'm an Indian, 1937 (Bruckman)
Whose Wife?, 1917 (Seitz)
Why?, 1972 (Garmes)
Why?. *See* Detenuto in attesa di giudizio, 1971
Why Aren't You Laughing?. *See* Proč se nesmeješ, 1922
Why Be Good?, 1929 (Grot)
Why Bother to Knock. *See* Don't Bother to Knock, 1961
Why Bri?, 1961 (Lassally)
Why Do You Smile, Mona Lisa?. *See* Proč se usmíváš, Mona Lisa?, 1966
Why Foxy Grandpa Escaped Ducking, 1903 (Bitzer)
Why Girls Love Sailors, 1927 (Roach)
Why Girls Say No, 1927 (Roach)
Why Go Home?, 1920 (Roach)
Why Husbands Go Mad, 1924 (Roach)
Why Is a Plumber?, 1929 (Roach)
Why Man Creates, 1968 (Bass)
Why Men Leave Home, 1924 (Booth; Polito)
Why Men Work, 1924 (Roach)
Why Mules Leave Home, 1934 (Terry)
Why Must I Die?, 1960 (Haller)
Why Pick on Me?, 1918 (Roach)
Why UNESCO?. *See* Proč UNESCO?, 1958
Why We Fight series, 1942-45 (Hornbeck; Tiomkin)
Why We Fight. *See* Divide and Conquer, 1943
Why We Fight. *See* **Battle of Britain**, 1943
Why We Fight. *See* **Battle of China**, 1944
Why We Fight. *See* **Battle of Russia**, 1944
Why We Fight. *See* **Nazis Strike**, 1943
Why We Fight. *See* **Prelude to War**, 1942
Why We Fight. *See* **War Comes to America**, 1945
Why Worry?, 1923 (Roach; Zukor)

Wichita, 1955 (Mirisch)
Wicked as They Come, 1957 (Arnold)
Wicked Lady, 1945 (Bryan; Rank)
Wicked Lady, 1983 (Cardiff; Golan and Globus)
Wicked West, 1929 (Lantz)
Wicked Willie, 1990 (Godfrey)
Wicked Wolf, 1946 (Terry)
Wicked Woman, 1934 (Mayer)
Wickedness Preferred, 1928 (Day; Gibbons; Mayer)
Wicket Wacky, 1951 (Lantz)
Wicky-Wacky Romance, 1939 (Terry)
Wide Open Spaces, 1924 (Roach)
Wide Open Spaces, 1950 (Terry)
Wide Open Town, 1941 (Harlan; Head)
Wideo Wabbit, 1956 (Blanc; McKimson; Stalling)
Widow, 1903 (Bitzer)
Widow and the Only Man, 1904 (Bitzer)
Widow and the Pig, 1960 (Halas and Batchelor)
Widow from Chicago, 1930 (Polito)
Widow from Monte Carlo, 1935 (Orry-Kelly)
Widow's Kids, 1913 (Loos)
Widow's Might, 1918 (Rosher)
Widows' Nest. *See* Nido de viudas, 1977
Wie aus Cocl Asta Pilsen wurde, 1913 (Kolowrat-Krakowsky)
Wie heirate ich meinen Chef, 1927 (Planer)
Wie konntest du, Veronika?, 1940 (Von Harbou)
Wie sag ich's meinem Mann, 1932 (Hoffmann)
Wie werde ich reich und glücklich?, 1930 (Reisch)
Wiedergefundene Freund. *See* Ami retrouvé, 1989
Wiegenlied, 1908 (Messter)
Wielka mloso Balzaka, 1973 (Stawiński)
Wien im Krieg, 1916 (Kolowrat-Krakowsky)
Wiener Blut, 1942 (Stallich)
Wiener Herzen. *See* Erzehog Otto und das Wäschermadel, 1930
Wiener Mädeln, 1945 (Stallich)
Wiezien Rio. *See* Prisoners of Rio, 1989
Wife against Wife, 1921 (Haller)
Wife and Woman Journalist. *See* Tsuma to onna kisha, 1950
Wife, Doctor, and Nurse, 1937 (Cronjager; Trotti)
Wife, Husband, and Friend, 1939 (Johnson; Zanuck)
Wife in Love. *See* Koisuru tsuma, 1947
Wife in Name Only, 1923 (Carré)
Wife of the Centaur, 1925 (Gibbons)
Wife Takes a Flyer, 1942 (Planer)
Wife Tamers, 1926 (Roach)
Wife vs. Secretary, 1936 (Gibbons; Krasna; Stothart; Stromberg)
Wife Wanted, 1907 (Bitzer)
Wiggle Your Ears, 1929 (Roach)
Wilbur the Lion, 1947 (Pal)
Wilcze echa, 1967 (ścibor-Rylski)
Wild About Hurry, 1959 (Blanc; Jones)
Wild and Free—Twice Daily, 1969 (Menges)
Wild and the Willing, 1962 (Rank)
Wild and Wonderful, 1963 (La Shelle)
Wild and Woolfy, 1945 (Avery)
Wild and Woolly, 1917 (Edeson; Loos)
Wild and Woolly, 1932 (Lantz)
Wild and Wooly Hare, 1959 (Blanc)
Wild at Heart, 1990 (Badalamenti)
Wild Babies, 1932 (Roach)
Wild Bill, 1995 (Zanuck)
Wild Bill Hickok Rides, 1942 (McCord)
Wild Blue Yonder, 1951 (Young)
Wild Boss. *See* Abarenbou taishou, 1960
Wild Boy, 1934 (Balcon; Junge; Rank)
Wild Boys of the Road, 1933 (Warner)

Woman across the Way. *See* Frau gegenüber, 1978
Woman Alone, 1917 (Edeson; Marion)
Woman Alone. *See* Sabotage, 1936
Woman and Pirates. *See* Onna to kauzoku, 1959
Woman at Her Window. *See* Femme a sa fenetre, 1976
Woman Between. *See* Woman I Love, 1937
Woman Chases Man, 1937 (Day; Goldwyn; Mandell; Newman; Toland)
Woman Commands, 1932 (Brown; Krasner; Mandell; Mohr)
Woman Destroyed. *See* Smash-Up, 1947
Woman Disputed, 1928 (Menzies; Schenck; Sullivan)
Woman from Hell, 1929 (Carré)
Woman from Mellon's, 1909 (Bitzer)
Woman from Monte Carlo, 1932 (Haller)
Woman for Joe, 1955 (Rank)
Woman God Forgot, 1917 (Buckland; Macpherson)
Woman Hater, 1948 (Dillon; Rank)
Woman He Loved, 1922 (Gaudio)
Woman Hungry, 1931 (Polito)
Woman Hunt, 1961 (Crosby)
Woman Hunter, 1972 (Duning)
Woman I Love, 1929 (Miller; Plunkett)
Woman I Love, 1937 (Plunkett; Polglase; Rosher; Veiller)
Woman in Black, 1914 (Gaudio)
Woman in Bondage. *See* Impassive Footman, 1932
Woman in Command. *See* Soldiers of the King, 1933
Woman in Green, 1945 (Miller)
Woman in Her Thirties. *See* Side Streets, 1934
Woman in Hiding, 1950 (Daniels; Orry-Kelly)
Woman in His House. *See* Animal Kingdom, 1932
Woman in His Life, 1933 (Adrian)
Woman in Question, 1950 (Dillon)
Woman in Red, 1935 (Orry-Kelly; Polito)
Woman in Room 13, 1932 (Friedhofer; Seitz)
Woman in the Dark, 1934 (Plunkett)
Woman in the Dunes. *See* Sunna no onna, 1963
Woman in the Hall, 1947 (Mathieson; Rank)
Woman in the Moon. *See* Frau im Mond, 1929
Woman in the Suitcase, 1919 (Barnes; Ince)
Woman in the Window, 1944 (Fields; Friedhofer; Johnson; Krasner)
Woman in Two Minds. *See* A ketlekü asszony, 1917
Woman in White, 1929 (Wilcox)
Woman in White, 1948 (Blanke; Burks; Steiner)
Woman in White. *See* Journal d'une femme en blanc, 1965
Woman Is a Woman. *See* Femme est une femme, 1961
Woman Is the Judge, 1939 (Brown)
Woman Next Door. *See* Femme d'à côté, 1981
Woman Obsessed, 1959 (Friedhofer; Lemaire; Smith; Wheeler)
Woman of Affairs, 1928 (Adrian; Daniels; Gibbons; Mayer)
Woman of Distinction, 1950 (Louis; Walker)
Woman of Dolwyn. *See* Last Days of Dolwyn, 1948
Woman of Experience, 1931 (Mohr)
Woman of No Importance. *See* Frau ohne Bedetung, 1936
Woman of Otowi Crossing, 1974 (Koch)
Woman of Rome. *See* Romana, 1954
Woman of Straw, 1964 (Adam; Heller; Mathieson)
Woman of Summer. *See* Stripper, 1963
Woman of the Rumor. *See* Uwasa no onna, 1954
Woman of the Town, 1943 (Harlan; Rozsa)
Woman of the Year, 1942 (Adrian; Lardner; Mayer; Ruttenberg; Waxman)
Woman of the Year, 1976 (Ames)
Woman of the World, 1925 (Glennon)
Woman on Pier 13, 1950 (Musuraca)
Woman on the Beach, 1947 (D'Agostino; Eisler)
Woman on the Run, 1950 (Leven; Mohr)
Woman on Trial, 1927 (Glennon)

Woman Opening a Door. *See* Tobira o hiraku onna, 1946
Woman Opening the Door. *See* Tobira o hiraku onna, 1946
Woman-Proof, 1923 (Haller)
Woman Racket, 1930 (Gibbons)
Woman Rebels, 1936 (Berman; Polglase; Vajda; Veiller)
Woman Scorned, 1911 (Bitzer)
Woman Tamer. *See* She Couldn't Take It, 1935
Woman the Flower. *See* Femme-Fleur, 1965
Woman Times Seven, 1967 (Evein; Levine; Matras)
Woman to Woman, 1923 (Balcon; Reville)
Woman to Woman, 1929 (Balcon)
Woman Trap, 1936 (Brackett; Head)
Woman Using a Small Sword. *See* Kodachi o tsukau onna, 1961
Woman, Wake Up!, 1922 (Barnes)
Woman Wanted, 1935 (Clarke)
Woman Who Convicts Men. *See* Otoko o sabaku onna, 1948
Woman Who Gave, 1918 (Ruttenberg)
Woman Who Knows What She Wants. *See* Zena, která ví, co chce, 1934
Woman Who Sinned, 1924 (Mohr)
Woman Who Walked Alone, 1922 (Glennon; Howe)
Woman Who Wouldn't Die, 1964 (Mainwaring)
Woman with Four Faces, 1923 (Howe)
Woman with No Name, 1950 (Heller)
Woman with the Orchid. *See* Frau mit den Orchiden, 1919
Woman's Face, 1941 (Adrian; Kaper; Mayer; Stewart)
Woman's Place, 1921 (Loos; Schenck)
Woman's Secret, 1949 (Mankiewicz)
Woman's Vengeance, 1947 (Lourié; Metty; Orry-Kelly; Rozsa)
Woman's Way, 1916 (Marion)
Woman's Woman, 1922 (Goodrich and Hackett)
Woman's World, 1954 (Brackett; Lemaire)
Womanhandled, 1925 (Cronjager)
Womb of Power, 1979 (Nihalani)
Women, 1939 (Adrian; Loos; Mayer; Ruttenberg; Stromberg)
Women & Men 2: In Love There Are No Rules, 1991 (Bernstein)
Women and Gold, 1925 (Daniels)
Women Are Like That, 1938 (Orry-Kelly)
Women Everywhere, 1930 (Biro; Korda)
Women Family. *See* Jokei kazoku, 1963
Women in Film, 2000 (Vachon)
Women in Limbo. *See* Limbo, 1972
Women in Love, 1969 (Delerue)
Women in Our Time, 1948 (Arnold)
Women in the Wind, 1939 (Orry-Kelly)
Women Love Diamonds, 1927 (Gibbons; Gillespie)
Women Love Once, 1931 (Struss)
Women Men Marry, 1931 (Shamroy)
Women Must Dress, 1935 (Krasner)
Women of All Nations, 1931 (Carré)
Women of Paris. *See* Parisiskor, 1928
Women of the Night. *See* Yoru no onnatachi, 1948
Women of Twilight, 1952 (de Grunwald)
Women: So We Are Made. *See* Noi donne siamo fatte cosi, 1971
Women Tend to . . . . *See* Tokaku omna to iu mono wa, 1932
Women Trouble. *See* Molti sogni per le strade, 1948
Women without Men, 1956 (Carreras)
Women without Names, 1940 (Dreier; Head; Lang)
Women, Women, 1918 (Ruttenberg)
Women's Origin. *See* Fukeizu, 1962
Women's Scroll. *See* Jokei, 1960
Wonder Bar, 1934 (Orry-Kelly; Polito)
Wonder Boys, 2000 (Allen)
Wonder Gloves, 1951 (Bosustow)
Wonder Kid, 1950 (Korda; Krasker)
Wonder Man, 1945 (Banton; Goldwyn; Mandell)
Wonder of Women, 1929 (Day; Gibbons)

Wonder of Wool, 1960 (Halas and Batchelor)
Wonder Woman, 1974 (Biroc)
Wonder World, 1972 (Takemitsu)
Wonderful Adventures of Herr Munchausen. *See* Monsieur de Crac, 1910
Wonderful Bad Woman. *See* Subarashii akujo, 1963
Wonderful Country, 1959 (Bernstein; Crosby; Horner; North; Parrish)
Wonderful Lie of Nina Petrovna. *See* Wunderbare Lüge der Nina Petrovna, 1929
Wonderful Lies of Nina Petrovna. *See* Underbare Lüge der Nina Poetrowna, 1929
Wonderful Story, 1922 (Wilcox)
Wonderful Thing, 1921 (Carré; Schenck)
Wonderful Things, 1958 (Wilcox)
Wonderful to Be Young. *See* Young Ones, 1961
Wonderful World of Jack Paar, 1959 (McClaren)
Wonderful World of the Brothers Grimm, 1962 (Pal)
Wonderful Years. *See* Restless Years, 1958
Wonderland, 1931 (Lantz)
Wonderland. *See* Fruit Machine, 1988
Wonders of Aladdin. *See* Meraviglie di Aladino, 1961
Wooden Horse, 1950 (Korda)
Wooden Indian, 1949 (Terry)
Wooden Leg, 1909 (Bitzer)
Woodland, 1932 (Terry)
Woodman Spare That Tree, 1951 (Terry)
Woodpecker in the Rough, 1952 (Lantz)
Woods Are Full of Cuckoos, 1937 (Stalling)
Woodstock, 1970 (Schoonmaker)
Woody Woodpecker, 1941 (Lantz)
Woody Woodpecker Polka, 1951 (Lantz)
Woolen Under Where, 1963 (Blanc; Jones)
Words and Music, 1929 (Clarke)
Words and Music, 1948 (Edens; Freed; Mayer; Rose; Rosher; Smith; Stradling)
Work Party, 1942 (Lye)
Worker and Warfront, 1945 (Alwyn)
Working, 1982 (Schwartz)
Working Class Goes to Heaven. *See* Classe operaia va in paradiso, 1971
Working Class Man. *See* Gung Ho, 1986
Working Girl, 1988 (Ballhaus; O'Ssteen; Von Brandenstein)
Working Man, 1933 (Orry-Kelly)
World According to Garp, 1982 (Bumstead; Ondříček)
World against Him, 1916 (Polito)
World and His Wife, 1920 (Marion)
World and His Wife. *See* State of the Union, 1948
World and Its Women, 1919 (Gibbons)
World and the Flesh, 1932 (Struss)
World Apart, 1987 (Menges)
World Apart, 1988 (Biziou; Zimmer)
World Belongs to Us. *See* Svet patří nám, 1937
World Changes, 1933 (Gaudio; Orry-Kelly; Wallis)
World Gardens, 1942 (Unsworth)
World in Flames, 1940 (Head)
World in His Arms, 1952 (Chase; Metty)
World is Not Enough, 1999 (Biddle)
World Is Peaceful. *See* Tenka taihei, 1955
World Moves On, 1934 (Friedhofer; Steiner)
World of Apu. *See* **Apur Sansar**, 1959
World of Dong Kingman . *See* Dong Kingman, 1955
World of Henry Orient, 1964 (Bernstein; Johnson; Kaufman; Smith)
World of Little Ig, 1956 (Halas and Batchelor)
World of Plenty, 1943 (Alwyn; Mayer)
World of Sam Smith, 1974 (Lassally)
World of Suzie Wong, 1960 (Cahn; Duning; Stark; Unsworth; van Heusen)
World Premiere, 1941 (Head)

World, the Flesh, and the Devil, 1959 (Rozsa)
World War II: When Lions Roared, 1994 (Alonzo)
World Window, 1937-40 (Cardiff)
World's a Stage, 1922 (Haskin)
World's Greatest Athlete, 1972 (Hamlisch)
Worldly Goods, 1924 (Glennon)
Worldly Madonna, 1922 (Edeson)
Worst Woman in Paris, 1933 (Mohr)
Worth of a Life, 1914 (Ince)
Wot Dot, 1970 (Halas and Batchelor)
Wot's All th' Shootin, Fer, 1940 (Terry)
Wotta Nitemare, 1939 (Fleischer)
Would You Forgive?, 1920 (Furthman)
Wozzeck, 1947 (Warm)
Wrath of God, 1972 (Schifrin)
Wrath of the Gods, 1914 (Ince)
Wreath in Time, 1908 (Bitzer)
Wreath of Orange Blossoms, 1910 (Bitzer)
Wreck of the Hesperus, 1927 (Adrian; Goosson)
Wreck of the Hesperus, 1944 (Terry)
Wreck of the Mary Deare, 1959 (Duning; Ruttenberg; Young)
Wrecker, 1928 (Balcon)
Wreckety Wrecks, 1933 (Roach)
Wrestling, N.Y. Athletic Club, 1905 (Bitzer)
Written on the Wind, 1956 (Cahn; Metty)
Wrong Arm Of The Law, 1962 (Bennett)
Wrong Blonde. *See* Mauvaise passe, 1999
Wrong Box, 1966 (Barry)
Wrong Man, 1956 (Burks; Herrmann)
Wrong Move. *See* Falsche Bewegung, 1974
Wrong Trousers, 1991 (Park)
Wrongfully Accused, 1998 (Conti)
W.S.P., 1974 (Lassally)
Wu Li Chang, 1930 (Gibbons; Marion)
Wünderbare Lüge der Nina Petrowna, 1929 (Herlth; Hoffmann; Jaubert; Röhrig)
Wunkanal Hinrichtung fur vier Stimmen, 1984 (Alekan)
WUSA, 1970 (Schifrin)
Wuthering Heights, 1939 (Basevi; Goldwyn; Hecht; MacArthur; Mandell; Newman; Toland)
Wuthering Heights, 1970 (Legrand)
W.V.S., 1942 (Alwyn)
W.W. and the Dixie Dancekings, 1975 (Grusin)
Wy brouwen, 1929 (van Dongen)
Wyatt Earp, 1994 (Littleton)
Wyoming, 1928 (Selznick)
Wyoming, 1947 (Alton; Canutt)
Wyoming Mail, 1950 (Metty)
Wyoming Outlaw, 1939 (Canutt)
Wyoming Whirlwind, 1932 (Canutt)

X, 1963 (Crosby)
X-Diagnosis. *See* Diagnoza X, 1933
X-Men, 2000 (Schamus)
X-Ray Glasses. *See* Lunettes féeriques, 1909
X the Unknown, 1956 (Bernard; Carreras)
Xeroscopy, 1971 (Halas and Batchelor)
Xochimilco. *See* María Candelária, 1943

Y a des jours . . . et des lunes, 1990 (Lai)
Y a longtemps que je t'aime, 1979 (Guillemot)
Y mañana seran mujeres!, 1954 (Alcoriza)
Ya Kuba, 1964 (Urusevsky)
Yacht on the High Seas, 1955 (Lemaire)
Yakuza, 1975 (Grusin; Towne)
Yale Laundry, 1907 (Bitzer)

Yamamoto Isoroku, 1968 (Tsuburaya)
Yamaneko rei jou, 1948 (Yoda)
Yamata, 1919 (Korda)
Yami no Kageboushi, 1938 (Miyagawa)
Yangtse Incident, 1957 (Wilcox)
Yank at Eton, 1942 (Freund; Kaper)
Yank at Oxford, 1938 (Balcon; Booth; Mayer; Rosson; Saunders)
Yank in London. See I Live in Grosvenor Square, 1945
Yank in Rome. See Americano in vacanza, 1946
 Yank in the R.A.F., 1941 (Banton; Basevi; Day; Newman;
    Shamroy; Zanuck)
Yank on the Burma Road, 1942 (Schary)
Yankee Buccaneer, 1952 (Boyle; Metty)
Yankee Clipper, 1927 (Sullivan)
Yankee Dood It, 1956 (Blanc)
Yankee Doodle Andy, 1941 (Bruckman)
Yankee Doodle Boy, 1929 (Fleischer)
Yankee Doodle Bugs, 1954 (Blanc)
Yankee Doodle Cricket, 1974 (Jones)
Yankee Doodle Daffy, 1943 (Blanc; Stalling)
Yankee Doodle Dandy, 1942 (Howe; Wallis)
Yankee Doodle Mouse, 1943 (Hanna and Barbera)
Yankee in London. See I Live in Grosvenor Square, 1945
Yanks, 1979 (Bennett; Bernstein)
Yanks Ahoy, 1942 (Roach)
Yaqui Cur, 1913 (Bitzer)
Yari no Gonza, 1985 (Miyagawa; Takemitsu)
Yari-odori gojusan-tsugi, 1946 (Miyagawa)
Yarn about Yarn, 1941 (Terry)
Ye Happy Pilgrims, 1934 (Lantz)
Ye Olde Melodies, 1929 (Fleischer)
Ye Olde Songs, 1932 (Terry)
Ye Olde Swap Shoppe, 1940 (Iwerks)
Ye Olde Toy Shop, 1935 (Terry)
Year Around, 1948 (Fleischer)
Year of Living Dangerously, 1982 (Boyd; Jarre; Seale)
Year of the Comet, 1992 (Goldman)
Year of the Dragon, 1985 (de Laurentiis)
Year of the Gun, 1991 (Allen; Conti)
Year of the Horse, 1966 (Hubley)
Year of the Mouse, 1965 (Jones)
Year's Blonde, 1980 (Kanin)
Yearling, 1946 (Gibbons; Irene; Mayer; Rosher; Stothart)
Years to Come, 1922 (Roach)
Years without Days. See Castle on the Hudson, 1940
Yeh Gulistan Hamara, 1972 (Burman)
Yellow Cab Man, 1950 (Deutsch; Stradling)
Yellow Canary, 1943 (Wilcox)
Yellow Canary, 1963 (Crosby)
Yellow Dust, 1936 (Cronjager)
Yellow Jack, 1938 (Vorkapich)
Yellow Lily, 1928 (Biro; Garmes; Korda)
Yellow Men and Gold, 1922 (Gibbons)
Yellow Mountain, 1954 (Hunter)
Yellow Passport, 1916 (Marion)
Yellow Passport. See Yellow Ticket, 1931
Yellow Peril, 1908 (Bitzer)
Yellow Rolls-Royce, 1964 (Fisher; Head; Korda; Rattigan; de Grunwald)
Yellow Sky, 1948 (Lemaire; Newman; Trotti; Zanuck)
Yellow Stain, 1922 (Furthman)
Yellow Submarine, 1968 (Dunning)
Yellow Ticket, 1931 (Friedhofer; Furthman; Howe)
Yellowbeard, 1983 (Fisher; Reynolds)
Yellowstone, 1936 (Krasner)
Yellowstone, 1994 (Conti)
Yentl, 1983 (Legrand; Watkin)

Yerma, 1999 (de Almeida)
Yes, Giorgio, 1982 (Williams)
Yes Mr. Brown, 1933 (Wilcox)
Yes, My Darling Daughter, 1939 (Rosher; Wallis)
Yes or No, 1920 (Haller)
Yes! We Have No Bananas, 1930 (Fleischer)
Yes, Yes, Nanette, 1925 (Roach)
Yesterday, Today and Tomorrow. See Levi, oggi, domani, 1963
Yesterday, Today, and Tomorrow. See Ieri, oggi, e domani, 1963
Yesterday's Enemy, 1959 (Carreras)
Yesterday's Heroes, 1940 (Clarke; Day)
Yesterday's Wife, 1924 (Cohn)
Yeux d'elstir, 1967 (Fradetal)
Yeux du dragon, 1924 (Starewicz)
Yeux noirs, 1935 (Andrejew; Lourié)
Yeux ouverts, 1913 (Gaumont)
Yeux sans visage, 1959 (Jarre; Schüfftan)
Yin shi nan nu, 1994 (Schamus)
Yip, Yip, Yippy, 1939 (Fleischer)
Yo quiero ser hombre, 1949 (Alcoriza)
Yoba, 1976 (Miyagawa)
Yogen, 1982 (Takemitsu)
Yogoreta hanazono, 1948 (Yoda)
Yoidore bayashi, 1955 (Yoda)
Yoidore tenshi, 1948 (Hayasaka)
Yojimbo, 1961 (Miyagawa; Muraki)
Yokel. See Boob, 1926
Yokel Boy Makes Good, 1938 (Lantz)
Yokel Duck Makes Good, 1943 (Terry)
Yoke's on Me, 1944 (Bruckman)
Yokihi, 1955 (Hayasaka; Yoda)
Yokohama Yankee, 1955 (Terry)
Yola, 1918 (Starewicz)
Yolanda, 1924 (Barnes)
Yolanda and the Thief, 1945 (Edens; Freed; Gibbons; Gillespie; Irene;
    Rosher; Sharaff; Smith)
Yoma Kidan, 1929 (Tsuburaya)
Yomigaeru daichi, 1970 (Takemitsu)
Yorck, 1931 (Herlth; Röhrig)
York, 1931 (Hoffmann)
Yoru no cho, 1957 (Miyagawa)
Yoru no kawa, 1956 (Miyagawa)
Yoru no onnatachi, 1948 (Yoda)
Yosei Goraith, 1962 (Tsuburaya)
Yosei Gorasu. See Yosei Goraith, 1962
Yoshiwara, 1937 (Barsacq; Schüfftan)
Yotsuya kaidan, 1965 (Takemitsu)
Yottsu no koi no monogatari, 1947 (Hayasaka)
Yotz 'im Kavua, 1979 (Golan and Globus)
You and Me, 1938 (Dreier; Head; Krasna; Lang)
You Are My Adventure. See Du är mitt äventry, 1958
You Belong to Me, 1934 (Head)
You Belong to Me, 1941 (Head; Trumbo; Walker)
You Belong to My Heart. See Mr. Imperium, 1950
You Bring the Ducks, 1934 (Roach)
You Came Along, 1945 (Dreier; Head; Wallis; Young)
You Came to My Rescue, 1937 (Fleischer)
You Can Draw, 1938 (van Dongen)
You Can't Beat Love, 1937 (Metty)
You Can't Buy Everything, 1934 (Nichols; Trotti)
You Can't Cheat an Honest Man, 1939 (Krasner)
You Can't Do without Love. See One Exciting Night, 1944
You Can't Escape, 1942 (Deutsch)
You Can't Escape Forever, 1942 (Gaudio)
You Can't Fool Your Wife, 1923 (Glennon)
You Can't Fool Your Wife, 1940 (Polglase)

You Can't Get Away with Murder, 1939 (Friedhofer; Polito)
You Can't Ration Love, 1944 (Dreier; Head)
You Can't Run Away from It, 1956 (Duning; Louis; Mercer; Wald)
You Can't Shoe a Horsefly, 1940 (Fleischer)
You Can't Take It with You, 1938 (Cohn; Goosson; Irene; Riskin; Tiomkin; Walker)
You Can't Win 'em All, 1970 (Mathieson)
You Don't Need Pajamas at Rosie's. *See* First Time, 1968
You Gotta Be a Football Hero, 1935 (Fleischer)
You Gotta Stay Happy, 1948 (Metty)
You Know What Sailors Are, 1954 (Arnold; Rank)
You Laugh. *See* Tu ridi, 1998
You Leave Me Breathless, 1938 (Fleischer)
You Must Be Joking!, 1965 (Godfrey; Unsworth)
You Nazty Spy!, 1940 (Bruckman)
You Never Know Women, 1926 (Vajda)
You Only Live Once, 1937 (Mandell; Newman; Shamroy; Wanger)
You Only Live Twice, 1967 (Adam; Barry; Broccoli; Young)
You Ought to Be in Pictures, 1940 (Blanc; Stalling)
You Said a Hatful!, 1934 (Roach)
You Said a Mouthful, 1932 (Orry-Kelly)
You Shouldn't Die. *See* Kimi shinitamau koto nakare, 1954
You Took the Words Right Out of My Heart, 1938 (Fleischer)
You Try Somebody Else, 1932 (Fleischer)
You Were Meant for Me, 1948 (Lemaire; Reynolds)
You Were Never Duckier, 1948 (Blanc; Jones; Stalling)
You Were Never Lovelier, 1942 (Cohn; Irene; Mercer)
You Will Send Me to Bed, Eh?, 1903 (Bitzer)
You'd Be Surprised, 1926 (Furthman)
You'll Find Out, 1940 (Mercer; Polglase)
You'll Never Get Rich, 1941 (Cohn; Porter)
You're Darn Tootin', 1928 (Roach)
You're Driving Me Crazy, 1931 (Fleischer)
You're in the Army Now. *See* O.H.M.S., 1937
You're in the Navy Now, 1951 (Lemaire; Wheeler)
You're My Everything, 1949 (Lemaire; Newman; Trotti)
You're Never Too Young, 1955 (Cahn; Head)
You're Next, 1921 (Roach)
You're Not Built That Way, 1936 (Fleischer)
You're Pinched, 1920 (Roach)
You're Telling Me!, 1932 (Roach)
You're Telling Me, 1934 (Banton)
You're the One, 1941 (Head; Mercer)
Youki no seidayo, 1932 (Yoda)
Young and Beautiful, 1934 (Schary)
Young and Innocent, 1937 (Junge; Reville)
Young and Innocent. *See* Girl Was Young, 1937
Young and the Damned. *See* **Olvidados**, 1950
Young and Willing, 1943 (Dreier; Head; Young)
Young and Willing. *See* Wild and the Willing, 1962
Young April, 1926 (Adrian; Grot; Macpherson)
Young As You Feel, 1940 (Clarke)
Young at Heart, 1954 (Blanke; Epstein; McCord; van Heusen)
Young Bess, 1953 (Plunkett; Rosher; Rozsa)
Young Bill Hickok, 1940 (Canutt)
Young Bride, 1932 (Miller; Steiner)
Young Captives, 1959 (Head)
Young Cassidy, 1964 (Cardiff)
Young Days. *See* Mladé dny, 1956
Young Dillinger, 1965 (Cortez)
Young Doctors, 1961 (Bernstein; Justin; Sylbert)
Young Doctors in Love, 1982 (Jarre)
Young Donovan's Kid, 1931 (Cronjager; Steiner)
Young Don't Cry, 1957 (Haller)
Young Dr. Kildare, 1938 (Mayer; Seitz)
Young Einstein, 1988 (Morricone)

Young Frankenstein, 1974 (Jeakins)
Young Girl at the University. *See* Daigaku no oneichan, 1959
Young Girl Dares to Pass. *See* Oneichan makari touru, 1959
Young Girls of Rochefort. *See* Demoiselles de Rochefort, 1967
Young Girls Turn 25. *See* Demoiselles ont eu 25 Ans, 1993
Young Guard. *See* Molodaya gvardiya, 1947
Young Guns, 1959 (Fraker)
Young Ideas, 1943 (Schary)
Young in Heart, 1938 (Menzies; Selznick; Shamroy; Waxman; Wheeler)
Young Indiana Jones and the Attack of the Hawkmen, 1995 (Burtt)
Young Indiana Jones Chronicles, 1992 (Burtt)
Young Invaders. *See* Darby's Rangers, 1957
Young Ironsides, 1932 (Roach)
Young Joe, the Forgotten Kennedy, 1977 (Barry)
Young Lady from the Riverside. *See* Slečna od vody, 1959
Young Lady in a Dream. *See* Yume no naka no ojousan, 1934
Young Land, 1957 (Hoch; Tiomkin)
Young Lawyers, 1969 (Schifrin)
Young Lions, 1958 (Friedhofer; Lemaire; Spencer; Wheeler)
Young Lord. *See* Bonchi, 1960
Young Love: Lemon Popsicle VII, 1988 (Golan and Globus)
Young Lovers, 1954 (Havelock-Allan; Rank)
Young Lovers, 1964 (Biroc)
Young Lovers. *See* Never Fear, 1950
Young Man of Music. *See* Young Man with a Horn, 1950
Young Man with a Horn, 1950 (Cahn; Carmichael; Foreman; McCord; Wald)
Young Man with Ideas, 1952 (Ruttenberg)
Young Man's Fancy, 1939 (Balcon; Ncame)
Young Medardus. *See* Junge Medardus, 1923
Young Mr. Jazz, 1919 (Roach)
Young Mr. Lincoln, 1939 (Day; Glennon; Macgowan; Miller; Newman; Parrish; Trotti; Zanuck)
Young Mr. Lincoln, 1962 (Newman)
Young Mr. Pitt, 1942 (Beaton; Vetchinsky; Young)
Young Nowheres, 1929 (Haller)
Young Oldfield, 1924 (Roach)
Young Ones, 1961 (Figueroa; Slocombe)
Young People, 1940 (Cronjager; Day; Newman)
Young Philadelphians, 1959 (Stradling)
Young Racers, 1963 (Crosby; Golan and Globus)
Young Rajah, 1922 (Mathis; Zukor)
Young Sherlock Holmes, 1985 (Marshall; Muren)
Young Sherlocks, 1922 (Roach)
Young Sinners, 1931 (Seitz)
Young Stranger, 1957 (Bass; Rosenman)
Young Teacher. *See* Wakai sensei, 1941
Young Tom Edison, 1940 (Schary)
Young Werther. *See* Jeune Werther, 1993
Young Whirlwind, 1928 (Miller)
Young Widow, 1946 (Garmes; Stromberg)
Young Winston, 1972 (Foreman)
Young World. *See* Mondo nuovo, 1966
Youngblood Hawke, 1964 (O'Ssteen; Steiner)
Younger and Younger, 1993 (Zimmer)
Younger Brothers, 1949 (Burks)
Younger Generation, 1929 (Cohn; Levien)
Youngest Profession, 1943 (Irene; Lederer; Schary)
Younita, (undated) (Barker)
Your Children and You, 1946 (Alwyn)
Your Children's Ears, 1945 (Alwyn)
Your Children's Eyes, 1944 (Alwyn)
Your Children's Sleep, 1948 (Alwyn)
Your Children's Teeth, 1945 (Alwyn)
Your Husband's Past, 1926 (Roach)
Your Key to the Future, 1956 (Kidd)

Zoë, 1953 (Alekan)
Zoku ningen kakumai, 1976 (Muraki)
Zolotoi klyuchik, 1939 (Ptushko)
Zombies on Broadway, 1943 (D'Agostino)
Zone de la mort, 1917 (Burel; Gaumont)
Zone, 1928 (Périnal)
Zoo, 1933 (Lantz)
Zoo, 1988 (Lanci)
Zoo. See Chiriakhana, 1967
Zoo and You, 1938 (Alwyn)
Zoo Babies, 1938 (Alwyn)
Zoo in Budapest, 1933 (Friedhofer; Garmes; Lasky)
Zoo Is Company, 1961 (Hanna and Barbera)
Zoo Zero, 1978 (Nuytten)
Zoom and Bored, 1957 (Blanc; Jones; Stalling)
Zoom at the Top, 1962 (Blanc; Jones)
Zoot Cat, 1944 (Hanna and Barbera)
Zorba the Greek, 1964 (Lassally; Theodorakis)
Zorro and Son, 1983 (Duning)
Zorro Rides Again, 1937 (Canutt)
Zorro's Black Whip, 1944 (Canutt)
Zorro's Fighting Legion, 1939 (Canutt)
Zouhei monogatari, 1963 (Miyagawa)
Zouzou, 1934 (Douy; Kaufman; Meerson)
Zoya, 1944 (Shostakovich)
Zpev zlata, 1920 (Heller)
Ztracená varta, 1956 (Brdečka)

Ztracenci, 1957 (Brdečka)
Zu spät, 1911 (Messter)
Zuckerkandl!, 1968 (Hubley)
Zuiderzee Dike, 1931 (van Dongen)
Zula Hula, 1937 (Fleischer)
Zulu, 1963 (Barry)
Zulu Dawn, 1979 (Bernstein)
Zulu-Land, 1911 (Selig)
Zulu's Heart, 1908 (Bitzer)
Zum Goldenen Anker. See Marius, 1931
Zum Tee bei Dr. Borsig, 1963 (Herlth)
Zuppa di pesce, 1992 (Age and Scarpelli; de Almeida)
Zur Chronik von Grieshuus, 1925 (Herlth; Röhrig; Von Harbou; Wagner)
Zut, chien des rues, 1955 (Kosma)
Zuyderzee, 1933 (van Dongen)
Zvířátka a Petrovští, 1946 (Trnka)
Zwei Frauen, 1911 (Messter)
Zwei Herzen im 3/4 Takt, 1930 (Reisch)
Zwei in einder grosser Stadt, 1942 (Hoffmann)
Zwei Kinder, 1924 (Courant)
Zwei Krawatten, 1930 (Metzner)
Zwei Menschen, 1930 (Pasternak)
Zwei rote Rosen, 1928 (Andrejew)
Zwei Welten, 1919 (Kolowrat-Krakowsky)
Zwischen Abends und Morgens, 1923 (Wagner)
Zwischen gestern und morgen, 1947 (Herlth; Pommer)